Full pronunciation key

The pronunciation of each word is shown just after the word, in this way:
ab bre vi ate (ə brē′vē āt).

The letters and signs used are pronounced as in the words below.

The mark ′ is placed after a syllable with primary or heavy accent, as in the example above.

The mark ′ after a syllable shows a secondary or lighter accent, as in
ab bre vi a tion (ə brē′vē ā′shən).

a	hat, cap		**p**	paper, cup
ā	age, face		**r**	run, try
ä	father, far		**s**	say, yes
			sh	she, rush
			t	tell, it
b	bad, rob		**th**	thin, both
ch	child, much		**ᴛʜ**	then, smooth
d	did, red			
			u	cup, butter
e	let, best		**u̇**	full, put
ē	equal, be		**ü**	rule, move
ėr	term, learn			
			v	very, save
f	fat, if		**w**	will, woman
g	go, bag		**y**	young, yet
h	he, how		**z**	zero, breeze
			zh	measure, seizure
i	it, pin			
ī	ice, five			
			ə	represents:
j	jam, enjoy			a in about
k	kind, seek			e in taken
l	land, coal			i in pencil
m	me, am			o in lemon
n	no, in			u in circus
ng	long, bring			
o	hot, rock			
ō	open, go			
ô	order, all			
oi	oil, voice			
ou	house, out			

Scott, Foresman
Intermediate Dictionary

by E.L. Thorndike/Clarence L. Barnhart

Scott, Foresman and Company

Editorial Offices: Glenview, Illinois

Regional Offices: Sunnyvale, California ·
Tucker, Georgia · Glenview, Illinois ·
Oakland, New Jersey · Dallas, Texas

ISBN: 0-673-12384-7

2345678910-RRW-969594939291908988887

CONTENTS

PREFACE

The Intermediate Dictionary is designed specifically for use in schools and for study at home by young people who are passing from the simple curriculum of the lower elementary grades to the more complex studies of high school. A staff of editors long experienced in writing school dictionaries has examined every entry for clarity. All material has been selected to reflect the pluralism of our society, and at the same time to avoid unfortunate stereotypes. Illustrations have been carefully chosen to augment definitions and to stimulate an interest in language. The striking and innovative use of graphics will encourage the user to browse through the book.

The selection of words and meanings in this dictionary was checked against current word frequency counts. To supplement these counts, a wide variety of contemporary textbooks and other literature was read to check for new words and meanings. This reading is backed up by Scott, Foresman's citation files, which contain more than one million examples of words in use continually collected from newspapers, children's and general magazines, books, and other publications.

The attractive format of the Intermediate Dictionary will encourage young people to notice and retain interesting facts and impressions about words. Since words that express feelings, qualities, ideas, and actions deserve to be illustrated as much as words for things, such entries as *pensive, enthrall, jubilation,* and *dapper* have been dramatized to broaden and deepen young people's conversational and written vocabulary. The hundreds of illustrations—photographs, drawings, movie stills, maps, collages, charts—were specially chosen to promote browsing and incidental learning in which the user absorbs more than the specific information being sought. Many of these illustrations are enhanced by the addition of color. All pictures and their captions are set full-column width. Definitions are not run around the illustrations, thereby avoiding short lines and excessive hyphenation that make reading difficult. Picture captions give the size of animals both in the customary way and in the metric system.

An important feature of the Intermediate Dictionary is the inclusion of about 1800 etymologies (word histories) to create an awareness of and interest in the origins of words. Some of these are featured in colored frames. The etymologies are simply written in sentence form and use no abbreviations. They were chosen for their interest, and often include the date that a word entered English, as well as the language it came from, and its meaning in that language.

For the first time in a dictionary, word families, showing many different English words that go back to a common root, are included. These word families are featured in colored frames. In an indirect way they can be a means of increasing vocabulary, since a student who knows the root and its meaning should be able to recognize this root in an unfamiliar word. Furthermore, the meaning of the root could be a clue to the meaning of the unfamiliar word. Word families, by helping students see the relationship between words and teaching them basic roots, are an important tool in language study.

To help students acquire the skills necessary to derive the greatest benefit from dictionary use, self-teaching lessons are included in the front of the book. They are illustrated with photographs and drawings, and are designed to appeal to students. These lessons have been successfully tested in the classroom. An answer key for the lesson section is in the back of the book on page 1063.

We have been guided at all times during our work on this dictionary by the basic principles that for more than fifty years have made the Thorndike-Barnhart series leaders in the development and improvement of dictionaries designed for every level of school use. We trust that this new edition of the Intermediate Dictionary will successfully carry on the tradition of excellence that has enabled millions of young people to improve their understanding of and their ability to speak and write American English.

The Editors

HOW TO USE THIS DICTIONARY

There are words to name almost everything you have seen or can imagine. Words name animals, people, parts of the body, places, machines, and ideas. There are words to tell almost everything that you can do. There are words to describe how things look or feel or act.

Quite often, we have questions or problems about words similar to those that the people in the drawings below have. What does a word mean, how is it pronounced, how is it spelled, and where did it come from? A dictionary helps answer these questions because it tells us so much about words.

The dictionary tells about:

MEANING

PRONUNCIATION

SPELLING

WORD HISTORY

A dictionary has to give many different kinds of information about thousands of words. All of this information has to be organized so that you can find it when you need it. These lessons will help you learn how to find words and understand what the dictionary says about them.

How to Find Words

ENTRY WORDS

The words that a dictionary explains are called entry words. Entry words are printed in heavy black type and start at the left of each column. Some entry words are made up of more than one word. All the words in the dictionary are listed in alphabetical order.

Below are eight entry words from this dictionary. Read them and their definitions. Then answer the questions that follow.

back gam mon (bak′gam′ən), game for two played on a special board with 12 spaces on each side. Each player has 15 pieces, which are moved according to the throw of the dice. *n.*

Bronx (brongks), **The,** borough of New York City, the only one on the mainland. *n.*

clav i chord (klav′ə kôrd), a musical instrument with strings and a keyboard. The piano developed from it. *n.*

etc., et cetera. *Etc.* is usually read "and so forth." The definition of *equality* reads "sameness in amount, size, number, value, rank, etc." *Etc.* in this and similar definitions shows that the definition applies to many similar items in addition to the ones mentioned.

Frank en stein (frang′kən stīn), **1** scientist in a novel, written in 1818 by Mary Wollstonecraft Shelley, who creates a monster that he cannot control. **2** the monster itself. *n.*

Ho mo sa pi ens (hō′mō sā′pē enz), the species including all existing races of human beings.

in fat u a tion (in fach′ü ā′shən), exaggerated fondness or passion; foolish love. *n.*

-or, *suffix added to verbs to form nouns.* person or thing that _____s: *Actor = person who acts. Accelerator = thing that accelerates.*

► *TEACH YOURSELF*

6

ALPHABETICAL ORDER

> We are lined up in alphabetical order.
>
> Al | Dot | Gus | Pat | Viv | Zac   Sis
>
> I belong between Pat and Viv.

The entry words in a dictionary are always in alphabetical order from A to Z. A dictionary has a section for each letter of the alphabet. The first letter of a word tells you which section of the dictionary to look in.

You will find words beginning with the letters *a through f* in the first ⅓ of this book. You will find words beginning with the letters *g through p* in the middle ⅓ of this book. You will find words beginning with the letters *q through z* in the last ⅓ of this book.

Suppose you wanted to look up the words *dense, doodle,* and *damage* in your dictionary. All three words start with the letter *d,* and you know you will find them in the section of the dictionary that lists words beginning with *d.*

But which of the words is listed first? To find out, look at the second letter in each word. Words with the same first letter are alphabetized by their second letters, then by their third letters, and so on. Now you know that *damage* will come first, then *dense,* then *doodle.*

EXERCISE

A. Here are the names of six students in a class. Find what city they live in by alphabetizing the names, writing the second letter of each in the circle, and reading the circled letters down.

Laura   1. _____○_____

Una   2. _____○_____

Craig   3. _____○_____

Wanda   4. _____○_____

Ebenezer   5. _____○_____

Buddy   6. _____○_____

B. Now copy the following words in alphabetical order and circle the letter in each indicated by the number on the line next to it. When you read the circled letters down, they will give you the name of the state the city is in.

peremptorily   _____ 8

perfectionist   _____ 6

perhaps   _____ 11

perennial   _____ 7

percolate   _____ 10

perfidy   _____ 9

perceptible   _____ 5

perfection   _____ 7

GUIDE WORDS

At the top of every page in this dictionary are two guide words printed in heavy black type. Guide words make it easier for you to find entry words. Turn to page 577 and you will see these guide words:

microscopic | midge

The first guide word is **microscopic** as that is the first entry word on the page. The other guide word is **midge,** the last entry word on the page. All the words found between these two guide words are listed in alphabetical order. *Middy blouse* follows *middy* in alphabetical order and comes before *Mideast.* It is an entry word on page 577.

▶ *TEACH YOURSELF*

1. Suppose you want to find *knickers* in your dictionary. Turn to the first page that has words starting with the letters *kn.* It is page 507. What are the guide words for the page?
2. Does *knickers* come between these guide words in alphabetical order?
3. Is *knickers* on this page?
4. Now use the guide words to find *puttee* in your dictionary.
5. On what page did you find *puttee?*
6. What are the guide words for the page?

EXERCISE

This **middy blouse** comes between microscopic and midge.

My **knickers** come between kisser and knight-errant.

My **puttees** come between pushy and PWA.

In the beach scene, various things are numbered and identified. Below are corresponding numbers with three guide word combinations. Write each number, and choose the letter of the guide words for the page on which you would find the word.

1. bathing suit   2. sea   3. boat   4. leg

5. child   6. sand   7. goatee   8. umbrella

1. a. baseboard | Bastille   b. bastion | batter   c. battered | bayonet

2. a. scrutiny | sea   b. sea anemone | seam   c. seaman | seat

3. a. boastful | bogey   b. bogeyman | bolt   c. bomb | boneless

4. a. lead | learned   b. learner | lectern   c. lecture | legalize

5. a. chew | childless   b. childlike | chink   c. chink | chloroform

6. a. saloon | Samoa   b. samovar | sandstorm   c. sandwich | Saracen

7. a. glue | go   b. goad | godchild   c. goddaughter | gondola

8. a. U | Ulysses   b. umbel | unapproachable   c. unarm | unbroken

HOMOGRAPHS

The **fan** fainted.

She was revived with a **fan**.

Sometimes two or more words have the same spelling but different origins and meanings. They are called homographs. A small raised number after an entry word tells you that at least one other entry word has the same spelling. If the first word is not the one you want, the number reminds you to look at the next one.

fan[1] (fan), instrument or device with which to stir the air in order to cool or ventilate a room, remove odors, cool one's face, etc. One kind of fan can be folded or spread out into part of a circle. Another kind consists of a series of revolving blades turned by an electric motor. . . . *n.* [*Fan*[1] is from Old English *fann*, which came from Latin *vannus*.]

fan[2] (fan), . . . person extremely interested in some sport, the movies, television, etc.: *A baseball fan would hate to miss the championship game.* . . . *n.* [*Fan*[2] was shortened from *fanatic*.]

▶*TEACH YOURSELF*

1. Which homograph of *fan* is pictured in the first cartoon?
2. Which one is being used in the second cartoon?

EXERCISES

1. How many homographs do you find in your dictionary for each of the following spellings?
   a. arm   b. bay   c. flag   d. grave   e. ring
2. Decide which homograph of each italicized word is used.
   a. The *cow's* mooing *cowed* the puppy.
   b. When they *alighted* from the plane, their faces were *alight* with happiness.
   c. I weighed the *scaled* fish on a *scale*.
   d. She *felt* disappointed when her *flight* was canceled.
   e. Take a *cue* from me and hold your *cue* like this.
   f. The official *closed* the document with a *seal*.
   g. I *jogged* for a mile down the *pike*.
   h. When he backed up the car, he *squashed* the *squash*.
   i. A *mole scuttled* across the road.
   j. Our *hosts* served *perch* for dinner.

WORDS THAT AREN'T ENTRY WORDS

Lonesome George, a giant Galápagos tortoise, was found *plodding* across one of the Galápagos Islands in 1971, just going about his usual *activities*. Up to that moment, scientists *believed* that tortoises of his type no longer *existed*. Lonesome George may be the *loneliest* animal in the world. As the only known creature of his kind, he is certainly the *rarest*. He is thought to be about 50 years old, and will probably live for another hundred years.

Lonesome George now lives at a research center, penned in with tortoises of another type. He seems happier now that he has company. Meanwhile, scientists are investigating the possibilities of locating a mate for him. He goes on with his life, not realizing that all over the world a search is going on. Female giant Galápagos tortoises in zoos are being scrutinized on the merest chance that one of them might have been wrongly identified, and might possibly be the same type of tortoise as Lonesome George.

Lonesome George

The words in italics in the story above are not entry words in your dictionary. Many words with the endings *-s, -es, -ed, -ing, -er,* and *-est* are not. To find the meaning of these words, which are called inflected forms, look up the root word to which the ending was added.

► *TEACH YOURSELF*

1. To find *plodding,* look up *plod.* Notice that the inflected forms are given in heavy type after the definition. What letter is added to plod before the endings?
2. To find *activities,* look up *activity.* What letter of *activity* changes when *-es* is added?
3. To find *believed,* look up *believe.* What letter is dropped from *believe* before an ending is added?
4. To find *loneliest,* look up *lonely.* What letter of *lonely* changes before *-est* is added?
5. To find *rarest,* look up *rare.* What letter is dropped from *rare* before the ending?
6. *Existed* is also italicized above. To find it, look up *exist.* There are no inflected forms after the definition. Why?

In answer to the last question, if you said that the inflected forms are not listed because the spelling of *exist* does not change when you add the endings, you were right. This dictionary gives inflected forms for a word only if its spelling changes when an ending is added.

EXERCISE

To look up the following words used in the story, what entry word do you have to find in your dictionary?

1. penned
2. happier
3. investigating
4. possibilities
5. locating
6. realizing
7. scrutinized
8. merest
9. identified

The island where Lonesome George was found was searched <u>intensively</u>, but no other tortoises were there. Many <u>dragonlike</u> iguanas and lizards lived on the island, which is Ecuadorian territory, and it was overpopulated with goats, which had been thoughtlessly introduced by sailors. The overabundant goats destroyed the previously unmarred plant life, which the nonaggressive tortoises needed to survive. The destructiveness of people also played a part. However, if Lonesome George does get a mate, his offspring will be carefully protected at the research center. Then tortoises will be reintroduced onto the island.

Many words in the story above are not entry words in your dictionary. They are formed by adding either prefixes or suffixes to other words. The prefixes and suffixes add new meaning to the basic word. A word with a suffix is sometimes found at the end of the entry for the basic word and is printed in heavy type. That word is called a run-on entry. To get the meaning of a run-on entry, combine the meaning of the entry word with the meaning of the suffix.

in ten sive (in ten′siv), **1** deep and thorough: *New laws were passed following an intensive study of the causes of pollution.* **2** (in grammar) giving force or emphasis; expressing intensity. In "I did it myself," *myself* is an intensive pronoun. **3** word, prefix, etc., that expresses intensity or gives force or emphasis. In "It's terribly late," *terribly* is an intensive. 1,2 *adj.*, 3 *n.* —**in ten′sive ly,** *adv.* —**in ten′sive ness,** *n.*

-ly[1], *suffix added to adjectives to form adverbs.* **1** in a _____ manner: *Cheerfully = in a cheerful manner.* **2** in _____ ways or respects: *Financially = in financial respects.* **3** to a _____ degree or extent: *Greatly = to a great degree.* **4** in, to, or from a _____ direction: *Northerly = to or from the north.* **5** in a _____ place: *Thirdly = in the third place.* **6** at a _____ time: *Recently = at a recent time.*

You can now see that *intensively*, the first underlined word in the story, means "in a deep and thorough manner."

The second underlined word, *dragonlike*, is not listed in this dictionary at all. But it is simple to find its meaning by looking up these two entry words:

drag on (drag′ən), (in old stories) a huge, fierce animal supposed to look like a winged snake with claws, which often breathed out fire and smoke. *n.*

-like, *suffix added to nouns to form adjectives.* **1** like: *Wolflike = like a wolf.* **2** like that of; characteristic of: *Childlike = like that of a child.*

EXERCISE

The following words are from the story above. What entry words would you have to look up to find the meaning of each word? Write down the number before each word and after it write your answer.

1. Ecuadorian
2. overpopulated
3. thoughtlessly
4. overabundant

5. unmarred
6. nonaggressive
7. destructiveness
8. reintroduced

WORD COMBINATIONS AND NAMES

Sometimes two or more words together are an entry word. Examples of such entry words are *battle royal* and *parlor car*.

Knowing the meaning of the words *battle* and *royal* does not make clear the meaning of *battle royal*. Knowing what *parlor* and *car* mean tells you little about *parlor car*. When a combination of words like these puzzles you, look to see if the combined form is an entry word.

Some entries of more than one word are names of places. These are easy to recognize because they are capitalized. On page 399 there are several such entry words: *Great Lakes, Great Plains, Great Salt Lake.*

Names of people are capitalized too. People are usually listed under their family names, not under their first names. For example, you will find *Marie Curie* in the *c*'s, not in the *m*'s.

EXERCISE

Look up each entry word printed in italics below. Answer each question yes or no and give the reason for your answer. Do it like this: 1. No, it's a muscle cramp.

1. Could you ride a *charley horse?*
2. Would a fisherman catch a *red herring?*
3. Does the postman deliver *chain mail?*
4. Can a person be a *lame duck?*
5. Is *aqueous humor* a kind of joke?
6. Does a *sea dog* bark?
7. Would a kitten sleep in a *cat's cradle?*
8. Would you eat an *honor roll* for breakfast?

IDIOMS

Have you ever been told to stop *pulling someone's leg?*

Were you ever *brought to your knees* by an opponent?

If so, you did not actually do the things the people are doing in the pictures. To *pull one's leg* has nothing to do with grabbing someone's leg and pulling it. You were being told to stop fooling someone.

The italicized phrases above are called idioms. Their meanings are not understood from the ordinary meanings of the words in them. An idiom is listed in the dictionary under its most important word. Idioms are at the end of an entry in heavy black type.

To find the meaning of the idiom *bring to one's knees,* you would look under the entry *knee.* Here is what you would find:

> **knee** (nē), **1** the joint between the thigh and the lower leg. **2** any joint in a four-footed animal corresponding to the human knee or elbow. **3** anything like a bent knee in shape or position. **4** part of a garment covering the knee. *n.*
> **bring to one's knees,** force to yield.

EXERCISE

The idioms below also involve parts of the body. Look up each one after determining the most important word in it. The picture should help you. On a piece of paper, write each number, and the word under which the idiom is listed. Then write the meaning of the idiom (a or b).

1. We always *see eye to eye.*   most important word   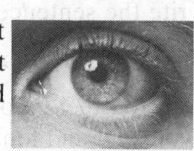   a. We always look at each other with our noses touching.   b. We agree entirely.

2. Don't *split hairs* about minor details.   most important word      a. If you cut your hair it's a minor detail.   b. Don't make fine distinctions about minor details.

3. She can *play the piano by ear.*   most important word   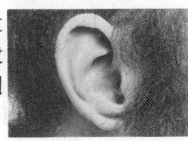   a. She can play the piano without written music.   b. She can use her ears to play the keys of the piano.

EXERCISE

Look up the following idioms in your dictionary. Write each number and after it write the entry word under which you found the idiom.

1. see red
2. no great shakes
3. up a tree
4. rub the wrong way
5. place on a pedestal
6. keep one's eyes peeled
7. eat crow
8. call it quits
9. lend a hand

Test Yourself

1. Suppose you had a friend named Winifred G. Whizdom who became famous and had her name added to the dictionary.

   a. Between what two entry words would her name be?
   b. Between what guide words would her name be?

2. For each of the following sentences, look up all the entries spelled the same as the word in italics. Decide which entry is used in the sentence. Write each letter, and after it write your answer.

   a. On May 16, 1975, Junko Tabei of Japan became the first woman to reach the *top* of Mount Everest, the world's highest mountain.
   b. Junko was one of 15 Japanese women mountaineers chosen to make an attempt to *scale* the peak.
   c. She had already climbed every major Japanese peak, as well as another *steep* mountain in the Himalayas.
   d. At one point in the month-long climb, an avalanche *left* 10 of the women injured.
   e. The group did not *let* high winds and harsh conditions stop them.
   f. Junko was selected to make the final part of the climb, because she was in better physical condition than the *rest.*
   g. After struggling through bad weather for five hours, she and a guide finally reached the *tip* of the peak.
   h. Afterward, when asked to comment on her great accomplishment, Junko insisted that the *real* credit belonged to the entire group.

3. Look up each of the animals in the sentence below. When you have found the plural for each animal, rewrite the sentence using the plural forms.

   The moose, the ox, the calf, and the goose were upset by the mouse.

4. The following paragraphs contain fourteen idioms that include parts of the body. Write down each idiom you find and look it up in your dictionary. Then underline the word under which you found the idiom. Do it like this: twiddle his <u>thumbs</u>.

   John couldn't decide if he should twiddle his thumbs and hope for a miracle or rack his brains for the right answers to the science test. He really had his hands full. He had passed the last test by the skin of his teeth, and the teacher had turned a cold shoulder to his excuses. "If you would take to heart my reading assignments, hold your tongue when I explain the lessons, and keep on your toes during class, you wouldn't lose your head every time we have a test," she said.

   John made no bones about the fact that he was in trouble. After this he would be all ears in science class. He would really knuckle down. But on this test he was risking his neck making wild guesses, even though he was trying to keep a stiff upper lip.

How to Use the Pronunciations

a shaky skater

a derailed train

a jay at play

a great steak

a veiled reindeer

eight n**eigh**bors

The gr**ey**hound ob**ey**ed.

Look at the examples above. Notice the different ways that this one sound (long *a*) is spelled.

It would be easy to pronounce words if each letter of the alphabet stood for only one sound. But that is not the case. The English language has more than 40 sounds, while its alphabet has only 26 letters.

This dictionary uses special symbols to help you pronounce words. There is one symbol for each sound. Twenty-three of the symbols are letters of the alphabet. Each letter stands for its most common sound.

► *TEACH YOURSELF*

> **fun** (fun)   **laugh** (laf)   **phone** (fōn)

Of course you know how to pronounce the words given above in heavy type.

1. Say each word. How many sounds do you hear in each word?
2. Look at the pronunciation given in parentheses after each word. Are the number of symbols the same as the number of sounds you heard?
3. Look carefully at each of the pronunciations in parentheses. There is one symbol that occurs in all three pronunciations. What symbol is it?

If you said the symbol (f) you were correct. The first sound in the word *phone* and the last sound in the word *laugh* are the same as the sound of the letter *f* in the word *fun.* The letter *f* is used in the pronunciations as the symbol for this sound, whether the sound is spelled *ph, gh,* or *f.*

THE PRONUNCIATION KEY AND VOWEL SOUNDS

Inside each cover of this dictionary is a pronunciation key. It tells you what sound each pronunciation symbol used in this dictionary stands for. Turn to the pronunciation key. Look at the first symbol (a) and the words *hat* and *cap* that follow it. The words *hat* and *cap* are called key words. They tell you that whenever you see the symbol (a) in a pronunciation, you say the same sound that you say for the letter *a* in the words *hat* and *cap*.

Now look at the symbols (e), (i), (o), and (u). Pronounce the key words for each of these symbols. The sounds that the symbols (a), (e), (i), (o), and (u) stand for are often called the short vowel sounds.

► *TEACH YOURSELF*

Pronounce the key words that tell you what to say when you see the pronunciation symbol (s). Now pronounce the following words: *sand, circle, silly, can, city, scene, psalm, coat, sugar.* Which of these words begin with the sound that you heard when you pronounced the key words for the symbol (s)?

When you become familiar with the pronunciation key inside the covers of your book, turn to any right-hand page of your dictionary. At the top of the outside column is a short pronunciation key. It, too, shows pronunciation symbols with a key word. If you forget what a pronunciation symbol stands for, you may find it here.

EXERCISE

wreck	rack
dance	dunce
sieve	salve
ledge	lodge
gnat	knot
gym	gem
calf	cuff
prince	prance
sick	sock

Each of the numbered pronunciations below stands for one of the words shown above. Using the pronunciation key, match each word to its pronunciation. Do it like this: 1. cuff

1. (kuf)	7. (duns)	13. (siv)
2. (not)	8. (rek)	14. (dans)
3. (jem)	9. (sik)	15. (jim)
4. (sav)	10. (nat)	16. (prins)
5. (loj)	11. (rak)	17. (lej)
6. (prans)	12. (kaf)	18. (sok)

VOWELS WITH SPECIAL MARKS

bait (bāt)　　**seed** (sēd)　　**kite** (kīt)　　**bone** (bōn)

You already know that the vowel letters *a, e, i, o,* and *u* without marks over them are used as pronunciation symbols. They stand for the short vowel sounds. Each of the pronunciations above has a symbol in it that stands for the long vowel sounds. These symbols (ā), (ē), (ī), and (ō) are vowel letters with special marks over them called diacritical marks. The long *u* is actually a combination of two sounds, so it takes two symbols to show its pronunciation.

EXERCISE

Look at the symbols and key words given to the right. Say all the key words to yourself several times. Make sure you can hear the difference in each pair on the same line. Pronounce the following groups of words.

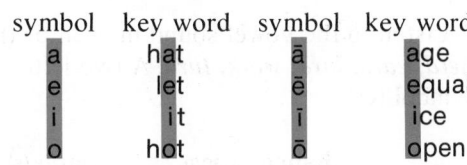

symbol	key word	symbol	key word
a	hat	ā	age
e	let	ē	equal
i	it	ī	ice
o	hot	ō	open

1. Jane ate dad's ham
   Which of these words have the sound (ā)?
2. we helped red hen eat bread
   Which of these words have the sound (ē)?
3. six nice tin mice
   Which of these words have the sound (ī)?
4. coal boat broke dock
   Which of these words have the sound (ō)?

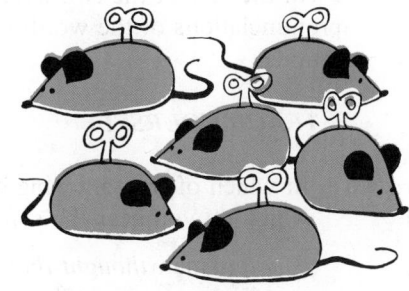

Four other pronunciation symbols are vowel letters with marks over them. They are (ä) as in *father* and *far,* (ô) as in *order* and *all,* (ù) as in *full* and *put,* and (ü) as in *rule* and *move.*

EXERCISE

Look at the symbols and key words given to the right.

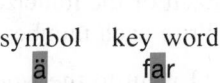
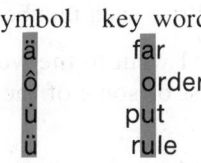

symbol	key word
ä	far
ô	order
ù	put
ü	rule

1. Which of these words have the sound (ä)?
   tan ants play cards and darts
2. Which of these words have the sound (ô)?
   tots crawl not walk
3. Which of these words have the sound (ù)?
   woods full of wolves
4. Which of these words have the sound (ü)?
   who put shoe in cook's soup
5. Pronounce the words *mule* and *fuel.* These words are pronounced with a long *u.* The symbols (yü) together stand for this pronunciation. Which of the following words have the pronunciation (yü)?
   few moose use tools

TWO-LETTER SYMBOLS

symbol	key word
ėr	tĕrm
oi	oil
ou	out

All but one of the remaining pronunciation symbols are made up of two letters. Two of these two-letter symbols are for the vowel sounds (oi) and (ou). The sound (oi) is the sound you hear in the words *oil* and *toy*. The sound (ou) is the sound you hear in *mouse* and *out*.

▶ *TEACH YOURSELF*

1. Tell which of the following words have the vowel sound (ou) in them:
   loud   crowd   bought   now   grow   group
2. Tell which of the following words have the vowel sound (oi) in them:
   coin   aisle   toy   count   noise

Listen to the vowel sound in each of the following words as you say them: *herd, earn, bird, work, turn.* A two-letter symbol stands for this sound. It is the symbol (ėr).

chance (chans)   **shop** (shop)   **breathe** (brēᵺH)
sing (sing)   **breath** (breth)   **rouge** (rüzh)

All the rest of the two-letter symbols used in this dictionary are in the pronunciations of the words above. These symbols all stand for consonant sounds.

▶ *TEACH YOURSELF*

symbol	key word
ch	child
ng	long
sh	she
th	thin
ᵺH	then
zh	measure

1. In which of the following italicized words do you hear the sound (th)? In which do you hear the sound (ᵺH)?

   The thin man *thought that this thrush thrived* on *thistles.*

2. In which of the following italicized words do you hear the sound (ch)? In which do you hear the sound (sh)? In which do you hear the sound (zh)?

   The *shop* had *cheap beige shoes* with *arch* supports.

EXERCISE

Each of the italicized words contains one of the numbered sounds listed below. Write each number and after it write the word which has this sound.

I went to the world's worst garage sale. I didn't spend a cent, but here is a list of some of the *junk* that was sold.

A *sketch* of a man with a beard
A rusty *scythe*
A moldy stuffed *owl*
Some music for bass *voice* and flute
A *fur* coat complete with a *moth*
A hat for a *chef*
A book on the life of *Jeanne* d'Arc

1. (ėr)	3. (ou)	5. (ng)	7. (th)	9. (zh)
2. (oi)	4. (ch)	6. (sh)	8. (ᵺH)	

SYLLABLES AND ACCENT

jump (jump) **jump y** (jum′pē)   **jump i ness** (jum′pē nis)
hand (hand) **hand ful** (hand′fŭl) **hand i work** (han′dē wėrk′)
half (haf)   **half way** (haf′wā′) **half heart ed** (haf′här′tid)

Say the three words in the first list above. Notice that in these words you hear only one vowel sound.

▶ *TEACH YOURSELF*

1. Say the words in the second list. How many vowel sounds do you hear in each word? Into how many parts is each word divided?
2. How many vowel sounds do you hear in each word in the third list? Into how many parts is each of these words divided?

 Each part of a word in which we hear one vowel sound is called a syllable. In the pronunciations, words are divided into syllables by a space. The words in the first list have only one syllable. Those in the second list have two. Those in the third list have three.

 When we say a word having two or more syllables, we accent at least one of the syllables. That is, we say it with more force or stress than we do the others. In the pronunciations above, some syllables are followed by the marks (′) and (′). The darker mark (′), called a primary accent, follows the syllable we say with the most force. The lighter mark (′), a secondary accent, follows the syllable we say with medium force. Syllables which are not followed by marks are unaccented or unstressed syllables. We say them with the least force.

EXERCISE

The words below are divided into syllables for you. Say each word, noticing where the stress falls. Then copy the words putting accent marks after the stressed syllable or syllables. (If a word has two stressed syllables, both primary and secondary accents will be needed.)

1. em ploy	3. laugh ing stock	5. ra di a tor	7. chem is try
2. chick en	4. pas sen ger	6. so lid i ty	8. tor na do

 Sometimes in an unaccented syllable we do not say a vowel sound. Instead we say the sound (l) or (n). In these syllables (l) and (n) are called syllabic consonants. Here are some words that have syllables without vowel sounds.

lit tle (lit′l)   **jour nal** (jėr′nl) **re cent** (rē′snt)
hast i ly (hā′stl ē) **cot ton** (kot′n) **sea son** (sē′zn)

THE SCHWA

a in **a bout** (ə bout′)
e in **tak en** (tā′kən)
i in **pen cil** (pen′səl)
o in **lem on** (lem′ən)
u in **cir cus** (sėr′kəs)

There is one more pronunciation symbol used in this dictionary. It is called schwa (shwä) and looks like this: (ə). It is a vowel sound heard only in unaccented syllables. See the symbol (ə) and its five key words given at the left. When you pronounce the key words, you hear the same sound for the *a* in *about,* the *e* in *taken,* the *i* in *pencil,* the *o* in *lemon,* and the *u* in *circus.* In an unaccented syllable, any of the five vowel letters can have the sound represented by (ə). Some combinations of vowel letters can have the sound (ə) too.

► *TEACH YOURSELF*

e nor mous (i nôr′məs)   **lunch eon** (lun′chən)   **fash ion** (fash′ən)
bar gain (bär′gən)   **tor toise** (tôr′təs)   **ep au let** (ep′ə let)

In each word above, what combination of vowel letters has the sound represented by (ə)?

EXERCISE

A psychologist named Sigmund Schwa became a famous vocational counselor. But he would only recommend and place his clients in jobs that had the sound of schwa in them.

Below are pictures of some of the satisfied people that he helped. The schwa symbol (ə) is used at least once in pronouncing the nine underlined words that appear under the picture or in the balloon caption. Write each word, and circle the vowel letter or letters in each which have the sound represented by (ə).

vō kā'shə nəl koun'sə lər

sig'mənd shwä sī kol'ə jist

I'm an authority on taxes.

accountant

I play in the orchestra.

clarinetist

I get specimens for the aquarium.

marine biologist

My work can be dangerous.

mountaineer

VARIANT PRONUNCIATIONS

Most entries in this dictionary give only one pronunciation. It is the pronunciation you will almost always hear. Some entries, however, give more than one pronunciation. For example, two pronunciations are given for *rodeo* (rō′dē ō *or* rō dā′ō). The pronunciation (rō′dē ō) is given first, not because it is more correct than (rō dā′ō), but because scholars think it is used by more people than (rō dā′ō). If you are one of the people who say (rō dā′ō), you are just as correct as those who say (rō′dē ō).

Sometimes when the meaning of a word changes, its pronunciation changes too. The word *separate* is pronounced one way when it is used as a verb and another way when it is used as an adjective. Here is the way this is shown in the pronunciation of *separate*.

sep a rate (sep′ə rāt′ *for 1-5;* sep′ər it *for 6-8*)

►*TEACH YOURSELF*

1. Look at the entry *separate* and read the definitions. Tell which pronunciation is correct for each sentence: a. (sep′ə rāt′) b. (sep′ər it).

    The mad scientist *separated* the acid and sulfur.
    He put them into *separate* containers.

2. Look up the entry *conduct* and read the definitions. Tell which pronunciation is correct for each sentence: a. (kon′dukt) b. (kən dukt′).

    He began to *conduct* his dangerous experiment.
    He did not realize that his *conduct* might be criticized if a murderous monster resulted.

EXERCISE

The pronunciation of each of the following words in italics changes when its meaning changes. Read each sentence and decide how the numbered italicized words are pronounced. Write the number of each word, and after it write *a* if the correct pronunciation is in column a, *b* if the correct pronunciation is in column b.

I (1) *rebel* at being called a (2) *rebel.*
Our dog was (3) *confined* to the house because he wouldn't stay within the (4) *confines* of the yard.
Would you (5) *object* if I painted that (6) *object* purple?
A skateboard is (7) *inclined* to go rapidly down an (8) *incline.*
(9) *Record* what is said at this meeting, so that we will have a (10) *record* for our next meeting.
And so on behalf of all of us, I (11) *present* this (12) *present* to you.
They (13) *suspect* that the (14) *suspect* is not telling the truth.
The players were (15) *upset* when their team suffered an (16) *upset.*

	a	b		a	b
rebel	(reb′əl)	(ri bel′)	**record**	(ri kôrd′)	(rek′ərd)
confine	(kən fīn′)	(kon′fīn)	**present**	(prez′nt)	(pri zent′)
object	(ob′jikt)	(əb jekt′)	**suspect**	(sə spekt′)	(sus′pekt)
incline	(in klīn′)	(in′klīn)	**upset**	(up′set′)	(up set′)

Test Yourself

1. Use your dictionary to answer these questions:
   a. Does *campanile* rhyme with *crocodile, repeal,* or *steely?*
   b. Does *bury* rhyme with *hurry, ferry,* or *fury?*
   c. Does *faille* rhyme with *mile, fail,* or *pal?*
   d. Does *coup* rhyme with *stoup, who,* or *taupe?*
   e. Does *chamois* rhyme with *tortoise, mammy,* or *patois?*

2. The clues for this crossword puzzle are the pronunciations of common words. Copy the puzzle or get a copy from your teacher. Fill in the puzzle with the words that the pronunciations stand for.

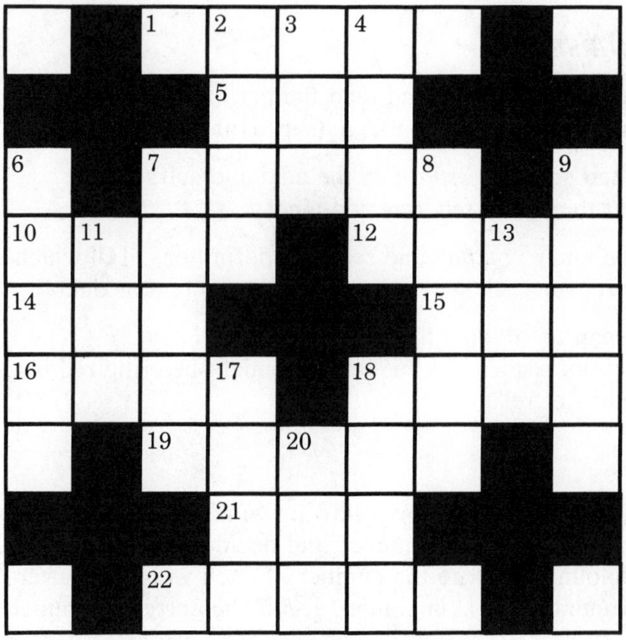

ACROSS

1. (spend)
5. (āj)
7. (krôs)
10. (rer *or* rar)
12. (thin)
14. (yü)
15. (ôr)
16. (els)
18. (ren)
19. (tas′it)
21. (rod)
22. (ang′gər)

DOWN

2. (per *or* par)
3. (ē′gō)
4. (nest)
6. (grēk)
7. (krest)
8. (shôrt)
9. (ə nent′)
11. (ôl)
13. (īr)
17. (ėrn)
18. (wīd)
20. (kog)

Test Yourself

In *The Canterville Ghost,* a story by Oscar Wilde, an American diplomat named Mr. Otis buys a historic house in England. When he and his family move in, the scary spook who has been living there for over three hundred years soon becomes only a ghost of his former self.

In the following sentences, which describe how Mr. Otis first meets the ghost, some of the words are written in pronunciation symbols. Read the sentences, using the pronunciation key whenever you need help. Then rewrite the story spelling out the words written in symbols.

Mr. Otis was (ə wā′kənd) by a curious (noiz) in the (hôl), (out′sīd′) his (rüm). It sounded (līk) the (klangk) of (met′l), and (sēmd) to be coming (nir′ər) every (mō′mənt). He (pùt) on his (slip′ərz), (tùk) a small (ob′lông) phial from his (dres′ər), and (ō′pənd) the (dôr). Right in (frunt) of him he (sô) an (ōld) man of (ter′ə bəl) aspect. Long (grā) (her) fell (ō′vər) his (shōl′dərz) in matted (koilz). His (gär′mənts) were of antique (kut), and from his (rists) and (ang′kəlz) hung (hev′ē) manacles and (rus′tē) fetters.

QUESTION: What kind of hair did the ghost have?

"My (dir) (sėr)," said Mr. Otis, "I really must insist on (yùr) oiling those (chānz) and have (brôt) you for (ᴛʜat) purpose a small (bot′l) of (lü′brə kā′- ting) oil."

QUESTION: Was Mr. Otis afraid of the ghost?

For a (mō′mənt) the (kan′tər vil) (gōst) stood (kwīt) motionless in natural (in′dig nā′shən). Then, dashing the bottle (vī′ə lənt lē) upon the (pol′isht) floor, he fled. On (rē′ching) the west wing, he (lēnd) up (ə genst′) a (mün′bēm′) to recover his (breth). Never, in a (bril′yənt) and (un′in tə rup′tid) career of (thrē) hundred (yirz), had he (bin) so grossly (in sul′tid).

QUESTION: Did the ghost like Mr. Otis's gift?

How to Find a Meaning

CONTEXT

From her earliest years, Jane Goodall's <u>paramount</u> interest was in animals and nature. "My idea of *utopia* was to go to the country and look at animals," she says of her childhood in England. "I always kept notes on the way animals behaved." Jane had a *comprehensive* nature collection which contained skulls of <u>sundry</u> animals. She even published a small magazine of animal quizzes and stories, which her mother typed. She used to *apprise* everyone of her ambition—to go to Africa and study wild animals.

After she finished school, Jane worked in an office for several years. She was able to *accumulate* enough money to go to Africa in 1957. There she worked for Dr. Louis Leakey, a scientist famous for his discoveries in the field of *anthropology.* Jane wanted to study the behavior of animals in the wild by subjecting them to close *scrutiny* over a *protracted* period. Dr. Leakey suggested that she study the chimpanzees in the Gombe Stream game reserve on Lake Tanganyika.

Jane agreed. However, the government authorities were *adamant* in refusing permission. Nothing could convince them to let a young English girl go into the *bush* alone. Finally, Jane's mother agreed to go with her, and permission was granted.

It was many months before Jane could get close to the chimps. But she did not give up, and she was able to see them through binoculars. Eventually they accepted her, and she was then able to observe them at close range, making many *momentous* discoveries.

Chris was reading the story above. In the first sentence, he did not know the meaning of the word *paramount.* But as he continued to read, he realized that he would not have to look it up. The words used with it, which are called its context, made its meaning clear to him. When he got to the end of the paragraph, after reading about Jane's making notes on animals, having a nature collection, and publishing a nature magazine, he had decided that *paramount* meant chief or most important.

Look up *paramount* in your dictionary. You can see that Chris was right. He had found the word's meaning from its context.

Further on, Chris did not know the meaning of *sundry.* This time, nothing gave him a clue. When the context does not help to explain a word, you need to look it up in the dictionary. The definition for an entry word can often be used in place of the word in a sentence. A definition is a substitute for an entry word. Chris found the following definition for the word *sundry:*

sun dry . . . several; various: *From sundry hints, I guessed I was to be given a bicycle for my birthday.*

In the definition are the words *several* and *various.* They are both synonyms of *sundry.* A synonym is a word that means the same as another word. When synonyms are included in the definition of a word, it is easy to substitute one of them for the word in a sentence. Chris was able to substitute either *several* or *various* in the sentence he was reading. Then he understood that Jane Goodall's colle ٫tion contained skulls of several animals or, if he wanted to use the second synonym, skulls of various animals.

EXERCISES

1. Read each of the following sentences, trying to figure out the meaning of the word in italics from its context. Choose the meaning below which is closest to the one you figured out.

   a. Scientists believed chimpanzees were not *carnivorous* until Jane Goodall saw them occasionally kill and eat other animals.
      carnival performers   meat-eating   transported by car
   b. Her most important discovery was that chimps *fashion* simple tools and use them to help in getting food and water.
      make   wear   break
   c. When a chimp gave birth to a baby, Jane had an *unprecedented* opportunity—she was the first scientist to observe the development of a wild chimpanzee from birth.
      interesting   not prepared for   never known before
   d. Each chimp's personality is *unique;* Jane can recognize each one by its actions, voice, and looks, and has given each a name.
      friendly   one of a kind   bad-tempered
   e. Jane Goodall has become such a *luminary* in the field of scientific research that people all over the world know and admire her work.
      famous person   electrician   hard worker

2. Look up the following words italicized in the story about Jane Goodall on the opposite page. Write each letter, and after it write the definition you found that substitutes for the word in the story.

a. utopia	d. accumulate	g. protracted	j. momentous
b. comprehensive	e. anthropology	h. adamant	
c. apprise	f. scrutiny	i. bush	

A   B

dia mond (dī′mənd *or* dī′ə mənd), **1** a colorless or tinted precious stone, formed of pure carbon in crystals. Diamond is the hardest natural substance known. Inferior diamonds are used to cut glass. **2** figure shaped like this: ◇. **3** a playing card marked with one or more red, diamond-shaped figures. **4 diamonds,** *pl.* suit of such playing cards. **5** (in baseball) the area bounded by home plate and three bases; infield. *n.* —**dia′mond like′,** *adj.*

C

Many words have more than one meaning. The people in the cartoons are all talking about different kinds of diamonds. To the right above is the entry **diamond** in this dictionary. Each definition is numbered to help you find the meaning you are looking for. Can you match the meaning used by each cartoon character with the correct definition?

Many words also have more than one use in a sentence. That is, they can be used as more than one part of speech. The parts of speech are summarized by definition number after the last definition.

► *TEACH YOURSELF*

tack le (tak′əl), **1** equipment; apparatus; gear. Fishing tackle means the rod, line, hooks, etc., used in catching fish. **2** set of ropes and pulleys for lifting, lowering, or moving heavy things. The sails of a ship are raised and moved by tackle. **3** try to deal with: *We have a difficult problem to tackle.* **4** lay hold of; seize: *He tackled the boy who was running away and pulled him to the ground.* **5** (in football) seize and stop, or throw to the ground (an opponent who has the ball). **6** act of tackling. **7** an offensive or defensive player between the guard and the end on either side of the line in football. 1,2,6,7 *n.,* 3-5 *v.,* **tack led, tack ling.**

1. Read the entry for *tackle.* Notice the part-of-speech summary after definition 7. How many noun definitions does *tackle* have? How many verb definitions?
2. What part of speech is *tackle* as used in the cartoons?
3. What definition of *tackle* is used in the first cartoon?
4. What definition of *tackle* is used in the second cartoon?

EXERCISE

On a piece of paper, write the number of each sentence. Then look up and read the entry for the underlined word. Write the number of the definition used, and its part of speech.
1. We sailed the boat into the *harbor.*
2. It is silly to *harbor* a grudge.
3. We *panned* for gold on our trip to Colorado.
4. He fried the fish in a *pan* over the open fire.
5. My house is on the *far* side of town.
6. It is *far* better to try again than to give up.

LABELS

Some words or meanings of words are labeled to tell you how, when, or where they are used. In the cartoons to the right, each character is using words that are labeled in your dictionary. These words are underlined.

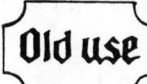 This label means that the word or meaning is not used much today. You may see it in stories or poems written long ago or about the past.

 Language labels mean that a word or meaning is used chiefly in certain countries or by people from those countries. The label LATIN means that the word is a Latin word.

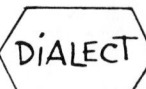 This label means that the word or meaning is used by people in a certain region of the United States, or by a certain group of people.

 This label means you might use the word or meaning in everyday talk, but you probably wouldn't use it in formal writing.

 This label means that you might use the word or meaning in familiar talk with your friends. It would not be appropriate in school themes, but is used in writing dialogue and to get a special effect.

Following are examples of the labels you will find in this dictionary:

y clept or **y cleped** (i klept/), OLD USE. called; named. *adj.*

right (rīt), . . . **22** DIALECT. extremely: *I am right glad to see you. . . . adv. . . .*

pad[1] (pad), . . . **10** SLANG. room, house, or apartment: *My pad is on the third floor.* 1,3-7,9,10 *n.,* 2,8 *v.*

burn[2] (bėrn), SCOTTISH. a small stream; brook. *n.*

a round (ə round/), . . . **8** INFORMAL. somewhere about; near: *I waited around for an hour* (*adv.*). *Stay around the house* (*prep.*).

EXERCISE

For each of the following sentences, look up the entry in italics in your dictionary. Then give its meaning and tell how it is labeled.

1. That car is a real *gas guzzler*.
2. I put my belongings in a *poke*.
3. She is a real hockey *buff*.
4. Thus *spake* the king.

5. That story is *bunk*.
6. Thou *wouldst* not betray me.
7. I'm tired of waiting. Let's *split*.
8. What a lovely wee *bairn*.

OLD USE

SCOTTISH

DIALECT

INFORMAL

SLANG

WORD HISTORIES

Word histories, also called etymologies, are listed for many of the words in this dictionary. Word histories tell such things as what language the word came from, how it is spelled in that language, and what it meant. Sometimes the modern English word has the same meaning as the word it came from. Notice the word history for *sparrow* below. In such cases, no meaning is shown for the original word.

The word history usually appears enclosed in brackets at the end of the entry, after the definition. However, some word histories in this dictionary are featured because they are of special interest. These featured word histories are enclosed in colored frames and usually appear right after or next to the entry. Some may also include a picture.

Some words started as English words, but over the years they may have changed a great deal.

spar row (spar′ō), any of various small, usually brownish songbirds common in North and South America but also found in Europe, Asia, and Africa. Sparrows are finches. *n.* [*Sparrow* comes from Old English *spearwa.*] **—spar′row like′,** *adj.*

game[1] (gām), **1** way of playing; pastime; amusement: *a game of tag, a game with bat and ball.* **2** things needed to play a game: *This store sells games.* **3** contest with certain rules: *a football game.* One person or side tries to win it. . . . [*Game*[1] comes from Old English *gamen,* meaning "joy."]

were wolf (wir′wu̇lf′), (in folklore) a person who changes into a wolf at certain times. *n., pl.* **were wolves** (wir′wu̇lvz′). Also, **werewolf.**

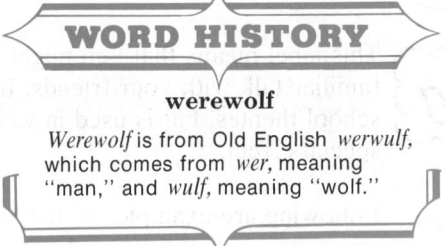

WORD HISTORY

werewolf

Werewolf is from Old English *werwulf,* which comes from *wer,* meaning "man," and *wulf,* meaning "wolf."

All the words above are derived from Old English, an earlier form of English spoken before the year 1100. If you look up the entry *Old English* in your dictionary, you will notice a chart next to it. This chart explains and gives some examples of Old English words, and shows how they have changed.

swap (swop), INFORMAL. **1** to exchange, barter, or trade: *The children swapped books.* **2** an exchange, barter, or trade. **1** *v.,* **swapped, swap ping; 2** *n.* Also, **swop.** [*Swap* comes from Middle English *swappen,* meaning "to strike." *Swap* probably got its present meaning from the practice of "striking hands" as a sign of agreement in bargaining.] **—swap′per,** *n.*

laun der (lôn′dər), **1** wash and iron (clothes, tablecloths, towels, etc.). **2** be able to be washed; stand washing: *Cotton materials usually launder well. v.* [*Launder* comes from Middle English *lander,* meaning "one who washes," and can be traced back to Latin *lavare,* meaning "to wash."] **—laun′der a ble,** *adj.* **—laun′der er,** *n.*

a ghast (ə gast′), struck with surprise or horror; filled with terror: *I was aghast when I saw the destruction caused by the earthquake. adj.*

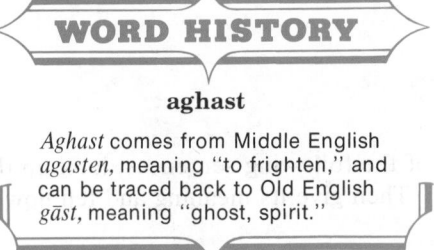

WORD HISTORY

aghast

Aghast comes from Middle English *agasten,* meaning "to frighten," and can be traced back to Old English *gāst,* meaning "ghost, spirit."

The entries above are derived from Middle English, the form of English used from about 1100 to about 1500. Next to the entry *Middle English* in your dictionary you will find a chart which explains and gives examples of that form of the language. You will notice that many of the Middle English words listed on the chart have not changed their spelling, and are used in the same form in modern English.

English has borrowed many of its words from other languages. In the word history of *launder,* shown above, the Middle English word was in turn derived from Latin. Many words pass from language to language, often changing spelling and meaning as they go.

li lac (līˈlək *or* līˈlak), **1** shrub with clusters of tiny, fragrant, pale pinkish-purple or white flowers. **2** a pale pinkish purple. **3** pinkish-purple. 1,2 *n.,* 3 *adj.* [*Lilac* came into English about 350 years ago from French *lilac,* and can be traced back to Sanskrit *nīla,* meaning "dark blue."]

um brel la (um brelˈə), a light, folding frame covered with cloth or plastic, used as a protection against rain or sun. *n., pl.* **um brel las.** [*Umbrella* comes from Italian *ombrella,* and can be traced back to Latin *umbra,* meaning "shade, shadow."] **—um brelˈla like**ˈ, *adj.*

bath y scaph or **bath y scaphe** (bathˈə skaf), a diving craft for deep-sea exploration consisting of a round steel chamber suspended from a large, cigar-shaped float. *n.* [*Bathyscaph* comes from Greek *bathys,* meaning "deep," and *skaphē,* meaning "bowl, tub."]

me sa (māˈsə), a small, high plateau with a flat top and steep sides, common in dry regions of the western and southwestern United States. *n.*

WORD HISTORY

mesa

Mesa was borrowed from Spanish *mesa,* which came from Latin *mensa,* meaning "table."

Some words are derived from the names of people or places. Some are a blend of other words or are composed of certain letters of other words.

sax o phone (sakˈsə fōn), a woodwind instrument having a curved metal body with keys for the fingers and a mouthpiece with a single reed. *n.* [*Saxophone* was formed in French from the name of its Belgian inventor, Adolphe *Sax,* 1814-1894, and Greek *phōnē,* meaning "sound."]

smog (smog), mixture of smoke and fog in the air: *Automobile exhaust fumes were blamed as one of the major causes of smog. n.* [*Smog* is a blend of *smoke* and *fog.*]

EXERCISE

Find the word history of each of the following entries in your dictionary. Write each number, and after it write the language, languages, or other source from which the word came.

1. boudoir
2. knit
3. badminton
4. catkin
5. simulcast
6. chop suey
7. squash²
8. tarantula
9. robot
10. yam

WORD FAMILIES

A root is a word in a prior, or older, language that developed into a modern word, or group of words, or family of words. About 60 word families are featured in this dictionary. These families are listed with the older root from which each family developed, whether from ancient Greek, Latin, or Old English. The word families featured in this dictionary include only a sampling of the word families in English.

Featured word families are enclosed in colored frames and are placed next to the entry for one of the words in the group. Here is one example:

WORD FAMILY

habit

Below are words related to *habit*. They can all be traced back to the Latin word *habere* (hä bā′re), meaning "to have, hold."

ability	duty	inhabit
able	endeavor	inhibit
avoirdupois	exhibit	malady
debt	habeas corpus	prohibit
disability	habitat	rehabilitate
due	habitual	uninhabited

All the words in the word family listed under *habit* can be traced back to one Latin word, *habere,* meaning "to have, hold." However, if you look up the meanings of these words, it may not always be clear to you just how the words can be related.

One way to think of a group of words like this is to compare it to a large group of cousins at a family reunion of a human family. If you trace cousins back far enough, you will find a common ancestor. Even distantly related cousins are related, but they may not look or act very much alike. On the other hand, some cousins may resemble each other.

Similarly, words such as *habitat* and *rehabilitate* resemble the word *habit,* and you may be able to see the connection in meaning. Some other words in the family, such as *able* and *endeavor,* seem very different and unrelated. However, if you trace their histories in a large reference dictionary, you will find that they indeed share a common root, Latin *habere.*

EXERCISE

Look up the word family listed under each of the following entries. Write each number, and after it write the word to which the family can be traced, and its language.

1. legible
2. health
3. bonus
4. nautical
5. point
6. plate

Test Yourself

1. Each numbered clue for the crossword puzzle below is a definition of one of these words:

| arena | era | eland | pinnate |
| polyp | lob | Nubia | placard |

Look up each word in your dictionary. Match it to its definition below and fill in a copy of the puzzle.

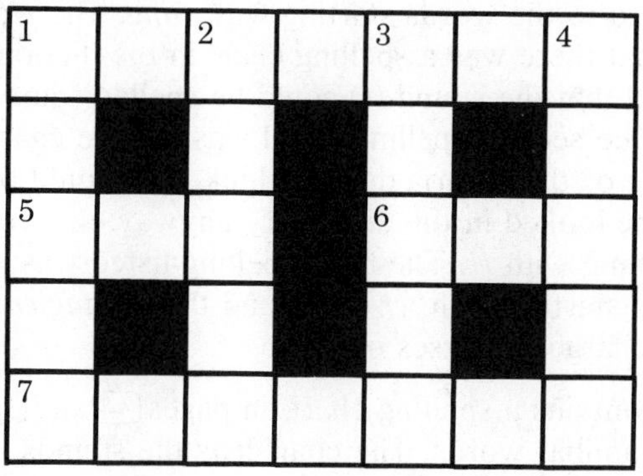

ACROSS

1. like a feather
5. to hit a ball in a high arc
6. an age in history
7. a posted notice; poster

DOWN

1. a small water animal
2. a region in northeast Africa
3. a place where contests took place
4. a large African antelope

2. Look up the clue word or the important word in each clue below. In its definition you will find a word with the same meaning that is spelled with letters used in the word *vocabulary*. EXAMPLE: Look up *kingly*. In its definition you will find the word *royal*. All its letters, *r, o, y, a,* and *l*, are in *vocabulary*. So royal is the answer.

a. constrictor
b. laurel
c. kinky

d. kind of crustacean
e. kind of reef
f. lad

g. caboose
h. rod
i. ringlet

3. Look up each of the following words in your dictionary and read the word history. Tell what person or place each word is derived from. Do it like this:
a. the island of Jersey.

a. jersey
b. curium
c. badminton
d. Conestoga wagon

e. cinchona
f. graham
g. diesel
h. sandwich

i. Chihuahua
j. maverick
k. denim
l. Queen Anne's lace

How To Use this Dictionary for Spelling

Maria's father was looking through a book about the old days of the American West. The book was illustrated with beautiful and very realistic pictures by Frederic Remington, and many of them were of cowboys and horses. They showed life as it really was in those days. Maria's parents were talking about the book, and she heard them mention something that sounded like (rang′glər). She had heard this mentioned before when people talked about ranches, but she didn't know exactly what the word meant. She decided to look it up in her dictionary.

First, Maria turned to the words starting with *rang.* The word was not there. She remembered that there was a spelling chart in the dictionary. Turning to the chart, she found that the sound (r) could be spelled four ways. The first she had already tried. The second spelling listed was *rr.* The chart gave the word *carry* as an example of this. Maria did not think that would be the answer to her problem, but she looked in the dictionary anyway, and found that there were no words starting with *rr.* The third spelling listed was *wr.* When Maria turned to the words starting with *wr* she found that *wrangler* was listed, and means a herder in charge of horses or cattle.

This dictionary contains a spelling chart on pages ③④ and ③⑤ to help you find the spellings of unfamiliar words. The chart lists the sounds of English, and then gives examples of the ways each sound can be spelled. The letters that spell the sounds are printed in heavy type. If you can find how to spell the first few sounds of an unfamiliar word, you will probably be able to find it in the dictionary. You will notice that certain words may be spelled in more than one way. Sometimes this is shown in a single dictionary entry:

bat tle-ax or **bat tle-axe** (bat′l aks′), ax with a broad blade, used in medieval times as a weapon in battle. *n.,* *pl.* **bat tle-ax es.**

However, sometimes the different spellings have to be entered in different places to be in alphabetical order. When this happens the definition is given under the more common spelling.

bron co (brong′kō), a wild or partly tamed horse of the western United States. *n., pl.* **bron cos.** Also, **broncho.**

bron cho (brong′kō), bronco. *n., pl.* **bron chos.**

Bronco Buster by Frederic Remington

► *TEACH YOURSELF*

Turn to the spelling chart on pages ③④ and ③⑤. Read the instructions for using the chart. Then answer the following questions.

1. How many ways can the sound (hw) be spelled?
2. How is the sound (f) spelled in the word pronounced (frāz)?
3. How is the sound (f) spelled in the word pronounced (laf)?
4. How is the sound (o) spelled in the word pronounced (nol′ij)?
5. Look up the word pronounced (grā) in your dictionary. What letters are used to spell the sound (ā)? Now read the rest of the entry. What other way is the word spelled? What letters are used to spell the sound (ā) in the alternate spelling?

EXERCISE

Following is a paragraph about Frederic Remington, the artist who illustrated the book Maria's father was reading. In certain words a part is missing, and has been replaced by the symbol for the sound spelled by the missing letter or letters. Read the paragraph, and then, using your spelling chart, find out how to spell the sound. Write each word, circling the letter or letters you used to spell the sound.

Even when he was still in school, Frederic Remington was fa(s)inated by the American West. His first dr(ô)ings were of horses and cowboys. As soon as he c(u̇)d, he traveled to the Western front(i)r, where his ske(ch)es made a (k)roni-cle of the rou(f) life of those days. He did hard (f)ysical work as a cowboy and a rancher before he was able to earn a living as an artist. Frederic Remington r(ō)med the West, traveling through deep c(ü)lees and crossing wide m(ā)sas where the only green was that of cactus and mes(k)ite. He painted the buffalo, the c(ī)use, and the cowboy with his bronco. He painted the Apache, the (sh)eyenne, and the Sioux. Often, dressed in (k)aki, he accompanied army troopers on scouting trips. He sketched these troopers on their long marches and in battle, recording the last stages of the Indian wars. In the early days of mo(sh)on pictures, costume and set de(z)igners studied his work to make the clothing and backgrounds as (ô)thentic as possible. Frederic Remington, in his paintings, sculptures, and books, cap(ch)ured the American West in vivid detail, creating for us a pictorial history of a vanishing world.

SPELLINGS OF ENGLISH SOUNDS

This chart shows all the sounds of the English language, and illustrates the ways in which each sound may be spelled. It can help you find words you can say, but do not know how to spell.

The pronunciation symbols used in this dictionary are shown in the colored boxes. Each symbol represents a different sound. Following each symbol are words showing different ways the sound may be spelled. The letters used to spell the sound are printed in heavy black type. Common spellings are listed first.

Some of the words used as examples are in more than one list. This is because the words are pronounced in more than one way.

Sound	Spelling and examples	Sound	Spelling and examples
a	at, plaid, half, laugh, aerial, ere, prayer, their, pear, heir	**g**	go, egg, league, guest, ghost
ā	age, aid, say, suede, eight, vein, they, break, bouquet, straight, gaol, gauge, éclair, eh	**gz**	exact, exhibit
		h	he, who
ä	father, heart, sergeant, ah, calm, bazaar	**hw**	wheat
b	bad, rabbit	**i**	in, enough, hymn, manage, ear, build, sieve, busy, marriage, been, women, weird, Aegean
ch	child, future, watch, question, righteous, cello, Czech	**ī**	ice, sky, lie, high, rye, eye, island, stein, height, buy, bayou, aisle, aye, geyser, coyote
d	did, filled, add		
e	end, bread, any, aerial, said, friend, leopard, says, heifer, bury, heir	**j**	gem, large, jam, bridge, region, gradual, badger, soldier, exaggerate
ē	equal, happy, each, bee, ski, believe, ceiling, key, algae, phoenix, people, quay	**k**	coat, kind, back, chemist, account, excite, quit, antique, liquor, acquire, khaki, saccharin, biscuit
ėr	stern, turn, first, word, earth, journey, myrtle, err, whirr, purr, myrrh, herb	**ks**	tax, tactics
f	fat, effort, phrase, laugh	**l**	land, tell

Sound	Spelling and examples	Sound	Spelling and examples
m	me, common, climb, solemn, phlegm	**th**	thin
n	no, manner, knife, gnaw, pneumonia	**ᴛʜ**	then, breathe
ng	ink, long, tongue, handkerchief	**u**	under, other, trouble, flood, does
o	odd, watch, honest, knowledge, yacht	**u̇**	full, good, detour, wolf, should, pleurisy
ō	old, oak, own, soul, toe, brooch, though, folk, beau, oh, chauffeur, owe, sew, yeoman	**ü**	food, rule, move, soup, threw, blue, fruit, shoe, maneuver, through, lieutenant, buoy
ô	order, all, auto, awful, oar, ought, walk, taught, cough, awe, Utah	**v**	very, have, of, Stephen, flivver
oi	oil, boy, buoy	**w**	will, quick, bivouac, choir
ou	out, owl, bough, hour	**wu**	one
p	pay, happy	**y**	opinion, yes, hallulujah, azalea
r	run, carry, wrong, rhythm	**yü**	use, few, feud, cue, view, beauty, adieu, yule, queue
s	say, cent, tense, dance, miss, scent, listen, psychology, waltz, sword, schism	**yu̇**	uranium, Europe
sh	nation, she, special, mission, tension, machine, conscience, issue, ocean, schwa, sugar, nauseous, pshaw, crescendo	**z**	has, zero, buzz, scissors, xylophone, discern, raspberry, asthma, czar
		zh	division, measure, garage, azure, regime, equation, jabot, brazier
t	tell, button, stopped, doubt, two, Thomas, receipt, indict, pizza	**ə**	occur, about, April, essential, cautious, circus, oxygen, bargain, gaiety, dungeon, tortoise, pageant, authority

How to Use this Dictionary for Writing

bas ket ball   thought   i de a   long-suf fer ing

Mike had to write a report about his favorite sport, and he wanted to do a good job. He wanted his report to look neat, too. As he got near the end of the line, the next word he had to write was *basketball.* There was no room to write the word on the line. However, if he started it on the following line, a large gap would be left at the end of the line above.

Then Mike remembered that his teacher had told the class how to handle such a situation. "It is all right to divide a word between syllables," she had said, "but put a hyphen at the end of the line to show that the word continues on the next line."

Mike looked up *basketball* in his dictionary, and found it written

bas ket ball

There were two places it could be divided. He decided to write *basket-* on one line and *ball* on the next.

Mike's teacher had also told the class that a word of one syllable could not be divided, and that a single letter could not be separated from the rest of the word. Later, he came to the word *thought* and realized right away that it could not be divided. He was thinking of dividing the word *idea,* but when he looked it up, it was written

i de a

so he knew there was no place to divide it without having one letter by itself. He would have to write the whole word on the line below.

Mike came to one other word, *long-suffering,* at the end of a line. His dictionary listed it as

long-suf fer ing

When he saw it was hyphenated, he remembered an additional rule his teacher had mentioned: a hyphenated word should be broken only at the hyphen.

EXERCISE

On the next page is Mike's report, with some of the words in italics. Look up each of these words. Then write each word in syllables, exactly like the entry word in your dictionary. In each word, circle the letter or letters after which it can be divided. If it cannot be divided, do not circle anything.

HOW BASKETBALL BEGAN

One *hundred* years ago no one had ever heard of basketball. The game was not invented until 1891. During that winter, Dr. James Naismith was working as a *physical* education *instructor* at the Y.M.C.A. training *school* in Springfield, Mass. It was hard to find *something* for the boys to play when they could not go outdoors. They were *bored*, and their long-suffering teachers felt the results in an outbreak of pranks. Dr. Naismith *decided* to create a new game—one that was not rough, and could be played indoors between the fall football *season* and the *spring* baseball season.

To cut down on roughness, Dr. Naismith wanted the goal to be above the heads of the players. He thought and thought, and *suddenly* an idea came to him.

Dr. Naismith's students got a *surprise* next day in the gym. An old peach basket was tacked to the edge of the *balcony,* and they were asked to throw a soccer ball into it. At first, a janitor stood on a ladder to *retrieve* the ball when it fell into the basket. Naturally *enough*, these first games were quite *different* from the fast, *exciting* basketball contests we see today. After some months, the bottoms of the peach baskets were cut out so the ball could drop *through*. It was years before the basketball court began to look as it does now.

Today, basketball is not only the most popular *spectator* sport in the world, it is also played by more people than any other game. Although it was invented for boys, it is enjoyed just as much by girls. *Children,* teenagers, and *adults* all like to play it. Basketball is also a popular game with people who are physically *handicapped.* It is enjoyed in countries all *over* the world, and is played both outdoors and indoors in all seasons. The game of basketball has come a long way since that first day in the winter of 1891.

A game of basketball played in 1892

Spain plays Canada in basketball at the Olympic Games for the Handicapped, 1972

The Parts of a Dictionary Entry

(1) **The entry word** is printed in boldface type. It shows how the word is spelled and how it may be divided in writing.

(2) **The homograph number** appears when successive entries are spelled the same way.

(3) **The pronunciation** is enclosed in parentheses. Letters used in the respelling for pronunciation have special sounds assigned to them. These are explained in the pronunciation key.

(4) **A restrictive label** shows that use of a word or meaning is limited to a particular region or level of usage.

(5) **The definition** of a word tells its meaning. A word with several different meanings has numbered definitions, one for each meaning.

(6) **An illustrative sentence** is printed in italic type following the definition. It shows how the entry word may be used with that particular meaning in a sentence.

(7) **The part-of-speech label** is an abbreviation in italic type naming the function of the entry word. When the word may function as more than one part of speech, definition numbers are added to each label.

(8) **Inflected forms,** in small boldface type, are given whenever their spelling or form might give you trouble.

(9) **The word history,** or etymology, appears in square brackets or in a colored frame. It tells the language the English word came from and, if its form or meaning was different, how it was spelled or what it meant there.

(10) **A run-on entry,** in small boldface type, is an undefined word. Its meaning combines the meaning of the entry word with that of its suffix. Each run-on entry has a part-of-speech label.

(11) **Idioms,** in small boldface type, follow the rest of an entry. Such word combinations have special definitions.

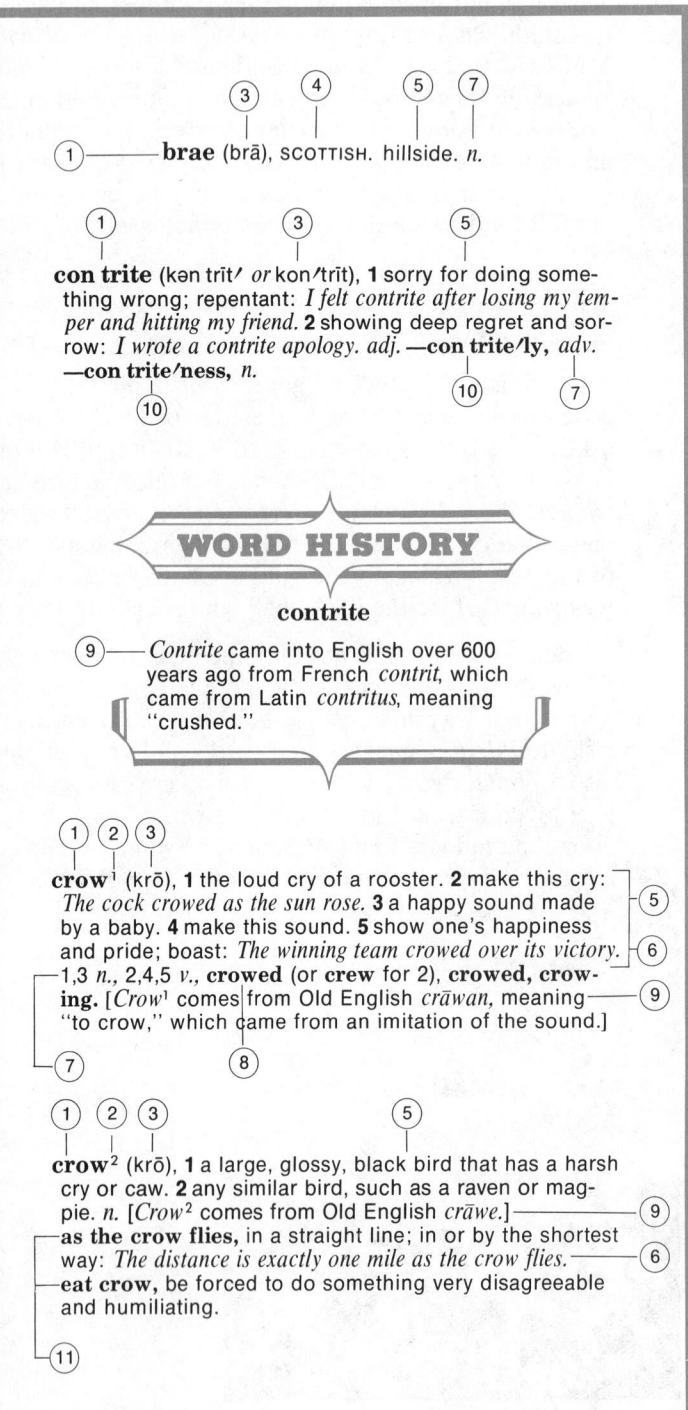

38

Aa

a hat	i it	oi oil	ch child	⎧ a in about
ā age	ī ice	ou out	ng long	e in taken
ä far	o hot	u cup	sh she	ə = ⎨ i in pencil
e let	ō open	u̇ put	th thin	o in lemon
ē equal	ô order	ü rule	ᴛͪн then	⎩ u in circus
ėr term			zh measure	

A or **a**[1] (ā), the first letter of the English alphabet. *n., pl.* **A's** or **a's.**

a[2] (ə; *stressed* ā), **1** any: *A tree has leaves.* **2** one: *Buy a dozen eggs and a pound of butter.* **3** every: *Thanksgiving comes once a year.* **4** one kind of: *Chemistry is a science. adj. or indefinite article.*

a-, *prefix.* in; on; to: *Abed = in bed.*

A, symbol for argon.

a., **1** acre or acres. **2** ampere or amperes.

AA, Alcoholics Anonymous.

aard vark (ärd′värk), a burrowing African mammal with a piglike snout, a long, sticky tongue, and very strong claws. It feeds on ants and termites. *n.*

WORD HISTORY

aardvark

Aardvark was borrowed from Afrikaans *aardvark*, which came from *aarde*, meaning "earth," and *varken*, meaning "pig."

about 6 ft. (1.8 m.) long, including tail

Aar on (er′ən *or* ar′ən), (in the Bible) the brother of Moses and the first high priest of the Hebrews. *n.*

A.B., Bachelor of Arts. Also, **B.A.**

a back (ə bak′). **taken aback,** suddenly surprised: *I was taken aback by my friend's angry reply. adv.*

ab a cus (ab′ə kəs), frame with rows of counters or beads that slide back and forth. Abacuses are sometimes used in China, Japan, Korea, etc., for adding and other tasks in arithmetic. *n., pl.* **ab a cus es, ab a ci** (ab′ə sī).

a baft (ə baft′), at or toward the back of a ship; aft. *adv.*

ab a lo ne (ab′ə lō′nē), shellfish that can be eaten, with a large, rather flat shell lined with mother-of-pearl. *n.* [*Abalone* is from American Spanish *abulón*, which came from a local Indian word for this shellfish.]

a ban don (ə ban′dən), **1** give up entirely: *We abandoned the idea of a picnic because of the rain.* **2** leave without intending to return to; desert: *The crew abandoned the ship before it sank.* **3** give (oneself) up completely (to a feeling, impulse, etc.): *The lost child abandoned all hope.* **4** freedom from restraint; carefree manner: *The students on the winning side cheered with abandon.* 1-3 *v.,* 4 *n.* —**a ban′don er,** *n.*

a ban doned (ə ban′dənd), **1** deserted. **2** wicked; immoral: *an abandoned life.* **3** unrestrained: *abandoned glee. adj.* —**a ban′doned ly,** *adv.*

a ban don ment (ə ban′dən mənt), an abandoning or a being abandoned. *n.*

a base (ə bās′), make lower in rank, condition, or character; degrade: *Public officials who take bribes abase themselves. v.,* **a based, a bas ing.**

a base ment (ə bās′mənt), an abasing or a being abased; degradation. *n.*

a bash (ə bash′), make uneasy, shy, and somewhat ashamed; embarrass and confuse: *I was abashed by the laughter of my classmates. v.* —**a bash′ment,** *n.*

a bate (ə bāt′), **1** make less; decrease: *Her confidence helped to abate my fear.* **2** become less; diminish: *Although the rain has abated somewhat the wind is still blowing very hard. v.,* **a bat ed, a bat ing.** —**a bat′a ble,** *adj.* —**a bat′er,** *n.*

a bate ment (ə bāt′mənt), **1** a decrease; lessening. **2** amount abated; reduction. *n.*

ab bé (ab′ā), a title used in France and Quebec for any clergyman, especially a priest. *n., pl.* **ab bés.**

ab bess (ab′is), woman who is the head of an abbey of nuns. *n., pl.* **ab bess es.**

ab bey (ab′ē), **1** the building or buildings where monks or nuns live, ruled by an abbot or abbess; monastery or convent. **2** church or building that was once an abbey or part of an abbey: *Westminster Abbey. n., pl.* **ab beys.**

ab bot (ab′ət), man who is the head of an abbey of monks. *n.*

abbrev. or **abbr.,** abbreviation.

ab bre vi ate (ə brē′vē āt), **1** make (a work or phrase) shorter so that a part stands for the whole: *We can abbreviate "hour" to "hr."* **2** make briefer. *v.,* **ab bre vi at ed, ab bre vi at ing.** —**ab bre′vi a′tor,** *n.*

ab bre vi a tion (ə brē′vē ā′shən), **1** a shortened form of a word or phrase standing for the whole: *"Dr." is an abbreviation for "Doctor."* **2** a making briefer. *n.*

abacus—When the beads are pushed toward the middle bar, the top ones count as 5 and the bottom ones as 1 each. The number shown is 964,708.

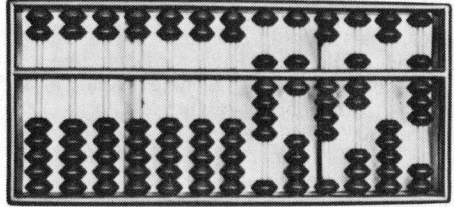

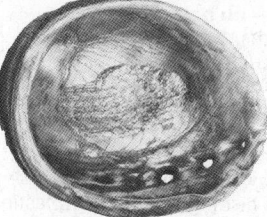

abalone
shell of an abalone

ABC, American Broadcasting Company.

A B C (ā′bē′sē′), **1** facts or skills to be learned first; basic principles: *We learned the ABC of swimming this summer at camp.* **2** ABC's, *pl.* the alphabet. *n., pl.* **ABC's** or **ABCs.**

ab di cate (ab′də kāt), give up or renounce (office, power, or authority) formally; resign: *When the king abdicated his throne, his brother became king.* v., **ab di cat ed, ab di cat ing.** —**ab′di ca′tor,** n.

ab di ca tion (ab′də kā′shən), an abdicating; resigning. n.

ab do men (ab′də mən *or* ab dō′mən), 1 the part of the body containing the stomach, the intestines, and other important organs; belly. 2 the last of the three parts of the body of an insect or a crustacean. n.

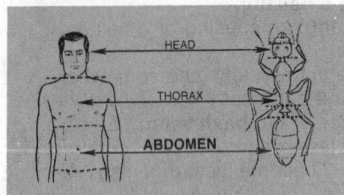

abdomen
(defs. 1 and 2)

ab dom i nal (ab dom′ə nəl), of the abdomen: *abdominal muscles.* adj. —**ab dom′i nal ly,** adv.

ab duct (ab dukt′), carry off (a person) by force or by trickery; kidnap: *The police are looking for the person who abducted the baby from its crib.* v.

ab duc tion (ab duk′shən), a kidnaping. n.

ab duc tor (ab duk′tər), kidnaper. n.

a beam (ə bēm′), opposite the middle of a ship's side: *They came abeam of the lighthouse.* adv.

a bed (ə bed′), in bed. adv.

A bel (ā′bəl), (in the Bible) the second son of Adam and Eve. Abel was killed by his older brother Cain. n.

Ab er deen (ab′ər dēn′), city in E Scotland. n.

ab er ra tion (ab′ə rā′shən), 1 a wandering from the normal or right practice: *A lie is an aberration from the truth.* 2 an abnormal structure or development. 3 a wandering of the mind: *His peculiarities are no more than harmless aberrations.* 4 failure of a lens or mirror to bring to a single focus the rays of light coming from one point: *Aberration in the mirror caused a blurred and crooked image.* n.

a bet (ə bet′), encourage or help, especially in doing something wrong: *The thief was abetted in the robbery by two accomplices.* v., **a bet ted, a bet ting.** —**a bet′ment,** n. —**a bet′tor, a bet′ter,** n.

ab hor (ab hôr′), shrink away from with horror; feel disgust or hate for; detest: *Most people abhor the thought of war.* v., **ab horred, ab hor ring.** [*Abhor* is from Latin *abhorrere,* which comes from *ab-,* meaning "from," and *horrere,* meaning "to shudder."] —**ab hor′rer,** n.

ab hor rence (ab hôr′əns), 1 a feeling of very great hatred; horror; disgust: *I have an abhorrence of snakes.* 2 something hated or detested. n.

ab hor rent (ab hôr′ənt), causing horror; disgusting; hateful: *Lying and stealing are abhorrent to someone who is honest.* adj. —**ab hor′rent ly,** adv.

a bide (ə bīd′), 1 put up with; endure: *I can't abide their always being late.* 2 stay; remain: *Abide with me for a time.* 3 dwell; reside. 4 OLD USE. wait for. v., **a bode** or **a bid ed, a bid ing.** —**a bid′er,** n.

abide by, 1 accept and carry out: *Both teams will abide by the umpire's decision.* 2 remain faithful to; fulfill: *You must abide by your promise.*

a bid ing (ə bī′ding), permanent; lasting: *The old sailor had an abiding love of the sea.* adj. —**a bid′ing ly,** adv.

Ab i djan (ab′i jän′), capital of the Ivory Coast, in the SE part. n.

Ab i lene (ab′ə lēn′), 1 city in central Texas. 2 town in central Kansas. n.

a bil i ty (ə bil′ə tē), 1 power to do or act: *A horse has the*

ability to work. 2 power to do some special thing; skill: *He has great ability in making jewelry.* 3 special natural gift; talent: *Musical ability often shows itself early in life.* n., pl. **a bil i ties.**

ab ject (ab′jekt), 1 so low or degraded as to be hopeless; wretched; miserable: *Many people in Asia still live in abject poverty.* 2 deserving contempt; despicable: *abject fear, abject flattery.* adj. —**ab ject′ly,** adv. —**ab ject′ness,** n.

ab jure (ab jùr′), swear to give up; renounce on oath: *An alien must abjure foreign citizenship before becoming an American citizen.* v., **ab jured, ab jur ing.** —**ab′ju ra′tion,** n. —**ab jur′er,** n.

ab late (ab lāt′), remove by burning away, wearing down, or cutting off. v., **ab lat ed, ab lat ing.**

a blaze (ə blāz′), 1 on fire: *The forest was set ablaze by lightning.* 2 shining brightly: *The hotel was ablaze with lights.* 3 in great excitement: *I was ablaze with anger when he kicked my dog.* adj.

a ble (ā′bəl), 1 having enough power, skill, or means to do something; capable: *A cat is able to see in the dark.* 2 having more power or skill than usual; skillful: *She is an able teacher.* 3 done with skill: *The audience applauded her able speech.* adj., **a bler, a blest.**

-able, suffix forming adjectives. 1 (added to verbs) able to be _____ed: *Enjoyable = able to be enjoyed.* 2 (added to nouns) suitable for _____: *Comfortable = suitable for comfort.* 3 (added to nouns) inclined to _____: *Peaceable = inclined to peace.*

a ble-bod ied (ā′bəl bod′ēd), strong and healthy; physically fit. adj.

able-bodied seaman or **able seaman,** an experienced seaman who can perform all the duties required of a seaman.

a bloom (ə blüm′), in bloom; blossoming. adj.

ab lu tion (ab lü′shən). Often, **ablutions,** pl. a washing or cleansing of one's person, especially as part of a religious ceremony. n.

a bly (ā′blē), in an able manner; with skill; capably. adv.

-ably, suffix forming adverbs. in a _____ manner: *Peaceably = in a peaceable manner. Pleasurably = in a pleasurable manner.*

ABM, antiballistic missile.

ab ne ga tion (ab′nə gā′shən), a giving up of one's own interests and desires; self-denial; self-sacrifice: *to lead a life of abnegation.* n.

ab nor mal (ab nôr′məl), different from the ordinary conditions, the standard, or a type; unusual: *an abnormal amount of rain.* adj. —**ab nor′mal ly,** adv.

ab nor mal i ty (ab′nôr mal′ə tē), 1 an abnormal thing or happening. 2 an abnormal condition. n., pl. **ab normal i ties.**

a board (ə bôrd′), on board; in or on a ship, train, bus, airplane, etc.: *"All aboard!" shouted the conductor, and everyone rushed for the train (adv.). Everybody was soon aboard the train (prep.).* adv., prep.

a bode (ə bōd′), 1 place to live in; dwelling; house: *A simple hut was their abode.* 2 a past tense and a past participle of **abide.** *She abode there one year.* 1 n., 2 v.

a bol ish (ə bol′ish), do away with completely; put an end to: *Many people wish that nations would abolish war.* v. —**a bol′ish a ble,** adj. —**a bol′ish er,** n.

ab o li tion (ab′ə lish′ən), a putting an end to; an abolishing: *The abolition of slavery in the United States occurred in 1865.* n.

ab o li tion ist (ab′ə lish′ə nist), person who wishes to abolish something. The people who wished to put an end to slavery in the United States were called **Abolitionists.**

A-bomb (ā′bom′), an atomic bomb. n.

a hat	i it	oi oil	ch child	⌈ a in about
ā age	ī ice	ou out	ng long	e in taken
ä far	o hot	u cup	sh she	ə = ⎱ i in pencil
e let	ō open	u̇ put	th thin	o in lemon
ē equal	ô order	ü rule	ᵮн then	⌊ u in circus
ėr term			zh measure	

abominable (def. 2)
The weather was **abominable,** with a cold wind driving the snow.

a bom i na ble (ə bom′ə nə bəl), **1** arousing disgust and hatred; loathsome: *Kidnaping is an abominable act.* **2** very unpleasant; disagreeable. *adj.* —**a bom′i na bly,** *adv.*

Abominable Snowman, an apelike creature supposed to inhabit the higher parts of the Himalayas; yeti.

a bom i nate (ə bom′ə nāt), **1** feel disgust and hatred for; loathe: *I abominate cruelty.* **2** dislike: *She abominates hot, humid weather.* *v.,* **a bom i nat ed, a bom i nat ing.**

a bom i na tion (ə bom′ə nā′shən), **1** a disgusting or loathsome thing. **2** a feeling of disgust; loathing. *n.*

ab o rig i nal (ab′ə rij′ə nəl), **1** existing from the beginning; original; native: *the aboriginal inhabitants of a continent.* **2** of the earliest known inhabitants: *an aboriginal custom. adj.* —**ab′o rig′i nal ly,** *adv.*

ab o rig i nes (ab′ə rij′ə nēz′), the earliest known inhabitants of a country or area. *n.pl. of* **aborigine.** [*Aborigines* was borrowed from Latin *aborigines,* which came from the Latin phrase *ab origine,* meaning "from the beginning." The word was originally used in Latin to refer to the people who inhabited Italy before the Romans.]

a bort (ə bôrt′), **1** fail to develop or come to completion: *The rocket flight aborted.* **2** cause to fail to come to completion: *abort a mission. v.*

a bor tion (ə bôr′shən), **1** the birth or removal of a developing embryo before it is able to live outside the mother's body. **2** failure to develop or to be completed. *n.*

a bor tive (ə bôr′tiv), **1** coming to nothing; unsuccessful; fruitless: *Early attempts to make airplanes fly proved abortive.* **2** born before the right time; born prematurely. *adj.* —**a bor′tive ly,** *adv.* —**a bor′tive ness,** *n.*

a bound (ə bound′), **1** be plentiful: *Fish abound in the ocean. Rock abounds under the soil.* **2** be well supplied; be filled; be rich: *The ocean abounds with fish. America abounds in natural resources. v.*

a bout (ə bout′), **1** of; having something to do with: *"Black Beauty" is a story about a horse.* **2** nearly; almost: *I have about finished my work.* **3** all around; around: *A collar goes about the neck* (prep.). *Look about and tell me what you see* (adv.). **4** in the opposite direction: *You are going the wrong way. Face about!* **5** one after another; by turns: *Turn about is fair play.* **6** moving around; active: *He is able to be up and about.* 1,3 *prep.,* 2-6 *adv.*
about to, on the point of; going to; ready to: *The plane is about to take off.*

a bout-face (ə bout′fās′ *for 1,2;* ə bout′fās′ *for 3*), **1** a turning or going in the opposite direction. **2** a shift to the opposite attitude or opinion. **3** turn or go in the opposite direction. 1,2 *n.,* 3 *v.,* **a bout-faced, a bout-fac ing.**

a bove (ə buv′), **1** in or at a higher place; overhead: *The sky is above.* **2** to or in a higher place than: *This elevator does not go above the third floor.* **3** higher than; over: *Look above the tall building to see the sun. A captain is above a sergeant.* **4** more than: *Our club has above thirty members—thirty-five, to be exact.* **5** beyond: *Turn at the first corner above the school.* **6** too great in importance for; superior to: *be above acting in such a childish manner.* **7** earlier in a book or article: *See what is written above* (adv.). *The above definition contains six words* (adj.). **8** above zero: *The temperature is five above.* 1,7,8 *adv.,* 2-6 *prep.,* 7 *adj.*

a bove board (ə buv′bôrd′), in open sight; without tricks or concealment: *Everything that the mayor did was open and aboveboard* (adj.). *Her campaign was run aboveboard* (adv.). *adj., adv.*

ab ra ca dab ra (ab′rə kə dab′rə), **1** word supposed to have magic power. **2** meaningless talk; gibberish. *n.*

a brade (ə brād′), wear down or away by rubbing; scrape off: *Glaciers abrade rocks. v.,* **a brad ed, a brad ing.**

A bra ham (ā′brə ham), (in the Bible) the ancestor of the Hebrews. *n.*

a bra sion (ə brā′zhən), **1** place scraped or worn by rubbing: *He had an abrasion on his knee from falling on gravel.* **2** a wearing down or away by rubbing; scraping off: *Coins become thinner by constant abrasion. n.*

a bra sive (ə brā′siv), **1** substance used for grinding, smoothing, or polishing. Sandpaper, pumice, and emery are abrasives. **2** wearing away by rubbing; causing abrasion. **3** harsh or crude in manner: *an abrasive person.* 1 *n.,* 2,3 *adj.* —**a bra′sive ly,** *adv.* —**a bra′sive ness,** *n.*

a breast (ə brest′), **1** side by side: *The soldiers marched four abreast* (adv.). *The airplane had four seats, two abreast on each side of the aisle* (adj.). **2** up with; alongside of; even with: *Read the newspapers to keep abreast of what is going on.* 1,2 *adv.,* 1 *adj.*

a bridge (ə brij′), **1** make shorter, especially by using fewer words: *A long story can be abridged by leaving out unimportant parts.* **2** make less: *The rights of citizens must not be abridged without proper cause. v.,* **a bridged, a bridg ing.** —**a bridg′a ble, a bridge′a ble,** *adj.* —**a bridg′er,** *n.*

a bridg ment or **a bridge ment** (ə brij′mənt), **1** a shortened form of a book, long article, etc.: *That one book is an abridgment of a three-volume history.* **2** a making shorter; an abridging. *n.*

a broad (ə brôd′), **1** outside one's country; to a foreign land: *I am going abroad next year to study in Italy.* **2** out in the open air; outdoors: *My grandfather walks abroad only on warm days.* **3** far and wide; widely: *The news that the circus was coming quickly spread abroad.* **4** going around; in motion; current: *A rumor is abroad that school will close.* 1-3 *adv.,* 4 *adj.*

ab ro gate (ab′rə gāt), do away with; repeal; cancel: *When war broke out, our government abrogated its trade agreements with the enemy country. v.,* **ab ro gat ed, ab ro gat ing.** —**ab′ro ga′tion,** *n.* —**ab′ro ga′tor,** *n.*

a brupt (ə brupt′), **1** showing sudden change; unexpected: *I made an abrupt turn to avoid another car.* **2** very steep: *The horse made an abrupt rise up the hill.* **3** short or sudden in speech or manner; blunt: *a gruff, abrupt way of speaking. adj.* [*Abrupt* is from Latin *abruptum,* meaning "broken off," which comes from *ab-,* meaning "off, from," and *rumpere,* meaning "to break."] **—a brupt′ly,** *adv.* **—a brupt′ness,** *n.*

Ab sa lom (ab′sə ləm), (in the Bible) David's favorite son. He rebelled against his father and was later killed in battle. *n.*

ab scess (ab′ses), a collection of pus in the tissues of some part of the body. An abscess results from an infection and is usually painful. *n., pl.* **ab scess es.**

ab scessed (ab′sest), having an abscess: *an abscessed tooth. adj.*

ab scond (ab skond′), go away suddenly and secretly, especially to avoid punishment; go off and hide: *An employee absconded with $50,000 of the bank's money. v.* **—ab scond′er,** *n.*

ab sence (ab′səns), **1** a being away: *Her absence from school was excused.* **2** time of being away: *I returned to school after an absence of two days.* **3** a being without; lack: *Darkness is the absence of light. n.*

ab sent (ab′sənt), **1** away; not present: *Three members of the class are absent today.* **2** lacking; not existing: *In certain fishes the ribs are entirely absent.* **3** absent-minded: *I knew you were daydreaming from your absent look. adj.*

ab sen tee (ab′sən tē′), person who is away or remains away. *n.*

absentee ballot, ballot of or for a voter who is permitted to vote by mail.

ab sent ly (ab′sənt lē), in an absent-minded manner; inattentively. *adv.*

ab sent-mind ed (ab′sənt mīn′did), not paying attention to what is going on around one; forgetful; inattentive: *The absent-minded man put salt in his coffee and sugar on his egg. adj.* **—ab′sent-mind′ed ly,** *adv.* **—ab′sent-mind′ed ness,** *n.*

ab so lute (ab′sə lüt), **1** free from any imperfection or lack; complete; whole; entire: *That is the absolute truth.* **2** with no limits or restrictions: *The dictator had absolute power.* **3** certain; positive: *I had absolute proof that the witness was lying. adj.* **—ab′so lute′ness,** *n.*

ab so lute ly (ab′sə lüt′lē *or* ab′sə lüt′lē), **1** completely; entirely: *My broken bicycle was absolutely useless.* **2** without doubt; certainly: *She is absolutely the finest person I know. adv.*

absolute zero, temperature at which substances would have no heat whatever, and all molecules would stop moving. Theoretically, it is −273.16 degrees Celsius or −459.69 degrees Fahrenheit.

ab so lu tion (ab′sə lü′shən), a freeing from sin, guilt, or blame; forgiveness; an absolving. *n.*

ab solve (ab solv′), **1** declare free from sin, guilt, or blame: *The judge absolved the accused of the crime.* **2** set free; release: *I absolve you from your promise. v.,* **ab solved, ab solv ing. —ab solv′er,** *n.*

ab sorb (ab sôrb′), **1** take in or suck up (liquids): *The sponge absorbed the spilled milk.* **2** take in and make part of itself; assimilate: *The United States has absorbed millions of immigrants. Digested food is absorbed into the bloodstream in the intestines.* **3** take in without reflecting: *Rugs absorb sounds and make a house quieter.* **4** take up all the attention of; interest very much: *Building a dam in the brook absorbed the children completely. v.*

ab sorbed (ab sôrbd′), very much interested; completely occupied: *I was so absorbed that I did not hear the bell ring. adj.* **—ab sorb′ed ly,** *adv.* **—ab sorb′ed ness,** *n.*

ab sorb ent (ab sôr′bənt), able to absorb moisture, light, or heat: *Absorbent paper towels are used to dry the hands. adj.*

ab sorb ing (ab sôr′bing), extremely interesting: *an absorbing book. adj.* **—ab sorb′ing ly,** *adv.*

ab sorp tion (ab sôrp′shən), **1** act or process of absorb-

ing: *A sponge picks up spilled water by absorption.* **2** a being absorbed; great interest: *The children's absorption in their game was so complete that they did not hear the doorbell. n.*

ab sorp tive (ab sôrp′tiv), able to absorb. *adj.* **—ab sorp′tive ness,** *n.*

ab stain (ab stān′), **1** do without something; hold oneself back; refrain: *To lose weight, abstain from eating rich foods.* **2** refrain from voting: *Six members voted in favor of the motion, five voted against it, and four abstained. v.* **—ab stain′er,** *n.*

ab ste mi ous (ab stē′mē əs), sparing in eating, drinking, etc.; moderate; temperate: *to be abstemious in one's eating habits. adj.* **—ab ste′mi ous ly,** *adv.* **—ab ste′mi ous ness,** *n.*

ab sten tion (ab sten′shən), **1** an abstaining; abstinence. **2** fact of not voting: *There were five votes in favor, four against, and three abstentions. n.*

ab sti nence (ab′stə nəns), partly or entirely giving up certain pleasures, food, drink, etc.: *The doctor recommended abstinence from coffee and tobacco. n.*

ab sti nent (ab′stə nənt), abstemious. *adj.* **—ab′sti nent ly,** *adv.*

ab stract (ab′strakt *or* ab strakt′ *for 1,3,6;* ab strakt′ *for 2,4;* ab′strakt *for 5*), **1** thought of apart from any particular object or real thing; not concrete: *Sweetness is abstract; a lump of sugar is concrete.* **2** think of (a quality) apart from any object or real thing having that quality: *We can abstract the idea of redness from the color of all red objects.* **3** hard to understand; difficult: *The atomic theory of matter is so abstract that it can be fully understood only by advanced students.* **4** take away; remove: *Iron is abstracted from ore.* **5** a brief statement of the main ideas in an article, book, case in court, etc.; summary. **6** not representing any actual object or concrete thing; having little or no resemblance to real or material things: *We saw many abstract paintings in the Museum of Modern Art.* **1,3,6** *adj.,* **2,4** *v.,* **5** *n.* **—ab stract′er, ab strac′tor,** *n.* **—ab′stract ly,** *adv.* **—ab′stract ness,** *n.*

abstract (def. 6)
an abstract work of art

ab stract ed (ab strak′tid), absent-minded. *adj.* **—ab stract′ed ly,** *adv.* **—ab stract′ed ness,** *n.*

ab strac tion (ab strak′shən), **1** the idea of a quality thought of apart from any particular object or real thing having that quality; abstract idea or term: *Hardness, bravery, and length are abstractions.* **2** a taking away; removal: *the abstraction of iron from ore.* **3** a being lost in thought; absent-mindedness. **4** a work of abstract art. *n.*

ab struse (ab strüs′), hard to understand: *an abstruse riddle. adj.* **—ab struse′ly,** *adv.* **—ab struse′ness,** *n.*

ab surd (ab sèrd′), plainly not true or sensible; foolish; ridiculous: *The idea that the number 13 brings bad luck is absurd. adj.* [*Absurd* comes from Latin *absurdus,* meaning "out of tune, senseless."] **—ab surd′ly,** *adv.* **—ab surd′ness,** *n.*

ab surd i ty (ab sėr′də tē), **1** absurd quality or condition; lack of sense; foolishness: *the absurdity of superstition.* **2** something absurd; something unreasonable or ridiculous: *Your explanation is an absurdity. n., pl.* **ab surd i ties.**

A bu Dha bi (ä′bü dä′bē), capital of the United Arab Emirates.

a bun dance (ə bun′dəns), quantity that is more than enough; great plenty: *There is an abundance of apples this year. n.*

a bun dant (ə bun′dənt), **1** more than enough; very plentiful: *an abundant supply of food.* **2** having more than enough; abounding: *a river abundant in salmon. adj.* —**a bun′dant ly,** *adv.*

a buse (ə byüz′ *for 1,3,6;* ə byüs′ *for 2,4,5,7*), **1** make wrong or bad use of; misuse: *The senator abused his office by doing favors for those who paid him.* **2** a wrong or bad use; misuse: *abuse of privileges.* **3** treat roughly or cruelly; mistreat: *to abuse an animal by beating it.* **4** rough or cruel treatment: *abuse of a helpless animal.* **5** a bad practice or custom: *Slavery is an abuse.* **6** use harsh and insulting language about or to; scold severely: *Instead of debating the issues the candidates abused each other.* **7** harsh and insulting language; severe scolding. *1,3,6 v.,* **a bused, a bus ing;** *2,4,5,7 n.* —**a bus′er,** *n.*

a bu sive (ə byü′siv), **1** using harsh and insulting language; scolding severely. **2** treating roughly or cruelly. *adj.* —**a bu′sive ly,** *adv.* —**a bu′sive ness,** *n.*

a but (ə but′), touch at one end or edge; border; end: *Our property abuts on the street. The shed abuts against a stone wall. v.,* **a but ted, a but ting.** —**a but′ter,** *n.*

a but ment (ə but′mənt), a support for an arch or bridge. *n.*

a bysm (ə biz′əm), abyss. *n.*

a bys mal (ə biz′məl), too deep to be measured; bottomless. *adj.* —**a bys′mal ly,** *adv.*

a byss (ə bis′), **1** a bottomless or very great depth; a very deep crack in the earth: *The mountain climber stood at the edge of a cliff overlooking an abyss four thousand feet deep.* **2** anything too deep or great to be measured; lowest depth: *an abyss of despair. n., pl.* **a byss es.** [*Abyss* comes from Latin *abyssus,* and can be traced back to Greek *a-,* meaning "without," and *byssos,* meaning "bottom."]

Ab ys sin i a (ab′ə sin′ē ə), Ethiopia. *n.* —**Ab′ys sin′i an,** *adj., n.*

Ac, symbol for actinium.

a.c., A.C., or **a-c,** alternating current.

a ca cia (ə kā′shə), **1** tree or shrub with finely divided leaves that grows in tropical or warm regions. Acacias are related to peas and beans, and some are used in making perfume, gum, and dyes. **2** a locust tree of North America. *n., pl.* **a ca cias.**

acad., 1 academic. **2** academy.

ac a dem ic (ak′ə dem′ik), **1** of schools, colleges, and their studies: *The academic year begins when school opens in September.* **2** concerned with general education rather than commercial, technical, or professional education: *History and French are academic subjects; typewriting and bookkeeping are commercial subjects.* **3** theoretical; not practical: *"Which came first, the chicken or the egg?" is an academic question. adj.*

ac a dem i cal ly (ak′ə dem′ik lē), in an academic manner. *adv.*

a cad e my (ə kad′ə mē), **1** place for instruction. **2** a private high school. **3** school where some special subject can be studied: *West Point is a military academy.* **4** group of authors, scholars, scientists, artists, etc., organized to encourage literature, science, or art. *n., pl.* **a cad e mies.**

A ca di a (ə kā′dē ə), former French colony, from 1604 until 1713, in SE Canada, including what is now Nova Scotia. *n.* —**A ca′di an,** *adj., n.*

a cap pel la or **a ca pel la** (ä′ kə pel′ə), (in music) without instrumental accompaniment.

acc., account.

ac cede (ak sēd′), **1** give in; agree: *Finally I acceded to their requests.* **2** come or attain: *When the king died, his daughter acceded to the throne. v.,* **ac ced ed, ac ced ing.**

accel., accelerando.

ac cel e ran do (ak sel′ə rän′dō), (in music) gradually increasing in speed. *adv., adj.* [*Accelerando* was borrowed from Italian *accelerando.*]

ac cel e rate (ak sel′ə rāt′), **1** go or cause to go faster; increase in speed; speed up: *The car accelerated as it went down the steep hill.* **2** cause to happen sooner; hasten: *Rest often accelerates recovery from sickness. v.,* **ac cel e rat ed, ac cel e rat ing.**

ac cel e ra tion (ak sel′ə rā′shən), **1** a speeding up or hastening. **2** a change in speed. *n.*

ac cel e ra tor (ak sel′ə rā′tər), **1** thing that causes an increase in the speed of anything. **2** pedal or lever that controls the speed of an automobile engine. **3** particle accelerator. *n.*

ac cent (ak′sent *for 1,2,4,5;* ak′sent *or* ak sent′ *for 3,6*), **1** greater force or stronger tone of voice used in pronouncing some syllables or words: *In "letter," the accent is on the first syllable.* **2** a mark (′) written or printed to show the spoken force of a syllable, as in *to day* (tə dā′). Some words have two accents, a primary or stronger accent (′) and a secondary or weaker accent (′), as in *ac cel e ra tor* (ak sel′ə rā′tər). **3** pronounce or mark with an accent: *Is "acceptable" accented on the first or second syllable?* **4** a characteristic manner of pronunciation heard in a particular section of a country, or in the speech of a person speaking a language not his or her own: *My father was born in Germany and still speaks English with a German accent.* **5** emphasis on certain musical notes or chords. **6** emphasize; accentuate. *1,2,4,5 n., 3,6 v.* [*Accent* comes from Latin *accentus,* originally meaning "song added to (speech)."]

accent mark, accent (def. 2).

ac cen tu ate (ak sen′chü āt), **1** call special attention to; emphasize: *Her black hair accentuated the whiteness of her skin.* **2** pronounce with an accent. **3** mark with an accent. *v.,* **ac cen tu at ed, ac cen tu at ing.**

ac cen tu a tion (ak sen′chü ā′shən), an accentuating; emphasis. *n.*

ac cept (ak sept′), **1** take what is offered or given to one; consent to take: *She accepted the job.* **2** agree to; consent to: *The United States accepted Japan's proposal for a con-*

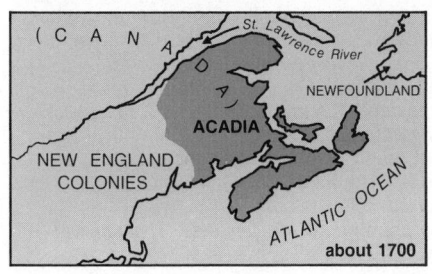
about 1700

ference on fishing rights. **3** say yes to an invitation, offer, etc.: *They asked me to go along and I accepted.* **4** take as true or satisfactory; believe: *The teacher accepted our excuse.* **5** receive with liking and approval; approve: *The design of the new car was not accepted by the public. v.* —**ac cept′er, ac cep′tor,** *n.*

ac cept a bil i ty (ak sep′tə bil′ə tē), quality of being acceptable or satisfactory. *n.*

ac cept a ble (ak sep′tə bəl), **1** likely to be well received; agreeable: *Flowers are an acceptable gift.* **2** good enough but not outstanding; satisfactory: *I received an acceptable mark on the test. adj.* —**ac cept′a ble ness,** *n.*

ac cept a bly (ak sep′tə blē), in a way that pleases. *adv.*

ac cept ance (ak sep′təns), **1** act of taking something offered or given: *the acceptance of added responsibility.* **2** favorable reception; approval: *the acceptance of a story for publication.* **3** the taking of something as true and satisfactory; belief: *The acceptance of the atomic theory by physicists has led to many scientific discoveries. n.*

ac cess (ak′ses), **1** right to approach, enter, or use; admittance: *All students have access to the library during the afternoon.* **2** approach to places, persons, or things; accessibility: *Access to mountain towns is often difficult because of poor roads.* **3** way or means of approach; entrance: *A ladder provided the only access to the attic.* **4** make (information) available by putting into or retrieving from a computer memory: *access a list of names.* 1-3 *n., pl.* **ac cess es;** 4 *v.*

ac ces si bil i ty (ak ses′ə bil′ə tē), condition of being easy to reach or get at. *n.*

accessible
(def. 2)
The village was **accessible** on foot only at low tide.

ac ces si ble (ak ses′ə bəl), **1** easy to get at; easy to reach or enter: *A telephone should be put where it will be accessible.* **2** able to be entered or reached. **3** able to be obtained: *Not many facts about the kidnaping were accessible. adj.* —**ac ces′si ble ness,** *n.* —**ac ces′si bly,** *adv.*

ac ces sion (ak sesh′ən), **1** act of attaining to a right, office, etc.: *The king's death was followed by the princess's accession to the throne.* **2** addition: *The accession of forty new pupils overcrowded the school. n.*

ac ces sor y (ak ses′ər ē), **1** an extra thing added to help something of more importance; subordinate part or detail: *Her new car has many accessories, including an air conditioner.* **2** added; extra: *His tie supplied an accessory bit of color.* **3** person who has helped in a crime or who has helped to hide it: *By not reporting the theft he became an accessory.* 1,3 *n., pl.* **ac ces sor ies;** 2 *adj.* —**ac ces′sor i ly,** *adv.*

ac ci dent (ak′sə dənt), **1** something harmful or unlucky that happens: *an automobile accident.* **2** something that happens without being planned, intended, wanted, or known in advance: *A series of lucky accidents led the scientist to the discovery. n.*

by accident, by chance; not on purpose: *I met an old friend by accident.*

ac ci den tal (ak′sə den′tl), **1** happening by accident; not planned; unexpected: *Our accidental meeting led to our becoming friends. Breaking the new dish was accidental; I did not mean to do it.* **2** a sign used in music to show a change of pitch. 1 *adj.,* 2 *n.* —**ac′ci den′tal ness,** *n.*

ac ci den tal ly (ak′sə den′tl ē), in an accidental manner; by chance. *adv.*

ac claim (ə klām′), **1** welcome with loud approval; praise highly; applaud: *The crowd acclaimed the winning team.* **2** a shout or show of approval; applause: *His new symphony was received with great acclaim.* 1 *v.,* 2 *n.*

ac cla ma tion (ak′lə mā′shən), a shout of welcome or show of approval by a crowd; applause: *The candidate was greeted by the acclamation of the crowd. n.*

by acclamation, with an overwhelming oral vote of approval in which the votes are not counted: *All the club members said "Aye," and so the officers were elected by acclamation.*

ac cli mate (ə klī′mit *or* ak′lə māt), accustom or become accustomed to a new climate, surroundings, or conditions: *Workers from warm climates acclimated slowly to arctic conditions. v.,* **ac cli mat ed, ac cli mat ing.** —**ac cli ma tion** (ak′lə mā′shən), *n.*

ac cli ma tize (ə klī′mə tīz), acclimate. *v.,* **ac cli ma tized, ac cli ma tiz ing.** —**ac cli′ma ti za′tion,** *n.*

ac cliv i ty (ə kliv′ə tē), an upward slope of ground. *n., pl.* **ac cliv i ties.**

ac co lade (ak′ə lād), something awarded as an honor; praise or recognition. *n.*

ac com mo date (ə kom′ə dāt), **1** have room for; hold comfortably. **2** help out; oblige: *I needed change for a ten-dollar bill, but the cashier couldn't accommodate me.* **3** supply with a place to sleep or live for a time: *Tourists are accommodated here.* **4** make fit or suitable; adjust: *My eyes soon accommodated themselves to the darkness. v.,* **ac com mo dat ed, ac com mo dat ing.**

accommodate (def. 1)—The bobsled was long enough to **accommodate** fifteen riders.

ac com mo dat ing (ə kom′ə dā′ting), willing to do favors; obliging: *My teacher was accommodating enough to lend me a dollar. adj.* —**ac com′mo dat′ing ly,** *adv.*

ac com mo da tion (ə kom′ə dā′shən), **1** anything that supplies a want or gives aid; a help, favor, or convenience: *It will be an accommodation to me if you will meet me tomorrow instead of today.* **2 accommodations,** *pl.* lodging and sometimes food as well: *Can we find accommodations at a motel for tonight?* **3** the fitting of something to a purpose or situation; adjustment: *The accommodation of our desires to a smaller income took some time.* **4** the automatic adjustment of the lens of the eye to see objects at various distances. *n.*

ac com pa ni ment (ə kum′pə nē mənt), **1** anything that goes along with something else: *The rain was an unpleasant accompaniment to our ride.* **2** a part in music that helps or enriches the main part: *We sang with piano accompaniment. n.*

ac com pa nist (ə kum′pə nist), person who plays a musical accompaniment. *n.*

ac com pa ny (ə kum′pə nē), **1** go along with: *May we accompany you on your walk?* **2** be or happen in connection with: *The rain was accompanied by a high wind.* **3** play a musical accompaniment for: *He accompanied the singer on the piano.* v., **ac com pa nied, ac com pa ny ing.** —**ac com′pa ni er,** *n.*

ac com plice (ə kom′plis), person who knowingly aids another in committing a crime or other wrong act: *Without an accomplice to open the door the thief could not have got into the building. n.*

ac com plish (ə kom′plish), succeed in completing; carry out; finish: *Did you accomplish your purpose? She can accomplish more in a day than anyone else in class. v.* —**ac com′plish a ble,** *adj.* —**ac com′plish er,** *n.*

ac com plished (ə kom′plisht), **1** carried out; completed; done: *The division of Germany is an accomplished fact.* **2** expert; skilled: *Only an accomplished dancer can perform with this ballet company. adj.*

ac com plish ment (ə kom′plish mənt), **1** something that has been done with knowledge, skill, or ability; achievement: *The teachers were proud of their pupils' accomplishments.* **2** skill in some social art or grace: *She was a person of many accomplishments; she could play the guitar, paint a picture, and change a tire equally well.* **3** a carrying out; completion: *The accomplishment of that project took two months. n.*

ac cord (ə kôrd′), **1** be in harmony; agree: *Her account of the accident accords with yours.* **2** agreement; harmony: *Most people are in accord in their desire for peace.* **3** grant (a favor, request, etc.): *accord praise for good work.* **1,3** v., **2** *n.*

of one's own accord or **on one's own accord,** without being asked; without suggestion from another: *We didn't ask for their help; they helped of their own accord.*

ac cord ance (ə kôrd′ns), agreement; harmony: *Play the game in accordance with the rules. n.*

ac cord ing ly (ə kôr′ding lē), **1** in a way that agrees with what is expected or stated: *These are the rules; you can act accordingly or leave the club.* **2** therefore; for this reason: *I was told to speak briefly; accordingly I cut short my talk. adv.*

ac cord ing to (ə kôr′ding), **1** in agreement with: *He came according to his promise.* **2** in proportion to; on the basis of: *You will be ranked according to the work you do.* **3** on the authority of: *According to this prediction we will have a hard winter.*

ac cor di on (ə kôr′dē ən), **1** a portable musical wind instrument with a bellows, metallic reeds, and keys. **2** having folds like the bellows of an accordion: *a skirt with accordion pleats.* **1** *n.*, **2** *adj.*

ac cost (ə kôst′), speak to first; come up and speak to: *A stranger accosted me and asked for directions. v.*

ac count (ə kount′), **1** statement telling in detail about an event or thing; explanation: *We gave them an account of everything that had happened.* **2** value; worth: *This torn notebook is of little account.* **3** statement of money received and spent: *I keep a written account of the way I spend my money.* **4** record of business dealings: *Businesses and factories keep accounts.* **5** statement of money due: *The office settles its accounts on the tenth of each month.* **6** hold to be; consider: *Solomon was accounted wise.* **1-5** *n.*, **6** *v.*

account for, 1 tell what has been done with; answer for: *The treasurer of the club had to account for all the dues paid.* **2** explain: *Can you account for your absence from class?* **3** be the cause of: *Late frosts accounted for the poor fruit crop.*

call to account, 1 demand an explanation of: *The*

treasurer was called to account for the shortage of funds. **2** scold; rebuke; reprimand: *We were called to account for our bad behavior.*

on account, as part payment: *I bought my new camera by paying $5 a week on account.*

on account of, because of: *The game was put off on account of rain.*

on any account, under any conditions; for any reason: *We were brought up not to lie on any account.*

on no account, under no conditions; for no reason: *On no account should you swim alone.*

on one's account, for one's sake: *Don't wait on my account.*

on one's own account, for one's own purposes and at one's own risk: *She left the law firm to go into business on her own account.*

take into account or **take account of,** make allowance for; consider: *You must take their wishes into account.*

turn to account, get advantage or profit from: *The new pitcher turned the coach's advice to good account in the next game.*

ac count a bil i ty (ə koun′tə bil′ə tē), state of being held responsible for carrying out one's obligations; responsibility. *n.*

ac count a ble (ə koun′tə bəl), liable to be called to account; responsible: *You are accountable for your own actions. adj.* —**ac count′a ble ness,** *n.* —**ac count′a bly,** *adv.*

ac count ant (ə koun′tənt), person who examines or manages business accounts. *n.*

ac count ing (ə koun′ting), **1** system or practice of keeping, analyzing, and interpreting business accounts. **2** statement of accounts. *n.*

accordion
(def. 1)

ac cou ter (ə kü′tər), furnish with clothing or equipment; equip; outfit: *Knights were accoutered in armor. v.*

ac cou ter ments (ə kü′tər mənts), **1** a soldier's equipment with the exception of weapons and clothing. A blanket and knapsack are parts of a soldier's accouterments. **2** clothes; outfit. *n.pl.*

ac cou tre (ə kü′tər), accouter. v., **ac cou tred, ac cou tring.**

ac cou tre ments (ə kü′tər mənts), accouterments. *n.pl.*

Ac cra (ə krä′), seaport in W Africa, capital of Ghana. *n.*

ac cred it (ə kred′it), 1 give authority to: *to accredit someone as a representative of the government.* 2 recognize as coming up to an official standard: *to accredit a college.* 3 accept as true; believe; trust. *v.* —**ac cred′i ta′tion,** *n.*

ac cred i ted (ə kred′ə tid), 1 recognized as coming up to an official standard: *Some colleges will accept without examination the graduates of accredited high schools.* 2 worthy of acceptance, belief, or trust: *an accredited authority in ancient history. adj.*

ac cre tion (ə krē′shən), 1 a growing together of separate things: *A glacier is formed by the accretion of many particles of frozen packed snow.* 2 something formed in this way. *n.*

ac crue (ə krü′), come as a growth or result: *Interest accrues from money left in a savings account. v.,* **ac crued, ac cru ing.** —**ac crue′ment,** *n.*

acct., 1 account. 2 accountant.

ac cu mu late (ə kyü′myə lāt), collect little by little; pile up; gather: *They accumulated enough money to buy a car. Dust had accumulated in the empty house. v.,* **ac cu mu lated, ac cu mu lat ing.**

ac cu mu la tion (ə kyü′myə lā′shən), 1 material collected; mass: *An accumulation of old papers filled the attic.* 2 a collecting together; an amassing: *the accumulation of knowledge. n.*

ac cu ra cy (ak′yər ə sē), a being without errors or mistakes; correctness; exactness: *I question the accuracy of that report. n.*

ac cu rate (ak′yər it), without errors or mistakes; precisely correct; exact: *an accurate report, an accurate watch. adj.* [*Accurate* comes from Latin *accuratum,* meaning "done with care."] —**ac′cur ate ly,** *adv.* —**ac′cur ate ness,** *n.*

ac curs ed (ə ker′sid *or* ə kerst′), 1 annoying and troublesome; detestable; hateful. 2 under a curse; doomed. *adj.* —**ac curs ed ness** (ə ker′sid nis), *n.*

ac cu sa tion (ak′yə zā′shən), a charge of having done something wrong, of being something bad, or of having broken the law: *The accusation against him was that he had stolen ten dollars from the store. n.*

ac cuse (ə kyüz′), 1 charge with having done something wrong, with being something bad, or with having broken the law: *The driver was accused of speeding.* 2 place the blame on: *The President accused Congress for the delay in passing his program. v.,* **ac cused, ac cus ing.**

ac cused (ə kyüzd′), **the accused,** the person or persons formally charged with an offense or a crime in a court of law. *n.*

ac cus er (ə kyü′zər), person who accuses another. *n.*

ac cus ing ly (ə kyü′zing lē), in an accusing manner. *adv.*

ac cus tom (ə kus′təm), make familiar by use or habit; get used: *When traveling you can accustom yourself to almost any kind of food. v.*

ac cus tomed (ə kus′təmd), usual; customary: *By Monday I was well again and was back in my accustomed seat in class. adj.*

accustomed to, used to; in the habit of: *I am accustomed to getting up early.*

ace (ās), 1 a playing card, domino, or side of a die having one spot. 2 (in tennis, handball, etc.) a point won on a serve which the opponent fails to return. 3 person expert at something: *She is an ace at basketball.* 4 very skilled; expert. 5 a combat pilot who has shot down five or more enemy planes. 1-3,5 *n.,* 4 *adj.*
within an ace of, on the very point of.

ac e tate (as′ə tāt), 1 a chemical substance formed from acetic acid. 2 fabric or other product made from cellulose acetate. *n.*

a ce tic acid (ə sē′tik), a very sour, colorless acid present in vinegar. It is a compound of hydrogen, carbon, and oxygen, used in making acetates, in drugs, etc.

a cet y lene (ə set′l ēn′), a colorless gas that burns with a bright light and very hot flame. It is used for lighting, for making plastics, and, when combined with oxygen, for welding metals. *n.*

ache (āk), 1 a dull, continuous pain: *Muscular aches often follow hard exercise.* 2 suffer continuous pain; be in pain; hurt: *My arm aches.* 3 INFORMAL. be eager; wish very much: *During the hot days of August we all ached to go swimming.* 1 *n.,* 2,3 *v.,* **ached, ach ing.** —**ach′ing ly,** *adv.*

a chieve (ə chēv′), 1 carry out to a successful end; accomplish; do: *Did you achieve your purpose?* 2 reach by one's own efforts; get by effort: *achieve high grades in mathematics. v.,* **a chieved, a chiev ing.** —**a chiev′a ble,** *adj.* —**a chiev′er,** *n.*

a chieve ment (ə chēv′mənt), 1 thing achieved; some plan or action carried out with courage or unusual ability; accomplishment; feat: *Landing astronauts on the moon was a great achievement.* 2 an achieving: *the achievement of success. n.*

A chil les (ə kil′ēz), (in Greek legends) a hero of the Greeks at the siege of Troy. No weapon could injure Achilles anywhere, except in the heel. *n.*

Achilles′ heel, a weak point.

ach y (ā′kē), full of aches. *adj.*

ac id (as′id), 1 any compound that yields hydrogen ions when dissolved in water. Acids turn blue litmus paper red and usually react with a base to form a salt. Hydrochloric acid and sulfuric acid are two common acids. 2 of acids; having the properties of an acid: *an acid solution.* 3 sharp or biting to the taste; sour: *Lemons are an acid fruit.* 4 sharp in manner or temper: *an acid comment.* 1 *n.,* 2-4 *adj.* [*Acid* comes from Latin *acidus,* meaning "sour."] —**ac′id ly,** *adv.* —**ac′id ness,** *n.*

a cid i fy (ə sid′ə fī), 1 make or become sour. 2 change into an acid. *v.,* **a cid i fied, a cid i fy ing.** —**a cid′i fi ca′tion,** *n.* —**a cid′i fi′er,** *n.*

a cid i ty (ə sid′ə tē), acid quality or condition; sourness. *n.*

acid rain, rain containing a weak solution of sulfuric and nitric acid, created by pollutants emitted during the burning of fossil fuels.

acid test, a decisive test.

ac knowl edge (ak nol′ij), 1 admit to be true: *to acknowledge one's own faults.* 2 recognize the authority or claims of: *Parliament acknowledged Elizabeth I to be queen.* 3 make known that one has received (a service, favor, gift, message, etc.): *I acknowledged her letter at once. v.,* **ac knowl edged, ac knowl edg ing.** —**ac knowl′edge a ble,** *adj.* —**ac knowl′edged ly,** *adv.* —**ac knowl′edg er,** *n.*

ac knowl edg ment *or* **ac knowl edge ment** (ak nol′ij mənt), 1 something given or done to show that one has received a service, favor, gift, message, etc.: *The winner waved in acknowledgment of the cheers.* 2 act of admitting that something is true: *acknowledgment of a mistake.* 3 recognition of authority, claims, or merit. *n.*

ac me (ak′mē), the highest point: *The acme of the development of spaceships probably lies in the future. n.*

ac ne (ak′nē), a skin disease in which the oil glands in the skin become clogged and inflamed, often causing pimples. *n.*

ac o lyte (ak′ə līt), person who helps a priest, deacon, etc., during certain religious services: *The acolyte lit the candles on the altar. n.*

A con ca gua (ä′kông kä′gwə), mountain in the Andes, in W Argentina, 22,834 feet (6960 meters) high. It is the highest mountain in the Western Hemisphere. *n.*

a corn (ā′kôrn *or* ā′kərn), the nut of an oak tree. *n.*

a cous tic (ə kü′stik), **1** having to do with the sense or the organs of hearing. **2** having to do with the science of sound. *adj.* —**a cous′ti cal ly,** *adv.*

a cous ti cal (ə kü′stə kəl), having to do with the science of sound. *adj.*

a cous tics (ə kü′stiks), **1** *pl. in form and use.* the qualities of a room, hall, auditorium, etc., that determine how well sounds can be heard in it: *The acoustics were so good that people in the last row could hear the speaker well.* **2** *pl. in form, sing. in use.* the science of sound: *Acoustics is taught in some colleges. n.*

ac quaint (ə kwānt′), make aware; let know; inform: *Let me acquaint you with your new duties. v.*

be acquainted with, have personal knowledge of; know: *I have heard about your friend, but I am not acquainted with him.*

ac quaint ance (ə kwān′təns), **1** person known to one, but not a close friend: *We have many acquaintances in our neighborhood.* **2** knowledge of persons or things gained from experience with them: *I have some acquaintance with French, but I do not know it well. n.*

make the acquaintance of, get to know (someone): *We soon made the acquaintance of our new neighbors.*

ac quaint ance ship (ə kwān′təns ship), **1** relation between acquaintances: *Their acquaintanceship lasted many years.* **2** personal knowledge; acquaintance. *n.*

ac qui esce (ak′wē es′), give consent by keeping silent or by not making objections; agree or submit quietly: *We acquiesced in their plan because we could not suggest a better one. v.,* **ac qui esced, ac qui esc ing.**

ac qui es cence (ak′wē es′ns), an agreeing or submitting quietly; consent given without objections. *n.*

ac qui es cent (ak′wē es′nt), quietly consenting or agreeing; acquiescing. *adj.* —**ac′qui es′cent ly,** *adv.*

ac quire (ə kwīr′), come to have; get as one's own; obtain: *I acquired the money for college by working summers. v.,* **ac quired, ac quir ing.** —**ac quir′a ble,** *adj.*

ac quire ment (ə kwīr′mənt), **1** act of acquiring: *the acquirement of wealth.* **2** something acquired; attainment: *Her musical acquirements are remarkable for a girl of her age. n.*

ac qui si tion (ak′wə zish′ən), **1** an acquiring; getting as one's own: *the acquisition of skill by practicing.* **2** something acquired: *The gallery's new acquisitions included two paintings by Picasso. n.*

ac quis i tive (ə kwiz′ə tiv), fond of acquiring; eager to get wealth, power, knowledge, etc.: *My acquisitive friend is too fond of money. adj.* —**ac quis′i tive ly,** *adv.* —**ac quis′i tive ness,** *n.*

ac quit (ə kwit′), declare not guilty; set free: *Both of the accused bank robbers were acquitted. v.,* **ac quit ted, ac quit ting.** —**ac quit′ter,** *n.*

acquit oneself, do one's part; behave: *You acquitted yourself well during the debate.*

acrostic with first letters forming the word "spring"

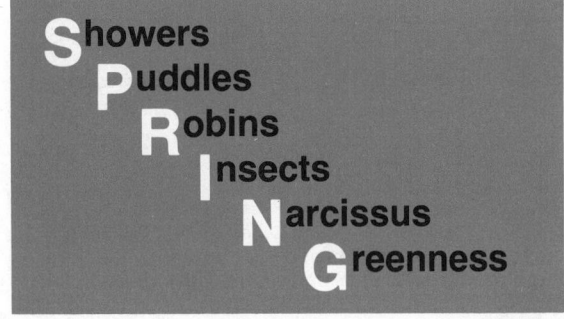

Showers	
Puddles	
Robins	
Insects	
Narcissus	
Greenness	

a hat	i it	oi oil	ch child	a in about
ā age	ī ice	ou out	ng long	e in taken
ä far	o hot	u cup	sh she	ə = i in pencil
e let	ō open	u̇ put	th thin	o in lemon
ē equal	ô order	ü rule	ŦH then	u in circus
ėr term			zh measure	

ac quit tal (ə kwit′l), a setting free by declaring not guilty; discharge; release: *The jury brought in a verdict of acquittal. n.*

a cre (ā′kər), **1** a unit of area equal to 160 square rods or 43,560 square feet (4047 square meters), used to measure land. **2 acres,** *pl.* lands; property. *n.*

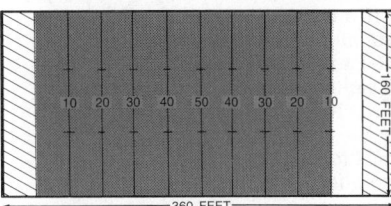

acre (def. 1)—An acre is smaller than a football field. The colored part of this football field is an acre.

a cre age (ā′kər ij), number of acres. *n.*

ac rid (ak′rid), **1** sharp, bitter, or stinging to the mouth, eyes, skin, or nose: *Acrid coal smoke made my eyes water.* **2** irritating in manner; sharp in temper: *an acrid disposition. adj.* —**ac′rid ly,** *adv.* —**ac′rid ness,** *n.*

Ac ri lan (ak′rə lan), trademark for an acrylic fiber that resembles wool and resists wrinkling. *n.*

ac ri mo ni ous (ak′rə mō′nē əs), sharp or bitter in temper, language, or manner: *An acrimonious dispute broke out between the drivers who had the accident. adj.* —**ac′ri mo′ni ous ly,** *adv.* —**ac′ri mo′ni ous ness,** *n.*

ac ri mo ny (ak′rə mō′nē), sharpness or bitterness in temper, language, or manner. *n.*

ac ro bat (ak′rə bat), person who can perform gymnastic feats, such as swinging on a trapeze, walking a tightrope, etc. *n.* [*Acrobat* is from French *acrobate,* which came from Greek *akrobatos,* meaning "walking on tiptoe."]

ac ro bat ic (ak′rə bat′ik), **1** of an acrobat: *Walking a tightrope is an acrobatic feat.* **2** like an acrobat's: *an acrobatic leap. adj.* —**ac′ro bat′i cal ly,** *adv.*

ac ro bat ics (ak′rə bat′iks), **1** tricks or performances of an acrobat; gymnastic feats. **2** feats like those of an acrobat: *a monkey's acrobatics. n. pl. in form, sometimes sing. in use.*

ac ro nym (ak′rə nim), word formed from the first letters or syllables of other words. EXAMPLE: scuba (self-contained underwater breathing apparatus). *n.* [*Acronym* comes from Greek *akros,* meaning "tip, outermost," and *onyma,* meaning "name." This word first appeared in English about 1943.]

a crop o lis (ə krop′ə lis), the high, fortified part of an ancient Greek city. The Parthenon was built on **the Acropolis** of Athens. *n., pl.* **a crop o lis es.**

a cross (ə krôs′), **1** from one side to the other of; over: *The cat walked across the street.* **2** from one side to the other: *What is the distance across?* **3** on the other side of; beyond: *The woods are across the river.* **4** on or to the other side: *When are you going across?* **1,3** *prep.,* **2,4** *adv.*

come across or **run across,** meet or fall in with; find: *We come across hard words in some books.*

a cros tic (ə krôs′tik), composition in verse or arrangement of words in which the first, last, or certain other letters in each line, taken in order, spell a word or phrase. *n.* —**a cros′ti cal ly,** *adv.*

a cryl ic (ə kril′ik), **1** a durable plastic used to make fabrics, optical lenses, taillights, etc. **2** made of such plastic. **3** paint made from a liquid plastic and used with water. **4** of such paint. 1,3 *n.*, 2,4 *adj.*

act (akt), **1** something done; deed: *Sharing your candy was a generous act.* **2** process of doing: *I was caught in the act of hiding the gifts.* **3** do something: *The fire department acted promptly and saved the burning house.* **4** have effect: *The medicine failed to act.* **5** behave: *I apologize for acting badly.* **6** behave like: *Most people act the fool now and then.* **7** perform on the stage, in motion pictures, on television, or over the radio; play a part: *He acts the part of the district attorney. She acts very well.* **8** a main division of a play or opera: *Most modern plays have three acts.* **9** one of several performances on a program: *We stayed to see the comedian's act.* **10** a legislative decision; decree. An act of Congress is a bill that has been passed by Congress. 1,2,8-10 *n.*, 3-7 *v.* —**act′a ble,** *adj.*

act for or **act as,** take the place of; do the work of: *While the principal was gone, the assistant principal acted for her.*

act on or **act upon, 1** follow; obey: *I will act on your suggestion.* **2** have an effect or influence on: *Yeast acted on the dough and made it rise.*

act up, INFORMAL. behave badly: *The children began to act up when company came.*

act ing (ak′ting), taking the place of another; serving temporarily as: *While the principal was sick, one of the teachers was acting principal. adj.*

ac tin i um (ak tin′ē əm), a radioactive chemical element somewhat like radium, found in pitchblende. *n.*

ac tion (ak′shən), **1** process of acting; doing something: *The quick action of the firemen saved the building from being burned down. The situation called for immediate action.* **2** something done; act: *Helping a small child to cross the street was a kind action.* **3 actions,** *pl.* conduct; behavior: *Her actions revealed her thoughtfulness.* **4** effect or influence of one thing on another: *the action of wind on a ship's sails.* **5** way of moving or working; movement: *a pulley with an easy action.* **6** battle; part of a battle: *to be wounded in action.* **7** series of events in a story or play. **8** lawsuit. *n.* —**ac′tion less,** *adj.*

take action, 1 begin to do something; start working: *The government decided to take action to prevent a flu epidemic.* **2** start a lawsuit; sue: *The people hurt in the accident have taken action to obtain payment for their injuries.*

ac ti vate (ak′tə vāt), **1** make active. **2** make radioactive. *v.,* **ac ti vat ed, ac ti vat ing.** —**ac′ti va′tor,** *n.*

ac ti va tion (ak′tə vā′shən), an activating. *n.*

ac tive (ak′tiv), **1** showing much action; moving rather quickly much of the time; lively: *The baby is very active.* **2** acting; working: *An active volcano may erupt at any time.* **3** working hard or with energy; busy and energetic: *We took an active part in organizing the stamp club.* **4** showing the subject of a verb as acting. In "She broke the window," *broke* is in the active voice. **5** a verb form that does this. 1-4 *adj.,* 5 *n.* —**ac′tive ly,** *adv.* —**ac′tive ness,** *n.*

ac tiv i ty (ak tiv′ə tē), **1** a being active; use of power; movement: *physical activity, mental activity.* **2** action; doing: *the activities of enemy spies.* **3** vigorous action; liveliness: *The activity of the children disturbed my sleep.* **4** thing to do: *Students who have too many outside activities may find it hard to keep up with their studies. n., pl.* **ac tiv i ties.**

ac tor (ak′tər), person who acts on the stage, in motion pictures, on television, or over the radio. *n.*

ac tress (ak′tris), girl or woman who acts on the stage, in motion pictures, on television, or over the radio. *n., pl.* **ac tress es.**

Acts (akts), the fifth book of the New Testament. Acts tells about the beginnings of the Christian church. *n.*

Acts of the Apostles, Acts.

ac tu al (ak′chü əl), existing as a fact; real: *What he told us was not a dream but an actual happening. adj.* —**ac′tu al ness,** *n.*

ac tu al i ty (ak′chü al′ə tē), an actual thing; fact; reality: *A trip to the moon is now an actuality. n., pl.* **ac tu al i ties.**

ac tu al ize (ak′chü ə līz), make (a plan or idea) actual. *v.,* **ac tu al ized, ac tu al iz ing.** —**ac′tu al i za′tion,** *n.*

ac tu al ly (ak′chü ə lē), really; in fact: *Are you actually going to camp this summer or just wishing to go? adv.*

ac tu ar y (ak′chü er′ē), person who figures risks, rates, premiums, etc., for insurance companies. *n., pl.* **ac tu ar ies.**

ac tu ate (ak′chü āt), **1** put into action: *This pump is actuated by a belt driven by an electric motor.* **2** influence to act: *Kindness actuated him to help the old woman with the heavy bundle. v.,* **ac tu at ed, ac tu at ing.** —**ac′tu a′tion,** *n.* —**ac′tu a′tor,** *n.*

a cu men (ə kyü′mən), sharpness and quickness in seeing and understanding; keen insight; discernment. *n.*

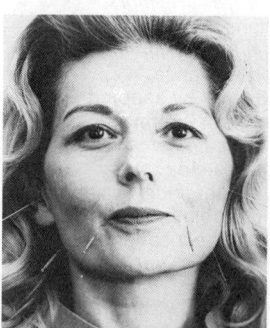

acupuncture

ac u punc ture (ak′yủ pungk′chər), an ancient Chinese practice of inserting needles into certain parts of the body. Acupuncture is used to treat some diseases and to relieve pain. *n.*

a cute (ə kyüt′), **1** sharp and severe: *A toothache can cause acute pain.* **2** brief and severe: *An acute disease like pneumonia reaches a crisis within a short time.* **3** threatening; critical: *The long drought caused an acute shortage of water in the city.* **4** quick in perceiving and responding to impressions; keen: *Dogs have an acute sense of smell.* **5** having a sharp point. *adj.* —**a cute′ly,** *adv.* —**a cute′ness,** *n.*

acute accent, mark (′) placed over a vowel letter to show the kind of sound, as in French *attaché,* or place of the accent, as in Spanish *Asunción.*

acute angle   right angle

acute angle, angle less than a right angle.

ad (ad), advertisement. *n.*

A.D., after the birth of Christ. From 63 B.C. to A.D. 14 is 77 years. [The abbreviation *A.D.* stands for the Latin phrase *Anno Domini,* meaning "in the year of the Lord."]

ad age (ad′ij), a wise saying that has been much used; proverb. "Haste makes waste" is a well-known adage. *n.*

a da gio (ə dä′jō), in music: **1** slowly. **2** slow. **3** a slow part. 1 *adv.*, 2 *adj.*, 3 *n., pl.* **a da gios.** [*Adagio* comes from the Italian phrase *ad agio,* meaning "at ease."]

Ad am (ad′əm), (in the Bible) the first man, the husband of Eve. *n.*

ad a mant (ad′ə mənt), not giving in readily; firm and unyielding: *Columbus was adamant in refusing the requests of his sailors to turn back. adj.* —**ad′a mant ly,** *adv.*

Ad ams (ad′əmz), **1 John,** 1735-1826, the second president of the United States, from 1797 to 1801. **2 John Quincy,** 1767-1848, the sixth president of the United States, from 1825 to 1829, son of John Adams. **3 Samuel,** 1722-1803, a leader of the American colonists' resistance to England at the time of the Revolutionary War. *n.*

Adam's apple, the slight lump in the front of a person's throat formed by the larynx.

a dapt (ə dapt′), **1** make fit or suitable; adjust: *Can you adapt your way of working to the new job?* **2** change so as to make suitable for a different use: *The story was adapted for the movies from a novel by Jane Austen. v.* —**a dapt′er, a dap′tor,** *n.*

a dapt a bil i ty (ə dap′tə bil′ə tē), power to change easily to fit different conditions. *n.*

a dapt a ble (ə dap′tə bəl), easily changed or changing easily to fit different conditions: *an adaptable person. My schedule is adaptable; I can see you anytime. adj.*

ad ap ta tion (ad′ap tā′shən), **1** a changing to fit different conditions; an adapting: *He made a good adaptation to high school.* **2** a being adapted or made to fit: *Mother's adaptation of an old bottle to a table lamp was clever.* **3** something made by adapting: *A motion picture is often an adaptation of a novel.* **4** a change in structure, form, or habits to fit different conditions: *Wings are adaptations of the upper limbs for flight. n.*

a dapt ed (ə dap′tid), fitted; suitable. *adj.*

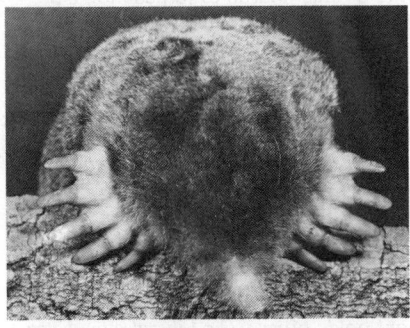

adapted—The front feet of the mole are well **adapted** for digging.

a dap tive (ə dap′tiv), able to adapt; showing adaptation. *adj.* —**a dap′tive ly,** *adv.* —**a dap′tive ness,** *n.*

add (ad), **1** find the sum of: *Add 73 and 27 and you have 100.* **2** say further; go on to say or write: *They said goodby and added that they had had a pleasant visit.* **3** join (one thing to another): *I tasted the lemonade, then added more sugar. v.* —**add′er,** *n.*

add to, make greater; increase: *The fine day added to our pleasure.*

add up to, amount to: *What do the profits add up to?*

ad dend (ad′end *or* ə dend′), a number or quantity to be added to another: *In 2 + 3 + 4 = 9, the addends are 2, 3, and 4. n.*

ad den dum (ə den′dəm), thing added; appendix. *n., pl.* **ad den da** (ə den′də).

ad der (ad′ər), **1** a small, poisonous snake of Europe. **2** hognose snake. **3** puff adder. *n.*

ad dict (ad′ikt), person who is a slave to a habit, especially to the use of a drug. *n.*

ad dict ed (ə dik′tid), slavishly following a habit or practice; strongly inclined: *addicted to drugs. adj.*

ad dic tion (ə dik′shən), condition of being a slave to a habit. *n.*

ad dic tive (ə dik′tiv), causing or tending to cause addiction: *Alcohol can be addictive. adj.*

Ad dis Ab a ba (ad′is ab′ə bə), capital of Ethiopia, in the central part.

ad di tion (ə dish′ən), **1** an adding of one number or quantity to another: $2 + 3 = 5$ *is a simple addition.* **2** an adding of one thing to another: *The addition of flour will thicken gravy.* **3** thing added: *Cream is a tasty addition to many desserts.* **4** part added to a building. *n.*

in addition or **in addition to,** besides; also: *In addition to her work as a composer, she is a music critic.*

ad di tion al (ə dish′ə nəl), added; extra; more: *I need some additional information. adj.* —**ad di′tion al ly,** *adv.*

ad di tive (ad′ə tiv), **1** substance added to another substance to preserve it, increase its effectiveness, etc. **2** involving addition. 1 *n.,* 2 *adj.* —**ad′di tive ly,** *adv.*

ad dled (ad′ld), **1** muddled; confused: *an addled brain.* **2** rotten: *addled eggs. adj.*

ad dress (ə dres′; *also* ad′res *for 4,7*), **1** a speech, especially a formal one: *The President gave an address to the nation over television.* **2** make an address to: *The speaker addressed the organization on the subject of ecology.* **3** speak to or write to: *She addressed me as though we were old friends. The king was addressed as "Your Majesty."* **4** the place to which one's mail is directed; place of residence or of business: *Write your name and address on this envelope.* **5** write on (a letter, package, etc.) where it is to be sent: *to address envelopes for greeting cards.* **6** apply or devote (oneself); direct one's energies: *She addressed herself to the task of learning French.* **7** symbol or symbols identifying the place where certain information is stored in a computer memory. **8** retrieve or store information by means of a computer address. 1,4,7 *n., pl.* **ad dress es;** 2,3,5,6,8 *v.* —**ad dress′er, ad dres′sor,** *n.*

ad dress ee (ə dre sē′), person to whom a letter, package, etc., is addressed. *n.*

ad duce (ə düs′ *or* ə dyüs′), offer as a reason; give as proof or evidence; bring up as an example: *The scientist adduced the results of several experiments to prove his point. v.,* **ad duced, ad duc ing.** —**ad duc′er,** *n.*

A den (äd′n *or* ād′n), capital of Southern Yemen. *n.*

ad e noids (ad′n oidz), growths of glandular tissue in the upper part of the throat, just back of the nose. Adenoids can swell up and make breathing and speaking difficult. *n.pl.*

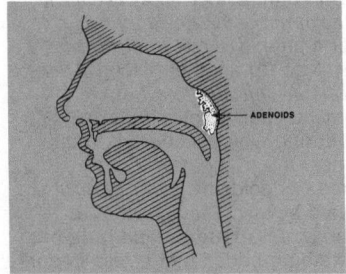

a dept (ə dept′), thoroughly skilled; expert: *She is adept at skiing. adj.* **—a dept′ly,** *adv.* **—a dept′ness,** *n.*

ad e qua cy (ad′ə kwə sē), a being adequate; as much as is needed for a particular purpose; sufficiency. *n.*

ad e quate (ad′ə kwit), **1** as much as is needed for a particular purpose; sufficient; enough: *To be healthy one must have an adequate diet.* **2** suitable; competent: *He is barely adequate for the job. adj.* **—ad′e quate ly,** *adv.* **—ad′e quate ness,** *n.*

ad here (ad hir′), **1** stick fast; remain attached: *Mud adheres to your shoes.* **2** hold closely or firmly: *The principal adhered to the plan for dropping Latin in spite of the opposition of some teachers.* **3** be a follower or upholder; give allegiance: *adhere to a political party. v.,* **ad hered, ad her ing. —ad her′er,** *n.*

ad her ence (ad hir′əns), a holding to and following closely; faithfulness: *The coach insisted on rigid adherence to the rules. n.*

ad her ent (ad hir′ənt), **1** a faithful supporter; follower: *He was an adherent of the conservative party.* **2** sticking fast; attached. **1** *n.,* **2** *adj.* **—ad her′ent ly,** *adv.*

ad he sion (ad hē′zhən), a sticking fast; attachment; an adhering. *n.*

ad he sive (ad hē′siv), **1** gummed tape used to hold bandages in place. **2** glue, paste, or other substance for sticking things together. **3** holding fast; adhering easily; sticky. **1,2** *n.,* **3** *adj.* **—ad he′sive ly,** *adv.* **—ad he′sive ness,** *n.*

a dieu (ə dü′ *or* ə dyü′), good-by. *interj., n., pl.* **a dieus** *or* **a dieux** (ə düz′ *or* ə dyüz′). [*Adieu* came into English about 600 years ago from French *adieu,* which is from the French phrase *a Dieu,* meaning "to God."]

a di os (ä′dē ōs′ *or* ad′ē ōs′), good-by. *interj., n.* [*Adios* is from Spanish *adiós,* which comes from the Spanish phrase *a Dios,* meaning "to God."]

ad i pose (ad′ə pōs), fat. *adj.* **—ad′i pose′ness,** *n.*

Ad i ron dack Mountains (ad′ə ron′dak), mountains of a large area in NE New York State.

Ad i ron dacks (ad′ə ron′daks), Adirondack Mountains. *n.pl.* [*Adirondacks* comes from a Mohawk word meaning "they eat trees." The Mohawks used the word in reference to a group of Canadian Indians.]

adj., adjective.

ad ja cent (ə jā′snt), lying near or close; adjoining; next: *The house adjacent to ours has been sold. adj.* **—ad ja′cent ly,** *adv.*

ad jec ti val (aj′ik tī′vəl), **1** of an adjective. **2** used as an adjective. *adj.* **—ad′jec ti′val ly,** *adv.*

ad jec tive (aj′ik tiv), **1** one of a class of words that qualify, limit, or add to the meaning of a noun or pronoun. In "a tiny brook," "The day is warm," "great happiness," and "this pencil," *tiny, warm, great,* and *this* are adjectives. **2** of an adjective. **3** used as an adjective. **1** *n.,* **2,3** *adj.* **—ad′jec tive ly,** *adv.*

ad join (ə join′), be next to; be close to; be side by side: *Canada adjoins the United States. v.*

ad join ing (ə joi′ning), being next to or in contact with; bordering: *The twins have adjoining rooms. adj.*

ad journ (ə jėrn′), **1** put off until a later time: *The members of the club voted to adjourn the meeting until two o'clock.* **2** stop activity for a time: *The court adjourned from Friday until Monday.* **3** go (to another place): *After the meeting we adjourned to the cafeteria to eat. v.*

ad journ ment (ə jėrn′mənt), **1** an adjourning or a being adjourned. **2** time during which a court, lawmaking body, etc., is adjourned. *n.*

ad judge (ə juj′), **1** decree or decide by law: *The accused was adjudged guilty.* **2** award by law: *The property was adjudged to the rightful owner. v.,* **ad judged, ad judg ing.**

ad junct (aj′ungkt), something added that is less impor-

tant or not necessary, but helpful: *Grammar is not merely an adjunct to composition; it is a study in itself. n.* **—ad′junct ly,** *adv.*

ad jure (ə jūr′), ask earnestly or solemnly: *I adjure you on your honor to tell the truth. v.,* **ad jured, ad jur ing.**

ad just (ə just′), **1** change to make fit: *These desks and seats can be adjusted to the height of any child.* **2** put in proper order, position, or relation; arrange: *Please adjust the TV so that the picture doesn't jump.* **3** arrange satisfactorily; set right; settle: *The girls adjusted their difference of opinion and were friends again.* **4** accommodate oneself; get used: *Some wild animals never adjust to life in a zoo. v.*

ad just a ble (ə jus′tə bəl), able to be adjusted: *This adjustable lamp can be placed in various positions. adj.* **—ad just′a bly,** *adv.*

ad just er *or* **ad jus tor** (ə jus′tər), **1** thing that adjusts something else. **2** person who adjusts claims. *n.*

ad just ment (ə just′mənt), **1** act or process of adjusting: *The adjustment of seats to the right height for children is necessary for their comfort.* **2** a means of adjusting: *All TVs have an adjustment for volume control.* **3** settlement of a dispute, a claim, etc. *n.*

ad ju tant (aj′ə tənt), **1** an army officer who assists a commanding officer by sending out orders, writing letters, etc. **2** assistant. *n.*

ad lib (ad lib′), **1** make up as one goes along; improvise: *The actor forgot some of his lines and had to adlib his part.* **2** on the spur of the moment; freely: *The orchestra played adlib.* **3** music or words made up as one goes along. **1** *v.,* **ad libbed, ad lib bing;** **2** *adv.,* **3** *n.*

Adm., **1** Admiral. **2** Admiralty.

ad min is ter (ad min′ə stər), **1** manage the affairs of; direct: *The Secretary of Defense administers a department of the government.* **2** give out; apply: *administer first aid to an injured person. Judges administer justice.* **3** offer formally: *The witness could not testify until the oath had been administered.* **4** settle or take charge of (an estate). **5** be helpful; contribute: *The government administered to the needs of the flood victims. v.*

ad min is tra tion (ad min′ə strā′shən), **1** the managing of the affairs of a business, an office, etc.: *The administration of a big business requires skill in dealing with people.* **2** group of persons in charge: *The principal and teachers of a school are part of the administration of the school.* **3** management of public affairs by government officials: *She is experienced in city administration.* **4** officials as a group; the government. **5 the Administration,** the President of the United States, the cabinet appointed by the President, and the departments of the government headed by cabinet members. **6** the period of time during which a government holds office: *The Liberal administration in Canada lasted many years.* **7** a giving out or applying: *The Red Cross handled the administration of aid to the refugees. n.*

ad min is tra tive (ad min′ə strā′tiv), having to do with administration; executive. *adj.* **—ad min′is tra′tive ly,** *adv.*

ad min is tra tor (ad min′ə strā′tər), **1** person who administers; manager. **2** person appointed to settle or take charge of an estate. *n.*

ad mir a ble (ad′mər ə bəl), worth admiring; very good; excellent: *She has an admirable character. adj.* **—ad′mir a ble ness,** *n.*

ad mir a bly (ad′mər ə blē), in an admirable manner; excellently. *adv.*

ad mir al (ad′mər əl), **1** the commander of a navy or a fleet. **2** officer in the United States Navy ranking next below a fleet admiral. **3** any of several colorful butterflies, especially one kind having reddish streaks on its wings. *n.*

ad mir al ty (ad′mər əl tē), branch of law dealing with affairs of the sea and of ships. *n., pl.* **ad mir al ties.**

ad mi ra tion (ad′mə rā′shən), **1** a feeling of wonder, pleasure, and approval: *The beauty of the performance excited admiration.* **2** person or thing that is admired: *a spectacular painting that was the admiration of all who viewed it. n.*

ad mire (ad mīr′), **1** regard with wonder, pleasure, or satisfaction: *We admired the beautiful painting.* **2** think highly of; respect: *I admire your courage. v.,* **ad mired, ad mir ing.**

ad mir er (ad mī′rər), person who admires: *The clever girl had many admirers. n.*

ad mir ing ly (ad mī′ring lē), with admiration: *I looked at the new bicycle admiringly. adv.*

ad mis si ble (ad mis′ə bəl), **1** capable or worthy of being admitted: *Any student is admissible to this club.* **2** permitted by a person in authority or by the rules; allowable: *Is it admissible to practice here? adj.* **—admis′si ble ness,** *n.* **—ad mis′si bly,** *adv.*

ad mis sion (ad mish′ən), **1** an allowing to enter; entrance: *His admission into the hospital was delayed for lack of beds.* **2** right of entering or using a place, an office, etc.; permission to enter: *apply for admission into a college.* **3** price paid for the right to enter: *Admission to the show is one dollar.* **4** an admitting to be true; acknowledging: *Their admission that they were to blame kept others from being punished. n.*

ad mit (ad mit′), **1** say (something) is real or true; acknowledge: *She admits now that she made a mistake. His opponent had to admit defeat.* **2** allow to enter; let in: *He was admitted to a trade school. Windows admit light and air.* **3** have room for; be large enough for: *This garage door will admit two cars abreast. v.,* **ad mit ted, ad mitting.**

ad mit tance (ad mit′ns), right to enter; permission to enter: *She had admittance to the theater free of charge. n.*

ad mit ted ly (ad mit′id lē), without denial; by general consent: *Admittedly the rules are strict. adv.*

ad mon ish (ad mon′ish), **1** advise (a person) against something in order that he may be guided to improve; warn: *The policeman admonished him not to drive so fast.* **2** scold gently; reprove: *The teacher admonished the student for careless work. v.* **—ad mon′ish er,** *n.*

ad mon ish ment (ad mon′ish mənt), admonition. *n.*

ad mo ni tion (ad′mə nish′ən), an admonishing; gentle reproof or warning: *They received an admonition from their parents for being late. n.*

ad mon i to ry (ad mon′ə tôr′ē), admonishing; warning: *The librarian raised an admonitory finger. adj.*

a do (ə dü′), **1** noisy activity; bustle: *There was much ado about the party by all the family.* **2** trouble; difficulty. *n.*

a do be (ə dō′bē), **1** brick made of clay baked in the sun.

a hat	i it	oi oil	ch child	a in about
ā age	ī ice	ou out	ng long	e in taken
ä far	o hot	u cup	sh she	ə = i in pencil
e let	ō open	u̇ put	th thin	o in lemon
ē equal	ô order	ü rule	ᵺ then	u in circus
ėr term			zh measure	

adobe (def. 2) adobe building and oven

2 built or made of adobe. **3** a building made of adobe. 1,3 *n.,* 2 *adj.* [*Adobe* was borrowed from Spanish *adobe,* which came from Arabic *aṭ-ṭūb,* meaning "the brick."]

ad o les cence (ad′l es′ns), period of growth from childhood to adulthood; youth. *n.*

ad o les cent (ad′l es′nt), **1** person growing up from childhood to adulthood, especially a person from about 12 to about 20 years of age. **2** growing up from childhood to adulthood; youthful: *He is still in the adolescent stage of development.* **3** of adolescents; characteristic of adolescents: *Adolescent friendships often do not last.* 1 *n.,* 2,3 *adj.* [*Adolescent* comes from Latin *adolescentem,* meaning "growing up."] **—ad′o les′cent ly,** *adv.*

A don is (ə don′is *or* ə dō′nis), **1** (in Greek and Roman myths) a handsome young man who was loved by Aphrodite (Venus). **2** any handsome young man. *n.*

a dopt (ə dopt′), **1** take as one's own choice: *I liked your idea and adopted it. Few Americans would find it easy to adopt Japanese customs.* **2** accept formally; approve: *The club adopted the motion by a vote of 20 to 5.* **3** take (a child of other parents) and bring up as one's own child: *The judge permitted the family to adopt both of the children. v.* **—a dopt′a ble,** *adj.* **—a dopt′er,** *n.*

a dop tion (ə dop′shən), **1** an adopting: *Our club voted for the adoption of some new rules.* **2** a being adopted: *The children were offered for adoption. n.*

a dor a ble (ə dôr′ə bəl), **1** worthy of being adored. **2** INFORMAL. attractive; delightful: *an adorable kitten. adj.* **—a dor′a ble ness,** *n.*

a dor a bly (ə dôr′ə blē), in an adorable manner. *adv.*

ad o ra tion (ad′ə rā′shən), **1** devoted love and admiration. **2** worship. *n.*

a dore (ə dôr′), **1** love and admire very greatly: *They adore their grandchildren.* **2** INFORMAL. like very much: *I just adore that song!* **3** worship: *"O! Come, let us adore Him," sang the choir at Christmas. v.,* **a dored, a dor ing.** **—a dor′er,** *n.*

a dor ing ly (ə dôr′ing lē), with adoration. *adv.*

a dorn (ə dôrn′), add beauty to; put ornaments on; decorate: *She adorned her hair with flowers. v.* **—a dorn′er,** *n.*

a dorn ment (ə dôrn′mənt), **1** something that adds beauty; ornament; decoration: *The park is an adornment to the neighborhood.* **2** an adorning: *They are busy with the adornment of the room for the party. n.*

ad re nal gland (ə drē′nl), one of the two glands, one on the upper part of each kidney, that secrete adrenalin.

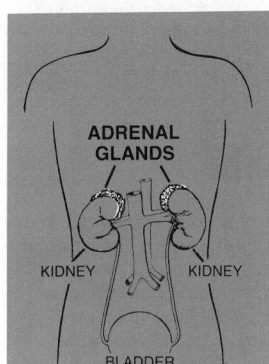

adrenal glands of a human being

ad ren a lin or **ad ren a line** (ə dren′l ən), hormone secreted by the adrenal glands. Adrenalin speeds up the heartbeat and increases bodily energy and resistance to fatigue. *n.*

A dri at ic Sea (ā′drē at′ik), sea between Italy and Yugoslavia. It is an arm of the Mediterranean.

a drift (ə drift′), **1** floating without being guided; drifting: *During the storm our boat was adrift on the lake.* **2** without guidance or direction; aimless: *He quit school, but without an education or special talents he found himself adrift. adj.*

a droit (ə droit′), **1** having or showing skill in using the hands or the body; skillful: *Monkeys are adroit climbers.* **2** having or showing skill in using the mind; clever: *A good teacher is adroit in asking questions. adj.* —**a droit′ly,** *adv.* —**a droit′ness,** *n.*

ad sorb (ad sôrb′), hold (a gas, liquid, or dissolved substance) spread out on a surface in a thin layer of molecules: *Dyes are adsorbed on fibers of cloth. v.*

ad sorp tion (ad sôrp′shən), an adsorbing; condensation of gases, liquids, or dissolved substances on the surface of solids. *n.*

ad u late (aj′ə lāt), praise excessively; flatter slavishly. *v.,* **ad u lat ed, ad u lat ing.** —**ad′u la′tor,** *n.*

ad u la tion (aj′ə lā′shən), too much praise; slavish flattery. *n.*

a dult (ə dult′ *or* ad′ult), **1** having full size and strength; fully developed; grown-up; mature: *an adult person.* **2** person who has reached full growth and development; grown-up person. **3** plant or animal grown to full size and development. **4** of, for, or by adults: *adult education, adult behavior.* 1,4 *adj.,* 2,3 *n.* [*Adult* is from Latin *adultum,* which comes from *adolescere,* meaning "to grow up."] —**a dult′ness,** *n.*

a dul te rate (ə dul′tə rāt′), make lower in quality by adding an inferior, impure, or improper substance: *It is against the law to adulterate milk with water. v.,* **a dul te rat ed, a dul te rat ing.** —**a dul′te ra′tor,** *n.*

a dul te ra tion (ə dul′tə rā′shən), **1** an adulterating: *We have laws against the adulteration of coffee and tea.* **2** product that has been adulterated. *n.*

a dul ter er (ə dul′tər ər), person who commits adultery. *n.*

a dul ter ous (ə dul′tər əs), guilty of adultery. *adj.* —**a dul′ter ous ly,** *adv.*

a dul ter y (ə dul′tər ē), unfaithfulness of a husband to his wife or a wife to her husband by having sexual intercourse with another. *n., pl.* **a dul ter ies.**

a dult hood (ə dult′hùd), condition of being an adult. *n.*

adv., 1 adverb. **2** advertisement.

ad vance (ad vans′), **1** move forward; push forward: *The troops advanced. The general advanced the troops.* **2** movement forward; progress: *The project's advance was very slow. We have made great advances in airplane design.* **3** ahead of time: *The teacher gave advance notice of the change of the date of our test.* **4** help forward; further: *The*

President's speech advanced the cause of peace. **5** put forward; suggest: *advance an opinion.* **6** raise to a higher rank; promote: *The teacher was advanced to principal.* **7** raise (prices); increase: *The grocer advanced the price of milk by two cents. Milk advanced two cents a quart.* **8** a rise in price or value: *There was an advance of two cents a quart in the price of milk.* **9** pay (money) before it is due or as a loan: *The company advanced the salesman funds for expenses.* **10** money paid before it is due or as a loan: *May I have an advance on next week's allowance?* **11 advances,** *pl.* attempts or offers to another or others to settle a difference, to make an acquaintance, etc.: *She made the first advances toward making up her quarrel with me.* 1,4-7,9 *v.,* **ad vanced, ad vanc ing;** 2,8,10,11 *n.,* 3 *adj.* —**ad vanc′er,** *n.*

in advance, 1 in front; ahead: *The leader of the band marched in advance.* **2** ahead of time: *I paid for my ticket in advance.*

ad vanced (ad vanst′), **1** in front of others; forward: *Our army is in an advanced position.* **2** ahead of most others in progress, ideas, etc.: *an advanced class in science, an advanced aircraft design.* **3** far along in life; very old: *Her grandmother lived to the advanced age of ninety years. adj.*

ad vance ment (ad vans′mənt), **1** advance; improvement: *Loyalty and hard work brought him an advancement in pay.* **2** promotion: *Good work won her advancement to a higher position. n.*

ad van tage (ad van′tij), anything that is in one's favor, or is a benefit; a help in getting something desired: *Good health is always a great advantage. n.*

take advantage of, 1 use to help or benefit oneself: *take advantage of a beautiful day by working in the garden.* **2** use unfairly; impose upon: *She was so good-natured that people often took advantage of her.*

to advantage, to a good effect; with a useful effect; favorably: *That frame sets off the painting to advantage.*

to one's advantage, to one's benefit or help: *It will be to your advantage to study Spanish before you visit Mexico.*

ad van ta geous (ad′vən tā′jəs), giving a benefit; favorable; helpful: *The agreement was advantageous to both sides. adj.* —**ad′van ta′geous ly,** *adv.* —**ad′van ta′geous ness,** *n.*

ad vent (ad′vent), **1** a coming or arrival, especially of someone or something seldom seen or unusually important. **2 Advent, a** the season including the four Sundays before Christmas. **b** the coming of Christ into the world. *n.*

adventure (def. 2) Sailing across the ocean on a boat made of reeds was a daring **adventure.**

ad ven ture (ad ven′chər), **1** an unusual or exciting experience: *The trip to Alaska was quite an adventure for her.* **2** a bold and difficult undertaking, usually exciting and dangerous. **3** readiness to take part in exciting or dangerous undertakings: *An explorer must have a spirit of adventure.* **4** dare to do; risk. 1-3 *n.,* 4 *v.,* **ad ven tured, ad ven tur ing.**

ad ven tur er (ad ven′chər ər), **1** person who has or

seeks adventures. **2** person who schemes for money or social position. *n.*

ad ven ture some (ad ven′chər səm), bold and daring; adventurous. *adj.*

ad ven tur ess (ad ven′chər is), woman who schemes for money or social position. *n., pl.* **ad ven tur ess es.**

ad ven tur ous (ad ven′chər əs), **1** fond of adventures; ready to take risks; daring: *a bold, adventurous explorer.* **2** full of risk; dangerous: *An expedition to the North Pole is an adventurous undertaking. adj.* **—ad ven′tur ous ly,** *adv.* **—ad ven′tur ous ness,** *n.*

ad verb (ad′vėrb′), one of a class of words that extend or limit the meaning of verbs (They sing *well*) but are also used to qualify adjectives (She is *very* intelligent) or other adverbs (They sing *quite* well), usually to express time, place, manner, degree, or circumstance. Words like *soon, here, very, gladly,* and *not* are adverbs. Most adverbs are made up of adjectives or participles plus the ending *-ly,* like *badly* in "The team played badly" and *deservedly* in "He was deservedly popular." *n.*

ad ver bi al (ad vėr′bē əl), **1** used as an adverb. In the sentence, "I worked as quickly as possible," *as quickly as possible* is an adverbial phrase. **2** of an adverb; forming adverbs: *"-ly" is an adverbial suffix. adj.* **—ad ver′- bi al ly,** *adv.*

ad ver sar y (ad′vər ser′ē), **1** person or group opposing or hostile to another person or group; enemy: *The two countries were adversaries in World War II.* **2** person or group on the other side in a game or contest; opponent. *n., pl.* **ad ver sar ies.**

ad verse (ad′vėrs′ *or* ad vėrs′), **1** unfriendly in purpose; hostile: *Adverse criticism discouraged me.* **2** acting against one's interests; unfavorable; harmful: *adverse circumstances.* **3** coming from or acting in a contrary direction; opposing: *Adverse winds delayed the voyage. adj.* **—ad verse′ly,** *adv.* **—ad verse′ness,** *n.*

ad ver si ty (ad vėr′sə tē), **1** condition of unhappiness, misfortune, or distress. **2** stroke of misfortune; unfavorable or harmful thing or event. *n., pl.* **ad ver si ties.**

ad ver tise (ad′vər tīz), **1** give public notice of in a newspaper, on the radio or television, etc.: *When people lose something valuable, they advertise it in the newspaper.* **2** ask for by public notice: *He advertised for a job.* **3** praise the good qualities of (something) in order to create a demand or promote sales: *Manufacturers advertise products that they wish to sell.* **4** seek to sell goods, etc., by advertising: *It pays to advertise. v.,* **ad ver tised, ad ver tis ing.**

ad ver tise ment (ad′vər tīz′mənt *or* ad vėr′tis mənt), a public notice or announcement recommending some product or service, or informing of some need: *The furniture store has an advertisement in the newspaper of a special sale. n.*

ad ver tis er (ad′vər tī′zər), person, organization, or business firm that advertises. *n.*

ad ver tis ing (ad′vər tī′zing), **1** business of preparing, publishing, or circulating advertisements. **2** advertisements: *Billboards carry advertising.* **3** a bringing to public notice by radio or television announcements, published notices, posters, or other means: *The store attracted many customers by advertising. n.*

ad vice (ad vīs′), opinion about what should be done; suggestion: *My advice is that you study more. n.*

ad vis a bil i ty (ad vī′zə bil′ə tē), fitness; suitability: *I asked about the advisability of buying a used car. n.*

ad vis a ble (ad vī′zə bəl), to be advised or recommended; wise; sensible; suitable: *It is not advisable for you to go to school while you are still sick. adj.*

ad vis a bly (ad vī′zə blē), wisely; sensibly. *adv.*

ad vise (ad vīz′), **1** give advice to; offer an opinion to; counsel: *Advise them to be cautious. I shall act as you*

advise. **2** give notice; inform: *We were advised of the dangers before we began our trip. v.,* **ad vised, ad vis ing.**

ad vis ed ly (ad vī′zid lē), after careful consideration; deliberately. *adv.*

ad vise ment (ad vīz′mənt), careful consideration: *The lawyer took our case under advisement and said she would give us an answer in two weeks. n.*

ad vis er *or* **ad vi sor** (ad vī′zər), **1** person who gives advice. **2** teacher appointed to advise students. *n.*

adversary (def. 2)
The two **adversaries** shook hands before the game began.

ad vi sor y (ad vī′zər ē), **1** having power to advise: *an advisory committee.* **2** containing advice: *an advisory opinion.* **3** bulletin or report to advise of developments: *An advisory by the Weather Bureau warned of a hurricane.* 1,2 *adj.,* 3 *n., pl.* **ad vi sor ies. —ad vi′sor i ly,** *adv.*

ad vo ca cy (ad′və kə sē), a speaking or writing in favor of something; public recommendation; support: *The senator's advocacy of the plan won votes for it. n., pl.* **ad vo ca cies.**

ad vo cate (ad′və kāt *for 1;* ad′və kit *or* ad′və kāt *for 2,3*), **1** speak or write in favor of; recommend publicly; support: *He advocates building more public housing.* **2** person who pleads or argues for; supporter: *She is an advocate of lower property taxes.* **3** lawyer who pleads in a court of law. 1 *v.,* **ad vo cat ed, ad vo cat ing;** 2,3 *n.* **—ad′vo ca′tion,** *n.* **—ad′vo ca′tor,** *n.*

advt., advertisement.

adz *or* **adze** (adz), a cutting tool for shaping heavy timbers. It is somewhat like an ax but with a blade set across the end of the handle and curving inward. *n., pl.* **adz es.** [*Adz* and *adze* come from Old English *adesa.*]

AEC *or* **A.E.C.,** Atomic Energy Commission.

Ae ge an Sea (i jē′ən), sea between Greece and Turkey. It is an arm of the Mediterranean. See **Adriatic Sea** for map.

Ae ne as (i nē′əs), (in Greek and Roman legends) a Trojan hero who after the fall of Troy and years of wandering reached Italy, where his descendants supposedly founded Rome. *n.*

Ae ne id (i nē′id), a long poem by Vergil telling the story of the wanderings of Aeneas. *n.*

ae on (ē′ən *or* ē′on), eon. *n.*

aer ate (er′āt *or* ar′āt), **1** expose to and mix with air: *Water in this reservoir is aerated and purified by being sprayed high into the air.* **2** fill with a gas: *Soda water is water that has been aerated with carbon dioxide.* **3** expose to chemical action with oxygen: *Blood is aerated in the lungs. v.,* **aer at ed, aer at ing.** —**aer′a tor,** *n.*

aer a tion (er′ā/shən *or* ar′ā/shən), an aerating: *the aeration of soil by plowing. n.*

aer i al (er′ē əl *or* ar′ē əl), **1** a long wire or set of wires or rods used in television or radio for sending out or receiving electromagnetic waves; antenna. **2** having to do with or done by aircraft: *aerial photography, aerial warfare.* **3** growing in air instead of in soil. **4** of or having to do with the air; atmospheric: *aerial currents.* **1** *n.,* **2-4** *adj.* —**aer′i al ly,** *adv.*

aer i al ist (er′ē ə list *or* ar′ē ə list), acrobat who performs feats on a trapeze, tightrope, etc. *n.*

aer ie (er′ē, ar′ē, *or* ir′ē), the lofty nest of an eagle, hawk, or other bird of prey. *n.* Also, **aery, eyrie,** or **eyry.**

aero-, *combining form.* **1** air or other gas: *Aerosol = fine particles in air or other gas.* **2** atmosphere: *Aerospace = the earth's atmosphere and outer space.* [The form *aero-* is from Greek *aëro-,* which comes from *aēr,* meaning "air."]

aer o bics (er′ō/biks *or* ar′ō/biks), a system of physical exercises that increases the body's consumption of oxygen and improves the functioning of the circulatory system. *n.*

aer o dy nam ics (er′ō dī nam′iks *or* ar′ō dī nam′iks), branch of physics that deals with the forces exerted by air or other gases in motion on both flying and wind-blown bodies. *n.*

aer o nau tic (er′ə nô′tik *or* ar′ə nô′tik), aeronautical. *adj.*

aer o nau ti cal (er′ə nô′tə kəl *or* ar′ə nô′tə kəl), of aeronautics. *adj.* —**aer′o nau′ti cal ly,** *adv.*

aer o nau tics (er′ə nô′tiks *or* ar′ə nô′tiks), science or art having to do with the design, manufacture, and operation of aircraft. *n.*

aer o plane (er′ə plān *or* ar′ə plān), airplane. *n.*

aer o sol (er′ə sol *or* ar′ə sol), **1** very fine particles of a solid or liquid substance suspended in the air or in some other gas. **2** product packaged under pressure to be released as a spray or mist. *n.*

aer o space (er′ō spās *or* ar′ō spās), the earth's atmosphere and the space beyond it, especially the space in which rockets, satellites, and other spacecraft operate. *n.*

aer y (er′ē, ar′ē, *or* ir′ē), aerie. *n., pl.* **aer ies.**

Ae sop (ē′səp *or* ē′sop), Greek writer of fables who lived about 600 B.C. *n.*

aes thet ic (es thet′ik), **1** having to do with the artistic or beautiful rather than the useful or practical. **2** having an appreciation of beauty in nature or art: *an aesthetic person.* **3** showing good taste; artistic: *an aesthetic wallpaper. adj.* Also, **esthetic.**

aes thet i cal ly (es thet′ik lē), in an aesthetic manner. *adv.* Also, **esthetically.**

ae ther e al (i thir′ē əl), ethereal. *adj.*

Aet na (et′nə), **Mount.** See **Etna.** *n.*

AF, Air Force.

A.F. *or* **a.f.,** audio frequency.

a far (ə fär′). **from afar,** from a distance: *I saw him from afar.*

AFB *or* **A.F.B.,** Air Force Base.

a feard *or* **a feared** (ə fird′), OLD USE. frightened; afraid. *adj.*

af fa bil i ty (af′ə bil′ə tē), quality that makes a person easy to talk to; courteous and pleasant ways. *n.*

af fa ble (af′ə bəl), easy to talk to; courteous and pleasant: *Our principal is very affable. adj.* [*Affable* came into English over 400 years ago from French *affable,* which is from Latin *affabilis,* meaning "easy to speak to," and can be traced back to Latin *ad-,* meaning "to," and *fari,* meaning "speak."]

aerial (def. 3)
The banyan tree
has **aerial** roots.

af fa bly (af′ə blē), in an affable manner; courteously. *adv.*

af fair (ə fer′ *or* ə far′), **1** matter of business; job; task: *Such a large project is a time-consuming affair.* **2** any thing or matter or happening: *The party was a delightful affair. n.*

af fect[1] (ə fekt′), **1** have a result on; have an effect on; influence: *The small amount of rain last year affected the growth of crops. The disease affected her eyesight.* **2** touch the heart of; stir the feelings of: *The sad story affected me deeply. v.*

af fect[2] (ə fekt′), **1** pretend to have or feel: *He affected ignorance of the fight, but we knew that he had seen it.* **2** use because one prefers to; choose: *affect carelessness in dress. v.*

af fec ta tion (af′ek tā′shən), an artificial way of talking or acting put on to impress others; pretense: *Her roughness is an affectation; she really is a quiet, gentle girl. n.*

af fect ed[1] (ə fek′tid), **1** acted upon; influenced: *Everyone felt affected by the war.* **2** influenced injuriously: *She froze her feet and the affected toes were numb. adj.*

af fect ed[2] (ə fek′tid), put on for effect; not natural; artificial: *an affected tone of voice, an affected welcome. adj.* —**af fect′ed ly,** *adv.* —**af fect′ed ness,** *n.*

af fect ing (ə fek′ting), touching the heart; moving the feelings: *The refugee told an affecting story of hunger and suffering. adj.* —**af fect′ing ly,** *adv.*

af fec tion (ə fek′shən), friendly feeling; tenderness; love: *the affection of parents for their children. n.*

af fec tion ate (ə fek′shə nit), showing or having affection; loving and tender: *an affectionate letter, an affectionate farewell. adj.* —**af fec′tion ate ly,** *adv.*

af fi ance (ə fī′əns), promise in marriage; engage: *James and Beth are affianced to each other. v.,* **af fi anced, af fi anc ing.**

af fi da vit (af′ə dā′vit), statement written down and sworn to be true. An affidavit is usually made before a judge or notary public. *n.*

af fil i ate (ə fil′ē āt *for* 1; ə fil′ē it *or* ə fil′ē āt *for* 2), **1** join in close association; connect: *That TV station recently affiliated with a national network.* **2** organization or group associated with another or larger organization or group: *Our local automobile club is an affiliate of the national automobile club.* **1** *v.,* **af fil i at ed, af fil i at ing;** **2** *n.* [*Affiliate* comes from a medieval Latin word *affiliatum,* meaning "adopted (as a son)."]

af fil i a tion (ə fil′ē ā′shən), association; connection: *Our hospital has an affiliation with the medical school of the university. n.*

af fin i ty (ə fin′ə tē), **1** a natural attraction to a person or liking for a thing: *She has an affinity for science.* **2** relationship; connection: *There is an affinity between the diseases smallpox and cowpox, which are caused by similar viruses. n., pl.* **af fin i ties.**

af firm (ə ferm′), **1** declare to be true; say firmly; assert: *The prisoner affirmed his innocence.* **2** confirm; ratify: *The higher court affirmed the lower court's decision. v.*

af fir ma tion (af/ər mā/shən), positive statement; assertion. *n.*

af firm a tive (ə fèr/mə tiv), **1** stating that a fact is so; saying yes: *His answer to my question was affirmative.* **2** word or statement that says yes or agrees: *"I will" is an affirmative.* **3** the side arguing in favor of a question being debated: *The affirmative presented a strong argument.* **1** *adj.*, **2,3** *n.* —**af firm/a tive ly,** *adv.*

in the affirmative, expressing agreement by saying yes: *She answered my question in the affirmative.*

affirmative action, a program that encourages the employment of women and minorities in order to compensate for past discrimination. The United States government requires that many employers carry out affirmative action.

af fix (ə fiks/ *for 1,2;* af/iks *for 3*), **1** stick on; fasten; attach: *She affixed a stamp to her letter.* **2** add at the end: *The President affixed his signature to the bill.* **3** a sound or group of sounds added to a word to change its meaning or use. Affixes are either prefixes like *un-* and *re-* or suffixes like *-ly, -ness, -s,* or *-ed.* **1,2** *v.,* **3** *n., pl.* **af fix es.** —**af/fix a/tion,** *n.* —**af fix/er,** *n.*

af flict (ə flikt/), cause pain to; trouble greatly; distress: *Our neighbor is afflicted with arthritis.* *v.*

af flic tion (ə flik/shən), **1** state of pain, trouble, or distress; misery: *the affliction of war.* **2** a cause of pain, trouble, or distress; misfortune: *Blindness is an affliction.* *n.*

af flu ence (af/lü əns), **1** wealth; riches: *The United States is a country of great affluence.* **2** a plentiful flow or abundant supply of tears, words, etc. *n.*

af flu ent (af/lü ənt), **1** having wealth; rich. **2** abundant; plentiful. *adj.* —**af/flu ent ly,** *adv.*

af ford (ə fôrd/), **1** spare the money for: *Can we afford a new car?* **2** manage to give, spare, or have: *A busy person cannot afford delay. He cannot afford to waste so much time.* **3** be able without difficulty or harm: *I can't afford to take the chance.* **4** give as an effect or a result; provide; yield: *Reading a good book affords real pleasure.* *v.*

af fray (ə frā/), a noisy quarrel; public fight; brawl. *n.*

af fright (ə frīt/), OLD USE. excite with sudden fear; frighten. *v.*

af front (ə frunt/), **1** word or act intended to show disrespect; open insult: *To be called a coward is an affront.* **2** insult openly; offend purposely: *The boy affronted his sister by calling her names.* **1** *n.,* **2** *v.* [*Affront* came into English over 600 years ago from French *afronter,* meaning "to strike on the forehead, to defy."]

Af ghan (af/gən), **1** person born or living in Afghanistan. **2** of Afghanistan or its people. **3 afghan,** blanket or shawl made of knitted or crocheted wool, nylon, etc. **1,3** *n.,* **2** *adj.*

Af ghan i stan (af gan/ə stan), country in SW Asia, between Pakistan and Iran. *Capital:* Kabul. See **India** for map. *n.*

a field (ə fēld/), **1** away from home; away: *She wandered far afield in foreign lands.* **2** out of the right way; astray: *We seem to have gone far afield; we are lost.* *adv.*

a fire (ə fīr/), **1** on fire; burning. **2** enthusiastic. *adv., adj.*

AFL, American Football League.

a flame (ə flām/), **1** in flames; on fire. **2** in a glow; glowing. *adv., adj.*

AFL-CIO, American Federation of Labor and Congress of Industrial Organizations.

a float (ə flōt/), **1** floating on the water or in the air. **2** on shipboard; at sea. **3** flooded. **4** being spread; going around: *Many rumors were afloat.* *adv., adj.*

a flut ter (ə flut/ər), **1** fluttering or waving: *The flags were aflutter in the breeze.* **2** in a flutter; excited: *The town was aflutter at the news.* *adv., adj.*

a hat	i it	oi oil	ch child	a in about
ā age	ī ice	ou out	ng long	e in taken
ä far	o hot	u cup	sh she ə =	i in pencil
e let	ō open	ů put	th thin	o in lemon
ē equal	ô order	ü rule	ŦH then	u in circus
ėr term			zh measure	

a foot (ə fůt/), **1** on foot; by walking. **2** going on; in progress: *There is mischief afoot.* *adv., adj.*

a fore (ə fôr/), OLD USE. before. *prep., adv., conj.*

a fore men tioned (ə fôr/men/shənd), spoken of before; mentioned earlier. *adj.*

a fore said (ə fôr/sed/), spoken of before; mentioned earlier. *adj.*

a fore thought (ə fôr/thôt/), thought out beforehand; deliberately planned: *The evil deed was planned with malice aforethought. adj.*

a foul (ə foul/), in a tangle; in a collision; entangled: *Raising the sail was impossible with the lines afoul. adj.*

run afoul of, get into trouble with: *A person who steals may run afoul of the law.*

Afr., **1** Africa. **2** African.

a fraid (ə frād/), **1** feeling fear; frightened: *afraid of the dark.* **2** sorry to have to say: *I'm afraid you are wrong about that. adj.*

a fresh (ə fresh/), once more; again: *If you spoil your drawing, start afresh. adv.*

Af ri ca (af/rə kə), continent south of Europe. It is the second largest continent. *n.*

Af ri can (af/rə kən), **1** of Africa or its people. **2** person born or living in Africa. **1** *adj.,* **2** *n.*

African violet

African violet, a tropical plant with violet, white, or pink flowers, often grown as a house plant.

Af ri kaans (af/rə käns/ *or* af/rə känz/), language spoken in South Africa which developed from the Dutch spoken by colonists who came to the area in the 1600's; South African Dutch. *n.*

Af ro (af/rō), a bushy hairdo like that worn in parts of Africa. *n., pl.* **Af ros.**

Af ro-A mer i can (af/rō ə mer/ə kən), **1** of American Negroes. **2** an American Negro. **1** *adj.,* **2** *n.*

aft (aft), **1** at or toward the stern of a ship, boat, or aircraft; abaft. **2** in or near the stern of a ship, boat, or aircraft. **1** *adv.,* **2** *adj.*

AFT, American Federation of Teachers.

af ter (af/tər), **1** later in time than: *After dinner we can go.* **2** following: *I ran so hard I panted for five minutes after (adv.). In after years she did not come to see us so often (adj.). Day after day I hoped to get a letter from my friend (prep.).* **3** later than the time that: *After he goes, we shall eat.* **4** behind: *You come after me in the line (prep.). Jill came tumbling after (adv.).* **5** in search of; in pursuit of:

The dog ran after the rabbit. **6** about; concerning: *Your aunt asked after you.* **7** because of; as a result of: *After such a big dinner, I couldn't finish my dessert.* **8** in spite of: *After all her suffering she is still cheerful.* **9** in honor of; for: *She is named after her grandmother.* **10** nearer or toward the stern of a ship: *the after sails.* 1,2,4-9 *prep.,* 2,4 *adv.,* 2,10 *adj.,* 3 *conj.* [*After* comes from Old English *æfter,* meaning "more to the rear, later."]

af ter deck (af′tər dek′), part of a deck at or near the stern of a ship. *n.*

af ter ef fect (af′tər i fekt′), **1** result or effect that follows later: *The aftereffect of the explosion was a great fire.* **2** secondary effect of a drug or disease. *n.*

af ter glow (af′tər glō′), **1** glow remaining after something bright has gone. **2** glow in the sky after sunset. **3** a pleasurable feeling following something greatly enjoyed. *n.*

af ter life (af′tər līf′), life after death. *n.*

af ter math (af′tər math), a result or consequence: *The aftermath of war is hunger and disease. n.*

af ter noon (af′tər nün′), the part of the day between noon and evening. *n.*

af ter thought (af′tər thôt′), **1** thought that comes too late to be used. **2** a second or later thought or explanation. *n.*

af ter ward (af′tər wərd), afterwards; later. *adv.*

af ter wards (af′tər wərdz), later: *Afterwards I regretted what I had said. adv.*

Ag, symbol for silver.

a gain (ə gen′), **1** another time; once more: *Come again to play. Say that again.* **2** on the other hand; yet: *It may rain, and again it may not.* **3** moreover; besides: *Again, I must say that you are wrong. adv.*

again and again, many times over; often: *I telephoned again and again before I finally reached him.*

a gainst (ə genst′), **1** in opposition to; contrary to: *Our team will debate against yours. It is against the rules of the game.* **2** in the opposite direction to, so as to meet; upon or toward: *We will sail against the wind. Rain beat against the window.* **3** in contact with: *The ladder is leaning against the wall.* **4** in preparation for: *Squirrels store up nuts against the winter.* **5** so as to defend or protect from: *An umbrella is a protection against rain. prep.*

Ag a mem non (ag′ə mem′non), (in Greek legends) the leader of the Greeks in the Trojan War. *n.*

a gape (ə gāp′), with the mouth wide open in wonder or surprise; gaping. *adj.*

a gar (ä′gər), a jellylike extract obtained from certain seaweeds, used in making cultures for bacteria and fungi. *n.* [*Agar* comes from Malay *agar-agar.*]

Ag as siz (ag′ə sē), **Louis,** 1807-1873, American zoologist and geologist, born in Switzerland. *n.*

ag ate (ag′it), **1** variety of quartz with variously colored stripes or clouded colors. **2** a playing marble that looks like this. *n.*

agate (def. 1)—a polished agate

agave

a ga ve (ə gä′vē), an American desert plant which has a dense cluster of rigid, fleshy leaves with spines along the edges and at the tips. *n.*

age (āj), **1** time of life: *He has reached the age of fourteen.* **2** length of life; time anything has existed: *A species of pine in California is said to have the greatest age of any living thing.* **3** a particular period or stage in life: *old age, middle age.* **4** the latter part of life; old age: *the wisdom of age.* **5** period in history: *the Bronze Age. This is the age of supersonic jets.* **6** ages, *pl.* **a** INFORMAL. a long time: *I haven't seen him for ages.* **b** hundreds of years: *the work of ages.* **7** grow old: *to age fast.* **8** make old: *Worry can age you.* **9** bring or come to full growth; mature: *This cheese must be aged for a year. Wine is put in casks to age.* 1-6 *n.,* 7-9 *v.,* **aged, ag ing** or **age ing.**

of age, at the time of life when a person is considered ready for adult rights and responsibilities, usually 18 years old.

-age, *suffix forming nouns from other nouns or from verbs.* **1** act of _____ing: *Breakage = act of breaking.* **2** group of _____s: *Baggage = a group of bags.* **3** condition or rank of _____s: *Peerage = rank of peers.* **4** cost of or fee for _____ing: *Postage = cost of posting (mailing).* **5** home for _____s: *Orphanage = home for orphans.*

a ged (ā′jid *for 1;* ājd *for 2,3*), **1** having lived a long time; old: *The aged couple lived on a small pension.* **2** having the age of: *She was aged six when she first went to school.* **3** improved by aging: *aged meat, aged cheese. adj.*
—**a ged ly** (ā′jid lē), *adv.* —**a ged ness** (ā′jid nis), *n.*

age ism (ā′jiz əm), discrimination against a certain age group, especially against the elderly with regard to jobs and housing. *n.*

age less (āj′lis), never growing old; never coming to an end: *the ageless wisdom of the Bible. adj.* —**age′less ly,** *adv.* —**age′less ness,** *n.*

a gen cy (ā′jən sē), **1** a person or company that has the authority to act for another: *An agency rented our house for us. Employment agencies help people to get jobs.* **2** office of such a person or company. **3** a special department of the government concerned with the administration of affairs within a specific field: *The agency which deals with pollution in the United States is the Environmental Protection Agency.* **4** means of producing effects; action: *Snow is drifted by the agency of the wind. n., pl.* **a gen cies.**

a gen da (ə jen′də), list of things to be dealt with or done: *The agenda for today's club meeting includes reading of committee reports and admission of new members. n., pl.* **a gen das.**

a gent (ā′jənt), **1** person or company having the authority to act for another: *She is a real-estate agent and can help you sell your house.* **2** any power or cause that produces an effect by its action: *Yeast is an important agent in causing bread to rise.* **3** means; instrument: *Graphite is sometimes used as a lubricating agent.* **4** a law enforcement officer. **5** member of the government secret service. *n.*

age-old (āj′ōld′), having existed for a very long time; very old; ancient: *age-old customs. adj.*

ag glu ti nate (ə glüt′n āt), stick together; join together. *v.*, **ag glu ti nat ed, ag glu ti nat ing.**

ag glu ti na tion (ə glüt′n ā′shən), process of sticking together, especially the clumping together of bacteria or blood cells, usually caused by the introduction of antibodies to such cells. *n.*

ag gran dize (ə gran′dīz *or* ag′rən dīz), make greater or larger in power; increase the rank or wealth of: *The dictator sought to aggrandize himself at the expense of his people. v.*, **ag gran dized, ag gran diz ing.** —**ag gran′-diz er**, *n.*

ag gran dize ment (ə gran′diz mənt), **1** a making greater, larger, or more powerful. **2** an increase in power, rank, or wealth. *n.*

ag gra vate (ag′rə vāt), **1** make worse or more severe: *His headache was aggravated by all the noise.* **2** annoy; irritate; exasperate: *She aggravated me by asking so many questions. v.*, **ag gra vat ed, ag gra vat ing.** —**ag′gra-vat′ing ly**, *adv.*

ag gra va tion (ag′rə vā′shən), **1** a making worse or more severe. **2** annoyance; irritation. **3** something that aggravates. *n.*

ag gre gate (ag′rə git *or* ag′rə gāt *for 1,3;* ag′rə gāt *for 2,4*), **1** total amount; sum: *The aggregate of all the gifts was over $100.* **2** amount to; come to; total: *The money collected will aggregate $1000.* **3** mass of separate things joined together: *A lump of sugar is an aggregate of sugar crystals.* **4** gather into one mass or whole; unite: *Granite is made of small particles aggregated together.* **1,3** *n.,* **2,4** *v.,* **ag gre gat ed, ag gre gat ing.** —**ag′gre gate ly**, *adv.* —**ag′gre gate ness,** *n.*

ag gre ga tion (ag′rə gā′shən), **1** the collecting of separate things into one mass or whole. **2** the group or mass collected. *n.*

ag gres sion (ə gresh′ən), **1** the first step in an attack or a quarrel; unprovoked attack: *A country that sends its army to occupy another country is guilty of aggression.* **2** practice of making assaults or attacks on the rights or territory of others as a method or policy. *n.*

ag gres sive (ə gres′iv), **1** taking the first step in an attack or a quarrel; ready to attack others: *a warlike and aggressive nation.* **2** very active; energetic: *They organized an aggressive campaign against pollution.* **3** too confident and certain; assertive: *An aggressive manner can be irritating to others. adj.* —**ag gres′sive ly**, *adv.* —**ag gres′-sive ness,** *n.*

ag gres sor (ə gres′ər), one that begins an attack or a quarrel, especially a nation that starts a war. *n.*

ag grieved (ə grēvd′), **1** feeling injured or wronged: *to make amends to an aggrieved person.* **2** feeling troubled or distressed: *I was aggrieved at having lost their friendship. adj.*

a ghast (ə gast′), struck with surprise or horror; filled with terror: *I was aghast when I saw the destruction caused by the earthquake. adj.*

WORD HISTORY

aghast

Aghast comes from Middle English *agasten*, meaning "to frighten," and can be traced back to Old English *gāst*, meaning "ghost, spirit."

a	hat	i	it	oi	oil	ch	child	a in about
ā	age	ī	ice	ou	out	ng	long	e in taken
ä	far	o	hot	u	cup	sh	she	ə = i in pencil
e	let	ō	open	u̇	put	th	thin	o in lemon
ē	equal	ô	order	ü	rule	₮H	then	u in circus
ėr	term					zh	measure	

ag ile (aj′əl), **1** moving quickly and easily; nimble: *as agile as a cat.* **2** quick in thinking; alert: *You need an agile mind to solve puzzles. adj.* —**ag′ile ly**, *adv.* —**ag′ile-ness,** *n.*

a gil i ty (ə jil′ə tē), **1** ability to move quickly and easily; nimbleness: *He has the agility of a monkey.* **2** alertness. *n.*

ag i tate (aj′ə tāt), **1** move or shake violently: *The slightest wind will agitate the leaves of some trees.* **2** disturb or excite very much: *He was agitated by the unexpected news of his friend's illness.* **3** argue about or discuss a matter vigorously to arouse public interest and feeling: *agitate for a shorter working day. v.,* **ag i tat ed, ag i tat ing.** [*Agitate* comes from Latin *agitatum,* meaning "moved to and fro."] —**ag′i tat′ed ly,** *adv.*

ag i ta tion (aj′ə tā′shən), **1** a violent moving or shaking: *The agitation of the sea almost turned the little boat over.* **2** a disturbed, upset, or troubled state: *Because of her agitation over losing her job, she could not sleep.* **3** argument or discussion to arouse public interest and feeling: *There was much agitation for and against gun control. n.*

ag i ta tor (aj′ə tā′tər), **1** person who stirs up public feeling for or against something. **2** device or machine for shaking or stirring. *n.*

a gleam (ə glēm′), gleaming. *adj.*

a glit ter (ə glit′ər), glittering. *adj.*

a glow (ə glō′), glowing: *The baby's cheeks were aglow with health. adj.*

Ag new (ag′nü *or* ag′nyü), **Spir o** (spir′ō) **T(heodore),** born 1918, vice-president of the United States from 1969 to 1973. *n.*

ag nos tic (ag nos′tik), person who believes that nothing is known or can be known about the existence of God. *n.* —**ag nos′ti cal ly,** *adv.*

a go (ə gō′), **1** gone by; past: *I met her two years ago.* **2** in the past: *He lived here long ago.* **1** *adj.,* **2** *adv.*

a gog (ə gog′), full of expectation or excitement; eager: *The children were all agog to see their presents. adj.*

ag o niz ing (ag′ə nī′zing), causing very great suffering. *adj.* —**ag′o niz′ing ly,** *adv.*

ag o ny (ag′ə nē), very painful suffering; very great anguish: *the agony of a severe toothache. The loss of their child filled them with agony. n., pl.* **ag o nies.**

a grar i an (ə grer′ē ən), **1** having to do with farming land, its use, or its ownership: *Most old countries had agrarian disputes between tenants and landlords.* **2** for the support and advancement of farmers or farming: *an agrarian movement. adj.*

a gree (ə grē′), **1** have the same feeling or opinion: *We all agree on that subject. I agree that we should try to be more careful.* **2** be in harmony; correspond: *All accounts of the accident seem to agree.* **3** get along well together: *My cousin and I don't always agree.* **4** say that one is willing; consent: *He agreed to go with us.* **5** come to an understanding, especially in settling a dispute: *The workers and employers agreed on the terms for settling the strike.* **6** say (something) is real or true; admit: *We agreed that we had been careless.* **7** (in grammar) have the same number, case, gender, or person. In the sentences "The woman is going," "The women are going," the subjects and the verbs agree in person and number. *v.,* **a greed, a gree ing.**

agree with, have a good effect on; suit: *This food does not agree with me; it makes me sick.*

a gree a ble (ə grē′ə bəl), **1** giving pleasure; pleasing: *She had an agreeable manner.* **2** ready to agree; willing: *If you are agreeable we can see the show together this afternoon. adj.* **—a gree′a ble ness,** *n.*

a gree a bly (ə grē′ə blē), in an agreeable manner; pleasingly. *adv.*

a gree ment (ə grē′mənt), **1** an understanding reached by two or more persons, groups of persons, or nations among themselves. Nations make treaties and individuals make contracts; both are agreements. **2** a coming to an understanding, especially in settling a dispute: *Every obstacle to agreement has been removed.* **3** harmony in feeling or opinion: *There was perfect agreement between the two friends.* **4** (in grammar) correspondence of words in number, case, gender, or person. There is agreement in "that man" but lack of agreement in "those man." *n.*

agric., agriculture.

ag ri cul tur al (ag′rə kul′chər əl), having to do with farming; of agriculture: *The Middle West is an important agricultural region. adj.* **—ag′ri cul′tur al ly,** *adv.*

ag ri cul tur al ist (ag′rə kul′chər ə list), agriculturist. *n.*

ag ri cul ture (ag′rə kul′chər), science or art of cultivating the soil, including the production of crops and the raising of livestock; farming. *n.*

ag ri cul tur ist (ag′rə kul′chər ist), **1** farmer. **2** an expert in farming. *n.*

aground
The boat ran **aground** on the rocks.

a ground (ə ground′), stranded on the shore or on the bottom in shallow water. *adv., adj.*

agt., agent.

ah (ä), exclamation of pain, sorrow, regret, pity, admiration, surprise, joy, dislike, contempt, etc. *interj.*

a ha (ä hä′), exclamation of triumph, satisfaction, surprise, joy, etc. *interj.*

A hab (ā′hab), king of Israel from about 873 to 853 B.C., who was led to worship idols by his wife Jezebel. *n.*

a head (ə hed′), **1** in front; before: *Walk ahead of me.* **2** forward: *Go ahead with this work for another week.* **3** in advance; earlier: *Columbus was ahead of his time in his belief that the world was round. adv..*

be ahead, 1 be winning: *Our team is ahead by 6 points.* **2** have more than is needed: *We're ahead $10 on the budget.*

get ahead, succeed: *I worked hard at my job in the hope that I would get ahead.*

get ahead of, do or be better than; surpass: *She worked hard trying to get ahead of the others in the class.*

a hem (ə hem′), a sound made by coughing or clearing the throat, sometimes used to attract attention, express doubt, or gain time. *interj.*

a hoy (ə hoi′), call used by sailors to attract the attention of persons at a distance: *The sailors in the lifeboat shouted "Ship ahoy!" to the passing freighter. interj.*

aid (ād), **1** give support to; help: *The Red Cross aids flood victims.* **2** a help; assistance: *When my arm was broken, I could not dress without aid.* **3** person or thing that helps; helper: *A dishwasher is an aid to housework.* **1** *v.,* **2,3** *n.* **—aid′er,** *n.*

aide (ād), **1** helper; assistant. **2** aide-de-camp. *n.*

aide-de-camp (ād′də kamp′), a military officer who acts as an assistant to a superior officer by taking and sending messages and acting as a secretary. *n., pl.* **aides-de-camp.**

AIDS (ādz), a deadly disease caused by a kind of virus which attacks the immune system, resulting in the body's inability to resist other serious infections. *n.* [*AIDS* comes from the words *acquired immune deficiency syndrome.* It was formed from the first letters of these words.]

ail (āl), **1** be the matter with; trouble: *What ails the child?* **2** be ill; feel sick: *Our cat is ailing again. v.*

ai le ron (ā′lə ron′), a hinged, movable part on the rear edge of an airplane wing, used for banking or balancing the airplane. *n.*

ail ment (āl′mənt), disorder of the body or mind; illness: *He has a serious heart ailment. n.*

aim (ām), **1** point or direct (a gun, blow, etc.) in order to hit a target: *She aimed carefully at the target.* **2** act of pointing or directing at something: *Take careful aim.* **3** ability to point or direct (a gun, blow, etc.): *She hit the target because her aim was good.* **4** direct (words or acts) at someone or something: *The teacher's talk was aimed at the students who cheated on the test.* **5** direct one's efforts; try: *He aimed to please his friends.* **6** have in mind as a purpose; intend: *I aim to go.* **7** purpose; intention: *Her aim was to do two years' work in one.* **1,4-6** *v.,* **2,3,7** *n.*

aim less (ām′lis), without purpose; pointless. *adj.* **—aim′less ly,** *adv.* **—aim′less ness,** *n.*

ain't (ānt), **1** am not; is not. **2** are not. **3** have not; has not. Careful speakers and writers do not use *ain't.*

Ai nu (ī′nü), member of an aboriginal, light-skinned people in northern Japan. *n., pl.* **Ai nu** or **Ai nus.**

air (er *or* ar), **1** the mixture of gases that surrounds the earth; atmosphere. Air has no smell, taste, or color. It consists chiefly of nitrogen and oxygen, along with argon, carbon dioxide, hydrogen, and small quantities of neon, helium, and other inert gases. **2** space overhead; sky: *Birds fly in the air.* **3** put out in the air: *We aired the sleeping bags in the backyard.* **4** fresh air: *He opened the window to let some air into the overheated room.* **5** let fresh air in: *Open the windows and air the room.* **6** airline; airplane: *We traveled by air on our vacation.* **7** make known: *Don't air your troubles too often.* **8** a simple melody or tune: *an old Scottish air.* **9** general character or appearance of a person or thing: *An air of mystery surrounds the deserted house.* **10** airs, *pl.* unnatural or showy manners: *Just act natural; don't put on airs.* **11** medium through which radio waves travel; airways: *to fill the air with advertising.* **12** of or having to do with aviation or aircraft: *air safety.* **1,2,4,6,8-11** *n.,* **3,5,7** *v.,* **12** *adj.*

in the air, being spread; going around: *Wild reports of revolt were in the air.*

off the air, 1 not engaged in broadcasting: *This station is off the air from midnight to six in the morning.* **2** not being broadcast: *We used to watch that show, but it's off the air now.*

on the air, 1 engaged in broadcasting: *This station has been on the air since 1958.* **2** being broadcast: *Is that show still on the air?*

take the air, go outdoors; take a walk or ride.

up in the air, uncertain or unsettled: *Plans for the picnic are still up in the air.*

walk on air, be very happy or pleased: *We were walking on air when everything worked out just as we had always planned.*

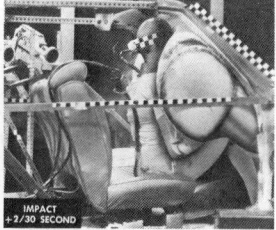

air bag—left, bag stored in front of passenger; right, bag opening to cushion passenger after a collision

a hat	**i** it	**oi** oil	**ch** child	a in about
ā age	**ī** ice	**ou** out	**ng** long	e in taken
ä far	**o** hot	**u** cup	**sh** she	**ə** = { i in pencil
e let	**ō** open	**ů** put	**th** thin	o in lemon
ē equal	**ô** order	**ü** rule	**ŦH** then	u in circus
ėr term			**zh** measure	

air bag, an inflatable bag that prevents automobile passengers from being thrown forward in the event of a collision. It is installed beneath the dashboard, and inflates instantaneously upon impact.

air base, headquarters and airfield for military aircraft.

air borne (er′bôrn′ *or* ar′bôrn′), **1** supported by the air; off the ground: *Within seconds the plane was airborne.* **2** carried in aircraft: *airborne troops.* **3** carried by air: *airborne dust, airborne pollen. adj.*

air brake, brake operated by forcing compressed air against a piston.

air-con di tion (er′kən dish′ən *or* ar′kən dish′ən), **1** supply (a building, room, car, etc.) with air conditioning. **2** treat air by means of air conditioning. *v.*

air-con di tioned (er′kən dish′ənd *or* ar′kən dish′ənd), having air conditioning. *adj.*

air conditioner, device used to air-condition a building, room, car, etc.

air conditioning, means of treating and circulating air in a building, room, car, etc., to regulate its temperature and amount of moisture and to free it from dust.

air-cooled (er′küld′ *or* ar′küld′), cooled by air forced on or around the cylinders of an internal-combustion engine: *This car has no radiator because the engine is air-cooled. adj.*

air craft (er′kraft′ *or* ar′kraft′), machine for flying in the air that is supported in flight by buoyancy (such as a balloon) or by the action of air on its surface (such as an airplane). Airplanes, airships, helicopters, and balloons are aircraft. *n., pl.* **air craft.**

aircraft carrier, warship designed as a base for aircraft, with a large, flat deck on which to land or take off.

air drome (er′drōm′ *or* ar′drōm′), airport. *n.*

air drop (er′drop′ *or* ar′drop′), **1** a delivering of food, supplies, or persons by parachute from aircraft in flight. **2** deliver (food, supplies, etc.) by parachute from aircraft in flight. 1 *n.,* 2 *v.,* **air dropped, air drop ping.**

Airedale
about 23 in. (58 cm.) high at the shoulder

Aire dale (er′dāl *or* ar′dāl), a large terrier having a wiry brown or tan coat with dark markings. *n.* [*Airedale* comes from the name *Airedale,* a valley in northern England.]

air field (er′fēld′ *or* ar′fēld′), the landing area of an airport or air base. *n.*

air foil (er′foil′ *or* ar′foil′), a wing, aileron, rudder, or other surface designed to help lift or control an aircraft. *n.*

air force, 1 branch of the military forces that uses aircraft. **2 Air Force,** branch of the armed forces of the United States that includes aviation personnel, equipment, etc.

air gun, 1 air rifle. **2** device that uses compressed air to force grease, putty, etc., into or onto something.

air i ly (er′ə lē *or* ar′ə lē), in an airy manner. *adv.*

air i ness (er′ē nis *or* ar′ē nis), airy quality. *n.*

air ing (er′ing *or* ar′ing), **1** exposure to air for drying, warming, etc.: *Give the rug a thorough airing.* **2** a walk, ride, or drive outdoors. **3** exposure to public notice or discussion: *The new bill is due for an airing in Congress. n.*

air lane, a regular route used by aircraft; airway.

air less (er′lis *or* ar′lis), **1** without fresh air; stuffy. **2** without a breeze; still. *adj.*

air lift (er′lift′ *or* ar′lift′), **1** system of using aircraft to transport passengers and freight to a place when existing land routes are closed or inadequate: *Medical supplies were brought by airlift to the flooded villages.* **2** transport by airlift: *Enough planes were provided to airlift two army divisions.* 1 *n.,* 2 *v.*

air line (er′lin′ *or* ar′lin′), company that carries passengers and freight by aircraft from one place to another. *n.*

air lin er (er′li′nər *or* ar′li′nər), a large passenger airplane. *n.*

air lock (er′lok′ *or* ar′lok′), an airtight compartment which allows workers on underwater tunnels, etc., to go between places where there is a difference in air pressure. The pressure in an airlock can be raised or lowered. *n.*

air mail (er′māl′ *or* ar′māl′), **1** mail sent by aircraft. **2** sent or to be sent by aircraft: *an airmail package.* **3** system for carrying mail by aircraft. **4** send by airmail. 1,3 *n.,* 2 *adj.,* 4 *v.*

air man (er′mən *or* ar′mən), **1** pilot of an aircraft; aviator. **2** an enlisted man or woman of the lowest rank in the Air Force. *n., pl.* **air men.**

air mass, a large body of air within the atmosphere that has nearly uniform temperature and humidity at any given level and moves horizontally over great distances without changing.

air mattress, pad that can be inflated to serve as a mattress.

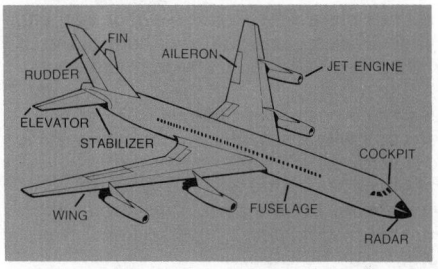

airplane
with
jet engines

FIN, AILERON, JET ENGINE, RUDDER, ELEVATOR, STABILIZER, WING, FUSELAGE, COCKPIT, RADAR

air plane (er′plān′ *or* ar′plān′), aircraft heavier than air, supported in flight by the action of air on its fixed wings and driven by propeller, jet propulsion, etc. *n.* Also, **aer o plane.**

air pocket, a downward current of air that causes an aircraft to lose altitude suddenly.

air pollution, the contamination of the air by waste gases from industry, fuel exhaust, and atomic fallout.

air port (er′pôrt′ *or* ar′pôrt′), area, especially on land, used regularly by aircraft to land or take off. An airport usually has buildings for passengers and aircraft and equipment for storing, repairing, and servicing aircraft. *n.*

air pressure, pressure caused by the weight of the air; atmospheric pressure. At sea level this pressure is 14.7 pounds per square inch (1.03 kilograms per square centimeter).

air pump, device for forcing air into or drawing air out of something.

air raid, attack by enemy aircraft, especially by bombers.

air rifle, gun that uses compressed air to shoot a single pellet or dart; air gun.

air sac, 1 one of the tiny pouches in the lungs through which oxygen passes into the blood and carbon dioxide is removed; alveolus. **2** an air-filled space in different parts of the body of a bird, connected with the lungs.

air ship (er′ship′ *or* ar′ship′), a kind of balloon that can be steered. An airship is filled with a gas that is lighter than air. Dirigibles and blimps are airships. *n.*

air sick (er′sik′ *or* ar′sik′), sick as a result of the motion of aircraft. *adj.* —**air′sick′ness,** *n.*

air speed, speed of an aircraft in relation to the speed of the air through which it moves.

air stream (er′strēm′ *or* ar′strēm′), the relative flow of air around or against an object in flight, usually in a direction opposite to that of the object's flight. *n.*

air strip (er′strip′ *or* ar′strip′), a paved or cleared runway, often temporary, on which aircraft land and take off; landing strip. *n.*

air tight (er′tīt′ *or* ar′tīt′), **1** so tight that no air or gas can get in or out. **2** having no weak points open to an opponent's attack: *an airtight alibi. adj.*

air waves (er′wāvz′ *or* ar′wāvz′), radio or television broadcasting. *n.pl.*

air way (er′wā′ *or* ar′wā′), **1** route for aircraft; air lane. **2** passage for air. **3 airways,** *pl.* channels for radio or television broadcasting. *n.*

air y (er′ē *or* ar′ē), **1** light as air; graceful: *an airy tune.* **2** light-hearted and gay: *airy laughter.* **3** open to currents of air; breezy: *a large, airy room.* **4** of air; in the air; aerial: *birds and other airy creatures.* **5** like air; not solid or substantial: *Such airy plans won't succeed. adj.,* **air i er, air i est.**

aisle (īl), **1** passage between rows of seats in a hall, theater, school, etc. **2** passage on either side of a church, often set off by pillars. **3** any long, narrow passage. *n.*

a jar (ə jär′), slightly open: *Please leave the door ajar. adj.*

A jax (ā′jaks), (in Greek legends) a Greek hero at the siege of Troy, second to Achilles in strength and courage. *n.*

AK, Alaska (used with postal Zip Code).

a kim bo (ə kim′bō), with the hands on the hips and the elbows bent outward. *adj.*

a kin (ə kin′), **1** of the same kind; similar: *His tastes in music seem akin to mine.* **2** of the same family; related: *Your cousins are akin to you. adj.*

Ak ron (ak′rən), city in NE Ohio. *n.*

-al[1], *suffix added to nouns to form adjectives.* of; like; having the nature of: *Ornamental = having the nature of ornament.*

-al[2], *suffix added to verbs to form nouns.* act of _____ing: *Refusal = act of refusing.*

Al, symbol for aluminum.

AL, Alabama (used with postal Zip Code).

Ala., Alabama.

A.L.A., American Library Association.

Al a bam a (al′ə bam′ə), one of the south central states of the United States. *Abbreviation:* Ala. or AL *Capital:* Montgomery. *n.* —**Al′a bam′an, Al′a bam′i an,** *adj., n.*

al a bas ter (al′ə bas′tər), **1** a smooth, white or delicately shaded, translucent mineral, often carved into ornaments and vases. **2** smooth and white like alabaster. **1** *n.,* **2** *adj.*

à la carte (ä′ lə kärt′ *or* al′ ə kärt′), with a stated price for each dish (instead of one price for the whole meal).

a lack (ə lak′), OLD USE. alas. *interj.*

a lac ri ty (ə lak′rə tē), brisk and eager action; liveliness: *She began making the arrangements for her trip with alacrity. n.*

A lad din (ə lad′n), a youth in *The Arabian Nights,* who found a magic lamp and a magic ring. By rubbing either one of them he could call either of two powerful spirits to do whatever he asked. *n.*

Al a mo (al′ə mō), a mission building in San Antonio, Texas, used as a fort by a band of Texas rebels fighting for independence from Mexico. Besieged by an army of Mexicans, the Texans were overwhelmed and killed on March 6, 1836. *n.*

à la mode or **a la mode** (ä′ lə mōd′ *or* al′ ə mōd′), **1** in style; fashionable. **2** served with ice cream; *pie à la mode.* **3** cooked with vegetables: *beef à la mode.*

a larm (ə lärm′), **1** sudden fear of danger; fright: *The deer darted off in alarm.* **2** fill with sudden fear; frighten: *The breaking of a branch under my foot alarmed the deer.* **3** a warning of approaching danger: *This is no false alarm.* **4** signal giving such a warning: *a fire alarm.* **5** device that makes noise to warn or awaken people: *a burglar alarm.* **6** call to arms or action: *Paul Revere gave the alarm to the towns near Boston.* **1,3-5,6** *n.,* **2** *v.*

alarm clock, clock that can be set to ring or sound at any fixed time.

a larm ing (ə lär′ming), causing alarm; frightening. *adj.* —**a larm′ing ly,** *adv.*

a larm ist (ə lär′mist), person who is easily alarmed or alarms others needlessly or on very slight grounds. *n.*

a lar um (ə lär′əm *or* ə lär′əm), OLD USE. alarm. *n.*

a las (ə las′), exclamation of sorrow, grief, regret, pity, or dread. *interj.* [*Alas* came into English about 700 years ago from French *a,* meaning "ah," and *las,* meaning "miserable."]

Alas., Alaska.

A las ka (ə las′kə), **1** one of the Pacific states of the United States, in the NW part of North America. *Abbreviation:* Alas. or AK *Capital:* Juneau. **2 Gulf of,** arm of the Pacific, off S Alaska. *n.* —**A las′kan,** *adj., n.*

Alaska Pipeline, pipeline that carries oil across Alaska from Prudhoe Bay on the Arctic Ocean south to Valdez on the Gulf of Alaska. Its official name is the **Trans Alaska Pipeline.** 800 miles (1287 kilometers) long.

a late (ā′lāt), having wings or winglike parts. *adj.*

a lat ed (ā′lā tid), alate. *adj.*

alb (alb), a white linen robe worn by Roman Catholic and some Anglican priests at the Communion service. *n.*

Alb., **1** Albanian. **2** Albany.

al ba core (al′bə kôr), a large tuna with long fins and light-colored flesh valued for canning. *n., pl.* **al ba cores** or **al ba core.**

Al ba ni a (al bā′nē ə), country in SE Europe, between Yugoslavia and Greece. *Capital:* Tirana. See **Adriatic Sea** for map. *n.* —**Al ba′ni an,** *adj., n.*

Al ba ny (ôl′bə nē), capital of New York State, on the Hudson River. *n.*

al ba tross (al′bə trôs), a very large web-footed sea bird related to petrels, that can fly long distances. *n., pl.* **al ba tross es** or **al ba tross.**

al be it (ôl bē′it), even though; even if; although: *Albeit we are late, we may still be able to catch the bus.* *conj.*

Al ber ta (al bėr′tə), province in W Canada. *Capital:* Edmonton. *n.* —**Al ber′tan,** *adj., n.*

al bi no (al bī′nō), **1** person that from birth has abnormally white or milky skin and hair, and pink eyes with red pupils. **2** animal or plant with pale, defective coloring. *n., pl.* **al bi nos.**

a	hat	i	it	oi	oil	ch	child		a in about
ā	age	ī	ice	ou	out	ng	long		e in taken
ä	far	o	hot	u	cup	sh	she	ə =	i in pencil
e	let	ō	open	ů	put	th	thin		o in lemon
ē	equal	ô	order	ü	rule	₮H	then		u in circus
ėr	term					zh	measure		

WORD HISTORY

albino

Albino was borrowed from Portuguese *albino*, and can be traced back to Latin *albus*, meaning "white."

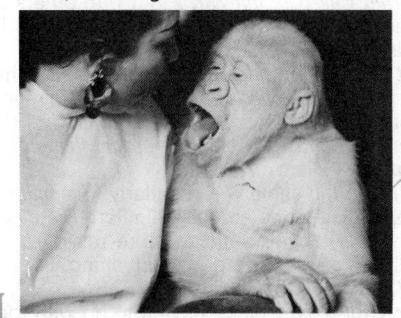

albino (def. 2)—an albino gorilla

Al bi on (al′bē ən), England. *n.*

al bum (al′bəm), **1** book with blank pages for holding photographs, stamps, autographs, etc. **2** case for or containing a phonograph record or records. **3** a single long-playing phonograph record. *n.*

al bu men (al byü′mən), the white of an egg, consisting mostly of albumin dissolved in water. *n.*

al bu min (al byü′mən), protein found in the white of an egg, milk, blood serum, lymph, and in many other animal and plant tissues and juices. *n.*

Al bu quer que (al′bə kėr′kē), city in central New Mexico. *n.*

al bur num (al bėr′nəm), sapwood. *n.*

al che mist (al′kə mist), person who studied or practiced a combination of chemistry and magic in the Middle Ages. Alchemists tried to find a way to turn cheaper metals into gold and silver and to produce a substance which would prolong human life. *n.*

al che my (al′kə mē), **1** combination of chemistry and magic studied and practiced in the Middle Ages. **2** magical power of transforming one thing into another. *n.*

al co hol (al′kə hôl), **1** the colorless liquid in whiskey, gin, wine, beer, etc., that makes them intoxicating; grain alcohol; ethyl alcohol. Alcohol is used in medicines, in manufacturing, and as a fuel. **2** whiskey, gin, or any other intoxicating liquor containing this liquid. **3** any of a group of similar organic compounds, reacting with certain acids to form esters. Wood alcohol is very poisonous. *n.*

al co hol ic (al′kə hô′lik), **1** consisting of alcohol: *alcoholic fumes.* **2** containing alcohol: *alcoholic drinks.* **3** person who suffers from alcoholism. **4** suffering from alcoholism. 1,2,4 *adj.,* 3 *n.* —**al′co hol′i cal ly,** *adv.*

al co hol ism (al′kə hô liz′əm), a diseased condition caused by continually drinking too much alcoholic liquor. *n.*

Al cott (ôl′kət), **Louisa May,** 1832-1888, American author. *n.*

al cove (al′kōv), **1** a small room opening out of a larger room. **2** recess or large, hollow space in a wall. *n.*

Ald., Alderman. Also, **Aldm.**

al der (ôl′dər), tree or shrub that usually grows in wet land and has clusters of catkins that develop into small, woody cones. *n.*

al der man (ôl′dər mən), person elected to represent a certain district on a council that governs a city. *n., pl.* **al der men.**

Al der ney (ôl′dər nē), one of the Channel Islands. *n.*

Aldm., Alderman. Also, **Ald.**

ale (āl), a bitter alcoholic beverage fermented from malt and flavored with hops. Ale is similar to beer but contains more alcohol. *n.*

a lee (ə lē′), on or toward the side of a ship that is away from the wind. *adv.*

a lert (ə lėrt′), **1** keen and watchful; wide-awake: *A good hunting dog is alert to every sound and movement in the field.* **2** quick in action; nimble: *A sparrow is very alert in its movements.* **3** signal warning of an attack by approaching enemy aircraft, a hurricane, or other threatening danger. **4** period of time after this warning until the attack is over or the danger has passed: *The hurricane alert is over.* **5** warn against an attack by aircraft, a hurricane, or other threatening danger. **6** notify (troops) to get ready for action. **7** make aware of; arouse: *to alert people to the dangers of smoking cigarettes.* 1,2 *adj.,* 3,4 *n.,* 5-7 *v.* —**a lert′ly,** *adv.* —**a lert′ness,** *n.*

on the alert, ready at any instant for what is coming; watchful: *A driver must be on the alert.*

Al e ut (al′ē üt), **1** person born or living in the Aleutian Islands. **2** the language spoken there, related to Eskimo. *n.*

A leu tian Islands (ə lü′shən), chain of about 150 small islands in the N Pacific, part of Alaska and extending southwest from the mainland for 1200 miles.

Al ex an der the Great (al′ig zan′dər), 356-323 B.C., king of Macedonia from 336 to 323 B.C. He conquered the Greek city-states and the whole Persian empire, from the coasts of Asia Minor and Egypt to India.

Al ex an dri a (al′ig zan′drē ə), seaport in N Egypt, on the Mediterranean. Alexandria was famous in ancient times for its library and scholars. *n.*

al fal fa (al fal′fə), plant, somewhat like clover, that has deep roots and bluish-purple flowers. Alfalfa is grown as food for horses and cattle. *n.* [*Alfalfa* was borrowed from Spanish *alfalfa,* which came from Arabic *alfasfas,* meaning "the best kind of fodder."]

Al fred the Great (al′frid), A.D. 849-899, king of England from A.D. 871 to 899, who defeated the Danes, united southern England, and led a revival of learning and literature.

alg., algebra.

al ga (al′gə), one of the algae. *n., pl.* **al gae.**

al gae (al′jē), group of water plants that can make their own food. Algae contain chlorophyll but lack true stems, roots, or leaves. Some algae are one-celled and form scum on rocks; others, such as the seaweeds, are very large. *n.pl.*

al gal (al′gəl), of or like algae. *adj.*

al ge bra (al′jə brə), branch of mathematics which deals with the relations and properties of quantities. In algebra quantities are denoted by letters, negative numbers as well as ordinary numbers are used, and problems are solved in the form of equations. $x + y = x^2$ is a way of stating, by algebra, that the sum of two numbers equals the square of one of them. *n.*

al ge bra ic (al′jə brā′ik), of or used in algebra: $(a+b)$ $(a-b) = a^2-b^2$ *is an algebraic statement. adj.*

al ge bra i cal ly (al′jə brā′ik lē), by means of algebra or of algebraic processes. *adv.*

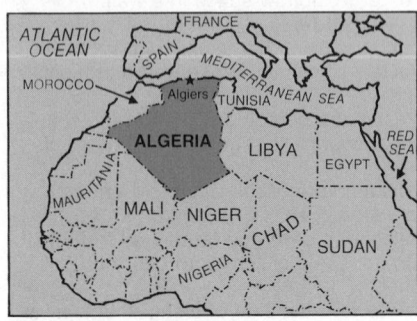

Al ger i a (al jir′ē ə), country in N Africa, on the Mediterranean, which became independent of France in 1962. *Capital:* Algiers. *n.* —**Al ger′i an,** *adj., n.*

Al ge rine (al′jə rēn′), Algerian. *adj., n.*

Al giers (al jirz′), capital of Algeria, on the Mediterranean. *n.*

Al gon ki an (al gong′kē ən), Algonquian. *n., adj.*

Al gon qui an (al gong′kē ən *or* al gong′kwē ən), **1** family of North American Indian languages, including the languages of the Arapaho, Blackfoot, Cheyenne, Ojibwa, Delaware, and Shawnee tribes. **2** of this family of languages. **3** person belonging to an Algonquian tribe. 1,3 *n., pl.* **Al gon qui an** or **Al gon qui ans** for 3; 2 *adj.*

Al gon quin (al gong′kən *or* al gong′kwən), member of a group of North American Indian tribes that lived in eastern Canada. *n., pl.* **Al gon quin** or **Al gon quins.**

Al ham bra (al ham′brə), palace of the Moorish kings at Granada, Spain. The Alhambra was the last stronghold of the Moors in Europe and was conquered in 1492. *n.*

a li as (ā′lē əs), **1** name other than a person's real name used to hide who he or she is; assumed name: *The spy's real name was Harrison, but he sometimes went by the alias of Johnson.* **2** otherwise called: *The thief's name was Jones, alias Williams.* 1 *n., pl.* **a li as es;** 2 *adv.*

A li Ba ba (ä′lē bä′bə *or* al′ē bab′ə), a poor woodcutter in *The Arabian Nights* who discovers a treasure hidden in a cave by forty thieves.

al i bi (al′ə bī), **1** the statement that an accused person was somewhere else when an offense was committed: *Immediately after the robbery the gang scattered to establish alibis.* **2** INFORMAL. an excuse: *What is your alibi for failing to do your homework?* **3** INFORMAL. make an excuse: *She alibied that she was very busy when they asked her why she didn't visit them.* 1,2 *n., pl.* **al i bis;** 3 *v.,* **al i bied, al i bi ing.** [*Alibi* comes from Latin *alibi,* meaning "elsewhere."]

al ien (ā′lyən), **1** person who is not a citizen of the country in which he or she lives. **2** of another country; foreign: *an alien language, alien conquerors.* **3** entirely different; not in agreement; strange: *Cruelty is alien to his nature.* 1 *n.,* 2,3 *adj.*

al ien ate (ā′lyə nāt), turn from affection to indifference, dislike, or hatred; make unfriendly: *The colonies were alienated from England by disputes over trade and taxation.* *v.,* **al ien at ed, al ien at ing.** —**al′ien a′tor,** *n.*

al ien a tion (ā′lyə nā′shən), **1** an alienating; making unfriendly. **2** a being alienated; not feeling interested in or involved with one's family, associates, or society. *n.*

a light¹ (ə līt′), **1** get down; get off; dismount: *She alighted from the bus.* **2** come down from the air and lightly settle; come down from flight: *The bird alighted on our window sill.* *v.,* **a light ed** or **a lit** (ə lit′), **a light ing.** [*Alight¹* comes from Old English *ālīhtan,* meaning "to get down."]

a light² (ə līt′), **1** on fire; lighted: *Is the kindling alight?* **2** lighted up; aglow: *Her face was alight with happiness.* *adj.* [*Alight²* comes from Old English *ālīht,* meaning "lighted up."]

a lign (ə līn′), **1** bring into line; arrange in a straight line: *I aligned the sights of my gun with the target. The mechanic aligned the front wheels of our car.* **2** join with others for or against a cause: *Germany was aligned with Japan in World War II. v.* Also, **aline.**

a lign ment (ə līn′mənt), **1** arrangement in a straight line: *The pictures were in perfect alignment.* **2** a joining with others for or against a cause: *The establishment of the Common Market resulted in a new European alignment. n.* Also, **alinement.**

a like (ə līk′), **1** in the same way; similarly: *She and her sister think alike.* **2** like one another; similar: *These twins are very much alike.* 1 *adv.,* 2 *adj.* —**a like′ness,** *n.*

al i men tal (al′ə men′tl), of food; nourishing. *adj.* —**al′ i men′tal ly,** *adv.*

al i men tar y (al′ə men′tər ē), having to do with food and nutrition. *adj.*

alimentary canal, the parts of the body through which food passes as it is digested and from which wastes are eliminated.

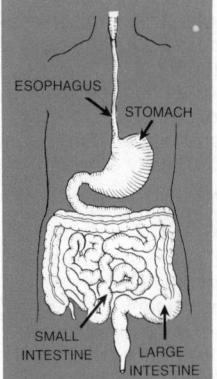

alimentary canal
of a human being—
a 30 ft. (9 m.) tube
beginning at the mouth,
where food enters, and
ending at the anus,
where undigested solids
leave the body

al i mo ny (al′ə mō′nē), a regular sum of money paid by one spouse to the other after a divorce or legal separation. The amount of alimony is fixed by a court. *n.*

a line (ə līn′), align. *v.,* **a lined, a lin ing.**

a line ment (ə līn′mənt), alignment. *n.*

a live (ə līv′), **1** having life; living: *Was the snake alive or dead?* **2** in continued activity; in full force; active: *We celebrate Memorial Day to keep alive the memory of those who have died for their country.* **3** of all living: *I was the happiest person alive.* **4** full of energy; lively. *adj.* —**a live′ness,** *n.*

alive to, awake to; sensitive to: *Are you alive to what is going on?*

alive with, full of; swarming with: *The streets were alive with people.*

look alive! hurry up! be quick!

al ka li (al′kə lī), **1** any of a group of substances that are soluble in water, neutralize acids and form salts with them, and turn red litmus paper blue. Lye and ammonia are alkalis. **2** any salt or mixture of salts found in some desert soils. *n., pl.* **al ka lis** or **al ka lies.**

al ka line (al′kə līn *or* al′kə lən), **1** of or like an alkali: *an alkaline reaction.* **2** containing alkali. *adj.*

al ka lin i ty (al′kə lin′ə tē), alkaline quality or condition. *n.*

all (ôl), **1** every one of: *All the children came.* **2** everyone: *All of us are going.* **3** everything: *All is well.* **4** the whole of: *The mice ate all the cheese.* **5** the whole amount: *All of the bread has been eaten.* **6** wholly; entirely: *The cake is all gone.* **7** the greatest possible: *I made all haste to reach home in time.* **8** nothing but; only: *This plane carries all cargo and no passengers.* **9** each; apiece: *The score was even at forty all.* 1,4,7,8 *adj.*, 2,3,5 *pron.*, 6,9 *adv.*

above all, before everything else: *Above all, she loves to travel.*

after all, when everything has been considered; nevertheless: *I see that you came after all.*

all but, nearly; almost: *This job is all but done.*

all in, INFORMAL. worn out; weary: *After the race, I was all in.*

all in all, when everything has been taken into account: *All in all, I think you did a good job.*

all over, 1 everywhere: *I looked all over for your glasses.* **2** done with; finished: *The game is all over.*

at all, 1 under any conditions: *Maybe I won't be able to go at all.* **2** in any way: *I was not at all surprised.*

for all that, in spite of that; notwithstanding.

in all, counting every person or thing; altogether: *There were five of us in all.*

Al lah (al′ə *or* ä′lə), the Moslem name for God. *n.*

all-A mer i can (ôl′ə mer′ə kən), **1** chosen as the best at a particular position in one year, from among all high-school, or collegiate, players of a team sport in the United States. **2** made up entirely of Americans or American elements: *The ship had an all-American crew.* **3** player that is chosen all-American. 1,2 *adj.*, 3 *n.*

all-a round (ôl′ə round′), able to do many things; not limited or specialized: *She is an all-around athlete—she plays tennis, golfs, and swims well. adj.*

al lay (ə lā′), **1** put at rest; quiet: *The parents' fears were allayed by the news that their children were safe.* **2** make less; weaken or relieve: *Her fever was allayed by the medicine. v.,* **al layed, al lay ing. —al lay′er,** *n.*

all clear, signal indicating the end of an air raid or other danger.

al le ga tion (al′ə gā′shən), a positive statement, especially one without proof; assertion: *Everyone knows better than to believe the allegations made against you. n.*

al lege (ə lej′), **1** state positively; assert: *Although he has no proof, this man alleges that the janitor stole his watch.* **2** give or bring forward as a reason, excuse, or argument: *Alleging illness, the mayor retired from office. v.,* **al leged, al leg ing. —al lege′a ble,** *adj.* **—al leg′er,** *n.*

al leged (ə lejd′), **1** stated positively to be, but without proof: *The alleged burglar was held for trial.* **2** doubtful: *an alleged cure for cancer. adj.*

al leg ed ly (ə lej′id lē), according to what is alleged. *adv.*

Al le ghe nies (al′ə gā′nēz), Allegheny Mountains. *n.pl.*

Al le ghe ny Mountains (al′ə gā′nē), mountain range of the Appalachian Mountain system, in Pennsylvania, Maryland, Virginia, and West Virginia.

Allegheny River, river in W Pennsylvania. It joins the Monongahela at Pittsburgh to form the Ohio River.

al le giance (ə lē′jəns), **1** the loyalty owed to one's

a hat	i it	oi oil	ch child		a in about
ā age	ī ice	ou out	ng long		e in taken
ä far	o hot	u cup	sh she	ə =	i in pencil
e let	ō open	ù put	th thin		o in lemon
ē equal	ô order	ü rule	ŦH then		u in circus
ėr term			zh measure		

country or government: *I pledge allegiance to the flag.* **2** loyalty to any person or thing: *We owe allegiance to our friends. n.*

al le go ri cal (al′ə gôr′ə kəl), explaining or teaching something by a story; using allegory. *adj.* **—al′le-go′ri cal ly,** *adv.*

al le go rize (al′ə gə rīz′), **1** make into allegory. **2** treat as an allegory. **3** use allegory. *v.,* **al le go rized, al le go riz ing. —al′le go′ri za′tion,** *n.* **—al′le go riz′er,** *n.*

al le go ry (al′ə gôr′ē), a story that is told to explain and teach something. The parables in the Bible are allegories. *n., pl.* **al le go ries.**

al leg ro (ə leg′rō *or* ə lā′grō), in music: **1** quick; lively. **2** in quick time. **3** a quick, lively part in a piece of music: 1 *adj.,* 2 *adv.,* 3 *n., pl.* **al leg ros.** [*Allegro* was borrowed from Italian *allegro.*]

al le lu ia (al′ə lü′yə), hallelujah. *interj., n., pl.* **al le lu ias.**

Al len (al′ən), Ethan, 1737-1789, American officer in the Revolutionary War. *n.*

al ler gic (ə lėr′jik), **1** having an allergy: *Some people who are allergic to eggs cannot eat them without breaking into a rash.* **2** of or caused by allergy: *Hay fever is an allergic reaction.* **3** INFORMAL. having a strong dislike: *She is allergic to physical exercise. adj.* **—al ler′gi cal ly,** *adv.*

al ler gist (al′ər jist), doctor who specializes in treating allergies. *n.*

al ler gy (al′ər jē), an unusual reaction of body tissue to certain substances such as particular kinds of pollen, food, hair, or cloth. Hay fever, asthma, headaches, and hives are common signs of allergy. *n., pl.* **al ler gies.**

al le vi ate (ə lē′vē āt), make easier to endure; relieve; lessen: *Heat often alleviates pain. v.,* **al le vi at ed, al le vi at ing. —al le′vi a′tor,** *n.*

al le vi a tion (ə lē′vē ā′shən), **1** an alleviating: *the alleviation of taxes.* **2** thing that alleviates: *Lower taxes were an alleviation to the taxpayers. n.*

al ley (al′ē), **1** a narrow back street in a city or town. **2** path in a park or garden, bordered by trees. **3** a long, narrow lane along which the ball is rolled in bowling. **4** building having a number of alleys for bowling. *n., pl.* **al leys.**

al ley way (al′ē wā′), **1** alley in a city or town. **2** a narrow passageway. *n.*

All Fools' Day, April 1; April Fools' Day.

All hal lows (ôl′hal′ōz), November 1; All Saints' Day. *n.*

al li ance (ə lī′əns), a union of persons, groups, or nations formed by agreement for some special purpose or benefit. An alliance may be a joining of national interests by treaty or a joining of family interests by marriage. *n.*

al lied (ə līd′ *or* al′īd), **1** united by agreement: *allied nations, allied armies.* **2** similar in some way; related; connected: *Painting, drawing, and sculpture are allied arts. adj.*

Al lies (al′īz *or* ə līz′), **1** the countries that fought against Germany, Austria-Hungary, Turkey, and Bulgaria in World War I. **2** the countries that fought against Germany, Italy, and Japan in World War II. *n.pl.*

al li ga tor (al′ə gā′tər), **1** a large reptile with a rather thick skin, related and similar to the crocodile but having a shorter and flatter head. Alligators live in the rivers and marshes of the warm parts of America and China. **2** leather prepared from its skin. *n.* [*Alligator* comes from

Spanish *el lagarto*, meaning "the lizard."]

alligator pear, avocado.

al lit e ra tion (ə lit/e rā/shən), repetition of the same sound or letter in a group of words or a line of poetry. *n.*

The **s**ilken **s**ad un**c**ertain ru**s**tling

alliteration—This quotation from a poem by Edgar Allan Poe contains alliteration of the "s" sound.

all-night (ôl/nīt/), **1** open all night: *an all-night drugstore.* **2** lasting all night: *an all-night card game. adj.*

al lo cate (al/ə kāt), set or lay aside for a special purpose; allot: *The federal government allocated millions of dollars for cancer research. v.*, **al lo cat ed, al lo cat ing.**

al lo ca tion (al/ə kā/shən), **1** an allocating; allotment. **2** share, portion, or thing allotted. *n.*

al lot (ə lot/), **1** divide and distribute in parts or shares: *The profits have been allotted among the owners of the company.* **2** give to as a share; assign: *The principal allotted each class a part in the school program. v.*, **al lot ted, al lot ting.** —**al lot/ter,** *n.*

al lot ment (ə lot/mənt), **1** division and distribution in parts or shares: *The allotment of profits was made Monday.* **2** share allotted: *Your allotment was $4. n.*

all-out (ôl/out/), **1** greatest possible; complete: *The team made an all-out effort to win.* **2** to the utmost extent: *go all-out to win.* **1** *adj.*, **2** *adv.*

all o ver (ôl/ō/vər), covering the whole surface: *an all-over pattern. adj.*

al low (ə lou/), **1** let (someone) do something; permit (something) to be done or happen: *They do not allow swimming at this beach.* **2** let have; give: *My parents allowed me a dollar to spend as I wish.* **3** accept as true; acknowledge; recognize: *The judge allowed the claim of the person whose property was damaged.* **4** add or subtract to make up for something: *The trip will cost you only $20; but you ought to allow $5 more for extra expenses. v.* —**al low/er,** *n.*

allow for, take into consideration; provide for: *I buy my jeans a little large to allow for shrinking.*

al low a ble (ə lou/ə bəl), allowed by law; permitted by the rules; not forbidden. *adj.* —**al low/a bly,** *adv.*

al low ance (ə lou/əns), **1** a sum of money given or set aside for expenses: *a household allowance for groceries of $50 a week. My weekly allowance is $1.* **2** amount subtracted to make up for something; discount: *The salesman offered us an allowance of $400 on our old car; so we got a $3000 car for $2600.* **3** an allowing; conceding: *allowance of a claim. n.*

make allowance for or **make allowances for,** take into consideration; allow for: *We made allowance for the heavy traffic by leaving half an hour early.*

al loy (al/oi *or* ə loi/ *for 1,3;* ə loi/ *for 2,4*), **1** metal made by melting and mixing two or more metals or a metal and another substance. An alloy may be harder, lighter, and stronger than the metals of which it is composed. Brass is an alloy of copper and zinc. **2** make into an alloy. **3** an inferior metal mixed with a more valuable one: *This ring is not pure gold; there is some alloy in it.* **4** make lower or less valuable by mixing with something bad: *Two days of rain somewhat alloyed their enthusiasm for camping.* **1,3** *n.*, **2,4** *v.*

all right, 1 without error; correct: *The answers were all right.* **2** satisfactory: *The work was not done very well; but it was all right.* **3** in a satisfactory way: *The engine seemed to be working all right.* **4** in good health: *The doctor says I am all right.* **5** yes: *"Will you come with me?" "All right."* **6** without doubt; certainly: *I am tired, all right!*

all-round (ôl/round/), all-around. *adj.*

All Saints' Day, November 1, a church festival honoring all the saints; Allhallows.

all spice (ôl/spīs/), spice having a flavor suggesting a mixture of cinnamon, nutmeg, and cloves, made from the berry of a tropical American tree. *n.*

all-star (ôl/stär/), made up of the best players or performers: *Two of our players have been named to the all-star team. adj.*

al lude (ə lüd/), refer indirectly to something; mention slightly in passing: *Don't tell them of our decision; don't even allude to it. v.*, **al lud ed, al lud ing.**

al lure (ə lür/), **1** tempt or attract very strongly; fascinate; charm: *City life allured her with its action and excitement.* **2** attractiveness; fascination; charm: *the allure of the sea.* **1** *v.*, **al lured, al lur ing; 2** *n.* —**al lur/er,** *n.*

al lure ment (ə lür/mənt), **1** attractiveness; fascination; charm. **2** thing that allures. *n.*

al lur ing (ə lür/ing), strongly attracting; tempting: *an alluring advertisement. adj.* —**al lur/ing ly,** *adv.* —**al lur/ing ness,** *n.*

al lu sion (ə lü/zhən), slight mention made in passing; indirect reference: *Don't make any allusion to the surprise party while they are present. n.*

al lu sive (ə lü/siv), containing an allusion; full of allusions. *adj.* —**al lu/sive ly,** *adv.* —**al lu/sive ness,** *n.*

al lu vi al (ə lü/vē əl), consisting of or formed by sand or mud left by flowing water. A delta is an alluvial deposit at the mouth of a river. *adj.*

al ly (al/ī *or* ə lī/ *for 1,2;* ə lī/ *for 3*), **1** person, group, or nation united with another for some special purpose: *England and France were allies in some wars and enemies in others.* See also **Allies. 2** helper; supporter. **3** combine for some special purpose; unite by agreement. Small nations sometimes ally themselves with larger ones for protection. **1,2** *n., pl.* **al lies; 3** *v.*, **al lied, al ly ing.**

-ally, suffix forming adverbs. in a _____ic manner: *Basically = in a basic manner. Tragically = in a tragic manner.*

al ma ma ter or **Al ma Ma ter** (al/mə mä/tər *or* äl/mə mä/tər), person's school, college, or university. [*Alma mater* comes from Latin *alma mater,* meaning "fostering mother."]

al ma nac (ôl/mə nak), **1** a booklike calendar published every year that also gives information about the weather, sun, moon, stars, tides, church days, and other facts. **2** a reference book published every year that has tables of facts and figures and summaries of information on many subjects. *n.*

al might y (ôl mī/tē), **1** having supreme power; omnipotent. **2 the Almighty,** God. **1** *adj.*, **2** *n.* —**al might/i ly,** *adv.* —**al might/i ness,** *n.*

al mond (ä/mənd *or* am/ənd), the oval-shaped nut of the peachlike fruit of a tree growing in warm regions. *n.* —**al/mond like/,** *adj.*

al most (ôl′mōst), very near to; all but; nearly: *It is almost ten o'clock. I almost missed the train. adv.*
almost never, scarcely ever.
almost no, scarcely any.
alms (ämz), money or gifts to help the poor. *n. sing. or pl.* [*Alms* comes from Old English *ælmysse,* and can be traced back to Greek *eleos,* meaning "pity."]
alms house (ämz′hous′), home for very poor persons supported at public expense or by private charity. *n., pl.* **alms hous es** (ämz′hou′ziz).
al ni co (al′nə kō), alloy of iron containing aluminum, nickel, cobalt, and other metals, used as a magnet. *n.*
al oe (al′ō), **1** plant related to the lily, having a long spike of flowers and thick, narrow leaves. It grows chiefly in South Africa. **2 aloes,** *pl.* a bitter drug made from the dried juice of this plant's leaves, used as a laxative. **3** century plant. *n.*
a loft (ə lôft′), **1** far above the earth; up in the air; high up: *Some birds fly thousands of feet aloft.* **2** high up among the sails, rigging, or masts of a ship: *The sailor went aloft to get a better view of the distant shore. adv.*
a lo ha (ə lō′ə *or* ä lō′hä), **1** greetings; hello. **2** good-by; farewell. *n., pl.* **a lo has;** *interj.* [*Aloha* comes from Hawaiian *aloha,* meaning "love."]
a lone (ə lōn′), **1** apart from other persons or things: *After my friends left, I was alone (adj.). One tree stood alone on the hill (adv.).* **2** without help from others: *I solved the problem alone.* **3** without anyone else; only: *She alone can do this work.* **4** without anything more: *Bread alone is not enough for lunch.* **5** and nothing more; only; merely: *I did the job for money alone.* 1,3,4 *adj.,* 1,2,5 *adv.* **—a lone′-ness,** *n.*
leave alone, not bother; not meddle with: *She's busy with her homework; you'd better leave her alone.*
let alone, 1 not bother; not meddle with: *If everyone will let him alone, he will get his work done.* **2** not to mention: *It would have been a hot day for summer, let alone early spring.*
let well enough alone, be satisfied with conditions and not try to change them: *You have done what you can to help, so why not just let well enough alone?*
a long (ə lông′), **1** from one end to the other end of; lengthwise of: *Trees are planted along the street.* **2** from one end to the other; lengthwise: *Cars are parked along by the stadium.* **3** forward; onward: *Let's walk along quickly.* **4** together with someone or something: *We took our dog along.* **5** INFORMAL. (of time) somewhere: *Be ready to leave along about four o'clock.* 1 *prep.,* 2-5 *adv.*
all along, all the time: *He knew the answer all along.*
along with, in company with; together with: *I'll go along with you.*
get along, 1 manage: *Can you get along without our help?* **2** agree: *They get along well as partners.* **3** move forward; advance: *Let's get along or we'll be late.* **4** succeed; prosper: *She is getting along well in her new business.*
a long side (ə lông′sīd′), **1** at the side; side by side: *A car pulled up alongside.* **2** by the side of; side by side with: *The boat was alongside the wharf.* 1 *adv.,* 2 *prep.*
alongside of, beside; next to: *If you stay alongside of me, you won't get lost.*
a loof (ə lüf′), **1** at a distance or apart: *One boy stood aloof from all the others.* **2** tending to keep to oneself; indifferent; reserved. 1 *adv.,* 2 *adj.* **—a loof′ly,** *adv.* **—a loof′ness,** *n.*
a loud (ə loud′), loud enough to be heard; not in a whisper: *The book I was reading was so funny I laughed aloud. The teacher read the story aloud to the class. adv.*
alp (alp), a high mountain. See **Alps.** *n.*
al pac a (al pak′ə), **1** a sheeplike animal of South America with long, soft, silky hair or wool. It is closely related

alpaca (def. 1)
about 4¹/₂ ft. (1.5 m.) long

to but somewhat smaller than the llama. **2** its wool. **3** cloth made from this wool. **4** a glossy, wiry cloth made of sheep's wool and cotton. *n., pl.* **al pac as** or **al pac a.** [*Alpaca* was borrowed from Spanish *alpaca,* which came from the local Indian name for this animal in Peru.]
al pha (al′fə), **1** the first letter of the Greek alphabet (A, α). **2** the first of a series. *n., pl.* **al phas.**
al pha bet (al′fə bet), **1** the letters of a language arranged in their usual order, not as they are in words. **2** set of letters or characters representing sounds, used in writing a language. The English alphabet has only 26 letters to represent more than 40 sounds. *n.* [*Alphabet* can be traced back to the names of the first two letters of the Greek alphabet: *alpha* A and *bēta* B.]
al pha bet ic (al′fə bet′ik), alphabetical. *adj.*
al pha bet i cal (al′fə bet′ə kəl), **1** arranged by letters in the order of the alphabet: *Dictionary entries are listed in alphabetical order.* **2** of the alphabet. *adj.* **—al′pha bet′i cal ly,** *adv.*
al pha bet ize (al′fə bə tīz), arrange in alphabetical order: *Alphabetize the words in your spelling lesson. v.,* **al pha bet ized, al pha bet iz ing. —al′pha bet′i za′tion,** *n.* **—al′pha bet iz′er,** *n.*
alpha particle, a positively charged particle consisting of two protons and two neutrons, released at a very high speed in the disintegration of radium and other radioactive substances.
alpha ray, a stream of alpha particles.
al pine (al′pīn), **1** of or like high mountains: *alpine plants, alpine terrain.* **2 Alpine,** of or like the Alps. *adj.*
Alps (alps), mountain system in S Europe, with ranges in France, Switzerland, West Germany, Italy, Austria, and Yugoslavia. *n.pl.*
al read y (ôl red′ē), before this time; by this time; even now: *You are half an hour late already. adv.*
Al sace (al sās′), region in NE France, on the Rhine. *n.*
Al sace-Lor raine (al sās′lə rān′), Alsace and Lorraine,

aloof (def. 2)
Her manner was cool and **aloof.**

---

region in NE France. It formed a German province from 1871 to 1919 and from 1940 to 1945. *n.*

Al sa tian (al sā′shən), **1** of Alsace or its people. **2** person born or living in Alsace. **3** a German shepherd dog. 1 *adj.*, 2,3 *n.*

al so (ôl′sō), in addition; besides; too: *That car is the latest model; it is also very expensive. adv.*

al so-ran (ôl′sō ran′), an unsuccessful contestant; loser. *n.*

alt., 1 alternate. **2** altitude.

Alta., Alberta, a province in Canada.

al tar (ôl′tər), **1** table or stand used in religious worship in a church or temple: *The worshipers received Communion from the priest at the altar.* **2** block of stone, mound of turf, etc., on which to place sacrifices or burn offerings to a god. *n.*

altar boy, man or boy who helps a priest during certain religious services; acolyte.

al ter (ôl′tər), make or become different; change; vary: *The coat can be altered to fit you. Since her summer on the farm, her whole outlook has altered.* v. —**al′ter a ble,** *adj.* —**al′ter a ble ness,** *n.* —**al′ter a bly,** *adv.*

al ter a tion (ôl′tə rā′shən), **1** change in the appearance or form of anything; altered or changed condition: *My coat fit better after the alterations were made.* **2** an altering: *The alteration of our house took three months. n.*

al ter cate (ôl′tər kāt), dispute angrily; quarrel. *v.*, **al ter cat ed, al ter cat ing.**

al ter ca tion (ôl′tər kā′shən), an angry dispute; noisy quarrel: *The two teams had an altercation over the umpire's decision. n.*

al ter e go (ôl′tər ē′gō), a very intimate friend; close associate. [*Alter ego comes from the Latin phrase alter ego,* meaning "other I, other self."]

al ter nate (ôl′tər nāt *for 1-3;* ôl′tər nit *for 4-6*), **1** happen or be arranged by turns. Squares and circles alternate in this row: □○□○□○□○. **2** arrange by turns: *We alternated work and pleasure.* **3** take turns: *The two of us will alternate in setting the table.* **4** first one and then the other by turns: *The United States flag has alternate stripes of red and white.* **5** every other: *Our dairy no longer delivers milk daily, but only on alternate days.* **6** person appointed to take the place of another if it should be necessary; substitute: *We have several alternates on our debating team.* 1-3 *v.*, **al ter nat ed, al ter nat ing;** 4,5 *adj.*, 6 *n.*

al ter nate ly (ôl′tər nit lē), by turns. *adv.*

alternating current, an electric current in which the electricity flows regularly in one direction and then the other, usually reversing 120 times per second.

al ter na tion (ôl′tər nā′shən), an alternating; occurring by turns, first one and then the other: *There is an alternation of red and white stripes in the flag of the United States. n.*

al ter na tive (ôl tėr′nə tiv), **1** choice from among two or more things: *She had the alternative of going to summer school or finding a summer job.* **2** one of the things to be chosen: *She chose the first alternative and went to summer school.* **3** giving or requiring a choice between two or more things: *I offered the alternative suggestions of having a picnic or taking a trip on a boat.* 1,2 *n.*, 3 *adj.* —**al ter′na tive ly,** *adv.* —**al ter′na tive ness,** *n.*

al though or **al tho** (ôl ᴛʜō′), in spite of the fact that; though: *Although it rained all morning, they went on the hike. conj.*

al tim e ter (al tim′ə tər), instrument for measuring altitude. Altimeters are used in aircraft to indicate height above the earth's surface. *n.*

al ti tude (al′tə tüd *or* al′tə tyüd), **1** height above the earth's surface: *What altitude did the airplane reach?* **2** height above sea level: *The altitude of Denver is 5300*

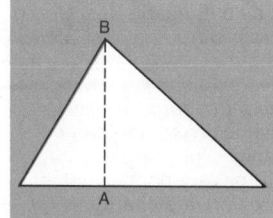 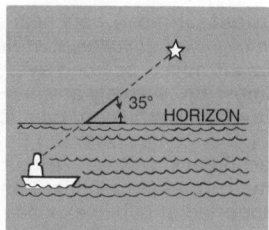

altitude (def. 4)
of the triangle is the
distance from A to B.

altitude (def. 5)
of the star
is 35°.

feet. **3** a high place: *At some altitudes snow never melts.* **4** the vertical distance from the base of a geometrical figure to its highest point. **5** the angular distance of a star, planet, etc., above the horizon. *n.*

al to (al′tō), **1** the lowest singing voice in women and boys. **2** singer with such a voice. **3** part in music for such a voice or for an instrument of similar range. **4** instrument playing such a part. **5** of or for an alto. 1-4 *n., pl.* **al tos;** 5 *adj.*

alto clef, the C clef when the clef symbol is placed on the third line of the staff. See **clef** for diagram.

al to geth er (ôl′tə geᴛʜ′ər), **1** to the whole extent; completely; entirely: *The house was altogether destroyed by fire.* **2** on the whole; considering everything: *Altogether, he was well pleased.* **3** all included: *Altogether there were 14 books. adv.*

al tru ism (al′trü iz′əm), unselfish devotion to the welfare of others; unselfishness. *n.*

al tru ist (al′trü ist), person who works for the welfare of others; unselfish person. *n.*

al tru is tic (al′trü is′tik), thoughtful of the welfare of others; unselfish. *adj.* —**al′tru is′ti cal ly,** *adv.*

al um (al′əm), **1** a white mineral substance used in medicine and in dyeing. Alum is sometimes used to stop the bleeding of a small cut. **2** a colorless, crystalline substance used in baking powder, in medicine, etc. *n.*

a lu mi num (ə lü′mə nəm), a very lightweight, silver-white, metallic element which does not readily tarnish. Aluminum is one of the most abundant metals, but it occurs only in combination with other elements. These aluminum compounds make up more than 15 percent of the earth's crust. Aluminum is used to make utensils, instruments, aircraft parts, etc. *n.*

a lum na (ə lum′nə), a woman graduate or former student of a school, college, or university. *n., pl.* **a lum nae** (ə lum′nē).

a lum ni (ə lum′nī), graduates or former students of a school, college, or university. "Alumni" may mean either men graduates or both men and women. *n.pl.*

a lum nus (ə lum′nəs), graduate or former student of a

altimeter—As an airplane climbs, air pressure on the flexible, airtight metal box decreases and its sides expand, forcing the pointer to move up from zero. With a loss in altitude, air pressure on the box increases and its sides contract, forcing the pointer to move back toward zero.

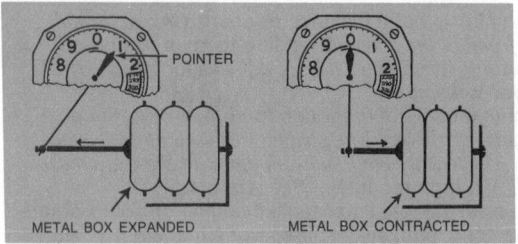

METAL BOX EXPANDED   METAL BOX CONTRACTED

school, college, or university. *n., pl.* **a lum ni.**

al ve o lus (al vē′ə ləs), **1** a small cavity, pit, or cell. The air sacs in the lung are alveoli. **2** socket of a tooth. *n., pl.* **al ve o li** (al vē′ə lī).

al way (ôl′wā), OLD USE. always. *adv.*

al ways (ôl′wiz *or* ôl′wāz), **1** at all times; every time: *Night always follows day.* **2** all the time; continually: *Home is always a cheerful place at holiday time. adv.* [*Always* comes from the Old English phrase *ealne weg,* meaning "all the way."]

am (am; *unstressed* əm), form of the verb **be** used with *I* in the present tense. *I am twelve years old. I am going to school. v.*

Am, symbol for americium.

Am., **1** America. **2** American.

AM or **A.M.,** amplitude modulation.

a.m. or **A.M.,** the time from midnight to noon: *School begins at 9 a.m.* [The abbreviations *a.m.* and *A.M.* stand for the Latin phrase *ante meridiem,* meaning "before noon."]

A.M., Master of Arts. Also, **M.A.**

A.M.A., American Medical Association.

a main (ə mān′), **1** at full speed. **2** with full force; violently. *adv.*

a mal gam (ə mal′gəm), **1** an alloy of mercury with some other metal or metals: *The dentist used silver amalgam to fill one of my teeth.* **2** mixture or blend of different things. *n.*

a mal gam ate (ə mal′gə māt), combine so as to form a whole; unite: *The two stores amalgamated to form one big store. The company amalgamated its three sales offices. v.,* **a mal gam at ed, a mal gam at ing.** —**a mal′gam a ble,** *adj.* —**a mal′ga ma′tor,** *n.*

a mal gam a tion (ə mal′gə mā′shən), an amalgamating; mixture; combination; union: *Our nation is an amalgamation of many different peoples. n.*

Am a ril lo (am′ə ril′ō), city in NW Texas. *n.*

am a ryl lis (am′ə ril′is), a lilylike plant with clusters of large red, white, purple, or pink flowers. *n., pl.* **am a ryl lis es.**

a mass (ə mas′), heap together; pile up; accumulate: *She invested her money wisely and amassed a fortune. v.* —**a mass′a ble,** *adj.* —**a mass′er,** *n.*

am a teur (am′ə chər *or* am′ə tər), **1** person who does something for pleasure, not for money or as a profession: *Only amateurs can compete in Olympic games.* **2** person who does something unskillfully or in an inexpert way: *This painting is the work of an amateur; it shows very little skill.* **3** of or by amateurs: *an amateur orchestra.* **4** being an amateur: *an amateur golfer.* **1,2** *n.,* **3,4** *adj.* [*Amateur* was borrowed from French *amateur,* which came from Latin *amator,* meaning "lover."]

am a teur ish (am′ə chůr′ish *or* am′ə tyůr′ish), done as an amateur might do it; not expert; not very skillful. *adj.* —**am′a teur′ish ly,** *adv.* —**am′a teur′ish ness,** *n.*

am a to ry (am′ə tôr′ē), of love; expressing love: *Valentine cards often have amatory verses on them. adj.*

a maze (ə māz′), surprise greatly; strike with sudden wonder; astound: *He was amazed at how different the strand of hair looked under a microscope. v.,* **a mazed, a maz ing.**

a maz ed ly (ə mā′zid lē), with wonder or astonishment. *adv.*

a maze ment (ə māz′mənt), great surprise; sudden wonder; astonishment: *I was filled with amazement when I saw the ocean for the first time. n.*

a maz ing (ə mā′zing), very surprising; wonderful; astonishing. *adj.* —**a maz′ing ly,** *adv.*

Am a zon (am′ə zon), **1** largest river in the world, in N South America. The Amazon flows from sources in the

a hat	i it	oi oil	ch child	a in about
ā age	ī ice	ou out	ng long	e in taken
ä far	o hot	u cup	sh she	ə = { i in pencil
e let	ō open	ů put	th thin	o in lemon
ē equal	ô order	ü rule	ŦH then	u in circus
ėr term			zh measure	

Andes Mountains of Peru across Brazil into the Atlantic. See **Andes Mountains** for map. **2** one of a race of women warriors in Greek legends. **3 amazon,** a tall, strong, aggressive woman. *n.*

Am a zo ni an (am′ə zō′nē ən), **1** of the Amazon River or the region it drains. **2** of the Amazons. **3 amazonian,** (of a woman) aggressive or warlike. *adj.*

Amb., ambassador.

am bas sa dor (am bas′ə dər), **1** a representative of highest rank sent by one government or ruler to another: *The U.S. ambassador to France lives in Paris and speaks and acts for the government of the United States.* **2** any messenger with a special errand; agent: *The famous musician was welcomed abroad as an ambassador of goodwill. n.*

am ber (am′bər), **1** a hard, yellow or yellowish-brown gum, used for jewelry, in making pipe stems, etc. Amber is the resin of fossil pine trees. **2** a yellow or yellowish brown. **3** yellow or yellowish-brown: *a black cat with amber eyes.* **1,2** *n.,* **3** *adj.*

am ber gris (am′bər grēs′ *or* am′bər gris), a waxlike, grayish substance produced in the intestines of the sperm whale. Ambergris is used in making perfumes. *n.*

am bi dex trous (am′bə dek′strəs), able to use both hands equally well. *adj.* —**am′bi dex′trous ly,** *adv.* —**am′bi dex′trous ness,** *n.*

am bi gu i ty (am′bə gyü′ə tē), **1** possibility of two or more meanings: *The ambiguity of the speaker's statement made it hard to tell which side she was on.* **2** word or expression that can have more than one meaning: *Answer me without ambiguities. n., pl.* **am bi gu i ties.**

am big u ous (am big′yü əs), having more than one possible meaning. The sentence "After John hit Dick he ran away" is ambiguous because we cannot tell which boy ran away. *adj.* —**am big′u ous ly,** *adv.* —**am big′u ous ness,** *n.*

am bi tion (am bish′ən), **1** a strong desire for fame, honor, wealth, etc.; seeking after a high position or great power: *Because he was filled with ambition, he worked after school and on Saturdays.* **2** thing strongly desired or sought after: *Her ambition is to be an oceanographer. n.* —**am bi′tion less,** *adj.*

am bi tious (am bish′əs), **1** having or guided by ambition; desiring strongly: *She is ambitious to get through high school in three years.* **2** showing or arising from ambition: *an ambitious plan. adj.* —**am bi′tious ly,** *adv.* —**am bi′tious ness,** *n.*

am biv a lence (am biv′ə ləns), a being ambivalent. *n.*

am biv a lent (am biv′ə lənt), acting in opposite ways; having or showing conflicting feelings: *He has an ambivalent attitude toward his friend; he likes him but always quarrels with him. adj.* —**am biv′a lent ly,** *adv.*

am ble (am′bəl), **1** an easy, slow pace in walking. **2** walk at an easy, slow pace. **1** *n.,* **2** *v.,* **am bled, am bling.** —**am′bler,** *n.*

am bro sia (am brō′zhə), **1** (in Greek and Roman myths) the food of the gods. **2** anything especially delicious. *n.* [*Ambrosia* was borrowed from Latin *ambrosia,* and can be traced back to Greek *a-,* meaning "not," and *brotos,* meaning "mortal."]

am bro sial (am brō′zhəl), like ambrosia; especially delicious. *adj.* —**am bro′sial ly,** *adv.*

am bu lance (am′byə ləns), an automobile, boat, or air-craft equipped to carry sick, injured, or wounded persons. *n.*

am bu la to ry (am′byə lə tôr′ē), capable of walking; not bedridden: *an ambulatory patient. adj.*

am bus cade (am′bə skād′), ambush. *n., v.,* **am bus-cad ed, am bus cad ing. —am′bus cad′er,** *n.*

am bush (am′bush), **1** soldiers or other persons hidden so that they can make a surprise attack on an approaching enemy. **2** a secret or hidden place where soldiers or others lie in wait to make such an attack: *The troops lay in ambush, waiting for the signal to open fire.* **3** attack unexpectedly from a hidden position: *The bandits ambushed the stagecoach.* **4** a lying in wait for the purpose of attacking by surprise: *The troops trapped the enemy by ambush.* 1,2,4 *n., pl.* **am bush es;** 3 *v.* **—am′bush er,** *n.*

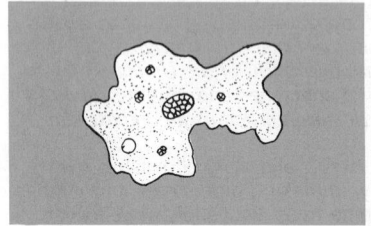

ameba

a me ba (ə mē′bə), a one-celled animal that moves by forming temporary projections that are constantly changing shape. Amebas are so small that they can be examined only with a microscope. Many amebas live in water; others live as parasites in other animals. *n.* Also, **amoeba.** [*Ameba* comes from Greek *amoibē,* meaning "a change." The animal was called this because its shape is always changing.]

a me bic (ə mē′bik), **1** of or like an ameba or amebas. **2** caused by amebas: *amebic dysentery. adj.* Also, **amoebic.**

a mel io rate (ə mē′lyə rāt′), make or become better; improve: *Stricter control of air pollution ameliorated living conditions in the city. v.,* **a mel io rat ed, a mel io rat ing. —a mel′io ra′tor,** *n.*

a mel io ra tion (ə mē′lyə rā′shən), an ameliorating; improvement. *n.*

a men (ā′men′ *or* ä′men′), so be it; may it become true. *Amen* is said after a prayer, a wish, or a statement with which one agrees. *interj.* [*Amen* was borrowed from Latin *amen,* and can be traced back to Hebrew *āmēn.*]

a me na ble (ə mē′nə bəl *or* ə men′ə bəl), **1** open to influence, suggestion, advice, etc.; responsive: *I am amenable to your plan.* **2** accountable; answerable: *People living in a country are amenable to its laws. adj.* **—a me′na ble ness,** *n.*

a me na bly (ə mē′nə blē *or* ə men′ə blē), in an amenable manner. *adv.*

a mend (ə mend′), **1** change (a law, bill, or motion) by addition, omission, or alteration of language: *The Constitution of the United States was amended so that women could vote.* **2** change for the better; improve: *make efforts to amend conditions in an overcrowded city. v.* **—a mend′a ble,** *adj.* **—a mend′er,** *n.*

a mend ment (ə mend′mənt), **1** change made in a law, bill, or motion by addition, omission, or alteration of language: *The Constitution of the United States has over twenty amendments.* **2** a change for the better; improvement. *n.*

a mends (ə mendz′), something given or paid to make up for a wrong or an injury done; payment for loss; compensation: *I bought my friend a new book to make amends for the one I lost. n. sing. or pl.*

a men i ty (ə men′ə tē *or* ə mē′nə tē), **1 amenities,** *pl.* pleasant ways; polite acts. Saying "Thank you" and holding the door open for a person to pass through are amenities. **2** quality of being pleasant; agreeableness: *We went to Hawaii to enjoy the amenity of a warm climate. n., pl.* **a men i ties.**

Amer., 1 America. **2** American.

A mer i ca (ə mer′ə kə), **1** the United States of America. **2** North America. **3** Also, **the Americas.** North America and South America; the Western Hemisphere. **4** South America. *n.*

A mer i can (ə mer′ə kən), **1** of or in the United States: *an American citizen.* **2** person born or living in the United States; citizen of the United States. **3** native only to the Western Hemisphere: *Corn and tobacco are American plants.* **4** of or in the Western Hemisphere: *the Amazon and other American rivers.* **5** person born or living in the Western Hemisphere: *The citizens of Mexico, Canada, and Argentina are Americans.* 1,3,4 *adj.,* 2,5 *n.*

American cheese, a deep yellow cheese made in America, similar to Cheddar.

American eagle, bald eagle. The coat of arms of the United States has a design of the American eagle on it.

American eagle
on the coat of arms
of the United States

American Indian, one of the people who have lived in America from long before the time of the first European settlers.

A mer i can ism (ə mer′ə kə niz′əm), **1** devotion or loyalty to the United States and to its customs and traditions. **2** word, phrase, or meaning originating in the United States. **3** custom or trait peculiar to the United States. *n.*

A mer i can i za tion (ə mer′ə kə nə zā′shən), an Americanizing. *n.*

A mer i can ize (ə mer′ə kə nīz), make or become American in habits, customs, or character: *Although she has lived in the United States for only a short time, she is already Americanized. v.,* **A mer i can ized, A mer i can iz ing.**

American Revolution, Revolutionary War.

am e ri ci um (am′ə rish′ē əm), a radioactive metallic element produced from plutonium. *n.*

am e thyst (am′ə thist), **1** a purple or violet variety of quartz, used for jewelry. **2** a purple or violet color. **3** purple; violet. 1,2 *n.,* 3 *adj.*

a mi a ble (ā′mē ə bəl), having a good-natured and friendly disposition; pleasant and agreeable: *She is an amiable girl who gets along with most people. adj.* **—a′mi a ble ness,** *n.*

a mi a bly (ā′mē ə blē), in an amiable manner. *adv.*

am i ca bil i ty (am′ə kə bil′ə tē), a being amicable. *n.*

am i ca ble (am′ə kə bəl), having or showing a friendly attitude; peaceable: *Instead of fighting, the company and the union settled their quarrel in an amicable way by arbitration. adj.* **—am′i ca ble ness,** *n.*

am i ca bly (am′ə kə blē), in an amicable manner. *adv.*

a mid (ə mid′), in the middle of; among: *One small house stood amid the tall buildings.* *prep.*

a mid ship (ə mid′ship), amidships. *adv.*

a mid ships (ə mid′ships), in or toward the middle of a ship; halfway between the bow and stern. *adv.*

a midst (ə midst′), amid. *prep.*

a mi go (ə mē′gō), friend. *n., pl.* **a mi gos.**

a mi no acid (ə mē′nō *or* am′ə nō), any of a group of complex organic compounds of nitrogen, hydrogen, carbon, and oxygen that combine in various ways to form the proteins that make up living matter.

a mir (ə mir′), emir. *n.*

Am ish (am′ish *or* ä′mish), **1** a very strict Mennonite sect. **2** of this sect. 1 *n.,* 2 *adj.*

a miss (ə mis′), not the way it should be; out of order; wrong: *Everything has gone amiss today* (*adv.*). *It would not be amiss to offer an apology, even though you may not have intended harm* (*adj.*). *adv., adj.*

take amiss, be offended at (something not intended to offend): *Don't take it amiss if I correct your grammar.*

am i ty (am′ə tē), peace and friendship; friendly relations: *If there were amity between nations, there would be no wars.* *n.*

Am man (ä′män *or* ä män′), capital of Jordan, in the NW part. *n.*

am me ter (am′ē′tər), instrument for measuring in amperes the strength of an electric current. *n.*

am mo ni a (ə mō′nyə), **1** a colorless gas, consisting of nitrogen and hydrogen, that has a sharp, suffocating smell and a strong alkaline reaction. **2** this gas dissolved in water. Ammonia is very useful for cleaning and for making fertilizers and other products. *n.*

am mu ni tion (am′yə nish′ən), **1** bullets, shells, gunpowder, bombs, etc., that can be exploded or fired from guns or other weapons; military explosives and missiles. **2** any means of attack or defense: *Her speech gave fresh ammunition to her opponents.* *n.*

am ne sia (am nē′zhə), loss of memory caused by injury to the brain, or by disease or shock. *n.*

am nes ty (am′nə stē), a general pardon for past offenses against a government. *n.*

am ni on (am′nē ən), a membrane forming the inner sac which encloses the embryos of reptiles, birds, and mammals. *n.*

am ni ot ic (am′nē ot′ik), of or inside the amnion. *adj.*

a moe ba (ə mē′bə), ameba. *n.*

a moe bic (ə mē′bik), amebic. *adj.*

a mok (ə muk′ *or* ə mok′). **run amok,** run about in a frenzy; behave wildly: *He ran amok, screaming and throwing things about.* *adv.* Also, **amuck.** [*Amok* comes from Malay *amok,* meaning "in a murderous frenzy."]

a mong (ə mung′), **1** one of: *The United States is among the largest countries in the world.* **2** in the company of; with: *to spend time among friends.* **3** surrounded by: *a house among the trees.* **4** with a portion for each of: *Divide the fruit among all of us.* **5** by the combined action of: *You have, among you, done a good job.* **6** by, with, or through the whole of: *There was political unrest among the people.* *prep.*

among ourselves, among yourselves, or **among themselves,** each with all the others; as a group: *They agreed among themselves to have a party.*

a mongst (ə mungst′), among. *prep.*

am or ous (am′ər əs), **1** inclined to love; loving; fond: *an amorous disposition.* **2** of love or courtship. *adj.* —**am′orous ly,** *adv.* —**am′or ous ness,** *n.*

a mor phous (ə môr′fəs), **1** having no definite form; shapeless; formless. **2** not consisting of crystals: *Glass is amorphous; sugar is crystalline.* *adj.* —**a mor′phous ly,** *adv.* —**a mor′phous ness,** *n.*

a	hat	i	it	oi	oil	ch	child		a in about
ā	age	ī	ice	ou	out	ng	long		e in taken
ä	far	o	hot	u	cup	sh	she	ə =	i in pencil
e	let	ō	open	u̇	put	th	thin		o in lemon
ē	equal	ô	order	ü	rule	ᴛʜ	then		u in circus
ėr	term					zh	measure		

am or ti za tion (am′ər tə zā′shən), **1** an amortizing of a debt, etc. **2** money regularly set aside for this purpose. *n.*

am or tize (am′ər tīz), set money aside regularly in a special fund for the future paying or settling of a debt. *v.,* **am or tized, am or tiz ing.**

A mos (ā′məs), **1** Hebrew prophet and social reformer who lived about 750 B.C. **2** book of the Old Testament containing his prophecies. *n.*

a mount (ə mount′), **1** the total of two or more numbers or quantities taken together; sum: *What is the amount of the bill for the groceries?* **2** the full value or extent: *The amount of evidence against them is great.* **3** portion or quantity: *No amount of coaxing would make the dog leave its owner.* **4** add up; reach: *The loss from the flood amounts to ten million dollars.* **5** be equal: *Keeping what belongs to another amounts to stealing.* 1-3 *n.,* 4,5 *v.*

a mour (ə mu̇r′), a love affair, especially a secret love affair. *n.*

amp., **1** amperage. **2** ampere.

am per age (am′pər ij), strength of an electric current measured in amperes. *n.*

am pere (am′pir), unit for measuring the strength of an electric current. It is the amount of current one volt can send through a resistance of one ohm. Ordinary light bulbs take from ¹/₂ to 1 ampere. *n.* [The *ampere* was named for André M. *Ampère,* 1775-1836, a French physicist.]

am per sand (am′pər sand), the sign (&) meaning "and." *n.*

am phet a mine (am fet′ə mēn′), **1** drug used for the relief of colds, hay fever, etc. **2** drug used as a stimulant to combat fatigue or reduce appetite. *n.*

am phib i an (am fib′ē ən), **1** one of a group of cold-blooded animals having a backbone and moist, scaleless skin. Their young usually have gills and live in water until they develop lungs for living on land. Frogs, toads, newts, and salamanders are amphibians. **2** plant that grows on land or in water. **3** able to live both on land and in water. **4** aircraft that can take off from and land on either land or water. **5** able to start from and land on either land or water. **6** tank, truck, or other vehicle able to travel across land or water. 1,2,4,6 *n.,* 3,5 *adj.*

am phib i ous (am fib′ē əs), **1** able to live both on land and in water: *Frogs are amphibious.* **2** able to travel across land or water: *Some tanks are amphibious.* **3** by the combined action of land, sea, and air forces: *The enemy launched an amphibious attack.* *adj.* —**am phib′i ous ly,** *adv.* —**am phib′i ous ness,** *n.*

amorphous (def. 1)
A piece of pottery
begins as an **amorphous**
lump of clay.

amphitheater (def. 1)—an ancient Roman amphitheater

am phi the a ter or **am phi the a tre** (am′fə thē′ə tər), **1** a circular or oval building with rows of seats around a central open space. Each row is higher than the one in front of it. **2** something like an amphitheater in shape: *The town was set in an amphitheater of hills. n.*

am phor a (am′fər ə), a two-handled jar used by the ancient Greeks and Romans. *n., pl.* **am phor ae** (am′fə-rē′), **am phor as.**

am ple (am′pəl), **1** more than enough; abundant: *We needn't hurry; there's ample time to catch our bus.* **2** as much as is needed; enough; sufficient: *My allowance is ample for carfare and lunches.* **3** having plenty of room; large; roomy: *A well-designed house has ample closets. adj.,* **am pler, am plest.** —**am′ple ness,** *n.*

am pli fi ca tion (am′plə fə kā′shən), **1** a making greater, stronger, or more extensive: *the amplification of knowledge.* **2** detail or example that amplifies: *Your argument needs amplification before I can understand it. n.*

am pli fi er (am′plə fī′ər), a transistor, vacuum tube, or other device in a radio, phonograph, etc., for strengthening electrical impulses. *n.*

am pli fy (am′plə fī), **1** make greater; make stronger: *When sound is amplified, it can be heard a greater distance.* **2** make fuller and more extensive; expand; enlarge: *Please amplify your description of the accident by giving us more details. v.,* **am pli fied, am pli fy ing.**

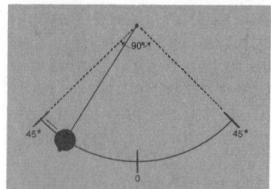

amplitude (def. 2)
The amplitude of the 90° swing of the pendulum is 45°.

am pli tude (am′plə tüd or am′plə tyüd), **1** quantity that is more than enough; abundance: *an amplitude of money.* **2** one half the range of a regular vibration. The distance between the position of rest and the highest position in the arc of a pendulum is its amplitude. **3** the peak strength of an alternating current in a given cycle. *n.*

amplitude modulation, deliberate change of the amplitude of radio waves in order to transmit sound or pictures. Ordinary broadcasting uses amplitude modulation.

am ply (am′plē), in an ample manner: *We were amply supplied with food. adv.*

am pu tate (am′pyə tāt), cut off (all or part of a leg, arm, etc.) by surgery. *v.,* **am pu tat ed, am pu tat ing.** [*Amputate* comes from Latin *amputatum,* meaning "cut around, pruned."] —**am′pu ta′tor,** *n.*

am pu ta tion (am′pyə tā′shən), a cutting off of all or a part of a leg, arm, etc. *n.*

am pu tee (am′pyə tē′), person who has had all or part of a leg or arm amputated. *n.*

Am ster dam (am′stər dam), the largest city and official capital of the Netherlands, on the North Sea. The unofficial capital is The Hague. *n.*

amt., amount.

Am trak (am′trak), a public corporation that receives financial support from the federal government to provide railroad passenger service on selected routes in the United States. *n.*

a muck (ə muk′), amok. *adv.*

am u let (am′yə lit), some object worn as a magic charm against evil or harm. *n.*

A mund sen (ä′mən sən), **Roald,** 1872-1928, Norwegian explorer who discovered the South Pole in 1911. *n.*

A mur (ä múr′), river in E Asia. *n.*

a muse (ə myüz′), **1** cause to laugh or smile: *The clown's jokes and antics amused everyone.* **2** keep pleasantly interested; cause to feel cheerful or happy; entertain: *The new toys amused the children. v.,* **a mused, a mus ing.** —**a mus′a ble,** *adj.* —**a mus′er,** *n.*

a mus ed ly (ə myü′zid lē), in an amused manner. *adv.*

a muse ment (ə myüz′mənt), **1** condition of being amused: *The boy's amusement was so great that we all had to laugh with him.* **2** anything that amuses, such as an entertainment or sport. *n.*

amusement park, an outdoor place of entertainment with booths for games, various rides, and other amusements.

a mus ing (ə myü′zing), **1** causing laughter or smiles: *an amusing joke.* **2** entertaining: *an amusing book. adj.* —**a mus′ing ly,** *adv.*

an (an; *unstressed* ən), **1** any: *Is there an apple in the box?* **2** one: *I'll have an egg for breakfast.* **3** every; each: *The job pays five dollars an hour. adj. or indefinite article.*

-an, suffix used to form adjectives and nouns, especially from proper nouns. **1** of _____: *Mohammedan = of Mohammed.* **2** of _____ or its people: *Asian = of Asia or its people.* **3** person born or living in _____: *American = person born or living in America.* Also, **-ian.**

PRES. WASHINGTON

anachronism (def. 1)—It is an anachronism to picture George Washington using a telephone.

a nach ro nism (ə nak′rə niz′əm), **1** a placing of anything in some time where it does not belong. **2** something placed or occurring out of its proper time. *n.* [*Anachronism* can be traced back to Greek *ana-,* meaning "back," and *chronos,* meaning "time."]

a nach ro nis tic (ə nak′rə nis′tik), having or involving an anachronism. *adj.* —**a nach′ro nis′ti cal ly,** *adv.*

an a con da (an′ə kon′də), a very large South American

snake related to the boa that crushes its prey in its coils. Anacondas live in tropical forests and rivers and are the longest snakes in America, sometimes over 30 feet (9 meters). *n., pl.* **an a con das.**

a nae mi a (ə nē′mē ə), anemia. *n.*

a nae mic (ə nē′mik), anemic. *adj.*

an ae ro bic (an′ə rō′bik), living or growing where there is no free oxygen. Anaerobic bacteria get their oxygen by decomposing compounds containing oxygen. *adj.* —**an′ae ro′bi cal ly,** *adv.*

an aes the sia (an′əs thē′zhə), anesthesia. *n.*

an aes thet ic (an′əs thet′ik), anesthetic. *adj., n.*

an aes the tist (ə nes′thə tist), anesthetist. *n.*

an aes the tize (ə nes′thə tīz), anesthetize. *v.,* **an aes the tized, an aes the tiz ing.** —**an aes′the ti za′tion,** *n.* —**an aes′the tiz′er,** *n.*

ANAGRAM

INSPIRED POET ∞ O SPIRITED PEN

ENDEARMENT ∞ TENDER NAME

SOFTHEARTEDNESS ∞ SHEDS TEARS OFTEN

ENRAGED CHUM ∞ MUCH ANGERED

anagram (def. 1)—four anagrams

an a gram (an′ə gram), **1** word or phrase formed from another by rearranging the letters. EXAMPLE: lived—devil. **2 anagrams,** *pl.* game in which the players make words by changing and adding letters. *n.*

a nal (ā′nl), **1** of the anus. **2** at or near the anus. *adj.* —**a′nal ly,** *adv.*

anal., 1 analogous. **2** analogy. **3** analysis. **4** analytic.

an al ge sic (an′l jē′zik), drug that relieves or lessens pain. *n.*

a nal o gous (ə nal′ə gəs), alike in some way; similar in the quality or feature that is being thought of; comparable: *The heart is analogous to a pump. adj.* —**a nal′o gous ly,** *adv.* —**a nal′o gous ness,** *n.*

a nal o gy (ə nal′ə jē), likeness in some ways between things that are otherwise unlike; similarity: *There is an analogy between the heart and a pump. n., pl.* **a nal o gies.**

an a lyse (an′l īz), BRITISH. analyze. *v.,* **an a lysed, an a lys ing.**

a nal y sis (ə nal′ə sis), **1** separation of anything into its parts or elements to find out what it is made of. A chemical analysis of ordinary table salt shows that it is made up of two elements, sodium and chlorine. **2** an examining carefully and in detail. An analysis can be made of a book, a person's character, etc. **3** psychoanalysis. *n., pl.* **a nal y ses** (ə nal′ə sēz′).

an a lyst (an′l ist), **1** person who analyzes. **2** psychoanalyst. *n.*

an a lyt ic (an′l it′ik), analytical. *adj.*

an a lyt i cal (an′l it′ə kəl), separating a whole into its parts; using analysis: *The methods of science are analytical. The detective had an analytical mind. adj.* —**an′a lyt′i cal ly,** *adv.*

an a lyze (an′l īz), **1** separate anything into its parts or elements to find out what it is made of: *The chemistry teacher analyzed water into two colorless gases, oxygen and hydrogen.* **2** examine carefully and in detail: *analyze a situation. The newspaper analyzed the results of the election.*

v., **an a lyzed, an a lyz ing.** —**an′a lyz′a ble,** *adj.* —**an′a ly za′tion,** *n.* —**an′a lyz′er,** *n.*

an ar chic (a när′kik), **1** favoring anarchy; lawless: *an anarchic age. adj.* —**an ar′chi cal ly,** *adv.*

an ar chism (an′ər kiz′əm), the political theory that all systems of government and law are harmful. *n.*

an ar chist (an′ər kist), **1** person who wants to destroy governments and laws. **2** person who promotes disorder and stirs up revolt. *n.*

an ar chy (an′ər kē), **1** absence of a system of government and law. **2** disorder and confusion; lawlessness. *n.* [*Anarchy* comes from a medieval Latin word *anarchia,* and can be traced back to Greek *an-,* meaning "without," and *archos,* meaning "ruler."]

a nath e ma (ə nath′ə mə), **1** a solemn curse by church authorities excommunicating some person from the church. **2** person or thing that has been cursed. **3** person or thing that is detested or condemned. *n., pl.* **a nath e mas.**

a nath e ma tize (ə nath′ə mə tīz), pronounce an anathema against; denounce; curse. *v.,* **a nath e ma tized, a nath e ma tiz ing.** —**a nath′e ma ti za′tion,** *n.*

An a to li a (an′ə tō′lē ə), Asia Minor. *n.* —**An′a to′li an,** *adj., n.*

an a tom i cal (an′ə tom′ə kəl), of anatomy. *adj.* —**an′a tom′i cal ly,** *adv.*

a nat o mist (ə nat′ə mist), an expert in anatomy. *n.*

a nat o my (ə nat′ə mē), **1** science of the structure of animals and plants. **2** the dissecting of animals or plants to study their structure. **3** structure of an animal or plant: *the anatomy of an earthworm. n., pl.* **a nat o mies.**

-ance, *suffix forming nouns chiefly from verbs.* **1** act or fact of _____ing: *Avoidance = act or fact of avoiding.* **2** quality or state of being _____ed: *Annoyance = quality or state of being annoyed.* **3** thing that _____s: *Conveyance = thing that conveys.* **4** what is _____ed: *Contrivance = what is contrived.* **5** quality or state of being _____ant: *Importance = quality or state of being important.*

an ces tor (an′ses′tər), **1** person from whom one is descended, such as one's great-grandparents: *Their ancestors came to America in 1812.* **2** the early form from which a species or group is descended: *Dinosaurs and snakes have the same ancestor. n.*

an ces tral (an ses′trəl), **1** of or having to do with ancestors: *England was the ancestral home of the Pilgrims.* **2** inherited from ancestors: *Black hair is an ancestral trait in that family. adj.* —**an ces′tral ly,** *adv.*

an ces try (an′ses′trē), **1** ancestors: *Many early settlers in California had Spanish ancestry.* **2** line of descent from ancestors; lineage: *The king was of noble ancestry. n., pl.* **an ces tries.**

an chor (ang′kər), **1** a heavy, shaped piece of iron or steel attached to a chain or rope and dropped into the water to hold a ship in place: *The anchor caught in the mud at the bottom of the lake and kept the boat from drifting.* **2** hold in place with an anchor: *Can you anchor the boat in this storm?* **3** stop or stay in place by using an anchor: *The ship anchored in the bay.* **4** hold in place; fix firmly: *The scouts anchored the tent to the ground.* **5** something that makes a person feel safe and secure: *The weekly talks with an understanding counselor were an anchor to the troubled child.* **6** thing for holding something else in place: *The anchors of the cables of this suspension bridge are set in concrete.* **1,5,6** *n.,* **2-4** *v.* [*Anchor* comes from Old English *ancor,* and can be traced back to Greek *ankyra.*]

at anchor, held by an anchor: *The ship was at anchor.*

cast anchor, drop the anchor: *The boat cast anchor near the shore.*

weigh anchor, take up the anchor: *They weighed anchor and sailed away.*

an chor age (ang′kər ij), **1** place to anchor. **2** something on which to depend. *n.*

An chor age (ang′kər ij), seaport in S Alaska. *n.*

an cho rite (ang′kə rīt′), person who lives alone in a solitary place for religious meditation; hermit. *n.*

anchor man, 1 the last person to run or swim on a relay team. **2** person on a television or radio program who coordinates reports from correspondents in several different cities, countries, etc.

an cho vy (an′chō vē), a very small fish that looks somewhat like a herring. Anchovies may be packed in oil or made into a paste. *n., pl.* **an cho vies.** [*Anchovy* comes from Spanish and Portuguese *anchova.*]

an cient (ān′shənt), **1** of times long past: *In Egypt, we saw the ruins of an ancient temple built six thousand years ago.* **2 the ancients,** people who lived long ago, such as the ancient Greeks, Romans, and Egyptians. **3** of great age; very old: *Rome is an ancient city.* **4** a very old person. **1,3** *adj.,* **2,4** *n.* —**an′cient ness,** *n.*

ancient history, 1 history from the earliest times to the fall of the western part of the Roman Empire in A.D. 476. **2** INFORMAL. a well-known fact or event of the recent past.

an cient ly (ān′shənt lē), in ancient times. *adv.*

an cil lar y (an′sə ler′ē), **1** subordinate; dependent. **2** assisting; auxiliary: *an ancillary engine in a boat. adj.*

and (and; *unstressed* ənd *or* ən), **1** as well as: *You can come and go in the car.* **2** added to; with: *4 and 2 make 6. She likes ham and eggs.* **3** as a result: *The sun came out and the grass dried.* **4** INFORMAL. to: *Try and do better. conj.*

An da lu sia (an′də lü′zhə), region in S Spain. *n.* —**An′da lu′sian,** *adj., n.*

an dan te (än dän′tā *or* an dan′tē), in music: **1** moderately slow. **2** a moderately slow movement in a piece of music. **1** *adj., adv.,* **2** *n.* [*Andante* comes from Italian *andante,* originally meaning "going, walking."]

An de an (an′dē ən *or* an dē′ən), of or having to do with the Andes Mountains. *adj.*

An der sen (an′dər sən), **Hans Christian,** 1805-1875, Danish writer of fairy tales. *n.*

An der son (an′dər sən), **Marian,** born 1902, American concert singer. *n.*

An des Mountains (an′dēz), mountain range in W South America. It is the longest continuous mountain system in the world.

and i ron (and′ī′ərn), one of a pair of metal supports for wood in a fireplace; firedog. *n.*

andirons

and/or, both or either. "To earn money from stocks and/or bonds" means to earn it from both stocks and bonds or from either stocks or bonds.

An dor ra (an dôr′ə), **1** small country between France and Spain. **2** its capital. *n.* —**An dor′ran,** *adj., n.*

An drew (an′drü), (in the Bible) one of Jesus' twelve apostles. *n.*

an droid (an′droid), robot that resembles a human being. *n.* [*Android* comes from Greek *andros,* meaning "man," and *eidos,* meaning "form."]

An drom e da (an drom′ə də), (in Greek legends) the wife of Perseus, who rescued her from a sea monster. *n.*

An dro pov (än drô′pôf), **Yuri V.,** 1914-1984, Russian political leader, general secretary of the Soviet Communist Party from 1982 to 1984, and president of the Soviet Union from 1983 to 1984. *n.*

an ec dote (an′ik dōt), a short account of some interesting incident or event, often humorous or biographical. *n.*

a ne mi a (ə nē′mē ə), a weak condition caused by not enough hemoglobin or red corpuscles in the blood or by a loss of blood. *n.* Also, **anaemia.** [*Anemia* can be traced back to Greek *an-,* meaning "without," and *haima,* meaning "blood."]

a ne mic (ə nē′mik), **1** of anemia; having anemia: *an anemic patient.* **2** lacking in vigor, strength, or spirit; weak: *an anemic defense. adj.* Also, **anaemic.**

anemometer
Wind catches the cups and moves them around causing the shaft to turn. The speed of the turning is shown on an indicator.

an e mom e ter (an′ə mom′ə tər), instrument for measuring the speed of wind. *n.*

a nem o ne (ə nem′ə nē), **1** plant with a slender stem and small white or colored flowers shaped like cups; windflower. It often blossoms early in the spring. **2** the sea anemone, a flowerlike polyp. *n.*

a nent (ə nent′), concerning; about. *prep.*

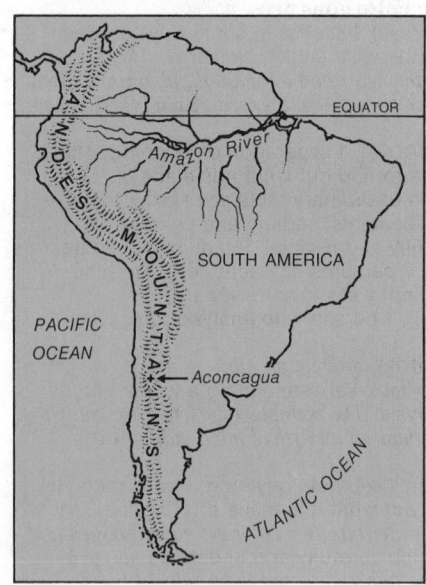

an e roid barometer (an′ə roid′), barometer worked by the pressure of air on the elastic lid of an airtight metal box from which the air has been pumped out.

an es the sia (an′əs thē′zhə), entire or partial loss of the feeling of pain, touch, cold, etc. *n.* Also, **anaesthesia.**

an es thet ic (an′əs thet′ik), **1** substance that causes entire or partial loss of the feeling of pain, touch, cold, etc. Ether is an anesthetic used by doctors so that patients will feel no pain. **2** causing anesthesia: *an anesthetic gas.* **1** *n.,* **2** *adj.* Also, **anaesthetic.** —**an′es thet′i cal ly,** *adv.*

an es tist (ə nes′tə tist), person specially trained to give anesthetics. *n.* Also, **anaesthetist.**

an es the tize (ə nes′thə tīz), make unable to feel pain, touch, cold, etc.; make insensible. *v.,* **an es the tized, an es the tiz ing.** Also, **anaesthetize.** —**an es′the ti za′tion,** *n.* —**an es′the tiz′er,** *n.*

a new (ə nü′ *or* ə nyü′), once more; again: *I made so many mistakes I had to begin the work anew. adv.*

an gel (ān′jəl), **1** messenger from God. **2** person as good or as lovely as an angel. *n.*

angelfish
about 6 in.
(15 cm.) long

an gel fish (ān′jəl fish′), any of several colorful tropical fishes with spiny fins. *n., pl.* **an gel fish es** or **an gel fish.**

an gel ic (an jel′ik), **1** of angels; heavenly: *an angelic vision.* **2** like an angel; pure, innocent, good, or lovely: *an angelic child. adj.*

an gel i cal (an jel′ə kəl), angelic. *adj.* —**an gel′i cal ly,** *adv.*

An gel i co (an jel′ə kō), **Fra,** 1387-1455, Italian painter. *n.*

an ge lus or **An ge lus** (an′jə ləs), **1** prayer said by Roman Catholics in memory of Christ's assuming human form. **2** the bell rung at morning, noon, and night to signal the times this prayer is said. *n.*

an ger (ang′gər), **1** the feeling that one has toward someone or something that hurts, opposes, offends, or annoys: *In a moment of anger, I hit my brother.* **2** make or become angry: *The girl's disobedience angered her parents. He angers easily.* **1** *n.,* **2** *v.* [*Anger* came into English about 700 years ago from Icelandic *angr,* meaning "grief, trouble."]

an gi o sperm (an′jē ə spėrm′), any plant having its seeds enclosed in an ovary or fruit; a flowering plant. Grasses, beans, strawberries, and oaks are angiosperms. *n.*

an gle[1] (ang′gəl), **1** the space between two lines or surfaces that meet. **2** the figure formed by two such lines or surfaces. **3** the difference in direction between two such lines or surfaces: *The two roads lie at an angle of about 45 degrees.* **4** move, turn, or bend at an angle: *The road angles to the right here.* **5** corner: *the northeast angle of a building.* **6** point of view: *We are treating the problem from a new angle.* **1-3,5,6** *n.,* **4** *v.,* **an gled, an gling.** [*Angle*[1] came into English about 600 years ago from French *angle.*]

an gle[2] (ang′gəl), **1** to fish with a hook and line. **2** try to get something by using tricks or schemes: *He angled for*

an invitation to the party by flattering her. *v.,* **an gled, an gling.** [*Angle*[2] comes from Old English *angel,* meaning "fishhook."]

An gle (ang′gəl), member of a Germanic tribe that, with the Jutes and Saxons, conquered England in the A.D. 400's and 500's. *n.*

an gler (ang′glər), person who fishes with a hook and line, especially one who does so for sport. *n.*

an gle worm (ang′gəl wėrm′), earthworm. *n.*

An gli can (ang′glə kən), **1** of the Church of England or other churches of the same faith elsewhere. **2** member of an Anglican church. **1** *adj.,* **2** *n.*

An gli cize (ang′glə sīz), make or become English in form, pronunciation, habits, customs, or character. *Cajole, lace,* and *cousin* are French words that have been Anglicized. *v.,* **An gli cized, An gli ciz ing.**

an gling (ang′gling), act or sport of fishing, especially with a hook and line. *n.*

An glo-Sax on (ang′glō sak′sən), **1** member of the Germanic tribes that invaded England in the A.D. 400's and 500's and ruled most of England until the Norman Conquest in 1066. **2** the language of these tribes; Old English. **3** of the Anglo-Saxons or their language. **4** person of English descent. **1,2,4** *n.,* **3** *adj.*

An go la (ang gō′lə), country in SW Africa. *Capital:* Luanda. *n.* —**An go′lan,** *adj., n.*

An go ra (ang gôr′ə), **1** Angora cat. **2** Angora goat. **3** Angora rabbit. **4** Ankara. **5** angora, **a** mohair. **b** a very fluffy yarn made partly or entirely from the hair of Angora goats or Angora rabbits. *n., pl.* **An go ras** for 1-3.

Angora cat, cat with long, silky hair.

Angora goat, goat with long, silky hair. This hair is used for wool and made into a cloth called angora or mohair.

Angora rabbit, rabbit with long, soft hair. This hair is used in making a very fluffy yarn or fabric.

an gri ly (ang′grə lē), in an angry manner; with anger. *adv.*

an gri ness (ang′grē nis), condition of being angry. *n.*

an gry (ang′grē), **1** feeling or showing anger: *I was very angry when you disobeyed. My friend's angry words hurt my feelings.* **2** stormy: *the dark clouds of an angry sky.* **3** inflamed and sore: *An infected cut looks angry. adj.,* **an gri er, an gri est.**

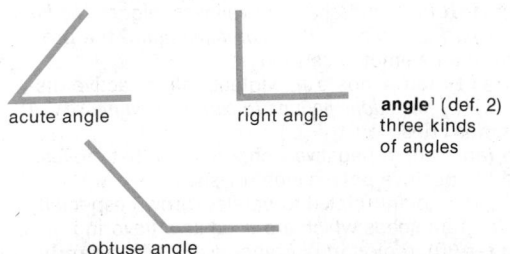

acute angle

right angle

angle[1] (def. 2)
three kinds
of angles

obtuse angle

an guish (ang′gwish), very great pain or grief; great distress: *He was in anguish until the doctor set his broken leg. n.*

an guished (ang′gwisht), full of grief or distress; showing anguish: *We saw the anguished faces of the parents whose child was lost. adj.*

a hat	i it	oi oil	ch child	a in about
ā age	ī ice	ou out	ng long	e in taken
ä far	o hot	u cup	sh she	ə = i in pencil
e let	ō open	u̇ put	th thin	o in lemon
ē equal	ô order	ü rule	ŦH then	u in circus
ėr term			zh measure	

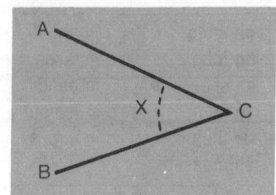

angular (def. 3)
The angular distance
of A from B,
when measured from C,
is the angle X.

an gu lar (ang′gyə lər), **1** having angles; having sharp corners: *an angular piece of rock.* **2** somewhat thin and bony; not plump: *Many basketball players have tall, angular bodies.* **3** measured by an angle: *angular distance. adj.* —**an′gu lar ly,** *adv.*

an gu lar i ty (ang′gyə lar′ə tē), condition of having sharp or prominent corners. *n.*

an i line or **an i lin** (an′l ən), a colorless, poisonous, oily liquid, obtained from coal tar. It is a compound of carbon, nitrogen, and hydrogen and is used in making dyes, medicines, plastics, etc. *n.*

aniline dye, 1 dye made from aniline. **2** any artificial dye.

an i mal (an′ə məl), **1** any living thing that is not a plant. Most animals can move about, feed upon other animals or plants, inhale oxygen and exhale carbon dioxide, and have a digestive cavity and a nervous system. A dog, a bird, a fish, a snake, a fly, and a worm are animals. **2** an animal other than a human being; beast. **3** any mammal, as distinguished from a bird, reptile, etc. Whales, apes, and horses are animals. **4** of animals: *the animal world.* **5** like that of animals: *animal cunning.* **6** person who acts more like a beast than a human being. 1-3,6 *n.,* 4,5 *adj.* [*Animal* is from Latin *animal,* meaning "a living being," which comes from *anima,* meaning "life, breath."]

animal kingdom, all animals.

animal spirits, natural liveliness.

an i mate (an′ə māt *for 1-4;* an′ə mit *for 5*), **1** make lively or vigorous: *Her arrival animated the whole party.* **2** be a motive or a reason for; inspire: *Love for her job animated her work.* **3** cause to move as if alive: *Wind animated the scarecrow, which appeared to wave at us.* **4** living; having life. Animate nature means all living plants and animals. 1-3 *v.,* **an i mat ed, an i mat ing;** 4 *adj.* —**an′i ma′tor,** *n.*

an i mat ed (an′ə mā′tid), **1** lively; vigorous: *The children had an animated discussion about yesterday's field trip.* **2** seeming to be alive: *animated dolls. adj.* —**an′i mat′ed ly,** *adv.*

animated cartoon, series of drawings arranged to be photographed and shown as a motion picture. Each drawing shows a slight change from the one before it, so that when projected in rapid sequence the figures appear to move.

an i ma tion (an′ə mā′shən), **1** liveliness; vigor: *The boy acted his part as a pirate with great animation.* **2** the production of an animated cartoon. *n.*

an i mos i ty (an′ə mos′ə tē), violent hatred; active dislike; ill will: *I have done nothing to earn your animosity. n., pl.* **an i mos i ties.**

an i on (an′ī′ən), a negatively charged ion that moves toward the positive pole in electrolysis. *n.*

an ise (an′is), plant related to parsley, grown especially for its fragrant seeds which are used as a flavoring. *n.*

An jou (an′jü), region in W France. *n.* See **Normandy** for map.

An kar a (ang′kər ə), capital of Turkey, in the central part. *n.* Also, **Angora.**

an kle (ang′kəl), **1** joint that connects the foot with the leg; tarsus. **2** the slender part of the leg between this joint and the calf. *n.*

an klet (ang′klit), **1** a short sock. **2** band or bracelet worn around the ankle. An anklet may be an ornament, a brace, or a fetter. *n.*

an nal ist (an′l ist), **1** writer of annals. **2** historian. *n.*

an nals (an′lz), **1** historical records; history: *Marie Curie holds an important place in the annals of science.* **2** a written account of events year by year. *n.pl.*

An na po lis (ə nap′ə lis), seaport and capital of Maryland. The United States Naval Academy is located there. *n.*

Anne (an), 1665-1714, queen of Great Britain and Ireland from 1702 to 1714. *n.*

an neal (ə nēl′), make (glass, metals, etc.) less brittle by heating and then gradually cooling. *v.* —**an neal′er,** *n.*

an ne lid (an′l id), worm with a body composed of a series of similar ringlike segments. Earthworms, leeches, and various sea worms are annelids. *n.*

an nex (ə neks′ *for 1;* an′eks *for 2*), **1** join or add (a smaller thing) to a larger thing: *The United States annexed Texas in 1845.* **2** something annexed; an added part: *We are building an annex to the school.* **1** *v.,* **2** *n., pl.* **an nex es.** —**an nex′a ble,** *adj.* —**an nex′ment,** *n.*

an nex a tion (an′ek sā′shən), **1** an annexing or a being annexed: *The annexation of Texas enlarged the United States.* **2** something annexed. *n.*

an ni hi late (ə nī′ə lāt), destroy completely; wipe out of existence: *An avalanche annihilated the village. v.,* **an ni hi lat ed, an ni hi lat ing.** [*Annihilate* comes from Latin *annihilatum,* meaning "brought to nothing."]

an ni hi la tion (ə nī′ə lā′shən), complete destruction. *n.*

an ni ver sar y (an′ə vėr′sər ē), **1** the yearly return of a special date: *Your birthday is an anniversary you like to have remembered.* **2** celebration of the yearly return of a special date. **3** having to do with an anniversary: *an anniversary dinner.* 1,2 *n., pl.* **an ni ver sa ries;** 3 *adj.*

an no Dom i ni (an′ō dom′ə nī), LATIN. in the year of the Lord; in the (specified) year since the birth of Christ. *Abbrev.:* A.D.

an no tate (an′ə tāt), **1** provide with notes or comments: *The Bible is often annotated to explain the meaning of certain words and events.* **2** write or insert notes or comments. *v.,* **an no tat ed, an no tat ing.** —**an′no ta′tor,** *n.*

an no ta tion (an′ə tā′shən), **1** a providing with notes or comments: *The annotation of this Shakespearean play required the explanation of many words no longer used.* **2** note added to explain or criticize: *The editor's annotations were printed in small type at the bottom of the page. n.*

an nounce (ə nouns′), **1** give public or formal notice of: *The teacher announced that there would be no school tomorrow.* **2** make known the presence or arrival of: *The loudspeaker announced each airplane as it landed at the airport.* **3** introduce programs, read news, etc., on the radio or television. *v.,* **an nounced, an nounc ing.**

an nounce ment (ə nouns′mənt), **1** an announcing; making known. We speak of the announcement of a speaker, a meeting, a wedding, a concert, etc. **2** what is announced or made known: *The principal made two announcements. The announcement was published in the newspapers. n.*

an nounc er (ə noun′sər), person who announces, especially on the radio or television. *n.*

an noy (ə noi′), make somewhat angry; disturb; trouble; vex: *The baby is always annoying me by pulling my hair. v.*

an noy ance (ə noi′əns), **1** a being annoyed; feeling of dislike or trouble; vexation: *He showed his annoyance at us by slamming the door.* **2** something that annoys; nuisance: *The heavy traffic on our street is an annoyance.* **3** an annoying: *Your annoyance of the class must stop. n.*

an noy ing (ə noi′ing), disturbing; troublesome. *adj.* —**an noy′ing ly,** *adv.* —**an noy′ing ness,** *n.*

an nu al (an′yü əl), **1** coming once a year: *Your birthday is an annual event.* **2** in a year; for a year: *For the last two years her annual salary has been $14,000.* **3** lasting for a whole year: *The earth makes an annual course around the sun.* **4** living but one year or season: *Corn and beans are annual plants.* **5** plant that lives but one year or season. **6** book, journal, etc., published once a year. 1-4 *adj.*, 5,6 *n.*

an nu al ly (an′yü ə lē), each year; yearly. *adv.*

an nu i ty (ə nü′ə tē *or* ə nyü′ə tē), **1** sum of money paid every year or at certain regular times: *Many businesses provide annuities for employees after they retire.* **2** an investment that provides a fixed yearly income during one's lifetime or for a specified time. *n.*, *pl.* **an nu i ties.**

an nul (ə nul′), do away with; destroy the force of; make void; cancel: *The judge annulled the contract because one of the signers was too young. v.*, **an nulled, an nul ling.**

an nu lar (an′yə lər), of or like a ring; ring-shaped. *adj.*

an nul ment (ə nul′mənt), an annulling or being annulled; declaring void: *An annulment of the marriage was granted by the court because the marriage was illegal. n.*

An nun ci a tion (ə nun′sē ā′shən), **1** (in the Bible) the announcement by the angel Gabriel to the Virgin Mary that she was to be the mother of Christ. **2** a church festival held on March 25 in memory of the Annunciation. *n.*

an ode (an′ōd), electrode by which electricity flows out of a device. The anode is the negative electrode of a battery but the positive electrode of most devices. *n.*

a noint (ə noint′), **1** put oil on; rub with a healing ointment; smear: *Anoint sunburned skin with cold cream.* **2** put oil on (a person) as part of a ceremony: *The bishop anointed the new king. v.* —**a noint′er,** *n.*

a noint ment (ə noint′mənt), an anointing or being anointed. *n.*

a nom a lous (ə nom′ə ləs), departing from the common rule; irregular: *It would be anomalous for a principal to have no authority. adj.* —**a nom′a lous ly,** *adv.*

a nom a ly (ə nom′ə lē), **1** something abnormal: *A dog with six legs would be an anomaly.* **2** departure from the common rule; irregularity: *"A lamb in school is an anomaly," said the teacher to Mary. n.*, *pl.* **a nom a lies.**

a non (ə non′), OLD USE. **1** in a little while; soon. **2** at another time; again. *adv.*

anon., anonymous.

an o nym i ty (an′ə nim′ə tē), condition of being anonymous. *n.*

a non y mous (ə non′ə məs), **1** by or from a person whose name is not known or given: *An anonymous letter is one which does not give the name of the writer.* **2** having no name; nameless: *This book was written by an anonymous author. adj.* —**a non′y mous ly,** *adv.*

an o rec tic (an′ə rek′tik), **1** having anorexia. **2** person who suffers from anorexia. 1 *adj.*, 2 *n.*

an o rex i a (an′ə rek′sē ə), condition in which a person deliberately eats very little, usually caused by emotional problems and producing extreme thinness and even starvation. *n.*

an oth er (ə nuŦH′ər), **1** one more: *Have another glass of milk (adj.). I ate a candy bar and then asked for another (pron.).* **2** a different: *Show me another kind of hat.* **3** a different one: *I don't like this book; give me another.* 1,2 *adj.*, 1,3 *pron.*

ans., **1** answer. **2** answered.

an swer (an′sər), **1** speak or write in return to a question: *I asked them a question, but they would not answer. He finally answered my question.* **2** words spoken or written in return to a question: *The girl gave a quick answer.* **3** gesture or act done in return: *A nod was her only answer.* **4** act in return to a call, signal, etc.; respond: *I*

knocked on the door, but no one answered. She answered the doorbell.* **5** solution to a problem: *What is the correct answer to this arithmetic problem?* **6** meet or satisfy a requirement, wish, etc.; serve: *On the picnic, a newspaper answered for a tablecloth.* **7** be responsible: *The bus driver must answer for the safety of the children in the bus.* **8** be similar to; agree with; correspond: *The dog we found answers to your description.* 1,4,6-8 *v.*, 2,3,5 *n.* [*Answer* is from Old English *andswaru,* which comes from *and-,* meaning "against," and *swerian,* meaning "to swear."]

answer back, reply in a rude, impertinent way: *When the teacher scolded the pupil he answered back.*

an swer a ble (an′sər ə bəl), **1** responsible: *The club treasurer is held answerable to the club for the money collected or spent.* **2** able to be answered: *That question is easily answerable. adj.* —**an′swer a ble ness,** *n.*

ant (ant), any of certain small insects living in large colonies either in the ground or in wood. Ants are black, brown, reddish, or yellowish. Ants, bees, and wasps belong to the same group of insects. *n.* —**ant′like′,** *adj.*

-ant, *suffix added to verbs.* **1** (*to form adjectives*) that _____s; _____ing: *Buoyant = that buoys or buoying. Compliant = that complies or complying.* **2** (*to form nouns*) one that _____s: *Assistant = one that assists.*

ant ac id (ant′as′id), substance that neutralizes acids. Baking soda is an antacid. *n.*

an tag o nism (an tag′ə niz′əm), active opposition; hostility: *During the argument, the boy's antagonism showed plainly in his face. n.*

an tag o nist (an tag′ə nist), person who fights, struggles, or contends against another in a combat or contest of any kind; adversary; opponent: *The knight defeated each antagonist who came against him. n.*

an tag o nis tic (an tag′ə nis′tik), acting against each other; opposing; hostile: *Cats and dogs are antagonistic. adj.* —**an tag′o nis′ti cal ly,** *adv.*

an tag o nize (an tag′ə nīz), make an enemy of; arouse dislike in: *Her unkind remarks antagonized people who had been her friends. v.*, **an tag o nized, an tag o niz ing.**

An ta na na ri vo (än′tä nä′nä rē′vō), capital of Madagascar, in the central part. *n.*

ant arc tic (ant′ärk′tik *or* ant′är′tik), **1** at or near the South Pole; of the south polar region. **2** the Antarctic, the south polar region. 1 *adj.*, 2 *n.*

Ant arc ti ca (ant′ärk′tə kə *or* ant′är′tə kə), continent around or near the South Pole. It is almost totally covered by ice and lies within the antarctic circle. *n.*

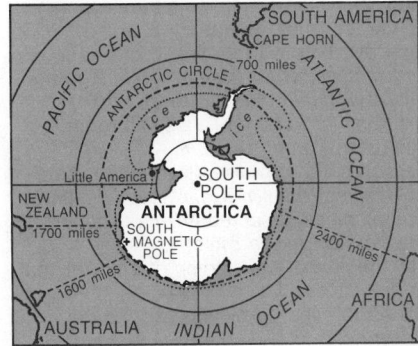

antarctic circle or **Antarctic Circle,** the imaginary boundary of the south polar region. It runs parallel to the equator at 23 degrees 30 minutes (23° 30′) north of the South Pole. See **Antarctica** for map.

Antarctic Continent, Antarctica.

Antarctic Ocean, the ocean of the south polar region.

Antarctic Zone, region between the antarctic circle and the South Pole.

ante-, *prefix.* before; in front of: *Antedate = to date before. Anteroom =a room in front of (another).* [The prefix *ante-* comes from Latin *ante*, meaning "before."]

ant eat er (ant/ē/tər), any of various mammals that eat ants and termites which they catch with their long, sticky tongues. *n.*

an te-bel lum (an/ti bel/əm), **1** before the war. **2** before the American Civil War. *adj.*

an te ced ent (an/tə sēd/nt), **1** the noun or noun phrase to which a pronoun refers. In "The dog which killed the rat is brown," *dog* is the antecedent of *which.* **2** coming or happening before; previous: *Cave dwellers lived in a period of history antecedent to written records.* **3** a previous happening or event. **4 antecedents,** *pl.* **a** past life or history: *No one knew the antecedents of the mysterious stranger.* **b** ancestors: *She has Polish antecedents.* 1,3,4 *n.*, 2 *adj.*

an te cham ber (an/ti chām/bər), a small waiting room; anteroom. *n.*

an te date (an/ti dāt), **1** be or happen before; precede: *Radio antedated television.* **2** give an earlier date to (a document, event, etc.). *v.*, **an te dat ed, an te dat ing.**

an te di lu vi an (an/ti də lü/vē ən), **1** very old; old-fashioned. **2** before the Flood. *adj.*

an te lope (an/tl ōp), **1** any of certain hoofed mammals of Africa and Asia that are related to the goat and cow but resemble the deer in appearance, grace, and speed. Antelopes chew the cud and usually have a single pair of hollow horns that curve backward and do not fork or branch. **2** pronghorn. *n.*, *pl.* **an te lope** or **an te lopes.**

antenna (def. 1) antennae of a grasshopper

an ten na (an ten/ə), **1** one of the long, slender feelers on the head of an insect, scorpion, lobster, etc. **2** the aerial of a radio or television set. *n.*, *pl.* **an ten nae** (an ten/ē) or **an ten nas** for 1, **an ten nas** for 2.

an ter i or (an tir/ē ər), **1** more to the front; fore: *The anterior part of a fish contains the head and gills.* **2** going before; earlier: *events anterior to the last war. adj.*

an te room (an/ti rüm/ or an/ti rùm/), a small room leading to a larger one; waiting room. *n.*

an them (an/thəm), **1** song of praise, devotion, or patriotism: *"The Star-Spangled Banner" is the national anthem of the United States.* **2** piece of sacred music, usually with words from some passage in the Bible. *n.*

an ther (an/thər), the part of the stamen of a flower that bears the pollen. *n.*

ant hill, heap of earth piled up by ants around the entrance to their tunnels.

an thol o gy (an thol/ə jē), collection of poems or prose selections, usually from various authors. *n.*, *pl.* **an thol o gies.** [*Anthology* is from Greek *anthologia*, meaning "collection of flowers."]

An tho ny (an/thə nē), Susan B., 1820-1906, American leader in the women's rights movement. *n.*

an thra cite (an/thrə sīt), coal that burns with very little smoke and flame; hard coal. It consists almost entirely of carbon. *n.*

anteater
This species is about 3½ ft. (1 m.) long, including the tail.

an thrax (an/thraks), an often fatal disease of cattle, sheep, etc., that may be caught by human beings. *n.*

an thro poid (an/thrə poid), **1** (of certain apes) resembling a human being. Anthropoid apes have no tail and lack cheek pouches. **2** ape that resembles a human being. Gorillas, chimpanzees, orangutans, and gibbons are anthropoids. 1 *adj.*, 2 *n.* [*Anthropoid* can be traced back to Greek *anthrōpos*, meaning "a human being."]

an thro po log i cal (an/thrə pə loj/ə kəl), of anthropology. *adj.* —**an/thro po log/i cal ly,** *adv.*

an thro pol o gist (an/thrə pol/ə jist), an expert in anthropology. *n.*

an thro pol o gy (an/thrə pol/ə jē), the science dealing with the origin, development, races, customs, and beliefs of human beings. *n.*

anti-, *prefix.* **1** against _____; opposed to _____: *Antiaircraft = against aircraft. Antislavery = opposed to slavery.* **2** preventing or counteracting _____: *Antirust = preventing or counteracting rust.* [The prefix *anti-* can be traced back to Greek *anti*, meaning "against."]

an ti air craft (an/tē er/kraft/ or an/tē ar/kraft/), used in defense against enemy aircraft. *adj.*

an ti-A mer i can (an/tē ə mer/ə kən), opposed to the interests or the people of the United States. *adj.*

an ti bi ot ic (an/ti bī ot/ik), substance produced by a living organism, especially a bacterium or fungus, that destroys or weakens germs. Penicillin is an antibiotic. *n.*

an ti bod y (an/ti bod/ē), a protein substance produced in the blood or tissues that destroys or weakens bacteria or neutralizes poisons produced by them. *n.*, *pl.* **an ti bod ies.**

an tic i pate (an tis/ə pāt), **1** look forward to; expect: *We are anticipating a good time at your party.* **2** do before others do; be ahead of in doing: *The Chinese anticipated the European discovery of gunpowder.* **3** take care of ahead of time; consider in advance: *We anticipated hot weather and took our bathing suits with us.* *v.*, **an tic i pat ed, an tic i pat ing.** —**an tic/i pa/tor,** *n.*

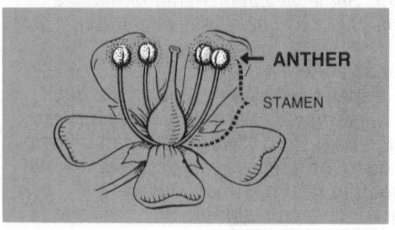

← ANTHER

STAMEN

an tic i pa tion (an tis′ə pā′shən), act of anticipating; looking forward to; expectation: *In anticipation of a cold winter, they cut extra firewood. n.*

an ti cli mac tic (an′ti klī mak′tik), of or like an anticlimax. *adj.* —**an′ti cli mac′ti cal ly,** *adv.*

an ti cli max (an′ti klī′maks), an abrupt descent from the important to the trivial or unimportant. *n., pl.* **an ti cli max es.**

an tics (an′tiks), funny gestures or actions; silly tricks: *The antics of the clown amused us. n.pl.*

an ti cy clone (an′ti sī′klōn), winds moving around and away from a center of high pressure, which also moves. *n.*

an ti dote (an′ti dōt), **1** medicine or remedy that counteracts the harmful effects of a poison: *Milk is an antidote for some poisons.* **2** remedy for anything that is harmful: *Education is an antidote for ignorance. n.*

An tie tam (an tē′təm), small creek in NW Maryland. A major battle of the Civil War was fought near it in 1862 between Lee and McClellan which resulted in Lee's retreat. *n.*

an ti freeze (an′ti frēz′), substance added to a liquid to lower its freezing point. Antifreeze in automobile radiators prevents the water from freezing. *n.*

an ti gen (an′tə jən), any protein substance that causes the body to produce antibodies to counteract it. Bacteria are antigens. *n.*

An ti gua and Bar bu da (an tē′gwə ənd bär bü′də or an tē′gə ənd bär bü′də), island country in the West Indies, a member of the Commonwealth of Nations. *Capital:* St. John's.

an ti his ta mine (an′ti his′tə mēn′), medicine that helps to relieve the symptoms of colds and allergies. *n.*

an ti knock (an′ti nok′), substance added to the fuel of an internal-combustion engine to reduce noise caused by too rapid combustion. *n.*

An til les (an til′ēz), chain of islands in the West Indies. The **Greater Antilles** are Cuba, Hispaniola, Puerto Rico, and Jamaica; the **Lesser Antilles** are smaller islands southeast of Puerto Rico, including the Windward and Leeward Islands. See **Caribbean Sea** for map. *n.pl.*

an ti mis sile (an′ti mis′əl), used in defense against ballistic missiles, rockets, etc.: *antimissile missiles. adj.*

an ti mo ny (an′tə mō′nē), a brittle, silver-white, metallic element. It occurs chiefly in combination with other elements. Antimony is used to make alloys harder and its compounds are used to make medicines, pigments, and glass. *n.*

an tip a thy (an tip′ə thē), **1** a strong dislike; a feeling against: *He felt an antipathy to snakes.* **2** anything that arouses such a feeling. *n., pl.* **an tip a thies.**

an ti per spir ant (an′ti pėr′spər ənt), a chemical preparation that is applied to the skin to decrease perspiration and control body odor. *n.*

an ti quar i an (an′tə kwer′ē ən), **1** of antiques or antiquaries: *the antiquarian section of a museum.* **2** antiquary. **1** *adj.,* **2** *n.*

an ti quar y (an′tə kwer′ē), student or collector of relics from ancient times. *n., pl.* **an ti quar ies.**

an ti quat ed (an′tə kwā′tid), **1** that has grown old but is no longer valued; old-fashioned; out-of-date: *Most science books written 20 years ago are now antiquated.* **2** too old for work or service. *adj.*

an tique (an tēk′), **1** of times long ago; from times long ago: *This antique chair was made in 1750.* **2** something made long ago: *This carved chest is a genuine antique.* **1** *adj.,* **2** *n.* —**an tique′ly,** *adv.* —**an tique′ness,** *n.*

an tiq ui ty (an tik′wə tē), **1** great age; oldness: *This vase is of such antiquity that it is priceless.* **2** times long ago, especially the period of history between 5000 B.C. and

A.D. 476: *Troy was a city of antiquity.* **3** the people of ancient times. **4 antiquities,** *pl.* things from times long ago: *antiquities in a museum. n., pl.* **an tiq ui ties.**

an ti-Se mit ic (an′ti sə mit′ik), prejudiced against Jews. *adj.*

an ti-Sem i tism (an′ti sem′ə tiz′əm), dislike or hatred for Jews; prejudice against Jews. *n.*

an ti sep tic (an′tə sep′tik), **1** substance that prevents the growth of germs that cause infection. Iodine, peroxide, Mercurochrome, alcohol, and boric acid are antiseptics. **2** preventing infection. **1** *n.,* **2** *adj.* [*Antiseptic* is from *anti-* and *septic. Septic* comes from Greek *sēptikos,* which is from *sēpein,* meaning "to rot."]

an ti sep ti cal ly (an′tə sep′tik lē), by the use of antiseptics. *adv.*

an ti slav er y (an′ti slā′vər ē), opposed to slavery; against slavery. *adj.*

an ti so cial (an′ti sō′shəl), **1** opposed to the principles upon which society is based: *Stealing is an antisocial act.* **2** opposed to friendly relationship and normal companionship with others: *Hermits are antisocial. adj.*

an tith e sis (an tith′ə sis), **1** the direct opposite: *Hate is the antithesis of love.* **2** contrast of ideas. EXAMPLE: "To err is human; to forgive, divine." **3** opposition; contrast: *the antithesis between theory and fact. n., pl.* **an tith e ses** (an tith′ə sēz′).

an ti tox in (an′ti tok′sən), **1** antibody formed in response to the presence of a toxin to prevent or reduce the effects of that toxin. **2** serum containing antitoxin, injected to create immunity to a disease. *n.*

an ti trust (an′ti trust′), opposed to large corporations that stifle competition and so control the trade practices of certain kinds of businesses. *adj.*

antler (def. 1)
antlers of a deer

ant ler (ant′lər), **1** horn of a deer, elk, or moose, usually having one or more branches. Antlers are shed once a year and grow back again during the next year. **2** branch of such a horn. *n.* [*Antler* came into English about 600 years ago from French *antoillier,* and can be traced back

antiquated (def. 2)
The engine of **the antiquated** truck would no longer run.

to Latin *ante,* meaning "in front of," and *oculus,* meaning "eye."]

ant lion, insect whose larva digs a pit, where it lies in wait to catch ants and other insects as they fall in and are trapped.

An toi nette (an′twə net′), **Marie.** See **Marie Antoinette.** *n.*

An to ny (an′tə nē), **Mark,** 83?-30 B.C., Roman general and statesman. *n.*

an to nym (an′tə nim), word that means the opposite of another word. "Hot" is the antonym of "cold." *n.*

Ant werp (ant′wərp), seaport in NW Belgium. *n.*

a nus (ā′nəs), the opening at the lower end of the alimentary canal, through which solid waste material passes from the body. *n.*

an vil (an′vəl), **1** an iron or steel block on which metals are hammered and shaped. **2** the central bone of three small bones in the middle ear of human beings and other mammals. It is shaped something like an anvil. *n.*

anx i e ty (ang zī′ə tē), **1** uneasy thoughts or fears about what may happen; troubled, worried, or uneasy feeling: *We all felt anxiety when the airplane was caught in the storm.* **2** eager desire: *Her anxiety to succeed led her to work hard. n., pl.* **anx i e ties.**

anx ious (angk′shəs *or* ang′shəs), **1** uneasy because of thoughts or fears of what may happen; troubled; worried: *I felt anxious about my final exams.* **2** causing uneasy feelings or troubled thoughts; distressing: *The week of the flood was an anxious time for all of us.* **3** wishing very much; eager: *He was anxious for a bicycle. She was anxious to learn to play chess. adj.* [*Anxious* is from Latin *anxius,* which comes from *angere,* meaning "to choke, to cause distress."] —**anx′ious ly,** *adv.* —**anx′ious ness,** *n.*

an y (en′ē), **1** one out of many: *Choose any book you like from the books on the shelf.* **2** some: *Have you any fresh fruit?* (*adj.*). *I need more ink; have you any?* (*pron.*). **3** every: *Any child knows that.* **4** even one or two: *Because of an allergy, I can't eat any chocolate.* **5** to some extent or degree; at all: *Have I improved any?* 1-4 *adj.,* 2 *pron.,* 5 *adv.*

an y bod y (en′ē bod′ē), **1** any person; anyone: *Has anybody been here?* **2** an important person: *Everybody who's anybody stays at that hotel.* 1 *pron.,* 2 *n., pl.* **an y bod ies.**

an y how (en′ē hou), **1** in any case; at least: *I can see as well as you can, anyhow.* **2** in any way whatever: *The answer is wrong anyhow you look at it.* **3** carelessly: *He dumped the tools into the box just anyhow. adv.*

an y more (en′ē môr′), at present; now; currently: *We seldom see them anymore. adv.*

an y one (en′ē wun), any person; anybody: *Can anyone go to this movie or is it just for adults? pron.*

an y place (en′ē plās), anywhere. *adv.*

an y thing (en′ē thing), **1** any thing: *Do you have anything to eat?* **2** a thing of any kind whatever: *My dog will eat almost anything.* **3** in any way; at all: *My bike isn't anything like yours.* 1 *pron.,* 2 *n.,* 3 *adv.*

anything but, not at all: *This old shack is anything but warm.*

an y time (en′ē tīm), at any time; no matter when: *You are welcome to visit us anytime. adv.*

an y way (en′ē wā), **1** in any case; at least: *I am coming anyway, no matter what you say.* **2** in any way whatever; carelessly; anyhow: *She stacked the books on the floor just anyway. adv.*

an y where (en′ē hwer), in, at, or to any place: *I'll meet you anywhere you say. adv.*

an y wise (en′ē wīz), in any way; to any degree; at all. *adv.*

a.o. or **a/o,** account of.

A-OK (ā′ō′kā′), INFORMAL. OK. *adj., adv., interj.*

a or ta (ā ôr′tə), the main artery that carries the blood from the left side of the heart to all parts of the body except the lungs. *n., pl.* **a or tas, a or tae** (ā ôr′tē′).

Ap., April.

AP or **A.P.,** Associated Press.

a pace (ə pās′), very soon; swiftly; fast: *The summer flew by, and the time for school was coming on apace. adv.*

A pach e (ə pach′ē), member of a tribe of American Indians living in the southwestern United States. *n., pl.* **A pach es** or **A pach e.**

a part (ə pärt′), **1** to pieces; in pieces; in separate parts: *They took the watch apart to see how it runs.* **2** away from each other: *Keep the dogs apart.* **3** to one side; aside: *I set some money apart for a vacation each year.* **4** away from others; separately; independently: *View each idea apart. adv.* —**a part′ness,** *n.*

apart from, besides: *Apart from that, it was a good plan.*

a part heid (ə pärt′hāt *or* ə pärt′hīt), racial segregation, especially as practiced in South Africa. *n.* [*Apartheid* comes from Afrikaans *apartheid,* originally meaning "separateness."]

a part ment (ə pärt′mənt), **1** room or group of rooms to live in; flat. **2** apartment house. *n.*

apartment house, building with a number of apartments in it.

ap a thet ic (ap′ə thet′ik), **1** with little interest or desire for action; indifferent: *The student's apathetic attitude toward schoolwork annoyed the teacher.* **2** lacking in feeling; unemotional. *adj.*

ap a thet i cal ly (ap′ə thet′ik lē), in an apathetic manner. *adv.*

ap a thy (ap′ə thē), **1** lack of interest or desire for action; indifference: *The citizens' apathy to local affairs resulted in poor government.* **2** lack of feeling *She reacted to her former friend's troubles with apathy. n.* [*Apathy* is from Greek *apatheia,* which comes from *a-,* meaning "without," and *pathos,* meaning "feeling."]

ape (āp), **1** any large, tailless monkey with long arms, able to stand almost erect and walk on two feet. Chimpanzees, gorillas, orangutans, and gibbons are apes. **2** any monkey. **3** imitate; mimic: *They aped the mannerisms of their favorite TV stars.* **4** person who imitates or mimics. 1,2,4 *n.,* 3 *v.,* **aped, ap ing.** —**ape′like′,** *adj.* —**ap′er,** *n.*

Ap en nines (ap′ə nīnz), the chief mountain range in Italy, extending north and south. *n.pl.*

ap er ture (ap′ər chər), an opening; gap; hole. A shutter regulates the size of the aperture through which light passes into a camera. *n.*

a pex (ā′peks), **1** the highest point; tip: *The apex of a triangle is the point opposite the base.* **2** climax: *Her role in that film was the apex of her career. n., pl.* **a pex es** or **ap i ces.**

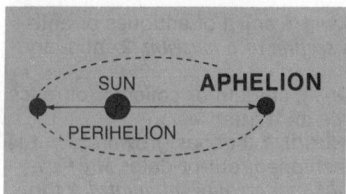

aphelion—a planet in orbit around the sun shown at aphelion and perihelion

a phe li on (ə fē′lē ən), the point farthest from the sun in the orbit of a planet or comet. *n., pl.* **a phe li a** (ə fē′lē ə).

a phid (ā′fid *or* af′id), a very small insect that lives by sucking juices from plants; plant louse. *n.*

aph o rism (af′ə riz′əm), a short sentence expressing a general truth or some practical wisdom; maxim; proverb. EXAMPLE: "A living dog is better than a dead lion." *n.*

Aph ro di te (af′rə dī′tē), (in Greek myths) the goddess of love and beauty. The Romans called her Venus. *n.*

A pi a (ä pē′ə *or* ä′pē ə), capital of Western Samoa. *n.*

a pi ar y (ā′pē er′ē), place where bees are kept; group of beehives. *n., pl.* **a pi ar ies.**

ap i ces (ap′ə sēz′ *or* ā′pə sēz′), a plural of **apex.** *n.*

a piece (ə pēs′), for each one; each: *These apples cost ten cents apiece. adv.*

ap ish (ā′pish), **1** foolish; silly: *I hid my embarrassment with an apish grin.* **2** like an ape. *adj.* —**ap′ish ly,** *adv.* —**ap′ish ness,** *n.*

a plomb (ə plom′), self-possession; assurance; poise. *n.*

APO or **A.P.O.,** Army Post Office.

A poc a lypse (ə pok′ə lips), the last book of the New Testament; the book of Revelation. *n.*

A poc ry pha (ə pok′rə fə), fourteen books included in the Roman Catholic Bible but not generally found in Jewish or Protestant Bibles. *n.pl.*

a poc ry phal (ə pok′rə fəl), **1** of doubtful genuineness; false: *apocryphal stories about a gigantic ape living in the hills.* **2 Apocryphal,** of or from the Apocrypha. *adj.* —**a poc′ry phal ly,** *adv.* —**a poc′ry phal ness,** *n.*

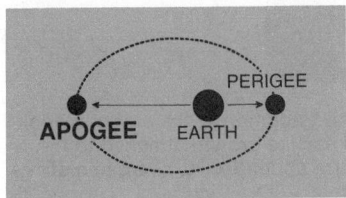

apogee—the moon in orbit around the earth shown at apogee and perigee

ap o gee (ap′ə jē), the point farthest from the earth in the orbit of the moon or any other earth satellite. *n.* [*Apogee* can be traced back to Greek *apo,* meaning "from," and *gē,* meaning "earth."]

A pol lo (ə pol′ō), (in Greek and Roman myths) the god of the sun, poetry, music, prophecy, and healing. Apollo was the highest type of youthful, manly beauty to the Greeks and Romans. *n.*

a pol o get ic (ə pol′ə jet′ik), **1** making an excuse; expressing regret: *He sent an apologetic note saying he could not attend the party.* **2** defending by speech or writing. *adj.*

a pol o get i cal ly (ə pol′ə jet′ik lē), in an apologetic manner. *adv.*

a pol o gist (ə pol′ə jist), person who defends an idea, belief, religion, etc., in speech or writing. *n.*

a pol o gize (ə pol′ə jīz), **1** make an apology; say one is sorry; offer an excuse: *I apologized for being so late.* **2** defend an idea, argument, belief, etc., in speech or writing. *v.,* **a pol o gized, a pol o giz ing.** —**a pol′o giz′er,** *n.*

a pol o gy (ə pol′ə jē), **1** words saying one is sorry for an offense, fault, or accident; explanation asking pardon: *Will you accept my apology for yelling at you?* **2** explanation of the truth or justice of something; defense: *Thomas Paine's "Common Sense" is an apology for American independence.* **3** a poor substitute; makeshift: *One piece of toast is a skimpy apology for a breakfast. n., pl.* **a pol o gies.**

ap o plec tic (ap′ə plek′tik), **1** of or causing apoplexy. **2** suffering from apoplexy. **3** showing symptoms of a tendency to apoplexy. *adj.* —**ap′o plec′ti cal ly,** *adv.*

ap o plex y (ap′ə plek′sē), a sudden loss of the power to feel or think or move; stroke. Apoplexy is caused by injury to the brain when a blood vessel breaks or the blood supply becomes obstructed. *n.*

a pos tle or **A pos tle** (ə pos′əl), **1** one of the twelve disciples, **the Apostles,** chosen by Christ to preach the gospel to all the world. **2** any early Christian leader or missionary: *Paul was frequently called the "Apostle to the Gentiles." n.*

ap os tol ic or **Ap os tol ic** (ap′ə stol′ik), **1** of the Apostles. **2** of the pope; papal. *adj.*

a pos tro phe (ə pos′trə fē), sign (') used: **1** to show the omission of one or more letters in contractions, as in *isn't* for *is not, thro'* for *through.* **2** to show the possessive forms of nouns or indefinite pronouns, as in *Lee's book, the lions' den,* and *everybody's business.* **3** to form plurals of letters and numbers: *There are two o's in apology and four 9's in 959,990. n.*

apothecaries' weight, system of weights used in mixing drugs and filling prescriptions.

a poth e car y (ə poth′ə ker′ē), person who prepares and sells drugs and medicines; druggist; pharmacist. *n., pl.* **a poth e car ies.**

app., 1 apparent. **2** appendix.

Ap pa la chia (ap′ə lā′chə), region in the E United States covering parts of 11 states from N Pennsylvania to N Alabama. *n.*

Ap pa la chian Mountains (ap′ə lā′chən), the chief mountain system in E North America, extending from Quebec Province in Canada to central Alabama.

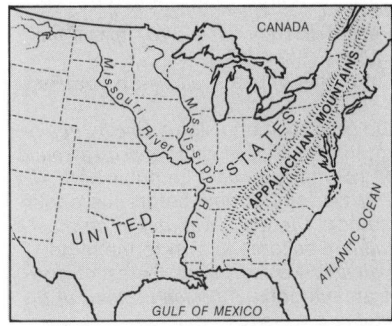

Ap pa la chians (ap′ə lā′chənz), Appalachian Mountains. *n.pl.*

ap pall or **ap pal** (ə pôl′), fill with horror or fear; dismay; terrify: *The thought of another war appalled us. v.,* **ap palled, ap pall ing.**

ap pall ing (ə pô′ling), causing horror; dismaying; terrifying. *adj.* —**ap pall′ing ly,** *adv.*

Ap pa loo sa (ap′ə lü′sə), a horse with dark spots, usually on the rump, on a roan background. *n.*

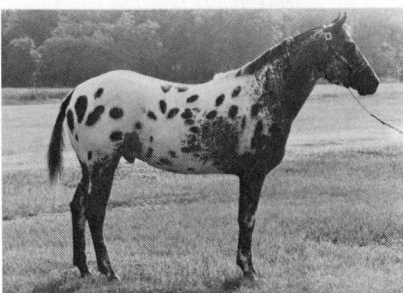

Appaloosa about 5 ft. (1.5 m.) high at the shoulder

---

a hat	i it	oi oil	ch child	a in about
ā age	ī ice	ou out	ng long	e in taken
ä far	o hot	u cup	sh she	ə = i in pencil
e let	ō open	u̇ put	th thin	o in lemon
ē equal	ô order	ü rule	⊤H then	u in circus
ėr term			zh measure	

ap pa ra tus (ap/ə rā/təs *or* ap/ə rat/əs), **1** the tools, machines, or other equipment necessary to carry out a purpose or for a particular use. Test tubes, beakers, and a Bunsen burner are part of the apparatus used in chemistry. **2** the organs of the body which together perform a particular function. The stomach and intestines are part of our digestive apparatus. *n., pl.* **ap pa ra tus** *or* **ap pa ra tus es.**

ap par el (ə par/əl), **1** clothing; dress: *Does this store sell women's apparel?* **2** clothe; dress up: *The circus performers were gaily appareled.* 1 *n.,* 2 *v.,* **ap par eled, ap par el ing** *or* **ap par elled, ap par el ling.**

ap par ent (ə par/ənt), **1** plain to see or understand; so plain that one cannot help seeing or understanding it: *The stain is apparent from across the room. It is apparent that she enjoys her work.* **2** appearing to be; seeming: *The apparent truth was really a lie. adj.* —**ap par/ent ly,** *adv.* —**ap par/ent ness,** *n.*

ap pa ri tion (ap/ə rish/ən), **1** ghost or phantom: *The apparition, clothed in white, glided through the wall.* **2** the appearance of something strange, remarkable, or unexpected. *n.*

ap peal (ə pēl/), **1** ask earnestly; ask for help, sympathy, etc.: *When the children were in trouble they appealed to their parents.* **2** a call for help, sympathy, etc.; earnest request: *an appeal for forgiveness, an appeal for money for the poor.* **3** call on some person to decide a matter in one's favor: *When one of my parents says "No," I appeal to the other.* **4** a call on some person to decide a matter in one's favor: *an appeal for another chance.* **5** ask that a case be taken to a higher court or judge to be heard again. **6** a request to have a case heard again before a higher court or judge. **7** be attractive, interesting, or enjoyable: *That blue and red wallpaper appeals to me.* **8** attraction or interest: *Television has a great appeal for most young people.* 1,3,5,7 *v.,* 2,4,6,8 *n.*

ap peal ing (ə pē/ling), that appeals. *adj.* —**ap peal/ing ly,** *adv.*

ap pear (ə pir/), **1** be seen; come in sight: *One by one the stars appear.* **2** seem; look as if: *The apple appeared sound on the outside, but it was rotten inside.* **3** be published: *Her latest book appeared a year ago.* **4** come before the public as a performer or author: *The singer will appear on the television program today.* **5** become known to the mind; be plain: *It appears that we were mistaken.* **6** present oneself formally before an authority: *A person accused of a crime must appear in court. v.*

ap pear ance (ə pir/əns), **1** act of coming in sight: *His sudden appearance in the doorway startled me.* **2** a coming before the public as a performer or author: *a singer's first appearance.* **3** outward look: *a pleasing appearance.* **4** outward show; pretense: *They buy things they can't afford in order to keep up an appearance of wealth. n.*

ap pease (ə pēz/), **1** put an end to by satisfying an appetite or desire: *A good dinner will appease your hunger.* **2** make calm or quiet; pacify: *We tried to appease the crying child by giving her candy.* **3** give in to the demands of: *The boy appeased his parents and returned to finish school. v.,* **ap peased, ap peas ing.** —**ap peas/er,** *n.*

ap pease ment (ə pēz/mənt), an appeasing or being appeased; pacification; satisfaction. *n.*

ap pel late court (ə pel/it), court having the power to examine again and reverse the decisions of a lower court.

ap pel la tion (ap/ə lā/shən), name or title describing some quality. In "John the Baptist," the appellation of *John* is *the Baptist. n.*

ap pend (ə pend/), add to a larger thing; attach as a supplement: *The amendments to the Constitution of the United States are appended to it. v.*

ap pend age (ə pen/dij), thing attached to something larger or more important; addition. Arms, tails, fins, legs, etc., are appendages. *n.*

ap pen dec to my (ap/ən dek/tə mē), removal of the appendix by a surgical operation. *n., pl.* **ap pen dec to mies.**

ap pen di ces (ə pen/də sēz/), a plural of **appendix.** *n.*

ap pen di ci tis (ə pen/də sī/tis), inflammation of the appendix. *n.*

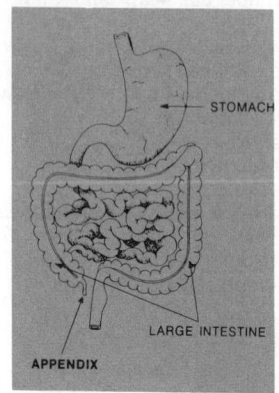

appendix
(def. 2)

ap pen dix (ə pen/diks), **1** addition at the end of a book or document. **2** a small saclike growth attached to the large intestine; vermiform appendix. *n., pl.* **ap pen dix es** *or* **ap pen di ces.**

ap per ceive (ap/ər sēv/), perceive clearly. *v.,* **ap perceived, ap per ceiv ing.**

ap per tain (ap/ər tān/), belong as a part; be connected; relate: *Forestry appertains to geography, to botany, and to agriculture. v.*

ap pe tite (ap/ə tīt), **1** desire for food: *Swimming increases my appetite.* **2** desire: *a great appetite for adventure. n.* [*Appetite* is from Latin *appetitus,* which comes from *appetere,* meaning "to long for, to seek."]

ap pe tiz er (ap/ə tī/zər), something that arouses the appetite, usually served before a meal. Pickles and olives are appetizers. *n.*

ap pe tiz ing (ap/ə tī/zing), arousing or exciting the appetite: *Appetizing food always smells delicious. adj.* —**ap/pe tiz/ing ly,** *adv.*

ap plaud (ə plôd/), **1** show approval by clapping hands, shouting, etc.: *The audience applauded at the end of the play.* **2** be pleased with; approve; praise: *My parents applauded my decision to remain in school. v.* —**ap plaud/a ble,** *adj.* —**ap plaud/er,** *n.*

ap plause (ə plôz/), **1** approval shown by clapping the hands, shouting, etc.: *Applause for the singer's good performance rang out from the audience.* **2** approval; praise. *n.*

ap ple (ap/əl), the firm, fleshy, somewhat round fruit of a tree widely grown in temperate regions. Apples have red, yellow, or green skin, and are eaten either raw or cooked. *n.* —**ap/ple like/,** *adj.*

apple of one's eye, person or thing that is cherished or valued.

ap ple sauce (ap/əl sôs/), apples cut in pieces and cooked with sugar, spices, and water until soft. *n.*

ap pli ance (ə plī/əns), instrument or machine designed for a particular purpose or operation. Vacuum cleaners, blenders, and refrigerators are household appliances. *n.*

ap pli ca ble (ap/lə kə bəl), capable of being applied; that can be put to practical use; appropriate; suitable: *The rule "Look before you leap" is almost always applicable. adj.*

ap pli cant (ap′lə kənt), person who applies (for a job, money, position, help, etc.). *n.*

ap pli ca tion (ap′lə kā′shən), **1** a putting to use; use: *the application of atomic energy to manufacturing. The application of what you know will help you solve new problems.* **2** way of using: *"Freedom" is a word of many applications.* **3** an applying; putting on: *The painter's careless application of paint spattered the floor.* **4** something applied. Cold cream and ointments are applications. **5** a request (for employment, an award, tickets, etc.): *I filled out an application for a job at the supermarket.* **6** continued effort; close attention: *Application to her work got her a promotion. n.*

ap pli ca tor (ap′lə kā′tər), instrument or device for applying a medicine, cosmetic, paint, etc. *n.*

ap plied (ə plīd′), put to practical use; used to solve actual problems: *The engineer used applied mathematics to solve the practical problems in building a bridge. adj.*

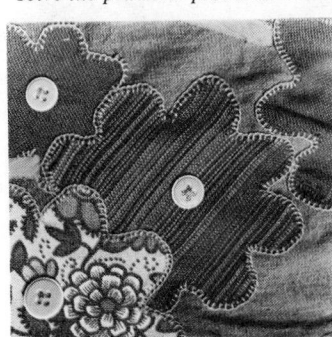
appliqué
(def. 1)

ap pli qué (ap′lə kā′), **1** ornament made of one material sewed or otherwise fastened on another. **2** trim or ornament with appliqué. 1 *n.,* 2 *v.,* **ap pli quéd, ap pli qué ing.**

ap ply (ə plī′), **1** put on; lay on or in contact with: *She applied two coats of paint to the table. He applied a wet cloth to the bump on my head.* **2** put to practical use; put into effect; use: *I know the rule but I don't know how to apply it.* **3** use (a word or expression) to refer to a person or object: *They applied the nickname "Slowpoke" to the pet turtle.* **4** be useful or suitable; fit: *When does this rule apply?* **5** make a request; ask: *She is applying for a summer job.* **6** set to work and stick to it: *He applied himself to learning to play the piano. v.,* **ap plied, ap ply ing. —ap pli′er,** *n.*

ap point (ə point′), **1** name for an office or position; choose: *The class president appointed five students to the clean-up committee.* **2** decide on; set: *to appoint a time for the meeting. v.* **—ap point′er,** *n.*

ap point ee (ə poin′tē′), person who is appointed to an office or position. *n.*

ap point ment (ə point′mənt), **1** act of naming for an office or position; choosing: *The President announced the appointment of his cabinet.* **2** office or position: *She has a government appointment.* **3** a meeting with someone at a certain time and place; engagement: *an appointment to see the doctor at four o'clock.* **4 appointments,** *pl.* furniture; equipment: *an old hotel with shabby appointments. n.*

Ap po mat tox (ap′ə mat′əks), town in central Virginia. Lee surrendered to Grant there on April 9, 1865. *n.*

ap por tion (ə pôr′shən), divide and give out in fair shares; distribute according to some rule: *Their property was to be apportioned among their children. v.*

ap por tion ment (ə pôr′shən mənt), a dividing and giving out in fair shares; distribution according to some rule. *n.*

a hat	i it	oi oil	ch child	a in about
ā age	ī ice	ou out	ng long	e in taken
ä far	o hot	u cup	sh she	ə = i in pencil
e let	ō open	u̇ put	th thin	o in lemon
ē equal	ô order	ü rule	ᴛH then	u in circus
ėr term			zh measure	

ap pose (a pōz′), **1** put next. **2** apply. *v.,* **ap posed, ap pos ing.**

ap po site (ap′ə zit), suitable; appropriate. *adj.*

ap po si tion (ap′ə zish′ən), the relationship to a noun of another noun or noun phrase which is placed after the first noun in order to explain it. In the sentence, "Mr. Brown, our neighbor, has a new car," *Mr. Brown* and *our neighbor* are in apposition. *n.*

ap pos i tive (ə poz′ə tiv), a noun or noun phrase placed after another noun in order to explain the first noun. In the sentence, "Mr. Brown, our neighbor, has a new car," *our neighbor* is an appositive. *n.*

ap prais al (ə prā′zəl), **1** estimate of value, amount, quality, etc.: *The bank's appraisal of the worth of our house was $30,000.* **2** an appraising; evaluating: *The coach gave a frank appraisal of the runner's ability. n.*

ap praise (ə prāz′), **1** estimate the value, amount, quality, etc., of: *An employer should be able to appraise an employee's ability.* **2** set a price on; fix the value of: *Property is appraised for taxation. v.,* **ap praised, ap prais ing. —ap prais′ing ly,** *adv.*

ap prais er (ə prā′zər), person authorized to fix the value of property, imported goods, etc. *n.*

ap pre ci a ble (ə prē′shē ə bəl), enough to be felt or estimated; noticeable: *The slight hill made an appreciable difference in the ease of walking. adj.*

ap pre ci a bly (ə prē′shē ə blē), to an appreciable degree; noticeably. *adv.*

ap pre ci ate (ə prē′shē āt), **1** think highly of; recognize the worth or quality of; value; enjoy: *Almost everybody appreciates good food.* **2** be thankful for: *We appreciate your help.* **3** have an opinion of the value, worth, or quality of; estimate: *Most people can appreciate the contributions of medical research to good health.* **4** be fully aware of; recognize: *A musician is able to appreciate small differences in sounds.* **5** rise in value: *This land will appreciate greatly as soon as good roads are built. v.,* **ap pre ci at ed, ap pre ci at ing. —ap pre′ci a′tor,** *n.*

ap pre ci a tion (ə prē′shē ā′shən), **1** a valuing highly; sympathetic understanding: *She has no appreciation of modern art.* **2** an appreciating; valuing: *They showed their appreciation by taking me to dinner.* **3** a rise in value. *n.*

ap pre ci a tive (ə prē′shē ā′tiv *or* ə prē′shə tiv), having or showing appreciation; recognizing the value: *The appreciative audience applauded the performer. adj.* **—ap pre′ci a′tive ly,** *adv.*

ap pre hend (ap′ri hend′), **1** arrest; seize. **2** grasp with

apprehend (def. 1)—The cattle rustler was **apprehended** by the ranchers and sent off to jail.

the mind; understand: *Though I couldn't hear him, I could apprehend his meaning from his gestures. v.* [*Apprehend* is from Latin *apprehendere*, which comes from *ad-*, meaning "upon," and *prehendere*, meaning "seize."] **—ap′pre-hend′er,** *n.*

ap pre hen sion (ap′ri hen′shən), **1** fear; dread: *The roar of the hurricane filled us with apprehension.* **2** a seizing or being seized; arrest: *The appearance of the suspect's picture in all the papers led to her apprehension.* **3** a grasping by the mind; understanding: *I have no apprehension of nuclear physics. n.*

ap pre hen sive (ap′ri hen′siv), feeling alarm; afraid, anxious, or worried: *I felt apprehensive before taking my first airplane trip. adj.* **—ap′pre hen′sive ly,** *adv.* **—ap′pre hen′sive ness,** *n.*

ap pren tice (ə pren′tis), **1** person learning a trade or art. In return for instruction the apprentice agrees to work for the employer a certain length of time with little or no pay. **2** bind or take as an apprentice: *Benjamin Franklin's father apprenticed him to a printer.* **3** beginner; learner. **1,3** *n.,* **2** *v.,* **ap pren ticed, ap pren tic ing.**

ap pren tice ship (ə pren′tis ship), **1** condition of being an apprentice. **2** time during which one is an apprentice. *n.*

ap prise (ə prīz′), give notice to; let know; inform: *Our teacher apprised us that there would be a test on Monday. v.,* **ap prised, ap pris ing.**

ap proach (ə prōch′), **1** come near or nearer to: *Walk softly as you approach the baby's crib. Winter is approaching. The wind was approaching a gale.* **2** act of coming near or nearer: *Sunset announces the approach of night.* **3** way by which a place or person can be reached; access: *The approach to the house was a narrow path. Our best approach to the senator lay through a mutual friend.* **4** method of starting work on a task or problem: *She seems to have a good approach to the problem.* **5** make advances or overtures to: *He approached his boss for a raise.* **1,5** *v.,* **2-4** *n., pl.* **ap proach es. —ap proach′er,** *n.*

ap proach a bil i ty (ə prō′chə bil′ə tē), approachable quality or condition. *n.*

ap proach a ble (ə prō′chə bəl), **1** able to be approached; accessible: *The house on the mountain is approachable only on foot.* **2** easy to approach and talk to; friendly and sociable: *No matter how busy she was, our principal was always approachable. adj.*

ap pro ba tion (ap′rə bā′shən), favorable opinion; approval; praise: *His new play received the approbation of audiences and critics. n.*

ap pro pri ate (ə prō′prē it *for 1;* ə prō′prē āt *for 2,3*), **1** right for the occasion; suitable; proper: *Plain, simple clothes are appropriate for school wear.* **2** set apart for some special use: *The state government appropriated money for a new road into our town.* **3** take for oneself; use as one's own: *You should not appropriate other people's belongings without their permission.* **1** *adj.,* **2,3** *v.,* **ap pro pri at ed, ap pro pri at ing. —ap pro′pri ate ly,** *adv.* **—ap pro′pri ate ness,** *n.* **—ap pro′pri a′tor,** *n.*

ap pro pri a tion (ə prō′prē ā′shən), **1** sum of money or other thing appropriated: *Our town received a state appropriation of five thousand dollars for a new playground.* **2** act of appropriating: *The appropriation of the land made it possible to have a park. n.*

ap prov al (ə prü′vəl), **1** favorable opinion; approving; praise: *We all like others to show approval of what we do.* **2** permission; consent: *I have my parents' approval to go on the trip. n.*

on approval, so that the customer can inspect the item and decide whether to buy or return it: *We bought the television set on approval.*

ap prove (ə prüv′), **1** think or speak well of; be pleased with: *The teacher read my science report and approved it.* **2** give a favorable opinion: *I'm not sure I can approve of what you propose to do.* **3** authorize or make legal; consent to: *The school board approved the budget. v.,* **ap proved, ap prov ing. —ap prov′ing ly,** *adv.*

ap prox i mate (ə prok′sə mit *for 1;* ə prok′sə māt *for 2*), **1** nearly correct: *The approximate length of a meter is 40 inches; the exact length is 39.37 inches.* **2** come near to; approach: *Your account of what happened approximates the truth, but there are several small errors.* **1** *adj.,* **2** *v.,* **ap prox i mat ed, ap prox i mat ing.**

ap prox i mate ly (ə prok′sə mit lē), by a close estimate; nearly; about: *We are approximately 200 miles from home. adv.*

ap prox i ma tion (ə prok′sə mā′shən), **1** a nearly correct amount; close estimate: *25,000 miles is an approximation of the circumference of the earth.* **2** an approximating; approach: *Her story was a close approximation to the truth. n.*

ap pur te nance (ə pėrt′n əns), addition to something more important; accessory. A radio in a car is an appurtenance; an engine is a necessity. *n.*

Apr., April.

a pri cot (ā′prə kot *or* ap′rə kot), **1** the round, pale, orange-colored fruit of a tree grown in mild climates. Apricots have a downy skin somewhat like that of a peach. **2** a pale orange yellow. **3** pale orange-yellow. **1,2** *n.,* **3** *adj.*

A pril (ā′prəl), the fourth month of the year. It has 30 days. *n.*

April fool, person who gets fooled on April Fools' Day.

April Fools' Day, April 1, a day on which tricks and jokes are played on people; All Fools' Day.

a pron (ā′prən), **1** garment worn over the front part of the body to cover or protect clothes: *a kitchen apron, a carpenter's apron.* **2** area in front of an airport terminal or hangar on which to park aircraft. **3** area of a stage in front of the curtain. *n.* **—a′pron like′,** *adj.*

ap ro pos (ap′rə pō′), to the point; fitting; suitable: *Your remark is certainly apropos to what we are discussing. adj.* [*Apropos* comes from the French phrase *à propos,* meaning "to the purpose."]

apropos of, with regard to: *Apropos of the party, what are you going to wear?*

apse (aps), a semicircular or many-sided recess in a church, usually at the east end. The roof of an apse is arched or vaulted. *n.*

apt (apt), **1** fitted by nature; likely: *A careless person is apt to make mistakes.* **2** right for the occasion; suitable; fitting: *His apt reply to the question showed that he had understood it very well.* **3** quick to learn: *Some pupils in our class are more apt than others. adj.* **—apt′ly,** *adv.* **—apt′-ness,** *n.*

apt., apartment. *pl.* **apts.**

ap ti tude (ap′tə tüd *or* ap′tə tyüd), **1** natural tendency or talent; ability; capacity. **2** readiness in learning; quick-

aptitude (def. 1)
Edison had a remarkable **aptitude** for inventing things. He is pictured here with his phonograph.

ness to understand: *She is a pupil of great aptitude. n.*

aq ua (ak′wə), **1** a light bluish green. **2** light bluish-green. **3** water. 1,3 *n.,* 2 *adj.*

Aqua-Lung (ak′wə lung′), trademark for an underwater breathing device used in skin diving; scuba. *n.*

aq ua ma rine (ak′wə mə rēn′), **1** a transparent, bluish-green, semiprecious stone that is a variety of beryl. **2** a light bluish green. **3** light bluish-green. 1,2 *n.,* 3 *adj.*

aq ua naut (ak′wə nôt), an underwater explorer. *n.*

aq ua plane (ak′wə plān′), **1** a wide board on which a person rides as it is towed by a speeding motorboat. **2** ride on an aquaplane. 1 *n.,* 2 *v.,* **aq ua planed, aq ua plan ing. —aq′ua plan′er,** *n.*

a quar i um (ə kwer′ē əm), **1** tank or glass bowl in which living fish or other water animals, and water plants are kept. **2** building used for showing collections of living fish, water animals, and water plants. *n., pl.* **a quar i ums, a quar i a** (ə kwer′ē ə). [*Aquarium* is from Latin *aquarium,* meaning "a watering place (for cattle)," which comes from *aqua,* meaning "water."]

a quat ic (ə kwat′ik *or* ə kwot′ik), **1** growing or living in water: *Water lilies are aquatic plants.* **2** taking place in or on water: *Swimming and sailing are aquatic sports. adj.*

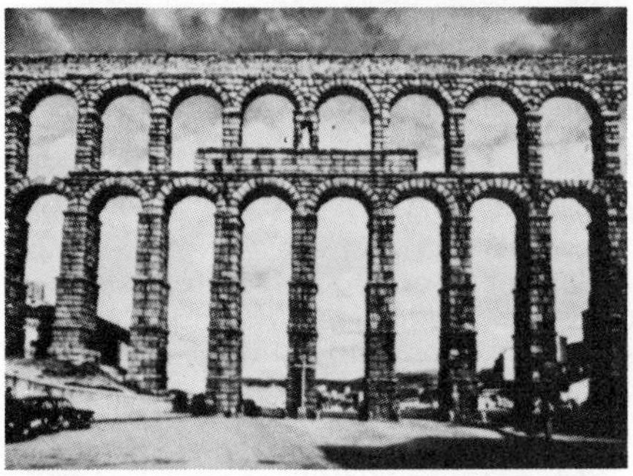

aqueduct (def. 2)

aq ue duct (ak′wə dukt), **1** an artificial channel or large pipe for bringing water from a distance. **2** structure that supports such a channel or pipe. *n.*

a que ous (ā′kwē əs), **1** of or made with water: *The druggist put the medicine in an aqueous solution.* **2** like water; watery: *Aqueous matter ran from the sore. adj.*

aqueous humor, the watery liquid which fills the space in the eye between the cornea and the lens.

aq ui line (ak′wə līn *or* ak′wə lən), curved like an eagle's beak; hooked. *adj.* [See **Word History.**]

A qui nas (ə kwī′nəs), **Saint Thomas,** 1225?-1274, Italian philosopher and Roman Catholic theologian. *n.*

A qui no (ä kē′nō), **Corazón,** born 1933, Philippine political leader, president of the Philippines since 1986. *n.*

Ar, symbol for argon. Also, **A.**

AR, Arkansas (used with postal Zip Code).

ar. or **ar, 1** arrival. **2** arrive.

Ar., 1 Arabic. **2** Aramaic.

Ar ab (ar′əb), **1** person born or living in Arabia. **2** member of a Semitic people now widely scattered over southwestern and southern Asia and northern Africa. **3** of the Arabs or Arabia. 1,2 *n.,* 3 *adj.*

Arab. or **Arab, 1** Arabia. **2** Arabian. **3** Arabic.

ar a besque (ar′ə besk′), **1** an elaborate and fanciful design of flowers, leaves, geometrical figures, etc. **2** carved or painted in arabesque. **3** a ballet pose in which the dancer stands on one leg, with the other at right angles to it, and with the arms held in any of various positions. 1,3 *n.,* 2 *adj.* **—ar′a besque′ly,** *adv.*

a hat	**i** it	**oi** oil	**ch** child	ə = a in about
ā age	**ī** ice	**ou** out	**ng** long	e in taken
ä far	**o** hot	**u** cup	**sh** she	i in pencil
e let	**ō** open	**ů** put	**th** thin	o in lemon
ē equal	**ô** order	**ü** rule	**ᴛʜ** then	u in circus
ėr term			**zh** measure	

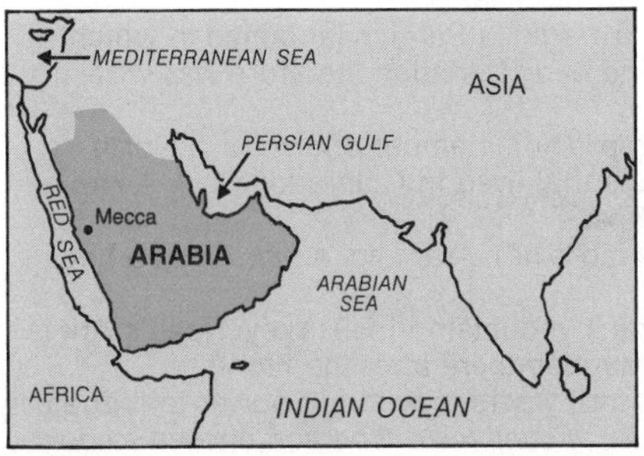

A ra bi a (ə rā′bē ə), large peninsula in SW Asia. *n.*

A ra bi an (ə rā′bē ən), **1** of Arabia or the Arabs. **2** person born or living in Arabia; Arab. 1 *adj.,* 2 *n.*

Arabian camel, dromedary.

Arabian horse, a swift, graceful saddle horse originally developed by the Arabs for use in the deserts.

Arabian Nights, The, collection of old tales from Arabia, Persia, and India, dating from the A.D. 900's. It contains tales of Ali Baba, Aladdin, and many others.

Arabian Sea, part of the Indian Ocean between Arabia and India.

Ar a bic (ar′ə bik), **1** the Semitic language of the Arabs, related to Hebrew. Arabic is spoken chiefly in Arabia, Iraq, Syria, Jordan, Lebanon, and North Africa. **2** of the language of the Arabs. **3** of the Arabs or Arabia; Arabian. 1 *n.,* 2,3 *adj.*

Arabic numerals or **Arabic figures,** the figures 1, 2, 3, 4, 5, 6, 7, 8, 9, 0. They are called Arabic because they were introduced into western Europe by Arabian scholars, but most probably they were derived from India.

ar a ble (ar′ə bəl), fit for plowing: *There is not much arable land on the side of a rocky mountain. adj.*

Ar a by (ar′ə bē), OLD USE. Arabia. *n.*

a rach nid (ə rak′nid), any of a large group of animals that includes spiders, scorpions, mites, ticks, and daddy-

WORD HISTORY

aquiline

Aquiline is from Latin *aquilinus,* meaning "of or like an eagle," which comes from *aquila,* meaning "eagle." *Aquiline* first came into English in reference to a nose which was hooked or curved like an eagle's beak.

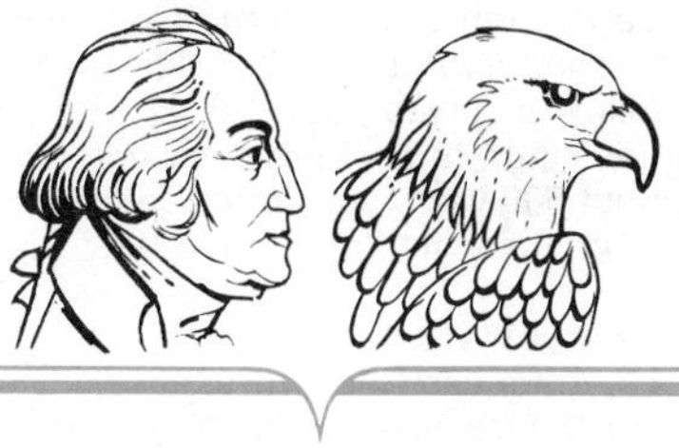

longlegs. Though they resemble insects, arachnids differ in having four pairs of legs, no wings, and a body usually divided into only two parts. *n.*

Ar a gon (ar′ə gon), region in NE Spain, formerly a kingdom. See **Castile** for map. *n.*

Ar al Sea (ar′əl), inland sea in the SW Soviet Union, east of the Caspian Sea. See **Assyria** for map.

Aram. or **Aram,** Aramaic.

Ar a ma ic (ar′ə mā′ik), a Semitic language in which much Jewish and early Christian literature was written. *n.*

Ar ap a ho (ə rap′ə hō), member of a tribe of North American Indians that lived in Colorado. *n., pl.* **A rap a- ho** or **A rap a hos.**

A rap a hoe (ə rap′ə hō), Arapaho. *n., pl.* **A rap a hoes** or **A rap a hoe.**

Ar a rat (ar′ə rat′), mountain in E Turkey. Noah's Ark is said to have grounded there after the Flood. *n.*

ar bi ter (är′bə tər), **1** person with full power to judge or decide: *an arbiter of good taste.* **2** person chosen to decide or settle a dispute; arbitrator. *n.*

ar bi trar i ly (är′bə trer′ə lē), in an arbitrary manner; at will. *adv.*

ar bi trar y (är′bə trer′ē), **1** based on one's own wishes, notions, or will; not going by any rule or law: *The judge tried to be fair and avoided arbitrary decisions.* **2** fixed or determined by chance: *an arbitrary choice.* **3** using or abusing unlimited power; tyrannical: *an arbitrary king.* *adj.* —**ar′bi trar′i ness,** *n.*

ar bi trate (är′bə trāt), **1** give a decision in a dispute; act as arbitrator; mediate: *The teacher arbitrated between the two girls in their quarrel.* **2** settle by arbitration; submit to arbitration: *The two nations finally agreed to arbitrate their dispute and war was avoided.* *v.,* **ar bi trat ed, ar bi trat- ing.**

ar bi tra tion (är′bə trā′shən), settlement of a dispute by the decision of a judge, umpire, or committee. *n.*

ar bi tra tor (är′bə trā′tər), **1** person chosen to decide or settle a dispute. **2** person with full power to judge or decide; arbiter. *n.*

ar bor (är′bər), a shaded place formed by trees or shrubs or by vines growing on a lattice. *n.*

Arbor Day, day set aside in many states of the United States for planting trees. The date varies in different states.

ar bo re al (är bôr′ē əl), **1** living in or among trees. A squirrel is an arboreal animal. **2** of trees; like trees. *adj.* —**ar bo′re al ly,** *adv.*

ar bo re tum (är′bə rē′təm), place where trees and shrubs are grown and exhibited for scientific and educational purposes. *n., pl.* **ar bo re tums, ar bo re ta** (är′bə- rē′tə).

ar bor vi tae (är′bər vī′tē), an evergreen tree often planted for ornament and for hedges. *n.*

ar bu tus (är byü′təs), a trailing plant of eastern North America that has clusters of fragrant, pink or white flowers that bloom very early in the spring; mayflower. *n., pl.* **ar bu tus es.**

arc (ärk), **1** any part of the circumference of a circle. **2** any part of any curved line. **3** a curved stream of brilliant light or sparks formed as a strong electric current jumps from one conductor to another. **4** form an electric arc. **5** take or follow a curved path. 1-3 *n.,* 4,5 *v.,* **arced** (ärkt), **arc ing** (är′king), or **arcked, arck ing.** [*Arc* came into English about 600 years ago from French *arc,* which is from Latin *arcus,* meaning "an arch, a bow, an arc."] —**arc′like′,** *adj.*

Arc (ärk). See **Joan of Arc.** *n.*

ARC or **A.R.C.,** American Red Cross.

ar cade (är kād′), **1** passageway with an arched roof.

2 any covered passageway: *This building has an arcade with small stores along either side.* **3** row of arches supported by columns. **4** a store in which customers pay to play games, especially video games. *n.*

Ar ca di a (är kā′dē ə), **1** mountainous district in the S part of ancient Greece. It was famous for the simple, contented life of its people. **2** Also, **arcadia.** any region of simple, quiet contentment. *n.* —**Ar ca′di an,** *adj., n.*

arch¹ (def. 1)

arch¹ (ärch), **1** a curved structure capable of bearing the weight of the material above it. Arches often form the tops of doors, windows, and gateways. **2** monument in the form of an arch or arches. **3** bend into an arch; curve: *The wind had arched the trees over the road.* **4** form an arch over; span: *A bridge arched the stream.* **5** archway. **6** the lower part of the foot which makes a curve between the heel and the toes: *Fallen arches cause flat feet.* 1,2,5,6 *n., pl.* **arch es;** 3,4 *v.* [*Arch*¹ came into English about 600 years ago from French *arche,* which is from Latin *arcus,* meaning "an arch, a bow."] —**arch′like′,** *adj.*

arch² (ärch), **1** playfully mischievous: *The little girl gave her mother an arch look and ran away.* **2** chief; principal; leading: *He was the arch rebel of them all. adj.* [*Arch*² can be traced back to Greek *archein,* meaning "to be first, to lead."] —**arch′ly,** *adv.* —**arch′ness,** *n.*

arch., **1** archipelago. **2** architecture.

ar chae o log i cal (är′kē ə loj′ə kəl), of or having to do with archaeology: *An archaeological expedition uncovered the lost city of Troy. adj.* Also, **archeological.**

ar chae ol o gist (är′kē ol′ə jist), an expert in archaeology. *n.* Also, **archeologist.**

ar chae ol o gy (är′kē ol′ə jē), the scientific study of the people, customs, and life of ancient times. Archaeologists study buildings, tools, pottery, weapons, and other objects in order to find out how people lived in the past when there were few or no written records. *n.* Also, **archeology.**

arc (def. 1)
arcs of circles

ar cha ic (är kā′ik), **1** no longer in general use. The words *forsooth* and *methinks* are archaic. **2** of an earlier time; out-of-date or ancient. *adj.* —**ar cha′i cal ly,** *adv.*

ar cha ism (är′kē iz′əm), word or expression no longer in general use. *n.*

arch an gel (ärk/ān/jəl), angel of high rank. *n.*

Arch an gel (ärk/ān/jəl), seaport in NW Soviet Union, on the White Sea. *n.*

arch bish op (ärch/bish/əp), bishop having the highest rank. *n.*

arch di o cese (ärch/dī/ə sis *or* ärch/dī/ə sēs/), a church district governed by an archbishop. *n.*

arch duch ess (ärch/duch/is), **1** wife or widow of an archduke. **2** princess of the former ruling house of Austria-Hungary. *n., pl.* **arch duch ess es.**

arch duke (ärch/dük/ *or* ärch/dyük/), prince of the former ruling house of Austria-Hungary. *n.*

arched (ärcht), having an arch or arches. *adj.*

arch en e my (ärch/en/ə mē), a principal enemy. *n., pl.* **arch en e mies.**

ar che o log i cal (är/kē ə loj/ə kəl), archaeological. *adj.* —**ar/che o log/i cal ly,** *adv.*

ar che ol o gist (är/kē ol/ə jist), archaeologist. *n.*

ar che ol o gy (är/kē ol/ə jē), archaeology. *n.*

arch er (är/chər), person who shoots with a bow and arrow; bowman. *n.*

arch er y (är/chər ē), **1** practice or sport of shooting with a bow and arrow. **2** archers: *The archery advanced, shooting steadily. n.*

Ar chi me des (är/kə mē/dēz), 287?-212 B.C., Greek mathematician, physicist, and inventor. He discovered the principles of specific gravity and of the lever. *n.*

ar chi pel a go (är/kə pel/ə gō *or* är/chə pel/ə gō), **1** group of many islands. The islands between southeast Asia and Australia form the Malay Archipelago. **2** sea having many islands in it. *n., pl.* **ar chi pel a gos** *or* **ar chi pel a goes.**

archit., architecture.

ar chi tect (är/kə tekt), **1** person who designs and makes plans for buildings and sees that these plans are followed by the people who actually put up the buildings. **2** maker; creator: *The architects of the United Nations hoped to bring about lasting world peace. n.* [*Architect* came into English about 400 years ago from French *architecte,* and can be traced back to Greek *archi-,* meaning "chief," and *tektōn,* meaning "builder."]

ar chi tec tur al (är/kə tek/chər əl), of architecture. *adj.* —**ar/chi tec/tur al ly,** *adv.*

ar chi tec ture (är/kə tek/chər), **1** science or art of planning and designing buildings. **2** style or special manner of building: *Greek architecture made much use of columns.* **3** construction: *the massive architecture of the Pyramids. n.*

ar chi trave (är/kə trāv), the main beam resting on the top of a column or row of columns. *n.*

ar chives (är/kīvz), **1** place where public records or historical documents are kept. **2** the public records or historical documents kept in such a place. *n.pl.*

arch way (ärch/wā/), **1** entrance or passageway with an arch above it. **2** arch covering a passageway. *n.*

arc tic (ärk/tik *or* är/tik), **1** at or near the North Pole; of the north polar region: *They explored the great arctic wilderness of northern Canada.* **2 the Arctic,** the north polar region. The Arctic has an extremely cold winter. **3** extremely cold; frigid. **4 arctics,** *pl.* warm, waterproof overshoes. **1,3** *adj.,* **2,4** *n.* —**arc/ti cal ly,** *adv.*

arctic circle *or* **Arctic Circle,** the imaginary boundary of the north polar region. It runs parallel to the equator at 66 degrees 30 minutes (66°30/) north latitude.

Arctic Ocean, ocean of the north polar region.

Arctic Zone, region between the arctic circle and the North Pole.

ar dent (ärd/nt), full of enthusiasm; eager: *an ardent believer in the benefits of health foods. adj.* —**ar/dent ly,** *adv.*

ar dor (är/dər), great enthusiasm; eagerness; zeal: *The*

a hat	i it	oi oil	ch child	(a in about
ā age	ī ice	ou out	ng long	e in taken
ä far	o hot	u cup	sh she	ə = { i in pencil
e let	ō open	u̇ put	th thin	o in lemon
ē equal	ô order	ü rule	ŦH then	u in circus
ėr term			zh measure	

senator spoke with ardor about the need for gun control. n.

ar du ous (är/jü əs), **1** hard to do; requiring much effort; difficult: *an arduous lesson.* **2** using up much energy; strenuous: *She enjoys an arduous workout in the gym. adj.* —**ar/du ous ly,** *adv.* —**ar/du ous ness,** *n.*

are (är; *unstressed* ər), form of the verb **be** used with *we, you,* and *they* and any plural noun to indicate the present tense. *We are ready. You are next. They are waiting. v.*

ar e a (er/ē ə *or* ar/ē ə), **1** amount of surface; extent of surface: *The area of this floor is 600 square feet.* **2** range of knowledge or interest; sphere of activity; field: *I took many courses in the areas of physics, chemistry, and related sciences.* **3** region or district: *The Rocky Mountain area is very mountainous.* **4** a level, open space: *a playground area. n., pl.* **ar e as.**

area code, combination of three numerals used to dial directly by telephone from one region of the United States and Canada to another.

ar e a way (er/ē ə wā/ *or* ar/ē ə wā/), **1** a sunken area or court at the entrance to a cellar or basement. **2** area used as a passageway between buildings. *n.*

a re na (ə rē/nə), **1** space in an ancient Roman amphitheater in which contests or shows took place: *Gladiators fought with lions in the arena at Rome.* **2** a similar space, surrounded by seats, used today for contests or shows: *a boxing arena.* **3** building in which indoor sports are played. **4** any place of conflict and trial: *The United Nations is an arena for world debate.* **5** field of endeavor: *the political arena. n., pl.* **a re nas.**

aren't (ärnt), **1** are not. **2** am not. In this meaning, *aren't* is used only in questions. *Why aren't I allowed to stay?*

Ar es (er/ēz *or* ar/ēz), (in Greek myths) the god of war. The Romans called him Mars. *n.*

ar gent (är/jənt), silvery. *adj.*

Ar gen ti na (är/jən tē/nə), country in S South America. *Capital:* Buenos Aires. *n.* —**Ar gen tin e an** *or* **Ar gen tin i an** (är/jən tin/ē ən), *adj., n.*

Ar gen tine (är/jən tēn/ *or* är/jən tīn), **1** of Argentina or its people. **2** person born or living in Argentina. **1** *adj.,* **2** *n.*

ar gon (är/gon), a colorless, odorless, element which is a gas that forms a very small part of the air. Argon is used in electric light bulbs and radio tubes. *n.*

Ar go naut (är/gə nôt), (in Greek legends) any of the men who sailed with Jason in search of the Golden Fleece. *n.*

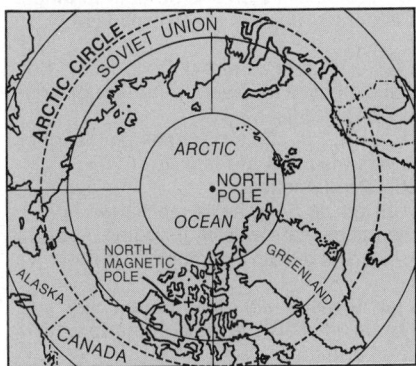

ar go sy (är′gə sē), OLD USE. **1** a large merchant ship. **2** fleet of such ships. *n., pl.* **ar go sies.**

ar gue (är′gyü), **1** discuss with someone who disagrees: *He argued with his sister about who should wash the dishes.* **2** give reasons for or against something: *One side argued for building a new school and the other side argued against it.* **3** persuade by giving reasons: *They argued me into going along on the trip.* **4** try to prove by reasoning; maintain: *Scientists argue that the oceans are endangered by pollution.* *v.,* **ar gued, ar gu ing.** —**ar′gu a ble,** *adj.* —**ar′gu a bly,** *adv.*

ar gu er (är′gyü ər), person who argues. *n.*

ar gu ment (är′gyə mənt), **1** discussion by persons who disagree; dispute: *She won the argument by producing facts to prove her point.* **2** reason or reasons offered for or against something: *His arguments in favor of a new school building are very convincing.* *n.*

ar gu men ta tive (är′gyə men′tə tiv), fond of arguing; quarrelsome: *an argumentative disposition.* *adj.* —**ar′gu men′ta tive ly,** *adv.* —**ar′gu men′ta tive ness,** *n.*

Ar gus (är′gəs), (in Greek myths) a giant with a hundred eyes. *n.*

a ri a (är′ē ə, er′ē ə, *or* ar′ē ə), song for a single voice, with accompaniment, in an opera, oratorio, or cantata. *n., pl.* **a ri as.**

Ar i ad ne (ar′ē ad′nē), (in Greek legends) the daughter of Minos, king of Crete. She fell in love with Theseus and helped him escape from Crete after he killed the Minotaur. *n.*

ar id (ar′id), **1** having very little rainfall; dry and barren: *Desert lands are arid.* **2** uninteresting and empty; dull: *an arid, boring speech.* *adj.* —**ar′id ly,** *adv.* —**ar′id ness,** *n.*

a rid i ty (ə rid′ə tē), **1** arid condition. **2** dullness. *n.*

a right (ə rīt′), correctly; rightly: *If I heard you aright, you said you would go.* *adv.*

a rise (ə rīz′), **1** rise up; get up: *They arose to greet us when we came in.* **2** move upward; ascend: *Smoke arises from the chimney.* **3** come into being; come about: *A great wind arose. Accidents often arise from carelessness.* *v.,* **a rose, a ris en, a ris ing.**

a ris en (ə riz′n), past participle of **arise.** *He awoke to find that a storm had arisen.* *v.*

ar is toc ra cy (ar′ə stok′rə sē), **1** class of people having a high position in society because of birth, rank, or title; nobility. Earls, duchesses, and princes belong to the aristocracy. **2** class of people considered superior because of intelligence, culture, or wealth; upper class. **3** government in which the nobility or any privileged upper class rules. *n., pl.* **ar is toc ra cies.**

a ris to crat (ə ris′tə krat), **1** person who belongs to the aristocracy; noble. **2** person like an aristocrat in tastes, opinions, and manners. *n.*

a ris to crat ic (ə ris′tə krat′ik), **1** belonging to the upper classes; considered superior because of birth, intelligence, culture, or wealth. **2** like an aristocrat in manners; proud. **3** of an aristocracy. *adj.* —**a ris′to crat′i cal ly,** *adv.*

Ar is to te li an (ar′ə stə tē′lē ən *or* ə ris′tə tē′lyən), **1** of Aristotle or his philosophy. **2** follower or student of Aristotle or his philosophy. **1** *adj.,* **2** *n.*

Ar is tot le (ar′ə stot′l), 384-322 B.C., Greek philosopher and scientist. He was the pupil of Plato. *n.*

arith., **1** arithmetic. **2** arithmetical.

a rith me tic (ə rith′mə tik *for 1;* ar′ith met′ik *for 2),* **1** branch of mathematics that deals with adding, subtracting, multiplying, and dividing numbers. **2** arithmetical. **1** *n.,* **2** *adj.*

ar ith met i cal (ar′ith met′ə kəl), of arithmetic. *adj.*

ar ith met i cal ly (ar′ith met′ik lē), according to arithmetic; by the use of arithmetic. *adv.*

arithmetical progression, series of numbers in which there is always the same difference between a number and the one next after it. 2, 4, 6, 8, 10 form an arithmetical progression; so do 8, 5, 2, −1.

a rith me ti cian (ə rith′mə tish′ən), an expert in arithmetic. *n.*

ar ith met ic mean (ar′ith met′ik), an average.

Ariz., Arizona.

Ar i zo na (ar′ə zō′nə), one of the southwestern states of the United States. *Abbreviation:* Ariz. or AZ *Capital:* Phoenix. *n.* —**Ar′i zo′nan, Ar′i zo′ni an,** *adj., n.*

ark (ärk), **1** (in the Bible) the large boat in which Noah saved himself, his family, and a pair of each kind of animal from the Flood. **2** the chest or box in which the Hebrews kept the two stone tablets containing the Ten Commandments. **3** a cabinet in a synagogue for housing scrolls of the Torah. *n.* [*Ark* is from Old English *earc,* which came from Latin *arca,* meaning "chest, box."] —**ark′like′,** *adj.*

Ark., Arkansas.

Ar kan sas (är′kən sô *for 1;* är′kən sô *or* är kan′zəs *for 2),* **1** one of the south central states of the United States. *Abbreviation:* Ark. or AR *Capital:* Little Rock. **2** river flowing from central Colorado southeast into the Mississippi. *n.* —**Ar kan san** (är kan′zən), *adj., n.*

Ar ling ton (är′ling tən), the largest national cemetery in the United States, in NE Virginia, across the Potomac from Washington, D.C. *n.*

arm¹ (ärm), **1** the part of a person's body between the shoulder and the hand. **2** forelimb of an animal. The front legs of a bear are sometimes called arms. **3** something shaped or used like an arm: *the arm of a chair, an arm of the sea.* **4** a division or branch: *The National Park Service is an arm of the United States government.* **5** power; authority: *The strong arm of the law keeps order in the city.* *n.* [*Arm¹* comes from Old English *earm.*] —**arm′less,** *adj.* —**arm′like′,** *adj.*

arm in arm, with arms linked: *She walked arm in arm with her sister.*

with open arms, in a warm, friendly way; cordially: *Her friends welcomed her with open arms.*

arm² (ärm), **1** **arms,** *pl.* weapons of any kind. Guns, swords, axes, or sticks might be arms for defense or attack. **2** supply with weapons: *During the American Revolutionary War the French helped arm the colonists.* **3** supply with any means of defense or attack: *The lawyer entered court armed with the evidence he planned to use to support his case.* **4** take up weapons; prepare for war: *The soldiers armed for battle.* **5** a combat branch of one of the armed forces, such as the infantry or artillery. **1,5** *n.,* **2-4** *v.* [*Arm²* came into English over 750 years ago from French *armer,* meaning "to arm," and can be traced back to Latin *arma,* meaning "weapons."] —**arm′er,** *n.* —**arm′less,** *adj.*

ar ma da (är mä′də), **1** a large fleet of warships. **2** the Armada, the Spanish fleet sent to attack England in 1588. It was defeated in the English Channel. **3** any large group of military vehicles. *n., pl.* **ar ma das.**

ar ma dil lo (är′mə dil′ō), a small, burrowing mammal with a protective shell of bony plates. Armadillos are

armadillo
about 2¹/₂ ft. (75 cm.) long, including tail

found in South America and southern North America. *n.,
pl.* **ar ma dil los.**

ar ma ment (är′mə mənt), **1** the weapons, ammunition,
and equipment used by the military; war equipment and
supplies. **2** the military forces of a country, including
both equipment and people. **3** act or process of arm-
ing. *n.*

ar ma ture (är′mə chər), **1** a revolving part of an electric
motor or dynamo, consisting of wire wound around an
iron core placed between opposite poles of a magnet.
2 armor. *n.*

arm band (ärm′band′), band of cloth worn around the
upper arm as a symbol or badge: *a mourning armband of
black. n.*

arm chair (ärm′cher′ *or* ärm′char′), chair with sidepieces to support a person's arms or elbows. *n.*

armed forces, all the military, naval, and air forces of
a country.

Ar me ni a (är mē′nē ə), **1** former country of SW Asia,
now divided among Turkey, Iran, and the Soviet Union.
See **Persia** for map. *n.* —**Ar me′ni an,** *adj., n.*

arm ful (ärm′fúl), as much as one arm or both arms can
hold: *an armful of groceries. n., pl.* **arm fuls.**

arm hole (ärm′hōl′), hole for the arm or sleeve in a
garment. *n.*

ar mi stice (är′mə stis), a stop in fighting; temporary
peace; truce. *n.* [*Armistice* can be traced back to Latin
arma, meaning "arms, weapons," and *sistere,* meaning
"to stop, to stand."]

Armistice Day, November 11, the anniversary of the
end of World War I, in 1918. As an official holiday it is
now called Veterans Day.

armor (def. 1)
of the 1400's.
A helmet completely
covers and protects
the head; chain mail
protects the upper
chest and inner
arms; metal plates
cover legs, hands,
and outside of the
arms.

Courtesy of The Metropolitan Museum of Art

ar mor (är′mər), **1** a covering, usually of metal or leather, worn to protect the body in fighting. **2** any kind of
protective covering. The steel plates of a warship and
the scales of a fish are armor. **3** the armored forces and
equipment, such as the tanks, of a military unit. *n.*
—**ar′mor like′,** *adj.*

ar mored (är′mərd), **1** covered or protected with armor:
an armored car. **2** using or equipped with armored vehicles: *He served in an armored division. adj.*

ar mor er (är′mər ər), **1** (in former times) a person who
made or repaired armor. **2** person in the armed forces
who takes care of revolvers, pistols, rifles, and other
firearms. *n.*

armor plate, steel or iron plating to protect warships,
tanks, forts, etc. Armor plate is now usually a specially
toughened alloy of steel.

ar mor y (är′mər ē), **1** place where weapons are kept or
manufactured; arsenal. **2** a building with a drill hall, offices, etc., for militia. *n., pl.* **ar mor ies.**

a hat	**i** it	**oi** oil	**ch** child	⎧ a in about
ā age	**ī** ice	**ou** out	**ng** long	⎪ e in taken
ä far	**o** hot	**u** cup	**sh** she	ə = ⎨ i in pencil
e let	**ō** open	**ú** put	**th** thin	⎪ o in lemon
ē equal	**ô** order	**ü** rule	**ᴛʜ** then	⎩ u in circus
ėr term			**zh** measure	

ar mour (är′mər), BRITISH. armor. *n.*

arm pit (ärm′pit′), the hollow place under the arm at
the shoulder. *n.*

arms (ärmz), **1** See **arm²** (def. 1). **2** fighting; war: *The
colonists were quick to answer the call to arms.* **3** symbols
and designs used in heraldry; coat of arms. *n.pl.*

bear arms, serve as a soldier; fight: *The soldier bore
arms for his country.*

take up arms, arm for attack or defense: *take up arms
against an enemy.*

up in arms, very angry; in rebellion: *The students were up
in arms when their after-school activities were canceled.*

Arm strong (ärm′strông′), Neil A., born 1930, American astronaut. He was the first human being to walk on
and explore the surface of the moon, on July 20, 1969. *n.*

ar my (är′mē), **1** a large, organized group of soldiers
trained and armed for war. **2** Often, **Army.** the military
land forces of a nation, in some countries including also
the air forces. **3** military unit made up of two or more
corps plus supporting troops, commanded by a general.
It is the largest tactical military unit. **4** any group of
people organized for a purpose: *an army of research
scientists, the Salvation Army.* **5** a very large number; multitude: *an army of ants. n., pl.* **ar mies.**

ar ni ca (är′nə kə), **1** a healing liquid formerly used on
bruises and sprains, prepared from a plant related to the
aster. **2** the plant itself, which has showy, yellow flowers.
n., pl. **ar ni cas** for 2.

Ar nold (är′nld), **Benedict,** 1741-1801, American general in the Revolutionary War who became a traitor. *n.*

a ro ma (ə rō′mə), spicy odor; fragrance: *Just smell the
aroma of the cake baking in the oven. n., pl.* **a ro mas.**

ar o mat ic (ar′ə mat′ik), spicy; fragrant: *The cinnamon
tree has an aromatic inner bark. adj.* —**ar′o mat′i cal ly,**
adv.

a rose (ə rōz′), past tense of **arise.** *She arose from her
chair. v.*

a round (ə round′), **1** in a circle about: *She has traveled
around the world.* **2** in a circle: *The top spun around.* **3** in
circumference: *The tree measures four feet around.* **4** on all
sides of: *Woods lay around the house.* **5** on all sides; in
every direction: *A dense fog lay around.* **6** on the far side
of; so as to round: *The store is just around the corner. I
drove too fast around the curve.* **7** here and there; about:
We walked around to see the town (adv.). *She leaves her
books around the house* (prep.). **8** INFORMAL. somewhere
about; near: *I waited around for an hour* (adv.). *Stay
around the house* (prep.). **9** INFORMAL. near in amount,
number, or time to; approximately; about: *That blouse
cost around ten dollars. I'll be home around six o'clock.*
10 in the opposite direction: *Turn around! You are going
the wrong way.* **11** from one to another: *If you pass the
class roll around, everyone can sign it.* **12** through a round
of time: *Summer will soon come around again.* 1,4,6-9
prep., 2,3,5,7,8,10-12 *adv.*

a rous al (ə rou′zəl), an arousing or a being aroused. *n.*

a rouse (ə rouz′), **1** stir to action; excite: *The mystery
story aroused my imagination.* **2** awaken: *The barking dog
aroused me from my sleep. v.,* **a roused, a rous ing.**
—**a rous′a ble,** *adj.* —**a rous′er,** *n.*

ar que bus (är′kwə bəs), harquebus. *n., pl.* **ar que-
bus es.**

ar raign (ə rān´), **1** bring before a court of law to answer a charge: *The cashier was arraigned on a charge of theft.* **2** find fault with; accuse. *v.* —**ar raign´er**, *n.*

ar raign ment (ə rān´mənt), a bringing before a court of law to answer a charge: *the arraignment of the suspects. n.*

ar range (ə rānj´), **1** put in the proper order: *Please arrange the books on the library shelf. I arranged my time so that I could work at my hobbies.* **2** form plans; prepare beforehand: *Can you arrange to meet me this evening?* **3** reach an understanding about; settle (a dispute): *The two neighbors have now arranged their differences.* **4** adapt (a piece of music) to voices or instruments for which it was not written: *This music for the violin is also arranged for the piano. v.,* **ar ranged, ar rang ing.** —**ar range´a ble,** *adj.*

ar range ment (ə rānj´mənt), **1** a putting or a being put in proper order: *Careful arrangement of books in a library makes them easier to find.* **2** way or order in which things or persons are put: *You can make six arrangements of the letters A, B, and C.* **3** something arranged in a particular way: *a beautiful flower arrangement.* **4** adjustment, settlement, or agreement: *No arrangement of the dispute could possibly please everybody.* **5 arrangements,** *pl.* plans; preparations: *All arrangements have been made for our trip to Chicago.* **6** adaptation of a piece of music to voices or instruments for which it was not written. *n.*

ar rang er (ə rān´jər), person who arranges. *n.*

ar rant (ar´ənt), thoroughgoing; downright: *Nobody will believe such an arrant liar. adj.* —**ar´rant ly,** *adv.*

ar ray (ə rā´), **1** proper order; regular arrangement: *The troops marched in battle array.* **2** put in order for some purpose: *The general arrayed his troops for the battle.* **3** display of persons or things: *The team had an impressive array of fine players.* **4** clothes, especially for some special occasion: *bridal array.* **5** dress in fine clothes; adorn: *He was arrayed in medieval costume for his role as King Richard the Lion-Hearted.* **6** (in mathematics) an orderly arrangement of objects or symbols in rows and columns. **1,3,4,6** *n.,* **2,5** *v.* —**ar ray´er,** *n.*

ar rears (ə rirz´), **1** money due but not paid; debts. **2** unfinished work; things not done on time. *n.pl.*

in arrears, behind in payments, work, etc.: *She is in arrears with her car payments.*

ar rest (ə rest´), **1** seize by authority of the law; take to jail or court: *A policeman arrested the woman for shoplifting.* **2** a seizing of a person by authority of the law; a taking to jail or court: *We saw the arrest of the burglary suspect.* **3** stop; check: *Filling a tooth arrests decay.* **4** a stopping; checking: *Machines can now take over after an arrest of the heart's function during an operation.* **5** catch and hold: *Our attention was arrested by the unusual sound.* **1,3,5** *v.,* **2,4** *n.* —**ar rest´a ble,** *adj.* —**ar rest´er,** *n.* —**ar rest´ment,** *n.*

under arrest, held by the police: *He was under arrest on suspicion of stealing.*

ar rest ing (ə res´ting), that catches and holds the attention; striking. *adj.* —**ar rest´ing ly,** *adv.*

ar riv al (ə rī´vəl), **1** an arriving: *She is waiting for the arrival of the plane.* **2** person or thing that arrives: *We greeted the new arrivals at the door. n.*

ar rive (ə rīv´), **1** reach the end of a journey; come to a place: *We arrived in Boston a week ago.* **2** come; occur: *Summer vacation finally arrived. v.,* **ar rived, ar riv ing.** —**ar riv´er,** *n.*

arrive at, come to; reach: *You should arrive at school before nine o'clock. We must arrive at a decision soon.*

ar ro gance (ar´ə gəns), a too great pride with contempt of others; haughtiness: *He was a talented actor, but his arrogance made him unpopular. n.*

ar ro gant (ar´ə gənt), too proud and contemptuous of others; haughty. *adj.* —**ar´ro gant ly,** *adv.*

ar row (ar´ō), **1** a slender, pointed shaft or stick which is shot from a bow. **2** anything like an arrow in shape or speed. **3** a sign (→) used to show direction or position in maps, on road signs, and in writing. *n.*

ar row head (ar´ō hed´), head or tip of an arrow. An arrowhead is usually shaped like a wedge and made of harder material than the shaft. *n.*

ar row root (ar´ō rüt´ *or* ar´ō rút´), an easily digested starch made from the roots of a tropical American plant. *n.*

ar roy o (ə roi´ō), in southwestern United States: **1** the dry bed of a stream; gully. **2** a small river. *n., pl.* **ar roy os.** [*Arroyo* was borrowed from Spanish *arroyo.*]

ar se nal (är´sə nəl), **1** a building for storing or manufacturing military weapons and ammunition. **2** storehouse. *n.*

ar se nic (är´sə nik), **1** a very brittle element which has the properties of both a metal and a nonmetal and occurs chiefly in combination with other elements. It forms poisonous compounds with oxygen and is used to make insecticides, weed killers, certain medicines, etc. **2** a very strong, tasteless poison that is a compound of this element. *n.*

ar son (är´sən), the crime of intentionally setting fire to a building or other property. *n.*

art[1] (ärt), **1** a branch or division of learning. History is usually considered one of the arts; chemistry is one of the sciences. **2** a branch of learning that depends more on special practice than on general principles. Writing compositions is an art; grammar is a science. The fine arts include painting, drawing, sculpture, architecture, music, and dancing. **3** painting, drawing, and sculpture: *I am studying both art and music.* **4** paintings, sculptures, and other works of art: *We went to an exhibit at the museum of art.* **5** working principles; methods: *She understands the art of making friends.* **6** some kind of skill or practical application of skill. Cooking, sewing, and housekeeping are household arts. **7** human skill or effort: *This well-kept garden owes more to art than to nature.* **8** skillful act; cunning; trick: *The magician's arts deceived the audience. n.*

art[2] (ärt), OLD USE. are. "Thou art" means "You are." *v.*

Ar te mis (är´tə mis), (in Greek myths) the goddess of the hunt and of the moon. She was the twin sister of Apollo and was called Diana by the Romans. *n.*

ar ter i al (är tir´ē əl), **1** of or in an artery or the arteries: *hardening of the arterial walls, arterial blood.* **2** serving as a major route of transportation, supply, or access: *an arterial highway. adj.* —**ar ter´i al ly,** *adv.*

ar ter i o scle ro sis (är tir´ē ō sklə rō´sis), an abnormal thickening and hardening of the walls of the arteries, causing a decrease or loss of circulation. Arteriosclerosis occurs chiefly in old age. *n.*

ar ter y (är´tər ē), **1** any of the tubes that carry blood from the heart to all parts of the body. **2** a main road; important channel: *Main Street and Broadway are the two arteries of traffic in our city. n., pl.* **ar ter ies.**

ar te sian well (är tē´zhən), a deep, drilled well, especially one from which water gushes up without pumping. *n.*

art ful (ärt´fəl), **1** slyly clever; crafty; deceitful: *A swindler uses artful tricks to get people's money away from them.* **2** skillful; clever: *The teacher's artful handling of the situation won the approval of the class. adj.* —**art´ful ly,** *adv.* —**art´ful ness,** *n.*

ar thrit ic (är thrit´ik), **1** of arthritis. **2** caused by arthritis. *adj.*

ar thri tis (är thrī´tis), inflammation of a joint or joints of the body. Gout is one kind of arthritis. *n.*

a hat	i it	oi oil	ch child	⎧ a in about
ā age	ī ice	ou out	ng long	e in taken
ä far	o hot	u cup	sh she	ə = ⎨ i in pencil
e let	ō open	u̇ put	th thin	o in lemon
ē equal	ô order	ü rule	ᵺ then	⎩ u in circus
ėr term			zh measure	

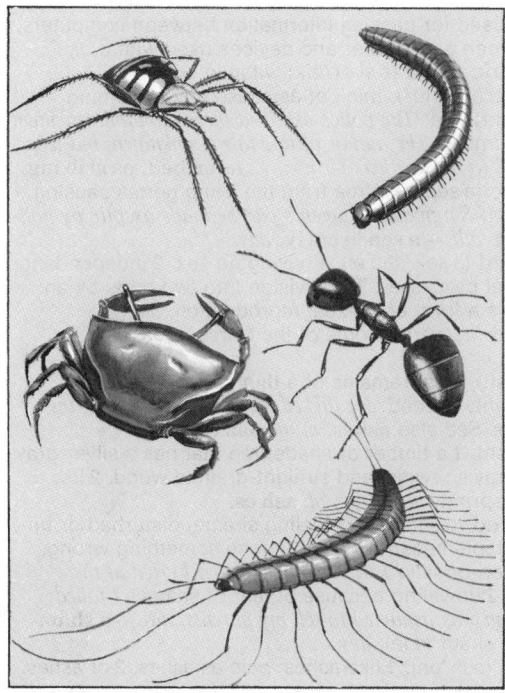

arthropods

ar thro pod (är′thrə pod), any animal without a backbone having a jointed body and jointed legs. Insects, spiders, and lobsters are three kinds of arthropods. *n.* [*Arthropod* can be traced back to Greek *arthron,* meaning "joint," and *podos,* meaning "foot."]

Ar thur (är′thər), **1** (in medieval legends) king of ancient Britain who gathered about him the knights of the Round Table. The real Arthur was probably a British chieftain about A.D. 500. **2 Chester A.,** 1830-1886, the 21st president of the United States, from 1881 to 1885. *n.*

ar ti choke (är′tə chōk), the flower bud of a thistlelike plant with large prickly leaves. Artichokes are cooked and eaten as a vegetable. *n.*

artichoke
left, mature
thistlelike flower;
right, bud

ar ti cle (är′tə kəl), **1** a written composition on a special subject, complete in itself, but forming part of a magazine, newspaper, or book: *This newspaper has a good article on gardening.* **2** a clause in a contract, treaty, statute, etc.: *When the Constitution of the United States was adopted it had seven articles.* **3** a particular thing; item: *Bread is an important article of food.* **4** one of the words *a, an,* or *the,* as in *a book, an egg, the boy. A* and *an* are indefinite articles; *the* is the definite article. *n.*

Articles of Confederation, the constitution adopted by the thirteen original states of the United States in 1781, replaced by the present Constitution in 1789.

ar tic u late (är tik′yə lit *for 1,3,4;* är tik′yə lāt *for 2,5*), **1** spoken in distinct syllables or words: *A baby cries and gurgles, but does not use articulate sounds.* **2** speak distinctly; express in clear sounds and words: *The speaker was careful to articulate his words so that everyone in the room could understand him.* **3** able to put one's thoughts into words easily and clearly: *She is the most articulate of the sisters.* **4** having joints; jointed. The backbone is an articulate structure. **5** fit together in a joint. The leg bones articulate at the knee. 1,3,4 *adj.,* 2,5 *v.,* **ar tic u lat ed, ar tic u lat ing.** —**ar tic u late ly** (är tik′yə lit lē), *adv.* —**ar tic′u la′tor,** *n.*

ar tic u la tion (är tik′yə lā′shən), **1** way of speaking; enunciation: *If you speak more slowly, your articulation will probably improve.* **2** a joint. **3** act or manner of connecting by a joint or joints: *The articulation of the bones of the hand is quite complex. n.*

ar ti fact (är′tə fakt), anything made by human skill or work, especially a tool or weapon. *n.*

artifact—A button, scissors, thimble, crochet hook, and needles were among the **artifacts** uncovered in an ancient Roman village.

ar ti fice (är′tə fis), **1** a clever device; trick; ruse: *The child used every artifice to avoid going to the dentist.* **2** trickery; craft: *Her conduct is free from artifice. n.*

ar tif i cer (är tif′ə sər), a skilled worker; craftsman. *n.*

ar ti fi cial (är′tə fish′əl), **1** made by human skill or labor; not natural: *At night, you read by artificial light.* **2** made as a substitute or imitation; not real: *We made artificial paper flowers.* **3** put on for effect; affected; pretended: *When nervous, he had an artificial laugh. adj.* —**ar′ti fi′cial ly,** *adv.* —**ar′ti fi′cial ness,** *n.*

artificial intelligence, ability of a computer to do things that require intelligence when done by human beings, such as playing chess.

artificial respiration, method of restoring normal breathing to a person who has stopped breathing by forcing air alternately into and out of the lungs.

ar til ler y (är til′ər ē), **1** mounted guns; cannon. **2** the part of an army that uses and manages cannon. *n.*

ar ti san (är′tə zən), person skilled in some industry or trade; craftsman. Carpenters, masons, plumbers, and electricians are artisans. *n.*

art ist (är′tist), **1** person who paints pictures. **2** person who is skilled in any of the fine arts, such as sculpture, music, or literature. **3** a public performer, especially an actor or singer. **4** person who does work with skill and good taste. *n.*

ar tis tic (är tis′tik), **1** of art or artists: *That museum has* *many artistic treasures.* **2** done with skill and good taste: *an artistic performance.* **3** having good color and design; pleasing to the senses: *an artistic wallpaper.* **4** having or showing appreciation of beauty: *You have an artistic way of arranging flowers.* adj.

ar tis ti cal ly (är tis′tik lē), **1** with skill and good taste. **2** from an artistic point of view. adv.

art ist ry (är′tə strē), artistic work; workmanship of an artist. n., pl. **art ist ries.**

art less (ärt′lis), **1** made or done without knowledge of social customs; simple and natural: *Small children ask many artless questions, such as, "Mom, did you want these people to come to see you?"* **2** without art; unskilled; ignorant. adj. —**art′less ly,** adv. —**art′less ness,** n.

as (az; *unstressed* əz), **1** to the same degree or extent; equally: *I am as tall as you.* **2** in the character of; doing the work of: *Who will act as teacher?* **3** during the time that; while: *As they were walking, it began to rain.* **4** in the same way that: *Treat others as you wish them to treat you.* **5** for example: *Some animals, as dogs and cats, eat meat.* **6** because: *As she was a skilled worker, she received good wages.* **7** though: *Brave as they were, the danger made them afraid.* **8** that: *Do the same thing as I do.* 1,5 adv., 2 prep., 3,4,6,7 conj., 8 pron.

as for, about; concerning; referring to: *As for politics, I am indifferent.*

as if, similar to what it would be if: *You sound as if you were angry.*

as is, in the present condition; without a guarantee of good or perfect quality: *If you buy the car as is, it will cost you very little.*

as of, beginning on or at (a certain date or time): *The new contract becomes effective as of January 1st.*

as though, similar to what it would be if: *It looks as though it might rain.*

as to, about; concerning; referring to: *I was uncertain as to which sweater to wear.*

as yet, up to this time; so far.

As, symbol for arsenic.

AS or **A.S.,** Anglo-Saxon.

as bes tos (as bes′təs), **1** mineral that does not burn or conduct heat and that usually comes in fibers. **2** a fireproof fabric made of these fibers. Asbestos is used to make insulating and roofing materials, brake linings, and fire-resistant clothing. n.

as cend (ə send′), go up; rise; climb: *She watched the airplane ascend higher and higher. A small party is planning to ascend Mount Everest.* v. —**as cend′a ble, as cend′i ble,** adj.

as cen sion (ə sen′shən), **1** a rising; ascent. **2** the Ascension, (in the Bible) the ascent of Christ from earth to heaven after the Resurrection. n.

as cent (ə sent′), **1** a going up; upward movement; rising: *The sudden ascent of the elevator made us dizzy.* **2** a climbing: *The ascent of Mount Everest is difficult.* **3** place or way that slopes up: *The gradual ascent of the hill made it easy to climb.* n.

as cer tain (as′ər tān′), find out; make sure of; determine: *The detective tried to ascertain the facts about the robbery.* v. —**as′cer tain′a ble,** adj.

as cet ic (ə set′ik), **1** person who practices unusual self-denial or discipline, especially for religious reasons. Fasting is a common practice of ascetics. **2** refraining from pleasures and comforts; practicing unusual self-denial. 1 n., 2 adj. —**as cet′i cal ly,** adv.

as cet i cism (ə set′ə siz′əm), unusual or extreme self-denial. n.

AS CII (as′kē), American Standard Code for Information Interchange, a system for coding letters, numbers, and other characters into groups of binary digits. It is widely used for passing information between computers, or between a computer and devices used with it. n.

a scor bic acid (ə skôr′bik), vitamin C.

as cribe (ə skrīb′), think of as caused by or coming from; attribute: *The police ascribed the automobile accident to fast driving. The author of this tale is unknown, but it is ascribed to the brothers Grimm.* v., **as cribed, as crib ing.**

a sep tic (ə sep′tik), free from the living germs causing infection: *Surgical instruments can be made aseptic by boiling them.* adj. —**a sep′ti cal ly,** adv.

a sex u al (ā sek′shü əl), **1** having no sex. **2** independent of sexual processes. The division into two parts by an ameba is a form of asexual reproduction. adj.

As gard (as′gärd), home of the Norse gods and heroes. n.

ash[1] (ash), what remains of a thing after it has been thoroughly burned: *He flicked his cigarette ash into the fireplace.* See also **ashes.** n., pl. **ash es.**

ash[2] (ash), **1** a timber or shade tree that has a silver-gray bark, grayish twigs, and straight-grained wood. **2** its tough, springy wood. n., pl. **ash es.**

a shamed (ə shāmd′), **1** feeling shame; disturbed or uncomfortable because one has done something wrong, improper, or silly: *I was ashamed when I cried at the movies.* **2** unwilling because of fear of shame: *I failed math and was ashamed to tell my parents.* adj. —**a shamed ly** (ə shām′id lē), adv.

ash en[1] (ash′ən), **1** like ashes; pale as ashes. **2** of ashes. adj.

ash en[2] (ash′ən), made from ash wood. adj.

ash es (ash′iz), **1** what remains of a thing after it has thoroughly burned: *Ashes have to be removed from the fireplace to make room for more wood.* **2** what remains of a dead body when burned. **3** a dead body; corpse. n.pl.

a shore (ə shôr′), **1** to the shore; to land: *The ship's passengers went ashore.* **2** on the shore; on land: *The sailor had been ashore for months.* adv.

ash tray (ash′trā′), a small dish to put tobacco ashes in. n.

Ash Wednesday, the first day of Lent; the seventh Wednesday before Easter.

A sia (ā′zhə), the largest continent, extending eastward from Europe and Africa to the Pacific Ocean. China, India, and most of the Soviet Union are in Asia. n.

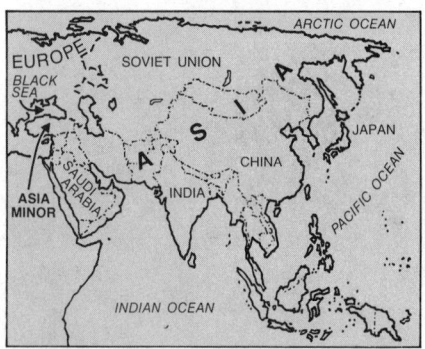

Asia Minor, peninsula of SW Asia, between the Black Sea and the Mediterranean Sea; Anatolia. It includes most of Asian Turkey.

A sian (ā′zhən), **1** person born or living in Asia. **2** of Asia or its people. 1 n., 2 adj.

A si at ic (ā′zhē at′ik), Asian. The word *Asian* should be used when referring to the people of Asia, because the word *Asiatic* is sometimes considered offensive. adj., n.

a side (ə sīd′), **1** on one side; to one side; away: *I stepped aside to let them pass.* **2** out of one's thoughts or consideration: *Swimming is easier if you can put your fears aside.*

3 remark that others who are present are not supposed to hear. An actor's asides are usually spoken to the audience. 1,2 *adv.*, 3 *n.*

aside from, except for: *Aside from arithmetic, I have finished my homework.*

as i nine (as′n īn), obviously silly; foolish and stupid. *adj.* [Asinine is from Latin *asininus*, meaning "of or like an ass," which comes from *asinus*, meaning "ass, donkey, fool."] —**as′i nine ly**, *adv.*

ask (ask), 1 try to find out by words; inquire: *Why don't you ask? She asked about our health. Ask the way.* 2 seek the answer to: *Ask any questions you wish.* 3 put a question to; inquire of: *Ask him how old he is.* 4 try to get by words; request: *Ask them to sing. Ask for help if you need it.* 5 invite: *She asked ten guests to the party.* *v.*

a skance (ə skans′), 1 with suspicion or disapproval: *The students looked askance at the plan to have classes on Saturday.* 2 to one side; sideways. *adv.*

a skew (ə skyü′), to one side; turned or twisted the wrong way; out of the proper position: *The wind blew her hat askew (adv.). Isn't that picture askew? (adj.).* *adv., adj.*

a slant (ə slant′), 1 in a slanting direction. 2 slantingly across. 3 slanting. 1 *adv.*, 2 *prep.*, 3 *adj.*

a sleep (ə slēp′), 1 not awake; sleeping: *The cat is asleep.* 2 into a condition of sleep: *The tired boy fell asleep.* 3 having lost the power of feeling; numb: *My foot is asleep.* 1,3 *adj.*, 2 *adv.*

asp (asp), any of several small, poisonous snakes of Africa and Europe. *n.*

as par a gus (ə spar′ə gəs), 1 plant with scalelike leaves. 2 its green, tender shoots, eaten as a vegetable. *n.*

A.S.P.C.A. or **ASPCA**, American Society for the Prevention of Cruelty to Animals.

as pect (as′pekt), 1 one of the ways in which a subject or situation may be looked at or thought about: *We must consider each aspect of this plan before we decide.* 2 look; appearance: *The judge has a solemn aspect.* 3 side fronting or facing in a given direction: *The southern aspect of the house is the warmest in winter.* *n.*

as pen (as′pən), 1 any of several poplar trees of North America and Europe whose leaves tremble and rustle in the slightest breeze. 2 of this tree. 1 *n.*, 2 *adj.*

as per sion (ə spėr′zhən), a damaging or false statement; slander: *She was accused of casting aspersions on the reputation of an innocent person.* *n.*

as phalt (as′fôlt), 1 a dark substance much like tar, found in various parts of the world or obtained by refining petroleum. 2 a mixture of this substance with crushed rock or sand. Asphalt is used in surfacing roads. *n.*

as phyx i ate (a sfik′sē āt), suffocate because of lack of oxygen in the blood: *The trapped miners were almost asphyxiated before help reached them.* *v.*, **as phyx i at ed, as phyx i at ing.** [Asphyxiate can be traced back to Greek *a-*, meaning "without," and *sphyxis*, meaning "the pulse."] —**as phyx′i a′tor**, *n.*

as phyx i a tion (a sfik′sē ā′shən), suffocation caused by lack of oxygen in the blood. *n.*

as pic (as′pik), kind of jelly made from meat or fish stock, tomato juice, etc., used as a garnish or in salads. *n.*

as pir ant (ə spī′rənt *or* as′pər ənt), person who aspires; person who seeks a position of honor: *There were many aspirants to the office of class president.* *n.*

as pi rate (as′pə rāt′ *for 1,2;* as′pər it *for 3,4*), 1 begin (a word or syllable) with a breathing or *h*-sound. *Hot* is aspirated; *honor* is not. 2 pronounce with such a sound. The *h* in *hot* is aspirated. 3 pronounced with a breathing or *h*-sound. The *h* in *here* is aspirate. 4 the sound of *h* in *hot.* 1,2 *v.*, **as pi rat ed, as pi rat ing;** 3 *adj.*, 4 *n.*

a hat	i it	oi oil	ch child	a in about
ā age	ī ice	ou out	ng long	e in taken
ä far	o hot	u cup	sh she	ə = i in pencil
e let	ō open	u̇ put	th thin	o in lemon
ē equal	ô order	ü rule	ŦH then	u in circus
ėr term			zh measure	

as pi ra tion (as′pə rā′shən), 1 earnest desire; longing; ambition: *She had aspirations to be a doctor.* 2 an aspirating: *Many people pronounce "where" with no aspiration.* 3 a drawing air into the lungs; breathing. *n.*

as pire (ə spīr′), have an ambition for something; desire earnestly; seek: *aspire to be captain of the team, aspire after knowledge.* *v.*, **as pired, as pir ing.** —**as pir′er**, *n.*

as pir in (as′pər ən), drug used to relieve pain or fever in headaches, colds, etc. *n.*

ass (as), 1 donkey. 2 a stupid, silly, or stubborn person; fool. *n., pl.* **ass es.** —**ass′like′**, *adj.*

as sail (ə sāl′), 1 set upon with violence; attack: *The soldiers assailed the fort.* 2 set upon vigorously with arguments or abuse: *The senators assailed the President on the subject of the treaty.* *v.* —**as sail′a ble**, *adj.*

as sail ant (ə sā′lənt), person who attacks: *The injured man did not know who his assailant was.* *n.*

as sas sin (ə sas′n), murderer; one who kills a well-known person, especially a political leader, by a sudden or secret attack. *n.*

as sas si nate (ə sas′n āt), murder by a sudden or secret attack: *President Kennedy was assassinated in 1963.* *v.*, **as sas si nat ed, as sas si nat ing.** —**as sas′si na′tor**, *n.*

as sas si na tion (ə sas′n ā′shən), a murdering by a sudden or secret attack. *n.*

as sault (ə sôlt′), 1 a sudden, vigorous attack: *The soldiers made an assault on the fort.* 2 make an assault on. 3 (in law) a threat or attempt to strike or otherwise harm a person. 1,3 *n.*, 2 *v.* —**as sault′er**, *n.*

as say (ə sā′), 1 analyze (an ore or alloy) to find out the quantity of gold, silver, or other metal in it. 2 an analysis to find out the amount of metal in an ore or alloy or of an ingredient in a drug. 1 *v.*, 2 *n.* —**as say′er**, *n.*

as sem blage (ə sem′blij), 1 group of persons or things collected or gathered together; assembly. 2 process of putting together; fitting together: *the assemblage of parts of an automobile engine.* *n.*

as sem ble (ə sem′bəl), 1 gather together; bring together: *The principal assembled all the students in the auditorium.* 2 come together; meet: *Congress assembles in January.* 3 put together; fit together: *Will you help me assemble my model airplane?* *v.*, **as sem bled, as sem bling.** —**as sem′bler**, *n.*

as sem bly (ə sem′blē), 1 a gathering of people for some purpose; meeting: *The principal addressed the school assembly.* 2 a meeting of lawmakers. 3 **Assembly,** the lower branch of the state legislature of some states of the United States. 4 a coming together; an assembling: *unlawful assembly.* 5 a putting together; fitting together: *the assembly of parts to make an automobile.* 6 the complete group of parts required to put something together: *the tail assembly of an airplane.* *n., pl.* **as sem blies.**

assembly language, computer programming language that uses numbers and letter codes, including shortened words, to control computer functions. Each small group of letters and numbers stands for a single data processing step.

assembly line, row of workers and machines along which work is passed until the final product is made: *Most automobiles are made on an assembly line.*

as sent (ə sent′), 1 express agreement; consent; agree: *Everyone assented to the plan.* 2 acceptance of a proposal, statement, etc.; agreement: *She gave her assent to the plan.* 1 *v.*, 2 *n.* —**as sen′tor**, as **sent′er**, *n.*

as sert (ə sėrt′), 1 state positively; declare firmly: *She asserts that her story is true.* 2 defend or insist on (a right, a claim, etc.): *Assert your independence.* *v.* —**as sert′er**, as **ser′tor**, *n.*

assert oneself, insist on one's rights; demand recognition: *If you feel you've been treated unfairly, you should assert yourself.*

as ser tion (ə sėr′shən), 1 a positive statement; firm declaration: *His assertion of innocence was believed by the jury.* 2 an insisting on a right, a claim, etc. *n.*

as ser tive (ə sėr′tiv), confident and certain; positive: *He is an assertive boy, always insisting on his rights and opinions.* *adj.* —**as ser′tive ly**, *adv.* —**as ser′tive ness**, *n.*

as sess (ə ses′), 1 estimate the value of (property or income) for taxation; value: *The town clerk has assessed our house at $20,000.* 2 fix the amount of (a tax, fine, damages, etc.): *Damages from last week's flood have been assessed at $150,000.* 3 put a tax on or call for a contribution from (a person, property, etc.): *Each member of the club will be assessed $5 to pay for the trip.* *v.* —**as sess′a ble**, *adj.*

as sess ment (ə ses′mənt), 1 an assessing. 2 amount assessed. *n.*

as ses sor (ə ses′ər), person who estimates the value of property or income for taxation. *n.*

as set (as′et), 1 something having value: *Ability to get along with people is an asset in business.* 2 **assets**, *pl.* **a** things of value; property, such as a house, a car, stocks, bonds, jewelry, etc. **b** property that can be used to pay debts. *n.*

as sev e rate (ə sev′ə rāt′), declare solemnly; state positively. *v.*, **as sev e rat ed**, **as sev e rat ing.** —**as sev′e ra′tion**, *n.*

as sid u ous (ə sij′ü əs), careful and attentive; diligent. *adj.* —**as sid′u ous ly**, *adv.* —**as sid′u ous ness**, *n.*

as sign (ə sīn′), 1 give as a share; allot: *The teacher has assigned the next ten problems for today.* 2 appoint (to a post or duty): *We were assigned to decorate the room for the party.* 3 name definitely; fix; set: *The judge assigned a day for the trial.* *v.* —**as sign′a ble**, *adj.* —**as sign′er**, *n.*

as sign ment (ə sīn′mənt), 1 something assigned, especially a piece of work to be done: *Today's assignment in arithmetic consists of ten examples.* 2 an assigning; appointment: *Homeroom assignments were made on the first day of school.* *n.*

as sim i late (ə sim′ə lāt), 1 take in and make part of oneself; absorb; digest: *to assimilate what one reads. The body assimilates sugars rapidly.* 2 become absorbed; be digested: *Fats assimilate slowly.* 3 make or become like the people of a nation in customs, viewpoint, character, etc.: *The United States has assimilated immigrants from many lands.* *v.*, **as sim i lat ed**, **as sim i lat ing.** —**as sim′i la′tor**, *n.*

as sim i la tion (ə sim′ə lā′shən), 1 an absorbing or a being absorbed: *the assimilation of food.* 2 a making or a becoming like. *n.*

as sist (ə sist′), 1 give aid to; help: *She assisted the science teacher with the experiment.* 2 act of assistance; aid; help: *If you will give me an assist I think I can reach the branch.* 1 *v.*, 2 *n.* —**as sist′er**, as **sis′tor**, *n.*

as sist ance (ə sis′təns), an assisting; aid; help: *I need your assistance.* *n.*

as sist ant (ə sis′tənt), 1 person who assists another; aid; helper: *He was my assistant in the library for a time.* 2 assisting; helping: *an assistant teacher.* 1 *n.*, 2 *adj.*

assn., ass′n, or **Assn.**, association.

assoc., 1 associate. 2 association.

as so ci ate (ə sō′shē āt *for 1,3,4;* ə sō′shē it *or* ə sō′-shē āt *for 2,5,6*), 1 connect in thought: *We associate turkey with Thanksgiving.* 2 joined with another or others: *I am an associate editor of the school paper.* 3 join as a companion, partner, or friend: *She is associated with her brothers in business.* 4 be friendly; keep company: *He associated with interesting people.* 5 companion, partner, or friend: *She is an associate in a law firm.* 6 admitted to some, but not all, rights and privileges: *After being an associate member of the glee club for a year I became a full member.* 1,3,4 *v.*, **as so ci at ed**, **as so ci at ing**; 2,6 *adj.*, 5 *n.* [Associate comes from Latin *associatum*, meaning "joined in companionship," and can be traced back to *ad-*, meaning "to," and *socius*, meaning "companion."] —**as so ci a tor** (ə sō′shē ā′tər), *n.*

as so ci a tion (ə sō′sē ā′shən *or* ə sō′shē ā′shən), 1 group of people joined together for some purpose; society: *Will you join the young people's association at our church?* 2 an associating: *association of ideas.* 3 a being associated: *Her association with that firm ended several years ago.* 4 companionship or friendship: *They had enjoyed a close association over many years.* 5 idea connected with another idea in thought: *Some people make the association of the color red with anger.* *n.*

association football, BRITISH. soccer.

as so ci a tive (ə sō′shē ā′tiv), 1 tending to associate. 2 having to do with association. 3 of or having to do with a rule that the combinations by which numbers are added or multiplied will not change their sum or product. EXAMPLE: $(2 \times 3) \times 5$ will give the same product as $2 \times (3 \times 5)$. *adj.* —**as so′ci a′tive ly**, *adv.*

as so nance (as′n əns), 1 resemblance in sound of words or syllables. EXAMPLE: W**a**ken l**o**rds and l**a**dies g**a**y. 2 a substitute for rhyme in which the vowels are alike but the consonants are different. EXAMPLES: br**a**ve—v**ai**n, l**o**ne—sh**o**w, m**a**n—h**a**t, pen**i**tent—ret**i**cence. *n.*

as sort ed (ə sôr′tid), 1 selected so as to be of different kinds; various: *She served assorted cakes.* 2 arranged by kinds; classified: *There were socks assorted by size on the shelf.* *adj.*

as sort ment (ə sôrt′mənt), collection of various kinds: *These scarves come in an assortment of colors.* *n.*

asst. or **Asst.**, assistant.

as suage (ə swāj′), 1 calm or soothe: *Her words assuaged the child's fears.* 2 make milder or easier: *Aspirin assuages pain.* 3 satisfy; appease; quench: *She took a drink of water to assuage her thirst.* *v.*, **as suaged**, **as suag ing.** —**as suag′er**, *n.* —**as suage′ment**, *n.*

as sume (ə süm′), 1 take for granted without proof; suppose: *He assumed that the train would be on time.* 2 take upon oneself; undertake: *She assumed the leadership of the project.* 3 take on; put on: *The problem has assumed a new form.* 4 pretend: *Although she was afraid, she assumed an air of confidence.* 5 take for oneself; appropriate; usurp: *The king's wicked brother tried to assume the throne.* *v.*, **as sumed**, **as sum ing.** —**as sum′a ble**, *adj.* —**as sum′a bly**, *adv.* —**as sum′er**, *n.*

as sumed (ə sümd′), false; not real; pretended: *an assumed name.* *adj.* —**as sum ed ly** (ə süm′id lē), *adv.*

as sump tion (ə sump′shən), 1 an assuming: *The clerk bustled about with an assumption of authority.* 2 thing assumed: *His assumption that he would win the prize proved incorrect.* *n.*

as sur ance (ə shur′əns), 1 statement intended to make a person more sure or certain: *Do I have your assurance that you will not do it again?* 2 security, certainty, or confidence: *We have the assurance of final victory.* 3 confidence in one's own ability: *The actor's careful preparation gave him assurance in performing.* *n.*

as sure (ə shur′), 1 tell positively: *They assured me that they would be on time.* 2 make sure or certain; convince:

She assured herself that the bridge was safe before she crossed it. **3** make safe; secure: *Victory was assured when the team scored in the final seconds of the game.* **4** give or restore confidence to; encourage: *The father assured his frightened son. v.,* **as sured, as sur ing.** —**as sur′er, as su′ror,** *n.*

as sur ed ly (ə shu̇r′id lē), **1** surely; certainly: *I will assuredly come.* **2** confidently; boldly: *I spoke more assuredly than I felt. adv.*

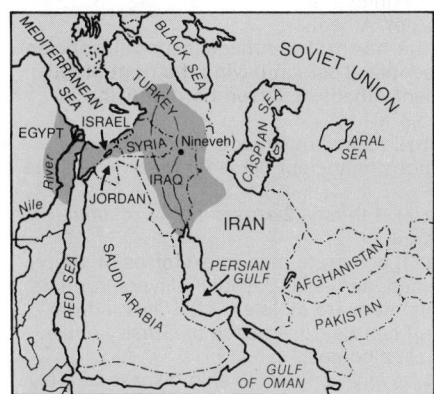

Assyria (670 B.C. (shown, by the darker area, on a modern map)

As syr i a (ə sir′ē ə), ancient country in SW Asia, once a great empire. The capital was Nineveh. *n.* —**As syr′i an,** *adj., n.*

as ta tine (as′tə tēn′), a radioactive nonmetallic element produced artificially from bismuth. *n.*

as ter (as′tər), a common plant having daisylike flowers with white, pink, or purple petals around a yellow center. *n.* —**as′ter like′,** *adj.*

as ter isk (as′tə risk′), a star-shaped mark (*) used in printing and writing to call attention to a footnote, indicate the omission of words or letters, etc. *n.* [*Asterisk* comes from Latin *asteriscus,* and can be traced back to Greek *astēr,* meaning "a star."]

a stern (ə stern′), **1** at or toward the rear; aft: *The captain went astern.* **2** backward: *The boat moved slowly astern.* **3** behind: *The yacht towed a small boat astern. adv.*

as ter oid (as′tə roid′), any of the thousands of very small planets that revolve about the sun, chiefly between the orbits of Mars and Jupiter; planetoid. *n.* [*Asteroid* is from Greek *asteroeidēs,* meaning "starlike," which comes from *astēr,* meaning "a star."]

asth ma (az′mə), a chronic disease characterized by difficulty in breathing accompanied by wheezing, a feeling of suffocation, and coughing. *n.*

a stig ma tism (ə stig′mə tiz′əm), defect of an eye or of a lens that makes objects look indistinct or gives imperfect images. *n.*

a stir (ə ster′), in motion; up and about: *The whole town was astir. adj.*

as ton ish (ə ston′ish), surprise greatly; amaze: *We were astonished by the child's remarkable memory. v.*

as ton ish ing (ə ston′i shing), very surprising; amazing. *adj.* —**as ton′ish ing ly,** *adv.*

as ton ish ment (ə ston′ish mənt), great surprise; sudden wonder; amazement. *n.*

as tound (ə stound′), surprise greatly; amaze: *She was astounded by the news that she had won the contest. v.*

as tound ing (ə stound′ing), amazing. *adj.* —**as tound′ing ly,** *adv.*

a strad dle (ə strad′l), astride. *adv.*

as tra khan (as′trə kən), **1** the curly furlike wool on the skin of young caracul lambs. **2** a rough woolen cloth that looks like this. *n.*

a hat	**i** it	**oi** oil	**ch** child	⎧ a in about
ā age	**ī** ice	**ou** out	**ng** long	⎪ e in taken
ä far	**o** hot	**u** cup	**sh** she	ə = ⎨ i in pencil
e let	**ō** open	**u̇** put	**th** thin	⎪ o in lemon
ē equal	**ô** order	**ü** rule	**ᴛ͟ʜ** then	⎩ u in circus
ėr term			**zh** measure	

a stray (ə strā′), out of the right way; off: *Your reasoning is astray on that subject* (adj.). *The cows have gone astray* (adv.). *adj., adv.*

a stride (ə strīd′), **1** with one leg on each side of: *She sat astride her horse.* **2** with one leg on each side: *The knight sat astride on his horse.* **1** *prep.,* **2** *adv.*

as trin gen cy (ə strin′jən sē), quality of being astringent. *n.*

as trin gent (ə strin′jənt), **1** substance that contracts body tissues and thus checks the flow of blood or other secretions. Alum is an astringent. **2** having the property of contracting tissues. **1** *n.,* **2** *adj.* —**as trin′gent ly,** *adv.*

astro-, *combining form.* **1** star or other heavenly body: *Astronomy = science of heavenly bodies.* **2** space: *Astronautics = space travel.* [The form *astro-* is from Greek *astro-,* which comes from *astron,* meaning "star."]

astrol., astrology.

aster

as tro labe (as′trə lāb), an astronomical instrument formerly used for measuring the altitude of the sun or stars. It has been replaced by the sextant. *n.*

as trol o ger (ə strol′ə jər), person who studies the stars and planets to determine their supposed influence on persons or events, and to foretell the future. *n.*

as tro log i cal (as′trə loj′ə kəl), of astrology. *adj.* —**as′tro log′i cal ly,** *adv.*

WORD HISTORY

astrology

Astrology came into English about 600 years ago from French *astrologie,* and can be traced back to Greek *astron,* meaning "a star," and *logos,* meaning "word, discussion."

as trol o gy (ə strol′ə jē), study of the stars and planets to determine their supposed influence on persons or events, and to foretell the future. *n.* [See **Word History.**]

astron., **1** astronomer. **2** astronomy.

as tro naut (as′trə nôt), pilot or member of the crew of a spacecraft. *n.*

as tro naut ic (as′trə nô′tik), of astronauts or astronautics. *adj.* —**as′tro naut′i cal ly,** *adv.*

as tro naut i cal (as′trə nô′tə kəl), astronautic. *adj.*

as tro naut ics (as′trə nô′tiks), **1** science or art having to do with the design, manufacture, and operation of spacecraft. **2** space travel. *n.*

as tron o mer (ə stron′ə mər), an expert in astronomy. *n.*

as tro nom ic (as′trə nom′ik), astronomical. *adj.*

as tro nom i cal (as′trə nom′ə kəl), **1** of astronomy: *astronomical calculations.* **2** enormous; very great: *The government has astronomical expenses. adj.* —**as′tro nom′i cal ly,** *adv.*

as tron o my (ə stron′ə mē), science that deals with the sun, moon, planets, stars, and other heavenly bodies. It studies their composition, motions, positions, distances, sizes, etc. *n.* [*Astronomy* came into English over 700 years ago from French *astronomie,* and can be traced back to Greek *astron,* meaning "a star," and *nomos,* meaning "distribution."]

as tro phys i cal (as′trō fiz′ə kəl), of astrophysics. *adj.*

as tro phys ics (as′trō fiz′iks), branch of astronomy that deals with the physical and chemical characteristics of heavenly bodies. *n.*

As tro Turf (as′trō térf′), trademark for a synthetic material made of nylon and plastic. It is used instead of grass on playing fields and lawns. *n.*

as tute (ə stüt′ *or* ə styüt′), shrewd with regard to one's own interests; clever: *He was an astute businessman. adj.* —**as tute′ly,** *adv.* —**as tute′ness,** *n.*

A sun ción (ä sün′syôn′), capital and a major port of Paraguay, on the Paraguay River. *n.*

a sun der (ə sun′dər), in pieces; into separate parts: *Lightning split the tree asunder. adv.*

As wan Dam (äs swän′), large dam in SE Egypt, built on the Nile for irrigation and flood control.

a sy lum (ə sī′ləm), **1** institution for the support and care of the mentally ill, the blind, orphans, or other people who need care. **2** refuge; shelter. In olden times a church might be an asylum for a debtor or a criminal, since no one was allowed to drag a person from the altar. Now asylum is sometimes given by one nation to persons of another nation who are accused of political crimes. *n.*

a sym met ric (ā′sə met′rik), not symmetrical; lacking symmetry. *adj.* —**a′sym met′ri cal ly,** *adv.*

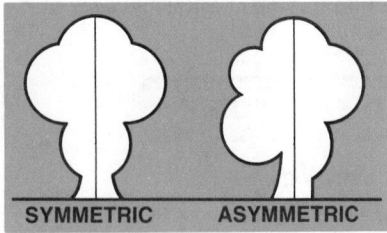

SYMMETRIC ASYMMETRIC

a sym me try (ā sim′ə trē), lack of symmetry. *n.*

at (at; *unstressed* ət *or* it), **1** in; on; by; near: *There is someone at the front door. I will be at home.* **2** in the direction of; to; toward: *The dog ran at the cat.* **3** on or near the time of: *She goes to bed at nine o'clock.* **4** in a place or condition of: *England and France were at war.* **5** through; by way of: *Smoke came out at the chimney.* **6** doing; trying to do; engaged in: *He is at work on a new project.* **7** for: *We bought two books at a dollar each.* **8** because of; with: *My friends were happy at my success.* **9** according to: *She can wiggle her ears at will. prep.*

At, symbol for astatine.

at., **1** atmosphere. **2** atomic.

ate (āt), past tense of **eat.** *The boy ate his dinner. v.*

a the ism (ā′thē iz′əm), belief that there is no God. *n.*

a the ist (ā′thē ist), person who believes that there is no God. *n.*

a the is tic (ā′thē is′tik), of atheism or atheists. *adj.* —**a′the is′ti cal ly,** *adv.*

A the na (ə thē′nə), (in Greek myths) the goddess of wisdom, arts, industries, and prudent warfare. The Romans called her Minerva. *n.*

A the ne (ə thē′nē), Athena. *n.*

A the ni an (ə thē′nē ən), **1** of Athens (especially ancient Athens) or its people. **2** person having the right of citizenship in ancient Athens. **3** person born or living in Athens. 1 *adj.,* 2,3 *n.*

Ath ens (ath′ənz), capital of Greece, in the SE part. Athens was famous in ancient times for its art and literature. *n.*

a thirst (ə thérst′), **1** thirsty. **2** eager: *They were athirst for new experiences. adj.*

ath lete (ath′lēt′), person trained in exercises of physical strength, speed, and skill. Baseball players, runners, boxers, and swimmers are athletes. *n.* [*Athlete* is from Latin *athleta,* and can be traced back to Greek *athlon,* meaning "a prize, a contest."]

athlete's foot, a very contagious skin disease of the feet, caused by a fungus; ringworm of the feet.

ath let ic (ath let′ik), **1** of or suited to an athlete. **2** having to do with active games and sports: *an athletic association.* **3** strong and active: *an athletic girl. adj.* —**ath let′i cal ly,** *adv.*

ath let ics (ath let′iks), **1** *pl. in form and use.* exercises of physical strength, speed, and skill; active games and sports. Athletics include baseball and basketball. **2** *pl. in form, sing. in use.* the practice and principles of physical training: *Athletics is recommended for every student. n.*

a thwart (ə thwôrt′), **1** across from side to side; crosswise. **2** across. **3** across the line or course of: *The tug steamed athwart the ship.* **4** in opposition to; against. 1 *adv.,* 2-4 *prep.*

-ation, suffix added mainly to verbs to form nouns. **1** act or process of _____ing: *Preparation = act or process of preparing.* **2** condition or state of being _____ed: *Cancellation = condition or state of being canceled.* **3** result of _____ing: *Civilization = result of civilizing.*

-ative, suffix added to verbs and nouns to form adjectives. **1** tending to _____: *Talkative = tending to talk.* **2** having to do with _____: *Qualitative = having to do with quality.*

At lan ta (at lan′tə), capital of Georgia, in the NW part. *n.*

At lan tic (at lan′tik), **1** ocean east of North and South America, west of Europe and Africa. **2** of the Atlantic Ocean. **3** on, in, over, or near the Atlantic Ocean: *Atlantic air routes.* **4** of or on the Atlantic coast of the United States: *New Jersey is one of the Atlantic states.* 1 *n.,* 2-4 *adj.*

At lan tis (at lan′tis), legendary island in the Atlantic Ocean said to have sunk beneath the sea. *n.*

at las (at′ləs), **1** book of maps. **2 Atlas,** (in Greek myths) a giant who supported the heavens on his shoulders. *n., pl.* **at las es** for 1.

atm., **1** atmosphere. **2** atmospheric.

at mo sphere (at′mə sfir), **1** air that surrounds the earth. **2** mass of gases that surrounds, or may surround, any heavenly body: *the cloudy atmosphere of Venus.* **3** air in any given place: *the damp atmosphere of a cellar.* **4** general character or mood of one's surroundings; surrounding influence: *a religious atmosphere, an atmosphere of excitement.* **5** unit of pressure equal to 14.7 pounds per square inch (1.03 kilograms per square centimeter). *n.*

at mo spher ic (at′mə sfir′ik *or* at′mə sfer′ik), in or of the atmosphere: *atmospheric conditions. adj.* —**at′mo- spher′i cal ly,** *adv.*

atmospheric pressure, pressure caused by the weight of the air. The normal atmospheric pressure on the earth's surface at sea level is 14.7 pounds per square inch (1.03 kilograms per square centimeter).

at oll (at′ol *or* ə tol′), a ring-shaped coral island or group of islands enclosing or partly enclosing a lagoon. *n.*

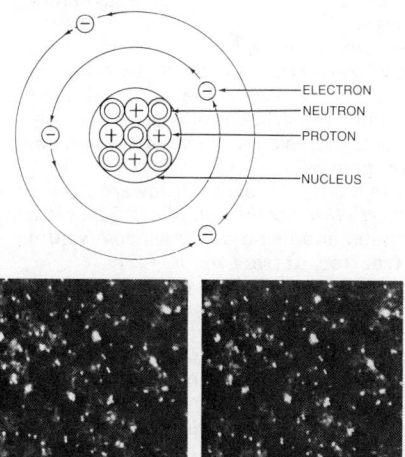

ELECTRON
NEUTRON
PROTON
NUCLEUS

atom (def. 1)—top, diagram of an atom of beryllium; below, uranium atoms magnified 5.5 million times. The picture on the right was taken 5 minutes after the one on the left. The slight changes in atom positions are due to the thermal motion of the atoms.

at om (at′əm), **1** the smallest particle of a chemical element that can take part in a chemical reaction without being permanently changed. An atom is made up of protons and neutrons in a central nucleus surrounded by electrons. A molecule of water consists of two atoms of hydrogen and one atom of oxygen. **2** a very small particle; tiny bit: *There is not an atom of truth in the whole story. n.* [*Atom* comes from Latin *atomus,* and can be traced back to Greek *a-,* meaning "not," and *tomos,* meaning "a cutting."]

atom bomb, atomic bomb.

a tom ic (ə tom′ik), **1** of atoms: *atomic research.* **2** using atomic energy: *an atomic submarine.* **3** extremely small; minute. *adj.* —**a tom′i cal ly,** *adv.*

atomic bomb, bomb in which the splitting of atomic nuclei results in an explosion of tremendous force and heat, accompanied by a blinding light; A-bomb.

atomic energy, energy that exists in atoms; nuclear energy. Some atoms can be made to release some of their energy, either slowly (in a reactor) or very suddenly (in a bomb), by the splitting or the fusion of their nuclei.

atomic number, the number of protons in the nucleus of an atom of an element: *The atomic number of hydrogen is 1, of uranium 92.*

atomic weight, the relative weight of an atom of a chemical element based on the weight of an atom of carbon, which is taken as 12: *The atomic weight of hydrogen is 1.00797, of uranium 238.03.*

at om ize (at′ə mīz), **1** change (a liquid) into a spray of very small drops. **2** reduce (anything) to small particles. **3** obliterate (anything) by an atomic explosion. *v.,* **at om- ized, at om iz ing.** —**at′om i za′tion,** *n.*

at om iz er (at′ə mī′zər), apparatus used to blow a liquid in a spray of tiny drops: *a perfume atomizer. n.*

a ton al (ā tō′nl), (in music) having no key. *adj.* —**a ton′al ly,** *adv.*

a tone (ə tōn′), make up; make amends: *He atoned for his unkindness to his sister by taking her to the movies. v.,* **a toned, a ton ing.**

a tone ment (ə tōn′mənt), **1** a making up for something; giving satisfaction for a wrong, loss, or injury; amends. **2 the Atonement,** the reconciliation of God with sinners through the sufferings and death of Christ. *n.*

a top (ə top′), on the top of: *He had a hat atop his head. prep.*

a tro cious (ə trō′shəs), **1** very wicked or cruel; very savage or brutal: *Kidnaping is an atrocious crime.* **2** INFOR- MAL. very bad or unpleasant: *atrocious weather. adj.* —**a tro′cious ly,** *adv.* —**a tro′cious ness,** *n.*

a troc i ty (ə tros′ə tē), **1** very great wickedness or cruelty: *acts of atrocity committed in war.* **2** a very cruel or brutal act: *the atrocities of war.* **3** INFORMAL. something very bad or unpleasant: *That suit is an atrocity. n., pl.* **a troc i ties.**

at ro phy (at′rə fē), **1** a wasting away; withering: *Some diseases cause atrophy of the muscles in the legs.* **2** waste away: *An ability may atrophy if it is not used.* **1** *n.,* **2** *v.,* **at ro phied, at ro phy ing.**

at tach (ə tach′), **1** fix in place; fasten: *We can attach the trailer to our car.* **2** add at the end; affix: *The signers attached their names to the Constitution.* **3** bind by affection: *She is very attached to her cousin.* **4** fasten itself; belong: *The blame for this accident attaches to the driver who did not stop.* **5** give to; attribute: *The world at first attached little importance to rockets.* **6** assign a military unit, soldiers, etc., for a short time to an organization or commander. **7** take property, etc., by order of a court of law: *If you don't pay them the money you owe, they can attach your salary. v.* —**at tach′a ble,** *adj.*

at ta ché (at′ə shā′), person on the official staff of an ambassador or minister to a foreign country: *a naval attaché. n., pl.* **at ta chés.** [*Attaché* comes from French *attaché,* meaning "attached."]

at tach ment (ə tach′mənt), **1** an attaching or a being attached; connection: *The attachment of the trailer to the car took half an hour.* **2** thing attached, such as an addi- tional device. Some sewing machines have attachments for making buttonholes. **3** means of attaching; fastening. **4** affection that binds a person to someone or some- thing; devotion: *The children have a great attachment to their pets.* **5** the legal taking of property, etc. *n.*

at tack (ə tak′), **1** use force or weapons against; set upon to hurt; begin fighting: *The dog attacked the cat. The enemy attacked at dawn.* **2** talk or write against: *The candidate angrily attacked his opponent's record as mayor.*

atomizer

3 go at with vigor: *attack a hard lesson.* **4** an attacking: *The attack took them by surprise.* **5** act harmfully on: *Locusts attacked the crops.* **6** a sudden occurrence of illness, discomfort, etc.: *an attack of flu.* 1-3,5 *v.*, 4,6 *n.* —at tack′er, *n.*

at tain (ə tān′), **1** arrive at; come to; reach: *Grandfather has attained the age of 80.* **2** gain by effort; accomplish: *She attained her goal. v.*

at tain a ble (ə tā′nə bəl), capable of being attained; able to be reached or achieved: *The office of President is the highest attainable in the United States. adj.* —at tain′a ble ness, *n.*

at tain der (ə tān′dər), loss of property and civil rights as the result of being sentenced to death or being outlawed. *n.*

at tain ment (ə tān′mənt), **1** an attaining: *Her main goal was the attainment of a medical degree.* **2** accomplishment; ability: *Benjamin Franklin was a man of varied attainments; he was a diplomat, statesman, writer, and inventor. n.*

at tempt (ə tempt′), **1** make an effort; try: *I will attempt to reply to your question.* **2** a putting forth of effort to accomplish something; endeavor: *an attempt to climb Mount Everest.* **3** an attack: *an attempt upon someone's life.* 1 *v.*, 2,3 *n.*

at tend (ə tend′), **1** be present at: *Children must attend school.* **2** give care and thought; apply oneself: *Attend to the instructions.* **3** go with as a servant: *Noble ladies attended the queen.* **4** go with as a result: *Success often attends hard work.* **5** wait on; care for; tend: *Nurses attend the sick. v.*

at tend ance (ə ten′dəns), **1** act of being present at a place; an attending: *Our class had perfect attendance today.* **2** number of people present; persons attending: *The attendance at the meeting last night was over 200. n.*
dance attendance on, wait on often and with much care; be too polite and obedient to.
take attendance, call the roll.

at tend ant (ə ten′dənt), **1** person who waits on another, such as a servant or follower. **2** employee who waits on customers. **3** waiting on another to help or serve: *An attendant nurse is at the patient's bedside.* **4** going with as a result; accompanying: *Coughing and sneezing are some of the attendant discomforts of a cold.* 1,2 *n.*, 3,4 *adj.*

at ten tion (ə ten′shən), **1** act of attending; heed: *Pay attention to the teacher.* **2** power of attending; notice: *She called my attention to the problem.* **3** care and thought; consideration: *Your letter will receive early attention.* **4** attentions, *pl.* acts of courtesy or devotion: *She received many attentions, such as invitations to parties, candy, and flowers.* **5** a military attitude of readiness: *The private came to attention. The private stood at attention during inspection. n.*

at ten tive (ə ten′tiv), **1** paying attention; observant: *an attentive pupil.* **2** courteous; polite: *They were attentive to their guests. adj.* —at ten′tive ly, *adv.* —at ten′tive ness, *n.*

at test (ə test′), **1** give proof of; certify: *Your good work attests the care you have taken.* **2** bear witness; testify: *The handwriting expert attested to the genuineness of the signature. v.* —at test′er, *n.*

at tic (at′ik), space in a house just below the roof; garret. *n.*

At ti ca (at′ə kə), district in SE Greece. Its chief city is Athens. Attica was famous in ancient times for its literature and art. *n.*

At ti la (at′l ə *or* ə til′ə), A.D. 406?-453, leader of the Huns in their invasions of Europe. He was defeated by the Romans and Goths in A.D. 451. *n.*

at tire (ə tīr′), **1** clothing or dress: *The queen wore rich attire to her coronation.* **2** clothe or dress; array: *The king*

was attired in a robe trimmed with ermine. 1 *n.*, 2 *v.*, **at tired, at tir ing.**

at ti tude (at′ə tüd *or* at′ə tyüd), **1** way of thinking, acting, or feeling: *As the family next door got to know us better, their attitude changed from formality to friendliness.* **2** position of the body suggesting an action, purpose, emotion, etc.: *He raised his fists in the attitude of a boxer ready to fight. n.*

attn., attention.

at tor ney (ə ter′nē), **1** lawyer. **2** person who has power to act for another in business or legal matters. *n., pl.* **at tor neys.**

attorney at law, lawyer.

attorney general, 1 the chief law officer of a country, state, or province. **2** Attorney General, the head of the United States Department of Justice and the chief legal adviser of the President. *n., pl.* **attorneys general** or **attorney generals.**

at tract (ə trakt′), **1** draw to or toward itself or oneself: *The magnet attracted the iron filings.* **2** be pleasing to; win the attention and liking of: *Bright colors attract children. v.* —at trac′tor, at tract′er, *n.*

at trac tion (ə trak′shən), **1** thing that delights or attracts people: *The elephants were the chief attraction at the circus.* **2** act or power of attracting: *the attraction of a magnet for iron filings. Sports have no attraction for him. n.*

at trac tive (ə trak′tiv), **1** winning attention and liking; pleasing: *an attractive young couple.* **2** attracting: *the attractive power of a magnet. adj.* —at trac′tive ly, *adv.* —at trac′tive ness, *n.*

attrib., 1 attribute. **2** attributive.

at trib ut a ble (ə trib′yə tə bəl), able to be attributed: *Some diseases are attributable to lack of cleanliness. adj.*

at trib ute (ə trib′yüt for *1,2;* at′rə byüt for *3*), **1** regard as an effect of: *She attributes her good health to a carefully planned diet.* **2** think of as belonging to or appropriate to: *We attribute courage to the lion and cunning to the fox.* **3** a quality considered as belonging to a person or thing; characteristic: *Patience is an attribute of a good teacher.* 1,2 *v.*, **at trib ut ed, at trib ut ing;** 3 *n.* —at trib′ut er, at trib′u tor, *n.*

at tri bu tion (at′rə byü′shən), **1** an attributing. **2** thing or quality attributed; an attribute. *n.*

at trib u tive (ə trib′yə tiv), **1** expressing a quality or attribute. An adjective used before or immediately after a noun is an attributive adjective, as in "a *white* shirt," "the ocean *blue.*" A noun placed immediately before another noun and serving as a modifier is an attributive noun, as in "*highway* patrol." **2** an attributive word. 1 *adj.*, 2 *n.* —at trib′u tive ly, *adv.*

at tri tion (ə trish′ən), a wearing away; gradual wearing down: *Pebbles become smooth by attrition. The long war of attrition exhausted the strength of both countries. n.*

at tune (ə tün′ *or* ə tyün′), put in tune or accord; tune: *Our ears became attuned to the noise of the city after several months. v.*, **at tuned, at tun ing.** —at tune′ment, *n.*

atty., attorney.

Atty. Gen., Attorney General.

at. wt., atomic weight.

a typ i cal (ā tip′ə kəl), not typical; irregular. *adj.* —a typ′i cal ly, *adv.*

Au, symbol for gold.

au burn (ô′bərn), **1** a reddish brown. **2** reddish-brown. 1 *n.*, 2 *adj.*

Auck land (ôk′lənd), important seaport in N New Zealand. *n.*

auc tion (ôk′shən), **1** a public sale in which each thing is sold to the person who offers the most money for it. **2** sell at an auction. 1 *n.*, 2 *v.*

auc tion eer (ôk′shə nir′), person whose business is conducting auctions. *n.*

au da cious (ô dā′shəs), **1** having the courage to take risks; bold; daring: *an audacious explorer.* **2** rudely bold; impudent: *The audacious waiter demanded a larger tip. adj.* —**au da′cious ly,** *adv.* —**au da′cious ness,** *n.*

au dac i ty (ô das′ə tē), **1** boldness; reckless daring: *The highest trapeze could not daunt the acrobat's audacity.* **2** rude boldness; impudence: *They had the audacity to go to the party without being invited. n., pl.* **au dac i ties.**

au di bil i ty (ô′də bil′ə tē), quality of being audible. *n.*

au di ble (ô′də bəl), able to be heard; loud enough to be heard: *Without a microphone the speaker was barely audible. adj.*

au di bly (ô′də blē), in an audible manner; so as to be heard. *adv.*

au di ence (ô′dē əns), **1** people gathered in a place to hear or see: *The audience at the theater enjoyed the play.* **2** any persons within hearing: *That television program has an audience of over ten million people.* **3** the readers of a book, newspaper, or magazine. **4** chance to be heard; hearing: *The committee will give you an audience so you may present your plan.* **5** formal interview with a person of high rank: *The queen granted an audience to the ambassador. n.*

au di o (ô′dē ō), **1** using or involving sound or hearing: *audio equipment.* **2** involving or used in transmitting or receiving sound in television. An audio problem is a sound problem; a video problem involves the picture. **3** sound reproduction: *Some of the audio for this film was very bad.* 1,2 *adj.,* 3 *n.* [*Audio* comes from Latin *audire,* meaning "to hear." See **Word Family.**]

audio frequency, a sound wave frequency that can be heard. For human beings this would be any such frequency from about 15 to about 20,000 cycles per second.

au di om e ter (ô′dē om′ə tər), instrument for measuring the keenness and range of hearing. *n.*

au di o-vis u al (ô′dē ō vizh′ü əl), of hearing and sight. Schools use motion pictures, slides, recordings, and other devices as audio-visual aids in teaching. *adj.* —**au′di o-vis′u al ly,** *adv.*

au dit (ô′dit), **1** examine and check (business accounts). **2** an examination and check of business accounts. **3** statement of an account that has been examined and checked. 1 *v.,* 2,3 *n.*

au di tion (ô dish′ən), **1** a hearing to test the ability, quality, or performance of a singer, actor, or other performer. **2** give (a singer, actor, or other performer) such a hearing. **3** sing, act, or perform at such a hearing. 1 *n.,* 2,3 *v.*

au di tor (ô′də tər), **1** person who audits business accounts. **2** hearer; listener. *n.*

au di to ri um (ô′də tôr′ē əm), **1** large room for an audience in a church, theater, school, etc. **2** a building especially designed for public meetings, concerts, lectures, etc. *n., pl.* **au di to ri ums, au di to ri a** (ô′də tôr′ē ə).

au di to ry (ô′də tôr′ē), of hearing or the organs of hearing: *The auditory nerve transmits impulses from the ear to the brain. adj.*

Au du bon (ô′də bon), **John James,** 1785-1851, American painter who made a study of birds. *n.*

Aug., August.

au ger (ô′gər), **1** tool for boring holes in wood. **2** a large tool for boring holes in the earth. *n.*

aught[1] (ôt), anything: *Has she done aught to help you? n.* [*Aught*[1] is from Old English *āwiht,* which comes from *ā,* meaning "ever," and *wiht,* meaning "thing."]

aught[2] (ôt), zero; cipher; nothing. *n.* [*Aught*[2] comes from *naught,* because *a naught* was read as *an aught.*]

aug ment (ôg ment′), make or become greater in size, number, amount, or degree; increase: *He augmented his income by working overtime three nights a week. v.* —**aug ment′a ble,** *adj.* —**aug ment′er,** *n.*

aug men ta tion (ôg′men tā′shən), **1** an augmenting; increase. **2** thing that augments; addition. *n.*

au gur (ô′gər), **1** be a sign or promise of: *Those storm clouds augur ill for our picnic.* **2** priest in ancient Rome who foretold future events and gave advice on the course of public business by interpreting such signs or omens as the flight of birds, thunder and lightning, etc. 1 *v.,* 2 *n.*

audio

Below are words related to *audio.* They can all be traced back to the Latin word *audire* (ou dē′re), meaning "to hear."

audible	auditor	inaudible
audibly	auditorium	obedience
audience	auditory	obedient
audiometer	disobedience	obeisance
audit	disobedient	obey
audition	disobey	oyez

au gust (ô gust′), inspiring reverence and admiration; majestic; venerable. *adj.* —**au gust′ness,** *n.*

Au gust (ô′gəst), the eighth month of the year. It has 31 days. *n.*

Au gus ta (ô gus′tə), **1** capital of Maine, in the SW part. **2** city in E Georgia. *n.*

Au gus tine (ô′gə stēn′), **Saint,** A.D. 354-430, one of the leaders in the early Christian church. *n.*

Au gus tus (ô gus′təs), 63 B.C.-A.D. 14, the first emperor of Rome, who reigned from 27 B.C. to A.D. 14. He was the grandnephew and heir of Julius Caesar. *n.*

auk (ôk), a sea bird found in arctic regions, with legs set so far back that it stands like a penguin. It has short wings used chiefly as paddles in swimming. *n.*

auld (ôld), SCOTTISH. old. *adj.*

aunt (ant), **1** sister of one's father or mother. **2** wife of one's uncle. *n.*

aunt ie (an′tē), INFORMAL. aunt. *n.*

au ra (ôr′ə), something that seems to come from or surround a person or thing as an atmosphere: *There was an aura of mystery about the stranger. n., pl.* **au ras.**

au ral (ôr′əl), of or perceived by the ear. *adj.* —**au′ral ly,** *adv.*

au re ole (ôr′ē ōl), ring of light surrounding a figure or object. *n.*

Au re o my cin (ôr′ē ō mī′sn), trademark for an antibiotic derived from a soil microorganism, used to check or kill certain bacterial infections and viruses. *n.*

au re voir (ō rə vwär′), FRENCH. good-by; till we see each other again.

au ri cle (ôr′ə kəl), **1** chamber of the heart that receives the blood from the veins and forces it into a ventricle. The heart of a bird, mammal, or reptile has two auricles. A fish has one auricle. **2** the outer part of the ear. *n.*

Au ro ra (ô rôr′ə), (in Roman myths) the goddess of the dawn. *n.*

au ro ra bo re al is (ô rôr′ə bôr′ē al′is), streamers or bands of light appearing in the northern sky at night; northern lights.

aus pic es (ô′spə siz), **1** helpful influence; approval or support; patronage: *The school fair was held under the auspices of the Parents' Association.* **2** omens; signs. The ancient Romans used the flight of birds as auspices. *n.pl.*

aus pi cious (ô spish′əs), with signs of success; favorable: *The popularity of her first book was an auspicious beginning for a new author. adj.* **—aus pi′cious ly,** *adv.* **—aus pi′cious ness,** *n.*

Aus ten (ô′stən), **Jane,** 1775-1817, English novelist. *n.*

aus tere (ô stir′), **1** stern in manner or appearance; harsh: *My father was a silent, austere man, very strict with us.* **2** strict in morals: *Some of the ideas of the Puritans seem too austere to us.* **3** severely simple: *The tall, plain columns stood against the sky in austere beauty. adj.* **—aus tere′ly,** *adv.* **—aus tere′ness,** *n.*

aus ter i ty (ô ster′ə tē), **1** sternness in manner or appearance; harshness; severity. **2** moral strictness. **3** severe simplicity. *n., pl.* **aus ter i ties.**

Aus tin (ô′stən), capital of Texas, in the central part. *n.*

Aus tral a sia (ô′strə lā′zhə), Australia, Tasmania, New Guinea, New Zealand, and other nearby islands. *n.* **—Aus′tral a′sian,** *adj., n.*

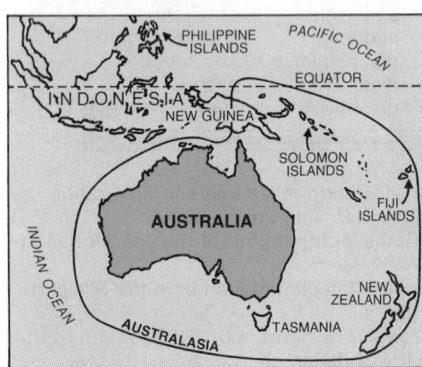

Aus tral ia (ô strā′lyə), **1** continent southeast of Asia. **2 Commonwealth of,** country that includes this continent and Tasmania. It is a member of the Commonwealth of Nations. *Capital:* Canberra. *n.*

Aus tral ian (ô strā′lyən), **1** of Australia or its people. **2** person born or living in Australia. **1** *adj.,* **2** *n.*

Aus tri a (ô′strē ə), country in central Europe. Before World War I it was an empire. *Capital:* Vienna. *n.* **—Aus′tri an,** *adj., n.*

Aus tri a-Hun gar y (ô′strē ə hung′gər ē), monarchy in central Europe from 1867 to 1918, composed of the Austrian empire and the kingdom of Hungary. *n.*

au then tic (ô then′tik), **1** worthy of trust or belief; reliable: *We heard an authentic account of the wreck, given by one of the ship's passengers.* **2** genuine; real: *That is her authentic signature, not a forgery. adj.*

au then ti cal ly (ô then′tik lē), **1** reliably. **2** genuinely. *adv.*

au then ti cate (ô then′tə kāt), establish the truth of; show to be valid or genuine: *Handwriting experts authenticated the signature on the will. v.,* **au then ti cat ed, au then ti cat ing. —au then′ti ca′tor,** *n.*

au then ti ca tion (ô then′tə kā′shən), an authenticating or a being authenticated. *n.*

au then tic i ty (ô′then tis′ə tē), **1** reliability: *The value of the evidence depends on its authenticity.* **2** genuineness: *The lawyer questioned the authenticity of the signature. n.*

au thor (ô′thər), **1** person who writes books, poems, stories, or articles; writer. **2** person who creates or begins anything: *Are you the author of this scheme? n.* [*Author* came into English about 600 years ago from French *autor,* which came from Latin *auctor,* originally meaning "one who creates, builds, or increases."]

au thor i tar i an (ə thôr′ə ter′ē ən), favoring obedience to authority instead of individual freedom: *An authoritarian government will often censor newspapers. adj.*

au thor i ta tive (ə thôr′ə tā′tiv), **1** having authority; officially ordered: *Authoritative orders came from the general.* **2** commanding: *In authoritative tones the policeman told us to keep back.* **3** having the authority of expert knowledge: *an authoritative article by a well-known scientist. adj.* **—au thor′i ta′tive ly,** *adv.* **—au thor′i ta′tive ness,** *n.*

au thor i ty (ə thôr′ə tē), **1** power to enforce obedience; right to command or act: *Parents have authority over their children. The police have the authority to arrest speeding drivers.* **2** person or group who has such power or right. **3 the authorities,** the officials in control: *Who are the proper authorities to give permits to hunt or fish?* **4** source of correct information or wise advice: *A good dictionary is an authority on the meanings of words.* **5** an expert on some subject: *She is an authority on the Revolutionary War. n., pl.* **au thor i ties.**

au thor i za tion (ô′thər ə zā′shən), **1** an authorizing; giving legal power to: *The authorization of the police to give tickets to jaywalkers cut down on the number of accidents.* **2** legal right; official permission: *I have the authorization of the owner to fish in this pond. n.*

au thor ize (ô′thə rīz′), **1** give power or right to: *The committee authorized her to proceed.* **2** give formal approval to; approve: *Congress authorized the spending of money for a new post-office building. This dictionary authorizes the two spellings "acknowledgment" and "acknowledgement." v.,* **au thor ized, au thor iz ing. —au′thor iz′er,** *n.*

au thor ship (ô′thər ship), origin as to author: *What is the authorship of that novel? n.*

au to (ô′tō), automobile. *n., pl.* **au tos.**

auto-, *combining form.* **1** self; by itself: *Automatic = moving or acting by itself.* **2** of or by oneself: *Autobiography = biography of oneself.* [The form *auto-* comes from Greek *autos,* meaning "self."]

Austria-Hungary in 1914
(shown, by the darker area, on a modern map)

au to bi o graph ic (ô′tə bī′ə graf′ik), autobiographical. *adj.*

au to bi o graph i cal (ô′tə bī′ə graf′ə kəl), **1** having to do with the story of one's own life. **2** telling or writing the story of one's own life. *adj.*

au to bi og ra phy (ô′tə bī og′rə fē), story of a person's life written by that person. *n., pl.* **au to bi og ra phies.**

au toc ra cy (ô tok′rə sē), **1** government by a single person having unlimited power. **2** absolute authority. *n., pl.* **au toc ra cies.**

au to crat (ô′tə krat), **1** ruler having unlimited power. **2** person who uses power over others in a harsh way: *A good teacher is never an autocrat. n.*

au to crat ic (ô′tə krat′ik), of or like an autocrat; having absolute power or authority; ruling without checks or limitations: *The principal's autocratic manner made him unpopular. adj.* —**au′to crat′i cal ly,** *adv.*

au to graph (ô′tə graf), **1** a person's signature: *Many people collect the autographs of celebrities.* **2** write one's name in or on: *The movie star autographed my program.* **1** *n.,* **2** *v.*

Au to harp (ô′tō härp′), a trademark for a musical instrument similar to the zither, that produces chords. A set of keys presses down on all strings except those required for the chord. *n.*

au to mat (ô′tə mat), restaurant in which food is obtained from compartments that open when coins are inserted in slots. *n.*

au to mate (ô′tə māt), convert to automation; operate by automation. *v.,* **au to mat ed, au to mat ing.**

au to mat ic (ô′tə mat′ik), **1** moving or acting by itself: *Our apartment house has an automatic elevator.* **2** done without thought or attention: *Breathing and swallowing are usually automatic.* **3** gun that throws out the empty shell and reloads by itself. An automatic continues to fire until the trigger is released. **1,2** *adj.,* **3** *n.*

au to mat i cal ly (ô′tə mat′ik lē), in an automatic manner: *Electric refrigerators work automatically. adv.*

au to ma tion (ô′tə mā′shən), the use of automatic controls in the operation of a machine or group of machines. In automation, electronic or mechanical devices do many of the tasks formerly performed by people. *n.*

au tom a ton (ô tom′ə ton), **1** person or animal whose actions are entirely mechanical. **2** machine or toy that moves by itself. *n., pl.* **au tom a tons, au tom a ta** (ô tom′ə tə).

au to mo bile (ô′tə mə bēl′), **1** a passenger vehicle, for use on roads and streets, that carries its own engine. **2** of or for automobiles: *an automobile mechanic.* **1** *n.,* **2** *adj.*

au to mo tive (ô′tə mō′tiv), **1** of cars, trucks, and other self-moving vehicles. Automotive engineering deals with the design and construction of motor vehicles. **2** furnishing its own power; moving by itself: *A truck is one type of automotive vehicle. adj.*

au to nom ic (ô′tə nom′ik), having to do with that part of the nervous system of vertebrates that controls digestive, reproductive, and other involuntary reactions. *adj.*

au ton o mous (ô ton′ə məs), self-governing; independent: *an autonomous nation. adj.* —**au ton′o mous ly,** *adv.*

au ton o my (ô ton′ə mē), self-government; independence: *Algeria achieved autonomy in 1962. n.*

au top sy (ô′top sē), medical examination of a dead body to find the cause of death; post-mortem: *The autopsy revealed that the patient died of a heart attack. n., pl.* **au top sies.**

au tumn (ô′təm), **1** season of the year between summer and winter; fall. **2** of autumn; coming in autumn: *autumn rains, autumn flowers.* **1** *n.,* **2** *adj.*

au tum nal (ô tum′nəl), of or coming in autumn: *autumnal frosts. adj.* —**au tum′nal ly,** *adv.*

aux il iar y (ôg zil′yər ē), **1** giving help or support; assisting: *Some sailboats have auxiliary engines.* **2** person or thing that helps; aid: *The microscope is a useful auxiliary to the human eye.* **3** additional; subsidiary: *The main*

Autoharp

library has several auxiliary branches. **4** a subsidiary group: *a men's club with a women's auxiliary.* **5** auxiliary verb. **1,3** *adj.,* **2,4,5** *n., pl.* **aux il iar ies.**

auxiliary verb, verb used to form the tenses, moods, or voices of other verbs; helping verb. *Be, can, do, have, may, must, shall,* and *will* are auxiliary verbs. EXAMPLES: I *am* going; she *will* go; they *are* lost; they *were* lost.

av., 1 avenue. **2** average. **3** avoirdupois.

a vail (ə vāl′), **1** be of use or value to; help: *Money will not avail you after you are dead.* **2** be of use or value: *Talk will not avail without work. v.*

avail oneself of, take advantage of; profit by; make use of: *He availed himself of the opportunity to learn French.*

of no avail or **to no avail,** of no use or value: *Crying is of no avail now. I complained about the clerk's rudeness, but to no avail.*

a vail a bil i ty (ə vā′lə bil′ə tē), a being available; being at hand; being ready: *The availability of water power helped make New England a manufacturing center. n.*

a vail a ble (ə vā′lə bəl), **1** able to be used: *She is not available for the job; she is out of town.* **2** able to be had: *All available tickets were sold. adj.* —**a vail′a ble ness,** *n.* —**a vail′a bly,** *adv.*

avalanche
(def. 1)

av a lanche (av′ə lanch), **1** a large mass of snow and ice, or of dirt and rocks, rapidly sliding or falling down the side of a mountain. **2** anything like an avalanche: *The reporters asked the governor an avalanche of questions. n.*

a vant-garde (ä′vänt gärd′), group of people, especially in the arts, who are ahead of all others in using or creating new ideas, methods, designs, etc. *n.*

av ar ice (av′ər is), too great a desire to acquire money or property; greed for wealth. *n.*

av a ri cious (av/ə rish/əs), greatly desiring money or property; greedy for wealth. *adj.* —**av/a ri/cious ly,** *adv.* —**av/a ri/cious ness,** *n.*

a vast (ə vast/), stop! stay! *"Avast there!" shouted the sailor. interj.*

a vaunt (ə vônt/), OLD USE. begone! get out! go away! *interj.*

Ave. or **ave.,** Avenue; avenue.

A ve Ma ri a (ä/vā mə rē/ə), 1 "Hail Mary!", the first words of the Latin form of a prayer of the Roman Catholic Church. 2 this prayer.

a venge (ə venj/), get revenge for: *avenge an insult. They fought to avenge the enemy's invasion of their country. v.,* **a venged, a veng ing.**

a veng er (ə ven/jər), person who avenges. *n.*

av e nue (av/ə nü *or* av/ə nyü), 1 a wide street. 2 road or walk bordered by trees. 3 way of approach: *Hard work is one avenue to success. n.*

a ver (ə vėr/), state positively to be true; assert: *They averred that they had nothing to do with breaking into the parked car. v.,* **a verred, a ver ring.**

av er age (av/ər ij), 1 quantity found by dividing the sum of all the quantities by the number of quantities. The average of 3 and 5 and 10 is 6 (3 + 5 + 10 = 18; 18 ÷ 3 = 6). 2 find the average of: *Will you average those numbers for me?* 3 obtained by averaging; being an average: *The average temperature for the week was 82.* 4 have as an average; amount on the average to: *The cost of our lunches at school averaged two dollars a week.* 5 usual sort or amount: *The amount of rain this year has been below average.* 6 usual; ordinary: *a person of average intelligence.* 7 do, get, yield, etc., on an average: *She averages six hours of work a day. The farmer averaged forty bushels of wheat to the acre.* 1,5 *n.,* 2,4,7 *v.,* **av er aged, av er ag ing;** 3,6 *adj.* —**av/er age ly,** *adv.* —**av/er age ness,** *n.*

on the average or **on an average,** considered on the basis of the average: *I work six hours a day on the average. The farm produces, on an average, forty bushels to the acre.*

a verse (ə vėrs/), having a strong or fixed dislike; opposed or unwilling: *I am averse to smoking. adj.* —**a verse/ly,** *adv.* —**a verse/ness,** *n.*

a ver sion (ə vėr/zhən), 1 a strong or fixed dislike: *I have an aversion to tea.* 2 thing or person disliked: *Impoliteness is his special aversion. n.*

a vert (ə vėrt/), 1 keep from happening; prevent; avoid: *The driver averted an accident by a quick turn of the steering wheel.* 2 turn away; turn aside: *I averted my eyes from the accident. v.* —**a vert/i ble, a vert/a ble,** *adj.*

avg., average.

a vi ar y (ā/vē er/ē), house, enclosure, or large cage in which many birds, especially wild birds, are kept. *n., pl.* **a vi ar ies.**

a vi a tion (ā/vē ā/shən *or* av/ē ā/shən), 1 art or science of operating and navigating aircraft. 2 the designing and manufacturing of aircraft, especially airplanes. *n.* [*Aviation* was borrowed from French *aviation,* which came from Latin *avis,* meaning "bird."]

a vi a tor (ā/vē ā/tər *or* av/ē ā/tər), person who flies an aircraft; pilot. *n.*

a vi a trix (ā/vē ā/triks *or* av/ē ā/triks), woman who flies an aircraft; pilot. *n., pl.* **a vi a trix es.**

av id (av/id), extremely eager: *an avid desire for fame. She is an avid golfer. adj.* —**av/id ly,** *adv.* —**av/id ness,** *n.*

a vid i ty (ə vid/ə tē), 1 great eagerness: *Our suggestion that they visit us was seized upon with avidity.* 2 greed for wealth; avarice. *n.*

av o ca do (av/ə kä/dō), the dark-green, pear-shaped fruit of a tree that grows in warm regions; alligator pear. Avocados have a large seed surrounded by yellow-green pulp which is used in salads, dips, etc. *n., pl.* **av o ca dos.** [*Avocado* is from Spanish *aguacate,* which came from Nahuatl *ahuacatl.*]

av o ca tion (av/ə kā/shən), something that a person likes to do in addition to a regular job; hobby: *He is a lawyer, but writing stories is his avocation. n.*

WORD HISTORY

avocation

Avocation is from Latin *avocationem,* and can be traced back to *a-,* meaning "away," and *vocare,* meaning "to call."

a void (ə void/), keep away from; keep out of the way of: *We avoided driving through large cities on our trip. v.*

a void a ble (ə voi/də bəl), able to be avoided. *adj.* —**a void/a bly,** *adv.*

a void ance (ə void/ns), an avoiding; keeping away from: *His avoidance of me made me wonder if I had offended him. n.*

av oir du pois (av/ər də poiz/), system of weights in which a pound containing 16 ounces is used. The avoirdupois system is used to weigh everything except gems, precious metals, and drugs. *n.*

A von (ā/vən), name of several rivers in central and southern England. *n.*

a vow (ə vou/), declare frankly or openly; admit; acknowledge: *The senator avowed that he had never favored higher taxes for low-income people. v.* —**a vow/a ble,** *adj.*

a vow al (ə vou/əl), a frank or open declaration; admission; acknowledgment: *She made a plain avowal of her opinions even though they were unpopular. n.*

a vowed (ə voud/), openly declared; admitted: *an avowed candidate for the office of president. adj.*

a vow ed ly (ə vou/id lē), admittedly; openly. *adv.*

a wait (ə wāt/), 1 wait for; look forward to: *I shall await your answer to my letter with eagerness.* 2 be ready for; be in store for: *Many pleasures await you on your trip. v.*

a wake (ə wāk/), 1 wake up; arouse: *I awoke from a sound sleep. The alarm clock awoke me.* 2 roused from sleep; not asleep: *She is always awake early.* 3 stir up: *My words awoke his anger.* 4 on the alert; watchful: *They were awake to possible danger.* 1,3 *v.,* **a woke** or **a waked, a waked, a wak ing;** 2,4 *adj.*

a wak en (ə wā/kən), wake up; stir up; arouse: *The sun was shining when he awakened. I was awakened late this morning. v.* —**a wak/en er,** *n.*

a wak en ing (ə wā/kə ning), a waking up; arousing. *n.*

a ward (ə wôrd/), 1 give after careful consideration; grant: *A medal was awarded to the best speller in the class.* 2 something given after careful consideration; prize: *My dog won the highest award.* 3 decide upon by law; adjudge: *The court awarded damages of $5000 to the injured man.* 4 decision by a judge: *We all thought the award was fair.* 1,3 *v.,* 2,4 *n.* —**a ward/a ble,** *adj.* —**a ward/er,** *n.*

a ware (ə wer/ *or* ə war/), having knowledge; realizing; conscious: *I was too sleepy to be aware how cold it was. She was not aware of her danger. adj.* —**a ware/ness,** *n.*

a wash (ə wosh/ *or* ə wôsh/), 1 level with the surface of the water; just covered with water: *The beach was awash with the flowing tide.* 2 carried about by water; floating: *The rising water set everything awash. adj.*

a way (ə wā/), 1 from a place; to a distance: *Stay away from the fire.* 2 at a distance; a way off: *The sailor was far away from home* (adv.). *His home is miles away* (adj.).

3 absent; gone: *My friend is away today.* **4** out of one's possession, notice, or use: *He gave his boat away.* **5** out of existence: *The sounds died away.* **6** in another direction; aside: *She turned her car away to avoid an accident.* **7** without stopping; continuously: *work away at a job.* **8** without delay; at once: *Fire away!* 1,2,4-8 *adv.,* 2,3 *adj.*
do away with, 1 put an end to; get rid of: *The United States did away with slavery in 1865.* **2** kill: *They had to do away with the sick animal.*

awe (ô), **1** great fear and wonder; fear and reverence: *The sight of the great waterfall filled us with awe.* **2** cause to feel awe; fill with awe: *The majesty of the mountains awed us.* 1 *n.,* 2 *v.,* **awed, aw ing.**

awe some (ô/səm), causing awe: *The great fire was an awesome sight. adj.* —**awe/some ness,** *n.*

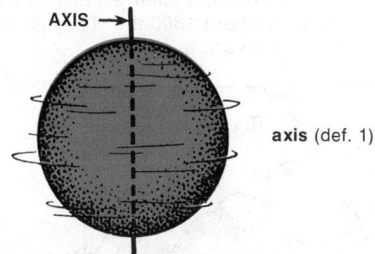

AXIS →

axis (def. 1)

awe-strick en (ô/strik/ən), awe-struck. *adj.*
awe-struck (ô/struk/), filled with awe: *She was awe-struck by the mountain's grandeur. adj.*
aw ful (ô/fəl), **1** causing fear; dreadful; terrible: *An awful storm with thunder and lightning came up.* **2** deserving great respect and reverence: *He felt the awful power of God.* **3** filling with awe; impressive: *The mountains rose to awful heights.* **4** INFORMAL. very bad, great, ugly, etc.: *an awful mess, an awful nuisance.* **5** INFORMAL. very: *She was awful mad.* 1-4 *adj.,* 5 *adv.* —**aw/ful ness,** *n.*
aw ful ly (ô/flē *or* ô/fə lē), **1** dreadfully; terribly: *The burn hurt awfully.* **2** INFORMAL. very: *I'm awfully sorry. adv.*
a while (ə hwīl/), for a short time: *Stay awhile. adv.*
awk ward (ôk/wərd), **1** not graceful or skillful in movement or shape; clumsy: *Seals are very awkward on land, but graceful in the water.* **2** not well suited to use: *The handle of this pitcher has an awkward shape.* **3** not easily managed: *This is an awkward corner to turn.* **4** inconvenient or embarrassing: *an awkward situation. He asked me such an awkward question that I did not know what to reply. adj.* —**awk/ward ly,** *adv.* —**awk/ward ness,** *n.*
awl (ôl), a pointed tool used for making small holes in leather or wood. *n.*
awn ing (ô/ning), piece of canvas, metal, wood, or plastic spread over or before a door, window, porch, patio, etc., for protection from the sun or rain. *n.*
a woke (ə wōk/), a past tense of **awake.** *I awoke late. v.*
a wry (ə rī/), **1** with a twist or turn to one side: *My hat was blown awry by the wind.* **2** wrong; out of order: *Our plans have gone awry. adv.*
ax or **axe** (aks), tool with a flat, sharp blade fastened on a handle, used for chopping, splitting, and shaping wood. *n., pl.* **ax es.** —**ax/like/, axe/like/,** *adj.*
ax es[1] (ak/siz), plural of **ax.** *n.*
ax es[2] (ak/sēz/), plural of **axis.** *n.*
ax i al (ak/sē əl), of or forming an axis. *adj.*
ax il (ak/səl), angle between the upper side of a leaf or stem and the supporting stem or branch. A bud is usually found in the axil. *n.*
ax i om (ak/sē əm), **1** statement taken to be true without proof; self-evident truth: *It is an axiom that if equals are added to equals the results will be equal.* **2** a well-established principle; rule or law. *n.*

ax i o mat ic (ak/sē ə mat/ik), accepted without proof; self-evident: *It is axiomatic that a whole is greater than any of its parts. adj.* —**ax/i o mat/i cal ly,** *adv.*
ax is (ak/sis), **1** a straight line about which an object turns or seems to turn. The axis of the earth is an imaginary line through the North Pole and the South Pole. **2** a central or principal line around which parts are arranged regularly. The axis of a cone is a straight line going from the center of its base to its peak. **3** one of the lines along which the coordinates of a point are measured. **4 the Axis,** Germany, Italy, Japan, and their allies, during World War II. *n., pl.* **ax es.**
ax le (ak/səl), **1** bar or shaft on which a wheel turns. Some axles turn with the wheel. **2** axletree. *n.*
ax le tree (ak/səl trē/), crossbar connecting two opposite wheels of a vehicle. The wheels turn on its ends. *n.*
ax on (ak/son), the long extension of a nerve cell that carries impulses away from the body of the cell. *n.*
a ya tol lah (ä/yä tō/lə), **1** a Moslem religious leader. **2** any leader. *n.* [*Ayatollah* can be traced back to Arabic *āya,* meaning "sign, reflection," and *āllah,* meaning "Allah, God."]
aye or **ay** (ī), **1** yes: *Aye, aye, sir.* **2** an affirmative answer, vote, or voter: *The ayes won the vote.* 1 *adv.,* 2 *n.*
Ayr shire (er/shər *or* ar/shər), any of a breed of dairy cattle that are red and white or brown and white, originating in Scotland. *n.*
AZ, Arizona (used with postal Zip Code).
a zal ea (ə zā/lyə), **1** any of a group of shrubs growing mainly in northeastern North America and in China. Azaleas are related to rhododendrons but are usually not evergreen. **2** its showy flower. *n., pl.* **a zal eas.**
A zores (ə zôrz/ *or* ā/zôrz), group of islands in the Atlantic, west of and belonging to Portugal. *n.pl.*
Az tec (az/tek), **1** member of an American Indian people of central Mexico. The Aztecs had a highly developed culture, and ruled a large empire during the 1400's, which fell to the Spanish in 1521. **2** their language; Nahuatl. **3** of the Aztecs or their language. 1,2 *n.,* 3 *adj.*
Az tec an (az/tek/ən), Aztec. *adj.*
az ure (azh/ər), **1** the blue color of the unclouded sky. **2** having this color; sky-blue. 1 *n.,* 2 *adj.*

WORD HISTORY

axil

Axil comes from Latin *axilla,* meaning "armpit." An axil was called this because of its appearance.

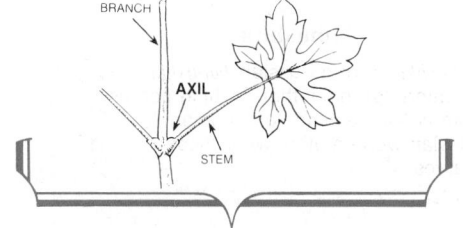

BRANCH

AXIL

STEM

Bb

B or **b** (bē), the second letter of the English alphabet. *n., pl.* **B's** or **b's.**

B, symbol for boron.

Ba, symbol for barium.

B.A., Bachelor of Arts. Also, **A.B.**

baa (bä *or* ba), **1** the sound a sheep makes; bleat. **2** make this sound; bleat. 1 *n., pl.* **baas;** 2 *v.,* **baaed, baa ing.**

Ba al (bā′əl), **1** the sun god of the Phoenicians. **2** a false god. *n., pl.* **Ba al im** (bā′ə lim) or **Ba als.**

bab ble (bab′əl), **1** make sounds like a baby: *The baby was babbling and cooing.* **2** talk that cannot be understood: *A confused babble filled the room.* **3** talk foolishly: *They babbled on and on about the weather.* **4** foolish talk. **5** talk too much; tell secrets. **6** make a murmuring sound: *The little brook babbled away just behind our tent.* **7** a murmuring sound: *The babble of the brook put me to sleep.* 1,3,5,6 *v.,* **bab bled, bab bling;** 2,4,7 *n.*

babe (bāb), baby. *n.*

Ba bel (bā′bəl *or* bab′əl), **1** (in the Bible) a city where a high tower, called the **Tower of Babel,** was built after the Flood to reach heaven. God punished its builders by changing their language into several new and different languages. Because they could not understand one another, they had to leave the tower unfinished. **2 babel,** noise; confusion. *n.*

baboon
about 3½ ft. (1 m.)
long with its tail

ba boon (ba bün′), kind of large, fierce monkey with a doglike face and a rather short tail. Baboons live in the rocky hills of Africa and Arabia in large groups. *n.*

ba bush ka (bə bush′kə), scarf worn on the head and tied under the chin. *n., pl.* **ba bush kas.**

WORD HISTORY

babushka

Babushka is from Russian *babushka,* meaning "grandmother," which comes from *baba,* meaning "old woman." Russian women often wear these scarves.

ba by (bā′bē), **1** child too young to walk or speak; infant. **2** the youngest of a family or group. **3** young: *a baby lamb.* **4** small for its kind; small: *my baby finger.* **5** of or for a baby: *baby shoes.* **6** childish: *baby talk.* **7** person who acts like a baby; childish person: *Don't be a baby.* **8** treat as a baby; pamper: *You are too old to be babied.* 1,2,7 *n., pl.* **ba bies;** 3-6 *adj.,* 8 *v.,* **ba bied, ba by ing.** **—ba′by like′,** *adj.*

ba by hood (bā′bē hud), condition or time of being a baby. *n.*

ba by ish (bā′bē ish), like a baby; childish. *adj.* **—ba′by ish ly,** *adv.* **—ba′by ish ness,** *n.*

Bab y lon (bab′ə lən), capital of ancient Babylonia, on the Euphrates. It was noted for its wealth, power, magnificence, and the wickedness of its people. *n.*

Bab y lo ni a (bab′ə lō′nē ə), ancient empire in SW Asia which reached its peak about 1800 B.C. The capital was Babylon. *n.* **—Bab′y lo′ni an,** *adj., n.*

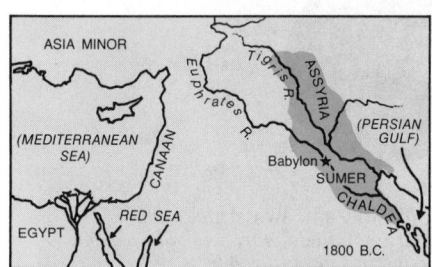

Babylonia—The darker area shows the Babylonian Empire at its greatest extent.

ba by-sit (bā′bē sit′), take care of a child or children while the parents are away for a while. *v.,* **ba by-sat** (bā′bē sat′), **ba by-sit ting.**

ba by-sit ter (bā′bē sit′ər), person who takes care of a child or children while the parents are away for a while. *n.*

baby teeth, one's first set of teeth.

Bach (bäk), **Johann Sebastian,** 1685-1750, German composer and organist. *n.*

bach e lor (bach′ə lər), **1** man who has not married. **2** person who has the first degree of a college or university. *n.*

bach e lor's-but ton (bach′ə lərz but′n), plant with a single, small, button-shaped flower that is blue, violet, pink, or white; cornflower. *n.*

ba cil lus (bə sil′əs), **1** any of the rod-shaped bacteria, especially one that forms spores: *the typhoid bacillus.* **2** any type of bacteria. *n., pl.* **ba cil li** (bə sil′ī).

back (bak), **1** the part of a person's body opposite the face or the front part of the body. **2** the upper part of an animal's body from the neck to the end of the backbone. **3** the backbone; spine. **4** the side of anything away from one; rear, upper, or farther part: *Put the chair in the back of the room. I had a bruise on the back of my hand.* **5** opposite the front; away from one: *The box is in the back seat of the car.* **6** part of a chair, couch, bench, or the like, which supports the back of a person sitting down. **7** support or help: *Many of her friends backed her plan.* **8** move or cause to move backward or in the opposite direction: *I backed the car out of the driveway. We backed away from the dog.* **9** behind in space or time: *Please walk back three steps (adv.). Have you read the back issues of this magazine? (adj.) Some years back this land was all in farms (adv.).* **10** in return: *They paid back what they borrowed.* **11** in the place from which something or someone came: *Put the books back.* **12** in check: *The police held the crowd back.* **13** (in football) a player whose position is behind the line of scrimmage. 1-4,6,13 *n.*, 5,9 *adj.*, 7,8 *v.*, 9-12 *adv.* [*Back* comes from Old English *bæc.*]

back and forth, first one way and then the other: *The dog ran back and forth across the field.*

back down, give up an attempt or claim; withdraw: *I said I would go swimming, but I backed down when I found out how cold the water was.*

back of, in the rear of; behind: *The barn is back of the house.*

back out or **back out of,** 1 break a promise: *I promised to buy everyone ice cream, but I backed out when I realized I had no money with me.* 2 withdraw from an undertaking: *The village backed out of building a pool when the cost got too high.*

back up, 1 move backward: *The freight train backed up onto the siding.* 2 support or help: *Most of the neighborhood backed up the city's plan for new street lights.*

behind one's back, without one's knowing it; secretly: *The cashier of the store stole money behind the owner's back.*

go back on, INFORMAL. break a promise to.

back ache (bak′āk′), a pain in the back. *n.*

back bite (bak′bīt′), say mean or spiteful things about; slander (an absent person). *v.*, **back bit** (bak′bit′), **back bit ten** (bak′bit′n) or **back bit**, **back bit ing.** —**back′bit′er,** *n.*

back board (bak′bôrd′), (in basketball) the upright, rectangular surface of wood, glass, or plastic, to which the basket is fastened. *n.*

back bone (bak′bōn′), **1** the main bone along the middle of the back in human beings and other mammals, birds, reptiles, amphibians, and fishes; spine. The backbone is made up of many separate bones, called vertebrae, held together by muscles and tendons. **2** the most important part; chief support; basis: *The Constitution is the backbone of our legal system.* **3** strength of character; firmness: *Although she is criticized, she has the backbone to stand up for her beliefs. n.*

back break ing (bak′brā′king), very exhausting or tiring; demanding great effort: *Shoveling snow all day is backbreaking work. adj.*

back drop (bak′drop′), curtain at the back of a stage, often painted and used as part of the scenery. *n.*

back er (bak′ər), person who supports another person, a plan, or an idea. *n.*

back field (bak′fēld′), (in football) the players whose position is behind the line of scrimmage. *n.*

back fire (bak′fīr′), **1** explosion of gas occurring at the wrong time or in the wrong place in a gasoline engine. **2** explode in this way. **3** fire set to check a forest or prairie fire by controlled burning off of the space in front of it. **4** have a result opposite to the expected result: *His scheme backfired, and instead of getting rich he lost all his money.* 1,3 *n.*, 2,4 *v.*, **back fired, back fir ing.**

back gam mon (bak′gam′ən), game for two played on a special board with 12 spaces on each side. Each player has 15 pieces, which are moved according to the throw of the dice. *n.*

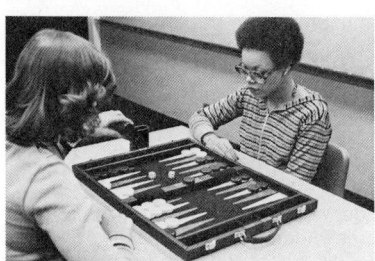

backgammon

back ground (bak′ground′), **1** the part of a picture or scene toward the back: *The cottage stands in the foreground with the mountains in the background.* **2** surface upon which things are made or placed: *Her dress had pink flowers on a white background.* **3** earlier conditions or events that help to explain some later condition or event: *This book gives the background of the Revolutionary War.* **4** past experience, knowledge, and training: *His early background included living on a farm. n.*

in the background, out of sight; not in clear view: *Stay in the background so you don't get into trouble.*

back hand (bak′hand′), **1** stroke in tennis and other games made with the back of the hand turned outward. **2** handwriting in which the letters slope to the left. **3** backhanded. 1,2 *n.*, 3 *adj.*

backhand writing

backhand (def. 2)

back hand ed (bak′han′did), **1** done or made with the back of the hand turned outward: *a backhanded stroke.* **2** indirect: *She means to help, even though she offers to do so in a backhanded way.* **3** sounding like praise but actually an insult; insincere: *He paid his opponent a backhanded compliment.* **4** slanting to the left: *backhanded writing. adj.* —**back′hand′ed ly,** *adv.* —**back′hand′ed ness,** *n.*

back ing (bak′ing), **1** support or help: *The candidate had the backing of several newspapers in the state.* **2** supporters or helpers. **3** something placed at the back of anything to support or strengthen it: *a quilt with new backing. n.*

back log (bak′lôg′), **1** an accumulation of orders, duties, etc., that have not yet been carried out: *After my illness I had a backlog of schoolwork to make up.* **2** a large log at the back of a wood fire. *n.*

back pack (bak′pak′), **1** a pack, often supported by a frame, that is worn on the back by hikers and campers to carry food, clothes, and equipment. **2** go hiking or camping while carrying a backpack. 1 *n.*, 2 *v.* —**back′pack′er,** *n.*

back rest (bak′rest′), a support at the back. *n.*

back seat, INFORMAL. place of inferiority.

back side (bak′sīd′), INFORMAL. rump; buttocks. *n.*

back slide (bak′slīd′), slide back into wrong ways, error, etc.; gradually return to old ways and practices. *v.*, **back slid** (bak′slid′), **back slid** or **back slid den** (bak′slid′n), **back slid ing.**

back slid er (bak′slī′dər), person who backslides. *n.*

back stage (bak′stāj′), in the part of a theater not seen by the audience; behind a backdrop, in the wings, or in a dressing room: *She went backstage (adv.). The star gave a backstage interview (adj.). adv., adj.*

back stop (bak′stop′), **1** wall, fence, or screen used in various games to keep the ball in the area of play. **2** catcher in baseball. **3** anything that supports. *n.*

back stroke (bak′strōk′), **1** a swimming stroke made by a swimmer lying on his back. **2** a backhanded stroke. *n.*

back talk, impudent answers, especially by a younger person to an older one.

back track (bak′trak′), **1** go back over a course or path. **2** withdraw from an undertaking, position, etc.: *He backtracked on the promise he made last week.* v.

back up (bak′up′), **1** reserve: *a backup of troops.* **2** accumulation: *a backup of traffic.* **3** kept in readiness or reserve: *a backup pilot.* 1,2 *n.,* 3 *adj.*

back ward (bak′wərd), **1** with the back first: *He tumbled over backward.* **2** toward the back: *He looked backward* (*adv.*). *She gave him a backward look* (*adj.*). **3** opposite to the usual way: *Can you read backward?* **4** from better to worse: *In some towns living conditions improved; in some they went backward.* **5** toward the past: *She looked backward forty years and talked about her childhood.* **6** slow in development: *a backward country.* **7** shy; bashful: *Shake hands with her; don't be backward.* 1-5 *adv.,* 2,6,7 *adj.* —**back′ward ly,** *adv.* —**back′ward ness,** *n.*

back wards (bak′wərdz), backward (defs. 1-5). *adv.*

back wash (bak′wosh′ *or* bak′wôsh′), **1** water thrown back by oars, a passing ship, etc. **2** a backward current of air. *n., pl.* **back wash es.**

back wa ter (bak′wô′tər *or* bak′wot′ər), **1** stretch of water that is held, thrown, or pushed back. **2** a backward place. *n.*

back woods (bak′wúdz′), **1** uncleared forests or wild regions far away from towns. **2** a remote area; backward place. *n.pl.*

back woods man (bak′wúdz′mən), person who lives in the backwoods. *n., pl.* **back woods men.**

back yard (bak′yärd′), yard behind a house or building. *n.*

ba con (bā′kən), salted and smoked meat from the back and sides of a hog. *n.*

Ba con (bā′kən), **Francis,** 1561-1626, English essayist, statesman, and philosopher. *n.*

bac ter i a (bak tir′ē ə), very tiny and simple plants, so small that they can usually be seen only through a microscope. Bacteria consist of single cells that are rod-shaped, spherical, or spiral, and have no chlorophyll. Most bacteria multiply by splitting apart. Certain bacteria cause diseases such as pneumonia and typhoid fever; others do useful things, such as turning cider into vinegar. *n.pl.* of **bacterium.**

WORD HISTORY

bacteria

Bacteria is the plural of *bacterium,* which comes from Greek *baktērion,* meaning "little rod."

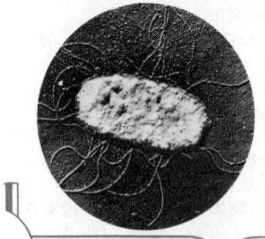

bacteria
the rod type
as seen through
a microscope

bac ter i al (bak tir′ē əl), **1** of bacteria: *bacterial life.* **2** caused by bacteria: *bacterial diseases.* *adj.* —**bac ter′i al ly,** *adv.*

bac ter i o log i cal (bak tir′ē ə loj′ə kəl), **1** of or having to do with bacteriology. **2** using bacteria: *bacteriological warfare.* *adj.* —**bac ter′i o log′i cal ly,** *adv.*

bac ter i ol o gist (bak tir′ē ol′ə jist), an expert in bacteriology. *n.*

bac ter i ol o gy (bak tir′ē ol′ə jē), science that deals with bacteria. *n.*

bac ter i um (bak tir′ē əm), singular of **bacteria.** *n.*

Bac tri an camel (bak′trē ən), camel having two humps and long hair, found in central Asia.

bad (bad), **1** not good; not as it ought to be: *It was hard to read in the bad light.* **2** evil; wicked: *Only someone bad would hurt a helpless person.* **3** not friendly; cross; unpleasant: *a bad temper.* **4** naughty; not behaving well: *My sister was bad when she ate my candy.* **5** unfavorable: *You have come at a bad time.* **6** severe: *A bad thunderstorm delayed the airplane.* **7** rotten; spoiled: *Don't use that egg; it's bad.* **8** sorry: *I feel bad about losing your baseball.* **9** sick: *Her cold made her feel bad.* **10** incorrect: *You made a bad guess.* **11** INFORMAL. badly. **12** something that is bad; bad condition or quality. 1-10 *adj.,* **worse, worst;** 11 *adv.,* 12 *n.* —**bad′ness,** *n.*

be in bad, INFORMAL. be in disfavor: *I'm in bad with the teacher, because I did not do my homework.*

not bad or **not half bad,** fairly good.

not so bad, rather good.

bad blood, unfriendly feeling; hate: *There is bad blood between the rival gangs.*

bade (bad), a past tense of **bid.** *The captain bade the soldiers go on.* v.

Ba den-Pow ell (bād′n pō′əl), Sir **Robert,** 1857-1941, English general who founded the Boy Scouts in 1908. *n.*

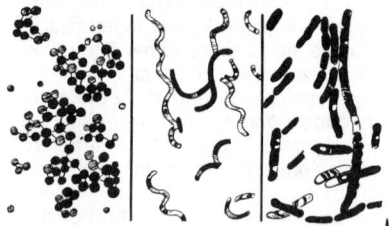

bacteria
the three
main types:
spherical, spiral,
and rod-shaped

badge (baj), **1** something worn to show that a person belongs to a certain occupation, school, class, club, society, etc.: *The Red Cross badge is a red cross on a white background.* **2** symbol or sign: *Chains are a badge of slavery.* *n.*

badg er (baj′ər), **1** a hairy, gray mammal that feeds at night and digs a hole in the ground to live in. Badgers are related to weasels but are larger and more heavily built. **2** its fur. **3** keep on annoying or teasing; bother or question persistently: *That salesman has been badgering us for the last two weeks to buy a new car.* 1,2 *n.,* 3 *v.*

Bad lands (bad′landz′), **1** rugged, barren region in SW South Dakota and NW Nebraska in which erosion has produced unusual land formations. **2 badlands,** any similar region. *n.pl.*

bad ly (bad′lē), **1** in a bad manner: *She sings badly.* **2** INFORMAL. very much: *He wants to go badly.* *adv.*

bad man (bad′man′), INFORMAL. an outlaw or villain. *n., pl.* **bad men.**

bad min ton (bad′min tən), game in which either two or four players use lightweight rackets to keep a shuttlecock moving back and forth over a high net. *n.* [*Badminton* was named after an estate belonging to the Duke of Beaufort in England, where the game was first played.]

bad-tem pered (bad′tem′pərd), having a bad temper; cross; irritable. *adj.*

baf fle (baf′əl), **1** hinder (a person) by being too hard to understand or solve; bewilder: *This puzzle baffles me. The absence of clues baffled the police.* **2** device for hindering or changing the flow of air, water, or sound waves: *a baffle for a jet engine.* 1 *v.*, **baf fled, baf fling;** 2 *n.* —**baf′fle ment,** *n.* —**baf′fler,** *n.*

bag (bag), 1 container made of paper, cloth, leather, etc., that can be pulled together to close at the top: *Fresh vegetables are sometimes sold in plastic bags.* 2 something like a bag in its use or shape; handbag, suitcase, etc.: *Mother calls her purse her bag.* 3 put into a bag or bags: *We bagged the cookies we had baked so we could sell them.* 4 bulge; swell: *These pants bag at the knees.* 5 game killed or caught at one time by a hunter. 6 kill or catch in hunting: *The hunter bagged many large ducks.* 7 base in baseball. 8 SLANG. something for which one has an interest, an ability, or a liking: *Tennis is my bag.* 1,2,5,7,8 *n.*, 3,4,6 *v.*, **bagged, bag ging.** —**bag′like′,** *adj.*

be left holding the bag, INFORMAL. 1 be left to take the blame. 2 be left empty-handed.

bag a telle (bag′ə tel′), a mere trifle; thing of no importance. *n.*

Bag dad (bag′dad), Baghdad. *n.*

ba gel (bā′gəl), a hard roll made of raised dough shaped into a ring. *n.* [*Bagel* comes from Yiddish *beigel.*]

bag gage (bag′ij), 1 the trunks, bags, suitcases, etc., that you take with you when you travel; luggage. 2 equipment that an army takes with it, such as tents, blankets, and dishes. *n.*

Bag gie (bag′ē), trademark for a small square bag made of transparent plastic, used for wrapping food. *n.*

bag gi ness (bag′ē nis), baggy condition. *n.*

bag gy (bag′ē), hanging loosely; baglike: *baggy trousers.* *adj.*, **bag gi er, bag gi est.** —**bag′gi ly,** *adv.*

Bagh dad (bag′dad), capital of Iraq, on the Tigris in SW Asia. Baghdad is an ancient city mentioned many times in *The Arabian Nights.* *n.* Also, **Bagdad.**

bag pipe (bag′pīp′). Often, **bagpipes,** *pl.* a musical instrument made of a tube to blow through, a leather bag for air, and four sounding pipes. Bagpipes produce shrill tones and are used especially in Scotland and Ireland. *n.*

bagpipe

bag pip er (bag′pī′pər), person who plays a bagpipe. *n.*

bah (bä), exclamation of scorn, contempt, or impatience. *interj.*

Ba ha mas (bə hä′məz *or* bə hā′məz), **the,** country consisting of more than 700 islands in the West Indies, southeast of Florida. It is a member of the Commonwealth of Nations. *Capital:* Nassau. See **Caribbean Sea** for map. *n.pl.*

Bah rein or **Bah rain** (bä rān′), island country in the Persian Gulf. *Capital:* Manama. *n.*

Bai kal (bī käl′), **Lake,** lake in S Siberia. It is the deepest freshwater lake in the world. *n.*

bail[1] (bāl), 1 guarantee of money necessary to release a person under arrest from jail or prison until a trial is

held: *They put up bail for their friend who was arrested for speeding.* 2 amount of money guaranteed. 3 obtain the release of (a person under arrest) by supplying bail: *They bailed out their friend.* 1,2 *n.*, 3 *v.* —**bail′a ble,** *adj.*

go bail for, supply bail for.

bail[2] (bāl), the curved handle of a kettle or pail. *n.*

bail[3] (bāl), throw (water) out of a boat with a bucket, pail, or any other container: *She bailed water from the sinking boat.* *v.*

bail out, jump from an airplane by parachute: *When the plane caught fire, the pilot bailed out.*

bail iff (bā′lif), 1 officer of a court of law who has charge of jurors and guards prisoners while they are in the courtroom. 2 (in England) an overseer of an estate: *The bailiff collected the rents from the tenants for the owner.* *n.*

bail i wick (bā′lə wik), a person's field of knowledge, work, or authority. *n.*

bails man (bālz′mən), person who gives bail. *n., pl.* **bails men.**

bairn (bern *or* barn), SCOTTISH. child. *n.*

bait (bāt), 1 anything, especially food, used to attract fish or other animals so that they may be caught. 2 put bait on (a hook) or in (a trap): *I baited the hook.* 3 thing used to tempt or attract. 4 set dogs to attack: *Men used to bait bulls and bears for sport.* 5 torment or worry by unkind or annoying remarks: *A group of troublemakers kept baiting the speaker.* 1,3 *n.*, 2,4,5 *v.* —**bait′er,** *n.*

baize (bāz), a thick woolen or cotton cloth like felt, used for the playing surface of pool and billiard tables. *n.*

bake (bāk), 1 cook (food) by dry heat without exposing it directly to the fire: *I am baking a cake in the oven. I bake every Saturday.* 2 dry or harden by heat: *Bricks and china are baked in a kiln.* 3 become baked: *Cookies bake quickly.* *v.*, **baked, bak ing.**

bak er (bā′kər), person who makes or sells bread, pies, cakes, etc. *n.*

baker's dozen, thirteen.

bak er y (bā′kər ē), store where bread, pies, cakes, etc., are made or sold; baker's shop. *n., pl.* **bak er ies.**

bake shop (bāk′shop′), bakery. *n.*

bak ing (bā′king), 1 a cooking in dry heat without exposing directly to the fire. 2 a drying or hardening by heat. 3 amount baked at one time; batch. *n.*

baking powder, mixture of sodium bicarbonate and cream of tartar, used instead of yeast to cause biscuits, cakes, etc., to rise.

baking soda, sodium bicarbonate.

bal ance (bal′əns), 1 instrument for weighing. 2 weigh

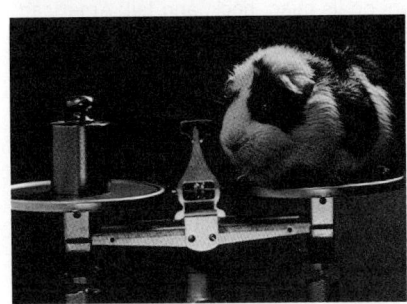

balance (def. 1) The guinea pig is balanced by a 1000-gram weight; therefore it weighs 1000 grams (about 2 pounds).

a hat	i it	oi oil	ch child	a in about
ā age	ī ice	ou out	ng long	e in taken
ä far	o hot	u cup	sh she	ə = { i in pencil
e let	ō open	ů put	th thin	o in lemon
ē equal	ô order	ü rule	ŦH then	u in circus
ėr term			zh measure	

two things against each other on scales, in one's hands, or in one's mind to see which is heavier or more important: *She balanced a trip to the mountains against a chance to go to a summer camp.* **3** condition of being equal in weight, amount, etc.: *Keep the balance between the two sides of the scale.* **4** steady condition or position: *I lost my balance and fell off the ladder.* **5** put or keep in a steady condition or position: *to balance a coin on its edge.* **6** be equal or equivalent in weight, amount, force, effect, etc.: *These scales balance.* **7** steadiness of character: *His balance kept him from losing his temper very often.* **8** make up for the effect, influence, etc., of; counteract. **9** difference between the amount one owes or has withdrawn from an account and the amount one is owed or deposits in an account: *I have a balance of $20 in the bank.* **10** (in an account) make the amount one owes and the amount one is owed equal. **11** part that is left over; remainder: *I will be away for the balance of the week.* **12** balance wheel. 1,3,4,7,9,11,12 *n.,* 2,5,6,8,10 *v.,* **bal anced, bal anc ing.** [*Balance* came into English about 700 years ago from French *balance,* which can be traced back to Latin *bi-,* meaning "two," and *lancem,* meaning "scale."]

in the balance, undecided: *The outcome of the baseball game was in the balance until the last inning.*

balance wheel, wheel for regulating motion. A clock or watch has a balance wheel that controls the movement of the hands.

Bal bo a (bal bō′ə), **Vasco de,** 1475?-1517, Spanish explorer who was the first European to visit the Pacific Ocean, in 1513. *n.*

bal brig gan (bal brig′ən), a knitted cotton cloth, once used for stockings and underwear. *n.*

balcony
(def. 1)

bal co ny (bal′kə nē), **1** an outside platform enclosed by a railing, that juts out from an upper floor of a building. **2** a projecting upper floor in a theater, hall, or church with seats for part of the audience; gallery. *n., pl.* **bal co nies.**

bald (bôld), **1** wholly or partly without hair on the head. **2** without its natural covering: *A mountaintop with no trees or grass is bald.* **3** obvious; plain: *the bald truth, a bald lie. adj.* —**bald′ly,** *adv.* —**bald′ness,** *n.*

bald eagle, a large, powerful, North American eagle with white feathers on its head, neck, and tail; American eagle. It is the national emblem of the United States.

bal der dash (bôl′dər dash), nonsense; foolishness. *n.*

bal dric (bôl′drik), belt for a sword, horn, etc., hung from one shoulder to the opposite side of the body. *n.*

bale (bāl), **1** a large bundle of merchandise or material securely wrapped or bound for shipping or storage: *a bale of cotton.* **2** make into bales: *We saw a big machine bale hay.* 1 *n.,* 2 *v.,* **baled, bal ing.**

Bal e ar ic Islands (bal′ē ar′ik), group of Spanish islands in the W Mediterranean. See **Castile** for map.

ba leen (bə lēn′), whalebone. *n.* [*Baleen* comes from Latin *ballena,* meaning "whale."]

bale ful (bāl′fəl), hostile; menacing: *The librarian gave the noisy children a baleful glance. adj.* —**bale′ful ly,** *adv.*

bal er (bā′lər), person or machine that makes up bales or bundles. *n.*

Ba li (bä′lē), island in Indonesia, east of Java. *n.*

Ba li nese (bä′lə nēz′), **1** person born or living in Bali. **2** of Bali or its people. 1 *n., pl.* **Ba li nese;** 2 *adj.*

balk (bôk), **1** stop short and stubbornly refuse to go on: *My horse balked at the fence.* **2** prevent from going on; hinder: *The police balked the robber's plans.* **3** hindrance. **4** (in baseball) an illegal motion made by a pitcher, especially one in which a throw that has been started is not completed. 1,2 *v.,* 3,4 *n.* Also **baulk.** —**balk′er,** *n.*

Bal kan (bôl′kən), **1** Balkans, *pl.* Balkan States. **2** of the people living in the Balkan States. **3** of the Balkan Peninsula or the countries on it. 1 *n.,* 2,3 *adj.*

Balkan Peninsula, peninsula in SE Europe.

Balkan
States

Balkan States, countries on the Balkan Peninsula; Yugoslavia, Romania, Bulgaria, Albania, Greece, and European Turkey.

balk y (bô′kē), stopping short and stubbornly refusing to go on; likely to balk: *Mules are balky animals. adj.,* **balk i er, balk i est.**

ball[1] (bôl), **1** a round or somewhat oval object that is thrown, hit, batted, kicked, rolled, or carried in various games. Different sizes and types of balls are used in tennis, golf, baseball, football, and soccer. **2** game in which some kind of ball is used, especially baseball. **3** anything round or roundish; something that is somewhat like a ball: *a ball of string. I have a blister on the ball of my foot.* **4** baseball pitched too high, too low, or not over the plate, that the batter does not strike at. **5** a round, solid object shot from a gun or cannon. **6** form into a ball: *to ball string or yarn.* 1-5 *n.,* 6 *v.* —**ball′-like′,** *adj.*

ball up, SLANG. get mixed up; confuse: *I balled up the keys on my chain. The speaker got his notes all balled up.*

bald eagle—about 3 ft. (1 m.) from head to tail

ball[2] (bôl), a large, formal party with dancing. *n.*

bal lad (bal′əd), **1** a simple song. **2** poem that tells a story in a simple verse form, especially one that tells a popular legend. Ballads are often sung. **3** a folk song. *n.*

ball-and-sock et joint (bôl′ən sok′it), joint formed by a ball or knob fitting into a socket, permitting circular motion. The shoulder and hip joints are ball-and-socket joints.

bal last (bal′əst), **1** something heavy carried in a ship to steady it. **2** weight carried in a balloon or dirigible to steady it or regulate its ascent: *The balloon used bags of sand for ballast.* **3** gravel or crushed rock used in making the bed for a road or railroad track. **4** furnish or steady with ballast. 1-3 *n.,* 4 *v.*

ball bearing, 1 bearing in which the shaft turns upon a number of freely moving steel balls. Ball bearings are used to lessen friction. **2** one of these steel balls.

bal le ri na (bal′ə rē′nə), a woman ballet dancer. *n., pl.* **bal le ri nas.**

bal let (bal′ā *or* ba lā′), **1** an elaborate dance by a group on a stage. A ballet tells a story through the movements of the dancing and is accompanied by music often written especially for it. **2** the dancers in a ballet. *n.*

bal lis tic (bə lis′tik), having to do with the motion of projectiles. *adj.* [*Ballistic* comes from Latin *ballista,* meaning "machine for hurling large stones in battle."] —**bal lis′ti cal ly,** *adv.*

ballistic missile, missile aimed at or before the time of launching. It differs from a guided missile, which can be aimed during flight.

bal lis tics (bə lis′tiks), science that deals with the motion of projectiles, such as bullets, shells, or bombs, and also rockets and missiles after thrust has ended. *n.*

bal loon (bə lün′), **1** an airtight bag filled with some gas lighter than air so that it will rise and float in the air. Some balloons have a basket or container for carrying persons or instruments high up in the air. **2** a child's toy made of thin rubber that may be blown up by mouth or filled with some gas lighter than air. **3** swell out like a balloon: *The sails of the boat ballooned in the wind.* 1,2 *n.,* 3 *v.* —**bal loon′like′,** *adj.*

bal lot (bal′ət), **1** piece of paper or other object used in voting: *Have you cast your ballot?* **2** the total number of votes cast. **3** method of secret voting that uses paper slips, voting machines, etc. **4** vote or decide by using ballots: *We will now ballot for president of the club.* 1-3 *n.,* 4 *v.*

ball park (bôl′pärk′), a baseball field. *n.*

ball play er (bôl′plā′ər), person who plays ball, especially baseball. *n.*

ball point pen (bôl′point′), pen that writes with a small metal ball which turns inside the end of a cartridge holding ink.

ball room (bôl′rüm′ *or* bôl′rùm′), a large room for dancing. *n.*

bal ly hoo (bal′ē hü), **1** sensational or noisy advertising. **2** uproar; outcry. **3** make exaggerated or false statements. 1,2 *n., pl.* **bal ly hoos;** 3 *v.,* **bal ly hooed, bal ly hoo ing.** —**bal′ly hoo′er,** *n.*

balm (bäm *or* bälm), **1** a fragrant, oily, sticky substance obtained from certain kinds of trees, used to heal or to relieve pain. **2** an ointment or similar preparation that heals or soothes. **3** anything that heals or soothes: *Your kindness was balm to my wounded feelings. n.*

balm i ly (bä′mə lē *or* bäl′mə lē), in a balmy manner. *adv.*

balm i ness (bä′mē nis *or* bäl′mē nis), balmy condition or quality. *n.*

balm y (bä′mē *or* bäl′mē), **1** mild; gentle; soothing: *A balmy breeze blew across the lake.* **2** fragrant. *adj.,* **balm i er, balm i est.**

ba lo ney (bə lō′nē), **1** SLANG. nonsense. **2** INFORMAL. bologna. *n.*

a hat	**i** it	**oi** oil	**ch** child	⎧ a in about
ā age	**ī** ice	**ou** out	**ng** long	⎮ e in taken
ä far	**o** hot	**u** cup	**sh** she	**ə** = ⎨ i in pencil
e let	**ō** open	**ù** put	**th** thin	⎮ o in lemon
ē equal	**ô** order	**ü** rule	**ŦH** then	⎩ u in circus
ėr term			**zh** measure	

bal sa (bôl′sə), **1** a tropical American tree with strong wood which is very light in weight. **2** its wood, used in making rafts, airplane models, etc. *n., pl.* **bal sas** for 1. [*Balsa* comes from Spanish *balsa,* meaning "raft."]

bal sam (bôl′səm), **1** balsam fir. **2** balm. *n.*

balsam fir, 1 an evergreen tree of North America, related to the pine, whose resin is used in making varnish and turpentine. Balsam firs are much used as Christmas trees. **2** its wood, used for lumber and in making paper.

Bal tic (bôl′tik), **1** of the Baltic Sea: *the Baltic coasts.* **2** of the Baltic States. *adj.*

Baltic Sea, sea in N Europe, north of Poland and southeast of Sweden. See **Lapland** for map.

Baltic States, Estonia, Latvia, Lithuania, and sometimes Finland.

Bal ti more (bôl′tə môr), city in N Maryland, near Chesapeake Bay. *n.*

bal us ter (bal′ə stər), one of the short posts or columns that support the railing of a staircase, balcony, etc. *n.*

WORD HISTORY

baluster

Baluster came into English about 300 years ago from French *balustre,* which can be traced back to Greek *balaustion,* meaning "pomegranate blossom." The shape of a baluster suggests the shape of the flower.

bal us trade (bal′ə strād), row of balusters and the railing on them. *n.*

Bam a ko (bam′ə kō), capital of Mali, in the SW part. *n.*

bam bi no (bam bē′nō), **1** baby. **2** a little child. *n., pl.* **bam bi ni** (bam bē′nē), **bam bi nos.**

bam boo (bam bü′), a woody or treelike grass with a very tall, stiff, hollow stem that has hard, thick joints. Bamboo grows in warm regions. Its stems are used for making canes, fishing poles, furniture, and even houses. *n., pl.* **bam boos.** [*Bamboo* is from Dutch *bamboe,* which comes from Malay *bambu.*]

bam boo zle (bam bü′zəl), INFORMAL. **1** impose upon; cheat; trick: *to bamboozle a customer.* **2** puzzle; perplex. *v.,* **bam boo zled, bam boo zling.** —**bam boo′zle ment,** *n.* —**bam boo′zler,** *n.*

ban (ban), **1** forbid by law or authority; prohibit: *Swimming is banned in this lake.* **2** the forbidding of an act or speech by authority: *The city has a ban on parking cars in this busy street.* 1 *v.,* **banned, ban ning;** 2 *n.*

ba nal (bā′nl *or* bə nal′), not new or interesting; commonplace; trite: *Their conversation was banal, full of uninteresting remarks such as "nice weather" and "slow traffic today."* *adj.* —**ba′nal ly,** *adv.*

ba nal i ty (bə nal′ə tē), **1** commonplaceness; triteness. **2** a banal remark, idea, etc. *n., pl.* **ba nal i ties.**

ba nan a (bə nan′ə), a slightly curved, yellow or red tropical fruit with firm, creamy flesh. Bananas are five to eight inches long and grow in clusters two or three feet

long. The treelike plant has great, long leaves. *n., pl.*
ba nan as. [*Banana* was borrowed from Spanish or Portuguese *banana*, which came from a west African word.]
go bananas, SLANG. become very excited.

band[1] (band), **1** number of persons or animals joined or acting together: *a band of robbers, a band of coyotes.*
2 unite in a group: *The children banded together to buy a present for their teacher.* **3** group of musicians performing together, especially on wind and percussion instruments: *The school band played several marches.* 1,3 *n.,* 2 *v.*

band[2] (band), **1** a thin, flat strip of material for binding, trimming, or some other purpose: *The oak box was strengthened with bands of iron.* **2** put a band on: *Students of birds often band them in order to identify them later.* **3** a stripe: *The white cup has a gold band.* **4** a particular range of wavelengths or frequencies in radio broadcasting. 1,3,4 *n.,* 2 *v.* —**band′er,** *n.*

band age (ban′dij), **1** strip of cloth or other material used in binding up and dressing a wound or injury. **2** bind or dress with a bandage. 1 *n.,* 2 *v.,* **band aged, band ag ing. —band′ag er,** *n.*

Band-Aid (band′ād′), trademark for a small adhesive bandage, used to cover and protect minor wounds. *n.*

ban dan a (ban dan′ə), bandanna. *n., pl.* **ban dan as.**

ban dan na (ban dan′ə), a large handkerchief, often worn on the head or neck. *n., pl.* **ban dan nas.** [*Bandanna* comes from Hindustani *bāndhnū,* meaning "a way of tying cloth so that dyeing the cloth produces designs."]

Ban dar Se ri Be ga wan (bän där′ se′rē be gä′wän), capital of Brunei, in the N part.

band box (band′boks′), a light cardboard box to put hats, collars, etc., in. *n., pl.* **band box es.**

ban deau (ban dō′), a narrow band worn about the head. *n., pl.* **ban deaux** or **ban deaus** (ban dōz′).

ban dit (ban′dit), robber or thief, especially one of a gang of outlaws. *n., pl.* **ban dits, ban dit ti** (ban dit′ē).

ban dit ry (ban′də trē), **1** the work of bandits. **2** bandits. *n.*

band mas ter (band′mas′tər), leader of a band of musicians. *n.*

ban do leer or **ban do lier** (ban′dl ir′), a broad belt worn over the shoulder and across the breast, often with loops for carrying cartridges or with small cases for bullets, gunpowder, etc. *n.*

band saw, saw in the form of an endless steel belt running over two pulleys.

band stand (band′stand′), an outdoor platform for band concerts. It usually has a roof. *n.*

band wag on (band′wag′ən), wagon that carries a musical band in a parade. *n.*
climb on the bandwagon, INFORMAL. join what appears to be a winning or successful group, movement, etc.

ban dy (ban′dē), **1** throw back and forth; toss about: *The team bandied the ball from player to player while waiting for the game to start.* **2** give and take; exchange: *bandy blows, bandy insults.* *v.,* **ban died, ban dy ing.**

ban dy-leg ged (ban′dē leg′id), having legs that curve outward like a bow; bowlegged. *adj.*

bane (bān), cause of death, ruin, or harm: *Frequent earthquakes were the bane of the mountain village.* *n.* [*Bane* comes from Old English *bana,* meaning "murderer."]

bane ful (bān′fəl), causing harm or destruction: *Air pollution has a baneful effect on trees in cities. adj.* —**bane′ful ly,** *adv.* —**bane′ful ness,** *n.*

bang (bang), **1** a sudden, loud noise: *the bang of firecrackers.* **2** make or cause to make a sudden, loud noise: *The door banged as it blew shut. He banged the door.* **3** a violent, noisy blow: *She gave the drum a bang.* **4** strike noisily or violently: *The baby was banging the pan with a spoon.* **5** violently and suddenly: *The bicyclist ran*

bang into a telephone pole. **6** a thrill: *I get a bang out of riding the roller coaster.* 1,3,6 *n.,* 2,4 *v.,* 5 *adv.*
bang up, damage: *My car was badly banged up in the accident.*

bangs (bangz), fringe of hair cut short and worn over the forehead. *n.pl.*

Bang kok (bang′kok), capital and chief port of Thailand. *n.*

Ban gla desh (bäng′glə desh′), country in S Asia, on the Bay of Bengal, a member of the Commonwealth of Nations. *Capital:* Dacca. See **India** for map. *n.*

ban gle (bang′gəl), **1** a small ornament suspended from a bracelet. **2** bracelet or anklet. *n.* [*Bangle* comes from Hindustani *bangrī,* meaning "glass bracelet."]

Ban gui (bäng′gē), capital of the Central African Republic, in the SW part. *n.*

ban ian (ban′yən), banyan. *n.*

ban ish (ban′ish), **1** force (a person) to leave a country; exile: *The king banished some of his enemies.* **2** force to go away; drive away; expel. *v.* —**ban′ish er,** *n.*

banish (def. 2)
He was **banished** into the cold.

ban ish ment (ban′ish mənt), **1** act of banishing. **2** condition of being banished; exile: *Their banishment was for twenty years. n.*

ban is ter (ban′ə stər). Often, **banisters,** *pl.* handrail of a staircase, balcony, etc., and its row of supports. *n.*

ban jo (ban′jō), a musical instrument having four or five strings, played by plucking the strings with the fingers or a pick. *n., pl.* **ban jos** or **ban joes.** [*Banjo* is probably of Bantu origin.]

banjo

Ban jul (bän′jül), capital of The Gambia, in the W part. *n.*

bank[1] (bangk), **1** a long pile or heap: *a bank of snow over ten feet deep.* **2** pile up; heap up: *The tractors banked the snow by the side of the road.* **3** ground bordering a river, lake, etc.; shore: *We fished from the bank.* **4** a shallow place in a body of water; shoal: *the fishing banks of*

Newfoundland. **5** cause to slope: *The bulldozers banked the curves of the new express highway.* **6** the sloping of an airplane to one side when making a turn. **7** make (an airplane) do this. **8** cover (a fire) with ashes or fresh fuel so that it will burn slowly: *The janitor banked the fire for the night.* 1,3,4,6 *n.,* 2,5,7,8 *v.*

bank² (bangk), **1** place of business for keeping, lending, exchanging, and issuing money: *A bank pays interest on money deposited in a savings account.* **2** keep or put money in a bank: *We bank at the First National. I bank the money I earn baby-sitting.* **3** a small container with a slot through which coins can be dropped to save money. **4** any place where reserve supplies are kept: *a bank for blood plasma.* 1,3,4 *n.,* 2 *v.* —**bank′a ble,** *adj.*
bank on, depend on: *I can bank on my teacher to help me.*

bank³ (bangk), **1** row or close arrangement of things: *a bank of machines.* **2** row of keys on an organ, typewriter, etc. **3** row or tier of oars. *n.*

bank book (bangk′bùk′), book in which a record of a person's account at a bank is kept; passbook. *n.*

bank er (bang′kər), person or company that manages a bank. *n.*

bank ing (bang′king), business of keeping, lending, exchanging, and issuing money. *n.*

bank rupt (bang′krupt), **1** person who is declared by a court of law to be unable to pay his or her debts, and whose property is distributed as far as it will go among the people who are owed money. **2** unable to pay one's debts. **3** make bankrupt: *Foolish expenditures will bankrupt the company.* 1 *n.,* 2 *adj.,* 3 *v.*

bank rupt cy (bang′krupt sē), bankrupt condition. *n., pl.* **bank rupt cies.**

Ban ne ker (ban′ə kər), **Benjamin,** 1731-1806, American astronomer, mathematician, surveyor, and almanac author. *n.*

ban ner (ban′ər), **1** flag: *The banners of many countries fly outside the headquarters of the United Nations.* **2** piece of cloth with some design or words on it: *The banner our school displays in parades is blue and white.* **3** leading or outstanding: *This has been a banner year for apple growers.* **4** a newpaper headline extending across the top of a page. 1,2,4 *n.,* 3 *adj.*

banns (banz), notice given three separate times in church that a certain man and woman are to be married. *n.pl.*

ban quet (bang′kwit), **1** a large meal with many courses, prepared for a special occasion or for many people; feast: *a wedding banquet.* **2** a formal dinner with speeches. **3** take part in a banquet; feast: *We banqueted on roast beef and duck.* 1,2 *n.,* 3 *v.* —**ban′quet er,** *n.*

ban shee or **ban shie** (ban′shē), (in Irish and Scottish folklore) a female spirit whose wail means that there will soon be a death in the family. *n.*

ban tam or **Ban tam** (ban′təm), a small kind of domestic fowl. The roosters are often spirited fighters. *n.*

ban tam weight (ban′təm wāt′), boxer who weighs more than 112 pounds (51 kilograms) and less than 118 pounds (54 kilograms). *n.*

ban ter (ban′tər), **1** playful teasing; joking: *There was much banter going on at the party.* **2** tease playfully; talk in a joking way. 1 *n.,* 2 *v.* —**ban′ter er,** *n.* —**ban′ter ing ly,** *adv.*

Ban tu (ban′tü), **1** member of a large group of peoples living in central and southern Africa. **2** any of the languages of these peoples. Swahili is a Bantu language. **3** of these peoples or their languages. 1,2 *n., pl.* **Ban tu** or **Ban tus;** 3 *adj.*

ban yan (ban′yən), an East Indian fig tree whose branches have hanging roots that grow down to the

---

ground and start new trunks. One tree may cover several acres. *n.* Also, **banian.**

ban zai (bän′zī′), a Japanese greeting, patriotic cheer, or battle cry. It means "May you live ten thousand years!" *interj.*

ba o bab (bā′ō bab), a tall, tropical tree of Africa, India, and Australia, with a very thick trunk and an oblong, gourdlike, woolly fruit. *n.*

bap tism (bap′tiz əm), **1** rite or ceremony in which a person is dipped in water or sprinkled with water, as a sign of washing away sin and admission to the Christian church. **2** an experience that tests a person or initiates one into a new kind of life. *n.*

bap tis mal (bap tiz′məl), of baptism: *a baptismal ceremony. adj.* —**bap tis′mal ly,** *adv.*

Bap tist (bap′tist), **1** member of a Christian church that believes in baptizing by dipping the whole person in water. **2 the Baptist,** John the Baptist. *n.*

bap tis ter y (bap′tə stər ē), building or part of a church where baptism is performed. *n., pl.* **bap tis ter ies.**

bap tis try (bap′tə strē), baptistery. *n., pl.* **bap tis tries.**

bap tize (bap tīz′ or bap′tīz), **1** dip (a person) into water or sprinkle with water as a sign of washing away sin and admission into the Christian church. **2** give a first name to (a person) at baptism; christen: *The baby was baptized Maria. v.,* **bap tized, bap tiz ing.** —**bap tiz′er,** *n.*

bar (bär), **1** an evenly shaped piece of some solid, longer than it is wide or thick: *a bar of iron, a bar of soap, a bar of chocolate.* **2** pole or rod put across a door, gate, window, or across any opening: *Let down the pasture bars for the cows to come in.* **3** put bars across; fasten or shut off: *Bar the door.* **4** anything that blocks the way or prevents progress: *A bar of sand kept boats out of the harbor. Shyness can be a bar to making friends.* **5** block; obstruct: *Fallen trees bar the road.* **6** exclude or forbid: *All talking is barred during a study period. Dogs are barred from that store.* **7** except; excluding: *He is the best student, bar none.* **8** band of color; stripe: *a dark bar of cloud across the setting sun.* **9** mark with stripes. **10** unit of rhythm in music. The regular accent falls on the first note of each bar. **11** the vertical line between two such units on a musical staff, dividing a composition into measures. A **double bar** marks the end of a movement or of an entire piece of music. **12** counter or place where drinks, usually alcoholic, and sometimes food are served to customers. **13** place where a prisoner stands in a court of law. **14** profession of a lawyer: *After you have passed your law examinations, you will be admitted to the bar.* **15** lawyers as a group: *Judges are chosen from the bar.* **16** court of law. 1,2,4,8,10-16 *n.,* 3,5,6,9 *v.,* **barred, bar ring;** 7 *prep.*

bar., **1** barometer. **2** barometric. **3** barrel.

barb (bärb), **1** point sticking out and curving backward from the main point of an arrow, fishhook, etc.

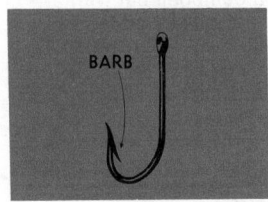

barb (def. 1)

2 something that wounds or stings: *the barb of sarcasm.* n. [*Barb* came into English about 600 years ago from French *barbe,* which comes from Latin *barba,* meaning "beard."]

Bar ba dos (bär bā′dōz), island country in the West Indies, a member of the Commonwealth of Nations. *Capital:* Bridgetown. n.

bar bar i an (bär ber′ē ən *or* bär bar′ē ən), **1** person belonging to a people or to a tribe that is not civilized: *The Roman Empire was conquered by barbarians.* **2** not civilized; cruel and coarse. **3** person who rejects or lacks interest in literature, the arts, etc. **4** of barbarians: *barbarian customs.* 1,3 n., 2,4 adj. [*Barbarian* comes from Latin *barbarus,* meaning "foreigner."]

bar bar ic (bär bar′ik), **1** like barbarians; suited to an uncivilized people; rough and rude. **2** rich or splendid in a crude way: *barbaric color, barbaric music.* adj. —**bar bar′i cal ly,** adv.

bar ba rism (bär′bə riz′əm), **1** condition of uncivilized people. **2** word or expression not in accepted use. EXAMPLE: "his'n" for "his." n.

bar bar i ty (bär bar′ə tē), **1** brutal or inhuman cruelty. **2** a cruel act. **3** barbaric manner or style; gaudy taste. n., pl. **bar bar i ties.**

bar ba rize (bär′bə rīz′), make or become barbarous. v., **bar ba rized, bar ba riz ing.** —**bar′ba ri za′tion,** n.

bar bar ous (bär′bər əs), **1** not civilized; savage. **2** savagely cruel; brutal: *Torturing prisoners is barbarous.* **3** rough and rude; coarse; unrefined: *barbarous manners.* adj. —**bar′bar ous ly,** adv. —**bar′bar ous ness,** n.

Bar bar y (bär′bər ē), Moslem countries west of Egypt on the N coast of Africa. n.

bar be cue (bär′bə kyü), **1** an outdoor meal in which meat is roasted over an open fire. **2** grill or open fireplace for cooking meat, usually over charcoal. **3** meat roasted over an open fire. **4** roast (meat) over an open fire. **5** cook (meat or fish) in a highly flavored sauce. **6** an outdoor feast at which animals are roasted whole. **7** animal roasted whole. 1-3,6,7 n., 4,5 v., **bar be cued, bar be cu ing.** Also, **barbeque.**

⟩⟩⟩ **WORD HISTORY** ⟨⟨⟨

barbecue

Barbecue was borrowed from Spanish *barbecue,* which comes from a Caribbean Indian word *barbacoa,* meaning "a framework of sticks." The sticks formed a primitive outdoor cooking device.

barbed (bärbd), **1** having a barb or barbs: *A fishhook is barbed.* **2** sharply critical; cutting: *a barbed remark.* adj.

barbed wire, wire with sharp points on it every few inches, used for fences.

bar bel (bär′bəl), a long, thin, fleshy growth on the mouths or nostrils of some fishes. n.

bar bell (bär′bel′), device like a dumbbell but with a much longer bar, to which weights may be added. n.

bar be que (bär′bə kyü), barbecue. n., v., **bar be qued, bar be que ing.**

bar ber (bär′bər), person whose business is cutting hair and shaving or trimming beards. n.

bar ber ry (bär′ber′ē), a low, thorny shrub with small, yellow flowers and sour, red berries. n., pl. **bar ber ries.**

bar bi can (bär′bə kən), tower for defense built over a gate or bridge to a castle or city. n.

bar bit ur ate (bär bich′ər it *or* bär bich′ə rāt′), drug used in medicine to induce sleep. n.

bar ca role *or* **bar ca rolle** (bär′kə rōl′), **1** a Venetian boat song, sung by gondoliers. **2** music imitating such a song. n.

Bar ce lo na (bär′sə lō′nə), seaport in NE Spain, on the Mediterranean. n.

bar chart, bar graph.

bar code, a set of short vertical lines that have differing lengths and differing amounts of space between them. Printed on any item, these lines can be read by a machine which turns them into numbers that stand for a price, an address, or similar information.

bard (bärd), **1** poet and singer of long ago: *The bard sang his own poems to the music of his harp.* **2** any poet. n. [*Bard* comes from Irish and Scottish Gaelic *bard.*]

Bard of Avon, William Shakespeare.

bare (ber *or* bar), **1** without covering; not clothed; naked: *The sun burned her bare shoulders. The top of the hill was bare.* **2** with the head uncovered; bareheaded. **3** not furnished; empty: *The room was bare of furniture.* **4** plain; not adorned: *a bare little cabin in the woods.* **5** just enough and no more; mere: *She earns only a bare living by her work.* **6** make bare; uncover; reveal: *to bare one's feelings. The dog bared its teeth.* 1-5 adj., **bar er, bar est;** 6 v., **bared, bar ing.** —**bare′ness,** n.

lay bare, uncover; expose; reveal: *The police laid bare the plot to rob the bank.*

bare back (ber′bak′ *or* bar′bak′), without a saddle; on a horse's bare back: *She likes to ride bareback* (adv.). *He is a bareback rider* (adj.). adv., adj.

bare faced (ber′fāst′ *or* bar′fāst′), shameless; impudent: *a barefaced lie.* adj. —**bare′fac′ed ly,** adv.

bare foot (ber′fut′ *or* bar′fut′), without shoes and stockings on: *A barefoot child played in the puddles* (adj.). *If you go barefoot, watch out for broken glass* (adv.). adj., adv.

bare foot ed (ber′fut′id *or* bar′fut′id), barefoot. adj., adv.

bare hand ed (ber′han′did *or* bar′han′did), **1** without any covering on the hands. **2** with no aid but one's own hands. adj., adv.

bare head ed (ber′hed′id *or* bar′hed′id), wearing nothing on the head: *You shouldn't be bareheaded in such cold weather.* adj., adv. —**bare′head′ed ness,** n.

bare leg ged (ber′leg′id *or* bar′leg′id), without stockings on. adj., adv.

bare ly (ber′lē *or* bar′lē), **1** with nothing to spare; only just; scarcely: *I have barely enough money to live on.* **2** poorly: *The room was furnished barely.* adv.

bar gain (bär′gən), **1** agreement to trade or exchange; deal: *You can't back out on our bargain.* **2** something offered for sale cheap or bought cheap: *This hat is a bargain.* **3** try to get good terms; try to make a good deal: *I bargained with the owner and bought the book for $5 instead of $8.* 1,2 n., 3 v. —**bar′gain er,** n.

bargain for, be ready for; expect: *I hadn't bargained for rain and have left my umbrella at home.*

into the bargain, besides; also: *My new sweater shrank and it faded into the bargain.*

strike a bargain, make or reach an agreement: *They finally struck a bargain: a mitt for two baseballs and a bat.*

barge (bärj), **1** a large, strongly built, flat-bottomed boat for carrying freight on rivers, canals, etc.: *a grain barge.* **2** a large boat used for excursions, pageants, and special occasions. **3** move clumsily like a barge: *He barged into the table and knocked the lamp over.* **4** INFORMAL. push oneself rudely: *Don't barge in where you're not wanted.* 1,2 n., 3,4 v., **barged, barg ing.**

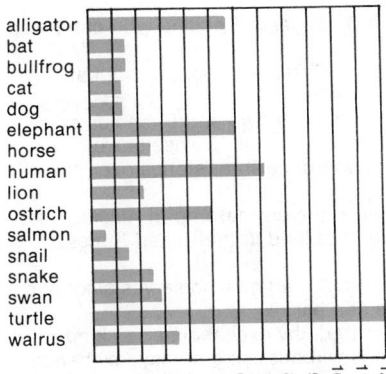

alligator
bat
bullfrog
cat
dog
elephant
horse
human
lion
ostrich
salmon
snail
snake
swan
turtle
walrus

YEARS 0 10 20 30 40 50 60 70 80 90 100 110 120

bar graph
This bar graph shows how long certain animals usually live.

bar graph, graph representing different quantities by rectangles of different lengths.

bar i tone (bar′ə tōn), **1** a male voice between tenor and bass. **2** singer with such a voice. **3** part to be sung by such a voice. **4** of or for a baritone. 1-3 *n.,* 4 *adj.* [*Baritone* comes from Italian *baritono,* meaning "a low voice," and can be traced back to Greek *barys,* meaning "deep," and *tonos,* meaning "tone."]

bar i um (ber′ē əm *or* bar′ē əm), a soft, silvery-white metallic element which occurs only in combination with other elements. Barium compounds are used in making pigments, safety matches, vacuum tubes, etc. *n.*

bark[1] (bärk), **1** the tough outside covering of the trunk and branches of trees. **2** scrape the skin from: *I fell down the steps and barked my shins.* 1 *n.,* 2 *v.*

bark[2] (bärk), **1** the short, sharp sound that a dog makes. **2** a sound like this: *the bark of a fox, the bark of a gun, the bark of a cough.* **3** make this sound: *The dog barked. Rifles barked.* **4** speak gruffly or sharply: *The police barked out orders.* 1,2 *n.,* 3,4 *v.*

bark[3] (bärk), **1** ship with three masts, square-rigged on the first two masts and fore-and-aft-rigged on the other. **2** OLD USE. boat; ship. *n.* Also, **barque.**

bar keep (bär′kēp′), barkeeper. *n.*

bar keep er (bär′kē′pər), bartender. *n.*

bark er (bär′kər), person who stands in front of a store, show, etc., urging people to go in. *n.*

bar ley (bär′lē), a cereal grass that has compact spikes of flowers and grows in cool climates. Its grain is used for food and for making malt. *n.*

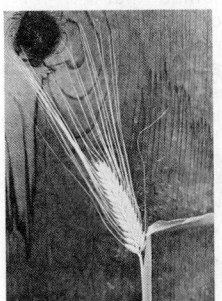 

barley—left, head of barley; right, stand of barley

bar magnet, magnet in the shape of a bar or rod, usually made of steel: *A bar magnet suspended from a string will serve as a simple compass.*

bar maid (bär′mād′), woman who serves alcoholic drinks to customers at a bar. *n.*

bar man (bär′mən), bartender. *n., pl.* **bar men.**

bar mitz vah (bär mits′və), **1** ceremony or celebration held when a Jewish boy becomes thirteen years old to affirm that he has reached the age of religious responsibility. **2** the boy himself.

barn (bärn), building for storing hay, grain, or other farm produce, and for sheltering cows, horses, and farm machinery. *n.* —**barn′like′,** *adj.*

bar na cle (bär′nə kəl), a small, saltwater animal with a shell, that attaches itself to rocks, the bottoms of ships, the timbers of wharves, etc. *n.*

barn dance, 1 an informal party for square dancing, formerly often held in a barn. **2** a lively square dance resembling a polka.

barn storm (bärn′stôrm′), travel from one small town or district to another, acting in plays, making political speeches, etc. *v.* —**barn′storm′er,** *n.*

barn swallow, swallow with a reddish breast and a long, forked tail. It usually nests in barns.

Bar num (bär′nəm), P(hineas) T(aylor), 1810-1891, American showman. *n.*

barn yard (bärn′yärd′), yard around or next to a barn for livestock. *n.*

barometer (def. 1)

ba rom e ter (bə rom′ə tər), **1** instrument for measuring the pressure of air, used in determining height above sea level and in predicting probable changes in the weather. **2** something that indicates changes: *Newspapers are often called barometers of public opinion. n.* [*Barometer* comes from Greek *baros,* meaning "weight," and English *meter,* meaning "device that measures."]

bar o met ric (bar′ə met′rik), **1** of a barometer. **2** indicated by a barometer: *Low barometric pressure is a sign of a possible storm. adj.* —**bar′o met′ri cal ly,** *adv.*

bar on (bar′ən), **1** nobleman of the lowest hereditary rank. In Great Britain, a baron ranks next below a viscount and has "Lord" before his name instead of "Baron." In other European countries "Baron" is used before his name. **2** an English nobleman during the Middle Ages who held his lands directly from the king. *n.*

bar on ess (bar′ə nis), **1** wife or widow of a baron. **2** woman whose rank is equal to that of a baron. *n., pl.* **bar on ess es.**

bar on et (bar′ə nit), man in Great Britain ranking next below a baron and next above a knight. He has "Sir" before his name and "Bart." after it. EXAMPLE: Sir John Brown, Bart. *n.*

ba ro ni al (bə rō′nē əl), **1** of a baron or barons: *a ring* *with a baronial crest on it.* **2** suitable for a baron; splendid, stately, and grand. *adj.*

bar on y (bar′ə nē), **1** lands of a baron. **2** rank or title of a baron. *n., pl.* **bar on ies.**

ba roque (bə rōk′), **1** having to do with a style of art or architecture characterized by the use of curved forms and lavish ornamentation. **2** having to do with a style of music characterized by complex rhythms and melodic ornamentation. **3** tastelessly odd; grotesque. **4** irregular in shape: *baroque pearls. adj.*

ba rouche (bə rüsh′), a four-wheeled carriage with a driver's seat, two passenger seats facing each other, and a folding top. *n.*

barque (bärk), bark³. *n.*

bar racks (bar′əks), a building or group of buildings for soldiers to live in, usually in a fort or camp. *n. pl. or sing.*

bar ra cu da (bar′ə kü′də), a saltwater fish with a long, narrow body, sharp teeth, and a jutting lower jaw. It sometimes attacks swimmers. *n., pl.* **bar ra cu das** or **bar ra cu da.**

bar rage (bə räzh′), **1** barrier of artillery fire to check the enemy or to protect one's own soldiers when advancing or retreating. **2** a large number of words, blows, etc., coming quickly one after the other: *The reporters kept up a barrage of questions for an hour.* **3** subject to a barrage. **1,2** *n.,* **3** *v.,* **bar raged, bar rag ing.**

barred (bärd), **1** having bars: *a barred window.* **2** marked with stripes: *a chicken with barred feathers. adj.*

bar rel (bar′əl), **1** container with a round, flat top and bottom and sides that curve out slightly. Barrels are usually made of boards held together by hoops. **2** amount that a barrel can hold: *They picked a barrel of apples.* **3** unit of measure for liquids and dry things. Its exact amount is not the same for all commodities, and is often fixed by law. **4** put in barrels: *to barrel cider.* **5** the metal tube of a gun through which the bullet is discharged. **6** INFORMAL. a great deal; much: *a barrel of fun.* **1-3,5,6** *n.,* **4** *v.,* **bar reled, bar rel ing** or **bar relled, bar rel ling.**

bar rel ful (bar′əl fůl′), amount that a barrel can hold. *n., pl.* **bar rel fuls.**

barrel organ, hand organ.

bar ren (bar′ən), **1** not able to produce offspring: *a barren fruit tree, a barren animal.* **2** not able to produce much: *a barren desert.* **3** without interest; unattractive; dull. **4** of no advantage; unprofitable: *the barren victories of war.* **5** barrens, *pl.* a barren stretch of land. **1-4** *adj.,* **5** *n.* —**bar′ren ly,** *adv.* —**bar′ren ness,** *n.*

bar rette (bə ret′), pin with a clasp for holding the hair in place. *n.*

bar ri cade (bar′ə kād′ *or* bar′ə kād), **1** a rough, hastily made barrier for defense: *The soldiers cut down trees to make a barricade across the road.* **2** any barrier or obstruction. **3** block or obstruct with a barricade: *The road was barricaded by fallen trees.* **1,2** *n.,* **3** *v.,* **bar ri cad ed, bar ri cad ing.**

bar ri er (bar′ē ər), **1** something that stands in the way; something stopping progress or preventing approach; obstacle: *A dam is a barrier holding back water. Lack of water was a barrier to settling much of New Mexico.* **2** something that separates or keeps apart: *The Isthmus of Panama forms a barrier between the Atlantic and Pacific oceans. n.*

bar ring (bär′ing), leaving out of consideration; excepting: *Barring poor weather, the plane will leave Chicago at twelve. prep.*

bar ri o (bär′ē ō *or* bar′ē ō), part of a city where mainly Spanish-speaking people live. *n., pl.* **bar ri os.** [*Barrio* was borrowed from Spanish *barrio,* which comes from Arabic *barri,* meaning "outside."]

bar ris ter (bar′ə stər), lawyer in England who can plead in any court. *n.*

bar room (bär′rüm′ *or* bär′rům′), room with a bar for the sale of alcoholic drinks. *n.*

bar row¹ (bar′ō), **1** frame with two short handles at each end, used for carrying a load. **2** wheelbarrow. *n.*

bar row² (bar′ō), mound of earth or stones over an ancient grave. *n.*

Bar row (bar′ō), **Point,** the northern tip of Alaska. It is the northernmost point of land in the United States. *n.*

Bart., Baronet.

bar tend er (bär′ten′dər), person who serves alcoholic drinks to customers at a bar. *n.*

bar ter (bär′tər), **1** to trade by exchanging one kind of goods for other goods without using money; exchange: *The trapper bartered furs for supplies.* **2** a bartering; trading by exchanging goods: *Nations sometimes trade by barter instead of paying money for the things they need.* **1** *v.,* **2** *n.* —**bar′ter er,** *n.*

Bar thol o mew (bär thol′ə myü), (in the Bible) one of Jesus' twelve apostles. *n.*

Bar tók (bär′tok), **Béla,** 1881-1945, Hungarian composer and pianist. *n.*

Bar ton (bärt′n), **Clara,** 1821-1912, American nurse who organized the American Red Cross in 1881. *n.*

bas al (bā′səl), fundamental; basic. *adj.* —**bas′al ly,** *adv.*

basal metabolism, amount of energy used by an animal or plant at rest.

ba salt (bə sôlt′), a hard, dark-colored rock of volcanic origin. It often occurs in a form resembling a group of columns. *n.*

ba sal tic (bə sôl′tik), of basalt. *adj.*

base¹ (bās), **1** the part on which anything stands or rests; bottom: *This big machine has a wide steel base.* **2** a starting place; headquarters: *The base for our hiking trip was a camp beside a brook.* **3** establish; found: *Their large business was based on good service.* **4** main or supporting part; basis; foundation: *The new law was a base on which to build needed reforms.* **5** the most important element of anything; essential part: *This paint has an oil base.* **6** place that is a station or goal in certain games, such as baseball or hide-and-seek: *A home run doesn't count if you fail to touch a base.* **7** a chemical compound that yields ions composed of hydrogen and oxygen when dissolved in water. Such substances turn red litmus paper blue and will usually react with an acid to form a salt. Sodium hydroxide is a base. **8** line or surface on which a geometrical figure is supposed to rest. Any side of a triangle can be its base. **9** the number that is a definite starting point for a system of numbers. 10 is the base of the decimal system of arithmetic. **10** the form of a word to which prefixes and suffixes can be attached; root. **1,2,4-10** *n.,* **3** *v.,* **based, bas ing.**

off base, INFORMAL. incorrect; wrong.

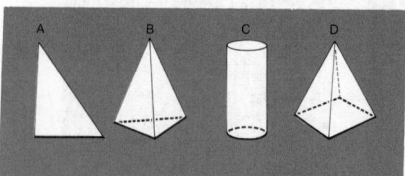

base (def. 8)

base² (bās), **1** morally low or mean; selfish and cowardly: *Betraying a friend is a base action.* **2** having little value when compared with something else; inferior: *Iron and lead are base metals; gold and silver are precious metals. adj.,* **bas er, bas est.** —**base′ly,** *adv.* —**base′ness,** *n.*

base ball (bās′bôl′), **1** game played with bat and ball by two teams of nine players each, on a field with four bases. A player who touches all the bases, under the rules, scores a run. **2** ball used in this game. *n.*

base board (bās′bôrd′), line of boards around the inside walls of a room, next to the floor. *n.*

base less (bās′lis), without foundation; groundless: *a baseless rumor. adj.* —**base′less ly,** *adv.*

base man (bās′mən), a baseball player guarding first, second, or third base. *n., pl.* **base men.**

base ment (bās′mənt), the lowest story of a building, partly or wholly below ground. *n.*

base runner, (in baseball) player on the team at bat who is on base or running between two bases.

bas es[1] (bā′siz), plural of **base**[1]. *n.*

ba ses[2] (bā′sēz′), plural of **basis.** *n.*

bash (bash), INFORMAL. **1** strike with a smashing blow. **2** a smashing blow. **3** SLANG. a big party or meal. 1 *v.,* 2, 3 *n., pl.* **bash es.**

bash ful (bash′fəl), uneasy in the presence of strangers; easily embarrassed; shy: *The child was too bashful to greet us. adj.* —**bash′ful ly,** *adv.* —**bash′ful ness,** *n.*

BA SIC (bā′sik), computer programming language that uses English words and algebraic notation. It is a simple language often used with smaller computers. *n.*

ba sic (bā′sik), **1** forming the basis; fundamental: *Addition, subtraction, multiplication, and division are the basic processes of arithmetic.* **2** (in chemistry) being, having the properties of, or containing a base; alkaline. *adj.*

ba si cal ly (bā′sik lē), as a basic principle; fundamentally. *adv.*

bas il (baz′əl), a sweet-smelling plant related to mint, used in cooking. *n.*

ba sil i ca (bə sil′ə kə), **1** an oblong hall with a row of columns at each side and a structure in the shape of a half circle at one end. The Romans used such buildings for courts of law and public meetings. **2** church built in this form. *n., pl.* **ba sil i cas.**

bas i lisk (bas′ə lisk), **1** (in old stories) a lizardlike reptile whose breath and look were thought to be fatal. **2** a tropical American lizard with a crest along its head and back which it can raise or lower. *n.*

ba sin (bā′sn), **1** a wide, shallow bowl for holding liquids. **2** amount that a basin can hold: *They have used up a basin of water already.* **3** a shallow area containing water: *Part of the harbor is a basin for yachts.* **4** all the land drained by a river and the streams that flow into it: *The Mississippi basin extends from the Appalachians to the Rockies. n.* —**ba′sin like′,** *adj.*

ba sis (bā′sis), **1** thing or part on which anything is established or supported; foundation: *The basis of their friendship was a common interest in sports.* **2** the main part; base: *The basis of this medicine is an oil. n., pl.* **ba ses.**

bask (bask), **1** warm oneself pleasantly: *The cat basks before the fire.* **2** feel great pleasure: *The author basked in the praise of the critics. v.*

bas ket (bas′kit), **1** container made of twigs, grasses, fibers, strips of wood, etc., woven together: *a clothes basket.* **2** amount that a basket holds: *We ate a basket of peaches.* **3** anything that looks like or is shaped like a basket: *a metal wastepaper basket.* **4** net shaped like a basket open at the bottom, used as a goal in basketball. **5** score made in basketball by tossing the ball through the basket. *n.* —**bas′ket like′,** *adj.*

bas ket ball (bas′kit bôl′), **1** game played with a large, round ball by two teams of five players each. The players try to toss the ball through a ring into a net shaped like a basket but open at the bottom. **2** ball used in this game. *n.*

bas ket ry (bas′kə trē), **1** art of making baskets. **2** baskets. *n.*

a hat	i it	oi oil	ch child	(a in about
ā age	ī ice	ou out	ng long	e in taken
ä far	o hot	u cup	sh she	ə = { i in pencil
e let	ō open	ů put	th thin	o in lemon
ē equal	ô order	ü rule	ᴛʜ then	u in circus
ėr term			zh measure	

bas mitz vah (bäs mits′və), bat mitzvah.

Basque (bask), **1** member of a people living in the Pyrenees region of northern Spain and southern France. **2** the language of the Basques. **3** of the Basques or their language. 1,2 *n.,* 3 *adj.*

bas-re lief (bä′ri lēf′), carving or sculpture in which the figures stand out only slightly from the background. *n.*

bass[1] (bās), **1** the lowest male voice in music. **2** singer with such a voice. **3** part in music for such a voice. **4** instrument playing such a part. **5** having a deep, low sound. 1-4 *n., pl.* **bass es;** 5 *adj.*

bass[2] (bas), North American freshwater or saltwater fish with spiny fins, used for food. *n., pl.* **bass es** or **bass.**

bass clef (bās), symbol in music showing that the pitch of the notes on a staff is below middle C; F clef. See **clef** for diagram.

bass drum (bās), a large drum that makes a deep, low sound when struck on one or both of its heads.

bas set (bas′it), dog with short legs and a long body, like a dachshund, but larger and heavier. *n.*

bass horn (bās), tuba.

bas si net (bas′n et′), a baby's basketlike cradle, usually with a hood over one end. *n.*

bas so (bas′ō), singer with a bass voice. *n., pl.* **bas sos.**

bassoon

bas soon (bə sün′), a deep-toned wind instrument with a doubled wooden body and a curved metal pipe to which a double reed is attached. *n.*

bass viol (bās), double bass.

bass wood (bas′wůd′), **1** the American linden tree. **2** its wood. *n.*

bast (bast), the tough fiber in the inner bark of certain trees, used in making rope, matting, etc. *n.*

bas tard (bas′tərd), child born of parents who are not married to each other. *n.*

baste[1] (bāst), drip or pour melted fat or butter on (meat, fowl, etc.) while roasting: *Baste the turkey to keep it from drying out. v.,* **bast ed, bast ing.** —**bast′er,** *n.*

baste[2] (bāst), sew with long, loose stitches. These stitches are usually removed after the final sewing. *v.,* **bast ed, bast ing.** —**bast′er,** *n.*

Bas tille (ba stēl′), an old fort in Paris used as a prison for enemies of the king. A mob captured and destroyed it on July 14, 1789, at the beginning of the French Revolution. *n.*

bas tion (bas/chən), **1** a part of a fortification that sticks out so that the defenders can fire at attackers from as many angles as possible. **2** stronghold; center of defense. *n.*

bat[1] (bat), **1** a stout wooden stick or club, used to hit the ball in baseball, cricket, etc. **2** hit with a bat; hit: *She bats well. I batted the balloon with my hand.* **3** a turn at batting: *Who goes to bat first?* **4** a stroke; blow. 1,3,4 *n.*, 2 *v.*, **bat ted, bat ting.**

at bat, in position to bat; having a turn at batting: *Our side is at bat.*

go to bat for, INFORMAL. support the cause of.

right off the bat, INFORMAL. without hesitation; immediately.

bat[2] (bat), a flying mammal with a mouselike body and wings made of thin skin that are supported by the long, slim bones of the forelimbs. Bats fly at night. There are over 1000 species, with bodies varying in size from one and a half inches to twelve inches. Most of them eat insects but some live on fruit and a few suck the blood of other mammals. *n.* —**bat/like/,** *adj.*

bat[3] (bat), INFORMAL. wink: *The ball nearly hit her, but she didn't bat an eye.* *v.*, **bat ted, bat ting.**

Ba taan (bə tan/), peninsula near Manila in the Philippines, where United States and Philippine troops surrendered to the Japanese in 1942. *n.*

batch (bach), **1** quantity of bread, cookies, etc., made at one baking. **2** quantity of anything made as one lot or set: *Our second batch of candy was better than the first.* **3** number of persons or things taken together: *We caught a fine batch of fish.* *n., pl.* **batch es.**

bate (bāt), deduct; lessen. *v.*, **bat ed, bat ing.**

with bated breath, holding the breath in great fear, wonder, interest, etc.: *We listened with bated breath to the exciting story.*

bath (bath), **1** a washing of the body: *I took a hot bath.* **2** water in a tub for a bath: *Your bath is ready.* **3** tub, room, or other place for bathing. In ancient Rome, baths were often elaborate public buildings, which were also used as clubs. **4** liquid in which something is washed or dipped: *a bath for developing photographic film.* **5** container holding the liquid. *n., pl.* **baths** (baᵀHz). [*Bath* comes from Old English *bæth.*] —**bath/less,** *adj.*

bathe (bāᵀH), **1** take a bath: *We wash our hair and bathe regularly.* **2** give a bath to: *She is bathing the dog.* **3** apply water to; wash or moisten with any liquid: *He bathed his swollen ankle.* **4** go swimming; go into a river, lake, ocean, etc., for pleasure or to get cool. **5** cover or surround: *The valley was bathed in sunlight.* *v.*, **bathed, bath ing.**

bath er (bā/ᵀHər), **1** person who bathes. **2** swimmer. *n.*

bath house (bath/hous/), **1** house or building fitted out for bathing. **2** building containing dressing rooms for swimmers. *n., pl.* **bath hous es** (bath/hou/ziz).

bathing suit, garment worn for swimming.

bath robe (bath/rōb/), a long, loose garment worn to and from a bath or when resting or lounging. *n.*

bath room (bath/rüm/ *or* bath/rùm/), **1** room fitted out for taking baths, usually equipped with a sink and a toilet. **2** a room containing a toilet. *n.*

bath tub (bath/tub/), tub to bathe in, especially one permanently fixed in a bathroom. *n.*

bath y scaph or **bath y scaphe** (bath/ə skaf), a diving craft for deep-sea exploration consisting of a round steel chamber suspended from a large, cigar-shaped float. *n.* [*Bathyscaph* comes from Greek *bathys,* meaning "deep," and *skaphē,* meaning "bowl, tub."]

bath y sphere (bath/ə sfir/), a watertight steel ball with observation windows, lowered by cables from a ship to study the depths of the sea. *n.*

ba tik (bə tēk/), method of making designs on cloth by covering the material with wax in a pattern, dyeing the parts left exposed, and then removing the wax. *n.* [*Batik* comes from Javanese *mbatik,* meaning "painted."]

ba tiste (bə tēst/), a fine, thin cloth made of cotton, rayon, or wool. *n.*

bat mitz vah (bät/ mits/və), **1** ceremony or celebration held when a Jewish girl becomes thirteen years old to affirm that she has reached the age of religious responsibility. **2** the girl herself. Also, **bas mitzvah.**

bat[2]
wingspread about
15 in. (38 cm.)

ba ton (ba ton/), **1** the light stick or wand used by the leader of an orchestra, chorus, or band to indicate the beat and direct the performance. **2** staff or stick used as a symbol of office or authority. **3** a stick passed from runner to runner in a relay race. **4** a light, hollow metal rod twirled by a drum major or majorette as a showy display. *n.*

Bat on Rouge (bat/n rüzh/), capital of Louisiana, in the SE part.

bats man (bats/mən), player whose turn it is to bat in cricket. *n., pl.* **bats men.**

bat tal ion (bə tal/yən), **1** military unit made up of two or more companies or batteries, usually commanded by a major or a lieutenant colonel. It is usually part of a group or a regiment. **2** any large group organized to act together: *A battalion of volunteers helped to rescue the flood victims.* *n.*

bat ten (bat/n), **1** strip of wood or steel used on shipboard to fasten tarpaulins over hatchways to keep out water. **2** narrow strip of wood or plastic inserted into a sail to keep it flat. **3** fasten down with, or as if with, such strips. 1,2 *n.*, 3 *v.*

bat ter[1] (bat/ər), strike with repeated blows so as to bruise, break, or get out of shape; pound: *They battered down the door with a heavy ax. Violent storms battered the coast for days.* *v.*

bat ter[2] (bat/ər), a liquid mixture of flour, milk, eggs, etc., that becomes solid when cooked. Cakes, pancakes, and muffins are made from batter. *n.*

bat ter[3] (bat/ər), player whose turn it is to bat in baseball, cricket, etc. *n.*

bathyscaph

bat tered (bat′ərd), damaged by hard use: *I found a battered old bookcase in the office. adj.*

battering ram, a heavy wooden beam with a mass of metal at the striking end. Battering rams were used in ancient and medieval warfare for battering down walls, gates, etc.

bat ter y (bat′ər ē), **1** container holding materials that produce electricity by chemical action; a single electric cell: *Most flashlights work on two batteries.* **2** set of two or more electric cells that produce electric current: *The car won't start because the battery is dead.* **3** any set of similar or connected things: *a battery of television cameras and microphones. If you want this job you will have to take a battery of tests.* **4** set of similar pieces of equipment, such as mounted guns, searchlights, mortars, etc., used as a unit. **5** a military unit of artillery, usually commanded by a captain. A battery corresponds to a company or troop in other branches of the army. **6** (in baseball) the pitcher and catcher together. **7** the unlawful beating of another person or any threatening touch to another person's clothes or body. *n., pl.* **bat ter ies.**

bat ting (bat′ing), cotton, wool, or synthetic material pressed into thin layers, used to line comforters, quilts, etc. *n.*

bat tle (bat′l), **1** a fight between opposing armies, air forces, or navies: *The battle for the island lasted six months.* **2** fighting or warfare: *The soldier received his wounds in battle.* **3** any fight or contest: *The candidates fought a battle of words during the campaign.* **4** take part in a battle; fight; struggle; contend: *The swimmer had to battle a strong current. Our team is battling for first place.* 1-3 *n.,* 4 *v.,* **bat tled, bat tling.**
join battle, begin to fight.

battle-ax

bat tle-ax or **bat tle-axe** (bat′l aks′), ax with a broad blade, used in medieval times as a weapon in battle. *n., pl.* **bat tle-ax es.**

battle cry, 1 shout of soldiers rushing into or engaged in battle. **2** motto or slogan in any contest.

bat tle field (bat′l fēld′), place where a battle is fought or has been fought. *n.*

bat tle front (bat′l frunt′), place where the fighting between armies takes place; front. *n.*

bat tle ground (bat′l ground′), battlefield. *n.*

bat tle ment (bat′l mənt), **1** a low wall for defense at the top of a tower or wall in which solid parts alternate with openings. Soldiers of ancient and medieval times stood on a platform behind the wall and shot through the openings. **2** wall built like this for ornament. *n.*

bat tler (bat′lər), person who battles; warrior; fighter. *n.*

battle royal, 1 fight in which several take part; riot. **2** a long, hard fight. *pl.* **battles royal.**

bat tle ship (bat′l ship′), type of warship having the heaviest armor and the most powerful guns, last built during World War II. *n.*

a hat	i it	oi oil	ch child	a in about
ā age	ī ice	ou out	ng long	e in taken
ä far	o hot	u cup	sh she	ə = i in pencil
e let	ō open	u̇ put	th thin	o in lemon
ē equal	ô order	ü rule	ŦH then	u in circus
ėr term			zh measure	

bat ty (bat′ē), SLANG. crazy. *adj.,* **bat ti er, bat ti est.**

bau ble (bô′bəl), a showy trifle having no real value; trinket. *n.*

baulk (bôk), balk. *v., n.*

baux ite (bôk′sīt), a claylike mineral from which aluminum is obtained. *n.* [*Bauxite* was borrowed from French *bauxite,* which gets its name from *Les Baux,* a town in southern France where it was discovered.]

Ba var i a (bə ver′ē ə *or* bə var′ē ə), state in S West Germany. In the past it has been a duchy, a kingdom, and a republic. *n.* —**Ba var′i an,** *n., adj.*

bawd y (bô′dē), not decent; lewd; obscene. *adj.,* **bawd i er, bawd i est.** —**bawd′i ly,** *adv.* —**bawd′i ness,** *n.*

bawl (bôl), **1** weep loudly: *The baby dropped his toy and started to bawl.* **2** shout or cry out in a noisy way: *a lost calf bawling for its mother.* **3** a shout at the top of one's voice. 1,2 *v.,* 3 *n.* —**bawl′er,** *n.*

bawl out, INFORMAL. scold loudly; reprimand: *She bawled me out for denting her bicycle.*

bay[1] (bā), part of a sea or lake extending into the land. A bay is usually smaller than a gulf and larger than a cove. *n.*

bay[2] (bā), **1** a long, deep barking, especially by a large dog: *The hunters heard the distant bay of the hounds.* **2** to bark with long, deep sounds: *Dogs sometimes bay at the moon.* **3** position of a hunted animal that turns to face its pursuers when escape is impossible: *The stag stood at bay against the hounds on the edge of the cliff.* **4** position of an enemy or pursuers thus faced or kept off: *The stag held the hounds at bay.* 1,3,4 *n.,* 2 *v.*

bay[3] (bā), a small evergreen tree with smooth, shiny leaves; laurel. Dried bay leaves are used in cooking. *n.*

bay[4] (bā), **1** reddish-brown: *a bay horse.* **2** a reddish-brown horse with black mane and tail. **3** a reddish brown. 1 *adj.,* 2,3 *n.*

bay[5] (bā), **1** space or division of a wall or building between columns, pillars, buttresses, etc. **2** bay window. **3** compartment in an airplane, especially one for carrying bombs. *n.*

bay ber ry (bā′ber′ē), a North American shrub with clusters of grayish-white berries coated with wax. Candles made from the wax of bayberries burn with a pleasant fragrance. *n., pl.* **bay ber ries.**

bay leaf, the dried leaf of a laurel or bay, used as a flavoring for foods.

bay o net (bā′ə nit *or* bā′ə net′), **1** knife attached to the muzzle of a rifle. It may be detached and used as a separate hand weapon. **2** pierce or stab with a bayonet. 1 *n.,* 2 *v.,* **bay o net ed, bay o net ing** or **bay o net ted,**

battlement (def. 1)

bay o net ting. [*Bayonet* is from French *baïonnette*, which comes from *Bayonne*, a city in southern France where the weapon was first made.]

bay ou (bī′ü), a marshy inlet or outlet of a lake, river, or gulf in the south central United States. The water in a bayou flows sluggishly. *n.* [*Bayou* was borrowed from the Louisiana French *bayou,* which comes from Choctaw *bayuk.*]

bay window, window or set of windows projecting from a wall to form an alcove or small space in a room.

ba zaar or **ba zar** (bə zär′), 1 street or streets full of small shops and booths in Oriental countries. 2 place for the sale of many kinds of goods. 3 sale of things contributed by various people, held for some charity or other special purpose. *n.* [*Bazaar* comes from Persian *bāzār.*]

ba zoo ka (bə zü′kə), a portable weapon used to fire rockets at tanks. *n., pl.* **ba zoo kas.**

B B (bē′bē′), 1 a standard, small size of shot, about .18 inch (.46 centimeter) in diameter. 2 shot of this size, used especially in an air rifle. *n.*

BBC, British Broadcasting Corporation.

BB gun, air rifle.

bbl., barrel. *pl.* **bbls.**

B.C., 1 before Christ. B.C. is used for times before the birth of Christ. A.D. is used for times after the birth of Christ. 350 B.C. is 100 years earlier than 250 B.C. From 20 B.C. to A.D. 50 is 70 years. 2 British Columbia.

B complex, vitamin B complex.

bd., 1 board. 2 bond. 3 bound.

bd. ft., board foot or board feet.

bdl., bundle. *pl.* **bdls.**

be (bē), *He will be here all year. She tries to be good. They will be punished. v.,* **was** or **were, been, be ing.**

be-, *prefix.* 1 thoroughly; all around: *Bespatter = spatter thoroughly.* 2 make; cause to seem: *Benumb = make numb.* 3 provide with: *Bespangle = provide with spangles.* 4 at; on; to; for; about; against: *Bewail = wail about.*

Be, symbol for beryllium.

beach (bēch), 1 an almost flat shore of sand or pebbles over which water washes when high. 2 run (a boat) ashore; pull up on the shore. 1 *n., pl.* **beach es;** 2 *v.* —**beach′less,** *adj.*

beach comb er (bēch′kō′mər), vagrant or loafer, especially on islands of the Pacific. *n.*

beach head (bēch′hed′), the first position established by an invading military force on an enemy beach or shore to make possible the landing of troops and supplies. *n.*

beach wagon, station wagon.

bea con (bē′kən), 1 fire or light used as a signal to guide or warn. 2 marker, signal light, or radio station that guides aircraft and ships through fogs, storms, etc. 3 a tall tower for a signal; lighthouse. *n.*

bead (bēd), 1 a small ball or bit of glass, metal, etc., with a hole through it, so that it can be strung on a thread with others like it. 2 **beads,** *pl.* **a** string of beads. **b** string of beads for keeping count in saying prayers; rosary. 3 put beads on; ornament with beads. 4 any small, round object like a drop or bubble: *Beads of sweat covered her forehead.* 5 piece of metal at the front end of a gun to aim by. 1,2,4,5 *n.,* 3 *v.* —**bead′like′,** *adj.*

draw a bead on, aim a gun at; take aim at.

say one's beads, tell one's beads, or **count one's beads,** say prayers, using a rosary.

bead ed (bēd′id), 1 trimmed with beads. 2 like beads. *adj.*

bead ing (bē′ding), 1 trimming made of beads. 2 pattern or edge on woodwork, silver, etc., made of small beads. *n.*

bea dle (bē′dl), a minor parish officer whose duties include helping the clergyman and keeping order. *n.*

bead work (bēd′wėrk′), beading. *n.*

bead y (bē′dē), small, round, and shiny: *The parakeet has beady eyes. adj.,* **bead i er, bead i est.**

bea gle (bē′gəl), a small dog with smooth hair, short legs, and drooping ears, bred for hunting. *n.*

beak (bēk), 1 bill of a bird. Eagles and hawks have strong, hooked beaks that are useful in striking or tearing. 2 a similar, often horny, part in other animals. Turtles and octopuses have beaks. 3 anything shaped like a beak, such as the projecting prow of an ancient warship or the spout of a pitcher, jug, etc. *n.* —**beak′like′,** *adj.*

beak er (bē′kər), 1 a large cup or drinking glass with a wide mouth. 2 a thin glass or metal cup used in laboratories. A beaker has a flat bottom, no handle, and a small lip for pouring. *n.*

beam (bēm), 1 a large, long piece of timber, iron, or steel, for use in building. 2 the main horizontal support of a building or ship. 3 any long piece or bar: *The beam of a balance supports a pair of scales.* 4 ray or rays of light: *The beam from the flashlight showed a kitten.* 5 send out rays of light; shine: *The sun was beaming brightly.* 6 a bright look or smile. 7 look or smile brightly: *Her face beamed with delight.* 8 a radio signal directed in a straight line, used to guide aircraft, ships, etc. 9 direct (a broadcast): *A program was beamed at England.* 10 the widest part of a ship: *This ship has a thirty-foot beam.* 1-4,6,8,10 *n.,* 5,7,9 *v.*

beam ing (bē′ming), 1 shining; bright. 2 looking or smiling brightly; cheerful. *adj.* —**beam′ing ly,** *adv.*

bean (bēn), 1 the smooth, somewhat flat seed of a bush or vine, eaten as a vegetable. Lima beans, kidney beans, and navy beans are three different varieties of beans. 2 the long pod containing such seeds. The green or yellow pods of some varieties are also used as a vegetable. 3 any seed shaped somewhat like a bean. Coffee beans are seeds of the coffee plant. *n.* —**bean′like′,** *adj.*

spill the beans, INFORMAL. reveal a secret.

bean bag (bēn′bag′), a small bag partly filled with dried beans, used to toss in play. *n.*

bean ie (bē′nē), a small, close-fitting cap, worn especially by schoolboys. *n.*

bean stalk (bēn′stôk′), stem of a bean plant. *n.*

bear[1] (ber *or* bar), 1 carry or support; hold up: *The hikers bore heavy packs on their backs. The ice is too thin to bear your weight.* 2 put up with; endure: *She can't bear the noise. He cannot bear any more pain.* 3 bring forth; produce: *This tree bears fine apples. That tree is too young to bear.* 4 give birth to: *Our cat will soon bear kittens. She was born on May 15.* 5 act in a certain way; behave; conduct: *The famous author bore himself with great dignity.* 6 hold in mind; hold: *bear a grudge, bear affection.* 7 move; go: *The ship bore north.* 8 take on oneself as a duty: *bear the cost, bear the responsibility. v.,* **bore, borne** or **born, bear ing.**

bear down or **bear down on,** 1 put pressure on; press down: *The lead will break if you bear down too hard on your pencil.* 2 put all one's efforts on; try hard: *I bore down on my homework and got it done on time.* 3 move toward; approach: *The hunters bore down on the wounded animal.*

bear on, have something to do with: *Your story does not bear on the question.*

bear out, back up; support; prove: *The facts bear out our claim.*

bear up, keep one's courage; not lose hope or faith: *bear up under troubles.*

bear with, put up with; be patient with: *Please bear with me while I ask some questions.*

bear[2] (ber *or* bar), 1 a large mammal with thick, coarse fur and a very short tail. A bear walks flat on the soles of its feet. The black bear, brown bear, grizzly bear, and polar bear are four kinds of bears. **2** a gruff or bad-tempered person. *n.* —**bear′like′**, *adj.*

bear a ble (ber′ə bəl *or* bar′ə bəl), able to be endured. *adj.* —**bear′a ble ness,** *n.*

bear a bly (ber′ə blē *or* bar′ə blē), in a way that can be endured; tolerably. *adv.*

beard (bird), **1** the hair growing on a man's chin and cheeks. **2** something resembling or suggesting this. The chin tuft of a goat is a beard; so are the stiff hairs on the heads of plants like oats, barley, and wheat. **3** face boldly; defy: *beard the lion in its den.* 1,2 *n.,* 3 *v.* —**beard′like′,** *adj.*

Beard (bird), **Daniel Carter,** 1850-1941, American naturalist who founded the Boy Scouts of America in 1910. *n.*

beard ed (bir′did), having a beard. *adj.*

beard less (bird′lis), **1** without a beard. **2** young or immature. *adj.* —**beard′less ness,** *n.*

bear er (ber′ər *or* bar′ər), **1** person or thing that carries. **2** person who holds or presents a check, draft, or note for payment. *n.*

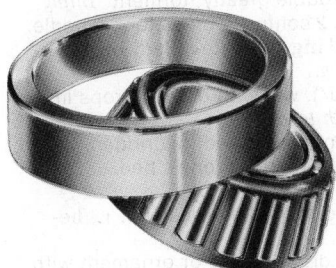

bearing (def. 4)
outer ring lifted and tilted to show the inner ring, which contains the bearings

bear ing (ber′ing *or* bar′ing), **1** way of standing, sitting, walking, or behaving; manner: *A general should have a military bearing.* **2** connection in thought or meaning; relation: *Do not ask questions that have no bearing on our discussion.* **3 bearings,** *pl.* position in relation to other things; direction: *We had no compass, so we got our bearings from the stars.* **4** part of a machine on which another part moves. A bearing supports the moving part and reduces friction by turning with the motion. *n.*

bear ish (ber′ish *or* bar′ish), like a bear in manner or temper; rough or surly. *adj.* —**bear′ish ly,** *adv.* —**bear′ish ness,** *n.*

bear skin (ber′skin′ *or* bar′skin′), **1** the skin of a bear with the fur on it. **2** rug, blanket, or the like made from this. **3** a tall, black fur cap worn by some soldiers and drum majors, especially in the British army. *n.*

beast (bēst), **1** any four-footed animal. Lions, bears, cows, and horses are beasts. **2** a brutal person. *n.* —**beast′like′,** *adj.*

beast li ness (bēst′lē nis), beastly condition, behavior, or quality. *n.*

beast ly (bēst′lē), **1** like a beast; brutal; vile. **2** INFORMAL. very bad or irritating; unpleasant: *I have a beastly headache.* **3** INFORMAL. very; unpleasantly. 1,2 *adj.,* beast-li er, beast li est; 3 *adv.*

beast of burden, animal used for carrying or pulling heavy loads.

beast of prey, animal that kills other animals for food.

beat (bēt), **1** strike again and again: *The baby beat the floor with the toy hammer.* **2** stroke or blow made again and again: *the beat of a drum.* **3** get the better of; defeat; overcome: *Their team beat ours by a huge score.* **4** make flat: *The jeweler beat gold into thin strips with a hammer.*

a hat	i it	oi oil	ch child	a in about
ā age	ī ice	ou out	ng long	e in taken
ä far	o hot	u cup	sh she	ə = i in pencil
e let	ō open	ù put	th thin	o in lemon
ē equal	ô order	ü rule	ŦH then	u in circus
ėr term			zh measure	

5 mix by stirring rapidly with a fork, spoon, or other utensil: *I helped make the cake by beating the eggs.* **6** sound made by the regular action of the heart as it pumps blood. **7** to throb: *Her heart beat fast with joy.* **8** a throb: *the beat of the heart.* **9** move up and down; flap: *The bird beat its wings.* **10** make a sound by being struck: *The drums beat loudly.* **11** unit of time or accent in music: *three beats to a measure. The dancer never missed a beat.* **12** mark time with drumsticks or by tapping with the hands, fingers, or feet. **13** stroke of the hand, baton, etc., showing a musical beat. **14** a regular round or route taken by a police officer or guard. **15** move against the wind by a zigzag course: *The sailboat beat along the coast.* **16** INFORMAL. worn out; tired; exhausted: *I was beat after running the race.* 1,3-5,7,9,10,12,15 *v.,* beat, beat en *or* beat, beat ing; 2,6,8,11,13,14 *n.,* 16 *adj.*

beat back, force or push back: *The police beat back the rioting crowd.*

beat down, INFORMAL. force to set a lower price.

beat it, SLANG. go away.

beat off, drive away by blows: *to beat off a savage dog.*

beat up, SLANG. thrash soundly.

beat en (bēt′n), **1** whipped; struck: *The beaten dog ran away from its owner.* **2** much walked on or traveled: *a beaten path across the grass.* **3** defeated; overcome: *a beaten army.* **4** exhausted. **5** shaped by blows of a hammer: *This bowl is made of beaten silver.* **6** a past participle of beat. *Our team was beaten in basketball on Saturday.* 1-5 *adj.,* 6 *v.*

beat er (bē′tər), **1** device or utensil for beating eggs, cream, etc. **2** person or thing that beats: *a rug beater. n.*

be a tif ic (bē′ə tif′ik), showing very great happiness; blissful. *adj.* —**be′a tif′i cal ly,** *adv.*

be at i fy (bē at′ə fī), **1** make supremely happy; bless. **2** declare by a decree of the pope that a dead person is among the blessed in heaven. *v.,* **be at i fied, be at i fy-ing.**

beat ing (bē′ting), **1** act of one that beats; a striking. **2** punishment by blows; whipping; thrashing. **3** state of being beaten; defeat. **4** throbbing. *n.*

be at i tude (bē at′ə tüd *or* bē at′ə tyüd), **1** supreme happiness; bliss. **2** a blessing. **3 the Beatitudes,** (in the Bible) the eight verses in the Sermon on the Mount which begin with "Blessed," as "Blessed are the poor in spirit." *n.*

beat-up (bēt′up′), worn out from long or hard use: *a beat-up car. adj.*

beau (bō), **1** a young man courting a young woman; suitor or lover. **2** man who pays much attention to the way he dresses and to the fashion of his clothes; dandy. *n., pl.* **beaus** *or* **beaux.**

Beau fort scale (bō′fərt), scale of wind velocities, ranging from 0 (calm) to 17 (hurricane), used in weather maps.

beau te ous (byü′tē əs), beautiful. *adj.* —**beau′te ous ly,** *adv.* —**beau′te ous ness,** *n.*

beau ti cian (byü tish′ən), a person that is skilled in the use of cosmetics, etc., especially one who works in a beauty shop. *n.*

beau ti fi ca tion (byü′tə fə kā′shən), a making beautiful or more beautiful; beautifying. *n.*

beau ti ful (byü′tə fəl), very pleasing to see or hear;

delighting the mind or senses. *adj.* —**beau′ti ful ly,** *adv.*
—**beau′ti ful ness,** *n.*

beau ti fy (byü′tə fī), make beautiful; make more beautiful: *Flowers beautify a room.* *v.,* **beau ti fied, beau ti fy ing.** —**beau′ti fi′er,** *n.*

beau ty (byü′tē), **1** good looks: *The child had beauty and intelligence.* **2** quality that pleases in flowers, pictures, music, etc. **3** something beautiful: *the beauties of nature.* **4** a beautiful woman. *n., pl.* **beau ties.**

beauty shop, beauty parlor, or **beauty salon,** place where women have their hair, skin, and nails cared for.

beaux (bōz), a plural of **beau.** *n.*

beaver[1] (def. 1)
about 3½ ft. (1 m.)
long with the tail

bea ver[1] (bē′vər), **1** a large rodent with soft fur, a broad, flat tail, and webbed hind feet for swimming. Beavers live both in water and on land and build dams across streams. **2** its soft brown fur. *n.* —**bea′ver like′,** *adj.*

bea ver[2] (bē′vər), the movable lower part of a helmet, protecting the chin and mouth. *n.*

bea ver board (bē′vər bôrd′), a building material made of compressed wood fibers, used for wall partitions and ceilings. *n.*

be calmed (bi kämd′ *or* bi kälmd′), kept from moving because there is no wind: *The sailboat lay becalmed on the lake.* *adj.*

be came (bi kām′), past tense of **become.** *The seed became a plant.* *v.*

be cause (bi kôz′), for the reason that; since: *Because we were late, we ran the whole way home.* *conj.*

because of, by reason of; on account of: *The game was called off because of rain.*

beck (bek). **at one's beck and call, 1** ready whenever wanted. **2** under one's complete control. *n.*

Beck et (bek′it), **Saint Thomas à,** 1118?-1170, archbishop of Canterbury. He was murdered in the cathedral there for resisting the policies of Henry II of England. *n.*

beck on (bek′ən), signal by motion of the head or hand: *He beckoned me to follow him.* *v.*

be cloud (bi kloud′), **1** hide by a cloud or clouds. **2** make obscure; hide: *Too many big words becloud the meaning.* *v.*

be come (bi kum′), **1** come to be; grow to be: *It is becoming colder. I became tired and fell asleep.* **2** seem proper or fitting for: *It does not become them to brag about their furniture.* **3** look well on; suit: *That blue sweater becomes you.* *v.,* **be came, be come, be com ing.**

become of, happen to: *What has become of the box of candy?*

be com ing (bi kum′ing), **1** fitting; suitable: *the high moral character becoming to a judge.* **2** pleasant to look at; attractive: *a very becoming new suit.* *adj.*

bed (bed), **1** anything to sleep or rest on. A bed usually consists of a mattress raised upon a support and covered with sheets and blankets. **2** any place where people or animals sleep or rest: *The cat made its bed by the fireplace.* **3** provide with a bed; put to bed; go to bed: *She bedded down her horse in the barn.* **4** a flat base on which

anything rests; foundation: *The tall flagpole was set in a bed of concrete.* **5** the ground under a body of water: *The river bed was soft and muddy.* **6** piece of ground in a garden in which plants are grown: *a bed of tulips.* **7** plant in a garden bed: *These tulips should be bedded in rich soil.* **8** layer; stratum: *a bed of coal deep in the earth.* **1,2,4-6,8** *n.,* **3,7** *v.,* **bed ded, bed ding.** [*Bed* comes from Old English *bedd.*]

get up on the wrong side of the bed, be bad-tempered or irritable.

be daz zle (bi daz′əl), dazzle completely; confuse by dazzling. *v.,* **be daz zled, be daz zling.** —**be daz′zle ment,** *n.* —**be daz′zling ly,** *adv.*

bed bug (bed′bug′), a small, wingless, reddish-brown insect that sucks blood, found in houses and especially in beds. Its bite is painful. *n.*

bed cham ber (bed′chām′bər), bedroom. *n.*

bed clothes (bed′klōz′ *or* bed′klōтʜz′), sheets, blankets, quilts, etc. *n.pl.*

bed ding (bed′ing), **1** bedclothes. **2** material for beds: *Straw is used as bedding for cows and horses.* *n.*

be deck (bi dek′), adorn; decorate: *The actor's magnificent robe was bedecked with jewels and fine lace.* *v.*

be dev il (bi dev′əl), **1** trouble greatly; torment: *Biting flies bedeviled the horses.* **2** confuse completely; muddle. *v.,* **be dev iled, be dev il ing** or **be dev illed, be dev il ling.** —**be dev′il ment,** *n.*

be dew (bi dü′ *or* bi dyü′), wet with dew or drops like dew: *cheeks bedewed with tears.* *v.*

bed fast (bed′fast′), confined to bed; bedridden. *adj.*

bed fel low (bed′fel′ō), **1** sharer of one's bed. **2** associate. *n.*

be dim (bi dim′), make dim; darken; obscure. *v.,* **be dimmed, be dim ming.**

be di zen (bi dī′zn *or* bi diz′n), dress or ornament with showy finery. *v.*

bed lam (bed′ləm), noisy confusion; uproar: *When our team won, there was bedlam in the gym.* *n.* [*Bedlam* comes from *Bedlam,* an old form of St. Mary of *Bethlehem,* an asylum in London.]

bed lam ite (bed′lə mīt), lunatic. *n.*

Bed ou in (bed′ü ən), **1** member of certain tribes of Arab nomads who live in the deserts of Arabia, Syria, and northern Africa. **2** any wanderer or nomad. *n.*

bed pan (bed′pan′), pan used as a toilet by sick people in bed. *n.*

be drag gled (bi drag′əld), **1** wet and hanging limp: *She tried to comb her bedraggled hair.* **2** soiled by being dragged in the dirt. *adj.*

bed rid (bed′rid′), bedridden. *adj.*

bed rid den (bed′rid′n), compelled to stay in bed for a long time because of sickness or weakness. *adj.*

bed rock (bed′rok′), **1** the solid rock under the soil and under looser rocks. **2** the lowest level; bottom. *n.*

bed roll (bed′rōl′), blankets or a sleeping bag that can be rolled up and tied for carrying. *n.*

bed room (bed′rüm′ *or* bed′rum′), a room to sleep in. *n.*

bed side (bed′sīd′), area by the side of a bed: *The nurse sat by the patient's bedside.* *n.*

bed spread (bed′spred′), cover for a bed that is spread over the blankets. *n.*

bed spring (bed′spring′), set of springs forming part of a bed and supporting a mattress. *n.*

bed stead (bed′sted′), the wooden or metal framework of a bed that supports the springs and mattress. *n.*

bed time (bed′tīm′), time to go to bed: *My regular bedtime is nine o'clock.* *n.*

bee (bē), **1** insect with four wings that produces wax to make honeycombs and gathers nectar and pollen to make honey; honeybee. Bees live in large, permanent colonies containing a queen, many workers, and drones. Only the queen and the workers have stings. **2** a related insect. There are over 20,000 species of bees in the world. **3** a gathering for work or amusement: *a spelling bee, a quilting bee. n. [Bee comes from Old English bēo.]*

bee bread (bē′bred′), a brownish, bitter substance consisting of pollen, or pollen mixed with honey, used by bees as food for their larvae or young. *n.*

beech (bēch), **1** tree with smooth, gray bark and glossy leaves. It bears a small, sweet nut which is good to eat. **2** its wood. *n., pl.* **beech es** or **beech** for 1.

beech nut (bēch′nut′), the small, triangular nut of the beech tree. *n.*

beef (bēf), **1** meat from a steer, cow, or bull. **2** steer, cow, or bull when full-grown and fattened for food. **3** SLANG. complain. **4** SLANG. complaint. 1,2,4 *n., pl.* **beeves** for 2, **beefs** for 4; 3 *v.* [*Beef* came into English about 700 years ago from French *boef*, which comes from Latin *bovem*, meaning "ox, cow."]

beef up, INFORMAL. make greater; enlarge; strengthen: *The company plans to beef up benefits to retired workers.*

beef cattle, cattle raised for meat.

beef steak (bēf′stāk′), slice of beef for broiling or frying; steak. *n.*

beef y (bē′fē), strong, solid, and heavy. *adj.,* **beef i er, beef i est.** —**beef′i ness,** *n.*

bee hive (bē′hīv′), **1** hive or house for bees. **2** a busy, swarming place. *n.*

bee keep er (bē′kē′pər), person who raises bees for their honey. *n.*

bee line (bē′līn′), the straightest way between two places, like the flight of a bee to its hive. *n.*

Be el ze bub (bē el′zə bub), **1** (in the Bible) the Devil; Satan. **2** a devil. *n.*

been (bin), past participle of **be.** *I have been sick. The books have been read by everyone in the room. v.*

beep (bēp), **1** a sharp, short sound. **2** cause to make sharp, short sounds. 1 *n.,* 2 *v.*

beeper
coins in foreground indicate the size of the beeper

beep er (bē′pər), an electronic radio device that signals with a beeping sound. A portable beeper signals a person to telephone his or her home or office. *n.*

beer (bir), **1** an alcoholic drink made from malted barley flavored with hops. **2** a soft drink made from roots or plants, such as root beer. *n.*

beer y (bir′ē), of or caused by beer. *adj.,* **beer i er, beer i est.**

bees wax (bēz′waks′), wax given out by bees, from which they make their honeycomb. *n.*

beet (bēt), the thick, fleshy root of a garden plant. Red beets and their green leaves are eaten as vegetables. Sugar is made from white beets. *n.* —**beet′like′,** *adj.*

Bee tho ven (bā′tō vən), Ludwig van, 1770-1827, German composer. *n.*

bee tle[1] (bē′tl), **1** insect that has its front pair of wings modified as hard, shiny cases that cover the delicate

a hat	**i** it	**oi** oil	**ch** child	a in about
ā age	**ī** ice	**ou** out	**ng** long	e in taken
ä far	**o** hot	**u** cup	**sh** she	ə = { i in pencil
e let	**ō** open	**u̇** put	**th** thin	o in lemon
ē equal	**ô** order	**ü** rule	**ŦH** then	u in circus
ėr term			**zh** measure	

rear pair of wings when at rest. **2** insect resembling a beetle. *n.*

bee tle[2] (bē′tl), to project or overhang. *v.,* **bee tled, bee tling.**

bee tle-browed (bē′tl broud′), **1** having projecting or overhanging eyebrows. **2** scowling; sullen. *adj.*

beeves (bēvz), plural of **beef** (def. 2). *Beeves are fattened before being sold. n.*

be fall (bi fôl′), **1** happen to: *I hope no harm befalls you.* **2** happen: *Whatever befell, the family held together. v.,* **be fell, be fall en, be fall ing.**

be fall en (bi fô′lən), past participle of **befall.** *An accident must have befallen them. v.*

be fell (bi fel′), past tense of **befall.** *Evil befell them. v.*

be fit (bi fit′), be suitable for; be proper for; suit: *He always wears clothes that befit the occasion. v.,* **be fit ted, be fit ting.** —**be fit′ting ly,** *adv.*

be fog (bi fog′), **1** surround with fog; make foggy. **2** make obscure; confuse. *v.,* **be fogged, be fog ging.**

be fool (bi fül′), deceive; fool. *v.*

be fore (bi fôr′), **1** earlier than: *Come before five o'clock.* **2** earlier: *Come at five o'clock, not before.* **3** until now; in the past: *You were never late before.* **4** in front of; ahead of: *Walk before me.* **5** in front; ahead: *She went before to see if the road was safe.* **6** rather than; sooner than: *I will starve before giving in* (prep.). *I will starve before I give in* (conj.). **7** previous to the time when: *I would like to talk to her before she goes.* 1,4,6 *prep.,* 2,3,5 *adv.,* 6,7 *conj.*

be fore hand (bi fôr′hand′), ahead of time; in advance: *Get everything ready beforehand* (adv.). *Aren't you a little beforehand with your request for your allowance?* (adj.). *adv., adj.*

be friend (bi frend′), act as a friend to; help: *The children befriended the lost dog. v.*

be fud dle (bi fud′l), confuse; bewilder. *v.,* **be fud dled, be fud dling.** —**be fud′dle ment,** *n.*

beg (beg), **1** ask for (food, money, clothes, etc.) as a charity: *The poor woman had to beg for food.* **2** ask a favor; ask earnestly or humbly: *I beg you to forgive me. The children begged for a ride on the pony.* **3** ask politely and courteously: *I beg your pardon. v.,* **begged, beg ging.**

beg off, make an excuse for not being able to keep a promise: *Although he had promised to come to my party, he begged off because of a headache.*

go begging, find no one that will accept.

be gan (bi gan′), past tense of **begin.** *Snow began to fall. v.*

be gat (bi gat′), OLD USE. begot; a past tense of **beget.** *v.*

be get (bi get′), **1** be the father of. **2** cause to be; produce: *Hate begets hate and love begets love. v.,* **be got, be got ten** or **be got, be get ting.** —**be get′ter,** *n.*

beg gar (beg′ər), **1** person who lives by begging. **2** a very poor person; pauper. **3** bring to poverty: *Your reckless spending will beggar your family.* **4** go beyond; outdo: *The grandeur of Niagara Falls beggars description.* 1,2 *n.,* 3,4 *v.*

beg gar ly (beg′ər lē), fit for a beggar; poor. *adj.* —**beg′gar li ness,** *n.*

beg gar y (beg′ər ē), very great poverty. *n.*

be gin (bi gin′), **1** do the first part; make a start: *begin on one's work. When shall we begin? Begin at the third chapter.* **2** come or bring into being: *The club began two years ago.*

Five people began the club two years ago. **3** be near; come near: *Your brother's suit wouldn't even begin to fit you.* v., **be gan, be gun, be gin ning.**

Be gin (bā′gin), **Menachem,** born 1913, Israeli political leader, prime minister of Israel from 1977 to 1983. *n.*

be gin ner (bi gin′ər), person who is doing something for the first time; person who lacks skill and experience: *You skate well for a beginner. n.*

be gin ning (bi gin′ing), **1** a start: *Make a good beginning.* **2** time when anything begins: *In the beginning our club had only ten members; now there are 40.* **3** first part: *I enjoyed this book from beginning to end.* **4** source; origin: *The idea of the airplane had its beginning in the flight of birds.* **5** that begins: *This is the beginning lesson of the spelling book.* 1-4 *n.,* 5 *adj.*

be gone (bi gôn′), go away: *"Begone!" said the prince (interj.). The prince bade him begone (v.).* *interj., v.*

be go nia (bi gō′nyə), a tropical plant often grown for its large, richly colored leaves and waxy flowers. *n., pl.* **be go nias.** [*Begonia* was named after Michel *Bégon,* 1638-1710, a French patron of botany.]

be got (bi got′), past tense and a past participle of **be-get.** *He begot a son. v.*

be got ten (bi got′n), a past participle of **beget.** *He has begotten a daughter. v.*

be grudge (bi gruj′), **1** give or allow (something) unwillingly; grudge: *She is so stingy that she begrudges her dog a bone.* **2** envy: *The neighbors begrudge us our swimming pool.* v., **be grudged, be grudg ing.**

be guile (bi gīl′), **1** trick or mislead (a person); deceive; cheat: *His flattery beguiled me into thinking that he was my friend.* **2** win the attention of; entertain; amuse: *The playful puppies beguiled the children with their antics.* v., **be-guiled, be guil ing.** —**be guile′ment,** *n.* —**be guil′er,** *n.*

be gun (bi gun′), past participle of **begin.** *It has begun to rain. v.*

be half (bi haf′), side, interest, or favor: *Her friends will act in her behalf. n.*

in behalf of or **on behalf of,** in the interest of; for: *I am speaking in behalf of my friend.*

be have (bi hāv′), **1** manage, handle, or conduct (one-self); act: *You behaved yourself well during the whole trip.* **2** act properly; do what is right: *If you behave today, we can come here again.* v., **be haved, be hav ing.**

be hav ior (bi hā′vyər), manner of behaving; way of acting: *Her sullen behavior showed that she was angry. n.*

be head (bi hed′), cut off the head of. *v.*

be held (bi held′), past tense and past participle of **be-hold.** *We beheld the beautiful sunset. v.*

be he moth (bi hē′məth), **1** (in the Bible) a huge and powerful animal. It may have been the hippopotamus. **2** anything very large and powerful. *n.*

be hest (bi hest′), command; order: *I am ready to act at your behest. n.*

be hind (bi hīnd′), **1** at the back of; in the rear of: *Stand behind me.* **2** at the back; in the rear: *The dog's tail hung down behind.* **3** in support of; supporting: *Your friends are behind you.* **4** farther back: *The rest of the hikers are still quite a ways behind.* **5** later than: *The milkman is behind his usual time today.* **6** not on time; late: *The class is behind in its work.* **7** inferior to; less advanced than: *If you miss too much school you will be behind your classmates.* **8** in the place that has been or is being left: *When my family went to New York, I stayed behind.* 1,3,5,7 *prep.,* 2,4,6,8 *adv.*

be hind hand (bi hīnd′hand′), behind time; late: *They are behindhand with their rent (adj.). She handed her assignment in behindhand (adv.). adj., adv.*

be hold (bi hōld′), look at; see; observe: *to behold a beautiful sunset (v.). Behold! the king! (interj.). v.,* **be held, be hold ing;** *interj.*

be hold en (bi hōl′dən), under obligation; in debt: *I am much beholden to you for your help. adj.*

be hold er (bi hōl′dər), onlooker; spectator. *n.*

be hoove (bi hüv′), be necessary or proper for: *It be-hooves you to work hard if you want to keep this job. v.,* **be hooved, be hoov ing.**

beige (bāzh), **1** pale-brown. **2** a pale brown. 1 *adj.,* 2 *n.*

Bei jing (bā′jing′) official spelling of **Peking.** *n.*

be ing (bē′ing), **1** present participle of **be.** *The dog is being fed.* **2** person; living creature: *a human being.* **3** life; existence: *The world came into being long ago.* 1 *v.,* 2,3 *n.*

Bei rut (bā rüt′), capital and chief seaport of Lebanon, on the Mediterranean. *n.*

be jew el (bi jü′əl), adorn with jewels, or as if with jew-els. v., **be jew eled, be jew el ing** or **be jew elled, be-jew el ling.**

be la bor (bi lā′bər), **1** beat vigorously; thrash: *The rider belabored the tired horse with a stick.* **2** set upon with too much talk, advice, etc.: *They belabored my mistake. v.*

be lat ed (bi lā′tid), happening or coming late; delayed: *Your belated letter has arrived at last. adj.* —**be lat′ed ly,** *adv.* —**be lat′ed ness,** *n.*

Be lau (bā lou′), island country in the W Pacific, east of the Philippines. *Capital:* Koror. *n.*

be lay (bi lā′), **1** fasten (a rope) by winding it around a pin or cleat. **2** stop: *"Belay there!" said the captain. v.*

belaying pin, sturdy metal or wooden pin in a rail of a ship around which ropes can be wound and fastened.

belch (belch), **1** throw out gas noisily from the stomach through the mouth. **2** throw out with force: *The volcano belched fire, smoke, and ashes.* **3** a belching. 1,2 *v.,* 3 *n., pl.* **belch es.** —**belch′er,** *n.*

bel dam or **bel dame** (bel′dəm), an ugly old woman; hag; witch. *n.*

be lea guer (bi lē′gər), **1** surround with troops; besiege: *The fort was beleaguered.* **2** surround; beset: *Our cities are beleaguered by problems. v.* [*Beleaguer* comes from Dutch *belegeren.*]

Bel fast (bel′fast), capital of Northern Ireland, a seaport on the E coast. *n.*

bel fry (bel′frē), **1** tower for a bell or bells. **2** space in a tower in which a bell or bells may be hung. *n., pl.* **bel fries.**

Belg., 1 Belgian. **2** Belgium.

Bel gian (bel′jən), **1** person born or living in Belgium. **2** of Belgium or its people. 1 *n.,* 2 *adj.*

Belgian hare, a large, reddish-brown, domestic rabbit.

Bel gium (bel′jəm), country in W Europe, north of France. *Capital:* Brussels. See **Gaul** for map. *n.*

Bel grade (bel′grād), capital of Yugoslavia, on the Dan-ube. *n.*

Be li al (bē′lē əl), the Devil. *n.*

be lie (bi lī′), **1** give a false idea of; misrepresent: *Her frown belied her usual good nature.* **2** fail to come up to; disappoint: *The failure of their new business belied their expectations.* v., **be lied, be ly ing.** —**be li′er,** *n.*

be lief (bi lēf′), **1** what is held to be true or real; thing believed; opinion: *It was once a common belief that the earth is flat.* **2** acceptance as true or real: *His belief in ghosts makes him afraid of the dark.* **3** confidence in any person or thing; faith; trust: *He expressed his belief in his friend's honesty.* **4** religious faith; creed: *Most children fol-low the belief of their parents. n.*

be liev a ble (bi lē′və bəl), able to be believed. *adj.* —**be-liev′a bly,** *adv.*

be lieve (bi lēv′), **1** think (something) is true or real: *Who doesn't believe that the earth is round?* **2** think (somebody) tells the truth: *Her friends believe her.* **3** have faith; trust: *We believe in our friends.* **4** think; suppose: *I believe I will go. v.,* **be lieved, be liev ing.** —**be liev′ing ly,** *adv.*

be liev er (bi lē′vər), **1** person who believes. **2** follower of some religion. *n.*

be like (bi līk′), OLD USE. perhaps. *adv.*

be lit tle (bi lit′l), cause to seem little or unimportant; makes less important: *They belittled your success because they were jealous. v.,* **be lit tled, be lit tling. —be lit′tle ment,** *n.* **—be lit′tler,** *n.*

Be lize (be lēz′), country in Central America. *Capital:* Belmopan. See **Yucatán** for map. *n.*

bell (bel), **1** a hollow metal cup that makes a musical sound when struck by a clapper or hammer. **2** anything that makes a ringing sound as a signal: *Did I hear the bell at the front door?* **3** stroke or sound of a bell: *Our teacher dismissed us before the bell.* **4** stroke of a bell used on shipboard to indicate a half hour of time. 1 bell = 12:30, 4:30, or 8:30; 2 bells = 1:00, 5:00, or 9:00; and so on up to 8 bells = 4:00, 8:00, or 12:00. **5** put a bell on: *We belled the cat.* **6** anything shaped like a bell. The flaring end of a funnel or of a musical wind instrument is a bell. **7** swell out like a bell. 1-4,6 *n.,* 5,7 *v.* **—bell′-like′,** *adj.*

Bell (bel), **Alexander Graham,** 1847-1922, American scientist who invented the telephone. *n.*

bel la don na (bel′ə don′ə), **1** a poisonous plant of Europe with black berries and red, bell-shaped flowers; deadly nightshade. **2** drug made from this plant. *n., pl.* **bel la don nas** for 1.

bell boy (bel′boi′), person whose work is carrying baggage and doing errands for the guests of a hotel or club; bellhop. *n.*

belle (bel), **1** a beautiful woman or girl. **2** the prettiest or most admired woman or girl: *She was the belle of the ball. n.*

bell hop (bel′hop′), bellboy. *n.*

bel li cose (bel′ə kōs), fond of fighting; warlike. *adj.* **—bel′li cose ly,** *adv.*

bel lig er ence (bə lij′ər əns), **1** fondness for fighting; being warlike. **2** act of fighting; being at war. *n.*

bel lig er en cy (bə lij′ər ən sē), belligerence. *n.*

belligerent (def. 3)—He shouted and waved his fist in a **belligerent** way.

bel lig er ent (bə lij′ər ənt), **1** at war; engaged in war; fighting: *Great Britain and Germany were belligerent powers in 1941.* **2** nation or state engaged in war: *France and Germany were belligerents in World War II.* **3** fond of fighting; quarrelsome: *a belligerent neighborhood gang.* **4** person engaged in fighting with another person. 1,3 *adj.,* 2,4 *n.* **—bel lig′er ent ly,** *adv.*

bell jar, a bell-shaped container or cover made of glass, used in laboratories.

bel low (bel′ō), **1** make a loud, deep noise; roar: *The bull bellowed.* **2** a loud, deep noise; roar. **3** shout loudly, angrily, or with pain. 1,3 *v.,* 2 *n.* **—bel′low er,** *n.*

bel lows (bel′ōz), **1** device for producing a strong current of air, used for blowing fires or sounding an organ, accordion, etc. **2** the folding part of some cameras, behind the lens. *n. sing. or pl.*

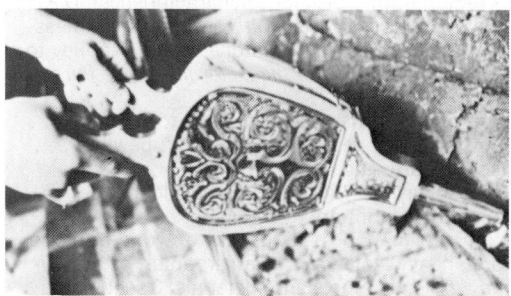

bellows (def. 1)

bell weth er (bel′weᵺ′ər), a male sheep that leads the flock, wearing a bell. *n.*

bel ly (bel′ē), **1** the lower part of the human body, which contains the stomach and intestines; abdomen. **2** the underpart of an animal's body. **3** stomach. **4** bulging part of anything, or the hollow in it: *the belly of a sail.* **5** swell out; bulge: *The sails bellied in the wind.* 1-4 *n., pl.* **bel lies;** 5 *v.,* **bel lied, bel ly ing.**

bel ly ache (bel′ē āk′), INFORMAL. **1** pain in the abdomen; stomach ache. **2** complain or grumble about small problems. 1 *n.,* 2 *v.,* **bel ly ached, bel ly ach ing.**

bel ly band (bel′ē band′), a strap around an animal's body to keep a saddle, harness, etc., in place. *n.*

bel ly but ton (bel′ē but′n), INFORMAL. navel. *n.*

bel ly land (bel′ē land′), land an airplane with the landing gear retracted. *v.*

belly laugh, INFORMAL. a hearty, unrestrained fit of laughter.

Bel mo pan (bel′mō pän′), capital of Belize, in the central part. *n.*

be long (bi lông′), have one's or its proper place: *That book belongs on this shelf. v.*

belong to, 1 be the property of: *Does this cap belong to you?* **2** be a part of: *That top belongs to this box.* **3** be a member of: *She belongs to the Girl Scouts.*

be long ings (bi lông′ingz), things that belong to a person; possessions. *n.pl.*

be lov ed (bi luv′id *or* bi luvd′), **1** dearly loved; dear. **2** person who is loved; darling. 1 *adj.,* 2 *n.*

be low (bi lō′), **1** in a lower place; to a lower place: *From the airplane we could see the fields below.* **2** on a lower floor or deck; downstairs: *The ship's cargo is stored below.* **3** lower than; under: *The dining room is below my bedroom.* **4** less than: *four degrees below zero.* **5** unworthy of: *below contempt.* **6** after or later in a book or article: *See the note below.* **7** below zero: *The temperature was five below last night.* 1,2,6,7 *adv.,* 3-5 *prep.*

be low decks (bi lō′deks′), inside the body of a vessel: *The cargo was securely stored belowdecks. adv.*

be low ground (bi lō′ground′), **1** below the surface of the earth. **2** buried. *adj.*

below stairs, BRITISH. on a lower floor or level; downstairs.

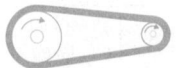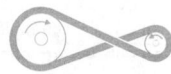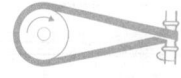

belt (def. 8)—belt used to transmit power in different directions, as indicated by the arrows

belt (belt), **1** strip of leather, cloth, etc., fastened around the waist to hold in or support clothes or weapons. **2** put a belt around: *I belted my jeans.* **3** fasten on with a belt: *to belt on a hunting knife.* **4** beat with a belt. **5** hit suddenly and hard: *The hitter belted the ball over the fence.* **6** any broad strip or band: *A belt of trees grew between the two fields.* **7** region having distinctive characteristics: *The cotton belt is the region where cotton is grown.* **8** an endless band that transfers motion from one wheel or pulley to another: *A belt connected to the motor moves the fan in an automobile.* 1,6-8 *n.,* 2-5 *v.*

be moan (bi mōn′), moan about; weep for; bewail. *v.*

be muse (bi myüz′), make very confused; bewilder. *v.,* **be mused, be mus ing.**

be mused (bi myüzd′), **1** confused; bewildered. **2** absorbed in thought or daydreaming. *adj.*

bench (bench), **1** a long seat, usually of wood or stone. **2** a strong, heavy table used by a carpenter, or by anyone who works with tools and materials. **3** seat where judges sit in a court of law. **4** judge or group of judges sitting in a court of law: *Bring the prisoner before the bench.* **5** position as a judge: *He was appointed to the bench last year.* **6** take (a player) out of a game. 1-5 *n., pl.* **bench es;** 6 *v.*

bench mark, a surveyor's mark made on an object lying in a fixed position at a known elevation. It is a reference point in determining differences in level and altitude.

bend (bend), **1** part that is not straight; curve; turn: *There is a sharp bend in the road here.* **2** make or become crooked; curve: *bend a wire. The branch began to bend as I climbed along it.* **3** turn or move in a certain direction; direct: *His steps were bent toward home now. She bent her mind to her homework.* **4** stoop; bow: *She bent down and picked up a stone.* **5** submit: *A stubborn person will not bend to the will of others.* **6** force to submit: *The spirit of the rebels could not be bent.* **7** the bends, cramps caused by changing too suddenly from an environment of high pressure to ordinary air pressure. 1,7 *n.,* 2-6 *v.,* **bent, bend ing.**

be neath (bi nēth′), **1** in a lower place; below; underneath; under: *The apple fell to the ground beneath (adv.). The dog sat beneath the tree (prep.).* **2** not even worthy of: *Your insulting remarks are beneath notice.* 1 *adv.,* 1,2 *prep.*

Ben e dict (ben′ə dikt), Saint, A.D. 480?-543?, Italian monk who founded the order of monks called the Benedictine order. *n.*

Ben e dic tine (ben′ə dik′tən *or* ben′ə dik′tēn′), **1** monk or nun following the rules of the order founded by Saint Benedict. **2** of Saint Benedict or his order. 1 *n.,* 2 *adj.*

be ne dic tion (ben′ə dik′shən), **1** the asking of God's blessing at the end of a religious service. **2** blessing. *n.*

ben e fac tor (ben′ə fak′tər), person who has given money or kindly help. *n.*

be nef i cent (bə nef′ə sənt), doing good; kind. *adj.* —**be nef′i cent ly,** *adv.*

ben e fi cial (ben′ə fish′əl), producing good; favorable; helpful: *Daily exercise is beneficial to your health. adj.* —**ben′e fi′cial ly,** *adv.* —**ben′e fi′cial ness,** *n.*

ben e fi ci ar y (ben′ə fish′ē er′ē), **1** person who receives benefit: *All the children are beneficiaries of the new playground.* **2** person who receives money or property from an insurance policy, a will, etc. *n., pl.* **ben e fi ci ar ies.**

ben e fit (ben′ə fit), **1** anything which is for the good of a person or thing; advantage: *Good roads are of great benefit to travelers.* **2** do good to; be good for: *Rest will benefit a sick person.* **3** receive good; profit: *I benefited from the medicine.* **4** performance at the theater, a game, etc., to raise money for a worthy cause. **5** Often, **benefits,** *pl.* money paid to a sick or disabled person by an insurance company, government agency, etc. 1,4,5 *n.,* 2,3 *v.*

be nev o lence (bə nev′ə ləns), **1** desire to promote the happiness of others; goodwill; kindly feeling. **2** act of kindness; something good that is done. *n.*

be nev o lent (bə nev′ə lənt), having a desire to promote the happiness of others; kindly; charitable. *adj.* —**be nev′o lent ly,** *adv.*

Ben gal (beng gôl′), **1** former province of India, in the NE part. Bengal is now divided into **West Bengal,** a part of India, and **East Bengal,** the country of Bangladesh. **2** of or from Bengal: *a Bengal tiger.* **3 Bay of,** bay between India and Burma, part of the Indian Ocean. See **India** for map. 1,3 *n.,* 2 *adj.*

Ben gha zi *or* **Ben ga si** (ben gä′zē), city in Libya, on the Mediterranean. *n.*

be night ed (bi nī′tid), not knowing right from wrong; ignorant. *adj.* —**be night′ed ness,** *n.*

be nign (bi nīn′), **1** having a kind disposition; gracious: *a benign neighbor with a friendly smile.* **2** favorable; mild: *Hawaii has a benign climate.* **3** not dangerous to health; not malignant: *a benign tumor. adj.* —**be nign′ly,** *adv.*

be nig ni ty (bi nig′nə tē), **1** kindliness; graciousness. **2** a kind act; favor. *n., pl.* **be nig ni ties.**

Be nin (be nēn′), country in W Africa, on the Atlantic. *Capital:* Porto-Novo. See **Nigeria** for map. *n.*

Ben ja min (ben′jə mən), **1** (in the Bible) the youngest son of Jacob. **2** one of the twelve tribes of Israel. *n.*

bent (bent), **1** past tense and past participle of **bend.** *I bent the wire.* **2** not straight; crooked; curved: *The farmer's back was bent from years of toil.* **3** determined: *She is bent on being a doctor.* **4** a natural inclination; tendency: *He has a decided bent for drawing.* 1 *v.,* 2,3 *adj.,* 4 *n.*

be numb (bi num′), make numb; deaden: *My fingers were benumbed by the cold. I was benumbed with fright when I got up to give my speech. v.* —**be numb′ing ly,** *adv.*

Ben ze drine (ben′zə drēn′), trademark for a drug that causes wakefulness. *n.*

ben zene (ben′zēn′), a colorless liquid easily set on fire, obtained chiefly from coal tar; benzol. It is used for removing grease stains and in making dyes. *n.*

ben zine (ben′zēn′), a colorless liquid easily set on fire, obtained in distilling petroleum. It is used in cleaning and dyeing and as a motor fuel. *n.*

ben zol (ben′zōl), benzene. *n.*

be queath (bi kwēŦH′), **1** give or leave by means of a will when one dies: *He bequeathed his fortune to his children.* **2** hand down; pass along: *One age bequeaths its knowledge to the next. v.* —**be queath′er,** *n.*

be queath al (bi kwē′ŦHəl), bequest. *n.*

be quest (bi kwest′), **1** something bequeathed; legacy: *When she died she left a bequest of ten thousand dollars to her niece.* **2** act of bequeathing. *n.*

be rate (bi rāt′), scold sharply; upbraid. *v.,* **be rat ed, be rat ing.**

Ber ber (bėr′bər), **1** member of a group of Moslem tribes living in northern Africa, west of Egypt. **2** their language. *n.*

be reave (bi rēv′), leave desolate and alone; deprive: *The family was bereaved by the death of the father. v.,* **be reaved** *or* **be reft, be reav ing.**

be reave ment (bi rēv′mənt), **1** loss of a relative or friend by death. **2** bereaved condition; great loss: *We sympathized with the family in their bereavement. n.*

be reft (bi reft′), **1** deprived: *The refugees were homeless and bereft.* **2** a past tense and a past participle of **bereave.** *They were bereft by the loss of their child.* 1 *adj.,* 2 *v.*

be ret (bə rā′), a soft, flat, round cap of wool, felt, etc., with no visor. *n.* [*Beret* comes from French *béret,* which can be traced back to Latin *birrus,* meaning "cloak."]

berg (bėrg), iceberg. *n.*

Ber gen (bėr′gən), seaport in SW Norway. *n.*

ber i ber i (ber′ē ber′ē), disease affecting the nervous system, accompanied by weakness and extreme loss of weight. It is caused by lack of vitamin B$_1$ in the diet. *n.*

WORD HISTORY

beriberi

Beriberi was borrowed from Singhalese (the language of Sri Lanka) *beriberi,* which comes from *beri,* meaning "weakness."

Ber ing Sea (bir′ing *or* ber′ing), N portion of the Pacific, between Alaska and Siberia.

Bering Strait, strait between the Bering Sea and the Arctic Ocean.

Ber keley (bėr′klē), city in W California, near San Francisco. *n.*

ber keli um (bėr′klē əm *or* bėr′kē′lē əm), a metallic element produced artificially from americium, curium, or plutonium. *n.*

Berk shires (bėrk′shərz), range of hills in W Massachusetts. *n.pl.*

Ber lin (bər lin′), former capital of Germany. Berlin is now divided into West Berlin, which belongs to West Germany, and East Berlin, the capital of East Germany. *n.*

Ber li oz (ber′lē ōz), **Hector,** 1803-1869, French composer. *n.*

Ber mu da (bər myü′də), group of British islands off the coast of the United States, in the N Atlantic. *n.*

Ber mu das (bər myü′dəz), Bermuda. *n.pl.*

Bermuda shorts, short trousers that end an inch or two above the knee.

Bern or **Berne** (bėrn), capital of Switzerland, in the W part. *n.*

Bern stein (bėrn′stīn), **Leonard,** born 1918, American composer and conductor. *n.*

ber ry (ber′ē), **1** any small, juicy fruit with many seeds. Strawberries and raspberries are berries. **2** a simple fruit having a skin or rind surrounding the seeds in the pulp. Botanists classify grapes, tomatoes, currants, and bananas as berries. **3** gather or pick berries: *During our vacation in Maine we went berrying one day.* 1,2 *n., pl.* **ber ries;** 3 *v.,* **ber ried, ber ry ing. —ber′ry like′,** *adj.*

ber serk (bėr′sėrk′ *or* bər sėrk′). **go berserk** or **run berserk,** be carried away by madness or wild fury; become violently angry: *The sick dog went berserk and tried to bite everyone in its way. adv.*

berth (bėrth), **1** place to sleep on a ship, train, or airplane. **2** a ship's place at a wharf. **3** place for a ship to anchor conveniently or safely. **4** position; job: *My sister has a berth as lifeguard for the summer.* **5** provide with a berth; have a berth. 1-4 *n.,* 5 *v.*

give a wide berth to, keep well away from: *Give a wide berth to her when she is angry.*

ber yl (ber′əl), a very hard mineral, usually green or

a hat	**i** it	**oi** oil	**ch** child	a in about
ā age	**ī** ice	**ou** out	**ng** long	e in taken
ä far	**o** hot	**u** cup	**sh** she	ə = { i in pencil
e let	**ō** open	**ú** put	**th** thin	o in lemon
ē equal	**ô** order	**ü** rule	**ᴛʜ** then	u in circus
ėr term			**zh** measure	

blue-green, used as a gem and as a source of beryllium. The emerald is a variety of beryl. *n.*

be ryl li um (bə ril′ē əm), a hard, light, metallic element found in various minerals. Beryllium is used in various alloys and in controlling the speed of neutrons in atomic reactors. *n.*

be seech (bi sēch′), ask earnestly; beg; implore: *I beseech you to listen to me. v.,* **be sought** or **be seeched, be seech ing. —be seech′er,** *n.* **—be seech′ing ly,** *adv.*

be set (bi set′), attack from all sides; surround or hem in: *We were beset by mosquitoes in the swamp. In the darkness they were suddenly beset by fear. v.,* **be set, be set ting.**

be set ting (bi set′ing), always present: *Constantly putting things off is her besetting sin. adj.*

be side (bi sīd′), **1** by the side of; close to; near: *Grass grows beside the fence.* **2** compared with: *My troubles seem small beside yours.* **3** away from; aside from: *That question is beside the point and shows that you were not listening.* **4** besides. *prep.*

beside oneself, out of one's mind; crazy or upset: *They were beside themselves with worry over their lost child.*

be sides (bi sīdz′), **1** more than that; moreover: *I don't want to go shopping; besides, I have no money to spend.* **2** in addition to; over and above: *Others came to the school picnic besides our own class.* **3** in addition; also: *We tried two other ways besides.* **4** other than; except: *They spoke of no one besides you.* 1,3 *adv.,* 2,4 *prep.*

be siege (bi sēj′), **1** surround and try to capture: *For ten years the Greeks besieged the city of Troy.* **2** crowd around: *Hundreds of admirers besieged the movie star.* **3** overwhelm with requests, questions, etc.: *During the flood, the Red Cross was besieged with calls for help. v.,* **be sieged, be sieg ing. —be sieg′er,** *n.*

be smirch (bi smėrch′), make dirty; soil; stain: *Crime and dishonesty will besmirch one's good name. v.*

be sought (bi sôt′), a past tense and a past participle of **beseech.** *She besought them to listen to her. v.*

be span gle (bi spang′gəl), adorn with spangles. *v.,* **be span gled, be span gling.**

be spat ter (bi spat′ər), spatter all over; soil by spattering. *v.* **—be spat′ter er,** *n.*

be speak (bi spēk′), be a sign of; show; indicate: *The neat appearance of the house bespeaks care. v.,* **be spoke** (bi spōk′), **be spo ken** or **be spoke, be speak ing.**

be sprin kle (bi spring′kəl), sprinkle all over. *v.,* **be sprin kled, be sprin kling.**

Bes se mer process (bes′ə mər), method of making steel by forcing a blast of air through molten iron in order to burn out carbon and other impurities.

best (best), **1** of the most desirable, valuable, or superior quality: *My work is good; your work is better; but her work is best. We have the best food to eat. I want to be one of the best students in the class.* **2** in the most excellent way: *Who reads best?* **3** in or to the highest degree: *I like this book best.* **4** person or thing that is best: *Most parents want the best for their children. He is the best in the class.* **5** largest: *I spent the best part of the day at school.* **6** the most that is possible; utmost: *I did my best to finish the work on time.* **7** outdo; defeat: *Our team was bested in the final game.* 1,5 *adj.,* superlative of **good;** 2,3 *adv.,* superlative of **well**[1]; 4,6 *n.,* 7 *v.*

all for the best, not so bad as it seems.

at best, under the most favorable circumstances: *Summer is at best very short.*

get the best of, defeat.

had best, ought to; will be wise to; should: *You had best leave before the storm breaks.*

make the best of, do as well as possible with: *Try to make the best of a bad job.*

bes tial (bes′chəl), like a beast; beastly; brutal. *adj.* —**bes′tial ly,** *adv.*

bes ti al i ty (bes′chē al′ə tē), bestial conduct. *n., pl.* **bes ti al i ties.**

be stir (bi stėr′), rouse to action; stir up; exert: *If we want to win this game we'll have to bestir ourselves. v.,* **be stirred, be stir ring.**

best man, the chief attendant of the bridegroom at a wedding.

be stow (bi stō′), give (something) as a gift; give: *The millionaire bestowed a large sum of money on the university. v.*

be stow al (bi stō′əl), a bestowing: *the bestowal of a large sum of money. n.*

be strew (bi strü′), **1** strew; scatter; sprinkle: *The park was bestrewed with litter.* **2** lie scattered over: *Papers bestrewed the park. v.,* **be strewed, be strewed** or **be strewn** (bi strün′), **be strew ing.**

bestride—statue of a man bestriding a horse

be stride (bi strīd′), get on, sit on, or stand over (something) with one leg on each side; straddle. You can bestride a horse, a chair, or a fence. *v.,* **be strode** (bi strōd′), **be strid den** (bi strid′n), **be strid ing.**

best seller, anything, especially a book, that has a very large sale.

bet (bet), **1** a promise between two people or groups that the one that is wrong will give something of value to the one that is right; wager: *We made a 25-cent bet on who would win the game.* **2** to promise something of value to another if you are wrong; wager: *I bet her a candy bar that my team would win.* **3** the money or thing promised: *My bet on the game was 25 cents.* **4** make a bet: *Which team did you bet on?* **5** be very sure: *I bet you are wrong about that.* **6** thing to bet on: *Which team is a good bet?* 1,3,6 *n.,* 2,4,5 *v.,* **bet** or **bet ted, bet ting.**

be ta (bā′tə), the second letter of the Greek alphabet (B, β). *n.*

be take (bi tāk′). **betake oneself,** go: *They betake themselves to the mountains every summer. v.,* **be took, be tak en** (bi tā′kən), **be tak ing.**

beta particle, electron released by the nucleus of a radioactive substance in the process of disintegration.

beta ray, stream of beta particles.

be ta tron (bā′tə tron), particle accelerator that greatly increases the speed of electrons. *n.*

Be tel geuse (bē′tl jüz), a very large red star in the constellation Orion. *n.*

be think (bi thingk′). **bethink oneself of,** think about; consider; remember. *v.,* **be thought** (bi thôt′), **be thinking.**

Beth le hem (beth′lə hem), the birthplace of Jesus, a town now in Jordan. *n.*

Be thune (bə thün′), **Mary McLeod,** 1875-1955, American educator. *n.*

be tide (bi tīd′), **1** happen to: *Woe betide you if you dare break your promise.* **2** happen: *No matter what betides, the family will hold together. v.,* **be tid ed, be tid ing.**

be times (bi tīmz′), OLD USE. early. *adv.*

be to ken (bi tō′kən), be a sign of; show: *His smile betokens his satisfaction. v.*

be took (bi tůk′), past tense of **betake.** *The queen betook herself to her summer palace. v.*

be tray (bi trā′), **1** hand over or expose to the power of an enemy by being disloyal: *The traitor betrayed his country.* **2** be unfaithful to: *She betrayed her promise.* **3** mislead; deceive: *He was betrayed by his own enthusiasm.* **4** show signs of; reveal: *The girl's wet shoes betrayed the fact that she had walked through puddles. v.* —**be tray′er,** *n.*

be tray al (bi trā′əl), act of betraying; violation of trust or confidence. *n.*

be troth (bi trōŦH′ or bi trôth′), promise in marriage; engage. *v.*

be troth al (bi trō′ŦHəl or bi trô′thəl), engagement to be married. *n.*

be trothed (bi trōŦHd′ or bi trôtht′), **1** person engaged to be married: *My sister introduced me to her betrothed.* **2** engaged to be married: *He and my sister are now betrothed.* 1 *n.,* 2 *adj.*

bet ter[1] (bet′ər), **1** more desirable, useful, or suitable than another: *She left her old job for a better one.* **2** in a more excellent way: *Try to read better next time.* **3** in a higher degree; more completely: *I know my old friend better than I know anyone else.* **4** more: *It is better than a mile to town.* **5** person or thing that is better: *Which is the better of these two coats?* **6 betters,** *pl.* one's superiors: *Listen to the advice of your betters.* **7** make better; improve: *We can better that work by being more careful next time.* **8** do better than; surpass: *The other team could not better our score.* **9** larger: *Four days is the better part of a week.* **10** improved in health: *The sick child is better today.* 1,9,10 *adj., comparative of* **good;** 2-4 *adv., comparative of* **well**[1]; 5,6 *n.,* 7,8 *v.*

better off, in a better condition: *He is better off now that he has a new job.*

for the better, toward improvement or recovery: *The patient took a turn for the better.*

get the better of or **have the better of,** be superior to; defeat: *In the race, the tortoise got the better of the hare.*

go one better, do better than; excel.

had better, ought to; will be wise to; should: *I had better go before it rains.*

think better of, think over and change one's mind about: *In the morning you will think better of your decision to go on such a long hike.*

bet ter[2] (bet′ər), bettor. *n.*

bet ter ment (bet′ər mənt), a making better; improvement: *to work for the betterment of living conditions. n.*

bet tor (bet′ər), person who bets. Also, **better.** *n.*

be tween (bi twēn′), **1** in the space or time separating two points, objects, places, etc.: *Many cities lie between New York and Chicago* (prep.). *We don't go to school between Friday and Monday* (prep.). *The bus from Main Street to Broadway stops at every corner between* (adv.). **2** in the range of: *She earned between ten and twelve dollars.* **3** connecting; joining: *There is a good highway between Chicago and Detroit.* **4** having to do with; involving: *A war between two countries can affect the whole world.* **5** either one or the other of: *We must choose between the two books.* **6** by the joint action of: *They caught twelve fish between them.* 1-6 *prep.*, 1 *adv.* —**be tween′ness,** *n.*

between you and me, as a secret; in confidence: *This is between you and me; don't tell anyone else.*

in between, 1 in the middle: *He studies either very hard or not at all, never anything in between.* **2** in the midst of; among: *In between the rows of corn there was a scarecrow.*

be twixt (bi twikst′), between. *prep., adv.*

betwixt and between, in the middle; neither one nor the other.

Bev or **BeV** (bev), a billion electron volts, used as a measure of energy in nuclear physics. *n.*

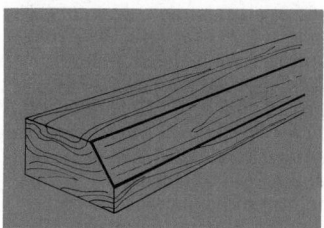

bevel (def. 1)

bev el (bev′əl), **1** a sloping edge. There is often a bevel on the frame of a picture, on a mirror, or on a piece of plate glass. **2** cut a square edge to a sloping edge; make slope: *The edges of the board have been beveled with a plane.* **3** instrument or tool for drawing or measuring angles. 1,3 *n.*, 2 *v.*, **bev eled, bev el ing** or **bev elled, bev el ling.**

bev er age (bev′ər ij), liquid used or prepared for drinking. Milk, tea, coffee, beer, and wine are beverages. *n.*

bev y (bev′ē), a small group or flock: *a bevy of quail. n., pl.* **bev ies.**

be wail (bi wāl′), mourn for; weep for; complain of: *The children bewailed the loss of their cat. v.* —**be wail′ing ly,** *adv.*

be ware (bi wer′ *or* bi war′), be on one's guard against; be careful: *Beware! there is a deep hole here. You must beware of swimming in a strong current. v.*

be wil der (bi wil′dər), confuse completely; puzzle: *The child was bewildered by the crowds. v.* —**be wil′der ing ly,** *adv.*

be wil der ment (bi wil′dər mənt), a bewildered condition; complete confusion. *n.*

be witch (bi wich′), **1** put under a spell; use magic on: *The wicked fairy bewitched the princess and made her fall into a long sleep.* **2** charm; fascinate; enchant: *We were all bewitched by our bright little cousin. v.* —**be witch′ing ly,** *adv.* —**be witch′ment,** *n.*

bey (bā), governor of a Turkish province or district. *n., pl.* **beys.**

be yond (bi yond′), **1** on or to the farther side of: *He lives beyond those tall trees.* **2** farther on than: *I fell asleep on the bus and rode beyond my stop.* **3** farther away: *Beyond the hills. Your ball did not fall here; look beyond for it.* **4** later than; past: *I stayed up beyond my usual bedtime.* **5** out of the reach, range, or understanding of: *This shirt is so worn that it is beyond repair. The meaning of this poem is beyond me.* **6** more than: *The price of the suit was beyond what I could pay. The day at the beach was beyond all we had hoped.* **7 the beyond** or **the great beyond,** life after death: *He has gone to the great beyond.* 1,2,4-6 *prep.*, 3 *adv.*, 7 *n.*

b.f. or **bf.,** (in printing) boldface.

bg., bag. *pl.* **bgs.**

Bhu tan (bü tän′), country between Tibet and NE India. Bhutan's foreign affairs are partly under Indian control. *Capital:* Thimbu. See **India** for map. *n.*

bi-, *prefix.* **1** twice a _____: *Biannual = twice a year.* **2** two _____s: *Bisect = divide into two parts.* **3** having two _____: *Biped = having two feet.* **4** once every two _____: *Bimonthly = once every two months.*

Bi, symbol for bismuth.

bi an nu al (bī an′yü əl), occurring twice a year: *Our school nurse recommends a biannual visit to the dentist. adj.*

bi an nu al ly (bī an′yü ə lē), twice a year. *adv.*

bi as (bī′əs), **1** a slanting or diagonal line. **2** tendency to favor one side too much; prejudice: *An umpire should have no bias.* **3** give a bias to; influence, usually unfairly; prejudice: *Judges cannot let their feelings bias their decisions.* 1,2 *n., pl.* **bi as es;** 3 *v.*, **bi ased, bi as ing** or **bi assed, bi as sing.**

on the bias, diagonally across the weave.

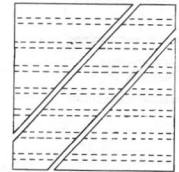

bias
This cloth is cut
on the bias.

bi ased (bī′əst), favoring one side too much, prejudiced. *Parents are often biased concerning their children. adj.*

bib (bib), **1** cloth worn under the chin, especially by babies and small children, to protect clothing during meals. **2** part of an apron or overalls above the waist. *n.*

Bib., 1 Bible. **2** Biblical.

bib and tucker, INFORMAL. clothes.

Bi ble (bī′bəl), **1** the book of sacred writings of the Christian religion, including the Old Testament and the New Testament. **2** the form of the Old Testament accepted by the Jews. **3** book of the sacred writings of any religion. The Koran is the Bible of the Moslems. **4 bible,** any book accepted as an authority. *n.*

bib li cal or **Bib li cal** (bib′lə kəl), **1** of the Bible: *biblical literature.* **2** according to the Bible: *biblical history.* **3** in the Bible: *a biblical reference to Solomon. adj.* —**bib′li cal ly, Bib′li cal ly,** *adv.*

bib li o graph i cal (bib′lē ə graf′ə kəl), having to do with bibliography. *adj.* —**bib′li o graph′i cal ly,** *adv.*

bib li og ra phy (bib′lē og′rə fē), list of books or articles by a certain author or about a particular subject or person. *n., pl.* **bib li og ra phies.**

bi cam er al (bī kam′ər əl), having two legislative chambers. The Congress of the United States is a bicameral legislature; it consists of the Senate and the House of Representatives. *adj.* [*Bicameral* comes from *bi-,* meaning "two," Latin *camera,* meaning "chamber," and *-al* meaning "of."]

---

bi car bo nate of soda (bī kär′bə nit), sodium bicarbonate.

bi cen ten ni al (bī′sen ten′ē əl), **1** of a period of 200 years or its anniversary. **2** a 200th anniversary: *The town is celebrating its bicentennial.* **3** celebration of the 200th anniversary. 1 *adj.*, 2,3 *n.*

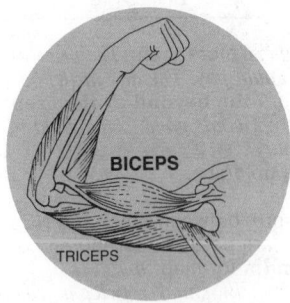

bi ceps (bī′seps), the large muscle in the front part of the upper arm. If you move your fist up to your shoulder, the biceps will stick out. *n., pl.* **bi ceps** or **bi ceps es.**

bick er (bik′ər), **1** take part in a petty, noisy quarrel; squabble: *The children bickered through the long, hot summer afternoon.* **2** a petty, noisy quarrel. 1 *v.*, 2 *n.*

bi cus pid (bī kus′pid), a double-pointed tooth that tears and grinds food. Adult human beings have eight bicuspids. *n.*

bi cy cle (bī′sik′əl), **1** a lightweight vehicle with two wheels, one behind the other, that support a metal frame on which there is a seat. The rider pushes two pedals to move the back wheel and steers with handlebars. **2** ride a bicycle. 1 *n.*, 2 *v.*, **bi cy cled, bi cy cling.**

WORD HISTORY

bicycle

Bicycle comes from bi-, meaning "two," and Greek kyklos, meaning "circle, wheel."

bi cy cler (bī′sik′lər), bicyclist. *n.*

bi cy clist (bī′sik′list), person who rides a bicycle. *n.*

bid (bid), **1** tell (someone) what to do, where to go, etc.; command: *We were bidden to assemble in the gym. Do as I bid you.* **2** say; tell: *My friends bade me good-by.* **3** offer to pay (a certain price): *She bid $5 for the table. He then bid $7.* **4** an offer to pay a certain price: *She made a bid on the table.* **5** state one's price for doing a certain piece of work: *Several companies will bid for the contract.* **6** amount offered or stated: *My bid for the table was $7. The contractor's bid for building the new bridge was $300,000.* **7** invite: *The king bade the nobles stay for the feast.* **8** invitation: *a bid to join the honor society.* **9** an attempt to secure, achieve, or win something: *The candidate was making a bid for reelection.* 1-3,5,7 *v.*, **bade** or **bid, bid den** or **bid, bid ding** (for 1,2,7), **bid, bid ding** (for 3,5); 4,6,8,9 *n.*

bid fair, seem likely; have a good chance.

bid den (bid′n), a past participle of **bid.** *Twelve guests were bidden to the feast. v.*

bid der (bid′ər), person who bids. The highest bidder at an auction is the person who offers to pay the highest price for something. *n.*

bid ding (bid′ing), **1** command; order: *The servant awaited the queen's bidding.* **2** invitation: *He joined the club at my bidding.* **3** the offering of a price for something: *The bidding at the auction was very slow at first. n.*

do one's bidding, obey one.

bid dy (bid′ē), hen. *n., pl.* **bid dies.**

bide (bīd), continue; wait; abide: *Bide here awhile. v.*, **bid ed** or **bode, bid ing.**

bi en ni al (bī en′ē əl), **1** living two years or seasons. A biennial plant begins its growth in the first season, then flowers, produces fruit, and dies in the second season. **2** plant that lives two years or seasons. Carrots and onions are biennials. **3** occurring every two years: *a biennial celebration.* **4** event that occurs every two years. 1,3 *adj.*, 2,4 *n.*

bi en ni al ly (bī en′ē ə lē), once in two years. *adv.*

bier (bir), a movable stand or framework on which a coffin or dead body is placed before burial. *n.*

bi fo cal (bī fō′kəl), **1** having two focuses. The lenses of bifocal glasses have two sections of different focal lengths, the upper part for distant vision, the lower for close vision. **2 bifocals,** *pl.* pair of glasses having bifocal lenses. 1 *adj.*, 2 *n.*

big (big), **1** great in amount or size; large: *a big room, a big book. Making automobiles is a big business. An elephant is a big animal.* **2** grown up: *You are a big girl now.* **3** important; great: *The election of the President is big news.* **4** full; loud: *a big voice.* **5** generous: *His brother had a big heart and forgave him for breaking the model airplane.* **6** boastful: *big talk.* **7** INFORMAL. boastfully: *She talks big.* 1-6 *adj.*, **big ger, big gest;** 7 *adv.* —**big′ness,** *n.*

big a my (big′ə mē), condition of having two wives or two husbands at the same time. Bigamy is unlawful in most countries. *n.*

Big Dipper, group of seven bright stars in the constellation Ursa Major.

Big foot (big′fút′), a large, hairy creature believed to live in the mountainous parts of the western United States. Large footprints and occasional visual sightings of this creature have been reported. *n.*

big gish (big′ish), somewhat big. *adj.*

big heart ed (big′här′tid), kindly; generous. *adj.*

big horn (big′hôrn′), a wild, grayish-brown sheep of the Rocky Mountains, having large, curving horns; Rocky Mountain sheep. *n., pl.* **big horns** or **big horn.**

big no ni a (big nō′nē ə), a woody vine with clusters of large, orange-red flowers shaped like trumpets; trumpet creeper; trumpet vine. *n., pl.* **big no ni as.**

big ot (big′ət), an intolerant, prejudiced person; bigoted person. *n.*

big ot ed (big′ə tid), sticking to an opinion, belief, party, etc., without reason and not tolerating other views; intolerant; prejudiced. *adj.* —**big′ot ed ly,** *adv.*

big ot ry (big′ə trē), bigoted conduct or attitude; intolerance; prejudice. *n., pl.* **big ot ries.**

big shot, SLANG. an important person.

big top, INFORMAL. circus.

big tree, giant sequoia.

bike (bīk), INFORMAL. **1** a bicycle. **2** ride a bicycle. 1 *n.*, 2 *v.*, **biked, bik ing.**

bike way (bīk′wā′), a graded or paved path, or a designated route through an urban area, to be used by bicyclists only. *n.*

bi ki ni (bə kē′nē), a very scant bathing suit in two pieces for women and girls. *n., pl.* **bi ki nis.**

bi lat er al (bī lat′ər əl), **1** on or having two sides. **2** binding both sides or parties: *The two nations signed a bilateral treaty. adj.* —**bi lat′er al ly,** *adv.*

bile (bīl), **1** a bitter, greenish-yellow liquid produced by the liver and stored in the gall bladder; gall. It aids in the digestion of fats in the small intestine. **2** ill humor; anger. *n.*

bilge (bilj), **1** the lowest part of a ship's hold; bottom of a ship's hull. **2** bilge water. **3** INFORMAL. nonsense. *n.*

bilge water, dirty water that collects in the bottom of a ship's hold.

bi lin gual (bī ling′gwəl), **1** able to speak another language as well or almost as well as one's own; knowing two languages. **2** containing or written in two languages: *a bilingual dictionary. adj.* —**bi lin′gual ly,** *adv.*

bil ious (bil′yəs), **1** suffering from or caused by some trouble with bile or the liver: *a bilious headache.* **2** cross; bad-tempered: *a bilious person. adj.* —**bil′ious ly,** *adv.*

bilk (bilk), cheat; swindle. *v.* —**bilk′er,** *n.*

bill[1] (bil), **1** statement of money owed for work done or things supplied: *The store sent me a $35 bill for clothing I had charged.* **2** send a bill to: *The dairy bills us on the first of each month.* **3** piece of paper money: *Do you have change for a five-dollar bill?* **4** a written or printed public notice, such as an advertisement, poster, or handbill: *Post no bills on this fence.* **5** announce by bills or public notice: *Many interesting television programs are billed for next week.* **6** a written or printed statement; list of items. **7** a proposed law presented to a lawmaking body for its approval: *This bill for gun control will be voted on by the Senate today.* 1,3,4,6,7 *n.,* 2,5 *v.* —**bill′er,** *n.*

fill the bill, satisfy requirements.

foot the bill, pay or settle the bill.

bill[2] (bil), **1** the horny part of the jaws of a bird; beak. **2** anything shaped somewhat like a bird's bill: *the bill of a turtle.* **3** join beaks; touch bills. 1,2 *n.,* 3 *v.*

bill and coo, kiss and talk softly, as pigeons touch bills and coo.

bill board (bil′bôrd′), a large board, usually outdoors, on which to display advertisements or notices. *n.*

bil let (bil′it), **1** a written order to provide board and lodging for a soldier. **2** place where a soldier is lodged. **3** assign to quarters by billet: *Soldiers were billeted in all the houses of the village.* 1,2 *n.,* 3 *v.*

bill fold (bil′fōld′), a small, flat case for carrying paper money, cards, etc., in one's pocket or handbag; wallet. *n.*

bil liards (bil′yərdz), game played with three hard balls on a special table with a raised, cushioned edge. A long stick called a cue is used to hit the balls. *n.*

bil lion (bil′yən), **1** (in the United States and Canada) one thousand millions; 1,000,000,000. **2** (in Great Britain, France, and Germany) one million millions; 1,000,000,000,000. *n., adj.*

bil lion aire (bil′yə ner′ or bil′yə nar′), an extremely wealthy person who has a billion or more dollars, francs, marks, pounds, etc. *n.*

bil lionth (bil′yənth), **1** last in a series of a billion. **2** one of a billion equal parts. 1 *adj.,* 2 *n.*

bill of fare, menu.

bill of goods, a shipment of merchandise.

sell a bill of goods, SLANG. mislead.

bill of rights, 1 statement of the fundamental rights of the people of a state or nation. **2 Bill of Rights,** the first ten amendments to the Constitution of the United States, adopted in 1791, which include a declaration of fundamental rights held by United States citizens.

bill of sale, a written statement transferring ownership of something from the seller to the buyer.

bil low (bil′ō), **1** a great, swelling wave or surge of the sea. **2** any great wave or swelling mass of smoke, flame, sound, or the like: *Billows of smoke rose from the chimney.* **3** rise or roll in big waves; surge: *The waves billowed toward the shore. Smoke billowed from the burning building.* **4** swell out; bulge: *The sheets on the clothesline billowed in the wind.* 1,2 *n.,* 3,4 *v.*

bil low y (bil′ō ē), **1** rising or rolling in big waves; surging. **2** swelling out; bulging. *adj.,* **bil low i er, bil low i est.**

bil ly (bil′ē), a policeman's club or stick. *n., pl.* **bil lies.**

billy goat, a male goat.

Bi lox i (bi luk′sē or bə lok′sē), city in SE Mississippi. *n.*

bi month ly (bī munth′lē), **1** once every two months: *A bimonthly magazine is issued six times a year (adj.). The magazine is issued bimonthly (adv.).* **2** twice a month: *The bimonthly meetings are on the first and third Wednesdays of each month (adj.). The meetings are held bimonthly (adv.).* **3** newspaper or magazine published bimonthly. 1,2 *adj., adv.,* 3 *n., pl.* **bi month lies.**

bin (bin), box or enclosed place for holding or storing grain, coal, etc. *n.*

bi nar y (bī′nər ē), made up of two; involving two. *adj.*

binary star, pair of stars that revolve around a common center of gravity.

binary system, system of numeration which counts only from 0 to 1 and then moves to a new number place, so that each place represents a quantity double that of the previous place. In this system, the decimal number 1 is written as 1, but the decimal number 2 is written as 10 (1 in the twos place, 0 in the ones place), while 5 is written as 101 (1 in the fours place, 0 in the twos place, 1 in the ones place). The binary system is used by electronic devices because 1 and 0 can easily be represented by the presence or absence of electric charge.

bin au ral (bī nôr′əl), having or using two sound speakers, in order to give a more realistic quality to what is heard: *binaural reception. adj.* —**bin au′ral ly,** *adv.*

bind (bīnd), **1** tie together; hold together; fasten: *bind a package with string.* **2** stick together: *Gravel in a roadway may be bound by tar.* **3** hold by some force; restrain: *Vines are binding the flowers and choking their growth.* **4** fasten (sheets of paper) into a cover; put a cover on (a book): *The loose pages were bound into a small book.* **5** hold by a promise, duty, law, etc.; oblige: *A doctor is in duty bound to help the sick. Parents are bound to send their children to school.* **6** put a bandage on: *bind up a wound.* **7** put a border or edge on to strengthen or ornament: *The sleeves were bound with leather.* **8** INFORMAL. a situation that binds or restricts: *We found we were in a bind when we were invited to two parties in the same evening.* 1-7 *v.,* **bound, bind ing;** 8 *n.*

bind er (bīn′dər), **1** person or business that binds books. **2** anything that ties or holds together. **3** cover for a loose-leaf notebook. **4** machine that cuts stalks of grain and ties them in bundles. *n.*

bind er y (bīn′dər ē), place where books are bound. *n., pl.* **bind er ies.**

bind ing (bīn′ding), **1** the covering of a book. **2** strip protecting or ornamenting an edge. Binding is used on the seams of dresses. **3** having force or power to hold to a promise, duty, law, etc.; obligatory. A contract is a binding agreement. 1,2 *n.,* 3 *adj.* —**bind′ing ly,** *adv.*

bind weed (bīnd′wēd′), plant with long stems that twine around fences, trees, or other plants. *n.*

bin go (bing′gō), game in which each player covers the numbers on a card as they are called out. The first player to cover a column of numbers is the winner. *n.*

bin na cle (bin′ə kəl), box or stand that contains a

ship's compass. The binnacle is placed near the helm. *n.*

bi noc u lar (bə nok′yə lər), 1 for both eyes at once: *a binocular microscope.* 2 using both eyes at once: *Most animals have binocular vision. adj.*

bi noc u lars (bə nok′yə lərz), a double telescope joined as a unit for use with both eyes. Field glasses and opera glasses are binoculars. *n.pl.*

WORD HISTORY

binoculars

Binoculars comes from Latin *bini*, meaning "two at a time," and *oculus*, meaning "eye."

bi no mi al (bī nō′mē əl), 1 expression in algebra made up of two terms connected by a plus or minus sign. *8a + 2b* is a binomial. 2 the scientific name of a plant or animal, made up of two terms. *Homo sapiens* is a binomial. 3 made up of two terms. 1,2 *n.,* 3 *adj.*

bio-, *combining form.* 1 life or living things: *Biology = science of life or living things.* 2 biological: *Biochemistry = biological chemistry.* [The form *bio-* comes from Greek *bios,* meaning "life."]

bi o chem i cal (bī′ō kem′ə kəl), having to do with biochemistry. *adj.* —**bi′o chem′i cal ly,** *adv.*

bi o chem ist (bī′ō kem′ist), an expert in biochemistry. *n.*

bi o chem is try (bī′ō kem′ə strē), science that deals with the chemical processes of living animals and plants. *n.*

bi o de grad a ble (bī′ō di grā′də bəl), capable of being broken down by the action of bacteria: *a biodegradable detergent. adj.*

bi o de grade (bī′ō di grād′), break down by the action of bacteria. *v.,* **bi o de grad ed, bi o de grad ing.**

bi og ra pher (bī og′rə fər), person who writes someone's biography. *n.*

bi o graph i cal (bī′ə graf′ə kəl), 1 of a person's life: *biographical details.* 2 having to do with biography. *adj.* —**bi′o graph′i cal ly,** *adv.*

bi og ra phy (bī og′rə fē), an account of a person's life. *n., pl.* **bi og ra phies.**

bi o log ic (bī′ə loj′ik), biological. *adj.*

bi o log i cal (bī′ə loj′ə kəl), 1 of plant and animal life; connected with the processes of life: *biological studies.* 2 having to do with biology: *a biological laboratory. adj.* —**bi′o log′i cal ly,** *adv.*

biological warfare, warfare in which disease germs are used against persons, animals, or crops.

bi ol o gist (bī ol′ə jist), an expert in biology. *n.*

bi ol o gy (bī ol′ə jē), the scientific study of plant and animal life, including its origin, structure, activities, and distribution. Botany, zoology, and ecology are branches of biology. *n.*

bi on ic (bī on′ik), 1 of or about bionics. 2 having both biological and electronic parts. 3 SLANG. artificial; contrived. *adj.*

bi on ics (bī on′iks), study of the anatomy and physiology of animals as a basis for designing new or improved electronic devices or systems. *n.* [*Bionics* is a blend of *biology* and *electronics.*]

bi op sy (bī′op sē), the removal of cells or tissue from a living body for medical examination. *n., pl.* **bi op sies.**

bi o sphere (bī′ə sfir), the region of the earth that can support life, including soil, water, and air. *n.*

bi o tech nol o gy (bī′ō tek nol′ə jē), 1 application of technological facts to biological science. 2 the industrial use of microorganisms to produce useful products and services. *n.*

bi par ti san (bī pär′tə zən), representing or supported by two political parties: *a bipartisan foreign policy. adj.*

bi par tite (bī pär′tīt), 1 having to do with two peoples, nations, etc.: *a bipartite treaty between the United States and Canada.* 2 having two parts: *A clam has a bipartite shell. adj.* —**bi par′tite ly,** *adv.*

bi ped (bī′ped), animal having two feet. Birds and human beings are bipeds. *n.*

bi plane (bī′plān′), airplane having two wings on each side of the fuselage, one above the other. *n.*

birch (bėrch), 1 a slender, hardy tree with a smooth bark that peels off in thin layers. 2 its hard, close-grained wood, often used in making furniture. 3 a birch stick used for whipping. *n., pl.* **birch es** for 1 and 3.

bird (bėrd), 1 any of a group of warm-blooded animals with a backbone and two legs and wings, that lay eggs and have a body covered with feathers. Most birds can fly. 2 shuttlecock. 3 SLANG. person: *He's an odd bird. n.* [*Bird* comes from Old English *bridd.*] —**bird′like′,** *adj.*

bird bath (bėrd′bath′), a shallow basin raised off the ground and filled with water for birds to bathe in or drink. *n., pl.* **bird baths** (bėrd′baŦHz′).

bird call (bėrd′kôl′), 1 sound that a bird makes. 2 instrument for imitating that sound. *n.*

bird dog, dog trained to find birds or bring back birds shot by hunters.

bird house (bėrd′hous′), a small box with a roof and one or more openings, raised off the ground for birds to nest in. *n., pl.* **bird hous es** (bėrd′hou′ziz).

bird ie (bėr′dē), 1 a little bird. 2 score of one stroke less than par for any hole on a golf course. 3 make such a score. 1,2 *n.,* 3 *v.,* **bird ied, bird y ing.**

bird of paradise, bird of New Guinea noted for its magnificent plumage.

bird of passage, bird that flies from one region to another as the seasons change.

bird of prey, any of a group of birds, including eagles, hawks, owls, and vultures, that hunt animals.

bird seed (bėrd′sēd′), mixture of small seeds often fed to caged birds. *n.*

bird's-eye (bėrdz′ī′), 1 seen from above or from a distance; general: *a bird's-eye view of the city from an airplane.* 2 having markings somewhat like birds' eyes. *Bird's-eye maple* is a wood used in furniture. *adj.*

bird watcher, person who observes and classifies wild birds in their natural environment. —**bird watching.**

bi ret ta (bə ret′ə), a stiff, square cap worn by Roman Catholic or Episcopal clergymen on certain occasions. *n., pl.* **bi ret tas.**

Bir ming ham (bėr′ming ham), 1 city in central England. 2 city in central Alabama. *n.*

birth (bėrth), 1 a coming into life; being born: *the birth* of a baby. **2** a beginning; origin: *the birth of a nation.* **3** a bringing forth: *the birth of a plan, the birth of a new age.* **4** descent; family: *a person of African birth, a woman of noble birth. n.*

give birth to, 1 bring forth; bear: *The dog gave birth to four puppies.* **2** be the origin or cause of: *The scientist's experiments gave birth to a new drug.*

birth control, 1 control of the birthrate by artificial means. **2** use of contraceptive methods or devices.

birth day (bėrth′dā′), **1** day on which a person was born. **2** day on which something began: *July 4, 1776, was the birthday of the United States.* **3** yearly return of the day on which a person was born, or on which something began: *Tomorrow is my birthday; I shall be ten years old. n.*

birth mark (bėrth′märk′), mark on the skin that was there at birth. *n.*

birth place (bėrth′plās′), **1** place where a person was born. **2** place in which something began; place of origin: *Philadelphia is the birthplace of the United States. n.*

birth rate (bėrth′rāt′), relationship of the number of births in a year to the total population. *n.*

birth right (bėrth′rīt′), right or privilege that a person is entitled to by birth. *n.*

birth stone (bėrth′stōn′), gem identified with a certain month of the year. A birthstone is supposed to bring good luck when worn by a person born in its month. *n.*

Bis cay (bis′kā), **Bay of,** bay north of Spain and west of France. It is part of the Atlantic. *n.*

bis cuit (bis′kit), **1** soft bread dough baked in small shapes. **2** BRITISH. cracker. *n., pl.* **bis cuits** or **bis cuit.**

bi sect (bī′sekt), divide into two equal parts: *You can bisect a 90-degree angle into two 45-degree angles. v.*

bi sec tor (bī sek′tər), line that bisects something, especially an angle. *n.*

bi sex u al (bī sek′shü əl), **1** of both sexes. **2** having both male and female reproductive organs in one plant or animal. **3** plant or animal that is bisexual. 1,2 *adj.,*3 *n.* —**bi sex′u al ly,** *adv.*

bish op (bish′əp), **1** clergyman of high rank who is the head of a church district or diocese. **2** one of the pieces in the game of chess that move diagonally. *n.*

bish op ric (bish′əp rik), **1** position, office, or rank of bishop. **2** church district under the charge of a bishop; diocese; see. *n.*

Bis marck (biz′märk), **1 Otto von,** 1815-1898, German statesman who united the German states into an empire in 1871. **2** capital of North Dakota, in the S part. *n.*

bis muth (biz′məth), a brittle, reddish-white metallic element, used in making medicine and in alloys. *n.*

bison
about 5¹/₂ ft.
(1.5 m.) high at
the shoulder

bi son (bī′sn *or* bī′zn), a wild ox of North America; buffalo. Bison have big, shaggy heads and strong front legs. *n., pl.* **bi son.**

bisque (bisk), a rich, thick soup. *n.*

Bis sau (bi sou′), capital of Guinea-Bissau. *n.*

bis tro (bis′trō *or* bē′strō), bar or nightclub. *n., pl.* **bistros.**

---

a hat	**i** it	**oi** oil	**ch** child
ā age	**ī** ice	**ou** out	**ng** long
ä far	**o** hot	**u** cup	**sh** she
e let	**ō** open	**ù** put	**th** thin
ē equal	**ô** order	**ü** rule	**ᴛʜ** then
ėr term			**zh** measure

ə = { a in about, e in taken, i in pencil, o in lemon, u in circus }

bit[1] (bit), **1** a small piece; small amount: *bits of broken glass. A pebble is a bit of rock.* **2** a short time: *Stay a bit.* **3** INFORMAL. 12¹/₂ cents. A quarter is two bits. *n.*

a bit, 1 a little; slightly: *I am a bit tired.* **2** somewhat: *That barking dog is a bit of a nuisance.*

bit by bit, little by little.

do one's bit, do one's share: *She did her share of the work, now you do your bit.*

bit[2] (bit), past tense and a past participle of **bite.** *The strong trap bit the leg of the fox. The postman was bit by our dog. v.*

bit[3] (bit), **1** tool for boring or drilling that fits into a brace, electric drill, etc. **2** the biting or cutting part of a tool. **3** the part of a bridle that goes in a horse's mouth. *n.*

champ at the bit, be impatient.

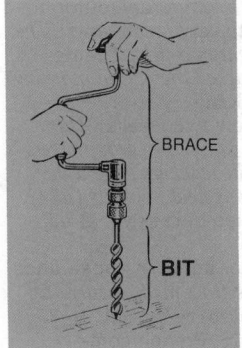

bit[3] (def. 1)

bit[4] (bit), the basic unit of information in an electronic computer. It is the same as a choice between two possibilities, such as "yes" or "no." *n.*

bitch (bich), a female dog, wolf, or fox. *n., pl.* **bitch es.**

bite (bīt), **1** seize, cut into, or cut off with the teeth: *She bit the apple. When I'm nervous I bite my fingernails.* **2** act of biting: *The dog gave a bite or two at the bone.* **3** a piece bitten off; mouthful: *Eat the whole apple, not just a bite.* **4** a light meal; snack: *Have a bite with me now or you'll get hungry later.* **5** wound with teeth, fangs, a sting, etc.: *My dog never bites.* **6** a wound made by biting or stinging: *Mosquito bites itch.* **7** a sharp, smarting pain: *We felt the bite of the cold wind.* **8** cause a sharp, smarting pain to: *Her fingers are bitten by frost.* **9** take a tight hold of; grip: *The jaws of a vise bite the wood they hold.* **10** take a bait; be caught: *The fish are biting well today.* 1,5,8-10 *v.,* **bit, bit ten** or **bit, bit ing;** 2-4,6,7 *n.* [*Bite* comes from Old English *bītan.*]

bit er (bī′tər), person or animal that bites. *n.*

bit ing (bī′ting), **1** sharp; cutting: *Dress warmly before you go out in that biting wind.* **2** sarcastic; sneering: *Biting remarks hurt people's feelings. adj.* —**bit′ing ly,** *adv.*

bit ten (bit′n), a past participle of **bite.** *Finish the apple, now that you have bitten into it. v.*

bit ter (bit′ər), **1** having a sharp, harsh, unpleasant taste: *Quinine is bitter medicine.* **2** causing pain or grief; hard to admit or bear: *a bitter defeat. The death of his father was a bitter loss.* **3** showing pain or grief: *bitter tears.* **4** harsh or cutting: *a bitter remark, bitter enemies.* **5** very cold: *The*

bitter winter killed our apple tree. adj. —**bit′ter ly,** *adv.*
—**bit′ter ness,** *n.*
to the bitter end, until the very last.

bit tern (bit′ərn), a wading bird which lives in marshes and has a peculiar booming cry. It is a small heron. *n.*

bit ter root (bit′ər rüt′ *or* bit′ər rut′), a small plant with fleshy roots and pink flowers, found in the northern Rocky Mountains. *n.*

bit ter sweet (bit′ər swēt′), **1** a climbing plant with purple flowers and poisonous, scarlet berries. **2** a climbing vine of North America with greenish flowers and orange seedcases that open and show red seeds. **3** sweet and bitter mixed: *bittersweet chocolate.* **4** pleasant and painful at once: *The movie had a bittersweet ending which left her uncertain whether to laugh or cry.* **1,2** *n.,* **3,4** *adj.*

bit ty (bit′ē), very small; tiny. *adj.,* **bit ti er, bit ti est.**

bi tu men (bə tü′mən *or* bə tyü′mən), any of a number of minerals that will burn, such as asphalt, petroleum, and naphtha. *n.*

bi tu mi nous coal (bə tü′mə nəs *or* bə tyü′mə nəs), coal that burns with much smoke and a yellow flame; soft coal.

bi valve (bī′valv′), any mollusk whose shell is made of two parts hinged together so that it will open and shut like a book. Oysters and clams are bivalves. *n.*

biv ouac (biv′wak *or* biv′ü ak), **1** a temporary, outdoor camp usually without tents or with very small tents: *The soldiers made a bivouac for the night in a field.* **2** camp outdoors in this way: *They bivouacked there until morning.* **1** *n.,* **2** *v.,* **biv ouacked, biv ouack ing.**

bi week ly (bī wēk′lē), **1** once every two weeks: *This magazine is a biweekly publication* (adj.). *The group meets biweekly* (adv.). **2** twice a week: *The teachers have a biweekly conference* (adj.). *That class is held biweekly* (adv.). **3** newspaper or magazine published biweekly. **1,2** *adj., adv.,* **3** *n., pl.* **bi week lies.**

bi zarre (bə zär′), strikingly odd or queer in appearance or style; fantastic; grotesque: *The frost made bizarre figures on the windowpanes. adj.* —**bi zarre′ly,** *adv.*

Bi zet (bē zā′), **Georges,** 1838-1875, French composer. *n.*

Bk, symbol for berkelium.

bk., 1 bank. **2** book. *pl.* **bks.**

blab (blab), tell (secrets); talk too much. *v.,* **blabbed, blab bing.**

blab ber (blab′ər), **1** person who blabs. **2** foolish talk. **3** blab. **1,2** *n.,* **3** *v.*

black (blak), **1** having the color of coal: *a black sweater.* **2** the color of coal. This sentence is printed in black. **3** a black paint, dye, or pigment. **4** make black; blacken: *I blacked my shoes before going to the party.* **5** without any light; very dark: *The room was black as night.* **6** dirty; filthy: *Her hands were black with soot.* **7** dismal; gloomy: *a black day.* **8** sullen; angry: *She gave her brother a black look.* **9** wicked: *black deeds of murder and treason.* **10** Also, **Black. a** having dark skin; Negro. **b** person who has dark skin; Negro. **1,5-10a** *adj.,* **2,3,10b** *n.,* **4** *v.* [*Black* comes from Old English *blæc.*] —**black′ly,** *adv.* —**black′ness,** *n.*

black out, 1 become temporarily blind or unconscious: *Her pain was so intense that she blacked out for several minutes.* **2** darken completely: *black out the stage.* **3** suppress; withhold: *to black out the news of a battle.*

black-and-blue (blak′ən blü′), discolored from a bruise. *adj.*

black art, evil magic; black magic.

black ball (blak′bôl′), **1** vote against; turn down as a candidate for membership: *One member of the club blackballed him, so he could not become a member.* **2** a vote against a person or thing. **1** *v.,* **2** *n.* —**black′ball′er,** *n.*

black bear, a large North American bear that has dense black fur.

black ber ry (blak′ber′ē), **1** a small, black or dark-purple fruit of certain thorny bushes and vines. It is sweet and juicy. **2** gather blackberries. **1** *n., pl.* **black ber ries; 2** *v.,* **black ber ried, black ber ry ing.**

black bird (blak′bėrd′), any of various American birds, the male of which is mostly black. The cowbird, grackle, and redwing are blackbirds. *n.*

black board (blak′bôrd′), a smooth piece of slate, glass, or painted wood on which to write or draw with chalk. *n.*

black bod y (blak′bod′ē), a theoretical surface or body capable of completely absorbing all the radiation falling on it. *n., pl.* **black bod ies.**

Black Death, the bubonic plague that spread through Europe in the 1300's and destroyed one fourth of its population.

black en (blak′ən), **1** make black: *Soot blackened the snow.* **2** become black: *The sky blackened and soon it began to rain.* **3** speak evil of: *blacken a person's reputation by spreading rumors about that person. v.* —**black′en er,** *n.*

black eye, 1 a bruise around an eye. **2** INFORMAL. cause of disgrace or discredit.

black-eyed pea (blak′īd′), seed of a plant closely related to peas and beans, widely grown in the southern United States for use as a vegetable.

black-eyed Su san (sü′zn), a yellow daisylike flower with a black center.

Black foot (blak′füt′), member of a tribe of American Indians that live in Montana, Alberta, and Saskatchewan. *n., pl.* **Black feet** (blak′fēt′), **Black foot.**

Black Forest, mountains covered with forests in SW West Germany.

black guard (blag′ärd), a low, contemptible person; scoundrel. *n.*

black head (blak′hed′), a small black-tipped lump of dead cells and oil plugging a pore of the skin. *n.*

Black Hills, group of mountains in W South Dakota and NE Wyoming.

black hole, a theoretical heavenly body whose mass is so great for its size that its extreme gravity keeps light from escaping and changes the basic properties of time and space in its area.

black ing (blak′ing), a black polish used on shoes, stoves, etc. *n.*

black ish (blak′ish), somewhat black. *adj.*

black jack (blak′jak′), **1** a small, weighted leather-covered weapon with a flexible handle, used for striking someone. **2** hit with a blackjack. **3** the black flag of a pirate. **4** a card game in which the players draw cards face down from the dealer, trying for a score of not more than 21 points. **1,3,4** *n.,* **2** *v.*

black list (blak′list′), **1** list of persons who are believed to deserve punishment, blame, suspicion, etc.: *That store keeps a blacklist of persons who do not pay their bills.* **2** put on a blacklist. **1** *n.,* **2** *v.*

black magic, evil magic; sorcery; witchcraft.

black mail (blak′māl′), **1** money gotten from a person by threatening to tell or reveal something bad about him or her. **2** get or try to get blackmail from. **3** an attempt to get money by threats. **1,3** *n.,* **2** *v.* —**black′mail′er,** *n.*

black mark, mark of criticism or punishment made against a person.

black market, 1 the selling of goods at unlawful prices or in unlawful quantities. **2** place where such selling is done.

black out (blak′out′), **1** a turning off or going out of all the lights of a city, district, etc., as a protection against an air raid or as the result of power failure. **2** temporary blindness or loss of consciousness resulting from lack of blood circulation in the brain. **3** the withholding of information usually printed or broadcast: *a news blackout. n.*

Black Power, power of collective action by Blacks, used to gain equality.

Black Sea, large sea between Turkey and S Soviet Union. See **Caucasia** for map.

black sheep, person considered by his or her group or family to be a disgrace.

black smith (blak′smith′), person who makes things out of iron by heating it in a forge and hammering it into shape on an anvil. Blacksmiths mend tools and shoe horses. *n.*

black snake (blak′snāk′), **1** a harmless dark or black snake of North America. **2** a heavy whip made of braided leather. *n.*

black top (blak′top′), **1** asphalt mixed with crushed rock, used as a pavement for highways, roads, and other surfaces. **2** surface covered with this substance. **3** surface or pave (a road) with blacktop. 1,2 *n.,* 3 *v.,* **black-topped, black top ping.**

black widow, spider, the female of which is poisonous and has a glossy black body with a reddish mark in the shape of an hourglass on the underside.

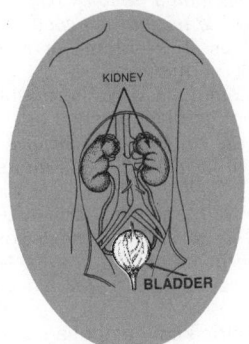

bladder (def. 1)

blad der (blad′ər), **1** a soft, thin bag in the body that receives urine from the kidneys. **2** anything like this. A football has a hollow rubber bladder that can be blown up with air. *n.*

blade (blād), **1** the cutting part of anything like a knife or sword: *A carving knife should have a very sharp blade. He had the blades of his skates sharpened.* **2** sword. **3** a smart, dashing fellow. **4** leaf of grass. **5** the flat, wide part of a leaf. **6** the flat, wide part of anything: *the blade of an oar or paddle, the shoulder blade. n.* [*Blade* comes from Old English *blæd.*] —**blade′like′,** *adj.*

blah (blä), SLANG. without spirit; dull; uninteresting: *a blah performance. adj.*

Blake (blāk), **William,** 1757-1827, English poet and artist. *n.*

blam a ble (blā′mə bəl), deserving blame; faulty. *adj.* —**blam′a bly,** *adv.*

blame (blām), **1** hold responsible for something bad or wrong: *The driver blamed the fog for his accident.* **2** responsibility for something bad or wrong: *Carelessness deserves the blame for many mistakes.* **3** find fault with: *The teacher will not blame us if we do our best.* **4** a finding fault; reproof. 1,3 *v.,* **blamed, blam ing;** 2,4 *n.*
be to blame, deserve to be blamed: *Each person said somebody else was to blame.*

blame less (blām′lis), not deserving blame; faultless. *adj.* —**blame′less ly,** *adv.* —**blame′less ness,** *n.*

blame wor thy (blām′wér′ŦHē), deserving blame; faulty. *adj.* —**blame′wor′thi ness,** *n.*

a hat	**i** it	**oi** oil	**ch** child	a in about
ā age	**ī** ice	**ou** out	**ng** long	e in taken
ä far	**o** hot	**u** cup	**sh** she	ə = { i in pencil
e let	**ō** open	**u̇** put	**th** thin	o in lemon
ē equal	**ô** order	**ü** rule	**ŦH** then	u in circus
ėr term			**zh** measure	

blanch (blanch), **1** make white; bleach. We blanch almonds by soaking off their skins in boiling water. **2** turn white; become pale: *We blanched with fear when we saw the bear coming. v.*

bland (bland), **1** gentle; soothing: *a bland smile.* **2** smoothly agreeable and polite: *a bland manner.* **3** mild; not irritating: *a bland diet of baby food. adj.* —**bland′ly,** *adv.* —**bland′ness,** *n.*

blan dish (blan′dish), persuade by gentle ways; coax; flatter. *v.* —**blan′dish er,** *n.*

blan dish ment (blan′dish mənt), a coaxing; flattery. *n.*

blank (blangk), **1** space left empty or to be filled in: *Leave a blank if you can't answer the question.* **2** not written or printed on: *blank paper.* **3** a paper with spaces to be filled in: *Fill out this application blank and return it at once.* **4** with spaces left for filling in: *a blank check, a blank form for you to fill in.* **5** an empty or vacant place: *When he read the hard questions his mind became a complete blank.* **6** empty; vacant: *There was a blank look on his face.* **7** cartridge containing gunpowder but no bullet. **8** keep from scoring. 1,3,5,7 *n.,* 2,4,6 *adj.,* 8 *v.* —**blank′ly,** *adv.* —**blank′ness,** *n.*
draw a blank, be unsuccessful: *I drew a blank when I tried to recall her name.*

blan ket (blang′kit), **1** a soft, heavy covering woven from wool, cotton, nylon, or other material, used to keep people or animals warm. **2** anything like a blanket: *A blanket of snow covered the ground.* **3** to cover with a blanket or anything like a blanket: *The snow blanketed the ground.* **4** covering several or all: *a blanket guarantee to repair defects of any kind.* 1,2 *n.,* 3 *v.,* 4 *adj.*

blank verse, 1 unrhymed poetry having five iambic feet in each line. **2** any unrhymed verse.

blank verse

What's in a name? that which we call a rose

By an y oth er name would smell as sweet.

blank verse—from Shakespeare's "Romeo and Juliet"

blare (bler *or* blar), **1** make a loud, harsh sound: *The trumpets blared.* **2** a loud, harsh sound. 1 *v.,* **blared, blaring;** 2 *n.*

blar ney (blär′nē), **1** flattering, coaxing talk. **2** flatter; coax. 1 *n., pl.* **blar neys;** 2 *v.*

Blarney Stone, a stone in a castle near Cork, Ireland. Anyone who kisses it is supposed to become skillful in flattering and coaxing people.

bla sé (blä zā′), tired of pleasures; bored. *adj.* [*Blasé* was borrowed from French *blasé.*]

blas pheme (bla sfēm′), speak about (God or sacred things) with abuse or contempt. *v.,* **blas phemed, blas phem ing.**

blas phem er (bla sfē′mər), person who blasphemes. *n.*

blas phe mous (blas′fə məs), speaking about God or sacred things with abuse or contempt. *adj.* —**blas′phemous ly,** *adv.* —**blas′phe mous ness,** *n.*

blas phe my (blas′fə mē), abuse or contempt for God or sacred things. *n., pl.* **blas phe mies.**

blast (blast), **1** a strong, sudden rush of wind or air: *the icy blasts of winter.* **2** the blowing of a trumpet, horn, whistle, etc.: *The warning blast of a bugle aroused the camp.* **3** sound made by blowing a trumpet, horn, whistle, etc. **4** current of air used in smelting, etc. **5** blow up (rocks, earth, etc.) with dynamite, gunpowder, etc.: *The old building was blasted.* **6** a blasting; explosion: *We heard the blast a mile away.* **7** charge of dynamite, gunpowder, etc., that blows up rocks, earth, etc. **8** cause to wither; blight; destroy: *The bad news blasted our hopes.* 1-4,6,7 *n.,* 5,8 *v.* —**blast′er,** *n.*

blast off, take off into flight propelled by rockets: *All parts of the spacecraft are carefully checked before it blasts off.*

full blast, in full operation: *The party was going full blast.*

blast furnace, furnace in which ores are smelted by forcing a strong current of air into the furnace from the bottom to make a very great heat.

blast off (blast′ôf′), a launching or taking off into rocket-propelled flight. *n.*

blat (blat), cry like a calf or sheep; bleat. *v.,* **blat ted, blat ting.**

bla tan cy (blāt′n sē), noisy or unpleasant intrusion: *Viewers object to the blatancy of some television commercials. n.*

bla tant (blāt′nt), **1** noisy; offensive: *a blatant fool.* **2** obvious; flagrant: *a blatant lie, a blatant disregard of others. adj.* —**bla′tant ly,** *adv.*

blaze[1] (blāz), **1** a bright flame or fire: *We could see the blaze of the campfire across the beach.* **2** burn with a bright flame: *A fire was blazing in the fireplace.* **3** a glow of brightness; intense light; glare: *the blaze of the noon sun.* **4** show bright colors or lights: *On New Year's Eve the big house blazed with lights.* **5** bright display: *The tulips made a blaze of color in the garden.* **6** burst out in anger or excitement: *She blazed up at the insult.* **7** a sudden or violent outburst: *a blaze of temper.* 1,3,5,7 *n.,* 2,4,6 *v.,* **blazed, blaz ing.**

blaze away, fire a gun continuously.

blaze[2] (blāz), **1** mark made on a tree by cutting off a piece of bark, to indicate a trail or boundary in a forest. **2** mark (a tree, trail, or boundary) by cutting off a piece of bark. **3** a white spot on the face of a horse, cow, etc. 1,3 *n.,* 2 *v.,* **blazed, blaz ing.**

blaze[3] (blāz), make known; proclaim. *v.,* **blazed, blazing.**

blaz er (blā′zər), a distinctively colored or decorated jacket. Blazers are sometimes worn as part of the uniform of a team or school. *n.*

bla zon (blā′zn), **1** make known; proclaim: *Big posters blazoned the wonders of the coming circus.* **2** decorate with designs, names, colors, etc. **3** coat of arms. 1,2 *v.,* 3 *n.*

bldg., building. *pl.* **bldgs.**

bleach (blēch), **1** whiten by exposing to sunlight or by using chemicals: *animal skulls bleached by the desert sun. We bleached the linen napkins in the wash.* **2** any chemical used in bleaching. 1 *v.,* 2 *n., pl.* **bleach es.**

bleach ers (blē′chərz), section of wooden or plastic benches for spectators at baseball or other outdoor events. Bleachers are not roofed, and are the lowest priced seats. *n.pl.*

bleak (blēk), **1** swept by winds; bare: *The rocky peaks of high mountains are bleak.* **2** chilly; cold: *The bleak winter wind made us shiver.* **3** cheerless and depressing; dismal:

A prisoner's life is bleak. adj. —**bleak′ly,** *adv.* —**bleak′ness,** *n.*

blear (blir), make dim or blurred: *The old dog's eyes were bleared by age. v.*

blear-eyed (blir′īd′), bleary-eyed. *adj.*

blear y (blir′ē), dim; blurred: *Her eyes were bleary from lack of sleep. adj.,* **blear i er, blear i est.** —**blear′i ly,** *adv.*

blear y-eyed (blir′ē īd′), having eyes dim with water, tears, etc. *adj.*

bleat (blēt), **1** cry made by a sheep, goat, or calf. **2** a sound like this: *a bleat of terror.* **3** make the cry of a sheep, goat, or calf. **4** make a sound like this. 1,2 *n.,* 3,4 *v.* —**bleat′er,** *n.*

bled (bled), past tense and past participle of **bleed.** *The cut bled for ten minutes. v.*

bleed (blēd), **1** lose blood: *The cut on your leg is bleeding.* **2** suffer wounds or death: *They fought and bled for their country.* **3** take blood from: *Doctors used to bleed sick people as a method of treating diseases.* **4** lose sap, juice, etc., from a surface that has been cut or scratched, as a tree or vine. **5** feel pity, sorrow, or grief: *My heart bleeds for the poor little orphan. v.,* **bled, bleed ing.**

bleed er (blē′dər), person who bleeds excessively when injured, because the blood fails to clot. *n.*

blem ish (blem′ish), **1** something that spoils beauty; defect; flaw: *A pimple is a blemish on a person's skin.* **2** injure; mar: *Scandal blemished the mayor's good reputation.* 1 *n., pl.* **blem ish es;** 2 *v.* —**blem′ish er,** *n.*

blench (blench), draw back; shrink away. *v.*

blend (blend), **1** mix or become mixed so thoroughly that the things mixed cannot be distinguished or separated; mix together: *Blend the butter and the sugar before adding the other ingredients of the cake.* **2** shade into each other, little by little; merge: *The colors of the rainbow blend into one another.* **3** go well together; harmonize. **4** a mixture of several kinds: *This coffee is a blend.* **5** word made by combining two words, often with a syllable in common. EXAMPLE: *Motel is a blend of motor and hotel.* 1-3 *v.,* 4,5 *n.*

blend er (blen′dər), an electric kitchen appliance for grinding, mixing, or beating various foods. *n.*

bless (bles), **1** make holy or sacred: *The bishop blessed the new church.* **2** ask God's favor for: *Bless these little children.* **3** wish good to; feel grateful to: *I bless her for her kindness.* **4** make happy or fortunate: *I have always been blessed with good health.* **5** praise; glorify: *to bless the Lord. v.,* **blessed** or **blest, bless ing.**

bless ed (bles′id *or* blest), **1** holy; sacred: *a blessed sacrament.* **2** happy; fortunate: *The birth of a baby is often called a blessed event. adj.* —**bless′ed ly,** *adv.* —**bless′ed ness,** *n.*

Bless ed Virgin (bles′id), the Virgin Mary.

bless ing (bles′ing), **1** prayer asking God's favor; benediction: *A religious service often ends with a blessing.* **2** a wish for happiness or success: *When I left home, I received my family's blessing.* **3** anything that makes one happy and contented; benefit: *A good temper is a great blessing.* **4** consent or approval: *The committee's proposal has my blessing. n.*

blest (blest), **1** a past tense and a past participle of **bless.** *He was blest with good health.* **2** blessed. 1 *v.,* 2 *adj.*

blew (blü), past tense of **blow**[2]. *All night long the wind blew. v.*

blight (blīt), **1** disease that causes plants or parts of plants to wither and die: *The apple crop was wiped out by blight.* **2** bacterium, fungus, or virus that causes such a disease. **3** anything that causes destruction or ruin. **4** cause to wither and die; destroy; ruin: *Mildew blighted the June roses. Rain blighted our hopes for a picnic.* 1-3 *n.,* 4 *v.*

blimp

a hat	i it	oi oil	ch child	a in about
ā age	ī ice	ou out	ng long	e in taken
ä far	o hot	u cup	sh she	ə = { i in pencil
e let	ō open	ủ put	th thin	o in lemon
ē equal	ô order	ü rule	₮H then	u in circus
ėr term			zh measure	

blimp (blimp), a kind of balloon that can be steered. It is filled with gas that is lighter than air. *n.*

blind (blīnd), **1** not able to see: *a blind person.* **2** make unable to see: *He was accidentally blinded in one eye.* **3** hard to see; hidden: *There is a blind curve on the highway.* **4** make temporarily unable to see: *The bright lights blinded me.* **5** without the help of sight; by means of instruments instead of the eyes: *blind flying of an aircraft at night (adj.). We flew blind through the storm (adv.).* **6** without thought, judgment, or good sense: *He was in a blind fury. I made a blind guess.* **7** take away the power to understand or judge: *Her prejudices blinded her.* **8** something that keeps out light or hinders sight. A window shade or shutter is a blind. **9** anything that conceals an action or purpose: *The shop was a blind for an illegal gambling ring.* **10** with only one opening. A blind alley is a passageway closed at one end. **11** without an opening: *a blind wall.* **12** a hiding place for a hunter. 1,3,5,6,10,11 *adj.*, 2,4,7 *v.*, 5 *adv.*, 8,9,12 *n.* —**blind′ly**, *adv.* —**blind′ness**, *n.*

blind to, unable to understand or appreciate.

blind date, 1 date between two people of opposite sex, who have not met before. **2** either of the two people.

blind er (blīn′dər), a leather flap on a horse's bridle to keep it from seeing sideways; blinker. *n.*

blind fold (blīnd′fōld′), **1** cover the eyes of: *We blindfolded her for a game of blindman's buff.* **2** with the eyes covered: *He walked the line blindfold.* **3** thing covering the eyes: *I put on the blindfold.* 1 *v.*, 2 *adj.*, 3 *n.*

blind man's buff (blīnd′manz buf′), game in which a blindfolded person tries to catch and name one of several other players.

blind spot, a point on the retina that is not sensitive to light. The optic nerve enters the eye there.

blink (blingk), **1** close the eyes and open them again quickly: *She blinked at the sudden light.* **2** shut the eyes to; look with indifference; ignore: *You cannot blink at this terrible injustice.* **3** shine with an unsteady light: *A little lantern blinked through the darkness.* **4** a sudden flash of light; gleam. 1-3 *v.*, 4 *n.*

on the blink, INFORMAL. not working properly: *My radio is on the blink.*

blink er (bling′kər), **1** blinder. **2** a device with flashing lights used as a warning signal. *n.*

blintz (blints), blintze. *n.*

blin tze (blin′tsə), a thin, rolled pancake filled with cheese, fruit, etc. *n.*

blip (blip), a small dot of light on a radar screen, showing the location of an object within its range. *n.*

bliss (blis), great happiness; perfect joy: *What bliss it is to plunge into the cool waves on a hot day! n.*

bliss ful (blis′fəl), very happy; joyful: *blissful memories of a summer vacation. adj.* —**bliss′ful ly**, *adv.*

blis ter (blis′tər), **1** a small swelling in the skin filled with watery matter. Blisters are often caused by burns or rubbing. *My new shoes have made blisters on my heels.* **2** a similar swelling on the surface of a plant, on metal, on painted wood, or in glass. **3** raise a blister or blisters on: *Sunburn has blistered my back.* **4** become covered with

blisters; have blisters. 1,2 *n.*, 3,4 *v.*

blithe (blī₮H *or* blīth), happy and cheerful; gay. *adj.*, **blith er, blith est.** —**blithe′ly**, *adv.* —**blithe′ness**, *n.*

blithe some (blī₮H′səm *or* blīth′səm), blithe. *adj.*

blitz (blits), **1** a sudden, violent attack using many airplanes and tanks. **2** any sudden, violent attack. **3** to attack or overcome by a blitz. 1,2 *n., pl.* **blitz es**; 3 *v.* [*Blitz* comes from German *Blitzkrieg*, meaning "lightning war."]

bliz zard (bliz′ərd), a blinding snowstorm with a very strong wind and very great cold. *n.*

bloat (blōt), swell up; puff up: *Overeating bloated their stomachs. v.*

blob (blob), a small, soft drop; sticky lump: *blobs of wax. n.*

bloc (blok), group of persons, companies, or nations combined for a purpose: *The farm bloc in Congress is a group from different political parties that favors laws to help farmers. n.*

block (blok), **1** a solid piece of wood, stone, metal, ice, etc., usually with one or more flat sides. **2** fill up so as to prevent passage or progress: *The country roads were blocked with snow.* **3** put things in the way of; obstruct; hinder: *Illness blocked our vacation plans.* **4** (in sports and games) hinder an opponent's play. **5** anything or any group of persons that keeps something from being done; obstruction; hindrance: *A block in traffic kept our car from moving on. Ever since the fire, she has had a block about remembering how it began.* **6** space in a city or town enclosed by four streets; square. **7** length of one side of a block in a city or town: *Walk one block east.* **8** number of buildings close together. **9** group of things of the same kind: *We bought a block of ten tickets for a play.* **10** platform where things are put up for sale at an auction. **11** holder with a hook or eye in which a pulley or pulleys are mounted. **12** shape with a mold: *Felt hats are blocked.* 1,5-11 *n.*, 2-4,12 *v.*

block in or **block out**, plan or sketch roughly without filling in the details; outline: *The artist blocked in parts of a portrait. The committee blocked out its plan.*

on the block, up for sale: *A collection of paintings will go on the block at the auction.*

block ade (blo kād′), **1** a blocking of a place by military means to control who or what goes into or out of it. **2** put under blockade. **3** anything that blocks up or obstructs. **4** block up; obstruct. 1,3 *n.*, 2,4 *v.*, **block ad ed**, **block ad ing.** —**block ad′er**, *n.*

block and tackle, combination of pulleys and ropes to lift or pull something.

block bust er (blok′bus′tər), INFORMAL. **1** a very destructive aerial bomb. **2** anything very large, forceful, or overwhelming. *n.*

block head (blok′hed′), a stupid person; fool. *n.*

block house (blok′hous′), a small fort or building with small openings to shoot from. *n., pl.* **block hous es** (blok′hou′ziz).

block ish (blok′ish), very dull or stupid. *adj.*

block y (blok′ē), like a block; chunky; *a blocky pony. adj.*, **block i er**, **block i est.**

blond or **blonde** (blond), **1** light in color: *blond hair, blond furniture.* **2** having yellow or light-brown hair and usually blue or gray eyes and fair skin. **3** person with such hair, eyes, and skin. A man or boy of this sort is usually referred to as a blond. A woman or girl of this sort is usually referred to as a blonde. 1,2 *adj.,* 3 *n.*

blood (blud), **1** the red liquid in the veins, arteries, and capillaries of vertebrates; the red liquid that flows from a cut. Blood is circulated by the heart, carrying oxygen and digested food to all parts of the body and carrying away waste materials. **2** the corresponding liquid in animals other than vertebrates. It may be colored or colorless. **3** relationship by descent from a common ancestor; family; parentage; descent: *We are related by blood.* **4** temper; state of mind: *There was bad blood between them. n.* [*Blood* comes from Old English *blōd.*]

curdle one's blood, frighten very much; horrify; terrify: *The piercing scream curdled my blood.*

draw blood, inflict damage or pain.

in cold blood, without feeling; cruelly and deliberately: *a murder committed in cold blood.*

blood bank, 1 place for storage of blood to be used in transfusions. **2** the blood kept in storage.

blood cur dling (blud′kėrd′ling), terrifying; horrible: *a bloodcurdling shriek. adj.*

blood ed (blud′id), coming from good stock; of good breed: *a blooded stallion. adj.*

blood group, any one of the groups into which human blood may be divided on the basis of the presence or absence of certain substances that cause red cells to clump together; blood type.

bloodhound
about 26 in.
(66 cm.) high
at the shoulder

blood hound (blud′hound′), a large, powerful dog with a keen sense of smell. *n.*

blood i ly (blud′l ē), in a bloody manner. *adv.*

blood i ness (blud′ē nis), condition of being bloody. *n.*

blood less (blud′lis), **1** without bloodshed: *a bloodless victory.* **2** without blood; pale: *a bloodless face.* **3** without energy; spiritless. *adj.* —**blood′less ly,** *adv.* —**blood′less ness,** *n.*

blood mo bile (blud′mə bēl′), a large motor vehicle with medical equipment and staff for collecting blood needed for transfusions. *n.*

blood poisoning, a diseased condition of the blood caused by poisonous matter or germs.

blood pressure, pressure of the blood against the inner walls of the arteries. Blood pressure varies with exertion, excitement, health, and age.

blood root (blud′rüt′ or blud′rùt′), a wild plant that has a red root, red sap, and a white flower that blooms in early spring. It is related to the poppy. *n.*

blood shed (blud′shed′), the shedding of blood; slaughter: *They captured the escaped convict without bloodshed. n.*

blood shot (blud′shot′), red and inflamed from broken or swollen blood vessels: *bloodshot eyes. adj.*

blood stained (blud′stānd′), stained with blood: *a bloodstained bandage. adj.*

blood stream (blud′strēm′), blood as it flows through the body. *n.*

blood suck er (blud′suk′ər), leech or other animal that sucks blood. *n.*

blood thirst i ly (blud′thėr′stl ē), in a bloodthirsty manner. *adv.*

blood thirst i ness (blud′thėr′stē nis), eagerness for bloodshed. *n.*

blood thirst y (blud′thėr′stē), eager for bloodshed; cruel and murderous: *a bloodthirsty pirate. adj.*

blood type, blood group.

blood-type (blud′tīp′), classify (blood or persons) according to blood group. *v.,* **blood-typed, blood-typ ing.**

blood vessel, any tube in the body through which the blood circulates. Arteries, veins, and capillaries are blood vessels.

blood y (blud′ē), **1** covered with blood; bleeding: *He came home with a bloody nose.* **2** accompanied by much killing: *It was a bloody battle.* **3** cause to bleed. **4** stain with blood: *Her knee was bloodied by her fall.* **5** stained with blood: *The sword was bloody.* **6** eager for bloodshed; cruel. 1,2,5,6 *adj.,* **blood i er, blood i est;** 3,4 *v.,* **blood ied, blood y ing.**

bloom (blüm), **1** have flowers; open into flowers; blossom: *Many plants bloom in the spring.* **2** a flower; blossom. **3** condition or time of flowering: *violets in bloom.* **4** condition or time of greatest health, vigor, or beauty: *in the bloom of youth.* **5** be in the condition or time of greatest health, vigor, or beauty; flourish: *Only water can make the desert bloom.* **6** glow of health and beauty. **7** the powdery coating on some fruits and leaves. There is a bloom on grapes and plums. 1,5 *v.,* 2-4,6,7 *n.*

bloom ers (blü′mərz), **1** loose trousers, gathered at the knee, formerly worn by women and girls for physical training. **2** underwear made like these. *n.pl.*

WORD HISTORY

bloomers

Bloomers were named for Amelia J. Bloomer, 1818-1894, an American magazine publisher who popularized the use of this type of trousers.

Amelia J. Bloomer

bloom y (blü′mē), covered with bloom, as a plum. *adj.,* **bloom i er, bloom i est.**

blos som (blos′əm), **1** flower, especially of a plant that produces fruit: *apple blossoms.* **2** condition or time of flowering: *The cherry trees are in blossom.* **3** have flowers; open into flowers: *All the orchards blossom in spring.* **4** open out; develop: *The shy child blossomed into an outgoing teenager.* 1,2 *n.,* 3,4 *v.*

blot (blot), **1** a spot of ink or stain of any kind. **2** make blots on; stain; spot: *My pen slipped and blotted the paper.* **3** dry with paper that soaks up ink: *Blot your page before you smear the ink.* **4** blemish; disgrace: *The field of rusting cars was a blot on the landscape.* 1,4 *n.,* 2,3 *v.,* **blot ted, blot ting.**

blot out, 1 cover up entirely; hide: *I blotted out the mistake with ink.* **2** wipe out; destroy: *When the dam broke, a village was blotted out by the violently rushing waters.*

blotch (bloch), **1** a large, irregular spot or stain. **2** place where the skin is red or broken out: *Too much sun can cause blotches on the skin.* **3** cover or mark with spots or stains. 1,2 *n., pl.* **blotch es;** 3 *v.*

blotch y (bloch′ē), having blotches. *adj.,* **blotch i er, blotch i est.**

blot ter (blot′ər), **1** piece of blotting paper. **2** book for recording happenings or transactions. A police station blotter is a record of arrests. *n.*

blotting paper, a soft paper used to dry writing by soaking up ink.

blouse (blous), **1** a loose upper garment worn by women and children as a part of their outer clothing. **2** a loosely fitting garment for the upper part of the body: *The sailor wore a wool blouse as a part of his uniform.* **3** a short, fitted coat worn as part of a military uniform. *n.*

blow¹ (blō), **1** a hard hit; knock; stroke: *strike a blow with the fist, strike a blow with a hammer.* **2** a sudden happening that causes misfortune or loss; severe shock: *His mother's death was a great blow to him.* **3** a sudden attack or assault: *The army struck a swift blow at the enemy.* n.

at one blow, by one act or effort.

come to blows, start fighting.

without striking a blow, with no effort.

blow² (blō), **1** send forth a strong current of air: *Blow on the fire or it will go out.* **2** move in a current; move rapidly or with power: *The wind blew in gusts.* **3** drive or carry by a current of air: *The wind blew the curtain.* **4** force a current of air into, through, or against: *The bellows blew the coals of the fire into flames.* **5** empty or clear by forcing air through: *The plumber blew the pipes.* **6** cause to pant: *He blew his horse by riding him hard.* **7** form or shape by air; swell with air: *blow glass, blow bubbles.* **8** make a sound by a current of air or steam: *The whistle blows at noon.* **9** break by an explosion: *The dynamite blew the wall to bits.* **10** melt: *The short circuit caused the fuse to blow.* **11** a blowing. **12** gale of wind: *Last night's big blow brought down several trees.* **13** spout water in the air: *"There she blows!"* was the sailor's cry when he spotted the whale.* **14** SLANG. ruin: *The team had a good chance to win, but they blew it in the last quarter by fumbling twice.* 1-10,13,14 *v.,* **blew, blown, blow ing;** 11,12 *n.*

blow one's stack or **blow one's top,** SLANG. become extremely angry; lose one's temper.

blow out, 1 put out or be put out by a current of air: *The candle blew out. I blew out the candle.* **2** have or cause a blowout in: *The worn tire blew out.*

blow over, 1 pass by or over: *The storm has blown over.* **2** be forgotten: *In time the scandal blew over.*

blow up, 1 explode: *The ammunition ship blew up and sank when it hit the rocks.* **2** fill with air: *blow up a bicycle tire.* **3** INFORMAL. become very angry: *I blew up at my sister for leaving our room in a mess.* **4** become stronger; arise: *A storm blew up suddenly.* **5** enlarge (a photograph).

blow-dry (blō′drī′), **1** dry (hair) with a blow dryer. **2** prepared with or dried by a blow dryer: *a blow-dry haircut.* 1 *v.,* **blow-dried, blow-dry ing;** 2 *adj.*

a hat	i it	oi oil	ch child	a in about
ā age	ī ice	ou out	ng long	e in taken
ä far	o hot	u cup	sh she	ə = i in pencil
e let	ō open	u̇ put	th thin	o in lemon
ē equal	ô order	ü rule	ŦH then	u in circus
ėr term			zh measure	

blow dryer, an electric hair dryer that dries the hair by a directed jet of warm air.

blow er (blō′ər), **1** person or thing that blows: *a glass blower.* **2** fan or other machine for forcing air into a building, furnace, mine, or other enclosed area. *n.*

blow fly (blō′flī′), any of various two-winged flies that lay their eggs on meat or in wounds. *n., pl.* **blow flies.**

blow gun (blō′gun′), tube through which a person blows something, such as darts or dried beans; blowpipe. *n.*

blow hard (blō′härd′), SLANG. a noisy boaster; bragger. *n.*

blow hole (blō′hōl′), hole for breathing, in the top of the head of whales, porpoises, and dolphins. *n.*

blown (blōn), past participle of **blow².** *My hat was blown away by the wind.* v.

blow out (blō′out′), **1** the bursting of a tire. **2** a sudden or violent escape of air, steam, or the like. *n.*

blow pipe (blō′pīp′), **1** tube for blowing air or gas into a flame to increase the heat. **2** blowgun. *n.*

blow torch (blō′tôrch′), a small torch that shoots out a very hot flame under pressure. A blowtorch is used to melt metal and burn off paint. *n., pl.* **blow torch es.**

blow up (blō′up′), **1** explosion. **2** INFORMAL. outburst of anger. **3** an enlargement of a photograph. *n.*

blow y (blō′ē), windy: *a blowy day.* adj., **blow i er, blow i est.**

blowz y (blou′zē), lacking neatness; untidy. *adj.,* **blowz i er, blowz i est.** —**blowz′i ly,** *adv.* —**blowz′i ness,** *n.*

blub ber (blub′ər), **1** fat of whales and some other sea animals. The oil obtained from whale blubber was formerly burned in lamps. **2** weep noisily. 1 *n.,* 2 *v.*

bludg eon (bluj′ən), **1** a short, heavy club. **2** strike with a bludgeon. **3** bully or threaten. 1 *n.,* 2,3 *v.* —**bludg′eon er,** *n.*

blue (blü), **1** the color of the clear sky in daylight. **2** having this color. **3** something having this color. **4** **the blue, a** the sky. **b** the sea. **5** having a dull-bluish color; livid: *Her hands were blue from cold.* **6** sad; gloomy; discouraged: *I felt blue when I failed.* See also **blues.** **7** use bluing on. 1,3,4 *n.,* 2,5,6 *adj.,* **blu er, blu est;** 7 *v.,* **blued, blu ing** or **blue ing.** —**blue′ness,** *n.*

out of the blue, completely unexpectedly: *His visit came out of the blue.*

blue bell (blü′bel′), a plant with blue bell-shaped flowers; harebell. *n.*

blue ber ry (blü′ber′ē), a small, round, sweet, blue berry which grows on a shrub. *n., pl.* **blue ber ries.**

blue bird (blü′bėrd′), a small songbird of North America, related to the robin. The male usually has a bright blue back and wings and a chestnut-brown breast. *n.*

blue blood, aristocrat.

blue bon net (blü′bon′it), plant with blue flowers resembling sweet peas. *n.*

blue bot tle (blü′bot′l), a large blowfly that has a blue abdomen and a hairy body. *n.*

blue-col lar (blü′kol′ər), of or having to do with industrial or factory work or workers. *adj.*

blue fish (blü′fish′), a saltwater food fish, bluish or greenish above and silvery below, of the Atlantic coast of North America. *n., pl.* **blue fish es** or **blue fish.**

blue flag, kind of iris with blue flowers.

blue grass (blü′gras′), grass with bluish-green stems. It is valuable for pasturage, hay, and lawns. *n., pl.* **blue-grass es.**

blue ing (blü′ing), bluing. *n.*

blue ish (blü′ish), bluish. *adj.*

blue jay, a North American bird with a crest and a blue back.

blue jeans, jeans, usually made of blue denim.

blue law, any very strict law regulating personal conduct. Laws prohibiting dancing or going to the theater on Sunday are blue laws.

blue print (blü′print′), **1** a photographic print that shows white outlines on a blue background. The process of making blueprints is used to copy original drawings of building plans, maps, etc. **2** a detailed plan for doing anything. *n.*

blue ribbon, the first prize; highest honor: *That sheep won a blue ribbon for best entry in its class at the fair.*

Blue Ridge, the SE range of the Appalachian Mountains, extending from NW Maryland to N Georgia.

blues (blüz), **1** a slow, melancholy song with jazz rhythm. **2 the blues,** INFORMAL. low spirits: *A rainy day always gives me the blues. n.pl.*

blu et (blü′it), a small plant of North America, with pale blue flowers. *n.*

blue whale, a blue-gray whale with yellowish underparts, sometimes growing to over 100 feet (30 meters) in length. It is the largest living animal.

bluff[1] (bluf), **1** a high, steep bank or cliff. **2** rising with a straight, broad front: *a bluff headland.* **3** abrupt, frank, and hearty in manner. **1** *n.,* **2,3** *adj.*

bluff[2] (bluf), **1** to fool or mislead, especially by pretending confidence: *She bluffed the robbers by convincing them that the police were on the way.* **2** something said or done to fool or mislead others in this way. Pretending to have better cards in a card game than you actually have is a bluff. **1** *v.,* **2** *n.* —**bluff′er,** *n.*

call one's bluff, ask for proof or for action when pretense is suspected.

blu ing (blü′ing), a blue liquid or powder put in the rinse water when doing laundry. It keeps white fabric from turning yellow. *n.* Also, **blueing.**

blu ish (blü′ish), somewhat blue. *adj.* Also, **blueish.**

blun der (blun′dər), **1** a stupid mistake: *Misspelling the title of a book is a silly blunder to make in a book report.* **2** make a stupid mistake: *Someone blundered in sending you to the wrong address.* **3** move clumsily or blindly; stumble: *I blundered through the dark house.* **1** *n.,* **2,3** *v.*

blun der buss (blun′dər bus), a short gun with a wide muzzle and large bore, formerly used to shoot at very close range. *n., pl.* **blun der buss es.**

blunt (blunt), **1** without a sharp edge or point; dull: *He sharpened the blunt knife.* **2** make less sharp; make less keen: *a knife blunted from use. A cold blunted my sense of smell.* **3** saying what one thinks very frankly, without trying to be tactful; outspoken: *When I asked if she liked my painting, her blunt answer was "No."* **1,3** *adj.,* **2** *v.* —**blunt′ly,** *adv.* —**blunt′ness,** *n.*

blur (blėr), **1** make less clear in form or outline: *Mist blurred the hills.* **2** dim: *Tears blurred my eyes. My eyes blurred with tears.* **3** blurred condition; dimness: *The blur in his vision was caused by old age.* **4** thing seen dimly or indistinctly: *When I don't have my glasses on, your face is just a blur.* **5** to smear; smudge: *You blurred the picture by touching it before the paint was dry.* **6** a smear; smudge: *The old, yellowed letter had many blurs.* **1,2,5** *v.,* **blurred, blur ring; 3,4,6** *n.*

blurb (blėrb), INFORMAL. advertisement or description, usually on the jacket of a book, album, etc., full of high praise. *n.*

blur ry (blėr′ē), **1** dim; indistinct: *The hills were a blurry outline in the dusk.* **2** full of smears and smudges. *adj.,* **blur ri er, blur ri est.**

blurt (blėrt), say suddenly or without thinking: *In my excitement I blurted out the secret. v.*

blush (blush), **1** become red in the face because of shame, confusion, or excitement: *The little boy blushed when everyone laughed at his mistake.* **2** a reddening of the face caused by shame, confusion, or excitement. **3** be ashamed: *I blushed at my sister's bad table manners.* **4** a rosy color: *The blush of dawn showed in the east.* **5** be or become red or rosy. **1,3,5** *v.,* **2,4** *n., pl.* **blush es.**

at first blush, on first glance; at first thought: *At first blush, I thought the job would be easy.*

blus ter (blus′tər), **1** storm noisily; blow violently: *The wind blustered around the corner of the house.* **2** stormy noise and violence: *We heard the bluster of the wind and rain.* **3** talk noisily and violently: *They were very excited and angry, and blustered for a while.* **4** noisy and violent talk with empty threats or protests: *angry bluster.* **1,3** *v.,* **2,4** *n.* —**blus′ter er,** *n.*

blus ter y (blus′tər ē), blustering. *adj.*

blvd., boulevard.

bo a (bō′ə), **1** a snake which is not poisonous, but kills its prey by crushing with its coils. Most boas are found in tropical regions and are very large, up to 30 feet (9 meters) in length. Anacondas, pythons, and boa constrictors are boas. **2** a long scarf made of fur or feathers, worn around a woman's neck. *n., pl.* **bo as.**

boa constrictor, a large boa of the tropical parts of America, up to 15 feet (4.5 meters) long.

boar (bôr), **1** a male pig or hog. **2** wild boar. *n., pl.* **boars** or **boar.** [*Boar* comes from Old English *bār.*]

board (bôrd), **1** a broad, thin piece of wood for use in building, etc.: *We used boards 10 inches wide, 1 inch thick, and 3 feet long for shelves in our new bookcase.* **2** cover with boards: *We board up the windows of our summer cottage in the fall.* **3** a flat piece of wood or other material used for one special purpose: *an ironing board, a drawing board.* **4** table to serve food on; table. **5** meals provided for pay: *The cost of going away to college includes room and board.* **6** provide with or get meals, or room and meals, for pay: *You will have to board elsewhere.* **7** group of persons managing something; council: *a school board, a board of directors.* **8** get on (a ship, train, bus, airplane, etc.): *We board the school bus at the corner.* **1,3-5,7** *n.,* **2,6,8** *v.*

go by the board, be given up or ignored.

on board, on a ship, train, bus, airplane, etc.: *When everybody was on board, the ship sailed.*

board er (bôr′dər), person who pays for meals, or for room and meals, at another's house. *n.*

board foot, unit of measure equal to a board one foot square and one inch thick; 144 cubic inches. It is used for measuring logs and lumber.

board ing (bôr′ding), boards. *n.*

board ing house (bôr′ding hous′), house where meals, or room and meals, are provided for pay. *n., pl.* **board-ing hous es** (bôr′ding hou′ziz).

boarding school, school with buildings where the pupils live during the school term.

board of health, department of a state or local government in charge of public health.

board sail ing (bôrd′sā′ling), the sport of riding a sailboard; windsurfing. *n.*

board walk (bôrd′wôk′), a wide sidewalk usually made of boards, along the beach at a shore resort. *n.*

boast (bōst), **1** speak too highly of oneself or what one owns; brag: *He boasts about his grades in school.* **2** statement speaking too highly of oneself or what one owns; bragging words: *I don't believe her boast that she can run faster than I can.* **3** something to be proud of: *The town's boast is its outstanding school system.* **4** have (something) to be proud of: *Our town boasts many fine parks.* 1,4 *v.*, 2,3 *n.* —**boast′er,** *n.* —**boast′ing ly,** *adv.*

boast ful (bōst′fəl), fond of bragging; boasting: *It is hard to listen very long to a boastful person.* *adj.*

boat (bōt), **1** a small, open vessel for traveling on water, such as a motorboat or a rowboat. **2** a large vessel, such as a steamboat or ocean liner; ship. **3** go in a boat. **4** dish shaped somewhat like a boat for gravy or sauce. 1,2,4 *n.*, 3 *v.* —**boat′er,** *n.* —**boat′like′,** *adj.*
in the same boat, in the same position or condition; taking the same chances.
miss the boat, INFORMAL. lose one's chances.
rock the boat, INFORMAL. disturb or upset the way things are: *If the mayor doesn't rock the boat by raising taxes, his supporters will vote for him again.*

boat house (bōt′hous′), house or shed for sheltering a boat or boats. *n., pl.* **boat hous es** (bōt′hou′ziz).

boat man (bōt′mən), **1** person who rents out boats or takes care of them. **2** person who rows, sails, or works on boats for pay. *n., pl.* **boat men.**

boat people, refugees who flee by boat, often by small fishing boats, to any country that will allow them to enter.

boat swain (bō′sn), a ship's officer in charge of the anchors, ropes, and rigging. He directs some of the work of the crew. *n.* Also, **bo's'n** or **bosun.**

bob[1] (bob), **1** move up and down, or to and fro, with short, quick motions: *The pigeon bobbed its head as it picked up crumbs.* **2** a short, quick motion up and down, or to and fro. 1 *v.*, **bobbed, bob bing;** 2 *n.*
bob up, appear suddenly or unexpectedly.

bob[2] (bob), **1** a child's or woman's haircut that is fairly short all around the head. **2** cut (hair) short. **3** weight on the end of a plumb line. **4** a float for a fishing line. 1,3,4 *n.*, 2 *v.*, **bobbed, bob bing.**

bob[3] (bob), BRITISH SLANG. shilling. *n., pl.* **bob.**

bob bin (bob′ən), reel or spool for holding thread, yarn, etc. Bobbins are used in spinning, weaving, machine sewing, and making lace. *n.*

bob ble (bob′əl), INFORMAL. fumble (a ball). *v.*, **bob bled, bob bling.**

bob by (bob′ē), BRITISH INFORMAL. policeman. *n., pl.* **bob bies.** [*Bobby* comes from the nickname of Sir *Robert Peel,* 1788-1850, who founded the London police force.]

bobby pin, a metal hairpin whose prongs close on and hold tightly to the hair.

bob by socks (bob′ē soks′), socks reaching just above the ankle, worn especially by girls. *n.pl.*

bob cat (bob′kat′), a small lynx of North America, having a reddish-brown coat with black spots. *n.*

bobcat
23 in. (58 cm.) high
at the shoulder

bob o link (bob′ə lingk), a common North American songbird that lives in fields and meadows. It is related to the blackbirds. *n.*

bob sled (bob′sled′), **1** a long sled with two sets of runners and a continuous seat. It has a steering wheel and brakes. **2** ride or coast on a bobsled. 1 *n.*, 2 *v.*, **bob sled ded, bob sled ding.** —**bob′sled′der,** *n.*

bob stay (bob′stā′), rope or chain to hold a bowsprit down. *n.*

bob tail (bob′tāl′), **1** a short tail, or a tail cut short. **2** horse or dog with its tail cut short. **3** having such a tail. 1,2 *n.*, 3 *adj.*

bob white (bob′hwīt′), an American quail that has a grayish body with brown and white markings. Its call sounds somewhat like its name. *n.*

bode[1] (bōd), be a sign of; indicate beforehand; foreshadow: *The rumble of thunder boded rain.* *v.*, **bod ed, bod ing.**
bode ill, be a bad sign: *The dark clouds boded ill for the success of our picnic.*
bode well, be a good sign: *The good weather bodes well for our trip to the zoo.*

bode[2] (bōd), a past tense of **bide.** *v.*

bo de ga (bō dā′gə), a grocery store in a Spanish-speaking neighborhood. *n., pl.* **bo de gas.** [*Bodega* was borrowed from Spanish *bodega,* which can be traced back to Greek *apothēkē,* meaning "storehouse."]

bod ice (bod′is), **1** the close-fitting upper part of a dress. **2** a kind of vest worn over a dress or blouse and laced up the front. *n.*

bod i less (bod′ē lis), without a body; not having material form: *Spirits are bodiless.* *adj.*

bod i ly (bod′l ē), **1** of the body; in the body: *bodily pain.* **2** in person: *She cannot be with us bodily, but is here in spirit.* **3** as a whole; altogether; entirely: *The audience rose bodily to cheer the great pianist.* 1 *adj.*, 2,3 *adv.*

bod kin (bod′kən), **1** a large, blunt needle. **2** a pointed tool for making holes. *n.*

bod y (bod′ē), **1** the whole material or physical structure of a person, animal, or plant: *I exercise to keep my body strong and healthy.* **2** the main part or trunk of an animal, apart from the head, limbs, or tail. **3** the main or central part of anything, such as the hull of a ship or the part of a vehicle that holds the passengers or the load. **4** group of persons or things: *The student body of our school gathered for an assembly. Congress is the lawmaking body of our government.* **5** a dead person or animal; corpse. **6** portion of matter; mass: *A lake is a body of water. The moon, the sun, and the stars are heavenly bodies.* **7** matter; substance; density: *Pea soup has more body than chicken broth.* *n., pl.* **bod ies.** [*Body* comes from Old English *bodig.*]

bod y guard (bod′ē gärd′), person or group of persons who guards someone: *A bodyguard accompanies the President at all public appearances.* *n.*

Boer (bôr *or* bōr), **1** person of Dutch descent living in South Africa. **2** of or having to do with the Boers. 1 *n.*, 2 *adj.*

Boer War, war between Great Britain and the Boers, from 1899 to 1902.

bog (bog), **1** piece of soft, wet, spongy ground; marsh; swamp. **2** sink or get stuck in a bog. 1 *n.*, 2 *v.*, **bogged, bog ging.** [*Bog* comes from Irish or Scottish Gaelic *bog,* meaning "soft."]
bog down, sink in or get stuck so that one cannot get out without help: *I am bogged down with my homework.*

bo gey (bō′gē *or* bu̇g′ē for 1; bō′gē for 2), **1** bogy. **2** score of one stroke over par for any hole on a golf course. *n., pl.* **bo geys.**

bo gey man (bō′gē man′ *or* bug′ē man′), a frightening imaginary creature. *n., pl.* **bo gey men.**

bog gle (bog′əl), **1** hold back; hesitate: *My parents boggled at my request for a pet snake.* **2** overwhelm or be overwhelmed with wonder, shock, etc.: *The vastness of the universe boggles the imagination. His mind boggled at the thought of his inheriting a million dollars. v.,* **bog gled, bog gling.**

bog gy (bog′ē), soft and wet like a bog; marshy; swampy: *boggy ground. adj.,* **bog gi er, bog gi est.**

bo gie (bō′gē *or* bug′ē), bogy. *n.*

Bo go tá (bō′gə tä′), capital of Colombia, in the central part. *n.*

bo gus (bō′gəs), not genuine; counterfeit; sham: *a bogus ten-dollar bill. adj.*

bo gy (bō′gē *or* bug′ē), **1** evil spirit; goblin. **2** person or thing, usually imaginary, that is feared without reason; bugbear; bugaboo. *n., pl.* **bo gies.** Also, **bogey** or **bogie.**

Bo he mi a (bō hē′mē ə), **1** former country in central Europe, now a region of Czechoslovakia. **2** Also, **bohe mia.** an unconventional, carefree place or way of living. *n.*

Bo he mi an (bō hē′mē ən), **1** of Bohemia, its people, or their language. **2** person born or living in Bohemia. **3** language of Bohemia; Czech. **4** Also, **bohemian.** **a** carefree and unconventional. **b** artist, writer, etc., who lives an unconventional, carefree sort of life. 1,4a *adj.,* 2,3,4b *n.*

Bohr (bôr), **Niels,** 1885-1962, Danish physicist who studied the atom. *n.*

boil[1] (boil), **1** bubble up and give off steam or vapor: *Water at sea level boils when heated to 212 degrees Fahrenheit or 100 degrees Celsius.* **2** cause (a liquid) to boil by heating it: *Boil some water for tea.* **3** cook by boiling: *We boil eggs four minutes.* **4** have its contents boil: *The pot is boiling.* **5** be very excited; be stirred up: *I boiled with anger.* **6** a boiling condition: *Bring the water to a boil.* 1-5 *v.,* 6 *n.*

boil down, 1 make less by boiling: *Boil down the sauce to half the amount.* **2** shorten by getting rid of unimportant parts: *The notes for her report were so long that the teacher asked her to boil them down.*

boil over, 1 come to the boiling point and overflow: *While I was answering the telephone, the soup boiled over.* **2** be unable to control anger: *I boiled over when someone took my bicycle without asking me first.*

boil[2] (boil), a painful, red swelling on the skin, formed by pus around a hard core. Boils are often caused by infection. *n.*

boil er (boi′lər), **1** tank for making steam to heat buildings or drive engines. **2** tank for heating and holding hot water. **3** container for heating liquids. *n.*

boiling point, temperature at which a liquid boils. The boiling point of water at sea level is 212 degrees Fahrenheit or 100 degrees Celsius.

Boi se (boi′sē), capital of Idaho, in the SW part. *n.*

bois ter ous (boi′stər əs), **1** noisily cheerful: *The room was filled with boisterous laughter.* **2** violent; rough: *a boisterous wind. adj.* —**bois′ter ous ly,** *adv.*

bo la (bō′lə), weapon consisting of stone or metal balls tied at the ends of long cords. South American cowboys throw it so that it winds around and entangles the animal aimed at. *n., pl.* **bo las.**

bold (bōld), **1** without fear; brave: *Lancelot was a bold knight.* **2** showing or requiring courage: *Climbing the steep mountain was a bold act.* **3** too free in manner; impudent: *The bold child made faces at us as we passed.* **4** sharp and clear to the eye; striking: *The mountains stood in bold outline against the sky.* **5** steep; abrupt: *Bold cliffs overlooked the sea. adj.* —**bold′ly,** *adv.* —**bold′ness,** *n.*

bold face (bōld′fās′), a heavy printing type that stands out clearly. **This sentence is in boldface.** *n.*

bole (bōl), stem or trunk of a tree. *n.*

bo ler o (bə ler′ō), **1** a lively Spanish dance in ³/₄ time. **2** music for it. **3** a short, loose jacket coming barely to the waist. *n., pl.* **bo ler os.**

Bo lí var (bō lē′vär *or* bol′ə vər), **Simón,** 1783-1830, Venezuelan general and statesman, who led revolts against Spanish rule in South America. Bolivia is named after him. *n.*

Bo liv i a (bə liv′ē ə), country in W South America. *Capitals:* La Paz and Sucre. See **Brazil** for map. *n.* —**Bo liv′i an,** *adj., n.*

boll (bōl), the rounded seed pod of a plant, especially that of cotton or flax. *n.*

boll weevil, a small beetle with a long snout whose larva is hatched in and does great damage to young cotton bolls.

boll weevil
about ¹/₅ in.
(5 mm.) long

bo lo (bō′lō), a long, heavy knife, used in the Philippines. *n., pl.* **bo los.**

bo lo gna (bə lō′nē *or* bə lō′nə), a large sausage usually made of beef, veal, and pork. *n., pl.* **bo lo gnas.** [*Bologna* was named for *Bologna,* Italy, where it was first made.]

Bo lo gna (bə lō′nyə), city in N Italy. *n.*

Bol she vik (bōl′shə vik), **1** member of a radical political party in Russia that seized power in November 1917. The Bolsheviks became the Communist Party in 1918. **2** member of any Communist Party. **3** of the Bolsheviks or Bolshevism. **4** Also, **bolshevik. a** any extreme radical. **b** extremely radical. 1,2,4a *n.,* 3,4b *adj.*

Bol she vism (bōl′shə viz′əm), **1** doctrines and methods of the Bolsheviks. **2** Also, **bolshevism.** extreme radicalism. *n.*

Bol she vist or **bol she vist** (bōl′shə vist), Bolshevik. *n., adj.*

bol ster (bōl′stər), **1** a long pillow or cushion for a couch or bed. **2** keep from falling; support; prop: *The walls of the church are bolstered up with buttresses. Her encouragement bolstered my confidence.* 1 *n.,* 2 *v.*

bolt (bōlt), **1** rod with a head at one end and a screw thread for a nut at the other. Bolts are used to fasten things together or hold something in place. **2** bar slid or dropped into a bracket to lock a door, gate, etc. **3** part of

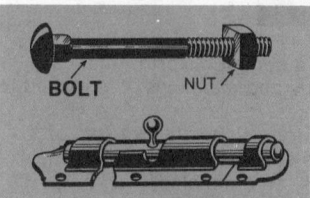

BOLT **NUT**

bolt
(top, def. 1)
(bottom, def. 2)

a lock moved by a key. **4** fasten with a bolt: *Bolt the doors.* **5** a short arrow with a thick head. Bolts were shot from crossbows. **6** discharge of lightning. **7** a sudden start; a running away: *When the rabbit saw us, it made a bolt for safety.* **8** dash off; run away: *The horse bolted at the sight of the car.* **9** break away from one's party or its candidates. **10** roll of cloth or wallpaper. **11** swallow (food) quickly without chewing: *The dog bolted its food.* 1-3,5-7,10 *n.*, 4,8,9,11 *v.* [Bolt comes from Old English *bolt*, meaning "arrow."]

bolt upright, stiff and straight: *A noise in the middle of the night made me sit bolt upright in bed.*

shoot one's bolt, do as much as one can.

bomb (bom), **1** container filled with an explosive. A bomb is set off by a fuse, a timing device, or by the force with which it hits something. **2** a similar device filled with gas, smoke, or other material: *a tear gas bomb.* **3** attack with bombs; hurl bombs at; drop bombs on. 1,2 *n.*, 3 *v.*

WORD HISTORY

bomb

Bomb comes from Italian *bomba,* which can be traced back to Greek *bombos,* meaning "a booming sound."

bom bard (bom bärd′), **1** attack with bombs or heavy fire of shot and shell from big guns: *The artillery bombarded the enemy all day.* **2** keep attacking vigorously: *The lawyer bombarded the witness with one question after another.* **3** strike (the nucleus of an atom) with a stream of fast-moving particles to change the structure of the nucleus. *v.*

bom bar dier (bom′bər dir′), member of the crew of a bomber who aims and releases the bombs over a target. *n.*

bom bard ment (bom bärd′mənt), **1** an attack with bombs or with heavy fire of shot and shell. **2** a vigorous attack. **3** the striking of the nucleus of an atom with a stream of fast-moving particles. *n.*

bom bas tic (bom bas′tik), using many showy or high-flown words with too little thought: *The speaker used bombastic language to cover up almost total ignorance of the subject. adj.*

bombastic

If elected, I solemnly vow to escalate the struggle against the pestilential effects of galloping inflation!

Does that mean prices are going up or down?

a hat	i it	oi oil	ch child	
ā age	ī ice	ou out	ng long	a in about
ä far	o hot	u cup	sh she	e in taken
e let	ō open	u̇ put	th thin	ə = i in pencil
ē equal	ô order	ü rule	ŦH then	o in lemon
ėr term			zh measure	u in circus

bom bas ti cal ly (bom bas′tik lē), in a bombastic manner. *adv.*

Bom bay (bom bā′), seaport in W India, on the Arabian Sea. *n.*

bom ba zine (bom′bə zēn′ *or* bom′bə zēn′), a twilled fabric with a silk warp and worsted filling, often dyed black. *n.*

bomb bay, compartment in the fuselage of a bomber in which bombs are carried and from which they are dropped.

bomb er (bom′ər), airplane used to drop bombs on enemy troops, factories, cities, etc. *n.*

bomb load (bom′lōd′), load of bombs carried by a bomber or other aircraft. *n.*

bomb proof (bom′prüf′), strong enough to be safe from the effects of bombs and shells. *adj.*

bomb shell (bom′shel′), **1** bomb (def. 1). **2** a sudden, unexpected happening; disturbing surprise: *The news of his accident was a bombshell to the family. n.*

bo na fide (bō′nə fid′ *or* bō′nə fi′dē), in good faith; without make-believe or fraud; genuine: *a bona fide offer.*

bo nan za (bə nan′zə), **1** a rich mass of ore in a mine. **2** any rich source of profit: *Their farm has turned out to be a bonanza, for oil has been found on it. n., pl.* **bo nan zas.**

Bo na parte (bō′nə pärt), Napoleon. See **Napoleon I.** *n.*

bon bon (bon′bon′), piece of candy, usually soft and often having a fancy shape. *n.*

bond (bond), **1** anything that ties, binds, or unites: *a bond of affection between sisters.* **2 bonds,** *pl.* chains; shackles: *the bonds of slavery.* **3** certificate issued by a government or private company which promises to pay back with interest the money borrowed from the buyer of the certificate: *The city issued bonds to raise money for new parks.* **4** a written agreement by which a person says he will pay a certain sum of money if he does not perform certain duties properly. **5** agree to pay a certain sum of money if a person does not perform certain duties properly: *An insurance company has bonded the city treasurer for one million dollars.* **6** bind together. 1-4 *n.*, 5,6 *v.* —**bond′a ble,** *adj.*

bond age (bon′dij), a being held against one's will under the control or influence of some person or thing; lack of freedom; slavery. *n.*

bond man (bond′mən), **1** slave. **2** (in the Middle Ages) a person who belonged with the land and was sold with it; serf. *n., pl.* **bond men.**

bonds man (bondz′mən), **1** person who becomes responsible for another by giving a bond. **2** bondman. *n., pl.* **bonds men.**

bone (bōn), **1** one of the pieces of the skeleton of an animal with a backbone: *the bones of the hand, a beef bone for soup.* **2** take bones out of: *I boned the fish before eating it.* **3** the hard substance of which bones are made. **4** something like bone. Ivory is sometimes called bone. 1,3,4 *n.*, 2 *v.*, **boned, bon ing.** —**bone′like′,** *adj.*

make no bones about, INFORMAL. show no hesitation about; acknowledge readily: *The tired children made no bones about wanting to go home.*

bone-dry (bōn′drī′), very dry. *adj.*

bone less (bōn′lis), **1** without bones. **2** without courage; cowardly. *adj.*

bon er (bō′nər), SLANG. a foolish mistake; stupid error; blunder. *n.*

bon fire (bon′fīr′), a large fire built outdoors. *n.*

bon go (bong′gō), a small drum played with flattened hands, especially in Latin-American and African music. Bongos usually come in pairs and are held between the knees. *n., pl.* **bon gos.**

bongo drum, bongo.

bo ni to (bə nē′tō), saltwater fish related to mackerel and tuna. *n., pl.* **bo ni tos, bo ni toes,** or **bo ni to.**

Bonn (bon), capital of West Germany, in the W part, on the Rhine. *n.*

bon net (bon′it), **1** a covering for the head usually tied under the chin with strings or ribbons, worn by women and children. **2** cap worn by men and boys in Scotland. **3** headdress of feathers worn by North American Indians. *n.*

bon ny or **bon nie** (bon′ē), fair to see; rosy and pretty: *a bonny baby. adj.,* **bon ni er, bon ni est. —bon′ni ly,** *adv.* **—bon′ni ness,** *n.*

bo nus (bō′nəs), something extra, given in addition to what is due: *The company gave each worker a vacation bonus. n., pl.* **bo nus es.** [*Bonus* comes from Latin *bonus,* meaning "good." See **Word Family.**]

bonus

Below are words related to *bonus.* They can all be traced back to the Latin word *bonus* (bō′nùs), meaning "good."

bona fide	bon voyage	bounty
bonanza	boon	debonaire
bonbon	bounteous	
bonny	bountiful	

bon vo yage (bon′ vwä yäzh′), good-by; good luck; pleasant trip.

bon y (bō′nē), **1** of bone. **2** like bone. **3** full of bones: *bony fish.* **4** having big bones that stick out; very thin: *bony hands, the bony hips of a thin horse. adj.,* **bon i er, bon i est. —bon′i ness,** *n.*

boo (bü), **1** sound made to show dislike or contempt, or to frighten: *Boos were heard from those who didn't like the concert* (n.). *We were frightened when she jumped from behind the door and shouted, "Boo!"* (interj.). **2** make such a sound; shout "boo" at: *He sang so badly that the audience booed him.* 1 *n., pl.* **boos;** 1 *interj.,* 2 *v.,* **booed, boo ing.**

boob (büb), SLANG. a stupid person; fool; dunce. *n.*

boo boo (bü′bü′), SLANG. a foolish mistake. *n., pl.* **boo-boos.**

boo by (bü′bē), **1** a stupid person; dunce. **2** kind of large tropical sea bird. *n., pl.* **boo bies.**

booby prize, prize given to the person or team that does the worst in a game or contest.

booby trap, 1 bomb arranged to explode when a harmless-looking object to which it is attached is touched or moved. **2** trick arranged to annoy some unsuspecting person.

boo by-trap (bü′bē trap′), catch with or in a booby trap. *v.,* **boo by-trapped, boo by-trap ping.**

boog ie (bùg′ē), **1** a lively dance, with rapid, rhythmic movements, to the accompaniment of rock'n'roll music. **2** dance the boogie. 1 *n.,* 2 *v.,* **boog ied, boog ie ing.**

boo hoo (bü′hü′), **1** weep or sob loudly. **2** a loud sob. 1 *v.,* **boo hooed, boo hoo ing;** 2 *n., pl.* **boo hoos.**

book (bùk), **1** a written or printed work of considerable length, especially on sheets of paper bound together between covers: *She read the first two chapters of her book.* **2** blank sheets bound together: *You can keep a record of what you spend in this book.* **3** a main division of a book: *Genesis is the first book of the Old Testament.* **4** something fastened together like a book: *a book of matches.* **5 the Book,** the Bible. **6** make reservations to get tickets or to engage service: *He had booked passage by airplane from New York to London.* **7** enter a charge against (a person) in a police record: *An officer booked the suspect at the police station.* 1-5 *n.,* 6,7 *v.* [*Book* comes from Old English *bōc.*] **—book′er,** *n.*

by the book, by rule; accurately: *She played the game carelessly and not by the book.*

keep books, keep a record of business accounts: *An accountant keeps books for the grocer.*

like a book, with fullness or accuracy; completely: *We are best friends; we know each other like a book.*

book case (bùk′kās′), piece of furniture with shelves for holding books. *n.*

book club, a business organization that regularly supplies selected books to subscribers, usually at a reduced rate.

book end, a prop or support placed at the end of a row of books to hold them upright.

book ish (bùk′ish), **1** fond of reading or studying; studious: *The bookish boy spent many hours in the library.* **2** knowing books better than real life: *The scholar was a bookish man who did not know the world of business.* **3** stiffly dignified or formal; scholarly in a dull and narrow way; stilted: *Her conversation was sprinkled with bookish phrases. adj.* **—book′ish ly,** *adv.* **—book′ish-ness,** *n.*

book keep er (bùk′kē′pər), person who keeps a record of business accounts. *n.*

book keep ing (bùk′kē′ping), work of keeping a record of business accounts. *n.*

book let (bùk′lit), a little book; thin book. Booklets often have paper covers. *n.*

book mark (bùk′märk′), piece of cloth, paper, etc., put between the pages of a book to mark the reader's place. *n.*

book mo bile (bùk′mə bēl′), bus or truck that serves as a traveling branch of a library. *n.*

Book of Mormon, a sacred book of the Church of Jesus Christ of Latter-day Saints.

book sell er (bùk′sel′ər), person whose business is selling books. *n.*

book shelf (bùk′shelf′), shelf for holding books. *n., pl.* **book shelves.**

book shop (bùk′shop′), bookstore. *n.*

book store (bùk′stôr′), store where books are sold. *n.*

book worm (bùk′wėrm′), **1** person who is very fond of reading and studying. **2** any insect larva that eats the bindings or leaves of books. *n.*

boom¹ (büm), **1** a deep hollow sound like the roar of cannon or of big waves: *The big bell tolled with a loud boom.* **2** make a deep hollow sound: *The big man's voice boomed out above the rest.* **3** a sudden activity and increase in business, prices, or values of property; rapid growth: *Our town is having such a boom that it is likely to double its size in two years.* **4** increase suddenly in activity; grow rapidly: *Business is booming.* 1,3 *n.,* 2,4 *v.*

boom² (büm), **1** a long pole or beam, used to extend the bottom of a sail. **2** the lifting and guiding pole of a derrick. **3** chain, cable, or line of timbers that keeps logs from floating away. *n.*

boo me rang (bü′mə rang′), **1** a curved piece of wood, used as a weapon by the original people of Australia. Certain boomerangs can be thrown so that they return to the thrower. **2** anything that recoils or reacts to harm the doer or user. **3** act as a boomerang: *Their scheme to get rich boomeranged and they were left with less money than ever.* 1,2 *n.,* 3 *v.*

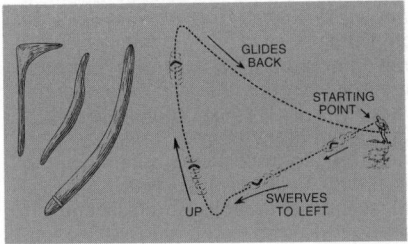

boomerang
(def. 1)
left, three types of boomerangs; right, the path of a boomerang

boon[1] (bün), **1** a great benefit; blessing: *Those warm boots were a boon to me in the cold weather.* **2** something asked for or granted as a favor. *n.*

boon[2] (bün), jolly; cheerful; merry: *boon companions. adj.*

boon docks (bün′doks′), SLANG. **1** a rough backwoods area. **2** a rural area outside cities and towns. *n.pl.* [*Boondocks* comes from Tagalog (a language of the Philippines) *bundók,* meaning "mountain."]

Boone (bün), **Daniel,** 1734-1820, American frontiersman who explored Kentucky. *n.*

boor (bür), a rude, bad-mannered person. *n.*

boor ish (bür′ish), having bad manners; rude. *adj.*

boost (büst), **1** a push or shove that helps a person in rising or advancing: *Give me a boost over the fence.* **2** lift or push from below or behind. **3** help by speaking well of: *The manufacturers are boosting the new cereal in a series of TV ads.* **4** an increase in degree, amount, price, pay, etc.: *a boost in food prices.* **5** to raise; increase: *The supermarket has boosted its prices.* 1,4 *n.,* 2,3,5 *v.*

boost er (bü′stər), **1** person or thing that boosts. **2** any of various devices for increasing the voltage in an electric circuit. **3** a rocket unit or engine which provides all or part of the thrust to an aircraft, missile, etc. *n.*

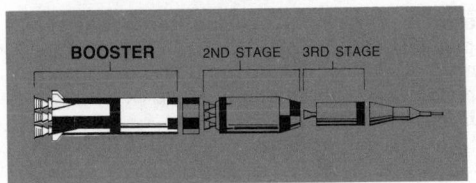

booster
(def. 3)

booster shot, an additional inoculation of a vaccine to continue the effectiveness of a previous inoculation.

boot[1] (büt), **1** a leather or rubber covering for the foot and lower part of the leg. **2** put boots on; supply with boots: *The horseback rider was booted and spurred.* **3** BRITISH. an automobile trunk. **4** a kick: *He gave the ball a boot.* **5** give a kick to: *She booted the ball.* 1,3,4 *n.,* 2,5 *v.*

boot[2] (büt). **to boot,** in addition; besides: *For my knife she gave me a compass and a dime to boot. n.*

boot[3] (büt), put into operation by means of a computer program that instructs the computer to take in other routines or information: *boot a computer, boot a disk. v.*

boot black (büt′blak′), person whose work is shining shoes and boots. *n.*

boot camp, camp at which U.S. Navy or Marine Corps recruits are trained.

a hat	i it	oi oil	ch child	(a in about
ā age	ī ice	ou out	ng long	e in taken
ä far	o hot	u cup	sh she	ə = { i in pencil
e let	ō open	ů put	th thin	o in lemon
ē equal	ô order	ü rule	ŦH then	(u in circus
ėr term			zh measure	

boot ee (bü′tē), a baby's soft shoe, often knitted. *n.*

booth (büth), **1** a covered stall or similar place where goods are sold or shown at a fair, market, convention, etc. **2** a small, enclosed place for a telephone, motion-picture projector, etc. **3** a small, enclosed place for voting at elections. **4** a partly enclosed space in a restaurant or café, containing a table and seats for a few persons. *n., pl.* **booths** (büŦHz *or* büths).

Booth (büth), **William,** 1829-1912, English clergyman who founded the Salvation Army. *n.*

boot leg (büt′leg′), **1** sell, transport, or make unlawfully: *Some people were bootlegging cigarettes into the state to avoid paying a tax.* **2** sold, transported, or made unlawfully. 1 *v.,* **boot legged, boot leg ging;** 2 *adj.*

boot leg ger (büt′leg′ər), person who bootlegs. *n.*

boot less (büt′lis), of no benefit or profit; useless. *adj.*

boo ty (bü′tē). **1** things taken from the enemy in war. **2** things seized by violence and robbery; plunder: *The pirates fought over the booty from the town they raided. n.*

booze (büz), INFORMAL. **1** any intoxicating liquor. **2** drink a lot of intoxicating liquor. 1 *n.,* 2 *v.,* **boozed, booz ing.**

bop (bop), SLANG. **1** a blow or punch with the hand, a club, etc. **2** hit; punch; strike. 1 *n.,* 2 *v.,* **bopped, bop-ping.**

Bo phu tha tswa na (bō pü′tä tswä′nä), country in S Africa, formerly part of the Republic of South Africa, and entirely surrounded by it. *Capital:* Mmabatho. *n.*

bo rax (bôr′aks), a white, crystalline powder used as an antiseptic, as a cleansing substance, in fusing metals, and in making heat-resistant glass. *n.*

Bor deaux (bôr dō′), **1** seaport in SW France. **2** a red or white wine made near Bordeaux. *n.*

bor der (bôr′dər), **1** the side, edge, or boundary of anything, or the part near it: *We pitched our tent on the border of the lake.* **2** form a boundary; bound: *The Rio Grande borders part of Texas.* **3** line which separates one country, state, or province from another; frontier: *We crossed the border between France and Germany.* **4** a strip on the edge of anything for strength or ornament: *napkins with a lace border.* **5** put a border on; edge: *We bordered our garden with shrubs.* 1,3,4 *n.,* 2,5 *v.*

border on or **border upon, 1** touch at the border; be next to: *Canada borders on the United States.* **2** be close to; resemble: *Such silly behavior borders on the ridiculous.*

bor der land (bôr′dər land′), **1** land forming, or next to, a border. **2** an uncertain range, extent, or region: *the borderland between sleeping and waking. n.*

bor der line (bôr′dər līn′), **1** a dividing line; boundary. **2** on a border or boundary. **3** in between; uncertain: *a borderline case of pneumonia.* 1 *n.,* 2,3 *adj.*

bore[1] (bôr), **1** make a hole by means of a tool that keeps turning, or as a worm does in fruit: *Bore through the handle of this brush so we can hang it up.* **2** make (a hole, passage, etc.) by pushing through or digging out: *A mole has bored its way under the hedge.* **3** hole made by a revolving tool. **4** the hollow space inside a pipe, tube, or gun barrel. **5** the distance across the inside of a hole or tube: *The bore of this pipe is two inches.* 1,2 *v.,* **bored, bor ing;** 3-5 *n.*

bore[2] (bôr), **1** make weary by tiresome talk or by being dull: *This book bores me, so I shall not finish it.* **2** a dull, tiresome person or thing: *It is a bore to have to wash* *dishes three times a day.* **1** *v.,* **bored, bor ing; 2** *n.*

bore[3] (bôr), past tense of **bear**[1]. *She bore her loss bravely. v.*

bore dom (bôr/dəm), a bored condition; weariness caused by dull, tiresome people or events. *n.*

bor er (bôr/ər), **1** insect or worm that bores into wood, fruit, etc. **2** tool for boring holes. *n.*

bo ric acid (bôr/ik), a white, crystalline substance used as a mild antiseptic.

born (bôrn), **1** brought into life; brought forth: *a recently born calf.* **2** by birth; by nature: *a born athlete.* **3** a past participle of **bear**[1]. *He was born on December 30, 1960.* **1,2** *adj.,* **3** *v.*

be born again, have a spiritual experience that gives one a new and better spiritual life.

born-a gain (bôrn/ə gen/), having been born again: *a born-again Christian. adj.*

borne (bôrn), a past participle of **bear**[1]. *I have borne the pack for three miles. She has borne three children. v.*

Bor ne o (bôr/nē ō), large island in the East Indies, between Java and the Philippines. Part of Borneo is a British protectorate, part belongs to Malaysia, and part belongs to Indonesia. See **East Indies** for map. *n.*

bo ron (bôr/on), a nonmetallic element which occurs only in borax and other compounds. Boron is used in alloys, nuclear reactors, etc. *n.*

bor ough (bėr/ō), **1** (in some states of the United States) an incorporated town with certain privileges, smaller than a city. **2** one of the five divisions of New York City. **3** (in Alaska) a district similar to a county. *n.*

bor row (bor/ō), **1** get (something) from another person with the understanding that it must be returned: *I borrowed his book and promised to return it in a week.* **2** take and use as one's own; adopt; take: *The English word for the vegetable "squash" was borrowed from a Narragansett Indian word.* **3** (in subtraction) take (one) from the digit immediately to the left and add its place value to the digit being subtracted from: *In 46 − 19, borrow 10 from 40 to add to the 6, making the subtraction in the first digit 9 from 16. v.* **—bor/row er,** *n.*

borrow (def. 2)—a sampling of the many words borrowed into English from languages all over the world

NOODLE
borrowed from **GERMAN** *(European)*
BOOMERANG
borrowed from **NATIVE AUSTRALIAN**
HICKORY
borrowed from **ALGONQUIAN** *(North American)*
CHIMPANZEE
borrowed from **BANTU** *(African)*
PAJAMAS
borrowed from **HINDUSTANI** *(Asian)*
POTATO
borrowed from **NAHUATL** *(South American)*

bosh (bosh), INFORMAL. nonsense: *She thought the new theories were bosh* (n.). *"Bosh," he responded when asked for an opinion* (interj.). *n., interj.* [*Bosh* comes from Turkish *bos,* meaning "empty, worthless."]

bosk ẏ (bos/kē) **1** wooded. **2** shady. *adj.,* **bosk i er, bosk i est.**

bo's'n (bō/sn), boatswain. *n.*

bos om (bůz/əm), **1** the upper, front part of the human body; breast. **2** part of a garment that covers the bosom: *the bosom of a dress.* **3** heart or feelings: *He kept the secret*

in his bosom. **4** center or inmost part: *He did not mention it even in the bosom of his family.* **5** close and trusted: *Very dear friends are bosom friends.* **1-4** *n.,* **5** *adj.*

Bos por us (bos/pər əs), strait connecting the Black Sea and the Sea of Marmara. See **Dardanelles** for map. *n.*

boss[1] (bôs), **1** person who hires workers or watches over or directs them; foreman; manager. **2** person who controls a political organization. **3** be the boss of; direct; control: *Who is bossing this job?* **1,2** *n., pl.* **boss es; 3** *v.* [*Boss*[1] comes from Dutch *baas,* meaning "master."]

boss[2] (bôs), **1** a raised ornament of silver, ivory, or other material on a flat surface. **2** decorate with ornamental nails, knobs, or studs. **1** *n.,* **2** *v.* [*Boss*[2] came into English about 600 years ago from French *boce.*]

boss y (bô/sē), INFORMAL. fond of telling others what to do and how to do it. *adj.,* **boss i er, boss i est.**

Bos ton (bô/stən), seaport and capital of Massachusetts, on the Atlantic. *n.*

bo sun (bō/sn), boatswain. *n.*

bo tan ic (bə tan/ik), botanical. *adj.*

bo tan i cal (bə tan/ə kəl), **1** of plants and plant life. **2** of botany. *adj.* **—bo tan/i cal ly,** *adv.*

bot a nist (bot/n ist), an expert in botany. *n.*

bot a ny (bot/n ē), science of plants; study of plants and plant life. Botany deals with the structure, growth, classification, diseases, etc., of plants. *n.* [*Botany* comes from Greek *botanē,* meaning "a plant."]

botch (boch), **1** spoil by poor work; bungle: *I botched my essay and had to rewrite it.* **2** a poor piece of work. **1** *v.,* **2** *n., pl.* **botch es. —botch/er,** *n.*

botch y (boch/ē), poorly made or done. *adj.,* **botch i er, botch i est.**

both (bōth), **1** the two; the one and the other: *Both houses are white.* **2** the two together: *Both belong to her.* **3** together; alike; equally: *He fears and hopes both at once* (adv.). *He is both strong and healthy* (conj.). **1** *adj.,* **2** *pron.,* **3** *adv., conj.*

both er (boᴛʜ/ər), **1** much fuss or worry about small matters; trouble: *What a lot of bother about nothing!* **2** take trouble; concern oneself: *Don't bother about my breakfast; I'll eat what is here.* **3** person or thing that causes worry, fuss, or trouble: *A door that will not shut is a bother.* **4** annoy; irritate: *Hot weather bothers me.* **1,3** *n.,* **2,4** *v.*

both er some (boᴛʜ/ər səm), causing worry or fuss; troublesome. *adj.*

Bot swa na (bot swä/nə), country in S Africa, a member of the Commonwealth of Nations. *Capital:* Gaborone. See **South Africa** for map. *n.*

Bot ti cel li (bot/ə chel/ē), Sandro, 1444?-1510, Italian painter. *n.*

bot tle (bot/l), **1** container for holding liquids, made of glass, plastic, etc. Bottles often have narrow necks fitted with caps or stoppers. **2** amount that a bottle can hold: *drink a bottle of milk.* **3** put into bottles: *Dairies bottle milk.* **1,2** *n.,* **3** *v.,* **bot tled, bot tling. —bot/tle like/,** *adj.*

bottle up, hold in; keep back; control: *I managed to bottle up my anger.*

bot tle neck (bot/l nek/), person, thing, or condition that hinders progress: *The narrow bridge was a bottleneck during heavy traffic. n.*

bot tom (bot/əm), **1** the lowest part: *These berries at the bottom of the basket are crushed.* **2** part on which anything rests: *The bottom of that glass is wet.* **3** ground under water: *Many wrecks lie at the bottom of the sea.* **4** Often, **bottoms,** *pl.* the low land along a river. **5** seat: *This chair needs a new bottom.* **6** basis; foundation; origin: *We will get to the bottom of the mystery.* **7** keel or hull of a ship. **8** lowest or last: *I see a robin on the bottom branch of that tree.* **1-7** *n.,* **8** *adj.*

bot tom less (bot/əm lis), **1** without a bottom. **2** so deep that the bottom cannot be reached; extremely deep: *the bottomless depths of the sea. adj.*

bot u lism (boch/ə liz/əm), poisoning caused by certain bacteria sometimes present in foods not properly canned or preserved. *n.*

bou doir (bü/dwär), a lady's private bedroom, dressing room, or sitting room. *n.*

WORD HISTORY

boudoir

Boudoir came into English about 400 years ago from French *boudoir*, meaning "a place to sulk in."

bouf fant (bü fänt/), puffed out: *a bouffant hairdo. adj.*

bough (bou), one of the main branches of a tree. *n.*

bought (bôt), past tense and past participle of **buy.** *We bought apples at the market. I have bought a new pen. v.*

bouil lon (bùl/yon), a clear, thin soup or broth. *n.*

boul der (bōl/dər), a large rock, rounded or worn by the action of water and weather. *n.*

Boulder Dam, Hoover Dam.

boul e vard (bùl/ə värd), a broad street or avenue, often planted with trees. *n.*

bounce (bouns), **1** spring into the air like a ball: *The baby likes to bounce up and down on the bed.* **2** cause to bounce: *Bounce the ball to me.* **3** a bound; a spring; a bouncing: *I caught the ball on the first bounce.* **4** INFORMAL. (of a check) be returned uncashed by the bank on which it was drawn due to lack of funds in the account of the person who signed it. **5** SLANG. throw out; eject. 1,2,4,5 *v.,* **bounced, bounc ing;** 3 *n.*

bounce back, begin again, especially with enthusiasm or vigor.

bounc ing (boun/sing), **1** that bounces: *a bouncing ball.* **2** vigorous; healthy: *a bouncing baby. adj.* —**bounc/ing-ly,** *adv.*

bound[1] (bound), **1** under some obligation; obliged: *I feel bound by my promise.* **2** certain; sure: *Everyone is bound to make a mistake sooner or later.* **3** INFORMAL. with one's mind firmly made up; determined; resolved: *He was bound to go, though we tried to stop him.* **4** past tense and past participle of **bind.** *I bound the package with string. They had bound my hands.* **5** put in covers: *a bound book.* 1-3,5 *adj.,* 4 *v.*

bound up with, closely connected with: *The price of meat is bound up with the price of feed.*

bound[2] (bound), **1** spring back; bounce: *The ball bounded from the wall.* **2** a springing back; bounce: *I caught the ball on the first bound.* **3** leap or spring lightly along; jump: *Mountain goats can bound from rock to rock.* **4** a leaping or springing lightly along; jump: *With one bound the deer went into the woods.* 1,3 *v.,* 2,4 *n.*

bound[3] (bound), **1** Usually, **bounds,** *pl.* a limiting line; boundary; limit: *Keep your hopes within bounds.* **2** bounds, *pl.* area included within boundaries. **3** form the boundary of; limit: *Canada bounds the United States on the north.* **4** name the boundaries of: *Can you bound the state of Maine?* 1,2 *n.,* 3,4 *v.*

out of bounds, outside the area allowed by rules, custom, or law: *I kicked the ball out of bounds.*

bound[4] (bound), on the way; going: *I am bound for home. adj.*

bound ar y (boun/dər ē), a limiting line or thing; limit; border: *Lake Superior forms part of the boundary between Canada and the United States. n., pl.* **bound ar ies.**

bound en (boun/dən), required: *It is our bounden duty as citizens to obey the laws. adj.*

bound less (bound/lis), **1** not limited; infinite: *Outer space is boundless.* **2** vast: *the boundless ocean. She has boundless energy. adj.* —**bound/less ly,** *adv.*

boun te ous (boun/tē əs), **1** given freely; generous: *The rich man gave bounteous gifts to the poor.* **2** plentiful; abundant: *a bounteous crop. adj.* —**boun/te ous ly,** *adv.* —**boun/te ous ness,** *n.*

boun ti ful (boun/tə fəl), **1** giving freely; generous: *the help of bountiful friends.* **2** more than enough; plentiful; abundant: *We put in so many plants that we have a bountiful supply of tomatoes. adj.* —**boun/ti ful ly,** *adv.* —**boun/ti ful ness,** *n.*

boun ty (boun/tē), **1** whatever is given freely; generous gift. **2** generosity in bestowing gifts and favors: *the bounty of Nature.* **3** reward; premium: *The state government used to give a bounty for killing coyotes. n., pl.* **boun ties.**

bou quet (bō kā/ *or* bü kā/ *for 1;* bü kā/ *for 2*), **1** bunch of flowers. **2** fragrance; aroma: *the bouquet of a wine. n.*

bour bon (bėr/bən), kind of whiskey, distilled mainly from corn mash. *n.*

Bour bon (bùr/bən), a former royal family of France, Spain, Sicily, and Naples. The Bourbons were in power when the French Revolution began. *n.*

bour geois (bùr zhwä/), **1** person of the middle class, such as a merchant or professional person. **2** of the middle class. **3** like the middle class in way of thinking, appearance, etc.; ordinary: *bourgeois taste.* 1 *n., pl.* **bourgeois;** 2,3 *adj.*

bour geoi sie (bùr/zhwä zē/), the middle class; people between the very wealthy class and the working class. *n.*

bourn[1] or **bourne**[1] (bôrn), a small stream; brook. *n.*

bourn[2] or **bourne**[2] (bôrn *or* bōrn), OLD USE. **1** boundary; limit. **2** goal. *n.*

bout (bout), **1** trial of strength; contest: *Those are the two boxers who will appear in the main bout.* **2** period spent in some particular way; spell: *I have just had a long bout of illness. n.*

bou tique (bü tēk/), a small shop that specializes in stylish clothes and accessories, especially for women. *n.* [*Boutique* was borrowed from French *boutique,* and can be traced back to Greek *apothēkē,* meaning "storehouse."]

bo vine (bō/vīn), **1** ox or cow. **2** of or like an ox or cow; slow; dull. **3** like that of an ox or cow; without emotion; stolid: *a bovine nature.* **4** any animal belonging to a group of mammals that chew the cud, including domestic cattle, bison, water buffaloes, and the like. **5** belonging to this group. 1,4 *n.,* 2,3,5 *adj.*

bow[1] (bou), **1** bend the head or body in greeting, respect, worship, or submission: *The people bowed before the queen. Let us bow our heads in prayer.* **2** a bending of the head or body in this way. **3** show by bowing: *The actors bowed their thanks at the end of the play.* **4** cause to stoop; bend: *The old man was bowed by age.* **5** submit; yield: *She bowed to her parents' wishes.* 1,3-5 *v.,* 2 *n.*

bow out, withdraw.

take a bow, accept praise or applause for something done.

bow[2] (def. 4)
The branches
were broken
and **bowed** by
snow and ice.

bow[2] (bō), **1** weapon for shooting arrows. A bow usually consists of a strip of flexible wood bent by a string. **2** a slender rod with horsehairs stretched on it, for playing a violin, cello, etc. **3** play (a violin, cello, etc.) with a bow. **4** to curve; bend. **5** something curved; curved part: *A rainbow is a bow.* **6** a looped knot: *The gift had a bow on top.* 1,2,5,6 *n.,* 3,4 *v.* —**bow′like′,** *adj.*

bow[3] (bou), the forward part of a ship, boat, or aircraft. *n.*

bow el (bou′əl), **1** part of the bowels; intestine. **2** bowels, *pl.* **a** the tube in the body into which food passes from the stomach; intestines. **b** the inner part of anything: *Miners dig for coal in the bowels of the earth. n.*

bow er (bou′ər), **1** shelter of leafy branches. **2** arbor. *n.*

bow ie knife (bō′ē *or* bü′ē), a long, single-edged hunting knife carried in a sheath.

bowl[1] (bōl), **1** a hollow, rounded dish, usually without handles: *Cake batter was in the mixing bowl.* **2** amount that a bowl can hold: *She had a bowl of soup for lunch.* **3** the hollow, rounded part of anything: *The bowl of a pipe holds the tobacco.* **4** structure shaped somewhat like a bowl: *The Yale Bowl is a stadium used for football and other sports.* **5** a special football game played when the season is over: *the Orange Bowl. n.* —**bowl′like′,** *adj.*

bowl[2] (bōl), **1** play the game of bowling or lawn bowling. **2** roll or move along rapidly and smoothly: *The new bus bowled along on the highway. v.* —**bowl′er,** *n.*

bowl over, 1 knock over: *The force of the wind nearly bowled me over.* **2** INFORMAL. make helpless and confused: *I was bowled over by the bad news.*

bow leg ged (bō′leg′id), having the legs curved outward: *a bowlegged cowboy. adj.*

bow line (bō′lən *or* bō′līn), knot used to tie a loop. *n.*

bowline

bowl ing (bō′ling), game played indoors, in which balls are rolled down an alley at bottle-shaped wooden pins; tenpins. *n.*

bowling alley, 1 a long, narrow lane for rolling the balls in bowling; alley. **2** building having a number of lanes for bowling.

bowling green, a smooth, flat stretch of grass for playing the game of bowls.

bowls (bōlz), lawn bowling. *n.*

bow man (bō′mən), person who shoots with a bow and arrow; archer. *n., pl.* **bow men.**

bow sprit (bou′sprit′), pole or spar projecting forward from the bow of a ship. Ropes attached to the bowsprit help to steady sails and masts and hold the jib. *n.*

bow string (bō′string′), a strong cord stretched from the ends of a bow, pulled back by the archer to send the arrow forward. *n.*

bow tie (bō), a small necktie tied in a bow.

box[1] (boks), **1** container, usually with four sides, a bottom, and a lid, to pack or put things in: *We packed the boxes full of books.* **2** amount that a box can hold: *a box of soap.* **3** pack in a box; put into a box: *She boxed the candy before she sold it.* **4** a small enclosed space with chairs in a theater, stadium, etc. **5** an enclosed space in a courtroom for a jury, witnesses, newspaper reporters, etc. **6** the driver's seat on a coach, carriage, etc. **7** a small shelter: *a box for a sentry.* **8** (in baseball) place where the pitcher, batter, or catcher stands. 1,2,4-8 *n., pl.* **box es;** 3 *v.* —**box′er,** *n.* —**box′like′,** *adj.*

box in or **box up,** close in or surround; keep from getting out: *The dog had the cat boxed in on the porch.*

box[2] (boks), **1** a blow with the open hand or fist: *A box on the ear hurts.* **2** strike with such a blow: *I will box your ears if you yell at me again.* **3** fight with the fists as a sport: *He had not boxed since he left school.* 1 *n., pl.* **box es;** 2,3 *v.*

box[3] (boks), an evergreen shrub or small, bushy tree, much used for hedges, borders, etc. *n., pl.* **box es.**

box car (boks′kär′), a railroad freight car enclosed on all sides. Most boxcars are loaded and unloaded through a sliding door on either side. *n.*

box elder, a North American maple tree, often grown for shade or ornament.

box er (bok′sər), **1** person who fights with the fists as a sport, usually in padded gloves and according to special rules. **2** a medium-sized dog with a smooth brown coat, related to the bulldog and terrier. *n.*

box ing (bok′sing), act or sport of fighting with the fists. *n.*

boxing gloves, padded leather gloves worn when boxing.

box office, office or booth in a theater, hall, etc., where tickets of admission are sold.

box wood (boks′wûd′), **1** the hard, fine-grained wood of the box tree. **2** the tree. *n.*

boy (boi), **1** a male child from birth to about eighteen. **2** a male servant. This meaning of *boy* is often considered offensive. *n.*

boy cott (boi′kot), **1** join together against and agree not to buy from, sell to, or associate with (a person, business, or nation) in order to force a change or to punish. **2** refuse to buy or use (a product or service). **3** act of boycotting. 1,2 *v.,* 3 *n.*

WORD HISTORY

boycott

Boycott comes from Captain Charles Boycott, 1832-1897, an Irish estate manager whose tenants would have nothing to do with him when he refused to lower rents in hard times.

boy friend (boi′frend′), INFORMAL. **1** a girl's sweetheart or steady male companion. **2** a male friend. *n.*

boy hood (boi′hùd), time of being a boy. *n.*

boy ish (boi′ish), **1** of a boy. **2** like a boy. **3** like a boy's;

suitable for a boy. *adj.* —**boy′ish ly,** *adv.*

boy scout, member of the Boy Scouts.

Boy Scouts, organization for boys that seeks to develop character, citizenship, usefulness to others, and outdoor skills.

boy sen ber ry (boi′zn ber′ē), a purple berry like a blackberry in size and shape, and like a raspberry in flavor. Boysenberries grow on trailing, thorny plants and are good to eat. *n., pl.* **boy sen ber ries.**

Br, symbol for bromine.

Br., **1** Britain. **2** British.

bra (brä), brassiere. *n., pl.* **bras.**

brace (brās), **1** thing that holds parts together or in place, such as a timber used to strengthen a building or a metal frame to hold the ankle straight. **2 braces,** *pl.*
a metal wires used to straighten crooked teeth.
b BRITISH. suspenders. **3** give strength or firmness to; support: *We braced the roof with four poles.* **4** prepare (oneself): *I braced myself for the crash.* **5** give strength and energy to; refresh: *The mountain air braced us after the long climb.* **6** a pair; couple: *a brace of ducks.* **7** handle for a tool or drill used for boring. **8** either of these signs { }, used to enclose words, figures, staffs in music, or a set in arithmetic. 1,2,6-8 *n.,* 3-5 *v.,* **braced, brac ing.**

brace up, gather one's strength or courage anew: *He braced up after his defeat and decided to run again in the next election.*

brace let (brās′lit), band or chain worn for ornament around the wrist or arm. *n.*

brac ing (brā′sing), giving strength and energy; refreshing. *adj.* —**brac′ing ly,** *adv.*

brack en (brak′ən), **1** a large, coarse fern common on hillsides, in woods, etc.; brake³. **2** thicket of these ferns. *n.*

brack et (brak′it), **1** a flat piece of stone, wood, or metal projecting from a wall as a support for a shelf, a statue, etc. **2** to support with a bracket: *She bracketed the shelves to make them stronger.* **3** shelf supported by brackets.
4 either of these signs [ ], used to enclose words or figures. The word histories in this dictionary are enclosed in brackets. *In the article, brackets were used to show which parts expressed the author's own opinion.*
5 enclose within brackets: *The teacher bracketed the mistakes in my homework.* **6** think of or mention together; group in the same class or category. **7** any group thought of or mentioned together; class or category: *a family in a low income bracket.* 1,3,4,7 *n.,* 2,5,6 *v.*

brack ish (brak′ish), **1** slightly salty. Coastal marshes often have brackish waters. **2** distasteful; unpleasant. *adj.*

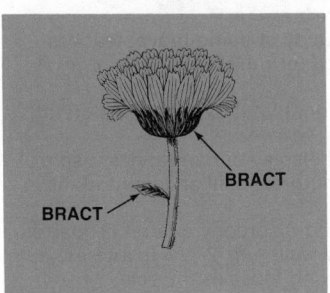

BRACT

BRACT

bract (brakt), a small leaf growing at the base of a flower or on a flower stalk. *n.*

brad (brad), a small, thin nail with a small head. *n.*

Brad dock (brad′ək), **Edward,** 1695-1755, British general, commander in America during the French and Indian War. *n.*

a hat	i it	oi oil	ch child	⎧ a in about
ā age	ī ice	ou out	ng long	⎪ e in taken
ä far	o hot	u cup	sh she	ə = ⎨ i in pencil
e let	ō open	u̇ put	th thin	⎪ o in lemon
ē equal	ô order	ü rule	ᴛʜ then	⎩ u in circus
ėr term			zh measure	

Brad ford (brad′fərd), **William,** 1590-1657, Pilgrim leader and second governor of Plymouth Colony. *n.*

brae (brā), SCOTTISH. hillside. *n.*

brag (brag), **1** praise oneself or what one has; boast: *They bragged about their new car.* **2** a boast. **3** boasting talk. 1 *v.,* **bragged, brag ging;** 2,3 *n.*

brag gart (brag′ərt), person who brags; boaster. *n.*

brag ger (brag′ər), person who brags; boaster. *n.*

Brah ma (brä′mə *for 1;* brā′mə *or* brä′mə *for 2*), **1** the Hindu god of creation. **2** Brahman, a kind of cattle. *n.*

Brah man (brä′mən), **1** member of the priestly caste, the highest caste in India. **2** kind of cattle, originally imported from India. *n.*

Brahms (brämz), **Johannes,** 1833-1897, German composer. *n.*

braid (brād), **1** band formed by weaving together three or more strands of hair, ribbon, straw, etc.: *She wore her hair in braids.* **2** weave or twine together (three or more strands of hair, ribbon, straw, etc.): *We braided strips of wool and made a rug.* **3** make by weaving such strands together: *to braid a rug.* **4** a narrow band of fabric used to trim or bind clothing: *a uniform trimmed with gold braid.* 1,4 *n.,* 2,3 *v.* —**braid′er,** *n.*

Braille or **braille** (brāl), system of writing and printing for blind people. The letters in Braille are represented by different arrangements of raised points and are read by touching them. *n.* [*Braille* comes from Louis *Braille,* 1809-1852, a French teacher of the blind who invented this system.]

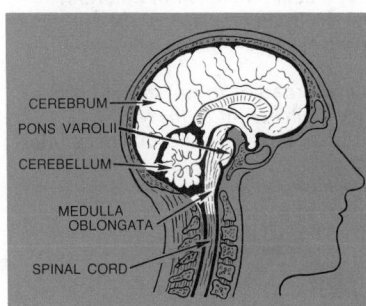

CEREBRUM
PONS VAROLII
CEREBELLUM

MEDULLA
OBLONGATA

SPINAL CORD

brain (def. 1)
parts of the
human brain

brain (brān), **1** the part of the central nervous system in humans and other vertebrates that is enclosed in the skull or head and consists of a soft mass of nerve cells and nerve fibers. The brain controls almost all the functions of the body and with it we can learn, think, and remember. **2** kill by smashing the skull of. **3** a large electronic computer or an electronic device to control some mechanism. **4** Often, **brains,** *pl.* intelligence: *It takes brains to get into that university.* **5** INFORMAL. a very intelligent person. 1,3-5 *n.,* 2 *v.* [*Brain* comes from Old English *brægen.*]

rack one's brains, try very hard to think: *He racked his brains for his friend's phone number, but he couldn't remember it.*

brain cell, a nerve cell in the brain.

brain less (brān′lis), without brains; stupid; foolish. *adj.* —**brain′less ly,** *adv.* —**brain′less ness,** *n.*

brain pan (brān′pan′), cranium. *n.*

brain storm (brān'stôrm'), INFORMAL. a sudden idea or inspiration. *n.*

brain wash (brān'wosh' *or* brān'wôsh'), destroy or weaken a person's beliefs and ideas through torture or other methods, so that one becomes willing to accept different or opposite beliefs and ideas. *v.* —**brain'-wash'er,** *n.*

brain y (brā'nē), INFORMAL. intelligent; clever. *adj.,* **brain i er, brain i est.** —**brain'i ness,** *n.*

braise (brāz), brown (meat or vegetables) quickly in fat and then cook long and slowly in a covered pan with very little water. *v.,* **braised, brais ing.**

brake¹ (brāk), **1** anything used to slow or stop the motion of a wheel or vehicle by pressing or scraping or by rubbing against. **2** slow or stop by using a brake: *The driver braked the speeding car and it slid to a stop.* 1 *n.,* 2 *v.,* **braked, brak ing.** —**brake'less,** *adj.*

brake² (brāk), a thick growth of bushes; thicket. *n.*

brake³ (brāk), bracken, a large, coarse fern. *n.*

brake man (brāk'mən), member of a train crew who helps the conductor; trainman. *n., pl.* **brake men.**

bram ble (bram'bəl), shrub related to the rose, with slender, drooping branches covered with little thorns that prick. Blackberry and raspberry plants are brambles. *n.*

bram bly (bram'blē), **1** full of brambles: *a brambly field.* **2** like brambles; prickly: *a brambly bush. adj.,* **bram bli er, bram bli est.**

bran (bran), the outer covering of the grains of wheat, rye, etc., which is often separated from the inner part in the process of milling flour. Bran is used in cereal, bread, and as food for farm animals. *n.*

branch (branch), **1** part of a tree growing out from the trunk; any wood part of a tree above the ground except the trunk. A bough is a large branch. A twig is a very small branch. **2** division; part: *a branch of a river, a branch of a family. History is a branch of learning.* **3** a local office: *a branch of a bank, a branch of a library.* **4** divide into branches: *The road branches at the bottom of the hill.* 1-3 *n., pl.* **branch es;** 4 *v.* —**branch'less,** *adj.* —**branch'like',** *adj.*

branch off, go off (a main road or route) in a different direction: *The new route branches off to the left.*

branch out, 1 put out branches. **2** extend business interests or activities: *They used to be only printers; now they are branching out into publishing books.*

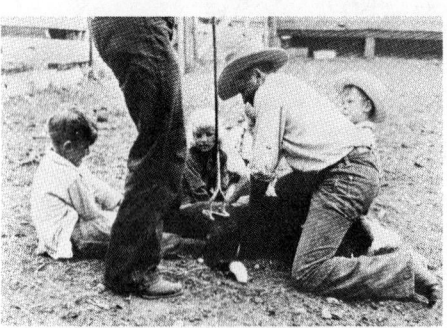

brand
(def. 5)
branding
a calf

brand (brand), **1** a certain kind, grade, or make: *Do you like this brand of flour?* **2** a name or mark that a company uses to distinguish its goods from the goods of others; trademark. **3** an iron stamp for burning a mark. **4** a mark made by burning the skin with a hot iron: *The cattle on this big ranch are identified by a brand which shows who owns them.* **5** to mark by burning the skin with a hot iron. In former times criminals were often branded. **6** a mark of disgrace: *He could never rid himself of the brand of*

coward. **7** put a mark of disgrace on: *She has been branded as a traitor.* **8** piece of wood that is burning or partly burned. 1-4,6,8 *n.,* 5,7 *v.* —**brand'er,** *n.*

bran dish (bran'dish), wave or shake in a threatening manner: *The knight brandished his sword at his enemy. v.*

brand-new (brand'nü' *or* brand'nyü'), very new; entirely new. *adj.*

bran dy (bran'dē), **1** a strong alcoholic liquor distilled from wine or fermented fruit juice. **2** mix, flavor, or preserve with brandy. 1 *n., pl.* **bran dies;** 2 *v.,* **bran died, bran dy ing.** [*Brandy* comes from Dutch *brandewijn,* meaning "burnt, or distilled, wine."]

brant (brant), a small, dark, wild goose. It breeds in arctic regions and migrates south in the autumn. *n., pl.* **brants** or **brant.**

brash (brash), **1** showing lack of respect; impudent; saucy: *The brash boy contradicted his parents all the time.* **2** hasty; rash: *When I got over being angry, I regretted my brash act. adj.* —**brash'ly,** *adv.* —**brash'ness,** *n.*

Bra sí lia (brə zē'lyə), capital of Brazil since 1960, in the central part. *n.*

brass (bras), **1** a yellowish metal that is an alloy of copper and zinc. **2** ornaments, dishes, or other things made of brass: *I polished all the brass.* **3** made of brass: *brass candlesticks.* **4** Also, **brasses,** *pl.* musical instruments made of metal. The trumpet, trombone, and French horn are brasses. **5** INFORMAL. rude boldness; impudence: *She had the brass to go to the party uninvited.* **6** SLANG. military officers of high rank. 1,2,4-6 *n., pl.* **brass es;** 3 *adj.*

bras siere (brə zir'), a woman's undergarment worn to support the breasts. *n.*

brass i ly (bras'ə lē), in a brassy manner. *adv.*

brass i ness (bras'ē nis), brassy quality or appearance. *n.*

brass y (bras'ē), **1** like brass: *a brassy green sky.* **2** loud and harsh: *The brassy music soon gave me a headache.* **3** INFORMAL. shameless; impudent: *a brassy manner. adj.,* **brass i er, brass i est.**

brat (brat), a rude, annoying, or unpleasant child. *n.*

brat ty (brat'ē), INFORMAL. disobedient; impudent. *adj.,* **brat ti er, brat ti est.**

bra va do (brə vä'dō), a great show of boldness without much real courage or real desire to fight. *n.*

brave (brāv), **1** without fear; having or showing courage: *The brave girl went into the burning house to save a baby.* **2** brave people: *The United States has been called "the land of the free and the home of the brave."* **3** meet without fear; defy: *The early settlers braved the hardships of life in a new land.* **4** a North American Indian warrior. 1 *adj.,* **brav er, brav est;** 2,4 *n.,* 3 *v.,* **braved, brav ing.** —**brave'ly,** *adv.* —**brave'ness,** *n.*

brav er y (brā'vər ē), quality of being brave; fearlessness; courage: *They owed their lives to the bravery of the firefighters. n.*

bra vo (brä'vō), **1** well done! fine! excellent! **2** a cry of "bravo!" 1 *interj.,* 2 *n., pl.* **bra vos.**

bra vur a (brə vyur'ə), **1** display of daring; dash; spirit. **2** piece of music requiring great skill and spirit in the performer. *n.*

brawl (brôl), **1** a noisy and disorderly quarrel. **2** quarrel in a noisy and disorderly way. 1 *n.,* 2 *v.* —**brawl'er,** *n.*

brawn (brôn), **1** firm, strong muscles; muscle. **2** muscular strength: *Football requires brains as well as brawn. n.*

brawn y (brô'nē), strong; muscular. *adj.,* **brawn i er, brawn i est.** —**brawn'i ness,** *n.*

bray (brā), **1** the loud, harsh cry or noise made by a donkey. **2** a sound like this. **3** make this sound: *The trumpets brayed.* 1,2 *n.,* 3 *v.* —**bray'er,** *n.*

bra zen (brā'zn), having no shame; shameless: *The bra-*

zen girl told lie after lie. adj. —**bra′zen ly,** adv. —**bra′zen-ness,** n.

brazen it out or **brazen it through,** act as if one did not feel ashamed of it: *Although he was caught lying, he tried to brazen it out by telling another lie.*

bra zier (brā′zhər), a large, metal pan or tray to hold burning charcoal or coal. n.

Bra zil (brə zil′), largest country in South America. *Capital:* Brasília. n.

Bra zil ian (brə zil′yən), **1** of Brazil or its people. **2** person born or living in Brazil. 1 adj., 2 n.

Brazil nut, a large, triangular nut of a tree growing in Brazil. It is good to eat.

Braz za ville (braz′ə vil), capital of Congo, in the S part. n.

breach (brēch), **1** an opening made by breaking down something solid; gap: *Cannon fire had made a breach in the wall of the fort.* **2** break through; make an opening in: *The wall had been breached in several places.* **3** a breaking or neglect: *For me to leave now would be a breach of duty.* **4** a breaking of friendly relations; quarrel: *There was never a breach between the two friends.* 1,3,4 n., pl. **breach es;** 2 v. —**breach′er,** n.

bread (bred), **1** food made of flour or meal mixed with milk or water and usually shortening and yeast. Bread is kneaded, set to rise, and baked in a loaf. **2** means of keeping alive; food; livelihood: *How will you earn your daily bread?* **3** cover with bread crumbs before cooking: *to bread chicken before frying it.* **4** SLANG. money. 1,2,4 n., 3 v. [Bread comes from Old English *brēad*.] —**bread′less,** adj.

break bread, share a meal.

bread and butter, things necessary to live; a living: *He earns his bread and butter by selling cars.*

bread fruit (bred′früt′), the large, round, starchy fruit of a tropical tree grown in the islands of the Pacific and much used for food. When baked, the fruit tastes somewhat like bread. n.

bread stuff (bred′stuf′), **1** Also **breadstuffs,** pl. grain, flour, or meal for making bread. **2** bread. n.

breadth (bredth), **1** how broad a thing is; distance across; width: *He has traveled the length and the breadth of this land.* **2** freedom from narrowness in outlook: *A tolerant person usually has breadth of mind.* n.

bread win ner (bred′win′ər), person who earns a living and supports a family. n.

break (brāk), **1** come apart or make come apart; smash: *The plate broke into pieces when it fell on the floor. I broke the window with a ball.* **2** a broken place; crack: *a break in the wall.* **3** damage; injure: *She broke her watch by winding it too tightly.* **4** crack or split the bone of: *to break*

one's arm. **5** fail to keep; act against: *to break a promise. People who break the law are punished.* **6** force one's way: *The lion broke loose from its cage.* **7** a forcing one's way out: *The prisoners made a break for freedom.* **8** come suddenly: *The storm broke within ten minutes.* **9** change suddenly: *The spell of rainy weather has broken. His voice broke with emotion.* **10** an abrupt or marked change: *a break in the weather.* **11** a short interruption in work, athletic practice, etc.: *a five-minute break between classes.* **12** decrease the force of; lessen: *The bushes broke my fall from the tree.* **13** become weak; give way; fail: *Her spirit broke when she lost her job.* **14** dawn; appear: *The day is breaking.* **15** put an end to; stop: *break one's fast, break a strike.* **16** train to obey; tame: *break a colt.* **17** go beyond; exceed: *The speed of the new train has broken all records.* **18** dig or plow: *to break ground for a new building.* **19** make known; reveal: *Someone must break the news of the girl's accident to her parents.* **20** SLANG. chance; opportunity: *Finding that money was a lucky break.* **21** (in baseball) to curve or swerve abruptly: *The pitcher threw a ball that broke over the plate.* **22** act of breaking. 1,3–6,8,9,12–19,21 v., **broke, bro ken, break ing;** 2,7,10,11,20,22 n.

break away, 1 start before the signal: *The excited horse broke away at a gallop.* **2** pull or run away from; escape: *The rabbit broke away from my arms.*

break down, 1 go out of order; fail to work: *The car's engine broke down.* **2** become weak; fail suddenly; collapse: *Her health broke down.* **3** begin to cry: *He broke down when he heard the bad news.* **4** separate or divide into parts, steps, etc.: *break down a chemical.*

break in, 1 prepare for work or use; train: *to break in a new salesperson.* **2** enter by force: *The thieves broke in through the cellar.* **3** interrupt: *She broke in with a funny remark.*

break into, 1 enter by force: *A robber broke into the house.* **2** begin suddenly: *She broke into a run.* **3** interrupt: *He broke into their conversation.*

break off, 1 stop suddenly: *He broke off in the middle of his speech to clear his throat.* **2** stop being friends: *She broke off with the old crowd when she went away to college.*

break out, 1 start suddenly; begin: *War broke out. A fire broke out in the garage.* **2** have pimples, rashes, etc., appear on the skin: *The child broke out with measles.* **3** burst out: *A cry of horror broke out among the spectators when someone yelled "Fire!"* **4** leave by force; escape: *The thief broke out of jail.*

break up, 1 scatter: *The fog is breaking up.* **2** come or bring to an end: *The committee broke up its meeting early. Their marriage is breaking up.* **3** disturb greatly; upset: *The news of his sister's death broke him up.* **4** laugh or cause to laugh, especially in a hearty or an uncontrollable manner: *The audience broke up at the comedian's jokes. The clown's antics broke us up.*

break with, stop being friends with: *They broke with me after our fight.*

break a ble (brā′kə bəl), able to be broken. adj.

break age (brā′kij), **1** a breaking; break. **2** damage or loss caused by breaking. **3** allowance made for such damage or loss. n.

break down (brāk′doun′), **1** failure to work: *Lack of oil caused a breakdown in the motor.* **2** failure of health; collapse: *If you don't stop worrying, you will have a nervous* *breakdown.* **3** separation or division of anything into parts, steps, etc. *n.*

break er (brā′kər), wave that breaks into foam on the beach or on rocks. *n.*

break fast (brek′fəst), **1** the first meal of the day. **2** eat breakfast: *I like to breakfast alone.* **1** *n.,* **2** *v.*

break-in (brāk′in′), burglary. *n.*

break neck (brāk′nek′), likely to cause a broken neck; very dangerous: *The car traveled at breakneck speed. adj.*

break of day, dawn.

break out (brāk′out′), **1** an escaping from a prison. **2** breakthrough (def. 1). *n.*

break through (brāk′thrü′), **1** a military attack that gets through the enemy defense system into the area in the rear. **2** achievement or solution of some baffling or technical problem: *an important breakthrough in medical research. n.*

break up (brāk′up′), **1** a scattering; separation. **2** a stopping; end. *n.*

breakwater

break wa ter (brāk′wô′tər *or* brāk′wot′ər), wall or barrier built to break the force of waves. *n.*

bream (brēm), **1** carp of inland European waters. **2** the common freshwater sunfish of the United States. *n., pl.* **breams** *or* **bream.**

breast (brest), **1** the upper, front part of the body between the shoulders and the stomach; chest. **2** gland that gives milk. **3** heart or feelings: *Pity tore his breast.* **4** struggle with; face or oppose: *The swimmer breasted the waves with powerful strokes.* **1-3** *n.,* **4** *v.*

make a clean breast of, confess completely: *When he was shown proof that he broke the window, he made a clean breast of it.*

breast bone (brest′bōn′), the thin, flat bone in the front of the chest to which the ribs are attached by cartilages; sternum. *n.*

breast-feed (brest′fēd′), feed milk to (a baby) at the breast; nurse. *v.,* **breast fed, breast feed ing.**

breast plate (brest′plāt′), piece of armor worn over the chest. *n.*

breast stroke (brest′strōk′), stroke in swimming in which the swimmer lies face downward, draws both arms at one time from in front of the head to the sides, and kicks like a frog. *n.*

breast work (brest′werk′), a low, sometimes hastily built wall for defense. *n.*

breath (breth), **1** air drawn into and forced out of the lungs. **2** act of breathing: *Hold your breath a moment.* **3** moisture in the air when a person breathes out: *You can see your breath on a very cold day.* **4** ability to breathe easily: *Running so fast made me lose my breath.* **5** a slight movement in the air; light breeze: *Not a breath was stirring.* **6** a slight trace or suggestion; hint: *a breath of scandal. n.*

below one's breath, in a whisper.

catch one's breath, 1 gasp; pant: *The dogs were catching* their breath after a long chase. **2** stop for breath; rest: *The hikers sat down to catch their breath.*

in the next breath or **in the same breath,** at the same time.

out of breath, short of breath; breathless: *At the end of the race the winner was out of breath.*

under one's breath, in a whisper: *She was talking under her breath so no one could hear.*

breathe (brēᴛʜ), **1** draw air into the lungs and force it out. One breathes through the nose or through the mouth. **2** stop for breath; rest; allow to rest and breathe: *At last there is time to breathe. At the top of the hill the rider breathed his horse.* **3** say softly; whisper; utter: *Don't breathe a word of this to anyone.* **4** be alive; live: *As long as I breathe, I will remember all you've done for me.* **5** send out; give: *Her enthusiasm breathed new life into our club. v.,* **breathed, breath ing.**

breathe one's last, die.

breath er (brē′ᴛʜər), a short stop for breath; rest. *n.*

breath less (breth′lis), **1** out of breath: *Running upstairs very fast made me breathless.* **2** holding one's breath because of fear, amazement, excitement, etc.: *The beauty of the scenery left us breathless. adj.* —**breath′less ly,** *adv.* —**breath′less ness,** *n.*

breath tak ing (breth′tā′king), thrilling; exciting: *a breathtaking ride on a roller coaster. adj.* —**breath′tak′ing ly,** *adv.*

Breck in ridge (brek′ən rij), **John C.,** 1821-1875, American statesman and Confederate general, vice-president of the United States from 1857 to 1861. *n.*

bred (bred), past tense and past participle of **breed.** *He bred cattle for market. Those parents have bred their children to be honest. v.*

breech (brēch), **1** part of a gun behind the barrel. **2** the lower part; back part. *n., pl.* **breech es.**

breech cloth (brēch′klôth′), loincloth. *n., pl.* **breech-cloths** (brēch′klôᴛʜz′ *or* brēch′klôths′).

breech es (brich′iz *or* brē′chiz), **1** short trousers fastened below the knees. **2** trousers. *n.pl.*

breeches (def. 1)

breeches buoy, pair of short canvas trousers fastened to a belt or life preserver. A breeches buoy slides along a rope on a pulley and is used to rescue people from sinking ships or to transfer people from one ship to another.

breed (brēd), **1** produce young: *Rabbits breed rapidly.* **2** raise or grow, especially to get new or improved kinds: *to breed new varieties of corn, to breed cattle and hogs for market.* **3** be the cause of; produce: *Careless driving breeds accidents.* **4** bring up; train: *The princess was born and bred to one day be queen.* **5** group of animals or plants looking much alike and having the same ancestry: *Terriers and spaniels are breeds of dogs.* **6** kind; sort: *The people of the early West were a hardy breed.* **1-4** *v.,* **bred, breeding; 5,6** *n.* —**breed′a ble,** *adj.*

breed er (brē′dər), person who breeds animals or plants: *a dog breeder. n.*

breeder reactor, reactor that produces at least as much fissionable material as it uses. In one type of reaction it consumes uranium and produces plutonium.

breed ing (brē′ding), **1** the producing of animals or new types of plants, especially to get improved kinds: *Breeding has produced types of wheat which can be grown in the far North.* **2** bringing up; training; behavior; manners: *Politeness is a sign of good breeding. n.*

breeze (brēz), **1** a light, gentle wind. **2** INFORMAL. move easily or briskly: *She breezed through her homework.* **3** INFORMAL. anything that is easily done: *The history test was a breeze.* 1,3 *n.,* 2 *v.,* **breezed, breez ing.**

breeze way (brēz′wā′), a roofed passage open at the sides between a house and a garage. *n.*

breez i ly (brē′zə lē), in a breezy manner. *adv.*

breez i ness (brē′zē nis), breezy condition. *n.*

breez y (brē′zē), **1** having many breezes; with light winds blowing: *It was a breezy day.* **2** lively and jolly: *We like her breezy, joking manner.* adj., **breez i er, breez i est.**

br'er (brėr), DIALECT. brother: *Br'er Rabbit. n.*

breth ren (breŦH′rən), **1** the fellow members of a church, society, or religious order. **2** OLD USE. brothers. *n.pl.*

Bret on (bret′n), **1** person born in Brittany. **2** language of Brittany. **3** of Brittany, its people, or their language: *Breton folklore.* 1,2 *n.,* 3 *adj.*

bre vi ar y (brē′vē er′ē), book of prayers to be said daily by Roman Catholic and Anglican clergymen. *n., pl.* **bre vi ar ies.**

brev i ty (brev′ə tē), shortness; briefness: *The brevity of the speech was appreciated by the audience. n.*

brew (brü), **1** make (beer, ale, etc.) by soaking, boiling, and fermenting malt, hops, etc. **2** make (a drink) by soaking, boiling, or mixing: *Tea is brewed in boiling water.* **3** a drink that is brewed: *The last brew of beer tasted bad.* **4** bring about; plan; plot: *The group whispering in the corner is brewing some mischief.* **5** begin to form; gather: *Dark clouds show that a storm is brewing.* 1,2,4,5 *v.,* 3 *n.*

brew er (brü′ər), person who brews beer, ale, etc. *n.*

brew er y (brü′ər ē), place where beer, ale, etc., is brewed. *n., pl.* **brew er ies.**

Brezh nev (brezh′nef), **Leonid I.,** 1906-1982, Russian political leader, first secretary of the Soviet Communist Party from 1964 to 1982, and president of the Soviet Union from 1977 to 1982. *n.*

bri ar[1] (brī′ər), brier[1]. *n.*

bri ar[2] (brī′ər), brier[2]. *n.*

bri ar wood (brī′ər wùd′), brierwood. *n.*

bribe (brīb), **1** money or other reward given or offered to a person to do something dishonest, unlawful, etc.: *The driver who caused the accident offered the police officer a bribe to let her go.* **2** a reward for doing something that a person does not want to do: *The stubborn child needed a bribe to go to bed.* **3** give or offer a bribe to: *A gambler bribed one of the boxers to lose the fight.* 1,2 *n.,* 3 *v.,* **bribed, brib ing. —brib′a ble,** *adj.* **—brib′er,** *n.*

brib er y (brī′bər ē), **1** the giving or offering of a bribe. **2** the taking of a bribe: *The dishonest detective was arrested for bribery. n., pl.* **brib er ies.**

bric-a-brac (brik′ə brak′), interesting or curious trinkets used as decorations; small ornaments, such as vases, old china, or small statues. *n.*

brick (brik), **1** block of clay baked by sun or fire. Bricks are used to build walls or houses, pave walks, etc. **2** these blocks used as building material: *Chimneys are usually built of brick.* **3** made of bricks: *a brick house.* **4** anything shaped like a brick: *Ice cream is often sold in bricks.* **5** build or pave with bricks; cover or fill in with

bricks: *The old window had been bricked up for many years.* 1,2,4 *n., pl.* **bricks** or **brick;** 3 *adj.,* 5 *v.*

brick bat (brik′bat′), **1** piece of broken brick: *The speaker was injured by brickbats hurled from the crowd.* **2** an insult. *n.*

brick lay er (brik′lā′ər), person whose work is building with bricks. *n.*

brick lay ing (brik′lā′ing), act or work of building with bricks. *n.*

brick work (brik′wėrk′), wall, foundation, or other structure made of bricks. *n.*

brid al (brī′dl), of a bride or a wedding: *a bridal veil, the bridal cake. adj.*

bride (brīd), woman just married or about to be married. *n.*

bride groom (brīd′grüm′ or brīd′grùm′), man just married or about to be married; groom. *n.*

brides maid (brīdz′mād′), a young woman who attends the bride at a wedding. *n.*

bridge[1] (brij), **1** something built over a river, road, railroad, or other obstacle, so that people, cars, trains, etc., can get across. **2** make a way over a river or other obstacle; make or form a bridge over: *The engineers bridged the river. Politeness will bridge many difficulties.* **3** platform above the deck of a ship for the officer in command: *The captain directed the course of his ship from the bridge.* **4** the upper, bony part of the nose. **5** the curved part of a pair of eyeglasses which rests on the nose. **6** false tooth or teeth in a mounting fastened to nearby natural teeth. **7** a thin, arched piece over which the strings of a violin or some other stringed instrument are stretched. 1,3-7 *n.,* 2 *v.,* **bridged, bridg ing.** [*Bridge*[1] comes from Old English *brycg.*] **—bridge′a ble,** *adj.* **—bridge′like′,** *adj.*

bridge[2] (brij), a card game for two pairs of players played with 52 cards. *n.*

bridge head (brij′hed′), position obtained and held by troops within enemy territory, used as a starting point for further attack. *n.*

Bridge town (brij′toun), capital of Barbados. *n.*

bridge work (brij′wėrk′), false teeth in a mounting fastened to real teeth nearby. *n.*

bridle (def. 1)

bri dle (brī′dl), **1** the part of a harness that fits around a horse's head including the bit and reins which control the animal. **2** put a bridle on: *I saddled and bridled my horse.* **3** anything that holds back or controls; curb. **4** hold back; bring under control; check: *Bridle your temper.* **5** hold the head up high with the chin drawn back to show pride, scorn, or anger: *She bridled when we criticized her ideas.* 1,3 *n.,* 2,4,5 *v.,* **bri dled, bri dling. —bri′dler,** *n.*

bridle path, path for riding horses.

brief (brēf), **1** lasting only a short time: *The meeting was brief. A brief shower fell in the afternoon.* **2** using few words: *She made a brief announcement. Be as brief as you can.* **3** a short statement; summary: *The lawyer prepared a brief of the facts and the points of law in the case.* **4** give detailed information to: *The park ranger briefed the campers on fire prevention.* 1,2 *adj.,* 3 *n.,* 4 *v.* —**brief′ly,** *adv.* —**brief′ness,** *n.*

in brief, in a few words: *Let me give you the facts in brief.*

brief case (brēf′kās′), a flat container for carrying loose papers, books, drawings, etc. A briefcase is often made of leather and has a handle. *n.*

bri er[1] (brī′ər), bush that has a thorny or prickly, woody stem. The blackberry plant and the wild rose are often called briers. *n.* Also, **briar.**

bri er[2] (brī′ər), **1** a white heath tree found in southern Europe. Its root is used in making tobacco pipes. **2** a tobacco pipe made of brierwood. *n.* Also, **briar.**

bri er wood (brī′ər wùd′), the wood of brier roots, used in making tobacco pipes. *n.* Also, **briarwood.**

brig (brig), **1** ship with two masts and square sails set at right angles across the ship. **2** prison on a warship. *n.*

Brig., 1 brigade. **2** Brigadier.

bri gade (bri gād′), **1** part of an army made up of two or more regiments or groups, commanded by a brigadier general or a colonel. **2** any group of people organized for some purpose. A fire brigade puts out fires. *n.*

brig a dier (brig′ə dir′), brigadier general. *n.*

brigadier general, a military officer next in rank above a colonel and below a major general.

brig and (brig′ənd), person who robs travelers on the road, especially one of a gang of robbers in mountain or forest regions; robber; bandit. *n.*

brig an tine (brig′ən tēn′), ship with two masts. The foremast is square-rigged; the mainmast is fore-and-aft-rigged. *n.*

bright (brīt), **1** giving much light; shining: *The stars are bright, but sunshine is brighter.* **2** very light or clear: *It is a bright day. Dandelions are bright yellow.* **3** clever; quick-witted: *A bright student learns quickly.* **4** lively or cheerful: *There was a bright smile on his face.* **5** likely to turn out well; favorable: *There is a bright outlook for the future.* **6** in a bright manner: *The fire shines bright.* 1-5 *adj.,* 6 *adv.* —**bright′ly,** *adv.* —**bright′ness,** *n.*

bright en (brīt′n), make or become bright or brighter: *Flowers brighten the fields in the spring. The sky brightened after the storm. v.*

brill (bril), a European flatfish related to the turbot. *n., pl.* **brills** or **brill.**

bril liance (bril′yəns), **1** great brightness; radiance; sparkle: *the brilliance of a fine diamond.* **2** splendor; magnificence: *the brilliance of the royal court.* **3** great ability: *His brilliance as a pianist was soon recognized. n.*

bril lian cy (bril′yən sē), brilliance. *n.*

bril liant (bril′yənt), **1** shining brightly; sparkling: *brilliant jewels, brilliant sunshine.* **2** splendid; magnificent: *The singer gave a brilliant performance.* **3** having great ability: *a brilliant musician.* **4** diamond or other gem cut to sparkle brightly. 1-3 *adj.,* 4 *n.* —**bril′liant ly,** *adv.*

brim (brim), **1** edge of a cup, bowl, etc.: *a glass filled to the brim.* **2** edge or border of anything; rim: *Don't go near the brim of the canyon.* **3** fill to the brim; be full to the brim: *The pond was brimming with water after the heavy rain.* **4** the projecting edge of something: *The hat's wide brim shaded my eyes from the sun.* 1,2,4 *n.,* 3 *v.,* **brimmed, brim ming.** —**brim′less,** *adj.*

brim ful (brim′fül′), full to the brim; full to the very top. *adj.*

brim stone (brim′stōn′), sulfur. *n.*

brin dle (brin′dl), **1** brindled. **2** a brindled color. **3** a brindled animal. 1 *adj.,* 2,3 *n.*

brin dled (brin′dld), gray, tan, or tawny with darker streaks and spots. *adj.*

brine (brīn), **1** very salty water. Some pickles are kept in brine. **2** a salt lake, sea, or ocean. *n.* —**brine′less,** *adj.*

bring (bring), **1** come with or carry (a thing or person) from another place; take along to a place or person: *The bus brought us home. Bring me a clean plate.* **2** cause to come: *What brings you into town today?* **3** win over to a belief or action; influence; persuade; convince: *Our arguments finally brought them to agree with us.* **4** sell for: *Tomatoes bring a high price in winter.* **5** present before a court of law: *He brought a charge against us in a lawsuit. v.,* **brought, bring ing.** —**bring′er,** *n.*

bring about, cause; cause to happen: *The flood was brought about by a heavy rain.*

bring around or **bring round, 1** restore to consciousness: *None of the doctor's efforts could bring him around.* **2** win over to a belief or action; convince; persuade: *At first my parents refused to let me go to the party, but I was able to bring them around.*

bring forth, 1 give birth to; bear: *In spring the ewes brought forth their young.* **2** make known something that has been hidden; reveal; show: *New evidence was brought forth by the lawyer.*

bring forward, 1 reveal; show: *The judge ordered the prisoner to be brought forward.* **2** (in accounting or bookkeeping) carry over from one page to another.

bring off, carry out successfully: *They brought off a good business deal.*

bring on, cause; cause to happen: *My headache was brought on by a cold.*

bring out, 1 reveal; show: *The lawyer brought out new evidence at the trial.* **2** offer to the public: *The company is bringing out a new product.*

bring over, win over to do or believe; persuade: *Try to bring her over to our way of thinking.*

bring to, 1 restore to consciousness: *The swimmer was unconscious when the lifeguards rescued her, but they finally brought her to.* **2** stop; check: *The captain brought the ship to.*

bring up, 1 care for in childhood: *My grandparents brought up four children.* **2** educate or train, especially in behavior or manners: *His good manners showed he was well brought up.* **3** suggest for action or discussion: *Please bring your plan up at the meeting.*

bring ing-up (bring′ing up′), care and training given to a child when growing up; upbringing. *n.*

brink (bringk), **1** edge at the top of a steep place: *the brink of the cliff.* **2** edge: *The business is on the brink of ruin. n.*

brin y (brī′nē), of or like brine; very salty: *Too much salt gives a briny taste. adj.,* **brin i er, brin i est.** —**brin′i-ness,** *n.*

bri quette or **bri quet** (bri ket′), a molded block of coal dust or charcoal used for fuel. *n.*

brisk (brisk), **1** quick and active; lively: *Grandmother likes to take a brisk walk every morning.* **2** keen; sharp: *A brisk wind was blowing from the north. adj.* —**brisk′ly,** *adv.* —**brisk′ness,** *n.*

bris ket (bris′kit), meat from the breast of an animal. *n.*

bris tle (bris′əl), **1** one of the short, stiff hairs of some animals or plants. Brushes are often made of the bristles of hogs. **2** stand up straight: *The dog growled and its hair bristled.* **3** have one's hair stand up straight: *The frightened kitten bristled when it saw the dog.* **4** show that one is aroused and ready to fight: *The insult made her bristle.* **5** be thickly set: *The harbor bristled with boats and ships.* 1 *n.,* 2-5 *v.,* **bris tled, bris tling.** —**bris′tle like′,** *adj.*

bristlecone pine—Though only about 45 ft. (13.5 m.) tall, some of these trees are believed to be more than 4000 years old.

a hat	**i** it	**oi** oil	**ch** child		⌠ a in about
ā age	**ī** ice	**ou** out	**ng** long		│ e in taken
ä far	**o** hot	**u** cup	**sh** she	ə = ⟨ i in pencil
e let	**ō** open	**u̇** put	**th** thin		│ o in lemon
ē equal	**ô** order	**ü** rule	**ᴛʜ** then		⌊ u in circus
ėr term			**zh** measure		

bris tle cone pine (bris′əl kōn′), a bushy or shrublike pine with cones that bear long prickles or bristles. Bristlecone pines are found in the western United States, and are among the oldest trees in existence.

bris tly (bris′lē), 1 rough with bristles or hair like bristles: *The trapper had a bristly chin after a week in the woods.* 2 like bristles: *bristly hair.* 3 likely to bristle: *a bristly temper.* adj., **bris tli er, bris tli est.**

Brit., 1 Britain. 2 British.

Brit ain (brit′n), England, Scotland, and Wales; Great Britain. n.

Bri tan ni a (bri tan′ē ə), Great Britain. n.

Bri tan nic (bri tan′ik), British. adj.

britch es (brich′iz), INFORMAL. breeches. n.pl.

Brit i cism (brit′ə siz′əm), word or phrase used especially by the British. *Lift* meaning *elevator* and *petrol* meaning *gasoline* are Briticisms. n.

Brit ish (brit′ish), 1 of Great Britain or its people. 2 the people of Great Britain. 3 the English spoken in Great Britain. 1 adj., 2 n.pl., 3 n.sing.

British Columbia, province in SW Canada, on the Pacific. *Capital:* Victoria.

British Commonwealth or **British Commonwealth of Nations,** Commonwealth of Nations.

British Empire, former empire consisting of all the countries and colonies owing allegiance to the British crown. At its height, in the late 1800's and early 1900's, it was the largest empire in the history of the world.

Brit ish er (brit′i shər), any British subject, especially an Englishman. n.

British Honduras, former name of **Belize.**

British Isles, Great Britain, Ireland, the Isle of Man, and other nearby islands.

British Isles

British thermal unit, unit for measuring heat. It is the amount of heat necessary to raise the temperature of a pound of water one degree Fahrenheit.

British West Indies, British islands in the West Indies.

Brit on (brit′n), 1 person born or living in Great Britain.

2 one of the Celtic people who inhabited southern Britain before the Roman conquest of Britain. n.

Brit ta ny (brit′n ē), region in NW France. See **Burgundy** for map. n.

brit tle (brit′l), very easily broken; breaking with a snap; apt to break: *Thin glass is brittle.* adj. —**brit′tle ness,** n.

bro. or **Bro.,** brother.

broach (brōch), 1 begin to talk about: *She broached the subject of a raise in her allowance.* 2 a pointed tool to make and shape holes with. 3 open by making a hole: *We broached a barrel of cider.* 1,3 v., 2 n., pl. **broach es.** —**broach′er,** n.

broad (brôd), 1 large across; wide: *a broad road.* 2 having wide range; extensive: *Our librarian has had broad experience with books.* 3 not limited or narrow; of wide range; liberal: *The police took a broad view of the children's prank and sent them home with only a warning.* 4 including only the most important parts; not detailed; general: *Give the broad outlines of today's lesson.* 5 clear; full: *The theft was made in broad daylight.* 6 plain; plain-spoken: *He gave his parents broad hints of what he wanted for his birthday.* adj. —**broad′ly,** adv. —**broad′ness,** n.

broad ax or **broad axe** (brôd′aks′), ax with a broad blade. n., pl. **broad ax es.**

broad cast (brôd′kast′), 1 something sent out by radio or television; a radio or television program of speech, music, etc.: *The broadcast was televised from Washington, D.C.* 2 send out by radio or television: *Some stations broadcast twenty-four hours a day.* 3 a sending out by radio or television: *a nation-wide broadcast.* 4 sent out by radio or television. 5 scatter or spread widely: *broadcast seed. Don't broadcast gossip.* 6 a scattering or spreading far and wide: *nature's broadcast of seed.* 7 scattered widely. 8 over a wide surface: *The seed was sown broadcast.* 1,3,6 n., 2,5 v., **broad cast** or **broad cast ed** for 2, **broad cast** for 5, **broad cast ing;** 4,7 adj., 8 adv. —**broad′cast′er,** n.

broad cloth (brôd′klôth′), 1 a closely woven cotton, silk, or synthetic cloth with a smooth finish, used in making shirts, dresses, pajamas, etc. 2 a closely woven woolen cloth with a smooth finish, used in making suits, coats, etc. n.

broad en (brôd′n), become or make broad or broader; widen: *The river broadens at its mouth. Travel broadens a person's experience.* v.

broad jump, an athletic contest or event in which the contestants jump from a standing or running position to cover as much ground as possible.

broad loom (brôd′lüm′), 1 woven on a wide loom: *a broadloom carpet.* 2 material woven in this way: *gray broadloom.* 1 adj., 2 n.

broad-mind ed (brôd′mīn′did), not prejudiced or bigoted; liberal; tolerant: *He tried to be broad-minded, but did not always succeed.* adj. —**broad′-mind′ed ly,** adv. —**broad′-mind′ed ness,** n.

broad side (brôd′sīd′), 1 the whole side of a ship above the water. 2 the firing of all the guns on one side of a ship at the same time: *The broadside caught the pirates by surprise.* 3 with the side turned: *The ship drifted broadside to the wharf.* 1,2 n., 3 adv.

broad sword (brôd′sôrd′), sword with a broad, flat cutting blade. n.

Broad way (brôd/wā/), street running northwest and southeast through New York City. Part of Broadway lies in the main theater district. *n.*

bro cade (brō kād/), **1** an expensive cloth woven with raised designs on it, used for clothing or upholstery: *silk brocade, velvet brocade.* **2** weave or decorate with raised designs. 1 *n.,* 2 *v.,* **bro cad ed, bro cad ing.**

broc co li (brok/ə lē), vegetable with green branching stems and flower heads. It belongs to the same family as the cabbage. *n., pl.* **broc co li.** [*Broccoli* comes from Italian *broccoli,* meaning "sprouts."]

bro chure (brō shùr/), pamphlet. *n.*

bro gan (brō/gən), a strong work shoe made of heavy leather. *n.*

brogue¹ (brōg), a strongly marked pronunciation or accent peculiar to a dialect: *She speaks English with an Irish brogue. n.*

brogue² (brōg), a shoe made for comfort and long wear, often with decorative perforations. *n.*

broil (broil), **1** cook by putting or holding directly over the fire or heat on a rack, or under it in a pan; grill: *We often broil steaks and chops.* **2** be or make very hot: *You will broil in this bright sunlight. v.*

broil er (broi/lər), **1** pan or rack for broiling. **2** a young chicken for broiling. *n.*

broke (brōk), **1** past tense of **break.** *I broke my watch.* **2** INFORMAL. without money. 1 *v.,* 2 *adj.*

bro ken (brō/kən), **1** past participle of **break.** *The window was broken by a ball.* **2** separated into parts by a break; in pieces: *a broken cup.* **3** not in working condition; damaged: *a broken watch.* **4** rough; uneven: *broken ground.* **5** acted against; not kept: *a broken promise.* **6** imperfectly spoken: *The French girl speaks broken English.* **7** weakened in strength, spirit, etc.; tamed; crushed: *broken by failure.* 1 *v.,* 2-7 *adj.* —**bro/ken ly,** *adv.* —**bro/ken ness,** *n.*

bro ken-down (brō/kən doun/), **1** shattered; ruined: *broken-down health.* **2** unfit for use: *broken-down furniture. adj.*

bro ken heart ed (brō/kən här/tid), crushed by sorrow or grief; heartbroken. *adj.* —**bro/ken heart/ed ly,** *adv.*

bro ker (brō/kər), person who buys and sells stocks, bonds, grain, cotton, etc., for other people. *n.*

bro ker age (brō/kər ij), **1** business of a broker. **2** money charged by a broker for services. *n.*

bro mide (brō/mīd), drug containing bromine, used to calm nervousness, cause sleep, etc. *n.*

bro mine (brō/mēn/), a dark, brownish-red, nonmetallic, liquid element. Bromine is somewhat like chlorine and iodine and gives off an irritating vapor. It is used in antiknock compounds for gasoline, in drugs, and in photography. *n.*

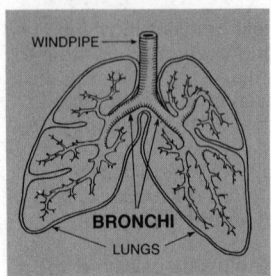

bronchi (def. 1)

bron chi (brong/kī), **1** the two large, main branches of the windpipe, one going to each lung. **2** the smaller branching tubes in the lungs. *n.pl.* of **bronchus.**

bron chi al (brong/kē əl), of the bronchi or their many branching tubes. *adj.* —**bron/chi al ly,** *adv.*

bronchial tubes, bronchi and their branching tubes.

bron chi tis (brong kī/tis), inflammation of the mucous membrane that lines the bronchial tubes. Bronchitis is usually accompanied by a deep cough and may be acute or chronic. *n.*

bron cho (brong/kō), bronco. *n., pl.* **bron chos.**

bron chus (brong/kəs), one of the bronchi. *n., pl.* **bron chi.**

bronco
cowgirl riding a bronco

bron co (brong/kō), a wild or partly tamed horse of the western United States. *n., pl.* **bron cos.** Also, **broncho.**

Bron të (bron/të), **1** Charlotte, 1816-1855, English novelist. **2** her sister, Emily, 1818-1848, English novelist. *n.*

bron to sau rus (bron/tə sôr/əs), a huge prehistoric plant-eating dinosaur. *n., pl.* **bron to sau ri** (bron/tə - sôr/ī), **bron to sau rus es.**

WORD HISTORY

brontosaurus

Brontosaurus comes from Greek *brontē,* meaning "thunder," and *sauros,* meaning "lizard."

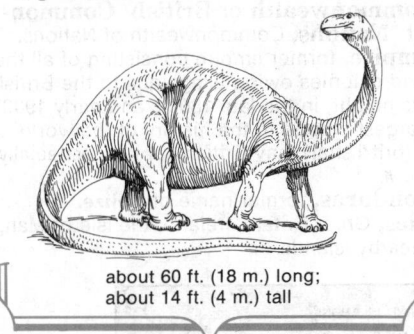

about 60 ft. (18 m.) long;
about 14 ft. (4 m.) tall

Bronx (brongks), **The,** borough of New York City, the only one on the mainland. *n.*

Bronx cheer, SLANG. raspberry (def. 3).

bronze (bronz), **1** a brown alloy of copper and tin. **2** a similar alloy of copper and zinc or another metal. **3** a statue, medal, disk, etc., made of bronze: *A bronze went to the swimmer who came in third.* **4** made of bronze: *a bronze bell.* **5** color of bronze; a dark yellowish brown. **6** dark yellowish-brown. **7** make or become a dark yellowish brown: *a lifeguard bronzed by the sun.* 1-3,5 *n.,* 4,6 *adj.,* 7 *v.,* **bronzed, bronz ing.**

Bronze Age, period after the Stone Age when bronze tools and weapons were used. It was followed by the Iron Age.

bronz y (bron′zē), **1** tinged with bronze color. **2** like bronze. *adj.*

brooch (brōch *or* brüch), an ornamental pin having the point fastened by a catch. Brooches are often made of gold, silver, or jewels. *n., pl.* **brooch es.**

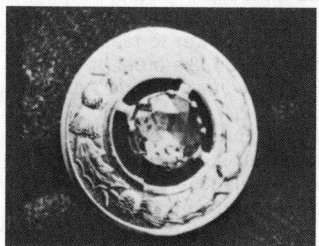

brooch

brood (brüd), **1** the young birds hatched at one time in the nest or cared for together: *a brood of chicks.* **2** young animals or humans who share the same mother or are cared for by the same person: *That father and mother have a brood of twelve children.* **3** sit on eggs in order to hatch; incubate. Hens and birds brood till the young are hatched. **4** worry a long time about some one thing: *They brooded over their lost dog.* **1,2** *n.,* **3,4** *v.*

brood er (brü′dər), **1** a closed place that can be heated, used in raising chicks, etc. **2** person who tends to worry a long time about some one thing. *n.*

brood y (brü′dē), **1** brooding: *broody hens.* **2** apt to brood; moody. *adj.,* **brood i er, brood i est. —brood′i ness,** *n.*

brook¹ (brük), a small stream; creek. *n.*

brook² (brük), put up with; endure; tolerate: *I will not brook any more of your insults.* *v.*

brook let (brük′lit), a little brook. *n.*

Brook lyn (brük′lən), borough of New York City, on Long Island. *n.*

Brooks (brüks), **Gwendolyn,** born 1917, American poet. *n.*

broom (brüm *or* brüm), **1** brush with a long handle for sweeping. **2** shrub with slender branches, small leaves, and yellow flowers. It is related to the pea. *n.*

broom stick (brüm′stik′ *or* brüm′stik′), the long handle of a broom. *n.*

bros. or **Bros.,** brothers.

broth (brôth), a thin soup made from water in which meat, fish, or vegetables have been boiled. *n., pl.* **broths** (brôᴛʜz *or* brôths).

broth er (bruᴛʜ′ər), **1** son of the same parents. A boy is a brother to the other children of his parents. **2** a close friend or companion. **3** a male member of the same union, club, religious organization, etc. **4** member of a religious order who is not a priest: *a lay brother.* *n., pl.* **broth ers** (or **breth ren** for **3,4**). **—broth′er less,** *adj.*

broth er hood (bruᴛʜ′ər hüd), **1** bond between brothers; feeling of brother for brother. **2** persons joined as brothers; association of men with some common aim or characteristic. *n.*

broth er-in-law (bruᴛʜ′ər in lô′), **1** brother of one's husband or wife. **2** husband of one's sister. *n., pl.* **brothers-in-law.**

broth er li ness (bruᴛʜ′ər lē nis), brotherly affection or sympathy. *n.*

broth er ly (bruᴛʜ′ər lē), **1** of a brother: *brotherly traits.* **2** like a brother; very friendly; kindly: *brotherly advice.* *adj.*

brougham (brüm *or* brü′əm), a closed carriage having an outside seat for the driver. *n.*

brought (brôt), past tense and past participle of **bring.** *I brought my lunch yesterday. They were brought to school in a bus.* *v.*

a hat	i it	oi oil	ch child	[a in about
ā age	ī ice	ou out	ng long	e in taken
ä far	o hot	u cup	sh she	ə = { i in pencil
e let	ō open	ù put	th thin	o in lemon
ē equal	ô order	ü rule	ᴛʜ then	[u in circus
ėr term			zh measure	

brow (brou), **1** part of the face above the eyes; forehead: *a wrinkled brow.* **2** arch of hair over the eye; eyebrow. **3** edge of a steep place; top of a slope: *Our house is on the brow of a hill.* *n.*

brow beat (brou′bēt′), frighten into doing something by overbearing looks or threats; bully. *v.,* **brow beat, brow beat en, brow beat ing.**

brown (broun), **1** the color of toast and coffee. **2** having this color: *Many people have brown hair.* **3** make or become brown: *The cook browned the onions in hot butter.* **1** *n.,* **2** *adj.,* **3** *v.* **—brown′ness,** *n.*

Brown (broun), **John,** 1800-1859, American Abolitionist who attempted to incite a slave rebellion but was captured at Harpers Ferry, West Virginia. *n.*

brown-bag (broun′bag′), SLANG. carry (lunch) to work or school, usually in a brown paper bag. *v.,* **brown-bagged, brown-bag ging. —brown′-bag′ger,** *n.*

brown bear, bear having brown fur that lives in northern Europe and North America, especially Alaska.

brown ie (brou′nē), **1** a good-natured elf, especially one supposed to help secretly at night. **2 Brownie,** member of the junior division of the Girl Scouts. **3** a small, flat, sweet chocolate cake, often containing nuts. *n.*

Brown ing (brou′ning), **1 Elizabeth Barrett,** 1806-1861, English poet, wife of Robert Browning. **2 Robert,** 1812-1889, English poet. *n.*

brown ish (brou′nish), somewhat brown. *adj.*

brown out (broun′out′), a partial lowering of electric power that causes lights to dim. *n.*

brown rice, rice that has not had the outer covering of bran removed.

brown stone (broun′stōn′), **1** a reddish-brown sandstone, used as a building material. **2** house with exterior walls built of this material. *n.*

brown sugar, sugar that is only partly refined.

browse—(left, def. 1)
The cows **browsed** in the meadow.

(right, def. 2)
She spent the afternoon **browsing** in a bookstore.

browse (brouz), **1** feed on growing grass or the leaves and shoots of trees and bushes by nibbling and eating here and there; graze. **2** read here and there in a book, library, etc. *v.,* **browsed, brows ing. —brows′er,** *n.*

Bruce (brüs), **Robert the,** 1274-1329, king of Scotland from 1306 to 1329. *n.*

bru in (brü′ən), bear² (def. 1). *n.*

bruise (brüz), **1** injury to the body, caused by a fall or a blow, that breaks blood vessels without breaking the skin: *The bruise on my arm turned black and blue.* **2** injury to the outside of a fruit, vegetable, plant, etc. **3** injure the outside of: *Rough handling bruised the apples before they* could be sold. **4** hurt; injure: *Your harsh words bruised my feelings.* **5** become bruised: *My flesh bruises easily.* 1,2 *n.,* 3-5 *v.,* **bruised, bruis ing.**

bruit (brüt), spread a report or rumor of: *News of their engagement was bruited about. v.*

brunch (brunch), meal taken late in the morning and intended to combine breakfast and lunch. *n., pl.* **brunch es.** [*Brunch* is a blend of *breakfast* and *lunch*.]

Bru nei (brü nī′), country in N Borneo. *Capital:* Bandar Seri Begawan. *n.*

bru nette or **bru net** (brü net′), **1** dark in color: *brunette hair.* **2** having dark-brown or black hair and usually brown or black eyes and dark skin. **3** person with such hair, eyes, and skin. 1,2 *adj.,* 3 *n.*

brunt (brunt), the main force or violence; hardest part: *The island felt the brunt of the hurricane. n.*

brush¹ (brush), **1** tool for cleaning, sweeping, scrubbing, painting, etc. A brush is made of bristles, hair, or wire set in a stiff back or fastened to a handle. **2** clean, sweep, scrub, or paint with a brush; use a brush on: *I brushed my hair.* **3** a brushing; a rub with a brush: *I gave my puppy a good brush.* **4** wipe away; remove: *The child brushed the tears from his eyes.* **5** touch lightly in passing: *No harm was done—your bumper just brushed our fender.* **6** a light touch in passing: *Give the desk a brush with the cloth.* **7** a short, brisk fight or quarrel: *The trespassers had a brush with the farmer.* **8** the bushy tail of an animal, especially of a fox. **9** piece of carbon, copper, etc., used to connect the electricity from the revolving part of an electric motor or generator to the outside circuit. 1,3,6-9 *n., pl.* **brush es;** 2,4,5 *v.* —**brush′a ble,** *adj.*

brush aside, put aside; refuse to consider: *She brushed aside their criticisms and continued her work.*

brush off, 1 refuse to see or listen to: *The mayor hurried into city hall, brushing off the reporters.* **2** dismiss as unimportant; make light of: *The mayor brushed off the reporter's question with a joke.*

brush up on or **brush up,** refresh one's knowledge of: *I brushed up on fractions before the arithmetic test.*

brush² (brush), **1** branches broken or cut off; brushwood. **2** shrubs, bushes, and small trees growing thickly; brushwood. **3** thinly settled country; backwoods. *n.*

brush off (brush′ôf′), INFORMAL. refusal or dismissal of a request, person, etc.: *The reporter got a polite brushoff when she asked the new mayor for an appointment. n.*

brush wood (brush′wùd′), brush² (defs. 1 and 2). *n.*

brush y (brush′ē), covered with bushes, shrubs, etc. *adj.,* **brush i er, brush i est.**

brusque (brusk), abrupt in manner or speech; blunt: *A brusque wave of the hand was her only reply to my question. adj.* —**brusque′ly,** *adv.* —**brusque′ness,** *n.*

Brus sels (brus′əlz), capital of Belgium, in the central part. *n.*

Brussels sprouts, vegetable that looks like small heads of cabbage. The heads grow along the stalk of a garden plant related to cabbage.

Brussels sprouts
about 2¹/₂ ft.
(75 cm.) tall

bru tal (brü′tl), savagely cruel; inhuman: *a brutal beating. adj.* —**bru′tal ly,** *adv.*

bru tal i ty (brü tal′ə tē), **1** brutal conduct; cruelty. **2** a brutal act. *n., pl.* **bru tal i ties.**

bru tal ize (brü′tl īz), make brutal: *War brutalizes many people. v.,* **bru tal ized, bru tal iz ing.** —**bru′tal i za′tion,** *n.*

brute (brüt), **1** an animal without power to reason. **2** like an animal; without power to reason. **3** a cruel or coarse person. **4** without feeling: *We are often powerless against the brute forces of nature.* 1,3 *n.,* 2,4 *adj.*

brut ish (brü′tish), like a brute; cruel or coarse. *adj.* —**brut′ish ly,** *adv.* —**brut′ish ness,** *n.*

Bru tus (brü′təs), **Marcus Junius,** 85-42 B.C., Roman political leader and one of the men who killed Julius Caesar. *n.*

Bry an (brī′ən), **William Jennings,** 1860-1925, American political leader and orator. *n.*

Bry ant (brī′ənt), **William Cullen,** 1794-1878, American poet. *n.*

b.s., bill of sale.

B.S., Bachelor of Science.

btl., bottle.

btry., battery.

Btu, B.t.u., or **B.T.U.,** British thermal unit or units.

bu., bushel or bushels.

bub ble (bub′əl), **1** a thin, round film of liquid enclosing air or gas. The surface of boiling water is covered with bubbles. **2** a round space filled with air in a liquid or solid. Sometimes there are bubbles in ice or in glass. **3** have bubbles; make bubbles; send up or rise in bubbles: *Water bubbled up between the stones.* **4** make sounds like water boiling; gurgle: *The baby bubbled and cooed.* **5** sound of bubbling. **6** plan or idea that looks good, but soon falls apart. 1,2,5,6 *n.,* 3,4 *v.,* **bub bled, bub bling.** —**bub′bling ly,** *adv.*

bubble over, 1 be very full; overflow: *The teakettle bubbled over on the stove.* **2** be very enthusiastic: *The children bubbled over at the idea of an overnight camping trip.*

bubble bath, a bath with a mass of bubbles on the surface, formed by adding a certain kind of soap.

bubble gum, a chewing gum that can be blown out through the lips so as to form a large bubble.

bub bly (bub′lē), full of bubbles. *adj.,* **bub bli er, bub bli est.**

bu bon ic plague (byü bon′ik), a very dangerous contagious disease, accompanied by fever, chills, and swelling of the lymph glands. It is carried to human beings by fleas from rats or squirrels.

buc ca neer (buk′ə nir′), pirate. *n.*

Bu chan an (byü kan′ən), **James,** 1791-1868, the 15th president of the United States, from 1857 to 1861. *n.*

Bu cha rest (bü′kə rest *or* byü′kə rest), capital of Romania, in the S part. *n.*

buck¹ (buk), **1** a male deer, goat, hare, rabbit, antelope, or sheep. **2** jump into the air with the back curved and come down with the front legs stiff: *My horse began to buck violently, but I managed to stay on.* **3** throw by bucking: *The cowboy was bucked by the bronco.* **4** a throw or attempt to throw by bucking. **5** charge against; work against: *The swimmer bucked the current with strong strokes.* 1,4 *n.,* 2,3,5 *v.* —**buck′er,** *n.*

buck for, work hard for.

buck up, INFORMAL. cheer up; be brave or energetic: *Buck up; everything will be all right.*

buck² (buk), SLANG. dollar. *n.*

Buck (buk), **Pearl,** 1892-1974, American novelist. *n.*

buck a roo (buk′ə rü′ *or* buk′ə rü′), cowboy. *n., pl.* **buck a roos.** [*Buckaroo* apparently comes from a west African word *buckra,* meaning "white man," with the ending from Spanish *vaquero*, meaning "cowboy."]

buck board (buk′bôrd′), an open four-wheeled carriage having the seat fastened to a platform of long, springy boards instead of a body and springs. *n.*

buck et (buk′it), **1** pail made of wood, metal, or plastic. Buckets are used for carrying such things as water, milk, or coal. **2** bucketful: *Pour in about four buckets of water. n.*

kick the bucket, SLANG. die.

buck et ful (buk′it fül), amount that a bucket can hold. *n., pl.* **buck et fuls.**

bucket seat, a small, low, single seat with a rounded back, used in some cars, small airplanes, etc.

buck eye (buk′ī′), **1** tree or shrub closely related to the horse chestnut, with showy clusters of small flowers, large divided leaves, and large brown seeds. **2** its seed. *n.*

Buck ing ham Palace (buk′ing əm), official London residence of all British sovereigns since 1837.

buck le (buk′əl), **1** catch or clasp used to hold together the ends of a belt, strap, or ribbon. **2** fasten together with a buckle: *buckle one's belt.* **3** a metal, plastic, etc., ornament for a shoe. **4** bend out of shape; bulge, kink, or wrinkle: *The heavy snowfall caused the roof of the shed to buckle.* **5** a bend, bulge, kink, or wrinkle. 1,3,5 *n.,* 2,4 *v.,* **buck led, buck ling.**

buckle down to, work hard at: *I buckled down to my studies before the test.*

buck ler (buk′lər), a small, round shield. *n.*

buck ram (buk′rəm), a coarse cloth made stiff with glue or something like glue. *n.*

bucksaw

buck saw (buk′sô′), saw set in a light frame and held with both hands. *n.*

buck shot (buk′shot′), a large lead shot used to shoot large game, such as deer. *n.*

buck skin (buk′skin′), **1** a strong, soft leather, yellowish or grayish in color, made from the skins of deer or sheep. **2** buckskins, *pl.* clothing made of buckskin. *n.*

buck tooth (buk′tüth′), tooth that sticks out beyond the other teeth. *n., pl.* **buck teeth.**

buck toothed (buk′tütht′), having a protruding tooth or teeth. *adj.*

buck wheat (buk′hwēt′), **1** plant with black or gray, triangular seeds and fragrant white flowers. **2** its seeds, used as food for animals or ground into flour for pancakes, etc. *n.*

bu col ic (byü kol′ik), **1** of shepherds; pastoral. **2** rustic; rural. *adj.* —**bu col′i cal ly,** *adv.*

bud (bud), **1** a small swelling on a plant that will grow into a flower, leaf, or branch: *Buds on the trees are a sign of spring.* **2** a partly opened flower or leaf. **3** put forth buds: *The rosebush has budded.* **4** begin to grow or develop. **5** anything in an undeveloped state or beginning stage. **6** a small swelling in certain plants and animals that grows into a new plant or animal. Sponges grow

from buds. 1,2,5,6 *n.,* 3,4 *v.,* **bud ded, bud ding.** —**bud′der,** *n.* —**bud′like′,** *adj.*

in bud, budding: *In the spring the pear tree is in bud.*

nip in the bud, stop at the very beginning: *I tried to nip their argument in the bud before it became a fight.*

Bu da pest (bü′də pest), capital of Hungary, on the Danube. *n.*

Bud dha (bü′də *or* bu̇d′ə), 563?-483? B.C., religious teacher of northern India, founder of Buddhism. *n.*

Bud dhism (bü′diz əm *or* bu̇d′iz əm), religion based on the teachings of Buddha. It developed during his lifetime in northern India and spread widely after his death over central, southeastern, and eastern Asia. *n.*

Bud dhist (bü′dist *or* bu̇d′ist), **1** person who believes in and follows the teachings of Buddha. **2** of Buddha, his followers, or the religion founded by him: *a Buddhist temple.* 1 *n.,* 2 *adj.*

bud ding (bud′ing), showing signs of becoming; developing: *She is a budding scientist. adj.*

bud dy (bud′ē), INFORMAL. a close friend; comrade; pal. *n., pl.* **bud dies.**

budge (buj), move even a little: *The stone was so heavy that we could not budge it. I was too tired to budge from my chair. v.,* **budged, budg ing.**

budg et (buj′it), **1** estimate of the amount of money that will probably be received and spent for various purposes in a given time. Governments, companies, schools, families, etc., make budgets. **2** make a plan for spending: *She budgeted her allowance so that she could save some money each week for a new tennis racket. Budget your time.* **3** put in a budget: *He budgeted three dollars a week for school lunches.* 1 *n.,* 2,3 *v.*

budg et ar y (buj′ə ter′ē), of a budget. *adj.*

Bue nos Ai res (bwā′nəs er′ēz *or* bwā′nəs ar′ēz), capital of Argentina, in the E part.

buff (buf), **1** dull-yellow. **2** a dull yellow. **3** a strong, soft, dull-yellow leather. Buff was formerly made from the skin of buffalo and is now made from the skin of oxen. **4** to polish with a wheel or stick covered with leather. **5** to polish; shine: *I buffed my shoes to make them shine.* **6** a polishing wheel or stick covered with leather. **7** INFORMAL. a fan or devotee: *a model-train buff.* 1 *adj.,* 2,3,6,7 *n.,* 4,5 *v.*

buf fa lo (buf′ə lō), **1** the bison of North America. **2** any of several kinds of oxen, such as the tame water buffalo of Asia and the wild Cape buffalo of Africa. *n., pl.* **buf fa loes, buf fa los,** *or* **buf fa lo.**

Buf fa lo (buf′ə lō), city in W New York State, a port on Lake Erie. *n.*

Buffalo Bill, 1846-1917, American frontier scout and showman. His real name was William F. Cody.

buff er¹ (buf′ər), anything that helps to soften the shock of a blow or to balance the effect of opposing forces: *He acted as a buffer between the quarreling children. n.*

buff er² (buf′ər), **1** stick or pad having a soft cloth or leather surface for polishing. **2** person who polishes. *n.*

buffer state, a small country between two larger countries that are enemies or competitors.

buf fet¹ (buf′it), **1** knock about, strike, or hurt: *The waves buffeted the small boat.* **2** a knock, stroke, or hurt: *The boat withstood the buffets of the waves.* 1 *v.,* 2 *n.* —**buf′fet er,** *n.*

buf fet[2] (bu fā′ *or* bú fā′), **1** a low cabinet with a flat top for dishes and with shelves or drawers for silver and table linen; sideboard. **2** counter where food and drinks are served. **3** restaurant with a counter like this. **4** meal at which guests serve themselves from food laid out on a table or sideboard. *n.*

buf foon (bu fün′), **1** person who amuses people with tricks, pranks, and jokes; clown. **2** person who makes undignified or rude jokes. *n.*

buf foon er y (bu fü′nər ē), **1** tricks, pranks, and jokes of a clown. **2** undignified or rude joking. *n., pl.* **buf foon-er ies.**

buf foon ish (bu fü′nish), like a buffoon. *adj.*

bug (bug), **1** insect without wings or with a front pair of wings thickened at the base, and a pointed beak for piercing and sucking. Bedbugs, lice, and chinch bugs are true bugs. **2** any insect or other invertebrate somewhat like a true bug. Ants, spiders, beetles, and flies are often called bugs. **3** INFORMAL. a disease germ: *the flu bug.* **4** INFORMAL. mechanical defect or difficulty: *The new engine needed repair because of a bug in the design of the fuel system.* **5** INFORMAL. person who is very enthusiastic about something: *She is a basketball bug, always practicing to better her game.* **6** a very small microphone hidden within a room, a telephone, etc., for overhearing conversation. **7** hide a small microphone within (a room, telephone, etc.): *The spy bugged enemy headquarters.* **8** SLANG. annoy; irritate: *His constant grumbling bugs me.* **1-6** *n.,* **7,8** *v.,* **bugged, bug ging.** —**bug′like′,** *adj.*

bug a boo (bug′ə bü), an imaginary or real thing that is feared; bogy. *n., pl.* **bug a boos.**

bug bear (bug′ber′ *or* bug′bar′), **1** bugaboo. **2** a difficulty, problem, or obstacle. *n.*

buggy (def. 1)

bug gy (bug′ē), **1** a light carriage with or without a top, pulled by one horse and having a single large seat. **2** a baby's carriage. *n., pl.* **bug gies.**

bu gle (byü′gəl), a musical instrument like a small trumpet, made of brass or copper, and sometimes having keys or valves. Bugles are used in the armed forces for sounding calls and orders, and for playing band music. *n.*

WORD HISTORY

bugle

Bugle came into English about 600 years ago from French *bugle,* which can be traced back to Latin *bovem,* meaning "ox." It was called this because the first musical horns were made from ox horns.

bu gler (byü′glər), person who plays a bugle. *n.*

build (bild), **1** make by putting materials together; construct: *People build houses, bridges, and machines. Birds build nests.* **2** form or produce gradually; develop: *build a business. The lawyer built her case on facts.* **3** form, style, or manner in which something is put together; structure: *a person with a heavy build.* **1,2** *v.,* **built, build ing; 3** *n.*

build up, 1 strengthen or develop: *When sick you must rest to build up your health.* **2** fill with houses: *The hill overlooking the town has been built up in the last five years.*

build er (bil′dər), **1** person or animal that builds. **2** person whose business is constructing buildings. *n.*

build ing (bil′ding), **1** thing built. Barns, factories, stores, houses, and hotels are all buildings. **2** business, art, or process of making houses, stores, bridges, ships, etc. *n.*

build up (bild′up′), **1** an increasing of strength, size, rate, etc.: *a military buildup, a buildup of pressure.* **2** enhancement or promotion, especially by the use of publicity: *The play has had a big buildup in the press. n.*

built (bilt), past tense and past participle of **build.** *The bird built a nest. It was built of twigs. v.*

built-in (bilt′in′), included in or provided for as part of the plan or design of anything; not movable: *a built-in bookcase. adj.*

Bu jum bur a (bü jəm bur′ə), capital of Burundi. *n.*

bulb (bulb), **1** a round, underground bud from which certain plants grow. Onions, tulips, and lilies grow from bulbs. **2** the thick part of an underground stem resembling a bulb; tuber: *a crocus bulb.* **3** any object with a rounded end or swelling part: *a light bulb, the bulb of a thermometer. n.* —**bulb′less,** *adj.* —**bulb′like′,** *adj.*

bulb ous (bul′bəs), **1** shaped like a bulb; rounded and swelling: *The clown had a bulbous red nose.* **2** having bulbs; growing from bulbs: *Daffodils are bulbous plants. adj.*

Bul gar i a (bul ger′ē ə), country in SE Europe, on the Black Sea. *Capital:* Sofia. See **Balkan States** for map. *n.* —**Bul gar′i an,** *adj., n.*

bulge (bulj), **1** swell outward: *My pockets bulged with candy.* **2** an outward swelling: *a can of soup with a bulge in it.* **1** *v.,* **bulged, bulg ing; 2** *n.*

bulg y (bul′jē), having a bulge or bulges. *adj.,* **bulg i er, bulg i est.** —**bulg′i ness,** *n.*

bulk (bulk), **1** size, especially large size: *An elephant has great bulk.* **2** the largest part of: *The oceans form the bulk of the earth's surface. n.*

in bulk, 1 lying loose in heaps, not in packages: *Some markets sell fresh fruit in bulk.* **2** in large quantities: *Grain goes to the mill in bulk.*

bulk head (bulk′hed′), **1** one of the upright partitions dividing a ship into compartments. **2** wall or partition built in a tunnel to hold back water, earth, rocks, gas, etc. *n.*

bulk y (bul′kē), **1** taking up much space; large: *Bulky shipments are often sent in freight cars.* **2** hard to handle; clumsy: *a bulky package of curtain rods. adj.,* **bulk i er, bulk i est.** —**bulk′i ly,** *adv.* —**bulk′i ness,** *n.*

bull[1] (bul), **1** the full-grown male of cattle. **2** the male of the whale, elephant, seal, and other large mammals. **3** male: *a bull moose.* **1,2** *n.,* **3** *adj.* —**bull′-like′,** *adj.*

bull[2] (bul), a formal announcement or official order from the pope. *n.*

bull., bulletin.

bull dog (bul′dôg′), **1** a heavy, muscular dog of medium height with a large head, very short nose, strong jaws, and short hair. **2** like a bulldog's: *a bulldog grip.* **3** bring (a steer) to the ground by grasping its horns and twisting its neck. **1** *n.,* **2** *adj.,* **3** *v.,* **bull dogged, bull dog-ging.**

bull doze (bùl/dōz/), **1** INFORMAL. frighten, sometimes by violence or threats; bully: *The chairman bulldozed the whole committee into voting for his proposal.* **2** move, clear, dig, or level with a bulldozer. *v.,* **bull dozed, bull doz-ing.**

bull doz er (bùl/dō/zər), a powerful crawler tractor with a wide steel blade that pushes rocks and earth, used for grading, road building, etc. *n.*

bulldozer

bul let (bùl/it), piece of lead, steel, or other metal shaped to be fired from a pistol, rifle, or other small gun. *n.* —**bul/let like/,** *adj.*

bul le tin (bùl/ə tən), **1** a short statement of news: *Sports bulletins and weather bulletins are published in most newspapers.* **2** magazine or newspaper appearing regularly, especially one published by a club or society for its members. *n.*

bulletin board, board on which notices are posted.

bull fiddle, INFORMAL. contrabass.

bull fight (bùl/fīt/), fight between men and a bull in an arena. Bullfights are popular in Spain, Portugal, Mexico, and parts of South America. *n.*

bull fight er (bùl/fī/tər), man who fights a bull in an arena. *n.*

bull fight ing (bùl/fī/ting), act or sport of fighting a bull in an arena. *n.*

bull finch (bùl/finch/), a European songbird with a blue and gray back and light-red breast, and a short, stout bill. *n., pl.* **bull finch es.**

bull frog (bùl/frog/), a large North American frog that makes a loud, croaking noise. *n.*

bull head (bùl/hed/), an American catfish with a large, broad head. *n.*

bull head ed (bùl/hed/id), stupidly stubborn; obstinate; headstrong. *adj.* —**bull/head/ed ly,** *adv.*

bul lion (bùl/yən), gold or silver in the form of lumps or bars. *n.*

bull ish (bùl/ish), like a bull in manner or temper. *adj.* —**bull/ish ly,** *adv.* —**bull/ish ness,** *n.*

bull ock (bùl/ək), ox; steer. *n.*

bull ring (bùl/ring/), arena for bullfights. *n.*

Bull Run, stream in NE Virginia where two Civil War battles took place in 1861 and 1862.

bull's-eye (bùlz/ī/), **1** center of a target. **2** shot that hits it. **3** a thick piece of dome-shaped glass in the deck or side of a ship to let in light. **4** a small lantern with a dome-shaped lens in its side to concentrate light. *n.*

bul ly (bùl/ē), **1** person who teases, frightens, threatens, or hurts smaller or weaker people. **2** frighten (into doing something) by noisy talk or threats: *Stop trying to bully me into doing what you want.* **3** INFORMAL. very good; excellent: *a bully plan (adj.). Bully for you!(interj.).* **1** *n., pl.* **bul lies; 2** *v.,* **bul lied, bul ly ing; 3** *adj.,* **bul li er, bul li est; 3** *interj.*

bully beef, canned or pickled beef.

bul rush (bùl/rush/), a tall, slender plant that grows in wet places. *n., pl.* **bul rush es.**

a hat	i it	oi oil	ch child	a in about
ā age	ī ice	ou out	ng long	e in taken
ä far	o hot	u cup	sh she	ə = i in pencil
e let	ō open	ù put	th thin	o in lemon
ē equal	ô order	ü rule	∓H then	u in circus
ėr term			zh measure	

bul wark (bùl/wərk), **1** person, thing, or idea that is a defense or a protection: *A free press and free speech are bulwarks of democracy.* **2** wall of earth or other material for defense against the enemy: *The city was protected by a moat and a bulwark surrounding it.* **3** breakwater for protection against the force of the waves. **4** Usually, **bulwarks,** *pl.* side of a ship above the deck. *n.*

bum (bum), INFORMAL. **1** an idle person; tramp. **2** get (food, money, etc.) by sponging on others; beg: *Let's try to bum a ride.* **3** loaf around; idle about. **4** of poor quality; worthless. **1** *n.,* **2,3** *v.,* **bummed, bum ming; 4** *adj.,* **bum mer, bum mest.**

on the bum, out of order.

bum ble bee (bum/bəl bē/), a large bee with a thick, hairy body, usually banded with gold. Bumblebees make a loud, buzzing sound. They live in small colonies in underground nests, old logs, etc. *n.*

bum mer (bum/ər), SLANG. any very unpleasant thing, happening, or experience. *n.*

bump (bump), **1** push, throw, or strike against something large or solid: *She bumped against the table in the dark.* **2** hit or come against heavily: *That truck bumped our car.* **3** a heavy blow or knock: *The bump knocked our car forward a few feet.* **4** move by bumping against things: *Our car bumped along the dirt road.* **5** a swelling caused by a bump: *He has a bump on his head from getting hit by a baseball.* **6** any swelling or lump: *Avoid the bump in the road.* **1,2,4** *v.,* **3,5,6** *n.*

bump er (bum/pər), **1** bar or bars of metal across the front and back of a car or truck that protect it from being damaged if bumped. **2** unusually large: *The farmer raised a bumper crop of wheat last year.* **1** *n.,* **2** *adj.*

bump i ly (bum/pə lē), in a bumpy manner. *adv.*

bump i ness (bum/pē nis), bumpy condition. *n.*

bump kin (bump/kən), an awkward or simple person from the country. *n.*

bump y (bum/pē), **1** having bumps; full of bumps: *a bumpy road.* **2** causing bumps; rough: *a bumpy ride.* *adj.,* **bump i er, bump i est.**

bun (bun), **1** bread or cake in small shapes. Buns are often slightly sweetened and may contain spice, raisins, etc. **2** hair coiled at the back of the head in a knot. *n.*

bunch (bunch), **1** group of things of the same kind growing, fastened, placed, or thought of together: *a bunch of grapes, a bunch of flowers, a bunch of sheep.* **2** INFORMAL. group of people: *They are a friendly bunch.* **3** come together in one place: *The sheep were all bunched in the shed to keep warm.* **4** bring together and make into a bunch: *We have bunched the flowers for you to carry home.* **1,2** *n., pl.* **bunch es; 3,4** *v.* —**bunch/er,** *n.*

Bunche (bunch), **Ralph,** 1904-1971, American educator and diplomat. He was the winner of the Nobel Peace Prize in 1950. *n.*

bunch y (bun/chē), **1** having bunches. **2** growing in bunches. *adj.,* **bunch i er, bunch i est.** —**bunch/i ly,** *adv.* —**bunch/i ness,** *n.*

bun dle (bun/dl), **1** number of things tied or wrapped together: *We gave away several bundles of old newspapers and magazines.* **2** parcel; package: *We sent my uncle a large bundle on his birthday.* **3** tie or wrap together; make into a bundle: *We bundled all our old newspapers for the school's paper drive.* **4** send or go in a hurry; hustle: *The*

children were bundled off to school. 1,2 *n.,* 3,4 *v.,* **bun-dled, bun dling. —bun′dler,** *n.*
bundle up, dress warmly: *You should bundle up on cold winter mornings.*

bung (bung), **1** stopper for closing the hole in the side or end of a barrel, keg, or cask. **2** bunghole. *n.*

bun ga low (bung′gə lō), a small one-story house. *n.* [*Bungalow* comes from Hindustani *banglā*, meaning "of Bengal." These houses were first observed in India, when it was part of the British Empire.]

bung hole (bung′hōl′), hole in the side or end of a barrel, keg, or cask through which it is filled and emptied. *n.*

bun gle (bung′gəl), **1** do or make in a clumsy, unskilled way: *I tried to make a birdhouse but bungled the job.* **2** a clumsy, unskilled performance or piece of work. **1** *v.,* **bun gled, bun gling; 2** *n.* **—bun′gling ly,** *adv.*

bun gler (bung′glər), person who bungles. *n.*

bun ion (bun′yən), a painful, inflamed swelling on the foot, especially on the first joint of the big toe. *n.*

bunk[1] (bungk), **1** a narrow bed, one of two or more stacked one above another: *My sister sleeps in the top bunk.* **2** sleep in a bunk; occupy a bunk. **3** any place to sleep. **4** sleep in rough quarters: *We bunked in a barn.* 1,3 *n.,* 2,4 *v.*

bunk[2] (bungk), SLANG. insincere talk; nonsense; humbug. *n.*

bunk[2]

Bunk[2] comes from *Buncombe* County in North Carolina. The local congressman in 1819-1821 made many long-winded speeches in Washington "for Buncombe."

bunk er (bung′kər), **1** place or bin for coal or oil on a ship. **2** a sandy hollow or mound of earth on a golf course, used as an obstacle. **3** a fortified shelter built partly or entirely below ground. *n.*

Bunker Hill, hill near Boston, Massachusetts. An early battle of the Revolutionary War was fought near there on June 17, 1775.

bunk house (bungk′hous′), a rough building with sleeping quarters or bunks, especially one provided for workers on a ranch. *n., pl.* **bunk hous es** (bungk′hou′ziz).

bun ny (bun′ē), a pet name for a rabbit. *n., pl.* **bun nies.**

Bun sen burner (bun′sən), a gas burner with a very hot, blue flame, used in laboratories. Air is let in at the base and mixed with gas.

bunt (bunt), **1** hit (a baseball) lightly with a bat so that the ball goes to the ground and rolls only a short distance. **2** act of bunting a baseball. **3** baseball that is bunted. 1 *v.,* 2,3 *n.* **—bunt′er,** *n.*

bun ting[1] (bun′ting), **1** a thin cloth used for flags. **2** long pieces of cloth having the colors and designs of a flag, used to decorate buildings and streets on holidays and special occasions. **3** a baby's warm, hooded, outer garment closed at the bottom. *n.*

bun ting[2] (bun′ting), a small, usually brightly colored bird with a stout bill. It is a kind of finch. *n.*

bunt line (bunt′lən *or* bunt′līn′), rope fastened to the bottom of a sail, used to haul the sail up to the yard for furling. *n.*

Bun yan (bun′yən), **Paul,** (in American folklore) a giant lumberjack with amazing strength. *n.*

buoy (boi *or* bü′ē), **1** a floating object anchored on the water to warn against hidden rocks or shallows or to show the safe part of a channel. **2** life buoy. *n.*

buoy up, 1 hold up; keep from sinking: *Life jackets buoyed them up until rescuers came.* **2** support or encourage: *Hope can buoy you up, even when something goes wrong.*

buoy an cy (boi′ən sē *or* bü′yən sē), **1** ability to float: *Wood has more buoyancy than iron, since it is less dense.* **2** power to keep things afloat: *Salt water has greater buoyancy than fresh water.* **3** tendency to be hopeful and cheerful: *Her buoyancy kept us from being downhearted.* *n.*

buoy ant (boi′ənt *or* bü′yənt), **1** able to float: *Wood and cork are buoyant in water; iron and lead are not.* **2** able to keep things afloat or aloft: *Salt water is more buoyant than fresh water.* **3** cheerful and hopeful; light-hearted: *I was in a buoyant mood.* *adj.* **—buoy′ant ly,** *adv.*

bur (bėr), **1** a prickly, clinging seedcase or flower of some plants. Burs stick to cloth and fur. **2** plant or weed that has burs. **3** remove burs from. 1,2 *n.,* 3 *v.,* **burred, bur ring.** Also, **burr.**

Bur bank (bėr′bangk), **Luther,** 1849-1926, American naturalist who bred new varieties of plants. *n.*

bur den[1] (bėrd′n), **1** something carried; load (of things, care, work, duty, or sorrow): *A light burden was laid on the mule's back. Everyone in my family shares the burden of housework.* **2** a load too heavy to carry easily; heavy load: *His debts are a burden that will bankrupt him.* **3** put a burden on; load too heavily; weigh down; oppress: *The mule was burdened with heavy bags of ore. I don't want to burden you with my troubles.* **4** quantity of freight that a ship can carry; weight of a ship's cargo. 1,2,4 *n.,* 3 *v.* **—bur′den er,** *n.* **—bur′den less,** *adj.*

bur den[2] (bėrd′n), **1** the main idea or message: *The need for more pollution control was the burden of her speech.* **2** a repeated verse in a song; chorus; refrain. *n.*

bur den some (bėrd′n səm), hard to bear; very heavy; oppressive: *burdensome duties.* *adj.* **—bur′den some ly,** *adv.* **—bur′den some ness,** *n.*

bur dock (bėr′dok′), a coarse weed with burs and broad leaves. *n.*

bur eau (byùr′ō), **1** chest of drawers for clothes; dresser. It often has a mirror. **2** office: *We asked about the airplane fares at the travel bureau.* **3** a division within a government department: *The Forest Service is a bureau of the Department of Agriculture.* *n., pl.* **bur eaus, bur eaux** (byùr′ōz).

bu reauc ra cy (byù rok′rə sē), **1** system of government by groups of officials, each dealing with its own kind of business under the direction of its chief. **2** the officials running government bureaus. **3** too much insistence on rigid routine, resulting in delay in making decisions; red tape. *n., pl.* **bu reauc ra cies.**

bur eau crat (byùr′ə krat), **1** official in a bureaucracy. **2** a government official who insists on rigid routine. *n.*

bur eau crat ic (byùr′ə krat′ik), of a bureaucracy or a bureaucrat. *adj.* **—bur′eau crat′i cal ly,** *adv.*

burg (bėrg), INFORMAL. town or city. *n.*

bur geon (bėr′jən), grow or shoot forth; sprout: *New suburbs have burgeoned all around the city.* *v.*

burg er (bėr′gər), INFORMAL. hamburger. *n.*

Bur ger (bėr′gər), **Warren Earl,** born 1907, chief justice of the United States Supreme Court from 1969 to 1986. *n.*

bur gess (bėr′jis), member of the lower house of the colonial legislature in Virginia or Maryland. *n., pl.* **bur gess es.**

burgh (bėrg *or* bėr′ō), a chartered town in Scotland. *n.*

burgh er (bėr′gər), citizen of a burgh or town; citizen. *n.*

bur glar (bėr′glər), person who breaks into a house or other building, usually at night, to steal. *n.*

bur glar ize (bėr′glə rīz′), INFORMAL. break into (a building) to steal. *v.*, **bur glar ized, bur glar iz ing.**

bur glar y (bėr′glər ē), a breaking into a house or other building, usually at night, to steal. *n., pl.* **bur glar ies.**

bur go mas ter (bėr′gə mas′tər), mayor of a town in Austria, Belgium, Germany, or the Netherlands. *n.*

Bur goyne (bər goin′), **John,** 1722-1792, English general. His defeat and surrender in 1777 marked the turning point of the Revolutionary War. *n.*

Bur gun di an (bər gun′dē ən), **1** of Burgundy or its people. **2** person born or living in Burgundy. 1 *adj.*, 2 *n.*

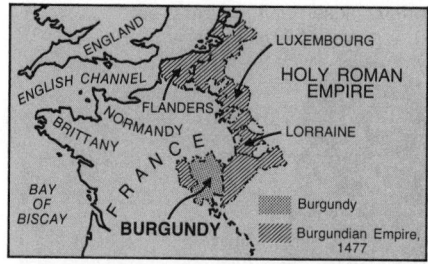

Burgundy
(def. 1)

Bur gun dy (bėr′gən dē), **1** region in E France. Once an independent kingdom, it became a duchy and later a province of France. **2** a red or white wine first made there. *n., pl.* **Bur gun dies** for 2.

bur i al (ber′ē əl), act of putting a dead body in a grave, in a tomb, or in the sea; burying: *The sailor was given a burial at sea. n.*

bur ied (ber′ēd), past tense and past participle of **bury.** *The dog buried a bone. Nuts were buried under the tree. v.*

Bur ki na Fa so (bủr′kē′nä fä′sō), country in W Africa, north of Ghana. *Capital:* Ouagadougou. Former name, **Upper Volta.** See **Nigeria** for map.

bur lap (bėr′lap), a coarse fabric made from jute or hemp, used to make bags. *n.*

bur lesque (bər lesk′), **1** a story, play, etc., that treats a serious subject ridiculously or a trivial subject as if it were important: *Mark Twain's story, "A Connecticut Yankee in King Arthur's Court," is a burlesque of the legends about King Arthur.* **2** imitate so as to make fun of. **3** a ridiculous imitation of something worthy or dignified; mockery. 1,3 *n.*, 2 *v.*, **bur lesqued, bur les quing.**

bur ly (bėr′lē), big and strong; sturdy: *a burly wrestler. adj.*, **bur li er, bur li est.**

Bur ma (bėr′mə), country in SE Asia, on the Indian Ocean. *Capital:* Rangoon. See **Indochina** for map. *n.*

Bur mese (bėr′mēz′), **1** person born or living in Burma. **2** language of Burma. **3** of Burma, its people, or their language. 1,2 *n., pl.* **Bur mese** for 1; 3 *adj.*

burn[1] (bėrn), **1** be on fire; be very hot: *The campfire burned all night.* **2** set on fire; cause to burn: *They burned wood in the fireplace to keep warm.* **3** destroy or be destroyed by fire: *Please burn those old papers.* **4** injure or be injured by fire, heat, or acid: *The flame from the candle burned her finger.* **5** injury caused by fire, heat, or acid; burned place: *I got a burn on my hand when I touched the hot pan. Don't lie too long in the sun or you will get a painful burn.* **6** make by fire, heat, acid, etc.: *The cigarette burned a hole in the rug.* **7** consume or change in chemical form by combining with oxygen: *The body burns food to produce heat and energy.* **8** feel hot; give a feeling of heat to: *The child's forehead burned with fever. Mustard burns the tongue.* **9** be inflamed with anger, passion, etc.: *She burned with fury at the unkind remarks. We were burning with enthusiasm.* **10** give light: *Lamps were burning in*

every room. **11** use to produce heat: *Our furnace burns oil.* **12** (of a rocket engine) fire or ignite. 1-4,6-12 *v.*, **burned** or **burnt, burn ing;** 5 *n.* —**burn′a ble,** *adj.*

burn[2] (bėrn), SCOTTISH. a small stream; brook. *n.*

burn er (bėr′nər), **1** part of a lamp, stove, furnace, etc., where the flame is produced. **2** thing or part that burns or works by heat: *Our furnace is an oil burner. n.*

bur nish (bėr′nish), **1** make shiny; polish: *burnish copper.* **2** a polish; shine. 1 *v.*, 2 *n.* —**bur′nish er,** *n.*

bur noose or **bur nous** (bər nüs′ *or* bėr′nüs), a cloak with a hood, worn by Moors and Arabs. *n.*

burnoose
The burnoose is a piece of cloth that is draped about the head and body.

Burns (bėrnz), **Robert,** 1759-1796, Scottish poet. *n.*

burnt (bėrnt), **1** burned; a past tense and a past participle of **burn**[1]. **2** injured or scorched by fire, heat, or acid: *I don't like burnt toast.* 1 *v.*, 2 *adj.*

burp (bėrp), INFORMAL. **1** a belch. **2** belch. **3** help (a baby) belch, as by patting it on the back. 1 *n.*, 2,3 *v.*

burr[1] (bėr), **1** bur. **2** a rough ridge or edge left by a tool on metal, wood, etc., after cutting or drilling it. 1,2 *n.*, 1 *v.*

burr[2] (bėr), **1** a rough pronunciation of *r: a Scottish burr.* **2** pronounce roughly: *He burrs his r's.* **3** a whirring sound. **4** make a whirring sound. 1,3 *n.*, 2,4 *v.*

Burr (bėr), **Aaron,** 1756-1836, American political leader, vice-president of the United States from 1801 to 1805. *n.*

bur ri to (bủ rē′tō), tortilla rolled around a seasoned filling, usually of beef, chicken, or beans. *n., pl.* **bur ri tos.** [*Burrito* comes from Mexican Spanish *burrito,* which originally meant "little burro."]

bur ro (bėr′ō *or* bủr′ō), a small donkey used to carry loads or packs in the southwestern United States. *n., pl.* **bur ros.** [*Burro* was borrowed from Spanish *burro.*]

bur row (bėr′ō), **1** hole dug in the ground by an animal for refuge or shelter. Rabbits live in burrows. **2** dig a hole in the ground: *The mole quickly burrowed out of sight.* **3** dig: *Rabbits have burrowed the ground for miles around.* **4** search: *She burrowed in the library for a book about insects.* **5** hide: *The runaway burrowed himself in the haystack.* 1 *n.*, 2-5 *v.* —**bur′row er,** *n.*

bur sa (bėr′sə), sac of the body, especially one containing a lubricating fluid that reduces friction between body parts. *n., pl.* **bur sae** (bėr′sē′), **bur sas.**

bur sar (bėr′sər), treasurer, especially of a college. *n.*

bur si tis (bər sī′tis), inflammation of a bursa, usually near the shoulder or hip. *n.*

burst (bėrst), **1** break open; break out suddenly: *They burst the lock. The trees had burst into bloom.* **2** fly apart or cause to fly apart suddenly with force; explode: *The balloon burst.* **3** go, come, do, etc., by force or suddenly: *Don't burst into the room without knocking.* **4** act or change suddenly in a way suggesting a break or explosion: *She burst into laughter.* **5** be very full: *The barn was bursting with grain. She was bursting with enthusiasm.* **6** a bursting; outbreak: *a burst of laughter.* **7** a sudden display of activity or energy: *In a burst of speed, she won the race at the last minute.* 1-5 *v.*, **burst, burst ing;** 6,7 *n.*

Bu run di (bü rün′dē), country in central Africa. *Capital:* Bujumbura. See **Congo** for map. *n.*

bur y (ber′ē), **1** put (a dead body) in the earth, in a tomb, or in the sea: *We buried the dead bird.* **2** cover up; hide: *The squirrels buried many nuts under the dead leaves.* **3** put or sink (oneself) deeply: *I buried myself in an interesting book.* **4** put far from one's mind: *I long ago buried any resentment caused by our argument.* *v.*, **bur ied, bur y ing.**

bus (bus), **1** a large motor vehicle with seats inside and formerly also on the roof. Buses are used to carry many passengers between fixed stations along a certain route. **2** take or go by bus: *The city bused the children to school.* 1 *n.*, *pl.* **bus es** or **bus ses;** 2 *v.*, **bused, bus ing** or **bussed, bus sing.** [*Bus* is short for *omnibus,* which came from French (*voiture*) *omnibus,* meaning "(vehicle) for all," which comes from Latin *omnibus,* meaning "for all."]

bus boy (bus′boi′), a waiter's assistant, who brings bread and butter, fills glasses, and carries off empty dishes. *n.*

bush (bush), **1** a woody plant smaller than a tree, often with many separate branches starting from or near the ground. Some bushes are used as hedges; others are cultivated for their fruit. **2** open forest or wild, unsettled land: *the Australian bush. n., pl.* **bush es.** —**bush′like′,** *adj.*

beat around the bush, avoid coming straight to the point: *Tell me the truth now; don't beat around the bush.*

Bush (bush), **George,** born 1924, vice-president of the United States since 1981. *n.*

bush., bushel.

bush el (bush′əl), **1** measure for grain, fruit, vegetables, and other dry things. It is equal to 4 pecks or 32 quarts. **2** container that holds a bushel. *n.*

bush ing (bush′ing), a removable metal lining used to protect parts of machinery from wear. *n.*

Bush man (bush′mən), member of a group of roving hunters of southern Africa. *n., pl.* **Bush men.**

bush mas ter (bush′mas′tər), the largest poisonous snake of Central and South America. *n.*

bush pilot, pilot who flies a small plane over unsettled country, such as parts of Alaska.

bush whack (bush′hwak′), to ambush or raid. *v.*

bush y (bush′ē), **1** spreading out like a bush; growing thickly: *a bushy beard.* **2** overgrown with bushes: *a bushy ravine. adj.,* **bush i er, bush i est.** —**bush′i ness,** *n.*

bus i ly (biz′ə lē), in a busy manner; actively: *Bees were busily collecting nectar in the clover. adv.*

busi ness (biz′nis), **1** thing that one is busy at; work; occupation: *A carpenter's business is building.* **2** matter; affair; concern: *I am tired of the whole business.* **3** buying and selling; commercial dealings; trade: *This hardware store does a big business in tools.* **4** of or having to do with business: *A business office usually has typewriters and other business machines.* **5** a store, factory, or other commercial enterprise; industrial establishment: *They own a bakery business.* **6** right to act; responsibility: *That is not your business.* 1-3,5,6 *n., pl.* **busi ness es** for 5; 4 *adj.*

mean business, INFORMAL. be in earnest; be serious: *When I say I'll do something, I mean business.*

busi ness like (biz′nis līk′), having system and method; well-managed; practical: *They ran a prosperous store in a businesslike manner. adj.*

busi ness man (biz′nis man′), man who is in business or who runs a business. *n., pl.* **busi ness men.**

busi ness wom an (biz′nis wùm′ən), woman who is in business or who runs a business. *n., pl.* **busi ness women.**

bus ing (bus′ing), transportation of students by bus from one residential area to another in order to achieve racial balance in schools. *n.*

bus man (bus′mən), conductor or driver of a bus. *n., pl.* **bus men.**

buss (bus), INFORMAL. kiss. *v., n., pl.* **buss es.**

bus ses (bus′iz), a plural of **bus.** *n.*

bust[1]
(def. 1)

bust[1] (bust), **1** statue of a person's head, shoulders, and upper chest. **2** a woman's breasts. *n.*

bust[2] (bust), SLANG. **1** burst; break. **2** punch; hit. **3** arrest or put in jail. *v.* —**bust′er,** *n.*

bus tle[1] (bus′əl), **1** be noisily busy and in a hurry: *The children bustled to get ready for the party.* **2** noisy or excited activity: *There was a great bustle as the children got ready for the party.* 1 *v.,* **bus tled, bus tling;** 2 *n.*

bus tle[2] (bus′əl), pad formerly used to puff out the upper back part of a woman's skirt. *n.*

bus y (biz′ē), **1** having plenty to do; working; active; not idle: *a busy person.* **2** full of work or activity: *Main Street is a busy place. Holidays are a busy time.* **3** make busy; keep busy: *The children busied themselves at drawing pictures.* **4** in use: *I tried to call you, but your phone was busy.* 1,2,4 *adj.,* **bus i er, bus i est;** 3 *v.,* **bus ied, bus y ing.** [*Busy* comes from Old English *bisig.*]

bus y bod y (biz′ē bod′ē), person who pries into the affairs of others; meddler. *n., pl.* **bus y bod ies.**

but (but; *unstressed* bət), **1** on the other hand; yet: *You may go, but you must come home at six o'clock.* **2** except; save: *I worked every day last week but Sunday. You were right but for one thing.* **3** unless; except that: *It never rains but it pours.* **4** no more than; only; merely: *He is but a small boy. We can but try.* **5** other than; otherwise than: *We cannot choose but listen.* **6** that: *I don't doubt but she will come.* 1,3,5,6 *conj.,* 2 *prep.,* 4 *adv.*

bu tane (byü′tān), a colorless gas, a hydrocarbon, much used as a fuel. *n.*

butch er (bùch′ər), **1** person who cuts up and sells meat. **2** person whose work is killing animals for food. **3** kill (animals) for food. **4** kill (people, wild animals, or birds) needlessly, cruelly, or in large numbers. **5** a brutal killer; murderer. **6** spoil by poor work: *Don't butcher that song by singing off key.* 1,2,5 *n.,* 3,4,6 *v.* —**butch′er er,** *n.*

butch er y (bùch′ər ē), brutal killing; murder in large numbers. *n., pl.* **butch er ies.**

but ler (but′lər), the head male servant in a household, in charge of the pantry and table service. *n.*

butt¹ (but), **1** the thicker end of a tool, weapon, ham, etc.: *the butt of a gun.* **2** end that is left; stub; stump: *a cigar butt. n.*

butt² (but), **1** object of ridicule or scorn: *to be made the butt of a joke.* **2** target. *n.*

butt³ (but), **1** to strike or push by knocking hard with the head: *A goat butts.* **2** a push or blow with the head. 1 *v.,* 2 *n.*

butt in, SLANG. meddle; interfere.

butte (byüt), (in the western United States) a steep hill that has a flat top and stands alone. *n.*

but ter (but′ər), **1** the solid yellowish fat separated from cream by churning. **2** put butter on: *Please butter my bread.* **3** any of various foods like butter in looks or use: *apple butter, peanut butter.* 1,3 *n.,* 2 *v.* —**but′ter less,** *adj.*

butter up, INFORMAL. flatter.

WORD HISTORY

butter

Butter is from Old English *butere,* which can be traced back to Greek *bous,* meaning "cow," and *tyros,* meaning "cheese."

butter bean, kind of lima bean grown in the southern United States.

but ter cup (but′ər kup′), a common plant with bright yellow flowers shaped like cups. *n.*

but ter fat (but′ər fat′), fat in milk. It can be made into butter. *n.*

but ter fin gers (but′ər fing′gərz), a careless or clumsy person. *n.*

but ter fly (but′ər flī′), **1** any of various insects with slender bodies and two pairs of large, usually brightly colored, overlapping wings. Butterflies fly mostly in the daytime. **2 butterflies,** *pl.* feelings of nervousness or sickness, especially in the stomach, because of fear, worry, or anticipation. *n., pl.* **but ter flies.**

but ter milk (but′ər milk′), the sour liquid left after butter has been separated from cream. Milk can also be changed to buttermilk artificially. *n.*

but ter nut (but′ər nut′), **1** an oily kind of walnut grown in North America, which is good to eat. **2** tree that bears butternuts. *n.*

but ter scotch (but′ər skoch′), **1** candy made from brown sugar and butter. **2** flavored with brown sugar and butter: *butterscotch pudding.* 1 *n.,* 2 *adj.*

but ter y (but′ər ē), **1** like butter. **2** containing or spread with butter. *adj.*

but tocks (but′əks), the fleshy hind part of the body where the legs join the back; rump. *n.pl.*

but ton (but′n), **1** a round, flat piece of metal, bone, glass, plastic, etc., fastened on garments to hold them closed or to decorate them. **2** fasten the buttons of; close with buttons: *Button your coat.* **3** knob or disk pushed, turned, etc., to cause something to work: *Push the button of the elevator to make it go up.* 1,3 *n.,* 2 *v.* —**but′ton less,** *adj.* —**but′ton like′,** *adj.*

but ton hole (but′n hōl′), **1** hole or slit through which a button is passed. **2** make buttonholes in. **3** hold in conversation or force to listen, as if holding someone by his or her coat. 1 *n.,* 2,3 *v.,* **but ton holed, but ton hol ing.** —**but′ton hol′er,** *n.*

a hat	**i** it	**oi** oil	**ch** child	a in about
ā age	**ī** ice	**ou** out	**ng** long	e in taken
ä far	**o** hot	**u** cup	**sh** she	ə = { i in pencil
e let	**ō** open	**u̇** put	**th** thin	o in lemon
ē equal	**ô** order	**ü** rule	**ᴛʜ** then	u in circus
ėr term			**zh** measure	

but ton wood (but′n wu̇d′), the sycamore tree of North America. *n.*

but tress (but′ris), **1** a support built against a wall or building to strengthen it. **2** a support like this; prop. **3** support and strenghten: *She buttressed her report with facts and figures.* 1,2 *n., pl.* **but tress es;** 3 *v.*

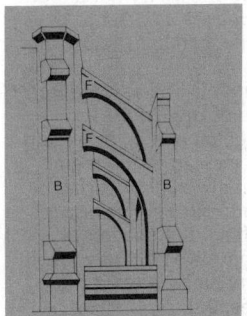

buttress (def. 1)
B, ordinary buttress
F, flying buttress

bux om (buk′səm), plump and good to look at; healthy and cheerful. *adj.* —**bux′om ly,** *adv.* —**bux′om ness,** *n.*

buy (bī), **1** get by paying a price; purchase: *You can buy a pencil for ten cents.* **2** INFORMAL. a bargain: *That book was a real buy.* **3** bribe: *It was charged that two members of the jury had been bought by the defendant.* **4** INFORMAL. believe or accept: *The jury didn't buy the witness's story.* 1,3,4 *v.,* **bought, buy ing;** 2 *n.* —**buy′a ble,** *adj.*

buy off, get rid of by paying money to; bribe: *The crook tried to buy off the judge.*

buy out, buy all the shares, rights, merchandise, etc., of: *buy out a business.*

buy er (bī′ər), **1** person who buys. **2** person whose work is buying goods for a department store or other business. *n.*

buzz (buz), **1** the humming sound made by flies, mosquitoes, or bees. **2** the low, confused sound of many people talking quietly: *The buzz of whispers stopped when the teacher entered the room.* **3** make a steady, humming sound; hum loudly: *The radio should be fixed; it buzzes when you turn it on.* **4** talk excitedly: *The whole class buzzed with the news of the holiday.* **5** fly an airplane very fast and low over (a place or person): *The pilot buzzed the treetops.* **6** to signal with a buzzer: *The editor buzzed her secretary.* 1,2 *n.,* 3-6 *v.*

buzz about, move about busily: *The children buzzed about the stage, getting ready to perform the play.*

buz zard (buz′ərd), **1** any of various large, heavy, slow-moving hawks. **2** turkey buzzard, a kind of vulture. *n.*

buzz er (buz′ər), an electrical device that makes a buzzing sound as a signal. *n.*

B.W.I., British West Indies.

bx., box. *pl.* **bxs.**

by (bī), **1** at the side or edge of; near; beside: *The garden is by the house. Sit by me.* **2** along; over; through: *They went by the main road.* **3** through the means, use, or action of: *We traveled by airplane. The house was destroyed by fire.* **4** in the measure of: *They sell eggs by the dozen.* **5** as soon as; not later than: *Try to be here by six o'clock.* **6** during: *The sun shines by day.* **7** past: *The Pilgrims lived in days gone by (adv.). A car raced by (adv.). They walked* *by our house* (*prep.*). **8** aside or away: *She puts money by every week to save for a new bicycle.* **9** according to: *to play by the rules.* **10** in relation to; concerning: *They did well by their children.* 1-7,9,10 *prep.*, 7,8 *adv.*

by and by, after a while; before long; soon: *Summer vacation will come by and by.*

by and large, for the most part: *By and large it is a good book.*

by the by, by the way; incidentally.

by-and-by (bī′ən bī′), the future. *n.*

Byel o rus sia (byel′ə rush′ə), republic in the W Soviet Union, just east of Poland. *Capital:* Minsk. *n.* Also, **White Russia. —Byel′o rus′sian,** *adj., n.*

by gone (bī′gôn′), **1** gone by; past; former: *The ancient Romans lived in bygone days.* **2 bygones,** *pl.* what is gone by and past: *Let bygones be forgotten.* 1 *adj.*, 2 *n.*

by law (bī′lô′), law made by a city, company, club, etc., for the control of its own affairs. *n.*

by-line (bī′līn′), line at the beginning of a newspaper or magazine article giving the name of the writer. *n.*

by pass (bī′pas′), **1** road, channel, pipe, etc., providing a secondary passage to be used instead of the main passage: *Drivers use the bypass to avoid the city when there is a lot of traffic.* **2** go around: *The new highway bypasses the entire city.* **3** the grafting of a section of blood vessel onto a blocked or narrowed blood vessel, usually a coronary artery, to carry blood around the obstruction. 1,3 *n.*, *pl.* **by pass es;** 2 *v.*

by path (bī′path′), a side path; byway. *n.*, *pl.* **by paths** (bī′paᴛHz′ *or* bī′paths′).

by play (bī′plā′), action that is not part of the main action, especially on the stage. *n.*

by-prod uct (bī′prod′əkt), something of value produced in making the principal product or doing something else: *Kerosene is a by-product of petroleum refining. n.*

Byrd (bėrd), **Richard Evelyn,** 1888-1957, American naval officer, aviator, and polar explorer. *n.*

by road (bī′rōd′), a side road. *n.*

By ron (bī′rən), **George Gordon,** Lord, 1788-1824, English poet. *n.*

by stand er (bī′stan′dər), person who stands near or looks on but does not take part; onlooker. *n.*

by-street (bī′strēt′), a side street. *n.*

byte (bīt), unit of computer information, equal to eight bits. *n.*

by way (bī′wā′), a side path or road. *n.*

by word (bī′wėrd′), **1** a common saying; proverb. **2** object of contempt; thing scorned: *Her cheating in class made her a byword to her classmates. n.*

Byz an tine (biz′n tēn′), **1** of the Byzantine Empire or Byzantium. **2** of or like a style of architecture developed in the Byzantine Empire, characterized by a circular dome over a square space, and the use of rich mosaics and frescoes. *adj.*

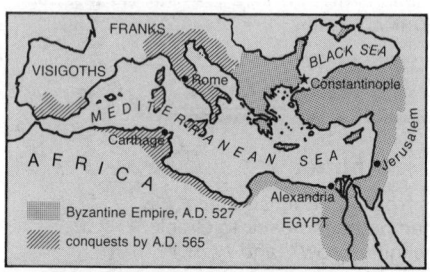

Byzantine Empire—The shaded areas show the Empire at its greatest extent.

Byzantine Empire, E part of the Roman Empire after its division in A.D. 395. The Byzantine Empire ended with the capture of its capital, Constantinople, by the Turks in 1453.

By zan ti um (bi zan′shē əm *or* bi zan′tē əm), ancient city where Istanbul (Constantinople) now is. It became the capital of the Roman Empire in A.D. 330. *n.*

Cc

a hat	i it	oi oil	ch child	⌈ a in about
ā age	ī ice	ou out	ng long	e in taken
ä far	o hot	u cup	sh she	ə = ⟨ i in pencil
e let	ō open	u̇ put	th thin	o in lemon
ē equal	ô order	ü rule	ŦH then	⌊ u in circus
ėr term			zh measure	

C or c (sē), **1** the third letter of the English alphabet. **2** the Roman numeral for 100. *n., pl.* **C's** or **c's.**

C, symbol for carbon.

c., 1 about; approximately. Also, **ca. 2** cent or cents. **3** centimeter. **4** cup or cups.

C., Centigrade.

CA, California (used with postal Zip Code).

Ca, symbol for calcium.

ca., about; approximately. Also, **c.** [The abbreviation *ca.* stands for the Latin word *circa.*]

C.A., Central America.

cab (kab), **1** automobile that can be hired with driver; taxicab: *We telephoned for a cab to take us to the airport.* **2** carriage that can be hired with driver, usually pulled by one horse: *We rode through the park in a cab.* **3** the enclosed part of a railroad engine where the engineer and fireman sit. **4** the enclosed part of a truck, crane, or other machine, where the driver or operator sits. *n.*

cab al ler o (kab/ə ler/ō *or* kab/ə lyer/ō), **1** (in Spain) a gentleman. **2** in southwestern United States: **a** horseman. **b** an ardent admirer. *n., pl.* **cab al ler os.** [*Caballero* was borrowed from Spanish *caballero,* and can be traced back to Latin *caballus,* meaning "horse."]

ca ban a (kə ban/ə), shelter like a small tent or cabin, used on a beach or near a swimming pool for dressing or to provide shade. *n., pl.* **ca ban as.** [*Cabana* is from Spanish *cabaña,* which comes from Latin *capanna,* meaning "hut."]

cab a ret (kab/ə rā/), restaurant offering singing and dancing as entertainment. *n.*

cab bage (kab/ij), vegetable whose thick leaves are closely folded into a round head that grows on a short stem. Cabbage is eaten either cooked or raw. *n.* **—cab/bage like/,** *adj.*

cab by or **cab bie** (kab/ē), INFORMAL. driver of a cab, especially a taxicab. *n., pl.* **cab bies.**

cab driv er (kab/drī/vər), person who drives a cab. *n.*

cab in (kab/ən), **1** a small, roughly built house; hut: *Last summer we stayed in a cabin in the Maine woods.* **2** a private room in a ship. **3** a room on a small boat containing the bunks. **4** place for passengers in an aircraft. *n.*

cabin boy, boy or man whose work is waiting on the officers and passengers on a ship.

cab i net (kab/ə nit), **1** piece of furniture with shelves or drawers, used to hold articles for use or display: *a medicine cabinet, a filing cabinet for letters. We keep our very best dishes in the china cabinet.* **2** Also, **Cabinet.** group of advisers chosen by the head of a nation, usually to administer particular departments of the government. The Attorney General and the Secretary of Defense are members of the cabinet of the President of the United States. *n.*

cab i net mak er (kab/ə nit mā/kər), person whose work is making fine furniture and woodwork. *n.*

ca ble (kā/bəl), **1** a strong, thick rope, usually made of wires twisted together: *The truck towed the automobile with a cable.* **2** an insulated bundle of wires which carries an electric current. Telegraph messages are sent across the ocean by underwater cable. **3** cablegram: *A transatlantic cable arrived from Paris.* **4** send (a message) across the ocean by underwater cable: *They cabled us from Paris.* 1-3 *n.,* 4 *v.,* **ca bled, ca bling. —ca/ble like/,** *adj.*

cable car, car pulled by a moving cable that is operated by an engine.

ca ble gram (kā/bəl gram), message sent across the ocean by underwater cable. *n.*

cable television, a system for direct transmission by coaxial cable of television programs that are not available by ordinary broadcast transmission.

ca boose (kə büs/), a small car on a freight train in which several of the train crew can work, rest, and sleep. It is usually the last car. *n.*

Cab ot (kab/ət), **1 John,** 1450?-1498, English navigator and explorer, born in Italy, who reached North America in 1497. **2** his son, **Sebastian,** 1474?-1557, English navigator and explorer in the service of England and Spain, born in Italy. *n.*

cacao (def. 1)
The broken pod reveals the seeds from which chocolate is made.

ca ca o (kə kā/ō *or* kə kä/ō), **1** the seeds from which cocoa and chocolate are made. **2** the small, tropical American evergreen tree that they grow on. *n., pl.* **ca ca os.**

cache (kash), **1** a hiding place to store food or other things: *The explorers dug a hole to serve as a cache for the supplies needed on the return trip.* **2** a hidden store of food or supplies: *Squirrels make caches of nuts for winter food.* **3** put in a cache; hide: *The bear had cached her cubs in a cave.* 1,2 *n.,* 3 *v.,* **cached, cach ing.**

cack le (kak/əl), **1** the shrill, broken sound that a hen makes, especially after laying an egg: *The cackle in the henhouse awoke the farmer.* **2** make this sound: *The hens started to cackle early in the morning.* **3** shrill, harsh, or broken laughter: *Before the comedian finished the joke, there were a few cackles from the audience.* **4** laugh in a shrill, harsh, or broken way: *The old man cackled at his own joke.* 1,3 *n.,* 2,4 *v.,* **cack led, cack ling.**

cable (def. 2)

ca coph o nous (kə kof′ə nəs), harsh and clashing in sound. *adj.* —**ca coph′o nous ly,** *adv.*

cac tus (kak′təs), plant with a thick, fleshy stem that usually has spines but no leaves. Most cactuses grow in very hot, dry regions of America and often have brightly colored flowers. *n., pl.* **cac tus es, cac ti** (kak′tī). —**cac′tus like′,** *adj.*

cad (kad), boy or man who does not act like a gentleman. *n.*

ca dav er (kə dav′ər), a dead body; corpse. *n.*

ca dav er ous (kə dav′ər əs), **1** pale and ghastly. **2** thin and worn. *adj.* —**ca dav′er ous ly,** *adv.*

cad die (kad′ē), **1** person who helps a golf player by carrying golf clubs, finding the ball, etc. **2** help a golf player in this way. 1 *n.,* 2 *v.,* **cad died, cad dy ing.** Also, **caddy.**

cad dis fly (kad′is), insect somewhat like a moth. Its larva lives under water and forms for itself a case of sand, bits of leaves, or the like.

cad dish (kad′ish), like a cad; ungentlemanly. *adj.* —**cad′dish ly,** *adv.* —**cad′dish ness,** *n.*

cad dy¹ (kad′ē), a small box, can, or chest, often used to hold tea. *n., pl.* **cad dies.** [*Caddy¹* comes from Malay *kati,* meaning "a small weight."]

cad dy² (kad′ē), caddie. *n., pl.* **cad dies;** *v.,* **cad died, cad dy ing.** [*Caddy²* comes from French *cadet,* meaning "younger brother," and can be traced back to Latin *caput,* meaning "head."]

ca dence (kād′ns), **1** the measure or beat of music, dancing, marching, or any movement regularly repeating itself; rhythm: *The cadence of the surf lulled us to sleep.* **2** fall of the voice: *the cadence at the end of a sentence.* **3** a rising and falling sound: *She speaks with a pleasant cadence.* **4** series of chords bringing part of a piece of music to an end. *n.*

ca den za (kə den′zə), flourish or showy passage, often improvised, usually near the end of a section of a musical composition. *n., pl.* **ca den zas.**

ca det (kə det′), **1** a young person in training for service as an officer in one of the armed forces: *The cadets from West Point will graduate next week.* **2** student in a high-school or grade-school military academy. *n.*

cadge (kaj), INFORMAL. beg shamelessly. *v.,* **cadged, cadg ing.** —**cadg′er,** *n.*

ca di (kä′dē), a minor Moslem judge, usually of a town or village. *n., pl.* **ca dis.**

cad mi um (kad′mē əm), a soft, bluish-white, metallic element resembling tin, used in plating to prevent corrosion and in making alloys. *n.*

cad re (kad′rē), an experienced staff that can set up, train, and form the core of an organization. *n.* [*Cadre* was borrowed from French *cadre,* and can be traced back to Latin *quadrum,* meaning "square."]

ca du ce us (kə dü′sē əs *or* kə dyü′sē əs), staff of Mercury with two snakes twined around it and a pair of wings on top. The caduceus is often used as an emblem of the medical profession. *n., pl.* **ca du ce i** (kə dü′sē ī *or* kə dyü′sē ī). —**ca du′ce an,** *adj.*

Cae sar (sē′zər), **1** Gaius Julius, 102?-44 B.C., Roman general, statesman, and historian. **2** title of the Roman emperors from Augustus to Hadrian, and later of the heir to the throne. **3** emperor. **4** dictator or tyrant. *n.*

Cae sa re a (sē′zə rē′ə), small seaport in NW Israel. It was the ancient Roman capital of Judea. *n.*

cae sur a (si zhür′ə), a pause in a line of verse. EXAMPLE: "To err is human, | to forgive, divine." *n., pl.* **cae sur as, cae sur ae** (si zhür′ē).

ca fe (ka fā′), café. *n., pl.* **ca fes.**

ca fé (ka fā′), **1** place to buy and eat a meal; restaurant. **2** barroom. *n., pl.* **ca fés.** [*Café* comes from French *café,*

cactus

which also means "coffee," and can be traced back to Arabic *qahwa,* meaning "coffee."]

caf e ter i a (kaf′ə tir′ē ə), restaurant where people serve themselves. *n., pl.* **caf e ter i as.**

caf feine or **caf fein** (kaf′ēn′), a slightly bitter, stimulating drug found in coffee and tea. *n.*

cage (kāj), **1** frame or place closed in with wires, strong iron bars, or wood. Birds and wild animals are kept in cages. **2** thing shaped or used like a cage. The car or closed platform of an elevator is a cage. Bank tellers often work in a cage. **3** put or keep in a cage: *After the lion was caught, it was caged.* 1,2 *n.,* 3 *v.,* **caged, cag ing.**

cage y or **cag y** (kā′jē), INFORMAL. shrewd and cautious; sharp and wary: *The cagey fox could not be easily trapped by the farmer.* *adj.,* **cag i er, cag i est.**

cag i ly (kā′jə lē), in a cagey manner; warily. *adv.*

cag i ness (kā′jē nis), cagey quality; wariness. *n.*

ca hoots (kə hüts′), SLANG. **in cahoots,** in partnership: *She did the mischief in cahoots with another.* *n.*

cai man (kā′mən), a large reptile of tropical America, similar to an alligator. *n., pl.* **cai mans.** Also, **cayman.** [*Caiman* comes from Spanish *caimán.*]

Cain (kān), **1** (in the Bible) the oldest son of Adam and Eve. He killed his brother Abel. **2** murderer. *n.*

raise Cain, SLANG. make a great disturbance: *When the teacher left the room, the students raised Cain.*

ca ique (kä ēk′), a long, narrow Turkish rowboat. *n., pl.* **ca iques.**

ca ïque (kä ēk′), caique. *n., pl.* **ca ïques.**

cairn (kern *or* karn), pile of stones, heaped up as a memorial, tomb, or landmark. *n.*

Cai ro (kī′rō), capital of Egypt, in the NE part. *n.*

caisson
(defs. 1 and 2)

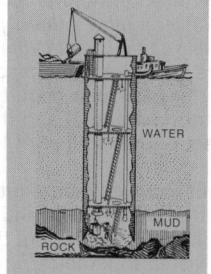

caisson (def. 3)
The weight of the caisson forces it into sand and mud below the water. Air under pressure is then forced into the caisson, driving out the water and permitting workers to enter through airtight compartments.

cais son (kā′sn *or* kā′son), **1** wagon to carry ammunition. **2** box for ammunition. **3** a watertight box or chamber in which men can work under ground or water to make foundations for buildings, tunnels, etc. **4** a watertight float used in raising sunken ships. *n.*

ca jole (kə jōl′), persuade by pleasant words, flattery, or false promises; coax: *He cajoled his friends into deciding in his favor. v.,* **ca joled, ca jol ing.** —**ca jol′er,** *n.* —**ca jol′ing ly,** *adv.*

ca jol er y (kə jō′lər ē), persuasion by pleasant words, flattery, or false promises; coaxing. *n., pl.* **ca jol er ies.**

Ca jun (kā′jən), person who is a descendant of the French-speaking people who came to Louisiana from the colony of Acadia in eastern Canada. *n.*

cake (kāk), **1** a baked mixture of flour, sugar, eggs, flavoring, and other things: *We baked a chocolate cake with white frosting for Mother's birthday.* **2** pancake. **3** a shaped mass of food or other substance: *a fish cake, a cake of soap.* **4** form into a solid mass; harden: *Mud cakes as it dries.* 1-3 *n.,* 4 *v.,* **caked, cak ing.**

take the cake, SLANG. **1** win first prize. **2** excel.

cake walk (kāk′wôk′), **1** a dance with prancing high steps that developed from an earlier march or promenade for couples. A cake was the prize for the most original steps. **2** do a cakewalk. 1 *n.,* 2 *v.* —**cake′-walk′er,** *n.*

cal., caliber.

Cal., California. The official abbreviation is **Calif.**

cal a bash (kal′ə bash), **1** gourd or gourdlike fruit whose dried shell is used to make bottles, bowls, drums, pipes, and rattles. **2** the tropical plant or tree that it grows on. **3** bottle, bowl, drum, pipe, or rattle made from such a dried shell. *n., pl.* **cal a bash es.**

cal a boose (kal′ə büs), INFORMAL. a jail; prison. *n.*

Cal ais (ka lā′), seaport in N France that is nearest England. *n.*

cal a mine (kal′ə mīn), compound of zinc oxide and iron oxide used in lotions to relieve skin irritations or sunburn. *n.*

ca lam i tous (kə lam′ə təs), causing calamity; accompanied by calamity; disastrous. *adj.* —**ca lam′i tous ly,** *adv.* —**ca lam′i tous ness,** *n.*

ca lam i ty (kə lam′ə tē), **1** a great misfortune such as a flood, a fire, the loss of one's sight or hearing, or of much money or property; disaster. **2** serious trouble; misery: *Many people still suffer from the calamity of hunger and poverty. n., pl.* **ca lam i ties.**

cal ca ne us (kal kā′nē əs), the heel bone. *n., pl.* **cal ca ne i** (kal kā′nē ī).

cal ci fi ca tion (kal′sə fə kā′shən), **1** process of calcifying. **2** a calcified part. *n.*

cal ci fy (kal′sə fī), make or become hard or bony by the deposit of calcium salts: *Cartilage often calcifies in older people. v.,* **cal ci fied, cal ci fy ing.**

cal ci mine (kal′sə mīn), **1** a white or tinted lime solution used as a wash for walls, ceilings, etc. **2** cover with calcimine. 1 *n.,* 2 *v.,* **cal ci mined, cal ci min ing.** —**cal′ci min′er,** *n.*

cal cine (kal′sīn), burn (something) to ashes or powder: *calcine bones. v.,* **cal cined, cal cin ing.**

cal cite (kal′sīt), mineral made up of calcium carbonate. It is the chief substance in limestone, chalk, and marble. *n.*

cal ci um (kal′sē əm), a soft, silvery-white metallic element. It is a part of limestone, chalk, milk, bone, shells, teeth, etc. Calcium is used in alloys and its compounds are used in making plaster, in cooking, and as bleaching agents. *n.*

calcium carbonate, compound of calcium occurring in rocks such as marble and limestone, in animals' bones, shells, and teeth, and to some extent in plants. *n.*

calcium hydroxide, slaked lime.

calcium oxide, lime[1].

cal cu la ble (kal′kyə lə bəl), able to be calculated. *adj.* —**cal′cu la bly,** *adv.*

a hat	i it	oi oil	ch child	a in about
ā age	ī ice	ou out	ng long	e in taken
ä far	o hot	u cup	sh she	ə = { i in pencil
e let	ō open	u̇ put	th thin	o in lemon
ē equal	ô order	ü rule	ŦH then	u in circus
ėr term			zh measure	

cal cu late (kal′kyə lāt), **1** find out by adding, subtracting, multiplying, or dividing; compute: *They calculated the cost of building a house.* **2** find out beforehand by any process of reasoning; estimate: *Calculate the day of the week on which New Year's Day will fall.* **3** rely; depend; count: *You can calculate on earning $50 a week if you take the job.* **4** plan or intend: *That remark was calculated to make me angry. v.,* **cal cu lat ed, cal cu lat ing.** —**cal′cu lat′ed ly,** *adv.*

cal cu lat ing (kal′kyə lā′ting), **1** that calculates: *a calculating machine.* **2** shrewd and careful. **3** scheming and selfish. *adj.* —**cal′cu lat′ing ly,** *adv.*

cal cu la tion (kal′kyə lā′shən), **1** act of adding, subtracting, multiplying, or dividing to find a result; computation. **2** result found by calculating. **3** careful thinking; deliberate planning: *The success of the expedition was the result of much calculation. n.*

cal cu la tor (kal′kyə lā′tər), **1** machine that calculates, especially one that solves difficult problems in calculation. **2** person who calculates. *n.*

cal cu lus (kal′kyə ləs), system of calculation in advanced mathematics, using algebraic symbols to solve problems dealing with changing quantities. *n., pl.* **cal cu li** (kal′kyə lī), **cal cu lus es.**

Cal cut ta (kal kut′ə), seaport in E India. *n.*

cal dron (kôl′drən), a large kettle or boiler. *n.* Also, **cauldron.**

Cal e do ni a (kal′ə dō′nē ə), Scotland. *n.* —**Cal′e do′ni an,** *adj., n.*

cal en dar (kal′ən dər), **1** table showing the months, weeks, and days of the year. A calendar shows the day of the week on which each day of the month falls. *The calendar shows that Memorial Day will fall on a Monday.* **2** system by which the beginning, length, and divisions of the year are fixed: *The Julian calendar was established during the reign of Julius Caesar.* **3** a list or schedule; record; register: *The clerk of the court announced the next case on the calendar. n.*

calf[1] (kaf), **1** a young cow or bull. **2** a young elephant, whale, deer, or seal. **3** calfskin: *The gloves are made of calf. n., pl.* **calves** for 1 and 2. [*Calf*[1] comes from Old English *cealf.*] —**calf′like′,** *adj.*

calf[2] (kaf), the thick, fleshy part of the back of the leg below the knee. *n., pl.* **calves.** [*Calf*[2] came into English about 650 years ago from Icelandic *kālfi.*]

calf skin (kaf′skin′), **1** skin of a calf. **2** leather made from it. *n.*

Cal gar y (kal′gər ē), city in SW Canada. *n.*

Cal houn (kal hün′), **John Caldwell,** 1782-1850, American statesman, vice-president of the United States from 1825 to 1832. *n.*

cal i ber or **cal i bre** (kal′ə bər), **1** the inside diameter of the barrel of a gun. A .45-caliber revolver has a barrel with an inside diameter of $^{45}/_{100}$ of an inch. **2** the diameter of a bullet or shell fired from a particular gun. **3** amount of ability: *a person of high caliber.* **4** quality: *improve the caliber of our schools. n.*

cal i brate (kal′ə brāt), **1** determine, check, or adjust the scale of (a thermometer, gauge, or other measuring instrument). Calibrating is usually done by comparison with a standard instrument. **2** find the caliber of. *v.,* **cal i brat ed, cal i brat ing.** —**cal′i bra′tor,** *n.*

cal i bra tion (kal′ə brā′shən), a calibrating or a being calibrated. *n.*

cal i co (kal′ə kō), **1** a cotton cloth that usually has colored patterns printed on one side. **2** made of calico: *a calico dress.* **3** spotted in colors: *a calico cat.* **1** *n., pl.* **cal i coes** or **cal i cos; 2,3** *adj.*

ca lif (kā′lif), caliph. *n.*

Calif., the official abbreviation of California.

cal if ate (kal′ə fāt), caliphate. *n.*

Cal i for nia (kal′ə fôr′nyə), **1** one of the Pacific states of the United States. *Abbreviation:* Calif. or CA *Capital:* Sacramento. **2 Gulf of,** arm of the Pacific between Lower California and the mainland of Mexico. *n.* —**Cal′i-for′nian,** *adj., n.*

cal i for ni um (kal′ə fôr′nē əm), a radioactive metallic element, produced artificially from curium, plutonium, or uranium. *n.* [This element was named in honor of *California* and the University of *California,* where it was first produced.]

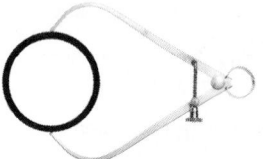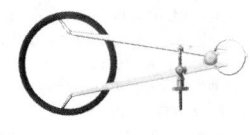

calipers—used to measure the outside diameter of a pipe

calipers—used to measure the inside diameter of a pipe

cal i pers (kal′ə pərz), instrument used to measure the diameter or thickness of something. *n.pl.* Also, **callipers.**

ca liph (kā′lif), the former title of religious and political heads of some Moslem states. *n.* Also, **calif.**

cal iph ate (kal′ə fāt), rank, reign, government, or territory of a caliph. *n.* Also, **califate.**

cal is then ics (kal′is then′iks), exercises to develop a strong and graceful body. Calisthenics are carried out simply by moving the body, without the use of special equipment. *n.pl.* Also, **callisthenics.**

calk[1] (kôk), a projecting piece on a horseshoe that catches in the ground or ice to prevent slipping. *n.* [*Calk*[1] can be traced back to Latin *calcem,* meaning "heel."]

calk[2] (kôk), caulk. *v.* [*Calk*[2] came into English about 500 years ago from French *cauquer,* meaning "to press in, tread," and can be traced back to Latin *calcem,* meaning "heel."]

call (kôl), **1** speak or say in a loud voice; shout or cry out: *He called from downstairs. The nurse called the names of the next three patients.* **2** a loud sound uttered by a person so as to be heard from a distance; shout: *I heard the swimmer's call for help.* **3** the special noise or cry an animal or bird makes: *The call of a moose came from the forest.* **4** make this noise or cry: *The crows called to each other from the trees around the meadow.* **5** give a signal to; arouse: *The bugle called the group to assemble. Call me at seven o'clock.* **6** command or ask to come; summon: *He called his dog with a loud whistle.* **7** invitation or summons: *Every farmer in the neighborhood answered the firemen's call for volunteers.* **8** give a name to; name: *They called the new baby "Olga."* **9** read over aloud: *The teacher called the roll of the class.* **10** talk to by telephone: *Did anyone call today? Call me at the office.* **11** a telephone call: *I want to make a call to Chicago.* **12** make a short visit or stop: *Our pastor called yesterday.* **13** a short visit or stop: *The doctor had six calls to make.* **14** consider; estimate: *Everyone called the party a success.* **15** a claim; demand: *I cannot rest with all these calls on my time.*

16 need; occasion: *You have no call to meddle in other people's business.* **17** (in sports) end; stop: *The ball game was called on account of rain.* **18** demand payment of: *The bank called their loan.* **19** (in sports) to make a spoken judgment about: *The umpire called the long drive a foul ball.* **20** a decision or ruling by a referee or umpire: *The batter was enraged at the umpire's call of strike three.* **1,4-6,8-10,12,14,17-19** *v.,* **2,3,7,11,13,15,16,20** *n.*

call down, scold: *Most people dislike being called down in front of others.*

call for, 1 go and get; stop and get: *The cab called for her at the hotel.* **2** need; require: *This recipe calls for two eggs.*

call in, 1 summon for advice or consultation: *Mother called in a doctor when I got a high fever.* **2** withdraw: *The library calls in books that are damaged.*

call off, 1 cancel: *We called off our trip.* **2** say or read over aloud in succession: *The teacher called off the names on the roll.* **3** order to withdraw: *Call off your dog.*

call on or **call upon, 1** pay a short visit to: *We must call on our new neighbors.* **2** appeal to: *He called upon his friends for help.*

call out, 1 say in a loud voice; shout: *She called out to the boys to stop quarreling.* **2** summon into service: *The governor called out the National Guard to help with the rescue work during the flood.*

call up, 1 telephone to: *He called me up at the office.* **2** draft into military service: *The army called him up when he finished school.* *n.*

on call, ready or available: *Doctors are expected to be on call day and night.*

within call, near enough to hear a call: *We are supposed to stay within call since supper is almost ready.*

cal la (kal′ə), plant with a large, white leaf like a petal around a thick spike of small yellow flowers. *n., pl.* **cal-las.**

calla lily, calla.

call boy (kôl′boi′), a hotel bellboy. *n.*

call er (kô′lər), **1** person who makes a short visit: *The doctor said that the patient was now able to receive callers.* **2** person who calls out names, steps at a square dance, etc. *n.*

cal lig ra phy (kə lig′rə fē), **1** handwriting. **2** beautiful handwriting: *Calligraphy is considered an art in China.* *n.*

call ing (kô′ling), **1** occupation, profession, or trade: *He chose to follow the calling of a teacher while his sister chose medicine as her calling.* **2** urge or summons: *She felt an inner calling to be a social worker.* *n.*

cal li o pe (kə lī′ə pē), a musical instrument having a series of steam whistles played by pressing keys on a keyboard. *n.*

cal li pers (kal′ə pərz), calipers. *n.pl.*

cal lis then ics (kal′is then′iks), calisthenics. *n.pl.*

call loan, loan that must be paid back on demand.

call number, number put on a library book to enable the user to identify and find it.

cal los i ty (kə los′ə tē), **1** callus. **2** lack of feeling or sensitivity. *n., pl.* **cal los i ties.**

cal lous (kal′əs), **1** having a callus; hard: *Going barefoot makes the bottoms of your feet callous.* **2** unfeeling; not sensitive: *Only a callous person can see suffering without trying to relieve it.* *adj.* —**cal′lous ly,** *adv.* —**cal′lous-ness,** *n.*

cal loused (kal′əst), made callous; hardened. *adj.*

cal low (kal′ō), not fully grown or developed; immature: *a callow youth. adj.* —**cal′low ness,** *n.*

call-up (kôl′up′), a calling to military training or duty. *n.*

cal lus (kal′əs), a hard, thickened place on the skin. *n., pl.* **cal lus es.**

calm (käm *or* kälm), **1** not stormy or windy; not stirred

up; quiet; still: *In fair weather, the sea is usually calm.*
2 not excited; peaceful: *Although she was frightened, she answered with a calm voice.* **3** absence of wind or motion; quietness; stillness: *There was a sudden calm as the wind dropped.* **4** absence of excitement; peacefulness: *The activity of the game was followed by an unusual calm.* **5** make or become calm: *I rocked the cradle to calm the crying baby. The storm ceased and the sea calmed.* 1,2 *adj.,* 3,4 *n.,* 5 *v.* —**calm′ly,** *adv.* —**calm′ness,** *n.*

cal o mel (kal′ə mel), a white, tasteless, crystalline powder, formerly used in medicine as a laxative. It is a compound of mercury and chlorine. *n.*

ca lo ric (kə lôr′ik), having to do with heat or calories. *adj.* —**ca lo′ri cal ly,** *adv.*

cal or ie (kal′ər ē), **1** unit for measuring the amount of heat. It is the quantity of heat needed to raise by one degree centigrade the temperature of either a gram of water (**small calorie**) or a kilogram of water (**large calorie**). **2** unit of the energy supplied by food, corresponding to the large calorie. An ounce of sugar will produce about one hundred such calories. *n., pl.* **cal ories.**

cal o rif ic (kal′ə rif′ik), caloric. *adj.*

cal or y (kal′ər ē), calorie. *n., pl.* **cal or ies.**

cal u met (kal′yə met), a long, ornamented tobacco pipe smoked by the American Indians in ceremonies as a symbol of peace. *n.* [*Calumet* was borrowed from Canadian French *calumet,* and can be traced back to Greek *kalamos,* meaning "reed."]

ca lum ni ate (kə lum′nē āt), say false and harmful things about; slander. *v.,* **ca lum ni at ed, ca lum ni at ing.** —**ca lum′ni a′tor,** *n.*

ca lum ni ous (kə lum′nē əs), slanderous. *adj.* —**ca lum′ni ous ly,** *adv.*

cal um ny (kal′əm nē), a false statement made on purpose to do harm to someone; slander. *n., pl.* **cal um nies.**

Cal var y (kal′vər ē), (in the Bible) a place near Jerusalem where Jesus died on the Cross; Golgotha. *n.*

calve (kav), give birth to a calf. *v.,* **calved, calv ing.**

calves (kavz), plural of **calf**[1] (defs. 1 and 2) and **calf**[2]. *n.*

Cal vin (kal′vən), **John,** 1509-1564, French leader of the Protestant Reformation at Geneva. *n.*

Cal vin ism (kal′və niz′əm), the religious teachings of Calvin and his followers. *n.*

Cal vin ist (kal′və nist), **1** person who follows the teachings of Calvin. **2** having to do with Calvinism or Calvinists. 1 *n.,* 2 *adj.*

ca lyp so (kə lip′sō), type of improvised song, usually about some matter of current interest, that originated in the West Indies. *n., pl.* **ca lyp sos.**

PETAL
SEPAL
calyx

ca lyx (kā′liks *or* kal′iks), the outer leaves that surround the unopened bud of a flower. The calyx is made up of sepals. *n., pl.* **ca lyx es, cal y ces** (kal′ə sēz′ *or* kā′lə sēz′).

cam (kam), a wheel that is not circular which is mounted on a shaft so that it changes circular motion into back-and-forth motion. Cams are used to vary the speed of some mechanisms or change the direction of their movement. *n.*

ca ma ra der ie (kä′mə rä′dər ē), friendliness and loyalty among comrades; comradeship: *the cheerful camaraderie of school days. n.*

cam bi um (kam′bē əm), layer of soft growing tissue between the bark and the wood of trees and shrubs. New bark and new wood grow from it. *n.*

Cam bo di a (kam bō′dē ə), country in SE Asia. *Capital:* Phnom Penh. See **Indochina** for map. *n.* Also, **Kampuchea.** —**Cam bo′di an,** *adj., n.*

cam bric (kām′brik), a fine, thin linen or cotton cloth. *n.*

cambric tea, drink made of hot water, milk, and sugar, sometimes flavored with a little tea. *n.*

Cam bridge (kām′brij), **1** city in SE England. **2** the old and famous English university located there. *n.*

cam cor der (kam′kor′dər), a hand-held combination of a camera and a video recorder. *n.* [*Camcorder* is a blend of the word *camera* and the phrase *video recorder.*]

Cam den (kam′dən), city in SW New Jersey. *n.*

came (kām), past tense of **come.** *I came home late. v.*

cam el (kam′əl), a large, four-footed, cud-chewing mammal with a long neck and cushioned feet. It is used as a beast of burden in the deserts of northern Africa and central Asia because it can go for a long time without drinking water. The Arabian camel, or dromedary, has one hump; the Bactrian camel has two humps. *n.*

ca mel lia (kə me′lyə), shrub or tree with glossy, evergreen leaves and waxy white, red, pink, or spotted flowers shaped like roses. *n., pl.* **ca mel lias.**

Cam e lot (kam′ə lot), legendary place in England where King Arthur had his palace and court. *n.*

Cam em bert (kam′əm ber), a rich, soft cheese. *n.* [This cheese was named for *Camembert,* a village in northwestern France, where it was first made.]

cam e o (kam′ē ō), a semiprecious stone carved so that there is a raised design on a background usually of a different color. *n., pl.* **cam e os.**

cam er a (kam′ər ə), **1** machine for taking photographs or motion pictures. A camera lens focuses light rays through the dark inside part of the camera onto film which is sensitive to light. **2** part of the transmitter which converts images into electronic impulses for television transmitting. *n., pl.* **cam er as.**

cam er a man (kam′ər ə man′), person who operates a motion-picture or television camera. *n., pl.* **cam er a men.**

Cam er oon or **Cam er oun** (kam′ə rün′), country in W central Africa. *Capital:* Yaoundé. See **Nigeria** for map. *n.* —**Cam′er oon′i an, Cam′er oun′i an,** *adj., n.*

cam i sole (kam′ə sōl), a woman's undergarment that is like the top part of a slip. *n.*

cam o mile (kam′ə mīl), chamomile. *n.*

cam ou flage (kam′ə fläzh), **1** a disguise or false appearance for the purpose of concealing. The white fur of

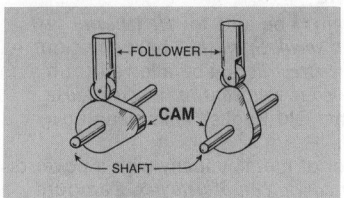

FOLLOWER
CAM
SHAFT

cam—As the cam turns with the shaft, the follower moves down (left) and up (right).

a polar bear is a natural camouflage, for it prevents the bear's being easily seen against the snow. **2** the practice of giving soldiers, weapons, etc., a false appearance to conceal them from the enemy. **3** materials or other means by which this is done: *The guns were hidden by a camouflage of earth and branches.* **4** give a false appearance to in order to conceal; disguise: *The hunters were camouflaged with shrubbery so that they blended with the green landscape.* 1-3 *n.*, 4 *v.*, **cam ou flaged, cam ou flag ing. —cam′ou flage′a ble,** *adj.* **—cam′ou flag′er,** *n.*

camp (kamp), **1** group of tents, huts, or other shelters where people live for a time: *Many people live in the camp near that large lake during the summer.* **2** live away from home for a time outdoors or in a tent or hut: *The scout troop camped at the foot of the mountain for two weeks.* **3** place where one lives in a tent or hut or outdoors: *Last year I spent two weeks at summer camp.* **4** area where an army sets up temporary shelter. **5** persons living in a camp: *The camp was awakened by the bugler.* **6** live simply, as one does in a tent: *We camped in the empty house until our furniture arrived.* **7** group of people who agree or work together: *The election of a new president divided the club into two opposing camps.* 1,3-5,7 *n.*, 2,6 *v.*
break camp, pack up tents and equipment: *We broke camp early in the morning to return home.*
camp out, spend the night outdoors.
in the same camp, in agreement.

cam paign (kam pān′), **1** series of related military operations in a war which are aimed at some special purpose: *The general planned a campaign to capture the enemy's most important city.* **2** series of connected activities to do or get something: *Our town had a campaign to raise money for a new hospital.* **3** take part or serve in a campaign: *She campaigned for mayor by giving speeches.* 1,2 *n.*, 3 *v.* **—cam paign′er,** *n.*

cam pa ni le (kam′pə nē′lē), tower built to contain a bell or bells. It may be a separate building. *n., pl.* **cam pa ni les, cam pa ni li** (kam′pə nē′lē).

camp er (kam′pər), **1** person who camps. **2** vehicle fitted out for camping, either self-propelled or pulled by an automobile. *n.*

camp fire (kamp′fīr′), **1** fire in a camp for cooking or warmth. **2** a social gathering of soldiers, scouts, etc. *n.*

campfire girl, member of the Camp Fire Girls.

Camp Fire Girls, organization for girls to help them develop character, health, and usefulness to others.

camp ground (kamp′ground′), **1** place for camping, especially a public park with campsites, fireplaces for cooking, etc. **2** place where a camp meeting is held. *n.*

cam phor (kam′fər), a white, crystalline substance with a strong odor, usually obtained from a laurel tree in eastern Asia. Camphor is used in medicine and to protect clothes from moths. *n.*

cam phor at ed (kam′fə rā′tid), containing camphor: *camphorated oil. adj.*

camp ing (kam′ping), the practice or recreation of living outdoors in a temporary shelter, or vehicle. *n.*

camp meeting, a religious gathering held outdoors or in a tent, sometimes lasting several days.

camp site (kamp′sīt′), place where people camp. *n.*

cam pus (kam′pəs), grounds of a college, university, or school. *n., pl.* **cam pus es.**

can[1] (kan; *unstressed* kən), **1** be able to: *He can run fast.* **2** know how to: *She can speak Spanish.* **3** have the right to: *Anyone can cross the street here.* **4** be allowed to; may: *Can I go now? You can go if you want to. v., past tense* **could.** [*Can*[1] comes from Old English *can,* meaning "know, know how, can."]

can[2] (kan), **1** a container of metal, usually with a cover or lid: *a trash can, a paint can, a can of peaches.* **2** amount that a can holds: *Add three cans of water to make the orange juice.* **3** put in an airtight can or jar to preserve: *We are going to can tomatoes.* 1,2 *n.*, 3 *v.*, **canned, canning.** [*Can*[2] comes from Old English *canne,* meaning "vessel, cup."]

Can., **1** Canada. **2** Canadian.

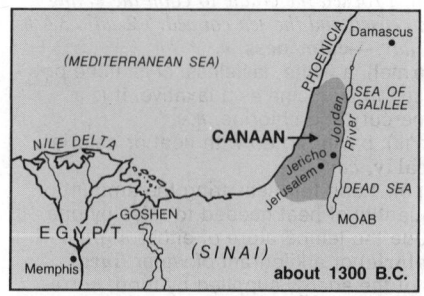

Ca naan (kā′nən), (in the Bible) a region in Palestine between the Jordan River and the Mediterranean. God promised Canaan to Abraham and his descendants. *n.*

Ca naan ite (kā′nə nīt), inhabitant of Canaan before it was conquered by the Hebrews. *n.*

Canad., Canadian.

Can a da (kan′ə də), country in the N part of North America, consisting of ten provinces and two territories and extending from the Atlantic to the Pacific and from the United States to the Arctic Ocean. It is a member of the Commonwealth of Nations. *Capital:* Ottawa. *n.*

Canada goose, a large, wild goose of North America, having a black head and neck, white throat, and a brownish-gray body.

Canada goose
up to 43 in.
(109 cm.) long

Ca na di an (kə nā′dē ən), **1** of Canada or its people. **2** person born or living in Canada. 1 *adj.,* 2 *n.*

ca nal (kə nal′), **1** waterway dug across land for ships or small boats to go through or to carry water for irrigation. **2** tube in the body of a person or an animal that carries food, liquid, air, etc.: *The food that we eat goes through the alimentary canal. n.*

Canal Zone, the Panama Canal and the land five miles (eight kilometers) on each side, governed by the United States from 1903 to 1979, and now governed by Panama. Also, **Panama Canal Zone.**

can a pé (kan′ə pā *or* kan′ə pē), cracker or thin piece of toast or bread spread with olives, meat, fish, cheese, etc., and served as an appetizer. *n., pl.* **can a pés.**

ca nard (kə närd′), a false rumor; hoax. *n.*

Ca nar ies (kə ner′ēz), Canary Islands. *n.pl.*

ca nar y (kə ner′ē), **1** a small, yellow songbird. It is a kind of finch and is often kept as a pet. **2** a light yellow. **3** light-yellow. 1,2 *n., pl.* **ca nar ies;** 3 *adj.*

Canary Islands, group of Spanish islands in the Atlantic, near the NW coast of Africa.

canary yellow, a light yellow.

Can ber ra (kan′ber ə), capital of Australia, in the SE part. *n.*

canc., 1 canceled. **2** cancellation.

can cel (kan′səl), **1** put an end to, set aside, or withdraw; do away with; stop: *The teacher canceled his order for the books. She canceled her appointment with the doctor.* **2** make up for; compensate for; balance: *If I vote "Yes" and you vote "No," we shall cancel out each other.* **3** cross out; mark, stamp, or punch so that it cannot be used again: *The post office cancels the stamp on a letter.* **4** in mathematics: **a** reduce (a fraction) by dividing both the numerator and the denominator by the same quantity. **b** reduce (an equation) by dividing both members by a common factor. *v.,* **can celed, can cel ing** or **can celled, can cel ling. —can′cel a ble, can′cel la ble,** *adj.* **—can′cel er, can′cel ler,** *n.*

can cel la tion (kan′sə lā′shən), **1** a canceling or a being canceled: *cancellation of a baseball game because of rain.* **2** marks made when something is canceled or crossed out: *The cancellation of that check consists of small holes punched through it.* **3** something that is canceled. *n.*

can cer (kan′sər), **1** a very harmful growth in the body; malignant tumor. Cancer tends to spread and destroy the healthy tissues and organs of the body. **2** an evil or harmful thing that tends to spread: *The existence of slums is a destructive cancer in many large cities.* **3 Cancer, a** tropic of Cancer. **b** group of stars shaped somewhat like a crab. *n.* [*Cancer* comes from Latin *cancer,* meaning "crab, tumor."]

can cer ous (kan′sər əs), **1** like cancer: *a cancerous tumor.* **2** having cancer: *a cancerous liver. adj.* **—can′cer ous ly,** *adv.*

can de la (kan dē′lə), unit for measuring the strength or intensity of light; candle. *n., pl.* **can de las.**

can de la bra (kan′dl ä′brə *or* kan′dl ā′brə), candelabrum. *n., pl.* **can de la bras.**

can de la brum (kan′dl ä′brəm *or* kan′dl ā′brəm), an ornamental candlestick with several branches for candles. *n., pl.* **can de la bra** or **can de la brums.**

can did (kan′did), **1** saying openly what one really thinks; frank and sincere; outspoken: *a candid reply. Please be candid with me.* **2** fair; impartial: *a candid decision.* **3** not posed: *a candid photograph of children playing. adj.* **—can′did ly,** *adv.* **—can′did ness,** *n.*

can di da cy (kan′də də sē), fact or condition of being a candidate: *Please support my candidacy for class treasurer. n., pl.* **can di da cies.**

can di date (kan′də dāt), person who seeks, or is proposed for, some office or honor: *There are three candidates for president of the club. n.*

can died (kan′dēd), **1** cooked in sugar; glazed with sugar: *candied sweet potatoes.* **2** preserved or encrusted with sugar: *candied ginger.* **3** made sweet or agreeable: *candied words of praise. adj.*

can dle (kan′dl), **1** stick of wax or tallow with a wick in it, burned to give light: *There are ten candles on the birthday cake.* **2** test (eggs) for freshness by holding them in front of a light: *The farmer candled the eggs before he sold them.* **3** candela. 1,3 *n.,* 2 *v.,* **can dled, can dling.**

burn the candle at both ends, use up one's strength and resources rapidly.

not hold a candle to, not compare with: *The cake from the bakery did not hold a candle to the homemade one.*

can dle light (kan′dl līt′), **1** light of a candle or candles.

a hat	**i** it	**oi** oil	**ch** child	ə = a in about
ā age	**ī** ice	**ou** out	**ng** long	e in taken
ä far	**o** hot	**u** cup	**sh** she	i in pencil
e let	**ō** open	**u̇** put	**th** thin	o in lemon
ē equal	**ô** order	**ü** rule	**ᴛʜ** then	u in circus
ėr term			**zh** measure	

2 time when candles are lighted; dusk; twilight; nightfall. *n.*

can dle lit (kan′dl lit′), lit by candle. *adj.*

Can dle mas (kan′dl məs), February 2, a church festival in honor of the purification of the Virgin Mary. It is celebrated with lighted candles. *n.*

can dle pow er (kan′dl pou′ər), strength or intensity of light, measured in candelas. *n.*

can dler (kan′dlər), person who tests eggs for freshness by holding them in front of a light. *n.*

can dle stick (kan′dl stik′), holder for a candle, to make it stand up straight. *n.*

can dle wick (kan′dl wik′), wick of a candle. *n.*

can dor (kan′dər), **1** a saying openly what one really thinks; honesty in giving one's view or opinion; frankness and sincerity: *She expressed her views with great candor.* **2** fairness: *We must weigh each argument with candor before coming to a decision. n.*

can dour (kan′dər), BRITISH. candor. *n.*

can dy (kan′dē), **1** sugar or syrup, boiled with water and flavoring, then cooled and made into small pieces for eating. Chocolate, butter, milk, nuts, fruits, etc., are often added. **2** piece of this: *Take a candy from the box.* **3** turn into sugar: *This honey has candied.* **4** cook in sugar; preserve by boiling in sugar: *She candied the peaches before canning them.* 1,2 *n., pl.* **can dies;** 3,4 *v.,* **can died, can dy ing. —can′dy like′,** *adj.*

can dy tuft (kan′dē tuft′), plant related to the mustard, with clusters of white, purple, pink, or red flowers. *n.*

cane (kān), **1** a slender stick used as an aid in walking: *On long walks the old woman took along her cane.* **2** stick used to beat with: *A blow with a cane was an old form of punishment.* **3** beat with a cane: *Some schoolmasters used to cane boys when they did not obey.* **4** a long, jointed stem, such as that of the bamboo. **5** plant having such stems. Sugar cane, bamboo, and rattan are canes. **6** material made of such stems, used for furniture, chair seats, etc.: *Our porch chairs have cane seats.* **7** make or repair with this material: *We are having all our porch furniture caned.* 1,2,4-6 *n.,* 3,7 *v.,* **caned, can ing. —cane′like′,** *adj.*

cane brake (kān′brāk′), thicket of cane plants. *n.*

cane sugar, sugar made from sugar cane.

ca nine (kā′nīn), **1** dog. **2** of or like a dog: *canine faithfulness.* **3** any animal belonging to a group of meat-eating animals including dogs, foxes, and wolves. **4** belonging to this group. The coyote is a canine animal. **5** canine tooth. 1,3,5 *n.,* 2,4 *adj.*

canine tooth, one of the four pointed teeth next to the incisors; cuspid.

can is ter (kan′ə stər), a small box or can, especially for tea, coffee, flour, or sugar. *n.*

can ker (kang′kər), a spreading sore, especially one in the mouth. *n.*

can ker ous (kang′kər əs), **1** of or like a canker. **2** causing a canker. *adj.*

can ker worm (kang′kər wėrm′), caterpillar that eats away the leaves of trees and plants. *n.*

can na (kan′ə), a tropical plant with large, pointed leaves and large red, pink, or yellow flowers. *n., pl.* **cannas.**

canned (kand), **1** put in a can; preserved by being put in airtight cans or jars: *canned peaches.* **2** SLANG. preserved on a phonograph record or on tape; recorded: *canned music. adj.*

can ner (kan′ər), person who cans food. *n.*

can ner y (kan′ər ē), factory where food is canned. *n., pl.* **can ner ies.**

Cannes (kan), resort in SE France, on the Mediterranean. *n.*

can ni bal (kan′ə bəl), **1** person who eats human flesh. **2** animal that eats others of its own kind: *Many fishes are cannibals.* **3** of or like cannibals: *Cannibal ants help control ants that destroy crops.* 1,2 *n.,* 3 *adj.*

can ni bal ism (kan′ə bə liz′əm), act or habit of eating the flesh of one's own kind: *Most animals do not practice cannibalism. n.*

can ni bal is tic (kan′ə bə lis′tik), of cannibals; characteristic of cannibals. *adj.* —**can′ni bal is′ti cal ly,** *adv.*

can ni ly (kan′l ē), in a canny manner. *adv.*

can ni ness (kan′ē nis), canny character or quality. *n.*

can ning (kan′ing), the preserving of meat, fish, fruit, etc., by cooking it and sealing it up in airtight cans or jars. *n.*

can non (kan′ən), a big gun, especially one that is too large to be carried by hand and is fixed to the ground or mounted on wheels. Artillery consists of cannons, such as howitzers and mortars. The old-fashioned cannon that fired cannonballs was much used during the Civil War. *n., pl.* **can nons** or **can non.**

can non ade (kan′ə nād′), **1** a continued firing of cannons. **2** attack with cannons. 1 *n.,* 2 *v.,* **can non ad ed, can non ad ing.**

can non ball (kan′ən bôl′), a large iron or steel ball, formerly fired from cannons. *n.*

can non eer (kan′ə nir′), gunner. *n.*

can not (kan′ot *or* ka not′), can not. *v.*

can ny (kan′ē), shrewd and cautious in dealing with others: *The canny trader made a large profit by buying goods when they were plentiful and selling them when they became scarce. adj.,* **can ni er, can ni est.**

ca noe (kə nü′), **1** a light boat pointed at both ends and moved with a paddle. **2** paddle a canoe; go in a canoe. 1 *n.,* 2 *v.,* **ca noed, ca noe ing.**

ca noe ist (kə nü′ist), person who paddles a canoe. *n.*

can on[1] (kan′ən), **1** rule by which a thing is judged; standard: *the canons of good taste.* **2** law of a church. **3** the official list of the books of the Bible accepted by the Christian church as genuine and inspired. *n.*

can on[2] (kan′ən), clergyman belonging to a cathedral. *n.*

ca ñon (kan′yən), canyon. *n., pl.* **ca ñons.** [*Cañon* comes from Mexican Spanish *cañón,* meaning "narrow passage, canyon."]

ca non i cal (kə non′ə kəl), **1** according to church laws: *canonical dress.* **2** in the canon of the Bible. *adj.* —**canon′i cal ly,** *adv.*

can on i za tion (kan′ə nə zā′shən), a canonizing or a being canonized. *n.*

can on ize (kan′ə nīz), declare (a dead person) to be a saint; place in the official list of saints: *Joan of Arc was canonized by the Roman Catholic Church in 1920. v.,* **can on ized, can on iz ing.** —**can′on iz′er,** *n.*

canopy
(def. 1)

can o py (kan′ə pē), **1** a covering fixed over a bed, throne, entrance, etc., or carried on poles over a person: *There is a striped canopy over the entrance to the hotel.* **2** a rooflike covering; shelter or shade: *The trees formed a canopy over the old road.* **3** cover with a canopy. 1,2 *n., pl.* **can o pies;** 3 *v.,* **can o pied, can o py ing.**

canst (kanst), OLD USE. can[1]. "Thou canst" means "you can." *v.*

cant[1] (kant), **1** talk that is not sincere; moral or religious statements that many people make, but few really believe or act upon. **2** the peculiar language of a special group, using many strange words; jargon: *"Jug" is one of the words for "jail" in thieves' cant. n.* [*Cant*[1] can be traced back to Latin *cantus,* meaning "song."]

cant[2] (kant), **1** give a slant or slope to; bevel: *He canted the edges of the board.* **2** put into a slant; tip; tilt: *The wind canted the ship to port.* **3** a sloping, slanting, or tilting; inclination: *The ship took on a dangerous cant to starboard.* 1,2 *v.,* 3 *n.* [*Cant*[2] came into English about 600 years ago from French *cant,* meaning "border, edge," which came from Latin *cantus,* meaning "iron ring or tire of a wheel."]

can't (kant), cannot or can not.

can ta loupe or **can ta loup** (kan′tl ōp), kind of muskmelon with a hard, rough rind and sweet, juicy, orange-colored flesh. *n.*

can tan ker ous (kan tang′kər əs), ready to make trouble and oppose anything suggested; ill-natured; quarrelsome. *adj.* —**can tan′ker ous ly,** *adv.* —**can tan′ker ous ness,** *n.*

can ta ta (kən tä′tə), musical composition consisting of a story or play which is sung by a chorus and soloists, but not acted. *n., pl.* **can ta tas.**

can teen (kan tēn′), **1** a small container for carrying water or other drinks. **2** a store in a school, camp, factory, etc., where food, drinks, and other articles are sold or given out. **3** recreation hall for members of the armed forces. *n.*

can ter (kan′tər), **1** gallop gently: *She cantered her horse down the road. The horse cantered across the meadow.* **2** a gentle gallop. 1 *v.,* 2 *n.*

Can ter bur y (kan′tər ber′ē), city in SE England. Many pilgrims traveled there during the Middle Ages to visit the shrine of Saint Thomas à Becket. *n.*

cant hook, pole with a movable hook at one end, used to grip and turn over logs.

can ti cle (kan′tə kəl), a short song, hymn, or chant used in church services. *n.*

can ti lev er (kan′tl ev′ər *or* kan′tl ē′vər), a large, projecting bracket or beam that is supported at one end only. *n.*

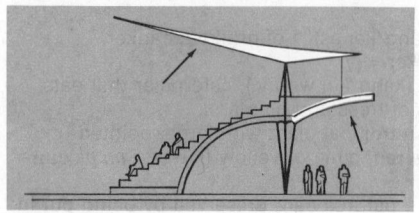

cantilever
two cantilevers
shown in a
cross section
of a football
grandstand

cantilever bridge

a hat	**i** it	**oi** oil	**ch** child		a in about
ā age	**ī** ice	**ou** out	**ng** long		e in taken
ä far	**o** hot	**u** cup	**sh** she	**ə** =	i in pencil
e let	**ō** open	**ú** put	**th** thin		o in lemon
ē equal	**ô** order	**ü** rule	**ŦH** then		u in circus
ėr term			**zh** measure		

cantilever bridge, bridge made of two cantilevers whose projecting ends meet but do not support each other.

can tle (kan′tl), the part of a saddle that sticks up at the back. *n.*

can to (kan′tō), one of the main divisions of a long poem. A canto of a poem is like a chapter of a novel. *n., pl.* **can tos.**

can ton (kan′tən *or* kan′ton), a small part or political division of a country. Switzerland is made up of 22 cantons. *n.*

Can ton (kan ton′), former name for **Kwangchow,** a city in China. *n.*

can ton al (kan′tə nəl), of a canton. *adj.*

Can ton ese (kan′tə nēz′), **1** person born or living in Canton. **2** the Chinese dialect spoken in or near Canton. **3** of Canton, its people, or their dialect. 1,2 *n., pl.* **Canton ese** for 1; 3 *adj.*

can ton ment (kan ton′mənt), place where soldiers live; temporary quarters for soldiers. *n.*

can tor (kan′tər), **1** man who leads the services in a synagogue. **2** man who leads the singing of a choir or congregation. *n.*

can vas (kan′vəs), **1** a strong cloth with a coarse weave made of cotton, flax, or hemp, used to make tents, sails, certain articles of clothing, etc., and for painting on. **2** made of canvas: *The boat had canvas sails.* **3** something made of canvas: *The artist painted on a large canvas.* **4** picture painted on canvas; oil painting: *A valuable canvas was stolen from the art gallery.* 1,3,4 *n., pl.* **can vas es;** 2 *adj.* —**can′vas like′,** *adj.*

the canvas, the floor of a boxing ring.

under canvas, 1 in tents: *The circus was held under canvas in an open field.* **2** with sails spread: *The schooner left the harbor under full canvas.*

can vas back (kan′vəs bak′), a large wild duck of North America with grayish feathers on its back. *n., pl.* **canvas backs** *or* **can vas back.**

can vass (kan′vəs), **1** go through a city, district, etc., asking for votes, orders, donations, etc.: *Volunteers canvassed the whole city for the candidate.* **2** an asking for votes, orders, donations, etc.: *During his canvass of the neighborhood, my father collected $100 for the cancer fund.* **3** examine the parts of carefully; inspect: *He canvassed the papers, hunting for notices of after-school jobs.* **4** discuss: *The city council canvassed the mayor's plan thoroughly.* **5** discussion. 1,3,4 *v.,* 2,5 *n., pl.* **can vass es.** —**can′vass er,** *n.*

can yon (kan′yən), a narrow valley with high, steep sides, usually with a stream at the bottom. *n.* Also, **ca ñon.**

cap (kap), **1** a soft, close-fitting covering for the head, with little or no brim, but often with a visor. **2** a special head covering worn to show rank or occupation: *a student's cap and gown.* **3** anything like a cap. The stopper or top of a jar, bottle, tube, or fountain pen is a cap. The top of a mushroom is called a cap. **4** the highest part;

top: *the polar cap at the North Pole.* **5** put a cap on; cover the top of: *I capped the bottle. Snow capped the mountain peak.* **6** an artificial crown fastened to a tooth. **7** fasten an artificial crown to (a tooth). **8** do or follow up with something as good or better: *Each of the two clowns capped the other's last joke.* **9** a small amount of explosive in a wrapper or covering: *They shot off caps in their toy guns.* 1-4,6,9 *n.,* 5,7,8 *v.,* **capped, cap ping.** —**cap′less,** *adj.* —**cap′like′,** *adj.*

cap., capital letter. *pl.* **caps.**

ca pa bil i ty (kā′pə bil′ə tē), **1** ability to learn or do; power or fitness; capacity: *With her background in Latin, she has the capability to learn French.* **2 capabilities,** *pl.* undeveloped properties; potential uses: *Atomic energy has many unexplored capabilities. n., pl.* **ca pa bil i ties.**

ca pa ble (kā′pə bəl), having fitness, power, or ability; able; efficient; competent: *She was such a capable teacher that the school appointed her principal the next year. adj.* —**ca′pa ble ness,** *n.*

capable of, 1 having ability, power, or fitness for: *Some airplanes are capable of going 1000 miles an hour.* **2** open to; ready for: *a statement capable of being misunderstood.*

ca pa bly (kā′pə blē), in a capable manner; with ability; ably: *a job capably done. adv.*

ca pa cious (kə pā′shəs), able to hold much; large and roomy; spacious: *a capacious closet. adj.* —**ca pa′cious ly,** *adv.* —**ca pa′cious ness,** *n.*

ca pac i tance (kə pas′ə təns), property of a capacitor that determines the amount of electrical charge it can receive and store; capacity. *n.*

ca pac i tor (kə pas′ə tər), device for receiving and storing a charge of electricity; condenser. *n.*

ca pac i ty (kə pas′ə tē), **1** amount of room or space inside; largest amount that can be held by a container: *This can has a capacity of 4 quarts.* **2** ability to receive and hold: *the capacity of a metal for retaining heat. The theater has a seating capacity of 400.* **3** ability to learn or do; power or fitness: *an intelligent student with a capacity for learning.* **4** position or relation. A person may act in the capacity of guardian, trustee, voter, friend, etc. **5** capacitance. *n., pl.* **ca pac i ties.**

cap and bells, cap trimmed with bells, worn by a jester.

cap and gown, a flat cap and loose gown, worn by teachers and students on certain occasions, especially at commencement exercises.

ca par i son (kə par′ə sən), **1** an ornamental covering for a horse. **2** any rich dress or outfit. **3** dress richly. 1,2 *n.,* 3 *v.*

caparison
(def. 1)

cape[1] (kāp), an outer garment, or part of one, without sleeves, worn falling loosely from the shoulders and often fastened at the neck. *n.* [*Cape*[1] was borrowed from French *cape*, which came from Latin *cappa*, meaning "cap, hood."]

cape[2] (kāp), point of land extending into the water. *n.* [*Cape*[2] came into English about 600 years ago from French *cap*, and can be traced back to Latin *caput*, meaning "head." See **Word Family**.]

Cape buffalo, a large, fierce buffalo of southern Africa.

Cape Ca nav er al (kə nav′ər əl), cape in E Florida from which the United States launches rockets.

Cape Horn, cape which forms the S tip of South America. See **Patagonia** for map.

Cape of Good Hope, cape near the S tip of Africa.

ca per[1] (kā′pər), **1** leap or jump about playfully: *The children capered and laughed in the park.* **2** a playful leap or jump: *the shouts and capers of children playing tag.* **3** prank; trick: *The child's capers made us laugh.* **4** SLANG. a crime, especially a burglary: *The jewel thieves pulled off a big caper at the art museum.* **1** *v.*, **2-4** *n.* [*Caper*[1] was probably shortened from earlier *capriole*, meaning "leap," and can be traced back to Latin *caper*, meaning "goat."] —**ca′per er**, *n.* —**ca′per ing ly**, *adv.*

cut a caper or **cut capers**, **1** play or do a trick. **2** leap about playfully.

ca per[2] (kā′pər), **1** a low, prickly shrub of the Mediterranean region. **2** capers, *pl.* the green flower buds and berries of this shrub, pickled and used for seasoning. *n.*

Cape town (kāp′toun′), Cape Town. *n.*

Cape Town, seaport near the S tip of Africa. The legislature for the Republic of South Africa meets there.

Cape Verde (vėrd), cape which is the westernmost point of Africa.

Cape Verde Islands, country consisting of a group of islands west of Cape Verde. *Capital:* Praia.

cap il lar y (kap′ə ler′ē), **1** a blood vessel with a very slender, hairlike opening. Capillaries join the end of an artery to the beginning of a vein. **2** of or in such tubes. **3** like a hair; very slender. **1** *n.*, *pl.* **cap il lar ies;** **2,3** *adj.*

capillary attraction, the force that causes a liquid to rise in a narrow tube or when in contact with a porous substance. A plant draws up water from the ground and a paper towel absorbs water by means of capillary attraction.

cap i tal[1] (kap′ə təl), **1** city where the government of a country, state, or province is located. Toronto is the capital of Ontario. Lincoln is the capital of Nebraska. **2** capital letter. A capital is used at the beginning of a sentence or a proper name. **3** very important; leading; chief: *The invention of the telephone was a capital advance in communication.* **4** of the best kind; excellent: *A maple tree gives capital shade.* **5** punishable by death: *Murder is a capital crime in many countries.* **6** money or property that companies or individuals use to increase their wealth: *The Smith Company has capital amounting to $300,000.* **1,2,6** *n.*, **3-5** *adj.* —**cap′i tal ness**, *n.*

make capital of, take advantage of: *He made capital of his father's fame to get the job.*

cap i tal[2] (kap′ə təl), the top part of a column or pillar. *n.*

cap i tal ism (kap′ə tə liz′əm), an economic system in which private individuals or groups of individuals own land, factories, and other means of production. They compete with one another, using the hired labor of other persons, to produce goods and services for profit. *n.*

cap i tal ist (kap′ə tə list), **1** person whose money and property are used in carrying on business. **2** a wealthy person. **3** person who favors or supports capitalism. *n.*

WORD FAMILY

cape[2]

Below are words related to *cape*[2]. They can all be traced back to the Latin word *caput* (kä′pút), meaning "head."

achieve	capitol	kerchief
biceps	capitulate	mischief
cad	captain	mischievous
caddie	cattle	neckerchief
caddy[2]	chapter	occipital
cadet	chattel	per capita
capital[1]	chef	precipice
capital[2]	chief	precipitate
capitalism	corporal[2]	precipitation
capitalist	decapitate	recapitulate
capitalize	handkerchief	triceps

cap i tal is tic (kap′ə tə lis′tik), **1** of capitalism or capitalists: *capitalistic production.* **2** favoring or supporting capitalism: *capitalistic policies.* *adj.* —**cap′i tal is′ti cal ly**, *adv.*

cap i tal i za tion (kap′ə tə lə zā′shən), **1** a capitalizing or a being capitalized. **2** amount at which a company is capitalized; capital stock of a business: *The company increased its capitalization to $10 million.* *n.*

cap i tal ize (kap′ə tə līz), **1** write or print with a capital letter: *You always capitalize the first letter of your name.* **2** turn into capital; use as capital: *The company capitalized its reserve funds.* **3** provide or furnish with capital. *v.*, **cap i tal ized, cap i tal iz ing.** —**cap′i tal iz′a ble**, *adj.* —**cap′i tal iz′er**, *n.*

capitalize on, take advantage of; use to one's own advantage: *capitalize on another's mistake.*

capital letter, the large form of a letter; A, B, C, D, etc., as distinguished from a, b, c, d, etc.

cap i tal ly (kap′ə tə lē), very well; excellently: *She did her job capitally.* *adv.*

capital punishment, the death penalty for a crime.

capital ship, a large warship, such as a battleship.

Cap i tol (kap′ə təl), **1** the building at Washington, D.C., in which Congress meets. **2** Also, **capitol.** the building in which a state legislature meets. *n.*

ca pit u late (kə pich′ə lāt), surrender on certain terms or conditions: *The men in the fort capitulated on condition that they be allowed to go away unharmed.* *v.*, **ca pit u lat ed, ca pit u lat ing.** —**ca pit′u la′tor**, *n.*

ca pit u la tion (kə pich′ə lā′shən), a surrender on certain terms or conditions. *n.*

Cap'n (kap′ən), Captain. *n.*

ca pon (kā′pon), rooster specially raised to be eaten. It is castrated and fattened. *n.*

Ca pri (kə prē′), small island in W Italy, near Naples. *n.*

ca price (kə prēs′), a sudden change of mind without reason; unreasonable notion or desire; whim: *The child's refusal to wear red clothes was pure caprice.* *n.*

ca pri cious (kə prish′əs), likely to change suddenly without reason; changeable; fickle: *capricious weather.* *adj.* —**ca pri′cious ly**, *adv.* —**ca pri′cious ness**, *n.*

Cap ri corn (kap′rə kôrn), **1** tropic of Capricorn. **2** group of stars shaped somewhat like a goat. *n.* [*Capricorn* is from Latin *capricornus*, which comes from *caper*, meaning "goat," and *cornu*, meaning "horn."]

caps., capital letters.

cap size (kap sīz′ or kap′sīz), turn bottom side up; up-

a hat	i it	oi oil	ch child	a in about
ā age	ī ice	ou out	ng long	e in taken
ä far	o hot	u cup	sh she	ə = i in pencil
e let	ō open	u̇ put	th thin	o in lemon
ē equal	ô order	ü rule	ŦH then	u in circus
ėr term			zh measure	

set; overturn: *The sailboat nearly capsized in the squall. The rough waves capsized the rowboat. v.*, **cap sized, cap siz ing. —cap siz′a ble,** *adj.*

cap stan (kap′stən), machine for lifting or pulling that revolves on an upright shaft or spindle. Sailors on old sailing ships hoisted the anchor by turning the capstan. *n.*

capstan
on large sailing vessel. As it is turned, it winds up the rope that hoists the anchor, or unwinds it.

capstan bar, pole used to turn a capstan.

cap su lar (kap′sə lər), **1** of a capsule. **2** shaped like a capsule. *adj.*

cap sule (kap′səl), **1** a small case or covering. Medicine is often given in capsules made of gelatin. **2** the enclosed front section of a rocket made to carry instruments, astronauts, etc., into space. In flight the capsule can separate from the rest of the rocket and go into orbit or be directed back to earth. **3** a dry seedcase that opens when ripe. **4** membrane enclosing an organ of the body. **5** enclose within a capsule. 1-4 *n.*, 5 *v.*, **cap suled, cap sul ing.**

capsule
(def. 2)

Capt., Captain.

cap tain (kap′tən), **1** head of a group; leader or chief: *the captain of a basketball team.* **2** commander of a ship. **3** an army, air force, or marine officer ranking below a major and above a first lieutenant. **4** a navy officer ranking below a rear admiral and above a commander. **5** a police officer or fire department officer ranking below a chief and above a lieutenant. **6** lead or command as captain: *She will captain the debating team next year.* 1-5 *n.*, 6 *v.*

cap tain cy (kap′tən sē), rank or authority of a captain. *n., pl.* **cap tain cies.**

cap tain ship (kap′tən ship), captaincy. *n.*

cap tion (kap′shən), **1** title or heading at the beginning of a page, article, chapter, etc., or under a picture explaining it. **2** (in motion pictures) a subtitle. **3** put a caption on. 1,2 *n.*, 3 *v.* **—cap′tion less,** *adj.*

cap tious (kap′shəs), hard to please; faultfinding. *adj.* **—cap′tious ly,** *adv.* **—cap′tious ness,** *n.*

cap ti vate (kap′tə vāt), hold captive by beauty or interest; charm; fascinate: *The children were captivated by the exciting story. v.*, **cap ti vat ed, cap ti vat ing. —cap′ti vat′ing ly,** *adv.* **—cap′ti va′tor,** *n.*

cap ti va tion (kap′tə vā′shən), **1** a captivating or a being captivated. **2** charm; fascination. *n.*

cap tive (kap′tiv), **1** person or animal captured and held against his or her will; prisoner: *The pirates took many captives during raids along the coast.* **2** made a prisoner; held against one's will: *a captive sparrow.* 1 *n.*, 2 *adj.*

cap tiv i ty (kap tiv′ə tē), **1** condition of being in prison. **2** condition of being held against one's will: *Some animals cannot bear captivity, and die after a few weeks in a cage. n., pl.* **cap tiv i ties.**

cap tor (kap′tər), person who takes or holds a prisoner. *n.*

cap ture (kap′chər), **1** make a prisoner of; take by force, skill, or trickery; seize: *We captured butterflies with a net.* **2** person or thing taken in this way: *Captain Jones's first capture was an enemy ship.* **3** a capturing or a being captured: *The capture of this ship took place on July 6.* **4** attract and hold; catch and keep: *The story "Alice in Wonderland" captures the imagination.* 1,4 *v.*, **cap tured, cap tur ing;** 2,3 *n.* **—cap′tur a ble,** *adj.* **—cap′tur er,** *n.*

cap u chin (kap′yə shən *or* kə pyü′shən), **1** a South American monkey with black hair on its head that looks like a hood. **2** Capuchin, a Franciscan monk belonging to an order that wears a long, pointed hood or cowl. *n.* [*Capuchin* came into English about 400 years ago from French *capuchin*, and can be traced back to Latin *cappa*, meaning "cap, hood."]

cap y ba ra (kap′ə bär′ə), a tailless rodent of South America. It is the world's largest rodent, growing up to two feet (60 centimeters) high and four feet (1.2 meters) long. *n., pl.* **cap y ba ras.**

car (kär), **1** automobile: *They made the trip by car.* **2** a railroad car or streetcar. **3** the closed platform of an elevator, balloon, or airship for carrying passengers or cargo. *n.* **—car′less,** *adj.*

ca ra ba o (kär′ə bä′ō), water buffalo of the Philippines. *n., pl.* **ca ra ba os** *or* **ca ra ba o.**

Ca ra cas (kə rä′kəs *or* kə rak′əs), capital of Venezuela, in the N part. *n.*

car a cul (kar′ə kəl), **1** a short, flat, loose, curly fur made from the skin of newborn or very young lambs of a breed of Asian sheep. **2** this sheep. *n.* Also, **karakul.**

ca rafe (kə raf′), a glass bottle for holding water, wine, coffee, etc. *n.*

car a mel (kar′ə məl *or* kär′məl), **1** sugar browned or burned over heat, used for coloring and flavoring food. **2** a small block of chewy candy flavored with this sugar. *n.*

car a mel ize (kär′ə mə līz *or* kär′mə līz), change into caramel. *v.*, **car a mel ized, car a mel iz ing. —car′a mel i za′tion,** *n.*

car a pace (kar′ə pās), shell or bony covering on the back of a turtle, armadillo, lobster, crab, etc. *n.*

car at (kar′ət), **1** unit of weight for precious stones, equal to $1/5$ gram. **2** karat. *n.*

car a van (kar′ə van), **1** group of merchants, pilgrims, etc., traveling together for safety through difficult or dangerous country: *A caravan of Arab merchants and* *camels, laden with spices and silks, moved across the desert.* **2** a closed truck or trailer, or formerly a large, covered wagon, for moving people or goods; van. *n.*

car a van sar y (kar/ə van/sər ē), inn or hotel in the Orient where caravans stop to rest. *n., pl.* **car a van sar ies.**

car a van se rai (kar/ə van/sə rī/), caravansary. *n., pl.* **car a van se rais** or **car a van se rai.**

car a vel (kar/ə vel), a small, fast sailing ship of the type used by Columbus, with a broad bow and a high stern. *n.*

car a way (kar/ə wā), the fragrant, spicy seed of a plant related to parsley, used to flavor bread, rolls, or cakes. *n.*

car bide (kär/bīd), compound of carbon with another element, usually a metal. *n.*

car bine (kär/bīn *or* kär/bēn/), a short, light rifle or musket. *n.*

car bo hy drate (kär/bō hī/drāt), substance made from carbon dioxide and water by green plants in sunlight. Carbohydrates are composed of carbon, hydrogen, and oxygen. Sugar and starch are carbohydrates. *n.*

car bo lat ed (kär/bə lā/tid), containing carbolic acid. *adj.*

car bol ic acid (kär bol/ik), a very poisonous acid obtained from coal tar, used in solution as a disinfectant and antiseptic; phenol.

car bon (kär/bən), **1** a very common nonmetallic element which occurs in combination with other elements in all plants and animals. Diamonds and graphite are pure carbon in the form of crystals; coal and charcoal are mostly carbon in uncrystallized form. **2** piece of carbon paper: *I put a carbon between the two sheets of paper.* **3** copy made with carbon paper: *I kept a carbon of each letter I typed. n.* —**car/bon less,** *adj.*

carbon 12, the most common isotope of carbon, now used as the standard for measuring atomic weights.

carbon 14, a radioactive isotope of carbon produced by the bombardment of nitrogen atoms by neutrons; radiocarbon. Since carbon 14 gives off radioactivity at a uniform rate in all animals and plants that have died, scientists are able to find out the age of many ancient remains of living things by measuring the amount of carbon 14 left in them.

car bon ate (kär/bə nāt), **1** saturate with carbon dioxide. Soda water is carbonated to make it bubble and fizz. **2** a chemical substance formed from carbonic acid. 1 *v.,* **car bon at ed, car bon at ing;** 2 *n.* —**car/bon a/tor,** *n.*

car bon at ed (kär/bə nā/tid), saturated with carbon dioxide. Soda water is carbonated water. *adj.*

car bon a tion (kär/bə nā/shən), act of carbonating. *n.*

carbon dioxide, a heavy, colorless, odorless gas, present in the atmosphere or formed when any fuel containing carbon is burned. The air that is breathed out of an animal's lungs contains carbon dioxide. Plants absorb it from the air and use it to make plant tissue. Carbon dioxide is used in soda water, in fire extinguishers, etc.

car bon ic (kär bon/ik), of or containing carbon. *adj.*

carbonic acid, acid made when carbon dioxide is dissolved in water. It gives the sharp taste to soda water.

car bon if er ous (kär/bə nif/ər əs), containing or producing coal. *adj.*

car bon ize (kär/bə nīz), **1** change into carbon by burning; char. **2** cover or combine with carbon. *v.,* **car bon ized, car bon iz ing.** —**car/bon i za/tion,** *n.*

carbon monoxide, a colorless, odorless, very poisonous gas, formed when carbon burns with an insufficient supply of air. It is part of the exhaust gases of automobile engines.

carbon paper, a thin paper having carbon or some other inky substance on one surface. It is used between sheets of paper to make a copy of what is written or typed on the upper sheet.

carbon tet ra chlo ride (tet/rə klôr/īd), a colorless liquid which does not burn, often used in fire extinguishers and in cleaning fluids. Its fumes are very dangerous if inhaled.

car bun cle (kär/bung kəl), a very painful, inflamed swelling under the skin. A carbuncle is larger than a boil and more serious in its effects. *n.*

car bu re tor (kär/bə rā/tər), device for mixing air with a liquid fuel to produce an explosive mixture. A carburetor is part of the gasoline engine of an automobile, lawn mower, etc. *n.*

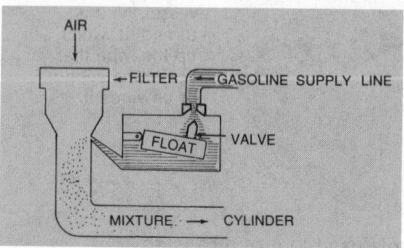

carburetor
A float and valve control the flow of gasoline, which sprays into the pipe and is mixed with air.

car bu ret tor (kär/byə ret/ər), BRITISH. carburetor. *n.*

car cass (kär/kəs), **1** body of a dead animal. **2** INFORMAL. a human body. *n., pl.* **car cass es.** —**car/cass less,** *adj.*

car cin o gen (kär sin/ə jən), any substance that produces cancer. *n.*

card[1] (kärd), **1** a flat piece of stiff paper, thin cardboard, or plastic, usually small and rectangular: *a post card, a credit card, a birthday card.* **2** playing card. **3 cards,** *pl.* **a** game or games played with a pack of playing cards. **b** a playing such a game or games: *Many people at the party were busy at cards.* **4** INFORMAL. an odd or amusing person. *n.* [*Card*[1] came into English about 600 years ago from French *carte*, and can be traced back to Greek *chartēs*, meaning "leaf of paper, papyrus."]

in the cards, likely to happen.

put one's cards on the table, show what one has or can do; be frank about something.

card[2] (kärd), **1** a toothed tool or wire brush used to separate, clean, and straighten the fibers of wool, cotton, flax, etc., before spinning. **2** clean or comb with such a tool: *She carded wool for spinning.* 1 *n.,* 2 *v.* [*Card*[2] came into English about 600 years ago from French *carde*, and can be traced back to Latin *carduus*, meaning "thistle."] —**card/er,** *n.*

card board (kärd/bôrd/), a stiff material made of layers of paper pressed together, used to make cards, boxes, etc. *n.*

card catalog, list of items in a library, entered on cards arranged alphabetically and filed in a set of drawers.

car di ac (kär/dē ak), of the heart: *cardiac arteries. adj.*

Car diff (kär/dif), seaport and capital of Wales, in the SE part. *n.*

car di gan (kär/də gən), a knitted jacket or sweater that buttons down the front. *n.* [*Cardigan* was named for the seventh Earl of *Cardigan*, 1797-1868, a British general.]

car di nal (kärd/n əl), **1** of first importance; chief; principal: *The cardinal value of his plan is that it is simple.* **2** one of the high officials of the Roman Catholic Church, appointed by the pope as his advisers, and ranking next below him. Cardinals wear red robes and red hats. **3** bright, rich red. **4** a bright, rich red. **5** a colorful songbird of North America. The male has bright-red feathers marked with a little gray and black. It is a kind of finch. 1,3 *adj.,* 2,4,5 *n.* —**car/di nal ly,** *adv.*

cardinal flower, the bright-red flower of a North American plant.

cardinal number, number which shows how many are meant. One, two, three, etc., are cardinal numbers; first, second, third, etc., are ordinal numbers.

cardinal points, the four main directions of the compass; north, south, east, and west.

car di o gram (kär′dē ə gram), electrocardiogram. *n.*

car di o graph (kär′dē ə graf), electrocardiograph. *n.*

car di o pul mo nar y resuscitation (kär′dē ō-pul′mə ner′ē), technique used to revive victims of heart attack, drowning, etc., involving mouth-to-mouth breathing and rhythmical pressure on the breastbone which forces the heart to pump.

care (ker *or* kar), **1** a troubled state of mind because of fear of what may happen; worry: *Few people are completely free from care.* **2** serious attention; heed: *A pilot's work requires great care.* **3** object of worry, concern, or attention: *The sick puppy was a care to its owners.* **4** be concerned; feel interest: *Musicians care about music.* **5** watchful keeping; charge: *The little girl was left in her older brother's care.* **6** food, shelter, and protection: *While you're away, we will give your pets the best of care.* **7** like; want; wish: *A cat does not care to be washed.* 1-3,5,6 *n.,* 4,7 *v.,* **cared, caring. —car′er,** *n.*

care for, 1 be fond of; like: *I don't care for her friends.* **2** want; wish: *I don't care for any dessert tonight.* **3** take charge of; attend to: *The nurse will care for him now.*

have a care, be careful.

in care of, at the address of: *All mail for the governor should be sent in care of the statehouse.*

take care, be careful: *Take care to be accurate.*

take care of, 1 take charge of; attend to: *Grandfather will take care of the children. My parents will take care of this bill.* **2** watch over; be careful with: *Take care of your money.*

ca reen (kə rēn′), lean to one side or sway sharply; tilt; tip: *The speeding car careened around the corner. v.*

ca reer (kə rir′), **1** a general course of action or progress through life: *It is interesting to read of the careers of great men and women.* **2** way of living; occupation or profession: *I plan to make law my career.* **3** rush along wildly; dash: *A runaway horse careered down the street.* 1,2 *n.* 3 *v.*

care free (ker′frē′ *or* kar′frē′), without worry; happy; gay: *The children spent a carefree summer sailing and swimming at the seashore. adj.* **—care′free′ness,** *n.*

care ful (ker′fəl *or* kar′fəl), **1** thinking what one says; watching what one does; taking pains; watchful; cautious: *She is a very careful driver. Please be careful with my new bicycle!* **2** showing care; done with thought or effort; exact; thorough: *Arithmetic requires careful work.* **3** full of care or concern; attentive: *Try to be careful of the feelings of others. adj.* **—care′ful ly,** *adv.* **—care′ful ness,** *n.*

care less (ker′lis *or* kar′lis), **1** not thinking what one says; not watching what one does; not careful: *I was careless and broke the cup.* **2** done without enough thought or effort; not exact or thorough: *careless work.* **3** not caring; not troubling oneself; indifferent: *a careless attitude toward school, careless about one's appearance. adj.* **—care′less ly,** *adv.* **—care′less ness,** *n.*

ca ress (kə res′), **1** a touch showing affection; tender embrace or kiss. **2** touch or stroke tenderly; embrace or kiss. 1 *n., pl.* **ca ress es;** 2 *v.* **—ca ress′a ble,** *adj.* **—ca ress′er,** *n.* **—ca ress′ing ly,** *adv.*

car et (kar′ət), a mark (∧) to show where something should be put in, used in writing or printing. *n.*

care tak er (ker′tā′kər *or* kar′tā′kər), person who takes care of another person, a place, or a thing, often for the owner or for another. *n.*

care worn (ker′wôrn′ *or* kar′wôrn′), showing signs of worry; tired or weary from care: *the careworn look on an old person's face. adj.*

car fare (kär′fer′ *or* kär′far′), money paid for riding on a bus or subway, in a taxicab, etc. *n.*

car go (kär′gō), load of goods carried by a ship or plane: *The freighter had docked to unload a cargo of wheat. n., pl.* **car goes** *or* **car gos.**

WORD HISTORY

cargo

Cargo comes from Spanish *cargo,* meaning "a load, weight," and can be traced back to Latin *carrus,* meaning "wagon."

car hop (kär′hop′), person who serves customers in their cars at a drive-in restaurant. *n.*

Car ib be an (kar′ə bē′ən *or* kə rib′ē ən), of the Caribbean Sea or the islands in it. *adj.*

Caribbean Sea, sea bordered by Central America, the West Indies, and South America.

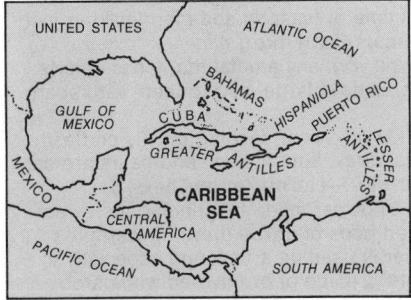

ca ri be (kä rē′bā), piranha. *n.*

car i bou (kar′ə bü), the North American reindeer. *n., pl.* **car i bous** *or* **car i bou.**

car i ca ture (kar′ə kə chùr), **1** picture, cartoon, or description that exaggerates the peculiarities of a person or the defects of a thing. **2** art of making such pictures, cartoons, or descriptions: *A person needs a good eye for*

caricature (def. 1)
caricature of
Abraham Lincoln

a hat	i it	oi oil	ch child	a in about
ā age	ī ice	ou out	ng long	e in taken
ä far	o hot	u cup	sh she	ə = i in pencil
e let	ō open	ů put	th thin	o in lemon
ē equal	ô order	ü rule	ŦH then	u in circus
ėr term			zh measure	

detail to become a master of caricature. **3** make a caricature of: *The artist caricatured the mayor.* 1,2 *n.,* 3 *v.,* **car i ca tured, car i ca tur ing. —car′i ca tur′a ble,** *adj.*

car i ca tur ist (kar′ə kə chür′ist), person who makes caricatures. *n.*

car ies (ker′ēz *or* kar′ēz), **1** decay of teeth or bones. **2** cavity formed in a tooth by such decay. *n., pl.* **car ies.**

car il lon (kar′ə lon), set of bells arranged for playing melodies. A carillon is usually played by a person sitting at a keyboard. *n.* [*Carillon* was borrowed from French *carillon,* and can be traced back to Latin *quattuor,* meaning "four." A carillon was called this because it originally consisted of four bells.]

car load (kär′lōd′), as much as a car can hold or carry. *n.*

Car lyle (kär līl′), **Thomas,** 1795-1881, Scottish essayist and historian. *n.*

Car mel (kär′məl), **Mount,** mountain in NW Israel. *n.*

car mine (kär′mən), **1** a deep red with a tinge of purple. **2** deep-red with a tinge of purple. **3** a light crimson. **4** light-crimson. 1,3 *n.,* 2,4 *adj.*

car nage (kär′nij), slaughter of a great number of people. *n.*

car nal (kär′nl), of or connected with bodily pleasures; sensual. *adj.* **—car′nal ly,** *adv.*

car na tion (kär nā′shən), **1** a red, white, or pink flower with a spicy fragrance, grown in gardens and greenhouses. **2** rosy-pink. 1 *n.,* 2 *adj.*

Car ne gie (kär nā′gē *or* kär′nə gē), **Andrew,** 1835-1919, American steel manufacturer and philanthropist, born in Scotland. *n.*

car ni val (kär′nə vəl), **1** place of amusement or a traveling show having merry-go-rounds, games, sideshows, etc. **2** an organized program of events involving a particular sport, institution, etc.: *a water carnival, a school carnival.* **3** feasting and merrymaking; noisy and unrestrained revels. **4** time of feasting and merrymaking just before Lent. *n.* **—car′ni val like′,** *adj.*

car ni vore (kär′nə vôr), any animal that feeds chiefly on flesh. Carnivores have large, strong teeth with sharp cutting edges. *n.*

car niv or ous (kär niv′ər əs), feeding chiefly on flesh; meat-eating. Cats, dogs, lions, tigers, and bears are carnivorous animals. *adj.* **—car niv′or ous ness,** *n.*

car ob (kar′əb), **1** powder made by grinding the sweet pulp from the seed pods of a tree grown in warm regions. The powder is used as a flavoring especially in place of chocolate. **2** made of or flavored with carob: *carob ice cream.* 1 *n.,* 2 *adj.*

car ol (kar′əl), **1** song of joy. **2** hymn of joy sung at Christmas. **3** sing joyously; sing: *The birds carol in the early morning.* **4** sing carols: *to go caroling at Christmastime.* 1,2 *n.,* 3,4 *v.,* **car oled, car ol ing** or **car olled, car ol ling. —car′ol er, car′ol ler,** *n.*

Car o li na (kar′ə lī′nə), **1** either North Carolina or South Carolina. **2 the Carolinas,** North Carolina and South Carolina. *n.*

Car o line Islands (kar′ə līn), group of over 500 islands in the W Pacific, east of the Philippines. See **Melanesia** for map.

Car o lin i an (kar′ə lin′ē ən), **1** of North Carolina and South Carolina, or either of them. **2** person born or living in North Carolina or South Carolina. 1 *adj.,* 2 *n.*

car om (kar′əm), **1** hit and bounce off: *The car went out of control and caromed off the wall.* **2** a hitting and bouncing off. 1 *v.,* 2 *n.*

ca rous al (kə rou′zəl), a noisy feast or drinking party. *n.*

ca rouse (kə rouz′), **1** drink heavily; take part in noisy feasts or merrymaking. **2** a noisy feast or drinking party. 1 *v.,* **ca roused, ca rous ing;** 2 *n.* **—ca rous′er,** *n.*

carillon—The keys, or levers, are connected by wires to bell clappers and are played by being struck with the fists. The heavy bass bells are played by the feet on a pedal board.

car ou sel (kar′ə sel′), carrousel. *n.*

carp[1] (kärp), find fault; complain. *v.* **—carp′er,** *n.*

carp[2] (kärp), a bony, freshwater fish which lives in ponds and slow streams. It feeds mostly on plants and sometimes grows quite large. *n., pl.* **carps** or **carp.**

car pal (kär′pəl), **1** of the carpus. **2** bone of the carpus. 1 *adj.,* 2 *n.*

car pel (kär′pəl), a modified leaf which forms a pistil or part of a pistil of a flower. *n.*

car pen ter (kär′pən tər), person whose work is building and repairing the wooden parts of houses, ships, etc. *n.*

car pen try (kär′pən trē), trade or work of a carpenter. *n.*

car pet (kär′pit), **1** a heavy, woven fabric for covering floors and stairs. **2** anything like a carpet: *a carpet of grass.* **3** cover with a carpet: *In the fall, the ground was carpeted with leaves.* 1,2 *n.,* 3 *v.*

on the carpet, being scolded or rebuked: *I was on the carpet for being tardy too often.*

car pet bag (kär′pit bag′), a traveling bag made of carpet. *n.*

car pet bag ger (kär′pit bag′ər), Northerner who went to the South to get political or other advantages during the time of disorganization that followed the American Civil War. *n.*

car pet ing (kär′pə ting), **1** fabric for carpets. **2** carpets: *The carpeting was worn and frayed in spots.* *n.*

carp ing (kär′ping), faultfinding; complaining. *adj.*

car pool, 1 arrangement made by a group of persons to take turns driving themselves or others to and from a place: *The parents formed a car pool to take their children to school.* **2** group of such persons: *Our car pool takes a different route to work every day.*

car port (kär′pôrt′), shelter for automobiles, usually attached to a house and open on at least one side. *n.*

car pus (kär′pəs), **1** wrist. **2** bones of the wrist. *n., pl.* **car pi** (kär′pī).

car riage (kar′ij), **1** vehicle that moves on wheels. Some carriages are pulled by horses and are used to carry people. Baby carriages are small and light, and can often be folded. **2** frame on wheels that supports a gun. **3** a moving part of a machine that supports another part: *a typewriter carriage.* **4** manner of holding the head and body; bearing: *She has a queenly carriage.* *n.*

car ri er (kar′ē ər), **1** person or thing that carries something. A postman is a mail carrier. A porter is a baggage carrier. Railroads, airlines, bus systems, and truck companies are common carriers. **2** person or thing that carries or transmits a disease. Carriers are often healthy persons who are immune to a disease, but carry its germs. **3** aircraft carrier. **4** carrier wave. *n.*

carrier pigeon, homing pigeon.

carrier wave, a radio wave whose intensity and frequency are varied in order to transmit a signal, usually in broadcasting radio and television programs and sending telephone and telegraph messages.

car ri on (kar′ē ən), dead and decaying flesh. *n.*

Car roll (kar′əl), **Lewis,** 1832-1898, English writer, author of *Alice in Wonderland.* His real name was Charles L. Dodgson. *n.*

car rot (kar′ət), the long, tapering, orange-red root of a garden plant, eaten cooked or raw as a vegetable. *n.*

car rou sel (kar′ə sel), merry-go-round. *n.* Also, **carousel.**

car ry (kar′ē), **1** take from one place to another: *Railroads carry coal from the mines to the factories. The man carried the child home. This story will carry your thoughts back to last winter.* **2** bear or have with one: *carry an umbrella in case of rain.* **3** hold up; support; sustain: *Rafters carry the weight of the roof.* **4** hold (one's body and head) in a certain way: *The dancer carried herself gracefully.* **5** capture or win: *Our side carried the election.* **6** get (a motion or bill) passed or adopted: *The motion to adjourn the meeting was carried.* **7** cover the distance: *The opera singer's voice carried clear to the back rows of the theater.* **8** have as a result; involve: *The expert's judgment carried great weight.* **9** sing (a melody, theme, or part) with correct pitch: *I can't carry a tune.* **10** keep in stock: *This store carries toys and games.* **11** transfer (a number) from one place or column in the sum to the next. **12** (in football) a running with the ball from scrimmage: *In three carries the speedy back made nearly 30 yards.* 1-11 *v.,* **car ried, car ry ing;** 12 *n., pl.* **car ries.**

carry away, arouse strong feeling in; influence beyond reason: *I was carried away by the sad movie, so I cried.*

carry off, 1 win (a prize, an honor, etc.): *The champion swimmer carried off two gold medals at the Olympic games.* **2** be the death of; kill: *Pneumonia carried him off.*

carry on, 1 do; manage; conduct: *She carried on a successful business.* **2** keep going; not stop; continue: *We must carry on in our effort to establish world peace.* **3** INFORMAL. behave wildly or foolishly: *The children carried on at the party.*

carry out, get done; do; accomplish; complete: *He carried out his job well.*

car ry all (kar′ē ôl′), a large bag or basket. *n.*

car ry-out (kar′ē out′), **1** food that is packaged to be taken away from its place of sale rather than eaten on the premises. **2** of or having to do with such food or the place where it is sold. 1 *n.,* 2 *adj.*

car sick (kär′sik′), nauseated as a result of the motion of a car, train, etc. *adj.* —**car′sick′ness,** *n.*

Car son (kär′sən), **1 Kit,** 1809-1868, American frontiersman, scout, and guide in the Far West. **2 Rachel,** 1907-1964, American marine biologist and writer who pioneered in the ecology movement. *n.*

Carson City, capital of Nevada, in the W part.

cart (kärt), **1** vehicle with two wheels, used in farming and for carrying heavy loads. Horses, donkeys, and oxen are often used to draw carts. **2** a light wagon, used to deliver goods. **3** a small vehicle on wheels, moved by

cartridge (def. 1)

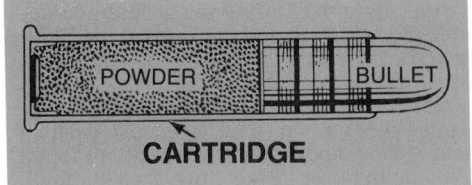

CARTRIDGE

hand: *a grocery cart.* **4** carry in a cart: *Cart away this rubbish.* 1-3 *n.,* 4 *v.*

put the cart before the horse, reverse the accepted or usual order of things.

cart age (kär′tij), **1** a carting or transporting. **2** cost or price of carting. *n.*

carte blanche (kärt′ blänch′), freedom to use one's own judgment; full authority. *pl.* **cartes blanches** (kärts′ blänch′).

carte blanche

Carte blanche comes from French *carte blanche,* which originally meant "blank paper."

car tel (kär tel′), a large group of business firms that agree to operate as a monopoly, especially to regulate prices and production. *n.*

cart er (kär′tər), person whose work is driving a cart or truck. *n.*

Car ter (kär′tər), **Jimmy (James Earl, Jr.),** born 1924, the 39th president of the United States, from 1977 to 1981. *n.*

Car thage (kär′thij), city and seaport of ancient times in N Africa, founded by the Phoenicians. It was destroyed by the Romans in 146 B.C., rebuilt in 29 B.C., and finally destroyed by the Arabs in A.D. 698. See **Byzantine Empire** for map. *n.*

Car tha gin i an (kär′thə jin′ē ən), **1** of Carthage. **2** person who was born or lived in Carthage. 1 *adj.,* 2 *n.*

Car tier (kär tyā′), **Jacques,** 1491-1557, French navigator who explored the St. Lawrence River. *n.*

car ti lage (kär′tl ij), a tough, elastic substance forming parts of the skeleton of vertebrates; gristle. Cartilage is more flexible than bone and not as hard. The external ear consists of cartilage and skin. *n.*

car ti lag i nous (kär′tl aj′ə nəs), **1** of or like cartilage; gristly. **2** having the skeleton formed mostly of cartilage: *Sharks are cartilaginous. adj.*

car tog ra pher (kär tog′rə fər), maker of maps or charts. *n.*

car tog ra phy (kär tog′rə fē), the making or study of maps or charts. *n.*

car ton (kärt′n), **1** box made of pasteboard or cardboard: *a candy carton. Pack the books in large cartons.* **2** amount that a carton holds: *a carton of milk. n.*

car toon (kär tün′), **1** sketch or drawing showing persons, things, or events in an amusing way: *Political cartoons often represent the United States as a tall man with chin whiskers, called Uncle Sam.* **2** animated cartoon. **3** comic strip. **4** a full-size drawing of a design or painting, used as a model for a fresco, tapestry, etc. *n.*

car toon ist (kär tü′nist), person who draws cartoons. *n.*

car tridge (kär′trij), **1** case made of metal, plastic, or cardboard for holding gunpowder and a bullet or shot.

2 a small container holding a roll of photographic film, ink for a pen, etc. **3** a small device with a plastic case containing electronic circuits. A cartridge put into a computer, a calculator, or a video game machine allows these machines to work in particular ways. *n.*

cart wheel (kärt′hwēl′), **1** wheel of a cart. **2** a sideways handspring or somersault. *n.*

Ca ru so (kə rü′sō), Enrico, 1873-1921, Italian operatic tenor. *n.*

carve (kärv), **1** cut into slices or pieces: *I carved the meat at the dinner table.* **2** make by cutting; cut: *Statues are often carved from marble, stone, or wood.* **3** decorate with figures or designs cut on the surface: *The oak chest was carved with flowers. v.,* **carved, carv ing.**

carv er (kär′vər), **1** person who carves. **2** carving knife. *n.*

Car ver (kär′vər), George Washington, 1864?-1943, American botanist and chemist. *n.*

carv ing (kär′ving), carved work: *a wood carving. n.*

carving knife, knife for cutting meat.

car y at id (kar′ē at′id), statue of a woman used as a column. *n.*

ca sa ba (kə sä′bə), kind of winter muskmelon with a yellow rind. *n., pl.* **ca sa bas.** Also, **cassaba.**

Cas a blan ca (kas′ə blang′kə), seaport in N Morocco, on the Atlantic. *n.*

cas cade (ka skād′), **1** a small waterfall. **2** anything like this: *A cascade of ivy hung from the flower box.* **3** fall or flow in a cascade: *The water cascaded off the roof in the thunderstorm.* **1,2** *n.,* **3** *v.,* **cas cad ed, cas cad ing.**

Cascade Range, mountain range in NW United States, extending from N California to British Columbia.

Cas cades (ka skādz′), Cascade Range. *n.pl.*

cas car a (ka sker′ə), **1** shrub or small tree of the northwestern United States. **2** medicine prepared from the dried bark of this tree, used as a laxative. *n., pl.* **cascar as.**

case[1] (kās), **1** any special condition of a person or thing; instance; example: *a case of poverty. A case of chicken pox kept me away from school.* **2** the actual condition; real situation; true state: *She said the work was done, but that was not the case.* **3** person who is being treated by a doctor; patient: *Hospitals had many cases of polio each summer before a vaccine to prevent it was developed.* **4** matter for a court of law to decide: *The case will be brought before the court tomorrow.* **5** a convincing argument: *The agent made a good case for buying insurance.* **6** (in grammar) one of the forms of a noun, pronoun, or adjective used to show its relation to other words. *I is in the nominative case; me is in the objective case; my is in the possessive case. n.*

in any case, no matter what happens; anyhow: *In any case, you should prepare for the worst.*

in case, if it should happen that; if; supposing: *What would you do in case fire broke out?*

in case of, if there should be: *In case of fire walk quietly to the nearest door.*

in no case, under no circumstances; never: *In no case should you panic.*

case[2] (kās), **1** thing to hold or cover something: *a typewriter case. Put the knife back in its case.* **2** box: *There is a big case full of books in the hall.* **3** amount that a case can hold: *The children drank a case of ginger ale at the party.* **4** frame. A window fits in a case. **5** put in a case; cover with a case: *He cased the books for shipping.* **6** INFORMAL. look over carefully; inspect or examine: *The thieves cased the bank before the robbery.* **1-4** *n.,* **5,6** *v.,* **cased, cas ing.**

ca sein (kā′sēn′), protein present in milk, used in making plastics, adhesives, and certain kinds of paints. Cheese is mostly casein. *n.*

case ment (kās′mənt), window which opens on hinges like a door. *n.*

cash (kash), **1** money in the form of coins and bills. **2** money paid at the time of buying something: *Do you want to pay cash for the clothes or charge them?* **3** give cash for: *The bank will cash your check.* **4** get cash for: *I cashed a check at the bank.* **1,2** *n.,* **3,4** *v.* —**cash′a ble,** *adj.*

cash in, INFORMAL. change into cash: *I cashed in a savings bond at the bank.*

cash in on, INFORMAL. **1** make a profit from: *After holding the land till the city needed it, we finally cashed in on our real estate investment.* **2** take advantage of; use to advantage: *She cashed in on her love of travel by becoming a tour guide.*

cash ew (kash′ü), the small, kidney-shaped nut of a tropical American tree. Cashews are good to eat. *n.*

cash ier[1] (ka shir′), person who has charge of money in a bank, or in any business. *n.* [*Cashier*[1] comes from French *caissier,* meaning "treasurer," and can be traced back to Latin *capsa,* meaning "box."]

cascade (def. 1)

cash ier[2] (ka shir′), dismiss from service; discharge in disgrace: *The dishonest officer was deprived of his rank and cashiered. v.* [*Cashier*[2] comes from Dutch *casseren,* and can be traced back to Latin *quassare,* meaning "to shatter, shake violently."]

cash mere (kash′mir *or* kazh′mir), a fine, soft wool, used in making sweaters, coats, etc. The finest cashmere is obtained from a breed of long-haired goats of Tibet and Kashmir. *n.*

cash on delivery, payment when goods are delivered.

cash register, machine which records and shows the amount of a sale. It usually has a drawer to hold money.

cas ing (kā′sing), **1** thing put around something; covering; case. The outermost part of a tire and the skin of a sausage are kinds of casings. **2** frame. A window fits in a casing. *n.*

ca si no (kə sē′nō), **1** building or room for public shows, dancing, gambling, etc. **2** cassino. *n., pl.* **ca si nos.**

cask (kask), **1** barrel. A cask may be large or small, and is usually made to hold liquids. **2** amount that a cask holds. *n.*

cas ket (kas′kit), **1** coffin. **2** a small box or chest used to hold jewels, letters, or other valuables. *n.*

Cas pi an Sea (kas′pē ən), inland sea between Europe and Asia in the Soviet Union and Iran, east of the Black Sea. See **Assyria** for map.

casque (kask), helmet. *n.*

cas sa ba (kə sä′bə), casaba. *n., pl.* **cas sa bas.**

Cas san dra (kə san′drə), (in Greek legends) a daughter of King Priam of Troy. Apollo gave her the power to foretell the future, but later in anger punished her by ordering that no one should believe her prophecies. *n.*

cas sa va (kə sä′və), **1** a tropical plant with starchy roots; manioc. **2** starch made from its roots. Tapioca is made from cassava. *n., pl.* **cas sa vas.**

cas se role (kas′ə rōl′), **1** a covered baking dish in which food can be both cooked and served. **2** food cooked and served in such a dish. *n.*

cas sette (ka set′), **1** container holding magnetic tape for playing or recording sound automatically. **2** cartridge for film. *n.*

cas sia (kash′ə), **1** tree native to China, with spicy bark which is sometimes used as a substitute for cinnamon. **2** plant yielding leaves and pods that are used in making senna. *n., pl.* **cas sias.**

cas si no (kə sē′nō), a card game in which cards in the hand are matched with cards on the table. *n.* Also, **casino.**

cas sock (kas′ək), a long outer garment, usually black, worn by a clergyman. *n.*

cas so war y (kas′ə wer′ē), a large bird of Australia and New Guinea like an ostrich, but smaller. Cassowaries run swiftly, but cannot fly. *n., pl.* **cas so war ies.**

cast (kast), **1** throw; fling or hurl: *cast a stone, cast a fishing line. The criminal was cast into jail.* **2** throw off; let fall; shed: *The snake cast its skin.* **3** the distance a thing is thrown; throw: *The fisherman made a long cast with his line.* **4** direct or turn: *She cast a glance of surprise at me.* **5** deposit (a ballot); give or record (a vote): *Voters cast their ballots for President of the United States in an election held every four years.* **6** to shape by pouring or squeezing into a mold to harden. Metal is first melted and then cast. **7** thing shaped in a mold: *The sculptor made a cast of an antelope.* **8** mold used to shape or support: *Her broken arm is in a plaster cast.* **9** select for a part in a play: *The director cast her in the role of the heroine.* **10** the actors in a play: *The cast was listed on the program.* **11** outward form or look; appearance: *His face had a gloomy cast.* **12** a slight amount of color; tinge: *a white shirt with a pink cast.* **13** a slight squint. 1,2,4-6,9 *v.*, **cast**, **cast ing;** 3,7,8,10-13 *n.*

cast about, search; look: *The company cast about for a long time until it found a good site for its new factory.*

cast aside, throw away; discard: *cast aside an old hat.*

cast away, 1 abandon: *We cast away the project as useless.* **2** to shipwreck.

cast down, 1 turn downward; lower: *He cast down his eyes to avoid looking at me.* **2** make sad or discouraged: *She was cast down by the bad news.*

cast off, 1 let loose; set free: *cast off a boat from its moorings.* **2** abandon or discard: *He cast off his old friends as soon as he left the old neighborhood.*

cast out, drive out forcibly; banish.

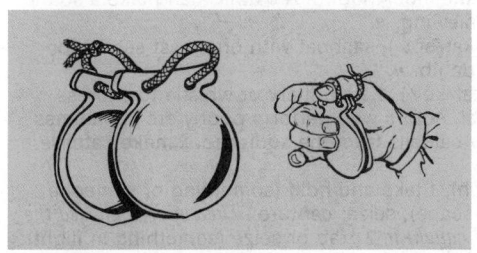

castanets

cas ta net (kas′tə net′), one of a pair of instruments held in the hand and clicked together to beat time for dancing or music. Castanets are made of hard wood or ivory. *n.*

cast a way (kast′ə wā′), **1** thrown away; cast adrift. **2** a shipwrecked person: *The castaways swam to the island.*

a hat	i it	oi oil	ch child	⎧ a in about
ā age	ī ice	ou out	ng long	⎪ e in taken
ä far	o hot	u cup	sh she	ə = ⎨ i in pencil
e let	ō open	u̇ put	th thin	⎪ o in lemon
ē equal	ô order	ü rule	ᴛʜ then	⎩ u in circus
ėr term			zh measure	

3 outcast; rejected. **4** an outcast. 1,3 *adj.*, 2,4 *n.*

caste (kast), **1** one of the social classes into which Hindus are divided. By tradition, a Hindu is born into a caste and cannot rise above it. **2** an exclusive social group; distinct class: *The priestly caste in ancient Egypt had great power.* **3** a social system having distinct classes separated by differences of rank, wealth, or position. *n.*

lose caste, lose social rank or position: *They had a fear of losing caste among their neighbors.*

cast er (kas′tər), **1** a small wheel on a swivel set into the base of a piece of furniture or other heavy object to make it easier to move. **2** shaker or bottle containing seasoning for table use: *a pepper caster.* **3** stand or rack for such bottles. **4** person or thing that casts. *n.* Also, **castor** for 1-3.

cas ti gate (kas′tə gāt), criticize severely or punish. *v.*, **cas ti gat ed, cas ti gat ing.** —**cas′ti ga′tion,** *n.* —**cas′ti ga′tor,** *n.*

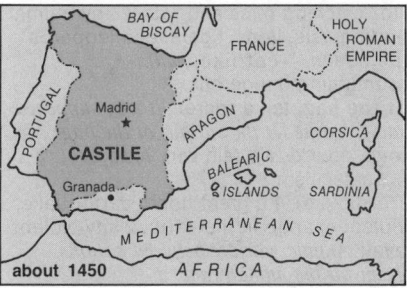

about 1450

Cas tile (ka stēl′), region in N and central Spain, formerly a kingdom. *n.*

Castile soap, a pure, hard soap made from olive oil and sodium hydroxide.

Cas til ian (ka stil′yən), **1** of Castile, its people, or their language. **2** Castilian Spanish. **3** person born or living in Castile. 1 *adj.*, 2,3 *n.*

Castilian Spanish, Spanish as spoken in Castile. It is the standard language of Spain.

cast ing (kas′ting), **1** thing shaped by being poured into a mold to harden. **2** act or process of shaping things by pouring into a mold: *Casting in bronze was practiced in ancient Greece. n.*

cast iron, a hard, brittle form of iron made by casting.

cast-i ron (kast′ī′ərn), **1** made of cast iron: *He fried ham and eggs in a cast-iron skillet.* **2** not yielding; hard: *It took cast-iron control to keep from losing my temper.* **3** hardy; strong: *Her cast-iron stomach could digest almost anything. adj.*

cas tle (kas′əl), **1** a large building or group of buildings with thick walls, turrets, battlements, and other defenses against attack: *The knight rode over the drawbridge into the castle.* **2** a large and stately residence. **3** rook². *n.*

castle in the air, something imagined but not likely to come true; daydream.

cast off (kast′ôf′), **1** thrown away; abandoned; discarded: *castoff clothes.* **2** person or thing that has been cast off. 1 *adj.*, 2 *n.*

cas tor (kas′tər), caster (defs. 1-3). *n.*

Cas tor (kas′tər), (in Greek and Roman myths) one of

the twin sons of Zeus. Castor was mortal; his brother, Pollux, was immortal. *n.*

castor oil, a thick, yellow oil obtained from the beans of a tall, tropical plant, used as a laxative and as a lubricant for machines.

cas trate (kas′trāt), remove the testicles of; emasculate. An ox is a castrated bull. *v.,* **cas trat ed, cas trat ing.** —**cas tra′tion,** *n.*

Cas tries (ka strē′), capital of St. Lucia. *n.*

Cas tro (kas′trō), **Fidel,** born 1927, premier of Cuba since 1959. *n.*

cas u al (kazh′ü əl), 1 happening by chance; not planned or expected; accidental: *Our long friendship began with a casual meeting at a party.* 2 without plan or method; careless: *She gave the note a casual glance and then threw it away.* 3 informal in manner; offhand: *Some people mistook his casual behavior for rudeness.* 4 designed for informal wear: *We dressed in casual clothes for the picnic. adj.* —**cas′u al ly,** *adv.* —**cas′u al ness,** *n.*

cas u al ty (kazh′ü əl tē), 1 member of the armed forces who has been wounded, killed, or captured as a result of enemy action: *The war produced many casualties.* 2 person injured or killed in an accident: *If drivers were more careful, there would be fewer casualties on the highways.* 3 accident, especially a fatal or serious one: *a casualty at sea. n., pl.* **cas u al ties.**

cat (kat), 1 a small, furry, flesh-eating mammal, often kept as a pet or for catching mice and rats. 2 any animal of the group including cats, lions, tigers, and leopards. 3 SLANG. fellow; person. *n.* —**cat′like′,** *adj.*

bell the cat, do something dangerous.

let the cat out of the bag, tell a secret: *It was supposed to be a surprise party, but he let the cat out of the bag.*

rain cats and dogs, pour down rain very hard.

cat., 1 catalogue. 2 catechism.

cat a clysm (kat′ə kliz′əm), 1 a great flood, earthquake, or any sudden, violent change in the earth. 2 any violent change or upheaval: *Atomic warfare between nations would be a cataclysm for the human race. n.*

cat a clys mic (kat′ə kliz′mik), of or like a cataclysm; sudden and violent. *adj.* —**cat′a clys′mi cal ly,** *adv.*

cat a combs (kat′ə kōmz), an underground network of galleries used as a burial place with recesses in which to place the dead. *n.pl.*

Cat a lan (kat′l ən), 1 of Catalonia, its people, or their language. 2 person born or living in Catalonia. 3 language spoken in Catalonia. 1 *adj.,* 2,3 *n.*

cat a log (kat′l ôg), 1 list of items in some collection. A library has a catalog of its books, arranged in alphabetical order. Some companies print catalogs with pictures and prices of the things they have for sale. 2 make a catalog of; put in a catalog: *to catalog an insect collection.* 1 *n.,* 2 *v.* Also, **catalogue.**

cat a log er (kat′l ô′gər), person who catalogs. *n.* Also, **cataloguer.**

cat a logue (kat′l ôg), catalog. *n., v.,* **cat a logued, cat a logu ing.**

cat a logu er (kat′l ô′gər), cataloger. *n.*

Cat a lo ni a (kat′l ō′nē ə), region in NE Spain. *n.*

ca tal pa (kə tal′pə), tree of America and Asia with large, heart-shaped leaves, clusters of bell-shaped flowers, and long pods. *n., pl.* **ca tal pas.** [*Catalpa* comes from Creek *kutuhlpa,* which originally meant "head with wings." The tree was called this because of the shape of its flowers.]

ca tal y sis (kə tal′ə sis), the causing or speeding up of a chemical reaction by the presence of a catalyst. *n., pl.* **ca tal y ses** (kə tal′ə sēz′).

cat a lyst (kat′l ist), 1 substance that causes or speeds up a chemical reaction while remaining practically unchanged itself. Enzymes are important catalysts in diges-

tion. 2 anything that brings about some change or changes without being directly affected itself: *The first successful heart transplant was the catalyst that sparked widespread scientific work in this field. n.*

cat a lyt ic (kat′l it′ik), 1 of catalysis. 2 causing catalysis. *adj.*

catalytic converter, an emission control device in the exhaust system of an automobile or other motor vehicle. It contains a catalyst which causes carbon monoxide and hydrocarbons to be converted to carbon dioxide and water vapor.

cat a lyze (kat′l īz), act upon by catalysis. *v.,* **cat a lyzed, cat a lyz ing.**

cat a lyz er (kat′l ī zer), catalyst. *n.*

cat a ma ran (kat′ə mə ran′), 1 boat with two hulls fitted side by side. 2 raft made of pieces of wood lashed together. *n.*

cat a mount (kat′ə mount), wildcat, such as a puma or lynx. *n.*

catapult (def. 1) By means of ropes, ancient soldiers drew this very heavy bow. It could send an arrow a great distance.

cat a pult (kat′ə pult), 1 weapon used in ancient times for shooting stones, arrows, etc. 2 slingshot. 3 device for launching an airplane from the deck of a ship. 4 throw; hurl: *He stopped his bicycle so suddenly that he was catapulted over the handlebars.* 5 shoot up suddenly; spring: *The frightened cat catapulted from the chair when the big dog came in.* 1-3 *n.,* 4,5 *v.*

cat a ract (kat′ə rakt′), 1 a large, steep waterfall. 2 a violent rush or downpour of water; flood: *Cataracts of rain flooded the streets.* 3 disease of the eye in which the lens develops a cloudy film, making a person partly or entirely blind. *n.*

ca tarrh (kə tär′), an inflamed condition of a mucous membrane, usually that of the nose or throat, causing a discharge of mucus. *n.*

ca tas tro phe (kə tas′trə fē), a sudden, widespread, or extraordinary disaster; great calamity or misfortune. An earthquake, flood, or fire is a catastrophe. *n.*

cat a stroph ic (kat′ə strof′ik), of or caused by disaster; calamitous. *adj.* —**cat′a stroph′i cal ly,** *adv.*

cat bird (kat′bėrd′), a grayish North American songbird related to the mockingbird. A catbird can make a sound like a cat mewing. *n.*

cat boat (kat′bōt′), sailboat with one mast set far forward and no jib. *n.*

cat call (kat′kôl′), 1 a shrill cry or whistle to express disapproval. Actors who perform poorly are sometimes greeted by catcalls from the audience. 2 make catcalls. 1 *n.,* 2 *v.*

catch (kach), 1 take and hold (something or someone trying to escape); seize; capture: *The children chased the puppy and caught it.* 2 grab or seize (something in flight): *Catch the ball with both hands.* 3 attract and hold the attention of: *Bright colors catch the baby's eye.* 4 take or get: *Paper catches fire easily. Put on a warm coat or you will catch cold. She caught a glimpse of her friend in the crowd.* 5 reach or get to in time: *You have just five minutes to catch your train.* 6 see, hear, or understand: *He spoke so rapidly that I didn't catch the meaning of what he* said. **7** become hooked or fastened: *My coat caught in the door.* **8** entangle or grip: *A nail caught her sleeve.* **9** come upon suddenly; surprise: *Mother caught me just as I was hiding her birthday present.* **10** act as catcher in baseball: *He catches for our school team.* **11** act of catching: *She made a fine catch with one hand.* **12** thing that fastens: *The catch on that door is broken.* **13** thing caught: *A dozen fish is a good catch.* **14** reach with a blow; hit; strike: *The stone caught her on the leg.* **15** game of throwing and catching a ball: *The children played catch on the lawn.* **16** check suddenly: *She caught her breath in surprise.* **17** a choking or stoppage of the breath: *He had a catch in his voice.* **18** INFORMAL. a hidden or tricky condition in a plan, etc.: *There is a catch to that question.* 1-10,14,16 *v.*, **caught, catch ing;** 11-13,15,17,18 *n.*, *pl.* **catch es.**

catch at, 1 try to catch. **2** seize eagerly.

catch it, INFORMAL. be scolded or punished: *He hadn't cleaned his room, and was afraid he would catch it.*

catch on, INFORMAL. **1** get the idea; understand: *The second time the teacher explained the problem, I caught on.* **2** become popular; be widely used or accepted: *That new song caught on quickly.*

catch up, come from behind and be even with.

catch up with, come up even with a person or thing while going the same way; overtake: *I was late, and had to run to catch up with my friends.*

catch er (kach′ər), **1** person or thing that catches. **2** a baseball player who stands behind the batter to catch the ball thrown by the pitcher. *n.*

catch ing (kach′ing), **1** spread by infection; contagious: *Colds are catching.* **2** likely to spread from one person to another: *Enthusiasm is catching.* *adj.*

catch up (kech′əp *or* kach′əp), catsup. *n.*

catch word (kach′wėrd′), word or phrase used again and again for effect; slogan: *"No taxation without representation" was a political catchword during the Revolutionary War.* *n.*

catch y (kach′ē), **1** pleasing and easy to remember: *The new musical has several catchy tunes.* **2** tricky; misleading; deceptive: *The third question on the test was catchy; everyone in the class gave the wrong answer.* *adj.*, **catch i er, catch i est.** —**catch′i ly,** *adv.* —**catch′i ness,** *n.*

cat e chism (kat′ə kiz′əm), **1** book of questions and answers about religion, used for teaching religious doctrine. **2** any long set of questions and answers about a subject. *n.*

cat e chis tic (kat′ə kis′tik), of a catechism. *adj.* —**cat′e chis′ti cal ly,** *adv.*

cat e chize (kat′ə kīz), **1** teach by questions and answers. **2** question closely. *v.*, **cat e chized, cat e chiz ing.** —**cat′e chi za′tion,** *n.* —**cat′e chiz′er,** *n.*

cat e gor i cal (kat′ə gôr′ə kəl), without conditions or qualifications; positive: *His categorical answer left no doubt about his opinion.* *adj.* —**cat′e gor′i cal ly,** *adv.*

cat e go rize (kat′ə gə rīz′), put in a category. *v.*, **cat e go rized, cat e go riz ing.** —**cat′e go ri za′tion,** *n.*

cat e go ry (kat′ə gôr′ē), group or general division in classification; class: *The characters in the story can be divided into two categories: good people and bad people.* *n.*, *pl.* **cat e go ries.**

ca ter (kā′tər), **1** provide food and supplies, and sometimes service: *They run a restaurant and also cater for weddings and parties.* **2** provide what is needed or wanted: *The new magazine caters to campers by printing stories about camping, hiking, and nature.* *v.*

cat er-cor ner (kat′ər kôr′nər), **1** diagonal: *a cater-corner walk across the park.* **2** diagonally: *My friend moved cater-corner across the park from our house.* 1 *adj.*, 2 *adv.* Also, **catty-corner** or **kitty-corner.**

cat er-cor nered (kat′ər kôr′nərd), cater-corner. *adj.*,

adv. Also, **catty-cornered** or **kitty-cornered.**

ca ter er (kā′tər ər), person who provides food and supplies, and sometimes service, for parties, weddings, etc. *n.*

cat er pil lar (kat′ər pil′ər), the wormlike larva of insects such as the butterfly and the moth. *n.*

caterpillar
about 1 in.
(2.5 cm.) long

cat er waul (kat′ər wôl), **1** howl like a cat; screech: *The bagpipes caterwauled.* **2** such a howl or screech. 1 *v.*, 2 *n.*

cat fish (kat′fish′), a fish without scales and with long, slender feelers around the mouth that look somewhat like a cat's whiskers. *n.*, *pl.* **cat fish es** or **cat fish.**

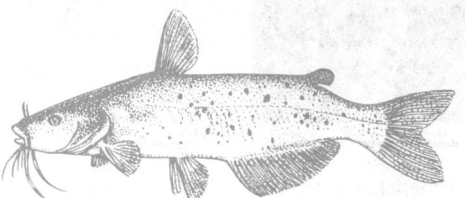

catfish—about 20 in. (50 cm.) long

cat gut (kat′gut′), a tough string made from the dried and twisted intestines of sheep or other animals, used to string violins and tennis rackets. It was formerly used by surgeons for stitching wounds. *n.*

Cath., Catholic.

ca thar tic (kə thär′tik), **1** a strong laxative. Epsom salts and castor oil are cathartics. **2** strongly laxative. 1 *n.*, 2 *adj.* —**ca thar′ti cal ly,** *adv.*

Ca thay (ka thā′), OLD USE. China. *n.*

ca the dral (kə thē′drəl), **1** the official church of a bishop. The bishop of a district or diocese has a throne in the cathedral. **2** a large or important church. *n.*

Cath er ine the Great (kath′ər ən), 1729-1796, empress of Russia from 1762 to 1796.

cath ode (kath′ōd), a negatively charged electrode. In a battery or vacuum tube, the electrical current flows from the negative cathode to the positive anode. *n.*

cathode rays, the invisible streams of electrons from the cathode in a vacuum tube. When cathode rays strike a solid substance, they produce X rays.

cath ode-ray tube (kath′ōd rā′), vacuum tube in which high-speed electrons are passed through magnetic fields in the form of a beam. Cathode-ray tubes are used in television receivers.

Cath o lic (kath′ə lik), **1** of the Christian church governed by the Pope; Roman Catholic. **2** of the ancient, undivided Christian church, or of its present representatives, including the Anglican, Orthodox, and Roman

Catholic churches. **3** member of a Catholic church, especially the Roman Catholic. **4 catholic,** of interest or use to all people; broad; universal: *Music has a catholic appeal to every type of person.* 1,2,4 *adj.,* 3 *n.*

Ca thol i cism (kə thol′ə siz′əm), the faith, doctrine, and organization of the Roman Catholic Church. *n.*

ca thol i cize (kə thol′ə sīz), make or become catholic or universal. *v.,* **ca thol i cized, ca thol i ciz ing.**

cat i on (kat′ī′ən), a positively charged ion that moves toward the negative pole in electrolysis. *n.*

cat kin (kat′kən), the soft, downy or scaly, pointed cluster of flowers, without petals, which grows on willows, birches, etc. *n.*

WORD HISTORY

catkin

Catkin comes from older Dutch *katteken*, originally meaning "kitten." It was called this because it is soft and downy and looks like a kitten's tail.

catkins

cat nap (kat′nap′), a short nap. *n.*

cat nip (kat′nip), plant somewhat like mint, with strongly scented leaves that cats like. *n.*

cat-o'-nine-tails (kat′ə nīn′tālz′), whip consisting of nine pieces of knotted cord fastened to a handle. It was formerly used as a means of punishment in the navy. *n., pl.* **cat-o'-nine-tails.**

cat's cradle, a child's game played with a string looped over the fingers of both hands.

Cats kill Mountains (kats′kil), range of Appalachian Mountains in SE New York State.

Cats kills (kats′kilz), Catskill Mountains. *n.pl.*

cat's-paw or **cats paw** (kats′pô′), person used by another to do something unpleasant or dangerous. *n.*

cat sup (kech′əp, kach′əp, *or* kat′səp), sauce made to use with meat, fish, etc. Tomato catsup is made of tomatoes, onions, salt, sugar, and spices. *n.* Also, **catchup** or **ketchup.**

cat tail (kat′tāl′), a tall marsh plant with flowers in long, round, furry, brown spikes. *n.*

cat ti ly (kat′l ē), in a catty manner. *adv.*

cat ti ness (kat′ē nis), catty quality. *n.*

cat tle (kat′l), **1** animals related to the ox that chew their cud, have hoofs, and are raised for meat, milk, hides, etc.; cows, bulls, and steers. **2** (formerly) farm animals; livestock. *n.pl.*

cat tle man (kat′l mən), person who raises or takes care of cattle. *n., pl.* **cat tle men.**

cat ty (kat′ē), mean and spiteful: *Catty comments about your classmates will not help you make friends.* adj., **cat ti er, cat ti est.**

cat ty-cor ner (kat′ē kôr′nər), cater-corner. *adj., adv.*

cat ty-cor nered (kat′ē kôr′nərd), cater-cornered. *adj., adv.*

cat walk (kat′wôk′), a narrow place to walk on a bridge, near the ceiling of a stage, in an airship, etc. *n.*

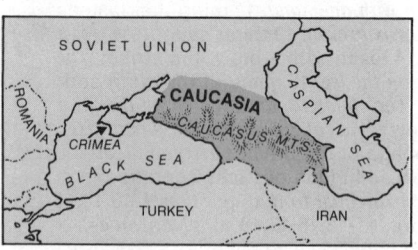

Cau ca sia (kô kā′zhə), region in the S Soviet Union, between the Black and Caspian Seas; Caucasus. *n.*

Cau ca sian (kô kā′zhən), **1** member of the division of the human race that includes the original inhabitants of Europe, southwestern Asia, and northern Africa, and their descendants throughout the world. **2** of this division of the human race. **3** person born or living in the Caucasus. **4** of the Caucasus or its inhabitants. 1,3 *n.,* 2,4 *adj.*

Cau ca sus (kô′kə səs), **1** mountain range in S Soviet Union, extending from the Black Sea to the Caspian Sea. **2** Caucasia. *n.*

cau cus (kô′kəs), **1** meeting of members or leaders of a political party to make plans, choose candidates, or decide how to vote. **2** hold such a meeting. 1 *n., pl.* **cau cus es;** 2 *v.*

cau dal (kô′dl), **1** of, at, or near the tail. **2** like a tail. *adj.* —**cau′dal ly,** *adv.*

caught (kôt), past tense and past participle of **catch.** *I caught the ball. The mouse was caught in a trap. v.*

caul dron (kôl′drən), caldron. *n.*

cau li flow er (kô′lə flou′ər), vegetable having a solid, white head with a few leaves around it. It is related to the cabbage. *n.*

caulk (kôk), fill up (a seam, crack, or joint) so that it will not leak; make watertight. Sailors caulk boats with oakum and tar. Plumbers caulk joints in pipe with lead. *v.* Also, **calk.** —**caulk′er,** *n.*

cat's cradle

cause (kôz), **1** person, thing, or event that makes something happen: *The flood was the cause of much damage.* **2** make happen; make do; bring about: *The fire caused much damage. A loud noise caused me to jump.* **3** reason or occasion for action: *The Olympic winner's return was a cause for celebration. You have no cause to complain.* **4** subject or movement in which many people are interested and to which they give their support: *World peace is the cause she works for.* 1,3,4 *n.,* 2 *v.,* **caused, caus ing.** —**caus′er,** *n.*

cause way (kôz′wā′), a raised road or path, usually

built across wet ground or shallow water: *A narrow causeway ran across the bog.* n.

caus tic (kô′stik), **1** substance that burns or destroys flesh; corrosive substance: *My warts were burned away by the caustic put on them.* **2** that burns or destroys flesh; corrosive. Lye is caustic soda or caustic potash. **3** very critical or sarcastic; stinging; biting: *The coach's caustic remarks made the football players angry.* 1 *n.,* 2,3 *adj.*

caus ti cal ly (kô′stik lē), very critically or sarcastically. *adv.*

caustic potash, potassium hydroxide.

caustic soda, sodium hydroxide.

cau ter i za tion (kô′tər ə zā′shən), a cauterizing or a being cauterized. *n.*

cau ter ize (kô′tə rīz′), burn with a hot iron or a caustic substance. Doctors sometimes cauterize wounds to prevent bleeding or infection. *v.,* **cau ter ized, cau ter iz ing.**

cau tion (kô′shən), **1** great care; regard for safety; unwillingness to take chances: *Always use caution when crossing streets.* **2** a warning: *A sign with "Danger" on it is a caution.* **3** urge to be careful; warn: *I cautioned them against playing in the street.* 1,2 *n.,* 3 *v.*

cau tious (kô′shəs), very careful; taking care to be safe; not taking chances: *A cautious driver never drives too fast.* *adj.* —**cau′tious ly,** *adv.* —**cau′tious ness,** *n.*

cav al cade (kav′əl kād′), **1** procession of persons riding on horses, in carriages, or in automobiles. **2** series of scenes or events: *a cavalcade of sports.* *n.*

cav a lier (kav′ə lir′), **1** horseman, mounted soldier, or knight. **2** a courteous gentleman. **3** a courteous escort for a lady. **4** careless in manner; free and easy; offhand: *She did not take me seriously and gave a cavalier reply.* **5** proud and scornful; haughty; arrogant: *People were often irritated by his cavalier attitude towards them.* **6 Cavalier,** person who supported Charles I of England in his struggle with Parliament from 1640 to 1649. 1-3,6 *n.,* 4,5 *adj.* —**cav′a lier′ly,** *adv.* —**cav′a lier′ness,** *n.*

cav al ry (kav′əl rē), **1** (formerly) soldiers who fought on horseback. **2** soldiers who fight from armored vehicles. *n.,* pl. **cav al ries.**

cav al ry man (kav′əl rē mən), soldier in the cavalry. *n.,* pl. **cav al ry men.**

cave (kāv), **1** a hollow space underground, especially one with an opening in the side of a hill or mountain. **2 cave in,** fall in; sink: *The weight of the snow caused the roof of the cabin to cave in.* 1 *n.,* 2 *v.,* **caved, cav ing.**

cave-in (kāv′in′), **1** a caving in; collapse: *a tunnel cave-in, the cave-in of a mine.* **2** place where something has caved in. *n.*

cave man, person who lived in a cave in prehistoric times.

cav ern (kav′ərn), a large cave. *n.*

cav ern ous (kav′ər nəs), **1** like a cavern; large and hollow: *a cavernous cellar, cavernous eyes.* **2** full of caverns: *cavernous mountains.* *adj.* —**cav′ern ous ly,** *adv.*

cav i ar or **cav i are** (kav′ē är), the salted eggs of sturgeon or of certain other large fish, eaten as an appetizer. *n.*

cav il (kav′əl), **1** find fault without good reason; raise trivial objections: *He cavils about minor points in the rules of the game.* **2** a trivial objection; petty criticism. 1 *v.,* **cav iled, cav il ing** or **cav illed, cav il ling;** 2 *n.* —**cav′il er, cav′il ler,** *n.*

cav i ty (kav′ə tē), **1** hollow place; hole. Cavities in teeth are caused by decay. **2** an enclosed space inside the body: *the abdominal cavity.* *n.,* pl. **cav i ties.**

ca vort (kə vôrt′), prance about; jump around: *The children cavorted about the field, racing and tumbling.* *v.*

caw (kô), **1** the harsh cry made by a crow or raven. **2** make this cry. 1 *n.,* 2 *v.*

---

cay (kē *or* kā), a low island; reef; key. *n.*

cay enne (kī en′ *or* kā en′), a very hot, biting powder made from the seeds or fruit of a pepper plant; red pepper. *n.*

cayenne pepper, cayenne.

cay man (kā′mən), caiman. *n.,* pl. **cay mans.**

Ca yu ga (kā yü′gə *or* kī yü′gə), **1** member of an Iroquois tribe of American Indians formerly living in western New York State. **2** of this tribe. 1 *n.,* pl. **Ca yu ga** or **Ca yu gas;** 2 *adj.*

cay use (kī yüs′ *or* kī′üs), in the western United States: **1** an Indian-bred pony. **2** any pony or horse. *n.*

CB, citizens band (radio).

CBC, Canadian Broadcasting Corporation.

CBS, Columbia Broadcasting System.

cc, cc., or **c.c.,** cubic centimeter or cubic centimeters.

C clef, symbol in music that shows the position of middle C. It is called the alto clef when placed on the third line of the staff, and the tenor clef when placed on the fourth line of the staff. See **clef** for diagram.

Cd, symbol for cadmium.

CD, compact disc.

cd., cord or cords.

C.D., civil defense.

Cdn., Canadian.

Ce, symbol for cerium.

cease (sēs), come to an end; put an end to; stop: *The music ceased suddenly. Cease trying to do more than you can.* *v.,* **ceased, ceas ing.**

cease-fire (sēs′fīr′), a halt in military operations, especially for the purpose of discussing peace. *n.*

cease less (sēs′lis), going on all the time; never stopping; continual: *the ceaseless roar of the falls.* *adj.*

cecropia moth
wingspread about
5 in. (13 cm.)

ce cro pi a moth (sə krō′pē ə), a large silkworm moth of the eastern United States. Its larvae feed on trees and shrubs.

ce dar (sē′dər), **1** an evergreen tree related to the pine, with branches that spread widely, and fragrant, durable, reddish wood. **2** the wood of this tree, used for lining clothes closets and making chests, pencils, and posts. *n.*

Cedar Rapids, city in E Iowa.

cedar waxwing, a small North American bird with a crest and small, red markings on its wings.

cede (sēd), hand over to another; give up; surrender: *Spain ceded the Philippines to the United States.* *v.,* **ced ed, ced ing.**

ce dil la (sə dil′ə), a mark somewhat like a comma (ç)

put under *c* before *a, o,* or *u* in certain words to show that it has the sound of *s.* EXAMPLE: façade. *n., pl.* **ce dil las.**

ceil ing (sē′ling), **1** the inside, top covering of a room; surface opposite the floor. **2** the greatest height to which an airplane can go under certain conditions: *That plane has a ceiling of more than 100,000 feet.* **3** distance between the earth and the lowest clouds: *The weather report said that the ceiling was only 300 feet.* **4** an upper limit set for prices, wages, rents, etc.: *There is a ceiling on the amount candidates can spend for election campaigns. n.*

Cel e bes (sel′ə bēz′), large island in Indonesia, between Borneo and New Guinea; Sulawesi. See **East Indies** for map. *n.*

cel e brant (sel′ə brənt), **1** person who performs a ceremony or rite. **2** priest who performs Mass. *n.*

cel e brate (sel′ə brāt), **1** observe (a special time or day) with the proper ceremonies or festivities: *We celebrated her birthday with cake, ice cream, and presents.* **2** perform publicly with the proper ceremonies and rites: *The priest celebrates Mass in church.* **3** praise; honor: *Her books are celebrated all over the world.* **4** INFORMAL. have a gay time: *When the children saw the snow, they celebrated. v.,* **cel e brat ed, cel e brat ing.** —**cel′e bra′tor,** *n.*

cel e brat ed (sel′ə brā′tid), much talked about; famous; well-known: *a celebrated author. adj.*

cel e bra tion (sel′ə brā′shən), **1** special services or activities in honor of a particular person, act, time, or day: *A Fourth of July celebration often includes a display of fireworks.* **2** act of celebrating: *celebration of a birthday. n.*

ce leb ri ty (sə leb′rə tē), **1** a famous person; person who is well known or much talked about: *Astronauts are celebrities around the world.* **2** a being well known or much talked about; fame: *Her celebrity brought her riches. n., pl.* **ce leb ri ties.**

ce ler i ty (sə ler′ə tē), swiftness; speed. *n.*

cel er y (sel′ər ē), vegetable related to parsley, with long, crisp stalks, which are sometimes covered as they grow to whiten them. Celery is eaten either raw or cooked. *n.*

ce les ta (sə les′tə), a musical instrument resembling a small, upright piano. Its bell-like tones are made by hammers hitting steel plates. *n., pl.* **ce les tas.**

ce les tial (sə les′chəl), **1** of the sky or the heavens: *The sun, moon, planets, and stars are celestial bodies.* **2** of or belonging to heaven as the place of God and the angels; heavenly; divine: *celestial joy. adj.* —**ce les′tial ly,** *adv.*

celestial sphere, the imaginary sphere which appears to enclose the universe. To an observer on earth, the visible sky forms half of the celestial sphere.

cel i bate (sel′ə bit), **1** an unmarried person who takes a vow to lead a single life: *Nuns and priests are celibates.* **2** unmarried; single: *to lead a celibate life.* **1** *n.,* **2** *adj.*

cell (sel), **1** a small room in a prison, convent, or monastery. **2** any small, hollow place: *Bees store honey in the cells of a honeycomb.* **3** the basic unit of living matter of which all plants and animals are made. Cells vary in size and shape but are generally microscopic. Most cells consist of protoplasm, have a nucleus near the center, and are enclosed by a cell wall or cell membrane. The body has blood cells, nerve cells, muscle cells, etc. **4** container holding materials which produce electricity by chemical action. A battery consists of one or more cells. *n.* —**cell′-like′,** *adj.*

cel lar (sel′ər), an underground room or rooms, usually under a building and often used for storage. *n.*

Cel li ni (chə lē′nē), **Benvenuto,** 1500-1571, Italian sculptor and artist in metalwork. *n.*

cel list (chel′ist), person who plays the cello; violoncellist. *n.*

cell membrane, the thin membrane that forms the outer surface of the protoplasm of a cell.

cel lo (chel′ō), a musical instrument like a violin, but very much larger and with a lower tone; violoncello. It is held between the knees while it is played. *n., pl.* **cel los.**

cello
played with a bow
or by plucking strings
with the fingers

cel lo phane (sel′ə fān), a transparent substance made from cellulose. It is used as a wrapping to keep food, candy, tobacco, etc., fresh and clean. *n.*

cel lu lar (sel′yə lər), **1** having to do with cells. **2** made up of cells. All animal and plant tissue is cellular. **3** of or having to do with cellular radio: *cellular telephones, cellular technology. adj.*

cellular radio, a communication system for use in phone-equipped cars in a city or metropolitan area that is divided into smaller areas or cells, each with a low-powered radio transmitter and receiver. As a car moves along, a call is transferred automatically from cell to cell.

Cel lu loid (sel′yə loid), trademark for a hard, transparent substance made from cellulose. It catches fire easily. Combs, toilet articles, camera films, etc., are often made of Celluloid. *n.*

cel lu lose (sel′yə lōs), substance that forms the walls of plant cells; the woody part of trees and plants. Wood, cotton, flax, and hemp are largely cellulose. Cellulose is used to make paper, rayon, plastics, explosives, etc. *n.*

cell wall, the hard outer covering of a plant cell, made up mostly of cellulose and surrounding the cell membrane.

Cel si us (sel′sē əs), of, based on, or according to the Celsius scale; centigrade. *adj.*

Celsius scale, a scale for measuring temperature on which 0 degrees marks the freezing point of water and 100 degrees marks the boiling point. [This scale was named for Anders *Celsius,* 1701-1744, a Swedish astronomer who invented it in 1742.]

Celt (selt *or* kelt), member of a people to which the Irish, Scottish Highlanders, Welsh, Bretons, and Manx belong. The ancient Gauls and Britons were Celts. *n.*

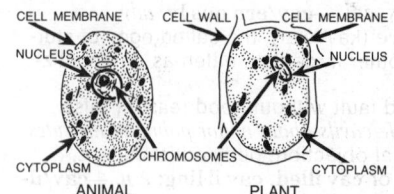

cell (def. 3)
two types,
greatly magnified

Celt ic (sel′tik *or* kel′tik), **1** of the Celts or their language. **2** the group of languages spoken by the Celts, including Irish, Gaelic, Welsh, Breton, and Manx. **1** *adj.,* **2** *n.*

ce ment (sə ment′), **1** a fine, gray powder made by burning clay and limestone. Cement is used to make concrete and mortar. **2** anything applied soft which hardens to make things stick together: *rubber cement.* **3** substance used to fill cavities in teeth. **4** fasten together with cement: *A broken plate can be cemented.* **5** spread cement over: *The workmen were cementing the sidewalk.* **6** join firmly; unite: *The marriage of our son to their daughter cemented the friendship of our two families.* 1-3 *n.,* 4-6 *v.* **—ce men ta′tion,** *n.* **—ce ment′er,** *n.*

cem e ter y (sem′ə ter′ē), place for burying the dead; graveyard. *n., pl.* **cem e ter ies.**

cen., central.

Cen o zo ic (sen′ə zō′ik), **1** the most recent era of geological history. The Cenozoic began about 60 or 70 million years ago, when mammals began to dominate the animal kingdom, and includes the present time. **2** of this era or its rocks. 1 *n.,* 2 *adj.*

cen ser (sen′sər), container in which incense is burned, especially during religious ceremonies. *n.*

cen sor (sen′sər), **1** person who examines and, if necessary, changes letters, books, newspapers, plays, motion pictures, etc., so as to make their content satisfactory to the government or to some institution or organization. **2** examine or change as a censor; make changes in; take out part of (news reports, books, letters, motion pictures, etc.): *All letters from the battlefield were censored to make sure military information did not fall into enemy hands. Two scenes in the movie had been censored for having too much violence.* 1 *n.,* 2 *v.*

cen so ri ous (sen sôr′ē əs), too ready to find fault; severely critical. *adj.* **—cen so′ri ous ly,** *adv.* **—cen so′ri ous ness,** *n.*

cen sor ship (sen′sər ship), act or system of censoring: *Censorship of news is common in time of war. n.*

cen sure (sen′shər), **1** expression of disapproval; unfavorable opinion; criticism: *Censure is sometimes harder to bear than punishment.* **2** find fault with; criticize: *I was censured by the club for not paying my dues.* 1 *n.,* 2 *v.,* **cen sured, cen sur ing. —cen′sur er,** *n.*

cen sus (sen′səs), an official count of the people of a country or district. It is taken to find out the number of people, their age, sex, what they do to make a living, and many other facts about them. *n., pl.* **cen sus es.**

cent (sent), coin of the United States and Canada, usually an alloy of copper; penny. 100 cents make one dollar. *n.*

cent., **1** centigrade. **2** central. **3** century.

cen taur (sen′tôr), (in Greek myths) a creature with the head, arms, and chest of a man, and the body and legs of a horse. *n.*

cen ta vo (sen tä′vō), coin used in many Latin-American countries and the Philippines. 100 centavos make a peso. *n., pl.* **cen ta vos.** [*Centavo* is from Spanish *centavo,* originally meaning "hundredth," which came from Latin *centum,* meaning "hundred."]

cen te nar i an (sen′tə ner′ē ən), person who is 100 years old or more. *n.*

cen ten ar y (sen ten′ər ē *or* sen′tə ner′ē), **1** a 100th anniversary: *The town was bustling with plans for its centenary.* **2** period of 100 years; century. **3** having to do with 100 years or a 100th anniversary: *a centenary celebration.* 1,2 *n., pl.* **cen ten ar ies;** 3 *adj.*

cen ten ni al (sen ten′ē əl), **1** of or having to do with 100 years or the 100th anniversary. **2** 100 years old: *centennial pines.* **3** a 100th anniversary: *The town is celebrating its centennial.* **4** celebration of the 100th anniversary: *I hope there will be a fair during our centennial.* 1,2 *adj.,* 3,4 *n.* **—cen ten′ni al ly,** *adv.*

cen ter (sen′tər), **1** point within a circle or sphere equally distant from all points of the circumference or surface. **2** the middle point, place, or part: *the center of a*

room. **3** person, thing, or group that is the central point of attraction: *The Egyptian mummy was the center of the exhibit.* **4** point toward which people or things go, or from which they come; main point: *New York City is one of the trade centers of the world.* **5** place in or at a center: *A bowl of fruit was centered on the kitchen table.* **6** concentrate; rest: *All his hopes are centered on being promoted.* **7** collect at a center: *The guests centered around the table.* **8** player in the middle of a forward line in football, basketball, hockey, etc. 1-4,8 *n.,* 5-7 *v.* Also, **centre.**

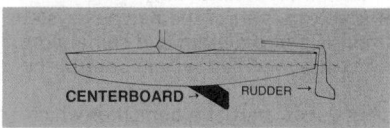

cen ter board (sen′tər bôrd′), a movable keel of a sailboat. It is lowered through a slot in the bottom of a boat to prevent drifting to leeward. *n.*

center field, (in baseball) the section of the outfield between left field and right field.

center of gravity, point in a body around which its weight is evenly balanced.

cen ter piece (sen′tər pēs′), an ornamental piece of glass, lace, etc., or an arrangement of flowers for the center of a dining table, buffet, mantel, etc. *n.*

centi-, combining form. **1** one hundred: *Centigrade = one hundred degrees.* **2** one hundredth part of: *Centimeter = one hundredth part of a meter.* [The form *centi-* comes from Latin *centum,* meaning "one hundred."]

cen ti grade (sen′tə grād), of, based on, or according to a scale for measuring temperature on which 0 degrees marks the freezing point of water and 100 degrees marks the boiling point; Celsius. The **centigrade thermometer** is marked off according to this scale. *adj.*

cen ti gram or **cen ti gramme** (sen′tə gram), 1/100 of a gram. *n.*

cen ti li ter or **cen ti li tre** (sen′tə lē′tər), 1/100 of a liter. *n.*

cen time (sän′tēm′), coin used in France, Belgium, Switzerland, Mali, Niger, Congo, and other countries. 100 centimes make a franc. *n.*

cen ti me ter or **cen ti me tre** (sen′tə mē′tər), 1/100 of a meter; .3937 inch. *n.*

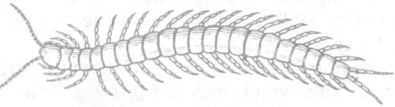

centipede—about 1 in. (2.5 cm.) long

cen ti pede (sen′tə pēd′), a flat, wormlike animal with many pairs of legs, the front pair of which are clawlike and contain poison glands. *n.*

cen tral (sen′trəl), **1** being or forming the center: *a central point, the central part of a wheel.* **2** at the center; near the center: *The park is in the central part of the city.* **3** equally distant from all points; easy to get to or from: *We shop at a central market.* **4** main; chief; principal: *The central library sends books to its branches. What is the central idea in this story? adj.* **—cen′tral ness,** *n.*

Central African Republic, country in central Africa, south of Chad. *Capital:* Bangui.

Central America, part of North America between Mexico and South America. Guatemala, El Salvador, Honduras, Belize, Nicaragua, Costa Rica, and Panama are the countries in Central America.

Central American, 1 of Central America or its people. **2** person born or living in Central America.

cen tral i za tion (sen′trə lə zā′shən), **1** a coming or bringing to a center. **2** a gathering together at a center: *centralization of medical services.* **3** a bringing together under the control of a single authority: *the centralization of government under a dictator. n.*

cen tral ize (sen′trə līz), **1** bring to or toward a center; locate in a center. **2** gather together in a center; concentrate. **3** bring or come under the control of a single authority. *v.,* **cen tral ized, cen tral iz ing.**

cen tral ly (sen′trə lē), at the center; near the center: *The business district is centrally located. adv.*

central nervous system, part of the nervous system of vertebrates that consists of the brain and spinal cord. The nerves from the central nervous system control the muscles.

central processing unit, part of a computer which carries out instructions and processes data. It also controls the operations of the computer as a whole.

Central Standard Time, the standard time in the central part of the United States and Canada. It is six hours behind Greenwich Time.

cen tre (sen′tər), BRITISH. center. *n., v.,* **cen tred, cen tring.**

cen trif u gal (sen trif′yə gəl), moving away from the center. *adj.* —**cen trif′u gal ly,** *adv.*

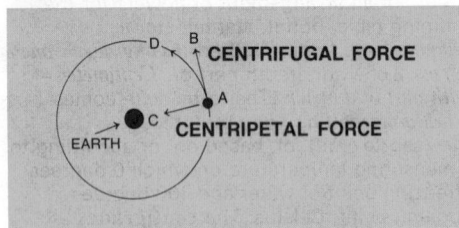

The tendency of the satellite A to move in a straight line toward B (**centrifugal force**) is overcome by the force exerted by gravity toward C (**centripetal force**), resulting in motion toward D.

centrifugal force, the inertia, or tendency to move in one direction, which causes a body turning around a center to move away from the center.

cen tri fuge (sen′trə fyüj), machine for separating two substances varying in density, as cream from milk or bacteria from a fluid, by means of centrifugal force. *n.*

cen trip e tal (sen trip′ə təl), moving toward the center. *adj.* —**cen trip′e tal ly,** *adv.*

centripetal force, the force that tends to move things toward the center around which they are turning. The earth's gravity exerts a centripetal force on an orbiting satellite and keeps it from flying off into space.

cen tur y (sen′chər ē), **1** each 100 years, counting from some special time, such as the birth of Christ. The first century is 1 through 100; the nineteenth century is 1801 through 1900; the twentieth century is 1901 through 2000. **2** period of 100 years. From 1824 to 1924 is a century. *n., pl.* **cen tur ies.**

century plant, a large plant with thick leaves, a kind of agave, growing in Mexico and the southwestern United States; aloe. It may reach thirty feet in height and is often wrongly supposed to bloom once every 100 years.

ce ram ic (sə ram′ik), **1** of or having to do with pottery, earthenware, porcelain, etc., or with making them. **2** article made of pottery, earthenware, porcelain, etc. 1 *adj.,* 2 *n.*

ce ram ics (sə ram′iks), art of making pottery, earthenware, porcelain, etc. *n.*

cer e al (sir′ē əl), **1** any grass that produces grain which is used as a food. Wheat, rice, corn, oats, and barley are cereals. **2** the grain. **3** food made from the grain. Oatmeal and corn meal are cereals. **4** of or having to do with grain or the grasses producing it: *cereal crops, cereal products.* 1-3 *n.,* 4 *adj.*

WORD HISTORY

cereal

Cereal comes from Latin *Cerealem,* meaning "of *Ceres*," the Roman goddess of agriculture.

cer e bel lum (ser′ə bel′əm), the part of the brain that controls the coordination of the muscles. *n., pl.* **cer e bel lums, cer e bel la** (ser′ə bel′ə).

ce re bral (sə rē′brəl *or* ser′ə brəl), **1** of the brain. **2** of the cerebrum. **3** characterized by thought and reason rather than emotion or action: *Chess is a cerebral game. adj.* —**ce re′bral ly,** *adv.*

cerebral palsy, paralysis caused by damage to the brain before or at birth. Persons suffering from cerebral palsy have trouble coordinating their muscles.

ce re brum (sə rē′brəm *or* ser′ə brəm), the part of the human brain that controls thought and voluntary muscular movements. *n., pl.* **ce re brums, ce re bra** (sə rē′brə *or* ser′ə brə).

cer e mo ni al (ser′ə mō′nē əl), **1** of or having to do with ceremony: *The emperor's ceremonial costumes were beautiful.* **2** very formal: *The queen receives guests in a ceremonial way.* **3** the formal actions proper to an occasion. Bowing the head and kneeling are ceremonials of religion. 1,2 *adj.,* 3 *n.* —**cer′e mo′ni al ly,** *adv.* —**cer′e mo′ni al ness,** *n.*

cer e mo ni ous (ser′ə mō′nē əs), **1** full of ceremony: *There was a ceremonious unveiling of the statue.* **2** very formal; extremely polite; *a ceremonious bow. adj.* —**cer′e mo′ni ous ly,** *adv.* —**cer′e mo′ni ous ness,** *n.*

cer e mo ny (ser′ə mō′nē), **1** a special act or set of acts to be done on special occasions such as weddings, funerals, graduations, or holidays: *The graduation ceremony was held in the gymnasium.* **2** very polite conduct; way of conducting oneself that follows all the rules of polite social behavior: *The old gentleman showed us to the door with a great deal of ceremony.* **3** attention to forms and customs; formality: *The princess disliked the traditional ceremony of the court. n., pl.* **cer e mo nies.**

stand on ceremony, be too polite; be very formal: *He is a hospitable person who does not stand on ceremony and so makes everyone feel at ease in his home.*

Cer es (sir′ēz), (in Roman myths) the goddess of agriculture. The Greeks called her Demeter. *n.*

ce rise (sə rēs′), **1** bright pinkish-red. **2** a bright pinkish red. 1 *adj.,* 2 *n.*

cer i um (sir′ē əm), a soft, grayish metallic element. Cerium is used in porcelain, glass, and alloys. *n.*

cer tain (sert′n), **1** without a doubt; sure: *It is certain that 2 and 3 do not make 6. I am certain that these are the facts.* **2** known but not named; some; particular: *Certain* *plants will not grow in this country.* **3** settled; fixed: *I earn a certain amount of money each week.* **4** that can be depended on; reliable: *I have certain information that school will end a day earlier this year.* *adj.* —**cer′tain ness,** *n.*

for certain, without a doubt; surely: *She will be here for certain.*

cer tain ly (sėrt′n lē), without a doubt; surely: *I will certainly be at the party. adv.*

cer tain ty (sėrt′n tē), **1** a being certain; freedom from doubt: *The man's certainty was amusing, for we could all see that he was wrong.* **2** something certain; a sure fact: *The coming of spring is a certainty. n., pl.* **cer tain ties.**

cer tif i cate (sər tif′ə kit), an official written or printed statement that declares something to be a fact. A birth certificate gives the date and place of a person's birth and the names of the parents. *n.*

cer ti fi ca tion (sėr′tə fə kā′shən), **1** a certifying or a being certified. **2** a certified statement. *n.*

cer ti fied (sėr′tə fīd), **1** guaranteed: *certified Grade A milk.* **2** having a certificate: *a certified teacher. adj.*

cer ti fy (sėr′tə fī), **1** declare (something) true or correct by an official spoken, written, or printed statement: *This diploma certifies that you have completed high school.* **2** guarantee the quality or value of: *The fire inspector certified the school building as fireproof. v.,* **cer ti fied, cer ti fy ing.** —**cer′ti fi′er,** *n.*

ce ru le an (sə rü′lē ən), **1** sky-blue. **2** a sky-blue color. 1 *adj.,* 2 *n.*

Cer van tes (sər van′tēz′), **Miguel de,** 1547-1616, Spanish author who wrote *Don Quixote. n.*

cer vi cal (sėr′və kəl), of the neck. *adj.*

ce si um (sē′zē əm), a soft, silvery, metallic element used in photoelectric cells, radio tubes, etc. *n.*

ces sa tion (se sā′shən), a ceasing; a stopping: *Both armies agreed on a cessation of the fighting. n.*

cess pool (ses′pül′), a pool or pit for house sewer pipes to empty into. *n.*

Cey lon (si lon′), former name of **Sri Lanka.** *n.*

Cey lo nese (sē′lə nēz′), **1** of Ceylon or its people. **2** person born or living in Ceylon. 1 *adj.,* 2 *n., pl.* **Cey lo nese.**

Cé zanne (sā zan′), **Paul,** 1839-1906, French painter. *n.*

Cf, symbol for californium.

cf., compare.

cg., centigram or centigrams.

cgm., centigram or centigrams.

ch., **1** chapter. **2** church.

Chad (chad), country in central Africa south of Libya. *Capital:* N'djamena. See **Algeria** for map. *n.*

chafe (chāf), **1** rub so as to wear away, scrape, or make sore: *The stiff collar chafed my neck.* **2** make or become angry: *His big sister's teasing chafed him. He chafed under his big sister's teasing. v.,* **chafed, chaf ing.**

chaff¹ (chaf), **1** the tough, outer skin of wheat, oats, rye, etc., especially when separated from grain by threshing. **2** worthless stuff; rubbish. *n.*

chaff² (chaf), **1** make fun of in a good-natured way to one's face: *Her friends chaffed the girl about her inability to sing on key.* **2** good-natured joking about a person to his face: *She did not mind her friend's chaff.* 1 *v.,* 2 *n.*

chaf finch (chaf′inch), a European songbird, often kept as a cage bird. *n.*

chaf ing dish (chā′fing), pan with a flame under it, used to cook food at the table or to keep it warm.

Cha gall (shə gäl′), **Marc,** 1887-1985, Russian painter who lived in France. *n.*

cha grin (shə grin′), **1** a feeling of disappointment, failure, or humiliation: *I felt chagrin because I did not pass the test.* **2** cause to feel chagrin: *She was chagrined by her failure.* 1 *n.,* 2 *v.*

a hat	**i** it	**oi** oil	**ch** child	a in about
ā age	**ī** ice	**ou** out	**ng** long	e in taken
ä far	**o** hot	**u** cup	**sh** she	**ə =** i in pencil
e let	**ō** open	**u̇** put	**th** thin	o in lemon
ē equal	**ô** order	**ü** rule	**ŦH** then	u in circus
ėr term			**zh** measure	

chain (chān), **1** series of links joined together: *The dog is fastened to a post by a chain.* **2** series of things linked together: *a chain of mountains, a chain of restaurants, a chain of events.* **3** join together with a chain; fasten with a chain: *The dog was chained to a post.* **4** anything that binds or restrains: *the chains of duty.* **5** bind; restrain: *Work chained him to his desk.* **6** keep in prison; make a slave of. **7** chains, *pl.* **a** bonds; fetters: *The rebels were brought back in chains.* **b** imprisonment or bondage: *Enemies of the government spent many years in chains.* 1,2,4,7 *n.,* 3,5,6 *v.* —**chain′like′,** *adj.*

chain mail, kind of flexible armor, made of metal rings linked together.

chain reaction, **1** process of releasing atomic energy by a series of nuclear fissions that continues automatically once it has been started. In a chain reaction, some of the neutrons given off by a nucleus that has been split collide with other nuclei, which, in turn, give off neutrons that collide with more nuclei. **2** any series of events or happenings, each caused by the preceding one or ones.

chain store, one of a group of stores owned and managed by the same company.

chair (cher *or* char), **1** seat that has a back and, sometimes, arms, usually for one person. **2** seat of rank, dignity, or authority. **3** position or authority of a person who has such a seat: *Professor Smith has the chair of astronomy at this college.* **4** chairman or chairwoman: *The chair called the meeting to order.* **5** conduct as chairman or chairwoman: *chair a meeting.* 1-4 *n.,* 5 *v.*

take the chair, preside at a meeting: *The vice-president took the chair when the president was ill.*

chairlift

chair lift (cher′lift′ *or* char′lift′), a series of chairs or seats, attached to an overhead cable. Skiers ride a chairlift to the top of a slope. *n.*

chair man (cher′mən *or* char′mən), **1** person who is in charge of a meeting. **2** person at the head of a committee. *n., pl.* **chair men.**

chair man ship (cher′mən ship *or* char′mən ship), position, duties, or term of office of a person who chairs (a meeting or committee). *n.*

chair per son (cher′pėr′sən *or* char′pėr′sən), **1** person who is in charge of a meeting. **2** person at the head of a committee. *n.*

chair wom an (cher′wu̇m′ən *or* char′wu̇m′ən),

1 woman in charge of a meeting. **2** woman at the head of a committee. *n., pl.* **chair wom en.**

chaise (shāz), **1** a light, open carriage, usually with a folding top. **2** chaise longue. *n.*

chaise longue (shāz′ lông′), chair with a long seat and a back at one end, somewhat like a couch. [*Chaise longue* comes from French *chaise longue,* which originally meant "long chair."]

chaise lounge (shāz′ lounj′), chaise longue.

Chal de a (kal dē′ə), ancient region in SW Asia, on the Tigris and Euphrates rivers. See **Babylonia** for map. *n.* —**Chal de′an,** *adj., n.*

cha let (sha lā′), **1** a Swiss house with wide, overhanging eaves. **2** any house like this. *n.*

chal ice (chal′is), **1** cup or goblet. **2** cup that holds the wine used in the Communion service. *n.*

chalk (chôk), **1** a soft, white or gray limestone, made up mostly of very small fossil seashells. Chalk is used for making lime and for writing or drawing. **2** a white or colored substance like chalk, used for writing or drawing on a blackboard or chalkboard. **3** mark, write, or draw with chalk. 1,2 *n.,* 3 *v.* —**chalk′like′,** *adj.*

chalk up, 1 credit: *You learned your lesson the hard way and you can chalk it up to experience.* **2** score: *Our team chalked up 10 points.*

chalk board (chôk′bôrd′), a smooth, hard surface, used for writing or drawing on with crayon or chalk. *n.*

chalk y (chô′kē), **1** of chalk; containing chalk. **2** like chalk; white as chalk: *a face chalky with fear. adj.,* **chalk i er, chalk i est. —chalk′i ness,** *n.*

chal lenge (chal′ənj), **1** a call to a game or contest: *The champions accepted our team's challenge.* **2** call to a game or contest; dare: *The champion swimmer challenged anyone in the world to beat her.* **3** call to fight: *The knight challenged his rival to a duel.* **4** a call to fight: *His rival accepted the challenge.* **5** a call to answer and explain: *"Who goes there?" was the challenge of the soldier on guard.* **6** stop and question a person about an action: *When I tried to enter the building, the guard at the door challenged me.* **7** call in question; doubt; dispute: *The teacher challenged my statement that rice grows in Oregon.* **8** a demand for proof of the truth of a statement; a doubting or questioning of the truth of a statement: *His challenge led me to read widely about Oregon.* **9** anything that claims or commands effort, interest, feeling, etc.: *Fractions are a real challenge to her.* **10** claim or command effort, interest, feeling, etc.: *How to prevent disease is a problem that challenges everyone's attention.* **11** object to: *The attorney for the defense challenged the juror.* **12** objection: *The judge upheld the challenge and dismissed the juror from duty.* 1,4,5,8,9,12 *n.,* 2,3,6,7,10,11 *v.,* **challenged, chal leng ing. —chal′lenge a ble,** *adj.*

chal leng er (chal′ən jər), person who challenges another or others. *n.*

cham ber (chām′bər), **1** a room, especially a bedroom. **2** hall where lawmakers meet: *the council chamber.* **3** group of lawmakers: *The Congress of the United States has two chambers, the Senate and the House of Representatives.* **4** an enclosed space in the body of an animal or plant, or in some kinds of machinery. The heart has four chambers. The part of a gun that holds the charge is called the chamber. **5 chambers,** *pl.* **a** office of a lawyer or judge: *The judge met the two lawyers in her chambers.* **b** set of rooms in a building arranged for living or for offices. *n.*

cham ber lain (chām′bər lən), person who manages the household of a king or great noble. *n.*

cham ber maid (chām′bər mād′), maid who takes care of bedrooms in a house, hotel, or motel. *n.*

chamber music, music suited for performance in a room or small hall, such as music for a trio or quartet.

chamber of commerce, group of people in business organized to protect and promote the business interests of a city, state, or country.

cham bray (sham′brā), a cotton cloth woven from white and colored threads, used for dresses and men's shirts. It is a kind of gingham. *n.*

chameleon (def. 1)
up to 1 ft.
(30 cm.) long

cha me le on (kə mē′lē ən), **1** a small lizard that can change the color of its skin to blend with the surroundings. **2** a changeable or fickle person. *n.*

cham ois (sham′ē), **1** a small, goatlike antelope that lives in the high mountains of Europe and southwestern Asia. **2** a soft leather made from its skin or the skin of sheep, goats, or deer. *n., pl.* **cham ois.**

chamois (def. 1)
about 2¹/₂ ft.
(75 cm.) high
at the shoulder

cham o mile (kam′ə mīl), plant related to the aster, with daisylike flowers. Its flowers and leaves are sometimes dried and used as a medicine. *n.* Also, **camomile.**

champ[1] (champ), bite and chew noisily: *champ food. The racehorse champed its bit. v.*

champ at the bit, be impatient or restless: *The children were champing at the bit as the parade approached.*

champ[2] (champ), INFORMAL. champion. *n.*

cham pagne (sham pān′), **1** a sparkling, bubbling white wine made in Champagne, a region in northern France. **2** any similar wine made elsewhere. *n.*

cham pi on (cham′pē ən), **1** person, animal, or thing that wins first place in a game or contest: *He is the swimming champion of our school.* **2** that has won first place; ahead of all others: *a champion runner.* **3** person who fights or speaks for another; person who defends a cause: *That writer is a great champion of peace.* **4** fight for; speak in behalf of; defend: *All his life he has championed freedom.* 1,3 *n.,* 2 *adj.,* 4 *v.* —**cham′pi on less,** *adj.*

cham pi on ship (cham′pē ən ship), **1** position of a champion; first place: *Our school won the championship in baseball.* **2** defense; support: *She undertook the championship of our cause. n.*

Cham plain (sham plān′), **1 Lake,** long, narrow lake between New York and Vermont. **2 Samuel de,** 1567-1635, French explorer who founded Quebec. *n.*

chance (chans), **1** favorable time; opportunity: *Now is your chance. I saw a chance to earn some money selling newspapers.* **2** likelihood of anything happening; possibility or probability: *There's a good chance that you will be well enough to return to school next week. The chances are against snow in May.* **3** fate, fortune, or luck: *Chance led* *to the finding of gold in California.* **4** have the fortune; happen: *I chanced to meet an old friend today.* **5** a risk; gamble: *He took a big chance when he swam the wide river.* **6** take the risk of: *I will not chance driving in this awful blizzard.* **7** not expected or planned; accidental: *We had a chance visit from Grandmother.* **8** ticket in a raffle or lottery: *She bought two chances in the car raffle at the fair.* 1-3,5,8 *n.*, 4,6 *v.*, **chanced, chanc ing;** 7 *adj.*

by chance, accidentally: *It was only by chance that I found the keys you lost.*

chance upon or **chance on,** happen to find or meet: *I chanced upon an old friend.*

on the off chance, depending on luck.

stand a chance, have favorable prospects.

chan cel lor (chan′sə lər), **1** the prime minister or other very high official of some European countries. **2** the chief judge of a chancery. **3** head or president of some universities. *n.*

chan cer y (chan′sər ē), court of law dealing with cases in which justice requires a settlement not covered by either common law or statute law. *n., pl.* **chan cer ies.**

chanc y (chan′sē), uncertain; risky. *adj.*, **chanc i er, chanc i est.**

chan de lier (shan′də lir′), fixture with branches for lights, usually hanging from the ceiling. *n.*

chand ler (chand′lər), **1** maker or seller of candles. **2** dealer in groceries and supplies: *Before sailing they bought provisions from a ship chandler. n.*

change (chānj), **1** make or become different: *She changed the room by painting the walls green. The wind changed from east to west.* **2** put or take (something) in place of another; substitute or exchange: *change soiled clothes for clean ones. Can you change a dollar bill for ten dimes? I changed seats with my brother.* **3** a changing; a passing from one form or place to another: *The change from flower to fruit is interesting to watch. Vacationing in the country is a pleasant change from city life.* **4** a changed condition: *Do you see any change in his behavior?* **5** thing to be used in place of another of the same kind: *He brought along a change of clothes.* **6** money returned to a person who has given a larger amount than the price of what is purchased. **7** money of smaller denomination given in place of money of larger denomination: *Can you give me change for a dollar?* **8** coins of small denomination: *She was carrying a dollar and some change.* **9** change one's clothes: *After swimming we went to the cabin and changed.* **10** transfer from one aircraft, train, bus, etc., to another: *Passengers must change here for Chicago.* 1,2,9, 10 *v.*, **changed, chang ing;** 3-8 *n.*

change a ble (chān′jə bəl), **1** that can change; likely to change; varying; fickle: *April weather is changeable.* **2** having a color or appearance that changes. Silk is called changeable when it shows different colors in different lights. *adj.* —**change′a ble ness,** *n.*

change a bly (chān′jə blē), in a changeable manner; with constant change or variety. *adv.*

change ful (chānj′fəl), full of changes; likely to change; changing. *adj.* —**change′ful ly,** *adv.* —**change′fulness,** *n.*

change less (chānj′lis), not changing; not likely to change; constant. *adj.* —**change′less ly,** *adv.* —**change′less ness,** *n.*

change ling (chānj′ling), **1** child secretly left in the place of another. **2** (in fairy tales) a child left by fairies in place of a child carried off by them. *n.*

chang er (chān′jər), person or thing that changes something, especially a device in a record player which automatically changes records. *n.*

Chang Jiang (chäng jyäng), official spelling of **Yangtze.**

a hat	**i** it	**oi** oil	**ch** child	a in about
ā age	**ī** ice	**ou** out	**ng** long	e in taken
ä far	**o** hot	**u** cup	**sh** she	ə = i in pencil
e let	**ō** open	**u̇** put	**th** thin	o in lemon
ē equal	**ô** order	**ü** rule	**ŦH** then	u in circus
ėr term			**zh** measure	

chan nel (chan′l), **1** the bed of a stream, river, etc.: *Rivers cut their own channels to the sea.* **2** body of water joining two larger bodies of water: *The English Channel lies between the North Sea and the Atlantic Ocean.* **3** the deeper part of a waterway: *There is shallow water on both sides of the channel in this river.* **4** passage for liquids; groove or canal: *the poison channel in a snake's fangs.* **5** the means by which something moves or is carried: *The information came through secret channels.* **6** form a channel in; wear or cut into a channel: *The river had channeled its way through the rocks.* **7** a narrow band of frequencies that carries the programs of a television or radio station. **8** course of action; field of activity: *She tried to find a suitable channel for her abilities.* **9** direct into a particular course: *Channel all your efforts into this one project, and you will succeed.* 1-5,7,8 *n.*, 6,9 *v.*, **channeled, chan nel ing** or **chan nelled, chan nel ling.** —**chan′nel er, chan′nel ler,** *n.*

Channel Islands, British islands near the NW coast of France.

chant (chant), **1** a short, simple song in which several syllables or words are sung in one tone. Chants are sometimes used in religious services. **2** sing in this way. A choir chants psalms or prayers. **3** sing: *chant a melody.* **4** a singsong way of talking. **5** keep talking about; say over and over again: *The football fans chanted, "Go, team, go!"* 1,4 *n.*, 2,3,5 *v.* —**chant′er,** *n.* —**chant′ing ly,** *adv.*

chan tey (shan′tē or chan′tē), song chanted by sailors in rhythm with the motions of their work. *n., pl.* **chanteys.** Also, **chanty** or **shanty.**

chan ti cleer (chan′tə klir), rooster. *n.*

chan ty (shan′tē or chan′tē), chantey. *n., pl.* **chan ties.**

Cha nu kah (hä′nə kə), Hanukkah. *n.*

cha os (kā′os), very great confusion; complete disorder: *The tornado left the town in chaos. n.*

cha ot ic (kā ot′ik), very confused; completely disordered: *The town was in a chaotic condition after the flood. adj.* —**cha ot′i cal ly,** *adv.*

chap¹ (chap), crack open; make or become rough: *A person's lips or skin often chap in cold weather. v.*, **chapped, chap ping.** [*Chap¹* comes from Middle English *chappen,* meaning "to cut, chop."]

chap² (chap), INFORMAL. fellow; man or boy. *n.* [*Chap²* was shortened from earlier *chapman,* meaning "peddler," which came from Old English *cēapman,* meaning "trader."]

chap. or **Chap., 1** chapter. **2** chaplain.

chap ar ral (chap′ə ral′ or shap′ə ral′), (in the southwestern United States) a dense, often thorny thicket of low, brushy vegetation. *n.*

cha peau (sha pō′), hat. *n., pl.* **cha peaux** or **cha peaus** (sha pōz′).

chap el (chap′əl), **1** a building for worship, not as large as a church. **2** a small place for worship in a building: *a hospital chapel.* **3** a religious s⸱ chapel, especially in a school or colle⸱ today. *n.*

chap e ron or **chap e rone** (s⸱ person who is present at a party of young people to see that good person, especially a married or an ⸱ accompanies a young unmarried wo⸱

the sake of good form. **3** act as a chaperon to. 1,2 *n.*, 3 *v.*, **chap e roned, chap e ron ing.**

chap lain (chap′lən), clergyman authorized or appointed to perform religious functions for a family, court, society, public institution, or unit in the armed forces: *a prison chaplain. n.*

chap lain cy (chap′lən sē), position of a chaplain. *n., pl.* **chap lain cies.**

chap let (chap′lit), **1** wreath worn on the head. **2** string of beads. *n.*

chaps (shaps *or* chaps), strong leather trousers without a back, worn over other trousers by cowhands. *n.pl.*

chap ter (chap′tər), **1** a main division of a book or other writing, dealing with a particular part of the story or subject. **2** anything like a chapter; part; section: *The first moon flight is an interesting chapter in space travel.* **3** a local division of an organization, which holds its own meetings; branch of a club, society, etc. *n.*

Cha pul te pec (chə pul′tə pek), fort on a rocky hill in SW Mexico City. United States troops captured the fort in 1847 during the Mexican War. *n.*

char (chär), **1** burn to charcoal. **2** burn enough to blacken; scorch: *After the fire a carpenter replaced the badly charred floor. v.*, **charred, char ring.**

char., **1** character. **2** charter.

char ac ter (kar′ik tər), **1** all the qualities or features of anything; kind; sort; nature: *The soil on the prairies is of a different character from that in the mountains.* **2** moral nature; moral strength or weakness; the special way in which any person feels, thinks, and acts: *She has an honest, dependable character.* **3** moral firmness, self-control, or integrity: *It takes character to endure hardship for very long.* **4** person or animal in a play, poem, story, or book: *His favorite character in "Charlotte's Web" is Wilbur, the pig.* **5** INFORMAL. person who attracts attention because he or she is different or odd: *My great-grandmother was considered a character because she smoked a corncob pipe.* **6** letter, mark, or sign used in writing or printing: *There are 52 characters in our alphabet, consisting of 26 small letters and 26 capital letters. n.*

in character, as expected; natural or usual: *It is in character for them to be late.*

out of character, not as expected; not natural or usual: *It is out of character for her to be so rude.*

char ac ter is tic (kar′ik tə ris′tik), **1** marking off or distinguishing one person or thing from others; special: *Bananas have their own characteristic smell.* **2** a special quality or feature; whatever distinguishes one person or thing from others; trait: *Cheerfulness is a characteristic that we admire in people. An elephant's trunk is its most noticeable characteristic.* 1 *adj.*, 2 *n.*

char ac ter is ti cal ly (kar′ik tə ris′tik lē), in a way that shows characteristics; specially; typically. *adv.*

char ac ter i za tion (kar′ik tər ə zā′shən), **1** a characterizing; description of characteristics. **2** creation of characters in a play or book. *n.*

char ac ter ize (kar′ik tə rīz′), **1** describe the special qualities or features of: *The story of "Red Riding Hood" characterizes the wolf as a cunning and savage beast.* **2** be a characteristic of; distinguish: *A camel is characterized by the humps on its back and its ability to go without water for several days. v.*, **char ac ter ized, char ac ter iz ing.** —char′ac ter iz′a ble, *adj.* —char′ac ter iz′er, *n.*

a rade (shə rād′). Often, **charades,** *pl.* game in which player acts out a word or phrase and the others try ꞏuess what it is. If the word is *penmanship*, the player ꞏ act out "pen," "man," and "ship." *n.*

ꞏal (chär′kōl′), a black, brittle form of carbon ꞏ partly burning wood or bones in a place from

chaps
cowboy wearing chaps

which the air is shut out. Charcoal is used as fuel, in filters, and for drawing. *n.*

charge (chärj), **1** ask as a price; demand payment: *The grocer charged 75 cents a dozen for eggs. This store charges for delivery.* **2** price asked for or put on something: *The charge for delivery is $3.* **3** put down as a debt to be paid: *We charged the table, so the store will send a bill for it.* **4** a debt to be paid: *Taxes are a charge on property.* **5** load or fill: *charge a gun with powder and shot.* **6** give an accumulation of electricity, which may be discharged, to: *charge a battery.* **7** amount needed to load or fill something. A gun is fired by exploding the charge of powder and shot. **8** an accumulation of electricity in a battery, condenser, etc., which may be discharged. **9** give a task, duty, or responsibility to: *My parents charged me to take good care of the baby.* **10** task; duty; responsibility: *I accepted the charge to take good care of the baby.* **11** care; management: *Doctors and nurses have charge of sick people.* **12** person or thing under the care or management of someone: *Sick people are the charges of doctors and nurses.* **13** give an order or command to; direct: *She charged us to keep the plan secret. The judge charged the jury to come to a fair decision.* **14** an order; command; direction: *a judge's charge to the jury to arrive at a verdict.* **15** accuse: *The driver was charged with speeding.* **16** accusation: *He admitted the truth of the charge and paid a fine.* **17** rush with force; attack: *A herd of elephants charged the hunters. The captain gave the order to charge.* **18** an attack: *The charge drove the enemy back.* 1,3,5,6,9,13,15,17 *v.*, **charged, charg ing;** 2,4,7,8,10-12,14,16,18 *n.* —**charge′less,** *adj.*

charge off, 1 subtract as a loss: *The store owner charged off all unpaid debts over three years old.* **2** put down as belonging: *A bad mistake must be charged off to experience.*

in charge, having the care or management: *The mate is in charge when the captain leaves the boat.*

in charge of, having the care or management of: *My sister-in-law is in charge of the book department of the store.*

charge a ble (chär′jə bəl), **1** capable of being charged: *The salesman's travel expenses are chargeable to the company.* **2** liable to be charged: *A person who steals is chargeable with theft. adj.* —**charge′a ble ness,** *n.* —**charge′a bly,** *adv.*

charge account, record kept at a store of things bought by a person on credit. A customer with a charge account receives and uses what he or she purchases and pays for it later.

charg er (chär′jər), **1** a war horse. **2** device that gives an electrical charge to storage batteries. *n.*

char i ly (cher′ə lē *or* char′ə lē), **1** cautiously. **2** shyly. **3** stingily. *adv.*

char i ness (cher′ē nis *or* char′ē nis), **1** caution. **2** shyness. **3** stinginess. *n.*

chariot
Roman chariot

a hat	i it	oi oil	ch child	⌠ a in about
ā age	ī ice	ou out	ng long	e in taken
ä far	o hot	u cup	sh she	ə = ⟨ i in pencil
e let	ō open	u̇ put	th thin	o in lemon
ē equal	ô order	ü rule	₮H then	⌊ u in circus
ėr term			zh measure	

char i ot (char'ē ət), a two-wheeled carriage pulled by horses. The chariot was used in ancient times for fighting, for racing, and in processions. *n.*

char i ot eer (char'ē ə tir'), person who drives a chariot. *n.*

cha ris ma (kə riz'mə), a mysterious power to fascinate and attract; great personal magnetism or glamor: *the charisma of a popular leader. n.*

char i ta ble (char'ə tə bəl), **1** generous in giving to poor, sick, or helpless people; benevolent and kind: *He was a charitable man who used his wealth to help others.* **2** of or for charity: *The Salvation Army is a charitable organization.* **3** kindly in judging people and their actions; lenient: *Grandparents are usually charitable toward the mistakes of their grandchildren. adj.* —**char'i ta ble ness,** *n.*

char i ta bly (char'ə tə blē), in a charitable manner; with charity. *adv.*

char i ty (char'ə tē), **1** generous giving to the poor, or to organizations which look after the sick, the poor, and the helpless: *The charity of our citizens enabled the hospital to purchase new beds.* **2** fund or organization for helping the sick, the poor, and the helpless: *She gives money regularly to the Red Cross and to other charities.* **3** kindness in judging people's faults. **4** love of other human beings. *n., pl.* **char i ties.** [*Charity* came into English about 800 years ago from French *charite,* and can be traced back to Latin *carus,* meaning "dear."] —**char'i ty less,** *adj.*

char la tan (shär'lə tən), person who pretends to have expert knowledge or skill; quack. *n.*

Char le magne (shär'lə mān), A.D. 742-814, king of the Franks from A.D. 768 to 814 and emperor of the Holy Roman Empire from A.D. 800 to 814. He made many reforms in government and education in western Europe. He was called "Charles the Great." *n.*

Charles I (chärlz), 1600-1649, king of England from 1625 until he was convicted of treason and executed in 1649.

Charles II, 1630-1685, king of England from 1660 to 1685. He was the son of Charles I.

Charles ton (chärlz'tən), **1** capital of West Virginia, in the W part. **2** seaport in SE South Carolina. **3** a lively ballroom dance, especially popular in the 1920's. *n.*

char ley horse (chär'lē), INFORMAL. stiffness or cramp in a muscle, especially of the leg or arm.

Char lotte town (shär'lət toun), capital of Prince Edward Island, Canada. *n.*

charm (chärm), **1** power of delighting or fascinating; attractiveness: *Our grandmother's house never lost its charm for our family.* **2** a pleasing quality or feature: *The book has many charms; the chief one is its delightful humor.* **3** please greatly; delight; fascinate; attract: *The children were charmed by the neighbor's pet raccoon.* **4** a small ornament or trinket worn on a bracelet, watch chain, etc. **5** word, verse, act, or thing supposed to have magic power to help or harm people. **6** act on as if by magic: *Their laughter charmed away our troubles.* 1,2,4,5 *n.,* 3,6 *v.*

—**charm'less,** *adj.* —**charm'less ly,** *adv.*

charmed (chärmd), protected as by a charm: *The pilot led a charmed life in which he narrowly survived many accidents. adj.* —**charm'ed ly,** *adv.*

charm er (chär'mər), one that charms, delights, or fascinates. *n.*

charm ing (chär'ming), very pleasing; delightful; fascinating; attractive: *We saw a charming play. They are a charming couple. adj.* —**charm'ing ly,** *adv.* —**charm'ing ness,** *n.*

char nel house (chär'nl), place where dead bodies or bones are laid.

Char on (ker'ən *or* kar'ən), (in Greek myths) the boatman who ferried the spirits of the dead across the river Styx to Hades. *n.*

chart (chärt), **1** map used by sailors to show the coasts, rocks, and shallow places of the sea. The course of a ship is marked on a chart. **2** an outline map showing special conditions or facts: *This weather chart shows where rain fell over the United States yesterday.* **3** sheet of information arranged in lists, pictures, tables, or diagrams: *Our history book has a chart of the major historic events of the last 200 years.* **4** make a chart of; show on a chart: *The navigator charted the course of the ship.* **5** plan in detail: *The explorers charted their expedition with great care.* 1-3 *n.,* 4,5 *v.* —**chart'a ble,** *adj.* —**chart'less,** *adj.*

char ter (chär'tər), **1** a written grant by a government to a colony, a group of citizens, a corporation, etc., bestowing the right of organization, with other privileges, and specifying the form of organization: *The proposed new airline must obtain a government charter.* **2** a written order from the authorities of a society, giving to a group of persons the right to organize a new chapter, branch, or lodge. **3** document setting forth aims and purposes of a group of nations, organizations, or individuals in a common undertaking: *the Charter of the United Nations.* **4** give a charter to: *The government chartered the new airline.* **5** hire: *Our school chartered a bus to take the class to the zoo.* 1-3 *n.,* 4,5 *v.* —**char'ter a ble,** *adj.* —**char'ter er,** *n.* —**char'ter less,** *adj.*

Char tres (shär'trə), city in N France. Its Gothic cathedral is over 700 years old. *n.*

char treuse (shär trüz'), **1** a light, yellowish green. **2** light yellowish-green. 1 *n.,* 2 *adj.*

char wom an (chär'wum'ən), woman who is hired to clean and scrub homes, offices, and public buildings. *n., pl.* **char wom en.**

char y (cher'ē *or* char'ē), **1** showing caution; careful; wary: *The cat was chary of getting its paws wet.* **2** sparing; stingy: *A jealous person is chary of praising those who do well. adj.,* **char i er, char i est.** [*Chary* is from Old English *cearig,* meaning "sorrowful," which comes from *caru,* meaning "care, sorrow."]

Cha ryb dis (kə rib'dis), **1** whirlpool supposedly located in the strait between Sicily and Italy, opposite the rock Scylla. **2** (in Greek myths) a monster that sucked down ships. *n.*

chase (chās), **1** run or follow after to catch or kill: *The cat chased the mouse.* **2** drive away: *The blue jay chased the squirrel from its nest.* **3** run after; follow; pursue: *I chased the ball as it rolled downhill.* **4** act of chasing: *We watched the children in their chase after butterflies.* **5** hunting as a sport; hunt: *The fox hunter was devoted to the chase.* **6** a hunted animal: *The chase escaped the hunter.* 1-3 *v.*, **chased, chas ing;** 4-6 *n.* —**chase′a ble, chas′a ble,** *adj.* **give chase,** run after; pursue: *The fox gave chase as soon as it spotted the rabbit.*

chas er (chā′sər), person or thing that chases. *n.*

chasm (kaz′əm), **1** a deep opening or crack in the earth; gap. **2** a wide difference of feelings or interests between two persons or groups: *The chasm between England and the American colonies finally led to the Revolutionary War.* *n.*

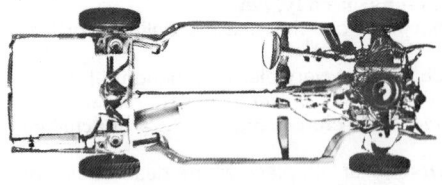

chassis
(def. 1)

chas sis (chas′ē *or* shas′ē), **1** the frame, wheels, and machinery of a motor vehicle that support the body. **2** the base or frame for the parts of a radio or television set. *n., pl.* **chas sis** (chas′ēz *or* shas′ēz).

chaste (chāst), **1** pure; virtuous. **2** decent; modest. **3** simple in taste or style; not too much ornamented. *adj.* —**chaste′ly,** *adv.* —**chaste′ness,** *n.*

chas ten (chā′sn), **1** punish to improve; discipline: *chasten a child.* **2** restrain from excess or crudeness; moderate. *v.* —**chas′ten er,** *n.* —**chas′ten ing ly,** *adv.*

chas tise (cha stīz′), **1** inflict punishment or suffering on to improve; punish. **2** criticize or rebuke severely. *v.*, **chas tised, chas tis ing.** —**chas tis′a ble,** *adj.*

chas tise ment (cha stīz′mənt), **1** punishment. **2** a severe criticism or rebuke. *n.*

chas ti ty (chas′tə tē), **1** purity; virtue. **2** decency; modesty. **3** simplicity of style or taste; absence of too much decoration. *n.*

chas u ble (chaz′yə bəl), a sleeveless outer vestment worn by the priest at Mass. *n.*

chat (chat), **1** easy, familiar talk: *The two friends had a pleasant chat about old times.* **2** talk in an easy, familiar way: *We sat chatting by the fire after supper.* **3** any of several birds with a chattering cry. 1,3 *n.*, 2 *v.*, **chat ted, chat ting.** —**chat′ta ble,** *adj.* —**chat′ting ly,** *adv.*

château (def. 2)

châ teau (sha tō′), **1** a large country house in France or elsewhere in Europe. **2** a French castle. *n., pl.* **châ teaux** (sha tōz′).

Chat ta noo ga (chat′n ü′gə), city in SE Tennessee. *n.*

chat tel (chat′l), piece of property that is not real estate; any movable possession. Furniture, automobiles, and animals are chattels. *n.*

chat ter (chat′ər), **1** talk constantly and quickly about

unimportant things: *The children chattered about the circus.* **2** constant, quick talk about unimportant things: *The pupils' chatter disturbed the classroom.* **3** make quick, indistinct sounds: *Monkeys chatter.* **4** quick, indistinct sounds: *the chatter of sparrows.* **5** rattle together: *Cold can make your teeth chatter.* **6** sound of rattling together: *the chatter of typewriters.* 1,3,5 *v.*, 2,4,6 *n.* —**chat′ter er,** *n.*

chat ter box (chat′ər boks′), person who chatters. *n., pl.* **chat ter box es.**

chat ti ly (chat′l lē), in a chatty manner. *adv.*

chat ty (chat′ē), **1** fond of friendly, familiar talk about unimportant things. **2** having the style or manner of friendly, familiar talk: *a chatty newspaper article about gardening.* *adj.*, **chat ti er, chat ti est.** —**chat′ti ness,** *n.*

Chau cer (chô′sər), Geoffrey, 1340?-1400, English poet, author of *The Canterbury Tales.* *n.*

chauf feur (shō′fər *or* shō fér′), **1** person whose work is driving an automobile. **2** act as a chauffeur to; drive around. 1 *n.*, 2 *v.*

chau vin ism (shō′və niz′əm), **1** boastful, warlike patriotism; an unreasoning enthusiasm for the military glory of one's country. **2** an excessive enthusiasm for one's sex, race, or group: *no lack of female chauvinism.* *n.*

WORD HISTORY

chauvinism

Chauvinism comes from French *chauvinisme,* which was named for Nicolas *Chauvin,* an early nineteenth-century soldier who was an enthusiastic admirer of Napoleon I.

chau vin ist (shō′və nist), **1** a boastful, warlike patriot. **2** person excessively enthusiastic about his or her sex, race, or group: *a male chauvinist.* *n.*

cheap (chēp), **1** costing little: *Eggs are cheap out in the country.* **2** costing less than it is worth: *My new sweater will be cheap, because I am going to buy the yarn and knit it myself.* **3** charging low prices: *He bought that suit at a very cheap department store.* **4** costing little effort; easily obtained: *He thinks that the cheapest way to make friends is to give them presents.* **5** of little value; not worth respect; common: *cheap jokes.* **6** at a low price; at small cost: *I sold the car cheap to get rid of it.* 1-5 *adj.*, 6 *adv.* —**cheap′ly,** *adv.* —**cheap′ness,** *n.*

feel cheap, feel inferior and ashamed: *I felt cheap about forgetting my best friend's birthday.*

cheap en (chē′pən), **1** make or become cheap; lower the price of. **2** cause to be thought little of. *v.* —**cheap′en er,** *n.*

cheap skate (chēp′skāt′), INFORMAL. person who is very stingy. *n.*

cheat (chēt), **1** play or do business in a way that is not honest; deceive or trick: *I hate to play games with a person who cheats. That cashier cheated me out of fifty-five cents in change.* **2** person who is not honest and does things to deceive or trick others. **3** fraud; trick. 1 *v.*, 2,3 *n.* —**cheat′er,** *n.* —**cheat′ing ly,** *adv.*

check (chek), **1** stop suddenly: *The tennis player checked her swing as the ball went out of bounds.* **2** a sudden stop: *The storm warning put a check to our plans for a picnic.* **3** hold back; control; restrain: *check one's anger, check a forest fire.* **4** a holding back; control; restraint: *Keep a check on your appetite.* **5** any person, thing, or event that controls or holds back action. **6** prove true or right by comparing or examining: *Check your watch with the school clock.* **7** examination or comparison to prove something true or right: *My work will be a check on yours.* **8** a mark (✓) to show that something has been examined or compared. Often it shows that the thing looked at was found to be true or right. *I put a check beside the correct answer.* **9** to mark (something examined or compared) with a check: *How many answers did the teacher check as wrong?* **10** ticket or metal piece given in return for a coat, hat, baggage, package, etc., left for safekeeping, to show ownership or the right to claim again later: *Give your check to the man in the checkroom when you want your coat.* **11** leave or take for safekeeping: *He checked his hat at the door of the club. The hotel checked our baggage.* **12** a written order directing a bank to pay money to the person named; cheque: *My parents pay most of their bills by check.* **13** a written statement of the amount owed in a restaurant: *After our meal the waitress brought the check to our table.* **14** to mark in a pattern of squares. **15** a pattern made of squares: *Do you want a check or a stripe for your new suit?* **16** a single one of these squares: *The checks in this dress are big.* **17** in chess: **a** position of an opponent's king when it is in danger. **b** put (an opponent's king) in this position. **18** (in hockey) a blocking of a player on the other team. 1,3,6,9,11,14,17b *v.*, 2,4,5,7,8,10,12,13,15-17a,18 *n.* —**check′a ble**, *adj.* —**check′less**, *adj.*

check in, arrive and register at a hotel, motel, etc.: *We checked in and were then shown to our rooms.*

check out, **1** pay one's bill at a hotel, motel, etc., when leaving: *They loaded the car while I checked out at the desk.* **2** inspect or examine to see if in proper order, condition, etc.: *The mechanic checked out the plane before takeoff.* **3** prove right or true: *check out a fact or statement.* **4** borrow from a library: *check out several books about camping.* **5** add up the prices of purchases in a supermarket or discount store and accept payment for them.

check up on, examine or compare to prove true or correct: *If you are not sure, you ought to check up on the facts.*

in check, held back; controlled: *He kept his temper in check.*

check book (chek′bùk′), book of blank checks on a bank. *n.*

checked (chekt), having checks; marked with checks: *a checked shirt. adj.*

check er[1] (chek′ər), **1** to mark in a pattern of squares of different colors. **2** pattern made of such squares. **3** one of these squares. **4** one of the flat, round pieces used in the game of checkers. 1 *v.*, 2-4 *n.* [*Checker*[1] came into English about 600 years ago from French *eschequier*, meaning "chessboard," and can be traced back to Persian *shāh*, meaning "king, king at chess."]

check er[2] (chek′ər), **1** person or thing that checks: *The checker in our supermarket checked out the merchandise at the counter. n.*

check er board (chek′ər bôrd′), board marked in a pattern of 64 squares of two alternating colors, used in playing checkers or chess; chessboard. *n.*

check ered (chek′ərd), **1** marked in a pattern of squares of different colors: *a checkered tablecloth.* **2** marked in patches. **3** often changing; varied; irregular: *a checkered career. adj.*

check ers (chek′ərz), game played by two people, each with 12 round, flat pieces to move on a checkerboard. The object of the game is to capture all the opponent's pieces or to prevent them from being able to move. *n.*

check list (chek′list′), list of names, titles, jobs, etc., arranged to form a ready means of reference, compari-

son, or checking: *The pilot went over the flight checklist before takeoff. n.*

check mate (chek′māt′), **1** in chess: **a** put (an opponent's king) in check from which there is no escape, and so win the game. **b** a move that ends the game by putting the opponent's king in check so that there is no way to escape. **2** defeat completely. **3** a complete defeat. 1a,2 *v.*, **check mat ed, check mat ing;** 1b,3 *n.*

check out (chek′out′), a checking out: *Careful checkouts were made on the new equipment. The time for checkout at the motel was 10 a.m. n.*

check point (chek′point′), place of inspection on a road, at a border, etc. *n.*

check rein (chek′rān′), **1** a short rein to keep a horse from lowering its head. **2** a short rein connecting the bit of one of a team of horses to the driving rein of the other. *n.*

check room (chek′rüm′ *or* chek′rùm′), place where coats, hats, baggage, etc., can be left for safekeeping until called for later. *n.*

check up (chek′up′), **1** a careful inspection or examination. **2** a thorough physical examination: *The doctor asked the patient to come to her office for a checkup. n.*

Ched dar or **ched dar** (ched′ər), kind of hard, white or yellow cheese. *n.* [This cheese was named for *Cheddar*, a village in southern England where it was first made.]

cheek (chēk), **1** side of the face below either eye. **2** INFORMAL. rude talk or behavior; impudence: *They had the cheek to barge into line ahead of everyone. n.* —**cheek′less**, *adj.*

cheek bone (chēk′bōn′), bone just below either eye. *n.*

cheek y (chē′kē), rude; impudent. *adj.*, **cheek i er, cheek i est.** —**cheek′i ly**, *adv.* —**cheek′i ness**, *n.*

cheep (chēp), **1** make a short, sharp sound such as a young bird makes; chirp; peep. **2** a young bird's cry. 1 *v.*, 2 *n.* —**cheep′er**, *n.*

cheer (chir), **1** a shout of encouragement, approval, praise, etc.: *Give three cheers for the winners.* **2** shout encouragement or praise to: *Everyone cheered our team. We all cheered loudly.* **3** joy or gladness; comfort: *The warmth of the fire and a good meal brought cheer to our hearts again.* **4** give joy to; make glad; comfort: *It cheered our sick friend to have us visit him.* **5** state of mind; condition of feeling: *His friends encouraged him to be of good cheer.* 1,3,5 *n.*, 2,4 *v.* —**cheer′er**, *n.* —**cheer′ing ly**, *adv.*

cheer up, brighten up; be or make glad; raise one's spirits: *The sick girl said that our visit cheered her up. Cheer up, perhaps we'll win the next game.*

cheer ful (chir′fəl), **1** full of cheer; joyful; glad: *She is a smiling, cheerful girl.* **2** filling with cheer; pleasant; bright: *This is a cheerful, sunny room.* **3** willing: *I appreciate a cheerful helper. adj.* —**cheer′ful ly**, *adv.* —**cheer′ful ness**, *n.*

cheer i ly (chir′ə lē), in a cheerful or cheery manner; cheerfully. *adv.*

cheer i ness (chir′ē nis), condition of being cheerful or cheery; cheerfulness. *n.*

cheer lead er (chir′lē′dər), person who leads a group in organized cheering, especially at high school or college athletic events. *n.*

cheer less (chir′lis), without joy or comfort; gloomy;

a hat	**i** it	**oi** oil	**ch** child	a in about
ā age	**ī** ice	**ou** out	**ng** long	e in taken
ä far	**o** hot	**u** cup	**sh** she	ə = i in pencil
e let	**ō** open	**ù** put	**th** thin	o in lemon
ē equal	**ô** order	**ü** rule	**ŦH** then	u in circus
ėr term			**zh** measure	

dreary. *adj.* —**cheer′less ly,** *adv.* —**cheer′less ness,** *n.*

cheer y (chir′ē), cheerful; pleasant; bright; gay: *a cheery smile. adj.,* **cheer i er, cheer i est.**

cheese (chēz), a solid food made from the curds of milk. Most cheeses are pressed or molded into a shape and are often covered with a rind. *n.* —**cheese′like′,** *adj.*

cheese burg er (chēz′bėr′gər), a hamburger sandwich with a slice of melted cheese on top of the meat. *n.*

cheese cloth (chēz′klôth′), a thin, loosely woven cotton cloth, first used for wrapping cheese. *n., pl.* **cheesecloths** (chēz′klôᴛʜz′ *or* chēz′klôths′).

chees y (chē′zē), **1** of or like cheese. **2** SLANG. of low quality; inferior. *adj.,* **chees i er, chees i est.** —**chees′i ly,** *adv.* —**chees′i ness,** *n.*

cheetah
about 2½ ft. (75 cm.) high at the shoulder

chee tah (chē′tə), a flesh-eating mammal somewhat like a leopard, found in southern Asia and Africa. Cheetahs run very fast and can be trained to hunt deer and antelope. *n.*

chef (shef), **1** a head cook: *the chef of a large restaurant.* **2** any cook. *n.*

che la (kē′lə), claw of a lobster, crab, scorpion, etc. *n., pl.* **che lae** (kē′lē).

chem., 1 chemical. **2** chemist. **3** chemistry.

chem i cal (kem′ə kəl), **1** of, having to do with, or in chemistry: *Chemical research has made possible many new products.* **2** made by or used in chemistry: *The burning of coal is a process of chemical change in which oxygen in the air unites with carbon from the coal, giving off light and heat.* **3** any substance obtained by or used in a chemical process. Sulfuric acid, sodium bicarbonate, and borax are chemicals. **4** working, operated, or done by using chemicals: *a chemical fire extinguisher.* 1,2,4 *adj.,* 3 *n.*

chemical change, a change in which the nature of a substance is made different from what it was. In a chemical change, atoms are rearranged into new molecules. Burning is a process of chemical change in which the oxygen of the air unites with wood or coal to give ashes, light, and heat.

chemical engineering, science or profession of using chemistry for industrial purposes.

chem i cal ly (kem′ik lē), **1** according to chemistry. **2** by chemical processes. *adv.*

che mise (shə mēz′), **1** a loose, shirtlike undergarment worn by women and girls. **2** a loosely fitting dress without a belt. *n.*

chem ist (kem′ist), **1** an expert in chemistry. **2** BRITISH. druggist. *n.*

chem is try (kem′ə strē), **1** science that deals with the characteristics of elements, the changes that take place when they combine to form substances, and the laws of their behavior under various conditions. **2** the application of this science to a certain subject: *the chemistry of foods. n., pl.* **chem is tries.**

che nille (shə nēl′), **1** a velvety cord, used in embroidery, fringe, etc. **2** fabric woven from this cord, used for rugs, bedspreads, etc. *n.*

Che ops (kē′ops), 2600? B.C., king of Egypt who built the largest of the Pyramids. *n.*

cheque (chek), BRITISH. check (def. 12). *n.*

Cher bourg (sher′bůrg), seaport in NW France, on the English Channel. *n.*

cher ish (cher′ish), **1** hold dear; treat with affection; care for tenderly: *Parents cherish their children.* **2** keep in mind; cling to: *We all cherished the hope of their safe return from the dangerous journey.* *v.* —**cher′ish a ble,** *adj.*

Cher o kee (cher′ə kē′), **1** member of a tribe of American Indians of the southern Appalachians, now living mostly in Oklahoma. **2** their language. *n., pl.* **Cher o kee** or **Cher o kees** for 1.

cher ry (cher′ē), **1** a small, round, juicy fruit with a stone or pit in it. Cherries are good to eat. **2** the tree that it grows on. **3** the wood of this tree. **4** a bright red. **5** bright-red. 1-4 *n., pl.* **cher ries;** 5 *adj.*

cher ub (cher′əb), **1** angel. **2** picture or statue of a child with wings, or of a child's head with wings. **3** a beautiful, innocent, or good child. *n., pl.* **cher u bim** for 1 and 2, **cher ubs** for 3. [*Cherub* was borrowed from Latin *cherub,* and can be traced back to Hebrew *kerūb.*]

che ru bic (chə rü′bik), **1** of or like a cherub; angelic. **2** innocent; good. *adj.* —**che ru′bi cal ly,** *adv.*

cher u bim (cher′ə bim), **1** a plural of **cherub** (defs. 1 and 2). **2** (formerly) cherub. 1 *n.pl.,* 2 *n.sing.*

Ches a peake Bay (ches′ə pēk′), bay of the Atlantic, in Maryland and Virginia.

Chesh ire cat (chesh′ər), **1** the grinning cat in *Alice in Wonderland.* It faded away until finally only its grin was left. **2** any creature that grins fixedly. [This cat was named for *Cheshire,* a county in western England.]

Cheshire cat
(def. 1)

chess (ches), game played by two people, each with 16 pieces to move on a checkerboard. The object of the game is to checkmate the other's king. *n.*

chess board (ches′bôrd′), checkerboard. *n.*

chess man (ches′man′), one of the pieces used in playing chess. *n., pl.* **chess men.**

chest (chest), **1** part of a person's or an animal's body enclosed by ribs. **2** a large box with a lid, used for holding things: *a linen chest, a medicine chest, a tool chest.* **3** piece of furniture with drawers. **4** place where money is kept; treasury. *n.*

ches ter field (ches′tər fēld′), a single-breasted overcoat with the buttons hidden and a velvet collar. *n.*

chest nut (ches′nut), **1** a large tree that bears nuts in prickly burs. The chestnut belongs to the same family as the beech. **2** the sweet nut of this tree. **3** the wood of this tree. **4** a reddish brown. **5** reddish-brown. **6** a reddish-brown horse. 1-4,6 *n.,* 5 *adj.*

chev i ot (shev′ē ət *for 1 and 2;* chev′ē ət *or* chē′vē ət *for 3*), **1** a rough, woolen cloth. **2** a cotton cloth like it. **3** Cheviot, a hardy breed of sheep. *n.*

chev ron (shev′rən), a cloth design shaped like Λ or V, worn on the sleeve by noncommissioned officers, the police, etc., to show rank or length of service. *n.*

chew (chü), **1** crush or grind with the teeth: *We chew food.* **2** a chewing: *The puppy gave the rag a good chew.* **3** thing chewed; piece for chewing. 1 *v.,* 2,3 *n.* —**chew′a ble,** *adj.* —**chew′er,** *n.*

chew out, SLANG. criticize severely or bitterly; scold: *The sergeant chewed out the new recruit for not keeping his equipment clean.*

chew i ness (chü′ē nis), chewy quality: *the chewiness of caramel. n.*

chewing gum, gum for chewing. It is usually chicle that has been sweetened and flavored.

che wink (chi wingk′), towhee. *n.*

chew y (chü′ē), requiring much chewing: *chewy caramels. adj.,* **chew i er, chew i est.**

Chey enne (shī an′ *or* shī en′ *for 1,2;* shī en′ *for 3,4*), **1** capital of Wyoming, in the SE part. **2** river flowing from E Wyoming into the Missouri River in South Dakota. **3** member of an Algonquian tribe of Indians, now living in Montana and Oklahoma. **4** their language. *n., pl.* **Chey enne** *or* **Chey ennes** *for 3.*

Chiang Kai-shek (chyäng′ kī′shek′), 1886-1975, Chinese general and political leader, president of Nationalist China from 1948 to 1975.

chic (shēk), **1** up-to-date in fashion; stylish: *a chic new suit.* **2** style: *She is famous for her chic.* 1 *adj.,* 2 *n.* —**chic′ly,** *adv.* —**chic′ness,** *n.*

Chi ca go (shə kô′gō *or* shə kä′gō), city in NE Illinois, on Lake Michigan. Chicago is the second largest city in the United States. *n.* —**Chi ca′go an,** *n.*

Chi ca na (chi kä′nä), a female American of Mexican descent. *n., pl.* **Chi ca nas.**

chi can er y (shi kā′nər ē), low trickery; unfair practice: *He used chicanery to outwit his partner and take over the business. n., pl.* **chi can er ies.**

Chi ca no (chi kä′nō), an American of Mexican descent; Mexican American. *n., pl.* **Chi ca nos.**

chick (chik), **1** a young chicken. **2** a young bird. **3** child. *n.*

chick a dee (chik′ə dē′), a small bird with black, white, and gray feathers, and usually a black head. Its cry sounds somewhat like its name. *n.*

Chick a mau ga (chik′ə mô′gə), a small creek flowing from NW Georgia into the Tennessee River. The Confederates defeated the Union army there in 1863. *n.*

Chick a saw (chik′ə sô), **1** member of a tribe of American Indians, now living in western Oklahoma. **2** their language. *n., pl.* **Chick a saw** *or* **Chick a saws** *for 1.*

chick en (chik′ən), **1** a common domestic fowl raised for food; hen or rooster. **2** flesh of a chicken used for food: *fried chicken.* **3** SLANG. afraid of risk; cowardly. 1,2 *n.,* 3 *adj.*

chicken out, SLANG. fail to do something because of fear.

chick en-heart ed (chik′ən här′tid), timid; cowardly. *adj.* —**chick′en-heart′ed ly,** *adv.* —**chick′en-heart′ed ness,** *n.*

chicken pox, a mild, contagious disease of children, accompanied by a rash on the skin.

chick pea (chik′pē′), the seed of a plant related to the pea, used as a vegetable; garbanzo. *n., pl.* **chick peas.**

chick weed (chik′wēd′), a common weed with small white flowers. The leaves and seeds are eaten by birds. *n.*

chic le (chik′əl), a tasteless, gummy substance used in making chewing gum. It is the dried milky juice of a tree of tropical America. *n.*

chic or y (chik′ər ē), **1** plant with bright blue flowers whose leaves are used for salad. **2** its root, roasted and used as a substitute for coffee or for mixing with coffee. *n., pl.* **chic or ies.**

a hat	**i** it	**oi** oil	**ch** child	a in about
ā age	**ī** ice	**ou** out	**ng** long	e in taken
ä far	**o** hot	**u** cup	**sh** she	ə = { i in pencil
e let	**ō** open	**u̇** put	**th** thin	o in lemon
ē equal	**ô** order	**ü** rule	**ᵀH** then	u in circus
ėr term			**zh** measure	

chide (chīd), find fault with; blame; scold: *My uncle chided me for playing in his flower garden. v.,* **chid ed** *or* **chid** (chid), **chid ing.** —**chid′er,** *n.* —**chid′ing ly,** *adv.*

chief (chēf), **1** head of a group; person highest in rank or authority; leader: *a police chief.* **2** at the head; in authority; leading: *the chief engineer of a building project.* **3** most important; main: *the chief town in the county. The chief thing on my mind was dinner.* 1 *n.,* 2,3 *adj.* —**chief′less,** *adj.*

in chief, at the head; of the highest rank or authority: *editor in chief of a book.*

chief executive, 1 head of the executive branch of a government. **2 Chief Executive,** the President of the United States or the governor of a state.

chief justice, 1 judge who acts as chairman of a group of judges in a court. **2 Chief Justice,** the presiding judge of the United States Supreme Court.

chief ly (chēf′lē), **1** for the most part; mainly; mostly: *This juice is made up chiefly of tomatoes.* **2** first of all; above all: *We visited Washington chiefly to see the Capitol and the White House. adv.*

Chief of Staff, the senior officer of the Army or Air Force of the United States.

chief tain (chēf′tən), **1** chief of a clan or tribe: *a Highland chieftain.* **2** head of a group; leader. *n.*

chief tain cy (chēf′tən sē), position or rank of a chieftain. *n., pl.* **chief tain cies.**

chif fon (shi fon′), **1** a very thin silk or rayon cloth, used for dresses. **2** whipped light and fluffy: *lemon chiffon pie.* 1 *n.,* 2 *adj.*

chif fo nier (shif′ə nir′), a high chest of drawers, often having a mirror. *n.*

chig ger (chig′ər), larva of certain mites. Chiggers stick to the skin and suck the blood, causing severe itching. *n.*

chi gnon (shē′nyon), knot or roll of hair worn at the back of the head by women. *n.*

chi hua hua (chi wä′wä), Chihuahua. *n., pl.* **chi hua-huas.**

Chi hua hua (chi wä′wä), a very small dog of an ancient Mexican breed, usually weighing from one to six pounds. *n., pl.* **Chi hua huas.** [*Chihuahua* was borrowed from Mexican Spanish *Chihuahua,* which was named for a state and a city in Mexico where the modern breed was discovered.]

chil blain (chil′blān′). Usually, **chilblains,** *pl.* an itching sore or redness on the hands or feet caused chiefly by exposure to cold. *n.*

child (chīld), **1** a young boy or girl: *games for children.* **2** son or daughter: *Parents love their children.* **3** baby; infant. *n., pl.* **chil dren.**

with child, pregnant.

child birth (chīld′bėrth′), act of giving birth to a child. *n.*

child hood (chīld′hud), **1** condition of being a child. **2** time during which one is a child. *n.*

child ish (chīl′dish), **1** of a child. **2** like a child. **3** not suitable for a grown person; weak; silly: *Crying for things you can't have is childish. adj.* —**child′ish ly,** *adv.* —**child′ish ness,** *n.*

child less (chīld′lis), having no child. *adj.* —**child′less-ness,** *n.*

child like (chīld′līk′), like a child; innocent; frank; simple: *He has a childlike love of the circus. adj.* —**child′like′-ness,** *n.*

child proof (chīld′prüf′), not able to be opened, used, or damaged by a child because of its design: *childproof locks, childproof containers. adj.*

chil dren (chil′drən), plural of **child.** *n.*

child's play, something very easy to do: *I found it child's play to do that puzzle.*

chil e (chil′ē), chili. *n., pl.* **chil es.**

Chil e (chil′ē), country in SW South America, on the Pacific coast. *Capital:* Santiago. *n.* —**Chil′e an,** *adj., n.*

chil i (chil′ē), **1** a hot-tasting pod of red pepper, used for seasoning. **2** a highly seasoned Mexican dish of chopped meat cooked with red peppers and, usually, kidney beans. *n., pl.* **chil ies.** Also, **chile** or **chilli.** [*Chili* is from Mexican Spanish *chile,* which came from Nahuatl *chilli.*]

chili sauce, sauce made of red peppers, tomatoes, and spices, used on meat, fish, etc.

chill (chil), **1** unpleasant coldness: *feel a sudden chill. There was a chill in the air.* **2** unpleasantly cold: *A chill wind blew across the lake.* **3** make or become cold: *The icy wind chilled us to the bone. Her blood chilled as she read the horror story.* **4** a sudden coldness of the body with shivering: *I caught a chill yesterday and today I have a fever.* **5** cold in manner; unfriendly: *a chill greeting.* 1,4 *n.,* 2,5 *adj.,* 3 *v.* —**chill′er,** *n.* —**chill′ness,** *n.*

chil li (chil′ē), chili. *n., pl.* **chil lies.**

chill i ness (chil′ē nis), chilly quality. *n.*

chill ing (chil′ing), that chills. *adj.* —**chill′ing ly,** *adv.*

chill y (chil′ē), **1** unpleasantly cool; rather cold: *It is a rainy, chilly day. You'll feel chilly if you don't wear a coat.* **2** cold in manner; unfriendly: *We gave a chilly reception to the people who came to our party uninvited. adj.,* **chill i er, chill i est.** —**chill′i ly,** *adv.*

chi maer a (kə mir′ə *or* kī mir′ə), chimera. *n., pl.* **chi maer as.**

chime (chīm), **1** set of bells tuned to a musical scale and played by hammers or simple machinery. **2** the musical sound made by a set of tuned bells. **3** ring out musically: *The bells of the town clock chime on the hour.* 1,2 *n.,* 3 *v.,* **chimed, chim ing.** —**chim′er,** *n.*

chime in, 1 be in harmony; agree: *Her ideas chimed in perfectly with mine.* **2** break into a conversation, especially to express one's agreement: *I said I would like to go to the circus and my brother chimed in.*

chi mer a (kə mir′ə *or* kī mir′ə), **1** Also, **Chimera.** (in Greek legends) a monster with a lion's head, a goat's body, and a serpent's tail, supposed to breathe out fire. **2** a horrible creature of the imagination. **3** an absurd or impossible idea; wild fancy: *The hope of changing lead to gold was a chimera. n., pl.* **chi mer as.** Also, **chimaera.**

chi mer i cal (kə mer′ə kəl), **1** unreal; imaginary. **2** wildly fanciful; absurd; impossible: *Pay no attention to chimerical schemes for getting rich quick. adj.* —**chi mer′i cal ly,** *adv.*

chim ney (chim′nē), **1** an upright structure of brick or stone, connected with a fireplace, furnace, etc., to make a draft and carry away smoke. **2** part of this that rises above a roof: *We could see the town's chimneys from afar.* **3** a glass tube placed around the flame of a lamp. *n., pl.* **chim neys.** —**chim′ney less,** *adj.*

chimney sweep, person whose work is cleaning out chimneys.

chimney swift, bird of North America that often builds its nest in unused chimneys.

chimp (chimp), INFORMAL. chimpanzee. *n.*

chim pan zee (chim′pan zē′ *or* chim pan′zē), a highly intelligent ape of Africa, smaller than a gorilla. *n.*

chin (chin), **1** the front of the lower jaw below the

mouth. **2 chin oneself,** hang by the hands from an overhead bar and pull up until one's chin reaches the bar. 1 *n.,* 2 *v.,* **chinned, chin ning.** —**chin′less,** *adj.*

Chin., Chinese.

chi na (chī′nə), **1** a fine, white pottery baked by a special process, first used in China; porcelain. Colored designs can be baked into china. **2** dishes, vases, ornaments, etc., made of china. **3** pottery dishes of any kind. *n.*

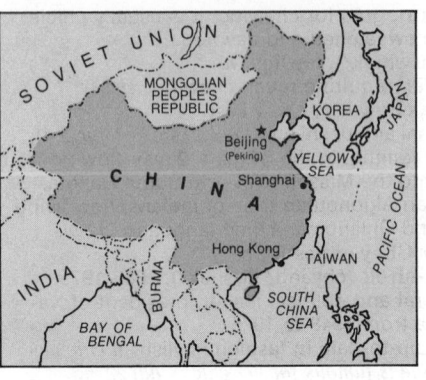

China (def. 1)

Chi na (chī′nə), **1 People's Republic of,** large country in E Asia. *Capital:* Peking (Beijing). **2** country consisting of the island of Taiwan; Nationalist China. *Capital:* Taipei. *n.*

China Sea, part of the Pacific Ocean, east and southeast of Asia. It is divided into the **South China Sea** and the **East China Sea** by the island of Taiwan.

chi na ware (chī′nə wer′ *or* chī′nə war′), china. *n.*

chinch (chinch), **1** bedbug. **2** chinch bug. *n., pl.* **chinch es.**

chinch bug, a small, black-and-white bug that does much damage to grain in dry weather.

chin chil la (chin chil′ə), **1** a South American rodent that looks somewhat like a squirrel. **2** its very valuable soft, bluish-gray fur. **3** a thick woolen fabric woven in small, closely set tufts, used for overcoats. *n., pl.* **chin chil las.**

Chi nese (chī nēz′), **1** of China, its people, or their language. **2** person born or living in China. **3** person of Chinese descent. **4** language of China. 1 *adj.,* 2-4 *n., pl.* **Chi nese** for 2 and 3.

Chinese lantern, lantern of thin colored paper that can be folded up like an accordion.

Chinese puzzle, something that is very complicated and hard to solve, like a kind of puzzle with interlocking pieces invented by the Chinese.

chink[1] (chingk), **1** a narrow opening; crack: *Wind and snow came through the chinks between the logs of the cabin.* **2** fill up the chinks in: *The trapper chinked the cracks in the walls of the cabin with mud.* 1 *n.,* 2 *v.*

chimpanzee—up to 4½ ft. (1.5 m.) tall when standing

chink² (chingk), **1** a short, sharp, ringing sound like coins or drinking glasses hitting together. **2** make or cause to make such a sound. **1** *n.*, **2** *v.*

chi no (chē′nō), **1** a strong cotton fabric, used especially in making trousers. **2 chinos,** *pl.* trousers made of this fabric. *n., pl.* **chi nos.**

chi nook (shə nůk′ *or* chə nük′), **1** a warm, moist wind blowing from the sea to the land in winter and spring in the northwestern United States. **2** a warm, dry wind that comes down the eastern slope of the Rocky Mountains. *n.* [This wind was named for the *Chinook,* American Indians. Early settlers called it this because they thought that the wind blew from the area of the Chinook.]

Chi nook (shə nůk′ *or* chə nük′), **1** member of a group of American Indian tribes living along the Columbia River in the northwestern United States. **2** language of these Indians. *n., pl.* **Chi nook** or **Chi nooks** for 1.

chintz (chints), a cotton cloth printed in patterns of various colors and often glazed. *n., pl.* **chintz es.**

chintz y (chint′sē), **1** of or like chintz. **2** INFORMAL. cheap and showy. *adj.,* **chintz i er, chintz i est.**

chip (chip), **1** a small, thin piece cut or broken off: *They used chips of wood to light a fire.* **2** place where a small, thin piece has been cut or broken off: *This plate has a chip on the edge.* **3** cut or break off in small, thin pieces: *She chipped off the old paint. These cups chip if they are not handled carefully.* **4** shape by cutting at the surface or edge with an ax or chisel. **5** a small, thin piece of food or candy. Potato chips are fried slices of potatoes. **6** a round, flat piece used for counting or to represent money in games: *poker chips.* **7** a small piece of a semiconductor, usually silicon, that holds an integrated circuit. **1,2,5-7** *n.*, **3,4** *v.*, **chipped, chip ping.**

chip in, INFORMAL. join with others in giving (money or help): *We all chipped in to buy our teacher a gift.*

chip off the old block, boy who is much like his father.

chip munk (chip′mungk), a small, striped, North American rodent related to the squirrel; ground squirrel. Chipmunks live in burrows in the ground. *n.*

chipmunk
about 10 in.
(25 cm.) long
with the tail

chip per (chip′ər), INFORMAL. lively and cheerful. *adj.*

Chip pe wa (chip′ə wä *or* chip′ə wā), Ojibwa. *n., pl.* **Chip pe wa** or **Chip pe was.**

chipping sparrow, a small sparrow of eastern and central North America.

Chi ron (kī′ron), (in Greek legends) a wise and kindly centaur, teacher of many Greek heroes. He was famous for his medical skill. *n.*

chi rop o dist (kə rop′ə dist), person who removes corns and treats other troubles of the feet. *n.*

chi ro prac tor (kī′rə prak′tər), person who treats diseases by manipulating parts of the body, especially the spine. *n.*

chirp (chėrp), **1** a short, sharp sound made by some small birds and insects: *the chirp of a sparrow.* **2** make a chirp: *The crickets chirped outside the house.* **1** *n.*, **2** *v.*

chir rup (chir′əp *or* chėr′əp), **1** chirp again and again:

She chirruped to her horse to make it go faster. **2** the sound of chirruping. **1** *v.*, **2** *n.*

chis el (chiz′əl), **1** a cutting tool with a sharp edge at the end of a strong blade, used to cut or shape wood, stone, or metal. **2** cut or shape with a chisel: *The sculptor was at work chiseling a statue.* **3** SLANG. to cheat or swindle. **1** *n.*, **2,3** *v.*, **chis eled, chis el ing** or **chis elled, chis el ling.** —**chis′el like′,** *adj.*

chisel
(def. 1)

chis el er or **chis el ler** (chiz′ə lər), **1** person or thing that chisels. **2** SLANG. a cheat. *n.*

Chis holm Trail (chiz′əm), famous western cattle trail from San Antonio, Texas, to Abilene, Kansas.

chit chat (chit′chat′), **1** friendly, informal talk; chat. **2** talk in a friendly, informal way. **3** idle talk; gossip. **1,3** *n.*, **2** *v.*, **chit chat ted, chit chat ting.**

chi tin (kīt′n), a horny substance forming the hard outer covering of beetles, lobsters, crabs, etc. *n.*

chi tin ous (kīt′n əs), of or like chitin. *adj.*

chit lings (chit′linz), chitterlings. *n.pl.*

chit lins (chit′linz), chitterlings. *n.pl.*

chit ter lings (chit′linz), parts of the small intestines of pigs, cooked as food. *n.pl.*

chiv al rous (shiv′əl rəs), **1** having the qualities of an ideal knight; brave, courteous, helpful, and honorable. **2** having to do with the rules and customs of knights in the Middle Ages. *adj.* —**chiv′al rous ly,** *adv.* —**chiv′al rous ness,** *n.*

chiv al ry (shiv′əl rē), **1** the qualities of an ideal knight in the Middle Ages; bravery, honor, courtesy, protection of the weak, respect for women, and fairness to enemies. **2** rules and customs of knights in the Middle Ages. **3** knights as a group. *n.*

chive (chīv), plant related to the onion, having a very small bulb. Its long, slender leaves are used as seasoning. *n.*

chlo ride (klôr′īd), compound of chlorine with another element or radical. Sodium chloride is a compound of sodium and chlorine. *n.*

chlo rin ate (klôr′ə nāt), combine or treat with chlorine, especially to disinfect: *chlorinate water in a swimming pool.* *v.*, **chlo rin at ed, chlo rin at ing.**

chlo rin a tion (klôr′ə nā′shən), act or process of chlorinating. *n.*

chlo rine (klôr′ēn′), a greenish-yellow, bad-smelling, poisonous gas. It is a chemical element which occurs chiefly in combination with sodium as common salt. Chlorine is very irritating to the nose, throat, and lungs. It is used in bleaching and disinfecting, and in making plastics, explosives, and dyes. *n.*

chlo ro form (klôr′ə fôrm), **1** a colorless liquid with a sharp, sweetish smell and taste. When its vapor is inhaled, it makes a person unconscious or unable to feel pain. It is also used to dissolve rubber, resin, wax, and many other substances. **2** make unconscious or unable to feel pain by giving chloroform. **3** kill with chloroform. 1 *n.*, 2,3 *v.*

chlo ro phyll or **chlo ro phyl** (klôr′ə fil), the green coloring matter of plant cells. In the presence of light it makes carbohydrates, such as starch and sugar, from carbon dioxide and water. *n.*

chlo ro plast (klôr′ə plast), a tiny body in the cells of green plants that contains chlorophyll. *n.*

chm. or **chmn.**, chairman.

chock (chok), **1** block or wedge put under a barrel or wheel to keep it from rolling or under a boat to keep it in place. **2** provide or fasten with chocks: *chock a boat on a ship's deck.* 1 *n.*, 2 *v.*

chock-full (chok′fùl′), as full as can be; stuffed full: *The boy's pockets were chock-full of marbles. adj.* Also, **chuck-full.**

choc o late (chôk′lit or chôk′ə lit), **1** substance made by roasting and grinding cacao seeds. It has a strong, rich flavor and much value as food. **2** drink made of chocolate with hot milk or water and sugar. **3** candy made of chocolate. **4** made of or flavored with chocolate: *chocolate cake.* **5** a dark brown. **6** dark-brown. 1-3,5 *n.*, 4,6 *adj.*

Choc taw (chok′tô), **1** member of a tribe of American Indians, now living mostly in Oklahoma. **2** the language of these Indians. *n., pl.* **Choc taw** or **Choc taws** for 1.

choice (chois), **1** act of choosing: *She was careful in her choice of friends.* **2** power or chance to choose: *I have my choice between a radio and a camera for my birthday.* **3** person or thing chosen: *This camera is my choice.* **4** thing among several things to be chosen; alternative: *Their action left no choice but to adjourn the meeting.* **5** quantity and variety to choose from: *We found a wide choice of vegetables in the market.* **6** of fine quality; excellent; superior: *The choicest fruit had the highest price.* 1-5 *n.*, 6 *adj.*, **choic er, choic est.** —**choice′less,** *adj.* —**choice′ly,** *adv.* —**choice′ness,** *n.*

choir (kwīr), **1** group of singers who sing together in a church service. **2** part of a church set apart for such a group. **3** any group of singers; chorus. *n.* —**choir′like′,** *adj.*

choir boy (kwīr′boi′), boy who sings in a choir; chorister. *n.*

choke (chōk), **1** stop the breath of (an animal or person) by squeezing or blocking up the throat; suffocate: *The smoke from the burning building almost choked the firefighters.* **2** be unable to breathe: *I choked when a piece of meat stuck in my throat.* **3** act or sound of choking: *After a few chokes I got my breath.* **4** check or put out by cutting off air; smother: *A bucket of sand will choke a fire.* **5** fill up or block; clog: *Sand is choking the river.* **6** valve that reduces the supply of air to an internal-combustion engine. **7** kill or injure (a plant) by depriving it of air and light or of room to grow. 1,2,4,5,7 *v.*, **choked, chok ing;** 3,6 *n.* —**choke′a ble,** *adj.* —**chok′ing ly,** *adv.*

choke back, hold back, control, or suppress: *I choked back a sharp reply.*

choke off, put an end to; stop: *The break in the water main choked off the city's supply of water.*

choke up, 1 block up; fill up; clog up: *A traffic jam choked up the highway.* **2** fill with emotion; be or cause to be on the verge of tears: *I was choked up by the movie's sad ending.*

choke cher ry (chōk′cher′ē), bitter wild cherry of a North American tree or shrub. *n., pl.* **choke cher ries.**

chok er (chō′kər), **1** person or thing that chokes. **2** something that fits tightly around the neck, such as a necklace or high collar. *n.*

chol er (kol′ər), an irritable disposition; anger. *n.*

chol er a (kol′ər ə), an acute, infectious disease of the stomach and intestines, characterized by vomiting, cramps, and diarrhea. *n.*

chol er ic (kol′ər ik), having an irritable disposition; easily made angry. *adj.*

cho les te rol (kə les′tə rol′ or kə les′tə rōl′), a white, fatty substance, found in the blood and tissues of the body and also in foods such as eggs and meat. It is important in metabolism. *n.*

chomp (chomp), champ¹. *v.*

Chong qing (chông′ching′), official spelling of **Chungking.** *n.*

choose (chüz), **1** pick out; select from a number: *to choose a book, to choose wisely.* **2** prefer and decide; think fit: *The cat did not choose to go out in the rain. v.,* **chose, cho sen, choos ing.** —**choos′er,** *n.*

choos y or **choos ey** (chü′zē), INFORMAL. particular or fussy: *They are so choosy about their food that no one invites them to dinner. adj.,* **choos i er, choos i est.** —**choos′i ness,** *n.*

chop¹ (chop), **1** cut by hitting with something sharp: *You can chop wood with an ax. We chopped down the dead tree.* **2** cut into small pieces: *chop up cabbage for coleslaw.* **3** a cutting blow or stroke: *I split the log with one chop of the ax.* **4** slice of meat, especially of lamb, pork, or veal on a piece of rib. **5** (in tennis, cricket, etc.) swing at or hit with a downward stroke: *The batter chopped at the ball.* **6** make by cutting: *The hikers had to chop their way through the bushes.* 1,2,5,6 *v.*, **chopped, chop ping;** 3,4 *n.*

chop² (chop), **1** jaw. **2 chops,** *pl.* jaws or cheeks: *The cat is licking the milk off its chops. n.*

chop³ (chop), change suddenly; shift quickly; veer. *v.*, **chopped, chop ping.**

Cho pin (shō′pan), Frédéric François, 1810-1849, Polish pianist and composer who lived in France. *n.*

chop per (chop′ər), **1** person, tool, or machine that chops: *a wood chopper.* **2** SLANG. helicopter. *n.*

chop py¹ (chop′ē), **1** making quick, sharp movements; jerky: *The speaker made nervous, choppy gestures.* **2** moving in short, irregular, broken waves: *The wind made the water choppy. adj.,* **chop pi er, chop pi est.** —**chop′pi ness,** *n.*

chop py² (chop′ē), changing suddenly; shifting quickly: *A choppy wind tossed the ship about. adj.,* **chop pi er, chop pi est.**

chops (chops). See def. 2 under **chop². n.pl.**

chop sticks (chop′stiks′), pair of small, slender sticks used by the Chinese and Japanese to raise food to the mouth. *n.pl.*

chop su ey (chop′ sü′ē), fried or stewed meat and vegetables cut up and cooked together in a sauce. It is usually served with rice.

WORD HISTORY

chop suey

Chop suey comes from Chinese *tsap sui,* meaning "odds and ends."

---

cho ral (kôr′əl), **1** of a choir or chorus: *Our choral society meets on Wednesdays.* **2** sung by a choir or chorus: *a choral hymn. adj.* —**cho′ral ly,** *adv.*

cho rale (kə ral′), a simple hymn sung in unison. *n.*

chord¹ (kôrd), combination of two or more musical

notes sounded together in harmony. *n.* [*Chord*[1] comes from Middle English *cord,* which was shortened from *accord.*]

chord[2] (kôrd), **1** a straight line segment connecting two points on a curve. **2** feeling or emotion: *The stray and hungry puppy touched a tender chord in us. n.* [*Chord*[2] can be traced back to Greek *chordē,* meaning "gut, string of a musical instrument."]

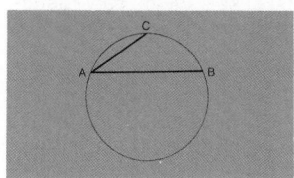

chord[2] (def. 1)
AB and AC are chords.

chor date (kôr′dāt), one of the large group of animals that have backbones. Chordates include human beings and all other vertebrates. *n.*

chore (chôr), **1** an odd job; small task: *Feeding the dog is my daily chore.* **2** a difficult or disagreeable thing to do: *Painting the house is a real chore. n.*

cho re a (kô rē′ə), St. Vitus's dance. *n.*

cho re o graph (kôr′ē ə graf), arrange or design dancing for. *v.*

cho re og ra pher (kôr′ē og′rə fər), planner or creator of dances in a ballet, motion picture, or musical play. *n.*

cho re o graph ic (kôr′ē ə graf′ik), of choreography. *adj.* —**cho′re o graph′i cal ly,** *adv.*

cho re og ra phy (kôr′ē og′rə fē), **1** art of planning or creating the dances in a ballet, motion picture, or musical play. **2** dancing, especially ballet dancing. *n.*

cho ris ter (kôr′ə stər), **1** singer in a choir. **2** choirboy. **3** leader of a choir. *n.*

chor tle (chôr′tl), **1** chuckle or snort with glee: *He chortled at the joke.* **2** a gleeful chuckle or snort. 1 *v.,* **chortled, chor tling;** 2 *n.* —**chor′tler,** *n.*

cho rus (kôr′əs), **1** group of singers who sing together, such as a choir: *Our school chorus gave a concert at the town hall.* **2** a musical composition to be sung by all singers together. A chorus is often a part of an opera or oratorio. **3** the repeated part of a song coming after each stanza: *Everybody knew the chorus by heart.* **4** sing or speak all at the same time: *The audience chorused its approval by loud cheering.* **5** anything sung by many people at once: *The children greeted the teacher with a chorus of "Happy Birthday."* **6** a saying all together at the same time: *My question was answered by a chorus of no's.* **7** group of singers and dancers: *the chorus in a musical comedy.* 1-3,5-7, *n., pl.* **cho rus es;** 4 *v.*

in chorus, all together at the same time: *The whole class replied in chorus to the teacher's questions.*

chose (chōz), past tense of **choose.** *I chose the red shirt. v.*

cho sen (chō′zn), **1** past participle of **choose.** *Have you chosen a book from the library?* **2** picked out; selected from a group: *Six chosen scouts marched at the front of the parade.* 1 *v.,* 2 *adj.*

Chou En-lai (jō′ en′lī′), 1898-1976, premier of the People's Republic of China from 1949 to 1976.

chow[1] (chou), dog of medium size, first bred in China, with a short, compact body, large head, and thick coat of one color. Chows have a black tongue and a tail that curls over the back. *n.*

chow[2] (chou), SLANG. food. *n.*

chow der (chou′dər), a thick soup or stew usually made of clams or fish with potatoes, onions, etc., and milk. *n.*

chow mein (chou′ mān′), a thickened stew of onions, celery, meat, etc., served with fried noodles. [*Chow mein*

comes from Chinese *ch'au min,* meaning "fried noodles."]

Christ (krīst), Jesus, the founder of the Christian religion. *n.*

chris ten (kris′n), **1** give a first name to (a person) at baptism: *The child was christened Maria.* **2** give a name to: *The new ship was christened before it was launched.* **3** baptize as a Christian. *v.*

Chris ten dom (kris′n dəm), **1** Christian countries; the Christian part of the world: *Many of the monarchs of Christendom took part in the Crusades.* **2** all Christians: *Christendom everywhere celebrates Christmas. n.*

chris ten ing (kris′n ing), act or ceremony of baptizing and naming; baptism. *n.*

Chris tian (kris′chən), **1** person who believes in and follows the teachings of Christ. **2** believing in or belonging to the religion of Christ: *the Christian church, the Christian gospel.* **3** showing a gentle, humble, helpful spirit: *Christian kindness.* **4** of Christians or Christianity: *the Christian faith.* 1 *n.,* 2-4 *adj.* —**Chris′tian like′,** *adj.* —**Chris′tian ly,** *adj., adv.*

Chris ti an i ty (kris′chē an′ə tē), **1** the religion based on the teachings of Christ as they appear in the Bible; Christian religion. **2** condition of being a Christian. **3** all Christians; Christendom. *n.*

Chris tian ize (kris′chə nīz), make Christian; convert to Christianity. *v.,* **Chris tian ized, Chris tian iz ing.** —**Chris′tian i za′tion,** *n.* —**Chris′tian iz′er,** *n.*

Christian name, first name; given name: *"Mary" is the Christian name of "Mary Smith."*

Christian Science, religion and system of healing founded by Mary Baker Eddy in 1866. It treats disease by mental and spiritual means.

Christian Scientist, believer in Christian Science.

Christ like (krīst′līk′), like Christ; like that of Christ; showing the spirit of Christ. *adj.* —**Christ′like′ness,** *n.*

Christ mas (kris′məs), the yearly celebration of the birth of Christ; December 25. *n., pl.* **Christ mas es.**

Christmas Day, December 25.

Christ mas time (kris′məs tīm′), the Christmas season. *n.*

Christmas tree, an evergreen or artificial tree hung with decorations at Christmastime.

Chris to pher (kris′tə fər), **Saint,** died A.D. 250?, legendary Christian martyr. He is the patron saint of travelers. *n.*

chro mat ic (krō mat′ik), **1** of color or colors. **2** progressing only by half steps instead of by the regular intervals of the musical scale. There are twelve chromatic tones in an octave. *adj.* —**chro mat′i cal ly,** *adv.*

chromatic scale, a musical scale that progresses by half steps.

chro ma tin (krō′mə tən), a protein substance in the nucleus of an animal or plant cell. The chromosomes are made up in part of chromatin. *n.*

chrome (krōm), chromium. *n.*

chro mi um (krō′mē əm), a grayish, hard, brittle metallic element that does not rust or become dull easily when exposed to air. Chromium occurs in compounds that are used as plating, as part of stainless steel and other alloys, for making dyes and paints, in photography, etc. *n.*

a hat	i it	oi oil	ch child	(a in about
ā age	ī ice	ou out	ng long		e in taken
ä far	o hot	u cup	sh she	ə = { i in pencil
e let	ō open	u̇ put	th thin		o in lemon
ē equal	ô order	ü rule	ᵺ then	(u in circus
ėr term			zh measure	

chro mo some (krō′mə sōm), any of the rod-shaped bodies found in the nucleus of a cell that appear when the cell divides. Chromosomes carry the genes that determine heredity. *n.*

chron ic (kron′ik), **1** lasting a long time: *a chronic disease.* **2** never stopping; constant; habitual: *a chronic tease. adj.* —**chron′i cal ly,** *adv.*

chron i cle (kron′ə kəl), **1** record of events in the order in which they took place; history; story: *Columbus kept a chronicle of his voyages.* **2** write the history of; tell the story of: *Many of the old monks chronicled the Crusades.* **1** *n.,* **2** *v.,* **chron i cled, chron i cling.**

chron i cler (kron′ə klər), writer of a chronicle; recorder; historian. *n.*

Chron i cles (kron′ə kəlz), two books of the Old Testament, called I and II Chronicles. *n.*

chron o log i cal (kron′ə loj′ə kəl), arranged in the order in which the events happened: *In telling a story a person usually follows chronological order. adj.* —**chron′o log′i cal ly,** *adv.*

chro nol o gy (krə nol′ə jē), **1** science of measuring time and determining the proper order and dates of events. **2** table or list that gives the exact dates of events arranged in the order in which they happened. *n., pl.* **chro nol o gies.**

chro nom e ter (krə nom′ə tər), clock or watch that keeps very accurate time. A ship's chronometer is used in determining longitude. *n.*

chrys a lid (kris′ə lid), chrysalis. *n.*

chrysalis of a monarch butterfly

chrys a lis (kris′ə lis), the stage in the development of butterflies between the larva and the adult; pupa. *n., pl.* **chrys a lis es, chry sal i des** (krə sal′ə dēz′).

chry san the mum (krə san′thə məm), the round flower of any of several cultivated plants that are related to the aster and bloom in the fall. Chrysanthemums have many petals and various shades, especially white, yellow, red, and brown. *n.*

chub (chub), any of various small, freshwater fishes of central and eastern United States and Canada. *n., pl.* **chubs** or **chub.**

chub bi ness (chub′ē nis), a being chubby. *n.*

chub by (chub′ē), round and plump: *Most babies have chubby cheeks. adj.,* **chub bi er, chub bi est.**

chuck¹ (chuk), **1** give a slight blow or tap; pat: *He chucked the baby under the chin.* **2** a slight blow or tap: *He gave the baby a chuck under the chin.* **3** throw or toss: *She chucked the stones into the pond.* **4** a throw or toss. **1,3** *v.,* **2,4** *n.*

chuck² (chuk), **1** device for holding a tool or piece of work in a machine. **2** cut of beef between the neck and the shoulder. *n.*

chuck-full (chuk′fùl′), chock-full. *adj.*

chuck le (chuk′əl), **1** laugh softly or quietly: *She kept chuckling to herself throughout the funny movie.* **2** a soft laugh; quiet laughter. **1** *v.,* **chuck led, chuck ling; 2** *n.* —**chuck′ler,** *n.*

chuck wagon, (in the western United States) a wagon or truck that carries food and cooking equipment for cowhands or harvest workers.

chug (chug), **1** a short, loud burst of sound: *We heard the chug of a steam engine.* **2** make such sounds. **3** go or move with such sounds: *The old truck chugged along.* **1** *n.,* **2,3** *v.,* **chugged, chug ging.**

chum (chum), INFORMAL. **1** a very close friend. **2** be very close friends. **1** *n.,* **2** *v.,* **chummed, chum ming.**

chum my (chum′ē), INFORMAL. like a chum; very friendly; intimate. *adj.,* **chum mi er, chum mi est.** —**chum′mi ly,** *adv.* —**chum′mi ness,** *n.*

chump (chump), INFORMAL. a foolish or stupid person; blockhead. *n.*

Chung king (chùng′king′), city in central China, on the Yangtze River. Officially, **Chongqing.** *n.*

chunk (chungk), a thick piece or lump: *Here's a chunk of wood for the fire. n.*

chunk y (chung′kē), **1** like a chunk; short and thick: *She threw a chunky log on the fire.* **2** stocky: *The child had a chunky build. adj.,* **chunk i er, chunk i est.** —**chunk′i ly,** *adv.* —**chunk′i ness,** *n.*

church (chėrch), **1** building for public Christian worship. **2** public worship of God in a church: *Don't be late for church.* **3** Usually, **Church.** group of Christians with the same beliefs and under the same authority; denomination: *the Methodist Church, the Presbyterian Church.* **4** the **Church,** all Christians. **5** profession of a clergyman: *He is going into the church as a career. n.* —**church′less,** *adj.* —**church′like′,** *adj.*

church go er (chėrch′gō′ər), person who goes to church regularly. *n.*

Church ill (chėr′chil), Sir **Winston,** 1874-1965, British statesman and writer, prime minister of Great Britain from 1940 to 1945 and from 1951 to 1955. *n.*

church man (chėrch′mən), **1** clergyman. **2** member of a church. *n., pl.* **church men.**

Church of England, the Episcopal Church in England that is recognized as a national institution by the government; Anglican Church.

Church of Jesus Christ of Latter-day Saints, the official name of the Mormon Church.

church ward en (chėrch′wôrd′n), a lay official in the Church of England or the Protestant Episcopal Church who manages the business, property, and money of a church. *n.*

church wom an (chėrch′wùm′ən), a woman member of a church. *n., pl.* **church wom en.**

church yard (chėrch′yärd′), the ground around a church. Part of a churchyard is sometimes used as a burial ground. *n.*

churl (chėrl), **1** a rude, surly person. **2** person of low birth; peasant. *n.*

churl ish (chėr′lish), rude or surly; bad-tempered. *adj.* —**churl′ish ly,** *adv.* —**churl′ish ness,** *n.*

churn (chėrn), **1** container or machine in which butter is made from cream or milk by beating and shaking. **2** beat

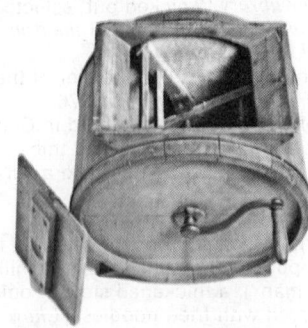
churn (def. 1)

and shake (cream or milk) in a churn. **3** stir violently; make or become foamy: *The ship's propeller churned the waves.* **4** move as if beaten and shaken: *The water churns in the rapids.* **1** *n.,* 2-4 *v.* —**churn′er,** *n.*

chute (shüt), **1** a steep slide for dropping or sliding things down to a lower level. There are chutes for carrying mail, soiled clothes, coal, etc. A toboggan slide is called a chute. **2** rapids in a river; waterfall. **3** INFORMAL. parachute. *n.*

chut ney (chut′nē), a spicy sauce or relish made of fruits, herbs, pepper, etc. *n., pl.* **chut neys.**

chyme (kīm), a pulpy mass into which food is changed by the action of the stomach. Chyme passes from the stomach into the small intestine. *n.*

CIA, Central Intelligence Agency (an agency of the United States government that deals with matters involving national security).

ci ca da (sə kā′də), a large insect with two pairs of thin, transparent wings. The male makes a shrill sound in hot, dry weather. Cicadas are commonly called locusts. *n., pl.* **ci ca das.**

Cic e ro (sis′ə rō′), **Marcus Tullius,** 106-43 B.C., Roman orator, writer, and statesman. *n.*

ci der (sī′dər), juice pressed out of apples, used as a drink and in making vinegar. *n.*

ci gar (sə gär′), a tight roll of tobacco leaves for smoking. *n.*

cig a rette or **cig a ret** (sig′ə ret′ or sig′ə ret′), a small roll of finely cut tobacco enclosed in a thin sheet of paper for smoking. *n.*

cil i a (sil′ē ə), very small, hairlike parts of leaves, wings, insects, etc. Some microscopic animals use cilia to move themselves. *n.pl.* of **cil i um** (sil′ē əm).

cinch (sinch), **1** a strong strap for fastening a saddle or pack on a horse. **2** fasten on with a cinch; bind firmly. **3** INFORMAL. a firm hold or grip. **4** SLANG. make certain of. **5** SLANG. something sure and easy: *It's a cinch to ride a bike once you know how.* 1,3,5 *n., pl.* **cinch es;** 2,4 *v.*

cin cho na (sin kō′nə), an evergreen tree native to the Andes Mountains, now also grown in the East Indies. It is valuable for its bark from which quinine and other drugs are obtained; Peruvian bark. *n., pl.* **cin cho nas.** [*Cinchona* was named in honor of the Countess of *Chinchón,* 1576-1639, wife of a Spanish viceroy to Peru. She was said to have been cured of a fever by the bark.]

Cin cin nat i (sin′sə nat′ē), city in SW Ohio, on the Ohio River. *n.*

cinc ture (singk′chər), **1** belt or girdle. **2** encircle; surround. **1** *n.,* 2 *v.,* **cinc tured, cinc tur ing.**

cin der (sin′dər), **1** piece of wood or coal that has burned up. **2** cinders, *pl.* wood or coal partly burned but no longer flaming. Cinders are made up of larger and coarser pieces than ashes are. *n.*

cinder block, a rectangular building block of cement and pressed coal cinders, usually hollow. It is used in walls and partitions.

cin e ma (sin′ə mə), **1** a motion-picture theater. **2** the cinema, motion pictures. *n., pl.* **cin e mas.**

cin na bar (sin′ə bär), a reddish or brownish mineral that is the chief source of mercury. *n.*

cin na mon (sin′ə mən), **1** spice made from the dried inner bark of a small tree of the East Indies. **2** light reddish-brown: *a cinnamon bear.* **3** a light, reddish brown. 1,3 *n.,* 2 *adj.*

CIO or **C.I.O.,** Congress of Industrial Organizations. It merged with the AFL in 1955. See **AFL-CIO.**

ci pher (sī′fər), **1** secret writing; code: *Part of his letter is in cipher.* **2** zero; 0. **3** person or thing of no importance. **4** do arithmetic; use figures: *She can read, write, and cipher.* 1-3 *n.,* 4 *v.* Also, **cypher.**

a hat	i it	oi oil	ch child		a in about
ā age	ī ice	ou out	ng long		e in taken
ä far	o hot	u cup	sh she	ə =	i in pencil
e let	ō open	ù put	th thin		o in lemon
ē equal	ô order	ü rule	ᴛʜ then		u in circus
ėr term			zh measure		

cir ca (sėr′kə), about; approximately: *Mohammed was born circa A.D. 570. prep.*

Cir ce (sėr′sē), (in Greek legends) an enchantress who changed men into swine. Ulysses withstood her spell and forced her to set free his companions, whom she had changed to swine. *n.*

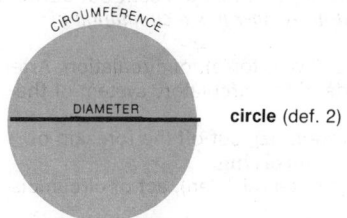

circle (def. 2)

cir cle (sėr′kəl), **1** a round line. Every point on a circle is the same distance from the center. **2** a plane figure bounded by such a line. **3** anything shaped like a circle or part of one: *a circle around the moon.* **4** ring: *We sat in a circle around the teacher.* **5** go around in a circle; revolve around: *The moon circles the earth. The airplane circled before it landed.* **6** form a circle around; surround; encircle: *A ring of trees circled the clearing.* **7** a complete series or course: *A year is a circle of twelve months.* **8** group of people held together by the same interests: *the family circle, a circle of friends.* 1-4,7,8 *n.,* 5,6 *v.,* **cir cled, cir cling.** —**cir′cler,** *n.*

cir clet (sėr′klit), **1** a small circle. **2** a round ornament worn on the head, neck, arm, or finger. *n.*

cir cuit (sėr′kit), **1** a going around; a moving around: *It takes a year for the earth to make its circuit of the sun.* **2** route over which a person or group makes repeated journeys at certain times: *Some judges make a circuit, stopping at certain towns along the way to hold court.* **3** the district through which such journeys are made. **4** distance around any space. **5** line enclosing any space. **6** the complete path over which an electric current flows. **7** arrangement of wiring, tubes, etc., forming electrical connections; hookup. **8** number of theaters under the same management and presenting the same shows. *n.*

circuit breaker, switch that automatically interrupts an electric circuit when the current gets too strong.

cir cu i tous (sər kyü′ə təs), not direct; roundabout: *We took a circuitous route home to avoid poor roads. adj.* —**cir cu′i tous ly,** *adv.* —**cir cu′i tous ness,** *n.*

circuit rider, preacher who rides from place to place over a circuit to preach. Methodist circuit riders were common in the 1800's.

cir cu lar (sėr′kyə lər), **1** round like a circle: *The full moon has a circular shape.* **2** moving in a circle; going around a circle: *A merry-go-round makes a circular trip.* **3** of a circle. **4** letter, notice, or advertisement sent to each of a number of people. 1-3 *adj.,* 4 *n.* —**cir′cu lar ly,** *adv.*

cir cu lar ize (sėr′kyə lə rīz′), send circulars to. *v.,* **cir cu lar ized, cir cu lar iz ing.** —**cir′cu lar i za′tion,** *n.* —**cir′cu lar iz′er,** *n.*

cir cu late (sėr′kyə lāt), **1** go around; pass from place to place or from person to person: *Water circulates in the pipes of a building. Money circulates as it goes from person* *to person. A newspaper circulates among people who read it.* **2** send around from person to person or from place to place: *circulate news. This book has been widely circulated among children.* **3** (of the blood) flow from the heart through the arteries and veins back to the heart. *v.,* **cir cu lat ed, cir cu lat ing.** —**cir′cu la′tor,** *n.*

circulating library, library whose books can be rented or borrowed.

cir cu la tion (sėr′kyə lā′shən), **1** a going around; circulating: *Open windows increase the circulation of air in a room.* **2** flow of the blood from the heart through the arteries and veins back to the heart. **3** a sending around of books, papers, news, etc., from person to person or from place to place. **4** the number of copies of a book, newspaper, magazine, etc., that are sent out during a certain time: *That newspaper has a circulation of 500,000. n.*

cir cu la to ry (sėr′kyə lə tôr′ē), of circulation. Arteries and veins are parts of the circulatory system of the human body. *adj.*

cir cum cise (sėr′kəm sīz), cut off the foreskin of. *v.,* **cir cum cised, cir cum cis ing.**

cir cum ci sion (sėr′kəm sizh′ən), act of circumcising. *n.*

cir cum fer ence (sər kum′fər əns), **1** the boundary line of a circle or of certain other surfaces. Every point in the circumference of a circle is at the same distance from the center. **2** the distance around: *The circumference of the earth at the equator is almost 25,000 miles. n.*

cir cum flex (sėr′kəm fleks), **1** (in the pronunciations in this book) a mark used over *o* to show that it is pronounced as in *order* (ôr′dər). **2** mark (ˆ or ˇ or ˜) placed over a vowel to tell something about its pronunciation, as in the French word *fête. n., pl.* **cir cum flex es.** [*Circumflex* comes from Latin *circumflexum,* meaning "bent around."]

cir cum lo cu tion (sėr′kəm lō kyü′shən), **1** the use of several or many words instead of one or a few: *The witness's account of the accident was so full of circumlocution that it was difficult to understand it.* **2** a roundabout expression: *"The wife of your father's brother" is a circumlocution for "Your aunt." n.*

cir cum nav i gate (sėr′kəm nav′ə gāt), sail around: *Magellan's ship circumnavigated the earth. v.,* **cir cum nav i gat ed, cir cum nav i gat ing.** —**cir′cum nav′i ga′tor,** *n.*

cir cum nav i ga tion (sėr′kəm nav′ə gā′shən), act of sailing around. *n.*

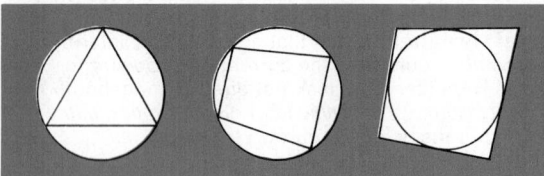

circumscribe (def. 4)—circumscribed figures

cir cum scribe (sėr′kəm skrīb′), **1** draw a line around; mark the boundaries of; bound: *The horizon circumscribed my view of the sea.* **2** surround: *the atmosphere circumscribing the earth.* **3** put limits on; restrict: *Poor health circumscribes a person's activities.* **4** draw (a figure) around another figure so as to touch as many points as possible. **5** be drawn around so as to touch as many points as possible: *A circle that circumscribes a square touches·the four corners of the square. v.,* **cir cum scribed, cir cum scrib ing.**

cir cum spect (sėr′kəm spekt), watchful on all sides; careful; cautious; prudent: *She was circumspect in all her purchases. adj.* —**cir′cum spect′ly,** *adv.* —**cir′cum spect′ness,** *n.*

cir cum spec tion (sėr′kəm spek′shən), circumspect action or conduct; care; caution; prudence. *n.*

cir cum stance (sėr′kəm stans), **1** condition that accompanies an act or event: *Unfavorable circumstances such as fog and rain often delayed us on our trip to the mountains.* **2** fact or event: *It was a lucky circumstance that I found my money.* **3** full detail: *The speaker told of her adventures with great circumstance.* **4 circumstances,** *pl.* **a** financial condition: *A rich person is in good circumstances; a poor person is in bad circumstances.* **b** the existing condition or state of affairs: *He was forced by circumstances to resign.* **5** ceremony; display: *The royal procession advanced with pomp and circumstance. n.*

under no circumstances, never: *Under no circumstances should you reveal that we are planning a surprise party.*

under the circumstances, because of these conditions: *Tickets to that show were sold out; under the circumstances we had no choice but to go to another show.*

cir cum stan tial (sėr′kəm stan′shəl), **1** depending on or based on circumstances: *Stolen jewels found on a person are circumstantial evidence that the person stole them.* **2** not essential; not important; incidental: *Minor details are circumstantial compared with the main fact.* **3** giving full and exact details; complete: *a circumstantial report of an accident. adj.* —**cir′cum stan′tial ly,** *adv.*

cir cum vent (sėr′kəm vent′), **1** get the better of or defeat by trickery; outwit: *The dishonest official was always trying to circumvent the law.* **2** go around: *He took a roundabout route to circumvent the traffic. v.* —**cir′cum ven′tion,** *n.*

cir cus (sėr′kəs), **1** a traveling show of acrobats, clowns, horses, riders, and wild animals. The performers who give the show and the performances they give are both called the circus. **2** (in ancient Rome) an arena with seats around it in rows, each row higher than the one in front of it. *n., pl.* **cir cus es.**

cir rho sis (sə rō′sis), a chronic disease of the liver marked by the breakdown of liver cells and formation of too much connective tissue between cells. *n.*

cir rus (sir′əs), a cloud formation consisting of thin, featherlike white clouds of ice crystals formed very high in the air. *n., pl.* **cir ri** (sir′ī).

WORD HISTORY

cirrus

Cirrus comes from Latin *cirrus,* meaning "a curl."

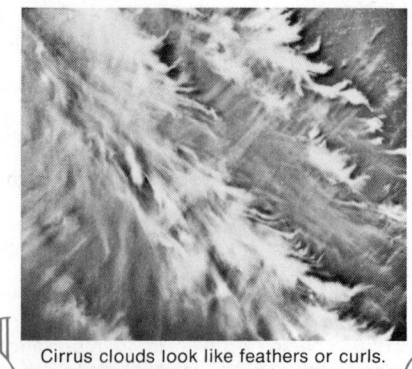

Cirrus clouds look like feathers or curls.

cis tern (sis′tərn), an artificial reservoir for storing water, especially a tank below ground. *n.*

cit a del (sit′ə dəl), **1** fortress, especially one in a city. **2** a strongly fortified place; stronghold. **3** a strong, safe place; refuge. *n.*

ci ta tion (sī tā′shən), **1** quotation or reference given as an authority for facts or opinions. **2** act of citing. **3** honorable mention for bravery in war: *The soldier received a citation from the President.* **4** official praise or commendation for public service: *The mayor gave her a citation for her role in planning the new museum.* **5** summons to appear before a court of law. *n.*

cite (sīt), **1** quote (a passage, book, or author), especially as an authority: *She cited the U.S. Constitution to prove her statement.* **2** refer to; mention as an example: *The lawyer cited another case similar to the one being tried.* **3** give honorable mention for bravery in war. **4** commend publicly for service to the community. **5** summon to appear before a court of law. *v.,* **cit ed, cit ing.**

cit i zen (sit′ə zən), **1** person who by birth or by choice is a member of a nation. A citizen owes loyalty to that nation and is given certain rights by it. *Many immigrants have become citizens of the United States.* **2** inhabitant of a city or town. *n.*

cit i zen ry (sit′ə zən rē), citizens as a group. *n., pl.* **cit i zen ries.**

citizens band, one of two bands of radio frequencies available for the use of private citizens, especially for communications over a short distance.

cit i zen ship (sit′ə zən ship), **1** the duties, rights, and privileges of a citizen. **2** condition of being a citizen: *Voting is a right of citizenship. n.*

cit rate (sit′rāt *or* sī′trāt), a chemical substance formed from citric acid. *n.*

cit ric acid (sit′rik), a white, odorless acid with a sour taste, found in the juice of oranges, lemons, limes, and similar fruits. It is used as a flavoring, as a medicine, and in making dyes.

cit ron (sit′rən), **1** a pale-yellow fruit somewhat like a lemon but larger, with less acid and a thicker rind. **2** the shrub or small tree that it grows on. **3** its rind, candied and used in fruit cakes, plum pudding, candies, etc. *n.*

cit ro nel la (sit′rə nel′ə), oil obtained from a fragrant grass of Asia and Central America. It is used in making perfume, soap, liniment, etc., and for keeping mosquitoes away. *n.*

cit rus (sit′rəs), **1** any tree bearing lemons, grapefruit, limes, oranges, or similar fruits. Citruses usually grow in warm climates. **2** fruit of such a tree. **3** of such trees. Citrus fruits contain much vitamin C. 1,2 *n., pl.* **cit rus es;** 3 *adj.*

cit y (sit′ē), **1** a large and important center of population and business activity. New York, Buenos Aires, London, Cairo, and Shanghai are major cities of the world. **2** division of local government in the United States having a charter from the state that fixes its boundaries and powers. A city is usually governed by a mayor and a board of aldermen or councilmen. **3** people living in a city: *The whole city was alarmed by the great fire.* **4** of or in a city. 1-3 *n., pl.* **cit ies;** 4 *adj.* [*City* came into English about 750 years ago from French *cite,* and can be traced back to Latin *civis,* meaning "citizen."]

city hall, the headquarters of the officials, bureaus, etc., of a city government: *The mayor's office is in city hall.*

city manager, person appointed by a city council or commission to manage the government of a city.

cit y-state (sit′ē stāt′), an independent state consisting of a city and the territories depending on it. Athens was a city-state in ancient Greece. *n.*

a hat	**i** it	**oi** oil	**ch** child	(a in about
ā age	**ī** ice	**ou** out	**ng** long	e in taken
ä far	**o** hot	**u** cup	**sh** she	ə = { i in pencil
e let	**ō** open	**u̇** put	**th** thin	o in lemon
ē equal	**ô** order	**ü** rule	**ᵺ** then	u in circus
ėr term			**zh** measure	

civ et (siv′it), **1** a yellowish substance produced by certain glands of the civet cat. It has a musky odor and is used in making perfume. **2** civet cat. *n.*

civet cat, a small, spotted mammal of Africa and Asia, having glands that produce civet.

civet cat
about 4 ft.
(1 m.) long
with tail

civ ic (siv′ik), **1** of a city: *She is interested in civic affairs and will be a candidate for mayor.* **2** of citizens or citizenship. A person's civic duties include such things as obeying the laws, voting, and paying taxes. *adj.* —**civ′i cal ly,** *adv.*

civ ics (siv′iks), study of the duties, rights, and privileges of citizens. *n.*

civ il (siv′əl), **1** of a citizen or citizens: *civil duties.* **2** of the government, state, or nation: *Police departments are civil institutions to protect local citizens.* **3** occurring among citizens of one community, state, or nation: *civil strife.* **4** of a citizen or the public; not connected with the armed forces or the church: *The accused soldier was tried in a military rather than in a civil court. The couple had both a civil and a religious marriage ceremony.* **5** polite; courteous: *I pointed out the way in a very civil manner.* **6** having to do with the private rights of individuals and with laws protecting these rights. Civil lawsuits deal with such things as contracts, ownership of property, and payment for personal injury. *adj.*

civil defense, a civilian emergency program for protecting people and property from disasters such as fire, flood, or enemy attack.

civil disobedience, deliberate, public refusal to obey a law that one considers unjust. Civil disobedience is often used as a form of protest.

civil engineering, the planning and directing of the construction of bridges, roads, harbors, canals, dams, and other public works.

ci vil ian (sə vil′yən), **1** person who is not enrolled in any of the armed forces. **2** of civilians; not of the armed forces: *civilian clothes.* 1 *n.,* 2 *adj.*

ci vil i ty (sə vil′ə tē), **1** polite behavior; courtesy: *Thank you for your civility in replying to my letter so promptly.* **2** act or expression of politeness or courtesy. *n., pl.* **ci vil i ties.**

civ i li za tion (siv′ə lə zā′shən), **1** civilized condition; advanced stage in social development. **2** a civilizing or a becoming civilized: *The civilization of a primitive society is a gradual process which takes centuries.* **3** nations and peoples that have reached advanced stages in social development: *All civilization should be aroused against war.* **4** the ways of living of a people or nation: *There are differences between Chinese civilization and that of the United States. n.*

civ i lize (siv′ə līz), change from a primitive way of life; train in culture, science, and art: *The Romans civilized a* *great part of their world.* v., **civ i lized, civ i liz ing.**

civ i lized (siv′ə līzd), **1** advanced in social customs, art, and science: *The ancient Greeks were a civilized people.* **2** showing culture and good manners; refined: *civilized behavior, a civilized attitude.* adj.

civil liberty, the freedom of a person to enjoy the rights guaranteed by the laws or constitution of a country without any undue restraint or interference by the government.

civ il ly (siv′ə lē), politely; courteously. adv.

civil rights, the rights of a citizen, especially the rights guaranteed to all U.S. citizens, regardless of race, color, religion, or sex.

civil servant, person who is employed in the civil service.

civil service, branch of government service concerned with affairs not military, naval, legislative, or judicial. It includes all civilian government workers who are appointed rather than elected. Forest rangers and postal service employees belong to the United States civil service.

civil war, 1 war between opposing groups of citizens of one nation. **2 Civil War,** war between the northern and southern states of the United States from 1861 to 1865; War Between the States.

Cl, symbol for chlorine.

cl., 1 centiliter. **2** class. **3** clerk.

clab ber (klab′ər), **1** thick, sour milk. **2** become thick in souring; curdle. 1 n., 2 v.

clack (klak), **1** make or cause to make a short, sharp sound: *The train clacked over the rails.* **2** a short, sharp sound: *the clack of typewriters.* 1 v., 2 n. **—clack′er,** n.

clad (klad), clothed; a past tense and a past participle of **clothe.** v.

claim (klām), **1** demand as one's own or one's right: *The settlers claimed the land beyond the river as theirs. Does anyone claim this pencil?* **2** such a demand: *She made a claim to the pencil.* **3** a right or title to something; right to demand something: *He has a legal claim to the property. There are too many claims on my time.* **4** something that is claimed, such as a piece of public land which a settler or prospector marks out for himself. **5** require; call for; deserve: *Practicing the clarinet claims his full attention.* **6** say strongly; declare as a fact; maintain: *She claimed that her answer was correct.* **7** declaration of something as a fact: *Careful study showed that the claims that Salk vaccine prevented polio were correct.* 1,5,6 v., 2-4,7 n. **—claim′a ble,** adj. **—claim′er,** n.

jump a claim, seize a piece of land claimed by another.

lay claim to, assert one's right to; claim: *The settlers laid claim to the piece of land they occupied.*

claim ant (klā′mənt), person who makes a claim. n.

clair voy ance (kler voi′əns or klar voi′əns), the supposed power of seeing or knowing about things that are out of sight. n.

clair voy ant (kler voi′ənt or klar voi′ənt), **1** supposedly having the power of seeing or knowing about things that are out of sight. **2** person who has, or claims to have, such power: *The clairvoyant claimed to be able to locate lost articles and to give news of faraway people.* 1 adj., 2 n. **—clair voy′ant ly,** adv.

clam (klam), **1** shellfish somewhat like an oyster, with a soft body and a shell in two hinged halves. Clams burrow in sand along the seashore or at the edges of rivers, lakes, etc. Many kinds are good to eat. **2** go out after clams; dig for clams. 1 n., 2 v., **clammed, clam ming. —clam′like′,** adj.

clam up, INFORMAL. stop talking.

clam bake (klam′bāk′), picnic where clams are baked or steamed. n.

clam ber (klam′bər), climb, using both hands and feet; climb awkwardly or with difficulty; scramble: *The children clambered up the cliff.* v.

clam mi ly (klam′ə lē), in a clammy manner. adv.

clam mi ness (klam′ē nis), clammy condition or quality: *We felt an uncomfortable clamminess in the old castle's damp dungeon.* n.

clam my (klam′ē), cold and damp: *The walls of the cellar were clammy.* adj., **clam mi er, clam mi est.**

clam or (klam′ər), **1** a loud noise, especially of voices; continual uproar: *The clamor of the crowd filled the air.* **2** make a loud noise or continual uproar; shout. **3** a noisy demand. **4** demand noisily: *The children were clamoring for candy.* 1,3 n., 2,4 v.

clam or ous (klam′ər əs), **1** loud and noisy; shouting: *clamorous criticism.* **2** making noisy demands or complaints: *The mayor gave in to the clamorous parents and agreed to discuss building a new school with them.* adj. **—clam′or ous ly,** adv. **—clam′or ous ness,** n.

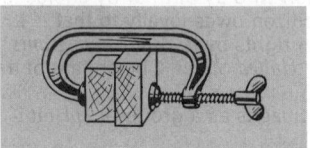
clamp (def. 1)

clamp (klamp), **1** brace, band, wedge, or other device for holding things tightly together: *She used a clamp to hold the arm on the chair until the glue dried.* **2** fasten together with a clamp; put in a clamp; strengthen with a clamp: *A picture frame must be clamped together while the glue is drying.* 1 n., 2 v.

clamp down, INFORMAL. become more strict; impose strict control: *The police clamped down on speeders.*

clan (klan), **1** group of related families that claim to be descended from a common ancestor. **2** group of people closely joined together by some common interest: *The whole clan of jazz fans was at the concert.* n. **—clan′like′,** adj.

clan des tine (klan des′tən), arranged or made in a stealthy or underhanded manner; secret; concealed: *The spy's clandestine plans to enter the country went undetected.* adj. **—clan des′tine ly,** adv. **—clan des′tine ness,** n.

clang (klang), **1** a loud, harsh, ringing sound like metal being hit: *The clang of the fire bell aroused the town.* **2** make or cause to make such a sound: *The fire bell clanged. The firemen clanged the bell.* 1 n., 2 v.

clan gor (klang′ər or klang′gər), **1** a continued clanging. **2** clang. n.

clan gor ous (klang′ər əs or klang′gər əs), clanging. adj.

clank (klangk), **1** a sharp, harsh sound like the rattle of a heavy chain: *The clank of heavy machinery filled the factory.* **2** make or cause to make such a sound: *The old bridge rattled and clanked as we drove over it. The dishwasher clanked the pots and pans.* 1 n., 2 v.

clan nish (klan′ish), **1** having to do with a clan: *the clannish customs of the Scottish Highlanders.* **2** closely united; not liking outsiders: *The older settlers were clannish and avoided their new neighbors.* adj. **—clan′nish ly,** adv. **—clan′nish ness,** n.

clans man (klanz′mən), member of a clan. n., pl. **clansmen.**

clap (klap), **1** strike together loudly: *clap the cymbals, clap one's hands.* **2** applaud by striking the hands together: *When the show was over, we all clapped.* **3** a sudden noise, such as a single burst of thunder, the sound of the hands struck together, or the sound of a loud slap. **4** strike with a quick blow; slap: *I clapped my friend on the back.* **5** a loud, quick blow; slap: *a clap on the shoulder.*

6 put or place quickly and effectively: *The police clapped the escaped prisoner back into jail.* 1,2,4,6 *v.*, **clapped, clap ping;** 3,5 *n.*

clap board (klab′ərd *or* klap′bôrd′), **1** a thin board, thicker along one edge than along the other. Clapboards are used to cover the outer walls of wooden buildings. **2** cover with clapboards. 1 *n.*, 2 *v.*

clap per (klap′ər), the movable part inside a bell that strikes against and rings the outer part. *n.*

clar et (klar′ət), **1** kind of red wine. **2** a dark purplish red. **3** dark purplish-red: *a claret coat.* 1,2 *n.*, 3 *adj.*

clar i fi ca tion (klar′ə fə kā′shən), act or process of clarifying. *n.*

clar i fy (klar′ə fī), **1** make clearer; explain: *The teacher's explanation clarified the difficult instructions.* **2** make or become clear; purify: *The cook clarified the fat by heating it with a little water and straining it through cloth.* *v.*, **clar i fied, clar i fy ing.**

clarinet

clar i net (klar′ə net′), a woodwind instrument, having a mouthpiece with a single reed and played by means of holes and keys. *n.*

clar i net ist *or* **clar i net tist** (klar′ə net′ist), person who plays a clarinet. *n.*

clar i on (klar′ē ən), **1** a trumpet with clear, shrill tones. **2** sound made by this trumpet or a sound like it. **3** clear and shrill: *a clarion call.* 1,2 *n.*, 3 *adj.*

clar i ty (klar′ə tē), clearness: *He writes with great clarity.* *n.*

Clark (klärk), **1 George Rogers,** 1752-1818, American soldier and frontiersman. **2** his brother, **William,** 1770-1838, American soldier and explorer of the American northwest together with Meriwether Lewis. *n.*

clash (klash), **1** a loud, harsh sound like that of two things running into each other, of striking metal, or of bells rung together but not in tune: *He heard the clash of cymbals.* **2** hit or strike with a clash: *The metal gate clashed shut.* **3** a strong disagreement; conflict: *There are many clashes of opinion between the opposing candidates.* **4** come into conflict; disagree strongly: *The freshmen clashed with the sophomores. Red pants and a purple shirt clash.* 1,3 *n.*, *pl.* **clash es;** 2,4 *v.* —**clash′er,** *n.*

clasp (klasp), **1** thing to fasten two parts or pieces together. A buckle on a belt is one kind of clasp. **2** fasten together with a clasp. **3** hold closely with the arms; embrace: *I clasped the kitten.* **4** a close hold with the arms: *The hunter escaped from the bear's clasp.* **5** grip firmly with the hand; grasp: *I clasped the railing as I climbed the stairs.* **6** a firm grip with the hand: *She gave my hand a warm clasp.* 1,4,6 *n.*, 2,3,5 *v.* —**clasp′er,** *n.*

class (klas), **1** group of persons or things alike in some way; kind; sort: *That magazine has an intelligent class of readers.* **2** group of students taught together: *The art class meets in room 202.* **3** a meeting of such a group: *When I was absent I missed a great many classes.* **4** group of pupils entering a school together and graduating in the same year: *The class of 1968 graduated in 1968.* **5** rank or division of society: *the upper class, the middle class, the lower class.* **6** put or be in a class or group; classify: *She is classed with the best swimmers in the school.* **7** grade or quality: *First class is the most costly way to travel.* **8** INFORMAL. high quality; excellence; style: *That singer has never really showed much class.* **9** group of animals or plants ranking below a phylum or division and above an order. Crustaceans and insects are two classes in the phylum of arthropods. 1-5,7-9 *n.*, *pl.* **classes;** 6 *v.*

class action, a legal action brought by one or more individuals who represent the whole class of persons having the same interest in the action.

clas sic (klas′ik), **1** work of literature or art of the highest rank or quality: *Louisa May Alcott's book "Little Women" is a classic.* **2** author or artist of acknowledged excellence whose works serve as a standard, model, or guide: *Shakespeare is a classic.* **3** of the highest rank or quality; serving as a standard, model, or guide: *The "Mona Lisa" is a classic work of art.* **4** simple and fine in form: *the classic design of a Greek temple.* **5** contest of great importance: *The World Series is a baseball classic.* **6** of the literature, art, and life of ancient Greece and Rome. **7 the classics,** the literature of ancient Greece and Rome. 1,2,5,7 *n.*, 3,4,6 *adj.*

clas si cal (klas′ə kəl), **1** of or having to do with the literature, art, and life of ancient Greece and Rome: *Classical languages include ancient Greek and the Latin of the ancient Romans.* **2** excellent; first-class. **3** simple and fine in form. **4** of high musical quality and enjoyed especially by serious students of music. Symphonies, concertos, and operas are considered classical music. *adj.*

clas si fi a ble (klas′ə fī′ə bəl), able to be classified. *adj.*

clas si fi ca tion (klas′ə fə kā′shən), arrangement in classes or groups; grouping according to some system: *the classification of books in a library.* *n.*

clas si fied (klas′ə fīd), **1** sorted or arranged in classes. A classified telephone directory lists names according to classes of business, services, and professions. **2** (of certain public documents of the United States) having a classification as secret, confidential, or restricted. **3** secret: *The airplane was on a classified flight.* *adj.*

classified ad, want ad.

clas si fy (klas′ə fī), arrange in classes or groups; group according to some system: *Botanists have attempted to classify all plants.* *v.*, **clas si fied, clas si fy ing.**

class mate (klas′māt′), member of the same class in school. *n.*

class room (klas′rüm′ *or* klas′rům′), room in which classes are held; schoolroom. *n.*

clat ter (klat′ər), **1** a confused noise like that of many plates being struck together: *The clatter in the cafeteria made it hard for us to hear one another talk.* **2** move or fall with confused noise; make a confused noise: *The horse's hoofs clattered over the stones.* 1 *n.*, 2 *v.* —**clat′ter er,** *n.*

clause (klôz), **1** part of a sentence having a subject and predicate. In "He came before we left," "He came" is a main clause that can stand alone as a sentence, and "before we left" is a subordinate clause that depends upon the main clause for completion of its meaning. **2** a single provision of a law, treaty, or any other written agreement: *A clause in our lease says we may not keep a dog in this building.* n. [*Clause* came into English about 750 years ago from French *clause,* and can be traced back to Latin *claudere,* meaning "to close."]

claus tro pho bi a (klô′strə fō′bē ə), an abnormal fear of enclosed spaces: *Elevators give me claustrophobia.* n.

clav i chord (klav′ə kôrd), a musical instrument with strings and a keyboard. The piano developed from it. n.

clav i cle (klav′ə kəl), collarbone. n. [*Clavicle* comes from Latin *clavicula,* meaning "a small key." The bone was called this because of its shape.]

cla vier (klə vir′), 1 keyboard or set of keys of a piano, organ, etc. 2 any musical instrument with a keyboard. The harpsichord and piano are two kinds of claviers. n.

claw (klô), 1 a sharp, hooked nail on a bird's or animal's foot. 2 foot with such sharp, hooked nails. 3 the pincers of a lobster, crab, etc. 4 anything like a claw. The part of a hammer used for pulling nails is the claw. 5 scratch, tear, seize, or pull with claws or hands: *The kitten was clawing the rug.* 1-4 n., 5 v. —**claw′like′,** adj.

clay (klā), a stiff, sticky kind of earth, that can be easily shaped when wet and hardens when it is dried or baked. Bricks, dishes, and vases may be made from clay. n. —**clay′like′,** adj.

Clay (klā), **Henry,** 1777-1852, American statesman. n.

clay ey (klā′ē), 1 of, like, or containing clay. 2 covered or smeared with clay. adj., **clay i er, clay i est.**

clay pigeon, a saucerlike clay target thrown in the air or released from the trap in trapshooting.

clean (klēn), 1 free from dirt or filth; not soiled or stained: *clean clothes. Soap and water make us clean.* 2 guiltless; free from wrong: *a politician with a clean record.* 3 having clean habits: *Cats are clean animals.* 4 make clean: *clean a room. Washing cleans clothes.* 5 do cleaning: *I am going to clean this morning.* 6 clear, even, or regular: *a clean cut with no ragged edges, the clean features of a handsome face.* 7 well-shaped; trim: *an airplane with clean, sleek lines.* 8 clever; skillful: *a clean performance.* 9 complete; entire; total: *After leaving the company, she made a clean break with everyone she had known there.* 10 completely; entirely; totally: *The horse jumped clean over the brook.* 1-3,6-9 adj., 4,5 v., 10 adv.

clean out, 1 make clean by emptying: *Clean out your desk.* 2 empty; use up: *The children cleaned out a whole box of cookies.* 3 SLANG. deprive of money: *I was cleaned out in the card game.*

clean up, 1 make clean by removing dirt, rubbish, etc.: *clean up a campsite.* 2 put in order: *clean up a cluttered drawer.* 3 INFORMAL. finish; complete: *Let's clean up this work.*

clean-cut (klēn′kut′), 1 having clear, sharp outlines; distinct; definite: *a clean-cut profile.* 2 having a neat and wholesome look: *a clean-cut young man.* adj.

clean er (klē′nər), 1 person whose work is keeping buildings, windows, or other objects clean. 2 anything that removes dirt, grease, or stains. 3 dry cleaner. n.

clean li ness (klen′lē nis), a being clean; cleanness: *Cleanliness is good for health.* n.

clean ly[1] (klen′lē), clean: *Our cat is a cleanly animal.* adj., **clean li er, clean li est.**

clean ly[2] (klēn′lē), in a clean manner: *The butcher's knife cut cleanly through the meat.* adv.

cleanse (klenz), 1 make clean: *cleanse a wound before bandaging.* 2 make pure: *cleanse the soul.* v., **cleansed, cleans ing.** —**cleans′a ble,** adj.

cleans er (klen′zər), substance for cleaning or scouring. n.

clean up (klēn′up′), 1 a cleaning up: *The cleanup of the school auditorium took an hour.* 2 (in baseball) batting fourth in the lineup: *the cleanup hitter.* 1 n., 2 adj.

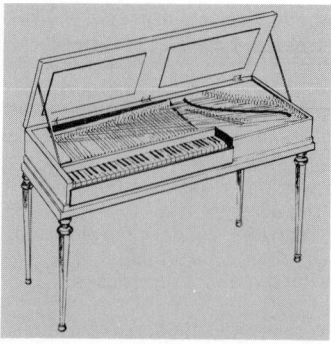

clavichord
made in Germany
about 1760

clear (klir), 1 not cloudy, misty, or hazy; bright; light: *A clear sky is free of clouds.* 2 easy to see through; transparent: *clear glass.* 3 easily heard, seen, or understood; plain; distinct: *a clear voice, a clear view, a clear account of the accident.* 4 free from blemishes: *a clear skin.* 5 sure; certain: *It is clear that it is going to rain.* 6 make clean and free; get clear: *clear land of trees.* 7 become clear: *It rained and then it cleared.* 8 remove to leave a space clear: *clear the dishes from the table.* 9 pass by or over without touching: *The horse cleared the fence.* 10 free from blame or guilt; innocent: *a clear conscience.* 11 make free from blame or guilt; prove to be innocent: *The jury's verdict cleared the accused.* 12 free from debts or charges: *He made a clear profit after taking money out to pay taxes and expenses.* 13 make as profit free from debts or charges: *The company cleared a million dollars last year.* 14 in a clear manner; completely; entirely: *We could see clear to the bottom of the lake.* 1-5,10,12 adj., 6-9,11,13 v., 14 adv. —**clear′er,** n. —**clear′ly,** adv. —**clear′ness,** n.

clear away or **clear off,** 1 remove to leave a space clear: *I cleared away the snow with a shovel.* 2 disappear; go away: *The fog cleared away.*

clear out, 1 make clear by throwing out or emptying: *I cleared out my closet.* 2 INFORMAL. go away; leave: *The audience cleared out of the theater quickly.*

clear up, 1 make or become clear: *Stay indoors until the weather clears up.* 2 explain: *She cleared up our problems by telling us what we had done wrong.*

in the clear, free of guilt or blame; innocent: *The testimony of the witness puts the suspect in the clear.*

clear ance (klir′əns), 1 act of clearing: *Clearance of the theater was quick during the fire.* 2 a clear space; distance between things that pass by each other without touching: *There was only a foot of clearance between the top of the truck and the roof of the tunnel.* 3 a certifying that a person considered for a position of trust is reliable. 4 sale of goods at reduced prices. n.

clear-cut (klir′kut′), 1 having clear, sharp outlines: *a face with clear-cut features.* 2 clear; definite; distinct: *She had clear-cut ideas about what she wanted.* adj.

clear ing (klir′ing), an open space of cleared land in a forest or in an area of dense undergrowth. n.

cleat (klēt), 1 strip of wood or iron fastened across anything for support or for sure footing: *The gangway had cleats to keep the passengers from slipping.* 2 piece of wood or iron used for securing ropes or lines to a flagpole, a mast, a dock, etc. 3 piece of metal, wood, or stiff leather

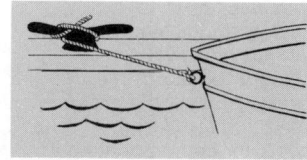

cleat (def. 2)

attached to the sole or heel of a shoe to prevent slipping. *n.*

cleav age (klē′vij), **1** a cleaving or a being cleft; split; division. **2** the property of a crystal or rock of splitting along planes: *Slate shows a marked cleavage and can easily be separated into layers. n.*

cleave[1] (klēv), **1** cut, divide, or split open: *A blow of the whale's tail caused the whaling boat to cleave in two.* **2** pass through; pierce; penetrate: *The airplane swept across the sky, cleaving the clouds.* *v.*, **cleft** or **cleaved** or **clove**, **cleft** or **cleaved** or **clo ven**, **cleav ing.** —**cleav′a ble,** *adj.*

cleave[2] (klēv), hold fast; cling; adhere: *cleave to an old-fashioned idea.* *v.*, **cleaved, cleav ing.**

cleav er (klē′vər), a cutting tool with a heavy blade and a short handle. A butcher uses a cleaver to chop through meat or bone. *n.*

clef (klef), symbol in music indicating the pitch of the notes on a staff. *n.*

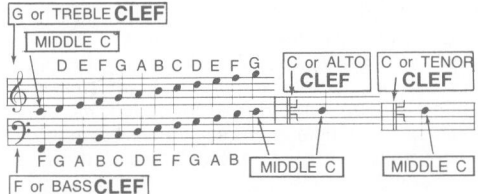

cleft (kleft), **1** a past tense and a past participle of **cleave**[1]. *A blow of the ax cleft the log in two.* **2** split; divided: *a cleft stick.* **3** space or opening made by splitting; crack: *a cleft in the rocks.* **1** *v.*, **2** *adj.*, **3** *n.*

cleft palate, a narrow opening running lengthwise in the roof of the mouth, caused by failure of the two parts of the palate to join before birth.

clem a tis (klem′ə tis), a climbing vine with clusters of white, red, pink, blue, or purple flowers. *n.*, *pl.* **clem a tis es** or **clem a tis.**

clem en cy (klem′ən sē), **1** gentleness in the use of power or authority; mercy: *The government showed clemency to the defeated rebels.* **2** mildness: *The clemency of the weather allowed them to live outdoors. n.*

Clem ens (klem′ənz), **Samuel Langhorne,** the real name of **Mark Twain.** *n.*

clem ent (klem′ənt), **1** merciful toward those in one's power. **2** mild: *Hawaii usually has clement weather. adj.*

clench (klench), **1** close tightly together: *clench one's teeth, clench one's fist.* **2** grasp firmly: *I clenched the bat and swung at the ball.* **3** a firm grasp; tight grip: *the clench of a hand.* **4** clinch (a nail, staple, etc.). **1,2,4** *v.*, **3** *n.*, *pl.* **clench es.** —**clench′er,** *n.*

Cle o pat ra (klē′ə pat′rə *or* klē′ə pä′trə), 69?-30 B.C., last queen of ancient Egypt, from 47 to 30 B.C. *n.*

cler gy (klėr′jē), persons ordained for religious work; ministers, pastors, priests, and rabbis. *n.*, *pl.* **cler gies.**

cler gy man (klėr′jē mən), member of the clergy; a minister, pastor, priest, or rabbi. *n.*, *pl.* **cler gy men.**

cler ic (kler′ik), clergyman. *n.*

cler i cal (kler′ə kəl), **1** of a clerk or clerks; for clerks: *Keeping records and typing letters are clerical jobs in an office.* **2** of a clergyman or the clergy: *clerical duties, clerical robes. adj.* —**cler′i cal ly,** *adv.*

clerk (klėrk), **1** person employed in a store or shop to sell goods; salesperson in a store. **2** person employed in an office to file records, type letters, or keep accounts. **3** work as a clerk: *I clerk in a drugstore after school.* **4** a public official who keeps the records and superintends the routine business of a court of law, legislature, town or county government, etc. **1,2,4** *n.*, **3** *v.*

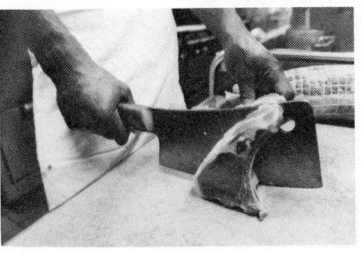

cleaver

Cleve land (klēv′lənd), **1** city in NE Ohio, on Lake Erie. **2** **(Stephen) Grover,** 1837-1908, the 22nd and 24th president of the United States, from 1885 to 1889 and from 1893 to 1897. *n.*

clev er (klev′ər), **1** having a quick mind; bright; intelligent: *a clever student.* **2** skillful in doing some particular thing: *clever at working with wood.* **3** showing skill or intelligence: *The magician did a clever trick. Her answer to the riddle was clever. adj.* —**clev′er ly,** *adv.* —**clev′er ness,** *n.*

clew (klü), clue. *n.*

cliché—a conversation in clichés

cli ché (klē shā′), expression or idea worn out by long use. *n.*, *pl.* **cli chés.**

click (klik), **1** a short, sharp sound like that of a key turning in a lock: *We heard a click as the dime went down the coin slot.* **2** make or cause to make such a sound: *The key clicked in the lock. I clicked my tongue.* **3** SLANG. come to an understanding; be in harmony: *I clicked with them from the start.* **4** SLANG. be successful: *The new play clicked with the critics.* **1** *n.*, **2-4** *v.*

cli ent (klī′ənt), **1** person for whom a lawyer, accountant, or other professional person acts. **2** customer. *n.*

cli en tele (klī′ən tel′), **1** clients as a group. **2** customers. *n.*

cliff (klif), a very steep slope of rock, clay, etc. *n.* —**cliff′like′,** *adj.*

cliff dweller, member of a group of prehistoric people who lived in the southwestern United States in caves or houses built in a cliff. The cliff dwellers were ancestors of the Pueblos.

cli mate (klī′mit), **1** the kind of weather a place has. Climate includes conditions of heat and cold, moisture and dryness, clearness and cloudiness, wind and calm. **2** region with certain conditions of heat and cold, rainfall, wind, sunlight, etc.: *to live in a dry climate.* **3** condition or feeling that exists at some time: *The climate of public opinion favored tax reforms. n.*

cli mat ic (klī mat′ik), of or having to do with climate. *adj.* —**cli mat′i cal ly,** *adv.*

cli max (klī′maks), **1** the highest point of interest; most exciting part: *A visit to the Grand Canyon was the climax of our vacation.* **2** bring or come to a climax: *Her election to the Senate climaxed a long career in politics.* **3** series of ideas arranged so that there is a steady rise of force and interest. **1,3** *n., pl.* **cli max es; 2** *v.*

WORD HISTORY

climax

Climax was borrowed from Latin *climax,* which came from Greek *klimax,* originally meaning "ladder."

climb (klīm), **1** go up, especially by using the hands or feet, or both; ascend: *She climbed the stairs quickly.* **2** go in any direction, especially with the help of the hands: *climb over a fence, climb down a ladder.* **3** move upward; rise: *Smoke climbed slowly from the chimney. The price of gasoline has climbed during the past year.* **4** grow upward by holding on or twining around: *Ivy and honeysuckle climbed over the wall.* **5** a climbing: *Our climb up the mountain took ten hours.* **6** place to be climbed: *The path ended in a difficult climb.* **1-4** *v.,* **5,6** *n.* —**climb′a ble,** *adj.*

climb er (klī′mər), **1** person or thing that climbs. **2** a climbing plant; vine. *n.*

clime (klīm), **1** region. **2** climate. *n.*

clinch (klinch), **1** fasten (a driven nail, a bolt, etc.) firmly by bending over the point that sticks out. **2** fix firmly; settle decisively: *A deposit of five dollars clinched our bargain.* **3** grasp one another tightly in boxing or wrestling; grapple. **4** act of clinching: *The boxers went into a clinch.* **1-3** *v.,* **4** *n., pl.* **clinch es.** [*Clinch* is a different form of *clench.*]

clinch er (klin′chər), INFORMAL. a decisive argument, statement, etc. *n.*

cling (kling), stick or hold fast; adhere: *A vine clings to the wall. Wet clothes cling to the body. The child clung to its parent's hand. People sometimes cling to tradition. v.,* **clung, cling ing.**

clin ic (klin′ik), **1** place connected with a hospital or medical school where people can receive medical treatment, usually free or at low cost. **2** place for medical treatment or study of certain people or diseases: *The children's clinic is open during school hours.* **3** place where practical instruction on any subject is given: *a football clinic, a reading clinic.* **4** practical instruction of medical students by examining or treating patients in the presence of the students. *n.*

clin i cal (klin′ə kəl), **1** of or having to do with a clinic. **2** used or performed in a sickroom: *Doctors learn clinical procedure. adj.* —**clin′i cal ly,** *adv.*

clink (klingk), **1** a light, sharp, ringing sound like that of drinking glasses hitting together. **2** make or cause to make this sound: *The spoon clinked in the glass.* **1** *n.,* **2** *v.*

clink er (kling′kər), a large, rough cinder. *n.*

clip[1] (klip), **1** trim with shears, scissors, or clippers; cut short; cut: *A sheep's fleece is clipped off to get wool.* **2** cut the hair or fleece of: *Our dog is clipped every summer.* **3** act of clipping: *My hair needs a clip around the back of my neck.* **4** cut out of a magazine, newspaper, etc.: *She clipped the cartoon and passed it around the class.* **5** piece clipped from a reel of film or videotape, a newspaper, magazine, etc. **6** INFORMAL. a fast motion: *Our bus passed through the village at quite a clip.* **7** move fast: *The car clipped down the road at seventy miles an hour.* **8** INFORMAL. hit or punch sharply: *The boxer clipped his opponent on the jaw.* **9** INFORMAL. a sharp blow or punch. **1,2,4,7,8** *v.,* **clipped, clip ping; 3,5,6,9** *n.* [*Clip*[1] came into English about 800 years ago from Icelandic *klippa.*]

clip[2] (klip), **1** hold tight; fasten: *The teacher clipped the papers together.* **2** something used for clipping things together. A paper clip is made of a piece of bent wire. **3** a metal holder for cartridges used in some firearms. **1** *v.,* **clipped, clip ping; 2,3** *n.* [*Clip*[2] comes from Old English *clyppan,* meaning "to encircle, embrace."]

clip board (klip′bôrd′), board with a heavy spring clip at one end for holding papers while writing. *n.*

clip per (klip′ər), **1** person who clips or cuts. **2** Often, **clippers,** *pl.* tool for cutting: *hair clippers, a nail clipper.* **3** a large sailing ship built and rigged for speed. *n.*

clip ping (klip′ing), **1** article, picture, or advertisement cut out of a newspaper, magazine, etc. **2** piece cut off from or out of something else. *n.*

clique (klēk *or* klik), **1** a small, exclusive group of people within a larger group. **2** form or associate in a clique. **1** *n.,* **2** *v.,* **cliqued, cli quing.**

cli quish (klē′kish *or* klik′ish), **1** like a clique. **2** tending to form a clique. *adj.* —**cli′quish ly,** *adv.* —**cli′quish ness,** *n.*

clk., 1 clerk. **2** clock.

cloak (klōk), **1** a loose outer garment with or without sleeves. **2** cover with a cloak. **3** anything that covers or conceals: *They hid their dislike of us behind a cloak of friendship.* **4** cover up; conceal: *I tried to cloak my fear by whistling and pretending to be unafraid.* **1,3** *n.,* **2,4** *v.*

cloak room (klōk′rüm′ *or* klōk′rum′), room where coats, hats, etc., can be left for a time; coatroom. *n.*

clob ber (klob′ər), SLANG. **1** strike or beat heavily. **2** defeat severely. *v.*

clock[1] (klok), **1** instrument for measuring and showing time. A clock is not made to be carried around as a watch is. **2** measure or record the time of; time: *I clocked the runners with a stopwatch to see who was the fastest.* **1** *n.,* **2** *v.* [*Clock*[1] came into English about 600 years ago from Dutch *clocke,* meaning "clock, bell," and can be traced back to Latin *clocca,* meaning "bell."] —**clock′er,** *n.* —**clock′like′,** *adj.*

clock[2] (klok), an ornamental pattern on the side of a stocking or sock, extending from the ankle up. *n.*

clock wise (klok′wīz′), in the direction in which the hands of a clock move; from left to right: *Turn the key clockwise to unlock the door* (*adv.*). *He opened the faucet with a clockwise turn* (*adj.*). *adv., adj.*

clock work (klok′werk′), **1** the machinery by which a clock is run. **2** any similar machinery, consisting of gears, wheels, and springs. Mechanical toys are run by clockwork. *n.*

like clockwork, with great regularity and smoothness: *The launching of the rocket went off like clockwork.*

clod (klod), **1** lump of earth. **2** a stupid person; blockhead. *n.*

clod dish (klod′ish), like a clod; stupid. *adj.* —**clod′dish ness,** *n.*

clog (klog), **1** fill up; choke up: *Grease clogged the drain.* **2** hinder; hold back: *An accident clogged traffic.* **3** anything that hinders. **4** shoe with a thick, wooden sole. 1,2 *v.*, **clogged, clog ging;** 3,4 *n.*

clois ter (kloi′stər), **1** a covered walk, often along the wall of a building, with a row of pillars on the open side or sides. A cloister is sometimes built around the courtyard of a monastery, church, or college building. **2** place of religious retirement; convent or monastery. **3** a quiet place shut away from the world. **4** shut away in a quiet place: *He cloistered himself in his room to work.* 1-3 *n.,* 4 *v.*

cloister (def. 1)

clomp (klomp), walk heavily and clumsily; clump. *v.*

clone (klōn), **1** group of plants or animals produced from a single ancestor without sexual reproduction. **2** a living being with the same genes as another, from which it has been produced asexually. **3** reproduce without sexual reproduction. 1,2 *n.,* 3 *v.* **cloned, clon ing.** [*Clone* comes from Greek *klōn,* meaning "twig."]

close¹ (klōz), **1** bring together or move the parts of so as to leave no opening; shut: *Close the door. The sleepy child's eyes are closing.* **2** stop up; fill; block: *close a crack in the wall with plaster.* **3** bring together; come together: *The troops closed ranks.* **4** bring or come to an end; finish: *The meeting closed with a speech by the president.* **5** an end; finish: *She spoke at the close of the meeting.* 1-4 *v.,* **closed, clos ing;** 5 *n.* —**clos′a ble,** *adj.* —**clos′er,** *n.*

close down, shut completely; stop: *The factory closed down because it had no orders from customers.*

close in, come near and shut in on all sides: *The zoo keepers closed in on the escaped tiger.*

close out, sell in order to get rid of: *The store closed out the old models in a special sale.*

close up, 1 shut completely; stop up; block: *The windows of the warehouse were closed up with brick.* **2** bring or come nearer together.

close² (klōs), **1** with little space between; near together; near: *These two houses are close.* **2** fitting tightly; tight; narrow: *They live in very close quarters.* **3** having its parts near together; compact: *This sweater has a close weave.* **4** intimate; dear: *We are close friends.* **5** careful; exact: *You need to take closer measurements before ordering the lumber.* **6** thorough; strict: *Pay close attention.* **7** having little fresh air; stuffy: *With the windows shut, the room was hot and close.* **8** near the surface; short: *a close haircut.* **9** stingy: *He is as close as a miser with his money.* **10** nearly equal: *The last game was a close contest.* **11** not fond of talking; not open; reserved: *She is very close about her own affairs.* **12** near: *The two farms lie close together. The end of the year is drawing close.* 1-11 *adj.,* **clos er, clos est;** 12 *adv.* —**close′ly,** *adv.* —**close′ness,** *n.*

close call (klōs), INFORMAL. a narrow escape.

close fist ed (klōs′fis′tid), stingy; miserly. *adj.*

close mouthed (klōs′mouᴛHd′ *or* klōs′moutht′), not fond of talking; reserved; reticent. *adj.*

clos et (kloz′it), **1** a small room for storing clothes or household supplies. **2** shut up in a private room for a secret talk: *We were closeted with our lawyer for over an hour.* 1 *n.,* 2 *v.*

close-up (klōs′up′), **1** picture taken with a camera at close range. **2** a close view. *n.*

clo sure (klō′zhər), **1** a closing or a being closed: *the closure of a shop.* **2** thing that closes. **3** cloture. *n.*

clot (klot), **1** a half-solid lump; thickened mass: *A clot of blood formed in the cut and stopped the bleeding.* **2** form into clots; coagulate: *Blood clots when it is exposed to the air.* 1 *n.,* 2 *v.,* **clot ted, clot ting.**

cloth (klôth), **1** material made from wool, cotton, silk, rayon, or other fiber, by weaving, knitting, or rolling and pressing. **2** piece of this material used for a special purpose: *a cloth for the table.* **3** **the cloth,** clergymen; the clergy. *n., pl.* **cloths** (klôᴛHz *or* klôths).

clothe (klōᴛH), **1** put clothes on; cover with clothes; dress: *We clothed the child warmly in a heavy sweater and pants.* **2** provide with clothes: *It costs quite a bit to clothe a family of six.* **3** cover: *The sun clothes the earth with light.* **4** provide; furnish; equip: *Congress is clothed with the authority to make laws.* **5** express: *Her ideas are clothed in simple words.* *v.,* **clothed** or **clad, cloth ing.**

clothes (klōz *or* klōᴛHz), **1** coverings for a person's body: *I bought some new clothes for my trip.* **2** bedclothes. *n.pl.*

clothes line (klōz′līn′), rope or wire to hang clothes on to dry or air them. *n.*

clothes pin (klōz′pin′), a wooden or plastic clip to hold clothes on a clothesline. *n.*

cloth ier (klō′ᴛHyər), **1** seller or maker of clothing. **2** seller of cloth. *n.*

cloth ing (klō′ᴛHing), **1** clothes. **2** covering. *n.*

clo ture (klō′chər), a limiting of debate by a legislature in order to get an immediate vote on the question being discussed; closure. *n.*

cloud (kloud), **1** mass of tiny drops of water or ice particles floating in the air high above the earth. Clouds may be white, rounded heaps, fleecy streamers, or dark, almost black, masses. **2** mass of smoke or dust in the air. **3** cover with a cloud or clouds: *A mist clouded our view.* **4** grow or become cloudy: *The sky clouded over. My eyes clouded with tears.* **5** a great number of things moving close together: *A cloud of locusts descended upon the wheat field.* **6** anything that darkens or dims: *A cloud of disappointment was reflected in his face.* **7** darken; dim; make or become gloomy: *a face clouded with anger.* **8** a cause of suspicion or disgrace: *The former convict found it hard to get a job because a cloud always hung over his reputation.* **9** bring under suspicion or disgrace. 1,2,5,6,8 *n.,* 3,4,7,9 *v.* —**cloud′like′,** *adj.*

in the clouds, 1 unrealistic or fanciful; not practical. **2** daydreaming; absent-minded.

under a cloud, under suspicion.

cloud burst (kloud′bėrst′), a sudden, violent rainfall. *n.*

cloud i ness (klou′dē nis), cloudy condition. *n.*

cloud less (kloud′lis), without a cloud; clear and bright; sunny: *a cloudless sky. adj.* —**cloud′less ly,** *adv.* —**cloud′less ness,** *n.*

cloud y (klou′dē), **1** covered with clouds; having clouds in it: *a cloudy sky.* **2** not clear: *The stream is cloudy with mud.* **3** not carefully thought out; confused; indistinct: *cloudy ideas.* **4** gloomy; frowning: *The unhappy child had a cloudy expression. adj.,* **cloud i er, cloud i est.** —**cloud′i ly,** *adv.*

clout (klout), **1** INFORMAL. hit with the hand; rap; knock. **2** INFORMAL. a rap or knock; cuff. 1 *v.*, 2 *n.*

clove¹ (klōv), **1** a strong, fragrant spice made from the dried flower buds of a tropical tree. **2** the dried flower bud. *n.*

WORD HISTORY

clove¹

Clove¹ came into English about 750 years ago from French *clou*, originally meaning "nail," which came from Latin *clavus*. The bud was called this because it is shaped like a nail.

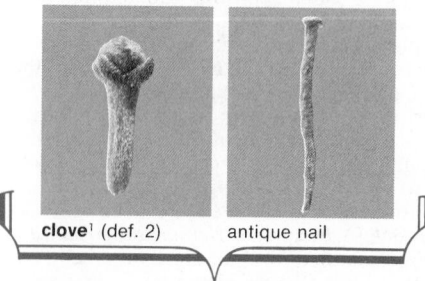

clove¹ (def. 2)   antique nail

clove² (klōv), a small, separate section of a bulb: *a clove of garlic. n.* [*Clove²* comes from Old English *clufu*.]

clove³ (klōv), cleft; a past tense of **cleave¹**. *v.*

clo ven (klō′vən), **1** cleft; a past participle of **cleave¹**. **2** split; divided. Cows and sheep have cloven hoofs. 1 *v.*, 2 *adj.*

clo ver (klō′vər), a low plant related to the pea with leaves having three leaflets and sweet-smelling rounded heads of small red, white, yellow, or purple flowers. Clover is grown as food for horses and cattle and to improve the soil. *n.*

in clover, enjoying a life of pleasure and luxury without work or worry.

clo ver leaf (klō′vər lēf′), intersection of two highways, with one passing over the other. A series of curving ramps in the shape of a four-leaf clover permits traffic to move from one highway to the other without having to cross in front of other traffic. *n., pl.* **clo ver leafs, clo ver leaves** (klō′vər lēvz′).

cloverleaf

clown (kloun), **1** performer in a circus, carnival, etc., who makes people laugh by wearing funny costumes and makeup and by playing tricks and jokes. **2** act like a clown; play tricks and jokes; act silly. **3** person who acts like a clown; silly person. 1,3 *n.*, 2 *v.*

clown ish (kloun′ish), like a clown; like a clown's: *clownish behavior. adj.* —**clown′ish ly,** *adv.* —**clown′ish ness,** *n.*

cloy (kloi), make or become weary by too much of anything pleasant. *v.* —**cloy′ing ly,** *adv.* —**cloy′ing ness,** *n.*

club (klub), **1** a heavy stick of wood, thicker at one end, used as a weapon. **2** stick or bat used in some games to hit a ball: *golf clubs.* **3** beat or hit with a club or something similar. **4** group of people joined together for some special purpose: *a tennis club, a yacht club, a nature-study club.* **5** building or rooms used by a club. **6** join together for some special purpose: *The neighborhood children clubbed together to put on a show.* **7** figure shaped like this: ♣. **8** a playing card with one or more black, club-shaped figures. **9** clubs, *pl.* suit of such playing cards. 1,2,4,5,7-9 *n.*, 3,6 *v.*, **clubbed, club bing.**

club foot (klub′fut′), **1** a deformed foot, short and distorted. **2** deformity of the foot caused by faulty development before birth. *n., pl.* **club feet** (klub′fēt′).

club house (klub′hous′), building used by a club. *n., pl.* **club hous es** (klub′hou′ziz).

club moss, a flowerless plant that grows along the ground and looks much like a vine covered with pine needles.

club soda, soda water.

cluck (kluk), **1** the sound that a hen makes in calling to her chicks. **2** make this sound. **3** SLANG. a simple-minded person. 1,3 *n.*, 2 *v.*

clover

clue (klü), **1** fact or object which aids in solving a mystery or problem: *The police could find no fingerprints or other clues to help them solve the robbery.* **2** show (something) by means of a clue. **3** INFORMAL. give a clue to: *The note clued us to what was going on.* 1 *n.*, 2,3 *v.*, **clued, clu ing** or **clue ing.**

clump (klump), **1** number of things of the same kind growing or grouped together; cluster: *The girl hid in a clump of bushes.* **2** lump or mass: *a clump of earth.* **3** sound of heavy, clumsy walking. **4** walk with a heavy, clumsy, noisy tread; clomp: *The weary hikers clumped along in their heavy boots.* **5** form a clump; form into a clump. 1-3 *n.*, 4,5 *v.*

clump y (klum′pē), full of clumps. *adj.*

clum si ly (klum′zə lē), in a clumsy manner; awkwardly. *adv.*

clum si ness (klum′zē nis), a being clumsy; awkwardness. *n.*

clum sy (klum′zē), **1** awkward in moving; not graceful or skillful: *The cast on my broken leg made me walk in a clumsy manner.* **2** awkwardly done; tactless: *a clumsy reply.* **3** not well shaped or well made: *The stage for the puppet show was a clumsy structure made out of old boxes. adj.*, **clum si er, clum si est.**

clung (klung), past tense and past participle of **cling.** *The child clung to his sister. Mud had clung to my boots. v.*

clus ter (klus′tər), **1** number of things of the same kind growing or grouped together: *a cluster of grapes, a little cluster of houses in the valley.* **2** any group of persons or things: *Protesters stood in a cluster before the mayor's house.* **3** form into a cluster; gather in a group: *The students clustered around their teacher.* 1,2 *n.,* 3 *v.*

clutch[1] (kluch), **1** a tight grasp; hold: *I lost my clutch on the rope and fell.* **2** grasp tightly: *I clutched the railing to keep my balance.* **3** seize eagerly; snatch: *clutch at an opportunity.* **4** Often, **clutches,** *pl.* **a** a grasping claw, paw, hand, etc.: *The fish wiggled out of the hungry bear's clutches and swam away.* **b** control; power: *That country is in the clutches of a dictator.* **5** device in a machine for transmitting motion from one shaft to another or for disconnecting related moving parts. The clutch in an automobile is used to connect the engine with the transmission or to disconnect it from the transmission. **6** lever or pedal that operates this device. 1,4-6 *n., pl.* **clutch es;** 2,3 *v.*

clutch[2] (kluch), nest of eggs. *n., pl.* **clutch es.**

clut ter (klut′ər), **1** number of things scattered or left in disorder; litter: *It was hard to find the lost pen in the clutter of his room.* **2** litter with things in confusion: *Her desk drawer was cluttered with old papers.* 1 *n.,* 2 *v.*

Cly tem nes tra (klī′təm nes′trə), (in Greek legends) the wife of Agamemnon. She killed him on his return from Troy and was afterwards slain by their son Orestes. *n.*

Cm, symbol for curium.

cm., centimeter or centimeters.

co-, *prefix.* **1** with; together: *Coexist = exist together or exist with.* **2** joint: *Coauthor = joint author.* **3** equally: *Coextensive = equally extensive.*

Co, symbol for cobalt.

CO, Colorado (used with postal Zip Code).

Co., **1** Company. **2** County.

c/o or **c.o.,** in care of.

coach
(def. 1)

coach (kōch), **1** a large, usually closed carriage with seats inside and often on top, pulled by horses. In former times, most coaches carried passengers, and sometimes mail, along a regular route, stopping for meals and fresh horses. **2** a passenger car of a railroad train. **3** bus. **4** a class of passenger accommodations on a commercial aircraft at lower rates than first class. **5** person who teaches or trains athletic teams, singers, etc.: *a swimming coach, a drama coach.* **6** teach or train: *She coaches Olympic swimmers. He coaches at a university.* 1-5 *n., pl.* **coach es;** 6 *v.* [*Coach* came into English over 400 years ago from French *coche,* and can be traced back to *Kocs,* a village in Hungary, where it originated. This word was first used in a phrase meaning "wagon of Kocs."]

coach dog, Dalmatian.

coach man (kōch′mən), man whose work is driving a coach or carriage. *n., pl.* **coach men.**

co ag u late (kō ag′yə lāt), change from a liquid to a thickened mass; thicken: *Cooking coagulates the whites of eggs. v.,* **co ag u lat ed, co ag u lat ing.**

co ag u la tion (kō ag′yə lā′shən), **1** act of coagulating. If coagulation of the blood does not take place in a cut

or wound, the injured person may bleed to death. **2** a coagulated mass; clot. *n.*

coal (kōl), **1** a black mineral that burns and gives off heat, composed mostly of carbon. It is formed from partly decayed vegetable matter under great pressure in the earth. Anthracite and bituminous coal are two kinds of coal. **2** piece or pieces of this mineral for burning: *a bag of coal.* **3** supply or be supplied with coal: *The ship stopped just long enough to coal.* **4** piece of burning wood, coal, etc.; ember: *The big log had burned down to a few glowing coals.* 1,2,4 *n.,* 3 *v.*

co a lesce (kō′ə les′), **1** grow together. **2** unite into one body, mass, party, etc.; combine: *The thirteen colonies coalesced to form a nation. v.,* **co a lesced, co a lesc ing.**

co a les cence (kō′ə les′ns), **1** a growing together. **2** union; combination. *n.*

coal gas, **1** gas made from coal, used for heating and lighting. **2** gas given off by burning coal.

co a li tion (kō′ə lish′ən), **1** union; combination. **2** alliance of statesmen, political parties, etc., for some special purpose. In wartime several countries may form a temporary coalition against a common enemy. *n.*

coal oil, **1** kerosene. **2** petroleum.

coal scuttle, bucket for holding or carrying coal.

coal tar, a black, sticky substance left after bituminous coal has been distilled to make coal gas. Coal tar is used to make roofing and paving materials and is a source of chemicals used in dyes, medicines, paints, perfumes, etc.

coarse (kôrs), **1** made up of fairly large parts; not fine: *coarse sand.* **2** heavy or rough in looks or texture: *The old fisherman had coarse, weathered features. Burlap is a coarse cloth.* **3** common; poor; inferior: *coarse food.* **4** not delicate or refined; crude; vulgar: *coarse manners. adj.,* **coars er, coars est. —coarse′ly,** *adv.* **—coarse′ness,** *n.*

coars en (kôr′sən), make or become coarse: *skin coarsened by wind and sun. v.*

coast (kōst), **1** land along the sea; seashore: *Maine has a rocky coast.* **2** sail along or near the coast of: *The disabled ship coasted the island, looking for a harbor to make repairs.* **3** sail from port to port along a coast. **4** ride or slide without the use of effort or power: *You can coast downhill on a sled. She shut off the engine and the car coasted into the driveway.* **5** move or advance with little effort or exertion: *The test was so easy that I was able to just coast through it.* 1 *n.,* 2-5 *v.*

coast al (kō′stl), of the coast; near or along a coast: *coastal shipping. adj.*

coast er (kō′stər), **1** person or thing that coasts. **2** ship that sails or trades along a coast. **3** sled to coast on. **4** a little tray for holding a glass or bottle. A coaster protects surfaces of furniture from moisture. *n.*

coaster brake, brake in the hub of the rear wheel of a bicycle, worked by pushing back on the pedals.

coast guard, **1** group whose work is protecting lives and property and preventing smuggling along the coast of a country. **2** member of any such group. **3 Coast Guard,** the government organization whose work is protecting lives and property and preventing smuggling along the coasts of the United States. It is under the Navy Department in wartime and under the Department of Transportation in peacetime.

coast line (kōst′līn′), outline of a coast. *n.*

coat (kōt), **1** an outer garment of cloth, fur, etc., with sleeves: *a winter coat. Father wears a coat and tie to work.* **2** a natural outer covering: *a dog's coat of hair, the silky coat of a kitten.* **3** a thin layer covering a surface: *a coat of paint.* **4** cover with a thin layer: *The old books were coated with dust. The floor is coated with varnish.* 1-3 *n.,* 4 *v.* —**coat′less,** *adj.*

coat ing (kō′ting), layer covering a surface: *a coating of dust. n.*

coat of arms, shield, or drawing of a shield, bearing symbols or designs which show the marks of distinction of a noble family, a government, a city, etc. In the Middle Ages, each knight or lord had his own coat of arms. *pl.* **coats of arms.**

coat of mail, garment made of metal rings or plates, worn as armor. *pl.* **coats of mail.**

coat room (kōt′rüm′ *or* kōt′rùm′), cloakroom. *n.*

co au thor (kō ô′thər), a joint author. *n.*

coax (kōks), **1** persuade by soft words; influence by pleasant ways: *She coaxed me into letting her borrow my bicycle.* **2** get by coaxing: *The baby-sitter coaxed a smile from the baby. v.* —**coax′er,** *n.* —**coax′ing ly,** *adv.*

co ax i al (kō ak′sē əl), having a common axis. *adj.* —**co-ax′i al ly,** *adv.*

coaxial cable, an electric cable consisting of a tube of conducting materials surrounding an insulated central conductor. It is used for transmitting many telegraph, telephone, and television signals at the same time.

cob (kob), **1** corncob. **2** a strong horse with short legs. **3** a male swan. *n.*

co balt (kō′bôlt), **1** a hard, silver-white metallic element with a pinkish tint, which occurs only in combination with other elements. It is used in making alloys, paints, etc. **2** a dark-blue coloring matter made from cobalt. *n.*

WORD HISTORY

cobalt

Cobalt comes from German *Kobold,* meaning "goblin." The substance was called this because miners believed it caused evil or mischievous things to happen.

cob ble (kob′əl), mend (shoes, etc.); repair; patch. *v.,* **cob bled, cob bling.**

cob bler[1] (kob′lər), person whose work is mending shoes. *n.*

cob bler[2] (kob′lər), a fruit pie baked in a deep dish, usually with a crust only on top. *n.*

cob ble stone (kob′əl stōn′), a naturally rounded stone formerly much used in paving. *n.*

CO BOL (kō′bôl), language for programming computers, especially to process business data. *n.*

co bra (kō′brə), a very poisonous snake of Asia and Africa. When excited, it flattens its neck so that the head takes on the appearance of a hood. *n., pl.* **co bras.**

cob web (kob′web′), **1** a spider's web, or the stuff it is made of. **2** anything thin and slight or entangling like a spider's web: *caught in a cobweb of lies. n.*

co caine or **co cain** (kō kān′ *or* kō′kān), drug used to deaden pain and as a stimulant. It is obtained from the dried leaves of a tropical shrub. When used in excess, it can cause addiction and poisoning. *n.*

coc cus (kok′əs), bacterium shaped like a sphere. *n., pl.* **coc ci** (kok′sī).

coc cyx (kok′siks), a small triangular bone forming the lower end of the backbone. *n., pl.* **coc cy ges** (kok-sī′jēz′).

coch le a (kok′lē ə), a spiral-shaped cavity of the inner ear, containing the nerve endings that transmit sound impulses along the auditory nerve. *n., pl.* **coch le ae** (kok′lē ē′), **coch le as.**

cock[1] (kok), **1** a male chicken; rooster. **2** the male of other birds: *a turkey cock.* **3** faucet used to turn the flow of a liquid or gas on or off. **4** hammer of a gun. **5** position of the hammer or firing pin of a gun when it is pulled back ready to fire. **6** pull back the hammer or firing pin of (a gun), ready to fire: *There was a click as the sheriff cocked his revolver.* 1-5 *n.,* 6 *v.*

cock[2] (kok), **1** turn or stick up, especially in a carefree, defiant, or inquiring manner: *The little bird cocked its eye at me. The dog cocked its ears when it heard the approaching footsteps. He cocked his hat jauntily on the back of his head.* **2** an upward turn or bend of the eye, ear, hat, etc. 1 *v.,* 2 *n.*

cock[3] (kok), **1** a small, cone-shaped pile of hay, turf, etc., in a field. **2** to pile in cocks. 1 *n.,* 2 *v.*

cock ade (ko kād′), knot of ribbon or a rosette worn on the hat as a badge. *n.*

cock-a-doo dle-doo (kok′ə dü′dl dü′), imitation of the loud cry of a rooster. *n., pl.* **cock-a-doo dle-doos.**

cockatoo
about 18 in.
(46 cm.) long

cock a too (kok′ə tü′ *or* kok′ə tü′), a large, brightly colored parrot of Australia, the East Indies, etc., with a crest which it can raise and lower. *n., pl.* **cock a toos.**

cock boat (kok′bōt′), a small rowboat. *n.*

cocked hat, 1 hat with the brim turned up in three places. **2** hat pointed in front and in back.

cock er el (kok′ər əl), a young rooster, not more than one year old. *n.*

cock er spaniel (kok′ər), a small dog with long, silky hair and drooping ears.

cock eye (kok′ī′), eye that squints. *n.*

cock eyed (kok′īd′), **1** cross-eyed. **2** SLANG. tilted or

cobra
about 6 ft.
(2 m.) long

twisted to one side. **3** SLANG. foolish; silly. *adj.*

cock horse (kok′hôrs′), rocking horse. *n.*

cock i ness (kok′ē nis), INFORMAL. a cocky manner; cocksureness. *n.*

cock le (kok′əl), **1** a small, saltwater shellfish that is good to eat. It has two ridged, heart-shaped shells. **2** cockleshell. *n.*

warm the cockles of one's heart, make one feel much pleased and encouraged: *The friendly welcome into the new neighborhood warmed the cockles of her heart.*

cock le bur (kok′əl bėr′), any of several weeds with spiny burs. *n.*

cock le shell (kok′əl shel′), **1** shell of the cockle. **2** a small, light, shallow boat. *n.*

cock ney (kok′nē), **1** person born or living in the eastern section of London who speaks a particular dialect of English. **2** this dialect. **3** of cockneys or their dialect. 1,2 *n., pl.* **cock neys;** 3 *adj.*

cock pit (kok′pit′), **1** place where the pilot sits in an airplane. **2** the open place in a boat where the pilot and passengers sit. *n.*

cock roach (kok′rōch′), a small, brownish or yellowish insect often found in kitchens and around water pipes. Cockroaches usually come out at night to feed. *n., pl.* **cock roach es.**

cocks comb (koks′kōm′), **1** the fleshy, red part on the top of a rooster's head. **2** plant with crested or feathery clusters of red or yellow flowers. *n.*

cock sure (kok′shur′), **1** too sure; overly confident. **2** perfectly sure; absolutely certain. *adj.* —**cock′sure′ly,** *adv.* —**cock′sure′ness,** *n.*

cock tail (kok′tāl′), **1** a chilled alcoholic drink of gin, whiskey, rum, etc., mixed with vermouth, fruit juices, etc., and sometimes sugar or a dash of bitters. **2** an appetizing drink served just before a meal: *a tomato-juice cocktail.* **3** shellfish or mixed fruits served as an appetizer: *a shrimp cocktail. n.*

cock y (kok′ē), INFORMAL. conceited or swaggering; cocksure: *He is a cocky fellow. adj.,* **cock i er, cock i est.**

co co (kō′kō), **1** coconut palm. **2** coconut. *n., pl.* **co cos.** Also, **cocoa.**

co coa[1] (kō′kō), **1** powder made by roasting and grinding the kernels of cacao seeds, and removing some of the fat. **2** drink made of this powder with milk or water and sugar. **3** a dull-brown color, lighter than chocolate. **4** dull-brown. 1-3 *n., pl.* **co coas;** 4 *adj.*
[*Cocoa*[1] is a different form of *cacao,* which was borrowed from Spanish *cacao.*]

co coa[2] (kō′kō), coco. *n., pl.* **co coas.**

co co nut or **co coa nut** (kō′kə nut′), the large, round, hard-shelled fruit of the coconut palm that contains a sweet, white liquid called **coconut milk,** which is used as a drink. Coconuts have a brown shell with a sweet, white, pulpy meat which is often shredded for use in cakes, puddings, and pies. *n.*

WORD HISTORY

coconut

Coco of *coconut* comes from Portuguese *coco,* which originally meant "grinning face, grin." It was called this because the base of the shell of the nut was thought to look like a grinning face.

a hat	i it	oi oil	ch child	a in about
ā age	ī ice	ou out	ng long	e in taken
ä far	o hot	u cup	sh she	ə = { i in pencil
e let	ō open	u̇ put	th thin	o in lemon
ē equal	ô order	ü rule	ᴛʜ then	u in circus
ėr term			zh measure	

coconut oil, oil obtained from coconuts, used for making soap, candles, etc.

coconut palm, a tall, tropical palm tree on which coconuts grow; coco palm.

co coon (kə kün′), **1** case of silky thread spun by the larvae of various insects to live in while they are developing into adults. Most moth larvae form cocoons. Silk is obtained from the cocoons of silkworms. **2** any similar protective case or covering. *n.*

coco palm, coconut palm.

cod (kod), an important food fish found in the cold parts of the northern Atlantic; codfish. *n., pl.* **cods** or **cod.**

Cod (kod), **Cape,** hook-shaped peninsula in SE Massachusetts. *n.*

c.o.d. or **C.O.D.,** cash on delivery; collect on delivery.

cod dle (kod′l), **1** treat tenderly; pamper: *coddle a sick child.* **2** cook in hot water without boiling: *coddle an egg.* *v.,* **cod dled, cod dling.**

code (kōd), **1** system of secret writing; arrangement of words, figures, etc., to keep a message short or secret: *The enemy could not understand the code in which the message was sent.* **2** change into a code: *The spy coded a message to headquarters.* **3** a collection of laws arranged according to a system so that they can be understood and used: *The punishments for robbery and murder are found in the penal code.* **4** any set of accepted manners or rules. A traffic code contains rules for driving. A moral code is made up of the notions of right and wrong conduct held by a person, a group of persons, or a society. **5** system of signals for sending messages by telegraph, flags, etc. The Morse code is used in telegraphy. 1,3-5 *n.,* 2 *v.,* **cod ed, cod ing.**

co deine or **co dein** (kō′dēn′), a white, crystalline drug obtained from opium, used to relieve pain and cause sleep. *n.*

cod fish (kod′fish′), cod. *n., pl.* **cod fish es** or **cod fish.**

codg er (koj′ər), INFORMAL. an odd or peculiar person. *n.*

cod i fi ca tion (kod′ə fə kā′shən *or* kō′də fə kā′shən), arrangement of laws, etc., according to a system. *n.*

cod i fy (kod′ə fī *or* kō′də fī), arrange (laws, etc.) according to a system: *The laws of France were codified by order of Napoleon I. v.,* **cod i fied, cod i fy ing.** —**cod′i fi′er,** *n.*

cod ling moth (kod′ling), a small moth whose larvae destroy apples, pears, etc.

cod-liv er oil (kod′liv′ər), oil extracted from the liver of cod or of related species, used in medicine as a source of vitamins A and D.

Co dy (kō′dē), **William F(rederick),** the real name of **Buffalo Bill.** *n.*

co ed or **co-ed** (kō′ed′), INFORMAL. a girl or woman student at a coeducational school. *n.*

co ed u ca tion al (kō′ej ə kā′shə nəl), educating boys and girls or men and women together in the same school or classes. *adj.* —**co′ed u ca′tion al ly,** *adv.*

co ef fi cient (kō′ə fish′ənt), number or symbol put with and multiplying another. In $3x$, 3 is the coefficient of x, and x is the coefficient of 3. *n.*

co erce (kō ėrs′), compel; force: *The prisoner was coerced into confessing the crime. v.,* **co erced, co erc ing.** —**co erc′er,** *n.* —**co erc′i ble,** *adj.*

co er cion (kō ėr′shən), use of force; compulsion: *Dictators rule by coercion. n.*

co er cive (kō ėr′siv), using force; compelling. *adj.* —**co- er′cive ly,** *adv.* —**co er′cive ness,** *n.*

co ex ist (kō′ig zist′), exist together or at the same time. *v.*

co ex ist ence (kō′ig zis′təns), existence together or at the same time. *n.*

cof fee (kô′fē), **1** a dark-brown drink made from the roasted and ground seeds of a tall, tropical shrub. **2** coffee beans. **3** the color of coffee; a dark brown, darker than chocolate. **4** having the color of coffee; dark-brown. 1-3 *n.,* 4 *adj.*

coffee bean, seed of the coffee plant. Coffee beans are roasted and ground to make coffee.

cof fee house (kô′fē hous′), place where coffee and other refreshments are served. *n., pl.* **cof fee hous es** (kô′fē hou′ziz).

cof fee pot (kô′fē pot′), container for making or serving coffee. *n.*

coffee table, a low table for serving coffee and other refreshments. It is often placed in front of a sofa or chair.

cof fer (kô′fər), **1** box, chest, or trunk, especially one used to hold money or other valuable things. **2 coffers,** *pl.* treasury; funds: *The revenue from the sales tax goes into the city's coffers. n.*

cof fin (kô′fən), box into which a dead person is put to be buried; casket. *n.*

cog (kog), one of a series of teeth on the edge of a gear. *n.*

cogs on gears

co gen cy (kō′jən sē), forcible quality; power of convincing: *The cogency of her argument helped her win the debate. n.*

co gen er a tion (kō′jen ə rā′shən), the production of electricity from steam that is not completely used in an industrial process. *n.*

co gent (kō′jənt), having the power to convince; forcible or convincing: *The lawyer used cogent arguments to persuade the jury that his client was innocent. adj.* —**co′gent-ly,** *adv.*

cog i tate (koj′ə tāt), think over; consider with care; ponder; meditate: *The judge cogitated a long time before making any decision. v.,* **cog i tat ed, cog i tat ing.** —**cog′i ta′tor,** *n.*

cog i ta tion (koj′ə tā′shən), deep thought; careful consideration; pondering; meditation. *n.*

cog i ta tive (koj′ə tā′tiv), given to thinking; thoughtful. *adj.* —**cog′i ta′tive ly,** *adv.*

co gnac (kō′nyak), a French brandy of superior quality. *n.* [*Cognac* was borrowed from French *cognac,* which was named for *Cognac,* a town and region in France where it is made.]

cog nate (kog′nāt), **1** related by family or origin. English, Dutch, and German are cognate languages. **2** anything related to another by having a common source. The German word *Wasser* and the English word *water* are cognates. 1 *adj.,* 2 *n.*

coffee beans

cog ni zance (kog′nə zəns), knowledge obtained by observation or information; perception; awareness: *The queen had cognizance of plots against her. n.*

cog ni zant (kog′nə zənt), aware: *When the queen became cognizant of the plot to overthrow her, she acted swiftly to crush it. adj.*

co hab it (kō hab′it), live together as husband and wife do. *v.* —**co hab′i ta′tion,** *n.*

co here (kō hir′), **1** stick together; hold together: *Brick and mortar cohere.* **2** be well connected; be consistent: *The various details of the witness's story failed to cohere. v.,* **co hered, co her ing.**

co her ence (kō hir′əns), **1** logical connection; consistency: *The excited girl's story lacked coherence.* **2** a sticking together; tendency to hold together: *the coherence of atoms of the same element. n.*

co her ent (kō hir′ənt), **1** logically connected; consistent: *He was so excited that he could not give a coherent account of the accident.* **2** sticking together; holding together. *adj.* —**co her′ent ly,** *adv.*

co he sion (kō hē′zhən), **1** a sticking together; tendency to hold together: *Wet sand has more cohesion than dry sand.* **2** attraction between molecules of the same kind: *Drops of water are a result of cohesion. n.*

co he sive (kō hē′siv), sticking together; tending to hold together: *Magnetized iron filings form a cohesive mass. The members of a family are a cohesive unit in our society. adj.* —**co he′sive ly,** *adv.* —**co he′sive ness,** *n.*

co ho (kō′hō), a salmon of the Pacific coast of North America, recently introduced into the Great Lakes. *n., pl.* **co hos** or **co ho.**

co hort (kō′hôrt), companion; associate; follower. *n.*

coif (koif), cap or hood that fits closely around the head. *n.*

coif fure (kwä fyùr′), style or manner of arranging a woman's hair. *n.*

coil (koil), **1** wind around and around in a circular or spiral shape: *The snake coiled around a branch. The sailor coiled the rope evenly.* **2** anything that is coiled: *a coil of rope.* **3** one wind or turn of a coil. **4** series of connected pipes arranged in a coil or row: *the coils in a radiator.* **5** wire wound round and round into a spiral for carrying electric current. 1 *v.,* 2-5 *n.*

coil (def. 4)
coils
in refrigerator

coil (def. 5)—coils
in electromagnet
of electric bell

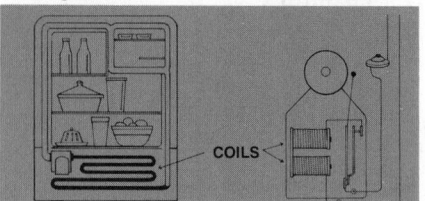

COILS

coin (koin), **1** piece of metal stamped by a government for use as money. Pennies, nickels, dimes, and quarters are coins. **2** metal money. A government makes coin by stamping metal. **3** make (money) by stamping metal: *The mint coins millions of nickels and dimes each year.* **4** make (metal) into money: *to coin copper and zinc into pennies.* **5** make up; invent: *We often coin new words or phrases to name new products. Alfred Nobel coined the word "dynamite."* 1,2 *n.,* 3-5 *v.* —**coin′er,** *n.*

coin age (koi′nij), **1** the making of coins. The United States mint is in charge of coinage. **2** metal money; coins. **3** a making up; inventing: *Travel in outer space has led to the coinage of many new words.* **4** word, phrase, etc., invented: *"Transistor" and "laser" are fairly new coinages. n.*

co in cide (kō′in sīd′), **1** occupy the same place in space: *If these two triangles △△ were placed one on top of the other, they would coincide.* **2** occupy the same time: *The working hours of the two friends coincide.* **3** be just alike; correspond exactly; agree: *Her opinion coincides with mine. v.,* **co in cid ed, co in cid ing.**

co in ci dence (kō in′sə dəns), **1** the chance occurrence of two things at the same time or place in such a way as to seem remarkable, fitting, etc.: *It is a coincidence that my cousin and I were born on the very same day.* **2** a coinciding: *the coincidence of two triangles. n.*

co in ci dent (kō in′sə dənt), **1** happening at the same time: *My cousin's birthday is coincident with mine.* **2** in exact agreement: *Our views were often coincident. adj.* —**co in′ci dent ly,** *adv.*

co in ci den tal (kō in′sə den′tl), showing coincidence; occurring by chance. *adj.* —**co in′ci den′tal ly,** *adv.*

coke (kōk), **1** fuel made from bituminous coal that has been heated in an oven from which most of the air has been shut out. Coke burns with much heat and little smoke, and is used in furnaces, for melting metal, etc. **2** change into coke. 1 *n.,* 2 *v.,* **coked, cok ing.**

col., column.

Col., 1 Colonel. **2** Colorado. The official abbreviation is **Colo.**

co la (kō′lə), a soft drink flavored with a nut from a tropical evergreen tree. *n., pl.* **co las.**

col an der (kul′ən dər *or* kol′ən dər), a wire or metal dish full of small holes for draining off liquids from foods. *n.*

cold (kōld), **1** much less warm than the body: *Snow and ice are cold.* **2** less warm than usual: *The weather is cold for April.* **3** feeling cold or chilly: *Put on a sweater, or you will be cold.* **4** coldness; being cold: *Warm clothes protect against the cold of winter.* **5** a common illness that causes a running at the nose and a sore throat. **6** lacking in feeling; unfriendly: *Since our argument she has remained cold and aloof.* **7** faint; weak: *The hunting dogs could not trail the cold scent of the fox.* **8** (in games, treasure hunts, etc.) far from what one is searching for. **9** suggesting coolness. Blue, green, and gray are called cold colors. 1-3, 6-9 *adj.,* 4,5 *n.* —**cold′ly,** *adv.* —**cold′ness,** *n.*

catch cold or **take cold,** become ill with a cold: *I caught cold and stayed home from school.*

in the cold or **out in the cold,** all alone; neglected.

cold-blood ed (kōld′blud′id), **1** having blood that is about the same temperature as the air or water around the animal. The blood of such animals is colder in winter than in summer. Turtles, snakes, and many other animals are cold-blooded; birds and mammals are warm-blooded. **2** lacking in feeling; cruel: *a cold-blooded murder.* **3** feeling the cold because of poor circulation. *adj.* —**cold′-blood′ed ly,** *adv.* —**cold′-blood′ed ness,** *n.*

cold cream, a creamy, soothing salve for the skin.

cold front, the advancing edge of a cold air mass as it

a hat	i it	oi oil	ch child	a in about
ā age	ī ice	ou out	ng long	e in taken
ä far	o hot	u cup	sh she	ə = { i in pencil
e let	ō open	u̇ put	th thin	o in lemon
ē equal	ô order	ü rule	ᵺ then	u in circus
ėr term			zh measure	

overtakes and passes under a warmer one. Showers usually form along a cold front.

cold-heart ed (kōld′här′tid), lacking in feeling; unsympathetic; unkind. *adj.* —**cold′-heart′ed ly,** *adv.* —**cold′-heart′ed ness,** *n.*

cold sore, blister near or on the mouth, caused by a virus which infects the skin; fever blister.

cold war, 1 a prolonged contest between nations or groups of nations, conducted by political, economic, and other means rather than by direct military action. **2 Cold War,** the contest for world leadership between the communist and democratic nations that began after World War II.

cold wave, period of very cold weather.

cole slaw (kōl′slô′), salad made of finely shredded raw cabbage; slaw. *n.*

col ic (kol′ik), severe pains in the stomach and intestines. *n.*

col ick y (kol′i kē), having colic. *adj.*

col i se um (kol′ə sē′əm), **1** a large building or stadium for games, contests, etc. **2 Coliseum,** Colosseum. *n.*

coll., 1 college. **2** colloquial.

col lab o rate (kə lab′ə rāt′), **1** work together: *The two authors collaborated in writing a history of the United States.* **2** aid or cooperate with enemies of one's country: *The traitor collaborated with the enemy. v.,* **col lab o rat ed, col lab o rat ing.**

col lab o ra tion (kə lab′ə rā′shən), **1** act of working together. **2** an aiding or cooperating with enemies of one's country. *n.*

col lab o ra tor (kə lab′ə rā′tər), **1** person who works with another, especially in literary or scientific work. **2** person who aids or cooperates with enemies of one's country. *n.*

col lage (kə läzh′), picture made by pasting on a background such things as parts of photographs and newspapers, fabric, and string. *n.*

WORD HISTORY

collage

Collage comes from French *collage,* meaning "a pasting, gluing," and can be traced back to Greek *kolla,* meaning "glue."

col lapse (kə laps′), **1** fall in; shrink together suddenly: *Sticking a pin into the balloon caused it to collapse.* **2** a falling in; sudden shrinking together: *A heavy flood caused the collapse of the bridge.* **3** break down; fail: *The business collapsed because it was run poorly.* **4** breakdown; failure: *Overwork can cause the collapse of a person's health.* **5** fold or push together: *to collapse a telescope.* 1,3,5 *v.,* **col lapsed, col laps ing;** 2,4 *n.*

col laps i ble (kə lap′sə bəl), made so that it can be folded or pushed together: *a collapsible table. adj.*

col lar (kol′ər), **1** the part of a coat, dress, or shirt that makes a band around the neck. **2** a separate band of linen, lace, or other material worn around the neck: *a fur collar.* **3** a leather or metal band for the neck of a dog or other pet animal. **4** a leather roll for a horse's neck to bear the weight of the loads it pulls. **5** any of various kinds of rings, bands, or pipes in machinery. A collar on a shaft is a metal ring that keeps the shaft from moving sideways. Sometimes a collar is a short pipe connecting two other pipes. **6** seize by the collar; capture: *The police collared the thief after a long chase.* 1-5 *n.*, 6 *v.* —**col′lar-less,** *adj.* —**col′lar like′,** *adj.*

col lar bone (kol′ər bōn′), the bone connecting the breastbone and the shoulder blade; clavicle. *n.*

col lard (kol′ərd). Usually, **collards,** *pl.* a kind of kale with fleshy leaves, cooked as greens. *n.*

col late (kə lāt′ *or* kol′āt), arrange in order; put together. *v.*, **col lat ed, col lat ing.**

collate
She operated a device that could rapidly **collate** ten pages at a time.

col lat er al (kə lat′ər əl), **1** aside from the main thing; secondary: *The teacher listed ten books about explorers as collateral reading for the chapter on exploring America.* **2** side by side; parallel. **3** stocks, bonds, etc., pledged as security for a loan: *The bank will not make a loan without collateral.* 1,2 *adj.*, 3 *n.* —**col lat′er al ly,** *adv.*

col league (kol′ēg′), fellow worker; associate. *n.*

col lect (kə lekt′), **1** bring or come together; gather together: *We collected sticks of wood to make a fire. A crowd soon collected at the scene of the accident.* **2** gather together for a set: *I collect stamps as a hobby.* **3** heap up; accumulate: *Dust is collecting under the bed.* **4** ask and receive payment of (bills, debts, dues, or taxes): *My scout troop collects dues each week.* **5** to be paid for at the place of delivery: *a collect telephone call (adj.). Telephone me collect (adv.).* **6** regain control of: *We soon collected ourselves after the slight accident.* 1-4,6 *v.*, 5 *adj.*, 5 *adv.*

col lect ed (kə lek′tid), not confused or disturbed; calm: *Throughout all the excitement she remained cool and collected. adj.* —**col lect′ed ly,** *adv.* —**col lect′ed ness,** *n.*

col lec tion (kə lek′shən), **1** a bringing together; coming together: *The collection of these stamps took ten years.* **2** group of things gathered from many places and belonging together: *Our library has a large collection of books.* **3** money gathered from people: *A church takes up a collection to help pay its expenses.* **4** a large quantity; mass or heap: *There is a collection of dust in the attic. n.*

col lec tive (kə lek′tiv), **1** of a group; as a group; taken all together: *Our fifth-grade class made a collective decision to write to a similar class in Italy.* **2** owned, worked, and managed by a group: *a collective farm.* **3** farm, factory, or other organization operated and worked by a group cooperatively: *There are many collectives in the Soviet Union.* 1,2 *adj.*, 3 *n.*

collective bargaining, negotiation about wages, hours, and working conditions between workers organized as a group and their employer or employers.

col lec tive ly (kə lek′tiv lē), **1** as a group; all together. **2** in a singular form, but with a plural meaning. In the sentence "We caught many fish," *fish* is used collectively. *adv.*

collective noun, noun that is singular in form, but plural in meaning. *Crowd, people, troop,* and *herd* are collective nouns.

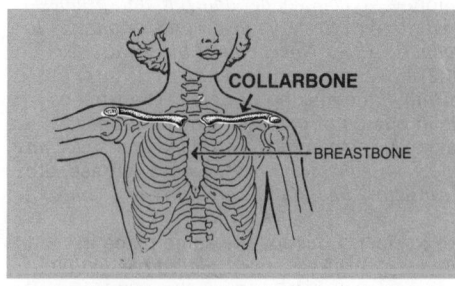

col lec tiv ize (kə lek′ti vīz), transfer ownership of, from an individual to the state. *v.*, **col lec tiv ized, col lec tiv iz ing.** —**col lec′tiv i za′tion,** *n.*

col lec tor (kə lek′tər), **1** person or thing that collects: *I am a stamp collector.* **2** person hired to collect money owed: *He works for the government as a tax collector.* **3** solar collector. *n.*

col leen (kol′ēn′ *or* kə lēn′), IRISH. girl. *n.*

col lege (kol′ij), **1** school of higher learning that gives degrees or diplomas. A college is often a part of a university. **2** school for special training: *a business college.* **3** group of persons with the same duties and privileges: *Many large hospitals have a college of surgeons. n.*

col le giate (kə lē′jit), **1** of or like a college: *a collegiate library.* **2** of or like college students: *She enjoyed collegiate life. adj.*

col lide (kə līd′), **1** hit or strike violently together; crash: *Two ships collided in the harbor and sank.* **2** to clash; conflict. *v.*, **col lid ed, col lid ing.**

col lie (kol′ē), a large, intelligent, long-haired dog used for tending sheep and as a pet. *n.*

col lier (kol′yər), **1** ship for carrying coal. **2** a coal miner. *n.*

col lier y (kol′yər ē), a coal mine and its buildings and equipment. *n., pl.* **col lier ies.**

col li sion (kə lizh′ən), **1** a hitting or striking violently together; crash: *The car was badly damaged in the collision.* **2** a clash; conflict: *There was a collision of interests on how to spend the city's gasoline tax money. n.*

colloq., **1** colloquial. **2** colloquialism.

col lo qui al (kə lō′kwē əl), used in common talk; belonging to everyday, familiar talk; informal. Such expressions as *clip* for *punch* and *close call* for *narrow escape* are colloquial. *adj.* —**col lo′qui al ly,** *adv.*

col lo qui al ism (kə lō′kwē ə liz′əm), a colloquial word or phrase. *n.*

col lo quy (kol′ə kwē), a talking together; conversation; conference. *n., pl.* **col lo quies.**

col lude (kə lüd′), act together secretly; conspire in a fraud. *v.*, **col lud ed, col lud ing.**

col lu sion (kə lü′zhən), secret agreement for some wrong or harmful purpose; secret or crafty understanding for the purposes of trickery or fraud. *n.*

col lu sive (kə lü′siv), involving collusion; fraudulent. *adj.* —**col lu′sive ly,** *adv.*

Colo., the official abbreviation of Colorado.

co logne (kə lōn′), a fragrant liquid, not so strong as perfume. *n.*

Co logne (kə lōn′), city in W West Germany, on the Rhine. *n.*

Co lom bi a (kə lum′bē ə), country in NW South America. *Capital:* Bogotá. *n.* —**Co lom′bi an,** *adj., n.*

Co lom bo (kə lum′bō), seaport and capital of Sri Lanka, on the W coast. *n.*

co lon[1] (kō′lən), mark (:) of punctuation used before lists, explanations, long quotations, etc., to set them off from the rest of the sentence. *n.*

co lon[2] (kō′lən), the lower part of the large intestine. *n., pl.* **co lons, co la** (kō′lə).

colo nel (kėr′nl), an army, air force, or marine officer ranking next below a brigadier general and next above a lieutenant colonel. *n.*

co lo ni al (kə lō′nē əl), **1** of a colony or colonies. **2** of the thirteen British colonies which became the United States of America. **3** person who lives in a colony. 1,2 *adj.,* 3 *n.* —**co lo′ni al ly,** *adv.*

co lo ni al ism (kə lō′nē ə liz′əm), policy of a nation that rules or seeks to rule weaker or dependent nations. *n.*

col o nist (kol′ə nist), **1** person who lives in a colony; settler: *Early colonists in New England suffered from cold and hunger.* **2** person who helped to found a colony. *n.*

col o ni za tion (kol′ə nə zā′shən), establishment of a colony or colonies: *The English, French, Dutch, and Spanish took part in the colonization of North America. n.*

col o nize (kol′ə nīz), **1** establish a colony or colonies in: *The English colonized New England.* **2** form a colony; settle in a colony. *v.,* **col o nized, col o niz ing.**

col o niz er (kol′ə nī′zər), person who colonizes. *n.*

colonnade of an ancient Greek temple

col on nade (kol′ə nād′), series of columns set the same distance apart. *n.*

col o ny (kol′ə nē), **1** group of people who leave their own country and go to settle in another land, but who still remain citizens of their own country: *The Pilgrim colony came from England to America in 1620.* **2** the settlement made by such a group of people: *The Pilgrims founded a colony at Plymouth, Massachusetts.* **3** the Colonies, the thirteen British colonies that became the United States of America; New Hampshire, Massachusetts, Rhode Island, Connecticut, New York, New Jersey, Pennsylvania, Delaware, Maryland, Virginia, North Carolina, South Carolina, and Georgia. **4** territory distant from the country that governs it: *Hong Kong has been a British colony since 1842.* **5** group of people having the same background or occupation who live together in a certain part of a city: *a colony of artists.* **6** group of animals or plants of the same kind, living or growing together: *a colony of ants. Coral grows in colonies. n., pl.* **col o nies.**

col or (kul′ər), **1** sensation produced by the effect of waves of light striking the retina of the eye. Different colors are produced by rays of light having different wavelengths. **2** any color except black, white, or gray; red, yellow, blue, or any combination of them. The color green is a mixture of yellow and blue. **3** any color including black, white, or gray. The color gray is a mixture of black and white. **4** give color to; put color on; change the color of: *I colored the picture with crayons.* **5** a paint; dye; pigment: *The color was so thick on the canvas that it*

began to peel off. **6** coloring of the skin; complexion: *She has a healthy color.* **7** become or make red in the face; blush: *He colored when I teased him.* **8** an outward appearance; show: *Though imaginative, his plays always have the color of truth.* **9** change to give a wrong idea: *The fisherman colored the facts to make his catch seem the biggest of all.* **10** distinguishing quality; vividness: *The author's gift for description adds color to her stories.* **11** give a distinguishing or vivid quality to: *A love of nature colored the author's works.* **12** the colors, the flag of a nation, regiment, etc.: *Salute the colors.* 1-3,5,6,8,10,12 *n.,* 4,7,9,11 *v.* —**col′or er,** *n.*

change color, 1 turn pale. **2** blush.

give color to or **lend color to,** cause to seem true or likely.

lose color, turn pale.

show one's true colors, show oneself as one really is: *When he saw that he was losing, he showed his true colors and gave up.*

with flying colors, successfully; victoriously: *He passed the test with flying colors.*

Col o rad an (kol′ə rad′n *or* kol′ə räd′n), **1** of the state of Colorado. **2** person born or living in Colorado. 1 *adj.,* 2 *n.*

Col o rad o (kol′ə rad′ō *or* kol′ə rä′dō), **1** one of the western states of the United States. *Abbreviation:* Colo. or CO *Capital:* Denver. **2** river flowing from N Colorado through Utah, Arizona, Nevada, California, and NW Mexico into the Gulf of California. *n.*

col or a tion (kul′ə rā′shən), way in which a person or thing is colored; coloring: *The coloration of some animals is like that of their surroundings. n.*

col or a tur a (kul′ər ə tu̇r′ə *or* kul′ər ə tyu̇r′ə), **1** ornamental passages in vocal music, such as trills or runs. **2** soprano who sings such passages. *n., pl.* **col or a tur as.**

col or-blind (kul′ər blīnd′), unable to tell certain colors apart; unable to perceive certain colors. *adj.* —**col′or-blind′ness,** *n.*

col or cast (kul′ər kast′), **1** a television broadcast in color. **2** broadcast (a television program) in color. 1 *n.,* 2 *v.,* **col or cast** or **col or cast ed, col or cast ing.**

col ored (kul′ərd), **1** having color: *This book has colored pictures.* **2** having a certain kind of color: *a green-colored leaf.* **3** of the black race or any race other than white. This meaning of *colored* is often considered offensive. **4** tinged by prejudice, emotion, or desire for effect; biased: *She gave a highly colored description of the size of the fish she had caught. adj.*

col or ful (kul′ər fəl), **1** having excitement, variety, or interest; picturesque; vivid: *Her letters give colorful descriptions of her travels abroad.* **2** full of color. *adj.* —**col′or ful ly,** *adv.* —**col′or ful ness,** *n.*

col or ing (kul′ər ing), **1** way in which a person or thing is colored; coloration: *Our cat has a tan coloring.* **2** substance used to color; pigment. **3** an outward or false appearance: *Her story had the coloring of truth, but we knew we could not believe her. n.*

col or less (kul′ər lis), **1** without color: *Pure water is colorless.* **2** without excitement or variety; uninteresting: *a colorless person, a colorless description. adj.* —**col′or less ly,** *adv.* —**col′or less ness,** *n.*

co los sal (kə los/əl), of huge size; gigantic; vast: *Sky-scrapers are colossal structures. adj.* —**co los/sal ly,** *adv.*

Col os se um (kol/ə sē/əm), a large amphitheater in Rome, completed in A.D. 80. The Colosseum was used for games and contests. *n.* Also, **Coliseum.**

co los sus (kə los/əs), **1** a huge statue. The **Colossus of Rhodes** was a huge statue of Apollo made at Rhodes about 280 B.C. It was one of the seven wonders of the ancient world. **2** anything huge; gigantic person or thing. *n., pl.* **co los si** (kə los/ī), **co los sus es.**

colt (kōlt), a young horse, donkey, zebra, etc., especially a male less than four or five years old. *n.*

colt ish (kōl/tish), like a colt; lively and frisky. *adj.* —**colt/ish ly,** *adv.* —**colt/ish ness,** *n.*

Co lum bi a (kə lum/bē ə), **1** capital of South Carolina, in the central part. **2** river flowing from British Columbia through E Washington and between Washington and Oregon into the Pacific. **3** a name for the United States of America. Columbia is often represented as a woman dressed in red, white, and blue. *n.*

col um bine (kol/əm bīn), plant whose flowers have petals shaped like hollow spurs. Wild columbines have red-and-yellow or blue-and-white flowers. *n.*

Co lum bus (kə lum/bəs), **1 Christopher,** 1451?-1506, Italian navigator in the service of Spain who sailed to America in 1492, making its existence known to Europeans. **2** capital of Ohio, in the central part. *n.*

Columbus Day, October 12, the anniversary of Columbus's arrival in America. It is observed as a legal holiday on the second Monday in October in most states of the United States.

col umn (kol/əm), **1** a slender, upright structure; pillar. Columns are usually made of stone, wood, or metal, and are used as supports or ornaments to a building. Sometimes a column stands alone as a monument. **2** anything that seems slender and upright like a column: *a column of smoke, a column of figures.* **3** soldiers or ships following one another in a single line. **4** a narrow division of a page reading from top to bottom, kept separate by lines or by blank spaces. Some newspapers have eight columns on a page. **5** part of a newspaper used for a special subject or written by a special writer: *the sports column. n.*

col umn ist (kol/əm nist), person who writes a special column in a newspaper or magazine. *n.*

com-, *prefix.* with; together: *Commingle = mingle with one another. Compress = press together.*

com., **1** commerce. **2** common.

Com., **1** Commissioner. **2** Committee.

co ma (kō/mə), a prolonged unconsciousness caused by disease, injury, or poison. *n., pl.* **co mas.**

Co man che (kə man/chē), member of a tribe of American Indians that formerly occupied territory from Nebraska to northern Mexico and now live in Oklahoma. *n., pl.* **Co man che** or **Co man ches.**

comb (kōm), **1** piece of metal, plastic, rubber, bone, etc., with teeth, used to arrange the hair or to hold it in place. **2** anything shaped or used like a comb, especially an instrument for combing wool or flax. **3** arrange with a comb. **4** take out tangles in (wool, flax, etc.) with a comb. **5** search through; look everywhere in: *We had to comb the neighborhood before we found our lost dog.* **6** the red, fleshy piece on top of the head of chickens and some other fowls. **7** honeycomb. 1,2,6,7 *n.,* 3-5 *v.* —**comb/like/,** *adj.*

com bat (kəm bat/ *or* kom/bat *for 1;* kom/bat *for 2,3*), **1** fight against; struggle with: *Doctors combat disease.* **2** armed fighting between opposing forces; battle. **3** any fight or struggle; conflict. 1 *v.,* **com bat ed, com bat ing** or **com bat ted, com bat ting;** 2,3 *n.*

com bat ant (kəm bat/nt *or* kom/bə tənt), one that takes part in combat; fighter. *n.*

com bat ive (kəm bat/iv), ready to fight; fond of fighting: *A good football team has a combative spirit. adj.* —**com bat/ive ly,** *adv.* —**com bat/ive ness,** *n.*

comb er (kō/mər), **1** breaker (def. 1). **2** person or thing that combs. *n.*

com bi na tion (kom/bə nā/shən), **1** one whole made by combining two or more different things: *The color purple is a combination of red and blue.* **2** series of numbers or letters dialed in opening a certain kind of lock: *Do you know the combination of the safe?* **3** a combining or a being combined; union: *The combination of flour and water makes paste. n.*

com bine (kəm bīn/ *for 1,2;* kom/bīn *for 3,4*), **1** join two or more things together; unite: *Our club combined the offices of secretary and treasurer.* **2** unite to form a chemical compound: *Two atoms of hydrogen combine with one of oxygen to form water.* **3** group of persons joined together for business or political purposes. **4** machine for harvesting and threshing grain. 1,2 *v.,* **com bined, com bin ing;** 3,4 *n.* —**com bin/a ble,** *adj.* —**com bin/er,** *n.*

combine (def. 4) combines harvesting sorghum

combining form, form of a word used for combining with words or with other combining forms to make new words. EXAMPLE: *micro- + second = microsecond; psycho- + -logy = psychology.*

com bo (kom/bō), INFORMAL. a small group of jazz musicians that play together regularly. *n., pl.* **com bos.**

com bust (kəm bust/), burn up. *v.*

com bus ti ble (kəm bus/tə bəl), **1** capable of taking fire and burning: *Gasoline is highly combustible.* **2** a combustible substance. Wood and coal are combustibles. 1 *adj.,* 2 *n.* —**com bus/ti bly,** *adv.*

com bus tion (kəm bus/chən), act or process of burning. Many houses are heated by the rapid combustion of coal, oil, or gas. By slow combustion, the cells of the body transform food into energy and heat. *n.*

Comdr., Commander.

Comdt., Commandant.

come (kum), **1** move toward: *Come this way.* **2** arrive: *The train comes at noon.* **3** reach; extend: *The drapes come to the floor.* **4** take place; happen: *Snow comes in winter.* **5** be born; descend: *come from a musical family.* **6** turn out to be; become: *My wish came true.* **7** be obtainable or sold: *This soup comes in a can.* **8** be equal; amount: *The bill comes to $5.00. v.,* **came, come, com ing.**

come about, 1 take place; happen: *Many changes have come about in the past year.* **2** turn around; change direction: *The sailboat came about, heading back to the dock.*

come around or **come round, 1** return to consciousness or health; recover. **2** change direction or opinion.

come at, rush toward; attack: *The barking dog came at me and I ran away.*

come back, return: *Come back home.*

come by, get; obtain; acquire: *They came by the money honestly.*

come down, 1 be handed down: *Many fables have come down through the ages.* **2** lose position, rank, money, etc.

come down on, INFORMAL. scold; blame.

come down with, become ill with: *She came down with the measles.*

come forward, offer oneself for work or duty; volunteer.

come in, 1 arrive: *When did you come in this morning?* **2** enter: *Come in, please.*

come in for, get; receive; acquire.

come into, inherit: *She came into a great deal of money when her aunt died.*

come off, 1 take place; happen; occur: *The rocket launching comes off next week.* **2** turn out to be: *Our first meeting did not come off as I had expected.* **3** finish in a certain way: *Our team came off with a great victory in last week's game.*

come on, 1 find or meet by chance. **2** improve; progress: *She is coming on well and will be out of the hospital next week.* **3** SLANG. have an effect; give an impression: *Some people come on very strong when you first meet them.* **4** please; if you don't mind: *Come on now, pick up all this stuff on the floor.*

come out, 1 be revealed or shown: *The sun came out from behind the clouds.* **2** take place in the end; result: *The ball game came out in our favor.* **3** be offered to the public: *The singer's new recording will come out next fall.* **4** put in an appearance: *How many people came out to cheer the team?* **5** declare oneself: *One candidate came out for lower taxes.* **6** make a debut.

come to, return to consciousness: *He came to slowly after the accident.*

come up, come into being; arise: *The question is not likely to come up.*

come upon, find or meet by chance: *We came upon a rabbit in the woods.*

come back (kum/bak/), **1** INFORMAL. return to a former condition or position: *The team made a comeback after several losses.* **2** SLANG. a clever answer; sharp reply. *n.*

co me di an (kə mē/dē ən), **1** actor in comedies. **2** person who amuses others with funny talk and actions. *n.*

co me dic (kə mē/dik), comic. *adj.*

come down (kum/doun/), loss of position, rank, money, etc. *n.*

com e dy (kom/ə dē), **1** an amusing play or show having a happy ending. **2** an amusing happening. *n., pl.* **com e dies.**

come li ness (kum/lē nis), pleasant appearance; attractiveness. *n.*

come ly (kum/lē), pleasant to look at; attractive: *a comely girl. adj.,* **come li er, come li est.**

come-on (kum/on/), INFORMAL. something that lures or entices. *n.*

com er (kum/ər), **1** person who arrives or comes. **2** INFORMAL. person who seems likely to succeed or who shows promise. *n.*

com et (kom/it), a bright heavenly body with a starlike center and often with a cloudy tail of light. Comets move around the sun like planets, but in a long oval course. *n.*

com fort (kum/fərt), **1** ease the grief or sorrow of; cheer: *comfort a crying child.* **2** anything that makes trouble or sorrow easier to bear: *Your friendship brought me comfort while I was in the hospital.* **3** person or thing that makes life easier or takes away hardship: *The warm bonfire was a comfort to the cold campers.* **4** freedom from hardship; ease: *live in comfort.* **1** *v.,* **2-4** *n.* —**com/fort ing ly,** *adv.*

com fort a ble (kum/fər tə bəl), **1** giving comfort: *A soft, warm bed is comfortable.* **2** in comfort; at ease: *We felt comfortable in the warm house after a cold day outdoors.* **3** enough for one's needs: *a comfortable income. adj.*

<table>
<tr><td>**a** hat</td><td>**i** it</td><td>**oi** oil</td><td>**ch** child</td><td>a in about</td></tr>
<tr><td>**ā** age</td><td>**ī** ice</td><td>**ou** out</td><td>**ng** long</td><td>e in taken</td></tr>
<tr><td>**ä** far</td><td>**o** hot</td><td>**u** cup</td><td>**sh** she</td><td>ə = { i in pencil</td></tr>
<tr><td>**e** let</td><td>**ō** open</td><td>**u̇** put</td><td>**th** thin</td><td>o in lemon</td></tr>
<tr><td>**ē** equal</td><td>**ô** order</td><td>**ü** rule</td><td>**ᵮн** then</td><td>u in circus</td></tr>
<tr><td>**ėr** term</td><td></td><td></td><td>**zh** measure</td><td></td></tr>
</table>

com fort a bly (kum/fər tə blē), in a comfortable manner. *adv.*

com fort er (kum/fər tər), **1** person or thing that gives comfort. **2** a padded or quilted covering for a bed. *n.*

com fort less (kum/fərt lis), **1** bringing no comfort or ease of mind. **2** having none of the comforts of life. *adj.*

com fy (kum/fē), INFORMAL. comfortable. *adj.,* **com fi er, com fi est.**

com ic (kom/ik), **1** causing laughter or smiles; amusing; funny. **2** comedian. **3** of comedy; in comedies: *a comic actor.* **4** comics, *pl.* comic strips; funnies. **1,3** *adj.,* **2,4** *n.*

com i cal (kom/ə kəl), amusing; funny: *You look comical in that battered old hat. adj.* —**com/i cal ly,** *adv.* —**com/i cal ness,** *n.*

comic book, magazine containing comic strips.

comic strip, series of drawings that tell a funny story, a series of happenings, or a story of adventure.

com ing (kum/ing), **1** a drawing near; approach; arrival: *the coming of summer.* **2** approaching; next: *this coming spring.* **1** *n.,* **2** *adj.*

com i ty (kom/ə tē), courtesy. *n., pl.* **com i ties.**

com ma (kom/ə), mark (,) of punctuation that sets off or separates the parts of a sentence or the parts of an address, a date, or other series of words or numbers. *n., pl.* **com mas.**

com mand (kə mand/), **1** give an order to; direct: *The queen commanded the admiral to set sail at once.* **2** an order; direction: *The admiral obeyed the queen's command.* **3** be in authority over; have power over; be master of: *A captain commands a ship.* **4** possession of authority; power; control: *She took command and led everyone from the burning building.* **5** soldiers, ships, or region over which an officer has control or authority: *The captain knew every man in his command.* **6** position of control or authority: *The general has held several commands.* **7** control by position; rise high above; overlook: *The castle stands on a hill that commands the entire valley.* **8** be able to have and use: *That lawyer commands a high fee for his services.* **9** ability to have and use: *A good speaker has an excellent command of words.* **10** deserve and get: *a person who commands our respect.* **1,3,7,8,10** *v.,* **2,4-6,9** *n.*

comet

com man dant (kom/ən dant/), **1** commander. **2** officer in command of a fort, naval station, military school, etc. *n.*

com man deer (kom/ən dir/), seize (private property) for military or public use: *The police commandeered a taxicab to chase the bank robber. v.*

com mand er (kə man/dər), **1** person who commands: *a commander of rebel forces.* **2** officer in the navy ranking next below a captain and above a lieutenant commander. *n.*

commander in chief, **1** person who has complete command of the armed forces of a country. In the United States, the President is the commander in chief. **2** officer in command of part of an army or navy. *pl.* **commanders in chief.**

com mand ing (kə man′ding), **1** in command: *a commanding officer.* **2** controlling; powerful: *commanding influences.* **3** authoritative; impressive: *a commanding voice. adj.* —**com mand′ing ly,** *adv.*

com mand ment (kə mand′mənt), **1** (in the Bible) one of the ten laws that God gave to Moses; one of the Ten Commandments. **2** any law or command. *n.*

com man do (kə man′dō), **1** soldier trained to make brief, daring, surprise raids upon enemy territory. **2** group of such soldiers. *n., pl.* **com man dos** or **com man does.**

com mem o rate (kə mem′ə rāt′), preserve or honor the memory of: *a stamp commemorating the landing of the Pilgrims. v.,* **com mem o rat ed, com mem o rat ing.** —**com mem′o ra′tor,** *n.*

com mem o ra tion (kə mem′ə rā′shən), **1** act of commemorating. **2** service or celebration in memory of some person or event. *n.*

commemorative
This commemorative postage stamp honors the art of the Pueblos.

com mem o ra tive (kə mem′ə rā′tiv), preserving or honoring the memory of some person or event. *adj.* —**com mem′o ra′tive ly,** *adv.*

com mence (kə mens′), begin; start: *The play commenced at eight o'clock. v.,* **com menced, com menc ing.**

com mence ment (kə mens′mənt), **1** a beginning; start. **2** day when a school or college gives diplomas and degrees to students who have completed the required course of study. **3** ceremonies on this day. *n.*

com mend (kə mend′), **1** speak well of; praise: *The teacher commended the pupils who did well on the test.* **2** hand over for safekeeping; entrust: *The child's parents commended her to her aunt's care for a few days. v.*

com mend a ble (kə men′də bəl), deserving praise or approval. *adj.* —**com mend′a bly,** *adv.*

com men da tion (kom′ən dā′shən), praise; approval. *n.*

com men sur ate (kə men′shər it *or* kə men′sər it), **1** in the proper proportion: *The pay should be commensurate with the work.* **2** of the same size or extent; equal: *The amount I earn and the amount I spend are nearly commensurate. adj.* —**com men′sur ate ly,** *adv.* —**com men′sur ate ness,** *n.* —**com men′sur a′tion,** *n.*

com ment (kom′ent), **1** a short statement, note, or remark that explains, praises, or finds fault with something that has been written, said, or done: *The teacher made some helpful comments about my work.* **2** make a comment or comments: *Everyone commented on my new coat.* **3** talk; gossip: *The scandal has been causing much comment.* **1,3** *n.,* **2** *v.*

com men tar y (kom′ən ter′ē), **1** series of notes explaining the hard parts of a book; explanation. **2** series of comments: *a news commentary on television. n., pl.* **com men tar ies.**

com men ta tor (kom′ən tā′tər), **1** writer of comments. **2** person who reports and comments on news, sporting events, plays, concerts, etc.: *a television commentator. n.*

com merce (kom′ərs), the buying and selling of goods, especially in large amounts between different places; business; trade. *n.* [*Commerce* came into English about 400 years ago from French *commerce,* and can be traced back to Latin *com-,* meaning "with," and *mercem,* meaning "wares."]

com mer cial (kə mėr′shəl), **1** having to do with trade or business: *a store or other commercial establishment.* **2** made to be sold for a profit: *Anything you can buy in a store is a commercial product.* **3** supported by an advertiser or sponsor: *a commercial television program.* **4** an advertising message on radio or television, broadcast between or during programs. **1-3** *adj.,* **4** *n.* —**com mer′cial ly,** *adv.*

com mer cial ize (kə mėr′shə līz), make a matter of business or trade: *Charging admission to church services would commercialize religion. v.,* **com mer cial ized, com mer cial iz ing.** —**com mer′cial i za′tion,** *n.*

com mie or **Com mie** (kom′ē), INFORMAL. communist. *n.*

com min gle (kə ming′gəl), mingle with one another; blend. *v.,* **com min gled, com min gling.**

com mis e rate (kə miz′ə rāt′), feel or express sorrow for another's suffering or trouble; pity; sympathize. *v.,* **com mis e rat ed, com mis e rat ing.**

com mis e ra tion (kə miz′ə rā′shən), pity; sympathy. *n.*

com mis sar (kom′ə sär), (formerly) a head of a government department in the Soviet Union. *n.*

com mis sar y (kom′ə ser′ē), store handling food and supplies in a mining camp, lumber camp, army camp, etc. *n., pl.* **com mis sar ies.**

com mis sion (kə mish′ən), **1** a written order giving certain powers, rights, and duties: *She held a commission as United States ambassador to Italy.* **2** give (a person) the power, right, or duty (to do something); give authority to: *They commissioned a real estate agent to sell their house.* **3** a written order giving rank or authority in the armed forces: *A captain in the United States Army has a commission signed by the President.* **4** give such a rank or authority to. **5** group of people appointed or elected with authority to do certain things: *A commission was appointed to investigate the assassination of the President.* **6** a committing; doing; performance: *People are punished for the commission of crimes.* **7** a percentage of the amount of business done, paid to the agent who does it: *She gets a commission of 10 percent on all the sales that she makes.* **8** working order; service; use: *A flat tire has put my bicycle out of commission.* **9** put into active service; make ready for use. A new warship is commissioned when it has the officers, sailors, and supplies needed for a sea trip. **1,3,5-8** *n.,* **2,4,9** *v.*

commissioned officer, officer holding the rank of second lieutenant or above in the United States Army, Air Force, or Marine Corps, or of ensign or above in the United States Navy.

com mis sion er (kə mish′ə nər), **1** member of a commission. **2** official in charge of some department of a government: *a health commissioner. n.*

com mit (kə mit′), **1** do or perform (usually something wrong): *commit a crime.* **2** hand over for safekeeping; deliver: *The convicted thief was committed to the penitentiary.* **3** give over; carry over; transfer: *commit a poem to memory.* **4** bind or involve (oneself); pledge: *I* *have committed myself now and must keep my promise.* v., **com mit ted, com mit ting.** —**com mit′ta ble,** *adj.*

com mit ment (kə mit′mənt), **1** a committing or a being committed: *the commitment of a prisoner to jail.* **2** a pledge; promise. *n.*

com mit tal (kə mit′l), commitment. *n.*

com mit tee (kə mit′ē), group of persons appointed or elected to do some special thing: *Our teacher appointed a committee to plan the class picnic. n.*

com mode (kə mōd′), **1** chest of drawers. **2** washstand. **3** toilet. *n.*

com mo di ous (kə mō′dē əs), having plenty of room; spacious; roomy. *adj.* —**com mo′di ous ly,** *adv.* —**com mo′di ous ness,** *n.*

com mod i ty (kə mod′ə tē), anything that is bought and sold; article of trade or commerce: *Groceries are commodities. n., pl.* **com mod i ties.**

com mo dore (kom′ə dôr), **1** (formerly) an officer in the United States Navy ranking next below a rear admiral and next above a captain. **2** title given to the president of a yacht club. *n.*

com mon (kom′ən), **1** belonging equally to all; joint: *The house was the common property of the three sisters.* **2** of all; from all; by all; to all; general: *By common consent of the class, she was chosen president.* **3** often met with; ordinary; usual: *Snow is common in cold countries.* **4** having no special rank or position: *the common people. A common soldier is a private.* **5** below ordinary; having poor quality; inferior: *cloth of a common sort.* **6** coarse; vulgar: *His speech was very common.* **7** belonging to or representing the entire community; public: *A common council of twelve persons governs our city.* **8** Also, **commons,** *pl.* land owned or used by all the people of a town, village, etc. **1-7** *adj.,* **8** *n.* —**com′mon ness,** *n.*

in common, equally with another or others; owned, used, or done by both or all: *They have many interests in common.*

common cold, a cold.

common denominator, a common multiple of the denominators of a group of fractions: *15 is the common denominator of* $^3/_5$ *and* $^2/_3$ *because these fractions can be expressed as* $^9/_{15}$ *and* $^{10}/_{15}$.

common divisor, number that will divide a group of two or more other numbers without a remainder: *2 is a common divisor of 4, 6, 8, and 10.*

com mon er (kom′ə nər), one of the common people; person who is not a noble. *n.*

common fraction, fraction expressed as the ratio of two whole numbers. $^1/_2$ and $^7/_8$ are common fractions.

common law, law based on custom and usage.

com mon ly (kom′ən lē), usually; generally: *Arithmetic is commonly taught in elementary schools. adv.*

Common Market, an association established in 1958 to promote free trade among its members. It includes Belgium, Denmark, France, Great Britain, Ireland, Italy, Luxembourg, the Netherlands, and West Germany.

common multiple, number that can be divided by two or more other numbers without a remainder: *12 is a common multiple of 2, 3, 4, and 6.*

common noun, name for any one of a class. *Boy* and *city* are common nouns. *Carlos* and *Boston* are proper nouns.

com mon place (kom′ən plās′), **1** not new or interesting; everyday; ordinary: *The plots of television movies are often commonplace.* **2** an ordinary or everyday thing: *Forty years ago television was a novelty; today it is a commonplace.* **3** an ordinary statement; obvious remark: *boring talk full of commonplaces about the weather.* **1** *adj.,* **2,3** *n.* —**com′mon place′ness,** *n.*

com mons (kom′ənz), **1** a dining hall or building where food is served to many at large tables. **2 the Commons,** House of Commons. *n., pl. in form, sometimes sing. in use.*

common sense, good sense in everyday affairs; practical intelligence.

com mon weal (kom′ən wēl′), **1** the general welfare; public good. **2** OLD USE. commonwealth. *n.*

com mon wealth (kom′ən welth′), **1** the people who make up a nation; citizens of a state. **2** nation in which the people have the right to make the laws; republic. Brazil, Australia, and the United States are commonwealths. **3** any state of the United States, especially Kentucky, Massachusetts, Pennsylvania, and Virginia. **4 the Commonwealth,** the Commonwealth of Nations. *n.*

Commonwealth of Nations, association of the United Kingdom, the independent member states (such as Canada, Australia, New Zealand, India, Sri Lanka, Ghana, Nigeria, Cyprus), and various associated states, dependent territories, protectorates, and protected states; the Commonwealth. It was formerly called **British Commonwealth of Nations** or **British Commonwealth.**

com mo tion (kə mō′shən), violent movement; confusion; disturbance; tumult: *Their fight caused quite a commotion in the hall. n.*

com mu nal (kə myü′nl *or* kom′yə nəl), **1** of a community; public: *communal property.* **2** of or in a commune: *communal living. adj.* —**com mu′nal ly,** *adv.*

com mune[1] (kə myün′), **1** talk intimately. **2** receive Holy Communion. *v.,* **com muned, com mun ing.**

com mune[2] (kom′yün), **1** the smallest division for local government in France, Belgium, and several other European countries. **2** group of people living together. *n.*

com mu ni ca ble (kə myü′nə kə bəl), that can be transferred or passed along to others: *a communicable disease. Ideas are communicable by words. adj.* —**com mu′ni ca ble ness,** *n.* —**com mu′ni ca bly,** *adv.*

com mu ni cate (kə myü′nə kāt), **1** give or exchange information or news by speaking, writing, etc.; send and receive messages: *She communicated her ideas to her friend. We communicate with them often by letter.* **2** pass along; transfer: *communicate a disease.* **3** be connected: *The dining room communicates with the kitchen. v.,* **com mu ni cat ed, com mu ni cat ing.** —**com mu′ni ca′tor,** *n.*

com mu ni ca tion (kə myü′nə kā′shən), **1** a giving or exchanging information or news by speaking, writing, etc.; communicating: *Sign language is a means of communication.* **2** information or news given; letter, message, etc., which gives information or news: *Your communication came in time to change my plans.* **3** means of going from one place to another; passage; connection: *There is no communication between these two rooms.* **4** act or fact of passing along; transfer. **5 communications,** *pl.* **a** system of communicating by telephone, telegraph, radio, television, etc.: *A network of communications links all parts of the civilized world.* **b** system of routes or facilities for transporting military supplies, vehicles, and troops. *n.*

communications satellite, an artificial satellite that relays microwave signals between two points on earth.

com mu ni ca tive (kə myü′nə kā′tiv), ready to give information; talkative. *adj.* —**com mu′ni ca′tive ly,** *adv.* —**com mu′ni ca′tive ness,** *n.*

---

a hat	i it	oi oil	ch child	a in about
ā age	ī ice	ou out	ng long	e in taken
ä far	o hot	u cup	sh she	ə = i in pencil
e let	ō open	u̇ put	th thin	o in lemon
ē equal	ô order	ü rule	̅TH then	u in circus
ėr term			zh measure	

com mun ion (kə myü′nyən), **1** a having in common; sharing: *The partners had a communion of interests.* **2** exchange of thoughts and feelings; fellowship. **3** group of people having the same religious beliefs. **4 Communion,** Holy Communion. *n.*

com mu ni qué (kə myü′nə kā′), an official bulletin, statement, or other communication. *n.* [*Communiqué* was borrowed from French *communiqué,* and can be traced back to Latin *communem,* meaning "common."]

com mu nism (kom′yə niz′əm), **1** an economic and social system in which most or all property is owned by the state or community as a whole and is shared by all. **2 Communism,** the principles and practices of members of a Communist party. *n.*

com mu nist (kom′yə nist), **1** person who favors or supports communism. **2** communistic. **3 Communist,** member of a Communist party. **4 Communist,** of a Communist party. 1,3 *n.,* 2,4 *adj.*

com mu nis tic (kom′yə nis′tik), **1** of communists or communism. **2** favoring communism. *adj.*

com mu ni ty (kə myü′nə tē), **1** all the people living in the same place and subject to the same laws; people of any district or town: *This lake provides water for six communities.* **2** group of people living together or sharing common interests: *a monastery and its community of monks, the scientific community.* **3 the community,** the public: *To be successful a new product needs the approval of the community.* **4** ownership together; sharing together: *community of food supplies.* **5** group of animals and plants living together. **6** likeness; similarity: *community of interests. n., pl.* **com mu ni ties.**

community chest, fund of money given voluntarily by people to support charity and welfare in their community.

community college, junior college serving the needs of local students, usually supported by public funds.

com mu ta tion (kom′yə tā′shən), **1** the changing (of a penalty, obligation, etc.) to a less severe one: *The prisoner obtained a commutation of his sentence from death to life imprisonment.* **2** regular travel to and from work by train, bus, automobile, etc. *n.*

com mu ta tive (kom′yə tā′tiv), of a rule in mathematics that the order in which numbers are added or multiplied will not change the result. EXAMPLE: $2 + 3$ will give the same result as $3 + 2.$ *adj.*

com mu ta tor (kom′yə tā′tər), device for reversing the direction of an electric current. *n.*

com mute (kə myüt′), **1** change (a penalty, obligation, etc.) to a less severe one: *The governor commuted the prisoner's sentence from death to life imprisonment.* **2** travel regularly to and from work by train, bus, automobile, etc. **3** the distance or trip ordinarily traveled by a commuter: *a long commute, an easy commute.* 1,2 *v.,* **commut ed, com mut ing;** 3 *n.* —**com mut′a ble,** *adj.*

com mut er (kə myü′tər), person who travels regularly to and from work by train, bus, automobile, etc. *n.*

Com o ros (kom′ə rōz), country consisting of a group of islands in the Indian Ocean, east of N Mozambique. *Capital:* Moroni. *n.*

com pact[1] (kəm pakt′ *or* kom′pakt *for 1,2,4;* kəm pakt′ *for 3;* kom′pakt *for 5,6*), **1** firmly packed together, closely joined: *Cabbage leaves are folded into a compact head.* **2** having the parts neatly or tightly arranged within a small space; not scattered or sprawling: *a compact portable TV set.* **3** pack firmly together; compress. **4** using few words; brief: *a compact report.* **5** a small case containing face powder or rouge. **6** automobile smaller than most models. 1,2,4 *adj.,* 3 *v.,* 5,6 *n.* [*Compact*[1] is from Latin *compactum,* meaning "confined, fastened together," which comes from *com-,* meaning "together," and

pangere, meaning "to fasten."] —**com pact′ly,** *adv.* —**com pact′ness,** *n.*

com pact[2] (kom′pakt), agreement; contract: *The United Nations is a result of a compact among nations. n.* [*Compact*[2] is from Latin *compactum,* which comes from *com-,* meaning "together," and *pacisci,* meaning "to make an agreement."]

com pact disc (kom′pakt), a small, plastic-coated, metallic disc on one side of which sound has been digitally recorded at very high speed. The data is read by a laser beam, producing sound of high quality with no surface noise and little background noise.

com pac tor (kom pak′tər), an electrically powered device that compacts or crushes garbage and rubbish to a fraction of its original volume. *n.*

com pan ion (kəm pan′yən), **1** one who goes along with or accompanies another; one who shares in what another is doing; comrade: *The twin sisters were companions in work and play.* **2** person paid to live or travel with another as a friend and helper. **3** anything that matches or goes with another in kind, size, and color: *I can't find the companion to this shoe. n.*

com pan ion a ble (kəm pan′yə nə bəl), pleasant as a companion; agreeable; friendly. *adj.*

com pan ion a bly (kəm pan′yə nə blē), in a companionable manner. *adv.*

com pan ion ship (kəm pan′yən ship), a being a companion; fellowship: *the companionship of a friend. n.*

com pan ion way (kəm pan′yən wā′), stairway from the deck of a ship down to the rooms or area below. *n.*

com pa ny (kum′pə nē), **1** group of people, especially a group joined together for some purpose: *a company of actors, the Ford Motor Company.* **2** companion or companions: *You are known by the company you keep.* **3** companionship: *I've greatly enjoyed your company.* **4** one or more guests or visitors: *Are you expecting company for dinner?* **5** a military unit made up of two or more platoons, usually commanded by a captain. **6** a ship's crew. *n., pl.* **com pa nies.**

keep company, 1 go with; remain with for companionship: *My dog kept me company while I was alone.* **2** go together; date regularly.

part company, 1 go separate ways: *The friends parted company at the gate.* **2** end companionship: *They parted company forever.*

com pa ra ble (kom′pər ə bəl), **1** able to be compared: *two actors of comparable ability.* **2** fit to be compared: *A small car is not comparable to a larger one for comfort. adj.*

com pa ra bly (kom′pər ə blē), in a comparable manner; to a comparable degree. *adv.*

com par a tive (kəm par′ə tiv), **1** that compares: *She made a comparative study of the habits of bees and wasps.* **2** measured by comparison with something else; relative: *Screens give us comparative freedom from flies.* **3** the second of three degrees of comparison of an adjective or adverb. *Fairer* is the comparative of *fair. More slowly* is the comparative of *slowly.* **4** showing the second degree of comparison of an adjective or adverb. *Better* is the comparative form of *good.* 1,2,4 *adj.,* 3 *n.*

com par a tive ly (kəm par′ə tiv lē), by comparison; relatively; somewhat: *Mountains are comparatively free of mosquitoes. adv.*

com pare (kəm per′ *or* kəm par′), **1** find out or point out how persons or things are alike and how they are different: *I compared my answers with the teacher's and found I had made a mistake.* **2** say (two things) are alike; consider as similar; liken: *The fins of a fish may be compared to the wings of a bird; both are used in moving.* **3** be considered like or equal: *Canned fruit cannot compare with fresh fruit.* **4** name the positive, comparative, and superlative degrees of an adjective or adverb. *v.*, **com pared, com par ing.**

beyond compare, without an equal; most excellent: *The food at this restaurant is beyond compare.*

com par i son (kəm par′ə sən), **1** act or process of comparing; finding the likenesses and differences: *The teacher's comparison of the heart to a pump helped the students to understand how the heart works.* **2** likeness; similarity: *There is no comparison between these two cameras; one is much better than the other.* **3** change in an adjective or adverb to show degrees. The three degrees of comparison are positive, comparative, and superlative. EXAMPLE: cold, colder, coldest; helpful, more helpful, most helpful; good, better, best. *n.*

in comparison with, compared with: *Even a large lake is small in comparison with an ocean.*

com part ment (kəm pärt′mənt), a separate division or section of anything; part of an enclosed place set off by walls or partitions: *The ship's hold has watertight compartments so that a leak will fill up only part of the ship. n.*

compass (def. 1)
Even though the dial may be turned, the needle remains fixed on north.

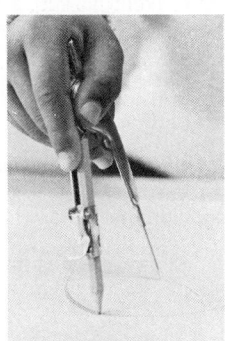
compass (def. 2)
The sharply pointed arm remains fixed as the drawing arm revolves.

com pass (kum′pəs), **1** instrument for showing directions, especially one consisting of a needle that points to the North Magnetic Pole. **2** instrument consisting of two legs hinged together at one end, used for drawing circles and curved lines and for measuring distances. **3** boundary; circumference: *within the compass of four walls.* **4** space within limits; extent; range: *There have been many scientific discoveries within the compass of her lifetime.* **5** range of a voice or musical instrument. **6** go around; move around: *Bold explorers compassed the earth in wooden ships.* **7** hem in; surround: *The lake is compassed by a ring of mountains.* 1-5 *n., pl.* **com pass es;** 6,7 *v.*

com pas sion (kəm pash′ən), feeling for another's sorrow or hardship that leads to help; sympathy; pity: *Compassion for the earthquake victims brought a flood of contributions. n.*

com pas sion ate (kəm pash′ə nit), wishing to help those that suffer; sympathetic; pitying. *adj.*

com pat i bil i ty (kəm pat′ə bil′ə tē), agreement; harmony. *n.*

com pat i ble (kəm pat′ə bəl), **1** able to exist or get on well together; agreeing; in harmony: *My new roommate and I are quite compatible.* **2** (in electronics) able to be used with another item or items: *a printer compatible with several computers. adj.*

com pat i bly (kəm pat′ə blē), in a compatible manner; harmoniously. *adv.*

com pa tri ot (kəm pā′trē ət), person born or living in one's own country. *n.*

com pel (kəm pel′), **1** drive or urge with force; force: *Rain compelled us to stop our ball game.* **2** bring about by force; command: *A policeman can compel obedience to the law. v.*, **com pelled, com pel ling.** —**com pel′ling ly,** *adv.*

com pen di um (kəm pen′dē əm), summary that gives much information in little space. *n., pl.* **com pen di ums, com pen di a** (kəm pen′dē ə).

com pen sate (kom′pən sāt), **1** make an equal return to; give an equivalent to: *The children mowed our lawn to compensate us for the window they broke playing ball.* **2** balance by equal weight or power; make up: *Skill sometimes compensates for lack of strength.* **3** pay: *The company compensated her for her extra work. v.*, **com pen sat ed, com pen sat ing.** —**com′pen sa′tor,** *n.*

com pen sa tion (kom′pən sā′shən), **1** something given to make up for something else; something which makes up for a loss, injury, etc.: *I was given a day off as compensation for working overtime.* **2** pay: *Equal compensation should be given for equal work. n.*

com pete (kəm pēt′), **1** try hard to win or gain something wanted by others; be rivals; contend: *She competed against many fine athletes for the gold medal. It is difficult for a small grocery store to compete with a supermarket.* **2** take part (in a contest): *Will you compete in the final race? v.*, **com pet ed, com pet ing.**

com pe tence (kom′pə təns), a being competent; ability: *No one doubted the guide's competence. n.*

com pe ten cy (kom′pə tən sē), competence. *n.*

com pe tent (kom′pə tənt), properly qualified; able: *a competent secretary. adj.* —**com′pe tent ly,** *adv.*

com pe ti tion (kom′pə tish′ən), **1** a trying hard to win or gain something wanted by others; rivalry: *competition among stores for customers.* **2** contest: *She won first place in the swimming competition. n.*

com pet i tive (kəm pet′ə tiv), decided by competition; using competition: *A competitive examination for the job will be held January 10. adj.* —**com pet′i tive ly,** *adv.*

com pet i tor (kəm pet′ə tər), person who competes; rival. *n.*

com pi la tion (kom′pə lā′shən), **1** act of compiling. **2** book, list, or table that has been compiled. *n.*

com pile (kəm pīl′), **1** collect and bring together in one list or account: *I compiled a list of the supplies and equipment we needed.* **2** make (a book, a report, etc.) out of various materials: *It takes many experts to compile an encyclopedia. v.*, **com piled, com pil ing.**

com pil er (kəm pī′lər), **1** person who compiles. **2** computer program that converts programs written in normal words, numbers, and mathematical symbols into programs in the machine language that a computer can use directly. *n.*

com pla cence (kəm plā′sns), complacency. *n.*

com pla cen cy (kəm plā′sn sē), a being pleased with oneself or what one has; self-satisfaction: *She solved the difficult puzzle easily and smiled with complacency. n.*

com pla cent (kəm plā′snt), pleased with oneself or what one has; self-satisfied: *The winner's complacent smile annoyed the loser. adj.* —**com pla′cent ly,** *adv.*

com plain (kəm plān′), **1** say that something is wrong; find fault: *We complained that the room was too cold.* **2** talk about one's pain, troubles, etc.: *He is always complaining.* **3** make an accusation or charge: *I com-*

plained to the police about the barking of my neighbor's dog.
v. —**com plain′er,** *n.* —**com plain′ing ly,** *adv.*

com plain ant (kəm plā′nənt), person who brings a lawsuit against another. *n.*

com plaint (kəm plānt′), **1** a complaining; a voicing of dissatisfaction; finding fault: *His letter is filled with complaints about the food at camp.* **2** accusation; charge: *The judge heard the complaint and ordered an investigation.* **3** a cause for complaining: *Her main complaint is that she has too much work to do.* **4** illness; disease: *A cold is a very common complaint.* *n.*

com plai sance (kəm plā′sns), a being complaisant or obliging; graciousness. *n.*

com plai sant (kəm plā′snt), inclined to do what is asked; obliging; gracious. *adj.* —**com plai′sant ly,** *adv.*

com ple ment (kom′plə mənt *for 1-3;* kom′plə ment *for 4*), **1** something that completes or makes perfect: *The teacher considers homework a necessary complement to classroom work.* **2** number required to complete or make perfect: *The plane had its full complement of passengers; all seats were taken.* **3** word or group of words completing a predicate. In "The bus is late" *late* is a complement. **4** supply a lack of any kind; complete: *The salty flavor of the olives and pickles complemented the blandness of the cheese.* 1-3 *n.,* 4 *v.*

com ple men tar y (kom′plə men′tər ē), forming a complement; completing: *The four seasons are complementary parts of a year. adj.*

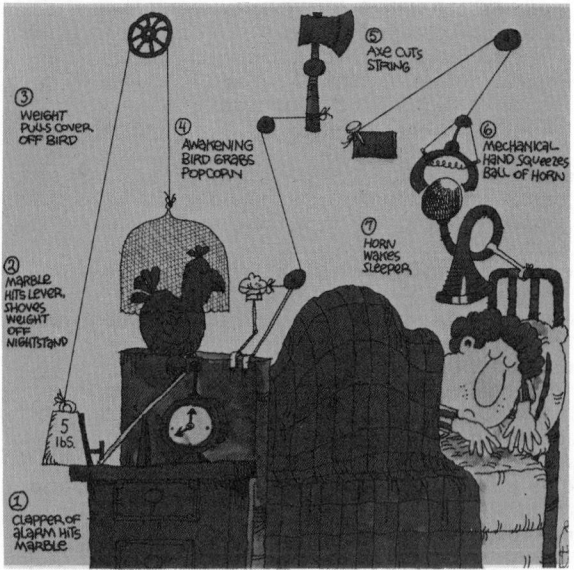

complementary angle
Angle ACB and angle BCD
are complementary angles.

complementary angle, either of two angles which together form an angle of 90 degrees.

com plete (kəm plēt′), **1** with all the parts; whole; entire: *We have a complete set of garden tools.* **2** make whole or entire; make up the full number or amount of: *I completed the set of dishes by buying the cups and saucers.* **3** perfect; thorough: *a complete surprise.* **4** make perfect or thorough: *The good news completed his happiness.* **5** finished; done: *My homework is complete.* **6** get done; finish: *She completed her homework before dinner.* 1,3,5 *adj.,* 2,4,6 *v.* —**com plete′ly,** *adv.* —**com plete′ness,** *n.*

com ple tion (kəm plē′shən), **1** act of completing; finishing: *After the completion of the job, the workers went home.* **2** condition of being completed: *The work is near completion. n.*

com plex (kəm pleks′ *or* kom′pleks *for 1,2;* kom′pleks *for 3,4*), **1** made up of a number of parts: *A watch is a complex device.* **2** hard to understand: *The instructions for building the radio were so complex we could not follow them.* **3** group of related or connected buildings, structures, units, etc.: *The new cultural complex built in our city includes a library, a museum, and a concert hall.* **4** a strong prejudice; unreasonable dislike or fear: *He has a complex about cats.* 1,2 *adj.,* 3,4 *n., pl.* **com plex es.** —**com plex′ly,** *adv.* —**com plex′ness,** *n.*

complex fraction, fraction having a fraction in the numerator, in the denominator, or in both; compound fraction. EXAMPLES: $\frac{1\frac{3}{4}}{3}$, $\frac{1}{3\frac{3}{4}}$, $\frac{\frac{3}{4}}{1\frac{7}{8}}$.

com plex ion (kəm plek′shən), **1** color, quality, and general appearance of the skin, particularly of the face.

2 general appearance of anything; nature; character: *The complexion of the little farm town was changed when two big factories were built nearby. n.*

com plex i ty (kəm plek′sə tē), **1** a complex quality or condition; intricacy: *The complexity of the road map puzzled me.* **2** something complex; complication. *n., pl.* **com plex i ties.**

complex sentence, sentence having one main clause and one or more subordinate clauses. EXAMPLE: When the traffic light turns red, traffic must stop.

com pli ance (kəm plī′əns), **1** a complying; yielding to a request or command: *I appreciated the clerk's ready compliance with my request to exchange the sweater.* **2** tendency to yield to others: *His refusal was all the more surprising in view of his usual compliance. n.*

in compliance with, complying with; according to: *She sent the package by airmail in compliance with my request.*

com pli an cy (kəm plī′ən sē), compliance. *n.*

com pli ant (kəm plī′ənt), complying; yielding; obliging. *adj.* —**com pli′ant ly,** *adv.*

com pli cate (kom′plə kāt), **1** make hard to understand or settle; mix up; make complex; confuse: *Too many rules complicate a game.* **2** make worse or more mixed up: *Headaches can be complicated by eye trouble. v.,* **com pli cat ed, com pli cat ing.**

com pli cat ed (kom′plə kā′tid), hard to understand; involved; complex: *These directions are too complicated. adj.* —**com′pli cat′ed ly,** *adv.* —**com′pli cat′ed ness,** *n.*

com pli ca tion (kom′plə kā′shən), **1** a complex or confused condition that is hard to understand or settle: *Various complications delayed the start of our camping trip.* **2** something that makes matters worse or harder to untangle or settle: *Pneumonia was the complication the doctor feared most after the operation.* **3** act of complicating. *n.*

com plic i ty (kəm plis′ə tē), a being an accomplice; partnership in wrongdoing: *Knowingly receiving stolen goods is complicity in theft. n., pl.* **com plic i ties.**

com pli ment (kom′plə mənt *for 1,2,4;* kom′plə ment *for 3*), **1** something good said about one; something said in praise of one's work: *She received many compliments on her science project.* **2** a courteous act: *The town paid the old artist the compliment of a large attendance at his*

complex (def. 2)
He had a **complex** system for waking up in the morning.

exhibit. **3** pay a compliment to; congratulate: *The coach complimented the winner of the race.* **4 compliments,** *pl.* greetings: *In the box of flowers was a card saying "With the compliments of a friend."* 1,2,4 *n.*, 3 *v.*

com pli men tar y (kom′plə men′tər ē), **1** expressing a compliment; praising: *a complimentary remark.* **2** given free: *a complimentary ticket to the circus.* adj. —**com′pli men tar′i ly,** adv.

com ply (kəm plī′), act in agreement with a request or a command: *I will comply with the doctor's orders.* v., **com plied, com ply ing.** —**com pli′er,** n.

com po nent (kəm pō′nənt), **1** a necessary or essential part: *Quartz and feldspar are the chief components of granite.* **2** forming a necessary part; making up; constituent: *component parts.* 1 *n.*, 2 *adj.*

com port (kəm pôrt′), conduct (oneself) in a certain manner; behave: *Judges should comport themselves with dignity.* v.

com pose (kəm pōz′), **1** make up; form: *The ocean is composed of salt water. Our party was composed of three grown-ups and four children.* **2** put together. To compose a story or poem is to construct it from words. To compose a piece of music is to invent the tune and write down the notes. To compose in a printing office is to set up type to form words or sentences. To compose a picture is to arrange the things in it artistically. **3** make calm: *Stop crying and compose yourself.* **4** settle; arrange: *The union and the company composed their differences and agreed on a contract.* v., **com posed, com pos ing.**

com posed (kəm pōzd′), calm; quiet. adj. —**com pos′ed ly,** adv. —**com pos′ed ness,** n.

com pos er (kəm pō′zər), **1** person who composes. **2** writer of music. n.

com pos ite (kəm poz′it), **1** made up of various parts; compound: *She made a composite photograph by putting together parts of several others.* **2** belonging to a group of plants having flower heads consisting of many very tiny flowers. Daisies and dandelions are composite flowers. **3** any composite thing. 1,2 *adj.*, 3 *n.* —**com pos′ite ly,** adv.

composite number, number exactly divisible by some counting number other than itself or one. 4, 6, and 9 are composite numbers; 2, 3, 5, and 7 are prime numbers.

com po si tion (kom′pə zish′ən), **1** the makeup of anything; what is in it: *The composition of this candy includes sugar, chocolate, and milk.* **2** a putting together of a whole. Writing sentences, making pictures, and setting type in printing are all forms of composition. **3** thing composed. A symphony, poem, or painting is a composition. A piece of writing composed as a school exercise is also a composition. **4** mixture of substances; compound. n.

com post (kom′pōst), mixture of decaying leaves, manure, etc., for fertilizing soil. n.

com po sure (kəm pō′zhər), calmness; quietness; self-control: *She always keeps her composure, even during a crisis.* n.

com pound¹ (kom′pound *for 1-4;* kom pound′ *for 5,6*), **1** having more than one part: *a compound medicine.* **2** something made by combining parts; mixture: *Many medicines are compounds.* **3** word made up of two or more words which keep their separate forms. *Steamship* is a compound made up of the two words *steam* and *ship.* **4** substance formed by chemical combination of two or more elements in definite proportions: *Water is a compound of hydrogen and oxygen.* **5** mix; combine: *The druggist compounded several medicines to fill the prescription.* **6** add to; increase; multiply: *I compounded my troubles by forgetting to bring my homework to school.* 1 *adj.*, 2-4 *n.*, 5,6 *v.* [*Compound*¹ came into English about

600 years ago from French *compondre,* meaning "to put together."] —**com pound′a ble,** adj. —**com pound′er,** n.

com pound² (kom′pound), an enclosed yard with buildings in it. n. [*Compound*² comes from Malay *kampong,* meaning "village, enclosure."]

compound eye, the eye of certain insects and crustaceans. It is composed of many tiny units, each of which receives part of the image.

compound fraction, complex fraction.

compound fracture, fracture in which a broken bone cuts through the flesh.

compound interest, interest paid on both the original sum of money borrowed or invested and the interest added to it.

compound leaf, leaf composed of two or more leaflets on a single stalk.

compound sentence, sentence made up of two or more main clauses. EXAMPLE: The winds blew, the rains fell, and the water covered the earth.

com pre hend (kom′pri hend′), **1** understand the meaning of: *If you can use a word correctly, you comprehend it.* **2** include; contain: *Your report comprehended all the facts.* v. —**com′pre hend′i ble,** adj. —**com′pre hend′ing ly,** adv.

com pre hen si ble (kom′pri hen′sə bəl), understandable. adj. —**com′pre hen′si bly,** adv.

com pre hen sion (kom′pri hen′shən), act or power of understanding: *Arithmetic is beyond the comprehension of a baby.* n.

com pre hen sive (kom′pri hen′siv), of large scope or extent; including much: *The month's schoolwork ended with a comprehensive review.* adj. —**com′pre hen′sive ly,** adv. —**com′pre hen′sive ness,** n.

compress (def. 1)—The cars on the trailer have been **compressed** for processing as scrap.

com press (kəm pres′ *for 1;* kom′pres *for 2*), **1** squeeze together; make smaller by pressure: *Cotton is compressed into bales. Can you compress the story into a few short sentences?* **2** pad of cloth applied to some part of the body to prevent bleeding, lessen inflammation, etc.: *I put a cold compress on my forehead to relieve my headache.* 1 *v.*, 2 *n.*, *pl.* **com press es.**

com press i bil i ty (kəm pres′ə bil′ə tē), compressible quality. n.

com press i ble (kəm pres′ə bəl), that can be compressed. adj.

com pres sion (kəm presh′ən), **1** act or process of compressing. **2** compressed condition. n.

com pres sor (kəm pres′ər), machine for compressing air, gas, etc. *n.*

com prise (kəm prīz′), **1** be made up of; consist of; include: *The United States comprises 50 states.* **2** make up; compose: *Five members comprise the committee.* *v.*, **com prised, com pris ing.**

com pro mise (kom′prə mīz), **1** settle a quarrel or difference of opinion by agreeing that each will give up a part of what he demands: *A good politician knows how to compromise.* **2** settlement of a quarrel or difference of opinion in which both sides agree to give up a part of what each demands: *They both wanted the apple; their compromise was to share it.* **3** result of any such settlement. **4** put under suspicion; put in danger: *You will compromise your reputation if you go around with such a bad crowd.* **1,4** *v.*, **com pro mised, com pro mis ing; 2,3** *n.* —**com′pro mis′er,** *n.*

comp trol ler (kən trō′lər), person employed to look after expenditures and accounts; controller. *n.*

com pul sion (kəm pul′shən), **1** a compelling or being compelled; use of force; force: *A contract signed under compulsion is not legal.* **2** impulse that is hard to resist: *Some people have a compulsion to gamble.* *n.*

com pul sive (kəm pul′siv), of or having to do with an impulse that is hard to resist: *a compulsive desire for neatness.* *adj.* —**com pul′sive ly,** *adv.*

com pul sor y (kəm pul′sər ē), **1** compelled; required: *Attendance at school is compulsory for children over seven years old.* **2** compelling; using force. *adj.*

com punc tion (kəm pungk′shən), uneasiness of the mind because of wrongdoing; regret; remorse: *She had no compunction about copying her friend's work.* *n.*

com pu ta tion (kom′pyə tā′shən), a computing; calculation. *Addition and subtraction are forms of computation.* *n.*

com pute (kəm pyüt′), find out by arithmetical or other mathematical work; calculate: *Mother computed the cost of our trip.* *v.*, **com put ed, com put ing.**

com put er (kəm pyü′tər), **1** an electronic machine that can store, recall, or process information. A computer performs these tasks according to instructions which can easily be changed, so it is able to do many different kinds of work. Computers keep files, solve mathematical problems, play games, and control the operations of other machines. **2** person skilled or trained in computing. *n.*

com put er ize (kəm pyü′tə rīz′), adapt to a computer; operate by means of a computer. *v.*, **com put er ized, com put er iz ing.** —**com put′er i za′tion,** *n.*

computer literacy, an understanding of the basic concepts of computer use and operation; knowledge of computers equivalent to the knowledge of language necessary to read and write.

com rade (kom′rad), **1** a close companion and friend. **2** fellow worker; partner. *n.*

comrade in arms, a fellow soldier.

con[1] (kon), **1** against: *The two groups argued the question pro and con.* **2** a reason against: *The pros and cons of a question are the arguments for and against it.* **1** *adv.*, **2** *n.* [*Con*[1] was shortened from Latin *contra*, meaning "against."]

con[2] (kon), SLANG. **1** swindle (someone) after gaining his or her confidence: *They were conned into investing money in a company that did not exist.* **2** a swindle. **3** swindling: *a con game.* **1** *v.*, **conned, con ning; 2** *n.*, **3** *adj.*

con., **1** against. **2** conclusion.

Con a kry (kon′ə krē), capital of Guinea, in the W part. *n.*

con cave (kon kāv′ *or* kon′kāv), hollow and curved like the inside of a circle or sphere: *The palm of one's hand is concave.* *adj.* —**con cave′ly,** *adv.*

con cav i ty (kon kav′ə tē), **1** concave condition or quality. **2** a concave surface or thing. *n.*, *pl.* **con cav i ties.**

con ceal (kən sēl′), **1** put out of sight; hide: *He concealed the surprise gift in the closet.* **2** keep secret: *They concealed their identities by wearing masks.* *v.* —**con ceal′a ble,** *adj.*

con ceal ment (kən sēl′mənt), **1** a concealing or keeping secret: *The witness's concealment of facts prevented a fair trial.* **2** means or place for concealing. *n.*

con cede (kən sēd′), **1** admit as true; acknowledge: *I conceded that I had made a mistake.* **2** allow (a person) to have; grant: *They conceded us the right to use their driveway.* *v.*, **con ced ed, con ced ing.** —**con ced′er,** *n.*

con ceit (kən sēt′), too high an opinion of oneself or of one's ability; vanity: *In his conceit, the track star thought that no one could outrun him.* *n.*

con ceit ed (kən sē′tid), having too high an opinion of oneself or of one's ability; vain. *adj.*

con ceiv a ble (kən sē′və bəl), able to be conceived or thought of; imaginable: *We take every conceivable precaution against fire.* *adj.*

con ceiv a bly (kən sē′və blē), in a conceivable way. *adv.*

con ceive (kən sēv′), **1** form in the mind; think up; imagine: *She conceived a plan for earning some spending money.* **2** have an idea or feeling; think: *It is difficult to conceive of life without conveniences such as automobiles and telephones.* **3** become pregnant with: *conceive a child.* *v.*, **con ceived, con ceiv ing.** —**con ceiv′er,** *n.*

con cen trate (kon′sən trāt), **1** bring or come together in one place: *A magnifying glass can concentrate enough sunlight to scorch paper. The audience at the music festival concentrated around the stage.* **2** pay close attention; focus the mind: *He concentrated on his reading so that he would understand the story.* **3** make stronger. An acid solution is concentrated when it has a lot of acid in it. **4** something that has been concentrated: *Lemon juice with the water removed is a concentrate.* **1-3** *v.*, **con cen trat ed, con cen trat ing; 4** *n.*

con cen tra tion (kon′sən trā′shən), **1** a concentrating or a being concentrated. **2** close attention: *When she gave the problem her full concentration, she figured out the answer.* **3** (of a solution) strength: *The acid solution was of weak concentration because so much water had been added.* *n.*

concentration camp, a prison camp where political enemies, prisoners of war, or members of minority groups are held by government order.

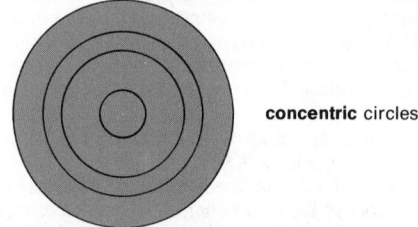

concentric circles

con cen tric (kən sen′trik), having the same center. *adj.* —**con cen′tri cal ly,** *adv.*

con cept (kon′sept), idea of a thing or class of things; general notion; idea: *the concept of equal treatment under law.* *n.*

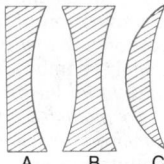

concave lenses
A, concave surface opposite plane surface
B, double concave
C, concave and convex

con cep tion (kən sep′shən), **1** idea; thought; notion: *Her conception of the problem was different from mine.* **2** act of forming an idea or thought. **3** a becoming pregnant. *n.*

con cep tu al ize (kən sep′chü ə līz), form concepts or ideas about. *v.*, **con cep tu al ized, con cep tu al iz ing.** —**con cep′tu al i za′tion,** *n.*

con cern (kən sėrn′), **1** have to do with; be the business or affair of; belong to; interest: *The school play concerns every member of the class.* **2** anything which has to do with one's work or one's interests; business; affair: *The party decorations are my concern; you pay attention to refreshments.* **3** troubled interest; worry; anxiety: *Their concern over their sick child kept them awake all night.* **4** make anxious; cause to worry; trouble: *We didn't want to concern you with the bad news.* **5** a business company; firm: *We wrote to two big concerns for their catalogs.* 1,4 *v.*, 2,3,5 *n.*

con cerned (kən sėrnd′), **1** worried; anxious: *His parents are quite concerned about his poor health.* **2** interested: *Concerned citizens exercise their right to vote. adj.*

con cern ing (kən sėr′ning), having to do with; about: *The reporter asked many questions concerning the accident. prep.*

con cert (kon′sərt), a musical performance in which several musicians or singers take part: *The school orchestra gave a concert last night. n.*

in concert, all together; in agreement: *The class worked in concert.*

con cert ed (kən sėr′tid), arranged by agreement; combined: *a concerted effort. adj.* —**con cert′ed ly,** *adv.*

concertina

con cer ti na (kon′sər tē′nə), a small musical instrument somewhat like an accordion. *n., pl.* **con cer ti nas.**

con cer to (kən cher′tō), a long musical composition for one or more principal instruments, such as a violin or piano, with the accompaniment of an orchestra. It usually has three movements. *n., pl.* **con cer tos, con cer ti** (kən cher′tē). [*Concerto* was borrowed from Italian *concerto,* and can be traced back to Latin *com-,* meaning "with," and *certare,* meaning "to strive."]

con ces sion (kən sesh′ən), **1** a conceding; granting: *As a concession to their pleas, the children were allowed to stay up past bedtime.* **2** anything conceded or granted; admission: *I have made all the concessions that I intend to make.* **3** something conceded or granted by a government or controlling authority; grant. Land or privileges given by a government to a business company are called concessions. **4** the right or space leased for a specific use: *the hot-dog concession at the amusement park. n.*

conch (kongk *or* konch), **1** a soft-bodied sea animal of tropical waters having a large, spiral shell. **2** its shell. *n., pl.* **conchs** (kongks), **conch es** (kon′chiz).

con cil i ate (kən sil′ē āt), **1** win over; soothe: *She conciliated her angry little sister with a candy bar.* **2** bring into harmony; reconcile. *v.*, **con cil i at ed, con cil i at ing.** —**con cil′i a′tor,** *n.*

con cil i a tion (kən sil′ē ā′shən), **1** a winning over or

a hat	i it	oi oil	ch child	(a in about
ā age	ī ice	ou out	ng long	e in taken
ä far	o hot	u cup	sh she	ə = { i in pencil
e let	ō open	u̇ put	th thin	o in lemon
ē equal	ô order	ü rule	ŦH then	(u in circus
ėr term			zh measure	

soothing; reconciling. **2** a being won over or soothed; being reconciled. *n.*

con cil i a to ry (kən sil′ē ə tôr′ē), tending to win over, soothe, or reconcile: *Shaking hands after a fight is a conciliatory gesture. adj.*

con cise (kən sīs′), expressing much in few words; brief but full of meaning: *He gave a concise report of the meeting. adj.* —**con cise′ly,** *adv.* —**con cise′ness,** *n.*

con clave (kon′klāv), a private meeting. *n.*

con clude (kən klüd′), **1** come or bring to an end; finish: *The play concluded with a happy ending and the curtain came down. We concluded the meeting at six o'clock.* **2** reach (certain decisions or opinions) by reasoning; infer: *From the tracks we saw, we concluded that the animal must have been a bear.* **3** arrange; settle: *The two countries concluded a trade agreement. v.,* **con clud ed, con clud ing.** —**con clud′er,** *n.*

con clu sion (kən klü′zhən), **1** final part; end: *The end of each chapter in our science book has a conclusion summing up all the important facts.* **2** decision or opinion reached by reasoning; inference: *Researchers came to the conclusion that the disease was caused by a virus.* **3** arrangement; settlement: *the conclusion of a peace treaty between two countries.* **4** a final result; outcome: *bring work to a good conclusion. n.*

in conclusion, finally; lastly; to conclude: *I will say, in conclusion, that it was an honor to be the speaker at this meeting.*

con clu sive (kən klü′siv), decisive; convincing; final: *The evidence against the suspect was conclusive. adj.* —**con clu′sive ly,** *adv.* —**con clu′sive ness,** *n.*

con coct (kon kokt′), prepare; make up: *He concocted a drink made of grape juice and ginger ale. They concocted an excuse for being late to school. v.* —**con coct′er,** *n.*

con coc tion (kon kok′shən), **1** a concocting: *The concoction of the milk shake took several minutes.* **2** thing concocted. *n.*

con cord (kon′kôrd *or* kong′kôrd), agreement; harmony; peace: *concord between friends. n.* [*Concord* came into English about 650 years ago from French *concorde,* and can be traced back to Latin *com-,* meaning "with," and *cordis,* meaning "heart." See **Word Family.**]

WORD FAMILY

concord

Below are words related to *concord.* They can all be traced back to the Latin word *cor* (kōr), meaning "heart."

accord	cordial	discourage
accordance	courage	encourage
accordion	discord	record

Con cord (kong′kərd), **1** town in E Massachusetts. The second battle of the Revolutionary War was fought there on April 19, 1775. **2** capital of New Hampshire, in the S part. *n.*

con cord ance (kon kôrd′ns), an alphabetical list of the principal words of a book with references to the passages in which they occur. *n.*

con course (kon′kôrs), **1** a flowing or coming together: *The fort was built on a wedge of land at the concourse of two rivers.* **2** a crowd. **3** a place where crowds come: *the main concourse of the railroad station. n.*

con crete (kon′krēt′ *or* kon krēt′), **1** existing as an actual object, not merely as an idea or as a quality; real: *A painting is concrete; its beauty is not.* **2** specific; particular; not general: *A daisy is a concrete example of a composite flower.* **3** mixture of crushed stone or gravel, sand, cement, and water that hardens as it dries. Concrete is used for foundations, buildings, sidewalks, roads, dams, and bridges. **4** made of this mixture: *a concrete sidewalk.* **1,2,4** *adj.,* **3** *n.* —**con crete′ly,** *adv.* —**con crete′ness,** *n.*

con cu bine (kong′kyə bīn), **1** woman who lives with a man without being legally married to him. **2** (in countries where one man can legally have many wives) a wife having inferior rank or rights. *n.*

con cur (kən kėr′), **1** be of the same opinion; agree: *The contest judges all concurred in giving her the prize.* **2** happen at the same time; coincide: *Two weeks of rain concurred with high tides, causing coastal flooding.* *v.,* **con curred, con cur ring.**

con cur rence (kən kėr′əns), **1** agreement. **2** a happening at the same time. *n.*

con cur rent (kən kėr′ənt), **1** happening at the same time: *concurrent events.* **2** agreeing; harmonious: *concurrent ideas.* **3** coming together; meeting at a point. *adj.* —**con cur′rent ly,** *adv.*

con cus sion (kən kush′ən), **1** a sudden, violent shaking; shock: *The concussion caused by the explosion broke many windows.* **2** injury to the brain caused by a blow, fall, etc. *n.*

con demn (kən dem′), **1** express strong disapproval of: *We condemn cruelty to animals.* **2** pronounce guilty of crime or wrong: *The accused was condemned by the jury.* **3** sentence; doom: *condemned to a life of loneliness.* **4** declare not sound or suitable for use: *This bridge was condemned as unsafe.* **5** take for public use under special provision of the law: *Two neighborhood streets have been condemned to make room for the new expressway. v.*

con dem na tion (kon′dem nā′shən), a condemning or a being condemned: *the condemnation of an unsafe bridge. His condemnation made him an outcast. n.*

con den sa tion (kon′den sā′shən), **1** a condensing or a being condensed: *the condensation of milk, the condensation of steam into water.* **2** something condensed; condensed mass. A cloud is a condensation of water vapor in the atmosphere. *n.*

con dense (kən dens′), **1** make or become denser or more compact: *Milk is condensed by removing much of the water from it.* **2** change from a gas or vapor to a liquid. If steam touches cold surfaces, it condenses or is condensed into water. **3** put into fewer words; say briefly: *A long story can sometimes be condensed into a few sentences. v.,* **con densed, con dens ing.** —**con den′sa ble,** *adj.*

condensed milk, a thick, sweetened, canned milk, prepared by evaporating some of the water from ordinary milk.

con dens er (kən den′sər), **1** person or thing that condenses something. **2** capacitor. **3** apparatus for changing gas or vapor into a liquid. *n.*

con de scend (kon′di send′), **1** come down willingly or graciously to the level of one's inferiors in rank: *The queen condescended to eat with the beggars.* **2** grant a favor with a haughty or patronizing attitude: *The little boy's older sister finally condescended to take him to the movies. v.* —**con′de scend′ing ly,** *adv.*

con de scen sion (kon′di sen′shən), **1** pleasantness to one's inferiors in rank. **2** a haughty or patronizing attitude. *n.*

con di ment (kon′də mənt), something used to give flavor and relish to food, such as mustard and spices. *n.*

con di tion (kən dish′ən), **1** state in which a person or thing is: *The condition of the house is better than when I bought it.* **2** good condition; good health: *People who take part in sports must keep in condition.* **3** put in good condition: *Exercise conditions your muscles.* **4** social position; rank: *Lincoln's parents were poor settlers of humble condition.* **5** thing on which something else depends; thing without which something else cannot be: *One of the conditions of the peace treaty was the return of all prisoners.* **6** conditions, *pl.* set of circumstances: *Icy roads make for poor driving conditions.* **7** shape the behavior of; accustom: *This dog has been conditioned to expect food when it hears a bell.* **8** a requirement that is expressed by an open mathematical sentence. $3 + x = 5$ expresses the condition that a number you are to find, added to 3, must equal 5. **1,2,4-6,8** *n.,* **3,7** *v.*

on condition that, with the understanding that; if: *I'll go on condition that you will go, too.*

con di tion al (kən dish′ə nəl), **1** depending on something else; limited. "You may go if the sun shines" is a conditional promise. **2** expressing or containing a condition: *Conditional statements in the sales agreement limited the use of the land. adj.*

con di tion al ly (kən dish′ə nə lē), under a condition or conditions: *She accepted the invitation conditionally, until she could check her calendar. adv.*

con di tion er (kən dish′ə nər), **1** device or substance that maintains or improves the quality of something: *water conditioner.* **2** air conditioner. *n.*

con do (kon′dō), INFORMAL. condominium. *n., pl.* **con dos.**

con dole (kən dōl′), express sympathy; grieve: *Friends condoled with the family at the funeral. v.,* **con doled, con dol ing.**

con do lence (kən dō′ləns), expression of sympathy: *Their friends sent the family many condolences. n.*

con do min i um (kon′də min′ē əm), **1** an apartment house in which each apartment is owned rather than rented. **2** apartment in a building like this. *n.*

con done (kən dōn′), forgive or overlook: *Good friends will condone each other's faults. v.,* **con doned, con don ing.** —**con′do na′tion,** *n.* —**con don′er,** *n.*

condor—about 4 ft. (1.5 m.) long; wingspread up to about 10 ft. (3 m.)

con dor (kon′dər), a large vulture with a ruffed neck and bare head. Condors live on high mountains in South America and California. *n.*

con duce (kən düs′ *or* kən dyüs′), be favorable; lead; contribute: *Darkness and quiet conduce to sleep. v.,* **con duced, con duc ing.**

con du cive (kən dü′siv *or* kən dyü′siv), favorable; helpful: *Exercise and proper eating habits are conducive to good health. adj.*

con duct (kon′dukt *for 1,4;* kən dukt′ *for 2,3,5-7*), **1** way of acting; behavior thought of as good or bad: *Her conduct was rude and inexcusable.* **2** act in a certain way; behave: *When company came, the children were expected to conduct themselves properly.* **3** direct; manage: *The board of directors conducts the affairs of this large business.* **4** direction; management. **5** direct (an orchestra, choir, etc.) as leader: *He conducts a band of one hundred instruments.* **6** go along with and show the way to; guide: *She conducted tours through the museum.* **7** transmit; be a channel for: *Those pipes conduct steam to the radiators upstairs. Metals conduct heat and electricity.* 1,4 *n.,* 2,3, 5-7 *v.*

con duc tion (kən duk′shən), **1** transmission of heat, electricity, etc., by the transferring of energy from one particle to another. Heat travels through metal by conduction. **2** a conveying: *the conduction of water through a pipe. n.*

con duc tiv i ty (kon′duk tiv′ə tē), power of conducting heat, electricity, sound, etc. *n.*

con duc tor (kən duk′tər), **1** person who conducts; leader or guide: *the conductor of a tour.* **2** director of an orchestra, chorus, etc. **3** a railroad worker in charge of a train and its crew. On a passenger train, the conductor may also collect tickets. **4** thing that transmits heat, electricity, light, or sound. Copper is a good conductor of heat and electricity. *n.*

con du it (kon′dü it *or* kon′dit), **1** channel or pipe for carrying liquids long distances; aqueduct or canal. **2** pipe or underground passage for electric wires or cables. *n.*

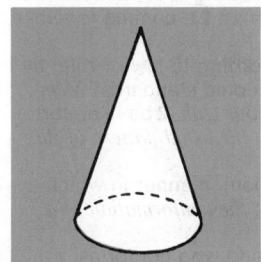

cone (def. 1)

cone (def. 3)

cone (kōn), **1** a solid object that has a flat, round base that narrows to a point at the top. **2** anything shaped like a cone: *an ice-cream cone, the cone of a volcano.* **3** a cone-shaped, scaly growth that bears the seeds on pine, cedar, fir, and other evergreen trees. **4** one of a group of cells of the retina of the eye that responds to light. *n.*

Con es to ga wagon (kon′ə stō′gə), a covered wagon with broad wheels, used by the American pioneers for traveling on soft ground or on the prairie. [This wagon was named for the *Conestoga* Valley, Pennsylvania, where it was first built.]

conf., **1** compare. **2** conference.

con fec tion (kən fek′shən), piece of candy, candied fruit, jam, etc. *n.*

con fec tion er (kən fek′shə nər), person who makes or sells candies, ice cream, and cakes. *n.*

con fec tion er y (kən fek′shə ner′ē), **1** candies or sweets; confections. **2** place where confections, ice cream, and cakes are made or sold. *n., pl.* **con fec tion er ies.**

con fed er a cy (kən fed′ər ə sē), **1** union of countries or states; group of people joined together for a special

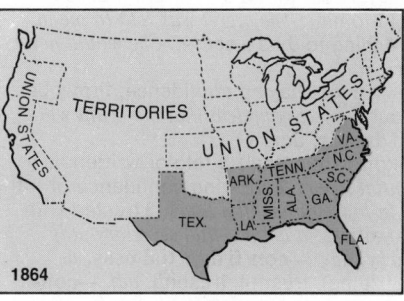

the Confederacy (def. 2) the darker area

1864

a hat	i it	oi oil	ch child	a in about
ā age	ī ice	ou out	ng long	e in taken
ä far	o hot	u cup	sh she	ə = i in pencil
e let	ō open	u̇ put	th thin	o in lemon
ē equal	ô order	ü rule	ŦH then	u in circus
ėr term			zh measure	

purpose; league. **2 the Confederacy,** group of eleven southern states that seceded from the United States in 1860 and 1861. *n., pl.* **con fed er a cies.**

con fed er ate (kən fed′ər it *for 1,2,4;* kən fed′ə rāt′ *for 3*), **1** country, person, etc., joined with another for a special purpose; ally: *The hijacker told his confederate to guard the passengers.* **2** joined together for a special purpose; allied. **3** join together for a special purpose; ally: *When the Civil War began in 1861, only six states had confederated.* **4 Confederate, a** of or belonging to the Confederacy. **b** person who lived in, supported, or fought for the Confederacy. 1,4b *n.,* 2,4a *adj.,* 3 *v.,* **con fed er at ed, con fed er at ing.**

Confederate States of America, the Confederacy.

con fed e ra tion (kən fed′ə rā′shən), **1** a joining together in a league or alliance: *The conference devised a plan for a confederation of the colonies.* **2** league; confederacy; alliance. *n.*

con fer (kən fėr′), **1** talk things over; consult together; exchange ideas: *The President often confers with advisers.* **2** give; bestow: *to confer a medal on a hero. v.,* **conferred, con fer ring. —con fer′rer, n.**

con fer ence (kon′fər əns), **1** meeting of interested persons to discuss a particular subject: *A conference was called to discuss the fuel shortage.* **2** act of consulting together: *The teacher was in conference with parents after school.* **3** association of athletic teams, churches, etc., joined together for some special purpose. *n.*

con fess (kən fes′), **1** own up; acknowledge; admit: *I confess you are right on one point.* **2** admit one's guilt: *The thief decided to confess.* **3** tell one's sins to a priest in order to obtain forgiveness. **4** hear (a person) tell his or her sins in order to obtain forgiveness, as a priest does. *v.*

con fes sion (kən fesh′ən), **1** act of confessing; owning up; telling one's mistakes or sins. **2** thing confessed. *n.*

con fes sion al (kən fesh′ə nəl), a small booth in which a priest hears confessions. *n.*

con fes sor (kən fes′ər), **1** person who confesses. **2** priest who has the authority to hear confessions. *n.*

con fet ti (kən fet′ē), bits of colored paper thrown about at carnivals, weddings, or parades. *n.* [*Confetti* comes from Italian *confetti,* meaning "bonbons, candies," and can be traced back to Latin *con-,* meaning "with, together," and *facere,* meaning "to make, do." Confetti was called this because of the colored paper in which the candies were wrapped.]

con fi dant (kon′fə dant′), person trusted with one's secrets or private affairs; close friend. *n.*

con fide (kən fīd′), **1** tell as a secret: *He confided his troubles to his brother.* **2** show trust by telling secrets: *She always confided in her friend.* v., **con fid ed, con fid ing.** —**con fid′er,** *n.*

con fi dence (kon′fə dəns), **1** firm belief or trust: *I have complete confidence in his honesty.* **2** firm belief in oneself; self-confidence: *Years of experience at her work have given her great confidence.* **3** trust that a person will not tell others what is told to him: *The secret was told to me in strict confidence.* **4** thing told as a secret: *She would never reveal a confidence.* *n.*

con fi dent (kon′fə dənt), having confidence; firmly believing; certain; sure: *I feel confident that our team will win.* *adj.* —**con′fi dent ly,** *adv.*

con fi den tial (kon′fə den′shəl), **1** told or written as a secret: *a confidential report.* **2** showing confidence or intimacy: *She spoke in low, confidential tones.* **3** trusted with secrets or private affairs: *a confidential secretary.* *adj.* —**con′fi den′tial ly,** *adv.* —**con′fi den′tial ness,** *n.*

con fid ing (kən fī′ding), trustful; trusting. *adj.* —**con fid′ing ly,** *adv.*

con fig u ra tion (kən fig′yə rā′shən), manner of arrangement; form; shape; outline: *Geographers study the configuration of the surface of the earth.* *n.*

con fine (kən fīn′ *for 1,2;* kon′fīn *for 3*), **1** keep within limits; restrict: *She confined her reading to biography.* **2** keep in; shut in: *A cold confined him to the house. For two years he was confined in prison.* **3** Often, **confines,** *pl.* boundary; border; limit: *I have never been beyond the confines of my own state.* **1,2** *v.,* **con fined, con fin ing; 3** *n.* —**con fin′er,** *n.*

confinement (def. 1)
The kitten tried to escape from its **confinement** in the yard.

con fine ment (kən fīn′mənt), **1** a confining or a being confined. **2** period of childbirth. *n.*

con firm (kən fėrm′), **1** prove to be true or correct; make certain: *The mayor confirmed the report that taxes would be increased.* **2** make more certain; place beyond all doubt; verify: *The airline office telephoned to confirm an airplane reservation that I had requested last week.* **3** make firmer; strengthen: *A sudden storm confirmed my decision not to leave.* **4** admit to full membership in a church or synagogue after required study and preparation. *v.* —**con firm′a ble,** *adj.*

con fir ma tion (kon′fər mā′shən), **1** a making certain by more information or evidence: *She telephoned the store for confirmation that it was open evenings.* **2** thing that confirms; proof: *Don't believe rumors that lack confirmation.* **3** ceremony of admitting a person to full membership in a church or synagogue after required study and preparation. *n.*

con firmed (kən fėrmd′), **1** firmly established; proved: *a confirmed rumor.* **2** settled; habitual: *a confirmed bachelor.* *adj.*

con fis cate (kon′fə skāt), **1** seize for the public treasury:

The traitor's property was confiscated. **2** seize by authority; take and keep: *The teacher confiscated several comic books.* *v.,* **con fis cat ed, con fis cat ing.** —**con′fis ca′tor,** *n.*

con fis ca tion (kon′fə skā′shən), a confiscating or a being confiscated. *n.*

con fla gra tion (kon′flə grā′shən), a big and destructive fire. *n.*

conflagration—In 1871, a **conflagration** leveled much of the city of Chicago.

con flict (kon′flikt *for 1,2;* kən flikt′ *for 3*), **1** a fight or struggle, especially a long one: *The UN General Assembly discussed the conflict in the Middle East.* **2** active opposition of persons or ideas; clash: *A conflict of opinion arose over the need for a new highway.* **3** be actively opposed; differ in thought or action; clash: *The testimony of the witnesses conflicted on whether the robber had blond or dark hair.* **1,2** *n.,* **3** *v.*

con flu ence (kon′flü əns), **1** a flowing together: *the confluence of two streams to form a river.* **2** a coming together of people or things; throng. *n.*

con form (kən fôrm′), **1** act according to law or rule; be in agreement with generally accepted standards: *Members must conform to the rules of our club.* **2** be like; correspond: *Her symptoms conform to the usual pattern of flu.* *v.* —**con form′er,** *n.*

con for ma tion (kon′fôr mā′shən), manner in which a thing is formed; structure; form: *the conformation of a flower.* *n.*

con form ist (kən fôr′mist), person who conforms. *n.*

con form i ty (kən fôr′mə tē), **1** action in agreement with generally accepted standards. **2** likeness; similarity; agreement. *n., pl.* **con form i ties.**

con found (kon found′), confuse; perplex: *I was confounded by their rude behavior.* *v.* —**con found′er,** *n.*

con front (kən frunt′), **1** meet face to face; stand facing. **2** face boldly; oppose: *We crept downstairs with baseball bats in hand to confront the prowler.* **3** bring face to face; place before: *The teacher confronted the student with his failing grade.* *v.*

con fron ta tion (kon′frən tā′shən), a confronting or a being confronted. *n.*

Con fu cius (kən fyü′shəs), 551?-479 B.C., Chinese philosopher and moral teacher. *n.*

con fuse (kən fyüz′), **1** throw into disorder; mix up; bewilder: *So many people talking to me at once confused me.* **2** be unable to tell apart; mistake (one thing or person for another): *People often confuse this girl with her twin sister.* *v.,* **con fused, con fus ing.** —**con fus′ing ly,** *adv.*

con fu sion (kən fyü′zhən), **1** a disordered condition of things: *the confusion in an untidy room.* **2** a mistaking one thing or person for another: *Words like "believe" and "receive" sometimes cause confusion in spelling.* **3** a being perplexed or bewildered: *His confusion over the exact* *address caused him to go to the wrong house. n.*

con fute (kən fyüt′), **1** prove (an argument, testimony, etc.) to be false or incorrect: *The lawyer confuted the testimony of the witness by showing actual photographs of the accident.* **2** prove (a person) to be wrong: *The speaker confuted her opponents by facts and logic. v.,* **con fut ed, con fut ing.** —**con fut′er,** *n.*

con geal (kən jēl′), **1** harden or make solid by cold; freeze. **2** thicken; coagulate: *The pudding congealed as it cooled. v.* —**con geal′ment,** *n.*

con gen ial (kən jē′nyəl), **1** having similar tastes and interests; getting on well together: *Congenial companions made the trip pleasant.* **2** agreeable; suitable: *The young scientist found laboratory work more congenial than teaching science. adj.* —**con gen′ial ly,** *adv.*

con gen i tal (kən jen′ə təl), present at birth: *a congenital defect. adj.* —**con gen′i tal ly,** *adv.*

con ger (kong′gər), a large ocean eel that is caught for food along the coasts of Europe. *n.*

conger eel, conger.

congest (def. 1)
The street was **congested** with traffic.

con gest (kən jest′), **1** fill too full; overcrowd. **2** become or cause to become too full of blood or mucus. In pneumonia, the lungs become congested. *v.*

con ges tion (kən jes′chən), **1** an overcrowded or congested condition: *Many drivers were caught in Sunday's traffic congestion and were late getting home.* **2** too much blood or mucus in one part of the body: *Nose drops often relieve nasal congestion. n.*

con glom er ate (kən glom′ər it *for 1-4;* kən glom′ə rāt′ *for 5*), **1** made up of various parts or materials gathered into a mass: *a conglomerate rock.* **2** mass formed of fragments. **3** rock made up of pebbles, gravel, etc., held together by a cementing material. **4** group of unrelated corporations operating under a single ownership. **5** gather in a rounded mass; collect together. **1** *adj.,* **2-4** *n.,* **5** *v.,* **con glom er at ed, con glom er at ing.**

con glom e ra tion (kən glom′ə rā′shən), a mixed-up mass of various things or persons; mixture. *n.*

Con go (kong′gō), **1** river in central Africa, flowing from SE Zaïre to the Atlantic. Also, **Zaïre. 2** former name of **Zaïre. 3 Republic of,** country in central Africa on the Atlantic. *Capital:* Brazzaville. *n.*

con grat u late (kən grach′ə lāt), express one's pleasure at the happiness or good fortune of: *The judge congratulated the winner of the race. v.,* **con grat u lat ed, con grat u lat ing.**

con grat u la tion (kən grach′ə lā′shən), **1** a congratulating; wishing a person joy. **2 congratulations,** *pl.* expression of pleasure at another's happiness or good fortune: *Congratulations on your high grades. n.*

con gre gate (kong′grə gāt), come together into a crowd or mass; assemble: *They congregated around the campfire. v.,* **con gre gat ed, con gre gat ing.** —**con′gre ga′tor,** *n.*

a hat	i it	oi oil	ch child
ā age	ī ice	ou out	ng long
ä far	o hot	u cup	sh she
e let	ō open	ù put	th thin
ē equal	ô order	ü rule	ᴛʜ then
ėr term			zh measure

ə = { e in ... / i in ... / o in ... / u in ... }

con gre ga tion (kong′grə gā′shən), **1** act of coming together into a crowd or mass; an assembling. **2** group of people gathered together for religious worship or instruction: *The congregation joined together in prayer.* **3** a gathering of people or things; assembly. *n.*

con gre ga tion al (kong′grə gā′shə nəl), **1** of a congregation: *congregational singing.* **2 Congregational,** of a form of church government in which each individual church governs itself. *adj.*

Con gre ga tion al ist (kong′grə gā′shə nə list), member of a Congregational church. *n.*

con gress (kong′gris), **1** the lawmaking body of a nation, especially of a republic. **2 Congress,** the national lawmaking body of the United States, consisting of the Senate and House of Representatives, with members elected from every state. **3** a meeting of representatives for the discussion of some subject; conference: *Doctors came from all over the world to the medical congress on heart transplants. n., pl.* **con gress es.**

con gres sion al (kən gresh′ə nəl), **1** of or having to do with a congress. **2 Often, Congressional.** of or having to do with Congress. *adj.* —**con gres′sion al ly,** *adv.*

con gress man (kong′gris mən). Often, **Congressman.** member of Congress, especially of the House of Representatives. *n., pl.* **con gress men.**

con gress wom an (kong′gris wùm′ən). Often, **Congresswoman.** a woman member of Congress, especially of the House of Representatives. *n., pl.* **con gress wom en.**

con gru ence (kən grü′əns *or* kong′grü əns), a being congruent. *n.*

con gru ent (kən grü′ənt *or* kong′grü ənt), exactly coinciding: *Congruent triangles have the same size and shape. adj.* —**con gru′ent ly,** *adv.*

con ic (kon′ik), conical. *adj.*

con i cal (kon′ə kəl), **1** shaped like a cone: *Volcanic mountains are conical.* **2** of a cone. *adj.* —**con′i cal ly,** *adv.*

con i fer (kon′ə fər *or* kō′nə fər), tree or shrub that bears cones. The pine, fir, spruce, hemlock, and larch are conifers. *n.* [*Conifer* comes from Latin *conifer,* meaning "bearing cones."]

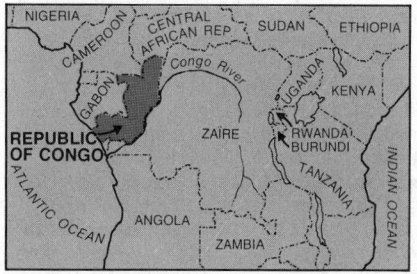

Congo (def. 3)

co nif er ous (kō nif′ər əs), **1** bearing cones. **2** belonging to the conifers. *adj.*

conj., conjunction (def. 1).

con jec tur al (kən jek′chər əl), involving a guess; depending on conjecture: *His statement was merely conjectural, not proved. adj.* —**con jec′tur al ly,** *adv.*

con jec ture (kən jek′chər), **1** conclusion reached by

193

height of that mountain is ... a conjecture; guess: conjecture about the next ... v., con jec tured, con-...ble, adj. —con jec'tur er, n. ... together; unite; combine. v. ..., united; combined. adj. —con-

...jə gəl), **1** of or having to do with mar-...gal life. **2** of husband and wife: *conjugal love.* ...'ju gal ly, *adv.*

...gate (kon'jə gāt), give the forms of (a verb) in ...er: *The past tense of "to be" is conjugated: I was, you were, he, she, or it was; we were, you were, they were. v.,* **con ju gat ed, con ju gat ing.** [*Conjugate* comes from Latin *conjugatum*, meaning "yoked together, united."]

con ju ga tion (kon'jə gā'shən), **1** a systematic arrangement of the forms of a verb. **2** a joining together; coupling. Some one-celled animals reproduce by the conjugation of one cell with another. *n.*

con junc tion (kən jungk'shən), **1** word that connects words, phrases, clauses, or sentences. *And, but, or, though,* and *if* are conjunctions. **2** a joining together; union; combination: *Our school, in conjunction with two other schools, will hold a large bazaar next week. n.*

con jure (kon'jər *or* kun'jər), **1** compel (a spirit, devil, etc.) to appear or disappear by a set form of words. **2** cause to appear as if by magic: *Grandmother conjured up a bag of old-fashioned toys from the attic to our delight.* **3** perform tricks by very quick, deceiving movements of the hands. *v.,* **con jured, con jur ing.**

con jur er *or* **con jur or** (kon'jər ər *or* kun'jər ər), **1** person who performs tricks with quick, deceiving movements of the hands; juggler. **2** magician. *n.*

conk (kongk), SLANG. **1** hit, especially on the head. **2** a blow on the head. **1** *v.,* **2** *n.*
conk out, SLANG. break down; stall: *The old car conked out.*

Conn., Connecticut.

con nect (kə nekt'), **1** join one thing to another; link two things together; join: *connect a hose to a faucet. The telephone operator connected us. These two rooms connect.* **2** think of one thing with another: *We usually connect spring with sunshine and flowers.* **3** join with others in some business or interest; bring into some relation: *This store is connected with a chain of stores. v.* —**con nec'tor, con nect'er,** *n.*

Con nect i cut (kə net'ə kət), one of the northeastern states of the United States. *Abbreviation:* Conn. or CT *Capital:* Hartford. *n.*

con nec tion (kə nek'shən), **1** act of connecting: *The connection of our telephone took several hours.* **2** a being joined together or connected; association: *His connection with our business firm has lasted over thirty years.* **3** thing that connects; connecting part: *The connection between the radiator and the pipe has become loose.* **4** any kind of relation with another: *I had no connection with that prank.* **5** a thinking of persons or things together; linking together of words or ideas in proper order: *His last remark had no connection with the earlier part of his talk.* **6** an influential, wealthy, or prominent associate or friend: *I got a summer job through my friend's connections.* **7** the meeting of trains, ships, etc., at definite times so that passengers can change from one to the other without delay: *The bus arrived late at the airport and we missed our airplane connection.* **8** a related person; relative: *My sister-in-law is a connection of mine by marriage. n.*
in connection with, in relation with; in regard to: *He read a biography of Booker T. Washington in connection with his study of American history.*

con nec tive (kə nek'tiv), **1** that connects. **2** anything that connects. Conjunctions and relative pronouns are connectives that join together words, phrases, or clauses. **1** *adj.,* **2** *n.* —**con nec'tive ly,** *adv.*

connective tissue, tissue that connects, supports, or encloses other tissues and organs in the body.

con ning tower (kon'ing), tower on the deck of a submarine, used as an entrance and as a place for observation.

con niv ance (kə nī'vəns), a conniving; pretended ignorance or secret encouragement of wrongdoing. *n.*

con nive (kə nīv'), **1** avoid noticing what one might have to condemn; pretend not to see something wrong; give aid to wrongdoing by not telling of it: *The dishonest sheriff connived at gambling.* **2** cooperate secretly: *connive with the enemy. v.,* **con nived, con niv ing.** —**con niv'ing ly,** *adv.*

con niv er (kə nī'vər), person who connives. *n.*

con nois seur (kon'ə sėr'), person able to give critical judgments in art or in matters of taste; expert: *a connoisseur of antique furniture. n.*

con no ta tion (kon'ə tā'shən), what is suggested in addition to the simple or literal meaning. When Elaine is described in legends about King Arthur as "the lily maid," the connotation is that she was pale, delicate, and pure. *n.*

con note (kə nōt'), suggest in addition to the simple or literal meaning; mean besides; imply. Red is a color that can connote feelings of passion, anger, or hatred. *v.,* **con not ed, con not ing.**

con nu bi al (kə nü'bē əl *or* kə nyü'bē əl), of marriage; conjugal. *adj.* —**con nu'bi al ly,** *adv.*

con quer (kong'kər), **1** get by fighting; win in war: *The Romans conquered much of the ancient world.* **2** overcome by force; get the better of; defeat: *conquer an enemy, conquer a bad habit.* **3** be victorious; be the conqueror: *The general said he would conquer or die. v.* —**con'quer a ble,** *adj.* —**con'quer ing ly,** *adv.*

con quer or (kong'kər ər), person who conquers. *n.*

con quest (kon'kwest *or* kong'kwest), **1** act of conquering: *the conquest of a country, the conquest of disease.* **2** thing conquered; land, people, etc., conquered: *The city was an easy conquest for the invaders. n.*

con quis ta dor (kon kwis'tə dôr *or* kon kē'stə dôr), **1** a Spanish conqueror in North or South America during the 1500's. **2** conqueror. *n., pl.* **con quis ta dors, con quis ta do res** (kon kē'stə dôr'ēz).

cons., consolidated.

con science (kon'shəns), sense of right and wrong; ideas and feelings within you that tell you when you are doing right and warn you of what is wrong. *n.* —**con'science less,** *adj.*

con sci en tious (kon'shē en'shəs), **1** careful to do what one knows is right; controlled by conscience. **2** done with care to make it right: *Conscientious work is careful and exact. adj.* —**con'sci en'tious ly,** *adv.* —**con'sci en'tious ness,** *n.*

conscientious objector, person with moral or religious objections to serving in the armed forces or to taking up arms in warfare.

con scious (kon'shəs), **1** having experience; aware; knowing: *I was conscious of a sharp pain.* **2** able to feel or perceive; awake: *About five minutes after fainting he became conscious again.* **3** known to oneself; felt: *The young woman had a conscious desire to see her family again.* **4** meant; intended; intentional: *She told a conscious lie when she denied that she had broken the vase. adj.* —**con'scious ly,** *adv.*

con scious ness (kon'shəs nis), **1** condition of being conscious; awareness: *The injured woman did not regain* *consciousness for two hours.* **2** all the thoughts and feelings of a person. *n.*

con script (kən skript′ *for 1;* kon′skript *for 2*), **1** force by law to serve in the armed forces; draft. **2** a conscripted soldier or sailor. 1 *v.,* 2 *n.*

con scrip tion (kən skrip′shən), forced service in the armed forces; the draft. *n.*

con se crate (kon′sə krāt), **1** set apart as sacred; make holy: *The new chapel in the church was consecrated by the bishop.* **2** devote to a purpose; dedicate: *The doctor consecrated her life to helping the sick.* *v.,* **con se crat ed, con se crat ing.** —**con′se cra′tor, con′se crat′er,** *n.*

con se cra tion (kon′sə krā′shən), **1** a consecrating or a being consecrated. **2** ordination to a sacred office, especially that of bishop. *n.*

con sec u tive (kən sek′yə tiv), following one right after another; successive: *Monday, Tuesday, and Wednesday are consecutive days of the week.* *adj.* —**con sec′u tive ly,** *adv.* —**con sec′u tive ness,** *n.*

con sen sus (kən sen′səs), general agreement; opinion of all or most of the people consulted: *The club members finally reached a consensus about adopting the proposal.* *n., pl.* **con sen sus es.**

con sent (kən sent′), **1** give approval or permission; agree: *My father would not consent to my staying up past 10 p.m.* **2** approval; permission: *We have mother's consent to go swimming.* 1 *v.,* 2 *n.* —**con sent′er,** *n.*

con se quence (kon′sə kwens), **1** a result or effect: *The consequence of the fall was a broken leg.* **2** importance: *The loss of her ring is a matter of great consequence to her.* *n.*
take the consequences, accept what happens because of one's action: *She did not study for the test, so she had to take the consequences.*

con se quent (kon′sə kwent), following as an effect; resulting: *His long illness and consequent absence put him far behind in his work.* *adj.*

con se quen tial (kon′sə kwen′shəl), **1** following as an effect; resulting; consequent. **2** self-important. *adj.* —**con′se quen′tial ly,** *adv.* —**con′se quen′tial ness,** *n.*

con se quent ly (kon′sə kwent′lē), as a result; therefore: *He overslept and, consequently, he was late.* *adv.*

con ser va tion (kon′sər vā′shən), a preserving from harm or decay; protecting from loss or from being used up: *The conservation of our mineral resources is important because they can never be replaced.* *n.*

con ser va tion ist (kon′sər vā′shə nist), person who wants to preserve and protect the forests, rivers, and other natural resources of a country. *n.*

con serv a tism (kən sér′və tiz′əm), inclination to keep things as they are or were in the past; opposition to abrupt change, especially any major change in established traditions. *n.*

con serv a tive (kən sér′və tiv), **1** inclined to keep things as they are or were in the past; opposed to abrupt change, especially any major change in established traditions. **2** person opposed to change. **3** not inclined to take risks; cautious; moderate: *This old, reliable company has conservative business methods.* **4** Often, **Conservative. a** of a political party that favors the preservation of established traditions and opposes major changes in national institutions. **b** member of a conservative political party. **5** conserving; preserving. 1,3,4a,5 *adj.,* 2,4b *n.* —**con serv′a tive ly,** *adv.* —**con serv′a tive ness,** *n.*

con serv a to ry (kən sér′və tôr′ē), **1** school for instruction in music. **2** greenhouse for growing and displaying plants and flowers. *n., pl.* **con serv a to ries.**

con serve (kən sérv′ *for 1;* kon′sérv′ *for 2*), **1** keep from harm or decay; keep from loss or from being used up; preserve: *She conserved her strength for the end of the race.* **2** Often, **conserves,** *pl.* fruit preserved in sugar, often as

jam. 1 *v.,* **con served, con serv ing;** 2 *n.* —**con serv′- er,** *n.*

con sid er (kən sid′ər), **1** think about in order to decide; think about carefully: *Before you dash off an answer, take time to consider the problem.* **2** think to be; regard as: *I consider him a very able student.* **3** allow for; take into account: *This watch runs very well, when you consider how old it is.* **4** be thoughtful of: *A kind person considers the feelings of others.* *v.*

con sid er a ble (kən sid′ər ə bəl), **1** worth thinking about; important: *Pollution is a considerable problem.* **2** not a little; much: *$500 is a considerable sum of money.* *adj.*

con sid er a bly (kən sid′ər ə blē), a good deal; much: *The boy was considerably older than he looked.* *adv.*

con sid er ate (kən sid′ər it), thoughtful of others and their feelings: *She is considerate enough to tell her parents where she is going and with whom.* *adj.* —**con sid′er ate ly,** *adv.* —**con sid′er ate ness,** *n.*

con sid er a tion (kən sid′ə rā′shən), **1** a thinking about in order to decide: *Before writing your answers please give careful consideration to the questions on the test.* **2** something thought of as a reason: *Price and quality are two considerations in buying anything.* **3** thoughtfulness for others and their feelings: *Playing the radio loud at night shows a lack of consideration for the neighbors.* **4** money or other payment: *I will do the work for you for a small consideration.* *n.*
in consideration of, 1 because of: *In consideration of my bad cold, the teacher let me leave school early.* **2** in return for: *The neighbor gave the girl a dollar in consideration of her helpfulness.*
take into consideration, allow for; take into account; consider: *The teacher took my week's absence into consideration in grading my test.*
under consideration, being thought about: *Her request for a higher salary is under consideration.*

con sid ered (kən sid′ərd), carefully thought out: *That is my considered opinion.* *adj.*

con sid er ing (kən sid′ər ing), taking into account; making allowance for: *Considering her age, the little girl reads well.* *prep.*

con sign (kən sīn′), **1** hand over; deliver: *The dog was consigned to the pound. His will consigned his property to his sister.* **2** send: *We will consign the goods to him by express.* *v.* —**con sign′a ble,** *adj.*

con sign ment (kən sīn′mənt), **1** a consigning: *The Red*

conservatory
(def. 2)

Cross ordered the consignment of food and clothing to the flooded area. **2** something consigned: *The store received a consignment of fall clothing.* n.

con sist (kən sist′), be made up; be formed: *A week consists of seven days.* v.

consist in, be contained in; be made up of: *He believes that happiness consists in being easily pleased or satisfied.*

con sist ence (kən sis′təns), consistency. n.

con sist en cy (kən sis′tən sē), **1** degree of firmness or stiffness: *Frosting for a cake must be of the right consistency to spread easily without dripping.* **2** a keeping to the same principles, course, etc.: *He showed no consistency when he did excellent work the first part of the year and very poor work after that.* n., pl. **con sist en cies.**

con sist ent (kən sis′tənt), **1** thinking or acting today in agreement with what you thought yesterday; keeping to the same principles and habits. **2** in agreement; in accord: *Driving at high speed on a rainy night is not consistent with safety.* adj. —**con sist′ent ly,** adv.

con sis tor y (kən sis′tər ē), court of clergymen to decide church matters; church council. n., pl. **con sis tor ies.**

con so la tion (kon′sə lā′shən), **1** a consoling; comfort. **2** a comforting person, thing, or event. n.

console[1]
He tried to
console his
grieving friend.

con sole[1] (kən sōl′), ease the grief or sorrow of; comfort. v., **con soled, con sol ing.** [*Console*[1] comes from French *consoler,* and can be traced back to Latin *com-,* meaning "together," and *solari,* meaning "to soothe, comfort."] —**con sol′a ble,** adj. —**con sol′er,** n. —**con sol′ing ly,** adv.

con sole[2] (kon′sōl), **1** part of an organ containing the keyboard, stops, and pedals. **2** a radio, television, or phonograph cabinet made to stand on the floor. **3** panel of buttons, switches, dials, etc., used to control electrical or electronic equipment in a computer, missile, etc. n. [*Console*[2] comes from French *console,* meaning "beam, support."]

con sol i date (kən sol′ə dāt), **1** combine into one; unite; merge: *The three banks consolidated and formed a single large bank.* **2** make solid or firm; strengthen: *The political party consolidated its power by winning many state elections.* v., **con sol i dat ed, con sol i dat ing.** —**con sol′i da′tor,** n.

con sol i da tion (kən sol′ə dā′shən), a consolidating or a being consolidated. n.

con som mé (kon′sə mā′), a clear soup made by boiling meat in water. n., pl. **con som més.** [*Consommé* comes from French *consommé,* which originally meant "consumed, finished."]

con so nance (kon′sə nəns), **1** agreement; accordance. **2** harmony of sounds. n.

con so nant (kon′sə nənt), **1** a speech sound formed by completely or partially stopping the breath. The two consonants in *ship* are spelled by the letters *sh* and *p.* **2** any letter or combination of letters that stands for such a

sound. All the letters that are not vowels (*b, c, d, f,* etc.) are consonants. n.

con sort (kon′sôrt *for 1,3;* kən sôrt′ *for 2*), **1** husband or wife. The husband of a queen is sometimes called the prince consort. **2** keep company; associate: *The soldier was jailed for consorting with the enemy.* 1 n., 2 v.

con spic u ous (kən spik′yü əs), **1** easily seen: *A traffic light should be placed where it is conspicuous.* **2** attracting notice; remarkable: *conspicuous bravery.* adj. —**con spic′u ous ly,** adv. —**con spic′u ous ness,** n.

con spir a cy (kən spir′ə sē), secret planning with others to do something unlawful or wrong; plot: *The leaders of the conspiracy against the government were caught.* n., pl. **con spir a cies.**

con spir a tor (kən spir′ə tər), person who conspires; plotter: *A group of conspirators planned to overthrow the government.* n.

con spire (kən spīr′), **1** plan secretly with others to do something unlawful or wrong; plot: *The spies conspired to steal secret government documents.* **2** act together: *All things conspired to make her birthday a happy one.* v., **con spired, con spir ing.** —**con spir′er,** n. —**con spir′ing ly,** adv.

con sta ble (kon′stə bəl *or* kun′stə bəl), a police officer; policeman. n.

con stan cy (kon′stən sē), firmness in belief or feeling; steadfastness: *the constancy of Christopher Columbus in looking for a new route to India.* n.

con stant (kon′stənt), **1** going on without stopping: *Three days of constant rain caused flooding.* **2** continually happening; repeated again and again: *a constant ticking sound.* **3** always the same; not changing: *The ship held a constant course due north.* **4** thing that is always the same; value or quantity that does not change: *The speed of light is an important constant in physics.* **5** faithful; loyal; steadfast: *a constant friend.* 1-3,5 adj., 4 n.

Con stan tine the Great (kon′stən tēn *or* kon′stən-tīn), A.D. 288?-337, Roman emperor from A.D. 306 to 337, who granted liberty of worship to Christians and established the city of Constantinople.

Con stan ti no ple (kon′stan tə nō′pəl), large city in SE Europe, now called **Istanbul.** It was the capital of the Byzantine Empire and later the capital of Turkey. See **Byzantine Empire** for map. n.

con stant ly (kon′stənt lē), **1** without change; always: *He is constantly late.* **2** without stopping: *If a clock is kept wound it runs constantly.* **3** often; again and again: *She has to be reminded constantly to clean her room.* adv.

con stel la tion (kon′stə lā′shən), group of stars usually having a recognized shape. The Big Dipper is the easiest constellation to locate. n.

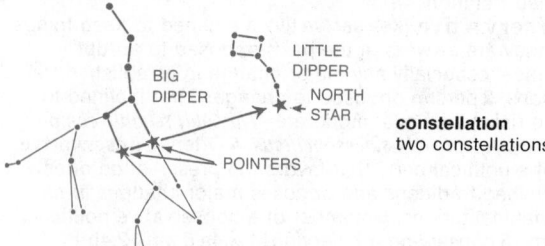

LITTLE
DIPPER
BIG
DIPPER
NORTH
STAR
POINTERS

constellation
two constellations

con ster na tion (kon′stər nā′shən), great dismay; paralyzing terror: *To our consternation the child darted out in front of the speeding car.* n.

con sti pate (kon′stə pāt), cause constipation in. v., **con sti pat ed, con sti pat ing.**

con sti pa tion (kon′stə pā′shən), a condition in which it is difficult to empty the bowels. n.

con stit u en cy (kən stich′ü ən sē), **1** the voters in a district; constituents: *The congresswoman was reelected to office by her constituency.* **2** this district. *n., pl.* **con stit u en cies.**

con stit u ent (kən stich′ü ənt), **1** forming a necessary part: *Carbon is a constituent element in all living cells.* **2** part of a whole; necessary part: *Sugar is the main constituent of candy.* **3** voter: *A senator receives many letters from constituents.* 1 *adj.,* 2,3 *n.*

con sti tute (kon′stə tüt *or* kon′stə tyüt), **1** make up; form: *Seven days constitute a week.* **2** set up; establish: *Schools are constituted by law to teach boys and girls.* **3** appoint; elect: *The group constituted one member as its leader.* *v.,* **con sti tut ed, con sti tut ing.** **—con′sti tut′- er,** *n.*

con sti tu tion (kon′stə tü′shən *or* kon′stə tyü′shən), **1** way in which a person or thing is organized; nature; makeup: *A person with a good constitution is strong and healthy.* **2** system of fundamental principles according to which a nation, state, or group is governed: *The United States has a written constitution.* **3** the Constitution, the written set of fundamental principles by which the United States is governed. *n.*

con sti tu tion al (kon′stə tü′shə nəl *or* kon′stə tyü′- shə nəl), **1** of or in the constitution of a person or thing: *A constitutional weakness makes him catch a cold easily.* **2** of, in, or according to the constitution of a nation, state, or group: *The Supreme Court must decide whether this law is constitutional.* **3** a walk taken for one's health: *After Sunday dinner my grandparents always take a constitutional.* 1,2 *adj.,* 3 *n.*

con sti tu tion al i ty (kon′stə tü′shə nal′ə tē *or* kon′- stə tyü′shə nal′ə tē), accordance with the constitution of a nation, state, or group: *The constitutionality of freedom of speech has been upheld in the courts many times.* *n.*

con sti tu tion al ly (kon′stə tü′shə nə lē *or* kon′stə- tyü′shə nə lē), **1** in or by constitution; naturally. **2** according to the constitution. *adv.*

con strain (kən strān′), **1** force to do something; compel: *I felt constrained to question them further.* **2** confine; restrain: *The wild animal was constrained.* *v.* **—con- strain′a ble,** *adj.* **—con strain′er,** *n.*

con straint (kən strānt′), **1** a holding back of natural feelings; embarrassment: *They felt a little constraint with the new teacher for the first day or so.* **2** force; compulsion: *The witness testified under constraint.* *n.*

con strict (kən strikt′), make smaller by squeezing; contract; compress: *A tourniquet stops the flow of blood by constricting the blood vessels.* *v.*

con stric tion (kən strik′shən), **1** a constricting; compression. **2** a feeling of tightness; constricted condition: *He coughed and complained of a constriction in his chest.* **3** a constricted part. *n.*

con stric tive (kən strik′tiv), contracting; compressing. *adj.*

con stric tor (kən strik′tər), snake that kills its prey by squeezing it with its coils. The boa is a constrictor. *n.*

con struct (kən strukt′), put together; fit together; build: *construct a bridge.* *v.* **—con struc′tor,** *n.*

con struc tion (kən struk′shən), **1** act of constructing; building: *The city council provided funds for the construction of a new gym.* **2** way in which a thing is constructed: *Cracks and leaks are signs of poor construction.* **3** thing built or put together; structure: *The dollhouse was a construction of wood and cardboard.* **4** arrangement or relation of words in a sentence, phrase, clause, etc. **5** meaning; interpretation: *You put an unfair construction on what I said.* *n.*

con struc tive (kən struk′tiv), **1** tending to be useful; helpful: *During the experiment the teacher gave some con-* structive suggestions that prevented accidents. **2** having to do with construction; structural. *adj.* **—con struc′tive ly,** *adv.* **—con struc′tive ness,** *n.*

con strue (kən strü′), show the meaning of; explain; interpret: *Different lawyers may construe the same law differently.* *v.,* **con strued, con stru ing.** **—con stru′a ble,** *adj.* **—con stru′er,** *n.*

con sul (kon′səl), **1** official appointed by a government to live in a foreign city in order to look after its business interests and to protect its citizens who are traveling or living there. **2** either of two chief magistrates of the ancient Roman republic. *n.*

con su lar (kon′sə lər), **1** of a consul. **2** serving as a consul: *the consular representative of the United States at Frankfurt.* *adj.*

con su late (kon′sə lit), the official residence or the offices of a consul: *the Canadian consulate in New York.* *n.*

con sult (kən sult′), **1** seek information or advice from; refer to. You can consult persons, books, or maps to find out what you wish to know. **2** exchange ideas; talk things over: *He consulted with his lawyer before signing the contract.* **3** take into consideration; have regard for: *A good teacher consults the interests of the class.* *v.* **—con- sult′a ble,** *adj.* **—con sult′er,** *n.*

con sult ant (kən sult′nt), **1** person who gives professional or technical advice. **2** person who consults another. *n.*

con sul ta tion (kon′səl tā′shən), **1** act of consulting; seeking information or advice. **2** a meeting to exchange ideas or talk things over: *The three doctors held a consultation to discuss the patient's condition.* *n.*

con sum a ble (kən sü′mə bəl), **1** able to be consumed: *consumable products.* **2** something meant to be consumed or used up: *Some workbooks are consumables.* 1 *adj.,* 2 *n.*

con sume (kən süm′), **1** use up; spend: *A student consumes much time in studying. I consumed almost all the money I earned last summer.* **2** eat or drink up: *We will each consume at least two sandwiches on our hike.* **3** destroy; burn up: *A huge fire consumed the entire forest.* *v.,* **con sumed, con sum ing.** **—con sum′ing ly,** *adv.* **consumed with,** absorbed by curiosity, envy, etc.: *She was consumed with the desire to travel.*

con sum er (kən sü′mər), **1** person who uses food, clothing, or anything grown or made by producers: *A low price for wheat should reduce the price of flour to the consumer.* **2** person or thing that consumes. *n.*

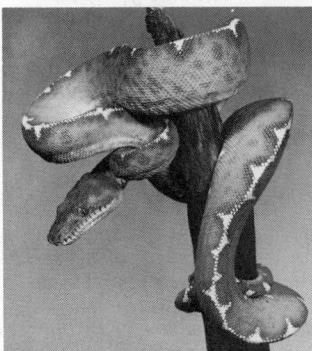

constrictor
a tree boa constrictor
from South America

con sum er ism (kən sü′mə riz′əm), trend toward increased protection of consumers from unsafe manufacturing processes and from misleading labeling, packaging, and promotion practices, and toward protection of the environment as far as possible. *n.*

con sum mate (kon′sə māt *for 1;* kən sum′it *for 2*), **1** bring to completion; realize; fulfill: *My ambition was consummated when I won the first prize.* **2** in the highest degree; complete; perfect: *The orchestra played with consummate skill.* 1 *v.,* **con sum mat ed, con sum mat ing;** 2 *adj.* —**con sum′mate ly,** *adv.* —**con′sum ma′tor,** *n.*

con sum ma tion (kon′sə mā′shən), completion; fulfillment: *the consummation of an ambition. n.*

con sump tion (kən sump′shən), **1** a using up; use: *We took along some food for consumption on our trip.* **2** amount used up: *The consumption of fuel oil is much greater in winter than in summer.* **3** tuberculosis of the lungs. *n.*

con sump tive (kən sump′tiv), **1** having or likely to have tuberculosis of the lungs. **2** person who has tuberculosis of the lungs. **3** tending to consume; destructive; wasteful. 1,3 *adj.,* 2 *n.* —**con sump′tive ly,** *adv.* —**consump′tive ness,** *n.*

cont., continued.

Cont., Continental.

con tact (kon′takt), **1** condition of touching; a touching together: *A magnet will draw iron filings into contact with it.* **2** condition of being in communication: *The control tower lost radio contact with the airplane pilot.* **3** connection: *The reporter had several important contacts in the government.* **4** get in touch with: *I've been trying to contact you for two days.* **5** put or bring into contact. 1-3 *n.,* 4,5 *v.*

contact lens, a very small, thin, plastic lens fitted on the front of the eyeball. Contact lenses take the place of eyeglasses.

con ta gion (kən tā′jən), **1** the spreading of disease by contact: *Contagion is hard to prevent in crowded areas.* **2** disease spread in this way. **3** the spreading of any influence from one person to another: *At the cry of "Fire!" a contagion of fear swept through the audience. n.*

con ta gious (kən tā′jəs), **1** spreading by contact; catching: *Mumps is a contagious disease.* **2** easily spreading from one person to another: *Yawning is often contagious. adj.* —**con ta′gious ly,** *adv.* —**con ta′gious ness,** *n.*

con tain (kən tān′), **1** have within itself; hold as contents: *Books contain information. My wallet contains two dollars.* **2** be capable of holding: *That pitcher will contain a quart of milk.* **3** be equal to: *A pound contains 16 ounces.* **4** control; hold back; restrain: *She could not contain her excitement over winning the contest. v.* —**con tain′a ble,** *adj.*

con tain er (kən tā′nər), box, can, jar, etc., used to hold or contain something. *n.*

con tam i nant (kən tam′ə nənt), something that contaminates; pollutant. *n.*

con tam i nate (kən tam′ə nāt), make impure by contact; defile; pollute: *The drinking water had been contaminated by sewage. v.,* **con tam i nat ed, con tam i nat ing.** —**con tam′i na′tor,** *n.*

con tam i na tion (kən tam′ə nā′shən), a contaminating or being contaminated; pollution: *The river was free of contamination. n.*

contd., continued.

con temn (kən tem′), treat with contempt; despise; scorn. *v.* —**con temn′er,** *n.*

con tem plate (kon′təm plāt), **1** look at or think about for a long time; study carefully: *I will contemplate your offer. We contemplated the beautiful mountain landscape.* **2** have in mind; consider, intend, or expect: *She is con-*

templating a trip to Europe. **3** meditate. *v.,* **con tem plated, con tem plat ing.** —**con′tem plat′ing ly,** *adv.* —**con′tem pla′tor,** *n.*

con tem pla tion (kon′təm plā′shən), **1** a looking at or thinking about something for a long time; deep thought: *I was sunk in contemplation and did not hear the doorbell.* **2** expectation or intention: *We are buying tents and other equipment in contemplation of a camping trip next summer. n.*

con tem pla tive (kon′təm plā′tiv), deeply thoughtful; meditative: *The monks lived a quiet, contemplative life in the monastery. adj.* —**con′tem pla′tive ly,** *adv.* —**con′tem pla′tive ness,** *n.*

con tem po ra ne ous (kən tem′pə rā′nē əs), belonging to the same period of time; contemporary: *contemporaneous eighteenth-century composers. adj.* —**con tem′po ra′ne ous ly,** *adv.* —**con tem′po ra′ne ous ness,** *n.*

con tem po rar y (kən tem′pə rer′ē), **1** belonging to or living in the same period of time: *Dickinson and Whitman were contemporary poets. The telephone and the phonograph were contemporary inventions.* **2** person living in the same period of time: *Abraham Lincoln and Robert E. Lee were contemporaries.* **3** of the present time; modern: *The book had contemporary children's stories in addition to the old fairy tales.* 1,3 *adj.,* 2 *n., pl.* **con tem po rar ies.**

con tempt (kən tempt′), **1** the feeling that a person, act, or thing is mean, low, or worthless; despising; scorn: *feel contempt for a cheat.* **2** condition of being despised or scorned; disgrace: *The traitor was held in contempt.* **3** disobedience to or open disrespect for the rules or decisions of a court of law or a lawmaking body. A person can be put in jail for contempt of court. *n.*

con tempt i ble (kən temp′tə bəl), deserving contempt or scorn: *a contemptible lie. adj.* —**con tempt′i ble ness,** *n.*

con tempt i bly (kən temp′tə blē), in a contemptible manner. *adv.*

con temp tu ous (kən temp′chü əs), showing contempt; scornful: *a contemptuous look. adj.* —**con temp′tu ous ly,** *adv.* —**con temp′tu ous ness,** *n.*

con tend (kən tend′), **1** work hard against difficulties; fight; struggle: *The first settlers in America had to contend with harsh winters, sickness, and lack of food.* **2** take part in a contest; compete: *Five runners were contending in the first race.* **3** declare to be true; argue: *The children contended about whose turn it was. Most doctors contend that cigarette smoking is dangerous to one's health. v.* —**contend′er,** *n.*

con tent¹ (kon′tent), **1** Often, **contents,** *pl.* what is contained in anything; all things inside: *An old chair, a desk, and a bed were the only contents of the room. The contents of the box fell out in my lap.* **2** facts and ideas stated; what is written in a book and in a speech: *I didn't understand the content of her speech.* **3** amount contained: *Maple syrup has a high sugar content. n.*

con tent² (kən tent′), **1** give satisfaction; please; make easy in mind: *Nothing contents me when I'm in a bad mood.* **2** satisfied; pleased; easy in mind; contented: *Will you be content to wait until tomorrow?* **3** contentment; satisfaction; ease of mind: *The cat lay stretched out beside the fire in complete content.* 1 *v.,* 2 *adj.,* 3 *n.*

con tent ed (kən ten′tid), satisfied; pleased; easy in mind. *adj.* —**con tent′ed ly,** *adv.* —**con tent′ed ness,** *n.*

con ten tion (kən ten′shən), **1** statement or point that one has argued for; statement maintained as true: *Galileo's contention that the earth goes around the sun proved to be true.* **2** an arguing; disputing; quarreling: *There was some contention about the choice of a new captain of the baseball team. n.*

con ten tious (kən ten′shəs), fond of arguing; given to

disputing; quarrelsome: *A contentious person argues about trifles. adj.* —**con ten′tious ly,** *adv.* —**con-ten′tious ness,** *n.*

con tent ment (kən tent′mənt), a being satisfied or pleased; ease of mind. *n.*

con tents (kon′tents). See def. 1 of **content**[1]. *n.pl.*

con test (kon′test *for 1,2;* kən test′ *for 3,4*), **1** trial of skill to see which can win. A game or race is a contest; so is a debate. **2** a fight, struggle, or dispute: *The contest between France and England for North America ended in a victory for England.* **3** fight for; struggle for: *The soldiers contested every inch of ground.* **4** argue against; dispute about: *The lawyer contested the claim and tried to prove that it was false.* *1,2 n., 3,4 v.* —**con test′a ble,** *adj.*

con test ant (kən tes′tənt), person who contests; person who takes part in a contest: *My sister was a contestant in the 100-yard dash. n.*

con text (kon′tekst), the parts directly before and after a word or sentence that influence its meaning. You can often tell the meaning of a word from its use in context. *n.*

con tig u ous (kən tig′yü əs), **1** in actual contact; touching: *a long row of contiguous houses.* **2** very close together; near. *adj.* —**con tig′u ous ly,** *adv.* —**con tig′u ous ness,** *n.*

con ti nence (kon′tə nəns), control of one's actions and feelings; self-restraint; moderation. *n.*

con ti nent (kon′tə nənt), **1** one of the seven great masses of land on the earth. The continents are North America, South America, Europe, Africa, Asia, Australia, and Antarctica. **2 the Continent,** the mainland of Europe. It does not include the British Isles. *n.* [*Continent* comes from Latin *continentem,* meaning "a continuous mass of land, mainland," and can be traced back to Latin *com-,* meaning "together," and *tenere,* meaning "to hold."]

con ti nent al (kon′tə nen′tl), **1** of or like a continent. **2 Continental, a** of or like the mainland of Europe: *Continental customs differ from those of England.* **b** person living on the Continent; European. **c** of the American colonies at the time of the Revolutionary War: *The Second Continental Congress adopted the Declaration of Independence in 1776.* **d** soldier of the American army during the Revolutionary War. *1,2a,2c adj., 2b,2d n.*

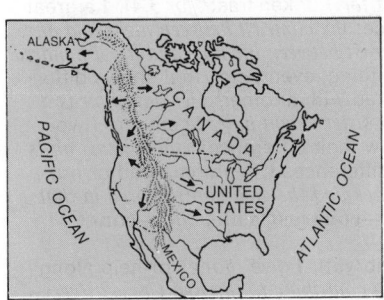

Continental Divide

Continental Divide, ridge in W North America which separates streams flowing toward the Pacific Ocean from those flowing toward the Atlantic or the Arctic Oceans; Great Divide. The Rocky Mountains form a major part of the Continental Divide.

con tin gen cy (kən tin′jən sē), **1** a happening or event depending on something that is uncertain; possibility: *The explorer carried supplies for every contingency.* **2** an accidental happening; chance. *n., pl.* **con tin gen cies.**

con tin gent (kən tin′jənt), **1** share of soldiers, laborers, etc., to be furnished: *The United States sent a large contingent of troops to Europe in World War II.* **2** group that is part of a larger group: *The New York contingent sat* together at the national convention. **3** depending on something not certain; conditional: *Our plans for a picnic are contingent upon fair weather.* **4** liable to happen or not to happen; possible; uncertain: *The traveler set aside five dollars a day for contingent expenses.* **5** happening by chance; accidental; unexpected. *1,2 n., 3-5 adj.*

con tin u al (kən tin′yü əl), **1** never stopping: *the continual flow of the river.* **2** repeated many times; very frequent: *continual interruptions. adj.* —**con tin′u al ness,** *n.*

con tin u al ly (kən tin′yü ə lē), **1** always; without stopping: *Time is continually passing.* **2** again and again; very frequently: *I am continually losing things. adv.*

con tin u ance (kən tin′yü əns), **1** a continuing; going on: *the continuance of a friendship.* **2** act of remaining; stay: *The senator's continuance in office depends on the voters.* **3** adjournment or postponement of legal proceedings until a future time. *n.*

con tin u a tion (kən tin′yü ā′shən), **1** act of going on with a thing after stopping; beginning again: *Continuation of my reading was difficult after so many interruptions.* **2** anything by which a thing is continued; added part: *The continuation of the story will be seen on next week's program.* **3** act or fact of not stopping. *n.*

con tin ue (kən tin′yü), **1** keep up; keep on; go on; go on with: *The rain continued all day. The road continues for miles.* **2** go on after stopping; take up; carry on: *The story will be continued next week. The class begged the teacher to continue with the reading.* **3** last: *The queen's reign continued for 20 years.* **4** stay: *The children must continue in school till the end of June.* **5** cause to stay; maintain: *The club members voted to continue the president in office for another term.* **6** put off until a later time; postpone; adjourn: *The judge continued the case until next month. v.,* **con tin ued, con tin u ing.** —**con tin′u a ble,** *adj.*

con ti nu i ty (kon′tə nü′ə tē *or* kon′tə nyü′ə tē), a going on without stopping; continuing without interruption: *The continuity of her story was broken when the telephone rang. n.*

con tin u ous (kən tin′yü əs), without a stop or break; connected; unbroken: *a continuous sound, a continuous line of cars. adj.* —**con tin′u ous ly,** *adv.* —**con tin′u ous ness,** *n.*

con tort (kən tôrt′), twist or bend out of shape; distort: *The clown contorted his face. v.*

con tor tion (kən tôr′shən), **1** a twisting or bending out of shape. **2** twisted condition: *The acrobat went through various contortions. n.*

contortion
(def. 2)

contour
(def. 2)
contour
plowing

con tour (kon′tuṙ), **1** outline of a figure: *The contour of the Atlantic coast of America is very irregular.* **2** following natural ridges and furrows to avoid erosion. **1** *n.*, **2** *adj.*

contour line, line on a map, showing height above sea level. All points on a contour line have the same elevation.

contour map, map showing heights above sea level by means of contour lines.

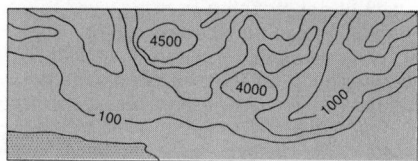

contour map
Mountains in landscape sketch (above) appear on the contour map (below).

con tra band (kon′trə band), **1** goods imported or exported contrary to law; smuggled goods: *Customs officials went through each bag looking for contraband.* **2** a smuggling. **3** against the law; prohibited: *to smuggle contraband drugs into a country.* **1,2** *n.*, **3** *adj.*

con tra bass (kon′trə bās′), **1** the lowest bass instrument. **2** double bass. *n.*

con tra cep tion (kon′trə sep′shən), prevention of conception or becoming pregnant. *n.*

con tra cep tive (kon′trə sep′tiv), of or for contraception: *contraceptive information. adj.*

con tract (kən trakt′ *for 1-4;* kon′trakt *for 5,6;* kon′trakt *or* kən trakt′ *for 7*), **1** draw together; make shorter: *The earthworm contracted its body.* **2** become shorter or smaller; shrink: *Wool fibers contract in hot water.* **3** shorten (a word, phrase, etc.) by omitting some of the letters or sounds: *In talking and writing we often contract "do not" to "don't."* **4** bring on oneself; get; form: *Bad habits are easy to contract and hard to get rid of. She contracted a cold.* **5** agreement. In a contract two or more people agree to do or not to do certain things. **6** a written agreement that can be enforced by law. **7** make a contract: *The builder contracted to build the new house.* **1-4,7** *v.*, **5,6** *n.*

con trac tion (kən trak′shən), **1** a contracting: *Cold causes the contraction of substances; heat causes their expansion.* **2** a being contracted; decrease in size or volume: *The contraction of mercury by cold makes it go down in thermometers.* **3** something contracted; shortened

form: *"Can't" is a contraction of "cannot." n.*

con trac tor (kon′trak tər *or* kən trak′tər), person who agrees to furnish materials or to do a piece of work for a certain price: *a building contractor. n.*

con trac tu al (kən trak′chü əl), of or like a contract. *adj.* —**con trac′tu al ly,** *adv.*

con tra dict (kon′trə dikt′), **1** say that a statement is not true; deny: *They contradicted the rumor that they were moving to another town.* **2** say the opposite of what (a person) has said: *I seldom contradict my parents.* **3** be contrary to; disagree with: *Your story and her story contradict each other. v.* —**con′tra dict′a ble,** *adj.* —**con′tra dict′er, con′tra dic′tor,** *n.*

con tra dic tion (kon′trə dik′shən), **1** a denying of what has been said; saying the opposite: *The expert spoke without fear of contradiction by his listeners.* **2** statement or act that contradicts another; denial. **3** disagreement. *n.*

con tra dic tor y (kon′trə dik′tər ē), in disagreement; contradicting; contrary: *First reports of the election results were so contradictory we could not tell who won. adj.* —**con′tra dic′tor i ly,** *adv.* —**con′tra dic′tor i ness,** *n.*

con tral to (kən tral′tō), **1** the lowest singing voice of a woman; alto. **2** singer with such a voice. **3** part in music for such a voice. **4** of or for a contralto. **1-3** *n., pl.* **con tral tos; 4** *adj.*

con trap tion (kən trap′shən), INFORMAL. device or gadget; contrivance. *n.*

con tra ri ly (kon′trer ə lē *or* kən trer′ə lē), in a contrary manner; on the contrary. *adv.*

con tra ri ness (kon′trer ē nis *or* kən trer′ē nis), a being contrary. *n.*

con tra ri wise (kon′trer ē wīz′), **1** in the opposite way or direction. **2** on the contrary. *adv.*

con tra ry (kon′trer ē *for 1,2;* kən trer′ē *for 3*), **1** completely different; opposed; opposite: *Your taste in music is contrary to mine.* **2** the opposite: *After promising to come early, she did the contrary and came late.* **3** opposing others; stubborn: *The contrary boy often refused to do what was asked of him.* **1,3** *adj.,* **2** *n.*

on the contrary, exactly opposite to what has been said: *He is not stingy; on the contrary, no one could be more generous.*

to the contrary, with the opposite effect.

con trast (kon′trast *for 1,2;* kən trast′ *for 3,4*), **1** a great difference; difference: *the contrast between night and day. There is a great contrast between life now and life a hundred years ago.* **2** person, thing, event, etc., that shows differences when compared with another: *Her dark hair is a sharp contrast to her sister's light hair.* **3** compare (two things) so as to show their differences: *to contrast birds with fishes.* **4** show differences when compared or put side by side: *The black and the gold contrast well in that design.* **1,2** *n.,* **3,4** *v.* —**con trast′a ble,** *adj.* —**con trast′ing ly,** *adv.*

con trib ute (kən trib′yüt), **1** give money or help along with others: *Will you contribute to the Red Cross? Everyone was asked to contribute suggestions.* **2** write (articles, stories, etc.) for a newspaper or magazine. *v.,* **con trib ut ed, con trib ut ing.** —**con trib′ut a ble,** *adj.*

contribute to, help bring about: *A poor diet contributed to the child's bad health.*

con tri bu tion (kon′trə byü′shən), **1** act of contributing; giving of money or help along with others: *Contribution to worthy causes is one of their pet projects.* **2** money or help contributed; gift: *Our contribution to the picnic was the lemonade.* **3** article, story, etc., written for a newspaper or magazine. *n.*

con trib u tor (kən trib′yə tər), person or thing that contributes. *n.*

con trib u to ry (kən trib′yə tôr′ē), helping to bring

about; contributing: *The worker's own carelessness was a contributory cause of the accident. adj.*

con trite (kən trīt′ *or* kon′trīt), **1** sorry for doing something wrong; repentant: *I felt contrite after losing my temper and hitting my friend.* **2** showing deep regret and sorrow: *I wrote a contrite apology. adj.* —**con trite′ly**, *adv.* —**con trite′ness**, *n.*

WORD HISTORY

contrite

Contrite came into English over 600 years ago from French *contrit*, which came from Latin *contritus*, meaning "crushed."

con tri tion (kən trish′ən), **1** sorrow for one's sins or guilt; being contrite; repentance. **2** deep regret. *n.*

con triv ance (kən trī′vəns), **1** thing invented; mechanical device: *A can opener is a handy contrivance.* **2** act or manner of contriving: *By careful contrivance she repaired the old clock and made it go.* **3** plan; scheme. *n.*

con trive (kən trīv′), **1** plan with cleverness or skill; invent; design: *The inventor had contrived a new kind of engine.* **2** plan; scheme; plot: *to contrive a robbery.* **3** arrange to have something happen; manage: *I will contrive to be there by ten o'clock. v.,* **con trived, con triv ing.** —**con triv′a ble**, *adj.* —**con triv′er**, *n.*

con trol (kən trōl′), **1** have power or authority over; direct: *The government controls the printing of money.* **2** power to direct or guide; authority: *Children are under their parents' control.* **3** hold back; keep down; restrain: *I was so upset by the accident that I couldn't control my tears.* **4** a holding back; a keeping down; restraint: *to lose control of one's temper.* **5** means of restraint; check: *The President's power to veto is a control over the legislation passed by Congress.* **6** device on or connected to a machine, that regulates its operation: *This control starts the dishwasher. There is a control for the furnace in our kitchen.* **7 controls,** *pl.* the instruments and devices by which an aircraft, locomotive, car, etc., is operated. **8** individual or group serving as a standard of comparison for testing the results of a scientific experiment performed on a similar individual or group. **1,3** *v.,* **con trolled, con trolling; 2,4-8** *n.* —**con trol′la ble**, *adj.*

con trol ler (kən trō′lər), **1** person employed to supervise expenditures; comptroller: *The mayor directed the city controller to examine the expenses of the fire department.* **2** person who controls, directs, or restrains: *air-traffic controller. n.*

control tower, tower at an airfield for controlling the traffic of aircraft taking off and landing.

con tro ver sial (kon′trə vėr′shəl), **1** of or having to do with controversy: *controversial writing.* **2** open to controversy; debatable; disputed: *a controversial question.* **3** fond of disputing. *adj.* —**con′tro ver′sial ly**, *adv.*

con tro ver sy (kon′trə vėr′sē), act of arguing a question about which differences of opinion exist; debate; dispute; argument: *The long controversy over slavery was one of the causes of the Civil War. n., pl.* **con tro ver sies.**

con tu sion (kən tü′zhən *or* kən tyü′zhən), a bruise. *n.*

co nun drum (kə nun′drəm), **1** riddle whose answer involves a pun or play on words. EXAMPLE: "When is a door not a door?" ANSWER: "When it's ajar." **2** any puzzling problem. *n.*

con va lesce (kon′və les′), recover health and strength

a hat	i it	oi oil	ch child	a in about
ā age	ī ice	ou out	ng long	e in taken
ä far	o hot	u cup	sh she	ə = i in pencil
e let	ō open	u̇ put	th thin	o in lemon
ē equal	ô order	ü rule	ᵺ then	u in circus
ėr term			zh measure	

after illness: *I convalesced at home for three weeks after my operation. v.,* **con va lesced, con va lesc ing.**

con va les cence (kon′və les′ns), **1** the gradual recovery of health and strength after illness. **2** time during which one is convalescing: *The doctor prescribed a three-week convalescence at home for her patient. n.*

con va les cent (kon′və les′nt), **1** recovering health and strength after illness. **2** of or for recovering after illness: *a convalescent home.* **3** person recovering after illness. **1,2** *adj.,* **3** *n.* —**con′va les′cent ly**, *adv.*

con vec tion (kən vek′shən), the transfer of heat from one place to another by the movement of heated particles of a gas or liquid. *n.*

con vene (kən vēn′), **1** meet for some purpose; gather together; assemble: *Congress convenes in the Capitol at Washington, D.C., at least once a year.* **2** call together: *Any member may convene our club in an emergency. v.,* **convened, con ven ing.** —**con ven′a ble**, *adj.* —**con ven′er**, *n.*

con ven ience (kən vē′nyəns), **1** fact or quality of being convenient: *The convenience of packaged meats and other foods helps to increase their sales.* **2** comfort; advantage: *Many stores have a delivery service for the convenience of shoppers.* **3** anything handy or easy to use; thing that saves trouble or work: *A folding table is a convenience in a small room. n.*

at one's convenience, when it is convenient for one; at a suitable time or place, or under suitable conditions: *Come by to pick me up at your convenience.*

con ven ient (kən vē′nyənt), **1** saving trouble; well arranged; easy to use: *live in a convenient house.* **2** easily done; not troublesome; suitable: *Will it be convenient for you to meet me?* **3** within easy reach; handy: *Would my house be a convenient place to meet? adj.* —**con ven′iently**, *adv.*

con vent (kon′vent), **1** group of nuns living together according to fixed rules and under religious vows. **2** building or buildings in which they live. *n.*

con ven tion (kən ven′shən), **1** a meeting arranged for some particular purpose; gathering; assembly: *The Democratic and Republican parties hold conventions every four years to choose candidates for President.* **2** general agreement; common consent; custom: *Convention influences how we dress.* **3** custom or practice approved by general agreement: *Using the right hand to shake hands is a convention.* **4** agreement signed by two or more countries about matters less important than those in a treaty. *n.*

con ven tion al (kən ven′shə nəl), **1** depending on conventions; customary: *"Good morning" is a conventional greeting.* **2** acting or behaving according to commonly accepted and approved ways: *Our neighbors are quiet, conventional people.* **3** of the usual type or design; commonly used or seen: *conventional furniture.* **4** (in the arts) following custom and traditional models; formal: *The ode and the sonnet are conventional forms of English poetry. adj.* —**con ven′tion al ly**, *adv.*

con ven tion al i ty (kən ven′shə nal′ə tē), conventional quality or character; adherence to custom: *His conventionality made his reaction quite predictable. n.*

con ven tion al ize (kən ven′shə nə līz), make conventional. *v.,* **con ven tion al ized, con ven tion al iz ing.** —**con ven′tion al i za′tion**, *n.*

con verge (kən vėrj′), **1** tend to meet in a point. **2** turn toward each other: *If you look at the end of your nose, your eyes converge.* **3** come together; center: *A large group converged on the city hall. The attention of all the children converged upon the kitten.* v., **con verged, con verg ing.**

con ver gence (kən vėr′jəns), **1** act or process of converging; tendency to meet in a point. **2** point of converging. n.

con ver gent (kən vėr′jənt), converging. adj. —**converg′ent ly,** adv.

con ver sant (kən vėr′sənt), familiar by use or study; acquainted: *Our music teacher is conversant with all the instruments of the orchestra.* adj. —**con ver′sant ly,** adv.

con ver sa tion (kon′vər sā′shən), friendly talk; exchange of thoughts by talking informally together. n.

con ver sa tion al (kon′vər sā′shə nəl), **1** of conversation. **2** fond of conversation; good at conversation. adj. —**con′ver sa′tion al ly,** adv.

con ver sa tion al ist (kon′vər sā′shə nə list), person who is fond of or who is good at conversation. n.

con verse[1] (kən vėrs′), talk together in an informal way. v., **con versed, con vers ing.** —**con vers′er,** n.

con verse[2] (kən vėrs′ or kon′vėrs′ for 1,2; kon′vėrs′ for 3), **1** opposite or contrary in direction or action: *A converse wind slowed down the airplane.* **2** reversed in order; turned about: *The converse order of the alphabet is from "z" to "a."* **3** thing that is turned around, opposite, or contrary to something else: *The converse of a hamburger without onions is onions without a hamburger.* 1,2 adj., 3 n.

con verse ly (kən vėrs′lē), if turned the other way around: *Six is more than five; conversely, five is less than six.* adv.

con ver sion (kən vėr′zhən), **1** a changing or a turning; change: *Heat causes the conversion of water into steam.* **2** a change from unbelief to faith; change from one religion, party, etc., to another. **3** (in football) one or two extra points scored after a touchdown. n.

con vert (kən vėrt′ for 1,2,4,5; kon′vėrt′ for 3), **1** turn to another or a particular use or purpose; change: *The generators at the dam convert water power into electricity.* **2** cause to change from one belief to another or from lack of belief to faith: *Missionaries tried to convert the villagers.* **3** person who has been converted to a different belief or faith. **4** exchange for an equivalent: *She converted her dollars into pounds upon arriving in London.* **5** (in football) score a conversion: *convert after a touchdown.* 1,2,4,5 v., 3 n.

con vert er (kən vėr′tər), person or thing that converts. n.

con vert i ble (kən vėr′tə bəl), **1** able to be converted. **2** automobile with a folding top. 1 adj., 2 n. —**con vert′i bly,** adv.

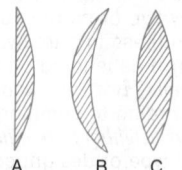

convex lenses
A, convex surface opposite plane surface
B, convex and concave
C, double convex

con vex (kon veks′ or kon′veks), curved out like the outside of a circle or sphere; curving out: *The lens of an automobile headlight is convex on the outside.* adj. —**con vex′ly,** adv. —**con vex′ness,** n.

con vex i ty (kon vek′sə tē), **1** convex condition or quality. **2** a convex surface or thing. n., pl. **con vex i ties.**

con vey (kən vā′), **1** take from one place to another; carry: *A bus conveyed the passengers from the city to the airport.* **2** transmit; conduct: *A wire conveys an electric*

converge (def. 1)—The railroad tracks seemed to **converge** in the distance.

circuit. **3** make known; communicate: *Do the author's words convey any meaning to you?* **4** transfer ownership of; hand over; give: *convey property by a will.* v.

con vey ance (kən vā′əns), **1** a carrying; transmission: *Freighters engage in the conveyance of goods from one port to another.* **2** thing that carries people and goods; vehicle: *Trains and buses are public conveyances.* **3** transfer of property from one person to another. n.

con vey or or **con vey er** (kən vā′ər), **1** person or thing that conveys. **2** a mechanical device that carries things from one place to another, especially by means of a moving, endless belt. n.

con vict (kən vikt′ for 1; kon′vikt for 2), **1** prove, find, or declare guilty: *The jury convicted the accused woman of stealing.* **2** person serving a prison sentence for some crime. 1 v., 2 n. —**con vict′a ble,** adj.

con vic tion (kən vik′shən), **1** act of proving or declaring guilty: *The trial resulted in the conviction of the accused man.* **2** condition of being proved or declared guilty: *The thief's conviction meant a year in prison.* **3** firm belief: *It often takes courage to act according to one's convictions.* n.

con vince (kən vins′), make (a person) feel sure; cause to believe; persuade by argument or proof: *The mistakes she made convinced me she had not studied her lesson.* v., **con vinced, con vinc ing.** —**con vinc′er,** n. —**con vin′ci ble,** adj.

con vinc ing (kən vin′sing), able to convince; persuasive: *The lawyer's convincing argument influenced the jury.* adj. —**con vinc′ing ly,** adv. —**con vinc′ing ness,** n.

con viv i al (kən viv′ē əl), **1** fond of eating and drinking with friends; sociable: *They were a convivial couple who enjoyed having friends drop in.* **2** festive; gay: *a convivial party.* adj. —**con viv′i al ly,** adv.

con vo ca tion (kon′və kā′shən), **1** a calling together. **2** assembly: *The convocation of clergymen passed a resolution condemning violence.* n.

con voke (kən vōk′), call together; notify to assemble. v., **con voked, con vok ing.** —**con vok′er,** n.

con vo lu tion (kon′və lü′shən), **1** a coiling, winding, or twisting together: *the convolutions of a snake slithering through the grass.* **2** a coil; winding; twist. **3** an irregular fold or ridge on the surface of the brain. n.

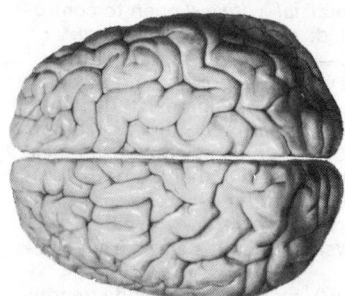

convolutions (def. 3)

con voy (kən voi′ *or* kon′voi *for 1;* kon′voi *for 2-4*), **1** go with in order to protect; escort: *Warships convoy unarmed merchant ships during time of war.* **2** an escort; protection: *The gold was moved from the truck to the bank's vault under convoy of armed guards.* **3** warships, soldiers, etc., that escort. **4** ship, fleet, supplies, etc., that are escorted. 1 *v.*, 2-4 *n.*

con vulse (kən vuls′), **1** shake violently: *An earthquake convulsed the island, damaging many buildings.* **2** cause violent disturbance in: *to be convulsed with rage.* **3** throw into convulsions; shake with muscular spasms. **4** throw into fits of laughter; cause to shake with laughter: *The clown's funny antics convulsed the audience.* *v.*, **convulsed, con vuls ing.**

con vul sion (kən vul′shən), **1** Often, **convulsions,** *pl.* a violent, involuntary contracting and relaxing of the muscles; spasm; fit: *We called the veterinarian when our dog had convulsions.* **2** a fit of laughter. **3** a violent disturbance: *An earthquake is a convulsion of the earth.* *n.*

con vul sive (kən vul′siv), **1** violently disturbing. **2** having convulsions. *adj.* —**con vul′sive ly,** *adv.* —**convul′sive ness,** *n.*

coo (kü), **1** the soft, murmuring sound made by doves or pigeons. **2** make this sound. **3** murmur softly; speak in a soft, loving manner: *to coo to a baby.* 1 *n., pl.* **coos;** 2,3 *v.,* **cooed, coo ing.** —**coo′er,** *n.* —**coo′ing ly,** *adv.*

cook (kük), **1** prepare (food, etc.) by using heat. Boiling, frying, broiling, roasting, and baking are forms of cooking. **2** undergo cooking; be cooked: *Let the meat cook slowly.* **3** person who cooks. 1,2 *v.,* 3 *n.* —**cook′a ble,** *adj.*
cook up, INFORMAL. make up or prepare, especially falsely: *We cooked up an excuse for being late.*

cook book (kük′bük′), book of directions for cooking various kinds of food; book of recipes. *n.*

cook er (kük′ər), apparatus or container to cook things in. *n.*

cook er y (kük′ər ē), art or occupation of cooking. *n.*

cook ie (kük′ē), a small, flat, sweet cake. *n.* Also, **cooky.**

cook out (kük′out′), meal where the food is cooked and eaten outdoors. *n.*

cook y (kük′ē), cookie. *n., pl.* **cook ies.**

cool (kül), **1** somewhat cold; more cold than hot: *a cool, cloudy day.* **2** allowing or giving a cool feeling: *a cool, thin dress.* **3** not excited; calm: *Everyone kept cool when paper in the wastebasket caught fire.* **4** having little enthusiasm or interest; not cordial: *My former friend gave me a cool greeting.* **5** something cool; cool part, place, or time: *in the cool of the evening.* **6** make or become cool: *Ice cools water. The ground cools off after the sun goes down.* **7** bold or impudent in a calm way. **8** INFORMAL. without exaggeration: *a cool million dollars.* **9** SLANG. admirable; excellent. **10** SLANG. calm restraint; presence of mind: *Don't lose your cool.* 1-4,7-9 *adj.,* 5,10 *n.,* 6 *v.* —**cool′ly,** *adv.* —**cool′ness,** *n.*

cool ant (kü′lənt), a cooling substance, used to reduce heat in machinery. *n.*

cool er (kü′lər), container that cools foods or drinks, or keeps them cool. *n.*

cool-head ed (kül′hed′id), not easily excited; calm. *adj.* —**cool′-head′ed ly,** *adv.* —**cool′-head′ed ness,** *n.*

Coo lidge (kü′lij), (**John**) **Calvin,** 1872-1933, the 30th president of the United States, from 1923 to 1929. *n.*

coo lie *or* **coo ly** (kü′lē), formerly, an unskilled laborer in China, India, etc., hired for very low wages. *n., pl.* **coo lies.**

coon (kün), raccoon. *n.*

coop (küp *or* kup), **1** a small cage or pen for chickens, rabbits, etc. **2** keep or put in a coop. **3** confine, especially in a small space: *The children were cooped up indoors by the rain.* 1 *n.,* 2,3 *v.*

co-op (kō′op), INFORMAL. cooperative. *n.*

coop er (kü′pər *or* kup′ər), person who makes or repairs barrels, casks, etc. *n.*

Coo per (kü′pər *or* kup′ər), **James Fenimore,** 1789-1851, American novelist who wrote stories about American Indian and frontier life, and about the sea. *n.*

co op e rate (kō op′ə rāt′), work together: *Everyone cooperated in helping to clean up after the class party.* *v.,* **co op e rat ed, co op e rat ing.** —**co op′e ra′tor,** *n.*

co op e ra tion (kō op′ə rā′shən), a working together; united effort or labor: *Cooperation can accomplish many things which no individual could do alone.* *n.*

co op er a tive (kō op′ər ə tiv *or* kō op′ə rā′tiv), **1** wanting or willing to work together with others: *Most of the pupils were helpful and cooperative.* **2** store where merchandise is sold to members who share in the profits and losses according to the amounts they buy. **3** union of farmers for buying and selling their produce at the best price. **4** an apartment house owned and operated by the tenants. **5** apartment in such a building. 1 *adj.,* 2-5 *n.* —**co op′er a tive ly,** *adv.* —**co op′er a tive ness,** *n.*

co or di nate (kō ôrd′n āt *for 1,3;* kō ôrd′n it *for 2,4-6*), **1** arrange in proper order; put in proper relation; harmonize; adjust: *Coordinating the movements of the arms and legs is the hardest part of learning to swim.* **2** equal in importance; of equal rank. **3** make equal in importance. **4** a coordinate person or thing; an equal. **5** joining words, phrases, or clauses of equal grammatical importance. *And* and *but* are coordinate conjunctions. **6** any of a set of numbers that give the position of a point by reference to fixed lines or axes. 1,3 *v.,* **co or di nat ed, co or di nat ing;** 2,5 *adj.,* 4,6 *n.* —**co or′di nate ly,** *adv.* —**co or′di nate ness,** *n.*

co or di na tion (kō ôrd′n ā′shən), **1** harmonious adjustment or working together: *Poor coordination in the hands makes drawing difficult.* **2** arrangement in proper order or proper relation: *An outline often helps in the coordination of ideas.* *n.*

co or di na tor (kō ôrd′n ā′tər), person or thing that coordinates. *n.*

coot
about 13 to 16 in.
(33 to 41 cm.) long

coot (küt), a wading and swimming bird with short wings and webbed feet. *n.*

coot ie (kü′tē), SLANG. louse. *n.*

cop¹ (kop), INFORMAL. a police officer. *n.*

cop² (kop), SLANG. take; steal. *v.,* **copped, cop ping.**
cop out, SLANG. refuse to become involved; back out.

co part ner (kō pärt′nər), a fellow partner; associate. *n.*

cope[1] (kōp), struggle with some degree of success; struggle on even terms; deal successfully: *She was busy but she was still able to cope with the extra work.* *v.,* **coped, cop ing.** [*Cope*[1] came into English about 600 years ago from French *coper,* meaning "to strike," and can be traced back to Greek *kolaphos,* meaning "a blow, stroke."]

cope[2] (kōp), a long cape worn by priests during certain religious rites. *n.* [*Cope*[2] comes from Old English (*cantel*)-*cāp,* and can be traced back to Latin *cappa,* meaning "cap, hood."]

co peck (kō′pek), kopeck. *n.*

Co pen ha gen (kō′pən hā′gən), capital of Denmark and its largest city. *n.*

co pe pod (kō′pə pod), any of a large group of very small animals that live in great numbers in fresh and salt water. They are an important source of food for other water animals. *n.*

Co per ni can (kə pėr′nə kən), of Copernicus or his system of astronomy. *adj.*

Co per ni cus (kə pėr′nə kəs), **Nikolaus,** 1473-1543, Polish astronomer who demonstrated that the earth rotates on its axis and that the planets revolve around the sun. *n.*

cop i er (kop′ē ər), **1** person who copies; imitator. **2** person who makes written copies. **3** machine that makes copies. *n.*

co pi lot (kō′pī′lət), the assistant or second pilot in an aircraft. *n.*

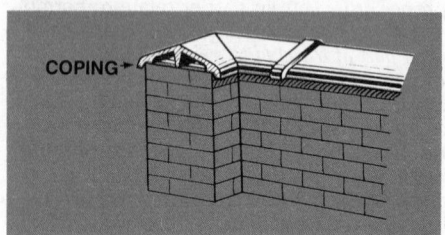

COPING

cop ing (kō′ping), the top layer of a brick or stone wall. It is usually built with a slope to shed water. *n.*

coping saw, a narrow saw in a U-shaped frame, used to cut curves.

co pi ous (kō′pē əs), more than enough; plentiful; abundant: *a copious harvest.* *adj.* —**co′pi ous ly,** *adv.* —**co′pi ous ness,** *n.*

Co pland (kō′plənd), **Aaron,** born 1900, American composer. *n.*

cop out (kop′out′), SLANG. a refusing to become involved; a backing out. *n.*

cop per (kop′ər), **1** a tough, reddish-brown metallic element which occurs in various ores. Copper resists rust and is easily shaped into thin sheets or fine wire. It is an excellent conductor of heat and electricity. **2** coin made of copper or bronze, especially a penny. **3** of copper: *a copper kettle.* **4** cover or coat with copper. **5** reddish-brown. **6** a reddish brown. 1,2,6 *n.,* 3,5 *adj.,* 4 *v.*

cop per head (kop′ər hed′), **1** a poisonous snake with a copper-colored head, found in the eastern United States. It is related to the water moccasin and the rattlesnake. **2 Copperhead,** person in the North who sympathized with the South during the Civil War. *n.*

cop per plate (kop′ər plāt′), **1** a thin, flat piece of copper on which a design, writing, or the like is engraved or etched. **2** an engraving, picture, or print made from such a plate. *n.*

cop per y (kop′ər ē), **1** of or containing copper. **2** like copper: *a coppery sky at sunset.* *adj.*

cop pice (kop′is), copse. *n.*

co pra (kō′prə), the dried meat of coconuts. Coconut oil is obtained from copra. *n.*

copse (kops), a number of small trees, bushes, or shrubs growing together; coppice. *n.*

cop ter (kop′tər), INFORMAL. helicopter. *n.*

cop u la (kop′yə lə), a linking verb, often a form of the verb *be.* EXAMPLE: John *is* a boy. *n., pl.* **cop u las.**

cop y (kop′ē), **1** thing made to be just like another; thing made on the pattern or model of another. A written page, a picture, a dress, or a piece of furniture can be an exact copy of another. **2** make a copy of: *Copy this page. I copied the painting.* **3** be a copy of; be like; follow as a model or example; imitate: *to copy someone's way of dressing.* **4** one of a number of books, newspapers, magazines, pictures, etc., made at the same printing: *six copies of today's paper.* **5** written material ready to be set in print in a newspaper, magazine, or book. 1,4,5 *n., pl.* **cop ies;** 2,3 *v.,* **cop ied, cop y ing.**

cop y book (kop′ē bùk′), book with models of handwriting to be copied in learning to write. *n.*

cop y right (kop′ē rīt′), **1** the exclusive right to publish or sell a certain book, picture, etc., granted by a government for a certain number of years. **2** protect by getting a copyright. Books, pieces of music, plays, etc., are usually copyrighted. 1 *n.,* 2 *v.*

co que try (kō′kə trē *or* kō ket′rē), behavior of a coquette; flirting. *n., pl.* **co que tries.**

co quette (kō ket′), woman who tries to attract men; flirt. *n.*

co ra cle (kôr′ə kəl), a small, light boat made by covering a wooden frame with waterproof material. *n.*

co ral (kôr′əl), **1** a stony substance consisting of the skeletons of certain kinds of tiny sea animals called polyps. Reefs and small islands consisting of coral are common in tropical seas and oceans. Red, pink, and white coral is often used for jewelry. **2** tiny sea animal that secretes a skeleton of coral and forms large branching colonies by budding. **3** deep-pink or red. **4** a deep pink or red. 1,2,4 *n.,* 3 *adj.* —**cor′al like′,** *adj.*

coral reef, a narrow ridge of coral at or near the surface of the water.

coral snake, a small, poisonous American snake whose body is banded with alternating rings of red, yellow, and black.

coral snake
about 18 in. to 4 ft. (46 cm. to 1.2 m.) long

copperhead (def. 1)—about 2½ ft. (75 cm.) long

cord (kôrd), **1** a thick string; very thin rope: *She tied the package with a cord.* **2** fasten or tie up with a cord: *They corded bundles of papers.* **3** anything resembling a cord, such as an insulated cable fitted with a plug to connect a lamp or other electrical appliance with an electrical outlet. **4** nerve, tendon, or other structure in an animal body that is somewhat like a cord. The spinal cord is in the backbone. The vocal cords are in the throat. **5** ridge or ridged pattern on cloth. **6** cloth with such ridges on it, especially corduroy. **7** measure of quantity for cut wood equal to 128 cubic feet. A pile of wood 4 feet wide, 4 feet high, and 8 feet long is a cord. **8** pile (wood) in cords. 1,3-7 *n.*, 2,8 *v.* —**cord′er**, *n.* —**cord′like′**, *adj.*

cord age (kôr′dij), **1** cords or ropes: *Most of the cordage on a sailing ship is in its rigging.* **2** quantity of wood measured in cords. *n.*

cor date (kôr′dāt), heart-shaped. *adj.* —**cor′date ly**, *adv.*

cord ed (kôr′did), **1** having ridges on it; ribbed: *corded cloth.* **2** fastened with a cord; bound with cords: *corded bundles of newspaper. adj.*

cor dial (kôr′jəl), **1** warm and friendly in manner; hearty: *Her friends gave her a cordial welcome.* **2** liqueur. 1 *adj.*, 2 *n.* —**cor′dial ly**, *adv.* —**cor′dial ness**, *n.*

cor di al i ty (kôr′jē al′ə tē), cordial quality or feeling; heartiness: *The cordiality of our host's welcome made us feel at home. n., pl.* **cor di al i ties.**

cor dil ler a (kôr′də lyer′ə), a long mountain range; chain of mountains. *n., pl.* **cor dil ler as.** —**cor′dil-ler′an**, *adj.*

Cór do ba (kôr′də bə), **1** city in S Spain. **2** city in central Argentina. *n.* Also, **Cordova.**

cor don (kôrd′n), **1** line or circle of soldiers, policemen, forts, etc., enclosing or guarding a place: *A cordon of troops surrounded the burned-out area of the city.* **2** a cord, braid, or ribbon worn as an ornament or as a badge of honor. *n.*

Cor do va (kôr′də və), Córdoba. *n.*

cor do van (kôr′də vən), **1** kind of soft, fine-grained leather. **2** shoe made from this leather. *n.* [*Cordovan* comes from Spanish *cordobán,* which was named for *Córdoba,* a city in southern Spain where it was first made.]

cor du roy (kôr′də roi′), **1** a thick, cotton cloth with close, velvetlike ridges. **2** made of corduroy: *a corduroy jacket.* **3** **corduroys,** *pl.* corduroy trousers. 1,3 *n.*, 2 *adj.*

corduroy road, road made of logs laid crosswise, usually across low, wet land.

cord wood (kôrd′wùd′), **1** wood sold by the cord. **2** firewood piled in cords. **3** wood cut in 4-foot lengths. *n.*

core (kôr), **1** the hard, central part containing the seeds of fruits like apples and pears. **2** the central or most important part: *He is honest to the core. The core of her argument against the plan is its costliness.* **3** the central or innermost part of the earth lying below the mantle. **4** take out the core of (fruit): *I cored the apples before baking them.* 1-3 *n.*, 4 *v.*, **cored, cor ing.** —**cor′er**, *n.*

Cor inth (kôr′inth), seaport in S Greece. In ancient times, Corinth was a center of commerce noted for its art and luxury. See **Sparta** for map. *n.*

Co rin thi an (kə rin′thē ən), **1** of Corinth or its people. **2** person born or living in Corinth. **3** having to do with the most elaborate style of Greek architecture. 1,3 *adj.*, 2 *n.*

Co rin thi ans (kə rin′thē ənz), either of two books of the New Testament, consisting of letters written by Saint Paul to the Christians of Corinth. *n.*

cork (kôrk), **1** the light, thick, outer bark of the cork oak. Cork is used for bottle stoppers, floats for fishlines, filling for some kinds of life preservers, and some floor coverings. **2** a shaped piece of cork: *the cork of a bottle.* **3** any stopper for a bottle, flask, etc., made of glass, rubber, etc. **4** stop up with a cork: *Fill these bottles and cork them tightly.* 1-3 *n.*, 4 *v.* —**cork′like′**, *adj.*

cork oak, the oak tree of the Mediterranean area, from which cork is obtained.

cork screw (kôrk′skrü′), **1** tool used to pull corks out of bottles. **2** shaped like a corkscrew; spiral: *corkscrew curls.* 1 *n.*, 2 *adj.*

cork y (kôr′kē), of or like cork. *adj.*, **cork i er, cork i est.** —**cork′i ness**, *n.*

cor mor ant (kôr′mər ənt), a very large sea bird that has a pouch under its beak for holding captured fish. *n.*

corn[1] (kôrn), **1** kind of grain that grows on large ears; maize; Indian corn. **2** plant, a kind of cereal grass, that it grows on. **3** preserve (meat) with strong salt water or with dry salt. **4** SLANG. something trite, outdated, or sentimental. 1,2,4 *n.*, 3 *v.* [*Corn*[1] comes from Old English *corn,* meaning "grain, seed, wheat."]

corn[2] (kôrn), a small, hard, shiny thickening of the outer layer of the skin, caused by pressure or rubbing: *Painful corns on the toes can be caused by shoes that do not fit properly. n.* [*Corn*[2] came into English over 500 years ago from French *corn,* meaning "horn," which came from Latin *cornu.*]

corn bread (kôrn′bred′), bread made of corn meal. *n.*

corn cob (kôrn′kob′), the central, woody part of an ear of corn, on which the kernels grow; cob. *n.*

corn crib (kôrn′krib′), bin or small, ventilated building for storing unshelled corn. *n.*

cor ne a (kôr′nē ə), the transparent part of the outer coat of the eyeball. The cornea covers the iris and the pupil. *n., pl.* **cor ne as.**

corned (kôrnd), preserved with strong salt water or with dry salt: *corned beef. adj.*

cor ner (kôr′nər), **1** place where two lines or surfaces meet: *the corner of a room.* **2** the place where two streets meet: *There is a traffic light at the corner.* **3** at or on a corner: *a corner house, a corner lot.* **4** for a corner: *a corner cupboard.* **5** piece to form, protect, or decorate a corner: *The leather box has gold corners.* **6** place away from crowds; secret place: *Her money was hidden in odd corners all over the house.* **7** place that is far away; distant region or quarter: *People have searched in all corners of the earth for gold.* **8** an awkward or difficult position; place from which escape is impossible: *His enemies had driven him into a corner.* **9** force into an awkward or difficult position; drive into a corner: *Workers at the zoo cornered the escaped lion.* **10** a buying up of large amounts of some stock or article to raise its price: *a corner in wheat.* **11** buy up large amounts of (some stock or article) to raise its price: *Some speculators have tried to corner wheat.* **12** (of a car) to round sharp corners at relatively high speeds without sway. 1,2,5-8,10 *n.*, 3,4 *adj.*, 9,11,12 *v.*

cut corners, save money by reducing effort, time, labor, etc.: *We had to cut corners to make a profit.*

turn the corner, pass the worst or most dangerous point.

cor nered (kôr′nərd), without hope of escape or relief: *A cornered animal will fight. adj.*

cor ner stone (kôr′nər stōn′), **1** stone at the corner of two walls that holds them together. **2** such a stone built into the corner of a building as its formal beginning. The laying of a cornerstone is often accompanied by ceremonies. **3** something of fundamental importance; foundation; basis: *The cornerstone of most religions is the belief in a creator. n.*

cornet

cor net (kôr net′), a musical wind instrument somewhat like a trumpet, usually made of brass. It has three valves that control the pitch. *n.*

cor net ist or **cor net tist** (kôr net′ist), person who plays a cornet. *n.*

corn field (kôrn′fēld′), field in which corn is grown. *n.*

corn flow er (kôrn′flou′ər), bachelor's-button. *n.*

corn husk (kôrn′husk′), husk of an ear of corn. *n.*

cor nice (kôr′nis), **1** an ornamental molding along the top of a wall, pillar, or side of a building. **2** a molding around the walls of a room just below the ceiling. **3** furnish with a cornice. 1,2 *n.*, 3 *v.*, **cor niced, cor nic ing.**

Cor nish (kôr′nish), **1** of Cornwall, its people, or the language formerly spoken by them. **2** a Celtic language spoken in Cornwall until the late 1700's. 1 *adj.*, 2 *n.*

corn meal, coarsely ground dried corn.

corn pone, (in the southern United States) cornbread shaped by hand into a small flat loaf, and cooked in a frying pan or griddle.

corn stalk (kôrn′stôk′), stalk of corn. *n.*

corn starch (kôrn′stärch′), a starchy flour made from corn, used to thicken puddings, custard, etc. *n.*

corn syrup, syrup made from cornstarch.

cor nu co pi a (kôr′nə kō′pē ə), **1** horn-shaped container represented in art as overflowing with fruits, vegetables, and flowers; horn of plenty. It is a symbol of fruitfulness and plenty. **2** a horn-shaped container or ornament. *n., pl.* **cor nu co pi as.**

Corn wall (kôrn′wôl), county in SW England. *n.*

Corn wal lis (kôrn wô′lis), **Charles,** 1738-1805, British general who surrendered to Washington at Yorktown on October 19, 1781. *n.*

corn y (kôr′nē), INFORMAL. trite, outdated, or sentimental: *corny jokes, corny music. adj.*, **corn i er, corn i est.**

co rol la (kə rol′ə), the petals of a flower. The petals which make up the corolla may be either separate from each other or fused together. *n., pl.* **co rol las.**

co rol lar y (kôr′ə ler′ē), **1** something proved by inference from something else already proved. **2** a natural consequence or result: *Crop failure was a corollary of the drought. n., pl.* **co rol lar ies.**

co ro na (kə rō′nə), **1** ring of light seen around the sun, moon, or other luminous body. **2** halo of light around the sun, seen only during an eclipse. *n., pl.* **co ro nas, co ro nae** (kə rō′nē).

Co ro na do (kôr′ə nä′dō), **Francisco Vásquez de,** 1510-1554, Spanish conquistador who explored the

southwestern part of what is now the United States. *n.*

co ro nar y (kôr′ə ner′ē), **1** of or having to do with either of the two arteries (**coronary arteries**) that supply blood to the muscular tissue of the heart. **2** coronary thrombosis. 1 *adj.*, 2 *n., pl.* **co ro nar ies.**

coronary thrombosis, the stopping up of a coronary artery or one of its branches by a blood clot.

co ro na tion (kôr′ə nā′shən), ceremony of crowning a king, queen, emperor, etc. *n.*

co ro ner (kôr′ə nər), official of a local government who investigates any death not clearly due to natural causes. *n.*

co ro net (kôr′ə net′), **1** a small crown indicating a rank of nobility below that of a king or queen. **2** a circle of gold, jewels, or flowers worn around the head as an ornament. *n.*

Corp., **1** Corporal. **2** Corporation.

cor por al[1] (kôr′pər əl), of the body: *Spanking someone is corporal punishment. adj.* [*Corporal*[1] came into English about 600 years ago from French *corporal,* and can be traced back to Latin *corpus,* meaning "body." See **Word Family.**] —**cor′por al ly,** *adv.*

WORD FAMILY

corporal[1]

Below are words related to *corporal*[1]. They can all be traced back to the Latin word *corpus* (kôr′pùs), meaning "body."

corporate	corpulent	corset
corporation	corpuscle	habeas corpus
corps	corsage	incorporate
corpse	corselet	unincorporated

cor por al[2] (kôr′pər əl), the lowest-ranking noncommissioned officer in the army, ranking next below a sergeant and next above a private first class. *n.* [*Corporal*[2] was borrowed from French *corporal,* which came from Italian *caporale,* and can be traced back to Latin *caput,* meaning "head."]

cor por ate (kôr′pər it), **1** forming a corporation; incorporated: *Most car manufacturers are corporate companies.* **2** of a corporation: *corporate property.* **3** united; combined: *The corporate will of the majority prevailed. adj.* —**cor′por ate ly,** *adv.* —**cor′por ate ness,** *n.*

cor po ra tion (kôr′pə rā′shən), **1** group of persons who obtain a charter giving them as a group the right to buy and sell, own property, manufacture and ship products, etc., as if it were one person. **2** group of persons with authority to act as a single person. The governing body

corona (def. 2) seen during a total eclipse of the sun

of a college or the mayor and aldermen of a city are a corporation. *n.*

corps (kôr), **1** group of soldiers, trained for specialized military service: *the Medical Corps, the Signal Corps.* **2** a military unit made up of two or more divisions plus supporting troops, usually commanded by a lieutenant general. It is smaller than an army. **3** group of people with special training, organized for working together: *A large hospital has a corps of nurses. n., pl.* **corps** (kôrz).

corpse (kôrps), a dead human body. *n.*

cor pu lence (kôr′pyə ləns), fatness; stoutness. *n.*

cor pu lent (kôr′pyə lənt), fat; stout. *adj.*

cor pus cle (kôr′pus′əl), any of the cells that form a large part of the blood, lymph, etc. Red corpuscles carry oxygen to the tissues and remove carbon dioxide; some white corpuscles destroy disease germs. *n.*

corral (def. 1)

cor ral (kə ral′), **1** pen for horses, cattle, etc. **2** drive into or keep in such a pen: *The cowhands corralled the herd of wild ponies.* **3** hem in; surround; capture: *The reporters corralled the candidate and asked for a statement.* **4** a circular camp formed by wagons for defense against attack. **5** form (wagons) into such a circular camp. 1,4 *n.,* 2,3,5 *v.,* **cor ralled, cor ral ling.**

cor rect (kə rekt′), **1** free from mistakes; right: *give the correct answer.* **2** agreeing with a good standard of taste; proper: *correct manners.* **3** change to what is right; remove mistakes or faults from: *Correct any misspellings that you find.* **4** alter or adjust to agree with some standard: *correct the reading of a barometer.* **5** point out or mark the errors of; check: *The teacher corrected our tests and returned them to us.* **6** set right by punishing; find fault with in order to improve; punish: *correct a child for misbehaving.* 1,2 *adj.,* 3-6 *v.* **—cor rect′a ble,** *adj.* **—cor rect′ly,** *adv.* **—cor rect′ness,** *n.* **—cor rec′tor,** *n.*

cor rec tion (kə rek′shən), **1** correcting; setting right: *The correction of all my mistakes took nearly an hour.* **2** a change to correct an error or mistake: *Write in your corrections neatly.* **3** punishment. A prison is sometimes called a house of correction. *n.*

cor rec tive (kə rek′tiv), **1** tending to correct; setting right; making better: *Corrective exercises can make weak muscles strong.* **2** something that corrects. 1 *adj.,* 2 *n.* **—cor rec′tive ly,** *adv.*

cor re late (kôr′ə lāt), **1** put in relation: *Try to correlate your knowledge of history with your knowledge of geography.* **2** be related one to the other: *Increasing cancer rates appear to correlate with rising levels of pollution. v.,* **cor re lat ed, cor re lat ing.** **—cor′re lat′a ble,** *adj.*

cor re la tion (kôr′ə lā′shən), **1** the mutual relation of two or more things: *There is a close correlation between annual rainfall and crop yield.* **2** act or process of correlating. *n.*

a hat	i it	oi oil	ch child	a in about
ā age	ī ice	ou out	ng long	e in taken
ä far	o hot	u cup	sh she	ə = { i in pencil
e let	ō open	u̇ put	th thin	o in lemon
ē equal	ô order	ü rule	ŦH then	u in circus
ėr term			zh measure	

cor rel a tive (kə rel′ə tiv), **1** having a mutual relation. Conjunctions used in pairs, such as *either . . . or,* are correlative. **2** either of two things having a mutual relation and commonly used together. Pairs of words like *husband* and *wife, mother* and *father,* are correlatives. 1 *adj.,* 2 *n.* **—cor rel′a tive ly,** *adv.*

cor re spond (kôr′ə spond′), **1** be in harmony; agree: *The answers she got on the test correspond with those I got.* **2** be similar: *The fins of a fish correspond to the wings of a bird.* **3** exchange letters; write letters to each other: *Will you correspond with me while I am away? v.*

cor re spond ence (kôr′ə spon′dəns), **1** a being in harmony; agreement: *Your account of the accident has little correspondence with the story the other driver told.* **2** similarity: *There is a correspondence of form in the skeletons of most mammals.* **3** exchange of letters; practice of letter writing: *The boy kept up a correspondence with his friend in Europe.* **4** letters: *Bring me the correspondence concerning that order. n.*

cor re spond ent (kôr′ə spon′dənt), **1** person who exchanges letters with another: *My cousin and I are correspondents.* **2** person employed by a newspaper, magazine, radio or television network, etc., to send news from a particular place or region: *reports from correspondents in China and Great Britain.* **3** person or company that has regular business with another in a distant place: *Many American banks have correspondents in European cities.* **4** in agreement; corresponding. 1-3 *n.,* 4 *adj.*

cor re spond ing (kôr′ə spon′ding), similar: *The wings of a bird and the fins of a fish have corresponding functions. adj.* **—cor′re spond′ing ly,** *adv.*

cor ri dor (kôr′ə dər), a long hallway; passage in a large building into which rooms open: *Our classroom is at the end of a corridor. n.*

cor rob o rate (kə rob′ə rāt′), make more certain; confirm: *Eyewitnesses corroborated her testimony in court. v.,* **cor rob o rat ed, cor rob o rat ing.** **—cor rob′o ra′tor,** *n.*

cor rob o ra tion (kə rob′ə rā′shən), additional proof; confirmation: *The police have an eyewitness's corroboration of the victim's statement. n.*

cor rode (kə rōd′), wear or eat away gradually: *Moist air corrodes iron. Acid caused the pipes to corrode. v.,* **cor rod ed, cor rod ing.**

cor ro sion (kə rō′zhən), **1** act or process of corroding. **2** a corroded condition. *n.*

cor ro sive (kə rō′siv), **1** eating away gradually; tending to corrode: *Most acids are corrosive.* **2** substance that corrodes. 1 *adj.,* 2 *n.* **—cor ro′sive ly,** *adv.* **—cor ro′sive ness,** *n.*

cor ru gate (kôr′ə gāt), bend or shape into wavy folds or ridges; wrinkle. *v.,* **cor ru gat ed, cor ru gat ing.**

cor ru gat ed (kôr′ə gā′tid), bent or shaped into wavy folds or ridges; wrinkled: *corrugated paper, corrugated iron. adj.*

cor ru ga tion (kôr′ə gā′shən), **1** a corrugating or a being corrugated. **2** one of a series of wavy folds or ridges; wrinkle. *n.*

cor rupt (kə rupt′), **1** influenced by bribes; dishonest: *a corrupt judge.* **2** influence by bribes: *That judge cannot be corrupted.* **3** morally bad; evil; wicked: *to lead a corrupt life.* **4** make evil or wicked: *Bad companions may corrupt a* *person.* **5** make or become rotten or decayed. **6** rotten; decayed. 1,3,6 *adj.*, 2,4,5 *v.* —**cor rupt′er, cor rup′tor,** *n.* —**cor rupt′ly,** *adv.* —**cor rupt′ness,** *n.*

cor rupt i ble (kə rup′tə bəl), able to be corrupted. *adj.* —**cor rupt′i ble ness,** *n.* —**cor rupt′i bly,** *adv.*

cor rup tion (kə rup′shən), **1** a being influenced by bribes; dishonesty: *The police force must be kept free from corruption.* **2** a making or a being made evil or wicked. **3** evil conduct; wickedness. **4** rot; decay. *n.*

cor sage (kôr säzh′), bouquet to be worn on the waist or shoulder of a woman's dress. *n.*

cor sair (kôr′ser *or* kôr′sar), **1** pirate. **2** a pirate ship. *n.*

corse let (kôrs′lit), armor for the upper part of the body. *n.* Also, **corslet.**

cor set (kôr′sit), a close-fitting undergarment worn about the waist and hips to support or shape the body. *n.*

Cor si ca (kôr′sə kə), island in the Mediterranean, southeast of and belonging to France. See **Castile** for map. *n.* —**Cor′si can,** *adj., n.*

cors let (kôrs′lit), corselet. *n.*

cor tege (kôr tezh′), **1** procession: *a funeral cortege.* **2** group of followers or attendants; retinue. *n.* [*Cortege* comes from French *cortège,* and can be traced back to Latin *cohortem,* meaning "crowd, enclosure."]

cor tège (kôr tezh′), cortege. *n., pl.* **cor tèg es** (kôr tezh′iz).

Cor tés *or* **Cor tez** (kôr tez′), **Hernando,** 1485-1547, Spanish soldier who conquered Mexico. *n.*

cor tex (kôr′teks), **1** the layer of gray matter which covers most of the surface of the brain. **2** the outer layer of an internal organ: *the cortex of the kidney.* **3** the bark of a tree. *n., pl.* **cor ti ces** (kôr′tə sēz′).

cor ti cal (kôr′tə kəl), of or having to do with a cortex, especially of the brain or kidneys. *adj.* —**cor′ti cal ly,** *adv.*

cor ti sone (kôr′tə sōn), hormone produced by the cortex of the adrenal glands or produced synthetically, used in the treatment of arthritis and other ailments. *n.*

co run dum (kə run′dəm), an extremely hard mineral. The dark-colored variety is used for polishing and grinding. Sapphires and rubies are transparent varieties of corundum. *n.*

cor vette *or* **cor vet** (kôr vet′), **1** a former warship with sails and only one tier of guns. **2** gunboat used against submarines and in convoy work. *n.*

cos, cosine.

cos., 1 companies. **2** counties.

co sign (kō′sīn′), **1** sign (a document, treaty, contract, loan, etc.) jointly with another person. One who cosigns a document assumes full responsibility if the other signer fails to fulfill the terms of the document. **2** sign jointly. *v.* —**co′sign′er,** *n.*

co si ly (kō′zə lē), cozily. *adv.*

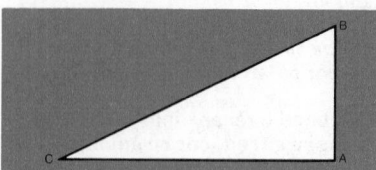

cosine

In a right triangle with hypotenuse BC,

the cosine of angle ACB is $\dfrac{AC}{BC}$,

and the cosine of angle ABC is $\dfrac{AB}{BC}$.

co sine (kō′sīn), the ratio of the length of the side next to an acute angle of a right triangle to the length of the hypotenuse. *n.*

co si ness (kō′zē nis), coziness. *n.*

cos met ic (koz met′ik), **1** preparation for beautifying the skin, hair, nails, etc. Powder, rouge, lipstick, and face creams are cosmetics. **2** beautifying the skin, hair, nails, etc.: *a cosmetic cream.* 1 *n.,* 2 *adj.* —**cos met′i cal ly,** *adv.*

cos mic (koz′mik), **1** having to do with the whole universe: *Cosmic forces produce stars and meteors.* **2** vast: *a cosmic explosion. adj.* —**cos′mi cal ly,** *adv.*

cosmic dust, fine particles of matter in outer space.

cosmic rays, rays of very short wavelengths and very great penetrating power that come to the earth from beyond the earth's atmosphere.

cos mo naut (koz′mə nôt), a Soviet astronaut. *n.*

cos mo pol i tan (koz′mə pol′ə tən), **1** free from national or local prejudices; feeling at home in all parts of the world: *Diplomats are usually cosmopolitan people.* **2** person who feels at home in all parts of the world. **3** belonging to all parts of the world; not limited to any one country or its inhabitants; widely spread: *Music is a cosmopolitan art.* 1,3 *adj.,* 2 *n.*

cos mos (koz′məs), **1** the universe thought of as an orderly, harmonious system. **2** any complete, harmonious system. **3** a tall, tropical American plant with showy flowers of many colors, that blooms in the fall or late summer. It is related to the aster. *n., pl.* **cos mos** *or* **cos mos es** for 2 and 3.

Cos sack (kos′ak), one of a people living in the southwestern Soviet Union, noted as horsemen. *n.*

cost (kôst), **1** price paid: *The cost of this watch was $10.* **2** be obtained at the price of: *This watch costs $10.* **3** loss or sacrifice: *The poor fox escaped from the trap at the cost of a leg.* **4** cause the loss or sacrifice of: *A thoughtless remark almost cost me a friend.* **5 costs,** *pl.* expenses of a lawsuit or case in court: *The guilty party was ordered to pay a $1000 fine and $50 costs.* 1,3,5 *n.,* 2,4 *v.,* **cost, cost ing.** —**cost′less,** *adj.*

at all costs *or* **at any cost,** regardless of expense; by all means; no matter what must be done: *Let's catch that bus at all costs; it's the last one today.*

Cos ta Ri ca (kos′tə rē′kə), country in Central America, northwest of Panama. *Capital:* San José. —**Cos′ta Ri′can.**

cos tive (kos′tiv), **1** constipated. **2** producing constipation. *adj.* —**cos′tive ly,** *adv.* —**cos′tive ness,** *n.*

cost li ness (kôst′lē nis), great cost; expensiveness. *n.*

cost ly (kôst′lē), **1** of great value: *costly jewels.* **2** costing much: *a costly mistake. adj.,* **cost li er, cost li est.**

cost of living, the average price paid for food, rent, clothing, transportation, and other necessities by a person, family, etc., within a given period.

cos tume (kos′tüm *or* kos′tyüm *for 1,2;* ko stüm′ *or* ko styüm′ *for 3*), **1** way of dressing, including the way the hair is worn, kind of jewelry worn, etc.: *a hunting costume. The kimono is part of the national costume of Japan.* **2** dress belonging to another time or place, worn on the stage, at masquerades, etc.: *The actors wore colonial costumes.* **3** provide a costume for; dress: *costumed in red satin.* 1,2 *n.,* 3 *v.,* **cos tumed, cos tum ing.**

cos tum er (ko stü′mər *or* ko styü′mər), person who makes, sells, or rents costumes. *n.*

co sy (kō′zē), cozy. *adj.,* **co si er, co si est;** *n., pl.* **co sies.**

cot[1] (kot), a narrow bed, sometimes made of canvas stretched on a frame that folds together. *n.* [*Cot*[1] comes from Hindustani *khāt.*]

cot[2] (kot), **1** cottage. **2** cote. *n.* [*Cot*[2] comes from Old English *cot.*]

cote (kōt), shelter or shed for small animals or birds. *n.*

co ter ie (kō′tər ē), set or circle of close acquaintances; group of people who often meet socially. *n.*

co til lion (kə til′yən), **1** a dance with complicated steps

and much changing of partners, led by one couple.
2 any large, formal party for dancing. *n.*

Co to pax i (kō/tə pak/sē), volcano in the Andes Mountains in N Ecuador, the highest active volcano in the world. 19,347 feet (5897 meters) high. *n.*

cot tage (kot/ij), **1** a small house. **2** house at a summer resort. *n.*

cottage cheese, a soft, white cheese made from the curds of sour skim milk.

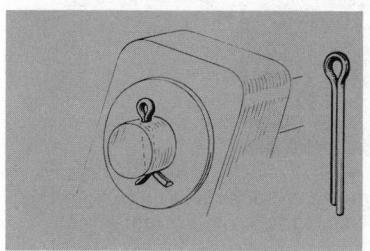

cotter pin

cotter pin (kot/ər), a split pin inserted through a slot to hold small parts of machinery together. The ends are bent back to keep it in the slot.

cot ton (kot/n), **1** the soft, white fibers in a fluffy mass around the seeds of a tall plant, used in making fabrics, thread, etc. **2** the plant that produces these fibers. **3** thread or cloth made of cotton. **4** made of cotton: *a cotton handkerchief.* 1-3 *n.,* 4 *adj.* —**cot/ton like/,** *adj.*

cotton (def. 2)

cotton gin, machine for separating the fibers of cotton from the seeds; gin.

cot ton mouth (kot/n mouth/), water moccasin. *n., pl.* **cot ton mouths** (kot/n mouᵀHz/).

cot ton seed (kot/n sēd/), seed of cotton, used for making cottonseed oil, fertilizer, cattle fodder, etc. *n., pl.* **cot ton seeds** or **cot ton seed.**

cottonseed oil, oil pressed from cottonseed, used for cooking, for making soap, etc.

cot ton tail (kot/n tāl/), a common American wild rabbit with a fluffy, white tail. *n.*

cot ton wood (kot/n wud/), **1** kind of American poplar tree with cottonlike tufts on the seeds. **2** its soft wood. *n.*

cot ton y (kot/n ē), **1** of cotton. **2** like cotton; soft; fluffy; downy. *adj.*

cot y le don (kot/l ēd/n), the first leaf, or one of the first pair of leaves, growing from a seed; an embryo leaf in the seed of a plant. *n.*

couch (kouch), **1** a long seat, usually upholstered and having a back and arms; sofa. **2** any place for rest or sleep: *The deer sprang up from its grassy couch.* **3** put in words; express: *His thoughts were couched in beautiful*

language. 1,2 *n., pl.* **couch es;** 3 *v.* —**couch/like/,** *adj.*

cou gar (kü/gər), puma. *n.*

cough (kôf), **1** force air from the lungs with sudden effort and noise. **2** act of coughing. **3** sound of coughing. **4** condition or symptom of repeated coughing: *He had a bad cough.* **5** expel from the throat by coughing: *I coughed up the candy that was stuck in my throat.* **6** to make a noise something like a cough: *The airplane engine coughed before starting.* 1,5,6 *v.,* 2-4 *n.* —**cough/er,** *n.*

could (kud), **1** past tense of **can**[1]. *Years ago she could sing beautifully.* **2** might be able to: *Perhaps I could go with you. v.*

could n't (kud/nt), could not.

couldst (kudst), OLD USE. could. "Thou couldst" means "You could." *v.*

cou lee (kü/lē), a deep ravine or gulch, usually dry in summer. *n.*

coun cil (koun/səl), **1** group of people called together to give advice and to discuss or settle questions. **2** group of persons elected by citizens to make laws for and manage a city or town. *n.*

coun cil lor (koun/sə lər), councilor. *n.*

coun cil man (koun/səl mən), member of the council of a city or town. *n., pl.* **coun cil men.**

coun ci lor (koun/sə lər), member of a council. *n.* Also, **councillor.**

coun sel (koun/səl), **1** act of exchanging ideas; talking things over; consultation: *We benefited from our frequent counsel.* **2** advice: *A wise person gives good counsel.* **3** lawyer or group of lawyers: *Each side of a case in a court of law has its own counsel.* **4** give advice to; advise: *She counsels sophomores to help them choose their courses.* **5** recommend: *The doctor counseled operating at once.* 1-3 *n.,* 4,5 *v.,* **coun seled, coun sel ing** or **coun selled, coun sel ling.**

keep one's own counsel, not tell one's secrets.

take counsel, exchange ideas; talk things over; consult together: *I took counsel with my friends as to what I should do.*

coun se lor or **coun sel lor** (koun/sə lər), **1** person who gives advice; adviser. **2** teacher appointed to advise students; adviser (def. 2). **3** lawyer. **4** instructor or leader in a summer camp. *n.*

count[1] (kount), **1** name numbers in order: *The child can count from one to ten.* **2** add up; find the number of: *I counted the books and found there were fifty.* **3** an adding up; a finding out how many: *The count showed that more than 5000 votes had been cast.* **4** the total number; amount: *The exact count was 5170 votes.* **5** include or be included in the total number; take or be taken into account: *Let's not count that practice game. Your first race is only for practice; it won't count.* **6** have an influence; be of account or value: *Every vote counts in an election. Every penny counts.* **7** think of as; consider: *You can count yourself lucky in having good health.* **8** depend; rely: *We count on your help.* **9** (in law) each charge in a formal accusation: *The accused was found guilty on all four counts.* 1,2,5-8 *v.,* 3,4,9 *n.* [*Count*[1] came into English about 650 years ago from French *conter,* which came from Latin *computare,* meaning "to calculate, reckon."]

count for, be worth.

count in, include: *Count me in on the picnic.*

count off, divide into equal groups by counting: *For the spelling bee, you may count off from the left.*

count out, 1 fail to consider or include: *If you go skiing, count me out.* **2** declare (a fallen boxer) the loser for failing to rise after 10 seconds have been counted.

count[2] (kount), a European nobleman having a rank about the same as that of an English earl. *n.* [*Count*[2] came into English about 400 years ago from French *conte,* and can be traced back to Latin *com-,* meaning "with," and *ire,* meaning "to go."]

count down (kount′doun′), **1** period of time before the launching of a missile, rocket, etc. **2** the calling out of the passing minutes or seconds of this period as they pass. *n.*

coun te nance (koun′tə nəns), **1** expression of the face. **2** face; features: *a person with a noble countenance.* **3** approve; support; encourage: *I will not countenance such rude behavior.* **4** approval; support; encouragement: *I gave countenance to the plan, but no active help.* 1,2,4 *n.,* 3 *v.,* **coun te nanced, coun te nanc ing. —coun′te nanc er,** *n.*

count er[1] (koun′tər), **1** a long table in a store, restaurant, bank, etc., on which money is counted out, and across which goods, food, or drinks are given to customers. **2** a flat space in a kitchen, usually over a cabinet, used to prepare food on. **3** thing used for counting. The beads on an abacus are called counters. *n.* [*Counter*[1] came into English about 650 years ago from French *conteour,* and can be traced back to Latin *computare,* meaning "to calculate, count."]

count er[2] (koun′tər), person or thing that counts. *n.* [*Counter*[2] came into English about 650 years ago from French *conteour,* which came from *compter,* meaning "to count."]

coun ter[3] (koun′tər), **1** in the opposite direction; opposite; contrary: *He acted counter to his promise (adv.). Your plans are counter to ours (adj.).* **2** oppose: *She countered my plan with one of her own.* **3** give a blow while receiving or blocking an opponent's blow: *The boxer countered with a right to the jaw.* **4** blow given while receiving or blocking an opponent's blow. 1 *adv., adj.,* 2,3 *v.,* 4 *n.* [*Counter*[3] came into English over 500 years ago from French *countre,* which came from Latin *contra,* meaning "against."]

counter-, *prefix.* **1** in opposition to; against: *Counteract = act against.* **2** in return: *Counterattack = attack in return.* **3** corresponding: *Counterpart = corresponding part.* [The prefix *counter-* can be traced back to Latin *contra,* meaning "against."]

coun ter act (koun′tər akt′), act against; neutralize the action or effect of: *A hot bath will sometimes counteract a chill. She tried to counteract her former rudeness by being especially polite now. v.*

coun ter at tack (koun′tər ə tak′), **1** attack made to counter another attack. **2** make an attack in return. 1 *n.,* 2 *v.*

coun ter bal ance (koun′tər bal′əns *for 1,2;* koun′tər bal′əns *for 3*), **1** weight balancing another weight. **2** influence or power balancing or offsetting another: *The captain's coolness was a counterbalance to the crew's panic in the gale.* **3** act as a counterbalance to; offset: *By studying hard, I was able to counterbalance my difficulty with arithmetic.* 1,2 *n.,* 3 *v.,* **coun ter bal anced, coun ter bal anc ing.**

coun ter claim (koun′tər klām′), an opposing claim; claim made by a person to offset a claim made against him: *A counterclaim for damages was filed by the other driver. n.*

coun ter clock wise (koun′tər klok′wīz′), in the direction opposite to that in which the hands of a clock go; from right to left. *adv., adj.*

counterance (def. 1)
The general was
a man of stern
countenance.

coun ter es pi o nage (koun′tər es′pē ə nij *or* koun′-tər es′pē ə näzh′), measures taken to prevent or confuse enemy espionage. *n.*

coun ter feit (koun′tər fit), **1** copy (money, handwriting, pictures, etc.) in order to deceive or defraud: *They were arrested for counterfeiting twenty-dollar bills.* **2** a copy made to deceive or defraud and passed as genuine: *This twenty-dollar bill looks genuine, but it is a counterfeit.* **3** not genuine: *a counterfeit coin.* **4** pretend: *She counterfeited interest to be polite.* **5** pretended; dissembled. 1,4 *v.,* 2 *n.,* 3,5 *adj.* **—coun′ter feit′er,** *n.* **—coun′ter feit′ness,** *n.*

coun ter in tel li gence (koun′tər in tel′ə jəns), system or activity of counteracting the intelligence or spy activities of an enemy. *n.*

coun ter man (koun′tər man′), person who serves at a counter, especially in a lunchroom. *n., pl.* **coun ter men.**

coun ter mand (koun′tər mand′), withdraw or cancel (an order or command). *v.* **—coun′ter mand′a ble,** *adj.*

coun ter of fen sive (koun′tər ə fen′siv), an attack by a defending force against an attacking force. *n.*

coun ter pane (koun′tər pān′), an outer covering for a bed; bedspread. *n.*

coun ter part (koun′tər pärt′), **1** person or thing closely resembling another: *She is the counterpart of her twin sister.* **2** person or thing that complements or corresponds to another: *Night is the counterpart of day. n.*

coun ter plot (koun′tər plot′), **1** a plot to defeat another plot. **2** plot against (another plot or plotter). 1 *n.,* 2 *v.,* **coun ter plot ted, coun ter plot ting.**

coun ter point (koun′tər point′), **1** melody added to another as an accompaniment. **2** art of adding melodies to a given melody according to fixed rules. *n.*

coun ter rev o lu tion (koun′tər rev′ə lü′shən), revolution against a government established by a previous revolution. *n.*

coun ter sign (koun′tər sīn′), **1** a secret signal; password; watchword: *The spy was caught when he could not give the countersign to the sentry.* **2** sign (something already signed by another) to confirm it: *The check was signed by the treasurer and countersigned by the president.* 1 *n.,* 2 *v.*

coun ter sink (koun′tər singk′), **1** enlarge the upper part of (a hole) to make room for the head of a screw or bolt. **2** sink the head of (a screw or bolt) into such a hole so that it is even with or below the surface. *v.,* **coun ter sunk** (koun′tər sungk′), **coun ter sink ing.**

coun ter spy (koun′tər spī′), spy who works to uncover or oppose the activities of enemy spies. *n., pl.* **coun ter spies.**

coun ter weight (koun′tər wāt′), weight that balances another weight. *n.*

count ess (koun′tis), **1** wife or widow of a count or an earl. **2** woman whose rank is equal to that of a count or an earl. *n., pl.* **count ess es.**

count ing house (koun′ting hous′), building or office used for keeping accounts and doing business. *n., pl.* **count ing hous es** (koun′ting hou′ziz).

*Be not the first by whom the new are tried,
Nor yet the last to lay the old aside.*

count less (kount′lis), too many to count; very many; innumerable: *the countless stars. adj.*

coun tri fied (kun′tri fid), **1** looking or acting like a person from the country. **2** like the country; rural. *adj.*

coun try (kun′trē), **1** land, region, or district: *The country around the mining town was rough and hilly.* **2** all the land of a nation: *France is a country in Europe.* **3** land where a person was born or where he or she is a citizen: *The United States is my country.* **4** people of a nation: *The country rejoiced when the war ended.* **5** land outside of cities and towns: *the farms and fields of the country.* **6** of the country; in the country; rural: *hearty country meals and fresh country air.* 1-5 *n., pl.* **coun tries;** 6 *adj.*

coun try man (kun′trē mən), person of one's own country. *n., pl.* **coun try men.**

country music, folk music that originated in the southern United States, played with a guitar and other stringed instruments.

coun try side (kun′trē sīd′), a rural area; country. *n.*

coun try wom an (kun′trē wùm′ən), woman of one's own country. *n., pl.* **coun try wom en.**

coun ty (koun′tē), **1** one of the districts into which a state, country, province, or other large political unit is divided for purposes of local government. The county officers collect taxes, hold court, keep county roads in repair, and maintain county schools. **2** people of a county: *The whole county voted against the plan.* **3** the officials of a county. *n., pl.* **coun ties.**

county agent, a United States government specialist who informs and advises farmers and rural communities about agriculture and home economics.

county seat, town or city where the county government is located.

coup (kü), **1** a sudden, brilliant action; unexpected, clever move; master stroke. **2** coup d'état. *n., pl.* **coups** (küz).

coup d'é tat (kü′ dā tä′), a sudden, decisive act in politics, usually bringing about a change in government unlawfully or by force. *pl.* **coups d'é tat** (kü′ dā tä′). [*Coup d'état* comes from French *coup d'état,* which originally meant "stroke of state."]

coupe (küp), a closed, two-door automobile, usually seating two to six people. *n., pl.* **coupes.**

cou pé (kü pā′), **1** coupe. **2** a four-wheeled, closed carriage with a seat for two people inside and a seat for the driver outside. *n., pl.* **cou pés.**

cou ple (kup′əl), **1** two things of the same kind that go together; pair: *I bought a couple of tires for my bicycle.* **2** INFORMAL. a small number; a few: *Give me a couple of those apples—about four of them.* **3** man and woman who are married, engaged, partners in a dance, etc. **4** join together: *The brakeman coupled the freight cars.* 1-3 *n.,* 4 *v.,* **cou pled, cou pling.**

cou pler (kup′lər), **1** person or thing that couples. **2** device used to join two railroad cars; coupling. *n.*

cou plet (kup′lit), two successive lines of poetry, especially two that rhyme and have the same number of feet. *n.*

cou pling (kup′ling), **1** a joining together. **2** device for joining together parts of machinery. **3** coupler. *n.*

cou pon (kü′pon *or* kyü′pon), **1** part of a ticket, advertisement, package, etc., that gives the person who holds it certain rights: *If she saves the coupons that come with each box of soap, she can get a free camera.* **2** a printed statement of interest due on a bond, which can be cut from the bond and presented for payment. *n.* —**cou′pon less,** *adj.*

cour age (kėr′ij), a meeting danger without fear; bravery; fearlessness: *The pioneers faced the hardships of the westward trek with courage. n.*

cou ra geous (kə rā′jəs), full of courage; brave; fearless. *adj.* —**cou ra′geous ly,** *adv.* —**cou ra′geous ness,** *n.*

cour i er (kėr′ē ər *or* kùr′ē ər), messenger sent in haste: *Government dispatches were sent by courier. n.*

course (kôrs), **1** onward movement; forward progress; advance: *Our history book traces the course of human development from the cave to modern city living.* **2** direction taken: *Our course was straight to the north.* **3** line of action; way of doing: *The only sensible course was to go home.* **4** way, path, track, or channel: *the winding course of the stream.* **5** number of like things arranged in some regular order: *a course of lectures.* **6** regular order: *the course of nature.* **7** series of studies in a school, college, or university. A student must complete a certain course in order to graduate. **8** one of the studies in such a series: *Each course in history lasts one year.* **9** part of a meal served at one time: *Soup was the first course and dessert was the last course.* **10** area marked out for races or games: *a golf course, an automobile racing course.* **11** run: *The blood courses through the arteries.* 1-10 *n.,* 11 *v.,* **coursed, cours ing.**

in the course of, during; in the process of: *He mentioned you a few times in the course of our discussion.*

of course, 1 surely; certainly: *Of course you can go!* **2** naturally; as should be expected: *She gave me a gift, and, of course, I accepted it.*

coupe

cours er (kôr′sər), OLD USE. a swift horse. *n.*

course ware (kôrs′wer′ or kôrs′wãr′), lessons written for use on a computer or with a computer: *The algebra courseware includes a computer game and a book of problems. n.*

court (kôrt), **1** space partly or wholly enclosed by walls or buildings: *The four apartment houses were built around a court of grass.* **2** a short street. **3** place marked off for a game: *a tennis court, a basketball court.* **4** place where a king, queen, or other ruler lives; royal palace. **5** household and followers of a king, queen, or other ruler: *The court of King Solomon was noted for its splendor.* **6** ruler and his or her advisers as a ruling body or power: *"By order of the Court of St. James's" is by order of the British government.* **7** assembly held by a king, queen, or other ruler: *The queen held court to hear from her advisers.* **8** place where justice is administered; court of law: *The case will be heard in court next week.* **9** persons who are chosen to administer justice; judge or judges: *The court found her guilty.* **10** assembly of such persons to administer justice: *Court is now in session.* **11** seek the favor of; try to please: *The nobles courted the king to get power.* **12** pay loving attention to in order to marry; woo: *The young man courted the young woman by bringing her flowers every day.* **13** try to get; seek: *It is foolish to court danger.* 1-10 *n.,* 11-13 *v.*
pay court to, pay attention to (a person) to get favor; try to please: *pay court to a high official.*

cour te ous (kėr′tē əs), thoughtful of others; polite: *The clerks are always courteous at this store.* adj. —**cour′te ous ly,** *adv.* —**cour′te ous ness,** *n.*

cour te sy (kėr′tə sē), **1** polite behavior; thoughtfulness for others: *It is a sign of courtesy to give one's seat to an old person on a crowded bus.* **2** a courteous act or expression: *Thanks for all your courtesies. n., pl.* **cour te sies.**

court house (kôrt′hous′), **1** building in which courts of law are held. **2** building used for the government of a county. *n., pl.* **court hous es** (kôrt′hou′ziz).

cour ti er (kôr′tē ər), **1** person often present at a royal court; court attendant. **2** person who tries to win the favor of another through flattery. *n.*

court li ness (kôrt′lē nis), a being courtly; politeness, elegance, or polish. *n.*

court ly (kôrt′lē), having manners fit for a royal court; polite, elegant, or polished: *The courtly gentleman was a favorite with the ladies.* adj., **court li er, court li est.**

court-mar tial (kôrt′mär′shəl), **1** a military court for trying offenders against the laws of the armed forces. **2** trial by a military court. **3** try by a military court. 1,2 *n., pl.* **courts-mar tial;** 3 *v.,* **court-mar tialed, court-mar tial ing** or **court-mar tialled, court-mar tial ling.**

court of law, place where justice is administered; law court.

court room (kôrt′rüm′ or kôrt′rùm′), room where a court of law is held. *n.*

court ship (kôrt′ship), condition or time of courting in order to marry; wooing: *Their brief courtship was a very happy one. n.*

court yard (kôrt′yärd′), space enclosed by walls, in or near a large building. *n.*

cous in (kuz′n), **1** son or daughter of one's uncle or aunt. First cousins have the same grandparents; second cousins have the same great-grandparents; and so on for third and fourth cousins, etc. **2** a distant relative. **3** citizen of a related nation. *n.*

cous in-ger man (kuz′n jėr′mən), a first cousin. *n., pl.* **cous ins-ger man.**

cove (kōv), **1** a small, sheltered bay; inlet on the shore. **2** a sheltered place among hills or woods. *n.*

cov e nant (kuv′ə nənt), a solemn agreement between two or more persons or groups: *The rival nations signed a covenant to reduce their armaments. n.*

cov er (kuv′ər), **1** put something over: *I covered the child with a blanket.* **2** be over; occupy the surface of; spread over: *Snow covered the ground.* **3** anything that covers. Books have covers. A box, can, or jar usually has a cover. A blanket is a cover. **4** hide: *She tried to cover her mistake.* **5** protect; shelter: *Our insurance covers our belongings against loss by fire.* **6** protection; shelter: *We took cover in an old shed during the storm. The burglar escaped under cover of darkness.* **7** go over; travel: *The travelers covered 400 miles a day by car.* **8** take in; include: *The math review covers everything we studied.* **9** be enough for; provide for: *My allowance covers my lunch at school.* **10** (in sports) protect defensively: *The shortstop covered second base on all throws from right field.* **11** report or photograph (events, meetings, etc.): *A reporter covered the fire for the newspaper.* 1,2,4,5,7-11 *v.,* 3,6 *n.* —**cov′er a ble,** *adj.* —**cov′er er,** *n.* —**cov′er less,** *adj.*
break cover, come out in the open.
cover up, 1 cover completely. **2** hide; conceal.
under cover, 1 hidden; secret: *He kept his activities under cover.* **2** secretly: *Spies work under cover.*

cov er age (kuv′ər ij), **1** risks covered by an insurance policy: *She has fire coverage on her belongings.* **2** way of presenting information by a reporter, newspaper, etc.: *The President's inauguration got broad coverage on radio and television. n.*

cov er all (kuv′ər ôl′). Often, **coveralls,** *pl.* a one-piece work garment that includes shirt and trousers. *n.*

covered wagon, wagon having a canvas cover that can be taken off.

cov er ing (kuv′ər ing), thing that covers: *bed coverings. n.*

cov er let (kuv′ər lit), a covering, especially a covering for a bed. *n.*

cov ert (kuv′ərt or kō′vərt), kept from sight; secret; hidden: *The children cast covert glances at the box of candy they were told not to touch.* adj. —**cov′ert ly,** *adv.*

cov er-up (kuv′ər up′), something that covers up or hides an evil or criminal act: *Legally, a cover-up of a crime is itself a crime. n.*

cov et (kuv′it), desire eagerly (something that belongs to another): *Her friends coveted her new bicycle. v.*

cov et ous (kuv′ə təs), desiring things that belong to others. adj. —**cov′et ous ly,** *adv.* —**cov′et ous ness,** *n.*

cov ey (kuv′ē), a small flock of partridges, quail, etc. *n., pl.* **cov eys.**

cow[1] (kou), **1** the full-grown female of domestic cattle that gives milk. **2** female of the buffalo, moose, and other large mammals: *an elephant cow. n.* [*Cow*[1] comes from Old English *cū.*] —**cow′like′,** *adj.*

cow[2] (kou), make afraid; frighten: *I was cowed by their threats and stayed out of their sight. v.* [*Cow*[2] probably comes from Icelandic *kūga.*]

cow ard (kou′ərd), person who lacks courage or is easily made afraid; person who runs from danger, trouble, etc. *n.*

cow ard ice (kou′ər dis), lack of courage; being easily made afraid: *to be guilty of cowardice in the presence of danger. n.*

cow ard li ness (kou′ərd lē nis), a being cowardly. *n.*

cow ard ly (kou′ərd lē), **1** lacking courage. **2** of a coward; suitable for a coward. **3** in a cowardly manner. 1,2 adj., 3 adv.

cow bell (kou′bel′), bell hung around a cow's neck to indicate its whereabouts. *n.*

cow bird (kou′bėrd′), a small American blackbird that is often found with cattle. Most cowbirds lay their eggs in the nests of other birds. *n.*

cow boy (kou′boi′), man whose work is looking after cattle on a ranch. *n.*

cow catch er (kou′kach′ər), a metal frame on the front of a locomotive, streetcar, etc., to clear the tracks of anything in the way. *n.*

cow er (kou′ər), crouch or draw back in fear or shame: *The dog cowered under the table after being scolded. v.*

cow girl (kou′gėrl′), woman or girl who works on a ranch, at rodeos, etc. *n.*

cow hand (kou′hand′), person who works on a cattle ranch. *n.*

cow herd (kou′hėrd′), person whose work is looking after cattle at pasture. *n.*

cow hide (kou′hīd′), 1 the hide of a cow. 2 leather made from it. 3 a strong, heavy whip made of rawhide or braided leather. 4 whip with a cowhide; flog. 1-3 *n.*, 4 *v.*, **cow hid ed, cow hid ing.**

cowl (koul), 1 a monk's cloak with a hood. 2 the hood itself. 3 the part of an automobile body that includes the windshield, the dashboard, and sometimes the hood. 4 cowling. *n.*

cow lick (kou′lik′), a small tuft of hair that will not lie flat. *n.*

cowl ing (kou′ling), a metal covering over the engine of an airplane; cowl. *n.*

cow man (kou′mən), 1 owner of cattle. 2 cowboy. *n., pl.* **cow men.**

co-work er (kō′wėr′kər), person who works with another. *n.*

cow poke (kou′pōk′), SLANG. cowboy. *n.*

cow pox (kou′poks′), a contagious disease of cows. Vaccine for smallpox is obtained from cows that have cowpox. *n.*

cow punch er (kou′pun′chər), INFORMAL. cowboy. *n.*

cow rie or **cow ry** (kou′rē), the brightly colored, smooth shell of a tropical mollusk, used as money in some parts of Africa and Asia. *n., pl.* **cow ries.**

cow slip (kou′slip), 1 a wild plant with bright, yellow flowers that bloom in early spring. 2 marsh marigold. *n.*

cox (koks), INFORMAL. coxswain. *n.*

cox comb (koks′kōm′), a vain, empty-headed man; conceited dandy. *n.*

cox swain (kok′sən or kok′swān′), person who steers a rowboat, racing boat, etc. *n.* Also, **cockswain.**

coy (koi), 1 shy or modest; bashful. 2 acting more shy than one really is. *adj.* —**coy′ly,** *adv.* —**coy′ness,** *n.*

coy o te (kī ō′tē or kī′ōt), a small wolflike mammal living on the prairies of western North America; prairie wolf. It is noted for loud howling at night. *n., pl.* **coy o tes** or **coy o te.**

coyote
about 21 in.
(53 cm.) high
at the shoulder

coy pu (koi′pü), a large water rodent of South America; nutria. Its fur resembles beaver. *n., pl.* **coy pus** or **coy pu.**

coz en (kuz′n), deceive or trick; cheat. *v.* —**coz′en er,** *n.*

co zi ly (kō′zə lē), in a warm and comfortable manner. *adv.* Also, **cosily.**

a hat	i it	oi oil	ch child	⎧ a in about
ā age	ī ice	ou out	ng long	e in taken
ä far	o hot	u cup	sh she	ə = ⎨ i in pencil
e let	ō open	u̇ put	th thin	o in lemon
ē equal	ô order	ü rule	ᴛʜ then	⎩ u in circus
ėr term			zh measure	

cowl (def. 2)

co zi ness (kō′zē nis), cozy condition or quality. *n.* Also, **cosiness.**

co zy (kō′zē), 1 warm and comfortable; snug: *The cat lay in a cozy corner near the fireplace.* 2 a padded cloth cover to keep a teapot warm. 1 *adj.*, **co zi er, co zi est;** 2 *n., pl.* **co zies.** Also, **cosy.**

cp., compare.

C.P., Communist Party.

C.P.A., Certified Public Accountant.

Cpl., corporal.

cps, cycles per second.

CPU, central processing unit.

Cr, symbol for chromium.

C.R., Costa Rica.

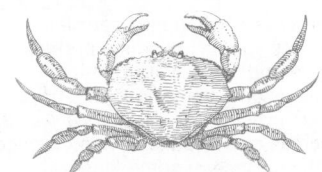

crab¹ (def. 1)
shell about 4 in.
(10 cm.) wide

crab[1] (krab), 1 a broad, flat shellfish that has four pairs of legs and one pair of claws. Many kinds of crabs are good to eat. 2 catch crabs for eating. 3 a cross, sour person. 4 INFORMAL. find fault; criticize: *Don't crab so much.* 1,3 *n.*, 2,4 *v.*, **crabbed, crab bing.** —**crab′ber,** *n.* —**crab′like′,** *adj.*

crab[2] (krab), crab apple. *n.*

crab apple, 1 a small, sour apple, used to make jelly. 2 tree on which it grows.

crab bed (krab′id), 1 hard to read or decipher because irregular: *crabbed handwriting.* 2 crabby. *adj.* —**crab′bed ly,** *adv.* —**crab′bed ness,** *n.*

crab by (krab′ē), cross, peevish, or ill-natured; crabbed. *adj.*, **crab bi er, crab bi est.**

crab grass (krab′gras′), a coarse grass that spreads rapidly and spoils lawns. *n.*

crack (krak), 1 split or opening made by breaking without separating into parts: *There is a crack in this cup.* 2 break without separating into parts: *You have cracked the mirror. The glass cracked when I poured hot water into it.* 3 a narrow opening: *I can see between the cracks in the old floor boards.* 4 a sudden, sharp noise like that made by something breaking, by a whip, or by loud thunder. 5 make or cause to make a sudden, sharp noise: *The*

whip cracked. *The stagecoach driver cracked the whip.*
6 break with a sudden, sharp noise: *The tree cracked and fell. We cracked the nuts.* **7** INFORMAL. a hard, sharp blow: *The falling branch gave me a crack on the head.* **8** hit with a hard, sharp blow: *The falling branch cracked me on the head.* **9** make or become harsh, broken, or shrill: *His voice cracked with emotion.* **10** give way; break down: *His mind cracked under the strain of working for three days without sleep.* **11** break into: *The burglar cracked the safe.* **12** INFORMAL. excellent; first-rate: *a crack train. She was a crack shot.* **13** INFORMAL. a try; effort: *She took a crack at the job and succeeded.* **14** SLANG. a funny or clever remark; joke: *If you make another crack about my singing, you'll be sorry.* **15** INFORMAL. tell or say (something funny or clever): *She cracked a joke.* **16** figure out the meaning of (a code); decipher: *In wartime each enemy tries to crack the other's code.* 1,3,4,7,13,14 *n.*, 2,5,6,8-11,15,16 *v.*, 12 *adj.*

crack down, INFORMAL. take stern measures: *The police intend to crack down on speeders.*

crack up, 1 crash; smash: *The driver skidded off the road and cracked up his car against a tree.* **2** suffer a mental or physical collapse: *She was in danger of cracking up under the strain of overwork.* **3** INFORMAL. praise: *That book is not what it is cracked up to be.* **4** INFORMAL. burst out laughing.

crack down (krak′doun′), act of taking stern measures or swift disciplinary action: *The police began a crackdown on speeders. n.*

cracked (krakt), **1** broken without separating into parts: *a cracked cup.* **2** broken into parts: *cracked corn, cracked ice.* **3** having harsh notes; uneven; broken: *a cracked voice.* **4** INFORMAL. crazy. *adj.*

crack er (krak′ər), **1** a thin, crisp biscuit. **2** firecracker. *n.*

crack er jack (krak′ər jak′), SLANG. **1** person or thing of superior ability or grade: *She is a crackerjack at dominoes.* **2** of superior ability or grade: *a crackerjack motorboat.* 1 *n.*, 2 *adj.*

crack ing (krak′ing), process of changing petroleum and other oils into products such as gasoline and jet fuel, by heat and pressure and a catalyst. *n.*

crack le (krak′əl), **1** make slight, sharp sounds: *A fire crackled in the fireplace. Twigs crackled beneath her feet.* **2** a slight, sharp sound, such as paper makes when crushed. **3** very small cracks on the surface of some kinds of china or glass. 1 *v.*, **crack led, crack ling;** 2,3 *n.*

crack ling (krak′ling), the crisp, browned skin of roasted pork. *n.*

crack pot (krak′pot′), SLANG. **1** a very eccentric or crazy person. **2** eccentric or impractical. 1 *n.*, 2 *adj.*

crack up (krak′up′), **1** a crash; smash-up: *That fast driver has been in more than one automobile crackup.*
2 INFORMAL. a mental or physical collapse; breakdown. *n.*

cra dle (krā′dl), **1** a small bed for a baby, usually mounted on rockers. **2** put or rock in a cradle; hold as in a cradle: *She cradled the baby in her arms.* **3** place where anything begins its growth: *The sea is thought to have been the cradle of life.* **4** frame to support a ship or other large object while it is being built, repaired, or lifted. **5** the part of the telephone that supports the receiver. **6** box on rockers to wash earth from gold or other metals. **7** wash (earth from gold or other metals) in a cradle. 1,3-6 *n.*, 2,7 *v.*, **cra dled, cra dling. —cra′dle like′,** *adj.*

craft (kraft), **1** special skill: *The expert carpenter shaped and fitted the wood into a cabinet with great craft.* **2** trade or art requiring skilled work: *Carpentry is a craft.*
3 members of a trade requiring special skill: *the craft of electricians.* **4** skill in deceiving others; slyness; trickiness: *By craft the gambler tricked them out of all their money.* **5** work, make, or finish with skill or art: *woodwork*

crafted by expert cabinetmakers. **6** boats, ships, or aircraft: *Craft of all kinds come into New York every day.* **7** a boat, ship, or aircraft: *A strange craft sailed into the harbor.* 1-4,6,7 *n.*, 5 *v.*

craft i ly (kraf′tə lē), in a crafty manner; cunningly. *adv.*

craft i ness (kraf′tē nis), skill in deceiving others; being crafty; cunning. *n.*

crafts man (krafts′mən), **1** person skilled in a craft or trade. **2** artist. *n., pl.* **crafts men.**

crafts man ship (krafts′mən ship), work or skill of a craftsman. *n.*

craft union, a labor union made up of persons in the same craft. Unions of carpenters, plumbers, or bricklayers are craft unions.

craft y (kraf′tē), skillful in deceiving others; sly; tricky: *a crafty schemer. adj.,* **craft i er, craft i est.**

crag (krag), a steep, rugged rock rising above others. *n.* **—crag′like′,** *adj.*

crag gi ness (krag′ē nis), quality of being craggy; ruggedness. *n.*

crag gy (krag′ē), **1** having many crags; steep and rugged: *The craggy hill was difficult to climb.* **2** rough; uneven: *The old fisherman had a craggy, weathered face. adj.,* **crag gi er, crag gi est.**

cram (kram), **1** force into; force down; stuff: *I crammed all my books and papers into my locker.* **2** fill too full; crowd: *The bus was crammed, with many people standing.*
3 eat too fast or too much: *She felt ill after she crammed down her lunch.* **4** INFORMAL. try to learn too much in a short time: *Having studied very little during the year, he has to cram for his finals. v.,* **crammed, cram ming. —cram′mer,** *n.*

cramp (kramp), **1** shut into a small space; limit: *In only three rooms, the family was cramped.* **2** a sudden, painful contracting or pulling together of muscles, often from chill or strain: *The swimmer was seized with a cramp and had to be helped from the pool.* **3 cramps,** *pl.* very sharp pains in the abdomen. **4** cause to have a cramp: *The green apples she ate cramped her stomach.* **5** a metal bar bent at both ends. It is used for holding together blocks of stone, timbers, etc. **6** turn sharply to one side or the other; steer: *The driver had to cramp the front wheels to get out of the tight parking space.* 1,4,6 *v.*, 2,3,5 *n.*

cran ber ry (kran′ber′ē), a firm, sour, dark-red berry, used for jelly and sauce. It grows on a creeping shrub found in marshes or bogs. *n., pl.* **cran ber ries.**

crane (krān), **1** machine with a long, swinging arm, for lifting and moving heavy weights. **2** a swinging metal arm in a fireplace, used to hold a kettle over the fire. **3** a large wading bird with long legs, neck, and bill. **4** stretch (the neck) as a crane does, in order to see better: *The little girl craned her neck to see the parade over the heads of the crowd.* 1-3 *n.*, 4 *v.*, **craned, cran ing. —crane′like′,** *adj.*

crane (def. 1)

cra ni al (krā′nē əl), of or having to do with the skull: *cranial nerves. adj.* —**cra′ni al ly,** *adv.*

cra ni um (krā′nē əm), **1** the skull of an animal with a backbone. **2** the part of the skull that encloses the brain. *n., pl.* **cra ni ums, cra ni a** (krā′nē ə).

crank (krangk), **1** part or handle of a machine connected at right angles to a shaft to set it in motion: *the crank of a pencil sharpener.* **2** work or start by means of a crank: *Car engines used to be cranked by hand.* **3** INFORMAL. person who has strange ideas or habits; odd person. **4** INFORMAL. a cross or ill-tempered person. 1,3,4 *n.,* 2 *v.* —**crank′less,** *adj.*

crank case (krangk′kās′), a heavy, metal case forming the bottom of an internal-combustion engine. It contains lubricating oil and encloses the crankshaft. *n.*

crank i ly (krang′kə lē), in a cranky manner. *adv.*

crank i ness (krang kē nis), quality or condition of being cranky. *n.*

crank shaft (krangk′shaft′), shaft turning or turned by a crank. The crankshaft of an internal-combustion engine is connected to the pistons by piston rods. *n.*

crank y (krang′kē), cross; irritable. *adj.,* **crank i er, crank i est.**

cran nied (kran′ēd), full of crannies. *adj.*

cran ny (kran′ē), a small, narrow opening; crack; crevice: *She looked in all the nooks and crannies of the house for the misplaced book. n., pl.* **cran nies.**

crap pie (krap′ē), a small freshwater fish of North America, used for food. *n.*

crash (krash), **1** a sudden, loud noise like many dishes falling and breaking: *The lightning was followed by a crash of thunder.* **2** make a sudden, loud noise: *The cymbals crashed.* **3** fall, hit, or break with force and a loud noise: *The dishes crashed to the floor.* **4** a falling, hitting, or breaking with force and a loud noise: *the crash of dishes on the floor.* **5** the violent striking of one thing against another; collision: *There was a crash of two cars at the corner.* **6** strike violently and shatter: *The baseball crashed through the window.* **7** fall to the earth in such a way as to be damaged or wrecked: *The airplane went out of control and crashed.* **8** such a fall or landing: *an airplane crash.* **9** sudden ruin; severe failure in business: *They lost their money in the stock market crash.* **10** INFORMAL. go to (a party or dance) without being invited. 1,4,5,8,9 *n., pl.* **crash es;** 2,3,6,7,10 *v.* —**crash′er,** *n.*

crash-land (krash′land′), land in an airplane so that a crash results. *v.*

crass (kras), gross or stupid: *crass ignorance, a crass person. adj.* —**crass′ly,** *adv.* —**crass′ness,** *n.*

crate (krāt), **1** a large frame or box made of strips of wood. Crates are often used to pack furniture, glass, china, or fruit for shipping or storage. **2** pack in a crate: *crate a mirror for moving.* 1 *n.,* 2 *v.,* **crat ed, crat ing.**

cra ter (krā′tər), **1** a bowl-shaped hole around the opening of a volcano. **2** hole on the surface of the earth, moon, etc., shaped like this: *The meteor crashed to earth, forming a huge crater. n.* —**cra′ter like′,** *adj.*

cra vat (krə vat′), necktie, especially a wide one. *n.*

crave (krāv), **1** long for greatly; desire strongly: *The thirsty hiker craved water.* **2** ask earnestly for; beg: *He craved a favor of the king. v.,* **craved, crav ing.**

cra ven (krā′vən), **1** cowardly. **2** coward. 1 *adj.,* 2 *n.* —**cra′ven ly,** *adv.* —**cra′ven ness,** *n.*

crav ing (krā′ving), a strong desire; great longing; yearning: *a craving for alcohol. n.*

craw (krô), **1** crop of a bird or insect. **2** stomach of any animal. *n.*

craw fish (krô′fish′), crayfish. *n., pl.* **craw fish es or craw fish.**

crawl (krôl), **1** move slowly by pulling the body along

the ground: *Worms and snakes crawl.* **2** creep on hands and knees: *We crawled through a hole in the fence.* **3** move slowly: *The heavy traffic crawled through the narrow tunnel.* **4** a crawling; slow movement: *Traffic had slowed to a crawl.* **5** swarm with crawling things: *The ground under the garbage can was crawling with ants.* **6** feel creepy: *My flesh crawled when I saw a big snake.* **7** a fast way of swimming by overarm strokes and rapid kicking of the feet. **8** swim this way. 1-3,5,6,8 *v.,* 4,7 *n.* —**crawl′er,** *n.*

crawler tractor, tractor that can travel over very rough ground on its two endless tracks.

crawl y (krô′lē), INFORMAL. creepy. *adj.,* **crawl i er, crawl i est.**

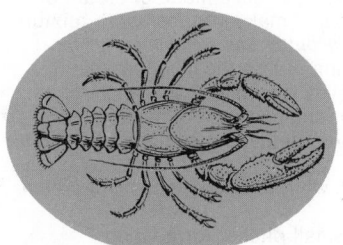

crayfish
about 3 to 6 in.
(7.5 to 15 cm.)
long

cray fish (krā′fish′), any of numerous freshwater crustaceans looking much like a small lobster. *n., pl.* **crayfish es or cray fish.** Also, **crawfish.**

Cray o la (krā ō′lə), trademark for a set of crayons. *n.*

cray on (krā′on *or* krā′ən), **1** stick or pencil of chalk, charcoal, or a waxlike, colored substance, used for drawing or writing. **2** draw with a crayon or crayons. **3** drawing made with a crayon or crayons. 1,3 *n.,* 2 *v.*

craze (krāz), **1** a short-lived, eager interest in doing some one thing; fad: *The craze for flying kites was soon replaced by another for skateboards.* **2** make or become crazy: *to be crazed with pain.* **3** make very small cracks on the surface of (a dish, vase, etc.); crackle. 1 *n.,* 2,3 *v.,* **crazed, craz ing.**

crater
(def. 2)

cra zi ly (krā′zə lē), in a crazy manner: *The driver zigzagged crazily through traffic. adv.*

cra zi ness (krā′zē nis), quality or condition of being crazy. *n.*

cra zy (krā′zē), **1** mentally ill; mad; insane. **2** greatly distressed or shaken by strong emotion: *The parents of the kidnaped child were crazy with worry.* **3** unwise or senseless; foolish: *It was a crazy idea to jump out of such a high tree.* **4** INFORMAL. very eager or enthusiastic: *She is so crazy about cats that she brings home every stray she finds.* **5** not strong or sound; shaky: *That crazy light blinks on and off whenever anyone slams the door.* *adj.,* **cra zi er, cra zi est.**

like crazy, SLANG. like mad.

crazy bone, funny bone.

crazy quilt, quilt made of pieces of cloth of various shapes, colors, and sizes, sewed together with no definite pattern.

creak (krēk), **1** squeak loudly: *The hinges on the door creaked because they needed oiling.* **2** a creaking noise: *The creak of the stairs in the old house was spooky.* **1** *v.,* **2** *n.*

creak i ly (krē′kə lē), in a creaky manner. *adv.*

creak y (krē′kē), likely to creak; creaking: *a creaky floor.* *adj.,* **creak i er, creak i est.** —**creak′i ness,** *n.*

cream (krēm), **1** the oily, yellowish part of milk. Cream rises to the top when milk that is not homogenized is allowed to stand. Butter is made from cream. **2** a fancy sweet dessert or candy made of cream: *chocolate creams.* **3** cook with cream, milk, or a sauce made of cream or milk with butter and flour. **4** make into a smooth mixture like cream: *I creamed the butter and sugar together for a cake.* **5** an oily preparation put on the skin to make it smooth and soft. **6** a yellowish white. **7** yellowish-white: *cream lace.* **8** the best or choicest part of anything: *the cream of the crop.* **9** SLANG. defeat completely. **1,2,5,6,8** *n.,* **3,4,9** *v.,* **7** *adj.*

cream cheese, a soft, white cheese made from cream, or milk and cream.

cream er (krē′mər), a small pitcher for holding cream. *n.*

cream er y (krē′mər ē), **1** place where butter and cheese are made. **2** place where cream, milk, and butter are bought and sold. *n., pl.* **cream er ies.**

cream i ness (krē′mē nis), creamy condition or quality. *n.*

cream of tartar, a white powder obtained from the deposit in wine casks, used in baking powder and in medicine.

cream y (krē′mē), **1** like cream; smooth and soft. **2** having much cream in it: *pie with a rich, creamy filling.* *adj.,* **cream i er, cream i est.** —**cream′i ly,** *adv.*

crease (krēs), **1** line or mark made by folding or pressing cloth, paper, etc.; ridge; fold: *She likes a sharp crease in her slacks.* **2** a wrinkle: *The creases on his face showed that he was very old.* **3** make a crease or creases in: *Mother creased the pleats in her skirt with an iron.* **4** become creased: *Some cloth is too thick to crease well.* **1,2** *n.,* **3,4** *v.,* **creased, creas ing.** —**creas′er,** *n.*

cre ate (krē āt′), **1** make a thing which has not been made before; cause to be; bring into being; make: *Composers create music.* **2** be the cause of; cause: *The noise created a disturbance.* *v.,* **cre at ed, cre at ing.**

cre a tion (krē ā′shən), **1** a creating; act of making a thing which has not been made before: *The gasoline engine led to the creation of the modern automobile.* **2** all things created; the world and everything in it; the universe: *Let all creation praise the Lord.* **3** thing produced by intelligence or skill, usually something important or original: *Art, drama, and music are creations of the imagination.* **4** **the Creation,** the creating of the universe by God: *The Bible says the Creation took six days.* *n.*

cre a tive (krē ā′tiv), having the power to create; inventive: *a creative person.* *adj.* —**cre a′tive ly,** *adv.* —**cre a′tive ness,** *n.*

cre a tor (krē ā′tər), **1** person who creates: *Leonardo da Vinci was the creator of many ideas for inventions.* **2 the Creator,** God. *n.*

crea ture (krē′chər), **1** any living person or animal. **2** anything created: *Ghosts are creatures of the imagination.* **3** person who is strongly influenced or controlled by another person or thing: *I am a creature of habit.* *n.*

crèche (kresh), model of the Christ child in the manger, with attending figures, often displayed at Christmas. *n., pl.* **crèch es** (kresh′iz). [*Crèche* comes from French *crèche,* meaning "manger, crib."]

cre dence (krēd′ns), belief: *Don't give credence to that gossip.* *n.*

cre den tials (kri den′shəlz), letters of introduction; references: *The new ambassador from England presented his credentials to the President.* *n.pl.*

cred i bil i ty (kred′ə bil′ə tē), quality of being believable. *n.*

cred i ble (kred′ə bəl), worthy of belief; believable: *Her excuse for being absent was hardly credible.* *adj.* —**cred′i ble ness,** *n.*

cred i bly (kred′ə blē), in a credible manner; so as to be believed. *adv.*

cred it (kred′it), **1** belief in the truth of something; faith; trust: *I know he is sure of his facts and put great credit in what he says.* **2** believe in the truth of something; have faith in; trust: *I can credit your story because I had a similar experience.* **3** a trust in a person's ability and intention to pay: *This store will extend credit to you by opening a charge account in your name.* **4** amount of money in a person's account: *When I deposit this check, I will have a credit of fifty dollars in my savings account.* **5** add to one's credit in a bank account, business record, etc.: *The bank credited fifty dollars to my savings account.* **6** delayed payment; time allowed for delayed payment: *The store allowed us six months' credit on our purchase.* **7** reputation in money matters: *If you pay your bills on time, your credit will be good.* **8** good reputation: *The mayor is a man of credit in the community.* **9** honor; praise: *The person who does the work should get the credit.* **10** person or thing that brings honor or praise: *I entered college, determined to be a credit to my family.* **11** entry on a student's record showing that he or she has passed a course of study: *You must pass the examination to get credit for the course.* **12** unit of work entered in this way: *She needs three credits to graduate.* **1,3,4,6-12** *n.,* **2,5** *v.*

credit with, think that someone has; attribute to: *I credit you with the ability to do well.*

do credit to, bring honor or praise to: *The winning team did credit to the school.*

on credit, on a promise to pay later: *buy a car on credit.*

cred it a ble (kred′ə tə bəl), bringing credit or honor: *She has a creditable record as a senator.* *adj.* —**cred′it a ble ness,** *n.*

cred it a bly (kred′ə tə blē), in a creditable manner; with credit to oneself. *adv.*

credit card, card that identifies its holder, and allows that person to charge the cost of goods or services from one or many businesses.

cred i tor (kred′ə tər), person to whom a debt is owed. *n.*

cre do (krē′dō *or* krā′dō), creed. *n., pl.* **cre dos.** [*Credo* comes from Latin *credo,* meaning "I believe."]

cre du li ty (krə dü′lə tē *or* krə dyü′lə tē), a too great readiness to believe. *n.*

cred u lous (krej′ə ləs), too ready to believe: *She was so credulous that the other children could easily fool her.* *adj.* —**cred′u lous ly,** *adv.* —**cred′u lous ness,** *n.*

Cree (krē), member of a tribe of American Indians living in Montana and in central and southern Canada. *n., pl.* **Cree** or **Crees.**

creed (krēd), **1** a brief statement of the main points of religious belief of some church. **2** any statement of faith, belief, or opinions: *"Honesty is the best policy"* was his creed in all his business dealings. *n.*

creek (krēk *or* krik), **1** a small stream. **2** a narrow bay, running inland for some distance. *n.*

Creek (krēk), **1** member of a group of American Indian tribes formerly living in Alabama and Georgia, and now living in Oklahoma. **2** their language. *n., pl.* **Creek** or **Creeks** for 1.

creel (krēl), basket for holding fish that have been caught. *n.*

creep (krēp), **1** move slowly with the body close to the ground or floor; crawl: *Babies creep on their hands and knees before they begin to walk.* **2** move slowly or little by little: *The traffic crept over the narrow bridge. The fog crept in while we were asleep.* **3** move in a timid or stealthy way: *They didn't see me creeping up on them. The dog crept into the room.* **4** grow along the ground or over a wall by means of clinging stems: *Ivy had crept up the wall of the old house.* **5** feel as if things were creeping over the skin: *It made my flesh creep to hear the wolves howl.* **6** a creeping; slow movement. **7 the creeps,** INFORMAL. a feeling of horror, as if things were creeping over one's skin: *Movies about werewolves give me the creeps.* **8** SLANG. an unpleasant or annoying person. 1-5 *v.,* **crept, creep ing;** 6-8 *n.*

creep er (krē′pər), **1** person or thing that creeps. **2** any plant that grows along a surface, sending out rootlets from the stem, such as the Virginia creeper and ivy. **3** a small bird that creeps around on trees and bushes looking for food. *n.*

creep i ly (krē′pə lē), in a creepy manner. *adv.*

creep i ness (krē′pē nis), creepy quality or condition. *n.*

creep y (krē′pē), **1** having a feeling of horror, as if things were creeping over one's skin; frightened: *The ghost stories made the children creepy.* **2** causing such a feeling: *The wind howling through the old house was creepy. adj.,* **creep i er, creep i est.**

cre mate (krē′māt), burn (a dead body) to ashes. *v.,* **cre mat ed, cre mat ing.** —**cre′ma tor,** *n.*

cre ma tion (kri mā′shən), the burning of a dead body to ashes. *n.*

cre ma to ry (krē′mə tôr′ē), **1** furnace for cremating. **2** building having such a furnace. *n., pl.* **cre ma to ries.**

Cre ole or **cre ole** (krē′ōl), **1** descendant of the early French or Spanish settlers in Louisiana. **2** the French language as spoken in Louisiana. **3** a French or Spanish person born in Latin America or the West Indies. **4** person who is part Negro and part Creole. **5** of or having to do with the Creoles: *Creole customs, Creole cooking.* **6** cooked in sauce made of stewed tomatoes, peppers, etc. 1-4 *n.,* 5,6 *adj.*

cre o sote (krē′ə sōt), **1** a poisonous, oily liquid, made by distilling coal tar. It is used to preserve wood. **2** a similar liquid made by distilling wood tar. It is used as an antiseptic. *n.*

crepe or **crêpe** (krāp), **1** a thin, light cloth with a finely crinkled surface. **2** crepe paper. **3** a very thin pancake, usually served folded around a filling. *n.*

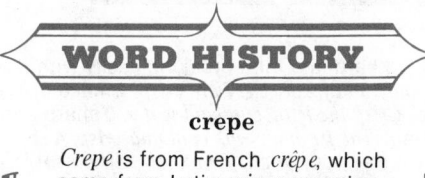

WORD HISTORY

crepe

Crepe is from French *crêpe,* which came from Latin *crispa,* meaning "curled."

a hat	i it	oi oil	ch child	a in about
ā age	ī ice	ou out	ng long	e in taken
ä far	o hot	u cup	sh she	ə = i in pencil
e let	ō open	u̇ put	th thin	o in lemon
ē equal	ô order	ü rule	ŦH then	u in circus
ėr term			zh measure	

crepe paper, a thin, crinkled paper that looks like crepe, used for making decorations.

crepe rubber, a crude rubber with a crinkled surface, used for the soles of shoes.

crept (krept), past tense and past participle of **creep.** *We crept up on them from behind. v.*

cre scen do (krə shen′dō), **1** (in music) with a gradual increase in force or loudness. **2** a gradual increase in force or loudness, especially in music. 1 *adj., adv.,* 2 *n., pl.* **cre scen dos.**

cres cent (kres′nt), **1** shape of the moon in its first or last quarter. **2** anything that curves in a similar way. **3** shaped like the moon in its first or last quarter: *a crescent pin.* **4** growing; increasing: *the crescent darkness.* 1,2 *n.,* 3,4 *adj.* —**cres′cent like′,** *adj.*

cress (kres), any of various plants whose leaves have a peppery taste and are used as a garnish or in salad. *n., pl.* **cress es.**

cres set (kres′it), a metal container for burning oil, wood, etc., to give light. Cressets are mounted on poles or hung from above. *n.*

crest (krest), **1** tuft or comb on the head of a bird or other animal. **2** decoration of plumes or feathers worn on the top of a helmet. **3** decoration at the top of a coat of arms. A family crest is sometimes put on silverware, dishes, or letter paper. **4** the top part; peak; summit: *the crest of a wave, the crest of the hill. n.* —**crest′like′,** *adj.*

crest ed (kres′tid), having a crest: *a crested bird, a crested shield. adj.*

crest fall en (krest′fô′lən), in low spirits; discouraged: *Several students went home crestfallen because they had failed the examination. adj.* —**crest′fall′en ly,** *adv.* —**crest′fall′en ness,** *n.*

Cret an (krēt′n), **1** of Crete or its inhabitants. **2** person born or living in Crete. 1 *adj.,* 2 *n.*

Crete (krēt), Greek island in the Mediterranean, southeast of Greece. See **Balkan States** for map. *n.*

cre tin (krēt′n), person in whom a thyroid gland deficiency has caused severe mental and physical retardation. *n.*

crevasse (def. 1)
The climbers used ropes to cross a **crevasse.**

cre vasse (krə vas′), **1** a deep crack or split in the ice of a glacier, or in the ground after an earthquake. **2** a break in a levee, dike, or dam. *n.*

crev ice (krev′is), a narrow split or crack; fissure: *Tiny ferns grew in crevices in the stone wall. n.*

crew[1] (krü), **1** the sailors who work aboard a ship. **2** the group of persons who fly and work on an aircraft. **3** any group of people working or acting together: *a crew of loggers, a railroad maintenance crew.* **4** the members of a rowing team. *n.* [*Crew*[1] came into English over 500 years ago from French *creüe*, meaning "an increase, recruit," and can be traced back to Latin *crescere*, meaning "to grow."]

crew[2] (krü), crowed; a past tense of **crow**[1]. *The cock crew. v.*

crew cut, kind of very short haircut for men and boys.

crew el (krü′əl), **1** a loosely twisted, woolen yarn, used for embroidery. **2** embroidery done with this yarn. *n.*

crew man (krü′mən), member of a crew. *n., pl.* **crewmen.**

crib (krib), **1** a small bed with high barred sides to keep a baby from falling out. **2** rack or manger for horses and cows to eat from. **3** building or box for storing grain, salt, etc.: *Rats damaged much of the corn in the crib.* **4** framework of logs or timbers used in building. The wooden lining inside a mine shaft is a crib. **5** INFORMAL. use (another's words or ideas) as one's own: *She cribbed from the encyclopedia to write her report.* **6** INFORMAL. notes or helps that are unfair to use in doing schoolwork. **7** INFORMAL. use notes or helps unfairly in doing schoolwork. 1-4,6 *n.,* 5,7 *v.,* **cribbed, crib bing.** —**crib′ber,** *n.*

crib bage (krib′ij), a card game for two, three, or four people. The players keep score by moving pegs along a narrow board. *n.*

crick (krik), a muscular cramp; painful stiffness of muscles: *I got a crick in the neck from sleeping in the chair. n.*

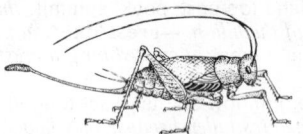

cricket[1]
about 1 in.
(2.5 cm.) long

crick et[1] (krik′it), a black insect related to the grasshopper. Male crickets make a chirping noise by rubbing their front wings together. *n.* [See **Word History.**]

crick et[2] (krik′it), **1** an outdoor game played by two teams of eleven players each, with a ball, bats, and wickets. Cricket is very popular in England. **2** INFORMAL. fair play; good sportsmanship: *It's not cricket to push ahead of others in line. n.* [See **Word History.**]

cried (krīd), past tense and past participle of **cry.** *He cried when he fell down. The baby has cried all day. v.*

cri er (krī′ər), **1** official who shouts out public announcements. **2** person who cries or shouts. *n.*

cries (krīz), **1** plural of **cry. 2** a present tense of **cry.** *The baby cries when she is hungry.* 1 *n.,* 2 *v.*

crime (krīm), **1** a harmful or grave offense against the law. Theft, kidnaping, murder, and arson are crimes. **2** activity of criminals; violation of law: *Police forces combat crime.* **3** an evil or wrong act: *It is a crime to ignore suffering. n.*

Cri me a (krī mē′ə), peninsula in the SW part of the Soviet Union in Europe, on the N coast of the Black Sea. See **Caucasia** for map. *n.* —**Cri me′an,** *adj., n.*

crim i nal (krim′ə nəl), **1** person who has committed a crime: *The criminal was sentenced to prison for theft.* **2** guilty of wrongdoing: *a criminal person.* **3** of or having to do with crime or its punishment: *A criminal court hears criminal cases.* **4** like crime; wrong: *It is criminal to neglect a pet.* 1 *n.,* 2-4 *adj.* —**crim′i nal ly,** *adv.*

crim i no log i cal (krim′ə nə loj′ə kəl), of criminology. *adj.*

crim i nol o gist (krim′ə nol′ə jist), an expert in criminology. *n.*

crim i nol o gy (krim′ə nol′ə jē), the scientific study of crime, its prevention and treatment, and criminals. *n.*

crimp (krimp), **1** press into small, regular, narrow folds; make wavy: *The children crimped tissue paper to make paper flowers.* **2** something crimped; fold or wave. 1 *v.,* 2 *n.* —**crimp′er,** *n.*

crimp y (krim′pē), having small, narrow folds; wavy. *adj.,* **crimp i er, crimp i est.**

crim son (krim′zən), **1** a deep red. **2** deep-red. **3** turn deep-red: *Her face crimsoned with embarrassment.* 1 *n.,* 2 *adj.,* 3 *v.*

cringe (krinj), **1** shrink from danger or pain; crouch in fear: *I cringed when the nurse gave me a shot.* **2** act of cringing. 1 *v.,* **cringed, cring ing;** 2 *n.* —**cring′er,** *n.*

crin kle (kring′kəl), **1** wrinkle or ripple: *Crepe paper is crinkled.* **2** rustle: *Paper crinkles when it is crushed.* **3** a wrinkle or ripple: *There is a crinkle in the tablecloth.* **4** a rustle. 1,2 *v.,* **crin kled, crin kling;** 3,4 *n.*

crin kly (kring′klē), full of crinkles. *adj.,* **crin kli er, crin kli est.**

crin o line (krin′l ən), **1** a stiff cloth used as a lining to hold a skirt out, make a coat collar stand up, etc. **2** petticoat of crinoline to hold a skirt out. **3** a hoop skirt. *n.*

crip ple (krip′əl), **1** person or animal that cannot use an arm or leg properly because of injury or deformity; lame person or animal. **2** make a cripple of; make lame. **3** damage; disable; weaken: *The ship was crippled by the storm.* 1 *n.,* 2,3 *v.,* **crip pled, crip pling.** —**crip′pler,** *n.*

cri sis (krī′sis), **1** an important or deciding event; point at which a change must come, either for the better or the worse: *The scandal was a crisis in the senator's career.* **2** time of difficulty, lack of security, and of anxious waiting: *Because of the scarcity of oil the country faces an energy crisis.* **3** the turning point in a disease, toward life or death: *After the fever broke the doctor said the patient had passed the crisis and would recover. n., pl.* **cri ses** (krī′sēz′).

WORD HISTORY

cricket[1]

Cricket[1] came into English about 650 years ago from French *criquet,* which came from an imitation of the insect's sound.

cricket[2]

Cricket[2] came into English about 400 years ago from French *criquet,* meaning "goal post, stick," which came from an imitation of the sound of the ball hitting the post.

crisp (krisp), **1** hard and thin; breaking easily with a snap: *Dry toast and fresh celery are crisp.* **2** make or become crisp: *Crisp the lettuce in cold water.* **3** sharp and clear; bracing: *The fresh air was cool and crisp.* **4** short and decisive; clear-cut: *a crisp manner.* "*Sit down!*" was her crisp command. 1,3,4 *adj.,* 2 *v.* —**crisp′ly,** *adv.* —**crisp′ness,** *n.*

crisp y (kris′pē), crisp. *adj.,* **crisp i er, crisp i est.** —**crisp′i ness,** *n.*

criss cross (kris′krôs′), **1** mark or cover with crossed lines: *Little cracks crisscrossed the wall.* **2** come and go across: *Buses and cars crisscross the city.* **3** made or marked with crossed lines; crossed; crossing: *Plaids have a crisscross pattern.* **4** a mark or pattern of crossed lines: *The messy paper was a crisscross of lines and scribbles.* 1,2 *v.*, 3 *adj.*, 4 *n.*, *pl.* **criss cross es.** [*Crisscross* comes from Middle English *cristcross,* which originally meant "Christ's cross." Middle English *cross* can be traced back to Latin *crux.*]

cri ter i a (krī tir′ē ə), a plural of **criterion.** *n.*

cri ter i on (krī tir′ē ən), rule or standard for making a judgment; test: *Wealth is only one criterion of success. n., pl.* **cri ter i a** or **cri ter i ons.**

crit ic (krit′ik), **1** person who makes judgments of the merits and faults of books, music, pictures, plays, acting, etc.: *We went to see the movie because we read that the critics liked it.* **2** person who disapproves or finds fault; faultfinder. *n.*

crit i cal (krit′ə kəl), **1** inclined to find fault or disapprove: *a critical disposition.* **2** coming from one who is skilled as a critic: *a critical judgment, critical essays.* **3** of a crisis; being important to the outcome of a situation: *Help arrived at the critical moment.* **4** full of danger or difficulty: *The patient was in a critical condition. adj.* —**crit′i cal ly,** *adv.* —**crit′i cal ness,** *n.*

crit i cism (krit′ə siz′əm), **1** unfavorable remarks or judgments; finding fault: *I could not let their rudeness pass without criticism.* **2** the making of judgments; analysis of merits and faults: *literary criticism, drama criticism.* **3** a critical comment, essay, review, etc.: *The editor wrote a criticism of the author's new book. n.*

crit i cize (krit′ə sīz), **1** find fault with; disapprove of; blame: *Do not criticize him until you know all the circumstances.* **2** judge or speak as a critic: *The editor criticized the author's new novel, comparing it with her last one. v.,* **crit i cized, crit i ciz ing.** —**crit′i ciz′er,** *n.*

crit ter (krit′ər), DIALECT. creature. *n.*

croak (krōk), **1** the deep, hoarse sound made by a frog, crow, or raven. **2** make this sound. **3** utter in a deep, hoarse voice: *to croak a reply.* **4** be dissatisfied; grumble. 1 *n.,* 2-4 *v.* —**croak′er,** *n.*

Cro at (krō′at), person born or living in Croatia. *n.*

Cro a tia (krō ā′shə), district in NW Yugoslavia. *n.* —**Cro a′tian,** *adj., n.*

crochet (def. 1)

cro chet (krō shā′), **1** make (sweaters, lace, etc.) by looping thread or yarn into links with a single hooked needle. **2** needlework done in this way. 1 *v.,* **cro cheted** (krō shād′), **cro chet ing** (krō shā′ing); 2 *n.*

crock (krok), pot or jar made of baked clay. *n.*

crock er y (krok′ər ē), earthenware. *n.*

Crock ett (krok′it), **Davy,** 1786-1836, American hunter, scout, and Congressman, killed at the defense of the Alamo. *n.*

croc o dile (krok′ə dīl), a large, lizardlike reptile with thick skin, a long narrow head, and webbed feet. Crocodiles live in the rivers and marshes of the warm parts of Africa, Asia, Australia, and America. *n.*

crocodile tears, pretended or insincere grief. [The tears are called this because of the story that crocodiles shed tears while eating their victims.]

a hat	i it	oi oil	ch child	a in about
ā age	ī ice	ou out	ng long	e in taken
ä far	o hot	u cup	sh she	ə = { i in pencil
e let	ō open	ů put	th thin	o in lemon
ē equal	ô order	ü rule	ŦH then	u in circus
ėr term			zh measure	

cro cus (krō′kəs), a small plant related to the iris, that grows from a bulblike base and has white, yellow, or purple flowers. Most crocuses bloom very early in the spring. *n., pl.* **cro cus es, cro ci** (krō′sī).

Croe sus (krē′səs), **1** king in Asia Minor from 560 to 546 B.C., famous for his great wealth. **2** any very rich person. *n.*

Cro-Mag non (krō mag′nən), **1** belonging to a group of prehistoric people who lived in southwestern Europe. They used stone and bone implements, and some of them were skilled artists. **2** person of this group. 1 *adj.,* 2 *n.*

Crom well (krom′wel), **Oliver,** 1599-1658, English general, statesman, and Puritan leader. *n.*

crone (krōn), a withered old woman. *n.*

cro ny (krō′nē), a very close friend; chum. *n., pl.* **cro nies.**

crook (krúk), **1** make a hook or curve in; bend: *I crooked my leg around the branch to keep from falling.* **2** a hooked, curved, or bent part: *the crook of the elbow. There is a crook in the stream.* **3** a shepherd's hooked staff. Its upper end is curved or bent into a hook. **4** INFORMAL. a dishonest person; thief or swindler: *The crook stole all my money.* 1 *v.,* 2-4 *n.*

crook ed (krúk′id), **1** not straight; bent; curved; twisted: *a crooked toe.* **2** dishonest: *a crooked scheme. adj.* —**crook′ed ly,** *adv.* —**crook′ed ness,** *n.*

croon (krün), **1** hum, sing, or murmur in a low tone: *I crooned a lullaby to the baby.* **2** sing in a low voice with exaggerated emotion. *v.* —**croon′er,** *n.*

crop (krop), **1** plants grown or gathered by people for their use, especially as food: *Wheat, corn, and cotton are three main crops of the United States.* **2** the whole amount (of wheat, corn, or the produce of any plant or tree) that one season yields: *The drought made the potato crop very small this year.* **3** plant, cultivate, or yield a crop or crops. **4** anything like a crop; group; collection: *a crop of lies.* **5** cut or bite off the top of: *Sheep had cropped the grass very short.* **6** cut short; clip: *to crop a horse's tail.* **7** act or result of cropping. A short haircut is a crop. **8** a baglike swelling of a bird's or insect's food passage where food is prepared for digestion; craw. **9** a short whip with a loop instead of a lash: *a riding crop.* 1,2,4,7-9 *n.,* 3,5,6 *v.,* **cropped, crop ping.**

crop up, turn up unexpectedly: *Unless you plan carefully, all sorts of difficulties may crop up.*

crocodile—up to 30 ft. (9 m.) long

crop per (krop/ər). **come a cropper,** INFORMAL. meet with misfortune; fail or collapse. *n.*

cro quet (krō kā/), an outdoor game played by knocking wooden balls through small wire arches with mallets. *n.*

cro quette (krō ket/), a small mass of chopped meat, fish, or vegetables, coated with crumbs and fried. *n.*

cross (krôs), **1** stick or post with another across it like a T or an X. **2 the Cross,** the cross on which Christ died. **3** thing, design, or mark shaped like a cross. A cross is the symbol of the Christian religion. A person who cannot write makes a cross instead of a signature. **4** draw a line across: *In writing you cross the letter "t."* **5** cancel by marking with a cross or by drawing a line or lines across: *cross off a name on a list.* **6** put or lay across: *He crossed his arms.* **7** lie across; intersect: *Main Street crosses Market Street. Parallel lines cannot cross.* **8** go or move across: *Let's cross the street. The bridge crosses the river.* **9** meet and pass: *My letter to her and hers to me crossed in the mail.* **10** lying or going across; crossing: *We stood at the intersection of the cross streets.* **11** make the sign of the cross on or over: *She crossed herself as she went into the church.* **12** act against; get in the way of; oppose: *If anyone crosses him, he gets very angry.* **13** in a bad temper; complaining: *People are often cross when they don't feel well.* **14** burden of duty or suffering; trouble: *bear one's cross without complaining.* **15** mix kinds or breeds of: *A new plant is sometimes made by crossing two others.* **16** a mixing or mixture of kinds or breeds: *A mule is a cross between a horse and a donkey.* 1-3,14,16 *n., pl.* **cross es;** 4-9,11,12,15 *v.,* 10,13 *adj.* [*Cross* comes from Old English *cros,* and can be traced back to Latin *crux.*] —**cross/ly,** *adv.* —**cross/ness,** *n.*

cross bar (krôs/bär/), bar, line, or stripe going crosswise. *n.*

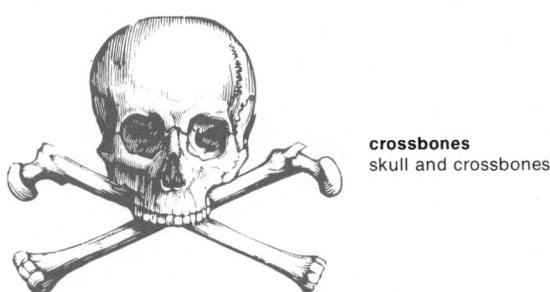

crossbones
skull and crossbones

cross bones (krôs/bōnz/), two bones placed crosswise, usually below a skull, to mean death: *Poisonous medicines are sometimes marked with a skull and crossbones. n.pl.*

cross bow (krôs/bō/), a medieval weapon for shooting arrows, stones, etc., consisting of a bow fixed across a wooden stock, with a groove in the middle to direct the arrows, stones, etc. *n.*

cross breed (krôs/brēd/), **1** to breed by mixing kinds or breeds: *You can crossbreed a horse and a donkey to get a mule.* **2** individual or breed produced by crossbreeding. The loganberry is a crossbreed of the dewberry and the red raspberry. 1 *v.,* **cross bred** (krôs/bred/), **cross-breed ing;** 2 *n.*

cross-coun try (krôs/kun/trē), **1** across fields or open country instead of by road: *a cross-country race.* **2** across an entire country, not merely a part: *a cross-country flight from New York to Seattle. adj.*

cross cut (krôs/kut/), **1** a cut, course, or path going across. **2** used or made for cutting across. **3** to cut across. 1 *n.,* 2 *adj.,* 3 *v.,* **cross cut, cross cut ting.**

crosscut saw, saw used or made for cutting across the grain of wood.

cross-ex am i na tion (krôs/eg zam/ə nā/shən), examination to check a previous examination, especially the questioning of a witness by the lawyer of the opposing side to test the truth of the witness's testimony. *n.*

cross-ex am ine (krôs/eg zam/ən), question closely (a witness of the opposing side) to check the truth of his or her testimony. *v.,* **cross-ex am ined, cross-ex am in ing.** —**cross/-ex am/in er,** *n.*

cross-eyed (krôs/īd/), having both eyes turned toward the nose, and unable to focus on the same point. *adj.*

cross-grained (krôs/grānd/), having the grain arranged in crossing directions, or irregularly, instead of running straight: *cross-grained wood. adj.*

cross ing (krô/sing), **1** place where lines, tracks, etc., cross: *a railroad crossing.* **2** place at which a street, river, etc., may be crossed: *White lines mark the crossing.* **3** a going across, especially a voyage across water: *The ocean liner made a crossing from New York to England every two weeks. n.*

cross piece (krôs/pēs/), piece of wood, metal, etc., that is placed across something. *n.*

cross-pol li na tion (krôs/pol/ə nā/shən), transfer of pollen from the anther of one flower to the stigma of another, usually by insects or currents of air. *n.*

cross-prod uct (krôs/prod/əkt), (in a mathematical proportion) the product of the first number of one ratio and the second number of the other ratio. For $^3/_4$ and $^9/_{12}$, the cross-products are 3×12 and 9×4, both of which equal 36. *n.*

cross-pur pose (krôs/pėr/pəs), an opposing or contrary purpose. *n.*

at cross-purposes, misunderstanding each other's purpose: *We cannot accomplish anything while we are at cross-purposes.*

cross-ques tion (krôs/kwes/chən), question closely; cross-examine. *v.*

cross-re fer (krôs/ri fėr/), refer from one part to another. *v.,* **cross-re ferred, cross-re fer ring.**

cross-ref er ence (krôs/ref/ər əns), reference from one part of a book, index, etc., to another. "See **clef** for diagram" under **alto clef** is a cross-reference. *n.*

cross road (krôs/rōd/), **1** road that crosses another. **2** road that connects main roads. **3 crossroads,** *pl.* place where roads cross: *At the crossroads we stopped and read the signs. n.*

cross section, 1 act of cutting anything across: *I sliced the tomatoes by making a series of cross sections.* **2** piece cut in this way. **3** small selection of people, things, etc., with the same qualities as the entire group; sample: *They interviewed a cross section of the population in their survey of public opinion.*

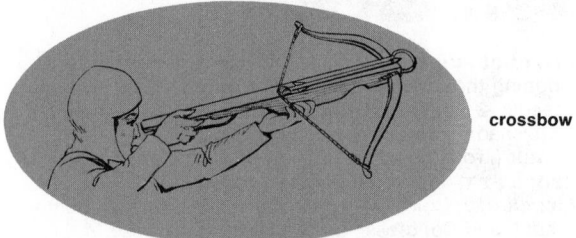

crossbow

cross trees (krôs/trēz/), two horizontal bars of wood or metal near the top of a ship's mast. *n.pl.*

cross walk (krôs/wôk/), area marked with lines, used by pedestrians in crossing a street. *n.*

cross way (krôs/wā/), crossroad. *n.*

cross ways (krôs/wāz/), crosswise. *adv.*

cross wise (krôs/wīz/), **1** so as to cross; across: *The tree* *fell crosswise over the stream.* **2** in the form of a cross: *The streets come together crosswise at the intersection. adv.*

cross word puzzle (krôs′wėrd′), puzzle with sets of numbered squares to be filled in with words, one letter to each square, so that the words may be read both across and down. Synonyms, definitions, or other clues are given with numbers corresponding to the numbers in the squares.

crotch (kroch), **1** place where a tree, bough, etc., divides into two limbs or branches: *The bird's nest was in the crotch of a tree.* **2** place where the human body divides into the two legs. *n., pl.* **crotch es.**

crotch et y (kroch′ə tē), full of odd notions or unreasonable whims. *adj.* —**crotch′et i ness,** *n.*

crouch (krouch), **1** stoop low with bent legs as though ready to spring: *The cat crouched in the corner, waiting for the mouse to come out of its hole.* **2** shrink down in fear. **3** a crouching. **4** a crouching position. 1,2 *v.*, 3,4 *n., pl.* **crouch es.**

croup (krüp), a children's disease of the throat and windpipe that causes a hoarse cough and difficult breathing. *n.* [*Croup* comes from earlier *croup*, meaning "to cry hoarsely, croak," which came from an imitation of the sound.]

croup y (krü′pē), sick with croup: *the wheeze of a croupy baby. adj.,* **croup i er, croup i est.**

crou ton (krü′ton), a small piece of toasted or fried bread, often served in soup. *n.*

crow[1] (krō), **1** the loud cry of a rooster. **2** make this cry: *The cock crowed as the sun rose.* **3** a happy sound made by a baby. **4** make this sound. **5** show one's happiness and pride; boast: *The winning team crowed over its victory.* 1,3 *n.*, 2,4,5 *v.*, **crowed** (or **crew** for 2), **crowed, crowing.** [*Crow*[1] comes from Old English *crāwan,* meaning "to crow," which came from an imitation of the sound.]

crow[2] (krō), **1** a large, glossy, black bird that has a harsh cry or caw. **2** any similar bird, such as a raven or magpie. *n.* [*Crow*[2] comes from Old English *crāwe.*]

as the crow flies, in a straight line; in or by the shortest way: *The distance is exactly one mile as the crow flies.*

eat crow, be forced to do something very disagreeable and humiliating.

Crow (krō), member of a tribe of American Indians who formerly lived in Montana and Wyoming and now live in Montana. *n., pl.* **Crow** or **Crows.**

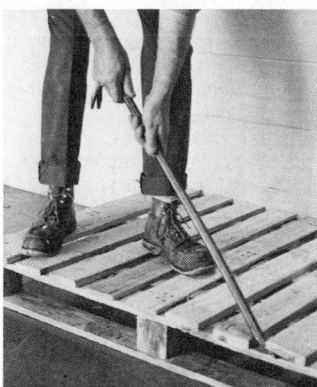

crowbar

crow bar (krō′bär′), a strong iron or steel bar, used to lift things or pry them apart. *n.*

crowd (kroud), **1** a large number of people together: *A crowd gathered at the scene of the fire.* **2** people in general; the masses: *Advertisements seek to appeal to the crowd.* **3** INFORMAL. group; set: *Our crowd wasn't invited to the party.* **4** collect in large numbers: *crowd around a TV star.*

a hat	i it	oi oil	ch child	
ā age	ī ice	ou out	ng long	a in about
ä far	o hot	u cup	sh she	e in taken
e let	ō open	ù put	th thin	ə = { i in pencil
ē equal	ô order	ü rule	ᵮH then	o in lemon
ėr term			zh measure	u in circus

5 fill; fill too full: *Christmas shoppers crowded the store.* **6** push; shove: *The big man crowded the child out of his way.* **7** press forward; force one's way: *She crowded into the subway car.* 1-3 *n.*, 4-7 *v.*

crown (kroun), **1** a head covering of precious metal and jewels, worn by a king or queen. **2 the Crown,** the governing power and authority in a monarchy; royal power: *The Crown granted lands in colonial America to William Penn.* **3** a king or queen: *Always address the crown respectfully.* **4** make king or queen: *The princess was crowned in London.* **5** of a crown: *the crown jewels.* **6** wreath for the head: *The winner of the race received a crown.* **7** an honor; reward: *He won the amateur boxing crown in his last bout.* **8** to honor; reward: *Her hard work was crowned with success.* **9** head: *"Jack fell down and broke his crown."* **10** the highest part; top: *the crown of the head, the crown of a hat. The Olympic victory was the crown of her athletic career.* **11** be on top of; cover the highest part of: *A fort crowns the hill.* **12** make perfect or complete; add the finishing touch to: *Success crowned her efforts.* **13** part of a tooth which appears beyond the gum, or an artificial substitute for it. **14** put an artificial crown on (a tooth). **15** a British coin worth 5 shillings or 25 new pence. 1-3,6,7,9,10,13,15 *n.*, 4,8,11,12,14 *v.*, 5 *adj.*

crown prince, the oldest living son of a king or queen; the male heir to a throne.

crown princess, 1 wife of a crown prince. **2** the female heir to a throne.

crow's-feet (krōz′fēt′), the tiny wrinkles at the outer corners of the eyes. *n.pl.*

crow's-nest (krōz′nest′), a small, enclosed platform near the top of a ship's mast, used by the lookout. *n.*

CRT, cathode-ray tube.

cru cial (krü′shəl), very important or decisive; critical: *This is a crucial game, for it will decide the championship. adj.* —**cru′cial ly,** *adv.*

cru ci ble (krü′sə bəl), container in which metals, ores, etc., can be melted. *n.*

cru ci fix (krü′sə fiks), cross with a figure of the crucified Christ on it. *n., pl.* **cru ci fix es.**

cru ci fix ion (krü′sə fik′shən), **1** a crucifying or a being crucified. **2 Crucifixion, a** the crucifying of Christ on the Cross. **b** picture, statue, etc., of this. *n.*

cru ci form (krü′sə fôrm), shaped like a cross. *adj.*

cru ci fy (krü′sə fī), **1** put to death by nailing or binding the hands and feet to a cross. **2** persecute or torture. *v.,* **cru ci fied, cru ci fy ing.**

crude (krüd), **1** in a natural or raw state; unrefined: *crude oil, crude rubber.* **2** rough; coarse. **3** lacking finish, grace,

crude (def. 2)
A **crude** wooden horse was the children's favorite toy.

taste, or refinement: *crude manners. adj.,* **crud er,
crud est. —crude′ly,** *adv.* **—crude′ness,** *n.*

cru di ty (krü′də tē), **1** a being crude; lack of finish;
roughness: *The crudity of the homemade furniture fit in
with the rustic charm of the summer cabin.* **2** a crude action or thing. *n., pl.* **cru di ties.**

cru el (krü′əl), **1** ready to give pain to others or to delight in their suffering; hardhearted: *Kicking a dog is
cruel.* **2** showing a cruel nature: *cruel acts.* **3** causing pain
and suffering: *a cruel war. adj.* **—cru′el ly,** *adv.* **—cru′el-
ness,** *n.*

cru el ty (krü′əl tē), **1** readiness to give pain to others or
to delight in their suffering. **2** a cruel act or acts: *an
organization that seeks to prevent cruelty to animals. n., pl.*
cru el ties.

cruet

cru et (krü′it), a glass bottle to hold vinegar, oil, etc., for
the table. *n.*

cruise (krüz), **1** sail about from place to place on pleasure or business; sail over or about: *We cruised to Bermuda on our vacation. Freighters and tankers cruise the oceans
of the world. The coast guard cruised along the shore.* **2** a
voyage from place to place for pleasure: *We went for a
cruise on the Great Lakes last summer.* **3** to travel or journey from place to place: *The taxicab cruised the city
streets in search of passengers.* **4** to travel in a car, airplane, boat, etc., at the speed at which it operates best.
1,3,4 *v.,* **cruised, cruis ing;** 2 *n.* [*Cruise* comes from
Dutch *kruisen,* meaning "to cross, cruise," and can be
traced back to Latin *crux,* meaning "a cross."]

cruis er (krü′zər), **1** warship with less armor and greater
speed than a battleship. **2** motorboat having a cabin and
equipped with facilities for living on board. **3** a police car
used for patrolling streets and highways. *n.*

crul ler (krul′ər), piece of rich, sweet dough fried brown
in deep fat. The dough is usually shaped in twists and
cut in short pieces. *n.* [*Cruller* is from Dutch *kruller,*
which comes from *krullen,* meaning "to curl."]

crumb (krum), **1** a very small piece of bread, cake, etc.,
broken from a larger piece: *I fed crumbs to the birds.*
2 break into crumbs; crumble. **3** cover with crumbs for
frying or baking. **4** a little bit: *a crumb of comfort.* 1,4 *n.,*
2,3 *v.*

crum ble (krum′bəl), **1** break into very small pieces or
crumbs: *I crumbled the bread for the birds.* **2** fall to pieces;
decay: *The old wall was crumbling away at the edges. v.,*
crum bled, crum bling.

crum bly (krum′blē), tending to crumble; easily crumbled. *adj.,* **crum bli er, crum bli est. —crum′bli ness,** *n.*

crum my (krum′ē), SLANG. **1** disgusting; dirty; filthy: *a
crummy neighborhood.* **2** having little quality or value;
poor: *a crummy movie, a crummy idea. adj.,* **crum mi er,
crum mi est.**

crum pet (krum′pit), a round, flat cake, thicker than a
pancake, baked on a griddle. Crumpets are usually
toasted and eaten while hot. *n.*

crum ple (krum′pəl), **1** crush together; wrinkle: *She
crumpled the paper into a ball.* **2** fall down: *He crumpled to
the floor in a faint. v.,* **crum pled, crum pling.**

crunch (krunch), **1** crush noisily with the teeth: *He was
crunching celery.* **2** make or move with a crunching noise:
*The frozen crust of snow crunched under our feet. The
children crunched through the snow.* **3** act or sound of
crunching. **4** INFORMAL. a critical time or situation; crisis:
*The crunch came when we ran out of food on our camping
trip.* 1,2 *v.,* 3,4 *n., pl.* **crunch es.**

crunch y (krun′chē), INFORMAL. brittle and crackling:
crunchy candy. adj., **crunch i er, crunch i est.**
—crunch′i ness, *n.*

cru sade (krü sād′), **1** Often, **Crusade.** any one of the
Christian military expeditions between the years 1096
and 1272 to recover the Holy Land from the Moslems.
2 a vigorous campaign against a public evil or in favor of
some new idea: *Everyone was asked to join the crusade
against cancer.* **3** take part in a crusade: *We crusaded
against cancer.* 1,2 *n.,* 3 *v.,* **cru sad ed, cru sad ing.**
[*Crusade* comes from French *croisade* and Spanish *cruza-
da,* and can be traced back to Latin *crux,* meaning "a
cross."]

cru sad er (krü sā′dər), person who takes part in a crusade. The **Crusaders** of the Middle Ages tried to recover
the Holy Land from the Moslems. *n.*

cruse (krüz), jug, pot, or bottle made of earthenware. *n.*

crush (krush), **1** squeeze together violently so as to
break or bruise: *The car door slammed and crushed his
fingers.* **2** wrinkle or crease by wear or rough handling:
My suitcase was so full that my clothes were crushed.
3 break into fine pieces by grinding, pounding, or pressing: *The ore is crushed between steel rollers.* **4** act of crushing; violent pressure like grinding or pounding: *She
pushed her way through the crush of the crowd.* **5** mass of
people crowded close together: *There was a crush at the
narrow exits after the football game.* **6** subdue; conquer:
The revolt was crushed, and its leaders were imprisoned.
7 INFORMAL. a sudden, strong liking for a person: *I once
had a crush on my fifth-grade teacher.* 1-3,6 *v.,* 4,5,7 *n., pl.*
crush es. —crush′er, *n.*

Cru soe (krü′sō), **Robinson,** hero of Daniel Defoe's
novel of the same name, a sailor shipwrecked on a
desert island. *n.*

crust (krust), **1** the hard, outside part of bread. **2** piece of
this. **3** any hard, dry piece of bread. **4** rich dough rolled
out thin and baked for pies. **5** any hard outside covering:
*The frozen crust on the snow was thick enough for us to
walk on it.* **6** the solid outside part of the earth: *Volcanoes
form below the crust of the earth.* **7** cover or become covered with a crust; form into a crust: *By the next day the
snow had crusted over. The rocks were crusted with moss.*
1-6 *n.,* 7 *v.* **—crust′like′,** *adj.*

crus ta cean (krus tā′shən), **1** any of a group of animals
with hard shells and jointed bodies and legs, living
mostly in the water. Crabs, lobsters, and shrimps are
crustaceans. **2** of this group. 1 *n.,* 2 *adj.*

crust i ly (krus′tl ē), in a crusty manner. *adv.*

crust y (krus′tē), **1** of or like a crust; having a crust;
hard: *crusty bread.* **2** harsh in manner or speech: *The
crusty sea captain has a quick temper. adj.,* **crust i er,
crust i est. —crust′i ness,** *n.*

crutch (kruch), **1** a support to help a lame or injured
person walk. It is a stick with a padded crosspiece at the
top that fits under a person's arm and supports part of
the weight in walking. **2** anything like a crutch in shape
or use; support; prop: *She must learn to make her own*

decisions and not to lean on her friend as a crutch. n., pl. **crutch es.**

crux (kruks), **1** the essential part; most important point: *the crux of an argument.* **2** a puzzling or perplexing question; difficult point to explain. *n., pl.* **crux es.**

cry (krī), **1** call loudly; shout: *"Wait!" she cried from behind me.* **2** a loud call; shout: *a cry of rage. We heard his cry for help.* **3** shed tears; weep: *The child cried when the toy broke.* **4** spell of shedding tears; fit of weeping: *I feel better now that I have had a good cry.* **5** noise or call of an animal: *the cry of hounds, the hungry cry of the wolf.* **6** make such a noise: *The crows cried to one another from the treetops.* **7** a call to action; slogan: *"Forward" was the army's cry as it attacked.* **8** a call for help; appeal. **9** offer for sale by calling out: *Peddlers cry their wares in the street.* **10** a call that means things are for sale: *a peddler's cry.* 1,3,6,9 *v.,* **cried, cry ing;** 2,4,5,7,8,10 *n., pl.* **cries.**

cry for, 1 ask earnestly for; beg for: *The captives cried for mercy.* **2** need very much: *The run-down old house cried for a coat of paint.*

in full cry, in close pursuit: *The hounds were in full cry after the fox.*

cry ba by (krī′bā′bē), person who cries easily or pretends to be hurt. *n., pl.* **cry ba bies.**

cry ing (krī′ing), **1** that cries. **2** demanding attention; very bad: *The slums in that city are a crying shame. adj.*

crypt (kript), an underground room or vault. *The crypt beneath the main floor of a church was formerly often used as a burial place. n.*

cryp tic (krip′tik), having a hidden meaning; secret; mysterious: *We could not fully understand his cryptic remark. adj.* —**cryp′ti cal ly,** *adv.*

cryp to gram (krip′tə gram), something written in secret code or cipher. *n.*

crys tal (kris′tl), **1** a clear, transparent mineral that looks like ice. It is a kind of quartz. **2** piece of crystal cut into form for use or ornament. Crystals may be hung around lights or worn as beads. **3** clear and transparent like crystal: *crystal spring water.* **4** a very transparent glass from which drinking glasses, serving dishes, etc., are made: *goblets of crystal.* **5** made of crystal: *crystal beads, crystal water goblets.* **6** the transparent glass or plastic cover over the face of a watch. **7** a regularly shaped piece with angles and flat surfaces, into which many substances solidify. Crystals of sugar are different in form from crystals of snow. 1,2,4,6,7 *n.,* 3,5 *adj.* —**crys′tal like′,** *adj.*

crys tal line (kris′tl ən), **1** made of crystals: *Sugar and salt are crystalline.* **2** made of crystal. **3** clear and transparent like crystal: *A crystalline sheet of ice covered the pond. adj.*

crystalline lens, lens of the eye.

crys tal li za tion (kris′tl ə zā′shən), **1** a crystallizing or a being crystallized: *the crystallization of water by freezing.* **2** a crystallized substance or formation. **3** the taking on of a real, concrete, or permanent form: *The meeting resulted in the crystallization of our plans. n.*

crys tal lize (kris′tl īz), **1** form into crystals; solidify into crystals: *Water crystallizes to form snow.* **2** form into definite shape: *After much thought her ideas crystallized into a clear plan. v.,* **crys tal lized, crys tal liz ing.** —**crys′tal liz′a ble,** *adj.*

Cs, symbol for cesium.

CST or **C.S.T.,** Central Standard Time.

CT, Connecticut (used with postal Zip Code).

ct., 1 cent. *pl.* **cts. 2** court.

Cu, symbol for copper.

cu., cubic.

cub (kub), **1** a young bear, fox, lion, etc. **2** a young or inexperienced person. **3** a cub scout. *n.*

Cu ba (kyü′bə), country on the largest island in the West Indies, south of Florida. *Capital:* Havana. See **Caribbean Sea** for map. *n.* —**Cu′ban,** *adj., n.*

cub by hole (kub′ē hōl′), a small, enclosed space. *n.*

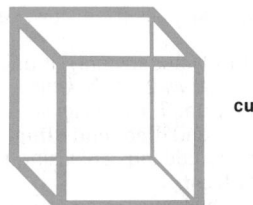

cube (def. 1)

cube (kyüb), **1** a solid object with 6 square faces or sides, all equal. **2** anything shaped like a cube: *ice cubes, a cube of sugar.* **3** make or form into the shape of a cube: *The beets we had for supper were cubed instead of sliced.* **4** use (a number) three times as a factor: *5 cubed is 125, because 5 × 5 × 5 = 125.* **5** product obtained when a number is cubed: *The cube of 4 is 64.* 1,2,5 *n.,* 3,4 *v.,* **cubed, cub ing.** —**cube′like′,** *adj.*

cube root, number that produces a given number when multiplied twice by itself: *The cube root of 27 is 3.*

cu bic (kyü′bik), **1** shaped like a cube: *the cubic form of a block of ice.* **2** having length, breadth, and thickness. A cubic inch is the volume of a cube whose edges are each one inch long. The cubic content of a room is the number of cubic feet it contains. **3** having to do with or involving the cubes of numbers. *adj.*

cu bi cal (kyü′bə kəl), shaped like a cube; cubic. *adj.* —**cu′bi cal ly,** *adv.*

cu bi cle (kyü′bə kəl), a very small room or compartment. *n.*

cubism

cub ism (kyü′biz′əm), style of painting, drawing, and sculpture in which objects are represented by cubes and other geometric forms rather than by realistic details. *n.*

cub ist (kyü′bist), artist or sculptor whose art is based on cubism. *n.*

cu bit (kyü′bit), an ancient measure of length, about 18 to 22 inches or 46 to 56 centimeters. Once a cubit meant the length from the elbow to the tip of the middle finger. *n.*

cub scout, member of the junior division of the Boy Scouts. Cub scouts are 8 to 10 years of age.

cuck oo (kü′kü or kůk′ü), **1** bird whose call sounds much like its name. The common European cuckoo lays its eggs in the nests of other birds instead of hatching them itself. The American cuckoo builds its own nest and has a call less like the name. **2** the call of the cuckoo. **3** SLANG. crazy; silly. 1,2 *n., pl.* **cuck oos;** 3 *adj.*

cu cum ber (kyü′kum bər), the fruit of a garden vine related to the squash. It is a long, green vegetable with firm flesh inside, used in salads and for pickles. *n.*
cool as a cucumber, 1 very cool. **2** calm; not excited.

cud (kud), mouthful of food brought back from the first stomach of cattle or similar animals for a slow, second chewing in the mouth. *n.*

cud dle (kud′l), **1** hold closely and lovingly in one's arms or lap; hug tenderly: *The child cuddled the kittens.* **2** lie close and comfortably; curl up: *The two puppies cuddled together near the radiator.* *v.,* **cud dled, cud dling.**

cud dly (kud′lē), **1** given to cuddling. **2** pleasing to cuddle. *adj.,* **cud dli er, cud dli est.**

cudg el (kuj′əl), **1** a short, thick stick used as a weapon; club. **2** beat with a cudgel. 1 *n.,* 2 *v.,* **cudg eled, cudg el ing** or **cudg elled, cudg el ling.**

cue¹ (kyü), **1** action, word, or last part of a speech by an actor which serves as the signal for another actor to come on the stage or begin speaking. **2** a signal like this to a singer or musician. **3** hint or suggestion as to what to do or when to act: *Take your cue from me at the party about when it is time to leave.* **4** provide (a person) with a cue or hint: *During the rehearsal the director cued the actors.* 1-3 *n.,* 4 *v.,* **cued, cue ing** or **cu ing.** [*Cue¹* may be a spelling for *q.* or *qu.,* which were abbreviations of Latin *quando,* meaning "when." This Latin word was used in directions to actors.]

cue² (kyü), **1** a long, tapering stick used for striking the ball in the game of billiards or pool. **2** queue. *n.* [*Cue²* is a different form of *queue.*]

cuff¹ (kuf), **1** band of material attached to a sleeve and worn around the wrist. **2** a turned-up fold around the bottom of the legs of trousers. **3** handcuff. *n.*

cuff² (kuf), **1** hit with the hand; slap. **2** a hit with the hand; slap. 1 *v.,* 2 *n.*

cuff link, link for the cuff of a shirt.

cu. ft., cubic foot or cubic feet.

cu. in., cubic inch or cubic inches.

cui rass (kwi ras′), **1** piece of armor for the body made of a breastplate and a plate for the back fastened together. **2** the breastplate alone. *n., pl.* **cui rass es.**

cui sine (kwi zēn′), **1** style of cooking or preparing food; cooking; cookery: *Italian cuisine.* **2** food: *The cuisine is excellent at that restaurant. n.*

cu li nar y (kyü′lə ner′ē), having to do with cooking or the kitchen: *We praised the cook's culinary skill. adj.*

cull (kul), **1** pick out; select: *The lawyer culled important facts from the mass of evidence.* **2** pick over; make selections from: *We culled the berries, discarding the bad ones.* **3** something picked out as inferior or worthless. Poor fruit, stale vegetables, and animals not up to standard are called culls. 1,2 *v.,* 3 *n.* —**cull′er,** *n.*

cul mi nate (kul′mə nāt), reach its highest point; reach a climax: *Weeks of unsuccessful bargaining for wage increases culminated in a strike. v.,* **cul mi nat ed, cul mi nat ing.**

cul mi na tion (kul′mə nā′shən), **1** the highest point; climax: *The fireworks display was the culmination of the Fourth of July celebration.* **2** a reaching of the highest point. *n.*

cu lottes (kü′lots), a woman's skirt divided and sewed like trousers, but cut so full as to look like a skirt. *n.pl.*

cul pa bil i ty (kul′pə bil′ə tē), fact or condition of being culpable. *n.*

cul pa ble (kul′pə bəl), deserving blame: *The policeman was dismissed for culpable neglect of duty. adj.* —**cul′pa ble ness,** *n.*

cul pa bly (kul′pə blē), in a culpable manner. *adv.*

cul prit (kul′prit), **1** person guilty of a fault or crime; offender: *Someone broke the window; are you the culprit?* **2** prisoner in court accused of a crime. *n.*

cult (kult), **1** system of religious worship. **2** great admiration for a person, thing, or idea; worship. **3** group showing such admiration; worshipers. *n.*

cul ti vate (kul′tə vāt), **1** prepare and use (land) to raise crops by plowing it, planting seeds, and taking care of the growing plants; till. **2** help (plants) grow by labor and care. **3** loosen the ground around (growing plants) to kill weeds, etc. **4** improve or develop by study or training: *cultivate one's mind, cultivate good manners.* **5** seek the friendship of: *She cultivated people who could help her. v.,* **cul ti vat ed, cul ti vat ing.** —**cul′ti vat′a ble,** *adj.*

cul ti vat ed (kul′tə vā′tid), **1** prepared and used to raise crops: *A field of wheat is cultivated land; a pasture is not.* **2** produce by cultivation; not wild: *a cultivated flower.* **3** improved or developed. **4** cultured; refined: *cultivated tastes. adj.*

cul ti va tion (kul′tə vā′shən), **1** preparing land and growing crops by plowing, planting, and necessary care: *Better cultivation of soil will result in better crops.* **2** condition of being prepared by plowing, planting, etc.: *Only half the farm was under cultivation.* **3** giving time and thought to improving and developing (the body, mind, or manners): *the cultivation of good study habits.* **4** result of improvement or growth through education and experience; culture. *n.*

cul ti va tor (kul′tə vā′tər), **1** person or thing that cultivates. **2** tool or machine used to loosen the ground and destroy weeds. A cultivator is pulled or pushed between rows of growing plants. *n.*

cul tur al (kul′chər əl), of or having to do with culture: *Literature, art, and music are cultural studies. adj.* —**cul′tur al ly,** *adv.*

cul ture (kul′chər), **1** fineness of feelings, thoughts, tastes, manners, etc.; refinement: *A person of culture appreciates art, music, and literature.* **2** the customs, arts, and conveniences of a nation or people at a given time: *The culture of the ancient Incas is noted for its art, its fine buildings, and its religion.* **3** development of the mind or body by education or training: *a course in physical culture.* **4** preparation of land and producing of crops; cultivation. **5** the cultivating or breeding of animals or plants, especially to get new or improved kinds: *bee culture.* **6** growth of bacteria in a special medium for scientific use. *n.*

cul tured (kul′chərd), **1** having or showing culture; refined. **2** produced or raised by culture: *cultured pearls. adj.*

cul vert (kul′vərt), a small channel or drain for water crossing under a road, railroad, etc. *n.*

cum ber (kum′bər), burden or hinder; encumber. *v.*

Cum ber land (kum′bər lənd), river flowing from SE Kentucky through N Tennessee and W Kentucky into the Ohio River. *n.*

Cumberland Mountains or **Cumberland Plateau,** plateau of the Appalachian Mountains, extending from S West Virginia to N Alabama.

cum ber some (kum′bər səm), hard to manage; clumsy, unwieldy, or burdensome: *The armor worn by knights was often so cumbersome they had to be helped onto their horses. adj.* —**cum′ber some ly,** *adv.* —**cum′ber some ness,** *n.*

cum brous (kum′brəs), cumbersome. *adj.* —**cum′-brous ly,** *adv.* —**cum′brous ness,** *n.*

cu mu la tive (kyü′myə lə tiv), increasing or growing by additions; accumulated: *The cumulative effects of many illnesses made the patient weak. adj.* —**cu′mu la tive ly,** *adv.* —**cu′mu la tive ness,** *n.*

cumulonimbus

cu mu lo nim bus (kyü′myə lō nim′bəs), a very large, high cloud formation with very tall peaks that sometimes flatten at the top to resemble anvils; thundercloud; thunderhead. *n., pl.* **cu mu lo nim bus es, cu mu lo nim bi** (kyü′myə lō nim′bī).

cu mu lus (kyü′myə ləs), cloud made up of rounded heaps with a flat bottom. Cumuli are seen in fair weather. *n., pl.* **cu mu li** (kyü′myə lī).

NUMERAL 1   10   TAP   BE   ME

cuneiform (def. 1)

cu ne i form (kyü nē′ə fôrm), **1** the wedge-shaped characters used in the writing of ancient Babylonia, Assyria, Persia, etc. **2** composed of cuneiform inscriptions: *cuneiform tablets.* 1 *n.,* 2 *adj.*

cun ning (kun′ing), **1** clever in deceiving; sly: *The cunning fox outwitted the dogs and got away.* **2** slyness in getting what one needs or wants or in deceiving one's enemies: *The fox has a great deal of cunning.* **3** clever; skillful: *With cunning hand the sculptor shaped the little statue.* **4** skill; cleverness: *The old sculptor's hand never lost its cunning.* **5** INFORMAL. pretty and dear; cute: *Kittens and babies are cunning.* 1,3,5 *adj.,* 2,4 *n.* —**cun′ning ly,** *adv.* —**cun′ning ness,** *n.*

cup (kup), **1** dish to drink from. Most cups have handles. **2** as much as a cup holds; cupful. In cooking, a cup equals a half pint: *He drank a cup of milk.* **3** thing shaped like a cup. The petals of some flowers form a cup. **4** shape like a cup: *She cupped her hands to catch the ball.* **5** take or put in a cup: *I cupped the flour from the bag.* **6** an ornamental cup, vase, etc., given to the winner of a contest. 1-3,6 *n.,* 4,5 *v.,* **cupped, cup ping.** —**cup′like′,** *adj.*

cup board (kub′ərd), **1** closet or cabinet with shelves, especially for dishes and food supplies. **2** any small closet. *n.*

cup cake (kup′kāk′), a small cake baked in a pan shaped like a cup. *n.*

cup ful (kup′fùl), as much as a cup holds. In cooking, a cupful equals a half pint. *n., pl.* **cup fuls.**

a hat	i it	oi oil	ch child		a in about
ā age	ī ice	ou out	ng long		e in taken
ä far	o hot	u cup	sh she	ə =	i in pencil
e let	ō open	ù put	th thin		o in lemon
ē equal	ô order	ü rule	₮H then		u in circus
ėr term			zh measure		

Cu pid (kyü′pid), **1** (in Roman myths) the god of love, son of Mercury and Venus. The Greeks called him Eros. Cupid is usually represented as a winged child with bow and arrows. **2 cupid,** a winged child used as a symbol of love: *a valentine covered with little cupids. n.*

cu pid i ty (kyü pid′ə tē), eager desire to possess something; greed. *n.*

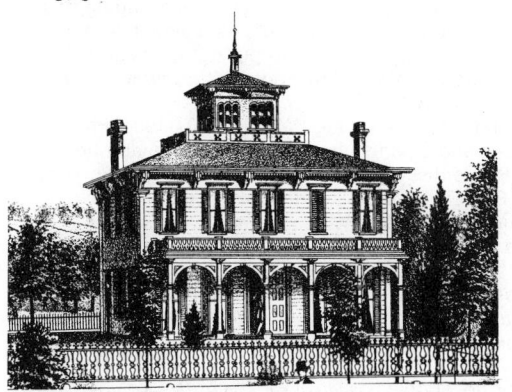

cupola (def. 2)

cu po la (kyü′pə lə), **1** a rounded roof; dome: *The Capitol at Washington, D.C., has a cupola.* **2** a small dome or tower on a roof. *n., pl.* **cu po las.**

cur (kėr), **1** dog of mixed breed; mongrel. **2** a bad-tempered, contemptible person. *n.*

cur a ble (kyúr′ə bəl), able to be cured: *With proper care and medicine tuberculosis is a curable disease. adj.* —**cur′a ble ness,** *n.* —**cur′a bly,** *adv.*

cur ate (kyúr′it), clergyman who assists a pastor, rector, or vicar. *n.*

cur a tive (kyúr′ə tiv), **1** having the power to cure; tending to cure; curing. **2** means of curing; remedy. 1 *adj.,* 2 *n.* —**cur′a tive ly,** *adv.*

cu ra tor (kyú rā′tər), person in charge of all or part of a museum, library, art gallery, zoo, etc. *n.*

curb (kėrb), **1** a raised border of concrete or stone along the edge of a pavement or sidewalk: *Park the car close to the curb.* **2** hold in check; restrain: *I curbed my hunger by eating a piece of cheese.* **3** a check; restraint: *Put a curb on your temper.* **4** chain or strap fastened to a horse's bit and passed under its lower jaw. When the reins are pulled tight, the curb checks the horse. **5** cause (a driver) to pull his or her car over to the curb, usually because of a traffic violation. **6** lead (a dog) to the curb, gutter, or other place away from a sidewalk where it may defecate. 1,3,4 *n.,* 2,5,6 *v.*

curb ing (kėr′bing), **1** material for making a curb. **2** a curb. *n.*

curb stone (kėrb′stōn′), stone or stones forming a curb along the edge of a pavement or sidewalk. *n.*

curd (kėrd). **1** Often, **curds,** *pl.* the thick part of milk that separates from the watery part when milk sours. Cheese is made from curds. **2** any food that resembles this: *bean curd. n.*

cur dle (kėr′dl), **1** form into curds: *Milk curdles when kept too long.* **2** thicken. *v.,* **cur dled, cur dling.**

cure (kyúr), **1** make well; bring back to health: *The medicine cured the sick child.* **2** get rid of: *cure a cold. Only*

great determination can cure a bad habit like smoking.
3 means of curing; treatment intended to relieve or remove disease or any bad condition: *a cure for sore eyes, a cure for laziness.* **4** medicine that is a means of curing; remedy: *Quinine is a cure for malaria.* **5** a successful medical treatment; restoration to health. **6** preserve (bacon, fish, etc.) by drying, salting, smoking, pickling, etc. **7** be or become cured: *Tobacco leaves are often hung in barns to cure.* 1,2,6,7 *v.,* **cured, cur ing;** 3,4,5 *n.* **—cure′less,** *adj.* **—cur′er,** *n.*

cu ré (kyů rā′), a parish priest. *n., pl.* **cu rés.**

cure-all (kyůr′ôl′), remedy supposed to cure all diseases or ills; panacea. *n.*

cur few (kėr′fyü), **1** rule requiring certain persons to be off the streets or at home before a fixed time: *There is a 10 p.m. curfew for children in our city.* **2** the ringing of a bell at a fixed time every evening as a signal. In the Middle Ages, it was a signal to put out lights and cover fires. **3** time when a curfew begins: *The curfew at our summer camp is ten o'clock. n.*

Cur ie (kyůr′ē *or* kyů rē′), **1 Marie,** 1867-1934, French physicist and chemist, born in Poland. She and her husband Pierre discovered radium in 1898. **2 Pierre,** 1859-1906, French physicist and chemist. **3 curie,** unit for measuring radioactivity. *n.*

cur i o (kyůr′ē ō), object valued as a curiosity: *a curio from the Orient. n., pl.* **cur i os.**

cur i os i ty (kyůr′ē os′ə tē), **1** an eager desire to know: *She satisfied her curiosity about animals by visiting the zoo every week.* **2** a being too eager to know: *Curiosity got the better of me, and I opened the unmarked box.* **3** a strange, rare, or novel object: *One of the curiosities we saw was a basket made from an armadillo's shell. n., pl.* **cur i os i ties.**

cur i ous (kyůr′ē əs), **1** eager to know: *Small children are very curious and they ask many questions.* **2** too eager to know; prying: *Some people are always curious about their neighbors' business.* **3** strange, odd, or unusual: *I found a curious old box in the attic. adj.* **—cur′i ous ly,** *adv.* **—cur′i ous ness,** *n.*

cur i um (kyůr′ē əm), a radioactive metallic element produced artificially from plutonium or americium. *n.* [*Curium* was named for Marie and Pierre *Curie* when it was discovered in 1944.]

curl (kėrl), **1** twist into ringlets; roll into coils: *curl someone's hair. My hair curls naturally.* **2** twist out of shape; bend into a curve: *Paper curls as it burns.* **3** rise in rings: *Smoke is curling slowly from the chimney.* **4** a curled lock of hair. **5** anything curled or bent into a curve: *Wood shavings form curls.* 1-3 *v.,* 4,5 *n.*

curl up, draw up one's legs: *I curled up on the sofa.*

curl er (kėr′lər), device on which hair is twisted or wound to make it curl. *n.*

cur lew (kėr′lü), a wading bird with a long, thin bill curved downward. *n., pl.* **cur lews** *or* **cur lew.**

curlew
a long-billed curlew, about 2 ft. (61 cm.) long

curl i cue (kėr′lə kyü), a fancy twist, curl, or flourish: *Curlicues in handwriting often make it hard to read. n.*

curl i ness (kėr′lē nis), curly quality or condition. *n.*

curl ing (kėr′ling), game in which large, smooth, rounded stones with handles are slid over ice at a target. *n.*

curl y (kėr′lē), **1** curling; wavy: *curly hair.* **2** having curls or curly hair: *a curly head. adj.,* **curl i er, curl i est.**

cur rant (kėr′ənt), **1** a small raisin without seeds made from certain small, sweet grapes grown chiefly in the countries on the eastern Mediterranean Sea. Currants are used in puddings, cakes, and buns. **2** a small, sour, red, black, or white berry that grows on a bush and is used for jelly and preserves. *n.*

cur ren cy (kėr′ən sē), **1** money in actual use in a country: *Coins and paper money are currency in the United States.* **2** a passing from person to person; circulation: *People who spread a rumor give it currency.* **3** general use or acceptance; common occurrence: *Words such as "couldst" and "thou" have little currency now. n., pl.* **cur ren cies.**

cur rent (kėr′ənt), **1** a flow of water, air, or any liquid; running stream: *The current swept the stick down the river. The draft created a current of cold air over my feet.* **2** flow of electricity through a wire, etc.: *The current went off when lightning hit the power lines.* **3** rate or amount of such a flow, usually expressed in amperes: *Heating requires much more current than lighting does.* **4** course or movement (of events or of opinions): *Newspapers influence the current of public opinion.* **5** of the present time. *The current issue of a magazine is the latest one published. We discuss current events in social studies class.* **6** generally used or accepted: *Long ago the belief was current that the earth was flat.* **7** going around; passing from person to person: *A rumor is current that school will close a week early this year.* 1-4 *n.,* 5-7 *adj.* **—cur′rent ness,** *n.*

cur rent ly (kėr′ənt lē), at the present time; now: *The flu is currently going around school. adv.*

cur ri cle (kėr′ə kəl), a two-wheeled carriage drawn by two horses. *n.*

cur ric u lar (kə rik′yə lər), having to do with a curriculum. *adj.*

cur ric u lum (kə rik′yə ləm), course of study: *At our school the curriculum in Grade 6 includes mathematics, science, social studies, reading, and spelling. n., pl.* **cur ric u lums, cur ric u la** (kə rik′yə lə).

cur ry[1] (kėr′ē), rub and clean (a horse) with a curry-comb. *v.,* **cur ried, cur ry ing.** [*Curry*[1] came into English about 700 years ago from French *correier,* meaning "to put in order."] **—cur′ri er,** *n.*

curry favor, seek favor by insincere flattery, constant attentions, etc.: *Most students disliked him because he tried to curry favor with the teacher.*

cur ry[2] (kėr′ē), **1** a peppery sauce or powder made from a mixture of spices, seeds, and vegetables. Curry is a popular seasoning in India. **2** food flavored with it. **3** prepare or flavor (food) with curry. 1,2 *n., pl.* **cur ries;** 3 *v.,* **cur ried, cur ry ing.** [*Curry*[2] comes from Tamil *kari,* meaning "sauce." Tamil is a language spoken in parts of India and Sri Lanka.]

cur ry comb (kėr′ē kōm′), a comb or brush with metal teeth for rubbing and cleaning a horse. *n.*

curse (kėrs), **1** ask God to bring evil or harm on: *The evil witch cursed the prince.* **2** the words that a person says when asking God to curse someone or something: *to utter a curse against an enemy.* **3** bring evil or harm on; trouble greatly; torment: *cursed with blindness. He is cursed with a bad temper.* **4** trouble; harm: *My quick temper has been a curse to me all my life.* **5** use profane language; swear. **6** swear at. **7** words used in swearing:

Their talk was full of curses. 1,3,5,6 *v.,* **cursed** or **curst,** **curs ing;** 2,4,7 *n.*

curs ed (kėr′sid *or* kėrst), **1** under a curse. **2** deserving a curse; evil; hateful. *adj.* —**curs′ed ly,** *adv.*

cur sive (kėr′siv), written with the letters joined together. Ordinary handwriting is cursive. *adj.*

cur sor (kėr′sər), a movable mark on a computer screen. It shows where the next letter or number can be made to appear on the screen, or which data already on the screen can be changed or processed. *n.*

cur sor i ly (kėr′sər ə lē), in a cursory manner. *adv.*

cur sor y (kėr′sər ē), without attention to details; hasty and superficial: *She gave the lesson a cursory glance, expecting to study it later. adj.* —**cur′sor i ness,** *n.*

curst (kėrst), cursed; a past tense and past participle of **curse.** *v.*

curt (kėrt), rudely brief; short; abrupt: *The impatient clerk gave a curt reply. adj.* —**curt′ly,** *adv.* —**curt′ness,** *n.*

cur tail (kėr′tāl′), cut short; cut off part of; reduce; lessen: *During the drought it was necessary to curtail the use of water. v.* —**cur′tail′er,** *n.*

cur tail ment (kėr′tāl′mənt), a curtailing; reduction; lessening: *The Bill of Rights forbids the curtailment of free speech. n.*

cur tain (kėrt′n), **1** cloth hung at windows or in doors for protection or ornament. **2** the drapery or hanging screen which separates the stage of a theater from the part where the audience sits. **3** the fall or closing of the curtain at the end of an act or scene. **4** provide or shut off with a curtain or curtains: *They took two sheets and curtained off a space in the corner.* **5** cover; hide: *Darkness curtained the entire winter countryside.* **6** thing that covers or hides: *A curtain of fog fell over the harbor.* 1-3,6 *n.,* 4,5 *v.*

curt sey (kėrt′sē), curtsy. *n., pl.* **curt seys;** *v.*

curt sy (kėrt′sē), **1** bow of respect or greeting by women and girls, made by bending the knees and lowering the body slightly. **2** make a curtsy: *The actress curtsied when the audience applauded.* 1 *n., pl.* **curt sies;** 2 *v.,* **curt sied,** **curt sy ing.**

cur va ture (kėr′və chər), **1** a curving. **2** a curved condition: *curvature of the spine. n.*

curve (kėrv), **1** line that has no straight part. A circle is a closed curve. **2** something having the shape of a curve; bend: *The automobile had to slow down to go around the curves in the road.* **3** bend so as to form a curve; bend in a curve: *The highway curved to the right in a sharp turn.* **4** baseball thrown to swerve just before it reaches the batter. 1,2,4 *n.,* 3 *v.,* **curved, curv ing.**

cush ion (kush′ən), **1** a soft pillow or pad used to sit, lie, or kneel on: *I rested my head on a cushion.* **2** anything that makes a soft place: *a cushion of moss under a tree.* **3** put or rest on a cushion: *The nurse cushioned the patient's head.* **4** provide with a cushion: *cushion a chair.* **5** anything that softens, lessens, or protects from a shock, jar, or jolt. Air or steam forms a protective cushion in some machines. *The bush acted as a cushion to my fall.* **6** soften or ease the effects of: *Nothing could cushion the shock of my friend's death.* 1,2,5 *n.,* 3,4,6 *v.*

cush y (kush′ē), SLANG. soft; easy. *adj.,* **cush i er, cush i est.**

cusp (kusp), **1** a pointed end; point: *A crescent has two cusps.* **2** a pointed end on the crown of a tooth. *n.*

cus pid (kus′pid), canine tooth. *n.*

cus pi dor (kus′pə dôr), spittoon. *n.*

cuss (kus), INFORMAL. curse. *v., n., pl.* **cuss es.**

cus tard (kus′tərd), a baked, boiled, or frozen mixture of eggs, milk, and sugar. Custard is used as a dessert or as a food for sick people. *n.*

a hat	i it	oi oil	ch child	(a in about
ā age	ī ice	ou out	ng long	e in taken
ä far	o hot	u cup	sh she	ə = { i in pencil
e let	ō open	ů put	th thin	o in lemon
ē equal	ô order	ü rule	ᵺ then	u in circus
ėr term			zh measure	

Cus ter (kus′tər), **George Armstrong,** 1839-1876, United States Army officer in the Civil War and in many Indian wars. *n.*

cus to di an (ku stō′dē ən), **1** person in charge; guardian; keeper: *He is the custodian of the library's collection of rare books.* **2** person who takes care of a building or offices; janitor: *a school custodian. n.*

cus to dy (kus′tə dē), watchful keeping; charge; care: *Parents have the custody of their young children. All the important papers are in the lawyer's custody. n.*

in custody, in the care of the police; under arrest: *The person accused of the robbery is now in custody.*

take into custody, arrest: *The suspect was taken into custody by the police.*

cus tom (kus′təm), **1** any usual action or practice; habit: *It was her custom to rise early.* **2** a long-established habit having the force of law: *The social customs of many countries differ from ours.* **3** made to order; custom-made: *custom clothes.* **4** making things to order: *He had that suit made by a custom tailor.* **5 customs,** *pl.* **a** taxes paid to the government on things brought in from foreign countries: *I paid $4 in customs on the $100 Swiss watch.* **b** department of the government that collects these taxes. 1,2,5 *n.,* 3,4 *adj.*

cus tom ar i ly (kus′tə mer′ə lē), in a customary manner; usually: *She customarily walks to work. adv.*

cus tom ar y (kus′tə mer′ē), according to custom; usual: *Ten o'clock is her customary bedtime. adj.* —**cus′tom ar′i ness,** *n.*

cus tom er (kus′tə mər), **1** person who buys, especially a regular shopper at a particular store. **2** INFORMAL. person; individual: *He can be a rough customer when he gets angry. n.*

custom house, a government building or office, usually at a seaport, airport, or border-crossing point, where taxes on things brought into a country are collected.

cus tom-made (kus′təm mād′), made to order; made specially for an individual customer; not ready-made: *a custom-made suit. adj.*

cut (kut), **1** divide, separate, open, or remove with a knife or any tool that has a sharp edge: *I cut the meat with a knife. We cut a branch from the tree.* **2** pierce or wound with something sharp: *She cut her finger on the broken glass.* **3** opening made by something sharp: *bandage a cut.* **4** passage or channel that has been made by cutting or digging: *The train went through a deep cut in the side of the mountain.* **5** piece cut off or cut out: *A leg of lamb is a tasty cut of meat.* **6** make a cut, opening, channel, etc.: *This knife cuts well.* **7** make by cutting: *They cut a hole through the wall with an ax.* **8** be cut: *Cheese cuts easily.* **9** way in which a thing is cut; style; fashion: *the narrow, close-fitting cut of his coat.* **10** make a recording on: *cut a record, cut tape.* **11** have (teeth) grow through the gums. **12** reduce; decrease: *We must cut our expenses to save money.* **13** reduction; decrease: *The store made a cut in prices to attract more customers.* **14** shorten by removing a part or parts: *cut a speech, cut the hedge, cut one's hair.* **15** shortcut. **16** go by a shortcut: *She cut across the field to save time.* **17** divide by crossing: *A brook cuts through that field.* **18** hit or strike sharply: *The cold wind cut me to the bone.* **19** a sharp blow or stroke: *He took a cut at the ball and missed.* **20** hurt the feelings of: *His mean remark*

cut me. **21** action or speech that hurts the feelings.
22 stop: *cut an engine. The director said, "Cut!"* **23** INFOR-
MAL. act as if one does not know (a person): *After our
fight, she cut me whenever we met.* **24** INFORMAL. be absent
from (a class, lecture, etc.): *cut a history class.* **25** block
or plate with a picture engraved on it, used in printing.
26 INFORMAL. a share: *Each partner has a cut of the
profits.* 1,2,6-8,10-12,14,16-18,20,22-24 *v.,* **cut, cut ting;**
3-5,9,13,15,19,21,25,26 *n.*

cut and dried, dull; uninteresting: *The speech was cut
and dried.*

cut back, reduce or curtail: *The company had to cut back
production because orders fell off.*

cut down, 1 cause to fall by cutting: *cut down a tree.*
2 reduce; decrease: *cut down one's allowance.*

cut in, 1 break in; interrupt: *She cut in suddenly with a
remark while I was talking.* **2** interrupt a dancing couple to
take the place of one of them. **3** move a vehicle suddenly
into a line of moving traffic: *The driver cut in, just missing
another car.*

cut off, 1 remove by cutting: *Cut off that branch.* **2** shut
off: *cut off the water.* **3** stop suddenly: *cut off all hope of
success.* **4** break; interrupt: *cut off a conversation.* **5** dis-
inherit: *The will cut her off without a cent.* **6** intercept: *The
posse cut off the cattle rustlers near the river. The shortstop
cut off the throw from right field to third base.*

cut out, 1 remove by cutting: *He cut out the picture from
a newspaper.* **2** take out; leave out: *Why did you cut out
this part of the play?* **3** designate as necessary: *She has
her work cut out for her.* **4** stop doing, using, making, etc.:
Please cut out the noise.

cut up, 1 cut to pieces. **2** INFORMAL. hurt. **3** SLANG. show
off; play tricks.

cut a way (kut′ə wā′), **1** man's formal coat with the lower part cut back in a curve or slope from the waist in
front to the tails in back. **2** object, or a model or drawing
of an object, having part of its covering removed to
show a section of its working parts for examination.
3 showing or representing an object in this way: *a cutaway drawing of an engine.* 1,2 *n.,* 3 *adj.*

cut back (kut′bak′), reduction: *a cutback in expenditures,
a cutback in production. n.*

cute (kyüt), INFORMAL. **1** pretty and dear: *a cute baby.*
2 handsome; good-looking. **3** clever; shrewd: *a cute trick.*
adj., **cut er, cut est.** [*Cute* is a different form of *acute.*]
—cute′ly, *adv.* **—cute′ness,** *n.*

cu ti cle (kyü′tə kəl), the hard skin around the sides and
base of a fingernail or toenail. *n.*

cut las (kut′ləs), cutlass. *n., pl.* **cut las es.**

cut lass (kut′ləs), a short, heavy, slightly curved sword,
used in former times especially by sailors. *n., pl.* **cutlass es.**

cut ler y (kut′lər ē), **1** cutting instruments, such as
knives and scissors. **2** knives, forks, and spoons, for
table use. *n.*

cut let (kut′lit), **1** slice of meat cut from the leg or ribs
for broiling or frying: *a veal cutlet.* **2** a flat, fried cake of
chopped meat or fish. *n.*

cut off (kut′ôf′), **1** a short way across or through; shortcut: *We'll save time if we take the cutoff across the park.*
2 valve or other device that stops the passage of liquid,
gas, etc., through a pipe or opening. **3** at or in which
anything is cut off: *a cutoff period. A cutoff date ends this
agreement.* 1,2 *n.,* 3 *adj.*

cut out (kut′out′), shape or design to be cut out: *Some
books for children have cutouts. n.*

cut purse (kut′pėrs′), pickpocket. *n.*

cut ter (kut′ər), **1** person who cuts: *A garment cutter cuts
out pieces of fabric to be made into clothes.* **2** tool or machine for cutting: *The blade of a meat cutter is very sharp.*

cutter
(def. 3)

3 a small, light sleigh, usually pulled by one horse. **4** a
small, armed ship used for patrolling by the coast guard.
5 boat belonging to a ship, used to carry people and
supplies to and from the ship. *n.*

cut throat (kut′thrōt′), **1** person who kills; murderer.
2 murderous: *a cutthroat band of pirates.* **3** without mercy;
relentless or severe: *cutthroat competition.* 1 *n.,* 2,3 *adj.*

cut ting (kut′ing), **1** a small shoot cut from a plant to
grow a new plant. **2** a newspaper or magazine clipping.
3 able to cut; sharp: *the cutting edge of a knife. A cutting
wind whistled over the frozen lake.* **4** hurting the feelings: *a
cutting remark.* 1,2 *n.,* 3,4 *adj.* **—cut′ting ly,** *adv.*

cut tle bone (kut′l bōn′), the hard inside shell of cuttlefish. It is used for making polishing powder and as food
for canaries, etc. *n.*

cut tle fish (kut′l fish′), a saltwater mollusk that has
eight short arms with suckers, two long tentacles, and a
hard inside shell. When frightened, cuttlefishes squirt
out an inky fluid. *n., pl.* **cut tle fish es** or **cut tle fish.**

cut up (kut′up′), SLANG. person who shows off or plays
tricks. *n.*

cut worm (kut′wėrm′), caterpillar that cuts off the
stalks of young plants near or below the ground when
feeding on them at night. *n.*

cwt., hundredweight. [The *c* of the abbreviation *cwt.*
stands for Latin *centum,* meaning "hundred," and *wt.* for
English *weight.*]

-cy, *suffix added to nouns or adjectives to form nouns.*
1 office, position, or rank of _____: *Captaincy = rank of
a captain.* **2** quality, condition, or fact of being _____:
Bankruptcy = condition of being bankrupt.

cy a nide (sī′ə nīd), any of various metal salts used in
making plastics and insecticides, in extracting gold and
silver from ores, and in treating metals. Some kinds of
cyanide are extremely poisonous. *n.*

cy ber net ics (sī′bər net′iks), science which studies
and compares systems of communication and control,
such as those in the brain and those in electronic or
mechanical devices. *n.*

cyc la men (sik′lə mən), plant with heart-shaped leaves
and showy white, purple, pink, or deep-red flowers,
whose five petals bend backward. *n.*

cy cle (sī′kəl), **1** period of time or complete process of
growth or action that repeats itself in the same order.
The seasons of the year—spring, summer, autumn, and
winter—make a cycle. **2** a complete set or series: *a cycle
of songs.* **3** all the stories or legends told about a certain
hero or event: *There is a cycle of stories about the adventures of King Arthur and his knights.* **4** a very long period
of time; age. **5** bicycle, tricycle, or motorcycle. **6** ride a
bicycle, tricycle, or motorcycle. 1-5 *n.,* 6 *v.,* **cy cled, cy-
cling. —cy′cler,** *n.*

cy clic (sī′klik), **1** of a cycle: *the cyclic motion of a piston.*
2 moving in cycles; coming in cycles: *the cyclic nature of
the seasons. adj.* **—cy′cli cal ly,** *adv.*

cy clist (sī′klist), rider of a bicycle, tricycle, or motorcycle. *n.*

cy clone (sī′klōn), **1** a very violent windstorm; tornado. **2** winds moving around and toward a calm center of low pressure, which also moves. *n.*

cy clon ic (sī klon′ik), **1** of a cyclone: *a cyclonic wind.* **2** like a cyclone. *adj.* —**cy clon′i cal ly,** *adv.*

cy clo pae di a (sī′klə pē′dē ə), encyclopedia. *n., pl.* **cy clo pae di as.**

cy clo pae dic (sī′klə pē′dik), encyclopedic. *adj.*

cy clo pe di a (sī′klə pē′dē ə), encyclopedia. *n., pl.* **cy clo pe di as.**

cy clo pe dic (sī′klə pē′dik), encyclopedic. *adj.*

Cy clops (sī′klops), (in Greek legends) one of a race of giants, each having only one eye in the center of the forehead. *n., pl.* **Cy clo pes** (sī klō′pēz).

cy clo tron (sī′klə tron), particle accelerator that greatly increases the speed and energy of protons and other atomic particles. *n.*

cyg net (sig′nit), a young swan. *n.*

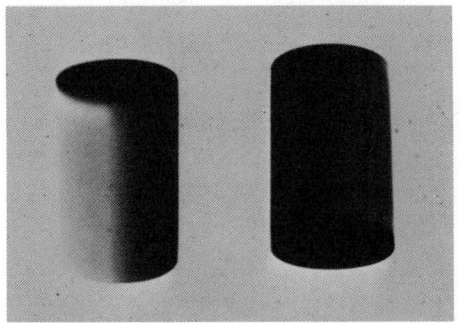

cylinders
(def. 1)

cyl in der (sil′ən dər), **1** any long, round object, solid or hollow, with flat ends. Rollers and tin cans are cylinders. **2** a solid bounded by two equal, parallel circles and by a curved surface, formed by moving a straight line of fixed length so that its ends always lie on the two parallel circles. **3** the rotating part of a revolver that contains chambers for cartridges. **4** the piston chamber of an automobile engine. *n.*

cy lin dri cal (sə lin′drə kəl), shaped like a cylinder; having the form of a cylinder. Silos, candles, and water pipes are often cylindrical. *adj.* —**cy lin′dri cal ly,** *adv.*

cym bal (sim′bəl), one of a pair of brass plates, used as a musical instrument. When cymbals are struck together, they make a loud, ringing sound. *n.*

cymbals

cyn ic (sin′ik), person inclined to doubt the sincerity and goodness of human motives and to show this doubt by sneers and sarcasm. *n.*

cyn i cal (sin′ə kəl), **1** doubting the sincerity and goodness of others. **2** sneering; sarcastic: *It is hard to befriend*

someone who is cynical about friendship. adj. —**cyn′i cal ly,** *adv.* —**cyn′i cal ness,** *n.*

cyn i cism (sin′ə siz′əm), **1** cynical disposition. **2** a cynical remark. *n.*

cy no sure (sī′nə shu̇r), center of attraction, interest, or attention. *n.*

cy pher (sī′fər), cipher. *n., v.*

cy press (sī′prəs), **1** an evergreen tree with hard wood and dark leaves. **2** its wood. Cypress is much used for boards and shingles and for doors. *n., pl.* **cy press es.**

Cyp ri an (sip′rē ən), Cypriot. *adj., n.*

Cyp ri ot (sip′rē ət), **1** person born or living in Cyprus. **2** of Cyprus. 1 *n.,* 2 *adj.*

Cyp ri ote (sip′rē ōt), Cypriot. *n., adj.*

Cy prus (sī′prəs), island country in the E Mediterranean, south of Turkey. Cyprus is a member of the Commonwealth of Nations. *Capital:* Nicosia. See **Balkan States** for map. *n.*

Cy rus (sī′rəs), died 529 B.C., king of Persia and founder of the Persian empire. He was called "Cyrus the Great." *n.*

cyst (sist), a small saclike growth in animals or plants, usually containing diseased matter. *n.*

cy tol o gist (sī tol′ə jist), an expert in cytology. *n.*

cy tol o gy (sī tol′ə jē), branch of biology that deals with the formation, structure, and function of cells. *n.*

cy to plasm (sī′tə plaz′əm), the living substance or protoplasm of a cell, outside of the nucleus. *n.*

C.Z., Canal Zone.

czar (zär), **1** emperor. It was the title of the former emperors of Russia. **2** person having absolute power. *n.* Also, **tsar** or **tzar.**

WORD HISTORY

czar

Czar comes from Russian *tsar,* and can be traced back to Latin *Caesar,* meaning "Caesar, emperor," which was used as a title by the Roman emperors.

cza ri na (zä rē′nə), wife of a czar; Russian empress. *n., pl.* **cza ri nas.** Also, **tsarina** or **tzarina.**

Czech (chek), **1** member of a branch of the Slavs. Bohemians, Moravians, and Silesians are Czechs. **2** their language; Bohemian. **3** Czechoslovak. **4** of Czechoslovakia, its people, or the language of the Czechs. 1-3 *n.,* 4 *adj.*

Czech ish (chek′ish), Czech. *adj.*

Czech o slo vak (chek′ə slō′vak *or* chek′ə slō′väk), **1** of Czechoslovakia or its people. **2** person born or living in Czechoslovakia. 1 *adj.,* 2 *n.*

Czech o slo va ki a (chek′ə slō vä′kē ə), country in central Europe, surrounded by West Germany, Poland, the Soviet Union, Hungary, and Austria. *Capital:* Prague. See **Bohemia** for map. *n.* —**Czech′o slo va′ki an,** *adj., n.*

Dd

D or **d** (dē), **1** the fourth letter of the English alphabet. **2** the Roman numeral for 500. *n., pl.* **D's** or **d's.**

D, diameter.

d., **1** date. **2** daughter. **3** day. **4** degree. **5** density. **6** died. **7** dime. **8** dollar.

D., **1** December. **2** Democrat. **3** Dutch.

D.A., District Attorney.

dab (dab), **1** touch lightly; pat with something soft or moist; tap: *I dabbed my lips with a napkin.* **2** a quick, light touch or blow; pat or tap: *The cat made a dab at the butterfly with its paw.* **3** put on with light strokes: *She dabbed paint on the canvas.* **4** a small, soft or moist mass: *a dab of butter.* **5** a little bit: *This spot needs a dab of paint.* 1,3 *v.,* **dabbed, dab bing;** 2,4,5 *n.*

dab ble (dab'əl), **1** dip in and out of water; splash: *We sat and dabbled our feet in the pool.* **2** do anything in a slight or superficial manner; work at a little: *He dabbled at painting but soon gave it up.* *v.,* **dab bled, dab bling.**

dab bler (dab'lər), person who dabbles. *n.*

Dac ca (dak'ə), Dhaka. *n.*

dace (dās), a small freshwater fish, related to the carp. *n., pl.* **dac es** or **dace.**

dachs hund (däks'hunt' or daks'hund'), a small dog with a long body and very short legs. *n.*

Da cron (dā'kron or dak'ron), trademark for an artificial fiber or fabric that does not wrinkle or fade easily. It is used for shirts, dresses, suits, etc. *n.*

dad (dad), INFORMAL. father. *n.*

dad dy (dad'ē), INFORMAL. father. *n., pl.* **dad dies.**

dad dy-long legs (dad'ē lông'legz'), animal that looks much like a spider, but does not bite. It has a small body and long, thin legs. *n., pl.* **dad dy-long legs.**

da do (dā'dō), the part of a pedestal between the base and the cap. *n., pl.* **da does** or **da dos.**

Daed a lus (ded'l əs), (in Greek legends) a skillful worker who made wings for flying and built the Labyrinth in Crete. *n.*

daf fo dil (daf'ə dil), plant with long, slender leaves and yellow flowers that bloom in the spring. It grows from a bulb. *n.*

daff y (daf'ē), INFORMAL. daft. *adj.,* **daff i er, daff i est.**

daft (daft), **1** crazy; insane. **2** without sense or reason; silly; foolish. *adj.* [*Daft* comes from Old English *gedæfte,* meaning "gentle."] —**daft'ly,** *adv.* —**daft'ness,** *n.*

da Gam a (də gam'ə or də gä'mə), Vasco, 1469?-1524, Portuguese navigator who discovered a route from Europe to India by sailing around southern Africa.

dag ger (dag'ər), **1** a small weapon with a short, pointed blade, used for stabbing. **2** sign (†) used in printing to refer the reader to a note someplace else in the book. *n.*

da guerre o type (də ger'ə tīp), **1** an early method of photography. The pictures were made on silvered metal plates made sensitive to light. **2** picture made in this way. *n.* [*Daguerreotype* is from French *daguerréotype,* which comes from Louis *Daguerre,* 1789-1851, who invented this photographic method.]

dahl ia (dal'yə), **1** a tall plant with large, showy flowers of many colors and varieties that bloom in autumn. It is related to the aster. *n., pl.* **dahl ias.**

dai ly (dā'lē), **1** done, happening, or appearing every day, or every day but Sunday: *a daily newspaper, a daily visit.* **2** every day; day by day: *She rides her bike daily.* **3** newspaper printed every day, or every day but Sunday. 1 *adj.,* 2 *adv.,* 3 *n., pl.* **dai lies.**

dai mio (dī'myō), one of the feudal nobles of Japan. *n., pl.* **dai mio** or **dai mios.**

dain ti ly (dān'tl ē), in a dainty manner. *adv.*

dain ti ness (dān'tē nis), a being dainty. *n.*

dain ty (dān'tē), **1** having delicate beauty; fresh and pretty: *The violet is a dainty spring flower.* **2** delicate in tastes and feeling; particular: *a dainty eater.* **3** good to eat; delicious: *"Wasn't that a dainty dish to set before the king?"* **4** something very good to eat; delicious bit of food: *Candy and nuts are dainties.* 1-3 *adj.,* **dain ti er, dain ti est;** 4 *n., pl.* **dain ties.**

dair y (der'ē), **1** room or building where milk and cream are kept and made into butter and cheese. **2** farm where milk and cream are produced and sometimes butter and cheese are made. **3** store or company that sells milk, cream, butter, and cheese. *n., pl.* **dair ies.**

dairy cattle, cows bred and kept for the milk they give.

dair y maid (der'ē mād'), girl or woman who works in a dairy. *n.*

dair y man (der'ē mən), **1** man who works in a dairy. **2** person who owns or manages a dairy. *n., pl.* **dair y-men.**

da is (dā'is), a raised platform at one end of a hall or large room. A throne, seats of honor, a desk, etc., may be set on a dais. *n., pl.* **da is es.**

daisy

dai sy (dā'zē), plant whose flowers or petals are usually white or pink around a yellow center. It is related to the aster. *n., pl.* **dai sies.** —**dai'sy like',** *adj.*

Da kar (dä kär'), seaport and capital of Senegal, on the Atlantic. *n.*

Da ko ta (də kō'tə), **1** North Dakota or South Dakota. **2** the former territory of the United States that became North Dakota and South Dakota. *n., pl.* **Da ko tas.** —**Da ko'tan,** *adj., n.*

Da lai La ma (dä lī' lä'mə), the chief priest of the religion of the Buddhist priests in Tibet and Mongolia.

dale (dāl), valley. *n.*

Dal las (dal'əs), city in NE Texas. *n.*

dal li ance (dal'ē əns), a dallying; trifling. *n.*

dal ly (dal'ē), **1** act in a playful manner: *The spring breeze dallies with the flowers.* **2** talk, act, or think about without being serious; trifle: *For over a month she dallied with the idea of buying a new car.* **3** linger idly; loiter: *They dallied along the way and were late for dinner.* **4** waste (time): *He dallied the afternoon away looking out the window and daydreaming.* *v.,* **dal lied, dal ly ing.** —**dal'li er,** *n.*

Dal ma tia (dal mā'shə), region in W Yugoslavia, along the Adriatic. *n.*

Dal ma tian (dal mā'shən), a large, short-haired dog, usually white with black spots; coach dog. *n.*

dam¹ (def. 1)

dam¹ (dam), **1** wall built to hold back the water of a stream or any flowing water: *There was a flood when the dam burst.* **2** provide with a dam; hold back or block up with anything: *Beavers had dammed the stream.* 1 *n.,* 2 *v.,* **dammed, dam ming.**

dam² (dam), the female parent of sheep, cattle, horses, and other four-footed animals. *n.*

dam age (dam′ij), **1** harm or injury that lessens value or usefulness: *The accident did some damage to the car.* **2** harm or injure so as to lessen value or usefulness: *High winds damaged the wheat crop.* **3 damages,** *pl.* money claimed or paid by law to make up for some harm done to a person or his property: *The person who was hit by the car asked for $25,000 in damages.* 1,3 *n.,* 2 *v.,* **dam aged, dam ag ing. —dam′ag er,** *n.*

Da mas cus (də mas′kəs), capital of Syria, in the SW part. It is one of the world's oldest cities. *n.*

dam ask (dam′əsk), **1** a firm, shiny, reversible linen, silk, or cotton fabric with woven designs: *hangings of damask.* **2** made of damask: *a damask tablecloth.* 1 *n.,* 2 *adj.* [*Damask* comes from Greek *Damaskos,* which means "Damascus," where the fabric is supposed to have first been made.]

dame (dām), **1** lady: *Dame Fortune.* **2** title of honor given in Great Britain to a woman, corresponding to the rank of a knight. **3** SLANG. woman. *n.*

damn (dam), **1** declare (something) to be bad or inferior; condemn: *The critics damned the new book.* **2** doom to hell. **3** swear or swear at by saying "damn"; curse. **4** INFORMAL. very. 1-3 *v.,* 4 *adv.*

dam na ble (dam′nə bəl), hateful or outrageous; detestable. *adj.* **—dam′na ble ness,** *n.*

dam na bly (dam′nə blē), in a damnable manner. *adv.*

dam na tion (dam nā′shən), a damning or a being damned; condemnation. *n.*

damned (damd), **1** cursed; hateful. **2** INFORMAL. very. 1 *adj.,* 2 *adv.*

Dam o cles (dam′ə klēz′), (in Greek legends) a courtier of the king of Syracuse who praised kings. The king made Damocles aware of the dangers of a king's life by seating him at a banquet under a sword suspended by a single hair. *n.*

Da mon (dā′mən), (in Roman legends) a man who pledged his life for his friend Pythias, who was sentenced to death. Because of their devotion, the lives of both were spared. *n.*

damp (damp), **1** slightly wet; moist: *This house is damp in rainy weather.* **2** moisture: *When it's foggy you can feel the damp in the air.* **3** make moist or slightly wet; dampen: *Damp the cloth and wipe up the spilled milk.* **4** thing that checks or deadens; damper: *Our argument cast a damp over the evening.* **5** check or deaden: *Weariness damped the traveler's enthusiasm.* **6** any poisonous or explosive gas that collects in mines. Firedamp is one kind. 1 *adj.,* 2,4,6 *n.,* 3,5 *v.* **—damp′ly,** *adv.* **—damp′ness,** *n.*

damp en (dam′pən), **1** make or become damp; moisten: He sprinkled water over the clothes to dampen them before ironing. **2** cast a chill over; depress; discourage: *The sad news dampened our spirits.* *v.* **—damp′en er,** *n.*

damp er (dam′pər), **1** person or thing that discourages or checks. **2** a movable plate to control the draft in a stove or furnace. *n.*

dam sel (dam′zəl), OLD USE. a young girl; maiden. *n.*

dam son (dam′zən), **1** a small, dark-purple plum. **2** tree that it grows on. *n.*

Dan (dan), **1** (in the Bible) a Hebrew tribe that migrated to northern Palestine. **2** city in ancient Palestine. *n.*

Dan., **1** Daniel. **2** Danish.

dance (dans), **1** move in rhythm, usually in time with music: *She can dance very well.* **2** movement in rhythm, usually in time with music. **3** some special group of steps: *The waltz is a well-known dance.* **4** party where people dance: *My older brother is going to the high-school dance.* **5** one round of dancing: *Will you be my partner in the next dance?* **6** do, perform, or take part in (a dance): *They danced a waltz.* **7** piece of music for dancing. **8** jump up and down; move in a lively way: *The children danced with delight.* **9** cause to dance: *He danced me around the room.* 1,6,8,9 *v.,* **danced, danc ing;** 2-5,7 *n.*

danc er (dan′sər), **1** person who dances. **2** person whose occupation is dancing. *n.*

dan de li on (dan′dl ī′ən), a common weed with deeply notched leaves and bright-yellow flowers that bloom in the spring. *n.*

dan dle (dan′dl), move (a child) up and down on one's knees or in one's arms. *v.,* **dan dled, dan dling.** **—dan′dler,** *n.*

dan druff (dan′drəf), small, whitish scales of dead skin that flake off the scalp. *n.*

dan dy (dan′dē), **1** man who is too concerned about his clothing and appearance; fop. **2** INFORMAL. an excellent or first-rate thing: *That new car is a dandy.* **3** INFORMAL. excellent; first-rate: *She got a dandy new bike.* 1,2 *n., pl.* **dan dies;** 3 *adj.,* **dan di er, dan di est.**

Dane (dān), person born or living in Denmark. *n.*

dan ger (dān′jər), **1** chance of harm; nearness to harm; risk; peril: *The trip through the jungle was full of danger.* **2** thing that may cause harm: *Hidden rocks are a danger to ships.* *n.*

dan ger ous (dān′jər əs), likely to cause harm; not safe; risky: *Shooting off firecrackers can be dangerous. adj.* **—dan′ger ous ly,** *adv.* **—dan′ger ous ness,** *n.*

dan gle (dang′gəl), **1** hang and swing loosely: *The cord of the window shade dangled in the wind.* **2** hold or carry (a thing) so that it swings loosely: *The cat played with the string I dangled in front of it.* **3** hang about; follow: *The popular novelist always had people dangling after her. v.,* **dan gled, dan gling. —dan′gler,** *n.*

Dan iel (dan′yəl), **1** (in the Bible) a Hebrew prophet whose great faith in God kept him unharmed in a den of lions. **2** book in the Old Testament which tells about him. *n.*

Dan ish (dā′nish), **1** of Denmark, its people, or their language. **2** people of Denmark. **3** language of Denmark. **4** kind of rich pastry. 1 *adj.,* 2 *n.pl.,* 3,4 *n.sing.*

dank (dangk), unpleasantly damp or moist: *The cave was dark, dank, and chilly. adj.* **—dank′ly,** *adv.* **—dank′ness,** *n.*

Dan te (dan′tē), 1265-1321, Italian poet, author of the *Divine Comedy. n.*

Dan ube (dan′yüb), river flowing from S West Germany into the Black Sea. *n.*

Dan zig (dant′sig), seaport in N Poland, on the Baltic Sea. *n.*

Daph ne (daf′nē), (in Greek myths) a nymph pursued by Apollo, from whom she was saved by being changed into a laurel tree. *n.*

dap per (dap′ər), 1 neat, trim, or spruce. 2 small and active. *adj.* [*Dapper* comes from Dutch *dapper,* meaning "agile, strong."] —**dap′per ly,** *adv.* —**dap′per ness,** *n.*

dapper (def. 1)
He was a **dapper** fellow.

dap ple (dap′əl), 1 mark or become marked with spots: *The bleach dappled the dark cloth.* 2 dappled. 1 *v.,* **dap-pled, dap pling;** 2 *adj.*

dap pled (dap′əld), marked with spots; spotted. *adj.*

Dar da nelles (därd′n elz′), strait in NW Turkey which connects the Sea of Marmara with the Aegean Sea, and separates European from Asian Turkey. In ancient times it was called the Hellespont. *n.*

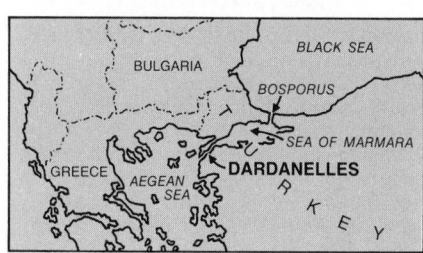

dare (der *or* dar), 1 have courage; be bold; be bold enough: *The children dared to explore the haunted house.* 2 have courage to try; not be afraid of; face or meet boldly: *The pioneers dared the dangers of a strange land.* 3 to challenge: *I dare you to jump the puddle.* 4 a challenge: *I took their dare to jump.* 1-3 *v.,* **dared, dar ing;** 4 *n.* —**dar′er,** *n.*

dare dev il (der′dev′əl *or* dar′dev′əl), 1 a reckless person. 2 recklessly daring: *The speeder's daredevil driving caused an accident.* 1 *n.,* 2 *adj.*

dare say (der′sā′ *or* dar′sā′), believe: *I daresay you will be late if you don't hurry. v.*

Dar es Sa laam (där es sə läm′), seaport in Tanzania.

dar ing (der′ing *or* dar′ing), 1 courage to take risks; boldness: *The lifeguard's daring saved a swimmer's life.* 2 bold; fearless; courageous: *Performing on a trapeze high above a crowd is a daring act.* 1 *n.,* 2 *adj.* —**dar′ing ly,** *adv.* —**dar′ing ness,** *n.*

Da ri us I (də rī′əs), 558?-486? B.C., Persian emperor who was defeated by the Athenians at Marathon in 490 B.C.

dark (därk), 1 without light; with very little light: *A night*

without a moon is dark. 2 not light-colored; near to black in color: *He has dark-brown eyes and dark hair.* 3 gloomy; dull; dismal: *It was a dark day, rainy and cold.* 4 absence of light; darkness: *Don't be afraid of the dark.* 5 night; nightfall: *The dark comes on early in the winter.* 6 secret or hidden: *The spy had a dark plan.* 7 without knowledge or culture; ignorant: *The years after the Roman Empire broke up were dark years for Europe.* 8 evil; wicked: *The assassination of the ambassador was a dark deed.* 1-3,6-8 *adj.,* 4,5 *n.* —**dark′ly,** *adv.* —**dark′ness,** *n.*

in the dark, in ignorance; without knowledge or information: *She said nothing, leaving me in the dark about her plans.*

Dark Ages or **dark ages,** the early part of the Middle Ages, from about A.D. 400 to about A.D. 1000, when learning and culture were in a decline in western Europe.

dark en (där′kən), make or become dark or darker: *We darkened the room by drawing the shades. As the storm approached, the sky darkened. v.* —**dark′en er,** *n.*

dark horse, 1 an unexpected winner about whom little is known. 2 person who is unexpectedly nominated for a political office.

dark ish (där′kish), somewhat dark. *adj.*

dark ling (därk′ling), 1 in the dark. 2 dark. 1 *adv.,* 2 *adj.*

dark room (därk′rüm′ *or* därk′rùm′), room cut off from all outside light, arranged for developing photographs. It usually has a very dim, colored light. *n.*

dar ling (där′ling), 1 person or animal very dear to another; person or animal much loved: *You are a darling.* 2 a favorite: *The baby is everyone's darling.* 3 very dear; much loved: *"My darling daughter," his letter began.* 4 INFORMAL. pleasing or attractive: *What a darling puppy!* 1,2 *n.,* 3,4 *adj.* [*Darling* is from Old English *dēorling,* which comes from *dēore,* meaning "dear."]

darn[1] (därn), 1 mend by making rows of stitches back and forth across a hole or torn place. 2 place mended by darning. 1 *v.,* 2 *n.* —**darn′er,** *n.*

darn[2] (därn), INFORMAL. damn. *v., n., adv.*

dart (därt), 1 a slender, pointed weapon thrown by hand or shot from a blowgun. 2 **darts,** *pl.* game in which darts are thrown at a target. 3 move suddenly and swiftly: *The deer saw us and darted away.* 4 send suddenly: *She darted an angry glance at her sister.* 1,2 *n.,* 3,4 *v.* —**dart′er,** *n.*

Dar win (där′wən), **Charles,** 1809-1882, English naturalist famous for his theory of evolution which maintains that present-day forms of plants and animals have developed from simpler forms through slight changes. Those with changes best suited to their surroundings are those which survived. *n.*

dash (dash), 1 throw, drive, or strike: *In a fit of anger he dashed his ruler against the door. The waves dashed against the rocks.* 2 splash: *The car sped by and dashed muddy water all over me.* 3 a splash: *She was sprayed by a dash of salt water.* 4 to rush: *They dashed by in a hurry.* 5 a rush: *We made a dash for safety.* 6 strike violently so as to break; smash: *I was so angry I dashed the glass to bits on the tile floor.* 7 a forceful blow or stroke: *the dash of the* *oar against the water.* **8** ruin or destroy: *Our hopes were dashed by the bad news.* **9** a small amount: *Put in just a dash of pepper.* **10** a short race: *the fifty-yard dash.* **11** energy; spirit; liveliness: *The winning team played with dash against the losers.* **12** a mark (—) used in writing or printing to show a break in thought, omitted letters or words, etc. **13** a long sound used in sending messages by telegraph or radiotelegraph. **14** dashboard. 1,2,4,6,8 *v.*, 3,5,7,9-14 *n.*

dash off, do, make, write, etc., quickly: *He dashed off a letter to his friend.*

date palm

dash board (dash′bôrd′), panel with instruments, gauges, and certain controls in front of the driver in an automobile, aircraft, etc. *n.*

dash ing (dash′ing), **1** full of energy and spirit; lively: *a dashing young couple.* **2** showy: *The members of the band wore bright, dashing uniforms. adj.* —**dash′ing ly,** *adv.*

das tard (das′tərd), **1** a mean coward; sneak. **2** mean and cowardly; dastardly. 1 *n.*, 2 *adj.*

das tard ly (das′tərd lē), mean and cowardly: *a dastardly act. adj.* —**das′tard li ness,** *n.*

da ta (dā′tə *or* dat′ə), facts from which conclusions can be drawn; things known or admitted; information: *Names, ages, grades, and other data about the class are written in the teacher's notebook. n.pl.* of **datum.**

da ta base (dā′tə bās′ *or* dat′ə bās′), a large collection of information, organized and kept and made available by a computer or computers, including such items as newspaper stories, airplane schedules, or inventory lists. *n.*

data processing, the handling and storing of data, or coded information, by means of computers.

date[1] (dāt), **1** time when something happens or happened; a particular day, month, or year: *Give the date of your birth. July 4, 1776, is the date of the signing of the Declaration of Independence.* **2** statement of time: *There is a date stamped on every piece of United States money.* **3** mark the time of; put a date on: *Please date your papers before handing them in.* **4** find out the date of; give a date to: *The historian was able to date the letter by its reference to Woodrow Wilson's election.* **5** period of time: *At that date there were no airplanes.* **6** belong to a certain period of time; have its origin: *The oldest house in town dates from the early 1800's.* **7** make old-fashioned or out of date: *Wearing a stiff collar dates Grandpa.* **8** appointment for a certain time: *Don't forget to keep your Monday morning date with the dentist.* **9** make a social appointment with (a person of the opposite sex): *They have been dating one another for several weeks.* **10** person of the opposite sex with whom a social appointment is made: *Will you be my date Friday for the school dance?* 1,2,5,8,10 *n.*, 3,4,6,7,9 *v.*, **dat ed, dat ing.** [*Date*[1] came into English about 600 years ago from French *date,* which can be traced back to Latin *data* (*epistola Romae*), meaning "(a

letter) given, that is, written (at Rome)."] —**dat′er,** *n.*

out of date, old-fashioned; not in present use: *I refused to wear the suit because it was out of date.*

up to date, 1 according to the latest style or idea; in fashion; modern: *His clothes are always up to date.* **2** up to the present time: *The teacher entered our latest grades on our report cards to bring them up to date.*

date[2] (dāt), the oblong, fleshy, sweet fruit of the date palm. *n.* [*Date*[2] came into English about 700 years ago from French *date,* which can be traced back to Greek *daktylos,* meaning "finger, date." The leaves of the date tree resemble fingers.]

dat ed (dā′tid), **1** marked with or showing a date. **2** out-of-date. *adj.*

date less (dāt′lis), **1** without a date; not dated. **2** endless; unlimited. *adj.*

date line, International Date Line.

date palm, the palm tree on which dates grow.

da tum (dā′təm *or* dat′əm), singular of **data.** *n.*

daub (dôb), **1** coat or cover with plaster, clay, mud, or any greasy or sticky material: *She filled the cracks in the wall by daubing them with cement.* **2** anything daubed on: *Just a few daubs of glue will mend the broken plate.* **3** make dirty; soil; stain: *Your skirt is daubed with mud.* **4** paint unskillfully: *She is no artist; she just daubs.* **5** a badly painted picture. 1,3,4 *v.*, 2,5 *n.* —**daub′er,** *n.*

daugh ter (dô′tər), **1** a female child. A girl or woman is the daughter of her father and mother. **2** a female descendant. *n.*

daugh ter-in-law (dô′tər in lô′), wife of one's son. *n.*, *pl.* **daugh ters-in-law.**

daunt (dônt), frighten or discourage: *Rain did not daunt the campers. v.*

daunt less (dônt′lis), not to be frightened or discouraged; brave: *a dauntless mountain climber. adj.*

dau phin (dô′fən), title of the oldest son of the king of France, used from 1349 to 1830. *n.*

dav en port (dav′ən pôrt), a long, upholstered sofa, frequently convertible into a bed. *n.*

Da vid (dā′vid), died 970? B.C., Hebrew warrior, poet, and second king of Israel, who organized the Jewish tribes into a national state. According to tradition, he wrote many Psalms of the Bible. *n.*

da Vin ci (də vin′chē), **Leonardo,** 1452-1519, Italian painter, musician, sculptor, architect, engineer, and scientist.

Da vis (dā′vis), **Jefferson,** 1808-1889, president of the Confederacy from 1861 to 1865. *n.*

dav it (dav′it *or* dā′vit), one of a pair of metal or wooden arms at the side of a ship, used to hold or lower a small boat. *n.*

davits

Da vy Jones (dā′vē), spirit of the sea.

Davy Jones's locker, grave of those who die at sea; bottom of the ocean.

daw (dô), jackdaw. *n.*

daw dle (dô′dl), waste time; idle; loiter: *Don't dawdle so long over your work. I dawdled the afternoon away.* *v.,* **daw dled, daw dling.**

daw dler (dô′dlər), person who wastes time; idler. *n.*

dawn (dôn), **1** beginning of day; the first light in the east: *The sun rose at dawn.* **2** beginning: *Dinosaurs roamed the earth before the dawn of human life.* **3** grow bright or clear in the morning: *It was dawning when I awoke.* **4** grow clear to the eye or mind: *When they didn't leave, it dawned on me that they expected dinner.* **5** begin; appear: *Day dawns in the east.* 1,2 *n.,* 3-5 *v.*

day (dā), **1** time of light between sunrise and sunset: *Days are longer in summer than in winter.* **2** the 24 hours of day and night; time it takes for the earth to make one rotation on its axis. **3** day or date set aside for a particular purpose or celebration: *a school day, a feast day.* **4** hours for work; working day: *Our company has a seven-hour day.* **5** time; period: *the present day. In days of old they used candles instead of electric lights.* **6** period of life, activity, power, or influence: *Great Britain has had its day as a great colonial power.* **7** contest; conflict: *Our side won the day.* *n.* [*Day* comes from Old English *dæg.*]

call it a day, INFORMAL. stop work: *After rehearsing the play for three hours, the director called it a day.*

day break (dā′brāk′), time when it first begins to get light in the morning; dawn. *n.*

day-care center (dā′ker′ *or* dā′kar′), a place where small children may be cared for during the day while their parents are at work.

day dream (dā′drēm′), **1** dreamy thinking about pleasant things. **2** think dreamily about pleasant things. **3** something imagined but not likely to come true. 1,3 *n.,* 2 *v.* —**day′dream′er,** *n.*

Day-Glo (dā′glō′), trademark for a kind of paint that gives off a brilliant, fluorescent color. *n.*

day light (dā′līt′), **1** light of day: *It is easier to read by daylight than by lamplight.* **2** daytime. **3** dawn; daybreak: *We were up at daylight.* *n.*

see daylight, INFORMAL. get the meaning; understand.

day light-sav ing time (dā′līt′sā′ving), time that is one hour ahead of standard time. It gives more daylight after working hours. Clocks are set ahead one hour when they are changed from standard to daylight-saving time.

Day of Atonement, Yom Kippur.

day school, 1 school held in the daytime. **2** a private school for students who live at home. **3** an elementary school held on weekdays.

day star (dā′stär′), **1** morning star. **2** sun. *n.*

day time (dā′tīm′), time when it is day and not night: *A baby sleeps even in the daytime.* *n.*

Day ton (dāt′n), city in SW Ohio. *n.*

daze (dāz), **1** make unable to think clearly; bewilder; stun: *A blow on the head dazed him so that he could not find his way home.* **2** hurt (one's eyes) with light; dazzle: *The child was dazed by the bright sun.* **3** a dazed condition: *I was in a daze from the accident and could not understand what was happening.* 1,2 *v.,* **dazed, daz ing;** 3 *n.*

daz zle (daz′əl), **1** hurt (the eyes) with too bright light or with quick-moving lights: *It dazzles the eyes to look straight at the sun.* **2** overcome the sight or the mind of with anything very bright or splendid: *The children were dazzled by the richness of the palace.* **3** a dazzling; bewildering brightness: *the dazzle of flashbulbs going off all around.* 1,2 *v.,* **daz zled, daz zling;** 3 *n.* —**daz′zler,** *n.*

daz zling (daz′ling), brilliant or splendid: *dazzling lights,*

a dazzling display of skill. adj. —**daz′zling ly,** *adv.*

DC, District of Columbia (used with postal Zip Code).

d.c., direct current.

D.C., 1 direct current. **2** District of Columbia.

D.D., Doctor of Divinity.

D.D.S., Doctor of Dental Surgery.

DDT or **D.D.T.,** a very powerful, odorless insecticide.

de-, prefix. **1** do the opposite of: *Decentralize = do the opposite of centralize.* **2** down; lower: *Depress = press down.* **3** take away; remove: *Defrost = remove the frost.*

DE, Delaware (used with postal Zip Code).

dea con (dē′kən), **1** officer of a church who helps the minister in church duties not connected with preaching. **2** member of the clergy next below a priest in rank. *n.* [*Deacon* comes from Old English *diacon,* and can be traced back to Greek *diakonos,* meaning "servant."]

de ac ti vate (dē ak′tə vāt), make inactive. *v.,* **de ac ti vat ed, de ac ti vat ing.** —**de ac′ti va′tion,** *n.*

dead (ded), **1** no longer living: *The flowers in my garden are dead.* **2 the dead,** person or persons no longer living: *We remember the dead of our wars on Memorial Day.* **3** without life: *Stone and water are dead matter.* **4** like death: *I fell over in a dead faint.* **5** not active; dull or quiet: *The summer resort was a dead town in winter.* **6** without force, power, spirit, or feeling: *The car won't start because the battery is dead.* **7** no longer in use: *The language of the ancient Romans is a dead language.* **8** INFORMAL. very tired; worn-out: *Dead from exhaustion, the children fell fast asleep.* **9** sure: *She was a dead shot with a rifle.* **10** complete; absolute: *There was dead silence in the library.* **11** completely; absolutely: *You are dead wrong. I was dead tired.* **12** directly; straight: *Walk dead ahead two miles.* **13** time when there is the least life stirring: *The plane landed in the dead of night.* 1,3-10 *adj.,* 2,13 *n.,* 11,12 *adv.* —**dead′ness,** *n.*

dead beat (ded′bēt′), SLANG. **1** person who avoids paying bills. **2** a lazy person; loafer. *n.*

dead en (ded′n), **1** make dull or weak; lessen the force of: *Some medicines deaden pain. The force of the wind was deadened by the row of trees.* **2** make soundproof: *The curtains, carpets, and thick walls deadened the room.* *v.*

dead end, street, passage, etc., closed at one end.

dead heat, race that ends in a tie.

dead letter, 1 letter that cannot be delivered or returned because of a wrong address, not enough stamps, etc. **2** law or rule that is no longer observed.

dead line (ded′līn′), the latest possible time to do something: *The teacher made Friday afternoon the deadline for handing in all book reports. n.*

dead li ness (ded′lē nis), deadly quality or character. *n.*

dead lock (ded′lok′), **1** a stopping of activity between two opposing sides because they are equally strong and neither one will give in; complete standstill: *Employers and strikers had reached a deadlock in their dispute over higher wages; neither group would give in to the other.* **2** bring or come to a complete standstill: *The two groups have been deadlocked for almost a week.* 1 *n.,* 2 *v.*

dead ly (ded′lē), **1** causing or likely to cause death; fatal: *a deadly disease, deadly toadstools.* **2** like death; deathly: *deadly pale* (adv.), *deadly stillness* (adj.). **3** filled with hatred that lasts till death: *deadly enemies.* **4** causing death of the soul: *Envy and pride are deadly sins.* **5** extremely: *"Washing dishes is deadly dull,"* she said. **6** dull; boring: *a deadly lecture by a tiresome speaker.* **7** absolutely accurate: *The hunter was a deadly shot.* 1-4, 6,7 *adj.,* **dead li er, dead li est;** 2,5 *adv.*

deadly nightshade, belladonna.

dead pan (ded′pan′), INFORMAL. **1** an expressionless face or manner. **2** showing no expression or feeling. 1 *n.,* 2 *adj.*

dead reckoning, 1 calculation of the position of a ship or aircraft without observations of the sun, stars, etc., by using a compass and studying the navigator's record. **2** calculation of one's location by natural landmarks.

Dead Sea, a salt lake between Israel and Jordan. Its surface is the lowest on earth, almost 1300 feet below sea level.

Dead Sea Scrolls, collection of ancient scrolls discovered in several caves near the Dead Sea. Some contain the oldest known copies of books in the Bible.

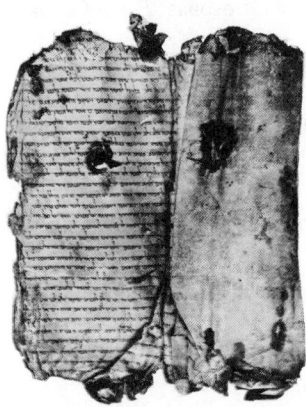

Dead Sea Scrolls
one of the
Dead Sea Scrolls

dead weight (ded′wāt′), **1** the weight of anything lifeless, rigid, and heavy. **2** a very great burden. *n.*

dead wood (ded′wùd′), **1** dead branches or trees. **2** useless people or things. *n.*

deaf (def), **1** not able to hear: *A deaf person can learn to read people's lips.* **2** not able to hear well. **3** not willing to hear: *He is deaf to any criticism of his work. adj.* [Deaf comes from Old English *dēaf.*] —**deaf′ly,** *adv.* —**deaf′ness,** *n.*

deaf en (def′ən), **1** make deaf: *A hard blow on the ear can deafen someone for life.* **2** stun with noise: *A sudden explosion deafened us for a moment. v.* —**deaf′en ing ly,** *adv.*

deaf-mute (def′myüt′), person who is unable to hear and speak, usually because of deafness from birth or from early childhood. *n.*

deal (dēl), **1** have to do: *Arithmetic deals with numbers.* **2** act; behave: *Deal kindly with them so you don't hurt their feelings.* **3** occupy oneself; take action: *The courts deal with those who break the laws.* **4** carry on business; buy and sell: *A butcher deals in meat.* **5** INFORMAL. a business arrangement; bargain: *If you buy this television on sale you can get a good deal.* **6** give or deliver: *One fighter dealt the other a blow.* **7** give out among several; distribute: *The Red Cross dealt out food to the victims of the flood.* **8** INFORMAL. arrangement; plan: *She is proposing that we substitute a new deal for the old one.* **9** a secret or underhanded agreement: *The corrupt mayor was caught in a deal to take public money.* **10** distribute playing cards: *It's your turn to deal.* **11** the distribution of playing cards. 1-4,6,7,10 *v.,* **dealt, deal ing;** 5,8,9,11 *n.*

a good deal or **a great deal, 1** a large part, portion, or amount: *A great deal of her money goes for rent.* **2** to a great extent or degree; much: *She is always going to the beach because she likes to swim a good deal.*

deal er (dē′lər), **1** person who makes his living by buying and selling: *a used-car dealer, a dealer in antique furniture.* **2** person who distributes the playing cards in a card game. *n.*

deal ing (dē′ling), **1** way of doing business: *The grocer is respected for his honest dealing.* **2** way of acting; behavior toward others: *The judge is known for her fair dealings.*

3 dealings, *pl.* **a** business relations: *That company has dealings with firms all over the world.* **b** friendly relations. *n.*

dealt (delt), past tense and past participle of **deal.** *The knight dealt his enemy a blow. The cards have been dealt. v.*

dean (dēn), **1** member of the faculty of a school, college, or university who has charge of the behavior or studies of the students: *the dean of women.* **2** head of a division or school in a college or university: *the dean of the law school.* **3** a high official of a church. A dean is often in charge of a cathedral. **4** a respected, long-time member of a group: *the dean of sports writers. n.*

dear (dir), **1** much loved; precious: *His sister was very dear to him.* **2** dear one; darling: *"Come, my dear," said his grandmother.* **3** much valued; highly esteemed. *Dear* is used as a form of polite address at the beginning of letters: *Dear Sir, Dear Madam.* **4** high in price; costly; expensive: *Fresh strawberries are dear in winter.* **5** at a high price; very much; much: *That mistake will cost you dear.* **6** exclamation of surprise, trouble, etc.: *Oh, dear! I lost my pencil.* 1,3,4 *adj.,* 2 *n.,* 5 *adv.,* 6 *interj.* —**dear′ness,** *n.*

dear ly (dir′lē), **1** fondly: *We love our parents dearly.* **2** at a high price: *She bought her new car quite dearly.* **3** very much: *You will regret your foolish behavior dearly in years to come. adv.*

dearth (dėrth), too small a supply; great scarcity or lack: *A dearth of food caused the prices to go up. n.*

dear y or **dear ie** (dir′ē), INFORMAL. a dear one; darling. *n., pl.* **dear ies.**

death (deth), **1** act or fact of dying; the ending of life: *The old man's death was calm and peaceful.* **2** any ending that is like dying: *the death of an empire, the death of one's hopes.* **3** condition of being dead: *In death he looked peaceful.* **4** any condition like being dead. **5** cause of dying: *Her high blood pressure was her death. n.*

at death's door, dying.

put to death, kill or execute.

to death, beyond endurance; excessively: *She was bored to death.*

death bed (deth′bed′), **1** bed on which a person dies. **2** the last hours of life. **3** during the last hours of life: *We tried to honor the patient's deathbed request.* 1,2 *n.,* 3 *adj.*

death blow (deth′blō′), **1** blow that kills: *He received a deathblow early in the battle.* **2** thing that puts an end (to something): *My illness was the deathblow to hopes for a trip to Europe. n.*

death less (deth′lis), never dying; living forever; immortal; eternal. *adj.* —**death′less ly,** *adv.* —**death′less ness,** *n.*

death like (deth′līk′), like that of death: *There was a deathlike silence before the storm. adj.*

death ly (deth′lē), **1** like death: *Long illness had brought a deathly pallor to his face (adj.). The sick woman grew deathly pale (adv.).* **2** extremely: *I am deathly afraid of deep water.* 1 *adj.,* 1,2 *adv.*

death rate, proportion of the number of deaths per year to the total population.

death's-head (deths′hed′), a human skull, used as a symbol of death. *n.*

Death Valley, valley in E California. It is the lowest land in the Western Hemisphere.

a hat	i it	oi oil	ch child	a in about
ā age	ī ice	ou out	ng long	e in taken
ä far	o hot	u cup	sh she	ə = i in pencil
e let	ō open	ù put	th thin	o in lemon
ē equal	ô order	ü rule	ᵺ then	u in circus
ėr term			zh measure	

de ba cle (dā bä′kəl *or* di bak′əl), a sudden downfall or collapse; disaster; overthrow: *The election was a great debacle for the party in power since most of its candidates lost. n.*

de bar (di bär′), bar out; shut out; prevent; prohibit: *School rules debarred me from playing. v.,* **de barred, de bar ring. —de bar′ment,** *n.*

de bark (di bärk′), go or put ashore from a ship; disembark: *The passengers debarked in port. v.* **—de′bar ka′tion,** *n.*

de base (di bās′), make low or lower; lessen the value of: *They debased themselves through greed. The nation's paper money was debased when the government printed more than it could back with gold. v.,* **de based, de bas ing. —de bas′er,** *n.*

de base ment (di bās′mənt), a debasing or a being debased: *the debasement of silver money by increasing the amount of alloy in it. n.*

de bat a ble (di bā′tə bəl), 1 capable of being debated; open to debate. To be debatable a topic must have at least two sides. 2 not decided; in dispute; questionable: *The results of your experiment are debatable. adj.*

WORD FAMILY

decade

Below are words related to *decade.* They can all be traced back to the Greek word *deka* (de′kä), meaning "ten."

decaliter   decameter
Decalogue   decathlon

de bate (di bāt′), 1 talk about reasons for and against; consider; discuss: *I am debating buying a new car.* 2 discussion of reasons for and against: *There has been much debate about the safety of atomic energy.* 3 a public argument for and against a question in a meeting. A formal debate is a contest between two sides to see which one has more skill in speaking and reasoning. 4 argue about (a question, topic, etc.) in a public meeting: *The two candidates debated the right of government employees to go out on strike for higher wages.* 1,4 *v.,* **de bat ed, de bat ing;** 2,3 *n.*

de bat er (di bā′tər), person who debates. *n.*

de bauch (di bôch′), 1 lead away from duty, virtue, or morality; corrupt or seduce: *debauched by bad companions.* 2 period of excessive eating, drinking, etc.: *a drunken debauch.* 1 *v.,* 2 *n.* **—de bauch′er,** *n.*

de bauch er y (di bô′chər ē), 1 excessive eating, drinking, etc. 2 departure from duty, virtue, or morality. *n., pl.* **de bauch er ies.**

de bil i tate (di bil′ə tāt), make weak or feeble; weaken: *A hot, wet, tropical climate debilitates those who are not used to it. v.,* **de bil i tat ed, de bil i tat ing. —de bil′i ta′tion,** *n.*

de bil i ty (di bil′ə tē), weakness; feebleness: *Long illness may cause general debility. n., pl.* **de bil i ties.**

deb it (deb′it), 1 entry of something owed in an account. 2 charge with or as a debt: *The bank debited her account $500.* 1 *n.,* 2 *v.*

deb o nair *or* **deb o naire** (deb′ə ner′ *or* deb′ə nar′), pleasant, courteous, and cheerful: *a carefree and debonair manner. adj.* [*Debonair* came into English about 700 years ago from French *debonaire,* which comes from *de bon aire,* meaning "of good disposition." French *bon,*

meaning "good," comes from Latin *bonus.*]

de brief (dē brēf′), question (a pilot, astronaut, intelligence officer, etc.) after a mission has been completed, in order to record information. *v.*

de bris (də brē′), scattered fragments; ruins; rubbish: *The street was covered with broken glass, stone, and other debris from the explosion. n.*

debt (det), 1 something owed to another: *Having borrowed money a few times, he had debts to pay back to several people. My debt for her kindness can never be repaid.* 2 condition of owing; indebtedness: *The loan from the bank has put her in debt.* 3 a sin; trespass: *Forgive us our debts against others. n.*

debt or (det′ər), person who owes something to another. *n.*

de bug (dē bug′), find and correct the mistakes in a computer program. *v.,* **de bugged, de bug ging.**

De bus sy (də byü′sē), Claude, 1862-1918, French composer. *n.*

de but (dā′byü *or* dā byü′), 1 a first public appearance: *a young actor's debut on the stage.* 2 the first formal appearance of a young woman in society. *n.*

dé but (dā′byü *or* dā byü′), debut. *n., pl.* **dé buts.**

deb u tante (deb′yə tänt), a young woman during her first season in society. *n.*

dé bu tante (dā′byü tänt *or* deb′yə tänt), debutante. *n., pl.* **dé bu tantes.**

dec., 1 deceased. 2 decimeter.

Dec., December.

dec ade (dek′ād), period of ten years. From 1967 to 1977 is a decade. Two decades ago means twenty years ago. *n.* [*Decade* came into English about 500 years ago from French *décade,* and can be traced back to Greek *deka,* meaning "ten." See **Word Family.**]

dec a dence (dek′ə dəns *or* di kād′ns), a falling off; growing worse; decline; decay: *a decadence in literature. The decadence of morals was one of the causes of the fall of Rome. n.* [*Decadence* came into English about 400 years ago from French *décadence,* and can be traced back to Latin *de-,* meaning "down," and *cadere,* meaning "fall."]

dec a dent (dek′ə dənt *or* di kād′nt), 1 falling off; growing worse; declining; decaying: *a decadent nation.* 2 a decadent person. 1 *adj.,* 2 *n.* **—dec′a dent ly,** *adv.*

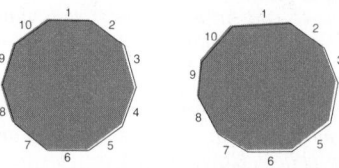

regular **decagon**   irregular **decagon**

dec a gon (dek′ə gon), a plane figure having 10 angles and 10 sides. *n.*

de cal (dē′kal *or* di kal′), design or picture treated so that it will stick fast when it is put on glass, wood, plastic, or metal. *n.*

dec a li ter *or* **dec a li tre** (dek′ə lē′tər), unit of volume equal to 10 liters. *n.* Also, **dekaliter.**

Dec a logue *or* **Dec a log** (dek′ə lôg), (in the Bible) the Ten Commandments. *n.*

dec a me ter *or* **dec a me tre** (dek′ə mē′tər), unit of length equal to 10 meters. *n.* Also, **dekameter.**

de camp (di kamp′), 1 leave quickly and secretly; run away; flee: *The strangers decamped during the night, taking two of our horses. v.* 2 leave a camp. **—de camp′ment,** *n.*

de cant (di kant′), 1 pour off (liquor or a solution) gently without disturbing the sediment: *The waiter decanted the wine.* 2 pour from one container to another. *v.*

de cant er (di kan′tər), a glass bottle with a stopper, used for serving wine, liquor, or other liquids. *n.*

de cap i tate (di kap′ə tāt), cut off the head of; behead. *v.*, **de cap i tat ed, de cap i tat ing.** —**de cap′i ta′tion,** *n.* —**de cap′i ta′tor,** *n.*

de cath lon (di kath′lon), an athletic contest with ten different parts, such as racing, jumping, throwing the javelin, etc. The person who scores the most points for all ten parts is the winner. *n.* [*Decathlon* comes from Greek *deka,* meaning "ten," and *athlon,* meaning "contest."]

de cay (di kā′), **1** become rotten; rot: *The old apples got moldy and decayed. My teeth decayed because I ate too many sweets.* **2** a rotting: *The decay in the tree trunk proceeded so rapidly the tree fell over in a year.* **3** grow less in power, strength, wealth, or beauty: *Many nations have grown great and then decayed.* **4** a growing less in power, strength, wealth, or beauty: *the gradual decay of a person's health as one grows older.* **5** change in a radioactive substance resulting from the giving off of particles. 1,3 *v.,* 2,4,5 *n.* —**de cay′a ble,** *adj.* —**de cay′less,** *adj.*

de cease (di sēs′), **1** act or fact of dying; death: *the unexpected decease of a famous writer.* **2** die. 1 *n.,* 2 *v.,* **deceased, de ceas ing.** [*Decease* is from Latin *decessus,* meaning "departure, death," and can be traced back to *de-,* meaning "away," and *cedere* meaning "go."]

de ceased (di sēst′), **1** no longer living; dead. **2 the deceased,** a (particular) dead person or persons: *The deceased had been a famous writer.* 1 *adj.,* 2 *n.*

de ce dent (di sēd′nt), (in law) a dead person. *n.*

de ceit (di sēt′), **1** a making a person believe as true something that is false; deceiving; lying: *He was a truthful person, incapable of deceit.* **2** a dishonest trick; lie spoken or acted. **3** quality that makes a person tell lies or cheat; deceitfulness: *The dishonest trader was full of deceit.* *n.*

de ceit ful (di sēt′fəl), **1** ready or willing to deceive or lie: *a deceitful person.* **2** meant to deceive; deceiving; misleading: *She told a deceitful story to avoid punishment. adj.* —**de ceit′ful ly,** *adv.* —**de ceit′ful ness,** *n.*

de ceive (di sēv′), **1** make (a person) believe as true something that is false; mislead: *The magician deceived her audience into thinking she had really pulled a rabbit from a hat.* **2** use deceit; lie. *v.,* **de ceived, de ceiv ing.** —**de ceiv′a ble,** *adj.* —**de ceiv′a ble ness,** *n.* —**de ceiv′a bly,** *adv.* —**de ceiv′ing ly,** *adv.*

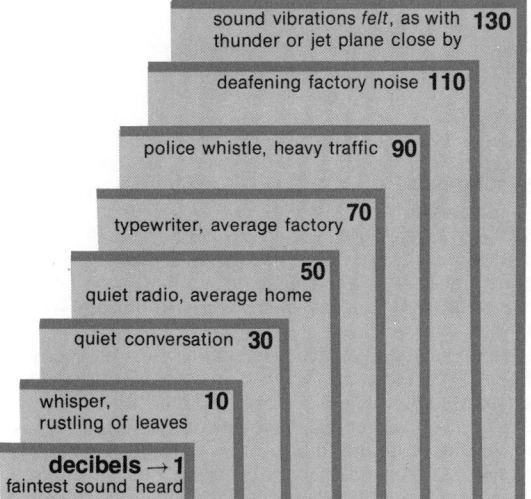

decibel—the decibels of various sounds

sound vibrations *felt*, as with thunder or jet plane close by	**130**
deafening factory noise	**110**
police whistle, heavy traffic	**90**
typewriter, average factory	**70**
quiet radio, average home	**50**
quiet conversation	**30**
whisper, rustling of leaves	**10**
decibels → 1 faintest sound heard	

a hat	**i** it	**oi** oil	**ch** child		a in about
ā age	**ī** ice	**ou** out	**ng** long		e in taken
ä far	**o** hot	**u** cup	**sh** she	ə =	i in pencil
e let	**ō** open	**u̇** put	**th** thin		o in lemon
ē equal	**ô** order	**ü** rule	**ᴛʜ** then		u in circus
ėr term			**zh** measure		

de ceiv er (di sē′vər), person who deceives. *n.*

de cel e rate (dē sel′ə rāt′), decrease the velocity of; slow down: *By firing small rockets the astronauts decelerated the spaceship. v.,* **de cel e rat ed, de cel e rat ing.** —**de cel′e ra′tor,** *n.*

de cel e ra tion (dē sel′ə rā′shən), a decrease in velocity. *n.*

De cem ber (di sem′bər), the 12th and last month of the year. It has 31 days. *n.* [*December* was borrowed from Latin *December,* which comes from *decem,* meaning "ten." December was the tenth month in the ancient Roman calendar. See **Word Family.**]

WORD FAMILY

December

Below are words related to *December.* They can all be traced back to the Latin word *decem* (de′kem), meaning "ten."

dean	decimate	dicker
decibel	decimation	dime
decimal	decimeter	dozen

de cen cy (dē′sn sē), **1** a being decent; proper behavior: *Common decency requires that you pay for the window you broke.* **2** a regard for modesty or delicacy; respectability. **3 decencies,** *pl.* **a** suitable acts; proper observances: *courtesy, tolerance, kindness, and other decencies of life.* **b** things required for a proper standard of living. *n., pl.* **de cen cies.**

de cent (dē′snt), **1** proper and right; respectable; modest: *The decent thing to do is to pay for the damage you have done.* **2** good enough; fairly good; adequate: *He is not rich but he earns a decent living.* **3** not severe; rather kind: *It's very decent of you to forgive me.* **4** dressed; not naked: *"Are you decent?" my sister called through the door. adj.* —**de′cent ly,** *adv.* —**de′cent ness,** *n.*

de cen tral ize (dē sen′trə līz), spread or distribute (authority, power, etc.) among more groups or local governments. *v.,* **de cen tral ized, de cen tral iz ing.** —**de cen′tral i za′tion,** *n.*

de cep tion (di sep′shən), **1** a deceiving: *The twins' deception in exchanging places fooled everybody except their parents.* **2** a being deceived: *The deception of the magician's audience was almost complete.* **3** trick meant to deceive; fraud; sham: *The scheme is all a deception. n.*

de cep tive (di sep′tiv), **1** deceiving or misleading: *Travelers on the desert are often fooled by the deceptive appearance of water where there is none.* **2** meant to deceive: *The deceptive friendliness of the fox fooled the rabbit. adj.* —**de cep′tive ly,** *adv.* —**de cep′tive ness,** *n.*

deci-, *combining form.* one tenth of: *Decimeter = one tenth of a meter.* [The form *deci-* is from Latin *decimus,* meaning "tenth," which comes from *decem,* meaning "ten."]

dec i bel (des′ə bəl), unit for measuring the relative loudness of sounds. *n.*

de cide (di sīd′), **1** settle (a question, dispute, etc.):

Fighting is not the best way to decide an argument. **2** give judgment or decision: *The jury heard the evidence and decided in favor of the defendant.* **3** make up one's mind; resolve: *She decided to be a scientist.* **4** cause (a person) to reach a decision: *What decided you to vote for him? v.,* **de cid ed, de cid ing. —de cid′a ble,** *adj.* **—de cid′er,** *n.*

de cid ed (di sī′did), **1** clear or definite; unquestionable: *There was a decided change in the temperature.* **2** firm; determined; resolute: *I studied hard because I had a decided wish to go to college. adj.* **—de cid′ed ness,** *n.*

de cid ed ly (di sī′did lē), without question; clearly; definitely: *One painting was decidedly better than the others. adv.*

de cid u ous (di sij′ü əs), **1** shedding leaves each year. Maples, elms, and most oaks are deciduous trees. **2** falling off at a particular season or stage of growth: *Maples have deciduous leaves that fall in autumn. Antlers are deciduous horns. adj.* **—de cid′u ous ly,** *adv.* **—de cid′u ous ness,** *n.*

dec i mal (des′ə məl), **1** decimal fraction. **2** number containing a decimal fraction. EXAMPLES: 75.24, 3.062, .091. **3** of tens; proceeding by tens. The metric system is a decimal system of measurement. 1,2 *n.,* 3 *adj.* **—dec′i mal ly,** *adv.*

decimal fraction, fraction whose denominator is ten or a multiple of ten, expressed by placing a decimal point to the left of the numerator. EXAMPLES: $.04 = {}^4/_{100}$, $.2 = {}^2/_{10}$.

decimal point, period placed before a decimal fraction, as in 2.03, .623.

decimal system, system of numeration which is based on units of 10.

dec i mate (des′ə māt), destroy much of; kill a large part of: *War decimated the nation. v.,* **dec i mat ed, dec i mat ing. —dec′i ma tor,** *n.*

dec i ma tion (des′ə mā′shən), a decimating or a being decimated. *n.*

dec i me ter (des′ə mē′tər), measure of length equal to $^1/_{10}$ of a meter, or 3.937 inches. *n.*

de ci pher (di sī′fər), **1** make out the meaning of (something that is not clear): *I can't decipher this poor handwriting.* **2** change (something in cipher or code) to ordinary language; decode: *The spy deciphered the secret message. v.* **—de ci′pher a ble,** *adj.* **—de ci′pher er,** *n.* **—de ci′pher ment,** *n.*

de ci sion (di sizh′ən), **1** a making up of one's mind; deciding: *I have not yet come to a decision about buying the property.* **2** judgment reached or given: *The jury brought in a decision of not guilty.* **3** firmness and determination: *She is a woman of decision who makes up her mind what to do and then does it. n.*

de ci sive (di sī′siv), **1** having or giving a clear result; settling something beyond question: *The team won by 20 points, which was a decisive victory.* **2** having or showing decision: *When I asked for a decisive answer, he said flatly, "No." adj.* **—de ci′sive ly,** *adv.* **—de ci′sive ness,** *n.*

deck (dek), **1** one of the floors or platforms extending from side to side and often from end to end of a ship. Often the upper deck has no roof over it. **2** part or floor resembling this: *the deck of an airplane.* **3** a pack of playing cards: *She shuffled the deck and dealt the cards.* **4** cover, dress, or adorn: *deck the halls with holly.* 1-3 *n.,* 4 *v.* **—deck′er,** *n.*

on deck, ready to do something.

deck hand (dek′hand′), sailor who works on deck; a common sailor. *n.*

decl., declension.

de claim (di klām′), **1** recite in public; make a formal speech. **2** speak like an orator in a loud and emotional manner; speak for effect: *The politician declaimed against* the opposing party. *v.* **—de claim′er,** *n.*

dec la ma tion (dek′lə mā′shən), **1** act of declaiming; making formal speeches. **2** a formal speech or selection of poetry, prose, etc., for reciting: *a long declamation given before an audience.* **3** loud and emotional talk. *n.*

dec la ra tion (dek′lə rā′shən), **1** a declaring: *rejoice at the declaration of a truce.* **2** thing declared; open or public statement: *The royal declaration was announced in every city and town.* **3** statement of goods, etc., for taxation: *a declaration stating the goods one is bringing into a country. n.*

Declaration of Independence, the public statement adopted by the Second Continental Congress on July 4, 1776, in which the American colonies declared themselves free and independent of Great Britain.

de clar a tive (di klar′ə tiv), making a statement; explaining. "I'm eating" and "The dog has four legs" are declarative sentences. *adj.* **—de clar′a tive ly,** *adv.*

de clare (di kler′ *or* di klar′), **1** announce publicly or formally; make known; proclaim: *Congress has the power to declare war.* **2** say openly; state strongly: *I declared that I would never do anything so foolish again.* **3** make a statement of (goods, etc.) for taxation: *Travelers returning to the United States must declare the things which they bought abroad. v.,* **de clared, de clar ing. —de clar′a ble,** *adj.* **—de clar′er,** *n.*

de clas si fy (dē klas′ə fī), remove (documents, codes, etc.) from the list of restricted, confidential, or secret information. *v.,* **de clas si fied, de clas si fy ing. —de clas′si fi ca′tion,** *n.*

de clen sion (di klen′shən), **1** the giving of the different endings to nouns, pronouns, and adjectives according to their case or their relation to other words in the sentence. The declension of *who* is: nominative case, *who;* possessive case, *whose;* objective case, *whom.* **2** group of words whose endings for the different cases are alike. *n.*

dec li na tion (dek′lə nā′shən), deviation of the needle of a compass from true north. *n.*

de cline (di klīn′), **1** turn away from doing; refuse (to do something): *The children declined to do as they were told.* **2** refuse politely: *I declined her offer of help.* **3** grow less in power, strength, wealth, beauty, etc.; grow worse; decay: *Great nations have risen and declined. A person's strength declines in old age.* **4** a losing of power, strength, wealth, beauty, etc.; growing worse: *Lack of money led to a decline in the condition of the school.* **5** a falling to a lower level; sinking: *a decline in prices, the decline of the sun as it nears the horizon.* **6** the last part of anything: *the decline of a person's life.* **7** bend or slope down: *The hill declines to a fertile valley.* **8** a downward incline or slope: *The wagon rolled down the decline.* **9** give the different cases or case endings of (a noun, pronoun, or adjective). 1-3,7,9 *v.,* **de clined, de clin ing;** 4-6,8 *n.* [*Decline is from Latin* declinare, *which comes from* de-, *meaning "from," and* clinare, *meaning "to bend."*] **—de clin′a ble,** *adj.* **—de clin′er,** *n.*

de cliv i ty (di kliv′ə tē), a downward slope. *n., pl.* **de cliv i ties.**

de code (dē kōd′), translate (secret writing) from code into ordinary language. *v.,* **de cod ed, de cod ing. —de cod′er,** *n.*

de com pose (dē′kəm pōz′), **1** separate (a substance) into what it is made of: *The prism decomposed the sunlight into its many colors.* **2** rot or become rotten; decay: *Bodies decompose after death. v.,* **de com posed, de com pos ing. —de′com pos′a ble,** *adj.* **—de′com pos′er,** *n.*

de com po si tion (dē′kom pə zish′ən), **1** act or process of decomposing: *the decomposition of water into hydrogen and oxygen.* **2** decay; rot. *n.*

de com pres sion (dē/kəm presh/ən), removal or lessening of pressure, especially of air pressure: *Gradual decompression is necessary as deep-sea divers surface.* *n.*

de con ges tant (dē/kən jes/tənt), drug used to relieve nasal congestion. *n.*

dec o rate (dek/ə rāt/), **1** make beautiful; adorn; trim: *We decorated the gymnasium for the dance.* **2** paint or paper (a room, etc.): *The old rooms looked like new after they had been decorated.* **3** give a medal, ribbon, or badge to (a person) as an honor: *The general decorated the soldier for bravery.* *v.,* **dec o rat ed, dec o rat ing.**

decoration (def. 2)—He wore seven **decorations**.

dec o ra tion (dek/ə rā/shən), **1** thing used to decorate; ornament: *We put pictures and other decorations up in the classroom.* **2** medal, ribbon, or badge given as an honor. **3** act of decorating: *Decoration of the gymnasium took most of the day before the dance.* *n.*

Decoration Day, Memorial Day.

dec o ra tive (dek/ə rā/tiv), helping to adorn; ornamental; decorating: *Wallpaper gives a decorative effect to a room.* *adj.* —**dec/o ra/tive ly,** *adv.* —**dec/o ra/tiveness,** *n.*

dec o ra tor (dek/ə rā/tər), **1** person who decorates. **2** interior decorator. *n.*

dec or ous (dek/ər əs *or* di kôr/əs), acting properly; in good taste; well-behaved; dignified: *decorous behavior.* *adj.* —**dec/or ous ly,** *adv.* —**dec/or ous ness,** *n.*

de co rum (di kôr/əm), proper behavior; good taste in conduct, speech, dress, etc.: *act with decorum, observe decorum in a court of law.* *n.*

de cou page or **dé cou page** (dā/kü päzh/), the technique of decorating a surface by gluing down paper cutouts and then coating it all with a finish such as varnish. *n.* [*Decoupage* comes from French *découpage,* which originally meant "act of cutting out."]

decoy (def. 2)

de coy (di koi/ *for 1,3;* dē/koi *or* di koi/ *for 2,4*), **1** lure (wild birds, animals, etc.) into a trap or near the hunter: *I decoyed the rats with cheese.* **2** an artificial bird used to lure birds into a trap or near the hunter: *The duck hunter floated wooden decoys on the water.* **3** lead or tempt (a person) into danger by trickery; entice. **4** any person or thing used to lead or tempt into danger; lure. 1,3 *v.,* 2,4 *n.* —**de coy/er,** *n.*

de crease (di krēs/ *for 1;* dē/krēs/ *or* di krēs/ *for 2,3*),

a hat	i it	oi oil	ch child	a in about
ā age	ī ice	ou out	ng long	e in taken
ä far	o hot	u cup	sh she	ə = i in pencil
e let	ō open	u̇ put	th thin	o in lemon
ē equal	ô order	ü rule	ŦH then	u in circus
ėr term			zh measure	

1 make or become less; lessen: *Hunger decreases as one eats.* **2** a growing less; lessening: *Toward night there was a decrease of heat.* **3** amount by which a thing becomes less or is made less: *The decrease in temperature was 10 degrees.* 1 *v.,* **de creased, de creas ing;** 2,3 *n.*

on the decrease, decreasing.

de cree (di krē/), **1** something ordered or settled by authority; official decision; law: *The new state holiday was declared by a decree of the governor.* **2** order or settle by authority: *The city government decreed that all dogs must be licensed.* 1 *n.,* 2 *v.,* **de creed, de cree ing.**

de crep it (di krep/it), broken down or weakened by old age; old and feeble: *He was too decrepit to climb stairs.* *adj.* —**de crep/it ly,** *adv.*

de crep i tude (di krep/ə tüd *or* di krep/ə tyüd), feebleness, usually from old age; weakness. *n.*

de cre scen do (dē/krə shen/dō), in music: **1** a gradual decrease in force or loudness; diminuendo. **2** with a gradual decrease in force or loudness; diminuendo. 1 *n.,* pl. **de cre scen dos,** 2 *adj., adv.*

de cry (di krī/), express strong disapproval of; condemn: *The taxpayers decried the increase in federal spending.* *v.,* **de cried, de cry ing.** —**de cri/er,** *n.*

ded i cate (ded/ə kāt), **1** set apart for a purpose; devote: *The library was dedicated to the memory of a great writer. The doctor dedicated her life to improving hospital care.* **2** address (a book, poem, etc.) to a friend or patron as a mark of affection, respect, or gratitude. *v.,* **ded i cat ed, ded i cat ing.** —**ded/i ca/tor,** *n.*

ded i ca tion (ded/ə kā/shən), **1** a setting apart or a being set apart for a purpose: *the dedication of a park.* **2** words dedicating a book, poem, etc., to a friend or patron. *n.*

ded i ca to ry (ded/ə kə tôr/ē), of dedication; as a dedication. *adj.*

de duce (di düs/ *or* di dyüs/), reach (a conclusion) by reasoning; infer: *I deduced from your loss of appetite what had happened to the cookies.* *v.,* **de duced, de duc ing.**

de duc i ble (di dü/sə bəl *or* di dyü/sə bəl), able to be deduced. *adj.*

de duct (di dukt/), take away; subtract: *When I broke the window, my parents deducted its cost from my allowance.* *v.*

de duct i ble (di duk/tə bəl), able to be deducted. *adj.*

de duc tion (di duk/shən), **1** a taking away; subtraction: *No deduction from one's pay is made for absence due to illness.* **2** amount deducted: *There was a deduction of $50 from the bill for damage caused by the movers.* **3** a reaching of conclusions by reasoning; inference. A person using deduction reasons from general laws to particular cases. **4** thing deduced; conclusion: *The detective reached her clever deduction by careful study of the facts.* *n.*

de duc tive (di duk/tiv), of or using deduction; reasoning by deduction. *adj.* —**de duc/tive ly,** *adv.*

deed (dēd), **1** thing done; act; action: *a good deed. Deeds, not words, are needed.* **2** a written or printed statement of ownership. The buyer of real estate receives a deed to the property from the former owner. **3** transfer by deed: *She deeded the land to her son.* 1,2 *n.,* 3 *v.*

dee jay (dē/jā/), INFORMAL. disk jockey. *n.*

deem (dēm), think, believe, or consider: *Doctors prescribe the medicines they deem necessary to cure their patients.* *v.*

deep (dēp), **1** going a long way down from the top or

surface: *a deep well. The pond is deep in the middle.* **2** far down or back: *We dug deep before we could find water.* **3** going a long way back from the front: *The lot on which our house stands is 100 feet deep.* **4** a deep place. **5** low in pitch: *a deep voice.* **6** hard to understand: *a deep book.* **7** earnest; heartfelt: *deep sorrow. Deep feeling is hard to put into words.* **8** strong; great; intense; extreme: *I fell into a deep sleep after the hike.* **9** strong and dark in color: *a deep red.* **10** in depth: *a tank 8 feet deep.* **11** with the mind fully taken up: *deep in thought.* **12** well along in time; far on: *I studied deep into the night.* **13** the most intense part: *the deep of winter.* **14 the deep,** the sea: *Frightened sailors thought they saw monsters from the deep.* 1,3,5-11 *adj.,* 2,12 *adv.,* 4,13,14 *n.* [*Deep* comes from Old English *dēop.*] —**deep′ly,** *adv.* —**deep′ness,** *n.*

deep en (dē′pən), make or become deeper: *We deepened the hole. The water deepened as the tide came in. v.*

deep-root ed (dēp′rü′tid *or* dēp′rút′id), **1** deeply rooted: *a tall and deep-rooted tree.* **2** firmly fixed: *a deep-rooted fear of snakes. adj.* —**deep′-root′ed ness,** *n.*

deep-sea (dēp′sē′), of or in the deeper parts of the sea: *a deep-sea diver. adj.*

deep-seat ed (dēp′sē′tid), **1** far below the surface. **2** firmly fixed: *She has a deep-seated love of nature. adj.*

deep-set (dēp′set′), **1** set deeply: *He has deep-set eyes.* **2** firmly fixed. *adj.*

deer (dir), a swift, graceful mammal that has hoofs and chews the cud. All male deer and some female deer have antlers, which are shed and grow again every year. *n., pl.* **deer.** [*Deer* comes from Old English *dēor,* meaning "animal."] —**deer′like′,** *adj.*

deer mouse, a small American mouse with white feet and large ears.

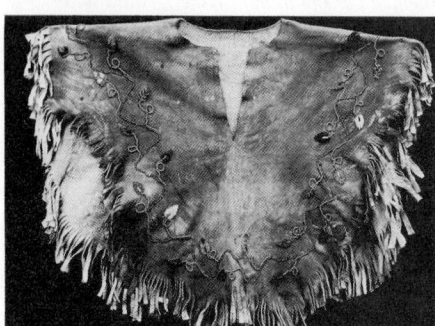

deerskin
(def. 3)

deer skin (dir′skin′), **1** skin of a deer. **2** leather made from it. **3** clothing made of this leather. *n.*

def., definition. *pl.,* **defs.**

de face (di fās′), spoil the appearance of; mar: *Scribbled pictures and notes defaced the pages of the book. v.,* **de faced, de fac ing.** —**de face′a ble,** *adj.* —**de fac′er,** *n.*

de face ment (di fās′mənt), **1** a defacing or a being defaced. **2** thing that defaces. *n.*

de fac to (di fak′tō), in fact; in reality; actually existing, whether lawful or not: *de facto racial segregation.*

def a ma tion (def′ə mā′shən), a defaming or a being defamed; slander or libel. *n.*

de fam a to ry (di fam′ə tôr′ē), that defames; slanderous or libelous. *adj.*

de fame (di fām′), attack the good name of; harm the reputation of; speak evil of; slander or libel. *v.,* **de famed, de fam ing.** —**de fam′er,** *n.*

de fault (di fôlt′), **1** failure to do something or to appear somewhere when due; neglect. If, in any contest, one side does not appear, it loses by default. **2** fail to do something or appear somewhere when due: *They de-*

faulted in the tennis tournament. She defaulted in the payment of her debt. 1 *n.,* 2 *v.* —**de fault′er,** *n.*

de feat (di fēt′), **1** win a victory over; overcome: *defeat an enemy in battle, defeat another softball team.* **2** cause to fail; frustrate: *defeat someone's plans.* **3** a defeating; an overcoming in a contest: *The crowd cheered their team's defeat of the visiting team.* **4** a being defeated; failing to win: *We were unhappy about our team's defeat.* 1,2 *v.,* 3,4 *n.* —**de feat′er,** *n.*

de feat ism (di fē′tiz′əm), attitude or behavior of a defeatist. *n.*

de feat ist (di fē′tist), person who expects or admits defeat. *n.*

def e cate (def′ə kāt), discharge intestinal waste from the body. *v.,* **def e cat ed, def e cat ing.** —**def′e ca′tion,** *n.*

de fect (dē′fekt *or* di fekt′ *for 1,2;* di fekt′ *for 3*), **1** a shortcoming or failing in a person or thing; fault or blemish: *The cloth had holes and other defects. A hearing aid helps to overcome defects in hearing.* **2** lack of something necessary for completeness: *an error caused by a defect in reasoning.* **3** forsake one's own country, group, etc., for another, especially another that is opposed to it: *The traitor defected to the enemy.* 1,2 *n.,* 3 *v.*

de fec tion (di fek′shən), a falling away from loyalty, duty, etc.; desertion. *n.*

de fec tive (di fek′tiv), having a flaw or blemish; not perfect; not complete; faulty: *A watch with defective parts will not keep time. adj.* —**de fec′tive ly,** *adv.* —**de fec′tive ness,** *n.*

de fec tor (di fek′tər), person who defects. *n.*

de fence (di fens′), BRITISH. defense. *n.*

de fend (di fend′), **1** guard from attack or harm; keep safe; protect: *defend a fort.* **2** act, speak, or write in favor of: *The newspapers defended the governor's action. Lawyers defend people charged with crimes.* **3** fight or contest (a claim or a lawsuit). *v.* —**de fend′er,** *n.*

de fend ant (di fen′dənt), person accused or sued in a court of law: *The defendant is charged with theft. n.*

de fense (di fens′ *for 1-3,5;* di fens′ *or* dē′fens *for 4*), **1** thing that defends or protects; thing to guard against attack or harm: *A wall around the city was a defense against enemies.* **2** a guarding against attack or harm; defending or protecting: *The armed forces are responsible for the defense of the country.* **3** action, speech, or writing in favor of something. **4** team or players defending a goal in a game. **5** side that speaks and acts for the accused, or the defendant, in a court of law. *n.* Also, **defence.**

de fense less (di fens′lis), helpless against attack or harm; having no defense; unprotected: *a defenseless village, a defenseless child. adj.* —**de fense′less ly,** *adv.* —**de fense′less ness,** *n.*

de fen si ble (di fen′sə bəl), able to be defended or justified. *adj.* —**de fen′si ble ness,** *n.* —**de fen′si bly,** *adv.*

de fen sive (di fen′siv), **1** of or for defense; intended to defend: *defensive armor, a defensive attitude.* **2** position or attitude of defense. 1 *adj.,* 2 *n.* —**de fen′sive ly,** *adv.* —**de fen′sive ness,** *n.*

on the defensive, ready to defend, apologize, or explain.

de fer¹ (di fėr′), put off; delay: *The test was deferred because so many students were sick. v.,* **de ferred, de fer ring.** —**de fer′a ble, de fer′ra ble,** *adj.* —**de fer′rer,** *n.*

de fer² ((di fėr′), yield in judgment or opinion: *The children deferred to their parents' wishes. v.,* **de ferred, de fer ring.**

def er ence (def′ər əns), respect for the judgment, opinion, wishes, etc., of another: *People often show deference to others who are older and wiser. n.*

in deference to, out of respect for the wishes or authority of.

def e ren tial (def/ə ren/shəl), showing deference; respectful. *adj.* —**def/e ren/tial ly,** *adv.*

de fer ment (di fėr/mənt), a putting off; delay. *n.*

de fi ance (di fī/əns), a defying; standing up against authority and refusing to recognize or obey it; open resistance to power: *The colonists' defiance of the king led to war. n.*

in defiance of, without regard for; in spite of: *We played baseball all day in defiance of the rain.*

de fi ant (di fī/ənt), showing defiance; openly resisting: *She told us in a defiant manner that she was against our plans. adj.* —**de fi/ant ly,** *adv.*

de fi cien cy (di fish/ən sē), **1** lack of something needed or required; incompleteness: *A deficiency of calcium in your diet can cause soft bones and teeth.* **2** amount by which something is not sufficient; shortage: *If a bill to be paid is $10 and you have only $6, the deficiency is $4. n., pl.* **de fi cien cies.**

de fi cient (di fish/ənt), **1** not complete; defective: *The child's knowledge of arithmetic is deficient.* **2** not sufficient in quantity, force, etc.; lacking: *a diet deficient in vitamin C. adj.* —**de fi/cient ly,** *adv.*

def i cit (def/ə sit), amount by which a sum of money falls short; shortage: *Since the club owed $15 and had only $10 in the treasury, there was a deficit of $5 to be made up by the members. n.*

de fi er (di fī/ər), person who defies. *n.*

de file¹ (di fīl/), **1** make filthy or dirty; make disgusting in any way. **2** destroy the purity or cleanness of (anything sacred); desecrate: *The barbarians defiled the church by using it as a stable. v.,* **de filed, de fil ing.** —**de fil/er,** *n.*

de file² (di fīl/), **1** a steep and narrow valley. **2** march in single file or a narrow column. 1 *n.,* 2 *v.,* **de filed, de fil ing.**

de file ment (di fīl/mənt), a defiling or a being defiled; pollution: *The defilement of the air by industrial wastes is a growing problem. n.*

de fine (di fīn/), **1** make clear the meaning of; explain: *A dictionary defines words.* **2** make clear; make distinct: *The shape of the building was defined against the dark sky.* **3** fix; settle: *The powers of the courts are defined by law.* **4** settle the limits of: *The boundary between the United States and Canada is defined by treaty. v.,* **de fined, de fin ing.** [*Define comes from Latin definire,* meaning "to limit," and can be traced back to *de-,* meaning "down," and *finis,* meaning "the end."] —**de fin/a ble,** *adj.* —**de fin/a bly,** *adv.* —**de fin/er,** *n.*

def i nite (def/ə nit), **1** clear or exact; not vague: *definite proof. I expect a definite answer, either yes or no.* **2** having settled limits: *a definite boundary line. adj.*

definite article, the article *the.* "A dog" means "any dog"; "the dog" means "a certain or particular dog."

def i nite ly (def/ə nit lē), **1** in a definite manner: *Say definitely what you have in mind.* **2** certainly: *Will you go? Definitely. adv.*

def i ni tion (def/ə nish/ən), **1** an explaining of the nature of a thing; making clear the meaning of a word. **2** statement in which the nature of a thing is explained or the meaning of a word is made clear. One definition of "home" is "the place where a person or family lives." **3** clearness; distinctness. Good photographs have definition. *n.*

de fin i tive (di fin/ə tiv), deciding or settling a question; conclusive; final: *The school issued a definitive statement of policy regarding unexcused absences. adj.* —**de fin/i tive ly,** *adv.* —**de fin/i tive ness,** *n.*

de flate (di flāt/), **1** let air or gas out of (a balloon, tire, football, etc.): *A nail had deflated the tire.* **2** reduce (inflat-

ed prices or currency). **3** injure or destroy the conceit or confidence of: *I was deflated by their criticisms. v.,* **de flat ed, de flat ing.** —**de fla/tor,** *n.*

de fla tion (di flā/shən), **1** a letting the air or gas out: *the deflation of a tire.* **2** reduction of the amount of available money in circulation so that the value of money increases and prices go down. *n.*

de flect (di flekt/), bend or turn aside; change the direction of: *The wind deflected the arrow's flight. v.* —**de flec/tor,** *n.*

de flec tion (di flek/shən), **1** a bending or turning aside: *Strong winds caused some deflection from the plane's charted course.* **2** amount of bending or turning. *n.*

De foe (di fō/), **Daniel,** 1660?-1731, English author who wrote *Robinson Crusoe. n.*

de fo rest (dē fôr/ist), remove the trees from; clear of trees: *The land had to be deforested before the settlers could farm it. v.* —**de fo/rest er,** *n.*

de fo res ta tion (dē fôr/ə stā/shən), a deforesting or a being deforested. *n.*

de form (di fôrm/), **1** spoil the form or shape of: *Wearing shoes that are too tight may deform the feet.* **2** make ugly: *a face deformed by hate and anger. v.* —**de form/er,** *n.*

de for ma tion (dē/fôr mā/shən), **1** act of deforming. **2** deformed condition; disfigurement. *n.*

deformed—a deformed tree

de formed (di fôrmd/), not properly formed: *The baby's deformed foot was corrected by surgery. adj.*

de form i ty (di fôr/mə tē), **1** part that is not properly formed. **2** condition of being improperly formed. *n., pl.* **de form i ties.**

de fraud (di frôd/), take money, rights, etc., away from by fraud; cheat: *The company was accused of defrauding the government of millions of dollars in taxes. v.* —**de/frau da/tion,** *n.* —**de fraud/er,** *n.*

de fray (di frā/), pay (costs or expenses): *The expenses of national parks are defrayed by the taxpayers. v.* —**de fray/a ble,** *adj.* —**de fray/er,** *n.* —**de fray/ment,** *n.*

de frost (di frôst/), **1** remove frost or ice from: *defrost the refrigerator.* **2** thaw out: *Cooking defrosts frozen foods. v.*

de frost er (di frôs/tər), device that removes frost or ice. *n.*

defs., definitions.

deft (deft), quick and skillful in action; nimble: *The fingers of a violinist must be deft. adj.* —**deft/ly,** *adv.* —**deft/ness,** *n.*

a hat	**i** it	**oi** oil	**ch** child		a in about
ā age	**ī** ice	**ou** out	**ng** long		e in taken
ä far	**o** hot	**u** cup	**sh** she	**ə =**	i in pencil
e let	**ō** open	**u̇** put	**th** thin		o in lemon
ē equal	**ô** order	**ü** rule	**ŦH** then		u in circus
ėr term			**zh** measure		

de funct (di fungkt/), no longer in existence; dead; extinct: *A business that fails is defunct. adj.*

de fuse (dē fyüz/), remove the fuse from (a bomb, etc.). *v.,* **de fused, de fus ing.**

de fy (di fī/), **1** set oneself openly against (authority); resist boldly: *defy the law, defy one's parents.* **2** withstand; resist: *The beauty of the forest defies description.* **3** challenge (a person) to do or prove something; dare: *I defy you to do that again. v.,* **de fied, de fy ing.**

deg., degree or degrees.

de Gaulle (də gōl/), **Charles,** 1890-1970, French general and political leader, president of France from 1959 to 1969.

de gen er a cy (di jen/ər ə sē), degenerate condition or character. *n.*

de gen e rate (di jen/ə rāt/ *for 1,2;* di jen/ər it *for 3,4*), **1** grow worse; decline in physical, mental, or moral qualities: *Her health degenerated with disease.* **2** (in biology) sink to a lower type; lose the normal or more highly developed characteristics of one's race or kind. **3** that has degenerated; showing a decline in physical, mental, or moral qualities: *a degenerate person.* **4** person having an evil and unwholesome character. 1,2 *v.,* **de gen e rat- ed, de gen e rat ing;** 3 *adj.,* 4 *n.* —**de gen/e rate ly,** *adv.* —**de gen/e rate ness,** *n.*

de gen e ra tion (di jen/ə rā/shən), **1** process of degenerating. **2** a degenerate condition. *n.*

deg ra da tion (deg/rə dā/shən), **1** a degrading: *A poor diet may cause a gradual degradation of health.* **2** a being degraded: *a corporal's degradation to the rank of private.* **3** a degraded condition. *n.*

de grade (di grād/), **1** reduce in rank as a punishment; take away a position, rank, or honor from: *The corporal was degraded to private for disobeying orders.* **2** make worse; lower; debase: *to degrade oneself by cheating on a test. v.,* **de grad ed, de grad ing.** —**de grad/er,** *n.*

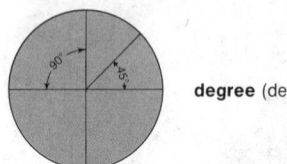

degree (def. 4)

de gree (di grē/), **1** a step in a scale; stage in a process: *By degrees I improved my ability to swim and dive.* **2** amount; extent: *To what degree are you interested in reading?* **3** unit for measuring temperature: *The freezing point of water is 32 degrees (32°) Fahrenheit, or 0 degrees (0°) Celsius.* **4** unit for measuring an angle or an arc of a circle. A degree is ¹/₉₀ of a right angle or ¹/₃₆₀ of the circumference of a circle. 45 degrees (45°) is half a right angle or one eighth of the line bounding a circle. **5** rank: *A noble is a person of high degree.* **6** rank or title given by a college or university to a student whose work fulfills certain requirements, or to a noted person as an honor: *a bachelor's degree, a master's degree.* **7** (in grammar) one of the three stages in the comparison of adjectives or adverbs. The positive degree of *fast* is *fast;* the comparative degree is *faster;* the superlative degree is *fastest.* **8** (in law) a relative measure of the seriousness of a crime: *murder in the first degree. n.* —**de gree/less,** *adj.*

de gree-day (di grē/dā/), unit that represents a change of one degree below a standard (usually 65 degrees) in the mean outdoor temperature for one day. Degree-days are used to determine fuel requirements. *n.*

de hu mid i fy (dē/hyü mid/ə fī), remove moisture from. *v.,* **de hu mid i fied, de hu mid i fy ing.**

de hy drate (dē hī/drāt), **1** take water or moisture from;

dry: *to dehydrate vegetables. High fever dehydrates the body.* **2** lose water or moisture. *v.,* **de hy drat ed, de hy- drat ing.** —**de hy/dra tor, de hy/drat er,** *n.*

de hy dra tion (dē/hī drā/shən), removal or loss of water or moisture from the body or from vegetables, fruits, etc. *n.*

de i fi ca tion (dē/ə fə kā/shən), **1** a deifying: *The deification of the emperor was customary in ancient Rome.* **2** a being deified: *After the emperor's deification, altars were erected to him throughout the empire. n.*

de i fy (dē/ə fī), **1** make a god of: *Ancient peoples often deified and worshiped the sun, animals, and other objects of nature.* **2** worship or regard as a god: *Some people deify wealth. v.,* **de i fied, de i fy ing.** —**de/i fi er,** *n.*

deign (dān), think fit; lower oneself: *So great a novelist would never deign to quarrel with such trifling critics. v.*

de i ty (dē/ə tē), **1** god or goddess: *Juno was the queen of the ancient Roman deities.* **2** divine nature; being a god: *Christians believe in the deity of Jesus.* **3 the Deity,** God. *n., pl.* **de i ties.**

de ject ed (di jek/tid), in low spirits; sad; discouraged: *I was feeling dejected and unhappy until I heard the good news. adj.* —**de ject/ed ly,** *adv.* —**de ject/ed ness,** *n.*

de jec tion (di jek/shən), lowness of spirits; sadness; discouragement: *Her face showed her dejection at missing the airplane. n.*

dek a li ter (dek/ə lē/tər), decaliter. *n.*

dek a me ter (dek/ə mē/tər), decameter. *n.*

del., **1** delegate. **2** delete. **3** delivery.

Del., Delaware.

de la Ma drid Hur ta do (dā/lä mä drēd/ ür tä/dō), **Miguel,** born 1934, president of Mexico since 1982.

Del a ware (del/ə wer *or* del/ə wär), **1** one of the southeastern states of the United States. *Abbreviation:* Del. or DE *Capital:* Dover. **2** river flowing from SE New York State between Pennsylvania and New Jersey into the Atlantic. **3** member of a tribe of American Indians, most of whom formerly lived in the valley of the Delaware River. *n., pl.* **Del a ware** *or* **Del a wares** for 3. —**Del/a- war/e an, Del/a war/i an,** *adj., n.*

de lay (di lā/), **1** put off till a later time: *We will delay the party for a week and hold it next Saturday.* **2** a putting off till a later time: *The delay upset our plans.* **3** make late; keep waiting; hinder the progress of: *The accident delayed the train for two hours.* **4** be late; go slowly; stop along the way: *Do not delay on this errand.* **5** a stopping along the way; wait; hindering: *We were so late we could afford no further delay.* 1,3,4 *v.,* 2,5 *n.* —**de lay/er,** *n.*

de lec ta ble (di lek/tə bəl), very pleasing; delightful: *the delectable taste of freshly baked bread. adj.* —**de lec/ta ble- ness,** *n.* —**de lec/ta bly,** *adv.*

del e gate (del/ə git *or* del/ə gāt *for 1;* del/ə gāt *for 2,3*), **1** person given power or authority to act for others; representative: *Our club sent two delegates to the meeting.* **2** appoint or send (a person) as a representative: *The club delegated her to buy the equipment.* **3** give over (one's power or authority) to another so that he or she may act for one: *The teacher delegated the task of keeping order to the class president.* 1 *n.,* 2,3 *v.,* **del e gat ed, del e gat ing.**

del e ga tion (del/ə gā/shən), **1** act of delegating. **2** fact of being delegated. **3** group of delegates: *Each state sent a delegation to the national convention. n.*

de lete (di lēt/), strike out or take out (anything written or printed); cross out: *I deleted the unnecessary words from my theme. v.,* **de let ed, de let ing.**

del e ter i ous (del/ə tir/ē əs), causing harm; injurious. *adj.* —**del/e ter/i ous ly,** *adv.* —**del/e ter/i ous ness,** *n.*

Del hi (del/ē), city in N India, former capital of India. *n.*

del i (del/ē), INFORMAL. delicatessen. *n., pl.* **del is.**

de lib er ate (di lib/ər it *for 1-3;* di lib/ə rāt/ *for 4,5*),

1 carefully thought out beforehand; made or done on purpose; intended: *Their excuse was a deliberate lie.* **2** slow and careful in deciding what to do: *Deliberate persons do not make up their minds quickly.* **3** not hurried; slow: *to walk with deliberate steps.* **4** think over carefully; consider: *I am deliberating where to put up my new picture. He was slow to answer, deliberating over each question.* **5** talk over reasons for and against; discuss; debate: *In a long session, Congress deliberated the question of raising taxes.* 1-3 *adj.,* 4,5 *v.,* **de lib er at ed, de lib er at ing.** —**de lib′er ate ly,** *adv.* —**de lib′er ate ness,** *n.* —**de lib′e ra′tor,** *n.*

de lib e ra tion (di lib′ə rā′shən), **1** careful thought: *After long deliberation she decided not to go.* **2** a talking about reasons for and against something; discussion; debate: *the deliberations of Congress over raising taxes.* **3** slowness and care: *She drove the car over the icy bridge with great deliberation. n.*

de lib e ra tive (di lib′ə rā′tiv), for deliberation; having to do with deliberation: *Congress is a deliberative body. adj.* —**de lib′e ra′tive ly,** *adv.* —**de lib′e ra′tive ness,** *n.*

del i ca cy (del′ə sē), **1** fineness of weave, quality, or make; slightness and grace: *the delicacy of lace, the delicacy of a flower, the delicacy of a baby's skin.* **2** fineness of feeling for small differences: *The pianist had great delicacy of touch.* **3** need of care, skill, or tact: *His refusal required great delicacy, since he did not wish to hurt his friend's feelings.* **4** thought for the feelings of others. **5** a shrinking from what is offensive or not modest. **6** a being easily hurt or made ill; weakness: *The parents often worried about their child's delicacy.* **7** a choice kind of food; dainty. Nuts and candy are delicacies. *n., pl.* **del i ca cies.**

del i cate (del′ə kit), **1** pleasing to the taste; lightly flavored; mild or soft: *delicate foods, delicate colors. Roses have a delicate fragrance.* **2** of fine weave, quality, or make; easily torn; thin: *A spider's web is very delicate.* **3** requiring care, skill, or tact: *a delicate situation, a delicate question.* **4** very quickly responding to slight changes of condition; finely sensitive: *delicate instruments, a delicate sense of touch.* **5** easily hurt or made ill: *a weak and delicate child. adj.* —**del′i cate ly,** *adv.* —**del′i cate ness,** *n.*

del i ca tes sen (del′ə kə tes′n), store that sells prepared foods, such as cooked meats, smoked fish, cheese, salads, pickles, sandwiches, etc. *n.* [*Delicatessen* comes from German *Delikatessen,* meaning "delicacies."]

de li cious (di lish′əs), very pleasing or satisfying, especially to the taste or smell; delightful: *delicious cake. adj.* —**de li′cious ly,** *adv.* —**de li′cious ness,** *n.*

de light (di līt′), **1** great pleasure; joy: *The children took delight in their toys.* **2** something which gives great pleasure: *Swimming is her delight.* **3** please greatly: *The circus delighted us.* **4** have great pleasure: *Most people delight in surprises.* 1,2 *n.,* 3,4 *v.* —**de light′er,** *n.* —**de light′ing ly,** *adv.* —**de light′less,** *adj.*

de light ed (di lī′tid), greatly pleased; very glad: *I am delighted to be here. adj.* —**de light′ed ly,** *adv.* —**de light′ed ness,** *n.*

de light ful (di līt′fəl), very pleasing; giving joy: *a delightful visit from an old friend. adj.* —**de light′ful ly,** *adv.* —**de light′ful ness,** *n.*

de lin e ate (di lin′ē āt), **1** trace the outline of: *The map clearly delineated the boundary between Mexico and Texas.* **2** draw; sketch. **3** describe in words; portray: *He delineated his plan in a thorough report. v.,* **de lin e at ed, de lin e at ing.** —**de lin′e a′tor,** *n.*

de lin e a tion (di lin′ē ā′shən), **1** act of delineating. **2** thing delineated; diagram, sketch, portrait, or description. *n.*

---

a hat	**i** it	**oi** oil	**ch** child	a in about
ā age	**ī** ice	**ou** out	**ng** long	e in taken
ä far	**o** hot	**u** cup	**sh** she	ə = i in pencil
e let	**ō** open	**ù** put	**th** thin	o in lemon
ē equal	**ô** order	**ü** rule	**ŦH** then	u in circus
ėr term			**zh** measure	

de lin quen cy (di ling′kwən sē), **1** failure in a duty; neglect of an obligation; guilt. **2** condition or habit of behaving unlawfully: *to take measures to check delinquency in children.* **3** juvenile delinquency. *n., pl.* **de lin quen cies.**

de lin quent (di ling′kwənt), **1** failing in a duty; neglecting an obligation: *He was delinquent in paying his overdue taxes.* **2** guilty of a fault or an offense: *The delinquent children had to pay for the windows they broke.* **3** due and unpaid; overdue: *The owner lost her house when it was sold for delinquent taxes.* **4** a delinquent person; offender. **5** juvenile delinquent. 1-3 *adj.,* 4,5 *n.* —**de lin′quent ly,** *adv.*

de lir i ous (di lir′ē əs), **1** out of one's senses for a short time; wandering in mind; raving: *The patient with the high fever was delirious.* **2** wildly excited: *The students were delirious with joy when their team won the tournament. adj.* —**de lir′i ous ly,** *adv.* —**de lir′i ous ness,** *n.*

de lir i um (di lir′ē əm), **1** a temporary disorder of the mind that occurs during fevers, insanity, drunkenness, etc. Delirium is characterized by restlessness, excitement, wild talk, and hallucinations. **2** wild excitement. *n.*

WORD HISTORY

delirium

Delirium was borrowed from Latin *delirium,* and can be traced back to *de lira ire,* meaning "to go out of the furrow while plowing."

de liv er (di liv′ər), **1** carry and give out; distribute: *deliver mail.* **2** hand over; give up: *The defeated army delivered the fort to the enemy.* **3** give forth in words: *deliver a talk. The jury delivered its verdict.* **4** strike; throw: *The boxer delivered a blow.* **5** set free; rescue; save: *A passing ship delivered the shipwrecked passengers from a certain death at sea.* **6** help a woman give birth to a child. *v.* —**de liv′er a ble,** *adj.* —**de liv′er er,** *n.*

de liv er ance (di liv′ər əns), a setting free or a being set free; rescue; release: *The shipwrecked passengers rejoiced at their deliverance. n.*

de liv er y (di liv′ər ē), **1** a carrying and giving out of letters, goods, etc.: *There is one delivery of mail a day in our city.* **2** a giving up; handing over: *The captive was released upon the delivery of the ransom.* **3** manner of speaking; way of giving a speech or lecture: *The speaker had an excellent delivery.* **4** act or way of striking, throwing, etc.: *That pitcher has a fast delivery.* **5** a rescue; release. **6** a giving birth to a child; childbirth. *n., pl.* **de liv er ies.**

dell (del), a small, sheltered glen or valley, usually with trees in it. *n.*

Del phi (del′fī), ancient town in Greece where a famous oracle of Apollo was located. See **Sparta** for map. *n.*

Del phic (del′fik), **1** having to do with the oracle of Apollo at Delphi. **2** having a double meaning; obscure. *adj.*

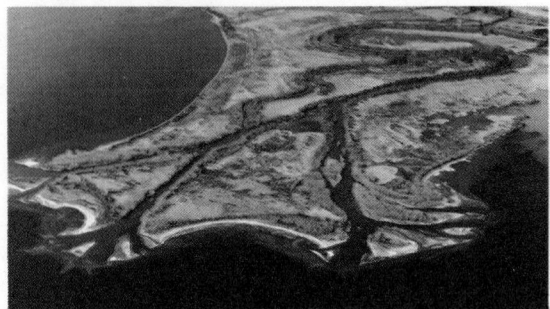

delta (def. 1)

del ta (del′tə), **1** deposit of earth and sand that collects at the mouths of some rivers and is usually three-sided. **2** the fourth letter of the Greek alphabet (Δ or δ). **3** anything shaped like Δ. *n., pl.* **del tas.**

de lude (di lüd′), mislead the mind or judgment of; trick or deceive: *He deluded me into thinking he was on my side.* *v.,* **de lud ed, de lud ing.** —**de lud′er,** *n.* —**de lud′ing ly,** *adv.*

del uge (del′yüj), **1** a great flood: *After the dam broke, the deluge washed away the bridge.* **2 the Deluge,** (in the Bible) the great flood in the days of Noah; the Flood. **3** a heavy fall of rain: *We were caught in a deluge on the way home.* **4** to flood or overflow: *Water deluged our cellar.* **5** overwhelm: *The rock singers were deluged with requests for their autographs.* **6** any overwhelming rush: *The post office always has a deluge of mail just before Christmas.* 1-3,6 *n.,* 4,5 *v.,* **del uged, del ug ing.**

de lu sion (di lü′zhən), a false belief or opinion: *She was under the delusion that she could pass any test without studying for it.* *n.*

de lu sive (di lü′siv), misleading the mind or judgment; deceptive; false. *adj.* —**de lu′sive ly,** *adv.* —**de lu′sive ness,** *n.*

de luxe (də lüks′ *or* də luks′), of exceptionally good quality; elegant. *adj.*

delve (delv), search carefully for information: *The scholar delved into many books for facts to support her theory.* *v.,* **delved, delv ing.** —**delv′er,** *n.*

Dem., 1 Democrat. **2** Democratic.

de mag net ize (dē mag′nə tīz), deprive of magnetism. *v.,* **de mag net ized, de mag net iz ing.** —**de mag′net i za′tion,** *n.* —**de mag′net iz′er,** *n.*

dem a gogue or **dem a gog** (dem′ə gog), a popular leader who stirs up the people by appealing to their emotions and prejudices. The chief aim of most demagogues is to get power and money for themselves alone. *n.*

de mand (di mand′), **1** ask for as a right: *demand a trial by jury.* **2** ask for with authority: *The teacher demanded the name of the student who rang the fire alarm.* **3** call for; require; need: *Training a puppy demands patience.* **4** act of demanding: *a demand for a bigger allowance.* **5** thing demanded; claim: *Parents have many demands upon their time.* **6** desire and ability to buy: *Because of the large crop, the supply of apples is greater than the demand.* 1-3 *v.,* 4-6 *n.* —**de mand′a ble,** *adj.* —**de mand′er,** *n.*

in demand, wanted: *Taxicabs are much in demand on rainy days.*

de mar ca tion (dē′mär kā′shən), **1** a setting and marking the limits: *the demarcation of a country's authority.* **2** separation; distinction: *the demarcation of infancy from childhood.* *n.*

de mean[1] (di mēn′), to lower in dignity or standing; humble; degrade: *Public officials who take bribes demean themselves.* *v.*

de mean[2] (di mēn′), behave or conduct (oneself): *He demeans himself well.* *v.*

de mean or (di mē′nər), way a person looks and acts; behavior; manner: *He has a quiet, modest demeanor.* *n.*

de ment ed (di men′tid), mentally ill; insane; crazy. *adj.* —**de ment′ed ly,** *adv.* —**de ment′ed ness,** *n.*

de mer it (di mer′it), **1** fault or defect. **2** a mark against a person's record for bad behavior or poor work. *n.*

De me ter (di mē′tər), (in Greek myths) the goddess of agriculture, fruitfulness, and marriage. The Romans called her Ceres. *n.*

dem i god (dem′i god), one who is partly divine and partly human. Hercules was a demigod. *n.*

dem i john (dem′i jon), a large bottle of glass or earthenware enclosed in wicker. *n.*

de mil i ta rize (dē mil′ə tə rīz′), to free from military control: *demilitarize a zone or boundary between enemy countries.* *v.,* **de mil i ta rized, de mil i ta riz ing.** —**de mil′i tar i za′tion,** *n.*

de mise (di mīz′), death. *n.*

dem i tasse (dem′i tas′), **1** a very small cup of black coffee. **2** a small cup for serving black coffee. *n.*

de mo bi lize (dē mō′bə līz), remove or disband from military service, status, or control: *When a war is over, the soldiers are demobilized and sent home.* *v.,* **de mo bi lized, de mo bi liz ing.** —**de mo′bi li za′tion,** *n.*

de moc ra cy (di mok′rə sē), **1** government that is run by the people who live under it. In a democracy the people rule either directly through meetings that all may attend, such as the town meetings in New England, or indirectly through the election of certain representatives to attend to the business of government. **2** country, state, or community having such a government. **3** treatment of other people as one's equals. *n., pl.* **de moc ra cies.**

WORD HISTORY

democracy

Democracy is from Greek *dēmokratia,* which comes from *dēmos,* meaning "people," and *kratos,* meaning "rule."

dem o crat (dem′ə krat), **1** person who believes that a government should be run by the people who live under it. **2** person who treats other people as equals. **3 Democrat,** member of the Democratic Party. *n.*

dem o crat ic (dem′ə krat′ik), **1** of a democracy; like a democracy. **2** treating other people as one's equals: *The queen's democratic ways made her dear to her people.* **3 Democratic,** of the Democratic Party. *adj.*

dem o crat i cal ly (dem′ə krat′ik lē), in a democratic manner. *adv.*

Democratic Party, one of the two main political parties in the United States. The other is the Republican Party.

de moc ra tize (di mok′rə tīz), make democratic. *v.,* **de moc ra tized, de moc ra tiz ing.** —**de moc′ra ti za′tion,** *n.*

de mol ish (di mol′ish), pull or tear down; destroy: *The old building was demolished to make room for a new one.* *v.* —**de mol′ish er,** *n.* —**de mol′ish ment,** *n.*

dem o li tion (dem′ə lish′ən), a destroying; destruction: *The demolition of several buildings was necessary to clear the land for a new highway.* *n.*

de mon (dē′mən), **1** an evil spirit; devil; fiend. **2** a very wicked or cruel person. **3** person who has great energy

or vigor: *My music teacher is a demon for practicing.* n.
—**de′mon like′,** *adj.*

de mo ni ac (di mō′nē ak), **1** of or like demons. **2** devilish; fiendish: *Burning people at the stake was a demoniac
custom.* **3** raging; frantic. **4** person supposed to be possessed by an evil spirit. 1-3 *adj.,* 4 *n.*

de mo ni a cal (dē′mə nī′ə kəl), demoniac. *adj.* —**de′-
mo ni′a cal ly,** *adv.*

de mon stra ble (di mon′strə bəl), able to be shown or
proved. *adj.* —**de mon′stra ble ness,** *n.* —**de mon′stra-
bly,** *adv.*

dem on strate (dem′ən strāt), **1** show clearly; prove:
Can you demonstrate that the earth is round? **2** explain by
carrying out experiments, or by using samples or specimens; show how (a thing) is done: *The science teacher
demonstrated the use of a magnet in class.* **3** show the
merits of (a thing for sale); advertise or make known by
carrying out a process in public: *The saleswoman played
a record to demonstrate the stereo to us.* **4** show (feeling)
openly: *to demonstrate affection by hugging someone.*
5 take part in a parade or meeting to protest or to make
demands: *An angry crowd demonstrated in front of the
mayor's office for more police protection.* v., **dem on strat-
ed, dem on strat ing.**

dem on stra tion (dem′ən strā′shən), **1** clear proof: *The
ease with which she solved the hard problem was a demonstration of her ability in math.* **2** a showing or explaining
something by carrying out experiments or by using samples or specimens: *A compass was used in a demonstration of the earth's magnetism.* **3** a showing of the merits of
a thing for sale; advertising or making known by carrying out a process in a public place: *the demonstration of
a new vacuum cleaner.* **4** an open show or expression of
feeling: *a demonstration of affection.* **5** parade or meeting
to protest or make demands: *The tenants held a demonstration against the raise in rent.* n.

de mon stra tive (di mon′strə tiv), **1** expressing one's
affections freely and openly: *a demonstrative greeting.*
2 pointing out the object referred to. *This* and *that* are
demonstrative pronouns. *adj.* —**de mon′stra tive ly,** *adv.*
—**de mon′stra tive ness,** *n.*

dem on stra tor (dem′ən strā′tər), **1** person or thing
that demonstrates. **2** person who takes part in a parade
or meeting to protest or make demands. *n.*

de mor al i za tion (di môr′ə lə zā′shən), a demoralizing
or a being demoralized. *n.*

de mor al ize (di môr′ə līz), **1** lower the morals of; corrupt: *The drug habit demoralizes its victims.* **2** lower the
morale of; weaken the spirit, courage, or discipline of;
dishearten: *The villagers were demoralized by the long
famine.* v., **de mor al ized, de mor al iz ing.** [*Demoralize*
was first used by Noah Webster. It comes from French
démoraliser, and can be traced back to Latin *de-,* meaning "away," and *mores,* meaning "manners."] —**de-
mo′ral iz′er,** *n.*

De mos the nes (di mos′thə nēz′), 384?-322 B.C., the
most famous orator of ancient Greece. *n.*

de mote (di mōt′), put back to a lower grade; reduce in
rank: *The student who had trouble doing fourth-grade work
was demoted to third grade.* v., **de mot ed, de mot ing.**

de mo tion (di mō′shən), a demoting or a being demoted. *n.*

de mur (di mėr′), **1** show disapproval or dislike; object:
The clerk demurred at working overtime without extra pay.
2 a demurring; objection; exception: *The clerk's demur
was ignored by the boss.* 1 v., **de murred, de mur-
ring.** 2 *n.*

de mure (di myur′), **1** seeming more modest and proper
than one really is; coy: *a demure smile.* **2** serious;
thoughtful; sober: *their restrained and demure conduct.*

adj., **de mur er, de mur est.** —**de mure′ly,** *adv.* —**de-
mure′ness,** *n.*

den (den), **1** place where a wild animal lives; lair: *The
bear's den was in a cave.* **2** place where thieves or the like
have their headquarters. **3** a small, dirty room. **4** one's
private room for reading and work, usually small and
cozy. **5** group of eight to ten cub scouts. *n.* [*Den* comes
from Old English *denn.*] —**den′like′,** *adj.*

Den., Denmark.

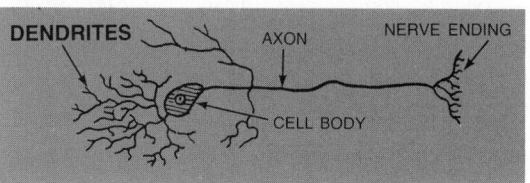

dendrite—A nerve impulse is received by the dendrites and
travels through the cell body and axon to another cell.

den drite (den′drīt), the branching part at the receiving
end of a nerve cell. *n.*

de ni al (di nī′əl), **1** a saying that something is not true: *a
denial of the existence of ghosts.* **2** a saying that one does
not hold to or accept a belief: *Galileo was forced to make
a public denial of his belief that the earth goes around the
sun.* **3** a refusing: *Their quick denial of our request was very
unkind.* **4** a refusing to acknowledge; disowning. *n.*

de ni er (di nī′ər), person who denies. *n.*

den im (den′əm), **1** a heavy, coarse cotton cloth with a
diagonal weave, used for overalls, sports clothes, etc.
2 denims, *pl.* overalls or pants made of this cloth. *n.*
[*Denim* comes from French *serge de Nîmes,* meaning
"serge from Nîmes," a town in France where the fabric
was made.]

den i zen (den′ə zən), person or animal that lives in a
place; inhabitant; occupant: *Fish are denizens of the
sea.* n.

Den mark (den′märk), country in N Europe, between
the Baltic Sea and the North Sea. *Capital:* Copenhagen.
See **Prussia** for map. *n.*

de nom i nate (di nom′ə nāt *for 1;* di nom′ə nit *for 2*),
1 give a name to; name. **2** called by a specific name. 6
ft., 4 oz., 10 in., and 9 lbs. are **denominate numbers.** 1
v., **de nom i nat ed, de nom i nat ing;** 2 *adj.*

de nom i na tion (di nom′ə nā′shən), **1** name for a
group or class of things; name. **2** a religious group or
sect: *Methodists and Baptists are two large Protestant
denominations.* **3** class or kind of units: *Reducing* $5/12$, $1/3$,
and $1/6$ *to the same denomination gives* $5/12$, $4/12$, *and* $2/12$.
The United States coin of lowest denomination is a cent. n.

de nom i na tion al (di nom′ə nā′shə nəl), having to do
with or controlled by some religious denomination: *a
denominational school.* *adj.* —**de nom′i na′tion al ly,** *adv.*

de nom i na tor (di nom′ə nā′tər), the number below or
to the right of the line in a fraction: *In* $3/4$, *4 is the
denominator, and 3 is the numerator.* n.

de no ta tion (dē′nō tā′shən), **1** meaning, especially the
exact, literal meaning. The denotation of *home* is "place
where one lives," but it has many connotations. **2** a de-
noting or marking out; indication. *n.*

de note (di nōt′), **1** be the sign of; indicate: *A fever usu-*

ally denotes sickness. If the teacher puts an "A" on your paper, it denotes very good work. **2** be a name for; mean: *The word "stool" denotes a small chair without a back. v.,* **de not ed, de not ing. —de not′a ble,** *adj.*

de noue ment or **dé noue ment** (dā′nü män′), solution of a plot in a story, play, situation, etc.; outcome; end. *n.*

de nounce (di nouns′), **1** speak against; express strong disapproval of: *The mayor denounced crime in the streets.* **2** give information against; accuse: *denounce someone to the FBI as a spy. v.,* **de nounced, de nounc ing. —denounce′ment,** *n.* **—de nounc′er,** *n.*

dense (dens), **1** closely packed together; thick: *a dense forest, a dense fog.* **2** stupid: *The dense looks of the students showed that they did not understand. adj.,* **dens er, dens est. —dense′ly,** *adv.* **—dense′ness,** *n.*

den si ty (den′sə tē), **1** a being dense; having parts very close together; compactness; thickness: *The density of the forest prevented us from seeing more than a little way ahead.* **2** the quantity of matter in a unit of volume or of area: *The density of lead is greater than the density of wood.* **3** the quantity of anything in a given area: *Population density in the state is 197 per square mile.* **4** stupidity. *n., pl.* **den si ties.**

dent (dent), **1** a hollow made by a blow or pressure: *The fall put a dent in my bicycle fender.* **2** make a dent in: *The fall dented my bicycle fender.* **3** become dented: *Soft wood dents easily.* **1** *n.,* **2,3** *v.*

dent., **1** dentist. **2** dentistry.

den tal (den′tl), **1** of or for the teeth: *Proper dental care can prevent tooth decay.* **2** of or for a dentist's work: *a dental drill. adj.* **—den′tal ly,** *adv.*

dental hygienist, person who assists a dentist by performing such duties as examining and cleaning a patient's teeth, taking X rays, etc.

den ti frice (den′tə fris), paste, powder, or liquid for cleaning the teeth. *n.* [*Dentifrice is from Latin dentifricium, which comes from dentem, meaning "tooth," and fricare, meaning "to rub."*]

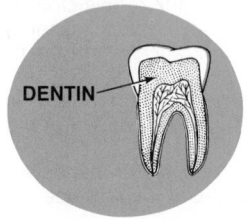

DENTIN

dentin
shown in a cross
section of a molar

den tin (den′tən), the hard, bony material beneath the enamel of a tooth. It forms the main part of a tooth. *n.*

den tine (den′tēn′), dentin. *n.*

den tist (den′tist), doctor whose work is the care of teeth. A dentist fills cavities in teeth, cleans, straightens, or extracts them, and supplies artificial teeth. *n.*

den tist ry (den′tə strē), work, art, or profession of a dentist. *n.*

den ture (den′chər), set of artificial teeth. *n.*

de nude (di nüd′ *or* di nyüd′), make bare; strip (something) of its clothing or covering: *Most trees are denuded of their leaves in winter. v.,* **de nud ed, de nud ing.**

de nun ci a tion (di nun′sē ā′shən), **1** expression of strong disapproval; condemnation; denouncing: *the mayor's denunciation of crime.* **2** an informing against; accusation: *The denunciation of our neighbor as a foreign spy shocked everyone. n.*

Den ver (den′vər), capital of Colorado, in the central part. *n.*

de ny (di nī′), **1** say (something) is not true: *The prisoners denied the charges against them.* **2** say that one does not

hold to or accept: *deny a belief in ghosts.* **3** refuse to give or grant: *I could not deny the stray cat some milk.* **4** refuse to acknowledge; disown: *They denied their debts and refused to pay their bills. v.,* **de nied, de ny ing.**

deny oneself, do without the things one wants: *Some people deny themselves candy, cake, and other rich foods in order to lose weight.*

de o dor ant (dē ō′dər ənt), preparation that destroys bad odors. *n.*

de o dor ize (dē ō′də rīz′), destroy the odor of. *v.,* **de o dor ized, de o dor iz ing. —de o′dor i za′tion,** *n.* **—de o′dor iz′er,** *n.*

de ox y ri bo nu cle ic acid (dē ok′sə rī′bō nü klē′ik), DNA.

dep., **1** department. **2** deputy.

de part (di pärt′), **1** go away; leave: *Your flight departs at 6:15.* **2** turn away; change: *She departed from her usual way of working. v.*

de part ment (di pärt′mənt), a separate part of some whole; special branch; division: *the toy department of a store. Our city government has a fire department, a police department, and a sanitation department. n.*

de part men tal (dē′pärt men′tl), **1** having to do with a department: *departmental policies.* **2** divided into departments: *Their business is so large that it must be handled on a departmental basis. adj.* **—de′part men′tal ly,** *adv.*

department store, store that sells many different kinds of articles arranged in separate departments.

de par ture (di pär′chər), **1** act of going away; leaving: *The airplane's departure for New York was delayed by a blizzard.* **2** a turning away; change: *a departure from our old custom.* **3** a starting on a course of action or thought: *Attending this dancing class will be a new departure for me, for I have never done anything like it. n.*

de pend (di pend′), **1** be a result of; be controlled or influenced by something else: *The success of our picnic will depend partly upon the weather.* **2** get support; rely for help: *Children depend on their parents for food and clothing.* **3** rely; trust: *I depend on my alarm clock to wake me in time for school. v.*

de pend a bil i ty (di pen′də bil′ə tē), reliability; trustworthiness. *n.*

de pend a ble (di pen′də bəl), reliable; trustworthy: *a dependable person. adj.* **—de pend′a ble ness,** *n.*

de pend a bly (di pen′də blē), in a dependable manner. *adv.*

de pend ence (di pen′dəns), **1** fact or condition of being dependent: *the dependence of crops on good weather.* **2** a trusting or relying on another for support or help: *I am going to work so that I can end my dependence on my parents.* **3** reliance; trust: *Do not put your dependence on the bus, for it is often late. n.*

de pend en cy (di pen′dən sē), **1** country or territory controlled by another country: *The Virgin Islands is a dependency of the United States.* **2** a trusting or relying on another for support; dependence. *n., pl.* **de pend en cies.**

de pend ent (di pen′dənt), **1** trusting to another for support; relying on another for help: *A child is dependent on its parents.* **2** person who is supported by another. **3** possible if something else takes place; depending: *Good crops are dependent on the right amount of rainfall and sunshine.* **1,3** *adj.,* **2** *n.* **—de pend′ent ly,** *adv.*

dependent clause, (in grammar) clause in a complex sentence that cannot act alone as a sentence; subordinate clause. In "If I go home, my dog will follow me," *If I go home* is a dependent clause.

de pict (di pikt′), represent by drawing, painting, or describing; portray: *The artist and the poet both tried to depict the splendor of the sunset. v.* **—de pic′tion,** *n.*

de plete (di plēt′), reduce the fullness of; empty; exhaust: *Rapid consumption of our natural resources can quickly deplete them. v.,* **de plet ed, de plet ing.**

de ple tion (di plē′shən), an emptying; exhausting: *Years of mining have caused a depletion of coal deposits in the mines. n.*

de plor a ble (di plôr′ə bəl), **1** regrettable; lamentable: *a deplorable accident.* **2** wretched; miserable: *Deplorable living conditions exist in slums. adj.* **—de plor′a ble ness,** *n.*

de plor a bly (di plôr′ə blē), in a deplorable manner; lamentably. *adv.*

de plore (di plôr′), be very sorry about; express great sorrow for; regret deeply: *We deplore the accident. v.,* **de plored, de plor ing.**

de ploy (di ploi′), **1** spread out (troops, etc.) from a column into a long battle line. **2** spread out or extend (anything): *A fleet of ships was deployed over the area in which the astronauts were expected to land. v.* **—de ploy′ment,** *n.*

de pop u late (dē pop′yə lāt), get rid of the inhabitants of: *The conquerors depopulated the enemy's capital by driving most of the inhabitants away. v.,* **de pop u lat ed, de pop u lat ing.** **—de pop′u la′tor,** *n.*

de pop u la tion (dē pop′yə lā′shən), **1** act of depopulating. **2** condition of being depopulated. *n.*

de port (di pôrt′), **1** force to leave; banish; expel. Deported aliens are sent out of the country, usually back to their native land. **2** behave or conduct (oneself) in a particular manner: *The children deport themselves well when we have guests. v.* [*Deport* is from Latin *deportare,* which comes from *de-,* meaning "away," and *portare,* meaning "carry."] **—de port′a ble,** *adj.*

de por ta tion (dē′pôr tā′shən), removal from a country by banishment or expulsion: *Deportation of criminals from England to Australia was once common. n.*

de port ment (di pôrt′mənt), way a person acts; behavior; conduct. *n.*

de pose (di pōz′), **1** put out of office or a position of authority, especially a high one like that of king: *The king was deposed by the revolution.* **2** declare under oath, especially in writing; testify: *The witness deposed that she had seen the accused on the day of the murder. v.,* **de posed, de pos ing.** **—de pos′a ble,** *adj.* **—de pos′er,** *n.*

de pos it (di poz′it), **1** put down; lay down; leave lying: *She deposited the bundles on the table. The flood deposited a layer of mud in the streets.* **2** material laid down or left lying by natural means: *There is often a deposit of mud and sand at the mouth of a river.* **3** put in a place for safekeeping: *Deposit your money in the bank.* **4** something put in a certain place for safekeeping: *Money put in a bank is a deposit.* **5** pay as a pledge to do something or to pay more later: *If you deposit part of the price, a store will keep an article for you until you pay the rest.* **6** money paid as a pledge to do something or to pay more later: *I put down a $25 deposit on the coat, and will pay the balance of $50 on the first of next month.* **7** mass of some mineral in rock or in the ground: *deposits of coal.* 1,3,5 *v.,* 2,4,6,7 *n.* **on deposit,** in a bank.

dep o si tion (dep′ə zish′ən), **1** act of putting out of office or a position of authority; removal from power. **2** testimony, especially a sworn statement in writing: *The prisoner made a deposition to use in appealing his case.* **3** a depositing: *the deposition of silt from the floodwaters. n.*

de pos i tor (di poz′ə tər), person who deposits: *Depositors in savings banks may receive interest on their money. n.*

de pos i to ry (di poz′ə tôr′ē), place where anything is stored for safekeeping; storehouse. *n., pl.* **de pos i to ries.**

de pot (dē′pō *for 1;* dep′ō *for 2,3*), **1** a railroad or bus station. **2** storehouse; warehouse. **3** place where military supplies are stored. *n.*

de prave (di prāv′), make bad; injure morally; corrupt:

Drug addiction can deprave a person's character. v., **de praved, de prav ing.** **—de prav′er,** *n.*

de praved (di prāvd′), morally bad; wicked; corrupt: *The murder was committed by a depraved person. adj.* **—de praved′ly,** *adv.* **—de praved′ness,** *n.*

de prav i ty (di prav′ə tē), **1** a being depraved; wickedness; viciousness; corruption. **2** a corrupt act; bad practice. *n., pl.* **de prav i ties.**

dep re cate (dep′rə kāt), express strong disapproval of: *Lovers of peace deprecate war. v.,* **dep re cat ed, dep re cat ing.** **—dep′re cat′ing ly,** *adv.* **—dep′re ca′tor,** *n.*

dep re ca tion (dep′rə kā′shən), a strong expression of disapproval. *n.*

de pre ci ate (di prē′shē āt), **1** lessen in value: *The government has the power to depreciate currency. The longer an automobile is driven the more it depreciates.* **2** speak slightingly of; belittle: *He depreciated the gift I got, saying that his was much nicer. v.,* **de pre ci at ed, de pre ci at ing.** **—de pre′ci at′ing ly,** *adv.* **—de pre′ci a′tor,** *n.*

de pre ci a tion (di prē′shē ā′shən), a lowering or a being lowered in price, value, or estimation. *n.*

dep re da tion (dep′rə dā′shən), act of plundering; robbery; ravaging. *n.*

de press (di pres′), **1** make sad or gloomy: *I was depressed by the bad news from home.* **2** press down; lower: *When you play the piano, you depress the keys.* **3** make less active; weaken: *Some medicines depress the action of the heart. v.* **—de press′i ble,** *adj.* **—de press′ing ly,** *adv.*

de pres sant (di pres′nt), drug or other substance that slows or reduces the body's reactions and relaxes muscles: *an appetite depressant. n.*

de pressed (di prest′), **1** gloomy; low-spirited; sad: *The rain made us depressed.* **2** pressed down; lowered. *adj.*

de pres sion (di presh′ən), **1** a pressing down; sinking or lowering: *A rapid depression of the mercury in a barometer usually means a storm is coming.* **2** a low place; hollow: *Rain formed puddles in the depressions in the ground.* **3** sadness or gloominess; low spirits: *Failure usually brings on a feeling of depression.* **4** a severe reduction of business activity: *Many people lose their jobs during a depression. n.*

dep ri va tion (dep′rə vā′shən), **1** act of depriving. **2** condition of being deprived; loss; privation. *n.*

de prive (di prīv′), **1** take away from by force: *The people deprived the cruel queen of her power.* **2** keep from having or doing: *Worrying deprived us of sleep. v.,* **de prived, de priv ing.** **—de priv′a ble,** *adj.* **—de priv′er,** *n.*

dept., department.

depth (depth), **1** distance from top to bottom: *the depth of a hole, the depth of a lake.* **2** distance from front to back: *The depth of our playground is 250 feet.* **3** the deepest or most central part: *the darkest depth of the jungle, the depths of despair.* **4** deep quality; deepness: *The students admired their teacher's depth of understanding.* **5** deep understanding; profoundness: *This story has a good plot, but it has no depth at all.* **6** lowness of pitch. *n.*

depth charge, an explosive charge dropped from a ship or airplane and set to explode at a certain depth under water.

dep u ta tion (dep′yə tā′shən), group of persons sent to represent others: *The neighborhood sent a deputation of citizens to the meeting of the town council. n.*

dep u tize (dep/yə tīz), appoint as deputy. *v.*, **dep u-tized, dep u tiz ing.**

dep u ty (dep/yə tē), person appointed to do the work of or take the place of another: *A sheriff's deputies help him enforce the law. n., pl.* **dep u ties.**

der., 1 derivation. 2 derivative.

de rail (di rāl/), 1 cause (a train, etc.) to run off the rails. 2 run off the rails. *v.*

de rail leur (di rā/lər), a spring-driven mechanism on a bicycle that changes gears by causing the chain to move from one sprocket wheel to another. *n.*

derailleur

derailment—the derailment of a steam engine

de rail ment (di rāl/mənt), a derailing or a being de-railed. *n.*

de range (di rānj/), make insane: *deranged by grief. v.*, **de ranged, de rang ing. —de range/a ble,** *adj.*

de range ment (di rānj/mənt), mental disorder or insan-ity. *n.*

Der by (dėr/bē), 1 a famous horse race run every year since 1780 near London. 2 a horse race of similar impor-tance: *the Kentucky Derby.* 3 **derby,** a stiff hat with a rounded crown and narrow brim. *n., pl.* **Der bies** for 2, **der bies** for 3. [This race was named after the 12th Earl of *Derby,* who died in 1834. He founded this horse race.]

der e lict (der/ə likt), 1 abandoned by its crew or owner; forsaken: *a derelict ship.* 2 ship abandoned at sea. 3 a penniless person who is homeless, jobless, and aban-doned by others. 4 failing in one's duty; negligent: *The guard was found derelict in letting the prisoner escape.* 1,4 *adj.,* 2,3 *n.*

der e lic tion (der/ə lik/shən), 1 failure in one's duty; negligence. 2 abandonment; forsaking. *n.*

de ride (di rīd/), make fun of; laugh at: *They derided me for my fear of the dark. v.,* **de rid ed, de rid ing.**

de ri sion (di rizh/ən), laughter; ridicule: *Their derision hurt my feelings. n.*

de ri sive (di rī/siv), showing ridicule; mocking. *adj.* **—de ri/sive ly,** *adv.* **—de ri/sive ness,** *n.*

deriv., 1 derivation. 2 derivative.

der i va tion (der/ə vā/shən), 1 act or fact of deriving. 2 origin: *The celebration of Halloween is of Scottish deriva-tion.* 3 system in a language for making new words from old words by adding prefixes and suffixes and by other methods. EXAMPLE: *Quickness = quick +* suffix *-ness.* 4 statement of how a word was formed; etymology. *n.*

de riv a tive (di riv/ə tiv), 1 not original; derived. 2 some-thing derived: *Many medicines are derivatives of roots and herbs.* 3 word formed by adding a prefix or suffix to another word. *Quickness* and *quickly* are derivatives of *quick.* 1 *adj.,* 2,3 *n.* **—de riv/a tive ly,** *adv.*

de rive (di rīv/), 1 obtain from a source or origin; get; receive: *I derive much enjoyment from reading.* 2 come from a source or origin; originate: *This story derives from an old legend.* 3 trace (a word, custom, etc.) from or to a source or origin: *The word "December" is ultimately de-rived from the Latin word "decem," which means "ten." v.,* **de rived, de riv ing.** [See **Word History.**]

der ma (dėr/mə), dermis. *n.*

der ma tol o gist (dėr/mə tol/ə jist), doctor who treats the skin and its diseases. *n.*

der mis (dėr/mis), the sensitive layer of skin beneath the outer skin; derma. *n.*

de rog a to ry (di rog/ə tôr/ē), lessening the value of; belittling; unfavorable: *People resent derogatory remarks about their personal appearance. adj.* **—de rog/a to/ri ly,** *adv.* **—de rog/a to/ri ness,** *n.*

der rick (der/ik), 1 machine for lifting and moving heavy objects. A derrick has a long arm that swings at an angle from the base of an upright post or frame. 2 a towerlike framework over an oil well that holds the drill-ing and hoisting machinery. *n.*

der ring-do (der/ing dü/), daring deeds. *n.*

derby (def. 3)

der vish (dėr/vish), member of a Moslem religious order that practices unusual self-denial and devotion. Some members dance and spin about violently. *n., pl.* **der-vish es.** [*Dervish* was borrowed from Turkish *dervish,* which came from Persian *darvīsh.*] **—der/vish like/,** *adj.*

de salt (dē sôlt/), remove salt from: *desalt sea water for human use. v.* **—de salt/er,** *n.*

de scend (di send/), 1 go or come down from a higher to a lower place: *The river descends from the mountains to the sea. We descended the stairs to get to the basement.* 2 go or come down from an earlier to a later time: *a supersti-tion descended from the Middle Ages.* 3 go from greater to less numbers; go from higher to lower on any scale:

WORD HISTORY

derive

Derive is from Latin *derivare,* meaning "lead off, draw off," which comes from *de-,* meaning "away," and *rivus,* mean-ing "stream."

75-50-25 form a series that descends. **4** make a sudden attack: *The wolves descended on the sheep and killed them.* **5** be handed down from parent to child: *This land has descended from my grandfather to my mother and now to me.* **6** come down or spring from: *He is descended from pioneers.* **7** lower oneself; stoop: *In order to eat she descended to stealing.* v. —**de scend′a ble, de scend′i ble,** *adj.* —**de scend′er,** *n.*

descendant (def. 2)—Grandmother sat on the sofa, surrounded by her **descendants.**

de scend ant (di sen′dənt), **1** person born of a certain family or group: *a descendant of the Pilgrims.* **2** offspring; child, grandchild, great-grandchild, etc. You are a direct descendant of your parents, grandparents, great-grandparents, and earlier ancestors. *n.*

de scent (di sent′), **1** a coming or going down from a higher to a lower place: *the descent of a helicopter.* **2** a downward slope: *We climbed down a steep descent.* **3** a handing down from parent to child: *The descent of certain physical characteristics can sometimes be traced back several generations.* **4** family line; ancestors: *They traced their descent back to a family in Spain.* **5** a sinking to a lower condition; decline; fall. **6** a sudden attack: *The descent of the bandits on the village was unexpected. n.*

de scribe (di skrīb′), **1** tell in words how a person looks, feels, or acts, or how a place, a thing, or an event looks; tell or write about: *The reporter described the accident in detail.* **2** draw the outline of; trace: *The spinning top described a figure 8.* v., **de scribed, de scrib ing.** —**de scrib′a ble,** *adj.* —**de scrib′er,** *n.*

de scrip tion (di skrip′shən), **1** a telling in words how a person, place, thing, or an event looks or behaves; describing. **2** composition or account that describes or gives a picture in words: *The reporter's vivid description of the hotel fire made me feel as if I were right at the scene.* **3** kind; sort: *I have seen no dog of any description today. n.*

de scrip tive (di skrip′tiv), using description; describing: *A descriptive booklet tells about the places to be seen on the trip.* adj. —**de scrip′tive ly,** *adv.* —**de scrip′tive ness,** *n.*

des e crate (des′ə krāt), treat or use without respect; disregard the sacredness of: *The enemy desecrated the church by using it as a stable.* v., **des e crat ed, des e crat ing.** —**des′e crat′er, des′e cra′tor,** *n.*

des e cra tion (des′ə krā′shən), **1** act of desecrating: *The Puritans felt that work or amusement on Sunday was a desecration of the Sabbath.* **2** condition of being desecrated. *n.*

de seg re gate (dē seg′rə gāt), do away with racial segregation in: *desegregate a public school.* v., **de seg re gat ed, de seg re gat ing.**

de seg re ga tion (dē seg′rə gā′shən), a doing away with the practice of racial segregation. *n.*

des ert[1] (dez′ərt), **1** a dry, barren region that is usually sandy and without trees. The Sahara Desert is a great

desert in northern Africa. **2** dry and barren: *Arabia is largely desert land.* **3** not inhabited or cultivated; wild: *They were shipwrecked on a desert island.* **1** *n.,* **2,3** *adj.*

de sert[2] (di zėrt′), go away and leave a person or a place, especially one that should not be left; forsake: *She deserted her old friends when she became famous. A soldier who deserts is punished. v.*

de sert[3] (di zėrt′). Usually, **deserts,** *pl.* what one deserves; suitable reward or punishment: *The reckless driver got his just deserts; he was fined and his driver's license was suspended. n.*

de sert er (di zėr′tər), **1** person who deserts. **2** member of the armed forces who runs away from duty. *n.*

de ser tion (di zėr′shən), **1** act of deserting. **2** condition of being deserted: *Desertion caused the old house to fall into ruin.* **3** a running away from duty, especially from military service. *n.*

de serve (di zėrv′), have a claim or right to; be worthy of: *A hard worker deserves good pay. A naughty child deserves punishment.* v., **de served, de serv ing.**

de serv ed ly (di zėr′vid lē), according to what is deserved; justly; rightly. *adv.*

de serv ing (di zėr′ving), worth helping: *The deserving student received a scholarship.* adj. —**de serv′ing ly,** *adv.*

des ic cate (des′ə kāt), deprive of moisture or water; dry thoroughly: *The soil in a desert is desiccated.* v., **des ic cat ed, des ic cat ing.** —**des′ic ca′tion,** *n.*

de sign (di zīn′), **1** a drawing, plan, or sketch made to serve as a pattern from which to work: *The design showed how to build the machine.* **2** arrangement of details, form, and color in painting, weaving, building, etc.: *a wallpaper design in tan and brown.* **3** make a first sketch of; arrange form and color of; draw in outline: *design a dress.* **4** make drawings, sketches, or plans: *He designs for our dress department.* **5** art of making designs, patterns, or sketches: *Architects study and become skilled in design.* **6** scheme of attack; evil plan: *The thief had designs upon the safe.* **7** plan out; form in the mind: *The author of this detective story has designed an exciting plot.* **8** purpose; aim; intention: *Whether by accident or design, she spilled water on me.* **9** have in mind to do; purpose: *Did you design this result?* **10** set apart; intend: *That room was designed to be her studio.* **1,2,5,6,8** *n.,* **3,4,7,9,10** *v.*

des ig nate (dez′ig nāt), **1** mark out; point out; indicate definitely; show: *Red lines designate main roads on this map.* **2** name: *Historians designate the period A.D. 400 to A.D. 1000, the Dark Ages.* **3** select for duty, office, etc.; appoint: *She has been designated ambassador to Italy by the President.* v., **des ig nat ed, des ig nat ing.**

designated hitter, (in baseball) a player who does not play in the field but is designated at the start of a game to bat in place of the pitcher.

des ig na tion (dez′ig nā′shən), **1** act of marking out; pointing out: *The designation of places on a map should be clear.* **2** a descriptive title; name: *"Your honor" is a designation given to a judge.* **3** appointment to an office or position; selection for a duty: *The designation of cabinet officers is one of the powers of the President. n.*

de sign ed ly (di zī′nid lē), on purpose; intentionally. *adv.*

de sign er (di zī′nər), person who designs. *n.*

de sign ing (di zī′ning), **1** scheming; plotting. **2** showing plan or forethought. **3** art of making designs, patterns, sketches, etc. 1,2 *adj.*,   3 *n.* —**de sign′ing ly**, *adv.*

de sir a bil i ty (di zī′rə bil′ə tē), desirable quality; condition to be wished for: *Nobody doubts the desirability of good health. n.*

de sir a ble (di zī′rə bəl), worth wishing for; worth having; pleasing; good: *The creek valley was a very desirable location for the state park. adj.* —**de sir′a ble ness**, *n.*

de sir a bly (di zī′rə blē), in a desirable manner. *adv.*

de sire (di zīr′), **1** a wanting or longing; strong wish: *feel a desire to travel.* **2** wish earnestly for; long for: *The people of the warring nations desire peace.* **3** express a wish for; ask for: *The principal desires your presence in her office.* **4** a wish expressed in words; request. **5** thing wished for: *His greatest desire was a bicycle.* 1,4,5 *n.*, 2,3 *v.*, **de sired**, **de sir ing.** —**de sir′er**, *n.*

de sir ous (di zī′rəs), desiring; wishing; eager: *She is desirous of going to Europe sometime. adj.* —**de sir′ous ly**, *adv.* —**de sir′ous ness**, *n.*

de sist (di zist′), stop doing something; cease. *v.*

desk (desk), **1** piece of furniture with a flat or sloping top on which to write or to rest books for reading. A desk often has drawers. **2** department of work at a certain location or at a desk: *the information desk of a library. n.* [*Desk* comes from a medieval Latin word *desca,* and can be traced back to Greek *diskos,* meaning "dish."]

Des Moines (də moin′), capital of Iowa, in the central part.

des o late (des′ə lit *for 1,2,4,6,7;* des′ə lāt *for 3,5*), **1** not producing anything; laid waste; devastated; barren: *desolate land.* **2** not lived in; deserted: *a desolate house.* **3** make unfit to live in; lay waste: *The earthquake desolated the business district.* **4** unhappy; forlorn: *The lost child looked very desolate.* **5** make unhappy: *We are desolated to hear that you are going away.* **6** left alone. **7** dreary; dismal: *a desolate life.* 1,2,4,6,7 *adj.*, 3,5 *v.*, **des o lat ed**, **des o lat ing.** —**des′o late ly**, *adv.* —**des′o late ness**, *n.* —**des′o lat′er**, **des′o la′tor**, *n.*

desolation (def. 2)—After the fire, the forest land was in complete **desolation.**

des o la tion (des′ə lā′shən), **1** a making desolate: *the desolation of the country by an invading army.* **2** a ruined, lonely, or deserted condition. **3** a desolate place. **4** lonely sorrow; sadness: *desolation at the loss of loved ones. n.*

De So to (di sō′tō), **Hernando**, 1500?-1542, Spanish explorer in North America who discovered the Mississippi River.

de spair (di sper′ *or* di spar′), **1** loss of hope; a being without hope; a dreadful feeling that nothing good can happen to one: *Despair overcame us as we felt the boat sinking.* **2** person or thing that causes loss of hope: *Another week without rain was the despair of the farmers.*

3 lose hope; be without hope: *The doctors despaired of saving the patient's life.* 1,2 *n.*, 3 *v.*

des patch (dis pach′), dispatch. *v., n., pl.* **des patch es.** —**des patch′er**, *n.*

des pe ra do (des′pə rä′dō), a bold, reckless criminal; dangerous outlaw. *n., pl.* **des pe ra does** or **des pe ra dos.**

desperado—A gang of **desperadoes** threatened the townspeople.

des per ate (des′pər it), **1** showing recklessness caused by despair; violent: *Suicide is a desperate act.* **2** ready to run any risk: *a desperate criminal.* **3** having little chance for hope or cure; very dangerous: *a desperate illness.* **4** extremely bad: *People in the slums live in desperate circumstances. adj.* —**des′per ate ly**, *adv.* —**des′per ate ness**, *n.*

des pe ra tion (des′pə rā′shən), **1** a hopeless and reckless feeling; readiness to try anything: *He jumped out of the window in desperation when he saw that the stairs were on fire.* **2** despair. *n.*

des pi ca ble (des′pi kə bəl *or* des pik′ə bəl), to be despised; contemptible: *It is despicable to go away and leave a cat behind to starve. adj.* —**des′pi ca ble ness**, *n.* —**des′pi ca bly**, *adv.*

de spise (di spīz′), look down on; feel contempt for; scorn: *They were despised for their dishonesty. v.,* **de spised**, **de spis ing.** —**de spis′er**, *n.*

de spite (di spīt′), **1** in spite of: *She will go for a walk despite the rain.* **2** insult or injury. 1 *prep.,* 2 *n.*

de spoil (di spoil′), strip of possessions; rob; plunder. *v.* —**de spoil′er**, *n.* —**de spoil′ment**, *n.*

de spond ence (di spon′dəns), despondency. *n.*

de spond en cy (di spon′dən sē), loss of heart, courage, or hope; discouragement; dejection. *n.*

de spond ent (di spon′dənt), having lost heart, courage, or hope; discouraged; dejected. *adj.* —**de spond′ent ly**, *adv.*

des pot (des′pət), **1** monarch having unlimited power; absolute ruler. **2** person who does just as he or she likes; tyrant. *n.*

des pot ic (di spot′ik), of a despot; having unlimited power; tyrannical. *adj.* —**des pot′i cal ly**, *adv.* —**des pot′i cal ness**, *n.*

des pot ism (des′pə tiz′əm), **1** government by a monarch having unlimited power. **2** tyranny or oppression. *n.*

des sert (di zėrt′), course of pie, cake, ice cream, cheese, fruit, etc., served at the end of a meal. *n.* [*Dessert* came into English about 300 years ago from French *dessert,* and can be traced back to Latin *dis-,* meaning "not," and *servire,* meaning "serve."]

des ti na tion (des′tə nā′shən), place to which a person or thing is going or is being sent. *n.*

des tine (des′tən), **1** set apart for a particular purpose or use; intend: *The princess was destined from birth to be a queen.* **2** cause by fate: *My letter was destined never to reach her. v.,* **des tined**, **des tin ing.**

destined for, intended to go to; bound for: *ships destined for England.*

des ti ny (des′tə nē), **1** what becomes of a person or thing in the end; one's lot or fortune: *It was young Washington's destiny to become the first President of the United States.* **2** what will happen, believed to be determined beforehand in spite of all later efforts to change or prevent it: *She felt that destiny had been unkind to her in making her poor. n., pl.* **des ti nies.**

des ti tute (des′tə tüt *or* des′tə tyüt), lacking necessary things such as food, clothing, and shelter: *Many families were destitute after the earthquake. adj.*

destitute of, having no; without: *The land was dry and destitute of trees.*

des ti tu tion (des′tə tü′shən *or* des′tə tyü′shən), lack of the means of living; extreme poverty. *n.*

de stroy (di stroi′), **1** break to pieces; make useless; ruin; spoil: *A tornado destroyed the farmhouse.* **2** put an end to; do away with: *A heavy rain destroyed all hope of a picnic.* **3** kill: *Fire destroys many trees every year. v.*

destroyer (def. 2)

de stroy er (di stroi′ər), **1** person or thing that destroys. **2** a small, fast warship with guns, torpedoes, and other weapons. *n.*

de struct (di strukt′), **1** blow up a rocket or other missile that fails to work properly. **2** the deliberate blowing up of a rocket or missile. **1** *v.,* **2** *n.*

de struct i ble (di struk′tə bəl), capable of being destroyed. *adj.*

de struc tion (di struk′shən), **1** a destroying: *A bulldozer was used in the destruction of the old barn.* **2** ruin: *The storm left destruction behind it.* **3** thing that destroys. *n.*

destructive (def. 1)
A house is being battered by a **destructive** hurricane.

de struc tive (di struk′tiv), **1** destroying; causing destruction. **2** tearing down; not helpful; not constructive: *Destructive criticism shows things to be wrong, but does not show how to correct them. adj.* —**de struc′tive ly,** *adv.* —**de struc′tive ness,** *n.*

des ul to ry (des′əl tôr′ē), jumping from one thing to another; without aim or method; unconnected: *He read the book in a desultory manner, skipping chapters as he pleased. adj.*

a hat	**i** it	**oi** oil	**ch** child	a in about	
ā age	**ī** ice	**ou** out	**ng** long	e in taken	
ä far	**o** hot	**u** cup	**sh** she	ə = i in pencil	
e let	**ō** open	**u̇** put	**th** thin	o in lemon	
ē equal	**ô** order	**ü** rule	**ᴛʜ** then	u in circus	
ėr term			**zh** measure		

de tach (di tach′), **1** loosen and remove; unfasten; separate: *I detached a key from the chain.* **2** send away on special duty: *One squad of soldiers was detached to guard the road. v.*

de tach a ble (di tach′ə bəl), able to be detached: *A loose-leaf notebook has detachable pages. adj.*

de tached (di tacht′), **1** separate from others; isolated: *A detached house is separated by land from neighboring houses.* **2** not influenced by others or by one's own interests and prejudices; impartial: *The judge listened to the claims of both sides with a detached air. adj.* —**de tach′ed ly,** *adv.* —**de tach′ed ness,** *n.*

de tach ment (di tach′mənt), **1** a taking apart; separation. **2** a standing apart; lack of interest; aloofness: *He watched the dull motion picture with detachment.* **3** freedom from prejudice or bias; impartial attitude. **4** troops or ships sent away on some special duty. *n.*

de tail (di tāl′ *or* dē′tāl), **1** a small or unimportant part: *Her report was complete; it didn't leave out a single detail.* **2** a dealing with small things one by one: *I do not enjoy the details of housekeeping.* **3** tell fully; tell even the small and unimportant parts of: *Our neighbors detailed to us all the things they had done on their vacation.* **4** a small group selected for or sent on some special duty: *A detail of six scouts was sent out to find firewood.* **5** select for or send on special duty: *Several police officers were detailed to direct traffic after the football game.* **1,2,4** *n.,* **3,5** *v.*

in detail, with all the details; part by part.

de tailed (di tāld′ *or* dē′tāld), **1** full of details: *The witness gave a detailed account of the accident.* **2** minute: *With a microscope a scientist can make a detailed examination of bacteria. adj.*

de tain (di tān′), **1** keep from going ahead; hold back; delay: *The heavy traffic detained us for almost an hour.* **2** keep from going away; hold as a prisoner: *The police detained the suspected thief for further questioning. v.* —**de tain′ment,** *n.*

de tect (di tekt′), find out; discover; catch: *I detected my friends hiding in the bushes. Can you detect any odor in the room? v.* [*Detect* comes from Latin *detectum,* meaning "uncovered."]

de tec tion (di tek′shən), a finding out; discovery. *n.*

de tec tive (di tek′tiv), **1** member of a police force or other person whose work is finding information secretly, solving crimes, etc. **2** having to do with detectives and their work: *She writes detective stories.* **3** used in discovering or finding out: *detective methods, a detective device.* **1** *n.,* **2,3** *adj.*

de tec tor (di tek′tər), **1** person or thing that detects: *a smoke detector.* **2** a vacuum tube or crystal in a radio that helps in the change of radio waves into sound waves. *n.*

de ten tion (di ten′shən), **1** act of detaining; holding back. **2** condition of being detained: *Detention after hours is a common punishment in school.* **3** a keeping in custody; confinement: *A jail is used for the detention of persons who have been arrested. n.*

de ter (di tėr′), keep back; discourage or hinder: *The barking dog deterred me from crossing the neighbor's yard. v.,* **de terred, de ter ring.** —**de ter′ment,** *n.*

de ter gent (di tėr′jənt), **1** substance used for cleansing. Many detergents are chemical compounds that act like soap. **2** cleansing. **1** *n.,* **2** *adj.* [*Detergent* comes from Latin *detergentem,* meaning "wiping off."]

de ter i o rate (di tir′ē ə rāt′), make or become lower in quality or value: *A hot, damp climate deteriorates leather. Machinery deteriorates rapidly if it is not taken care of. v.,* **de ter i o rat ed, de ter i o rat ing.**

de ter i o ra tion (di tir′ē ə rā′shən), a deteriorating; a making or becoming lower in quality or value: *We had the book rebound because of the deterioration of the cover. n.*

de ter mi nant (di tėr′mə nənt), determining; deciding: *The higher pay offered was the determinant factor in her changing jobs. adj.*

de ter mi na tion (di tėr′mə nā′shən), **1** great firmness in carrying out a purpose; fixed purpose: *His determination was not weakened by the difficulties he met.* **2** a finding out the exact amount or kind, by weighing, measuring, or calculating: *the determination of the gold in a sample of rock.* **3** a deciding; settling beforehand: *The determination of what things we needed to take on our camping trip took a long time. n.*

de ter mine (di tėr′mən), **1** make up one's mind very firmly; resolve: *He determined to become the best player on the team.* **2** find out exactly: *The pilot determined how far she was from the airport.* **3** be the deciding fact in reaching a certain result: *The number of answers you get right determines your mark in this test. Tomorrow's weather will determine whether we go to the beach or stay home.* **4** decide or settle beforehand; fix: *Can we now determine the date for our next meeting?* **5** limit; define: *The meaning of a word is partly determined by its use in a particular sentence. v.,* **de ter mined, de ter min ing.**

de ter mined (di tėr′mənd), firm; resolute: *Her determined look showed that she had made up her mind. adj.* **—de ter′mined ly,** *adv.* **—de ter′mined ness,** *n.*

de ter min er (di tėr′mə nər), an adjective that points out the thing named, or indicates quantity or number. *A* in *a hat, the* in *the big house,* and *every* in *every little thing* are determiners. *n.*

deterrent (def. 1)
A warning sign and a strong fence are **deterrents** to intruders.

de ter rent (di tėr′ənt), **1** something that hinders or discourages. **2** hindering or discouraging: *a deterrent influence.* 1 *n.,* 2 *adj.*

de test (di test′), dislike very much; hate: *I detest liars. v.* **—de test′er,** *n.*

de test a ble (di tes′tə bəl), deserving to be detested; hateful: *Murder is a detestable crime. adj.* **—de test′a ble ness,** *n.*

de test a bly (di tes′tə blē), in a detestable manner; hatefully. *adv.*

de tes ta tion (dē′tes′tā′shən), very strong dislike; hatred. *n.*

de throne (di thrōn′), put off a throne or a high position; remove from ruling power; depose: *The rebels dethroned the weak king. v.,* **de throned, de thron ing. —de thron′er,** *n.*

de throne ment (di thrōn′mənt), removal from a throne or a high position. *n.*

det o nate (det′n āt), explode with a loud noise: *The workers detonated the dynamite. Suddenly the bomb detonated. v.,* **det o nat ed, det o nat ing.**

det o na tion (det′n ā′shən), explosion with a loud noise. *n.*

det o na tor (det′n ā′tər), fuse, percussion cap, or similar device used to set off an explosive. *n.*

de tour (dē′tur), **1** road that is used when the main or direct road cannot be traveled. **2** a roundabout way or course: *I took several detours before I got the right answer.* **3** use a detour: *We detoured around the bridge that had been washed out.* **4** cause to use a detour: *The police detoured all traffic on Broadway to keep it open for the parade.* 1,2 *n.,* 3,4 *v.*

de tract (di trakt′), take away a part; remove some of the quality or worth: *The ugly frame detracts from the beauty of the picture. v.*

de trac tion (di trak′shən), a taking away of some quality or worth; a speaking evil of; belittling. *n.*

de trac tor (di trak′tər), person who speaks evil of or belittles another. *n.*

det ri ment (det′rə mənt), **1** loss, damage, or injury: *She worked her way through college without detriment to her studies.* **2** something that causes loss, damage, or injury: *His poor diet was a detriment to his health. n.*

det ri men tal (det′rə men′tl), harmful; injurious: *Smoking is detrimental to one's health. adj.* **—det′ri men′tal ly,** *adv.*

de tri tus (di trī′təs), particles of rock or other material worn away from a mass. *n.*

De troit (di troit′), city in SE Michigan. *n.*

deuce (düs *or* dyüs), **1** a playing card or a side of a die having two spots. **2** (in tennis) a tie score at 40 each in a game, or 5 or more games each in a set. **3** exclamation of annoyance meaning "bad luck" or "the devil." 1,2 *n.,* 3 *interj.*

deu ter i um (dü tir′ē əm *or* dyü tir′ē əm), an isotope of hydrogen; heavy hydrogen. Its atoms weigh about twice as much as those of ordinary hydrogen. *n.*

Deu te ron o my (dü′tə ron′ə mē *or* dyü′tə ron′ə mē), the fifth book of the Old Testament. *n.*

de Va ler a (dev′ə ler′ə *or* dev′ə lir′ə), **Eamon,** 1882-1975, Irish political leader.

de val u ate (dē val′yü āt), devalue. *v.,* **de val u at ed, de val u at ing.**

de val u a tion (dē val′yü ā′shən), a devaluing or a being devalued. *n.*

de val ue (dē val′yü), reduce the value of; fix a lower legal value on; devaluate: *When a country devalues its money, other countries can buy its products more cheaply. v.,* **de val ued, de val u ing.**

dev as tate (dev′ə stāt), lay waste; destroy; ravage: *A long war devastated the country. v.,* **dev as tat ed, dev as tat ing.**

dev as tat ing (dev′ə stā′ting), **1** causing destruction or devastation: *a devastating earthquake.* **2** very effective: *a devastating criticism. adj.*

dev as ta tion (dev′ə stā′shən), a devastating or a being devastated; destruction; desolation: *Every year fires cause the devastation of valuable forests. n.*

de vel op (di vel′əp), **1** come into being or activity; grow: *Plants develop from seeds.* **2** bring into being or activity: *Scientists have developed many new drugs to fight disease.* **3** come to have: *She developed an interest in collecting stamps.* **4** make or become bigger, better, more useful, etc.: *Exercise develops the muscles. His business developed very slowly.* **5** work out in greater and greater detail: *Gradually we developed our plans for the club.* **6** treat (a photographic film or plate) with chemicals to bring out the picture: *We shall print all the films we developed.*

7 make or become known: *The detective's investigation did not develop any new facts.* v. —**de vel'op a ble,** *adj.*

de vel op er (di vel'ə pər), **1** person or thing that develops: *a housing developer.* **2** chemical used to bring out the picture on a photographic film or plate. *n.*

de vel op ing (di vel'ə ping), advancing in production, technology, medicine, and overall standard of living after becoming self-governing: *developing nations.* *adj.*

de vel op ment (di vel'əp mənt), **1** process of developing; growth: *The doctor followed the child's development closely.* **2** outcome; result; new event: *The newspaper described the latest developments in the elections.* **3** a working out in greater and greater detail: *The development of plans for a flight to the moon took many years.* **4** group of similar houses or apartment buildings built on open land or in place of old buildings. *n.*

de vel op men tal (di vel'əp men'tl), of development. *adj.* —**de vel'op men'tal ly,** *adv.*

de vi ate (dē'vē āt), turn aside (from a way, course, rule, truth, etc.): *I deviated from my routine and walked to work.* v., **de vi at ed, de vi at ing.** —**de'vi a'tor,** *n.*

de vi a tion (dē'vē ā'shən), a turning aside from a way, course, rule, truth, etc.: *deviation from one's usual schedule, a deviation in the needle of a compass.* *n.*

de vice (di vīs'), **1** something invented, devised, or fitted for a particular use or special purpose. A can opener is a device. *Our car has a device to control pollution from exhaust.* **2** a plan, scheme, or trick: *In order to stay outside she used the device of pretending not to hear her mother calling her.* *n.*

leave to one's own devices, leave to do as one thinks best: *The teacher left us to our own devices in choosing the books for our reports.*

dev il (dev'əl), **1 the Devil,** the evil spirit; the enemy of goodness; Satan. **2** any evil spirit; fiend; demon. **3** a wicked or cruel person. **4** a very clever, energetic, or reckless person: *a mischievous devil.* **5** an unfortunate or wretched person: *That poor devil hasn't eaten a good meal in weeks.* **6** a young helper in a printing office. **7** bother; tease; torment: *My friends deviled me all day because I wore socks that didn't match.* 1-6 *n.,* 7 *v.*

dev iled (dev'əld), highly seasoned: *deviled eggs.* *adj.*

dev il fish (dev'əl fish'), **1** a large ray of warm seas that moves by a flapping motion of its broad fins. **2** octopus. *n., pl.* **dev il fish es** or **dev il fish.**

dev il ish (dev'ə lish), **1** like a devil; worthy of the Devil; very evil: *a devilish temper.* **2** mischievous or daring: *The children played devilish pranks on Halloween.* *adj.* —**dev'il ish ly,** *adv.* —**dev'il ish ness,** *n.*

dev il-may-care (dev'əl mā ker' or dev'əl mā kar'), very careless or reckless. *adj.*

dev il ment (dev'əl mənt), devilish action or behavior; mischief. *n.*

devil's food cake, a rich, dark, chocolate cake.

dev il try (dev'əl trē), **1** evil action; wicked or cruel behavior. **2** mischievous or daring behavior: *The children are full of deviltry today.* *n., pl.* **dev il tries.**

de vi ous (dē'vē əs), **1** out of the direct way; winding; roundabout: *We took a devious route through side streets and alleys to avoid the crowded main streets.* **2** straying from the right course; not straightforward: *a devious scheme for finding out the answers to the test beforehand.* *adj.* —**de'vi ous ly,** *adv.* —**de'vi ous ness,** *n.*

de vise (di vīz'), think out; plan or contrive; invent: *She devised a way of raising boards up to her tree house by using a pulley.* v., **de vised, de vis ing.**

de void (di void'), entirely without; empty; lacking: *A well devoid of water is useless.* *adj.*

de volve (di volv'), **1** be handed down to someone else; be transferred: *If the president is unable to handle his*

duties, they devolve upon the vice-president. **2** transfer (duty, work, etc.) to someone else. v., **de volved, de volv ing.**

de vote (di vōt'), give up (oneself, one's money, time, or efforts, etc.) to some person, purpose, or service: *She devoted herself to her studies. He is devoting his efforts to improving the environment.* v., **de vot ed, de vot ing.**

de vot ed (di vō'tid), very loyal; faithful: *devoted friends.* *adj.* —**de vot'ed ly,** *adv.* —**de vot'ed ness,** *n.*

dev o tee (dev'ə tē'), person who is strongly devoted to something: *Many Americans are devotees of football.* *n.*

de vo tion (di vō'shən), **1** deep, steady affection; loyalty; faithfulness: *the devotion of parents to their children.* **2** a giving up or being given up to some person, purpose, or service: *the devotion of much time to study.* **3 devotions,** *pl.* worship, prayers, or praying. *n.*

de vo tion al (di vō'shə nəl), of or for religious devotion; used in worship: *devotional hymns.* *adj.*

de vour (di vour'), **1** eat (usually said of animals): *The lion devoured the sheep.* **2** eat like an animal; eat very hungrily: *The hungry girl devoured her dinner.* **3** consume, waste, or destroy: *The raging fire devoured the forest.* **4** take in with eyes or ears in a hungry, greedy way: *He devoured the new book about airplanes.* **5** absorb wholly: *I was devoured by curiosity about my birthday presents.* v.

de vout (di vout'), **1** active in worship and prayer; religious: *a devout Moslem, a devout Christian.* **2** earnest; sincere; hearty: *You have my devout wishes for a safe trip.* *adj.* —**de vout'ly,** *adv.* —**de vout'ness,** *n.*

dew (dü or dyü), **1** moisture from the air that condenses in small drops on cool surfaces during the night: *In the morning there was dew on the grass and flowers.* **2** something fresh or refreshing like dew: *the dew of youth, the dew of sleep.* *n.* [Dew comes from Old English *dēaw.*]

dew ber ry (dü'ber'ē or dyü'ber'ē), the sweet, black berry of various trailing vines related to the blackberry. *n., pl.* **dew ber ries.**

dew drop (dü'drop' or dyü'drop'), a drop of dew. *n.*

Dew ey decimal system (dü'ē), system for classifying books, pamphlets, etc., in many libraries. Each subject and its subdivisions are assigned specific three-digit numbers and decimals. Books on language are numbered in the 400's. [This system was named for Melvil *Dewey,* 1851-1931, American librarian who devised it.]

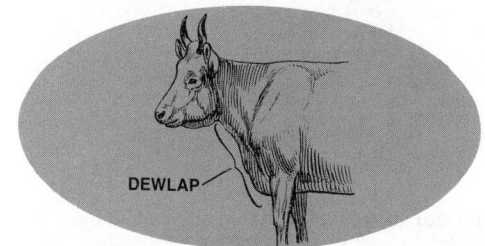

DEWLAP

dew lap (dü'lap' or dyü'lap'), the loose fold of skin under the throat of cattle and some other animals. *n.*

dew point, the temperature of the air at which dew begins to form.

dew y (dü'ē or dyü'ē), **1** wet with dew. **2** fresh or refreshing like dew. *adj.*, **dew i er, dew i est. —dew′i ness,** *n.*

dex ter i ty (dek ster′ə tē), skill in using the hands, body, or mind: *The jeweler's dexterity was shown in the quick, sure way he repaired the watch.* *n.* [*Dexterity* is from Latin *dexteritas*, which comes from *dexter*, meaning "on the right hand, skillful."]

dex ter ous (dek′stər əs), 1 having skill with the hands: *A typist needs to be dexterous.* 2 quick and skillful in bodily movements: *a dexterous acrobat.* 3 having skill with the mind; clever: *A successful manager must be dexterous in handling people.* *adj.* —**dex′ter ous ly,** *adv.*

dex trose (dek′strōs), a crystalline sugar less sweet than cane sugar, occurring in many plant and animal tissues and fluids; grape sugar. It is a form of glucose. *n.*

Dha ka (dak′ə), the capital of Bangladesh. *n.* Also, **Dacca.**

di-, *prefix.* two; twice; double, as in *dicotyledon, digraph, dioxide.*

dia-, *prefix.* through; across, as in *diameter, diaphragm.*

di a be tes (dī′ə bē′tis *or* dī′ə bē′tēz), disease in which a person's system cannot properly absorb normal amounts of sugar and starch because the pancreas fails to secrete enough insulin. *n.* [*Diabetes* is from Greek *diabētēs*, and can be traced back to *dia-*, meaning "through," and *bainein*, meaning "go." In this disease sugar passes through the body and is excreted in the urine.]

di a bet ic (dī′ə bet′ik), 1 of or for diabetes. 2 having diabetes. 3 person having diabetes. 1,2 *adj.*, 3 *n.*

di a bol ic (dī′ə bol′ik), very cruel or wicked; devilish; fiendish: *The police discovered a diabolic plot to poison the city's drinking water.* *adj.* —**di′a bol′i cal ly,** *adv.*

di a bol i cal (dī′ə bol′ə kəl), diabolic. *adj.*

di a crit ic (dī′ə krit′ik), a diacritical mark. *n.*

diacritical marks

∧	(circumflex)	ôrder
‾	(macron)	ēqual
~	(tilde)	cañon
••	(dieresis)	naïve
⸜	(cedilla)	façade
•	(single dot)	pùt
′	(acute accent)	attaché
`	(grave accent)	à la mode

di a crit i cal mark (dī′ə krit′ə kəl), a small mark put over or next to a letter to indicate pronunciation, accent, etc. The pronunciation key in this dictionary contains several types of diacritical marks.

di a dem (dī′ə dem), 1 a crown. 2 an ornamental band of cloth formerly worn as a crown. *n.*

di ag nose (dī′əg nōs′), find out the nature of by examination and careful study; identify: *The doctor diagnosed*

the disease as measles. *v.*, **di ag nosed, di ag nos ing.**

di ag no sis (dī′əg nō′sis), 1 act or process of finding out what disease a person or animal has by examination and careful study of the symptoms: *The doctors used X rays and blood samples in their diagnosis.* 2 a careful study of the facts about something to find out its essential features, faults, etc.: *The candidate made a diagnosis of the political situation at the start of his campaign.* 3 conclusion reached after a careful study of symptoms or facts: *The doctor's diagnosis was that I had measles.* *n.*, *pl.* **di ag no ses** (dī′əg nō′sēz′).

di ag nos tic (dī′əg nos′tik), 1 of diagnosis. 2 helping in diagnosis: *diagnostic tests.* *adj.*

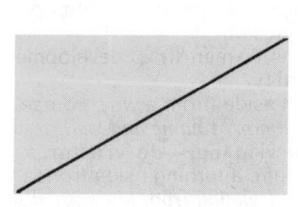

diagonal (def. 1)
Line AB is a diagonal.

di ag o nal (dī ag′ə nəl), 1 a line segment connecting two corners that are not next to each other in a four-sided or many-sided figure; line that cuts across in a slanting direction. 2 taking the direction of a diagonal; slanting: *diagonal stripes in cloth.* 3 any slanting part, course, or arrangement of things. 4 connecting two corners that are not next to each other in a four-sided or many-sided figure: *a diagonal line.* 1,3 *n.*, 2,4 *adj.* —**di ag′o nal ly,** *adv.*

di a gram (dī′ə gram), 1 drawing or sketch showing important parts of something. A diagram may be an outline, a plan, a figure, a chart, or a combination of any of these, made to show clearly what something is, how it works, or the relation between the parts. Diagrams are used in geometry to help in the proof of the problems. 2 put on paper, a blackboard, etc., in the form of a drawing or sketch; make a diagram of: *The architect diagramed the floor plan to show how she would divide the office space.* 1 *n.*, 2 *v.*

di a gram mat ic (dī′ə grə mat′ik), in the form of a diagram: *a diagrammatic sketch.* *adj.* —**di′a gram mat′i cal ly,** *adv.*

di al (dī′əl), 1 plate or disk with numbers, letters, or marks on it and a moving pointer that shows amount, time, degree, direction, etc. The face of a clock or of a compass is a dial. A dial may show the amount of water in a tank or the amount of steam pressure in a boiler. 2 plate or disk with numbers or letters on it for tuning in to a radio or television station. 3 tune in by using a radio or television dial: *He dials his favorite station every morning.* 4 a movable disk on some telephones mounted over a larger disk with letters and numbers and used to signal the number being called. 5 call by means of a telephone dial: *She dialed the wrong number.* 6 plate or disk on a lock, with numbers or letters on it, used for opening the lock. 7 turn such a dial in order to open a lock: *She dialed the combination to open her locker.* 8 sundial. 1,2,4,6,8 *n.*, 3,5,7 *v.*

di a lect (dī′ə lekt), a form of speech spoken in a certain district or by a certain group of people: *The Scottish dialect of English has many words and pronunciations that Americans do not use. A dialect of French is spoken in southern Louisiana by descendants of French Canadians.* *n.*

di a lec tal (dī′ə lek′təl), of a dialect; like that of a dialect. *adj.*

di a logue or **di a log** (dī′ə lôg), **1** conversation: *Two actors had a dialogue in the middle of the stage.* **2** conversation written out: *That book has a good plot and much clever dialogue.* n. [*Dialogue* is from Greek *dialogos,* which comes from *dia-,* meaning "between," and *logos,* meaning "speech."]

di am e ter (dī am′ə tər), **1** a line segment passing from one side through the center of a circle, sphere, etc., to the other side. **2** the length of such a line segment; measurement from one side to the other through the center; width; thickness: *The diameter of the earth is about 8000 miles.* n.

diameter (def. 1)
Line AB is a diameter.

di a met ric (dī′ə met′rik), **1** of or along a diameter. **2** exactly opposite: *The two candidates have diametric opinions on that issue.* adj.

di a met ri cal (dī′ə met′rə kəl), diametric. adj.

di a met ri cal ly (dī′ə met′rik lē), **1** as a diameter. **2** directly; exactly; entirely: *You and I have diametrically opposed views.* adv.

dia mond (dī′mənd or dī′ə mənd), **1** a colorless or tinted precious stone, formed of pure carbon in crystals. Diamond is the hardest natural substance known. Inferior diamonds are used to cut glass. **2** figure shaped like this: ◇. **3** a playing card marked with one or more red, diamond-shaped figures. **4 diamonds,** pl. suit of such playing cards. **5** (in baseball) the area bounded by home plate and the three bases; infield. n. —**dia′mond like′,** adj.

dia mond back (dī′mənd bak′ or dī′ə mənd bak′), a large rattlesnake with diamond-shaped markings on its back, found in the southern and western United States. n.

diamondback
3 to 6 ft.
(1 to 2 m.) long

Di an a (dī an′ə), (in Roman myths) the goddess of the hunt and of the moon. The Greeks called her Artemis. n.

di a per (dī′ə pər or dī′pər), **1** piece of cloth or other soft material folded and used as underpants for a baby. **2** put a diaper on: *diaper the baby after his bath.* 1 n., 2 v.

di aph a nous (dī af′ə nəs), transparent: *Gauze is a diaphanous fabric.* adj. —**di aph′a nous ly,** adv.

di a phragm (dī′ə fram), **1** a partition of muscles and tendons separating the cavity of the chest from the cavity of the abdomen. **2** a thin dividing partition. **3** a thin disk that vibrates rapidly when receiving or producing sounds, used in telephones, loudspeakers, microphones, and other instruments. **4** disk with a hole in the center

a hat	i it	oi oil	ch child	a in about
ā age	ī ice	ou out	ng long	e in taken
ä far	o hot	u cup	sh she	ə = i in pencil
e let	ō open	u̇ put	th thin	o in lemon
ē equal	ô order	ü rule	ŦH then	u in circus
ėr term			zh measure	

for controlling the amount of light entering a camera, microscope, etc. n.

di ar rhe a (dī′ə rē′ə), condition of having too many and too loose movements of the bowels. n.

di ar y (dī′ər ē), **1** account written down each day of what has happened to one, or what one has done or thought, during that day. **2** book for keeping such a daily account. It has a blank space for each day of the year. n., pl. **di ar ies.**

di a stol ic pressure (dī′ə stol′ik), the blood pressure measured when the heart is at rest as it refills after pumping blood. Diastolic pressure is lower than systolic pressure.

di a tom (dī′ə tom), any of numerous microscopic, one-celled algae that have hard shells. n.

di a ton ic (dī′ə ton′ik), of or using only the eight tones of a standard major or minor musical scale. adj.

di a tribe (dī′ə trīb), a speech or discussion bitterly and violently denouncing some person or thing. n.

dibs (dibz), SLANG. a claim: *I have dibs on the cake.* n.pl.

dice (dīs), **1** small cubes with a different number of spots (one to six) on each side. Dice are used in playing some games and in gambling. **2** game played with these. **3** cut into small cubes: *Carrots are sometimes diced before they are cooked.* 1,2 n. pl. of **die²;** 3 v., **diced, dic ing.**

Dick ens (dik′ənz), **Charles,** 1812-1870, English novelist. n.

dick er (dik′ər), **1** trade by barter or by petty bargaining; haggle: *She dickered with the butcher over the price of the steaks.* **2** a petty bargain. 1 v., 2 n.

WORD HISTORY

dicker

Dicker used to mean "a group of ten hides" in English. Hides were often used in bartering or trading. *Dicker* is from Latin *decuria,* meaning "a set of ten," which comes from *decem,* meaning "ten."

dick ey (dik′ē), **1** a shirt front that can be detached. **2** an insert worn at the neck opening of a blouse, jacket, etc. n., pl. **dick eys.**

Dick in son (dik′ən sən), **Emily,** 1830-1886, American poet. n.

di cot y le don (dī kot′l ēd′n), a flowering plant that has two cotyledons or seed leaves. Many trees and most cultivated plants are dicotyledons. n.

dict., dictionary.

dic ta (dik′tə), a plural of **dictum.** n.

dic tate (dik′tāt), **1** say or read aloud to another person who writes down the words: *The teacher dictated a list of books to the students. She dictates letters to her secretary each morning.* **2** speak with authority; give a direction or order that must be carried out or obeyed: *The country that won the war dictated the terms of peace to the country that lost.* **3** command given with authority; order that must be obeyed: *the dictates of a ruler.* **1,2** *v.,* **dic tat ed, dic tat ing; 3** *n.*

dic ta tion (dik tā′shən), **1** words said or read aloud to another person who writes them down: *The secretary took the dictation in shorthand and typed it out later.* **2** act of giving orders or making rules: *She was tired of her sister's constant dictation and refused to obey her.* *n.*

dic ta tor (dik′tā tər), **1** person who uses absolute authority: *The dictator seized control of the government and took complete power over the people of the country.* **2** person who says or reads something aloud for another to write down. *n.*

dic ta to ri al (dik′tə tôr′ē əl), **1** of or like that of a dictator: *That country has a dictatorial government.* **2** fond of commanding and giving orders; domineering; overbearing: *I dislike anyone who has a dictatorial manner. adj.* —**dic′ta to′ri al ly,** *adv.*

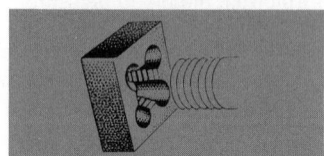

die[2] (def. 1)
for cutting
threads of bolts

dic ta tor ship (dik′tā tər ship), **1** position or rank of a dictator. **2** period of time a dictator rules. **3** absolute authority; power to give orders that must be obeyed. *n.*

dic tion (dik′shən), **1** manner of expressing ideas in words; style of speaking or writing. Good diction implies a skillful choice of words accurately used to express clearly the speaker's or writer's ideas. **2** manner of pronouncing words; enunciation: *That radio announcer is easy to understand because of her clear diction. n.*

dic tion ar y (dik′shə ner′ē), book that explains the words of a language or of some special subject. It is arranged alphabetically. You can use this dictionary to find out the meaning, spelling, or pronunciation of a word. A medical dictionary explains words used in medicine. A German-English dictionary translates German words into English. A biographical dictionary has accounts of people's lives arranged in alphabetical order of their names. *n., pl.* **dic tion ar ies.**

dic tum (dik′təm), **1** a formal comment; authoritative opinion: *The dictum of the critics was that the play was excellent.* **2** maxim; saying: *The old dictum says that love is blind. n., pl.* **dic tums** or **dic ta.** [*Dictum* is from Latin *dictum,* meaning "(a thing) said," which comes from *dicere,* meaning "to say." See **Word Family.**]

WORD FAMILY

dictum

Below are words related to *dictum.* They can all be traced back to the Latin word *dicere* (dē′ke re), meaning "to say."

addict	ditto	jurisdiction
adjudge	ditty	malediction
benediction	edict	predict
condition	indict	vendetta
contradict	interdict	vengeance
dictate	judge	verdict
dictator	judgment	vindicate
diction	judiciary	vindictive
dictionary	judicious	

did (did), past tense of **do**[1]. *I did my work yesterday. v.*

di dac tic (dī dak′tik), **1** meant to instruct: *Aesop's "Fables" are didactic stories; each one has a moral.* **2** inclined to instruct others; teacherlike: *They called their older brother "Professor" because of his didactic manner. adj.* —**di dac′ti cal ly,** *adv.*

did n't (did′nt), did not.

didst (didst), OLD USE. did. "Thou didst" means "You did." *v.*

die[1] (dī), **1** stop living; become dead: *The flowers in the garden died from frost.* **2** lose force or strength; come to an end; stop: *The motor sputtered and died.* **3** INFORMAL. want very much: *I'm dying for an ice-cream cone. v.,* **died, dy ing.**

die away or **die down,** stop or end little by little: *The music died away.*

die[2] (dī), **1** tool for shaping, cutting, punching, or stamping things. It is usually a carved metal block or plate. Dies are used for coining money and for raising printing up from the surface of paper. **2** one of a set of dice. *n., pl.* **dies** for 1, **dice** for 2.

the die is cast, the decision is made and cannot be changed.

die-hard (dī′härd′), **1** resisting to the very end; refusing to give in: *The Senator was a die-hard opponent of any changes in the Constitution.* **2** person who refuses to give in. 1 *adj.,* 2 *n.*

di er e sis (dī er′ə sis), two dots (¨) placed over the second of two consecutive vowels to indicate that the second vowel is to be pronounced in a separate syllable. EXAMPLES. Noël, naïve. *n., pl.* **di er e ses** (dī er′ə sēz′).

die sel or **Die sel** (dē′zəl), **1** a diesel engine. **2** equipped with or run by a diesel engine: *a diesel locomotive, a diesel tractor.* **3** truck, locomotive, train, etc., with a diesel engine. **4** of or for a diesel engine: *diesel fuel.* 1,3 *n.,* 2,4 *adj.* [*Diesel* was named after Rudolf *Diesel,* 1858-1913, a German engineer, who invented this form of engine.]

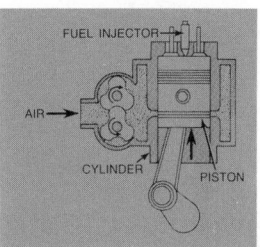

diesel engine
Air entering the cylinder is compressed by the piston and gets very hot. A jet of oil sprayed into the compressed air burns, causing a forceful expansion of the gas, which forces the piston downward.

diesel engine or **Diesel engine,** an internal-combustion engine that burns oil with heat caused by the compression of air.

di et[1] (dī′ət), **1** the usual kind of food and drink: *My diet is made up of meat, fish, vegetables, fruits, water, and milk. Grass is a large part of a cow's diet.* **2** a special kind of food eaten because one is sick, or to lose or gain weight: *While I was sick I was on a liquid diet.* **3** have a special kind of food as a part of a doctor's treatment, or in order to lose or gain weight: *I'm dieting, so don't give me any cake.* 1,2 *n.,* 3 *v.* [*Diet*[1] came into English about 700 years ago from French *diete,* and can be traced back to Greek *diaita,* meaning "way of life."] —**di′et er,** *n.*

di et[2] (dī′ət), **1** a formal assembly for discussion. **2** the national lawmaking body in certain countries. Switzerland and Japan are governed by diets. *n.* [*Diet*[2] is from a medieval Latin word *dieta,* meaning "day's work, meeting of councilors," which comes from *dies,* meaning "day."]

di e tar y (dī′ə ter′ē), of diet: *Dietary rules tell what foods to eat for healthy living and how to prepare them. adj.*

di e tet ic (dī/ə tet/ik), of diet or dietetics: *Many dietetic foods are without sugar, salt, or fats. adj.* —**di/e tet/i cal ly,** *adv.*

di e tet ics (dī/ə tet/iks), science that deals with the amount and kinds of food needed by the body. *n.*

di e ti tian or **di e ti cian** (dī/ə tish/ən), person trained to plan meals that have the right amount of various kinds of food. Many hospitals and schools employ dietitians. *n.*

dif fer (dif/ər), **1** be unlike; be different: *My answer to the arithmetic problem differs from yours.* **2** have or express a different opinion; disagree: *The two of us differ about how we should spend the money. v.*

dif fer ence (dif/ər əns), **1** a being different: *the difference between night and day.* **2** way of being different; point in which people or things are different: *The only difference between the twins is that Jane weights five pounds more than Sue.* **3** amount by which one quantity is different from another; what is left after subtracting one number from another: *The difference between 6 and 15 is 9.* **4** condition of having a different opinion; disagreement; quarrel: *The children had a difference over a name for the new puppy. n.*

make a difference, have an effect or influence; be important; matter: *Your vote will make a difference in the election.*

dif fer ent (dif/ər ənt), **1** not alike; not like: *We saw different kinds of animals at the zoo. A boat is different from an automobile.* **2** not the same; separate; distinct: *I saw her three different times today.* **3** not like others or most others; unusual: *Our teacher is quite different; he never gives us homework. adj.* —**dif/fer ent ly,** *adv.*

dif fe ren tial (dif/ə ren/shəl), of a difference; showing a difference; depending on a difference: *The differential rates in freight charges are for carrying heavier packages longer distances. adj.* —**dif/fe ren/tial ly,** *adv.*

differential gear, arrangement of gears in an automobile that allows one of the rear wheels to turn faster than the other in going around a corner or curve.

dif fe ren ti ate (dif/ə ren/shē āt), **1** make different; cause to have differences: *Consideration for others differentiates a thoughtful person from a thoughtless one.* **2** tell the difference in or between; find or show to be different: *Some color-blind people cannot differentiate red from green. v.,* **dif fe ren ti at ed, dif fe ren ti at ing.**

dif fe ren ti a tion (dif/ə ren/shē ā/shən), act or process of differentiating; alteration; modification; distinction. *n.*

dif fi cult (dif/ə kult), **1** hard to do or understand: *Cutting down the tree was difficult. Arithmetic is difficult for some pupils.* **2** hard to deal with or get along with; not easy to please: *My cousins are difficult and always want their own way. adj.* —**dif/fi cult ly,** *adv.*

dif fi cul ty (dif/ə kul/tē), **1** fact or condition of being difficult; degree to which something is difficult: *The difficulty of the job prevented us from finishing it on time.* **2** hard work; much effort: *I walked with difficulty after I sprained my ankle.* **3** something which stands in the way of getting things done; thing that is hard to do or understand: *Lack of time and money were difficulties we had to overcome.* **4** trouble: *Some children have difficulty learning how to spell. She has been in financial difficulty since she lost her job. n., pl.* **dif fi cul ties.**

dif fi dence (dif/ə dəns), lack of self-confidence; shyness: *His diffidence disappeared after he knew us awhile. n.*

dif fi dent (dif/ə dənt), lacking in self-confidence; shy. *adj.* —**dif/fi dent ly,** *adv.*

dif frac tion (di frak/shən), **1** a spreading of light around an obstacle into a series of light and dark bands or into the colored bands of the spectrum. **2** a similar spreading of sound waves, electricity, etc. *n.*

a hat	**i** it	**oi** oil	**ch** child	a in about	
ā age	**ī** ice	**ou** out	**ng** long	e in taken	
ä far	**o** hot	**u** cup	**sh** she	ə = i in pencil	
e let	**ō** open	**u** put	**th** thin	o in lemon	
ē equal	**ô** order	**ü** rule	**ŦH** then	u in circus	
ėr term			**zh** measure		

dif fuse (di fyüz/ *for 1;* di fyüs/ *for 2,3*), **1** spread out so as to cover a large space or surface; scatter widely: *The sun diffuses light and heat. Schools and libraries diffuse knowledge.* **2** not drawn together at a single point; spread out: *a diffuse light.* **3** using many words where a few would do; wordy: *A diffuse book is often tiresome to read.* **1** *v.,* **dif fused, dif fus ing;** **2,3** *adj.* —**dif fuse/ly,** *adv.*

dif fu sion (di fyü/zhən), **1** a spreading or scattering widely: *The invention of printing greatly increased the diffusion of knowledge.* **2** a being widely spread or scattered. **3** a mixing together by spreading into one another: *the diffusion of gases or liquids.* **4** use of too many words; wordiness. *n.*

dig (dig), **1** use a shovel, spade, hands, claws, or snout to make a hole or to turn over the ground: *Dogs bury bones and dig for them later.* **2** make by digging: *dig a well. The workers dug a cellar.* **3** make a way by digging: *They dug through the mountain to build a tunnel.* **4** get by digging: *dig potatoes. We dug clams at the beach yesterday.* **5** make a thrust or stab into; prod: *The cat dug its claws into my hand.* **6** a thrust or poke: *I gave my friend a dig in the ribs.* **7** a sarcastic remark: *The candidate made a dig at his opponent.* **8** make a careful search or inquiry: *The writer dug into the family records for the story of her pioneer ancestors.* **9** INFORMAL. work or study hard. **10** SLANG. understand; appreciate: *I dig what you're trying to tell me. I dig that group's music.* **1-5,8-10** *v.,* **dug, dig ging; 6,7** *n.*

di gest (də jest/ *or* dī jest/ *for 1,2;* dī/jest *for 3*), **1** change (food) in the stomach and intestines so that the body can use it: *The body digests fats slowly.* **2** think over (something) until you understand it clearly, or until it becomes a part of your thoughts: *It often takes a long time to digest new ideas.* **3** a brief statement of what is in a longer book, article, or statement; summary. **1,2** *v.,* **3** *n.*

di gest i ble (də jes/tə bəl *or* dī jes/tə bəl), capable of being digested; easily digested. *adj.*

di ges tion (də jes/chən *or* dī jes/chən), **1** the digesting of food: *Proper digestion is necessary for good health.* **2** ability to digest food: *A person's digestion can be affected by illness. n.*

di ges tive (də jes/tiv *or* dī jes/tiv), **1** of or for digestion: *The stomach is an important digestive organ.* **2** helping digestion: *digestive tablets. adj.*

dig gings (dig/ingz), **1** mine, archaeological site, or other place where digging is being done. **2** material that is dug out. **3** INFORMAL. place to live. *n.pl.*

dig it (dij/it), **1** any of the figures 0, 1, 2, 3, 4, 5, 6, 7, 8, 9. Sometimes 0 is not called a digit. **2** finger or toe. *n.*

dig it al (dij/ə təl), **1** of or made up of digits: *Digital telephone numbers, such as 223-2000, have replaced most of the old letter and number combinations.* **2** showing time, temperature, or other information by digits, rather than by positions of hands on a dial: *a digital clock. adj.*

digital computer, kind of computer which represents all information and instructions in the form of numbers, usually binary digits.

dig i tal is (dij/ə tal/is), **1** medicine used for stimulating the heart, obtained from the dried leaves of some varieties of foxglove. **2** foxglove. *n.*

dig ni fied (dig/nə fīd), having dignity; noble; stately: *The queen has a dignified manner. adj.*

dig ni fy (dig/nə fī), give dignity to; make noble, worthwhile, or worthy: *The simple farmhouse was dignified by the great elms around it.* v., **dig ni fied, dig ni fy ing.**

dig ni tar y (dig′nə ter′ē), person who has a position of honor: *We saw several foreign dignitaries when we visited the United Nations.* n., pl. **dig ni tar ies.**

dig ni ty (dig′nə tē), **1** proud and self-respecting character or manner; stateliness: *the dignity of a cathedral. The candidate maintained her dignity during the heated debate.* **2** degree of worth, honor, or importance: *A judge should maintain the dignity of his or her position.* **3** a high office, rank, or title; position of honor: *The candidate hoped to attain the dignity of the presidency.* **4** worth; nobleness: *Honest work has dignity.* n., pl. **dig ni ties.**

di gress (də gres′ or dī gres′), turn aside from the main subject in talking or writing: *I lost interest in the book because the author digressed too much.* v.

di gres sion (də gresh′ən or dī gresh′ən), a digressing; turning aside from the main subject in talking or writing: *The speaker's many digressions made the lecture longer than usual.* n.

dike (dīk), **1** a bank of earth or a dam built as a defense against flooding by a river or the sea. **2** provide with a dike or dikes. **1** n., **2** v., **diked, dik ing.** Also, **dyke.** [*Dike* comes from Old English *dīc.*] **—dik′er,** n.

di lap i dat ed (də lap′ə dā′tid), falling to pieces; partly ruined or decayed through neglect: *The ghost town was full of dilapidated houses.* adj.

di lap i da tion (də lap′ə dā′shən), a partial ruin; a falling to pieces. n.

di late (dī lāt′), make or become larger or wider: *When you take a deep breath, you dilate your nostrils. The pupil of the eye dilates when the light gets dim.* v., **di lat ed, di lat ing.**

di la tion (dī lā′shən), a dilating or a being dilated; enlargement; widening: *The dilation of her pupils was the result of applying drops to her eyes.* n.

dil a to ry (dil′ə tôr′ē), **1** tending to delay; not prompt: *People who are dilatory in paying their bills are poor customers.* **2** causing delay: *The carpenter's dilatory work habits held up the completion of the building for weeks.* adj. **—dil′a to′ri ly,** adv.

di lem ma (də lem′ə), situation requiring a choice between two evils; difficult choice: *She was faced with the dilemma of either telling a lie or betraying a friend.* n., pl. **di lem mas.**

dil et tante (dil′ə tänt or dil′ə tan′tē), person who follows some art or science without knowing or learning much about it; dabbler: *He was a dilettante in a dozen fields, an expert in none.* n., pl. **dil et tantes, dil et tan ti** (dil′ə tän′tē or dil′ə tan′tē).

dil i gence (dil′ə jəns), working hard; careful and steady effort; industry: *The student's diligence was rewarded with high marks.* n.

dil i gent (dil′ə jənt), **1** hard-working; industrious: *The diligent student kept on working until he had finished his homework.* **2** careful and steady: *The detective made a diligent search for clues.* adj. **—dil′i gent ly,** adv.

dill (dil), **1** plant whose spicy seeds or leaves are used to flavor pickles. **2** its seeds or leaves. n. [*Dill* comes from Old English *dile.*]

dill pickle, a cucumber pickle flavored with dill.

dil ly dal ly (dil′ē dal′ē), waste time; loiter; trifle: *Let's not dillydally over such unimportant matters.* v., **dil ly dal lied, dil ly dal ly ing.**

di lute (də lüt′ or dī lüt′), **1** make weaker or thinner by adding water or some other liquid: *You must dilute the concentrated orange juice with several cups of water.* **2** weakened or thinned by the addition of water or some other liquid: *a dilute acid.* **3** weaken; lessen: *The high price of a new car diluted our enthusiasm for buying one.*

1,3 v., **di lut ed, di lut ing;** 2 adj. **—di lut′er,** n.

di lu tion (də lü′shən or dī lü′shən), **1** a diluting or a being diluted. **2** something diluted. n.

dim (dim), **1** not bright; not clear; not distinct: *the dim light of dusk. With the shades drawn, the room was dim.* **2** not clearly seen, heard, or understood; faint: *We could see only the dim outline of the mountain in the distance. That happened so long ago that I have only a dim recollection of it.* **3** not seeing, hearing, or understanding clearly: *Grandfather's eyesight is getting dim.* **4** INFORMAL. unfavorable: *She takes a dim view of our chances of winning the game.* **5** make or become dim: *She dimmed the car's headlights as the other car approached. The lights in the house dimmed several times during the storm.* 1-4 adj., **dim mer, dim mest;** 5 v., **dimmed, dim ming.** **—dim′ly,** adv. **—dim′ness,** n.

dime (dīm), **1** a copper and nickel coin of the United States, worth 10 cents. **2** a similar coin of Canada, worth 10 cents. n. [*Dime* came into English about 600 years ago from French *disme,* meaning "a tenth part," and can be traced back to Latin *decem,* meaning "ten."]

di men sion (də men′shən), **1** measurement of length, breadth, or thickness: *I need wallpaper for a room of the following dimensions: 16 ft. long, 12 ft. wide, 9 ft. high.* **2** Also, **dimensions,** pl. size; extent: *Building a park in the slum area was a project of large dimensions.* n.

dime store, store selling a large variety of low-priced things.

di min ish (də min′ish), make or become smaller; lessen; reduce; decrease: *The poor harvest so diminished the food supply that people were starving. A sound diminishes as you get farther and farther away from it.* v.

di min u en do (də min′yü en′dō), decrescendo. n., pl. **di min u en dos;** adj., adv.

dim i nu tion (dim′ə nü′shən or dim′ə nyü′shən), a diminishing; lessening; reduction; decrease: *The colonists fought to prevent any diminution of their rights by the king.* n.

di min u tive (də min′yə tiv), very small; tiny; minute: *The dollhouse contained diminutive furniture.* adj. **—di min′u tive ly,** adv. **—di min′u tive ness,** n.

"I dabble in so many things—
I paint, I write, I strum on strings.
I do exactly what I want;
I'm not an expert but a **dilettante**."

dim i ty (dim′ə tē), a thin cotton cloth woven with heavy threads in striped or checked arrangement, used for dresses, curtains, etc. n., pl. **dim i ties.**

dim mer (dim′ər), **1** person or thing that dims. **2** device that dims an electric light. n.

dimples (def. 1)

a hat	**i** it	**oi** oil	**ch** child	a in about
ā age	**ī** ice	**ou** out	**ng** long	e in taken
ä far	**o** hot	**u** cup	**sh** she	ə = i in pencil
e let	**ō** open	**ù** put	**th** thin	o in lemon
ē equal	**ô** order	**ü** rule	**ŦH** then	u in circus
ėr term			**zh** measure	

dim ple (dim′pəl), **1** a small hollow place in the skin. A dimple is usually in a person's cheek or chin. **2** any small, hollow place. **3** make or show dimples in: *The shower dimpled the surface of the pond.* **4** form dimples: *He dimples whenever he smiles.* 1,2 *n.*, 3,4 *v.*, **dim pled, dim pling.**

din (din), **1** a loud, confused noise that lasts: *The din of the cheering crowd was deafening.* **2** make a din. **3** say over and over again; repeat in a tiresome way: *Our boss was always dinning into our ears the importance of hard work.* 1 *n.*, 2,3 *v.* **dinned, din ning.**

di nar (di när′), unit of money in Yugoslavia, Iraq, Jordan, Kuwait, Southern Yemen, Algeria, and Tunisia. *n.*

dine (dīn), **1** eat dinner: *We usually dine at six o'clock.* **2** give dinner to; give a dinner for: *The Chamber of Commerce dined the famous traveler.* *v.*, **dined, din ing.** [*Dine* came into English about 700 years ago from French *disner,* meaning "to breakfast," and can be traced back to Latin *dis-,* meaning "not," and *jejunus,* meaning "fasting."]

din er (dī′nər), **1** person who is eating dinner. **2** a railroad car in which meals are served. **3** a small eating place, that often looks like such a car. *n.*

di nette (dī net′), a small dining room. *n.*

ding (ding), **1** make the sound of a bell; ring continuously. **2** this sound. 1 *v.*, 2 *n.*

ding-dong (ding′dông′), sound made by the continuous ringing of a bell. *n.*

din ghy (ding′ē), **1** a small rowboat. **2** a small boat used as a tender by a large boat. *n., pl.* **din ghies.** [*Dinghy* comes from Hindustani *dingī.*]

din gi ness (din′jē nis), a being dingy; lack of cleanness and freshness. *n.*

dingo
about 2 ft. (60 cm.)
at the shoulder

din go (ding′gō), a wolflike wild dog of Australia. *n., pl.* **din goes.**

ding us (ding′əs), SLANG. thing whose name is unknown, unfamiliar, or forgotten. *n.*

din gy (din′jē), lacking brightness or freshness; dirty-looking; dull: *Dingy curtains covered the windows of the dusty old room. adj.,* **din gi er, din gi est. —din′gi ly,** *adv.*

dining car, diner.

dining room, room in which dinner and other meals are served.

dink y (ding′kē), INFORMAL. small and insignificant. *adj.,* **dink i er, dink i est.**

din ner (din′ər), **1** the main meal of the day: *In the city we have dinner at night, but in the country we have dinner at noon.* **2** a formal meal in honor of some person or occasion: *The city officials gave the mayor a dinner to celebrate his reelection. n.*

di no saur (dī′nə sôr), any of a group of extinct reptiles that dominated the earth many millions of years ago. Dinosaurs walked on two or four feet. Some dinosaurs were bigger than elephants; others were smaller than cats. *n.*

dint (dint), force: *By dint of hard work we finished the job on time. n.*

di o cese (dī′ə sis *or* dī′ə sēs′), church district over which a bishop has authority; bishopric; see. *n.*

Di og e nes (dī oj′ə nēz′), 412?-323 B.C., Greek philosopher who lived in a tub to show his belief in simplicity. *n.*

diorama—Features of daily life are shown in this diorama of an early North American village.

di o ram a (dī′ə ram′ə), scene or exhibit showing a group of lifelike sculptured figures of animals, people, etc., and surrounding objects against a painted or modeled background. *n., pl.* **di o ram as.**

di ox ide (dī ok′sīd), oxide having two atoms of oxygen for each molecule. *n.*

dip (dip), **1** put under water or any liquid and lift quickly out again: *She dipped her hand into the pool to see how cold the water was.* **2** go under water and come quickly out again: *She dipped a few times in the ocean to cool herself off.* **3** a dipping of any kind, especially a quick plunge into and out of a tub of water, the sea, etc.: *She felt refreshed after her dip in the ocean.* **4** liquid in which to dip something for washing or cleaning: *The sheep were driven through a dip to disinfect their coats.* **5** make (a candle) by putting a wick over and over into hot tallow or wax. **6** take up in the hollow of the hand or with a pail, pan, or other container: *dip water from a bucket, dip up a sample of wheat.* **7** put (one's hand, a spoon, etc.) into to take out something: *He dipped into the jar and snatched a handful of cookies.* **8** a creamy mixture of foods eaten by dipping into with a cracker, piece of bread, etc.: *a cheese dip.* **9** lower and raise again quickly: *The ship's flag was dipped as a salute.* **10** sink or drop

down: *The bird dipped low over the water in its flight.*
11 slope downward: *The road dips into the valley.* **12** a
sudden drop: *a dip in prices. The dip in the road made the
car bounce.* 1,2,5-7,9-11 *v.,* **dipped, dip ping;** 3,4,8,12 *n.*
[*Dip* comes from Old English *dyppan.*]

dip into, read or look at for a short time; glance at: *dip
into a book on astronomy.*

diph ther i a (dif thir′ē ə *or* dip thir′ē ə), a dangerous,
infectious disease of the throat caused by bacteria. It is
usually accompanied by a high fever and formation of a
membrane that hinders respiration. *n.*

diph thong (dif′thông *or* dip′thông), a vowel sound
made up of two vowel sounds pronounced in one syllable, such as *ou* in *house* or *oi* in *noise. n.*

di plo ma (də plō′mə), a written or printed paper given
by a school, college, or university, which states that a
person has completed a certain course of study or has
been graduated after a certain amount of work. *n., pl.*
di plo mas.

di plo ma cy (də plō′mə sē), **1** the handling of relations
between nations. The making of treaties and international agreements is an important part of diplomacy. **2** skill
in handling such relations: *The statesman's great diplomacy prevented an outbreak of war between the two countries.*
3 skill in dealing with people; tact: *By using diplomacy we
got to use the family car that night. n., pl.* **di plo ma cies.**

dip lo mat (dip′lə mat), **1** person whose work is to handle the relations between his or her nation and other
nations. **2** person who is skillful in dealing with others;
tactful person. *n.*

dip lo mat ic (dip′lə mat′ik), **1** of or having to do with
diplomacy: *Ambassadors are the highest-ranking members
of the diplomatic service.* **2** having or showing skill in
dealing with others; tactful: *He gave a diplomatic answer
to avoid hurting his friend's feelings. adj.* —**dip′lo mat′i-
cal ly,** *adv.*

dip per (dip′ər), **1** a cup-shaped container with a long
handle for dipping water or other liquids. **2 Dipper,**
either of two groups of stars in the northern sky somewhat resembling the shape of a dipper; Big Dipper or
Little Dipper. *n.*

dire (dīr), causing great fear or suffering; dreadful: *the
dire results of an earthquake, people in dire poverty. adj.,*
dir er, dir est. —**dire′ly,** *adv.* —**dire′ness,** *n.*

di rect (də rekt′ *or* dī rekt′), **1** have authority or control
over; manage or guide: *The teacher directs the work of the
class.* **2** order; command: *The policeman directed the traffic to stop.* **3** tell or show the way: *Can you direct me to
the airport?* **4** point or aim: *Direct the hose at the flames.
We should be directing our efforts to the problem at hand.*
5 put the address on (a letter or package). **6** address
(words, etc.) to a person: *Direct all your questions to her.*
7 without a stop or turn; straight: *A bee makes a direct
flight to the hive.* **8** in an unbroken line of descent: *That
man is a direct descendant of John Adams.* **9** without anyone or anything in between; not through others; immediate: *Selling door to door is direct selling. The new teacher
took direct charge of the library.* **10** straightforward; frank;
plain; truthful: *She gave direct answers to all the questions.*

11 exact; absolute: *the direct opposite.* **12** directly: *This
plane flies direct from Chicago to Los Angeles without
stopping.* 1-6 *v.,* 7-11 *adj.,* 12 *adv.* —**di rect′ness,** *n.*

direct current, an electric current that flows in one
direction only. Batteries produce direct current.

di rec tion (də rek′shən *or* dī rek′shən), **1** a directing;
managing or guiding: *the direction of a play or movie. The
school is under the direction of the principal.* **2** order; command: *It was her direction that I prepare a report.* **3** Also,
directions, *pl.* a knowing or telling what to do, how to
do something, where to go, etc.; instructions: *Can you
give me directions for driving to Chicago?* **4** course taken
by a moving body, such as a ball or a bullet. **5** any way
in which one may face or point. North, south, east, and
west are directions. *The school is in one direction from our
house and the post office is in another.* **6** course along
which something moves; way of moving; tendency: *The
town shows improvement in many directions. n.* —**di-
rec′tion less,** *adj.*

di rec tion al (də rek′shə nəl *or* dī rek′shə nəl), **1** of, having to do with, or indicating direction: *the directional
signals of an automobile.* **2** sending or receiving radio,
television, or radar signals in or from a particular direction: *a directional antenna. adj.*

di rec tive (də rek′tiv *or* dī rek′tiv), order or instruction
telling what to do, how to do something, where to go,
etc.: *The principal sent a directive to all the teachers. n.*

di rect ly (də rekt′lē *or* dī rekt′lē), **1** in a direct line or
manner; straight: *This road runs directly into the center of
town.* **2** exactly; absolutely: *directly opposite.* **3** at once;
immediately: *Come home directly! adv.*

direct object, (in grammar) word or words showing
the person or thing undergoing the action expressed by
the verb.

di rec tor (də rek′tər *or* dī rek′tər), **1** person who directs;
manager. A person who directs the performance of a
play, a motion picture, or a television or radio show is
called a director. **2** one of a group of persons who direct
the affairs of a company or institution. *n.*

di rec tor y (də rek′tər ē *or* dī rek′tər ē), list of names
and addresses, usually in alphabetical order. A telephone book is a directory of people who have telephones. *n., pl.* **di rec tor ies.**

dire ful (dīr′fəl), dire; dreadful; terrible. *adj.* —**dire′ful-
ly,** *adv.* —**dire′ful ness,** *n.*

dirge (dėrj), a funeral song or tune. *n.* [*Dirge* comes from
Latin *dirige,* meaning "direct," the first word in a church
prayer for the dead.] —**dirge′like′,** *adj.*

dir i gi ble (dir′ə jə bəl), a kind of balloon that can be
steered. It has a rigid inner framework and is filled with
gas that is lighter than air. *n.*

dirigible

dirk (dėrk), dagger. *n.*

dirt (dėrt), **1** mud, dust, earth, or anything like them. Dirt soils skin, clothing, houses, or furniture. **2** loose earth or soil. **3** an unclean action, thought, or speech. **4** scandal; gossip. *n.*

dirt-cheap (dėrt′chēp′), very cheap. *adj.*

dirt i ness (dėr′tē nis), dirty condition. *n.*

dirt y (dėr′tē), **1** soiled by dirt; not clean: *Children playing in the mud get dirty.* **2** not clean or pure in action, thought, or speech; low; base. **3** stormy or windy; rough: *The hurricane was the dirtiest weather I ever saw.* **4** not clear or pure in color: *a dirty red.* **5** make or become dirty; soil: *You will dirty your new clothes if you play in the mud.* 1-4 *adj.,* **dirt i er, dirt i est;** 5 *v.,* **dirt ied, dirt y ing.** —**dirt′i ly,** *adv.*

dis-, *prefix.* **1** opposite of; lack of; not: *Dishonest = not honest; opposite of honest. Discomfort = lack of comfort.* **2** do the opposite of: *Disentangle = do the opposite of entangle. Disallow = do the opposite of allow.*

dis., **1** distance. **2** distant.

dis a bil i ty (dis′ə bil′ə tē), **1** lack of ability or power: *The player's disability was due to illness.* **2** something that disables: *Deafness is a disability for a musician. n., pl.* **dis a bil i ties.**

dis a ble (dis ā′bəl), make unable; make unfit for use, action, etc.; cripple: *A sprained wrist disabled the tennis player for three weeks. He was disabled by polio. v.,* **dis a bled, dis a bling.** —**dis a′ble ment,** *n.* —**dis a′bler,** *n.*

dis ad van tage (dis′əd van′tij), **1** lack of advantage; unfavorable condition: *Her shyness was a disadvantage in company.* **2** loss or injury: *The candidate's enemies spread rumors that were to his disadvantage. n.*

dis ad van taged (dis′əd van′tijd), lacking advantages; being in an unfavorable condition: *a disadvantaged child. adj.*

dis ad van ta geous (dis ad′vən tā′jəs), causing disadvantage; unfavorable. *adj.* —**dis ad′van ta′geous ly,** *adv.* —**dis ad′van ta′geous ness,** *n.*

dis af fect ed (dis′ə fek′tid), unfriendly, disloyal, or discontented: *The disaffected crew decided to mutiny. adj.*

dis af fec tion (dis′ə fek′shən), unfriendliness, disloyalty, or discontent: *Poor working conditions caused disaffection among the employees. n.*

dis a gree (dis′ə grē′), **1** fail to agree; be different: *Your account of the accident disagrees with hers.* **2** have unlike opinions; differ: *Doctors sometimes disagree about the proper method of treating a patient.* **3** quarrel; dispute: *The two neighbors never spoke to each other again after they disagreed about their boundary line.* **4** have a bad effect; be harmful: *I can't eat strawberries because they disagree with me. v.,* **dis a greed, dis a gree ing.**

dis a gree a ble (dis′ə grē′ə bəl), **1** not to one's liking; unpleasant: *A headache is disagreeable.* **2** not friendly; bad-tempered; cross: *People often become disagreeable when they're tired. adj.* —**dis′a gree′a ble ness,** *n.*

dis a gree a bly (dis′ə grē′ə blē), in a disagreeable manner; unpleasantly. *adv.*

dis a gree ment (dis′ə grē′mənt), **1** failure to agree; difference of opinion: *The disagreement that existed between members of the jury led to a new trial.* **2** quarrel; dispute: *Their disagreement led to blows.* **3** difference; unlikeness: *There is a disagreement between his account of the accident and mine. n.*

dis al low (dis′ə lou′), refuse to allow; deny the truth or value of; reject: *The court disallowed my claim to the property. v.* —**dis′al low′a ble,** *adj.*

dis ap pear (dis′ə pir′), **1** pass from sight; stop being seen: *The dog disappeared around the corner.* **2** pass from existence; stop being: *When spring comes, the snow disappears. v.*

a hat	i it	oi oil	ch child	a in about
ā age	ī ice	ou out	ng long	e in taken
ä far	o hot	u cup	sh she	ə = { i in pencil
e let	ō open	u̇ put	th thin	o in lemon
ē equal	ô order	ü rule	ᴛʜ then	u in circus
ėr term			zh measure	

dis ap pear ance (dis′ə pir′əns), act of disappearing: *The disappearance of the airplane brought about a search of the entire area. n.*

dis ap point (dis′ə point′), **1** fail to satisfy or please; leave wanting or expecting something: *The circus disappointed me because there were no elephants.* **2** fail to keep a promise to: *You said you would help; do not disappoint me. v.* —**dis′ap point′ing ly,** *adv.*

dis ap point ment (dis′ə point′mənt), **1** a being disappointed; the feeling you have when you do not get what you expected or hoped for: *When she did not get a new bicycle her disappointment was very great.* **2** person or thing that causes disappointment: *The boring movie was a disappointment.* **3** act or fact of disappointing: *Finding that we had not saved enough money led to the disappointment of our hopes for a trip to Europe. n.*

dis ap prov al (dis′ə prü′vəl), opinion or feeling against; expression of an opinion against; dislike: *Hisses from the audience showed its disapproval of the speaker's remarks. n.*

dis ap prove (dis′ə prüv′), **1** have or express an opinion against; show dislike: *Parents often disapprove of rough games in the house.* **2** refuse consent to; reject: *The mayor disapproved the plan. v.,* **dis ap proved, dis ap prov ing.**

dis ap prov ing ly (dis′ə prü′ving lē), in a disapproving manner; with disapproval: *The librarian looked disapprovingly at the children who were talking. adv.*

dis arm (dis ärm′), **1** take weapons away from: *The police captured the robbers and disarmed them.* **2** stop having an army, navy, etc.; reduce a country's armed forces or their weapons: *The nations agreed to disarm.* **3** remove anger or suspicion from; make friendly: *The little boy's smile could always disarm those who were about to scold him.* **4** make harmless: *disarm a bomb by removing the fuse. v.* —**dis arm′er,** *n.* —**dis arm′ing ly,** *adv.*

dis ar ma ment (dis är′mə mənt), reduction of a country's armed forces or their weapons. *n.*

dis ar range (dis′ə rānj′), disturb the arrangement of; put out of order: *The wind disarranged my hair. v.,* **dis ar ranged, dis ar rang ing.** —**dis′ar rang′er,** *n.*

dis ar range ment (dis′ə rānj′mənt), a disarranging or a being disarranged. *n.*

dis ar ray (dis′ə rā′), lack of order; disorder; confusion: *There was disarray on the busy street after the accident. n.*

dis as sem ble (dis′ə sem′bəl), take apart: *The mechanic disassembled the motor to repair it. v.,* **dis as sem bled, dis as sem bling.**

dis as so ci ate (dis′ə sō′shē āt), break association with; separate. *v.,* **dis as so ci at ed, dis as so ci at ing.** —**dis′as so′ci a′tion,** *n.*

dis as ter (də zas′tər), event that causes much suffering or loss; great misfortune such as a destructive fire or an earthquake. *n.*

dis as trous (də zas′trəs), bringing disaster; causing much suffering or loss: *A disastrous hurricane struck the city. adj.* —**dis as′trous ly,** *adv.* —**dis as′trous ness,** *n.*

dis a vow (dis′ə vou′), deny that one knows about, approves of, or is responsible for; disclaim: *The driver disavowed any responsibility for the accident. v.* —**dis′a vow′er,** *n.*

dis a vow al (dis′ə vou′əl), a disavowing; denial. *n.*

dis band (dis band′), **1** break up; dismiss from service:

When peace is declared, armies are disbanded. **2** break ranks; become scattered: *The class disbanded for the summer vacation.* v. —**dis band′ment,** n.

dis bar (dis bär′), take away from (a lawyer) the right to practice law. v., **dis barred, dis bar ring.**

dis bar ment (dis bär′mənt), a disbarring or a being disbarred. n.

dis be lief (dis′bi lēf′), lack of belief; refusal to believe: *When she heard the shocking rumor she immediately expressed disbelief.* n.

dis be lieve (dis′bi lēv′), have no belief in; refuse to believe: *I disbelieved the foolish story.* v., **dis be lieved, dis be liev ing.**

dis be liev er (dis′bi lē′vər), person who disbelieves. n.

dis bur den (dis bėrd′n), relieve of a burden; unburden. v. —**dis bur′den ment,** n.

dis burse (dis bėrs′), pay out: *The treasurer is in charge of disbursing money to pay the club's bills.* v., **dis bursed, dis burs ing.** [*Disburse* came into English about 400 years ago from French *desbourser*, which can be traced back to Latin *dis-*, meaning "not," and *bursa*, meaning "purse."] —**dis burs′er,** n.

dis burse ment (dis bėrs′mənt), **1** a paying out: *Our club treasurer attends to the disbursement of funds.* **2** money paid out: *Disbursements must stay within the budget.* n.

disc (disk), disk. n.

disc., discount.

dis card (dis kärd′ for 1,4; dis′kärd for 2,3,5), **1** give up as useless or not wanted; throw aside: *discard a broken toy, discard a belief.* **2** act of throwing aside as useless or not wanted: *The discard of superstition comes with learning.* **3** thing or things thrown aside as useless or not wanted: *That old book is a discard from the library.* **4** get rid of (playing cards not wanted) by throwing them aside or playing them. **5** the cards thrown aside or played as not wanted. 1,4 v., 2,3,5 n.

dis cern (də zėrn′ or də sėrn′), see clearly; perceive the difference between (two or more things); distinguish or recognize: *Through the fog I could discern a person walking toward me. When there are many conflicting opinions, it is hard to discern the truth.* v. —**dis cern′er,** n.

dis cern i ble (də zėr′nə bəl or də sėr′nə bəl), capable of being discerned: *The island was just discernible through the mist.* adj. —**dis cern′i bly,** adv.

dis cern ing (də zėr′ning or də sėr′ning), keen in seeing and understanding; with good judgment; shrewd. adj. —**dis cern′ing ly,** adv.

dis cern ment (də zėrn′mənt or də sėrn′mənt), **1** keenness in seeing and understanding; good judgment; shrewdness. **2** act of discerning. n.

dis charge (dis chärj′ for 1,3,5,8,11-13,15; dis chärj′ or dis′chärj for 2,4,6,7,9,10,14,16), **1** unload (cargo or passengers) from a ship, train, bus, etc.: *The ship discharged its passengers at the dock.* **2** an unloading: *The discharge of this cargo will not take long.* **3** fire off; shoot: *The policeman discharged his gun at the fleeing robbers. The pistol discharged accidentally.* **4** a firing off of a gun, a blast, etc.: *The discharge of dynamite could be heard for a mile.* **5** release; let go; dismiss: *discharge a patient from a hospital, discharge a lazy employee.* **6** a release; a letting go; a dismissing: *I expect my discharge from the hospital in a few days.* **7** writing that shows a person's release or dismissal; certificate of release: *Many members of the armed services got discharges when the war ended.* **8** give off; let out: *The infection discharged pus.* **9** a giving off; a letting out: *Lightning is a discharge of electricity from the clouds.* **10** thing given off or let out: *a watery discharge from an eye.* **11** come or pour forth: *The river discharged into a bay.* **12** rid of an electric charge; withdraw electricity

from. **13** perform: *I have discharged all the errands I was given.* **14** performance: *All public officials should be honest in the discharge of their duties.* **15** pay: *You discharge a loan when you return the money.* **16** payment: *Money was set aside for the discharge of the debt.* 1,3,5,8,11-13,15 v., 2,4,6,7,9,10,14,16 n. —**dis charge′a ble,** adj. —**dis charg′er,** n.

dis ci ple (də sī′pəl), **1** believer in the thought and teaching of any leader; follower. **2** (in the Bible) one of the followers of Jesus. n.

dis ci pli nar i an (dis′ə plə ner′ē ən), person who enforces discipline or who believes in strict discipline. n.

dis ci pli nar y (dis′ə plə ner′ē), **1** having to do with discipline: *The well-behaved children presented no disciplinary problems.* **2** for discipline; intended to improve discipline: *I will have to take disciplinary measures if you continue to come to work late.* adj.

dis ci pline (dis′ə plin), **1** training, especially training of the mind or character: *Children who have had no discipline are often hard to teach.* **2** a trained condition of order and obedience; order kept among school pupils, soldiers, or members of any group: *When the fire broke out, the students showed good discipline.* **3** bring to a condition of order and obedience; bring under control; train: *The teacher was unable to discipline the unruly class.* **4** a particular system of rules for conduct: *The discipline of a military school is usually strict.* **5** punishment: *A little discipline would do them a world of good.* **6** punish: *They have never disciplined their children unfairly.* 1,2,4,5 n., 3,6 v., **dis ci plined, dis ci plin ing.** —**dis′ci plin er,** n.

disc jockey, INFORMAL. disk jockey.

dis claim (dis klām′), **1** refuse to recognize as one's own; deny connection with: *The motorist disclaimed responsibility for the accident.* **2** give up all claim to: *She disclaimed any share in the inheritance.* v.

dis claim er (dis klā′mər), a disclaiming; denial. n.

dis close (dis klōz′), **1** open to view: *The lifting of the curtain disclosed a beautiful painting.* **2** make known: *This letter discloses a secret.* v., **dis closed, dis clos ing.**

dis clo sure (dis klō′zhər), **1** a disclosing: *disclosure of a secret.* **2** thing disclosed: *The newspaper's disclosures shocked the public.* n.

dis co (dis′kō), INFORMAL. discotheque. n., pl. **dis cos.**

dis col or (dis kul′ər), **1** change or spoil the color of; stain: *Smoke and grime had discolored the building.* **2** become changed in color: *Many materials fade and discolor if exposed to bright sunshine.* v.

dis col or a tion (dis kul′ə rā′shən), **1** a discoloring or a being discolored. **2** a stain. n.

dis com bob u late (dis′kəm bob′yə lāt), INFORMAL. confuse. v., **dis com bob u lat ed, dis com bob u lat ing.**

dis com fit (dis kum′fit), **1** defeat the plans or hopes of; frustrate. **2** embarrass; confuse. v.

dis com fort (dis kum′fərt), **1** lack of comfort; uneasiness: *Embarrassing questions cause discomfort.* **2** thing that causes discomfort: *Mud and cold were the discomforts the campers minded most.* n.

dis com pose (dis′kəm pōz′), disturb the self-possession of; make uneasy; confuse: *The grins of his friends discomposed him when he tried to make his report before the class.* v., **dis com posed, dis com pos ing.**

dis com po sure (dis′kəm pō′zhər), condition of being discomposed; confusion; uneasiness. n.

dis con cert (dis′kən sėrt′), disturb the self-possession of; embarrass greatly; confuse: *I was disconcerted to find that I was wearing two different shoes.* v. —**dis′con cert′ing ly,** adv.

dis con nect (dis′kə nekt′), undo or break the connection of; separate; unfasten: *I pulled out the plug to disconnect the toaster.* v. —**dis′con nec′tion,** n.

dis con nect ed (dis/kə nek/tid), **1** not connected; separate: *Our house and the garage are entirely disconnected.* **2** without order or connection; incoherent; broken: *I cannot tell from her disconnected account of the accident what really happened. adj.* —**dis/con nect/ed ly,** *adv.* —**dis/con nect/ed ness,** *n.*

dis con so late (dis kon/sə lit), without hope; forlorn; unhappy; cheerless: *disconsolate over the death of a friend. adj.* —**dis con/so late ly,** *adv.* —**dis con/so late ness,** *n.*

dis con tent (dis/kən tent/), **1** a dislike of what one has and a desire for something different; uneasy feeling; dissatisfaction: *Low pay and long hours caused discontent among the workers.* **2** dissatisfy; displease. 1 *n.*, 2 *v.* —**dis/con tent/ment,** *n.*

dis con tent ed (dis/kən ten/tid), not contented; not satisfied; displeased and restless: *The discontented workers went on strike. adj.* —**dis/con tent/ed ly,** *adv.* —**dis/con tent/ed ness,** *n.*

dis con tin ue (dis/kən tin/yü), put an end or stop to; give up; stop: *Railroad service discontinued during the strike. I discontinued my subscription to that magazine. v.,* **dis con tin ued, dis con tin u ing.** —**dis/con tin/u a/tion,** *n.*

dis con tin u ous (dis/kən tin/yü əs), not continuous; broken; interrupted. *adj.* —**dis/con tin/u ous ly,** *adv.* —**dis/con tin/u ous ness,** *n.*

dis cord (dis/kôrd), **1** difference of opinion; disagreement; disputing: *Constant argument caused angry discord that spoiled the meeting.* **2** (in music) a lack of harmony in notes sounded at the same time. **3** harsh, clashing sounds. *n.* [*Discord* came into English about 700 years ago from French *discord,* and can be traced back to Latin *dis-,* meaning "apart," and *cordis,* meaning "heart."]

dis cord ance (dis kôrd/ns), discord. *n.*

dis cord ant (dis kôrd/nt), **1** not in agreement; differing; disagreeing: *A quarrel started after several discordant opinions had been expressed.* **2** not in harmony: *a discordant note in music.* **3** harsh; clashing: *the discordant sound of automobile horns honking in a traffic jam. adj.* —**dis cord/ant ly,** *adv.*

dis co theque (dis/kə tek), nightclub where phonograph records are played for dancing. *n.*

dis count (dis/kount), **1** take off a certain amount from (a price): *The store discounts all clothes ten percent.* **2** the amount taken off from a price: *We bought our new TV on sale at a 20 percent discount.* **3** allow for exaggeration in; believe only part of: *You must discount some of what he tells you, for he likes to make up stories.* **4** selling goods at prices below those suggested by manufacturers: *a discount store, a discount house.* 1,3 *v.,* 2 *n.,* 4 *adj.*

dis cour age (dis kėr/ij), **1** take away the courage of; lessen the hope or confidence of; dishearten: *Failing again and again discourages anyone.* **2** try to prevent by disapproving; frown upon: *All their friends discouraged them from sailing their small boat on the ocean.* **3** prevent or hinder: *Fear that it might rain discouraged us from camping out. v.,* **dis cour aged, dis cour ag ing.** —**dis cour/ag ing ly,** *adv.*

dis cour age ment (dis kėr/ij mənt), **1** condition of being or feeling discouraged. **2** something that discourages. **3** act of discouraging. *n.*

dis course (dis/kôrs for 1,2; dis kôrs/ for 3), **1** a formal speech or writing: *Lectures and sermons are discourses.* **2** talk; conversation. **3** to talk; converse. 1,2 *n.,* 3 *v.,* **dis coursed, dis cours ing.**

dis cour te ous (dis kėr/tē əs), not courteous; rude; impolite. *adj.* —**dis cour/te ous ly,** *adv.* —**dis cour/te ous ness,** *n.*

dis cour te sy (dis kėr/tə sē), **1** lack of courtesy; rudeness; impoliteness. **2** a rude or impolite act: *It is a discourtesy to interrupt another person's remarks. n., pl.* **dis cour te sies.**

dis cov er (dis kuv/ər), see or learn of for the first time; find out: *discover a new drug, discover a secret. v.* —**dis cov/er a ble,** *adj.* —**dis cov/er er,** *n.*

dis cov er y (dis kuv/ər ē), **1** act of discovering: *Marie and Pierre Curie's discovery of the element radium occurred in 1898.* **2** something discovered: *One of Benjamin Franklin's discoveries was that lightning is electricity. n., pl.* **dis cov er ies.**

dis cred it (dis kred/it), **1** cast doubt on; destroy belief, faith, or trust in: *The lawyer discredited the witnesses by proving they had been bribed.* **2** loss of belief, faith, or trust; doubt: *cast discredit on a theory.* **3** refuse to believe: *We discredit her because she has lied so often.* **4** do harm to the good name or standing of; give a bad reputation to: *His cheating during tests discredited him among his classmates.* **5** loss of good name or standing: *The player who took a bribe brought discredit upon the team.* **6** person or thing that causes loss of good name or standing: *A dishonest politician is a discredit to all politicians.* 1,3,4 *v.,* 2,5,6 *n.*

dis cred it a ble (dis kred/ə tə bəl), bringing discredit; disgraceful. *adj.*

dis cred it a bly (dis kred/ə tə blē), in a discreditable manner. *adv.*

dis creet (dis krēt/), very careful in speech and action; having or showing good judgment; wisely cautious: *a discreet person, a discreet answer. adj.* —**dis creet/ly,** *adv.* —**dis creet/ness,** *n.*

dis crep an cy (dis krep/ən sē), lack of consistency; difference: *There was a discrepancy in the two reports of the accident. n., pl.* **dis crep an cies.**

dis crete (dis krēt/), distinct from others; separate; individual: *An apple and a stone are discrete objects. adj.*

dis cre tion (dis kresh/ən), **1** great carefulness in speech or action; good judgment; wise caution: *It requires discretion to criticize others without hurting their feelings.* **2** freedom to decide or choose: *It is within the principal's discretion to punish a pupil. n.*

dis cre tion ar y (dis kresh/ə ner/ē), with freedom to decide or choose; left to one's own judgment: *The law gave the mayor certain discretionary powers. adj.*

dis crim i nate (dis krim/ə nāt), **1** make or see a difference; distinguish: *People who are color-blind usually cannot discriminate between red and green.* **2** show a difference in treatment: *It is wrong to discriminate against people because of their race, religion, nationality, or sex. v.,* **dis crim i nat ed, dis crim i nat ing.** —**dis crim/i nate ly,** *adv.* —**dis crim/i na/tor,** *n.*

dis crim i na tion (dis krim/ə nā/shən), **1** the ability to make fine distinctions; good judgment: *I think they showed lack of discrimination when they painted their house a bright purple.* **2** a difference in attitude or treatment shown to a particular person, class, etc.: *Racial or religious discrimination in hiring employees is against the law. n.*

dis crim i na to ry (dis krim/ə nə tôr/ē), showing partiality or prejudice: *discriminatory hiring practices. adj.*

dis cur sive (dis kėr/siv), wandering from one subject to another; rambling: *a long, discursive speech. adj.* —**dis- cur′sive ly,** *adv.* —**dis cur′sive ness,** *n.*

dis cus (dis′kəs), a heavy, circular plate of wood with a metal rim. It is used in an athletic contest to see who can throw it farthest. *n., pl.* **dis cus es.**

discus—athlete about to throw the discus

dis cuss (dis kus′), consider from different points of view; talk over: *The class discussed several problems. Congress is discussing tax rates. v.*

dis cus sion (dis kush′ən), a considering from different points of view; discussing things; talk: *After hours of discussion, we came to a decision. n.*

dis dain (dis dān′), **1** look down on; consider beneath oneself; scorn: *The policewoman disdained the offer of a bribe. Now that they are rich, they disdain to speak to their old friends.* **2** a looking down on a person or an act as beneath one; scorn: *The older students tended to treat the younger ones with disdain.* **1** *v.,* **2** *n.*

dis dain ful (dis dān′fəl), feeling or showing disdain; proud and scornful. *adj.* —**dis dain′ful ly,** *adv.* —**dis- dain′ful ness,** *n.*

dis ease (də zēz′), **1** condition of poor health; condition in which an organ, system, or part does not function properly; sickness; illness: *People, animals, and plants are all liable to disease.* **2** any particular illness: *Measles and chicken pox are two diseases of children. n.*

dis eased (də zēzd′), having a disease; showing signs of sickness: *a diseased lung, a diseased pet. adj.*

dis em bark (dis′em bärk′), go or put ashore from a ship; land from a ship. *v.* —**dis′em bar ka′tion,** *n.*

dis em bod ied (dis′em bod′ēd), separated from the body: *Ghosts are usually thought of as disembodied spirits. adj.*

dis em bow el (dis′em bou′əl), take or rip out the bowels of. *v.,* **dis em bow eled, dis em bow el ing** or **dis em- bow elled, dis em bow el ling.** —**dis′em bow′el- ment,** *n.*

dis en chant (dis′en chant′), free from enchantment or illusion; disillusion: *I thought that living in the city would be exciting, but I soon became disenchanted. v.*

dis en chant ment (dis′en chant′mənt), a disenchant- ing or a being disenchanted. *n.*

dis en cum ber (dis′ən kum′bər), free from a burden, annoyance, or trouble. *v.*

dis en fran chise (dis′en fran′chīz), disfranchise. *v.,* **dis en fran chised, dis en fran chis ing.** —**dis′en- fran′chise ment,** *n.*

dis en gage (dis′en gāj′), **1** free or release from any- thing that holds; detach; loosen: *He disengaged his hand from that of the sleeping child. She shifted gears and disen- gaged the clutch.* **2** free from an engagement, pledge, or obligation. *v.,* **dis en gaged, dis en gag ing.** —**dis′en- gage′ment,** *n.*

dis en tan gle (dis′en tang′gəl), free from tangles or complications; untangle: *disentangle a confusing story,*

disentangle a fishline. v., **dis en tan gled, dis en tan gling.**

dis en tan gle ment (dis′en tang′gəl mənt), a disentan- gling or a being disentangled. *n.*

dis fa vor (dis fā′vər), **1** unfavorable regard; dislike or disapproval: *The workers looked with disfavor on any at- tempt to lower their wages.* **2** dislike or disapprove. **3** condition of having lost favor or trust: *The government was in disfavor with the people.* **1,3** *n.,* **2** *v.*

dis fig ure (dis fig′yər), spoil the appearance of; hurt the beauty of: *Large billboards disfigure the countryside. A scar may disfigure a person's face. v.,* **dis fig ured, dis fig- ur ing.**

dis fig ure ment (dis fig′yər mənt), **1** a disfiguring or a being disfigured. **2** something that disfigures; defect. *n.*

dis fran chise (dis fran′chīz), **1** take the right to vote, hold office, etc., away from. **2** take any right or privilege away from. *v.,* **dis fran chised, dis fran chis ing.** Also, **disenfranchise.**

dis fran chise ment (dis fran′chiz mənt), a disfranchis- ing or a being disfranchised. *n.*

dis gorge (dis gôrj′), **1** throw up what has been swal- lowed. **2** pour forth; discharge: *Swollen streams disgorged their waters into the river.* **3** give up unwillingly: *force someone to disgorge secrets. v.,* **dis gorged, dis gorg ing.**

dis grace (dis grās′), **1** loss of honor or respect; shame: *the disgrace of being sent to jail.* **2** loss of favor or trust: *The king's former adviser is now in disgrace.* **3** cause dis- grace to; bring shame upon: *The embezzler disgraced her family.* **4** person or thing that causes disgrace: *The slums in our city are a disgrace.* **1,2,4** *n.,* **3** *v.,* **dis graced, dis- grac ing.** —**dis grac′er,** *n.*

dis grace ful (dis grās′fəl), causing loss of honor or re- spect; shameful. *adj.* —**dis grace′ful ly,** *adv.* —**dis- grace′ful ness,** *n.*

dis grun tled (dis grunt′ld), in bad humor; discontent- ed. *adj.*

dis guise (dis gīz′), **1** make changes in clothes or ap- pearance to hide who one really is or to look like some- one else: *On Halloween I disguised myself as a ghost.* **2** the use of such changes: *Detectives sometimes depend on disguise.* **3** clothes, actions, etc., used in making such changes: *Glasses and a wig formed the spy's disguise.* **4** hide what (a thing) really is; make (a thing) seem like something else: *The pirates disguised their ship as a trad- ing vessel. She disguised her handwriting by writing with her left hand.* **5** a false or misleading appearance; deception: *My outward show of indifference was only a disguise for my disappointment.* **1,4** *v.,* **dis guised, dis guis ing;** **2,3,5** *n.*

dis gust (dis gust′), **1** strong dislike; sickening dislike: *We feel disgust for bad odors or tastes.* **2** cause to feel disgust: *The smell of rotten eggs disgusts many people.* **1** *n.,* **2** *v.*

dis gust ed (dis gus′tid), filled with disgust. *adj.* —**dis- gust′ed ly,** *adv.* —**dis gust′ed ness,** *n.*

dis gust ing (dis gus′ting), unpleasant; distasteful. *adj.* —**dis gust′ing ly,** *adv.*

dish (dish), **1** anything to serve food in. Plates, platters, bowls, cups, and saucers are all dishes. **2** amount of food served in a dish: *I ate two dishes of ice cream.* **3** food served: *Chicken is the dish I like best.* **4** put (food) into a dish for serving at the table: *You may dish up the dinner now.* **5** antenna shaped like a dish or having a dish- shaped reflector. **1-3,5** *n.,* **4** *v.* [*Dish* comes from Old English *disc*, and can be traced back to Greek *diskos*.]

dis heart en (dis härt′n), cause to lose hope; discour- age; depress: *Long illness is disheartening. v.* —**dis- heart′en ing ly,** *adv.* —**dis heart′en ment,** *n.*

di shev el (də shev′əl), disarrange or rumple (hair, cloth- ing, etc.). *v.,* **di shev eled, di shev el ing** or **di shev- elled, di shev el ling.**

disheveled
Her hair was **disheveled** by the wind.

a hat	i it	oi oil	ch child	⎧ a in about
ā age	ī ice	ou out	ng long	e in taken
ä far	o hot	u cup	sh she	ə = ⎨ i in pencil
e let	ō open	u̇ put	th thin	o in lemon
ē equal	ô order	ü rule	ᴛʜ then	⎩ u in circus
ėr term			zh measure	

di shev eled or **di shev elled** (də shev′əld), not neat; rumpled; mussed; disordered. *adj.*

dis hon est (dis on′ist), **1** showing lack of honesty or fair play: *Lying, cheating, and stealing are dishonest.* **2** ready to cheat; not upright: *A person who lies or steals is dishonest.* **3** arranged to work in an unfair way: *dishonest scales weighted to cheat the customer. adj.* —**dis hon′est ly,** *adv.*

dis hon es ty (dis on′ə stē), **1** lack of honesty. **2** a dishonest act. *n., pl.* **dis hon es ties.**

dis hon or (dis on′ər), **1** loss of honor or reputation; shame; disgrace: *The robbers brought dishonor to their families.* **2** person or thing that causes dishonor: *The team's poor sportsmanship was a dishonor to the school.* **3** bring reproach or shame to; cause dishonor to: *The player who cheated dishonored the entire team.* 1,2 *n.,* 3 *v.*

dis hon or a ble (dis on′ər ə bəl), without honor; disgraceful; shameful. *adj.* —**dis hon′or a ble ness,** *n.*

dis hon or a bly (dis on′ər ə blē), in a dishonorable manner. *adv.*

dish tow el (dish′tou′əl), towel to dry dishes with. *n.*

dish wash er (dish′wosh′ər or dish′wôsh′ər), **1** machine for washing dishes, pots, glasses, etc. **2** person who washes dishes, especially in a restaurant, etc. *n.*

dish wa ter (dish′wô′tər or dish′wot′ər), water in which dishes have been or are to be washed. *n.*

dis il lu sion (dis′i lü′zhən), **1** to free from illusion: *Immigrants who expected America to have streets of gold were disillusioned.* **2** freedom from illusion. 1 *v.,* 2 *n.*

dis il lu sion ment (dis′i lü′zhən mənt), a disillusioning or a being disillusioned. *n.*

dis in cli na tion (dis in′klə nā′shən), unwillingness. *n.*

dis in clined (dis′in klīnd′), unwilling: *I was watching TV and was disinclined to clean up my room. adj.*

dis in fect (dis′in fekt′), destroy the disease germs in or on: *disinfect surgical instruments. v.* —**dis′in fec′tion,** *n.*

dis in fect ant (dis′in fek′tənt), **1** substance used to destroy disease germs. Alcohol and iodine are disinfectants. **2** used to destroy disease germs: *a disinfectant soap.* 1 *n.,* 2 *adj.*

dis in her it (dis′in her′it), prevent from inheriting; take away an inheritance from: *She disinherited her son by leaving him out of her will. v.*

dis in te grate (dis in′tə grāt), **1** break up; separate into small parts or bits: *The old papers had disintegrated into a pile of fragments and dust.* **2** (of the nucleus of an atom) undergo a change in structure by giving off particles or rays. *v.,* **dis in te grat ed, dis in te grat ing.**

dis in te gra tion (dis in′tə grā′shən), **1** a breaking up; separation into small parts or bits: *Rain and frost had caused the gradual disintegration of the rock.* **2** a change in the structure of an atomic nucleus by.its giving off particles or rays. *n.*

dis in ter (dis′in tėr′), take out of a grave or tomb; dig up. *v.,* **dis in terred, dis in ter ring.** —**dis′in ter′ment,** *n.*

dis in ter est (dis in′tər ist), lack of interest; indifference. *n.*

dis in ter est ed (dis in′tər ə stid), free from selfish motives; impartial; fair: *An umpire makes disinterested decisions. adj.* —**dis in′ter est ed ly,** *adv.*

dis joint (dis joint′), **1** take apart at the joints: *The butcher disjointed the chicken for me.* **2** break up; put out of order: *War disjoints a nation's affairs.* **3** (in mathematics) having no common members. (0,1,2) and (3,4,5) are disjoint sets. 1,2 *v.,* 3 *adj.*

dis joint ed (dis join′tid), broken up; disconnected; incoherent: *I was so nervous that my speech became disjointed. adj.* —**dis joint′ed ly,** *adv.*

disk (disk), **1** a round, flat, thin object shaped like a coin. **2** a round, flat surface that the sun, moon, and other planets seem to have. **3** a round, flat part of a plant or animal: *The yellow center of a daisy is a disk.* **4** a phonograph record. **5** object like a phonograph record, made of metal or plastic and with a magnetic surface, used to store information and instructions for computers. *n.* Also, **disc.**

disk brake, brake in which flat pads are pressed against both sides of a disk attached to the wheel.

disk drive, an electronic device that transfers information back and forth between a computer and magnetic storage disks.

disk ette (dis ket′), floppy disk. *n.*

disk harrow
towed by a tractor

disk harrow, harrow with a row of sharp, revolving disks, used in preparing ground for planting or sowing.

disk jockey, announcer for a radio program that consists chiefly of recorded popular music. Also, **disc jockey.**

dis like (dis līk′), **1** not like; object to; have a feeling against: *He dislikes studying and would rather play football.* **2** a feeling of not liking; a feeling against: *I have a dislike of thunder.* 1 *v.,* **dis liked, dis lik ing;** 2 *n.*

dis lo cate (dis′lō kāt), put out of joint: *She dislocated her shoulder when she fell down the stairs. v.,* **dis lo cat ed, dis lo cat ing.**

dis lo ca tion (dis′lō kā′shən), a dislocating or a being dislocated. *n.*

dis lodge (dis loj′), drive or force out of a place, position, etc.: *She used a crowbar to dislodge a heavy stone. Heavy gunfire dislodged the enemy from the fort. v.,* **dis lodged, dis lodg ing.** —**dis lodg′ment,** *n.*

dis loy al (dis loi′əl), not loyal; unfaithful: *a disloyal friend, a disloyal act. adj.* —**dis loy′al ly,** *adv.*

dis loy al ty (dis loi′əl tē), **1** lack of loyalty; unfaithfulness: *The traitor was imprisoned for disloyalty to his country.* **2** a disloyal act: *Revealing a friend's secret is a disloyalty.* *n., pl.* **dis loy al ties.**

dis mal (diz′məl), **1** dark and gloomy; dreary: *A rainy day is dismal.* **2** depressed; miserable: *Sickness often makes a person feel dismal.* *adj.* —**dis′mal ly,** *adv.*

WORD HISTORY

dismal

Dismal came into English about 700 years ago from French *dis mal,* meaning "evil days."

dis man tle (dis man′tl), **1** to strip of covering, equipment, furniture, guns, rigging, etc.: *The ship was dismantled before the hull was sold for scrap iron.* **2** pull down; take apart: *We had to dismantle the bookcases in order to move them.* *v.,* **dis man tled, dis man tling.** —**dis man′tle ment,** *n.*

dis may (dis mā′), **1** sudden loss of courage because of fear of danger: *They were filled with dismay when they saw the rattlesnake.* **2** trouble greatly; make afraid: *The thought that she might fail the test dismayed her.* **1** *n.,* **2** *v.* —**dis may′ing ly,** *adv.*

dis mem ber (dis mem′bər), **1** separate or divide into parts: *After the war the defeated country was dismembered.* **2** cut or tear the limbs from; divide limb from limb: *The wolves dismembered the deer's carcass.* *v.* —**dis mem′ber ment,** *n.*

dis miss (dis mis′), **1** send away; allow to go: *At noon the teacher dismissed the class for lunch.* **2** remove from office or service; not allow to keep a job: *We dismissed the painters because their work was so poor.* **3** put out of mind; stop thinking about: *Dismiss your troubles and be happy with what you have.* **4** refuse to consider in a court of law: *The judge dismissed the case because of lack of evidence.* *v.*

dis miss al (dis mis′əl), **1** act of dismissing: *The dismissal of those five workers caused a strike.* **2** condition or fact of being dismissed: *The company refused to announce the reason for the workers' dismissal.* **3** a written or spoken order dismissing someone: *The workers received their dismissal last Friday.* *n.*

dis mount (dis mount′), **1** get off a horse, bicycle, etc.: *The riders dismounted and led their horses across the stream.* **2** take (a thing) from its setting or support: *The cannons were dismounted for shipping to another fort.* *v.*

dis o be di ence (dis′ə bē′dē əns), refusal to obey; failure to obey: *The child was punished for disobedience.* *n.*

dis o be di ent (dis′ə bē′dē ənt), refusing to obey; failing to obey: *The disobedient child would not do as she was told.* *adj.* —**dis′o be′di ent ly,** *adv.*

dis o bey (dis′ə bā′), refuse to obey; fail to obey: *The student who disobeyed the teacher was punished.* *v.*

dis or der (dis ôr′dər), **1** lack of order; confusion: *Our whole house was in disorder after the birthday party.* **2** put out of order; destroy the order of; throw into confusion: *A series of accidents disordered traffic.* **3** a public disturbance; riot: *The National Guard was called to put an end to the disorder in the streets.* **4** sickness; disease: *Eating the wrong food can cause a stomach disorder.* **5** cause sickness in: *A severe emotional shock may disorder the mind.* **1,3,4** *n.,* **2,5** *v.*

dis or der li ness (dis ôr′dər lē nis), disorderly condition. *n.*

dis or der ly (dis ôr′dər lē), **1** not orderly; in confusion: *I can never find anything in this disorderly closet.* **2** causing disorder; making a disturbance; breaking rules; unruly: *A disorderly mob ran through the streets, shouting and breaking windows.* *adj.*

dis or gan i za tion (dis ôr′gə nə zā′shən), a disorganizing or a being disorganized; confusion; disorder. *n.*

dis or gan ize (dis ôr′gə nīz), throw into confusion or disorder; upset the order and arrangement of: *Heavy snowstorms delayed all flights and disorganized the airline schedule.* *v.,* **dis or gan ized, dis or gan iz ing.**

dis own (dis ōn′), refuse to recognize as one's own; cast off: *They disowned their daughter.* *v.*

dis par age (dis par′ij), **1** speak slightingly of; say (something) is of less value or importance than it actually is; belittle: *Perhaps you disparage her accomplishments because you are jealous of them.* **2** lower the reputation of; discredit. *v.,* **dis par aged, dis par ag ing.** —**dis par′ag er,** *n.*

dis par age ment (dis par′ij mənt), **1** act of disparaging. **2** something that lowers a thing or person in value or importance. **3** a lessening in esteem or standing; discredit: *Say nothing that will be to his disparagement with his new employer.* *n.*

dis par ag ing ly (dis par′ə jing lē), so as to disparage; slightingly. *adv.*

disparity (def. 1) There is great **disparity** in size between the girl and her dog.

dis par i ty (dis par′ə tē), **1** lack of equality. **2** quality of being unlike; difference: *The disparity in the accounts of the two witnesses puzzled the police.* *n., pl.* **dis par i ties.**

dis pas sion ate (dis pash′ə nit), free from emotion or prejudice; calm and impartial: *To a dispassionate observer, both drivers were to blame for the accident.* *adj.* —**dis pas′sion ate ly,** *adv.* —**dis pas′sion ate ness,** *n.*

dis patch (dis pach′), **1** send off to some place or for some purpose: *The captain dispatched a boat to bring a doctor on board ship.* **2** a sending off of a letter, a messenger, etc.: *Please hurry the dispatch of this telegram.* **3** a written message or communication: *a dispatch from the ambassador in France. The correspondent in Paris rushed news dispatches to her newspaper in New York.* **4** get done promptly or speedily: *The teacher dispatched the roll call and began the lesson.* **5** promptness in doing anything; speed: *They work with neatness and dispatch.* **6** kill: *dispatch an animal that has rabies.* **1,4,6** *v.,* **2,3,5** *n., pl.* **dis patch es.** Also, **despatch.**

dis patch er (dis pach′ər), person who dispatches. A train dispatcher is in charge of sending off the trains on schedule. *n.*

dis pel (dis pel′), drive away and scatter; disperse: *dispel one's fears.* *v.,* **dis pelled, dis pel ling.** —**dis pel′ler,** *n.*

dis pen sar y (dis pen′sər ē), place where medicines, medical care, and medical advice are given out. *n., pl.* **dis pen sar ies.** [*Dispensary* is from a medieval Latin word *dispensarius,* which comes from *dis-,* meaning "out," and *pendere,* meaning "weigh."]

dis pen sa tion (dis′pən sā′shən), **1** a giving out; distributing: *the dispensation of food and clothing to the flood victims.* **2** rule; management: *From 1558 to 1603 England was under the dispensation of Elizabeth I.* **3** official permission to disregard a rule. *n.*

dis pense (dis pens´), **1** give out; distribute: *The Red Cross dispensed food and clothing to the flood victims.* **2** carry out; put in force; apply: *Judges and courts of law dispense justice.* **3** prepare and give out: *Druggists must dispense medicine with the greatest care. v.,* **dis pensed, dis pens ing.**

dispense with, do without; get along without: *I shall dispense with these crutches as soon as my leg heals.*

dis pens er (dis pen´sər), person or thing that dispenses: *a dispenser of law, a paper-cup dispenser. n.*

dis per sal (dis pèr´səl), a scattering or a being scattered; dispersing: *the dispersal of a crowd. n.*

dis perse (dis pèrs´), spread in different directions; scatter: *The police dispersed the onlookers. The crowd dispersed when it began raining. v.,* **dis persed, dis pers ing. —dis per´ser,** *n.*

dis per sion (dis pèr´zhən), a dispersing or a being dispersed. *n.*

dispirit—The player was **dispirited** by defeat and fatigue.

dis pir it (dis pir´it), lower the spirits of; discourage; depress; dishearten. *v.* **—dis pir´it ed ly,** *adv.* **—dis pir´it ed ness,** *n.*

dis place (dis plās´), **1** take the place of; replace: *The automobile has displaced the horse and buggy.* **2** remove from a position of authority: *The mayor displaced the police chief.* **3** move from its usual place or position: *Someone has displaced my tools. A floating object displaces its own weight of liquid. v.,* **dis placed, dis plac ing. —dis place´a ble,** *adj.*

displaced person, person forced out of his or her own country by war, famine, political disturbance, etc.

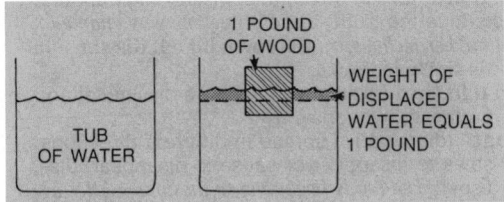

displacement (def. 2)—One pound (0.45 kg.) of wood, floating in water, displaces its own weight but not its own volume of water.

dis place ment (dis plās´mənt), **1** a displacing or a being displaced. **2** weight of the volume of water displaced by a ship or other floating object. This weight is equal to that of the floating object. *n.*

dis play (dis plā´), **1** put on view; show: *The American flag is displayed on the Fourth of July. The lecturer dis-*

played her good nature by patiently answering all our questions. **2** a showing; exhibition: *a display of bad temper.* **3** show in a special way, so as to attract attention: *The stores are displaying the new spring clothes in their windows.* **4** a showing off; ostentation: *Their fondness for display led them to buy flashy cars.* **5** a planned showing of a thing, for some special purpose; exhibit: *Grade 6 had two displays of children's drawings.* **6** a showing of information in visual form, as on the screen of a computer or calculator. **7** device that produces such a display. 1,3 *v.,* 2,4-7 *n.* **—dis play´er,** *n.*

dis please (dis plēz´), not please; annoy; offend: *You displease your parents when you disobey them. v.,* **displeased, dis pleas ing. —dis pleas´ing ly,** *adv.*

dis pleas ure (dis plezh´ər), the feeling of being displeased; annoyance; dislike. *n.*

dis port (dis pôrt´), amuse or entertain oneself: *People laughed at the clumsy bears disporting themselves in the water. v.*

dis pos a ble (dis pō´zə bəl), able to be disposed of or thrown away after use: *disposable paper napkins. adj.*

dis pos al (dis pō´zəl), **1** a getting rid (of something): *The city takes care of the disposal of garbage.* **2** a giving away or selling: *His will provided for the disposal of his property after his death.* **3** a dealing with; settling: *Her disposal of the difficulty satisfied everybody. n.*

at one's disposal, ready for one's use or service at any time: *My car is at your disposal.*

dis pose (dis pōz´), **1** put in a certain order or position; arrange: *The flags were disposed in a straight line for the parade.* **2** make ready or willing; incline: *More pay and shorter hours of work disposed him to take the new job.* **3** make liable or subject: *Getting overly tired disposes you to catching cold. v.,* **dis posed, dis pos ing. —dispos´er,** *n.*

dispose of, 1 get rid of: *Dispose of that rubbish.* **2** give away: *The Salvation Army will dispose of this clothing among the poor.* **3** sell: *The owner disposed of her house for $35,000.* **4** eat or drink: *They quickly disposed of the picnic lunch.* **5** arrange; settle: *The committee disposed of all its business in an hour.*

dis posed (dis pōzd´), willing; inclined: *They are more disposed to play than to work. adj.*

dis po si tion (dis´pə zish´ən), **1** one's habitual ways of acting toward others or of thinking about things; nature: *His cheerful disposition made him popular.* **2** tendency; inclination: *A quarrelsome person has a disposition to start trouble.* **3** a putting in a certain order or position; arrangement: *The teacher changed the disposition of the desks in the classroom.* **4** a disposing; settlement: *What disposition did the court make of the case?* **5** disposal: *She had a large sum of money at her disposition. n.*

dis pos sess (dis´pə zes´), force to give up the possession of a house, land, etc.: *The tenant was dispossessed for not paying the rent. v.* **—dis´pos ses´sor,** *n.*

dis proof (dis prüf´), **1** a disproving; refutation. **2** fact or reason that disproves something. *n.*

dis pro por tion (dis´prə pôr´shən), lack of proper proportion. *n.*

dis pro por tion ate (dis´prə pôr´shə nit), out of relation in size, number, etc. (to something else); not well proportioned: *A penny would be disproportionate pay for a* *day's work. adj.* —**dis′pro por′tion ate ly,** *adv.* —**dis′-pro por′tion ate ness,** *n.*

dis prove (dis prüv′), prove false or incorrect: *She disproved her brother's claim that he had less candy by weighing both boxes.* *v.,* **dis proved, dis prov ing.**

dis put a ble (dis pyü′tə bəl *or* dis′pyə tə bəl), liable to be disputed; uncertain; questionable: *The existence of flying saucers is disputable. adj.* —**dis put′a bly,** *adv.*

dis pu tant (dis′pyə tənt *or* dis pyüt′nt), person who takes part in a dispute or debate. *n.*

dis pu ta tion (dis′pyə tā′shən), 1 debate; controversy. 2 dispute. *n.*

dis pute (dis pyüt′), 1 give reasons or facts for or against something; argue; debate; discuss: *Congress disputed over the need for new taxes.* 2 argument; debate: *There is a dispute over where to build the new school.* 3 quarrel: *The children disputed over the last piece of cake.* 4 a quarrel: *The dispute between the two neighbors threatened their friendship.* 5 disagree with (a statement); declare to be false or wrong; call in question: *The insurance company disputed his claim for damages to his car.* 6 fight for; fight over; contest: *The soldiers disputed every inch of ground when the enemy attacked.* 7 try to win: *The losing team disputed the victory up to the last minute of play.* 1,3,5-7 *v.,* **dis put ed, dis put ing;** 2,4 *n.* —**dis put′er,** *n.*

dis qual i fi ca tion (dis kwol′ə fə kā′shən), 1 a disqualifying or a being disqualified. 2 something that disqualifies. *n.*

dis qual i fy (dis kwol′ə fī), 1 make unfit; make unable to do something: *Her broken leg disqualified her from all sports.* 2 declare unfit or unable to do something: *The principal disqualified two members of the school play because they had low marks.* *v.,* **dis qual i fied, dis qual i fy ing.**

dis qui et (dis kwī′ət), 1 make uneasy or anxious; disturb: *The child's strange actions disquieted the parents.* 2 uneasy feelings; anxiety: *Her disquiet made the rest of us uneasy, too.* 1 *v.,* 2 *n.* —**dis qui′et ing ly,** *adv.*

dis qui e tude (dis kwī′ə tüd *or* dis kwī′ə tyüd), uneasiness; anxiety. *n.*

dis re gard (dis′ri gärd′), 1 pay no attention to; take no notice of: *Disregarding the cold weather, we played outside all day.* 2 lack of attention; neglect: *The reckless driver was arrested for disregard of the traffic laws.* 1 *v.,* 2 *n.*

dis re pair (dis′ri per′ *or* dis′ri par′), bad condition; need of repair: *The house was in disrepair. n.*

dis rep u ta ble (dis rep′yə tə bəl), 1 having a bad reputation: *Police closed the disreputable barroom.* 2 not fit to be used or seen; in poor condition: *a disreputable old hat. adj.* —**dis rep′u ta ble ness,** *n.* —**dis rep′u ta bly,** *adv.*

dis re pute (dis′ri pyüt′), disgrace; discredit; disfavor: *Many old remedies for illness have fallen into disrepute among doctors. n.*

dis re spect (dis′ri spekt′), lack of respect; rudeness; impoliteness: *I meant no disrespect by my remark. n.*

dis re spect ful (dis′ri spekt′fəl), showing no respect; lacking in courtesy to elders or superiors; rude; impolite: *Making fun of your elders is disrespectful. adj.* —**dis′-re spect′ful ly,** *adv.* —**dis′re spect′ful ness,** *n.*

dis robe (dis rōb′), undress. *v.,* **dis robed, dis rob ing.**

dis rupt (dis rupt′), break up; split: *Troublemakers tried to disrupt the assembly. v.* —**dis rupt′er,** *n.*

dis rup tion (dis rup′shən), 1 a breaking up; splitting: *Arguments led to the disruption of their partnership.* 2 a being broken up; a being split: *There was a disruption of telephone service during the storm. n.*

dis rup tive (dis rup′tiv), causing disruption: *Their whispering was a disruptive influence in the library. adj.* —**dis rup′tive ly,** *adv.*

dis sat is fac tion (dis′sat i sfak′shən), discontent; displeasure: *Poor working conditions caused dissatisfaction among the employees. n.*

dis sat is fied (dis sat′i sfīd), discontented; displeased: *The dissatisfied workers voted to strike for higher pay. adj.*

dis sat is fy (dis sat′i sfī), fail to satisfy; make discontented; displease: *My teacher was dissatisfied with the paper I wrote. v.,* **dis sat is fied, dis sat is fy ing.**

dis sect (di sekt′ *or* dī sekt′), 1 cut apart (an animal, plant, etc.) in order to examine or study the structure. 2 examine carefully part by part; analyze: *Let us dissect that statement and find out just what it means. v.* —**dis sec′tor,** *n.*

dis sec tion (di sek′shən *or* dī sek′shən), 1 act of cutting apart an animal, plant, etc., in order to examine or study the structure. 2 examination of something in detail or point by point; analysis. *n.*

dis sem ble (di sem′bəl), 1 hide (one's real feelings, thoughts, plans, etc.); disguise: *She dissembled her anger with a smile.* 2 put on the appearance of; pretend; feign: *The bored listener dissembled an interest he didn't feel. v.,* **dis sem bled, dis sem bling.** —**dis sem′bler,** *n.*

dis sem i nate (di sem′ə nāt), scatter widely; spread abroad: *Television and radio stations disseminated news of the hurricane. v.,* **dis sem i nat ed, dis sem i nat ing.** —**dis sem′i na tor,** *n.*

dis sem i na tion (di sem′ə nā′shən), a scattering or a being scattered widely; spreading abroad; diffusion: *Dissemination of the news is the function of a newspaper. n.*

dis sen sion (di sen′shən), violent disagreement; strong difference of opinion; quarreling; disputing: *The club broke up because of dissension among its members. n.*

dis sent (di sent′), 1 differ in opinion; disagree: *Two of the judges dissented from the decision of the other three.* 2 difference of opinion; disagreement: *Dissent among the members broke up the club meeting.* 1 *v.,* 2 *n.* —**dis sent′er,** *n.*

dis ser ta tion (dis′ər tā′shən), a formal oral or written discussion of a subject. A university student who is working for a doctor's degree is required to write a dissertation. *n.*

dis serv ice (dis sėr′vis), bad treatment; harm; injury: *You do a disservice to him when you fail to give him credit for his efforts. n.*

dis si dent (dis′ə dənt), 1 disagreeing in opinion; dissenting: *dissident members of a jury.* 2 person who disagrees or dissents. 1 *adj.,* 2 *n.*

dis sim i lar (di sim′ə lər), not similar; unlike; different. *adj.* —**dis sim′i lar ly,** *adv.*

dis sim i lar i ty (di sim′ə lar′ə tē), lack of similarity; unlikeness; difference. *n., pl.* **dis sim i lar i ties.**

dis sim u late (di sim′yə lāt), disguise or hide under a pretense; hide the truth; dissemble: *She was unable to dissimulate her feelings. v.,* **dis sim u lat ed, dis sim u lat ing.** —**dis sim′u la′tor,** *n.*

dis sim u la tion (di sim′yə lā′shən), a dissimulating; deceit; pretense; hypocrisy. *n.*

dis si pate (dis′ə pāt), 1 spread in different directions; scatter so as to disappear or cause to disappear; disperse; dispel: *The fog is beginning to dissipate. After a brisk morning wind dissipated the clouds, the sky was clear all day.* 2 spend foolishly; waste on things of little value: *In a short time she had dissipated her inheritance.* 3 indulge too much in harmful or foolish pleasures. *v.,* **dis si pat ed, dis si pat ing.**

dis si pat ed (dis′ə pā′tid), indulging too much in harmful or foolish pleasures; dissolute: *a dissipated life spent drinking and gambling. adj.* —**dis′si pat′ed ly,** *adv.* —**dis′si pat′ed ness,** *n.*

dis si pa tion (dis′ə pā′shən), 1 a scattering in different directions. **2** a wasting by misuse. **3** too much indulgence in harmful or foolish pleasures; intemperance. *n.*

dis so ci ate (di sō′shē āt), break the connection or association with; separate: *When the lawyer discovered that his client was lying, he immediately dissociated himself from the case. v.,* **dis so ci at ed, dis so ci at ing.**

dis so ci a tion (di sō′sē ā′shən *or* di sō′shē ā′shən), a dissociating or a being dissociated. *n.*

dis so lute (dis′ə lüt), living an evil life; very wicked; immoral: *dissolute companions with bad reputations. adj.* —**dis′so lute ly,** *adv.* —**dis′so lute ness,** *n.*

dis so lu tion (dis′ə lü′shən), **1** a breaking up; an ending: *The partners arranged for the dissolution of their partnership.* **2** a making or becoming liquid; dissolving. **3** ruin; destruction. *n.*

dis solve (di zolv′), **1** change from a solid or gas to a liquid; form into a solution in a liquid: *Salt or sugar will dissolve in water.* **2** break up; end: *The two partners dissolved their partnership because they could not agree on how to conduct the business.* **3** fade away: *The dream dissolved when she woke up. v.,* **dis solved, dis solv ing.**

dis so nance (dis′n əns), **1** harshness and unpleasantness of sound; discord. **2** lack of harmony; disagreement. *n.*

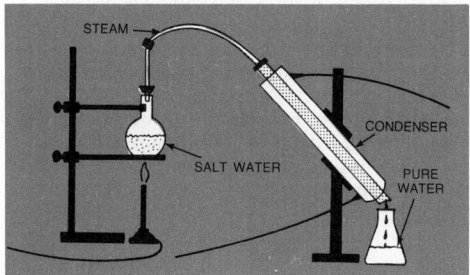

distill (def. 1)—Pure water is distilled from salt water by heating it until the water turns to vapor. It is changed back to liquid form by cooling it in the condenser.

dis so nant (dis′n ənt), **1** harsh and unpleasant in sound; not harmonious; clashing: *dissonant chords.* **2** out of harmony with other conditions, persons, etc.: disagreeing: *Two dissonant groups caused a split in the political party. adj.* —**dis′so nant ly,** *adv.*

dis suade (di swād′), persuade not to do something: *I dissuaded her from quitting the school band. v.,* **dis suaded, dis suad ing.**

dis sua sive (di swā′siv), attempting or tending to dissuade. *adj.* —**dis sua′sive ly,** *adv.* —**dis sua′sive ness,** *n.*

dist., **1** distance. **2** district.

dis taff (dis′taf), **1** a stick, split at the tip, to hold wool or flax for spinning by hand. **2** staff on a spinning wheel for holding wool or flax. *n.*

distaff side, the mother's side of a family: *My cousin and I are related on the distaff side.*

dis tance (dis′təns), **1** space in between: *The distance from the farm to the town is five miles.* **2** a being far away: *Because of the lake's distance, we will have to stop overnight on the way.* **3** a place far away: *He saw a light in the distance. n.*

at a distance, a long way: *The farm is at a distance from the road.*

keep at a distance, refuse to be friendly or familiar with; treat coldly: *The teacher kept the students at a distance.*

keep one's distance, be not too friendly or familiar: *The shy boy kept his distance and did not mingle with his new classmates.*

dis tant (dis′tənt), **1** far away in space: *The sun is distant from the earth.* **2** away: *The town is three miles distant.* **3** far apart in time, relationship, likeness, etc.; not close: *A third cousin is a distant relative. We may take a trip to Europe in the distant future.* **4** not friendly: *I gave him only a distant nod. adj.* [*Distant* is from Latin *distantem,* which comes from *dis-,* meaning "off," and *stare,* meaning "to stand."] —**dis′tant ly,** *adv.* —**dis′tant ness,** *n.*

dis taste (dis tāst′), dislike: *I have always had a distaste for Brussels sprouts. n.*

dis taste ful (dis tāst′fəl), unpleasant; disagreeable; offensive: *a distasteful task. adj.* —**dis taste′ful ly,** *adv.* —**dis taste′ful ness,** *n.*

dis tem per (dis tem′pər), an infectious disease of dogs and other animals, accompanied by fever, a short, dry cough, and a loss of strength. *n.*

dis tend (dis tend′), stretch out; swell out; expand: *The balloon was distended almost to the bursting point. n.* —**dis tend′er,** *n.*

dis ten tion (dis ten′shən), a distending or a being distended. *n.*

dis till *or* **dis til** (dis til′), **1** heat (a liquid or other substance) and condense the vapor given off by cooling it. A substance is distilled in order to purify it, to separate its liquid parts from its solid parts, or to break it down into separate substances. **2** obtain by distilling: *Gasoline is distilled from crude oil. Alcoholic liquor is distilled from mash made from grain.* **3** get out the essential principle; extract: *A jury must distill the truth from the testimony of witnesses.* **4** give off in drops: *These flowers distill a sweet nectar. v.,* **dis tilled, dis till ing.** —**dis till′a ble,** *adj.*

dis til la tion (dis′tl ā′shən), **1** act of distilling: *the distillation of water to purify it.* **2** process of distilling. **3** something distilled. *n.*

dis till er (dis til′ər), **1** person or thing that distills. **2** person or company that makes whiskey, rum, brandy, etc. *n.*

dis till er y (dis til′ər ē), **1** place where distilling is done. **2** place where whiskey, rum, brandy, etc., are made; still. *n., pl.* **dis till er ies.**

distaff (def. 1) Fibers attached to the distaff, on the woman's left, are drawn out and twisted onto the spindle in her right hand to make thread.

dis tinct (dis tingkt′), **1** not the same; separate: *She asked me about it three distinct times.* **2** different in quality or kind: *Mice are distinct from rats.* **3** easily seen, heard, or understood; clear: *Large, distinct print is easy to read.* **4** unmistakable; definite; decided: *A tall player has a distinct advantage in basketball. adj.* —**dis tinct′ly,** *adv.* —**dis tinct′ness,** *n.*

dis tinc tion (dis tingk′shən), **1** a distinguishing from others; making a difference: *They treated all their children alike without distinction.* **2** difference: *The distinction between hot and cold is easily noticed.* **3** special quality or feature; point of difference: *He has the distinction of being the best chess player in his school.* **4** honor: *The senator had served his country with distinction.* **5** mark or sign of honor: *The scientist received many awards as distinctions for her achievements.* **6** excellence; superiority: *a person of great distinction. n.*

dis tinc tive (dis tingk′tiv), distinguishing from others; special; characteristic: *Police officers wear a distinctive uniform. adj.* —**dis tinc′tive ly,** *adv.* —**dis tinc′tive ness,** *n.*

dis tin guish (dis ting′gwish), **1** see or show the differences in; tell apart: *Can you distinguish silk from nylon?* **2** see or show the difference: *to distinguish between right and wrong.* **3** see or hear clearly; make out plainly: *On a clear, bright day you can distinguish things far away.* **4** make different; be a special quality or feature of: *A trunk distinguishes the elephant.* **5** make famous or well known: *She distinguished herself by winning three prizes. v.*

dis tin guish a ble (dis ting′gwi shə bəl), able to be distinguished. *adj.* —**dis tin′guish a bly,** *adv.*

dis tin guished (dis ting′gwisht), **1** famous; well-known: *a distinguished American poet.* **2** looking important or superior: *Your new suit gives you a distinguished look. adj.*

dis tort (dis tôrt′), **1** pull or twist out of shape; change the normal appearance of: *Rage distorted his face.* **2** change from the truth; misrepresent: *The driver distorted the facts of the accident to escape blame. v.* —**dis tort′er,** *n.*

dis tor tion (dis tôr′shən), **1** a distorting; twisting out of shape: *Exaggeration is a distortion of the truth.* **2** condition of being distorted. **3** anything distorted: *Her story was full of distortions. n.*

dis tract (dis trakt′), **1** draw away (the mind, attention, etc.): *Noise distracts my attention from study.* **2** confuse; disturb: *Several people talking at once distract a listener.* **3** put out of one's mind; make insane: *distracted with fear and anxiety. v.* —**dis tract′ed ly,** *adv.* —**dis tract′ing ly,** *adv.*

dis trac tion (dis trak′shən), **1** act of drawing away the mind, attention, etc. **2** thing that draws away the mind, attention, etc.: *Noise is a distraction when you are trying to study.* **3** confusion of mind; disturbance of thought: *The parents of the lost child scarcely knew what they were doing in their distraction.* **4** relief from continued thought, grief, or effort; amusement: *Movies and television are popular distractions. n.*

dis trac tive (dis trak′tiv), distracting; tending to distract. *adj.*

dis traught (dis trôt′), **1** in a state of mental conflict and confusion; distracted: *distraught with fear.* **2** crazed. *adj.*

dis tress (dis tres′), **1** great pain or sorrow; anxiety; trouble: *The loss of our kitten caused us much distress.* **2** cause great pain or sorrow to; make unhappy: *Your tears distress me.* **3** something that causes distress; misfortune: *The failure of his business was a great distress to him.* **4** a dangerous condition; difficult situation: *A burning or sinking ship is in distress.* 1,3,4 *n.,* 2 *v.* —**dis tress′ing ly,** *adv.*

dis tress ful (dis tres′fəl), causing distress; painful. *adj.* —**dis tress′ful ly,** *adv.* —**dis tress′ful ness,** *n.*

dis trib ute (dis trib′yüt), **1** give some of to each; divide and give out in shares; deal out: *I distributed the candy among my friends.* **2** spread; scatter: *A painter should distribute the paint evenly over a wall.* **3** divide into parts: *The books were distributed into groups according to subject.* **4** arrange; sort out: *A mail clerk distributes mail by putting each letter into the proper bag. v.,* **dis trib ut ed, dis trib ut ing.** —**dis trib′ut a ble,** *adj.*

dis tri bu tion (dis′trə byü′shən), **1** act of distributing: *After the contest the distribution of prizes to the winners took place.* **2** way of being distributed: *If some get more than others, there is an uneven distribution.* **3** thing distributed. **4** a distributing to consumers of goods grown or made by producers. *n.*

dis trib u tive (dis trib′yə tiv), **1** of distribution. **2** referring to each individual of a group considered separately. *Each, every,* and *either* are distributive pronouns. **3** of a rule that the same product results in multiplication when performed on a set of numbers as when performed on the members of the set individually. EXAMPLE: $3(4+5) = (3 \times 4) + (3 \times 5)$. *adj.* —**dis trib′u tive ly,** *adv.* —**dis trib′u tive ness,** *n.*

dis trib u tor (dis trib′yə tər), **1** person or thing that distributes. **2** person or company that distributes goods to consumers. **3** part of a gasoline engine that distributes electric current to the spark plugs. *n.*

dis trict (dis′trikt), **1** part of a larger area; region: *The leading farming district of the United States is in the Middle West.* **2** part of a country, state, or city marked off for a special purpose such as providing schools or courts of law, or electing certain government officials. **3** divide into districts. 1,2 *n.,* 3 *v.*

district attorney, lawyer who handles cases for the government for a certain district of a state or the country.

District of Columbia, district in E United States between Maryland and Virginia, governed by the Federal government. It is entirely occupied by the national capital, Washington. *Abbreviation:* D.C. or DC

dis trust (dis trust′), **1** have no confidence in; not trust; be suspicious of; doubt: *Many people distrust statements made in advertisements.* **2** lack of trust or confidence; suspicion: *I could not explain my distrust of the stranger.* 1 *v.,* 2 *n.*

dis trust ful (dis trust′fəl), not trusting; suspicious. *adj.* —**dis trust′ful ly,** *adv.* —**dis trust′ful ness,** *n.*

dis turb (dis tėrb′), **1** destroy the peace, quiet, or rest of: *Heavy truck traffic disturbed the neighborhood all day long.* **2** break in upon with noise or change: *Please don't disturb her while she's studying.* **3** put out of order: *Someone has disturbed my books; I can't find the one I want.* **4** make uneasy; trouble: *He was disturbed to hear of his friend's illness.* **5** inconvenience: *Don't disturb yourself; I can do it. v.* —**dis turb′er,** *n.*

dis turb ance (dis tėr′bəns), **1** a disturbing or a being disturbed. **2** thing that disturbs. **3** confusion; disorder: *The police were called to quiet the disturbance at the street corner.* **4** uneasiness; trouble; worry. *n.*

dis un ion (dis yü′nyən), **1** separation; division. **2** lack of unity; disagreement; unfriendliness. *n.*

dis u nite (dis′yü nīt′), destroy the unity of; cause to disagree or to become unfriendly. *v.,* **dis u nit ed, dis u nit ing.**

dis u ni ty (dis yü′nə tē), lack of unity; disunion; dissension. *n.*

dis use (dis yüs′), lack of use; not being used: *The old tools were rusted from disuse. n.*

ditch (dich), **1** a long, narrow hole dug in the earth. Ditches are usually used to carry off water. **2** dig a ditch in or around. **3** drive or throw into a ditch: *The careless driver skidded off the road and ditched the car.* **4** INFORMAL. get rid of: *The robber ditched the gun in a sewer.* 1 *n., pl.* **ditch es;** 2-4 *v.* [*Ditch* comes from Old English *dīc.*] —**ditch′er,** *n.*

dith er (diᴛн′ər), a confused, excited condition: *He's in a dither about tomorrow's test. n.*

dit to (dit′ō), **1** the same; exactly the same as appeared or was said before. **2** ditto mark. **3** a copy; duplicate. **4** as said before; likewise. 1-3 *n., pl.* **dit tos;** 4 *adv.* [*Ditto* comes from Italian *ditto,* meaning "said," and can be traced back to Latin *dicere,* meaning "say."]

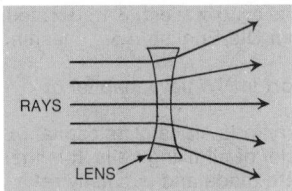

diverge (def. 1)
The lens causes the light rays to diverge.

ditto mark, a small mark (″) used to avoid repeating something written immediately above. Ditto marks are often used on long lists, bills, tables, etc. EXAMPLE:

6 lb. apples at 75 ¢ $4.50
4 ″ ″ ″ ″ ″ 3.00

dit ty (dit′ē), a short, simple song or poem. *n., pl.* **dit ties.**

di ur nal (dī ėr′nl), **1** occurring every day; daily: *Sunrise is a diurnal event.* **2** of or belonging to the daytime: *Diurnal temperatures are usually higher than those of the night.* **3** active in the daytime: *Butterflies are diurnal. adj.* —**di ur′nal ly,** *adv.*

div., 1 dividend. **2** division.

di van (dī′van *or* də van′), a long, low, soft couch or sofa. *n.* [*Divan* is from Turkish *divān,* which came from Persian *dēvān.*]

He **dived** into the water. He **dove** into the water.

dive—Whether he **dived** or **dove** into the water, he still came up wet. (Either form is correct.)

dive (dīv), **1** plunge headfirst into water. **2** act of diving: *The crowd applauded the girl's graceful dive.* **3** go down or out of sight suddenly: *The gopher dived into its hole and disappeared.* **4** plunge the hand suddenly into anything: *He dived into his pockets and brought out a dollar.* **5** plunge with the mind; begin with energy and zeal: *She dived into her work with enthusiasm.* **6** plunge downward at a steep angle: *The hawk dived straight at the field mouse.* **7** a downward plunge at a steep angle: *The submarine made a dive toward the bottom.* **8** INFORMAL. a low, cheap tavern or night club. 1,3-6 *v.,* **dived** or **dove, dived, div ing;** 2,7,8 *n.*

dive bomber, bomber that releases its load of bombs just before it pulls out of a dive toward the target.

div er (dī′vər), **1** person that dives. **2** person whose occupation is working or diving under water. **3** a diving bird. Loons, penguins, and auks are divers. *n.*

a	hat	i	it	oi	oil	ch	child		a in about
ā	age	ī	ice	ou	out	ng	long		e in taken
ä	far	o	hot	u	cup	sh	she	ə =	i in pencil
e	let	ō	open	u̇	put	th	thin		o in lemon
ē	equal	ô	order	ü	rule	ŦH	then		u in circus
ėr	term					zh	measure		

di verge (də vėrj′ *or* dī vėrj′), **1** move or lie in different directions from the same point; branch off: *Their paths diverged at the fork in the road; he turned left, and she turned right.* **2** differ; vary; deviate: *Contestants who diverge from the rules will be eliminated from the competition. v.,* **di verged, di verg ing.**

di ver gence (də vėr′jəns *or* dī vėr′jəns), a diverging; difference: *The committee couldn't come to an agreement because of the wide divergence of opinion among its members. n.*

di ver gent (də vėr′jənt *or* dī vėr′jənt), diverging; different. *adj.* —**di ver′gent ly,** *adv.*

di vers (dī′vərz), more than one; several different; various: *A well-balanced diet is made up of divers foods. adj.*

di verse (də vėrs′), not alike; different; varied: *Many diverse opinions were expressed at the meeting. adj.* —**di verse′ly,** *adv.* —**di verse′ness,** *n.*

di ver si fy (də vėr′sə fī), make diverse; give variety to; vary: *diversify one's interests. Mountains, plains, trees, and lakes diversify the landscape. v.,* **di ver si fied, di ver si fy ing.** —**di ver′si fi′a ble,** *adj.* —**di ver′si fi′er,** *n.*

di ver sion (də vėr′zhən), **1** a turning aside; a diverting: *A magician's talk creates a diversion of attention so that people do not see how the tricks are done.* **2** distraction from work, care, etc.; amusement; entertainment; pastime: *Golf is my parents' favorite diversion. n.*

di ver si ty (də vėr′sə tē), **1** complete difference; unlikeness: *The quiet student and the active athlete were friends in spite of the diversity of their dispositions.* **2** variety: *The diversity of food on the menu made it hard to decide what to order. n., pl.* **di ver si ties.**

di vert (də vėrt′), **1** turn aside: *A ditch diverted water from the stream into the fields. The siren of the fire engine diverted the audience's attention from the play.* **2** amuse; entertain: *Listening to music diverted him after a hard day's work. v.*

di vest (də vest′), **1** rid or free; strip: *We divested ourselves of our clothes and dived into the water.* **2** force to give up; deprive: *A person in prison is divested of the right to vote. v.* [*Divest* came into English about 300 years ago from French *desvestir,* which can be traced back to Latin *dis-,* meaning "from," and *vestis,* meaning "clothing."]

di vide (də vīd′), **1** separate into parts: *A brook divides the field. The road divides and forms two roads.* **2** separate into equal parts: *When you divide 8 by 2, you get 4.* **3** give some of to each; share: *The children divided the candy.* **4** disagree or cause to disagree; separate in feeling, opinion, etc.: *The school divided on the choice of a motto.* **5** ridge of land between two regions drained by different river systems: *The Rocky Mountains form part of the Continental Divide.* 1-4 *v.,* **di vid ed, di vid ing;** 5 *n.*

div i dend (div′ə dend), **1** number or quantity to be divided by another: *In 728 ÷ 16, 728 is the dividend.* **2** money earned by a company and divided among the owners or stockholders as their share of the profits. **3** share of such money. *n.*

di vid er (də vī′dər), **1** something that divides: *There is a concrete divider in the center of the parkway.* **2 dividers,** *pl.* compass used for dividing lines, measuring distances, etc. *n.*

div i na tion (div′ə nā′shən), **1** act of foreseeing the future or foretelling the unknown by inspiration, by magic, or by signs and omens. **2** a skillful guess or prediction. *n.*

di vine (də vīn′), **1** of God or a god: *The Bible describes the creation of the world as a divine act.* **2** given by or coming from God: *The queen believed that her power to rule was a divine right.* **3** to or for God; sacred; holy: *divine worship.* **4** like God or a god; heavenly. **5** INFORMAL. excellent or delightful; unusually good or great: *Oh, what a divine vacation we had!* **6** clergyman who knows a great deal about theology; minister; priest. **7** foresee or foretell by inspiration, by magic, or by signs and omens; predict. **8** find out without actually knowing; guess correctly: *We divined who had eaten the cake from the guilty looks on the children's faces.* 1-5 *adj.*, 6 *n.*, 7,8 *v.*, **di vined, di vin ing.** —**di vine′ly,** *adv.* —**di vine′ness,** *n.*

di vin er (də vī′nər), person who foresees or foretells things; prophet. *n.*

diving bell, a large, hollow container filled with air and open at the bottom. People can work in it under water.

diving suit, a waterproof suit with a helmet into which air can be pumped through a tube. Diving suits are worn by persons working under water.

di vin i ty (də vin′ə tē), **1** a divine being; god or goddess. **2** the Divinity, God. **3** divine nature or quality. **4** study of God, religion, and divine things; theology. *n., pl.* **di vin i ties.**

di vis i ble (də viz′ə bəl), **1** able to be divided. **2** able to be divided without leaving a remainder: *12 is divisible by 1, 2, 3, 4, 6, and 12. adj.* —**di vis′i ble ness,** *n.* —**di vis′i bly,** *adv.*

di vi sion (də vizh′ən), **1** a dividing or a being divided. **2** a giving some to each; sharing: *The making of automobiles in large numbers is made possible by a division of labor, in which each worker has a certain part of the work to do.* **3** operation of dividing one number by another: *26 ÷ 2 = 13 is a simple division.* **4** thing that divides. A boundary or a partition is a division. **5** one of the parts into which a thing is divided; group; section: *the research division of a drug company.* **6** a military unit made up of several brigades or regiments plus supporting troops, usually commanded by a major general. It is smaller than a corps. **7** a difference of opinion, thought, or feeling; disagreement: *There was a division in our class over the date for our spring trip. n.*

di vi sive (də vī′siv), tending to cause disagreement. *adj.* —**di vi′sive ly,** *adv.* —**di vi′sive ness,** *n.*

di vi sor (də vī′zər), number or quantity by which another is to be divided: *In 728 ÷ 16, 16 is the divisor. n.*

di vorce (də vôrs′), **1** the legal ending of a marriage. **2** end legally a marriage between: *The judge divorced the husband and wife.* **3** separate from by a divorce: *She divorced her husband.* **4** to separate: *The writers of the Constitution wanted to divorce government and religion in the United States.* **5** separation: *In the United States there is a complete divorce of government and religion.* 1,5 *n.*, 2-4 *v.*, **di vorced, di vorc ing.** —**di vorce′ment,** *n.*

di vor cé (də vôr sā′), a divorced man. *n., pl.* **di vor cés.**

di vor cée (də vôr sā′), a divorced woman. *n., pl.* **di vor cées.**

di vulge (də vulj′ or dī vulj′), make known; tell; reveal: *At the end of the story Sherlock Holmes divulged the name of the murderer. v.,* **di vulged, di vulg ing.** —**di vulg′er,** *n.*

div vy (div′ē), SLANG. share or divide: *We divvied up the money we won between us. v.,* **div vied, div vy ing.**

Dix ie (dik′sē), the southern states of the United States. *n.*

diz zi ly (diz′ə lē), in a dizzy manner. *adv.*

diz zi ness (diz′ē nis), dizzy condition. *n.*

diz zy (diz′ē), **1** likely to fall, stagger, or spin around; not steady: *When you spin round and round, and stop suddenly, you feel dizzy.* **2** confused; bewildered: *The noise and crowds of the city streets made the little boy dizzy.* **3** make dizzy: *The ride on the merry-go-round dizzied her.* **4** likely to make dizzy; causing dizziness: *The airplane climbed to a dizzy height.* 1,2,4 *adj.*, **diz zi er, diz zi est;** 3 *v.*, **diz zied, diz zy ing.** [*Dizzy* comes from Old English *dysig,* meaning "foolish."]

Dja kar ta (jə kär′tə), seaport in NW Java, capital of Indonesia. *n.* Also, **Jakarta.**

Dji bou ti (ji bü′tē), **1** country in E Africa. **2** its capital. *n.*

DNA, acid found in the nuclei of all living cells. It is the substance of which genes are made and is chiefly responsible for the transmission of inherited characteristics; deoxyribonucleic acid.

do¹ (dü), **1** carry through to an end any action or piece of work; carry out; perform: *Do your work well.* **2** produce; make: *She did a book on her travels in Africa.* **3** act; behave: *You did very well in ignoring the insult.* **4** be the cause of; bring about: *Your work does you credit.* **5** deal with; take care of: *do the dishes, do one's hair.* **6** get along; manage; fare: *My sister is doing well in her new job.* **7** be satisfactory: *This hat will do.* **8** *Do* is used: **a** to ask questions: *Do you like milk?* **b** to make what one says stronger: *I do want to go.* **c** to stand for another verb already used: *My dog goes where I do.* **d** in expressions that contain *not: People talk; animals do not. v.,* **did, done, do ing.** [*Do¹* comes from Old English *dōn.*] —**do′a ble,** *adj.*

do away with, 1 put an end to; abolish: *do away with a rule.* **2** kill: *The trap did away with the rat.*

do up, 1 wrap up; tie up: *Please do up this package more securely.* **2** arrange: *do up one's hair.*

do without, get along without.

do² (dō), (in music) the first and last tone of the scale. *do, re, mi, fa, sol, la, ti, do* are the names of the tones of the scale. *n.* [*Do²* is borrowed from Italian *do.*]

do., ditto.

dob bin (dob′ən), a slow, gentle, plodding horse. *n.*

Doberman pinscher
24 to 28 in.
(61 to 71 cm.)
high at the shoulder

Do ber man pin scher (dō′bər mən pin′shər), a medium-sized, slender dog with short, dark hair. [The name of this dog comes from Ludwig *Dobermann,* a German dog breeder of the 1800's, and German *Pinscher,* meaning "terrier."]

doc ile (dos′əl), easily trained or managed; obedient: *a docile horse, a docile student. adj.* —**doc′ile ly,** *adv.*

do cil i ty (do sil′ə tē), docile quality. *n.*

dock¹ (dok), **1** platform built on the shore or out from the shore; wharf; pier. Ships load and unload beside a dock. **2** water between two piers, permitting the entrance of ships. **3** place where a ship may be repaired, often built watertight so that the water may be kept high or pumped out. **4** platform for loading and unloading trucks or freight cars. **5** bring (a ship) to a dock: *The crew docked the ship and began to unload it.* **6** come into a dock: *The ship docked during the night.* **7** join (two space-craft) while in space. 1-4 *n.*, 5-7 *v.*

dock² (dok), **1** cut down; cut some off of: *Workers' wages are docked if they are late.* **2** cut short; cut off the end of. Horses' and dogs' tails are sometimes docked. *v.*

dock³ (dok), the place where an accused person stands or sits in a court of law. *n.*

dock⁴ (dok), a large weed with sour or bitter leaves and clusters of greenish flowers. *n.*

dock et (dok′it), **1** list of lawsuits to be tried by a court. **2** any list of matters to be considered by some person or group. **3** enter on a docket. **4** label or ticket giving the contents of a package, document, etc. 1,2,4 *n.*, 3 *v.*

dock yard (dok′yärd′), shipyard. *n.*

doc tor (dok′tər), **1** person trained in treating diseases or injuries. Physicians, surgeons, dentists, and veterinarians are doctors. **2** treat disease in: *My sister doctored me when I had a cold.* **3** person who has the highest degree given by a university: *a Doctor of Philosophy.* **4** falsify; tamper with: *The dishonest cashier doctored the accounts.* 1,3 *n.*, 2,4 *v.* [*Doctor* comes from Latin *doctor,* meaning "teacher."]

doc tor ate (dok′tər it), a doctor's degree given by a university. *n.*

doc tri nal (dok′trə nəl), of or having to do with doctrine. *adj.* —**doc′tri nal ly,** *adv.*

doc trine (dok′trən), **1** what is taught as true by a church, nation, or group of persons; belief: *religious doctrine.* **2** what is taught; teachings. *n.*

doc u ment (dok′yə mənt *for 1;* dok′yə ment *for 2*), **1** something written or printed that gives information or proof of some fact; any object used as evidence. Letters, maps, and pictures are documents. **2** prove or support by means of documents or the like: *Can you document your theory with facts?* 1 *n.*, 2 *v.*

doc u men tar y (dok′yə men′tər ē), **1** consisting of documents; in writing, print, etc.: *The photographs were used as documentary evidence at the trial.* **2** presenting or recording factual information in an artistic way: *a documentary film about the history of Boston.* **3** a documentary motion picture, book, or radio or television program. 1,2 *adj.*, 3 *n.*, *pl.* **doc u men tar ies.**

doc u men ta tion (dok′yə men tā′shən), **1** preparation and use of documentary evidence. **2** written material that comes with computer equipment or a computer program to explain its use. *n.*

dod der (dod′ər), be unsteady; shake; tremble; totter. *v.*

dodge (doj), **1** move or jump quickly to one side: *As I looked, they dodged behind a bush.* **2** avoid by jumping or moving to one side; get away from by twisting or turning quickly aside: *She dodged the ball as it came flying at her.* **3** a sudden movement to one side. **4** avoid by cleverness; get away from by some trick: *She dodged our question by changing the subject.* **5** a trick to cheat: *a clever dodge.* 1,2,4 *v.*, **dodged, dodg ing;** 3,5 *n.*

dodg er (doj′ər), person who dodges. *n.*

Dodg son (doj′sən), **Charles L.,** the real name of **Lewis Carroll.** *n.*

do do (dō′dō), a large, clumsy bird that could not fly. Dodos lived on several islands in the Indian Ocean until they became extinct in the 1600's. *n.*, *pl.* **do dos** or **do-does.** [See **Word History.**]

Do do ma (dō′dō mä), capital of Tanzania. *n.*

doe (dō), a female deer, goat, hare, rabbit, or antelope. *n.*

a hat	i it	oi oil	ch child	a in about
ā age	ī ice	ou out	ng long	e in taken
ä far	o hot	u cup	sh she	ə = { i in pencil
e let	ō open	ů put	th thin	o in lemon
ē equal	ô order	ü rule	ŦH then	u in circus
ėr term			zh measure	

do er (dü′ər), person who does something, especially with energy and drive: *He is a doer, not a dreamer. n.*

does (duz), a present tense of **do¹.** *He does all his work. Does she sing well? v.*

doe skin (dō′skin′), **1** a soft leather, now usually made from lambskin. **2** a smooth, soft woolen cloth, used for clothing. *n.*

does n't (duz′nt), does not.

doff (dof), take off; remove: *He doffed his hat as the flag passed by. v.*

dog (dôg), **1** a four-legged, flesh-eating mammal kept as a pet and used for hunting and for guarding property. Dogs are related to wolves, foxes, and jackals. **2** hunt or follow like a dog: *Bill collectors dogged them for over a month.* 1 *n.*, 2 *v.*, **dogged, dog ging.** —**dog′like′,** *adj.* **go to the dogs,** be ruined.

dog cart (dôg′kärt′), **1** a small cart pulled by dogs. **2** a small, open, horse-drawn carriage with two seats that are placed back to back. *n.*

dog catch er (dôg′kach′ər), person whose work is to catch stray dogs. *n.*

dog days, period of very hot and uncomfortable weather during July and August.

doge (dōj), the chief magistrate of Venice or Genoa when they were republics. *n.*

dog-ear (dôg′ir′), **1** a folded-down corner of a page in a book. A dog-ear is often made to mark the page where the reader has stopped. **2** fold down the corner of (a page in a book). 1 *n.*, 2 *v.*

dog-eared (dôg′ird′), badly worn: *dog-eared carpets. adj.*

dog fight (dôg′fit′), **1** combat between individual fighter planes at close quarters. **2** brawl. *n.*

dog fish (dôg′fish′), any of several kinds of small shark. *n.*, *pl.* **dog fish es** or **dog fish.**

dog ged (dô′gid), not giving up; stubborn; persistent: *Her dogged determination helped her to win the prize. adj.* —**dog′ged ly,** *adv.* —**dog′ged ness,** *n.*

WORD HISTORY

dodo

Dodo comes from Portuguese *doudo,* meaning "fool."

4 ft. (1 m.) long

dog ger el (dô′gər əl), 1 very poor poetry; poetry that is not artistic. 2 crude; poor; not artistic: *doggerel verses.* 1 *n.,* 2 *adj.*

dog gie bag or **dog gy bag** (dôg′ē), a small bag furnished by a restaurant to a customer who has not finished a meal, so that the uneaten food may be carried home.

dog gy (dôg′ē), like a dog. *adj.,* **dog gi er, dog gi est.**

dog house (dôg′hous′), a small house or shelter for a dog. *n., pl.* **dog hous es** (dôg′hou′ziz).
in the doghouse, SLANG. out of favor: *I am in the doghouse with my parents for staying out too late last night.*

do gie (dō′gē), (in the western United States and Canada) a motherless calf on the range or in a range herd. *n.* Also, **dogy.**

dog ma (dôg′mə), 1 belief taught or held as true, especially by authority of a church; doctrine. 2 opinion stated in a positive manner as if it were of the highest authority. *n., pl.* **dog mas.**

dog mat ic (dôg mat′ik), 1 of or having to do with dogma; doctrinal. 2 positive and emphatic in stating opinions: *The audience disliked the speaker's dogmatic manner in stating his opinions as if they were facts.* 3 stated in a positive and emphatic manner: *She gave no evidence to prove her dogmatic statement that the textbook was wrong. adj.* —**dog mat′i cal ly,** *adv.*

dog ma tism (dôg′mə tiz′əm), positive and emphatic statement of opinion. *n.*

Dog Star, Sirius.

dog-tired (dôg′tīrd′), very tired. *adj.*

dog trot (dôg′trot′), a gentle, easy trot. *n.*

dog wood (dôg′wùd′), tree with large white or pinkish flowers in the spring and red berries in the fall. *n.*

do gy (dō′gē), dogie. *n., pl.* **do gies.**

Do ha (dō′hä), capital of Qatar. *n.*

doi ly (doi′lē), a small piece of linen, lace, paper, or plastic, used on a table. Doilies are put under plates, bowls, vases, etc. *n., pl.* **doi lies.** [*Doily* was the name of an English dry-goods dealer in the 1700's.]

do ings (dü′ingz), 1 things done; actions. 2 behavior; conduct. *n.pl.*

do-it-your self (dü′it yər self′), designed for use, construction, or assembly by an amateur. *adj.*

dol drums (dol′drəmz or dōl′drəmz), 1 gloomy feeling; low spirits: *My brother has been in the doldrums since he failed the history test.* 2 region of the ocean near the equator where the wind is very light or constantly shifting. When a sailing ship gets in the doldrums, it makes little headway. *n.pl.*

dole (dōl), 1 portion of money, food, etc., given in charity. 2 give out in portions to the poor. 3 a small portion. 4 give in small portions: *The teacher doled out a dab of paste to each student.* 5 money given by a government to unemployed workers. 1,3,5 *n.,* 2,4 *v.,* **doled, dol ing.**

dole ful (dōl′fəl), very sad or dreary; mournful; dismal. *adj.* —**dole′ful ly,** *adv.* —**dole′ful ness,** *n.*

doll (dol), 1 a child's toy made to look like a baby, child, or grown person. 2 a pretty child, girl, or woman. 3 SLANG. dress in a stylish or showy way: *They were all dolled up in party clothes.* 1,2 *n.,* 3 *v.* [*Doll* is a nickname for *Dorothy.*] —**doll′-like′,** *adj.*

dol lar (dol′ər), 1 unit of money in the United States. 100 cents make one dollar. 2 a similar unit of money in Canada, Australia, and some other countries. 3 a silver coin or piece of paper money equal to 100 cents. *n.*

doll house (dol′hous′), a toy house for children to use in playing with dolls. *n., pl.* **doll hous es** (dol′hou′ziz).

dol lop (dol′əp), INFORMAL. portion or serving, either large or small. *n.*

doll y (dol′ē), 1 a child's name for a doll. 2 a small, low frame on wheels, used to move heavy things: *The refrigerator was moved into the house on a dolly. n., pl.* **doll ies.**

do lor (dō′lər), sorrow; grief. *n.*

dol or ous (dol′ər əs or dō′lər əs), 1 full of or expressing sorrow; mournful. 2 causing or giving rise to sorrow; grievous; painful. *adj.* —**dol′or ous ly,** *adv.* —**dol′or ous ness,** *n.*

dol phin (dol′fən), 1 a sea mammal related to the whale, but smaller. It has a beaklike snout and remarkable intelligence. 2 either of two large saltwater fishes that change color when taken from the water. *n.*

dolt (dōlt), a dull, stupid person. *n.*

dolt ish (dōl′tish), like a dolt; dull and stupid. *adj.* —**dolt′ish ly,** *adv.* —**dolt′ish ness,** *n.*

-dom, *suffix forming nouns.* 1 (*added to nouns*) position, rank, or realm of a ____: *Kingdom = realm of a king.* 2 (*added to adjectives*) condition of being ____: *Freedom = condition of being free.*

do main (dō mān′), 1 territory under the control of one ruler or government. 2 land owned by one person; estate. 3 field of thought or action: *the domain of science, the domain of religion. n.*

dome (def. 1)—of the Capitol in Washington, D.C.

dome (dōm), 1 a large, rounded roof or ceiling on a circular or many-sided base. 2 something high and rounded: *the dome of a hill. n.* —**dome′like′,** *adj.*

do mes tic (də mes′tik), 1 of the home, household, or family affairs: *domestic problems, a domestic scene.* 2 fond of home and family life: *He is a domestic man who enjoys being with his children.* 3 servant in a household. A butler or a maid is a domestic. 4 not wild; tame. Cats, dogs, cows, horses, and pigs are domestic animals. 5 of or made in one's own country; not foreign: *Most newspapers publish both domestic and foreign news.* 1,2,4,5 *adj.,* 3 *n.* —**do mes′ti cal ly,** *adv.*

do mes ti cate (də mes′tə kāt), 1 change from a wild to a tame or cultivated state: *People have domesticated many plants and animals.* 2 make fond of home and family life. *v.,* **do mes ti cat ed, do mes ti cat ing.**

do mes ti ca tion (də mes′tə kā′shən), a domesticating or a being domesticated. *n.*

do mes tic i ty (dō′mes tis′ə tē), 1 home and family life. 2 fondness for home and family life. *n., pl.* **do mes tic i ties.**

domestic science, home economics.

dom i cile (dom′ə sil), 1 a dwelling place; house; home. 2 place of permanent residence. A person may have several residences, but only one legal domicile at a time. 3 settle in a domicile. 4 dwell; reside: *They domiciled in Italy part of the year.* 1,2 *n.,* 3,4 *v.,* **dom i ciled, dom i cil ing.**

dom i cil i ar y (dom′ə sil′ē er′ē), of a domicile. *adj.*

dom i nance (dom′ə nəns), controlling influence; supreme authority; rule; control. *n.*

dom i nant (dom′ə nənt), 1 most powerful or influential; controlling; ruling; governing: *She was a dominant figure in local politics.* 2 rising high above its surroundings;

towering over: *Dominant hills sheltered the bay.* **3** the fifth note in a musical scale. G is the dominant in the key of C. **1,2** *adj.,* **3** *n.* —**dom′i nant ly,** *adv.*

dom i nate (dom′ə nāt), **1** control or rule by strength or power: *She spoke with the authority needed to dominate the meeting.* **2** rise high above; tower over: *The mountain dominates the city and its harbor.* *v.,* **dom i nat ed, dom i‐ nat ing.** —**dom′i na′tor,** *n.*

dom i na tion (dom′ə nā′shən), a dominating; control; rule: *The champion's long domination of archery ended when the challenger defeated her.* *n.*

dom i neer (dom′ə nir′), rule or assert one's authority or opinions in an arrogant way: *The oldest child in a family may sometimes domineer over the younger chil‐ dren.* *v.*

dom i neer ing (dom′ə nir′ing), inclined to domineer; arrogant; overbearing: *I dislike the domineering attitude of people who always want things done their own way.* *adj.* —**dom′i neer′ing ly,** *adv.* —**dom′i neer′ing ness,** *n.*

Dom i nic (dom′ə nik), **Saint,** 1170-1221, Spanish priest who founded an order of preaching friars. *n.*

Do min i can (də min′ə kən), **1** of Saint Dominic or the religious order founded by him. **2** friar belonging to the Dominican order. **3** of or having to do with the Domini‐ can Republic. **4** person born or living in the Dominican Republic. **1,3** *adj.,* **2,4** *n.*

Dominican Republic, country in the E part of the island of Hispaniola, in the West Indies. *Capital:* Santo Domingo.

dom i nie (dom′ə nē), SCOTTISH. schoolmaster. *n.*

do min ion (də min′yən), **1** power or right of governing and controlling; rule; control: *The ancient Romans had dominion over a large part of the world.* **2** territory under the control of one ruler or government. **3 Dominion,** name formerly used for a self-governing country within the British Commonwealth. *n.*

dom i no (dom′ə nō), **1 dominoes,** *pl.* game played with flat, oblong pieces of bone, wood, etc., that are either blank or marked with dots. Players try to match pieces having blanks or the same number of dots. **2** one of the pieces used in the game of dominoes. **3** a loose cloak with a small mask covering the upper part of the face. It was formerly worn as a disguise at masquerades. **4** the small mask. *n., pl.* **dom i noes** or **dom i nos.**

don[1] (don), put on (clothing, etc.): *The knight donned his armor.* *v.,* **donned, don ning.** [*Don*[1] is short for *do on,* meaning "put on (clothes)."]

don[2] (don), **1 Don,** a Spanish title meaning Mr. or Sir: *Don Felipe.* **2** a head, fellow, or tutor of a college at Oxford or Cambridge University in England. *n.* [*Don*[2] was borrowed from Spanish *Don,* which came from Latin *dominus,* meaning "lord, master."]

Don (don), river in SW Soviet Union. *n.*

do nate (dō′nāt), give money or help, especially to a fund or institution; contribute: *She donated $20 to the community chest.* *v.,* **do nat ed, do nat ing.** —**do′na‐ tor,** *n.*

do na tion (dō nā′shən), **1** gift; contribution: *The class decided to make a donation to UNICEF.* **2** a giving; donat‐ ing. *n.*

done (dun), **1** finished or completed; through: *He is done with his assignments.* **2** INFORMAL. worn out; exhausted. **3** cooked: *I want my steak well done.* **4** past participle of **do**[1]. *Have you done all your chores?* **1-3** *adj.,* **4** *v.*

don jon (dun′jən), a large, strongly fortified tower of a castle. *n.*

Don Juan (don wän′), a legendary Spanish nobleman who led an immoral life.

don key (dong′kē), **1** a small animal somewhat like a horse but with longer ears and a shorter mane; ass. **2** a

stubborn person. **3** a silly fool; stupid person. *n., pl.* **don‐ keys.**

don nish (don′ish), like a university don; scholarly in a dull way. *adj.* —**don′nish ly,** *adv.* —**don′nish ness,** *n.*

do nor (dō′nər), person who donates; giver; contributor. A blood donor is a person who gives blood for a transfu‐ sion. *n.*

Don Qui xo te (don ki hō′tē *or* don kwik′sət), hero of a famous novel of the same name by the Spanish writer Cervantes. Don Quixote is chivalrous and idealistic, but also foolish and impractical.

don't (dōnt), do not.

doo dle (dü′dl), **1** make drawings or marks absent‐ mindedly while talking or thinking. **2** drawing or mark made absent-mindedly. **1** *v.,* **doo dled, doo dling; 2** *n.*

doo dle bug (dü′dl bug′), larva of the ant lion. *n.*

doo dler (düd′lər), person who doodles. *n.*

doom (düm), **1** fate. **2** an unhappy or terrible fate; ruin or death: *As the ship sank, the voyagers faced their doom.* **3** condemn to an unhappy or terrible fate: *The prisoner was doomed to death. Poor health doomed my cousin to an inactive life.* **4** judgment; sentence: *The judge pronounced the prisoner's doom.* **5** make a bad or unwelcome out‐ come certain: *The weather doomed our hopes for a picnic.* **1,2,4** *n.,* **3,5** *v.* [*Doom* comes from Old English *dōm,* meaning "law, judgment."]

dooms day (dümz′dā′), end of the world; Judgment Day. *n.*

door (dôr), **1** a movable barrier that opens and shuts by turning on hinges or sliding on tracks. Doors may be set into the walls of buildings or rooms, into vehicles, up‐ right furniture cabinets, stoves, etc. **2** doorway: *The salesman had a foot in the door.* **3** room, house, or build‐ ing to which a door belongs: *Her house is three doors down the street from ours.* **4** way to go in or out; way to get something: *a door to opportunity. The door to knowl‐ edge is study. n.* [*Door* comes from Old English *duru,* meaning "door," and *dur,* meaning "gate."] —**door′‐ like′,** *adj.*

lay at the door of, blame for.

out of doors, not in a house or building; outside.

door bell (dôr′bel′), bell that a caller may ring by press‐ ing a button or pulling a handle on the outside of a door to a house. *n.*

door knob (dôr′nob′), handle on either side of a door, used for opening or closing the door. *n.*

door man (dôr′mən), person whose work is opening or guarding the door of a hotel, store, apartment house, etc., for people going in or out. *n., pl.* **door men.**

door mat (dôr′mat′), mat placed near a door for wiping off the dirt from the bottom of one's shoes before enter‐ ing. *n.*

door post (dôr′pōst′), the upright piece forming the side of a doorway. *n.*

door sill (dôr′sil′), threshold. *n.*

door step (dôr′step′), step leading from an outside door to the ground. *n.*

door way (dôr′wā′), an opening in a wall where a door is. *n.*

door yard (dôr′yärd′), yard near the door of a house; yard around a house. *n.*

dope (dōp), **1** SLANG. a narcotic drug, such as opium or

---

a hat	i it	oi oil	ch child	a in about
ā age	ī ice	ou out	ng long	e in taken
ä far	o hot	u cup	sh she	ə = { i in pencil
e let	ō open	ů put	th thin	o in lemon
ē equal	ô order	ü rule	ŦH then	u in circus
ėr term			zh measure	

morphine. **2** SLANG. give dope to. **3** SLANG. information.
4 SLANG. a very stupid person. **5** a thick varnish or similar
liquid applied to a fabric to strengthen or waterproof it.
1,3-5 *n.,* 2 *v.,* **doped, dop ing.** [*Dope* comes from Dutch
doop, meaning "dipping, sauce."] —**dop′er,** *n.*

dope y or **dop y** (dō′pē), SLANG. **1** drugged; drowsy.
2 very stupid. *adj.,* **dop i er, dop i est.** —**dop′i ness,** *n.*

Do ric (dôr′ik), of the oldest and simplest kind of Greek
architecture. *adj.*

dorm (dôrm), INFORMAL. dormitory. *n.*

dor mant (dôr′mənt), **1** sleeping; seeming to sleep; not
moving or feeling: *Bears and other animals that hibernate
are dormant during the winter.* **2** without activity; inactive:
Many volcanoes are dormant. adj.

dor mer (dôr′mər), **1** an upright window that sticks out
from a sloping roof. **2** the part of a roof that sticks out
and contains such a window. *n.*

dor mi to ry (dôr′mə tôr′ē), **1** a building with many
rooms for sleeping in. Many colleges have dormitories
for students whose homes are elsewhere. **2** room for
sleeping that has several beds. *n., pl.* **dor mi to ries.**

dormouse
about 5 in. (13 cm.)
long with the tail

dor mouse (dôr′mous′), a small rodent that looks
somewhat like a squirrel and sleeps all winter. *n., pl.*
dor mice (dôr′mīs′).

dor sal (dôr′səl), of, on, or near the back: *A shark has a
dorsal fin. adj.* —**dor′sal ly,** *adv.*

do ry (dôr′ē), rowboat with a narrow, flat bottom and
high sides. It is often used by fishermen. *n., pl.* **do ries.**

dory

dos age (dō′sij), **1** amount of a medicine to be given or
taken at one time. **2** the giving of medicine in doses. *n.*

dose (dōs), **1** amount of a medicine to be given or taken
at one time: *a dose of cough medicine.* **2** give medicine to
in doses; treat with medicine: *The doctor dosed the sick
child with penicillin.* **3** something unpleasant or disagreeable: *We had a dose of freezing rain this morning.* 1,3 *n.,* 2
v., **dosed, dos ing.**

dost (dust), OLD USE. do[1]. "Thou dost" means "you do"
(singular). *v.*

Dos to ev ski (dos′tə yef′skē), **Feodor,** 1821-1881,
Russian novelist. *n.*

dot (dot), **1** a tiny, round mark; point. There is a dot over
each *i* in this line. **2** a small spot: *a blue necktie with white
dots.* **3** mark with a dot or dots: *Dot your i's and j's.* **4** be
here and there in: *Trees and bushes dotted the broad lawn.*

5 a short sound used in sending messages by telegraph
or radio. 1,2,5 *n.,* 3,4 *v.,* **dot ted, dot ting.** —**dot′ter,** *n.*
on the dot, INFORMAL. at exactly the right time: *Our train
arrived on the dot.*

dot age (dō′tij), a weak-minded and childish condition
that sometimes accompanies old age. *n.*

dormer (def. 2) and window

dot ard (dō′tərd), person who is weak-minded and
childish from old age. *n.*

dote (dōt). **dote on** or **dote upon,** be foolishly fond of;
be too fond of: *The parents dote on their only son, giving
him everything he wants. v.,* **dot ed, dot ing.**

doth (duth), OLD USE. does. "She doth" means "she
does." *v.*

dot ing (dō′ting), foolishly fond; too fond: *Doting parents
see no fault in their children. adj.* —**dot′ing ly,** *adv.*

dot ty (dot′ē), INFORMAL. feeble-minded; partly insane.
adj., **dot ti er, dot ti est.**

dou ble (dub′əl), **1** twice as much, as many, as large, as
strong, etc.: *She was given double pay for working on
Sunday.* **2** twice; doubly: *I was paid double by mistake.*
3 number or amount that is twice as much: *Four is the
double of two.* **4** make twice as much or twice as many:
He doubled his money in ten years by investing it wisely.
5 become twice as much or twice as many: *Money left in
a bank account can double in less than ten years.* **6** made
of two like parts; in a pair: *Double doors open wide.* **7** having
two unlike parts; having two meanings, characters, etc.
The spelling *b-e-a-r* has a double meaning: *carry* and *a
certain animal.* **8** two (of everything) instead of one: *The
blow on the head made him see double.* **9** take the place of
another; substitute: *The principal is doubling for the teacher today.* **10** person or thing just like another. In a motion
picture an actor often has a double to do the dangerous
scenes. **11** serve two purposes; play two parts: *The chair
doubled as a stepladder.* **12** fold; bend: *She doubled her
slice of bread to make a sandwich.* **13** a fold; bend.
14 close tightly together; clench: *He doubled his fists in
anger.* **15** bend or turn sharply backward: *The fox doubled
on its tracks to get away from the dogs.* **16** go around: *The
ship doubled Cape Horn.* **17** having more than one set of
petals: *Some roses are double; others are single.* **18** hit by
which a batter gets to second base in baseball. **19** hit a
double in baseball. **20 doubles,** *pl.* game of tennis, etc.,
with two players on each side. 1,6,7,17 *adj.,* 2,8 *adv.,*
3,10,13,18,20 *n.,* 4,5,9,11,12,14-16,19 *v.,* **dou bled, doubling.** —**dou′bler,** *n.*

double back, 1 fold over: *It ruins a book to double back
the pages as a bookmark.* **2** go back the same way that
one came: *The fox doubled back to avoid capture.*

double up, 1 bend over: *I doubled up with laughter.*
2 share room, bed, or quarters with another: *Since there
was only one room left at the hotel, the girls doubled up.*

on the double, quickly: *The teacher warned us to stop
talking and get to work on the double.*

double bass
The four strings are played with a bow or by plucking with the fingers.

a hat	i it	oi oil	ch child	a in about
ā age	ī ice	ou out	ng long	e in taken
ä far	o hot	u cup	sh she	ə = { i in pencil
e let	ō open	ủ put	th thin	o in lemon
ē equal	ô order	ü rule	ŦH then	u in circus
ėr term			zh measure	

double bass (bās), a deep-toned stringed instrument shaped like a cello but much larger; bass viol; contrabass.

double cross, INFORMAL. act of treachery.

dou ble-cross (dub′əl krôs′), INFORMAL. promise to do one thing and then do another; be treacherous to. *v.* —**dou′ble-cross′er,** *n.*

dou ble-deal er (dub′əl dē′lər), person guilty of double-dealing. *n.*

dou ble-deal ing (dub′əl dē′ling), 1 a pretending to do one thing and then doing another; deceitful action or behavior. 2 ready to deceive; deceitful. 1 *n.*, 2 *adj.*

dou ble-dig it (dub′əl dij′it), consisting of a numeral from 10 through 99: *double-digit inflation of 12 percent. adj.*

dou ble head er (dub′əl hed′ər), two games played one after another on the same day. *n.*

dou ble-joint ed (dub′əl join′tid), having joints that let fingers, arms, legs, etc., bend in unusual ways. *adj.*

dou ble knit (dub′əl nit′), 1 a knitted fabric with two interlocked layers. 2 knitted with two interlocked layers: *doubleknit slacks.* 1 *n.*, 2 *adj.*

dou ble-park (dub′əl pärk′), park (a car, etc.) beside another car that is occupying a legal parking area. *v.*

double play, a play in baseball in which two base runners are put out.

dou ble-quick (dub′əl kwik′), 1 the next quickest step to a run in marching. 2 very quick. 1 *n.*, 2 *adj.*

doublet

dou blet (dub′lit), a man's close-fitting jacket. Men in Europe wore doublets from the 1400's to the 1600's. *n.*

dou ble-talk (dub′əl tôk′), speech that is purposely meaningless, but seems meaningful because normal words and intonations are mixed in. *n.*

dou bloon (du blün′), a former Spanish gold coin. *n.*

dou bly (dub′lē), twice as; twice: *Be doubly careful when driving during a storm. adv.*

doubt (dout), 1 not believe or trust; not be sure of; feel uncertain about: *She doubted if we would arrive home on time.* 2 difficulty in believing: *Our faith helped overcome*

our doubt. 3 an uncertain state of mind: *We were in doubt as to the right road.* 4 an uncertain condition of affairs: *The ship's fate is still in doubt.* 1 *v.*, 2-4 *n.* —**doubt′a ble,** *adj.* —**doubt′er,** *n.* —**doubt′ing ly,** *adv.*

no doubt or **without doubt,** surely; certainly: *No doubt it will rain today.*

doubt ful (dout′fəl), 1 full of doubt; not sure; uncertain: *We are doubtful about the weather for tomorrow.* 2 causing doubt; open to question or suspicion: *His sly answers made his sincerity doubtful. adj.* —**doubt′ful ly,** *adv.* —**doubt′ful ness,** *n.*

doubt less (dout′lis), 1 without doubt; surely. 2 probably. *adv.* —**doubt′less ly,** *adv.* —**doubt′less ness,** *n.*

dough (dō), 1 a soft, thick mixture of flour, milk, fat, and other materials for baking. Bread, biscuits, cake, and pie crust are made from dough. 2 INFORMAL. money. *n.* [*Dough* comes from Old English *dāg.*] —**dough′like′,** *adj.*

dough nut (dō′nut′), a small cake of sweetened dough cooked in deep fat. A doughnut is usually made in the shape of a ring. *n.*

dough ty (dou′tē), strong and bold; stout; brave; hardy: *a doughty knight. adj.,* **dough ti er, dough ti est.** —**dough′ti ly,** *adv.* —**dough′ti ness,** *n.*

dough y (dō′ē), of or like dough; soft and thick; pale and flabby. *adj.,* **dough i er, dough i est.**

Doug lass (dug′ləs), Frederick, 1817-1895, American author, orator, and Abolitionist who was once a slave. *n.*

dour (dủr *or* dour), 1 gloomy or sullen: *They sulked in dour silence.* 2 stern; severe: *Her dour remarks frightened me. adj.* —**dour′ly,** *adv.* —**dour′ness,** *n.*

douse (dous), 1 plunge into water or any other liquid. 2 throw water over; drench: *We quickly doused the flames.* 3 INFORMAL. put out; extinguish: *Douse the lights. v.,* **doused, dous ing.**

dove[1] (duv), pigeon, especially one of the smaller wild kinds. The dove is often a symbol of peace. *n.*

dove[2] (dōv), dived; a past tense of **dive.** *v.*

dove cot (duv′kot′), dovecote. *n.*

dove cote (duv′kōt′), a small house or shelter for doves or pigeons. *n.*

Do ver (dō′vər), 1 seaport in SE England, the nearest English port to France. 2 **Strait of,** narrow channel or strait between N France and SE England. 3 capital of Delaware, in the central part. *n.*

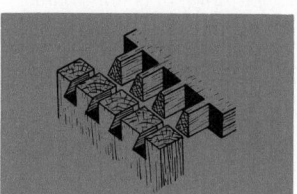

dovetails (def. 1)

dove tail (duv′tāl′), 1 projection at the end of a piece of wood, metal, etc., that can be fitted into a corresponding opening at the end of another piece to form a joint. 2 the joint formed in this way. 3 fasten, join, or fit together with dovetails. 4 fit together exactly: *The various pieces of evidence dovetailed so completely that the mystery was solved at once.* 1,2 *n.*, 3,4 *v.*

dow a ger (dou′ə jər), **1** woman who holds some title or property from her dead husband: *The queen and her mother-in-law, the queen dowager, were present.* **2** a dignified, elderly woman, usually of high social position. *n.*

dow di ly (dou′dl ē), in a dowdy manner; shabbily. *adv.*

dow di ness (dou′dē nis), dowdy quality or condition; shabbiness. *n.*

dow dy (dou′dē), poorly dressed; not neat; not stylish; shabby. *adj.*, **dow di er, dow di est.**

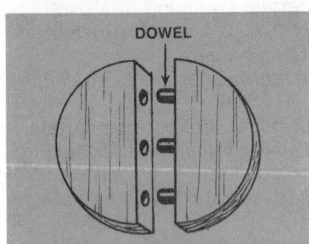

dowel (def. 1)

dow el (dou′əl), **1** peg on a piece of wood, metal, etc., made to fit into a corresponding hole on another piece, so as to form a joint fastening the two pieces together. **2** fasten with dowels. 1 *n.*, 2 *v.*, **dow eled, dow el ing** or **dow elled, dow el ling.**

dow er (dou′ər), a widow's share for life of her dead husband's property. *n.*

down[1] (doun), **1** from a higher to a lower place or condition: *They ran down from the top of the hill. The temperature has gone down.* **2** in a lower place or condition: *Down in the valley the fog still lingers* (adv.). *The sun is down* (adj.). **3** from an earlier to a later time: *The story has come down through many years.* **4** down along, through, or into: *ride down a hill, walk down a street, sail down a river.* **5** going or pointed down: *the down elevator.* **6** put down; throw down; get down: *She downed the medicine with one swallow. I was downed in a fight. Down, Fido!* **7** sick; ill: *We are both down with colds. I felt down about my grades.* **9** out of order: *Our computer is down.* **10** piece of bad luck: *the ups and downs of life.* **11** actually; really: *Stop talking, and get down to work.* **12** on paper; in writing: *Take down what I say.* **13** in cash when bought: *You can pay $10 down and the rest later* (adv.). *We made a down payment on a new car* (adj.). **14** (in football) a play from scrimmage. A team has four downs to make at least ten yards. 1,3,9,11-13 *adv.*, 4 *prep.*, 2,5,7,8,13 *adj.*, 6 *v.*, 10,14 *n.*

down and out, completely without health, money, friends, etc.; wretched; forsaken.

down on, INFORMAL. angry at; having a grudge against: *The other players were down on him for quitting the game.*

down with, put down; throw down: *Down with tyranny!*

down[2] (doun), **1** soft feathers: *the down of a young bird.* **2** soft hair or fluff: *the down on a boy's chin. n.*

down[3] (doun). Usually, **downs,** *pl.* rolling, grassy land. *n.*

down beat (doun′bēt′), (in music) the first beat in a measure. *n.*

down cast (doun′kast′), **1** directed downward: *They were downcast and stood before us with downcast eyes.* **2** dejected; sad; discouraged: *After all our plans failed, we felt very downcast. adj.*

down fall (doun′fôl′), **1** a coming to ruin; sudden overthrow: *the downfall of an empire. Pride caused their downfall.* **2** a heavy rain or snow. *n.*

down grade (doun′grād′), **1** a downward slope. **2** lower in position, importance, reputation, etc.: *downgrade an employee. He downgrades people he does not like, in spite of their merits.* 1 *n.*, 2 *v.*, **down grad ed, down grad ing.**

on the downgrade, growing less in strength, power, etc.

down heart ed (doun′här′tid), in low spirits; discouraged; dejected; depressed. *adj.* **—down′heart′ed ly,** *adv.* **—down′heart′ed ness,** *n.*

down hill (doun′hil′), **1** down the slope of a hill; downward. **2** going or sloping downward: *a downhill race.* 1 *adv.*, 2 *adj.*

go downhill, get worse: *Our business has been going downhill since we raised our prices.*

down pour (doun′pôr′), a heavy rain. *n.*

down right (doun′rīt′), **1** thorough; complete: *a downright fool, a downright lie.* **2** thoroughly; completely: *They were downright rude to me.* **3** plain; positive: *Her downright answer left no doubt as to what she thought.* 1,3 *adj.*, 2 *adv.*

down shift (doun′shift′), to shift from a higher to a lower gear. *v.*

down stairs (doun′sterz′ or doun′starz′), **1** down the stairs: *I hurried downstairs.* **2** on or to a lower floor: *Look downstairs for my glasses* (adv.). *The downstairs rooms are dark* (adj.). **3** the lower floor or floors: *My room is in the downstairs of the house.* 1,2 *adv.*, 2 *adj.*, 3 *n.*

down stream (doun′strēm′), with the current of a stream; down a stream: *The raft floated downstream* (adv.). *The downstream current was swift after the flood* (adj.). *adv.*, *adj.*

down-to-earth (doun′tə ėrth′), matter-of-fact; realistic. *adj.*

down town (doun′toun′), to or in the central or main business section of a town or city: *My parents went downtown shopping* (adv.). *Her office is in downtown Chicago* (adj.). *adv.*, *adj.*

down trod den (doun′trod′n), trampled upon; oppressed. *adj.*

down ward (doun′wərd), **1** toward a lower place or condition: *The bird swooped downward on its prey* (adv.). *The downward trip on the elevator was very slow* (adj.). **2** toward a later time: *There has been great progress in science from the 18th century downward.* 1 *adv.*, *adj.*, 2 *adv.*

down wards (doun′wərdz), downward. *adv.*

down wind (doun′wind′), in the same direction as the wind: *a downwind drift* (adj.). *The boat glided easily downwind* (adv.). *adj.*, *adv.*

down y (dou′nē), **1** made of soft feathers or hair: *a downy pillow.* **2** covered with soft feathers or hair: *a downy chick.* **3** like down; soft and fluffy: *A kitten's fur is downy. adj.*, **down i er, down i est. —down′i ness,** *n.*

dow ry (dou′rē), money or property that a woman brings to the man she marries. *n.*, *pl.* **dow ries.**

dox ol o gy (dok sol′ə jē), hymn or statement praising God. One familiar doxology begins: "Praise God from whom all blessings flow." *n.*, *pl.* **dox ol o gies.**

Doyle (doil), Sir **Arthur Conan,** 1859-1930, English writer, author of the Sherlock Holmes detective stories. *n.*

doz., dozen or dozens.

doze (dōz), **1** sleep lightly; be half asleep: *After dinner I dozed on the couch.* **2** a light sleep; nap. 1 *v.*, **dozed, doz ing;** 2 *n.* **—doz′er,** *n.*

doze off, fall into a doze: *The cat dozed off by the fire.*

doz en (duz′n), group of 12; 12: *We had to have dozens of chairs for the party. We will need three dozen eggs and a dozen rolls. n.*, *pl.* **doz ens** or (*after a number*) **doz en.** [*Dozen* came into English about 700 years ago from French *dozeine*, which can be traced back to Latin *duodecim*, meaning "twelve," which comes from *duo*, meaning "two," and *decem*, meaning "ten."]

DP or **D.P.,** displaced person.

dpt., department.

Dr., Doctor.

drab (drab), **1** not attractive; dull; monotonous: *the drab houses of the smoky, dingy mining town.* **2** dull brownish-gray. **3** a dull brownish-gray color. 1,2 *adj.*, **drab ber, drab best;** 3 *n.* —**drab′ly,** *adv.* —**drab′ness,** *n.*

drach ma (drak′mə), **1** unit of money of modern Greece, worth about 3½ cents. **2** an ancient Greek silver coin. *n., pl.* **drach mas, drach mae** (drak′mē), or **drach mai** (drak′mī).

draft (draft), **1** current of air: *I caught cold sitting in a draft.* **2** device for controlling a current of air. Opening the draft of a furnace makes the fire burn faster. **3** a plan; sketch: *Before starting to build, we had the architect make a draft of how the finished house would look.* **4** make a plan or sketch of. **5** a rough copy: *She made two drafts of her book report before she handed in the final form.* **6** write out a rough copy of: *Three members of the club drafted a new set of rules to be discussed and voted on by the membership.* **7** selection of persons for some special purpose. Men needed as soldiers are supplied to the army by draft during periods of war. **8** persons selected for some special purpose. **9** select for some special purpose: *If nobody volunteers to help me, I will draft someone.* **10** a pulling of loads. **11** for pulling loads: *A big, strong horse or ox is a draft animal.* **12** a written order from one person or bank to another, requiring the payment of a stated amount of money. **13** depth of water that a ship needs for floating; depth to which a ship sinks in water. A ship's draft is greater when it is loaded than when it is empty. **14** a single act of drinking: *He emptied the glass at one draft.* **15** amount taken in a single drink. 1-3,5,7,8,10, 12-15 *n.*, 4,6,9 *v.*, 11 *adj.* Also, **draught.** —**draft′er,** *n.*

draft ee (draf tē′), person who is drafted for military service. *n.*

draft i ness (draf′tē nis), drafty condition. *n.*

drafts man (drafts′mən), person who makes plans or sketches. A draftsman draws designs or diagrams from which buildings and machines are made. *n., pl.* **draftsmen.** Also, **draughtsman.**

drafts man ship (drafts′mən ship), work of a draftsman. *n.* Also, **draughtsmanship.**

draft y (draf′tē), **1** in a current of air: *I had a drafty seat near the window.* **2** having many currents of air: *a drafty room. adj.*, **draft i er, draft i est.** —**draft′i ly,** *adv.*

drag (drag), **1** pull or move along heavily or slowly; pull or draw along the ground: *A team of horses dragged the big log out of the forest. I dragged along on my sprained ankle.* **2** go too slowly: *Time drags when you have nothing to do.* **3** pull a net, hook, harrow, etc., over or along for some purpose: *They dragged the lake for fish.* **4** net, hook, harrow, etc., used in dragging. **5** anything that holds back; obstruction; hindrance: *If you don't practice, you'll be a drag on the team.* **6** SLANG. take part in a drag race. **7** SLANG. a boring person or situation. 1-3,6 *v.*, **dragged, drag ging;** 4,5,7 *n.* —**drag′ger,** *n.*

drag gle (drag′əl), make or become wet or dirty by dragging through mud, water, dust, etc. *v.*, **drag gled, drag gling.**

drag gy (drag′ē), dragging; slow-moving; boring. *adj.*, **drag gi er, drag gi est.**

drag net (drag′net′), **1** net pulled over the bottom of a river, pond, etc., or along the ground. Dragnets are used to catch fish and small game. **2** set of plans for catching or gathering in: *The criminals were caught in a police dragnet. n.*

drag on (drag′ən), (in old stories) a huge, fierce animal supposed to look like a winged snake with claws, which often breathed out fire and smoke. *n.*

drag on fly (drag′ən flī′), a large, harmless insect, with a long, slender body and two pairs of gauzy wings, which darts about catching flies, mosquitoes, etc. *n., pl.* **drag on flies.**

dra goon (drə gün′), **1** a mounted soldier trained to fight

on foot or on horseback. **2** compel; force: *The prisoner was dragooned into signing a false confession.* 1 *n.*, 2 *v.*

drag race, race between cars to determine which can accelerate faster over a given distance.

drag ster (drag′stər), SLANG. a car used in a drag race, especially one built with reduced wind resistance and increased engine power. *n.*

drain (drān), **1** draw off or flow off slowly: *That ditch drains water from the swamp. The water drains into the river.* **2** draw water or other liquid from; empty or dry by draining: *The farmers drained the swamps to get more land for crops. In one drink she drained the cup. Set the dishes here to drain.* **3** channel or pipe for carrying off water or waste of any kind. **4** take away from slowly; use up little by little: *The war drained the country of its people and money.* **5** a slow taking away; using up little by little; draining: *Working too hard is a drain on your strength.* 1,2,4 *v.*, 3,5 *n.* [*Drain* comes from Old English *drēahnian.*]

drain age (drā′nij), **1** act or process of draining; drawing off or flowing off of water: *The drainage of swamps improved the land.* **2** system of channels or pipes for carrying off water or waste of any kind. **3** what is drained off. *n.*

drain pipe (drān′pīp′), pipe for carrying off water or other liquid. *n.*

drake (drāk), a male duck. *n.*

Drake (drāk), Sir **Francis,** 1540?-1596, English admiral. He was the first Englishman to sail around the world. *n.*

dram (dram), **1** a small weight. In apothecaries' weight, 8 drams make one ounce; in avoirdupois weight, 16 drams make one ounce. **2** a small drink of intoxicating liquor. *n.*

WORD HISTORY

drama

Drama is from Greek *drama*, meaning "play, deed," which comes from *dran*, meaning "do."

dra ma (drä′mə *or* dram′ə), **1** a play such as one sees in a theater; story written to be acted out by actors on the stage. **2** the art of writing, acting, or producing plays: *He is studying drama.* **3** series of happenings in real life that seem like those of a play: *The history of America is a thrilling drama. n., pl.* **dra mas.** [See **Word History.**]

dragonfly
about
life-size

Dram a mine (dram′ə mēn′), trademark for a drug used against nausea caused by motion, especially while traveling. *n.*

dra mat ic (drə mat′ik), **1** of drama; having to do with plays: *a dramatic actor.* **2** seeming like a play; full of action or feeling; exciting: *the dramatic reunion of a family separated during wartime.* **3** striking; impressive: *a dramatic use of color. adj.* —**dra mat′i cal ly,** *adv.*

dra mat ics (drə mat′iks), **1** *pl. in form, sing. in use.* art of acting or producing plays: *Dramatics is taught in some colleges.* **2** *pl. in form and use.* tendency to show off. *n.*

dram a tist (dram′ə tist), writer of plays; playwright. *n.*

dram a ti za tion (dram′ə tə zā′shən), **1** act of dramatizing. **2** what is dramatized: *That play is a dramatization of the life of Joan of Arc. n.*

dram a tize (dram′ə tiz), **1** make a drama of; arrange in the form of a play: *dramatize a novel.* **2** show or express in a dramatic way; make seem exciting and thrilling: *The speaker dramatized her story with many actions and gestures. v.,* **dram a tized, dram a tiz ing.**

drank (drangk), past tense of **drink.** *The hungry cat drank its milk rapidly. v.*

drape (drāp), **1** cover or hang with cloth falling loosely in folds, especially as a decoration: *The buildings were draped with red, white, and blue bunting.* **2** arrange (clothes, hangings, etc.) to hang loosely in folds: *The actor draped the cape over his shoulders.* **3** cloth hung in folds: *There were heavy drapes at the windows.* **1,2** *v.,* **draped, drap ing;** **3** *n.*

dra per y (drā′pər ē), **1** hangings or clothing arranged in folds, especially such hangings hung as curtains: *The gay colors of the drapery made the living room bright and cheery.* **2** cloths or fabrics; dry goods. *n., pl.* **dra per ies.**

dras tic (dras′tik), acting with force or violence; extreme: *The police took drastic measures to put a stop to the wave of robberies. adj.* —**dras′ti cal ly,** *adv.*

WORD HISTORY

drastic

Drastic is from Greek *drastikos,* meaning "effective," which comes from *dran,* meaning "do."

draught (draft), draft. *n., v., adj.* —**draught′er,** *n.*

draughts (drafts), BRITISH. the game of checkers. *n.*

draughts man (drafts′mən), draftsman. *n., pl.* **draughts men.**

draughts man ship (drafts′mən ship), draftsmanship. *n.*

draw (drô), **1** cause to move by the use of force or effort; pull or drag; haul: *The horses drew the wagon.* **2** pull out; pull up; cause to come out; take out; get: *Draw a pail of water from the well. She drew ten dollars from the bank. Until you hear both sides of the argument, draw no conclusions.* **3** act of pulling or taking out: *The cowgirl was skilled with guns and quick on the draw.* **4** come or go; move: *We drew near the fire to get warm.* **5** attract: *A parade draws a crowd.* **6** make a picture or likeness of with pencil, pen, chalk, crayon, etc.: *Draw a circle. He draws very well for a six-year-old.* **7** describe: *The characters in this novel are not fully drawn; they seem unreal.* **8** make a current of air to carry off smoke: *The chimney does not draw well.* **9** breathe in; inhale; take in: *Draw a deep breath.* **10** a tie in a game. If neither side wins, it is a draw. **11** stretch: *The girls drew the rope taut.*

12 sink to a depth of; need for floating: *A ship draws more water when it is loaded than when it is empty.* **13** a small land basin into or through which water drains; kind of valley: *We found the stray cattle grazing in a draw.* **1,2,4-9,11,12** *v.,* **drew, drawn, draw ing;** **3,10,13** *n.* [*Draw* comes from Old English *dragan.*]

draw oneself up, stand up straight: *She drew herself up to her full height.*

draw out, 1 make long or longer: *His speech was much too drawn out.* **2** persuade to talk: *It is hard to draw out a shy person.*

draw up, 1 arrange in order: *The marchers were drawn up in formation for the parade.* **2** write out in proper form: *draw up a will.* **3** stop: *A car drew up in front of the house.*

draw back (drô′bak′), something that makes a situation or experience less complete or satisfying; unfavorable condition; disadvantage: *Our trip was interesting but the rainy weather was a drawback. n.*

draw bridge (drô′brij′), bridge that can be entirely or partly lifted, lowered, or moved to one side. In old castles drawbridges were lifted to keep out enemies. A drawbridge over a river is lifted to let boats pass. *n.*

drawer (drôr *for 1,3;* drô′ər *for 2*), **1** box with handles built to slide in and out of a table, desk, or bureau: *He kept his shirts in the dresser drawer.* **2** person or thing that draws. **3 drawers,** *pl.* undergarment fitting over the legs and around the waist. *n.*

draw ing (drô′ing), **1** picture, sketch, plan, or design done with pencil, pen, chalk, crayon, etc. **2** the making of such a picture, sketch, plan, or design; representing objects by lines. **3** lottery. *n.*

drawing room, room for receiving or entertaining guests; parlor.

drawl (drôl), **1** talk in a slow way, drawing out the vowels: *He drawled his words in imitation of his favorite movie cowboy.* **2** such a way of talking; speech of someone who drawls: *a southern drawl, a soft-spoken drawl.* **1** *v.,* **2** *n.* [*Drawl* apparently comes from Dutch *dralen,* meaning "linger, delay."] —**drawl′er,** *n.* —**drawl′ing ly,** *adv.*

drawn (drôn), **1** past participle of **draw.** *That old horse has drawn many loads.* **2** made tense; strained: *a face drawn and stiff with pain.* **1** *v.,* **2** *adj.*

draw string (drô′string′), string or cord threaded through the folded border of a bag, jacket, etc., so that it can be tightened or loosened. *n.*

dray (drā), a low, strong cart for carrying heavy loads. *n.*

dray man (drā′mən), person who drives a dray. *n., pl.* **dray men.**

dread (dred), **1** fear greatly; feel terror or uneasiness about: *I dreaded my visits to the dentist. My cat dreads water.* **2** great fear; feeling of terror or uneasiness about what may happen. **3** dreaded; fearful; terrible: *The dread day of the trial was approaching.* **4** held in awe; awe-inspiring: *the dread sight of the immense, glowing volcano.* **1** *v.,* **2** *n.,* **3,4** *adj.*

dread ful (dred′fəl), **1** causing dread; fearful; terrible: *a fairy tale about a dreadful dragon.* **2** very bad; very unpleasant: *I have a dreadful cold. adj.* —**dread′ful ness,** *n.*

dread ful ly (dred′fə lē), **1** in a dreadful manner. **2** very; exceedingly. *adv.*

dread nought or **dread naught** (dred′nôt′), a big, powerful battleship with heavy armor and large guns. *n.* [*Dreadnought* was the name of the first battleship of this kind, launched by the British in 1906.]

dream (drēm), **1** images passing through the mind during sleep: *I had a bad dream last night.* **2** something unreal like a dream; daydream: *Sometimes I sit at my desk and have dreams about faraway places.* **3** imagine with the mind during sleep; have a dream or dreams: *I dreamed that I was flying.* **4** have daydreams; form fancies: *For* *years they dreamed of fame and riches.* **5** think of (something) as possible; imagine: *The day seemed so bright that we never dreamed it would rain.* **6** something having great beauty or charm: *It was a dream of a vacation.* 1,2,6 *n.,* 3-5 *v.,* **dreamed** or **dreamt, dream ing.** [*Dream* comes from Old English *drēam,* meaning "joy, music."] —**dream′less,** *adj.* —**dream′like′,** *adj.*

dream er (drē′mər), **1** person who dreams. **2** person whose ideas do not fit real conditions. *n.*

dream i ly (drē′mə lē), in a dreamy manner. *adv.*

dream i ness (drē′mē nis), a dreamy condition. *n.*

dream land (drēm′land′), unreal place. *n.*

dreamt (dremt), dreamed; a past tense and a past participle of **dream.** *v.*

dream y (drē′mē), **1** full of dreams: *a dreamy sleep.* **2** like a dream; vague; dim: *a dreamy recollection.* **3** fond of daydreaming; fanciful; not practical: *a dreamy person.* **4** causing dreams; soothing: *a dreamy lullaby. adj.,* **dream i er, dream i est.**

drear (drir), dreary. *adj.*

drear i ly (drir′ə lē), in a dreary manner; dismally. *adv.*

drear i ness (drir′ē nis), dreary condition; cheerlessness. *n.*

drear y (drir′ē), without cheer; dull; gloomy: *A cold, rainy day is dreary. adj.,* **drear i er, drear i est.** [*Dreary* comes from Old English *drēorig.*]

dredge[1] (drej), **1** machine with a scoop or a suction pipe for cleaning out or deepening a body of water. **2** clean out or deepen with a dredge: *dredge a harbor.* **3** apparatus with a net, used for gathering oysters, etc. It is dragged along the bottom of a river or the sea. **4** bring up or gather with a dredge. **5** dig up; collect: *dredge up all the facts.* 1,3 *n.,* 2,4,5 *v.,* **dredged, dredg ing.**

dredge[2] (drej), sprinkle: *dredge meat with flour. v.,* **dredged, dredg ing.**

dregs (dregz), **1** the solid bits of matter that settle to the bottom of a liquid: *After pouring the coffee I rinsed the dregs out of the coffeepot.* **2** the least desirable part: *the dregs of humanity. n.pl.*

drench (drench), wet thoroughly; soak: *A heavy rain drenched us. v.* [*Drench* is from Old English *drencan,* which comes from *drincan,* meaning "to drink."]

Dres den (drez′dən), city in SE East Germany, on the Elbe River. *n.*

dress (def. 5)
The store windows were **dressed** for Christmas.

dress (dres), **1** an outer garment worn by women and girls. **2** clothes; clothing: *Everyone wore casual dress.* **3** put clothes on: *Please dress the baby. I dressed quickly.* **4** wear clothes properly and attractively: *Some people don't know how to dress.* **5** decorate; adorn. **6** make ready for use; prepare: *The butcher dressed the chicken by pulling out the feathers, cutting off the head and feet, and taking out the insides.* **7** comb, brush, and arrange (hair). **8** put medicine, bandages, etc., on (a wound or sore). **9** form in a straight line: *The soldiers dressed their ranks.* **10** smooth; finish: *to dress leather.* 1,2 *n., pl.* **dress es;**

3-10 *v.,* **dressed** or **drest, dress ing.**

dress down, scold; rebuke.

dress up, put on one's best clothes.

dress er[1] (dres′ər), person who dresses (himself, another person, a shop window, etc.). *n.*

dress er[2] (dres′ər), **1** piece of furniture with drawers for clothes and usually a mirror; bureau. **2** piece of furniture with shelves for dishes. *n.*

dress ing (dres′ing), **1** medicine, bandage, etc., put on a wound or sore. **2** mixture of bread crumbs, seasoning, etc., used to stuff chicken, turkey, etc. **3** sauce for salads, fish, meat, etc. **4** act of one that dresses. *n.*

dressing gown, a loose robe worn while dressing or resting.

dressing table, table with a mirror, at which a person sits to comb the hair, put on makeup, etc.

dress mak er (dres′mā′kər), person whose work is making women's or children's clothing. *n.*

dress mak ing (dres′mā′king), the work of making women's or children's clothing. *n.*

dress rehearsal, rehearsal of a play with costumes and scenery just as for a regular performance.

dress y (dres′ē), **1** fancy and suited to formal occasions; elegant: *I'm going to buy something dressy for the party.* **2** stylish; fashionable. *adj.,* **dress i er, dress i est.**

drest (drest), dressed; a past tense and a past participle of **dress.** *v.*

drew (drü), past tense of **draw.** *He drew a picture of his mother. v.*

drib ble (drib′əl), **1** flow or let flow in drops or small amounts; trickle: *Gasoline dribbled from the leak in the tank.* **2** let saliva run from the mouth; drool: *Babies dribble on their bibs.* **3** a dropping; dripping; trickle: *There's a dribble of milk running down your chin.* **4** move (a ball) along by bouncing it or giving it short kicks: *dribble a basketball, dribble a soccer ball.* **5** act of dribbling a ball. 1,2,4 *v.,* **drib bled, drib bling;** 3,5 *n.* —**drib′bler,** *n.*

drib let (drib′lit), a small amount: *She paid off her big debt in driblets, a dollar or two a week. n.*

dried (drīd), past tense and past participle of **dry.** *I dried my hands. The dishes have already been dried. v.*

dri er (drī′ər), **1** more dry: *This towel is drier than that one.* **2** person or thing that dries. **3** dryer (def. 2). 1 *adj.,* comparative of **dry;** 2,3 *n.*

dries (drīz), a present tense of **dry.** *Dad washes the dishes and Mom dries them. v.*

dri est (drī′ist), most dry: *Which is the driest towel? adj.,* superlative of **dry.**

drift (drift), **1** carry or be carried along by currents of air or water: *The wind drifted the boat onto the rocks. A raft drifts if it is not steered.* **2** move or appear to move aimlessly: *People drifted in and out of the meeting.* **3** go along without knowing or caring where one is going: *Some people have a purpose in life; others just drift.* **4** movement caused by currents of air or water: *the drift of an iceberg.* **5** direction of such movement: *The drift of the Gulf Stream is to the north.* **6** tendency or trend: *Many politicians watch the drift of public opinion carefully.* **7** direction of thought; meaning: *Please explain that again; I did not quite get the drift of your words.* **8** anything carried along by wind, water, or ice. **9** heap or be heaped up by the wind: *The strong wind drifted the snow. The snow drifted* along the fence. **10** snow, sand, etc., heaped up by the wind: *After the heavy snow there were deep drifts in the yard.* **11** distance that a ship or aircraft is off course because of currents. 1-3,9 *v.*, 4-8,10,11 *n.* —**drift′er,** *n.*

drift wood (drift′wùd′), wood carried along by water or washed ashore from the water. *n.*

drill (dril), **1** tool or machine for boring holes. **2** bore a hole in; pierce with a drill. **3** teach by having the learner do a thing over and over: *The sergeant drilled the new soldiers.* **4** teaching or training by having the learners do a thing over and over for practice: *The teacher gave the class plenty of drill in arithmetic.* 1,4 *n.*, 2,3 *v.* —**drill′er,** *n.*

dri ly (drī′lē), dryly. *adv.*

drink (dringk), **1** swallow anything liquid: *Kittens like to drink milk. We drank from paper cups.* **2** liquid swallowed or to be swallowed: *Water is a good drink to quench one's thirst.* **3** portion of a liquid: *Please give me a drink of milk.* **4** suck up; absorb: *The dry soil drank up the rain.* **5** alcoholic liquor. **6** drink alcoholic liquor. 1,4,6 *v.*, **drank, drunk, drink ing;** 2,3,5 *n.* [*Drink* comes from Old English *drincan.*]

drink in, take in through the senses with eagerness and pleasure: *Our ears drank in the music.*

drink to, drink in honor of; drink with good wishes for: *The guests drank to the happiness of the bride and groom.*

drink er (dring′kər), **1** person who drinks. **2** person who drinks alcoholic liquor often or too much. *n.*

drip (drip), **1** fall or let fall in drops: *Rain drips from an umbrella. The awning dripped water onto her head.* **2** a falling in drops. **3** be so wet that drops fall: *My forehead was dripping with perspiration.* **4** liquid that falls in drops. 1,3 *v.*, **dripped, drip ping;** 2,4 *n.*

drip-dry (drip′drī′), **1** wash and hang to dry without wringing and with little or no ironing: *drip-dry a shirt or blouse.* **2** able to be drip-dried; wash-and-wear: *drip-dry fabrics.* 1 *v.*, **drip-dried, drip-dry ing;** 2 *adj.*

drip pings (drip′ingz), the melted fat and juice that have dripped down from meat while it was being cooked. *n.pl.*

drive (drīv), **1** make go: *Drive the dog away. Drive the nails into the board. The wind drives the windmill. The noise of the drums almost drove me mad.* **2** make go where one wishes; control the movement of: *drive a team of horses. Can you drive a car?* **3** go or carry in an automobile or carriage: *We want to drive through the mountains on the way home. She drove us to the station.* **4** trip in an automobile or carriage: *On Sunday we took a drive in the country.* **5** road: *He built a drive from the street to his house.* **6** force; urge on: *Hunger drove them to steal.* **7** a strong force; pressure: *She has a drive to succeed.* **8** bring about or obtain by cleverness or force: *He drove a good bargain at the store.* **9** vigor; energy: *a person with drive.* **10** a special effort of a group for some purpose; campaign: *The town had a drive to get money for charity.* **11** work hard or compel to work hard: *They said their boss drove them too hard.* **12** dash or rush with force; dash violently: *The ship drove on the rocks.* **13** (in sports) hit very hard and fast: *drive a golf ball.* **14** a very hard, fast hit: *The batter's drive went into deep left field.* **15** act of driving. **16** the thing or things driven: *a drive of cattle.* **17** get or make by drilling, boring, etc.: *drive a well.* **18** part that drives machinery. **19** the means by which power is transmitted to the wheels in a motor vehicle: *rear-wheel drive, four-wheel drive.* 1-3,6,8,11-13,17 *v.*, **drove, driv en, driv ing;** 4,5,7,9,10,14-16,18,19 *n.*

drive at, mean; intend: *What are you driving at?*

let drive, strike; aim: *The fighter let drive a left to the jaw.*

drive-in (drīv′in′), **1** arranged and equipped so that customers may drive in and be served or entertained while remaining seated in their cars: *a drive-in movie, a drive-*

in bank. **2** place so arranged and equipped. 1 *adj.*, 2 *n.*

driv el (driv′əl), **1** let saliva run from the mouth. **2** saliva running from the mouth. **3** talk or say in a stupid, foolish manner; talk nonsense. **4** silly talk; nonsense. 1,3 *v.*, 2,4 *n.* —**driv′el er,** *n.*

driv en (driv′ən), past participle of **drive.** *Mom has just driven to work. v.*

driv er (drī′vər), **1** person who drives, especially one who drives an automobile or other vehicle. **2** person who makes people who are lower in rank work very hard. **3** a golf club with a wooden head. It is used in hitting the ball off the tee. **4** a machine part that transmits force or motion. *n.*

drive shaft, a shaft that transmits power from an engine to the various working parts of a machine. In an automobile, a drive shaft connects the transmission to the rear or front axle.

drive way (drīv′wā′), a privately owned road to drive on, usually leading from a house or garage to the road. *n.*

driz zle (driz′əl), **1** rain gently, in very small drops like mist. **2** very small drops of rain like mist: *A steady drizzle made it hard to see across the muddy football field.* 1 *v.*, **driz zled, driz zling;** 2 *n.*

driz zly (driz′lē), drizzling. *adj.*, **driz zli er, driz zli est.**

droll
Santa Claus has a **droll** appearance in this picture.

droll (drōl), odd and amusing; quaint and laughable. *adj.* —**droll′ness,** *n.*

drom e dar y (drom′ə der′ē), a swift camel with one hump and short hair, found in parts of India, Arabia, and northern Africa and used for riding; Arabian camel. *n.*, *pl.* **drom e dar ies.**

WORD HISTORY

dromedary

Dromedary is from Latin *dromedarius,* which came from Greek *dromados kamēlos,* meaning "running camel."

7½ ft. (2.3 m.) high at the hump

drone (drōn), **1** a male bee, especially a male honey bee, that fertilizes the queen. Drones do not sting, gather honey, or help in the upkeep of the hive. **2** make a deep, continuous humming sound: *The bees droned among the flowers.* **3** a deep, continuous humming sound: *the drone of mosquitoes. The hikers heard the drone of a far-off automobile.* **4** talk or say in a monotonous voice: *Several people in the audience fell asleep as the speaker droned on.* **5** person not willing to work; idler; loafer. **6** spend time idly; loaf. 1,3,5 *n.*, 2,4,6 *v.*, **droned, dron ing.**

drool (drül), let saliva run from the mouth as a baby does. *v.*

droop (drüp), **1** hang down; bend down: *These flowers will soon droop if they are not put in water.* **2** a bending position; hanging down: *The droop of the branches brought them within our reach.* **3** become weak; lose strength and energy: *The hikers were drooping by the end of the walk in the hot sun.* **4** become discouraged; be sad and gloomy. 1,3,4 *v.*, 2 *n.* —**droop'ing ly,** *adv.*

droop y (drü'pē), **1** hanging down; drooping: *a droopy hat.* **2** discouraged; depressed. *adj.*, **droop i er, droop i est.**

drop (drop), **1** a small amount of liquid in a somewhat round shape: *a drop of rain, a drop of blood.* **2** a very small amount of liquid: *Take a few drops of this medicine.* **3 drops,** *pl.* liquid medicine given in drops: *eye drops, nose drops.* **4** a very small amount of anything: *At the end of the two-mile race, the runners didn't have a drop of strength left.* **5** fall or let fall in very small amounts. **6** a sudden fall: *a drop in temperature, a drop in prices.* **7** the distance down; a sudden fall in level; length of a fall: *From the top of the cliff to the water is a drop of 200 feet.* **8** fall or let fall suddenly: *The acrobat dropped from the high rope into the net below. The price of sugar may drop soon.* **9** fall or cause to fall: *It was so quiet you could hear a pin drop.* **10** let fall: *He dropped his package.* **11** fall dead, wounded, or tired out: *After working all day I was ready to drop.* **12** cause to fall dead; kill: *The hunter dropped the deer with a single shot.* **13** go lower; sink: *Her voice dropped to a whisper.* **14** make lower: *Drop your voice.* **15** let go; dismiss: *Members who do not pay their dues will be dropped from the club.* **16** leave out; omit: *Drop the "e" in "drive" before adding "ing."* **17** stop; end: *The matter is not important; let it drop.* **18** send (a letter, etc.): *While you are away on your trip, drop me a card.* **19** give or express: *He dropped a hint that he would like to be invited to the party.* **20** go with the current or tide: *The raft dropped down the river.* **21** set down from an automobile, ship, carriage, etc.: *Drop me at the corner of Main Street.* 1-4,6,7 *n.*, 5,8-21 *v.*, **dropped** or **dropt, dropping.** —**drop'like',** *adj.*

drop in, visit informally: *Drop in and see me some day.*

drop out, leave school or college before completing a course or a term.

drop-forge (drop'fôrj'), beat (hot metal) into shape with a very heavy hammer or weight. *v.*, **drop-forged, drop-forg ing.** —**drop'-forg'er,** *n.*

drop let (drop'lit), a tiny drop. *n.*

drop out (drop'out'), **1** student who leaves school or college before completing a course or a term. **2** person who withdraws or drops out: *a dropout from the Democratic Party, a dropout from middle-class society.* *n.*

drop per (drop'ər), a small glass tube with a hollow rubber cap at one end and a small opening at the other end from which a liquid can be made to fall in drops. *n.*

drop sy (drop'sē), edema. *n.*

dropt (dropt), dropped; a past tense and a past participle of **drop.** *v.*

dross (drôs), **1** waste or scum that comes to the surface of melting metals. **2** waste material; rubbish. *n.*

a hat	i it	oi oil	ch child	⎧ a in about
ā age	ī ice	ou out	ng long	⎪ e in taken
ä far	o hot	u cup	sh she	ə = ⎨ i in pencil
e let	ō open	ù put	th thin	⎪ o in lemon
ē equal	ô order	ü rule	ᵀH then	⎩ u in circus
ėr term			zh measure	

drought (drout), **1** a long period of dry weather; continued lack of rain: *A drought of three months during the summer caused the brooks and streams to dry up.* **2** lack of moisture; dryness. *n.*

drought y (drou'tē), suffering from drought; dry. *adj.*, **drought i er, drought i est.**

drove¹ (drōv), past tense of **drive.** *We drove two hundred miles today.* *v.*

drove² (drōv), **1** group of cattle, sheep, hogs, etc., moving or driven along together; flock; herd: *The rancher sent a drove of cattle to market.* **2** many people moving along together; crowd. *n.*

drov er (drō'vər), **1** person who drives cattle, sheep, hogs, etc., to market. **2** dealer in cattle. *n.*

drown (droun), **1** die under water or other liquid because of lack of air to breathe: *We almost drowned when our sailboat suddenly overturned.* **2** kill by keeping under water or other liquid: *The flood drowned many cattle in the lowlands.* **3** be stronger or louder than; keep from being heard: *The boat's whistle drowned out what she was trying to tell us.* *v.*

drowse (drouz), **1** be sleepy; be half asleep: *I drowsed, but did not quite fall asleep.* **2** a being half asleep; sleepiness. 1 *v.*, **drowsed, drows ing;** 2 *n.*

drow si ly (drou'zə lē), in a drowsy manner. *adv.*

drow si ness (drou'zē nis), drowsy condition; sleepiness. *n.*

drow sy (drou'zē), **1** half asleep; sleepy. **2** making one sleepy: *It was a warm, quiet, drowsy afternoon.* *adj.*, **drow si er, drow si est.**

drub (drub), **1** beat with a stick; whip soundly; thrash. **2** defeat by a large margin in a fight, game, contest, etc. *v.*, **drubbed, drub bing.** —**drub'ber,** *n.*

drudge (druj), **1** person who does hard, tiresome, or disagreeable work. **2** do hard, tiresome, or disagreeable work. 1 *n.*, 2 *v.*, **drudged, drudg ing.** —**drudg'er,** *n.*

drudg er y (druj'ər ē), work that is hard, tiresome, or disagreeable: *I think that washing dishes every day is drudgery.* *n.*, *pl.* **drudg er ies.**

drug (drug), **1** substance used as a medicine or in preparing medicines. Drugs are obtained from plants, chemicals, minerals, etc. Aspirin is a drug. **2** substance taken for its effect and not for medical reasons. Such drugs speed up or slow down the activity of the body or affect the senses. Marijuana is a drug. **3** give drugs to, particularly drugs that are harmful or cause sleep: *The spy drugged the guard and then searched for the secret documents.* **4** mix harmful drugs with (food or drink): *The spy drugged the guard's coffee.* **5** affect or overcome (the body or the senses) in a way that is not natural: *The wine had drugged her.* 1,2 *n.*, 3-5 *v.*, **drugged, drug ging.**

drug gist (drug'ist), **1** person who sells drugs, medicines, etc. **2** person licensed to fill prescriptions; pharmacist. *n.*

drug store (drug'stôr'), store that sells drugs and other medicines and often also soft drinks, cosmetics, magazines, etc. *n.*

dru id or **Dru id** (drü'id), member of an order of priests among the ancient Celts of Britain, Ireland, and France. The druids were very powerful leaders and judges until the Christian religion was accepted by the Celts. *n.*

drum (drum), **1** a musical instrument that makes a sound when it is beaten. A drum is a hollow cylinder with a covering stretched tightly over the ends. **2** sound made by beating a drum. **3** any sound like this: *the drum of rain on a roof.* **4** beat or play the drum: *I drum in the school band.* **5** beat, tap, or strike again and again: *Stop drumming on the table with your fingers.* **6** teach or drive into one's head by repeating over and over: *Arithmetic had to be drummed into me because I couldn't understand it.* **7** container or other thing shaped somewhat like a drum: *an oil drum.* **8** a thick bar or cylinder in a machine on which something is wound: *a drum of cable.* 1-3,7,8 *n.,* 4-6 *v.,* **drummed, drum ming.** —**drum′like′,** *adj.*

drum out of, send away from in disgrace: *The corrupt politician was drummed out of office.*

drum up, 1 call together: *We could not drum up enough players to make a baseball team.* **2** get by asking again and again; obtain: *The company's advertising campaign drummed up more business.*

drum major, man who leads a marching band, often twirling a baton.

drum ma jor ette (mā′jə ret′), a girl or woman who leads parades, twirling a baton; majorette.

drum mer (drum′ər), person who plays a drum. *n.*

drum stick (drum′stik′), **1** stick for beating a drum. **2** the lower half of the leg of a cooked chicken, turkey, etc. *n.*

drunk (drungk), **1** affected by alcoholic liquor; intoxicated: *People who are drunk often have trouble standing up straight.* **2** person who is drunk. **3** very much excited or affected: *drunk with success.* **4** past participle of **drink.** *I have drunk several glasses of milk already.* 1,3 *adj.,* 2 *n.,* 4 *v.*

drunk ard (drung′kərd), person who is often drunk; person who drinks too much alcoholic liquor. *n.*

drunk en (drung′kən), **1** overcome by alcoholic liquor; drunk. **2** caused by being drunk: *a drunken act, drunken words. adj.* —**drunk′en ly,** *adv.* —**drunk′en ness,** *n.*

dry (drī), **1** not wet; not moist: *Dust is dry.* **2** make or become dry: *We washed and dried the dishes after dinner. Clothes dry in the sun.* **3** having little or no rain: *Arizona has a dry climate.* **4** not giving milk: *That cow has been dry for a month.* **5** empty of water or other liquid: *I can't write with a dry pen.* **6** wanting a drink; thirsty: *I'm awfully dry after that hike.* **7** not under, in, or on water: *I was glad to be on dry land and away from the swamp.* **8** not shedding tears: *After the sad play there wasn't a dry eye in the theater.* **9** not fresh: *The cook used dry bread to make turkey stuffing.* **10** quietly humorous in a sharp, biting way: *a dry wit, a dry remark.* **11** not interesting; dull: *A book full of facts and figures is dry.* **12** free from sweetness or fruity flavor: *dry wine.* **13** without butter: *dry toast.* **14** INFORMAL. forbidding the sale of alcoholic drinks: *a dry city, a dry state.* 1,3-14 *adj.,* **dri er, dri est;** 2 *v.,* **dried, dry ing.** [*Dry* comes from Old English *drȳge.*] —**dry′ness,** *n.*

dry up, SLANG. stop talking.

dry ad or **Dry ad** (drī′əd), (in Greek myths) a nymph that lives in a tree; wood nymph. *n., pl.* **dry ads, dry a des** (drī′ə dēz).

dry cell, an electric cell in which the chemicals producing the current are made into a paste, so that they cannot spill.

dry-clean (drī′klēn′), clean (clothes, etc.) with a chemical cleaning fluid instead of water. *v.*

dry cleaner, person or business that does dry cleaning.

dry cleaning, cleaning of cloth without water, using a chemical cleaning fluid.

dry dock, dock built watertight so that the water may be pumped out or kept high. Dry docks are used for building or repairing ships.

dry er (drī′ər), **1** device or machine that removes water by heat, air, etc.: *a clothes dryer, a hair dryer.* **2** substance mixed with paint, varnish, ink, etc., to make it dry more quickly. *n.* Also, **drier** for 2.

dry goods, cloth, ribbons, laces, etc., and similar textile fabrics.

Dry Ice, trademark for a very cold, white solid formed when carbon dioxide is greatly compressed and then cooled. It is used for cooling because it changes from a solid back to a gas without becoming liquid.

dry ly (drī′lē), in a dry manner. *adv.* Also, **drily.**

dry measure, system for measuring the volume of such things as grain, vegetables, or fruit. In the United States:

    2 pints = 1 quart
    8 quarts = 1 peck
    4 pecks = 1 bushel

dry run, a practice test or session.

dry-shod (drī′shod′), having dry shoes; without getting the feet wet. *adj.*

D.S. or **D.Sc.,** Doctor of Science.

D.S.C., Distinguished Service Cross.

D.S.T., daylight-saving time.

du al (dü′əl or dyü′əl), **1** consisting of two parts; double; twofold: *The automobile had dual controls, one set for the learner and one for the teacher.* **2** of two; showing two. *adj.* —**du′al ly,** *adv.*

du al i ty (dü al′ə tē or dyü al′ə tē), dual condition or quality. *n., pl.* **du al i ties.**

dub[1] (dub), **1** give a title, name, or nickname to; name; call: *My sister dubbed our new sailboat "Sea Breeze."* **2** make (a person) a knight by striking his shoulder lightly with a sword. *v.,* **dubbed, dub bing.** [*Dub*[1] comes from Old English *dubbian.*]

dub[2] (dub), add music, voices, or other sounds to (a motion-picture film, a radio or television broadcast, a recording, etc.): *The Italian film was dubbed with English dialogue. v.,* **dubbed, dub bing.** [*Dub*[2] is short for *double.*]

du bi ous (dü′bē əs or dyü′bē əs), **1** filled with or being in doubt; doubtful; uncertain: *The senator was dubious about his chances of reelection.* **2** of questionable character; probably bad: *The police are investigating the swindler's dubious schemes for making money. adj.* —**du′bi ous ly,** *adv.* —**du′bi ous ness,** *n.*

Dub lin (dub′lən), capital of the Republic of Ireland, in the E part. *n.*

Du Bois (dü bois′), **W(illiam) E(dward) B(urghardt),** 1868-1963, American sociologist and author.

du cal (dü′kəl or dyü′kəl), of a duke or dukedom. *adj.*

duc at (duk′ət), any of various gold or silver coins once used in Europe. *n.*

duch ess (duch′is), **1** wife or widow of a duke. **2** woman whose rank is equal to that of a duke. *n., pl.* **duch ess es.**

duch y (duch′ē), lands ruled by a duke or a duchess. *n., pl.* **duch ies.**

duck[1] (duk), **1** a wild or tame swimming bird with a short neck, short legs, webbed feet, and a broad, flat bill. **2** the female duck. The male is called a drake. **3** flesh of a duck used for food. *n., pl.* **ducks** or **duck.** [*Duck*[1] comes from Old English *dūce.*] —**duck′like′,** *adj.*

duck[2] (duk), **1** dip or plunge suddenly under water and out again. **2** a sudden dip or plunge under water and out again. **3** lower the head or bend the body suddenly to keep from being hit, seen, etc.: *She ducked to avoid a low branch.* **4** a sudden lowering of the head or bending of the body to keep from being hit, seen, etc. **5** get or keep away from; avoid; dodge: *duck a blow. He ducked my* question. 1,3,5 *v.*, 2,4 *n.* [*Duck²* comes from Middle English *duken.*]

duck³ (duk), **1** a strong cotton or linen cloth with a lighter and finer weave than canvas. Duck is used to make small sails, tents, and clothing. **2 ducks,** *pl.* trousers made of duck. *n.* [*Duck³* comes from Dutch *doek,* meaning "cloth."]

duck bill (duk′bil′), platypus. *n.*

duck billed platypus (duk′bild′), platypus.

duck ling (duk′ling), a young duck. *n.*

duck weed (duk′wēd′), a very small plant having no stem, that grows in water and often forms dense, green scum on the surface. *n.*

duct (dukt), **1** tube, pipe, or channel for carrying liquid, air, etc. **2** a single pipe for electric cables. **3** tube in the body for carrying a bodily fluid: *tear ducts. n.* [*Duct* is from Latin *ductus,* meaning "a leading," which comes from *ducere,* meaning "to lead." See **Word Family.**] —**duct′like′,** *adj.*

WORD FAMILY

duct

Below are words related to *duct.* They can all be traced back to the Latin word *ducere* (dü′ke re), meaning "to lead."

abduct	ducal	produce
adduce	duchess	product
aqueduct	duchy	reduce
conducive	ductile	reproduce
conduct	duke	reproduction
conduit	induce	seduce
deduce	induct	subdue
deduct	inductive	traduce
deductive	introduce	viaduct

duc tile (duk′təl), **1** capable of being hammered out thin or drawn out into a wire: *Gold and copper are ductile metals.* **2** capable of being easily molded or shaped; flexible: *Wax is ductile when it is warm.* **3** easily managed or influenced; docile. *adj.*

duct less (dukt′lis), having no duct. *adj.*

ductless gland, endocrine gland.

dud (dud), **1** shell or bomb that fails to explode. **2** INFORMAL. failure: *The rocket test was a complete dud.* **3 duds,** *pl.* INFORMAL. clothes. *n.*

dude (düd *or* dyüd), **1** man who pays too much attention to his clothes; dandy. **2** (in the western parts of the United States and Canada) person raised in the city, especially an easterner who vacations on a ranch. **3** SLANG. guy; fellow. *n.*

dude ranch, ranch which is run as a tourist resort.

dudg eon (duj′ən), a feeling of anger or resentment. *n.*

in high dudgeon, very angry; resentful: *He was in high dudgeon when he found out that we had left without him.*

due (dü *or* dyü), **1** owed as a debt; to be paid as a right; owing: *The money due her for her work was paid today. Respect is due to older people.* **2** what is owed to a person; a person's right: *Courtesy is their due as long as they are your guests.* **3** proper; suitable; rightful: *You will receive a due reward for your good work.* **4** as much as needed; enough: *Use due care in crossing streets.* **5 dues,** *pl.* amount of money it costs to be a member of a club; fee or tax for some purpose: *Members who do not pay their dues will be suspended from the club.* **6** promised to come

or be ready; looked for; expected: *The train is due at noon. Your report is due tomorrow.* **7** straight; directly: *The ship sailed due west.* 1,3,4,6 *adj.,* 2,5 *n.,* 7 *adv.*

due to, 1 caused by: *The accident was due to the driver's carelessness.* **2** because of: *The game was called off due to rain.*

fall due, be required to be paid.

du el (dü′əl *or* dyü′əl), **1** a formal fight between two persons armed with guns or swords. Duels are arranged to settle quarrels, avenge insults, etc., and are fought in the presence of two witnesses called seconds. **2** any fight or contest between two opponents: *The two opposing lawyers fought a duel of wits.* **3** fight a duel. 1,2 *n.,* 3 *v.,* **du eled, du el ing** *or* **du elled, du el ling.** —**du′el er, du′el ler,** *n.*

du el ist *or* **du el list** (dü′ə list *or* dyü′ə list), person who fights a duel or duels. *n.*

du en na (dü en′ə *or* dyü en′ə), **1** an elderly woman who is the governess and chaperon of young girls in a Spanish or Portuguese family. **2** governess or chaperon. *n., pl.* **du en nas.**

du et (dü et′ *or* dyü et′), **1** piece of music for two voices or instruments. **2** two singers or players performing together. *n.* [*Duet* is from Italian *duetto,* which comes from *duo,* meaning "two."]

duf fel bag (duf′əl), a large canvas sack used by soldiers, campers, etc., for carrying clothing and other belongings.

dug (dug), past tense and past participle of **dig.** *The dog dug a hole under the garden fence. The potatoes have all been dug. v.*

dugout (def. 3)

dug out (dug′out′), **1** a rough shelter or dwelling formed by digging into the side of a hill, trench, etc. During war, soldiers use dugouts for protection against bullets and bombs. **2** a small shelter at the side of a baseball field. It is used by players who are not at bat or not in the game. **3** boat made by hollowing out a large log. *n.*

duke (dük *or* dyük), **1** nobleman of the highest title, ranking just below a prince. **2** prince who rules a duchy. *n.*

duke dom (dük′dəm *or* dyük′dəm), **1** lands ruled by a duke; duchy. **2** title or rank of a duke. *n.*

dul cet (dul′sit), soothing, especially to the ear; sweet or pleasing: *the dulcet voice of a famous singer. adj.*

a	hat	i	it	oi	oil	ch	child		a in about
ā	age	ī	ice	ou	out	ng	long		e in taken
ä	far	o	hot	u	cup	sh	she	ə =	i in pencil
e	let	ō	open	ů	put	th	thin		o in lemon
ē	equal	ô	order	ü	rule	ᵺ	then		u in circus
ėr	term					zh	measure		

dulcimer (def. 2)

dul ci mer (dul′sə mər), **1** a musical instrument with metal strings, played by striking the strings with two hammers. **2** a stringed musical instrument plucked with a goose quill, the fingers, etc. It is used to play folk music in the Appalachian Mountain region. *n.* [*Dulcimer* came into English about 500 years ago from French *doulcemer,* and can be traced back to Latin *dulcis,* meaning "sweet," and *melos,* meaning "song."]

dull (dul), **1** not sharp or pointed; blunt: *It is hard to cut with a dull knife.* **2** not bright or clear: *dull eyes, a dull day, a dull color.* **3** slow in understanding; stupid: *a dull mind. A dull person often fails to get the meaning of a joke.* **4** not felt sharply; vague: *the dull pain of a bruise.* **5** not interesting; tiresome; boring: *a dull book, a dull joke.* **6** having little life, energy, or spirit; not active: *The fur coat business is usually dull in summer.* **7** make or become dull: *Chopping wood dulled the blade of the ax. This cheap knife dulls very easily.* 1-6 *adj.,* 7 *v.*

dull ness (dul′nis), dull condition or quality. *n.*

dul ly (dul′ē), in a dull manner. *adv.*

du ly (dü′lē *or* dyü′lē), **1** in a proper way; as due; properly; rightly; suitably: *The documents were duly signed before a lawyer.* **2** when due; at the proper time: *The debt will be duly paid. adv.*

Du mas (dü mä′), **1** Alexandre, 1802-1870, French novelist and dramatist. **2** his son, **Alexandre,** 1824-1895, French dramatist. *n.*

dumb (dum), **1** not able to speak: *Even intelligent animals are dumb.* **2** silenced for the moment by fear, surprise, shyness, etc.: *When I heard the news, I was struck dumb with astonishment.* **3** unwilling to speak; not speaking; silent. **4** INFORMAL. slow in understanding; stupid. *adj.*

dumb bell (dum′bel′), **1** a short bar of wood or iron with large, heavy, round ends. Dumbbells are generally used in pairs and are lifted or swung around to exercise the muscles of the arms, back, etc. **2** SLANG. a very stupid person. *n.*

dumbbell (def. 1)
A circus strongman hoists a heavy dumbbell.

dumb found (dum′found′), dumfound. *v.*
dumb show, pantomime.
dumb wait er (dum′wā′tər), a box with shelves that

can be pulled up or down a shaft. A dumbwaiter is used to send dishes, food, rubbish, etc., from one floor of a building to another. *n.*

dum found (dum′found′), amaze and make unable to speak; bewilder; confuse. *v.* Also, **dumbfound.**

dum my (dum′ē), **1** a life-size figure of a person used in place of a real person. Dummies are used to display clothing in store windows, to shoot at in rifle practice, to tackle in football practice, etc. **2** INFORMAL. a stupid person with no more sense than such a figure; blockhead. **3** person who has nothing to say or who takes no active part in affairs. **4** anything made to resemble a real thing; an imitation. **5** made to resemble the real thing; imitation: *We had a sword fight with dummy swords made of wood.* **6** corporation, person, or group that seems to be acting for itself, but is really acting for another. **7** a card player whose cards are laid face up on the table and played by his or her partner. 1-4,6,7 *n., pl.* **dum mies;** 5 *adj.*

dump (dump), **1** empty out; throw down in a heap; unload in a mass: *The truck backed up to the hole and dumped the dirt in it.* **2** place for throwing rubbish: *Garbage is taken to the city dump.* **3** SLANG. a dirty, shabby, or untidy place. **4** INFORMAL. get rid of; reject: *The party dumped the unpopular candidate.* **5** sell in large quantities at a very low price or below cost. **6** place for storing military supplies: *an ammunition dump.* 1,4,5 *v.,* 2,3,6 *n.*

dump ling (dump′ling), **1** a rounded piece of dough, boiled or steamed and usually served with meat. **2** a small pudding made by enclosing fruit in a piece of dough and baking or steaming it. *n.*

dumps (dumps), INFORMAL. **in the dumps,** feeling gloomy or sad: *She was in the dumps because her bike was broken. n.pl.*

Dump ster (dump′stər), trademark for a large, metal receptacle, often fitted with a lid, for holding garbage and having a means for easy dumping into a truck. *n.*

dump truck, truck which can be unloaded of waste, sand, etc., by tipping or by opening downward.

dump y (dum′pē), short and fat. *adj.,* **dump i er, dump i est.** —**dump′i ly,** *adv.* —**dump′i ness,** *n.*

dun[1] (dun), **1** demand payment of a debt from (someone) again and again: *The store dunned him until his overdue bills were finally paid.* **2** a demand for payment of a debt. 1 *v.,* **dunned, dun ning;** 2 *n.*

dun[2] (dun), **1** dull, grayish-brown. **2** a dull, grayish brown. 1 *adj.,* 2 *n.*

dunce (duns), person who is stupid or slow to learn. *n.*

dunes

dune (dün *or* dyün), mound or ridge of loose sand heaped up by the wind. *n.*

dung (dung), waste matter from the intestines of animals, much used as a fertilizer; manure. *n.*

dun ga ree (dung′gə rē′), **1** a coarse cotton cloth, used for work clothes. **2** **dungarees,** *pl.* trousers, work clothes, or overalls made of this cloth. *n.*

dun geon (dun′jən), a dark underground room or cell to keep prisoners in. *n.*

dung hill (dung′hil′), heap of dung or refuse: *a dunghill in the farmyard. n.*

dunk (dungk), dip (something to eat) into a liquid: *I like to dunk doughnuts in coffee. v.* [*Dunk* comes from a Pennsylvania German dialect word *dunken,* meaning "to dip."] —**dunk′er,** *n.*

dunk shot, (in basketball) a shot made by leaping so that the hands are above the rim of the basket, and throwing the ball down through the netting.

dun lin (dun′lən), a small sandpiper of northern regions. *n., pl.* **dun lins** or **dun lin.**

du o (dü′ō or dyü′ō), 1 duet. 2 pair. *n., pl.* **du os.**

du o de nal (dü′ō dē′nl or dyü′ō dē′nl), of or having to do with the duodenum: *a duodenal ulcer. adj.*

du o de num (dü′ō dē′nəm or dyü′ō dē′nəm), the first part of the small intestine, just below the stomach. *n., pl.* **du o de na** (dü′ō dē′nə or dyü′ō dē′nə).

dup., duplicate.

dupe (düp or dyüp), 1 person easily deceived or tricked. 2 deceive or trick: *They were dishonest and duped their customers.* 1 *n.,* 2 *v.,* **duped, dup ing.** —**dup′er,** *n.*

du plex (dü′pleks or dyü′pleks), 1 having two parts; double; twofold. A **duplex apartment** has rooms on two floors. A **duplex house** is a house accommodating two families. 2 a duplex house or apartment. 1 *adj.,* 2 *n., pl.* **du plex es.**

du pli cate (dü′plə kit or dyü′plə kit *for 1,2,4;* dü′plə kāt or dyü′plə kāt *for 3*), 1 exactly like something else: *We have duplicate keys for the front door.* 2 one of two things exactly alike; an exact copy: *I mailed the letter, but kept a duplicate.* 3 make an exact copy of; repeat exactly: *duplicate a picture, duplicate a mistake.* 4 having two corresponding parts; twofold; double: *A human being has duplicate lungs but only one heart.* 1,4 *adj.,* 2 *n.,* 3 *v.,* **du pli cat ed, du pli cat ing.**

in duplicate, in two copies exactly alike: *Using carbon paper, he typed the application in duplicate.*

du pli ca tion (dü′plə kā′shən or dyü′plə kā′shən), 1 a duplicating or a being duplicated: *Duplication of effort is a waste of time.* 2 a duplicate copy: *Her answers were a duplication of her sister's. n.*

du pli ca tor (dü′plə kā′tər or dyü′plə kā′tər), machine for making many exact copies of anything that is written, typed, or drawn. *n.*

du plic i ty (dü plis′ə tē or dyü plis′ə tē), an acting secretly in one way and openly in another in order to deceive; deceitfulness: *the duplicity of a friend who talks about you behind your back. n., pl.* **du plic i ties.**

dur a bil i ty (dùr′ə bil′ə tē or dyùr′ə bil′ə tē), lasting quality; ability to withstand wear. *n.*

dur a ble (dùr′ə bəl or dyùr′ə bəl), 1 able to withstand wear, decay, etc.: *durable fabric.* 2 lasting a long time: *a durable peace. adj.* —**dur′a ble ness,** *n.*

dur a bly (dùr′ə blē or dyùr′ə blē), in a durable manner; lastingly. *adv.*

dur ance (dùr′əns or dyùr′əns), imprisonment. *n.*

du ra tion (dù rā′shən or dyù rā′shən), length of time; time during which anything continues: *The storm was sudden and of short duration. n.*

Dü rer (dü′rər), **Albrecht,** 1471-1528, German painter and engraver. *n.*

du ress (dù res′ or dyù res′), use of force; compulsion. *The law does not require a person to fulfill a contract signed under duress. n.*

dur ing (dùr′ing or dyùr′ing), 1 through the whole time of; throughout: *The children played inside during the storm.* 2 at some time in; in the course of: *Come to see me during my office hours. prep.*

a hat	**i** it	**oi** oil	**ch** child	⎧ a in about
ā age	**ī** ice	**ou** out	**ng** long	⎪ e in taken
ä far	**o** hot	**u** cup	**sh** she	ə = ⎨ i in pencil
e let	**ō** open	**ù** put	**th** thin	⎪ o in lemon
ē equal	**ô** order	**ü** rule	**ŦH** then	⎩ u in circus
ėr term			**zh** measure	

durst (dėrst), OLD USE. dared; a past tense of **dare.** *v.*

dusk (dusk), 1 the darker stage of twilight; time just before dark: *We saw the evening star at dusk.* 2 shade; gloom: *the dusk of a forest.* 3 dark-colored; dusky. 1,2 *n.,* 3 *adj.* [*Dusk* comes from Old English *dox,* meaning "dark."]

dusk i ly (dus′kə lē), in a dusky manner; with partial darkness. *adv.*

dusk i ness (dus′kē nis), dusky condition; partial darkness. *n.*

dusk y (dus′kē), 1 somewhat dark; dark-colored. 2 dim; obscure: *the dusky light of the late afternoon. adj.,* **dusk i er, dusk i est.**

dust (dust), 1 fine, dry earth: *Dust lay thick on the road.* 2 any fine powder: *The old papers had turned to dust. The bee is covered with yellow dust from the flowers.* 3 brush or wipe the dust from; get dust off: *He dusted the furniture.* 4 sprinkle (with dust, powder, etc.): *to dust powder over a baby. The cook dusted the cake with sugar.* 5 what is left of a dead body after decay: *The tomb contains the dust of royalty.* 1,2,5 *n.,* 3,4 *v.* —**dust′less,** *adj.* —**dust′like′,** *adj.*

bite the dust, 1 fall dead or wounded. 2 be defeated, dismissed, or eliminated: *The other team bit the dust.*

shake the dust off one's feet, go away feeling angry or scornful.

throw dust in one's eyes, deceive or mislead a person.

dust bowl, area, especially in the western plains of the United States and Canada, where dust storms are frequent and violent.

dust er (dus′tər), 1 person or thing that dusts. 2 cloth or brush used to get the dust off things. 3 a long, light garment worn over the clothes to keep dust off them. *n.*

dust i ness (dus′tē nis), dusty condition. *n.*

dust jacket, an outer paper cover for protecting a book; jacket.

dust pan (dust′pan′), a flat, broad pan with a handle, onto which dust can be swept from the floor. *n.*

dust storm, a strong wind carrying clouds of dust across or from a dry region.

dust y (dus′tē), 1 covered with dust; filled with dust: *She found some dusty old books in the attic.* 2 like dust; dry and powdery: *dusty chalk.* 3 having the color of dust; grayish: *a dusty brown. adj.,* **dust i er, dust i est.** —**dust′i ly,** *adv.*

Dutch (duch), 1 of the Netherlands, its people, or their language. 2 people of the Netherlands. 3 their language. 4 Germans: *The ancestors of the Pennsylvania Dutch came from Germany, not from the Netherlands.* 1 *adj.,* 2,4 *n.pl.,* 3 *n.sing.*

go Dutch, INFORMAL. have each one pay for oneself: *Since neither one of us could afford to take the other to the movies we went Dutch.*

in Dutch, SLANG. in trouble or disgrace: *I am in Dutch with my parents for tearing my new jacket.*

Dutch man (duch′mən), 1 person born or living in the Netherlands; Hollander; Netherlander. 2 OLD USE. a German. *n., pl.* **Dutch men.**

Dutch treat, INFORMAL. meal or entertainment at which one pays for oneself.

du te ous (dü′tē əs or dyü′tē əs), dutiful; obedient. *adj.* —**du′te ous ly,** *adv.* —**du′te ous ness,** *n.*

du ti a ble (dü′tē ə bəl or dyü′tē ə bəl), on which a duty or tax must be paid: *Perfumes imported into the United States are dutiable goods. adj.*

du ti ful (dü′tə fəl *or* dyü′tə fəl), doing the duties required of one; obedient: *Dutiful children help their parents. adj.* —**du′ti ful ly,** *adv.* —**du′ti ful ness,** *n.*

du ty (dü′tē *or* dyü′tē), **1** thing that is right to do; what a person ought to do; obligation: *It is your duty to obey the laws.* **2** the binding force of what is right; moral obligation: *A sense of duty sometimes makes people do what they think is right even when they don't want to do it.* **3** thing that one must do in one's work: *One of the duties of a class treasurer is to keep records of the money in the treasury.* **4** a tax, especially a tax on articles brought into or taken out of a country. *n., pl.* **du ties.**

off duty, not working at one's job or position.

on duty, working at one's job or position.

Dvoř ák (dvôr′zhäk), **Anton,** 1841-1904, Czech composer. *n.*

dwarf (def. 4)—This tree has been **dwarfed.**

dwarf (dwôrf), **1** person, animal, or plant much smaller than the usual size for its kind. **2** (in fairy tales) an ugly little man with magic power. **3** much smaller than the usual size for its kind; stopped from growing: *dwarf trees.* **4** keep from growing large; check the growth of. **5** cause to look or seem small. 1,2 *n., pl.* **dwarfs, dwarves** (dwôrvz); 3 *adj.,* 4,5 *v.* [*Dwarf* comes from Old English *dweorg.*] —**dwarf′ness,** *n.*

dwarf (def. 5)
Giant equipment **dwarfs** the figure of a man.

dwarf ish (dwôr′fish), like a dwarf; much smaller than usual. *adj.* —**dwarf′ish ly,** *adv.* —**dwarf′ish ness,** *n.*

dwell (dwel), make one's home; live: *They dwell in the city. v.,* **dwelt** *or* **dwelled, dwell ing.** —**dwell′er,** *n.*

dwell on *or* **dwell upon, 1** think, write, or speak about for a long time: *Her mind dwelt on the pleasant day she had spent in the country.* **2** put stress on: *The speaker dwelt especially on the great need for teachers.*

dwell ing (dwel′ing), place in which one lives; house; residence. *n.*

dwelling place, dwelling.

dwelt (dwelt), a past tense and a past participle of **dwell.** *We dwelt there a long time. We have dwelt in the country for years. v.*

dwin dle (dwin′dl), become smaller and smaller; shrink; diminish: *During the blizzard the campers' supply of food dwindled day by day. v.,* **dwin dled, dwin dling.**

Dy, symbol for dysprosium.

dye (dī), **1** a coloring matter used to color cloth, hair, etc. Some dyes are vegetable, others chemical. **2** a color produced by such coloring matter: *A good dye will not fade or run.* **3** color (cloth, hair, etc.) by dipping in a liquid containing coloring matter: *have a shirt dyed.* **4** become colored when treated with a dye: *This material dyes evenly and quickly.* **5** to color or stain: *Grape juice dyed the tablecloth purple.* 1,2 *n.,* 3-5 *v.,* **dyed, dye ing.**

dyed-in-the-wool (dīd′in ᴛнə wu̇l′), thoroughgoing; complete: *a dyed-in-the-wool conservative in politics. adj.*

dye ing (dī′ing), the coloring of fabrics with dye. *n.*

dy er (dī′ər), person whose work or business is dyeing cloth, etc. *n.*

dye stuff (dī′stuf′), substance yielding a dye or used as a dye. *n.*

dy ing (dī′ing), **1** about to die: *a dying old man.* **2** coming to an end: *the dying year.* **3** of death; at death: *dying words.* **4** present participle of **die**[1]. *The storm is dying down.* 1-3 *adj.,* 4 *v.*

dyke (dīk), dike. *n., v.,* **dyked, dyk ing.**

dy nam ic (dī nam′ik), **1** of energy or force in motion. **2** active; energetic; forceful: *a dynamic personality. adj.* [*Dynamic* is from Greek *dynamikos,* which comes from *dynamis,* meaning "force."] —**dy nam′i cal ly,** *adv.*

dy nam ics (dī nam′iks), **1** branch of physics dealing with the action of forces on bodies either in motion or at rest. **2** the forces at work in any field: *the new dynamics of education. n.*

dy na mite (dī′nə mīt), **1** a powerful explosive made of nitroglycerin mixed with an absorbent material and pressed into round sticks. It is used in blasting rock, tree stumps, etc. **2** blow up or destroy, especially with dynamite. 1 *n.,* 2 *v.,* **dy na mit ed, dy na mit ing.** —**dy′na mit′er,** *n.*

dy na mo (dī′nə mō), machine that produces electricity; generator, especially one that produces direct current. *n., pl.* **dy na mos.**

dy nas tic (dī nas′tik), having to do with a dynasty. *adj.* —**dy nas′ti cal ly,** *adv.*

dy nas ty (dī′nə stē), succession of rulers who belong to the same family: *The Bourbon dynasty ruled France for more than 200 years. n., pl.* **dy nas ties.**

dyne (dīn), unit of force required to give a mass of one gram an acceleration of one centimeter per second for each second the force is applied. *n.*

dys en ter y (dis′n ter′ē), disease of the intestines, producing diarrhea with blood and mucus. *n.*

dys lex i a (dis lek′sē ə), difficulty in reading or in understanding what is read. *n.* [*Dyslexia* can be traced back to Greek *dys-,* meaning "bad," and *lexis,* meaning "word, speech," which comes from *legein,* meaning "to speak, say."]

dys pep si a (dis pep′sē ə), poor digestion; indigestion. *n.*

dys pep tic (dis pep′tik), **1** of dyspepsia. **2** suffering from dyspepsia. **3** person who has dyspepsia. **4** gloomy; pessimistic. 1,2,4 *adj.,* 3 *n.* —**dys pep′ti cal ly,** *adv.*

dys pro si um (dis prō′sē əm), a metallic element found in various minerals which forms highly magnetic compounds. *n.*

dz., dozen or dozens.

E or **e** (ē), the fifth letter of the English alphabet. *n., pl.*
E's or **e's.**

E or **E.**, **1** east. **2** eastern.

each (ēch), **1** every one (of two or more persons or
things) considered separately or one by one: *Each child
has a name.* **2** every one: *Each of the students has a pencil.*
3 for each; apiece: *These apples cost ten cents each.* 1 *adj.,*
2 *pron.,* 3 *adv.*

each other, 1 each one the other one: *They struck each
other.* **2** one another: *They struck at each other.*

ea ger (ē′gər), wanting very much; desiring very strongly: *The child was eager to have the candy. adj.* —**ea′ger ly,**
adv. —**ea′ger ness,** *n.*

eagle (def. 1)
3 ft. (1 m.)
from head to tail

ea gle (ē′gəl), **1** any of a group of large birds of prey that
are related to hawks and have keen eyesight and powerful wings. There are many kinds of eagles and they live
in every part of the world. The bald eagle is the national
emblem of the United States. **2** like that of an eagle: *The
eagle eye of the guide saw every move the deer made.* 1 *n.,* 2
adj.

ea glet (ē′glit), a young eagle. *n.*

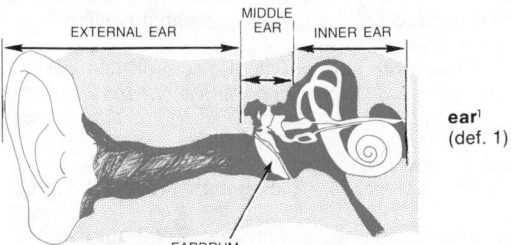

MIDDLE
EAR

EXTERNAL EAR   INNER EAR

ear¹
(def. 1)

EARDRUM

ear¹ (ir), **1** part of the body by which people and animals
hear. It consists of the external ear, the middle ear, and
the inner ear. **2** the outer part of the ear; auricle. **3** thing
shaped like the outer part of the ear. The handle of a
pitcher is called an ear. **4** Also, **ears,** *pl.* sense of hearing: *There is no need to shout; we have good ears.* **5** ability
to hear small differences in sounds: *I have a good ear for
music.* **6** attention: *Please give ear to my request. n.*
—**ear′less,** *adj.* —**ear′like′,** *adj.*

be all ears, INFORMAL. listen eagerly; pay careful attention: *The children were all ears while their teacher read them
the exciting story.*

play by ear, play (a piece of music or a musical instrument) without using written music: *She can't read notes
but she can play any tune on the piano by ear.*

prick up one's ears, 1 point the ears upward: *The dog
pricked up its ears at the sudden noise.* **2** give sudden
attention: *I pricked up my ears when I heard my name
mentioned.*

set by the ears, cause to disagree.

ear² (ir), the part of certain plants on which the grain
grows. The grains of corn, wheat, oats, barley, and rye
come from ears. *n.*

ear ache (ir′āk′), pain in the ear. *n.*

ear drum (ir′drum′), a thin membrane across the middle ear that vibrates when sound waves strike it. *n.*

eared (ird), having ears. *adj.*

ear ful (ir′fu̇l), a startling or important disclosure. *n., pl.*
ear fuls.

Ear hart (er′härt *or* ar′härt), **Amelia,** 1897-1937?,
American aviator. *n.*

earl (ėrl), a British nobleman ranking below a marquis
and above a viscount. *n.*

earl dom (ėrl′dəm), **1** lands ruled by an earl. **2** title or
rank of an earl. *n.*

ear lobe (ir′lōb′), the hanging lower part of the external
ear. *n.*

ear ly (ėr′lē), **1** near the beginning; in the first part: *The
sun is not hot early in the day (adv.). In his early years he
liked ships (adj.).* **2** before the usual or expected time:
Please come early (adv.). We had an early dinner (adj.).
3 before very long: *Spring may come early this year (adv.).
We expect an answer at an early date (adj.). adv., adj.,*
ear li er, ear li est. —**ear′li ness,** *n.*

early bird, INFORMAL. person who gets up or arrives
early.

ear mark (ir′märk′), **1** mark made on the ear of an animal to show who owns it. **2** a special mark, quality, or
feature that gives information about a person or thing;
sign: *Truthfulness is an earmark of an honest person.*
3 make an earmark on; identify or give information
about: *Careless work earmarks a poor student.* **4** set aside
for some special purpose: *A certain amount of money is
earmarked to buy books for the library; it cannot be spent
for anything else.* 1,2 *n.,* 3,4 *v.*

ear muffs (ir′mufs′), pair of coverings worn over the
ears in cold weather to keep them warm. *n.pl.*

earn (ėrn), **1** get in return for work or service; be paid:
She earns 25 dollars a day. **2** do enough to get; do good
enough work for; deserve: *Considering all the work he
does, he is paid less than he earns.* **3** bring or get as
deserved; win: *Her hard work earned her the respect of her
teachers.* **4** gain as a profit or return: *Money well invested
earns good interest. v.* —**earn′er,** *n.*

ear nest¹ (ėr′nist), strong and firm in purpose; eager
and serious: *Earnest pupils try very hard to do their best.
adj.* [*Earnest¹* comes from Old English *eornost.*] —**ear′-
nest ly,** *adv.* —**ear′nest ness,** *n.*

in earnest, strong and firm in purpose; eager and serious: *The art student is in earnest about her ambition to
become a famous painter.*

ear nest² (ėr′nist), part given or done in advance as a
pledge for the rest; pledge: *Part of the price he paid to the
seller was an earnest that the rest would be paid at a later*

date. n. [*Earnest²* comes from Middle English *ernes*, and can be traced back to Hebrew *'ērābōn*.]

earn ings (ėr′ningz), money earned; wages or profits. *n.pl.*

ear phone (ir′fōn′), receiver for a telephone, telegraph, radio, television set, or hearing aid that is fastened or placed over the ear. *n.*

ear ring (ir′ring′), ornament for the ear. *n.*

ear shot (ir′shot′), distance at which a sound can be heard; range of hearing: *We shouted, but he was already out of earshot and could not hear us. n.*

ear split ting (ir′split′ing), very noisy and loud; deafening: *The bomb exploded with an earsplitting sound. adj.*

earth (ėrth), 1 Also, **Earth.** the planet on which we live; the globe. The earth is the fifth largest planet in the solar system, and the third in distance from the sun. 2 all the people who live on this planet: *People have often wished that the whole earth spoke only one language.* 3 dry land: *the earth, the sea, and the sky.* 4 ground; soil; dirt: *The earth in the garden is soft. n.*
  down to earth, seeing things as they really are; practical.

earth en (ėr′thən), 1 made of baked clay: *an earthen jug.* 2 made of earth. *adj.*

earth en ware (ėr′thən wer′ *or* ėr′thən war′), 1 dishes or containers made of baked clay; crockery. Coarse pottery is earthenware. 2 made of baked clay: *an earthenware pot.* 1 *n.,* 2 *adj.*

earth ling (ėrth′ling), person who lives on the earth; human being; mortal. *n.*

earth ly (ėrth′lē), 1 having to do with the earth, not with heaven. 2 possible: *That rubbish is of no earthly use. adj.,* **earth li er, earth li est. —earth′li ness,** *n.*

earthquake
houses damaged by the San Francisco earthquake in 1906

earth quake (ėrth′kwāk′), a shaking or sliding of a portion of the earth's crust. It is caused by the sudden movement of masses of rock along a fault or by changes in the size and shape of masses of rock far beneath the earth's surface. Earthquakes are often related to volcanic activity. *n.*

earth satellite, satellite of the earth made by human beings.

earth science, any of the sciences dealing with the origin, composition, and physical features of the earth. Geology, geography, meteorology, and oceanography are earth sciences.

earth station, a dish-shaped antenna, especially one used to receive television signals transmitted from satellites.

earth ward (ėrth′wərd), toward the earth: *The burning airplane hurtled earthward (adv.). The eagle started its earthward descent (adj.). adv., adj.*

earth wards (ėrth′wərdz), earthward. *adv.*

earth work (ėrth′wėrk′), bank of earth piled up for a fortification. *n.*

earth worm (ėrth′wėrm′), a reddish-brown or grayish worm that lives in and helps loosen the soil; angleworm. It has minute bristles on each segment that aid in locomotion. *n.*

earth y (ėr′thē), 1 of earth or soil: *Potatoes have an earthy smell.* 2 like earth or soil: *The color of the field was a rich, earthy brown.* 3 down to earth; realistic; practical: *an earthy person.* 4 not refined; coarse: *earthy language. adj.,* **earth i er, earth i est. —earth′i ness,** *n.*

ear wig (ir′wig′), a slender insect somewhat like a beetle. *n.* [*Earwig* is from Old English *ēarwicga*, which comes from *ēare*, meaning "ear," and *wicga*, meaning "insect, beetle." Earwigs were called this because they were once thought to crawl into people's ears.]

earthenware
(def. 2)

ease (ēz), 1 freedom from pain or trouble; comfort: *When school is out, I am going to live a life of ease for a whole week.* 2 make free from pain or trouble; give comfort to: *Her reassuring words helped ease my worried mind.* 3 freedom from trying hard: *The reporter writes with great ease. You can do this lesson with ease.* 4 freedom from embarrassment; natural or easy manner: *He spoke to the class with ease and humor.* 5 lessen; lighten: *Aspirin eased my headache.* 6 loosen: *The belt is too tight; ease it a notch or two.* 7 move slowly and carefully: *We eased the big box through the narrow door.* 1,3,4 *n.,* 2,5-7 *v.,* **eased, eas ing.** [*Ease* came into English about 750 years ago from French *aise,* meaning "comfort, opportunity," and can be traced back to Latin *adjacentem,* meaning "lying near."] **—eas′er,** *n.*
  at ease, 1 free from pain or trouble; comfortable: *The doctor soon made the worried patient feel at ease.* 2 with the body relaxed and the feet apart: *Soldiers standing at ease are permitted to talk.*
  ease off or **ease up,** lessen; lighten.

ea sel (ē′zəl), a stand for holding a picture, blackboard, etc. *n.*

eas i ly (ē′zə lē), 1 in an easy manner. 2 without trying hard; with little effort: *The simple tasks were quickly and easily done.* 3 without pain or trouble; comfortably: *The patient was resting easily.* 4 by far; without question: *He is easily the best singer in the choir.* 5 very likely; probably: *She is a good writer and may easily become famous. adv.*

eas i ness (ē′zē nis), quality or condition of being easy. *n.*

east (ēst), 1 direction of the sunrise. 2 toward the east; farther toward the east: *Walk east to find the road (adv.). Take the east road (adj.).* 3 from the east: *an east wind.* 4 in the east: *the east wing of a house.* 5 Also, **East.** the part of any country toward the east. 6 **the East, a** the eastern part of the United States; region from Maine

through Maryland. **b** the countries in Asia; the Orient: *China and Japan are in the East.* 1,5,6 *n.,* 2-4 *adj.,* 2 *adv.*
east of, further east than: *Ohio is east of Indiana.*

East Berlin, capital of East Germany, in the E part.

east bound (ēst′bound′), going east: *an eastbound express. adj.*

Eas ter (ē′stər), the yearly Christian celebration of Jesus' rising from the dead. Easter comes between March 22 and April 25, on the first Sunday after the first full moon on or after March 21. *n.*

---

a hat	**i** it	**oi** oil	**ch** child	⎧ a in about
ā age	**ī** ice	**ou** out	**ng** long	⎪ e in taken
ä far	**o** hot	**u** cup	**sh** she	ə = ⎨ i in pencil
e let	**ō** open	**u̇** put	**th** thin	⎪ o in lemon
ē equal	**ô** order	**ü** rule	**ᵾH** then	⎩ u in circus
ėr term			**zh** measure	

WORD HISTORY

Easter

Easter comes from Old English *ēastre,* which was originally the name of a goddess of the dawn. Her feast was celebrated in the spring.

Easter lily, lily with large, white, trumpet-shaped flowers. Easter lilies symbolize purity and are often used at Easter to decorate church altars.

east er ly (ē′stər lē), **1** toward the east: *an easterly exposure.* **2** from the east: *an easterly wind.* **3** wind that blows from the east. 1,2 *adj., adv.,* 3 *n., pl.* **east er lies.**

east ern (ē′stərn), **1** toward the east: *an eastern trip.* **2** from the east: *eastern tourists.* **3** of or in the east: *eastern schools.* **4 Eastern, a** of or in the eastern part of the United States. **b** of or in the countries in Asia; Asian. *adj.*

Eastern Church, group of Christian churches in eastern Europe, western Asia, and Egypt that give the greatest honor to the patriarch of Constantinople; Greek Orthodox Church; Orthodox Church; Eastern Orthodox Church.

east ern er (ē′stər nər), **1** person born or living in the east. **2 Easterner,** person born or living in the eastern part of the United States. *n.*

Eastern Hemisphere, the half of the world that includes Europe, Asia, Africa, and Australia.

east ern most (ē′stərn mōst), farthest east. *adj.*

Eastern Orthodox Church, Eastern Church.

Eastern Standard Time, the standard time in the eastern part of the United States and most of eastern Canada. It is five hours behind Greenwich Time.

Easter Sunday, the Sunday on which Easter is celebrated.

East Germany, country in central Europe, consisting of much of the eastern part of pre-World War II Germany. *Capital:* East Berlin. See **Prussia** for map.

East Indian, 1 of the East Indies. **2** person born or living in the East Indies.

East Indies, 1 the islands of the Malay Archipelago. **2** these islands, India, and southeastern Asia.

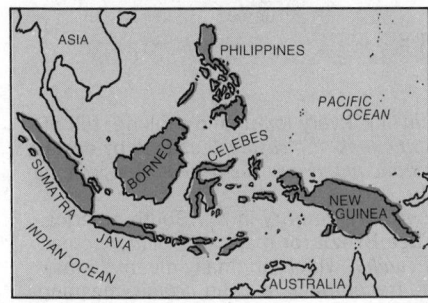

East Indies
(def. 1)

east ward (ēst′wərd), **1** toward the east; east: *She walked eastward (adv.). He sat on the eastward slope of the hill watching the sun rise (adj.).* **2** an eastward part, direction, or point. 1 *adv., adj.,* 2 *n.*

east wards (ēst′wərdz), eastward. *adv.*

eas y (ē′zē), **1** not hard to do or get: *an easy victory. Today's arithmetic lesson was easy.* **2** free from pain or trouble; comfortable: *a wealthy person who has an easy life.* **3** giving comfort or rest: *an easy chair.* **4** not strict or harsh: *We bought our new car on easy terms of payment. The new teacher is an easy grader.* **5** smooth and pleasant; not awkward: *She has an easy way of speaking to everyone.* **6** slow; not fast: *The old horse moved at an easy pace.* **7** INFORMAL. without much trouble; easily. 1-6 *adj.,* **eas i er, eas i est;** 7 *adv.*

go easy on, 1 be cautious or sparing of: *The doctor advised me to go easy on sweets.* **2** treat gently or carefully: *The lawyer went easy on the witness.*

take it easy or **take things easy,** act calmly; move slowly and carefully.

eas y go ing (ē′zē gō′ing), taking matters easily; not worrying: *an easygoing person. adj.*

eat (ēt), **1** chew and swallow (food): *Cows eat grass and grain.* **2** have a meal: *Where shall we eat?* **3** gnaw or devour: *Termites have eaten the posts and ruined the fence.* **4** destroy as if by eating; wear away: *The sea has eaten into the north shore. This acid eats metal.* **5** make by eating: *Moths ate holes in my wool coat.* **6** INFORMAL. bother; annoy: *What's eating him today? v.,* **ate, eat en, eat ing.** **—eat′er,** *n.*

eat up, use up; waste away: *Extravagant spending ate up our savings.*

eat a ble (ē′tə bəl), **1** fit to eat; edible. **2 eatables,** *pl.* things fit to eat; food. 1 *adj.,* 2 *n.*

eat en (ēt′n), past participle of **eat.** *Have you eaten your dinner? v.*

eaves (ēvz), the lower edge of a roof that projects over the side of a building. *n.pl.*

eaves drop (ēvz′drop′), listen to talk one is not supposed to hear; listen secretly to a private conversation. *v.,* **eaves dropped, eaves drop ping.**

eaves drop per (ēvz′drop′ər), person who eavesdrops. *n.*

ebb (eb), **1** a flowing of the tide away from the shore; fall of the tide. **2** flow out; fall: *We waded farther out as the tide ebbed.* **3** a growing less or weaker; decline: *His fortunes were at an ebb because of his long illness and a lack of money.* **4** grow less or weaker; decline: *Her courage began to ebb as she neared the haunted house.* 1,3 *n.,* 2,4 *v.*

ebb tide, a flowing of the tide away from the shore. Ebb tide occurs twice every 24 hours in most parts of the world.

eb on (eb′ən), OLD USE. ebony. *n., adj.*

eb on y (eb′ə nē), **1** the hard, black wood of a tropical tree, used for the black keys of a piano, for the backs and handles of brushes, and for ornamental woodwork. **2** made of ebony: *an ebony cane.* **3** like ebony; black; dark. 1 *n.,* 2,3 *adj.* [*Ebony* is from Greek *ebenos,* which came from Egyptian *hbnj.*]

e bul lient (i bul′yənt), overflowing with excitement or liveliness; very enthusiastic. *adj.* **—e bul′lient ly,** *adv.*

ec cen tric (ek sen′trik), **1** out of the ordinary; not usual;

odd; peculiar: *People stared at the artist's eccentric clothes.*
2 person who behaves in an unusual manner: *The behavior of an eccentric is hard to predict.* **3** not having the same center: *These circles ⊙ are eccentric.* **4** not perfectly circular: *The planets are in eccentric orbits around the sun.* **5** off center; having its axis set off center: *an eccentric wheel.* 1,3-5 *adj.,* 2 *n.* —**ec cen′tri cal ly,** *adv.*

ec cen tric i ty (ek′sen tris′ə tē), **1** something out of the ordinary; oddity; peculiarity: *One of my cousin's most noticeable eccentricities was to carry around an open umbrella on sunny days.* **2** eccentric condition; being unusual or out of the ordinary: *The clock's eccentricity became noticeable when it struck three, whatever the hour. n., pl.* **ec cen tric i ties.**

Eccl. or **Eccles.,** Ecclesiastes.

Ec cle si as tes (i klē′zē as′tēz), book of the Old Testament, supposed to have been written by Solomon. *n.*

ec cle si as tic (i klē′zē as′tik), **1** member of the clergy. **2** ecclesiastical. 1 *n.,* 2 *adj.*

ec cle si as ti cal (i klē′zē as′tə kəl), of the church or the clergy. *adj.* —**ec cle′si as′ti cal ly,** *adv.*

ECG., electrocardiogram.

ech e lon (esh′ə lon), level of command or authority. A unit of an army, such as a company, battalion, division, or corps, is called an echelon. *n.*

e chid na (i kid′nə), a small, egg-laying, ant-eating mammal of Australia with a long, slender snout, no teeth, and a covering of spines. *n., pl.* **e chid nas, e chid nae** (i kid′nē).

e chi no derm (i kī′nə dėrm′), any of a group of small sea animals, including starfish and sea urchins. An echinoderm has a spiny, stony shell and a body whose parts are arranged like the spokes of a wheel. *n.*

e chi nus (i kī′nəs), sea urchin. *n., pl.* **e chi ni** (i kī′nī).

ech o (ek′ō), **1** a sounding again; repeating of a sound. You hear an echo when a sound you make bounces back from a distant hill or wall so that you hear it again. **2** sound again; repeat or be repeated in sound: *The gunshot echoed through the valley.* **3** repeat or imitate what another says or does: *Small children sometimes echo their parents' words and actions.* **4 Echo,** (in Greek myths) a nymph who pined away with love for Narcissus until only her voice was left. 1,4 *n., pl.* **ech oes** for 1; 2,3 *v.*

e cho ic (e kō′ik), like an echo. *adj.*

é clair (ā kler′ or ā klar′), an oblong piece of pastry filled with whipped cream or custard and covered with icing. *n.* [*Éclair* comes from French *éclair,* which also means "lightning."]

é clat (ā klä′), **1** a brilliant success. **2** fame; glory. *n., pl.* **é clats.**

e clipse (i klips′), **1** a complete or partial blocking of light passing from one heavenly body to another. A **solar eclipse** occurs when the moon passes between the sun and the earth. A **lunar eclipse** occurs when the moon enters the earth's shadow. **2** cut off or dim the light from; darken. **3** make dim by comparison; surpass; outshine: *In sports he eclipsed his older brother.* **4** loss of importance or reputation: *The former champion has suffered an eclipse.* 1,4 *n.,* 2,3 *v.,* **e clipsed, e clips ing.** [*Eclipse* can be traced back to Greek *ex-,* meaning "out," and *leipein,* meaning "to leave."]

e clip tic (i klip′tik), path that the sun appears to travel in one year. *n.*

ec o log i cal (ek′ə loj′ə kəl or ē′kə loj′ə kəl), of or about ecology: *ecological studies. adj.* —**ec′o log′i cal ly,** *adv.*

e col o gist (ē kol′ə jist), an expert in ecology. *n.*

e col o gy (ē kol′ə jē), branch of biology that deals with the relation of living things to their environment and to each other. *n.*

e co nom ic (ē′kə nom′ik or ek′ə nom′ik), **1** having to do with economics. Economic problems have to do with the production, distribution, and consumption of goods and services. **2** having to do with the management of the income, supplies, and expenses of a household, community, government, etc. *adj.*

e co nom i cal (ē′kə nom′ə kəl or ek′ə nom′ə kəl), avoiding waste; saving; thrifty: *We can finish early if we are economical in the use of our time. adj.* —**e′co nom′i cal ly,** *adv.*

e co nom ics (ē′kə nom′iks or ek′ə nom′iks), science of the production, distribution, and consumption of goods and services. Economics studies the problems of capital, labor, wages, prices, taxes, etc. *n.*

e con o mist (i kon′ə mist), an expert in economics. *n.*

e con o mize (i kon′ə mīz), **1** manage so as to avoid waste; use to the best advantage: *If you can economize your time, you will get more done in less time.* **2** cut down expenses: *We must economize or we will go into debt. v.,* **e con o mized, e con o miz ing.** —**e con′o miz′er,** *n.*

echidna
about 1½ ft.
(45 cm.) long

e con o my (i kon′ə mē), **1** a making the most of what one has; avoiding waste in the use of anything; thrift: *By using economy in buying food and clothes, we were able to save enough money for our vacation.* **2** management of affairs and resources of a country, area, or business: *Under the new administration, the country's economy improved greatly. n., pl.* **e con o mies.** [*Economy* can be traced back to Greek *oikos,* meaning "house," and *nemein,* meaning "to manage."]

ec ru (ek′rü), **1** pale-brown. **2** a pale brown. 1 *adj.,* 2 *n.* [*Ecru* comes from French *écru,* meaning "raw, unbleached." Ecru was called this because of the color of unbleached linen.]

ec sta sy (ek′stə sē), condition of very great joy; thrilling or overwhelming delight; rapture: *She was speechless with ecstasy after winning the gold medal. n., pl.* **ec sta sies.**

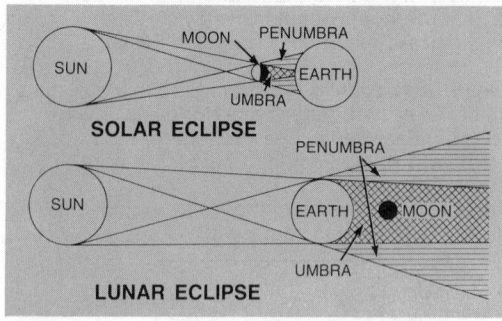

eclipse (def. 1)

ec stat ic (ek stat′ik), **1** very joyful and thrilling; full of ecstasy: *an ecstatic look of pleasure.* **2** caused by ecstasy: *He was in an ecstatic mood over the prize he had won. adj.* —**ec stat′i cal ly,** *adv.*

Ec ua dor (ek′wə dôr), country in NW South America. *Capital:* Quito. See **Brazil** for map. *n.* [*Ecuador* comes from Spanish *Ecuador,* which originally meant "equator," and can be traced back to Latin *aequus,* meaning "even, level."] —**Ec′ua do′ri an, Ec′ua do′re an,** or **Ec′ua do′ran,** *adj., n.*

ec u men i cal (ek′yə men′ə kəl), **1** general; universal. **2** of or representing the whole Christian Church: *an ecumenical council stressing unity among Christians. adj.* —**ec′u men′i cal ly,** *adv.*

ec ze ma (ek′sə mə *or* eg zē′mə), inflammation of the skin with itching and the formation of scaly, encrusted sores. *n.*

-ed¹, *suffix forming the past tense of many verbs,* as in *wanted, tried, dropped.*

-ed², 1 *suffix forming the past participle of many verbs,* as in *has echoed.* **2** *suffix forming adjectives from nouns:* **a** having _____: *Long-legged = having long legs.* **b** having the characteristics of _____: *Bigoted = having the characteristics of a bigot.*

ed., 1 edited. **2** edition. **3** editor.

ed dy (ed′ē), **1** water, air, smoke, etc., moving against the main current, especially when having a whirling motion; small whirlpool or whirlwind: *The wind moved in an eddy near the sails.* **2** move against the main current in a whirling motion; whirl: *The water eddied out of the sink.* **1** *n., pl.* **ed dies; 2** *v.,* **ed died, ed dy ing.**

Ed dy (ed′ē), **Mary Baker,** 1821-1910, American who founded Christian Science. *n.*

e del weiss (ā′dl vīs), a small plant that grows in high places. It has heads of very small, white flowers in the center of star-shaped leaf clusters. *n., pl.* **e del weiss** or **e del weiss es.**

e de ma (i dē′mə), disease in which a watery fluid collects in certain tissues or cavities of the body, often accompanied by swelling; dropsy. *n.*

E den (ēd′n), **1** (in the Bible) the garden where Adam and Eve first lived. **2** a delightful place; paradise. *n.*

edge (ej), **1** line or place where something ends or begins; side: *This page has four edges. We walked to the edge of the water.* **2** rim; brink: *The stag stood on the edge of the cliff.* **3** the thin side that cuts: *The knife had a very sharp edge.* **4** put an edge on; form an edge on: *The gardener edged the path with white stones.* **5** move sideways: *She edged through the narrow passageway.* **6** move little by little: *The dog edged nearer to the fire.* **1-3** *n.,* **4-6** *v.,* **edged, edg ing.**

on edge, disturbed; irritated; tense: *My nerves were on edge from the constant noise.*

take the edge off, take away the force, strength, or pleasure of: *The severe injury suffered by the winning pitcher took the edge off the team's victory.*

edged (ejd), sharp. *adj.*

edge ways (ej′wāz′), with the edge forward; in or along the direction of the edge. *adv.*

edge wise (ej′wīz′), edgeways. *adv.*

edg ing (ej′ing), thing forming an edge or put on along an edge; border or trimming for an edge: *an edging of lace on a tablecloth. n.*

edg y (ej′ē), irritable; tense: *The long wait in the dentist's office had made him edgy. adj.,* **edg i er, edg i est.** —**edg′i ly,** *adv.* —**edg′i ness,** *n.*

ed i ble (ed′ə bəl), fit to eat. *adj.*

e dict (ē′dikt), a public order or command by some authority; decree: *The queen issued an edict creating a new national holiday. n.*

ed i fi ca tion (ed′ə fə kā′shən), moral improvement; spiritual benefit: *Many fables were written for the edification of children. n.*

ed i fice (ed′ə fis), a building, especially a large or impressive one. *n.*

ed i fy (ed′ə fī), improve morally; benefit spiritually; instruct and uplift. *v.,* **ed i fied, ed i fy ing.** [*Edify* came into English over 600 years ago from French *edifier,*

a hat	**i** it	**oi** oil	**ch** child	a in about
ā age	**ī** ice	**ou** out	**ng** long	e in taken
ä far	**o** hot	**u** cup	**sh** she	ə = { i in pencil
e let	**ō** open	**ů** put	**th** thin	o in lemon
ē equal	**ô** order	**ü** rule	**ŦH** then	u in circus
ėr term			**zh** measure	

which came from Latin *aedificare,* meaning "to build."] —**ed′i fi′er,** *n.*

Ed in burgh (ed′n bėr′ō), capital of Scotland, in the SE part. *n.*

Ed i son (ed′ə sən), **Thomas Alva,** 1847-1931, American inventor. *n.*

ed it (ed′it), **1** prepare (another's writings, etc.) for publication or presentation by correcting errors, checking facts, etc.: *edit a manuscript.* **2** have charge of (a newspaper, magazine, etc.) and decide what shall be printed in it. **3** put into final form by selecting and reassembling the parts of: *edit a film, edit a tape recording. v.* [*Edit* was shortened from *editor.*]

edit., 1 edited. **2** edition. **3** editor.

e di tion (i dish′ən), **1** all the copies of a book, newspaper, etc., printed just alike and issued at or near the same time: *The second edition of the book had many corrections for the errors in the first edition.* **2** form in which a book is printed or published: *Some books appear in paperback editions. n.*

ed i tor (ed′ə tər), **1** person who edits: *She is the editor of our school paper.* **2** person who writes editorials. *n.* [*Editor* can be traced back to Latin *ex-,* meaning "out," and *dare,* meaning "to give."]

ed i to ri al (ed′ə tôr′ē əl), **1** article in a newspaper or magazine giving the editor's or publisher's opinion on some subject. **2** of an editor: *editorial work.* **3** of an editorial: *an editorial comment.* **1** *n.,* **2,3** *adj.* —**ed′i to′ri al ly,** *adv.*

ed i to ri al ize (ed′ə tôr′ē ə līz), include comment and criticisms in news articles. *v.,* **ed i to ri al ized, ed i to ri al iz ing.** —**ed′i to′ri al i za′tion,** *n.*

ed i tor ship (ed′ə tər ship), position, duties, or authority of an editor. *n.*

Ed mon ton (ed′mən tən), capital of Alberta, Canada, in the central part. *n.*

EDT, e.d.t., or **E.D.T.,** Eastern daylight time.

ed u cate (ej′ə kāt), **1** develop in knowledge or skill by teaching, training, or study; teach: *The job of teachers is to educate people.* **2** send to school: *My cousin is being educated in England. v.,* **ed u cat ed, ed u cat ing.** [*Educate* comes from Latin *educatum,* meaning "brought up, raised."] —**ed′u cat′a ble,** *adj.*

ed u cat ed (ej′ə kā′tid), **1** having an education: *an educated person.* **2** based on facts or training: *The forecaster made an educated guess about next week's weather. adj.*

ed u ca tion (ej′ə kā′shən), **1** development in knowledge or skill by teaching, training, or study: *In the United States, public schools offer an education to all children.* **2** knowledge or skill developed by teaching, training, or study: *A person with education knows how to speak, write, and read well.* **3** study of the methods, principles, problems, etc., of teaching and learning. *n.*

ed u ca tion al (ej′ə kā′shə nəl), **1** of education: *The teachers in our school belong to the state educational associations.* **2** giving education: *an educational movie about wild animals. adj.* —**ed′u ca′tion al ly,** *adv.*

ed u ca tor (ej′ə kā′tər), **1** person whose profession is education; teacher. **2** leader in education; authority on methods and principles of education. *n.*

e duce (i düs′ *or* i dyüs′), bring out; draw forth. *v.,* **e duced, e duc ing.**

-ee, *suffix added to verbs to form nouns.* **1** person who is
_____: *Absentee = person who is absent.* **2** person who is
_____ed: *Appointee = person who is appointed.* **3** person
to whom something is _____ed: *Mortgagee = person to
whom something is mortgaged.*

E.E., Electrical Engineer.

eel (ēl), a long, slippery fish shaped like a snake. *n., pl.*
eels or **eel.** —**eel´like´,** *adj.*

e'en (ēn), OLD USE. even. *adv.*

e'er (er), OLD USE. ever. *adv.*

eer ie (ir´ē), causing fear because of strangeness or
weirdness: *a dark and eerie old house. adj.,* **eer i er, eer i-
est.** Also, **eery.** [*Eerie* comes from Old English *earg,*
meaning "cowardly."]

eer i ly (ir´ə lē), in an eerie manner: *The wind whistled
eerily in the chimney. adv.*

eer i ness (ir´ē nis), eerie quality or condition. *n.*

eer y (ir´ē), eerie. *adj.,* **eer i er, eer i est.**

efface (def. 2)—The shy boy **effaced** himself by staying
in the background.

ef face (ə fās´), **1** rub out; blot out; do away with; wipe
out; destroy: *The inscriptions on many ancient monuments
have been effaced by time.* **2** keep (oneself) from being
noticed; make inconspicuous. *v.,* **ef faced, ef fac ing.**
—**ef face´a ble,** *adj.* —**ef fac´er,** *n.*

ef face ment (ə fās´mənt), an effacing or a being effaced. *n.*

ef fect (ə fekt´), **1** whatever is produced by a cause;
something made to happen by a person or thing; result:
The effect of their research was a new kind of plastic.
2 make happen; bring about: *Florence Nightingale effected
many changes in nursing.* **3** power to produce results;
force; influence: *The medicine had an immediate effect.*
4 impression produced on the mind or senses: *The room
was painted yellow for a light, sunny effect.* **5** something
which produces such an impression: *The movie used
many special effects to make its scenes appear real.* **6** effects, *pl.* belongings; goods: *We lost all of our personal
effects in the fire.* 1,3-6 *n.,* **2** *v.* —**ef fect´er,** *n.*
for effect, for show; in order to impress or influence
others: *He said that only for effect; he really didn't mean it.*
in effect, 1 almost the same as; practically; virtually: *By
not speaking out against this plan you are saying, in effect,
that you approve it.* **2** in force or operation; active: *That
law has been in effect for two years.*
take effect, begin to operate; become active: *That pill
takes effect as soon as you swallow it.*

ef fec tive (ə fek´tiv), **1** able to produce an effect: *She is
a principal who knows how to make effective rules.* **2** producing the desired effect; getting results: *Penicillin is
an effective medicine in the treatment of many diseases.*

3 in operation; active: *The law passed by Congress became
effective as soon as the President signed it.* **4** striking; impressive: *Her skillful use of bright colors resulted in a very
effective picture. adj.* —**ef fec´tive ly,** *adv.* —**ef fec´tive-
ness,** *n.*

ef fec tu al (ə fek´chü əl), producing the desired effect;
capable of producing the desired effect: *Quinine is an
effectual remedy for malaria. adj.* —**ef fec´tu al ly,** *adv.*
—**ef fec´tu al ness,** *n.*

ef fec tu ate (ə fek´chü āt), make happen; bring about.
v., **ef fec tu at ed, ef fec tu at ing.** —**ef fec´tu a´tion,** *n.*

ef fem i na cy (ə fem´ə nə sē), effeminate quality or
character in a man or boy. *n.*

ef fem i nate (ə fem´ə nit), (of a man or boy) having
qualities or characteristics traditionally considered to be
feminine. *adj.* —**ef fem´i nate ly,** *adv.* —**ef fem´i nate-
ness,** *n.*

ef fer vesce (ef´ər ves´), **1** give off bubbles of gas; bubble: *Ginger ale effervesces.* **2** be lively and gay. *v.,* **ef fer-
vesced, ef fer vesc ing.**

ef fer ves cence (ef´ər ves´ns), **1** act or process of giving off bubbles of gas; bubbling. **2** liveliness and gaiety. *n.*

ef fer ves cent (ef´ər ves´nt), **1** giving off bubbles of
gas; bubbling: *Ginger ale is effervescent.* **2** lively and gay:
an effervescent personality. adj. —**ef´fer ves´cent ly,** *adv.*

ef fi ca cious (ef´ə kā´shəs), producing the desired results; effective: *Vaccination is efficacious in preventing
smallpox. adj.* —**ef´fi ca´cious ly,** *adv.* —**ef´fi ca´cious-
ness,** *n.*

ef fi ca cy (ef´ə kə sē), power to produce the effect
wanted: *The efficacy of aspirin in relieving headaches is
well known. n., pl.* **ef fi ca cies.**

ef fi cien cy (ə fish´ən sē), **1** ability to produce the effect
wanted without waste of time, energy, etc.: *The carpenter
worked with great efficiency.* **2** efficient operation: *Friction
reduces the efficiency of a machine.* **3** a very small apartment, usually just one room and a bathroom. *n., pl.*
ef fi cien cies.

ef fi cient (ə fish´ənt), able to produce the effect wanted
without waste of time, energy, etc.; capable: *An efficient
worker deserves good pay. adj.* —**ef fi´cient ly,** *adv.*

ef fi gy (ef´ə jē), image or statue, usually of a person:
The dead woman's monument bore her effigy. n., pl. **ef fi-
gies.**
burn in effigy or **hang in effigy,** burn or hang an
image of a person to show hatred or contempt: *The
unpopular ruler was burned in effigy by a mob.*

ef fort (ef´ərt), **1** use of energy and strength to do something; trying hard: *Climbing a steep hill takes effort.* **2** a
hard try; strong attempt: *He did not win, but at least he
made an effort.* **3** result of effort; thing done with effort;
achievement: *Works of art are artistic efforts. n.*

ef fort less (ef´ərt lis), requiring or showing little or no
effort; easy: *The cat pounced on the mouse with an effort-
less leap. adj.* —**ef´fort less ly,** *adv.* —**ef´fort less ness,** *n.*

ef fron ter y (ə frun´tər ē), shameless boldness; impudence: *My neighbor had the effrontery to say that I talk too
much. n., pl.* **ef fron ter ies.**

ef ful gent (i ful´jənt), shining brightly; radiant. *adj.* —**ef-
ful´gent ly,** *adv.*

ef fu sion (i fyü´zhən), **1** a pouring out: *There was an
effusion of blood from the deep wound.* **2** unrestrained expression of feeling, etc., in talking or writing. *n.*

ef fu sive (i fyü´siv), showing too much feeling; too demonstrative and emotional. *adj.* —**ef fu´sive ly,** *adv.*
—**ef fu´sive ness,** *n.*

eft (eft), a small newt. An eft lives on land until it ma-
tures. *n.*

eft soon (eft sün´), OLD USE. soon afterward. *adv.*

e.g., for example; for instance. [The abbreviation *e.g.* stands for the Latin phrase *exempli gratia.*]

egg[1] (eg), **1** the round or oval body, covered with a shell or membrane, which is laid by the female of birds, many reptiles, amphibians, fishes, insects, and other types of animals. Young animals hatch from these eggs. **2** the contents of an egg, especially a hen's egg, used as food: *She likes two boiled eggs for breakfast.* **3** a female reproductive cell; ovum. *n.* —**egg′less,** *adj.* —**egg′like′,** *adj.*

egg[2] (eg), urge or encourage: *We egged the team on to victory. v.*

egg beat er (eg′bē′tər), device with revolving blades for beating eggs, cream, etc. *n.*

egg cell, a female reproductive cell; ovum.

egg nog (eg′nog′), drink made of eggs beaten up with milk and sugar. It often has whiskey, brandy, or wine in it. *n.*

egg plant (eg′plant′), the large, purple fruit of a garden plant, cooked and eaten as a vegetable. *n.*

egg roll, a small tube of egg dough, filled with a mixture of minced vegetables and sometimes shrimp or meat, and fried.

egg shell (eg′shel′), **1** shell covering an egg. **2** a yellowish white. **3** yellowish-white. 1,2 *n.,* 3 *adj.*

e go (ē′gō), **1** the individual as a whole with the capacity to think, feel, and act; self. **2** sense of one's worth; self-esteem: *Their criticism punctured my ego.* **3** conceit; self-importance. *n., pl.* **e gos.** [*Ego* comes from Latin *ego,* meaning "I."]

e go ism (ē′gō iz′əm), **1** seeking the welfare of oneself only; selfishness. **2** conceit. *n.*

e go ist (ē′gō ist), **1** person who seeks the welfare of himself only; selfish person. **2** a conceited person. *n.*

e go tism (ē′gə tiz′əm), **1** a thinking, talking, or writing too much of oneself; conceit. **2** selfishness. *n.*

e go tist (ē′gə tist), **1** person who thinks, talks, or writes about himself or herself too much; conceited person. **2** a selfish person. *n.*

e go tis tic (ē′gə tis′tik), **1** characterized by egotism; conceited. **2** selfish. *adj.* —**e′go tis′ti cal ly,** *adv.*

e go tis ti cal (ē′gə tis′tə kəl), egotistic. *adj.*

e gre gious (i grē′jəs), very great: *an egregious waste of time.* —**e gre′gious ly,** *adv.* —**e gre′gious ness,** *n.*

e gret (ē′gret), a white wading bird with a long neck and a long bill. It grows beautiful, long plumes during the mating season. *n.*

E gypt (ē′jipt), country in NE Africa. *Capital:* Cairo. See **Nile** for map. *n.*

E gyp tian (i jip′shən), **1** of Egypt or its people. **2** person born or living in Egypt. **3** language of the ancient Egyptians. 1 *adj.,* 2,3 *n.*

eh (ā *or* e), exclamation expressing doubt, surprise, failure to hear exactly, or suggesting "Yes" for an answer: *Eh? What's that you said? That's a good joke, eh? interj.*

ei der (ī′dər), **1** a large, northern sea duck, usually black and white, with very soft feathers on its breast. **2** eiderdown (def. 1). *n.*

ei der down (ī′dər doun′), **1** the soft feathers from the breasts of eiders, used to stuff pillows and bed quilts. **2** quilt stuffed with these feathers. *n.*

eight (āt), one more than seven; 8. *n., adj.*

eight een (ā′tēn′), eight more than ten; 18. *n., adj.*

eight eenth (ā′tēnth′), **1** next after the 17th; last in a series of 18. **2** one of 18 equal parts. *adj., n.*

eighth (ātth), **1** next after the seventh; last in a series of 8. **2** one of 8 equal parts. *adj., n.*

eighth note, (in music) a note played for one eighth as long a time as a whole note.

eight i eth (ā′tē ith), **1** next after the 79th; last in a series of 80. **2** one of 80 equal parts. *adj., n.*

a hat	**i** it	**oi** oil	**ch** child	(a in about
ā age	**ī** ice	**ou** out	**ng** long	e in taken
ä far	**o** hot	**u** cup	**sh** she	ə = i in pencil
e let	**ō** open	**u̇** put	**th** thin	o in lemon
ē equal	**ô** order	**ü** rule	**ŦH** then	u in circus
ėr term			**zh** measure	

eight y (ā′tē), eight times ten; 80. *n., pl.* **eight ies;** *adj.*

Ein stein (īn′stīn), **Albert,** 1879-1955, American physicist, born in Germany. He developed the theory of relativity. *n.*

ein stein i um (īn stī′nē əm), a rare, radioactive element produced artificially from plutonium or uranium. *n.* [*Einsteinium* was named in honor of Albert *Einstein.*]

Eir e (er′ə *or* ar′ə), Republic of Ireland. *n.*

Ei sen how er (ī′zn hou′ər), **Dwight D(avid),** 1890-1969, American general, the 34th president of the United States, from 1953 to 1961. *n.*

ei ther (ē′ŦHər *or* ī′ŦHər), **1** one or the other of two: *You may read either book* (adj.). *Choose either of the candy bars* (pron.). *Either come in or go out* (conj.). **2** each of two: *There are cornfields on either side of the river.* **3** any more than another: *If you don't go, I won't go either.* 1 *adj., pron., conj.,* 2 *adj.,* 3 *adv.*

e jac u late (i jak′yə lāt), **1** say suddenly and briefly; exclaim. **2** discharge a fluid suddenly. *v.,* **e jac u lat ed, e jac u lat ing.**

e jac u la tion (i jak′yə lā′shən), **1** something said suddenly and briefly; exclamation. **2** the sudden discharge of a fluid. *n.*

e ject (i jekt′), throw out; force out; drive out: *The volcano ejected lava and ashes. The landlady ejected the tenants who did not pay their rent. v.* —**e ject′ment,** *n.*

e jec tion (i jek′shən), **1** an ejecting or a being ejected: *The audience demanded the ejection of the hecklers. The pilot's life was saved by his automatic ejection from the burning plane.* **2** something ejected: *Lava is a volcanic ejection. n.*

e jec tor (i jek′tər), person or thing that ejects. *n.*

eke (ēk). **eke out, 1** add to; increase: *The clerk eked out her regular wages by working evenings.* **2** barely manage to make (a living): *He eked out a living doing various odd jobs. v.,* **eked, ek ing.**

el (el), INFORMAL. elevated. *n.*

El Aai ún (el′ ä yün′), capital of Western Sahara.

e lab or ate (i lab′ər it *for 1;* i lab′ə rāt′ *for 2,3*), **1** worked out with great care; having many details: *The scientists made elaborate plans for launching a new satellite.* **2** work out with great care; add details to: *The author spent months elaborating plans for a new book.* **3** talk or write in great detail; give added details: *The witness was asked to elaborate on one of his statements.* 1 *adj.,* 2,3 *v.,* **e lab o rat ed, e lab o rat ing.** —**e lab′or ate ly,** *adv.* —**e lab′o rate ness,** *n.* —**e lab′o ra′tor,** *n.*

e lab o ra tion (i lab′ə rā′shən), **1** an elaborating or a being elaborated. **2** something elaborated. *n.*

e land (ē′lənd), a large, heavy African antelope with twisted horns. *n.* [*Eland* was borrowed from Afrikaans *eland,* which came from Dutch *eland,* meaning "elk."]

e lapse (i laps′), slip away; glide by; pass: *Many hours elapsed while I slept. v.,* **e lapsed, e laps ing.**

e las tic (i las′tik), **1** able to spring back to its original shape after being stretched, squeezed, bent, etc.: *Rubber bands, sponges, and steel springs are elastic.* **2** springing back; springy: *an elastic step.* **3** recovering quickly from weariness, low spirits, or misfortune: *Her elastic spirits kept her from being discouraged for long.* **4** easily changed to suit conditions; flexible; adaptable: *I have an elastic schedule.* **5** tape or cloth woven partly of rubber. **6** a rubber band. 1-4 *adj.*, 5,6 *n.* —e las'ti cal ly, *adv.*

e las tic i ty (i las tis'ə tē *or* ē'las tis'ə tē), elastic quality: *Rubber has elasticity. n.*

e late (i lāt'), raise the spirits of; make joyful or proud: *Her success in the writing contest elated her. v.*, **e lat ed**, **e lat ing.** —e lat'er, *n.*

e lat ed (i lā'tid), in high spirits; joyful: *We were elated about the good news. adj.* —e lat'ed ly, *adv.* —e lat'edness, *n.*

elation—The happy children are filled with **elation**.

e la tion (i lā'shən), high spirits; joy or pride. *n.*

El ba (el'bə), Italian island between Italy and Corsica. Napoleon I was in exile there from 1814 to 1815. *n.*

El be (el'bə), river flowing from W Czechoslovakia through East Germany and West Germany into the North Sea. See **Rhine** for map. *n.*

el bow (el'bō), **1** joint between the upper and lower arm. **2** anything like a bent arm in shape or position. A bent joint for connecting pipes or a sharp turn in a road or river may be called an elbow. **3** push with the elbow; make one's way by pushing: *Don't elbow me off the sidewalk. 1,2 n., 3 v.*

out at the elbow, ragged; shabby.

rub elbows, mingle.

elbow grease, INFORMAL. hard work.

el bow room (el'bō rüm' *or* el'bō rum'), plenty of room; enough room or space to move or work in. *n.*

eld (eld), OLD USE. **1** old age. **2** ancient times. *n.*

eld er[1] (el'dər), **1** older; senior: *my elder sister, an elder statesman.* **2** an older person: *to take the advice of one's elders.* **3** one of the older and more influential members of a tribe or community. **4** any of various officers in certain churches. 1 *adj.*, 2-4 *n.*

el der[2] (el'dər), **1** shrub or small tree with flat clusters of white flowers and black or red berries. **2** its berry, used in making wine, pies, etc. *n.*

el der ber ry (el'dər ber'ē), elder[2]. *n., pl.* **el der ber ries.**

eld er ly (el'dər lē), somewhat old; beyond middle age. *adj.*

eld est (el'dist), oldest. *adj.*

El do ra do (el'də rä'dō), El Dorado. *n., pl.* **El do ra dos.**

El Do ra do (el də rä'dō), **1** an imaginary place supposed to be full of treasure, sought by early Spanish explorers in South America. **2** any wealthy place. *pl.* **El Do ra dos.** [*El Dorado* comes from Spanish *El Dorado*, which originally meant "the gilded one."]

elec., **1** electric. **2** electrical. **3** electricity.

e lect (i lekt'), **1** choose or select for an office by voting: *We elect our class officers every autumn.* **2** elected but not yet in office: *the governor-elect.* **3** choose; select: *The children elected to play baseball. 1,3 v., 2 adj.*

elect., **1** electric. **2** electrical. **3** electricity.

e lec tion (i lek'shən), **1** a choosing or selecting for an office by vote: *In our city we have an election for mayor every four years.* **2** a being chosen or selected for an

office by vote: *The candidate's excellent and honest campaign resulted in her election.* **3** choice; selection. *n.*

e lec tion eer (i lek'shə nir'), to work for the success of a candidate or party in an election. *v.*

e lec tive (i lek'tiv), **1** chosen by an election: *Senators are elective officials.* **2** filled by an election: *The office of President of the United States is elective.* **3** open to choice; not required: *Spanish is an elective subject in many high schools.* **4** subject or course of study which may be taken, but is not required. 1-3 *adj.*, 4 *n.* —e lec'tive ly, *adv.*

e lec tor (i lek'tər), **1** person who has the right to vote in an election. **2** member of the electoral college. *n.*

e lec tor al (i lek'tər əl), **1** of electors: *electoral votes.* **2** of an election. *adj.* —e lec'tor al ly, *adv.*

electoral college, group of people chosen by the voters to elect the President and Vice-President of the United States.

e lec tor ate (i lek'tər it), the persons having the right to vote in an election. *n.*

e lec tric (i lek'trik), **1** of electricity: *an electric light, an electric current.* **2** charged with electricity: *an electric battery.* **3** run by electricity: *an electric stove.* **4** exciting; thrilling: *an electric feeling. adj.*

e lec tri cal (i lek'trə kəl), electric. *adj.*

e lec tri cal ly (i lek'trik lē), by electricity. *adv.*

electric cell, container holding materials which produce electricity by chemical action. A battery consists of one or more electric cells.

electric eel, a large South American freshwater fish resembling an eel, that can give strong electric shocks.

electric eye, photoelectric cell.

e lec tri cian (i lek'trish'ən), person whose work is installing or repairing electric wiring, lights, motors, etc. *n.*

e lec tric i ty (i lek'tris'ə tē), **1** form of energy which can produce light, heat, motion, and magnetic force. Electricity is produced in generators for people to buy and use, but can be produced in small amounts by running a comb through your hair or by chemical change in a flashlight battery. **2** electric current: *Most refrigerators are run by electricity. n.*

WORD HISTORY

electricity

Electricity can be traced back to Greek *ēlektron,* meaning "amber." It was called this because amber becomes charged with electricity when it is rubbed.

electric light bulb, incandescent lamp.

electric storm, thunderstorm.

e lec tri fi ca tion (i lek'trə fə kā'shən), an electrifying or a being electrified. *n.*

e lec tri fy (i lek'trə fī), **1** charge with electricity. **2** equip for the use of electric power: *Some railroads once run by steam are now electrified.* **3** give an electric shock to. **4** excite; thrill: *The spectators were electrified by the team's performance. v.*, **e lec tri fied**, **e lec tri fy ing.**

electro-, *combining form.* **1** electric: *Electromagnet = an electric magnet.* **2** electricity: *Electroscope = device that detects electricity.* [The form *electro-* comes from Greek *ēlektron,* meaning "amber."]

e lec tro car di o gram (i lek'trō kär'dē ə gram), the tracing or record made by an electrocardiograph; cardiogram. *n.*

e lec tro car di o graph (i lek′trō kär′dē ə graf), instrument that detects and records the electrical impulses produced by the action of the heart with each beat; cardiograph. It is used to diagnose diseases of the heart. *n.*

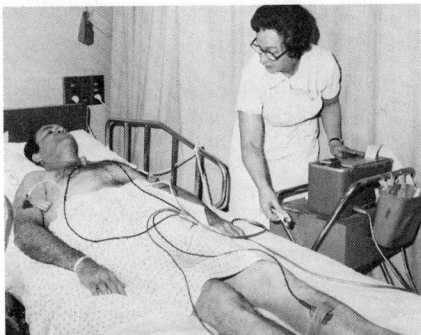

electrocardiograph—Electrical impulses from the heart are received from four points on the body and recorded on paper tape.

e lec tro cute (i lek′trə kyüt), kill or execute by electricity: *A live wire can electrocute a person who touches it. v.,* **e lec tro cut ed, e lec tro cut ing.**

e lec tro cu tion (i lek′trə kyü′shən), a killing or execution by electricity. *n.*

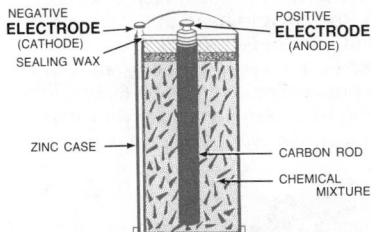

electrodes of a dry cell—The chemical mixture reacts with the zinc, causing positive ions to flow toward the carbon rod, and electrons to flow toward the zinc. When the electrodes are connected in a circuit, an electric current leaves the cell at the cathode and returns to it at the anode.

e lec trode (i lek′trōd), either of the two terminals of a battery or any other source of electricity; conductor by which a current is brought into a liquid or a gas. The anode and cathode of an electric cell are electrodes. *n.*

e lec trol y sis (i lek′trol′ə sis), decomposition of a chemical compound into its ions by the passage of an electric current through a solution of it. The electrolysis of metallic solutions is useful in putting metal coatings on objects. *n.*

e lec tro lyte (i lek′trə līt), a chemical compound whose water solution will conduct an electric current; chemical compound that ionizes. Acids, bases, and salts are electrolytes. *n.*

e lec tro mag net (i lek′trō mag′nit), piece of soft iron that becomes a strong magnet when an electric current is passing through wire coiled around it. *n.*

e lec tro mag net ic (i lek′trō mag net′ik), of or caused by an electromagnet. *adj.*

electromagnetic wave, wave of energy made up of an electric and a magnetic field. Light waves and radio waves are electromagnetic waves.

e lec tro mag net ism (i lek′trō mag′nə tiz′əm), **1** mag-

a hat	**i** it	**oi** oil	**ch** child	a in about
ā age	**ī** ice	**ou** out	**ng** long	e in taken
ä far	**o** hot	**u** cup	**sh** she	ə = i in pencil
e let	**ō** open	**ù** put	**th** thin	o in lemon
ē equal	**ô** order	**ü** rule	**ᵀH** then	u in circus
ėr term			**zh** measure	

netism produced by a current of electricity. **2** branch of physics that deals with electricity and magnetism. *n.*

e lec tron (i lek′tron), a tiny particle carrying one unit of negative electricity. All atoms have electrons arranged about a nucleus. *n.*

electron gun, device that produces and guides a flow of electrons. In a television set, an electron gun directs a stream of electrons to the screen.

e lec tron ic (i lek′tron′ik), of electronics. *adj.*

e lec tron i cal ly (i lek′tron′ik lē), by electronic means; in an electronic manner. *adv.*

electronic mail, 1 system of sending messages using computers linked by telephone wires or radio signals. **2** messages sent by such a system.

e lec tron ics (i lek′tron′iks), branch of physics that deals with the production, flow, motion, and use of electrons in vacuums and gases. Electronics has made possible the development of television, radio, radar, and computers. *n.*

electron microscope, microscope that uses beams of electrons instead of beams of light, and has much higher power than any ordinary microscope.

electron tube, vacuum tube.

e lec tro plate (i lek′trə plāt), cover (silverware, printing plates, etc.) with a coating of metal by means of electrolysis. *v.,* **e lec tro plat ed, e lec tro plat ing.**

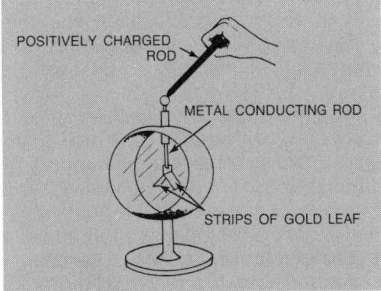

electroscope—When a positively charged rod touches the metal conducting rod, the strips of gold leaf repel each other. When a negative charge is brought into contact with the metal conducting rod, the strips of gold leaf come together again.

e lec tro scope (i lek′trə skōp), device that indicates the presence of minute charges of electricity and shows whether they are positive or negative. *n.*

el e gance (el′ə gəns), good taste; refined grace and richness; luxurious beauty: *We admired the elegance of the clothes worn to the formal dinner. n.*

el e gan cy (el′ə gən sē), elegance. *n., pl.* **el e gan cies.**

el e gant (el′ə gənt), having or showing good taste; gracefully and richly refined; beautifully luxurious: *The palace had elegant furnishings. adj.* **—el′e gant ly,** *adv.*

el e gize (el′ə jīz), write an elegy (about). *v.,* **el e gized, el e giz ing.**

el e gy (el′ə jē), a mournful or melancholy poem, usually a lament for the dead. *n., pl.* **el e gies.**

el e ment (el′ə mənt), **1** one of the simple substances from which all other things are made up. An element cannot be separated into simpler parts by chemical means. Gold, iron, carbon, sulfur, oxygen, and hydrogen are elements. There are more than 100 known elements, each composed of atoms that are chemically alike. **2** one of the parts of which anything is made up: *I like a story that has an element of surprise to it.* **3** a simple or necessary part to be learned first; first principle: *Most of us learn the elements of arithmetic before the seventh grade.* **4 the elements,** the forces of the atmosphere, especially in bad weather: *The raging storm seemed to be a war of the elements.* **5** natural or suitable surroundings: *He loves books, and is in his element in a library.* **6** member of a set in mathematics. **7** the part that does the work in an electrical device. *n.*

el e men tal (el′ə men′tl), **1** of the forces of the atmosphere, especially the weather: *The storm showed elemental fury in its violence.* **2** natural; simple but powerful: *Hunger is an elemental feeling.* **3** elementary. *adj.*

el e men tar y (el′ə men′tər ē *or* el′ə men′trē), of or dealing with the simple, necessary parts to be learned first; having to do with first principles; introductory: *Addition, subtraction, multiplication, and division are taught in elementary arithmetic. adj.* —**el′e men tar′i ly,** *adv.*

elementary school, 1 school of usually six grades for pupils from about six to twelve years of age, followed by junior high school. **2** school of eight grades for pupils from about six to fourteen years of age, followed by a four-year high school.

el e phant (el′ə fənt), a huge, heavy mammal, the largest living land animal, with ivory tusks and a long, muscular snout called a trunk. **African elephants** have large ears and both the males and females have tusks. **Asian** or **Indian elephants** have smaller ears and the females often have no tusks. *n., pl.* **el e phants** or **el e phant.**

el e phan tine (el′ə fan′tēn′ *or* el′ə fan′tīn), **1** like an elephant; huge, heavy, and clumsy. **2** of elephants. *adj.*

el e vate (el′ə vāt), lift up; raise: *elevate the stage in a theater, elevate one's mind by studying philosophy. She was elevated to an important position in the company. v.,* **el e-vat ed, el e vat ing.**

el e vat ed (el′ə vā′tid), **1** lifted up; raised: *an elevated platform.* **2** dignified: *elevated conversation.* **3** INFORMAL. an electric railroad raised above street level on a supporting frame, allowing traffic to pass underneath; el. **1,2** *adj.,* **3** *n.*

el e va tion (el′ə vā′shən), **1** a raised place; high place: *A hill is an elevation.* **2** height above the earth's surface: *The airplane flew at an elevation of 20,000 feet.* **3** height above sea level: *The elevation of Denver is 5300 feet.* **4** an elevating or a being elevated: *The elevation of a clerk to store manager surprised us. n.*

el e va tor (el′ə vā′tər), **1** something which raises or lifts up. **2** a moving platform or cage to carry people and things up and down in a building, mine, etc. **3** grain elevator. **4** an adjustable, flat piece on the tail of an airplane to cause it to go up or down. *n.*

e lev en (i lev′ən), **1** one more than ten; 11. **2** a football or cricket team. **1,2** *n.,* **1** *adj.*

e lev enth (i lev′ənth), **1** next after the 10th; last in a series of 11. **2** one of 11 equal parts. *adj., n.*

eleventh hour, the latest possible moment; time just before it is too late.

elf (elf), a tiny fairy that is full of mischief. *n., pl.* **elves.**

elf in (el′fən), of or suitable for elves; like an elf's: *an elfin smile. adj.*

elf ish (el′fish), like an elf; elfin; mischievous. *adj.*

El Grec o (el grek′ō), 1541?-1614, Spanish painter born in Crete. [Although the painter was born in Crete and had a Greek name, he did most of his work in Spain. The Spaniards called him *El Greco,* meaning "the Greek."]

e lic it (i lis′it), draw forth; bring out: *The comedian's joke elicited laughter from the audience. v.*

el i gi bil i ty (el′ə jə bil′ə tē), fitness to be chosen; qualification. *n., pl.* **el i gi bil i ties.**

el i gi ble (el′ə jə bəl), fit to be chosen; properly qualified: *Pupils had to pass all subjects to be eligible for the team. adj.* —**el′i gi bly,** *adv.*

E li jah (i lī′jə), Hebrew prophet who lived in the 800's B.C. *n.*

e lim i nate (i lim′ə nāt), **1** get rid of; remove: *The losing team was eliminated from the semifinals.* **2** leave out; omit: *Eliminate unnecessary details from your report.* **3** expel (waste) from the body; excrete. *v.,* **e lim i nat ed, e lim i-nat ing.** —**e lim′i na′tor,** *n.*

e lim i na tion (i lim′ə nā′shən), an eliminating or a being eliminated. *n.*

El i ot (el′ē ət *or* el′yət), **1 George,** 1819-1880, pen name of Mary Ann Evans, English novelist. **2 T(homas) S(tearns),** 1888-1965, British poet, essayist, and critic, born in the United States. *n.*

e lite or **é lite** (i lēt′ *or* ā lēt′), the choice or distinguished part; those thought of as the best people: *Only the elite attended the reception for the visiting queen. n.*

e lix ir (i lik′sər), **1** substance supposed to have the power of changing lead, iron, etc., into gold or of lengthening life indefinitely. The alchemists of the Middle Ages sought for it. **2** a universal remedy; cure-all. *n.*

E liz a beth I (i liz′ə bəth), 1533-1603, queen of England from 1558 to 1603, daughter of Henry VIII.

Elizabeth II, born 1926, since 1952 queen of Great Britain and Northern Ireland, and head of the Commonwealth of Nations; daughter of George VI.

E liz a be than (i liz′ə bē′thən *or* i liz′ə beth′ən), **1** of the time when Elizabeth I ruled England (1558-1603): *Elizabethan drama.* **2** an English person, especially a writer, of the time of Elizabeth I: *Shakespeare is a famous Elizabethan.* **1** *adj.,* **2** *n.*

elk
(def. 2)
5 ft. (1.5 m.)
high at
the shoulder

elk (elk), **1** a large deer of northern Europe and Asia. It has spreading antlers like those of a moose. **2** a large reddish deer of North America with long, slender antlers; wapiti. *n., pl.* **elks** or **elk.**

ell (el), a former measure of length, equal to 45 inches (1.14 meters) in England. *n.*

El ling ton (el′ing tən), **Edward Kennedy,** 1899-1974, American jazz composer, called "Duke" Ellington. *n.*

el lipse (i lips′), a figure shaped like an oval with both ends alike. *n.*

ellipses

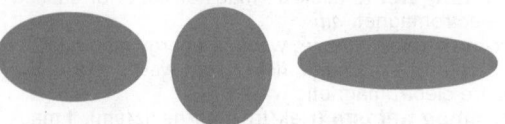

el lip sis (i lip′sis), marks (. . . or ***) used to show an omission in writing or printing. *n., pl.* **el lip ses** (i lip′sēz′).

el lip tic (i lip′tik), elliptical. *adj.*

el lip ti cal (i lip′tə kəl), shaped like an ellipse. *adj.* —**el lip′ti cal ly,** *adv.*

elm (elm), **1** a tall shade tree with high, spreading branches. **2** its hard, heavy wood. *n.*

el o cu tion (el′ə kyü′shən), art of speaking or reading clearly and effectively in public. Elocution includes the correct use of the voice and of gestures. *n.*

e lon gate (i lông′gāt), **1** make or become longer; lengthen; extend; stretch: *The balloon elongated as it became filled with air.* **2** long and thin: *Earthworms have elongate bodies.* **1** *v.,* **e lon gat ed, e lon gat ing; 2** *adj.*

e lon ga tion (ē′lông gā′shən), a lengthening; extension. *n.*

e lope (i lōp′), run away to get married. *v.,* **e loped, e lop ing.** —**e lop′er,** *n.*

e lope ment (i lōp′mənt), an eloping. *n.*

el o quence (el′ə kwəns), **1** flow of speech that has grace and force: *The jury was moved by the eloquence of the lawyer's words.* **2** power to win by speaking; art of speaking so as to stir the feelings. *n.*

el o quent (el′ə kwənt), **1** having the power of expressing one's feelings or thoughts with grace and force; having eloquence: *an eloquent speaker.* **2** very expressive: *eloquent eyes. adj.* —**el′o quent ly,** *adv.*

El Sal va dor (el sal′və dôr′), country in W Central America. *Capital:* San Salvador.

else (els), **1** other than the person, place, thing, etc., mentioned; different; instead: *Will somebody else speak? What else could I say?* **2** in addition; more; besides: *The Browns are here; do you expect anyone else?* **3** differently: *How else can it be done?* **4** otherwise; if not: *Hurry, else you will be late.* **1,2** *adj.,* **3,4** *adv.*

else where (els′hwer *or* els′hwar), in, at, or to some other place; somewhere else. *adv.*

e lu ci date (i lü′sə dāt), make clear; explain: *The scientist was asked to elucidate her theory. v.,* **e lu ci dat ed, e lu ci dat ing.** —**e lu′ci da′tor,** *n.*

e lu ci da tion (i lü′sə dā′shən), a making clear; explanation. *n.*

e lude (i lüd′), **1** avoid or escape by cleverness or quickness; slip away from: *The fox eluded the dogs.* **2** remain undiscovered or unexplained by; baffle: *The answer to the problem eluded me. v.,* **e lud ed, e lud ing.**

e lu sive (i lü′siv), **1** hard to describe or understand; baffling: *I had an idea that was too elusive to put in words.* **2** tending to elude or escape: *The elusive fox got away. adj.* —**e lu′sive ly,** *adv.* —**e lu′sive ness,** *n.*

elves (elvz), plural of **elf.** *n.*

'em (əm), INFORMAL. them. *pron.pl.*

e ma ci ate (i mā′shē āt), make unnaturally thin; cause to lose flesh or waste away: *A long illness had emaciated the patient. v.,* **e ma ci at ed, e ma ci at ing.**

e ma ci a tion (i mā′shē ā′shən), an unnatural thinness from loss of flesh; wasting away. *n.*

em a nate (em′ə nāt), come forth; spread out: *Light and heat emanate from the sun. The story emanated from the mayor's office. v.,* **em a nat ed, em a nat ing.**

em a na tion (em′ə nā′shən), **1** a coming forth; spreading out. **2** anything that comes forth or spreads out from a source: *Light and heat are emanations from the sun. n.*

e man ci pate (i man′sə pāt), set free from slavery or restraint; release: *Lincoln emancipated the slaves. Women have been emancipated from many old restrictions. v.,* **e man ci pat ed, e man ci pat ing.** [*Emancipate* can be traced back to Latin *ex-*, meaning "from, away," *manus,* meaning "hand," and *capere,* meaning "to take."]

e man ci pa tion (i man′sə pā′shən), a setting free from slavery or restraint; release: *The emancipation of slaves in the United States was proclaimed in 1863. The discoveries of science have led to people's emancipation from many old superstitions. n.*

Emancipation Proclamation, proclamation issued by Abraham Lincoln on January 1, 1863, declaring free all persons held as slaves in any state then in armed rebellion against the United States.

e man ci pa tor (i man′sə pā′tər), person who emancipates. *n.*

e mas cu late (i mas′kyə lāt), **1** remove the testicles of; castrate. **2** destroy the force of; weaken: *The editor emasculated the speech by cutting out its strongest passages. v.,* **e mas cu lat ed, e mas cu lat ing.** —**e mas′cu la′tor,** *n.*

e mas cu la tion (i mas′kyə lā′shən), an emasculating or a being emasculated. *n.*

em balm (em bäm′ *or* em bälm′), treat (a dead body) with chemicals to keep it from decaying. *v.*

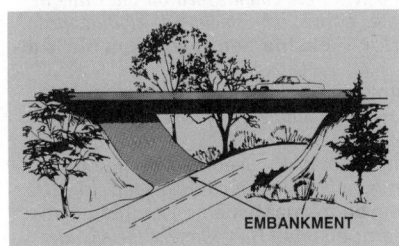

EMBANKMENT

em bank ment (em bangk′mənt), a raised bank of earth, stones, etc., used to hold back water, support a road, etc. *n.*

em bar go (em bär′gō), **1** an order of a government forbidding ships to enter or leave its ports. **2** any restriction put on commerce by law. **3** put under an embargo; forbid to enter or leave port: *The government embargoed all foreign ships.* **1,2** *n., pl.* **em bar goes; 3** *v.*

em bark (em bärk′), **1** go or put on board a ship or an aircraft: *to embark for Europe. The general embarked his troops.* **2** set out; start: *After leaving college, the young woman embarked upon a business career. v.*

em bar ka tion (em′bär kā′shən), an embarking. *n.*

em bar rass (em bar′əs), **1** make uneasy and ashamed; make self-conscious: *She embarrassed me by asking me if I really liked her.* **2** hamper; hinder: *Lack of trucks embarrassed the army's movements.* **3** burden with debt: *The company was financially embarrassed and could not pay its employees last week. v.*

em bar rass ing (em bar′ə sing), causing embarrassment: *an embarrassing situation. adj.*

em bar rass ment (em bar′əs mənt), **1** condition of being embarrassed; uneasiness; shame: *He blushed in embarrassment at such a stupid mistake.* **2** thing that embarrasses: *Forgetting the name of an old friend is a great embarrassment. n.*

em bas sy (em′bə sē), **1** ambassador and his or her staff of assistants. An embassy ranks next above a legation. **2** the official residence and offices of an ambassador in a foreign country. **3** position or duties of an ambassador. *n., pl.* **em bas sies.**

em bat tled (em bat′ld), **1** drawn up ready for battle; prepared for battle. **2** fortified. *adj.*

em bed (em bed′), enclose in a surrounding mass; fasten or fix firmly: *Precious stones are often found embedded in rock. Every detail is embedded in my memory. v.,* **em bed ded, em bed ding.** Also, **imbed.**

em bel lish (em bel′ish), **1** add beauty to; decorate; adorn; ornament: *embellish a room with flowers. He embellished his letters with clever sketches.* **2** make more interesting by adding real or imaginary details: *The speaker embellished the old stories, so that they sounded new. v.*

em bel lish ment (em bel′ish mənt), **1** decoration; adornment; ornament. **2** detail, often imaginary, added to make a story or account more interesting. *n.*

em ber (em′bər), **1** piece of wood or coal still glowing in the ashes of a fire. **2 embers,** *pl.* ashes in which there is still some fire: *She stirred the embers to make them blaze up again. n.*

em bez zle (em bez′əl), steal (money entrusted to one's care): *The cashier embezzled $50,000 from the bank. v.,* **em bez zled, em bez zling.**

em bez zle ment (em bez′əl mənt), theft of money entrusted to one's care. *n.*

em bez zler (em bez′lər), person who embezzles. *n.*

em bit ter (em bit′ər), make bitter: *embittered by constant failure. v.* **—em bit′ter ment,** *n.*

em bla zon (em blā′zn), **1** display conspicuously; picture in bright colors: *Posters were emblazoned on the walls of the room.* **2** decorate; adorn: *The shield was emblazoned with a coat of arms. v.* **—em bla′zon er,** *n.* **—em bla′zon ment,** *n.*

em blem (em′bləm), sign that stands for an idea; symbol; token: *The dove is an emblem of peace. The Stars and Stripes and the eagle are emblems of the United States. n.*

em blem at ic (em′blə mat′ik), used as an emblem; symbolic: *The lion is emblematic of courage. adj.*

em bod i ment (em bod′ē mənt), person or thing symbolizing some idea or quality: *They thought their leader was the embodiment of authority. n.*

em bod y (em bod′ē), **1** put into a form that can be seen; express in definite form: *A building embodies the idea of an architect.* **2** bring together in a single book, law, system, etc.; include: *The scout handbook embodies the information needed to become a good scout.* **3** make part of an organized book, law, system, etc.; incorporate: *embody suggestions in a revised plan. v.,* **em bod ied, em bod y ing.**

em bold en (em bōl′dən), make bold; encourage. *v.*

em bo lism (em′bə liz′əm), a blocking of a blood vessel by a clot, a bit of fat, or some other obstacle carried there by the blood. *n.*

em boss (em bôs′), **1** decorate with a design or pattern that stands out from the surface. **2** cause to stand out from the surface: *He ran his finger over the letters on the book's cover to see if they had been embossed. v.* **—em boss′er,** *n.* **—em boss′ment,** *n.*

emboss (def. 1)
The surface of the old cash register was elaborately **embossed.**

em brace (em brās′), **1** hold in the arms to show love or friendship; hug: *I embraced my old friend.* **2** a clasping in the arms; hug: *My old friend gave me a fond embrace.* **3** take up; take for oneself; accept: *She eagerly embraced the offer of a trip to Europe.* **4** include; contain: *The cat family embraces cats, lions, tigers, and similar animals.* **5** surround; enclose: *Vines embraced the hut.* 1,3-5 *v.,* **em braced, em brac ing;** 2 *n.* [*Embrace* came into English about 600 years ago from French *embracer,* and can be traced back to Latin *in-,* meaning "in," and *brachium,* meaning "arm."] **—em brace′a ble,** *adj.* **—em brace′ment,** *n.* **—em brac′er,** *n.*

em bra sure (em brā′zhər), an opening in a wall for a gun, with sides that spread outward to permit the gun to swing through a greater arc. *n.*

em broi der (em broi′dər), **1** ornament (cloth, leather, etc.) with a raised design or pattern of stitches: *embroider a shirt with a colorful design.* **2** make (an ornamental design or pattern) on cloth, leather etc., with stitches: *I embroidered silver stars on my blue jeans.* **3** add imaginary details to; exaggerate: *She often embroiders her stories to make them more interesting. v.* **—em broi′der er,** *n.*

em broi der y (em broi′dər ē), **1** act or art of embroidering. **2** embroidered work or material; ornamental designs sewn in cloth, leather, etc., with a needle. *n., pl.* **em broi der ies.**

em broil (em broil′), involve in a quarrel: *Even bystanders became embroiled in our argument. v.* **—em broil′ment,** *n.*

em bry o (em′brē ō), **1** animal in the earlier stages of its development, before birth or hatching. A chicken within an egg is an embryo. A human embryo more than three months old is usually called a fetus. **2** an undeveloped plant within a seed. *n., pl.* **em bry os.**

in embryo, in an undeveloped stage: *a plan in embryo.*

WORD HISTORY

embryo

Embryo was borrowed from a medieval Latin word *embryo,* and can be traced back to Greek *en-,* meaning "in," and *bryein,* meaning "to swell."

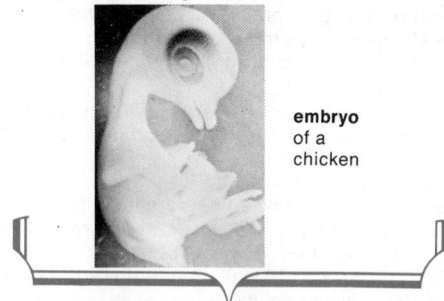

embryo
of a
chicken

em bry ol o gy (em′brē ol′ə jē), branch of biology that deals with the formation and development of embryos. *n.*

em bry on ic (em′brē on′ik), **1** of the embryo. **2** not mature; undeveloped: *an embryonic leaf, an embryonic plan. adj.*

em cee (em′sē′), INFORMAL. **1** master of ceremonies. **2** act as master of ceremonies of. 1 *n.,* 2 *v.,* **em ceed, em cee ing.**

e mend (i mend′), to free from faults or errors; correct. *v.*

e men da tion (ē′men dā′shən), an emending; correction. *n.*

em er ald (em′ər əld), **1** a clear, hard, deep-green precious gem. Emeralds are a variety of beryl. **2** a bright green. **3** bright-green. 1,2 *n.,* 3 *adj.*

e merge (i mėrj′), **1** come into view; come out; come up: *The sun emerged from behind a cloud.* **2** become known: *New facts emerged as a result of a second investigation. v.,* **e merged, e merg ing.**

e mer gence (i mėr′jəns), act or fact of emerging: *the emergence of a chick from its egg. n.*

e mer gen cy (i mėr′jən sē), **1** a sudden need for immediate action: *I keep a box of tools in my car for use in an emergency.* **2** for a time of sudden need: *When the brakes failed, the driver put on the emergency brake and stopped the car. The surgeon performed an emergency operation.* 1 *n., pl.* **e mer gen cies;** 2 *adj.*

e mer gent (i mėr′jənt), emerging. *adj.*

e mer i tus (i mer′ə təs), retired from active service, but still holding one's rank and title: *At the age of seventy, Professor Arnold became professor emeritus. adj.*

Em er son (ėm′ər sən), **Ralph Waldo,** 1803-1882, American essayist, poet, and philosopher. *n.*

em er y (em′ər ē), a hard, dark mineral used in powdered form to grind, smooth, and polish metals, stones, etc. *n.*

emery board, a thin, flat piece of wood with a coating of powdered emery. It is used to file fingernails.

e met ic (i met′ik), **1** causing vomiting. **2** medicine that causes vomiting. 1 *adj.,* 2 *n.*

em i grant (em′ə grənt), person who leaves his or her own country to settle in another: *My grandparents were emigrants from Japan. n.*

em i grate (em′ə grāt), leave one's own country to settle in another: *My grandparents emigrated from Ireland to the United States. v.,* **em i grat ed, em i grat ing.**

em i gra tion (em′ə grā′shən), **1** a leaving one's own country to settle in another: *There has been much emigration from Italy to the United States.* **2** body of emigrants: *The largest emigration from Europe came to the United States in 1907. n.*

ém i gré (em′ə grā), **1** emigrant. **2** member of a refugee group. *n., pl.* **ém i grés** (em′ə grāz).

em i nence (em′ə nəns), **1** rank or position above all or most others; high standing; fame: *to achieve eminence in the field of medicine.* **2** a high place; high point of land: *The lighthouse was built on an eminence rising many feet above the shore.* **3 Eminence,** title of honor given to a cardinal in the Roman Catholic Church. *n.*

em i nent (em′ə nənt), above all or most others; outstanding; famous; distinguished: *an eminent writer. adj.*

em i nent ly (em′ə nənt lē), to an eminent degree; so as to be distinguished from others: *Because of her long experience in the state legislature, she was eminently qualified to run for Congress. adv.*

e mir (ə mir′), **1** an Arabian chief, prince, or military leader. **2** title of honor of the descendants of Mohammed. *n.* [*Emir* comes from Arabic *amīr.*] Also, **amir.**

em is sar y (em′ə ser′ē), **1** person sent on a mission or errand. **2** a secret agent; spy. *n., pl.* **em is sar ies.**

e mis sion (i mish′ən), **1** act or fact of emitting: *the emission of light from the sun.* **2** thing emitted. *n.*

emission control, control or limitation of the quantity of polluting gases or particles given off by burning fuels, industrial processes, etc.

e mit (i mit′), give off; send out: *The sun emits light and heat. Volcanoes emit lava. The trapped lion emitted roars of rage. v.,* **e mit ted, e mit ting.**

Em man u el (i man′yü əl), Christ. *n.* Also, **Immanuel.**

e mol lient (i mol′yənt), **1** softening or soothing: *an emollient hand lotion.* **2** something that softens and soothes: *Cold cream is an emollient for the skin.* 1 *adj.,* 2 *n.*

a hat	**i** it	**oi** oil	**ch** child	⎧ a in about
ā age	**ī** ice	**ou** out	**ng** long	⎪ e in taken
ä far	**o** hot	**u** cup	**sh** she	ə = ⎨ i in pencil
e let	**ō** open	**ù** put	**th** thin	⎪ o in lemon
ē equal	**ô** order	**ü** rule	**ᴛʜ** then	⎩ u in circus
ėr term			**zh** measure	

e mo tion (i mō′shən), a strong feeling of any kind. Joy, grief, fear, hate, love, anger, and excitement are emotions. *n.*

e mo tion al (i mō′shə nəl), **1** of the emotions: *His constant fears show that he is suffering from a serious emotional disorder.* **2** showing emotion: *My reaction to the movie was so emotional that I began to cry.* **3** appealing to the emotions: *The speaker made an emotional plea for money to help crippled children.* **4** easily excited: *Emotional people are likely to cry if they hear sad music or read sad stories. adj.* —**e mo′tion al ly,** *adv.*

e mo tion al ism (i mō′shə nə liz′əm), tendency to show emotion too easily. *n.*

em pan el (em pan′l), impanel. *v.*

em per or (em′pər ər), man who is the ruler of an empire. *n.* [*Emperor* came into English about 700 years ago from French *empereor,* which came from Latin *imperator,* originally meaning "commander."]

em pha sis (em′fə sis), **1** special force; stress; importance: *That school puts emphasis on arithmetic and reading.* **2** special force put on particular syllables, words, or phrases: *A speaker puts emphasis on important words by stressing them. n., pl.* **em pha ses** (em′fə sēz′).

em pha size (em′fə sīz), **1** give special force to; make important; stress: *He emphasized her name by saying it very loudly.* **2** call attention to: *The large number of automobile accidents emphasizes the need for careful driving. v.,* **em pha sized, em pha siz ing.**

em phat ic (em fat′ik), **1** said or done with force; strongly expressed: *Her answer was an emphatic "No!"* **2** attracting attention; very noticeable; striking: *The club made an emphatic success of its party. adj.*

em phat i cal ly (em fat′ik lē), in an emphatic manner; to an emphatic degree. *adv.*

em phy se ma (em′fə sē′mə), an abnormal increase in size of the air sacs in the lungs. Emphysema makes breathing difficult, because the lungs cannot easily exhale waste carbon dioxide. *n.*

em pire (em′pīr), **1** group of countries or states under one ruler or government: *The Roman Empire consisted of many separate territories and different peoples.* **2** country that has an emperor or empress: *the Japanese Empire.* **3** absolute power; supreme authority. **4** a large business or group of businesses under the control of a single person, family, syndicate, etc. *n.*

em pir i cal (em pir′ə kəl), based on experiment and observation: *Chemistry is largely an empirical science. adj.* —**em pir′i cal ly,** *adv.*

em place ment (em plās′mənt), space or platform for a heavy gun or guns. *n.*

em ploy (em ploi′), **1** give work and pay to: *That big factory employs many workers.* **2** service for pay; employment: *There are many workers in the employ of that big factory.* **3** use: *You employ a knife, fork, and spoon in eating. She employs her time wisely.* **4** keep busy; occupy: *He employed himself in growing roses after he retired.* 1,3,4 *v.,* 2 *n.* —**em ploy′a ble,** *adj.*

em ploy ee or **em ploy e** (em ploi′ē *or* em′ploi ē′), person who works for some person or firm for pay. *n.*

em ploy er (em ploi′ər), person or firm that employs one or more persons. *n.*

em ploy ment (em ploi′mənt), **1** work; job: *She had no* difficulty finding employment. **2** an employing or a being employed: *A large office requires the employment of many people.* **3** use: *The painter was clever in his employment of brushes and colors. n.*

em po ri um (em pôr′ē əm), **1** center of trade; marketplace. **2** a large store selling many different things. *n., pl.* **em po ri ums, em po ri a** (em pôr′ē ə).

em pow er (em pou′ər), give power or authority to; authorize: *The secretary was empowered to sign certain contracts. v.*

em press (em′pris), **1** wife of an emperor. **2** woman who is the ruler of an empire. *n., pl.* **em press es.**

emp ti ly (emp′tə lē), in an empty manner. *adv.*

emp ti ness (emp′tē nis), a being empty; lack of contents. *n.*

emp ty (emp′tē), **1** with nothing or no one in it: *an empty house. The birds had gone and their nest was empty.* **2** pour out or take out all that is in (a thing); make empty: *She emptied her glass quickly. He emptied the trash from the wastebasket.* **3** become empty: *The hall emptied as soon as the concert was over.* **4** flow out: *The Mississippi River empties into the Gulf of Mexico.* **5** not real; meaningless: *An empty promise is one that you do not plan to keep. An empty threat has no force behind it.* **6** INFORMAL. something with nothing in it, such as a container, freight car, etc. **1,5** *adj.,* **emp ti er, emp ti est; 2-4** *v.,* **emp tied, emp ty ing; 6** *n.,* **emp ties.** [*Empty* is from Old English *ǣmtig,* which comes from *ǣmetta,* meaning "leisure."]

emp ty-hand ed (emp′tē han′did), having nothing in the hands; bringing or taking nothing of value. *adj.*

empty set, a set that has no elements; null set.

emu
6 ft. (2 m.) tall

e mu (ē′myü), a large, three-toed Australian bird like an ostrich, but smaller. Emus cannot fly, but they can run very fast. *n.* [*Emu* probably comes from Portuguese *ema.*]

em u late (em′yə lāt), imitate in order to equal or excel the achievements or qualities of an admired person: *to try to emulate the style of a famous author. v.,* **em u lat ed, em u lat ing.** —**em′u la′tor,** *n.*

em u la tion (em′yə lā′shən), imitation in order to equal or excel: *deeds done in emulation of heroic ancestors. n.*

e mul si fy (i mul′sə fī), make into an emulsion: *emulsify oil and water. v.,* **e mul si fied, e mul si fy ing.**

e mul sion (i mul′shən), mixture of liquids that do not dissolve in each other. In an emulsion one of the liquids contains minute droplets of the other evenly distributed throughout. *n.*

en a ble (en ā′bəl), give ability, power, or means to; make able: *Airplanes enable people to travel great distances rapidly. v.,* **en a bled, en a bling.** —**en a′bler,** *n.*

en act (en akt′), **1** make into law: *Congress enacted a bill to restrict the sale of guns.* **2** act out; play: *He enacted the part of Long John Silver very well. v.* —**en act′a ble,** *adj.*

en act ment (en akt′mənt), **1** an enacting or a being enacted: *After the House and Senate agreed on a compromise the enactment of the bill followed quickly.* **2** a law. *n.*

e nam el (i nam′əl), **1** a glasslike substance melted and then cooled to make a smooth, hard surface. Different colors of enamel are used to cover or decorate metal, pottery, etc. **2** paint or varnish used to make a smooth, hard, glossy surface. **3** the smooth, hard, glossy outer layer of the teeth. **4** cover or decorate with enamel. **1-3** *n.,* **4** *v.,* **e nam eled, e nam el ing** or **e nam elled, e nam el ling.** —**e nam′el er, e nam′el ler,** *n.* —**e nam′el like′,** *adj.*

en am ored (en am′ərd), in love: *She was enamored of the young man. adj.*

en camp (en kamp′), **1** make a camp: *It took the soldiers only an hour to encamp.* **2** live in a camp for a time: *The Girl Scouts encamped all week by the river. v.*

en camp ment (en kamp′mənt), **1** an encamping. **2** place where a camp is; camp. *n.*

en case (en kās′), **1** put into a case. **2** cover completely; enclose: *A cocoon encased the caterpillar. v.,* **en cased, en cas ing.** Also, **incase.** —**en case′ment,** *n.*

-ence, *suffix forming nouns.* **1** (*added to verbs*) act or fact of _____ing: *Abhorrence = act or fact of abhorring.* *Dependence = act or fact of depending.* **2** (*added to adjectives ending in* -ent) quality or condition of being _____ent: *Prudence = quality of being prudent. Absence = condition of being absent.*

en ceph a li tis (en sef′ə lī′tis), inflammation of the brain caused by injury, infection, poison, etc. Sleeping sickness is one kind of encephalitis. *n.* [*Encephalitis* can be traced back to Greek *en-,* meaning "in," and *kephalē,* meaning "head."]

en chant (en chant′), **1** use magic on; put under a spell: *The witch enchanted the princess so that she slept for a month.* **2** delight greatly; charm: *The music enchanted us all. v.* —**en chant′er,** *n.*

en chant ing (en chan′ting), very delightful; charming. *adj.* —**en chant′ing ly,** *adv.*

en chant ment (en chant′mənt), **1** use of magic spells; spell or charm: *In "The Wizard of Oz" Dorothy finds herself at home again by the enchantment of the Good Witch.* **2** delight; rapture. **3** thing that delights or charms: *We felt the enchantment of the moonlight on the lake. n.*

en chan tress (en chan′tris), **1** woman who enchants; witch. **2** a very delightful, charming woman. *n., pl.* **en chan tress es.**

en chi la da (en′chi lä′də), tortilla rolled around a filling of meat or cheese and served with a peppery sauce. *n., pl.* **en chi la das.**

en cir cle (en sér′kəl), **1** form a circle around; surround: *Trees encircled the pond.* **2** go in a circle around: *The moon encircles the earth. v.,* **en cir cled, en cir cling.**

en cir cle ment (en sér′kəl mənt), an encircling. *n.*

en clave (en′klāv), country or district surrounded by territory of a foreign country: *West Berlin is an enclave in East Germany. n.*

en close (en klōz′), **1** shut in on all sides; surround: *The little park was enclosed by tall apartment buildings.* **2** put a wall or fence around: *We are going to enclose our backyard to keep dogs out.* **3** put in an envelope along with a letter, etc.: *He enclosed a check when he mailed his order.* **4** contain: *a letter enclosing a dollar's worth of stamps. v.,* **en closed, en clos ing.** Also, **inclose.**

en clo sure (en klō′zhər), **1** an enclosed place: *A corral is an enclosure for horses.* **2** thing that encloses. A wall or fence is an enclosure. **3** thing enclosed: *The envelope contained a letter and $5 as an enclosure.* **4** an enclosing or a being enclosed. *n.* Also, **inclosure.**

en code (en kōd′), put into code: *The spy encoded his message and gave it to a courier for delivery. v.,* **en cod ed, en cod ing.** —**en cod′er,** *n.*

en co mi um (en kō′mē əm), an elaborate expression of

praise; high praise. *n., pl.* **en co mi ums, en co mi a** (en-kō′mē ə).

en com pass (en kum′pəs), **1** go or reach all the way around; encircle: *The atmosphere encompasses the earth.* **2** include; contain: *Our history book encompasses all the important events in American history since 1607. v.* —**en com′pass ment,** *n.*

en core (äng′kôr *or* än′kôr), **1** once more; again: *The audience liked the song so much they shouted, "Encore! Encore!"* **2** a demand by the audience for the repetition of a song, etc., or for another appearance of the performer or performers. **3** the repetition by the performer. **4** an extra song, appearance, etc., by the performer. 1 *interj.,* 2-4 *n.*

en coun ter (en koun′tər), **1** meet unexpectedly: *What if we should encounter a bear?* **2** an unexpected meeting: *A fortunate encounter brought the two friends together after a long separation.* **3** be faced with: *She encountered many difficulties before the job was done.* **4** meet as an enemy; meet in a fight or battle: *He encountered the strange knight in hand-to-hand conflict.* **5** a meeting of enemies; fight; battle: *The two armies had a desperate encounter.* 1,3,4 *v.,* 2,5 *n.* [*Encounter* came into English about 700 years ago from French *encontrer,* and can be traced back to Latin *in-,* meaning "in," and *contra,* meaning "against."]

en cour age (en kėr′ij), **1** give courage; increase the hope or confidence of; urge on: *The cheers of their schoolmates encouraged the players to try to win the game.* **2** be favorable to; help; support: *Sunlight encourages the growth of green plants. v.,* **en cour aged, en cour ag ing.**

en cour age ment (en kėr′ij mənt), **1** condition of being or feeling encouraged: *The singer drew her encouragement from the audience.* **2** something that encourages: *The faith of his teacher in his ability to draw was his only encouragement.* **3** act of encouraging: *Her encouragement was a great help to me. n.*

en cour ag ing (en kėr′ə jing), giving courage, hope, or confidence: *an encouraging smile, an encouraging report. adj.*

en croach (en krōch′), **1** go beyond proper or usual limits: *The sea encroached upon the shore and submerged the beach.* **2** trespass upon the property or rights of another; intrude: *Our neighbor's irrigation system is encroaching on our land. v.* —**en croach′er,** *n.*

en croach ment (en krōch′mənt), an encroaching: *The cliff is being worn away by the encroachments of the sea. n.*

en crust (en krust′), **1** cover with a crust or hard coating: *The inside of the kettle was encrusted with rust.* **2** decorate with a layer of costly material. *v.* Also, **incrust.**

encrust (def. 2) This crown is **encrusted** with jewels.

en cum ber (en kum′bər), **1** hold back; hinder; hamper: *Heavy shoes encumber a runner in a race.* **2** block up; fill: *Their yard was encumbered with old boxes and other rubbish.* **3** burden with weight, difficulties, cares, debt, etc.: *The farm was encumbered with a heavy mortgage. v.*

en cum brance (en kum′brəns), something useless or in the way; hindrance; burden: *Shoes would be an encumbrance to a swimmer. n.*

a hat	i it	oi oil	ch child	a in about
ā age	ī ice	ou out	ng long	e in taken
ä far	o hot	u cup	sh she	ə = i in pencil
e let	ō open	u̇ put	th thin	o in lemon
ē equal	ô order	ü rule	ŦH then	u in circus
ėr term			zh measure	

-ency, *suffix forming nouns.* **1** (*added to verbs*) act or fact of _____ ing: *Dependency = act or fact of depending.* **2** (*added to adjectives ending in* -ent) quality or condition of being _____ent: *Frequency = condition of being frequent.*

ency. *or* **encyc.,** encyclopedia.

en cyc li cal (en sik′lə kəl), letter from the Pope to his bishops, stating the position of the church on important questions. *n.*

en cy clo pae di a (en sī′klə pē′dē ə), encyclopedia. *n., pl.* **en cy clo pae di as.**

en cy clo pae dic (en sī′klə pē′dik), encyclopedic. *adj.*

en cy clo pe di a (en sī′klə pē′dē ə), **1** book or set of books giving information on all branches of knowledge, with its articles arranged alphabetically. **2** book treating one subject very thoroughly, with its articles arranged alphabetically: *an encyclopedia of art. n., pl.* **en cy clo pe di as.** [*Encyclopedia* comes from the Greek phrase *enkyklios paideia,* meaning "general education."]

en cy clo pe dic (en sī′klə pē′dik), **1** covering a wide range of subjects; possessing wide and varied information. **2** having to do with an encyclopedia. *adj.*

encroach (def. 1) On the outskirts of towns and cities, new housing developments **encroach** on farmland.

end (end), **1** the last part; conclusion: *She read to the end of the book.* **2** the part where a thing begins or stops: *Drive to the end of this road.* **3** bring or come to its last part; stop; finish: *Let us end this fight. The fight ended in a draw.* **4** form the end of; be the end of: *This scene ends the play.* **5** purpose; object: *The end he had in mind was to skip a grade.* **6** result; outcome: *It is hard to tell what the end will be.* **7** death; destruction: *He met his end in the accident.* **8** an offensive or defensive player at either end of the line in football. 1,2,5-8 *n.,* 3,4 *v.* —**end′er,** *n.*

at loose ends, 1 not settled or established: *The boy was at loose ends until he was put to work cleaning his room.* **2** in confusion or disorder.

end to end, with the ends placed so that they touch; endways.

end up, wind up; come out: *Where will I end up if I take this path?*

in the end, in the long run; ultimately: *In the end, he had to admit his mistake.*

make both ends meet, spend no more than one has; live within one's income: *The family had a hard time making both ends meet.*

on end, 1 upright: *Place the log on end. His hair stood on* *end.* **2** one after another: *It snowed for days on end.*

put an end to, do away with; stop.

en dan ger (en dān′jər), cause danger to: *Fire endangered the hotel's guests, but no lives were lost. v.*

en dan gered (en dān′jərd), liable to become extinct: *an endangered species. adj.*

en dear (en dir′), make dear: *Her kindness endeared her to all of us. v.* —**en dear′ing ly,** *adv.*

en dear ment (en dir′mənt), act or word showing love or affection. *n.*

en deav or (en dev′ər), **1** make an effort; try hard; attempt strongly: *Each time she endeavored to do better than before.* **2** a strong attempt; hard try; effort: *With each endeavor she did better.* **1** *v.,* **2** *n.*

en dem ic (en dem′ik), regularly found among a particular people or in a particular locality: *Cholera is endemic in India. adj.* —**en dem′i cal ly,** *adv.*

end ing (en′ding), **1** the last part; end: *The story has a sad ending.* **2** letter or syllable added to a word to change its meaning; suffix: *The common plural ending is "s" or "es." n.*

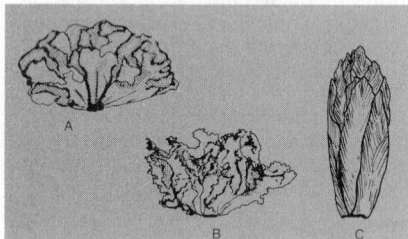

endive
(A, def. 1;
B, def. 2;
C, def. 3)

en dive (en′dīv), **1** kind of chicory with broad, smooth leaves, used for salads; escarole. **2** kind of chicory with finely divided, curly leaves, used for salads. **3** kind of chicory which looks like very smooth white celery, used for salads. *n.*

end less (end′lis), **1** having no end; never stopping; lasting or going on forever: *the endless rotation of the earth around the sun.* **2** seeming to have no end: *an endless scolding.* **3** with the ends joined; without ends: *The chain that turns the rear wheel of a bicycle is an endless chain. adj.* —**end′less ly,** *adv.* —**end′less ness,** *n.*

end most (end′mōst), most distant; farthest. *adj.*

en do crine gland (en′dō krən *or* en′dō krīn), any of various glands that produce secretions that pass directly into the bloodstream or lymph instead of into a duct; ductless gland. The thyroid and the pituitary are endocrine glands.

en dorse (en dôrs′), **1** write one's name on the back of (a check, note, or other document): *She had to endorse the check before the bank would cash it.* **2** approve; support: *Parents endorsed the plan for a school playground. v.,* **en dorsed, en dors ing.** Also, **indorse.**

en dorse ment (en dôrs′mənt), **1** person's name or other writing on the back of a check, note, bill, or other document. **2** approval; support: *Her idea received endorsement by the entire club. n.* Also, **indorsement.**

en dors er (en dôr′sər), person who endorses. *n.* Also, **indorser.**

en do skel e ton (en′dō skel′ə tən), the internal skeleton that animals with backbones and related animals have. *n.*

en do sperm (en′dō spėrm′), food material for the embryo of a plant, enclosed in the seed. *n.*

en dow (en dou′), **1** give money or property to provide an income for: *The rich man endowed the college he had attended.* **2** give from birth; provide with some ability, quality, or talent: *Nature endowed him with good looks. v.*

en dow ment (en dou′mənt), **1** money or property given a person or institution to provide an income: *This college has a large endowment.* **2** gift from birth; ability; talent: *Artistic ability is a natural endowment.* **3** an endowing. *n.*

end table, a small table suitable for placing beside a couch or chair.

en due (en dü′ *or* en dyü′), **1** provide with a quality or power; furnish; supply. **2** clothe. *v.,* **en dued, en du ing.**

en dur a ble (en dür′ə bəl *or* en dyür′ə bəl), **1** that can be endured; bearable: *The pain was barely endurable.* **2** likely to endure or last. *adj.* —**en dur′a bly,** *adv.*

en dur ance (en dür′əns *or* en dyür′əns), **1** power to last and to withstand hard wear: *It takes great endurance to run 30 miles in a day. Thin, cheap cloth has little endurance.* **2** power to stand something without giving out; holding out; bearing up: *Her endurance of pain is remarkable. n.*

en dure (en dür′ *or* en dyür′), **1** keep on; last: *Metal and stone endure for a long time.* **2** put up with; bear; stand: *The pioneers endured many hardships. v.,* **en dured, en dur ing.**

en dur ing (en dür′ing *or* en dyür′ing), lasting; permanent: *an enduring peace. adj.* —**en dur′ing ly,** *adv.*

end ways (end′wāz′), **1** on end; upright. **2** with the end forward; in the direction of the end. **3** lengthwise. **4** with the ends placed so that they touch; end to end. *adv.*

end wise (end′wīz′), endways. *adv.*

end zone, (in football) the part of the field between the goal line and the end of the field.

en e ma (en′ə mə), injection of liquid into the rectum to flush the bowels. *n., pl.* **en e mas.**

en e my (en′ə mē), **1** person or group that hates and tries to harm another: *They have many friends and few enemies.* **2** a force, nation, army, fleet, or air force that opposes another; person, ship, etc., of a hostile nation. Two countries at war with each other are enemies. **3** anything harmful: *Drought is an enemy of farmers. n., pl.* **en e mies.**

WORD HISTORY

enemy

Enemy came into English about 700 years ago from French *enemi,* and can be traced back to Latin *in-,* meaning "not," and *amicus,* meaning "friendly."

en er get ic (en′ər jet′ik), full of energy; eager to work; full of force; active; vigorous: *Cool autumn days make us feel energetic. adj.*

en er get i cal ly (en′ər jet′ik lē), with energy; vigorously. *adv.*

en er gize (en′ər jīz), give energy to; make active. *v.,* **en er gized, en er giz ing.** —**en′er giz′er,** *n.*

en er gy (en′ər jē), **1** will to work; vigor: *The boy is so full of energy that he cannot keep still.* **2** power to work or act; force: *All our energies were used in keeping the fire from spreading.* **3** capacity for doing work, such as lifting or moving an object. Light, heat, and electricity are different forms of energy: *A steam engine changes heat into mechanical energy. n., pl.* **en er gies.**

en er vate (en′ər vāt), lessen the vigor or strength of; weaken: *A hot, damp climate enervates people who are not used to it. v.,* **en er vat ed, en er vat ing.**

en er va tion (en′ər vā′shən), an enervating or a being enervated. *n.*

en fee ble (en fē′bəl), make feeble; weaken. *v.,* **en fee-**

bled, **en fee bling. —en fee′ble ment,** *n.*

en fold (en fōld′), **1** fold in; wrap up: *The old woman was enfolded in a shawl.* **2** embrace; clasp: *The little boy enfolded the puppy in his arms.* *v.* **—en fold′er,** *n.*

en force (en fôrs′), **1** force obedience to; cause to be carried out: *Monitors help enforce school regulations.* **2** force; compel: *We have laws to enforce the payment of income taxes.* *v.,* **en forced, en forc ing. —en force′a ble,** *adj.* **—en forc′er,** *n.*

en force ment (en fôrs′mənt), an enforcing; carrying out: *Strict enforcement of the laws against speeding will reduce automobile accidents.* *n.*

en fran chise (en fran′chīz), give the right to vote to: *The 19th amendment to the Constitution enfranchised American women.* *v.,* **en fran chised, en fran chis ing. —en fran′chise ment,** *n.*

eng., **1** engineer. **2** engineering.

Eng., **1** England. **2** English.

en gage (en gāj′), **1** keep oneself busy; be occupied; be active; take part: *He engages in politics. They engaged in conversation.* **2** keep busy; occupy: *Work engages much of her time.* **3** take for use or work; hire: *We engaged two rooms in the hotel. She engaged a carpenter to repair the porch.* **4** promise or pledge to marry: *He is engaged to my sister.* **5** catch and hold; attract: *Bright colors engage a baby's attention.* **6** bind by a promise or contract; pledge: *He engaged himself as an apprentice to a printer.* **7** fit into; lock together. **8** start a battle with; attack: *The soldiers engaged the enemy.* *v.,* **en gaged, en gag ing. —en gag′er,** *n.*

en gaged (en gājd′), **1** promised or pledged to marry: *A party was given for the engaged couple.* **2** busy; occupied: *Engaged in conversation, they did not see us.* *adj.*

en gage ment (en gāj′mənt), **1** an engaging or a being engaged. **2** a promise; pledge: *She tries to fulfill all of her engagements.* **3** a promise or pledge to marry: *Their parents announced the young couple's engagement.* **4** a meeting with someone at a certain time; appointment: *I have a dinner engagement tonight.* **5** period of being hired; time of use or work: *The actor had an engagement of three weeks in a play.* **6** a fight; battle. *n.*

en gag ing (en gā′jing), very attractive; pleasing; charming: *an engaging smile.* *adj.* **—en gag′ing ly,** *adv.*

en gen der (en jen′dər), bring into existence; produce; cause: *Filth engenders disease.* *v.*

en gine (en′jən), **1** machine that changes energy from fuel, steam, water pressure, etc., into motion and power. An engine is used to apply power to some work, such as running other machines. **2** machine that pulls a railroad train; locomotive. **3** anything used to bring about a result; machine; instrument: *Cannons are engines of war.* *n.*

WORD HISTORY

engine

Engine came into English about 650 years ago from French *engin,* meaning "skill," which came from Latin *ingenium,* meaning "inborn qualities, talent."

engine block, the main part of an engine, cast as a single unit, containing the cylinders.

en gi neer (en′jə nir′), **1** person who takes care of or runs engines. The person who runs a locomotive is an engineer. **2** an expert in engineering: *a mining engineer.* **3** plan, build, direct, or work as an engineer. **4** manage

cleverly; guide skillfully: *Against much opposition, she engineered the plan through to final approval.* **1,2** *n.,* **3,4** *v.*

en gi neer ing (en′jə nir′ing), science, work, or profession of planning, building, or managing engines, machines, roads, bridges, canals, railroads, etc.: *The Golden Gate bridge is a triumph of engineering.* *n.*

en gine ry (en′jən rē), engines or machinery. *n.*

Eng land (ing′glənd), the largest division of Great Britain, in the S part. *Capital:* London. See **United Kingdom** for map. *n.*

engage (def. 7) left, gears engaged; right, gears disengaged

Eng lish (ing′glish), **1** of England, its people, or their language. **2** the people of England. **3** the language of England. English is also spoken in the United States, Canada, Australia, New Zealand, the Republic of South Africa, and many other countries. **4** english, a spinning motion given to a ball by hitting, throwing, kicking, etc., on one side of its center. **1** *adj.,* **2** *n.pl.,* **3,4** *n.sing.* [*English* is from Old English *Englisc,* which comes from *Engle,* meaning "the English people, Angles."]

English Channel, strait between England and France. See **Normandy** for map.

English horn

English horn, a woodwind instrument resembling an oboe, but larger and having a lower tone.

Eng lish man (ing′glish mən), man born or living in England. *n., pl.* **Eng lish men.**

English sparrow, a small, brownish-gray, European bird, now very common in America. It is a kind of finch.

Eng lish wom an (ing′glish wùm′ən), woman born or living in England. *n., pl.* **Eng lish wom en.**

en gorge (en gôrj′), **1** swallow greedily. **2** congest with blood. *v.,* **en gorged, en gorg ing. —en gorge′ment,** *n.*

engr., engineer.

a hat	**i** it	**oi** oil	**ch** child	a in about
ā age	**ī** ice	**ou** out	**ng** long	e in taken
ä far	**o** hot	**u** cup	**sh** she	ə = i in pencil
e let	**ō** open	**ù** put	**th** thin	o in lemon
ē equal	**ô** order	**ü** rule	**ŦH** then	u in circus
ėr term			**zh** measure	

en grave (en grāv′), **1** cut deeply in; carve in; carve in an artistic way: *The jeweler engraved my initials on the back of the watch.* **2** cut (a picture, design, map, etc.) in lines on a metal plate, block of wood, etc., for printing. **3** print from such a plate, block, etc. **4** fix firmly: *The incident was engraved in her mind.* v., **en graved, en grav ing.**

en grav er (en grā′vər), person who engraves metal plates, blocks of wood, etc., for printing. n.

en grav ing (en grā′ving), **1** act or art of an engraver. **2** picture printed from an engraved plate, block, etc.; print. n.

en gross (en grōs′), occupy wholly; take up all the attention of: *The artist was so engrossed in his painting that he didn't notice the people watching him.* v. —**en gross′- ment,** n.

en gulf (en gulf′), swallow up; overwhelm: *A wave engulfed the small boat.* v. —**en gulf′ment,** n.

en hance (en hans′), make greater; add to; heighten: *The gardens enhanced the beauty of the house. The growth of a city often enhances the value of land close to it.* v., **en hanced, en hanc ing.**

en hance ment (en hans′mənt), an enhancing or a being enhanced. n.

e nig ma (i nig′mə), a baffling or puzzling problem, situation, person, etc.; riddle: *How the magician had been able to get out of the locked trunk was an enigma to the audience.* n., pl. **e nig mas.**

en ig mat ic (en′ig mat′ik), like an enigma or riddle; baffling; puzzling: *We could not understand their enigmatic answers to our questions.* adj. —**en′ig mat′i cal ly,** adv.

en ig mat i cal (en′ig mat′ə kəl), enigmatic. adj.

en join (en join′), **1** order, direct, or urge: *The father enjoined his children to always be honest.* **2** forbid; prohibit: *The judge enjoined the contractor from building a factory in an area set aside for homes.* v. [*Enjoin* came into English about 750 years ago from French *enjoindre,* and can be traced back to Latin *in-,* meaning "in, on," and *jungere,* meaning "to join."] —**en join′er,** n.

en joy (en joi′), **1** have or use with joy; be happy with; take pleasure in: *The children enjoyed their visit to the museum.* **2** have as an advantage or benefit: *She enjoys good health.* v.

enjoy oneself, have a good time; be happy: *Enjoy yourself at the party.*

en joy a ble (en joi′ə bəl), able to be enjoyed; giving joy; pleasant. adj. —**en joy′a ble ness,** n. —**en joy′a bly,** adv.

en joy ment (en joi′mənt), **1** pleasure; joy; delight. **2** a having as an advantage or benefit; possession or use: *the enjoyment of good health. Laws protect the enjoyment of our rights.* n.

en kin dle (en kin′dl), kindle. v., **en kin dled, en kin dling.**

en large (en lärj′), make or become larger; increase in size: *enlarge a photograph. The school auditorium was enlarged. The balloon enlarged as we pumped air into it.* v., **en larged, en larg ing.** —**en larg′er,** n.

enlarge on, talk or write about in more detail: *The principal enlarged on his plans for a new school.*

en large ment (en lärj′mənt), **1** an enlarging or a being enlarged. **2** thing that enlarges something else; addition. **3** photograph or other thing which has been made larger. n.

en light en (en līt′n), give truth and knowledge to; inform; instruct: *The book enlightened me on the subject of medicine.* v. —**en light′en er,** n.

en light en ment (en līt′n mənt), an enlightening or a being enlightened; information; instruction. n.

en list (en list′), **1** join the army, navy, or some other branch of the armed forces: *He enlisted in the Air Force.*

2 get to join some branch of the armed forces; induct: *Many men were enlisted during the war.* **3** get to join in some cause or undertaking; get the help or support of: *We enlisted her help in building our clubhouse.* **4** join in some cause or undertaking; give help or support: *Many members of our class enlist in the Red Cross drive each year.* v. —**en list′er,** n.

enlisted man, man in the armed forces who is not a commissioned officer or warrant officer.

en list ment (en list′mənt), **1** an enlisting or a being enlisted. **2** time for which a person enlists. n.

en liv en (en lī′vən), make lively, active, gay, or cheerful: *enliven a speech with humor.* v.

en mesh (en mesh′), catch in a net; enclose in meshes; entangle. v.

en mi ty (en′mə tē), the feeling that enemies have for each other; hostility or hatred. n., pl. **en mi ties.**

en no ble (en nō′bəl), **1** raise the respect of others for; make noble; dignify: *A good deed ennobles the person who does it.* **2** raise to a noble rank; give a title of nobility to. v., **en no bled, en no bling.** —**en no′ble ment,** n. —**en no′bling ly,** adv.

en nui (än′wē), a feeling of weariness and discontent from having no occupation or interest; boredom. n.

e nor mi ty (i nôr′mə tē), **1** extreme wickedness: *The enormity of the crime made it likely that the criminal was not sane.* **2** an extremely wicked crime. n., pl. **e nor mi ties.**

e nor mous (i nôr′məs), extremely large; huge: *an enormous animal, an enormous appetite.* adj. —**e nor′mous ness,** n.

WORD HISTORY

enormous

Enormous is from Latin *enormis,* which comes from *ex-,* meaning "out of," and *norma,* meaning "pattern, rule."

e nor mous ly (i nôr′məs lē), in or to an enormous degree; extremely; vastly. adv.

e nough (i nuf′), **1** as much or as many as needed or wanted; sufficient: *Buy enough food for the picnic. Are there enough seats for all?* **2** quantity or number needed or wanted; sufficient amount: *I have had enough to eat.* **3** sufficiently; adequately: *Have you played enough?* **4** quite; fully: *He was willing enough to go.* **5** rather; fairly: *She talks well enough for a baby.* **1** adj., **2** n., **3-5** adv. [*Enough* comes from Old English *genōg.*]

en quire (en kwīr′), inquire. v., **en quired, en quir ing.**

en quir y (en kwī′rē or en′kwər ē), inquiry. n., pl. **en quir ies.**

en rage (en rāj′), make very angry; make furious: *The dog was enraged by the teasing.* v., **en raged, en rag ing.**

en rap ture (en rap′chər), move to rapture; fill with great delight: *The audience was enraptured by the singer's beautiful voice.* v., **en rap tured, en rap tur ing.**

en rich (en rich′), make rich or richer: *An education enriches your mind. Adding vitamins or minerals to food enriches it. Fertilizer enriches the soil.* v.

en rich ment (en rich′mənt), **1** an enriching or a being enriched. **2** thing that enriches. n.

en roll or **en rol** (en rōl′), **1** write in a list; register: *The secretary enrolled our names.* **2** have one's name written in a list. **3** make a member: *He enrolled his daughter and son in a music school.* **4** become a member: *Her mother* *enrolled in a boating class.* **5** enlist: *He enrolled in the navy.* v., **en rolled, en roll ing.**

en roll ment or **en rol ment** (en rōl′mənt), **1** an enrolling: *Enrollment took place in the fall.* **2** number enrolled: *The school has an enrollment of 200 students. n.*

en route (än rüt′), on the way: *We shall stop at Philadelphia en route from New York to Washington.*

Ens., Ensign.

en sconce (en skons′), **1** shelter safely; hide: *The family was ensconced in the cellar when the tornado hit.* **2** settle comfortably and firmly: *The cat ensconced itself in the armchair. v.,* **en sconced, en sconc ing.**

en sem ble (än säm′bəl), **1** all the parts of a thing considered together; general effect. **2** group of musicians playing or singing together: *Two violins, a cello, and a harp made up the string ensemble.* **3** a complete, harmonious costume: *Her dress and coat made an attractive ensemble. n.*

en shrine (en shrīn′), **1** enclose in a shrine: *A statue is enshrined in the cathedral.* **2** keep sacred; cherish: *happy memories enshrined in one's heart. v.,* **en shrined, en shrin ing. —en shrine′ment,** n.

en shroud (en shroud′), cover or hide; veil: *Fog enshrouded the ship. v.*

en sign (en′sīn *or* en′sən for *1,3,4;* en′sən for *2*), **1** a flag or banner: *The ensign of the United States is the Stars and Stripes.* **2** a navy officer ranking next below a lieutenant junior grade and next above a warrant officer. An ensign is the lowest commissioned officer in the United States Navy. **3** a former British army officer whose duty was carrying the flag. **4** sign of one's rank, position, or power; symbol of authority: *The ensign of the queen was her crown and scepter. n.*

en si lage (en′sə lij), silage. *n.*

en slave (en slāv′), make a slave or slaves of; take away freedom from. *v.,* **en slaved, en slav ing.**

en slave ment (en slāv′mənt), an enslaving or a being enslaved. *n.*

en snare (en sner′ *or* en snar′), catch in a snare; trap. *v.,* **en snared, en snar ing.** Also, **insnare.**

en sue (en sü′), **1** come after; follow. The ensuing year means the year following this. **2** happen as a result: *Our discussion became heated, and an argument ensued. v.,* **en sued, en su ing. —en su′ing ly,** *adv.*

en sure (en shùr′), **1** make sure or certain: *Careful planning and hard work ensured the success of the party.* **2** make sure of getting; secure: *A letter of introduction will ensure you an interview.* **3** make safe; protect: *Proper clothing ensured us against suffering from the cold. v.,* **en sured, en sur ing. —en sur′er,** *n.*

-ent, suffix added to verbs. **1** (*to form adjectives*) _____ing: *Absorbent = absorbing. Indulgent = indulging.* **2** (*to form nouns*) one that _____s: *Correspondent = one that corresponds. President = one that presides.* **3** (*to form adjectives*) other meanings, as in *competent, confident.*

en tail (en tāl′), impose or require: *Owning an automobile entailed greater expense than we had expected. v.*

en tan gle (en tang′gəl), **1** get twisted up and caught; tangle: *He entangled his feet in the coil of rope and fell down.* **2** get into difficulty; involve: *Don't get entangled in their scheme. v.,* **en tan gled, en tan gling.**

en tan gle ment (en tang′gəl mənt), **1** an entangling or a being entangled: *The new nation avoided an entanglement with foreign countries.* **2** thing that entangles; snare: *The trenches were protected by barbed wire entanglements. n.*

en ter (en′tər), **1** go into; come into: *She entered the house.* **2** go in; come in: *Let them enter.* **3** become a part or member of; join: *She entered the contest.* **4** cause to join or enter; enroll: *Parents enter their children in school.*

a hat	i it	oi oil	ch child	⎧ a in about
ā age	ī ice	ou out	ng long	e in taken
ä far	o hot	u cup	sh she	ə = ⎨ i in pencil
e let	ō open	u̇ put	th thin	o in lemon
ē equal	ô order	ü rule	ᴛʜ then	⎩ u in circus
ėr term			zh measure	

5 begin; start: *After years of training, the doctor entered the practice of medicine.* **6** write or print in a book, list, etc.: *Words are entered alphabetically in a dictionary.* **7** put in regular form; make a record of; record: *The teller entered the deposit in my bankbook. The injured man entered a complaint in court. v.* **—en′ter a ble,** *adj.*

enter into, take part in; join in: *The two speakers entered into a debate.*

enter on or **enter upon,** begin; start: *She entered on her professional duties as soon as she finished law school.*

en ter prise (en′tər prīz), **1** an important, difficult, or dangerous plan to be tried; great or bold undertaking: *A trip into space is a daring enterprise.* **2** any undertaking; project: *a business enterprise.* **3** readiness to try important, difficult, or dangerous plans; willingness to undertake great or bold projects: *The American pioneers were people of great enterprise. n.*

en ter pris ing (en′tər prī′zing), likely to start projects; ready to face difficulties: *an enterprising young businessman. adj.* **—en′ter pris′ing ly,** *adv.*

en ter tain (en′tər tān′), **1** keep pleasantly interested; please or amuse: *The circus entertained the children.* **2** have as a guest: *They entertained ten people at dinner.* **3** have guests; provide entertainment for guests: *He entertains a great deal.* **4** take into the mind; consider: *I refuse to entertain such a foolish idea.* **5** hold in the mind; maintain: *Even after failing twice, we still entertained a hope of success. v.*

en ter tain er (en′tər tā′nər), **1** person who entertains. **2** singer, musician, etc., who performs in public. *n.*

en ter tain ing (en′tər tā′ning), interesting; pleasing or amusing. *adj.* **—en′ter tain′ing ly,** *adv.*

en ter tain ment (en′tər tān′mənt), **1** thing that interests, pleases, or amuses. A show or a circus is an entertainment. **2** act of entertaining: *The host and hostess devoted themselves to the entertainment of their guests.* **3** condition of being entertained: *He played the piano for our entertainment. n.*

enthrall (def. 1)—The children are **enthralled** by the daring aerialists.

en thrall or **en thral** (en thrôl′), **1** hold captive by beauty or interest; fascinate; charm. **2** make a slave of; enslave: *The captive peoples were enthralled by their conquerors. v.,* **en thralled, en thrall ing.**

en throne (en thrōn′), **1** set on a throne. **2** place highest of all; exalt. *v.,* **en throned, en thron ing. —en throne′ment,** *n.*

en thuse (en thüz′), INFORMAL. **1** show enthusiasm: *She enthused over the idea of going away to college.* **2** fill with enthusiasm: *The plan for a trip out West enthused the family.* *v.*, **en thused, en thus ing.**

en thu si asm (en thü′zē az′əm), eager interest; zeal: *The pep talk filled the team with enthusiasm.* *n.*

WORD HISTORY

enthusiasm

Enthusiasm can be traced back to Greek *en-*, meaning "in," and *theos*, meaning "god."

en thu si ast (en thü′zē ast), person who is filled with enthusiasm: *a football enthusiast.* *n.*

en thu si as tic (en thü′zē as′tik), full of enthusiasm; eagerly interested: *My little brother is very enthusiastic about going to kindergarten.* *adj.*

en thu si as ti cal ly (en thü′zē as′tik lē), with enthusiasm. *adv.*

en tice (en tīs′), attract by arousing hopes or desires; tempt: *The smell of food enticed the hungry children into the house.* *v.*, **en ticed, en tic ing.** **—en tic′ing ly,** *adv.*

en tice ment (en tīs′mənt), **1** an enticing or a being enticed. **2** thing that entices: *Enticements of milk and meat brought the frightened cat down from the tree.* *n.*

en tire (en tīr′), **1** having all the parts; whole; complete: *The entire class behaved very well on the trip.* **2** not broken; in one piece: *The original property is still entire even though it has had many owners.* *adj.* **—en tire′ly,** *adv.*

en tire ty (en tīr′tē), the whole; completeness. *n.*, *pl.* **en tire ties.**

in its entirety, wholly; completely: *I enjoyed the concert in its entirety.*

en ti tle (en tī′tl), **1** give a claim or right: *The one who wins is entitled to first prize.* **2** give the title of; call by the name of: *I entitled my theme "Looking for Treasure."* *v.*, **en ti tled, en ti tling.** **—en ti′tle ment,** *n.*

en ti ty (en′tə tē), something that has a real and separate existence. Persons, mountains, languages, and beliefs are distinct entities. *n.*, *pl.* **en ti ties.**

en tomb (en tüm′), place in a tomb; bury. *v.* **—en tomb′ment,** *n.*

en to mo log i cal (en′tə mə loj′ə kəl), of entomology. *adj.* **—en′to mo log′i cal ly,** *adv.*

en to mol o gist (en′tə mol′ə jist), an expert in entomology. *n.*

en to mol o gy (en′tə mol′ə jē), branch of zoology that deals with insects. *n.*

en tou rage (än′tü räzh′), group of attendants; people usually accompanying a person: *a queen and her entourage.* *n.*

en trails (en′trālz *or* en′trəlz), the inner parts of the body of a human being or animal, especially the intestines. *n.pl.*

en trance[1] (en′trəns), **1** act of entering: *The actor's entrance was greeted with applause.* **2** place by which to enter; door, passageway, etc.: *The entrance to the hotel was blocked with baggage.* **3** freedom or right to enter; permission to enter: *Entrance to the exhibit is on weekdays only.* *n.*

en trance[2] (en trans′), **1** fill with joy; delight; charm: *From the first note the singer's voice entranced the audience.* **2** put into a trance. *v.*, **en tranced, en tranc ing.** **—en trance′ment,** *n.* **—en tranc′ing ly,** *adv.*

en trant (en′trənt), person who takes part in a contest: *There were many entrants in the spelling contest.* *n.*

en trap (en trap′), **1** catch in a trap. **2** bring into difficulty or danger; trick: *By clever questioning, the lawyer entrapped the witness into contradicting himself.* *v.*, **en trapped, en trap ping. —en trap′ment,** *n.*

en treat (en trēt′), keep asking earnestly; beg and pray: *The prisoners entreated their captors to let them go.* *v.* **—en treat′ing ly,** *adv.*

en treat y (en trē′tē), an earnest request; prayer. *n.*, *pl.* **en treat ies.**

en tree (än′trā), **1** freedom or right to enter; access. **2** the main dish of food at dinner or lunch. *n.*

en trée (än′trā), entree. *n.*, *pl.* **en trées.**

en trench (en trench′), **1** surround with a trench; fortify with trenches: *Our soldiers were entrenched opposite the enemy.* **2** establish firmly: *a custom entrenched by long tradition.* *v.* Also, **intrench. —en trench′er,** *n.*

entrenchment (def. 2)

en trench ment (en trench′mənt), **1** an entrenching. **2** an entrenched position. **3** defense consisting of a trench and a wide bank of earth or stone. *n.* Also, **intrenchment.**

en tre pre neur (än′trə prə nėr′), person who organizes and manages a business or industrial undertaking. *n.*

en trust (en trust′), **1** charge with a trust: *We entrusted the class treasurer with all the money for bus fares on our class trip.* **2** give the care of; hand over for safekeeping: *They entrusted the child to her grandparents for a few days.* *v.* Also, **intrust.**

en try (en′trē), **1** act of entering: *His sudden entry startled me.* **2** place by which to enter; way to enter: *The entry to the hotel was blocked with luggage.* **3** thing written or printed in a book, list, etc. Each word explained in a dictionary is an entry or **entry word.** **4** person or thing that takes part in a contest: *The car race had thirty entries.* *n.*, *pl.* **en tries.**

en twine (en twīn′), twine together or around: *Two hearts were entwined on the valentine. Vines entwined the cottage.* *v.*, **en twined, en twin ing.**

e nu me rate (i nü′mə rāt′ *or* i nyü′mə rāt′), **1** name one by one; list: *She enumerated the capitals of the 50 states.* **2** find out the number of; count. *v.*, **e nu me rat ed, e nu me rat ing. —e nu′me ra′tor,** *n.*

e nu me ra tion (i nü′mə rā′shən *or* i nyü′mə rā′shən), **1** an enumerating; listing or counting: *A census is an official enumeration of the people of a country.* **2** a list. *n.*

e nun ci ate (i nun′sē āt′), **1** speak or pronounce words: *Radio and television announcers must enunciate very clearly.* **2** state definitely; announce: *After performing many experiments, the scientist enunciated a new theory.* *v.*, **e nun ci at ed, e nun ci at ing. —e nun′ci a′tor,** *n.*

e nun ci a tion (i nun′sē ā′shən), **1** manner of pronouncing words. **2** a definite statement; announcement. *n.*

envelop
Fog **enveloped** the village.

a hat	i it	oi oil	ch child	a in about
ā age	ī ice	ou out	ng long	e in taken
ä far	o hot	u cup	sh she	ə = i in pencil
e let	ō open	u̇ put	th thin	o in lemon
ē equal	ô order	ü rule	ᵀH then	u in circus
ėr term			zh measure	

en vel op (en vel′əp), wrap, cover, or hide: *The baby was enveloped in blankets.* v. [*Envelop* came into English about 600 years ago from French *enveloper*, which is from *en-*, meaning "in," and *voloper*, meaning "to wrap."] —**en vel′op ment**, *n.*

en ve lope (en′və lōp *or* än′və lōp), **1** a paper cover in which a letter or anything flat can be mailed. It can usually be folded over and sealed by wetting a gummed edge. **2** a covering; wrapper. *n.*

en vi a ble (en′vē ə bəl), to be envied; worth having; desirable: *an enviable position.* adj. —**en′vi a ble ness**, *n.*

en vi a bly (en′vē ə blē), in an enviable manner. *adv.*

en vi ous (en′vē əs), feeling or showing envy; full of envy: *envious of another's good fortune.* adj. —**en′vi ous ly**, *adv.* —**en′vi ous ness**, *n.*

en vi ron ment (en vī′rən mənt), **1** all the surrounding things, conditions, and influences affecting the growth of living things: *A child's character is greatly influenced by the environment at home. A plant will often grow differently in a different environment.* **2** surroundings: *an environment of poverty.* **3** condition of the air, water, soil, etc.; natural surroundings: *a pollution-free environment.* *n.*

en vi ron men tal (en vī′rən men′tl), having to do with environment. *adj.* —**en vi′ron men′tal ly**, *adv.*

en vi ron men tal ist (en vī′rən men′tl ist), person involved in trying to solve environmental problems, such as pollution, the improper use of natural resources, and overpopulation. *n.*

en vi rons (en vī′rənz), surrounding districts; suburbs: *We visited Boston and its environs.* n.pl.

en vis age (en viz′ij), form a mental picture of: *The architect looked at the plans and envisaged the finished house.* *v.*, **en vis aged, en vis ag ing.** —**en vis′age ment**, *n.*

en vi sion (en vizh′ən), picture in one's mind: *envision oneself as famous.* v.

en voy (en′voi), **1** messenger or representative. **2** diplomat ranking next below an ambassador and next above a minister. *n.*

en vy (en′vē), **1** feeling of discontent, dislike, or desire because another has what one wants: *The children were filled with envy when they saw her new bicycle.* **2** the object of such feeling; person or thing envied: *Their new car was the envy of the neighborhood.* **3** feel envy toward: *Some people envy the rich.* **4** feel envy because of: *He envied his friend's success.* 1,2 *n.*, *pl.* **en vies;** 3,4 *v.*, **en vied, en vy ing.** —**en′vy ing ly**, *adv.* [*Envy* came into English about 700 years ago from French *envie*, and can be traced back to Latin *in-*, meaning "against," and *videre*, meaning "to see."]

en wrap (en rap′), wrap. *v.*, **en wrapped, en wrap ping.**

en zyme (en′zīm), substance produced in living cells that influences a chemical reaction within the body without being changed itself. Some enzymes, such as pepsin, help break down food so that it can be digested. *n.*

e o hip pus (ē′ō hip′əs), an extinct horse that was the ancestor of modern horses. It was about 11 inches (28

centimeters) high at the shoulder and had toes instead of hoofs. n., pl. **e o hip pus es**. [*Eohippus* comes from Greek *ēōs*, meaning "dawn," and *hippos*, meaning "horse."]

e on (ē′ən), a very long period of time; many thousands of years: *Eons passed before life existed on the earth.* n. Also, **aeon**.

ep au let or **ep au lette** (ep′ə let), ornament on the shoulder of a uniform. Epaulets are now usually worn only as a part of a military uniform. *n.*

epaulet

e phed rine (i fed′rən), drug used to relieve hay fever, asthma, head colds, etc. *n.*

e phem er al (i fem′ər el), lasting for only a day; lasting for only a very short time; very short-lived. *adj.* —**e phem′er al ly**, *adv.*

E phe sians (i fē′zhənz), book of the New Testament. It consists of a letter by Saint Paul to the Christians at Ephesus. *n.*

Eph e sus (ef′ə səs), an ancient Greek city in what is now W Turkey. *n.*

ep ic (ep′ik), **1** a long poem that tells the adventures of one or more great heroes. It is written in a dignified, majestic style and often shows the ideals of a nation or race. Homer's *Odyssey* is an epic. **2** any writing having the qualities of an epic. Some very long novels are sometimes called epics. **3** of or like an epic; grand; heroic: *The first flight over the Atlantic was an epic deed.* 1,2 *n.*, 3 *adj.* [*Epic* can be traced back to Greek *epos*, meaning "story, word."] —**ep′ic like′**, *adj.*

ep i cen ter (ep′ə sen′tər), **1** point on the earth's surface directly above the true center of an earthquake. **2** any central point. *n.*

ep i cure (ep′ə kyur), person who enjoys eating and drinking and who is very particular in choosing fine foods, wines, etc. *n.* [*Epicure* comes from the name *Epicurus*, 342?-270 B.C., a Greek philosopher who taught that pleasure is the highest good.]

ep i cu re an (ep′ə kyu rē′ən), **1** of or fit for an epicure: *an epicurean banquet.* **2** person who is fond of pleasure and luxury; epicure. 1 *adj.*, 2 *n.*

ep i dem ic (ep′ə dem′ik), **1** the rapid spread of a disease so that many people have it at the same time: *an epidemic of measles.* **2** the rapid spread of an idea, fashion, etc.: *The city suffered from an epidemic of strikes by different labor unions.* **3** affecting many people at the same time; widespread: *An outbreak of the flu became epidemic last winter.* 1,2 *n.*, 3 *adj.* —**ep′i dem′i cal ly**, *adv.*

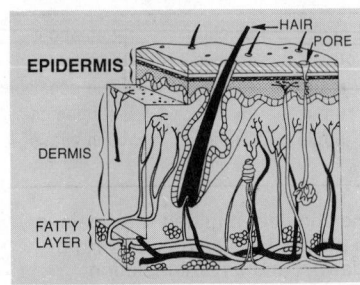

epidermis (def. 1)

ep i der mis (ep′ə dėr′mis), **1** the outer layer of the skin. **2** a skinlike layer of cells in plants. *n.*

ep i glot tal (ep′ə glot′l), of the epiglottis. *adj.*

ep i glot tis (ep′ə glot′is), a thin, triangular plate of cartilage that covers the entrance to the windpipe during swallowing, so that food and drink do not get into the lungs. *n.*

ep i gram (ep′ə gram), **1** a short, pointed or witty saying. EXAMPLE: "Speech is silver, but silence is golden." **2** a short poem ending in a witty or clever turn of thought. *n.*

epigram

Here lies our sovereign lord the King,

Whose word no man relies on;

He never said a foolish thing,

Nor ever did a wise one.

epigram (def. 2)—written by the Earl of Rochester about King Charles II of England

ep i gram mat ic (ep′ə grə mat′ik), **1** like an epigram; short and witty. **2** full of epigrams. *adj.* —**ep′i gram-mat′i cal ly,** *adv.*

ep i lep sy (ep′ə lep′sē), disorder of the nervous system which may cause periods of unconsciousness and convulsions. *n.*

ep i lep tic (ep′ə lep′tik), **1** of or having epilepsy. **2** person having epilepsy. **1** *adj.,* **2** *n.*

ep i logue or **ep i log** (ep′ə lôg), **1** a concluding part added to a novel, poem, etc. An epilogue may be used to round out or interpret the work. **2** speech or poem at the end of a play. It is addressed to the audience by one of the actors. *n.*

ep i neph rine (ep′ə nef′rən), adrenaline. *n.*

E piph a ny (i pif′ə nē), January 6, the anniversary of the coming of the Three Wise Men to honor the infant Jesus at Bethlehem. *n.*

e pis co pal (i pis′kə pəl), **1** of or governed by bishops. **2** **Episcopal,** of the Church of England or the Protestant Episcopal Church. *adj.*

E pis co pa lian (i pis′kə pā′lyən), **1** member of the Protestant Episcopal Church. **2** Episcopal. **1** *n.,* **2** *adj.*

ep i sode (ep′ə sōd), a single happening or group of happenings in real life or in a story: *Being named the best athlete of the year was an important episode in the baseball player's life. n.*

e pis tle (i pis′əl), **1** letter. Epistles are usually long, instructive, and written in formal or elegant language. **2 Epistle,** (in the Bible) any of the letters written by the

Apostles to various churches and individuals. The Epistles make up 21 books of the New Testament. *n.* [*Epistle* came into English about 750 years ago from French *epistle,* and can be traced back to Greek *epi-,* meaning "to," and *stellein,* meaning "send."]

ep i taph (ep′ə taf), a short statement in memory of a dead person. It is often put on a gravestone or tombstone. *n.*

ep i the li um (ep′ə thē′lē əm), a thin layer of cells forming a tissue that covers body surfaces and lines hollow organs. *n., pl.* **ep i the li ums, ep i the li a** (ep′ə thē′lē ə).

ep i thet (ep′ə thet), a descriptive expression; word or phrase expressing some quality or attribute. In "Honest Abe" and "Richard the Lion-Hearted" the epithets are "Honest" and "the Lion-Hearted." *n.*

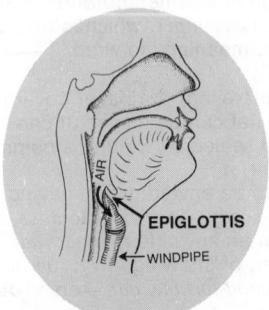

epiglottis
normal raised position for breathing. During the act of swallowing, the epiglottis lowers and closes the top of the windpipe.

e pit o me (i pit′ə mē), person or thing that is typical or representative of something: *Solomon is often spoken of as the epitome of wisdom. n.*

e pit o mize (i pit′ə mīz), be typical or representative of: *Helen Keller epitomizes the human ability to overcome handicaps. v.,* **e pit o mized, e pit o miz ing.**

e plu ri bus u num (ē plùr′ə bəs yü′nəm), LATIN. out of many, one. It is the motto inscribed on the official seal of the United States. It was once the official motto of the United States, but since 1956 the official motto has been "In God We Trust."

ep och (ep′ək), **1** period of time; era: *There have been few peaceful epochs in the history of our country.* **2** period of time in which striking things happened: *The years of the Civil War were an epoch in the United States.* **3** the starting point of such a period: *The invention of the steam engine marked an epoch in the growth of industry. n.*

ep och al (ep′ək əl), **1** having to do with an epoch. **2** epoch-making: *the epochal discovery of electricity. adj.*

ep och-mak ing (ep′ək mā′king), beginning an epoch; causing important changes: *the epoch-making discovery of America. adj.*

ep ox y (e pok′sē), kind of synthetic resin used in plastics and adhesives. *n., pl.* **ep ox ies.**

Ep som salts (ep′səm), a bitter, white, crystalline powder taken in water as a laxative and mixed with warm water to soak sore parts of the body. [This powder gets its name from *Epsom,* a town in England, where it was first obtained from springs.]

eq ua ble (ek′wə bəl), changing little; uniform; even; tranquil: *The good-natured traffic officer had an equable disposition. The Gulf Stream makes England's climate fairly equable. adj.*

eq ua bly (ek′wə blē), uniformly; evenly: *Laws should be equably enforced. adv.*

e qual (ē′kwəl), **1** the same in amount, size, number, value, or rank: *Ten dimes are equal to one dollar. All persons are considered equal before the law.* **2** be the same as: *Four times five equals twenty.* **3** person or thing that is equal: *In spelling she had no equal.* **4** make or do something equal to: *Our team equaled the other team's score, and the game ended in a tie.* **5** the same throughout; even; uniform: *an equal mixture.* 1,5 *adj.*, 2,4 *v.*, **e qualed, e qual ing** or **e qualled, e qual ling; 3** *n.* [*Equal* is from Latin *aequalis*, which comes from *aequus*, meaning "even, just." See **Word Family.**]

equal to, strong enough for: *One horse is not equal to pulling a load of five tons.*

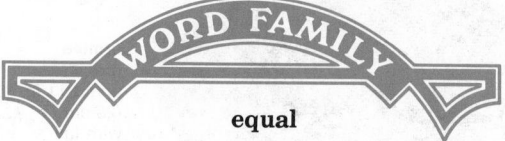

equal

Below are words related to *equal*. They can all be traced back to the Latin word *aequus* (ī′kwŭs), meaning "even, just."

adequate	equator	equitable
equable	equidistant	equity
equality	equilateral	equivalent
equanimity	equilibrium	equivocal
equate	equinox	iniquity
equation	equipoise	unequaled

e qual i ty (i kwol′ə tē), sameness in amount, size, number, value, rank, etc.; being equal. *n., pl.* **e qual i ties.**

e qual i za tion (ē′kwə lə zā′shən), an equalizing or a being equalized. *n.*

e qual ize (ē′kwə līz), **1** make equal. **2** make even or uniform. *v.*, **e qual ized, e qual iz ing.**

e qual iz er (ē′kwə lī′zər), **1** person or thing that equalizes. **2** device for equalizing forces, pressures, etc. *n.*

e qual ly (ē′kwə lē), in equal shares; in an equal manner; to an equal degree: *Divide the pie equally. My sister and brother are equally talented. adv.*

e qua nim i ty (ē′kwə nim′ə tē *or* ek′wə nim′ə tē), evenness of mind or temper; calmness; composure: *The speaker endured the insults of the heckler with equanimity. n.*

e quate (i kwāt′), **1** state to be equal; put into the form of an equation: *I equated 30 inches to 2½ feet.* **2** make equal; treat as equal. *v.*, **e quat ed, e quat ing.**

e qua tion (i kwā′zhən), **1** statement of the equality of two quantities. EXAMPLES: $(4 \times 8) + 12 = 44$. $C = 2\pi r$. **2** expression using chemical formulas and symbols to show the substances used and produced in a chemical change. EXAMPLE: $HCl + NaOH = NaCl + H_2O$. **3** an equating or a being equated. *n.*

e qua tor (i kwā′tər), an imaginary circle around the middle of the earth, halfway between the North Pole and the South Pole. The United States is north of the equator; Australia is south of it. *n.*

e qua to ri al (ē′kwə tôr′ē əl *or* ek′wə tôr′ē əl), **1** of, at, or near the equator: *Ecuador is an equatorial country.* **2** like conditions at or near the equator: *The weather was humid and hot enough to be equatorial. adj.*

Equatorial Guinea, country in W Africa consisting of two parts, one on the mainland and the other an island. *Capital:* Malabo.

e ques tri an (i kwes′trē ən), **1** having to do with horseback riding, horses, or horseback riders: *equestrian skill.* **2** on horseback. An equestrian statue shows a person riding a horse. **3** rider or performer on horseback. 1,2 *adj.*, **3** *n.*

equi-, *combining form.* **1** equal: *Equivalent = equal in value or force.* **2** equally: *Equidistant = equally distant.* [The form *equi-* comes from Latin *aequus*, meaning "equal, even, level."]

e qui dis tant (ē′kwə dis′tənt), equally distant: *All points

of the circumference of a circle are equidistant from the center. adj.* —**e′qui dis′tant ly,** *adv.*

e qui lat er al (ē′kwə lat′ər əl), having all sides equal. *adj.* —**e′qui lat′er al ly,** *adv.*

e qui lib ri um (ē′kwə lib′rē əm), **1** balance: *The acrobat in the circus maintained equilibrium on a tightrope. Scales are in equilibrium when the weights on each side are equal.* **2** mental poise: *My mother does not let quarrels between my brother and me upset her equilibrium. n.*

e quine (ē′kwīn), **1** of horses. **2** like a horse; like that of a horse. *adj.* [*Equine* is from Latin *equinus*, which comes from *equus*, meaning "horse."]

e qui noc tial (ē′kwə nok′shəl), of or occurring at an equinox: *an equinoctial storm. adj.*

e qui nox (ē′kwə noks), either of the two times in the year when the center of the sun crosses the equator, and day and night are of equal length in all parts of the earth. It occurs about March 21 (**vernal equinox**) and about September 22 (**autumnal equinox**). *n., pl.* **e qui nox es.**

e quip (i kwip′), supply with all that is needed; fit out; provide; furnish: *We were equipped with canteens and food for the hike. v.,* **e quipped, e quip ping.** —**e quip′per,** *n.* [*Equip* came into English about 450 years ago from French *equiper,* and can probably be traced back to Icelandic *skip,* meaning "a ship."]

e quip ment (i kwip′mənt), **1** act of equipping; fitting out: *The equipment of the expedition took six months.* **2** what a person or thing is equipped with; outfit; furnishings; supplies: *camping equipment. n.*

e qui poise (ē′kwə poiz *or* ek′wə poiz), **1** equal distribution of weight or force; even balance. **2** a balancing force; counterbalance. *n.*

eq ui ta ble (ek′wə tə bəl), fair; just: *It is equitable to pay a person good wages for work well done. adj.*

eq ui ta bly (ek′wə tə blē), in an equitable manner; fairly; justly. *adv.*

eq ui ta tion (ek′wə tā′shən), horseback riding; horsemanship. *n.*

eq ui ty (ek′wə tē), fairness; justice: *The judge was noted for the equity of her decisions. n.*

e quiv a lence (i kwiv′ə ləns), condition of being equivalent. *n.*

e quiv a lent (i kwiv′ə lənt), **1** equal; the same in value, force, effect, meaning, etc.: *Nodding your head is equivalent to saying yes.* **2** something equivalent: *Five pennies are the equivalent of a nickel.* 1 *adj.*, 2 *n.*

e quiv o cal (i kwiv′ə kəl), **1** having two or more meanings; ambiguous: *His equivocal answer puzzled us.* **2** undecided; uncertain: *Nothing was proved because the result of the experiment was equivocal. adj.* —**e quiv′o cal ly,** *adv.* —**e quiv′o cal ness,** *n.*

e quiv o cate (i kwiv′ə kāt), use expressions of double meaning in order to mislead: *When asked if he had finished his arithmetic, he equivocated by saying, "I was working on that an hour ago." v.,* **e quiv o cat ed, e quiv o cat ing.** —**e quiv′o cat′ing ly,** *adv.* —**e quiv′o ca′tor,** *n.*

e quiv o ca tion (i kwiv′ə kā′shən), **1** the use of expressions with double meaning in order to mislead. **2** an equivocal expression. *n.*

-er[1], *suffix forming nouns.* **1** (*added to verbs*) person or thing that ____s: *Admirer = a person who admires.*

a hat	**i** it	**oi** oil	**ch** child	a in about
ā age	**ī** ice	**ou** out	**ng** long	e in taken
ä far	**o** hot	**u** cup	**sh** she	ə = i in pencil
e let	**ō** open	**u̇** put	**th** thin	o in lemon
ē equal	**ô** order	**ü** rule	**ŦH** then	u in circus
ėr term			**zh** measure	

Burner = thing that burns. **2** (*added to nouns*) person living in _____: *New Yorker = a person living in New York. Villager = a person living in a village.* **3** (*added to nouns*) person who makes or works with _____: *Hatter = a person who makes hats.*

-er², *suffix forming the comparative degree of adjectives and adverbs.* more: *Softer = more soft. Slower = more slow.*

Er, symbol for erbium.

er a (ir′ə), **1** an age in history; historical period: *The years from 1817 to 1824 in United States history are often called the Era of Good Feelings.* **2** period of time starting from an important or significant happening, date, etc.: *We live in the 20th century of the Christian era.* **3** one of the five very large divisions of time in geological history. *n., pl.* **er as.**

e rad i cate (i rad′ə kāt), get rid of entirely; destroy completely: *Yellow fever has been eradicated in the United States. v.,* **e rad i cat ed, e rad i cat ing.**

e rad i ca tion (i rad′ə kā′shən), an eradicating; complete destruction; uprooting. *n.*

e rase (i rās′), **1** rub out; remove by rubbing, wiping, or scraping: *She erased the wrong answer and wrote in the right one.* **2** remove all trace of; blot out: *The blow on his head erased the details of the accident from his memory. v.,* **e rased, e ras ing. —e ras′a ble,** *adj.*

e ras er (i rā′sər), something used to erase marks made with pencil, ink, chalk, etc. *n.*

E ras mus (i raz′məs), 1466?-1536, Dutch scholar and religious teacher. *n.*

e ra sure (i rā′shər), **1** an erasing: *the erasure of a typing error.* **2** an erased word, letter, etc. **3** place where a word, letter, etc., has been erased. *n.*

er bi um (ėr′bē əm), a soft, lustrous, grayish metallic element which occurs as a minute part of various minerals. *n.* [*Erbium* gets its name from *Ytterby,* a town in Sweden, where it was first discovered in 1843.]

ere (er *or* ar), OLD USE. before. *prep., conj.*

e rect (i rekt′), **1** straight up; not bending; not tipping; upright: *erect posture.* **2** put straight up; set upright: *They erected a television antenna on the roof. The mast was erected on a firm base.* **3** put up; build: *That house was erected forty years ago.* **1** *adj.,* **2,3** *v.* **—e rect′a ble,** *adj.* **—e rect′er,** *n.* **—e rect′ly,** *adv.* **—e rect′ness,** *n.*

e rec tion (i rek′shən), **1** a setting up; raising; erecting: *The erection of the tent took only a few minutes.* **2** thing erected; building or other structure. *n.*

erg (ėrg), unit for measuring work or energy. It is the amount of work done by a force of one dyne acting through a distance of one centimeter. *n.* [*Erg* comes from Greek *ergon,* meaning "work." See **Word Family.**]

er go (ėr′gō), LATIN. therefore. *adv., conj.*

Er ic son (er′ik sən), **Leif,** Viking chieftain who probably discovered North America about A.D. 1000. *n.*

Er ie (ir′ē), **1 Lake,** one of the five Great Lakes. **2** city in NW Pennsylvania on Lake Erie. *n.*

Erie Canal, canal in New York State between Buffalo and Albany, connecting Lake Erie with the Hudson River.

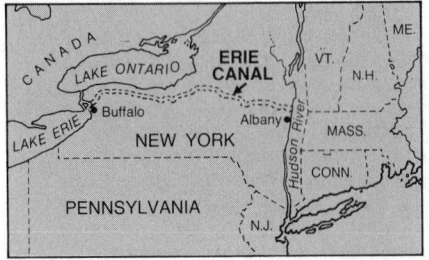

Er in (er′ən), Ireland. *n.*

er mine (ėr′mən), **1** weasel of northern regions that is brown in summer but white with a black tip on its tail in winter. **2** its soft, white fur, used for coats, trimming, etc. The official robes of English judges are trimmed with ermine as a symbol of purity and fairness. *n., pl.* **er mines** or **er mine.**

ermine (def. 1) about 11 in. (28 cm.) with tail

e rode (i rōd′), eat or wear away gradually; eat into: *Running water eroded the soil. v.,* **e rod ed, e rod ing.**

Er os (ir′os *or* er′os), (in Greek myths) the god of love, son of Aphrodite. The Romans called him Cupid. *n.*

erosion (def. 2)—The shape of this rock was caused by erosion.

e ro sion (i rō′zhən), **1** a gradual eating or wearing away by glaciers, running water, waves, or wind: *Trees help prevent the erosion of soil.* **2** a being eaten or worn away. *n.*

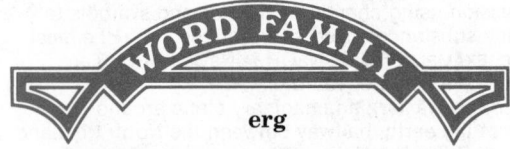

WORD FAMILY

erg

Below are words related to *erg.* They can all be traced back to the Greek word *ergon* (er′gon), meaning "work."

allergy	energize	liturgy
argon	energy	metallurgy
energetic	lethargy	surgery

err (ėr *or* er), **1** go wrong; make a mistake: *Everyone errs at some time or other.* **2** be wrong; be mistaken or incorrect: *to err in an opinion or belief.* **3** do wrong; sin: *To err is human; to forgive, divine. v.* [*Err* came into English about 700 years ago from French *errer,* which came from Latin *errare,* meaning "to wander, err."]

er rand (er′ənd), **1** a trip to do something: *She has gone on an errand to the store.* **2** what one is sent to do: *I did ten errands in one trip. n.* [*Errand* comes from Old English ǣrende.]

er rant (er′ənt), **1** wandering; roving: *an errant knight seeking adventures.* **2** wrong; mistaken: *errant conduct.* **3** doing what is considered wrong; erring: *an errant child. adj.* [*Errant* came into English about 600 years ago from French *errant,* and can be traced back to Latin *ire,* meaning "to go."] —**er′rant ly,** *adv.*

er rat ic (ə rat′ik), **1** uncertain; irregular: *An erratic clock is not dependable.* **2** strange; odd: *erratic behavior. adj.* —**er rat′i cal ly,** *adv.*

er ro ne ous (ə rō′nē əs), not correct; wrong; mistaken: *Years ago many people held the erroneous belief that the earth was flat. adj.* —**er ro′ne ous ly,** *adv.*

er ror (er′ər), **1** something done that is wrong; something that is not the way it ought to be; mistake: *I failed my test because of errors in spelling.* **2** condition of being wrong or mistaken: *You are in error; your answer is wrong.* **3** (in baseball) a fielder's mistake that allows either a batter to reach first or a runner to advance one or more bases. *n.* —**er′ror less,** *adj.*

erst while (èrst′hwīl′), **1** former; past: *an erstwhile companion.* **2** OLD USE. in time past; formerly. **1** *adj.,* **2** *adv.*

er u dite (er′ů dīt *or* er′yə dīt), having much knowledge; scholarly; learned: *an erudite teacher, an erudite book. adj.* —**er′u dite′ly,** *adv.* —**er′u dite′ness,** *n.*

er u di tion (er′ů dish′ən *or* er′yə dish′ən), scholarship; learning: *The professor's erudition came from long years of study. n.*

e rupt (i rupt′), **1** burst forth: *Hot water erupted from the geyser. Headlines erupted around the world.* **2** throw forth: *The volcano erupted lava and ashes.* **3** break out in a rash: *My skin erupted when I had measles. v.*

e rup tion (i rup′shən), **1** a bursting or throwing forth: *There was an eruption of glowing melted rock from the mountain top.* **2** a breaking out in a rash. **3** red spots on the skin; rash: *Chicken pox causes an eruption on the body. n.*

e rup tive (i rup′tiv), **1** bursting forth. **2** causing the skin to break out: *Measles is an eruptive disease. adj.*

-ery, *suffix forming nouns.* **1** (*added to verbs*) place for _____ing: *Cannery = place for canning.* **2** (*added to nouns*) place for _____s: *Nunnery = place for nuns.* **3** (*added to nouns*) art or occupation of a _____: *Cookery = art or occupation of a cook.* **4** (*added to nouns*) condition of a _____: *Slavery = condition of a slave.* **5** (*added to nouns*) qualities, actions, etc., of a _____: *Knavery = qualities, actions, etc., of a knave.* **6** (*added to nouns*) group of _____s: *Machinery = group of machines.*

Es, symbol for einsteinium.

E sau (ē′sô),(in the Bible) the older son of Isaac and Rebecca, who sold his birthright to his twin brother Jacob. *n.*

es ca late (es′kə lāt), increase or expand by stages: *The commotion in the prison almost escalated into a riot. To send in more troops would only escalate the war. v.,* **es ca lat ed, es ca lat ing.**

es ca la tion (es′kə lā′shən), an escalating or a being escalated. *n.*

es ca la tor (es′kə lā′tər), a moving stairway. *n.*

es cal lop (e skol′əp), scallop. *v.*

es ca pade (es′kə pād), a breaking loose from rules or restraint; wild prank. *n.*

es cape (e skāp′), **1** get out and away; get free: *to escape from prison. The bird escaped from its cage.* **2** get free from: *He thinks he will never escape hard work.* **3** keep free or safe from; avoid: *We all escaped the measles.* **4** act of escaping: *Their escape was aided by the thick fog.* **5** way of escaping: *There was no escape from the trap.* **6** come out or find a way out from a container; leak: *Gas had been escaping from the cylinder all night.* **7** come out without

being intended: *A cry escaped her lips.* **8** fail to be noticed or remembered by: *I knew his face, but the name escaped me.* **9** relief from boredom, trouble, etc.: *Some people find escape in mystery stories.* **1-3,6-8** *v.,* **es caped, es cap ing; 4,5,9** *n.* —**es cap′a ble,** *adj.* —**es cape′less,** *adj.* —**es cap′er,** *n.*

escape velocity, the velocity that a body such as a rocket must reach to break away permanently from the gravitational pull of the earth or other attracting body. Once a rocket's speed reaches 25,000 miles (40,225 kilometers) per hour, it can escape the pull of the earth without further power.

es cap ism (e skā′piz′əm), an avoiding of unpleasant things by daydreaming or by entertainment, such as motion pictures. *n.*

es car ole (es′kə rōl′), endive (def. 1). *n.*

es carp ment (e skärp′mənt), **1** a steep slope; cliff. **2** ground made into a steep slope as part of a fortification. *n.*

es chew (es chü′), keep away from; avoid; shun: *The doctor advised me to eschew rich foods. v.* —**es chew′er,** *n.*

es cort (es′kôrt for 1-3; e skôrt′ for 4), **1** person or group of persons going with another to give protection, show honor, etc.: *An escort of several city officials accompanied the famous visitor.* **2** one or more ships or airplanes serving as a guard. **3** man who goes on a date with a woman: *Her escort to the party was a tall young man.* **4** go with as an escort: *Three police cars escorted the governor's limousine in the parade. I enjoyed escorting my cousin to the movies.* **1-3** *n.,* **4** *v.*

es crow (es′krō *or* e skrō′), deed, bond, or other written agreement held by a third person until certain conditions are met by two other parties. *n.*

in escrow, held by a third party in accordance with an agreement.

es cutch eon (e skuch′ən), shield on which a coat of arms is put. *n.*

-ese, *suffix added to nouns.* **1** (*to form adjectives*) of _____: *Japanese = of Japan.* **2** (*to form nouns*) person born or living in _____: *Portuguese = person born or living in Portugal.* **3** (*to form nouns*) language of _____: *Chinese = language of China.*

Es ki mo (es′kə mō), **1** member of a people living in the arctic regions of North America and northeastern Asia. **2** language of the Eskimos. **3** of the Eskimos or their language. **1,2** *n., pl.* **Es ki mos** *or* **Es ki mo** for 1; **3** *adj.*

Eskimo dog, a strong, broad-chested dog of the arctic regions, used for pulling sleds; husky. Eskimo dogs have furry outer hair with another coat of fine hair near the skin.

e soph a gus (ē sof′ə gəs), passage for food from the throat to the stomach; gullet. *n., pl.* **e soph a gi** (ē sof′ə jī).

es o ter ic (es′ə ter′ik), understood only by a select few; intended for an inner circle of disciples, scholars, etc.: *esoteric literature. adj.* —**es′o ter′i cal ly,** *adv.*

ESP, extrasensory perception.

esp. or **espec.,** especially.

es pe cial (e spesh′əl), more than others; special: *my especial friend, of no especial value. Your birthday is an especial day for you. adj.* —**es pe′cial ness,** *n.*

es pe cial ly (e spesh′ə lē), more than others; specially;

particularly; principally; chiefly: *This book is designed especially for students.* *adv.*

es pi o nage (es′pē ə nij *or* es′pē ə näzh), the use of spies; spying. Nations use espionage to find out the military and political secrets of other nations. *n.*

es pla nade (es′plə nād′ *or* es′plə näd′), any open level space used for public walks or drives, especially along a shore. *n.*

es pous al (e spou′zəl), **1** Also, **espousals,** *pl.* ceremony of becoming engaged or married. **2** an espousing; adoption (of a cause, etc.): *The candidate's espousal of the campaign for a new park made her very popular.* *n.*

es pouse (e spouz′), **1** marry. **2** take up or make one's own; adopt: *Late in life he espoused a new religion.* *v.,* **es poused, es pous ing.** —**es pous′er,** *n.*

es prit (e sprē′), FRENCH. lively wit; spirit. *n.*

es prit de corps (e sprē′ də kôr′), FRENCH. group spirit; comradeship: *The club's strong esprit de corps showed itself in the intense loyalty, devotion, and enthusiasm of its members.*

es py (e spī′), see at a distance; catch sight of; spy: *They espied the castle from afar.* *v.,* **es pied, es py ing.**

Esq., Esquire: *Henry Smith, Esq.*

e squire (e skwīr′ *or* es′kwīr), **1** (in the Middle Ages) a knight's attendant; squire. **2** Englishman ranking next below a knight. **3 Esquire,** title of respect placed after a person's last name: *John Jones, Esquire = Mr. John Jones.* *n.*

-ess, *suffix added to nouns to form other nouns.* female _____: *Lioness = a female lion.*

es say (es′ā *for 1;* e sā′ *for 2;* es′ā *or* e sā′ *for 3),* **1** a short composition written on a certain subject. **2** to try; attempt: *The student essayed her first solo flight.* **3** a try; an attempt. **1,3** *n.,* **2** *v.* —**es say′er,** *n.*

es say ist (es′ā ist), writer of essays. *n.*

es sence (es′ns), **1** that which makes a thing what it is; necessary part or parts: *Being thoughtful of others is the essence of politeness.* **2** a concentrated substance that has the characteristic flavor, fragrance, or effect of the plant or fruit from which it is taken: *Essence of peppermint is a solution of peppermint in alcohol.* **3** perfume. *n.*

es sen tial (ə sen′shəl), **1** needed to make a thing what it is; very important; necessary: *Good food and enough rest are essential to good health.* **2** an absolutely necessary element or quality: *Learn the essentials first; then learn the details.* **3** of or making up the essence of a substance: *The essential oil of a plant or fruit is what gives it its own peculiar flavor or fragrance.* **1,3** *adj.,* **2** *n.*

es sen tial ly (ə sen′shə lē), in essentials; in an essential manner. *adv.*

-est, *suffix forming the superlative degree of adjectives and adverbs.* most: *Warmest = most warm. Slowest = most slow.*

E.S.T., Eastern Standard Time.

es tab lish (e stab′lish), **1** set up on a firm or lasting basis: *The early settlers from Europe established colonies in America.* **2** settle in a position; set up in a business: *A new doctor has established herself on our street.* **3** cause to be accepted and used for a long time: *to establish a custom.* **4** show beyond dispute; prove: *He established his innocence to the satisfaction of the jury.* *v.* —**es tab′lish a ble,** *adj.* —**es tab′lish er,** *n.*

es tab lish ment (e stab′lish mənt), **1** an establishing or a being established: *The establishment of the business took several years.* **2** something established. A household, business, church, or army is an establishment. **3 the Establishment,** group that holds all the positions of influence or authority in a country, society, etc. *n.*

es tan cia (e stän′syä), a large ranch or estate in Latin America. *n., pl.* **es tan cias.**

es tate (e stāt′), **1** a large piece of land belonging to a person; landed property: *They have a beautiful estate with a country house and a swimming pool on it.* **2** that which a person owns; property; possessions: *When the rich woman died, she left an estate of two million dollars.* **3** condition or stage in life: *The boy has reached man's estate.* *n.*

es teem (e stēm′), **1** have a very favorable opinion of; think highly of; value: *We esteem courage.* **2** a very favorable opinion; high regard: *Courage is held in esteem.* **3** think; consider: *She esteemed it an honor to be chosen for the award.* **1,3** *v.,* **2** *n.*

es ter (es′tər), compound produced by the reaction of an acid and an alcohol. Animal and vegetable fats and oils are esters. *n.*

Es ther (es′tər), **1** (in the Bible) the Jewish wife of a Persian king, who saved her people from massacre. **2** book of the Old Testament that tells her story. *n.*

es thet ic (es thet′ik), aesthetic. *adj.*

es thet i cal ly (es thet′ik lē), aesthetically. *adv.*

es ti ma ble (es′tə mə bəl), worthy of esteem; deserving high regard: *Unselfishness is an estimable trait.* *adj.*

es ti mate (es′tə mit *or* es′tə māt *for 1,3;* es′tə māt *for 2*), **1** judgment or opinion about how much, how many, how good, etc.: *My estimate of the length of the room was 15 feet; it actually measured 14 feet, 9 inches.* **2** form a judgment or opinion (about how much, how many, how good, etc.): *We estimated that it would take four hours to weed the garden.* **3** statement of what certain work will cost, made by one willing to do the work: *The painter's estimate for painting the house was $500.* **1,3** *n.,* **2** *v.,* **es ti mat ed, es ti mat ing.** —**es′ti ma′tor,** *n.*

es ti ma tion (es′tə mā′shən), **1** judgment or opinion: *In my estimation, your plan will not work.* **2** esteem; respect: *The doctor was held in high estimation by the community.* **3** act or process of estimating. *n.*

Es to ni a (e stō′nē ə), Soviet republic in N Europe, on the Baltic Sea. *n.* —**Es to′ni an,** *adj., n.*

es trange (e strānj′), turn (a person) from affection to indifference, dislike, or hatred; make unfriendly; keep apart; separate: *A quarrel had estranged him from his family.* *v.,* **es tranged, es trang ing.**

es trange ment (e strānj′mənt), a turning away in feeling; becoming distant or unfriendly: *A misunderstanding had caused the estrangement of the two friends.* *n.*

estuary (def. 1)

es tu ar y (es′chü er′ē), **1** a broad mouth of a river into which the tide flows. **2** inlet of the sea. *n., pl.* **es tu ar ies.**

etc., et cetera. *Etc.* is usually read "and so forth." The definition of *equality* reads "sameness in amount, size, number, value, rank, etc." *Etc.* in this and similar definitions shows that the definition applies to many similar items in addition to the ones mentioned.

et cet er a (et set′ər ə), and so forth; and others; and the rest; and so on; and the like. [*Et cetera* comes from the Latin phrase *et cetera,* meaning "and all the rest."]

etch (ech), **1** engrave (a drawing or design) on a metal plate, glass, etc., by means of acid that eats away the lines. When filled with ink, the lines of the design will reproduce a copy on paper. **2** make drawings or designs by this method. **3** impress deeply; fix firmly: *Her face was etched in my memory. v.* [*Etch* is from Dutch *etsen,* which came from German *ätzen,* meaning "to feed, etch."] —**etch′er,** *n.*

etch ing (ech′ing), **1** picture or design printed from an etched plate. **2** an etched plate; etched drawing or design. **3** art or process of engraving a drawing or design on a metal plate, glass, etc., by means of acid. *n.*

e ter nal (i tér′nl), **1** without beginning or ending; lasting throughout all time. **2** always and forever the same: *the eternal truths.* **3** seeming to go on forever; constant: *When will we have an end to this eternal noise?* **4** the **Eternal,** God. 1-3 *adj.,* 4 *n.* —**e ter′nal ness,** *n.*

Eternal City, Rome.

e ter nal ly (i tér′nl ē), **1** without beginning or ending; throughout all time. **2** always and forever. **3** constantly. *adv.*

e ter ni ty (i tér′nə tē), **1** all time; all the past and all the future. **2** the endless period after death. **3** a period of time that seems endless: *I waited in the dentist's office for an eternity. n., pl.* **e ter ni ties.**

-eth, *suffix added to numbers.* number _____ in order or position in a series: *Sixtieth = number sixty in order or position in a series.* The suffix *-th* is used to form numbers like *sixth.*

e ther (ē′thər), **1** a colorless, sweet-smelling liquid that burns and evaporates readily. Its fumes cause unconsciousness when deeply inhaled. Ether is used as an anesthetic and as a solvent for fats and resins. **2** the upper regions of space beyond the earth's atmosphere; clear sky. *n.*

e ther e al (i thir′ē əl), **1** light; airy; delicate: *the ethereal beauty of a butterfly, the ethereal music of a harp.* **2** not of the earth; heavenly: *An angel is an ethereal messenger. adj.* Also, **aethereal.** —**e ther′e al ly,** *adv.* —**e ther′e al ness,** *n.*

e ther e al ize (i thir′ē ə līz), make ethereal. *v.,* **e ther e al ized, e ther e al iz ing.**

eth i cal (eth′ə kəl), **1** having to do with standards of right and wrong; of ethics or morals. **2** morally right: *ethical conduct.* **3** in accordance with formal or professional rules of right and wrong: *It is not considered ethical for a doctor to gossip about a patient. adj.* —**eth′i cal ly,** *adv.* —**eth′i cal ness,** *n.*

eth ics (eth′iks), **1** *pl. in form, sing. in use.* the study of standards of right and wrong; the part of philosophy dealing with moral conduct, duty, and judgment. **2** *pl. in form and use.* formal or professional rules of right and wrong: *It is against medical ethics for doctors to advertise. n.*

E thi o pi a (ē′thē ō′pē ə), **1** country in E Africa; Abyssinia. *Capital:* Addis Ababa. See **Nile** for map. **2** ancient region in NE Africa, south of Egypt. *n.* —**E′thi o′pi an,** *adj., n.*

eth nic (eth′nik), **1** of the various racial or cultural groups of people and the characteristics, language, and customs of each; of or peculiar to a people. **2** of people of foreign birth or descent: *There are many ethnic groups in our large cities. adj.* —**eth′ni cal ly,** *adv.*

eth no log i cal (eth′nə loj′ə kəl), of ethnology. *adj.*

eth nol o gy (eth nol′ə jē), science that deals with the various races or cultural groups of people, their origin and distribution, distinctive characteristics, customs, institutions, and culture. *n.*

eth yl alcohol (eth′əl), ordinary alcohol, made by the fermentation of grain, sugar, etc. It is in alcoholic beverages, and is also used in drugs, dyes, cleaning solutions, etc.

eth yl ene (eth′ə lēn′), a colorless, flammable gas with an unpleasant odor. It is used in the manufacture of ethyl alcohol, plastics, and many other compounds, and to ripen fruit. *n.*

et i quette (et′ə ket), **1** the customary rules for behavior in polite society: *Etiquette requires that we eat peas with a fork, not a knife.* **2** formal rules for governing behavior in a profession, official ceremony, etc.: *Ambassadors observe diplomatic etiquette. n.* [*Etiquette* comes from French *étiquette,* which also means "ticket," and can be traced back to Dutch *stikken,* meaning "to stick."]

Et na (et′nə), **Mount,** active volcano in NE Sicily, 10,902 feet (3325 meters) high. *n.* Also, **Aetna.**

E ton (ēt′n), an English school for boys, at Eton, a town near London. *n.*

E trur i a (i trür′ē ə), ancient country in W Italy. *n.*

about 700 B.C.

E trus can (i trus′kən), **1** of Etruria, its people, their language, art, or customs. **2** person who was born or lived in Etruria. **3** language of Etruria. 1 *adj.,* 2,3 *n.*

-ette, *suffix often added to nouns to form new nouns.* **1** little _____: *Kitchenette = a little kitchen.* **2** female _____: *Usherette = a female usher.* **3** substitute for _____: *Leatherette = a substitute for leather.*

é tude (ā′tüd *or* ā′tyüd), piece of music intended to develop skill in technique. *n., pl.* **é tudes.** [*Étude* comes from French *étude,* which also means "study," and can be traced back to Latin *studium,* meaning "eagerness, study."]

et y mol o gy (et′ə mol′ə jē), **1** the derivation of a word. **2** account or explanation of the origin and history of a word. **3** the study dealing with the origin and history of words. *n., pl.* **et y mol o gies.**

Eu, symbol for europium.

eu ca lyp tus (yü′kə lip′təs), a very tall evergreen tree that grows mainly in Australia and neighboring islands. It is valued for its timber and for a medicinal oil made from its leaves. *n., pl.* **eu ca lyp tus es, eu ca lyp ti** (yü′kə lip′tī).

Eu char ist (yü′kər ist), **1** sacrament of the Lord's Supper; Holy Communion. **2** the consecrated bread and wine used in this sacrament. *n.*

Eu clid (yü′klid), Greek mathematician who wrote a famous book on geometry about 300 B.C. *n.*

eu gen ic (yü jen′ik), of eugenics. *adj.*

eu gen ics (yü jen′iks), science of improving the human race. Eugenics would apply the same principles of careful selection of parents that have long been applied to animals and plants, and develop healthier and more intelligent children. *n. sing. or pl.*

eu gle na (yü glē′nə), a microscopic, one-celled organism, usually green, that moves by a whiplike tail in fresh water. It is easily grown in a culture for study. *n., pl.* **eu gle nas.**

eu lo gist (yü′lə jist), person who eulogizes. *n.*

eu lo gis tic (yü′lə jis′tik), of or like a eulogy; praising very highly. *adj.* —**eu′lo gis′ti cal ly,** *adv.*

eu lo gize (yü′lə jīz), praise very highly. *v.,* **eu lo gized, eu lo giz ing.** —**eu′lo giz′er,** *n.*

eu lo gy (yü′lə jē), speech or writing in praise of a person or thing; high praise: *He delivered the eulogy at the mayor's funeral. n., pl.* **eu lo gies.**

eu nuch (yü′nək), **1** a castrated man. **2** such a man in charge of a harem or the household of an Oriental ruler. *n.*

eu phe mism (yü′fə miz′əm), a mild or indirect expression used instead of one that is harsh or unpleasantly direct. "Pass away" is a common euphemism for "die"; "not very bright" is a euphemism for "stupid." *n.*

eu phe mis tic (yü′fə mis′tik), using mild or indirect words instead of harsh or unpleasant ones. *adj.*

eu pho ni ous (yü fō′nē əs), pleasing to the ear; sounding agreeable; harmonious: *Our door chimes have a euphonious sound. adj.* —**eu pho′ni ous ly,** *adv.*

eu pho ny (yü′fə nē), pleasing effect to the ear; agreeable sound. *n., pl.* **eu pho nies.**

eu pho ri a (yü fôr′ē ə), a feeling of happiness and bodily well-being. *n.*

Eu phra tes (yü frā′tēz), river in SW Asia, flowing from E Turkey through Syria and Iraq into the Persian Gulf. It joins the Tigris River in SE Iraq. *n.*

Eur a sia (yùr ā′zhə), Europe and Asia, thought of as a single continent. The Soviet Union is the largest country in Eurasia.

Eur a sian (yùr ā′zhən), **1** person of mixed European and Asian parentage. **2** of mixed European and Asian parentage. 1 *n.,* 2 *adj.*

eu re ka (yù rē′kə), I have found it! (an exclamation of triumph at any discovery). *interj.*

Eur ope (yùr′əp), continent east of the North Atlantic Ocean and west of Asia. France, Sweden, and Spain are countries in Europe. *n.*

Eur o pe an (yùr′ə pē′ən), **1** of Europe or its people. **2** person born or living in Europe. 1 *adj.,* 2 *n.*

eu ro pi um (yù rō′pē əm), a soft, grayish metallic element which occurs only in combination with other elements. Europium compounds are used in coating color television screens. *n.* [*Europium* was named in honor of *Europe.*]

Eus ta chi an tube (yü stā′kē ən *or* yü stā′shən), a slender canal between the pharynx and the middle ear. It

equalizes the air pressure on the two sides of the eardrum. [The *Eustachian tube* was named for Bartolommeo *Eustachio,* 1520?-1574, an Italian anatomist who described it.]

eu tha na sia (yü′thə nā′zhə), a painless killing, especially to end a painful and incurable disease. *n.*

e vac u ate (i vak′yü āt), **1** leave empty; withdraw from: *The tenants evacuated the burning apartment house.* **2** withdraw; remove: *Efforts were made to evacuate all civilians from the war zone.* **3** make empty, especially to discharge intestinal waste. *v.,* **e vac u at ed, e vac u at ing.** —**e vac′u a′tor,** *n.*

e vac u a tion (i vak′yü ā′shən), **1** a leaving empty; withdrawal from. **2** removal; withdrawal: *Volunteers helped in the evacuation of the townspeople from their flooded homes.* **3** a making empty. **4** a discharge. *n.*

e vac u ee (i vak′yü ē′), person who is removed to a place of greater safety: *The evacuees from the flood were housed in the schools and churches. n.*

e vade (i vād′), get away from by trickery; avoid by cleverness: *The thief evaded the police and escaped. When they asked who broke the lamp, she evaded the question by saying, "I wonder who!" v.,* **e vad ed, e vad ing.**

e val u ate (i val′yü āt), find out the value or the amount of; estimate the worth or importance of; appraise: *An expert will evaluate the old furniture you wish to sell. v.,* **e val u at ed, e val u at ing.** —**e val′u a′tor,** *n.*

e val u a tion (i val′yü ā′shən), **1** an evaluating: *The jury began its careful evaluation of the evidence.* **2** an estimated value; valuation. *n.*

e van gel i cal (ē′van jel′ə kəl), **1** of or according to the four Gospels or the New Testament. **2** of the Protestant churches that emphasize Christ's atonement and man's salvation by faith as the most important parts of Christianity. Methodists and Baptists are evangelical; Unitarians and Universalists are not. *adj.*

e van gel ism (i van′jə liz′əm), a preaching of the Gospel; earnest effort for the spread of the Gospel. *n.*

e van gel ist (i van′jə list), **1** preacher of the Gospel. **2** a traveling preacher who stirs up religious feeling in revival services. **3 Evangelist,** writer of one of the four Gospels; Matthew, Mark, Luke, or John. *n.*

e van gel is tic (i van′jə lis′tik), of or by evangelists. *adj.*

Evans (ev′ənz), **Mary Ann,** the real name of **George Eliot.** *n.*

e vap o rate (i vap′ə rāt′), **1** change from a liquid into a vapor: *Boiling water evaporates rapidly. Heat evaporates water.* **2** remove water or other liquid from: *Heat is used to evaporate milk.* **3** vanish; disappear: *My good resolutions evaporated soon after New Year. v.,* **e vap o rat ed, e vap o rat ing.**

evaporated milk, a thick, unsweetened, canned milk, prepared by evaporating some of the water from ordinary milk.

e vap o ra tion (i vap′ə rā′shən), act or process of evaporating: *Wet clothes on a line become dry by evaporation of the water in them. n.*

e vap o ra tor (i vap′ə rā′tər), apparatus for removing water or other liquid from a substance: *an evaporator for drying fruits. n.*

e va sion (i vā′zhən), **1** a getting away from something by trickery; avoiding by cleverness: *I had no excuse for the evasion of my responsibilities.* **2** an attempt to escape an argument, a charge, a question, etc.: *The prisoner's evasions of the lawyer's questions convinced the jury that he was guilty. n.*

e va sive (i vā′siv), tending or trying to evade: *"I really haven't given it much thought" is an evasive answer. adj.* —**e va′sive ly,** *adv.* —**e va′sive ness,** *n.*

eve (ēv), **1** the evening or day before a holiday or some other special day: *New Year's Eve, Christmas Eve, the eve of my birthday.* **2** time just before something happens: *The campaign ended on the eve of the election.* **3** OLD USE. evening. *n.*

Eve (ēv), (in the Bible) the first woman, the wife of Adam. *n.*

e ven[1] (ē′vən), **1** having the same height everywhere; level; flat; smooth: *The countryside is even, with no hills or slopes.* **2** at the same level: *The snow was even with the windowsill.* **3** keeping about the same; uniform: *an even temper, an even motion, an even temperature.* **4** no more or less than; equal: *They divided the money in even shares.* **5** make level or equal; make even: *I evened the edges by trimming them.* **6** able to be divided by 2 without a remainder: *2, 4, 6, 8, and 10 are even numbers.* **7** neither more nor less; exact: *Twelve apples make an even dozen.* **8** just: *She left even as you came.* **9** indeed: *I am ready, even eager, to go.* **10** though one would not expect it; as one would not expect: *Even young children can operate this machine. Even the smallest noise disturbs them.* **11** still; yet: *You can read even better if you try.* 1-4,6,7 *adj.*, 5 *v.*, 8-11 *adv.* —**e′ven er**, *n.* —**e′ven ly**, *adv.* —**e′ven ness**, *n.*
break even, INFORMAL. have equal gains and losses.
even if, in spite of the fact that; although: *I will come, even if it rains.*
even though, although.
get even, have revenge.

e ven[2] (ē′vən), OLD USE. evening. *n.*

e ven hand ed (ē′vən han′did), impartial; fair. *adj.* —**e′ven hand′ed ly**, *adv.* —**e′ven hand′ed ness**, *n.*

eve ning (ēv′ning), the last part of day and early part of night; time between sunset and bedtime. *n.*

evening star, a bright planet seen in the western sky after sunset. Venus is often the evening star.

e ven song (ē′vən sông′), vespers. *n.*

e vent (i vent′), **1** a happening, especially an important happening: *Newspapers report all new and unexpected events. The discovery of the polio vaccine was a great event in medicine.* **2** one item in a program of sports: *The 100-yard dash was the last event. n.* [*Event* comes from Latin *eventus*, meaning "event, consequence," and can be traced back to *ex-*, meaning "out," and *venire*, meaning "to come." See **Word Family**.]
in any event, in any case; whatever happens: *In any event, you can always count on my friendship.*
in the event of, if there should be; in case of; if there is: *In the event of rain, the party will be held indoors.*

event

Below are words related to *event*. They can all be traced back to the Latin word *venire* (we nē′re), meaning "to come."

advent	convention	misadventure
adventure	conventional	prevent
avenue	covenant	revenue
convene	intervene	souvenir
convenient	invent	supervene
convent	inventory	venture

e vent ful (i vent′fəl), **1** full of events; having many unusual events: *The class spent an eventful day touring the new zoo.* **2** having important results; important: *The discovery of atomic energy began an eventful period in history. adj.* —**e vent′ful ly**, *adv.* —**e vent′ful ness**, *n.*

a hat	i it	oi oil	ch child	a in about
ā age	ī ice	ou out	ng long	e in taken
ä far	o hot	u cup	sh she	ə = { i in pencil
e let	ō open	u̇ put	th thin	o in lemon
ē equal	ô order	ü rule	ŦH then	u in circus
ėr term			zh measure	

e ven tide (ē′vən tīd′), OLD USE. evening. *n.*

e ven tu al (i ven′chü əl), coming in the end; final: *After several failures, their eventual success surprised us. adj.*

e ven tu al i ty (i ven′chü al′ə tē), a possible occurrence or condition; possibility: *They were prepared for the eventuality of a drought. n., pl.* **e ven tu al i ties.**

e ven tu al ly (i ven′chü ə lē), in the end; finally: *We waited more than an hour for them but eventually we had to leave without them. adv.*

ev er (ev′ər), **1** at any time: *Is she ever at home?* **2** at all times; always: *She is ever ready to accept a new challenge.* **3** by any chance; in any case; at all: *What did you ever do to make him so angry? adv.*
ever so, INFORMAL. very: *The ocean is ever so deep.*

Ev er est (ev′ər ist), **Mount**, mountain in the Himalayas between Tibet and Nepal, 29,028 feet (8853 meters) high. It is the highest mountain in the world. *n.*

everglade
(def. 1)

ev er glade (ev′ər glād), **1** a large tract of low, wet ground partly covered with tall grass; large swamp or marsh. **2** the Everglades, a swampy region in S Florida. *n.*

ev er green (ev′ər grēn′), **1** having green leaves or needles all year round. **2** an evergreen plant. Pine, spruce, cedar, ivy, box, rhododendrons, etc., are evergreens. **3 evergreens**, *pl.* evergreen twigs or branches used for decoration, especially at Christmas. 1 *adj.*, 2,3 *n.*

ev er last ing (ev′ər las′ting), **1** lasting forever; never stopping: *the everlasting beauty of nature.* **2** lasting a long time: *We wished them everlasting happiness.* **3** lasting too long; tiresome: *Their everlasting complaints annoyed me.* **4** the Everlasting, God. 1-3 *adj.*, 4 *n.* —**ev′er last′ing ly**, *adv.* —**ev′er last′ing ness**, *n.*

ev er more (ev′ər môr′), always; forever. *adv.*
for evermore, for all time; for eternity; forever.

ev er y (ev′rē), **1** each one of the entire number of persons or things: *Read every word on the page. Every student must have a book.* **2** all possible: *We showed them every consideration. adj.*
every now and then, from time to time: *Every now and then we have a frost that ruins the crop.*
every other, every second: *Every other day it's my turn to do the dishes.*
every which way, INFORMAL. in all directions.

ev er y bod y (ev′rə bud′ē *or* ev′rē bod′ē), every person; everyone: *Everybody likes the new principal. pron.*

eve ry day (ev′rē dā′), **1** of every day; daily: *Accidents are everyday occurrences.* **2** for every ordinary day; not for

Sundays or holidays: *She wears everyday clothes to work.*
3 not exciting; usual: *He had only an everyday story to tell.*
adj.

eve ry one (ev′rē wun *or* ev′rē wən), each one; everybody: *Everyone in the class is here. pron.*

eve ry thing (ev′rē thing), **1** every thing; all things: *She did everything she could to help her friend.* **2** something extremely important; very important thing: *This news means everything to us.* 1 *pron.,* 2 *n.*

eve ry where (ev′rē hwer *or* ev′rē hwar), in every place; in all places: *A smile is understood everywhere. We looked everywhere for our lost dog. adv.*

e vict (i vikt′), expel by law from land, a building, etc.; eject: *They were evicted for not paying their rent. v.*

e vic tion (i vik′shən), an evicting or a being evicted; expulsion: *They were threatened with eviction if they didn't pay their rent. n.*

ev i dence (ev′ə dəns), **1** anything that shows what is true and what is not; facts; proof: *The evidence showed that he had not been near the place.* **2** facts established and accepted in a court of law: *Before deciding the case, the judge and jury heard all the evidence given by both sides.* **3** indication; sign: *A smile gives evidence of pleasure.* **4** show clearly: *Their smiles evidenced their obvious pleasure.* 1-3 *n.,* 4 *v.,* **ev i denced, ev i denc ing.**
in evidence, easily seen or noticed: *The damage caused by the flood was much in evidence.*

ev i dent (ev′ə dənt), easy to see or understand; clear; plain: *It was evident that the shattered vase could never be repaired. adj.*

ev i dent ly (ev′ə dənt lē), plainly; clearly: *If he hasn't arrived yet, he evidently missed his train. adv.*

e vil (ē′vəl), **1** causing harm; bad; wrong; wicked: *an evil life, an evil character, an evil plan.* **2** bad or evil quality; wickedness: *Their thoughts were full of evil.* **3** thing causing harm: *Crime and poverty are some of the evils of society.* 1 *adj.,* 2,3 *n.* —**e′vil ly,** *adv.* —**e′vil ness,** *n.*

e vil do er (ē′vəl dü′ər), person who does evil. *n.*

e vil-mind ed (ē′vəl mīn′did), having an evil mind; wicked; malicious. *adj.* —**e′vil-mind′ed ly,** *adv.* —**e′vil-mind′ed ness,** *n.*

e vince (i vins′), show clearly: *The dog evinced its dislike of strangers by growling. v.,* **e vinced, e vinc ing.**

e vis ce rate (i vis′ə rāt′), remove the internal organs, especially the intestines, from: *The butcher eviscerated a chicken. v.,* **e vis ce rat ed, e vis ce rat ing.** —**e vis′ce ra′tion,** *n.*

e voke (i vōk′), call forth; bring out: *The speaker's witty remarks evoked many smiles from the audience. v.,* **e voked, e vok ing.**

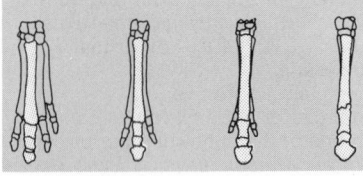

evolution (def. 1)—of the horse's forefoot from four toes to a single toe (hoof). The toe which became the hoof is white.

ev o lu tion (ev′ə lü′shən), **1** a gradual development: *the evolution of transportation from horse and buggy to jet aircraft.* **2** the theory that all living things developed from a few simple forms of life. *n.*

ev o lu tion ar y (ev′ə lü′shə ner′ē), **1** having to do with evolution. **2** in accordance with the theory of evolution. *adj.*

ev o lu tion ist (ev′ə lü′shə nist), person who believes in and supports the theory of evolution. *n.*

e volve (i volv′), develop gradually; unfold: *Buds evolve into flowers. The automobile evolved from the horse and buggy. The girls evolved a plan for earning money during their summer vacation. v.,* **e volved, e volv ing.**

ewe (yü), a female sheep. *n.*

ex-, *prefix.* **1** former; formerly: *Ex-president = former president.* **2** out of; from; out: *Express = press out.* **3** thoroughly: *Exterminate = terminate (finish or destroy) thoroughly.*

Ex., Exodus.

ex act (eg zakt′), **1** without any mistake; correct; accurate; precise: *an exact measurement, the exact amount.* **2** demand and get: *If you do the work, you can exact payment for it.* 1 *adj.,* 2 *v.*

ex act ing (eg zak′ting), **1** requiring much; hard to please: *An exacting teacher will not permit careless work.* **2** requiring effort, care, or attention: *Flying an airplane is exacting work. adj.*

ex act i tude (eg zak′tə tüd *or* eg zak′tə tyüd), exactness. *n.*

ex act ly (eg zakt′lē), **1** accurately; precisely. **2** just so; quite right. *adv.*

ex act ness (eg zakt′nis), a being exact: *She recalled the story with exactness, down to every detail. n.*

ex ag ge rate (eg zaj′ə rāt′), **1** make too large; say or think something is greater than it is; go beyond the truth: *The little boy exaggerated when he said there were a million cats in the backyard.* **2** increase or enlarge beyond what is normal: *The artist exaggerated parts of the drawing to make them clearer. v.,* **ex ag ge rat ed, ex ag ge rat ing.**

ex ag ge ra tion (eg zaj′ə rā′shən), **1** an exaggerated statement: *It is an exaggeration to say that you would rather die than touch a snake.* **2** an exaggerating: *His constant exaggeration made people distrust him. n.*

ex alt (eg zôlt′), **1** make high in rank, honor, power, character, or quality: *The queen exalted the commoner to the rank of earl.* **2** fill with pride, joy, or noble feeling: *He was exalted by success.* **3** praise; honor; glorify: *The worshipers exalted their god. v.* —**ex alt′er,** *n.*

ex am (eg zam′), INFORMAL. examination. *n.*

ex am i na tion (eg zam′ə nā′shən), **1** an examining or a being examined: *The doctor made a thorough examination of my eyes.* **2** test of knowledge or qualifications; list of questions; test: *The teacher gave us an examination in arithmetic. n.*

ex am ine (eg zam′ən), **1** look at closely and carefully: *The doctor examined the wound.* **2** test the knowledge or qualifications of; ask questions of; test: *The lawyer examined the witness. v.,* **ex am ined, ex am in ing.**

ex am in er (eg zam′ə nər), person who examines: *a medical examiner. n.*

ex am ple (eg zam′pəl), **1** one thing taken to show what others are like; sample: *New York is an example of a busy city.* **2** person or thing to be imitated; model; pattern: *to set a good example. Children often follow the example set by their parents.* **3** problem in arithmetic, etc.: *She wrote the example on the blackboard.* **4** warning to others: *The principal made an example of the students who cheated by suspending them for a week. n.*
for example, as an example; for instance: *Many flowers are fragrant: lilacs, for example.*

ex as pe rate (eg zas′pə rāt′), irritate very much; annoy greatly; make angry: *Her continual lateness exasperated me. v.,* **ex as pe rat ed, ex as pe rat ing.**

ex as pe ra tion (eg zas′pə rā′shən), extreme annoyance; irritation; anger. *n.*

Ex cal i bur (ek skal′ə bər), the magic sword of King Arthur. *n.*

ex ca vate (ek′skə vāt), **1** make hollow; hollow out: *The tunnel was made by excavating the side of a mountain.* **2** make by digging; dig: *The workmen excavated a tunnel for the new subway.* **3** dig out; scoop out: *Power shovels excavated the dirt and loaded it into trucks.* **4** uncover by digging: *They excavated an ancient buried city.* *v.,* **ex ca vat ed, ex ca vat ing.**

ex ca va tion (ek′skə vā′shən), **1** an excavating; a digging out: *The excavation for the basement of our new house took three days.* **2** hole made by digging: *The excavation for the new building was fifty feet across.* *n.*

ex ca va tor (ek′skə vā′tər), person or thing that excavates. A power shovel is an excavator. *n.*

ex ceed (ek sēd′), **1** be more or greater than: *The sum of 5 and 7 exceeds 10. Lifting that heavy trunk exceeds my strength.* **2** do more than; go beyond: *Drivers are not supposed to exceed the speed limit.* *v.*

ex ceed ing (ek sē′ding), **1** very great; unusual: *She is a girl of exceeding talent.* **2** exceedingly: *He has done exceeding well.* **1** *adj.,* **2** *adv.*

ex ceed ing ly (ek sē′ding lē), very greatly; to an unusual degree; very: *Yesterday was an exceedingly hot day.* *adv.*

ex cel (ek sel′), **1** be better than; do better than: *He excelled his class in spelling.* **2** be better than others; do better than others: *She excels in arithmetic.* *v.,* **ex celled, ex cel ling.**

ex cel lence (ek′sə ləns), unusually good quality; being better than others; superiority: *His teacher praised him for the excellence of his report.* *n.*

Ex cel len cy (ek′sə lən sē), title of honor used in speaking to or of a prime minister, governor, bishop, ambassador, or other high official: *Your Excellency, His Excellency, the British Ambassador.* *n., pl.* **Ex cel len cies.**

ex cel lent (ek′sə lənt), of unusually good quality; better than others; superior: *Excellent work deserves high praise.* *adj.* —**ex′cel lent ly,** *adv.*

ex cept (ek sept′), **1** leaving out; other than: *He works every day except Sunday.* **2** leave out; exclude: *Those who passed the first test were excepted from the second.* **3** only; but: *I would have had a perfect score except I missed the last question.* **1** *prep.,* **2** *v.,* **3** *conj.*

ex cept ing (ek sep′ting), leaving out; other than; except; but: *School is open every day excepting Saturday and Sunday.* *prep.*

ex cep tion (ek sep′shən), **1** a leaving out; excepting: *I like all my studies, with the exception of arithmetic.* **2** person or thing left out: *She praised the pictures, with two exceptions.* **3** thing that is different from the rule: *He comes on time every day; today is an exception.* **4** objection: *a statement liable to exception.* *n.*

take exception, 1 object: *Several teachers and students took exception to the plan of having classes on Saturdays.* **2** be offended: *I took exception to their rude remarks.*

ex cep tion a ble (ek sep′shə nə bəl), liable to exception; objectionable. *adj.* —**ex cep′tion a bly,** *adv.*

ex cep tion al (ek sep′shə nəl), **1** out of the ordinary; unusual: *This warm weather is exceptional for January. She is an exceptional student.* **2** in need of special training or handling, especially because of below-average mental or physical capabilities: *exceptional children.* *adj.* —**ex cep′tion al ly,** *adv.*

ex cerpt (ek′sėrpt′ *for 1;* ek sėrpt′ *for 2*), **1** passage taken out of a book, etc.; quotation; extract: *The English teacher read the class excerpts from several plays.* **2** take out (passages) from a book, etc.; quote: *In his report on Eleanor Roosevelt, he included some passages excerpted from her speeches.* **1** *n.,* **2** *v.*

ex cess (ek ses′ *for 1,2;* ek′ses *or* ek ses′ *for 3*), **1** part that is too much; more than enough: *The tailor trimmed off the excess from the cloth being measured for the two sleeves.* **2** amount by which one thing is greater than another: *The excess of five quarts over a gallon is one quart.* **3** beyond the usual amount; extra: *Passengers must pay for excess baggage taken on an airplane.* **1,2** *n., pl.* **ex cess es; 3** *adj.*

in excess of, more than: *a gift in excess of $5000.*

to excess, too much: *He eats candy to excess.*

ex ces sive (ek ses′iv), too much; too great; going beyond what is necessary or right: *Some teenagers spend an excessive amount of time on the phone.* *adj.* —**ex ces′sive ly,** *adv.* —**ex ces′sive ness,** *n.*

ex change (eks chānj′), **1** give for something else; change: *He exchanged the tight coat for one that was a size larger.* **2** give and take (things of the same kind): *We exchanged letters. They exchanged blows.* **3** an exchanging; giving and taking: *During the truce there was an exchange of prisoners.* **4** place where people trade. Stocks are bought, sold, and traded in a stock exchange. **5** a central station or office. A telephone exchange handles telephone calls. **1,2** *v.,* **ex changed, ex chang ing; 3-5** *n.* —**ex change′a ble,** *adj.*

ex cheq uer (eks chek′ər), **1** treasury, especially of a state or nation. **2 Exchequer,** department of the British government in charge of its finances and the public revenues. **3** INFORMAL. finances; funds. *n.*

ex cise¹ (ek′sīz *or* ek′sīs), tax on the manufacture, sale, or use of certain articles made, sold, or used within a country: *The government has placed an excise on tobacco.* *n.*

ex cise² (ek sīz′), cut out; remove: *The doctor excised some scar tissue after the burn was healed.* *v.,* **ex cised, ex cis ing.**

ex ci sion (ek sizh′ən), a cutting out; removal. *n.*

ex cit a bil i ty (ek sī′tə bil′ə tē), quality of being excitable. *n.*

ex cit a ble (ek sī′tə bəl), easily excited. *adj.* —**ex cit′a ble ness,** *n.* —**ex cit′a bly,** *adv.*

ex cite (ek sīt′), **1** stir up the feelings of: *News of the wedding excited the entire family.* **2** arouse: *Plans for a field trip excited the students' interest.* **3** stir to action: *Do not excite the dog; keep away from it.* *v.,* **ex cit ed, ex cit ing.**

ex cit ed (ek sī′tid), stirred up; aroused: *The excited mob rushed into the mayor's office.* *adj.* —**ex cit′ed ly,** *adv.*

ex cite ment (ek sīt′mənt), **1** an excited condition: *Birth of twins caused great excitement in the family.* **2** thing that excites: *We enjoyed the excitement of camping out in the high mountains.* *n.*

ex cit ing (ek sī′ting), causing excitement; arousing; stirring: *We read an exciting story about pirates and buried treasure.* *adj.* —**ex cit′ing ly,** *adv.*

ex claim (ek sklām′), speak suddenly in surprise or strong feeling; cry out: *"Here you are at last!" exclaimed her mother.* *v.* —**ex claim′er,** *n.*

ex cla ma tion (ek′sklə mā′shən), something said suddenly as the result of surprise or strong feeling: *Oh!, Hurrah!, Well!,* and *Look!* are common exclamations. *n.*

exclamation mark or **exclamation point,** mark (!) of punctuation used after a word, phrase, or sentence to show that it was exclaimed. EXAMPLE: *Hurrah! It's snowing.*

ex clam a to ry (ek sklam′ə tôr′ē), using, containing, or expressing exclamation. *adj.*

---

a hat	i it	oi oil	ch child	a in about
ā age	ī ice	ou out	ng long	e in taken
ä far	o hot	u cup	sh she	ə = i in pencil
e let	ō open	u̇ put	th thin	o in lemon
ē equal	ô order	ü rule	ᴛʜ then	u in circus
ėr term			zh measure	

ex clude (ek sklüd′), shut out; keep out: *The club's rules exclude from membership anyone who lives out of town.* v., **ex clud ed, ex clud ing.** —**ex clud′a ble,** adj. —**exclud′er,** n.

ex clu sion (ek sklü′zhən), **1** act of excluding: *We voted for the exclusion of large trucks from residential streets.* **2** condition of being excluded: *Her exclusion from the meeting hurt her feelings.* n.

ex clu sive (ek sklü′siv or ek sklü′ziv), **1** not divided or shared with others; single; sole: *exclusive rights to sell a product.* **2** limited to a single object: *exclusive attention to instructions.* **3** very particular about choosing friends, members, etc.: *It is hard to get admitted to an exclusive club.* **4** each shutting out the other. "Tree" and "animal" are exclusive terms; a thing cannot be both a tree and an animal. adj. —**ex clu′sive ly,** adv. —**ex clu′siveness,** n.

exclusive of, excluding; leaving out; not counting: *There are 26 days in that month, exclusive of Sundays.*

ex com mu ni cate (ek′skə myü′nə kāt), cut off from membership in the church; shut out from communion with the church. v., **ex com mu ni cat ed, ex com mu nicat ing.** —**ex′com mu′ni ca′tor,** n.

ex com mu ni ca tion (ek′skə myü′nə kā′shən), **1** a cutting off from membership in the church and from any part in its ceremonies. **2** an official statement announcing this. n.

ex cre ment (ek′skrə mənt), waste matter that is discharged from the body, especially from the intestines. n.

ex crete (ek skrēt′), discharge (waste matter) from the body; separate (waste matter) from the blood or tissues: *The sweat glands excrete sweat.* v., **ex cret ed, ex cret ing.**

ex cre tion (ek skrē′shən), **1** discharge of waste matter from the body; separation of waste matter from the blood or tissues. **2** the waste matter that is separated and discharged: *Sweat is an excretion.* n.

ex cre to ry (ek′skrə tôr′ē), excreting; having the task of excreting: *The kidneys are excretory organs.* adj.

ex cru ci at ing (ek skrü′shē ā′ting), causing great suffering; very painful. adj. —**ex cru′ci at′ing ly,** adv.

ex cur sion (ek skėr′zhən), **1** a short trip taken for interest or pleasure, often by a number of people together: *Our club went on an excursion to the mountains.* **2** trip on a train, ship, or aircraft, at fares lower than those usually charged. n.

ex cus a ble (ek skyü′zə bəl), able to be excused; deserving pardon. adj.

ex cuse (ek skyüz′ for 1,3-5; ek skyüs′ for 2,6), **1** offer an apology for; try to remove the blame of: *He excused his being upset yesterday on a headache from having too little sleep.* **2** reason, real or pretended, that is given; explanation: *Sickness was his excuse for being absent from school.* **3** be a reason or explanation for: *Sickness excuses absence from school.* **4** pardon; forgive: *Excuse me, I have to go now.* **5** free from duty; let off: *Those who passed the first test will be excused from the second one.* **6** act of excusing. 1,3-5 v., **ex cused, ex cus ing;** 2,6 n. —**ex cus′er,** n.

excuse oneself, 1 ask to be pardoned: *She excused herself for bumping into me by saying that she was in a hurry.* **2** ask permission to leave: *I excused myself from the table.*

ex e cute (ek′sə kyüt), **1** carry out; do: *The workers executed the foreman's orders and finished the job quickly.* **2** put into effect; enforce: *Congress makes the laws; the President executes them.* **3** put to death according to law: *The murderer was executed.* **4** make according to a plan or design: *The artist took several months to execute the statue.* **5** make (a deed, lease, contract, will, etc.) legal by signing, sealing, etc. v., **ex e cut ed, ex e cut ing.** —**ex′ecut′er,** n.

ex e cu tion (ek′sə kyü′shən), **1** a carrying out; doing:

She was prompt in the execution of her duties. **2** a putting into effect; enforcing: *the execution of a law.* **3** way of carrying out or doing; skill. **4** a putting to death according to law. **5** a making according to a plan or design. **6** a making legal by signing, sealing, etc.: *the execution of a deed or contract.* n.

ex e cu tion er (ek′sə kyü′shə nər), person who puts criminals to death according to law. n.

ex ec u tive (eg zek′yə tiv), **1** having to do with carrying out or managing affairs: *A principal has an executive position.* **2** person who carries out or manages affairs: *The president of a business firm is an executive.* **3** having the duty and power of putting the laws into effect: *The President of the United States is the head of the executive branch of the government.* **4** person, group, or branch of government that has the duty and power of putting the laws into effect: *The highest executive of a state is the governor.* 1,3 adj., 2,4 n. —**ex ec′u tive ly,** adv.

ex ec u tor (eg zek′yə tər), person named in a will to carry out the wishes of the person making the will. n.

ex em plar y (eg zem′plər ē), **1** worth imitating: *exemplary conduct.* **2** serving as a warning to others: *exemplary punishment.* **3** serving as an example; typical: *an exemplary incident.* adj.

ex em pli fy (eg zem′plə fī), show by example; be an example of: *Ballet dancers exemplify grace and skill.* v., **ex em pli fied, ex em pli fy ing.**

ex empt (eg zempt′), **1** make free (from a duty, obligation, rule, etc.); release: *Students who get high marks all year are exempted from final examinations.* **2** freed from a duty, obligation, rule, etc.; released: *School property is exempt from all taxes.* 1 v., 2 adj.

ex emp tion (eg zemp′shən), **1** act of exempting. **2** freedom from a duty, obligation, rule, etc.; release: *exemption from jury duty.* n.

ex er cise (ek′sər sīz), **1** active use; practice: *Exercise of the body is good for the health.* **2** make active use of: *When you vote you exercise your right as a citizen. Exercise caution in crossing streets.* **3** something that gives practice and training or causes improvement: *He performs physical exercises each day to strengthen his body. Study the lesson, and then do the exercises at the end.* **4** give exercise to; train: *She exercises her horse after school every day. Studying exercises the mind.* **5** take exercise; go through exercises: *I exercise for ten minutes each morning.* **6** carry out in action; perform: *The mayor exercises the duties and powers of his office.* **7** Often, **exercises,** pl. ceremony: *She gave the farewell address at the graduation exercises.* 1,3,7 n., 2,4-6 v., **ex er cised, ex er cis ing.** —**ex′er cis′a ble,** adj. —**ex′er cis′er,** n.

ex ert (eg zėrt′), put into use; use fully; use: *A gymnast exerts both strength and skill. A ruler exerts authority.* v.

exert oneself, make an effort; try hard; strive: *You must exert yourself to make up the work you missed.*

ex er tion (eg zėr′shən), **1** effort: *Our exertions kept the fire from spreading.* **2** a putting into action; active use; use: *exertion of the mind, exertion of authority.* n.

ex ha la tion (eks′hə lā′shən), **1** an exhaling. **2** something exhaled; air, vapor, smoke, odor, etc. n.

ex hale (eks hāl′), **1** breathe out: *We exhale air from our lungs.* **2** give off (air, vapor, smoke, odor, etc.). v., **exhaled, ex hal ing.**

ex haust (eg zôst′), **1** empty completely: *exhaust an oil well.* **2** use up: *exhaust the supply of water, exhaust one's strength.* **3** tire very much: *The long, hard climb up the hill exhausted us.* **4** find out or say everything important about: *Her detailed lecture on ways to earn money just about exhausted the subject.* **5** the escape of used steam, spent gases, etc., from an engine. **6** pipe or other means for used steam, spent gases, etc., to escape from an engine. **7** the used steam, spent gases, etc., that escape: *The exhaust from an automobile engine is poisonous.* 1-4 *v.,* 5-7 *n.*

ex haust ed (eg zô′stid), **1** used up: *Our patience was exhausted by everyone's trying to talk at once.* **2** worn out; very tired: *The exhausted hikers did not have the energy to continue the long walk home.* *adj.*

ex haus tion (eg zôs′chən), **1** act of exhausting. **2** condition of being exhausted. **3** extreme fatigue. *n.*

ex haus tive (eg zô′stiv), tending to exhaust or use up (resources, strength, or a subject); thorough: *The students were given an exhaustive examination covering the major points of the year's work.* *adj.* **—ex haus′tive ly,** *adv.* **—ex haus′tive ness,** *n.*

ex hib it (eg zib′it), **1** show; display: *Both of their children exhibit a talent for music.* **2** show publicly; put on display: *She hopes to exhibit her paintings in New York.* **3** an exhibiting; public showing: *The village art exhibit drew 10,000 visitors.* **4** thing or things shown publicly. **5** thing shown in court as evidence: *The defendant's glove was labeled Exhibit A.* 1,2 *v.,* 3-5 *n.*

ex hib it er (eg zib′ə tər), exhibitor. *n.*

ex hi bi tion (ek′sə bish′ən), **1** a showing; display: *Pushing and shoving in line is an exhibition of bad manners.* **2** a public show: *The art school holds an exhibition every year.* **3** thing or things shown publicly; exhibit. *n.*

ex hi bi tion ist (ek′sə bish′ə nist), person who tends to show off or behave in an unusual way in order to attract attention. *n.*

ex hib i tor (eg zib′ə tər), person, company, or group that exhibits. *n.*

ex hil a rate (eg zil′ə rāt′), make merry; make lively; cheer: *Seeing friends and exchanging gifts at the holiday season exhilarates us all.* *v.,* **ex hil a rat ed, ex hil a rat ing.**

ex hil a ra tion (eg zil′ə rā′shən), high spirits; lively joy. *n.*

ex hort (eg zôrt′), urge strongly; advise or warn earnestly: *The preacher exhorted the congregation to love one another.* *v.* **—ex hort′er,** *n.*

ex hor ta tion (eg′zôr tā′shən *or* ek′sôr tā′shən), **1** strong urging; earnest advice or warning. **2** speech, sermon, etc., that exhorts. *n.*

ex hume (eks hyüm′), dig (a dead body) out of a grave or the ground. *v.,* **ex humed, ex hum ing.**

WORD HISTORY

exhume

Exhume is from a medieval Latin word *exhumare,* which comes from Latin *ex-,* meaning "out of," and *humus,* meaning "ground."

ex i gen cy (ek′sə jən sē), **1** situation demanding prompt action or attention; emergency: *The fire department measured up to the exigency of two fires within an hour, and put them both out.* **2** Often, **exigencies,** *pl.* an urgent need; demand for prompt action or attention: *The exigencies of business kept him from taking a vacation.* *n., pl.* **ex i gen cies.**

ex i gent (ek′sə jənt), demanding prompt action or attention; urgent: *The exigent pangs of hunger sent the bear on a search for food.* *adj.* **—ex′i gent ly,** *adv.*

ex ile (eg′zīl *or* ek′sīl), **1** force to leave one's country or home, often by law as a punishment; banish: *Napoleon*

a hat	**i** it	**oi** oil	**ch** child	a in about
ā age	**ī** ice	**ou** out	**ng** long	e in taken
ä far	**o** hot	**u** cup	**sh** she	ə = i in pencil
e let	**ō** open	**u̇** put	**th** thin	o in lemon
ē equal	**ô** order	**ü** rule	**ŦH** then	u in circus
ėr term			**zh** measure	

exhibit (def. 4) a museum exhibit of the first giraffes brought to England

was exiled to Elba. **2** person who is exiled: *She has been an exile for ten years.* **3** condition of being exiled; banishment: *be sent into exile for life.* 1 *v.,* **ex iled, ex il ing;** 2,3 *n.*

ex ist (eg zist′), **1** have being; be: *Travel in space has existed for only a few years.* **2** be real: *She believes that ghosts exist.* **3** have life; live: *A person cannot exist without air.* **4** be found; occur: *Cases exist of persons who live completely alone.* *v.*

ex ist ence (eg zis′təns), **1** being: *When we are born, we come into existence.* **2** a being real: *Most people do not now believe in the existence of ghosts.* **3** life: *Drivers of racing cars lead a dangerous existence.* **4** occurrence: *The newspapers report the existence of many new cases of flu in the city.* *n.*

ex ist ent (eg zis′tənt), **1** existing. **2** now existing; of the present time. *adj.*

ex it (eg′zit *or* ek′sit), **1** way out: *The theater had six exits.* **2** a going out; departure: *When the cat came in, the mice made a hasty exit.* **3** act of leaving the stage: *a graceful exit. n.* [*Exit* is from Latin *exit,* meaning "he goes out," which comes from *ex-,* meaning "out," and *ire,* meaning "to go."]

ex o dus (ek′sə dəs), **1** a going out; departure: *Every June there is an exodus of students from the colleges.* **2 the Exodus,** the departure of the Israelites from Egypt under Moses. **3 Exodus,** the second book of the Old Testament, containing an account of this departure. *n., pl.* **ex o dus es** for 1.

ex of fi ci o (eks ə fish′ē ō), because of one's office: *The Vice-President is, ex officio, the presiding officer of the Senate.*

ex on e rate (eg zon′ə rāt′), free from blame: *Witnesses to the accident completely exonerated the truck driver. v.,* **ex on e rat ed, ex on e rat ing.**

ex on e ra tion (eg zon′ə rā′shən), an exonerating or a being exonerated. *n.*

ex or bi tant (eg zôr′bə tənt), much too high; unreasonably excessive: *One dollar is an exorbitant price for a pack of bubble gum. adj.* **—ex or′bi tant ly,** *adv.*

ex or cise (ek′sôr sīz), **1** drive out (an evil spirit) by prayers, ceremonies, etc. **2** free (a person or place) from an evil spirit. *v.,* **ex or cised, ex or cis ing.** **—ex′or cis′er,** *n.*

ex or cism (ek′sôr siz′əm), **1** an exorcising. **2** the prayers, ceremonies, etc., used in exorcising. *n.*

ex or cist (ek′sôr sist), a person who exorcises evil spirits. *n.*

ex o skel e ton (ek′sō skel′ə tən), any hard, external covering which protects or supports an animal body. A turtle shell is an exoskeleton. *n.*

ex o sphere (ek′sō sfir), the outermost region of the atmosphere, beginning about 300 miles (483 kilometers) above the earth's surface. *n.*

ex ot ic (eg zot′ik), 1 foreign; strange; not native: *We saw many exotic plants at the flower show.* 2 anything exotic. 1 *adj.,* 2 *n.* —**ex ot′i cal ly,** *adv.*

ex pand (ek spand′), 1 make or grow larger; increase in size; enlarge: *The balloon expanded as it was filled with air. Our country was expanded by the addition of new territory. Heat expanded the metal.* 2 spread out; open out; unfold: *A bird expands its wings before flying. As the plant grew, its leaves and flowers gradually expanded.* 3 express in fuller form or greater detail: *The writer expanded one sentence into a paragraph. v.* —**ex pand′er,** *n.*

ex pand a ble (ek span′də bəl), able to be expanded. *adj.*

ex panse (ek spans′), open or unbroken stretch; wide, spreading surface: *The Pacific Ocean is a vast expanse of water. n.*

ex pan sion (ek span′shən), 1 an expanding: *Heat causes the expansion of gas.* 2 a being expanded; increase in size, volume, etc.: *The expansion of the factory made room for more machines.* 3 an expanded part or form: *That book is an expansion of a magazine article. n.*

ex pan sive (ek span′siv), 1 capable of expanding; tending to expand: *expansive gases.* 2 wide; spreading: *an expansive lake.* 3 taking in much or many things; broad; extensive: *an expansive view of history.* 4 showing one's feelings freely and openly; unrestrained; demonstrative: *Her expansive personality made it easy for her to make friends. adj.* —**ex pan′sive ly,** *adv.* —**ex pan′sive ness,** *n.*

ex pa ti ate (ek spā′shē āt), write or talk much: *He expatiated on the thrills of his trip to Hawaii. v.,* **ex pa ti at ed, ex pa ti at ing.** —**ex pa′ti a′tion,** *n.* —**ex pa′ti a′tor,** *n.*

ex pa tri ate (ek spā′trē āt *for 1,2;* ek spā′trē it *or* ek spā′trē āt *for 3*), 1 force to leave one's country; banish. 2 withdraw from one's country or citizenship: *Some Americans expatriate themselves and live in Europe.* 3 an expatriated person. 1,2 *v.,* **ex pa tri at ed, ex pa tri at ing;** 3 *n.* [*Expatriate* can be traced back to Latin *ex-,* meaning "out of," and *patria,* meaning "native land."]

ex pa tri a tion (ek spā′trē ā′shən), 1 exile. 2 withdrawal from one's country or citizenship. *n.*

ex pect (ek spekt′), 1 think something will probably come or happen; look forward to: *I expect to take a vacation in May.* 2 count on as necessary or right: *I expect you to keep your promise.* 3 INFORMAL. think; suppose; guess: *I expect you're right about that. v.*

ex pect an cy (ek spek′tən sē), expectation. *n., pl.* **ex pect an cies.**

ex pect ant (ek spek′tənt), thinking something will come or happen; looking for; expecting: *She opened her package with an expectant smile. adj.* —**ex pect′ant ly,** *adv.*

ex pec ta tion (ek′spek tā′shən), 1 an expecting or a being expected; anticipation: *the expectation of a good harvest.* 2 something expected. 3 good reason for expecting something; prospect: *They have expectations of money from a rich aunt. n.*

ex pec to rate (ek spek′tə rāt′), cough up and spit out (phlegm, etc.); spit. *v.,* **ex pec to rat ed, ex pec to rat ing.**

ex pe di ence (ek spē′dē əns), expediency. *n.*

ex pe di en cy (ek spē′dē ən sē), 1 a helping to bring about a desired result; desirability under the circumstances: *I enjoy traveling by train, but when I haven't much*

time *I prefer the expediency of air travel.* 2 personal advantage; self-interest: *The salesclerk was influenced more by the expediency of making a sale than by the needs of the buyer. n., pl.* **ex pe di en cies.**

ex pe di ent (ek spē′dē ənt), 1 helping to bring about a desired result; desirable under the circumstances: *It is expedient to be friendly and pleasant if you want to have friends.* 2 means of bringing about a desired result: *When the truth wouldn't convince them I used the expedient of telling a believable lie.* 3 giving or seeking personal advantage; based on self-interest: *No honest judge would make a decision that was expedient rather than fair and just.* 1,3 *adj.,* 2 *n.* —**ex pe′di ent ly,** *adv.*

ex pe dite (ek′spə dīt), make easy and quick; speed up: *Airplanes expedite travel. The telephone expedites business. v.,* **ex pe dit ed, ex pe dit ing.**

WORD HISTORY

expedite

Expedite is from Latin *expeditum,* meaning "freed from entanglement," which comes from *ex-,* meaning "out," and *pedem,* meaning "foot." The Latin word was originally used of freeing the feet from a trap or chains.

ex pe di tion (ek′spə dish′ən), 1 journey for some special purpose, such as exploration, scientific study, or for military purposes. 2 the people, ships, etc., making such a journey. 3 quickness; speed: *He completed his work with expedition. n.*

expedition (def. 2) The **expedition** climbed the mountain peak.

ex pe di tion ar y (ek′spə dish′ə ner′ē), of or making up an expedition, especially for military purposes: *an expeditionary force. adj.*

ex pe di tious (ek′spə dish′əs), efficient and prompt; quick; speedy: *an expeditious method of packing. adj.*

ex pel (ek spel′), 1 drive out with much force; force out; eject: *When we exhale we expel air from our lungs.* 2 put (a person) out; dismiss permanently: *A student caught cheating may be expelled from school. v.,* **ex pelled, ex pelling.** —**ex pel′la ble,** *adj.*

ex pend (ek spend′), use up; spend: *He expended thought, work, and money on his project. v.*

ex pend a ble (ek spen′də bəl), able to be expended or used up. *adj.*

ex pend i ture (ek spen′də chùr *or* ek spen′də chər), 1 a using up; a spending: *Building a sailboat requires the expenditure of much money, time, and effort.* 2 amount of money, etc., spent; expense: *Her expenditures for Christmas presents were $2 and fourteen hours of work. n.*

ex pense (ek spens'), **1** amount of money, etc., spent; cost; charge: *The expense of the trip was slight. He traveled at his uncle's expense.* **2** an expending; a paying out of money; outlay: *Supporting a child at college puts parents to considerable expense.* **3** cause of spending: *Running an automobile is an expense.* **4 expenses,** *pl.* money to repay charges brought about by doing a job: *In addition to his salary, the traveling salesman received expenses.* **5** loss; sacrifice: *The town was captured at great expense to the victors. n.*

ex pen sive (ek spen'siv), costly; high-priced: *She has an expensive automobile. adj.* **—ex pen'sive ly,** *adv.*

ex per i ence (ek spir'ē əns), **1** what happens to a person; what is seen, done, or lived through: *We had several pleasant experiences on our trip. People often learn by experience.* **2** knowledge or skill gained by seeing, doing, or living through things; practice: *Have you had any experience in this kind of work?* **3** have happen to one; feel: *experience great pain.* 1,2 *n.,* 3 *v.,* **ex per i enced, ex per i enc ing.**

ex per i enced (ek spir'ē ənst), **1** having experience; taught by experience: *The job calls for a person experienced in teaching children.* **2** skillful or wise because of experience: *an experienced teacher. adj.*

ex per i ment (ek sper'ə ment *for 1;* ek sper'ə mənt *for 2*), **1** try in order to find out; make trials or tests: *The painter is experimenting with different paints to get the color she wants.* **2** trial or test to find out something: *a chemistry experiment. Scientists test out theories by experiments.* 1 *v.,* 2 *n.* **—ex per'i ment'er,** *n.*

ex per i men tal (ek sper'ə men'tl), **1** based on experiments: *Chemistry is an experimental science.* **2** used for experiments: *A new variety of wheat was developed at the experimental farm.* **3** for testing or trying out: *an experimental engine, a young bird's experimental attempts to fly. adj.* **—ex per'i men'tal ly,** *adv.*

ex per i men ta tion (ek sper'ə men tā'shən), an experimenting: *Cures for diseases are often found by experimentation on animals. n.*

ex pert (ek'spèrt' *for 1;* ek spèrt' *or* ek'spèrt' *for 2,3*), **1** a very skillful person; person who knows a great deal about some special thing: *She is an expert at fishing.* **2** very skillful; knowing a great deal about some special thing: *He is an expert chemist.* **3** requiring or showing special skill: *expert workmanship, expert testimony.* 1 *n.,* 2,3 *adj.* **—ex pert'ly,** *adv.* **—ex pert'ness,** *n.*

ex pert ise (ek'spər tēz'), expert skill. *n.*

ex pi a ble (ek'spē ə bəl), able to be expiated. *adj.*

ex pi ate (ek'spē āt), pay the penalty of; make amends for a wrong, sin, etc.; atone for. *v.,* **ex pi at ed, ex pi at ing. —ex'pi a'tor,** *n.*

ex pi a tion (ek'spē ā'shən), **1** a making amends for a wrong, sin, etc.; atonement. **2** means of atonement; amends. *n.*

ex pi ra tion (ek'spə rā'shən), **1** a coming to an end: *We shall move at the expiration of our lease.* **2** a breathing out; exhalation: *the expiration of air from the lungs. n.*

ex pire (ek spīr'), **1** come to an end: *You must obtain a new driver's license when the old one expires.* **2** die. **3** breathe out; exhale: *Air is expired from the lungs. v.,* **ex pired, ex pir ing. —ex pir'er,** *n.*

ex plain (ek splān'), **1** make plain or clear; tell the meaning of: *The teacher explained long division to the class. Will you explain this poem to me?* **2** give reasons for; state the cause of; account for: *Can you explain your friend's absence? v.* **—ex plain'er,** *n.*

ex plain a ble (ek splā'nə bəl), able to be explained. *adj.*

ex pla na tion (ek'splə nā'shən), **1** an explaining; clearing up a difficulty or mistake: *I did not understand the teacher's explanation of long division.* **2** something that ex-

a hat	i it	oi oil	ch child	a in about
ā age	ī ice	ou out	ng long	e in taken
ä far	o hot	u cup	sh she	ə = { i in pencil
e let	ō open	u̇ put	th thin	o in lemon
ē equal	ô order	ü rule	₮H then	u in circus
èr term			zh measure	

plains: *This diagram is a good explanation of how an automobile engine works. n.*

ex plan a to ry (ek splan'ə tôr'ē), helping to explain; helping to make clear: *Read the explanatory part of the lesson before you try to do the problem. adj.*

ex ple tive (ek'splə tiv), **1** word or phrase used for filling out a sentence or a line of verse, without adding to the sense. In the sentence "There is a book on the table," *there* is an expletive. **2** exclamation or oath. "Damn" and "My goodness!" are expletives. *n.*

ex pli ca ble (ek splik'ə bəl *or* ek'splə kə bəl), able to be explained. *adj.*

ex pli cate (ek'splə kāt), make clear the meaning of; explain. *v.,* **ex pli cat ed, ex pli cat ing. —ex'pli ca'tor,** *n.*

ex plic it (ek splis'it), clearly expressed; distinctly stated; definite: *She gave such explicit directions that everyone understood them. adj.* **—ex plic'it ly,** *adv.* **—ex plic'it ness,** *n.*

ex plode (ek splōd'), **1** burst with a loud noise; blow up: *The building was destroyed when the defective boiler exploded.* **2** cause to explode: *Some people explode firecrackers on the Fourth of July.* **3** burst forth noisily: *The speaker's remark was so funny the audience exploded with laughter.* **4** cause to be rejected; destroy belief in: *Columbus and other navigators helped to explode the theory that the earth is flat. v.,* **ex plod ed, ex plod ing.**

ex ploit (ek'sploit *for 1;* ek sploit' *for 2,3*), **1** a bold, unusual act; daring deed: *This book tells about the exploits of Robin Hood.* **2** make use of: *A mine is exploited for its minerals.* **3** make unfair or selfish use of: *Nations exploited their colonies, taking as much wealth out of them as they could.* 1 *n.,* 2,3 *v.* **—ex ploit'er,** *n.*

ex ploi ta tion (ek'sploi tā'shən), **1** use: *the exploitation of the ocean as a source for food.* **2** selfish or unfair use: *There are laws against the exploitation of child labor. n.*

ex plo ra tion (ek'splə rā'shən), **1** a traveling in little-known lands or seas for the purpose of discovery. **2** a going over carefully; a looking into closely; examining. *n.*

ex plor a to ry (ek splôr'ə tôr'ē), of exploration. *adj.*

ex plore (ek splôr'), **1** travel over little-known lands or seas for the purpose of discovery: *explore the ocean's depths.* **2** go over carefully; look into closely; examine: *explore a subject, explore a possibility. v.,* **ex plored, ex plor ing.**

ex plor er (ek splôr'ər), person who explores. *n.*

ex plo sion (ek splō'zhən), **1** a bursting with a loud noise; a blowing up: *The explosion of the bomb shook the whole neighborhood.* **2** a loud noise caused by this: *People five miles away heard the explosion.* **3** a noisy bursting forth; outbreak; outburst: *explosions of anger, an explosion of laughter.* **4** a sudden or rapid increase or growth: *The explosion of the world's population has created a shortage of food in many countries. n.*

ex plo sive (ek splō'siv), **1** of or for explosion; tending to explode: *Gunpowder is explosive.* **2** an explosive substance: *Explosives are used in making fireworks.* **3** tending to burst forth noisily: *an explosive temper, explosive laughter.* 1,3 *adj.,* 2 *n.* **—ex plo'sive ly,** *adv.* **—ex plo'sive ness,** *n.*

ex po nent (ek spō'nənt), **1** person or thing that explains. **2** person or thing that stands as an example, type, or symbol of something: *Martin Luther King was a famous exponent of civil rights.* **3** a small number written above and to the right of a symbol or quantity to show how many times the symbol or quantity is to be used as a factor. EXAMPLES: $2^2 = 2 \times 2$. $a^3 = a \times a \times a$. *n.*

ex po nen tial (ek′spō nen′shəl), of algebraic exponents. *adj.* —**ex′po nen′tial ly,** *adv.*

ex port (ek spôrt′ *or* ek′spôrt *for 1;* ek′spôrt *for 2,3*), **1** send (goods) out of one country for sale and use in another: *The United States exports many kinds of machinery.* **2** article exported: *Cotton is an important export of the United States.* **3** act or fact of exporting: *the export of oil from the Arab nations.* 1 *v.,* 2,3 *n.*

ex por ta tion (ek′spôr tā′shən), an exporting: *the exportation of wheat from Canada to India.* *n.*

ex port er (ek spôr′tər *or* ek′spôr tər), person or company whose business is exporting. *n.*

ex pose (ek spōz′), **1** lay open; leave without protection; uncover: *We were exposed to the hot sun all day while fishing. All the children have been exposed to mumps.* **2** show openly; display: *Goods are exposed for sale in a store.* **3** make known; reveal: *She exposed the plot to the police.* **4** allow light to reach and act on (a photographic film or plate). *v.,* **ex posed, ex pos ing.** —**ex pos′er,** *n.*

ex po sé (ek′spō zā′), a showing up of crime, dishonesty, fraud, etc.: *a public exposé of graft.* *n., pl.* **ex po sés.**

ex po si tion (ek′spə zish′ən), **1** a public show or exhibition. *A world's fair with exhibits from many countries is an exposition.* **2** a detailed explanation. **3** speech or writing explaining a process, thing, or idea. *n.*

ex pos i tor (ek spoz′ə tər), person that explains. *n.*

ex pos i to ry (ek spoz′ə tôr′ē), explanatory. *adj.*

ex pos tu late (ek spos′chə lāt), reason earnestly with a person, protesting against something that person means to do or has done; remonstrate in a friendly way: *The teacher expostulated with the student about her poor work.* *v.,* **ex pos tu lat ed, ex pos tu lat ing.**

ex pos tu la tion (ek spos′chə lā′shən), earnest protest; friendly remonstrance: *The teacher's expostulations were wasted, for the student made no effort to improve.* *n.*

ex po sure (ek spō′zhər), **1** an exposing; laying open; making known: *The exposure of the real criminal cleared the innocent suspect. Movie stars have a great deal of public exposure.* **2** a being exposed: *Exposure to the rain has ruined this machinery.* **3** position in relation to the sun and wind. *A house with a southern exposure is open to sun and wind from the south.* **4** time during which light reaches and acts on a photographic film or plate. **5** part of a photographic film for one picture. *n.*

ex pound (ek spound′), **1** make clear; explain: *The teacher expounds each new principle in arithmetic to the class.* **2** set forth or state in detail: *The Senator expounded her objections to the bill.* *v.* —**ex pound′er,** *n.*

ex-pres i dent (eks′prez′ə dənt), a former president; living person who once was president, but no longer is. *n.*

ex press (ek spres′), **1** put into words: *Try to express your ideas clearly.* **2** show by look, voice, or action; reveal: *Your smile expresses joy.* **3** clear and definite: *It was his express wish that we should go without him.* **4** special; particular: *She came for the express purpose of seeing you.* **5** a quick or direct means of sending things. *Packages and money can be sent by express in trains or airplanes.* **6** system or company that carries packages, money, etc. **7** send by some quick means: *Express this trunk to Chicago.* **8** by express; directly: *Please send this package express to Boston.* **9** traveling fast and making few stops: *an express train.* **10** train, bus, elevator, etc., traveling fast and making few stops. **11** for fast traveling: *an express highway.* 1,2,7 *v.,* 3,4,9,11 *adj.,* 5,6,10 *n., pl.* **ex press es** for 10; 8 *adv.* —**ex press′er,** *n.*

express oneself, say what one thinks: *The speaker expressed himself clearly.*

ex press i ble (ek spres′ə bəl), able to be expressed. *adj.*

ex pres sion (ek spresh′ən), **1** a putting into words: *the expression of an idea.* **2** word or group of words used as a unit: *"Wise guy" is a slang expression.* **3** a showing by look, voice, or action: *A sigh is often an expression of sadness.* **4** look that shows feeling: *The winners had happy expressions on their faces.* **5** a bringing out of the meaning or beauty of something read, spoken, sung, or played: *Try to read with more expression.* **6** any combination of constants, variables, and symbols expressing some mathematical operation or quantity. *n.*

ex pres sion less (ek spresh′ən lis), without expression: *an expressionless face, an expressionless voice.* *adj.*

ex pres sive (ek spres′iv), **1** expressing: *"Alas!" is a word expressive of sadness.* **2** full of expression; having much feeling, meaning, etc.: *"The cat's skin hung on its bones" is a more expressive sentence than "The cat was very thin."* *adj.* —**ex pres′sive ly,** *adv.* —**ex pres′sive ness,** *n.*

ex press ly (ek spres′lē), **1** plainly; definitely: *The package is not for you; you are expressly forbidden to touch it.* **2** on purpose; specially: *She came expressly to see you.* *adv.*

ex press way (ek spres′wā′), highway built for motor-vehicle travel at high speeds. *n.*

ex pro pri ate (ek sprō′prē āt), take (land, possessions, etc.) from the owner, especially for public use. *A city can expropriate land for a public park.* *v.,* **ex pro pri at ed, ex pro pri at ing.** —**ex pro′pri a′tor,** *n.*

ex pro pri a tion (ek sprō′prē ā′shən), the taking of land, possessions, etc., from the owner, especially for public use. *n.*

ex pul sion (ek spul′shən), **1** a forcing out: *Expulsion of air from the lungs is part of breathing.* **2** a being forced out: *Expulsion from school is a punishment for bad behavior.* *n.*

ex punge (ek spunj′), remove completely; erase: *to expunge certain remarks from the record.* *v.,* **ex punged, ex pung ing.** —**ex pung′er,** *n.*

express (defs. 1, 2, 10, 11)

ex pur gate (ek′spər gāt), remove objectionable passages or words from (a book, letter, etc.). *v.*, **ex pur gat ed, ex pur gat ing. —ex′pur ga′tion**, *n.* **—ex′pur ga′tor**, *n.*

ex qui site (ek′skwi zit *or* ek skwiz′it), **1** very lovely; delicate: *These violets are exquisite.* **2** sharp; intense: *A toothache causes exquisite pain.* **3** of highest excellence; most admirable: *They have exquisite taste and manners. adj.* **—ex′qui site ly**, *adv.* **—ex′qui site ness**, *n.*

ext., 1 extension. **2** extract.

ex tant (ek′stənt *or* ek stant′), still existing: *Some of George Washington's letters are extant. adj.*

ex tem po ra ne ous (ek stem′pə rā′nē əs), spoken or done without preparation; offhand: *an extemporaneous speech. adj.* [*Extemporaneous* is from Latin *extemporaneus*, which comes from the phrase *ex tempore*, meaning "on the spur of the moment."] **—ex tem′po ra′ne ous ly**, *adv.* **—ex tem′po ra′ne ous ness**, *n.*

ex tend (ek stend′), **1** stretch out: *extend your hand. This road extends to New York.* **2** lengthen: *I am extending my vacation another week.* **3** increase or enlarge: *They plan to extend their research in that field.* **4** offer; give; grant: *This organization extends help to poor people. v.*

extended family, family consisting of parents, children, and other near relatives of varying generations and relationships, all living together in one household.

ex ten sion (ek sten′shən), **1** an extending: *the extension of one's arm, the extension of a road.* **2** a being extended: *The railroad is in the process of extension.* **3** an extended part; addition: *The new extension to our school will make room for more students.* **4** telephone connected with the main telephone or with a switchboard but in a different location. *n.*

extension cord, length of electric cord fitted with a plug and a socket, used to connect a short cord to an outlet or other source of power.

ex ten sive (ek sten′siv), of great extent; far-reaching; large: *an extensive park, extensive changes. adj.* **—ex ten′sive ly**, *adv.* **—ex ten′sive ness**, *n.*

ex tent (ek stent′), **1** size, length, amount, or degree to which a thing extends: *The extent of a judge's power is limited by law. I agree with your plans, but only to a certain extent.* **2** something extended; extended space: *a vast extent of prairie. n.*

ex ten u ate (ek sten′yü āt), make the seriousness of (a fault or an offense) seem less; excuse in part. *v.*, **ex ten u at ed, ex ten u at ing.**

ex ten u at ing (ek sten′yü āt ing), making the seriousness of a fault or an offense seem less; partially excusing: *The teacher realized that there were extenuating circumstances causing the unhappy student's poor schoolwork. adj.*

ex te ri or (ek stir′ē ər), **1** outer part; outward appearance; outside: *The exterior of the house was made of brick. The gruff man has a harsh exterior but a kind heart.* **2** on or for the outside; outer: *Exterior paint should be durable.* **3** coming from without; happening outside: *exterior influences.* **1** *n.*, **2,3** *adj.* **—ex ter′i or ly**, *adv.*

ex ter mi nate (ek stėr′mə nāt), destroy completely: *This poison will exterminate rats. v.*, **ex ter mi nat ed, ex ter mi nat ing.**

ex ter mi na tion (ek stėr′mə nā′shən), complete destruction: *Poison is useful for the extermination of rats. n.*

ex ter mi na tor (ek stėr′mə nā′tər), person or thing that exterminates, especially a person whose business is exterminating fleas, cockroaches, bedbugs, rats, etc. *n.*

ex ter nal (ek stėr′nl), **1** on the outside; outer: *An ear of corn has an external husk.* **2** an outer surface or part; outside. **3 externals**, *pl.* clothing, manners, or other outward acts or appearances: *Don't judge people by mere externals rather than by their characters.* **4** to be used only on the outside of the body: *Liniment and rubbing alcohol*

are external remedies. **5** easily seen but not essential; superficial: *an external display of concern, external beauty.* **6** having to do with international affairs; foreign: *War affects a nation's external trade.* **1,4-6** *adj.*, **2,3** *n.* **—ex ter′nal ly**, *adv.*

external ear, the outer part of the ear, including the passage leading to the middle ear.

extinct (def. 1)
The great auk has been **extinct** since 1844.

ex tinct (ek stingkt′), **1** no longer existing. **2** no longer active; extinguished: *an extinct volcano. adj.*

ex tinc tion (ek stingk′shən), **1** an extinguishing: *The sudden extinction of the lights left the room in darkness.* **2** bringing to an end; wiping out; destruction: *Physicians are working toward the extinction of many serious diseases. n.*

ex tin guish (ek sting′gwish), **1** put out: *Water extinguished the fire.* **2** bring to an end; wipe out; destroy: *One failure after another extinguished my hopes. v.* **—ex tin′-guish a ble**, *adj.*

ex tin guish er (ek sting′gwish ər), a device for putting out fires; fire extinguisher. *n.*

ex tir pate (ek′stər pāt), remove completely; destroy totally: *extirpate disease and poverty. v.*, **ex tir pat ed, ex tir pat ing. —ex′tir pa′tion**, *n.* **—ex′tir pa′tor**, *n.*

ex tol *or* **ex toll** (ek stōl′), praise highly; commend: *The newspapers extolled the mayor's plan for a new park. v.*, **ex tolled, ex tol ling. —ex tol′ler**, *n.* **—ex tol′ment**, *n.*

ex tort (ek stôrt′), obtain (money, a promise, etc.) by threats, force, fraud, or wrong use of authority: *Blackmailers try to extort money from their victims. v.* **—ex tort′er**, *n.*

ex tor tion (ek stôr′shən), **1** an extorting: *Collecting very high interest on loans is considered extortion and is forbidden by law.* **2** something extorted. *n.*

ex tor tion ate (ek stôr′shə nit), much too great: *Fifty dollars for a softball glove is an extortionate price. adj.*

ex tor tion ist (ek stôr′shə nist), person who is guilty of extortion. *n.*

ex tra (ek′strə), **1** beyond what is usual, expected, or needed; additional: *extra fare, extra pay, extra favors.* **2** something extra; anything beyond what is usual, expected, or needed: *a luxurious new car equipped with many extras.* **3** a special edition of a newspaper: *The paper published an extra to announce the end of the war.* **4** person who is employed by the day to play minor parts in motion pictures: *Two hundred extras were hired for the* *crowd scene.* **5** more than usually: *extra fine quality. I am extra busy on Saturdays.* 1 *adj.,* 2-4 *n., pl.* **ex tras;** 5 *adv.* [*Extra* was probably shortened from *extraordinary.*]

extra-, *prefix.* outside ____; beyond ____: *Extracurricular = outside the curriculum.*

ex tract (ek strakt′ *for 1-4;* ek′strakt *for 5,6),* **1** pull out or draw out, usually with some effort: *extract a tooth, extract iron from the earth, extract a confession.* **2** obtain by pressing, squeezing, etc.: *extract oil from olives.* **3** derive; obtain: *extract pleasure from a party.* **4** take out (a passage) from a book, speech, etc.: *He extracted several sections of the article to read at the meeting.* **5** passage taken out of a book, speech, etc.: *He read several extracts from a book of poems.* **6** a concentrated preparation of a substance: *Vanilla extract, made from vanilla beans, is used as flavoring.* 1-4 *v.,* 5,6 *n.*

ex tract a ble (ek strak′tə bəl), able to be extracted. *adj.*

ex trac tion (ek strak′shən), **1** an extracting or a being extracted: *the extraction of a tooth.* **2** origin; descent: *Miss del Rio is of Spanish extraction; her parents came from Spain. n.*

ex trac tor (ek strak′tər), person or thing that extracts. *n.*

ex tra cur ric u lar (ek′strə kə rik′yə lər), outside the regular course of study: *Football, dramatics, and debating are extracurricular activities in our high school. adj.*

ex tra dite (ek′strə dīt), **1** give up (a fugitive or prisoner) to another state, nation, or authority. **2** obtain the surrender of (such a person). *v.,* **ex tra dit ed, ex tra dit ing. —ex′tra dit′a ble,** *adj.*

ex tra di tion (ek′strə dish′ən), surrender of a fugitive or prisoner by one state, nation, or authority to another. *n.*

ex tra ne ous (ek strā′nē əs), **1** not belonging or proper to a thing; foreign: *Sand and some other extraneous matter had got into the butter and ruined it.* **2** not essential: *The speaker made many extraneous remarks. adj.*

ex traor di nar i ly (ek strôr′də ner′ə lē), most unusually. *adv.*

ex traor di nar y (ek strôr′də ner′ē), beyond what is ordinary; very unusual; very remarkable: *Eight feet is an extraordinary height for a person. adj.*

ex tra sen sor y perception (ek′strə sen′sər ē), the perceiving of thoughts or actions through something other than the usual five senses.

ex tra ter res tri al (ek′strə tə res′trē əl), beyond or outside the earth or its atmosphere. *adj.*

ex trav a gance (ek strav′ə gəns), **1** careless and lavish spending; wastefulness: *Their extravagance kept them always in debt.* **2** a going beyond the bounds of reason: *The extravagance of the claims in the advertisement caused me to doubt the worth of the product.* **3** an extravagant action, idea, purchase, etc.: *A mink coat is an extravagance. n.*

ex trav a gant (ek strav′ə gənt), **1** spending carelessly and lavishly; wasteful: *An extravagant person has extravagant tastes and habits.* **2** beyond the bounds of reason: *an extravagant price, extravagant praise. adj.* [*Extravagant* can be traced back to Latin *extra-,* meaning "outside," and *vagari,* meaning "to wander."] **—ex trav′a gant ly,** *adv.*

ex treme (ek strēm′), **1** much more than usual; very great; very strong: *She drove with extreme caution during the snowstorm.* **2** at the very end; farthest possible; last: *the extreme north.* **3** something extreme; one of two things as far as or as different as possible from each other: *Love and hate are two extremes of feeling.* **4** the highest degree: *Joy is happiness in the extreme.* 1,2 *adj.,* **ex trem er, ex trem est;** 3,4 *n.* **—ex treme′ly,** *adv.* **—extreme′ness,** *n.*

go to extremes, do or say too much: *A person who owns twenty cats is going to extremes.*

ex trem ist (ek strē′mist), person who goes to extremes; supporter of extreme doctrines or practices. *n.*

ex trem i ty (ek strem′ə tē), **1** the very end; farthest possible place; last part or point: *Alaska is at the western extremity of North America.* **2 extremities,** *pl.* the hands and feet. **3** very great danger or need: *People on a sinking ship are in extremity.* **4** extreme degree: *Joy is the extremity of happiness.* **5** an extreme action or measure: *The government was forced to the extremity of rationing gas during the fuel shortage. n., pl.* **ex trem i ties.**

ex tri cate (ek′strə kāt), set free from entanglements, difficulties, embarrassing situations, etc.; release: *I extricated the kitten that was caught in the net. v.,* **ex tri cat ed, ex tri cat ing.**

ex tri ca tion (ek′strə kā′shən), an extricating or a being extricated. *n.*

ex trin sic (ek strin′sik), **1** not essential: *extrinsic differences.* **2** outside of a thing; coming from without; external: *extrinsic influences. adj.* **—ex trin′si cal ly,** *adv.*

ex tro vert (ek′strə vėrt′), person tending to act rather than think. Extroverts are more interested in what is going on around them than in their own thoughts and feelings. *n.*

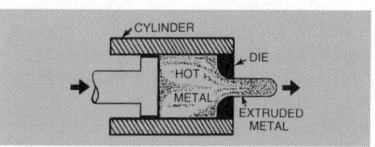

extrude (def. 2)—Cutaway drawing of cylinder shows the shaping of metal by extruding it. Hot metal is compressed in a cylinder and forced through a die; the extruded metal will have the shape of the die opening.

ex trude (ek strüd′), **1** thrust out; push out: *to extrude toothpaste from a tube.* **2** shape (metal, plastics, rubber, or ceramics) by forcing through dies. *v.,* **ex trud ed, ex trud ing. —ex trud′er,** *n.*

ex tru sion (ek strü′zhən), an extruding or a being extruded. *n.*

ex u ber ance (eg zü′bər əns), **1** a great abundance: *an exuberance of joy.* **2** an abounding in health and good cheer; high spirits: *Some people wake up every morning with a feeling of exuberance. n.*

ex u ber ant (eg zü′bər ənt), **1** very abundant; overflowing; lavish: *exuberant health, an exuberant welcome.* **2** abounding in health and high spirits; overflowing with good cheer: *I was in an exuberant mood all day. adj.* **—ex u′ber ant ly,** *adv.*

ex u da tion (ek′syə dā′shən), **1** an exuding. **2** something exuded. *n.*

ex ude (eg züd′ *or* ek syüd′), **1** come or send out in drops; ooze: *Sweat exudes from the pores in the skin.* **2** give forth: *Some people exude self-confidence. v.,* **ex ud ed, ex ud ing.**

ex ult (eg zult′), be very glad; rejoice greatly: *The winners exulted in their victory. v.* **—ex ult′ing ly,** *adv.*

ex ult ant (eg zult′nt), rejoicing greatly; exulting; triumphant: *an exultant shout. adj.* **—ex ult′ant ly,** *adv.*

ex ul ta tion (eg′zul tā′shən *or* ek′sul tā′shən), an exulting; great rejoicing; triumph: *There was exultation over our team's victory. n.*

ex ur bi a (ek sėr′bē ə), region between a city's suburbs and the country. *n.*

-ey, *suffix forming adjectives from nouns.* full of, containing, or like ____: *Clayey = like or containing clay. Gooey = like goo.*

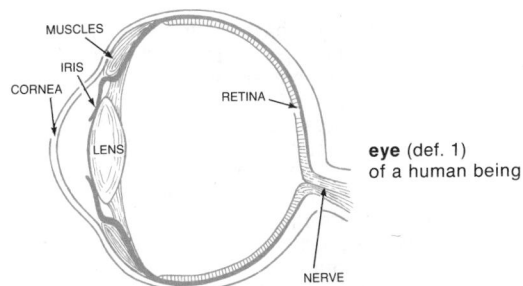

eye (def. 1)
of a human being

a	hat	i	it	oi	oil	ch	child		a in about
ā	age	ī	ice	ou	out	ng	long		e in taken
ä	far	o	hot	u	cup	sh	she	ə =	i in pencil
e	let	ō	open	u̇	put	th	thin		o in lemon
ē	equal	ô	order	ü	rule	₮H	then		u in circus
ėr	term					zh	measure		

eye (ī), **1** the organ of the body by which people and animals see. **2** the colored part of the eye; iris: *He has brown eyes.* **3** region surrounding the eye: *The blow gave her a black eye.* **4** Often, **eyes,** *pl.* sense of seeing; vision; sight: *A jet pilot must have good eyes.* **5** ability to see small differences in things: *A good artist must have an eye for color.* **6** a look; glance: *I cast an eye over the books and quickly found one I liked.* **7** look at; watch; observe: *The child eyed the monkey with great interest.* **8** Often, **eyes,** *pl.* way of thinking or considering; view; opinion; judgment: *Stealing is a crime in the eyes of the law.* **9** thing shaped like, resembling, or suggesting an eye. The little spots on potatoes, the hole for thread in a needle, and the loop in which a hook fastens are all called eyes. **10** the relatively calm, clear area at the center of a hurricane. 1-6,8-10 *n.,* 7 *v.,* **eyed, ey ing** or **eye ing.** [*Eye* comes from Old English *ēage.*] —**eye′a ble,** *adj.* —**eye′like′,** *adj.*
an eye for an eye, punishment as severe as the injury.
catch one's eye, attract one's attention: *The bright red sign caught my eye.*
in the public eye, 1 often seen in public. **2** widely known.
keep an eye on, look after; watch carefully: *Keep an eye on the baby while I go to the store.*
lay eyes on or **set eyes on,** look at; see: *I never laid eyes on these people until today.*
make eyes at, flirt with: *He was making eyes at the girl across the room.*
open one's eyes, make one see what is really happening.
see eye to eye, agree entirely: *My parents and I do not see eye to eye on my weekly allowance.*
shut one's eyes to, refuse to see or consider; ignore: *We often shut our eyes to the faults of our friends.*
with an eye to, for; considering.
eye ball (ī′bôl′), the eye without the surrounding lids and bony socket. It is shaped like a ball. *n.*
eye brow (ī′brou′), **1** hair that grows along the bony ridge just above the eye. **2** the bony ridge above the eye. *n.*
eye glass (ī′glas′), **1** a lens to aid poor vision. **2 eyeglasses,** *pl.* pair of such lenses, mounted in a frame, to correct defective eyesight; glasses; spectacles. *n., pl.* **eye glass es.**

eye hole (ī′hōl′), the bony socket for the eyeball. *n.*
eye lash (ī′lash′), **1** one of the hairs on the edge of the eyelid. **2** fringe of such hairs. *n., pl.* **eye lash es.**
eye less (ī′lis), without eyes. *adj.*
eye let (ī′lit), **1** a small, round hole for a lace or cord to go through. **2** a metal ring around such a hole to strengthen it. **3** a small, round hole with stitches around it, used to make a pattern in embroidery. *n.*
eye lid (ī′lid′), the movable fold of skin, upper or lower, by means of which we can shut and open the eyes. *n.*
eye-o pen er (ī′ō′pə nər), INFORMAL. a surprising happening or discovery. *n.*
eye piece (ī′pēs′), lens or set of lenses in a telescope, microscope, etc., nearest to the eye of the user. *n.*
eye shadow, a cosmetic used to color the eyelids.
eye shot (ī′shot′), eyesight (def. 2). *n.*
eye sight (ī′sīt′), **1** power of seeing; sight: *A hawk has keen eyesight.* **2** range of vision; view: *The water was within eyesight. n.*
eye sore (ī′sôr′), something unpleasant to look at: *That garbage heap is an eyesore. n.*
eye spot (ī′spot′), a simple organ for sensing light, found in certain lower animals. *n.*
eye strain (ī′strān′), a tired or weak condition of the eyes caused by using them too much, reading in a dim light, etc. *n.*

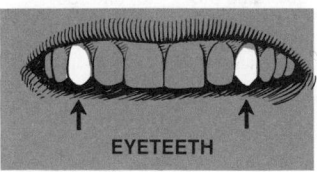

EYETEETH

eye tooth (ī′tüth′), an upper canine tooth. *n., pl.* **eyeteeth.**
eye wash (ī′wosh′ *or* ī′wôsh′), **1** a liquid preparation to clean or heal the eyes. **2** SLANG. deceiving flattery. *n.*
eye wit ness (ī′wit′nis), person who actually sees or has seen some act or happening, and thus can give testimony concerning it. *n., pl.* **eye wit ness es.**
eyr ie or **eyr y** (er′ē, ar′ē, *or* ir′ē), aerie. *n., pl.* **eyr ies.**
E ze ki el (i zē′kē əl), **1** Hebrew prophet who lived in the 500's B.C. **2** book of the Old Testament containing his prophecies. *n.*
Ez ra (ez′rə), **1** Hebrew scribe who led a revival of Judaism in the 400's or 300's B.C. **2** book of the Old Testament that tells about him. *n.*

F or f (ef), the sixth letter of the English alphabet. *n., pl.* F's or f's.

f, forte.

F, symbol for fluorine.

f., 1 female. 2 feminine. 3 forte. 4 franc.

F., 1 Fahrenheit. 2 February. 3 Friday.

fa (fä), the fourth tone of the musical scale. *n.*

fa ble (fā′bəl), 1 story which is made up to teach a lesson. Fables are often about animals who can talk, such as *The Hare and the Tortoise* and *The Fox and the Crow.* 2 an untrue story; falsehood. 3 legend; myth. *n.* [*Fable* came into English about 700 years ago from French *fable,* and can be traced back to Latin *fari,* meaning "to speak."]

fa bled (fā′bəld), 1 told about in fables, legends, or myths. 2 not real; made up. *adj.*

fab ric (fab′rik), 1 woven or knitted material; cloth. Velvet, canvas, linen, and flannel are fabrics. 2 way in which a thing is put together; frame or structure: *The fabric of a person's character may be weak or strong. n.*

fab ri cate (fab′rə kāt), 1 make by putting parts together; build or manufacture: *Automobiles are fabricated from parts made in different factories.* 2 make up; invent (a story, lie, excuse, etc.). *v.,* fab ri cat ed, fab ri cat ing. —fab′ri ca′tor, *n.*

fab ri ca tion (fab′rə kā′shən), 1 a fabricating; manufacture. 2 something fabricated; false story, lie, excuse, etc. *n.*

fab u lous (fab′yə ləs), 1 not believable; amazing: *Ten dollars is a fabulous price for a pencil.* 2 of a fable; imaginary: *The centaur is a fabulous monster.* 3 like a fable. 4 INFORMAL. wonderful; exciting. *adj.* —fab′u lous ly, *adv.* —fab′u lous ness, *n.*

facade
(def. 1)
of a
church

fa cade (fə säd′), 1 the front part of a building, especially the part that faces a street or an open space. 2 outward appearance. *n.* [*Facade* comes from French *façade,* and can be traced back to Latin *facies,* meaning "a form, face."]

fa çade (fə säd′), facade. *n., pl.* fa çades.

face (fās), 1 the front part of the head. The eyes, nose, and mouth are parts of the face. 2 look; expression: *His face was sad.* 3 an ugly or funny look made by twisting the face: *We made faces at each other.* 4 the front part; the right side; surface: *The face of a clock or watch has numbers on it.* 5 outward appearance: *The tall buildings*

changed the face of the city. 6 have the front toward; be opposite to: *The house faces the street. The picture faces page 60 in my book.* 7 meet bravely or boldly: *face danger, face the enemy.* 8 present itself to: *A crisis faced us.* 9 dignity; self-respect; personal importance: *to lose face.* 10 cover with a different material: *A wooden house is sometimes faced with brick.* 11 cover the inside or outside edges of cuffs, a collar, etc., with the same or different material for protection or trimming: *The lapels of my jacket are faced with velvet.* 12 any of the planes or surfaces that bound a solid figure. A cube has six faces. 1-5,9,12 *n.,* 6-8,10,11 *v.,* faced, fac ing.

face down, face fearlessly; meet boldly.

face to face, 1 with faces toward each other: *The enemies stood face to face.* 2 in the actual presence.

face up to, meet boldly; admit and accept.

fly in the face of, disobey openly; defy.

in the face of, 1 in the presence of. 2 in spite of: *He insisted he was right in the face of facts that proved he was wrong.*

to one's face, in one's presence; openly; boldly.

face card, king, queen, or jack of playing cards.

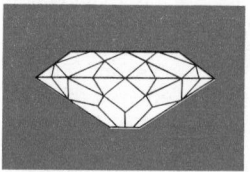

facet (def. 1)—gem with many facets

fac et (fas′it), 1 one of the small, polished surfaces of a cut gem. 2 any one of several sides or views: *Selfishness was a facet of her character that we seldom saw.* 3 cut facets on. 1,2 *n.,* 3 *v.,* fac et ed, fac et ing or fac et ted, fac et ting.

fa ce tious (fə sē′shəs), 1 having the habit of joking; being slyly humorous. 2 said in fun; not to be taken seriously: *facetious remarks. adj.* —fa ce′tious ly, *adv.* —fa ce′tious ness, *n.*

face value, 1 value stated on a bond, check, note, bill, etc. 2 apparent worth, meaning, etc.

fa cial (fā′shəl), 1 of or for the face. 2 massage or treatment of the face. 1 *adj.,* 2 *n.* —fa′cial ly, *adv.*

fac ile (fas′əl), 1 easily done or used; taking little effort: *facile tasks, facile methods.* 2 moving, acting, or working easily or rapidly: *a facile tongue for gossip, to write in a facile style.* 3 gentle; easygoing; agreeable; yielding: *Her facile nature adapted itself to any group of people without effort. adj.* —fac′ile ly, *adv.* —fac′ile ness, *n.*

fa cil i tate (fə sil′ə tāt), make easy; lessen the labor of; help bring about; assist: *A good vacuum cleaner facilitates housework. v.,* fa cil i tat ed, fa cil i tat ing. —fa cil′i ta′tion, *n.*

fa cil i ty (fə sil′ə tē), 1 absence of difficulty; ease: *The twins ran and dodged with such facility that no one could catch them.* 2 power to do anything easily and quickly; skill in using the hands or mind: *She has the facility to become a fine composer.* 3 Usually, facilities, *pl.* something that makes an action easy; aid; convenience: *research facilities. n., pl.* fa cil i ties.

fac ing (fā′sing), 1 a covering of different material for ornament, protection, etc.: *a wooden house with a brick facing.* 2 material put around the inside or outside edge of cloth to protect or trim it: *a blue coat with red facings on the collar and cuffs. n.*

fac sim i le (fak sim′ə lē), an exact copy or likeness. *n.* [*Facsimile* comes from Latin *facere,* meaning "to make, do," and *simile,* meaning "similar, like."]

fact (fakt), 1 thing known to be true or to have really happened: *It is a fact that the Pilgrims sailed to America*

on the Mayflower in 1620. **2** what is true; truth: *The fact of the matter is, I did want to go to the dance.* **3** thing said or supposed to be true or to have really happened: *We doubted his facts.* n. [*Fact* is from Latin *factum*, meaning "(a thing) done," which comes from *facere*, meaning "to make, do." See **Word Family**.]
as a matter of fact, in fact.
in fact, truly; really.

fact

Below are words related to *fact*. They can all be traced back to the Latin word *facere* (fä′ke re), meaning "to make, do."

affect	facsimile	officer
artificial	feature	pacify
benefit	glorify	perfect
chafe	hacienda	profit
confection	infect	qualify
confetti	justify	ratify
counterfeit	liquefy	sacrifice
defeat	magnificent	satisfy
effect	manufacture	suffice
efficient	notify	unify

fac tion (fak′shən), **1** group of persons who stand up for their side or act together for some common purpose against the rest of a larger group: *A faction in our club tried to make the president resign.* **2** strife among the members of a political party, church, club, or neighborhood. n.
fac tion al (fak′shə nəl), of factions; partisan. adj.
fac tious (fak′shəs), fond of stirring up disputes. adj. —**fac′tious ly,** adv. —**fac′tious ness,** n.
fac tor (fak′tər), **1** any one of the causes that helps bring about a result; one element in a situation: *The low price was a factor in my decision to buy this car.* **2** any of the numbers or expressions which, when multiplied together, form a product: *5, 3, and 4 are factors of 60.* **3** separate into factors. 1,2 n., 3 v.
fac tor y (fak′tər ē), building or group of buildings where things are made with machines, or by hand. n., pl. **fac tor ies.**
fac to tum (fak tō′təm), person employed to do all kinds of work. n. [*Factotum* comes from Latin *facere*, meaning "to make, do," and *totum*, meaning "the whole, everything."]
fac tu al (fak′chü əl), concerned with fact; consisting of facts: *I kept a detailed factual account of the trip in my diary.* adj. —**fac′tu al ly,** adv.
fac ul ty (fak′əl tē), **1** power to do some special thing, especially a power of the mind; ability: *the faculty of hearing, the faculty of memory, a faculty for arithmetic.* **2** the teachers of a school, college, or university. n., pl. **fac ul ties.**
fad (fad), something everybody is very much interested in for a short time; fashion or craze: *No one plays that game anymore; it was only a fad.* n.
fade (fād), **1** become less bright; lose color: *Daylight fades when the sun sets. My blue jeans faded after they were washed several times.* **2** lose freshness or strength; wither: *The flowers in our garden faded at the end of the summer.* **3** die away; disappear little by little: *The sound of the train faded after it went by.* **4** cause to fade: *Sunlight faded the new curtains.* v., **fad ed, fad ing.**

fade less (fād′lis), not fading; permanent. adj. —**fade′less ly,** adv.
fade-out (fād′out′), **1** the gradual fading from the screen of a scene in a motion picture or television show. **2** a gradual disappearance. n.
faer ie or **faer y** (fer′ē or far′ē), OLD USE. fairy. n., pl. **faer ies.**
fag (fag), tire by work: *After climbing to the top of the mountan we were completely fagged.* v., **fagged, fag ging.**
fag ot or **fag got** (fag′ət), bundle of sticks or twigs tied together for fuel: *to build a fire with fagots.* n.
Fahr., Fahrenheit.
Fahr en heit (far′ən hīt), of, based on, or according to a scale for measuring temperature on which 32 degrees marks the freezing point of water and 212 degrees marks the boiling point. The **Fahrenheit thermometer** is marked off according to this scale. adj. [The *Fahrenheit* scale was named for Gabriel D. *Fahrenheit*, 1686-1736, a German physicist who introduced it.]
fail (fāl), **1** not succeed; not be able to do or become what is wanted, expected, or attempted; come to nothing: *He tried hard to learn to skate, but he failed. After a long drought, the crops failed.* **2** not do; neglect: *She failed to follow our advice.* **3** be of no use to when needed: *When I needed their help, they failed me.* **4** be missing; be not enough: *When our supplies failed, we had no food.* **5** lose strength; grow weak; die away: *The patient's heart was failing.* **6** not be able to pay what one owes; become bankrupt: *The company lost all its money and failed in business.* **7** be unsuccessful in an examination, etc.; receive a mark of failure: *You failed the test because you didn't study.* **8** give the mark of failure to (a student). v.
without fail, surely; certainly: *You must do your homework without fail.*
fail ing (fā′ling), **1** failure. **2** fault; weakness; defect: *We all have our failings; none of us is perfect.* **3** in the absence of; lacking; without: *Failing good weather, the tennis match will be played indoors.* 1,2 n., 3 prep.
faille (fīl), a soft, ribbed cloth of silk, rayon, or cotton. n.
fail ure (fā′lyər), **1** a being unable to do or become what is wanted, expected, or attempted; not succeeding; failing: *failure in one's work.* **2** a not doing; neglecting: *Failure to obey orders on a ship is mutiny.* **3** a being not enough; falling short: *failure of supplies.* **4** a losing strength; becoming weak: *heart failure.* **5** a being unable to pay what one owes. **6** person or thing that has failed: *The picnic was a failure because it rained.* n.
fain (fān), OLD USE. **1** gladly; willingly. **2** glad; willing. 1 adv., 2 adj.
faint (fānt), **1** not clear or plain; dim: *faint colors, a faint idea.* **2** weak; feeble: *a faint voice, a faint attempt.* **3** a temporary loss of consciousness, often brought on by great hunger, sudden fear, illness, etc. In a faint, a person seems to be asleep and does not know what is going on around one. **4** lose consciousness temporarily. **5** about to lose consciousness; dizzy and weak: *I felt quite faint.* **6** lacking courage; cowardly: *a faint heart.* 1,2,5,6 adj., 3 n., 4 v. —**faint′ly,** adv. —**faint′ness,** n.
faint heart ed (fānt′här′tid), lacking courage; cowardly; timid. adj. —**faint′heart′ed ly,** adv. —**faint′heart′ed ness,** n.
fair[1] (fer or far), **1** not favoring one more than others;

just; honest: *a fair judge. Every person is entitled to a fair hearing in court.* **2** according to the rules: *fair play.* **3** not good and not bad; average: *a fair student. There is a fair crop of wheat this year.* **4** not dark; light: *A blond person has fair hair and skin.* **5** not cloudy or stormy; clear; sunny: *The weather will be fair today.* **6** pleasing to see; beautiful: *a fair lady.* **7** without spots or stains; clean: *He typed a fair copy of the letter.* **8** in a just manner; honestly: *to play fair.* 1-7 *adj.,* 8 *adv.*

bid fair, seem likely; have a good chance.

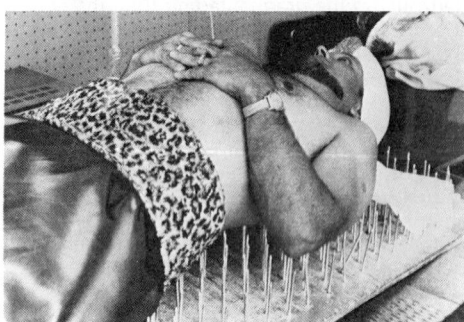

fakir lying unhurt on a bed of nails

fair² (fer *or* far), **1** a showing of farm products and goods of a certain region: *Prizes were given for the best livestock at the county fair.* **2** a gathering of buyers and sellers, often held at the same time and place every year: *a trade fair, an art fair.* **3** sale of articles; bazaar: *Our church held a fair to raise money for charity. n.*

fair ball, (in baseball) a batted ball that is not a foul, permitting the batter to start around the bases.

fair game, 1 animals or birds that it is lawful to hunt. **2** a suitable object of attack: *The playful puppy thought I was fair game.*

fair ground (fer′ground′ *or* far′ground′), place outdoors where fairs are held. *n.*

fair ly (fer′lē *or* far′lē), **1** in a fair manner; justly; honestly: *That salesperson deals fairly with all customers.* **2** moderately; rather: *She is a fairly good pupil, neither bad nor very good.* **3** absolutely; positively: *He was fairly beside himself with anger. adv.*

fair-mind ed (fer′mīn′did *or* far′mīn′did), not prejudiced; just; impartial. *adj.* —**fair′-mind′ed ness,** *n.*

fair ness (fer′nis *or* far′nis), a being fair: *Our teacher is known for fairness in grading pupils. n.*

fair way (fer′wā′ *or* far′wā′), the part of a golf course between the tee and putting green where the grass is kept short. *n.*

fair y (fer′ē *or* far′ē), **1** (in stories) a tiny being with magic powers. Fairies were supposed to help or harm people. **2** of fairies. **3** like a fairy; lovely; delicate. 1 *n., pl.* **fair ies;** 2,3 *adj.* [*Fairy* came into English about 650 years ago from French *faerie,* and can be traced back to Latin *fari,* meaning "to speak."] —**fair′y like′,** *adj.*

fair y land (fer′ē land′ *or* far′ē land′), **1** place where the fairies are supposed to live. **2** a very pleasant or delightful place. *n.*

fairy tale, 1 story about fairies. **2** something said that is not true; falsehood; lie.

faith (fāth), **1** belief without proof; trust: *We have faith in our friends.* **2** belief in God or in God's promises. **3** what a person believes. **4** religion: *the Jewish faith, the Christian faith.* **5** a being loyal. *n.*

break faith, break one's promise.

in bad faith, dishonestly.

in good faith, honestly; sincerely.

keep faith, keep one's promise.

faith ful (fāth′fəl), **1** worthy of trust; loyal: *a faithful friend. Several workers were given awards for long and faithful service.* **2** true to fact; accurate: *The witness gave a faithful account of what happened.* **3 the faithful, a** true believers. **b** loyal followers or supporters. 1,2 *adj.,* 3 *n.* —**faith′ful ly,** *adv.* —**faith′ful ness,** *n.*

faith less (fāth′lis), **1** failing in one's duty; breaking one's promises; not loyal: *a faithless lover, a faithless traitor.* **2** without faith; unbelieving: *live a faithless life doubting everything and everyone. adj.* —**faith′less ly,** *adv.* —**faith′less ness,** *n.*

fake (fāk), **1** make something false appear real in order to deceive; counterfeit: *to fake someone else's signature. They faked the picture by pasting two photographs together.* **2** pretend: *to fake illness. I wasn't really crying; I was only faking.* **3** fraud; deception: *The diamond ring was a fake.* **4** person who fakes: *Anyone who claims to be able to fly like a bird is a fake.* **5** intended to deceive; not real; false: *a fake fur, fake money.* 1,2 *v.,* **faked, fak ing;** 3,4 *n.,* 5 *adj.*

fak er (fā′kər), person who fakes. *n.*

fak er y (fā′kər ē), INFORMAL. deceit; fraud. *n., pl.* **fak er ies.**

fa kir (fə kir′ *or* fā′kər), a Moslem or Hindu holy man who lives by begging. Fakirs sometimes do extraordinary things, such as lying upon sharp knives. *n.* [*Fakir* comes from Arabic *faqīr,* meaning "poor or poor man."]

fal con (fôl′kən, fal′kən, *or* fô′kən), **1** hawk trained to hunt and kill birds and small game. In the Middle Ages, hunting with falcons was a popular sport. **2** a swift-flying hawk having a short, curved bill and long claws and wings. *n.*

falconer (def. 2) with a **falcon** (def. 1; wingspread about 3 ft. or 1 m.) trained to perch on the hand

fal con er (fôl′kə nər, fal′kə nər, *or* fô′kə nər), **1** person who hunts with falcons. **2** person who breeds and trains falcons. *n.*

fal con ry (fôl′kən rē, fal′kən rē, *or* fô′kən rē), **1** sport of hunting with falcons. **2** the training of falcons to hunt. *n.*

Falk land Islands, (fôk′lənd *or* fôlk′lənd), group of British islands in the S Atlantic, east of the Strait of Magellan, claimed also by Argentina. See **Patagonia** for map.

fall (fôl), **1** drop or come down from a higher place: *The snow falls fast. Leaves fall from the trees.* **2** a dropping from a higher place: *a fall from a horse.* **3** amount that comes down: *We had a heavy fall of snow last winter.* **4** distance that anything drops or comes down: *The fall of the river here is two feet.* **5** Usually, **falls,** *pl.* fall of water; waterfall: *Niagara Falls. Many tourists come to see the falls.* **6** come down suddenly from a standing position: *A baby who is learning to walk often falls.* **7** a coming down suddenly from a standing position: *The child had a bad fall.* **8** hang down: *The draperies in the living room fall to the floor.* **9** be directed downward: *He blushed, and his eyes fell. She placed the lamp so the light would fall on her book.* **10** do wrong; become bad or worse: *In the Bible, Adam was tempted by Eve and he fell.* **11** a becoming bad or worse; downfall: *Adam's fall.* **12** lose position, power, dignity, etc.; be taken by any evil: *The ruler fell from the people's favor. The fort fell to the enemy.* **13** drop wounded or dead; be killed: *Many fell in the battle.* **14** pass into some condition, position, etc.: *She fell sick. The baby fell asleep. The boy and girl fell in love.* **15** come as if by dropping: *When night falls, the stars appear.* **16** come by chance or lot: *Our choice fell on her.* **17** come to pass; happen; occur: *My birthday falls on Sunday this year.* **18** have proper place or position: *The accent of "over" falls on the first syllable.* **19** proper place or position: *The fall of the accent is on the first syllable.* **20** become lower or less: *Prices fell sharply. The water in the river has fallen two feet. When they saw me, their voices fell.* **21** a becoming lower or less: *a fall in prices, the fall of the tide.* **22** be divided: *The story falls into five parts.* **23** look sad or disappointed: *His face fell at the news.* **24** to slope downward: *The land falls gradually to the beach.* **25** a downward slope. **26** season of the year between summer and winter; autumn. **27** way of throwing or being thrown to the mat in wrestling. 1,6,8-10,12-18,20,22-24 *v.*, **fell, fall en, fall ing;** 2-5,7,11,19,21,25-27 *n.*

fall back, go toward the rear; retreat: *The enemy fell back as our army advanced.*

fall back on, 1 go back to for safety. **2** turn to for help or support.

fall behind, fail to keep up.

fall in, 1 take a place in line: *"Fall in!" said the officer to the soldiers.* **2** meet: *On our trip, we fell in with some interesting people.* **3** agree: *They fell in with our plans.*

fall off, become less; drop: *The profits of the business fell off last month.*

fall on or **fall upon,** attack: *The invading army fell on the city during the night.*

fall out, 1 leave a place in line: *"Fall out!" said the officer to the soldiers.* **2** stop being friends; quarrel: *She has fallen out with her friends.*

fall short of, fail to equal: *The sale wasn't a failure, but it did fall short of the success we had expected.*

fall through, fail: *Her plans fell through.*

fall to, 1 begin: *They fell to and worked with a will.* **2** begin to attack, eat, etc.: *When food was served, they fell to.*

fall under, belong under; be classified as: *Whales fall under the class of mammals.*

ride for a fall, act so as to invite danger or trouble.

fal la cious (fə lā′shəs), not logical: *It is fallacious reasoning to base a general rule on just two or three instances.* *adj.* —**fal la′cious ly,** *adv.* —**fal la′cious ness,** *n.*

fal la cy (fal′ə sē), **1** a false idea; mistaken belief; error: *It is a fallacy to suppose that riches always bring happiness.* **2** mistake in reasoning; misleading or unsound argument. *n., pl.* **fal la cies.**

fall en (fô′lən), **1** past participle of **fall.** *Much rain has fallen.* **2** dropped: *feet with fallen arches.* **3** face down; down on the ground; down flat: *a fallen tree.* **4** that has become bad or worse; degraded. **5** overthrown; destroyed: *a fallen fortress.* **6** dead: *fallen heroes.* 1 *v.*, 2-6 *adj.*

fal li bil i ty (fal′ə bil′ə tē), fallible condition or quality. *n.*

fal li ble (fal′ə bəl), liable to be deceived or mistaken; liable to err. *adj.* —**fal′li bly,** *adv.*

fall ing-out (fô′ling out′), disagreement; quarrel. *n., pl.* **fall ings-out.**

a hat	**i** it	**oi** oil	**ch** child		a in about
ā age	**ī** ice	**ou** out	**ng** long		e in taken
ä far	**o** hot	**u** cup	**sh** she	**ə =**	i in pencil
e let	**ō** open	**u̇** put	**th** thin		o in lemon
ē equal	**ô** order	**ü** rule	**ŦH** then		u in circus
ėr term			**zh** measure		

falling star, meteor.

fall out (fôl′out′), the radioactive particles or dust that fall to the earth after a nuclear explosion. *n.*

fal low (fal′ō), plowed and left unseeded for a season or more; uncultivated: *We shall let the north forty acres lie fallow next spring.* *adj.* [*Fallow* comes from Old English *fealg.*] —**fal′low ness,** *n.*

fallow deer, a small European deer with a yellowish coat that is spotted with white in the summer. [*Fallow* (in *fallow deer*) comes from Old English *fealu,* meaning "brownish-yellow, tawny."]

false (fôls), **1** not true; not correct; wrong: *false statements.* A **false step** is a stumble or mistake. **2** not truthful; lying: *a false witness.* **3** not loyal; not faithful; deceitful: *a false friend, be false to a promise.* **4** used to deceive; deceiving: *false weights, false signals.* A ship sails under **false colors** when it raises the flag of a country other than its own. A **false bottom** in a trunk or drawer is used to form a secret compartment. **5** (in music) not true in pitch: *a false note.* **6** not real; artificial: *false teeth, false diamonds.* **7** based on wrong notions; ill-founded: *False pride kept her from accepting help from her friends when she was out of money.* 1-7 *adj.*, **fals er, fals est;** 8 *adv.* —**false′ly,** *adv.* —**false′ness,** *n.*

play one false, deceive, cheat, trick, or betray one: *My memory played me false; I called him by the wrong name.*

false hood (fôls′hud), **1** a false statement; lie. **2** quality of being false. **3** something false. *n.*

fal set to (fôl set′ō), **1** an unnaturally high-pitched voice, especially in a man. **2** of or for such a voice. 1 *n.*, **fal set tos;** 2 *adj.*

WORD HISTORY

falsetto

Falsetto was borrowed from Italian *falsetto,* and can be traced back to Latin *fallere,* meaning "to deceive."

fal si fi ca tion (fôl′sə fə kā′shən), **1** a falsifying; change made to deceive. **2** a being falsified: *The falsification of the will was not discovered for three months. n.*

fal si fy (fôl′sə fī), **1** make false; change to deceive; misrepresent: *falsify tax records.* **2** make false statements; lie. *v.*, **fal si fied, fal si fy ing.** —**fal′si fi′a ble,** *adj.* —**fal′si fi′er,** *n.*

fal si ty (fôl′sə tē), **1** a being false: *Education often shows the falsity of superstitions.* **2** something false; falsehood. *n., pl.* **fal si ties.**

Fal staff (fôl′staf), Sir **John,** a fat, jolly, swaggering soldier, brazen and without scruples, in three of Shakespeare's plays. *n.*

fal ter (fôl′tər), **1** not go straight on; draw back or hesitate; waver: *I faltered for a moment before I made my decision.* **2** move unsteadily; stumble; totter: *I faltered up the rocky path in the dark.* **3** speak in hesitating or broken words; stammer: *Greatly embarrassed, he faltered out his thanks. v.* —**fal′ter er,** *n.* —**fal′ter ing ly,** *adv.*

fame (fām), fact or condition of being very well known; having much said or written about one. *n.*

famed (fāmd), famous. *adj.*

fa mil iar (fə mil′yər), **1** well-known; common: *a familiar face. French was as familiar to him as English.* **2** well-acquainted: *She is familiar with French and English.* **3** close; personal; intimate: *She spent her vacation visiting old and familiar friends.* **4** not formal; friendly: *a familiar attitude.* **5** too friendly; presuming; forward: *His manner is too familiar. adj.* —**fa mil′iar ly,** *adv.*

fa mil iar i ty (fə mil′yar′ə tē), **1** close acquaintance; knowledge: *Her familiarity with French was a great help to us in Paris.* **2** thing done or said in a familiar way: *I dislike such familiarities as the use of my nickname by people that I have just met.* **3** lack of formality or ceremony. *n., pl.* **fa mil iar i ties.**

fa mil iar i za tion (fə mil′yər ə zā′shən), a making or becoming familiar. *n.*

fa mil iar ize (fə mil′yə rīz′), **1** make (a person) well acquainted with something: *Before playing the new game, familiarize yourself with the rules.* **2** make well known: *Exploration in space has familiarized the word "astronaut." v.,* **fa mil iar ized, fa mil iar iz ing.** —**fa mil′iar iz′er,** *n.*

fam i ly (fam′ə lē), **1** a father, mother, and their children: *Our town has about a thousand families.* **2** children of a father and mother; offspring: *bring up a large family.* **3** group of people living in the same house. **4** all of a person's relatives: *His family holds an annual reunion.* **5** group of related people; tribe or clan: *the Roosevelt family.* **6** group of related animals or plants. Lions, tigers, and leopards belong to the cat family. A family ranks below an order and above a genus. **7** any group of related or similar things. *n., pl.* **fam i lies.**

family name, a last name; surname.

family tree, diagram showing how all the members and ancestors of a family are related.

fam ine (fam′ən), **1** lack of food in a place; a time of starving: *Many people died during the famine in India.* **2** starvation: *Many people died of famine. n.*

fam ished (fam′isht), very hungry; starving: *We were famished after not eating anything for ten hours. adj.*

fa mous (fā′məs), very well known; much talked about or written about; noted: *The famous singer was greeted by a large crowd. adj.*

fa mous ly (fā′məs lē), INFORMAL. excellently; very well: *The new neighbors are getting along famously with everyone. adv.*

fan[1] (fan), **1** instrument or device with which to stir the air in order to cool or ventilate a room, remove odors, cool one's face, etc. One kind of fan can be folded or spread out into part of a circle. Another kind consists of a series of revolving blades turned by an electric motor. **2** stir (the air) with a fan. **3** direct a current of air toward with a fan or anything like a fan: *She fanned herself. Fan the fire to make it burn faster.* **4** stir up; arouse: *Bad treatment fanned their dislike into hate.* **5** anything spread out like an open fan: *The peacock spread out its tail into a beautiful fan.* **6** spread out like an open fan: *He fanned the cards.* **7** (in baseball) to strike out. 1,5 *n.,* 2-4,6,7 *v.,* **fanned, fan ning.** [*Fan*[1] is from Old English *fann,* which came from Latin *vannus.*] —**fan′like′,** *adj.* —**fan′ner,** *n.*

fan[2] (fan), INFORMAL. **1** person extremely interested in some sport, the movies, television, etc.: *A baseball fan would hate to miss the championship game.* **2** admirer of an actor, writer, etc. *n.* [*Fan*[2] was shortened from *fanatic.*]

fa nat ic (fə nat′ik), **1** person who is carried away beyond reason because of feelings or beliefs: *My friend is a fanatic about fresh air and refuses to stay in a room with the windows closed.* **2** unreasonably enthusiastic; extremely zealous: *a fanatic follower of some leader or belief.*

1 *n.,* 2 *adj.* [*Fanatic* is from Latin *fanaticus,* meaning "inspired by divinity, frantic," which comes from *fanum,* meaning "temple."]

fa nat i cal (fə nat′ə kəl), unreasonably enthusiastic; extremely zealous. *adj.* —**fa nat′i cal ly,** *adv.* —**fa nat′i cal ness,** *n.*

fa nat i cism (fə nat′ə siz′əm), unreasonable enthusiasm; extreme zeal. *n.*

fan cied (fan′sēd), imagined. *adj.*

fan ci er (fan′sē ər), person who is especially interested in something: *A dog fancier is interested in breeding and raising dogs. n.*

fan ci ful (fan′sə fəl), **1** led by fancy; using fancies; imaginative: *a fanciful writer.* **2** suggested by fancy; imaginary; unreal: *Her story about a trip to a nearby star is fanciful.* **3** showing fancy in design; quaint or odd in appearance: *fanciful decorations. adj.* —**fan′ci ful ly,** *adv.* —**fan′ci ful ness,** *n.*

fan ci ly (fan′sə lē), in a fancy manner. *adv.*

fan cy (fan′sē), **1** picture to oneself; imagine: *Can you fancy yourself on the moon?* **2** power to imagine; imagination: *Dragons, fairies, and giants are creatures of fancy.* **3** something imagined or supposed; idea; notion: *I had a sudden fancy to go swimming.* **4** have an idea or belief; suppose: *I fancy that is right, but I am not sure.* **5** a liking; fondness: *She has a fancy for bright colors. They took a great fancy to each other and became close friends.* **6** be fond of; like: *Neither of us fancies the idea of having a picnic.* **7** not plain or simple; decorated; ornamental: *a fancy dinner for guests, fancy trimming.* **8** requiring much skill: *fancy skating.* **9** of high quality or of an unusual kind: *fancy fruit.* **10** much too high: *fancy prices.* 1,4,6 *v.,* **fan cied, fan cy ing;** 2,3,5 *n., pl.* **fan cies;** 7-10 *adj.,* **fan ci er, fan ci est.** [*Fancy* is a different form of *fantasy.*] —**fan′ci ness,** *n.*

fan fare (fan′fer *or* fan′fär), **1** a short tune or call played on trumpets, bugles, or the like. **2** a loud show of activity, talk, etc.: *The new bridge was opened with great fanfare by the mayor and city officials. n.*

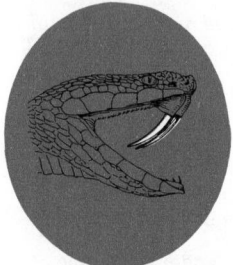

fang (def. 1)—fangs of a poisonous snake

fang (fang), **1** a long, pointed tooth of a dog, wolf, snake, etc. Poisonous snakes have hollow or grooved fangs for injecting venom. **2** something like it. *n.* —**fang′less,** *adj.* —**fang′like′,** *adj.*

fanged (fangd), having fangs. *adj.*

fan tail (fan′tāl′), **1** tail, end, or part spread out like an open fan. **2** pigeon, goldfish, or other animal whose tail spreads out like an open fan. *n.*

fan tas tic (fan tas′tik), **1** very odd; wild and strange in shape or manner; due to fancy: *People often see fantastic things in their dreams. The firelight cast weird, fantastic shadows on the walls.* **2** very fanciful; imaginary; unreal: *The idea that machines could be made to fly seemed fantastic a hundred years ago.* **3** INFORMAL. unbelievably good, quick, high, etc.: *That store charges fantastic prices. adj.* —**fan tas′ti cal ly,** *adv.* —**fan tas′ti cal ness,** *n.*

fan ta sy (fan′tə sē), **1** play of the mind; product of the imagination; fancy. Many stories, such as *Gulliver's Travels* and *Alice in Wonderland,* are fantasies. **2** picture existing only in the mind; any strange mental image or illusion: *I have a fantasy in which I walk about in a lovely garden.* **3** a wild, strange fancy: *This tale of talking horses is merely fantasy.* *n., pl.* **fan ta sies.** Also, **phantasy.** [*Fantasy* came into English over 600 years ago from French *fantasie,* and can be traced back to Greek *phainein,* meaning "to show."]

far (fär), **1** a long way; a long way off: *She studied far into the night. Far in the past, the Norsemen began sailing westward.* **2** not near; distant: *They live in a far country. The moon is far from the earth.* **3** more distant: *We live on the far side of the hill.* **4** very much: *It is far better to go by train.* 1,4 *adv.,* **far ther, far thest** or **fur ther, fur thest;** 2,3 *adj.,* **far ther, far thest** or **fur ther, fur thest.**
as far as, to the distance, point, or degree that.
by far, very much.
far and away, very much.
far and near, everywhere.
far and wide, everywhere; even in distant parts.
how far, to what distance, point, or degree; how much.
in so far as, to the extent that.
so far as, to the extent that.

Far a day (far′ə dā), **Michael,** 1791-1867, English physicist and chemist. *n.*

far a way (fär′ə wā′), **1** far away; distant; remote: *He read of faraway places in geography books.* **2** dreamy: *A faraway look in her eyes showed that she was thinking of something else. adj.*

farce (färs), **1** a play full of ridiculous happenings, absurd actions, and unreal situations, meant to be very funny. **2** a ridiculous mockery; absurd pretense: *The trial was a mere farce. n.*

far ci cal (fär′sə kəl), of or like a farce; ridiculous; absurd. *adj.* —**far′ci cal ly,** *adv.*

far cry, a long way.

fare (fer *or* far), **1** the money that a person pays to ride in a taxi, bus, train, airplane, etc. **2** passenger. **3** food: *plain and simple fare.* **4** get along; get on; do: *She is faring well in school.* **5** turn out; happen: *It will fare hard with her if she ignores parking tickets.* **6** OLD USE. go; travel: *fare forth on a journey.* 1-3 *n.,* 4-6 *v.,* **fared, far ing.**

Far East, China, Japan, and other parts of E Asia, including Korea and E Siberia. —**Far Eastern.**

fare well (fer′wel′ *or* fär′wel′), **1** good luck; good-by. **2** good wishes at parting. **3** departure; leave-taking. **4** of farewell; parting; last: *a farewell kiss. The singer gave a farewell performance.* 1,2,3 *n.,* 1,2 *interj.,* 4 *adj.*

far fetched (fär′fecht′), not closely related to the topic; forced; strained: *His excuse was too farfetched for anyone to believe. adj.*

far-flung (fär′flung′), covering a large area; widely spread: *Many American banks have far-flung operations in Europe, Asia, and South America. adj.*

farm (färm), **1** piece of land which a person uses to raise crops or animals. **2** raise crops or animals either to eat or to sell: *Her parents farm for a living.* **3** cultivate (land): *They farm fifty acres.* **4** anything like a farm. A tract of water for cultivating oysters is an oyster farm. 1,4 *n.,* 2,3 *v.* [*Farm* came into English about 650 years ago from French *ferme,* meaning "fixed rent or charge," and can be traced back to Latin *firmus,* meaning "firm, strong."]
farm out, 1 let for hire: *He farms out the right to pick berries on his land.* **2** assign to a baseball team in a minor league. **3** send out (work) to be done elsewhere: *The company farms out small jobs to free-lance editors and designers.*

farm er (fär′mər), person who owns or works on a farm. *n.*

farm hand (färm′hand′), person who works on a farm. *n.*

farm house (färm′hous′), house to live in on a farm. *n., pl.* **farm hous es** (färm′hou′ziz).

farm ing (fär′ming), business of raising crops or animals on a farm; agriculture. *n.*

farm land (färm′land′), land used or suitable for raising crops or grazing. *n.*

farm stead (färm′sted), farm with its buildings. *n.*

farm yard (färm′yärd′), yard connected with the farm buildings or enclosed by them. *n.*

far-off (fär′ôf′), far away; distant. *adj.*

far-out (fär′out′), INFORMAL. **1** very unusual; not at all customary: *a far-out idea.* **2** very difficult to understand: *far-out research.* **3** extreme: *far-out political views. adj.*

far-reach ing (fär′rē′ching), having a wide influence or effect; extending far: *The use of atomic energy is having far-reaching effects today. adj.* —**far′-reach′ing ness,** *n.*

far ri er (far′ē ər), blacksmith who shoes horses. *n.*

far row (far′ō), **1** litter of pigs. **2** give birth to a litter of pigs. 1 *n.,* 2 *v.*

far see ing (fär′sē′ing), **1** able to see far. **2** looking ahead; planning wisely for the future. *adj.*

far sight ed (fär′sī′tid), **1** seeing distant things more clearly than near ones; not seeing nearby objects clearly. Farsighted people usually wear glasses to correct their vision. **2** looking ahead; planning wisely for the future; shrewd; prudent: *Farsighted people save money while their wages are high. adj.* —**far′sight′ed ly,** *adv.* —**far′sight′ed ness,** *n.*

far ther (fär′ᴛʜər), **1** more distant: *Three miles is farther than two.* **2** at or to a greater distance: *We walked farther than we meant to.* **3** at or to a more advanced point: *She has investigated the subject farther than anyone else.* **4** in addition; also. **5** more; additional: *Do you need farther help?* 1,5 *adj., comparative of* **far;** 2-4 *adv., comparative of* **far.**

far ther most (fär′ᴛʜər mōst), most distant; farthest: *He has traveled to the farthermost points of the earth. adj.*

far thest (fär′ᴛʜist), **1** most distant: *the farthest journey of the space age. Ours is the house farthest down the road.* **2** to or at the greatest distance: *She hit the ball farthest.* **3** most: *Their ideas were the farthest advanced at that time.* 1 *adj., superlative of* **far;** 2,3 *adv., superlative of* **far.**

far thing (fär′ᴛʜing), a British coin equal to a fourth of a British penny. It is no longer used. *n.* [*Farthing* is from Old English *fēorthung,* which comes from *fēortha,* meaning "fourth."]

Far West, the part of the United States between the Rocky Mountains and the Pacific Ocean. —**Far Western.**

fas ci nate (fas′n āt), **1** attract very strongly; enchant by charming qualities; charm: *She was fascinated by the designs and colors in African art.* **2** hold motionless by strange power or by terror: *Snakes are said to fascinate small birds. v.,* **fas ci nat ed, fas ci nat ing.** —**fas′ci nat′ing ly,** *adv.*

fas ci na tion (fas′n ā′shən), **1** a fascinating. **2** very strong attraction; charm; enchantment. *n.*

fas cism or **Fas cism** (fash′iz′əm), **1** the form of government in Italy from 1922 to 1943, under Benito Mussolini. **2** the principles or methods of this or any similar government, or of a political party favoring such a government. Under fascism, a country is ruled by a dictator, with strong control of industry and labor by the central government, great restrictions upon the freedom of individuals, and extreme nationalism and militarism. *n.* [*Fascism* comes from Italian *fascismo,* and can be traced back to Latin *fasces,* meaning "bundle of rods," carried before a Roman magistrate as a symbol of authority.]

fas cist or **Fas cist** (fash′ist), **1** person who favors and supports fascism. **2** of fascism or fascists. **1** *n.,* **2** *adj.*

fash ion (fash′ən), **1** way a thing is made, shaped, or done; manner: *to walk in a peculiar fashion.* **2** current custom in dress, manners, speech, etc.; style: *the latest fashion in shoes.* **3** make, shape, or form: *to fashion a whistle out of wood.* **1,2** *n.,* **3** *v.* —**fash′ion er,** *n.*

after a fashion or **in a fashion,** in some way or other; not very well: *He plays the violin, after a fashion.*

fash ion a ble (fash′ə nə bəl), **1** following the fashion; in fashion; stylish: *fashionable clothes.* **2** of, like, or used by people who set the styles: *They are members of a fashionable club. adj.* —**fash′ion a ble ness,** *n.*

fash ion a bly (fash′ə nə blē), in a fashionable manner. *adv.*

fast[1] (fast), **1** moving, acting, or doing with speed; quick; rapid; swift: *She is a fast runner.* **2** quickly; rapidly; swiftly: *Airplanes go fast.* **3** showing a time ahead of the correct time: *My watch is fast.* **4** concerned only with pleasure; too wild: *lead a fast life of drinking and gambling.* **5** firm; secure; tight: *a fast hold on a rope.* **6** firmly; securely; tightly: *He held fast as the sled went on down the hill.* **7** loyal; faithful: *They have been fast friends for years.* **8** not fading easily: *Good cloth is dyed with fast color.* **9** adapted for speed: *a fast track.* **10** thoroughly; soundly: *The baby is fast asleep.* **1,3-5,7-9** *adj.,* **2,6,10** *adv.*

fast[2] (fast), **1** go without food; eat little or nothing; go without certain kinds of food: *Some people fast for religious reasons.* **2** a fasting. **3** day or time of fasting. **1** *v.,* **2,3** *n.*

fast back (fast′bak′), automobile with a roof that slopes down toward the rear in a single curve. *n.*

fas ten (fas′n), **1** tie, lock, or make hold together in any way; fix firmly in place: *fasten a seat belt, fasten a door.* **2** attach; connect: *try to fasten the blame on others.* **3** direct; fix: *The dog fastened its eyes on the stranger. v.*

fas ten er (fas′n ər), **1** person who fastens. **2** attachment or device used to fasten a door, garment, etc. A zipper is a fastener. *n.*

fas ten ing (fas′n ing), thing used to fasten something. Locks, bolts, clasps, hooks, buttons, etc., are all fastenings. *n.*

fast-food (fast′füd′), of or serving food that is prepared quickly, such as hamburgers, pizza, or fried chicken: *fast-food restaurants. adj.*

fas tid i ous (fa stid′ē əs), hard to please; dainty in taste; easily disgusted: *a fastidious dresser, a fastidious eater. adj.* —**fas tid′i ous ly,** *adv.* —**fas tid′i ous ness,** *n.*

fast ness (fast′nis), **1** a strong, safe, place; stronghold: *The bandits hid in their mountain fastness.* **2** a being fast or firm; firmness. **3** a being quick or rapid; swiftness. *n., pl.* **fast ness es** for 1.

fat (fat), **1** a white or yellow oily substance formed in the bodies of animals. Fat is also found in plants, especially in some seeds. Fats are made up chiefly of carbon, hydrogen, and oxygen. **2** animal tissue composed mainly of such a substance. **3** consisting of or containing fat; oily: *fat meat.* **4** having much flesh; fleshy; plump; well-fed: *a fat baby, a fat pig.* **5** large or larger than usual; plentiful: *a fat contract, a fat salary.* **6** make or become fat: *The farmer is fatting the pigs for market. The pigs fatted on corn.* **7** too fat; obese. **1,2** *n.,* **3-5,7** *adj.,* **fat ter, fat test; 6** *v.,* **fat ted, fat ting.** —**fat′like′,** *adj.* —**fat′ly,** *adv.* —**fat′ness,** *n.*

live off the fat of the land, have the best of everything.

fa tal (fā′tl), **1** causing death: *a fatal accident.* **2** causing destruction or ruin: *The loss of all our money was fatal to our plans.* **3** important; decisive; fateful: *At last the fatal day for the contest arrived. adj.*

fa tal ism (fā′tl iz′əm), **1** belief that fate controls everything that happens. **2** acceptance of everything that happens because of this belief. *n.*

fa tal ist (fā′tl ist), believer in fatalism. *n.*

fa tal is tic (fā′tl is′tik), of fatalism or fatalists. *adj.* —**fa′tal is′ti cal ly,** *adv.*

fa tal i ty (fā tal′ə tē), **1** a fatal accident or happening; death: *Careless driving causes thousands of fatalities every year.* **2** a fatal influence or effect: *Doctors are trying to reduce the fatality of diseases. n., pl.* **fa tal i ties.**

fa tal ly (fā′tl ē), in a manner leading to death or disaster: *The driver was fatally injured in the accident. adv.*

fat back (fat′bak′), salt pork from the upper part of a side of pork. *n.*

fate (fāt), **1** power supposed to fix beforehand and control what is to happen. Fate is beyond any person's control. **2** one's lot or fortune; what happens to a person, group, etc.: *History shows the fate of many nations.* **3** what becomes of a person or thing: *The jury decided the fate of the accused.* **4 Fates,** *pl.* (in Greek and Roman myths) the three goddesses who controlled human life. One spun the thread of life, one decided how long it should be, and one cut it off. *n.* [*Fate* is from Latin *fatum,* originally meaning "thing spoken," which comes from *fari,* meaning "to speak." See **Word Family.**]

fate

Below are words related to *fate.* They can all be traced back to the Latin word *fari* (fä′rē), meaning "to speak."

affable	fame	infant
fable	famous	infantry
fabulous	fatal	preface
fairy	infamous	

fat ed (fā′tid), **1** controlled by fate. **2** destined: *A fortune-teller told me that I was fated to be a great leader. adj.*

fate ful (fāt′fəl), **1** controlled by fate. **2** determining what is to happen; important; decisive: *Yorktown was the site of a fateful battle of the Revolutionary War.* **3** showing what will happen according to fate; prophetic: *fateful words.* **4** causing death, destruction, or ruin; disastrous: *a fateful blow. adj.* —**fate′ful ly,** *adv.* —**fate′ful ness,** *n.*

fath., fathom.

fa ther (fä′ᵺər), **1** a male parent. **2 Father,** God. **3** be the father of: *He fathered four daughters.* **4** take care of; act as father to: *father an orphan.* **5** person who is like a father. **6** a male ancestor; forefather: *the customs of our fathers.* **7** man who did important work as a maker or leader: *George Washington is often called the father of our country.* **8** be the cause of; make; originate: *Edison fathered many inventions.* **9 Father,** title of respect for a priest: *Father Walker.* **10** priest. **1,2,5-7,9,10** *n.,* **3,4,8** *v.* —**fa′ther like′,** *adj.*

fa ther hood (fä′ᵺər hůd), condition of being a father. *n.*

fa ther-in-law (fä′ᵺər in lô′), father of one's husband or wife. *n., pl.* **fathers-in-law.**

fa ther land (fä′ғнər land′), **1** one's native country. **2** land of one's ancestors. *n.*

fa ther less (fä′ғнər lis), having no father: *a fatherless child. adj.*

fa ther li ness (fä′ғнər lē nis), fatherly quality. *n.*

fa ther ly (fä′ғнər lē), **1** of a father. **2** like a father; like a father's; kindly: *a fatherly person, a fatherly smile. adj.*

Father's Day, the third Sunday in June, set apart in the United States in honor of fathers.

fath om (faтн′əm), **1** unit of measure equal to 6 feet. It is used mostly in measuring the depth of water and the length of ships' ropes, cables, etc. **2** measure the depth of. **3** get to the bottom of; understand fully: *I can't fathom what you mean.* 1 *n., pl.* **fath oms** or **fath om;** 2,3 *v.* —**fath′om a ble,** *adj.*

fath om less (faтн′əm lis), **1** too deep to be measured; bottomless: *The stream disappeared into a fathomless abyss.* **2** impossible to be fully understood: *the fathomless riddle of the origin of the universe. adj.* —**fath′om less- ness,** *n.*

fa tigue (fə tēg′), **1** weariness caused by hard work or effort: *I felt extreme fatigue after studying for four hours.* **2** make weary or tired; cause fatigue in. **3 fatigues,** *pl.* work clothes or uniform worn by soldiers for routine work. 1,3 *n.,* 2 *v.,* **fa tigued, fa ti guing.**

fat ten (fat′n), **1** make fat: *The farmer fattened beef cattle for market.* **2** become fat: *The pigs fattened on corn. v.* —**fat′ten a ble,** *adj.* —**fat′ten er,** *n.*

fat ty (fat′ē), **1** of or containing fat. **2** like fat; oily; greasy. *adj.,* **fat ti er, fat ti est.** —**fat′ti ly,** *adv.* —**fat′ti- ness,** *n.*

fat u ous (fach′ü əs), stupid but self-satisfied; foolish; silly. *adj.* —**fat′u ous ly,** *adv.* —**fat′u ous ness,** *n.*

fau cet (fô′sit), device containing a valve for turning on or off a flow of liquid from a pipe or a container holding it; tap; spigot. *n.*

Faulk ner (fôk′nər), **William,** 1897-1962, American writer of novels and short stories. *n.*

fault (fôlt), **1** something that is not as it should be: *Carelessness is her greatest fault. A fault in the wire started the fire.* **2** mistake; error: *a fault in the answer to an arithmetic problem.* **3** cause for blame; responsibility: *Whose fault was it?* **4** a break in the earth's crust, with the mass of rock on one side of the break pushed up, down, or sideways. **5** failure to serve the ball properly or into the right place in tennis and similar games. **6** find fault with: *The teacher could not fault us on our knowledge of the assignment.* 1-5 *n.,* 6 *v.* [Fault came into English about 700 years ago from French *faute,* and can be traced back to Latin *fallere,* meaning "to deceive."]

at fault, deserving blame; wrong.

find fault, find mistakes; complain.

find fault with, object to; criticize.

to a fault, too much; excessively: *She is generous to a fault.*

fault find er (fôlt′fīn′dər), person who finds fault; person who complains. *n.*

fault find ing (fôlt′fīn′ding), **1** act of finding fault. **2** finding fault; complaining. 1 *n.,* 2 *adj.*

fawn[1] (def. 1)

fault i ly (fôl′tə lē), in a faulty manner. *adv.*

fault i ness (fôl′tē nis), condition of being faulty; imperfection. *n.*

fault less (fôlt′lis), without a single fault or defect; perfect. *adj.* —**fault′less ly,** *adv.* —**fault′less ness,** *n.*

fault y (fôl′tē), having faults; wrong; imperfect; defective: *The leak in the faucet was caused by a faulty valve. adj.,* **fault i er, fault i est.**

faun

faun (fôn), (in Roman myths) a minor god that lived in fields and woods. A faun was supposed to look like a man, but to have the ears, horns, tail, and legs of a goat. *n.*

fau na (fô′nə), animals: *the fauna of Australia. n., pl.* **fau nas** or **fau nae** (fô′nē′).

Faust (foust), (in German legends) a man who sold his soul to the devil in return for youth, knowledge, and magic powers. *n.*

fa vor (fā′vər), **1** act of kindness: *Will you do me a favor?* **2** show kindness to; oblige: *Favor us with a song.* **3** liking; approval: *They will look with favor on your plan.* **4** like; approve; prefer: *We favor her plan.* **5** more than fair treatment: *He divided the candy among the children without favor to any one.* **6** give more than fair treatment to: *The teacher favors you.* **7** help; aid: *The sunny day favored the success of our picnic.* **8** a small token given to every guest at a party, dinner, etc.: *Small hats were used as favors at the birthday party.* **9** look like: *That girl favors her mother.* 1,3,5,8 *n.,* 2,4,6,7,9 *v.* —**fa′vor er,** *n.*

in favor of, 1 on the side of; supporting. **2** to the advantage of; helping.

in one's favor, for one; to one's benefit.

fa vor a ble (fā′vər ə bəl), **1** favoring; approving: *"Yes" is a favorable answer to a request.* **2** being to one's advantage; helping; promising: *A favorable wind made the boat go faster. adj.* —**fa′vor a ble ness,** *n.*

fa vor a bly (fā′vər ə blē), with consent or approval. *adv.*

fa vor ite (fā′vər it), **1** liked better than others: *What is your favorite flower?* **2** the one liked better than others; person or thing liked very much: *He is a favorite with everybody.* **3** person, horse, etc., expected to win a contest. 1 *adj.,* 2,3 *n.*

fa vor it ism (fā′vər ə tiz′əm), a favoring a certain one or some more than others; having favorites: *A teacher should try not to show favoritism. n.*

fawn[1] (fôn), **1** deer less than a year old. **2** a light, yellowish brown. **3** light yellowish-brown. 1,2 *n.,* 3 *adj.* —**fawn′like′,** *adj.*

fawn² (fôn), **1** try to get favor or notice by slavish acts: *Many flattering relatives fawned on the rich old woman.* **2** (of dogs, etc.) show fondness by crouching, wagging the tail, licking the hand, etc. *v.* —**fawn′er,** *n.* —**fawn′ing ly,** *adv.*

fay (fā), fairy. *n.*

faze (fāz), INFORMAL. disturb; worry; bother: *Nothing we said fazed her; she did as she pleased. v.,* **fazed, faz ing.**

FBI or **F.B.I.,** Federal Bureau of Investigation (a bureau of the United States Department of Justice, established to investigate violations of federal laws and safeguard national security).

F clef, bass clef.

F.D., Fire Department.

FDR, Franklin Delano Roosevelt.

Fe, symbol for iron.

fe al ty (fē′əl tē), **1** loyalty and duty owed by a vassal to his feudal lord: *The nobles swore fealty to the king.* **2** loyalty; faithfulness; allegiance. *n., pl.* **fe al ties.** [*Fealty* came into English about 650 years ago from French *feauté,* and can be traced back to Latin *fides,* meaning "faith."]

fear (fir), **1** a feeling that danger or evil is near; being afraid: *cry out in fear, a fear of heights, shake with fear.* **2** be afraid of: *Our cat fears big dogs.* **3** feel fear; have an uneasy feeling or idea: *I fear that my friends are in danger. I fear that I am late.* **4** cause for fear; danger; chance: *There is no fear of our losing.* **5** an uneasy feeling: *a fear for one's life.* **1,4,5** *n.,* **2,3** *v.* —**fear′er,** *n.*

fear ful (fir′fəl), **1** causing fear; terrible; dreadful: *a fearful dragon.* **2** feeling fear; frightened: *fearful of the dark.* **3** showing fear; caused by fear: *fearful cries.* **4** INFORMAL. very bad, unpleasant, ugly, etc.: *I have a fearful cold. adj.* —**fear′ful ly,** *adv.* —**fear′ful ness,** *n.*

fear less (fir′lis), without fear; afraid of nothing; brave; daring. *adj.* —**fear′less ly,** *adv.* —**fear′less ness,** *n.*

fear some (fir′səm), **1** causing fear; frightful: *a fearsome sight.* **2** afraid: *We were fearsome of danger. adj.*

fea si bil i ty (fē′zə bil′ə tē), feasible quality. *n.*

fea si ble (fē′zə bəl), **1** that can be done easily; possible without difficulty or damage: *The committee selected the plan that seemed most feasible.* **2** likely; probable: *The witness's explanation of the accident sounded feasible. adj.* —**fea′si ble ness,** *n.* —**fea′si bly,** *adv.*

feast (fēst), **1** a rich meal prepared for some special occasion, usually a joyous one; banquet: *We went to the wedding feast.* **2** eat a rich meal; have a feast: *They feasted on goose.* **3** provide a rich meal for: *The king feasted his friends.* **4** give pleasure or joy to; delight: *We feasted our eyes on the sunset.* **5** a religious festival or celebration: *Easter is an important Christian feast; Passover is an important Jewish feast.* **1,5** *n.,* **2-4** *v.* —**feast′er,** *n.*

feat (fēt), a great or unusual deed; act showing great skill, strength, or daring. *n.*

feath er (feᴛн′ər), **1** one of the light, thin growths that cover a bird's skin. Because feathers are soft and light, they are used to fill pillows. **2** something like a feather in shape or lightness. **3** supply or cover with feathers. **4** turn edgeways: *feather an oar.* **1,2** *n.,* **3,4** *v.* —**feath′er like′,** *adj.*

feather in one's cap, something to be proud of.

feather bed, 1 a very soft, warm mattress filled with feathers. **2** bed with such a mattress.

feath er bed ding (feᴛн′ər bed′ing), the practice of forcing employers to hire more workers than are needed for a particular job. *n.*

feath er less (feᴛн′ər lis), without feathers. *adj.*

feath er weight (feᴛн′ər wāt′), boxer who weighs more than 118 pounds (54 kilograms) and less than 126 pounds (57 kilograms). *n.*

feath er y (feᴛн′ər ē), **1** having feathers; covered with feathers. **2** like feathers; soft. **3** light; flimsy. *adj.* —**feath′er i ness,** *n.*

fea ture (fē′chər), **1** part of the face. The eyes, nose, mouth, chin, and forehead are features. **2** a distinct part or quality; thing that stands out and attracts attention: *Your plan has many good features. The main features of southern California are the climate and the scenery.* **3** a full-length motion picture: *They are showing a good feature this week.* **4** a special article, comic strip, etc., in a newspaper. **5** be or make a feature of: *The local newspapers featured the mayor's speech.* **1-4** *n.,* **5** *v.,* **fea tured, fea tur ing.** [*Feature* came into English about 650 years ago from French *feture,* and can be traced back to Latin *facere,* meaning "to make, do."]

fea ture less (fē′chər lis), without features; not distinctive. *adj.*

Feb., February.

Feb ru ar y (feb′rü er′ē *or* feb′yü er′ē), the second month of the year. It has 28 days except in leap years, when it has 29. *n., pl.* **Feb ru ar ies.**

fe cal (fē′kəl), of feces. *adj.*

fe ces (fē′sēz), waste matter discharged from the intestines. *n.pl.*

feck less (fek′lis), **1** useless; futile. **2** SCOTTISH. spiritless; worthless. *adj.* —**feck′less ly,** *adv.* —**feck′less ness,** *n.*

fe cund (fē′kənd *or* fek′ənd), able to produce much; fruitful; productive; fertile: *a fecund mind. adj.*

fe cun di ty (fi kun′də tē), a being fertile; fruitfulness; productiveness; fertility. *n.*

fed (fed), past tense and past participle of **feed.** *We fed the birds. Have they been fed today? v.*

fed up, INFORMAL. bored or disgusted.

fed., **1** federal. **2** federation.

fed er al (fed′ər əl), **1** formed by an agreement between states establishing a central government to handle their common affairs while the states keep separate control of local affairs: *Switzerland and the United States both became nations by federal union.* **2** of the central government formed in this way: *Congress is the federal lawmaking body of the United States.* **3** Also, **Federal.** of the central government of the United States, not of any state or city alone: *Coining money is a federal power.* **4 Federal, a** of the Federalist Party. **b** supporting the Union during the Civil War. **c** supporter of the Union during the Civil War. **1-3,4a,4b** *adj.,* **4c** *n.* [*Federal* comes from Latin *foederis,* meaning "a compact, league, treaty."] —**fed′er al ly,** *adv.*

fed er al ism (fed′ər ə liz′əm), the federal principle of government. *n.*

fed er al ist (fed′ər ə list), **1 Federalist,** member of the Federalist Party. **2** supporter of the federal principle of government. *n.*

Federalist Party, a political party in the United States that favored the adoption of the Constitution and a strong central government. It existed from about 1791 to about 1816.

Federal Party, Federalist Party.

fed e rate (fed′ə rāt′), form into a union or federation: *a plan to federate the provinces. v.,* **fed e rat ed, fed e rat ing.**

fed e ra tion (fed′ə rā′shən), union by agreement, often a union of states, nations, groups, etc.; league: *Each member of the federation keeps control over its own affairs. n.*

fee (fē), **1** money asked for or paid for some service or privilege; charge: *an admission fee. Doctors and lawyers receive fees for their services.* **2** right to keep and use land; fief. **3** an inherited estate in land. **4** ownership. **5** give a fee to. **1-4** *n.,* **5** *v.,* **feed, fee ing.**

fee ble (fē′bəl), lacking strength; weak: *A sick person is often feeble. A feeble attempt is liable to fail.* *adj.*, **fee bler, fee blest.** —**fee′ble ness,** *n.*

WORD HISTORY

feeble

Feeble came into English about 800 years ago from French *feble*, and can be traced back to Latin *flere*, meaning "to weep."

fee ble-mind ed (fē′bəl mīn′did), weak in mind; lacking normal intelligence. *adj.* —**fee′ble-mind′ed ly,** *adv.* —**fee′ble-mind′ed ness,** *n.*

fee bly (fē′blē), in a feeble manner; weakly. *adv.*

feed (fēd), **1** give food to: *We feed babies because they cannot feed themselves.* **2** give as food: *Feed this grain to the chickens.* **3** eat: *We put cows to feed in the pasture. Cows feed on hay.* **4** food for animals: *Give the chickens their feed.* **5** INFORMAL. meal for a person. **6** supply with material: *Feed the fire.* 1-3,6 *v.,* **fed, feed ing;** 4,5 *n.*

feed back (fēd′bak′), **1** process by which a system, machine, etc., regulates itself by feeding back to itself part of its output. **2** INFORMAL. response: *Was there much feedback to your advertisement for baby-sitting?* *n.*

feed er (fē′dər), **1** person or thing that feeds. **2** thing that supplies something else with material: *These brooks are feeders of the big river.* *n.*

feel (fēl), **1** put the hand or some other part of the body on or against; touch: *Feel this cloth.* **2** quality sensed by touch; way something seems to the touch; feeling: *I like the feel of silk.* **3** try to find or make (one's way) by touch: *I felt my way across the room when the lights went out.* **4** test or examine by touching: *feel a person's pulse.* **5** try to find by touching: *He felt in his pockets for a dime.* **6** find out by touching: *Feel how cold my hands are.* **7** be aware of: *He felt the cool breeze. She felt the heat.* **8** have the feeling of being; be: *She feels sure. He feels angry. We felt hot.* **9** give the feeling of being; seem: *The air feels cold. Your shirt feels wet.* **10** have in one's mind; experience: *I felt pain.* **11** have a feeling: *Try to feel more kindly toward them. I feel that we shall win.* 1,3-11 *v.,* **felt, feeling;** 2 *n.*

feel like, INFORMAL. have a desire or preference for: *Even though it was raining they felt like going out for a walk.*

feel out, find out from in a cautious way: *Feel them out on this matter.*

feel up to, think one is capable of: *I don't feel up to working just now.*

feel er (fē′lər), **1** a special part of an animal's body for sensing by touch. The long feelers on the heads of insects help them find their way. **2** remark, hint, or question made to find out what others are thinking or planning. *n.*

feel ing (fē′ling), **1** sense of touch. By feeling we tell what is hard from what is soft. **2** a being conscious; awareness; sensation: *I had a feeling that someone was watching me.* **3** emotion. Joy, sorrow, fear, and anger are feelings. *The loss of the ball game stirred up much feeling.* **4** feelings, *pl.* tender or sensitive side of one's nature: *You hurt my feelings when you yelled at me.* **5** that feels; sensitive: *a feeling heart.* **6** pity; sympathy: *Have you no feeling for that poor, sick creature?* **7** opinion; idea: *I have no feeling about the plan, one way or the other.* 1-4,6,7 *n.,* 5 *adj.*

feel ing ly (fē′ling lē), with emotion: *She spoke feelingly of her old friend.* *adv.*

feet (fēt), plural of **foot.** *A dog has four feet.* *n.*

feign (fān), **1** put on a false appearance of; make believe; pretend: *Some animals feign death when in danger. He isn't sick; he is only feigning.* **2** make up to deceive: *feign an excuse.* *v.* —**feign′er,** *n.*

feint (fānt), **1** a false appearance; pretense: *The girl made a feint of studying hard, though actually she was listening to the radio.* **2** movement intended to deceive; sham attack; pretended blow: *The fighter made a feint at his opponent with his right hand and struck with his left.* **3** make a feint: *The fighter feinted with his right hand.* 1,2 *n.,* 3 *v.*

feis ty (fī′stē), INFORMAL. full of spirit and energy. *adj.*

feld spar (feld′spär′), kind of crystalline mineral composed of silicate of aluminum. Feldspars are the most abundant minerals near the surface of the earth. They are used in making glass and pottery. *n.* Also, **felspar.**

fe lic i tate (fə lis′ə tāt), express good wishes to formally; congratulate: *The young woman's friends felicitated her upon her promotion.* *v.,* **fe lic i tat ed, fe lic i tat ing.**

fe lic i ta tion (fə lis′ə tā′shən), a formal expression of good wishes; congratulation. *n.*

fe lic i tous (fə lis′ə təs), well chosen for the occasion; appropriate; well-worded; apt: *The poem was full of striking and felicitous phrases.* *adj.* —**fe lic′i tous ly,** *adv.* —**fe lic′i tous ness,** *n.*

fe lic i ty (fə lis′ə tē), **1** great happiness; bliss. **2** good fortune; blessing. **3** a pleasing ability in expression; appropriateness or gracefulness: *The famous writer phrased his ideas with felicity.* **4** an unusually appropriate or graceful expression; well-chosen phrase. *n., pl.* **fe lic i ties.**

fe line (fē′līn), **1** cat. **2** of a cat: *feline eyes.* **3** like that of a cat: *feline stealth.* **4** any animal belonging to a group of meat-eating animals including domestic cats, lions, tigers, leopards, panthers, etc. **5** belonging to this group. 1,4 *n.,* 2,3,5 *adj.* —**fe′line ly,** *adv.*

fell[1] (fel), past tense of **fall.** *Snow fell last night.* *v.*

fell[2] (fel), **1** cause to fall; knock down: *The blow felled her to the ground.* **2** cut down (a tree). **3** turn down and stitch one edge of (a seam) over the other. *v.* —**fell′a ble,** *adj.*

fell[3] (fel), **1** extremely bad; cruel; fierce; terrible: *a fell blow.* **2** deadly; destructive: *a fell disease. adj.*

fell[4] (fel), skin or hide of an animal. *n.*

fel low (fel′ō), **1** a male person; man or boy. **2** a person; anybody; one: *What can a fellow do?* **3** companion; comrade: *He was cut off from his fellows.* **4** the other one of a pair; mate; match: *I have the fellow of your glove.* **5** being in the same or a like condition, class, etc.: *fellow citizens, fellow sufferers.* **6** person who has a fellowship from a university or college. **7** member of a learned society. 1-4,6,7 *n.,* 5 *adj.* [*Fellow* is from Old English *fēolaga,* meaning "partner, comrade," which came from Icelandic *fēlagi.*]

fellow man, fellow human being.

fel low ship (fel′ō ship), **1** companionship; friendliness. **2** a being one of a group; membership: *I have enjoyed my fellowship with you in this club.* **3** group of people having similar tastes or interests; brotherhood. **4** position or money given by a university or college to a student to

a hat	**i** it	**oi** oil	**ch** child		a in about
ā age	**ī** ice	**ou** out	**ng** long		e in taken
ä far	**o** hot	**u** cup	**sh** she	ə =	i in pencil
e let	**ō** open	**u̇** put	**th** thin		o in lemon
ē equal	**ô** order	**ü** rule	**ᵺ** then		u in circus
ėr term			**zh** measure		

enable him or her to continue studying. *n.*

fel on (fel′ən), person who has committed a felony; criminal. Murderers and thieves are felons. *n.*

fe lo ni ous (fə lō′nē əs), having to do with a felony; criminal: *break into a house with felonious intent. adj.*

fel o ny (fel′ə nē), crime more serious than a misdemeanor. Murder and burglary are felonies. *n., pl.* **fel o nies.**

fel spar (fel′spär′), feldspar. *n.*

felt[1] (felt), past tense and past participle of **feel.** *I felt the cat's soft fur. It was felt the picnic should be postponed. v.*

felt[2] (felt), **1** cloth made by rolling and pressing together wool, hair, or fur. Felt is used to make hats, slippers, and pads. **2** made of felt: *a felt hat.* **1** *n.,* **2** *adj.*

fe male (fē′māl), **1** woman or girl. **2** of women or girls. **3** belonging to the sex that can give birth to young or lay eggs. Mares, cows, and hens are female animals. **4** animal belonging to this sex. **5** flower having a pistil or pistils but no stamens. **6** plant bearing only flowers with pistils. **1,4,6** *n.,* **2,3,5** *adj.* —**fe′male ness,** *n.*

fem i nine (fem′ə nən), **1** of women or girls. **2** like a woman; womanly. **3** of or belonging to the female sex. **4** (in grammar) of the gender to which nouns and adjectives referring to females belong. *She* is a feminine pronoun; *he* is a masculine pronoun. *adj.* —**fem′i nine ly,** *adv.* —**fem′i nine ness,** *n.*

fem i nin i ty (fem′ə nin′ə tē), feminine quality or condition. *n.*

fem i nism (fem′ə niz′əm), **1** belief in increased rights and activities for women in their economic, social, political, and private life. **2** movement to obtain these rights. *n.*

fem i nist (fem′ə nist), **1** person who believes in or favors feminism. **2** believing in or favoring feminism. **1** *n.,* **2** *adj.*

fe mur (fē′mər), thighbone. *n., pl.* **fe murs, fem or a** (fem′ər ə).

fen (fen), low, wet land; marsh. *n.*

fence (fens), **1** railing, wall, or similar enclosure put around a yard, garden, field, farm, etc., to show where it ends or to keep people or animals out or in. Most fences are made of wood, wire, or metal. **2** put a fence around; keep out or in with a fence. **3** fight with long, slender swords or foils. **4** person who buys and sells stolen goods. **1,4** *n.,* **2,3** *v.,* **fenced, fenc ing.** —**fence′less,** *adj.* **on the fence,** not having made up one's mind which side to take; doubtful.

fenc er (fen′sər), person who knows how to fight with a sword or foil. *n.*

fencing
(def. 1)

fenc ing (fen′sing), **1** art or sport of fighting with swords or foils. **2** material for fences. **3** fences. *n.*

fend (fend), **1 fend for oneself,** provide for oneself; get along by one's own efforts: *While traveling alone I had to fend for myself.* **2 fend off,** ward off; keep off: *fend off a blow. v.*

fend er (fen′dər), **1** metal frame over the wheel of a car, truck, bicycle, etc., that protects the wheel and reduces splashing in wet weather. **2** cowcatcher. **3** bar, frame, or screen in front of a fireplace to keep hot coals and sparks from the room. *n.*

fen nel (fen′l), a tall, perennial plant related to parsley, with yellow flowers. Its fragrant seeds are used in medicine and cooking. *n.*

Fer di nand V (ferd′n and), 1452-1516, king of Spain from 1474 to 1516. He and his queen, Isabella I, encouraged Christopher Columbus in his voyages.

fer ment (fər ment′ *for 1,5;* fer′ment *for 2-4*), **1** undergo or produce a gradual chemical change in which bacteria, yeast, etc., change sugar into alcohol and produce carbon dioxide. Vinegar is formed when cider ferments. **2** substance that causes others to ferment. Yeast is a ferment. **3** a chemical change caused by a ferment; fermentation. **4** excitement; agitation; unrest: *Rumors of war caused ferment throughout the country.* **5** cause unrest in; excite; agitate. **1,5** *v.,* **2-4** *n.* —**fer ment′a ble,** *adj.*

fer men ta tion (fer′men tā′shən), **1** act or process of fermenting: *Fermentation causes milk to sour and bread to rise.* **2** a chemical change caused by a ferment. **3** excitement; ferment. *n.*

Fer mi (fer′mē), Enrico, 1901-1954, American physicist, born in Italy. *n.*

fer mi um (fer′mē əm), a radioactive metallic element produced artificially from plutonium or uranium. *n.* [*Fermium* was named in honor of Enrico *Fermi.*]

fern (fern), kind of plant that has roots, stems, and feathery leaves, but does not have flowers or seeds. The plant reproduces by means of spores which grow in little brown clusters on the backs of the leaves. *n.* —**fern′less,** *adj.* —**fern′like′,** *adj.*

fe ro cious (fə rō′shəs), **1** very cruel; savage; fierce: *The bear's ferocious growl terrified the hunter.* **2** INFORMAL. intense: *a ferocious headache. adj.* —**fe ro′cious ly,** *adv.* —**fe ro′cious ness,** *n.*

fe roc i ty (fə ros′ə tē), great cruelty; savageness; fierceness: *The wolves fought with great ferocity. n., pl.* **fe roc i ties.**

fer ret (fer′it), **1** kind of weasel with black feet, found in western North America. **2** a white or yellowish-white European polecat used for killing rats and driving rabbits from their holes. **3** hunt with ferrets. **4** hunt; search: *It took the detectives over a year to ferret out the criminal.* **1,2** *n.,* **3,4** *v.* [*Ferret* came into English about 600 years ago from French *fuiret,* and can be traced back to Latin *fur,* meaning "thief."] —**fer′ret er,** *n.*

Fer ris wheel (fer′is), a large, revolving wheel with hanging seats, used in carnivals, amusement parks, fairs, etc. [The *Ferris wheel* was named for George W. G. *Ferris,* 1859-1896, an American engineer who invented it.]

Ferris wheel

fer ry (fer′ē), **1** carry (people, vehicles, and goods) across a river or narrow stretch of water. **2** boat that carries people, vehicles, and goods on such a trip; ferryboat. **3** place where boats carry people, vehicles, and goods across a river or narrow stretch of water. **4** go across in a ferryboat. **5** carry back and forth in an airplane. **6** fly an airplane to a destination for delivery. 1,4-6 *v.*, **fer ried, fer ry ing;** 2,3 *n., pl.* **fer ries.**

fer ry boat (fer′ē bōt′), boat that carries people, vehicles, and goods across a river or narrow stretch of water. *n.*

fer tile (fer′tl), **1** able to bear seeds, fruit, young, etc.: *a fertile animal or plant.* **2** able to develop into a new individual; fertilized: *Chicks hatch from fertile eggs.* **3** able to produce much; producing crops easily: *Fertile soil yields good crops.* **4** producing ideas; creative: *a fertile mind. adj.* [*Fertile* is from Latin *fertilis,* which comes from *ferre,* meaning "to bear, carry."] —**fer′tile ly,** *adv.* —**fer′tile ness,** *n.*

fer til i ty (fər til′ə tē), **1** the bearing, or abundant bearing, of seeds, fruits, crops, or young. **2** power to produce: *The fertility of his imagination made him a first-class writer of mystery stories. n.*

fer ti li za tion (fer′tl ə zā′shən), **1** a fertilizing or a being fertilized. **2** the union of a male reproductive cell and a female reproductive cell to form a cell that will develop into a new individual. *n.*

fer ti lize (fer′tl īz), **1** make fertile; make able to produce much. **2** unite with (an egg cell) in fertilization; impregnate. **3** put fertilizer on: *fertilize a lawn. v.,* **fer ti lized, fer ti liz ing.** —**fer′ti liz′a ble,** *adj.*

fer ti liz er (fer′tl ī′zər), substance such as manure, chemicals, etc., spread over or put into the soil to make it able to produce more. *n.*

fer ven cy (fer′vən sē), fervor. *n.*

fer vent (fer′vənt), showing great warmth of feeling; very earnest: *She made a fervent plea for more food and medical supplies for the earthquake victims. adj.* —**fer′vent ly,** *adv.*

fer vid (fer′vid), full of strong feeling; very emotional; ardent; spirited: *The speaker's fervid words stirred the crowd to action. adj.* —**fer′vid ly,** *adv.* —**fer′vid ness,** *n.*

fer vor (fer′vər), great warmth of feeling; enthusiasm or earnestness: *patriotic fervor. n.*

WORD HISTORY

fervor

Fervor was borrowed from Latin *fervor,* which comes from *fervere,* meaning "to boil, glow."

fes tal (fes′tl), of a feast, festival, or holiday; gay; festive: *A wedding is a festal occasion. adj.* —**fes′tal ly,** *adv.*

fes ter (fes′tər), **1** form pus: *The neglected wound festered and became very painful.* **2** cause pain or resentment; rankle: *The hurt of the insult festered in her mind. v.*

fes ti val (fes′tə vəl), **1** day or special time of rejoicing or feasting, often in memory of some great happening: *Christmas is a Christian festival; Hanukkah is a Jewish festival.* **2** celebration or entertainment: *Every year the city has a music festival.*

fes tive (fes′tiv), of or suitable for a feast, festival, or holiday; gay; merry: *A birthday is a festive occasion. adj.* —**fes′tive ly,** *adv.* —**fes′tive ness,** *n.*

a hat	i it	oi oil	ch child	a in about
ā age	ī ice	ou out	ng long	e in taken
ä far	o hot	u cup	sh she	ə = i in pencil
e let	ō open	u̇ put	th thin	o in lemon
ē equal	ô order	ü rule	ᵺ then	u in circus
ėr term			zh measure	

fes tiv i ty (fe stiv′ə tē), **1** festive activity; thing done to celebrate: *The festivities on the Fourth of July included a parade and fireworks.* **2** gaiety; merriment. *n., pl.* **fes tiv i ties.**

fes toon (fe stün′), **1** a string or chain of flowers, leaves, ribbons, etc., hanging in a curve between two points: *The bunting was draped on the wall in colorful festoons.* **2** decorate with festoons: *The gym was festooned with crepe paper for the dance.* **3** form into festoons; hang in curves: *Draperies were festooned over the window.* 1 *n.,* 2,3 *v.* [*Festoon* comes from French *feston,* and can be traced back to Latin *festum,* meaning "festival."]

festoon (def. 1)

fe tal (fē′tl), of or like a fetus: *a fetal heartbeat. adj.* Also, **foetal.**

fetch (fech), **1** go and get; bring: *Please fetch me my glasses.* **2** cause to come; succeed in bringing: *Her call fetched me at once.* **3** be sold for: *These eggs will fetch a good price. v.* —**fetch′er,** *n.*

fetch ing (fech′ing), attractive; charming: *a fetching new outfit. adj.* —**fetch′ing ly,** *adv.*

fete (fāt), **1** festival or party, especially an elaborate one and often one held outdoors: *A large fete was given for the benefit of the town hospital.* **2** honor with a fete; entertain: *My parents were feted by their friends on their twentieth anniversary.* 1 *n.,* 2 *v.,* **fet ed, fet ing.** [*Fete* comes from French *fête,* and can be traced back to Latin *festum,* meaning "festival."]

fête (fāt), fete. *n., pl.* **fêtes;** *v.,* **fêt ed, fêt ing.**

fet id (fet′id), smelling very bad; stinking. *adj.* —**fet′id ly,** *adv.* —**fet′id ness,** *n.*

fe tish (fē′tish *or* fet′ish), **1** thing supposed to have magic powers: *The tribe worshiped a fetish that was a hideous snake carved out of stone.* **2** any object of unreasoning reverence or blind devotion: *Some people make a fetish of stylish clothes. n., pl.* **fe tish es.**

fet lock (fet′lok), **1** tuft of hair above a horse's hoof on the back part of its leg. **2** the part of a horse's leg where this tuft grows. *n.*

fet ter (fet′ər), **1** chain or shackle for the feet: *Fetters prevented the prisoner's escape.* **2** bind with chains; chain the feet of. **3** anything that shackles or binds; restraint. **4** bind; restrain: *Fetter your temper.* 1,3 *n.,* 2,4 *v.*

fet tle (fet′l), condition; state: *The horse is in fine fettle and should win the race. n.*

fe tus (fē′təs), an animal embryo during the later stages of its development in the womb or in the egg, especially a human embryo more than three months old. *n., pl.* **fe tus es.** Also, **foetus.**

feud (fyüd), **1** a long and deadly quarrel between families or tribes. Feuds are often passed down from generation to generation. **2** bitter hatred between two persons or groups. **3** carry on a long and deadly quarrel. 1,2 *n.*, 3 *v.*

feu dal (fyü′dl), of or having to do with feudalism: *the feudal system, feudal laws. adj.* **—feu′dal ly,** *adv.*

feu dal ism (fyü′dl iz′əm), the social, economic, and political system of Europe in the Middle Ages. Under this system vassals gave military and other services to their lord in return for his protection and the use of land. *n.*

fe ver (fē′vər), **1** an unhealthy condition in which the body temperature is higher than normal (98.6 degrees Fahrenheit or 37.0 degrees Celsius in human beings). **2** any sickness that causes or is accompanied by fever: *scarlet fever, typhoid fever.* **3** an excited, restless condition; agitation: *When gold was discovered the miners were in a fever of excitement. n.* **—fe′ver less,** *adj.*

fever blister, cold sore.

fe vered (fē′vərd), **1** having fever. **2** excited; restless. *adj.*

fe ver ish (fē′vər ish), **1** having fever. **2** having a slight degree of fever. **3** caused by fever: *a feverish thirst.* **4** causing fever: *a feverish climate.* **5** infested with fever: *a feverish swamp.* **6** excited; restless: *I packed in feverish haste. adj.* **—fe′ver ish ly,** *adv.* **—fe′ver ish ness,** *n.*

fever sore, cold sore.

few (fyü), **1** not many: *Few people attended the meeting.* **2** a small number: *I haven't many friends, only a few.* **3** the few, the minority. 1 *adj.*, 2,3 *n.* **—few′ness,** *n.*

quite a few, INFORMAL. a good many: *Quite a few of us went to the game.*

fez (fez), a felt cap, usually red and ornamented with a long, black tassel. *n., pl.* **fez zes.** [*Fez gets its name from Fez, a city in northern Morocco, where it was first made.*]

ff, fortissimo.

ff., and the following pages, sections, etc.; and what follows.

fi an cé (fē′än sā′), man engaged to be married. *n., pl.* **fi an cés.**

fi an cée (fē′än sā′), woman engaged to be married. *n., pl.* **fi an cées.**

fi as co (fē as′kō), a complete or ridiculous failure; humiliating breakdown: *The play was a fiasco and closed after only three performances. n., pl.* **fi as cos** or **fi as coes.**

fi at (fī′ət *or* fī′at), an authoritative order or command; decree. *n.* [*Fiat comes from Latin fiat, meaning "let it be done."*]

fib (fib), **1** a lie about some small matter. **2** tell such a lie. 1 *n.,* 2 *v.,* **fibbed, fib bing.**

fib ber (fib′ər), person who fibs. *n.*

fi ber (fī′bər), **1** a threadlike part; thread. A muscle is made up of many fibers. **2** substance made up of threads or threadlike parts: *Hemp fiber can be spun or woven.* **3** any part of food, such as the cellulose in vegetables, that cannot be digested, and so stimulates the movement of food and waste products through the intestines. **4** texture: *cloth of coarse fiber.* **5** character; nature: *a person of strong moral fiber. n.* Also, **fibre.**

fi ber board (fī′bər bôrd′), a building material made by compressing wood fibers and other material into flat sheets. *n.*

Fi ber glas (fī′bər glas′), trademark for fiberglass. *n.*

fi ber glass (fī′bər glas′), very fine, flexible filaments of glass used for insulating materials or woven into fabrics; spun glass. *n.*

fi bre (fī′bər), fiber, *n.*

fi brin (fī′brən), a white, tough, elastic substance formed when blood clots. *n.*

fi broid (fī′broid), made up of fibers or fibrous tissue: *a fibroid tumor. adj.*

fi brous (fī′brəs), **1** made up of fibers; having fibers. **2** like fiber; stringy. *adj.*

fib u la (fib′yə lə), the outer and thinner of the two

bones in the human lower leg. It extends from knee to ankle. *n., pl.* **fib u lae** (fib′yə lē′), **fib u las.**

WORD HISTORY

fibula

Fibula comes from Latin *fibula,* meaning "a clasp, brooch." It was probably called this because of its shape, since the fibula and the tibia together look like a clasp.

fick le (fik′əl), likely to change without reason; changing; not constant: *a fickle friend. adj.* **—fick′le ness,** *n.*

fic tion (fik′shən), **1** novels, short stories, and other prose writings that tell about imaginary people and happenings. **2** something imagined or made up: *They exaggerate so much in telling about their experiences that it is impossible to separate fact from fiction. n.*

fic tion al (fik′shə nəl), of fiction: *Dorothy and Aunt Em in "The Wizard of Oz" are fictional characters. adj.* **—fic′tion al ly,** *adv.*

fic tion al ize (fik′shə nə līz), give a fictional form to; make into fiction. *v.,* **fic tion al ized, fic tion al iz ing.** **—fic′tion al i za′tion,** *n.*

fic ti tious (fik tish′əs), **1** not real; imaginary: *a fictitious story.* **2** used in order to deceive; false: *a fictitious name. adj.* **—fic ti′tious ly,** *adv.* **—fic ti′tious ness,** *n.*

fid dle (fid′l), **1** violin. **2** INFORMAL. play on a violin. **3** make aimless movements; play nervously; toy: *The shy child fiddled with crayons and paid no attention to the guests.* **4** waste; trifle: *He fiddled away the whole day doing absolutely nothing.* 1 *n.,* 2-4 *v.,* **fid dled, fid dling.**

fid dler (fid′lər), person who plays a violin. *n.*

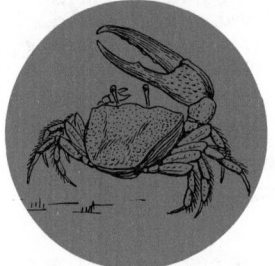

fiddler crab—shell width up to 1²/₃ in. (45 mm.)

fiddler crab, a small, burrowing crab found along coasts in warm regions. The male has one much enlarged claw.

fid dle stick (fid′l stik′), INFORMAL. **1** the bow with which a violin is played. **2 fiddlesticks,** nonsense! rubbish! 1 *n.,* 2 *interj.*

fi del i ty (fī del′ə tē *or* fə del′ə tē), **1** steadfast faithfulness; loyalty: *a dog's fidelity to its owner.* **2** exactness; accuracy: *The reporter wrote the story with absolute fidelity.* **3** the ability of a radio, phonograph, etc., to transmit or reproduce sound accurately. *n., pl.* **fi del i ties.**

fidg et (fij′it), **1** move about restlessly; be uneasy: *Many people fidget if they have to sit still a long time.* **2 the fidgets,** a fit of restlessness or uneasiness: *The long speech gave us the fidgets.* 1 *v.,* 2 *n.*

fidg et y (fij′ə tē), restless; uneasy: *That fidgety child keeps twisting and moving. adj.*

fie (fī), for shame! shame!: *Fie upon you! interj.*

fief (fēf), piece of land held on condition of giving military and other services to the feudal lord owning it, in return for his protection and the use of the land. *n.*

field (fēld), **1** land with few or no trees; open country: *They drove through the woods until they came to a field covered with wild flowers.* **2** piece of land used for crops or for pasture. **3** piece of land used for some special purpose: *a baseball field.* **4** battlefield: *the field of Gettysburg.* **5** land yielding some product: *the coal fields of Pennsylvania.* **6** a flat space; broad surface: *A field of ice surrounds the North Pole.* **7** surface on which something is pictured or painted; background: *Their flag shows a red circle on a white field.* **8** range of opportunity or interest; sphere of activity: *the field of politics, the field of art, the field of science.* **9** (in physics) the space throughout which a force operates. A magnet has a magnetic field around it. **10** space or area in which things can be seen through a telescope, microscope, etc. **11** area where contests in jumping, throwing, etc., are held. **12** all those in a game, contest, or outdoor sport. **13** (in baseball, cricket, etc.) to stop or catch (a batted ball) and throw it in. **14** send (a player, team, etc.) to the playing area. **15** of a field or fields. 1-12 *n.,* 13,14 *v.,* 15 *adj.*

take the field, begin a battle, campaign, game, etc.

Field (fēld), **Eugene,** 1850-1895, American journalist and poet. *n.*

field day, 1 day for athletic contests and outdoor sports. **2** day when soldiers perform drills, mock fights, etc. **3** day of unusual activity or display.

field er (fēl′dər), (in baseball, cricket, etc.) a player who stops or catches and throws the ball in. A fielder is stationed around or outside the diamond in baseball. *n.*

field glasses or **field glass,** small binoculars for use outdoors.

field goal, goal in football counting three points, made by a place kick.

field hockey, hockey played on a field.

field house, building near an athletic field, used for storing equipment, for dressing rooms, etc.

field magnet, magnet used to produce or maintain a magnetic field, especially in a dynamo or electric motor.

field marshal, officer ranking next below the commander in chief in the British, French, German, and some other armies.

field mouse, mouse which lives in open fields.

field trip, trip away from school to give students an opportunity to learn by seeing things closely and at first hand.

fiend (fēnd), **1** an evil spirit; devil. **2** a very wicked or cruel person. **3** INFORMAL. person who gives himself or herself up to some habit, practice, game, etc.: *a tennis fiend. n.* **—fiend′like′,** *adj.*

fiend ish (fēn′dish), very cruel; wicked; devilish: *fiendish tortures, a fiendish yell. adj.* **—fiend′ish ly,** *adv.*

fierce (firs), **1** savagely cruel; ferocious; wild: *A wounded lion can be fierce.* **2** raging; violent: *fierce anger. A fierce wind blows very hard.* **3** very eager or active: *a fierce determination to win. adj.,* **fierc er, fierc est.** **—fierce′ly,** *adv.* **—fierce′ness,** *n.*

fie ry (fī′rē), **1** containing fire; burning; flaming: *a fiery furnace.* **2** like fire; very hot; glowing: *a fiery red, fiery heat.* **3** full of feeling or spirit: *a fiery speech.* **4** easily aroused or excited: *a fiery temper. adj.,* **fie ri er, fie ri est.**

fi es ta (fē es′tə), **1** a religious festival; saint's day. **2** holiday or festivity. *n., pl.* **fi es tas.** [*Fiesta* was borrowed from Spanish *fiesta,* and can be traced back to Latin *festum,* meaning "festival."]

fife (fīf), **1** a small, shrill musical instrument like a flute, played by blowing. Fifes are used with drums to make music for marching. **2** play on a fife. 1 *n.,* 2 *v.,* **fifed, fif ing.** [*Fife* comes from German *Pfeife,* meaning "pipe."]

fife (def. 1)

fif teen (fif′tēn′), five more than ten; 15. *n., adj.*

fif teenth (fif′tēnth′), **1** next after the 14th; last in a series of 15. **2** one of 15 equal parts. *adj., n.*

fifth (fifth), **1** next after the fourth; last in a series of 5. **2** one of 5 equal parts. *adj., n.*

Fifth Amendment, the fifth amendment to the United States Constitution, which protects people from having to testify against themselves in criminal cases. It is part of the Bill of Rights.

fifth column, persons living within a country who secretly aid its enemies.

fifth ly (fifth′lē), in the fifth place. *adv.*

fif ti eth (fif′tē ith), **1** next after the 49th; last in a series of 50. **2** one of 50 equal parts. *adj., n.*

fif ty (fif′tē), five times ten; 50. *n., pl.* **fif ties;** *adj.*

fif ty-fif ty (fif′tē fif′tē), INFORMAL. in two equal parts; with two equal shares: *a fifty-fifty chance of winning* (adj.), *go fifty-fifty on expenses* (adv.). *adj., adv.*

fig (fig), **1** a small, soft, sweet fruit of a tree that grows in warm regions. Figs are sometimes eaten fresh or canned, but usually are dried like dates and raisins. **2** a very small amount: *I don't care a fig for their opinion. n.*

fig., figure.

fight (fīt), **1** a violent struggle; combat; contest: *A fight ends when one side gives up.* **2** an angry dispute; quarrel: *Their fights were always over money.* **3** take part in a violent struggle, quarrel, etc.; have a fight: *When people fight, they hit one another. Soldiers fight by shooting with guns. Countries fight with armies.* **4** take part in a struggle against; try to overcome: *fight disease, fight one's fear of the dark.* **5** carry on (a struggle, conflict, etc.): *fight a duel.* **6** get or make by struggling: *She had to fight her way through the crowd.* **7** power or will to struggle or combat: *There was not much fight in the defeated team.* 1,2,7 *n.,* 3-6 *v.,* **fought, fight ing.**

fight it out, struggle or battle until one side wins.

fight off, to battle or take action against with success: *to fight off an invading army, to fight off the flu.*

fight shy of, keep away from; avoid.

show fight, be ready to fight; resist.

fight er (fī′tər), **1** a person that fights. **2** a boxer. *n.*

fig ment (fig′mənt), something imagined; made-up story: *I don't believe it; it's just a figment of your imagination. n.*

---

fig ur a tive (fig′yər ə tiv), **1** using words out of their literal or ordinary meaning to add beauty or force. **2** having many figures of speech. Much poetry is figurative. *adj.* —**fig′ur a tive ly**, *adv.* —**fig′ur a tive ness**, *n.*

figure (defs. 1, 2, 5, 8, and 13)

fig ure (fig′yər), **1** symbol for a number. 1, 2, 3, 4, etc., are figures. **2** use numbers to find out the answer to some problem; calculate: *figure out one's taxes. Can you figure the cost of painting this room?* **3** **figures**, *pl.* calculations using figures; arithmetic: *She is very good at figures.* **4** amount or value given in figures; price: *The figure for that house is very high.* **5** form enclosing a surface or space: *Circles, triangles, squares, cubes, and spheres are geometric figures.* **6** form or shape: *In the darkness she saw dim figures moving.* **7** way in which a person looks or appears: *The survivor of the earthquake was a figure of distress.* **8** person; character: *Napoleon is a well-known figure in history.* **9** stand out; appear: *The names of great leaders figure in the story of human progress.* **10** picture; drawing; diagram; illustration: *This book has many figures to help explain words.* **11** a design or pattern: *the figures in the wallpaper.* **12** outline traced by movements: *figures made by an airplane.* **13** set of movements in dancing or skating. **14** figure of speech. **15** INFORMAL. think; consider: *I figured I should stop where I was.* **16** INFORMAL. to seem likely or to be expected: *They didn't come to our party; well, it figured.* 1,3-8,10-14 *n.*, 2,9,15,16 *v.*, **fig ured, fig ur ing.** [*Figure* came into English about 700 years ago from French *figure*, and can be traced back to Latin *fingere*, meaning "to form, shape."]

figure on, depend on; plan on: *I can figure on my parents' help to pay my way through college.*

figure out, think out; understand: *Even the repairman couldn't figure out what had gone wrong with the washer.*

fig ured (fig′yərd), decorated with a design or pattern; not plain: *figured silk. adj.*

fig ure head (fig′yər hed′), **1** person who is the head of a business, government, etc., in name only, without real authority. **2** ornamental figure on the bow of a ship. *n.*

figure of speech, expression in which words are used out of their literal meaning or out of their ordinary use to add beauty or force. Similes and metaphors are figures of speech.

fig u rine (fig′yə rēn′), a small, ornamental figure made of stone, pottery, metal, etc.; statuette. *n.*

Fi ji (fē′jē), island country in the S Pacific, consisting of the **Fiji Islands.** It is a member of the Commonwealth of Nations. *Capital:* Suva. See **Australasia** for map. *n.* —**Fi′ji an,** *adj., n.*

fil a ment (fil′ə mənt), **1** a very fine thread; very slender, threadlike part. The wire that gives off light in an electric light bulb is a filament. **2** the heated wire that acts as the negative electrode in a vacuum tube. **3** (in plants) the stalklike part of a stamen that supports the anther. *n.*

fil bert (fil′bərt), a sweet, thick-shelled kind of cultivated hazelnut. *n.* [The *filbert* was named for Saint *Philibert*, a French Benedictine priest who lived about A.D. 650. It was called this because the nuts ripen near his feast day, August 20.]

filch (filch), steal in small quantities; pilfer: *She filched cookies from the pantry. v.* —**filch′er,** *n.*

file[1] (fīl), **1** container, drawer, folder, etc., for keeping memorandums, letters, or other papers in order. **2** set of papers kept in order: *a file of receipts.* **3** information or instructions which a computer keeps together under a single name. A file can be placed in memory, recalled from memory, or processed all at once. **4** put away in order: *Please file those letters.* **5** row of persons or things one behind another: *a file of soldiers.* **6** march or move in a file: *The pupils filed out of the room during the fire drill.* **7** place among the records of a court, public office, etc.: *The deed to our house is filed with the county clerk.* 1-3,5 *n.*, 4,6,7 *v.* **filed, fil ing.** —**fil′er,** *n.*

in file, one after another: *ships sailing in file.*

file[2] (fīl), **1** a steel tool with many small ridges or teeth on it. Its rough surface is used to smooth rough materials or wear away hard substances. **2** smooth or wear away with a file. 1 *n.*, 2 *v.*, **filed, fil ing.** —**fil′er,** *n.*

file clerk, person whose work is taking care of office files.

fi let (fi lā′ *or* fil′ā), a fillet of fish or meat. *n.*

fil i al (fil′ē əl), due from a son or daughter toward a mother or father: *filial affection. adj.* [*Filial* is from Latin *filialis*, which comes from *filius*, meaning "son," and *filia*, meaning "daughter."] —**fil′i al ly,** *adv.* —**fil′i al ness,** *n.*

fil i bus ter (fil′ə bus′tər), **1** the deliberate hindering of the passage of a bill in a legislature by long speeches or other means of delay. **2** deliberately hinder the passage of a bill by such means. 1 *n.*, 2 *v.* —**fil′i bus′ter er,** *n.*

filigree (def. 1)

fil i gree (fil′ə grē), **1** very delicate, lacelike, ornamental work of gold or silver wire. **2** anything very lacy, delicate, or fanciful: *The frost made a beautiful filigree on the windowpane. n.*

fil ings (fĭ/lĭngz), small pieces of iron, wood, etc., which have been removed by a file. *n.pl.*

Fil i pi no (fil/ə pē/nō), 1 person born or living in the Philippines. 2 Philippine. 1 *n.*, *pl.* **Fil i pi nos;** 2 *adj.*

fill (fil), 1 make full; put into until there is room for nothing more: *Fill this bottle with water. We filled the pots with soil before planting the seeds.* 2 become full: *The well filled with water.* 3 take up all the space in; spread throughout: *The crowd filled the hall. Smoke filled the room.* 4 all that is needed or wanted: *There is plenty of food, so eat your fill.* 5 supply with all that is needed or wanted for: *The druggist filled the doctor's prescription.* 6 stop up or close by putting something in: *After the dentist had taken out the decayed part, he filled my tooth.* 7 hold and do the duties of (a position, office, etc.); occupy: *We need someone to fill the office of vice-president.* 8 something that fills. Earth or rock used to make uneven land level is called fill. 9 (of the wind) stretch out (a sail) by blowing fully into it. 1-3,5-7,9 *v.*, 4,8 *n.*

fill in, 1 put in to complete something; insert: *fill in the date of an application.* 2 be a substitute.

fill out, 1 grow larger; swell: *Her cheeks have filled out.* 2 supply what is needed in; complete: *My sister filled out an application for a summer job.*

fill up, fill; fill completely.

fill er (fil/ər), thing put in to fill something. A pad of paper for a notebook and a preparation used to fill holes and cracks in wood before painting it are fillers. *n.*

fil let (fi lā/, fil/ā, *or* fil/it), 1 slice of fish or meat without bones or fat; filet. 2 cut (fish or meat) into such slices. 1 *n.*, 2 *v.* [*Fillet* came into English about 650 years ago from French *filet,* and can be traced back to Latin *filum,* meaning "thread."]

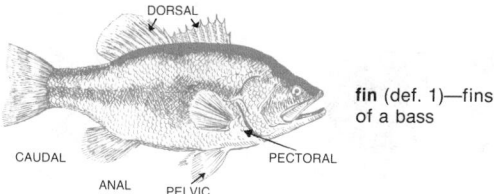

fin (def. 1)—fins of a bass

DORSAL
CAUDAL
ANAL
PELVIC
PECTORAL

fill ing (fil/ing), thing put in to fill something: *a filling in a tooth.*

filling station, place where gasoline and oil for automobiles, trucks, etc., are sold; gas station; service station.

fil lip (fil/əp), thing that rouses, revives, or excites: *The relishes served as a fillip to my appetite. n.*

Fill more (fil/môr), **Millard,** 1800-1874, the 13th president of the United States, from 1850 to 1853. *n.*

fil ly (fil/ē), a young female horse or donkey; mare that is less than four or five years old. *n.*, *pl.* **fil lies.**

film (film), 1 a very thin layer, sheet, surface, or coating, often of liquid: *The tanker sank, leaving a film of oil on the water.* 2 cover or become covered with a film; dim: *Her eyes filmed over with tears.* 3 roll or sheet of thin, flexible material covered with a coating that is sensitive to light, used in taking photographs. 4 a motion picture. 5 make a motion picture of: *They filmed "The Wizard of Oz."* 6 photograph for motion pictures: *They filmed the scene three times.* 1,3,4 *n.*, 2,5,6 *v.* —**film/like/,** *adj.*

film strip (film/strip/), series of still pictures printed on a reel of film. *n.*

film y (fil/mē), 1 like a film; very thin. 2 covered with a film. *adj.*, **film i er, film i est.** —**film/i ness,** *n.*

fil ter (fil/tər), 1 device for straining out substances from a liquid or a gas by passing it slowly through cloth, paper, sand, charcoal, etc. A filter is used to remove impurities from water. 2 material through which the liquid or gas passes in a filter. 3 device for allowing only certain light rays, frequencies, etc., to pass while blocking all others. A yellow filter placed in front of a camera lens allows less blue light to reach the film. 4 pass or flow very slowly: *Water filters through the sandy soil and into the well.* 5 put through a filter; strain: *We filter this water for drinking.* 6 act as a filter for: *The charcoal filtered the water.* 7 remove by a filter: *Filter out all the dirt before using this water.* 1-3 *n.*, 4-7 *v.* —**fil/ter er,** *n.*

fil ter a ble (fil/tər ə bəl), 1 able to be filtered. 2 capable of passing through a filter which traps bacteria: *a filterable virus. adj.* Also, **filtrable.**

filter tip, 1 cigarette with an attached filter for removing impurities from the smoke before it is inhaled. 2 the filter itself.

filth (filth), 1 foul dirt: *The alley was filled with garbage and filth.* 2 dirty words or thoughts. *n.*

filth y (fil/thē), very dirty; foul: *a filthy shirt. adj.,* **filth i er, filth i est.** —**filth/i ly,** *adv.* —**filth/i ness,** *n.*

fil tra ble (fil/trə bəl), filterable. *adj.*

fil trate (fil/trāt), 1 liquid that has been passed through a filter. 2 pass through a filter. 1 *n.*, 2 *v.*, **fil trat ed, fil trat ing.**

fil tra tion (fil trā/shən), a filtering or a being filtered. *n.*

fin (fin), 1 one of the movable winglike or fanlike parts of a fish's body. By moving its fins a fish can swim and balance itself in the water. 2 thing shaped or used like a fin. Some aircraft have fins to help balance them in flight. *n.* —**fin/less,** *adj.* —**fin/like/,** *adj.*

fi na gle (fə nā/gəl), INFORMAL. 1 get (something) by trickery or fraud. 2 cheat; swindle. 3 use trickery; practice fraud. *v.*, **fi na gled, fi na gling.** —**fi na/gler,** *n.*

fi nal (fī/nl), 1 at the end; coming last: *The book was interesting from the first to the final chapter.* 2 deciding completely; settling the question: *The one with the highest authority makes the final decisions.* 3 Often, **finals,** *pl.* the last or deciding set in a series of games or examinations: *If you pass your finals at the end of the term, you will be promoted.* 1,2 *adj.*, 3 *n.* [*Final* is from Latin *finalis,* which comes from *finis,* meaning "end." See **Word Family.**]

WORD FAMILY

final

Below are words related to *final.* They can all be traced back to the Latin word *finis* (fē/nis), meaning "end, limit."

affinity	fine[1]	finite
confine	fine[2]	infinite
define	finery	infinitesimal
definite	finesse	infinity
finale	finicky	paraffin
finance	finish	refine

fi na le (fə nä′lē), **1** the concluding part of a piece of music or a play. **2** the last part; end. *n.*

fi nal ist (fī′nl ist), person who takes part in the last or deciding set in a series of contests. *n.*

fi nal i ty (fī nal′ə tē), condition of being final, finished, or settled: *She refused with finality; we knew that she would not change her mind. n., pl.* **fi nal i ties.**

fi nal ize (fī′nl īz), make final or conclusive: *finalize an agreement. v.,* **fi nal ized, fi nal iz ing.** —**fi′na li za′- tion,** *n.*

fi nal ly (fī′nl ē), **1** at the end; at last. **2** in such a way as to decide or settle the question. *adv.*

fi nance (fə nans′ *or* fī′nans), **1** money matters: *A successful banker must have skill in finance.* **2** system by which the income of a nation, state, corporation, etc., is raised and managed. **3 finances,** *pl.* financial condition; money; funds; revenues: *New taxes were needed to increase the nation's finances.* **4** provide money for: *A part-time job helped finance my college education.* 1-3 *n.,* 4 *v.,* **fi nanced, fi nanc ing.** [Finance came into English about 600 years ago from French *finance,* meaning "end, settlement of a debt," and can be traced back to Latin *finis,* meaning "end."]

fi nan cial (fə nan′shəl *or* fī nan′shəl), **1** having to do with money matters: *Their financial affairs are in bad condition.* **2** having to do with the management of large sums of public or private money. *adj.* —**fi nan′cial ly,** *adv.*

fin an cier (fin′ən sir′ *or* fī′nən sir′), **1** person occupied or skilled in finance. Bankers are financiers. **2** person who is active in matters involving large sums of money. *n.*

finch (finch), any of several small songbirds with a bill shaped like a cone. Sparrows, buntings, grosbeaks, canaries, and cardinals are finches. *n., pl.* **finch es.**

find (find), **1** come upon by chance; happen on; meet with: *He found a dime in the road. They find friends everywhere.* **2** look for and get: *Please find my hat for me.* **3** discover; learn: *We found that he could not swim.* **4** get; get the use of: *Can you find time to do this?* **5** arrive at; reach: *Water finds its level. The arrow found its mark.* **6** decide and declare: *The jury found the defendant guilty.* **7** gain or recover the use of: *find one's tongue.* **8** something found. 1-7 *v.,* **found, find ing;** 8 *n.*

find oneself, learn one's abilities and how to make good use of them.

find out, learn about; come to know; discover.

find er (fīn′dər), **1** person or thing that finds. **2** a small, extra lens on the outside of a camera that shows what is being photographed. **3** a small telescope attached to a larger one to help find objects more easily. *n.*

find ing (fīn′ding), **1** discovery. **2** thing found. **3** decision reached after an examination or inquiry. The verdict of a jury is its finding. *n.*

fine[1] (fīn), **1** of very high quality; very good; excellent: *Everybody praised his fine singing. She is a fine scholar.* **2** very small or thin: *Thread is finer than rope. Sand is finer than gravel.* **3** sharp: *a tool with a fine edge.* **4** not coarse or heavy; delicate: *fine linen.* **5** refined; elegant: *fine manners.* **6** subtle: *The law makes fine distinctions.* **7** without impurities. Fine gold is gold not mixed with any other metal. **8** INFORMAL. very well; excellently: *I'm doing fine.* 1-7 *adj.,* **fin er, fin est;** 8 *adv.* [Fine[1] came into English about 700 years ago from French *fin,* meaning "perfected, finished," and can be traced back to Latin *finis,* meaning "end."] —**fine′ly,** *adv.* —**fine′ness,** *n.*

fine[2] (fīn), **1** sum of money paid as a punishment for breaking a law or regulation. **2** make pay such a sum: *The judge fined her ten dollars.* 1 *n.,* 2 *v.,* **fined, fin ing.** [Fine[2] came into English about 800 years ago from

French *fin,* meaning "end, settlement, payment," and can be traced back to Latin *finis,* meaning "end."]

fine arts, arts depending upon taste and appealing to the sense of beauty; painting, drawing, sculpture, and architecture.

fine-drawn (fīn′drôn′), **1** drawn out until very small or thin. **2** very subtle: *a fine-drawn distinction. adj.*

fin er y (fī′nər ē), showy clothes or ornaments. *n., pl.* **fin er ies.**

fi nesse (fə nes′), **1** delicacy of execution; skill: *That young artist shows wonderful finesse.* **2** the skillful handling of a delicate situation to one's advantage: *A successful diplomat must be a master of finesse.* **3** use finesse. 1,2 *n.,* 3 *v.,* **fi nessed, fi ness ing.**

fin ger (fing′gər), **1** one of the five slender divisions that end the hand, especially the four besides the thumb. **2** part of a glove that covers a finger. **3** anything shaped or used like a finger; thing that reaches out and touches: *a long finger of light.* **4** touch or handle with the fingers; use the fingers on: *finger the keyboard of a piano.* **5** perform or mark (a passage of music) with a certain fingering. **6** width of a finger; ³/₄ inch. 1-3,6 *n.,* 4,5 *v.* —**fin′ger like′,** *adj.*

put one's finger on, point out exactly: *The inspector was able to put his finger on the weak point in the suspect's alibi.*

fin ger ing (fing′gər ing), **1** way of using the fingers in playing a musical instrument. **2** signs marked on a piece of music to show how the fingers are to be used in playing it. *n.*

fin ger nail (fing′gər nāl′), a hard layer of horn on the upper side of the end of each finger. *n.*

finger painting, 1 method of painting pictures or designs on large sheets of paper, with fingers or hands instead of brushes. **2** picture or design painted in this way.

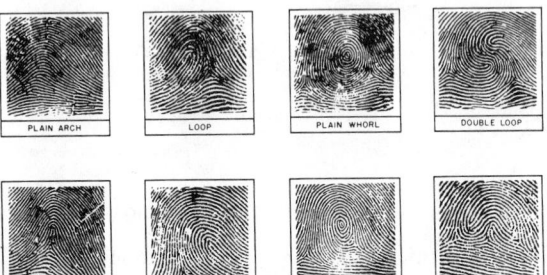

PLAIN ARCH LOOP PLAIN WHORL DOUBLE LOOP

TENTED ARCH LOOP CENTRAL POCKET LOOP ACCIDENTAL

fingerprint (def. 1)—the eight basic types of fingerprints

fin ger print (fing′gər print′), **1** an impression of the markings on the inner surface of the last joint of a finger or thumb. A person can be identified from fingerprints because no two fingers have identical markings. **2** take the fingerprints of. 1 *n.,* 2 *v.*

fin i cal (fin′ə kəl), finicky. *adj.* —**fin′i cal ly,** *adv.* —**fin′i cal ness,** *n.*

fin ick i ness (fin′ə kē nis), finicky quality or condition. *n.*

fin ick ing (fin′ə king), finicky. *adj.*

fin ick y (fin′ə kē), too dainty or particular; too precise; fussy. *adj.*

fi nis (fin′is *or* fī′nis), the end. *n.*

fin ish (fin′ish), **1** bring to an end; reach the end of; complete: *finish one's dinner, finish sewing a dress.* **2** come to an end: *There was so little wind that the sailing race didn't finish until after dark.* **3** an end: *fight to a finish.* **4** use up completely: *finish a bottle of milk, finish a spool of thread.* **5** way in which the surface is prepared: *a* *smooth finish on furniture.* **6** prepare the surface of in some way: *finish metal with a dull surface.* **7** polished condition or quality; perfection: *the finish of a person's manners.* **8** to perfect in detail; polish. 1,2,4,6,8 *v.,* 3,5,7 *n., pl.* **fin ish es.** —**fin′ish er,** *n.*

finish off, 1 complete. **2** overcome completely; destroy; kill.

finish up, 1 complete: *finish up a job.* **2** use up completely: *I've finished up all the paint.*

finish with, 1 complete. **2** stop being friends with; have nothing to do with.

fin ished (fin′isht), **1** ended or completed. **2** brought to the highest degree of excellence; perfected; polished: *It takes years of study and practice to become a finished musician. adj.*

fi nite (fī′nīt), **1** having limits or bounds; not infinite: *Human understanding is finite.* **2** in mathematics: **a** able to be reached or passed in counting: *a finite number.* **b** (of a set) having a limited number of elements. *adj.* —**fi′nite ly,** *adv.* —**fi′nite ness,** *n.*

fink (fingk), SLANG. **1** informer. **2** an undesirable or inferior person. *n.*

Fin land (fin′lənd), **1** country in N Europe, east of Sweden. *Capital:* Helsinki. See **Lapland** for map. **2 Gulf of,** part of the Baltic Sea, south of Finland. *n.*

Fin land er (fin′lən dər), Finn. *n.*

Finn (fin), person born or living in Finland. *n.*

fin nan had die (fin′ən had′ē), smoked and dried haddock. [*Finnan haddie* is from earlier *Findon haddock,* which comes from *Findon,* a village in Scotland, and *haddock.*]

finnan haddock, finnan haddie.

finned (find), having a fin or fins. *adj.*

Finn ish (fin′ish), **1** of Finland, its people, or their language. **2** the people of Finland. **3** language of Finland. 1 *adj.,* 2 *n.pl.,* 3 *n.sing.*

fin ny (fin′ē), **1** filled with fish. **2** having fins. **3** like a fin. *adj.,* **fin ni er, fin ni est.**

fiord (fyôrd), a long, narrow bay of the sea bordered by steep cliffs. Norway has many fiords. *n.* Also, **fjord.** [*Fiord* was borrowed from Norwegian *fiord,* which came from Icelandic *fjörthr.*]

fir (fėr), an evergreen tree related to the pine, having needles distributed evenly around the branch. Some firs are valued for their timber. Small firs are often used for Christmas trees. *n.*

fire (fīr), **1** flame, heat, and light caused by something burning. **2** something burning. **3** destruction by burning: *A cigarette thrown into the woods in dry weather may start a fire.* **4** make burn; set on fire. **5** fuel burning or arranged so that it will burn quickly: *A fire was laid in the fireplace.* **6** supply with fuel; tend the fire of: *fire a furnace.* **7** dry with heat; bake: *Bricks are fired to make them hard.* **8** heat of feeling; readiness to act; passion, fervor, enthusiasm, or excitement: *Their hearts were full of patriotic fire.* **9** arouse; excite; inflame: *Stories about adventures fire the imagination.* **10** the shooting or discharge of guns, etc.: *The enemy's fire forced the troops to take shelter in a ravine.* **11** discharge (a gun, etc.): *I fired my rifle four times.* **12** shoot: *fire a rocket. The soldiers fired from the fort.* **13** INFORMAL. throw: *The shortstop fired the ball to first base for the out.* **14** INFORMAL. dismiss from a job, etc. 1-3,5,8,10 *n.,* 4,6,7,9,11-14 *v.,* **fired, fir ing.** —**fir′er,** *n.*

between two fires, attacked from both sides.

catch fire, begin to burn.

hang fire, be slow in going off or acting; be delayed.

lay a fire, build a fire ready to be lit.

miss fire, 1 fail to go off. **2** fail to do what was attempted.

on fire, 1 burning. **2** full of a feeling or spirit like fire; excited.

open fire, begin shooting.

under fire, 1 exposed to shooting from the enemy's guns. **2** attacked; blamed.

fire arm (fīr′ärm′), gun, pistol, or other weapon to shoot with. It is usually one that can be carried and used by one person. *n.*

fire ball (fīr′bôl′), the great, glowing cloud of hot gases, water vapor, and dust produced by a nuclear explosion. *n.*

fire boat (fīr′bōt′), boat with equipment for putting out fires. *n.*

fire bomb, an incendiary bomb.

fire box (fīr′boks′), place for the fire in a furnace, boiler, etc. *n., pl.* **fire box es.**

fire brand (fīr′brand′), **1** piece of burning wood. **2** person who arouses angry feelings in others. *n.*

fire bug (fīr′bug′), INFORMAL. person who purposely sets houses or property on fire; person who commits arson. *n.*

fire crack er (fīr′krak′ər), a paper roll containing gunpowder and a fuse. Firecrackers explode with a loud noise. *n.*

fire damp (fīr′damp′), gas formed in coal mines, dangerously explosive when mixed with certain proportions of air. *n.*

fire dog (fīr′dôg′), andiron. *n.*

fiord

fire engine, truck with equipment for pumping and spraying water, chemicals, etc., to put out fires; fire truck.

fire escape, stairway or ladder in or on a building, to use when the building is on fire.

fire extinguisher, container filled with chemicals which can be sprayed on a fire to put it out.

fire fight er (fīr′fī′tər), person whose work is putting out fires. *n.*

fire fly (fīr′flī′), a small beetle that gives off flashes of light which can be seen when it flies at night; lightning bug. *n., pl.* **fire flies.**

fire house (fīr′hous′), building where fire trucks are kept; fire station. *n., pl.* **fire hous es** (fīr′hou′ziz).

fire light (fīr′līt′), light from a fire. *n.*

fire man (fīr′mən), **1** person who belongs to a fire company, trained to put out fires. **2** person whose work is looking after fires in a furnace, boiler, locomotive, etc. *n., pl.* **fire men.**

fire place (fīr′plās′), place built to hold a fire. Indoor

---

a hat	i it	oi oil	ch child	⎛ a in about
ā age	ī ice	ou out	ng long	⎜ e in taken
ä far	o hot	u cup	sh she ə =	⎨ i in pencil
e let	ō open	u̇ put	th thin	⎜ o in lemon
ē equal	ô order	ü rule	ŦH then	⎝ u in circus
ėr term			zh measure	

fireplaces are usually made of brick or stone, with a chimney leading up through the roof. *n.*

fire plug (fīr'plug'), hydrant. *n.*

fire proof (fīr'prüf'), very resistant to fire; almost impossible to burn: *A building made entirely of steel and concrete is fireproof.* **2** make fireproof: *fireproof a theater curtain.* **1** *adj.,* **2** *v.*

fire side (fīr'sīd'), **1** space around a fireplace or hearth. **2** home; hearth: *We were weary of traveling and longed to be back at our own fireside.* **3** home life: *a happy fireside. n.*

fire station, firehouse.

fire tower, tower from which forest rangers can watch for forest fires.

fire trap (fīr'trap'), building that could burn very easily and would be hard to get out of if it were on fire. *n.*

fire truck, fire engine.

fire wa ter (fīr'wô'tər *or* fīr'wot'ər), a strong alcoholic drink. *n.* [*Firewater* is a translation of the North American Indians' name for whiskey, gin, rum, etc.]

fire wood (fīr'wùd'), wood to make a fire. *n.*

fire work (fīr'werk'), **1** a firecracker, bomb, rocket, etc., that makes a loud noise or a beautiful, fiery display at night. **2 fireworks,** *pl.* a firework display. *n.*

firm[1] (ferm), **1** not yielding when pressed; solid; hard: *firm flesh, firm ground.* **2** not easily moved or shaken; fixed in place: *a tree firm in the earth.* **3** not easily changed; determined; resolute; positive: *a firm voice, a firm character, a firm belief.* **4** not changing; staying the same; steady: *a firm price. adj.* [*Firm*[1] came into English about 600 years ago from French *ferme,* which came from Latin *firmus,* meaning "firm, strong."] **—firm'ly,** *adv.* **—firm'ness,** *n.*

firm[2] (ferm), company of two or more persons in business together. *n.* [*Firm*[2] is from German *Firma,* which came from Italian *firma,* meaning "signature," and can be traced back to Latin *firmus,* meaning "firm, strong."]

fisher (def. 2)—about 2 ft. (60 cm.) long without the tail

fir ma ment (fer'mə mənt), arch of the heavens; sky. *n.*

first (ferst), **1** coming before all others: *She is first in her class.* **2** before all others; before anything else: *We eat first and then feed the cat.* **3** person, thing, place, etc., that is first: *We were the first to get here.* **4** the beginning: *At first I did not like school.* **5** for the first time: *When I first met her, she was a child.* **6** instead of something else; rather; sooner: *I won't give up; I will die first.* **7** (in music) playing or singing the chief part or the part highest in pitch: *first flute, first soprano.* **8** the first day of the month: *I'll see you on the first.* **1,7** *adj.,* **2,5,6** *adv.,* **3,4,8** *n.*

first aid, emergency treatment given to an injured or sick person before a doctor sees the person.

first-aid (ferst'ād'), of or for first aid: *a first-aid kit. adj.*

first-born (ferst'bôrn'), **1** born first; oldest. **2** the first-born child. **1** *adj.,* **2** *n.*

first class, the best and most expensive passenger seating and service offered for travel by ship, airplane, or train.

first-class (ferst'klas'), **1** of the highest class or best quality; excellent: *a first-class singer.* **2** by the best and most expensive passenger seating and service offered

by ship, airplane, or train: *We could not afford to travel first-class.* **1** *adj.,* **2** *adv.*

first hand (ferst'hand'), from the original source; direct: *This is firsthand information* (*adj.*). *We got our information firsthand* (*adv.*). *adj., adv.*

first lady, the official hostess (usually the wife) of the President of the United States or of the governor of a state.

first lieutenant, an army, air force, or marine officer ranking below a captain and above a second lieutenant.

first person, form of a pronoun or verb used to refer to the speaker. *I, me, we,* and *us* are pronouns of the first person.

first quarter, 1 period of time between the new moon and the first half moon. **2** phase of the moon represented by the first half moon after the new moon.

first-rate (ferst'rāt'), **1** of the highest class; excellent; very good: *a first-rate actor.* **2** excellently; very well: *He did first-rate on the test.* **1** *adj.,* **2** *adv.*

firth (ferth), a narrow arm of the sea; estuary of a river. *n.*

fis cal (fis'kəl), **1** financial. **2** having to do with public finance: *Important changes were made in the government's fiscal policy. adj.* **—fis'cal ly,** *adv.*

fiscal year, time between one yearly settlement of financial accounts and another. The fiscal year of the United States government begins July 1 and ends June 30.

fish (fish), **1** animal with a backbone that lives in the water and has gills instead of lungs for breathing. Fish are usually covered with scales and have fins for swimming. Some fishes lay eggs in the water; others produce living young. **2** flesh of fish used for food. **3** catch fish; try to catch fish. **4** try for something as if with a hook: *The boy fished with a stick for his watch which had fallen through a grating.* **5** search: *She fished in her purse for a coin.* **6** find and pull: *She fished an old map out of a box.* **7** try to get by means of cunning: *fish for compliments.* **1,2** *n., pl.* **fish es** *or* **fish; 3-7** *v.* **—fish'like',** *adj.*

fish and chips, pieces of fish and slices of potato fried in deep fat.

fish er (fish'ər), **1** person or animal that fishes. **2** a slender, meat-eating mammal of North America. It is related to the weasel. **3** its dark-brown fur. *n.*

fish er man (fish'ər mən), person who fishes, especially one who makes a living by catching fish. *n., pl.* **fish er men.**

fish er y (fish'ər ē), **1** occupation of catching fish. **2** place for catching fish. **3** place for breeding fish. *n., pl.* **fish er ies.**

fish hawk, osprey.

fish hook (fish'húk'), hook with a barb used for catching fish. *n.*

fish ing (fish'ing), the catching of fish for a living or for pleasure. *n.*

fishing ground, place where fish are plentiful.

fishing rod, a long, light pole with a line and hook attached to it, and often having a reel, used in catching fish.

fishing tackle, rods, lines, hooks, etc., used in catching fish.

fish line (fish'līn'), cord used with a fishhook for catching fish. *n.*

fish mon ger (fish'mung'gər), dealer in fish. *n.*

fish stick, a boneless piece of cod, perch, etc., dipped in batter and breaded, usually sold in frozen form.

fish wife (fish'wīf'), **1** woman who uses coarse and abusive language. **2** woman who sells fish. *n., pl.* **fish wives** (fish'wīvz').

fish y (fish'ē), **1** like a fish in smell, taste, or shape.

2 INFORMAL. not probable; doubtful; unlikely; suspicious: *Her excuse sounds fishy; I don't believe it.* **3** without expression or luster; dull: *fishy eyes.* adj., **fish i er, fish i est.** —**fish′i ly,** adv. —**fish′i ness,** n.

fis sion (fish′ən), **1** a splitting apart; division into parts. **2** method of reproduction in which the body of the parent divides to form two or more independent individuals. Many simple animals and plants reproduce by fission. **3** the splitting of an atomic nucleus into two parts, especially when bombarded by a neutron; nuclear fission. Fission releases huge amounts of energy when the nuclei of heavy elements, especially uranium and plutonium, are split. Fission is used to induce the chain reaction in an atomic bomb. n.

fis sion a ble (fish′ə nə bəl), capable of nuclear fission. adj.

fission bomb, atomic bomb.

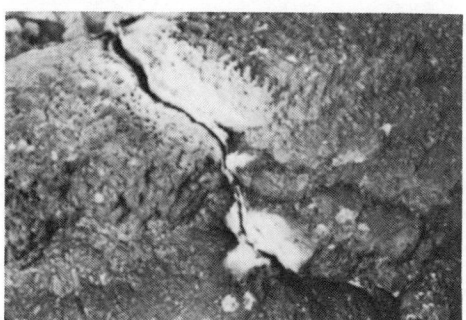

fissure

fis sure (fish′ər), a long, narrow opening; split; crack: *Water dripped from a fissure in the rock.* n.

fist (fist), hand closed tightly with the fingers bent against the palm: *He shook his fist at me.* n. —**fist′like′,** adj.

fist i cuffs (fis′tə kufs′), a fight with the fists. n.pl.

fis tu la (fis′chə lə), a deep, tubelike passage connecting the skin with some internal cavity or organ. It is caused by a wound, abscess, disease, etc. n., pl. **fis tu las, fis tu lae** (fis′chə lē′). [*Fistula* comes from Latin *fistula,* meaning "pipe, tube, ulcer." It was called this because it looks like a narrow tube or pipe.]

fit¹ (fit), **1** having the necessary qualities; suitable: *Grass is a fit food for cows; it is not fit for people.* **2** right; proper: *It is fit that we give thanks.* **3** in good physical condition; healthy and strong: *I am now well and fit for work.* **4** be right, proper, or suitable to: *a punishment that fits the crime.* **5** make right, proper or suitable; suit: *fit the action to the word.* **6** have the right size or shape; have the right size or shape for: *Does this glove fit? The dress fitted her.* **7** make the right size or shape; adjust: *I had my new jacket fitted at the store.* **8** way that something fits: *The coat was not a very good fit; it was too tight.* **9** supply with everything needed; equip: *fit a store with counters, fit out a room.* 1-3 adj., **fit ter, fit test;** 4-7,9 v., **fit ted** or **fit, fit ting;** 8 n. —**fit′ly,** adv.

see fit or **think fit,** prefer and decide; choose.

fit² (fit), **1** a sudden, sharp attack of disease: *a fit of colic.* **2** any sudden, sharp attack: *In a fit of anger I broke the dish.* **3** a short period of doing some one thing; spell: *a fit of coughing, a fit of laughter.* n.

by fits and starts, irregularly; starting, stopping, beginning again, and so on: *He does his homework by fits and starts instead of steadily.*

fitch (fich), **1** polecat of Europe. **2** its fur. n., pl. **fitch es.**

fitch et (fich′it), fitch. n.

fitch ew (fich′ü), fitch. n.

fit ful (fit′fəl), going on and then stopping for a while;

a hat	i it	oi oil	ch child	a in about
ā age	ī ice	ou out	ng long	e in taken
ä far	o hot	u cup	sh she	ə = i in pencil
e let	ō open	u̇ put	th thin	o in lemon
ē equal	ô order	ü rule	ŦH then	u in circus
ėr term			zh measure	

irregular: *She had a fitful sleep during the storm, waking up every few minutes.* adj. —**fit′ful ly,** adv. —**fit′ful ness,** n.

fit ness (fit′nis), a being fit. n.

fit ter (fit′ər), **1** person whose work is fitting clothes on people. **2** person who supplies and fixes anything necessary for some purpose: *a pipe fitter.* n.

fit ting (fit′ing), **1** proper and right; suitable: *a fitting reward.* **2** a small, metal part, used to connect things: *a pipe fitting.* 1 adj., 2 n. —**fit′ting ly,** adv. —**fit′ting ness,** n.

five (fīv), one more than four; 5. n., adj.

Five Nations, a former confederacy of Iroquois Indian tribes made up of the Mohawk, Oneida, Onondaga, Cayuga, and Seneca tribes.

fix (fiks), **1** make firm; fasten tightly: *We fixed the post in the ground. She fixed the spelling lesson in her mind.* **2** settle; set: *I fixed the price at one dollar. Did you fix on a day for the picnic?* **3** direct or hold steadily (eyes, attention, etc.); be directed or held steadily. **4** make or become stiff or rigid: *eyes fixed in death.* **5** put or place definitely: *She fixed the blame on them.* **6** treat to prevent fading or other changes: *fix a dye or a photograph with chemicals.* **7** put in order; set right; arrange: *fix one's hair.* **8** mend; repair: *fix a watch.* **9** prepare (a meal or food): *fix dinner.* **10** to bribe someone to decide something favorable to you and unfavorable to your opponents: *fix a jury, fix a game.* **11** INFORMAL. **a** get revenge upon; get even with; punish. **b** position hard to get out of; awkward state of affairs: *He got himself into a bad fix.* **c** narcotic, or an injection of a narcotic, such as heroin. 1-11a v., 11b, 11c n., pl. **fix es.** —**fix′a ble,** adj. —**fix′er,** n.

fix on or **fix upon,** choose; select.

fix up, INFORMAL. **1** mend; repair. **2** put in order; arrange.

fix a tion (fik sā′shən), **1** a fixing or a being fixed. **2** treatment to prevent something from fading or otherwise changing. n.

fix a tive (fik′sə tiv), substance used to prevent something from fading or otherwise changing. n.

fixed (fikst), **1** not movable; made firm: *The seats in some modern classrooms are not fixed.* **2** definitely assigned; settled; set: *fixed charges for taxicabs.* **3** steady; not moving: *a fixed gaze.* adj.

fix ed ly (fik′sid lē), in a fixed manner; without change; intently: *She stared fixedly at the ring.* adv.

fixed star, star whose position in relation to other stars appears not to change.

fix ings (fik′singz), INFORMAL. trimmings: *We had turkey and all the fixings for Thanksgiving dinner.* n.pl.

fix ture (fiks′chər), **1** thing put in place to stay: *a bathroom fixture, light fixtures.* **2** person or thing that stays in one place, job, etc.: *He is a fixture in the office.* n.

fiz (fiz), fizz. v., **fizzed, fiz zing;** n., pl. **fiz zes.**

fizz (fiz), **1** make a hissing sound. **2** a hissing sound; bubbling: *the fizz of soda water.* 1 v., 2 n., pl. **fizz es.** [*Fizz* comes from an imitation of the sound.]

fiz zle (fiz′əl), **1** make a hissing sound that dies out weakly: *The firecracker just fizzled instead of exploding.* **2** a fizzling or hissing. **3** INFORMAL. come to a poor end; fail: *The picnic fizzled out when it began to rain.* **4** INFORMAL. failure. 1,3 v., **fiz zled, fiz zling;** 2,4 n.

fizz y (fiz′ē), bubbly; effervescent. adj., **fizz i er, fizz i est.**

fjord (fyôrd), fiord. n.

Fl, symbol for fluorine.

FL, Florida (used with postal Zip Code).

fl., 1 florin. **2** flourished. **3** fluid.

Fla., Florida.

flab ber gast (flab′ər gast), INFORMAL. make speechless with surprise; astonish greatly; amaze. *v.*

flab bi ness (flab′ē nis), flabby quality or condition. *n.*

flab by (flab′ē), lacking firmness or force; soft; weak: *flabby cheeks, flabby arguments. adj.,* **flab bi er, flab bi est. —flab′bi ly,** *adv.*

flac cid (flak′sid), limp; weak: *flaccid muscles, a flaccid will. adj.* **—flac′cid ly,** *adv.*

flag¹ (flag), **1** piece of cloth, usually with square corners, with a pattern or picture on it that stands for some country, city, etc.: *the flag of the United States.* Flags are hung on poles over buildings, ships, army camps, etc. **2** cloth or banner, often used as a signal: *a red flag showing danger.* **3** stop or signal (a person, train, etc.), especially by waving a flag: *The train was flagged at the bridge.* **4** communicate by a flag: *flag a message.* 1,2 *n.,* 3,4 *v.,* **flagged, flag ging.**

flag² (flag), iris with blue, purple, yellow, or white flowers and sword-shaped leaves. *n.*

flag³ (flag), get tired; grow weak; droop: *My horse was flagging, but I urged him on. v.,* **flagged, flag ging.**

Flag Day, June 14, the anniversary of the day in 1777 when the Second Continental Congress adopted the Stars and Stripes as the flag of the United States.

flag el late (flaj′ə lāt *for 1;* flaj′ə lāt *or* flaj′ə lət *for 2-4*), **1** whip; flog. **2** like a whip; long, thin, and flexible. **3** having a flagellum or flagella. **4** any of a group of tiny, one-celled animals that have flagella. 1 *v.,* **flag el lat ed, flag el lat ing;** 2,3 *adj.,* 4 *n.*

flag el la tion (flaj′ə lā′shən), a whipping; flogging. *n.*

fla gel lum (flə jel′əm), a long, whiplike tail or part. Certain cells, bacteria, etc., have flagella to enable them to move. *n., pl.* **fla gel la** (flə jel′ə), **fla gel lums.** [*Flagellum* comes from Latin *flagellum,* meaning "a whip." It was called this because of its appearance.]

flag man (flag′mən), person who signals with a flag or lantern at a railroad crossing, etc. *n., pl.* **flag men.**

flag on (flag′ən), container for liquids, usually having a handle, a spout, and a cover. *n.*

flag pole (flag′pōl′), pole from which a flag is flown; flagstaff. *n.*

fla grant (flā′grənt), **1** notorious; outrageous; scandalous: *a flagrant crime.* **2** glaring: *a flagrant error. adj.* **—fla′grant ly,** *adv.*

flag ship (flag′ship′), ship that carries the officer in command of a fleet or squadron and displays a flag indicating that officer's rank. *n.*

flag staff (flag′staf′), flagpole. *n.*

flag stone (flag′stōn′), a large, flat stone, used for paving paths, etc. *n.*

flail (flāl), **1** instrument for threshing grain by hand. A flail consists of a wooden handle with a short, heavy stick fastened at one end by a strip of leather. **2** strike with a flail. **3** beat; thrash. 1 *n.,* 2,3 *v.*

flair (fler *or* flar), natural talent: *The poet had a flair for making clever rhymes. n.*

flak (flak), **1** shellfire from antiaircraft cannon. **2** INFORMAL. criticism. *n.*

flake (flāk), **1** a flat, thin piece, usually not very large: *a flake of snow, flakes of rust, corn flakes.* **2** come off in flakes; separate into flakes: *Dirty, gray spots showed where the paint had flaked off.* 1 *n.,* 2 *v.,* **flaked, flak ing. —flake′like′,** *adj.*

flak i ness (flā′kē nis), flaky quality or condition. *n.*

flak y (flā′kē), **1** consisting of flakes. **2** easily broken or separated into flakes. **3** SLANG. very strange or peculiar:

That group has some pretty flaky ideas. adj., **flak i er, flak i est. —flak′i ly,** *adv.*

flam boy ant (flam boi′ənt), **1** gorgeously brilliant; flaming; showily striking: *Some tropical flowers have flamboyant colors.* **2** very ornate; much decorated: *flamboyant architecture.* **3** given to display; showy: *a flamboyant person. adj.* **—flam boy′ant ly,** *adv.*

flame (flām), **1** one of the glowing tongues of light, usually red or yellow, that rise when a fire blazes up: *The burning house went up in flames.* **2** a burning gas or vapor. **3** rise up in flames; blaze. **4** a burning with flames; blaze: *The dying fire suddenly burst into flame.* **5** shine brightly; flash: *Her eyes flamed with rage.* **6** burst out quickly and hotly; be or act like a flame. **7** something like flame. 1,2,4,7 *n.,* 3,5,6 *v.,* **flamed, flam ing. —flame′like′,** *adj.*

flame throw er (flām′thrō′ər), weapon that throws a stream of burning fuel through the air. *n.*

flamingo—about 4¹/₂ ft. (1.5 m.) tall

fla min go (flə ming′gō), a tropical wading bird with very long legs and neck, and feathers that vary from pink to scarlet. *n., pl.* **fla min gos** *or* **fla min goes.**

flam ma ble (flam′ə bəl), easily set on fire; inflammable. *adj.*

Flan ders (flan′dərz), region in N Europe. It is now divided among Belgium, France, and the Netherlands. See **Burgundy** for map. *n.*

flange (flanj), a raised edge, collar, or rim on a wheel, pulley, pipe, or other object. It is used to keep an object in place, fasten it to another, strengthen it, etc. Railroad cars have wheels with flanges to keep them on the track. *n.*

flank (flangk), **1** side of an animal or person between the ribs and the hip. **2** piece of beef cut from this part. **3** side of a mountain, building, etc. **4** be at the side of: *A garage flanked the house.* **5** the far right or the far left side of an army, fort, or fleet. **6** get around the far right or the far left side of. **7** attack from or on the side. 1-3,5 *n.,* 4,6,7 *v.*

flan nel (flan′l), **1** a soft, warm, woolen or cotton cloth. **2 flannels,** *pl.* clothes made of flannel. **3** made of flannel. 1,2 *n.,* 3 *adj.*

flan nel ette (flan′l et′), a soft, warm, cotton cloth with a nap that looks like flannel. *n.*

flap (flap), **1** swing or sway about loosely and with some noise: *The sails flapped in the wind.* **2** move (wings, arms, etc.) up and down: *The goose flapped its wings but could not rise from the ground.* **3** fly by flapping the wings: *The bird flapped away.* **4** a flapping motion; flapping noise: *the flap of a bird's wing.* **5** strike noisily with something broad and flat: *The clown's big shoes flapped along the ground.* **6** piece hanging or fastened at one edge only: *a coat with flaps on the pockets.* 1-3,5 *v.,* **flapped, flap ping;** 4,6 *n.*

flap jack (flap′jak′), pancake. *n.*

flap per (flap′ər), **1** something that flaps. **2** a young woman of the 1920's who dressed unconventionally and behaved with considerable freedom. *n.*

flare (fler *or* flar), **1** flame up briefly or unsteadily, sometimes with smoke: *A gust of wind made the torches flare.* **2** a bright, brief, unsteady flame; blaze: *The flare of a match showed us the switch.* **3** a dazzling light that burns for a short time, used for signaling, lighting, etc.: *The Coast Guard vessel responded to the flare sent up from the lifeboat.* **4** a sudden outburst. **5** spread out in the shape of a bell: *These pants flare at the bottom.* **6** a spreading out into a bell shape: *the flare of a skirt.* 1,5 *v.*, **flared, flar ing;** 2-4,6 *n.*

flare up, burst out into open anger, violence, etc.

flash (flash), **1** a sudden, brief light or flame: *a flash of lightning.* **2** give out such a light or flame: *The lighthouse flashes signals twice a minute.* **3** come suddenly; pass quickly: *A train flashed by. A thought flashed across my mind.* **4** a sudden, short feeling or display: *a flash of hope, a flash of wit.* **5** a very brief time; instant: *It all happened in a flash.* **6** give out or send out like a flash: *His eyes flashed defiance.* **7** send by telegraph, radio, etc.: *flash the news across the country.* **8** a news report sent by telegraph, radio, etc. 1,4,5,8 *n.*, *pl.* **flash es;** 2,3,6,7 *v.*

flash back (flash′bak′), a break in the continuous series of events of a novel, motion picture, etc., to introduce some earlier event or scene. *n.*

flash bulb (flash′bulb′), an electric bulb which gives out a brilliant flash of light for a very short time. It is used in taking photographs indoors or at night. *n.*

flash card (flash′kärd′), card bearing a letter, word, number, simple problem or picture. In drills in elementary reading, arithmetic, etc., the teacher displays a flashcard briefly and the student gives a quick answer. *n.*

flash cube (flash′kyüb′), device shaped like a cube containing a set of four small flashbulbs. When attached to a camera, it can be used to take several photographs rapidly. *n.*

flash flood, a very sudden, violent flooding of a river, stream, etc.

flash-for ward (flash′fôr′wərd), a break in the continuous series of events of a novel, motion picture, etc., to show some later event or scene. *n.*

flash light (flash′līt′), a portable electric light, operated by batteries. *n.*

flash y (flash′ē), **1** brilliant or sparkling, especially in a superficial way or for a short time; flashing: *a flashy dance routine.* **2** showy; gaudy: *a flashy outfit.* adj., **flash i er, flash i est.** —**flash′i ly,** adv. —**flash′i ness,** n.

flask (flask), a glass or metal bottle, especially one with a narrow neck. n.

flat¹ (flat), **1** smooth and level; even: *flat land.* **2** at full length; horizontal: *The storm left the trees flat on the ground.* **3** the flat part: *The flat of one's hand is the palm.* **4** land that is flat and level. **5** not very deep or thick: *A plate is flat.* **6** a shallow box or basket: *I started the plants in flats, transplanting them in warm weather.* **7** with little air in it: *A nail or sharp stone can cause a flat tire.* **8** INFORMAL. a tire with little air in it. **9** not to be changed; positive: *a flat refusal.* **10** not varied; fixed: *a flat rate with no extra charges.* **11** without much life, interest, flavor, etc.; dull: *a flat voice. Plain food tastes flat.* **12** not shiny or glossy: *a flat yellow.* **13** in music: **a** below the true pitch: *sing flat.* **b** one half step or half note below natural pitch: *Play a B flat.* **c** such a tone or note. **d** sign (♭) that shows such a tone. **e** (of a key) having flats in the signature. **f** to lower in pitch. **14** in a flat manner; flatly: *I fell flat on the floor.* **15** exactly: *Her time for the race was two minutes flat.* 1,2,5,7,9-12,13b,e *adj.*, **flat ter, flat test;** 3,4,6,8,13c,d *n.*, 13a,14,15 *adv.*, 13f *v.*, **flat ted, flat ting.** —**flat′ly,** adv. —**flat′ness,** n.

fall flat, fail completely: *His attempts at clowning fell flat.*

flat² (flat), apartment or set of rooms on one floor. n.

flat boat (flat′bōt′), a large boat with a flat bottom, used especially for carrying goods on a river or canal. *n.*

flat car (flat′kär′), a railroad freight car without a roof or sides. *n.*

flat fish (flat′fish′), any of a group of fishes having a flat body, and swimming on one side, with both eyes on the upper side of the head; fluke. Halibut, flounder, and sole are flatfishes. *n., pl.* **flat fish es** or **flat fish.**

flatfish

flat-foot ed (flat′fut′id), having feet with flattened arches. *adj.* —**flat′-foot′ed ness,** *n.*

flat i ron (flat′ī′ərn), iron (def. 7). *n.*

flat land (flat′land′), level land, not broken by hills and valleys. *n.*

flat ten (flat′n), make or become flat: *Use a rolling pin to flatten the pie dough.* *v.* —**flat′ten er,** *n.*

flat ter (flat′ər), **1** praise too much or beyond the truth; praise insincerely: *Were you only flattering me when you said I sang well, or did you mean it?* **2** show as more beautiful or better looking than is the truth: *This picture flatters me.* **3** try to please or win over by flattering words or actions: *flatter someone with compliments and gifts.* **4** cause to be pleased or feel honored: *You flatter me with your concern for my welfare.* *v.* —**flat′ter er,** *n.* —**flat′ter ing ly,** *adv.*

flat ter y (flat′ər ē), **1** act of flattering. **2** praise that is too much or untrue: *Some people use flattery to get favors.* *n., pl.* **flat ter ies.**

flat tish (flat′ish), somewhat flat. *adj.*

flat top (flat′top′), INFORMAL. an aircraft carrier. *n.*

flat worm (flat′werm′), any of a group of worms with thin, flat bodies, that live in water or as parasites on some animals. Tapeworms are flatworms. *n.*

flaunt (flônt), **1** show off to impress others: *flaunt expensive new clothing before one's friends.* **2** wave proudly: *Flags and pennants flaunted from the masts of the ship.* *v.* —**flaunt′ing ly,** *adv.*

flau tist (flô′tist), flutist. *n.*

fla vor (flā′vər), **1** taste, especially a particular taste: *Chocolate and vanilla have different flavors.* **2** give added taste to; season: *The onion flavors the whole stew.* **3** thing used to give a certain taste to food or drink; flavoring. **4** a special quality: *Stories about ships have a flavor of the sea.* 1,3,4 *n.,* 2 *v.* —**fla′vor less,** *adj.*

fla vor ful (flā′vər fəl), having flavor and interest. *adj.*

fla vor ing (flā′vər ing), thing used to give a particular taste to food or drink: *chocolate flavoring.* *n.*

fla vor some (flā′vər səm), full of flavor; flavorful. *adj.*

flaw (flô), **1** a slight defect; fault; blemish: *A flaw in the dish caused it to break. Her quick temper is a flaw in her* *character.* **2** make or become defective: *A tiny chip flawed the diamond.* 1 *n.,* 2 *v.*

flaw less (flô′lis), without a flaw; perfect. *adj.* —**flaw′-less ly,** *adv.* —**flaw′less ness,** *n.*

flax (flaks), **1** a slender, upright plant with small, narrow leaves, blue or white flowers, and slender stems. Linseed oil is made from its seeds. **2** the threadlike parts into which the stems of this plant separate. Flax is spun into thread and woven into linen. *n.*

flax en (flak′sən), **1** made of flax. **2** like the color of flax; pale-yellow: *Flaxen hair is very light. adj.*

flax seed (flaks′sēd′), seed of flax; linseed. Flaxseed is used to make linseed oil and in medicine. *n.*

flay (flā), **1** strip off the skin or outer covering of. **2** scold severely; criticize without pity or mercy. *v.* —**flay′er,** *n.*

flea (flē), a small, jumping insect without wings. Fleas live in the fur of dogs, cats, and other animals and feed on their blood. *n., pl.* **fleas.**

fleck (flek), **1** a small spot or patch of color or light; speck; mark: *Freckles are brown flecks on the skin.* **2** a small particle; flake: *a fleck of dust.* **3** mark with spots of color or light; speckle: *The bird's breast is flecked with brown.* 1,2 *n.,* 3 *v.*

fled (fled), past tense and past participle of **flee.** *The enemy fled when we attacked. The prisoner has fled. v.*

fledge (flej), **1** (of a young bird) grow the feathers needed for flying. **2** provide or cover with feathers: *She fledged her arrows carefully. v.,* **fledged, fledg ing.**

fledg ling or **fledge ling** (flej′ling), **1** a young bird that has just grown feathers needed for flying. **2** a young, inexperienced person. *n.*

flee (flē), **1** run away; get away by running: *The robbers tried to flee, but they were caught.* **2** run away from: *They fled the burning house.* **3** go quickly; move away swiftly: *The summer days were fleeing. v.,* **fled, flee ing.** —**fle′-er,** *n.*

fleece (flēs), **1** wool that covers a sheep or similar animal. **2** the amount of wool cut off or shorn from a sheep at one time. **3** cut the fleece from. **4** strip of money or belongings; rob; cheat: *The gamblers fleeced him of all his money.* 1,2 *n.,* 3,4 *v.,* **fleeced, fleec ing.** —**fleec′er,** *n.*

fleec y (flē′sē), **1** like a fleece; soft and white: *fleecy clouds.* **2** covered with or made of fleece. *adj.,* **fleec i er, fleec i est.** —**fleec′i ness,** *n.*

fleer (flir), jeer. *v., n.*

fleet[1] (flēt), **1** group of ships under one command: *the United States fleet.* **2** group of ships sailing together: *a fleet of fishing boats.* **3** group of airplanes, automobiles, or the like, moving or working together: *a fleet of trucks. n.* [*Fleet*[1] is from Old English *flēot,* meaning "a ship," which comes from *flēotan,* meaning "to float."]

fleet[2] (flēt), swiftly moving; rapid: *a fleet horse. adj.* [*Fleet*[2] came into English about 450 years ago, and probably can be traced back to Icelandic *fliōtr,* meaning "swift."] —**fleet′ly,** *adv.* —**fleet′ness,** *n.*

fleet admiral, the naval officer of the highest rank in the United States Navy.

fleet ing (flē′ting), passing swiftly; soon gone: *a fleeting smile. adj.* —**fleet′ing ly,** *adv.* —**fleet′ing ness,** *n.*

Flem ing (flem′ing), **1** person born or living in Flanders. **2** a Belgian whose native language is Flemish. **3** Sir **Alexander,** 1881-1955, Scottish bacteriologist who discovered penicillin. *n.*

Flem ish (flem′ish), **1** of Flanders, its people, or their language. **2** the people of Flanders. **3** the language of Flanders. 1 *adj.,* 2 *n.pl.,* 3 *n.sing.*

flesh (flesh), **1** the soft tissue of the body that covers the bones and is covered by skin. Flesh consists mostly of muscles and fat. **2** meat. **3** the body, not the soul or spirit. **4** the soft part of fruits or vegetables; the part of

fruits that can be eaten: *The flesh of a peach is yellow or white. n.* —**flesh′less,** *adj.*

flesh and blood, family or relatives by birth.

in the flesh, in person; really present.

flesh ly (flesh′lē), **1** of the flesh; bodily. **2** sensual. *adj.,* **flesh li er, flesh li est.** —**flesh′li ness,** *n.*

flesh y (flesh′ē), **1** having much flesh; plump; fat. **2** of flesh; like flesh. *adj.,* **flesh i er, flesh i est.** —**flesh′i-ness,** *n.*

fleur-de-lis (def. 1)

fleur-de-lis (flėr′də lē′), **1** design or device used in heraldry to represent an iris. A fleur-de-lis was formerly used as the coat of arms of the royal family of France. **2** the iris flower or plant. *n., pl.* **fleurs-de-lis** (flėr′də-lēz′). [*Fleur-de-lis* comes from French *fleur de lis,* which also means "lily flower."]

flew (flü), past tense of **fly**[2]. *The bird flew high in the air. v.*

flex (fleks), bend: *She flexed her stiff arm slowly. v.*

flex i bil i ty (flek′sə bil′ə tē), flexible quality: *The flexibility of rubber bands lessens as they become old. n.*

flex i ble (flek′sə bəl), **1** easily bent; not stiff; bending without breaking: *Leather, rubber, and wire are flexible.* **2** easily adapted to fit various conditions; easily managed: *The actor's flexible voice accommodated itself to every emotion. adj.*

flex i bly (flek′sə blē), in a flexible manner; with flexibility. *adv.*

flex ile (flek′səl), flexible. *adj.*

flick (flik), **1** a quick, light blow; sudden, snapping stroke: *By a flick of his whip, he drove the fly from the horse's head.* **2** the light, snapping sound of such a blow or stroke: *the flick of an electric light switch.* **3** strike lightly with a quick, snapping blow: *She flicked the dust from her shoes with a handkerchief.* **4** make a sudden, snapping stroke with: *The children flicked wet towels at each other.* **5** move quickly and lightly; flutter. 1,2 *n.,* 3-5 *v.*

flick er[1] (flik′ər), **1** shine or burn with a wavering, unsteady light: *The firelight flickered on the walls.* **2** a wavering, unsteady light or flame: *the flicker of an oil lamp.* **3** move quickly and lightly in and out or back and forth: *We heard the birds flicker among the leaves.* **4** a quick, light movement: *the flicker of an eyelash.* **5** a brief flash; spark: *The speaker failed to arouse the least flicker of enthusiasm in his audience.* 1,3 *v.,* 2,4,5 *n.* —**flick′er ing ly,** *adv.*

flick er[2] (flik′ər), large, common woodpecker of North America, with a brownish back and yellow markings on its wings and tail. *n.*

flied (flīd), a past tense and past participle of **fly**[2] (def. 12). *The batter flied to center field. v.*

fli er (flī′ər), **1** person or thing that flies: *That eagle is a high flier.* **2** pilot of an airplane; aviator. **3** a very fast train, ship, bus, etc. **4** a small handbill. *n.* Also, **flyer.**

flies[1] (flīz), plural of **fly**[1] and **fly**[2]. *There are many flies on the window. Both batters hit flies to the outfield. n.*

flies[2] (flīz), a present tense of **fly**[2]. *A bird flies. She flies an airplane. v.*

flight[1] (flīt), **1** act or manner of flying: *the flight of a bird across the sky.* **2** distance a bird, bullet, airplane, etc., can fly: *a flight of 500 miles.* **3** group of things flying through the air together: *a flight of pigeons.* **4** trip in an aircraft, especially a scheduled trip on an airline. **5** airplane that makes a scheduled trip: *She took the three o'clock flight to Boston.* **6** a soaring above or beyond the ordinary: *a flight of fancy, a flight of the imagination.* **7** set of stairs or steps from one landing or story of a building to the next. *n.*

flight[2] (flīt), act of fleeing; running away; escape: *The flight of the prisoners was discovered. n.*

put to flight, force to flee: *They put the enemy to flight.*

flight attendant, a person employed on an airplane to look after passengers.

flight i ness (flī′tē nis), quality or condition of being flighty. *n.*

flight less (flīt′lis), unable to fly: *An ostrich is a flightless bird. adj.*

flight y (flī′tē), likely to have sudden fancies; full of whims; frivolous. *adj.*, **flight i er, flight i est.** —**flight′i ly,** *adv.*

flim si ly (flim′zə lē), in a flimsy manner. *adv.*

flim si ness (flim′zē nis), flimsy quality. *n.*

flim sy (flim′zē), **1** light and thin; slight; frail: *I accidentally tore the flimsy paper.* **2** lacking seriousness or sense; feeble; shallow: *Their excuse was so flimsy that no one believed it. adj.*, **flim si er, flim si est.**

flinch (flinch), **1** draw back from difficulty, danger, or pain; shrink: *He flinched when he touched the hot radiator.* **2** act of drawing back. **1** *v.*, **2** *n.* —**flinch′er,** *n.*

flin ders (flin′dərz), small pieces; fragments; splinters. *n.pl.*

fling (fling), **1** throw with force; throw: *fling a stone.* **2** a throw. **3** move hastily or violently; rush; dash: *In a rage the child flung out of the room.* **4** plunge or kick: *The excited horse flung about in its stall.* **5** time of doing as one pleases: *to have a brief fling before settling down.* **6** a lively Scottish dance. **7** a try; attempt: *He had a fling at acting, but discovered he had no talent.* **1,3,4** *v.*, **flung, fling ing; 2,5-7** *n.*

flint (flint), **1** a very hard, gray or brown stone which makes a spark when struck against steel. It is a kind of quartz. **2** piece of this used with steel to light fires, explode gunpowder, etc. **3** anything very hard or unyielding: *a heart of flint. n.*

Flint (flint), city in SE Michigan. *n.*

flint lock (flint′lok′), **1** gunlock in which a flint striking against steel makes sparks that explode the gunpowder. **2** an old-fashioned gun with such a gunlock. *n.*

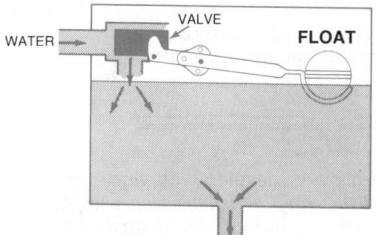

float (def. 7) regulating water level.
As water is used, the float drops, opening the valve and permitting more water to enter the tank.

flint y (flin′tē), **1** made of flint; containing flint. **2** like flint; very hard; unyielding: *flinty stubbornness. adj.*, **flint i er, flint i est.** —**flint′i ly,** *adv.* —**flint′i ness,** *n.*

flip (flip), **1** toss or move with a snap of a finger and thumb: *He flipped a coin on the counter.* **2** move with a

a	hat	i	it	oi	oil	ch child
ā	age	ī	ice	ou	out	ng long
ä	far	o	hot	u	cup	sh she
e	let	ō	open	u̇	put	th thin
ē	equal	ô	order	ü	rule	ŦH then
ėr	term					zh measure

ə = { a in about / e in taken / i in pencil / o in lemon / u in circus }

jerk or toss: *flip the pages of a book. The branch flipped back and scratched her face.* **3** a snap; tap; sudden jerk: *The cat gave the kitten a flip on the ear. Since there was a tie, the winner was picked by the flip of a coin.* **1,2** *v.*, **flipped, flip ping; 3** *n.*

flip pan cy (flip′ən sē), flippant quality or behavior. *n.*, *pl.* **flip pan cies.**

flip pant (flip′ənt), too free in speech or manner; not respectful: *Her flippant answer to my question annoyed me. adj.* —**flip′pant ly,** *adv.*

flip per (flip′ər), **1** a broad, flat limb especially adapted for swimming. Seals have flippers. **2** a molded rubber attachment for the human foot, used as an aid to swimming. *n.*

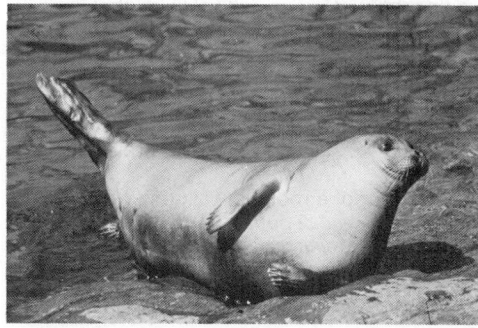

flipper
(def. 1)

flirt (flėrt), **1** play at courtship; be romantic in a light-hearted way. **2** person who plays at courtship. **3** trifle; toy: *He flirted with the idea of going to Europe, even though he couldn't afford it.* **4** move quickly; flutter: *The bird flirted from branch to branch.* **5** a quick movement or flutter: *With a flirt of its tail the squirrel ran off.* **1,3,4** *v.*, **2,5** *n.*

flir ta tion (flėr′tā′shən), **1** act of flirting. **2** a courtship that is not serious. *n.*

flir ta tious (flėr′tā′shəs), **1** inclined to flirt: *a flirtatious teenager.* **2** having to do with flirtation: *a flirtatious glance. adj.* —**flir′ta′tious ly,** *adv.* —**flir′ta′tious ness,** *n.*

flit (flit), **1** fly lightly and quickly; flutter: *Birds flitted from tree to tree.* **2** pass lightly and quickly: *Many thoughts flitted through my mind as I sat daydreaming. v.*, **flit ted, flit ting.**

flit ter (flit′ər), flutter. *v., n.*

float (flōt), **1** stay on top of or be held up by air, water, or other liquid. *A cork will float, but a stone sinks.* **2** anything that stays up or holds up something else in water. *A raft is a float. A cork on a fishline is a float.* **3** move with a moving liquid; drift: *The boat floated out to sea.* **4** rest or move in a liquid, the air, etc.: *Clouds floated in the sky.* **5** cause to float: *float logs downstream.* **6** set going (a company, scheme, etc.); launch: *To get money the government floated an issue of bonds.* **7** a hollow, metal ball that floats on and regulates the level, supply, or outlet of a liquid in a tank, boiler, etc. **8** a low, flat car that carries something to be shown in a parade. **1,3-6** *v.*, **2,7,8** *n.* —**float′a ble,** *adj.* —**float′er,** *n.*

flock (flok), **1** group of animals of one kind keeping, feeding, or herded together: *a flock of geese, a flock of sheep, a flock of birds.* **2** a large group; crowd: *Visitors* *came in flocks to the zoo to see the new gorilla.* **3** go or gather in a flock; come crowding: *Sheep usually flock together. The children flocked around the ice-cream stand.* **4** people of the same church group. 1,2,4 *n.*, 3 *v.*

floe (flō), field or sheet of floating ice. *n.*

flog (flog), whip very hard; beat with a whip or stick. *v.*, **flogged, flog ging. —flog′ger,** *n.*

flood (flud), **1** a great flow of water over what is usually dry land: *The heavy rains caused a serious flood in the riverside district.* **2 the Flood,** (in the Bible) the water that covered the earth in the time of Noah. **3** flow over: *The river flooded our fields.* **4** fill much fuller than usual; fill to overflowing: *A wave flooded the holes I had dug in the sand.* **5** a great outpouring of anything: *a flood of light, a flood of words.* **6** fill, cover, or overcome like a flood: *The TV star was flooded with requests for autographs. The room was flooded with moonlight.* **7** become covered or filled with water: *During the thunderstorm, our cellar flooded.* **8** rise of the tide; flow. 1,2,5,8 *n.*, 3,4,6,7 *v.*

flood gate (flud′gāt′), gate in a canal, river, stream, etc., to control the flow of water. *n.*

flood light (flud′līt′), **1** lamp that gives a broad beam of light. **2** a broad beam of light from such a lamp. **3** to light with a floodlight: *The baseball field was brightly floodlighted for the night game.* 1,2 *n.*, 3 *v.*, **flood light ed** or **flood lit** (flud′līt′), **flood light ing.**

flood plain (flud′plān′), plain bordering a river and made of soil deposited during floods. *n.*

flood tide, the flowing of the tide toward the shore. *n.*

flood wa ter (flud′wô′tər *or* flud′wot′ər), water flooding dry land. *n.*

floor (flôr), **1** the part of a room to walk on: *The floor of this room is made of wood.* **2** put a floor in or on: *The carpenter will floor this room with oak.* **3** a flat surface at the bottom: *They dropped their net to the floor of the ocean.* **4** story of a building: *Five families live on the fourth floor.* **5** right to speak: *"You may have the floor," said the chairman.* **6** knock down: *The boxer floored his opponent with one blow.* **7** INFORMAL. confuse; puzzle: *The last question on the examination completely floored us.* 1,3-5 *n.*, 2,6,7 *v.*

floor ing (flôr′ing), **1** floor. **2** floors. **3** material for making or covering floors, such as wood, linoleum, or tile. *n.*

floor walk er (flôr′wô′kər), person employed in a large store to direct the work of salesclerks and give assistance to customers. *n.*

flop (flop), **1** move loosely or heavily; flap around clumsily: *The fish flopped helplessly on the deck.* **2** fall, drop, throw, or move heavily or clumsily: *The tired girl flopped down into a chair.* **3** a flopping: *I threw myself on the bed with a flop.* **4** a dull, heavy sound made by flopping. **5** change or turn suddenly. **6** INFORMAL. failure: *His last book was a flop.* **7** INFORMAL. fail: *Her first business venture flopped.* 1,2,5,7 *v.*, **flopped, flop ping;** 3,4,6 *n.* [*Flop* is a different form of *flap.*] **—flop′per,** *n.*

flop py (flop′ē), INFORMAL. tending to flop; flopping: *a floppy hat. adj.,* **flop pi er, flop pi est. —flop′pi ly,** *adv.*

floppy disk, a small, bendable plastic disk with a magnetic surface, used to store information and instructions for computers; diskette.

flo ra (flôr′ə), plants: *the flora of the West Indies. n.*

flo ral (flôr′əl), of or resembling flowers: *floral decorations, floral patterns. adj.* **—flo′ral ly,** *adv.*

Flo rence (flôr′əns), city in central Italy. *n.*

Flo ren tine (flôr′ən tēn′), **1** of Florence or its people. **2** person born or living in Florence. 1 *adj.*, 2 *n.*

flo ret (flôr′it), a small flower. *n.*

flo rid (flôr′id), **1** reddish; ruddy: *a florid complexion.* **2** much ornamented; flowery; showy: *florid language, florid architecture. adj.* **—flo′rid ly,** *adv.* **—flo′rid ness,** *n.*

Flo ri da (flôr′ə də), one of the southeastern states of the United States. *Abbreviation:* Fla. or FL *Capital:* Tallahassee. *n.* **—Flor′i dan, Flo rid′i an,** *adj.*, *n.*

flo rin (flôr′ən), any of various gold or silver coins used in different countries of Europe, especially an English silver and nickel coin worth ten pence. *n.*

flo rist (flôr′ist), person who raises or sells flowers. *n.*

floss (flôs), **1** short, loose, silk fibers. **2** a shiny, untwisted silk thread made from such fibers. It is used for embroidery. Floss, often waxed, is used for cleaning between the teeth. **3** soft, silky fluff or fibers. Milkweed pods contain white floss. **4** use dental floss, or use dental floss on: *I flossed my teeth this morning.* 1-3 *n.*, 4 *v.*

floss y (flôs′ē), of or like floss. *adj.*, **floss i er, floss i est.**

flo til la (flō til′ə), **1** a small fleet. **2** fleet of small ships. *n., pl.* **flo til las.** [*Flotilla* was borrowed from Spanish *flotilla,* and can be traced back to Icelandic *floti,* meaning "a fleet, raft."]

flot sam (flot′səm), wreckage of a ship or its cargo found floating on the sea. *n.*

flounce¹ (flouns), **1** go with an angry or impatient fling of the body: *flounce out of the room in a rage.* **2** an angry or impatient fling of the body. 1 *v.*, **flounced, flounc ing;** 2 *n.*

flounce² (flouns), **1** a wide strip of cloth, gathered along the top edge and sewed to a dress, skirt, etc., for trimming; a wide ruffle. **2** trim with a flounce or flounces. 1 *n.*, 2 *v.*, **flounced, flounc ing.**

floun der¹ (floun′dər), **1** struggle awkwardly without making much progress; plunge about: *After the blizzard, we found cattle floundering in snowdrifts.* **2** be clumsy or confused and make mistakes: *I was so nervous I floundered through my speech. v.*

floun der² (floun′dər), a saltwater flatfish much used for food. *n., pl.* **floun ders** or **floun der.**

flour (flour), **1** the fine meal made by grinding and sifting wheat or other grain. It is used to make bread, rolls, cake, etc. **2** cover or sprinkle with flour. 1 *n.*, 2 *v.*

WORD HISTORY

flour

Flour comes from a special use of *flower.* It was called this because flour is "the finest part" of the meal.

flour ish (flėr′ish), **1** grow or develop with vigor; do well; thrive: *Your radishes are flourishing. Our newspaper business flourished.* **2** wave in the air: *She flourished the letter when she saw us.* **3** a waving about: *He removed his hat with a flourish.* **4** an extra ornament or curve in handwriting. **5** a showy trill or passage in music: *a flourish of trumpets.* **6** a showy display: *The agent showed us about the house with much flourish.* 1,2 *v.*, 3-6 *n., pl.* **flour ish es.** [*Flourish* can be traced back to Latin *florem,* meaning "a flower."] **—flour′ish ing ly,** *adv.*

flour y (flou′rē), **1** of or like flour. **2** covered or white with flour. *adj.*

flout (flout), treat with contempt or scorn; scoff at;

flourish (def. 4)—She signed her name with a bold **flourish.**

mock: *You are foolish to flout such good advice. v.*
—**flout′er,** *n.* —**flout′ing ly,** *adv.*

flow (flō), **1** run like water; move in a current or stream: *Blood flows through our bodies.* **2** current; stream: *There is a constant flow of water from the spring.* **3** pour out; pour along: *The crowd flowed out of the town hall and down the main street.* **4** move easily or smoothly; glide: *a flowing movement in a dance, flowing verse.* **5** any smooth, steady movement: *a rapid flow of speech.* **6** hang loose and waving: *flowing robes.* **7** act or way of flowing: *a flow of blood.* **8** rate of flowing: *a flow of two feet per second.* **9** the flowing of the tide toward the shore; rise of the tide. 1,3,4,6 *v.,* 2,5,7-9 *n.*

flow chart (flō′chärt), diagram that shows, step by step, each thing a computer must do to perform a particular task. *n.*

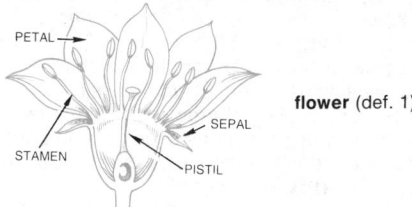

flower (def. 1)

flow er (flou′ər), **1** part of a plant that produces the seed; blossom. A flower is a shortened branch with modified leaves called petals. Flowers are often beautifully colored or shaped. **2** plant grown for its blossoms. **3** have flowers; produce flowers; bloom. **4** the finest part: *the flower of the country's youth.* **5** time when a thing is at its best: *a person in the flower of life.* **6** be at its best. 1,2,4,5 *n.,* 3,6 *v.* —**flow′er like′,** *adj.*

flow ered (flou′ərd), **1** having flowers. **2** covered or decorated with flowers: *flowered wallpaper. adj.*

flow er et (flou′ər it), floret. *n.*

flow er ing (flou′ər ing), having flowers. *adj.*

flow er pot (flou′ər pot′), pot to hold soil for a plant to grow in. *n.*

flow er y (flou′ər ē), **1** having many flowers. **2** full of fine words and fanciful expressions: *a flowery speech. adj.,* **flow er i er, flow er i est.** —**flow′er i ly,** *adv.*

flown (flōn), past participle of **fly²**. *The bird has flown. v.*

fl. oz., fluid ounce or fluid ounces.

flu (flü), influenza. *n.*

fluc tu ate (fluk′chü āt), rise and fall; change continually; waver: *The temperature fluctuates from day to day. v.,* **fluc tu at ed, fluc tu at ing.** [*Fluctuate* can be traced back to Latin *fluere,* meaning "to flow."]

fluc tu a tion (fluk′chü ā′shən), a rising and falling; continual change; wavering. *n.*

flue (flü), tube, pipe, or other enclosed passage for smoke or hot air. A chimney often has several flues. *n.*

flu en cy (flü′ən sē), **1** a smooth, easy flow: *The senator had great fluency of speech.* **2** easy, rapid speaking or writing. *n.*

flu ent (flü′ənt), **1** flowing smoothly or easily: *to speak fluent French.* **2** speaking or writing easily and rapidly: *She is a fluent lecturer. adj.* [*Fluent* is from Latin *fluentem,* which comes from *fluere,* meaning "to flow."] —**flu′ent ly,** *adv.*

fluff (fluf), **1** soft, light, downy particles: *Woolen blankets often have fluff on them.* **2** a soft, light, downy mass: *The kitten was a fluff of fur.* **3** shake or puff out (hair, feathers, etc.) into a soft, light, downy mass: *fluff a pillow.* **4** make a mistake in reading or speaking: *I fluffed my lines in the play.* 1,2 *n.,* 3,4 *v.*

fluff i ness (fluf′ē nis), fluffy quality or condition. *n.*

fluff y (fluf′ē), **1** soft and light like fluff: *a fluffy shawl.* **2** covered or filled with fluff; downy: *fluffy baby chicks, a fluffy pillow. adj.,* **fluff i er, fluff i est.** —**fluff′i ly,** *adv.*

flu id (flü′id), **1** any liquid or gas; something that will flow. Water, mercury, air, and oxygen are fluids. **2** like a liquid or gas; flowing: *She poured the fluid mass of hot metal into a mold to harden.* **3** changing easily; not fixed: *The situation on the battlefield was fluid.* 1 *n.,* 2,3 *adj.*

flu id ize (flü′ə dīz), make fluid. *v.,* **flu id ized, flu id iz ing.** —**flu′id i za′tion,** *n.*

fluid ounce, unit for measuring liquids. There are 16 fluid ounces in 1 pint.

fluke¹ (flük), **1** the flat, three-cornered piece at the end of each arm of an anchor, which catches in the ground and holds the anchor fast. **2** the barbed head of an arrow or harpoon. **3** either of the two halves of a whale's tail. *n.*

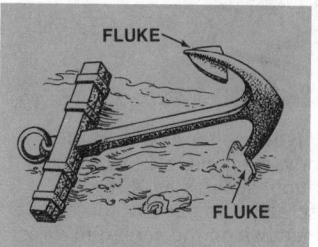

fluke¹ (def. 1)

fluke² (flük), a lucky stroke in games, business, or life. *n.*

fluke³ (flük), **1** flatfish. **2** a parasitic flatworm shaped somewhat like a flatfish. *n.*

fluk y (flü′kē), **1** obtained by chance rather than by skill. **2** uncertain: *fluky weather. adj.,* **fluk i er, fluk i est.**

flume (flüm), **1** a deep and very narrow valley with a stream running through it. **2** a large, inclined trough or chute for carrying water. Flumes are used to transport logs or to furnish water for power. *n.*

flum mox (flum′əks), INFORMAL. bring to confusion; bewilder. *v.*

flung (flung), past tense and past participle of **fling**. *I flung my coat on the chair. The paper was flung into the fire. v.*

flunk (flungk), INFORMAL. **1** fail in schoolwork: *She flunked the history examination.* **2** cause to fail or grade as having failed: *The teacher flunked him. v.*

flunk out, INFORMAL. dismiss or be dismissed from school or college for failing work.

flunk ey (flung′kē), flunky. *n., pl.* **flunk eys.**

flunk y (flung′kē), **1** a flattering, fawning person. **2** footman. *n., pl.* **flunk ies.**

fluo res cence (flù res′ns *or* flü′ə res′ns), **1** a giving off of light by a substance exposed to X rays, ultraviolet rays, or certain other rays, which continues only as long as exposure to these rays continues. **2** property of a substance that causes this. It is an ability to transform radiation so as to emit rays of a different wavelength or color. **3** light given off in this way. *n.*

fluo res cent (flù res′nt *or* flü′ə res′nt), able to give off light by fluorescence. Fluorescent substances glow in the dark when exposed to X rays. *adj.*

fluorescent lamp, an electric lamp consisting of a tube in which a coating of fluorescent powder exposed to ultraviolet rays gives off a light that is cooler and less glaring than incandescent light.

fluor i date (flür′ə dāt), add small amounts of a fluorine compound to drinking water to decrease tooth decay. *v.*, **fluor i dat ed, fluor i dat ing.**

fluor i da tion (flür′ə dā′shən), act or process of fluoridating. *n.*

fluo ride (flür′īd *or* flü′ə rīd′), compound of fluorine and another element or radical. *n.*

fluo rine (flür′ēn *or* flü′ə rēn′), a pale-yellow, bad-smelling, poisonous gas, an element which occurs only in combination with certain other elements. It is the most active of all the chemical elements and is used in small amounts in water to prevent tooth decay. *n.*

fluoroscope

fluor o scope (flür′ə skōp), device for examining the inner parts of a human body, machine, etc., by placing it between a source of radiation, such as an X-ray machine, and a fluorescent screen. The parts of the object under examination cast shadows on the screen in direct proportion to the amount of radiation they absorb. *n.*

flur ry (flėr′ē), **1** a sudden gust: *A flurry of wind upset the small sailboat.* **2** a light fall of rain or snow. **3** a sudden commotion: *a flurry of alarm.* **4** fluster; excite; agitate: *Noise in the audience flurried the actor so that he forgot his lines.* 1-3 *n.*, *pl.* **flur ries;** 4 *v.*, **flur ried, flur ry ing.**

flush (flush), **1** become red suddenly; blush; glow: *Her face flushed when they laughed at her.* **2** cause to blush or glow: *Exercise flushed her face.* **3** a rosy glow or blush: *The flush of sunrise was on the clouds.* **4** rush suddenly; flow rapidly: *Embarrassment caused the blood to flush to my cheeks.* **5** a sudden rush; rapid flow. **6** send a sudden flow of water over or through: *The city streets were flushed to make them clean.* **7** make joyful and proud; excite: *The team was flushed with its first victory.* **8** an excited condition or feeling: *the flush of victory.* **9** glowing vigor; freshness: *the first flush of youth.* **10** cause to fly or start up suddenly: *The hunter's dog flushed a partridge in the woods.* **11** even; level: *The edge of the new shelf must be flush with the old one.* **12** so as to be level; evenly: *The two edges met flush.* **13** well supplied; having plenty: *Payday is the only day I am flush with money.* 1,2,4,6,7,10 *v.*, 3,5,8,9 *n.*, *pl.* **flush es;** 11,13 *adj.*, 12 *adv.*

flus ter (flus′tər), **1** make nervous and excited; confuse: *The honking of horns flustered the driver, and he stalled his automobile.* **2** nervous excitement; confusion. 1 *v.*, 2 *n.*

flute (flüt), **1** a long, slender, pipelike musical instrument, played by blowing across a hole near one end. Different notes are made by opening and closing holes along its side with the fingers or with keys. **2** play on a flute. **3** sing or whistle so as to sound like a flute. **4** a long, round groove. Some columns have flutes. **5** make long, round grooves in. 1,4 *n.*, 2,3,5 *v.*, **flut ed, flut ing.**

flut ed (flü′tid), having long, round grooves: *fluted columns. adj.*

flut ing (flü′ting), decoration made of long, round grooves. *n.*

flut ist (flü′tist), person who plays a flute. *n.* Also, **flautist.**

flut ter (flut′ər), **1** wave back and forth quickly and lightly: *The flag fluttered in the breeze.* **2** move or flap the wings rapidly without flying or with short flights: *The chickens fluttered excitedly when they saw the dog.* **3** come or go with a trembling or wavy motion: *The falling leaves fluttered to the ground.* **4** move restlessly: *They fluttered about making preparations for the party.* **5** move quickly and unevenly; tremble: *My heart fluttered when I rose to give my speech.* **6** a fluttering: *the flutter of curtains in a breeze.* **7** a confused or excited condition: *The appearance of the queen caused a great flutter in the crowd.* 1-5 *v.*, 6,7 *n.* —**flut′ter er,** *n.*

flut ter y (flut′ər ē), fluttering. *adj.*

flux (fluks), **1** a flow; a flowing. **2** continuous change: *New words and meanings keep the English language in a state of flux.* **3** an abnormal discharge of liquid matter from the body. **4** rosin or other substance used in soldering, welding, etc., to clean the surfaces of metals and help them join. *n.*, *pl.* **flux es.**

fly¹ (flī), **1** any of a large group of insects that have two wings, especially the housefly. **2** any insect with transparent wings, such as a May fly. **3** fishhook with feathers, silk, tinsel, etc., on it to make it look like an insect. *n.*, *pl.* **flies.**

fly¹ (def. 3)—The shape and movement of these flies in the water attract fish.

fly² (flī), **1** move through the air with wings: *These birds fly long distances.* **2** float or wave in the air: *Our flag flies every day.* **3** cause to float or wave in the air: *The children are flying kites.* **4** travel in an aircraft. **5** pilot (an aircraft). **6** carry in an aircraft: *The government flew supplies to the flooded city.* **7** move swiftly; go rapidly: *She flew to my rescue.* **8** run away; flee: *fly from one's enemies.* **9** flap to cover buttons or a zipper on clothing. **10** piece of canvas, nylon, etc., forming an extra, outer top for a tent.

flute (def. 1)

11 baseball batted high in the air. 12 bat a baseball high in the air. 1-8,12 *v.*, **flew, flown, fly ing** for 1-8, **flied, fly ing** for 12; 9-11 *n., pl.* **flies.**
fly at, attack violently.
let fly, shoot or throw: *The archer let fly an arrow.*
on the fly, while still in the air: *He caught the ball on the fly.*
fly catch er (flī′kach′ər), any of several birds that catch flies and other insects while flying. The kingbird and the phoebe are flycatchers. *n.*
fly er (flī′ər), flier. *n.*
fly ing (flī′ing), 1 able to fly. 2 floating or waving in the air. 3 swift. 4 action of piloting or traveling in an aircraft. 1-3 *adj.*, 4 *n.*
flying buttress, an arched support or brace built between the wall of a building and a supporting column to bear some of the weight of the roof. See **buttress** for picture.
flying colors, success; victory: *The team finished the tournament with flying colors.*
flying disk, flying saucer.
flying fish, a tropical sea fish that has winglike fins and can leap for some distance through the air.
flying jib, a small, triangular sail set in front of the regular jib. *n.*
flying machine, aircraft.
flying saucer, UFO.
fly leaf (flī′lēf′), a blank sheet of paper at the beginning or end of a book. *n., pl.* **fly leaves.**
fly pa per (flī′pā′pər), paper covered with a sticky or poisonous substance, used to catch or kill flies. *n.*
fly speck (flī′spek′), 1 a tiny spot left by a fly. 2 any tiny speck. 3 mark with flyspecks. 1,2 *n.*, 3 *v.*
fly way (flī′wā′), route usually followed by migrating birds. *n.*
fly weight (flī′wāt′), boxer who weighs less than 112 pounds (51 kilograms). *n.*
fly wheel (flī′hwēl′), a heavy wheel attached to a machine to keep it and its parts moving at an even speed. *n.*
fm., fathom.
Fm, symbol for fermium.
FM or **F.M.,** frequency modulation.
fo., folio.
foal (fōl), 1 a young horse, donkey, etc.; colt or filly. 2 give birth to (a foal): *Our mare foaled twin colts last spring. When is she due to foal again?* 1 *n.*, 2 *v.*
foam (fōm), 1 mass of very small bubbles formed in a liquid by agitation, fermentation, boiling, etc. 2 form or gather foam; froth: *The soda foamed over the glass.* 3 break into foam: *The stream foams over the rocks.* 4 a frothy mass formed in the mouth as saliva or on the skin of animals as sweat: *The dog with foam around its mouth has rabies.* 1,4 *n.*, 2,3 *v.* —**foam′like′,** *adj.*
foam rubber, a soft, spongy rubber used for mattresses, cushions, etc.
foam y (fō′mē), 1 covered with foam; foaming. 2 made of foam. 3 like foam. *adj.*, **foam i er, foam i est.** —**foam′i ly,** *adv.* —**foam′i ness,** *n.*
fob (fob), 1 a small pocket for holding a watch, etc. 2 a short watch chain, ribbon, etc., that hangs out of such a pocket. 3 ornament worn at the end of such a chain, ribbon, etc. *n.*
f.o.b. or **F.O.B.,** free on board. The price $2500, f.o.b. Detroit, means that the $2500 does not pay for freight or other expenses after the article has been put on board a freight car at Detroit.
fo cal (fō′kəl), of a focus. The focal length of a lens is the distance of its focus from the optical center of the lens. *adj.* —**fo′cal ly,** *adv.*

a hat	i it	oi oil	ch child	a in about
ā age	ī ice	ou out	ng long	e in taken
ä far	o hot	u cup	sh she	ə = i in pencil
e let	ō open	ů put	th thin	o in lemon
ē equal	ô order	ü rule	ŦH then	u in circus
ėr term			zh measure	

focal distance, focal length.
focal length, distance from the optical center of a lens or mirror to the principal point of focus.
fo ci (fō′sī), a plural of **focus.** *n.*
fo cus (fō′kəs), 1 point at which rays of light, heat, etc., meet after being reflected from a mirror or bent by a lens. 2 bring (rays of light, heat, etc.) to a focus: *The lens focused the sun's rays on a piece of paper and burned a hole in it.* 3 distance from a lens or mirror to the point where rays from it meet: *A nearsighted eye has a shorter focus than a normal eye.* 4 the correct adjustment of a lens, the eye, etc., to make a clear image: *If the camera is not brought into focus, the photograph will be blurred.* 5 adjust (a lens, the eye, etc.) to make a clear image: *A nearsighted person cannot focus accurately on distant objects.* 6 make (an image, etc.) clear by adjusting a lens, the eye, etc. 7 the central point of attraction, attention, activity, etc.: *The new baby was the focus of attention.* 8 concentrate: *When studying, he focused his mind on his lessons.* 1,3,4,7 *n., pl.* **fo cus es** or **fo ci**; 2,5,6,8 *v.*, **fo cused, fo cus ing** or **fo cussed, fo cus sing.**
fod der (fod′ər), coarse food for horses, cattle, etc. Hay and cornstalks with their leaves are fodder. *n.*
foe (fō), enemy. *n.*
foe tal (fē′tl), fetal. *adj.*
foe tus (fē′təs), fetus. *n., pl.* **foe tus es.**
fog (fog), 1 cloud of fine drops of water just above the earth's surface; thick mist. 2 cover with fog. 3 make or become misty or cloudy: *Something fogged six of our photographs. My breath caused the window to fog.* 4 a confused or puzzled condition: *a fog of ignorance.* 5 confuse; puzzle. 1,4 *n.*, 2,3,5 *v.*, **fogged, fog ging.**
fog bank a dense mass of fog seen at a distance.
fo gey (fō′gē), fogy. *n., pl.* **fo geys.**
fog gi ness (fog′ē nis), foggy or misty condition. *n.*
fog gy (fog′ē), 1 having much fog; misty. 2 not clear; dim; blurred: *Their ideas are confused and rather foggy.* *adj.*, **fog gi er, fog gi est.** —**fog′gi ly,** *adv.*
fog horn (fog′hôrn′), horn that warns ships in foggy weather. *n.*
fo gy (fō′gē), old-fashioned person; person who is behind the times. *n., pl.* **fo gies.** Also, **fogey.**
foi ble (foi′bəl), a weak point; weakness: *Talking too much is one of my foibles.* *n.*
foil¹ (foil), prevent from carrying out plans; get the better of; outwit: *Quick thinking by the bank clerk foiled the robbers, and they were captured.* *v.*
foil² (foil), 1 metal beaten, hammered, or rolled into a very thin sheet: *Candy is sometimes wrapped in foil to keep it fresh.* 2 anything that makes something else look or seem better by contrast: *The colorful pillows were a perfect foil for the beige couch.* *n.*
foil³ (foil), a long, narrow sword with a knob or button on the point to prevent injury, used in fencing. *n.*
foist (foist), palm off as genuine; impose by fraud: *The dishonest shopkeeper foisted inferior goods on customers.* *v.*
fold¹ (fōld), 1 bend or double over on itself: *fold a letter, fold a napkin.* 2 layer of something folded; pleat: *The kitten played in the folds of the curtain.* 3 mark or line made by folding. 4 bend until close to the body: *You fold your arms. A bird folds its wings.* 5 put the arms around and hold tenderly: *He folded the crying child to him.*

6 wrap: *She folded her bathing suit in a towel.* 1,4-6 *v.*, 2,3 *n.*

fold[2] (fōld), **1** pen to keep sheep in. **2** a church group; congregation. *n.*

-fold, suffix forming adjectives and adverbs. **1** _____ times as many; _____ times as great: *Tenfold = ten times as many.* **2** formed or divided into _____ parts: *Manifold = formed in many parts.*

fold er (fōl/dər), **1** holder for papers made by folding a piece of stiff paper once. **2** pamphlet made of one or more folded sheets. **3** person or thing that folds. *n.*

fo li age (fō/lē ij), leaves of a plant. *n.*

fo li o (fō/lē ō), **1** a large sheet of paper folded once to make two leaves, or four pages, of a book. **2** volume consisting of sheets folded in this way; volume having pages of the largest size. **3** the page number of a printed book. *n., pl.* **fo li os.** [*Folio* comes from Latin *folium,* meaning ''a leaf.'']

folk (fōk), **1** people: *Most city folk know very little about farming.* **2** tribe or nation. **3** folks, *pl.* **a** people. **b** INFORMAL. relatives: *How are all your folks?* **c** INFORMAL. parents: *My folks aren't home tonight.* **4** of the common people, their beliefs, legends, customs, etc.: *folk laws, folk tunes.* 1-3 *n., pl.* **folk** or **folks** for 1,2; **4** *adj.*

folk dance, 1 dance originating and handed down among the common people. **2** music for it.

folk lore (fōk/lôr/), beliefs, legends, customs, etc., of a people or tribe. *n.*

folk music, music originating and handed down among the folk, or the common people.

folk singer, person who sings folk songs.

folk song, 1 song originating and handed down among the common people. **2** song imitating a real folk song: *''Oh! Susanna'' is a folk song written by Stephen Foster.*

folk sy (fōk/sē), INFORMAL. **1** sociable; friendly. **2** simple; unpretentious. *adj.,* **folk si er, folk si est.** —**folk/si ly,** *adv.* —**folk/si ness,** *n.*

folk tale, story or legend originating and handed down among the common people.

fol li cle (fol/ə kəl), a small cavity, sac, or gland in the body. Hair grows from follicles. *n.*

fol low (fol/ō), **1** go or come after: *Sheep follow a leader. April follows March. You lead; we'll follow.* **2** result from; result: *Misery follows war. If you eat too much candy, a stomach ache will follow.* **3** go along: *Follow this road to the corner.* **4** pursue: *The dogs followed the fox.* **5** act according to; take as a guide; use; obey: *Follow her advice.* **6** keep the eyes or attention on: *I could not follow that bird's flight.* **7** keep the mind on; keep up with and understand: *Try to follow the mayor's speech.* **8** take as one's work: *She expects to follow a career in law. v.*

follow through, continue a stroke, motion, plan, etc., through to the end.

follow up, 1 follow closely and steadily. **2** carry out to the end. **3** act upon with energy.

fol low er (fol/ō ər), **1** person or thing that follows. **2** person who follows the ideas or beliefs of another. *n.*

fol low ing (fol/ō ing), **1** group of followers. **2** next after: *If that was Sunday, then the following day must have been Monday.* **3 the following,** persons or things now to be named or described. 1,3 *n.,* **2** *adj.*

fol ly (fol/ē), **1** a being foolish; lack of sense; unwise conduct: *It was folly to eat too much on the picnic.* **2** a foolish act, practice, or idea; something silly: *To take that course would be a folly.* *n., pl.* **fol lies.**

fo ment (fō ment/), stir up (trouble, rebellion, etc.); promote: *Three sailors were fomenting a mutiny on the ship. v.*

fond (fond), **1** loving or liking: *a fond look, fond of children.* **2** loving foolishly or too much. **3** cherished: *fond hopes. adj.* —**fond/ly,** *adv.* —**fond/ness,** *n.*

fon dle (fon/dl), handle or treat with fondness; pet; caress: *They fondled the baby kittens.* *v.,* **fon dled, fon dling.**

font (font), **1** basin holding water for baptism. **2** basin for holy water. **3** fountain; source. *n.*

food (füd), **1** anything that plants, animals, or people eat, drink, or take in that makes them live and grow: *Milk and green vegetables are valuable foods for young people.* **2** what is eaten: *Give him food and drink.* **3** anything that causes growth: *Books are food for the mind. n.*

food chain, several kinds of living things that are linked because each uses another as food. Cats, birds, caterpillars, and plants are a food chain because each eats the one named next.

food stamp, stamp given or sold by the United States government to persons or families whose income is below a certain amount of money. The stamps may be used instead of cash to buy food.

food stuff (füd/stuf/), material for food. Grain and meat are foodstuffs. *n.*

fool (fül), **1** person without sense; person who acts unwisely. **2** clown formerly kept by royalty or nobility to amuse people; jester. **3** act like a fool for fun; play; joke: *I was only fooling.* **4** make a fool of; deceive; trick: *You can't fool me.* 1,2 *n.,* 3,4 *v.*

fool with, INFORMAL. meddle foolishly with.

fool har di ness (fül/här/dē nis), foolish boldness; rashness. *n.*

fool har dy (fül/här/dē), foolishly bold; rash. *adj.,* **fool har di er, fool har di est.** —**fool/har/di ly,** *adv.*

fool ish (fü/lish), without sense; unwise; silly: *foolish notions. adj.* —**fool/ish ly,** *adv.* —**fool/ish ness,** *n.*

fool proof (fül/prüf/), so safe or simple that even a fool can use or do it: *a foolproof device, a foolproof scheme. adj.*

fools cap (fülz/kap/), writing paper in sheets from 12 to 13¹/₂ inches wide and 15 to 17 inches long. *n.*

fool's gold, mineral that looks like gold, especially an iron pyrite.

foot (füt), **1** the end part of a leg; part that a person, animal, or thing stands on. **2** part opposite the head of something; end toward which the feet are put: *the foot of a bed.* **3** the lowest part; bottom; base: *the foot of a column, the foot of a hill, the foot of a page.* **4** part of a stocking that covers the foot. **5** unit of length equal to 12 inches. 3 feet = 1 yard. **6** one of the parts into which a line of poetry is divided. This line has four feet: ''The boy/stood on/the burn/ing deck.'' **7** INFORMAL. pay (a bill, etc.): *I'll foot the bill for lunch.* 1-6 *n., pl.* **feet;** 7 *v.*

on foot, standing or walking.

put one's foot down, make up one's mind and act firmly.

under foot, in the way.

foot age (füt/ij), length in feet. *n.*

foot ball (füt/bôl/), **1** game played with an inflated leather ball by two teams of eleven players each, on a field with a goal at each end. A player scores by carrying

folly (def. 1)—His plan to fly like a bat was sheer **folly.**

the ball over the goal line by a run or pass, or by kicking it through the goal posts. **2** ball used in this game. *n.*

foot board (fút/bôrd/), **1** board or small platform on which to support the feet. **2** an upright piece across the foot of a bed. *n.*

foot bridge (fút/brij/), bridge for people on foot only. *n.*

foot-can dle (fút/kan/dl), unit for measuring illumination. It is the amount of light produced by a standard candle on a surface at a distance of one foot. *n.*

foot ed (fút/id), having a foot or feet. *adj.*

foot fall (fút/fôl/), sound of steps coming or going. *n.*

foot hill (fút/hil/), a low hill at the base of a mountain or mountain range. *n.*

foot hold (fút/hōld/), **1** place to put a foot; support for the feet: *I climbed the steep cliff by getting footholds in cracks in the rock.* **2** a firm footing or position: *It is hard to break a habit after it has a foothold. n.*

foot ing (fút/ing), **1** a firm placing or position of the feet: *He lost his footing and fell down on the ice.* **2** place to put a foot; support for the feet: *The steep cliff gave us no footing.* **3** a secure position: *The new business has gained a footing in the community and is doing well.* **4** condition; position; relationship: *The United States and Canada are on a friendly footing. n.*

foot lights (fút/līts/), row of lights at the front of a stage. *n.pl.*

foot loose (fút/lüs/), free to go anywhere or do anything. *adj.*

foot man (fút/mən), a uniformed male servant who answers the bell, waits on the table, goes with an automobile or carriage to open the door, etc. *n., pl.* **foot men.**

foot mark (fút/märk/), footprint. *n.*

foot note (fút/nōt/), note at the bottom of a page about something on the page. *n.*

foot path (fút/path/), path for people on foot only. *n., pl.* **foot paths** (fút/paᴛHz/ *or* fút/paths/).

foot print (fút/print/), mark made by a foot. *n.*

foot rest (fút/rest/), support to rest the feet on. *n.*

foot soldier, infantryman.

foot sore (fút/sôr/), having sore feet from much walking: *The hike left us footsore and hungry. adj.*

foot step (fút/step/), **1** a person's step. **2** distance covered in one step. **3** sound of steps. **4** footprint. *n.*

follow in someone's footsteps, do as someone else has done.

foot stool (fút/stül/), a low stool on which to place the feet when seated. *n.*

foot work (fút/wėrk/), way of using the feet: *Footwork is important in boxing and dancing. n.*

fop (fop), a vain man who is very fond of fine clothes and has affected manners; dandy. *n.*

fop per y (fop/ər ē), behavior or dress of a fop. *n., pl.* **fop per ies.**

fop pish (fop/ish), **1** of a fop; suitable for a fop. **2** vain; affected. *adj.* —**fop/pish ly,** *adv.* —**fop/pish ness,** *n.*

for (fôr; *unstressed* fər), **1** in place of: *We used boxes for chairs.* **2** in support of; in favor of: *She is for changing the tax laws.* **3** in consideration of; in return: *These apples are twelve for a dollar. We thanked him for his kindness.* **4** with the object or purpose of: *She went for a walk.* **5** in order to become, have, keep, get to, etc.: *He ran for his life. She is hunting for her cat. He has just left for New York.* **6** meant to belong to or be used with; suited to: *a box for gloves, a present for you, books for children.* **7** with a feeling toward: *She has an eye for beauty. We longed for home.* **8** with respect or regard to: *It is warm for April. Eating too much is bad for one's health.* **9** because of; by reason of: *shout for joy. They were punished for stealing. A party was given for her.* **10** because: *We can't go, for it is raining.* **11** as far as: *We walked for a mile.* **12** as long as: *She*

worked for an hour. **13** as being: *They know it for a fact.* **14** in spite of: *For all her faults, we still like her.* **15** in proportion to: *For one poisonous snake there are many harmless ones.* **16** to the amount of: *a check for $20.* 1-9, 11-16 *prep.,* 10 *conj.*

for., **1** foreign. **2** forestry.

fo rage (fôr/ij), **1** hay, grain, or other food for horses, cattle, etc. **2** hunt or search for food: *Rabbits forage in our garden.* **3** get by hunting or searching about. **4** search about; hunt: *The boys foraged for old metal.* **5** plunder: *The soldiers foraged nearby villages.* 1 *n.,* 2-5 *v.,* **fo raged, fo rag ing.**

fo rag er (fôr/i jər), person who forages. *n.*

fo ray (fôr/ā), **1** a raid for plunder: *Armed bandits made forays on the villages and took away cattle.* **2** lay waste; plunder; pillage. 1 *n.,* 2 *v.*

for bade *or* **for bad** (fər bad/), past tense of **forbid.** *My parents forbade me to stay out past ten o'clock. v.*

for bear[1] (fôr ber/ *or* fôr bar/), **1** hold back; keep from doing, saying, using, etc.: *I forbore telling her the truth because I knew it would upset her.* **2** be patient; control oneself. *v.,* **for bore, for borne, for bear ing.** —**for bear/er,** *n.* —**for bear/ing ly,** *adv.*

for bear[2] (fôr/ber *or* fôr/bar), forebear; ancestor. *n.*

for bear ance (fôr ber/əns *or* fôr bar/əns), **1** act of forbearing. **2** patience; self-control. *n.*

for bid (fər bid/), not allow; say one must not do; make a rule against; prohibit: *The teacher forebade running in the halls. v.,* **for bade** *or* **for bad, for bid den** *or* **for bid, for bid ding.**

for bid den (fər bid/n), **1** not allowed; against the law or rules: *Eve ate the forbidden fruit.* **2** a past participle of **forbid.** *My parents have forbidden me to swim in that river.* 1 *adj.,* 2 *v.*

for bid ding (fər bid/ing), causing fear or dislike; looking dangerous or unpleasant: *The coast was rocky and forbidding. adj.* —**for bid/ding ly,** *adv.*

for bore (fôr bôr/), past tense of **forbear**[1]. *She forbore from showing her disappointment. v.*

for borne (fôr bôrn/), past participle of **forbear**[1]. *We have forborne from vengeance. v.*

force (fôrs), **1** active power; strength: *The speeding car struck the tree with great force.* **2** strength used against a person or thing; violence: *We had to use force to open the locked suitcase.* **3** power to control, influence, persuade, convince, etc.; effectiveness: *She writes with force.* **4** make (a person) act against his or her will; make do by force: *Give it to me at once, or I will force you to.* **5** get or take by force: *They forced their way in.* **6** break open or through by force: *force a lock, force a door.* **7** make by an unusual or unnatural effort; strain: *The unhappy child forced a smile.* **8** hurry the growth or development of (flowers, fruits, a child's mind, etc.). **9** group of people working or acting together: *our office force, the police force.* **10 forces,** *pl.* army, navy, etc. **11** cause that produces, changes, or stops the motion of a body: *the force of gravitation, magnetic force.* 1-3,9-11 *n.,* 4-8 *v.,* **forced, forc ing.** [*Force* came into English about 700 years ago from French *force,* and can be traced back to Latin *fortis,* meaning "strong."] —**force/less,** *adj.* —**forc/er,** *n.*

by main force, by using full strength: *lift a heavy object by main force.*

in force, 1 in effect or operation: *The old rules are still in force.* **2** with full strength: *The enemy attacked in force.*

forced (fôrst), **1** made, compelled, or driven by force: *The work of slaves was forced labor.* **2** done by unusual effort: *The soldiers made a forced march of three days.* **3** not natural; strained: *She hid her dislike with a forced smile. adj.*

force ful (fôrs′fəl), having much force; strong; powerful; vigorous: *a forceful manner. adj.* **—force′ful ly,** *adv.* **—force′ful ness,** *n.*

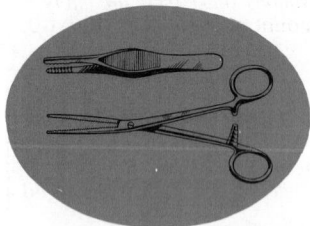

forceps—two kinds used in surgery

for ceps (fôr′seps), small pincers or tongs used by surgeons, dentists, etc., for grasping and pulling. *n., pl.* **for ceps.**

for ci ble (fôr′sə bəl), **1** made or done by force; using force: *a forcible entrance into a house.* **2** having or showing force; strong; powerful; convincing: *a forcible speaker. adj.* **—for′ci ble ness,** *n.*

for ci bly (fôr′sə blē), in a forcible manner. *adv.*

ford (fôrd), **1** place where a river, stream, etc., is not too deep to cross by walking or driving through the water. **2** cross (a river, etc.) by walking or driving through the water. 1 *n.,* 2 *v.* **—ford′a ble,** *adj.*

Ford (fôrd), **1 Gerald R(udolph),** born 1913, the 38th president of the United States, from 1974 to 1977, vice-president from 1973 to 1974. **2 Henry,** 1863-1947, American automobile manufacturer. *n.*

fore[1] (fôr), **1** at the front; toward the beginning or front; forward: *The fore wall of a house faces the street.* **2** at or toward the bow or front: *Several of the crew went fore.* **3** the forward part; front. 1 *adj.,* 2 *adv.,* 3 *n.*

to the fore, into full view; into a conspicuous place or position: *The question of new taxes will soon come to the fore.*

fore[2] (fôr), (in golf) a shout of warning to persons ahead who are liable to be struck by the ball. *interj.*

fore-, *prefix.* **1** front; in front; at or near the front: *Fore-paw = a front paw. Foremast = mast near the front of a ship.* **2** before; beforehand: *Foregoing = going before.*

fore and aft, 1 at or toward both bow and stern of a ship. **2** lengthwise on a ship; from bow to stern; placed lengthwise.

fore-and-aft (fôr′ən aft′), lengthwise on a ship; from bow to stern. Fore-and-aft sails are set lengthwise. *adj.*

fore arm[1] (fôr′ärm′), the part of the arm between the elbow and the wrist. *n.*

fore arm[2] (fôr ärm′), prepare for trouble ahead of time; arm beforehand. *v.*

fore bear (fôr′ber or fôr′bar), ancestor; forefather. *n.* Also, **forbear.**

fore bode (fôr bōd′), **1** give warning of; predict: *Those black clouds forebode a storm.* **2** have a feeling that something bad is going to happen. *v.,* **fore bod ed, fore bod ing. —fore bod′er,** *n.*

fore bod ing (fôr bō′ding), **1** prediction; warning. **2** a feeling that something bad is going to happen. *n.*

fore cast (fôr′kast), **1** tell what is coming; prophesy; predict: *Cooler weather is forecast for tomorrow.* **2** statement of what is coming; prophecy; prediction: *What is the forecast for the weather today?* 1 *v.,* **fore cast**

or **fore cast ed, fore cast ing;** 2 *n.* **—fore′cast′er,** *n.*

fore cas tle (fōk′səl or fôr′kas′əl), **1** the upper deck in front of the foremast. **2** the crew's quarters in the forward part of a merchant ship. *n.*

fore close (fôr klōz′), **1** shut out; prevent; exclude: *The club voted to foreclose further discussion of the subject.* **2** take away the right to redeem (a mortgage): *When the conditions of the mortgage were not met, the holder foreclosed and took possession of the house. v.,* **fore closed, fore clos ing.**

fore clo sure (fôr klō′zhər), act of foreclosing a mortgage. *n.*

fore doom (fôr düm′), doom beforehand: *Their plans were foredoomed to fail. v.*

fore fa ther (fôr′fä′ᵺər), ancestor. *n.*

fore fin ger (fôr′fing′gər), finger next to the thumb; index finger. *n.*

fore foot (fôr′füt′), one of the front feet of an animal having four or more feet. *n., pl.* **fore feet.**

fore front (fôr′frunt′), place of greatest importance, activity, etc.; foremost part; extreme front: *She was at the forefront of the citizens' campaign for cleaner living conditions. n.*

fore go[1] (fôr gō′), forgo. *v.,* **fore went, fore gone, fore go ing. —fore go′er,** *n.*

fore go[2] (fôr gō′), go before. *v.,* **fore went, fore gone, fore go ing.**

fore go ing (fôr′gō′ing), going before; preceding; previous: *There are many pictures in the foregoing pages. adj.*

fore gone[1] (fôr gôn′), past participle of **forego**[1]. *He has foregone his trip. v.*

fore gone[2] (fôr′gôn for 1,2; fôr gôn′ for 3), **1** known or decided beforehand; inevitable: *That one of the good students in the class would win the prize was a foregone conclusion.* **2** having gone before; previous. **3** past participle of **forego**[2]. *The tale of his heroic deeds had foregone his arrival.* 1,2 *adj.,* 3 *v.*

fore ground (fôr′ground′), the part of a picture or scene nearest the observer; the part in the front: *The cottage stands in the foreground with the mountains in the background. n.*

forehand (def. 1)

fore hand (fôr′hand′), **1** stroke in tennis and other games made with the palm of the hand turned forward. **2** done or made with the palm of the hand turned forward. 1 *n.,* 2 *adj.*

fore hand ed (fôr′han′did), providing for the future; prudent; thrifty. *adj.* **—fore′hand′ed ly,** *adv.***—fore′hand′ed ness,** *n.*

fore head (fôr′id or fôr′hed′), the part of the face above the eyes. *n.*

fo reign (fôr′ən), **1** outside one's own country: *He has traveled a lot in foreign countries.* **2** coming from outside one's own country: *a foreign language, foreign money.* **3** having to do with other countries; carried on or dealing with other countries: *foreign trade, foreign affairs.*

4 not belonging; not related: *Sitting still all day is foreign to that healthy girl's nature. adj.* —**fo′reign ness,** *n.*

foreign

Foreign came into English about 700 years ago from French *forain*, and can be traced back to Latin *foras*, meaning "outside."

a hat	**i** it	**oi** oil	**ch** child	a in about
ā age	**ī** ice	**ou** out	**ng** long	e in taken
ä far	**o** hot	**u** cup	**sh** she	ə = i in pencil
e let	**ō** open	**u̇** put	**th** thin	o in lemon
ē equal	**ô** order	**ü** rule	**ŦH** then	u in circus
ėr term			**zh** measure	

fo reign er (fôr′ə nər), person from another country; alien; outsider. *n.*

fore know (fôr nō′), know beforehand. *v.,* **fore knew** (fôr nü′ *or* fôr nyü′), **fore known** (fôr nōn′), **fore know ing.**

fore knowl edge (fôr′nol′ij *or* fôr nol′ij), knowledge of a thing before it exists or happens. *n.*

fore leg (fôr′leg′), one of the front legs of an animal having four or more legs. *n.*

fore limb (fôr′lim′), one of the front limbs of an animal having four or more limbs. *n.*

fore lock (fôr′lok′), lock of hair that grows just above the forehead. *n.*

fore man (fôr′mən), **1** person in charge of a group of workers or of some part of a factory. **2** chairman of a jury. *n., pl.* **fore men.**

fore mast (fôr′mast′ *or* fôr′məst), mast nearest the front of a ship. *n.*

fore most (fôr′mōst), **1** first: *I am foremost in line (adj.). He stumbled and fell head foremost (adv.).* **2** chief; leading: *one of the foremost scientists of this century.* 1,2 *adj.,* 1 *adv.*

fore noon (fôr′nün′), time between early morning and noon; part of the day from sunrise to noon. *n.*

fore or dain (fôr′ôr dān′), ordain beforehand; determine beforehand; predestine. *v.* —**fore′or dain′ment,** *n.*

fore part (fôr′pärt′), the front part; early part. *n.*

fore paw (fôr′pô′), a front paw. *n.*

fore quar ter (fôr′kwôr′tər), a front leg, shoulder, and nearby ribs of beef, lamb, pork, etc. *n.*

fore run ner (fôr′run′ər), **1** person who is sent ahead to prepare for and announce another's coming; herald. **2** sign or warning that something is coming: *Black clouds are forerunners of a storm.* **3** predecessor; ancestor. *n.*

fore sail (fôr′sāl′ *or* fôr′səl), **1** the principal sail on the foremast of a schooner. **2** the lowest sail on the foremast of a square-rigged ship. *n.*

fore saw (fôr sô′), past tense of **foresee.** *We foresaw that we would be late and called to tell our friends. v.*

fore see (fôr sē′), see or know beforehand: *We didn't take our bathing suits, because we could foresee that the water would be cold. v.,* **fore saw, fore seen, fore see ing.** —**fore se′er,** *n.*

fore see a ble (fôr sē′ə bəl), that can be foreseen. *adj.*

fore seen (fôr sēn′), past participle of **foresee.** *Nobody could have foreseen how cold it would be. v.*

fore shad ow (fôr shad′ō), indicate beforehand; be a warning of: *Those dark clouds foreshadow a storm. v.* —**fore shad′ow er,** *n.*

fore short en (fôr shôrt′n) shorten (lines, objects, etc.) in a drawing or painting in order to give the impression of depth and distance to the eye. Foreshortening helps give perspective to a drawing or painting. *v.*

fore sight (fôr′sīt′), **1** power to see or know beforehand what is likely to happen: *No one had enough foresight to predict the winner.* **2** careful thought for the future; prudence: *A spendthrift does not use foresight.* **3** a looking ahead; view into the future. *n.*

fore sight ed (fôr′sī′tid), having or showing foresight. *adj.* —**fore′sight′ed ly,** *adv.* —**fore′sight′ed ness,** *n.*

fore skin (fôr′skin′), fold of skin that covers the end of the penis. *n.*

fo rest (fôr′ist), **1** a large piece of land covered with trees; thick woods. **2** the trees themselves. **3** of a forest; in a forest: *Help prevent forest fires.* 1,2 *n.,* 3 *adj.* [*Forest* came into English about 700 years ago from French *forest*, and can be traced back to Latin *foris*, meaning "outside."]

fore stall (fôr stôl′), **1** prevent by acting first: *The mayor forestalled a strike by starting to negotiate early with the union.* **2** act sooner than and so get the better of; get ahead of: *By settling the deal over the telephone, she had forestalled all her competitors. v.* —**fore stall′er,** *n.*

fo rest ed (fôr′ə stid), covered with trees; thickly wooded. *adj.*

fo rest er (fôr′ə stər), person in charge of a forest to guard against fires, look after timber, etc. *n.*

fo rest ry (fôr′ə strē), science and art of planting and taking care of forests. *n.*

fore taste (fôr′tāst′), a taste beforehand: *The boy got a foretaste of business life by working during his vacation from school. n.*

fore tell (fôr tel′), tell or show beforehand; predict; prophesy: *Who can foretell what the future will be? v.,* **fore told, fore tell ing.**

fore thought (fôr′thôt′), careful thought or planning for the future; prudence; foresight: *A great deal of forethought went into their trip. n.*

fore told (fôr tōld′), past tense and past participle of **foretell.** *She foretold the future. The Weather Bureau had foretold the cold wave. v.*

fore top (fôr′top′ *or* fôr′təp), platform at the top of the bottom section of a foremast. *n.*

for ev er (fər ev′ər), **1** without ever coming to an end; for always; for ever: *Nobody lives forever.* **2** all the time; always: *She is forever telling me that I should take more exercise. adv.*

for ev er more (fər ev′ər môr′), forever. *adv.*

fore warn (fôr wôrn′), warn beforehand: *We should have been forewarned of his illness when he began to lose weight. v.*

fore went (fôr went′), past tense of **forego.** *v.*

fore wing (fôr′wing′), one of the front wings of an insect having four wings. *n.*

fore word (fôr′werd′), a brief introduction or preface to a book, speech, etc. *n.*

for feit (fôr′fit), **1** lose or have to give up by one's own act, neglect, or fault: *Careless drivers sometimes forfeit their lives.* **2** thing lost or given up because of some act, neglect, or fault; penalty; fine: *His life was the forfeit he paid for being careless.* 1 *v.,* 2 *n.* —**for′feit a ble,** *adj.* —**for′feit er,** *n.*

for fei ture (fôr′fi chər), **1** loss by forfeiting. **2** thing forfeited; penalty; fine. *n.*

for gath er (fôr gaŦH′ər), **1** gather together; assemble;

meet. **2** meet by accident. **3** be friendly; associate. *v.*

for gave (fər gāv′), past tense of **forgive.** *She forgave my mistake. v.*

forge[1] (fôrj), **1** place with a furnace or open fire where metal is heated very hot and then hammered into shape. **2** a blacksmith's shop; smithy. **3** heat (metal) very hot and then hammer into shape: *The blacksmith forged a bar of iron into a big, strong hook.* **4** place where iron or other metal is melted and refined. **5** make, shape, or form. **6** make or write (something false) to deceive; sign falsely: *forge a letter of recommendation, forge checks.* 1,2,4 *n.,* 3,5,6 *v.,* **forged, forg ing.** [*Forge*[1] came into English about 600 years ago from French *forge,* and can be traced back to Latin *faber,* meaning "worker."]

forge[1] (def. 1)—a forge in a blacksmith's shop a hundred years ago

forge[2] (fôrj), move forward slowly but steadily: *One runner forged ahead of the others and won the race. v.,* **forged, forg ing.**

forg er (fôr′jər), **1** person who forges metals. **2** person who forges another person's name or makes any fraudulent imitation. *n.*

forg er y (fôr′jər ē), **1** act of forging another person's name or making or writing something false. Forgery is a crime and is punishable by law. **2** something made or written falsely to deceive: *The painting was a forgery. The signature on the check was not mine but a forgery. n., pl.* **forg er ies.**

for get (fər get′), **1** let go out of the mind; fail to remember: *I forgot the poem which I had memorized.* **2** fail to think of; fail to do, take, notice, etc.: *I forgot to call the dentist. He had forgotten his umbrella. v.,* **for got, for got ten** or **for got, for get ting.** —**for get′ta ble,** *adj.* —**for get′ter,** *n.*

forget oneself, forget what one should do or be; say or do something improper: *The angry man forgot himself and started to shout in front of everybody on the bus.*

for get ful (fər get′fəl), **1** apt to forget; having a poor memory: *If I get overly tired I become forgetful.* **2** neglecting; heedless: *forgetful of the law. adj.* —**for get′ful ly,** *adv.* —**for get′ful ness,** *n.*

for get-me-not (fər get′mē not′), a small plant with hairy stems and clusters of small blue, pink, or white flowers. *n.*

for giv a ble (fər giv′ə bəl), able to be forgiven; excusable. *adj.*

for give (fər giv′), give up the wish to punish; not have hard feelings at or toward; pardon; excuse: *She forgave me for breaking her tennis racket. v.,* **for gave, for giv en, for giv ing.** —**for giv′er,** *n.*

for giv en (fər giv′ən), past participle of **forgive.** *Your mistakes are forgiven, but be more careful. v.*

for give ness (fər giv′nis), **1** act of forgiving; pardon. **2** willingness to forgive. *n.*

for giv ing (fər giv′ing), willing to forgive. *adj.* —**for giv′ing ly,** *adv.* —**for giv′ing ness,** *n.*

for go (fôr gō′), do without; give up: *She decided to forgo the movies and do her lessons. v.,* **for went, for gone, for go ing.** Also, **forego.**

for gone (fôr gôn′), past participle of **forgo.** *I have forgone dessert for a month in an effort to lose weight. v.*

for got (fər got′), past tense and a past participle of **forget.** *She was so busy that she forgot to eat her lunch. v.*

for got ten (fər got′n), a past participle of **forget.** *He has forgotten much of what he learned. v.*

fork (fôrk), **1** instrument with a handle and two or more long, pointed parts at one end. A small fork is used to lift food. A much larger fork, called a pitchfork, is used to lift and throw hay. Another kind is used for digging. **2** lift, throw, or dig with a fork: *fork hay into a wagon.* **3** anything shaped like a fork; any branching. The place where a tree, road, or stream divides into branches is a fork. **4** one of the branches into which anything is divided: *Take the right-hand fork.* **5** have a fork or forks; divide into forks: *There is a garage where the road forks.* 1,3,4 *n.,* 2,5 *v.* —**fork′like′,** *adj.*

fork out, fork over, or **fork up,** INFORMAL. hand over; pay out: *He forked over the money.*

forked (fôrkt), **1** having a fork or forks; divided into branches: *a forked stick.* **2** zigzag: *forked lightning. adj.*

fork lift (fôrk′lift′), device often attached to one end of a truck or small vehicle, with horizontal metal prongs that can be inserted under a load to lift it or put it down. *n.*

for lorn (fôr lôrn′), miserable and hopeless because left alone and neglected: *The lost kitten, a forlorn little animal, was wet and dirty. adj.* —**for lorn′ly,** *adv.*

form (fôrm), **1** appearance apart from color or materials; shape: *Circles and triangles are simple forms.* **2** to shape; make: *Bakers form dough into loaves.* **3** be formed; take shape: *Clouds form in the sky.* **4** become: *Water forms ice when it freezes.* **5** make up; compose: *Parents and children form a family.* **6** organize; establish: *We formed a club.* **7** develop: *She formed the good habit of doing her homework before watching television.* **8** kind; sort; variety: *Ice, snow, and steam are forms of water.* **9** way of doing something; manner; method: *He is a fast runner, but his form in running is bad.* **10** a set way of behaving according to custom or rule; formality; ceremony: *She said "Good morning" as a matter of form, although she hardly noticed me.* **11** piece of printed paper with blank spaces to be filled in: *We filled out a form to get a license for our dog.* **12** arrangement: *In what form was the list of words?* **13** mold; pattern: *Ice cream is often made in forms.* **14** good condition of body or mind: *Athletes exercise to keep in form.* **15** (in grammar) any of the ways in which a word is spelled or pronounced to show its different meanings. *Toys* is the plural form of *toy. Saw* is the past form of *see. My* and *mine* are the possessive forms of *I.* **16** grade in certain schools: *My cousin goes to an English school, and is now in the fifth form.* 1,8-16 *n.,* 2-7 *v.*

for mal (fôr′məl), **1** not familar and homelike; stiff: *a formal greeting. A judge has a formal manner in a court of law.* **2** according to set customs or rules: *The ambassador paid a formal call on the prime minister.* **3** done with the proper forms; clear and definite: *A written contract is a formal agreement to do something.* **4** very regular; symmetrical; orderly: *a formal arrangement of furniture, a formal poem.* **5** having to do with the form, not the content of a thing. **6** a dance, party, or other social affair at which women often wear long, fancy dresses and men wear elegant suits. **7** gown worn to such a social affair: *The women wore formals to the banquet.* 1-5 *adj.,* 6,7 *n.* —**for′mal ly,** *adv.*

for mal de hyde (fôr mal′də hīd), a colorless gas with a sharp, irritating odor. It is used in a water solution to disinfect and to preserve. *n.*

for mal i ty (fôr mal′ə tē), **1** something required by custom or rule; outward form; ceremony: *At a wedding there are many formalities.* **2** attention to forms and customs: *The queen received her visitors with much formality.* **3** stiffness of manner, behavior, or arrangement: *The formality of the party made me uneasy. n., pl.* **for mal i ties.**

for mal ize (fôr′mə līz), **1** make formal. **2** give a definite form to. *v.,* **for mal ized, for mal iz ing.**

for mat (fôr′mat), **1** shape, size, and general arrangement of a book, magazine, etc. **2** the design, plan, arrangement, form, or manner of anything: *the format of a television show.* **3** arrange; put in a format or give a format to: *to format a new magazine.* 1,2 *n.,* 3 *v.,* **for matted, for mat ting.**

for ma tion (fôr mā′shən), **1** the forming, making, or shaping (of something): *Heat causes the formation of steam from water.* **2** way in which something is arranged; arrangement; order: *The band marched in perfect parade formation. Football players line up in various formations for their plays.* **3** thing formed: *Clouds are formations of tiny drops of water in the sky. n.*

form a tive (fôr′mə tiv), having to do with formation or development; forming; molding: *Home and school are the chief formative influences in a child's life. adj.*

for mer (fôr′mər), **1** the first of two: *When I am offered ice cream or pie, I always choose the former.* **2** earlier; past; long past: *In former times, cooking was done in fireplaces instead of stoves. adj.*

for mer ly (fôr′mər lē), in the past; some time ago: *Our teacher formerly taught at a different school. adv.*

For mi ca (fôr mī′kə), trademark for a plastic that resists water, heat, and most chemicals. It is used on kitchen and bathroom surfaces, tables and other furniture, etc. *n.*

for mi da ble (fôr′mə də bəl), hard to overcome; hard to deal with; to be dreaded: *a formidable opponent. adj.*

for mi da bly (fôr′mə də blē), in a formidable manner. *adv.*

form less (fôrm′lis), without definite or regular form; shapeless. *adj.* —**form′less ly,** *adv.* —**form′less ness,** *n.*

form letter, letter copied from a pattern so that copies may be made easily and sent to many different people.

For mo sa (fôr mō′sə), Taiwan. *n.* —**For mo′san,** *adj., n.*

for mu la (fôr′myə lə), **1** a set form of words, especially one which by much use has partly lost its meaning: *"How do you do?" is a polite formula.* **2** recipe or prescription: *a formula for making soap.* **3** mixture made by following a recipe or prescription: *a baby's formula.* **4** combination of symbols used in chemistry to show the composition of a compound: *The formula for water is H_2O.* **5** combination of symbols used in mathematics to state a rule or principle: $(a+b)^2 = a^2 + 2ab + b^2$ *is an algebraic formula. n., pl.* **for mu las** *or* **for mu lae.**

for mu lae (fôr′myə lē), a plural of **formula.** *n.*

for mu late (fôr′myə lāt), state definitely or systematically; express in a formula: *Our country formulates its laws according to its constitution. v.,* **for mu lat ed, for mu lating.**

for mu la tion (fôr′myə lā′shən), a definite expression or statement; expression in a formula. *n.*

for sake (fôr sāk′), give up; leave alone; leave; abandon: *The Pilgrims forsook their homes and friends to settle in the American wilderness. v.,* **for sook, for sak en, for sak ing.**

for sak en (fôr sā′kən), **1** past participle of **forsake.** *That girl has forsaken her old friends.* **2** deserted; abandoned: *We found an old, forsaken graveyard out in the country.* 1 *v.,* 2 *adj.*

a hat	**i** it	**oi** oil	**ch** child	⎧ a in about
ā age	**ī** ice	**ou** out	**ng** long	⎪ e in taken
ä far	**o** hot	**u** cup	**sh** she	ə = ⎨ i in pencil
e let	**ō** open	**ù** put	**th** thin	⎪ o in lemon
ē equal	**ô** order	**ü** rule	**ŦH** then	⎩ u in circus
ėr term			**zh** measure	

for sook (fôr sùk′), past tense of **forsake.** *He forsook his family. v.*

for sooth (fôr süth′), OLD USE. in truth; indeed. *adv.*

for swear (fôr swer′ *or* fôr swar′), **1** swear solemnly to give up: *The coach asked the team to forswear smoking.* **2** be untrue to one's sworn word or promise; perjure (oneself). *v.,* **for swore, for sworn, for swear ing.**

for swore (fôr swôr′), past tense of **forswear.** *The team forswore smoking. v.*

for sworn (fôr swôrn′), past participle of **forswear.** *They have forsworn liquor and cigarettes. v.*

for syth i a (fôr sith′ē ə), shrub having many bell-shaped, yellow flowers in early spring before its leaves come out. *n., pl.* **for syth i as.** [*Forsythia* was named for William *Forsyth,* 1737-1804, a British botanist.]

fort (fôrt), a strong building or place that can be defended against an enemy; fortified place; stronghold. *n.*

forte[1] (fôrt), something a person does very well; strong point: *Bowling is her forte. n.*

for te[2] (fôr′tā), (in music) loud. *adj., adv.*

forth (fôrth), **1** forward; onward: *From this day forth I'll try to do better.* **2** into view; out: *The sun came forth from behind the clouds. adv.*

and so forth, and so on; and the like: *We ate cake, candy, nuts, and so forth.*

forth com ing (fôrth′kum′ing), **1** about to appear; approaching: *The forthcoming week will be busy.* **2** ready when wanted; coming forth: *I needed help, but none was forthcoming. adj.*

forth right (fôrth′rīt′), frank and outspoken; straightforward; direct: *The speaker did not like the plan and made forthright objections to it. adj.* —**forth′right′ly,** *adv.*

forth with (fôrth′with′ *or* fôrth′wiŦH′), at once; immediately: *The judge's summons ordered the witness to appear forthwith in court. adv.*

for ti eth (fôr′tē ith), **1** next after the 39th; last in a series of 40. **2** one of 40 equal parts. *adj., n.*

for ti fi ca tion (fôr′tə fə kā′shən), **1** a making strong; adding strength to; fortifying: *The general was responsible for the fortification of the town.* **2** wall or fort built to make a place strong. **3** place made strong by building walls and forts. *n.*

for ti fy (fôr′tə fī), **1** build forts, walls, etc.; protect a place against attack; strengthen against attack. **2** give support to; strengthen: *They fortified each other against the coming ordeal.* **3** enrich with vitamins and minerals: *fortify bread. v.,* **for ti fied, for ti fy ing.** —**for′ti fi er,** *n.*

for tis si mo (fôr tis′ə mō), (in music) very loud. *adj., adv.*

for ti tude (fôr′tə tüd *or* fôr′tə tyüd), courage in facing pain, danger, or trouble; firmness of spirit. *n.*

fort night (fôrt′nīt), two weeks. *n.*

fort night ly (fôrt′nīt lē), **1** once in every two weeks. **2** happening once in every two weeks. 1 *adv.,* 2 *adj.*

FOR TRAN (fôr′tran), computer programming language that uses algebraic notation, designed for mathematical tasks. *n.*

for tress (fôr′tris), place built with walls and defenses; large fort or fortification. *n., pl.* **for tress es.**

for tu i tous (fôr tü′ə təs *or* fôr tyü′ə təs), happening by chance; accidental: *The fortuitous falling of an apple led Newton to formulate the law of gravitation. adj.* —**for tu′i tous ly,** *adv.* —**for tu′i tous ness,** *n.*

for tu nate (fôr′chə nit), **1** having good luck; lucky: *You are fortunate in having such a fine family.* **2** bringing good luck; having favorable results: *a fortunate decision. adj.* —**for′tu nate ly,** *adv.*

for tune (fôr′chən), **1** a great deal of money or property; riches; wealth: *They made a fortune in oil.* **2** what happens; luck; chance: *Fortune was against us; we lost.* **3** good luck; prosperity; success. **4** what is going to happen to a person; fate: *I know someone who claims to be able to tell people's fortunes. n.*

for tune tell er (fôr′chən tel′ər), person who claims to be able to tell what is going to happen to people. *n.*

Fort Wayne (wān), city in NE Indiana.

Fort Worth (wėrth), city in N Texas.

for ty (fôr′tē), four times ten; 40. *n., pl.* **for ties;** *adj.*

for ty-nin er (fôr′tē nī′nər), person who went to California in 1849 to seek gold during the gold rush that had started there in 1848. *n.*

forum (def. 1)—ruins of an ancient Roman forum

fo rum (fôr′əm), **1** the public square or market place of an ancient Roman city. There business was done, and courts and public assemblies were held. **2** assembly for the discussion of questions of public interest. **3** court of law; tribunal. *n.*

for ward (fôr′wərd), **1** toward the front; onward; ahead: *Forward, march! From this time forward we shall be good friends.* **2** to the front: *come forward (adv.), the forward part of a ship (adj.).* **3** advanced; far ahead: *A child of four years who can read is forward for his age.* **4** into view or consideration; out: *In her talk she brought forward several new ideas.* **5** help along: *She did everything she could to forward her friend's plan.* **6** send on farther: *Please forward my mail to my new address.* **7** ready; eager: *He knew his lesson and was forward with his answers.* **8** impudent; bold: *Don't be so forward as to interrupt the speaker.* **9** player whose position is in the front line in games such as basketball, hockey, or soccer. 1,2,4 *adv.,* 2,3,7,8 *adj.,* 5,6 *v.,* 9 *n.* —**for′ward er,** *n.* —**for′ward ly,** *adv.*

for ward ness (fôr′wərd nis), **1** a being far ahead. **2** readiness; eagerness. **3** impudence; boldness. *n.*

for wards (fôr′wərdz), forward. *adv.*

for went (fôr went′), past tense of **forgo.** *She forwent the movies in order to do her lessons. v.*

fos sil (fos′əl), **1** the hardened remains or traces of an animal or plant of a former age. Fossils of ferns are found in coal. **2** forming a fossil; of the nature of a fossil: *the fossil remains of a dinosaur.* **3** a very old-fashioned person with out-of-date ideas. 1,3 *n.,* 2 *adj.* [See **Word History.**]

fossil fuel, a fuel found in the earth and formed from the remains of things that lived millions of years ago. Coal, oil, and natural gas are fossil fuels.

fos sil ize (fos′ə līz), change into a fossil. *v.,* **fos sil ized, fos sil iz ing.** —**fos′sil i za′tion,** *n.*

fos ter (fô′stər), **1** help the growth or development of; encourage: *Our city fosters libraries and parks.* **2** care for

fondly; cherish. **3** bring up; help to grow; make grow; rear. **4** in the same family, but not related by birth. A **foster child** is a child brought up by a person not his or her parent. A **foster father, foster mother,** and **foster parent** are persons who bring up the child of another. 1-3 *v.,* 4 *adj.* —**fos′ter er,** *n.*

Fos ter (fô′stər), **Stephen Collins,** 1826-1864, American composer. *n.*

fought (fôt), past tense and past participle of **fight.** *They fought for their rights. A battle was fought there. v.*

foul (foul), **1** very dirty, nasty, or smelly: *We opened the windows to let out the foul air.* **2** make or become dirty; soil; defile: *The oil spilled by the damaged ship fouled the harbor.* **3** very wicked; vile: *Murder is a foul crime.* **4** offending modesty or decency; obscene; profane: *foul language.* **5** done against the rules; unfair. **6** (in football, basketball, etc.) an unfair play; thing done against the rules. **7** make an unfair play against. **8** foul ball. **9** hit (a foul ball). **10** hit against: *One boat fouled the other.* **11** get tangled up with; catch: *The rope they threw fouled our anchor chain.* **12** tangled up; caught: *The ship's anchor was foul.* **13** clog up: *Grease fouled the drain.* **14** unfavorable; stormy: *Foul weather delayed us for several days.* 1,3-5,12,14 *adj.,* 2,7,9-11,13 *v.,* 6,8 *n.* —**foul′ly,** *adv.*

run foul of, get into trouble or difficulties with: *run foul of the law.*

fou lard (fù lärd′), a soft, thin fabric made of silk, rayon, or cotton, usually with a printed pattern. It is used for neckties, dresses, etc. *n.*

foul ball, (in baseball) a batted ball that lands outside the foul lines.

foul line, 1 (in baseball) either one of two straight lines extending from home plate through first base and third base to the limits of the playing field. **2** (in basketball) line ten feet in front of each basket from which foul shots are thrown.

foul play, 1 unfair play; thing or things done against the rules. **2** treachery; violence.

found[1] (found), past tense and past participle of **find.** *We found the treasure. The lost child was found. v.*

found[2] (found), **1** set up; establish: *The Pilgrims founded a colony at Plymouth.* **2** rest for support; base: *He founded his claim on facts. v.*

foun da tion (foun dā′shən), **1** part on which the other parts rest for support; base: *the foundation of a house.*

WORD HISTORY

fossil

Fossil comes from French *fossile,* and can be traced back to Latin *fodere,* meaning "to dig."

fossil (def. 1)—dug from shale in Wyoming

2 basis: *This report has no foundation in fact.* **3** a founding or establishing: *The foundation of the United States began in 1776.* **4** a being founded or established. **5** institution founded and endowed. **6** fund given to support an institution. *n.*

foun der[1] (foun′dər), **1** fill with water and sink: *The ship foundered in the storm.* **2** fall down; stumble: *The pony foundered in the swamp.* **3** break down; fail: *Their business has foundered. v.*

found er[2] (foun′dər), person who founds or establishes something. *n.*

found ling (found′ling), baby or little child found deserted. *n.*

found ry (foun′drē), place where metal is melted and molded; place where things are made of molten metal. *n., pl.* **found ries.**

fount (fount), **1** fountain. **2** source; origin. *n.*

foun tain (foun′tən), **1** water flowing or rising into the air in a spray. **2** pipes through which the water is forced and the basin built to receive it. **3** spring of water. **4** place to get a drink: *a drinking fountain, a soda fountain.* **5** source; origin: *My friend is a fountain of information about football. n.*

foun tain head (foun′tən hed′), **1** source of a stream. **2** an original source. *n.*

fountain pen, pen for writing that gives a steady supply of ink from a rubber or plastic tube.

four (fôr), one more than three; 4. *n., adj.*
on all fours, 1 on all four feet. **2** on hands and knees.

four-foot ed (fôr′fůt′id), having four feet; quadruped: *A dog is a four-footed animal. adj.*

Four-H clubs or **4-H clubs** (fôr′āch′), a national system of clubs to teach agriculture and home economics to children in rural areas.

four-post er (fôr′pō′stər), bed with four tall corner posts for supporting a canopy. *n.*

four score (fôr′skôr′), four times twenty; 80. *adj., n.*

four some (fôr′səm), **1** group of four people. **2** game played by four people, two on each side. **3** the players. *n.*

four square (fôr′skwer′ *or* fôr′skwar′), **1** square. **2** frank; outspoken. **3** firm. *adj.*

four teen (fôr′tēn′), four more than ten; 14. *n., adj.*

four teenth (fôr′tēnth′), **1** next after the 13th; last in a series of 14. **2** one of 14 equal parts. *adj., n.*

fourth (fôrth), **1** next after the third; last in a series of 4. **2** one of 4 equal parts; quarter. *adj., n.*

Fourth of July, Independence Day.

fowl (foul), **1** any of several kinds of large birds used for food. The hen, rooster, and turkey are fowls. **2** flesh of these birds used for food. **3** wild fowl. *n., pl.* **fowls** or **fowl.**

fowl er (fou′lər), person who hunts or traps wild birds. *n.*

fowling piece, a light gun for shooting wild birds.

fox (def. 1)—about 16 in. (40 cm.) high at the shoulder

fox (foks), **1** a wild animal somewhat like a dog, having a pointed muzzle and bushy tail. In many stories the fox gets the better of other animals by its cleverness. **2** its fur. **3** a clever or crafty person. *n., pl.* **fox es. —fox′like′, adj.*

fox glove (foks′gluv′), plant with tall stalks having many bell-shaped purple or white flowers; digitalis. *n.*

fox hole (foks′hōl′), hole in the ground, large enough for one or two soldiers, for protection against enemy fire. *n.*

fox hound (foks′hound′), hound with a keen sense of smell, bred and trained to hunt foxes. *n.*

fox i ly (fok′sə lē), in a foxy manner; slyly; craftily. *adv.*

fox i ness (fok′sē nis), foxy quality; slyness; craftiness. *n.*

fox terrier, a small, active dog kept as a pet, once trained to drive foxes from their holes. Fox terriers are white with brown or black spots and may have smooth or rough coats.

fox trot, 1 dance having short, quick steps. **2** music for it.

fox-trot (foks′trot′), dance the fox trot. *v.,* **fox-trot ted, fox-trot ting.**

fox y (fok′sē), sly; crafty; as a fox is considered to be. *adj.,* **fox i er, fox i est.**

foy er (foi′ər), **1** a lounging room in a theater, apartment house, or hotel; lobby. **2** an entrance hall. *n.*

fp, f.p., or **F.P.,** freezing point.

FPC, Federal Power Commission.

fpm or **f.p.m.,** feet per minute.

fps or **f.p.s.,** feet per second.

Fr, symbol for francium.

fr., 1 fragment. **2** franc. **3** from.

Fr., 1 Father. **2** France. **3** French. **4** Friar. **5** Friday.

fra cas (frā′kəs), a noisy quarrel or fight; disorderly noise; uproar; brawl. *n., pl.* **fra cas es.**

frac tion (frak′shən), **1** one or more of the equal parts of a whole. $\frac{1}{2}$, $\frac{1}{3}$, and $\frac{3}{4}$ are fractions; so are $\frac{4}{3}$ and $\frac{10}{6}$. **2** a very small part, amount, etc.; not all of a thing; fragment: *She has done only a fraction of her homework. n.*

frac tion al (frak′shə nəl), **1** having to do with fractions. **2** forming a fraction: *440 yards is a fractional part of a mile.* **3** small by comparison; insignificant. *adj.* —**frac′tion al ly,** *adv.*

frac tious (frak′shəs), **1** cross; fretful; peevish. **2** hard to manage; unruly. *adj.* —**frac′tious ly,** *adv.* —**frac′tious ness,** *n.*

frac ture (frak′chər), **1** a breaking of a bone or cartilage. **2** a breaking or a being broken: *a fracture of friendly relations.* **3** result of breaking; a break; crack: *The fracture in the foundation is widening.* **4** break; crack: *I fractured my arm.* 1-3 *n.,* 4 *v.,* **frac tured, frac tur ing.**

frag ile (fraj′əl), easily broken, damaged, or destroyed; delicate; frail: *Be careful; that thin glass is fragile. adj.* —**frag′ile ly,** *adv.*

fra gil i ty (frə jil′ə tē), fragile quality; delicacy; frailness. *n.*

frag ment (frag′mənt), **1** piece of something broken; part broken off: *After I broke the vase, I tried to put the fragments back together.* **2** an incomplete or disconnected part: *Because of the noise he could hear only fragments of the conversation. n.*

frag men tar y (frag′mən ter′ē), made up of fragments; incomplete; disconnected: *fragmentary remains of a temple, a fragmentary account of an accident. adj.* —**frag′men tar′i ness** *n.*

fra grance (frā′grəns), a sweet smell; pleasing odor: *the fragrance of flowers, the fragrance of perfume. n.*

fra grant (frā′grənt), having or giving off a pleasing odor; sweet-smelling: *Fragrant roses perfumed the air. adj.* —**fra′grant ly,** *adv.*

frail (frāl), 1 slender and not very strong; weak: *a frail old man.* 2 easily broken or giving way: *Be careful; those little branches are a very frail support.* 3 morally weak; liable to yield to temptation. *adj.* —**frail′ly,** *adv.* —**frail′ness,** *n.*

frail ty (frāl′tē), 1 a being frail; weakness: *concern about a sick person's physical frailty, frailty of character.* 2 fault caused by weakness: *Nobody is perfect; we all have our frailties. n., pl.* **frail ties.**

frame (frām), 1 support over which something is stretched or built: *the frame of a house.* 2 body: *a person of small frame.* 3 way in which a thing is put together; structure; system: *the frame of the Constitution.* 4 put together; plan; make: *frame an answer to a difficult question. Thomas Jefferson helped to frame the Constitution.* 5 border in which a thing is set: *a window frame, a picture frame.* 6 put a border around: *frame a picture.* 7 INFORMAL. make seem guilty by some false arrangement: *frame an innocent person.* 8 one turn at bowling. 1-3,5,8 *n.,* 4,6,7 *v.,* **framed, fram ing.** —**fram′er,** *n.*

frame house, house made of a wooden framework covered with boards.

frame of mind, way one is thinking or feeling; disposition; mood.

frame-up (frām′up′), INFORMAL. 1 a secret and dishonest arrangement made beforehand. 2 arrangement made to have a person falsely accused. *n.*

frame work (frām′wėrk′), 1 support or skeleton; stiff part which gives shape to a thing: *A bridge often has a steel framework.* 2 way in which a thing is put together; structure; system: *the framework of government. n.*

franc (frangk), 1 unit of money in France, Belgium, Switzerland, Mali, Niger, Congo, and some other countries. 2 coin worth one franc. *n.*

France (frans), country in W Europe. *Capital:* Paris. See Gaul for map. *n.*

fran chise (fran′chīz), 1 privilege or right granted by a government: *The city granted the company a franchise to operate its buses on the city streets.* 2 right to vote: *The United States gave women the franchise in 1920.* 3 privilege of selling the products of a manufacturer in a given area. *n.* —**fran′chis er,** *n.*

Fran cis (fran′sis), **Saint,** 1181?-1226, Italian founder of the Franciscan order of friars. *n.*

Fran cis can (fran sis′kən), 1 of Saint Francis or the religious order founded by him in 1209. 2 friar belonging to the Franciscan order. 1 *adj.,* 2 *n.*

fran ci um (fran′sē əm), a radioactive, metallic element produced artificially from actinium or thorium. *n.*

Fran co (frang′kō), **Francisco,** 1892-1975, Spanish general, ruler of Spain from 1936 to 1975. *n.*

fran gi ble (fran′jə bəl), breakable. *adj.*

frank[1] (frangk), 1 free in expressing one's real thoughts, opinions, and feelings; not hiding what is in one's mind; not afraid to say what one thinks; open: *She was frank in telling me that she did not like my new hat.* 2 send (a letter, package, etc.) without charge. 3 mark to show that a letter, package, etc., is to be sent without charge. 4 right to send letters, packages, etc., without charge. 1 *adj.,* 2 *v.,* 3,4 *n.* —**frank′ly,** *adv.* —**frank′ness,** *n.*

frank[2] (frangk), INFORMAL. frankfurter. *n.*

Frank (frangk), member of the German tribes that conquered Gaul in the A.D. 500's. *n.*

Frank en stein (frang′kən stīn), 1 scientist in a novel, written in 1818 by Mary Wollstonecraft Shelley, who creates a monster that he cannot control. 2 the monster itself. *n.*

Frank fort (frangk′fərt), capital of Kentucky, in the N part. *n.*

Frank furt (frangk′fərt, frängk′fərt), Frankfurt am Main. *n.*

Frank furt am Main (frängk′fúrt äm mīn′), city in central West Germany.

frank furt er (frangk′fər tər), a reddish sausage made of beef and pork, or of beef alone; wiener. Frankfurters on buns are called hot dogs. *n.* [*Frankfurter* comes from German *Frankfurter,* meaning "of Frankfurt," where this type of sausage is a specialty.]

frank in cense (frang′kən sens), a fragrant resin from certain Asian or African trees. It gives off a sweet, spicy odor when burned. *n.*

Frank ish (frang′kish) of the Franks. *adj.*

Frank lin (frang′klən), **Benjamin,** 1706-1790, American statesman, author, scientist, printer, and inventor. *n.*

fran tic (fran′tik), very much excited; wild with rage, fear, pain, or grief: *The trapped animal made frantic efforts to escape. adj.* —**fran′tic ness,** *n.*

fran ti cal ly (fran′tik lē), in a frantic manner; with wild excitement. *adv.*

frappe (frap), 1 milk shake. 2 frappé. *n.*

frap pé (fra pā′), fruit juice sweetened and partially frozen, or shaken with finely cracked ice. *n.*

fra ter nal (frə tėr′nl), 1 of brothers or a brother; brotherly. 2 having to do with a group organized for mutual fellowship: *a fraternal association. adj.* —**fra ter′nal ly,** *adv.*

fraternal twins

fraternal twins, twins of the same or opposite sex coming from two separately fertilized egg cells rather than from one egg cell as identical twins do.

fra ter ni ty (frə tėr′nə tē), 1 group of men or boys joined together for fellowship or for some other purpose. There are student fraternities in many American colleges. 2 group having the same interests, kind of work, etc.: *the musical fraternity.* 3 fraternal feeling; brotherhood. *n., pl.* **fra ter ni ties.**

frat er nize (frat′ər nīz), associate in a brotherly way; be friendly. *v.,* **frat er nized, frat er niz ing.**

Frau (frou), GERMAN. 1 Mrs. 2 wife. *n., pl.* **Frau en** (frou′ən).

fraud (frôd), 1 dishonest dealing; trickery; cheating: *obtain a prize by fraud, win an election by fraud.* 2 a dishonest act, statement, etc.; something which is not what it seems to be; trick. 3 person who is not what he or she pretends to be. *n.*

fraud u lent (frô′jə lənt), 1 cheating; dishonest: *a fraudulent dealer at cards.* 2 done by fraud; gotten by trickery: *fraudulent gains. adj.* —**fraud′u lent ly,** *adv.*

fraught (frôt), loaded; filled: *The attempt to climb Mount Everest was fraught with danger. adj.*

Fräu lein (froi′līn), GERMAN. 1 Miss. 2 an unmarried woman. *n., pl.* **Fräu lein.**

fray[1] (frā), 1 separate into threads; make or become ragged or worn along the edge: *Long wear had frayed the collar and cuffs of several old shirts. Those trousers are beginning to fray at the cuffs.* **2** wear away; rub. *v.*

fray² (frā), a noisy quarrel; fight. *n.*

fraz zle (fraz′əl), **1** wear to shreds; fray; ravel: *The edges of the rug were completely frazzled.* **2** tire out; weary. **3** INFORMAL. a frazzled condition. 1,2 *v.,* **fraz zled, fraz-zling;** 3 *n.*

freak (frēk), **1** something very odd or unusual: *A green leaf growing in the middle of a rose would be called a freak of nature.* **2** animal, plant, or person that has developed abnormally. **3** very odd or unusual: *a freak storm.* **4** a sudden change of mind without reason. **5** a person who is especially interested in or devoted to something: *a movie freak, a sports-car freak.* 1,2,4,5 *n.,* 3 *adj.*

freak ish (frē′kish), full of freaks; very odd or unusual. *adj.* —**freak′ish ly,** *adv.* —**freak′ish ness,** *n.*

freck le (frek′əl), **1** a small, light-brown spot on the skin, often caused by exposure to the sun. **2** make freckles on. **3** become marked or spotted with freckles. 1 *n.,* 2,3 *v.,* **freck led, freck ling.**

freck led (frek′əld), marked with freckles. *adj.*

Fred er ick the Great (fred′ər ik), 1712-1786, king of Prussia from 1740 to 1786.

Fred er ic ton (fred′rik tən), capital of New Brunswick, in SE Canada. *n.*

free (frē), **1** not under another's control; not a captive or slave: *a free people, a free nation, free speech.* **2** not held back, fastened, or shut up; released; loose: *We set free the bear cub caught in the trap. Let the captives go free.* **3** not hindered; easy: *a free step.* **4** make free; let loose; let go: *We freed the bird from its cage. She freed her foot from the vine that tripped her.* **5** open to all: *a free port.* **6** to clear: *The judge freed her of all charges after hearing the testimony.* **7** without anything to pay: *These tickets are free (adj.). Children under 12 attend free (adv.).* **8** having no tax or duty: *free trade.* **9** not following rules, forms, or words exactly; not strict: *a free translation.* **10** not combined with something else: *Oxygen exists free in air.* **11** in a free manner; freely: *The animals ran free around the farm.* 1-3,5,7-10 *adj.,* **fre er, fre est;** 4,6 *v.,* **freed, free ing;** 7,11 *adv.* —**free′ly,** *adv.* —**free′ness,** *n.*

free and easy, paying little attention to rules and customs.

free from or **free of,** without; having no; lacking: *free from fear, air free of dust.*

free boot er (frē′bü′tər), pirate. *n.* [*Freebooter* is from Dutch *vrijbuiter,* which comes from *vrij,* meaning "free," and *buit,* meaning "booty."]

freed man (frēd′mən), person freed from slavery. *n., pl.* **freed men.**

free dom (frē′dəm), **1** condition of being free. **2** power to do, say, or think as one pleases; liberty. **3** free use: *We gave our guest the freedom of the house.* **4** too great liberty; lack of restraint; frankness: *We did not like the freedom of his manner.* **5** ease of movement or action: *A fine athlete performs with freedom.* **6** a freeing or a releasing from unfavorable or undesirable conditions: *freedom from fear.*

free enterprise, the right of private business to select and operate undertakings for profit with little control or regulation by the government; private enterprise.

free-for-all (frē′fər ôl′), a fight, race, etc., open to all. *n.*

free hand (frē′hand′), done by hand without using instruments, measurements, etc.: *freehand drawing. adj.*

free-lance (frē′lans′), **1** work as an independent, selling one's professional skills to whoever will buy them, rather than as an employee of a single firm. **2** of such work: *free-lance designers, free-lance editing.* 1 *v.,* **free-lanced, free-lanc ing;** 2 *adj.*

a hat	**i** it	**oi** oil	**ch** child	a in about
ā age	**ī** ice	**ou** out	**ng** long	e in taken
ä far	**o** hot	**u** cup	**sh** she	ə = { i in pencil
e let	**ō** open	**u̇** put	**th** thin	o in lemon
ē equal	**ô** order	**ü** rule	**ŦH** then	u in circus
ėr term			**zh** measure	

free man (frē′mən), **1** person who is not a slave or a serf. **2** citizen. *n., pl.* **free men.**

Free ma son (frē′mā′sn), member of a worldwide secret society, whose purpose is mutual aid and fellowship; Mason. *n.*

free stone (frē′stōn′), **1** stone, such as limestone or sandstone, that can easily be cut without splitting. **2** having a fruit stone that is easily separated from the pulp: *freestone peaches.* 1 *n.,* 2 *adj.*

free style (frē′stīl′), **1** unrestricted as to style or method: *A freestyle swimmer may choose his or her own stroke.* **2** a freestyle race or figure-skating contest. 1 *adj.,* 2 *n.*

free think er (frē′thing′kər), one who forms religious opinions independently of authority or tradition. *n.*

Free town (frē′toun), capital of Sierra Leone, in the W part. *n.*

free verse, poetry that does not have the usual conventions of meter and rhyme.

free way (frē′wā′), a high-speed highway on which no tolls are charged. *n.*

free will (frē′wil′), of one's own accord; voluntary: *a freewill offering to the Red Cross. adj.*

free will, will free from outside restraints; voluntary choice; freedom of decision.

freeze (frēz), **1** harden by cold; turn into a solid by removal of heat. Water becomes ice when it freezes. **2** make or become very cold: *The north wind froze the spectators. We will freeze at the football game in this weather.* **3** kill or injure by frost; be killed or injured by frost: *This cold weather will freeze the flowers. The flowers froze last night.* **4** cover or become covered with ice; clog with ice: *The snow and hail will freeze the pond. The pipes froze.* **5** fix or become fixed to something by freezing: *His fingers froze to the tray of ice cubes.* **6** a freezing or a being frozen. **7** period during which there is freezing weather. **8** make or become stiff and unfriendly: *The reporter's prying questions froze her and she would not answer. The new boy froze up when I tried to be friendly.* **9** chill or be chilled with fear, etc.: *The howling of the wolves froze him with terror. She froze at the sight of the ghostly hand.* **10** become motionless: *The baby rabbit froze with fear at the strange sound.* **11** set at a definite amount, usually by governmental decree: *freeze prices, freeze rents.* 1-5,8-11 *v.,* **froze, fro zen, freez ing;** 6,7 *n.*

freeze-dry (frēz′drī′), dry (food) by freezing and evaporating the liquid content in a vacuum. Freeze-dried food keeps well without being refrigerated. *v.,* **freeze-dried, freeze-dry ing.**

freeze-frame (frēz′frām′), (in a motion-picture or television sequence) a single image repeated for some seconds, giving the illusion of a still picture. *n.*

freez er (frē′zər), **1** an insulating chamber or cabinet that freezes foods and refrigerates frozen foods. **2** machine that freezes ice cream. *n.*

freezing point, temperature at which a liquid freezes. The freezing point of water at sea level is 32 degrees Fahrenheit or 0 degrees Celsius.

freight (frāt), **1** goods that a train, truck, ship, or aircraft carries. **2** the carrying of goods on a train, ship, aircraft, or truck: *She sent the box by freight.* **3** price paid for carrying goods. **4** train for carrying goods. **5** load with freight. **6** carry as freight. **7** send as freight. 1-4 *n.,* 5-7 *v.*

freight car, a railroad car for carrying freight.

freight er (frā′tər), ship that carries mainly freight. *n.*

freight train, a railroad train of freight cars; freight.

Fré mont (frē′mont), **John Charles,** 1813-1890, American explorer and politician. *n.*

French (french), **1** of France, its people, or their language. **2** the people of France. **3** their language. 1 *adj.*, 2 *n.pl.*, 3 *n.sing.*

French and Indian War, war between Great Britain and France, fought in North America from 1754 to 1763. The French were greatly aided by Indian allies.

French Canada, the part of Canada inhabited mainly by French Canadians, especially the province of Quebec.

French Canadian, 1 Canadian whose ancestors came from France. **2** of French Canadians.

French fries, potatoes cut into thin strips and fried in deep fat until crisp on the outside.

French-fry (french′frī′), fry in deep fat. *v.*, **French-fried, French-fry ing.**

French Guiana, French territory in N South America. See **Brazil** for map.

French horn—It has three valves for changing pitch.

French horn, a brass wind instrument that has a mellow tone.

French man (french′mən), man born or living in France. *n.*, *pl.* **French men.**

French Revolution, revolution in France from 1789 to 1799 which ousted the monarchy and set up a republic.

French wom an (french′wům′ən), woman born or living in France. *n.*, *pl.* **French wom en.**

fre net ic (frə net′ik), **1** frenzied. **2** insane. *adj.* —**fre net′i cal ly,** *adv.*

fren zied (fren′zēd), very much excited; frantic; wild. *adj.* —**fren′zied ly,** *adv.*

fren zy (fren′zē), **1** a state of near madness; frantic condition: *They were in a frenzy when they heard that their child was missing.* **2** a condition of very great excitement: *The crowd was in a frenzy after the home team scored the winning goal. n.*, *pl.* **fren zies.** [*Frenzy* came into English over 600 years ago from French *frenesie*, and can be traced back to Greek *phrēn*, meaning "the mind."]

freq., 1 frequent. **2** frequently.

fre quen cy (frē′kwən sē), **1** rate of occurrence: *The flashes of light came with a frequency of three per minute.* **2** a frequent occurrence: *The frequency of their visits began to annoy us.* **3** number of complete cycles per second of an alternating current or other electric wave. Different radio and television stations broadcast at different frequencies so that their signals can be received distinctly. *n.*, *pl.* **fre quen cies.**

frequency modulation, a deliberate changing of the frequency of radio waves in order to agree with the changes in the sounds being transmitted. Frequency modulation reduces static.

fre quent (frē′kwənt *for 1;* fri kwent′ *for 2*), **1** happening often, near together, or every little while: *In my part of the country storms are frequent in March.* **2** go to often; be often in: *Frogs frequent ponds, streams, and marshes.* 1 *adj.*, 2 *v.* —**fre quent′er,** *n.*

fre quent ly (frē′kwənt lē), often; repeatedly; every little while. *adv.*

fres co (fres′kō), **1** act or art of painting with water colors on damp, fresh plaster. **2** picture or design so painted: *Beautiful frescoes covered the walls and ceiling of the cathedral. n.*, *pl.* **fres coes** or **fres cos.** [*Fresco* comes from Italian *fresco*, which also means "cool, fresh."]

fresh¹ (fresh), **1** newly made, grown, or gathered: *fresh footprints, fresh vegetables.* **2** not known, seen, or used before; new; recent: *Is there any fresh news from home?* **3** additional; further; another: *After her failure she made a fresh start.* **4** not salty: *Rivers are usually fresh water.* **5** not spoiled; not stale: *Is this milk fresh?* **6** not artificially preserved: *Fresh foods usually have more flavor than canned ones.* **7** not tired out; vigorous; lively: *Put in fresh horses.* **8** not faded or worn; bright: *The long trip abroad was fresh in his memory.* **9** looking healthy or young: *Grandmother is as hale and fresh in appearance as she was ten years ago.* **10** pure; cool; refreshing: *a fresh breeze. adj.* —**fresh′ly,** *adv.* —**fresh′ness,** *n.*

fresh² (fresh), INFORMAL. too bold; impudent. *adj.*

fresh en (fresh′ən), make or become fresh: *The rest freshened my spirits. v.* —**fresh′en er,** *n.*

fresh et (fresh′it), **1** flood caused by heavy rains or melted snow. **2** rush of fresh water flowing into the sea. *n.*

fresh man (fresh′mən), student in the first year of high school or college. *n.*, *pl.* **fresh men.**

fresh wa ter (fresh′wô′tər *or* fresh′wot′ər), of or living in water that is not salty: *a freshwater fish. adj.*

fret¹ (fret), **1** be peevish, unhappy, discontented, or worried: *The baby frets in hot weather. Don't fret over your mistakes.* **2** make peevish, unhappy, or worried: *His failures fretted him.* **3** condition of worry or discontent: *She is in a fret about her examinations.* **4** eat away; wear; rub. 1,2,4 *v.*, **fret ted, fret ting;** 3 *n.* —**fret′ter,** *n.*

fret² (fret), any of a series of ridges of wood, ivory, or metal on a guitar, banjo, etc., to show where to put the fingers in order to produce certain tones. *n.*

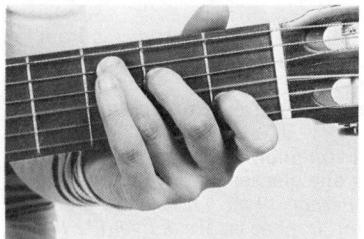

fret²—frets on a guitar

fret ful (fret′fəl), ready to fret; peevish, unhappy, discontented, or worried: *My baby brother is fretful because he is cutting his teeth. adj.* —**fret′ful ly,** *adv.* —**fret′ful ness,** *n.*

fret work (fret′wèrk′), ornamental openwork or carving. *n.*

Freud (froid), **Sigmund,** 1856-1939, Austrian physician who developed a theory and technique of psychoanalysis. *n.*

Fri., Friday.

fri a ble (frī′ə bəl), easily crumbled. *adj.* —**fri′a ble ness,** *n.*

fri ar (frī′ər), man who belongs to one of certain religious brotherhoods of the Roman Catholic Church. *n.*

[*Friar* came into English about 700 years ago from French *frere,* also meaning "brother," which came from Latin *frater,* meaning "brother."]

fric as see (frik′ə sē′), **1** meat cut up, stewed, and served in a sauce made with its own gravy. **2** prepare (meat) in this way. 1 *n.,* 2 *v.,* **fric as seed, fric as see ing.**

fric tion (frik′shən), **1** a rubbing of one thing against another; rubbing: *Matches are lighted by friction.* **2** resistance to motion of surfaces that touch: *Oil reduces friction. A sled moves more easily on smooth ice than on rough ground because there is less friction.* **3** conflict of differing ideas, opinions, etc.; disagreement; clash: *Constant friction between the two families almost created a feud.* *n.* —**fric′tion less,** *adj.*

Fri day (frī′dē), the sixth day of the week, following Thursday. *n.*

fried (frīd), **1** cooked in hot fat. **2** past tense and past participle of **fry.** *I fried the ham. The potatoes had been fried.* 1 *adj.,* 2 *v.*

friend (frend), **1** person who knows and likes another. **2** person who favors and supports: *She was a generous friend to the poor.* **3** person who belongs to the same side or group: *Are you friend or foe?* **4 Friend,** member of the Society of Friends; Quaker. *n.*
be friends with, be a friend of.
make friends with, become a friend of.

friend less (frend′lis), without friends. *adj.*

friend li ness (frend′lē nis), friendly feeling or behavior. *n.*

friend ly (frend′lē), **1** of a friend; having the attitude of a friend; kind: *a friendly teacher.* **2** like a friend; like a friend's: *a friendly greeting.* **3** on good terms; not hostile: *friendly relations between countries.* **4** favoring and supporting; favorable. *adj.,* **friend li er, friend li est.**

friend ship (frend′ship), **1** condition of being friends. **2** a liking between friends. **3** friendliness. *n.*

frieze (frēz), a horizontal band of decoration around a room, building, or mantel. *n.*

frig ate (frig′it), **1** a fast, three-masted, square-rigged sailing warship of medium size. Frigates were much used from 1750 to 1850. **2** a small, modern warship equipped to destroy submarines. *n.*

fright (frīt), **1** sudden and extreme fear; sudden terror or alarm: *The howl filled me with fright.* **2** INFORMAL. person or thing that is ugly, shocking, or ridiculous: *You look like a fright in that Halloween costume!* *n.*

fright en (frīt′n), **1** fill with fright; make or become afraid; scare or terrify: *Thunder frightened the puppy.* **2** drive or force by terrifying: *The sudden noise frightened the deer away.* *v.* —**fright′en ing ly,** *adv.*

fright ful (frīt′fəl), **1** likely to frighten; dreadful; terrible: *a frightful experience.* **2** ugly; shocking: *the frightful destruction caused by a fire.* **3** INFORMAL. very great: *I'm in a frightful hurry. adj.* —**fright′ful ly,** *adv.* —**fright′ful ness,** *n.*

frig id (frij′id), **1** very cold: *Arctic regions have a frigid climate.* **2** cold in feeling or manner; stiff; chilling: *He received a frigid greeting from the man he had insulted. adj.* —**frig′id ly,** *adv.* —**frig′id ness,** *n.*

fri gid i ty (fri jid′ə tē), condition of being frigid. *n.*

Frigid Zone, either of the two polar regions, north of the arctic circle and south of the antarctic circle.

fri jol (frē′hōl), kind of bean much used for food in Mexico and the southwestern United States. *n., pl.* **fri joles** (frē′hōlz or fri hō′lēz).

fri jole (frē′hōl or fri hō′lē), frijol. *n., pl.* **fri joles.**

frill (fril), **1** a ruffle. **2** thing added merely for show; useless ornament. *n.*

frill y (fril′ē), full of frills; like frills. *adj.,* **frill i er, frill i est.**

---

a hat	**i** it	**oi** oil	
ā age	**ī** ice	**ou** out	ng
ä far	**o** hot	**u** cup	sh s
e let	**ō** open	**u̇** put	**th** thin
ē equal	**ô** order	**ü** rule	ℑH then
ėr term			**zh** measure

fringe (frinj), **1** border or trimming made of thre, cords, etc., either loose or tied together in small L es. **2** anything like this; border: *A fringe of hair hung her forehead.* **3** make a fringe for. **4** be a fringe for: *Bus fringed the road.* 1,2 *n.,* 3,4 *v.,* **fringed, fring ing.**

Fris bee (friz′bē), trademark for a saucer-shaped disk of colored plastic for skimming back and forth in play. *n.*

frisk (frisk), **1** run and jump about playfully; dance and skip joyously: *Our lively puppy frisks all over the house.* **2** search for concealed weapons or stolen goods by running a hand quickly over a person's clothes. *v.* —**frisk′er,** *n.*

frisk i ly (fris′kə lē), in a frisky manner; briskly. *adv.*

frisk i ness (fris′kē nis), a frisky quality or condition; briskness. *n.*

frisk y (fris′kē), playful; lively. *adj.,* **frisk i er, frisk i est.**

frit ter[1] (frit′ər), waste little by little: *fritter away a day watching TV. v.*

frit ter[2] (frit′ər), sliced fruit, vegetables, meat, or fish covered with batter and fried. *n.* —**frit′ter er,** *n.*

fri vol i ty (fri vol′ə tē), **1** a being frivolous; silly behavior; trifling. **2** a silly thing; frivolous act. *n., pl.* **fri vol i ties.**

friv o lous (friv′ə ləs), **1** lacking in seriousness or sense; silly: *Frivolous behavior is out of place in a courtroom.* **2** of little worth or importance; trivial: *Don't waste time on frivolous matters. adj.* —**friv′o lous ly,** *adv.*

frizz or **friz** (friz), **1** form into small, crisp curls; curl. **2** hair curled in small, crisp curls or a very close crimp. 1 *v.,* **frizzed, friz zing;** 2 *n., pl.* **friz zes.**

friz zle[1] (friz′əl), **1** curl (hair) in small, crisp curls. **2** a small, crisp curl. 1 *v.,* **friz zled, friz zling;** 2 *n.*

friz zle[2] (friz′əl), **1** make a hissing, sputtering noise when cooking; sizzle: *The ham frizzled in the frying pan.* **2** a hissing, sputtering noise; sizzle. 1 *v.,* **friz zled, friz zling;** 2 *n.*

friz zly (friz′lē), full of small, crisp curls; curly. *adj.,* **friz zli er, friz zli est.**

friz zy (friz′ē), frizzly. *adj.* **friz zi er, friz zi est.**

fro (frō). **to and fro,** first one way and then back again; back and forth: *A rocking chair goes to and fro. adv.*

frock (frok), **1** a woman's or girl's dress; gown. **2** robe worn by a member of the clergy. *n.*

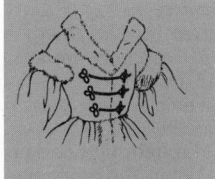

frog (def. 1)—about   frog (def. 2)
3 in. (75 mm.) long

frog (frog), **1** a small, leaping animal with webbed feet, that lives in or near water. Frogs hatch from eggs as tadpoles and live in the water until they grow legs. Some frogs live in trees. **2** an ornamental fastener on a garment, consisting of a loop and a button which passes through it. *n.* —**frog′like′,** *adj.*

frog man (frog′man′), scuba diver trained for underwa-

itary or scientific operations. *n., pl.* **frog men.**

c (frol′ik), **1** a joyous game or party; play; fun.
y about joyously; have fun together; make merry:
children frolicked with the puppy. 1 *n.,* 2 *v.,* **frol icked,**
ol ick ing. —**frol′ick er,** *n.*

ol ic some (frol′ik səm), full of fun; playful; merry. *adj.*
:om (from *or* frum; *unstressed* frəm), **1** out of: *a train
from New York. Steel is made from iron.* **2** out of the
possession of: *Take the book from her.* **3** starting at; beginning with: *from that time forward. Three weeks from
today is a holiday.* **4** because of; by reason of: *act from a
sense of duty. He was suffering from a cold.* **5** as being
unlike; as distinguished from: *Anyone can tell apples from
oranges.* **6** off: *He took a book from the table.* *prep.*

fronds of
a fern

frond (frond), the leaf of a fern or of a palm tree. *n.*
front (frunt), **1** the first part: *The title page is in the front
of a book.* **2** part that faces forward: *the front of a dress.*
3 thing fastened or worn on the front. **4** place where
fighting is going on; line of battle. **5** land facing a street,
river, etc.: *We have a house on the lake front.* **6** of, on, in,
or at the front: *a front door.* **7** have the front toward;
face: *Her house fronts the park.* **8** be in front of. **9** meet
face to face; meet as an enemy; defy; oppose.
10 manner of looking or behaving: *a genial front.*
11 INFORMAL. an outward appearance of wealth, importance, etc.: *The newcomer put up an impressive front.*
12 INFORMAL. person or thing that serves as a cover for
unlawful activities. **13** the dividing surface between two
dissimilar air masses: *A cold front is moving toward this
area from Canada.* 1-5,10-13 *n.,* 6 *adj.,* 7-9 *v.*
fron tal (frun′tl), **1** of, on, in, or at the front: *The soldiers
charged ahead and made a frontal attack.* **2** of the forehead: *frontal bones. adj.* —**fron′tal ly,** *adv.*
fron tier (frun tir′), **1** the farthest part of a settled country, where the wilds begin. **2** part of a country next to
another country; border. **3** the farthest limits: *explore the
frontiers of science. n.*
fron tiers man (frun tirz′mən), man who lives on the
frontier. *n., pl.* **fron tiers men.**
front-wheel (frunt′hwēl′), acting only on the front
wheels of a vehicle: *front-wheel brakes, front-wheel drive.
adj.*
frost (frôst), **1** a freezing condition; very cold weather;
temperature below the point at which water freezes:
Frost came early last winter. **2** moisture frozen on or in a
surface; feathery crystals of ice formed when water
vapor in the air condenses at a temperature below freezing: *On cold fall mornings, there is frost on the grass.*
3 cover with frost or something that suggests frost.
4 cover with frosting: *The cook frosted the cake.* **5** kill or
injure by frost or freezing: *A sudden drop in temperature
frosted the tomato plants.* 1,2 *n.,* 3-5 *v.* —**frost′less,** *adj.*
—**frost′like′,** *adj.*
Frost (frôst), **Robert,** 1874-1963, American poet. *n.*

frost bite (frôst′bīt′), **1** injury to a part of the body
caused by freezing. **2** injure (a part of the body) by frost;
harm by severe cold: *My ears were frostbitten.* 1 *n.,* 2 *v.,*
frost bit (frôst′bit′), **frost bit ten** (frôst′bit′n), **frost biting.**
frost ed (frô′stid), **1** covered with frost: *a frosted window.*
2 having a surface like frost: *Frosted glass has a rough
surface.* **3** covered with frosting; iced: *a frosted cake.*
4 frozen. *adj.*
frost i ly (frô′stl ē), in a frosty manner. *adv.*
frost i ness (frô′stē nis), condition or quality of being
frosty. *n.*
frost ing (frô′sting), **1** mixture of sugar and some liquid,
often with the beaten whites of eggs, flavoring, etc., to
cover a cake; icing. **2** a dull, rough finish on a glass or
metal. *n.*
frost y (frô′stē), **1** cold enough for frost; freezing: *a
frosty morning.* **2** covered with frost: *The glass is frosty.*
3 cold and unfriendly; with no warmth of feeling: *a frosty
greeting. adj.,* **frost i er, frost i est.**
froth (frôth), **1** mass of very small bubbles formed in
liquid; foam: *There was froth at the edge of the wave.*
2 give out froth; foam. **3** something light and trifling;
unimportant talk. 1,3 *n.,* 2 *v.*
froth i ness (frô′thē nis), condition or quality of being
frothy. *n.*
froth y (frô′thē), **1** of, like, or having froth; foamy: *frothy
soapsuds.* **2** light; trifling; unimportant: *frothy conversation. adj.,* **froth i er, froth i est.** —**froth′i ly,** *adv.*
frown (froun), **1** a wrinkling of the forehead to show
disapproval, anger, etc. **2** wrinkle the forehead to show
disapproval, anger, etc.; look displeased or angry: *The
teacher frowned when I came in late.* **3** look with disapproval: *The principal frowned on our plan for a class picnic
just before finals.* 1 *n.,* 2,3 *v.* —**frown′ing ly,** *adv.*
frow zi ness (frou′zē nis), condition or quality of being
frowzy. *n.*
frow zy (frou′zē), **1** dirty and untidy; slovenly. **2** smelling
bad; musty. *adj.* **frow zi er, frow zi est.**
froze (frōz), past tense of **freeze.** *The water in the pond
froze last week.* *v.*
fro zen (frō′zn), **1** hardened by cold; turned into ice:
frozen sherbet. **2** very cold: *My hands are frozen; I need
some gloves.* **3** preserved by being subjected to low temperatures: *frozen foods.* **4** killed or injured by frost: *frozen
flowers.* **5** covered or clogged with ice: *frozen water pipes.*
6 cold and unfeeling: *a frozen heart, a frozen stare.* **7** too
frightened or stiff to move: *frozen to the spot in horror.*
8 past participle of **freeze.** *The water has frozen to ice.* 1-7
adj., 8 *v.*
frt., freight.
fruc tose (fruk′tōs), sugar present in many fruits and in
honey; fruit sugar. It is sweeter than glucose or sucrose. *n.*
fru gal (frü′gəl), **1** without waste; saving; using things
well: *My parents are frugal—they buy and use carefully only
what they need.* **2** costing little; barely enough: *He ate a
frugal supper of bread and milk. adj.* —**fru′gal ly,** *adv.*
fru gal i ty (frü gal′ə tē), avoidance of waste; tendency
to save money. *n., pl.* **fru gal i ties.**
fruit (früt), **1** a juicy or fleshy product of a tree, bush,
shrub, or vine which consists of the seed and its covering and is usually sweet and good to eat. Apples, pears,
oranges, bananas, peaches, and plums are fruits. **2** part
of a seed plant which contains the seeds. Pea pods,
acorns, cucumbers, and grains of wheat are fruits.
3 group or selection of fruits. **4** a useful product of plant
growth: *The fruits of the earth are used mostly for food.*
5 result of anything; product: *This invention was the fruit
of much effort.* **6** produce fruit. 1-5 *n.,* 6 *v.* [*Fruit* came

into English about 800 years ago from French *fruit*, and can be traced back to Latin *frui*, meaning "to enjoy, make use of."] —**fruit′like′**, *adj.*

fruit cake (früt′kāk′), a rich cake usually containing many fruits and sometimes nuts and spices. *n.*

fruit fly, a small fly whose larvae feed on decaying fruits and vegetables.

fruit ful (früt′fəl), **1** producing much fruit. **2** producing much of anything: *a fruitful mind.* **3** having good results; bringing benefit or profit: *a fruitful idea.* *adj.* —**fruit′ful ly,** *adv.* —**fruit′ful ness,** *n.*

fru i tion (frü ish′ən), **1** condition of having results; fulfillment; attainment: *After years of hard work their plans came to fruition.* **2** pleasure that comes from possession or use. **3** condition of producing fruit. *n.*

fruit less (früt′lis), **1** having no results; useless; unsuccessful: *Our search was fruitless; we could not find the lost book.* **2** producing no fruit; barren: *fruitless soil.* *adj.* —**fruit′less ly,** *adv.* —**fruit′less ness,** *n.*

fruit sugar, fructose.

fruit y (frü′tē), tasting or smelling like fruit: *the fruity odor of jam.* *adj.*, **fruit i er, fruit i est.**

frus trate (frus′trāt), **1** make useless or worthless; block; defeat: *Heavy rain frustrated our plans for a picnic.* **2** thwart; oppose: *The struggling artist was often frustrated in her ambition to paint.* *v.*, **frus trat ed, frus trat ing.** —**frus′trat er,** *n.*

frus tra tion (fru strā′shən), a frustrating or a being frustrated. *n.*

fry¹ (frī), **1** cook in hot fat in a deep or shallow pan, often over a flame: *He is frying potatoes.* **2** dish of something cooked in this way. **3** an outdoor social gathering at which food is fried and eaten: *a fish fry.* 1 *v.*, **fried, fry ing;** 2,3 *n.*, *pl.* **fries.**

fry² (frī), young fishes. *n.*, *pl.* **fry.**

ft., **1** foot or feet. **2** fort.

fuch sia (fyü′shə), **1** shrub with handsome pink, red, or purple flowers that droop from the stems. **2** a purplish red. **3** purplish-red. 1,2 *n.*, *pl.* **fuch sias;** 3 *adj.* [*Fuchsia* was named for Leonhard *Fuchs,* 1501-1566, a German botanist.]

fud dle (fud′l), **1** make stupid with liquor; intoxicate. **2** confuse; muddle. *v.*, **fud dled, fud dling.**

fudge (fuj), **1** a soft candy made of sugar, milk, chocolate, butter, etc. **2** nonsense. *n.*

Fueh rer (fyür′ər), Führer. *n.*

fu el (fyü′əl), **1** anything that can be burned to produce useful heat or power. Coal, wood, and oil are fuels. **2** atomic matter that can produce heat in a nuclear reactor. **3** anything that keeps up or increases a feeling: *Her success was fuel to his resentment.* **4** supply with fuel. **5** get fuel: *The ship will have to fuel at the nearest port.* 1-3 *n.*, 4,5 *v.*, **fu eled, fu el ing,** or **fu elled, fu el ling.**

fu gi tive (fyü′jə tiv), **1** person who is running away or who has run away: *The murderer became a fugitive from justice.* **2** running away; having run away: *a fugitive serf.* **3** lasting only a very short time; passing swiftly: *fugitive thoughts.* 1 *n.*, 2,3 *adj.* —**fu′gi tive ly,** *adv.* —**fu′gi tive ness,** *n.*

fugue (fyüg), a musical composition based on one or more short themes in which different voices or instruments repeat the same melody with slight variations. *n.*

Füh rer (fyür′ər), a German word meaning leader. It was the title given to Adolf Hitler, the dictator of Nazi Germany. *n.* Also, **Fuehrer.**

Fu ji (fü′jē), Fujiyama. *n.*

Fu ji ya ma (fü′jē yä′mə), extinct volcano in S Japan, near Tokyo, 12,395 feet (3780 meters) high. It is the highest mountain in Japan. *n.*

-ful, *suffix added to nouns to form adjectives or other*

nouns. **1** full of____: *Cheerful = full of cheer.* **2** showing ____: *Careful = showing care.* **3** having a tendency to ____: *Harmful = having a tendency to harm.* **4** enough to fill a ____: *Cupful = enough to fill a cup.*

ful crum (ful′krəm), support on which a lever turns or is supported in moving or lifting something. *n.*, *pl.* **fulcrums, ful cra** (ful′krə).

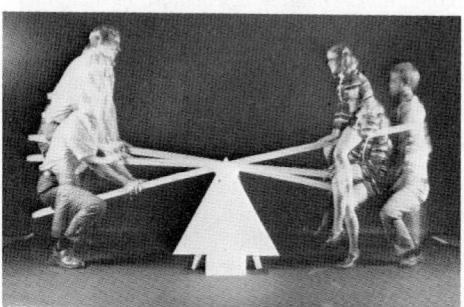

fulcrum—The seesaw works as a lever; the fulcrum is the triangle on which the board rests.

ful fill or **ful fil** (ful fil′), **1** carry out (a promise, prophecy, etc.); cause to happen or take place. **2** perform or do (a duty, command, etc.): *She fulfilled all the teacher's requests.* **3** satisfy (a requirement, condition, etc.): *This diet will fulfill all your needs in food.* **4** bring to an end; finish or complete (a period of time, work, etc.): *fulfill a contract.* *v.*, **ful filled, ful fill ing.**

ful fill ment or **ful fil ment** (ful fil′mənt), a fulfilling; completion; performance; accomplishment. *n.*

full (ful), **1** able to hold no more; with no empty space; filled: *a full cup. This suitcase is full.* **2** complete; entire: *a full supply of clothes. I ran a full mile.* **3** completely: *Fill the pail full.* **4** completeness; greatest degree: *Her new job satisfies her ambition to the full.* **5** more than enough to satisfy; well supplied: *He ate three full meals a day.* **6** well filled out; plump; round: *a full face.* **7** having wide folds or much cloth: *a full skirt.* **8** strong, rich, and distinct: *An orator should have a full voice.* **9** straight; directly: *The ball hit me full in the face.* 1,2,5-8 *adj.*, 3,9 *adv.*, 4 *n.*

full of, filled with: *The child's room is full of toys.*

full well, very well.

in full, 1 to or for the complete amount: *They made payment in full for the furniture.* **2** not abbreviated or shortened: *a document reproduced in full.*

full back (ful′bak′), a football player who is a member of the offensive backfield and usually lines up behind the offensive line. *n.*

full-fledged (ful′flejd′), **1** fully developed. **2** of full rank or standing: *He is now a full-fledged doctor.* *adj.*

full-grown (ful′grōn′), fully grown; mature. *adj.*

full-length (ful′lengkth′ or ful′length′), **1** showing the entire human body: *a full-length portrait.* **2** of considerable length: *I watched a full-length movie on television.* *adj.*

full moon, the moon seen from the earth as a whole circle.

full ness (ful′nis), condition of being full. *n.*

full-rigged (ful′rigd′), **1** having three or four masts, all completely square-rigged. **2** completely equipped. *adj.*

ful ly (fùl′ē), **1** completely; entirely: *The watchdog was fully alert.* **2** abundantly; plentifully: *The gymnasium was fully equipped.* **3** quite; exactly: *He could not fully describe what he had seen. adv.*

ful mi nate (ful′mə nāt), **1** thunder forth censure, threats, etc.; denounce something violently. **2** explode violently. *v.* —**ful′mi na′tion,** *n.* —**ful′mi na′tor,** *n.*

ful some (fùl′səm), so much as to be excessive and offensive: *fulsome flattery. adj.* —**ful′some ly,** *adv.* —**ful′some ness,** *n.*

Ful ton (fùlt′n), **Robert,** 1765-1815, American inventor who built the first successful steamboat in 1803. *n.*

fum ble (fum′bəl), **1** feel or grope about clumsily; search awkwardly: *I fumbled in the darkness for the doorknob.* **2** handle awkwardly. **3** let (a ball) drop instead of catching and holding it: *The quarterback fumbled the ball, and the other team recovered it.* **4** an awkward attempt to find or handle something. 1-3 *v.*, **fum bled, fum bling;** 4 *n.* —**fum′bler,** *n.*

fume (fyüm), **1** vapor, gas, or smoke, especially if harmful, strong, or giving out odor: *The fumes from the automobile exhaust nearly choked me.* **2** give off vapor, gas, or smoke: *The candle fumed, sputtered, and went out.* **3** let off one's rage in angry comments: *We fumed about the slowness of the train.* 1 *n.*, 2,3 *v.*, **fumed, fum ing.**

fu mi gate (fyü′mə gāt), disinfect with fumes; expose to fumes: *fumigate a building to kill the cockroaches. v.*, **fu mi gat ed, fu mi gat ing.** —**fu′mi ga′tor,** *n.*

fu mi ga tion (fyü′mə gā′shən), a fumigating or a being fumigated. *n.*

fun (fun), merry play; playfulness; amusement; joking: *They had a lot of fun at the party. n.*

for fun or **in fun,** as a joke; playfully.

make fun of or **poke fun at,** laugh at; ridicule.

func tion (fungk′shən), **1** proper work; normal action or use; purpose: *The function of the stomach is to help digest food.* **2** work; act: *One of the older students can function as teacher. This old fountain pen does not function very well.* **3** a formal public or social gathering: *The hotel ballroom is often used for weddings and other functions.* **4** in mathematics: **a** a quantity whose value depends on the value given to another related quantity: *The area of a circle is a function of its radius.* **b** a relationship between two sets such that each element in the first set is associated with exactly one element in the second set. 1,3,4 *n.*, 2 *v.*

func tion al (fungk′shə nəl), **1** of a function. **2** having a function; working; acting: *The functional wings of an insect are those used for flying. adj.* —**func′tion al ly,** *adv.*

func tion ar y (fungk′shə ner′ē), an official. *n.*, *pl.* **func tion ar ies.**

fund (fund), **1** sum of money set aside for a special purpose: *The school has a fund of $2000 to buy books with.* **2 funds,** *pl.* **a** money ready to use: *We took $10 from the club's funds to buy a flag.* **b** money: *I used up my allowance and am low on funds.* **3** stock or store ready for use; supply: *There is a fund of information in our new library.* **4** change (a debt) from a short term to a long term. 1-3 *n.*, 4 *v.*

fun da men tal (fun′də men′tl), **1** of or forming a foundation or basis; essential; basic: *Reading is a fundamental skill.* **2** something fundamental; essential part: *the fundamentals of grammar.* 1 *adj.*, 2 *n.* —**fun′da men′tal ly,** *adv.*

fu ner al (fyü′nər əl), **1** ceremonies performed when a dead person's body is buried or burned. A funeral usually includes a religious service and taking the body to the place where it is buried or burned. **2** of a funeral; suitable for a funeral: *a funeral procession. A funeral march is very slow.* 1 *n.*, 2 *adj.*

fu ner e al (fyü nir′ē əl), of or like a funeral; gloomy; dismal. *adj.* —**fu ner′e al ly,** *adv.*

fun gi (fun′jī), a plural of **fungus.** *n.*

fun gi cide (fun′jə sīd), any substance that destroys harmful fungi. *n.*

fun gous (fung′gəs), **1** of a fungus or fungi; like a fungus. **2** growing or springing up suddenly like a mushroom. **3** caused by a fungus: *Wheat rust is a fungous disease. adj.*

fungus on a tree trunk

fun gus (fung′gəs), any of a group of living things that are like plants but have no flowers, leaves, or green coloring matter. Fungi get their nourishment from dead or living organic matter. Yeasts and many mushrooms are useful fungi and can be eaten as food. Smuts, rusts, and mildews are harmful fungi. Certain fungi, such as molds, are used in medicine. *n.*, *pl.* **fun gi** or **fun gus es.**

funk (fungk), INFORMAL. **1** condition of panic or fear. **2** be afraid of. 1 *n.*, 2 *v.*

funnel (def. 2) funnel of a tornado

fun nel (fun′l), **1** a tapering tube with a wide, cone-shaped mouth. A funnel is used to prevent spilling in pouring liquids, powder, grain, etc., into containers with small openings. **2** anything shaped like a funnel: *a funnel of smoke.* **3** smokestack or chimney on a steamship or steam engine. **4** pass or feed through a funnel: *funnel gasoline into a can. The crowd funneled through the gate.* 1-3 *n.*, 4 *v.* **fun neled, fun nel ing** or **fun nelled, fun nel ling.**

fun nies (fun′ēz), **1** comic strips; comics. **2** section of a newspaper carrying comic strips. *n.pl.*

fun ny (fun′ē), **1** causing laughter; amusing: *The clown's funny jokes and antics kept us laughing.* **2** INFORMAL. strange; queer; odd: *It's funny that they are so late. adj.*, **fun ni er, fun ni est.** —**fun′ni ly,** *adv.* —**fun′ni ness,** *n.*

funny bone, place at the bend of the elbow over which a nerve passes. When it is struck, a sharp, tingling sensation is felt in the arm and hand; crazy bone.

fur (fėr), **1** the soft hair covering the skin of many animals. **2** skin with such hair on it. Fur is used to make, cover, trim, or line clothing. **3** Usually, **furs,** *pl.* clothes made of fur: *dressed in furs.* **4** made of fur: *a fur collar.* **5** a coating of foul or waste matter like fur. A sick person's tongue often has fur on it. 1-3,5 *n.*, 4 *adj.* —**fur′-less,** *adj.* —**fur′like′,** *adj.*

fur bish (fèr′bish), **1** brighten by rubbing or scouring; polish: *I furbished the tarnished silver until it shone like new.* **2** restore to good condition; make usable again: *Before going to France, she furbished up her half-forgotten French. v.* —**fur′bish er,** *n.*

Fur ies (fyür′ēz), (in Greek and Roman myths) the three spirits of revenge. *n.pl.*

fur i ous (fyür′ē əs), **1** full of wild, fierce anger: *The owner of the house was furious when she learned of the broken window.* **2** violent; raging: *A hurricane is a furious storm.* **3** of unrestrained energy, speed, etc.: *furious activity, a furious gallop. adj.* —**fur′i ous ly,** *adv.* —**fur′i ous-ness,** *n.*

furl (fèrl), roll up; fold up: *furl a sail, furl a flag. v.*

fur long (fèr′lông), measure of distance equal to one eighth of a mile; 220 yards. *n.* [*Furlong* is from Old English *furlang,* which comes from *furh,* meaning "furrow," and *lang,* meaning "long."]

fur lough (fèr′lō), **1** leave of absence: *The soldier has two weeks' furlough.* **2** give leave of absence to. 1 *n.,* 2 *v.* [*Furlough* comes from Dutch *verlof,* which also means "permission, leave."]

fur nace (fèr′nis), an enclosed chamber or box to make a very hot fire in. Furnaces are used to heat buildings, melt metals, make glass, etc. *n.*

fur nish (fèr′nish), **1** supply with something necessary, useful, or wanted; provide: *furnish an army with blankets. The sun furnishes heat.* **2** supply (a room, house, etc.) with furniture or equipment. *v.* —**fur′nish er,** *n.*

fur nish ings (fèr′ni shingz), **1** furniture or equipment for a room or a house. **2** articles of clothing: *That store sells men's furnishings. n.pl.*

fur ni ture (fèr′nə chər), movable articles needed in a room or house. Beds, chairs, tables, and desks are furniture. *n.*

furor (def. 2)—A **furor** for marathon running swept the country.

fur or (fyür′ôr), **1** wild enthusiasm or excitement: *The news that the first astronauts had orbited the moon caused great furor everywhere.* **2** a craze; mania. **3** a rage; fury. *n.*

fur ri er (fèr′ē ər), **1** dealer in furs. **2** person whose work is preparing furs or making and repairing fur coats, etc. *n.*

fur row (fèr′ō), **1** a long, narrow groove or track cut in the earth by a plow. **2** any long, narrow groove or track: *Heavy trucks made deep furrows in the muddy road.* **3** make furrows in. **4** a wrinkle: *a furrow in one's brow.* **5** make wrinkles in; wrinkle: *The old man's face was furrowed with age.* 1,2,4 *n.,* 3,5 *v.* —**fur′row like′,** *adj.*

fur ry (fèr′ē), **1** of fur; consisting of fur. **2** covered with fur. **3** soft like fur. *adj.,* **fur ri er, fur ri est.** —**fur′ri-ness,** *n.*

fur ther (fèr′тнər), **1** more distant: *on the further side.* **2** at or to a greater distance: *Go no further than a mile*

and you will find it. **3** to a more advanced point: *Inquire further into the matter.* **4** more: *Do you need further help?* **5** help forward; promote: *Let us further the cause of peace.* **6** also; in addition: *My teacher told me to study more and said further that I must cut down on sports.* 1,4 *adj.,* comparative of **far;** 2,3,6 *adv.,* comparative of **far;** 5 *v.*

fur ther ance (fèr′тнər əns), act of furthering; helping forward; advancement; promotion. *n.*

fur ther more (fèr′тнər môr), in addition; moreover; also; besides. *adv.*

fur ther most (fèr′тнər mōst), furthest. *adj.*

fur thest (fèr′тнist), **1** most distant. **2** to or at the greatest distance. **3** to the greatest degree or extent; most. 1 *adj.,* superlative of **far;** 2,3 *adv.,* superlative of **far.**

fur tive (fèr′tiv), **1** done quickly and with stealth to avoid being noticed; secret: *a furtive snatch at the candy, a furtive glance into the forbidden room.* **2** sly; shifty; stealthy: *I suspected them because of their furtive manner. adj.* —**fur′tive ly,** *adv.* —**fur′tive ness,** *n.*

fur y (fyür′ē), **1** wild, fierce anger. **2** violence; fierceness: *the fury of a battle, the fury of a hurricane.* **3** a raging or violent person. *n.,pl.* **fur ies.**

furze (fèrz), a low, prickly, evergreen shrub with yellow flowers, common on waste lands in Europe; gorse. *n.*

fuse[1] (fyüz), a slow-burning wick or other device used to set off a shell, bomb, a blast of gunpowder, or other explosive charge. *n.* Also, **fuze.** [*Fuse*[1] is from Italian *fuso,* meaning "spindle," which came from Latin *fusus.*]

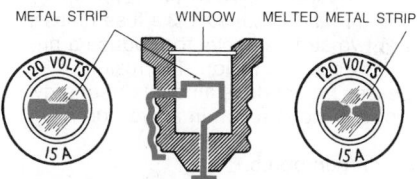

METAL STRIP   WINDOW   MELTED METAL STRIP

120 VOLTS   15 A   120 VOLTS   15 A

TOP VIEW   CROSS SECTION

fuse[2] (def. 1)—This plug fuse screws into an electric circuit. When an overload of current melts the metal strip (as at the right), the fuse must be replaced to restore the circuit.

fuse[2] (fyüz), **1** wire or strip of metal inserted in an electric circuit that melts and breaks the connection when the current becomes dangerously strong. **2** join together by melting; melt: *Copper and zinc are fused to make brass.*

furrow (def. 1)

3 blend; unite: *The intense heat fused the rocks together. Two political parties fused to form a new third party.* 1 *n.,* 2,3 *v.,* **fused, fus ing.** [*Fuse²* is from Latin *fusum,* meaning "poured, melted," which comes from *fundere,* meaning "to pour, melt." See **Word Family.**] —**fuse′less,** *adj.*

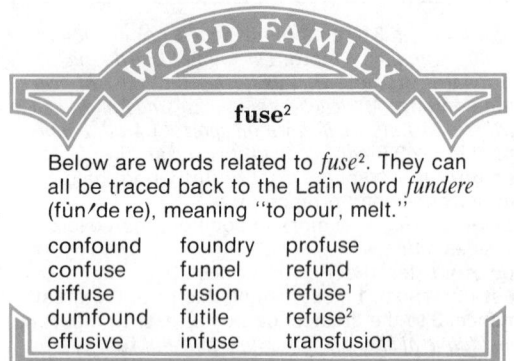

fuse²

Below are words related to *fuse².* They can all be traced back to the Latin word *fundere* (fun′de re), meaning "to pour, melt."

confound	foundry	profuse
confuse	funnel	refund
diffuse	fusion	refuse¹
dumfound	futile	refuse²
effusive	infuse	transfusion

fu se lage (fyü′sə läzh *or* fyü′sə lij), body of an airplane, to which the wings, tail, etc., are fastened. The fuselage holds the passengers, crew, and cargo. *n.*

fu si bil i ty (fyü′zə bil′ə tē), condition or quality of being fusible. *n.*

fu si ble (fyü′zə bəl), able to be fused or melted. *adj.*

fu sil lade (fyü′sə lād′), **1** a rapid or continuous discharge of many firearms at the same time. **2** any rapid discharge or burst: *The reporters greeted the mayor with a fusillade of questions. n.*

fu sion (fyü′zhən), **1** a melting together; melting; fusing: *Bronze is made by the fusion of copper and tin.* **2** a blending; union: *A third party was formed by the fusion of independent Republicans and Democrats.* **3** a fused mass. **4** the combining of two atomic nuclei to produce a nucleus of greater mass; nuclear fusion. The fusion of atomic nuclei releases tremendous amounts of energy and is used to produce the reaction in a hydrogen bomb. *n.*

fusion bomb, hydrogen bomb.

fuss (fus), **1** much bother about small matters; useless talk and worry; attention given to something not worth

it. **2** make a fuss: *He fussed nervously about his work.* 1 *n., pl.* **fuss es;** 2 *v.* —**fuss′er,** *n.*

fuss i ly (fus′ə lē), in a fussy manner. *adv.*

fuss i ness (fus′ē nis), quality or condition of being fussy. *n.*

fuss y (fus′ē), **1** hard to please; never satisfied: *A sick person is likely to be fussy about food.* **2** elaborately made; much trimmed: *fussy clothes.* **3** full of details; requiring much care: *a fussy job. adj.,* **fuss i er, fuss i est.**

fust y (fus′tē), **1** having a stale smell; moldy; stuffy. **2** too old-fashioned; out-of-date. *adj.,* **fust i er, fust i est.** —**fust′i ly,** *adv.* —**fust′i ness,** *n.*

fu tile (fyü′tl), **1** not successful; useless: *He fell down after making futile attempts to keep his balance.* **2** not important; trifling: *futile tasks. adj.* —**fu′tile ly,** *adv.*

fu til i ty (fyü til′ə tē), **1** uselessness. **2** unimportance. *n., pl.* **fu til i ties.**

fu ton (fü′ton), a padded sleeping mat, placed directly on the floor, originally used in Japan. *n.*

fu ture (fyü′chər), **1** time to come; what is to come; what will be: *You cannot change the past, but you can do better in the future.* **2** that is to come; that will be; coming: *We hope your future years will be happy.* **3** chance of success or prosperity: *She has a job with a future.* **4** expressing something expected to happen or exist in time to come: *the future tense of a verb.* **5** the verb form with *shall* or *will* that expresses something taking place in time to come. "I shall go" or "I will go" is the future of "I go." 1,3,5 *n.,* 2,4 *adj.*

fu tu ris tic (fyü′chə ris′tik), of or like the future; not traditional: *futuristic car design. adj.*

fu tur i ty (fyü tür′ə tē *or* fyü tyür′ə tē), **1** future. **2** a future state or event. **3** quality of being future. *n., pl.* **fu tur i ties.**

fuze (fyüz), fuse¹. *n.*

fuzz (fuz), loose, light fibers or hairs; fine down: *the fuzz on a caterpillar. Peach fuzz washes off easily. n.*

fuzz i ly (fuz′ə lē), in a fuzzy manner. *adv.*

fuzz i ness (fuz′ē nis), quality of being fuzzy. *n.*

fuzz y (fuz′ē), **1** of fuzz. **2** like fuzz. **3** covered with fuzz. **4** blurred; indistinct: *This photograph is too fuzzy for me to identify the people in it. adj.,* **fuzz i er, fuzz i est.**

fwd., forward.

-fy, *suffix forming verbs chiefly from adjectives.* **1** make _____; cause to be _____: *Simplify = make simple.* **2** become _____: *Solidify = become solid.*

a hat	i it	oi oil	ch child		a in about
ā age	ī ice	ou out	ng long		e in taken
ä far	o hot	u cup	sh she	ə =	i in pencil
e let	ō open	u̇ put	th thin		o in lemon
ē equal	ô order	ü rule	ᵺ then		u in circus
ėr term			zh measure		

G or **g** (jē), **1** the seventh letter of the English alphabet. **2** unit of force exerted on a body by the pull of gravity. The force exerted on a body at rest is one G. An accelerating body may experience a force of several G's. *n., pl.* **G's** or **g's.**

G or **G., 1** German. **2** gravity. **3** Gulf.

G, General (a rating for a motion picture that is recommended for all age groups).

g., gram or grams.

Ga, symbol for gallium.

GA, Georgia (used with postal Zip Code).

Ga., Georgia.

G.A., General Assembly.

gab (gab), INFORMAL. **1** talk too much; chatter; gabble. **2** idle talk; chatter. **1** *v.,* **gabbed, gab bing;** 2 *n.*

gab ar dine (gab/ər dēn/), a closely woven wool, cotton, or rayon cloth used for raincoats, suits, etc. *n.*

gab ble (gab/əl), **1** talk rapidly and noisily with little or no meaning; jabber. **2** rapid and noisy talk with little or no meaning. **1** *v.,* **gab bled, gab bling;** 2 *n.* —**gab/bler,** *n.*

gab by (gab/ē), INFORMAL. very talkative. *adj.,* **gab bi er, gab bi est.**

gable—a house with three gables

ga ble (gā/bəl), end of a ridged roof, with the three-cornered piece of wall that it covers. *n.*

ga bled (gā/bəld), built with a gable or gables; having or forming gables. *adj.*

Ga bon (gä bôn/), country in central Africa, on the Atlantic. *Capital:* Libreville. See **Congo** for map. *n.*

Ga bo ro ne (gä/bə rō/nä), capital of Botswana, in the SE part. *n.*

Ga bri el (gā/brē əl), (in the Bible) an archangel who acts as God's messenger. He is the angel of comfort and good news. *n.*

gad (gad), move about restlessly; go about looking for pleasure or excitement: *They were out all day gadding about town. v.,* **gad ded, gad ding.** —**gad/der,** *n.*

gad a bout (gad/ə bout/), person who moves about restlessly or goes about looking for pleasure or excitement. *n.*

gad fly (gad/flī/), **1** fly that bites cattle, horses, and other animals. The horsefly is one kind. **2** person who constantly irritates or annoys, especially to bring about changes in the way things are. *n., pl.* **gad flies.**

gadg et (gaj/it), a small mechanical device or contrivance; any ingenious device: *Can openers and cookie cutters are kitchen gadgets. n.*

gad o lin i um (gad/l in/ē əm), a highly magnetic metallic element which occurs in combination with certain minerals. *n.*

Gael (gāl), **1** a Scottish Highlander. **2** Celt born or living in Scotland, Ireland, or the Isle of Man. *n.*

Gael ic (gā/lik), **1** of the Gaels or their language. **2** language of the Gaels. **3** Irish. **1** *adj.,* 2,3 *n.*

gaff (gaf), **1** a strong hook on a handle or barbed spear for pulling large fish out of the water. **2** hook or pull (a fish) out of the water with a gaff. **3** spar or pole used to extend the upper edge of a fore-and-aft sail. 1,3 *n.,* 2 *v.*

gag (gag), **1** something put in a person's mouth to prevent talking or crying out. **2** stop up the mouth of with a gag: *The robbers tied their victims' arms and gagged them.* **3** choke or strain in an effort to vomit; retch: *Bad-tasting medicines make us gag.* **4** INFORMAL. joke; amusing remark or trick: *The comedian's gags made the audience laugh.* 1,4 *n.,* 2,3 *v.,* **gagged, gag ging.**

Ga ga rin (gə gär/ən), **Yuri,** 1934-1968, Soviet cosmonaut. He was the first human being to travel in outer space. *n.*

gage¹ (gāj), pledge; security: *The knight left a diamond as gage for the horse and armor. n.*

gage² (gāj), gauge. *n., v.,* **gaged, gag ing.**

Gage (gāj), **Thomas,** 1721-1787, British commander-in-chief at the beginning of the Revolutionary War. *n.*

gai e ty (gā/ə tē), **1** cheerful liveliness; joyousness: *Her gaiety helped to make the party a success.* **2** bright appearance: *gaiety of dress. n., pl.* **gai e ties.** Also, **gayety.**

gai ly (gā/lē), **1** merrily; happily. **2** brightly; showily: *They were gaily dressed in colorful costumes. adv.* Also, **gayly.**

gain (gān), **1** come to have; get; obtain: *The farmer gained possession of more land.* **2** what is gained; increase, addition, or advantage: *a gain of ten percent over last year's earnings.* **3** gains, *pl.* profits; earnings; winnings. **4** get as an increase, addition, or advantage; profit: *How much did she gain by that?* **5** make progress; improve: *The sick child is gaining and will soon be well.* **6** be the victor in; win: *The stronger team gained the victory.* **7** get to; arrive at; reach: *The swimmer gained the shore.* 1,4-7 *v.,* 2,3 *n.*

gain on, come closer to; catch up with: *One boat is gaining on another.*

gain over, persuade to join one's side.

gain er (gā/nər), **1** person or thing that gains. **2** dive in which the diver turns a back somersault in the air. *n.*

gain ful (gān/fəl), bringing in money or advantage; profitable: *a gainful occupation. adj.* —**gain/ful ly,** *adv.*

gain said (gān/sed/), past tense and past participle of **gainsay.** *Most people gainsaid the contention that the earth is round. Her athletic ability cannot be gainsaid. v.*

gain say (gān/sā/), deny; contradict; dispute: *We could not gainsay his opinion. v.,* **gain said, gain say ing.** —**gain/say/er,** *n.*

Gains bor ough (gānz/bėr/ō), **Thomas,** 1727-1788, English painter. *n.*

gait (gāt), the kind of steps used in going along; manner of walking or running: *A gallop is one of the gaits of a horse. n.*

gai ter (gā/tər), **1** an outer covering for the lower leg or ankle, made of cloth, leather, etc., for outdoor wear. **2** shoe with an elastic strip in each side. *n.*

gal., gallon. *pl.* **gal.** or **gals.**

ga la (gā′lə *or* gal′ə), **1** of festivity; festive: *In our family, Christmas and the Fourth of July are gala days.* **2** a festive occasion; festival. **1** *adj.,* **2** *n., pl.* **ga las.**

ga lac tic (gə lak′tik), of or having to do with the Milky Way or with other galaxies. *adj.*

Gal a had (gal′ə had), the noblest and purest knight of King Arthur's Round Table, who found the Holy Grail. *n.*

Ga lá pa gos Islands (gə lä′pə gəs *or* gə lä′pə gōs), group of islands in the Pacific, west of and belonging to Ecuador.

Ga la tians (gə lā′shənz), book of the New Testament, written by Saint Paul. *n.*

gal ax y (gal′ək sē), **1** group of billions of stars forming one system. The earth and sun are part of one galaxy. Many galaxies outside our own can be seen with a telescope. **2 Galaxy,** the Milky Way. **3** a brilliant or splendid group, especially of very attractive or distinguished persons. *n., pl.* **gal ax ies.**

WORD HISTORY

galaxy

Galaxy comes from Greek *galaxias,* and can be traced back to *galaktos,* meaning "milk." To the Greeks, a cluster of stars resembled a streak of milk against the night sky.

gale (gāl), **1** a very strong wind. A gale blows with a velocity of 32 to 63 miles (51 to 101 kilometers) per hour. **2** a noisy outburst: *gales of laughter. n.*

ga le na (gə lē′nə), a metallic, gray mineral containing lead and sulfur. It is the chief source of lead. *n.*

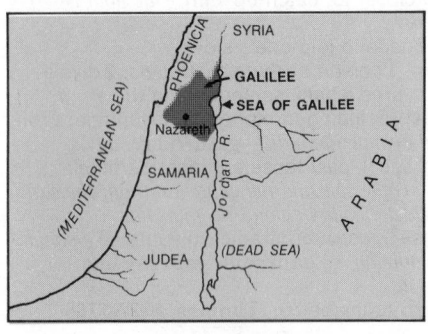

Galilee
(defs. 1 and 2)

Gal i lee (gal′ə lē′), **1** region in N Israel that was a Roman province in the time of Christ. **2 Sea of,** a small freshwater lake in NE Israel. *n.*

Gal i le o (gal′ə lē′ō), 1564-1642, Italian astronomer and physicist. He was the first to use the telescope to study the heavens. *n.*

gall¹ (gôl), **1** bile (def. 1). **2** anything very bitter or harsh. **3** bitterness; hate. **4** INFORMAL. too great boldness; impudence. *n.* [*Gall¹* comes from Old English *gealla.*]

gall² (gôl), **1** make or become sore by rubbing: *The rough strap galled the horse's skin.* **2** annoy; irritate: *It galls me that they are always late for dinner.* **3** a sore spot on the skin caused by rubbing, especially one on a horse's back. **1,2** *v.,* **3** *n.* [*Gall²* comes from Latin *galla,* meaning "gall-nut, gall³."]

gall³—The galls on this twig were caused by insects.

gall³ (gôl), lump or ball that forms on the leaves, stems, or roots of plants where they have been injured by insects, bacteria, or fungi. *n.* [*Gall³* came into English about 600 years ago from French *galle,* which comes from Latin *galla.*]

gal lant (gal′ənt *for 1-3;* gal′ənt *or* gə lant′ *for 4,5*), **1** noble in spirit or in conduct; brave: *King Arthur was a gallant knight.* **2** grand; fine; stately: *A ship with all of its sails spread is a gallant sight.* **3** very polite and attentive to women. **4** man who is very polite and attentive to women. **5** man who wears showy, stylish clothes. **1-3** *adj.,* **4,5** *n.* —**gal′lant ly,** *adv.* —**gal′lant ness,** *n.*

gal lant ry (gal′ən trē), **1** noble spirit or conduct; bravery. **2** great politeness and attention to women. **3** a gallant act or speech. *n., pl.* **gal lant ries.**

gall bladder, sac attached to the liver, in which bile is stored until needed.

gal le on (gal′ē ən), a large, high ship with three or four decks, used especially in the 1400's and 1500's. *n.*

gal ler y (gal′ər ē), **1** a hall or long, narrow passage, often with windows along one side. **2** balcony looking down into a large hall or room. **3** the highest balcony of a theater. It contains the cheapest seats. **4** people who sit there. **5** room or building used to show collections of pictures and statues. **6** room or building used for a particular purpose, such as taking photographs or practicing shooting. *n., pl.* **gal ler ies.** [*Gallery* came into English about 500 years ago from French *galerie,* and can be traced back to a medieval Latin word *galilea,* meaning "porch of a church."]

gal ley (gal′ē), **1** a long, narrow ship with oars and sails, used in ancient and medieval times. Galleys were often rowed by slaves or convicts. **2** kitchen of a ship or airplane. *n., pl.* **gal leys.**

galley slave, person forced or condemned to row a galley.

gall fly (gôl′flī′), insect that deposits its eggs in plants, causing galls to form. *n., pl.* **gall flies.**

Gal lic (gal′ik), **1** of Gaul or its people. **2** French: *Gallic wit. adj.*

gall ing (gô′ling), irritating; chafing. *adj.*

gal li um (gal′ē əm), a grayish-white metallic element similar to mercury, with a melting point slightly above room temperature. It is used in thermometers. *n.*

gal li vant (gal′ə vant), go about seeking pleasure; gad about. *v.*

gal lon (gal′ən), measure for liquids equal to 4 quarts. *n.*

gal lop (gal′əp), **1** the fastest gait of a horse or other four-footed animal. In a gallop, all four feet are off the ground together at each leap. **2** ride or cause to go at a gallop: *The hunters galloped after the hounds. She galloped her horse across the field.* **3** go at a gallop: *The wild horse galloped off when it saw us.* **4** go very fast; hurry: *gallop through a speech or book.* 1 *n.,* 2-4 *v.* —**gal′lop er,** *n.*

gal lows (gal′ōz), **1** a wooden frame made of a crossbar on two upright posts, used for hanging criminals. **2** punishment by hanging: *The judge sentenced the murderer to the gallows. n., pl.* **gal lows es** or **gal lows.**

gall stone (gôl′stōn′), a pebblelike mass of cholesterol, mineral salts, etc., that sometimes forms in the gall bladder or its duct. *n.*

ga lore (gə lôr′), many: *At the carnival she found that there were games and rides galore. adj.* [*Galore* comes from Irish *go leōr,* meaning "to sufficiency."]

ga losh es (gə losh′iz), rubber or plastic overshoes covering the ankles, worn in wet or snowy weather. *n.pl.*

gal van ic (gal van′ik), **1** of, caused by, or producing an electric current by chemical action. **2** startling. *adj.*

gal van ism (gal′və niz′əm), electricity produced by chemical action. *n.*

gal va nize (gal′və nīz), **1** apply an electric current produced by chemical action to. **2** arouse suddenly; startle: *The ringing of the alarm bell galvanized the dozing firemen into action.* **3** cover (iron or steel) with a thin coating of zinc to prevent rust. *v.,* **gal va nized, gal va niz ing.** —**gal′va ni za′tion,** *n.,* —**gal′va niz′er,** *n.*

gal va nom e ter (gal′və nom′ə tər), instrument for detecting, measuring, and determining the direction of a small electric current. *n.*

Gam bi a (gam′bē ə), **The,** country in W Africa, a member of the Commonwealth of Nations. *Capital:* Banjul. *n.* —**Gam′bi an,** *adj., n.*

gam bit (gam′bit), way of opening a game of chess by purposely sacrificing a pawn or a piece to gain some advantage. *n.* [*Gambit* is from Italian *gambetto,* meaning "a tripping up," which comes from *gamba,* meaning "leg."]

gam ble (gam′bəl), **1** play games of chance for money: *gamble at cards.* **2** take a risk; take great risks in business or speculation: *to gamble in stocks and bonds.* **3** to risk (money or other things of value): *The daredevil gambled his life on the chance he could leap the deep canyon.* **4** a risky act or undertaking: *Putting money into a new business is often a gamble.* 1-3 *v.,* **gam bled, gam bling;** 4 *n.*

gam bler (gam′blər), **1** person who gambles a great deal. **2** person whose occupation is gambling. *n.*

gam bol (gam′bəl), **1** a running and jumping about in play; frolic. **2** run and jump about in play; frolic. 1 *n.,* 2 *v.*

gambrel roof

gam brel roof (gam′brəl), roof with two slopes on each side. The lower slope is steeper than the upper one.

game¹ (gām), **1** way of playing; pastime; amusement: *a game of tag, a game with bat and ball.* **2** things needed to play a game: *This store sells games.* **3** contest with certain rules: *a football game.* One person or side tries to win it. **4** number of points that wins a game: *In volleyball, a*

game is fifteen points. **5** plan; scheme: *She tried to trick us, but we saw through her game.* **6** wild animals, birds, or fish hunted or caught for sport or for food. **7** flesh of wild animals or birds used for food. **8** having to do with game, hunting, or fishing: *Game laws protect wildlife.* **9** brave; plucky: *The losing team put up a game fight.* **10** having spirit or will enough: *The children were game for any adventure.* **11** to gamble. 1-7 *n.,* 8-10 *adj.* **gam er, gam est;** 11 *v.,* **gamed, gam ing.** [*Game¹* comes from Old English *gamen,* meaning "joy."] —**game′ly,** *adv.* —**game′ness,** *n.*

play the game, be fair; follow the rules; be a good sport.

the game is up, the plan or scheme has failed.

game² (gām), INFORMAL. lame; crippled; injured: *a game leg. adj.*

game cock (gām′kok′), rooster bred and trained for fighting. *n.*

game keep er (gām′kē′pər), person employed to take care of wild animals and birds on a private estate and prevent anyone from stealing them or killing them without permission. *n.*

game ster (gām′stər), gambler. *n.*

gam ete (gam′ēt *or* gə mēt′), a mature reproductive cell that can unite with another to form a fertilized cell that can develop into a new plant or animal; an egg or sperm cell; germ cell. *n.*

game warden, official whose duty is to enforce the game laws in a district.

gam in (gam′ən), a neglected child left to roam about the streets. *n.*

gambol (def. 2)—The children **gamboled** in the field.

gam ing (gā′ming), the playing of games of chance for money; gambling. *n.*

gam ma (gam′ə), the third letter of the Greek alphabet (Γ, γ). *n.*

gamma glob u lin (glob′yə lən), part of the human blood. Gamma globulin contains many antibodies which protect against infectious diseases.

gamma ray, electromagnetic radiation of very high frequency given off spontaneously by radium and other radioactive substances. Gamma rays are like X rays but have a shorter wavelength.

gam ut (gam′ət), **1** the whole series of notes on the musical scale. **2** the whole range of anything: *Her feelings about the contest ran the gamut from hope to despair. n.*

gam y (gā′mē), **1** having a strong taste or smell like the flesh of wild animals or birds. **2** brave; plucky. *adj.,* **gam·i er, gam i est.** **—gam′i ly,** *adv.* **—gam′i ness,** *n.*

gan der (gan′dər), a male goose. *n.*

Gan dhi (gän′dē *or* gan′dē), **1 Indira,** 1917-1984, prime minister of India from 1966 to 1977 and from 1980 to 1984. **2 Mohandas K.,** 1869-1948, Hindu political, social, and religious leader. **3 Rajiv,** born 1944, prime minister of India since 1984. *n.*

gang (gang), **1** group of people acting or going around together: *A whole gang of us went swimming.* **2** group engaged in wrongdoing: *A gang of hoodlums broke several windows along our street.* **3** group of people working together under one foreman: *A gang of workmen was mending the road.* **4** INFORMAL. form a gang: *The boys ganged together to build a raft.* 1-3 *n.,* 4 *v.*

gang up on, oppose as a group.

Gan ges (gan′jēz′), river flowing across N India and Bangladesh into the Bay of Bengal. It is regarded as sacred by the Hindus. *n.*

gan gli a (gang′glē ə), a plural of **ganglion.** *n.*

gan gling (gang′gling), awkwardly tall and slender. *adj.*

gan gli on (gang′glē ən), group of nerve cells forming a nerve center, especially outside of the brain or spinal cord. *n., pl.* **gan gli a** or **gan gli ons.**

gan gly (gang′glē), gangling. *adj.,* **gan gli er, gan gli-est.**

gang plank (gang′plangk′), a movable bridge used in getting on and off a ship. *n.*

gan grene (gang′grēn′), **1** decay of living tissue when its blood supply is interfered with by injury, infection, or freezing. **2** be or become affected with gangrene; decay. 1 *n.,* 2 *v.,* **gan grened, gan gren ing.**

gan gre nous (gang′grə nəs), of or having gangrene; decaying: *The wounded leg became gangrenous and had to be amputated. adj.*

gang ster (gang′stər), member of a gang of criminals or racketeers. *n.*

gang way (gang′wā′), **1** passageway. **2** passageway on a ship: *This ship has a gangway between the rail and the cabins.* **3** gangplank. **4** get out of the way! stand aside and make room! 1-3 *n.,* 4 *interj.*

gan net (gan′it), a large, fish-eating sea bird which resembles a goose but has a sharper bill, long, pointed wings, and a shorter tail. *n.*

gant let[1] (gônt′lit), gauntlet[1]. *n.*

gant let[2] (gônt′lit), gauntlet[2]. *n.*

←**gantry** (def. 1)

gantry (def. 2)
supporting a crane

gan try (gan′trē), **1** a movable framework used for setting up and servicing rockets. **2** a bridgelike framework for supporting a kind of suspended crane, signal lights over railway tracks, etc. *n., pl.* **gan tries.**

gaol (jāl), BRITISH. jail. *n., v.* **—gaol′er,** *n.*

gap (gap), **1** a broken place; opening: *The cows got out of the field through a gap in the fence.* **2** an empty part; unfilled space; blank: *The record is not complete; there are several gaps in it.* **3** a wide difference of opinion, character, etc. **4** a pass through mountains. *n.*

gape (gāp), **1** open wide: *A deep hole in the earth gaped before us.* **2** a wide opening. **3** open the mouth wide; yawn. **4** act of opening the mouth wide; yawning. **5** stare with the mouth open: *The crowd gaped at the daring tricks performed by the tightrope walkers.* 1,3,5 *v.,* **gaped, gaping;** 2,4 *n.* **—gap′er,** *n.* **—gap′ing ly,** *adv.*

gar (gär), fish with a long, slender body covered with hard scales and having a long narrow jaw. *n., pl.* **gars** or **gar.**

ga rage (gə räzh′ *or* gə räj′), **1** place where automobiles are kept. **2** shop for repairing automobiles. **3** put or keep in a garage. 1,2 *n.,* 3 *v.,* **ga raged, ga rag ing.**

garage sale, sale of used furniture, clothing, tools, etc., held in the seller's garage, yard, or basement.

garb (gärb), **1** the way one is dressed; kind of clothing: *stylish garb, official garb, priestly garb.* **2** clothe: *The doctor was garbed in white.* 1 *n.,* 2 *v.*

gar bage (gär′bij), scraps of food to be thrown away. *n.*

gar ban zo (gär ban′zō), chickpea. *n., pl.* **gar ban zos.**

gar ble (gär′bəl), make unfair or misleading selections from (facts, statements, writings, etc.); omit parts of, often in order to misrepresent; distort: *The paper gave a garbled account of the speech. v.,* **gar bled, gar bling.**

gar den (gärd′n), **1** piece of ground used for growing vegetables, herbs, flowers, or fruits. **2** take care of a garden; make a garden; work in a garden: *She liked to garden as a hobby.* **3** park or place where people go for amusement or to see things that are displayed: *the botanical garden.* 1,3 *n.,* 2 *v.* **—gar′den like′,** *adj.*

gar den er (gärd′nər), **1** person employed to take care of a garden, lawn, etc. **2** person who makes a garden or works in a garden. *n.*

gar de nia (gär dē′nyə), an evergreen shrub or small tree bearing fragrant, white flowers with smooth, waxy petals. *n., pl.* **gar de nias.** [*Gardenia* was formed from the name of Alexander *Garden,* 1730-1791, an American botanist.]

Gar field (gär′fēld′), **James A.,** 1831-1881, the 20th president of the United States. He was assassinated in 1881, his first year in office. *n.*

gar gle (gär′gəl), **1** wash or rinse the throat with a liquid kept in motion by the outgoing breath: *He gargled with hot salt water to relieve his sore throat.* **2** liquid used for gargling. 1 *v.,* **gar gled, gar gling;** 2 *n.*

gar goyle (gär′goil), figure in the shape of a grotesque animal or human being, often for draining water from the gutter of a building. *n.*

gargoyle—This gargoyle decorates a famous cathedral in Paris, France.

Gar i bal di (gär′ə bôl′dē), **Giuseppe,** 1807-1882, Italian patriot and general. *n.*

gar ish (ger′ish *or* gar′ish), unpleasantly bright; glaring; showy; gaudy: *The circus performer was dressed in garish colors. adj.* **—gar′ish ly,** *adv.* **—gar′ish ness,** *n.*

gar land (gär′lənd), **1** wreath or string of flowers, leaves, etc. **2** decorate with garlands. 1 *n.,* 2 *v.*

gar lic (gär′lik), plant of the same family as the onion, whose strong-smelling bulb is made up of small sections called cloves which are used to season meats, salads, etc. *n.* [*Garlic* is from Old English *gārlēac*, which comes from *gār*, meaning "spear," and *lēac*, meaning "leek."]

gar ment (gär′mənt), any article of clothing. *n.*

gar ner (gär′nər), gather and store away: *Wheat is cut and garnered at harvest time. Squirrels garner nuts in the fall. v.* [*Garner* came into English about 800 years ago from French *gernier*, meaning "granary," which comes from Latin *granarium*.]

gar net (gär′nit), **1** a hard mineral occurring in many varieties. A deep-red, transparent variety is used for jewelry and as an abrasive. **2** a deep red. **3** deep-red. **1,2** *n.*, **3** *adj.* —**gar′net like′,** *adj.*

gar nish (gär′nish), **1** something laid on or around food as a decoration: *The turkey was served with a garnish of cranberries and parsley.* **2** decorate (food). **3** decoration; trimming. **4** decorate; trim: *a gold ring garnished with rubies.* **1,3** *n., pl.* **gar nish es; 2,4** *v.*

gar nish ee (gär′ni shē′), withhold (a person's money or property) by legal authority in payment of a debt. If a creditor garnishees a debtor's salary, a certain portion of the salary is withheld and paid to the creditor. *v.*, **gar nish eed, gar nish ee ing.**

gar ret (gar′it), space in a house just below a sloping roof; attic. *n.*

gar ri son (gar′ə sən) **1** group of soldiers stationed in a fort, town, etc., to defend it. **2** place that has a garrison. **3** station soldiers in (a fort, town, etc.) to defend it. **4** occupy (a fort, town, etc.) as a garrison. **1,2** *n.*, **3,4** *v.*

gar ru lous (gar′ə ləs), **1** talking too much; talkative. **2** using too many words; wordy: *garrulous comments. adj.*

gar ter (gär′tər), **1** an elastic band or strap to hold up a stocking or sock. **2** fasten with a garter. **1** *n.*, **2** *v.*

garter snake—20 to 30 in. (50 to 75 cm.) long

garter snake, a small, harmless, brownish or greenish snake with light stripes that run along its body.

Gar y (ger′ē *or* gar′ē), city in NW Indiana, on Lake Michigan. It is famous for its steel production. *n.*

gas (gas), **1** substance that is not a solid or a liquid; substance that has no shape or size of its own and can expand without limit. Oxygen and nitrogen are gases at ordinary temperatures. **2** any mixture of gases that can be burned, obtained from coal and other substances. Gas was once much used for lighting, but is now used for cooking and heating. **3** any gas used as an anesthetic. Nitrous oxide is such a gas. **4** substance in the form of a gas that poisons, suffocates, or stupefies. Tear gas is one kind. Poisonous gas has been used in warfare. **5** injure or kill by poisonous gas. **6** INFORMAL. gasoline. **7** INFORMAL. supply with gasoline: *gas up the car.* **8** SLANG. talk idly or in a boasting way. **1-4,6** *n., pl.* **gas es; 5,7,8** *v.*, **gassed, gas sing.**

a hat	**i** it	**oi** oil	**ch** child	a in about
ā age	**ī** ice	**ou** out	**ng** long	e in taken
ä far	**o** hot	**u** cup	**sh** she	i in pencil
e let	**ō** open	**u̇** put	**th** thin	o in lemon
ē equal	**ô** order	**ü** rule	**ŦH** then	u in circus
ėr term			**zh** measure	

ə = { a in about / e in taken / i in pencil / o in lemon / u in circus }

gas e ous (gas′ē əs), in the form of gas; of or like a gas: *Steam is water in a gaseous condition. adj.*

gas guz zler (guz′lər), INFORMAL. automobile or other vehicle which gets low gasoline mileage.

gash (gash), **1** a long, deep cut or wound. **2** make a long, deep cut or wound in. **1** *n., pl.* **gash es; 2** *v.*

gas ket (gas′kit), ring or piece of rubber, plastic, etc., packed around a pipe joint or placed between machine parts to keep a liquid or a gas from escaping. *n.*

gas light (gas′līt′), **1** light made by burning gas. **2** lamp which burns gas. *n.*

gas mask, helmet or mask that covers the mouth and nose and is supplied with a filter to prevent breathing poisonous gas or smoke.

gas o hol (gas′ə hôl), a fuel for internal-combustion engines, composed of ninety percent unleaded gasoline and ten percent ethyl alcohol. *n.* [*Gasohol* is a blend of *gasoline* and *alcohol.*]

gas o line or **gas o lene** (gas′ə lēn′ *or* gas′ə lēn′), a colorless, liquid mixture of hydrocarbons which evaporates and burns very easily. It is made from petroleum or from gas formed in the earth. Gasoline is used chiefly as a fuel to run automobiles, airplanes, etc. *n.*

gasp (gasp), **1** try hard to get one's breath with open mouth. A person gasps when out of breath or surprised. **2** a trying hard to get one's breath with open mouth. **3** utter with gasps: *"Help! Help!" gasped the drowning man.* **1,3** *v.*, **2** *n.* —**gasp′ing ly,** *adv.*

gas station, filling station.

gas sy (gas′ē), **1** full of gas; containing gas: *a gassy atmosphere.* **2** like gas: *a gassy smell. adj.*, **gas si er, gas si est.** —**gas′si ness,** *n.*

gas tric (gas′trik), of or near the stomach. *adj.*

gastric juice, the digestive fluid produced by glands in the lining of the stomach. It contains pepsin and other enzymes and hydrochloric acid.

gas tro pod (gas′trə pod), any of a group of mollusks having eyes and feelers on a distinct head, a muscular foot used for moving, and usually a shell that is spiral or cone-shaped. Snails and slugs are gastropods. *n.*

WORD HISTORY

gastropod

Gastropod comes from Greek *gastros*, meaning "stomach," and *podos*, meaning "foot."

This gastropod is a snail.

gat (gat), OLD USE. got; a past tense of **get.** *v.*

gate (gāt), **1** a movable frame or door to close an opening in a wall or fence. It turns on hinges or slides open and shut. **2** an opening in a wall or fence where a door is; gateway. **3** door or valve to stop or control the flow of water in a pipe, dam, canal, lock, etc. **4** number of people who pay to see a contest, exhibition, etc. **5** the total amount of money received from them: *The two teams divided a gate of $3250. n.* [*Gate* comes from Old English *geat.*] —**gate′less,** *adj.* —**gate′like′,** *adj.*

gate post (gāt′pōst′), post on either side of a gate. A swinging gate is fastened to one gatepost and closes against the other. *n.*

gate way (gāt′wā′), **1** an opening in a wall or fence where a gate is. **2** way to go in or out; way to get to something: *A good education can be a gateway to success. n.*

gaunt (def. 1)—The guitar player was pale and **gaunt**.

gath er (gaTH′ər), **1** bring into one place; collect: *He gathered his books and papers and started to school.* **2** come together; assemble: *A crowd gathered at the scene of the accident.* **3** pick and collect from the place of growth; glean or pluck: *to gather crops.* **4.** get or gain little by little: *The train gathered speed as it left the station.* **5** put together in the mind; conclude: *I gather from the excitement that something important has happened.* **6** pull together in folds: *The dressmaker gathered the skirt at the waist. She gathered her brows in a frown.* **7** one of the little folds between stitches when cloth is gathered. **8** come to a head and form pus: *A boil is a painful swelling that gathers under the skin.* 1-6,8 *v.,* 7 *n.* —**gath′er er,** *n.*

gath er ing (gaTH′ər ing), **1** a group of people met together; meeting; assembly: *We had a large family gathering at our house on Thanksgiving Day.* **2** swelling that comes to a head and forms pus. *n.*

gauche (gōsh), awkward; clumsy. *adj.* —**gauche′ly,** *adv.* —**gauche′ness,** *n.*

gau cho (gou′chō), cowboy in the southern plains of South America, usually of mixed Spanish and Indian descent. *n., pl.* **gau chos.**

gaud i ly (gô′dl ē), in a gaudy manner. *adv.*

gaud i ness (gô′dē nis), gaudy condition or quality. *n.*

gaud y (gô′dē), too bright and gay to be in good taste; cheap and showy: *gaudy jewelry, a gaudy tie. adj.,* **gaud i er, gaud i est.**

gauge (gāj), **1** a standard measure; scale of standard measurements; measure. There are gauges of the capacity of a barrel, the thickness of sheet iron, the diameter of a shotgun bore or of a wire, etc. **2** instrument for measuring. A steam gauge measures the pressure of steam. **3** measure accurately; find out the exact measurement of with a gauge. **4** estimate; judge: *It's difficult to gauge the educational value of television.* **5** distance be-

tween the rails of a railroad. Standard gauge between rails is 56½ inches (1.44 meters). 1,2,5 *n.,* 3,4 *v.,* **gauged, gaug ing.** Also, **gage.** —**gauge′a ble,** *adj.*

Gau guin (gō gan′), **Paul,** 1848-1903, French painter. *n.*

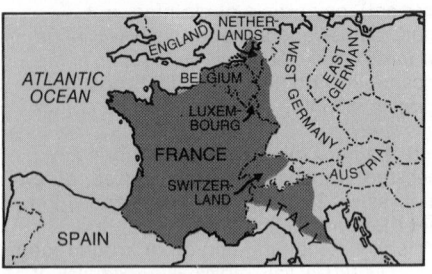

Gaul (def. 1), about 300 B.C., shown by the darker area on a modern map

Gaul (gôl), **1** ancient region of W Europe. It included what is now France, Belgium, Luxembourg, and parts of Switzerland, West Germany, the Netherlands, and N Italy. **2** one of the Celtic inhabitants of ancient Gaul. **3** Frenchman. *n.*

gaunt (gônt), **1** very thin and bony; with hollow eyes and a starved look. **2** looking bare and gloomy; desolate: *the gaunt slopes of a high mountain in winter. adj.* —**gaunt′ly,** *adv.* —**gaunt′ness,** *n.*

gaunt let[1] (gônt′lit), a former punishment or torture in which the offender had to run between two rows of men who struck him with clubs or other weapons as he passed. *n.* Also, **gantlet.**

run the gauntlet, 1 pass between two rows of men each of whom strikes the runner as he passes. **2** be exposed to unfriendly attacks or severe criticism.

gaunt let[2] (gônt′lit), **1** a stout, heavy glove with a wide, flaring cuff covering the wrist and lower part of the arm. Gauntlets, usually of leather covered with plates of iron or steel, were part of a knight's armor. **2** a stout, heavy glove with a wide, flaring cuff covering part of the arm. *n.* Also, **gantlet.**

throw down the gauntlet, challenge.

gauze (gôz), a very thin, light cloth, easily seen through. Gauze is often used for bandages. *n.* [*Gauze* came into English about 400 years ago from French *gaze,* which can be traced back to Arabic *qazz,* meaning "silk."] —**gauze′like′,** *adj.*

gauz y (gô′zē), like gauze; thin and light as gauze: *a gauzy mist, gauzy wings. adj.,* **gauz i er, gauz i est.** —**gauz′i ness,** *n.*

gave (gāv), past tense of **give.** *She gave me some of her candy. v.*

gav el (gav′əl), a small mallet used by a presiding officer to signal for attention or order or by an auctioneer to announce that the bidding is over: *The club's president rapped on the table twice with a gavel. n.*

ga votte (gə vot′), **1** an old French dance somewhat like a minuet but much more lively. **2** the music for it. *n.*

Ga wain (gä′wān *or* gä′win), one of the knights of the Round Table and nephew of King Arthur. *n.*

gawk (gôk), stare idly, rudely, or stupidly. *v.*

gawk i ly (gô′kə lē), in a gawky manner. *adv.*

gawk i ness (gô′kē nis), gawky condition or quality. *n.*

gawk y (gô′kē), awkward; clumsy. *adj.,* **gawk i er, gawk i est.**

gay (gā), **1** happy and full of fun; merry: *The children were cheerful and gay on the day of the first snowfall.* **2** bright-colored; showy: *a gay scarf. adj.* —**gay′ness,** *n.*

gay e ty (gā′ə tē), gaiety. *n., pl.* **gay e ties.**

gay ly (gā′lē), gaily. *adv.*

gaze (gāz), **1** look long and steadily: *For hours we sat gazing at the stars.* **2** a long, steady look. **1** *v.,* **gazed, gaz ing; 2** *n.* —**gaz′er,** *n.*

ga zelle (gə zel′), a small, swift, and graceful antelope of Africa and Asia, having soft, lustrous eyes. *n., pl.* **gazelles** or **ga zelle.** [*Gazelle* was borrowed from French *gazelle,* and can be traced back to Arabic *ghazāl.*] —**gazelle′like′,** *adj.*

gazelle—about 2 ft. (60 cm.) high at the shoulder

ga zette (gə zet′), **1** newspaper: *the "Emporia Gazette."* **2** an official government journal containing lists of appointments, promotions, etc. **3** publish, list, or announce in a gazette. **1,2** *n.,* **3** *v.,* **ga zet ted, ga zet ting.**

gaz et teer (gaz′ə tir′), dictionary of geographical names. Names of places, seas, mountains, etc., are arranged alphabetically. *n.*

G.B., Great Britain.

G clef, treble clef.

Gd, symbol for gadolinium.

Ge, symbol for germanium.

gear (gir), **1** wheel having teeth that fit into the teeth of another wheel. If the wheels are of different sizes they will turn at different speeds. **2** set of such wheels working together to transmit power or change the direction of motion in a machine. In an automobile, power is transmitted from the motor to the wheels by means of gears. **3** connect by gears: *The motor is geared to the rear wheels of the automobile.* **4** any arrangement of gears or moving parts; mechanism; machinery: *The car ran off the road when the steering gear broke.* **5** equipment needed for some purpose: *camping gear.* **6** make fit; adjust; adapt: *Steel production is geared to the needs of our industries.* **1,2,4,5** *n.,* **3,6** *v.* —**gear′less,** *adj.*

in gear, connected to the motor, etc.

out of gear, disconnected from the motor, etc.

shift gears, change from one gear to another; connect a motor, etc., to a different set of gears.

gears (def. 1)

gear ing (gir′ing), set of gears, chains, or parts of machinery for transmitting motion or power; gear. *n.*

gear shift (gir′shift′), device for connecting a motor, etc., to any of several sets of gears. *n.*

gear wheel (gir′hwēl′), cogwheel; gear. *n.*

geck o (gek′ō), a small, harmless, insect-eating lizard with adhesive pads on its feet for walking on ceilings,

a hat	i it	oi oil	ch child		a in about
ā age	ī ice	ou out	ng long		e in taken
ä far	o hot	u cup	sh she	ə =	i in pencil
e let	ō open	u̇ put	th thin		o in lemon
ē equal	ô order	ü rule	ᴛʜ then		u in circus
ėr term			zh measure		

walls, etc. *n., pl.* **geck os** or **geck oes.** [*Gecko* comes from Malay *gekok.*]

gee (jē), **1** word of command to horses or oxen directing them to turn to the right. **2** turn to the right. **3** exclamation or mild oath. **1,3** *interj.,* **2** *v.,* **geed, gee ing.**

geese (gēs), plural of **goose.** *n.*

Gei ger counter (gī′gər), device which detects and counts ionizing particles. It is used to measure or detect radioactivity, cosmic-ray particles, etc.

Gei sel (gī′zəl), **Theodor Seuss,** born 1904, American writer of children's books. His pen name is Dr. Seuss. *n.*

gei sha (gā′shə *or* gē′shə), a Japanese girl trained to be a professional entertainer. Geisha are hired to provide singing, dancing, and dinnertime conversation. *n., pl.* **gei sha** or **gei shas.**

gel a tin or **gel a tine** (jel′ə tən), **1** an odorless, tasteless substance like glue or jelly, obtained by boiling the bones, hoofs, and other tissues of animals. It is used in making jellied desserts, glue, camera film, etc. **2** any of various vegetable substances like this. *n.*

WORD HISTORY

gelatin

Gelatin comes from French *gélatine,* and can be traced back to Latin *gelare,* meaning "to freeze."

ge lat i nous (jə lat′n əs), **1** of or like jelly. **2** of, like, or containing gelatin. *adj.*

ge la to (jə lä′tō), a soft, creamy, Italian ice cream. *n., pl.* **ge la ti** (jə lä′tē). [*Gelato* was borrowed from Italian *gelato,* meaning "frozen."]

geld ing (gel′ding), a castrated horse or other animal. *n.*

gem (jem), **1** a precious or semiprecious stone, especially when cut and polished for ornament; jewel. Diamonds, rubies, and opals are gems. **2** person or thing that is very precious, beautiful, etc.: *The gem of the collection was a rare Persian stamp.* *n.*

Gen., General.

gen darme (zhän′därm), member of the police in France and several other European countries who has had military training. *n., pl.* **gen darmes** (zhän′därmz).

gen der (jen′dər), **1** the grouping of words into certain classes, such as masculine, feminine, or neuter. In English, except in pronouns (*him, her, it*) and a few nouns with endings such as -*ess* (*actress*), gender is now indicated only by the meaning of the word: *man—woman, nephew—niece, rooster—hen.* **2** one of such classes. **3** sex: *the female gender. n.*

gene (jēn), a minute part of a chromosome that influences the inheritance and development of some characteristic. The genes inherited from its parents determine what kind of plant or animal will develop from a fertilized egg cell. [*Gene* comes from German *Gen,* and can be traced back to Greek *genea,* meaning "breed, kind."]

ge ne a log i cal (jē′nē ə loj′ə kəl), of genealogy. A genealogical chart is called a family tree. *adj.*

ge ne al o gist (jē′nē al′ə jist *or* jē′nē ol′ə jist), a person who makes a study of or traces genealogies. *n.*

ge ne al o gy (jē′nē al′ə jē *or* jē′nē ol′ə jē), 1 account of the descent of a person or family from an ancestor or ancestors. 2 descent of a person or family from an ancestor; pedigree. 3 study of pedigrees. *n., pl.* **ge ne al o gies.**

gen er a (jen′ər ə), a plural of **genus.** *n.*

gen er al (jen′ər əl), 1 of all; for all; from all: *A government takes care of the general welfare.* 2 common to many or most; not limited to a few; widespread: *In our school there is a general interest in sports.* 3 not detailed: *The teacher gave us only general instructions.* 4 not special: *a general store. A general reader reads different kinds of books.* 5 chief; of highest rank: *The Attorney General is the head of the Justice Department.* 6 a military officer ranking above a colonel, such as a lieutenant general or a major general. 7 (in the United States Army and Air Force) an officer ranking next below a General of the Army or a General of the Air Force and next above lieutenant general. 8 (in the United States Marine Corps) an officer of the highest rank. 1-5 *adj.,* 6-8 *n.*

in general, for the most part; usually; commonly: *He is friendly in general, but he was particularly friendly today.*

General Assembly, 1 legislature of certain states of the United States. 2 the main body of the United Nations, made up of delegates from every member nation.

gen er al is si mo (jen′ər ə lis′ə mō), commander in chief of all the military forces in certain countries. *n., pl.* **gen er al is si mos.**

gen e ral i ty (jen′ə ral′ə tē), 1 a general or vague statement; word or phrase not definite enough to have much meaning or value: *The candidates spoke in generalities; not once did they say what they would do if elected.* 2 a general principle or rule: *"Nothing happens without a cause" is a generality. n., pl.* **gen e ral i ties.**

gen er al i za tion (jen′ər ə lə zā′shən), 1 act or process of generalizing: *Don't be hasty in generalization; be sure you have the necessary facts first.* 2 a general idea, statement, principle, or rule: *"A rainbow appears when the sun shines after a shower" is a generalization. n.*

gen er al ize (jen′ər ə līz), 1 make into a general rule; conclude from particular facts: *If you know that cats, lions, leopards, and tigers eat meat, you can generalize that the cat family eats meat.* 2 talk or write indefinitely or vaguely; use generalities: *The commentators generalized because they knew no details.* 3 bring into general use or knowledge; popularize. *v.,* **gen er al ized, gen er al iz ing.** —**gen′er al iz′er,** *n.*

gen er al ly (jen′ər ə lē), 1 in most cases; usually: *I am generally on time.* 2 for the most part; widely: *It was once generally believed that the earth is flat.* 3 in a general way; without giving details; not specially: *Generally speaking, our coldest weather comes in January. adv.*

General of the Air Force, general of the highest rank in the United States Air Force.

General of the Army, general of the highest rank in the United States Army.

general practitioner, physician who does not specialize in any single field of medicine.

gen er al ship (jen′ər əl ship), 1 ability as a general; skill in commanding an army. 2 skillful management; leadership. 3 rank, commission, or authority of a general. *n.*

gen e rate (jen′ə rāt′), cause to be; bring into being; produce: *Burning coal can generate steam. v.,* **gen e rat ed, gen e rat ing.**

gen e ra tion (jen′ə rā′shən), 1 all the people born about the same time. Your parents and their friends belong to one generation; you and your friends belong to the next generation. 2 about thirty years, or the time from the birth of one generation to the birth of the next generation. There are three generations in a century. 3 one step or degree in the descent of a family: *The picture showed four generations—great-grandmother, grandfather, mother, and baby.* 4 a bringing into being; generating: *Steam and water power are used for the generation of electricity. n.*

generation gap, differences in attitudes and values between the people of one generation and those of the next.

gen e ra tive (jen′ə rā′tiv), 1 of production of offspring. 2 having the power of producing. *adj.*

gen e ra tor (jen′ə rā′tər), 1 machine that changes mechanical energy into electrical energy and produces either direct or alternating current. 2 apparatus for producing gas or steam. 3 person or thing that generates. *n.*

ge ner ic (jə ner′ik), 1 characteristic of a genus, kind, or class: *Cats and lions show generic differences.* 2 general; not specific or special: *"Liquid" is a generic term, but "milk" is a specific term.* 3 not sold under a trademark or brand name: *generic drugs, generic canned goods. adj.*

gen e ros i ty (jen′ə ros′ə tē), 1 a being generous; willingness to share with others; unselfishness: *That wealthy family is known for its generosity.* 2 nobleness of heart or of mind; willingness to forgive. 3 generous behavior; generous act. *n., pl.* **gen e ros i ties.**

gen er ous (jen′ər əs), 1 willing to share with others; unselfish: *a generous giver. Our teacher is always generous with his time.* 2 noble and forgiving; not mean: *He was generous in accepting their apology.* 3 large; plentiful: *a generous piece of pie. adj.* —**gen′er ous ly,** *adv.*

gen e sis (jen′ə sis), origin; creation; coming into being: *the genesis of an idea. n., pl.* **gen e ses** (jen′ə sēz′).

Gen e sis (jen′ə sis), the first book of the Old Testament. Genesis gives an account of the creation of the world. *n.*

ge net ic (jə net′ik), 1 of a gene or genes: *a genetic mutation.* 2 of genetics. *adj.*

ge net i cal ly (jə net′ik lē), 1 with respect to origin. 2 according to genetics. *adv.*

ge net i cist (jə net′ə sist), an expert in genetics. *n.*

ge net ics (jə net′iks), branch of biology dealing with the principles of heredity and variation in animals and plants of the same or related kinds. *n.*

Ge ne va (jə nē′və), 1 city in SW Switzerland. 2 Lake, long, narrow lake in SW Switzerland and E France. *n.*

Gen ghis Khan (jeng′gis kän′), 1162-1227, Mongol conqueror of central Asia.

gen ial (jē′nyəl), 1 smiling and pleasant; cheerful and friendly; kindly: *She was glad to see us again and gave us a genial welcome.* 2 helping growth; pleasantly warming; comforting: *a genial climate. adj.* —**gen′ial ly,** *adv.*

ge ni al i ty (jē′nē al′ə tē), genial quality or behavior. *n.*

ge nie (jē′nē), spirit or jinni: *When Aladdin rubbed his lamp, the genie came and did what Aladdin asked. n., pl.* **ge nies** or **ge ni i.** [*Genie* is from French *génie,* which comes from Arabic *jinnī.*]

ge ni i (jē′nē ī), 1 a plural of **genius** (def. 5). 2 a plural of **genie.** *n.*

gen i tal (jen′ə təl), of reproduction or the sex organs. *adj.*

gen i tals (jen′ə təlz), the external sex organs. *n.pl.*

gen ius (jē′nyəs), 1 very great natural power of mind: *Important discoveries are usually made by men and women of genius.* 2 person having such power: *Shakespeare was a genius.* 3 great natural ability: *to have a genius for composing music.* 4 person having such natural ability: *She is a genius at playing the violin.* 5 a guardian spirit of a person, place, institution, etc. 6 person who powerfully influences another: *an evil genius. n., pl.* **gen ius es** for 1-4,6, **ge ni i** for 5.

WORD FAMILY

genus

Below are words related to *genus*. They can all be traced back to Latin *genus, generis* (ge′nùs, ge′ne ris), meaning "kind, sort, class."

degenerate generate generic
gender generation generous
general generator regenerate

Gen o a (jen′ō ə), seaport in NW Italy. *n.*

gen o cid al (jen′ə sī′dl), of genocide. *adj.*

gen o cide (jen′ə sīd), the extermination of a cultural or racial group. *n.*

Gen o ese (jen′ō ēz′), **1** of Genoa or its people. **2** person born or living in Genoa. 1 *adj.*, 2 *n., pl.* **Gen o ese.**

gent (jent), INFORMAL. man. *n.*

gen teel (jen tēl′), **1** belonging or suited to polite society. **2** polite; well-bred; fashionable; elegant. **3** artificially polite and courteous. *adj.* —**gen teel′ly,** *adv.*

gen tian (jen′shən), plant with usually blue flowers and stemless leaves. *n.*

gen tile or **Gen tile** (jen′tīl), **1** person who is not a Jew. **2** not Jewish. 1 *n.*, 2 *adj.*

gen til i ty (jen til′ə tē), **1** gentle birth; being of good family and social position. **2** good manners; politeness; refinement: *The gracious couple greeted us with gentility. n., pl.* **gen til i ties.**

gen tle (jen′tl), **1** not severe, rough, or violent; mild: *a gentle tap.* **2** soft; low: *a gentle sound.* **3** not too much or too fast; not harsh or extreme; moderate: *gentle heat, a gentle slope.* **4** kindly; friendly: *a gentle disposition.* **5** easily handled or managed: *a gentle dog.* **6** of good family and social position; wellborn. **7** having or showing good manners; refined; polite. *adj.*, **gen tler, gen tlest.** —**gen′tle ness,** *n.*

gen tle folk (jen′tl fōk′), people of good family and social position. *n.pl.*

gen tle man (jen′tl mən), **1** man of good family and social position. **2** a well-bred man. **3** a polite term for any man: *"Gentlemen" is often used in speaking or writing to a group of men. n., pl.* **gen tle men.** —**gen′tle man like′,** *adj.*

gen tle man ly (jen′tl mən lē), like a gentleman; suitable for a gentleman; well-bred; polite. *adj.*

gentleman's agreement or **gentlemen's agreement,** an informal agreement that is not legally binding. The people or countries that make it are bound only by their promise to keep it.

gen tle wom an (jen′tl wüm′ən), **1** woman of good family and social position. **2** a well-bred woman; lady. **3** a woman attendant of a lady of rank. *n., pl.* **gen tle wom en.**

gent ly (jent′lē), **1** in a gentle way; tenderly; softly: *Handle the baby gently.* **2** gradually: *a gently sloping hillside. adv.*

gen try (jen′trē), people of good family and social position. The English gentry are next below the nobility. *n.*

gen u flect (jen′yə flekt), bend the knee as an act of reverence or worship. *v.* —**gen′u flec′tion,** *n.*

gen u ine (jen′yü ən), **1** actually being what it seems or is claimed to be; real; true: *The table is genuine mahogany, not wood stained to look like it.* **2** without pretense; sincere; frank: *genuine sorrow. adj.* —**gen′u ine ly,** *adv.*

ge nus (jē′nəs), **1** any group of similar things; kind; sort; class. **2** group of related animals or plants ranking below a family and above a species. *n., pl.* **gen er a** or **ge nus es.** [*Genus* was borrowed from Latin *genus.* See **Word Family.**]

geo-, *combining form.* earth; of the earth: *Geology = science of the (crust of the) earth.* [The form *geo-* comes from Greek *gē,* meaning "the earth."]

ge o cen tric (jē′ō sen′trik), **1** viewed or measured from the earth's center. **2** having or representing the earth as a center: *a geocentric universe. adj.* —**ge′o cen′tri cal ly,** *adv.*

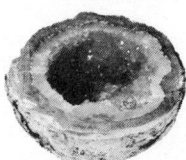

geode—left, uncut; right, cut to show cavity

ge ode (jē′ōd), rock with a cavity lined with crystals or other mineral matter. *n.*

ge o des ic dome (jē′ə des′ik), a dome having the shape of a hemisphere, supported by a lightweight framework of connected triangles.

geodesic domes

geog., 1 geographer. **2** geography.

ge og ra pher (jē og′rə fər), an expert in geography. *n.*

ge o graph ic (jē′ə graf′ik), geographical. *adj.*

ge o graph i cal (jē′ə graf′ə kəl), of geography. *adj.* —**ge′o graph′i cal ly,** *adv.*

geographical mile, nautical mile.

ge og ra phy (jē og′rə fē), **1** study of the earth's surface, climate, continents, countries, peoples, industries, and products. **2** the surface features of a place or region: *the geography of New England. n., pl.* **ge og ra phies.**

geol., geology.

ge o log ic (jē′ə loj′ik), geological. *adj.*

ge o log i cal (jē′ə loj′ə kəl), of geology. *adj.* —**ge′o log′i cal ly,** *adv.*

ge ol o gist (jē ol′ə jist), an expert in geology. *n.*

ge ol o gy (jē ol′ə jē), **1** science that deals with the earth's crust, the layers of which it is composed, and their history. **2** features of the earth's crust in a place or region; rocks, rock formation, etc., of a particular area. *n., pl.* **ge ol o gies.**

geom., 1 geometric. **2** geometry.

ge o met ric (jē ə met′rik), **1** of geometry; according to the principles of geometry: *geometric proof.* **2** consisting of straight lines, circles, triangles, etc.; regular and symmetrical. *adj.* —**ge′o met′ri cal ly,** *adv.*

ge o met ri cal (jē′ə met′rə kəl), geometric. *adj.*

geometric progression, sequence of numbers in which each number is multiplied by the same factor in order to obtain the following number. 2, 4, 8, 16, and 32 form a geometric progression.

ge om e try (jē om′ə trē), branch of mathematics which studies the relationship of points, lines, angles, and surfaces of figures in space; the mathematics of space. Geometry includes the definition, comparison, and measurement of squares, triangles, circles, cubes, cones, spheres, and other plane and solid figures. *n., pl.* **ge om e tries.**

ge o phys i cal (jē′ō fiz′ə kəl), of or concerning geophysics. *adj.*

ge o phys i cist (jē′ō fiz′ə sist), an expert in geophysics. *n.*

ge o phys ics (jē′ō fiz′iks), study of the relations between the features of the earth and the forces that change or produce them. Geophysics includes geology, meteorology, and similar sciences. *n.*

ge o po lit i cal (jē′ō pə lit′ə kəl), of geopolitics. *adj.* —**ge′o po lit′i cal ly,** *adv.*

ge o pol i tics (jē′ō pol′ə tiks), study of government and its policies as affected by physical geography. *n.*

George (jôrj), **Saint,** died A.D. 303?, Christian martyr, the patron saint of England. *n.*

George III, 1738-1820, king of England from 1760 to 1820. The Revolutionary War took place during his reign.

George V, 1865-1936, king of England from 1910 to 1936.

George VI, 1895-1952, king of England from 1936 to 1952.

George town (jôrj′toun′), capital of Guyana. *n.*

Geor gia (jôr′jə), one of the southeastern states of the United States. *Abbreviation:* Ga. or GA *Capital:* Atlanta. *n.* —**Geor′gian,** *adj., n.*

ge o ther mal (jē′ō thėr′məl), of or produced by the internal heat of the earth: *geothermal springs, geothermal energy. adj.*

ge ot ro pism (jē ot′rə piz′əm), response by various parts of plants to the action of gravity. *n.*

Ger., 1 German. **2** Germany.

ge ra ni um (jə rā′nē əm), **1** plant with fragrant leaves and large clusters of showy red, pink, or white flowers, often grown in pots for window plants. **2** a similar wild plant with pink or purple flowers. *n.* [*Geranium* was borrowed from Latin *geranium,* and can be traced back to Greek *geranos,* meaning "crane." The seed pod of the flower looks like a crane's bill.]

ger bil (jėr′bəl), a small rodent with long hind legs, native to desert regions. Gerbils are used in scientific research and are kept as pets. *n.*

ger i at rics (jer′ē at′riks), branch of medicine dealing with the study of the process of aging and the diseases and treatment of the aged. *n.*

germ (jėrm), **1** a microscopic animal or plant, especially one which causes disease; microbe: *the scarlet fever germ.* **2** the earliest form of a living thing; seed or bud; spore. **3** the beginning of anything; origin: *The germ of the idea for the phonograph came to Edison when he thought of ways of recording telegraph messages automatically. n.* —**germ′less,** *adj.* —**germ′like′,** *adj.*

Ger man (jėr′mən), **1** of Germany, its people, or their

geometric (def. 2) blanket with a geometric pattern

language: *German culture.* **2** person born or living in Germany. **3** language of Germany. **1** *adj.,* **2,3** *n.*

ger mane (jər mān′), closely connected; to the point; pertinent: *Her statement is not germane to the discussion. adj.*

Ger man ic (jər man′ik), **1** German. **2** of the people of northwestern Europe, such as the Germans, Scandinavians, and English, and their languages. English, German, Dutch, and Swedish are Germanic languages. **3** Teutonic. *adj.*

ger ma ni um (jər mā′nē əm), a brittle, silver-white element which occurs in zinc ores. It has the properties of both a metal and a nonmetal and is used as a semiconductor in transistors. *n.*

German measles, a contagious disease resembling measles, but much less serious; rubella.

German shepherds about 2 ft. (61 cm.) high at the shoulder

German shepherd, a large, strong, intelligent dog of a breed developed in Germany, often trained to work with soldiers and police or to guide blind persons; police dog.

German silver, nickel silver.

Ger ma ny (jėr′mə nē), former country in central Europe. Since 1949 Germany has been divided into West Germany and East Germany. *Capital of West Germany:* Bonn. *Capital of East Germany:* East Berlin. *n.*

germ cell, 1 an egg or sperm cell; gamete. **2** a primitive cell from which an egg or sperm cell develops.

gerbil—about 8 in. (20 cm.) long with the tail

ger mi cid al (jer′mə sī′dl), killing germs. *adj.*

ger mi cide (jer′mə sīd), any substance which kills germs, especially disease germs. Disinfectants and fungicides are germicides. *n.*

ger mi nate (jer′mə nāt), **1** begin to grow or develop; sprout: *Seeds germinate in the spring.* **2** cause to grow or develop: *Warmth and moisture germinate seeds. v.*, **ger mi nat ed, ger mi nat ing.** —**ger′mi na′tor,** *n.*

ger mi na tion (jer′mə nā′shən), a starting to grow or develop; a sprouting. Germination takes place when seeds are warm and moist. *n.*

germ plasm, substance in germ cells that transmits hereditary characteristics to the offspring.

germ warfare, the spreading of germs to produce disease among the enemy in time of war.

Ge ron i mo (jə ron′ə mō), 1829-1909, American Indian leader who was chief of the Apaches. *n.*

ger ry man der (jer′ē man′dər *or* ger′ē man′dər), **1** arrange the political divisions of (a state, county, etc.) to give one political party an unfair advantage in elections. **2** act of gerrymandering. 1 *v.*, 2 *n.*

WORD HISTORY

gerrymander

Gerrymander comes from Elbridge *Gerry,* 1744-1814, an American politician, and the word *(sala)mander.* While Gerry was governor of Massachusetts from 1810 to 1812, his party changed the lines of the voting districts in the state, so that in Essex county one district became shaped much like a salamander.

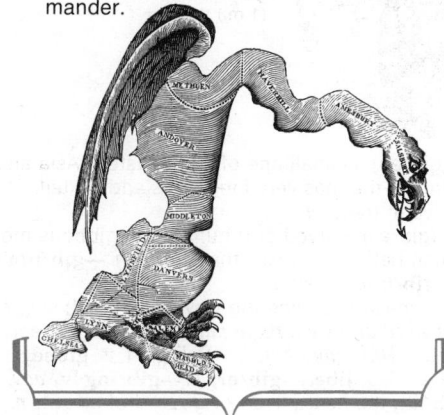

ger und (jer′ənd), a verb form ending in *-ing* and used as a noun. In "Watching them carefully was hard work," *watching* is a gerund used as the subject of *was;* like a verb it takes an object *them* and is modified by an adverb *carefully. n.*

ges ta tion (je stā′shən), **1** a having young developing in the uterus; pregnancy. **2** period of pregnancy. **3** formation and development of a project, idea, plan, etc. *n.* [*Gestation* comes from Latin *gestationem,* which can be traced back to *gerere,* meaning "to carry." See **Word Family.**]

ges tic u late (je stik′yə lāt), make or use gestures to show ideas or feelings: *The excited speaker gesticulated by raising his arms and then pounding the desk. v.*, **ges tic u lat ed, ges tic u lat ing.**

ges tic u la tion (je stik′yə lā′shən), **1** a making lively or excited gestures. **2** a lively or excited gesture. *n.*

ges ture (jes′chər), **1** movement of any part of the body to help express an idea or a feeling: *Speakers often make gestures with their hands to stress something that they are saying.* **2** anything said or done to impress or influence others: *Their refusal was merely a gesture; they really wanted to go.* **3** make gestures; use gestures. 1,2 *n.*, 3 *v.*, **ges tured, ges tur ing.**

get (get), **1** come to have; obtain: *I got a new coat yesterday.* **2** reach: *I got home early last night.* **3** catch; get hold of: *I got the cat by one leg.* **4** cause to be or do: *Get the windows open. They got the fire under control.* **5** be; become: *get sick. Don't get nervous when you take the test.* **6** persuade; influence: *Try to get them to come, too.* **7** make ready; prepare: *Should I help them get dinner?* **8** possess: *What have you got in your hand?* **9** to be obliged; need: *We have got to win.* **10** INFORMAL. hit; strike: *The ball got the batter on the arm.* **11** INFORMAL. understand: *Do you get me? I don't get it. v.*, **got, got** or **got ten, get ting.**

get about, 1 go from place to place. **2** become widely known.

get along, 1 be friendly: *to get along with others.* **2** manage: *I got along without their help.*

get around, 1 go from place to place: *The new roads will allow people to get around faster.* **2** become widely known; spread. **3** overcome: *He found the problem hard to get around.* **4** deceive; trick: *You can't get around that child; she's too smart to be fooled.*

get at, 1 reach: *We could not get at the cat on the tree without a ladder.* **2** find out.

get away, 1 go away: *Let's get away from here.* **2** escape: *The prisoner got away.*

get away with, INFORMAL. take or do something and escape safely: *get away with lying.*

get back, 1 return. **2** recover.

get back at, SLANG. take revenge on.

get by, INFORMAL. **1** pass: *Let me get by, as I'm in a hurry.* **2** not be noticed or caught. **3** manage: *She has just enough money to get by.*

get in, 1 go in. **2** put in: *They kept talking, and I couldn't get in a word.* **3** arrive: *Our train should get in at 9 p.m.*

get it, be scolded or punished.

get off, 1 come down from or out of: *She got off the horse.* **2** take off. **3** escape punishment. **4** help to escape punishment. **5** start.

get on, 1 go up on or into: *I got on the train.* **2** put on:

WORD FAMILY

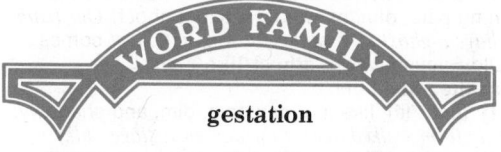

gestation

Below are words related to *gestation.* They can all be traced back to the Latin word *gerere* (ge′re re), meaning "to bear, carry."

belligerent	gesture	register
congest	indigestion	registrar
digest	jest	suggest

Pronunciation key

a hat	i it	oi oil	ch child	a in about
ā age	ī ice	ou out	ng long	e in taken
ä far	o hot	u cup	sh she	ə = i in pencil
e let	ō open	u̇ put	th thin	o in lemon
ē equal	ô order	ü rule	ꞙн then	u in circus
ėr term			zh measure	

Get on your boots; it's snowing outside. **3** advance: *get on in years.* **4** manage: *We can't get on without their help.* **5** succeed: *How are you getting on in your new job?* **6** agree: *The roommates get on with each other very well.*

get out, 1 go out: *Let's get out of here!* **2** take out. **3** go away. **4** escape. **5** help to escape. **6** become known. **7** publish.

get out of, 1 escape. **2** help to escape.

get over, recover from.

get there, succeed.

get through, finish.

get to, be allowed to: *I got to stay up late last night.*

get together, 1 bring or come together; meet; assemble. **2** come to an agreement.

get up, 1 arise: *They got up at six o'clock.* **2** stand up. **3** prepare; arrange.

get a way (get′ə wā′), **1** act of getting away; escape. **2** a start from a complete stop: *a racing car's fast getaway.* *n.*

Geth sem a ne (geth sem′ə nē), (in the Bible) a garden near Jerusalem, the scene of Jesus's agony, betrayal, and arrest. *n.*

get-to geth er (get′tə geŦH′ər), an informal social gathering or party. *n.*

Get tys burg (get′ēz bėrg′), town in S Pennsylvania. An important battle of the Civil War was fought there. *n.*

get-up (get′up′), INFORMAL. **1** way a thing is put together; arrangement or style. **2** dress or costume. *n.*

get-up-and-go (get′up′ən gō′), INFORMAL. energy; initiative. *n.*

gew gaw (gyü′gô), **1** a showy trifle; gaudy, useless ornament or toy; bauble. **2** showy but trifling. **1** *n.*, **2** *adj.*

gey ser (gī′zər), a spring that spouts a fountain or jet of hot water and steam into the air at regular intervals. There are geysers in Iceland, New Zealand, and Yellowstone National Park. *n.* [*Geyser* was named for *Geysir*, a spring like this in Iceland, which comes from Icelandic *geysa*, meaning "to gush."]

Gha na (gä′nə), country in W Africa, a member of the Commonwealth of Nations. *Capital:* Accra. See **Nigeria** for map. *n.*

ghast li ness (gast′lē nis), ghastly quality or condition. *n.*

ghast ly (gast′lē), **1** causing terror; horrible; shocking: *Murder is a ghastly crime.* **2** like a dead person or ghost; deathly pale: *The sick man looked ghastly.* **3** INFORMAL. very bad: *a ghastly failure.* *adj.*, **ghast li er, ghast li est.**

gher kin (gėr′kən), a small, prickly cucumber often used for pickles. *n.* [*Gherkin* comes from Dutch *gurken*, meaning "cucumbers."]

ghet to (get′ō), **1** part of a city where any racial group or nationality lives. **2** (formerly) a part of a city in Europe where Jews were required to live. *n.*, *pl.* **ghet tos.** [*Ghetto* is borrowed from Italian *ghetto.*]

ghost (gōst), **1** spirit of a dead person, supposed to appear to living people as a pale, dim, shadowy form. *The ghost of the murdered servant was said to haunt the house.* **2** anything pale, dim, or shadowy like a ghost: *Our team didn't have a ghost of a chance to win.* *n.* [*Ghost* comes from Old English *gāst.*] —**ghost′like′,** *adj.*

give up the ghost, die.

ghost ly (gōst′lē), like a ghost; pale, dim, and shadowy: *A ghostly form walked across the darkened stage.* *adj.*, **ghost li er, ghost li est.** —**ghost′li ness,** *n.*

ghost town, a once-flourishing town that has become empty and lifeless.

ghost writ er (gōst′rī′tər), person who writes something for another person who pretends to be the author. *n.*

ghoul (gül), **1** (in Oriental stories) a horrible demon that robs graves and feeds on corpses. **2** person who robs

graves or corpses. **3** person who enjoys what is revolting, brutal, and horrible. *n.* [*Ghoul* comes from Arabic *ghūl.*]

ghoul ish (gü′lish), like a ghoul; revolting, brutal, and horrible. *adj.* —**ghoul′ish ly,** *adv.* —**ghoul′ish ness,** *n.*

GI or **G.I.** (jē′ī′), **1** government issue: *GI shoes, GI socks.* **2** of or for a member of the armed forces: *a GI loan.* **3** INFORMAL. an enlisted soldier in the United States Army; serviceman. **1,2** *adj.*, **3** *n.*, *pl.* **GI's** or **G.I.'s** (jē′īz′).

gi ant (jī′ənt), **1** an imaginary being having human form, but larger and more powerful than a person. **2** person or thing of great size, strength, or importance. **3** like a giant; huge: *a giant potato.* **1,2** *n.*, **3** *adj.*

gi ant ess (jī′ən tis), a female giant. *n.*

giant sequoia, a very large evergreen tree of California; big tree. Though not as tall as the largest redwoods, giant sequoias are the most massive trees in the world, with trunks up to 100 feet (30.5 meters) in circumference.

gib ber (jib′ər), **1** chatter senselessly; talk in a confused, meaningless way: *The monkeys gibbered angrily at each other.* **2** senseless chattering. **1** *v.*, **2** *n.*

gib ber ish (jib′ər ish), senseless chatter; confused, meaningless talk or writing. *n.*

gib bet (jib′it), **1** an upright post with a projecting arm at the top, from which the bodies of criminals were hung after execution. **2** hang on a gibbet. **3** hold up to public scorn or ridicule. **4** gallows. **5** put to death by hanging. **1,4** *n.*, **2,3,5** *v.*

gibbon—about 3 ft. (1 m.) tall

gib bon (gib′ən), a small ape of southeastern Asia and the East Indies that has very long arms and no tail. Gibbons live in trees. *n.*

gib bous (gib′əs), curved out; humped. A gibbous moon is more than half full but less than full. *adj.* —**gib′bous ly,** *adv.* —**gib′bous ness,** *n.*

gibe (jīb), **1** speak in a sneering way; jeer; scoff; sneer: *My family gibed at my efforts to paint a picture.* **2** a jeer; taunt; sneer: *Their gibes hurt her feelings.* **1** *v.*, **gibed, gib ing; 2** *n.* Also, **jibe.** —**gib′er,** *n.* —**gib′ing ly,** *adv.*

gib let (jib′lit), the heart, liver, or gizzard of a fowl. *n.*

Gi bral tar (jə brôl′tər), **1** seaport and fortress on the Mediterranean Sea, near the S tip of Spain. It is a British colony. **2 Rock of,** the large rock on which this fortress stands. **3 Strait of,** strait between Africa and Europe, connecting the Mediterranean Sea with the Atlantic. *n.*

gid di ly (gid′ə lē), in a giddy manner. *adv.*

gid di ness (gid′ē nis), giddy condition or quality. *n.*

gid dy (gid′ē), **1** having a whirling feeling in one's head; dizzy: *It makes me giddy to go on a merry-go-round.* **2** likely to make dizzy; causing dizziness: *a giddy ride on a roller coaster.* **3** never serious; frivolous; fickle: *That giddy crowd thinks only of parties.* *adj.*, **gid di er, gid di est.** [*Giddy* is from Old English *gydig,* meaning "mad, possessed (by an evil spirit)," which comes from *god,* meaning "a god."]

gift (gift), **1** something given freely; present: *a birthday gift, the gift of a million dollars to a university.* **2** act of

giving freely: *The land came to her by gift from an aunt.*
3 natural ability; special talent: *A great artist must have a gift for painting. n.*

gift ed (gif′tid), having natural ability or special talent; unusually able: *a gifted musician. adj.*

gift-wrap (gift′rap′), wrap (a parcel or gift) in fancy paper and with decorative trimmings. *v.,* **gift-wrapped, gift-wrap ping.**

gig[1] (gig), **1** a light, open, two-wheeled carriage drawn by one horse. **2** a long, light ship's boat moved by oars or sails. *n.*

gig[2] (gig), **1** a fish spear. **2** spear (fish) with a gig. 1 *n.,* 2 *v.,* **gigged, gig ging.**

gi gan tic (jī gan′tik), big like a giant; huge: *An elephant is a gigantic animal. adj.* —**gi gan′ti cal ly,** *adv.*

gig gle (gig′əl), **1** laugh in a silly or undignified way. **2** a silly or undignified laugh. 1 *v.,* **gig gled, gig gling;** 2 *n.* —**gig′gler,** *n.* —**gig′gling ly,** *adv.*

gig gly (gig′lē), having the habit of giggling. *adj.*

Gi la monster (hē′lə), a large, poisonous lizard of the southwestern United States and northern Mexico. It has a thick tail, a heavy, clumsy body, and is covered with beadlike, orange-and-black scales.

gild (gild), **1** cover with a thin layer of gold or similar material; make golden. **2** make (something) look bright and pleasing. **3** make (something) seem better than it is. *v.,* **gild ed** or **gilt, gild ing.**

gill[1] (gil), part of the body of a fish, tadpole, or crab by which it breathes in water. Oxygen passes in and carbon dioxide passes out through the thin walls of the gills. *n.*

gill[2] (jil), a small measure for liquids, equal to one fourth of a pint, or about half a cup. *n.*

gilt (gilt), **1** a thin layer of gold or similar material with which a surface is gilded: *The gilt is coming off this frame.* **2** gilded: *a gilt sword.* **3** a past tense and a past participle of **gild.** 1 *n.,* 2 *adj.,* 3 *v.*

gim crack (jim′krak′), a showy, useless trifle; knickknack. *n.*

gim crack er y (jim′krak′ər ē), gimcracks collectively. *n., pl.* **gim crack er ies.**

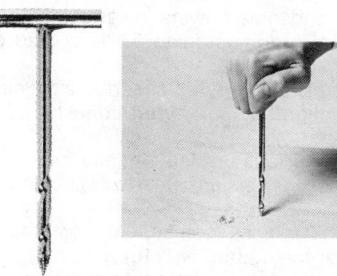

gimlet

gim let (gim′lit), a small tool with a screw point, for boring holes. *n.*

gim mick (gim′ik), SLANG. a clever or tricky idea, stunt, or device. *n.*

gin[1] (jin), a strong alcoholic drink, distilled from grain and usually flavored with juniper berries. *n.*

gin[2] (jin), **1** cotton gin. **2** separate (cotton) from its seeds. 1 *n.,* 2 *v.,* **ginned, gin ning.** —**gin′ner,** *n.*

gin[3] (jin), gin rummy. *n.*

gin ger (jin′jər), **1** spice made from the root of a tropical plant. The root is often preserved in syrup or candied. **2** INFORMAL. liveliness; energy. *n.*

ginger ale, a bubbling drink flavored with ginger. It contains no alcohol.

ginger beer, drink similar to ginger ale, but made with fermenting ginger.

gin ger bread (jin′jər bred′), **1** cake flavored with gin-

ger and sweetened with molasses. Gingerbread is often made in fancy shapes. **2** something showy and elaborate; tasteless ornamentation. Cheap carvings glued on furniture are gingerbread. **3** showy; gaudy. Gingerbread work on a house is fussy ornamentation. 1,2 *n.,* 3 *adj.*

gin ger ly (jin′jər lē), **1** with extreme care or caution. **2** extremely cautious or wary. 1 *adv.,* 2 *adj.* —**gin′ger li ness,** *n.*

gin ger snap (jin′jər snap′), a thin, crisp cookie flavored with ginger and sweetened with molasses. *n.*

ging ham (ging′əm), a cotton cloth made from colored threads. Its patterns are usually in stripes, plaids, or checks. *n.*

gink go (ging′ko), a large, ornamental tree native to China and Japan, with fan-shaped leaves and nuts that can be eaten. *n., pl.* **gink goes.**

gin rummy, a card game like rummy, usually played by two persons.

gin seng (jin′seng), a low plant of China and North America, with a thick, branched root much used in medicine by the Chinese. *n.*

Giot to (jot′ō), 1266?-1337, Italian painter and architect whose works mark the beginning of the Renaissance in painting. *n.*

gip sy (jip′sē), gypsy. *n., pl.* **gip sies;** *adj.*

gi raffe (jə raf′), a large African mammal that chews its cud and has hoofs, a very long neck, long legs, and a spotted skin. Giraffes are the tallest living animals. *n.* [*Giraffe* is from Italian *giraffa,* which comes from Arabic *zarāfah.*]

gird (gėrd), **1** put a belt, cord, etc., around. **2** fasten with a belt, cord, etc.: *gird on one's sword.* **3** surround; enclose. **4** get ready: *She girded herself to face the final examination. v.,* **gird ed** or **girt, gird ing.**

gird er (gėr′dər), a horizontal beam of steel, concrete, or wood, used as a main support. The weight of a floor is usually supported by girders. A tall building or big bridge often has steel girders for its frame. *n.*

girder—man walking across a girder

gir dle (gėr′dl), **1** belt, sash, cord, etc., worn around the waist. **2** anything that surrounds or encloses: *a girdle of trees around the pond.* **3** a light corset worn about the hips or waist. **4** put a girdle on or around. **5** surround; encircle: *Wide roads girdle the city.* **6** cut away the bark so as to make a ring around (a tree, branch, etc.). 1-3 *n.,* 4-6 *v.,* **gir dled, gir dling.** —**gir′dler,** *n.*

girl (gėrl), **1** a female child from birth to about eighteen. **2** a young, unmarried woman. **3** a female servant. This

---

meaning of *girl* is often considered offensive. **4** INFOR-
MAL. sweetheart. **5** INFORMAL. woman. *n.*

girl friend (gėrl/frend/), INFORMAL. **1** boy's sweetheart
or steady female companion. **2** a female friend. *n.*

girl hood (gėrl/hůd), time of being a girl. *n.*

girl ish (gėr/lish), **1** of a girl. **2** like a girl. **3** like a girl's;
suitable for a girl. *adj.* —**girl/ish ly,** *adv.* —**girl/ish-
ness,** *n.*

girl scout, member of the Girl Scouts.

Girl Scouts, organization for girls that seeks to develop character, citizenship, usefulness to others, and various skills.

girt (gėrt), girded; a past tense and a past participle of
gird. *v.*

girth (gėrth), **1** the measure around anything: *a man of
large girth, the girth of a tree.* **2** strap or band that keeps a
saddle, pack, etc., in place on a horse's back. *n.*

Gi scard d'Es taing (zhē skär/ des tang/), **Valéry,**
born 1926, president of France from 1974 to 1981.

gis mo (giz/mō), gizmo. *n.,* *pl.* **gis mos.**

gist (jist), the essential part; real point; main idea; substance of a longer statement: *The gist of the discussion
was that we should build a new school. n.*

give (giv), **1** hand over as a gift; make a present of: *My
parents gave me ice skates for my birthday.* **2** hand over:
Give me that pencil. **3** hand over in return for something;
pay: *She gave three dollars for the wagon.* **4** let have; cause
to have: *She gave us permission to go. Don't give me any
trouble.* **5** deal; administer: *give medicine, give hard blows.*
6 offer; present: *give a lecture. This newspaper gives a full
story of the game.* **7** put forth; utter: *He gave a cry of pain.*
8 yield; furnish; supply: *Lamps give light.* **9** yield to force:
The lock gave when they pushed hard against the door. **10** a
yielding to force. 1-9 *v.,* **gave, giv en, giv ing;** 10 *n.*

give away, 1 give as a present: *He gave away his best
toy.* **2** present (a bride) to a bridegroom at a wedding.
3 cause to be known; reveal; betray: *The spy gave away
secrets to the enemy.*

give back, return: *Give back the book.*

give in, stop fighting and admit defeat; yield: *A stubborn
person will not give in easily even when wrong.*

give it to, INFORMAL. punish or scold.

give off, send out; put forth: *This lamp gives off a very
bright light.*

give out, 1 send out; put forth. **2** distribute: *The supplies
will be given out tomorrow.* **3** make known: *Who has given
out this information?* **4** become used up or worn out: *My
strength gave out after the long climb.*

give over, 1 hand over; deliver. **2** set aside for a certain
purpose.

give up, 1 hand over; deliver; surrender. **2** stop having
or doing: *We gave up the search when it got dark.* **3** stop
trying: *Don't give up so soon.* **4** have no more hope for.

give-and-take (giv/ən tāk/), **1** an even or fair exchange.
2 good-natured banter; exchange of talk. *n.*

give a way (giv/ə wā/), INFORMAL. **1** something revealed
or made known unintentionally. **2** something given away
or sold at a cheap price to promote business or good
relations. *n.*

giv en (giv/ən), **1** that has been stated; fixed; specified:
You must finish the test in a given time. **2** having a fondness or habit; inclined; disposed: *A braggart is given to
boasting.* **3** past participle of **give.** *That book was given to
me.* 1,2 *adj.,* 3 *v.*

given name, name given to a person in addition to a
family name. *Judith is the given name of Judith Stein.*

giv er (giv/ər), person who gives. *n.*

giz mo (giz/mō), SLANG. a gadget; device. *n.,* *pl.* **giz mos.**
Also, **gismo.**

giz zard (giz/ərd), a bird's second stomach, where the

food from the first stomach is ground up. The gizzard
usually contains bits of sand or gravel. *n.*

Gk., Greek.

gla cial (glā/shəl), **1** of ice or glaciers; having much ice
or many glaciers. **2** like ice; very cold; icy. *adj.* —**gla/-
cial ly,** *adv.*

glacier—a glacier in the state of Washington

gla cier (glā/shər), a large mass of ice moving very
slowly down a mountain or along a valley, or spreading
slowly over a large area of land. Glaciers are formed
over many years from snow on high ground wherever
winter snowfall exceeds summer melting. *n.*

glad (glad), **1** feeling joy, pleasure, or satisfaction; happy; pleased: *I am glad to see you.* **2** bringing joy; pleasant: *The glad news made us happy.* **3** willing; ready: *I will
be glad to go if you need me. adj.,* **glad der, glad dest.**
—**glad/ly,** *adv.* —**glad/ness,** *n.*

glad den (glad/n), make or become glad. *v.*

glade (glād), a little open space in a wood or forest. *n.*

glad i a tor (glad/ē ā/tər), slave, captive, or paid fighter
who fought at the public shows in the arenas in ancient
Rome. *n.* [*Gladiator* was borrowed from Latin *gladiator,*
which comes from *gladius,* meaning "sword."]

glad i o la (glad/ē ō/lə), gladiolus. *n.,* *pl.* **glad i o las.**

glad i o lus (glad/ē ō/ləs), plant that grows from bulblike, underground stems and has sword-shaped leaves
and spikes of large, handsome flowers in various colors.
It is a kind of iris. *n.,* *pl.* **glad i o li** (glad/ē ō/lē or glad/ē-
ō/lī), **glad i o lus es.**

glad some (glad/səm), **1** glad; joyful; cheerful. **2** causing
gladness; pleasant; delightful. *adj.* —**glad/some ly,** *adv.*
—**glad/some ness,** *n.*

glam or (glam/ər), mysterious fascination; alluring
charm; magic attraction: *the glamor of circus life. n.* Also,
glamour.

glam or ize (glam/ə rīz/), make (someone or something)
glamorous. *v.,* **glam or ized, glam or iz ing.**

glam or ous (glam/ər əs), full of glamor; fascinating;
charming: *a glamorous job in a foreign city. adj.* —**glam/-
or ous ly,** *adv.* —**glam/or ous ness,** *n.*

glam our (glam/ər), glamor. *n.*

glance (glans), **1** a quick look: *She gave him only a
glance.* **2** look quickly: *He glanced out of the window to see
if the rain had stopped.* **3** a flash of light; gleam. **4** flash
with light; gleam. **5** hit and go off at a slant: *The spear
glanced against the wall and missed the target.* **6** a glancing
off; slanting movement. 1,3,6 *n.,* 2,4,5 *v.,* **glanced,
glanc ing.**

gland (gland), organ in the body which separates materials from the blood and changes them into some secretion for use in the body or into a product to be discharged from the body. The salivary glands make saliva.
The liver, the kidneys, the pancreas, and the thyroid are
glands. *n.* —**gland/like/,** *adj.*

glan du lar (glan/jə lər), of or like a gland; having

glands; made up of glands. *adj.* —**glan′du lar ly,** *adv.*

glare (gler *or* glar), **1** a strong, bright light; light that shines so brightly that it hurts the eyes. **2** give off a strong, bright light; shine so brightly as to hurt the eyes. **3** a bright, smooth surface. **4** bright and smooth. **5** a fierce, angry stare. **6** stare fiercely and angrily. 1,3,5 *n.*, 2,6 *v.*, **glared, glar ing;** 4 *adj.*

glar ing (gler′ing *or* glar′ing), **1** very bright; shining so brightly that it hurts the eyes; dazzling. **2** staring fiercely and angrily. **3** too bright and showy: *a shirt with glaring colors.* **4** very easily seen; conspicuous: *a glaring error in spelling. adj.* —**glar′ing ly,** *adv.*

glar y (gler′ē *or* glar′ē), dazzling; glaring. *adj.*, **glar i er, glar i est.**

Glas gow (glas′gō *or* glas′kō), the largest city and chief seaport in Scotland. *n.*

glass (glas), **1** a hard substance that breaks easily and can usually be seen through. It is made by melting sand with soda, potash, lime, or other substances. Windows are made of glass. **2** container to drink from made of glass: *I filled the glass with water.* **3** amount a glass can hold: *drink a glass of water.* **4** mirror: *Look at yourself in the glass.* **5** lens, telescope, thermometer, windowpane, or other thing made of glass. **6 glasses,** *pl.* eyeglasses. **7** made of glass: *a glass dish.* **8** cover or protect with glass. 1-6 *n., pl.* **glass es;** 7 *adj.,* 8 *v.* [*Glass* comes from Old English *glæs.*] —**glass′like′,** *adj.*

glass blowing

glass blowing, art or process of shaping glass objects by blowing air from the mouth through a tube into a blob of molten glass at the other end of the tube. —**glass blower.**

glass ful (glas′fůl), as much as a glass holds. *n., pl.* **glass fuls.**

glass i ness (glas′ē nis), glassy appearance or condition. *n.*

glass snake, a limbless, snakelike lizard whose tail breaks off easily.

glass ware (glas′wer′ *or* glas′war′), articles made of glass. *n.*

glass y (glas′ē), **1** like glass; smooth; easily seen through. **2** having a fixed, stupid stare: *glassy eyes. adj.,* **glass i er, glass i est.** —**glass′i ly,** *adv.*

glau co ma (glô kō′mə), disease of the eye common in old age in which increasing internal pressure causes damage resulting in a gradual loss of sight. *n.*

glaze (glāz), **1** put glass in; cover with glass. Pieces of glass cut to the right size are used to glaze windows and picture frames. **2** a smooth, glossy surface or coating: *the glaze on a china cup. A glaze of ice on the walk is dangerous.* **3** substance used to make such a surface or coating on things. **4** make a glossy or glassy surface on (china, food, etc.). **5** become glossy or glassy: *eyes glazed with fever.* 1,4,5 *v.,* **glazed, glaz ing;** 2,3 *n.* —**glaz′er,** *n.*

gla zier (glā′zhər), person whose work is putting glass in windows, picture frames, etc. *n.*

gleam (glēm), **1** a flash or beam of light: *We saw the gleam of headlights through the rain.* **2** to flash or beam with light: *The car's headlights gleamed through the rain.* **3** a short or faint light: *the gleam of a candle.* **4** send out a short or faint light: *A candle gleamed in the dark.* **5** a reflected light: *the gleam of polished silver.* **6** give off a reflected light: *The silver gleamed on the table.* **7** a short appearance; faint show: *a gleam of hope.* 1,3,5,7 *n.*, 2,4,6 *v.*

glean (glēn), **1** gather grain left on a field by reapers. **2** gather little by little: *I was able to glean some information from each book. v.* —**glean′er,** *n.*

glee (glē), a being merry and gay; lively joy; great delight: *They laughed with glee at the clown's antics. n.*

glee club, group organized for singing songs.

glee ful (glē′fəl), filled with glee; merry and gay; joyous. *adj.* —**glee′ful ly,** *adv.* —**glee′ful ness,** *n.*

glen (glen), a small, narrow valley. *n.*

Glenn (glen), **John,** born 1921, American astronaut and politician. He was the first American to orbit the earth, in 1962. *n.*

glib (glib), speaking or spoken too smoothly and easily: *No one believed their glib excuses. adj.,* **glib ber, glib best.** —**glib′ly,** *adv.* —**glib′ness,** *n.*

glide (glīd), **1** move along smoothly, evenly, and easily: *Birds, ships, dancers, and skaters glide.* **2** a smooth, even, easy movement. **3** pass gradually, quietly, or without being noticed: *The years glided past.* **4** come down slowly at a slant without using a motor. **5** a coming down in this way. 1,3,4 *v.,* **glid ed, glid ing;** 2,5 *n.*

glid er (glī′dər), **1** airplane without a motor. Rising air currents keep it up in the air. **2** a swinging seat suspended on a frame. Gliders are usually placed on porches or outdoors. *n.*

glim mer (glim′ər), **1** a faint, unsteady light. **2** shine with a faint, unsteady light: *The candle glimmered and went out.* **3** a faint idea or feeling: *The doctor's report gave us only a glimmer of hope.* 1,3 *n.,* 2 *v.*

glimpse (glimps), **1** a short, quick view or look: *I caught a glimpse of the falls as our train went by.* **2** catch a short, quick view of: *I glimpsed the falls as our train went by.* **3** look quickly; glance: *I glimpsed at the headlines, but I didn't read the paper.* **4** a short, faint appearance: *There was a glimpse of truth in what they said.* 1,4 *n.,* 2,3 *v.,* **glimpsed, glimps ing.**

glint (glint), **1** a gleam; flash: *The glint in her eye showed that she was angry.* **2** to gleam; flash. 1 *n.,* 2 *v.*

glis san do (gli sän′dō), (in music) part performed with a gliding effect. A pianist plays a glissando by running one finger rapidly over the white keys or the black keys on a piano. *n., pl.* **glis san di** (gli sän′dē), **glis san dos.**

glis ten (glis′n), **1** shine with a twinkling light; glitter; sparkle: *The stars glistened in the sky.* **2** a glitter; sparkle. 1 *v.,* 2 *n.*

glit ter (glit′ər), **1** shine with a bright, sparkling light: *The jewels glittered.* **2** a bright, sparkling light: *The glitter of the harsh lights hurt my eyes.* **3** be bright and showy. **4** brightness; showiness. 1,3 *v.,* 2,4 *n.*

glit ter y (glit′ər ē), glittering. *adj.*

gloam ing (glō′ming), evening twilight; dusk. *n.*

gloat (glōt), think about or gaze at with great satisfaction: *She gloated over her success. The miser gloated over his gold. v.* —**gloat′er,** *n.* —**gloat′ing ly,** *adv.*

a hat	i it	oi oil	ch child		a in about
ā age	ī ice	ou out	ng long		e in taken
ä far	o hot	u cup	sh she	ə =	i in pencil
e let	ō open	ů put	th thin		o in lemon
ē equal	ô order	ü rule	ŦH then		u in circus
ėr term			zh measure		

glob (glob), a shapeless mass; blob. *n.*

glob al (glō′bəl), **1** of the earth as a whole; worldwide: *the threat of global war.* **2** shaped like a globe: *a global map. adj.* —**glob′al ly,** *adv.*

globe (glōb), **1** anything round like a ball; sphere. **2** the earth; world. **3** sphere with a map of the earth or sky on it. **4** anything rounded like a globe. An electric light bulb is a globe. *n.*

glob u lar (glob′yə lər), **1** shaped like a globe or globule; round; spherical. **2** made up of globules. *adj.*

glob ule (glob′yül), a very small sphere or ball; tiny drop: *Globules of sweat stood out on the worker's forehead. n.*

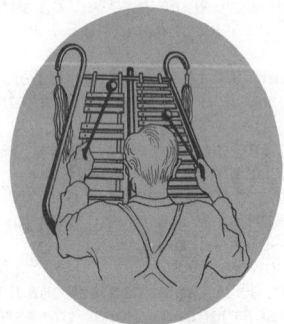

glockenspiel

glock en spiel (glok′ən spēl′), a percussion instrument made up of a series of tuned metal bells, bars, or tubes mounted in a frame and played by striking with two little hammers. *n.* [*Glockenspiel* was borrowed from German *Glockenspiel,* which comes from *Glocke,* meaning "bell," and *Spiel,* meaning "play."]

gloom (glüm), **1** deep shadow; darkness; dimness. **2** dark thoughts and feelings; low spirits; sadness. *n.*

gloom i ly (glü′mə lē), in a gloomy manner. *adv.*

gloom i ness (glü′mē nis), a being gloomy; gloom. *n.*

gloom y (glü′mē), **1** dark; dim: *a gloomy winter day.* **2** in low spirits; sad; melancholy: *a gloomy mood.* **3** causing low spirits; discouraging; dismal: *a gloomy scene of poverty. His views about the future are gloomy. adj.,* **gloom i er, gloom i est.**

glo ri a (glôr′ē ə), Gloria. *n., pl.* **glo ri as.**

Glo ri a (glôr′ē ə), **1** song of praise to God. **2** the music for it. *n., pl.* **Glo ri as.**

glo ri fi ca tion (glôr′ə fə kā′shən), a glorifying or a being glorified. *n.*

glo ri fy (glôr′ə fī), **1** give glory to; make glorious: *glorify a hero or a saint.* **2** to praise; worship: *singing hymns to glorify God.* **3** make more beautiful or splendid than it usually appears: *The sunset glorified the valley. v.,* **glo ri fied, glo ri fy ing.** —**glo′ri fi′er,** *n.*

glo ri ous (glôr′ē əs), **1** having or deserving glory; illustrious. **2** giving glory: *a glorious victory.* **3** magnificent; splendid: *a glorious day. adj.* —**glo′ri ous ly,** *adv.* —**glo′ri ous ness,** *n.*

glo ry (glôr′ē), **1** great praise and honor given to a person or thing by others; fame: *The heroic act won her glory.* **2** something that brings praise and honor; source of pride and joy: *America's great men and women are its glory.* **3** adoring praise and thanksgiving: *"Glory be to God on high!"* **4** be proud; rejoice: *The teachers gloried in their classes' achievements.* **5** brightness; splendor: *the glory of the royal palace.* **6** condition of greatest magnificence, splendor, or prosperity: *The British Empire reached its greatest glory in the 1800's, during the reign of Queen Victoria.* **7** heaven. 1-3,5-7 *n., pl.* **glo ries;** 4 *v.,* **glo ried, glo ry ing.** —**glo′ry ing ly,** *adv.*

go to glory, die.

in one's glory, having one's greatest satisfaction or enjoyment: *He is in his glory when he can perform before an audience.*

gloss (glôs), **1** a smooth, shiny surface; luster: *Varnished furniture has a gloss.* **2** put a smooth, shiny surface on. **3** an outward appearance or surface that covers wrong underneath. 1,3 *n.,* 2 *v.* —**gloss′er,** *n.* —**gloss′less,** *adj.*

gloss over, make (something) seem right even though it is really wrong; smooth over: *They tried to gloss over their mistakes.*

gloss., glossary.

glos sar y (glos′ər ē), list of special, technical, or hard words, usually in alphabetical order, with explanations or comments: *a glossary of terms used in chemistry. Textbooks sometimes have glossaries at the end. n., pl.* **glos sar ies.** [*Glossary* is from Latin *glossarium,* which comes from *glossa,* meaning "a hard word that needs to be explained."]

gloss i ness (glô′sē nis), glossy condition. *n.*

gloss y (glô′sē), smooth and shiny. *adj.,* **gloss i er, gloss i est.** —**gloss′i ly,** *adv.*

glot tis (glot′is), an opening at the upper part of the windpipe, between the vocal cords. *n., pl.* **glot tis es.**

Glouces ter (glos′tər), **1** city in SW England. **2** seaport and fishing center in NE Massachusetts. *n.*

glove (gluv), **1** a covering for the hand, usually with separate places for each of the four fingers and the thumb. Gloves are worn to keep the hands warm or clean. Boxers and baseball players use specially padded gloves for protection. **2** cover with a glove; provide with gloves. 1 *n.,* 2 *v.,* **gloved, glov ing.** —**glove′less,** *adj.* —**glove′like′,** *adj.*

glow (glō), **1** shine because of heat; be red-hot or white-hot: *Embers glowed in the fireplace after the fire had died down.* **2** the shine from something that is red-hot or white-hot: *the glow of embers in the fireplace.* **3** a similar shine without heat: *the glow of gold.* **4** give off light without heat: *The cat's eyes glowed in the dark.* **5** a bright, warm color; brightness: *the glow of sunset.* **6** the warm feeling or color of the body: *the glow of health on her cheeks.* **7** show a warm color; look warm; be red or bright: *His cheeks glowed as he skated.* **8** an eager look on the face: *a glow of excitement.* **9** look or be eager: *Their eyes glowed at the thought of a trip.* **10** warmth of feeling or passion; ardor: *The team was filled with the glow of success.* 1,4,7,9 *v.,* 2,3,5,6,8,10 *n.*

glower (def. 1)
He **glowered** at me as I passed.

glow er (glou′ər), **1** stare angrily; scowl fiercely. **2** an angry stare; fierce scowl. 1 *v.,* 2 *n.*

glow worm (glō′wėrm′), any insect larva or insect which glows in the dark. Fireflies develop from some glowworms. *n.*

glu cose (glü′kōs), **1** kind of sugar occurring in plant and animal tissues. Carbohydrates are present in the blood mainly in the form of glucose. Glucose is not as

sweet as cane sugar. **2** syrup made from starch. *n.*
[*Glucose* was borrowed from French *glucose*, which came
from Greek *gleukos*, meaning "sweet wine."]

glue (glü), **1** substance used to stick things together,
made by boiling the hoofs, skins, and bones of animals
in water. **2** any similar sticky substance made of casein,
rubber, etc.; adhesive. **3** stick together with glue. **4** fasten
tightly; attach firmly: *Her hands were glued to the steering
wheel as she drove down the dangerous mountain road.* **1,2**
n., **3,4** *v.,* **glued, glu ing. —glue′like′,** *adj.* **—glu′er,** *n.*

glue y (glü′ē), **1** like glue; sticky. **2** full of glue; smeared
with glue. *adj.,* **glu i er, glu i est. —glu′ey ness,** *n.*

glum (glum), gloomy; dismal; sullen: *I felt very glum
when my friend moved away. adj.,* **glum mer, glum mest.**
—glum′ly, *adv.* **—glum′ness,** *n.*

glut (glut), **1** fill full; feed or satisfy fully: *The children
glutted themselves with cake. A year of working aboard ship
glutted my appetite for adventure.* **2** supply more than there
is a demand for: *The prices for wheat dropped when the
market was glutted with it.* **3** too great a supply. **1,2** *v.,*
glut ted, glut ting; 3 *n.* **—glut′ting ly,** *adv.*

glu ten (glüt′n), a tough, sticky protein substance in the
flour of wheat and other grains. *n.*

glu ti nous (glüt′n əs), sticky. *adj.* **—glu′ti nous ly,** *adv.*
—glu′ti nous ness, *n.*

glut ton (glut′n), **1** a greedy eater; person who eats too
much: *Sometimes I go off my diet and eat like a glutton.*
2 person who never seems to have enough of something: *That boxer is a glutton for punishment. n.*

glut ton ous (glut′n əs), greedy about food; having the
habit of eating too much. *adj.* **—glut′ton ous ly,** *adv.*
—glut′ton ous ness, *n.*

glut ton y (glut′n ē), excess in eating. *n., pl.* **glut ton ies.**

glyc er in or **glyc er ine** (glis′ər ən), a colorless, syrupy, sweet liquid obtained from fats and oils. Glycerin is
used in ointments, lotions, antifreeze solutions, and explosives. *n.*

glyc e rol (glis′ə rōl′ *or* glis′ə rol′), glycerin. *n.*

gly co gen (glī′kə jən), a starchlike carbohydrate stored
in the liver and other animal tissues. It is changed into
glucose when needed. *n.*

gm., gram or grams.

G-man (jē′man′), INFORMAL. a special agent of the United States Department of Justice; agent of the FBI. *n., pl.*
G-men.

Gmc or **Gmc.,** Germanic.

GMT or **G.M.T.,** Greenwich mean time.

gnarl (närl), knot in wood; hard, rough lump: *Wood with
gnarls is hard to cut. n.*

gnarled (närld), containing gnarls; knotted; twisted: *The
farmer's gnarled hands grasped the plow firmly. adj.*

gnash (nash), strike or grind together: *I gnashed my teeth
in rage. v.* **—gnash′ing ly,** *adv.*

gnat (nat), any of various small, two-winged flies. Most
gnats suck blood and give bites that itch. *n.* [*Gnat* comes
from Old English *gnætt.*] **—gnat′like′,** *adj.*

gnaw (nô), **1** bite at and wear away: *to gnaw a bone. A
mouse has gnawed the cover of this box.* **2** make by biting:
A rat can gnaw a hole through wood. **3** trouble; harass;
torment: *A feeling of guilt gnawed at the prisoner's conscience day and night. v.,* **gnawed, gnawed** *or* **gnawn**
(nôn), **gnaw ing. —gnaw′a ble,** *adj.* **—gnaw′er,** *n.*

gneiss (nīs), a very dense rock which occurs in layers
and is composed of quartz and feldspar and any of
several other minerals. *n.*

gnome (nōm), (in folklore) a dwarf supposed to live in
the earth and guard treasures of precious metals and
stones. *n.*

gnu (nü *or* nyü), a large African antelope with an oxlike
head, curved horns, and a long tail. *n., pl.* **gnus** or **gnu.**

a hat	**i** it	**oi** oil	**ch** child	⎧ a in about
ā age	**ī** ice	**ou** out	**ng** long	⎜ e in taken
ä far	**o** hot	**u** cup	**sh** she	ə = ⎨ i in pencil
e let	**ō** open	**ù** put	**th** thin	⎜ o in lemon
ē equal	**ô** order	**ü** rule	**ŦH** then	⎩ u in circus
ėr term			**zh** measure	

go (gō), **1** move along: *Cars go on the road.* **2** move away;
leave: *Don't go yet.* **3** be in motion or action; act; work;
run: *Electricity makes the washing machine go.* **4** get to be;
become: *go mad.* **5** be habitually; be: *go hungry for a
week.* **6** proceed; advance: *go to New York.* **7** take part in
the activity of: *to go skiing, go swimming.* **8** put oneself:
Don't go to any trouble for me. **9** extend; reach: *Does your
memory go back that far?* **10** pass: *Summer had gone. Vacation goes quickly.* **11** be given: *First prize goes to you.*
12 be sold: *The painting goes to the highest bidder.* **13** turn
out; have a certain result: *How did the game go?* **14** have
its place; belong: *This book goes on the top shelf.* **15** make
a certain sound: *The cork went "pop!"* **16** have certain
words; be said: *How does that song go?* **17** break down;
give way; fail: *My grandfather's eyesight is going. The engine in the old car finally went.* **18** INFORMAL. try; attempt;
chance: *Let's have another go at this problem.* **19** something successful; a success: *She made a go of the new
store.* **20** INFORMAL. in perfect order and ready to proceed: *All systems are go for the rocket launching.* **1-17** *v.,*
went, gone, go ing; 18,19 *n., pl.* **goes; 20** *adj.* **—go′er,** *n.*

go about, 1 be busy at; work on: *She went about her work
with energy.* **2** turn around; change direction.

go along, cooperate: *The club members decided to go
along with the president's recommendation.*

go around, satisfy everyone; give some for all: *There
were enough apples and nuts to go around.*

go at, 1 attack: *I went at the dog with a stick.* **2** take in
hand with energy; work at: *Let's go at this problem in a
different way.*

go back on, INFORMAL. not be faithful or loyal to; betray:
She went back on her promise.

go by, 1 pass: *We went by that store often. He let the insult
go by.* **2** be guided by; follow: *Go by what she says.* **3** be
known by: *He goes by the name of Smith.*

go down, 1 descend; decline; sink: *The wrecked ship went
down.* **2** be defeated; lose: *Their team went down as a result of our superior playing.*

go for, 1 try to get: *Our athletes went for the gold medal.*
2 favor; support: *The public goes for her ideas.* **3** INFORMAL.
attack: *That dog goes for anyone who gets near it.*

go in for, INFORMAL. take part in; spend time and energy
at: *Our whole family goes in for touch football.*

go into, 1 enter into a condition, activity, or occupation:
to go into a rage. She went into law. **2** be contained in:
How many pints go into a gallon? **3** investigate: *The police
have gone into the case and made an arrest.*

go off, 1 leave; depart: *My sister has gone off to college.*
2 be fired; explode: *The pistol went off unexpectedly.*
3 take place; happen: *The picnic went off as planned.*
4 start to ring; sound: *The alarm went off at 6:30 a.m.*

go on, 1 go ahead; continue: *After a pause she went on*

gnu—about 4½ ft.
(1.5 m.) high at
the shoulder

reading. **2** happen: *What goes on here?* **3** behave: *You shouldn't go on in this manner.*

go out, 1 go to a party, show, etc.: *We had a very good time when we went out Saturday night.* **2** stop burning: *Don't let the candle go out.*

go over, 1 look at carefully: *go over a problem.* **2** do or read again; repeat: *I went over the explanation several times. Go over the poem till you memorize it.* **3** INFORMAL. succeed: *The play went over very well and became a hit.*

go through, 1 go to the end of; do all of: *Let's go through the rehearsal without any interruption.* **2** undergo; experience: *I went through a serious operation.* **3** search: *Going through his pockets he found the missing key.* **4** be accepted or approved: *The new schedule did not go through.*

go through with, carry out to the end; complete: *The contractor went through with his bargain to build the house in three months.*

go together, 1 harmonize; match: *These colors go together.* **2** keep steady company as sweethearts: *That couple has been going together for a long time.*

go under, be ruined; fail: *Poor management caused the business to go under.*

go up, 1 rise; ascend: *The thermometer is going up.* **2** increase: *The price of milk has gone up.*

go with, 1 go steadily with; accompany: *The girl he had gone with moved out of town.* **2** belong with; go well with: *Cheese goes with salad.*

go without, do without; not have: *You can eat what is on the table or go without.*

let go, 1 allow to escape: *Let me go.* **2** give up one's hold: *Let go of my shirt.*

let oneself go, 1 give way to one's feelings or desires: *He is much too shy to let himself go.* **2** fail to keep oneself in good condition: *The coach warned the team not to let themselves go during vacation.*

no go, INFORMAL. useless; worthless: *I knew that the idea would be no go from the start.*

on the go, INFORMAL. busily occupied; active or restless: *Some people are always on the go.*

to go, INFORMAL. to be eaten outside, rather than within, a restaurant: *two pizzas to go.*

goblet

goad (gōd), **1** a sharp-pointed stick for driving cattle. **2** anything which drives or urges one on. **3** drive or urge on; act as a goad to: *Hunger can goad a person to steal.* **1,2** *n.,* **3** *v.* —**goad′like′,** *adj.*

go-a head (gō′ə hed′), INFORMAL. permission to go ahead or begin: *The train engineer got the go-ahead from the signal tower. n.*

goal (gōl), **1** place where a race ends. **2** place to which players try to advance a ball or puck in certain games in order to make a score. **3** score or points won by reaching this place. **4** something for which an effort is made; something desired: *The goal of her ambition was to be a scientist. n.* —**goal′less,** *adj.*

goal ie (gō′lē), goalkeeper. *n.*

goal keep er (gōl′kē′pər), player who tries to prevent the ball or puck from crossing the goal in certain games. *n.*

goal post, one of a pair of posts with a bar across them, forming a goal in football, soccer, etc.

goat (gōt), **1** a lively, cud-chewing mammal with hollow horns and usually a beard. Goats are closely related to sheep but are stronger, less timid, and more active than sheep. They are raised for their milk and their hides. **2** INFORMAL. person made to take the blame or suffer for the mistakes of others; scapegoat. *n., pl.* **goats** or **goat.** —**goat′like′,** *adj.*

get one's goat, INFORMAL. make a person angry or annoyed; tease a person.

goatee

goat ee (gō tē′), a pointed beard on a man's chin. *n.*

goat herd (gōt′hėrd′), person who tends goats. *n.*

goat skin (gōt′skin′), **1** skin of a goat. **2** leather made from it. **3** container made from this leather, used especially for holding wine. *n.*

gob¹ (gob), SLANG. sailor in the United States Navy. *n.*

gob² (gob), lump; mass. *n.*

gob ble¹ (gob′əl), eat fast and greedily; swallow quickly in big pieces. *v.,* **gob bled, gob bling.**

gobble up, INFORMAL. seize upon eagerly.

gob ble² (gob′əl), **1** make the throaty sound of a male turkey or a sound like it. **2** the throaty sound that a male turkey makes. **1** *v.,* **gob bled, gob bling; 2** *n.*

gob ble dy gook or **gob ble de gook** (gob′əl dē-gùk′), INFORMAL. speech or writing which is hard to understand because it is full of long, involved sentences and big words. *n.*

gob bler (gob′lər), a male turkey. *n.*

go-be tween (gō′bi twēn′), person who goes back and forth between others with messages, proposals, suggestions, etc. *n.*

Go bi (gō′bē), desert in E Asia. Most of it is in Mongolia. *n.* —**Go′bi an,** *adj.*

gob let (gob′lit), a drinking glass with a base and stem. *n.*

gob lin (gob′lən), (in folklore) a mischievous spirit or elf in the form of an ugly-looking dwarf. *n.*

go cart or **go-cart** (gō′kärt′), a low seat on wheels to take a small child around on. *n.*

god (god), **1** a being thought to have supernatural or superhuman powers and considered worthy of worship. **2** likeness or image of a god; idol. **3** person or thing greatly admired and respected or thought of as very important: *Wealth and power are his gods. n.*

God (god), the Supreme Being worshiped in most religions as the maker and ruler of the world. *n.* [*God* comes from Old English *god.*]

god child (god′chīld′), child whom a grown-up person sponsors at its baptism. *n., pl.* **god chil dren** (god′chil′-drən).

god daugh ter (god/dô/tər), a female godchild. *n.*

god dess (god/is), **1** a female god. **2** a very beautiful or charming woman. *n., pl.* **god dess es.**

god fa ther (god/fä/ᴛʜər), man who sponsors a child when it is baptized. *n.*

god head (god/hed/), **1** divine nature; divinity. **2 God-head,** God. *n.*

god less (god/lis), **1** not believing in God; not religious. **2** ungodly; wicked; evil. *adj.* —**god/less ness,** *n.*

god like (god/līk/), **1** like God or a god; divine. **2** suitable for God or a god. *adj.* —**god/like/ness,** *n.*

god li ness (god/lē nis), a being religious; obedience to God's laws; piety; righteousness. *n.*

god ly (god/lē), obeying, loving, and fearing God; religious; pious. *adj.*, **god li er, god li est.**

god moth er (god/muᴛʜ/ər), woman who sponsors a child when it is baptized. *n.*

god par ent (god/per/ənt *or* god/par/ənt), godfather or godmother. *n.*

god send (god/send/), something unexpected and very welcome, as if sent from God; sudden piece of good luck: *The money I received on my birthday was a godsend. n.*

god son (god/sun/), a male godchild. *n.*

God speed (god/spēd/), a wish of success to a person starting on a journey or undertaking. *n.*

goes (gōz), a present tense of go. *He goes to school. v.*

Goe the (gėr/tə), **Johann Wolfgang von,** 1749-1832, German poet, prose writer, and dramatist. *n.*

go-get ter (gō/get/ər), ɪɴꜰᴏʀᴍᴀʟ. an energetic and ambitious person. *n.*

gog gle (gog/əl), **1** roll one's eyes; stare with bulging eyes: *The children goggled at the magician pulling a rabbit out of the empty hat.* **2** rolling; bulging: *A frog has goggle eyes.* **3 goggles,** *pl.* large, close-fitting eyeglasses to protect the eyes from light or dust. 1 *v.*, **gog gled, gog-gling;** 2 *adj.*, 3 *n.*

gog gle-eyed (gog/əl īd/), having rolling, bulging, or staring eyes. *adj.*

Gogh (gō). See **Van Gogh.** *n.*

go ing (gō/ing), **1** a going away; leaving: *Her going was very sudden.* **2** moving; acting; working; running: *Set the clock going.* **3** condition of the ground or road for walking or riding: *The going is bad on a muddy road.* **4** that goes well; operating with success: *Her new business is a going concern.* 1,3 *n.*, 2,4 *adj.*

be going to, will; be about to: *It is going to rain soon.*

go ings-on (gō/ingz on/), actions or events: *the goings-on at the convention. n.pl.*

goi ter *or* **goi tre** (goi/tər), enlargement of the thyroid gland which is often seen as a large swelling in the front of the neck. A goiter is usually caused by a diet with too little iodine. *n.*

gold (gōld), **1** a shiny, bright-yellow, precious metallic element which resists rust and other chemical changes and can easily be drawn out into fine wire or hammered into thin sheets. Gold is used chiefly for making coins and jewelry. **2** coins made of gold. **3** money in large sums; wealth; riches. **4** made of gold: *a gold watch.* **5** of or like gold. **6** a bright yellow. **7** bright-yellow. 1-3,6 *n.*, 4,5,7 *adj.* —**gold/less,** *adj.*

gold brick (gōld/brik/), ɪɴꜰᴏʀᴍᴀʟ. **1** avoid duties by any evasion or excuse, such as pretended illness. **2** person, especially in the armed forces, who avoids duty or shirks work. 1 *v.*, 2 *n.* —**gold/brick/er,** *n.*

Gold Coast, region in W Africa, a former British colony, now largely included in Ghana.

gold en (gōl/dən), **1** made of gold: *a golden medal.* **2** shining like gold; bright-yellow: *golden hair.* **3** very good; excellent; extremely favorable, valuable, or impor-

tant: *a golden opportunity.* **4** very happy and prosperous; flourishing: *a golden age. adj.* —**gold/en ness,** *n.*

Golden Fleece, (in Greek legends) a fleece of gold taken from a ram. It was guarded by a dragon until Jason carried it away with the help of Medea.

Golden Gate, strait forming the entrance to San Francisco Bay from the Pacific.

golden mean, avoidance of extremes; sensible way of doing things.

gold en rod (gōl/dən rod/), plant related to the aster, which blooms in the late summer or early autumn and has many small, yellow flowers on tall, slender stalks. *n.*

golden rule, rule of conduct which states that you should treat others as you would have them treat you.

gold-filled (gōld/fild/), made of cheap metal covered with a layer of gold. *adj.*

gold finch (gōld/finch/), **1** a small American songbird. The male is yellow marked with black. **2** a European songbird with a patch of yellow on its wings. *n., pl.* **gold finch es.**

gold fish (gōld/fish/), a small, usually reddish-golden fish, often kept in garden pools or in glass bowls indoors. *n., pl.* **gold fish es** *or* **gold fish.**

gold leaf, gold beaten into very thin sheets, used in gilding.

gold rush, a sudden rush of people to a place where gold has just been found.

gold smith (gōld/smith/), person who makes or sells things made of gold. *n.*

Gold smith (gōld/smith/), **Oliver,** 1730?-1774, British poet, novelist, and dramatist. *n.*

golf (golf), **1** game played on an outdoor course with a small, hard ball and a set of long-handled clubs having wooden or iron heads. The player tries to hit the ball into each of a series of holes with as few strokes as possible. **2** play this game. 1 *n.*, 2 *v.* —**golf/er,** *n.*

Gol go tha (gol/gə thə), (in the Bible) the place of Christ's crucifixion; Calvary. *n.*

Go li ath (gə lī/əth), (in the Bible) a giant whom David killed with a stone from a sling. *n.*

gol ly (gol/ē), exclamation of wonder, pleasure, joy, etc. *interj.*

Go mor rah *or* **Go mor rha** (gə môr/ə), (in the Bible) a wicked city destroyed, together with Sodom, by fire from heaven. *n.*

go nad (gō/nad), organ in which reproductive cells develop in the male or female. Ovaries and testicles are gonads. *n.*

gon do la (gon/dl ə), **1** a long, narrow boat with a high peak at each end, used on the canals of Venice. **2** a

gondola
(def. 1)

railroad freight car which has low sides and no top.
3 car which hangs under an airship and holds the passengers, instruments, etc. *n., pl.* **gon do las.**

gon do lier (gon′dl ir′), person who rows or poles a gondola. *n.*

gone (gôn), **1** away: *The students are gone on their vacation.* **2** dead: *Great-grandmother is gone now.* **3** used up; consumed: *Is all the candy gone?* **4** weak; faint: *Not eating all day gave me a gone feeling.* **5** past participle of **go.** *They have gone far away.* 1-4 *adj.,* 5 *v.*

far gone, much advanced; deeply involved: *The business was far gone in debt and could not be saved.*

gon er (gô′nər), INFORMAL. person or thing that is dead, ruined, or past help. *n.*

gong (gông), a large piece of metal shaped like a bowl or a saucer which makes a loud noise when struck. *n.* [*Gong* was borrowed from Malay *gong.*]

gon or rhe a or **gon or rhoe a** (gon′ə rē′ə), a contagious venereal disease caused by a particular type of bacteria, resulting in inflammation of the genital and urinary organs. *n.*

goo (gü), SLANG. thick, sticky matter. *n.*

goo ber (gü′bər), INFORMAL. (in the southern United States) a peanut. *n.* [*Goober* comes from a west African word *nguba.*]

good (gud), **1** having high quality; superior: *a good piece of work.* **2** as it ought to be; right; proper; satisfactory: *good health, good weather. Do what seems good to you.* **3** well-behaved: *a good girl.* **4** kind; friendly: *Say a good word for me.* **5** desirable: *a good book for children.* **6** honorable; worthy: *my good friend, a good reputation.* **7** reliable; dependable: *good judgment.* **8** real; genuine: *It is hard to tell counterfeit money from good money.* **9** agreeable; pleasant: *Have a good time.* **10** beneficial; advantageous; useful: *drugs good for a fever.* **11** benefit; advantage; use: *work for the common good.* **12** satisfying; enough; full: *a good meal.* **13** skillful; clever: *a good manager, be good at arithmetic.* **14** fairly great; more than a little: *work a good while.* **15** that which is good: *find the good in people.* **16** that is good! 1-10,12-14 *adj.,* **bet ter, best;** 11,15 *n.,* 16 *interj.*

as good as, almost the same as; almost: *The game was as good as won.*

for good, forever; finally; permanently: *They have moved out for good.*

good and, very: *Get the water good and hot.*

good for, 1 able to do, live, or last: *Our car is good for another year.* **2** able to pay or contribute: *He is good for about $10.*

make good, 1 make up for; pay for: *The girls made good the damage they had done.* **2** fulfill; carry out: *Will you make good your promise?* **3** succeed in doing: *The soldiers made good their retreat.* **4** succeed: *She made good in business.* **5** prove: *Can you make good your accusation?*

to the good, on the side of profit or advantage; in one's favor: *By winning the second game our team is now two games to the good in the finals.*

good afternoon, form of greeting or farewell in the afternoon; hello or good-by.

Good all (gud′ôl), **Jane,** born 1934, English zoologist known for her research on primates. *n.*

good by (gud′bī′), good-by. *interj., n., pl.* **good bys.**

good-by (gud′bī′), farewell: *We say "Good-by" to friends when they go away. interj., n., pl.* **good-bys.**

good-bye (gud′bī′), good-by. *interj., n., pl.* **good-byes.**

good day, form of greeting or farewell; hello or good-by.

good evening, form of greeting or farewell in the evening; hello or good-by.

good-for-noth ing (gud′fər nuth′ing), **1** worthless; useless. **2** person who is worthless or useless. 1 *adj.,* 2 *n.*

Good Friday, the anniversary of Christ's crucifixion, observed on the Friday before Easter.

good-heart ed (gud′här′tid), kind and generous. *adj.* —**good′-heart′ed ly,** *adv.* —**good′-heart′ed ness,** *n.*

good-hu mored (gud′hyü′mərd), having good humor; cheerful; pleasant; amiable. *adj.* —**good′-hu′mored ly,** *adv.* —**good′-hu′mored ness,** *n.*

good-look ing (gud′luk′ing), having a pleasing appearance; handsome or pretty. *adj.*

good ly (gud′lē), **1** good-looking: *a goodly youth.* **2** considerable; rather large; fairly great: *a goodly quantity. adj.,* **good li er, good li est.** —**good′li ness,** *n.*

good man (gud′mən), OLD USE. **1** master of a household; husband. **2** title of respect for a man ranking below a gentleman: *Goodman Brown. n., pl.* **good men.**

good morning, form of greeting or farewell in the morning; hello or good-by.

good-na tured (gud′nā′chərd), having a pleasant disposition; kindly; cheerful; obliging. *adj.* —**good′-na′tured ly,** *adv.* —**good′-na′tured ness,** *n.*

good ness (gud′nis), **1** a being good; kindness. **2** exclamation of surprise: *My goodness!* 1 *n.,* 2 *interj.*

good night, form of farewell said at night.

goods (gudz), **1** personal property; belongings: *household goods.* **2** thing or things for sale; wares. **3** material for clothing; cloth. *n.pl.*

Good Samaritan, 1 (in the Bible) a traveler who rescued another traveler who had been beaten and robbed by thieves. **2** person who is unselfish in helping others.

Good Shepherd, Jesus.

good-sized (gud′sīzd′), somewhat large. *adj.*

good-tem pered (gud′tem′pərd), easy to get along with; cheerful; agreeable. *adj.* —**good′-tem′pered ly,** *adv.* —**good′-tem′pered ness,** *n.*

good turn, a kind or friendly act; favor.

good wife (gud′wīf′), OLD USE. **1** mistress of a household. **2** title of respect for a woman ranking below a lady: *Goodwife Brown. n., pl.* **good wives.**

good will (gud′wil′), **1** kindly or friendly feeling. **2** cheerful consent; willingness. **3** the good reputation that a business has with its customers. *n.*

good y (gud′ē), INFORMAL. **1** something very good to eat; piece of candy or cake. **2** exclamation of pleasure: *Oh, goody!* 1 *n., pl.* **good ies;** 2 *interj.*

goo ey (gü′ē), SLANG. like goo; sticky. *adj.,* **goo i er, goo i est.**

goof (güf), SLANG. **1** make a stupid mistake; blunder. **2** a blunder. **3** waste time or avoid work: *goof off during class.* **4** simpleton; fool. 1,3 *v.,* 2,4 *n.*

goof-off (güf′ôf′), SLANG. person who wastes time or avoids work. *n.*

goof y (gü′fē), SLANG. silly. *adj.,* **goof i er, goof i est.**

goose (güs), **1** a wild or tame swimming bird, like a duck but larger and having a longer neck. A goose has webbed feet. **2** a female goose. The male is called a gander. **3** flesh of a goose used for food. **4** a silly person. *n., pl.* **geese.** —**goose′like′,** *adj.*

cook one's goose, INFORMAL. ruin one's reputation, plan, chances, etc.

goose ber ry (güs′ber′ē), a small, sour berry somewhat like a currant but larger, that grows on a thorny bush. Gooseberries are used to make pies, tarts, jam, etc. *n., pl.* **goose ber ries.**

goose flesh (güs′flesh′), a rough condition of the skin, like that of a plucked goose, caused by cold or fear; goose pimples. *n.*

goose neck (güs′nek′), something long and curved like a goose's neck, such as a movable support for a lamp or a support for bicycle handlebars. *n.*

goose pimples, gooseflesh.

goose step, a marching step in which the leg is swung high with straight, stiff knee.

G.O.P. or **GOP,** Grand Old Party; the Republican Party in the United States.

go pher (gō′fər), **1** a burrowing rodent of North America with large cheek pouches and long claws, especially on the front feet. **2** a striped ground squirrel of the western plains of the United States. *n.*

Gor ba chev (gôr′bə chof), **Mikhail,** born 1930, Russian political leader, general secretary of the Soviet Communist Party since 1985. *n.*

Gor di an knot (gôr′dē ən). **cut the Gordian knot,** find and use a quick, easy way out of a difficulty.

gore[1] (gôr), blood that is shed; thick blood; clotted blood: *The battlefield was covered with gore. n.*

gore[2] (gôr), wound with a horn or tusk: *The angry bull gored the farmer in the leg. v.,* **gored, gor ing.**

gore[3] (gôr), **1** a long, three-sided piece of cloth put or made in a skirt, sail, etc., to give greater width or change the shape. **2** put or make a gore in. **1** *n.,* **2** *v.,* **gored, gor ing.**

gorge (gôrj), **1** a deep, narrow valley, usually steep and rocky, especially one with a stream. **2** eat greedily until full; stuff with food: *I gorged myself with cake at the party.* **1** *n.,* **2** *v.,* **gorged, gorg ing.** —**gorge′a ble,** *adj.*

gor geous (gôr′jəs), richly colored; splendid: *a gorgeous sunset. The peacock spread its gorgeous tail. adj.* —**gor′geous ly,** *adv.* —**gor′geous ness,** *n.*

Gor gon (gôr′gən), (in Greek legends) any of three sisters having snakes for hair and faces so horrible that anyone who looked at them turned to stone. *n.*

go ril la (gə ril′ə), the largest and most powerful ape. It is found in the forests of central Africa. *n., pl.* **go ril las.**

gorilla—up to 6 ft. (2 m.) tall when standing

gorse (gôrs), furze. *n.*

gor y (gôr′ē), **1** covered with gore; bloody. **2** with much bloodshed: *a gory accident, a gory tale. adj.,* **gor i er, gor i est.** —**gor′i ly,** *adv.* —**gor′i ness,** *n.*

gosh (gosh), exclamation or mild oath: *Gosh, it's cold out today! interj.*

gos hawk (gos′hôk′), a powerful, short-winged hawk, formerly much used in falconry. *n.*

Go shen (gō′shən), **1** (in the Bible) a fertile part of Egypt where the Israelites lived before the Exodus. See **Canaan** for map. **2** any land of plenty and comfort. *n.*

gos ling (goz′ling), a young goose. *n.*

gos pel (gos′pəl), **1** the teachings of Jesus and the Apostles. **2** of or like the gospel. **3** in agreement with the gospel; evangelical. **4** marked by spiritual enthusiasm: *gospel music, gospel hymns.* **5 Gospel, a** any one of the first four books of the New Testament, by Matthew, Mark, Luke, and John. They tell about the life and teachings of Christ. **b** part of one of these books read during a religious service. **6** anything earnestly believed or taken as a guide for action: *Drink plenty of water: that is my gospel.* **1,5,6** *n.,* **2-4** *adj.*

gos sa mer (gos′ə mər), **1** film or thread of cobweb. **2** any very thin, light cloth or substance. **3** like gossamer; very light and thin; filmy. **1,2** *n.,* **3** *adj.*

gos sip (gos′ip), **1** idle talk, not always true, about other people and their private affairs. **2** repeat what one knows or hears about other people and their private affairs. **3** person who gossips a good deal. **1,3** *n.,* **2** *v.* —**gos′sip er,** *n.* —**gos′sip ing ly,** *adv.*

gos sip y (gos′ə pē), **1** fond of gossip. **2** full of gossip: *a gossipy letter. adj.* —**gos′sip i ness,** *n.*

got (got), past tense and a past participle of **get.** *She got the letter yesterday. We had got tired of waiting for it. v.*

Goth (goth), member of a Germanic people who invaded the Roman Empire in the A.D. 200's, 300's, and 400's. The Goths settled mainly in southern and eastern Europe. *n.*

Gothic (def. 2)—a Gothic cathedral in France

Goth ic (goth′ik), **1** style of architecture using pointed arches, flying buttresses, and high, steep roofs. It was developed in western Europe during the Middle Ages from about 1150 to 1550. **2** of this kind of architecture. **3** of the Goths or their language. **4** language of the Goths. **5** of a kind of literature that emphasizes the supernatural and the grotesque, usually having a medieval setting: *Gothic tales.* **1,4** *n.,* **2,3,5** *adj.*

got ten (got′n), got; a past participle of **get.** *v.*

gouge (gouj), **1** chisel with a curved, hollow blade. Gouges are used for cutting round grooves or holes in wood. **2** cut with a gouge. **3** groove or hole made by gouging. **4** dig out; tear out; force out. **5** INFORMAL. to trick; cheat; swindle. **1,3** *n.,* **2,4,5** *v.,* **gouged, goug ing.**

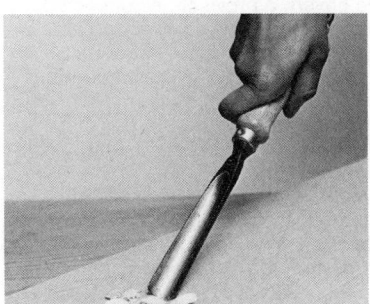

gouge (def. 1)

gou lash (gü′läsh), stew made of beef or veal and vegetables, usually highly seasoned. *n.* [*Goulash* comes from Hungarian *gulyás* (*hús*), meaning "herdsman's (meat)."]

Gou nod (gü′nō), **Charles François,** 1818-1893, French composer. *n.*

gourds
(def. 1)

gourd (gôrd), **1** any of various fleshy fruits that grow on vines and are related to squash. Gourds have hard rinds and are often dried and hollowed out for use as cups, bowls, etc. **2** cup, bowl, etc., made from the dried shell of a gourd. *n.* —**gourd′like′,** *adj.*

gour mand (gùr′mənd), person who is fond of good eating. *n.*

gour met (gùr′mā), person who is expert in judging and choosing fine foods, wines, etc. *n.*

gout (gout), a painful disease of the joints, especially of the big toe. *n.*

gout y (gou′tē), **1** diseased or swollen with gout. **2** of gout; caused by gout. *adj.,* **gout i er, gout i est.**

gov., **1** government. **2** governor.

Gov., governor.

gov ern (guv′ərn), **1** direct or manage with authority; rule or control: *The election determined which party would govern the United States for four years.* **2** determine or guide: *What were the motives governing the king's decision to give up his throne?* **3** hold back; restrain: *Govern your temper. v.*

gov ern a ble (guv′ər nə bəl), able to be governed. *adj.*

gov ern ess (guv′ər nis), woman who teaches and trains children in their home. *n.*

gov ern ment (guv′ərn mənt), **1** the ruling of a country, state, district, etc.; direction of the affairs of state; rule, control, or management: *federal government, municipal government.* **2** person or persons ruling a country, state, district, etc., at any time: *The government of the United States consists of the President, the cabinet, the Congress, and the Supreme Court.* **3** system of ruling: *The United States has a democratic form of government. n.*

gov ern men tal (guv′ərn men′tl), of or having to do with government. *adj.* —**gov′ern men′tal ly,** *adv.*

gov er nor (guv′ər nər), **1** official elected as the executive head of a state of the United States. The governor of a state carries out the laws made by the state legislature. **2** official appointed to govern a province, colony, city, fort, etc. **3** person who manages or directs a club, society, institution, etc. **4** an automatic device that controls the supply of fuel or power and keeps a machine going at a certain speed. *n.*

gov er nor ship (guv′ər nər ship), position, duties, or term of office of governor. *n.*

govt. or **Govt.,** government.

gown (goun), **1** a woman's dress. **2** a loose outer garment worn by college graduates, judges, clergymen, lawyers, and others to show their position, profession, etc. **3** nightgown or dressing gown. *n.* —**gown′less,** *adj.*

Go ya (gô′yə), **Francisco,** 1746-1828, Spanish painter and etcher. *n.*

gph or **g.p.h.,** gallons per hour.

gpm or **g.p.m.,** gallons per minute.

G.P.O. or **GPO, 1** General Post Office. **2** Government Printing Office.

G.Q. or **GQ,** General Quarters.

gr. or **gr, 1** grain or grains. **2** gram or grams. **3** gross (12 dozen).

Gr., 1 Grecian. **2** Greece. **3** Greek.

grab (grab), **1** seize suddenly; snatch: *I grabbed the child before she fell.* **2** a snatching; sudden seizing: *He made a grab at the butterfly.* **3** something which is grabbed. 1 *v.,* **grabbed, grab bing;** 2,3 *n.*

grab bag, bag containing various unseen and unknown objects from which a person can take out one.

grace (grās), **1** beauty of form, movement, or manner; pleasing or agreeable quality: *The ballerina danced with much grace.* **2** give or add grace to: *A vase of flowers graced the room.* **3** the favor and love of God: *fall from grace.* **4** a short prayer of thanks given before or after a meal. **5** favor shown by granting a delay. **6** time of the delay: *three days' grace.* **7** give grace or honor to: *The queen graced the ball with her presence.* **8** behavior put on to seem attractive: *serve tea with little airs and graces.* **9 Grace,** title of a duke, duchess, or archbishop: *May I assist Your Grace?* **10 Graces,** *pl.* (in Greek myths) three sister goddesses who give beauty, charm, and joy to people and nature. 1,3-6,8-10 *n.,* 2,7 *v.,* **graced, gracing.** [*Grace* came into English about 800 years ago from French *grace,* and can be traced back to Latin *gratus,* meaning "pleasing."] —**grace′like′,** *adj.*

in one's bad graces, disfavored or disliked by.

in one's good graces, favored or liked by: *I wonder if I am in the teacher's good graces.*

with bad grace, unpleasantly; unwillingly: *The apology was made with bad grace.*

with good grace, pleasantly; willingly: *He obeyed the order with good grace.*

grace ful (grās′fəl), beautiful in form, movement, or manner; pleasing; agreeable: *a graceful dancer. adj.* —**grace′ful ly,** *adv.* —**grace′ful ness,** *n.*

grace less (grās′lis), **1** ugly in form, movement, or manner: *awkward, graceless movements.* **2** without any sense of what is right or proper; impolite: *a graceless rascal. adj.* —**grace′less ly,** *adv.* —**grace′less ness,** *n.*

grace note, (in music) a note or group of notes not essential to the harmony or melody, added for ornament.

gra cious (grā′shəs), **1** pleasant and kindly; courteous: *He welcomed his guests in a gracious manner which made them feel at ease.* **2** pleasant and kindly to people of lower social position: *The queen greeted the crowd with a gracious smile.* **3** exclamation of surprise. 1,2 *adj.,* 3 *interj.* —**gra′cious ly,** *adv.* —**gra′cious ness,** *n.*

grack le (grak′əl), a large blackbird with shiny, black feathers. *n.*

grad., 1 graduate. **2** graduated.

gra da tion (grā dā′shən), **1** a change by steps or stages; gradual change: *A camera lens allows gradation of the light that reaches the film.* **2** one of the steps in a series: *the gradations of color in a rainbow. n.*

grade (grād), **1** division of elementary school or high school, arranged according to the pupils' progress and covering a year's work: *the seventh grade.* **2 the grades,** elementary school. **3** degree in rank, quality, or value: *Grade A milk is the best milk.* **4** group of persons or things having the same rank, quality, or value. **5** place in classes; arrange in grades; sort: *These apples are graded by size.* **6** number or letter that shows how well one has done: *Her grade in English is B.* **7** give a grade to: *The teacher graded the papers.* **8** slope of a road or railroad track: *a steep grade.* **9** amount of slope. **10** make more nearly level: *The road up the steep hill was graded.* 1-4, 6,8,9 *n.,* 5,7,10 *v.,* **grad ed, grad ing.** [*Grade* comes from Latin *gradus,* meaning "step, degree."]

make the grade, be successful: *It takes a lot of hard work to make the grade in business.*

grade crossing, place where a railroad crosses a street or another railroad on the same level.

grad er (grā′dər), **1** person or thing that grades. **2** person who is in a certain grade at school: *a fifth grader. n.*

grade school, elementary school.

gra di ent (grā′dē ənt), **1** rate of upward or downward slope of a road, railroad track, etc.: *steep gradients.* **2** the sloping part of a road, railroad, etc.; grade. **3** rate at which temperature, pressure, etc., changes. *n.*

grad u al (graj′ü əl), happening by small steps or degrees; changing step by step; moving little by little: *This low hill has a gradual slope. A child's growth into an adult is gradual. adj.* —**grad′u al ly,** *adv.* —**grad′u al ness,** *n.*

grad u ate (graj′ü āt *for 1,2,6;* graj′ü it *for 3-5*), **1** finish a course of study at a school, college, or university and be given a diploma or paper saying so: *Her brother graduated from the University last year.* **2** give a diploma to for finishing a course of study: *She was graduated with honors.* **3** person who has graduated and has a diploma. **4** that has graduated: *a graduate student.* **5** of or for graduates: *A graduate school is for students continuing their studies after college.* **6** mark out in equal spaces for measuring: *Rulers are graduated in inches and centimeters.* 1,2,6 *v.,* **grad u at ed, grad u at ing;** 3 *n.,* 4,5 *adj.* —**grad′u a′tor,** *n.*

grad u a tion (graj′ü ā′shən), **1** a graduating from a school, college, or university. **2** ceremony of graduating; graduating exercises. **3** division into equal spaces. **4** mark or set of marks to show degrees for measuring. *n.*

graf fi ti (grə fē′tē), drawings or writings scratched or scribbled on a wall or other surface. *n.pl.* of **graf fi to** (grə fē′tō).

graft[1]
(defs. 1 and 2)
three types.
The pieces are tied
or taped together
and kept moist
until they join.

graft[1] (graft), **1** put (a shoot, bud, etc., from one tree or plant) into a slit in another tree or plant, so it will grow there permanently; engraft. **2** shoot, bud, etc., used in grafting. A graft from a fine apple tree may be put on an inferior one to improve it. **3** act of grafting. **4** transfer (a piece of skin, bone, etc.) from one part of the body to another, or to a new body, so that it will grow there permanently. **5** piece of skin, bone, etc., so transferred. 1,4 *v.,* 2,3,5 *n.* —**graft′er,** *n.*

graft[2] (graft), **1** the taking of money dishonestly in connection with city or government business: *The crooked inspector was guilty of accepting bribes and other forms of graft.* **2** money dishonestly taken. *n.* —**graft′er,** *n.*

gra ham (grā′əm), made from whole-wheat flour, including all the bran: *graham crackers. adj.* [*Graham* was named for Sylvester *Graham,* 1794-1851, an American minister and dietary reformer, who urged the use of this flour.]

Grail (grāl), (in medieval legends) the cup or dish used by Christ at the Last Supper, and by one of His followers to catch the last drops of Christ's blood at the Cross; Holy Grail. The knights of the Round Table vowed to search for the Grail. *n.*

grain (grān), **1** the seed of wheat, corn, oats, and similar cereal grasses. **2** plants that these seeds grow on. **3** one of the tiny bits of which sand, sugar, salt, etc., are made up. **4** a very small unit of weight. One pound avoirdupois equals 7000 grains; one pound troy equals 5760 grains. **5** the smallest possible amount; tiniest bit: *There isn't a grain of truth in the charge.* **6** the little lines and other markings in wood, marble, etc.; arrangement of the particles of anything: *That mahogany table has a fine grain.* **7** natural character; disposition: *Laziness went against his grain. n.* —**grain′less,** *adj.* —**grain′like′,** *adj.*

with a grain of salt, with some doubt or allowance: *Her story must be taken with a grain of salt.*

grain alcohol, ordinary alcohol, made by the fermentation of grain.

grained (grānd), **1** having little lines and markings. **2** painted to look like the grain in wood, marble, etc. *adj.*

grain elevator, building for storing grain.

grain y (grā′nē), **1** like the grain of wood, marble, etc. **2** made up of grains; granular. *adj.,* **grain i er, grain i est.** —**grain′i ness,** *n.*

gram (gram), unit of weight or mass in the metric system. Twenty-eight grams weigh about one ounce. *n.* Also, **gramme.**

-gram[1], *combining form.* something drawn or written; message: *Cablegram = a message sent by cable.* [The form *-gram* comes from Greek *gramma.*]

-gram[2], *combining form.* **1** grams: *Kilogram = one thousand grams.* **2** part of a gram: *Centigram = 1/100 part of a gram.* [The form *-gram* comes directly from *gram,* which comes from Greek *gramma,* meaning "small weight."]

gram., **1** grammar. **2** grammatical.

gram mar (gram′ər), **1** the study of the forms and uses of words in sentences in a particular language. **2** rules describing the use of words in a language. **3** the use of words according to these rules: *My teacher's grammar is excellent. n.* —**gram′mar less,** *adj.*

gram mar i an (grə mer′ē ən), an expert in grammar. *n.*

grammar school, **1** (in the United States) an elementary school. **2** (in England) a secondary school that prepares students for university.

gram mat i cal (grə mat′ə kəl), **1** according to the correct use of words: *Our French teacher speaks grammatical English but has a French accent.* **2** of grammar: *"You should have saw it" is a grammatical mistake. adj.* —**gram mat′i cal ness,** *n.*

gram mat i cal ly (grə mat′ik lē), according to the rules of grammar; as regards grammar. *adv.*

gramme (gram), gram. *n.*

gram pus (gram′pəs), **1** a large sea mammal related to the dolphin, with a blunt nose. **2** killer whale. *n., pl.* **gram pus es.**

Gra na da (grə nä′də), city in S Spain, last stronghold of the Moors till they were driven out of Spain in 1492. See **Castile** for map. *n.*

gran ar y (gran′ər ē *or* grā′nər ē), **1** place or building where grain is stored. **2** region producing much grain. *n., pl.* **gran ar ies.**

grand (grand), **1** large and of fine appearance: *grand mountains.* **2** of very high or noble quality; dignified: *a very grand palace, grand music, a grand old man.* **3** highest or very high in rank; chief: *grand duchess.* **4** great; important; main: *the grand staircase.* **5** complete; comprehensive: *grand total.* **6** INFORMAL. very satisfactory: *a grand time, grand weather.* **7** SLANG. a thousand dollars. 1-6 *adj.,* 7 *n.* —**grand′ly,** *adv.* —**grand′ness,** *n.*

grand aunt (grand′ant′), aunt of one's father or mother; great-aunt. *n.*

Grand Bank or **Grand Banks,** shoal off the SE coast of Newfoundland. It is important for cod fishing.

Grand Canyon, deep gorge of the Colorado River, in N Arizona.

grand child (grand′chīld′), child of one's son or daughter. *n., pl.* **grand chil dren.**

grand chil dren (grand′chil′drən), plural of **grand-child.** *n.*

Grand Cou lee (kü′lē), large dam on the Columbia River, in E Washington.

grand dad (grand′dad′), INFORMAL. grandfather. *n.*

grand daugh ter (grand′dô′tər), daughter of one's son or daughter. *n.*

gran dee (gran dē′), **1** a Spanish or Portuguese nobleman of the highest rank. **2** person of high rank or great importance. *n.*

grandeur
the grandeur of
Niagara Falls

gran deur (gran′jər), greatness; majesty; nobility; dignity; splendor. *n.*

grand fa ther (grand′fä′ᴛHər), father of one's father or mother. *n.*

grandfather clock, grandfather's clock.

grand fa ther ly (grand′fä′ᴛHər lē), like or characteristic of a grandfather. *adj.*

grandfather's clock, clock in a tall, wooden case, which stands on the floor.

gran dil o quence (gran dil′ə kwəns), the use of lofty or pompous words. *n.*

gran dil o quent (gran dil′ə kwənt), using lofty or pompous words. *adj.* —**gran dil′o quent ly,** *adv.*

gran di ose (gran′dē ōs), **1** grand in an imposing or impressive way; magnificent. **2** grand in a showy or pompous way; not really magnificent, but trying to seem so. *adj.* —**gran′di ose ly,** *adv.*

grand jury, jury of from 6 to 23 persons chosen to investigate accusations of crime and decide whether there is enough evidence for a trial in court.

grand ma (grand′mä′ or gram′ə), INFORMAL. grandmother. *n.*

grand moth er (grand′muᴛH′ər), mother of one's father or mother. *n.*

grand moth er ly (grand′muᴛH′ər lē), like or characteristic of a grandmother. *adj.*

grand neph ew (grand′nef′yü), son of one's nephew or niece. *n.*

grand niece (grand′nēs′), daughter of one's nephew or niece. *n.*

grand pa (grand′pä′ or gram′pə), INFORMAL. grandfather. *n.*

grand par ent (grand′per′ənt or grand′par′ənt), grandfather or grandmother. *n.*

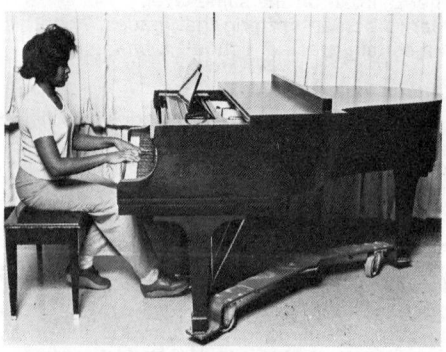

grand piano

grand piano, a large, harp-shaped piano with horizontal strings.

Grand Rapids, city in SW Michigan.

grand sire (grand′sīr′), OLD USE. **1** grandfather. **2** forefather. **3** an old man. *n.*

grand son (grand′sun′), son of one's son or daughter. *n.*

grand stand (grand′stand′), the main seating place for people at an athletic field, racetrack, parade, etc. *n.*

grand un cle (grand′ung′kəl), uncle of one's father or mother; great-uncle. *n.*

grange (grānj), **1** farm with its barns and other buildings. **2 Grange,** an association of farmers for the improvement of their welfare. *n.*

gran ite (gran′it), a hard rock made of grains of other rocks, chiefly quartz and feldspar. It is an igneous rock, much used for buildings and monuments. *n.* —**gran′ite-like′,** *adj.*

gran ny or **gran nie** (gran′ē), INFORMAL. **1** grandmother. **2** an old woman. *n., pl.* **gran nies.**

granny knot   square knot

granny knot, knot differing from a square knot in having the ends crossed the opposite way.

gra no la (grə nō′lə), a dry breakfast cereal of rolled oats, flavored with other things such as honey, chopped dried fruit, and nuts. *n.*

grant (grant), **1** give what is asked; allow: *grant a request, grant permission.* **2** admit to be true; accept without proof; concede: *I grant that you are right so far.* **3** give or confer (a right, etc.) by formal act. **4** gift, especially land or rights given by the government. **5** act of granting. 1-3 *v.,* 4,5 *n.* —**grant′a ble,** *adj.* —**grant′er,** *n.*

take for granted, 1 assume to be true; regard as proved or agreed to: *We take the law of gravitation for granted.* **2** accept as probable: *We took for granted that the sailor could swim.*

Grant (grant), Ulysses S(impson), 1822-1885, Union general during the Civil War, and 18th president of the United States, from 1869 to 1877. *n.*

grant ee (gran′tē′), person to whom a grant is made. *n.*

grant or (gran′tər or gran′tôr′), person who makes a grant. *n.*

gran u lar (gran′yə lər), **1** consisting of or containing grains or granules; grainy: *granular stone.* **2** like grains or granules. *adj.* —**gran′u lar ly,** *adv.*

gran u late (gran′yə lāt), **1** make into grains; form grains or granules. **2** roughen the surface of. *v.,* **gran u lat ed, gran u lat ing.** —**gran′u lat′er, gran′u la′tor,** *n.*

gran u lat ed (gran′yə lā′tid), **1** formed into grains or granules: *granulated sugar.* **2** roughened on the surface: *granulated leather. adj.*

gran u la tion (gran′yə lā′shən), formation into grains or granules. *n.*

gran ule (gran′yül), **1** a small grain. **2** a small bit or spot like a grain. *n.*

grape (grāp), **1** a small, round fruit, red, purple, or pale-green, that grows in bunches on a vine. Grapes are eaten raw or made into raisins or wine. **2** grapeshot. *n.* —**grape′like′,** *adj.*

grape fruit (grāp′früt′), a pale-yellow, roundish, juicy, citrus fruit of a tree grown in warm climates. Grapefruits are like oranges, but are larger and sourer. *n.*

grape shot (grāp′shot′), cluster of small iron balls formerly used as a charge for cannon. *n.*

grape sugar, dextrose.

grape vine (grāp′vīn′), **1** vine that grapes grow on. **2** way in which news or rumors are mysteriously spread. *n.*

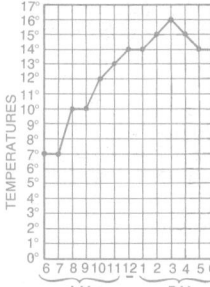

graph (def. 1)
of the temperature of a
winter day for 12 hours

graph (graf), **1** line or diagram showing how one quantity depends on or changes with another. You could draw a graph to show how your weight has changed each year with your change in age. **2** a curve or other line representing the mathematical relations of the elements in an equation or function. **3** make a graph of. 1,2 *n.,* 3 *v.*

-graph, *combining form.* **1** instrument that writes, draws, or records: *Seismograph=instrument that records earthquake data.* **2** something written, drawn, or recorded: *Autograph=something written by oneself.* [The form *-graph* comes from Greek *graphein,* meaning "to write."]

graph ic (graf′ik), **1** producing by words the effect of a picture; lifelike; vivid: *Her graphic description of the English countryside made me feel as though I had been there myself.* **2** shown by a graph: *The school board kept a graphic record of school attendance for a month.* **3** of or about drawing, painting, engraving, etching, etc.: *the graphic arts.* **4** of or using pictures or diagrams. **5** of or used in handwriting: *graphic symbols. adj.* [*Graphic* comes from Latin *graphicus,* and can be traced back to Greek *graphein,* meaning "to write."]

graph i cal ly (graf′ik lē), in a graphic manner; by a diagram or pictures; vividly. *adv.*

graph ics (graf′iks), pictures or diagrams made by a computer or video game. *n.*

graph ite (graf′īt), a soft, black form of carbon used for lead in pencils and for greasing machinery. *n.*

graph paper, paper ruled in squares, for making graphs, diagrams, etc.

grap nel (grap′nəl), **1** instrument with one or more hooks for seizing and holding something; grapple; grappling iron. Grapnels thrown by ropes were once used to catch on an enemy's ship. **2** a small anchor with three or more hooks. *n.*

grap ple (grap′əl), **1** seize and hold fast; grip or hold firmly. **2** a seizing and holding fast; firm grip or hold. **3** struggle; fight: *The wrestlers grappled in the center of the ring. I grappled with the problem for an hour before I solved it.* **4** grapnel. 1,3 *v.,* **grap pled, grap pling;** 2,4 *n.*

grappling iron, grapnel.

grasp (grasp), **1** seize and hold fast by closing the fingers around: *I grasped the tree limb to keep from falling.* **2** a seizing and holding tightly; clasp of the hand. **3** power of seizing and holding; reach: *Success is within her grasp.* **4** control; possession: *The people regained power from the grasp of the dictator.* **5** understand: *She grasped my meaning at once.* **6** understanding: *He has a good grasp of mathematics.* 1,5 *v.,* 2-4,6 *n.* —**grasp′a ble,** *adj.* —**grasp′er,** *n.*

grasp at, 1 try to take hold of; try to grasp. **2** accept eagerly: *She grasped at the opportunity.*

grasp ing (gras′ping), eager to get all that one can; greedy. *adj.* —**grasp′ing ly,** *adv.* —**grasp′ing ness,** *n.*

grass (gras), **1** plants with green blades which cover fields, lawns, and pastures. Horses, cows, and sheep eat grass. **2** plant which has jointed stems and long, narrow leaves. Wheat, corn, sugar cane, and bamboo are grasses. **3** land covered with grass; pasture. **4** SLANG. marijuana. *n., pl.* **grass es.** [*Grass* comes from Old English *græs.*] —**grass′less,** *adj.* —**grass′like′,** *adj.*

grass hop per (gras′hop′ər), a winged insect with strong hind legs for jumping. Locusts and katydids are grasshoppers. *n.*

grass land (gras′land′), land with grass on it, used for pasture. *n.*

grass roots, the ordinary citizens of a region or state taken all together: *The senator is certain to get support from the grass roots.*

grass y (gras′ē), **1** covered with grass; having much grass. **2** of or like grass. *adj.,* **grass i er, grass i est.**

grate¹ (grāt), **1** framework of iron bars to hold burning fuel in a furnace, fireplace, etc. **2** fireplace. **3** framework of bars over a window or opening; grating. *n.* —**grate′like′,** *adj.*

grate² (grāt), **1** have an annoying or unpleasant effect: *Their loud voices grate on my nerves.* **2** make a harsh, jarring noise by rubbing: *The door grated on its rusty hinges.* **3** wear down or grind off in small pieces: *The cook grated the cheese before melting it. v.,* **grat ed, grat ing.**

grate ful (grāt′fəl), **1** feeling kindly because of a favor received; wanting to do a favor in return; thankful: *I am grateful for your help.* **2** pleasing; welcome: *a grateful breeze on a hot day. adj.* —**grate′ful ly,** *adv.* —**grate′ful ness,** *n.*

grat er (grā′tər), utensil with a rough, sharp surface used to grate cheese, vegetables, and other food. *n.*

grat i fi ca tion (grat′ə fə kā′shən), **1** a gratifying: *The gratification of a person's every wish is not always possible.* **2** a being gratified. **3** something that satisfies or pleases: *Your faith in my ability is a gratification to me. n.*

grat i fy (grat′ə fī), **1** give pleasure to; please: *Praise gratifies most people.* **2** give satisfaction to; satisfy; indulge: *gratify a craving for sweets.* v., **grat i fied, grat i fy-ing.** —**grat′i fi′a ble,** *adj.* —**grat′i fi′er,** *n.* —**grat′i-fy′ing ly,** *adv.*

grat ing[1] (grā′ting), framework of parallel or crossed bars; grate. Windows in a prison, bank, or ticket office usually have gratings over them. *n.*

grat ing[2] (grā′ting), **1** not pleasant; annoying; irritating. **2** harsh or jarring in sound. *adj.* —**grat′ing ly,** *adv.*

grat is (grat′is *or* grā′tis), for nothing; free of charge: *I will give it to you gratis* (adv.). *The service was gratis to club members* (adj.). *adv., adj.*

grat i tude (grat′ə tüd *or* grat′ə tyüd), kindly feeling because of a favor received; desire to do a favor in return; thankfulness. *n.*

gra tu i tous (grə tü′ə təs *or* grə tyü′ə təs), **1** freely given or obtained; free: *a gratuitous gift.* **2** without reason or cause; unnecessary; uncalled-for: *a gratuitous insult. adj.* —**gra tu′i tous ly,** *adv.* —**gra tu′i tous ness,** *n.*

gra tu i ty (grə tü′ə tē *or* grə tyü′ə tē), present of money in return for service; tip. *n., pl.* **gra tu i ties.**

grave[1] (grāv), **1** hole dug in the ground where a dead body is to be buried. **2** any place of burial: *a watery grave.* **3** death. *n.* [Grave[1] comes from Old English *græf.*] —**grave′like′,** *adj.*

grave[2] (grāv), **1** important; weighty; momentous: *grave cares, a grave decision.* **2** serious; threatening; critical: *a grave illness, grave news.* **3** sober; dignified; solemn: *a grave face. adj.,* **grav er, grav est.** [Grave[2] came into English about 400 years ago from French *grave,* which comes from Latin *gravis,* meaning "heavy, serious."] —**grave′ly,** *adv.* —**grave′ness,** *n.*

grave[3] (grāv), engrave; carve. *v.,* **graved, grav en** or **graved, grav ing.** [Grave[3] comes from Old English *grafan.*]

grave accent, mark (`) placed over a vowel to show pitch, quality of sound, etc. The phrase *à la mode* has a grave accent. In English poetry a grave accent may be used to indicate that a word is pronounced with one more syllable than usual, as in *wreathèd* (rē′ŦHid).

grav el (grav′əl), **1** pebbles and pieces of rock coarser than sand. Gravel is much used for roads and walks. **2** lay or cover with gravel. **1** *n.,* **2** *v.,* **grav eled, grav el-ing** or **grav elled, grav el ling.**

grave less (grāv′lis), without a grave; unburied. *adj.*

grav el ly (grav′ə lē), **1** having much gravel. **2** of or like gravel. **3** rough; rasping; grating: *a gravelly voice. adj.*

grav en (grā′vən), **1** engraved; carved: *graven images.* **2** a past participle of **grave**[3]. *Figures had been graven in the rock.* **1** *adj.,* **2** *v.*

grave stone (grāv′stōn′), stone that marks a grave. *n.*

grave yard (grāv′yärd′), cemetery. *n.*

grav i tate (grav′ə tāt′), **1** move or tend to move toward a body by the force of gravity: *The planets gravitate toward the sun.* **2** settle down; sink; fall: *The sand and dirt in the water gravitated to the bottom of the bottle.* **3** tend to go; be strongly attracted: *The attention of the audience gravitated to the stage as the lights dimmed. v.,* **grav i tat-ed, grav i tat ing.** —**grav′i tat′er,** *n.*

grav i ta tion (grav′ə tā′shən), **1** the force or pull that makes all objects in the universe tend to move toward one another. Gravitation keeps the planets in their orbits around the sun. **2** a moving or tendency to move caused by this force. **3** a settling down; sinking; falling. **4** a natural tendency toward some point or object of influence: *The gravitation of people to the cities leaves many farms vacant. n.*

grav i ta tion al (grav′ə tā′shə nəl), of gravitation. *adj.* —**grav′i ta′tion al ly,** *adv.*

grav i ty (grav′ə tē), **1** the natural force that causes objects to move or tend to move toward the center of the earth. Gravity causes objects to have weight. **2** the natural force that makes objects move or tend to move toward each other; gravitation. **3** heaviness; weight: *He balanced the long pole at its center of gravity.* **4** seriousness; earnestness: *The gravity of her expression told us that the news was bad.* **5** serious or critical character; importance: *The gravity of the situation was greatly increased by threats of war. n., pl.* **grav i ties.**

gra vy (grā′vē), **1** juice that comes out of meat in cooking. **2** sauce for meat, potatoes, etc., made from this juice, usually by thickening it with flour. *n., pl.* **gra vies.**

gray (grā), **1** color made by mixing black and white. **2** having a color between black and white: *gray hair.* **3** make or become gray: *His hair is graying fast.* **4** having gray hair. **5** dark; gloomy; dismal: *a gray, rainy day.* **1** *n.,* **2,4,5** *adj.,* **3** *v.* Also, **grey.** —**gray′ly,** *adv.* —**gray′-ness,** *n.*

gray beard (grā′bird′), an old man. *n.*

gray ish (grā′ish), somewhat gray. *adj.*

gray ling (grā′ling), a freshwater fish related to the trout and much valued as a food and game fish. *n.*

gray matter, 1 the grayish tissue in the brain and spinal cord that contains nerve cells and some nerve fibers. **2** INFORMAL. intelligence; brains.

graze[1] (grāz), **1** feed on growing grass: *Cattle were grazing in the field.* **2** put (cattle, sheep, etc.) to feed on growing grass or a pasture: *The farmer grazed his sheep. v.,* **grazed, graz ing.** —**graze′a ble, graz′a ble,** *adj.* —**graz′er,** *n.*

graze[2] (grāz), **1** touch lightly in passing; rub lightly against: *The car grazed the garage door.* **2** scrape the skin from: *She fell and grazed her knee.* **3** a grazing. **4** a slight wound made by grazing. **1,2** *v.,* **grazed, graz ing; 3,4** *n.* —**graz′er,** *n.* —**graz′ing ly,** *adv.*

graz ing (grā′zing), the growing grass that cattle, sheep, etc., feed on; pasture. *n.*

Gr. Br. or **Gr. Brit.,** Great Britain.

grease (grēs), **1** soft, melted animal fat. **2** any thick, oily substance. **3** rub grease on: *grease a cake pan.* **4** put grease or oil on or in: *Please grease my car.* **1,2** *n.,* **3,4** *v.,* **greased, greas ing.** —**greas′er,** *n.*

grease paint (grēs′pānt′), mixture of tallow or grease and a pigment, used by actors in painting their faces. *n.*

greas i ly (grē′sə lē), in a greasy manner. *adv.*

greas i ness (grē′sē nis), greasy quality or condition. *n.*

greas y (grē′sē), **1** smeared with grease; having grease on it. **2** containing much grease; oily: *Greasy food is hard to digest.* **3** like grease; smooth; slippery. *adj.,* **greas i er, greas i est.**

great (grāt), **1** large in extent, amount, size, or number; big: *a great forest, a great crowd.* **2** more than is usual; much: *great pain, great kindness.* **3** high in rank; important; remarkable; famous: *a great writer, a great event.* **4** much in use; favorite: *Her great sport was tennis.* **5** very much of a: *a great talker.* **6** INFORMAL. very good; fine: *We had a great time at the party. adj.*

great-aunt (grāt′ant′), grandaunt. *n.*

Great Barrier Reef, the longest coral reef in the world, in the S Pacific along the NE coast of Australia.

Great Bear, Ursa Major.

Great Britain, England, Scotland, and Wales. Great Britain is the largest island of Europe. See **British Isles** for map.

great circle, any circle on the surface of a sphere having its plane passing through the center of the sphere. The equator is one of the great circles of the earth.

great coat (grāt′kōt′), a heavy overcoat. *n.*

Great Dane—about
32 in. (81 cm.) high
at the shoulder

a hat	**i** it	**oi** oil	**ch** child		a in about
ā age	**ī** ice	**ou** out	**ng** long		e in taken
ä far	**o** hot	**u** cup	**sh** she	ə =	i in pencil
e let	**ō** open	**u̇** put	**th** thin		o in lemon
ē equal	**ô** order	**ü** rule	**ŦH** then		u in circus
ėr term			**zh** measure		

grebe
about 14 in.
(35.5 cm.) long

Great Dane, a large, powerful, short-haired dog.

Great Divide, Continental Divide.

great-grand child (grāt′grand′chīld′), grandchild of one's son or daughter. *n., pl.* **great-grand chil dren** (grāt′grand′chil′drən).

great-grand daugh ter (grāt′gran′dô′tər), granddaughter of one's son or daughter. *n.*

great-grand fa ther (grāt′grand′fä′thər), grandfather of one's father or mother. *n.*

great-grand moth er (grāt′grand′muŦH′ər), grandmother of one's father or mother. *n.*

great-grand par ent (grāt′grand′per′ənt *or* grāt′grand′par′ənt), great-grandfather or great-grandmother. *n.*

great-grand son (grāt′grand′sun′), grandson of one's son or daughter. *n.*

great heart ed (grāt′här′tid), **1** noble; generous. **2** brave; fearless. *adj.* —**great′heart′ed ness,** *n.*

Great Lakes, series of five lakes between the United States and Ontario, Canada; Lakes Ontario, Erie, Huron, Michigan, and Superior.

great ly (grāt′lē), **1** much: *greatly feared. She greatly desired to be successful.* **2** in a great manner: *Solomon ruled greatly and wisely. adv.*

great-neph ew (grāt′nef′yü), grandnephew. *n.*

great ness (grāt′nis), **1** a being great; bigness. **2** high place or power. **3** great mind or character. *n.*

great-niece (grāt′nēs′), grandniece. *n.*

Great Plains, semiarid region just east of the Rocky Mountains in the United States and SW Canada. It is mostly pasture land.

Great Salt Lake, shallow lake in NW Utah. Its water is much saltier than ocean water.

Great Spirit, English name for the chief god worshiped by certain tribes or groups of American Indians.

great-un cle (grāt′ung′kəl), granduncle. *n.*

Great Wall of China

Great Wall of China, a stone wall about 1500 miles long between China and Mongolia. It was begun in the 200's B.C. for defense.

greave (grēv). Often, **greaves,** *pl.* armor for the leg below the knee. *n.*

grebe (grēb), a diving bird somewhat like a duck, having feet not completely webbed and a pointed bill. *n.*

Gre cian (grē′shən), **1** Greek. **2** a Greek. **1** *adj.,* **2** *n.*

Greece (grēs), country in SE Europe, on the Mediterranean. *Capital:* Athens. See **Balkan States** for map. *n.*

greed (grēd), a wanting to get more than one's share; greedy behavior; greedy desire. *n.*

greed y (grē′dē), **1** wanting to get more than one's share; wanting to get a great deal. **2** wanting to eat or drink a great deal in a hurry; piggish. *adj.,* **greed i er, greed i est.** [*Greedy* comes from Old English *grǣdig.*] —**greed′i ly,** *adv.* —**greed′i ness,** *n.*

Greek (grēk), **1** of Greece, its people, or their language. **2** person born or living in Greece. **3** language of Greece. **1** *adj.,* **2,3** *n.*

Greek Orthodox Church, 1 Eastern Church. **2** the part of the Eastern Church forming the established church in Greece.

green (grēn), **1** the color of most growing plants, grass, and the leaves of trees in summer; color in the spectrum between yellow and blue. **2** having this color; of this color: *green paint. An emerald is green.* **3** covered with growing plants, grass, leaves, etc.: *green fields.* **4** not ripe; not fully grown: *Most green fruit is not good to eat.* **5** not dried, cured, seasoned, or otherwise prepared for use: *green wood.* **6** not trained or experienced: *green players.* **7** ground covered with grass; grassy land: *the village green.* **8 greens,** *pl.* **a** green leaves and branches used for decoration. **b** leaves and stems of plants used for food: *beet greens.* **9** a putting green of a golf course. **1,7-9** *n.,* **2-6** *adj.* —**green′ly,** *adv.* —**green′ness,** *n.*

green back (grēn′bak′), piece of United States paper money having the back printed in green. *n.*

green er y (grē′nər ē), green plants, grass, or leaves. *n., pl.* **green er ies.**

green gro cer (grēn′grō′sər), person who sells fresh vegetables and fruit. *n.*

green horn (grēn′hôrn′), INFORMAL. **1** person without training or experience. **2** person easy to trick or cheat. *n.*

green house (grēn′hous′), building with a glass roof and glass sides kept warm for growing plants; hothouse. *n., pl.* **green hous es** (grēn′hou′ziz).

greenhouse effect, the effect of carbon dioxide and water vapor in the atmosphere. They act to trap solar radiation much as the glass of a greenhouse does, causing warming. With increasing carbon dioxide from pollutants, this effect could cause a change in climate.

green ish (grē′nish), somewhat green. *adj.*

Green land (grēn′lənd), arctic island northeast of North

America. It is the largest island in the world and belongs to Denmark. See **Arctic Circle** for map. *n.*

Green Mountains, part of the Appalachian Mountains extending north and south through Vermont.

green pepper, the unripe fruit of a red pepper plant. It is used as a vegetable.

green sward (grēn′swôrd′), green grass; turf. *n.*

green thumb, a remarkable ability to grow flowers, vegetables, etc.: *You certainly must have a green thumb to have such a beautiful garden.*

Green wich (gren′ich), borough in SE London, England. Longitude is measured east and west of Greenwich. *n.*

Greenwich Time, the standard time used in England and the basis for setting standard time elsewhere. It is determined by setting noon as the time at which the sun is directly overhead at the meridian which passes through Greenwich, England.

green wood (grēn′wůd′), forest in spring and summer when the trees are green with leaves. *n.*

greet (grēt), **1** speak or write to in a friendly, polite way; address in welcome; hail: *She greeted us at the door with a friendly "Hello."* **2** respond to: *His speech was greeted with cheers.* **3** present itself to; meet: *When we opened the door, an icy wind greeted us. v.* —**greet′er,** *n.*

greet ing (grē′ting), **1** act or words of a person who greets another; welcome. **2** greetings, *pl.* friendly wishes on a special occasion: *Season's greetings. n.*

gre gar i ous (grə ger′ē əs *or* grə gar′ē əs), **1** fond of being with others: *He is not gregarious, and spends most of his time alone.* **2** living in flocks, herds, or other groups: *Sheep are gregarious, raccoons are not. adj.*

Gre go ri an (grə gôr′ē ən), **1** of Pope Gregory I. The **Gregorian chant** is a kind of vocal music introduced by Gregory I and still used in the Roman Catholic Church. **2** of Pope Gregory XIII. The **Gregorian calendar,** introduced by Gregory XIII in 1582, is still used today. *adj.*

Greg or y I (greg′ər ē), **Saint,** A.D. 540?-604, pope from A.D. 590 to 604. He was called "Gregory the Great."

Gregory XIII, 1502-1585, pope from 1572 to 1585.

grem lin (grem′lən), an imaginary creature that causes trouble in an aircraft, its engines, parts, etc. *n.*

Gre na da (grə nā′də), island country in the West Indies, a member of the Commonwealth of Nations. *Capital:* St. George's. *n.*

gre nade (grə nād′), a small bomb, which is thrown by hand or fired from a rifle. *n.* [See **Word History.**]

gren a dier (gren′ə dir′), **1** (formerly) a soldier who threw grenades. **2** (later) a member of a specially chosen unit of foot soldiers. **3** (now) a member of a special regiment of guards in the British army. *n.*

grew (grü), past tense of **grow.** *It grew colder as the sun went down. v.*

grey (grā), gray. *n., adj., v.*

grey hound (grā′hound′), a tall, slender hunting dog with a long nose. Greyhounds can run very fast. *n.*

grid (grid), **1** a pattern of evenly spaced vertical and

griffin

horizontal lines. Grids are used on maps to locate places, and in mathematics to locate pairs of numbers. **2** framework of parallel iron bars with spaces between them; grating; gridiron. **3** electrode consisting of wires or a screen which controls the flow of electrons from cathode to anode in a vacuum tube. *n.*

grid dle (grid′l), a heavy, flat plate, usually of metal, on which to cook pancakes, bacon, etc. *n.*

grid dle cake (grid′l kāk′), pancake. *n.*

grid i ron (grid′ī′ərn), **1** grill for broiling. **2** frame or structure like this. A frame for supporting scenery in a theater is a gridiron. **3** a football field. *n.*

grid lock (grid′lok′), **1** a complete tie-up of traffic, which prevents vehicles from moving in any direction. **2** any tie-up, blockage or standstill: *an information gridlock. n.*

grief (grēf), **1** great sadness caused by trouble or loss; heavy sorrow. **2** cause of sadness or sorrow. *n.*

come to grief, have trouble; fail.

grief, come to grief
When he tried out his flying machine, the inventor **came to grief.**

Grieg (grēg), **Edvard,** 1843-1907, Norwegian composer. *n.*

griev ance (grē′vəns), a real or imagined wrong; reason for being angry or annoyed: *Report any grievances you may have to your supervisor. n.*

WORD HISTORY

grenade

Grenade came into English about 400 years ago from French *grenade,* which comes from *pomme grenate,* meaning "pomegranate." The shape of the bomb resembled the shape of the fruit.

grieve (grēv), **1** feel grief; be very sad: *The children grieved over their kitten's death.* **2** cause to feel grief; make very sad: *The news of your illness grieved me. v.,* **grieved, griev ing.** —**griev′er,** *n.* —**griev′ing ly,** *adv.*

griev ous (grē′vəs), **1** hard to bear; causing great pain or suffering; severe: *grievous cruelty.* **2** very evil or offensive; outrageous: *Murder is a grievous crime.* **3** causing grief: *a grievous loss.* **4** full of grief; showing grief: *a grievous cry. adj.* —**griev′ous ly,** *adv.* —**griev′ous ness,** *n.*

grif fin or **grif fon** (grif′ən), an imaginary creature with the head, wings, and forelegs of an eagle, and the body, hind legs, and tail of a lion. *n.*

grill (gril), **1** a cooking utensil with parallel iron bars or wires for broiling meat, fish, etc.; gridiron. **2** cook by holding near the fire; broil. **3** dish of broiled meat, fish, etc. **4** restaurant or dining room that specializes in serving broiled meat, fish, etc. **5** question severely and persistently: *The detectives grilled several suspects concerning the crime.* 1,3,4 *n.*, 2,5 *v.* —**grill′er,** *n.*

grille (gril), an openwork, metal structure or screen, used as a gate, door, window, or to cover the opening in front of the radiator of an automobile; grating. *n.*

grill work (gril′wėrk′), pattern of grilles. *n.*

grim (grim), **1** without mercy; stern, harsh, or fierce: *grim, stormy weather.* **2** not yielding; not relenting: *The losing team fought on with grim resolve.* **3** looking stern, fierce, or harsh: *My parents were grim when they heard about the broken window.* **4** horrible; frightful; ghastly: *It was my grim task to tell them of their friend's death.* *adj.,* **grim mer, grim mest.** —**grim′ly,** *adv.* —**grim′ness,** *n.*

gri mace (grə mās′ *or* grim′is), **1** a twisting of the face; ugly or funny smile: *a grimace caused by pain.* **2** make faces: *The clown grimaced at the children.* 1 *n.*, 2 *v.*, **gri maced, gri mac ing.** —**gri mac′er,** *n.*

grime (grīm), dirt rubbed deeply and firmly into a surface. *n.*

grim i ness (grī′mē nis), grimy condition. *n.*

Grimm (grim), **Jakob,** 1785-1863, and his brother, **Wilhelm,** 1786-1859, German dictionary makers and collectors of fairy tales. *n.*

grim y (grī′mē), covered with grime; very dirty: *grimy hands.* *adj.,* **grim i er, grim i est.** —**grim′i ly,** *adv.*

grin (grin), **1** smile broadly. **2** a broad smile. 1 *v.,* **grinned, grin ning;** 2 *n.* —**grin′ner,** *n.* —**grin′ning ly,** *adv.*

grind (grīnd), **1** crush into bits or powder: *That mill grinds corn into meal and wheat into flour.* **2** crush by harshness or cruelty: *The serfs were ground down by their lords.* **3** sharpen, smooth, or wear by rubbing on something rough: *grind an ax on a grindstone.* **4** make a harsh sound by rubbing; grate: *grind one's teeth in anger.* **5** force by rubbing or pressing: *grind one's heel in the dirt.* **6** work by turning a handle; produce by turning a crank: *grind a pepper mill.* **7** act of grinding. **8** something made by grinding: *a fine grind of coffee.* **9** INFORMAL. long, hard work or study: *To some of the students, mathematics was a grind.* **10** INFORMAL. work or study long and hard. **11** INFORMAL. person who studies long and hard. 1-6,10 *v.,* **ground, grind ing;** 7-9,11 *n.* —**grind′a ble,** *adj.*

grind er (grīn′dər), **1** person or thing that grinds. **2** person or machine that sharpens tools. *n.*

grind stone (grīnd′stōn′), a flat, round stone set in a frame and turned by hand, foot, or a motor. It is used to sharpen tools, such as axes and knives, or to smooth and polish things. *n.*

grip (grip), **1** a firm hold; seizing and holding tight; tight grasp. **2** take a firm hold on; seize and hold tight: *The dog gripped the stick.* **3** power of gripping: *the grip of a bear.* **4** part to take hold of; handle. **5** a certain way of gripping the hand as a sign of belonging to some secret society. **6** a small suitcase or handbag. **7** firm control: *in the grip of poverty.* **8** mental grasp; understanding: *She has a grip of the subject.* **9** get and keep the interest and attention of: *The exciting story gripped the whole class.* 1,3-8 *n.*, 2,9 *v.,* **gripped, grip ping.** —**grip′less,** *adj.* —**grip′per,** *n.*

come to grips, 1 fight hand to hand; struggle close together: *come to grips with an enemy.* **2** work hard and seriously; struggle: *come to grips with a problem.*

gripe (grīp), **1** INFORMAL. annoy; irritate. **2** cause pain in the bowels: *Too much unripe fruit can gripe a person.* **3 gripes,** *pl.* pain in the bowels. **4** INFORMAL. complain: *He was always griping about something.* **5** INFORMAL. complaint. 1,2,4 *v.,* **griped, grip ing;** 3,5 *n.* —**grip′er,** *n.*

grippe (grip), influenza. *n.*

a	hat	i	it	oi	oil	ch	child		a in about
ā	age	ī	ice	ou	out	ng	long		e in taken
ä	far	o	hot	u	cup	sh	she	ə =	i in pencil
e	let	ō	open	u̇	put	th	thin		o in lemon
ē	equal	ô	order	ü	rule	ŦH	then		u in circus
ėr	term					zh	measure		

gris ly (griz′lē), causing horror; frightful; horrible; ghastly. *adj.,* **gris li er, gris li est.** —**gris′li ness,** *n.*

grist (grist), **1** grain to be ground. **2** grain that has been ground; meal or flour. *n.*

gris tle (gris′əl), a tough, elastic tissue, such as is found in meat; cartilage. *n.*

gris tly (gris′lē), of, containing, or like gristle. *adj.,* **gris tli er, gris tli est.** —**gris′tli ness,** *n.*

grist mill (grist′mil′), mill for grinding grain. *n.*

grit (grit), **1** very fine bits of gravel or sand. **2** a coarse sandstone. **3** courage; pluck; endurance. **4** grate; grind: *The swimmer gritted her teeth and plunged into the cold water.* 1-3 *n.*, 4 *v.,* **grit ted, grit ting.** —**grit′less,** *adj.*

grits (grits), corn, oats, wheat, etc., husked and coarsely ground. Grits are eaten boiled. *n.pl.*

grit ti ness (grit′ē nis), condition or quality of being gritty. *n.*

grit ty (grit′ē), **1** of or containing grit; like grit; sandy. **2** courageous; plucky. *adj.,* **grit ti er, grit ti est.**

griz zled (griz′əld), **1** grayish; gray: *a grizzled beard.* **2** gray-haired. *adj.*

griz zly (griz′lē), **1** grayish; gray. **2** grizzly bear. 1 *adj.,* **griz zli er, griz zli est;** 2 *n.,* *pl.* **griz zlies.**

grizzly bear, a large, fierce, gray or brownish-gray bear of western North America.

gro. or **gro,** gross (12 dozen).

groan (grōn), **1** sound made deep in the throat that expresses grief, pain, or disapproval; deep, short moan: *We heard the groans of the injured people.* **2** give a groan or groans: *The movers groaned as they lifted the piano.* **3** make a deep, creaking sound: *The rickety stairs groaned as I climbed them.* **4** express by groaning: *He groaned his disapproval.* 1 *n.*, 2-4 *v.* —**groan′er,** *n.* —**groan′ing ly,** *adv.*

gro cer (grō′sər), person who sells food and household supplies. *n.* [*Grocer* came into English about 800 years ago from French *grossier*, meaning "wholesaler," and can be traced back to Latin *grossus*, meaning "bulky, gross."]

gro cer y (grō′sər ē), **1** store that sells food and household supplies. **2 groceries,** *pl.* articles of food and household supplies sold by a grocer. *n.,* *pl.* **gro cer ies.**

grog (grog), **1** drink made of rum and water, or whisky and water. **2** any strong, alcoholic drink. *n.*

grog gi ly (grog′ə lē), in a groggy manner; shakily. *adv.*

grog gi ness (grog′ē nis), condition of being groggy. *n.*

grog gy (grog′ē), not steady; shaky: *A blow on the head made me groggy.* *adj.,* **grog gi er, grog gi est.**

groin (groin), **1** the hollow on either side of the body where the thigh joins the abdomen. **2** the curved edge where two vaults of a roof intersect. *n.*

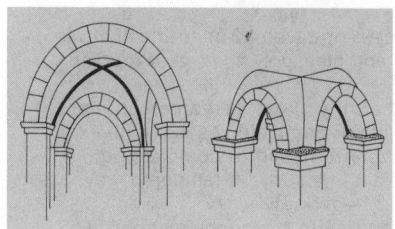

groins (def. 2) shown from the inside and outside of the vaults. (The groins are indicated by heavy lines.)

grom met (grom′it), 1 a metal eyelet. 2 ring of rope, used as an oarlock, to hold a sail on its stays, etc. *n.*

groom (grüm *or* grum), 1 person whose work is taking care of horses. 2 feed, rub down, brush, and generally take care of (horses). 3 take care of the appearance of; make neat and tidy: *He was grooming himself for the party.* 4 prepare (a person) for an office: *The lawyer was being groomed as a candidate for mayor.* 5 bridegroom. 1,5 *n.*, 2-4 *v.* —**groom′er**, *n.*

groove (grüv), 1 a long, narrow channel or furrow, especially one cut by a tool: *My desk has a groove for pencils.* 2 any similar channel; rut: *Wheels leave grooves in a dirt road.* 3 make a groove in. 4 a fixed way of doing things: *It is hard to get out of a groove.* 1,2,4 *n.*, 3 *v.*, **grooved, groov ing.** —**groove′less**, *adj.* —**groove′like′**, *adj.* —**groov′er**, *n.*

groov y (grü′vē), SLANG. excellent; perfect; just right: *a groovy party. adj.*, **groov i er, groov i est.**

grope (grōp), 1 feel about with the hands: *I groped for a flashlight when the lights went out.* 2 search blindly and uncertainly: *The detectives groped for some clue to the mysterious crime.* 3 find by feeling about with the hands; feel (one's way) slowly: *She groped her way down the dark, narrow hall. v.*, **groped, grop ing.** —**grop′er**, *n.* —**grop′ing ly**, *adv.*

gros beak (grōs′bēk′), a colorful bird with a large, stout bill. It is a kind of finch. *n.*

gros grain (grō′grān′), a closely woven silk or rayon cloth with heavy cross threads and a dull finish, used for ribbons, etc. *n.*

gross (grōs), 1 with nothing taken out; total; whole; entire. Gross receipts are all the money taken in before costs are deducted. 2 the whole sum; total amount. 3 make a gross profit of; earn a total of: *gross $20,000 per year.* 4 twelve dozen; 144. 5 very easily seen; glaring; flagrant: *gross misconduct, gross superstition. She makes gross errors in pronouncing words.* 6 coarse; vulgar: *a book with gross language, gross manners.* 7 too big and fat; overfed. 1,5-7 *adj.*, 2,4 *n.*, *pl.* **gross es** for 2, **gross** for 4; 3 *v.* —**gross′ly**, *adv.* —**gross′ness**, *n.*

gro tesque (grō tesk′), 1 odd or unnatural in shape, appearance, manner, etc.; fantastic; odd: *a grotesque monster.* 2 ridiculous; absurd: *The monkey's grotesque antics made us laugh. adj.* —**gro tesque′ly**, *adv.* —**grotesque′ness**, *n.*

◁▷ WORD HISTORY ◁▷

grotesque

Grotesque was borrowed from French *grotesque*, which came from Italian *grottesco*, meaning "of caves," and can be traced back to Greek *kryptē*, meaning "vault, crypt." Medieval underground ruins were often decorated with strange interwoven pictures.

grot to (grot′ō), 1 cave or cavern. 2 an artificial cave made for coolness and pleasure. *n.*, *pl.* **grot toes** or **grot tos.**

grouch (grouch), 1 a surly, ill-tempered person; person who tends to grumble or complain. 2 a surly, ill-tempered mood; fit of grumbling or complaining. 3 grumble or complain in a surly, ill-tempered way. 1,2 *n.*, *pl.* **grouch es;** 3 *v.* —**grouch′er**, *n.*

grouch i ly (grou′chə lē), in a grouchy manner. *adv.*

grouch i ness (grou′chē nis), a grouchy manner. *n.*

grouch y (grou′chē), tending to grumble or complain; surly; ill-tempered. *adj.*, **grouch i er, grouch i est.**

ground[1] (ground), 1 the solid part of the earth's surface; soil: *A blanket of snow covered the ground.* 2 Often, **grounds**, *pl.* any piece of land or region used for some special purpose: *fishing grounds. The school band practices daily on the parade ground.* 3 **grounds**, *pl.* **a** land, lawns, and gardens around a house, school, etc. **b** small bits that sink to the bottom of a drink such as coffee or tea; dregs; sediment. 4 of, on, at, or near the ground: *the ground floor of a building.* 5 run aground; hit the bottom or shore: *The boat grounded in shallow water.* 6 foundation for what is said, thought, claimed, or done; basis; reason: *What are your grounds for that statement?* 7 fix firmly; establish: *Their beliefs are grounded on facts.* 8 instruct in the first principles or elements: *The class is well grounded in arithmetic.* 9 underlying surface; background: *The cloth has a blue pattern on a white ground.* 10 the connection of an electrical conductor with the earth. 11 connect (an electric wire or other conductor) with the earth. 12 keep (a pilot or an aircraft) from flying: *The pilot was grounded by injury.* 13 INFORMAL. keep (a child or teenager) from going out of the home for entertainment, as a discipline or punishment. 14 (in baseball) hit a ball that rolls or bounces along the ground. 1-3,6, 9,10 *n.*, 4 *adj.*, 5,7,8,11-14 *v.* [*Ground*[1] comes from Old English *grund.*]

break ground, 1 turn up soil with a plow, shovel, etc.; dig; plow. 2 begin building.

cover ground, 1 go over a certain distance or area: *Did you cover much ground on your hike?* 2 do a certain amount of work, etc.: *We covered considerable ground in our history class today.*

gain ground, 1 go forward; advance; progress. 2 become more common or widespread: *His ideas are gaining ground.*

give ground, retreat; yield.

lose ground, 1 fail to move forward or progress; go backward: *We lost ground because of the storm.* 2 become less common or widespread: *Superstition loses ground as people become more educated.*

ground[2] (ground), past tense and past participle of **grind**. *The miller ground the corn into meal. The wheat was ground to make flour. v.*

ground crew, mechanics and other nonflying personnel responsible for conditioning and maintenance of aircraft.

ground er (groun′dər), baseball hit so as to bounce or roll along the ground. *n.*

ground hog (ground′hôg′), woodchuck. *n.*

Groundhog Day, February 2, the day when the groundhog is believed to come out of its hole. If it sees its shadow, it goes back in the hole and winter continues for six more weeks.

ground less (ground′lis), without foundation, basis, or reason: *a groundless rumor. adj.* —**ground′less ly**, *adv.* —**ground′less ness**, *n.*

ground pine, a low, creeping evergreen plant with stalks that look like tiny trees. It is a kind of club moss.

ground squirrel, any of several burrowing squirrels, such as the chipmunk.

ground swell, a broad, deep wave or swell of the ocean caused by a distant storm or earthquake.

ground water, water that flows or seeps downward and saturates the soil. The upper level of this saturated zone is called the water table. Ground water supplies springs and wells.

ground work (ground′wėrk′), foundation; basis. *n.*

group (grüp), 1 number of persons or things together: *A* group of children were playing tag. **2** number of persons or things belonging or classed together: *Wheat, rye, and oats belong to the grain group.* **3** form into a group: *The children grouped themselves at the monkey's cage.* **4** put in a group; arrange in groups: *Group the numbers to form three columns.* **5** a military unit made up of two or more battalions of supporting personnel, usually commanded by a colonel. **6** an air-force unit smaller than a wing and composed of two or more squadrons. 1,2,5,6 *n.,* 3,4 *v.*

grouse[1] (grous), any of several brown game birds with feathered legs. The prairie chicken and ruffed grouse are two different kinds of grouse. *n., pl.* **grouse.** —**grouse′like′,** *adj.*

grouse[2] (grous), INFORMAL. grumble; complain. *v.,* **groused, grous ing.** —**grous′er,** *n.*

grove (grōv), group of trees standing together. An orange grove is an orchard of orange trees. *n.*

grov el (gruv′əl *or* grov′əl), **1** lie face downward; crawl at someone's feet; cringe: *The dog groveled before its master when it saw the whip.* **2** humble oneself: *I will apologize when I am wrong, but I will grovel before no one.* *v.,* **grov eled, grov el ing** *or* **grov elled, grov el ling.** —**grov′el er, grov′el ler,** *n.* —**grov′el ing ly, grov′el- ling ly,** *adv.*

grow (grō), **1** become bigger by taking in food, as plants and animals do; develop toward full size or age: *Plants grow from seeds.* **2** exist; thrive: *Few trees grow in the desert.* **3** become bigger; increase: *Her fame grew. Their business has grown fast.* **4** cause to grow; produce; raise: *We grow cotton in the southern part of the United States.* **5** come to be; become: *grow rich. It grew cold.* **6** become attached or united by growth: *The vine has grown fast to the wall.* *v.,* **grew, grown, grow ing.** —**grow′a ble,** *adj.* —**grow′ing ly,** *adv.*

grow on, have an increasing effect or influence on: *The habit grew on me.*

grow out of, 1 grow too large for; outgrow: *When I grew out of my jacket, I gave it to my little brother.* **2** result from; develop from: *Several interesting ideas grew out of the discussion.*

grow up, become full-grown; become an adult: *What will you be when you grow up?*

grow er (grō′ər), **1** person who grows something: *a fruit grower.* **2** plant that grows in a certain way: *a quick grower.* *n.*

growl (groul), **1** make a deep, low, angry sound: *The dog growled at the stranger.* **2** a deep, low, angry sound; deep, warning snarl. **3** complain angrily; grumble: *The sailors growled about the poor food.* **4** an angry complaint; grumble. **5** rumble: *Thunder growled in the distance.* **6** a rumble. 1,3,5 *v.,* 2,4,6 *n.* —**growl′er,** *n.* —**growl′ing ly,** *adv.*

grown (grōn), **1** arrived at full growth. A grown person is an adult. **2** past participle of **grow.** *This corn has grown very tall.* 1 *adj.,* 2 *v.*

grown-up (grōn′up′), **1** adult: *a grown-up person, grown-up manners.* **2** an adult: *The child behaved like a grown-up.* 1 *adj.,* 2 *n.* —**grown′-up′ness,** *n.*

growth (grōth), **1** process of growing; development. **2** amount grown; increase: *one year's growth.* **3** what has grown or is growing: *A thick growth of bushes covered the ground.* **4** an abnormal mass of tissue formed in or on the body. A tumor is a growth. *n.*

grub (grub), **1** a soft, thick, wormlike larva of an insect, especially that of a beetle. **2** root out of the ground; dig up; dig: *Pigs grub for roots.* **3** toil; drudge. **4** SLANG. food. 1,4 *n.,* 2,3 *v.,* **grubbed, grub bing.** —**grub′ber,** *n.*

grub bi ly (grub′ə lē), in a grubby manner. *adv.*

grub bi ness (grub′ē nis), grubby condition or quality. *n.*

grub by (grub′ē), dirty; grimy. *adj.,* **grub bi er, grub bi- est.**

grub stake (grub′stāk′), INFORMAL. **1** food, equipment, money, etc., supplied to a prospector on the condition of sharing in whatever is found. **2** supply with a grub- stake. 1 *n.,* 2 *v.,* **grub staked, grub stak ing.** —**grub′- stak′er,** *n.*

grudge (gruj), **1** feeling of anger or dislike against be- cause of a real or imaginary wrong; ill will: *She has a grudge against the neighbors who built the fence.* **2** feel anger or dislike toward (a person) because of (some- thing); envy the possession of: *He grudged me my little prize even though he had won a bigger one.* **3** give or let have unwillingly: *My boss grudged me a small raise.* 1 *n.,* 2,3 *v.,* **grudged, grudg ing.** —**grudge′less,** *adj.* —**grudg′er,** *n.*

grudg ing ly (gruj′ing lē), unwillingly. *adj.*

gru el (grü′əl), a thin, almost liquid food made by boil- ing oatmeal, etc., in water or milk. *n.*

gru el ing *or* **gru el ling** (grü′ə ling), very tiring; ex- hausting: *Mountain climbing can be grueling. adj.* —**gru′el ing ly, gru′el ling ly,** *adv.*

grue some (grü′səm), causing fear or horror; horrible; revolting. *adj.* —**grue′some ly,** *adv.* —**grue′some- ness,** *n.*

gruff (gruf), **1** deep and harsh; hoarse: *a gruff voice.* **2** rough, rude, or unfriendly; bad-tempered: *a gruff manner. adj.* [*Gruff* comes from Dutch *grof.*] —**gruff′ly,** *adv.* —**gruff′ness,** *n.*

grum ble (grum′bəl), **1** mutter in discontent; complain in a bad-tempered way; find fault: *Everyone was grum- bling about the rainy weather.* **2** a mutter of discontent; bad-tempered complaint. **3** make a low, heavy sound like far-off thunder; rumble. **4** a rumble. 1,3 *v.,* **grum bled, grum bling;** 2,4 *n.* —**grum′bler,** *n.*

grump i ly (grum′pə lē), in a grumpy manner. *adv.*

grump i ness (grum′pē nis), grumpy condition, behav- ior, or quality. *n.*

grump y (grum′pē), surly; ill-humored; gruff: *Grumpy people can find fault with almost anything. adj.,* **grump i- er, grump i est.**

grunt (grunt), **1** the deep, hoarse sound that a hog makes. **2** a sound like this: *She picked up the heavy carton with a grunt.* **3** make this sound: *He grunted in discontent.* **4** say with this sound: *The sullen teenager grunted an apology.* 1,2 *n.,* 3,4 *v.* —**grunt′er,** *n.* —**grunt′ing ly,** *adv.*

G.S., GS, or **g.s.,** general secretary.

GSA or **G.S.A.,** Girl Scouts of America.

gt. or **gt,** great.

Gt. Br. or **Gt. Brit.,** Great Britain.

grubs
(def. 1)

Gua de loupe (gwä′dl üp′), French islands in the West Indies. *n.*

Guam (gwäm), island in the W Pacific, east of the Philippines. Guam belongs to the United States. *n.*

Guang zhou (gwäng′jō′), official spelling of **Kwangchow.** *n.*

gua no (gwä′nō), waste matter from sea birds, used as a fertilizer. It is found especially on islands near Peru. *n.*, *pl.* **gua nos.** [*Guano* was borrowed from Spanish *guano,* which comes from Quechua *huanu,* meaning "manure."]

guar an tee (gar′ən tē′), **1** a promise or pledge to replace or repair a purchased product, return the money paid, etc., if the product is not as represented: *We have a one-year guarantee on our new car.* **2** stand back of; give a guarantee for: *This company guarantees its clocks for a year.* **3** guaranty. **4** undertake to secure for another: *The landlady will guarantee us possession of the house by May.* **5** make secure; protect: *Our home insurance guarantees us against loss in case of fire or theft.* **6** promise (to do something); pledge that (something) has been or will be: *The store guaranteed to deliver my purchase by next Friday.* 1,3 *n.,* 2,4-6 *v.,* **guar an teed, guar an tee ing.**

guar an tor (gar′ən tôr), person who makes or gives a guarantee. *n.*

guar an ty (gar′ən tē), **1** a pledge or promise by which a person gives security for the payment of a debt or the performance of an obligation by another person; guarantee. **2** property, money, or goods given or taken as security. **3** act or fact of giving security. **4** to guarantee. 1-3 *n.,* *pl.* **guar an ties;** 4 *v.,* **guar an tied, guar an ty ing.**

guard (gärd), **1** watch over; take care of; keep safe; defend; protect: *The dog guarded the child day and night.* **2** keep from getting out; hold back; check: *Guard the prisoners.* **3** person or group that guards. A soldier or group of soldiers guarding a person or place is a guard. **4** take precautions: *Guard against cavities by brushing your teeth regularly.* **5** anything that gives protection; arrangement to give safety: *A helmet is a guard against head injuries.* **6** careful watch: *The shepherd kept guard over the sheep.* **7** position in which one is ready to defend in boxing, fencing, or cricket. **8** an offensive player at either side of the center in football. **9** either of two players in basketball stationed near the center of the court. 1,2,4 *v.,* 3,5-9 *n.* **—guard′a ble,** *adj.* **—guard′er,** *n.* **—guard′less,** *adj.* **—guard′like′,** *adj.*

on guard, ready to defend or protect; watchful.

guard ed (gär′did), **1** kept safe; carefully watched over; defended; protected. **2** careful; cautious: *"Maybe" was the guarded answer to my question. adj.*

guard house (gärd′hous′), **1** building used by soldiers on guard. **2** building used as a jail for soldiers. *n.,* *pl.* **guard hous es** (gärd′hou′ziz).

guard i an (gär′dē ən), **1** person who takes care of another or of some special thing. **2** person appointed by law to take care of the affairs of someone who is young or who cannot take care of his or her own affairs. **3** protecting: *guardian angel.* 1,2 *n.,* 3 *adj.*

guard i an ship (gär′dē ən ship), position or care of a guardian. *n.*

guard room (gärd′rüm′ or gärd′rùm′), room used by soldiers on guard. *n.*

guards man (gärdz′mən), **1** guard. **2** soldier who belongs to the National Guard. *n.,* *pl.* **guards men.**

Guat., Guatemala.

Gua te ma la (gwä′tə mä′lə), country in NW Central America. *Capital:* Guatemala City. See **Yucatán** for map. *n.* **—Gua′te ma′lan,** *adj., n.*

Guatemala City, capital of Guatemala, in the central part.

gua va (gwä′və), small, yellow or red fruit of a tropical American tree or shrub, used for jelly, jam, etc. *n.,* *pl.* **gua vas.** [*Guava* is from Spanish *guayaba,* which comes from an American Indian word of the Caribbean region.]

gu ber na to ri al (gü′bər nə tôr′ē əl), of a governor. *adj.*

gudg eon (guj′ən), a small European freshwater fish that is often used for bait. It is related to the carp. *n.*

gue ril la (gə ril′ə), guerrilla. *n.,* *pl.* **gue ril las;** *adj.*

Guern sey (gėrn′zē), **1** one of the Channel Islands. **2** one of a breed of tan-and-white dairy cattle which came from this island. Guernseys give rich, cream-colored milk. *n.,* *pl.* **Guern seys** for 2.

guer ril la (gə ril′ə), **1** member of a band of fighters who harass the enemy by sudden raids, ambushes, plundering supply trains, etc. Guerrillas are not part of a regular army. **2** of or by guerrillas: *a guerrilla attack.* 1 *n.,* *pl.* **guer ril las;** 2 *adj.* Also, **guerilla.**

guess (ges), **1** form an opinion of something without really knowing: *Do you know this or are you just guessing?* **2** opinion formed without really knowing: *My guess is that it will rain tomorrow.* **3** get right or find out by guessing: *Can you guess the answer to that riddle?* **4** think; believe; suppose: *I guess he was serious after all.* 1,3,4 *v.,* 2 *n.,* *pl.* **guess es. —guess′a ble,** *adj.* **—guess′er,** *n.*

guess work (ges′wèrk′), work, action, or results based on guessing; guessing. *n.*

guest (gest), **1** person who is received and entertained at another's home, club, etc.; visitor. **2** person staying at a hotel or motel. *n.* [*Guest* came into English about 800 years ago from Icelandic *gestr.*] **—guest′less,** *adj.*

guf faw (gu fô′), **1** burst of loud, coarse laughter. **2** laugh loudly and coarsely. 1 *n.,* 2 *v.*

guid ance (gīd′ns), a guiding; leadership; direction: *Under her mother's guidance, she learned how to swim. n.*

guide (gīd), **1** show the way; lead; direct: *The scout guided us through the pass. The counselor guided her in the choice of a career.* **2** person or thing that shows the way, leads, or directs: *Tourists sometimes hire guides.* **3** part of a machine for directing or regulating motion or action. **4** guidebook. 1 *v.,* **guid ed, guid ing;** 2-4 *n.* **—guid′a ble,** *adj.* **—guide′less,** *adj.* **—guid′er,** *n.* **—guid′ing ly,** *adv.*

guide book (gīd′bùk′), book of directions and information for travelers, tourists, etc. *n.*

guided missile, missile that can be guided in flight to its target by means of radio signals from the ground or by automatic devices inside the missile which direct its course.

guide line (gīd′līn′). Usually, **guidelines,** *pl.* guide, principle, or policy for determining a future course of action: *guidelines for foreign trade. n.*

guide post (gīd′pōst′), post with signs and directions on it. A guidepost where roads meet tells travelers what places each road goes to and how far it is to each place. *n.*

guide word, word put at the top of a page as a guide to the contents of the page. The guide words for this page are *Guadeloupe* and *guile.*

guild (gild), **1** association formed by people having the same interests, work, etc., for some useful or common purpose: *The author is a member of the Writers Guild.* **2** (in the Middle Ages) a union of the men in one particular trade or craft, formed to keep its standards high and to protect the interests of its members. *n.*

guil der (gil′dər), a silver coin or unit of money in the Netherlands, worth about 40½ cents. *n.*

guild hall (gild′hôl′), **1** hall in which a guild meets. **2** BRITISH. town hall or city hall. *n.*

guile (gīl), crafty deceit; sly tricks; cunning: *By guile the girl got the candy from her younger brother. n.*

guile ful (gīl'fəl), crafty and deceitful; sly and tricky. *adj.*
—**guile'ful ly,** *adv.* —**guile'ful ness,** *n.*

guile less (gīl'lis), without guile; honest; frank; straightforward. *adj.* —**guile'less ly,** *adv.* —**guile'less ness,** *n.*

guillotine (def. 1)

guil lo tine (gil'ə tēn'), **1** machine for beheading people
by means of a heavy blade that slides down between two
grooved posts. The guillotine was used during the
French Revolution. **2** behead with this machine. 1 *n.,* 2
v., **guil lo tined, guil lo tin ing.** [*Guillotine* was named for
Joseph-Ignace *Guillotin,* 1738-1814, a French doctor who
proposed that it be used in executions.]

guilt (gilt), **1** fact or condition of having done wrong;
being guilty; being to blame: *The evidence proved the
accused person's guilt.* **2** guilty action or conduct; crime;
offense; wrongdoing. **3** a feeling of having done wrong
or being to blame. *n.*

guilt i ly (gil'tə lē), in a guilty manner. *adv.*

guilt less (gilt'lis), free from guilt; not guilty; innocent.
adj. —**guilt'less ly,** *adv.* —**guilt'less ness,** *n.*

guilt y (gil'tē), **1** having done wrong; deserving to be
blamed and punished: *The jury pronounced the defendant
guilty of theft.* **2** knowing or showing that one has done
wrong: *a guilty conscience, a guilty look. adj.,* **guilt i er,
guilt i est.** —**guilt'i ness,** *n.*

guin ea (gin'ē), **1** a British gold coin, not made since
1813, worth 21 shillings. **2** amount equal to 21 shillings,
formerly used in Great Britain in stating prices, fees, etc.
n., pl. **guin eas.**

Guin ea (gin'ē), country in W Africa on the Atlantic.
Capital: Conakry. See **Nigeria** for map. *n.* —**Guin'e an,**
adj., n.

Guin ea-Bis sau (gin'ē bi sou'), country in NW Africa.
Capital: Bissau. *n.*

guinea fowl, a domestic fowl somewhat like a pheasant, having dark-gray feathers with small, white spots. Its
flesh and its eggs are eaten.

guinea hen, 1 guinea fowl. **2** a female guinea fowl.

guinea pig, 1 a small, fat, harmless rodent with short
ears and a short tail or no tail. Guinea pigs make good
pets and are often used for laboratory experiments.
2 any person or thing serving as a subject for experiment or observation.

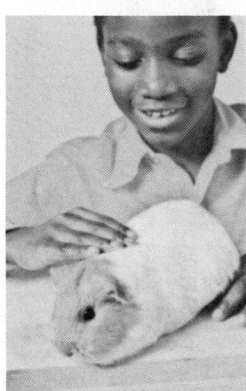

guinea pig (def. 1)
about 6 in.
(15 cm.) long

Guin e vere (gwin'ə vir), King Arthur's queen, who was
loved by Lancelot. *n.*

guise (gīz), **1** style of dress; garb: *The spy went in the
guise of a nurse and was not recognized by the enemy.*
2 outward appearance: *That theory is nothing but an old
idea in a new guise.* **3** assumed appearance; pretense:
Under the guise of friendship he plotted treachery. n.

gui tar (gə tär'), a musical instrument usually having six
strings, played with the fingers or with a pick. *n.*

guitar

gulch (gulch), a very deep, narrow ravine with steep
sides, especially one marking the course of a stream or
torrent. *n., pl.* **gulch es.**

gulf (gulf), **1** a large bay; arm of an ocean or sea extending into the land: *The Gulf of Mexico is between Florida
and Mexico.* **2** a very deep break or cut in the earth: *The
earthquake made a gulf in the earth.* **3** separation too great
to be closed; wide gap: *The quarrel created a gulf between
the old friends. n.* —**gulf'like',** *adj.*

Gulf Stream, current of warm water in the Atlantic. It
flows out of the Gulf of Mexico, north along the East
coast of the United States, and then northeast across
the Atlantic toward the British Isles.

gull[1]
about 23 in.
(58 cm.) long

gull[1] (gul), a graceful, gray-and-white bird living on or
near large bodies of water. A gull has long wings,
webbed feet, and a thick, strong beak. *n.*

gull[2] (gul), **1** deceive; cheat. **2** person who is easily deceived or cheated. 1 *v.,* 2 *n.*

gul let (gul'it), **1** esophagus. **2** throat. *n.*

gul li bil i ty (gul'ə bil'ə tē), tendency to be easily deceived or cheated. *n.*

gul li ble (gul'ə bəl), easily deceived or cheated. *adj.*

Gul li ver (gul'ə vər), **Lemuel,** hero of voyages to four imaginary regions in Jonathan Swift's satire, *Gulliver's Travels. n.*

gul ly (gul'ē), a narrow gorge; small ravine; ditch made by heavy rains or running water. *n., pl.* **gul lies.**

gulp (gulp), **1** swallow eagerly or greedily: *The hungry girl gulped down the bowl of soup.* **2** act of swallowing: *He ate the cookie in one gulp.* **3** amount swallowed at one time; mouthful: *I took a gulp of the wine.* **4** keep in; choke back: *The disappointed boy gulped down a sob and tried to smile.* **5** to gasp or choke: *The spray of cold water made me gulp.* 1,4,5 *v.,* 2,3 *n.* —**gulp'er,** *n.*

gum[1] (gum), **1** a sticky juice given off by certain trees and plants that hardens in the air and dissolves in water. Gum is used to make mucilage, candy, drugs, etc. **2** gum tree. **3** chewing gum. **4** the sticky substance on the back of a stamp, the flap of an envelope, etc.; mucilage. **5** rubber. **6** smear, stick together, or stiffen with gum. **7** make or become sticky: *Her jacket pocket was all gummed with candy.* 1-5 *n.,* 6,7 *v.,* **gummed, gum ming.**

gum[2] (gum). Often, **gums,** *pl.* the firm tissue around the teeth. *n.*

gum arabic, gum obtained from acacia trees, used in making candy, medicine, and mucilage.

gum bo (gum'bō), **1** the okra plant. **2** its sticky pods. **3** soup usually made of chicken and rice and thickened with these pods. **4** kind of fine soil that becomes very sticky when wet. *n., pl.* **gum bos.** [*Gumbo* is of Bantu origin.]

gum drop (gum'drop'), a stiff, jellylike piece of candy made of gum arabic, gelatin, etc., sweetened and flavored. *n.*

gum my (gum'ē), **1** sticky like gum. **2** covered with gum. **3** giving off gum. *adj.,* **gum mi er, gum mi est.**

gump tion (gump'shən), INFORMAL. **1** initiative; energy. **2** common sense; good judgment. *n.*

gum resin, mixture of gum and resin, obtained from certain plants.

gum tree, tree that yields gum. The eucalyptus is one kind of gum tree.

gun (gun), **1** weapon with a metal tube for shooting bullets or shells. Cannons, rifles, pistols, and revolvers are guns. **2** anything resembling a gun in use or shape: *a spray gun.* **3** the shooting of a gun as a signal or salute: *a salute of 21 guns.* **4** shoot with a gun; hunt with a gun: *They went gunning for rabbits.* **5** increase the speed of; accelerate: *gun a sports car around a corner.* 1-3 *n.,* 4,5 *v.,* **gunned, gun ning.** [*Gun* came into English about 600 years ago from Icelandic *Gunnhildr,* a woman's name. Personal names were often given to cannons.]

stick to one's guns, keep one's position; refuse to retreat or yield.

gun boat (gun'bōt'), a small warship that can be used in shallow water. *n.*

gun cot ton (gun'kot'n), an explosive made by treating cotton or other cellulose fibers with a mixture of nitric and sulfuric acids. *n.*

gun fire (gun'fīr'), the shooting of a gun or guns. *n.*

gung-ho (gung'hō'), INFORMAL. eager; enthusiastic: *a gung-ho student. adj.*

gun lock (gun'lok'), the part of a gun that controls the hammer and fires the charge. *n.*

gun man (gun'mən), person who uses a gun to rob or kill. *n., pl.* **gun men.**

gun ner (gun'ər), **1** person trained to fire artillery; soldier who handles and fires cannon. **2** (in the Navy) a warrant officer in charge of a ship's guns. **3** person who hunts with a gun. *n.*

gun ner y (gun'ər ē), **1** the construction and manage-

ment of large guns. **2** use of guns; shooting of guns. *n.*

gun ny (gun'ē), **1** a strong, coarse fabric made of jute, used for sacks, bags, etc. **2** gunnysack. *n., pl.* **gun nies.** [*Gunny* comes from Hindustani *gōnī.*]

gun ny sack (gun'ē sak'), sack, bag, etc., made of gunny. *n.*

gun pow der (gun'pou'dər), powder that explodes when brought into contact with fire, used in guns, blasting, and fireworks. Modern gunpowder is made of saltpeter, sulfur, and charcoal. *n.*

gun shot (gun'shot'), **1** shot fired from a gun. **2** the shooting of a gun: *We heard gunshots.* **3** distance that a gun will shoot: *The deer was within gunshot. n.*

gun smith (gun'smith'), person whose work is making or repairing small guns. *n.*

gun wale (gun'l), the upper edge of the side of a ship or boat. *n.*

gup py (gup'ē), a very small, brightly colored fish of tropical fresh water, often kept in aquariums. The female bears live young instead of laying eggs. *n., pl.* **gup pies.**

gur gle (gėr'gəl), **1** flow or run with a bubbling sound: *Water gurgles when it is poured out of a bottle or flows over stones.* **2** a bubbling sound. **3** make a bubbling sound: *The baby gurgled happily.* 1,3 *v.,* **gur gled, gur gling;** 2 *n.*

gur ney (gėr'nē), cart for moving patients in a hospital. It has a flat top, an adjustable back rest, and movable side rails. *n., pl.* **gur neys.**

gu ru (gü'rü *or* gü rü'), **1** a religious teacher or guide in Hinduism. **2** any guide or leader, in the spiritual, political, literary, or musical field. *n.*

gush (gush), **1** rush out suddenly; pour out: *Oil gushed from the new well.* **2** rush of water or other liquid from an enclosed space: *If you get a deep cut, there usually is a gush of blood.* **3** talk in a way that shows too much silly feeling: *The children gushed about the puppy.* 1,3 *v.,* 2 *n.*

gush er (gush'ər), an oil well which spouts a steady stream of oil without pumping. *n.*

gush y (gush'ē), showing too much silly feeling. *adj.,* **gush i er, gush i est.** —**gush'i ness,** *n.*

gus set (gus'it), a triangular piece of material inserted in a garment to give greater strength or more room. *n.*

gust (gust), **1** a sudden, violent rush of wind: *A gust upset the small sailboat.* **2** a sudden burst of rain, smoke, sound, etc. **3** a sudden bursting forth of anger, enthusiasm, or other feeling: *Gusts of laughter greeted the clown. n.*

gus to (gus'tō), hearty enjoyment; keen relish: *The hungry boy ate his dinner with gusto. n.*

gust y (gus'tē), coming in gusts; windy; stormy. *adj.,* **gust i er, gust i est.** —**gust'i ly,** *adv.* —**gust'i ness,** *n.*

gut (gut), **1** the whole alimentary canal or one of its parts, such as the intestines or stomach. **2 guts,** *pl.* **a** intestines. **b** SLANG. courage. **3** catgut. **4** remove the intestines of; disembowel. **5** destroy the inside of. 1-3 *n.,* 4,5 *v.,* **gut ted, gut ting.**

gut (def. 5)
Fire **gutted** the building and left only the brick walls standing.

Gu ten berg (güt′n bėrg′), **Johann**, 1398?-1468, German printer. He is supposed to have been the first European to print from movable type. *n.*

gut ta-per cha (gut′ə pėr′chə), substance like rubber, made from the thick, milky juice of certain tropical trees. It is used in temporary tooth fillings, in insulating electric wires, etc. *n.* [*Gutta-percha* comes from Malay *getah percha*.]

gut ter (gut′ər), **1** channel or ditch along the side of a street or road to carry off water; low part of a street beside the sidewalk. **2** channel or trough along the lower edge of a roof to carry off rain water. **3** a channel; groove: *the gutters on either side of a bowling alley.* **4** form gutters in. **5** flow or melt in streams: *Water guttered down the side of the hill. The candle guttered when the melted wax ran down its sides.* 1-3 *n.*, 4,5 *v.*

gut tur al (gut′ər əl), **1** of the throat. **2** formed in the throat; harsh: *a deep, guttural voice.* **3** formed between the back of the tongue and the soft palate. The *g* in *go* is a guttural sound. **4** sound formed between the back of the tongue and the soft palate. The sound *k* is a guttural in the word *cool.* 1-3 *adj.*, 4 *n.* —**gut′tur al ly**, *adv.*

guy[1] (gī), **1** rope, chain, or wire attached to something to steady or secure it. **2** steady or secure with a guy or guys: *The mast was guyed by four ropes.* 1 *n.*, 2 *v.*, **guyed, guy ing.**

guy[2] (gī), INFORMAL. fellow. *n.*

Guy an a (gī an′ə), country in N South America, a member of the Commonwealth of Nations. *Capital:* Georgetown. *n.*

guz zle (guz′əl), drink greedily; drink too much: *guzzle soft drinks.* *v.*, **guz zled, guz zling.** —**guz′zler,** *n.*

gym (jim), INFORMAL. **1** gymnasium. **2** physical education. *n.*

gym na si um (jim nā′zē əm), room, building, etc., fitted up for physical exercise or training and for indoor athletic sports. *n.*, *pl.* **gym na si ums, gym na si a** (jim nā′zē ə). [*Gymnasium* comes from Latin *gymnasium,* meaning "gymnastic school, school," and can be traced back to Greek *gymnos,* meaning "naked." In ancient times athletes exercised while naked.]

gym nast (jim′nast), an expert in gymnastics. *n.*

gym nas tic (jim nas′tik), having to do with physical exercises or activities. *adj.* —**gym nas′ti cal ly,** *adv.*

gymnastics

gym nas tics (jim nas′tiks), exercises for developing the muscles and improving physical fitness and health, such as are done in a gymnasium. *n.pl.*

gym no sperm (jim′nə spėrm′), any plant having its seeds exposed, not enclosed in an ovary or fruit. The pine, fir, and spruce are gymnosperms. *n.*

gyp (jip), SLANG. **1** to cheat; swindle. **2** a cheating; swindle. **3** person who cheats; swindler. 1 *v.*, **gypped, gyp ping;** 2,3 *n.* —**gyp′per,** *n.*

gyp sum (jip′səm), mineral used to make fertilizer and plaster of Paris. *n.*

gyp sy (jip′sē), **1** Also, **Gypsy.** person belonging to a wandering group of people who came originally from India. **2 Gypsy,** language of the gypsies; Romany. **3** of gypsies: *gypsy music.* 1,2 *n.*, *pl.* **gyp sies;** 3 *adj.* Also, **gipsy.** [*Gypsy* can be traced back to the word *Egyptian.* It was formerly believed that gypsies came from Egypt.]

gypsy moth, a brownish or white moth whose larvae damage trees by eating their leaves.

gy rate (jī′rāt), move in a circle or spiral; whirl; rotate: *A spinning top gyrates.* *v.*, **gy rat ed, gy rat ing.**

gy ra tion (jī rā′shən), circular or spiral motion; whirling; rotation. *n.*

gyrfalcon—about 2 ft. (60 cm.) long

gyr fal con (jėr′fôl′kən, jėr′fal′kən, *or* jėr′fô′kən), a large falcon of the Arctic, with white, black, or gray feathers. *n.*

gy ro com pass (jī′rō kum′pəs), compass using a gyroscope instead of a magnetic needle. It points to true north instead of to the North Magnetic Pole and is not affected by nearby objects of iron or steel. *n.*, *pl.* **gy ro com pass es.**

gyr os (hir′os *or* gir′ōs), pressed, seasoned lamb and beef formed into a cone on a vertical rotating grill and roasted over a charcoal fire. The crisp crust is cut off for serving, often on round bread. *n.*, *pl.* **gyr os.**

gyroscope

gy ro scope (jī′rə skōp), instrument consisting of a heavy, rotating wheel so mounted that its axis can turn freely in one or more directions. A spinning gyroscope tends to resist any change in the direction of its axis, no matter which way its base is turned. Gyroscopes are used to keep ships and airplanes steady. *n.*

gy ro scop ic (jī′rə skop′ik), of a gyroscope. *adj.*

H or h (āch), the eighth letter of the English alphabet. *n., pl.* **H's** or **h's.**

H, symbol for hydrogen.

ha (hä), **1** exclamation of surprise, joy, or triumph: *"Ha! I've caught you!" he shouted.* **2** sound of a laugh: *"Ha! ha! ha!" laughed the boys. interj.* Also, **hah.**

Ha, symbol for hahnium.

ha be as cor pus (hā′bē əs kôr′pəs), writ or order requiring that a prisoner be brought before a judge or into court to decide whether he or she is being held lawfully. The right of habeas corpus is a protection against unjust imprisonment. [*Habeas corpus* is from the medieval Latin phrase *habeas corpus,* meaning "you may have the body," which comes from Latin *habere,* meaning "to have," and *corpus,* meaning "body." It is called this because *habeas corpus* were the first words of the medieval writ.]

hab er dash er (hab′ər dash′ər), dealer in the things men wear, such as hats, ties, shirts, socks, etc. *n.*

hab er dash er y (hab′ər dash′ər ē), **1** store of a haberdasher. **2** articles sold by a haberdasher. *n., pl.* **hab er-dash er ies.**

hab it (hab′it), **1** tendency to act in a certain way; usual way of acting; custom; practice. Doing a thing over and over again makes it a habit. **2** the clothing worn by members of some religious orders. Monks and nuns often wear habits. **3** the clothing worn for horseback riding: *a black riding habit. n.* [*Habit* came into English about 750 years ago from French *habit,* and can be traced back to Latin *habere,* meaning "to have, hold." See **Word Family.**]

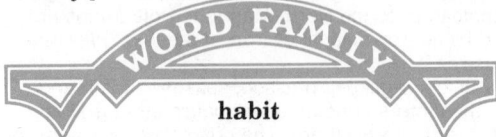

habit

Below are words related to *habit.* They can all be traced back to the Latin word *habere* (hä bā′re), meaning "to have, hold."

ability	duty	inhabit
able	endeavor	inhibit
avoirdupois	exhibit	malady
debt	habeas corpus	prohibit
disability	habitat	rehabilitate
due	habitual	uninhabited

hab it a ble (hab′ə tə bəl), fit to live in; able to be inhabited: *repair an abandoned house to make it habitable. adj.* —**hab′it a ble ness,** *n.* —**hab′it a bly,** *adv.*

hab i tat (hab′ə tat), place where an animal or plant naturally lives or grows: *The jungle is the habitat of monkeys. n.* [*Habitat* comes from Latin *habitat,* meaning "it inhabits," and can be traced back to *habere,* meaning "to have, hold."]

hab i ta tion (hab′ə tā′shən), **1** place or building to live in; home; dwelling. **2** a living in; inhabiting: *A barn is not fit for human habitation. n.*

ha bit u al (hə bich′ü əl), **1** done by habit; caused by habit: *a habitual smile. Habitual courtesy is always being polite to others.* **2** being or doing something by habit;

regular; steady: *A habitual reader reads a great deal.* **3** often done, seen, or used; usual; customary: *a habitual sight. adj.* —**ha bit′u al ly,** *adv.* —**ha bit′u al ness,** *n.*

ha bit u ate (hə bich′ü āt), make used; accustom: *The pioneers were habituated to the hardships of frontier life. v.,* **ha bit u at ed, ha bit u at ing.** —**ha bit′u a′tion,** *n.*

ha ci en da (hä′sē en′də), (In Spanish America) a ranch or country house. *n., pl.* **ha ci en das.** [*Hacienda* was borrowed from Spanish *hacienda,* and can be traced back to Latin *facere,* meaning "to make, do."]

hack[1] (hak), **1** cut roughly: *She hacked the meat into jagged pieces.* **2** a rough cut. **3** give frequent, short, dry coughs. **4** a short, dry cough. 1,3 *v.,* 2,4 *n.*

hack[2] (hak), **1** carriage for hire: *We rode around the park in a hack.* **2** INFORMAL. taxicab. **3** horse for hire. **4** an old or worn-out horse. **5** person hired to do routine work, especially literary work; drudge. **6** working just for money; hired; drudging: *a hack writer.* **7** done just for money: *a hack job.* 1-5 *n.,* 6,7 *adj.*

hack er (hak′ər), person who is especially interested in computers and skilled in using them. *n.*

hack le (hak′əl), **1** one of the long, slender feathers on the neck of a rooster, pigeon, etc. **2 hackles,** *pl.* hairs on the back of a dog's neck that can become erect. *n.* **raise the hackles,** INFORMAL. arouse anger; make mad.

hack ney (hak′nē), **1** horse for ordinary riding. **2** carriage for hire. *n.*

hack neyed (hak′nēd), used too often; commonplace: *"White as snow" is a hackneyed comparison. adj.*

hacksaw

hack saw (hak′sô′), saw for cutting metal, consisting of a narrow, fine-toothed blade fixed in a frame. *n.*

had (had), past tense and past participle of **have.** *She had a party. A fine time was had by all who came. v.*

had dock (had′ək), a food fish of the northern Atlantic, related to the cod, but smaller. *n., pl.* **had docks** or **had dock.**

Ha des (hā′dēz′), **1** (in Greek myths) the home of the dead, a gloomy place below the earth. **2** Also, **hades.** hell. *n.*

had n't (had′nt), had not.

hadst (hadst), OLD USE. had. "Thou hadst" means "you had." *v.*

haf ni um (haf′nē əm), a silvery metallic element which occurs in zirconium ores and is used to control the rate of reaction in nuclear reactors. *n.*

haft (haft), handle of a knife, sword, dagger, etc. *n.*

hag (hag), **1** a very ugly old woman, especially one who is vicious or malicious. **2** witch. *n.*

Hag ga i (hag′ē ī), **1** (in the Bible) a Hebrew prophet. **2** book of the Old Testament. *n.*

hag gard (hag′ərd), looking worn from pain, fatigue, worry, hunger, etc.; careworn: *the haggard faces of the rescued miners. adj.* —**hag′gard ly,** *adv.*

hag gle (hag′əl), to dispute, especially about a price or the terms of a bargain. *v.,* **hag gled, hag gling.**

hag gler (hag′lər), person who haggles. *n.*

Hague (hāg), **The,** unofficial capital of the Netherlands, in the SW part. The official capital is Amsterdam. *n.*

hah (hä), ha. *interj.*

hahn i um (hä′nē əm), proposed name for a radioactive metallic element, produced artificially from californium. *n.*

hai ku (hī′kü), a poem of three lines and containing only 17 syllables. *n., pl.* **hai ku.** [*Haiku* was borrowed from Japanese *haiku,* which comes from *hai,* meaning "sport, play," and *ku,* meaning "poem, verse."]

hail¹ (hāl), **1** small, round pieces of ice formed in thunderclouds and falling like rain; hailstones: *Hail fell with such violence that it broke windows.* **2** fall in hail: *Sometimes it hails during a summer thunderstorm.* **3** a shower like hail: *a hail of bullets.* **4** pour down in a shower like hail: *The mob hailed insults at the speaker.* 1,3 *n.,* 2,4 *v.*

hail² (hāl), **1** shout in welcome to; greet; cheer: *The crowd hailed the winner.* **2** a shout of welcome; greeting; cheer. **3** greetings! welcome!: *Hail to the winner!* **4** call out or signal to: *I hailed a taxi to take me to the airport.* 1,4 *v.,* 2 *n.,* 3 *interj.* **—hail′er,** *n.*

hail from, come from: *She hails from Boston.*

Hail Mary, Ave Maria.

hail stone (hāl′stōn′), a ball or pellet of hail. Hailstones are usually very small, but sometimes they are as big as marbles. *n.*

hail storm (hāl′stôrm′), storm with hail. *n.*

hair (her *or* har), **1** a fine, threadlike growth from the skin of people and animals. **2** mass of such growths covering the human head or forming the coat of an animal. **3** a fine, threadlike growth from the outer layer of plants. **4** hair's-breadth: *The ball missed his head by a hair. n.* **—hair′like′,** *adj.*

split hairs, make too fine distinctions.

hair breadth (her′bredth′ *or* har′bredth′), hair's-breadth. *adj., n.*

hair brush (her′brush′ *or* har′brush′), a stiff brush for smoothing the hair. *n.*

hair cloth (her′klôth′ *or* har′klôth′), a scratchy fabric made of cotton and horsehair or camel's hair, used to cover furniture, stiffen garments, etc. *n.*

hair cut (her′kut′ *or* har′kut′), act or manner of cutting the hair. *n.*

hair do (her′dü′ *or* har′dü′), way of arranging the hair. *n., pl.* **hair dos.**

hair dress er (her′dres′ər *or* har′dres′ər), person whose work is arranging or cutting women's hair. *n.*

hair i ness (her′ē nis *or* har′ē nis), hairy condition. *n.*

hair less (her′lis *or* har′lis), without hair. *adj.*

hair line (her′līn′ *or* har′līn′), **1** a very thin line. **2** the irregular outline where hair growth ends on the head or forehead. *n.*

hair pin (her′pin′ *or* har′pin′), **1** a small, thin piece of metal or plastic, usually shaped like a U, used by women and girls to keep their hair in place. **2** shaped like a hairpin: *a hairpin turn.* 1 *n.,* 2 *adj.*

hair-rais ing (her′rā′zing *or* har′rā′zing), making the hair stand on end from fright; terrifying: *a hair-raising ghost story. adj.* **—hair′-rais′ing ly,** *adv.*

hair's-breadth or **hairs breadth** (herz′bredth′ *or* harz′bredth′), **1** very narrow; extremely close: *When the tree fell, we had a hair's-breadth escape.* **2** a very narrow space or distance: *Our team was within a hair's-breadth of winning the game.* 1 *adj.,* 2 *n.* Also, **hairbreadth.**

hair split ting (her′split′ing *or* har′split′ing), **1** act of making too fine distinctions. **2** making too fine distinctions. 1 *n.,* 2 *adj.*

hair spring (her′spring′ *or* har′spring′), a fine, hairlike spring which regulates the motion of the balance wheel in a watch or clock. *n.*

a hat	i it	oi oil	ch child	a in about
ā age	ī ice	ou out	ng long	e in taken
ä far	o hot	u cup	sh she	i in pencil
e let	ō open	ù put	th thin	o in lemon
ē equal	ô order	ü rule	ŦH then	u in circus
ėr term			zh measure	

hair trigger, trigger that operates by very slight pressure.

hair y (her′ē *or* har′ē), **1** covered with hair; having much hair: *hairy hands, a plant with hairy leaves.* **2** of or like hair. **3** SLANG. **a** frightening or risky: *a hairy undertaking.* **b** difficult: *a hairy problem. adj.,* **hair i er, hair i est.**

Hai ti (hā′tē), **1** country in the W part of the island of Hispaniola in the West Indies. *Capital:* Port-au-Prince. **2** former name of Hispaniola. *n.* **—Hai ti an** (hā′tē ən *or* hā′shən), *adj., n.*

hake (hāk), a sea fish related to the cod but more slender. *n., pl.* **hakes** or **hake.**

hal berd (hal′bərd), weapon that is both a spear and a battle-ax, used in warfare in the 1400's and 1500's. *n.*

hal bert (hal′bert), halberd. *n.*

hal cy on (hal′sē ən), calm; peaceful; happy: *The elderly couple liked to recall the halcyon days of their youth. adj.*

hale¹ (hāl), strong and well; healthy: *Grandpa is still hale and hearty at seventy. adj.,* **hal er, hal est.**

hale² (hāl), **1** force to go: *The company was haled into court for polluting the river with chemicals.* **2** drag by force. *v.,* **haled, hal ing.**

Hale (hāl), Nathan, 1755-1776, American patriot hanged as a spy by the British. *n.*

half (haf), **1** one of two equal parts: *A half of 4 is 2. Two halves make a whole.* **2** making half of; being one of two equal parts: *a half pound, a half hour.* **3** to half of the full amount or degree: *a glass half full of milk.* **4** one of two nearly equal parts: *the bigger half of a candy bar.* **5** one of the two equal periods of active play in certain games. **6** not complete; being only part of: *A half truth is often no better than a lie.* **7** not completely; partly: *The potatoes were half cooked.* 1,4,5 *n., pl.* **halves;** 2,6 *adj.,* 3,7 *adv.*

in half, into two equal parts.

not half bad, fairly good.

half back (haf′bak′), (in football) a player who runs with the ball, blocks for another runner, or tries to catch a pass. *n.*

half-baked (haf′bākt′), **1** INFORMAL. not fully worked out or planned; foolish: *a half-baked scheme for getting rich quick.* **2** not cooked enough. *adj.*

half-breed (haf′brēd′), person whose parents are of different races. The word *half-breed* is often considered offensive. *n.*

half brother, brother related through one parent only.

half-caste (haf′kast′), **1** person who has one European parent and one Asian parent. **2** half-breed. The word *half-caste* is often considered offensive. *n.*

half dollar, a coin of the United States and Canada, worth 50 cents.

half heart ed (haf′här′tid), lacking courage, interest, or enthusiasm; not earnest. *adj.* **—half′heart′ed ly,** *adv.*

half hour, **1** thirty minutes. **2** the halfway point in an hour: *The train stops here on the half hour.*

half-hour (haf′our′), of a half hour; lasting a half hour: *a half-hour trip. adj.* **—half′-hour′ly,** *adv.*

half-life (haf′līf′), length of time it takes for half the atoms of a particular radioactive substance to break down or decay. The half-life of a particular radioactive substance is always the same, and it is therefore used to distinguish one radioactive substance from another and to measure radioactivity. *n.*

half-line (haf′līn′), the part of a line on one side of a fixed point of the line; ray. *n.*

half-mast (haf′mast′), position halfway or part way down from the top of a mast, staff, etc.; half-staff. A flag is lowered to half-mast as a mark of respect for someone who has died or as a signal of distress. *n.*

half-moon (haf′mün′), moon when only half of its surface appears bright. *n.*

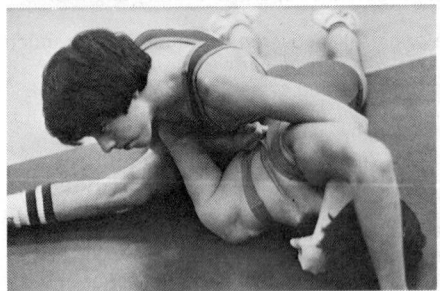

half nelson
applied by
the wrestler
on top

half nelson, hold used in wrestling. It is done by hooking one arm under an opponent's armpit and putting a hand on the back of his neck.

half note, (in music) a note played for one half as long a time as a whole note.

half pen ny (hā′pə nē *or* hāp′nē), a former British coin worth half a penny. *n., pl.* **half pence** (hā′pəns), **half-pen nies.**

half-plane (haf′plān′), the part of a plane on one side of a fixed line of the plane. *n.*

half sister, sister related through one parent only.

half sole, sole of a shoe or boot from the toe to the instep.

half-sole (haf′sōl′), put a new half sole on. *v.*, **half-soled, half-sol ing.**

half-staff (haf′staf′), half-mast. *n.*

half step, difference in pitch between two keys next to each other on a piano; semitone.

half tone, half step.

half-track or **half track** (haf′trak′), a military motor vehicle with wheels in front and short tracks in the rear, used to carry troops and weapons. *n.*

half way (haf′wā′), **1** half the way: *The rope reached only halfway around the tree.* **2** not completely; partially: *a job that is halfway finished, a halfway satisfactory answer.* **3** midway: *a halfway point in our trip.* **4** not going far enough; incomplete: *Halfway measures often fail.* 1,2 *adv.,* 3,4 *adj.*

meet halfway or **go halfway,** do one's share to agree or be friendly with.

half-wit (haf′wit′), **1** a feeble-minded person. **2** a stupid, foolish person. *n.*

half-wit ted (haf′wit′id), **1** feeble-minded. **2** very stupid; foolish. *adj.*

hal i but (hal′ə bət), a large flatfish, much used for food. Halibuts sometimes weigh several hundred pounds. *n., pl.* **hal i buts** or **hal i but.** [*Halibut* is from Middle English *halybutte,* which comes from *haly,* meaning "holy," and *butte,* meaning "flatfish." The fish was called this because it was eaten on holy days.]

Hal i fax (hal′ə faks), seaport in SE Canada, the capital of Nova Scotia. *n.*

hal ite (hal′īt *or* hā′līt), rock salt. *n.*

hall (hôl), **1** way for going through a building; passageway: *A hall ran the length of the upper floor of the house.* **2** passage or room at the entrance of a building: *Leave your umbrella in the hall.* **3** a large room for holding meetings, parties, banquets, etc. **4** building for public busi-

ness, meetings, etc.: *a village hall.* **5** building of a school, college, or university in which students live or classes are held. **6** house of an English landowner. *n.*

hal lah (hä′lə), loaf of white bread, usually shaped like a braid, eaten by Jews on the Sabbath and holidays. *n., pl.* **hal lahs, hal loth** (hä lōt′).

hal le lu jah or **hal le lu iah** (hal′ə lü′yə), **1** praise ye the Lord! **2** song of praise. 1 *interj.,* 2 *n.* Also, **alleluia.**

Hal ley's comet (hal′ēz), comet seen about every 76 years. It was last seen in 1986. [*Halley's comet* was named for Edmund *Halley,* 1656-1742, an English astronomer who first predicted the year of its return.]

hal liard (hal′yərd), halyard. *n.*

hall mark (hôl′märk′), **1** an official mark indicating standard of purity, put on gold or silver articles. **2** any mark or sign of genuineness or good quality. **3** put a hallmark on. **4** any distinguishing feature: *Self-control is a hallmark of maturity.* 1,2,4 *n.,* 3 *v.*

hal lo (hə lō′), **1** a call or shout to attract attention: *"Hallo!" she called from across the street.* **2** a call of greeting or surprise: *Hallo! what's that noise?* **3** a shout or call of hallo: *His hallo stopped me in the middle of the street.* **4** to shout or call. 1,2 *interj.,* 3 *n., pl.* **hal los;** 4 *v.,* **halloed, hal lo ing.**

hal loa (hə lō′), hallo. *interj., n., pl.* **hal loas;** *v.,* **halloaed, hal loa ing.**

hal loo (hə lü′), hallo. *interj., n., pl.* **hal loos;** *v.,* **hallooed, hal loo ing.**

hal low (hal′ō), **1** make holy; make sacred. **2** honor as holy or sacred: *"Hallowed be Thy name."* *v.*

Hal low een or **Hal low e'en** (hal′ō ēn′), evening of October 31, before All Saints' Day. It is observed especially by children, who masquerade, beg for treats, play pranks, etc. *n.*

hal lu ci nate (hə lü′sn āt), have hallucinations. *v.,* **hal lu ci nat ed, hal lu ci nat ing.**

hal lu ci na tion (hə lü′sn ā′shən), **1** a seeing or hearing things that exist only in a person's imagination. **2** an imaginary thing seen or heard. *n.*

hal lu cin o gen (hə lü′sn ə jen), drug that produces or tends to produce hallucinations. LSD and marijuana are hallucinogens. *n.*

hal lu cin o gen ic (hə lü′sn ə jen′ik), producing or tending to produce hallucinations: *hallucinogenic drugs.* *adj.*

hall way (hôl′wā′), **1** passage in a building; corridor; hall. **2** passageway or room at the entrance of a building. *n.*

halo (def. 2)

ha lo (hā′lō), **1** ring of light around the sun, moon, or other shining body. **2** a golden circle or disk of light represented about the head of a saint or angel in pictures or statues; nimbus. **3** glory or glamor that surrounds a person or thing. *n., pl.* **ha los** or **ha loes.**

halt[1] (hôlt), **1** stop for a time: *The hikers halted and rested from their climb. The store halted deliveries during the strike.* **2** a stop for a time: *During a strike work comes to a halt.* 1 *v.,* 2 *n.*

call a halt, order a stop.

halt[2] (hôlt), **1** be in doubt; hesitate; waver. **2** lame; crippled; limping. **3** OLD USE. be lame or crippled; limp. 1,3 *v.*, 2 *adj.*

hal ter (hôl′tər), **1** rope or strap with a noose or headstall for leading or tying an animal. **2** rope for hanging a person; noose. **3** a blouse worn by women and girls which fastens behind the neck and across the back and leaves the arms and back bare. *n.*

halter (def. 1)

halt ing (hôl′ting), slow and uncertain; wavering; hesitating: *to speak in a halting manner. adj.* —**halt′ing ly,** *adv.*

halve (hav), **1** divide into two equal parts; share equally: *He and I agreed to halve expenses on our trip.* **2** cut in half; reduce to half: *The new machine will halve the time and cost of doing the work by hand. v.*, **halved, halv ing.**

halves (havz), plural of **half.** *n.*
by halves, not completely; partly.
go halves, share equally.

hal yard (hal′yərd), rope or tackle used on a ship to raise or lower a sail, yard, or flag. *n.* Also, **halliard.**

ham (ham), **1** meat from the upper part of a hog's hind leg, usually salted and smoked. **2** the back of the thigh; thigh and buttock. **3** SLANG. actor or performer who plays poorly and in an exaggerated manner. **4** SLANG. play or act (a part) in this manner. **5** INFORMAL. an amateur radio operator. 1-3,5 *n.*, 4 *v.*, **hammed, ham ming.**

ham burg (ham′bėrg′), hamburger. *n.*

Ham burg (ham′bėrg′), city in N West Germany, on the Elbe River. *n.*

ham burg er (ham′bėr′gər), **1** ground beef, usually shaped into round, flat cakes and fried or broiled. **2** sandwich made with hamburger, usually in a roll or bun. *n.* [*Hamburger* comes from German *Hamburger,* meaning "of Hamburg."]

Ham il ton (ham′əl tən), **Alexander,** 1757-1804, American statesman, the first Secretary of the Treasury. *n.*

ham let (ham′lit), a small village; little group of houses in the country. *n.*

Ham let (ham′lit), **1** play by Shakespeare. **2** the principal character in this play, a prince of Denmark, who avenges his father's murder. *n.*

ham mer (ham′ər), **1** tool with a metal head set crosswise on a handle, used to drive nails and to beat metal into shape. **2** something shaped or used like a hammer. The hammer of a gun explodes the charge. **3** drive, hit, or work with a hammer. **4** beat into shape with a hammer: *The silver was hammered into bowls.* **5** fasten by using a hammer. **6** hit again and again: *The teacher hammered on the desk with a ruler to get the class to quiet down.* **7** force by repeated efforts: *to hammer common*

sense into someone's head. **8** a metal ball attached to a wire with a handle on the other end. It is used by athletes, who twirl it and throw it for distance. **9** the outermost of three small bones in the middle ear of human beings and other mammals. It is shaped something like a hammer. 1,2,8,9 *n.*, 3-7 *v.* —**ham′mer er,** *n.*

hammer and tongs, with all one's force and strength: *The boxers punched at each other hammer and tongs.*
hammer at, work hard at.
hammer away, keep working hard.
hammer out, work out with much effort: *to hammer out a new policy.*

ham mer head (ham′ər hed′), a fierce shark whose wide head looks somewhat like a double-headed hammer. *n.*

ham mer lock (ham′ər lok′), a hold in wrestling in which an opponent's arm is twisted and held behind his back. *n.*

ham mock (ham′ək), a hanging bed or couch made of canvas, netted cord, etc. It has cords or ropes at each end for hanging it between two trees, posts, etc. *n.* [*Hammock* is from Spanish *hamaca,* which came from a native South American Indian word.]

ham my (ham′ē), SLANG. acting like a ham. *adj.*, **ham mi er, ham mi est.**

ham per[1] (ham′pər), hold back; hinder: *Wet wood hampered our efforts to start the campfire. v.* [*Hamper*[1] comes from Middle English *hampren.*]

ham per[2] (ham′pər), a large container, often a wicker basket, usually having a cover: *a picnic hamper, a laundry hamper. n.* [*Hamper*[2] came into English about 600 years ago from French *hanapier,* which comes from *hanap,* meaning "cup."]

ham ster (ham′stər), a small rodent with a short tail and large cheek pouches. Hamsters are used in scientific research and are often kept as pets. *n.*

hamster
about 5 in. (13 cm.) long

ham string (ham′string′), **1** one of the two tendons at the back of the knee in human beings. **2** the great tendon at the back of the hock in a four-footed animal. **3** cripple by cutting a hamstring. **4** destroy the activity, efficiency, etc., of; cripple; disable: *Our building plans have been hamstrung by bad weather.* 1,2 *n.*, 3,4 *v.*, **hamstrung** (ham′strung′), **ham string ing.**

Han cock (han′kok), **John,** 1737-1793, American statesman, the first signer of the Declaration of Independence. *n.*

hand (hand), **1** the end part of the arm, below the wrist, which takes and holds objects. Each hand has four fingers and a thumb. **2** end of any limb that grasps, holds, or clings. We call a monkey's feet hands. **3** something like a hand in shape, appearance, or use: *The hands of a clock or watch show the time.* **4** a hired worker who uses his or her hands: *a factory hand.* **5** give with the hand; pass: *Please hand me a spoon.* **6** help with the hand: *I handed the old woman into the bus.* **7 hands,** *pl.* possession; control: *The property is no longer in my hands.* **8** part or share in doing something: *She had no hand in the matter.* **9** side: *There was a small table at my left hand.* **10** style of handwriting: *He writes in a clear hand.* **11** skill; ability: *The artist's work showed a master's hand.* **12** round of applause or clapping: *The crowd gave the winner a big hand.* **13** promise of marriage. **14** the breadth of a hand; 4 inches: *This horse is 18 hands high.* **15** cards held by a player in one round of a card game. **16** a single round in a card game. **17** player in a card game. **18** of, for, by, or in the hand: *a hand mirror, hand weaving, a hand pump.* 1-4,7-17 *n.,* 5,6 *v.,* 18 *adj.* —**hand'-like',** *adj.*

at first hand, from direct knowledge or experience.

at hand, 1 within reach; near. **2** ready.

at second hand, from the knowledge or experience of another; not directly: *He heard the story at second hand.*

at the hand of or **at the hands of,** through the act or deed of: *We have received many favors at the hands of our neighbors.*

by hand, by using the hands, not machinery: *embroidered by hand.*

change hands, pass from one person to another: *That building changed hands many times.*

from hand to mouth, without providing for the future: *Many poor people are forced to live from hand to mouth.*

give a hand, help: *Please give me a hand with this trunk.*

hand down, pass along: *The family heirloom is handed down to the oldest child in each generation.*

hand in, give; deliver: *Notebooks should be handed in at the end of class.*

hand in glove or **hand and glove,** in close relations; intimately: *All the members worked hand in glove with the planning committee.*

hand in hand, 1 holding hands. **2** together.

hand on, pass along.

hand out, give out; distribute.

hand over, give to another; deliver.

hands down, easily: *She won the contest hands down.*

hand to hand, close together: *The soldiers fought hand to hand.*

have one's hands full, be very busy; be able to do no more; have all one can do: *She has her hands full with a job and classes in night school.*

in hand, 1 under control. **2** in one's possession; ready: *cash in hand.*

lay hands on, 1 get hold of; seize. **2** attack; harm.

lend a hand, help: *I asked my brother to lend me a hand with my homework.*

off one's hands, out of one's care or charge.

on hand, 1 within reach; near: *Try to be on hand when I need you.* **2** ready: *have cash on hand.* **3** present: *I will be on hand again tomorrow.*

on the one hand, from this point of view: *On the one hand I want to buy this new car.*

on the other hand, from the opposite point of view: *On the other hand, it costs too much money.*

out of hand, out of control: *Your temper is getting out of hand.*

play into the hands of, act so as to give the advantage to.

hand (defs. 1, 3, 4, 14, 15, and 18)

the upper hand, a better position; advantage.

turn one's hand to, work at: *You would not turn your hand to making the punch, so I did it.*

wash one's hands of, have no more to do with; refuse to be responsible for: *I washed my hands of that job when I discovered what I'd have to do.*

hand bag (hand'bag'), **1** a woman's small bag for money, keys, cosmetics, etc.; purse. **2** a small traveling bag to hold clothes, etc. *n.*

hand ball (hand'bôl'), **1** game played by hitting a small, hard ball against a wall with the hand. **2** ball used in this game. *n.*

hand bill (hand'bil'), notice or advertisement, usually printed on one page, that is to be handed out to people. *n.*

hand book (hand'bùk'), a small book of directions or reference, especially in some field of study: *a handbook of engineering. n.*

hand car (hand'kär'), a light, open car moved by pumping a handle, used on railroads by workmen. *n.*

hand cart (hand'kärt'), a small cart pulled or pushed by hand; barrow. *n.*

hand clasp (hand'klasp'), the grasp of a person's hand in friendship, agreement, greeting, etc. *n.*

hand craft (hand'kraft'), **1** handicraft. **2** make or work by hand. 1 *n.,* 2 *v.*

hand cuff (hand'kuf'), **1** one of a pair of metal rings joined by a short chain and locked around the wrists of a prisoner. **2** put handcuffs on: *handcuff a prisoner.* 1 *n.,* 2 *v.*

Han del (han'dl), George Frederick, 1685-1759, English composer, born in Germany. *n.*

hand ful (hand'fùl), **1** as much or as many as the hand can hold: *a handful of candy.* **2** a small number: *Only a handful of football fans sat watching the game in the cold rain.* **3** INFORMAL. person or thing that is hard to manage: *That spirited horse is quite a handful. n., pl.* **handfuls.**

hand gun (hand'gun'), pistol. *n.*

hand i cap (han'dē kap'), **1** something that puts a person at a disadvantage; hindrance: *A sore throat was a* *handicap to the singer.* **2** put at a disadvantage; hinder: *A sore arm handicapped our pitcher.* **3** race, contest, or game in which better contestants are given special disadvantages and the rest are given certain advantages, so that all have an equal chance to win. **4** the disadvantage or advantage given in such a race, contest, or game: *a runner with a 5-yard handicap.* **5** give a handicap to. 1,3,4 *n.,* 2,5 *v.,* **hand i capped, hand i cap ping.**

hand i capped (han'dē kapt'), **1** having a physical or mental disability. **2 the handicapped,** people with physical or mental disabilities. **3** having an assigned handicap in a race, contest, etc. 1,3 *adj.,* 2 *n.*

hand i craft (han'dē kraft'), **1** skill with the hands. **2** trade or art requiring skill with the hands. Weaving baskets from rushes is a handicraft. *n.* Also, **handcraft.**

hand i ly (han'dl ē), in a handy manner. *adv.*

hand i ness (han'dē nis), skill with the hands; being handy. *n.*

hand i work (han'dē wėrk'), **1** work done by a person's hands. **2** work of a specific person. *n.*

hand ker chief (hang'kər chif), **1** a soft, usually square piece of cloth used for wiping the nose, face, hands, eyes, etc. **2** kerchief. *n.*

han dle (han'dl), **1** a part of a thing made to be held or grasped by the hand. Spoons, pitchers, hammers, and pails have handles. **2** touch, feel, hold, or use with the hand: *I handled the cat gently, feeling its soft fur.* **3** manage; direct: *The rider handled the horse well.* **4** behave or act when handled: *This car handles easily.* **5** deal with; treat: *handle complaints.* **6** deal in; trade in: *That store handles meat.* 1 *n.,* 2-6 *v.* **han dled, han dling.**

fly off the handle, INFORMAL. get angry or excited; lose one's temper or self-control.

han dle bar (han'dl bär'). Often, **handlebars,** *pl.* the curved bar on a bicycle, motorcycle, etc., that the rider holds and steers by. *n.*

han dler (han'dlər), **1** person or thing that handles. **2** person who helps train or manage a boxer. *n.*

hand made (hand'mād'), made by hand, not by machine: *handmade pottery. adj.*

hand maid (hand'mād'), a female servant. *n.*

hand-me-down (hand'mē doun'), something handed down from one person to another, such as a used garment. *n.*

hand organ

hand organ, a large, portable music box which is made to play tunes by turning a crank; barrel organ.

hand out (hand'out'), **1** portion of food, clothing, or money handed out: *The beggar asked for a handout.* **2** a news story or piece of publicity issued to the press by a business organization, government agency, etc. *n.*

hand rail (hand'rāl'), railing used as a guard or as a support to the hand on a stairway, platform, etc. *n.*

hand saw (hand'sô'), saw used with one hand. *n.*

hand shake (hand'shāk'), act of clasping and shaking

a hat	i it	oi oil	ch child		a in about
ā age	ī ice	ou out	ng long		e in taken
ä far	o hot	u cup	sh she	ə =	i in pencil
e let	ō open	u̇ put	th thin		o in lemon
ē equal	ô order	ü rule	ᴛʜ then		u in circus
ėr term			zh measure		

of each other's hands in friendship, agreement, greeting, etc. *n.*

hand some (han'səm), **1** pleasing in appearance; good-looking. We usually say that a man is handsome, but that a woman is pretty or beautiful. **2** fairly large; considerable: *A thousand dollars is a handsome sum of money.* **3** generous: *a handsome donation, a handsome reward. adj.,* **hand som er, hand som est. —hand'some ly,** *adv.*

hands-on (handz'ôn' *or* handz'on'), using or involving personal action or close participation; direct: *hands-on experience with computers. adj.*

handspring

hand spring (hand'spring'), spring or leap in which a person lands on one or both hands and then back on the feet, making a complete turn of the body. *n.*

hand stand (hand'stand'), the act of balancing on one's hands with one's feet in the air. *n.*

hand-to-hand (hand'tə hand'), close together; at close quarters: *a hand-to-hand fight. adj.*

hand-to-mouth (hand'tə mouth'), not providing for the future; having nothing to spare; not thrifty: *a hand-to-mouth existence. adj.*

hand work (hand'wėrk'), work done by hand, not by machinery. *n.*

hand writ ing (hand'rī'ting), **1** writing by hand; writing with pen, pencil, etc. **2** manner or style of writing: *He recognized his mother's handwriting on the envelope. n.*

hand y (han'dē), **1** easy to reach or use; saving work; useful; convenient: *a handy device.* **2** skillful with the hands: *My aunt is handy with tools. adj.,* **hand i er, hand i est.**

come in handy, be useful or helpful.

Han dy (han'dē), **W(illiam) C.,** 1873-1958, American jazz composer. *n.*

hand y man (han'dē man'), person who can do many kinds of odd jobs. *n., pl.* **hand y men.**

hang (hang), **1** fasten or be fastened to something above: *Hang your hat on the hook. The swing hangs from a tree.* **2** fasten or be fastened so as to swing or turn freely: *hang a door on its hinges.* **3** put to death by hanging with a rope around the neck. **4** die by hanging. **5** bend down; droop: *He hung his head in shame.* **6** cover or decorate with things that are fastened to something above: *hang a window with curtains. The walls were hung with pictures.* **7** attach (paper, etc.) to walls. **8** depend: *His future hangs on the court's decision.* **9** keep (a jury) from making a decision or reaching a verdict. One member can hang a jury by refusing to agree with the others. **10** way that a thing hangs: *There is something wrong with the hang of* *this coat.* **11** INFORMAL. way of using or doing: *Riding a bicycle is easy after you get the hang of it.* **12** INFORMAL. idea; meaning: *After studying an hour I finally got the hang of the lesson.* **13** loiter; linger: *hang about a place.* 1-9,13 *v.*, **hung** (or, usually, **hanged** for 3 and 4), **hanging**; 10-12 *n.*

hang back, be unwilling to go forward; be backward.

hang in there, SLANG. keep on; be unwilling to let go, stop, or leave: *Don't give up now; hang in there.*

hang on, 1 hold tightly: *Hang on to my hand going down these steep stairs.* **2** be unwilling to let go, stop, or leave: *The children hung on to their hope that the lost dog would be found.*

hang out, 1 lean out: *hang out of a window.* **2** SLANG. live or stay: *This is the corner where that gang hangs out.*

hang over, be about to happen to; threaten: *The prospect of defeat hangs over that political party.*

hang together, 1 stick together; support each other. **2** be coherent or consistent: *The story is confusing and does not hang together.*

hang up, 1 put on a hook, peg, etc. **2** put a telephone receiver back in place.

hang ar (hang′ər), a storage building for aircraft. *n.*

hang dog (hang′dôg′), ashamed or sneaking: *a guilty, hangdog look.* *adj.*

hang er (hang′ər), **1** thing on which something else is hung: *a coat hanger.* **2** person who hangs things. *n.*

hang er-on (hang′ər on′), **1** follower or dependent. **2** an undesirable follower. *n.*, *pl.* **hang ers-on.**

hang glider

hang glider, device like a large kite, from which a person hangs in a harness while gliding down from a high place.

hang gliding, act or sport of riding a hang glider.

hang ing (hang′ing), **1** death by hanging with a rope around the neck. **2** Often, **hangings,** *pl.* thing that hangs from a wall, bed, etc. Curtains and draperies are hangings. **3** fastened to something above: *a hanging basket of flowers.* 1,2 *n.*, 3 *adj.*

hang man (hang′mən), man who puts condemned criminals to death by hanging them. *n.*, *pl.* **hang men.**

hang nail (hang′nāl′), bit of skin that hangs partly loose near a fingernail. *n.*

hang out (hang′out′), SLANG. place one lives in or goes to often. *n.*

hang o ver (hang′ō′vər), **1** something that remains from an earlier time or condition. **2** headache, nausea, etc., resulting from drinking too much alcoholic liquor. *n.*

hang-up (hang′up′), SLANG. problem, worry, etc., that a person cannot get rid of. *n.*

hank (hangk), **1** coil or loop: *a hank of hair.* **2** bundle of yarn containing a definite number of yards. There are 840 yards in a hank of cotton yarn. *n.*

han ker (hang′kər), have a longing or craving; yearn: *The lonely child hankered for friends.* *v.* —**han′ker er,** *n.*

Han ni bal (han′ə bəl), 247-183? B.C., general of Car-

thage who fought the Romans and invaded Italy by crossing the Alps. *n.*

Ha noi (hä noi′), capital of Vietnam, in the N part. It was formerly the capital of North Vietnam. *n.*

Han sen's disease (han′sən), leprosy.

hansom

han som (han′səm), a two-wheeled cab for two passengers, pulled by one horse. The driver sits on a seat high up behind the cab, and the reins pass over the roof. *n.* [*Hansom* was named for Joseph *Hansom*, 1803-1882, a British architect who designed such cabs.]

Ha nuk kah (hä′nə kə), a yearly Jewish festival celebrating in November or December the rededication of the temple in Jerusalem after a victory over the Syrians in 165 B.C. Candles are lighted on each of the eight days of Hanukkah. *n.* Also, **Chanukah.** [*Hanukkah* comes from Hebrew *ḥanukkāh*, meaning "dedication."]

hap (hap), OLD USE. **1** chance; luck. **2** happen. 1 *n.*, 2 *v.*, **happed, hap ping.**

hap haz ard (hap haz′ərd), **1** not planned; random: *Haphazard answers are often wrong.* **2** by chance; at random: *papers scattered haphazard on the desk.* 1 *adj.*, 2 *adv.* —**hap haz′ard ly,** *adv.* —**hap haz′ard ness,** *n.*

hap less (hap′lis), unlucky; unfortunate. *adj.* —**hap′less ly,** *adv.* —**hap′less ness,** *n.*

hap ly (hap′lē), OLD USE. by chance; perhaps. *adv.*

hap pen (hap′ən), **1** come about; take place; occur: *What happened at the party yesterday?* **2** be or take place by chance: *Accidents will happen.* **3** have the fortune; chance: *I happened to sit beside him at dinner.* **4** be done: *What happened to my book? It's all dirty.* *v.*

happen on, 1 meet: *The two friends happened on each other by chance.* **2** find: *She happened on a dime while looking for her ball.*

hap pen ing (hap′ə ning), something that happens; event; occurrence: *The evening newscast reviewed the happenings of the day. n.*

hap pen stance (hap′ən stans), a chance occurrence; accident. *n.*

hap pi ly (hap′ə lē), **1** in a happy manner: *The cousins played happily together.* **2** by luck; with good fortune: *Happily, I found my lost wallet. adv.*

hap pi ness (hap′ē nis), **1** a being happy; gladness. **2** good luck; good fortune. *n.*

hap py (hap′ē), **1** feeling as you do when you are well and are having a good time; glad; pleased; contented: *She is happy in her new work.* **2** showing that one is glad; showing pleasure and joy: *a happy smile, a happy look.* **3** lucky; fortunate: *By a happy chance, I found my book just where I had left it in the theater.* **4** clever and fitting; successful and suitable: *That writer has a happy way of expressing his ideas. adj.*, **hap pi er, hap pi est.**

hap py-go-luck y (hap′ē gō luk′ē), taking things easily as they come; trusting to luck. *adj.*

Haps burg (haps′berg′), member of a German princely family, prominent since about 1100. Many rulers of the Holy Roman Empire, Austria, and Spain were Hapsburgs. *n.*

har a-kar i (har′ə kar′ē), hara-kiri. *n.*

har a-kir i (har′ə kir′ē), suicide by ripping open the abdomen with a knife. It was the national form of honorable suicide in Japan for the warrior class. *n.* [*Hara-kiri* is from Japanese *harakiri,* which comes from *hara,* meaning "belly," and *kiri,* meaning "a cutting."]

ha rangue (hə rang′), **1** a noisy speech. **2** a long, pompous speech. **3** address in a harangue. **4** deliver a harangue. 1,2 *n.,* 3,4 *v.,* **ha rangued, ha rangu ing.**

Ha ra re (hä rä′rā), capital of Zimbabwe, in the NE part. *n.*

har ass (har′əs *or* hə ras′), **1** trouble by repeated attacks; harry: *Pirates harassed the villages along the coast.* **2** disturb; worry; torment: *Flies harassed the hikers. v.*

har ass ment (har′əs mənt *or* hə ras′mənt), **1** a harassing or a being harassed; worry. **2** something that harasses. *n.*

har bin ger (här′bən jər), one that goes ahead to announce another's coming; forerunner: *The robin is a harbinger of spring. n.*

har bor (här′bər), **1** area of deep water protected from winds, currents, etc., forming a place of shelter for ships and boats: *Many yachts are in the harbor.* **2** any place of shelter: *The child fled to the harbor of her father's arms.* **3** give shelter to; give a place to hide: *The dog's shaggy hair harbors fleas.* **4** have and keep in the mind: *Don't harbor a grudge against her; she didn't mean to hurt you.* 1,2 *n.,* 3,4 *v.* [*Harbor* is from Middle English *herebeorg,* meaning "lodgings," which comes from Old English *here,* meaning "army," and *beorg,* meaning "a shelter."]

hard (härd), **1** like steel, glass, and rock; not yielding to touch; not soft: *a hard nut, hard wood.* **2** so as to be hard, solid, or firm: *The river is frozen hard.* **3** firm; tight: *a hard knot.* **4** firmly; tightly: *Don't hold my hand so hard.* **5** needing much ability, effort, or time; difficult or troublesome: *a hard problem, a hard job, a hard person to get on with.* **6** acting or done with energy, persistence, etc.: *a hard worker.* **7** with steady effort or much energy: *Try hard.* **8** vigorous or violent: *a hard storm, a hard run.* **9** with vigor or violence: *It is raining hard.* **10** causing much pain, trouble, care, etc.; bad; severe: *a hard winter. When my parents were out of work, we had a hard time.* **11** so as to cause trouble, pain, care, etc.; severely; badly: *It will go hard with those kidnapers if they are caught.* **12** not pleasant; harsh; ugly: *a hard face, a hard laugh.* **13** not yielding to influence; stern; unfeeling: *a hard master, a hard heart.* **14** close; near: *The house stands hard by the bridge.* **15** containing mineral salts that keep soap from forming suds: *hard water.* **16** containing much alcohol: *hard liquor.* **17** causing addiction and damaging one's health: *Heroin is a hard drug.* **18** sounded like the *c* in *corn* or the *g* in *get,* rather than like the soft *c* and *g* in *city* and *gem.* 1,3,5,6,8,10,12,13,15-18 *adj.,* 2,4,7,9,11,14 *adv.* —**hard′ness,** *n.*

hard and fast, that cannot be changed or broken; strict: *hard and fast rules.*

hard of hearing, somewhat deaf.

hard put, having much difficulty or trouble: *I am hard put to solve this problem.*

hard up, INFORMAL. needing money or anything very badly.

hard ball (härd′bôl′), baseball. *n.*

hard-bit ten (härd′bit′n), stubborn; unyielding. *adj.*

hard-boiled (härd′boild′), **1** (of an egg) boiled until the white and yolk are firm. **2** INFORMAL. not easily moved by one's feelings; tough; rough: *a hard-boiled sergeant. adj.*

hard coal, anthracite.

hard copy, copy that can be read or viewed without the use of any special equipment. Computer printouts are hard copy, words on a computer screen are not.

hard core, the firm, unyielding, central part, resistant to pressure or change.

a hat	i it	oi oil	ch child	⎧ a in about
ā age	ī ice	ou out	ng long	⎪ e in taken
ä far	o hot	u cup	sh she	ə = ⎨ i in pencil
e let	ō open	u̇ put	th thin	⎪ o in lemon
ē equal	ô order	ü rule	₮H then	⎩ u in circus
ėr term			zh measure	

hard-core (härd′kôr′), **1** stubbornly unyielding; habitual: *a hard-core criminal.* **2** firmly established and hard to get rid of: *hard-core unemployment. adj.*

hard en (härd′n), make or become hard: *When the candy cooled, it hardened. v.* —**hard′en er,** *n.*

hard head ed (härd′hed′id), **1** not easily excited or deceived; practical; shrewd. **2** stubborn; obstinate. *adj.*

hard heart ed (härd′här′tid), without pity; cruel. *adj.*

har di hood (här′dē hu̇d), boldness; daring. *n.*

har di ness (här′dē nis), **1** endurance; strength. **2** hardihood. *n.*

Har ding (här′ding), **Warren Gamaliel,** 1865-1923, the 29th president of the United States, from 1921 to 1923. *n.*

hard ly (härd′lē), **1** only just; not quite; barely: *We hardly had time to eat breakfast. I am hardly strong enough to lift this heavy box.* **2** probably not: *They will hardly come in all this rain.* **3** with trouble or effort: *a hardly fought game.*

hard palate, the bony front part of the roof of the mouth.

hard pan (härd′pan′), a hard, firm layer of subsoil through which roots cannot grow; pan. *n.*

hard ship (härd′ship), something hard to bear; hard condition of living: *Hunger, cold, and sickness were among the hardships of pioneer life. n.*

hard tack (härd′tak′), a very hard, dry biscuit, formerly eaten on shipboard; ship biscuit. *n.*

hard top (härd′top′), a passenger car with a rigid metal or plastic top but with window space comparable to that of a convertible. *n.*

hard ware (härd′wer′ *or* härd′war′), **1** articles made from metal. Locks, hinges, nails, screws, etc., are hardware. **2** the mechanical parts of a computer system. *n.*

hard wood (härd′wu̇d′), **1** the hard, compact wood of such trees as oak, cherry, maple, ebony, or mahogany. **2** any of such trees, having broad leaves instead of needles. **3** made of such wood: *hardwood floors.* 1,2 *n.,* 3 *adj.*

har dy (här′dē), **1** able to bear hard treatment, fatigue, etc.; strong; robust: *Cold weather did not kill the hardy plants.* **2** bold; daring: *hardy mountain climbers. adj.,* **har di er, har di est.** —**har′di ly,** *adv.*

Har dy (här′dē), **Thomas,** 1840-1928, English novelist and poet. *n.*

hare (her *or* har), a gnawing mammal that resembles a rabbit but is larger, has longer ears, and does not live in a burrow. The jack rabbit is a hare; the cottontail is a rabbit. *n., pl.* **hares** or **hare.**

hare
about 2 ft.
(60 cm.) long

hare bell (her'bel' *or* har'bel'), a slender plant with blue, bell-shaped flowers; bluebell. *n.*

hare brained (her'brānd' *or* har'brānd'), giddy, heedless, or reckless: *a harebrained scheme. adj.*

hare lip (her'lip' *or* har'lip'), deformity existing from birth, in which the upper lip is divided. It resembles the lip of a hare. *n.*

hare lipped (her'lipt' *or* har'lipt'), having a harelip. *adj.*

har em (her'əm *or* har'əm), **1** part of a Moslem house where the women live. **2** the wives, female relatives, and female servants of a Moslem household. *n.* [*Harem* comes from Arabic *harīm.*]

har i cot (har'ə kō), string bean. *n.*

hark (härk). **hark back**, go back; turn back: *Those ideas hark back twenty years. v.*

hark en (här'kən), hearken. *v.*

Har lem (här'ləm), part of New York City in northern Manhattan. *n.*

har le quin (här'lə kwən *or* här'lə kən), **1** Harlequin, character in comedy and pantomime who is usually masked and wears a costume of varied colors. **2** a mischievous person; buffoon. *n.*

har lot (här'lət), prostitute. *n.*

har lot ry (här'lə trē), prostitution. *n.*

harm (härm), **1** something that causes pain, loss, etc.; injury; damage: *He slipped and fell down but suffered no harm.* **2** evil; wrong: *It was an accident; she meant no harm.* **3** damage; injure; hurt: *Do not pick or harm the flowers in the park.* 1,2 *n.*, 3 *v.* [*Harm* comes from Old English *hearm.*]

harm ful (härm'fəl), causing harm; injurious; hurtful: *harmful germs. adj.* —**harm'ful ly,** *adv.* —**harm'ful ness,** *n.*

harm less (härm'lis), causing no harm; not harmful: *It's only a harmless spider. adj.* —**harm'less ly,** *adv.* —**harm'less ness,** *n.*

har mon ic (här mon'ik), **1** having to do with harmony in music. **2** overtone. **3** having to do with such tones. **4** musical. 1,3,4 *adj.*, 2 *n.* —**har mon'i cal ly,** *adv.*

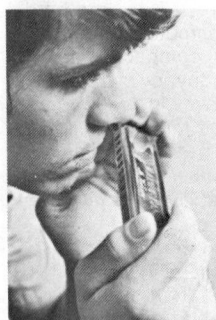

harmonica

har mon i ca (här mon'ə kə), a small musical instrument with metal reeds, played by breathing in and out through a set of openings; mouth organ. *n., pl.* **har mon i cas.**

har mon ics (här mon'iks), science of musical sounds. *n.*

har mo ni ous (här mō'nē əs), **1** agreeing in feelings, ideas, or actions; getting on well together: *harmonious neighbors.* **2** arranged so that the parts are orderly or pleasing; going well together: *A beautiful picture has harmonious colors.* **3** sweet-sounding; musical: *the harmonious sounds of a choir singing Christmas carols. adj.* —**har mo'ni ous ly,** *adv.* —**har mo'ni ous ness,** *n.*

har mo nize (här'mə nīz), **1** bring into harmony, accord, or agreement; make harmonious: *She harmonized the two plans by using parts of each one.* **2** be in harmony or agreement: *The colors in the room harmonized to give a*

pleasing effect. **3** add tones to (a melody) to make chords in music. *v.,* **har mo nized, har mo niz ing.** —**har'mo ni za'tion,** *n.*

har mo niz er (här'mə nī'zər), person who harmonizes. *n.*

har mo ny (här'mə nē), **1** agreement of feeling, ideas, or actions; getting on well together: *The two brothers lived and worked in perfect harmony.* **2** an orderly or pleasing arrangement of parts; going well together: *In a beautiful landscape there is harmony of the different colors.* **3** the sounding together of musical tones in a chord. **4** study of chords in music and of relating them to successive chords. **5** sweet or musical sound; music. *n., pl.* **har mo nies.**

har ness (här'nis), **1** leather straps, bands, and other pieces used to hitch a horse or other animal to a carriage, wagon, plow, etc. **2** any similar arrangement of straps, bands, etc., especially a combination of straps by which a parachute is attached to a person. **3** put harness on: *Harness the horse.* **4** cause to produce power: *Windmills harness the power of the wind.* 1,2 *n., pl.* **har ness es;** 3,4 *v.*

in harness, in one's regular work: *I was glad to get back in harness again after my long vacation.*

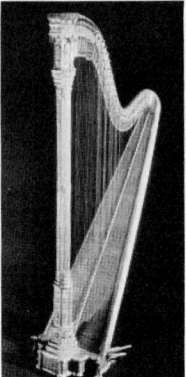

harp (def. 1)

harp (härp), **1** a large, stringed musical instrument played by plucking the strings with the fingers. **2** play on the harp. 1 *n.,* 2 *v.* [*Harp* comes from Old English *hearpe.*] —**harp'er,** *n.* —**harp'like',** *adj.*

harp on, talk about very much or too much.

Har pers Ferry (här'pərz), town in NE West Virginia. John Brown's raid on a government arsenal was made there in 1859.

harp ist (här'pist), person who plays the harp. *n.*

har poon (här pün'), **1** a barbed spear with a rope tied to it, used for catching whales and other sea animals. It is thrown by hand or fired from a gun. **2** strike, catch, or kill with a harpoon. 1 *n.,* 2 *v.* —**har poon'er,** *n.* —**harpoon'like',** *adj.*

harpoon (def. 1)

harp si chord (härp′sə kôrd), a stringed musical instrument like a piano, used especially from about 1550 to 1750. It has a tinkling sound from its strings being plucked by leather or quill points instead of being struck by hammers. *n.*

harpsichord

a hat	**i** it	**oi** oil	**ch** child	(a in about
ā age	**ī** ice	**ou** out	**ng** long	{ e in taken
ä far	**o** hot	**u** cup	**sh** she	ə = { i in pencil
e let	**ō** open	**u̇** put	**th** thin	{ o in lemon
ē equal	**ô** order	**ü** rule	**ŦH** then	(u in circus
ėr term			**zh** measure	

Har py (här′pē), **1** (in Greek and Roman myths) any of various filthy, greedy monsters with women's heads and birds' bodies. **2 harpy,** a cruel, greedy person; person who preys upon others. *n., pl.* **Har pies.**

har que bus (här′kwə bəs), an old form of portable gun used before muskets were invented. *n., pl.* **har que bus es.** Also, **arquebus.**

har ri er (har′ē ər), a small hound of the kind used to hunt hares. *n.*

Har ris burg (har′is bėrg′), capital of Pennsylvania, in the S part. *n.*

Har ri son (har′ə sən), **1 Benjamin,** 1833-1901, the 23rd president of the United States, from 1889 to 1893. **2** his grandfather, **William Henry,** 1773-1841, American general and ninth president of the United States, in 1841. *n.*

harrow (def. 1) pulled by a tractor

har row (har′ō), **1** a heavy frame with iron teeth or upright disks. Harrows are used by farmers to break up ground into fine pieces before planting seeds. **2** pull a harrow over (land, etc.). **3** cause pain or torment to; distress: *be harrowed with grief.* 1 *n.,* 2,3 *v.* —**har′row er,** *n.*

har row ing (har′ō ing), very painful or distressing: *a harrowing experience. adj.*

har ry (har′ē), **1** raid and rob with violence: *The pirates harried the towns along the coast, burning what they could not carry off.* **2** keep troubling; worry; torment: *Fear of losing her voice harried the ailing opera singer. v.,* **har ried, har ry ing.**

harsh (härsh), **1** rough to the touch, taste, eye, or ear; sharp and unpleasant: *a harsh voice, a harsh climate.* **2** without pity; unfeeling; cruel; severe: *a harsh judge. adj.* —**harsh′ly,** *adv.* —**harsh′ness,** *n.*

hart (härt), a male deer, especially the male red deer after its fifth year. *n., pl.* **harts** or **hart.**

har te beest (här′tə bēst′), a large, swift African antelope with ringed, curved horns bent backward at the tips. *n., pl.* **har te beests** or **har te beest.**

Hart ford (härt′fərd), capital of Connecticut, in the central part. *n.*

har um-scar um (her′əm sker′əm *or* har′əm skar′əm), **1** too hasty; reckless; rash: *a harum-scarum decision.* **2** recklessly; rashly: *He rushed harum-scarum down the street.* 1 *adj.,* 2 *adv.* [*Harum-scarum* may come from earlier *hare,* meaning "to frighten," *scare,* and *'em.*]

har vest (här′vist), **1** a reaping and gathering in of grain and other food crops. **2** time or season of the harvest, usually in the late summer or early autumn. **3** gather in and bring home for use: *harvest wheat.* **4** one season's yield of any natural product; crop: *The oyster harvest was small this year.* **5** result; consequences: *She is reaping the harvest of her hard work.* 1,2,4,5 *n.,* 3 *v.*

har vest er (här′və stər), **1** person who works in a harvest field; reaper. **2** machine for harvesting crops, especially grain. *n.*

harvest moon, the full moon at harvest time or about September 23.

Har vey (här′vē), **William,** 1578-1657, English physician who discovered that blood circulates through the body. *n.*

has (haz), a present tense of **have.** *Who has my book? He has been sick. v.*

has-been (haz′bin′), INFORMAL. person or thing whose best days are past. *n.*

hash¹ (hash), **1** mixture of cooked meat, potatoes, and other vegetables, chopped into small pieces and fried or baked. **2** chop into small pieces. **3** mixture. **4** a mess; muddle: *I made such a hash of the job that it had to be done over.* 1,3,4 *n., pl.* **hash es;** 2 *v.*

hash over, INFORMAL. discuss or review; reminisce about: *hash over the old days.*

hash² (hash), SLANG. hashish. *n.*

hash ish or **hash eesh** (hash′ēsh′), an extract prepared from the flowering tops of the hemp plant. Hashish is smoked or chewed for its intoxicating effect. *n.* [*Hashish* comes from Arabic *hashīsh,* meaning "dried hemp leaves."]

Has i dim (has′i dim), members of a Jewish group founded in the 1700's in Poland. Hasidim favor religious piety and devotion over formal learning. *n.pl.* of **Has id** (has′id).

has n't (haz′nt), has not.

hasp on a door

hasp (hasp), clasp or fastening for a door, window, trunk, box, etc., especially a hinged metal clasp that fits over a staple or into a hole and is fastened by a peg or padlock. *n.*

has sle (has′əl), INFORMAL. **1** a struggle or contest. **2** struggle; tussle. 1 *n.,* 2 *v.,* **has sled, has sling.**

has sock (has/ək), a thick cushion or cushioned footstool to rest the feet on, sit on, or kneel on. *n.*

hast (hast), OLD USE. have. "Thou hast" means "you have." *v.*

haste (hāst), **1** a trying to be quick; hurrying: *All my haste was of no use; I missed the bus anyway.* **2** quickness without thought or care; rashness: *Haste makes waste.* **3** hasten. 1,2 *n.*, 3 *v.*, **hast ed, hast ing.**

make haste, be quick; hurry: *Make haste or you will miss your train.*

has ten (hā/sn), **1** cause to be quick; speed; hurry: *Sunshine and rest hastened his recovery.* **2** be quick; go fast: *She hastened to explain that she had not meant to be rude.* *v.* —**hast/en er,** *n.*

hast i ly (hā/stl ē), **1** in a hurried manner. **2** rashly. **3** in a quick-tempered manner. *adv.*

hast i ness (hā/stē nis), **1** quickness of motion. **2** rashness. **3** quick temper. *n.*

Has tings (hā/stingz), town in SE England, where William I defeated the Saxons to become king of England in 1066. *n.*

hast y (hā/stē), **1** done or made in a hurry; quick: *She gave her watch a hasty glance and ran for the train.* **2** not well thought out; rash: *Their hasty decisions caused many mistakes.* **3** easily angered; quick-tempered. *adj.*, **hast i er, hast i est.**

hasty pudding, mush made of corn meal.

hat (hat), **1** a covering for the head when outdoors. A hat usually has a crown and a brim. **2** provide with a hat; put a hat on. 1 *n.*, 2 *v.*, **hat ted, hat ting.** —**hat/less,** *adj.*

pass the hat, ask for contributions; take up a collection.

take off one's hat to, admire; respect; honor.

talk through one's hat, talk foolishly; speak ignorantly.

under one's hat, INFORMAL. as a secret; to oneself: *Keep this information under your hat; tell it to no one.*

hat band (hat/band/), band around the crown of a hat, just above the brim. *n.*

hat box (hat/boks/), box or case for a hat. *n.*, *pl.* **hatbox es.**

hatch[1] (hach), **1** bring forth (young) from an egg or eggs: *A hen hatches chickens.* **2** keep (an egg or eggs) warm until the young come out: *The heat of the sun hatches turtles' eggs.* **3** come out from the egg: *Three of the chickens hatched today.* **4** develop to be young animals; bring forth young: *Not all eggs hatch properly.* **5** the brood hatched: *There are twelve chickens in this hatch.* **6** arrange; plan. **7** plan secretly; plot: *The spies hatched a scheme to steal government secrets.* 1-4,6,7 *v.*, 5 *n.*, *pl.* **hatch es.**

hatch[2] (hach), **1** an opening in a ship's deck or in the floor or roof of a building, etc.; hatchway. A ship's cargo is loaded through the hatch. The escape hatch in an airplane permits passengers to get out in an emergency. **2** a trapdoor covering such an opening: *The hatches were closed tightly during the storm.* *n.*, *pl.* **hatch es.**

hatch back (hach/bak/), **1** having a sloping back section that opens upward: *a hatchback coupe.* **2** an automobile having this feature. 1 *adj.*, 2 *n.*

hatch er y (hach/ər ē), place for hatching eggs of fish, hens, etc. *n.*, *pl.* **hatch er ies.**

hatch et (hach/it), a small ax with a short handle, for use with one hand. *n.* —**hatch/et like/,** *adj.*

bury the hatchet, stop quarreling or fighting; make peace.

dig up the hatchet, make war.

hatch way (hach/wā/), hatch. *n.*

hate (hāt), **1** dislike intensely; feel hostile towards: *I hated them for hurting my friend.* **2** a very strong dislike: *feel hate toward an enemy.* **3** be very unwilling; dislike: *I hate to study.* 1,3 *v.*, 2 *n.* —**hat/er,** *n.*

hate ful (hāt/fəl), **1** causing hate: *hateful behavior.* **2** feeling hate; showing hate: *a hateful comment. adj.* —**hate/ful ly,** *adv.* —**hate/ful ness,** *n.*

hath (hath), OLD USE. has. "He hath" means "he has." *v.*

hat pin (hat/pin/), a long pin used by women to fasten a hat to their hair. *n.*

ha tred (hā/trid), very strong dislike; hate. *n.*

hat ter (hat/ər), person who makes or sells hats. *n.*

Hat ter as (hat/ər əs), **Cape,** cape on an island off E North Carolina. *n.*

hau berk (hô/bėrk/), a long coat of mail. *n.*

haugh ti ly (hô/tl ē), in a haughty manner. *adv.*

haugh ti ness (hô/tē nis), a being haughty; disdainful pride; arrogance. *n.*

haugh ty (hô/tē), **1** too proud of oneself and too scornful of others: *A haughty person is often unpopular.* **2** showing too great pride of oneself and scorn for others: *a haughty glance, haughty words. adj.*, **haugh ti er, haugh ti est.**

haul (hôl), **1** pull or drag with force: *We hauled the heavy trunk out of the house.* **2** transport; carry: *Trucks, trains, and ships haul freight.* **3** act of hauling; hard pull. **4** load hauled: *Powerful trucks are used for heavy hauls.* **5** distance that a load is hauled: *Long hauls cost more than short ones.* **6** amount won, taken, etc., at one time; catch: *The fishing boats made a good haul and came back fully loaded.* 1,2 *v.*, 3-6 *n.* —**haul/er,** *n.*

haul off, draw back one's arm to give a blow.

haunch (hônch), **1** the fleshy part of the body around the hip; hip. **2 haunches,** *pl.* the hindquarters of an animal: *The dog sat on its haunches.* **3** the leg and loin of an animal, used for food: *a haunch of venison. n., pl.* **haunch es.**

haunt (hônt), **1** go often to; visit frequently: *People say ghosts haunt that old house.* **2** place often gone to or visited: *The swimming pool was the children's favorite haunt on hot summer days.* **3** be often with; come often to: *Memories of his youth haunted the old man.* 1,3 *v.*, 2 *n.* —**haunt/ing ly,** *adv.*

haunt ed (hôn/tid), visited by ghosts: *a haunted house. adj.*

haut boy (hō/boi), oboe. *n.*

hau teur (hō tėr/), a being proud and overbearing; haughtiness. *n.*

Ha van a (hə van/ə), capital of Cuba, on the NW coast. *n.*

have (hav; *unstressed* həv *or* əv), **1** hold in one's hand; hold in one's keeping; hold in one's possession: *We have a farm. A house has windows. He has a cheerful disposition.* **2** be forced; be compelled: *All animals have to sleep. I have to go now or I'll be late.* **3** cause (somebody to do something or something to be done): *Please have the store deliver my order.* **4** take; get: *You need to have a rest.* **5** experience: *Have a pleasant time. They had trouble with their car.* **6** engage in; carry on; perform: *Have a talk with him.* **7** allow; permit: *She won't have any noise while she is reading.* **8** hold in the mind: *have an idea.* **9** give birth to: *She had a girl.* **10** be the parent or parents of: *They have three children.* **11** *Have* is used with words like *asked, been, broken, done,* or *called* to express completed action. *They have eaten. She had gone before. I have called her. They will have seen her by Sunday. v.*, **had, hav ing.**

have at, attack; hit.

have done, be through; stop: *Let's have done with this quarreling.*

have had it, SLANG. become fed up.

have it out, fight or argue until a question is settled: *We have had it out, and now we are friends once more.*

have on, be wearing.

have to do with, relate to; deal with: *Botany has to do with the study of plants.*

ha ven (hā′vən), **1** harbor or port. **2** place of shelter and safety: *The warm cabin was a haven from the storm. n.*

have n't (hav′ənt), have not.

hav er sack (hav′ər sak), bag used by soldiers and hikers for carrying food when on a march or hike. *n.*

a hat	i it	oi oil	ch child	a in about
ā age	ī ice	ou out	ng long	e in taken
ä far	o hot	u cup	sh she	ə = i in pencil
e let	ō open	u̇ put	th thin	o in lemon
ē equal	ô order	ü rule	ŦH then	u in circus
ėr term			zh measure	

WORD HISTORY

haversack

Haversack comes from French *havre-sac,* and can be traced back to German *Haber,* meaning "oats," and *Sack,* meaning "bag." It was called this because cavalry originally carried oats for their horses in such a bag.

hav oc (hav′ək), very great destruction or injury: *Tornadoes can create widespread havoc. n.*

play havoc with, injure severely; ruin; destroy.

haw¹ (hô), **1** the red berry of the hawthorn. **2** hawthorn. *n.*

haw² (hô), a stammering sound between words. *interj., n.*

haw³ (hô), word of command to horses, oxen, etc., directing them to turn to the left. *interj.*

Ha wai i (hə wī′ē), **1** state of the United States in the N Pacific, consisting of the Hawaiian Islands. *Abbreviation:* HI *Capital:* Honolulu. **2** the largest of the Hawaiian Islands. *n.*

Ha wai ian (hə wī′yən), **1** of Hawaii, its people, or their language. **2** person born or living in Hawaii. **3** the Polynesian language of Hawaii. **1** *adj.,* **2,3** *n.*

Hawaiian Islands, group of islands in the N Pacific. See **Melanesia** for map.

hawk¹ (def. 1)—about 2 ft. (60 cm.) long

hawk¹ (hôk), **1** bird of prey with a strong, hooked beak, long claws, broad wings, and keen sight. Some hawks are trained to hunt and kill other birds and small animals. **2** hunt with trained hawks. **1** *n.,* **2** *v.* —**hawk′like′,** *adj.*

hawk² (hôk), carry (goods) about and offer them for sale by shouting: *Peddlers hawked their wares in the street. v.*

hawk³ (hôk), clear the throat noisily. *v.*

hawk er¹ (hô′kər), person who carries wares around and offers them for sale by shouting; peddler. *n.*

hawk er² (hô′kər), person who hunts with trained hawks. *n.*

hawk-eyed (hôk′īd′), having sharp eyes like a hawk. *adj.*

haw ser (hô′zər), a large rope or small cable, used for mooring or towing ships. *n.*

haw thorn (hô′thôrn), shrub or tree with many thorns and clusters of fragrant white, red, or pink flowers and small, red berries; haw. *n.*

Haw thorne (hô′thôrn), **Nathaniel,** 1804-1864, American writer of novels and short stories. *n.*

hay (hā), **1** grass, alfalfa, clover, etc., cut and dried for use as food for cattle and horses. **2** cut and dry grass, alfalfa, clover, etc., for hay: *They are haying in the east field.* **1** *n.,* **2** *v.*

hit the hay, SLANG. go to bed.

hay cock (hā′kok′), a small, cone-shaped pile of hay in a field. *n.*

haycock—They leaped over the **haycock.**

Hay dn (hīd′n), **Franz Joseph,** 1732-1809, Austrian composer. *n.*

Hayes (hāz), **Rutherford B.,** 1822-1893, the 19th president of the United States, from 1877 to 1881. *n.*

hay fever, allergy caused by the pollen of ragweed and other plants, characterized by itching and running eyes and nose and fits of sneezing.

hay field (hā′fēld′), field in which grass, alfalfa, clover, etc., are grown for hay. *n.*

hay fork (hā′fôrk′), **1** pitchfork. **2** a mechanical device equipped with hooks for moving hay into or out of a hayloft. *n.*

hay loft (hā′lôft′), place in a barn or stable where hay is stored. *n.*

hay mow (hā′mou′), **1** hayloft. **2** heap of hay stored in a barn or stable. *n.*

hay rick (hā′rik′), haystack. *n.*

hay ride (hā′rīd′), outing in a wagon partly filled with hay. *n.*

hay stack (hā′stak′), a large pile of hay outdoors. *n.*

hay wire (hā′wīr′), **1** wire used to tie up bales of hay. **2** SLANG. out of order; wrong. **3** SLANG. confused or crazy. **1** *n.,* **2,3** *adj.*

haz ard (haz′ərd), **1** chance of harm; risk; danger; peril: *Mountain climbing is full of hazards.* **2** a possible source of harm; likely cause of harm by: *a fire hazard.* **3** take a chance with; risk; venture: *I won't even hazard a guess.*

4 any obstruction on a golf course. 1,2,4 *n.*, 3 *v.* [*Hazard* came into English about 650 years ago from French *hasard*, meaning "a game of dice," which came from Arabic *az-zahr*, meaning "the die."]

haz ard ous (haz′ər dəs), full of risk; dangerous; perilous: *Flying across the ocean in a small plane was a hazardous undertaking. adj.* —**haz′ard ous ly,** *adv.*

haze[1] (hāz), **1** a small amount of mist, smoke, dust, etc., in the air: *A thin haze veiled the distant hills.* **2** slight confusion; vagueness: *Everything happened so fast that my mind is in a haze. n.*

haze[2] (hāz), (in schools, universities, etc.) force to do humiliating or ridiculous tasks; bully: *The freshmen resented being hazed by the sophomores. v.*, **hazed, haz ing.** —**haz′er,** *n.*

ha zel (hā′zəl), **1** shrub or small tree related to the birch, whose light-brown nuts are good to eat. **2** a light brown. **3** light-brown. 1,2 *n.*, 3 *adj.*

ha zel nut (hā′zəl nut′), nut of a hazel; filbert. *n.*

ha zi ly (hā′zə lē), in a hazy manner. *adv.*

ha zi ness (hā′zē nis), hazy quality or condition. *n.*

ha zy (hā′zē), **1** full of haze; misty; smoky: *a hazy sky.* **2** slightly confused; vague; dim; obscure: *It was so long ago, I have only a hazy memory of what happened. adj.*, **ha zi er, ha zi est.**

H-bomb (āch′bom′), a hydrogen bomb. *n.*

H.C., House of Commons.

hd., head. *pl.* **hds.**

hdqrs., headquarters.

he (hē; *unstressed* ē), **1** boy, man, or male animal spoken about or mentioned before: *He works hard, but is paid well.* **2** a male: *Is your dog a he or a she?* **3** anyone: *He who hesitates is lost.* 1,3 *pron.*, *pl.* **they;** 2 *n.*

He, symbol for helium.

H.E., 1 His Eminence. **2** His Excellency.

head (hed), **1** the top part of the human body or the front part of most animal bodies where the eyes, nose, ears, mouth, and brain are. **2** the top part of anything: *the head of a pin, the head of a page.* **3** the front part of anything: *the head of a procession, the head of a comet.* **4** at the top or front: *the head division of a parade.* **5** be or go at the top or front of: *head a parade.* **6** coming from in front: *a head sea, head tides.* **7** move toward; face toward: *Our ship headed south. It's getting late; we'd better begin to head for home.* **8** chief person; leader: *the head of the school.* **9** chief; leading: *a head nurse.* **10** be the head or chief of; lead: *head a business. Who heads the army?* **11** one or ones; individual or individuals: *ten head of cattle.* **12** anything rounded like a head: *a head of cabbage.* **13** the part of a boil or pimple where pus is about to break through the skin. **14** the striking or cutting part of a tool or implement: *You hit the nail with the head of a hammer.* **15** piece of skin stretched tightly over the end of a drum, etc. **16** mind; understanding; intelligence; intellect: *She has a good head for figures.* **17** topic; point: *She arranged her speech under four main heads.* **18** crisis or conclusion; decisive point: *His sudden refusal brought matters to a head.* **19** pressure of water, gas, etc.: *a full head of steam.* **20** source of a river or stream. **21** put a head on; furnish with a head: *head a letter with a date.* **22 heads,** *pl.* the top side of a coin. **23** part of a tape recorder or disk drive that produces, detects, or erases magnetic signals on the tape or disk. 1-3,8,11-20,22 *n.*, *pl.* **heads** for 1-3,8,12-20,22,23, **head** for 11; 5,7,10,21 *v.*, 4,6,9 *adj.* —**head′like′,** *adj.*

go to one's head, 1 make one dizzy: *The wine went to my head.* **2** make one conceited: *I'm afraid all this praise will go to my head.*

head off, get in front of and turn back or aside: *She tried to head off the runaway horse.*

keep one's head, stay calm; not get excited.

lose one's head, get excited; lose one's self-control.

out of one's head, INFORMAL. crazy.

over one's head, 1 too hard for one to understand: *Einstein's theory of relativity is way over my head.* **2** passing over a person without giving that person a chance to act: *I went over my supervisor's head and complained to the president.*

put heads together or **lay heads together,** plan or plot together.

turn one's head, make one conceited.

head ache (hed′āk′), **1** pain in the head. **2** INFORMAL. something which causes great bother or annoyance. *n.*

head band (hed′band′), band worn around the head. *n.*

headdress

head dress (hed′dres′), covering or decoration for the head. *n.*, *pl.* **head dress es.**

head er (hed′ər), INFORMAL. a plunge, dive, or fall headfirst: *I slipped and took a header. n.*

head first (hed′fėrst′), **1** with the head first. **2** hastily; rashly. *adv.*

head fore most (hed′fôr′mōst), headfirst. *adv.*

head gear (hed′gir′), **1** covering for the head; hat, cap, helmet, etc. **2** the parts of a harness which fit around an animal's head. *n.*

head ing (hed′ing), **1** something written or printed at the top of a page or at the beginning of a chapter, topic, etc. A letterhead and a chapter title are headings. **2** direction toward which an aircraft or ship is moving. *n.*

head land (hed′lənd), point of high land jutting out into water; cape; promontory. *n.*

head less (hed′lis), **1** having no head. **2** without a leader. *adj.*

head light (hed′līt′), a bright light at the front of an automobile, locomotive, etc. *n.*

head line (hed′līn′), **1** words printed in heavy type at the top of a newspaper article telling what it is about. **2 headlines,** *pl.* publicity: *The invention got headlines.* **3** furnish with a headline. **4** give publicity to: *headline a story.* **5** list or be listed as the main attraction: *She is headlining in the new show. The last show headlined another performer.* 1,2 *n.*, 3-5 *v.*, **head lined, head lin ing.**

head long (hed′lông′), **1** with the head first: *plunge headlong into the sea* (*adv.*), *a headlong plunge or dive* (*adj.*). **2** with great speed and force: *rush headlong into the crowd* (*adv.*), *a headlong course* (*adj.*). **3** in too great a rush; without stopping to think: *The boy ran headlong across the busy street* (*adv.*). *One should not make a headlong decision about something important* (*adj.*). *adv.*, *adj.*

head man (hed′man′), chief; leader. *n.*, *pl.* **head men.**

head mas ter (hed′mas′tər), man in charge of a school, especially of a private school; principal. *n.*

head mis tress (hed′mis′tris), woman in charge of a school, especially of a private school. *n.*

head note (hed′nōt′), an explanatory note placed before a chapter, section, article, etc. *n.*

head-on (hed′on′), with the head or front first: *a head-on collision* (adj.), *collide head-on* (adv.). *adj., adv.*

head phone (hed′fōn′), earphone held against one or both ears by a band over the head. *n.*

head piece (hed′pēs′), **1** helmet worn with a suit of armor. **2** any covering for the head. *n.*

head quar ters (hed′kwôr′tərz), **1** place from which the chief or commanding officer of an army, police force, etc., sends out orders. **2** place from which any organization is controlled and directed; main office: *The headquarters of the company is in Washington. n. pl. or sing.*

head set (hed′set′), pair of headphones used by telephone and radio operators, etc. *n.*

head shrinker, SLANG. psychiatrist.

heads man (hedz′mən), man who cuts off the heads of people condemned to death. *n., pl.* **heads men.**

head stand (hed′stand′), a balancing on the head, with the hands placed in front of the head for support. *n.*

head stone (hed′stōn′), stone set at the head of a grave; gravestone. *n.*

head strong (hed′strông′), rashly or foolishly determined to have one's own way; hard to control or manage; obstinate: *a headstrong person. adj.*

head wait er (hed′wā′tər), man in charge of the waiters in a restaurant, hotel, etc. *n.*

head wa ters (hed′wô′tərz *or* hed′wot′ərz), the sources or upper parts of a river. *n.pl.*

head way (hed′wā′), **1** motion forward; progress: *The ship could make no headway against the strong wind and tide.* **2** progress with work, etc.: *Science has made much headway in fighting disease.* **3** a clear space overhead in a doorway or under an arch, bridge, etc.; clearance. *n.*

head wind, wind blowing from the direction in which a ship, etc., is moving.

head y (hed′ē), **1** hasty; rash; headlong. **2** apt to affect the head and make one dizzy; intoxicating: *a heady wine. adj.,* **head i er, head i est.** —**head′i ness,** *n.*

heal (hēl), **1** make whole, sound, or well; bring back to health; cure. **2** become whole or sound; get well; return to health; be cured: *My cut finger healed in a few days. v.*

health (helth), **1** a being well; freedom from sickness: *Rest is important to your health.* **2** condition of body or mind: *be in excellent health.* **3** a drink in honor of a person with a wish for that person's health and happiness. *n.* [*Health* is from Old English *hælth,* which comes from *hāl,* meaning "whole." See **Word Family.**]

health

Below are words related to *health.* They can all be traced back to the Old English word *hāl* (häl), meaning "whole."

Allhallows	heal	wholehearted
hale¹	hollyhock	wholesale
hallow	holy	wholesome
Halloween	whole	whole-wheat

health food, food grown without chemicals or prepared without preservatives, selected for its nutritional value and believed to have health-giving properties.

a hat	i it	oi oil	ch child	a in about
ā age	ī ice	ou out	ng long	e in taken
ä far	o hot	u cup	sh she	ə = i in pencil
e let	ō open	u̇ put	th thin	o in lemon
ē equal	ô order	ü rule	ŦH then	u in circus
ėr term			zh measure	

health ful (helth′fəl), **1** giving health; good for the health: *healthful exercise, a healthful diet.* **2** having good health. *adj.* —**health′ful ly,** *adv.* —**health′ful ness,** *n.*

health i ly (hel′thə lē), in a healthy manner. *adv.*

health i ness (hel′thē nis), healthy condition. *n.*

Health Maintenance Organization, a medical organization that provides complete health care services to all members for the same fixed monthly or yearly fee.

health y (hel′thē), **1** having good health: *a healthy baby.* **2** showing good health: *healthy looks.* **3** good for the health; healthful: *healthy exercise. adj.,* **health i er, health i est.**

heap (hēp), **1** pile of many things thrown or lying together in a confused way: *a heap of stones, a sand heap.* **2** form into a heap; gather in heaps: *I heaped the dirty clothes beside the washing machine. Snow heaped against the fence.* **3** INFORMAL. a large amount: *a heap of trouble.* **4** give generously or in large amounts: *to heap praise on someone.* **5** fill full or more than full: *heap a plate with food.* 1,3 *n.,* 2,4,5 *v.* —**heap′er,** *n.*

hear (hir), **1** take in a sound or sounds through the ear: *We couldn't hear in the back row.* **2** listen: *The town crier shouted "Hear ye!"* **3** listen to: *You must hear what I have to say.* **4** give a formal hearing to: *hear a complaint.* **5** receive news or information: *I heard from my parents. v.,* **heard, hear ing.** —**hear′a ble,** *adj.* —**hear′er,** *n.*

hear out, listen to till the end.

will not hear of, will not listen to, agree to, or allow.

heard (hėrd), past tense and past participle of **hear.** *I heard the noise. The sound was heard a mile away. v.*

hear ing (hir′ing), **1** sense by which sound is perceived: *Please speak up; my hearing is poor.* **2** act or process of taking in sound, listening, or receiving information: *Hearing the good news made her happy.* **3** a formal or official listening: *The judge gave both sides a hearing.* **4** a chance to be heard: *Give us a hearing.* **5** distance that a sound can be heard; earshot: *be within hearing. n.*

hearing aid, a small battery-powered device which amplifies sounds, worn by people who cannot hear well.

heark en (här′kən), pay attention to what is said; listen attentively; listen. *v.* Also, **harken.** —**heark′en er,** *n.*

hear say (hir′sā′), common talk; gossip or rumor. *n.*

hearse (hėrs), automobile, carriage, etc., for carrying a coffin to the cemetery. *n.* —**hearse′like′,** *adj.*

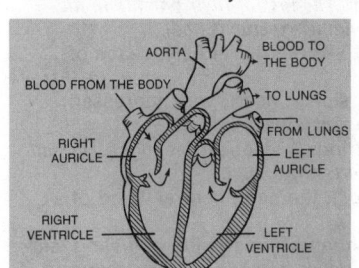

heart (def. 1)

heart (härt), **1** a hollow, muscular organ which pumps the blood throughout the body by contracting and relaxing. **2** the part that feels, loves, hates, and desires: *a heavy heart, a kind heart. He knew in his heart that he was wrong.* **3** love; affection: *give one's heart to someone.*

4 person loved or praised: *group of stout hearts.* **5** kindness; sympathy: *Have you no heart?* **6** spirit; courage; enthusiasm: *The losing team still had plenty of heart.* **7** the innermost part; middle; center: *in the heart of the forest.* **8** the main part; most important part: *the very heart of the matter.* **9** figure shaped like this: ♥ **10** a playing card marked with one or more red, heart-shaped figures. **11 hearts,** *pl.* suit of such playing cards. *n.*

after one's own heart, just as one likes it; pleasing one perfectly: *Now that's a meal after my own heart!*

at heart, in one's deepest thoughts or feelings: *He is kind at heart, though he appears to be gruff.*

by heart, 1 by memory: *I learned the poem by heart.* **2** from memory: *She can recite the poem by heart.*

lose one's heart (to), fall in love (with).

take heart, be encouraged.

take to heart, think seriously about; be deeply affected by.

with all one's heart, 1 sincerely: *He said that he loved her with all his heart.* **2** gladly.

heart ache (härt′āk′), great sorrow or grief; deep pain. *n.*

heart beat (härt′bēt′), pulsation of the heart, including one complete contraction and relaxation. *n.*

heart break (härt′brāk′), a crushing sorrow or grief. *n.*

heart break ing (härt′brā′king), crushing with sorrow or grief. *adj.* —**heart′break′ing ly,** *adv.*

heart bro ken (härt′brō′kən), crushed by sorrow or grief. *adj.* —**heart′bro′ken ly,** *adv.*

heart burn (härt′bėrn′), a burning feeling in the throat and chest caused by a rising up of acid from the stomach. *n.*

heart en (härt′n), cheer up; encourage: *This good news will hearten you.* *v.* —**heart′en er,** *n.*

heart felt (härt′felt′), with deep feeling; sincere; genuine: *heartfelt sympathy.* *adj.*

hearth (härth), **1** stone or brick floor of a fireplace, often extending into the room. **2** fireside; home: *The soldiers longed for their own hearths.* **3** the lowest part of a blast furnace, where the molten metal and slag collects. *n.*

hearth side (härth′sīd′), fireside; home. *n.*

hearth stone (härth′stōn′), **1** stone forming a hearth. **2** fireside; home. *n.*

heart i ly (här′tl ē), **1** in a warm, friendly way; sincerely: *express good wishes very heartily.* **2** with courage, spirit, or enthusiasm; vigorously: *set to work heartily.* **3** with a good appetite: *eat heartily.* **4** completely; extremely: *I heartily approve of her decision.* *adv.*

heart i ness (här′tē nis), **1** sincere feeling. **2** vigor. *n.*

heart less (härt′lis), without kindness or sympathy; unfeeling; cruel: *heartless words.* *adj.* —**heart′less ly,** *adv.*

heart-rend ing (härt′ren′ding), causing mental anguish; very distressing: *The loss of their parents in an accident was a heart-rending experience.* *adj.*

hearts ease or **heart's-ease** (härts′ēz′), peace of mind. *n.*

heart sick (härt′sik′), sick at heart; very depressed; very unhappy. *adj.* —**heart′sick′ness,** *n.*

heart strings (härt′stringz′), deepest feelings: *The sad story tugged at their heartstrings.* *n.pl.*

heart wood (härt′wùd′), the hard, central wood of a tree. *n.*

heart y (här′tē), **1** warm and friendly; full of feeling; sincere: *We gave our old friends a hearty welcome.* **2** strong and well; vigorous: *My grandmother was still hale and hearty at eighty.* **3** full of energy and enthusiasm; not restrained: *a hearty laugh.* **4** with plenty to eat; abundant: *a hearty meal.* **5** having a good appetite: *People who work outdoors are usually hearty eaters.* *adj.,* **heart i er, heart i est.**

heat (hēt), **1** condition of being hot; hotness; warmth; high temperature: *the heat of a fire.* **2** a form of energy that consists of the motion of the molecules of a substance. This energy can pass from one object to another and, when absorbed, produces an increase in temperature. **3** make or become warm or hot: *The stove heats the room. The soup is heating slowly.* **4** warmth or intensity of feeling; violence; excitement: *In the heat of the argument we lost our tempers.* **5** fill with strong feeling; excite or become excited: *The stirring speech heated the child's imagination.* **6** one trial in a race: *I won the first heat, but lost the final race.* 1,2,4,6 *n.,* 3,5 *v.* —**heat′less,** *adj.*

heat ed (hē′tid), angry, excited, or violent: *a heated argument.* *adj.* —**heat′ed ly,** *adv.* —**heat′ed ness,** *n.*

heat er (hē′tər), something that gives heat or warmth. A stove, furnace, or radiator is a heater. *n.*

heath (hēth), **1** open wasteland with heather or low bushes growing on it; moor. It has few or no trees. **2** a low bush growing on such land. Heather is a kind of heath. *n.* —**heath′like′,** *adj.*

hea then (hē′ᴛʜən), **1** person who does not believe in the God of the Bible; person who is not a Christian, Jew, or Moslem; pagan. **2** people who are heathens. **3** of heathens; not Christian, Jewish, or Moslem. **4** person who has no religion or culture. **5** not religious or cultured. 1,2,4 *n., pl.* **hea thens** or **hea then;** 3,5 *adj.* —**hea′then ness,** *n.*

hea then ish (hē′ᴛʜə nish), like heathens. *adj.*

heather

heath er (heᴛʜ′ər), a low, evergreen shrub with stalks of small, purple or pink, bell-shaped flowers, covering many heaths of Scotland and England. *n.*

heat lightning, lightning in broad flashes seen near the horizon, especially on hot summer evenings; sheet lightning. It is actually a reflection of lightning that occurs beyond the horizon.

heat shield, a coating or covering of special material on the nose cone of a missile or spacecraft. It absorbs or diffuses heat caused by friction during reentry into the earth's atmosphere.

heat wave, period of very hot weather.

heave (hēv), **1** lift with force or effort: *She heaved the heavy box into the station wagon.* **2** lift and throw: *The sailors heaved the anchor overboard.* **3** pull with force or effort; haul: *They heaved on the rope.* **4** give (a sigh, groan, etc.) with a deep, heavy breath: *She heaved a sigh of relief.* **5** rise and fall alternately: *The waves heaved in the storm.* **6** breathe hard; pant. **7** to vomit. **8** (of a ship) move in some direction. **9** to rise; swell; bulge: *The ground heaved from the earthquake.* **10** act of heaving: *With a mighty heave, we pushed the boat into the water.* 1-9 *v.,* **heaved** or **hove, heav ing;** 10 *n.* —**heav′er,** *n.*

heave ho! sailors' cry when pulling up the anchor, etc.

heave in sight, come into view.

heave to, stop a ship; stop.

heav en (hev′ən), **1** (in Christian and some other religious use) place where God and the angels live and where the blessed go after death. **2 Heaven,** God; Providence: *It was the will of Heaven.* **3** place or condition of greatest happiness. **4** Usually, **heavens,** *pl.* the upper air; sky: *Millions of stars were shining in the heavens. n.*

for heaven's sake! or **good heavens!** exclamation of surprise or protest.

heav en ly (hev′ən lē), **1** of or in heaven; divine: *heavenly angels, heavenly Father.* **2** like heaven; suitable for heaven; very happy, beautiful, or excellent: *a heavenly spot, heavenly peace.* **3** of or in the heavens: *The sun, moon, and stars are heavenly bodies. adj.* —**heav′en li ness,** *n.*

heav en ward (hev′ən wərd), toward heaven: *The rocket soared heavenward* (*adv.*). *The spaceship set out on its heavenward course* (*adj.*). *adv., adj.*

heav i ly (hev′ə lē), in a heavy manner. *adv.*

heav i ness (hev′ē nis), **1** a being heavy; great weight. **2** sadness. *n.*

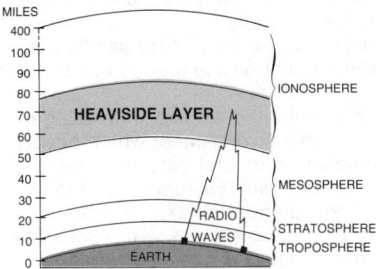

Heav i side layer (hev′ē sīd), a layer of the ionosphere which reflects low-frequency radio waves.

heav y (hev′ē), **1** hard to lift or carry; of great weight: *a heavy load.* **2** of more than usual weight for its kind: *heavy silk, heavy bread.* **3** of great amount, force, or intensity; greater than usual; large: *a heavy rain, a heavy meal, a heavy sea, a heavy vote.* **4** hard to bear or endure: *Their troubles became heavier.* **5** hard to deal with, manage, etc.; trying or difficult in any way: *heavy soil, a heavy job.* **6** hard to digest: *heavy food.* **7** weighted down; laden: *air heavy with moisture, eyes heavy with sleep.* **8** sorrowful; gloomy: *His heart was heavy.* **9** serious; deep; grave: *a heavy part in a play, a heavy discussion.* **10** SLANG. unpleasant; troublesome: *My being so late caused a heavy scene at home.* **11** cloudy; overcast: *a heavy sky.* **12** broad; thick; coarse: *heavy features.* **13** clumsy; sluggish; slow: *a heavy walk.* **14** uninteresting; dull; ponderous: *heavy reading.* **15** INFORMAL. villain: *the heavy in a play.* **16** in a heavy manner; heavily. 1-14 *adj.,* **heav i er, heav i est;** 15 *n.,* 16 *adv.*

hang heavy, pass slowly and dully: *Time hung heavy on her hands.*

heav y-hand ed (hev′ē han′did), **1** clumsy; awkward: *heavy-handed humor.* **2** treating others harshly. *adj.*

heav y-heart ed (hev′ē här′tid), sad; gloomy. *adj.*

heavy hydrogen, deuterium.

heavy water, water formed of oxygen and deuterium. Heavy water is much like ordinary water, but is about 1.1 times as heavy and has a higher freezing point. It occurs in very small amounts in ordinary water.

heav y weight (hev′ē wāt′), **1** person or thing of more than average weight. **2** boxer or wrestler who weighs 175 pounds (79 kilograms) or more. *n.*

Heb., Hebrew or Hebrews.

He bra ic (hi brā′ik), of the Hebrews or their language or culture. *adj.*

He brew (hē′brü), **1** Jew; Israelite. **2** the ancient Semitic language of the Jews, in which the Old Testament was

a hat	**i** it	**oi** oil	**ch** child	a in about
ā age	**ī** ice	**ou** out	**ng** long	e in taken
ä far	**o** hot	**u** cup	**sh** she	**ə** = i in pencil
e let	**ō** open	**u̇** put	**th** thin	o in lemon
ē equal	**ô** order	**ü** rule	**ᵀH** then	u in circus
ėr term			**zh** measure	

written. Citizens of Israel speak a modern form of Hebrew. **3** Jewish. 1,2 *n.,* 3 *adj.*

He brews (hē′brüz), book of the New Testament. *n.*

Heb ri des (heb′rə dēz′), group of Scottish islands off NW Scotland. *n.pl.*

He bron (hē′brən), town in W Jordan, near Jerusalem. *n.*

heck le (hek′əl), interrupt and annoy (a speaker, etc.) by asking bothersome questions, jeering, or making loud remarks. *v.,* **heck led, heck ling.**

heck ler (hek′lər), person who heckles. *n.*

hec tic (hek′tik), very exciting; feverish: *The children had a hectic time getting to school after the big snowstorm. adj.* —**hec′ti cal ly,** *adv.* —**hec′tic ness,** *n.*

hec tor (hek′tər), **1** a bragging, bullying fellow. **2** bluster; bully. **3** to tease. 1 *n.,* 2,3 *v.*

Hec tor (hek′tər), (in Greek legends) the bravest of the Trojan warriors. He was killed by Achilles. *n.*

he'd (hēd; *unstressed* ēd), **1** he had. **2** he would.

hedge (hej), **1** a thick row of bushes or small trees, planted as a fence or boundary. **2** any barrier or boundary. **3** put a hedge around: *hedge a garden.* **4** avoid giving a direct answer or taking a definite stand; evade questions. **5** bet on both sides in order to reduce one's possible losses. 1,2 *n.,* 3-5 *v.,* **hedged, hedg ing.** —**hedge′less,** *adj.* —**hedg′er,** *n.*

hedge in, hem in; surround on all sides: *The town was hedged in by mountains and a dense forest.*

hedgehog (def. 1)
about 9 in.
(23 cm.) long

hedge hog (hej′hog′), **1** a small, insect-eating mammal of Europe, Asia, and Africa, with spines on its back. When attacked, a hedgehog rolls up into a bristling ball. **2** porcupine of North America. *n.*

hedge hop (hej′hop′), fly an airplane very low. *v.,* **hedge hopped, hedge hop ping.**

hedge hop per (hej′hop′ər), pilot who hedgehops. *n.*

hedge row (hej′rō′), a thick row of bushes or small trees forming a hedge. *n.*

heed (hēd), **1** give careful attention to; take notice of: *Now heed what I say.* **2** careful attention: *Pay heed to her instructions.* 1 *v.,* 2 *n.* —**heed′er,** *n.*

heed ful (hēd′fəl), careful; attentive. *adj.* —**heed′ful ly,** *adv.* —**heed′ful ness,** *n.*

heed less (hēd′lis), careless; thoughtless. *adj.* —**heed′less ly,** *adv.* —**heed′less ness,** *n.*

hee haw (hē′hô′), **1** the braying sound made by a donkey. **2** make such a sound. 1 *n.,* 2 *v.*

heel[1] (hēl), **1** the back part of the foot, below the ankle. **2** the part of a stocking or shoe that covers the heel. **3** the part of a shoe or boot that is under the heel or raises the heel: *a pair of shoes with high heels.* **4** the part of the hind leg of an animal that corresponds to a per-

son's heel: *The horse kicked up its heels trying to throw the rider.* **5** put a heel or heels on: *heel a pair of shoes.*
6 touch the ground with the heel. **7** follow closely.
8 anything shaped, used, or placed at an end like a heel. The end crust of bread or the rear end of a ship's keel is a heel. **9** INFORMAL. a hateful person. 1-4,8,9 *n.*, 5-7 *v.*
at heel, near the heels; close behind.
down at the heel or **down at the heels, 1** with the heel of the shoe worn down. **2** shabby.
kick up one's heels, have a good time.
take to one's heels, run away.

heel² (hēl), **1** lean over to one side; tilt; tip: *The sailboat heeled as it turned.* **2** act of heeling. 1 *v.*, 2 *n.*

heft (heft), INFORMAL. **1** weight; heaviness. **2** lift; heave. **3** judge the weight of by lifting. 1 *n.*, 2,3 *v.*

heft y (hef′tē), INFORMAL. **1** weighty; heavy. **2** big and strong. *adj.*, **heft i er, heft i est.** —**heft′i ly,** *adv.*

Hei del berg (hī′dl bėrg′), city in S West Germany. A famous university is located there. *n.*

heif er (hef′ər), a young cow that has not had a calf. *n.*

heigh-ho (hī′hō′ or hā′hō′), sound made to express surprise, joy, sadness, or weariness. *interj.*

height (hīt), **1** measurement from top to bottom; how tall a person is; how high a thing is; how far up a thing goes: *the height of a mountain.* **2** a fairly great distance up: *rising at a height above the valley.* **3** a high point or place: *She stood on a height above the river.* **4** the highest part; top. **5** the highest point; greatest degree: *Fast driving on icy roads is the height of folly.* *n.*

height en (hīt′n), **1** make or become higher. **2** make or become stronger or greater; increase: *The wind whistling outside heightened the suspense of the ghost story.* *v.*

Heim lich maneuver, (hīm′lik), method used in first aid to save a person who is choking. You grasp the victim from behind, beneath the ribs, and squeeze hard with both hands clasped together. This will clear whatever is stuck in the person's windpipe. [The *Heimlich maneuver* is named for Henry J. *Heimlich,* born 1920, an American physician who developed it.]

hei nous (hā′nəs), very wicked; hateful. *adj.* [*Heinous* came into English about 600 years ago from French *haïnos,* and can be traced back to *haïr,* meaning "to hate."]

heir (er *or* ar), person who has the right to somebody's property or title after the death of its owner. *n.*

heir apparent, person who will be heir if he or she lives longer than the one holding the property or title: *The king's oldest son is heir apparent to the throne.* *pl.* **heirs apparent.**

heir ess (er′is *or* ar′is), **1** heir who is a woman or girl. **2** woman or girl inheriting great wealth. *n.*, *pl.* **heir ess es.**

heir loom (er′lüm′ *or* ar′lüm′), possession handed down from generation to generation: *This clock is a family heirloom.* *n.*

held (held), past tense and past participle of **hold¹.** *I held the kitten gently. The swing is held by strong ropes.* *v.*

Hel e na (hel′ə nə), capital of Montana, in the W part. *n.*

Hel en of Troy (hel′ən), (in Greek legends) a very beautiful Greek woman, the wife of King Menelaus of Sparta. Her kidnaping by Paris caused the Trojan War.

hel i ces (hel′ə sēz′), a plural of **helix.** *n.*

hel i cop ter (hel′ə kop′tər), aircraft without wings that is lifted from the ground and kept in the air by horizontal propellers. *n.* [*Helicopter* is from French *hélicoptère,* which came from Greek *helikos,* meaning "a spiral," and *pteron,* meaning "wing."]

he li o cen tric (hē′lē ō sen′trik), **1** viewed or measured from the center of the sun. **2** having or representing the sun as a center. *adj.*

heliograph (def. 1) used by armies in the late 1800's

he li o graph (hē′lē ə graf), **1** device for signaling by means of a movable mirror which flashes beams of sunlight to a distance. The flashes of the mirror represent the dots and dashes of the Morse code. **2** to signal by heliograph. **3** apparatus for taking photographs of the sun. 1,3 *n.*, 2 *v.*

he li o trope (hē′lē ə trōp), **1** plant with clusters of small, sweet-smelling purple or white flowers. **2** a pinkish purple. **3** pinkish-purple. 1,2 *n.*, 3 *adj.*

hel i port (hel′ə pôrt′), airport designed for use by helicopters. Heliports may be built on the tops of buildings. *n.*

he li um (hē′lē əm), a very light, colorless, odorless gas that will not burn. It is a chemical element which occurs in small amounts in the air, in natural gas, etc., and which is also produced artificially. Helium is used to inflate balloons and airships and, in the liquid state, as a refrigerant. *n.* [*Helium* comes from Greek *hēlios,* meaning "sun." It was called this because it was discovered to exist in the sun.]

he lix (hē′liks), anything having a spiral, coiled form. A screw thread, a watch spring, or a snail shell is a helix. *n.*, *pl.* **hel i ces** or **he lix es.**

hell (hel), **1** (in Christian and some other religious use) place where devils and evil spirits live and where wicked persons are punished after death. **2** home of the dead; Hades. **3** any place or condition of wickedness, torment, or misery. *n.*

he'll (hēl; *unstressed* hil), **1** he will. **2** he shall.

Hel las (hel′əs), Greece. *n.*

hell bend er (hel′ben′dər), a large salamander, common in the Ohio River and its tributaries. *n.*

hel le bore (hel′ə bôr), **1** a European plant related to the buttercup, with showy flowers that bloom before spring. Its root is dried and used in medicine. **2** a tall plant related to the lily, with clusters of purple or white flowers. Its root is used in medicine or as a powder to kill insects. *n.*

Hel lene (hel′ēn), a Greek. *n.*

Hel len ic (he len′ik), **1** Greek. **2** of Greek history, language, or culture from 776 B.C. to the death of Alexander the Great in 323 B.C. *adj.*

Hel len is tic (hel′ə nis′tik), of Greek history, language, or culture after 323 B.C. *adj.*

Hel les pont (hel′i spont), ancient name for the Dardanelles. *n.*

hell ish (hel′ish), fit to have come from hell; devilish; fiendish: *hellish shrieks, a hellish thing to do.* *adj.* —**hell′ish ly,** *adv.* —**hell′ish ness,** *n.*

hel lo (he lō′ *or* hə lō′), **1** a call or exclamation to attract attention, express greeting, etc. We usually say "hello" when we call or answer a call on the telephone. *"Hello, Mother!" the boy said.* **2** a call or shout: *She gave a loud hello to let us know where she was.* **3** say or call "hello"; shout; call: *He asked us to hello until somebody came.* 1 *interj.,* 2 *n.,* *pl.* **hel los;** 3 *v.*

helm¹ (helm), **1** handle or wheel by which a ship is steered. **2** the steering apparatus of a ship, including the wheel, rudder, and connecting parts. **3** position of control or guidance: *Upon the President's death, the Vice-President took the nation's helm. n.*

helm² (helm), OLD USE. helmet. *n.*

hel met (hel′mit), covering made of steel, leather, plastic, or some other sturdy material, worn to protect the head. *n.* —**hel′met like′,** *adj.*

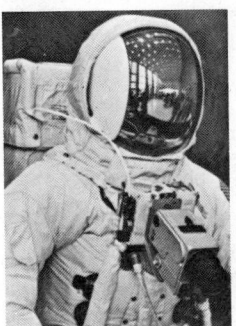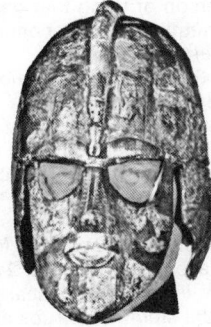

helmets—left, astronaut's helmet; right, ancient iron helmet

helms man (helmz′mən), person who steers a ship. *n.,* *pl.* **helms men.**

hel ot (hel′ət *or* hē′lət), **1** slave; serf. **2** Helot, member of a class of slaves or serfs in ancient Sparta. *n.*

help (help), **1** give or do what is needed or useful; give aid; assist: *My parents helped me with my homework. We could finish the job faster if you would help.* **2** act of helping; aid; assistance: *I need some help with my work. The dying woman was beyond help.* **3** person or thing that helps; helper: *A sewing machine is a help in making clothes.* **4** a hired helper or group of hired helpers: *The storekeeper treats her help well.* **5** make better; relieve: *This medicine will help your cough.* **6** means of making better; remedy: *The medicine was a help.* **7** prevent; stop: *It can't be helped.* **8** avoid; keep from: *I can't help yawning.* 1,5,7,8 *v.,* 2-4,6 *n.*

help oneself to, take for or serve oneself: *Help yourselves to some cake.*

help out, help; help in doing or getting: *The children were asked to help out around the house.*

help er (hel′pər), person or thing that helps. *n.*

help ful (help′fəl), giving help; useful. *adj.* —**help′ful ly,** *adv.* —**help′ful ness,** *n.*

help ing (help′ing), portion of food served to a person at one time. *n.*

helping verb, auxiliary verb.

help less (help′lis), **1** not able to help oneself: *A little baby is helpless.* **2** without help or protection: *Though he was alone and helpless, he managed to keep the boat from sinking until help arrived. adj.* —**help′less ly,** *adv.*

help mate (help′māt′), companion and helper, especially a wife or husband. *n.*

help meet (help′mēt′), helpmate. *n.*

Hel sin ki (hel′sing kē), seaport and capital of Finland, in the S part. *n.*

hel ter-skel ter (hel′tər skel′tər), **1** with headlong, disorderly haste: *The children ran helter-skelter when the dog rushed at them.* **2** disorderly; confused: *a helter-skelter way of playing a game.* 1 *adv.,* 2 *adj.*

hem¹ (hem), **1** border or edge on a garment; edge made on cloth by folding it over and sewing it down. **2** fold over and sew down the edge of (cloth): *I hemmed the curtains.* 1 *n.,* 2 *v.,* **hemmed, hem ming.** —**hem′mer,** *n.*

hem in, hem around, *or* **hem about,** close in or surround, and not let out.

hem² (hem), **1** sound like clearing the throat, used to

attract attention or show doubt or hesitation. **2** make this sound. 1 *interj., n.,* 2 *v.,* **hemmed, hem ming.**

hem and haw, 1 hesitate in speaking. **2** stall or put off.

he-man (hē′man′), INFORMAL. a virile, rugged man. *n.,* *pl.* **he-men.**

hem a tite (hem′ə tīt), an important iron ore that is reddish-brown when powdered. *n.* [*Hematite* is from Latin *haematites,* which comes from Greek *haimatitēs* (*lithos*), meaning "bloodlike (stone)," which is from *haimatos,* meaning "blood." The ore was called this because of its color, especially when scratched.]

hemi-, *prefix.* half: *Hemisphere = half a sphere.*

Hem ing way (hem′ing wā), **Ernest,** 1899-1961, American writer of novels and short stories. *n.*

hem i sphere (hem′ə sfir), **1** half of a sphere or globe. **2** half of the earth's surface. North America and South America are in the Western Hemisphere. Europe, Asia, Africa, and Australia are in the Eastern Hemisphere. All countries north of the equator are in the Northern Hemisphere, and the countries south of it are in the Southern Hemisphere. *n.*

hem i spher ic (hem′ə sfir′ik *or* hem′ə sfer′ik), hemispherical. *adj.*

hem i spher i cal (hem′ə sfir′ə kəl *or* hem′ə sfer′ə kəl), **1** shaped like a hemisphere. **2** of a hemisphere. *adj.*

hem lock (hem′lok), **1** an evergreen tree related to the pine, with flat needles, small cones, and reddish bark used in tanning. **2** its wood. **3** a poisonous plant with spotted stems, finely divided leaves, and small white flowers. It is related to the carrot. **4** poison made from it. *n.*

he mo glo bin (hē′mə glō′bən *or* hem′ə glō′bən), substance in the red blood cells made up of iron and protein. It carries oxygen from the lungs to the tissues, and carbon dioxide from the tissues to the lungs. Hemoglobin gives blood its red color. *n.*

he mo phil i a (hē′mə fil′ē ə), an inherited disorder of the blood in males in which clotting does not occur normally, making it difficult to stop bleeding even after the slightest injury. *n.*

hem or rhage (hem′ər ij), **1** discharge of blood, especially a heavy discharge from a damaged blood vessel. A nosebleed is a mild hemorrhage. **2** have a hemorrhage; lose much blood. 1 *n.,* 2 *v.,* **hem or rhaged, hem or rhag ing.** [*Hemorrhage* can be traced back to Greek *haima,* meaning "blood," and *rhēgnynai,* meaning "to break, burst." See **Word Family.**]

WORD FAMILY

hemorrhage

Below are words related to *hemorrhage.* They can all be traced back to Greek *haima, haimatos* (hī′mä, hī′mä tos), meaning "blood."

anemia hematite hemophilia
anemic hemoglobin leukemia

hem or rhoids (hem′ə roidz′), painful swellings formed by the enlargement of blood vessels near the anus. *n.pl.*

hemp (hemp), **1** a tall plant of Asia whose tough fibers are made into heavy string, rope, and coarse cloth. **2** hashish or other narcotic drug obtained from this plant. *n.* —**hemp′like′**, *adj.*

hemp en (hem′pən), of or like hemp. *adj.*

hem stitch (hem′stich′), **1** to hem along a line from which threads have been drawn out, gathering the cross threads into a series of little groups. **2** the stitch used. **3** ornamental needlework made by hemstitching. 1 *v.*, 2,3 *n.*, *pl.* **hem stitch es** for 2. —**hem′stitch′er**, *n.*

hen (hen), **1** a female domestic fowl: *a hen and her chicks.* **2** female of other birds. *n.* —**hen′like′**, *adj.*

hence (hens), **1** as a result of this; therefore: *The king died, and hence his son became king.* **2** from now; from this time onward: *Come back a week hence.* **3** from here: *"Go hence, I pray thee."* *adv.*

hence forth (hens′fôrth′), from this time on; from now on. *adv.*

hence for ward (hens′fôr′wərd), henceforth. *adv.*

hench man (hench′mən), **1** a trusted attendant or follower. **2** an obedient, unscrupulous follower. *n.*, *pl.* **hench men.** [*Henchman* is from Middle English *henxstman*, also meaning "groom," which comes from Old English *hengest*, meaning "horse," and *man*, meaning "man."]

hen house (hen′hous′), house for poultry. *n.*, *pl.* **hen hous es** (hen′hou′ziz).

hen na (hen′ə), **1** a reddish-brown dye used on the hair. **2** a small, thorny tree of Asia and Africa from whose leaves this dye is made. **3** a reddish brown. **4** reddish-brown. **5** dye or color with henna. 1-3 *n.*, *pl.* **hen nas**; 4 *adj.*, 5 *v.*, **hen naed, hen na ing.**

hen peck (hen′pek′), domineer over or rule (one's husband). *v.*

Hen ry (hen′rē), **Patrick,** 1736-1799, American patriot, orator, and statesman. *n.*

Henry II, 1133-1189, king of England from 1154 to 1189. His church policies were opposed by Thomas à Becket.

Henry VIII, 1491-1547, king of England from 1509 to 1547. He established the Church of England with himself as its head.

he pat i ca (hi pat′ə kə), a low plant with delicate purple, pink, or white flowers that bloom early in the spring; liverwort. *n.*, *pl.* **he pat i cas.** [*Hepatica* was borrowed from a medieval Latin word *hepatica*, and can be traced back to Greek *hēpatos*, meaning "liver." The plant was called this because its leaves were thought to look like livers.]

hep a ti tis (hep′ə tī′tis), inflammation of the liver. *n.*

hep ta gon (hep′tə gon), a plane figure having seven angles and seven sides. *n.* [*Heptagon* comes from Greek *hepta*, meaning "seven," and *gōnia*, meaning "angle."]

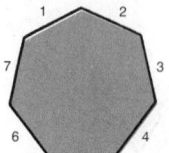

regular heptagon

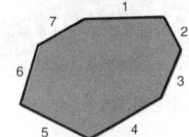

irregular heptagon

her (hėr; *unstressed* hər), **1** the girl, woman, or female animal spoken about: *She is not here; have you seen her? Find her.* **2** of her; belonging to her: *her book, her work.* 1 *pron.*, 2 *adj.*

Her a (hir′ə), (in Greek myths) a goddess who was the wife of Zeus. She was the goddess of marriage. The Romans called her Juno. *n.* Also, **Here.**

Her a cles (her′ə klēz′), Hercules. *n.*

her ald (her′əld), **1** person who carries messages and makes announcements; messenger. In former times, a herald was an official who made public announcements and carried messages between rulers, etc. **2** bring news of; announce: *The newspapers heralded the signing of the treaty.* **3** person or thing that goes or is sent before and shows something more is coming; harbinger: *Dawn is the herald of day.* 1,3 *n.*, 2 *v.*

he ral dic (he ral′dik), of heraldry or heralds. *adj.* —**he ral′di cal ly**, *adv.*

her ald ry (her′əl drē), science or art dealing with coats of arms. Heraldry determines a person's right to use a coat of arms, traces family descent, designs coats of arms for new countries, etc. *n.*

herb (ėrb *or* hėrb), **1** plant whose leaves or stems are used for medicine, seasoning, food, or perfume. Sage, mint, and lavender are herbs. **2** any flowering plant whose stem lives only one season and does not become woody as the stems of shrubs and trees do. Lilies, corn, and onions are herbs. *n.* —**herb′less**, *adj.* —**herb′like′**, *adj.*

her ba ceous (hėr′bā′shəs), of an herb; like an herb. *adj.*

herb age (ėr′bij *or* hėr′bij), herbs or grass. Cows graze on herbage in a pasture. *n.*

her bi vore (her′bə vôr), any animal that feeds mainly on plants. *n.*

her biv or ous (hėr′biv′ər əs), feeding on grass or other plants. Cattle are herbivorous animals. *adj.* [*Herbivorous* comes from Latin *herba*, meaning "grass, herb," and *vorare*, meaning "to devour."]

her cu le an or **Her cu le an** (her′kyü′lē ən *or* hėr′kyə lē′ən), **1** of great strength, courage, or size; very powerful: *a herculean warrior.* **2** requiring great strength, courage, or size; very hard to do: *a herculean task.* **3** *Herculean*, of Hercules. *adj.*

Her cu les (her′kyə lēz′), **1** (in Greek and Roman myths) a hero famous for his great strength and for the twelve great labors he performed. **2** Also, **hercules,** any person of great strength, courage, or size. *n.* Also, **Heracles.**

herd (hėrd), **1** group of animals of one kind, especially large animals, keeping, feeding, or moving together: *a herd of cows, a herd of horses, a herd of elephants.* **2** a large number of people. **3** join together; flock together: *We all herded under an awning to get out of the rain.* **4** form into a flock, herd, or group: *They herded the cows over to the barn door.* **5** tend or take care of (cattle, sheep, etc.). 1,2 *n.*, 3-5 *v.*

ride herd on, control strictly.

herd er (hėr′dər), herdsman. *n.*

herds man (hėrdz′mən), person who takes care of a herd. *n.*, *pl.* **herds men.**

here (hir), **1** in this place; at this place: *We will stop here. We live here in the summer.* **2** to this place: *Come here.* **3** this place: *Where do we go from here?* **4** at this time; now: *Here the speaker paused.* **5** this life: *the here and now.* **6** an answer showing that one is present when roll is called. **7** exclamation used to call attention to some person or thing: *"Here! take away the dishes."* 1,2,4 *adv.*, 3,5 *n.*, 6,7 *interj.*

here and there, in this place and that; at intervals.

here's to you! a wish for health or success.

neither here nor there, not to the point; off the subject; unimportant.

Her e (hir′ē), Hera.

here a bout (hir′ə bout′), about this place; around here; near here. *adv.*

here a bouts (hir/ə bouts/), hereabout. *adv.*

here af ter (hir af/tər), **1** after this; in the future. **2** the future. **3** the life or time after death. 1 *adv.*, 2,3 *n.*

here by (hir bī/), by this; by this means; in this way: *The license said, "You are hereby given the right to hunt and fish in Dover County." adv.*

he red i tar y (hə red/ə ter/ē), **1** coming by inheritance: *"Prince" and "princess" are hereditary titles.* **2** holding a position by inheritance: *The queen of England is a hereditary ruler.* **3** transmitted or caused by heredity: *Color-blindness is hereditary.* **4** taken from one's parents or ancestors: *a hereditary custom or belief.* **5** having to do with inheritance or heredity. *adj.* —**he red/i tar/i ly,** *adv.* —**he red/i tar/i ness,** *n.*

he red i ty (hə red/ə tē), **1** the passing on of physical or mental characteristics from parent to offspring by means of genes. **2** qualities of body and mind that have come to offspring from parents. *n., pl.* **he red i ties.**

Here ford (hèr/fərd), one of a breed of reddish-brown beef cattle having a white face and white markings under the body. *n.*

here in (hir in/), **1** in this place. **2** in this matter; in this way. *adv.*

here of (hir ov/ *or* hir uv/), of this; about this. *adv.*

here on (hir on/), **1** on this. **2** immediately after this. *adv.*

here's (hirz), here is.

her e sy (her/ə sē), **1** belief different from the accepted belief of a church or some other group. **2** the holding of such a belief. *n., pl.* **her e sies.** [*Heresy* came into English about 750 years ago from French *heresie*, and can be traced back to Greek *hairein*, meaning "to choose, take."]

her e tic (her/ə tik), person who holds a belief that is different from the accepted belief of a church or some other group. *n.*

he ret i cal (hə ret/ə kəl), **1** of heresy or heretics. **2** containing heresy; characterized by heresy. *adj.* —**he ret/i cal ly,** *adv.* —**he ret/i cal ness,** *n.*

here to (hir tü/), to this place, thing, document, etc. *adv.*

here to fore (hir/tə fôr/), before this time; until now. *adv.*

here un to (hir/un tü/), to this place, thing, document, etc.; hereto. *adv.*

here up on (hir/ə pon/), **1** upon this thing, point, subject, or matter. **2** immediately after this. *adv.*

here with (hir wiŦH/ *or* hir with/), with this: *I am sending ten cents in stamps herewith. adv.*

her it a ble (her/ə tə bəl), **1** capable of being inherited: *heritable diseases, heritable tendencies.* **2** capable of inheriting. *adj.* —**her/it a bly,** *adv.*

her it age (her/ə tij), what is handed down from one generation to the next; inheritance: *The heritage of freedom is precious to Americans. n.*

her maph ro dite (hər maf/rə dīt), animal or plant having both male and female reproductive organs. *n.*

Her mes (hèr/mēz), (in Greek myths) a god who was the messenger of Zeus and the other gods. He was the god of travel and commerce, of science and invention, of eloquence, luck, and cunning, and the patron of thieves and gamblers. The Romans called him Mercury. *n.*

her met ic (hər met/ik), closed tightly so that air cannot get in or out; airtight: *The bottle has a hermetic seal. adj.* —**her met/i cal ly,** *adv.*

her met i cal (hər met/ə kəl), hermetic. *adj.*

her mit (hèr/mit), person who goes away from others and lives alone. A hermit often lives a religious life. *n.* [*Hermit* came into English about 750 years ago from French *hermite*, and can be traced back to Greek *erēmos*, meaning "uninhabited, lonely."] —**her/mit like/,** *adj.*

her mit age (hèr/mə tij), home of a hermit. *n.*

hermit crab, crab with a soft body that lives in the empty shells of snails, whelks, etc., as a means of protection.

hermit thrush, a brown thrush of North America, with spotted breast and reddish tail, noted for its song.

her ni a (hèr/nē ə), an abnormal bulging out of a part of the intestine or some other organ through a break in its surrounding walls; rupture. *n., pl.* **her ni as, her ni ae** (hèr/nē ē).

he ro (hir/ō), **1** person admired for bravery, great deeds, or noble qualities: *Daniel Boone and Clara Barton are American heroes.* **2** the most important male person in a story, play, poem, motion picture, etc. *n., pl.* **her oes.**

Her od (her/əd), 73?-4 B.C., king of Judea from 37? to 4 B.C. Jesus was born during his reign. *n.*

he ro ic (hi rō/ik), **1** of, like, or suitable for a hero; brave, great, or noble: *the heroic deeds of our firemen.* **2** of or about heroes and their deeds: *The "Iliad" and the "Odyssey" are heroic poems.* **3** unusually daring or bold: *Heroic measures saved the town from the flood. adj.* —**he ro/i cal ly,** *adv.*

he ro i cal (hi rō/ə kəl), heroic. *adj.*

he ro ics (hi rō/iks), words or actions that seem grand or noble, but are only for effect. *n.pl.*

her o in (her/ō ən), a poisonous, habit-forming drug made from morphine. *n.*

her o ine (her/ō ən), **1** woman or girl admired for her bravery, great deeds, or noble qualities. **2** the most important female person in a story, play, poem, motion picture, etc. *n.*

her o ism (her/ō iz/əm), actions and qualities of a hero or heroine; great bravery; daring courage. *n.*

heron
about 4 ft. (1 m.) long

her on (her/ən), a wading bird with a long neck, a long bill, and long legs. Herons feed on fish, frogs, and small reptiles. *n.*

her pe tol o gist (hèr/pə tol/ə jist), an expert in herpetology. *n.*

her pe tol o gy (hèr/pə tol/ə jē), branch of zoology dealing with reptiles and amphibians. *n.* [*Herpetology* comes from Greek *herpeton*, meaning "reptile," and *-logia*, meaning "study or science of."]

Herr (her), GERMAN. **1** Mr.; Sir. **2** gentleman. *n., pl.* **Herren** (her/ən).

her ring (her/ing), a small food fish of the northern Atlantic. The grown fish are eaten fresh, salted, or smoked, and the young are canned as sardines. *n., pl.* **her rings** or **her ring.**

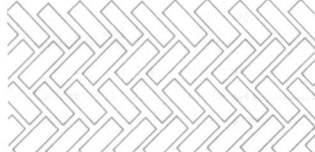

herringbone
(def. 2)

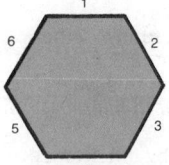
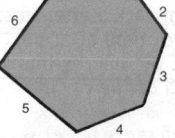

regular hexagon   irregular hexagon

her ring bone (her′ing bōn′), **1** having a zigzag pattern or arrangement like the spine of a herring. **2** a zigzag pattern, arrangement, or stitch. **3** a way of going up a slope on skis by setting the ski tips pointed outward. **1** *adj.,* **2,3** *n.*

hers (hėrz), the one or ones belonging to her: *This money is hers. Your answers are wrong; hers are right. pron.*

her self (hər self′), **1** form of *she* or *her* used to make a statement stronger: *She did it herself.* **2** form used instead of *she* or *her* in cases like: *She hurt herself.* **3** her real or true self: *She is so tired that she's not herself. pron.*

hertz (hėrts), unit of frequency equal to one cycle per second. *n., pl.* **hertz.** [*Hertz* was named for Heinrich R. Hertz, 1857-1894, a German physicist.]

he's (hēz; *unstressed* ēz), **1** he is. **2** he has.

hes i tan cy (hez′ə tən sē), hesitation; tendency to hesitate. *n., pl.* **hes i tan cies.**

hes i tant (hez′ə tənt), hesitating; doubtful; undecided: *I was hesitant about accepting the invitation. adj.* —**hes′i tant ly,** *adv.*

hes i tate (hez′ə tāt), **1** fail to act promptly; hold back because one feels doubtful or undecided; show that one has not yet made up one's mind: *I hesitated about taking his side until I knew the whole story.* **2** feel that perhaps one should not; be unwilling; not want: *I hesitated to ask you; you were so busy.* **3** stop for an instant; pause: *He hesitated before asking the question.* **4** speak with short stops or pauses; stammer. *v.,* **hes i tat ed, hes i tat ing.** [*Hesitate* comes from Latin *haesitatum,* meaning "stuck fast."] —**hes′i tat er, hes′i ta′tor,** *n.* —**hes′i tat′ing ly,** *adv.*

hes i ta tion (hez′ə tā′shən), **1** a hesitating; doubt; indecision. **2** a speaking with short stops or pauses. *n.*

Hesse (hes *or* hes′ə), district in central West Germany. *n.*

Hes sian (hesh′ən), **1** of Hesse or its people. **2** person born or living in Hesse. **3** a German soldier hired by England to fight against the Americans during the Revolutionary War. **1** *adj.,* **2,3** *n.*

het er o ge ne ous (het′ər ə jē′nē əs), **1** different in kind; unlike; varied: *a heterogeneous group of people.* **2** made up of unlike elements or parts; miscellaneous: *a heterogeneous mass of rubbish. adj.* [*Heterogeneous* comes from a medieval Latin word *heterogeneus,* and can be traced back to Greek *heteros,* meaning "other," and *genos,* meaning "kind, class."] —**het′er o ge′ne ous ly,** *adv.* —**het′er o ge′ne ous ness,** *n.*

het er o sex u al (het′ər ə sek′shü əl), **1** (in biology) of the different sexes. **2** having to do with or showing sexual feeling for a person of the opposite sex. **3** a heterosexual person. **1,2** *adj.,* **3** *n.*

hew (hyü), **1** cut with an ax, sword, etc.; chop: *He hewed down the tree.* **2** cut into shape; form by cutting with an ax, etc.: *hew stone for building, hew logs into beams. v.,* **hewed, hewed** *or* **hewn, hew ing.** —**hew′a ble,** *adj.* —**hew′er,** *n.*

hewn (hyün), hewed; a past participle of **hew.** *v.*

hex (heks), **1** practice witchcraft on; bewitch. **2** person or thing that brings bad luck. **3** a magic spell. **1** *v.,* **2,3** *n., pl.* **hex es.** [*Hex* is from Pennsylvania German *hexe,* which came from German *Hexe,* meaning "a witch."] —**hex′er,** *n.*

hex a gon (hek′sə gon), a plane figure having six angles and six sides. *n.* [*Hexagon* can be traced back to Greek *hex,* meaning "six," and *gōnia,* meaning "angle."]

hex ag o nal (hek sag′ə nəl), having the form of a hexagon. *adj.* —**hex ag′o nal ly,** *adv.*

hex a he dron (hek′sə hē′drən), a solid figure having six faces. *n., pl.* **hex a he drons, hex a he dra** (hek′sə hē′drə). [*Hexahedron* can be traced back to Greek *hex,* meaning "six," and *hedra,* meaning "base, seat."]

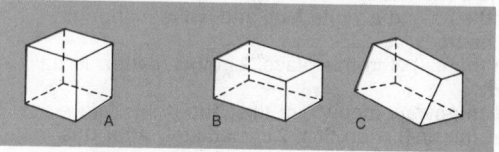

hexahedrons—A, regular; B,C irregular

hex am e ter (hek sam′ə tər), line of poetry having six feet or measures. EXAMPLE: "This′ | is the | fo′rest pri | me′val. The | mur′mur ing | pines′ and the | hem′locks." *n.*

hey (hā), sound made to attract attention, to express surprise or other feeling, or to ask a question: *"Hey! stop!" "Hey? what did you say?" interj.*

hey day (hā′dā′), period of greatest strength, vigor, success, prosperity, etc. *n.*

Hf, symbol for hafnium.

hf., half.

HF, H.F., or **h.f.,** high frequency.

Hg, symbol for mercury.

hgt., height.

hi (hī), a call of greeting; hello. *interj.*

HI, Hawaii (used with postal Zip Code).

H.I., Hawaiian Islands.

hi a tus (hī ā′təs), an empty space; space that needs to be filled; gap: *There was a five-year hiatus before we saw one another again. n., pl.* **hi a tus es** *or* **hi a tus.** [*Hiatus* was borrowed from Latin *hiatus,* which comes from *hiare,* meaning "to gape, yawn."]

Hi a wath a (hī′ə woth′ə), the young North American Indian hero of Longfellow's poem *The Song of Hiawatha. n.*

hibachi

hi ba chi (hi bä′chē), a small, cast-iron container covered by a grill, used to burn charcoal for cooking. *n., pl.* **hi ba chi** *or* **hi ba chis.**

hi ber nate (hī′bər nāt), spend the winter in sleep or in an inactive condition, as bears, woodchucks, and some other wild animals do. *v.*, **hi ber nat ed, hi ber nat ing.**

hi ber na tion (hī′bər nā′shən), a hibernating. *n.*

hi bis cus (hī bis′kəs), plant, shrub, or tree with large, red, pink, or white, bell-shaped flowers. *n., pl.* **hi bis cus es.**

hic cough (hik′up), hiccup. *n., v.*

hic cup (hik′up), **1** an involuntary catching of the breath with a sharp, clicking sound, caused by a muscular spasm of the diaphragm. **2 hiccups,** *pl.* condition of having one hiccup after another. **3** have the hiccups. 1,2 *n.*, 3 *v.*, **hic cupped, hic cup ping.** [*Hiccup* comes from an imitation of the sound.]

hick (hik), INFORMAL. **1** person who lives in the country or in a small town. **2** an ignorant, unsophisticated person. **3** of or like a hick: *a hick town.* 1,2 *n.*, 3 *adj.*

hick or y (hik′ər ē), **1** a North American tree whose nuts are good to eat. It is related to the walnut. **2** its tough, hard wood. *n., pl.* **hick or ies.**

hid (hid), past tense and a past participle of **hide**[1]. *The dog hid the bone. The money was hid in a safe place. v.*

hi dal go (hi dal′gō), a Spanish nobleman ranking below a grandee. *n., pl.* **hi dal gos.**

hid den (hid′n), **1** put or kept out of sight; concealed; secret: *The story is about hidden treasure.* **2** a past participle of **hide**[1]. *The moon was hidden behind a dark cloud.* 1 *adj.*, 2 *v.*

hide[1] (hīd), **1** put or keep out of sight; conceal: *Hide it where no one else will ever find it.* **2** cover up; shut off from sight: *Clouds hide the sun.* **3** keep secret: *He hid his disappointment.* **4** hide oneself: *I'll hide, and you find me. v.*, **hid, hid den** or **hid, hid ing.** —**hid′a ble,** *adj.*

hide[2] (hīd), **1** an animal's skin, either raw or tanned. Leather is made from the hides of cattle. **2** INFORMAL. a person's skin: *He tried to save his own hide by putting the blame on us. n.*

hide-and-go-seek (hīd′n gō sēk′), hide-and-seek. *n.*

hide-and-seek (hīd′n sēk′), a children's game in which one player tries to find the players who have hidden. *n.*

hide a way (hīd′ə wā′), place for hiding or being alone. *n.*

hide bound (hīd′bound′), narrow-minded and stubborn: *Some people are too hidebound to accept new ideas. adj.* —**hide′bound′ness,** *n.*

hid e ous (hid′ē əs), very ugly; frightful; horrible: *a hideous monster, a hideous crime. adj.* —**hid′e ous ly,** *adv.* —**hid′e ous ness,** *n.*

hide out (hīd′out′), place for hiding or being alone. *n.*

hid ing[1] (hī′ding), **1** a being hidden; concealment: *The fox remained in hiding.* **2** place to hide. *n.*

hid ing[2] (hī′ding), INFORMAL. a beating; thrashing. *n.*

hie (hī), go quickly; hasten; hurry: *hie oneself to work. v.*, **hied, hie ing** or **hy ing.**

hi e rar chy (hī′ə rär′kē), **1** organization of persons or things arranged one above the other according to rank, class, or grade. **2** group of church officials of different ranks. The church hierarchy is composed of archbishops, bishops, priests, etc. *n., pl.* **hi e rar chies.** [*Hierarchy* comes from a medieval Latin word *hierarchia*, and can be traced back to Greek *hieros,* meaning "sacred," and *archein,* meaning "to rule."]

hi er o glyph ic (hī′ər ə glif′ik), **1** picture, character, or symbol standing for a word, idea, or sound. The ancient Egyptians used hieroglyphics instead of an alphabet like ours. **2 hieroglyphics,** *pl.* writing that uses hieroglyphics. **3** of or written in hieroglyphics. 1,2 *n.*, 3 *adj.* [*Hieroglyphic* can be traced back to Greek *hieros,* meaning "sacred," and *glyphein,* meaning "to carve."] —**hi′er o glyph′i cal ly,** *adv.*

a hat	i it	oi oil	ch child	a in about
ā age	ī ice	ou out	ng long	e in taken
ä far	o hot	u cup	sh she	ə = i in pencil
e let	ō open	u̇ put	th thin	o in lemon
ē equal	ô order	ü rule	₮H then	u in circus
ėr term			zh measure	

hi-fi (hī′fī′), **1** high fidelity. **2** equipment for high fidelity. **3** of or for high fidelity. 1,2 *n.*, 3 *adj.*

hig gle (hig′əl), haggle. *v.*, **hig gled, hig gling.** —**hig′-gler,** *n.*

hig gle dy-pig gle dy (hig′əl dē pig′əl dē), **1** in jumbled confusion. **2** jumbled; confused. 1 *adv.*, 2 *adj.*

high (hī), **1** having height; rising up; tall: *a high tower. The mountain is over 20,000 feet high.* **2** above or far above the ground: *an airplane high in the air, a high leap, a high dive.* **3** up above others: *a high official. A general has high rank.* **4** greater or stronger than others; great: *a high price, high temperature, high winds, high speed.* **5** most important; chief; main: *the high altar.* **6** extreme of its kind; serious; grave: *high treason, high crimes.* **7** not low in pitch; shrill; sharp: *a high voice.* **8** at or to a high point, place, rank, amount, degree, price, pitch, etc.: *The eagle flies high. Strawberries come high in winter.* **9** INFORMAL. exhilarated or dazed from taking a drug or intoxicated due to drinking liquor. **10** a high point, level, position, etc.: *Food prices reached a new high last month.* **11** arrangement of gears to give the greatest speed. 1-7,9 *adj.*, 8 *adv.*, 10,11 *n.*

high and dry, 1 up out of water: *The boat ran ashore, high and dry.* **2** all alone; without help; stranded.

high and low, everywhere: *I searched high and low for my pen.*

high blood pressure, hypertension.

high born (hī′bôrn′), of noble birth. *adj.*

high boy (hī′boi′), a tall chest of drawers on legs. *n.*

high brow (hī′brou′), INFORMAL. **1** person who cares or claims to care a great deal about knowledge and culture. **2** of or fit for a highbrow. 1 *n.*, 2 *adj.*

high fa lu tin (hī′fə lüt′n), INFORMAL. high-sounding; pompous. *adj.*

high fidelity, reproduction of sound by a radio or phonograph with as little distortion of the original sound as possible. —**high′-fi del′i ty,** *adj.*

high-flown (hī′flōn′), **1** aspiring; extravagant: *high-flown ideas.* **2** attempting to be elegant or eloquent: *high-flown compliments. adj.*

high-grade (hī′grād′), of fine quality; superior: *high-grade oil. adj.*

high-hand ed (hī′han′did), acting or done in a bold, arbitrary way; overbearing: *high-handed methods. adj.* —**high′-hand′ed ly,** *adv.* —**high′-hand′ed ness,** *n.*

high hat, top hat.

high-hat (hī′hat′), INFORMAL. **1** treat as inferior; snub. **2** snobbish. 1 *v.*, **high-hat ted, high-hat ting;** 2 *adj.*

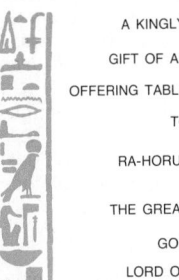

A KINGLY

GIFT OF AN

OFFERING TABLE

TO

RA-HORUS

THE GREAT

GOD

LORD OF

HEAVEN

hieroglyphics (defs. 1 and 2)
Egyptian hieroglyphics

high jump, 1 an athletic contest or event to determine how high each contestant can jump over a raised crossbar. **2** the jump itself. —**high jumper.**

high land (hī/lənd), **1** country or region that is higher and hillier than the neighboring country; land high above sea level. **2 Highlands,** pl. a mountainous region in N and W Scotland. **3** of or in a highland. **4 Highland,** of or in the Highlands. 1,2 n., 3,4 adj.

high land er (hī/lən dər), **1** person born or living in a highland. **2 Highlander,** person born or living in the Highlands of Scotland. n.

Highland fling, a lively dance of the Highlands of Scotland.

high-lev el language (hī/lev/əl), any computer programming language that is not written entirely in binary numbers, especially any language using common words and mathematical symbols.

high light (hī/līt/), **1** cast a bright light on. **2** effect or representation of bright light. **3** part of a painting, photograph, etc., in which light is represented as falling with greatest intensity. **4** the most prominent or interesting part, event, scene, etc.: *The highlight of our trip was seeing the Grand Canyon.* **5** make prominent. 1,5 v., **high lighted, high light ing;** 2-4 n.

high ly (hī/lē), **1** in a high degree; very much; very: *highly amusing, highly recommended.* **2** very favorably: *He spoke highly of his best friend.* **3** at a high rate or price: *highly paid.* **4** in or to a high position or rank: *a highly placed government official.* adv.

high-mind ed (hī/mīn/did), having or showing high principles; noble. adj. —**high/-mind/ed ly,** adv.

high ness (hī/nis), **1** a being high; height. **2 Highness,** title of honor given to members of royal families: *The Prince of Wales is addressed as "Your Highness."* n.

high noon, fully noon; exactly midday.

high-pitched (hī/picht/), **1** of high tone or sound; shrill: *a high-pitched voice.* **2** having a steep slope: *a high-pitched roof.* adj.

high-pow ered (hī/pou/ərd), having much power: *a high-powered car, a high-powered rifle.* adj.

high-pres sure (hī/presh/ər), **1** having, using, or resisting more than the usual pressure: *a high-pressure boiler.* **2** using strong, vigorous methods: *high-pressure selling.* **3** use strong, vigorous methods on, in selling, etc.: *high-pressure a customer.* 1,2 adj., 3 v., **high-pres sured, high-pres sur ing.**

high-rise (hī/rīz/), **1** having many stories; very tall. **2** a high-rise building. 1 adj., 2 n.

high road (hī/rōd/), a main road; highway. n.

high school, school attended after elementary school or junior high school; secondary school. High school consists of grades 9 through 12 or 10 through 12.

high seas, the open ocean. The high seas are outside the jurisdiction of any country.

high-sound ing (hī/soun/ding), having an imposing or pretentious sound. adj.

high-spir it ed (hī/spir/ə tid), **1** proud or courageous: *a high-spirited people.* **2** spirited; fiery: *a high-spirited horse.* adj. —**high/-spir/it ed ly,** adv. —**high/-spir/it ed ness,** n.

high spirits, happiness; cheerfulness; gaiety: *The team was in high spirits after winning the game.*

high-strung (hī/strung/), very sensitive or nervous; easily excited. adj.

high technology, advanced technology involving sophisticated devices and research in such fields as electronics, missiles, and computers.

high-ten sion (hī/ten/shən), having or using a high voltage: *high-tension wires.* adj.

high tide, 1 the highest level of the tide. **2** time when the tide is highest.

high time, time just before it is too late: *It is high time they got here.*

high way (hī/wā/), **1** a public road. **2** a main road or route. n.

high way man (hī/wā/mən), person who robs travelers on a public road. n., pl. **high way men.**

hi jack (hī/jak/), rob or take by force (goods in transit, an airplane in flight, etc.). v. —**hi/jack/er,** n.

hike (hīk), **1** take a long walk; tramp or march. **2** a long walk; tramp or march: *It was a four-mile hike to the camp.* **3** INFORMAL. raise with a jerk; hitch: *Hike up your socks.* **4** INFORMAL. raise; increase: *The company is going to hike wages.* 1,3,4 v., **hiked, hik ing;** 2 n.

hik er (hī/kər), person who hikes or goes on a hike. n.

hi lar i ous (hə ler/ē əs or hə lar/ē əs), very merry; very funny; noisy and cheerful: *a hilarious tale, a hilarious party.* adj. —**hi lar/i ous ly,** adv. —**hi lar/i ous ness,** n.

hi lar i ty (hə lar/ə tē), great merriment; noisy cheerfulness. n.

hill (hil), **1** a raised part of the earth's surface, smaller than a mountain. **2** a little heap or pile: *Ants and moles make hills.* **3** a plant with a little heap of soil over and around its roots: *a hill of corn.* n.

hill bil ly (hil/bil/ē), INFORMAL. person who lives in the backwoods or a mountain region, especially in the southern United States. The use of this word is often considered offensive. n., pl. **hill bil lies.**

hill i ness (hil/ē nis), hilly quality or condition. n.

hill ock (hil/ək), a little hill. n.

hill side (hil/sīd/), side of a hill. n.

hill top (hil/top/), top of a hill. n.

hill y (hil/ē), **1** having many hills: *hilly country.* **2** like a hill; steep: *a hilly slope.* adj., **hill i er, hill i est.**

hilt (hilt), handle of a sword, dagger, or tool. n.
to the hilt, thoroughly; completely: *She was involved to the hilt in politics.*

hi lum (hī/ləm), mark or scar on a seed at the point of attachment to the plant. n., pl. **hi la** (hī/lə).

him (him; *unstressed* im), the boy, man, or male animal spoken about: *Take him home. Give him a drink.* pron.

Him a la yan (him/ə lā/ən or hə mä/lyən), of the Himalayas. adj.

Him a la yas (him/ə lā/əz or hə mä/lyəz), mountain range along the N borders of India and Pakistan. Mount Everest, the world's highest mountain, is in the Himalayas. n.pl.

him self (him self/ or, except when following a pause, im self/), **1** form of he or him used to make a statement stronger: *He himself did it. Did you see John himself?* **2** form used instead of he or him in cases like: *He cut himself. He cared more for himself than for anybody else.* **3** his real or true self: *He feels like himself again.* pron.

hind[1] (hīnd), back; rear: *hind legs.* adj., **hind er, hindmost** or **hind er most.**

hind[2] (hīnd), a female deer, especially a female red deer in and after its third year. n., pl. **hinds** or **hind.**

hin der[1] (hin/dər), keep back; hold back; get in the way of; make hard to do; stop: *Deep mud hindered travel.* v.

hind er[2] (hīn/dər), hind; back; rear. adj.

hind er most (hīn/dər mōst), hindmost. adj.

Hin di (hin/dē), the official language of India. It is a form of Hindustani. n.

hind most (hīnd/mōst), farthest back; nearest the rear; last. adj.

hind quar ter (hīnd/kwôr/tər), **1** the rear half of a side of beef, veal, lamb, etc., including the leg, loin, and one or more ribs. **2 hindquarters,** pl. the rear part of an animal's body, including the lower back, buttocks, and thighs; haunches. n.

hin drance (hin/drəns), **1** person or thing that hinders;

obstacle: *Noise was a hindrance to our studying.* **2** act of hindering. *n.*

hind sight (hīnd′sīt′), ability to see, after the event is over, what should have been done. *n.*

Hin du (hin′dü), **1** person born or living in India. **2** of the Hindus, their language, or their religion. **3** person who believes in Hinduism. 1,3 *n., pl.* **Hin dus;** 2 *adj.* [*Hindu* is from Persian *Hindū*, which comes from *Hind*, meaning "India."]

Hin du ism (hin′dü iz′əm), the religion and social system of the Hindus. *n.*

Hin du stan i (hin′dü stan′ē), **1** of India, its people, or their languages. **2** the commonest language of northern India. 1 *adj.*, 2 *n.*

hinge (hinj), **1** joint on which a door, gate, cover, lid, etc., swings back and forth. **2** furnish with hinges; attach by hinges. **3** hang or turn on a hinge. **4** depend: *The success of the picnic hinges on the kind of weather we will have.* 1 *n.*, 2-4 *v.*, **hinged, hing ing. —hinge′less,** *adj.*

hint (hint), **1** a slight sign; indirect suggestion: *A small black cloud gave a hint of a coming storm.* **2** give a slight sign of; suggest indirectly: *She hinted that she was tired by yawning several times.* 1 *n.*, 2 *v.* **—hint′er,** *n.*

hin ter land (hin′tər land′), **1** land or district behind a coast. **2** region far from towns and cities; thinly settled country. *n.*

hip¹ (hip), **1** the fleshy part that sticks out on each side of the body below the waist, where the leg joins the body. **2** a similar part in animals, where the hind leg joins the body. *n.*

hip² (hip), seedcase containing the ripe seed of a rose. *n.*

hip³ (hip), SLANG. having up-to-date knowledge; informed. *adj.*, **hip per, hip pest.**

hip bone (hip′bōn′), either of the two wide, irregular bones which, with the lower backbone, form the pelvis. *n.*

hip pie (hip′ē), person who rejects the usual social customs. Most hippies are young, have long hair, live in groups, and wear unusual clothing. *n.*

Hip poc ra tes (hi pok′rə tēz′), 460?-377? B.C., Greek physician, called "the father of medicine." *n.*

hip po (hip′ō), INFORMAL. hippopotamus. *n., pl.* **hip pos.**

hip po drome (hip′ə drōm), **1** (in ancient Greece and Rome) an oval track for horse races and chariot races, surrounded by tiers of seats for spectators. **2** arena or building for a circus, rodeo, etc. *n.* [*Hippodrome* can be traced back to Greek *hippos,* meaning "horse," and *dromos,* meaning "racecourse."]

hip po pot a mus (hip′ə pot′ə məs), a huge, thick-skinned, almost hairless mammal found in and near the rivers of Africa. Hippopotamuses feed on plants and can stay under water for a long time. *n., pl.* **hip po pot a mus es, hip po pot a mi** (hip′ə pot′ə mī). [*Hippopotamus* can be traced back to Greek *hippos,* meaning "horse," and *potamos,* meaning "river."]

hippopotamus—about 13 ft. (4 m.) long

hip ster (hip′stər), SLANG. person who keeps up with new, unconventional ideas, styles, and attitudes; person who is or is considered hip. *n.*

hire (hīr), **1** pay for the use of (a thing) or the work or services of (a person): *They hired a car and a driver. The florist wants to hire someone to deliver flowers.* **2** payment for the use of a thing or the work or services of a person. 1 *v.*, **hired, hir ing;** 2 *n.* **—hir′er,** *n.*

for hire, for use or work in return for payment: *Are these boats for hire?*

hire out, give one's work in return for payment: *hire out as a house painter.*

hire ling (hīr′ling), person who works only for money, without interest or pride in the work. *n.*

Hir o hi to (hir′ō hē′tō), born 1901, emperor of Japan since 1926. *n.*

Hir o shi ma (hir′ō shē′mə), seaport in W Japan, largely destroyed by the first atomic bomb to be used in war, on August 6, 1945. *n.*

hir sute (hér′süt), hairy. *adj.* **—hir′sute ness,** *n.*

his (hiz; *unstressed* iz), **1** of him; belonging to him: *This is his book.* **2** the one or ones belonging to him: *My books are new; his are old.* 1 *adj.*, 2 *pron.*

His pan ic (hi span′ik), **1** Spanish. **2** Latin-American. **3** person of Spanish-speaking descent. 1,2 *adj.*, 3 *n.*

His pan io la (his′pə nyō′lə), the second largest island in the West Indies, between Cuba and Puerto Rico. It is divided into the Dominican Republic and Haiti. See **Caribbean Sea** for map. *n.*

hiss (his), **1** make a sound like *ss*, or like a drop of water on a hot stove: *Air or steam rushing out of a small opening hisses. Geese and snakes hiss.* **2** a sound like *ss*: *Hisses were heard from many who disliked what the speaker was saying.* **3** show disapproval of by hissing: *The audience hissed the dull play.* **4** force or drive by hissing: *They hissed her off the stage.* 1,3,4 *v.*, 2 *n., pl.* **hiss es.**

hist (hist), be still! listen!: *Hist! Did you hear that noise in the distance? interj.*

hist., 1 historian. **2** history.

his to ri an (hi stôr′ē ən), person who writes about history; expert in history. *n.*

his to ric (hi stôr′ik), **1** famous or important in history: *Plymouth Rock and Bunker Hill are historic spots.* **2** historical. *adj.*

his to ri cal (hi stôr′ə kəl), **1** of history: *historical documents.* **2** according to history; based on history: *a historical novel.* **3** known to be real or true; in history, not in legend: *a historical fact.* **4** famous in history; historic: *a historical town. adj.* **—his to′ri cal ness,** *n.*

his to ri cal ly (hi stôr′ik lē), according to history; as history. *adv.*

his tor y (his′tər ē), **1** story or record of important past events connected with a person or a nation: *the history of the United States.* **2** a known past: *This ship has a history.* **3** all past events considered together; course of human affairs: *the lessons of history.* **4** branch of knowledge or study that deals with past events: *a class in history.* **5** statement of what has happened; account. *n., pl.* **his tor ies.**

his tri on ic (his′trē on′ik), **1** having to do with actors or acting. **2** theatrical; insincere. *adj.* **—his′tri on′i cal ly,** *adv.*

histrionics
(def. 2)

his tri on ics (his′trē on′iks), **1** dramatic representation; theatricals; dramatics. **2** a theatrical or insincere manner, expression, etc. *n. sing. or pl.*

hit (hit), **1** come against with force; give a blow to; strike; knock: *He hit the ball with the bat. The ball hit against the window. She hit out at the fly buzzing around her head.* **2** a blow; stroke: *I drove the stake into the ground with one hit.* **3** get to (what is aimed at): *The second arrow hit the bull's-eye.* **4** a getting to what is aimed at. **5** come upon; meet with; reach or find: *We hit the right road in the dark. We hit upon a plan for making money.* **6** have a painful effect on; affect severely: *They were hard hit by the failure of their business.* **7** a successful attempt, performance, or production: *The new play is the hit of the season.* **8** a successful hitting of the baseball so that the batter gets at least to first base. 1,3,5,6 *v.,* hit, hit ting; 2,4,7,8 *n.*

hit it off, get along well together; agree: *My friend and I hit it off from the start.*

hit or miss, with no plan; at random.

hit-and-run (hit′n run′), having to do with hitting a person or vehicle and driving away without stopping to see what happened: *a hit-and-run driver, a hit-and-run accident. adj.*

hitch (def. 4)

hitch (hich), **1** fasten with a hook, ring, rope, strap, etc.: *She hitched her horse to a post.* **2** become fastened or caught; fasten; catch: *A knot made the rope hitch.* **3** a fastening; catch: *Our car has a hitch for pulling a trailer.* **4** kind of knot used for temporary fastening. **5** move or pull with a jerk: *He hitched his chair nearer to the fire.* **6** a short, sudden pull or jerk: *He gave his pants a hitch.* **7** obstacle; hindrance; delay: *A hitch in their plans made them miss the train.* **8** INFORMAL. get (a ride) by hitchhiking. **9** period of time, especially a period of service in the armed forces. 1,2,5,8 *v.,* 3,4,6,7,9 *n., pl.* **hitch es.**

hitch hike (hich′hīk′), travel by walking and getting free rides from passing automobiles, trucks, etc. *v.,* **hitch hiked, hitch hik ing.**

hitch hik er (hich′hī′kər), person who hitchhikes. *n.*

hith er (hiŦH′ər), to this place; here: *Come hither, child. adv.*

hither and thither, here and there.

hith er to (hiŦH′ər tü′), until now: *a fact hitherto unknown. adv.*

Hit ler (hit′lər), **Adolf,** 1889-1945, German dictator, born in Austria, ruler of Nazi Germany from 1933 to 1945. *n.*

hit-or-miss (hit′ər mis′), not planned; random. *adj.*

hit ter (hit′ər), person or thing that hits. *n.*

Hit tite (hit′īt), member of an ancient people in Asia Minor and Syria. Their civilization existed from about 2000 B.C. until about 1200 B.C. *n.*

hive (def. 1)
two kinds of hives

hive (hīv), **1** house or box for honeybees to live in; beehive. **2** a large number of bees living in such a place. **3** put (bees) in a hive. **4** a busy, swarming place full of people or animals: *a hive of industry.* 1,2,4 *n.,* 3 *v.,* **hived, hiv ing.**

hives (hīvz), condition in which the skin itches and shows raised patches of red. It is usually caused by an allergy to some food or drug. *n.*

hl., hectoliter or hectoliters.

hm., hectometer or hectometers.

H.M., 1 Her Majesty. **2** His Majesty.

ho (hō), **1** exclamation of surprise, joy, or scornful laughter. **2** exclamation to get attention: *Ho! Listen to this! interj.*

Ho, symbol for holmium.

hoar (hôr), hoary. *adj.*

hoard (hôrd), **1** save and store away: *A squirrel hoards nuts for the winter. The wealthy woman hoarded her money.* **2** what is saved and stored away; things stored: *They have a hoard of candy.* 1 *v.,* 2 *n.* —**hoard′er,** *n.*

hoar frost (hôr′frôst′), feathery crystals of ice formed when dew freezes; white frost; rime. *n.*

hoar hound (hôr′hound′), horehound. *n.*

hoarse (hôrs), **1** sounding rough and deep: *the hoarse croak of the bullfrog.* **2** having a rough voice: *A bad cold has made her hoarse. adj.,* **hoars er, hoars est.** —**hoarse′ly,** *adv.* —**hoarse′ness,** *n.*

hoar y (hôr′ē), **1** white or gray. **2** white or gray with age: *a hoary beard.* **3** old; ancient: *the hoary ruins of a castle. adj.,* **hoar i er, hoar i est.** —**hoar′i ness,** *n.*

hoax (hōks), **1** a mischievous trick, especially a made-up story passed off as true: *The report of an attack on the earth from Mars was a hoax.* **2** play a mischievous trick on; deceive. 1 *n., pl.* **hoax es;** 2 *v.* —**hoax′er,** *n.*

hob[1] (hob), shelf at the back or side of a fireplace. Food can be kept warm by placing it on the hob. *n.*

hob[2] (hob), hobgoblin; elf. *n.*

play hob or **raise hob,** INFORMAL. cause trouble: *The bad weather played hob with our plans for a picnic.*

hob ble (hob′əl), **1** walk awkwardly; limp: *hobble around with a broken toe.* **2** a limping walk. **3** tie the legs of (a horse, etc.) together: *They hobbled the horses at night so that they would not wander away.* **4** rope or strap used to hobble a horse or other animal. **5** hinder. 1,3,5 *v.,* **hob bled, hob bling;** 2,4 *n.* —**hob′bler,** *n.*

hob by (hob′ē), something a person especially likes to work at or study which is not the person's main business or occupation; favorite pastime: *Our teacher's hobby is gardening. n., pl.* **hob bies.** —**hob′by less,** *adj.*

hob by horse (hob′ē hôrs′), **1** stick with a horse's head, used as a toy horse by children. **2** rocking horse. *n.*

hob by ist (hob'ē ist), person who is very interested in a hobby or hobbies. *n.*

hob gob lin (hob'gob'lən), **1** goblin; elf. **2** ghost. *n.*

hob nail (hob'nāl'), a short nail with a large head to protect the soles of heavy boots and shoes. *n.*

hob nob (hob'nob'), be on familiar terms; associate intimately: *They hobnob with some important people. v.,* **hobnobbed, hob nob bing.** —**hob'nob'ber,** *n.*

ho bo (hō'bō), person who wanders about and lives by begging or doing odd jobs; tramp. *n., pl.* **ho bos** or **ho boes.**

Ho Chi Minh City (hō' chē min'), city in S Vietnam, formerly the capital of South Vietnam. Former name, **Saigon.**

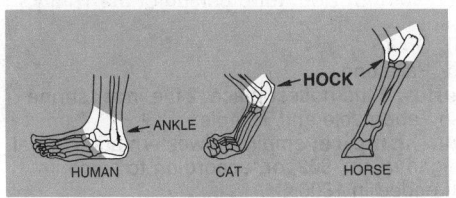

hock¹

hock¹ (hok), joint in the hind leg of a horse, cow, etc., corresponding to the human ankle. *n.*

hock² (hok), SLANG. pawn. *v., n.*
in hock, 1 in pawn. **2** in debt.

hock ey (hok'ē), game played by two teams on ice or on a field. The players hit a puck or ball with curved sticks to drive it across a goal. *n.*

ho cus-po cus (hō'kəs pō'kəs), **1** a meaningless form of words used in performing magic tricks. **2** trickery. *n.*

hod (hod), **1** trough or tray on top of a long, straight handle, used for carrying bricks, mortar, etc., on the shoulder. **2** coal scuttle. *n.*

hodge podge (hoj'poj'), a disorderly mixture; mess. *n.*

hoe (hō), **1** tool with a thin blade set across the end of a long handle, used for loosening soil, cutting weeds, etc. **2** loosen, dig, or cut with a hoe. **3** use a hoe. 1 *n.,* 2,3 *v.,* **hoed, hoe ing.** —**hoe'like',** *adj.* —**ho'er,** *n.*

hoe cake (hō'kāk'), kind of bread made of corn meal. *n.*

hoe down (hō'doun'), **1** a noisy, lively square dance. **2** music for such a dance. *n.*

hog (hog), **1** pig. **2** a full-grown pig, raised for its meat. **3** INFORMAL. a selfish, greedy, or dirty person. **4** SLANG. take more than one's share of. 1-3 *n.,* 4 *v.,* **hogged, hog ging.** —**hog'like',** *adj.*

hogan

ho gan (hō'gän'), dwelling used by the Navajos. Hogans are built with logs and covered with earth. *n.* [*Hogan* was borrowed from a Navajo word.]

hog gish (hog'ish), **1** very selfish or greedy. **2** dirty; filthy. *adj.* —**hog'gish ly,** *adv.* —**hog'gish ness,** *n.*

a hat	**i** it	**oi** oil	**ch** child		a in about
ā age	**ī** ice	**ou** out	**ng** long		e in taken
ä far	**o** hot	**u** cup	**sh** she	**ə =**	i in pencil
e let	**ō** open	**ù** put	**th** thin		o in lemon
ē equal	**ô** order	**ü** rule	**ŦH** then		u in circus
ėr term			**zh** measure		

hog nose snake (hog'nōz'), a harmless North American snake with an upturned snout; adder.

hogs head (hogz'hed'), **1** a large barrel or cask. In the United States, a hogshead contains from 63 to 140 gallons. **2** a liquid measure equal to 63 gallons. *n.*

hog-tie (hog'tī'), **1** tie all four feet, or the feet and hands, together; tie securely. **2** hinder; hold back. *v.,* **hog-tied, hog-ty ing.**

hoist (hoist), **1** raise on high; lift up, often with ropes and pulleys: *hoist a flag, hoist sails.* **2** a hoisting; lift; boost: *She gave me a hoist up the wall.* **3** elevator or other apparatus for hoisting heavy loads. 1 *v.,* 2,3 *n.* —**hoist'er,** *n.*

hold¹ (hōld), **1** grasp and keep: *Please hold my hat.* **2** a grasp or grip: *Take a good hold of this rope.* **3** thing to hold by: *The face of the cliff had enough holds for a good climber.* **4** keep in some place or position: *Hold the dish level. Hold the paper steady while you draw.* **5** stay strong or secure; not break, loosen, or give way: *The dike held during the flood.* **6** keep from acting; keep back: *Hold your breath.* **7** keep: *The soldiers held the fort against the enemy.* **8** contain: *How much water will this cup hold? This theater holds five hundred people.* **9** have: *Shall we hold a meeting of the club? She has held the office of mayor for ten years. I hold a high opinion of them.* **10** think; consider: *People once held that the world was flat.* **11** be faithful: *I held to my promise.* **12** be true; be in force or effect: *Will this rule hold in all cases?* **13** keep the same; continue: *The warm weather held all week.* **14** a controlling force or influence: *A habit has a hold on you.* **15** sign for a pause in music. 1,4-13 *v.,* 2,3,14,15 *n.* —**hold'a ble,** *adj.*

hold forth, 1 talk or preach. **2** offer.

hold in, 1 keep in; keep back. **2** restrain oneself.

hold off, keep at a distance: *hold off the enemy. The storm may hold off.*

hold on, 1 keep one's hold. **2** keep on; continue. **3** INFORMAL. stop!

hold out, 1 continue; last. **2** keep resisting; not give in.

hold over, 1 keep for future action or consideration; postpone: *The bill has been held over until next year.* **2** keep or stay longer than the expected time: *The play was so successful it was held over.*

hold up, 1 keep from falling; support: *The roof is held up by pillars.* **2** show; display: *She held up the sign for us to see.* **3** continue; last; endure: *If this wind holds up, we can go sailing.* **4** stop. **5** INFORMAL. stop by force and rob.

hold with, 1 side with. **2** agree with. **3** approve of.

lay hold of or **take hold of,** seize; grasp.

take hold, become attached; take root.

hold² (hōld), the part inside of a ship or airplane where the cargo is carried. A ship's hold is below the deck. *n.*

hold back (hōld'bak'), thing that holds back; restraint; hindrance. *n.*

hold er (hōl'dər), **1** person who holds something. An owner or possessor of property is a holder. **2** thing to hold something else: *a toothbrush holder. n.*

hold ing (hōl'ding), **1** piece of land or property. **2** Often, **holdings,** *pl.* property in stocks or bonds. *n.*

hold out (hōld'out'), INFORMAL. **1** person or group that refuses to accept terms or to comply with a trend or order. **2** a refusal to accept terms or comply. *n.*

hold up (hōld′up′), **1** act of stopping by force and robbing. **2** a stopping. *n.*

hole (hōl), **1** an open place; opening: *a hole in a sock.* **2** a hollow place in something solid: *Swiss cheese has holes in it.* **3** a hollow place in the earth in which an animal lives; burrow: *a rabbit hole.* **4** a small, dark, dirty room or place. **5** flaw; defect: *There's a hole in your argument.* **6** a small, round, hollow place on a golf course, into which a golf ball is hit. **7** one of the divisions of a golf course. A regular golf course has 18 holes. **8** hit or drive (a golf ball) into a hole. 1-7 *n.*, 8 *v.*, **holed, hol ing.**
hole up, 1 go or put into a hole: *In November the badgers all hole up for the winter.* **2** go or put into hiding.
in the hole, in debt.
pick holes in, find fault with.

hole y (hō′lē), full of holes. *adj.*

hol i day (hol′ə dā), **1** day when one does not work; day of pleasure and enjoyment: *Labor Day and the Fourth of July are holidays in the United States.* **2** Often, **holidays,** *pl.* vacation: *We plan to spend our holidays in the mountains.* **3** of or suited to a holiday: *holiday traffic.* **4** holy day; religious festival. 1,2,4 *n.*, 3 *adj.*

ho li ness (hō′lē nis), **1** a being holy. **2 Holiness,** title used in speaking to or of the pope: *The pope is addressed as "Your Holiness" and spoken of as "His Holiness."* *n.*

ho lis tic (hō lis′tik), having to do with or concerned with the physical, mental, emotional, and spiritual factors that affect health, rather than with isolated symptoms or diseases: *holistic medicine. adj.*

Hol land (hol′ənd), the Netherlands. *n.*

hol ler (hol′ər), INFORMAL. **1** cry or shout loudly. **2** a loud cry or shout. 1 *v.*, 2 *n.*

hol low (hol′ō), **1** having nothing, or only air, inside; with a hole inside; not solid; empty: *A tube or pipe is hollow. Most rubber balls are hollow.* **2** shaped like a bowl or cup: *a hollow dish for soup.* **3** a hollow place; hole: *a hollow in the road.* **4** make by hollowing; bend or dig out to a hollow shape: *She hollowed a whistle out of a piece of wood.* **5** make or become hollow. **6** a low place between hills; valley: *Sleepy Hollow.* **7** as if coming from something hollow; deep and dull: *the hollow boom of a foghorn.* **8** deep and sunken: *hollow eyes and cheeks.* **9** not real or sincere; false: *hollow promises.* 1,2,7-9 *adj.*, 3,6 *n.*, 4,5 *v.* —**hol′low ly,** *adv.* —**hol′low ness,** *n.*

hol ly (hol′ē), **1** an evergreen tree or shrub with shiny, sharp-pointed leaves and bright-red berries. **2** its leaves and berries, often used as Christmas decorations. *n., pl.* **hol lies.**

hol ly hock (hol′ē hok), a tall plant with large showy flowers of various colors that grow along the stem. *n.*

Hol ly wood (hol′ē wùd), district of Los Angeles, where many motion pictures are made. *n.*

Holmes (hōmz), **1 Oliver Wendell,** 1809-1894, American author, humorist, and physician. **2** his son, **Oliver Wendell,** 1841-1935, American lawyer, an associate justice of the United States Supreme Court from 1902 to 1932. **3 Sherlock,** a fictional detective with remarkable powers of observation and reasoning. *n.*

hol mi um (hōl′mē əm), a metallic element which occurs in combination with certain minerals. Its compounds are highly magnetic. *n.*

hol o caust (hol′ə kôst), **1** complete destruction by fire, especially of animals or human beings. **2** great or wholesale destruction. **3 the Holocaust,** the systematic annihilation by the Nazis of about six million European Jews from 1933 to 1945. *n.* [*Holocaust* can be traced back to Greek *holos,* meaning "whole," and *kaiein,* meaning "to burn."]

Hol stein (hōl′stēn′ *or* hōl′stīn), breed of large, black-and-white dairy cattle. *n.*

hol ster (hōl′stər), a leather case for a pistol, worn on the belt or under the shoulder. A holster for a rifle may be attached to a saddle. *n.*

ho ly (hō′lē), **1** belonging to God; set apart for God's service; coming from God; sacred: *the Holy Bible, holy sacraments.* **2** like a saint; spiritually perfect; very good; pure in heart: *a holy missionary.* **3** worthy of reverence: *Jerusalem is a holy place to Jews, Christians, and Moslems.* **4** a holy place. 1-3 *adj.*, **ho li er, ho li est;** 4 *n., pl.* **ho lies.**

Holy Communion, 1 a sharing in the Lord's Supper as a part of Christian worship. **2** celebration of the Lord's Supper.

holy day, a religious festival. Good Friday and Ash Wednesday are holy days.

Holy Father, the pope.

Holy Ghost, spirit of God; third person of the Trinity; Holy Spirit.

Holy Grail, Grail.

Holy Land, Palestine.

holy of holies, 1 the holiest place. **2** the inner shrine of the Jewish Tabernacle and Temple.

Holy Roman Empire, empire in western and central Europe. It began in A.D. 962, or, according to some, in A.D. 800, and ended in 1806.

Holy Saturday, Saturday before Easter.

Holy See, office or jurisdiction of the pope; the pope's court.

Holy Spirit, Holy Ghost.

ho ly stone (hō′lē stōn′), **1** piece of soft sandstone used for scrubbing the decks of ships. **2** scrub with a holystone. 1 *n.*, 2 *v.*, **ho ly stoned, ho ly ston ing.**

holy water, water blessed by a priest.

Holy Week, the week before Easter.

Holy Writ, the Bible.

hom age (hom′ij *or* om′ij), **1** dutiful respect; reverence; honor: *Everyone paid homage to the great leader.* **2** (in the Middle Ages) a pledge of loyalty and service by a vassal to a lord. *n.* [*Homage* came into English about 700 years ago from French *homage,* and can be traced back to Latin *hominem,* meaning "man, human being."]

hom bre (ôm′brā), SLANG. man; fellow. *n.* [*Hombre* was borrowed from Spanish *hombre,* which came from Latin *hominem,* meaning "man, human being."]

home (hōm), **1** place where a person or family lives; one's own house: *Her home is at 25 South Street.* **2** place where a person was born or brought up; one's own town or country: *His home is New York.* **3** place where a thing is very common: *Alaska is the home of fur seals.* **4** place where people who are homeless, poor, old, sick, blind, etc., may live: *a nursing home, a home for the aged.* **5** having to do with one's own home or country: *Write me all the home events.* **6** at or to one's own home or country: *I want to go home.* **7** goal in many games. **8** home plate in baseball. **9** to the thing aimed at: *The spear struck home. The criticism struck home.* **10** to the heart or center; deep in: *drive a nail home.* **11** go home. 1-4,7,8 *n.*, 5 *adj.*, 6,9,10 *adv.*, 11 *v.*, **homed, hom ing.**

at home, 1 at ease; comfortable: *to make oneself at home in a friend's house.* **2** ready to receive visitors.

bring home, make clear or emphatic.

home base, home plate.

home economics, science and art of managing a household. Home economics includes housekeeping, budgeting of finances, preparation of food, child care, etc.

home land (hōm′land′), country that is one's home; one's native land. *n.*

home less (hōm′lis), without a home: *a stray, homeless dog. adj.*

home like (hōm′līk′), familiar or comfortable; like home. *adj.*

home ly (hōm′lē), **1** not good-looking; ugly; plain. **2** suited to home life; simple; everyday: *homely pleasures, homely food.* **3** of plain manners; unpretending: *a simple, homely person. adj.*, **home li er, home li est. —home′li ness,** *n.*

home made (hōm′mād′), made at home: *homemade bread. adj.*

home mak er (hōm′mā′kər), woman who manages a home and its affairs; housewife. *n.*

home plate, flat, rubber slab beside which a player stands to bat the ball in baseball, and to which the runner must return, after getting on base, in order to score.

hom er (hō′mər), INFORMAL. a home run in baseball. *n.*

Ho mer (hō′mər), the great epic poet of ancient Greece. According to legend, Homer lived about the 800's B.C., and was the author of the *Iliad* and the *Odyssey.* *n.*

home room (hōm′rüm′ *or* hōm′rùm′), classroom where members of a class meet to answer roll call, hear announcements, etc. *n.*

home run, a hit in baseball which allows the batter to round the bases without a stop and reach home plate to score a run.

home sick (hōm′sik′), overcome by sadness because of being far away from home; ill with longing for home. *adj.* **—home′sick′ness,** *n.*

home spun (hōm′spun′), **1** spun or made at home. **2** cloth made of yarn spun at home. **3** a strong, loosely woven cloth similar to it. **4** made of homespun cloth. **5** not polished; plain; simple: *homespun manners.* 1,4,5 *adj.*, 2,3 *n.*

home stead (hōm′sted′), **1** house with its buildings and grounds; farm with its buildings. **2** public land granted to a settler under certain conditions by the United States government. **3** take and occupy as a homestead: *He homesteaded 160 acres of land.* 1,2 *n.*, 3 *v.*

home stead er (hōm′sted′ər), **1** person who has a homestead. **2** settler granted a homestead by the United States government. *n.*

home stretch (hōm′strech′), **1** the straight part of a racetrack between the last turn and the finish line. **2** the last part of anything. *n.*

home ward (hōm′wərd), toward home: *We turned homeward (adv.). The ship is on a homeward course (adj.). adv., adj.*

home wards (hōm′wərdz), homeward. *adv.*

home work (hōm′wėrk′), **1** work done at home. **2** lesson to be studied or prepared outside the classroom. *n.*

home y (hō′mē), homelike. *adj.*, **hom i er, hom i est. —hom′ey ness,** *n.*

hom i cid al (hom′ə sī′dl), **1** having to do with homicide. **2** murderous. *adj.* **—hom′i cid′al ly,** *adv.*

hom i cide (hom′ə sīd), **1** a killing of one human being

a	hat	i	it	oi	oil	ch	child		a in about
ā	age	ī	ice	ou	out	ng	long		e in taken
ä	far	o	hot	u	cup	sh	she	ə =	i in pencil
e	let	ō	open	ù	put	th	thin		o in lemon
ē	equal	ô	order	ü	rule	ᴛʜ	then		u in circus
ėr	term					zh	measure		

by another. **2** person who kills another human being. *n.* [*Homicide* came into English about 600 years ago from French *homicide,* and can be traced back to Latin *hominem,* meaning "man, human being," and *caedere,* meaning "to kill."]

homing pigeon, pigeon trained to fly home from great distances carrying written messages; carrier pigeon.

hom i ny (hom′ə nē), whole or coarsely ground hulled corn, usually eaten boiled. *n.*

homo-, *combining form.* same; the same: *Homogeneous = of the same kind. Homophone = (word with) the same sound (as another).* [The form *homo-* comes from Greek *homos,* meaning "same."]

ho mo ge ne ous (hō′mə jē′nē əs), **1** the same in kind; similar: *a homogeneous group of people.* **2** made up of similar elements or parts: *a homogeneous collection of books, all dealing with astronomy. adj.* [*Homogeneous* can be traced back to Greek *homos,* meaning "same," and *genos,* meaning "kind, class."] **—ho′mo ge′ne ous ly,** *adv.* **—ho′mo ge′ne ous ness,** *n.*

ho mog e nize (hə moj′ə nīz), make homogeneous. In **homogenized milk** the fat is distributed evenly throughout the milk and does not rise to the top in the form of cream. *v.*, **ho mog e nized, ho mog e niz ing. —ho mog′e ni za′tion,** *n.* **—ho mog′e niz′er,** *n.*

hom o graph (hom′ə graf), word having the same spelling as another word, but a different origin and meaning. *Bass* (bas), meaning "a kind of fish," and *bass* (bās), meaning "a male singing voice," are homographs. *n.* [*Homograph* can be traced back to Greek *homos,* meaning "same," and *graphein,* meaning "to write."]

hom o nym (hom′ə nim), word having the same pronunciation and often the same spelling as another word, but a different origin and meaning. *Mail,* meaning "letters," *mail,* meaning "armor," and *male,* meaning "masculine," are homonyms. *n.* [*Homonym* can be traced back to Greek *homos,* meaning "same," and *onyma,* meaning "a name."]

hom o phone (hom′ə fōn), word having the same pronunciation as another, but a different origin and meaning. *Ate* and *eight* are homophones. *n.* [*Homophone* can be traced back to Greek *homos,* meaning "same," and *phōnē,* meaning "a sound."]

Ho mo sa pi ens (hō′mō sā′pē enz), the species including all existing races of human beings.

ho mo sex u al (hō′mə sek′shü əl), **1** having to do with or showing sexual feeling for a person of the same sex. **2** a homosexual person. 1 *adj.*, 2 *n.*

Hon., Honorable.

Hon dur as (hon dùr′əs *or* hon dyùr′əs), country in N Central America. *Capital:* Tegucigalpa. *n.* **—Hon dur′an,** *adj., n.*

hone (hōn), **1** a fine-grained whetstone on which to sharpen cutting tools, especially straight razors. **2** sharpen on a hone. 1 *n.*, 2 *v.*, **honed, hon ing. —hon′er,** *n.*

hon est (on′ist), **1** fair and upright; truthful; not lying, cheating, or stealing: *honest people.* **2** without lying, cheating, or stealing: *make an honest profit.* **3** not hiding one's real nature; frank; open: *She has an honest face.* **4** not mixed with something of less value; genuine; pure: *Stores should sell honest goods. adj.*

hon est ly (on′ist lē), **1** in an honest way; with honesty: *The salesclerk dealt honestly with her customers.* **2** indeed; really: *Honestly! I never saw such rudeness.* 1 *adv.,* 2 *interj.*

hon es ty (on′ə stē), honest behavior; honest nature; honest quality. *n.*

hon ey (hun′ē), **1** a thick, sweet, yellow or golden liquid that bees make out of the nectar they collect from flowers. **2** the nectar of flowers, that draws bees to them. **3** something sweet like honey; sweetness. **4** darling; dear. *n., pl.* **hon eys.** —**hon′ey like′,** *adj.*

honeybee—about life-size

hon ey bee (hun′ē bē′), bee that makes honey. *n.*

hon ey comb (hun′ē kōm′), **1** a structure of wax containing rows of six-sided cells made by bees to store honey, pollen, and their eggs. **2** anything having a structure like this: *The village market was a honeycomb of tiny shops and passageways.* **3** like a honeycomb: *a honeycomb pattern in knitting.* **4** make like a honeycomb; pierce with many holes: *The old castle was honeycombed with passages.* 1,2 *n.,* 3 *adj.,* 4 *v.*

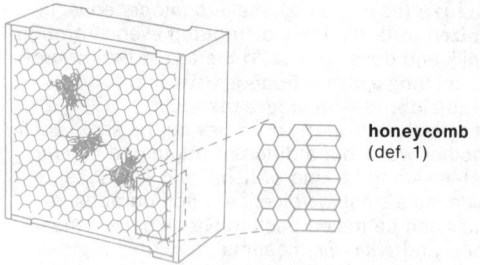

honeycomb (def. 1)

hon ey dew (hun′ē dü′ *or* hun′ē dyü′), **1** a sweet substance that oozes from the leaves of certain plants in hot weather. **2** a sweet substance on leaves and stems, secreted by aphids or other tiny insects. **3** honeydew melon. *n.*

honeydew melon, kind of muskmelon with sweet, green flesh and a smooth, pale-greenish skin.

hon eyed (hun′ēd), **1** sweetened with honey: *honeyed drinks.* **2** sweet as honey: *honeyed words. adj.*

hon ey moon (hun′ē mün′), **1** holiday spent together by a newly married couple. **2** the first month of marriage. **3** a period of good feeling or good relations. **4** spend or have a honeymoon. 1-3 *n.,* 4 *v.* —**hon′ey moon′er,** *n.*

hon ey suck le (hun′ē suk′əl), a climbing shrub with fragrant white, yellow, or red flowers; woodbine. *n.*

Hong Kong (hong′ kong′), British colony on the SE coast of China.

Ho ni a ra (hō′nē ä′rə), capital of the Solomon Islands. *n.*

honk (hongk), **1** the cry of a wild goose. **2** any similar sound: *the honk of a car horn.* **3** make or cause to make such a sound: *We honked as we drove past our friends' house. Stop honking that horn!* 1,2 *n.,* 3 *v.* —**honk′er,** *n.*

Hon o lu lu (hon′ə lü′lü), seaport and capital of Hawaii, in S Oahu. *n.*

hon or (on′ər), **1** credit for acting well; glory, fame, or reputation; good name: *It was greatly to his honor to be given the scholarship.* **2** honors, *pl.* special mention given to a student by a school for having done work much above the average. **3** source of credit; person or thing

that reflects honor: *to be an honor to one's family. It is an honor to be chosen class president.* **4** a sense of what is right or proper; nobility of mind: *A person of honor always keeps his or her promises.* **5** great respect; high regard: *She was held in honor by all who knew her.* **6** Honor, title of respect used in speaking to or of a judge, mayor, or other public official. **7** act that shows respect or high regard: *funeral honors, military honors.* **8** respect highly; think highly of. **9** show respect to: *We honor our country's dead soldiers on Memorial Day.* **10** give an honor to; favor: *be honored by a royal visit.* **11** accept and pay (a check, note, etc.) when due. 1-7 *n.,* 8-11 *v.* —**hon′or er,** *n.* —**hon′or less,** *adj.*

do the honors, act as host or hostess.

on one's honor, pledged to speak the truth and to do what is right.

hon or a ble (on′ər ə bəl), **1** having or showing a sense of what is right and proper; honest; upright: *It is not honorable to lie or cheat.* **2** causing honor; bringing honor to the one that has it: *honorable wounds.* **3** worthy of honor; noble: *to perform honorable deeds.* **4** showing honor or respect: *honorable burial.* **5** having a title, rank, or position of honor. **6** Honorable, title of respect before the names of certain officials. *adj.* —**hon′or a ble ness,** *n.*

hon or a bly (on′ər ə blē), in an honorable manner. *adv.*

hon or ar y (on′ə rer′ē), **1** given or done as an honor: *The university awarded honorary degrees to three well-known scientists.* **2** as an honor only; without pay or regular duties: *That association has an honorary secretary as well as a regular paid secretary who does the actual work. adj.* —**hon′o rar′i ly,** *adv.*

honor roll, list of students who have achieved the highest grades during the school term or year.

Hon shu (hon′shü), the largest and most important island of Japan. *n.*

hood[1] (hud), **1** a soft covering for the head and neck, either separate or as part of a coat: *My raincoat has a hood.* **2** anything like a hood in shape or use. **3** a metal covering over the engine of an automobile. **4** cover with a hood; furnish with a hood. 1-3 *n.,* 4 *v.* —**hood′less,** *adj.* —**hood′like′,** *adj.*

hood[2] (hud), SLANG. hoodlum. *n.*

-hood, *suffix added to nouns to form other nouns.* **1** state or condition of being: *Childhood = state of being a child.* **2** character or nature of: *Sainthood = the character of a saint.* **3** group or body of: *Priesthood = the body or group of priests.*

hood ed (hud′id), **1** having a hood. **2** shaped like a hood. *adj.* —**hood′ed ness,** *n.*

hood lum (hud′ləm), **1** criminal or gangster. **2** a young rowdy; street ruffian. *n.*

hood wink (hud′wingk), mislead by a trick; deceive. *v.*

hoo ey (hü′ē), SLANG. nonsense. *n.*

hoof (huf *or* hüf), **1** a hard, horny covering on the feet of horses, cattle, sheep, pigs, and some other animals. **2** the whole foot of such animals. **3** INFORMAL. to walk or dance. 1,2 *n., pl.* **hoofs** *or* **hooves;** 3 *v.* —**hoof′less,** *adj.* —**hoof′like′,** *adj.*

on the hoof, not butchered; alive.

hoof beat (huf′bēt′ *or* hüf′bēt′), sound made by an animal's hoof. *n.*

hoofed (huft *or* hüft), having hoofs. *adj.*

hook (huk), **1** piece of metal, wood, or other stiff material, curved or having a sharp angle, for catching hold of something or for hanging things on. **2** fasten with a hook or hooks: *Will you hook my dress for me?* **3** catch or take hold of with a hook. **4** a curved piece of wire, usually with a barb at the end, for catching fish. **5** catch (fish) with a hook. **6** anything curved or bent like a hook. **7** a sharp bend: *a hook in the river.* **8** a curved point of land. **9** be curved or bent like a hook. **10** throw or hit (a ball) so that it curves. **11** a curving throw or hit. **12** (in boxing) a short, swinging blow. **13** hit with such a blow. 1,4,6-8, 11,12 *n.*, 2,3,5,9,10,13 *v.* —**hook′less,** *adj.* —**hook′like′,** *adj.*

by hook or by crook, in any way at all; by fair means or foul.

hook up, arrange and connect the parts of (a radio set, telephone, etc.).

off the hook, INFORMAL. free of responsibility.

on one's own hook, INFORMAL. independently.

hook a (hůk′ə), hookah. *n., pl.* **hook as.**

hook ah (hůk′ə), an Oriental tobacco pipe with a long tube by which the smoke is drawn through water and cooled. *n.* [*Hookah* comes from Arabic *ḥuqqah,* meaning "vase, pipe."]

hooked (hůkt), **1** curved or bent like a hook. **2** having hooks. **3** made with a hook. A **hooked rug** is made by pulling loops of yarn or strips of cloth through a piece of canvas, burlap, etc., with a hook. **4** INFORMAL. slavishly dependent; addicted. *adj.*

hook up (hůk′up′), **1** arrangement and connection of the parts of a radio set, telephone, broadcasting facilities, etc.: *a nation-wide television hookup.* **2** INFORMAL. connection or combination. *n.*

hook worm (hůk′wėrm′), **1** a small roundworm that enters the body through the skin and fastens itself to the walls of the small intestine. **2** disease caused by this worm, characterized by weakness and apparent laziness. *n.*

hook y (hůk′ē). **play hooky,** INFORMAL. stay away from school without permission. *n.*

hoo li gan (hü′lə gən), INFORMAL. one of a gang of street hoodlums. *n.*

hoop (hůp *or* hüp), **1** ring or round, flat band: *a hoop for holding together the staves of a barrel.* **2** bind or fasten together with a hoop or hoops. **3** a large wooden, iron, or plastic ring used as a toy, especially for rolling around the ground. **4** a circular frame formerly used to hold out a woman's skirt. 1,3,4 *n.*, 2 *v.* —**hoop′er,** *n.* —**hoop′like′,** *adj.*

hoop skirt

hoop skirt, a woman's skirt worn over a frame of flexible hoops to hold out or expand the skirt; crinoline.

hoo ray (hů rā′), hurrah. *interj., n., v.*

hoot (hüt), **1** sound that an owl makes. **2** make this sound or one like it. **3** a shout to show disapproval or scorn. **4** make such a shout. **5** show disapproval of or scorn for by hooting: *The audience hooted the speaker's plan.* **6** force or drive by hooting: *What he said was so foolish that they hooted him off the platform.* **7** INFORMAL. the smallest thought; trifle: *She doesn't give a hoot about what happens to us.* 1,3,7 *n.*, 2,4-6 *v.* —**hoot′er,** *n.*

hoot e nan ny (hüt′n an′ē), an informal musical gathering featuring folk singing, especially one in which the audience joins in. *n., pl.* **hoot e nan nies.**

Hoo ver (hü′vər), **Herbert Clark,** 1874-1964, the 31st president of the United States, from 1929 to 1933. *n.*

Hoover Dam, dam on the Colorado River between Arizona and Nevada; Boulder Dam.

hooves (hůvz *or* hüvz), a plural of **hoof.** *n.*

hop¹ (hop), **1** spring, or move by springing, on one foot: *How far can you hop on your right foot?* **2** spring, or move by springing, with both or all feet at once: *Many birds hop.* **3** jump over: *hop a ditch.* **4** INFORMAL. jump on (a train, car, etc.). **5** a hopping; spring. **6** INFORMAL. fly in an airplane. **7** INFORMAL. flight in an airplane. **8** INFORMAL. a dancing party. 1-4,6 *v.*, **hopped, hop ping;** 5,7,8 *n.*

hop² (hop), **1** vine having flower clusters that look like small pine cones. **2 hops,** *pl.* the dried, ripe flower clusters of the hop vine, used to flavor beer and other malt drinks. *n.*

hope (hōp), **1** a feeling that what one desires will happen: *Your encouragement gave me hope.* **2** wish and expect: *I hope to do well in school this year.* **3** thing hoped for. **4** a cause of hope; person or thing that gives hope to others or that others have hope in: *She is the hope of the family.* 1,3,4 *n.*, 2 *v.*, **hoped, hop ing.** —**hop′er,** *n.*

hope ful (hōp′fəl), **1** feeling or showing hope; expecting to receive what one desires: *a hopeful attitude.* **2** giving hope; likely to succeed. **3** boy or girl thought likely to succeed: *a young hopeful.* 1,2 *adj.*, 3 *n.* —**hope′ful ly,** *adv.* —**hope′ful ness,** *n.*

hope less (hōp′lis), **1** feeling no hope: *He was disappointed so often that he became hopeless.* **2** giving no hope: *a hopeless illness. adj.* —**hope′less ly,** *adv.* —**hope′less ness,** *n.*

Ho pi (hō′pē), member of a tribe of Pueblo Indians living in adobe-built villages in northern Arizona. *n., pl.* **Ho pis** or **Ho pi.**

hopper (def. 3)

hop per (hop′ər), **1** person or thing that hops. **2** grasshopper or other hopping insect. **3** container having a narrow opening at the bottom, used to receive and hold coal, grain, or other material before feeding it into a machine or storage bin. *n.*

hop scotch (hop′skoch′), a children's game in which the players hop over the lines of a figure drawn on the ground and pick up an object thrown or kicked into one of the numbered squares of the figure. *n.*

ho ra (hôr′ə *or* hōr′ə), a lively Israeli folk dance performed by couples moving around to the left or right in a circle. *n.*

horde (hôrd), **1** multitude; crowd; swarm: *hordes of grasshoppers.* **2** a wandering tribe or troop: *Hordes of Mongols roamed Central Asia. n.*

hore hound (hôr′hound′), **1** plant related to mint, with woolly, whitish leaves. **2** candy or cough medicine flavored with a bitter extract made from the leaves of this plant. *n.* Also, **hoarhound.**

ho ri zon (hə rī′zn), **1** line where the earth and sky seem to meet. You cannot see beyond the horizon. **2** limit of one's thinking, experience, interest, or outlook. *n.*

ho ri zon tal (hôr′ə zon′tl), **1** parallel to the horizon; at right angles to a vertical line. **2** flat; level. **3** a horizontal line, plane, direction, position, etc. 1,2 *adj.,* 3 *n.* —**ho′ri zon′tal ly,** *adv.* —**hor′i zon′tal ness,** *n.*

hor mone (hôr′mōn), substance formed in the endocrine glands, which enters the bloodstream and affects or controls the activity of some organ or tissue. Adrenalin and insulin are hormones. *n.* [*Hormone* comes from Greek *hormōn,* meaning "a setting in motion."]

horn (hôrn), **1** a hard, hollow, permanent growth, usually curved and pointed, on the heads of cattle, sheep, goats, and some other animals. **2** anything that sticks up on the head of an animal: *a snail's horns, an insect's horns.* **3** the substance or material of horns. A person's fingernails, the beaks of birds, the hoofs of horses, and tortoise shells are all made of horn. **4** container made by hollowing out a horn. It was used to drink out of or to carry gunpowder in. **5** a musical instrument sounded by blowing into the smaller end. It was once made of horn, but now it is made of brass or other metal. **6** device sounded as a warning signal: *an automobile horn.* **7** anything that sticks out like a horn or is shaped like a horn: *a saddle horn.* **8** either pointed tip of a new or old moon, or of a crescent. *n.* —**horn′less,** *adj.* —**horn′like′,** *adj.*

horn in, SLANG. meddle or intrude.

Horn (hôrn), **Cape.** See **Cape Horn.** *n.*

horn blende (hôrn′blend′), a common black, darkgreen, or brown mineral found in granite and other rocks. *n.*

horn book (hôrn′bùk′), page with the alphabet, etc., on it, covered with a sheet of transparent horn and fastened in a frame with a handle, formerly used in teaching children to read. *n.*

horned (hôrnd), having a horn, horns, or hornlike growths. *adj.*

horned toad, a small lizard with a broad, flat body, short tail, and many hornlike spines.

hor net (hôr′nit), a large wasp that can give a very painful sting. *n.*

horn of plenty, cornucopia.

horn pipe (hôrn′pīp′), **1** a lively dance done by one person. It was formerly popular among sailors. **2** music for it. *n.*

horn y (hôr′nē), **1** made of horn or a substance like it. **2** hard like a horn; calloused: *A farmer's hands are horny from work.* **3** having a horn or horns; horned. *adj.,* **horn i er, horn i est.** —**horn′i ness,** *n.*

ho ro scope (hôr′ə skōp′), **1** diagram used in telling fortunes according to the relative position of the planets at a particular time, especially at the hour of a person's birth. **2** fortune told by using such a diagram. *n.* [*Horoscope* can be traced back to Greek *hōra,* meaning "hour," and *skopein,* meaning "to look at, watch."]

hor ren dous (hô ren′dəs), horrible; terrible; frightful. *adj.* —**hor ren′dous ly,** *adv.*

hor ri ble (hôr′ə bəl), **1** causing horror; terrible; dreadful; frightful; shocking: *a horrible crime, a horrible disease.*

2 extremely unpleasant: *a horrible noise. adj.* —**hor′ri ble ness,** *n.*

hor ri bly (hôr′ə blē), in a horrible manner. *adv.*

hor rid (hôr′id), **1** causing great fear; terrible; frightful. **2** very unpleasant: *a horrid person, a horrid day. adj.* —**hor′rid ly,** *adv.* —**hor′rid ness,** *n.*

hor rif ic (hô rif′ik), causing horror; horrifying. *adj.*

hor ri fy (hôr′ə fī), **1** cause to feel horror. **2** shock very much: *We were horrified by such rude behavior. v.,* **hor ri fied, hor ri fy ing.** —**hor′ri fy′ing ly,** *adv.*

hor ror (hôr′ər), **1** a shivering, shaking terror. **2** a very strong dislike: *I have a horror of high places.* **3** thing that causes horror. *n.*

hors d'oeuvre (ôr′ dėrv′), relish or light food served as an appetizer before the regular courses of a meal. Olives, celery, anchovies, etc., are hors d'oeuvres. *pl.* **hors d'oeuvres** (ôr′dėrvz′). [*Hors d'oeuvre* comes from French *hors d'oeuvre,* which originally meant "apart from (the main) work." French *oeuvre,* meaning "work," can be traced back to Latin *opus.*]

horse (def. 3)—The gymnast vaulted over the **horse.**

horse (hôrs), **1** a large, four-legged mammal with solid hoofs, and a mane and tail of long, coarse hair. Horses are used for riding and for carrying and pulling loads. **2** a full-grown male horse. **3** piece of gymnasium apparatus to jump or vault over. **4** a supporting frame with legs: *Five boards laid on two horses made our picnic table.*

5 horse around, SLANG. fool around; get into mischief. 1-4 *n., pl.* **hors es** *or* **horse;** 5 *v.,* **horsed, hors ing.** —**horse′less,** *adj.* —**horse′like′,** *adj.*

from the horse's mouth, from a well-informed source.

horse of a different color, something different.

horse back (hôrs′bak′), **1** the back of a horse. **2** on the back of a horse: *ride horseback.* 1 *n.,* 2 *adv.*

horse chestnut, 1 a shade tree with spreading branches, large leaves, clusters of showy white flowers, and glossy brown nuts. **2** its nut.

horse fly (hôrs′flī′), a large fly that bites animals, especially horses. *n., pl.* **horse flies.**

horse hair (hôrs′her′ *or* hôrs′har′), **1** hair from the mane or tail of a horse. **2** a stiff fabric made of this hair; haircloth. *n.*

horse hide (hôrs′hīd′), **1** hide of a horse. **2** leather made from this hide. *n.*

horse latitudes, two regions where the winds are usually calm or very light. They extend around the earth at about 30 degrees north and 30 degrees south of the equator.

horse man (hôrs′mən), **1** man who rides on horseback. **2** man who is skilled in riding or managing horses. *n., pl.* **horse men.**

horse man ship (hôrs′mən ship), skill in riding or managing horses: *She is proud of her horsemanship. n.*

horse opera, SLANG. western.

horse play (hôrs′plā′), rough, boisterous fun. *n.*

horse pow er (hôrs′pou′ər), unit for measuring the power of engines, motors, etc. One horsepower is the power to lift 550 pounds one foot in one second. *n.*

horse rad ish (hôrs′rad′ish), **1** a tall plant with a white, hot-tasting root. **2** its root, which is ground up and used as a relish with meat, fish, etc. *n.*

horse sense, INFORMAL. plain, practical good sense; common sense.

horse shoe (hôrs′shü′), **1** a metal plate shaped like a U, nailed to a horse's hoof to protect it. **2** thing shaped like a horseshoe. **3 horseshoes,** *pl.* game in which the players try to throw horseshoes over or near a stake 40 feet away. *n.* —**horse′sho′er,** *n.*

horseshoe crab—up to 20 in. (51 cm.) long

horseshoe crab, a crablike sea animal related to the spiders, with a horseshoe-shaped shell and a long, spiny tail.

horseshoe magnet, a steel magnet in the shape of a horseshoe.

horse whip (hôrs′hwip′), **1** whip for driving or controlling horses. **2** beat with a horsewhip. 1 *n.,* 2 *v.,* **horse-whipped, horse whip ping.**

horse wom an (hôrs′wum′ən), **1** woman who rides on horseback. **2** woman skilled in riding or managing horses. *n., pl.* **horse wom en.**

hors y or **hors ey** (hôr′sē), **1** of or like a horse or horses. **2** fond of horses or horse racing. **3** dressing or talking like people who spend much time with horses. *adj.,* **hors i er, hors i est.** —**hors′i ness,** *n.*

hort., horticulture.

hor ti cul tur al (hôr′tə kul′chər əl), having to do with the growing of flowers, fruits, vegetables, and plants: *a horticultural exhibit. adj.* —**hor′ti cul′tur al ly,** *adv.*

hor ti cul ture (hôr′tə kul′chər), **1** science or art of growing flowers, fruits, vegetables, and plants. **2** cultivation of a garden. *n.* [*Horticulture* comes from Latin *hortus,* meaning "garden," and English *culture.*]

hor ti cul tur ist (hôr′tə kul′chər ist), an expert in horticulture. *n.*

ho san na (hō zan′ə), a shout of praise to God: *The high priest cried, "Hosanna!" interj., n., pl.* **ho san nas.**

hose (hōz), **1** tube of rubber, plastic, or other flexible material for carrying liquid for short distances. A hose is used in pumping gasoline into automobiles. **2** stockings. **3** long, tight breeches formerly worn by men. **4** put water on with a hose. 1-3 *n., pl.* **hos es** for 1, **hose** for 2 and 3; 4 *v.,* **hosed, hos ing.** —**hose′like′,** *adj.*

Ho se a (hō zē′ə), **1** book of the Old Testament. **2** its author, a Hebrew prophet who lived in the 700's B.C. *n.*

ho sier y (hō′zhər ē), hose; stockings. *n.*

hosp., hospital.

hos pice (hos′pis), house where travelers can stop and rest. It is often kept by monks. *n.*

hos pi ta ble (hos′pi tə bəl *or* ho spit′ə bəl), **1** giving or liking to give a welcome, food and shelter, and friendly treatment to guests or strangers: *a hospitable family, a hospitable reception.* **2** with the mind open or receptive: *a person hospitable to new ideas. adj.*

hos pi ta bly (hos′pi tə blē *or* ho spit′ə blē), in a hospitable manner. *adv.*

hos pi tal (hos′pi təl), place for the care of the sick or injured. *n.*

hos pi tal i ty (hos′pə tal′ə tē), friendly reception; generous treatment of guests or strangers. *n., pl.* **hos pi tal i ties.**

hos pi tal i za tion (hos′pi tə lə zā′shən), a putting or a being put in a hospital for treatment. *n.*

hos pi tal ize (hos′pi tə līz), put in a hospital for treatment. *v.,* **hos pi tal ized, hos pi tal iz ing.**

host[1] (hōst), **1** person who receives another person as a guest. **2** a living plant or animal in or on which a parasite lives: *The oak tree is the host of the mistletoe that grows on it.* **3** receive or entertain at as a host does: *host a party.* 1,2 *n.,* 3 *v.* [*Host*[1] came into English about 700 years ago from French *hoste,* meaning "guest, host," which came from Latin *hospitem,* which is from *hostis,* meaning "stranger, enemy."]

host[2] (hōst), **1** a large number; multitude: *As it grew dark, a few stars appeared, then a host.* **2** army. *n.* [*Host*[2] came into English about 700 years ago from French *host,* which came from Latin *hostis,* meaning "stranger, enemy." See **Word Family.**]

host[2]

Below are words related to *host*[2]. They can all be traced back to the Latin word *hostis* (hōs′tis), meaning "stranger, enemy."

hospital	hostage	hostile
hospitality	hostel	hotel
host[1]	hostess	inhospitable

Host (hōst). Often, **host.** bread or wafer used in the Mass of the Roman Catholic Church. *n.* [*Host* came into English about 700 years ago from French *hoiste,* which came from Latin *hostia,* meaning "a sacrifice."]

hos tage (hos′tij), **1** person given up to another or held by an enemy as a pledge that certain promises, agreements, etc., will be carried out. **2** pledge; security. *n.*

hos tel (hos′tl), a lodging place, especially a supervised lodging place for young people on bicycle trips, hikes, etc.; inn; hotel. *n.*

hos tel ry (hos′tl rē), inn; hotel. *n., pl.* **hos tel ries.**

host ess (hō′stis), **1** woman who receives another person as her guest. **2** woman employed in a restaurant or on an airplane to welcome and serve people. *n., pl.* **host ess es.**

hos tile (hos′tl), **1** of an enemy or enemies: *the hostile army.* **2** opposed; unfriendly; unfavorable: *a hostile look. adj.* —**hos′tile ly,** *adv.*

hos til i ty (ho stil′ə tē), **1** the feeling that an enemy has;

being an enemy; unfriendliness; opposition: *He showed signs of hostility toward our plan.* **2 hostilities,** *pl.* acts of war; warfare; fighting: *The peace treaty brought hostilities between the two countries to an end. n., pl.* **hos til i ties.**

hos tler (os′lər *or* hos′lər), person who takes care of horses at an inn or stable. *n.* Also, **ostler.**

hot (hot), **1** having much heat; very warm: *Fire is hot. The sun is hot today. That long run has made me hot.* **2** having a sharp, burning taste: *Pepper and mustard are hot.* **3** fiery: *a hot temper, hot with rage.* **4** very eager: *The children were hot to go camping.* **5** new; fresh: *a hot scent, a hot trail.* **6** following closely: *We were in hot pursuit of the runaway horse.* **7** (in games, treasure hunts, etc.) very near or approaching what one is searching for. **8** radioactive: *the hot debris left by an atomic explosion.* **9** SLANG. obtained illegally; stolen: *hot diamonds.* **10** with much heat: *The sun beats hot upon the sand.* 1-9 *adj.,* **hot ter, hot test;** 10 *adv.* —**hot′ly,** *adv.* —**hot′ness,** *n.* **make it hot for,** INFORMAL. make trouble for.

hot air, SLANG. empty, showy talk or writing.

hot bed (hot′bed′), **1** bed of earth covered with glass and kept warm for growing plants. **2** place where anything grows and develops rapidly: *Dirty, crowded cities are hotbeds of disease and crime. n.*

hot-blood ed (hot′blud′id), **1** easily excited or angered. **2** passionate. *adj.* —**hot′-blood′ed ness,** *n.*

hot cake, pancake.

go like hot cakes or **sell like hot cakes,** sell well and rapidly; be in great demand.

hot dog, 1 INFORMAL. sandwich made with a hot frankfurter enclosed in a bun. **2** INFORMAL. frankfurter. **3** SLANG. an athlete who does stunts, especially while surfing or skiing.

hot-dog (hot′dôg′), SLANG. do stunts, especially while surfing or skiing. *v.,* **hot-dogged, hot-dog ging.**

ho tel (hō tel′), house or large building that supplies rooms and food for pay to travelers and others. *n.*

hot foot (hot′fut′), INFORMAL. go in great haste; hurry. *v.*

hot head ed (hot′hed′id), **1** having a fiery temper; easily angered. **2** hasty; rash. *adj.* —**hot′head′ed ly,** *adv.*

hot house (hot′hous′), greenhouse. *n., pl.* **hot hous es** (hot′hou′ziz).

hot line, a direct telephone or teletype line providing immediate communication in an emergency.

hot plate, a small, portable electric stove, with one or two burners, for cooking.

hot rod, automobile with a rebuilt motor for faster starts and higher speeds.

hot shot (hot′shot′), SLANG. person having more than ordinary skill at something and often being conceited about it. *n.*

Hot ten tot (hot′n tot), **1** member of a people who live mainly in southwestern Africa. The Hottentots are related to the Bushmen. **2** their language. *n.*

hot war, war that involves actual fighting.

hot water, INFORMAL. trouble.

hou dah (hou′də), howdah. *n.*

hound (hound), **1** dog of any of various breeds, most of which hunt by scent and have large, drooping ears and short tails. **2** any dog. **3** SLANG. person who is very fond of something: *a movie hound.* **4** keep on chasing or driving: *The police hounded the criminals and finally caught them.* **5** urge on; nag: *The children hounded their parents to buy a swimming pool.* 1-3 *n.,* 4,5 *v.*

hour (our), **1** one of the 12 equal periods of time between noon and midnight, or between midnight and noon; 60 minutes; ¹/₂₄ of a day. **2** the time of day: *This clock strikes the hours and the half hours.* **3** a particular or fixed time: *Our breakfast hour is at seven o'clock.* **4 hours,** *pl.* time for work, study, etc.: *What are the hours in this*

office? Our school hours are 9 to 12 and 1 to 4. **5** distance which can be traveled in an hour: *The concert hall is only an hour away. n.*

hour glass (our′glas′), device for measuring time, made up of two glass bulbs connected by a narrow neck. It takes an hour for sand in the top bulb to pass through the neck to the bottom bulb. *n., pl.* **hour glass es.**

hourglass
It takes just an hour for sand or mercury to pass through the narrow neck from the top bulb to the bottom bulb.

hour hand, the shorter hand on a clock or watch that indicates hours. It moves around the whole dial once in twelve hours.

hour i (hur′ē), one of the young, eternally beautiful girls of the Moslem paradise. *n., pl.* **hour is.**

hour ly (our′lē), **1** done, happening, or counted every hour: *There are hourly reports of the news and weather on this radio station.* **2** every hour; hour by hour: *Give two doses of the medicine hourly.* **3** coming very often; frequent: *hourly messages.* **4** very often; frequently: *Messages were coming from the front hourly.* 1,3 *adj.,* 2,4 *adv.*

house (hous *for 1-4,6-8;* houz *for 5*), **1** building in which people live. **2** people living in a house; household. **3** family with its ancestors and descendants, especially a noble family: *He was a prince of the house of David.* **4** building for any purpose: *an engine house.* **5** take or put into a house; provide with a house; shelter: *Where can we house all these children?* **6** place of business or a business firm: *a publishing house.* **7** assembly for making laws and considering questions of government; lawmaking body. In the United States, the House of Representatives is the lower house of Congress; the Senate is the upper house. **8** audience: *The singer sang to a large house.* 1-4, 6-8 *n., pl.* **hous es** (hou′ziz); 5 *v.,* **housed, hous ing.**

keep house, manage a home and its affairs; do housework.

on the house, paid for by the owner of the business; free.

house boat (hous′bōt′), boat fitted out for use as a place to live in. *n.*

house break (hous′brāk′), train (a dog, cat, etc.) to have clean habits for living indoors. *v.,* **house broke** (house′brōk′), **house bro ken, house break ing.**

house break er (hous′brā′kər), person who breaks into a house to steal or commit some other crime. *n.*

house break ing (hous′brā′king), act of breaking into a house to steal or commit some other crime. *n.*

house bro ken (hous′brō′kən), (of a dog, cat, etc.) trained to have clean habits for living indoors. *adj.*

house fly (hous′flī′), a two-winged fly that lives around and in houses in all parts of the world, feeding on food, garbage, and filth. Houseflies carry disease germs. *n., pl.* **house flies.**

house hold (hous′hōld), **1** all the people living in a house; family; family and servants. **2** a home and its affairs. **3** of a household; domestic: *household expenses, household chores.* 1,2 *n.,* 3 *adj.*

house hold er (hous′hōl′dər), **1** person who owns or lives in a house. **2** head of a family. *n.*

house hus band (hous′huz′bənd), married man who manages a home and its affairs for his family. *n.*

house keep er (hous′kē′pər), **1** woman who is hired to manage a home and its affairs and to do housework. **2** woman who is hired to direct the servants that do the housework in a home, hotel, etc. *n.*

house keep ing (hous′kē′ping), management of a home and its affairs; doing the housework. *n.*

house maid (hous′mād′), a woman servant who does housework. *n.*

House of Commons, the lower house of the Parliament of Great Britain or of Canada, composed of elected representatives; the Commons.

house of correction, place of confinement and reform for persons convicted of minor offenses.

House of Lords, the upper house of the Parliament of Great Britain, composed of nobles and clergymen of high rank; the Lords.

House of Representatives, the lower house of Congress or of the legislature of certain states of the United States.

house-sit (hous′sit′), live in and keep watch over a home during the absence of the owner or tenant. *v.,* **house-sat** (hous′sat′), **house-sit ting.**

house sparrow, English sparrow.

house top (hous′top′), top of a house; roof. *n.*

house warm ing (hous′wôr′ming), party given when a family moves into a home for the first time. *n.*

house wife (hous′wīf′), married woman who manages a home and its affairs for her family. *n., pl.* **house wives** (hous′wīvz′).

house wife ly (hous′wīf′lē), of or like a housewife. *adj.*

house work (hous′wėrk′), work to be done in housekeeping, such as washing, ironing, cleaning, and cooking. *n.*

hous ing[1] (hou′zing), **1** act of sheltering; providing shelter. **2** houses; dwellings: *There is not enough housing in that city.* **3** frame or plate to hold part of a machine in place. *n.*

hous ing[2] (hou′zing), an ornamental covering on an animal's back, especially a horse. *n.*

Hous ton (hyü′stən), **1 Samuel,** 1793-1863, American general and statesman who was twice president of Texas before it became a state in 1845. **2** city in SE Texas. *n.*

hove (hōv), heaved; a past tense and a past participle of **heave.** *v.*

hov el (huv′əl *or* hov′əl), house that is small, crude, and unpleasant to live in. *n.*

hov er (huv′ər *or* hov′ər), **1** stay in or near one place in the air: *The two birds hovered over their nest.* **2** stay in or near one place; wait nearby: *The dogs hovered around the kitchen door at mealtime.* **3** be in an uncertain condition; waver: *The patient hovered between life and death. v.*

hov er craft or **Hov er craft** (huv′ər kraft′ *or* hov′ər-kraft′), a vehicle that travels a few feet above the surface of land or water on a cushion of air. The air is created by jets or fans blowing downward. *n.*

hovercraft

how (hou), **1** in what way; by what means: *Tell me how to do it (adv.). I wonder how you get there (conj.).* **2** to what degree or amount: *How tall are you?* **3** in what condition: *How are you today? (adv.). Let me know how she is (conj.).* **4** for what reason; why: *How is it you don't like candy?* 1-4 *adv.,* 1,3 *conj.*

and how, INFORMAL. certainly.

how come, INFORMAL. why: *How come you didn't call me last night?*

howdah

how dah (hou′də), seat for persons riding on the back of an elephant. *n.* Also, **houdah.**

how dy (hou′dē), DIALECT. a call of greeting; hello. *interj.*

Howe (hou), **Elias,** 1819-1867, American inventor of the sewing machine. *n.*

how ev er (hou ev′ər), **1** in spite of that; nevertheless; yet: *We were very late for dinner; however, there was plenty left for us.* **2** to whatever extent, degree, or amount; no matter how: *I'll come however busy I am.* **3** in whatever way; by whatever means: *However did you get so dirty? adv.*

how it zer (hou′it sər), a short cannon for firing shells in a high curve. *n.* [*Howitzer* comes from Dutch *houwitser,* and can be traced back to Czech *houfnice,* meaning "a catapult, sling for hurling stones."]

howl (houl), **1** give a long, loud, mournful cry: *Our dog often howls at night. The winter winds howled around our cabin.* **2** a long, loud, mournful cry: *the howl of a wolf.* **3** give a long, loud cry of pain or rage. **4** a loud cry of pain or rage. **5** a yell or shout: *We heard howls of laughter.* **6** yell or shout: *It was so funny that we howled with laughter.* 1,3,6 *v.,* 2,4,5 *n.*

howl er (hou′lər), **1** person or thing that howls. **2** a tropical American monkey with a long, grasping tail. **3** INFORMAL. a ridiculous mistake or blunder. *n.*

howl ing (hou′ling), INFORMAL. very great: *a howling success. adj.* —**howl′ing ly,** *adv.*

how so ev er (hou′sō ev′ər), **1** to whatever extent, degree, or amount. **2** in whatever way. *adv.*

hoy den (hoid′n), a boisterous, romping girl; tomboy. *n.*

hp., h.p., HP, or **H.P.,** horsepower.

h.q. or **H.Q.,** headquarters.

hr., hour or hours. *pl.,* **hrs.**

H.R., House of Representatives.

H.R.H., 1 Her Royal Highness. **2** His Royal Highness.

ht., height.

Hua Guo feng (hwä′ gwō′fung′), born about 1920, Chinese political leader, chairman of the Chinese Communist Party from 1976 to 1981.

hub (hub), **1** the central part of a wheel. **2** center of interest, activity, etc.: *London is the hub of English life. n.*

hub bub (hub′ub), loud, confused noise; uproar: *There was a hubbub in the crowded street. n.*

hub by (hub′ē), INFORMAL. husband. *n., pl.* **hub bies.**

hub cap (hub′kap′), a removable, dish-shaped metal piece which covers the center of the outer side of a wheel. *n.*

huck le ber ry (huk′əl ber′ē), a small berry like a blueberry, but darker and with larger seeds. It grows on a shrub. *n., pl.* **huck le ber ries.**

huck ster (huk′stər), 1 peddler. 2 INFORMAL. person who is in the advertising business. *n.*

hud dle (hud′l), 1 to crowd close: *The sheep huddled together in a corner.* 2 put close together: *We huddled all the children into one bed.* 3 nestle in a heap: *The cat huddled itself on the cushion.* 4 a closely packed group or crowd. 5 INFORMAL. a secret consultation: *After the meeting, the lawyer went into a huddle with his partner.* 6 INFORMAL. confer secretly. 7 a grouping of football players behind the line of scrimmage to receive signals, plan the next play, etc. 1-3,6 *v.,* **hud dled, hud dling;** 4,5,7 *n.* —**hud′-dler,** *n.*

Hud son (hud′sən), 1 **Henry,** died 1611, English navigator and explorer in America. Hudson River and Hudson Bay were named for him. 2 river in E New York State. New York City is at its mouth. *n.*

Hudson Bay, large bay in central Canada. It is an extension of the Atlantic Ocean.

hue (hyü), color, shade, or tint: *all the hues of the rainbow, silk of a pinkish hue. n.*

hue and cry, shouts of alarm or protest.

huff (huf), 1 fit of anger or peevishness: *We had a heated argument, and she left in a huff.* 2 puff; blow: *He huffed up the stairs with the heavy packages.* 1 *n.,* 2,3 *v.*

huff i ly (huf′ə lē), in a huffy manner. *adv.*

huff i ness (huf′ē nis), huffy quality. *n.*

huff y (huf′ē), 1 in a huff; offended. 2 easily offended; touchy. *adj.,* **huff i er, huff i est.**

hug (hug), 1 put the arms around and hold close, especially to show love or friendship: *The girl hugged her big dog.* 2 a tight clasp with the arms: *She gave her dog a hug.* 3 cling firmly or fondly to: *hug an opinion or belief.* 4 keep close to: *The boat hugged the shore.* 1,3,4 *v.,* **hugged, hug ging;** 2 *n.* —**hug′ger,** *n.*

huge (hyüj), very big; extremely large or great: *A whale is a huge animal. He won a huge sum of money in the lottery. adj.,* **hug er, hug est.** —**huge′ly,** *adv.* —**huge′-ness,** *n.*

Hu go (hyü′gō), **Victor,** 1802-1885, French writer of poetry, novels, and plays. *n.*

Hu gue not (hyü′gə not), a French Protestant of the 1500's and 1600's. *n.*

huh (hu), sound made to express surprise, contempt, etc., or to ask a question. *interj.*

hu la (hü′lə), a native Hawaiian dance. *n., pl.* **hu las.**

hu la-hu la (hü′lə hü′lə), hula. *n., pl.* **hu la-hu las.**

hulk (hulk), 1 body of an old or wornout ship. 2 Often, **hulks,** *pl.* ship used as a prison. 3 a big, clumsy ship. 4 a big, clumsy person or thing. *n.*

hulk ing (hul′king), big and clumsy: *a large, hulking boy. adj.*

hull (hul), 1 body or frame of a ship. 2 the main body or frame of a seaplane, airship, etc. 3 the outer covering of a seed or fruit. 4 calyx of some fruits. We call the green leaves at the stem of a strawberry its hull. 5 remove the hull or hulls from. 6 any outer covering. 1-4,6 *n.,* 5 *v.* —**hull′er,** *n.*

hul la ba loo (hul′ə bə lü′), a loud noise or disturbance; uproar. *n., pl.* **hul la ba loos.**

hum (hum), 1 make a continuous murmuring sound like

that of a bee or of a spinning top: *The sewing machine hums busily.* 2 a continuous murmuring sound: *the hum of the bees. There was a hum of activity in the busy shop.* 3 make a low sound like *mm* or *hm* in hesitation, embarrassment, dissatisfaction, etc. 4 a low sound like *mm* or *hm* made in hesitation, embarrassment, etc.: *Hum, I don't know what to do.* 5 sing with closed lips, not sounding words. *She hummed a tune as she worked.* 6 a singing in this way. 7 put or bring by humming: *The father hummed the baby to sleep.* 8 INFORMAL. be busy and active: *Things hummed at campaign headquarters just before the election.* 1,3,5,7,8 *v.,* **hummed, hum ming;** 2,6 *n.,* 4 *interj.* —**hum′mer,** *n.*

hu man (hyü′mən), 1 of persons; that people have: *Kindness is a human trait. To know all that will happen in the future is beyond human power.* 2 being a person or persons; having the form or qualities of people: *Men, women, and children are human beings. Those monkeys look almost human.* 3 having or showing qualities (good or bad) natural to people: *She is a very human person, warm and understanding and not too perfect.* 4 belonging to all human beings: *The history of America has great human interest.* 5 a human being; person. 1-4 *adj.,* 5 *n.* —**hu′man ness,** *n.*

hu mane (hyü mān′), not cruel or brutal; kind; merciful: *We believe in the humane treatment of prisoners. adj.* —**hu-mane′ly,** *adv.* —**hu mane′ness,** *n.*

hu man ist (hyü′mə nist), 1 student of human nature or affairs. 2 student of the humanities. *n.*

hu man is tic (hyü′mə nis′tik), of humanists. *adj.*

hu man i tar i an (hyü man′ə ter′ē ən), 1 helpful to humanity; philanthropic. 2 person who is devoted to the welfare of all human beings. 1 *adj.,* 2 *n.*

hu man i ty (hyü man′ə tē), 1 human beings; people; mankind: *Advances in medicine should help all humanity.* 2 a being human; human nature: *Humanity is a mixture of good and bad qualities.* 3 a being humane; humane treatment; kindness; mercy: *Treat animals with humanity.* 4 the humanities, *pl.* cultural studies as opposed to the sciences, including languages, literature, philosophy, art, etc. *n., pl.* **hu man i ties.**

hu man ize (hyü′mə nīz), 1 make or become human. 2 make or become humane. *v.,* **hu man ized, hu man iz ing.** —**hu′man i za′tion,** *n.* —**hu′man iz′er,** *n.*

hu man kind (hyü′mən kīnd′), human beings; people; mankind. *n.*

hu man ly (hyü′mən lē), 1 by human means: *The doctor did everything humanly possible to save the patient.* 2 in a human manner: *Even a judge is humanly liable to make a mistake. adv.*

hu man oid (hyü′mə noid), 1 having human characteristics; of human form. 2 a being having human characteristics: *The Neanderthal man was a humanoid.* 1 *adj.,* 2 *n.*

hum ble (hum′bəl), 1 low in position or condition; not important or grand: *They lived in a humble, one-room cottage.* 2 not proud; modest: *a humble heart, to be humble in spite of success.* 3 make humble; make lower in position, condition, or pride: *humbled by defeat.* 1,2 *adj.,* **hum bler, hum blest;** 3 *v.,* **hum bled, hum bling.** [*Humble* came into English about 700 years ago from French *humble,* and can be traced back to Latin *humus,* meaning "earth."] —**hum′ble ness,** *n.* —**hum′bler,** *n.*

hum bly (hum′blē), in a humble manner. *adv.*

hum bug (hum′bug′), 1 person who tries to deceive or cheat; fraud. 2 deception or pretense: *There's no humbug about her; she speaks her mind straight out.* 3 deceive; cheat: *I won't be humbugged into buying inferior goods.* 1,2 *n.,* 3 *v.,* **hum bugged, hum bug ging.**

hum drum (hum′drum′), without variety; commonplace; dull: *a humdrum life. adj.*

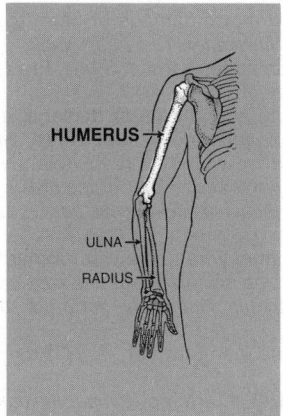

a hat	i it	oi oil	ch child	a in about
ā age	ī ice	ou out	ng long	e in taken
ä far	o hot	u cup	sh she	i in pencil
e let	ō open	ů put	th thin	o in lemon
ē equal	ô order	ü rule	ŦH then	u in circus
ėr term			zh measure	

ə = { a in about, e in taken, i in pencil, o in lemon, u in circus }

hu mer us (hyü′mər əs), the long bone in the upper part of the arm, from the shoulder to the elbow. *n., pl.* **hu mer i** (hyü′mə rī′).

hu mid (hyü′mid), slightly wet; moist; damp: *The air is very humid near the sea. adj.* —**hu′mid ly,** *adv.* —**hu′mid ness,** *n.*

hu mid i fi er (hyü mid′ə fī′ər), device for keeping air moist. *n.*

hu mid i fy (hyü mid′ə fī), make moist or damp. *v.,* **hu mid i fied, hu mid i fy ing.**

hu mid i ty (hyü mid′ə tē), **1** a being humid; moistness; dampness: *The humidity today is worse than the heat.* **2** amount of moisture in the air: *On a hot, sultry day the humidity is high. n.*

hu mil i ate (hyü mil′ē āt), lower the pride, dignity, or self-respect of; make ashamed: *We felt humiliated by our failure. They humiliated me by criticizing me in front of my friends. v.,* **hu mil i at ed, hu mil i at ing.**

hu mil i a tion (hyü mil′ē ā′shən), a lowering of pride, dignity, or self-respect; a making or a being made ashamed. *n.*

hu mil i ty (hyü mil′ə tē), humbleness of mind; lack of pride; meekness. *n., pl.* **hu mil i ties.**

hum ming bird (hum′ing bėrd′), a very small, brightly colored American bird with a long, narrow bill and narrow wings that move so rapidly they make a humming sound. *n.*

hum mock (hum′ək), **1** a very small, rounded hill; knoll; hillock. **2** a bump or ridge in a field of ice. *n.*

hu mor (hyü′mər), **1** funny or amusing quality: *I see no humor in your tricks.* **2** ability to see or show the funny or amusing side of things: *A sense of humor helps one overcome many problems.* **3** speech, writing, etc., showing this ability. **4** state of mind; mood; disposition; temper: *Is the teacher in a good humor this morning? I feel in the humor for working.* **5** give in to the fancies or whims of (a person); agree with; indulge: *to humor a sick child.* 1-4 *n.,* 5 *v.*

out of humor, in a bad mood; angry; displeased; cross.

hu mor ist (hyü′mər ist), a humorous talker or writer; person who tells or writes jokes and funny stories. *n.*

hu mor less (hyü′mər lis), without humor. *adj.* —**hu′mor less ly,** *adv.* —**hu′mor less ness,** *n.*

hu mor ous (hyü′mər əs), full of humor; funny; amusing: *We all laughed at the humorous story. adj.* —**hu′mor ous ly,** *adv.* —**hu′mor ous ness,** *n.*

hump (hump), **1** a rounded lump that sticks out: *Some camels have two humps on their backs.* **2** raise or bend up into a hump: *The cat humped its back when it saw the dog.* **3** mound. 1,3 *n.,* 2 *v.* —**hump′like′,** *adj.*

hump back (hump′bak′), **1** hunchback. **2** a back having a hump on it. *n.*

hump backed (hump′bakt′), hunchbacked. *adj.*

humph (humpf), exclamation expressing doubt, disgust, contempt, etc. *interj., n.*

Hum phrey (hum′frē), **Hubert Horatio,** 1911-1978, American political leader, vice-president of the United States from 1965 to 1969. *n.*

hump y (hum′pē), **1** full of humps. **2** humplike. *adj.,* **hump i er, hump i est.**

hu mus (hyü′məs), a dark-brown or black part of soil formed from decayed leaves and other vegetable matter. Humus contains valuable plant foods. *n.*

Hun (hun), **1** member of a warlike Asian people who invaded Europe in the A.D. 300's and 400's. **2** a barbarous, destructive person. *n.*

hunch (hunch), **1** a hump. **2** to hump: *hunch one's shoulders.* **3** draw, bend, or form into a hump: *She sat hunched up with her chin on her knees.* **4** move, push, or shove by jerks: *He hunched along in the rain.* **5** INFORMAL. a vague feeling or suspicion: *I had a hunch that it would rain, so I took along an umbrella.* 1,5 *n., pl.* **hunch es;** 2-4 *v.*

hunch back (hunch′bak′), **1** person whose back has a hump on it; humpback. **2** back having a hump on it. *n.*

hunch backed (hunch′bakt′), having a hump on the back; humpbacked. *adj.*

hun dred (hun′drəd), ten times ten; 100. There are one hundred cents in a dollar. *n., adj.*

hun dredth (hun′drədth), **1** next after the 99th; last in a series of 100. **2** one of 100 equal parts. *adj., n.*

hun dred weight (hun′drəd wāt′), unit of weight, equal to 100 pounds in the United States and Canada, and 112 pounds in Great Britain. *n., pl.* **hun dred weights** or (*as after a numeral*) **hun dred weight.**

hung (hung), a past tense and a past participle of **hang.** *He hung up his cap. Your coat has hung here all day. v.*

Hun gar i an (hung ger′ē ən), **1** of Hungary, its people, or their language. **2** person born or living in Hungary. **3** language of Hungary. 1 *adj.,* 2,3 *n.*

Hun gar y (hung′gər ē), country in central Europe. Hungary was formerly a part of the empire of Austria-Hungary. *Capital:* Budapest. See **Danube** for map. *n.*

hun ger (hung′gər), **1** an uncomfortable or painful feeling in the stomach caused by having had nothing to eat. **2** desire or need for food: *I ate an apple to satisfy my hunger.* **3** feel hunger; be hungry. **4** a strong desire; craving; longing: *to have a hunger for knowledge.* **5** have a strong desire; crave; long: *to hunger for affection, to hunger for friends.* 1,2,4 *n.,* 3,5 *v.*

hun gri ly (hung′grə lē), in a hungry manner. *adv.*

hun gri ness (hung′grē nis), condition of being hungry. *n.*

hun gry (hung′grē), **1** feeling a desire or need for food: *I missed breakfast and was hungry all morning.* **2** showing hunger: *The stray cat had a hungry look.* **3** having a strong desire or craving; eager: *Many young people are hungry for knowledge. adj.,* **hun gri er, hun gri est.**

hunk (hungk), INFORMAL. a big lump or piece: *a hunk of cheese. n.*

hunt (hunt), **1** go after (game and other wild animals) to catch or kill them for food or sport. **2** act of hunting. **3** group of persons hunting together. **4** search; seek; look for: *hunt through drawers, hunt for a lost book.* **5** an attempt to find something; search: *The hunt for the lost child continued until she was found.* 1,4 *v.*, 2,3,5 *n.*

hunt er (hun′tər), **1** person who hunts. **2** horse or dog trained for hunting. *n.*

hunt ing (hun′ting), act or sport of chasing game. *n.*

hunt ress (hun′tris), woman who hunts. *n., pl.* **hunt ress es.**

hunts man (hunts′mən), **1** hunter. **2** manager of a hunt. *n., pl.* **hunts men.**

hurdle (def. 2)—These athletes are competing in the **hurdles.**

hur dle (hėr′dl), **1** barrier for people or horses to jump over in a race. **2 hurdles,** *pl.* race in which the runners jump over hurdles. **3** jump over: *The horse hurdled both the fence and the ditch.* **4** obstacle, difficulty, etc. **5** overcome (an obstacle, difficulty, etc.). **6** frame made of sticks, used as a temporary fence. 1,2,4,6 *n.*, 3,5 *v.*, **hur dled, hur dling.**

hur dler (hėrd′lər), person who jumps over hurdles in a race. *n.*

hur dy-gur dy (hėr′dē gėr′dē), hand organ played by turning a handle. *n., pl.* **hur dy-gur dies.**

hurl (hėrl), **1** throw with much force; fling: *hurl a spear, hurl rocks.* **2** a forcible or violent throw. **3** throw forth (words, cries, etc.) violently: *They hurled insults at me.* 1,3 *v.*, 2 *n.* —**hurl′er,** *n.*

hur ly-bur ly (hėr′lē bėr′lē), disorder and noise; commotion; tumult. *n., pl.* **hur ly-bur lies.**

Hur on (hyur′ən), **Lake,** one of the five Great Lakes. *n.*

hur rah (hə rä′ *or* hə rô′), **1** a shout of joy, approval, etc.: *"Hurrah!" they shouted as the team scored again* (*interj.*). *Give a hurrah for the team!* (*n.*) **2** shout hurrahs; cheer. 1 *interj., n.*, 2 *v.* Also, **hooray.**

hur ray (hə rā′), hurrah. *interj., n., v.*

hur ri cane (hėr′ə kān), storm with violent wind and, usually, very heavy rain. Hurricanes are common in the West Indies. The wind in a hurricane blows with a speed of above 75 miles (121 kilometers) per hour. *n.*

hur ried (hėr′ēd), done or made in a hurry; hasty: *a hurried escape, a hurried reply.* *adj.* —**hur′ried ly,** *adv.*

hur ry (hėr′ē), **1** drive, carry, send, or move quickly: *They hurried the sick child to the doctor.* **2** move or act with more than an easy or natural speed: *If you hurry, your work may be poor. She hurried to get to work on time.* **3** a hurried movement or action: *In his hurry he dropped the bag of groceries.* **4** need to hurry; eagerness to have quickly or do quickly: *She was in a hurry to meet her friends.* **5** urge to act soon or too soon: *The salesman hurried the customer to make a choice.* **6** urge to great speed or to too great speed: *Don't hurry the driver.* **7** make go on or occur more quickly; hasten: *Please hurry dinner.* 1,2,5-7 *v.*, **hur ried, hur ry ing;** 3,4 *n., pl.* **hur ries.**

hurt (hėrt), **1** cause pain to; wound; injure: *The stone hurt my foot.* **2** a cut, bruise, or fracture; any wound or injury: *A scratch is not a serious hurt.* **3** suffer pain: *My hand*

hurts. **4** have a bad effect on; do damage or harm to: *Large price increases can hurt sales. Did I hurt your feelings?* **5** a bad effect; damage; harm. 1,3,4 *v.*, **hurt, hurt ing;** 2,5 *n.* —**hurt′er,** *n.*

hurt ful (hėrt′fəl), causing pain, harm, or damage; injurious: *a mean and hurtful remark.* *adj.* —**hurt′ful ly,** *adv.*

hur tle (hėr′tl), dash or drive violently; rush violently: *The express train hurtled past. The impact of the crash hurtled the driver against the windshield of the car.* *v.*, **hur tled, hur tling.**

hus band (huz′bənd), **1** man who has a wife; a married man. **2** manage carefully; be saving of: *to husband one's strength. They were husbanding their money for a vacation.* 1 *n.*, 2 *v.*

hus band man (huz′bənd mən), farmer. *n., pl.* **hus band men.**

hus band ry (huz′bən drē), **1** farming: *animal husbandry.* **2** careful management of one's affairs or resources; thrift: *To repair a leaking roof is good husbandry.* *n.*

hush (hush), **1** stop making a noise; make or become silent or quiet: *The wind has hushed. Hush your dog.* **2** a stopping of noise; silence; quiet; stillness. **3** stop the noise! be silent! keep quiet! 1 *v.*, 2 *n.*, 3 *interj.*

hush up, 1 keep from being told; stop discussion of: *The facts were hushed up to keep them secret.* **2** INFORMAL. hush!

husk (husk), **1** the dry outer covering of certain seeds or fruits. An ear of corn has a husk. **2** the dry or worthless outer covering of anything. **3** remove the husk from: *Husk the corn before cooking it.* 1,2 *n.*, 3 *v.* —**husk′er,** *n.*

husk i ly (hus′kə lē), in a husky voice; hoarsely. *adv.*

husk i ness (hus′kē nis), husky quality or condition. *n.*

husk y[1] (hus′kē), **1** big and strong: *a husky young man.* **2** dry in the throat; hoarse; rough of voice: *A cold can cause a husky cough.* *adj.*, **husk i er, husk i est.**

husky[2] (def. 1)
about 23 in. (58 cm.)
high at the shoulder

hus ky[2] *or* **Hus ky** (hus′kē), **1** a strong, medium-sized, arctic sled dog that has a thick coat and a bushy tail; Siberian husky. **2** any arctic sled dog. *n., pl.* **hus kies** *or* **Hus kies.**

hus sar (hù zär′), a light-armed cavalry soldier in various European armies. *n.* [*Hussar* comes from Hungarian *huszár,* which originally meant "pirate," and can be traced back to Latin *currere,* meaning "to run."]

hus sy (huz′ē *or* hus′ē), **1** a bad-mannered or pert girl. **2** an indecent or immoral woman. *n., pl.* **hus sies.**

hus tle (hus′əl), **1** to hurry: *Mother hustled the baby to bed.* **2** rush roughly; push one's way: *hustle along through the crowd.* **3** push or shove roughly; jostle rudely: *Guards hustled the demonstrators away from the mayor's office.* **4** go or work quickly or with energy: *He had to hustle to earn enough money to support his large family.* **5** tireless energy. **6** a hustling: *It was a hustle to get the dishes washed by seven o'clock.* 1-4 *v.*, **hus tled, hus tling;** 5,6 *n.*

hus tler (hus′lər), **1** person who hustles. **2** INFORMAL. a very energetic person. *n.*

hut (hut), a small, roughly made house; small cabin. *n.*

hutch (huch), **1** box or pen for small animals. Rabbits are kept in hutches. **2** hut. **3** box; chest; bin. **4** cupboard with open shelves on the upper part for holding dishes, etc. *n., pl.* **hutch es.**

huz za (hə zä′), huzzah. *n., pl.* **huzzas;** *v.*

huz zah (hə zä′), **1** a loud shout of joy, encouragement, or applause; hurrah. **2** shout huzzahs; cheer. **1** *interj., n.,* **2** *v.*

Hwang ho (hwäng′ hō′), Hwang Ho. *n.*

Hwang Ho (hwäng′ hō′), river in China flowing from central China into the Yellow Sea; Yellow River. See **Yangtze** for map.

hwy., highway.

hy a cinth (hī′ə sinth), a spring plant related to the lily, that grows from a bulb and has a spike of small, fragrant, bell-shaped flowers. *n.*

hy brid (hī′brid), **1** offspring of two animals or plants of different species, varieties, etc. The loganberry is a hybrid because it is a cross between the red raspberry and the dewberry. **2** bred from two different species, varieties, etc. A mule is a hybrid animal. **3** anything of mixed origin. A word formed of parts from different languages is a hybrid. **4** of mixed origin. **1,3** *n.,* **2,4** *adj.*

hy brid i za tion (hī′brə də zā′shən), production of hybrids; crossing of different species, varieties, etc. *n.*

hy dra (hī′drə), **1** kind of freshwater polyp with a tubelike body and stinging tentacles. When its body is cut into pieces, each piece forms a new individual. **2 Hydra,** (in Greek myths) a monster with many snakelike heads. When one head was cut off, two or three grew in its place. Hercules finally killed it. *n., pl.* **hy dras, hy drae** (hī′drē′).

hy dran gea (hī drān′jə), shrub with large, showy clusters of white, pink, or blue flowers. *n., pl.* **hy dran geas.**

hy drant (hī′drənt), a large, upright pipe with a valve for drawing water directly from a water main; hose connection on a street, road, etc.; fireplug. Hydrants are used to get water to put out fires and to wash the streets. *n.* [*Hydrant* is from *hydr-,* a form of *hydro-* used before vowels, which came from Greek *hydōr,* meaning "water." See **Word Family.**]

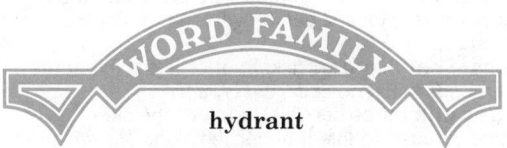

hydrant

Below are words related to *hydrant.* They can all be traced back to the Greek word *hydōr* (hü′dōr), meaning "water."

carbohydrate	hydraulic	hydrogenate
dehydrate	hydrocarbon	hydrometer
dropsy	hydrochloric	hydrophobia
formaldehyde	hydroelectric	hydroplane
hydra	hydrofoil	hydroponics
hydrangea	hydrogen	hydrosphere

hy drate (hī′drāt), **1** any chemical compound made when certain substances chemically unite with water. **2** become or cause to become a hydrate; combine with water to form a hydrate. **1** *n.,* **2** *v.,* **hy drat ed, hy drating.** —**hy dra′tion,** *n.*

hy drau lic (hī drô′lik), **1** of water or other liquids at rest or in motion. **2** operated by the pressure of water or other liquids in motion: *a hydraulic press.* **3** hardening under water: *hydraulic cement. adj.*

hy drau lics (hī drô′liks), science dealing with water

a hat	**i** it	**oi** oil	**ch** child	a in about
ā age	**ī** ice	**ou** out	**ng** long	e in taken
ä far	**o** hot	**u** cup	**sh** she	ə = { i in pencil
e let	**ō** open	**u̇** put	**th** thin	o in lemon
ē equal	**ô** order	**ü** rule	**ŦH** then	u in circus
ėr term			**zh** measure	

and other liquids at rest or in motion, their uses in engineering, and the laws of their actions. *n.*

hydro-, *combining form.* **1** water: *Hydroelectric = (developing) electricity from water (power).* **2** containing hydrogen: *Hydrochloric = containing hydrogen and chlorine.* [The form *hydro-* comes from Greek *hydōr,* meaning "water."]

hy dro car bon (hī′drō kär′bən), any of a class of chemical compounds containing only hydrogen and carbon. Gasoline is a mixture of hydrocarbons. *n.*

hy dro chlo ric acid (hī′drə klôr′ik), a clear, colorless liquid containing hydrogen and chlorine, with a strong, sharp odor. Hydrochloric acid is used in cleaning metals.

hy dro e lec tric (hī′drō i lek′trik), developing electricity from water power. *adj.*

hy dro foil (hī′drə foil), **1** fin just below the water line of a boat that raises the hull out of the water at high speeds, decreasing friction and increasing the speed of the boat. **2** boat with hydrofoils. *n.*

hy dro gen (hī′drə jən), a colorless, odorless gas that burns easily. Hydrogen is a chemical element that weighs less than any other element. It combines with oxygen to form water and is present in most organic compounds. *n.*

hy dro gen ate (hī′drə jə nāt), combine or treat with hydrogen. When vegetable oils are hydrogenated, they become solid fats. *v.,* **hy dro gen at ed, hy dro gen at ing.** —**hy′dro gen a′tion,** *n.*

hydrogen bomb, bomb that uses the fusion of atoms to cause an explosion of tremendous force; H-bomb; fusion bomb. It is many times more powerful than the atomic bomb.

hydrogen peroxide, a colorless compound of hydrogen and oxygen; peroxide. It is used in water solution as an antiseptic and to bleach hair.

hy drol y sis (hī drol′ə sis), a chemical process in which a compound is broken down and changed into other compounds by taking up the elements of water. *n., pl.* **hy drol y ses** (hī drol′ə sēz′).

hy dro lyze (hī′drə līz), break down by hydrolysis. *v.,* **hy dro lyzed, hy dro lyz ing.** —**hy′dro ly za′tion,** *n.*

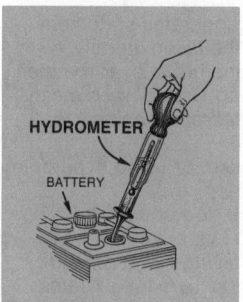

hydrometer being used to test an automobile battery. The amount that the weighted inner glass tube sinks in the liquid indicates the concentration of acid in the battery.

hy drom e ter (hī drom′ə tər), instrument for finding the specific gravity of a liquid. *n.*

hy dro pho bi a (hī′drə fō′bē ə), rabies. *n.*

hy dro plane (hī′drə plān), **1** a fast motorboat that glides on the surface of water. **2** seaplane. *n.*

hy dro pon ics (hī′drə pon′iks), the growing of plants

without soil by the use of water containing the necessary nutrients. *n.*

hy dro sphere (hī′drə sfir), water on the surface of the earth, sometimes also including the water vapor in the atmosphere. *n.*

hy drous (hī′drəs), containing water, usually in combination. *adj.*

hy drox ide (hī drok′sīd), a chemical compound that contains a radical made up of an oxygen and a hydrogen atom. *n.*

hyena
about 2 ft.
(60 cm.) high
at the shoulder

hy e na (hī ē′nə), a wild, flesh-eating, wolflike mammal of Africa and Asia which feeds at night. Hyenas avoid contact with other animals, and are noted for their terrifying yells. *n., pl.* **hy e nas.** [*Hyena* comes from Latin *hyaena,* and can be traced back to Greek *hys,* meaning "pig." The animal was called this because it has bristles on the neck and back like those of a pig.]

hy giene (hī′jēn′), rules of health; science of keeping well. *n.*

hy gien ic (hī jē′nik *or* hī jen′ik), 1 favorable to health; healthful; sanitary. 2 of health or hygiene. *adj.* —**hy-gien′i cal ly,** *adv.*

hy gien ist (hī jē′nist), 1 an expert in hygiene. 2 dental hygienist. *n.*

hy grom e ter (hī grom′ə tər), instrument for measuring the amount of moisture in the air. *n.*

hy ing (hī′ing), hieing; a present participle of **hie.** *v.*

hymn (him), 1 song in praise or honor of God. 2 any song of praise. *n.* —**hymn′like′,** *adj.*

hym nal (him′nəl), book of hymns. *n.*

hymn book (him′bůk′), hymnal. *n.*

hyper-, *prefix.* more than is normal; over; above; extremely; extreme: *Hypersensitive = extremely sensitive.*

hy per ac tive (hī′pər ak′tiv), overactive, especially to an abnormal or unhealthy degree. A **hyperactive child** may have difficulty with concentration, perception, muscular control, etc. *adj.*

hy per bo le (hī pėr′bə lē), an exaggerated statement used for effect and not meant to be taken literally. EXAMPLE: *Waves high as mountains broke over the reef.* *n.* [*Hyperbole* can be traced back to Greek *hyper,* meaning "above, over, beyond," and *ballein,* meaning "to throw."]

hy per bol ic (hī′pər bol′ik), of, like, or using hyperbole; exaggerated; exaggerating. *adj.*

hy per crit i cal (hī′pər krit′ə kəl), too critical. *adj.*

hy per sen si tive (hī′pər sen′sə tiv), extremely sensitive: *He was hypersensitive to the slightest criticism.* *adj.*

hy per sen si tiv i ty (hī′pər sen′sə tiv′ə tē), extreme sensitiveness. *n.*

hy per son ic (hī′pər son′ik), moving or able to move at a speed which is five or more times faster than the speed of sound in air. At sea level, hypersonic speed is at least 5435 feet (1657 meters) per second. *adj.*

hy per ten sion (hī′pər ten′shən), an abnormally high blood pressure. *n.*

hy per tro phy (hī pėr′trə fē), 1 enlargement of a body part or organ. 2 grow too big. 1 *n., pl.* **hy per tro phies,** 2 *v.,* **hy per tro phied, hy per tro phy ing.**

hy phen (hī′fən), 1 mark (-) used to join the parts of a compound word, or the parts of a word divided at the end of a line. 2 hyphenate. 1 *n.,* 2 *v.*

hy phen ate (hī′fə nāt), join by a hyphen; write or print with a hyphen. *v.,* **hy phen at ed, hy phen at ing.**

hy phen a tion (hī′fə nā′shən), act of joining by a hyphen; writing or printing with a hyphen. *n.*

hyp no sis (hip nō′sis), condition resembling deep sleep, but more active, in which a person has little will and sensation, and acts according to the suggestions of the person who brought about the condition. *n., pl.* **hyp no ses** (hip nō′sēz′).

hyp not ic (hip not′ik), 1 of hypnosis. 2 causing sleep. 3 drug or other means of causing sleep. 4 person who is hypnotized or easily hypnotized. 1,2 *adj.,* 3,4 *n.* —**hyp-not′i cal ly,** *adv.*

hyp no tism (hip′nə tiz′əm), 1 a putting into a hypnotic state; a hypnotizing. 2 science dealing with hypnosis. *n.*

hyp no tist (hip′nə tist), person who hypnotizes. *n.*

hyp no tize (hip′nə tīz), 1 put (a person) into a hypnotic state; cause hypnosis in. 2 dominate or control by suggestion; cast a spell over: *The candidate's speech hypnotized her audience.* *v.,* **hyp no tized, hyp no tiz ing.** —**hyp′no tiz′a ble,** *adj.* —**hyp′no tiz′er,** *n.*

hy po[1] (hī′pō), a chemical compound used to treat photographic negatives and prints to keep them from fading. *n., pl.* **hy pos.**

hy po[2] (hī′pō), INFORMAL. hypodermic. *n., pl.* **hy pos.**

hypo-, *prefix.* under; beneath; below: *Hypodermic = under the skin.*

hy po chon dri a (hī′pə kon′drē ə), abnormal anxiety over one's health; imaginary illness. *n.*

hy po chon dri ac (hī′pə kon′drē ak), person who imagines feeling ill, is often depressed, and worries unnecessarily about personal health. *n.*

hy poc ri sy (hi pok′rə sē), 1 a pretending to be very good or religious. 2 a pretending to be what one is not; pretense. *n., pl.* **hy poc ri sies.**

hyp o crite (hip′ə krit), 1 person who pretends to be very good or religious. 2 person who is not sincere; pretender. *n.*

hyp o crit i cal (hip′ə krit′ə kəl), of or like a hypocrite; insincere. *adj.* —**hyp′o crit′i cal ly,** *adv.*

hy po der mic (hī′pə dėr′mik), 1 under the skin. 2 injected or used to inject under the skin: *The doctor used a hypodermic needle.* 3 dose of medicine injected under the skin: *The doctor gave her a hypodermic to make her sleep.* 4 a hypodermic syringe. 1,2 *adj.,* 3,4 *n.* [*Hypodermic* can be traced back to Greek *hypo,* meaning "under," and *derma,* meaning "skin."]

hypodermic syringe, syringe fitted with a hollow needle, used to inject a dose of medicine beneath the skin, or to take out blood or other bodily fluid.

hypodermic syringe

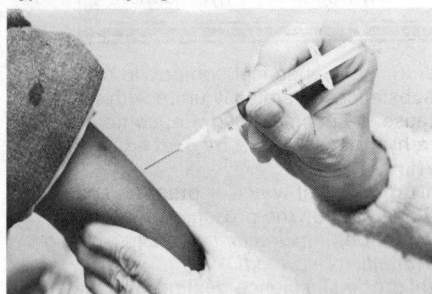

hy po gly ce mi a (hī′pō glī sē′mē ə), a condition caused by a lowered level of sugar in the blood, usually because of the presence of too much insulin. *n.*

hy po ten sion (hī′pō ten′shən), abnormally low blood pressure. *n.*

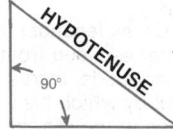

RIGHT ANGLE

hy pot e nuse (hī pot′n üs *or* hī pot′n yüs), the side of a right triangle opposite the right angle. *n.*

hy poth e sis (hī poth′ə sis), something assumed because it seems likely to be a true explanation; theory: *Let us act on the hypothesis that he is honest. n., pl.* **hy poth e ses** (hī poth′ə sēz′).

hy poth e size (hī poth′ə sīz), **1** make a hypothesis. **2** assume; suppose. *v.,* **hy poth e sized, hy poth e sizing.** **—hy poth′e siz′er,** *n.*

hy po thet i cal (hī′pə thet′ə kəl), of or based on a hypothesis; assumed; supposed: *a hypothetical case. adj.*

a hat	i it	oi oil	ch child	a in about
ā age	ī ice	ou out	ng long	e in taken
ä far	o hot	u cup	sh she	ə = i in pencil
e let	ō open	u̇ put	th thin	o in lemon
ē equal	ô order	ü rule	ŦH then	u in circus
ėr term			zh measure	

hys sop (his′əp), **1** a fragrant, bushy plant related to the mint, formerly used for medicine, flavoring, etc. **2** (in the Bible) a plant whose twigs were used in certain religious ceremonies. *n.*

hys ter i a (hi stir′ē ə *or* hi ster′ē ə), **1** a mental illness caused by anxiety or worry. Its physical symptoms may include blindness, paralysis, or stomach upsets. **2** unchecked excitement or emotion. *n.*

hys ter ic (hi ster′ik), hysterical. *adj.*

hys ter i cal (hi ster′ə kəl), **1** unnaturally excited; emotional: *hysterical weeping.* **2** showing an unnatural lack of self-control; suffering from hysteria: *The hysterical child was unable to stop crying.* **3** of or characteristic of hysteria: *a hysterical fit. adj.* **—hys ter′i cal ly,** *adv.*

hys ter ics (hi ster′iks), a fit of hysterical laughing and crying. *n.pl.*

I[1] or **i** (ī), **1** the ninth letter of the English alphabet. **2** the Roman numeral for 1. *n., pl.* **I's** or **i's.**

I[2] (ī), the person speaking or writing: *John said, "I am ten years old." I like my dog. pron., pl.* **we.**

I, symbol for iodine.

i., 1 intransitive. **2** island.

I., 1 Island. **2** Isle.

IA, Iowa (used with postal Zip Code).

Ia., Iowa.

The sun that brief De cem ber day

Rose cheer less o ver hills of gray.

i am bic (ī am′bik), **1** a foot or measure in poetry consisting of two syllables, an unaccented followed by an accented. **2** of or containing iambic measures. Much English poetry is iambic. 1 *n.,* 2 *adj.*

-ian, suffix meaning the same as **-an,** as in *mammalian, Italian,* etc.

I ber i a (ī bir′ē ə), peninsula in SW Europe, containing Spain and Portugal. *n.*

i bex (ī′beks), a wild goat of Europe, Asia, and Africa. The male has very large horns which curve backward. *n., pl.* **i bex es** or **i bex.**

ibid., in the same place; in the same book, chapter, page, etc. Ibid. is used in footnotes to refer to the work previously mentioned.

i bis (ī′bis), a large, long-legged wading bird of warm regions, having a long, downward-curving bill. The ancient Egyptians regarded the ibis as sacred. *n., pl.* **i bis es** or **i bis.**

-ible, *suffix added to verbs to form adjectives.* able to be _____ed: *Perfectible = able to be perfected. Reducible = able to be reduced.*

Ib sen (ib′sən), **Henrik,** 1828-1906, Norwegian dramatist. *n.*

-ic, *suffix added to nouns to form adjectives.* **1** of: *Atmo-*

iceboat
(def. 1)

spheric = of the atmosphere. Icelandic = of Iceland. **2** having the nature of: *Heroic = having the nature of a hero.* **3** containing; made up of: *Alcoholic = containing alcohol.* **4** like; like that of: *Meteoric = like a meteor.* **5** characterized by: *Rhythmic = characterized by rhythm.*

-ical, suffix meaning the same as **-ic,** as in *historical, geometrical, economical.*

Ic ar us (ik′ər əs), (in Greek legends) the son of Daedalus. Icarus and his father escaped from Crete by using wings that Daedalus had made. Icarus flew so high that the sun melted the wax by which his wings were attached, and he drowned in the sea. *n.*

ice (īs), **1** water made solid by cold; frozen water. **2** layer or surface of ice. **3** of ice. **4** something that looks or feels like ice. **5** make cool with ice; put ice in or around: *We iced the punch.* **6** cover with ice. **7** turn to ice; freeze. **8** a frozen dessert, usually one made of sweetened fruit juice. **9** a sugary covering for a cake; icing. **10** cover (cake) with icing. 1,2,4,8,9 *n.,* 3 *adj.,* 5-7,10 *v.,* **iced, ic ing.** [*Ice* comes from Old English *īs.*] —**ice′less,** *adj.* —**ice′like′,** *adj.*

break the ice, overcome first difficulties in talking or getting acquainted.

cut no ice, INFORMAL. have little or no effect.

on thin ice, in a dangerous or difficult position.

ice age, 1 any of the times when much of the earth was covered with glaciers. **2** Usually, **Ice Age.** the most recent such time, when most of the Northern Hemisphere was covered with glaciers.

ice berg (īs′bėrg′), a large mass of ice, detached from a glacier and floating in the sea. About 90 percent of its mass is below the surface of the water. *n.*

WORD HISTORY

iceberg

Iceberg comes from Dutch *ijsberg,* meaning "ice mountain."

ice boat (īs′bōt′), **1** a triangular frame on runners, fitted with sails or an engine for sailing on ice. **2** icebreaker. *n.*

ice bound (īs′bound′), **1** held fast by ice; frozen in. **2** shut in or obstructed by ice. *adj.*

ice box (īs′boks′), **1** refrigerator. **2** an insulated box in which food is kept cool with ice. *n., pl.* **ice box es.**

ice break er (īs′brā′kər), **1** a strong boat used to break a channel through ice; iceboat. **2** anything that helps overcome first difficulties in talking or getting acquainted. *n.*

ice cap (īs′kap′), a permanent covering of ice over an area, sloping down on all sides from an elevated center. *n.*

ice-cold (īs′kōld′), cold as ice. *adj.*

ice cream, a smooth, frozen dessert made of cream or milk, sweetened and flavored.

Ice land (īs′lənd), island country in the N Atlantic between Greenland and Norway, formerly a Danish possession. Iceland has been independent since 1944. *Capital:* Reykjavik. See **Lapland** for map. *n.*

Ice land er (īs′lan′dər), person born or living in Iceland. *n.*

Ice lan dic (īs lan′dik), **1** of Iceland, its people, or their language. **2** language of Iceland. 1 *adj.,* 2 *n.*

ice man (īs′man′), man who sells, delivers, or handles ice. *n., pl.* **ice men.**

ice pack, 1 a large area of masses of ice floating in the sea. **2** bag containing ice for application to the body.

ice pick, a sharp-pointed hand tool for breaking up ice.

ice sheet, a broad, thick sheet of ice covering a very large area for a long time.

ice skate, a shoe with a metal runner attached for skating on ice.

ice-skate (īs′skāt′), skate on ice. *v.,* **ice-skat ed, ice-skat ing.**

ice skater, person who ice-skates.

ice water, water cooled with ice.

ich thy ol o gist (ik′thē ol′ə jist), an expert in ichthyology. *n.*

ich thy ol o gy (ik′thē ol′ə jē), branch of zoology dealing with the study of fishes. *n.*

i ci cle (ī′si kəl), a pointed, hanging stick of ice formed by the freezing of dripping water. *n.* [Icicle is from Middle English *isykle,* which comes from Old English *īs,* meaning "ice," and *gicel,* meaning "icicle."]

i ci ly (ī′sə lē), in an icy manner. *adv.*

i ci ness (ī′sē nis), a being icy. *n.*

ic ing (ī′sing), frosting. *n.*

icon (def. 1)

i con (ī′kon), **1** picture or image of Christ, an angel, or a saint. Icons are sacred in the Eastern Church. **2** picture; image. *n., pl.* **i cons, i co nes** (ī′kə nēz′). Also, **ikon.**

i con o clast (ī kon′ə klast), **1** person who attacks cherished beliefs or institutions. **2** person opposed to worshiping images. *n.*

i con o clas tic (ī kon′ə klas′tik), of iconoclasts. *adj.* —**i con′o clas′ti cal ly,** *adv.*

ic tus (ik′təs), rhythmical or metrical stress. *n., pl.* **ic tus es** or **ic tus.**

i cy (ī′sē), **1** like ice; very cold: *icy fingers.* **2** covered with ice; slippery: *icy streets.* **3** of ice: *an icy snowball.* **4** without warm feeling; cold and unfriendly: *an icy stare. adj.,* **i ci er, i ci est.**

I'd (īd), **1** I should. **2** I would. **3** I had.

ID, Idaho (used with postal Zip Code).

Id., or **Ida.,** Idaho.

I da ho (ī′də hō), one of the western states of the United States. *Abbreviation:* Id., Ida., or ID *Capital:* Boise. *n.* —**I′da ho′an,** *n., adj.*

I.D. card, identification card.

a hat	i it	oi oil	ch child	(a in about
ā age	ī ice	ou out	ng long	e in taken
ä far	o hot	u cup	sh she	ə = { i in pencil
e let	ō open	u̇ put	th thin	o in lemon
ē equal	ô order	ü rule	ŦH then	u in circus
ėr term			zh measure	

i de a (ī dē′ə), **1** belief, plan, or picture in the mind: *Swimming is my idea of fun.* **2** thought, fancy, or opinion: *I had no idea that the job would be so difficult.* **3** point or purpose: *The idea of this vacation was to get a rest. n., pl.* **i de as.** —**i de′a less,** *adj.*

i de al (ī dē′əl), **1** a perfect type; model to be imitated; what one would wish to be: *a person with high ideals. Her mother is her ideal.* **2** just as one would wish; perfect: *A warm, sunny day is ideal for a picnic.* **3** existing only in thought; imaginary. 1 *n.,* 2,3 *adj.* —**i de′al less,** *adj.*

i de al ism (ī dē′ə liz′əm), **1** an acting according to one's ideals of what ought to be, regardless of what happens or of what other people may think; a cherishing of fine ideals. **2** a neglecting practical matters in following ideals; not being practical. **3** belief that reality is made up of ideas only and not of material objects. *n.*

i de al ist (ī dē′ə list), **1** person who has high ideals and acts according to them. **2** person who neglects practical matters in following ideals. *n.*

i de al is tic (ī′dē ə lis′tik or ī dē′ə lis′tik), **1** having high ideals and acting according to them. **2** forgetting or neglecting practical matters in trying to follow out one's ideals; not practical. **3** of idealism or idealists. *adj.* —**i de′al is′ti cal ly,** *adv.*

i de al i za tion (ī dē′ə lə zā′shən), **1** an idealizing or a being idealized. **2** result of idealizing. *n.*

i de al ize (ī dē′ə līz), make ideal; think of or represent as perfect rather than as is actually true: *He idealized his older sister and thought that everything she did was right. v.,* **i de al ized, i de al iz ing.** —**i de′al iz′er,** *n.*

i de al ly (ī dē′ə lē), **1** according to an ideal; perfectly. **2** only as an idea or theory; not really. *adv.*

i den ti cal (ī den′tə kəl), **1** the same: *Both events happened on the identical day.* **2** exactly alike: *identical bicycles. adj.* —**i den′ti cal ly,** *adv.* —**i den′ti cal ness,** *n.*

identical twins, twins of the same sex and physical appearance coming from a single fertilized egg cell rather than from two egg cells as fraternal twins do.

i den ti fi a ble (ī den′tə fī′ə bəl), able to be identified. *adj.* —**i den′ti fi′a bly,** *adv.*

i den ti fi ca tion (ī den′tə fə kā′shən), **1** an identifying or a being identified. **2** something used to identify a person or thing: *He offered his driver's license as identification. n.*

i den ti fy (ī den′tə fī), **1** recognize as being, or show to be, a particular person or thing; prove to be the same: *She identified the wallet as hers by describing it.* **2** make the same; treat as the same: *The king identified his people's good with his own.* **3** connect closely; associate: *identify with a political party. v.,* **i den ti fied, i den ti fy ing.** —**i den′ti fi′er,** *n.*

i den ti ty (ī den′tə tē), **1** a being oneself or itself, and not another; who or what one is: *The writer concealed her identity by signing her stories with a pen name.* **2** a being identical; exact likeness; sameness: *The identity of the two crimes led the police to think that the same person committed them.* **3** state or fact of being the same one: *The museum established the identity of the painting with one described in an old document.* **4** identity element. *n., pl.* **i den ti ties.**

identity element, an element of a set that does not change any other element it is combined with under a specific operation; identity. The identity element for addition is 0. EXAMPLE: 28 + 0 = 28. The identity element for multiplication is 1. EXAMPLE: 28 × 1 = 28.

id e o graph (id′ē ə graf *or* ī′dē ə graf), a graphic symbol that represents a thing or an idea directly, without representing the sounds of the word for the thing or idea. Most Egyptian hieroglyphics and some Chinese characters are ideographs. *n.*

i de o log i cal (ī′dē ə loj′ə kəl *or* id′ē ə loj′ə kəl), having to do with ideology. *adj.* —**i′de o log′i cal ly,** *adv.*

i de ol o gy (ī′dē ol′ə jē *or* id′ē ol′ə jē), set of doctrines or body of opinions that a group of people have. A political party or movement usually has an ideology. *n.,* *pl.* **i de ol o gies.**

ides (īdz), (in the ancient Roman calendar) the 15th day of March, May, July, and October, and the 13th day of the other months. *n. pl. or sing.*

id i o cy (id′ē ə sē), **1** a being an idiot. **2** great stupidity. *n., pl.* **id i o cies.**

id i om (id′ē əm), **1** phrase or expression whose meaning cannot be understood from the ordinary meanings of the words in it. "Hold one's tongue" is an English idiom meaning "keep still." **2** the language or dialect of a particular area or group: *the idiom of the French Canadians.* **3** a people's way of expressing themselves: *It is often hard to translate English into the French idiom. n.*

id i o mat ic (id′ē ə mat′ik), **1** containing an idiom; having or using idioms. **2** showing the individual character of a language; characteristic of a particular language: *The American spoke excellent idiomatic French. adj.* —**id′i-o mat′i cal ly,** *adv.*

id i o syn cra sy (id′ē ō sing′krə sē), a personal peculiarity: *One of his idiosyncrasies was eating a hamburger for breakfast. n., pl.* **id i o syn cra sies.**

id i o syn crat ic (id′ē ō sin krat′ik), of or caused by idiosyncrasy. *adj.* —**id′i o syn crat′i cal ly,** *adv.*

id i ot (id′ē ət), **1** person born with very little mental ability. Idiots never learn to read or count and can do only very simple tasks. **2** a very stupid or foolish person: *Like an idiot I lost my key. n.*

id i ot ic (id′ē ot′ik), very stupid or foolish. *adj.* —**id′i-ot′i cal ly,** *adv.*

i dle (ī′dl), **1** doing nothing; not busy; not working: *the idle hours of a holiday, idle hands.* **2** fond of doing nothing; not willing to work; lazy: *an idle student.* **3** useless; worthless: *to waste time in idle pleasures.* **4** without any good reason: *idle rumors.* **5** be idle; do nothing: *Are you going to spend your whole vacation just idling?* **6** cause (a person or thing) to be idle; take out of work or use: *A strike idled the factory workers.* **7** spend or waste (time): *She idled away many hours lying in the hammock.* **8** run slowly without transmitting power. The motor of a car idles when out of gear and running slowly. 1-4 *adj.,* **i dler, i dlest;** 5-8 *v.,* **i dled, i dling.** —**i′dle ness,** *n.*

i dler (ī′dlər), a lazy person. *n.*

i dly (ī′dlē), in an idle manner. *adv.*

i dol (ī′dl), **1** image or other object worshiped as a god. **2** person or thing that is loved or admired very much. *n.*

i dol a ter (ī dol′ə tər), person who worships idols. *n.*

i dol a tress (ī dol′ə tris), woman who worships idols. *n.,* *pl.* **i dol a tress es.**

i dol a trous (ī dol′ə trəs), **1** worshiping idols. **2** having to do with idolatry. **3** blindly adoring. *adj.* —**i dol′a-trous ly,** *adv.* —**i dol′a trous ness,** *n.*

i dol a try (ī dol′ə trē), **1** worship of idols. **2** worship of a person or thing; extreme devotion: *The queen was adored to the point of idolatry. n., pl.* **i dol a tries.**

i dol ize (ī′dl īz), **1** love or admire very much; be extremely devoted to: *Some baseball fans idolize their favorite players.* **2** worship as an idol; make an idol of: *The*

ancient Hebrews idolized the golden calf. v., **i dol ized, i dol iz ing.** —**i′dol i za′tion,** *n.* —**i′dol iz′er,** *n.*

i dyll or **i dyl** (ī′dl), **1** description in poetry or prose of a simple and charming scene or event of country life. **2** a simple and charming scene or event suitable for such a description. *n.*

idyllic—We visited an **idyllic** French village.

i dyl lic (ī dil′ik), suitable for an idyll; simple and charming. *adj.* —**i dyl′li cal ly,** *adv.*

i.e., that is; that is to say; namely.

if (if), **1** supposing that; on condition that; in case: *Come if you can. If it rains tomorrow, we shall stay at home.* **2** whether: *I wonder if they will go.* **3** although; even though: *It was a welcome if unexpected holiday. conj.*

if fy (if′ē), INFORMAL. having unknown qualities or conditions; doubtful: *an iffy undertaking. adj.,* **if fi er, if fi est.**

igloo—an igloo in northern Canada

ig loo (ig′lü), an Eskimo hut shaped like a dome, often built of blocks of hard snow. *n., pl.* **ig loos.** [*Igloo* comes from Eskimo *igdlu,* meaning "house."]

ig ne ous (ig′nē əs), **1** of fire; having to do with fire. **2** formed by the cooling of melted rock material either within or on the surface of the earth. Granite is an igneous rock. *adj.*

ig nite (ig nīt′), **1** set on fire: *A spark from the campfire ignited the dry grass.* **2** take fire; begin to burn: *Gasoline ignites easily. v.,* **ig nit ed, ig nit ing.** —**ig nit′a ble, ig-nit′i ble,** *adj.* —**ig nit′er,** *n.*

ig ni tion (ig nish′ən), **1** a setting on fire. **2** a catching on fire. **3** apparatus for igniting the fuel vapor in the cylinders of an internal-combustion engine. Spark plugs are part of the ignition of most cars. *n.*

ig no ble (ig nō′bəl), **1** without honor; disgraceful; base: *To betray a friend is ignoble.* **2** not of noble birth or position; humble: *Though of ignoble background, she was the queen's favorite. adj.* —**ig no′ble ness,** *n.*

ig no bly (ig nō′blē), in an ignoble manner. *adv.*

ig no min i ous (ig′nə min′ē əs), shameful; disgraceful; dishonorable: *After an ignominious defeat the army surrendered. adj.* —**ig′no min′i ous ly,** *adv.* —**ig′no-min′i ous ness,** *n.*

ig no min y (ig′nə min′ē), public shame and disgrace; dishonor. *n., pl.* **ig no min ies.**

ig no ra mus (ig′nə rā′məs), an ignorant person. *n., pl.* **ig no ra mus es.** [*Ignoramus* comes from Latin *ignoramus*, meaning "we do not know."]

ig nor ance (ig′nər əns), a being ignorant; lack of knowledge. *n.*

ig nor ant (ig′nər ənt), **1** knowing little or nothing; without knowledge. A person who has not had much chance to learn may be ignorant but not stupid. *People who live in the city are often ignorant of farm life.* **2** caused by or showing lack of knowledge: *Saying that the earth is flat is an ignorant remark.* **3** uninformed; unaware: *He was ignorant of the fact that Paris is the capital of France. adj.* —**ig′nor ant ly,** *adv.*

ig nore (ig nôr′), pay no attention to; disregard: *The driver ignored the traffic light and almost hit another car. v.,* **ig nored, ig nor ing.** —**ig nor′a ble,** *adj.* —**ig nor′er,** *n.*

iguana
about 5 ft.
(1.5 m.) long

i gua na (i gwä′nə), a large tropical American lizard having a spiny crest along its back. *n., pl.* **i gua nas.** [*Iguana* was borrowed from Spanish *iguana,* which came from an Indian word of the Caribbean area.]

i kon (ī′kon), icon. *n.*

il-, *prefix.* form of **in-**[1] before *l,* as in *illegal, illegible,* etc.

IL, Illinois (used with postal Zip Code).

Il i ad (il′ē əd), a Greek epic poem about the siege of Troy. Homer is supposed to be its author. *n.*

Il i um (il′ē əm), ancient Troy. *n.*

ilk (ilk), class; kind; sort: *cattle rustlers, bank robbers, and others of that ilk. n.*

ill (il), **1** in poor health; having some disease; not well; sick: *ill with a fever.* **2** sickness; disease. **3** bad; evil; harmful: *an ill wind, do a person an ill turn.* **4** badly; harmfully: *Strength is ill used in destroying property.* **5** Often, **ills,** *pl.* evil; harm; trouble: *the ills of poverty.* **6** something unfavorable or unkind: *I can think no ill of him.* **7** in an unkind manner; harshly; cruelly: *He speaks ill of his former friend.* **8** with trouble or difficulty; scarcely: *You can ill afford to waste your money.* **1,3** *adj.,* **worse, worst; 2,5,6** *n.,* **4,7,8** *adv.*

ill at ease, uncomfortable.

I'll (īl), **1** I shall. **2** I will.

ill., **1** illustrated. **2** illustration.

Ill., Illinois.

ill-ad vised (il′əd vīzd′), acting or done without enough thought; unwise. *adj.*

ill-bred (il′bred′), badly brought up; impolite; rude. *adj.*

il le gal (i lē′gəl), not lawful; against the law; forbidden by law. *adj.* —**il le′gal ly,** *adv.*

il le gal i ty (il′ē gal′ə tē), **1** a being illegal; unlawfulness. **2** an illegal act. *n., pl.* **il le gal i ties.**

il leg i ble (i lej′ə bəl), very hard or impossible to read; not plain enough to read: *The ink had faded so that many words were illegible. adj.* —**il leg′i ble ness,** *n.*

il leg i bly (i lej′ə blē), in an illegible manner. *adv.*

il le git i mate (il′i jit′ə mit), **1** not according to the law or the rules. **2** born of parents who are not married to each other. *adj.* —**il′le git′i mate ly,** *adv.*

ill-fat ed (il′fā′tid), **1** sure to have a bad fate or end. **2** bringing bad luck; unlucky. *adj.*

ill-fa vored (il′fā′vərd), **1** not pleasant to look at; ugly. **2** unpleasant; offensive. *adj.*

ill feeling, suspicious dislike; mistrust.

ill-got ten (il′got′n), acquired by evil or unfair means; dishonestly obtained. *adj.*

ill-hu mored (il′hyü′mərd), cross; unpleasant. *adj.* —**ill′-hu′mored ly,** *adv.*

il lib er al (i lib′ər əl), **1** not liberal; narrow-minded; prejudiced. **2** stingy; miserly. *adj.* —**il lib′er al ly,** *adv.*

il lic it (i lis′it), not permitted by law; forbidden. *adj.* —**il lic′it ly,** *adv.*

il lim it a ble (i lim′ə tə bəl), without limit; boundless; infinite. *adj.*

Il li nois (il′ə noi′ *or* il′ə noiz′), one of the north central states of the United States. *Abbreviation:* Ill. or IL *Capital:* Springfield. *n.*

il lit er a cy (i lit′ər ə sē), lack of knowledge of how to read and write. *n.*

il lit er ate (i lit′ər it), **1** not knowing how to read and write: *People who have never gone to school are usually illiterate.* **2** person who does not know how to read and write. **3** showing a lack of education: *illiterate writing.* **4** an uneducated person. **1,3** *adj.,* **2,4** *n.* —**il lit′er ate ly,** *adv.*

ill-man nered (il′man′ərd), having or showing bad manners; impolite; rude. *adj.* —**ill′-man′nered ly,** *adv.*

ill-na tured (il′nā′chərd), cross; disagreeable. *adj.* —**ill′na′tured ly,** *adv.*

ill ness (il′nis), an abnormal, unhealthy condition; disease; sickness. *n., pl.* **ill ness es.**

il log i cal (i loj′ə kəl), **1** contrary to the principles of sound reasoning; not logical: *Your illogical behavior worries me.* **2** not reasonable; foolish: *an illogical fear of the dark. adj.* —**il log′i cal ly,** *adv.* —**il log′i cal ness,** *n.*

ill-spent (il′spent′), spent badly; wasted; misspent. *adj.*

ill-starred (il′stärd′), unlucky; unfortunate. *adj.*

ill-tem pered (il′tem′pərd), having or showing a bad temper; often angry or annoyed; cross. *adj.* —**ill′-tem′pered ly,** *adv.*

ill-timed (il′tīmd′), coming at a bad time; not appropriate. *adj.*

ill-treat (il′trēt′), treat badly or cruelly; do harm to; abuse. *v.*

ill-treat ment (il′trēt′mənt), bad or cruel treatment; harm; abuse. *n.*

il lu mi nate (i lü′mə nāt), **1** light up; make bright: *The room was illuminated by four large lamps.* **2** make clear; explain: *Our teacher could illuminate almost any subject we studied.* **3** decorate with lights: *The streets were illuminated for the celebration.* **4** decorate with gold, colors, pictures, and designs. The letters and pages in some old books and manuscripts were illuminated. *v.,* **il lu mi nat ed, il lu mi nat ing.** —**il lu′mi na′tor,** *n.*

il lu mi na tion (i lü′mə nā′shən), **1** an illuminating; a lighting up; a making bright. **2** amount of light; light. **3** a making clear; explanation. **4** decoration with many lights. **5** decoration of letters or pages in books with gold, colors, pictures, and designs. *n.*

a	hat	i	it	oi	oil	ch	child		a in about
ā	age	ī	ice	ou	out	ng	long		e in taken
ä	far	o	hot	u	cup	sh	she	ə =	i in pencil
e	let	ō	open	u̇	put	th	thin		o in lemon
ē	equal	ô	order	ü	rule	ŦH	then		u in circus
ėr	term					zh	measure		

il lu mine (i lü′mən), make bright; illuminate: *A smile illumined his face.* v., **il lu mined, il lu min ing.**

illus., 1 illustrated. 2 illustration.

ill-us age (il′yü′sij), bad, cruel, or unfair treatment. *n.*

ill-use (il′yüz′ *for 1;* il′yüs′ *for 2*), 1 treat badly, cruelly, or unfairly. 2 bad, cruel, or unfair treatment. 1 *v.*, **ill-used, ill-us ing;** 2 *n.*

illusion (def. 1)—an optical illusion. The parallel vertical lines appear to go apart and come together because of the slanted lines.

il lu sion (i lü′zhən), 1 appearance or feeling that misleads because it is not real; thing that deceives by giving a false idea: *The highway gave the illusion of becoming narrower in the distance.* 2 a false notion or belief: *They have the illusion that wealth is the chief source of happiness.* *n.*

il lu sive (i lü′siv), illusory. *adj.* —**il lu′sive ly,** *adv.* —**il lu′sive ness,** *n.*

il lu sor y (i lü′sər ē), due to an illusion; misleading; deceptive. *adj.* —**il lu′sor i ly,** *adv.* —**il lu′sor i ness,** *n.*

il lus trate (il′ə strāt *or* i lus′trāt), 1 make clear or explain by stories, examples, comparisons, etc.: *The way that a pump works is used to illustrate how the heart sends blood around the body.* 2 provide with pictures, diagrams, maps, etc., that explain or decorate: *This book is well illustrated.* *v.*, **il lus trat ed, il lus trat ing.**

il lus tra tion (il′ə strā′shən), 1 picture, diagram, map, etc., used to explain or decorate something. 2 story, example, comparison, etc., used to make clear or explain something: *An apple cut into four equal pieces is a good illustration of what ¼ means.* 3 act or process of illustrating: *Her illustration of how to build a bookcase taught us a lot.* *n.*

il lus tra tive (i lus′trə tiv *or* il′ə strā′tiv), illustrating; used to illustrate; helping to explain: *A good teacher uses many illustrative examples to explain ideas that are hard to understand.* *adj.* —**il lus′tra tive ly,** *adv.*

il lus tra tor (il′ə strā′tər), artist who makes pictures to be used as illustrations. *n.*

il lus tri ous (i lus′trē əs), very famous; great; outstanding: *an illustrious leader.* *adj.* —**il lus′tri ous ly,** *adv.* —**il lus′tri ous ness,** *n.*

ill will, unkind or unfriendly feeling; dislike; spite: *I bear no ill will toward those who defeated me.*

I'm (īm), I am.

im-, *prefix.* form of **in-**¹ before *b, m,* and *p,* as in *imbibe, immoral, impatient.*

im age (im′ij), 1 likeness or copy: *She saw her image in the mirror. She is almost the exact image of her mother.* 2 likeness made of stone, wood, or some other material; statue: *The shelf was full of little images of all sorts of animals.* 3 picture in the mind; idea: *I no longer have a clear image of him.* 4 a comparison, description, or figure of speech that helps the mind to form forceful or beautiful pictures. Poetry often contains images. 5 impression that a person, group, or organization presents to the public. *n.*

im age ry (im′ij rē), 1 pictures formed in the mind; things imagined. 2 comparisons, descriptions, and figures of speech that help the mind to form forceful or beautiful pictures. Poetry often contains imagery. *n.*

i mag i na ble (i maj′ə nə bəl), able to be imagined; possible: *We had the best time imaginable at the party.* *adj.* —**i mag′i na bly,** *adv.*

i mag i nar y (i maj′ə ner′ē), existing only in the imagination; not real: *Elves are imaginary. The equator is an imaginary circle around the earth.* *adj.*

i mag i na tion (i maj′ə nā′shən), 1 power of forming pictures or images in the mind of things not present to the senses. A poet, artist, or inventor must have imagination to create new things or ideas or to combine old ones in new forms. 2 thing imagined; creation of the mind; fancy. *n.*

i mag i na tive (i maj′ə nə tiv), 1 full of imagination; showing imagination: *Fairy tales are imaginative.* 2 having a good imagination; able to imagine well; fond of imagining: *The imaginative child made up stories about life on other planets.* 3 of imagination. *adj.* —**i mag′i na tive ly,** *adv.* —**i mag′i na tive ness,** *n.*

i mag ine (i maj′ən), 1 picture in one's mind; form an image or idea of: *The girl likes to imagine herself a doctor.* 2 suppose; guess: *I cannot imagine what you mean.* *v.*, **i mag ined, i mag in ing.**

i ma go (i mā′gō), insect in the final adult, especially winged, stage. *n., pl.* **i ma gos, i mag i nes** (i maj′ə nēz).

im bal ance (im bal′əns), lack of balance. *n.*

im be cile (im′bə səl), 1 person born with very little mental ability. Imbeciles usually cannot learn to read but can do simple tasks. 2 lacking normal intelligence. 3 a very stupid or foolish person. 4 very stupid or foolish. 1,3 *n.*, 2,4 *adj.* —**im′be cile ly,** *adv.*

im be cil i ty (im′bə sil′ə tē), 1 a being an imbecile. 2 great stupidity. 3 a very stupid or foolish action, remark, etc. *n., pl.* **im be cil i ties.**

im bed (im bed′), embed. *v.*, **im bed ded, im bed ding.**

im bibe (im bīb′), 1 drink in; drink. 2 absorb. 3 take into one's mind: *A student imbibes a great deal of information during a school term.* *v.*, **im bibed, im bib ing.** —**im bib′er,** *n.*

im bro glio (im brō′lyō), 1 a complicated or difficult situation. 2 a complicated misunderstanding or disagreement. *n., pl.* **im bro glios.** [*Imbroglio* was borrowed from Italian *imbroglio.*]

im bue (im byü′), 1 fill the mind of; inspire: *They imbued their child with the ambition to succeed.* 2 fill with moisture or color; saturate or dye. *v.*, **im bued, im bu ing.**

imit., 1 imitation. 2 imitative.

im i tate (im′ə tāt), 1 try to be like or act like; follow the example of: *The little boy imitated his older brother.* 2 make or do something like; copy: *A parrot imitates the sounds it hears.* 3 act like; make fun of by acting like: *She amused the class by imitating a duck, a monkey, and a bear.* 4 be like; look like; resemble: *Wood is sometimes painted to imitate stone.* *v.*, **im i tat ed, im i tat ing.**

im i ta tion (im′ə tā′shən), 1 an imitating: *We learn many things by imitation.* 2 thing that imitates something else; likeness; copy: *Give as good an imitation as you can of a rooster crowing.* 3 made to look like something better; not real: *The imitation diamond was made of glass.* 1,2 *n.*, 3 *adj.*

im i ta tive (im′ə tā′tiv), 1 fond of imitating; likely to imitate others: *Monkeys are imitative.* 2 imitating; showing imitation: *"Whiz" is an imitative word.* *adj.* —**im′i ta′tive ly,** *adv.* —**im′i ta′tive ness,** *n.*

im i ta tor (im′ə tā′tər), person who imitates. *n.*

im mac u late (i mak′yə lit), 1 without a spot or stain; absolutely clean: *The newly washed shirts were immaculate.* 2 without sin; pure. *adj.* —**im mac′u late ly,** *adv.* —**im mac′u late ness,** *n.*

Im man u el (i man′yü əl), Christ. *n.* Also, **Emmanuel.**

im ma ter i al (im′ə tir′ē əl), 1 not important; insignificant: *This error is immaterial.* **2** not material; spiritual rather than physical. *adj.* —**im′ma ter′i al ly,** *adv.* —**im′ma ter′i al ness,** *n.*

im ma ture (im′ə chùr′, im′ə tùr′, *or* im′ə tyùr′), not mature; undeveloped. *adj.* —**im′ma ture′ly,** *adv.*

im ma tur i ty (im′ə chùr′ə tē, im′ə tùr′ə tē, *or* im′ə-tyùr′ə tē), immature condition or quality. *n.*

im meas ur a ble (i mezh′ər ə bəl), too large to be measured; very great; boundless: *the immeasurable vastness of the universe. She has immeasurable confidence in herself.* *adj.*

im meas ur a bly (i mezh′ər ə blē), beyond measure; to an extent too great to be measured: *They helped me immeasurably.* *adv.*

im me di a cy (i mē′dē ə sē), a being immediate. *n.*

im me di ate (i mē′dē it), **1** coming at once; without delay: *Please send an immediate reply.* **2** with nothing in between; direct: *Things that are touching are in immediate contact.* **3** closest; nearest; next: *Your immediate neighbors live next door.* **4** close; near: *I expect an answer today, tomorrow, or in the immediate future.* **5** having to do with the present; current: *What are your immediate plans? adj.*

im me di ate ly (i mē′dē it lē), **1** at once; without delay: *I answered his letter immediately.* **2** with nothing in between; directly. *adv.*

im me mo ri al (im′ə môr′ē əl), extending back beyond the bounds of memory; extremely old. *adj.* —**im′me-mo′ri al ly,** *adv.*

im mense (i mens′), **1** very large; huge; vast: *An ocean is an immense body of water.* **2** INFORMAL. very good; fine; excellent. *adj.* —**im mense′ness,** *n.*

im mense ly (i mens′lē), very greatly: *We enjoyed the party immensely.* *adv.*

im men si ty (i men′sə tē), **1** very great size or extent; vastness: *the ocean's immensity.* **2** infinite space or existence; infinity. *n., pl.* **im men si ties.**

im merse (i mèrs′), **1** dip or lower into a liquid until covered by it: *I immersed my aching feet in a bucket of hot water.* **2** baptize by dipping (a person) completely under water. **3** involve deeply; absorb: *The young pianist immersed herself in practice seven days a week.* *v.,* **im-mersed, im mers ing.**

im mer sion (i mèr′zhən *or* i mèr′shən), **1** an immersing or a being immersed. **2** baptism by dipping a person completely under water. *n.*

im mi grant (im′ə grənt), person who comes into a country or region to live there: *Canada has many immigrants from Europe. n.*

im mi grate (im′ə grāt), come into a country or region to live there. *v.,* **im mi grat ed, im mi grat ing.**

im mi gra tion (im′ə grā′shən), **1** a coming into a country or region to live there: *There has been immigration to America from many countries.* **2** the persons who immigrate; immigrants: *The immigration of 1956 included many people from Hungary. n.*

im mi nence (im′ə nəns), a being imminent. *n.*

im mi nent (im′ə nənt), likely to happen soon; about to occur: *The black clouds show that a storm is imminent. adj.* —**im′mi nent ly,** *adv.*

im mo bile (i mō′bəl), **1** not movable; firmly fixed. **2** not moving; not changing; motionless. *adj.*

im mo bil i ty (im′ō bil′ə tē), a being immobile. *n.*

im mo bi li za tion (i mō′bə lə zā′shən), a making immobile. *n.*

im mo bi lize (i mō′bə līz), make immobile. *v.,* **im mo bi-lized, im mo bi liz ing.**

im mod er ate (i mod′ər it), not moderate; going too far; extreme; more than is proper: *A fanatic has immoderate ideas. adj.* —**im mod′er ate ly,** *adv.* —**im mod′er ate-ness,** *n.* —**im mod′e ra′tion,** *n.*

a hat	**i** it	**oi** oil	**ch** child	a in about
ā age	**ī** ice	**ou** out	**ng** long	e in taken
ä far	**o** hot	**u** cup	**sh** she	ə = { i in pencil
e let	**ō** open	**ù** put	**th** thin	o in lemon
ē equal	**ô** order	**ü** rule	**ŦH** then	u in circus
ėr term			**zh** measure	

im mod est (i mod′ist), **1** not modest; bold and rude. **2** indecent; improper. *adj.* —**im mod′est ly,** *adv.*

im mod es ty (i mod′ə stē), **1** lack of modesty; boldness and rudeness. **2** lack of decency; improper behavior. *n.*

im mo late (im′ə lāt), **1** kill as a sacrifice. **2** offer in sacrifice. *v.,* **im mo lat ed, im mo lat ing.** —**im′mo la′tion,** *n.* —**im′mo la′tor,** *n.*

im mo ral (i môr′əl), **1** morally wrong; wicked: *Stealing is immoral.* **2** lewd; unchaste. *adj.* —**im mo′ral ly,** *adv.*

im mo ral i ty (im′ə ral′ə tē), **1** wickedness; wrongdoing; vice. **2** lewdness; lack of chastity. **3** an immoral act or practice. *n., pl.* **im mo ral i ties.**

im mor tal (i môr′tl), **1** living forever; never dying; everlasting: *Most religions teach that the soul is immortal.* **2** an immortal being. **3** remembered or famous forever: *A great hero is immortal.* **4** person remembered or famous forever: *Shakespeare is one of the immortals.* **1,3** *adj.,* **2,4** *n.* —**im mor′tal ly,** *adv.*

im mor tal i ty (im′ôr tal′ə tē), **1** life without death; a living forever. **2** fame that lasts forever. *n.*

im mor tal ize (i môr′tl īz), **1** make immortal. **2** cause to be remembered or famous forever: *Great authors are immortalized by their works. v.,* **im mor tal ized, im mor-tal iz ing.** —**im mor′tal i za′tion,** *n.* —**im mor′tal-iz′er,** *n.*

im mov a ble (i mü′və bəl), **1** not able to be moved; firmly fixed: *immovable mountains.* **2** not moving or changing; motionless. **3** firm; steadfast; unyielding: *She was immovable in her beliefs. adj.* —**im mov′a ble ness,** *n.*

im mov a bly (i mü′və blē), in an immovable manner. *adv.*

im mune (i myün′), **1** protected from disease, poison, etc.; having immunity: *Vaccination makes a person practically immune to polio.* **2** free; exempt: *immune from taxes. Nobody is immune from criticism. adj.* [*Immune* comes from Latin *immunis,* meaning "free from duties or obligations."]

immune system, system of antibodies and special white blood cells in a person or animal that recognize, attack, and destroy germs and other foreign material that enter the body.

im mu ni ty (i myü′nə tē), **1** resistance to disease, poison, etc.: *One attack of measles usually gives a person immunity to that disease.* **2** freedom; exemption: *The law gives schools and churches immunity from taxation. n., pl.* **im mu ni ties.**

im mu ni za tion (im′yə nə zā′shən), an immunizing or a being immunized. *n.*

im mu nize (im′yə nīz), protect from disease, poison, etc.; give immunity to; make immune: *Vaccination immunizes people against smallpox. v.,* **im mu nized, im mu niz-ing.** —**im′mu niz′er,** *n.*

im mu nol o gy (im′yə nol′ə jē), science dealing with the nature and causes of immunity from diseases. *n.*

im mure (i myùr′), shut up within walls; put in prison; confine. *v.,* **im mured, im mur ing.**

im mu ta ble (i myü′tə bəl), never changing; not changeable. *adj.* —**im mu′ta ble ness,** *n.*

im mu ta bly (i myü′tə blē), in an immutable manner. *adv.*

imp (imp), **1** a young or small devil or demon. **2** a mischievous child. *n.*

im pact (im′pakt), **1** a striking (of one thing against another); collision: *The impact of the heavy stone against the windowpane shattered the glass.* **2** a forceful or dramatic effect: *Her speech had a great impact on the audience.* *n.* —**im pac′tion,** *n.*

im pact ed (im pak′tid), **1** firmly wedged in place. **2** (of a tooth) wedged between the jawbone and another tooth. *adj.*

im pair (im per′ *or* im par′), make worse; damage; harm; weaken: *Poor eating habits impaired his health.* *v.* —**im pair′er,** *n.*

im pair ment (im per′mənt *or* im par′mənt), **1** an impairing or a being impaired. **2** injury; damage. *n.*

im pale (im pāl′), **1** pierce through with anything pointed; fasten upon anything pointed: *The dead butterflies were impaled on pins stuck in a sheet of cork.* **2** torture or punish by thrusting upon a pointed stake. *v.,* **im paled, im pal ing.** —**im pale′ment,** *n.* —**im pal′er,** *n.*

im pal pa ble (im pal′pə bəl), **1** not able to be felt by touching; intangible: *Color is impalpable.* **2** very hard to understand; not able to be grasped by the mind: *The impalpable distinctions in your argument only confuse me.* *adj.* —**im pal′pa bly,** *adv.*

im pan el (im pan′l), **1** put on a list for duty on a jury. **2** select (a jury) from the list. *v.* Also, **empanel.**

im part (im pärt′), **1** give a part or share of; give: *The new furnishings imparted an air of newness to the old house.* **2** communicate; tell: *They imparted the news of their engagement to their families.* *v.* —**im part′ment,** *n.*

im par tial (im pär′shəl), showing no more favor to one side than to the other; fair; just: *A judge should be impartial.* *adj.* —**im par′tial ly,** *adv.* —**im par′tial ness,** *n.*

im par ti al i ty (im′pär shē al′ə tē), fairness; justice. *n.*

im pass a ble (im pas′ə bəl), not passable; not able to be traveled over or across: *Snow and ice made the road impassable.* *adj.* —**im pass′a ble ness,** *n.* —**im pass′a bly,** *adv.*

im passe (im′pas), position from which there is no escape; deadlock. *n.*

im pas sioned (im pash′ənd), full of strong feeling; stirring; rousing: *She gave an impassioned speech in favor of equal rights for all people.* *adj.* —**im pas′sioned ly,** *adv.*

im pas sive (im pas′iv), **1** without feeling or emotion; unmoved: *Her face was impassive when we told her the news.* **2** not feeling pain or injury; insensible: *The injured man lay as impassive as if he were dead.* *adj.* —**im pas′sive ly,** *adv.* —**im pas′sive ness,** *n.*

im pa tience (im pā′shəns), **1** lack of patience; being impatient. **2** uneasiness and eagerness; restlessness. *n.*

im pa tient (im pā′shənt), **1** not patient; not willing to put up with delay, opposition, pain, bother, etc.: *She is impatient with her little sister.* **2** uneasy and eager; restless: *The horses are impatient to start the race.* **3** showing lack of patience; cross: *an impatient answer.* *adj.* —**im pa′tient ly,** *adv.* —**im pa′tient ness,** *n.*

im peach (im pēch′), **1** accuse (a public official) of wrong conduct during office before a competent tribunal: *The judge was impeached for taking a bribe.* **2** charge with wrongdoing; accuse. **3** cast doubt on; call in question: *impeach a person's honor.* *v.* —**im peach′a ble,** *adj.*

im peach ment (im pēch′mənt), **1** an impeaching: *The impeachment of the dishonest judge resulted in a verdict of "Guilty."* **2** a being impeached: *The verdict resulting from his impeachment destroyed his political career.* *n.*

im pec ca ble (im pek′ə bəl), faultless: *impeccable manners.* *adj.*

im pec ca bly (im pek′ə blē), faultlessly. *adv.*

im pe cu ni ous (im′pi kyü′nē əs), having little or no money; poor. *adj.* —**im′pe cu′ni ous ly,** *adv.*

impede

Impede is from Latin *impedire,* meaning "impede, entangle," which comes from *in-,* meaning "on," and *pedem,* meaning "foot." Something "on the foot" tends to hinder a person.

im pede (im pēd′), hinder; obstruct: *The deep snow impeded travel.* *v.,* **im ped ed, im ped ing.** [See **Word History.**] —**im ped′er,** *n.* —**im ped′ing ly,** *adv.*

im ped i ment (im ped′ə mənt), **1** hindrance; obstacle. **2** defect in speech: *Stuttering is a speech impediment.* *n.*

im pel (im pel′), **1** drive or force; cause: *The cold impelled her to go indoors.* **2** cause to move; drive forward; push along: *Wind and tide impelled the boat toward the shore.* *v.,* **im pelled, im pel ling.** —**im pel′ler,** *n.*

im pend (im pend′), **1** be likely to happen soon; be about to happen: *Black clouds are signs that a storm impends.* **2** hang threateningly; hang: *Great boulders impended over the narrow mountain path.* *v.*

im pend ing (im pen′ding), **1** likely to happen soon; threatening; about to occur: *an impending storm.* **2** overhanging: *Above her were impending cliffs.* *adj.*

im pen e tra bil i ty (im pen′ə trə bil′ə tē), a being impenetrable. *n.*

im pen e tra ble (im pen′ə trə bəl), **1** not able to be penetrated; so that one cannot get into or through: *The thorny branches made a thick, impenetrable hedge.* **2** that cannot be seen into or understood; impossible to explain or understand: *His sudden disappearance was hidden in an impenetrable mystery.* *adj.* —**im pen′e tra ble ness,** *n.*

im pen e tra bly (im pen′ə trə blē), in an impenetrable manner. *adv.*

im pen i tence (im pen′ə təns), lack of any sorrow or regret for doing wrong. *n.*

im pen i tent (im pen′ə tənt), not penitent; feeling no sorrow or regret for having done wrong. *adj.* —**im pen′i tent ly,** *adv.*

im per a tive (im per′ə tiv), **1** not to be avoided; urgent; necessary: *It is imperative that this very sick child should stay in bed.* **2** command: *The dog trainer issued sharp imperatives to the dog.* **3** (in grammar) having to do with a verb form which expresses a command, request, or advice. **4** form of a verb which expresses this. In "Try to be quiet" and "Make up your mind," *try* and *make* are imperatives. **5** mood of such a verb. 1,3 *adj.,* 2,4,5 *n.* —**im per′a tive ly,** *adv.* —**im per′a tive ness,** *n.*

impeccable—Their attire was **impeccable.**

im per cep ti ble (im/pər sep/tə bəl), not able to be perceived or felt; very slight; gradual: *There were imperceptible differences between the original painting and the copy.* *adj.*

im per cep ti bly (im/pər sep/tə blē), in an imperceptible manner. *adv.*

imperf., imperfect.

im per fect (im pėr/fikt), **1** not perfect; having some defect or fault: *A crack in the cup made it imperfect.* **2** not complete; lacking some part. **3** (in grammar) expressing incompleted, continued, or customary action in the past. English has no imperfect tense, but such constructions as *was studying* and *used to study* are like the imperfect verbs of other languages. *adj.* —**im per/fect ly,** *adv.* —**im per/fect ness,** *n.*

im per fec tion (im/pər fek/shən), **1** lack of perfection; imperfect condition or character. **2** fault; defect. *n.*

im per i al (im pir/ē əl), **1** of an empire or its ruler: *the imperial palace.* **2** having to do with the rule or authority of one country over other countries and colonies: *England had imperial power over many other countries.* **3** having the rank of an emperor. **4** supreme; majestic; magnificent. **5** of larger size or better quality. **6** a small, pointed beard growing beneath the lower lip. 1-5 *adj.,* 6 *n.* —**im per/i al ly,** *adv.*

im per i al ism (im pir/ē ə liz/əm), **1** policy of extending the rule or authority of one country over other countries and colonies. **2** an imperial system of government. *n.*

im per i al ist (im pir/ē ə list), person who favors imperialism. *n.*

im per i al is tic (im pir/ē ə lis/tik), **1** of imperialism or imperialists. **2** favoring imperialism. *adj.* —**im per/i al is/ti cal ly,** *adv.*

im per il (im per/əl), put in danger: *Children who play with matches imperil their lives.* *v.*

im per i ous (im pir/ē əs), **1** haughty or arrogant; domineering; overbearing: *The nobles treated the common people in an imperious way.* **2** not to be avoided; necessary; urgent: *the imperious demands of hunger.* *adj.* —**im per/i ous ly,** *adv.* —**im per/i ous ness,** *n.*

im per ish a ble (im per/i shə bəl), not perishable; unable to be destroyed; lasting forever; enduring. *adj.* —**im per/ish a ble ness,** *n.* —**im per/ish a bly,** *adv.*

im per ma nent (im pėr/mə nənt), not permanent; temporary. *adj.* —**im per/ma nent ly,** *adv.*

im per me a ble (im per/mē ə bəl), not allowing the passage of water, gas, etc.: *Gas masks are only impermeable to certain kinds of gas.* *adj.* —**im per/me a ble ness,** *n.* —**im per/me a bly,** *adv.*

im per son al (im pėr/sə nəl), **1** not referring to any one person in particular; not personal: *History is usually written from an impersonal point of view.* **2** having no existence as a person: *Electricity is an impersonal force.* **3** (of a verb) not requiring a subject or having indefinite *it* for a subject. EXAMPLE: *rained* in "It rained yesterday." *adj.* —**im per/son al ly,** *adv.*

im per son ate (im pėr/sə nāt), **1** play the part of: *We impersonated Pilgrims in the school play.* **2** pretend to be; mimic the voice, appearance, and manners of: *He impersonated several of his favorite TV stars to amuse us.* *v.,* **im per son at ed, im per son at ing.**

im per son a tion (im pėr/sə nā/shən), an impersonating: *The entertainer gave an impersonation of a famous movie actor.* *n.*

im per son a tor (im pėr/sə nā/tər), **1** person who pretends to be someone else. **2** actor who impersonates particular persons or types; professional mimic. *n.*

im per ti nence (im pėrt/n əns), **1** boldness and rudeness; impudence; insolence. **2** an impertinent act or speech. **3** lack of pertinence; irrelevance. *n.*

a hat	**i** it	**oi** oil	**ch** child	
ā age	**ī** ice	**ou** out	**ng** long	a in about
ä far	**o** hot	**u** cup	**sh** she	e in taken
e let	**ō** open	**u̇** put	**th** thin	ə = i in pencil
ē equal	**ô** order	**ü** rule	**ᴛʜ** then	o in lemon
ėr term			**zh** measure	u in circus

im per ti nent (im pėrt/n ənt), **1** rudely bold; impudent; insolent: *Talking back to older people is impertinent.* **2** not pertinent; not to the point; out of place: *His impertinent remarks wasted valuable time.* *adj.* —**im per/ti nent ly,** *adv.* —**im per/ti nent ness,** *n.*

im per turb a ble (im/pər tér/bə bəl), not easily excited or disturbed; calm. *adj.* —**im/per turb/a ble ness,** *n.*

im per turb a bly (im/pər tér/bə blē), in an imperturbable manner. *adv.*

im per vi ous (im pėr/vē əs), **1** not able to be penetrated; allowing no passage: *A coat made of rubber or vinyl is impervious to rain.* **2** not open to argument, suggestions, etc.: *Because they were impervious to our hints, we finally told them it was time to go.* *adj.* —**im per/vi ous ly,** *adv.* —**im per/vi ous ness,** *n.*

im pe ti go (im/pə tī/gō), an infectious skin disease characterized by pimples filled with pus. *n.*

im pet u os i ty (im pech/ü os/ə tē), **1** sudden or rash energy; hastiness: *The impetuosity of her temper got her into many arguments.* **2** rushing force or violence: *The impetuosity of the flood destroyed everything in its path.* *n.*

im pet u ous (im pech/ü əs), **1** acting or done with sudden or rash energy; hasty: *He was so angry that he made an impetuous decision.* **2** rushing with force and violence: *The dam broke and an impetuous torrent of water swept over the valley.* *adj.* —**im pet/u ous ly,** *adv.* —**im pet/u ous ness,** *n.*

im pe tus (im/pə təs), **1** the force with which a moving body tends to maintain its velocity and overcome resistance: *the impetus of a moving automobile. Anything that you can stop easily has little impetus.* **2** a driving force; cause of action or effort; incentive: *Ambition is an impetus to work for success.* *n., pl.* **im pe tus es.** [*Impetus* is from Latin *impetus*, meaning "rapid motion, attack," which comes from *in-*, meaning "in," and *petere*, meaning "aim for."]

im pi e ty (im pī/ə tē), **1** lack of piety or reverence for God. **2** an impious act. *n., pl.* **im pi e ties.**

im pinge (im pinj/), **1** hit; strike: *Rays of light impinge on the eye.* **2** trespass; encroach. *v.,* **im pinged, im ping ing.** —**im pinge/ment,** *n.* —**im ping/er,** *n.*

im pi ous (im/pē əs *or* im pī/əs), not pious; not having or not showing reverence for God. *adj.* —**im/pi ous ly,** *adv.* —**im/pi ous ness,** *n.*

imp ish (imp/ish), **1** of or like an imp. **2** mischievous. *adj.* —**imp/ish ly,** *adv.* —**imp/ish ness,** *n.*

im pla ca ble (im plā/kə bəl *or* im plak/ə bəl), unable to be appeased; refusing to be reconciled; unyielding: *The new nation was constantly threatened by its implacable enemies.* *adj.* —**im pla/ca ble ness,** *n.*

im pla ca bly (im plā/kə blē *or* im plak/ə blē), in an implacable manner. *adv.*

im plant (im plant/), **1** instill; fix deeply: *A good teacher implants high ideals in children.* **2** insert: *a steel tube implanted in a socket.* **3** set in the ground; plant. **4** graft or set (a piece of skin, bone, etc.) into the body. *v.* —**im/plan ta/tion,** *n.* —**im plant/er,** *n.*

im plau si ble (im plô/zə bəl), not plausible; not having the appearance of truth or reason. *adj.* —**im plau/si bly,** *adv.*

im ple ment (im/plə mənt *for 1;* im/plə ment *for 2,3*), **1** a useful piece of equipment; tool; instrument; utensil.

Plows and threshing machines are farm implements. An ax, a shovel, and a broom are implements. **2** provide with implements or other means. **3** carry out; get done: *Do not undertake a project unless you can implement it.* 1 *n.,* 2,3 *v.* [*Implement* comes from Latin *implementum,* meaning "that which fills a need."] —**im′ple ment′er,** *n.*

im ple men ta tion (im′plə men tā′shən), an implementing; a carrying out: *the implementation of a program. n.*

im pli cate (im′plə kāt), show to have a part or to be connected; involve: *She confessed to taking part in the theft and implicated two other students. v.,* **im pli cat ed, im pli cat ing.**

im pli ca tion (im′plə kā′shən), **1** an implying or a being implied. **2** something implied; indirect suggestion; hint: *She did not actually refuse, but the way that she frowned was an implication of her unwillingness.* **3** an implicating or a being implicated. *n.*

im plic it (im plis′it), **1** meant, but not clearly expressed; implied: *Her opposition to the present tax laws was implicit in her speech on tax reform.* **2** without doubting, hesitating, or asking questions; absolute: *He had implicit confidence in his friend. adj.* —**im plic′it ness,** *n.*

im plic it ly (im plis′it lē), **1** unquestioningly. **2** by implication. *adv.*

im plore (im plôr′), **1** beg earnestly for: *The prisoner implored pardon.* **2** beg (a person) to do something: *I implored my parents to let me go on the trip. v.,* **im plored, im plor ing.** —**im plor′er,** *n.* —**im plor′ing ly,** *adv.*

WORD HISTORY

implore

Implore is from Latin *implorare,* which comes from *in-,* meaning "toward," and *plorare,* meaning "to cry."

im ply (im plī′), mean without saying so; express indirectly; suggest: *The teacher's smile implied that she had forgiven us. v.,* **im plied, im ply ing.**

im po lite (im′pə līt′), not polite; having or showing bad manners; rude; discourteous. *adj.* —**im′po lite′ly,** *adv.* —**im′po lite′ness,** *n.*

im port (im pôrt′ *or* im′pôrt *for 1,4;* im′pôrt *for 2,3,5,6*), **1** bring in from a foreign country for sale or use: *The United States imports coffee from Brazil.* **2** article imported: *Rubber is a useful import.* **3** act or fact of importing; importation: *The import of diseased animals was forbidden.* **4** mean; signify: *Tell me what your remark imports.* **5** meaning; significance: *Explain your remark; I do not understand its import.* **6** importance; consequence: *matters of great import.* 1,4 *v.,* 2,3,5,6 *n.* —**im port′a ble,** *adj.*

im por tance (im pôrt′ns), a being important; consequence; value; significance: *Anybody can see the importance of good health. n.*

im por tant (im pôrt′nt), **1** meaning or mattering much; worth noticing or considering; having value or significance: *important business, an important occasion.* **2** having social position or influence: *Our mayor is an important person in our town.* **3** acting as if important; seeming to be important: *He ran around giving orders in an important manner. adj.* —**im por′tant ly,** *adv.*

im por ta tion (im′pôr tā′shən), **1** an importing; bringing in merchandise from foreign countries. **2** thing imported: *This pottery is a recent importation from Mexico. n.*

im port er (im pôr′tər *or* im′pôr tər), person or company whose business is importing goods. *n.*

im por tu nate (im pôr′chə nit), asking repeatedly; annoyingly persistent; urgent. *adj.* —**im por′tu nate ly,** *adv.* —**im por′tu nate ness,** *n.*

im por tune (im′pôr tün′ *or* im′pôr tyün′), ask urgently or repeatedly; annoy with pressing demands. *v.,* **im por tuned, im por tun ing.**

im por tu ni ty (im′pôr tü′nə tē *or* im′pôr tyü′nə tē), urgent or repeated asking; act of demanding again and again. *n., pl.* **im por tu ni ties.**

im pose (im pōz′), **1** put (a burden, tax, or punishment) on: *The judge imposed fines on each guilty person.* **2** force or thrust one's authority or influence on another or others. **3** force or thrust (oneself or one's company) on another or others; obtrude; presume. **4** palm off (something upon a person) to deceive. *v.,* **im posed, im pos ing.** —**im pos′a ble,** *adj.* —**im pos′er,** *n.*

impose on *or* **impose upon,** **1** take advantage of; use for selfish purposes: *Do not let them impose on you.* **2** deceive; cheat; trick.

imposing
Their home was an **imposing** structure.

im pos ing (im pō′zing), impressive because of size, appearance, dignity, etc. *adj.* —**im pos′ing ly,** *adv.*

im po si tion (im′pə zish′ən), **1** act of putting (a burden, tax, or punishment) on: *protest the imposition of heavy taxes.* **2** a burden, tax, or punishment. **3** an unfair burden, tax, or punishment. **4** an imposing by taking advantage of a person's good nature: *Would it be an imposition to ask her to mail this parcel?* **5** deception; fraud; trick. *n.*

im pos si bil i ty (im pos′ə bil′ə tē), **1** a being impossible: *We all realize the impossibility of living long without food.* **2** something impossible. *n., pl.* **im pos si bil i ties.**

im pos si ble (im pos′ə bəl), **1** not capable of being, being done, or happening; not possible: *It is impossible for two and two to be six.* **2** not possible to use; not to be done: *He proposed an impossible plan.* **3** known to be not possible; known to be untrue: *an impossible story.* **4** not possible to endure; very objectionable: *an impossible person. He said a summer without swimming would be impossible. adj.*

im pos si bly (im pos′ə blē), in an impossible manner. *adv.*

im post (im′pōst), a tax or duty, especially on goods brought into a country: *There is an impost on wool imported from other countries. n.*

im pos tor (im pos′tər), person who pretends to be someone else in order to deceive or defraud others. *n.*

im pos ture (im pos′chər), deception; fraud. *n.*

im po tence (im′pə təns), lack of power; helplessness; condition or quality of being impotent: *The government was overthrown because of its impotence when the crisis arose. n.*

im po ten cy (im′pə tən sē), impotence. *n.*

im po tent (im′pə tənt), not having power; helpless: *We were impotent against the force of the tornado. adj.* —**im′po tent ly,** *adv.*

im pound (im pound′), **1** shut up in a pen or pound: *The town impounds stray animals.* **2** enclose or confine within limits: *A dam impounds water.* **3** put in the custody of a court of law: *The court impounded the documents to use as evidence.* *v.* —**im pound'a ble,** *adj.* —**im pound'er,** *n.*

im pov er ish (im pov'ər ish), **1** make very poor: *A long war had impoverished the nation's treasury.* **2** exhaust the strength, richness, or resources of: *Careless farming impoverished the soil.* *v.* —**im pov'er ish er,** *n.*

im pov er ish ment (im pov'ər ish mənt), **1** an impoverishing or a being impoverished. **2** something that impoverishes. *n.*

im prac ti ca bil i ty (im prak'tə kə bil'ə tē), **1** a being impracticable. **2** something impracticable. *n.,* *pl.* **im prac ti ca bil i ties.**

im prac ti ca ble (im prak'tə kə bəl), not able to be done without greater difficulty, expense, etc., than is wise or sensible; impossible to put into practice: *impracticable suggestions.* *adj.*

im prac ti ca bly (im prak'tə kə blē), in an impracticable manner. *adv.*

im prac ti cal (im prak'tə kəl), **1** not practical; having to do with theory rather than actual practice; not useful. **2** not having good sense. *adj.* —**im prac'ti cal ly,** *adv.*

im pre ca tion (im'prə kā'shən), a curse: *The gardener shouted imprecations at the stray dogs.* *n.*

im pre cise (im'pri sīs'), not precise; lacking precision; inaccurate. *adj.* —**im'pre cise'ly,** *adv.* —**im'pre cise'ness,** *n.*

im preg na ble (im preg'nə bəl), able to resist attack; not yielding to force, persuasion, etc.: *an impregnable fortress, an impregnable argument.* *adj.* —**im preg'na bly,** *adv.*

im preg nate (im preg'nāt), **1** make pregnant; fertilize. **2** spread through the whole of; fill; saturate: *Seawater is impregnated with salt.* *v.,* **im preg nat ed, im preg nat ing.** —**im preg'na tor,** *n.*

im preg na tion (im'preg nā'shən), an impregnating or a being impregnated. *n.*

im pre sa ri o (im'prə sär'ē ō), the organizer, director, or manager of a concert tour, an opera or ballet company, etc. *n.,* *pl.* **im pre sa ri os.** [*Impresario* was borrowed from Italian *impresario,* which comes from *impresa,* meaning "undertaking."]

im press[1] (im pres' *for 1-4;* im'pres *for 5*), **1** have a strong effect on the mind or feelings of; influence deeply: *The movie impressed those who saw it.* **2** fix firmly in the mind: *She repeated the words to impress them in her memory.* **3** make marks on by pressing or stamping: *impress wax with a seal.* **4** to imprint; stamp. **5** a mark made by pressing or stamping. **1-4** *v.,* **5** *n.* —**im press'er,** *n.*

im press[2] (im pres'), **1** seize by force for public use: *The police impressed our car in order to pursue the escaping robbers.* **2** force (a person) to serve in the armed forces. *v.*

im pres sion (im presh'ən), **1** effect produced on a person: *Punishment seemed to make little impression on the stubborn child.* **2** idea; notion: *I have a vague impression*

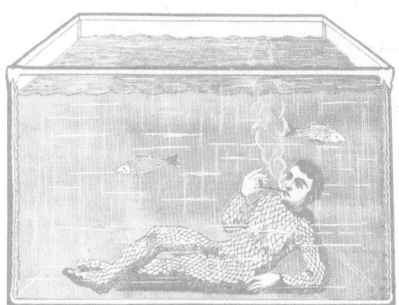

improbable
an improbable
sight

that I left the front door unlocked. **3** mark made by pressing or stamping: *A deer had left impressions of its hoofs in the soft dirt.* **4** imitation; impersonation: *The comedian did impressions of several movie stars.* *n.*

im pres sion a ble (im presh'ə nə bəl), sensitive to impression; easily impressed or influenced: *Children are more impressionable than adults.* *adj.* —**im pres'sion a bly,** *adv.*

impressionism

im pres sion ism (im presh'ə niz'əm), style of painting that conveys the impression of light striking and reflecting from a surface, rather than a photographic reproduction of the surface. *n.*

im pres sion ist (im presh'ə nist), artist who paints in the manner of impressionism. *n.*

im pres sion is tic (im presh'ə nis'tik), of impressionism or impressionists. *adj.* —**im pres'sion is'ti cal ly,** *adv.*

im pres sive (im pres'iv), able to impress the mind, feelings, conscience, etc.: *The actors gave an impressive performance.* *adj.* —**im pres'sive ly,** *adv.* —**im pres'sive ness,** *n.*

im print (im'print *for 1-3;* im print' *for 4-6*), **1** mark made by pressure; print: *Your foot made an imprint in the sand.* **2** mark; impression: *Suffering left its imprint on her face.* **3** the printer's or publisher's name, with the place and date of publication, on the title page or at the end of a book. **4** mark by pressing or stamping: *imprint a postmark on an envelope, imprint a letter with a postmark.* **5** put by pressing: *He imprinted a kiss on his grandmother's cheek.* **6** fix firmly in the mind: *His boyhood home was imprinted in his memory.* **1-3** *n.,* **4-6** *v.*

im pris on (im priz'n), **1** put in prison; keep in prison. **2** confine closely; restrain. *v.*

im pris on ment (im priz'n mənt), an imprisoning or a being imprisoned: *the imprisonment of a convicted criminal.* *n.*

im prob a bil i ty (im prob'ə bil'ə tē), **1** a being improbable; unlikelihood. **2** something improbable. *n.,* *pl.* **im prob a bil i ties.**

im prob a ble (im prob'ə bəl), not probable; not likely to happen; not likely to be true. *adj.* —**im prob'a ble ness,** *n.*

im prob a bly (im prob'ə blē), in an improbable manner. *adv.*

im promp tu (im promp'tü *or* im promp'tyü), **1** without previous thought or preparation; offhand: *a speech made impromptu.* **2** made or done without previous thought or preparation: *He gave an impromptu talk when asked to say a few words.* **1** *adv.,* **2** *adj.* [*Impromptu* was borrowed from French *impromptu,* which comes from Latin *in promptu,* meaning "in readiness."]

im prop er (im prop/ər), **1** not correct; wrong: *"You is" is an improper usage.* **2** not suitable: *A damp basement is an improper place to store books.* **3** not decent: *Reading another's mail is improper. adj.* —**im prop/er ly,** *adv.* —**im prop/er ness,** *n.*

improper fraction, fraction that is equal to or greater than 1. EXAMPLES: $^3/_2$, $^4/_3$, $^{27}/_4$, $^8/_5$, $^{21}/_{12}$, $^4/_4$, $^{12}/_{12}$.

im pro pri e ty (im/prə prī/ə tē), **1** lack of propriety; quality of being improper. **2** an improper act, expression, etc.: *Using "learn" to mean "teach" is an impropriety.* *n., pl.* **im pro pri e ties.**

im prove (im prüv/), **1** make or become better: *You could improve your handwriting if you tried. His health is improving.* **2** increase the value of: *Land is improved by using it for a farm or putting up a building on it.* **3** use well; make good use of: *We had two hours to wait and improved the time by seeing the city. v.,* **im proved, im prov ing.** —**im prov/a ble,** *adj.* —**im prov/er,** *n.*

improve on, make better than; do better than: *improve on one's earlier work.*

im prove ment (im prüv/mənt), **1** a making better or becoming better: *Her schoolwork shows much improvement since last term.* **2** an increase in value. **3** a change or addition that increases value: *The improvements in our house cost over a thousand dollars.* **4** better condition; thing that is better than another; a gain; advance: *The new lighting system is an improvement over the previous one. n.*

im prov i dence (im prov/ə dəns), lack of foresight; failure to look ahead; carelessness in providing for the future; lack of thrift. *n.*

im prov i dent (im prov/ə dənt), lacking foresight; not looking ahead; not careful in providing for the future; not thrifty: *Improvident people spend their money as fast as they can make it. adj.* —**im prov/i dent ly,** *adv.*

im prov i sa tion (im prov/ə zā/shən), **1** an improvising. **2** something improvised. *n.*

im pro vise (im/prə vīz), **1** make up (music, poetry, etc.) on the spur of the moment; sing, recite, speak, etc., without preparation: *We improvised a play for our parents.* **2** make for the occasion: *The girls improvised a tent out of blankets and long poles. v.,* **im pro vised, im pro vis ing.** —**im/pro vis/er,** *n.*

im pru dence (im prüd/ns), lack of prudence; imprudent behavior. *n.*

im pru dent (im prüd/nt), not prudent; rash; unwise: *It is imprudent to rush into something without thinking what may happen. adj.* —**im pru/dent ly,** *adv.* —**im pru/dent ness,** *n.*

im pu dence (im/pyə dəns), a being impudent; shameless boldness; great rudeness; insolence. *n.*

im pu dent (im/pyə dənt), shamelessly bold; very rude and insolent: *The impudent child made faces at us. adj.* —**im/pu dent ly,** *adv.*

im pugn (im pyün/), call in question; attack by words or arguments; challenge as false, worthless, etc.: *The attorney impugned the witness's testimony. v.* [See **Word History.**] —**im pugn/a ble,** *adj.* —**im pugn/er,** *n.*

im pulse (im/puls), **1** a sudden, driving force or influence; thrust; push: *the impulse of hunger, the impulse of curiosity.* **2** the effect of a sudden, driving force or influence. **3** a sudden inclination or tendency to act: *I had a strong impulse to contact my old friend.* **4** stimulus that is transmitted, especially by nerve cells, and influences action in the muscle, gland, or other nerve cells that it reaches. **5** surge of electrical current in one direction. *n.*

im pul sion (im pul/shən), **1** an impelling; driving force: *The impulsion of hunger drove her to steal food.* **2** impulse. **3** impetus. *n.*

im pul sive (im pul/siv), **1** acting or done upon impulse; with a sudden inclination or tendency to act: *Impulsive buyers often purchase things they don't need.* **2** driving with sudden force; able to impel; impelling. *adj.* —**im pul/sive ly,** *adv.* —**im pul/sive ness,** *n.*

im pu ni ty (im pyü/nə tē), freedom from punishment, injury, or other bad consequences: *If laws are not enforced, crimes are committed with impunity. n.*

im pure (im pyur/), **1** not pure; dirty; unclean: *The air in cities is often impure.* **2** mixed with something of lower value; adulterated: *The salt we use is slightly impure.* **3** bad; corrupt: *impure thoughts, impure acts. adj.* —**im pure/ly,** *adv.* —**im pure/ness,** *n.*

im pur i ty (im pyur/ə tē), **1** lack of purity; being impure. **2** impure thing; thing that makes something else impure: *Filtering the water removed some of its impurities. n., pl.* **im pur i ties.**

im pute (im pyüt/), consider as belonging; attribute; charge (a fault, etc.) to a person; blame. *v.,* **im put ed, im put ing.** —**im put/a ble,** *adj.*

in (in). *In* shows position with reference to space, time, state, circumstances, etc. **1** inside; within: *in the box. We live in the country.* **2** at, during, or after: *I'll be there in ten minutes. You can do this in an hour.* **3** into: *Go in the house.* **4** from among; out of: *one in a hundred.* **5** because of; for: *act in self-defense. The party is in honor of her birthday.* **6** to or at the position or condition of; affected by: *in trouble, in love.* **7** in or into some place; on the inside: *Come in. Lock the dog in.* **8** present, especially in one's home or office: *The doctor is not in today.* **9** having power or influence: *The in party has won another election.* **10** coming or leading in: *The train is on the in track.* **11** INFORMAL. in style; fashionable: *That's the in thing to do.* **12** a position of familiarity or influence: *have an in with the company president.* **1-6** *prep.,* **7,8** *adv.,* **9-11** *adj.,* **12** *n.* [*In* comes from Old English *in.*]

in for, unable to avoid; sure to get or have: *We are in for a storm.*

ins and outs, **1** turns and twists; nooks and corners: *He knows the ins and outs of the road because he has traveled it so often.* **2** different parts; details: *The manager knows the ins and outs of the business better than the owner.*

in that, because.

in with, **1** friendly with. **2** partners with: *She was in with him in the robbery.*

In, symbol for indium.

IN, Indiana (used with postal Zip Code).

in-¹, *prefix.* not; the opposite of; the absence of: *Inexpensive = not expensive. Inattention = the absence of attention.* Also, **il-, im-, ir-.**

in-², *prefix.* in; into; on; upon: *Incase = (put) into a case. Intrust = (give) in trust.*

WORD HISTORY

impugn

Impugn is from Latin *impugnare,* meaning "to assault," which comes from *in-,* meaning "against," and *pugnare,* meaning "to fight."

in-³, *prefix.* in; within; into; toward: *Indoors = within doors. Inland = toward land.*

in., inch or inches.

in a bil i ty (in′ə bil′ə tē), lack of ability, power, or means; being unable. *n.*

in ac ces si bil i ty (in′ak ses′ə bil′ə tē), lack of accessibility; being inaccessible. *n.*

in ac ces si ble (in′ak ses′ə bəl), **1** hard to get at; hard to reach or enter: *The house on top of the steep hill is inaccessible.* **2** not accessible; not able to be reached or entered at all. *adj.* —**in′ac ces′si ble ness,** *n.*

in ac ces si bly (in′ak ses′ə blē), so as to be inaccessible. *adv.*

in ac cu ra cy (in ak′yər ə sē), **1** lack of accuracy; being inaccurate. **2** error; mistake. *n., pl.* **in ac cur a cies.**

in ac cu rate (in ak′yər it), not accurate; not exact; containing mistakes. *adj.* —**in ac′cur ate ly,** *adv.* —**in ac′cur ate ness,** *n.*

in ac tion (in ak′shən), absence of action; idleness. *n.*

in ac ti vate (in ak′tə vāt), make inactive; destroy the action of: *inactivate a bomb, inactivate a virus.* *v.,* **in ac ti vat ed, in ac ti vat ing.**

in ac ti va tion (in ak′tə vā′shən), a making or becoming inactive. *n.*

in ac tive (in ak′tiv), not active; idle; slow: *Bears are inactive during the winter.* *adj.* —**in ac′tive ly,** *adv.* —**in ac′tive ness,** *n.*

in ac tiv i ty (in′ak tiv′ə tē), absence of activity; idleness; slowness. *n.*

in ad e qua cy (in ad′ə kwə sē), **1** a being inadequate. **2** something that is inadequate. *n., pl.* **in ad e qua cies.**

in ad e quate (in ad′ə kwit), not adequate; not enough; not as much as is needed: *The amount of food they ordered was inadequate for so many guests.* *adj.* —**in ad′e quate ly,** *adv.* —**in ad′e quate ness,** *n.*

in ad mis si ble (in′əd mis′ə bəl), not to be permitted; not allowable: *inadmissible evidence.* *adj.* —**in′ad mis′si bly,** *adv.*

in ad vert ence (in′əd vėrt′ns), **1** lack of attention; carelessness. **2** an inadvertent act; oversight; mistake. *n.*

in ad vert ent (in′əd vėrt′nt), **1** not attentive; careless; negligent. **2** not done on purpose; caused by oversight: *I forgave her inadvertent rudeness.* *adj.* —**in′ad vert′ent ly,** *adv.*

in ad vis a ble (in′əd vī′zə bəl), not advisable; unwise; not prudent. *adj.* —**in′ad vis′a bly,** *adv.*

in al ien a ble (in ā′lyə nə bəl), not able to be given or taken away: *an inalienable right.* *adj.*

in al ien a bly (in ā′lyə nə blē), in an inalienable manner. *adv.*

in ane (in ān′), silly or foolish; senseless: *an inane question.* *adj.* —**in ane′ly,** *adv.* —**in ane′ness,** *n.*

in an i mate (in an′ə mit), **1** lifeless: *Stones are inanimate objects.* **2** without liveliness or spirit; dull: *an inanimate face.* *adj.* —**in an′i mate ly,** *adv.* —**in an′i mate ness,** *n.*

in a ni tion (in′ə nish′ən), **1** weakness from lack of food. **2** emptiness. *n.*

in an i ty (in an′ə tē), **1** silliness; lack of sense. **2** a silly or senseless act, remark, etc. *n., pl.* **in an i ties.**

in ap pli ca ble (in ap′lə kə bəl *or* in′ə plik′ə bəl), not applicable; not suitable. *adj.* —**in ap′pli ca bly,** *adv.*

in ap pre ci a ble (in′ə prē′shē ə bəl), too small to be noticed or felt; very slight. *adj.* —**in′ap pre′ci a bly,** *adv.*

in ap pro pri ate (in′ə prō′prē it), not appropriate; not fitting. *adj.* —**in′ap pro′pri ate ly,** *adv.* —**in′ap pro′pri ate ness,** *n.*

in apt (in apt′), **1** not apt; not suitable; unfit. **2** unskillful; awkward. *adj.* —**in apt′ly,** *adv.* —**in apt′ness,** *n.*

in ap ti tude (in ap′tə tüd *or* in ap′tə tyüd), **1** unfitness. **2** lack of skill. *n.*

<table>
<tr><td>a hat</td><td>i it</td><td>oi oil</td><td>ch child</td><td rowspan="6">ə = {</td><td>a in about</td></tr>
<tr><td>ā age</td><td>ī ice</td><td>ou out</td><td>ng long</td><td>e in taken</td></tr>
<tr><td>ä far</td><td>o hot</td><td>u cup</td><td>sh she</td><td>i in pencil</td></tr>
<tr><td>e let</td><td>ō open</td><td>u̇ put</td><td>th thin</td><td>o in lemon</td></tr>
<tr><td>ē equal</td><td>ô order</td><td>ü rule</td><td>ᴛʜ then</td><td>u in circus</td></tr>
<tr><td>ėr term</td><td></td><td></td><td>zh measure</td><td></td></tr>
</table>

in ar tic u late (in′är tik′yə lit), **1** not distinct; not like regular speech: *an inarticulate mutter.* **2** unable to speak in words; unable to say what one thinks; dumb: *inarticulate with grief. Cats and dogs are inarticulate.* **3** not jointed: *A jellyfish's body is inarticulate.* *adj.* —**in′ar tic′u late ly,** *adv.* —**in′ar tic′u late ness,** *n.*

in ar tis tic (in′är tis′tik), not artistic; lacking good taste. *adj.* —**in′ar tis′ti cal ly,** *adv.*

in as much as (in′əz much′), because; since: *I stayed indoors, inasmuch as it was raining.*

in at ten tion (in′ə ten′shən), lack of attention; negligence; carelessness: *Her inattention was due to lack of sleep.* *n.*

in at ten tive (in′ə ten′tiv), not attentive; negligent; careless. *adj.* —**in′at ten′tive ly,** *adv.* —**in′at ten′tive ness,** *n.*

in au di ble (in ô′də bəl), not able to be heard. *adj.*

in au di bly (in ô′də blē), in an inaudible manner; so as not to be heard. *adv.*

in au gur al (in ô′gyər əl), **1** of or for an inauguration: *The President gave an inaugural address when he took office.* **2** the address or speech made by a person when formally admitted to office. **1** *adj.,* **2** *n.*

in au gu rate (in ô′gyə rāt′), **1** install in office with a ceremony: *A President of the United States is inaugurated every four years.* **2** make a formal beginning of; begin: *The invention of the airplane inaugurated a new era in transportation.* **3** open for public use with a ceremony or celebration: *The new city hall was inaugurated with a parade and speeches.* *v.,* **in au gu rat ed, in au gu rat ing.** —**in au′gu ra′tor,** *n.*

in au gu ra tion (in ô′gyə rā′shən), **1** act or ceremony of installing a person in office. The inauguration of a President of the United States takes place on January 20. **2** a formal beginning; beginning. **3** an opening for public use with a ceremony or celebration. *n.*

in aus pi cious (in′ô spish′əs), with signs of failure; unfavorable; unlucky. *adj.* —**in′aus pi′cious ly,** *adv.* —**in′aus pi′cious ness,** *n.*

in board (in′bôrd′), inside the hull of a ship or boat: *an inboard motor.* *adj.*

in born (in′bôrn′), born in a person; instinctive; natural: *The artist had an inborn talent for drawing.* *adj.*

in bound (in′bound′), inward bound: *an inbound flight.* *adj.*

in bred (in′bred′), **1** inborn; natural: *an inbred musical ability.* **2** produced by breeding between closely related ancestors: *an inbred strain of horses.* **3** past tense and past participle of **inbreed.** **1,2** *adj.,* **3** *v.*

in breed (in′brēd′ *or* in brēd′), breed closely related animals or plants. *v.,* **in bred, in breed ing.**

inc., incorporated.

In ca (ing′kə), member of an ancient people of South America. The Inca had a highly developed culture, and ruled a large empire in Peru and other parts of South America, which fell to the Spaniards in the 1500's. *n., pl.* **In ca** *or* **In cas.** —**In′can,** *n., adj.*

in cal cu la ble (in kal′kyə lə bəl), **1** too great in number to be calculated; innumerable: *The sands of the sea are incalculable.* **2** impossible to foretell or reckon beforehand: *A flood in the valley would cause incalculable losses.* *adj.*

in cal cu la bly (in kal′kyə lə blē), in an incalculable manner. *adv.*

in can des cence (in′kən des′ns), a glow produced by heat. *n.*

in can des cent (in′kən des′nt), **1** glowing with heat; red-hot or white-hot: *The embers of the fire were still incandescent even though the flames had disappeared.* **2** shining brightly; brilliant. *adj.* —**in′can des′cent ly,** *adv.*

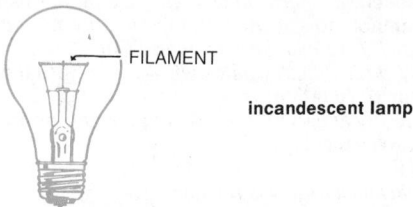

— FILAMENT

incandescent lamp

incandescent lamp, an electric lamp with a filament of very fine wire that becomes white-hot and gives off light when current flows through it.

in can ta tion (in′kan tā′shən), **1** set of words spoken as a magic charm or to cast a magic spell. "Double, double, toil and trouble, Fire burn and caldron bubble," is an incantation. **2** the use of such words. *n.*

in ca pa ble (in kā′pə bəl), having very little ability; not capable; not efficient; not competent: *An employer cannot afford to hire incapable workers. adj.* —**in ca′pa ble ness,** *n.* —**in ca′pa bly,** *adv.*

incapable of, 1 without the ability, power, or fitness for: *I felt incapable of playing such difficult piano music.* **2** not susceptible to; not open or ready for: *Gold is incapable of rusting.*

in ca pac i tate (in′kə pas′ə tāt), limit in ability, power, or fitness; disable: *Her injury incapacitated her for work.* *v.,* **in ca pac i tat ed, in ca pac i tat ing.** —**in′ca pac′i ta′tion,** *n.*

in ca pac i ty (in′kə pas′ə tē), lack of ability, power, or fitness; disability. *n., pl.* **in ca pac i ties.**

in car ce rate (in kär′sə rāt′), imprison. *v.,* **in car ce rat ed, in car ce rat ing.** —**in car′ce ra′tor,** *n.*

in car ce ra tion (in kär′sə rā′shən), imprisonment. *n.*

in car nate (in kär′nit *or* in kär′nāt *for 1;* in kär′nāt *for 2*), **1** embodied in flesh, especially in human form: *The villain was evil incarnate.* **2** make or be incarnate; embody: *Lancelot incarnated the spirit of chivalry.* 1 *adj.,* 2 *v.,* **in car nat ed, in car nat ing.**

in car na tion (in′kär nā′shən), **1** a taking on of human form by a divine being: *the incarnation of an angel.* **2** the **Incarnation,** (in Christian theology) the union of divine nature and human nature in the person of Jesus Christ; assumption of human form by the son of God. **3** person or thing that represents some quality or idea; embodiment: *The miser was an incarnation of greed. n.*

in case (in kās′), encase. *v.,* **in cased, in cas ing.** —**in case′ment,** *n.*

in cau tious (in kô′shəs), not cautious; reckless; rash: *In an incautious moment I revealed the secret I had sworn to keep. adj.* —**in cau′tious ly,** *adv.* —**in cau′tious ness,** *n.*

in cen di ar y (in sen′dē er′ē), **1** having to do with the setting of property on fire intentionally. **2** person who intentionally sets fire to property. **3** causing fires; used to start a fire: *The enemy town was set on fire with incendiary bombs.* **4** deliberately stirring up strife or rebellion: *The agitator was arrested for making incendiary speeches.* 1,3,4 *adj.,* 2 *n., pl.* **in cen di ar ies.**

in cense[1] (in′sens), **1** substance giving off a sweet smell when burned. **2** the perfume or smoke from it. **3** some-

thing sweet like incense: *the incense of flowers, the incense of flattery. n.* [*Incense*[1] came into English about 700 years ago from French *encens,* and can be traced back to Latin *incendere,* meaning "set on fire, burn."]

in cense[2] (in sens′), make very angry; fill with rage: *Their cruelty incensed me. v.,* **in censed, in cens ing.** [*Incense*[2] is from Latin *incensum,* meaning "inflamed, enraged, set on fire," which comes from *in-,* meaning "in," and *candere,* meaning "to glow white."] —**in cense′ment,** *n.*

in cen tive (in sen′tiv), thing that urges a person on; cause of action or effort; motive; stimulus: *The fun of playing the game was a greater incentive than the prize. n.*

in cep tion (in sep′shən), beginning: *the inception of a plan. n.*

in ces sant (in ses′nt), never stopping; continual: *The incessant noise from the factory kept me awake all night. adj.* —**in ces′sant ly,** *adv.* —**in ces′sant ness,** *n.*

in cest (in′sest), a sexual relationship between persons so closely related that their marriage is prohibited by law or custom, as between brother and sister or parent and child. *n.*

inch (inch), **1** unit of length, $\frac{1}{12}$ of a foot. **2** the amount of rainfall or snowfall that would cover a surface to the depth of one inch. **3** the smallest part, amount, or degree; a very little bit. **4** move slowly or little by little: *The worm inched along.* 1-3 *n., pl.* **inch es;** 4 *v.*

by inches, by slow degrees; gradually.

every inch, in every way; completely: *every inch a leader.*

inch by inch, little by little; slowly.

within an inch of, very near; very close to: *within an inch of death.*

WORD HISTORY

inch

Inch is from Old English *ynce,* which comes from Latin *uncia,* meaning "one twelfth," and can be traced back to *unus,* meaning "one."

inch worm (inch′wėrm′), the larva of certain moths; measuring worm. It moves by bringing the rear end of its body forward, forming a loop, and then advancing the front end. *n.*

in ci dence (in′sə dəns), **1** the way in which (a tax, disease, etc.) falls or distributes itself; range of occurrence or influence: *In an epidemic the incidence of a disease is widespread. The incidence of a tax is limited if only a few people must pay it.* **2** the falling or striking of a projectile, ray of light, etc., on a surface. *n.*

in ci dent (in′sə dənt), **1** happening; event: *an exciting incident.* **2** a less important happening: *She told us all of the main facts of her trip and a few of the amusing incidents.* **3** liable to happen; belonging: *Hardships were incident to the lives of the pioneers.* 1,2 *n.,* 3 *adj.* [*Incident* is from Latin *incidentem,* meaning "happening, befalling," which comes from *in-,* meaning "on," and *cadere,* meaning "to fall."]

in ci den tal (in′sə den′tl), **1** happening or likely to happen along with something else more important: *Certain discomforts are incidental to camping out.* **2** occurring by chance: *an incidental meeting of an old friend on the street.* **3** Often, **incidentals,** *pl.* something incidental: *On our trip we spent $52 for meals, room, and railroad fare, and $1.50 for incidentals, such as candy, magazines, and stamps.* 1,2 *adj.,* 3 *n.*

in ci den tal ly (in′sə den′tl ē), **1** in an incidental manner; as an incident along with something else: *She mentioned incidentally that she hadn't eaten.* **2** by the way: *Incidentally, are you coming to the meeting? adv.*

in cin e rate (in sin′ə rāt′), burn to ashes. *v.,* **in cin e rat ed, in cin e rat ing.**

in cin e ra tion (in sin′ə rā′shən), a burning or a being burned to ashes. *n.*

in cin e ra tor (in sin′ə rā′tər), furnace or other device for burning trash and other things to ashes. *n.*

in cip i ent (in sip′ē ənt), just beginning; in an early stage: *I hope this incipient cold doesn't become worse. adj.* —**in cip′i ent ly,** *adv.*

in cise (in sīz′), **1** cut into. **2** carve; engrave: *incise a figure or inscription. v.,* **in cised, in cis ing.**

in ci sion (in sizh′ən), **1** cut made in something; gash: *The doctor made a tiny incision to take out the splinter in my hand.* **2** act of incising. *n.*

in ci sive (in sī′siv), sharp; penetrating; piercing; cutting: *Incisive criticism goes directly to the point and uses plain words. adj.* —**in ci′sive ly,** *adv.* —**in ci′sive ness,** *n.*

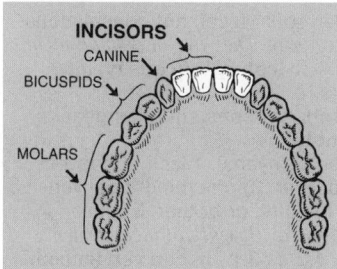

incisors
of a
human being

in ci sor (in sī′zər), tooth having a sharp edge for cutting; one of the front teeth between the canine teeth in either jaw. Humans have eight incisors. *n.*

in cite (in sīt′), urge on; stir up; rouse: *The speaker incited the audience to quick action. v.,* **in cit ed, in cit ing.** —**in cit′er,** *n.*

in cite ment (in sīt′mənt), **1** thing that urges on, stirs up, or rouses: *Poverty can be an incitement to steal.* **2** act of urging on, stirring up, or rousing. *n.*

inclement (def. 1)
He jogged even in
inclement weather.

in clem ent (in klem′ənt), **1** rough or stormy. **2** severe; harsh: *The dictator was an inclement ruler. adj.* —**in clem′ent ly,** *adv.*

in cli na tion (in′klə nā′shən), **1** natural bent; tendency: *My inclination is toward thinness.* **2** preference; liking: *That family has a strong inclination for sports.* **3** a leaning, bending, or bowing: *The inclination of his head showed that he approved.* **4** a slope; slant: *That high roof has a sharp inclination. n.*

in cline (in klīn′ for 1-3,6; in′klīn or in klīn′ for 4,5), **1** be favorable or willing; tend: *Dogs incline to eat meat as a*

food. **2** make favorable or willing; influence: *A hobby may incline a person toward a particular career.* **3** to slope; slant. **4** a slope; slant. **5** a sloping surface. The side of a hill is an incline. **6** lean, bend, or bow: *She inclined her head toward the sound.* 1-3,6 *v.,* **in clined, in clin ing;** 4,5 *n.* [*Incline* is from Latin *inclinare,* which comes from *in-,* meaning "in," and *clinare,* meaning "to lean."] —**in clin′er,** *n.*

in clined (in klīnd′), **1** favorable or willing; tending: *I am inclined to agree with you.* **2** sloping; slanting. *adj.*

inclined plane, plank or other plane surface placed at an angle to a horizontal surface and used to move heavy weights to a higher level with little force. It is a simple machine.

in close (in klōz′), enclose. *v.,* **in closed, in clos ing.**

in clo sure (in klō′zhər), enclosure. *n.*

in clude (in klüd′), **1** have within itself; contain; comprise: *Their farm includes 160 acres.* **2** put in a total, a class, or the like; reckon in a count: *The price includes the land, house, and furniture. v.,* **in clud ed, in clud ing.** —**in clud′a ble, in clud′i ble,** *adj.*

in clu sion (in klü′zhən), **1** an including or a being included. **2** thing included. *n.*

in clu sive (in klü′siv), **1** including; taking in; counting in; comprising: *"Read pages 10 to 20 inclusive" means "Begin with page 10 and read through to the very end of page 20."* **2** including much; including everything concerned: *Make an inclusive list of your expenses. adj.* —**in clu′sive ly,** *adv.* —**in clu′sive ness,** *n.*

in cog ni to (in′kog nē′tō or in kog′nə tō), with one's real name, character, rank, etc., hidden: *The prince traveled incognito to avoid crowds and ceremonies. adj.* [*Incognito* was borrowed from Italian *incognito,* which came from Latin *incognitus,* meaning "unknown."]

in co her ence (in′kō hir′əns), **1** disconnected thought or speech: *After she awoke from the surgery, her speech was marked by some incoherence.* **2** lack of logical connection. **3** failure to stick together; looseness. *n.*

in co her ent (in′kō hir′ənt), **1** having or showing no logical connection of ideas; not coherent; disconnected; confused: *rambling, incoherent talk.* **2** not sticking together. *adj.* —**in′co her′ent ly,** *adv.*

in com bus ti ble (in′kəm bus′tə bəl), not capable of being burned; fireproof. *adj.*

in come (in′kum′), money that comes in from property, business, work, etc.: *A person's yearly income is all the money earned in a year. n.*

income tax, tax on a person's or a corporation's income above a certain amount.

in com ing (in′kum′ing), coming in: *the incoming tide. The incoming tenant will pay more rent. adj.*

in com men sur ate (in′kə men′shər it or in′kə men′sər it), **1** not in proportion; not adequate: *Her salary is incommensurate to her ability.* **2** having no common measure; not able to be compared. *adj.* —**in′com men′sur ate ly,** *adv.* —**in′com men′sur ate ness,** *n.*

in com mu ni ca ble (in′kə myü′nə kə bəl), not able to be communicated or told. *adj.*

in com mu ni ca do (in′kə myü′nə kä′dō), without any way of communicating with others: *The prisoner was held incommunicado. adj.* [*Incommunicado* was borrowed from Spanish *incommunicado,* and can be traced back to Latin *in-*, meaning "not," and *communis*, meaning "common, shared."]

in com par a ble (in kom′pər ə bəl), **1** without equal; matchless: *incomparable beauty.* **2** not able to be compared; unsuitable for comparison. *adj.*

in com par a bly (in kom′pər ə blē), in an incomparable manner; beyond comparison. *adv.*

in com pat i bil i ty (in′kəm pat′ə bil′ə tē), quality of being incompatible; lack of harmony. *n.*

in com pat i ble (in′kəm pat′ə bəl), **1** not able to live or act together peaceably; opposed in character: *My cats and dogs are incompatible.* **2** inconsistent: *Bad eating habits are incompatible with good health.* *adj.* —**in′com pat′i bly,** *adv.*

in com pe tence (in kom′pə təns), lack of ability, power, or fitness: *The worker was discharged for incompetence.* *n.*

in com pe tent (in kom′pə tənt), **1** not competent; without ability, power, or fitness. **2** an incompetent person, especially a person suffering from some type of mental deficiency. **1** *adj.,* **2** *n.* —**in com′pe tent ly,** *adv.*

in com plete (in′kəm plēt′), not complete; lacking some part; unfinished. *adj.* —**in′com plete′ly,** *adv.* —**in′com plete′ness,** *n.*

in com pre hen si ble (in′kom pri hen′sə bəl), impossible to understand. *adj.* —**in′com pre hen′si ble ness,** *n.*

in com pre hen si bly (in′kom pri hen′sə blē), in an incomprehensible manner. *adv.*

in com press i ble (in′kəm pres′ə bəl), not able to be squeezed into a smaller size. *adj.*

in con ceiv a ble (in′kən sē′və bəl), **1** impossible to imagine: *A circle without a center is inconceivable.* **2** hard to believe; incredible: *It is inconceivable that two nations so friendly for centuries should now be at war.* *adj.* —**in′con ceiv a ble ness,** *n.*

in con ceiv a bly (in′kən sē′və blē), **1** in an inconceivable manner. **2** to an inconceivable degree. *adv.*

in con clu sive (in′kən klü′siv), not convincing; not settling or deciding something doubtful; not effective: *The result of my blood test was inconclusive, so I'll have to have another test.* *adj.* —**in′con clu′sive ly,** *adv.* —**in′con clu′sive ness,** *n.*

in con gru i ty (in′kən grü′ə tē), **1** a being out of place; inappropriateness; unfitness. **2** lack of agreement or harmony; inconsistency. **3** something that is incongruous. *n., pl.* **in con gru i ties.**

incongruous (def. 1)—It seems **incongruous** for a wedding ceremony to take place on top of an airplane.

in con gru ous (in kong′grü əs), **1** not appropriate; out of place. **2** lacking in agreement or harmony; inconsistent. *adj.* —**in con′gru ous ly,** *adv.* —**in con′gru ous ness,** *n.*

in con se quen tial (in′kon sə kwen′shəl), not important; trifling. *adj.* —**in′con se quen′tial ly,** *adv.*

in con sid er a ble (in′kən sid′ər ə bəl), not worth consideration; not important; insignificant. *adj.* —**in′con sid′er a ble ness,** *n.* —**in′con sid′er a bly,** *adv.*

in con sid er ate (in′kən sid′ər it), not thoughtful of others and their feelings; thoughtless. *adj.* —**in′con sid′er ate ly,** *adv.* —**in′con sid′er ate ness,** *n.*

in con sist en cy (in′kən sis′tən sē), **1** lack of agreement or harmony; variance: *There was a great inconsistency between what he said he would do and what he actually did.* **2** failure to keep to the same principles, course of action, etc.; changeableness: *She was accused of inconsistency in now defending what she had previously condemned.* **3** thing, act, etc., that is inconsistent. *n., pl.* **in con sist en cies.**

in con sist ent (in′kən sis′tənt), **1** not consistent; lacking in agreement with itself or something else: *Your failure to arrive on time is inconsistent with your usual promptness.* **2** failing to keep to the same principles, course of action, etc.; changeable: *An inconsistent person says one thing today and the opposite tomorrow.* *adj.* —**in′con sist′ent ly,** *adv.*

in con sol a ble (in′kən sō′lə bəl), not to be comforted; broken-hearted: *The girl was inconsolable at the loss of her kitten.* *adj.* —**in′con sol′a ble ness,** *n.*

in con sol a bly (in′kən sō′lə blē), in an inconsolable manner. *adv.*

in con spic u ous (in′kən spik′yü əs), not conspicuous; attracting little or no attention: *They live in a small inconspicuous gray house.* *adj.* —**in′con spic′u ous ly,** *adv.* —**in′con spic′u ous ness,** *n.*

in con stant (in kon′stənt), not constant; changeable; fickle. *adj.* —**in con′stant ly,** *adv.*

in con ven ience (in′kən vē′nyəns), **1** lack of convenience or ease; trouble; bother. **2** something inconvenient; cause of trouble, difficulty, or bother. **3** cause trouble, difficulty, or bother to: *It will not inconvenience me to wait a few minutes.* **1,2** *n.,* **3** *v.,* **in con ven ienced, in con ven ienc ing.**

in con ven ient (in′kən vē′nyənt), not convenient; causing trouble, difficulty, or bother; troublesome: *Shelves that are too high to reach easily are inconvenient.* *adj.* —**in′con ven′ient ly,** *adv.*

in cor po rate (in kôr′pə rāt′), **1** make (something) a part of something else; join or combine (something) with something else: *We will incorporate your suggestion in this new plan.* **2** make into a corporation: *When the business became large, the owners incorporated it.* **3** become a corporation. *v.,* **in cor po rat ed, in cor po rat ing.**

in cor po rat ed (in kôr′pə rā′tid), made into a corporation; chartered as a corporation. *adj.*

in cor po ra tion (in kôr′pə rā′shən), **1** an incorporating: *The new design reflected the incorporation of many revisions.* **2** a being incorporated. Incorporation gives a company the power to act as one person. *n.*

in cor po re al (in′kôr pôr′ē əl), not made of any material substance; spiritual. *adj.* —**in′cor po′re al ly,** *adv.*

in cor rect (in′kə rekt′), **1** containing errors or mistakes; not correct; wrong: *The newspaper gave an incorrect account of the accident.* **2** not agreeing with a good standard of taste; improper. *adj.* —**in′cor rect′ly,** *adv.* —**in′cor rect′ness,** *n.*

in cor ri gi ble (in kôr′ə jə bəl), **1** too firmly fixed in bad ways, an annoying habit, etc., to be reformed or changed: *Nothing could break her of her incorrigible habit of interrupting.* **2** an incorrigible person. **1** *adj.,* **2** *n.* —**in cor′ri gi ble ness,** *n.* —**in cor′ri gi bly,** *adv.*

in cor rupt i ble (in′kə rup′tə bəl), **1** not to be corrupted; honest: *An incorruptible judge cannot be bribed.* **2** not capable of decay; lasting forever: *Diamonds are incorruptible.* *adj.* —**in′cor rupt′i bly,** *adv.*

in crease (in krēs′ for 1,2; in′krēs for 3,4), **1** make greater, more numerous, more powerful, etc.; add to: *The driver increased the speed of the car.* **2** become greater; grow in numbers; advance in quality, power, etc.: *My*

weight has increased by ten pounds. These flowers will increase every year. **3** a gain in size, numbers, etc.; growth: *an increase in our family. There has been a great increase in student enrollment during the past year.* **4** result of increasing; amount added; addition. *1,2 v.,* **in creased, in creas ing;** *3,4 n.* —**in creas′a ble,** *adj.* —**in creas′er,** *n.*
on the increase, increasing: *The movement of people from the cities to the suburbs is on the increase.*

in creas ing ly (in krē′sing lē), to a greater degree; more and more: *As we traveled south, the weather became increasingly warm. adv.*

in cred i ble (in kred′ə bəl), hard to believe; seeming too extraordinary to be possible; unbelievable: *The racing car rounded the curve with incredible speed. Many old superstitions seem incredible to us. adj.*

in cred i bly (in kred′ə blē), so as to be incredible; beyond belief: *an incredibly swift flight. adv.*

in cre du li ty (in′krə dü′lə tē *or* in′krə dyü′lə tē), lack of belief; doubt. *n.*

in cred u lous (in krej′ə ləs), **1** not ready to believe; doubting: *Most people nowadays are incredulous about ghosts and witches.* **2** showing a lack of belief: *He listened to the neighbor's story with an incredulous smile. adj.* —**in cred′u lous ly,** *adv.*

in cre ment (in′krə mənt), **1** an increase; growth. **2** amount by which something increases: *The wages are $120 a week with an increment of $10 for each year of service. n.*

in crim i nate (in krim′ə nāt), accuse of a crime; show to be guilty: *The robber's confession incriminated two others who helped to rob the bank. v.,* **in crim i nat ed, in crim i nat ing.** —**in crim′i na′tion,** *n.* —**in crim′i na′tor,** *n.*

in crust (in krust′), encrust. *v.*

in crus ta tion (in′krus′tā′shən), **1** an encrusting or a being encrusted. **2** crust or hard coating. **3** a decorative layer of costly material. *n.*

in cu bate (ing′kyə bāt *or* in′kyə bāt), **1** sit on (eggs) in order to hatch them; brood. **2** keep (eggs, etc.) warm so that they will develop. *v.,* **in cu bat ed, in cu bat ing.**

in cu ba tion (ing′kyə bā′shən *or* in′kyə bā′shən), **1** an incubating or a being incubated. **2** stage of a disease from the time of infection until the first symptoms appear: *The period of incubation for measles is about ten days. n.*

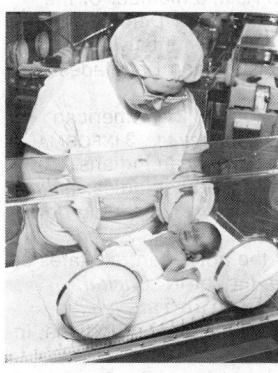

incubator (def. 2)

in cu ba tor (ing′kyə bā′tər *or* in′kyə bā′tər), **1** box or chamber for hatching eggs by keeping them warm and properly supplied with moisture and oxygen. **2** any similar box or chamber. *Very small babies and premature babies are sometimes kept for a time in incubators. n.*

in cul cate (in kul′kāt), impress by repetition; teach persistently: *Over the years she inculcated a love of books into her pupils. v.,* **in cul cat ed, in cul cat ing.** [*Inculcate* is

a hat	**i** it	**oi** oil	**ch** child	a in about
ā age	**ī** ice	**ou** out	**ng** long	e in taken
ä far	**o** hot	**u** cup	**sh** she	ə = i in pencil
e let	**ō** open	**u̇** put	**th** thin	o in lemon
ē equal	**ô** order	**ü** rule	**ŦH** then	u in circus
ėr term			**zh** measure	

from Latin *inculcatum,* meaning "impressed upon, trampled," which comes from *in-,* meaning "in," and *calcem,* meaning "heel."] —**in′cul ca′tion,** *n.* —**in′cul′ca tor,** *n.*

in cum ben cy (in kum′bən sē), term of office: *During his incumbency as governor the state prospered. n., pl.* **in cum ben cies.**

in cum bent (in kum′bənt), **1** lying, leaning, or pressing on something. **2** resting on a person as a duty: *She felt it incumbent upon her to answer the letter at once.* **3** currently holding an office, position, etc.: *the incumbent governor.* **4** person holding an office, position, etc.: *The former incumbent had been very popular in the district. 1-3 adj., 4 n.* —**in cum′bent ly,** *adv.*

in cur (in kėr′), run or fall into (something unpleasant or inconvenient); bring on oneself: *incur many expenses. The pioneers incurred great danger when they crossed the Rocky Mountains. v.,* **in curred, in cur ring.** —**in cur′ra ble,** *adj.*

in cur a ble (in kyu̇r′ə bəl), **1** not capable of being cured: *an incurable invalid, an incurable disease.* **2** person having an incurable disease: *a home for incurables. 1 adj., 2 n.* —**in cur′a ble ness,** *n.*

in cur a bly (in kyu̇r′ə blē), in an incurable manner; to an incurable degree. *adv.*

in cur sion (in kėr′zhən), a sudden attack; invasion; raid: *The pirates made incursions along the coast. n.*

in curve (in′kėrv′), **1** an inward curve. **2** curve inward. *1 n., 2 v.,* **in curved, in curv ing.**

ind., **1** independent. **2** index.

Ind., Indiana.

in debt ed (in det′id), owing money or gratitude; in debt; obliged: *We are indebted to science for many of our comforts. adj.*

in debt ed ness (in det′id nis), **1** condition of being in debt. **2** amount owed; debts. *n.*

in de cen cy (in dē′sn sē), **1** lack of decency; being indecent. **2** an indecent act or word. *n., pl.* **in de cen cies.**

in de cent (in dē′snt), **1** not decent; in very bad taste; improper: *They showed an indecent lack of gratitude to those who had helped them.* **2** not modest; morally bad; disgusting; obscene. *adj.* —**in de′cent ly,** *adv.*

in de ci sion (in′di sizh′ən), lack of decision; tendency to delay or to hesitate. *n.*

in de ci sive (in′di sī′siv), **1** having the habit of hesitating and putting off decisions: *an indecisive person.* **2** not deciding or settling the matter; without a clear result: *Neither side wins in an indecisive battle. "Maybe" is an indecisive answer. adj.* —**in′de ci′sive ly,** *adv.* —**in′de ci′sive ness,** *n.*

in deed (in dēd′), **1** in fact; in truth; really; surely: *She is hungry; indeed, she is almost starving. War is indeed terrible.* **2** expression of surprise, doubt, contempt, etc.: *Indeed! I never would have thought it. 1 adv., 2 interj.*

in de fat i ga ble (in′di fat′ə gə bəl), never getting tired or giving up; tireless: *An indefatigable worker keeps on working until the work is done. adj.* —**in′de fat′i ga ble ness,** *n.* —**in′de fat′i ga bly,** *adv.*

in de fen si ble (in′di fen′sə bəl), **1** not able to be defended: *an indefensible island.* **2** not justifiable: *an indefensible lie. adj.* —**in′de fen′si bly,** *adv.*

in de fin a ble (in′di fī′nə bəl), not able to be defined or described exactly: *It was a place of indefinable beauty. adj.*

in de fin a bly (in⁄di fī⁄nə blē), in an indefinable manner. *adv.*

in def i nite (in def⁄ə nit), **1** not clearly defined; not exact; vague: *"Maybe" is a very indefinite answer.* **2** not limited: *We have an indefinite time to finish this work. adj.* —**in def⁄i nite ly**, *adv.* —**in def⁄i nite ness**, *n.*

indefinite article, the article *a* or *an*. "A dog" or "an animal" means "any dog" or "any animal"; "the dog" means "a certain or particular dog."

in del i ble (in del⁄ə bəl), **1** not able to be erased or removed; permanent: *indelible ink. Her experiences in India left an indelible impression on her memory.* **2** making an indelible mark: *The papers were graded with an indelible pencil. adj.* —**in del⁄i ble ness**, *n.*

in del i bly (in del⁄ə blē), in an indelible manner. *adv.*

in del i ca cy (in del⁄ə kə sē), lack of delicacy; being indelicate. *n., pl.* **in del i ca cies.**

in del i cate (in del⁄ə kit), **1** not delicate; coarse; crude: *It is indelicate to talk back rudely to someone.* **2** improper; immodest. *adj.* —**in del⁄i cate ly**, *adv.*

in dem ni ty (in dem⁄nə tē), **1** payment for damage, loss, or hardship. Money demanded by a victorious nation at the end of a war as a condition of peace is an indemnity. **2** security against damage or loss; insurance. *n., pl.* **in dem ni ties.**

in dent[1] (in dent⁄), **1** make notches or jags in (an edge, line, border, etc.): *an indented coastline. The mountains indent the horizon.* **2** begin (a line) farther from the left margin than the other lines: *The first line of a paragraph is usually indented. v.*

in dent[2] (in dent⁄), **1** make a dent in; mark with a dent. **2** press in; stamp. *v.*

in den ta tion (in⁄den tā⁄shən), **1** an indenting or a being indented. **2** a dent, notch, or cut. *n.*

in den tion (in den⁄shən), **1** a beginning of a line farther from the left margin than the other lines. **2** the blank space left by doing this. **3** indentation. *n.*

in den ture (in den⁄chər), **1** contract by which a person is bound to serve someone else: *An apprentice has an indenture with the master from whom he is learning a trade.* **2** bind by a contract to serve someone else: *Many settlers who came to the American colonies were indentured for several years.* **1** *n.,* **2** *v.,* **in den tured, in den tur ing.** [*Indenture* came into English about 600 years ago from French *endenteüre,* meaning "indentation, an indented document," and can be traced back to Latin *in-,* meaning "in," and *dentem,* meaning "tooth." Originally, indenture documents were made in several copies with the edges indented alike so that they could be identified.]

in de pend ence (in⁄di pen⁄dəns), condition of being independent; freedom from the control, influence, support, or help of others: *The American colonies won independence from England. n.*

In de pend ence (in⁄di pen⁄dəns), city in W Missouri. *n.*

Independence Day, holiday in honor of the adoption of the Declaration of Independence on July 4, 1776; Fourth of July.

in de pend ent (in⁄di pen⁄dənt), **1** not influenced by others; thinking or acting for oneself: *an independent voter, an independent thinker.* **2** not under another's rule or control; ruling, guiding, or governing oneself: *The United States is an independent country.* **3** not connected with others; separate or distinct: *an independent investigation, independent work.* **4** not depending on others for one's support: *Now that I have a better-paying job, I can be completely independent.* **5** enough to live on without working: *an independent income.* **6** person who is independent in thought or behavior. **7** person who votes without re-

gard to party. 1-5 *adj.,* 6,7 *n.* —**in⁄de pend⁄ent ly,** *adv.*

independent clause, (in grammar) clause in a complex sentence that can act by itself as a sentence; main clause.

in-depth (in⁄depth⁄), thorough; detailed: *an in-depth report. adj.*

in de scrib a ble (in⁄di skrī⁄bə bəl), not able to be described; beyond description: *a scene of indescribable beauty. adj.* —**in⁄de scrib⁄a ble ness**, *n.*

in de scrib a bly (in⁄di skrī⁄bə blē), in an indescribable manner. *adv.*

in de struct i ble (in⁄di struk⁄tə bəl), not able to be destroyed. *adj.* —**in⁄de struct⁄i ble ness**, *n.* —**in⁄de struct⁄i bly,** *adv.*

in de ter mi nate (in⁄di tėr⁄mə nit), not determined; not fixed; indefinite; vague: *As the floodwaters rose, an indeterminate number of people were stranded. adj.* —**in⁄de ter⁄mi nate ly,** *adv.* —**in⁄de ter⁄mi nate ness,** *n.*

in dex (in⁄deks), **1** list of what is in a book, telling on what pages to find names, topics, etc. An index is usually put at the end of the book and arranged in alphabetical order. **2** provide with an index; make an index of. **3** thing that points out or shows; sign: *A person's face is often an index of his or her mood.* **4** pointer. A dial or scale usually has an index. 1,3,4 *n., pl.* **in dex es** or **in di ces;** 2 *v.* —**in⁄dex er,** *n.*

index finger, forefinger.

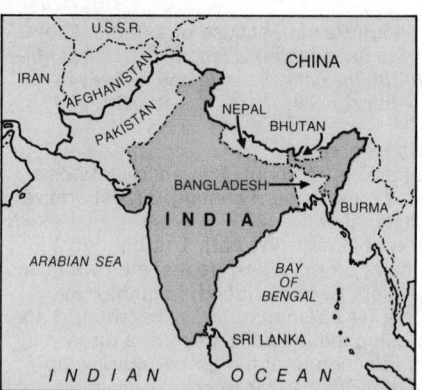

India (def. 1, the darker area; def. 2, the area within the heavy boundary line)

In di a (in⁄dē ə), **1** country in S Asia, a member of the Commonwealth of Nations. *Capital:* New Delhi. **2** region and former country in S Asia. It is now chiefly divided into the countries of India, Pakistan, and Bangladesh. *n.*

India ink, a black paint or ink.

In di an (in⁄dē ən), **1** American Indian. **2** of American Indians: *an Indian camp, an Indian language.* **3** INFORMAL. any one of the languages of the American Indians. **4** of, living in, or belonging to India or the East Indies: *Indian elephants, Indian temples, Indian costumes.* **5** person born or living in India or the East Indies. 1,3,5 *n.,* 2,4 *adj.*

In di an a (in⁄dē an⁄ə), one of the north central states of the United States. *Abbreviation:* Ind. or IN *Capital:* Indianapolis. *n.* —**In di an⁄an, In⁄di an⁄i an,** *adj., n.*

In di an ap o lis (in⁄dē ə nap⁄ə lis), capital of Indiana, in the central part. *n.*

Indian club, a bottle-shaped wooden club swung for exercise.

Indian corn, 1 kind of cereal grass first raised by American Indians; corn; maize. **2** grain or ears of this plant.

Indian meal, corn meal.

Indian Ocean, ocean south of Asia, east of Africa, and west of Australia.

Indian pipe, a waxy, leafless, white plant with a single flower. It looks somewhat like a tobacco pipe.

Indian summer, time of mild, dry, hazy weather in late October or early November, after the first frosts of autumn.

India paper, a thin, tough printing paper.

india rubber or **India rubber,** rubber.

indic., indicative.

in di cate (in′də kāt), **1** point out; make known; show: *The arrow on the sign indicates the right way to go.* **2** be a sign or hint of: *Fever indicates illness.* **3** give a sign or hint of: *People often indicate their feelings by facial expressions. v.,* **in di cat ed, in di cat ing.**

in di ca tion (in′də kā′shən), **1** act of indicating: *We use different words for the indication of different meanings.* **2** thing that indicates; sign: *There was no indication that the house was occupied. n.*

in dic a tive (in dik′ə tiv), **1** pointing out; showing; being a sign; suggestive: *A headache is sometimes indicative of eyestrain.* **2** (in grammar) of a verb form which expresses or denotes a state, act, or happening as actual, or which asks a simple question of fact. **3** form of a verb which expresses this. In "I go" and "Did you win?" *go* and *did win* are indicatives. **4** mood of such a verb. 1,2 *adj.,* 3,4 *n.*

in di ca tor (in′də kā′tər), **1** person or thing that indicates. **2** pointer on the dial of an instrument that shows the amount of heat, pressure, speed, etc. **3** a measuring or recording instrument. **4** substance which, by changing color, indicates the chemical condition of a solution. Litmus is an indicator. *n.*

in di ces (in′də sēz′), a plural of **index.** *n.*

in dict (in dīt′), **1** charge with an offense or crime; accuse. **2** charge (an accused person) with a crime and hold for trial on the recommendation of a grand jury which has heard the evidence and considered it sufficient. *v.* —**in dict′a ble,** *adj.* —**in dict′er, in dict′or,** *n.*

in dict ment (in dīt′mənt), **1** a formal written accusation, especially on the recommendation of a grand jury: *an indictment for murder.* **2** accusation. *n.*

In dies (in′dēz), **1** the East Indies. **2** the West Indies. *n.pl.*

in dif fer ence (in dif′ər əns), **1** lack of interest or attention; not caring: *The child's indifference to food worried its parents.* **2** lack of importance: *It is a matter of indifference to me whether we play ball or go swimming. n.*

in dif fer ent (in dif′ər ənt), **1** not caring one way or the other; having or showing no interest: *I was indifferent to their insults. I enjoyed the trip but she was indifferent.* **2** impartial; neutral; without preference: *The Supreme Court makes indifferent decisions.* **3** not mattering much; unimportant: *We can go whenever you please; the time for starting is indifferent to me.* **4** neither good nor bad; just fair: *an indifferent player. adj.*

in dif fer ent ly (in dif′ər ənt lē), **1** with indifference. **2** without distinction; equally. **3** moderately; tolerably; passably. **4** poorly; badly: *He did his work indifferently. adv.*

in di gence (in′də jəns), poverty. *n.*

in dig e nous (in dij′ə nəs), originating or produced in a particular country; growing or living naturally in a certain region, soil, climate, etc.; native: *Lions are indigenous to Africa. adj.* [See **Word History.**] —**in dig′e nous ly,** *adv.*

in di gent (in′də jənt), poor or needy. *adj.* [*Indigent* is from Latin *indigentem,* which comes from *indu,* meaning "in," and *egere,* meaning "be in need."] —**in′di gent ly,** *adv.*

in di gest i ble (in′də jes′tə bəl), not able to be digested; hard to digest. *adj.*

in di ges tion (in′də jes′chən), inability to digest food; difficulty in digesting food: *The rich food we ate gave us indigestion. n.*

a hat	i it	oi oil	ch child	a in about
ā age	ī ice	ou out	ng long	e in taken
ä far	o hot	u cup	sh she	ə = { i in pencil
e let	ō open	u̇ put	th thin	o in lemon
ē equal	ô order	ü rule	ŦH then	u in circus
ėr term			zh measure	

in dig nant (in dig′nənt), angry at something unworthy, unjust, or mean: *She was indignant when her sister threw cold water at her. adj.* —**in dig′nant ly,** *adv.*

in dig na tion (in′dig nā′shən), anger at something unworthy, unjust, or mean; anger mixed with scorn; righteous anger: *Cruelty to animals aroused his indignation. n.*

in dig ni ty (in dig′nə tē), an injury to one's dignity; lack of respect or proper treatment; insult: *Bill felt that being called "Willie dear" was an indignity. n., pl.* **in dig ni ties.**

in di go (in′də gō), **1** a blue dye formerly obtained from various plants, but now usually obtained artificially. **2** plant from which indigo was made. **3** a deep violet-blue. **4** deep violet-blue. 1-3 *n., pl.* **in di gos** or **in di goes;** 4 *adj.* [*Indigo* comes from Spanish *índigo,* and can be traced back to Greek *indikon,* meaning "indigo, Indian." The dye came originally from India.]

in di rect (in′də rekt′), **1** not straightforward and to the point: *She would not say yes or no but gave an indirect answer to my question.* **2** not directly connected; secondary: *Happiness is an indirect result of doing one's work well.* **3** not direct; not straight: *We walk to town by a road that is indirect, but very pleasant. adj.* —**in′di rect′ly,** *adv.* —**in′di rect′ness,** *n.*

indirect object, (in grammar) a word or group of words that usually comes before the direct object and shows the person or thing to which or for which something is done. In "Give me the book," *me* is the indirect object and *book* is the direct object.

in dis creet (in′dis krēt′), not discreet; not wise and judicious; imprudent: *You were indiscreet to tell them your secret. adj.* —**in′dis creet′ly,** *adv.* —**in′dis creet′ness,** *n.*

in dis cre tion (in′dis kresh′ən), **1** a being indiscreet; lack of good judgment; imprudence: *They were embarrassed at his indiscretion in talking about family matters in front of strangers.* **2** an indiscreet act or remark. *n.*

in dis crim i nate (in′dis krim′ə nit), **1** mixed up; confused: *She tipped everything out of her suitcase in an indiscriminate pile.* **2** without discrimination; not distinguishing carefully between persons, things, etc.: *an indiscriminate reader. adj.* —**in′dis crim′i nate ly,** *adv.* —**in′dis crim′i nate ness,** *n.*

in dis pen sa ble (in′dis pen′sə bəl), absolutely necessary: *Air is indispensable to life. adj.* —**in′dis pen′sa ble ness,** *n.*

in dis pen sa bly (in′dis pen′sə blē), to an indispensable degree; necessarily. *adv.*

in dis posed (in′dis pōzd′), **1** slightly ill: *I have been indisposed with a cold.* **2** unwilling; not inclined. *adj.*

WORD HISTORY

indigenous

Indigenous is from Latin *indigena,* meaning "a native," and can be traced back to *indu,* meaning "in," and *gignere,* meaning "to bear, to be the father of."

in dis po si tion (in/dis pə zish/ən), **1** a slight illness. **2** unwillingness. *n.*

in dis put a ble (in/dis pyü/tə bəl *or* in dis/pyə tə bəl), too evident to be disputed; undoubted; certain; unquestionable: *an indisputable fact. adj.* —**in/dis put/a ble ness,** *n.*

in dis put a bly (in/dis pyü/tə blē *or* in dis/pyə tə blē), in an indisputable manner; unquestionably. *adv.*

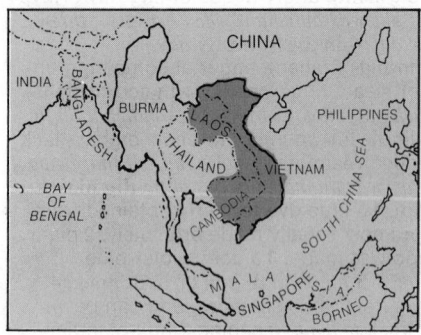

Indochina (def. 1, the area within the heavy boundary line; def. 2, the darker area)

in dis sol u ble (in/di sol/yə bəl), not able to be dissolved, undone, or destroyed; lasting; firm: *Let us make an indissoluble agreement. adj.* —**in/dis sol/u bly,** *adv.*

in dis tinct (in/dis tingkt/), not distinct; not clear to the eye, ear, or mind; confused: *an indistinct voice. I have an indistinct memory of the accident. adj.* —**in/dis tinct/ly,** *adv.* —**in/dis tinct/ness,** *n.*

in dis tin guish a ble (in/dis ting/gwi shə bəl), not able to be distinguished. *adj.* —**in/dis tin/guish a bly,** *adv.*

in di um (in/dē əm), a very soft, silvery metallic element found only in combination with other elements. It is used as a coating on bearings. *n.*

in di vid u al (in/də vij/ü əl), **1** person: *an extremely unpleasant individual.* **2** a single person, animal, or thing. **3** for or by one only; single; particular; separate: *Each student was given individual attention.* **4** belonging to or marking off one person or thing specially: *an individual style of writing.* 1,2 *n.,* 3,4 *adj.*

WORD HISTORY

individual

Individual comes from Latin *individualis,* and can be traced back to *in-,* meaning "not," and *dividere,* meaning "divide."

in di vid u al ism (in/də vij/ü ə liz/əm), **1** belief that individual freedom is as important as the welfare of the community or group as a whole. **2** absence of cooperation; wanting a separate existence for oneself. *n.*

in di vid u al ist (in/də vij/ü ə list), **1** person who lives independently and does not try to cooperate with or follow others. **2** supporter of individualism. *n.*

in di vid u al is tic (in/də vij/ü ə lis/tik), of individualism or individualists. *adj.* —**in/di vid/u al is/ti cal ly,** *adv.*

in di vid u al i ty (in/də vij/ü al/ə tē), **1** the character or sum of the qualities which distinguish one person or thing from another. **2** condition of being individual; existence as an individual. *n., pl.* **in di vid u al i ties.**

in di vid u al ly (in/də vij/ü ə lē), **1** one at a time; as individuals; personally: *Sometimes our teacher helps us individually.* **2** each from the others: *People differ individually. adv.*

in di vis i bil i ty (in/də viz/ə bil/ə tē), indivisible condition or quality. *n.*

in di vis i ble (in/də viz/ə bəl), **1** not able to be divided: *"One nation under God, indivisible, with liberty and justice for all."* **2** not able to be divided without a remainder: *Any odd number is indivisible by 2. adj.* —**in/di vis/i ble ness,** *n.*

in di vis i bly (in/də viz/ə blē), in an indivisible manner. *adv.*

In do chi na *or* **In do-Chi na** (in/dō chī/nə), **1** peninsula in SE Asia including Burma, Cambodia, Laos, Malaya, Singapore, Thailand, and Vietnam. **2** countries in the E part of this peninsula; Cambodia, Laos, and Vietnam. *n.*

In do chi nese *or* **In do-Chi nese** (in/dō chī nēz/), of Indochina, the peoples living there, or their languages. *adj.*

in doc tri nate (in dok/trə nāt), **1** teach a doctrine, belief, or principle to. **2** teach; instruct. *v.,* **in doc tri nat ed, in doc tri nat ing.** —**in doc/tri na/tor,** *n.*

in doc tri na tion (in dok/trə nā/shən), an indoctrinating or a being indoctrinated. *n.*

In do-Eur o pe an (in/dō yür/ə pē/ən), a group of related languages derived from a single prehistoric language, spoken in India, western Asia, and Europe. Indo-European includes English, German, Latin, Greek, Persian, Sanskrit, and other languages. *n.*

in do lence (in/dl əns), dislike of work; laziness; idleness. *n.* [*Indolence* comes from Latin *indolentia,* meaning "freedom from pain."]

in do lent (in/dl ənt), disliking work; lazy; idle. *adj.* —**in/do lent ly,** *adv.*

in dom i ta ble (in dom/ə tə bəl), not able to be discouraged, beaten, or conquered; unyielding: *The team's indomitable spirit helped them win a very close game. adj.* —**in dom/i ta ble ness,** *n.* —**in dom/i ta bly,** *adv.*

In do ne sia (in/də nē/zhə), **1** country in the East Indies that includes Java, Sumatra, Celebes, parts of Borneo and New Guinea, and over 3000 smaller islands. *Capital:* Djakarta. **2** Malay Archipelago. *n.* —**In/do ne/sian,** *adj., n.*

in door (in/dôr/), done, used, etc., in a house or building: *indoor tennis. adj.*

in doors (in/dôrz/), in or into a house or building: *Go indoors. adv.*

in dorse (in dôrs/), endorse. *v.,* **in dorsed, in dors ing.**

in dorse ment (in dôrs/mənt), endorsement. *n.*

in dors er (in dôr/sər), endorser. *n.*

in du bi ta ble (in dü/bə tə bəl *or* in dyü/bə tə bəl), too evident to be doubted; certain; unquestionable: *It is an indubitable truth that all living matter dies. adj.* —**in du/bi ta ble ness,** *n.*

in du bi ta bly (in dü/bə tə blē *or* in dyü/bə tə blē), in an indubitable manner; without doubt; unquestionably. *adv.*

in duce (in düs/ *or* in dyüs/), **1** lead on; influence; persuade: *Advertisements induce people to buy.* **2** cause; bring about: *The doctor says that this medicine will induce sleep.* **3** produce (an electric current, electric charge, or magnetic change) without direct contact. **4** infer by reasoning from particular facts to a general rule or principle. *v.,* **in duced, in duc ing.** —**in duc/er,** *n.* —**in duc/i ble,** *adj.*

in duce ment (in düs/mənt *or* in dyüs/mənt), **1** something that influences or persuades; incentive: *A new bicycle for the winner was an inducement to try hard to win the contest.* **2** act of influencing or persuading. *n.*

in duct (in dukt/), **1** put formally in possession of an office; install: *She was inducted as treasurer of the club.*

2 bring in; introduce (into a place, seat, position, etc.). **3** take into the armed forces. *v.*

in duct ance (in duk′təns), property of an electric circuit by which an electromotive force is induced in a nearby circuit. The tuner of a radio varies the inductance of its coils. *n.*

in duc tee (in duk′tē′), person who has been or soon will be inducted, especially into the armed forces. *n.*

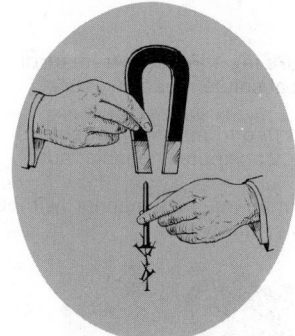

induction (def. 1)
Magnetic induction—the tacks stick to the nail and to each other because of induced magnetism.

in duc tion (in duk′shən), **1** process by which an object having electrical or magnetic properties produces similar properties in a nearby object, without direct contact. **2** a reasoning from particular facts to general truths or principles. **3** act of inducting; act or ceremony of installing a person in office. *n.* —**in duc′tion less,** *adj.*

in duc tive (in duk′tiv), **1** of or using induction; reasoning by induction. **2** of or caused by electric or magnetic induction. *adj.* —**in duc′tive ly,** *adv.* —**in duc′tive ness,** *n.*

in dulge (in dulj′), **1** give in to one's pleasure; let oneself have, use, or do what one wants: *A smoker indulges in tobacco. An easily angered person often indulges in fits of temper.* **2** give in to; let oneself have, use, or do: *to indulge one's fondness for candy.* **3** give in to the wishes or whims of; humor: *We often indulge a sick person. v.,* **indulged, in dulg ing.** —**in dulg′er,** *n.* —**in dulg′ing ly,** *adv.*

in dul gence (in dul′jəns), **1** act of indulging. **2** something indulged in: *Luxuries are indulgences.* **3** favor; privilege: *The student kept seeking the teacher's indulgence.* **4** (in the Roman Catholic Church) a freeing from the punishment still due for sin after the guilt has been forgiven. *n.*

in dul gent (in dul′jənt), **1** giving in to another's wishes or whims; too kind or agreeable: *Their indulgent parents gave them everything they wanted.* **2** making allowances; not critical; lenient: *Our indulgent teacher praised every poem we wrote. adj.* —**in dul′gent ly,** *adv.*

In dus (in′dəs), river flowing from W Tibet through Kashmir and Pakistan into the Arabian Sea. *n.*

in dus tri al (in dus′trē əl), **1** of or resulting from industry: *industrial products.* **2** having highly developed industries: *industrial nations.* **3** engaged in or connected with industry: *industrial workers, an industrial school.* **4** for use in industry: *industrial machines, industrial diamonds. adj.* —**in dus′tri al ly,** *adv.*

in dus tri al ist (in dus′trē ə list), person who manages or owns an industrial enterprise. *n.*

in dus tri al i za tion (in dus′trē ə lə zā′shən), development of large industries in a country or economic system. *n.*

in dus tri al ize (in dus′trē ə līz), make industrial; develop large industries in (a country or economic system). *v.,* **in dus tri al ized, in dus tri al iz ing.**

Industrial Revolution, the change from an agricultural to an industrial society and from home manufacturing to factory production, especially the one that took place in England from about 1750 to about 1850.

in dus tri ous (in dus′trē əs), working hard and steadily; diligent: *An industrious student usually has good grades. adj.* —**in dus′tri ous ly,** *adv.* —**in dus′tri ous ness,** *n.*

in dus try (in′də strē), **1** any branch of business, trade, or manufacture: *the automobile industry. Industries dealing with steel, copper, coal, and construction employ millions of people.* **2** all such business, trade, and manufacture taken as a whole: *Chicago is a center of industry.* **3** steady effort; hard work: *She became a lawyer through much industry. n., pl.* **in dus tries.**

in e bri ate (in ē′brē āt *for 1;* in ē′brē it *for 2*), **1** make drunk; intoxicate. **2** a drunken person. **1** *v.,* **in e bri at ed, in e bri at ing; 2** *n.* —**in e′bri a′tion,** *n.*

in ed i ble (in ed′ə bəl), not fit to eat: *Poisonous mushrooms are inedible. adj.*

in ef fa ble (in ef′ə bəl), not to be expressed in words; too great to be described in words: *the ineffable beauty of a sunset. adj.* —**in ef′fa ble ness,** *n.* —**in ef′fa bly,** *adv.*

in ef fec tive (in′ə fek′tiv), not producing the desired effect; of little use: *an ineffective medicine. adj.* —**in′ef fec′tive ly,** *adv.* —**in′ef fec′tive ness,** *n.*

in ef fec tu al (in′ə fek′chü əl), **1** without effect; failing to have the effect wanted; useless: *His attempts to become friends again after the quarrel were ineffectual.* **2** not able to produce the effect wanted; powerless. *adj.* —**in′ef fec′tu al ly,** *adv.* —**in′ef fec′tu al ness,** *n.*

in ef fi cien cy (in′ə fish′ən sē), **1** lack of efficiency; wastefulness. **2** a being incapable; inability to get things done. *n.*

in ef fi cient (in′ə fish′ənt), **1** not efficient; not able to produce an effect without waste of time or energy; wasteful: *A machine that uses too much fuel is inefficient.* **2** not able to get things done; incapable: *an inefficient worker. adj.* —**in′ef fi′cient ly,** *adv.*

in e las tic (in′i las′tik), not elastic; stiff; inflexible; unyielding. *adj.*

in el e gant (in el′ə gənt), not elegant; in poor taste; crude; vulgar. *adj.* —**in el′e gant ly,** *adv.*

in el i gi bil i ty (in el′ə jə bil′ə tē), lack of eligibility; being ineligible. *n.*

in el i gi ble (in el′ə jə bəl), not eligible; not suitable or qualified; unfit to be chosen: *A foreign-born citizen of the United States is ineligible for the Presidency. adj.* —**in el′i gi ble ness,** *n.* —**in el′i gi bly,** *adv.*

in ept (in ept′), **1** not suitable; out of place: *Such a poor player would be an inept choice as captain.* **2** awkward; clumsy: *an inept performance. adj.* —**in ept′ly,** *adv.* —**in ept′ness,** *n.*

in e qual i ty (in′i kwol′ə tē), **1** lack of equality; a being unequal in amount, size, value, rank, etc.: *There is a great inequality between the salaries of a bank president and a teller.* **2** lack of evenness, regularity, or uniformity: *There are many inequalities in the New England coastline.* **3** a mathematical expression showing that two quantities are unequal. EXAMPLE: $a > b$ means a is greater than b; $a < b$ means a is less than b; $a \neq b$ means a and b are unequal. *n., pl.* **in e qual i ties.**

in eq ui ta ble (in ek′wə tə bəl), not equitable; unfair; unjust. *adj.*

in eq ui ta bly (in ek′wə tə blē), not fairly; unjustly. *adv.*

in eq ui ty (in ek′wə tē), lack of equity; unfairness; injustice. *n., pl.* **in eq ui ties.**

in ert (in ėrt′), **1** having no power to move or act; lifeless: *A stone is an inert mass of matter.* **2** inactive; slow; sluggish: *He was sleepy and inert.* **3** with few or no active properties; rarely combining with other elements: *Helium and neon are inert gases. adj.* [*Inert* comes from Latin *inertem,* meaning "idle, unskilled."] —**in ert′ly,** *adv.* —**in ert′ness,** *n.*

in er tia (in ėr′shə), **1** tendency to remain in the state one is in, and not start changes. **2** tendency of all objects and matter in the universe to stay still, or, if moving, to go on moving in the same direction, unless acted on by some outside force. *n.*

in es cap a ble (in′ə skā′pə bəl), not able to be escaped or avoided; sure to happen. *adj.*

in es cap a bly (in′ə skā′pə blē), in an inescapable manner; inevitably. *adv.*

in es ti ma ble (in es′tə mə bəl), too great to be estimated; priceless; invaluable: *Freedom of speech is an inestimable privilege. adj.* —**in es′ti ma bly,** *adv.*

in ev i ta ble (in ev′ə tə bəl), not to be avoided; sure to happen; certain to come: *Death is inevitable. adj.*

in ev i ta bly (in ev′ə tə blē), in an inevitable manner. *adv.*

in ex act (in′ig zakt′), not exact; with errors or mistakes; not strictly correct; not just right. *adj.* —**in′ex act′ly,** *adv.* —**in′ex act′ness,** *n.*

in ex cus a ble (in′ik skyü′zə bəl), not to be excused; not able to be justified; unpardonable: *The winning team's poor sportsmanship was inexcusable. adj.* —**in′ex cus′a ble ness,** *n.*

in ex cus a bly (in′ik skyü′zə blē), in an inexcusable manner. *adv.*

in ex haust i ble (in′ig zô′stə bəl), **1** not able to be exhausted; very abundant: *The wealth of our country seems inexhaustible to many people abroad.* **2** tireless: *The new president is a woman of inexhaustible energy. adj.*

in ex haust i bly (in′ig zô′stə blē), in an inexhaustible manner. *adv.*

in ex or a ble (in ek′sər ə bəl), not influenced by prayers or pleading; relentless; unyielding: *The forces of nature are inexorable. adj.* [*Inexorable* is from Latin *inexorabilis,* which comes from *in-,* meaning "not," and *exorare,* meaning "pray earnestly."] —**in ex′or a ble ness,** *n.*

in ex or a bly (in ek′sər ə blē), in an inexorable manner. *adv.*

in ex pe di ent (in′ik spē′dē ənt), not expedient; not practicable, suitable, or wise. *adj.* —**in′ex pe′di ent ly,** *adv.*

in ex pen sive (in′ik spen′siv), not expensive; cheap; low-priced. *adj.* —**in′ex pen′sive ly,** *adv.* —**in′ex pen′sive ness,** *n.*

in ex per i ence (in′ik spir′ē əns), lack of experience; lack of practice; lack of skill or wisdom gained from experience. *n.*

in ex per i enced (in′ik spir′ē ənst), not experienced; without practice; lacking the skill and wisdom gained from experience. *adj.*

in ex pert (in′ik spėrt′ *or* in ek′spėrt′), not expert; unskilled. *adj.* —**in′ex pert′ly,** *adv.* —**in′ex pert′ness,** *n.*

in ex plic a ble (in′ik splik′ə bəl *or* in ek′splə kə bəl), not able to be explained; mysterious: *an inexplicable fire. adj.* —**in′ex plic′a ble ness,** *n.*

in ex plic a bly (in′ik splik′ə blē *or* in ek′splə kə blē), in an inexplicable manner. *adv.*

in ex press i ble (in′ik spres′ə bəl), not able to be expressed; impossible to express in words; indescribable. *adj.* —**in′ex press′i ble ness,** *n.*

in ex press i bly (in′ik spres′ə blē), beyond expression; indescribably. *adv.*

in ex tin guish a ble (in′ik sting′gwi shə bəl), not able to be put out or stopped: *an inextinguishable fire, an inextinguishable desire for knowledge. adj.*

in ex tri ca ble (in ek′strə kə bəl), **1** not able to be gotten out of: *an inextricable maze, inextricable difficulty.* **2** not able to be disentangled or solved: *inextricable confusion. adj.* —**in ex′tri ca bly,** *adv.*

inf., 1 infield. **2** infinitive.

Inf., infantry.

in fal li bil i ty (in fal′ə bil′ə tē), **1** freedom from error; inability to be mistaken. **2** absolute reliability; sureness. *n.*

in fal li ble (in fal′ə bəl), **1** free from error; not able to be mistaken: *an infallible rule.* **2** absolutely reliable; sure: *infallible obedience. adj.*

in fal li bly (in fal′ə blē), in an infallible manner; without failure or mistake; certainly; surely. *adv.*

infamous (def. 2)—a pair of infamous bank robbers

in fa mous (in′fə məs), **1** deserving or causing a very bad reputation; shamefully bad; very wicked: *To betray your country is an infamous deed.* **2** having a very bad reputation; in public disgrace: *A traitor's name is infamous. adj.* —**in′fa mous ly,** *adv.*

in fa my (in′fə mē), **1** a very bad reputation; public disgrace: *Traitors are held in infamy.* **2** shameful badness; extreme wickedness. **3** an infamous or disgraceful act. *n., pl.* **in fa mies.**

in fan cy (in′fən sē), **1** condition or time of being an infant; babyhood; early childhood. **2** an early stage; very beginning of development: *Space travel is still in its infancy. n., pl.* **in fan cies.**

in fant (in′fənt), **1** a very young child; baby. **2** of or for an infant: *an infant blanket, infant food.* **3** in an early stage; just beginning to develop: *an infant industry.* **4** person under the legal age of responsibility; minor. 1,4 *n.,* 2,3 *adj.* [*Infant* is from Latin *infantem,* originally meaning "not speaking," which comes from *in-,* meaning "not," and *fari,* meaning "to speak."]

in fan tile (in′fən tīl), **1** of an infant or infants: *Measles and chicken pox are infantile diseases.* **2** like an infant; babyish; childish: *an infantile display of temper.* **3** in an early stage; just beginning to develop. *adj.*

infantile paralysis, polio.

in fan try (in′fən trē), **1** soldiers trained, equipped, and organized to fight on foot. **2** branch of an army consisting of such troops. *n., pl.* **in fan tries.**

in fan try man (in′fən trē mən), soldier who fights on foot; foot soldier. *n., pl.* **in fan try men.**

in fat u at ed (in fach′ü ā′tid), having an exaggerated fondness or passion; foolishly in love. *adj.*

in fat u a tion (in fach′ü ā′shən), exaggerated fondness or passion; foolish love. *n.*

in fect (in fekt⁄), **1** cause disease or an unhealthy condition in by introducing germs or viruses: *Dirt infects an open cut. Anyone with a bad cold may infect others.* **2** influence in a bad way: *A noisy pupil may infect the behavior of a whole class.* **3** influence by spreading from one to another: *Her joy infected the rest of us.* *v.*

in fec tion (in fek⁄shən), **1** a causing of disease in people, animals, and plants by the introduction of germs or viruses. **2** disease caused in this manner, especially one that can spread from one person to another. **3** fact or condition of being infected. *n.*

in fec tious (in fek⁄shəs), **1** spread by germs or viruses: *an infectious disease.* **2** causing infection. **3** apt to spread from one to another: *an infectious laugh.* *adj.* —**in fec⁄tious ly,** *adv.* —**in fec⁄tious ness,** *n.*

in fer (in fėr⁄), **1** find out by reasoning; come to believe after thinking; conclude: *I inferred from the smoke that something was burning.* **2** be a sign or hint of; suggest indirectly; imply: *Ragged clothing infers poverty.* *v.,* **in ferred, in fer ring.** —**in fer⁄a ble,** *adj.* —**in fer⁄rer,** *n.*

in fer ence (in⁄fər əns), **1** the process of inferring; finding out by reasoning: *What happened is only a matter of inference; no one saw the accident.* **2** that which is inferred; conclusion: *What inference do you draw from smelling smoke?* *n.*

in fer i or (in fir⁄ē ər), **1** below most others; low in quality; below the average: *an inferior mind, an inferior grade of coffee.* **2** not so good or so great; lower in quality; worse: *This cloth is inferior to real silk.* **3** lower in position, rank, or importance: *A lieutenant is inferior to a captain.* **4** person who is lower in rank or station: *A good leader gets on well with inferiors.* **5** something that is below average. 1-3 *adj.,* 4,5 *n.*

in fer i or i ty (in fir⁄ē ôr⁄ə tē), inferior condition or quality. *n.*

inferiority complex, an abnormal feeling of being inferior to other people.

in fer nal (in fėr⁄nl), **1** of the lower world; of hell. **2** fit to have come from hell; hellish; devilish: *infernal cruelty.* **3** INFORMAL. hateful; shocking; outrageous: *Stop that infernal racket.* *adj.* —**in fer⁄nal ly,** *adv.*

in fer no (in fėr⁄nō), **1** hell. **2** place of torment or intense heat like hell: *The firefighters fought their way through a flaming inferno.* *n., pl.* **in fer nos.** [See **Word History.**]

in fer tile (in fėr⁄tl), not fertile; sterile. *adj.*

in fest (in fest⁄), trouble or disturb frequently or in large numbers: *Mosquitoes infest swamps. The national park was infested with tourists.* *v.* —**in⁄fes ta⁄tion,** *n.*

in fi del (in⁄fə dəl), **1** person who does not believe in religion. **2** not believing in religion. **3** person who does not accept a particular faith. During the Crusades, Moslems called Christians infidels. **4** person who does not accept Christianity. 1,3,4 *n.,* 2 *adj.*

in fi del i ty (in⁄fə del⁄ə tē), **1** unbelief in religion, especially in Christianity. **2** lack of faithfulness, especially to husband or wife; disloyalty. *n., pl.* **in fi del i ties.**

inflammable (def. 1)
Paper is inflammable.

in field (in⁄fēld⁄), **1** the part of a baseball field roughly bounded by the bases; diamond. **2** first, second, and third basemen and shortstop of a baseball team. *n.*

in field er (in⁄fēl⁄dər), player in the infield. *n.*

in fil trate (in fil⁄trāt), **1** pass into or through by filtering. **2** penetrate or slip through (an enemy's lines) individually or in small groups: *Enemy troops infiltrated the front lines.* **3** penetrate (an organization) for the purposes of spying, sabotage, or the like. **4** filter into or through; permeate. *v.,* **in fil trat ed, in fil trat ing.** —**in⁄fil tra⁄tor,** *n.*

in fil tra tion (in⁄fil trā⁄shən), **1** an infiltrating or a being infiltrated. **2** thing that infiltrates. *n.*

infin., infinitive.

in fi nite (in⁄fə nit), **1** without limits or bounds; endless: *the infinite reaches of outer space.* **2** extremely great: *Working a jigsaw puzzle sometimes takes infinite patience.* **3** that which is infinite. **4** in mathematics: **a** greater than can be reached in counting: *an infinite number.* **b** (of a set) having an unlimited number of elements. **5 the Infinite,** God. 1,2,4 *adj.,* 3,5 *n.* —**in⁄fi nite ly,** *adv.* —**in⁄fi nite ness,** *n.*

in fi ni tes i mal (in⁄fi nə tes⁄ə məl), so small as to be almost nothing: *Germs are infinitesimal. adj.* —**in⁄fi ni tes⁄i mal ly,** *adv.* —**in⁄fi ni tes⁄i mal ness,** *n.*

in fin i tive (in fin⁄ə tiv), (in grammar) form of a verb not limited by person and number, often preceded by *to.* In "I want to buy a hat," *to buy* is an infinitive. In "We must go now," *go* is an infinitive. *n.*

in fin i ty (in fin⁄ə tē), **1** condition of being infinite. **2** an infinite distance, space, time, or quantity. **3** an infinite extent, amount, or number. *n., pl.* **in fin i ties.**

WORD HISTORY

inferno

Inferno was borrowed from Italian *inferno,* which comes from Latin *infernus,* meaning "hell," and can be traced back to *inferus,* meaning "located below."

in firm (in fėrm⁄), **1** lacking strength or health; weak; feeble: *The patient was old and infirm.* **2** without a firm purpose; faltering: *infirm judgment. adj.* —**in firm⁄ly,** *adv.*

in fir mar y (in fėr⁄mər ē), place for the care of the infirm, sick, or injured; hospital in a school or institution. *n., pl.* **in fir mar ies.** [*Infirmary* comes from a medieval Latin word *infirmaria,* and can be traced back to *in-,* meaning "not," and *firmus,* meaning "firm, healthy."]

in fir mi ty (in fėr⁄mə tē), **1** weakness; feebleness. **2** sickness; illness: *the infirmities of age. n., pl.* **in fir mi ties.**

in flame (in flām⁄), **1** make more violent; excite: *Her stirring speech inflamed the crowd.* **2** become excited with strong feeling. **3** make or become unnaturally hot, red, sore, or swollen: *The thick smoke inflamed our eyes. v.,* **in flamed, in flam ing.**

in flam ma ble (in flam⁄ə bəl), **1** flammable. **2** easily excited or aroused; excitable: *an inflammable temper. adj.*

in flam ma tion (in/flə mā/shən), **1** a diseased condition of some part of the body, marked by heat, redness, swelling, and pain: *A boil is an inflammation of the skin.* **2** an inflaming or a being inflamed. *n.*

in flam ma to ry (in flam/ə tôr/ē), **1** tending to excite or arouse: *The crowd was stirred up by the inflammatory speech.* **2** of, causing, or accompanied by inflammation: *An inflammatory condition of the tonsils causes a sore throat. adj.*

in flat a ble (in flā/tə bəl), able to be inflated. *adj.*

in flate (in flāt/), **1** force air or gas into (a balloon, tire, ball, etc.) causing it to swell. **2** swell or puff out: *After his success he was inflated with pride.* **3** increase (prices or amount of currency) beyond the normal amount. *v.,* **in flat ed, in flat ing. —in flat/er, in fla/tor,** *n.*

in fla tion (in flā/shən), **1** a swelling (with air or gas). **2** a swollen state; too great expansion. **3** a sharp increase in prices resulting from too great an expansion in paper money or bank credit. *n.*

in fla tion ar y (in flā/shə ner/ē), of inflation; tending to inflate. *adj.*

in flect (in flekt/), **1** change the tone or pitch of (the voice). **2** vary the form of (a word) to show case, number, gender, person, tense, mood, voice, or comparison. By inflecting *who* we have *whose* and *whom.* **3** bend; curve. *v.* [*Inflect* is from Latin *inflectere,* which comes from *in-,* meaning "in," and *flectere,* meaning "to bend."] **—in flec/tor,** *n.*

in flec tion (in flek/shən), **1** a change in the tone or pitch of the voice: *We usually end questions with a rising inflection.* **2** variation in the form of a word to show case, number, gender, person, tense, mood, voice, or comparison. **3** suffix or ending used for this: *-est* and *-ed* are common inflections in English. **4** a bending; curving. **5** a bend; curve. *n.*

in flec tion al (in flek/shə nəl), of or showing grammatical inflection. *adj.* **—in flec/tion al ly,** *adv.*

in flex i bil i ty (in flek/sə bil/ə tē), lack of flexibility; being inflexible. *n.*

in flex i ble (in flek/sə bəl), **1** not yielding; firm; steadfast: *an inflexible decision.* **2** not able to be changed; unalterable. **3** not easily bent; stiff; rigid: *an inflexible rod. adj.* **—in flex/i bly,** *adv.*

in flict (in flikt/), **1** cause to have or suffer; give (a stroke, blow, or wound): *A knife can inflict a bad wound on a person.* **2** cause to be suffered or borne; impose (suffering, punishment, something unwelcome, etc.): *to inflict pain. Our unpleasant neighbors inflicted themselves on us all afternoon. v.*

in flic tion (in flik/shən), **1** act of inflicting: *the infliction of pain.* **2** something inflicted; pain; suffering; burden; punishment: *He endured many inflictions with patience. n.*

in flow (in/flō/), **1** a flowing in or into: *an inflow of money.* **2** that which flows in. *n.*

in flu ence (in/flü əns), **1** power of acting on others and having an effect without using force: *Use your influence to persuade your friends to join our club.* **2** person or thing that has such power: *My older sister was a good influence on me.* **3** have an influence on: *The moon influences the tides. What we read influences our thinking.* **4** use influence on: *We tried to influence the teacher by offering him our suggestions.* **1,2** *n.,* **3,4** *v.,* **in flu enced, in flu enc ing.**

in flu en tial (in/flü en/shəl), **1** having much influence: *Influential friends helped her get a good job.* **2** using influence; producing results. *adj.* **—in/flu en/tial ly,** *adv.*

in flu en za (in/flü en/zə), an acute, contagious disease caused by a virus. Its symptoms sometimes resemble those of a very bad cold, but it is much more dangerous and exhausting; flu; grippe. *n.* [See **Word History.**]

in flux (in/fluks), a flowing in; steady flow: *An influx of immigrants from Europe greatly increased the population of the United States. n.*

in form (in fôrm/), **1** give knowledge, facts, or news to; tell: *Her letter informed us of how and when she expected to arrive.* **2** make an accusation or complaint; accuse: *The criminal who was caught informed against the other robbers. v.*

in for mal (in fôr/məl), **1** not formal; without ceremony: *an informal party.* **2** used in everyday, common talk, but not used in formal talking or writing; colloquial. Such an expression as *kids* for *children* is informal. *adj.* **—in for/mal ly,** *adv.*

in for mal i ty (in/fôr mal/ə tē), **1** a being informal; lack of ceremony. **2** an informal act or behavior. *n., pl.* **in for mal i ties.**

in form ant (in fôr/mənt), person who gives information to another: *My informant told me what happened. n.*

in for ma tion (in/fər mā/shən), **1** knowledge given or received concerning some fact or circumstance; news: *We have just received information of the astronauts' safe landing.* **2** things known; facts; data: *A dictionary contains much information about words.* **3** an informing: *A guidebook is for the information of travelers. n.*

in for ma tion al (in/fər mā/shə nəl), having to do with or giving information: *A library's reference department provides informational services. adj.*

in form a tive (in fôr/mə tiv), giving information; instructive: *The class trip to see how a newspaper is printed was very informative. adj.* **—in form/a tive ly,** *adv.*

in formed (in fôrmd/), **1** having information. **2** educated; knowledgeable: *an informed opinion. adj.*

in form er (in fôr/mər), **1** person who tells authorities of violations of the law; person who informs on another: *An informer told the police that the store was selling stolen goods.* **2** informant. *n.*

in frac tion (in frak/shən), a breaking of a law or obligation; violation: *Reckless driving is an infraction of the law. n.*

in fra red (in/frə red/), of the invisible part of the spectrum whose rays have wavelengths longer than those of the red end of the visible spectrum. Most of the heat from sunlight and incandescent lamps is from infrared rays. *adj.*

in fre quen cy (in frē/kwən sē), a being infrequent; scarcity; rarity. *n.*

in fre quent (in frē/kwənt), occurring seldom or far apart; not frequent; scarce; rare. *adj.* **—in fre/quent ly,** *adv.*

in fringe (in frinj/), **1** violate (a law, obligation, right, etc.): *A false label infringes the food and drug law.* **2** go beyond the proper or usual limits; trespass; encroach: *Do not infringe upon the rights of others. v.,* **in fringed, in fring ing.** [*Infringe* is from Latin *infringere,* which comes from *in-,* meaning "in," and *frangere,* meaning "to break."] **—in fring/er,** *n.*

◆ WORD HISTORY ◆

influenza

Influenza was borrowed from Italian *influenza,* meaning "influenza, influence." The disease was thought to occur because of the influence of the stars on its victims.

in fringe ment (in frinj′mənt), **1** violation. **2** a trespassing. *n.*

in fur i ate (in fyůr′ē āt), fill with wild, fierce anger; make furious; enrage: *Their insults infuriated him. v.,* **in fur i at ed, in fur i at ing.** —**in fur′i at′ing ly,** *adv.* —**in fur′i a′tion,** *n.*

in fuse (in fyüz′), **1** pour in; put in; instill: *She infused her excitement into those who listened to her.* **2** inspire: *The crowd was infused with her excitement.* **3** steep or soak (a plant, leaves) in a liquid to get something out: *Tea leaves are infused in hot water to make tea. v.,* **in fused, in fus ing.** —**in fus′er,** *n.*

in fu sion (in fyü′zhən), **1** act or process of infusing: *The plan was improved by the infusion of new ideas.* **2** a liquid extract obtained by steeping or soaking: *Tea is an infusion of tea leaves in hot water. n.*

-ing[1], *suffix forming nouns chiefly from verbs.* **1** act of a person or thing that _____s: *Painting = act of a person that paints.* **2** product or result of such an act, as *a drawing, a painting.* **3** thing that _____s: *Lining = thing that lines.*

-ing[2], **1** *suffix forming the present participle of verbs,* as in *raining, staying, talking.* **2** *suffix forming adjectives from verbs, that* _____s: *Lasting happiness = happiness that lasts. Growing child = child that grows.*

in gen ious (in jē′nyəs), **1** with skill in planning or making; clever: *The ingenious boy made a radio set for himself.* **2** cleverly planned and made: *an ingenious device. adj.* [*Ingenious* is from Latin *ingeniosus,* which comes from *ingenium,* meaning "natural talent," and can be traced back to *in-,* meaning "in," and *gignere,* meaning "to be born."] —**in gen′ious ly,** *adv.* —**in gen′ious ness,** *n.*

in ge nue (an′zhə nü), **1** a simple, innocent girl or young woman. **2** actress who plays the part of such a girl or young woman. *n.* [*Ingenue* comes from French *ingénue,* originally meaning "ingenuous."]

in gé nue (an′zhə nü), ingenue. *n., pl.* **in gé nues.**

in ge nu i ty (in′jə nü′ə tē *or* in′jə nyü′ə tē), skill in planning or making; cleverness: *The girl showed ingenuity in making toys out of scraps of wood. n.*

in gen u ous (in jen′yü əs), **1** free from restraint or reserve; frank and open; sincere: *He gave an ingenuous account of his acts, concealing nothing.* **2** simple; natural; innocent: *an ingenuous child. adj.* [*Ingenuous* is from Latin *ingenuus,* meaning "frank, native," which comes from *in-,* meaning "in," and *gignere,* meaning "to be born."] —**in gen′u ous ly,** *adv.* —**in gen′u ous ness,** *n.*

in gest (in jest′), take (food, etc.) into the body for digestion: *Higher animals ingest food by swallowing. v.* —**in gest′i ble,** *adj.*

in ges tion (in jes′chən), act of taking food, etc., into the body for digesting. *n.*

in gle nook (ing′gəl nůk′), nook or corner beside a fireplace. *n.* [*Inglenook* comes from Scottish Gaelic *aingeal,* meaning "fire," and Middle English *noke,* meaning "nook, hidden corner."]

in glo ri ous (in glôr′ē əs), bringing no glory; shameful; disgraceful: *The tennis champion suffered an inglorious defeat at the hands of a mere amateur. adj.* —**in glo′ri ous ly,** *adv.* —**in glo′ri ous ness,** *n.*

in got (ing′gət), mass of metal, such as gold, silver, or steel, cast into a block or bar to be recast, rolled, or forged at a later time. *n.*

in grain (in grān′), fix deeply and firmly. *v.*

in grained (in grānd′), deeply and firmly fixed in one's very nature or being: *ingrained honesty. adj.*

in grate (in′grāt), an ungrateful person. *n.*

in gra ti ate (in grā′shē āt), bring (oneself) into favor; make (oneself) acceptable: *He tried to ingratiate himself with the teacher by cleaning the blackboards. v.,* **in gra ti-**

at ed, in gra ti at ing. —**in gra′ti at′ing ly,** *adv.* —**in gra′ti a′tion,** *n.*

in grat i tude (in grat′ə tüd *or* in grat′ə tyüd), lack of gratitude or thankfulness; being ungrateful. *n.*

in gre di ent (in grē′dē ənt), one of the parts of a mixture: *The ingredients of a cake usually include eggs, sugar, flour, and flavoring. n.* [*Ingredient* comes from Latin *ingredientem,* meaning "a going into."]

in-group (in′grüp′), group of people united by the same interests. An in-group often excludes outsiders. *n.*

in grown (in′grōn′), grown into the flesh: *an ingrown toenail. adj.*

in hab it (in hab′it), live in: *Fish inhabit the sea. v.* —**in hab′i ta′tion,** *n.* —**in hab′it er,** *n.*

in hab it a ble (in hab′ə tə bəl), **1** capable of being inhabited. **2** fit to live in; habitable. *adj.*

in hab it ant (in hab′ə tənt), person or animal that lives in a place: *Our town has ten thousand inhabitants. n.*

in hab it ed (in hab′ə tid), lived in: *an inhabited house. adj.*

in hal ant (in hā′lənt), medicine to be inhaled. *n.*

in ha la tion (in′hə lā′shən), an inhaling. *n.*

in ha la tor (in′hə lā′tər), apparatus for inhaling medicine, gas, anesthetic, etc.; inhaler. *n.*

in hale (in hāl′), draw (air, gas, fragrance, tobacco smoke, etc.) into the lungs; breathe in. *v.,* **in haled, in hal ing.**

in hal er (in hā′lər), inhalator. *n.*

in har mo ni ous (in′här mō′nē əs), not harmonious; disagreeing; conflicting; discordant. *adj.* —**in′har mo′ni ous ly,** *adv.* —**in′har mo′ni ous ness,** *n.*

in her ent (in hir′ənt), belonging to a person or thing as a quality or attribute; essential: *Her inherent curiosity about nature led her to study botany. adj.*

in her ent ly (in hir′ənt lē), by its own nature; essentially. *adv.*

in her it (in her′it), **1** get or have after someone dies; receive as an heir: *After Grandfather's death, Mother inherited all of his property.* **2** receive from one's parents or ancestors through heredity. **3** receive (anything) by succession from one who came before: *I inherited this old pen from the person who used to have my desk. v.*

in her it ance (in her′ə təns), **1** act or right of inheriting: *He obtained his house by inheritance from an aunt.* **2** anything inherited: *The house was her inheritance. n.*

in her i tor (in her′ə tər), person who inherits; heir. *n.*

in hib it (in hib′it), hold back; hinder or restrain; check:

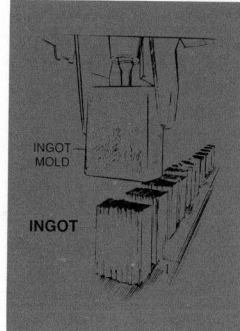

ingots—steel ingots just removed from molds by huge tongs suspended from a crane

Their aloof reception inhibited his usual friendliness. v. —**in hib′it a ble,** *adj.*

in hi bi tion (in′hə bish′ən), **1** a holding back; restraint; checking: *Some drugs can cause the inhibition of normal bodily activity.* **2** idea, emotion, attitude, habit, or other inner force holding back or checking one's impulses, desires, etc. *n.*

in hib i tor (in hib′ə tər), person or thing that inhibits. *n.*

in hib i to ry (in hib′ə tôr′ē), inhibiting; tending to inhibit. *adj.*

in hos pit a ble (in′ho spit′ə bəl *or* in hos′pi tə bəl), **1** not hospitable; not making visitors comfortable: *That inhospitable man never offers visitors any refreshments.* **2** providing no shelter; barren: *a rocky, inhospitable shore.* *adj.*

in hos pit a bly (in′ho spit′ə blē *or* in hos′pi tə blē), in an inhospitable manner. *adv.*

in hos pi tal i ty (in hos′pə tal′ə tē), lack of hospitality. *n.*

in hu man (in hyü′mən), **1** without kindness, mercy, or tenderness; cruel; brutal: *an inhuman lack of concern for the sufferings of others.* **2** not human; not having the qualities natural to a human being: *Some of the Olympic runners seem to have inhuman powers of endurance.* *adj.* —**in hu′man ly,** *adv.*

in hu mane (in′hyü mān′), not humane; lacking in kindness, mercy, or tenderness. *adj.* —**in′hu mane′ly,** *adv.*

in hu man i ty (in′hyü man′ə tē), **1** a being inhuman; lack of kindness, mercy, or tenderness; cruelty; brutality. **2** an inhuman, cruel, or brutal act. *n., pl.* **in hu man i ties.**

in im i cal (in im′ə kəl), **1** unfriendly; hostile: *The townspeople were inimical to strangers.* **2** unfavorable; harmful: *Censorship is inimical to freedom of the press. adj.* —**in im′i cal ly,** *adv.*

in im i ta ble (in im′ə tə bəl), impossible to imitate or copy; matchless. *adj.* —**in im′i ta ble ness,** *n.*

in im i ta bly (in im′ə tə blē), in an inimitable manner. *adv.*

in iq ui tous (in ik′wə təs), very unjust; wicked. *adj.* —**in iq′ui tous ly,** *adv.*

in iq ui ty (in ik′wə tē), **1** very great injustice; wickedness. **2** a wicked or unjust act: *the many iniquities of slavery. n., pl.* **in iq ui ties.** [*Iniquity* comes from Latin *iniquitatem,* and can be traced back to *in-,* meaning "not," and *aequus,* meaning "equal, favorable, just."]

i ni tial (i nish′əl), **1** occurring at the beginning; first; earliest: *His initial effort at skating was a failure.* **2** the first letter of a word: *The initials U.S. stand for United States.* **3** to mark or sign with initials: *Lee Ann Wong initialed the note L.A.W.* **1** *adj.,* **2** *n.,* **3** *v.*

i ni tial ly (i nish′ə lē), at the beginning. *adv.*

i ni ti ate (i nish′ē āt for *1-3;* i nish′ē it *or* i nish′ē āt *for 4*), **1** be the first one to start; set going; begin: *This year we shall initiate a series of free concerts for the public.* **2** admit (a person) with formal ceremonies into a group or society: *The old members initiated the new members.* **3** help to get a first understanding; introduce into the knowledge of some art or subject: *The teacher initiated the class into the wonders of science by telling a few interesting things about the earth and stars.* **4** person who is initiated. **1-3** *v.,* **i ni ti at ed, i ni ti at ing; 4** *n.* [*Initiate* comes from Latin *initiatum,* meaning "begun," and can be traced back to *in-,* meaning "in," and *ire,* meaning "to go." See **Word Family.**]

i ni ti a tion (i nish′ē ā′shən), **1** act or process of being the first one to start something; beginning. **2** formal admission into a group or society. **3** ceremonies by which one is admitted to a group or society: *All the club members attended the initiation. n.*

i ni ti a tive (i nish′ē ə tiv), **1** active part in taking the first

steps in any undertaking; lead: *She likes to take the initiative in planning class projects.* **2** readiness and ability to be the one to start something: *A good leader must have initiative.* **3** right of citizens outside the legislature to introduce or enact a new law by vote. **4** procedure for doing this. *n.*

i ni ti a tor (i nish′ē ā′tər), person or thing that initiates. *n.*

in ject (in jekt′), **1** force (liquid, medicine, etc.) into a passage, cavity, or tissue: *inject penicillin into a muscle, inject fuel into an engine.* **2** throw in; insert: *While she and I were talking he injected a remark into the conversation. v.* —**in jec′tor,** *n.*

in jec tion (in jek′shən), **1** act or process of injecting: *The medicine was given by injection rather than by mouth.* **2** liquid injected: *A nurse prepared the injection. n.*

in ju di cious (in′jü dish′əs), showing bad judgment; unwise; not judicious: *An injudicious person says or does things without thinking what their results may be. adj.* —**in′ju di′cious ly,** *adv.* —**in′ju di′cious ness,** *n.*

in junc tion (in jungk′shən), **1** a formal order from a court of law requiring a person or group to do or not to do something: *The injunction prohibited the teachers from striking before the end of the school year.* **2** command; order: *Injunctions of secrecy did not prevent the news from leaking out. n.*

in jure (in′jər), do damage to; harm; hurt: *I injured my arm while skiing. The misunderstanding injured their friendship. v.,* **in jured, in jur ing.**

in jur i ous (in jùr′ē əs), causing injury; harmful: *Hail is often injurious to crops. adj.* —**in jur′i ous ly,** *adv.* —**in jur′i ous ness,** *n.*

in jur y (in′jər ē), hurt or loss caused to or endured by a person or thing; harm; damage: *She escaped from the train wreck without injury. You did me an injury when you said I lied. n., pl.* **in jur ies.** [*Injury* is from Latin *injuria,* which comes from *in-,* meaning "not," and *juris,* meaning "a right, a law."]

in jus tice (in jus′tis), **1** lack of justice; being unjust. **2** an unjust act: *It is an injustice to send an innocent person to jail. n.*

initiate

Below are words related to *initiate.* They can all be traced back to the Latin word *ire* (ē′re), meaning "to go."

ambition	county	perish
circuit	errant	sedition
commence	exit	sudden
constable	initial	trance
count²	issue	transition
countess	obituary	transitive

ink (ingk), **1** a colored or black liquid used for writing, printing, or drawing. **2** put ink on; mark or stain with ink. **3** a dark liquid thrown out for protection by cuttlefish, squids, etc. **1,3** *n.,* **2** *v.* [*Ink* came into English about 700 years ago from French *enque,* which can be traced back to Greek *enkauston,* meaning "burnt in."] —**ink′er,** *n.* —**ink′like′,** *adj.*

ink blot (ingk′blot′), blot made with ink. *n.*

INKHORN

a hat	**i** it	**oi** oil	**ch** child		a in about
ā age	**ī** ice	**ou** out	**ng** long		e in taken
ä far	**o** hot	**u** cup	**sh** she	**ə** =	i in pencil
e let	**ō** open	**u̇** put	**th** thin		o in lemon
ē equal	**ô** order	**ü** rule	**ŦH** then		u in circus
ėr term			**zh** measure		

ink horn (ingk′hôrn′), a small container, often made of horn, formerly used to hold ink. *n.*

ink i ness (ing′kē nis), a being inky; blackness. *n.*

in kling (ing′kling), vague notion; slight suspicion; hint: *give a person an inkling of what is going on. n.*

ink stand (ingk′stand′), **1** stand to hold ink and pens. **2** container used to hold ink. *n.*

ink well (ingk′wel′), container used to hold ink on a desk or table. *n.*

ink y (ing′kē), **1** like ink; dark; black: *inky shadows.* **2** covered with ink; marked or stained with ink. **3** of ink. *adj.*, **ink i er, ink i est.**

inlaid (def. 1)—a wooden box with an inlaid design of ivory

in laid (in′lād′ *or* in lād′), **1** set in the surface as a decoration or design. **2** decorated with a design or material set in the surface: *The desk had an inlaid top of silver.* **3** past tense and past participle of **inlay.** *They inlaid tiles in the kitchen floor. The floor was inlaid with colored tiles.* 1,2 *adj.*, 3 *v.*

in land (in′lənd), **1** away from the coast or the border; situated in the interior: *Illinois is an inland state.* **2** interior of a country; land away from the border or the coast. **3** in or toward the interior: *He traveled inland from New York to Chicago.* **4** domestic; not foreign: *Commerce between the states of the United States is inland trade.* 1,4 *adj.*, 2 *n.*, 3 *adv.*

in-law (in′lô′), INFORMAL. person related by marriage. *n.*

in lay (in lā′ *or* in′lā′ *for 1,2;* in′lā′ *for 3,4*), **1** to set in the surface as a decoration or design: *The silversmith inlaid strips of gold in the top of the silver box.* **2** decorate with a design set in the surface: *inlay a wooden box with gold.* **3** an inlaid decoration, design, or material. **4** a shaped piece of gold, porcelain, etc., cemented in a tooth as a filling. 1,2 *v.*, **in laid, in lay ing;** 3,4 *n.* —**in′lay′er,** *n.*

in let (in′let), **1** a narrow strip of water running from a larger body of water into the land or between islands: *The fishing village was on a small inlet of the sea.* **2** entrance. *n.*

in mate (in′māt), person confined in a prison, asylum, hospital, etc. *n.*

in most (in′mōst), **1** farthest in; deepest: *We went to the inmost depths of the mine.* **2** most private; most secret: *one's inmost thoughts. adj.*

inn (in), **1** place where travelers and others can get meals and a room to sleep in. **2** restaurant or tavern. *n.*

in nards (in′ərdz), INFORMAL. **1** the internal organs of the body. **2** the internal workings or parts of a machine or structure. *n.pl.*

in nate (i nāt′ *or* in′āt), born in a person; natural: *an innate talent for drawing. adj.* —**in nate′ly,** *adv.* —**in nate′ness,** *n.*

in ner (in′ər), **1** farther in; inside: *The buildings formed a square surrounding an inner courtyard.* **2** more private; more secret: *He kept his inner thoughts to himself.* **3** of the mind or soul: *a person's inner life. adj.*

inner city, 1 the central part of a large city or metropolitan area. **2** the crowded, poor, run-down part of a city; the slums.

inner ear, the innermost part of the ear, behind the middle ear. In human beings it contains the organs of balance and the organs that change sound into nerve messages.

in ner most (in′ər mōst), farthest in; inmost: *the innermost parts of a machine. adj.*

inner tube, an inflatable rubber tube placed inside the casing of some tires.

in ning (in′ing), **1** division of a baseball game during which each team has a turn at bat. **2** the turn one team or group has to play and score in a game. **3** Usually, **innings,** *pl.* the time a person or party is in power; chance for action: *When our party lost the election, the other side had its innings. n.*

inn keep er (in′kē′pər), person who owns, manages, or keeps an inn. *n.*

in no cence (in′ə səns), **1** freedom from sin, wrong, or guilt; being innocent: *The accused woman proved her innocence of the crime.* **2** simplicity; lack of cunning: *the innocence of a little child. n.*

in no cent (in′ə sənt), **1** doing no wrong or evil; free from sin or wrong; not guilty: *In the United States a person is innocent until proved guilty.* **2** without knowledge of evil: *A baby is innocent.* **3** doing no harm; harmless: *innocent amusements.* **4** an innocent person. 1-3 *adj.*, 4 *n.* —**in′no cent ly,** *adv.*

in noc u ous (i nok′yü əs), harmless: *She took my innocuous remark as an insult. adj.* —**in noc′u ous ly,** *adv.* —**in noc′u ous ness,** *n.*

in no vate (in′ə vāt), make changes; bring in something new or new ways of doing things: *It is difficult to innovate when people feel that the old, familiar way of doing something is better. The scientist innovated new methods of research. v.,* **in no vat ed, in no vat ing.**

in no va tion (in′ə vā′shən), **1** change made in the established way of doing things: *The principal made many innovations.* **2** a making changes; bringing in new things or new ways of doing things: *Many people are opposed to innovation. n.*

in no va tive (in′ə vā′tiv), tending to innovate. *adj.*

in no va tor (in′ə vā′tər), person who makes changes or brings in new things or new ways of doing things. *n.*

in nu en do (in′yü en′dō), an indirect suggestion meant to discredit a person: *He was the victim of a vicious scandal spread by the use of lies and innuendoes. n., pl.* **in nu en does.** [*Innuendo* is from Latin *innuendo,* meaning "by nodding to."]

in nu mer a ble (i nü′mər ə bəl *or* i nyü′mər ə bəl), too many to count; very many; countless: *innumerable stars.* *adj.* —**in nu′mer a ble ness**, *n.*

in nu mer a bly (i nü′mər ə blē *or* i nyü′mər ə blē), in very great numbers; countlessly. *adv.*

in oc u late (in ok′yə lāt), **1** infect (a person or animal) with killed or weakened germs or viruses that will cause a mild form of a disease so that the individual will not get that disease or will suffer only a very mild form of the disease. **2** use disease germs to prevent diseases. Doctors inoculate against smallpox, diphtheria, typhoid fever, and other diseases. *v.,* **in oc u lat ed, in oc u lat ing.** [*Inoculate* is from Latin *inoculatum,* meaning "implanted," which comes from *in-,* meaning "in," and *oculus,* meaning "eye, bud of a plant."] —**in oc′u la′tor**, *n.*

in oc u la tion (in ok′yə lā′shən), **1** act or process of inoculating: *Inoculation has greatly reduced deaths from polio.* **2** bacteria, serums, etc., used in inoculating. *n.*

in of fen sive (in′ə fen′siv), not offensive; not arousing objections; harmless: *"Please try to be more quiet" is an inoffensive way of telling people to stop their noise. adj.* —**in′of fen′sive ly**, *adv.* —**in′of fen′sive ness**, *n.*

in op er a tive (in op′ər ə tiv *or* in op′ə rā′tiv), not operative; not working; without effect. *adj.*

in op por tune (in op′ər tün′ *or* in op′ər tyün′), not opportune; coming at a bad time; unsuitable: *An inopportune telephone call delayed us. adj.* —**in op′por tune′ly**, *adv.* —**in op′por tune′ness**, *n.*

in or di nate (in ôrd′n it), much too great; excessive: *an inordinate desire for sweets. adj.* —**in or′di nate ly**, *adv.* —**in or′di nate ness**, *n.*

in or gan ic (in′ôr gan′ik), **1** not organic; neither animal nor vegetable; not having the organized physical structure characteristic of animals and plants. Water and minerals are inorganic substances. **2** (in chemistry) not containing organic matter. Chemical compounds without carbon are inorganic. *adj.* —**in′or gan′i cal ly**, *adv.*

in pa tient (in′pā′shənt), patient who is lodged and fed in a hospital while undergoing treatment. *n.*

in put (in′pùt′), **1** put in; introduce. **2** what is put in or taken in. **3** power supplied to a machine. **4** information or instructions put into a computer. **1** *v.,* **in put, in put ting;** 2-4 *n.*

inscription (def. 1)
on a gravestone

in quest (in′kwest), a legal inquiry, especially before a jury: *An inquest was held to determine if his death was the result of a crime. n.*

in quire (in kwīr′), **1** try to find out by questions; ask: *The detective went from house to house, inquiring whether anyone had seen the lost girl.* **2** make a search for information, knowledge, or truth: *The scholar pored over old documents while inquiring into the history of the town. v.,* **in quired, in quir ing.** Also, **enquire.** —**in quir′a ble**, *adj.* —**in quir′ing ly**, *adv.*

in quir er (in kwī′rər), person who inquires. *n.*

in quir y (in kwī′rē *or* in′kwər ē), **1** act of inquiring; asking. **2** a search for information, knowledge, or truth. **3** question: *The guide answered all our inquiries. n., pl.* **in quir ies.** Also, **enquiry.**

in qui si tion (in′kwə zish′ən), **1** a thorough investigation; searching inquiry. **2** an official investigation; judicial inquiry. **3 the Inquisition,** court established by the Roman Catholic Church in the 1200's to discover and punish heresy. It was abolished in the 1800's. *n.*

in quis i tive (in kwiz′ə tiv), **1** asking many questions; curious: *an inquisitive person with a good mind.* **2** prying into other people's affairs; too curious: *Our neighbors are very inquisitive about what we do. adj.* —**in quis′i tive ly**, *adv.* —**in quis′i tive ness**, *n.*

in quis i tor (in kwiz′ə tər), **1** person who makes an inquisition; official investigator. **2 Inquisitor,** member of the Inquisition. *n.*

in road (in′rōd′), **1** an attack or raid. **2** encroachment by force: *The expenses of her trip made inroads upon the money that she had saved. n.*

in rush (in′rush′), a rushing in; inflow: *The inrush of water filled the pool. n.*

ins., **1** inches. **2** insurance.

in sane (in sān′), **1** not sane; mentally ill; crazy. **2** for insane people: *an insane asylum.* **3** extremely foolish; completely lacking in common sense: *Nobody paid any attention to their insane plan for crossing the ocean in a canoe. adj.* —**in sane′ly**, *adv.* —**in sane′ness**, *n.*

in san i tar y (in san′ə ter′ē), not sanitary; not healthful. *adj.* —**in san′i tar′i ness**, *n.*

in san i ty (in san′ə tē), **1** a being insane; madness; mental illness: *The lawyer insisted that the accused had fired the shot during a fit of temporary insanity.* **2** extreme folly; complete lack of common sense: *It is insanity to drive a car without any brakes. n., pl.* **in san i ties.**

in sa tia bil i ty (in sā′shə bil′ə tē), insatiable quality. *n.*

in sa tia ble (in sā′shə bəl), not able to be satisfied; extremely greedy: *The boy had an insatiable appetite for candy. adj.* —**in sa′tia ble ness**, *n.*

in sa tia bly (in sā′shə blē), in an insatiable manner. *adv.*

in sa ti ate (in sā′shē it), never satisfied: *A vain person has an insatiate desire for praise. adj.* —**in sa′ti ate ly**, *adv.* —**in sa′ti ate ness**, *n.*

in scribe (in skrib′), **1** write or engrave (words, names, etc.) on stone, metal, paper, etc.: *Her name was inscribed on the ring. Please inscribe my initials on the watch.* **2** mark (stone, metal, paper, etc.) with words, names, etc.: *The ring was inscribed with his name.* **3** address or dedicate (a book, picture, etc.) informally to a person. **4** impress deeply: *My father's words are inscribed in my memory.* **5** put in a list; enroll. *v.,* **in scribed, in scrib ing.** —**in scrib′a ble**, *adj.* —**in scrib′er**, *n.*

in scrip tion (in skrip′shən), **1** something inscribed; words, names, etc., written or engraved on stone, metal, paper, etc. A monument or a coin has an inscription on it. **2** an informal dedication in a book, on a picture, etc. **3** act of writing upon or in something. *n.* —**in scrip′tion less**, *adj.*

in scru ta bil i ty (in skrü′tə bil′ə tē), **1** a being inscrutable. **2** something inscrutable. *n.*

in scru ta ble (in skrü′tə bəl), not able to be understood; so mysterious or obscure that one cannot make out its meaning. *adj.* [*Inscrutable* is from Latin *inscrutabilis,* which comes from *in-,* meaning "not," and *scrutari,* meaning "examine, search through."] —**in scru′ta ble ness**, *n.*

in scru ta bly (in skrü′tə blē), in an inscrutable manner; mysteriously. *adv.*

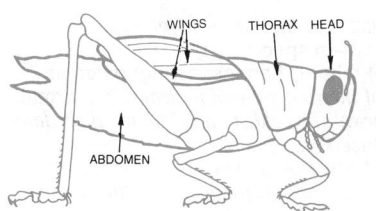

WINGS THORAX HEAD
ABDOMEN

insect (def. 1)
a grasshopper

a hat	**i** it	**oi** oil	**ch** child	a in about
ā age	**ī** ice	**ou** out	**ng** long	e in taken
ä far	**o** hot	**u** cup	**sh** she	ə = i in pencil
e let	**ō** open	**u̇** put	**th** thin	o in lemon
ē equal	**ô** order	**ü** rule	**ŦH** then	u in circus
ėr term			**zh** measure	

in sect (in′sekt), **1** any of a group of small animals with no backbone and with the body divided into three parts (head, thorax, and abdomen). Insects have three pairs of legs, and one or two pairs of wings. Flies, mosquitoes, butterflies, bees, grasshoppers, and beetles are insects. **2** any similar animal, especially a wingless one with four pairs of legs. Spiders, centipedes, mites, and ticks are often called insects. *n.* —**in′sect like′**, *adj.*

in sec ti cide (in sek′tə sīd), substance for killing insects. *n.*

in sec ti vore (in sek′tə vôr), any animal or plant that feeds mainly on insects. Moles and mantises are insectivores. *n.*

in sec tiv or ous (in′sek tiv′ər əs), insect-eating; feeding mainly on insects. *adj.*

in se cure (in′si kyu̇r′), **1** exposed to danger, loss, attack, etc.; not secure; unsafe: *a region where life is insecure.* **2** liable to give way; not firm: *an insecure support, an insecure lock. adj.* —**in′se cure′ly**, *adv.* —**in′se cure′ness**, *n.*

in se cur i ty (in′si kyu̇r′ə tē), **1** lack of security; being insecure; unsafe condition. **2** something insecure. *n., pl.* **in se cur i ties.**

in sem i nate (in sem′ə nāt), inject semen into; fertilize; impregnate. *v.,* **in sem i nat ed, in sem i nat ing.** —**in sem′i na′tion,** *n.*

in sen sate (in sen′sāt), **1** without sensation; lifeless; inanimate: *insensate stones.* **2** unfeeling; brutal: *insensate cruelty.* **3** senseless; stupid: *insensate folly. adj.* —**in sen′sate ly,** *adv.* —**in sen′sate ness,** *n.*

in sen si bil i ty (in sen′sə bil′ə tē), **1** lack of feeling; unawareness. **2** lack of consciousness; senselessness. *n., pl.* **in sen si bil i ties.**

in sen si ble (in sen′sə bəl), **1** not sensitive; not able to feel or notice: *She appeared to be insensible to cold.* **2** not aware; unmoved; indifferent: *The swimmers were insensible to the dangers of the high waves.* **3** not able to feel anything; unconscious; senseless: *The man hit by the truck was insensible for four hours. adj.* —**in sen′si ble ness,** *n.*

in sen si bly (in sen′sə blē), by insensible degrees; little by little. *adv.*

in sen si tive (in sen′sə tiv), **1** not sensitive: *an insensitive area of the skin.* **2** slow to feel or notice: *They were insensitive to the needs of others. adj.* —**in sen′si tive ly,** *adv.* —**in sen′si tive ness,** *n.*

in sen si tiv i ty (in sen′sə tiv′ə tē), insensitive condition or quality. *n.*

in sep ar a bil i ty (in sep′ər ə bil′ə tē), a being inseparable. *n.*

in sep ar a ble (in sep′ər ə bəl), not able to be separated; constantly together: *The two friends are inseparable companions. adj.* —**in sep′ar a ble ness,** *n.*

in sep ar a bly (in sep′ər ə blē), in an inseparable manner. *adv.*

in sert (in sėrt′ *for 1;* in′sėrt *for 2),* **1** put in; set in: *He inserted the key into the lock. She inserted a letter into the misspelled word.* **2** something put in or set in: *The newspaper had an insert of several pages of pictures.* 1 *v.,* 2 *n.* —**in sert′a ble,** *adj.* —**in sert′er,** *n.*

in ser tion (in sėr′shən), **1** act of inserting: *The insertion of one word can change the meaning of a whole sentence.* **2** something inserted. *n.*

in set (in set′ *for 1;* in′set′ *for 2),* **1** set in; insert. **2** something inserted. 1 *v.,* **in set, in set ting;** 2 *n.*

in shore (in′shôr′), **1** near the shore: *Inshore fishing is not allowed where people swim.* **2** in toward the shore: *The boat was driven inshore by the winds.* 1 *adj.,* 2 *adv.*

in side (in′sīd′ *for 1-3,6;* in′sīd′ *for 4,5),* **1** the part within; the inner surface: *The inside of the box was lined with colored paper.* **2** the contents: *The inside of the book was more interesting than the cover.* **3** being on the inside: *an inside seat.* **4** on or to the inside; within; in the inner part: *Please step inside.* **5** inside of; in: *The nut is inside the shell.* **6** done or known by those inside; secret: *The informer had inside information of the gang's plans.* 1,2 *n.,* 3,6 *adj.,* 4 *adv.,* 5 *prep.*

inside of, within the limits of; in.

inside out, 1 so that what should be inside is outside; with the inside showing: *He turned his pockets inside out.* **2** completely; thoroughly: *She learned her lessons inside out.*

in sid er (in′sī′dər), **1** person who belongs to a certain group, club, society, political party, etc. **2** person who has private or secret information about something not known to most others. *n.*

in sides (in′sīdz′), INFORMAL. the soft organs inside the body. *n.pl.*

in sid i ous (in sid′ē əs), **1** seeking to entrap or ensnare; wily or sly; crafty; tricky. **2** working secretly or subtly; developing without attracting attention: *Tuberculosis is an insidious disease; you can have it without knowing it. adj.* [*Insidious* is from Latin *insidiosus,* which comes from *insidiae,* meaning "an ambush."] —**in sid′i ous ly,** *adv.* —**in sid′i ous ness,** *n.*

in sight (in′sīt′), **1** a viewing of the inside with understanding: *Take the machine apart and get an insight into how it works.* **2** wisdom and understanding in dealing with people or with facts: *We study science to gain insight into the world we live in. n.*

in sig ne (in sig′nē), insignia. *n., pl.* **in sig ni a.**

insignia (def. 1)
of the United
States Navy

in sig ni a (in sig′nē ə), **1** medals, badges, or other distinguishing marks of a position, honor, military order, etc. **2** plural of **insigne.** *n., pl.* **in sig ni a** or **in sig ni as.**

in sig nif i cance (in′sig nif′ə kəns), **1** unimportance; uselessness. **2** meaninglessness. *n.*

in sig nif i cant (in′sig nif′ə kənt), **1** having little use or importance; trivial: *A tenth of a cent is an insignificant amount of money.* **2** having little meaning; meaningless: *insignificant chatter. adj.* —**in′sig nif′i cant ly,** *adv.*

in sin cere (in′sin sir′), not sincere; not honest or candid; deceitful. *adj.* —**in′sin cere′ly,** *adv.*

in sin cer i ty (in′sin ser′ə tē), lack of sincerity; being insincere; hypocrisy. *n., pl.* **in sin cer i ties.**

in sin u ate (in sin′yü āt), **1** suggest in an indirect way; hint: *To say "That worker can't do the job; it takes skill" is to insinuate that the worker is not skilled.* **2** push in or get in by an indirect, subtle way: *The spy insinuated himself into the confidence of important army officers.* *v.,* **in sin u at ed, in sin u at ing.** [*Insinuate* is from Latin *insinuatum,* meaning "wound or twisted into," which comes from *in-,* meaning "in," and *sinus,* meaning "a curve, a winding."] —**in sin′u at′ing ly,** *adv.* —**in sin′u a′tor,** *n.*

in sin u a tion (in sin′yü ā′shən), **1** an insinuating: *the insinuation of oneself into the confidence of others.* **2** an indirect suggestion meant to discredit someone: *The student objected strongly to the insinuation of dishonesty.* **3** hint; suggestion. **4** act or speech to gain favor in an indirect, subtle way. *n.*

in sip id (in sip′id), **1** without any particular flavor; tasteless: *A mixture of milk and water is an insipid drink.* **2** lacking interest or spirit; dull, colorless, or weak: *The insipid conversation bored everyone.* *adj.* —**in sip′id ly,** *adv.* —**in sip′id ness,** *n.*

in sist (in sist′), keep firmly to some demand, statement, or position; take a stand and refuse to give in: *He insists that he had a right to use his brother's tools. After her arrest she insisted on her innocence.* *v.* —**in sist′er,** *n.* —**in sist′ing ly,** *adv.*

in sist ence (in sis′təns), **1** act of insisting: *At the teacher's insistence the class became quiet.* **2** quality of being insistent. *n.*

in sist ent (in sis′tənt), **1** continuing to make a strong, firm demand or statement; insisting: *In spite of the rain she was insistent on going out.* **2** impossible to overlook or disregard; compelling attention or notice; pressing; urgent: *Her insistent knocking on the door woke us up.* *adj.* —**in sist′ent ly,** *adv.*

in snare (in sner′ *or* in snar′), ensnare. *v.,* **in snared, in snar ing.** —**in snare′ment,** *n.* —**in snar′er,** *n.*

in so far as (in′sō fär′), to such an extent or degree as: *Insofar as I can tell, the weather should be nice tomorrow.*

insol., insoluble.

in sole (in′sōl′), **1** the inner sole of a shoe or boot. **2** layer of warm or waterproof material put on the sole inside a shoe or boot. *n.*

in so lence (in′sə ləns), bold rudeness; insulting behavior or speech; intentional disregard of the feelings of others. *n.*

in so lent (in′sə lənt), boldly rude; intentionally disregarding the feelings of others; insulting: *You were insolent to turn your back on me while I was talking to you.* *adj.* [*Insolent* is from Latin *insolentem,* meaning "arrogant, contrary to custom."] —**in′so lent ly,** *adv.*

in sol u bil i ty (in sol′yə bil′ə tē), insoluble condition or quality. *n.*

in sol u ble (in sol′yə bəl), **1** not able to be dissolved: *Fats are insoluble in water.* **2** not able to be solved: *The detective finally gave up, declaring the mystery insoluble.* *adj.* —**in sol′u ble ness,** *n.* —**in sol′u bly,** *adv.*

in sol ven cy (in sol′vən sē), condition of not being able to pay one's debts; bankruptcy. *n., pl.* **in sol ven cies.**

in sol vent (in sol′vənt), unable to pay one's debts; bankrupt. *adj.*

in som ni a (in som′nē ə), inability to sleep; sleeplessness. *n.*

in so much as (in′sō much′), inasmuch; since.

in spect (in spekt′), **1** look over carefully; examine: *The engineers inspected the new dam.* **2** look over officially; examine formally: *Government officials inspect factories and mines to make sure that they are safe for workers.* *v.* —**in spect′a ble,** *adj.* —**in spect′ing ly,** *adv.*

in spec tion (in spek′shən), **1** an inspecting; examination: *An inspection of the roof showed no leaks.* **2** a formal or official examination: *The soldiers lined up for their daily inspection by their officers.* *n.*

in spec tor (in spek′tər), **1** person who inspects. **2** officer or official appointed to inspect: *a milk inspector.* **3** a police officer, usually ranking next below a superintendent. *n.*

in spi ra tion (in′spə rā′shən), **1** influence of thought and strong feelings on actions, especially on good actions: *Some people get inspiration from sermons, some from poetry.* **2** person or thing that puts life or force into others and arouses them to do well: *The teacher was an inspiration to her students.* **3** idea that is inspired; sudden, brilliant idea. **4** a breathing in; a drawing of air into the lungs. *n.*

in spi ra tion al (in′spə rā′shə nəl), **1** inspiring: *The sermon was both instructive and inspirational.* **2** of or having to do with inspiration. *adj.* —**in′spi ra′tion al ly,** *adv.*

in spire (in spīr′), **1** fill with a thought or feeling; influence: *A chance to try again inspired her with hope.* **2** cause (thought or feeling): *The leader's courage inspired confidence in others.* **3** put thought, feeling, life, force, etc., into: *The speaker inspired the crowd. The coach inspired the team with a desire to win.* **4** cause to be told or written; suggest: *Helen Keller's life story inspired a movie.* **5** draw air into the lungs; breathe in. *v.,* **in spired, in spir ing.** —**in spir′a ble,** *adj.* —**in spir′ing ly,** *adv.*

in spir er (in spī′rər), person or thing that inspires. *n.*

in spir it (in spir′it), put spirit into; encourage; hearten; cheer. *v.* —**in spir′i ter,** *n.* —**in spir′it ing ly,** *adv.* —**in spir′it ment,** *n.*

inst., instant (def. 6). "The 10th inst." means "the tenth day of the present month."

in sta bil i ty (in′stə bil′ə tē), lack of firmness; being unstable; unsteadiness. *n.*

in stall *or* **in stal** (in stôl′), **1** put (a person) in office with ceremonies: *The new judge was installed without delay.* **2** put in a place or position; settle: *The cat installed itself in a chair near the fireplace.* **3** put in place for use: *The new owner of the house had a telephone installed.* *v.,* **in stalled, in stall ing.** —**in stall′er,** *n.*

in stal la tion (in′stə lā′shən), **1** an installing: *Installation of more electric lights made the room brighter.* **2** a being installed: *I attended my mother's installation as president of the P.T.A.* **3** something installed, especially machinery placed in position for use. **4** a military base or camp, including personnel, equipment, buildings, etc. *n.*

in stall ment[1] *or* **in stal ment**[1] (in stôl′mənt), **1** part of a sum of money or of a debt to be paid at certain stated times: *The table cost $100; we paid for it in two installments of $50 each.* **2** one of several parts issued at different times as part of a series: *This magazine has a serial story in six installments.* *n.*

in stall ment[2] *or* **in stal ment**[2] (in stôl′mənt), **1** an installing: *the installment of electric lights in a house.* **2** a being installed: *our installment in our new home.* *n.*

installment plan, system of paying for goods in regular, usually monthly, installments.

in stance (in′stəns), **1** person or thing serving as an example; illustration; case: *Lincoln is an instance of a poor boy who became famous.* **2** give as an example; cite. **3** stage or step in an action; occasion: *I went in the first instance because I was asked to go.* **1,3** *n.,* **2** *v.,* **in stanced, in stanc ing.**

for instance, as an example: *Her many different hobbies include, for instance, skating and stamp collecting.*

in stant (in′stənt), **1** particular moment: *Stop talking this*

instant! **2** moment of time: *He paused for an instant.*
3 coming at once; without delay; immediate: *The medicine gave instant relief from pain.* **4** pressing; urgent: *When there is a fire, there is an instant need for action.* **5** prepared beforehand and requiring little or no cooking, mixing, or additional ingredients: *instant coffee, instant pudding.* **6** of the present month; present. 1,2 *n.*, 3-6 *adj.*

in stan ta ne ous (in′stən tā′nē əs), coming or done in an instant; happening or made in an instant: *A flash of lightning is instantaneous. adj.* —**in′stan ta′ne ous ly,** *adv.* —**in′stan ta′ne ous ness,** *n.*

in stant ly (in′stənt lē), in an instant; at once; immediately. *adv.*

in stead (in sted′), in another's place; as a substitute: *She stayed home, and her sister went riding instead. adv.*
instead of, rather than; in place of; as a substitute for: *Instead of studying, I watched television.*

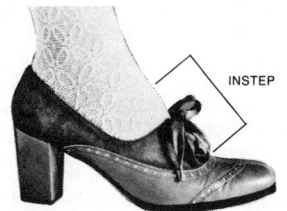

instep
(defs. 1 and 2)

in step (in′step), **1** the upper surface of the human foot between the toes and the ankle. **2** the part of a shoe, stocking, etc., over the instep. *n.*

in sti gate (in′stə gāt), urge on; stir up: *The older boy instigated a quarrel between his two younger brothers. v.,* **in sti gat ed, in sti gat ing.** —**in′sti gat′ing ly,** *adv.*

in sti ga tion (in′stə gā′shən), an urging on; stirring up. *n.*

in sti ga tor (in′stə gā′tər), person who instigates, especially one who stirs up evil or trouble. *n.*

in still or **in stil** (in stil′), put in little by little; cause to enter the mind, heart, etc., gradually: *Reading good books instills a love for fine literature. v.,* **in stilled, in still ing.** —**in′stil la′tion,** *n.* —**in still′er,** *n.* —**in still′ment, in stil′ment,** *n.*

in stinct (in′stingkt), **1** a natural feeling, knowledge, or power, such as that which guides animals; inborn tendency to act in a certain way: *Birds build their nests by instinct.* **2** a natural tendency or ability; talent: *Even as a child the artist had an instinct for drawing. n.*

in stinc tive (in stingk′tiv), of or having to do with instinct; caused or done by instinct; born in an animal or person, not learned: *The spinning of webs is instinctive in spiders. adj.* —**in stinc′tive ly,** *adv.*

in sti tute (in′stə tüt *or* in′stə tyüt), **1** organization or society for some special purpose. An art institute teaches or displays art. A technical school or college is often called an institute. **2** building used by such an organization or society: *We spent the afternoon in the Art Institute.* **3** set up; establish; begin; start: *The Pilgrims instituted Thanksgiving. After the accident, the police instituted an inquiry into its causes.* 1,2 *n.,* 3 *v.,* **in sti tut ed, in sti tut ing.** —**in′sti tut′er, in′sti tu′tor,** *n.*

in sti tu tion (in′stə tü′shən *or* in′stə tyü′shən), **1** society, club, college, or any organization established for some public or social purpose. A church, school, university, hospital, asylum, or prison is an institution. **2** a building used for the work of an institution. **3** an established law or custom: *Marriage is an institution among most of the world's people.* **4** a setting up; establishing; beginning; starting: *We hope for the institution of hot lunches at school this winter. n.*

a hat	**i** it	**oi** oil	**ch** child	a in about
ā age	**ī** ice	**ou** out	**ng** long	e in taken
ä far	**o** hot	**u** cup	**sh** she	ə = { i in pencil
e let	**ō** open	**ù** put	**th** thin	o in lemon
ē equal	**ô** order	**ü** rule	**ŦH** then	u in circus
ėr term			**zh** measure	

in sti tu tion al (in′stə tü′shə nəl *or* in′stə tyü′shə nəl), of or like an institution. *adj.* —**in′sti tu′tion al ly,** *adv.*

in sti tu tion al ize (in′stə tü′shə nə līz *or* in′stə tyü′shə nə līz), **1** make into an institution. **2** put into an institution. *v.,* **in sti tu tion al ized, in sti tu tion al iz ing.** —**in′sti tu′tion al i za′tion,** *n.*

instr., **1** instructor. **2** instrument.

in struct (in strukt′), **1** give knowledge to; show how to do; teach; train; educate: *We have one teacher who instructs us in reading, English, history, and arithmetic.* **2** give directions to; order: *The doctor instructed him to go to bed and rest. The owner of the house instructed her agent to sell it.* **3** inform; tell: *The family lawyer instructed them that the contract would be signed Monday. v.* —**in struct′i ble,** *adj.*

in struc tion (in struk′shən), **1** a teaching or educating. **2** knowledge or teaching given; lesson. **3 instructions,** *pl.* directions; orders. *n.*

in struc tion al (in struk′shə nəl), of or for instruction; educational. *adj.*

in struc tive (in struk′tiv), useful for instruction; giving knowledge or information; instructing: *A trip around the world can be an instructive experience. adj.* —**in struc′tive ly,** *adv.* —**in struc′tive ness,** *n.*

in struc tor (in struk′tər), **1** teacher. **2** teacher ranking below professors in American colleges and universities. *n.*

in stru ment (in′strə mənt), **1** a mechanical device that is portable, of simple construction, and usually operated by hand; tool: *a dentist's instruments.* **2** device for producing musical sounds: *wind instruments, stringed instruments. A violin, cello, and piano were the instruments in the trio.* **3** device for measuring, recording, or controlling. A thermometer is an instrument for measuring temperature. **4** thing with or by which something is done; person made use of by another; means: *The young king's wicked uncle used his influence as an instrument to gain power.* **5** a formal legal document, such as a contract, deed, or grant. *n.*

in stru men tal (in′strə men′tl), **1** acting or serving as a means; useful; helpful: *A friend was instrumental in getting me a job.* **2** played on or written for musical instruments: *The singer was accompanied by instrumental music. adj.* —**in′stru men′tal ly,** *adv.*

in stru men tal ist (in′strə men′tl ist), person who plays on a musical instrument. *n.*

in stru men tal i ty (in′strə men tal′ə tē), quality or condition of being instrumental; helpfulness; agency; means. *n., pl.* **in stru men tal i ties.**

in stru men ta tion (in′strə men tā′shən), **1** arrangement or composition of music for instruments. **2** use of instruments; work done with instruments. *n.*

in sub or di nate (in′sə bôrd′n it), not submitting to authority; refusing to obey; disobedient; rebellious. *adj.* —**in′sub or′di nate ly,** *adv.*

in sub or di na tion (in′sə bôrd′n ā′shən), resistance to authority; refusal to obey; disobedience; rebellion. *n.*

in sub stan tial (in′səb stan′shəl), **1** frail; flimsy: *A cobweb is very insubstantial.* **2** unreal; not actual; imaginary: *Dreams and ghosts are insubstantial. adj.* —**in′substan′tial ly,** *adv.*

in suf fer a ble (in suf′ər ə bəl), unbearable; intolerable: *The heat of the desert at noon was insufferable. adj.*

in suf fer a bly (in suf′ər ə blē), **1** in an insufferable manner. **2** to an insufferable degree. *adv.*

in suf fi cien cy (in′sə fish′ən sē), too small an amount; lack; deficiency. *n., pl.* **in suf fi cien cies.**

in suf fi cient (in′sə fish′ənt), not enough; less than is needed: *She was tired because she had had insufficient sleep. adj.* —**in′suf fi′cient ly,** *adv.*

in su lar (in′sə lər), **1** of islands or islanders. **2** living or situated on an island. **3** standing alone like an island; isolated: *No nation can now keep an insular position in world affairs.* **4** narrow-minded; prejudiced. *adj.*

in su lar i ty (in′sə lar′ə tē), **1** condition of being an island or of living on an island. **2** narrow-mindedness; prejudice. *n.*

in su late (in′sə lāt), **1** keep from losing or transferring electricity, heat, sound, etc., especially by covering, packing, or surrounding with a material that does not conduct electricity, heat, etc.: *Telephone wires are often insulated by a covering of rubber.* **2** set apart; separate from others; isolate: *Prisoners are insulated from the normal, everyday world. v.,* **in su lat ed, in su lat ing.** [*Insulate* comes from Latin *insula,* meaning "island."]

in su la tion (in′sə lā′shən), **1** an insulating: *The electrician checked the insulation of the wiring.* **2** a being insulated: *The insulation of the outer walls helps keep our house warm in the winter.* **3** material used in insulating: *Asbestos is often used as an insulation against fire. n.*

insulator—The glass insulators keep the electricity that goes through the wires from passing into the wooden pole.

in su la tor (in′sə lā′tər), that which insulates; something that prevents the passage of electricity, heat, or sound; nonconductor. *n.*

in su lin (in′sə lən), **1** hormone secreted by the pancreas that enables the body to use sugar and other carbohydrates. **2** drug containing insulin, used in treating diabetes. Insulin is obtained from the pancreas of slaughtered animals. *n.*

WORD HISTORY

insulin

Insulin comes from Latin *insula,* meaning "island." The hormone comes from small islandlike endocrine glands in the pancreas.

in sult (in sult′ *for 1;* in′sult *for 2*), **1** say or do something very scornful, rude, or harsh to: *She insulted me by calling me a liar.* **2** an insulting speech or action: *To be called stupid is an insult.* **1** *v.,* **2** *n.* —**in sult′a ble,** *adj.* —**in sult′er,** *n.* —**in sult′ing ly,** *adv.*

in su per a ble (in sü′pər ə bəl), not able to be passed over or overcome: *an insuperable barrier. adj.*

in su per a bly (in sü′pər ə blē), in an insuperable manner. *adv.*

in sup port a ble (in′sə pôr′tə bəl), not endurable; unbearable; intolerable. *adj.* —**in′sup port′a ble ness,** *n.*

in sur a ble (in shúr′ə bəl), capable of being insured; fit to be insured. *adj.*

in sur ance (in shúr′əns), **1** an insuring of property, person, or life. Fire insurance, burglary insurance, accident insurance, life insurance, and health insurance are some of the many kinds. **2** the business of insuring property, life, etc. **3** amount of money for which a person or thing is insured: *He has $10,000 in life insurance, which his wife will receive if he dies before she does.* **4** amount of money paid for insurance; premium: *The fire insurance on our house is $100 a year. n.*

in sure (in shúr′), **1** arrange payment of money in case of loss, accident, or death by paying a certain amount of money at intervals. An insurance company will insure your property, person, or life. **2** make safe from financial loss by paying money to an insurance company: *She insured her car against accident, theft, and fire. v.,* **in sured, in sur ing.**

in sured (in shúrd′), person who is insured. *n.*

in sur er (in shúr′ər), person or company that insures. *n.*

in sur gence (in sėr′jəns), a rising in revolt; rebellion. *n.*

in sur gent (in sėr′jənt), **1** person who rises in revolt; rebel: *The insurgents captured the town.* **2** rising in revolt; rebellious: *The insurgent peasants burned the landowners′ houses.* **1** *n.,* **2** *adj.* —**in sur′gent ly,** *adv.*

in sur mount a ble (in′sər moun′tə bəl), not able to be overcome. *adj.* —**in′sur mount′a ble ness,** *n.*

in sur rec tion (in′sə rek′shən), a rising against established authority; revolt; rebellion. *n.*

in sur rec tion ist (in′sə rek′shə nist), person who takes part in or favors an insurrection; rebel. *n.*

int., 1 interest. **2** interior. **3** internal.

in tact (in takt′), with no part missing; whole; untouched; uninjured: *dishes left intact after being dropped. The money was returned intact. adj.* —**in tact′ness,** *n.*

in take (in′tāk′), **1** place where water, air, gas, etc., enters a channel, pipe, or other narrow opening. **2** act or process of taking in. **3** amount or thing taken in: *The intake through the pipe was 5000 gallons a day. n.*

in tan gi ble (in tan′jə bəl), **1** not capable of being touched or felt: *Sound and light are intangible.* **2** not easily grasped by the mind; vague: *Charm is an intangible quality.* **3** something intangible. **1,2** *adj.,* **3** *n.* —**in tan′gi ble ness,** *n.* —**in tan′gi bly,** *adv.*

in te ger (in′tə jər), any positive or negative whole number, or zero. *n.*

in te gral (in′tə grəl), **1** necessary to make something complete; essential: *Steel is an integral part of a modern skyscraper.* **2** entire; complete. **3** of an integer; not fractional. *adj.* —**in′te gral ly,** *adv.*

in te grate (in′tə grāt), **1** make into a whole; complete. **2** put or bring together (parts) into a whole: *The committee will try to integrate the different ideas into one uniform plan.* **3** make (schools, parks, etc.) available to people of all races on an equal basis: *integrate a neighborhood. v.,* **in te grat ed, in te grat ing.** —**in′te gra′tor,** *n.*

integrated circuit, an electrical circuit designed for a single function and manufactured as a unit on or in a chip of semiconductor. An integrated circuit containing thousands of transistors may be less than an inch across.

in te gra tion (in′tə grā′shən), **1** an integrating: *the integration of the activities of all the people who are working on a project.* **2** inclusion of people of all races on an equal basis in schools, parks, neighborhoods, etc. *n.*

in te gra tion ist (in′tə grā′shə nist), person who believes in the integration of people of all races. *n.*

in teg ri ty (in teg′rə tē), **1** honesty or sincerity; upright-ness: *A person of integrity is respected.* **2** wholeness; com-pleteness: *to defend the integrity of a country against its enemies. n.*

in tel lect (in′tə lekt), **1** power of knowing; understand-ing; mind. *Our actions are influenced by our intellect, will, and feelings.* **2** great intelligence; high mental abil-ity: *Isaac Newton was a man of intellect.* **3** person of high mental ability: *Einstein was one of the greatest intellects of his time. n.*

in tel lec tu al (in′tə lek′chü əl), **1** needing or using in-telligence: *Teaching is an intellectual occupation.* **2** of the intellect: *Thinking is an intellectual process.* **3** having or showing intelligence: *an intellectual person.* **4** person who is well informed and intelligent. **1-3** *adj.*, **4** *n.*

in tel lec tu al ly (in′tə lek′chü ə lē), in an intellectual way. *adv.*

in tel li gence (in tel′ə jəns), **1** ability to learn and know; quickness of understanding; mind: *Many schools give tests to measure intelligence.* **2** knowledge, news, or infor-mation: *The spy gave secret intelligence to the enemy.* **3** secret information, especially about an enemy: *Spies supply our government with intelligence.* **4** group engaged in obtaining secret information: *Intelligence sent agents to infiltrate the enemy's missile bases. n.*

intelligence quotient, number that shows the rating of a person's intelligence. It is found by dividing the mental age shown in tests by the actual age (16 is the largest age used) and multiplying by 100.

intelligence test, any test used to measure mental development.

in tel li gent (in tel′ə jənt), **1** having or showing intelli-gence; able to learn and know; quick to understand. **2** in data processing: **a** containing a microprocessor and so able to perform functions often requiring a computer: *an intelligent terminal.* **b** having artificial intelligence. *adj.* [*In-telligent* is from Latin *intelligentem,* which comes from *inter-,* meaning "between," and *legere,* meaning "to choose."] **—in tel′li gent ly,** *adv.*

in tel li gent si a (in tel′ə jent′sē ə), persons represent-ing, or claiming to represent, the educated class; the intellectuals. *n.pl.*

in tel li gi ble (in tel′ə jə bəl), capable of being under-stood; clear. *adj.*

in tel li gi bly (in tel′ə jə blē), so as to be understood; clearly. *adv.*

in tem per ance (in tem′pər əns), **1** lack of moderation or self-control; excess: *Intemperance in eating can cause one to become very fat.* **2** too much drinking of intoxicat-ing liquor. *n.*

in tem per ate (in tem′pər it), **1** not moderate; lacking in self-control; excessive: *intemperate anger.* **2** drinking too much intoxicating liquor. **3** not temperate; extreme in temperature; severe: *an intemperate winter. adj.* **—in tem′per ate ly,** *adv.* **—in tem′per ate ness,** *n.*

in tend (in tend′), **1** have in mind as a purpose; plan: *I intend to go home soon. They intend that their children shall go to college.* **2** mean for a particular purpose or use: *That gift was intended for you. v.* **—in tend′er,** *n.*

in tend ed (in ten′did), **1** in mind as a purpose; meant; planned: *The medicine had the intended effect and stopped the pain.* **2** going to be; future: *A woman's intended hus-band is the man she is going to marry.* **3** INFORMAL. an intended husband or wife. **1,2** *adj.*, **3** *n.* **—in tend′ed ly,** *adv.* **—in tend′ed ness,** *n.*

in tense (in tens′), **1** very much; very great; very strong; extreme: *Intense heat melts iron. A bad burn causes intense pain.* **2** full of vigorous activity, strong feelings, etc. **3** having or showing strong feeling. An intense person is

one who feels things very deeply and is likely to be extreme in action. *adj.* [*Intense* is from Latin *intensum,* meaning "strained, stretched," which comes from *in-,* meaning "toward," and *tendere,* meaning "to stretch."] **—in tense′ly,** *adv.* **—in tense′ness,** *n.*

in ten si fi ca tion (in ten′sə fə kā′shən), a making or becoming more intense. *n.*

in ten si fi er (in ten′sə fī′ər), (in grammar) an inten-sive. *n.*

in ten si fy (in ten′sə fī), make or become intense or more intense; strengthen; increase: *Blowing on a fire intensifies the heat. My first failure only intensified my desire to succeed. v.,* **in ten si fied, in ten si fy ing.**

in ten si ty (in ten′sə tē), **1** quality of being intense; great strength: *the intensity of sunlight.* **2** extreme degree; great vigor; violence: *intensity of thought, intensity of feeling.* **3** amount or degree of strength of electricity, heat, light, sound, etc., per unit of area, volume, etc. *n., pl.* **in ten si ties.**

in ten sive (in ten′siv), **1** deep and thorough: *New laws were passed following an intensive study of the causes of pollution.* **2** (in grammar) giving force or emphasis; ex-pressing intensity. In "I did it myself," *myself* is an inten-sive pronoun. **3** word, prefix, etc., that expresses intensi-ty or gives force or emphasis. In "It's terribly late," *terri-bly* is an intensive. **1,2** *adj.*, **3** *n.* **—in ten′sive ly,** *adv.*

intensive care unit, a medical unit specially equipped to provide continuous hospital care for pa-tients who are very seriously ill or emergency care for accident or heart attack victims.

in tent (in tent′), **1** that which is intended; purpose; in-tention: *I'm sorry I hurt you; that wasn't my intent.* **2** meaning; significance: *What is the intent of that remark?* **3** very attentive; having the eyes or thoughts earnestly fixed on something; earnest: *an intent look. She was in-tent on a math problem.* **4** earnestly engaged; much inter-ested: *be intent upon making money. I am intent on doing my best.* **1,2** *n.,* **3,4** *adj.* **—in tent′ly,** *adv.*

to all intents and purposes, in almost every way; prac-tically; almost.

in ten tion (in ten′shən), **1** an intending; purpose; de-sign; plan: *If I hurt your feelings, it was without intention. Your intention to help is good, but first you must learn how.* **2** meaning. *n.*

in ten tion al (in ten′shə nəl), done on purpose; meant; planned; intended: *His lateness was intentional; he wanted to hear just the last two speakers. adj.* **—in ten′tion al ly,** *adv.*

in ter (in tėr′), put (a dead body) into a grave or tomb; bury. *v.,* **in terred, in ter ring.**

inter-, *prefix.* **1** one with the other; with or on each oth-er; together: *Intercommunicate = communicate with each other.* **2** between: *Interpose=put between.* **3** between or among a group: *International = between or among nations.*

in ter act (in′tər akt′), act on each other. *v.*

in ter ac tion (in′tər ak′shən), action on each other. *n.*

in ter breed (in′tər brēd′), breed by the mating of dif-ferent kinds; breed by using different varieties or species of animals or plants. *Many of our cultivated plants are hybrids developed by interbreeding various plants to combine their desirable qualities. v.,* **in ter bred** (in′tər-bred′), **in ter breed ing.**

---

a hat	**i** it	**oi** oil	**ch** child	a in about
ā age	**ī** ice	**ou** out	**ng** long	e in taken
ä far	**o** hot	**u** cup	**sh** she	ə = i in pencil
e let	**ō** open	**u̇** put	**th** thin	o in lemon
ē equal	**ô** order	**ü** rule	**ŦH** then	u in circus
ėr term			**zh** measure	

in ter cede (in′tər sēd′), **1** plead for another; ask a favor from one person for another: *The senator interceded with the governor to help us save the state park.* **2** interfere in order to bring about an agreement: *The debate between the lawyers became so heated that the judge had to intercede. v.,* **in ter ced ed, in ter ced ing.**

in ter cel lu lar (in′tər sel′yə lər), situated between or among cells. *adj.*

in ter cept (in′tər sept′), **1** take or seize on the way from one place to another: *intercept a letter, intercept a messenger, intercept a pass in a football game.* **2** check; stop: *The police intercepted the flight of the escaped criminal. v.*

in ter cep tion (in′tər sep′shən), an intercepting or a being intercepted. *n.*

in ter cep tor or **in ter cept er** (in′tər sep′tər), **1** person or thing that intercepts. **2** a fast-climbing airplane designed to intercept enemy aircraft. *n.*

in ter ces sion (in′tər sesh′ən), act or fact of interceding; pleading for another: *The girl's intercession for her brother won their parents' consent to his request. n.*

in ter ces sor (in′tər ses′ər), person who intercedes. *n.*

in ter change (in′tər chānj′ *for 1,3;* in′tər chānj′ *for 2,4, 5),* **1** put each of (two or more persons or things) in the other's place: *If you interchange those two pictures, they'll look better.* **2** a putting each of two or more persons or things in the other's place: *The word "team" becomes "meat" by the interchange of the first and last letters.* **3** give and take; exchange: *We interchanged our ideas and opinions before making a decision.* **4** a giving and taking; exchanging. **5** a point at which a highway, especially an express highway, connects with another main traffic route. *1,3 v.,* **in ter changed, in ter chang ing;** *2,4,5 n.*

in ter change a ble (in′tər chān′jə bəl), **1** capable of being used in place of each other: *interchangeable parts.* **2** able to change places. *adj.*

in ter change a bly (in′tər chān′jə blē), in an interchangeable manner. *adv.*

in ter col le giate (in′tər kə lē′jit), between colleges or universities: *intercollegiate football games. adj.*

in ter com (in′tər kom′), any apparatus, usually using microphones and loudspeakers, with which members of an office staff, the crew of an airplane, tank, ship, etc., can talk to each other. *n.*

in ter com mu ni cate (in′tər kə myü′nə kāt), communicate with each other. *v.,* **in ter com mu ni cat ed, in ter com mu ni cat ing.**

in ter com mu ni ca tion (in′tər kə myü′nə kā′shən), communication with each other. *n.*

in ter con nect (in′tər kə nekt′), connect with each other. *v.* **—in′ter con nec′tion,** *n.*

in ter con ti nen tal (in′tər kon′tə nen′tl), between continents; from one continent to another: *an intercontinental railroad. adj.*

in ter course (in′tər kôrs), **1** dealings between people; exchange of thoughts, services, and feelings; communication: *Airplanes, good roads, and telephones make intercourse with different parts of the country far easier than it was 50 years ago.* **2** sexual intercourse. *n.*

in ter de nom i na tion al (in′tər di nom′ə nā′shə nəl), between different religious denominations. *adj.*

in ter de pend ence (in′tər di pen′dəns), dependence upon each other. *n.*

in ter de pend ent (in′tər di pen′dənt), dependent upon each other. *adj.* **—in′ter de pend′ent ly,** *adv.*

in ter dict (in′tər dikt′ *for 1,3a;* in′tər dikt′ *for 2,3b),* **1** prohibit or forbid; restrain. **2** prohibition based on authority; formal order forbidding something. **3** in the Roman Catholic Church: **a** cut off from certain church privileges. **b** a cutting off from certain church privileges. *1,3a v., 2,3b n.*

in ter dic tion (in′tər dik′shən), an interdicting or a being interdicted. *n.*

in ter est (in′tər ist), **1** a feeling of wanting to know, see, do, own, share in, or take part in: *He has an interest in reading and in collecting stamps.* **2** power of arousing such a feeling: *A dull book lacks interest.* **3** arouse such a feeling in; make curious and hold the attention of: *An exciting mystery interests most people.* **4** a share or part in property and actions: *She bought a half interest in the business.* **5** cause (a person) to take a share or part in something; arouse the concern, curiosity, or attention of: *The salesman tried to interest us in buying a car. We were interested in the results of the election.* **6** thing in which a person has a share or part. Any business, activity, or pastime can be an interest. **7** group of people having the same business, activity, etc.: *the business interests of the town.* **8** advantage; benefit; profit: *The parents look after the interests of the family.* **9** money paid for the use of money, usually a percentage of the amount invested, borrowed, or loaned: *The interest on the loan was 7 percent a year.* *1,2,4,6-9 n., 3,5 v.* [*Interest* comes from Latin *interest,* meaning "it is of importance, it makes a difference."]

in the interest of, for; to help.

in ter est ed (in′tər ə stid *or* in′tə res′tid), **1** feeling or showing interest; with one's interest aroused: *an interested spectator.* **2** having an interest or share. *adj.*

in ter est ing (in′tər ə sting *or* in′tə res′ting), arousing interest; holding one's attention: *Stories about travel and adventure are interesting. adj.* **—in′ter est ing ly,** *adv.*

in ter face (in′tər fās′), **1** connection linking two or more separate items so they can work together. A computer program can be the interface for other programs. **2** connect; join. *1 n., 2 v.,* **in ter faced, in ter fac ing.**

in ter faith (in′tər fāth′), of or for different faiths or religions: *an interfaith chapel, an interfaith conference. adj.*

in ter fere (in′tər fir′), **1** get in the way of each other; come into opposition; clash: *The two plans interfere; one must be changed.* **2** mix in the affairs of others; meddle: *That neighbor is always interfering in other people's affairs. Don't interfere with your sister when she's busy.* **3** take part for a purpose: *The teacher interfered to stop the fight. v.,* **in ter fered, in ter fer ing.** **—in′ter fer′er,** *n.*

interference (def. 4)
Player 63 ran
interference for
player 40.

in ter fer ence (in′tər fir′əns), **1** act or fact of interfering: *Your interference spoiled our game.* **2** something that interferes. **3** in radio or television: **a** the interruption of a desired signal by other signals. **b** unwanted static, noise, signals, etc., that distort sounds or pictures and prevent clear reception. **4** (in football) the protecting of the player who has the ball by blocking opposing players. **5** (in football, hockey, and other sports) the obstruction of an opposing player in a way barred by the rules. *n.*

in ter fer on (in′tər fir′on), protein produced by animal cells that have been infected by a virus. It protects similar cells from infection by the same or other viruses. *n.*

in ter im (in′tər im), **1** time between; the meantime. **2** for the meantime; temporary. **1** *n.*, **2** *adj.*

in ter i or (in tir′ē ər), **1** inner surface or part; inside: *The interior of the house was beautifully decorated.* **2** on or for the inside; inner. **3** part of a region or country away from the coast or border: *There are deserts in the interior of Asia.* **4** away from the coast or border. **5** affairs within a country, regarded as separate from foreign affairs. In the United States, the Department of the Interior is responsible for managing federal land and the nation's natural resources. **1,3,5** *n.*, **2,4** *adj.*

interior decorator, person whose business is planning and arranging the furnishings, decoration, etc., of houses, offices, or public buildings.

interj., interjection (def. 1).

in ter ject (in′tər jekt′), throw in between other things; insert abruptly: *Every now and then the speaker interjected a joke to keep us interested. v.*

in ter jec tion (in′tər jek′shən), **1** an exclamation showing emotion. It is regarded as a part of speech. *Oh! ah! alas!* and *hurrah!* are interjections. **2** an interjecting; sudden throwing in; abrupt insertion: *The interjection of amusing stories into the speech made it more interesting.* **3** something interjected; remark thrown in; exclamation. *n.*

interlace (def. 2) a ring made of bands that interlace

in ter lace (in′tər lās′), **1** arrange (threads, strips, or branches) so that they go over and under each other; weave together; intertwine: *Baskets are made by interlacing reeds or fibers.* **2** cross each other over and under; mingle together in an intricate manner: *The branches of the trees interlaced above the path.* *v.*, **in ter laced, in ter lac ing.**

in ter lard (in′tər lärd′), give variety to; mix; intersperse: *The speaker interlarded the long speech with amusing stories to keep the listeners interested. v.*

in ter lin ing (in′tər lī′ning), an extra lining inserted between the outer cloth and the ordinary lining of a garment. *n.*

in ter lock (in′tər lok′), join or fit tightly together; lock together. *The two stags were fighting with their horns interlocked. The pieces of a jigsaw puzzle interlock. v.*

in ter lop er (in′tər lō′pər), person who interferes, unasked and unwanted; intruder. *n.*

in ter lude (in′tər lüd), **1** anything thought of as filling the time between two things; interval: *There was an interlude of sunshine between the two showers.* **2** piece of music played between the parts of a song, church service, or drama. *n.*

in ter lu nar (in′tər lü′nər), of the time when the moon is not seen at night, between the old moon and the new moon. *adj.*

in ter mar riage (in′tər mar′ij), marriage between members of different families, tribes, religions, or racial groups. *n.*

in ter mar ry (in′tər mar′ē), become connected by marriage (said of families, tribes, religions, or racial groups): *The families of this old town have intermarried for generations.* *v.*, **in ter mar ried, in ter mar ry ing.**

in ter med dle (in′tər med′l), meddle; interfere. *v.*, **in ter med dled, in ter med dling.** —**in′ter med′dler,** *n.*

in ter me di ar y (in′tər mē′dē er′ē), **1** person who acts between others to bring about an agreement; person who acts for another; go-between: *The teacher acted as intermediary for the students with the principal.* **2** acting between others; acting for another. **3** being between; intermediate: *A cocoon is an intermediary stage between caterpillar and butterfly.* **1** *n.*, *pl.* **in ter me di ar ies;** **2,3** *adj.*

in ter me di ate (in′tər mē′dē it), **1** being or occurring between; middle: *Classes are offered in beginning, intermediate, and advanced French. Gray is intermediate between black and white.* **2** something in between. **1** *adj.*, **2** *n.*

in ter ment (in tėr′mənt), act of interring; burial. *n.*

in ter mez zo (in′tər met′sō *or* in′tər med′zō), a short musical composition played between the main divisions of an opera, symphony, or other long musical work. *n.*, *pl.* **in ter mez zos, in ter mez zi** (in′tər met′sē *or* in′tər med′zē). [*Intermezzo* was borrowed from Italian *intermezzo,* and can be traced back to Latin *inter-,* meaning "between," and *medius,* meaning "in the middle."]

in ter mi na ble (in tėr′mə nə bəl), **1** never stopping; unceasing; endless. **2** so long as to seem endless; very long and tiring. *adj.*

in ter mi na bly (in tėr′mə nə blē), in an interminable manner; endlessly. *adv.*

in ter min gle (in′tər ming′gəl), mix together; mingle: *The hosts encouraged guests with different interests to intermingle.* *v.*, **in ter min gled, in ter min gling.**

in ter mis sion (in′tər mish′ən), **1** time between periods of activity; pause: *The band played from eight to twelve with a short intermission at ten.* **2** stopping for a time; interruption: *The rain continued all day without intermission. n.*

in ter mit tent (in′tər mit′nt), stopping for a time and beginning again; pausing at intervals: *The pilot watched for an intermittent red light, flashing on and off every 15 seconds. adj.* —**in′ter mit′tent ly,** *adv.*

in ter mix (in′tər miks′), mix together; blend: *Oil and water do not intermix. v.*

in tern[1] (in tėrn′), confine within a country or place; force to stay in a certain place, especially during wartime. *v.*

in tern[2] (in′tėrn′), **1** doctor acting as an assistant and undergoing training in a hospital. **2** be an intern. **1** *n.*, **2** *v.* Also, **interne** for 1.

in ter nal (in tėr′nl), **1** on the inside; inner: *The accident caused internal injuries.* **2** to be taken inside the body: *Pills are internal remedies.* **3** of affairs within a country; domestic: *internal politics. Internal revenue is money from taxes on business and income in a country. adj.*

in ter nal-com bus tion engine (in tėr′nl kəm bus′chən), engine in which power is produced by burning a mixture of fuel and air inside the engine itself, usually inside cylinders. Gasoline engines and diesel engines are internal-combustion engines; steam engines are not.

in ter nal ly (in tėr/nl ē), **1** inside. **2** inside the body: *This ointment must not be taken internally. adv.*

in ter na tion al (in/tər nash/ə nəl), **1** between or among nations: *A treaty is an international agreement.* **2** having to do with the relations between nations: *international law. adj.*

International Date Line, an imaginary line agreed upon as the place where each new calendar day begins. It runs north and south through the Pacific, mostly along the 180th meridian. When it is Sunday just east of the International Date Line, it is Monday just west of it.

in ter na tion al ism (in/tər nash/ə nə liz/əm), principle of international cooperation for the good of all nations. *n.*

in ter na tion al ize (in/tər nash/ə nə līz), make international; bring under the control of several nations. *v.,* **in ter na tion al ized, in ter na tion al iz ing. —in/ter na/tion al i za/tion,** *n.*

in ter na tion al ly (in/tər nash/ə nə lē), in an international manner. *adv.*

in terne (in/tėrn/), intern[2] (def. 1). *n.*

in ter ne cine (in/tər nē/sn *or* in/tər nē/sīn), **1** destructive to both sides. **2** deadly; destructive. *adj.*

in ter nee (in/tėr/nē/), person interned. Prisoners of war, enemy aliens, etc., may be internees. *n.*

in tern ist (in tėr/nist), doctor who treats internal organs or diseases. *n.*

in tern ment (in tėrn/mənt), an interning or a being interned; confinement within a country or place. *n.*

in ter plan e tar y (in/tər plan/ə ter/ē), situated or taking place between the planets: *interplanetary travel. adj.*

in ter play (in/tər plā/), action or influence on each other: *the interplay of light and shadow, the interplay of events and characters in a story. n.*

in ter po late (in tėr/pə lāt), **1** alter (a book, passage, etc.) by putting in new words or groups of words, especially without authorization or deceptively: *So many later writers had interpolated the old manuscript that it was hard to tell what parts were genuine.* **2** put in (new words, passages, etc.). **3** (in mathematics) find or insert a value between two known values by some method. *v.,* **in ter po lat ed, in ter po lat ing.** [Interpolate is from Latin *interpolatum,* meaning "freshened up," which comes from *inter-,* meaning "between," and *polire,* meaning "make smooth."] **—in ter/po la/tor, in ter/po lat/er,** *n.*

in ter po la tion (in tėr/pə lā/shən), **1** an interpolating. **2** something interpolated: *an old manuscript with many interpolations of later date. n.*

in ter pose (in/tər pōz/), **1** put between; insert. **2** come or be between other things. **3** put forward; break in with; interrupt: *I'd like to interpose an objection at this point.* **4** interfere in order to help; intervene: *I interposed in the dispute between my friends. v.,* **in ter posed, in ter pos ing. —in/ter pos/a ble,** *adj.* **—in/ter pos/er,** *n.* **—in/ter pos/ing ly,** *adv.*

in ter po si tion (in/tər pə zish/ən), **1** an interposing: *the interposition of a remark.* **2** something interposed. *n.*

in ter pret (in tėr/prit), **1** explain the meaning of: *interpret a hard passage in a book, interpret a dream.* **2** bring out the meaning of (a dramatic work, a character, music, etc.): *The actress interpreted the part of the queen with wonderful skill.* **3** understand: *We interpreted your silence as consent.* **4** serve as an interpreter; translate. *v.* **—in ter/pret a ble,** *adj.*

in ter pre ta tion (in tėr/prə tā/shən), **1** an interpreting; explanation: *People often give different interpretations to the same facts.* **2** a bringing out the meaning: *The newspapers praised the musician's interpretation of the piece. n.*

in ter pre ta tive (in tėr/prə tā/tiv), used for interpreting; explanatory. *adj.* **—in ter/pre ta/tive ly,** *adv.*

in ter pret er (in tėr/prə tər), **1** person who interprets. **2** person whose business is translating, especially orally, from a foreign language. *n.*

in ter pre tive (in tėr/prə tiv), interpretative. *adj.* **—in ter/pre tive ly,** *adv.*

in ter ra cial (in/tər rā/shəl), between or involving different racial groups. *adj.*

in ter reg num (in/tər reg/nəm), **1** time between the end of one ruler's reign and the beginning of the next ruler's reign. **2** period of inactivity; pause. *n., pl.* **in ter reg nums, in ter reg na** (in/tər reg/nə).

in ter re late (in/tər ri lāt/), bring into relation to each other. *v.,* **in ter re lat ed, in ter re lat ing.**

in ter re lat ed (in/tər ri lā/tid), closely connected with each other; mutually related. *adj.* **—in/ter re lat/ed ly,** *adv.* **—in/ter re lat/ed ness,** *n.*

in ter re la tion (in/tər ri lā/shən), close connection with each other; mutual relationship. *n.*

in ter re la tion ship (in/tər ri lā/shən ship), interrelation. *n.*

interrog., interrogative.

in ter ro gate (in ter/ə gāt), ask questions of; examine or get information from by asking questions; question thoroughly: *The lawyer took two hours to interrogate the witness. v.,* **in ter ro gat ed, in ter ro gat ing.**

in ter ro ga tion (in ter/ə gā/shən), **1** an interrogating; a questioning. The formal examination of a witness by asking questions is an interrogation. **2** a question. *n.*

interrogation mark *or* **interrogation point,** question mark; the mark (?).

in ter rog a tive (in/tə rog/ə tiv), **1** asking a question; having the form of a question: *an interrogative sentence, an interrogative tone of voice.* **2** (in grammar) a word used in asking a question. *Who, why,* and *what* are interrogatives. **1** *adj.,* **2** *n.* **—in ter rog/a tive ly,** *adv.*

in ter ro ga tor (in ter/ə gā/tər), person who interrogates; questioner. *n.*

in ter rog a to ry (in/tə rog/ə tôr/ē), questioning. *adj.*

in ter rupt (in/tə rupt/), **1** break in upon (talk, work, rest, a person speaking, etc.); keep from going on; stop for a time; hinder: *A fire drill interrupted the lesson.* **2** cause a break; break in: *It is not polite to interrupt when someone is talking.* **3** make a break in: *A dam interrupts the flow of the river. v.* **—in/ter rupt/er,** *n.* **—in/ter rupt/i ble,** *adj.*

in ter rup tion (in/tə rup/shən), **1** an interrupting; breaking in on. **2** a being interrupted; a break; stopping: *The rain continued without interruption all day.* **3** something that interrupts. **4** intermission. *n.*

in ter scho las tic (in/tər skə las/tik), between schools: *We won the interscholastic softball competition. adj.*

in ter sect (in/tər sekt/), **1** cut or divide by passing through or crossing: *A path intersects the field.* **2** cross each other: *Streets usually intersect at right angles. v.*

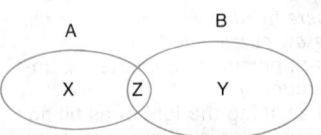

intersection (def. 3) If A has Z and X as members, and B has Z and Y as members, then Z is the intersection of A and B.

in ter sec tion (in/tər sek/shən), **1** an intersecting: *Bridges are used to avoid the intersection of a railroad and a highway.* **2** point, line, or place where one thing crosses another. **3** (in mathematics) the set that contains only those elements shared by two or more sets. *n.*

in ter sperse (in/tər spėrs/), **1** vary with something put here and there: *The grass was interspersed with beds of flowers.* **2** scatter here and there among other things:

Bushes were interspersed among trees. v., **in ter spersed, in ter spers ing.**

in ter state (in′tər stāt′), between persons or organizations in different states; between states: *The federal government regulates interstate commerce.* adj.

in ter stel lar (in′tər stel′ər), among the stars: *interstellar space.* adj.

in ter twine (in′tər twīn′), twine, one with another: *Two vines intertwined on the wall.* v., **in ter twined, in ter twin ing.**

in ter ur ban (in′tər ėr′bən), between cities or towns: *an interurban bus line.* adj.

in ter val (in′tər vəl), **1** time or space between: *There is an interval of six days between Christmas and New Year's Day.* **2** (in music) the difference in pitch between two tones. n. [*Interval* is from Latin *intervallum*, meaning "a space between palisades," which comes from *inter-*, meaning "between," and *vallum*, meaning "wall."] **at intervals, 1** now and then. **2** here and there.

in ter vene (in′tər vēn′), **1** come between; be between: *A week intervenes between my sister's birthday and mine.* **2** come between persons or groups to help settle a dispute: *The President was asked to intervene in the coal strike.* v., **in ter vened, in ter ven ing.** —**in′ter ven′er,** n.

in ter ven tion (in′tər ven′shən), **1** an intervening: *The strike was settled by the intervention of the President.* **2** interference, especially by one nation in the affairs of another. n.

in ter view (in′tər vyü), **1** a meeting, generally of persons face to face, to talk over something special: *My parents had an interview with the teacher about my work.* **2** a meeting between a reporter and a person from whom information is sought for publication or broadcast. **3** newspaper or magazine article, or broadcast containing the information given at such a meeting. **4** have an interview with; meet and talk with, especially to obtain information: *Reporters interviewed the mayor.* 1-3 n., 4 v. —**in′ter view′er,** n.

in ter weave (in′tər wēv′), **1** weave together: *interweave bamboo strips to make a basket.* **2** mix together; blend: *interweave truth with fiction in a story.* v., **in ter wove** (in′tər wōv′) or **in ter weaved, in ter wo ven** or **in ter wove** or **in ter weaved, in ter weav ing.**

in ter wo ven (in′tər wō′vən), **1** woven together. **2** mixed together; blended. **3** a past participle of **interweave.** *Various strands were interwoven to create a colorful pattern.* 1,2 adj., 3 v.

in tes tate (in tes′tāt), having made no will: *to die intestate.* adj.

in tes ti nal (in tes′tə nəl), of or in the intestines. adj. —**in tes′ti nal ly,** adv.

in tes tine (in tes′tən), either of two parts of the alimentary canal, extending from the stomach to the anus. Partially digested food passes from the stomach into the **small intestine,** a winding, narrow tube, where digestion is completed and nutrients are absorbed by the blood. The small intestine empties into the **large intestine,** a wide tube, where water is absorbed and wastes are eliminated. In humans, the small intestine is about twenty feet (6 meters) long and the large intestine is about five feet (1.5 meters) long. n.

in ti ma cy (in′tə mə sē), **1** a being intimate; close acquaintance; closeness. **2** a familiar or intimate act. n., pl. **in ti ma cies.**

in ti mate¹ (in′tə mit), **1** very familiar; known very well; closely acquainted: *They have been intimate friends since childhood.* **2** resulting from close familiarity; close: *an intimate connection, intimate knowledge of a matter.* **3** personal; private: *A diary is a very intimate book.* **4** a close friend. **5** far within; deepest; inmost: *a person's*

intimate thoughts. 1-3,5 adj., 4 n. —**in′ti mate ly,** adv.

in ti mate² (in′tə māt), **1** suggest indirectly; hint: *Her smile intimated that she was pleased.* **2** make known; announce; notify. v., **in ti mat ed, in ti mat ing.** —**in′ti mat′er,** n.

in ti ma tion (in′tə mā′shən), **1** indirect suggestion; hint: *His frown is an intimation of his disapproval.* **2** announcement; notice. n.

in tim i date (in tim′ə dāt), make afraid; frighten; influence by fear: *intimidate a witness.* v., **in tim i dat ed, in tim i dat ing.** —**in tim′i da′tor,** n.

in tim i da tion (in tim′ə dā′shən), a making or a being made afraid: *Intimidation of witnesses is illegal.* n.

in to (in′tü; *before consonants often* in′tə), **1** to the inside of; toward and inside: *Come into the house. We drove into the city. I will look into the matter.* **2** so as to become; to the form of: *Divide the apple into three parts. Cold weather turns water into ice.* **3** SLANG. involved with; interested in: *They were into rock music.* prep.

in tol er a ble (in tol′ər ə bəl), too much to be endured; unbearable: *The pain of the toothache was intolerable.* adj. —**in tol′er a ble ness,** n.

in tol er a bly (in tol′ər ə blē), in an intolerable manner; unbearably. adv.

in tol er ance (in tol′ər əns), **1** unwillingness to let others do and think as they choose, especially in religion: *The Pilgrims came to America because of intolerance and persecution.* **2** inability to tolerate; lack of tolerance: *She developed an intolerance to penicillin.* n.

in tol er ant (in tol′ər ənt), not tolerant; not willing to let others do and think as they choose, especially in religion: *Some Puritans were strict and intolerant.* adj. —**in tol′er ant ly,** adv. **intolerant of,** not able to endure; unwilling to endure: *intolerant of cold.*

in to na tion (in′tō nā′shən), **1** an intoning. **2** manner of producing musical notes, especially with regard to pitch. **3** manner of sounding words or speaking, especially with regard to the rise and fall of the pitch of the voice. n.

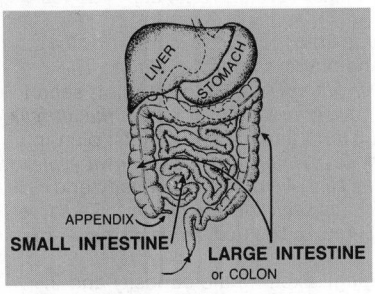

APPENDIX **SMALL INTESTINE** **LARGE INTESTINE** or COLON

in tone (in tōn′), read or recite in a singing voice; chant: *A cantor intones part of the service.* v., **in toned, in ton ing.** —**in ton′er,** n.

in tox i cant (in tok′sə kənt), **1** alcoholic liquor. **2** anything that intoxicates. n.

in tox i cate (in tok′sə kāt), **1** make drunk: *Too much wine intoxicates people.* **2** excite greatly; exhilarate: *The joy of winning intoxicated the team.* v., **in tox i cat ed, in tox i cat ing.**

in tox i cat ed (in tok′sə kā′tid), 1 drunk: *an intoxicated person.* 2 very much excited. *adj.*

in tox i ca tion (in tok′sə kā′shən), 1 an intoxicated condition; drunkenness. 2 great excitement. *n.*

in trac ta ble (in trak′tə bəl), hard to handle or manage; stubborn. *adj.*

intractable
The **intractable** cow refused to budge.

in tra mur al (in′trə myůr′əl), within the walls; inside: *Intramural games are games played between students of the same school. adj.*

in tran si tive (in tran′sə tiv), not taking a direct object. The verbs *belong, go,* and *seem* are intransitive. The verb *run* may be transitive or intransitive. In "I run to school" *run* is intransitive. In "I run the machine" *run* is transitive. *adj.* —**in tran′si tive ly,** *adv.*

in tra ve nous (in′trə vē′nəs), 1 within a vein or the veins. 2 into a vein: *When a person is too ill to digest food, an intravenous feeding is often given. adj.* —**in′tra ve′nous ly,** *adv.*

in trench (in trench′), entrench. *v.*

in trench ment (in trench′mənt), entrenchment. *n.*

in trep id (in trep′id), very brave; fearless; courageous; dauntless: *an intrepid adventurer. adj.* —**in trep′id ly,** *adv.*

in tre pid i ty (in′trə pid′ə tē), great bravery; dauntless courage; fearlessness. *n.*

in tri ca cy (in′trə kə sē), 1 intricate nature or condition; complexity: *The intricacy of the plan made it hard to understand.* 2 an intricate thing or event; complication: *The laws are full of intricacies. n., pl.* **in tri ca cies.**

in tri cate (in′trə kit), 1 with many twists and turns; puzzling, entangled, or complicated: *An intricate knot is very hard to tie or untie. A mystery story usually has a very intricate plot.* 2 very hard to understand: *The directions were so intricate that I made several errors. adj.* —**in′tri cate ly,** *adv.*

in trigue (in trēg′ *or* in′trēg′ *for 1,2,5;* in trēg′ *for 3,4*), 1 secret scheming and plotting; crafty dealings: *The royal palace was filled with intrigue.* 2 a crafty plot; secret scheme: *The king's younger brother took part in the intrigue to make himself king.* 3 form and carry out plots; plan in a secret or underhand way: *He pretended to be loyal while he intrigued against the king.* 4 excite the curiosity and interest of: *The book's unusual title intrigued me.* 5 a secret love affair. *1,2,5 n., 3,4 v.,* **in trigued, in tri guing.** —**in tri′guer,** *n.*

in tri guing (in trē′ging), exciting the curiosity and interest: *The book's intriguing title caught my attention. adj.* —**in tri′guing ly,** *adv.*

in trin sic (in trin′sik), belonging in a thing by its very nature; essential; inherent: *The intrinsic value of a dollar bill is the cost of the paper it's printed on. adj.* —**in trin′si cal ly,** *adv.*

intro. *or* **introd.,** 1 introduction. 2 introductory.

in tro duce (in′trə düs′ *or* in′trə dyüs′), 1 bring in: *She introduced a story into the conversation.* 2 put in; insert: *The doctor introduced a tube into the sick man's throat so*

he could breathe. 3 bring into use, notice, knowledge, etc.: *Television and space travel are introducing many new words into our language.* 4 bring into acquaintance with; make known: *The principal introduced the speaker to the students. I introduced my visiting cousin to our city by showing her the sights.* 5 bring forward for consideration: *introduce a question for debate.* 6 begin; start: *He introduced his speech by telling a joke. v.,* **in tro duced, in tro duc ing.** —**in′tro duc′er,** *n.*

in tro duc tion (in′trə duk′shən), 1 an introducing: *The introduction of steel made tall buildings easier to build.* 2 a being introduced: *She was confused by her introduction to so many strangers.* 3 thing that introduces; first part of a book, speech, piece of music, etc., leading up to the main part. 4 a first book for beginners. 5 thing introduced; thing brought into use: *Television is a later introduction than radio. n.*

in tro duc tor y (in′trə duk′tə rē), used to introduce; serving as an introduction; preliminary: *The speaker began her talk with a few introductory remarks about her subject. adj.*

in tro spec tion (in′trə spek′shən), examination of one's own thoughts and feelings. *n.*

in tro spec tive (in′trə spek′tiv), inclined to examine one's own thoughts and feelings. *adj.*

in tro vert (in′trə vėrt′), person tending to think rather than act. Introverts are more interested in their own thoughts and feelings than in what is going on around them. *n.*

in tro vert ed (in′trə vėr′tid), having a tendency to think rather than act and to be more interested in one's own thoughts and feelings than in what is going on around one. *adj.*

in trude (in trüd′), 1 force oneself in; come unasked and unwanted: *Do not intrude upon the privacy of your neighbors.* 2 give unasked and unwanted; force in: *Do not intrude your opinions upon others. v.,* **in trud ed, in trud ing.** —**in trud′er,** *n.*

in tru sion (in trü′zhən), an intruding; coming unasked and unwanted: *Excuse my intrusion; I didn't know that you were busy. n.*

in tru sive (in trü′siv), intruding; coming unasked and unwanted. *adj.*

in trust (in trust′), entrust. *v.*

in tu i tion (in′tü ish′ən *or* in′tyü ish′ən), 1 immediate perception or understanding without reasoning: *By experience with many kinds of people the doctor had developed great powers of intuition.* 2 truth, fact, etc., perceived or understood immediately and without reasoning. *n.* [Intuition comes from Latin *intuitionem,* meaning "a gazing at."]

in tu i tive (in tü′ə tiv *or* in tyü′ə tiv), 1 perceiving or understanding immediately and without reasoning: *an intuitive mind.* 2 acquired by intuition; instinctive; natural: *an artist's intuitive understanding of color. adj.* —**in tu′i tive ly,** *adv.*

in un date (in′un dāt), overflow; flood: *Heavy rains caused the river to rise and inundate the valley. v.,* **in un dat ed, in un dat ing.** —**in′un da′tor,** *n.*

in un da tion (in′un dā′shən), an overflowing; flood. *n.*

in ure (in yůr′), toughen or harden; accustom: *Nurses become inured to the sight of blood. v.,* **in ured, in ur ing.** —**in ure′ment,** *n.*

in vade (in vād′), 1 enter with force or as an enemy; attack: *Soldiers invaded the country to conquer it. Grasshoppers invade fields and eat the crops.* 2 enter as if to take possession: *Tourists invaded the city.* 3 interfere with; break in on; violate: *The law punishes people who invade the rights of others. v.,* **in vad ed, in vad ing.** —**in vad′er,** *n.*

in va lid[1] (in′və lid), **1** person who is weak because of sickness or injury. An invalid cannot get around and do things. **2** weak because of sickness or injury; not well; disabled. **3** for the use of invalids: *an invalid chair.* **4** make weak or sick; disable. 1 *n.*, 2,3 *adj.*, 4 *v.*

in val id[2] (in val′id), not valid; without force or effect; without value; worthless: *Unless a check is signed, it is invalid. adj.* —**in val′id ly,** *adv.*

in val i date (in val′ə dāt), make valueless; cause to be worthless; deprive of force or effect: *A contract is invalidated if only one party signs it. v.*, **in val i dat ed, in val i dat ing.** —**in val′i da′tion,** *n.* —**in val′i da′tor,** *n.*

in val u a ble (in val′yü ə bəl *or* in val′yə bəl), valuable beyond measure; very precious; priceless: *Good health is an invaluable blessing. adj.* —**in val′u a ble ness,** *n.* —**in val′u a bly,** *adv.*

in var i a bil i ty (in ver′ē ə bil′ə tē *or* in var′ē ə bil′ə tē), lack of variability; being invariable. *n.*

in var i a ble (in ver′ē ə bəl *or* in var′ē ə bəl), always the same; not changing: *After dinner it was her invariable habit to take a walk. adj.*

in var i a bly (in ver′ē ə blē *or* in var′ē ə blē), in an invariable manner; without change; without exception: *Spring invariably follows winter. adv.*

in va sion (in vā′zhən), an invading; entering by force or as an enemy; attack. *n.*

in vec tive (in vek′tiv), a violent attack in words; abusive speech: *His opponents were overcome by the fury of his invective. n.* [*Invective* comes from Latin *invectivus*, meaning "abusive," and can be traced back to *in-*, meaning "against," and *vehere*, meaning "carry."]

in veigh (in vā′), make a violent attack in words: *The agitator inveighed against the government. v.* —**in veigh′er,** *n.*

in vei gle (in vē′gəl *or* in vā′gəl), lead astray by trickery; entice; lure: *The saleswoman inveigled me into buying four magazine subscriptions. v.*, **in vei gled, in vei gling.** —**in vei′gle ment,** *n.* —**in vei′gler,** *n.*

in vent (in vent′), **1** make up for the first time; think out (something new): *Alexander Graham Bell invented the telephone.* **2** make up; think up: *Since they had no good reason for being late, they invented an excuse. v.*

in ven tion (in ven′shən), **1** a making something new: *the invention of gunpowder.* **2** thing invented: *Television is a modern invention.* **3** power of inventing: *An author must have invention to think up new ideas for stories.* **4** a made-up story; false statement: *That rumor is merely invention. n.*

in ven tive (in ven′tiv), **1** good at inventing; quick to invent things: *An inventive person thinks up ways to save time, money, and work.* **2** showing power of inventing. *adj.* —**in ven′tive ly,** *adv.* —**in ven′tive ness,** *n.*

in ven tor (in ven′tər), person who invents. *n.*

in ven to ry (in′vən tôr′ē), **1** a complete and detailed list of articles. An inventory of property or goods tells how many there are of each article and what they are worth. **2** all the articles listed or to be listed; stock: *The shoe store had a sale to reduce its inventory.* **3** make a complete and detailed list of; enter in a list: *Some stores inventory their stock once a month.* 1,2 *n., pl.* **in ven to ries;** 3 *v.*, **in ven to ried, in ven to ry ing.**

in verse (in vėrs′ *or* in′vėrs′), **1** exactly opposite; reversed in position, direction, or tendency; inverted: *DCBA is the inverse order of ABCD.* **2** something reversed: *Subtraction is the inverse of addition. The inverse of 3/4 is 4/3.* **3** direct opposite: *Evil is the inverse of good.* 1 *adj.*, 2,3 *n.* —**in verse′ly,** *adv.*

in ver sion (in vėr′zhən), **1** an inverting or a being inverted. **2** something inverted. **3** (in meteorology) an increase in air temperature at higher altitudes, instead of the usual decrease: *An inversion caused air pollution to build up over the city. n.*

in vert (in vėrt′), **1** turn upside down: *I inverted the pan and the cake dropped onto the rack.* **2** turn the other way; change to the opposite; reverse in position, direction, order, etc.: *If you invert "I can," you have "Can I?" v.* —**in vert′er,** *n.* —**in vert′i ble,** *adj.*

invertebrates (def. 2)

in ver te brate (in vėr′tə brit *or* in vėr′tə brāt), **1** without a backbone. **2** animal without a backbone. Worms and insects are invertebrates; fishes and mammals are vertebrates. 1 *adj.*, 2 *n.*

in vest (in vest′), **1** use (money) to buy something that is expected to produce a profit, or income, or both: *She invested her money in stocks, bonds, and land.* **2** spend or put in (time, energy, etc.) for later benefit: *Much time and energy has been invested in the cancer crusade.* **3** clothe; cover; surround: *Darkness invests the earth at night. The castle was invested with mystery and romance.* **4** give power, authority, or right to: *I invested my lawyer with power to act for me.* **5** give a quality or characteristic to: *The author invested the main character with every virtue.* **6** put in office with a ceremony: *A queen or king is invested by being crowned. v.*

in ves ti gate (in ves′tə gāt), look into thoroughly; search into carefully; examine closely: *Detectives investigate crimes to find out who did them. Scientists investigate nature to learn more about it. v.*, **in ves ti gat ed, in ves ti gat ing.**

in ves ti ga tion (in ves′tə gā′shən), a careful search; detailed or careful examination: *An investigation of the*

Pronunciation key

a hat	**i** it	**oi** oil	**ch** child			a in about	
ā age	**ī** ice	**ou** out	**ng** long			e in taken	
ä far	**o** hot	**u** cup	**sh** she	ə =		i in pencil	
e let	**ō** open	**u̇** put	**th** thin			o in lemon	
ē equal	**ô** order	**ü** rule	**ŦH** then			u in circus	
ėr term			**zh** measure				

accident by the police put the blame on the drivers of both cars. n.

in ves ti ga tor (in ves′tə gā′tər), person who investigates. *n.*

in ves ti ture (in ves′tə chŭr), a formal investing of a person with an office, dignity, power, right, etc. *n.*

in vest ment (in vest′mənt), **1** an investing; a laying out of money: *Getting an education is a wise investment of time and money.* **2** amount of money invested: *Their investments amount to thousands of dollars.* **3** something that is expected to yield money as income or profit or both: *She has a good income from wise investments. n.*

in ves tor (in ves′tər), person who invests money. *n.*

in vet er ate (in vet′ər it), **1** confirmed in a habit, practice, feeling, etc.; habitual: *It is very hard for an inveterate smoker to give up tobacco.* **2** long and firmly established; deeply rooted: *There was an inveterate distrust of newcomers in the old neighborhood. adj.*

in vid i ous (in vid′ē əs), likely to cause ill will or resentment; giving offense because unfair or unjust: *An invidious comparison of the skills of the two players increased the bitter rivalry between them.* adj. —**in vid′i ous ly,** *adv.* —**in vid′i ous ness,** *n.*

in vig o rate (in vig′ə rāt′), give vigor to; fill with life and energy: *Exercise invigorates the body.* v., **in vig o rat ed, in vig o rat ing.**

in vig o rat ing (in vig′ə rā′ting), giving vigor to; filling with life and energy: *An invigorating breeze made our hike enjoyable.* adj. —**in vig′o rat′ing ly,** *adv.*

in vig o ra tion (in vig′ə rā′shən), an invigorating. *n.*

in vin ci bil i ty (in vin′sə bil′ə tē), a being invincible. *n.*

in vin ci ble (in vin′sə bəl), impossible to overcome; unconquerable: *The champion team seemed invincible.* adj. —**in vin′ci ble ness,** *n.* —**in vin′ci bly,** *adv.*

in vi o la ble (in vī′ə lə bəl), **1** not to be violated or injured; sacred: *an inviolable vow.* **2** not able to be violated or injured: *The gods are inviolable.* adj. —**in vi′o la bly,** *adv.*

in vi o late (in vī′ə lit *or* in vī′ə lāt), not violated; uninjured; unbroken: *An inviolate promise is carried out.* adj.

in vis i bil i ty (in viz′ə bil′ə tē), condition of being invisible. *n.*

in vis i ble (in viz′ə bəl), not visible; not capable of being seen: *Thought is invisible. Germs are invisible to the naked eye.* adj. —**in vis′i ble ness,** *n.*

in vis i bly (in viz′ə blē), in an invisible manner; so as not to be seen. *adv.*

in vi ta tion (in′və tā′shən), **1** a polite request to come to some place or to do something: *The children received invitations to the party.* **2** act of inviting. *n.*

in vite (in vīt′), **1** ask (someone) politely to come to some place or to do something: *I invited some friends to a party. We invited them to join our club.* **2** make a polite request for: *She invited our opinion of her story.* **3** give a chance for; tend to cause: *New Year's Day invites good resolutions. Carelessness invites trouble.* **4** attract; tempt; encourage: *The cool water invited us to swim.* v., **in vit ed, in vit ing.**

in vit ing (in vī′ting), attractive; tempting: *The cool water looks inviting.* adj. —**in vit′ing ly,** *adv.*

in vo ca tion (in′və kā′shən), **1** a calling upon in prayer; appealing for help or protection: *A church service often begins with an invocation to God.* **2** a calling forth of spirits with magic words or charms. **3** set of magic words used to call forth spirits. *n.*

in voice (in′vois), **1** list of goods sent to a purchaser showing prices, amounts, shipping charges, etc. **2** make an invoice of; enter on an invoice. 1 *n.*, 2 *v.*, **in voiced, in voic ing.**

in voke (in vōk′), **1** call on in prayer; appeal to for help or protection: *The Pilgrims invoked God's help in their undertaking.* **2** ask earnestly for; beg for: *The condemned criminal invoked the judge's mercy.* **3** call forth with magic words or charms: *Aladdin invoked the powerful genie of the magic lamp.* v., **in voked, in vok ing.**

in vol un tar i ly (in vol′ən ter′ə lē), in an involuntary manner; without intention; against one's will. *adv.*

in vol un tar y (in vol′ən ter′ē), **1** not voluntary; not done of one's own free will; unwilling: *Taking gym was involuntary on my part; the school requires it.* **2** not done on purpose; not intended: *An accident is involuntary.* **3** not controlled by the will: *Breathing is mainly involuntary.* adj.

in volve (in volv′), **1** have as a necessary part, condition, or result; take in; include: *Housework involves cooking, washing dishes, sweeping, and cleaning.* **2** bring (into difficulty, danger, etc.): *One foolish mistake can involve you in a good deal of trouble.* **3** entangle; complicate: *Long, involved sentences are hard to understand.* **4** take up the attention of; occupy: *She was involved in working out a puzzle.* v., **in volved, in volv ing.** —**in volv′er,** *n.*

in volve ment (in volv′mənt), an involving or a being involved. *n.*

in vul ner a bil i ty (in vul′nər ə bil′ə tē), a being invulnerable. *n.*

in vul ner a ble (in vul′nər ə bəl), not able to be wounded or hurt; safe from attack: *Achilles was invulnerable except for his heel.* adj. —**in vul′ner a ble ness,** *n.* —**in vul′ner a bly,** *adv.*

in ward (in′wərd), **1** toward the inside: *a passage leading inward.* **2** on the inside; inner; internal: *inward surfaces of a hollow wall.* **3** directed toward the inside: *an inward flow of fresh air.* **4** into the mind or soul: *to turn one's thoughts inward.* **5** in mind or soul: *inward peace.* 1,4 *adv.*, 2,3,5 *adj.*

in ward ly (in′wərd lē), **1** on the inside; within. **2** toward the inside. **3** in the mind or soul. **4** not aloud or openly. *adv.*

in wards (in′wərdz), inward. *adv.*

i o dide (ī′ə dīd), a chemical compound of iodine with another element. *n.*

i o dine (ī′ə dīn), **1** a nonmetallic element in the form of grayish-black crystals which give off a dense, violet vapor with an irritating odor when heated. Iodine is used in medicine, in making dyes, in photography, etc. **2** a brown liquid containing iodine, used as an antiseptic. *n.*

WORD HISTORY

iodine

Iodine comes from French *iode*, and can be traced back to Greek *ion*, meaning "violet," and *eidos*, meaning "form."

i o dized salt (ī′ə dīzd), common salt containing iodide as a supplement to the diet, especially of persons with an iodine deficiency.

i on (ī′ən), atom or group of atoms having a negative or positive electric charge as a result of having lost or gained one or more electrons. A cation is a positive ion formed by the loss of electrons; an anion is a negative ion formed by the gain of one or more electrons. *n.*

-ion, *suffix added to verbs to form nouns.* **1** act of _____ing: *Attraction = act of attracting. Calculation = act of calculating.* **2** condition of being _____ed: *Adoption =*

condition of being adopted. Fascination = condition of being fascinated. **3** result of ＿＿＿ing: *Abbreviation = result of abbreviating. Collection = result of collecting.*

I o ni a (ī ō′nē ə), ancient region on the W coast of Asia Minor, with the islands near it. The Greeks colonized Ionia in very early times. *n.*

Ionia—about 1000 B.C. (the darker area)

I on ic (ī on′ik), **1** of or having to do with the order of Greek architecture having scrolls in the capitals of the columns. **2** of Ionia or its people. *adj.*

i on ize (ī′ə nīz), separate into ions; produce ions in. Acids, bases, and salts ionize when dissolved in a solution. *v.,* **i on ized, i on iz ing.** —**i′on iz′er,** *n.*

i on o sphere (ī on′ə sfir), region of ionized layers of air which extends from about 31 to 600 miles (50 to 965 kilometers) above the earth's surface. The ionosphere reflects certain radio waves, making transmission over long distances on earth possible. *n.*

i o ta (ī ō′tə), **1** a very small part or quantity; bit: *There is not an iota of truth in the story.* **2** the ninth letter of the Greek alphabet (I or ι). *n., pl.* **i o tas.**

I O U or **I.O.U.** (ī′ō′yü′), an informal note showing a debt: *Write me your IOU for ten dollars. n., pl.* **IOUs, IOU's, I.O.U.s,** or **I.O.U.'s.** [*IOU* comes from the pronunciation of the phrase *I owe you.*]

I o wa (ī′ə wə), one of the midwestern states of the United States. *Abbreviation:* Ia. or IA *Capital:* Des Moines. *n.* —**I′o wan,** *adj., n.*

IQ or **I.Q.,** intelligence quotient.

Ir, symbol for iridium.

ir-, *prefix.* form of **in-**[1] before *r,* as in *irrational, irregular,* etc.

IRA (ī′är ā′ *or* ī′rə), individual retirement account (a pension fund in which a person can deposit a certain amount of money each year and defer paying income tax on the savings and interest until after retirement). *n., pl.* **IRAs, IRA's.**

I ran (i ran′ *or* i rän′), country in SW Asia, south of the Caspian Sea. *Capital:* Teheran. Formerly called **Persia.** See **Assyria** for map. *n.*

I ra ni an (i rā′nē ən), **1** of Iran, its people, or their language. **2** person born or living in Iran. **3** language of Iran. 1 *adj.,* 2,3 *n.*

I raq (i rak′ *or* i räk′), country in SW Asia, west of Iran. *Capital:* Baghdad. See **Euphrates** for map. *n.*

I raq i (i rak′ē *or* i rä′kē), **1** of Iraq, its people, or their language. **2** person born or living in Iraq. **3** Arabic as spoken in Iraq. 1 *adj.,* 2,3 *n.*

i ras ci ble (i ras′ə bəl), easily made angry; with a quick temper; irritable. *adj.* —**i ras′ci bly,** *adv.*

i rate (ī′rāt *or* ī rāt′), angry. *adj.* —**i′rate ly,** *adv.*

ire (īr), anger; wrath. *n.*

Ire land (īr′lənd), **1** one of the British Isles, divided into the Republic of Ireland and Northern Ireland. **2 Republic of,** country in NW, central, and S Ireland; Irish Republic; Eire. *Capital:* Dublin. See **United Kingdom** for map. *n.*

ir i des cence (ir′ə des′ns), display of changing colors; change of color when moved or turned: *the iridescence of mother-of-pearl. n.*

ir i des cent (ir′ə des′nt), displaying changing colors; changing color when moved or turned: *Soap bubbles are iridescent. adj.* —**ir′i des′cent ly,** *adv.*

i rid i um (i rid′ē əm), a silver-white, hard metallic element which is used as an alloy with platinum for jewelry and the points of fountain pens. *n.*

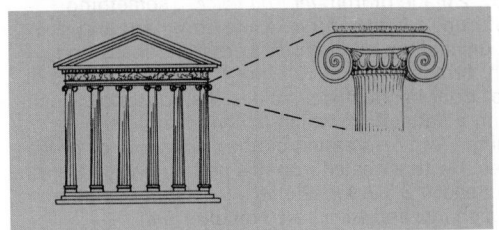

Ionic (def. 1) Ionic temple

i ris (ī′ris), **1** plant with sword-shaped leaves and large flowers with three upright parts and three drooping parts; fleur-de-lis. **2** the colored part of the eye around the pupil. *n., pl.* **i ris es.**

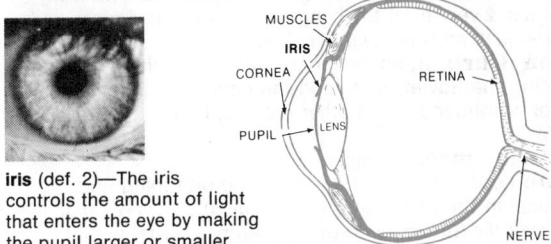

iris (def. 2)—The iris controls the amount of light that enters the eye by making the pupil larger or smaller.

MUSCLES
IRIS
CORNEA
RETINA
PUPIL
LENS
NERVE

I rish (ī′rish), **1** of Ireland, its people, or their language. **2** the people of Ireland. **3** the Celtic language spoken by some of the Irish; Gaelic. 1 *adj.,* 2 *n.pl.,* 3 *n.sing.*

I rish man (ī′rish mən), man born or living in Ireland. *n., pl.* **I rish men.**

Irish potato, another name for the potato.

irascible

Irish Republic, Republic of Ireland.

Irish Sea, part of the Atlantic between Ireland and England.

Irish terrier, a small dog with reddish-brown, wiry hair. It is somewhat like a small Airedale.

I rish wom an (ī′rish wům′ən), woman born or living in Ireland. *n., pl.* **I rish wom en.**

irk (ėrk), cause to feel disgusted, annoyed, or troubled; weary by being tedious or disagreeable; bore: *It irks us to wait for people who are late. v.*

irk some (ėrk′səm), tiresome; tedious: *Washing dishes all day would be an irksome task. adj.* —**irk′some ly,** *adv.* —**irk′some ness,** *n.*

i ron (ī′ərn), **1** a silver-gray, easily shaped, heavy metallic element. Iron is the most useful metal and is used to make steel. Iron occurs in the hemoglobin of the red blood cells where it serves to carry oxygen to all parts of the body. **2** made of iron: *an iron fence.* **3** something made of iron: *a branding iron.* **4** like iron; hard and strong; unyielding: *an iron will.* **5** great hardness and strength; firmness: *muscles of iron.* **6 irons,** *pl.* chains or bands of iron; handcuffs; shackles. **7** a household appliance with a flat surface which is heated and used for smoothing cloth or pressing clothes. **8** smooth or press (cloth, etc.) with a heated iron. **9** a golf club with an iron or steel head. 1,3,5-7,9 *n.,* 2,4 *adj.,* 8 *v.* [*Iron* comes from Old English *īren* and *īsern.*] —**i′ron like′,** *adj.*

iron out, smooth away or overcome (difficulties, differences, inconsistencies, etc.): *The dispute between the two players was ironed out by the coach.*

Iron Age, period after the Bronze Age, when people used iron tools, weapons, etc.

i ron clad (ī′ərn klad′), **1** warship protected with iron plates. **2** very hard to change or get out of: *An ironclad agreement must be kept.* 1 *n.,* 2 *adj.*

Iron Curtain, an imaginary wall or dividing line separating the Soviet Union and the countries under its control or influence from other nations, following World War II.

i ron ic (ī ron′ik), ironical. *adj.*

i ron i cal (ī ron′ə kəl), **1** expressing one thing and meaning the opposite: *Her ironical laugh showed that she wasn't the least bit amused.* **2** contrary to what would naturally be expected: *It was ironical that the man was run over by his own automobile. adj.* —**i ron′i cal ly,** *adv.*

iron lung

iron lung, device which applies periodic pressure on the chest wall in order to force air in and out of the lungs. It is used to enable people to breathe whose chest muscles are paralyzed.

iron oxide, compound of iron and oxygen, used especially as a pigment.

i ron wood (ī′ərn wůd′), any of various trees with hard, heavy wood. *n.*

i ron work (ī′ərn wėrk′), things made of iron; work in iron. *n.*

i ron work er (ī′ərn wėr′kər), **1** person whose work is making iron or iron articles. **2** person whose work is building the steel framework of bridges, skyscrapers, etc. *n.*

i ron works (ī′ərn wėrks′), place where iron is made or worked into iron articles. *n.pl. or sing.*

i ro ny (ī′rə nē), **1** way of speaking or writing in which the ordinary meaning of the words is the opposite of the thought in the speaker's mind: *The tallest person was called "Shorty" in irony.* **2** event or outcome which is the opposite of what would naturally be expected: *By the irony of fate the farmers had rain when they needed sun, and sun when they needed rain. n., pl.* **i ro nies.**

Ir o quois (ir′ə kwoi), member of a powerful confederacy of American Indian tribes called the Five Nations, formerly living mostly in what is now New York State. *n., pl.* **Ir o quois.**

ir ra di ate (i rā′dē āt), **1** shine upon; light up; make bright; illuminate. **2** shine. **3** radiate; give out. **4** treat with electromagnetic rays. *v.,* **ir ra di at ed, ir ra di at ing.**

ir ra di a tion (i rā′dē ā′shən), an irradiating or a being irradiated. *n.*

ir ra tion al (i rash′ə nəl), **1** not rational; contrary to reason; unreasonable: *It is irrational to be afraid of the number 13.* **2** unable to think and reason clearly. *adj.* —**ir ra′tion al ly,** *adv.*

irrational number, any real number that cannot be expressed as an integer or as a ratio between two integers. $\sqrt{2}$ and π are irrational numbers.

ir re claim a ble (ir′i klā′mə bəl), not able to be reclaimed. *adj.* —**ir′re claim′a bly,** *adv.*

ir rec on cil a ble (i rek′ən sī′lə bəl), not able to be reconciled; opposed: *irreconcilable enemies. Good and evil are irreconcilable. adj.* —**ir rec′on cil′a bly,** *adv.*

ir re deem a ble (ir′i dē′mə bəl), **1** not able to be redeemed or bought back. **2** not able to be exchanged for coin: *irredeemable paper money.* **3** impossible to change; beyond remedy; hopeless: *The auditor's mistake was serious, but not irredeemable. adj.*

ir re duc i ble (ir′i dü′sə bəl *or* ir′i dyü′sə bəl), impossible to make less, smaller, simpler, etc. *adj.*

ir ref u ta ble (i ref′yə tə bəl *or* ir′i fyü′tə bəl), not able to be refuted or disproved; undeniable; unanswerable: *irrefutable arguments. adj.* —**ir ref′u ta bly,** *adv.*

ir reg u lar (i reg′yə lər), **1** not regular; not according to rule; out of the usual order or natural way: *It would be quite irregular for a child of ten to drive a car.* **2** not even; not smooth or straight; broken and rough: *New England has a very irregular coastline.* **3** (of a word) not inflected in the usual way. *Be* is an irregular verb. *adj.* —**ir reg′u lar ly,** *adv.*

ir reg u lar i ty (i reg′yə lar′ə tē), **1** lack of regularity; being irregular. **2** something irregular. *n., pl.* **ir reg u lar i ties.**

ir rel e vance (i rel′ə vəns), **1** a being irrelevant. **2** something irrelevant. *n.*

ir rel e vant (i rel′ə vənt), not to the point; off the subject: *A question about arithmetic is irrelevant in a French lesson. adj.* —**ir rel′e vant ly,** *adv.*

ir re li gious (ir′i lij′əs), **1** not religious; indifferent to religion. **2** contrary to religious principles; impious. *adj.* —**ir′re li′gious ly,** *adv.*

ir rep ar a ble (i rep′ər ə bəl), not able to be repaired or put right: *irreparable damage. adj.*

ir rep ar a bly (i rep′ər ə blē), in an irreparable manner. *adv.*

ir re place a ble (ir′i plā′sə bəl), not replaceable; impossible to replace with another. *adj.*

ir re press i ble (ir′i pres′ə bəl), not able to be repressed or restrained; uncontrollable: *irrepressible laughter. adj.* —**ir′re press′i ble ness,** *n.*

ir re press i bly (ir/i pres/ə blē), in an irrepressible manner; uncontrollably. *adv.*

ir re proach a ble (ir/i prō/chə bəl), free from blame; faultless: *The Frenchman spoke excellent, irreproachable English. adj.*

ir re sist i ble (ir/i zis/tə bəl), not able to be resisted; too great to be withstood; overwhelming: *She had an irresistible desire for some ice cream. adj.*

ir re sist i bly (ir/i zis/tə blē), in an irresistible manner; overwhelmingly. *adv.*

ir res o lute (i rez/ə lüt), not resolute; unable to make up one's mind; not sure of what one wants; hesitating: *Irresolute persons make poor leaders. adj.* —**ir res/o lute ly,** *adv.* —**ir res/o lute ness,** *n.*

ir re spec tive (ir/i spek/tiv), regardless: *All pupils, irrespective of age, may join the club. adj.*

ir re spon si bil i ty (ir/i spon/sə bil/ə tē), lack of responsibility; being irresponsible. *n.*

ir re spon si ble (ir/i spon/sə bəl), 1 without a sense of responsibility; untrustworthy; unreliable. 2 not responsible; not able to be called to account: *A dictator is an irresponsible ruler. adj.*

ir re spon si bly (ir/i spon/sə blē), in an irresponsible manner. *adv.*

ir re triev a ble (ir/i trē/və bəl), not able to be retrieved or recovered; impossible to recall or restore to its former condition. *adj.* —**ir/re triev/a bly,** *adv.*

ir rev er ence (i rev/ər əns), 1 lack of reverence; disrespect. 2 an act showing irreverence. *n.*

ir rev er ent (i rev/ər ənt), not reverent; disrespectful. *adj.* —**ir rev/er ent ly,** *adv.*

ir re vers i ble (ir/i vėr/sə bəl), 1 not able to be turned the other way. 2 unable to be changed or repealed; unalterable. *adj.* —**ir/re vers/i bly,** *adv.*

ir rev o ca ble (i rev/ə kə bəl), 1 not able to be revoked; final: *Nothing could change his irrevocable decision to leave.* 2 impossible to call or bring back: *Yesterday belongs to the irrevocable past. adj.*

ir rev o ca bly (i rev/ə kə blē), in an irrevocable manner. *adv.*

irrigate
(def. 1)
This pipeline is used to irrigate crops.

ir ri gate (ir/ə gāt), 1 supply (land) with water by using ditches, by sprinkling, etc. 2 supply some part of the body with a continuous flow of some liquid: *The doctor showed her how to irrigate her nose and throat with warm water. v.,* **ir ri gat ed, ir ri gat ing.** —**ir/ri ga/tor,** *n.*

ir ri ga tion (ir/ə gā/shən), a supplying of land with water from ditches, sprinklers, etc.; irrigating: *Irrigation is needed to make crops grow in dry regions. n.*

ir ri ta bil i ty (ir/ə tə bil/ə tē), 1 a being irritable; impatience. 2 (in biology) the property that living plant or animal tissue has of responding to a stimulus. *n., pl.* **ir ri ta bil i ties.**

ir ri ta ble (ir/ə tə bəl), 1 easily made angry; impatient: *When the rain spoiled her plans, she was irritable for the rest of the day.* 2 more sensitive than is natural or normal:

a hat	i it	oi oil	ch child	⌈ a in about
ā age	ī ice	ou out	ng long	e in taken
ä far	o hot	u cup	sh she	ə = ⟨ i in pencil
e let	ō open	u̇ put	th thin	o in lemon
ē equal	ô order	ü rule	ŦH then	⌊ u in circus
ėr term			zh measure	

A baby's skin is often quite irritable. 3 (in biology) able to respond to stimuli. *adj.* —**ir/ri ta ble ness,** *n.*

ir ri ta bly (ir/ə tə blē), in an irritable manner. *adv.*

ir ri tant (ir/ə tənt), 1 thing that causes irritation: *Chlorine in swimming pools can be an irritant to the eyes.* 2 causing irritation. 1 *n.,* 2 *adj.*

ir ri tate (ir/ə tāt), 1 make impatient or angry; annoy; provoke; vex: *Their constant interruptions irritated me. Flies irritate horses.* 2 make unnaturally sensitive or sore: *Sunburn irritates the skin.* 3 (in biology) stimulate (an organ, muscle, tissue, etc.) to respond: *A muscle contracts when it is irritated by an electric shock. v.,* **ir ri tat ed, ir ri tat ing.** —**ir/ri tat/ing ly,** *adv.* —**ir/ri ta/tor,** *n.*

ir ri ta tion (ir/ə tā/shən), 1 act or process of irritating; annoyance; vexation. 2 irritated condition: *Irritation of your nose makes you sneeze. n.*

Ir ving (ėr/ving), **Washington,** 1783-1859, American writer, author of *Rip Van Winkle. n.*

is (iz), form of the verb **be** used with *he, she, it* or any singular noun to indicate the present tense. *The earth is round. He is at school. Flour is sold by the pound. v.* [*Is* comes from Old English *is.*]

is., 1 island or islands. 2 isle or isles.

I saac (ī/zək), (in the Bible) the son of Abraham and Sarah, and father of Jacob and Esau. *n.*

Is a bel la I (iz/ə bel/ə), 1451-1504, queen of Castile. She and her husband Ferdinand V were patrons of Columbus.

I sai ah (ī zā/ə), 1 Hebrew prophet of the late 700's B.C. 2 book of the Old Testament containing his prophecies. *n.*

ISBN, International Standard Book Number.

Is car i ot (is skar/ē ət), surname of Judas, the disciple who betrayed Jesus for money. *n.*

-ish, suffix added to adjectives or nouns to form adjectives. 1 somewhat _____: *Sweetish = somewhat sweet.* 2 like a _____: *Childish = like a child.* 3 like that of a _____: *Girlish = like that of a girl.* 4 of or having to do with _____: *English = of or having to do with England.*

i sin glass (ī/zn glas/), 1 kind of gelatin obtained from certain fishes, used for making glue. 2 mica. *n.*

I sis (ī/sis), the chief goddess of ancient Egypt, sister and wife of Osiris. She represented fertility. *n.*

Is lam (is/ləm *or* i släm/), 1 religion based on the teachings of Mohammed as they appear in the Koran; religion of the Moslems. 2 Moslems as a group. 3 the countries under Moslem rule. *n.*

Is lam a bad (iz lä/mə bäd), capital of Pakistan, in the northeast part. *n.*

Is lam ic (is slam/ik *or* i släm/ik), Moslem. *adj.*

is land (ī/lənd), 1 body of land smaller than a continent and completely surrounded by water: *Cuba is a large island. To reach the island you go by boat.* 2 something that suggests a body of land surrounded by water. Platforms in the middle of busy streets are called **safety islands.** *n.* [*Island* is from Old English *īgland.*]

is land er (ī/lən dər), person born or living on an island. *n.*

isle (īl), 1 a small island. 2 island. *n.* [*Isle* came into English about 700 years ago from French *ile,* which comes from Latin *insula,* meaning "island."]

Isle of Man. See **Man, Isle of.**

is let (ī′lit), a small island. *n.*

ism (iz′əm), doctrine, theory, system, or practice: *They dabbled in communism, socialism, and several other isms. n.*

-ism, *suffix forming nouns.* **1** (*added to verbs*) act or practice of _____ing: *Baptism = act or practice of baptizing.* **2** (*added to nouns or adjectives*) quality or condition of being a _____: *Heroism = quality of being a hero. Paganism = condition of being a pagan.* **3** (*added to nouns or adjectives*) illustration or instance of being _____: *Criticism = instance of being critical.* **4** (*added to nouns*) an unhealthy condition caused by _____: *Alcoholism = an unhealthy condition caused by alcohol.*

is n't (iz′nt), is not.

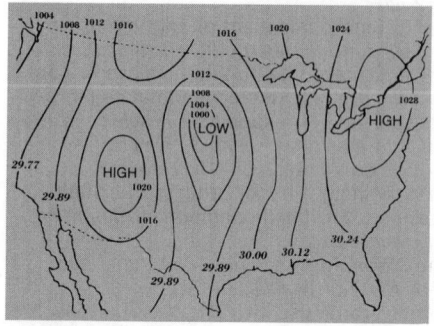

isobars
Pressure is given in inches at the bottom and millibars at the top.

i so bar (ī′sə bär), line on a weather map connecting places having the same average atmospheric pressure. Isobars show the distribution of atmospheric pressure at a particular time, and are used in making weather forecasts. *n.*

i so late (ī′sə lāt), set apart; separate from others; keep alone: *People with contagious diseases should be isolated. v.,* **i so lat ed, i so lat ing.**

i so la tion (ī′sə lā′shən), an isolating or a being isolated. *n.*

i so la tion ism (ī′sə lā′shə niz′əm), principles or policy of avoiding political alliances and economic relationships with other nations. *n.*

i so la tion ist (ī′sə lā′shə nist), person who believes in the principles or policy of isolationism. *n.*

i so met rics (ī′sə met′riks), physical exercises done without athletic activity, by pressing one part of the body against another or against an object. *n.pl.*

isosceles triangles

i sos ce les (ī sos′ə lēz′), (of a triangle) having two sides equal. *adj.*

i so therm (ī′sə thėrm′), line on a weather map connecting places having the same average temperature. *n.*

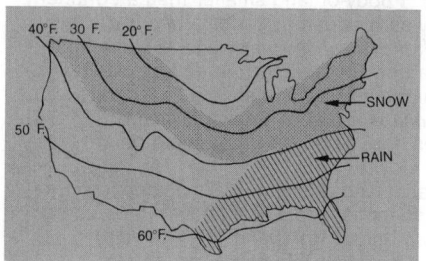

isotherms

i so tope (ī′sə tōp), any of two or more forms of a chemical element that have the same chemical properties and the same atomic number (number of protons), but different atomic weights (number of neutrons). Chlorine, whose atomic weight is 35.5, is a formation of two isotopes, one having an atomic weight of 37, the other, 35. Hydrogen and heavy hydrogen are isotopes. *n.*

Is ra el (iz′rē əl), **1** country in SW Asia, on the Mediterranean, including the major part of Palestine. It was declared a Jewish state May 14, 1948. *Capital:* Jerusalem. See **Roman Empire** for map. **2** ancient Jewish kingdom in N Palestine. See **Judah** for map. **3** (in the Bible) a name given to Jacob after he had wrestled with the angel. **4** name given to his descendants; the Jews; the Hebrews. *n.*

Is rae li (iz rā′lē), **1** person born or living in Israel. **2** of Israel. **1** *n., pl.* **Is rae lis** or **Is rae li; 2** *adj.*

Is ra el ite (iz′rē ə līt), Jew; Hebrew; descendant of Israel. *n.*

is su ance (ish′ü əns), an issuing; issue. *n.*

issue (defs. 2, 4, and 6)

is sue (ish′ü), **1** send out; put forth: *This magazine is issued every week. The government issues money and stamps.* **2** something sent out: *That newsstand sells the latest issues of all the popular magazines and newspapers.* **3** a sending out; a putting forth: *The government controls the issue of stamps.* **4** come out; go out; proceed: *Smoke issues from the chimney.* **5** a coming forth; a flowing out; a discharge: *the issue of blood from a deep flesh wound.* **6** point to be debated; problem: *Peace is one of the main issues of this political campaign.* **7** child or children; offspring. **1,4** *v.,* **is sued, is su ing; 2,3,5-7** *n.* [*Issue* came into English about 700 years ago from French *issue,* and can be traced back to Latin *ex-,* meaning "out," and *ire,* meaning "to go."] —**is′su a ble,** *adj.* —**is′su er,** *n.*

at issue, 1 in question; to be considered or decided. **2** in disagreement: *The children were at issue as to who would captain the team.*

take issue, disagree: *I must take issue with you on that point.*

-ist, *suffix forming nouns chiefly from other nouns.* **1** person who does or makes: *Tourist = a person who makes a tour.* **2** an expert in a science: *Botanist = an expert in botany.* **3** person who plays a musical instrument: *Organist = a person who plays the organ.* **4** person engaged in or working with: *Journalist = a person engaged in journalism. Machinist = a person working with machines.* **5** person who believes in: *Socialist = a person who believes in socialism.*

Is tan bul (is′tän bül′), city in NW Turkey, on the Bosporus. Formerly called **Constantinople.** *n.*

isthmus

isth mus (is′məs), a narrow strip of land with water on both sides, connecting two larger bodies of land: *The Isthmus of Panama connects North America and South America. n., pl.* **isth mus es.**

it (it), **1** the thing, part, animal, or person spoken about: *Look at it carefully. What is it you want? It snows in winter. It is now my turn.* **2** (in games) the player who must catch, find, guess, etc. **1** *pron., pl.* **they;** **2** *n.*

It., **1** Italian. **2** Italy.

ital., italic or italics.

Ital., **1** Italian. **2** Italy.

I tal ian (i tal′yən), **1** of Italy, its people, or their language. **2** person born or living in Italy. **3** language of Italy. **1** *adj.,* **2,3** *n.*

i tal ic (i tal′ik *or* ī tal′ik), **1** of or in type whose letters slant to the right: *These words are in italic type.* **2 italics,** *pl.* type whose letters slant to the right. **1** *adj.,* **2** *n.*

i tal i cize (i tal′ə sīz), **1** print in type in which the letters slant to the right: *This sentence is italicized.* **2** underline with a single line to indicate italics. We italicize expressions which we wish to distinguish or emphasize. **3** use italics. *v.,* **i tal i cized, i tal i ciz ing.**

It a ly (it′l ē), country in S Europe on the Mediterranean. *Capital:* Rome. See **Adriatic Sea** for map. *n.*

itch (ich), **1** a ticklish, prickling feeling in the skin that makes one want to scratch. **2** disease causing this feeling. **3** cause this feeling: *Mosquito bites itch.* **4** feel this way in the skin: *My nose itches.* **5** a restless, uneasy feeling, longing, or desire for anything: *Don't you ever have an itch to get away and explore?* **6** have an uneasy desire: *I itched to find out their secret.* **1,2,5** *n., pl.* **itch es;** **3,4,6** *v.* [*Itch* comes from Old English *giccan.*]

itch i ness (ich′ē nis), a being itchy. *n.*

itch y (ich′ē), **1** itching; like the itch. **2** restless; nervous: *I get itchy if I have to stay indoors all day. adj.,* **itch i er, itch i est.**

i tem (ī′təm), **1** a separate thing or article: *The list had twelve items on it.* **2** piece of news; bit of information: *There were several interesting items in today's paper. n.*

i tem ize (ī′tə mīz), give each item of; list by items: *The storekeeper itemized the bill to show each article and its cost. v.,* **i tem ized, i tem iz ing.**

it e rate (it′ə rāt′), say again or repeatedly; repeat. *v.,* **it e rat ed, it e rat ing.**

it e ra tion (it′ə rā′shən), repetition. *n.*

Ith a ca (ith′ə kə), small island west of Greece, the legendary home of Ulysses. See **Troy** for map. *n.*

i tin er ant (ī tin′ər ənt), **1** traveling from place to place. **2** person who travels from place to place. **1** *adj.,* **2** *n.*

i tin er ar y (ī tin′ə rer′ē), **1** route of travel; plan of travel. **2** record of travel. **3** guidebook for travelers. *n., pl.* **i tin e rar ies.**

it'll (it′l), **1** it will. **2** it shall.

its (its), of it; belonging to it: *The dog wagged its tail. adj.*

it's (its), **1** it is: *It's my turn.* **2** it has: *It's been a beautiful day.*

it self (it self′), **1** form of *it* used to make a statement stronger: *The land itself is worth the money, without the house.* **2** form used instead of *it* in cases like: *The horse tripped and hurt itself.* **3** its normal or usual self: *After a few minor repairs my car was itself again. pron.*

-ity, *suffix added to adjectives to form nouns.* quality, condition, or fact of being ____: *Sincerity = quality or condition of being sincere.* Also, **-ty.**

I've (īv), I have.

i vied (ī′vēd), covered or overgrown with ivy. *adj.*

i vor y (ī′vər ē), **1** a hard, white substance making up the tusks of elephants, walruses, etc. Ivory is used for piano keys, billiard balls, combs, ornaments, etc. **2** substance like ivory. **3** made of ivory. **4** of or like ivory. **5** a creamy white. **6** creamy-white. **1,2,5** *n., pl.* **i vor ies;** **3,4,6** *adj.*

Ivory Coast, country in W Africa, on the Atlantic. *Capital:* Abidjan. See **Nigeria** for map.

i vy (ī′vē), **1** a climbing plant with smooth, shiny, evergreen leaves. **2** any of various other climbing plants, such as poison ivy. *n., pl.* **i vies.** [*Ivy* comes from Old English *ifig.*]

-ize, *suffix added to adjectives and nouns to form verbs.* **1** make ____: *Legalize = make legal. Apologize = make an apology.* **2** become ____: *Crystallize = become crystal.* **3** engage in or use ____: *Criticize = engage in criticism.* **4** treat or combine with ____: *Oxidize = combine with oxygen.*

J or **j** (jā), the tenth letter of the English alphabet. *n., pl.* **J's** or **j's.**

Ja., January.

jab (jab), **1** thrust with something pointed; poke: *He jabbed his fork into the potato.* **2** a thrust with something pointed; poke: *She gave him a jab with her elbow.* **3** in boxing: **a** a blow in which the arm is extended straight from the shoulder. **b** to hit with a jab. 1,3b *v.,* **jabbed, jab bing;** 2,3a *n.*

jab ber (jab'ər), **1** talk very fast in a confused, senseless way; chatter. **2** very fast, confused, or senseless talk; chatter. 1 *v.,* 2 *n.*

ja bot (zha bō' *or* zhab'ō), ruffle or frill of lace, worn at the throat or down the front of a shirt, dress, or blouse. *n.*

jack (jak), **1** a portable tool or machine for lifting or pushing up heavy weights a short distance: *He raised the car off the ground with a jack to change the flat tire.* **2** lift or push up with a jack: *jack up a car.* **3** a playing card with a picture of a servant or soldier on it; knave. **4** pebble or small six-pointed metal piece used in the game of jacks; jackstone. **5 jacks,** *pl.* a children's game played with jacks; jackstones. Each player bounces the ball and picks up the jacks in between bounces. **6** a small flag used on a ship to show nationality or as a signal. **7** device for turning a spit in roasting meat. **8** a male donkey. **9** man or fellow. **10** an electrical device which can receive a plug to make a connection in a circuit. 1,3-10 *n.,* 2 *v.*

jack up, INFORMAL. raise (prices, wages, etc.): *Supermarkets have jacked up prices in recent months.*

WORD HISTORY

jack

Jack comes from *Jack*, a nickname for the name *John*. It was first applied to any common person. Then it came to be used for any commonly found animal, machine, etc.

jack (def. 1)

jack al (jak'əl *or* jak'ôl), a wild dog of Asia, Africa, and eastern Europe, about as big as a fox. Jackals hunt in packs at night and feed on small animals and animals they find dead. *n.*

jack a napes (jak'ə nāps), an impertinent, forward person. *n.*

jack ass (jak'as'), **1** a male donkey. **2** a very stupid or foolish person. *n., pl.* **jack ass es.**

jack boot (jak'büt'), a heavy military boot reaching above the knee. *n.*

jack daw (jak'dô'), a small European crow; daw. *n.*

jack et (jak'it), **1** a short coat. **2** an outer covering. The paper cover for a book, the casing around a steam pipe, and the skin of a potato are jackets. *n.*

Jack Frost, frost or freezing weather thought of as a person.

jack-in-the-box (jak'in ᴛʜə boks'), toy consisting of a figure that springs up from a box when the lid is opened. *n., pl.* **jack-in-the-box es.**

jack-in-the-pul pit (jak'in ᴛʜə pùl'pit), plant with a greenish, petallike sheath arched over the flower stalk. *n., pl.* **jack-in-the-pul pits.**

jack knife (jak'nīf'), **1** a large, strong pocketknife. **2** kind of dive in which a diver touches the feet with the hands in midair, and straightens out before entering the water. **3** double up like a jackknife. 1,2 *n., pl.* **jack- knives** (jak'nīvz'); 3 *v.,* **jack knifed, jack knif ing.**

jack of all trades, person who can do many different kinds of work fairly well.

jack-o'-lan tern (jak'ə lan'tərn), pumpkin hollowed out and cut to look like a face, used as a lantern at Halloween. *n.*

jack pot (jak'pot'), **1** stakes that accumulate in a game until some player wins. **2** the big prize of a game. *n.* **hit the jackpot, 1** get the big prize. **2** have a stroke of very good luck.

jack rabbit, a large hare of western North America, having very long hind legs and long ears.

Jack son (jak'sən), **1 Andrew,** 1767-1845, the seventh president of the United States, from 1829 to 1837. He was also a general in the War of 1812. **2 Thomas Jona than,** 1824-1863, Confederate general. He was called "Stonewall" Jackson. **3** capital of Mississippi, in the central part. *n.*

Jack son ville (jak'sən vil), city in NE Florida. *n.*

jack stone (jak'stōn'), **1** piece used in the game of jacks; jack. **2 jackstones,** *pl.* the game of jacks. *n.*

jack straw (jak'strô'), **1** straw, strip of wood, bone, etc., used in the game of jackstraws. **2 jackstraws,** *pl.* a children's game played with these. A set of jackstraws is thrown down in a pile and each player tries to pick them up one at a time without moving any of the others. *n.*

jack tar or **Jack Tar,** sailor.

Ja cob (jā'kəb), (in the Bible) the son of Isaac and Rebecca, and younger twin brother of Esau. The 12 tribes of Israel traced their descent from Jacob's 12 sons. *n.*

jade (jād), **1** a hard stone used for jewelry and ornaments. Most jade is green, but some is whitish. **2** a light green. **3** light-green. 1,2 *n.,* 3 *adj.* [*Jade* was borrowed from French *jade,* which came from Spanish (*piedra de*) *ijada,* meaning "(stone of) colic." The stone was called this because it was supposed to cure colic.] —**jade'- like',** *adj.*

jad ed (jā'did), worn out; tired; weary. *adj.* —**jad'ed ly,** *adv.* —**jad'ed ness,** *n.*

jag (jag), **1** a sharp point sticking out: *a jag of rock.* **2** cut or tear unevenly. 1 *n.,* 2 *v.,* **jagged, jag ging.**

jag ged (jag'id), with sharp points sticking out: *We cut our bare feet on the jagged rocks. adj.* —**jag'ged ly,** *adv.* —**jag'ged ness,** *n.*

jag uar (jag'wär), a fierce animal much like a leopard, but more heavily built. It lives in forests in tropical America. *n.*

jai alai

jai a lai (hī′ ä lī′), game similar to handball, played on a walled court with a hard ball. The ball is caught and thrown with a kind of curved wicker basket fastened to the arm.

jail (jāl), **1** prison, especially one for persons awaiting trial or being punished for some small offense. **2** put in jail; keep in jail. 1 *n.*, 2 *v.*

jail er or **jail or** (jā′lər), keeper of a jail. *n.*

Ja kar ta (jə kär′tə), Djakarta. *n.*

ja lop y (jə lop′ē), INFORMAL. an old automobile in bad condition. *n.*, *pl.* **ja lop ies.**

jal ou sie (jal′ə sē), shade or shutter made of horizontal slats which may be tilted to let in light and air but keep out sun and rain. *n.*

jam¹ (jam) **1** press or squeeze tightly between two surfaces: *The ship was jammed between two rocks.* **2** crush by squeezing; bruise: *I jammed my fingers in the door.* **3** press or squeeze (things or persons) tightly together: *A crowd jammed into the bus. They jammed us all into one bus.* **4** mass of people or things crowded together so that they cannot move freely: *She was delayed by the traffic jam.* **5** fill or block up (the way, etc.) by crowding: *The river was jammed with logs.* **6** stick or catch so that it cannot be worked: *The window has jammed; I can't open it.* **7** cause to stick or catch so that it cannot be worked: *The key broke off and jammed the lock.* **8** push or thrust (a thing) hard (into a place); shove: *jam one more book into the bookcase.* **9** INFORMAL. a difficulty or tight spot: *I was in a jam.* **10** make (radio signals, etc.) unintelligible by sending out others of approximately the same frequency. 1-3,5-8,10 *v.*, **jammed, jam ming;** 4,9 *n.*

jam² (jam), preserve made by boiling fruit with sugar until thick: *raspberry jam. n.* —**jam′like′,** *adj.*

Ja mai ca (jə mā′kə), island country in the West Indies, south of Cuba, a member of the Commonwealth of Nations. *Capital:* Kingston. *n.* —**Ja mai′can,** *adj., n.*

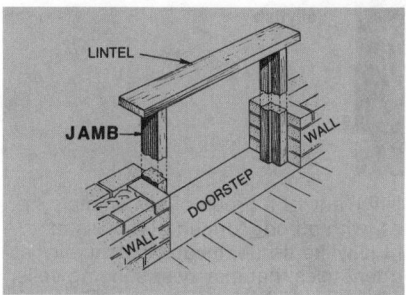

jamb (jam), an upright piece forming the side of a doorway, window, or fireplace. *n.*

jam bo ree (jam′bə rē′), **1** a large rally or gathering of Boy Scouts or Girl Scouts. **2** INFORMAL. a noisy party. *n.*

James (jāmz), **1** in the Bible: **a** one of the apostles of Jesus, sometimes called **James the Greater. b** another of the twelve apostles, sometimes called **James the Less. 2** book of the New Testament. **3 Henry,** 1843-1916 American novelist who lived in England. **4 Jesse,** 1847-1882, American bandit and outlaw. *n.*

James I, 1566-1625, the first Stuart king of England, from 1603 to 1625. The King James version of the Bible was written during his reign.

James town (jāmz′toun), restored village in SE Virginia. The first successful English settlement in North America was made there in 1607. *n.*

jam session, a gathering at which jazz musicians play compositions and improvise together.

Jan., January.

jan gle (jang′gəl), **1** sound harshly; make a loud, clashing noise: *The pots and pans jangled in the kitchen.* **2** cause to make a harsh, clashing sound: *The boys jangled cowbells.* **3** a harsh sound; clashing noise or ring: *the jangle of the telephone.* **4** have a harsh, unpleasant effect on: *All that racket jangles my nerves.* 1,2,4 *v.*, **jan gled, jan gling;** 3 *n.* —**jan′gler,** *n.*

jan i tor (jan′ə tər), person hired to take care of a building or offices; caretaker. *n.*

Jan u ar y (jan′yü er′ē), the first month of the year. It has 31 days. *n.*

Ja nus (jā′nəs), (in Roman myths) the god of gates and doors, and of beginnings and endings, represented with two faces, one looking forward and the other looking backward. *n.*

ja pan (jə pan′), **1** a hard, glossy varnish. Black japan is used on wood or metal. **2** put japan on. **3** articles varnished and ornamented in the Japanese manner. 1,3 *n.*, 2 *v.*, **ja panned, ja pan ning.**

Ja pan (jə pan′), **1** country made up of four large islands and many smaller ones, in the W Pacific east of the Asian mainland. The Japanese name for Japan is **Nippon.** *Capital:* Tokyo. See **China** for map. **2 Sea of,** sea between Japan and the Asian mainland. *n.*

Jap a nese (jap′ə nēz′), **1** of Japan, its people, or their language. **2** person born or living in Japan. **3** language of Japan. 1 *adj.*, 2,3 *n.*, *pl.* **Jap a nese** for 2. Also, **Nipponese.**

Japanese beetle, a small, green-and-brown beetle that eats fruits, leaves, and grasses. It causes much damage to crops in the United States.

jar¹ (jär), **1** a deep container made of glass, earthenware, or stone, with a wide mouth. **2** amount that it holds. *n.* [*Jar¹* came into English about 400 years ago from French *jarre,* meaning "an earthen vessel," and can be traced back to Arabic *jarrah.*] —**jar′less,** *adj.*

jar² (jär), **1** cause to shake or rattle; vibrate: *Your heavy footsteps jar my table.* **2** a shake, rattle. **3** make a harsh, grating noise. **4** a harsh, grating noise. **5** have a harsh, unpleasant effect on: *The children's screams jarred my nerves.* **6** a slight shock to the ears, nerves, feelings, etc. **7** clash; conflict: *We did not get on well together; our opinions always jarred.* 1,3,5,7 *v.*, **jarred, jar ring;** 2,4,6 *n.* [*Jar²* probably comes from an imitation of the sound of rattling.] —**jar′ring ly,** *adv.*

jar gon (jär′gən), **1** confused, meaningless talk or writing. **2** language that is a mixture of two or more languages. **3** language of a special group, profession, etc. Doctors, actors, and sailors have jargons. *n.*

jas mine (jas′mən), shrub or vine with clusters of fragrant yellow, white, or reddish flowers. *n.* Also, **jessamine.**

Ja son (jā′sn), (in Greek legends) the Greek hero who led the expedition of the Argonauts and secured the Golden Fleece. *n.*

jas per (jas′pər), an opaque variety of quartz, usually red, brown, or yellow in color. *n.*

jaun dice (jôn′dis), **1** an unhealthy yellowness of the skin, eyes, and body fluids. It is caused by too much bile pigment in the blood. **2** cause jaundice in. **3** a disturbed outlook due to envy, discontent, jealousy, etc. **4** prejudice the mind and judgment of, by envy, discontent, jealousy, etc. 1,3 *n.,* 2,4 *v.,* **jaun diced, jaun dic ing.** [*Jaundice* came into English about 700 years ago from French *jaunice,* and can be traced back to Latin *galbus,* meaning "yellow."]

jaunt (jônt), **1** a short journey or excursion, especially for pleasure: *a jaunt to the seashore.* **2** take such a trip. 1 *n.,* 2 *v.*

jaun ti ly (jôn′tl ē), in an easy, lively manner; smartly. *adv.*

jaun ti ness (jôn′tē nis), quality of being jaunty; airiness, sprightliness. *n.*

jaun ty (jôn′tē), **1** easy and lively; sprightly: *The happy children walked with jaunty steps.* **2** smart; stylish: *a jaunty hat. adj.,* **jaun ti er, jaun ti est.**

Ja va (jä′və *or* jav′ə), **1** large island southeast of Sumatra. It is the most important island of Indonesia. See **East Indies** for map. **2** kind of coffee obtained from Java and nearby islands. **3** SLANG. coffee. *n.*

Java man, a prehistoric human being, known from fossil remains found in Java.

Jav a nese (jav′ə nēz′), **1** of Java, its people, or their language. **2** person born or living in Java. **3** language of Java. 1 *adj.,* 2,3 *n., pl.* **Jav a nese** for 2.

jave lin (jav′lən), **1** a light spear thrown by hand. **2** a wooden or metal spear, thrown for distance in track and field contests. *n.*

jaw (jô), **1** the lower part of the face. **2** the upper or lower bone or set of bones, that together form the framework of the mouth. The lower jaw is movable. **3 jaws,** *pl.* the parts in a tool or machine that grip and hold. A vise has jaws. **4** SLANG. go on talking at great length, in a boring way. **5** SLANG. find fault; scold. 1-3 *n.,* 4,5 *v.* —**jaw′like′,** *adj.*

jaw bone (jô′bōn′), one of the bones in which the teeth are set, especially the lower jaw. *n.*

jay (jā), any of various crested birds of Europe and North America which are related to the crow. The blue jay is one kind of jay. *n.*

Jay (jā), **John,** 1745-1829, first chief justice of the United States Supreme Court, from 1789 to 1795. *n.*

jay walk (jā′wôk′), walk across a street without paying attention to traffic rules. *v.* —**jay′walk′er,** *n.*

jazz (jaz), **1** a popular kind of music in which the accents fall at unusual places. Jazz is native to the United States, and developed from early Afro-American spirituals and folk music. **2** of or like jazz: *a jazz band, jazz records.* **3** SLANG. worthless nonsense. **4** SLANG. similar things; stuff: *We had to give our age, height, color of hair, and all that jazz.* 1,3,4 *n.,* 2 *adj.* [*Jazz* may have been originally an American Negro word which came from a west African word.]

jazz up, SLANG. make lively; add flavor or interest to: *jazz up a speech with jokes and funny stories.*

jeal ous (jel′əs), **1** fearful that a person one loves may love or prefer someone else: *The child was jealous when* anyone paid attention to the new baby. **2** full of envy; envious: *She is jealous of her sister's good grades.* **3** watchful in keeping or guarding something; careful: *Our city is jealous of its rights within the State.* **4** close; watchful; suspicious: *The dog was such a jealous guardian of the little girl that he would not let her cross the street. adj.* —**jeal′ous ly,** *adv.* —**jeal′ous ness,** *n.*

jeal ous y (jel′ə sē), dislike or fear of rivals; jealous condition or feeling; envy. *n., pl.* **jeal ous ies.**

jean (jēn), **1** a strong, twilled cotton cloth, used for overalls, etc. **2 jeans,** *pl.* overalls or trousers made of this cloth: *The cowboy wore faded jeans. n.* [*Jean* is from Middle English *Jeane,* meaning "of Genoa," where the cloth was made.]

Jeanne d'Arc (zhän′ därk′), FRENCH. Joan of Arc.

jeep (jēp), a small, powerful, general-purpose motor vehicle in which power is transmitted to all four wheels. It was originally designed for use by the United States Army. *n.* [*Jeep* comes from a fast way of pronouncing the abbreviation *G.P.,* which stands for *General Purpose* Car.]

jeer (jir), **1** make fun rudely or unkindly; mock; scoff: *Do not jeer at the mistakes or misfortunes of others.* **2** a mocking or insulting remark. 1 *v.,* 2 *n.* —**jeer′er,** *n.*

Jef fer son (jef′ər sən), **Thomas,** 1743-1826, American statesman, third president of the United States, from 1801 to 1809. He drafted the Declaration of Independence. *n.*

Jefferson City, capital of Missouri, in the central part.

Je ho vah (ji hō′və), one of the names of God in the Old Testament. *n.* [*Jehovah* comes from Hebrew *Yahweh,* which was originally written without vowels as *JHVH.*]

jell (jel), **1** become jelly; thicken. **2** INFORMAL. take definite form; become fixed: *His hunch soon jelled into a plan. v.*

jel lied (jel′ēd), turned into jelly. *adj.*

Jell-O (jel′ō), trademark for a gelatin dessert, usually fruit-flavored. *n.*

jel ly (jel′ē), **1** a food, liquid when hot, but somewhat firm and partly transparent when cold. Jelly can be made by boiling fruit juice and sugar with some thickening agent like gelatin. **2** a jellylike substance. **3** become jelly or like jelly; thicken; congeal: *Some soup will jelly when it is chilled in the refrigerator.* 1,2 *n., pl.* **jel lies;** 3 *v.,* **jel lied, jel ly ing.** —**jel′ly like′,** *adj.*

jel ly bean (jel′ē bēn′), a small candy made of jellied sugar, often shaped like a bean. *n.*

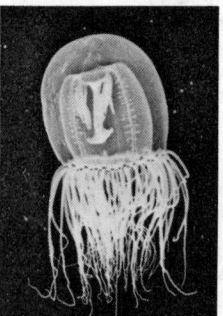

jellyfish

jel ly fish (jel′ē fish′), any of a group of sea animals without backbones, with a body formed of a mass of almost transparent jellylike tissue; medusa. Most jellyfish have long, trailing tentacles that may bear stinging cells. *n., pl.* **jel ly fish es** or **jel ly fish.**

Jen ner (jen′ər), **Edward,** 1749-1823, English physician who discovered vaccination. *n.*

jen net (jen′it), **1** a small Spanish horse. **2** a female donkey. *n.*

jen ny (jen′ē), **1** spinning jenny. **2** female of certain animals: *jenny wren. n., pl.* **jen nies.**

jeop ar dize (jep′ər dīz), put in danger; risk; endanger; imperil: *The raging forest fire jeopardized many lives. v.,* **jeop ar dized, jeop ar diz ing.**

jeop ar dy (jep′ər dē), risk; danger; peril: *Many lives were in jeopardy during the forest fire. n.* [Jeopardy came into English about 650 years ago from French *jeu parti,* meaning "an even or divided game."]

jer bo a (jər bō′ə), a small, jumping, mouselike mammal of Asia and northern Africa. *n., pl.* **jer bo as.**

Jer e mi ah (jer′ə mī′ə), **1** born 650 B.C.?, Hebrew prophet. **2** book of the Old Testament containing his prophecies. *n.*

Jer i cho (jer′ə kō), city in ancient Palestine. According to the Bible, its walls fell down at the noise made by the trumpets of Joshua's attacking army. See **Canaan** for map. *n.*

jerk¹ (jėrk), **1** a sudden, sharp pull, twist, or start: *The old car started with a jerk.* **2** a pull or twist of the muscles that one cannot control; twitch. **3** pull or twist suddenly: *If the water is unexpectedly hot, you jerk your hand out.* **4** move with a jerk: *The old wagon jerked along.* **5** SLANG. a stupid or simple-minded person. **1,2,5** *n.,* **3,4** *v.* —**jerk′er,** *n.*

jerk² (jėrk), preserve (meat) by cutting into long, thin slices and drying in the sun. *v.*

jerk i ly (jėr′kə lē), in a jerky manner; by fits and starts. *adv.*

jerkin
(worn by the man on the right)

jer kin (jėr′kən), a short, close-fitting coat or jacket without sleeves. *n.*

jerk y¹ (jėr′kē), with sudden starts and stops; with jerks. *adj.,* **jerk i er, jerk i est.** —**jerk′i ness,** *n.*

jerk y² (jėr′kē), strips of dried meat, usually beef. *n.*

Je rome (jə rōm′), **Saint,** A.D. 340?-420, monk and scholar, author of the Latin translation of the Bible known as the Vulgate. *n.*

jer sey (jėr′zē), **1** a machine-knitted cloth with a tight weave. **2** a close-fitting, pullover sweater made of this cloth. *n., pl.* **jer seys.** [Jersey gets its name from the island of *Jersey,* where this cloth had been made for a long time.]

Jer sey (jėr′zē), **1** one of the Channel Islands. **2** one of a breed of small, usually fawn-colored cattle that came from this island. Jerseys give very rich milk. *n., pl.* **Jerseys** for 2.

Je ru sa lem (jə rü′sə ləm), capital of Israel, in the E part. It is a holy city to Jews, Christians, and Moslems. *n.*

jes sa mine (jes′ə mən), jasmine. *n.*

jest (jest), **1** a joke. **2** to joke. **3** poke fun; make fun: *They jested at my idea until I proved it would work.* **1** *n.,* **2,3** *v.* [Jest came into English about 700 years ago from French *geste,* originally meaning "story, exploit," and can be

traced back to Latin *gerere,* meaning "to accomplish, bear, carry."] —**jest′ing ly,** *adv.*

in jest, in fun; not seriously: *His words were spoken in jest.*

jest er (jes′tər), person who jests. In the Middle Ages, royalty often had jesters to amuse them. *n.*

Je su (jē′zü *or* jē′sü), Jesus. *n.*

Jes u it (jezh′ü it *or* jez′yü it), member of the Society of Jesus, a Roman Catholic religious order of men founded by Saint Ignatius of Loyola in 1534. *n.*

Je sus (jē′zəs), 6 B.C.?-A.D. 29?, founder of the Christian religion. The name means "God is salvation." *n.*

Jesus Christ, Jesus.

jet¹ (jet), **1** stream of water, steam, gas, or any liquid, sent with force, especially from a small opening: *A fountain sends up a jet of water.* **2** spout or nozzle for sending out a jet. **3** shoot forth in a jet or forceful stream; gush out: *Water jetted from the broken pipe.* **4** jet plane. **5** fly by jet plane: *to jet from Chicago to New York.* **1,2,4** *n.,* **3,5** *v.,* **jet ted, jet ting.**

jet² (jet), **1** a hard, black kind of coal, glossy when polished, used for making beads, buttons, and ornaments. **2** made of jet. **3** a deep, glossy black. **4** deep, glossy black: *jet hair.* **1,3** *n.,* **2,4** *adj.*

jet airplane, jet plane.

jet-black (jet′blak′), very black. *adj.*

jet engine, engine using jet propulsion.

jet lag, the delayed effects, such as tiredness, that a person feels after a long flight through several time zones on a jet plane.

jet plane, airplane that is driven by jet propulsion; jet.

jet-pro pelled (jet′prə peld′), driven by jet propulsion. *adj.*

jet propulsion, propulsion in one direction caused by a jet of air, gas, etc., forced in the opposite direction.

jet sam (jet′səm), goods which are thrown overboard to lighten a ship in distress and often afterwards washed ashore. *n.*

jet stream, **1** current of air traveling at very high speed from west to east at altitudes of six to eight miles (10 to 13 kilometers). **2** the exhaust from a jet engine.

jet ti son (jet′ə sən), **1** throw (goods) overboard to lighten a ship in distress. **2** throw away; discard. *v.*

jet ty (jet′ē), **1** structure of stones or wooden piles projecting out from the shore to break the force of a current or waves; breakwater. **2** a landing place; pier. *n., pl.* **jet ties.**

Jew (jü), **1** person descended from the Semitic people led by Moses, who settled in Palestine and now live in Israel and many other countries; Hebrew; Israelite. **2** person whose religion is Judaism. *n.*

jew el (jü′əl), **1** a precious stone; gem. **2** a valuable ornament to be worn, often made of gold or silver and set with gems. **3** person or thing that is very precious. **4** gem or other hard material used as a bearing in a watch. **5** set or adorn with jewels or with things like jewels: *a jeweled comb, a sky jeweled with stars.* **1-4** *n.,* **5** *v.,* **jeweled, jew el ing** *or* **jew elled, jew el ling.** —**jew′el like′,** *adj.*

jew el er *or* **jew el ler** (jü′ə lər), person who makes, sells, or repairs jewelry and watches. *n.*

jew el ry *or* **jew el ler y** (jü′əl rē), **1** jewels and orna-

a hat	i it	oi oil	ch child	⎧ a in about
ā age	ī ice	ou out	ng long	⎪ e in taken
ä far	o hot	u cup	sh she	ə = ⎨ i in pencil
e let	ō open	u̇ put	th thin	⎪ o in lemon
ē equal	ô order	ü rule	ŦH then	⎩ u in circus
ėr term			zh measure	

ments set with gems: *She keeps her jewelry in a small, locked box.* **2** ring, bracelet, necklace, or other ornament to be worn, usually set with imitation gems or made of silver- or gold-colored metal, etc. *n.*

Jew ish (jü′ish), of the Jews or their religion: *the Jewish faith. adj.*

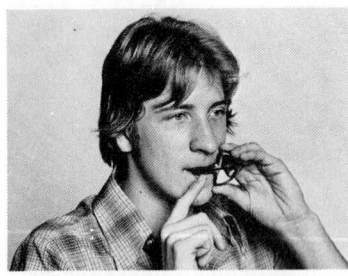

Jew's harp

Jew's harp, a simple musical instrument, held between the teeth and played by striking the free end of a flexible piece of metal with a finger.

jew's-harp (jüz′härp′), Jew's harp. *n.*

Jez e bel (jez′ə bəl), **1** (in the Bible) the wicked wife of Ahab, king of Israel. **2** a shameless, immoral woman. *n.*

jib[1] (jib), a triangular sail in front of the foremast. *n.*

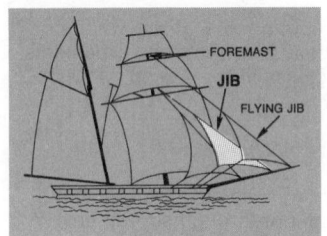

jib[1]

jib[2] (jib), jibe[3] *v.,* **jibbed, jib bing.**

jibe[1] (jīb), gibe. *v.,* **jibed, jib ing;** *n.* —**jib′er,** *n.*

jibe[2] (jīb), INFORMAL. be in harmony; agree: *Our opinions jibe; we both have the same idea. v.,* **jibed, jib ing.**

jibe[3] (jīb), **1** shift (a sail) from one side of a ship to the other when sailing before the wind. **2** shift itself in this way: *Be careful or your mainsail will jibe.* **3** change the course of a ship so that the sails shift in this way. *v.,* **jibed, jib ing.** Also, **jib.**

jif fy (jif′ē), INFORMAL. a very short time; moment: *He was on his bike in a jiffy, pedaling down the drive. n., pl.* **jif fies.**

jig[1] (jig), **1** a lively dance, often in triple time. **2** music for it. **3** dance a jig. **1,2** *n.,* **3** *v.,* **jigged, jig ging.**

the jig is up, it's all over; there is no more chance.

jig[2] (jig), **1** a fishing lure consisting of a fishhook or a set of fishhooks weighted with a piece of bright metal. It is bobbed up and down or pulled through the water. **2** any of various devices used to hold a piece of work and guide a drill, file, saw, etc., toward it. *n.*

jig ger (jig′ər), a small glass or metal cup, used to measure alcoholic liquor. It holds about 1¹/₂ ounces (44 milliliters). *n.*

jig gle (jig′əl), **1** shake or jerk slightly: *Don't jiggle the desk when I'm trying to write.* **2** a slight shake; light jerk. **1** *v.,* **jig gled, jig gling; 2** *n.*

jig saw (jig′sô′), saw with a narrow blade mounted in a frame and worked with an up-and-down motion. It is used to cut curves or irregular lines. *n.*

jigsaw puzzle, picture glued onto cardboard or wood and sawed into irregular pieces that can be fitted together again.

jilt (jilt), cast off (a lover or sweetheart) after giving encouragement. *v.*

jim my (jim′ē), **1** a short crowbar used especially by burglars to force open windows, doors, or other things. **2** force open with a jimmy. **1** *n., pl.* **jim mies; 2** *v.,* **jim mied, jim my ing.**

jim son weed or **jim son-weed** (jim′sən wēd′), a tall, coarse, bad-smelling weed with white flowers and poisonous, narcotic leaves. *n.* [*Jimson* (in *jimsonweed*) is a different form of *Jamestown,* where it was first found.]

jin gle (jing′gəl), **1** a sound like that of little bells, or of coins or keys striking together. **2** make a sound like bells, coins, or keys striking together: *The sleigh bells jingle as we ride.* **3** cause to jingle: *jingle one's money.* **4** verse or song that has repetition of similar sounds, or a catchy rhyme. "Higgledy, piggledy, my black hen" is a jingle. **1,4** *n.,* **2,3** *v.,* **jin gled, jin gling.**

jinn (jin), (in Moslem myths) spirit that can appear in human or animal form: *The good jinn helped Aladdin when he rubbed a magic lamp. n., pl.* **jinns** or **jinn.**

jin ni (ji nē′), jinn; genie. *n., pl.* **jinn.**

jin rick sha (jin rik′shə *or* jin rik′shô), jinrikisha. *n., pl.* **jin rick shas.**

jin rik i sha (jin rik′shə *or* jin rik′shô), a small, two-wheeled carriage with a folding top, pulled by a runner, formerly used in the Orient. *n., pl.* **jin rik i shas.** Also, **rickshaw** or **ricksha.**

WORD HISTORY

jinrikisha

Jinrikisha is from Japanese *jinrikisha,* which comes from *jin,* meaning "man," *riki,* meaning "strength," and *sha,* meaning "cart."

jinx (jingks), INFORMAL. **1** person or thing that brings bad luck. **2** bring bad luck to. **1** *n., pl.* **jinx es; 2** *v.*

jit ney (jit′nē), an automobile or small bus that carries passengers for a low fare. It usually travels along a regular route. *n., pl.* **jit neys.**

jit ter bug (jit′ər bug′), **1** a lively dance for couples, with

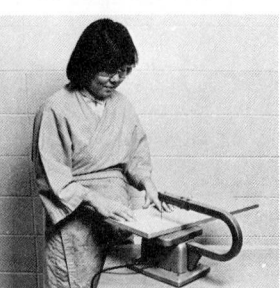

jigsaw

rapid twirling movements and acrobatics. It was especially popular in the 1940's. **2** dance the jitterbug. 1 *n.*, 2 *v.*, **jit ter bugged, jit ter bug ging.**

jit ters (jit′ərz), INFORMAL. extreme nervousness. *n.pl.*

jit ter y (jit′ər ē), INFORMAL. nervous. *adj.*

jiu jit su (jü jit′sü), jujitsu. *n.*

jive (jīv), SLANG. **1** swing music. **2** the latest slang. **3** misleading or tiresome talk. *n.*

Joan of Arc (jōn′ əv ärk′), 1412-1431, French heroine who led armies against the invading English. She was condemned as a witch and burned to death. In 1920 she was made a saint. Also FRENCH, **Jeanne d'Arc.**

job (job), **1** piece of work: *We had the job of painting the boat.* **2** a definite piece of work undertaken for a fixed price: *If you want your house painted, they will do the job for $900.* **3** work done for pay; employment: *My sister is hunting for a job.* **4** anything a person has to do: *I'm not going to wash the dishes; that's your job. n.*

Job (jōb), **1** (in the Bible) a very patient man who kept his faith in God in spite of many troubles. **2** book of the Old Testament that tells about him. *n.*

job ber (job′ər), person who buys goods from manufacturers in large quantities and sells them to retail dealers in small quantities. *n.*

job less (job′lis), having no job; unemployed. *adj.*

jock (jok), SLANG. athlete. *n.*

jock ey (jok′ē), **1** person whose occupation is riding horses in races. **2** ride (a horse) in a race. **3** trick; cheat: *Swindlers jockeyed them into buying some worthless land.* **4** maneuver so as to get advantage: *The crews were jockeying their boats to get into the best position for the race.* 1 *n.*, pl. **jock eys;** 2-4 *v.*

jo cose (jō kōs′), jesting; humorous; joking. *adj.* —**jo cose′ly,** *adv.* —**jo cose′ness,** *n.*

joc u lar (jok′yə lər), funny; joking. *adj.* —**joc′u lar ly,** *adv.*

joc u lar i ty (jok′yə lar′ə tē), **1** jocular quality. **2** jocular talk or behavior. **3** a jocular remark or act. *n., pl.* **joc u lar i ties.**

joc und (jok′ənd), cheerful; merry; gay. *adj.*

jodh purs (jod′pərz), breeches for horseback riding, loose above the knees and close-fitting below the knees. *n.pl.*

Jo el (jō′əl), **1** Hebrew prophet of the 400's B.C. **2** book of the Old Testament containing his prophecies. *n.*

jog[1] (jog), **1** shake with a push or jerk: *She jogged my elbow to get my attention.* **2** a shake, push, or nudge. **3** stir up with a hint or reminder: *He tied a string around his finger to jog his memory.* **4** a hint or reminder: *give one's memory a jog.* **5** move up or down with a jerk or a shaking motion: *The rider jogged up and down on the horse's back.* **6** walk or trot slowly: *I jog daily for exercise.* 1,3,5,6 *v.*, jogged, jog ging; 2,4,7 *n.*

jog[2] (jog), part that sticks out or in; unevenness in a line or surface: *We hid behind a jog in the wall. n.*

jog ger (jog′ər), one that jogs. *n.*

jog gle (jog′əl), **1** shake slightly. **2** a slight shake. 1 *v.*, **jog gled, jog gling;** 2 *n.*

Jo han nes burg (jō han′is bėrg′), city in NE South Africa, noted for its gold mines. *n.*

John (jon), **1** (in the Bible) one of Jesus' twelve apostles. **2** the fourth book of the New Testament. **3 King John,** 1167?-1216, king of England from 1199 to 1216. He signed the Magna Charta in 1215. *n.*

John XXIII, 1881-1963, pope from 1958 to 1963.

John Bull, 1 a typical Englishman. **2** the English nation.

John Doe, a made-up name used in legal forms or proceedings for the name of an unknown person.

John Hancock, a person's signature. [*John Hancock*

a hat	i it	oi oil	ch child	a in about
ā age	ī ice	ou out	ng long	e in taken
ä far	o hot	u cup	sh she	ə = { i in pencil
e let	ō open	u̇ put	th thin	o in lemon
ē equal	ô order	ü rule	ŦH then	u in circus
ėr term			zh measure	

comes from the bold and prominent signature of *John Hancock*, the first signer of the Declaration of Independence.]

john ny cake (jon′ē kāk′), cornbread in the form of a flat cake. *n.*

John Paul I, 1912-1978, pope in August and September 1978.

John Paul II, born 1920, pope since October 1978.

John son (jon′sən), **1 Andrew,** 1808-1875, the 17th president of the United States, from 1865 to 1869. **2 Lyndon Baines,** 1908-1973, the 36th president of the United States, from 1963 to 1969. **3 Samuel,** 1709-1784, English author, dictionary maker, and literary leader. *n.*

John the Baptist, died A.D. 29?, Hebrew prophet who foretold the coming of Christ and baptized Him.

join (join), **1** bring or put together; connect, fasten, or clasp together: *join hands, join an island to the mainland by a bridge.* **2** come together; meet: *The two roads join here. The brook joins the river just below the mill.* **3** make or become one; combine; unite: *join in marriage. The two clubs joined forces during the campaign.* **4** take part with others: *join in a song.* **5** become a member of: *She joined a tennis club. My uncle has joined the army.* **6** come into the company of: *Go now, and I'll join you later.* **7** be next to; adjoin: *Our farm joins theirs. v.*

join er (joi′nər), **1** person or thing that joins. **2** carpenter who makes doors, windows, molding, and other inside woodwork. *n.*

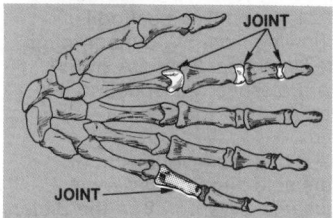

joint (def. 4)

joint (def. 5)

joint (joint), **1** the place at which two things or parts are joined together. A pocketknife has a joint to fold the blade inside the handle. **2** the way parts are joined: *The square ends of the wood made a perfect joint.* **3** connect by a joint or joints. **4** part in an animal where two bones join, allowing motion, and the way those bones are fitted together. **5** one of the parts of which a jointed thing is made up: *the middle joint of the finger.* **6** part of the stem of a plant from which a leaf or branch grows. **7** a large piece of meat for roasting, usually with a bone in it. **8** divide at the joints: *Please ask the butcher to joint the chicken.* **9** shared or done by two or more persons: *By our joint efforts we managed to push the car back on the road.* **10** joined together; sharing: *My sister and I are joint owners of this boat.* **11** SLANG. a cheap, low restaurant, bar, hotel, etc. 1,2,4-7,11 *n.*, 3,8 *v.*, 9,10 *adj.* —**joint′er,** *n.* —**joint′less,** *adj.*

out of joint, 1 out of place at the joint: *The fall put my shoulder out of joint.* **2** out of order; in bad condition.

joint ed (join′tid), having a joint or joints: *the jointed legs of a lobster. adj.*

joint ly (joint′lē), together; as partners: *The two girls owned the boat jointly. adv.*

joist (joist), one of the parallel beams of timber or steel which support the boards of a floor or ceiling. *n.*

joke (jōk), **1** something said or done to make somebody laugh; remark that is clever and funny; something funny; jest: *Looking for the hat that was on my head was a good joke on me.* **2** make jokes; say or do something as a joke; jest. **3** person or thing laughed at. 1,3 *n.,* 2 *v.,* **joked, jok ing.**

no joke, a serious matter: *The loss of my bicycle was no joke.*

jok er (jō′kər), **1** person who jokes. **2** an extra playing card used in some games. *n.*

jok ing ly (jō′king lē), in a joking manner. *adv.*

Jo li et (jō′lē et), **Louis,** 1645-1700, French-Canadian explorer of the Mississippi River. *n.*

jol li ty (jol′ə tē), fun; merriment. *n.*

jol ly (jol′ē), **1** full of fun; very cheerful; merry. **2** INFORMAL. pleasant or delightful. **3** INFORMAL. extremely; very: *a jolly good time.* 1,2 *adj.,* **jol li er, jol li est;** 3 *adv.*

Jolly Rog er (roj′ər), a pirates' black flag with a white skull and crossbones on it. *n.*

jolt (jōlt), **1** shake up; jar: *The wagon jolted us when the wheel went over a rock.* **2** a jar, shock, or jerk: *I put the brakes on suddenly and the car stopped with a jolt.* **3** a sudden surprise or shock: *News of the plane crash gave them a jolt.* **4** move with a shock or jerk: *The car jolted across the rough ground.* 1,4 *v.,* 2,3 *n.* —**jolt′er,** *n.*

Jo nah (jō′nə), **1** (in the Bible) a Hebrew prophet who was thrown overboard during a storm because he disobeyed God. He was swallowed by a large fish and later cast up on land. **2** book of the Old Testament that tells about him. *n.*

Jon a than (jon′ə thən), (in the Bible) a son of Saul, and devoted friend of David. *n.*

Jones (jōnz), **John Paul,** 1747-1792, American naval commander in the Revolutionary War. *n.*

jon quil (jong′kwəl), plant with yellow or white flowers and long slender leaves. It is much like a daffodil. *n.*

Jor dan (jôrd′n), **1** river flowing from SW Syria through Israel and Jordan into the Dead Sea. **2** country in SW Asia, east of Israel. Part of Palestine was added to it in 1950. *Capital:* Amman. See **Assyria** for map. *n.* —**Jor da ni an** (jôr dā′nē ən), *adj., n.*

Jo seph (jō′zəf), **1** (in the Bible) the favorite son of Jacob. His jealous brothers sold him into slavery in Egypt, where he finally became governor. **2** (in the Bible) the husband of Mary, mother of Jesus. **3 Chief,** 1840?-1904, American Indian leader of the Nez Percé tribe. *n.*

josh (josh), INFORMAL. make good-natured fun of; tease playfully. *v.* —**josh′er,** *n.*

Josh u a (josh′ü ə), **1** (in the Bible) the successor of Moses, who led the Israelites into the Promised Land. **2** book of the Old Testament. *n.*

joss stick, a slender stick of dried, fragrant paste, burned as incense.

jos tle (jos′əl), **1** shove, push, or crowd against; elbow roughly: *We were jostled by the big crowd at the entrance to the circus.* **2** a jostling; push; knock. 1 *v.,* **jos tled, jostling;** 2 *n.* Also, **justle.** —**jos′tler,** *n.*

jot (jot), **1** write briefly or in haste: *The clerk jotted down the order.* **2** a little bit; very small amount: *I do not care a jot.* 1 *v.,* **jot ted, jot ting;** 2 *n.*

joule (jül *or* joul), unit of work or energy used to measure the amount of work done. It is equal to ten million ergs. *n.* [*Joule* was named in honor of James P. *Joule,* 1818-1889, a British physicist.]

jounce (jouns), **1** shake up and down; bounce; bump; jolt: *The car jounced along on the rough road.* **2** a bump or jolt: *to sit down with a jounce.* 1 *v.,* **jounced, jouncing;** 2 *n.*

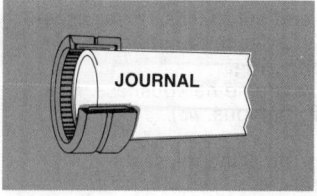

journal (def. 4)

jour nal (jėr′nl), **1** a daily record of events or occurrences. A diary is a journal of what a person does, thinks, feels, and notices. A ship's log is a journal of what happens on a ship. **2** newspaper, magazine, or other periodical. **3** (in bookkeeping) a book in which every item of business is written down, so that the item can be entered under the proper account. **4** the part of a shaft or axle that turns in a bearing. *n.*

jour nal ism (jėr′nl iz′əm), work of writing for, editing, managing, or publishing a newspaper or magazine. *n.*

jour nal ist (jėr′nl ist), person whose work is writing for, editing, managing, or publishing a newspaper or magazine. Editors and reporters are journalists. *n.*

jour nal is tic (jėr′nl is′tik), of or like journalism or journalists. *adj.* —**jour′nal is′ti cal ly,** *adv.*

jour ney (jėr′nē), **1** a traveling from one place to another; trip: *a journey around the world.* **2** distance traveled: *a week's journey.* **3** take a trip; travel: *to journey to Europe.* 1,2 *n., pl.* **jour neys;** 3 *v.* [*Journey* came into English about 750 years ago from French *journee,* meaning "a day's travel," and can be traced back to Latin *dies,* meaning "day."] —**jour′ney er,** *n.*

jour ney man (jėr′nē mən), **1** worker who knows a trade. **2** worker who has served an apprenticeship and is qualified to practice a trade. *n., pl.* **jour ney men.**

joust (joust *or* just), **1** combat between two knights on horseback, armed with lances. **2** fight with lances on horseback. Knights used to joust with each other for sport. 1 *n.,* 2 *v.* Also, **just.** —**joust′er,** *n.*

Jove (jōv), (in Roman myths) Jupiter. *n.*

by Jove, exclamation of surprise, pleasure, etc.

jo vi al (jō′vē əl), good-hearted and full of fun; merry: *Santa Claus is pictured as a jovial fellow.* adj.

jo vi al i ty (jō′vē al′ə tē), jollity; merriment. *n.*

jowl[1] (joul), **1** jaw, especially the lower jaw. **2** cheek. *n.*

jowl[2] (joul), fold of flesh hanging from the jaw. *n.*

joy (joi), **1** a strong feeling of pleasure; gladness; happiness: *They jumped for joy when they saw the circus.* **2** something that causes gladness or happiness: *On a hot day a cool swim is a joy. n.*

Joyce (jois), **James,** 1882-1941, Irish novelist, poet, and short-story writer. *n.*

joy ful (joi′fəl), **1** glad; happy: *a joyful heart.* **2** causing joy: *joyful news.* **3** showing joy: *a joyful look. adj.* —**joy′ful ly,** *adv.* —**joy′ful ness,** *n.*

joy less (joi′lis), without joy; sad; dismal. *adj.*

joy ous (joi′əs), joyful; glad; gay: *a joyous song, a joyous person. adj.* —**joy′ous ly,** *adv.* —**joy′ous ness,** *n.*

joy ride, INFORMAL. a ride in an automobile for pleasure, especially when the car is driven recklessly or without the owner's permission.

joy stick (joi′stik′), an electronic device used to control video games and computer games. It is an upright rod that can be tilted forward and back, from side to side, or in other directions. *n.*

J.P., Justice of the Peace.

jr. or **Jr.,** Junior.

Juan Car los I (hwän kär′lōs), born 1938, King of Spain since 1975.

ju bi lant (jü′bə lənt), expressing or showing joy; rejoicing: *She was jubilant when her team won the game. adj.*

jubilation
The crowd greeted the news that the war was over with **jubilation**.

a hat	i it	oi oil	ch child		a in about
ā age	ī ice	ou out	ng long	ə =	e in taken
ä far	o hot	u cup	sh she		i in pencil
e let	ō open	u̇ put	th thin		o in lemon
ē equal	ô order	ü rule	ŦH then		u in circus
ėr term			zh measure		

ju bi la tion (jü′bə lā′shən), a rejoicing. *n.*

ju bi lee (jü′bə lē), **1** an anniversary thought of as a time of rejoicing: *a twenty-fifth or fiftieth wedding jubilee.* **2** time of rejoicing or great joy; celebration. *n.*

Ju dae a (jü dē′ə), Judea. *n.*

Ju dah (jü′də), **1** in the Bible: **a** a son of Jacob and ancestor of the tribe of Judah. **b** the most powerful of the twelve tribes of Israel. **2** ancient Hebrew kingdom in S Palestine, made up of the tribes of Judah and Benjamin. *n.*

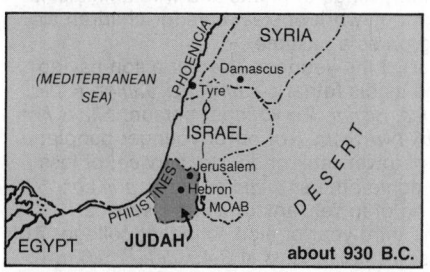

Judah
(def. 2)

about 930 B.C.

Ju da ic (jü dā′ik), of the Jews or Judaism. *adj.*

Ju da ism (jü′dē iz′əm), religion based on the teachings of Moses as found in the Old Testament and in the laws of the Talmud. *n.*

Ju das (jü′dəs), **1** (in the Bible) Judas Iscariot, the disciple who betrayed Jesus for money. **2** an utter traitor; person treacherous enough to betray a friend. *n.*

Jude (jüd), **1** (in the Bible) one of Jesus' twelve apostles. **2** book of the New Testament. *n.*

Ju de a (jü dē′ə), the S part of Palestine when it was a province of the Roman Empire. See **Galilee** for map. *n.* Also, **Judaea.**

judge (juj), **1** a public official appointed or elected to hear and decide cases in a court of law. **2** hear and decide (a case) in a court of law; act as a judge. **3** person chosen to settle a dispute or decide who wins a race, contest, etc. **4** settle a dispute; decide who wins a race, contest, etc. **5** person who can decide how good a thing is: *a good judge of character, a poor judge of poetry.* **6** form an opinion or estimate about: *judge the merits of a book.* **7** think; suppose; conclude: *I judged that you had forgotten to come.* **8** consider and blame; criticize; condemn: *You had little cause to judge him so harshly.* 1,3,5 *n.,* 2,4,6-8 *v.,* **judged, judg ing. —judg′er,** *n.*

judge ment (juj′mənt), judgment. *n.*

Judg es (juj′iz), book of the Old Testament dealing with the period in Jewish history between the death of Joshua and Saul's accession to the throne. *n.*

judge ship (juj′ship), position, duties, or term of office of a judge. *n.*

judg ment (juj′mənt), **1** result of judging; opinion or estimate: *In my judgment dogs make better pets than cats.* **2** ability to form sound opinions; power to judge well;

good sense: *Since she has judgment in such matters, we will ask her.* **3** act of judging, especially a decision, decree, or sentence given by a judge in a court of law. **4** decision made by anybody who judges. **5** criticism; condemnation: *pass judgment on one's neighbors.* *n.* Also, **judgement.**

Judgment Day, day of God's final judgment of all people at the end of the world; doomsday.

ju di cial (jü dish′əl), **1** of or by judges; of courts or the administration of justice: *a judicial decision.* **2** of or suitable for a judge; impartial; fair: *a judicial mind.* *adj.* **—ju di′cial ly,** *adv.*

ju di ci ar y (jü dish′ē er′ē), **1** branch of government that administers justice; system of courts of law of a country. **2** judges of a country, state, or city. **3** of courts, judges, or the administration of justice. 1,2 *n., pl.* **ju di ci ar ies;** 3 *adj.*

ju di cious (jü dish′əs), having, using, or showing good judgment; wise; sensible: *Judicious parents encourage their children to make their own decisions. A judicious historian selects and weighs facts carefully and critically. adj.* **—ju di′cious ly,** *adv.* **—ju di′cious ness,** *n.*

Ju dith (jü′dith), (in the Apocrypha) a Jewish woman who saved her people by killing a Babylonian general. *n.*

ju do (jü′dō), a modern form of jujitsu practiced as a sport or a means of self-defense. *n.* [*Judo* is from Japanese *jūdō,* which comes from *jū,* meaning "soft, gentle," and *dō,* meaning "art, way."]

Ju dy (jü′dē), wife of Punch in the puppet show *Punch and Judy. n.*

jug (jug), container for holding liquids. A jug usually has a short, narrow neck and a handle. *n.*

jug ger naut (jug′ər nôt), something to which a person blindly devotes himself or is cruelly sacrificed. *n.*

jug gle (jug′əl), **1** do tricks that require skill of hand or eye: *He juggled with knives by balancing them on his nose.* **2** do such tricks with: *She can juggle three balls, keeping them all in the air at one time.* **3** change by trickery: *The dishonest cashier juggled the store's accounts to hide his thefts.* *v.,* **jug gled, jug gling.**

jug gler (jug′lər), **1** person who can do juggling tricks. **2** person who uses tricks, deception, or fraud. *n.*

Ju go slav (yü′gō släv′), Yugoslav. *n., adj.*

Ju go sla vi a (yü′gō slä′vē ə), Yugoslavia. *n.*

jug u lar (jug′yə lər), **1** of the neck or throat. **2** of the jugular vein. **3** jugular vein. 1,2 *adj.,* 3 *n.*

jugular vein, one of the two large veins in each side of the neck and head that return blood from the head and neck to the heart.

juice (jüs), **1** the liquid part of fruits, vegetables, and meats: *the juice of a lemon, meat juice.* **2** fluid in the body. The juices of the stomach help to digest food. **3** SLANG. electricity. *n.* **—juice′less,** *adj.*

juic i ly (jü′sə lē), in a juicy manner. *adv.*

juic i ness (jü′sē nis), juicy quality or condition. *n.*

juic y (jü′sē), **1** full of juice; having much juice: *a juicy orange.* **2** INFORMAL. full of interest; lively. *adj.,* **juic i er, juic i est.**

ju jit su (jü jit′sü), a Japanese way of wrestling or of fighting without weapons that uses the strength and weight of an opponent to one's own advantage. *n.* Also, **jiujitsu.** [*Jujitsu* is from Japanese *jūjutsu,* which comes from *jū*, meaning "soft, gentle," and *jutsu*, meaning "art."]

juke box (jük′boks′), an automatic phonograph that plays records for money deposited in the coin slot. *n., pl.* **juke box es.**

Jul., July.

Jul ian (jü′lyən), of Julius Caesar. In the **Julian calendar,** which was introduced by Julius Caesar in 46 B.C., the average length of a year was 365¼ days. It was replaced by the Gregorian calendar in 1582. *adj.*

Ju li et (jü′lē et *or* jü′lyət), heroine of Shakespeare's play *Romeo and Juliet. n.*

Jul ius Caesar (jü′lyəs). See **Caesar.**

Ju ly (jü lī′), the seventh month of the year. It has 31 days. *n., pl.* **Ju lies.**

jum ble (jum′bəl), **1** mix or confuse: *She jumbled up everything in the drawer while hunting for a roll of tape.* **2** a mixed-up mess; state of confusion; muddle. 1 *v.,* **jumbled, jum bling;** 2 *n.*

jum bo (jum′bō), INFORMAL. **1** a big, clumsy person, animal, or thing; something unusually large of its kind. **2** very big: *a jumbo ice-cream cone.* 1 *n., pl.* **jum bos;** 2 *adj.*

WORD HISTORY

jumbo

Jumbo comes from *Jumbo,* the name of a large elephant exhibited by P.T. Barnum.

the original Jumbo

jump (jump), **1** spring from the ground; leap; bound: *Jump across the puddle.* **2** a spring from the ground; leap; bound: *The horse made a fine jump.* **3** leap over: *jump a stream. The speeding car jumped the curb and crashed.* **4** cause to jump: *jump a horse over a fence.* **5** thing to be jumped over: *The horse cleared the jump.* **6** distance jumped: *a ten-foot jump.* **7** contest in jumping for height or distance. **8** give a sudden start or jerk: *He jumped when the sudden noise startled him.* **9** a sudden nervous start or jerk: *She gave a jump at the crash of thunder.* **10** rise suddenly: *Prices jumped.* **11** a sudden rise: *a jump in the cost of living.* **12** pounce upon; attack. 1,3,4,8,10,12 *v.,* 2,5-7,9,11 *n.*

get the jump on or **have the jump on,** SLANG. get or have an advantage over.

jump at, accept eagerly and quickly: *jump at an offer.*

jump er[1] (jum′pər), person or thing that jumps. *n.*

jump er[2] (jum′pər), **1** a sleeveless dress to wear over a blouse. **2** a loose jacket. Jumpers are worn by workers to protect their clothes. *n.*

jumping jack, 1 a toy person or animal that can be made to jump by pulling a string. **2** a physical exercise performed by jumping from an erect position with feet

together and arms at the sides to a position with legs spread wide and hands touching overhead, and then returning to the original position.

jump suit, 1 a one-piece suit worn by parachutists. **2** any similar one-piece suit, usually for informal wear.

jump y (jum′pē), **1** moving by jumps; making sudden, sharp jerks. **2** easily excited or frightened; nervous. *adj.,* **jump i er, jump i est.**

jun co (jung′kō), a small, gray or brown bird of North America. It is a kind of finch. *n., pl.* **jun cos** or **jun coes.**

junc tion (jungk′shən), **1** a joining or a being joined: *The junction of the two rivers results in a large flow of water downstream.* **2** place of joining or meeting. A railroad junction is a place where railroad lines meet or cross. *n.*

junc ture (jungk′chər), **1** point or line where two things join; joint. **2** point of time, especially a critical time or state of affairs: *At this juncture we must decide what move to make next.* **3** a joining or a being joined. *n.*

June (jün), the sixth month of the year. It has 30 days. *n.*

Ju neau (jü′nō), capital of Alaska, in the SE part. *n.*

June bug, a large brown beetle of North America that appears in June.

jun gle (jung′gəl), wild land thickly overgrown with bushes, vines, trees, etc. Jungles are hot and humid regions with many kinds of plants and wild animals. *n.*

jungle gym, framework of steel bars for children to climb or swing on as a pastime.

jun ior (jü′nyər), **1** the younger (used of a son having the same name as his father): *Juan Roca, Junior, is the son of Juan Roca, Senior.* **2** a younger person: *She is her sister's junior by two years.* **3** of or for younger people: *a junior choir.* **4** of lower rank or shorter service; of less standing than some others: *a junior officer, a junior partner.* **5** person of lower rank or shorter service. **6** student in the third year of high school or college. **7** of these students: *the junior class.* 1,3,4,7 *adj.,* 2,5,6 *n.*

junior college, school giving only the first two years of a regular four-year college course.

junior high school, school consisting of grades 7, 8, and sometimes 6 or 9, attended after elementary school and followed by high school.

ju ni per (jü′nə pər), an evergreen shrub or tree with small berrylike cones. The cones of one kind of juniper contain an oil used in flavoring gin and in medicines. *n.*

junk[1] (jungk), **1** old metal, paper, rags, etc.; rubbish; trash. **2** INFORMAL. throw away or discard as junk. 1 *n.,* 2 *v.*

junk[2]

junk[2] (jungk), a Chinese sailing ship. *n.*

jun ket (jung′kit), **1** curdled milk, sweetened and flavored. **2** a pleasure trip. **3** go on a pleasure trip. 1,2 *n.,* 3 *v.* —**jun′ket er,** *n.*

junk food, SLANG. food that contains calories but has little other nutritional value.

junk ie (jung′kē), SLANG. person addicted to heroin or other drugs; drug addict. *n.*

junk mail, printed matter that consists mostly of circulars, catalogs, and advertising pieces, and is sent through the mail to a large number of addresses.

junk man (jungk′man′), person who buys and sells old

metal, paper, rags, etc. *n., pl.* **junk men.**

Ju no (jü′nō), (in Roman myths) the goddess who was the wife of Jupiter. She was the goddess of marriage. The Greeks called her Hera. *n.*

jun ta (jun′tə *or* hún′tə), **1** a political or military group holding power after a revolution. **2** an assembly or council for deliberation or administration, especially in Spain and Latin America. **3** junto. *n., pl.* **jun tas.**

jun to (jun′tō), group of plotters, partisans, etc.; faction; clique. *n., pl.* **jun tos.**

Ju pi ter (jü′pə tər), **1** (in Roman myths) the king of the gods and husband of Juno; Jove. The Greeks called him Zeus. **2** the largest planet in the solar system. It is the fifth in distance from the sun. *n.*

Ju ras sic (jù ras′ik), **1** a geological period of the Mesozoic era, when dinosaurs dominated the earth and birds first appeared. **2** of this period. 1 *n.,* 2 *adj.*

jur is dic tion (jür′is dik′shən), **1** right or power to give out justice; the giving out of justice. **2** authority; power; control: *The principal has jurisdiction over the teachers in a school.* **3** the things over which authority extends: *A school is the principal's jurisdiction.* **4** territory over which authority extends. *n.*

jur is pru dence (jür′i sprüd′ns), **1** science or philosophy of law. **2** system of laws. **3** branch of law. Medical jurisprudence deals with the use of medical knowledge in certain questions of law. *n.*

jur ist (jür′ist), **1** an expert in law. **2** a learned writer on law. *n.*

jur or (jür′ər), member of a jury. *n.*

jur y (jür′ē), **1** group of persons chosen to hear evidence in a court of law and sworn to give a decision in accordance with the evidence presented to them. A petit jury is made up of 12 jurors; a grand jury is made up of from 6 to 23 jurors. **2** group of persons chosen to give a judgment or to decide who is the winner in a contest: *The jury gave her poem the first prize. n., pl.* **jur ies.**

jur y man (jür′ē mən), member of a jury; juror. *n., pl.* **jur y men.**

just¹ (just), **1** no more than; only; merely: *He went just because his friend was going.* **2** barely: *The shot just missed the mark.* **3** INFORMAL. quite; truly; positively: *The weather is just glorious.* **4** exactly: *That is just a pound.* **5** almost exactly; nearly: *See the picture just above.* **6** a very little while ago: *She has just gone.* **7** right; fair: *a just price.* **8** deserved; merited: *a just reward.* **9** having good grounds; well-founded: *just anger.* **10** true; correct; exact: *just weights, a just description.* **11** good; righteous: *a just life.* 1-6 *adv.,* 7-11 *adj.* [*Just* came into English about 600 years ago from French *juste,* and can be traced back to Latin *jus,* meaning "a right, law." See **Word Family.**] —**just′ness,** *n.*

just now, only a very short time ago: *I saw her just now.*

just¹

Below are words related to *just¹*. They can all be traced back to Latin *jus, juris* (yüs, yü′ris), meaning "a right, law."

adjust	judicious	justify
conjure	jurisdiction	maladjusted
injury	jury	perjury
judge	justice	prejudice

just² (just), joust. *n., v.*

jus tice (jus′tis), **1** just conduct; fair dealing: *Judges should have a sense of justice.* **2** a being just; fairness; rightness: *the justice of a claim, uphold the justice of our cause.* **3** well-founded reason; rightfulness; lawfulness: *They complained with justice of the bad treatment they had received.* **4** just treatment; deserved reward or punishment. **5** administration of law; trial and judgment by process of law: *a court of justice.* **6** a judge. The Supreme Court has nine justices. *n.*

do justice to, 1 treat fairly. **2** see the good points of; show proper appreciation for.

do oneself justice, do as well as one really can do: *He did not do himself justice on the test.*

justice of the peace, a local magistrate who tries minor cases, administers oaths, performs civil marriages, etc.

jus ti fi a ble (jus′tə fī′ə bəl), capable of being justified; proper: *An act is justifiable if it can be shown to be just or right. adj.*

jus ti fi a bly (jus′tə fī′ə blē), in a justifiable manner. *adv.*

jus ti fi ca tion (jus′tə fə kā′shən), **1** a justifying or a being justified. **2** fact or circumstance that justifies; good reason or excuse: *What is your justification for being so late? n.*

jus ti fy (jus′tə fī), **1** give a good reason for: *The fine quality of the cloth justifies its high price.* **2** show to be just or right: *Can you justify your act?* **3** clear of blame or guilt: *The court ruled that he was justified in hitting the man in self-defense. v.,* **jus ti fied, jus ti fy ing.** —**jus′ti fi′er,** *n.*

jus tle (jus′əl), jostle. *v.,* **jus tled, jus tling.**

just ly (just′lē), **1** in a just manner: *deal justly with others.* **2** rightly: *You argue justly. adv.*

jut (jut), stick out; stand out; project: *The pier juts out from the shore into the water. v.,* **jut ted, jut ting.**

jute (jüt), **1** a strong fiber used for making coarse fabrics, rope, etc. Jute is obtained from two tropical plants. **2** either of these plants. *n.*

Jute (jüt), member of a Germanic tribe that, with the Angles and Saxons, conquered England in the A.D. 400's and 500's. *n.*

Jut ish (jü′tish), of the Jutes. *adj.*

juv., juvenile.

ju ve nile (jü′və nəl *or* jü′və nīl), **1** young; youthful: *a juvenile audience, to have a juvenile appearance.* **2** childish; infantile: *a display of juvenile behavior. That game is too juvenile for high-school seniors.* **3** a young person. **4** of or for boys and girls: *juvenile books.* **5** book for boys and girls. **6** actor who plays youthful parts. 1,2,4 *adj.,* 3,5,6 *n.*

juvenile delinquency, unlawful behavior by a boy or girl usually under 18 years of age.

juvenile delinquent, boy or girl usually under 18 years of age who has committed a legal offense.

jux ta pose (juk′stə pōz′), put close together; place side by side. *v.,* **jux ta posed, jux ta pos ing.**

jux ta po si tion (juk′stə pə zish′ən), **1** a putting close together; a placing side by side. **2** position close together or side by side. *n*

Jy., July.

K¹ or **k** (kā), the 11th letter of the English alphabet. *n.*, *pl.* **K's** or **k's.**

K² (kā), unit of computer memory size, equal to 1000 or to 1024. 8K bytes = 8000 bytes or 8192 (8 × 1024) bytes. *n.*, *pl.* **K.**

K, symbol for potassium.

k., 1 karat. 2 kilogram or kilograms. 3 kopeck.

Kabuki

Ka bu ki (kä bü′kē), a form of Japanese drama with song and dance, elegant costumes, and exaggerated acting. It dates from the 1600's. *n.*

Ka bul (kä′bùl), capital of Afghanistan, in the E part. *n.*

kai ak (kī′ak), kayak. *n.*

kai ser (kī′zər), 1 title of the rulers of Germany and Austria before 1918. 2 title of the emperors of the Holy Roman Empire. *n.*

kale (kāl), kind of cabbage that has loose, curled leaves which are eaten as a vegetable. *n.*

ka lei do scope (kə lī′də skōp), 1 tube containing bits of colored glass and two mirrors. As it is turned, it reflects continually changing patterns. 2 a continually changing pattern. *n.*

WORD HISTORY

kaleidoscope

Kaleidoscope comes from Greek *kalos,* meaning "pretty," *eidos,* meaning "form," and *skopein,* meaning "look at."

ka lei do scop ic (kə lī′də skop′ik), of or like a kaleidoscope; continually changing. *adj.*

Kam pa la (käm pä′lä), capital of Uganda, in the S part. *n.*

Kam pu che a (kam′pü chē′ə), Cambodia. —**Kam′pu che′an,** *adj., n.*

kan ga roo (kang′gə rü′), mammal of Australia and New Guinea having small forelegs, very strong hind legs which give it great leaping power, and a long, heavy tail for support. The female kangaroo has a pouch in front in which she carries her young. *n., pl.* **kan ga roos** or **kan ga roo.** —**kan′ga roo′like′,** *adj.*

kangaroo rat, a small, burrowing rodent of dry areas of North America. Kangaroo rats have cheek pouches and long hind legs and tails.

Kans., Kansas.

Kan san (kan′zən), 1 of Kansas. 2 person born or living in Kansas. 1 *adj.,* 2 *n.*

Kan sas (kan′zəs), one of the midwestern states of the United States. *Abbreviation:* Kans. or KS *Capital:* Topeka. *n.*

Kansas City, 1 city in W Missouri, on the Missouri River. **2** city in NE Kansas adjoining it.

ka o lin (kā′ə lən), a fine white clay, used in making porcelain. *n.*

ka pok (kā′pok), the silky fibers around the seeds of a tropical tree, used for stuffing mattresses and life preservers. *n.* [*Kapok* was borrowed from Malay *kapok.*]

Ka ra chi (kə rä′chē), city in S Pakistan, formerly the capital. *n.*

kar a kul (kar′ə kəl), caracul. *n.*

kar at (kar′ət), ¹/₂₄ part of gold by weight in an alloy. A gold ring of 18 carats is 18 parts pure gold and six parts alloy. *n.* Also, **carat.**

ka ra te (kə rä′tē), a Japanese method of fighting without weapons by striking with the hands, elbows, knees, and feet at vulnerable parts of the opponent's body. *n.*

ka sha (kä′shə *or* kash′ə), 1 a grain like buckwheat, wheat, or millet. 2 porridge or mush made with this hulled or crushed grain. *n.* [*Kasha* was borrowed from Russian *kasha.*]

Kash mir (kash mir′), area north of India, claimed by both India and Pakistan. *n.*

Kat man du (kät′män dü′), capital of Nepal, in the central part. *n.*

ka ty did (kā′tē did′), a large, green, long-horned grasshopper. The male makes a shrill noise by rubbing its front wings together. *n.*

Kau ai (kou ī′ *or* kou′ī), the fourth largest island of Hawaii. *n.*

kayak (def. 1)

kay ak (kī′ak), 1 an Eskimo canoe made of skins stretched over a light frame of wood or bone with an opening in the middle for a person. 2 a similar craft of other material. *n.* Also, **kaiak.**

ke a (kē′ə), a large, green parrot of New Zealand with a powerful, hooked bill which it uses to dig out insects. It will attack sheep when it is very hungry. *n., pl.* **ke as.**

Keats (kēts), **John,** 1795-1821, English poet. *n.*

keel (kēl), the main timber or steel piece that extends the whole length of the bottom of a ship or boat. The whole ship is built up on the keel. *n.*

keel over, 1 turn upside down; upset: *The sailboat keeled over in the storm.* 2 fall over suddenly: *keel over in a faint.*

on an even keel, horizontal: *The boat sailed on an even keel in good weather.*

keen¹ (kēn), 1 so shaped as to cut well: *a keen blade.* 2 sharp; cutting: *a keen wind, keen hunger, keen pain, keen* *wit.* **3** strong; vivid: *keen competition.* **4** highly sensitive; perceptive; acute: *She has a keen mind.* **5** full of enthusiasm; eager: *He is keen about sailing.* **6** SLANG. excellent; wonderful: *That's a keen bike.* *adj.* [**Keen**[1] comes from Old English *cēne.*] —**keen′ly,** *adv.* —**keen′ness,** *n.*

keen[2] (kēn), **1** a wailing lament for the dead. **2** wail; lament. **1** *n.,* **2** *v.* [**Keen**[2] comes from Irish *caoine.*]

keep (def. 14)

keep (kēp), **1** have for a long time or forever: *You may keep this book.* **2** have and not let go: *Can you keep a secret?* **3** have and take care of: *She keeps chickens. My aunt keeps two boarders.* **4** take care of and protect; guard: *The bank keeps money for people.* **5** have; hold: *Keep this in mind.* **6** hold back; prevent: *Keep the baby from crying. What is keeping her?* **7** maintain in good condition; preserve: *A refrigerator keeps food fresh.* **8** stay in good condition: *Milk does not keep long in hot weather.* **9** stay the same; continue: *Keep along this road for two miles.* **10** cause to continue; cause to stay the same: *The blanket keeps the baby warm. Keep the fire burning.* **11** do the right thing with; celebrate; observe: *keep Thanksgiving as a holiday.* **12** be faithful to: *keep a promise.* **13** food and a place to sleep: *He works for his keep.* **14** the strongest part of a castle or fort. **1-12** *v.,* **kept, keep ing; 13,14** *n.* [**Keep** comes from Old English *cēpan,* meaning "observe."]

for keeps, 1 for the winner to keep his or her winnings. **2** INFORMAL. forever.

keep on, continue; go on: *We kept on swimming in spite of the rain.*

keep to oneself, 1 avoid associating with others: *That man always keeps to himself.* **2** keep a secret.

keep up, 1 continue; prevent from ending: *We kept up a small fire.* **2** maintain in good condition. **3** not fall behind.

keep up with, not fall behind; go or move as fast as: *You walk so fast that I cannot keep up with you.*

keep er (kē′pər), one that watches, guards, or takes care of persons or things: *the keeper of an inn. n.*

keep ing (kē′ping), **1** care; charge: *The two older children were left in their grandparents' keeping.* **2** celebration; observance: *The keeping of Thanksgiving Day is an old American custom.* **3** agreement; harmony: *Don't trust him; his actions are not in keeping with his promises. n.*

keep sake (kēp′sāk′), thing kept in memory of the giver: *Before my friend went away, she gave me her picture as a keepsake. n.*

keg (keg), a small barrel, usually holding less than 10 gallons (38 liters). *n.*

Kel ler (kel′ər), **Helen (Adams),** 1880-1968, American writer and lecturer who was both deaf and blind. *n.*

kelp (kelp), **1** a large, tough, brown seaweed. **2** ashes of seaweed, used as a source of iodine. *n.*

Kel vin (kel′vən), of, based on, or according to a scale for measuring temperature on which 273 degrees marks

a hat	**i** it	**oi** oil	**ch** child	a in about
ā age	**ī** ice	**ou** out	**ng** long	e in taken
ä far	**o** hot	**u** cup	**sh** she	ə = i in pencil
e let	**ō** open	**u̇** put	**th** thin	o in lemon
ē equal	**ô** order	**ü** rule	**ŦH** then	u in circus
ėr term			**zh** measure	

the freezing point of water, 373 degrees marks the boiling point, and 0 degrees marks absolute zero. *adj.* [*Kelvin* was named for Lord *Kelvin,* 1824-1907, a British physicist.]

ken (ken), **1** range of sight. **2** range of knowledge: *What happens on Mars is no longer beyond our ken.* **3** SCOTTISH. know. **1,2** *n.,* **3** *v.,* **kenned** or **kent** (kent), **ken ning.**

Ken., Kentucky.

Ken ne dy (ken′ə dē), **1 Cape,** former name of **Cape Canaveral. 2 John F(itzgerald),** 1917-1963, the 35th president of the United States, 1961-1963. *n.*

Kennedy International Airport, a major international and domestic airport, in the borough of Queens in New York City.

ken nel (ken′l), **1** house for a dog or dogs. **2** Often, **kennels,** *pl.* place where dogs are bred or boarded. **3** put into or keep in a kennel. **1,2** *n.,* **3** *v.,* **ken neled, ken neling** or **ken nelled, ken nel ling.** [*Kennel* came into English about 600 years ago from French *kenil,* and can be traced back to Latin *canis,* meaning "dog."]

Kent (kent), county in SE England. *n.*

Ken tuck i an (kən tuk′ē ən), **1** of Kentucky or its people. **2** person born or living in Kentucky. **1** *adj.,* **2** *n.*

Ken tuck y (kən tuk′ē), one of the south central states of the United States. *Abbreviation:* Ky. or KY *Capital:* Frankfort. *n.*

Ken ya (ken′yə *or* kē′nyə), country in E Africa, a member of the Commonwealth of Nations. *Capital:* Nairobi. See **Congo** for map. *n.* —**Ken′yan,** *adj., n.*

Kep ler (kep′lər), **Johann,** 1571-1630, German astronomer. *n.*

kept (kept), past tense and past participle of **keep.** *I gave him the book and he kept it. The milk was kept in bottles. v.*

ker chief (kėr′chif), **1** piece of cloth worn over the head or around the neck. **2** handkerchief. *n.*

WORD HISTORY

kerchief

Kerchief came into English about 700 years ago from French *couvrechief,* which comes from *couvrir,* meaning "to cover," and *chief,* meaning "head." French *chief* comes from Latin *caput.*

ker nel (kėr′nl), **1** the softer part inside the hard shell of a nut or inside the stone of a fruit. **2** a grain or seed like that of wheat or corn. **3** the central or most important part of anything; core. *n.*

ker o sene or **ker o sine** (ker′ə sēn′), a thin, oily mixture of hydrocarbons distilled from petroleum; coal oil. It is used as fuel in lamps, stoves, and some kinds of engines. *n.*

ker sey (kėr′zē), a coarse, ribbed, woolen cloth. *n., pl.* **ker seys.**

ketch (kech), a small sailing ship with a large mainmast

toward the bow and a smaller mast toward the stern. *n.,
pl.* **ketch es.**

ketch up (kech/əp), catsup. *n.*

ket tle (ket/l), **1** any metal container for boiling liquids,
cooking fruit, etc. **2** teakettle. *n.*

kettle of fish, awkward state of affairs; mess; muddle.

ket tle drum (ket/l drum/), drum consisting of a hollow
brass or copper hemisphere and a parchment top. *n.*

kettledrums

key[1] (kē), **1** a small metal instrument for locking and
unlocking the lock of a door, a padlock, etc. **2** anything
shaped like it: *a roller-skate key.* **3** the answer to a puzzle
or a problem: *The key to this puzzle will be published next
week.* **4** sheet or book of answers: *a key to a test.* **5** a
systematic explanation of abbreviations, symbols, etc.,
used in a dictionary, map, etc. There is a pronunciation
key in this dictionary. **6** place that commands or gives
control of a sea, a district, etc., because of its position:
Gibraltar is the key to the Mediterranean. **7** controlling;
very important: *the key industries of a nation.* **8** an important or essential person, thing, etc. **9** pin, bolt, wedge, or
other piece put in a hole or space to hold parts together.
10 fasten or adjust with a key. **11** one of a set of levers
pressed down by the fingers in playing a piano, and in
operating a typewriter or other instruments. **12** scale or
system of related tones in music which are based on a
keynote: *a song written in the key of C.* **13** tone of voice;
style of thought or expression: *The poet wrote in a melancholy key.* **14** regulate the pitch of; tune: *key a musical
instrument.* 1-6,8,9,11-13 *n., pl.* **keys;** 7 *adj.,* 10,14 *v.* [*Key*[1]
comes from Old English *cǣg.*] —**key/less,** *adj.*

key up, excite; make nervous: *The actors were keyed up
on opening night.*

key[2] (kē), a low island; reef. There are keys south of
Florida. *n., pl.* **keys.** [*Key*[2] is from Spanish *cayo,*
meaning "shoal, rock," which comes from an American
Indian word of the Caribbean area.]

Key (kē), **Francis Scott,** 1779-1843, American author
who wrote the words to "The Star-Spangled Banner." *n.*

key board (kē/bôrd/), the set of keys in a piano, organ,
typewriter, computer, etc. *n.*

key hole (kē/hōl/), opening in a lock through which a
key is inserted. *n.*

key note (kē/nōt/), **1** tone on which a scale or system of
tones in music is based; tonic. **2** main idea; guiding
principle: *World peace was the keynote of the speech. n.*

key pad (kē/pad/), group of keys like the keys of a
typewriter or computer, but arranged like the keys of a
calculator and having a special purpose, such as entering large sets of numbers into a computer. *n.*

key punch, machine having a keyboard similar to that
of a typewriter, used to record and code information by
punching patterns of holes in cards or tapes.

key stone (kē/stōn/), **1** the middle stone at the top of an
arch, holding the other stones or pieces in place. **2** part
on which other related parts depend. *n.*

kg., **1** keg or kegs. **2** kilogram or kilograms.

Kha da fy (kä dä/fē), Qaddafi. *n.*

khak i (kak/ē *or* kä/kē), **1** a dull yellowish brown. **2** dull
yellowish-brown. **3** a heavy twilled cloth of this color,
much used for soldiers' uniforms. **4** khakis, *pl.* uniform
made of this cloth: *Khakis will be worn in the parade.*
1,3,4 *n., pl.* **khak is;** 2 *adj.* [*Khaki* is from Hindi *khākī,*
which comes from Persian *khāk,* meaning "dust."]

khan (kän), **1** (formerly) a title of a ruler among Tartar or
Mongol tribes. **2** title of respect in Iran, Afghanistan,
India, etc. *n.*

Khar kov (kär/kôf), city in SW Soviet Union. *n.*

Khar toum (kär tüm/), capital of Sudan, on the Nile. *n.*

Khru shchev (krüsh chôf/), **Nikita S.,** 1894-1971,
premier of the Soviet Union from 1958 to 1964. *n.*

Khy ber Pass (kī/bər), important mountain pass between N Pakistan and E Afghanistan.

kib butz (ki büts/), an Israeli communal settlement, especially a farm cooperative. *n., pl.* **kib butz im** (ki bü-
tsēm/).

kib itz er (kib/it sər), INFORMAL. person who gives unwanted advice; meddler. *n.* [*Kibitzer* is from Yiddish
kibitser, which comes from German *Kiebitz,* meaning
"busybody."]

kick (kik), **1** strike out with the foot: *That horse kicks
when anyone comes near it.* **2** strike with the foot: *The
horse kicked the boy.* **3** drive, force, or move by kicking:
*kick a ball along the ground, kick off one's shoes, kick up
dust.* **4** a blow with the foot: *The horse's kick knocked me
down.* **5** the recoil or backward motion of a gun when it
is fired. **6** spring back when fired; recoil: *This shotgun
kicks.* **7** INFORMAL. find fault; complain; grumble.
8 INFORMAL. complaint; objection. **9** excitement; thrill:
She got a kick out of winning the game. 1-3,6,7 *v..* 4,5,8,9 *n.*

kick around, INFORMAL. **1** treat roughly. **2** go about aimlessly. **3** consider or discuss (a plan, topic, etc.).

kick back, 1 INFORMAL. spring back suddenly and unexpectedly: *The gun kicked back with great force.* **2** SLANG.
return a portion of money received as a fee.

kick off, put a football in play with a kick at the beginning of each half and after a score has been made.

kick out, expel or turn out in a humiliating or disgraceful way: *be kicked out of school.*

kick up, SLANG. start; cause.

kick back (kik/bak/), SLANG. portion or amount of a fee
returned, especially as a bribe for having received a
contract. *n.*

kick ball (kik/bôl/), a game similar to baseball, in which
the ball is rolled instead of thrown and kicked instead of
hit. *n.*

kick off (kik/ôf/), kick that puts a football in play at the
beginning of each half and after a score has been
made. *n.*

kick stand (kik/stand/), a metal rod or other device
attached to the frame or rear axle of a bicycle or
motorcycle that holds the vehicle upright when not in
use. *n.*

kid[1] (kid), **1** a young goat. **2** leather made from the skin
of young goats, used for gloves and shoes. **3** INFORMAL.
child. *n.*

kid[2] (kid), INFORMAL. **1** tease playfully; talk in a joking
way; banter. **2** deceive; fool. *v.,* **kid ded, kid ding.**

Kidd (kid), **William,** 1645?-1701, Scottish privateer and
pirate, known as "Captain Kidd." *n.*

kid der (kid/ər), INFORMAL. person who kids. *n.*

kid gloves, gloves made of soft kidskin.
handle with kid gloves, treat with great care.

kid nap (kid/nap), steal (a child); carry off (a person) by
force. *v.,* **kid napped, kid nap ping** *or* **kid naped, kidnap ing.** —**kid/nap per, kid/nap er,** *n.*

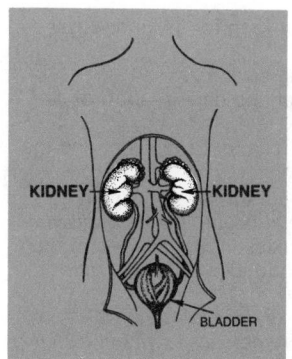

kidney (def. 1)
kidneys of a human being

a hat	i it	oi oil	ch child	a in about
ā age	ī ice	ou out	ng long	e in taken
ä far	o hot	u cup	sh she	ə = i in pencil
e let	ō open	u̇ put	th thin	o in lemon
ē equal	ô order	ü rule	₮H then	u in circus
ėr term			zh measure	

kid ney (kid′nē), **1** one of the pair of organs in the body that separates waste matter from the blood and passes it off through the bladder as urine. **2** kidney or kidneys of an animal, cooked for food. *n., pl.* **kid neys.** —**kid′ney- like′,** *adj.*

kidney bean, a large, red bean, shaped like a kidney and used as a vegetable.

kid skin (kid′skin′), leather made from the skin of young goats. *n.*

Kiel (kēl), seaport in N West Germany, on the Baltic Sea. *n.*

Kiel Canal, a ship canal in N West Germany from the North Sea to the Baltic Sea.

Ki ev (kē′ef *or* kē ev′), capital of the Ukraine, in SW Soviet Union. *n.*

Ki ga li (ki gä′lē), capital of Rwanda, in the central part. *n.*

Kil i man ja ro (kil′ə mən jär′ō), **Mount,** the highest mountain in Africa, in NE Tanzania, 19,340 feet (5895 meters) high. *n.*

kill (kil), **1** put to death; cause the death of: *A bolt of lightning killed the tree.* **2** cause death: *"Thou shalt not kill."* **3** act of killing. **4** animal killed. **5** put an end to; get rid of; destroy: *kill odors.* **6** cancel (a word, paragraph, item, etc.); delete. **7** defeat or veto (a legislative bill). **8** use up (time): *We killed an hour at the zoo.* **9** INFORMAL. cause pain or discomfort to: *My sore foot is killing me.* 1,2,5–9 *v.,* 3,4 *n.*

kill deer (kil′dir′), a North American bird which has two black bands across its breast. It has a loud, shrill cry. *n., pl.* **kill deers** or **kill deer.**

kill er (kil′ər), person, animal, or thing that kills. *n.*

killer whale, whale that travels in schools and kills and eats large fish, seals, and even other whales; grampus.

kill joy (kil′joi′), person who spoils other people's fun. *n.*

kiln (kil *or* kiln), furnace or oven for burning, baking, or drying something. Limestone is burned in a kiln to make lime. Bricks are baked in a kiln. *n.*

ki lo (kē′lō *or* kil′ō), **1** kilogram. **2** kilometer. *n., pl.* **ki los.**

kilo-, *combining form.* one thousand: *Kilogram = one thousand grams.* [The form *kilo-* is from French *kilo-,* which came from Greek *chilioi.*]

kil o cy cle (kil′ə sī′kəl), **1** 1000 cycles. **2** 1000 cycles per second, used formerly to express the frequency of radio waves, which are now expressed in kilohertz. *n.*

kil o gram or **kil o gramme** (kil′ə gram), the basic unit of weight or mass in the metric system, equal to 1000 grams, or 2.2046 pounds avoirdupois. *n.*

kil o hertz (kil′ə herts′), 1000 hertz, used to express the frequency of radio waves. *n., pl.* **kil o hertz.**

kil o li ter (kil′ə lē′tər), unit of volume equal to 1000 liters, or one cubic meter. *n.*

ki lom e ter (kə lom′ə tər *or* kil′ə mē′tər), unit of length equal to 1000 meters, or 3280.8 feet. *n.*

kil o ton (kil′ə tun′), **1** unit of weight equal to 1000 tons. **2** unit of atomic power equivalent to the energy released by one thousand tons of high explosive, specifically TNT. *n.*

kil o watt (kil′ə wot′), unit of electrical power equal to 1000 watts. *n.*

kil o watt-hour (kil′ə wot′our′), unit of electrical ener- gy equal to the work done by one kilowatt acting for one hour. *n.*

kilt (kilt), a pleated skirt reaching to the knees, worn especially by men in the Scottish Highlands. *n.*

kil ter (kil′tər). **out of kilter,** INFORMAL. out of working order; not in good condition: *Our radio is so out of kilter that we cannot tune in most stations. n.*

kimono (def. 1)

ki mo no (kə mō′nə), **1** a loose outer garment held in place by a sash, worn by Japanese men and women. **2** a woman's loose dressing gown. *n., pl.* **ki mo nos.**

kin (kin), **1** a person's family or relatives; kindred: *All our kin came to the family reunion.* **2** family relationship; con- nection by birth or marriage: *What kin is she to you?* **3** related: *Your cousin is also kin to me.* 1,2 *n.,* 3 *adj.*

next of kin, nearest living relative.

kind[1] (kīnd), **1** doing good rather than harm; friendly: *Kind people try to help others. Sharing your lunch was a kind thing to do.* **2** gentle: *Be kind to animals. adj.*

kind[2] (kīnd), **1** group of individuals or objects having characteristics in common; class; sort: *He likes many kinds of candy. A kilt is a kind of skirt.* **2** natural group; race: *The wolf hunted with others of its kind. n.*

in kind, 1 in goods or produce, not in money: *make payments in kind.* **2** in something of the same sort: *I returned their insults in kind by insulting them.* **3** in charac- teristic quality: *difference in kind, not merely in degree.*

kind of, INFORMAL. nearly; almost; somewhat; rather: *The room was kind of dark.*

of a kind, 1 of the same sort; alike: *The cakes were all of a kind—chocolate.* **2** of a poor or mediocre quality: *Two boxes and a plank make a table of a kind.*

kin der gar ten (kin′dər gärt′n), school or class for children from about 4 to 6 years old that educates them by games, toys, and pleasant occupations. *n.* [*Kinder- garten* is from German *Kindergarten,* which comes from *Kinder,* meaning "children," and *Garten,* meaning "garden."]

kin der gart ner or **kin der gar ten er** (kin′dər- gärt′nər), child who goes to kindergarten. *n.*

kind heart ed (kīnd′här′tid), having or showing a kind heart; kindly; sympathetic. *adj.* **—kind′heart′ed ly,** *adv.*

kin dle (kin′dl), **1** set on fire; light: *I used a match to kindle the wood.* **2** catch fire; begin to burn: *This damp wood will never kindle.* **3** stir up; arouse: *kindle anger, kindle enthusiasm.* **4** light up; brighten: *The girl's face kindled as she told about the circus. v.,* **kin dled, kin dling.**

kind li ness (kīnd′lē nis), **1** kindly feeling or quality. **2** a kindly act. *n., pl.* **kind li ness es.**

kin dling (kind′ling), small pieces of wood for starting a fire. *n.*

kind ly (kīnd′lē), **1** kind; friendly: *kindly faces, kindly people.* **2** in a kind or friendly way: *We thank you kindly for your help.* **3** pleasant; agreeable: *a kindly shower.* **4** pleasantly; agreeably: *He does not take kindly to criticism.* 1,3 *adj.,* **kind li er, kind li est;** 2,4 *adv.*

kind ness (kīnd′nis), **1** kind nature; being kind: *We admire her kindness.* **2** kind treatment: *Thank you for your kindness.* **3** a kind act: *They showed me many kindnesses. n., pl.* **kind ness es.**

kin dred (kin′drid), **1** like; similar; related: *We are studying about dew, frost, and kindred facts of nature.* **2** a person's family or relatives. *1 adj., 2 n.*

kin e scope (kin′ə skōp), **1** a record on film of a television broadcast. **2** the picture tube of a television, on which images are reproduced. *n.*

kin es thet ic (kin′əs thet′ik), having to do with sensations of motion from the muscles and joints. *adj.*

ki net ic (ki net′ik), **1** of motion. **2** caused by motion. *adj.*

kinetic energy, energy which a body has because it is in motion.

kin folk (kin′fōk′), kinsfolk. *n.pl.*

king (king), **1** the male ruler of a nation; male sovereign, usually with a hereditary position and with either absolute or limited power. **2** man supreme in a certain sphere: *a baseball king, a steel king.* **3** something best in its class: *The lion is the king of the beasts.* **4** an important piece in chess. **5** piece that has moved entirely across the board in checkers. **6** a playing card bearing a picture of a king. *n.* **—king′less,** *adj.* **—king′like′,** *adj.*

King (king), **Martin Luther, Jr.,** 1929-1968, American minister who led a nonviolent movement to end racial discrimination in the United States. *n.*

king bird (king′bėrd′), any of several American flycatchers, especially a bold, black-and-white flycatcher of the eastern United States. *n.*

king crab, 1 horseshoe crab. **2** a large crab found on the shores of the northern Pacific that is good to eat.

king dom (king′dəm), **1** nation that is governed by a king or a queen; land or territory ruled by one monarch. **2** a realm, domain, or province: *The mind is the kingdom of thought.* **3** one of the three divisions of the natural world; the animal kingdom, the vegetable kingdom, or the mineral kingdom. *n.*

king fish er (king′fish′ər), a bright-colored bird having a large head with a crest and a strong beak. Kingfishers eat fish and insects. *n.*

king li ness (king′lē nis), kingly quality; majesty. *n.*

king ly (king′lē), **1** of a king or kings; of royal rank. **2** fit for a king: *a kingly crown.* **3** like a king; royal; noble: *kingly pride.* **4** as a king does. 1-3 *adj.,* **king li er, king li est;** 4 *adv.*

Kings (kingz), **1** (in the Protestant Old Testament) either of two books (I Kings or II Kings) containing the history of the reigns of the Hebrew kings after David. **2** (in the Roman Catholic Old Testament) any of the four books that correspond to I and II Samuel and I and II Kings in the Protestant Bible. *n.*

king ship (king′ship), **1** position, rank, or dignity of a king. **2** rule of a king; government by a king. *n.*

king-size (king′sīz′), large or long for its kind: *a king-size cigarette. adj.*

king-sized (king′sīzd′), king-size. *adj.*

Kings ton (king′stən), capital and chief seaport of Jamaica, in the SE part. *n.*

Kings town (kingz′toun), capital of St. Vincent and the Grenadines. *n.*

kink (kingk), **1** a twist or curl in thread, rope, hair, etc. **2** form a kink or kinks; make kinks in: *The rope kinked as she rolled it up.* **3** pain or stiffness in the muscles of the neck, back, etc.; crick. **4** an odd idea; a mental quirk. 1,3,4 *n.,* 2 *v.*

kink y (king′kē), **1** full of kinks; twisted; curly. **2** INFORMAL. quite unusual; odd; extreme: *kinky styles in clothing. adj.,* **kink i er, kink i est. —kink′i ness,** *n.*

kins folk (kinz′fōk′), a person's family or relatives; kin. *n.pl.* Also, **kinfolk.**

Kin sha sa (kēn shä′sä), capital of Zaïre, in the W part. Formerly called **Léopoldville.** *n.*

kin ship (kin′ship), **1** a being kin; family relationship. **2** relationship. **3** resemblance. *n.*

kins man (kinz′mən), a male relative. *n., pl.* **kins men.**

kins wom an (kinz′wùm′ən), a female relative. *n., pl.* **kins wom en.**

kiosk (def. 2)

ki osk (kē osk′ *or* kī′osk), **1** a small building with one or more sides open, used as a newsstand, a bandstand, or an opening to a subway. **2** a cylindrical structure, usually placed on or near a sidewalk, on which advertisements, notices, etc., are displayed. *n.* [*Kiosk* is from French *kiosque,* which came from Turkish *köshk,* meaning "pavilion."]

Kip ling (kip′ling), **Rudyard,** 1865-1936, English writer of stories, novels, and poems. He was born in India. *n.*

kip per (kip′ər), **1** salt and dry or smoke (herring, salmon, etc.). **2** herring, salmon, etc., that has been kippered. 1 *v.,* 2 *n.*

Ki ri bati (kir′ə bäs), island country in the central Pacific near the equator. *Capital:* Tarawa. *n.*

kirk (kėrk), SCOTTISH. church. *n.*

kiss (kis), **1** touch with the lips as a sign of love, greeting, or respect: *The two sisters kissed. He kissed his mother goodby.* **2** a touch with the lips as a sign of love, greeting, or respect. **3** touch gently: *A soft wind kissed the treetops.* **4** a gentle touch. **5** put, bring, take, etc., by kissing: *kiss away tears.* **6** a small piece of candy, usually of chocolate. 1,3,5 *v.,* 2,4,6 *n., pl.* **kiss es. —kiss′a ble,** *adj.*

kiss er (kis′ər), 1 person who kisses. 2 SLANG. face or mouth. *n.*

kit (kit), 1 the parts of anything to be put together by the buyer: *a radio kit, a model airplane kit.* 2 a person's equipment packed for traveling: *a soldier's kit.* 3 outfit of tools or supplies: *a plumber's kit, a first-aid kit. n.*

kitch en (kich′ən), room or area where food is cooked. *n.* [*Kitchen* comes from Old English *cycene,* and can be traced back to Latin *coquere,* meaning "to cook."]

kitch en ette or **kitch en et** (kich′ə net′), 1 a very small kitchen. 2 part of a room fitted up as a kitchen. *n.*

kitchen police, a military duty of helping the cook prepare and serve food, wash dishes, and clean up the kitchen.

kitch en ware (kich′ən wer′ or kich′ən war′), kitchen utensils. Pots, kettles, and pans are kitchenware. *n.*

kite (kit), 1 a light wooden frame covered with paper, cloth, or plastic. Kites are flown in the air on the end of a long string. 2 hawk with long, pointed wings and often a long, forked tail. *n.*

kith (kith), friends; acquaintances. *n.*
kith and kin, friends and relatives.

kit ten (kit′n), a young cat. *n.*

kit ty (kit′ē), 1 kitten. 2 a pet name for a cat. *n., pl.* **kit ties.**

kit ty-cor ner (kit′ē kôr′nər), cater-corner. *adj., adv.*

kit ty-cor nered (kit′ē kôr′nərd), cater-cornered. *adj., adv.*

Kitty Hawk, village in NE North Carolina. Wilbur and Orville Wright made the first successful airplane flight there in 1903.

ki wi (kē′wē), bird of New Zealand with shaggy feathers, tiny undeveloped wings, and a long flexible bill. Kiwis cannot fly. *n., pl.* **ki wis.**

KKK or **K.K.K.,** Ku Klux Klan.

Klee nex (klē′neks), trademark for a disposable paper tissue used as a handkerchief, etc. *n.*

klep to ma ni a (klep′tə mā′nē ə), an abnormal, irresistible desire to steal, especially things which one does not need or cannot use. *n.*

klep to ma ni ac (klep′tə mā′nē ak), a person who has kleptomania. *n.*

Klon dike (klon′dīk), region in NW Canada, along the Yukon River, famous for its gold fields. *n.*

km., kilometer or kilometers.

knack (nak), special skill; power to do something easily: *That clown has the knack of making very funny faces. n.*

knap sack (nap′sak′), a canvas or leather bag with two shoulder straps, used for carrying clothes, equipment, etc., on the back; rucksack. *n.*

knave (nāv), 1 a tricky, dishonest person; rogue; rascal. 2 the jack, a playing card with a picture of a servant or soldier on it. 3 OLD USE. a male servant; man of humble birth or position. *n.*

knav ish (nā′vish), tricky; dishonest. *adj.* —**knav′ish ly,** *adv.* —**knav′ish ness,** *n.*

knead (nēd), 1 press or mix together (dough or clay) into a soft mass: *A baker kneads dough.* 2 make or shape by kneading. 3 press and squeeze with the hands; massage: *Kneading the muscles in a stiff shoulder helps to take away the stiffness. v.* —**knead′er,** *n.*

knee (nē), 1 the joint between the thigh and the lower leg. 2 any joint in a four-footed animal corresponding to the human knee or elbow. 3 anything like a bent knee in shape or position. 4 part of a garment covering the knee. *n.*
bring to one's knees, force to yield.

knee cap (nē′kap′), the flat, movable bone at the front of the knee; patella. *n.*

knee-deep (nē′dēp′), 1 so deep as to reach the knees:

a hat	**i** it	**oi** oil	**ch** child		a in about
ā age	**ī** ice	**ou** out	**ng** long		e in taken
ä far	**o** hot	**u** cup	**sh** she	**ə** =	i in pencil
e let	**ō** open	**u̇** put	**th** thin		o in lemon
ē equal	**ô** order	**ü** rule	**ᵀн** then		u in circus
ėr term			**zh** measure		

The snow was knee-deep. 2 sunk up to the knees: *I was knee-deep in mud. adj.*

kneel (nēl), 1 go down on one's knee or knees: *She knelt down to pull a weed from the flower bed.* 2 remain in this position: *They knelt in prayer for half an hour. v.,* **knelt** or **kneeled, kneel ing.** —**kneel′er,** *n.*

knell (nel), 1 sound of a bell rung slowly after a death or at a funeral. 2 ring slowly. 3 a warning sign of death, failure, etc.: *Their refusal rang the knell of our hopes.* 4 give such a warning sign. 1,3 *n.,* 2,4 *v.*

knelt (nelt), a past tense and a past participle of **kneel.** *She knelt and prayed. v.*

knew (nü or nyü), past tense of **know.** *She knew the right answer. v.*

knick er bock ers (nik′ər bok′ərz), knickers. *n.pl.*

knick ers (nik′ərz), short, loose-fitting trousers gathered in at, or just below, the knee. *n.pl.*

knick knack (nik′nak′), a pleasing trifle; ornament; trinket. *n.* Also, **nicknack.**

kiwi
up to 2 ft.
(60 cm.) long

knife (nīf), 1 a thin, flat metal blade fastened in a handle so that it can be used to cut or spread. 2 a sharp blade forming part of a tool or machine: *the knives of a lawn mower.* 3 cut or stab with a knife. 1,2 *n., pl.* **knives;** 3 *v.,* **knifed, knif ing.** —**knife′like′,** *adj.*

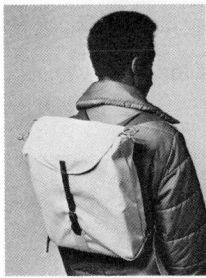

knapsack

knight (nīt), 1 (in the Middle Ages) a man raised to an honorable military rank and pledged to do good deeds. After serving as a page and squire, a man was made a knight by the king or a lord. 2 (in modern times) a man raised to an honorable rank because of great achievement or service. A British knight ranks just below a baronet and uses the title *Sir* before his name. EXAMPLE: Sir John Smith or Sir John. 3 raise to the rank of knight: *He was knighted by the queen.* 4 one of the pieces in the game of chess. 1,2,4 *n.,* 3 *v.*

knight-er rant (nīt′er′ənt), knight traveling in search of adventure. *n., pl.* **knights-er rant.**

knight hood (nīt′hùd), **1** rank of a knight. **2** profession or occupation of a knight. **3** character or qualities of a knight. **4** knights as a group or class: *All the knighthood of France came to the aid of the king.* *n.*

knight ly (nīt′lē), **1** of a knight. **2** having qualities admired in a knight; chivalrous. *adj.*

Knights Templars, a religious and military order of the Middle Ages. Its members were called Templars.

knit (nit), **1** make (cloth or an article of clothing) by looping yarn or thread together with long needles, or by machinery which forms loops instead of weaving: *knit a pair of socks.* **2** join closely and firmly together: *The players were all knit into a team that played together smoothly.* **3** grow together: *A broken bone knits.* **4** draw (the brows) together in wrinkles: *She knits her brows when she frowns.* *v.,* **knit ted** or **knit, knit ting.** [*Knit* is from Old English *cnyttan,* which comes from *cnotta,* meaning "knot."]

knit ter (nit′ər), person or thing that knits. *n.*

knit ting (nit′ing), knitted work. *n.*

knives (nīvz), plural of **knife.** *n.*

knob (nob), **1** a rounded lump: *The walking stick had a large knob at the top.* **2** handle on a door, drawer, etc.: *the knob on the dial of a television set.* *n.* —**knob′like′,** *adj.*

knob by (nob′ē), **1** covered with knobs. **2** rounded like a knob. *adj.,* **knob bi er, knob bi est.** —**knob′bi ness,** *n.*

knock (nok), **1** give a hard blow or blows to with the fist, knuckles, or anything hard; hit: *She knocked him on the head.* **2** a hit: *The hard knock made him angry.* **3** hit and cause to fall: *The speeding car knocked down several signs.* **4** hit with a noise: *He knocked on the door.* **5** a hit with a noise. **6** make a noise, especially a rattling or pounding noise: *The engine is knocking.* **7** act of knocking. **8** sound of knocking: *She did not hear the knock at the door.* **9** sound in an internal-combustion engine caused by loose parts or improper burning of fuel: *a knock in the engine.* **10** INFORMAL. find fault with; criticize: *The critics knocked the new book.* 1,3,4,6,10 *v.,* 2,5,7-9 *n.*

knock about, INFORMAL. wander from place to place.

knock down, take apart: *We knocked down the bookcases and packed them.*

knock off, INFORMAL. **1** take off; deduct: *He will knock off a dollar from the price if you pay cash.* **2** stop work: *We knock off at noon for lunch.* **3** stop; quit (doing something): *Knock off that noise!*

knock out, hit so hard as to make helpless or unconscious.

knock together, make or put together hastily: *The children knocked together a sort of raft out of old boards.*

knock a bout (nok′ə bout′), suitable for rough use. *adj.*

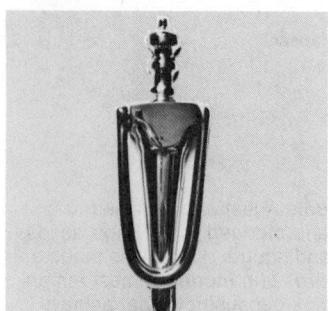

knocker (def. 2)

knock er (nok′ər), **1** person or thing that knocks. **2** a hinged knob, ring, or the like, usually of iron or brass, fastened on a door for use in knocking. *n.*

knock-kneed (nok′nēd′), having legs bent inward at the knees. *adj.*

knock out (nok′out′), a blow that makes an opponent helpless or unconscious: *The boxer won the fight by a knockout.* *n.*

knoll (nōl), a small, rounded hill; mound. *n.*

knot (not), **1** a fastening made by tying or twining together pieces of one or more ropes, cords, strings, etc.: *a square knot, a slip knot.* **2** tie or twine together in a knot: *He knotted two ropes together.* **3** tangle in knots: *My thread has knotted.* **4** bow or interlacing of ribbon, cord, braid, etc., worn as an ornament or badge of rank: *a shoulder knot.* **5** group; cluster: *A knot of students stood talking outside the classroom.* **6** the hard mass of wood formed in a tree where a branch grows out, which shows as a roundish, cross-grained piece in a board. **7** a hard lump. A knot sometimes forms in a tired muscle. **8** form into a hard lump. **9** joint where leaves grow out on the stem of a plant. **10** unit of speed used on ships and aircraft, equal to one nautical mile per hour: *The ship averaged 12 knots.* **11** nautical mile; 6076.11549 feet; 1.852 kilometers. **12** difficulty or problem. **13** unite closely in a way that is hard to undo. 1,4-7,9-12 *n.,* 2,3,8,13 *v.,* **knot ted, knot ting.** —**knot′less,** *adj.*

knot hole (not′hōl′), hole in a board where a knot has fallen out. *n.*

knot ty (not′ē), **1** full of knots: *knotty wood.* **2** difficult; puzzling: *a knotty problem.* *adj.,* **knot ti er, knot ti est.**

know (nō), **1** have the facts of; be skilled in: *She knows arithmetic. A carpenter must know his trade.* **2** have the facts and be sure that they are true: *We know that 2 and 2 are 4. She was there at the time; she will know.* **3** have knowledge: *I know from experience how to drive on icy roads.* **4** be acquainted with: *I know her very well, but I don't know her sister.* **5** tell apart from others; distinguish: *You will know his house by the red roof.* *v.,* **knew, known, know ing.** —**know′er,** *n.*

in the know, INFORMAL. having inside information.

know what's what, INFORMAL. be well-informed.

know-how (nō′hou′), INFORMAL. ability to do something. *n.*

know ing (nō′ing), **1** having knowledge; well-informed. **2** clever; shrewd. **3** suggesting shrewd or secret understanding of matters: *Her only answer was a knowing look.* *adj.*

know ing ly (nō′ing lē), **1** in a knowing way. **2** on purpose: *I would not knowingly hurt anyone.* *adv.*

knowl edge (nol′ij), **1** what one knows: *a gardener's knowledge of flowers.* **2** all that is known or can be learned: *Science is a part of knowledge.* **3** fact of knowing: *The knowledge of our victory caused great joy.* **4** act of knowing; familiarity with a thing, person, or subject: *a knowledge of the surrounding countryside.* *n.*

to the best of one's knowledge, as far as one knows: *I have never met them, to the best of my knowledge.*

knowl edge a ble (nol′i jə bəl), well-informed, especially about a particular subject. *adj.*

known (nōn), **1** past participle of **know.** *George Washington is known as the father of his country.* **2** familiar to all; generally recognized; well-known: *a known fact, a person of known ability.* 1 *v.,* 2 *adj.*

knuck le (nuk′əl), **1** a joint in a finger, especially one of the joints between a finger and the rest of the hand. **2** put the knuckles on the ground in playing marbles. **3** knee or hock joint of an animal used as food: *boiled pigs' knuckles.* 1,3 *n.,* 2 *v.,* **knuck led, knuck ling.**

knuckle down, 1 INFORMAL. work hard. **2** submit; yield: *She would not knuckle down under their attacks.*

knuckle under, submit; yield.

K O (kā′ō′), SLANG. **1** knock out. **2** knockout. 1 *v.,* **K O'd, K O'ing;** 2 *n.,* pl. **K O's.** Also, **kayo.**

K.O. or **k.o.,** knockout.

koala—about 2 ft. (60 cm.) long

a hat	i it	oi oil	ch child	a in about
ā age	ī ice	ou out	ng long	e in taken
ä far	o hot	u cup	sh she	i in pencil	ə =
e let	ō open	u̇ put	th thin	o in lemon
ē equal	ô order	ü rule	ғн then	u in circus
ėr term			zh measure	

ko a la (kō ä′lə), a gray, furry mammal of Australia that looks like a small bear and lives in trees. The female koala carries her young in a pouch. *n., pl.* **ko a las.**

Koch (kôk), **Robert,** 1843-1910, German bacteriologist and physician. *n.*

Ko dak (kō′dak), trademark for a small camera with rolls of film on which photographs are taken. *n.*

kohl ra bi (kōl′rä′bē), plant related to the cabbage that has a turnip-shaped stem which is eaten as a vegetable. *n., pl.* **kohl ra bies.**

koo doo (kü′dü), kudu. *n., pl.* **koo doos.**

kook (kük), SLANG. an odd or crazy person. *n.*

kook a bur ra (kük′ə bėr′ə), a large kingfisher of Australia that has a harsh cackling voice; laughing jackass. *n., pl.* **kook a bur ras.**

kook y (kü′kē), SLANG. crazy; odd; silly. *adj.,* **kook i er, kook i est.** —**kook′i ness,** *n.*

ko peck or **ko pek** (kō′pek), a coin of the Soviet Union. 100 kopecks make one ruble. Also, **copeck.** *n.*

Ko ran (kô rän′ or kô ran′), the sacred book of the Moslems. It consists of revelations to the prophet Mohammed and is the standard by which Moslems live. *n.*

Ko ran ic (kô ran′ik), of the Koran. *adj.*

Ko re a (kô rē′ə), former country on a peninsula in E Asia, divided into two countries, North Korea and South Korea, after World War II. *Capital of North Korea:* Pyongyang. *Capital of South Korea:* Seoul. See **China** for map. *n.*

Ko re an (kô rē′ən), **1** of Korea, its people, or their language. **2** person born or living in Korea. **3** language of Korea. 1 *adj.,* 2,3 *n.*

Korean War, war between South Korea, aided by the United Nations, and North Korea, aided by the People's Republic of China. The war lasted from June 1950 to July 1953.

Ko ror (kô′rôr), capital of Belau. *n.*

Kos ci us ko (kos′ē us′kō), **Thaddeus,** 1746-1817, Polish general who served in the American army during the Revolutionary War. *n.*

ko sher (kō′shər), **1** right or clean according to Jewish law: *kosher meat.* **2** prepare (food) according to the Jewish law. **3** SLANG. all right; fine: *It's not kosher to change the rules while you are playing the game.* 1,3 *adj.,* 2 *v.* [*Kosher* comes from Hebrew *kāshēr,* meaning "proper."]

Ko sy gin (kə sē′gin), **Aleksei N.,** 1904-1980, premier of the Soviet Union from 1964 to 1980. *n.*

kow tow (kou′tou′), show slavish respect or obedience. *v.*

K.P., kitchen police.

Kr, symbol for krypton.

kraal (kräl), **1** village of South African blacks. **2** pen for cattle or sheep in South Africa. *n.*

Krem lin (krem′lən), citadel of Moscow. The chief offices of the Soviet government are in the Kremlin. *n.*

krill (kril), a small, shrimplike shellfish that is eaten by whales and other sea animals. *n., pl.* **krill.**

Kriss Krin gle (kris′ kring′gəl), Santa Claus.

kryp ton (krip′ton), a colorless gas that forms a tiny part of the air. It is a chemical element. Krypton is used to fill some fluorescent lamps. *n.*

KS, Kansas (used with postal Zip Code).

kt., **1** karat (carat). **2** kiloton.

Kua la Lum pur (kwä′lə lùm′pùr′), capital of Malaysia, in W Malaya. *n.*

ku dos (kyü′dos or kü′dos), praise; glory; fame. *n., pl.* **ku dos.**

kudu
about 4¹/₂ ft. (1.5 m.) high at the shoulder

ku du (kü′dü), a large, grayish-brown African antelope with white stripes. *n.* Also, **koodoo.** [*Kudu* comes from Bantu *iqudu.*]

Ku Klux Klan (kü′ kluks′ klan′ or kyü′ kluks′ klan′), **1** a secret society of white people formed in the southern United States after the Civil War to suppress certain minority groups and maintain white supremacy. **2** a secret society founded in 1915 in the United States, violently opposed to Negroes, Jews, Catholics, and foreigners.

kum quat (kum′kwot), a yellow or orange fruit somewhat like a small orange. It has a sour pulp and a sweet rind, and is used in preserves and candy. *n.*

kung fu (kùng′ fü′), any of various styles of Chinese boxing, most of which use punches, kicks, and blocking actions similar to those of karate.

Ku wait (kü wāt′), **1** country in E Arabia, on the Persian Gulf. **2** its capital. *n.*

kw., kilowatt.

Kwang chow (kwäng′jō′), city in SE China. Officially, Guangzhou. It was formerly called **Canton.** *n.*

Kwan za (kwän′zə), a yearly Afro-American celebration commemorating various African festivals, especially one which marks the new planting season. It lasts from December 26 to January 1. *n.* [*Kwanza* is from Swahili *Kwanza,* originally meaning "first (fruits)," which comes from *kuanza,* meaning "to begin."]

K.W.H., kilowatt-hour or kilowatt-hours.

kwhr., kilowatt-hour or kilowatt-hours.

KY, Kentucky (used with postal Zip Code).

Ky., Kentucky.

Kyo to (kyō′tō), city in central Japan. It was formerly the capital. *n.*

Kyu shu (kyü′shü), large island at the SW end of Japan. *n.*

L or **l** (el), **1** the 12th letter of the English alphabet. **2** the Roman numeral for 50. *n., pl.* **L's** or **l's.**

L (el), anything shaped like the letter L. *n., pl.* **L's.**

l or **l.,** **1** book. **2** left. **3** length. **4** line. **5** lira or lire. **6** liter or liters.

L, **1** large. **2** Latin. **3** length. **4** longitude.

L., **1** lake. **2** Latin.

£ , pound or pounds sterling.

la (lä), the sixth tone of the musical scale. *n.*

La, symbol for lanthanum.

LA, Louisiana (used with postal Zip Code).

La., Louisiana.

L.A., Los Angeles.

lab (lab), INFORMAL. laboratory. *n.*

Lab., Labrador.

la bel (lā′bəl), **1** slip of paper or other material attached to anything and marked to show what or whose it is, or where it is to go: *Can you read the label on the bottle?* **2** put or write a label on: *The bottle is labeled "Poison."* **3** a word or phrase used to describe some person, thing, or idea: *In winter, Chicago deserves its label of "the Windy City."* **4** describe as; call; name: *label someone a liar.* 1,3 *n.,* 2,4 *v.,* **la beled, la bel ing** or **la belled, la bel ling.** —**la′bel er, la′bel ler,** *n.*

la bi al (lā′bē əl), **1** of the lips. **2** pronounced with the lips closed, nearly closed, or rounded. **3** sound made in this way. *B, p,* and *m* are labials. 1,2 *adj.,* 3 *n.*

la bor (lā′bər), **1** effort in doing or making something; work; toil: *Her understanding of the subject shows the amount of labor she puts into her homework.* **2** piece of work to be done; task: *The king gave Hercules twelve labors to perform.* **3** work, especially manual work, done by skilled and unskilled workers for wages: *Digging ditches is manual labor.* **4** workers as a group: *Labor favors safe working conditions.* **5** do work; work hard; toil: *I labored all day at the factory.* **6** move slowly and heavily: *The ship labored in the heavy seas.* **7** childbirth. 1-4,7 *n.,* 5,6 *v.* Also, **labour.**

lab o ra to ry (lab′rə tôr′ē), **1** place where scientific work is done; room or building fitted with apparatus for conducting scientific experiments, investigations, tests, etc.: *a chemical laboratory.* **2** place for manufacturing drugs, medicines, chemicals, etc. *n., pl.* **lab o ra to ries.**

Labor Day, the first Monday in September, a legal holiday throughout the United States in honor of labor and laborers.

la bored (lā′bərd), done with much effort; forced: *labored breathing, a labored attempt at humor.* *adj.*

la bor er (lā′bər ər), **1** person who does work that requires strength rather than skill or training. **2** worker. *n.*

la bo ri ous (lə bôr′ē əs), **1** needing or taking much effort; requiring hard work: *Climbing a mountain is laborious.* **2** showing signs of effort; labored: *The student who was always late made up laborious excuses.* **3** willing to work hard; industrious: *a careful and laborious painter.* *adj.* —**la bo′ri ous ly,** *adv.* —**la bo′ri ous ness,** *n.*

la bor-sav ing (lā′bər sā′ving), that takes the place of or lessens labor: *A washing machine is a labor-saving device.* *adj.*

labor union, group of workers joined together to protect and promote their interests by dealing as a group with their employers; union.

la bour (lā′bər), labor. *n., v.*

Lab ra dor (lab′rə dôr), **1** peninsula in NE North America, between Hudson Bay and the Atlantic Ocean. **2** the E part of this peninsula, part of the Canadian province of Newfoundland. *n.*

lab y rinth (lab′ə rinth′), **1** number of connecting passages so arranged that it is hard to find one's way from point to point; maze. **2 Labyrinth,** (in Greek myths) the maze built by Daedalus for King Minos of Crete to imprison the Minotaur. **3** any confusing, complicated arrangement: *We could not find our way out of the labyrinth of dark and narrow streets. n.*

lab y rin thine (lab′ə rin′thən), confusing and complicated; intricate. *adj.*

lac (lak), a sticky substance deposited on various trees by scale insects. Lac is used in making sealing wax, varnish, etc. *n.*

lace
(def. 1)

lace (lās), **1** an open weaving or net of fine thread in an ornamental pattern. **2** trim with lace: *a velvet cloak laced with gold.* **3** cord, string, or leather strip passed through holes to pull or hold together the opposite edges of a shoe, garment, etc.: *These shoes need new laces.* **4** put laces through; pull or hold together with a lace or laces: *Lace up your shoes.* **5** interlace; intertwine: *She sat with her fingers laced.* **6** beat; thrash. 1,3 *n.,* 2,4-6 *v.,* **laced, lac ing.** [*Lace* came into English about 750 years ago from French *laz,* which came from Latin *laqueus,* meaning "a noose."] —**lace′like′,** *adj.*

lace into, 1 strike again and again; lash: *The two angry children laced into each other until the teacher separated them.* **2** criticize severely: *The coach laced into the team for not trying hard enough to win.*

lace mak ing (lās′mā′king), art or process of making lace. *n.*

lac e rate (las′ə rāt′), **1** tear roughly; mangle: *The hawk's talons lacerated the field mouse.* **2** cause pain or suffering to; distress: *The coach's sharp words lacerated my feelings.* *v.,* **lac e rat ed, lac e rat ing.**

lac e ra tion (las′ə rā′shən), **1** a rough tearing or mangling. **2** a rough tear; mangled place. A torn, jagged wound is a laceration. *n.*

lac i ness (lā′sē nis), lacy condition or quality. *n.*

lack (lak), **1** have no; be without: *Some guinea pigs lack tails.* **2** a being without: *Lack of a fire made us cold.* **3** have not enough: *This book lacks excitement.* **4** not having enough: *Lack of rest made her tired.* **5** thing needed: *The campers' main lack was fuel for a fire.* 1,3 *v.,* 2,4,5 *n.*

lack a dai si cal (lak′ə dā′zə kəl), lacking interest or enthusiasm; languid; listless. *adj.*

lack ey (lak′ē), **1** a male servant; footman. **2** follower who obeys orders like a servant; toady. *n., pl.* **lack eys.** [*Lackey* can be traced back to Spanish *lacayo,* meaning "foot soldier."]

lack ing (lak′ing), **1** not having enough; deficient: *A weak person is lacking in strength.* **2** without; not having: *Lacking butter, we ate jam on our bread.* **3** absent; not here: *Water is lacking because the pipe is broken.* 1,3 *adj.,* 2 *prep.*

lack lus ter or **lack lus tre** (lak′lus′tər), lacking brightness; dull and drab. *adj.*

la con ic (lə kon′ik), using few words; brief in speech or expression; concise. *adj.* —**la con′i cal ly,** *adv.*

WORD HISTORY

laconic

Laconic is from Latin *Laconicus,* meaning "Spartan," which came from Greek *Lakōnikos.* It came to have this meaning because the Spartans were noted for speaking little.

lac quer (lak′ər), **1** varnish used to give a protective coating or a shiny appearance to metals, wood, paper, etc. Lacquers are made in all colors that are commonly found in paints. **2** coat with lacquer. 1 *n.,* 2 *v.* [*Lacquer* came into English about 400 years ago from French *lacre,* meaning "a sealing wax," and can be traced back to Sanskrit *lākshā,* meaning "lac."] —**lac′quer er,** *n.*

la crosse (lə krôs′), game played on a field with a ball and long-handled, loosely strung rackets by two teams, usually of 10 players each. The players carry the ball in the rackets, trying to send it into the other team's goal. *n.*

lac tase (lak′tās), enzyme present in mammals that breaks down lactose in milk into simpler sugars that can be absorbed into the blood. *n.*

lac te al (lak′tē əl), of milk; milky. *adj.*

lac tic acid (lak′tik), a colorless, odorless acid formed when milk sours, vegetable juices ferment, etc.

lac tose (lak′tōs), a crystalline sugar present in milk; milk sugar. *n.*

lac y (lā′sē), **1** of lace. **2** like lace: *the lacy leaves of a fern. adj.,* **lac i er, lac i est.**

lad (lad), boy; youth. *n.*

lad der (lad′ər), **1** set of rungs or steps fastened to two sidepieces for use in climbing up or down. **2** means of climbing higher: *Hard work is often a ladder to success. n.*

lad die (lad′ē), SCOTTISH. lad. *n.*

lade (lād), put a burden on; load. *v.,* **lad ed, lad en** or **lad ed, lad ing.**

lad en (lād′n), **1** loaded; burdened: *a ship laden with goods.* **2** a past participle of **lade.** *The camels were laden with bundles of silk.* 1 *adj.,* 2 *v.*

lad ing (lā′ding), **1** act of loading. **2** load; freight; cargo. *n.*

la dle (lā′dl), **1** a large cup-shaped spoon with a long handle, for dipping out liquids. **2** dip: *The cook ladled out the soup into large bowls.* 1 *n.,* 2 *v.,* **la dled, la dling.**

ladle (def. 1)

a hat	**i** it	**oi** oil	**ch** child	⎧ a in about
ā age	**ī** ice	**ou** out	**ng** long	⎪ e in taken
ä far	**o** hot	**u** cup	**sh** she	ə = ⎨ i in pencil
e let	**ō** open	**ù** put	**th** thin	⎪ o in lemon
ē equal	**ô** order	**ü** rule	**ŦH** then	⎩ u in circus
ėr term			**zh** measure	

la dy (lā′dē), **1** woman of good family and high social position: *a lady by birth.* **2** a well-bred woman. **3** a polite term for any woman. "Ladies" is often used in speaking or writing to a group of women. **4** woman who has the rights and authority of a lord. **5 Lady,** title used in writing or speaking about women of certain high ranks in Great Britain: *Lord and Lady Grey attended the Queen's reception.* **6 Our Lady,** a title of the Virgin Mary. *n., pl.* **la dies.** [*Lady* is from Old English *hlæfdīge,* originally meaning "one who kneads a loaf of bread" or "mistress of the house," which comes from *hlāf,* meaning "loaf," and *-dīge,* meaning "kneader (of dough)."]

lady beetle, ladybug.

la dy bird (lā′dē bėrd′), ladybug. *n.*

ladybug
about two times life-size

la dy bug (lā′dē bug′), a small beetle that has a rounded back and is often bright red or yellow with black spots. Ladybugs eat harmful insects. *n.*

la dy-in-wait ing (lā′dē in wā′ting), lady who accompanies or serves a queen or princess. *n., pl.* **la dies-in-wait ing.**

la dy like (lā′dē līk′), like a lady; suitable for a lady; well-bred; polite. *adj.*

la dy ship (lā′dē ship), **1** rank or position of a lady. **2 Ladyship,** title used in speaking to or of a woman having the rank of Lady: *your Ladyship, her Ladyship. n.*

la dy-slip per (lā′dē slip′ər), lady's-slipper. *n.*

la dy's-slip per (lā′dēz slip′ər), a wild orchid whose flower looks somewhat like a slipper. *n.*

La fa yette (lä′fē et′ or laf′ē et′), Marquis de, 1757-1834, French general and statesman who served in the American army during the Revolutionary War. *n.*

lag (lag), **1** move too slowly; fall behind: *The child lagged because he was tired.* **2** a falling behind; lagging: *There was a long lag in forwarding mail to us after we moved.* **3** amount by which a person or thing falls behind: *There was a month's lag between the order for our car and its delivery.* **4** become weaker; flag: *Our interest lagged as we watched the dull program.* 1,4 *v.,* **lagged, lag ging;** 2,3 *n.* —**lag′ger,** *n.*

lag gard (lag′ərd), **1** person who moves too slowly or falls behind; loiterer. **2** falling behind; slow; backward. 1 *n.,* 2 *adj.* —**lag′gard ly,** *adv.* —**lag′gard ness,** *n.*

la goon (lə gün′), **1** pond or small lake connected with a larger body of water. **2** shallow water separated from the sea by low ridges of sand. **3** water within a ring-shaped coral island. *n.* [*Lagoon* comes from Italian *laguna,* and can be traced back to Latin *lacus,* meaning "a lake, pond."]

La gos (lä′gōs or lā′gos), capital of Nigeria, in the SW part. *n.*

laid (lād), past tense and past participle of **lay**[1]. *He laid down the heavy bundle. Those eggs were laid this morning. v.*

lain (lān), past participle of **lie**[2]. *The snow has lain on the ground a week. v.*

lair (ler *or* lar), den or resting place of a wild animal. *n.*

laird (lerd *or* lard), SCOTTISH. owner of land. *n.*

lais sez faire or **lais ser faire** (les′ā fer′ or les′ā far′), principle that trade, business, industry, etc., should operate with a minimum of regulation and interference by government. *n.*

la i ty (lā′ə tē), persons who are not members of the clergy or of a particular profession; laymen: *Doctors use many words that the laity do not know. n.*

lake (lāk), **1** body of water entirely or nearly surrounded by land. A lake usually consists of fresh water and is larger than a pond. **2** pool of liquid. *n.*

lake dweller, person who lived in a house built on piles over a lake in prehistoric times.

lake shore (lāk′shôr′), lakeside. *n.*

lake side (lāk′sīd′), the edge or shore of a lake. *n.*

lake trout, a large, dark trout of the lakes of North America.

la ma (lä′mə), a Buddhist priest or monk in Tibet and Mongolia. *n., pl.* **la mas.**

la ma ser y (lä′mə ser′ē), a monastery of lamas in Tibet and Mongolia. *n., pl.* **la ma ser ies.**

lamb (lam), **1** a young sheep. **2** meat from a lamb: *roast lamb.* **3** lambskin. **4** give birth to a lamb or lambs. **5** a young, gentle, or dear person. 1-3,5 *n.*, 4 *v.* —**lamb′like′,** *adj.*

lam bast (lam bast′), lambaste. *v.*

lam baste (lam bāst′), INFORMAL. **1** strike again and again; beat severely; thrash. **2** scold roughly. *v.*, **lam bast ed, lam bast ing.**

lam bent (lam′bənt), **1** moving lightly over a surface: *a lambent flame.* **2** playing lightly and brilliantly over a subject: *lambent wit.* **3** shining with a soft, clear light: *Moonlight is lambent. adj.* —**lam′bent ly,** *adv.*

lamb kin (lam′kən), a little lamb. *n.*

lamb skin (lam′skin′), **1** skin of a lamb, especially with the wool on it. **2** leather made from the skin of a lamb. **3** parchment. *n.*

lame (lām), **1** not able to walk properly; having an injured leg or foot; crippled: *He limps because he has been lame since birth.* **2** stiff and sore: *My arm is lame from playing ball.* **3** make lame; cripple: *The accident lamed me for life.* **4** not very good; unsatisfactory; poor: *Oversleeping is a lame excuse for being late.* 1,2,4 *adj.*, **lam er, lam est;** 3 *v.*, **lamed, lam ing.** —**lame′ly,** *adv.* —**lame′ness,** *n.*

la mé (la mā′), a rich fabric made with gold or silver threads. *n.*

lame duck, 1 a public official who has been defeated for reelection and is serving the last part of a term. **2** a disabled or helpless person.

la ment (lə ment′), **1** feel or show grief for; mourn aloud for: *We lament the dead.* **2** feel or show grief; mourn aloud; weep: *Why do they lament so?* **3** expression of grief or sorrow; wail. **4** poem, song, or tune that expresses grief. **5** feel sorry about; regret: *We lamented her absence.* 1,2,5 *v.*, 3,4 *n.* —**la ment′er,** *n.* —**la ment′ing ly,** *adv.*

lam en ta ble (lam′ən tə bəl or lə men′tə bəl), **1** to be regretted or pitied; giving cause for sorrow: *It was a lamentable day when our dog was run over.* **2** not so good; inferior; pitiful: *The singer gave a lamentable performance. adj.*

lam en ta bly (lam′ən tə blē or lə men′tə blē), to a lamentable degree; regrettably; deplorably: *They are lamentably ignorant about world affairs. adv.*

lam en ta tion (lam′ən tā′shən), loud grief; cries of sorrow; mourning; wailing. *n.*

Lam en ta tions (lam′ən tā′shənz), book of the Old Testament. According to tradition it was written by Jeremiah. *n.*

lam i na (lam′ə nə), a thin plate, scale, or layer. *n., pl.* **lam i nae** (lam′ə nē′), **lam i nas.**

lam i nate (lam′ə nāt), **1** make (plywood, plastics, glass, etc.) by fastening together layer on layer of one or more materials. **2** beat or roll (metal) into a thin plate. *v.*, **lam i nat ed, lam i nat ing.** —**lam′i na′tor,** *n.*

lam i na tion (lam′ə nā′shən), a laminating or a being laminated. *n.*

lamp (lamp), **1** device that gives artificial light. Oil lamps hold oil and a wick by which the oil is burned. A gas or electric light, especially when covered by a glass globe or other shade, is called a lamp. **2** a similar device that gives heat or radiant energy: *an ultraviolet lamp. n.* [*Lamp* came into English about 800 years ago from French *lampe*, and can be traced back to Greek *lampein*, meaning "to shine."]

lamp black (lamp′blak′), a fine black soot that is deposited when oil, gas, etc., burn incompletely. Lampblack is used as a coloring matter in paint and ink. *n.*

lamp light (lamp′līt′), light from a lamp. *n.*

lamp light er (lamp′lī′tər), person formerly employed to light gas-burning street lamps. *n.*

lam poon (lam pün′), **1** piece of writing that attacks and makes fun of a person. **2** attack and make fun of in a lampoon. 1 *n.*, 2 *v.* [*Lampoon* is from French *lampon*, which comes from *lampons*, meaning "let us drink," used as a refrain in insulting poems and songs.]

lamp post (lamp′pōst′), post used to support a street lamp. *n.*

lam prey (lam′prē), a water animal having a body like an eel, gill slits like a fish, no jaws, and a large, round mouth. Lampreys attach themselves to fishes with their mouths, sucking the body fluids. *n., pl.* **lam preys.**

La nai (lä nī′), island in the central part of the Hawaiian Islands. *n.*

Lan ca shire (lang′kə shər), county in NW England. *n.*

Lan cas ter (lang′kə stər), **1** the English royal house from 1399 to 1461. Its emblem was a red rose. **2** Lancashire. *n.*

lance (lans), **1** a long, wooden spear with a sharp iron or steel head: *The knights carried lances as they rode into battle.* **2** lancer. **3** any instrument like a soldier's lance. A spear for harpooning a whale is called a lance. **4** pierce with a lance: *lance a fish.* **5** cut open with a lancet: *The doctor lanced the boil.* 1-3 *n.*, 4,5 *v.*, **lanced, lanc ing.**

Lan ce lot (lan′sə lot), the bravest of King Arthur's knights of the Round Table. *n.*

lanc er (lan′sər), a mounted soldier armed with a lance; lance. *n.*

lan cet (lan′sit), a small, pointed knife with two sharp edges, used by doctors and surgeons in opening boils, abscesses, etc. *n.*

land (land), **1** the solid part of the earth's surface: *After weeks at sea, the voyagers sighted land.* **2** come to land; bring to land: *The ship landed at the pier. The pilot landed the airplane in Seattle.* **3** come down from the air; come to rest: *The seaplane landed in the harbor. The eagle landed on a rock.* **4** put on land; set ashore: *The ship landed its passengers.* **5** go on shore from a ship or boat: *The passengers landed.* **6** ground; soil: *This is good land for a garden.* **7** ground or soil used as property: *People often buy land as an investment.* **8** country; region: *Switzerland* *is a mountainous land.* **9** people of a country; nation: *She collected folk songs from all the land.* **10** come to a stop; arrive: *The burglar landed in jail. The car landed in the ditch.* **11** cause to arrive: *This train will land you in London.* **12** INFORMAL. get; catch: *land a job, land a fish.* **13** INFORMAL. strike; hit: *I landed a blow on his chin.* 1,6-9 *n.*, 2-5,10-13 *v.*

land breeze, breeze blowing from the land toward the sea.

land ed (lan′did), owning land: *landed nobles. adj.*

land fall (land′fôl′), **1** a sighting of land. **2** the land sighted or reached. *n.*

land form (land′fôrm′), a physical feature of the earth's surface. Plains, plateaus, hills, and mountains are landforms. *n.*

land hold er (land′hōl′dər), person who owns or occupies land. *n.*

land ing (lan′ding), **1** a coming to land or something solid like land: *the landing of the Pilgrims at Plymouth. There are many millions of takeoffs and landings at the nation's airports each year.* **2** place where persons or goods are landed from a ship, helicopter, etc. A wharf, dock, or pier is a landing for boats. **3** platform between flights of stairs. *n.*

landing field, field large enough and smooth enough for airplanes to land on and take off from safely.

landing gear, wheels, pontoons, etc., under an aircraft. When on land or water an aircraft rests on its landing gear.

landing strip, airstrip.

land la dy (land′lā′dē), **1** woman who owns buildings or land that she rents to others. **2** woman who runs an inn or rooming house. *n., pl.* **land la dies.**

land less (land′lis), without land; owning no land. *adj.*

land locked (land′lokt′), **1** shut in, or nearly shut in, by land: *The landlocked harbor was protected from the full force of the wind and waves.* **2** living in waters shut off from the sea: *Landlocked salmon have to spend their lives in fresh water instead of making the migration to salt water. adj.*

land lord (land′lôrd′), **1** person who owns buildings or land for rent to others. **2** person who runs an inn or rooming house. *n.*

land lub ber (land′lub′ər), person not used to being on ships; person who is awkward on board ship because of lack of experience. *n.*

land mark (land′märk′), **1** something familiar or easily seen, used as a guide: *The traveler did not lose her way in the forest because the rangers' high tower served as a landmark.* **2** any important fact or event; any happening that stands out above others: *The inventions of the printing press, telephone, telegraph, radio, and television are landmarks in the history of communication.* **3** a building, monument, or place designated as important or interesting: *a historical landmark.* **4** stone or other object that marks the boundary of a piece of land. *n.*

land own er (land′ō′nər), person who owns land. *n.*

land scape (land′skāp), **1** view of scenery on land that can be taken in at a glance from one point of view: *From the church tower the two hills with the valley formed a beautiful landscape.* **2** painting, etching, etc., showing such a view. **3** make (land) more pleasant to look at by arranging trees, shrubs, flowers, etc.: *This park is landscaped.* 1,2 *n.*, 3 *v.*, **land scaped, land scap ing.**

land slide (land′slīd′), **1** a sliding down of a mass of earth or rock on a steep slope. **2** the mass that slides down. **3** an overwhelming majority of votes for one candidate or political party in an election. *n.*

land ward (land′wərd), toward the land or shore. *adv., adj.*

a hat	i it	oi oil	ch child	(a in about
ā age	ī ice	ou out	ng long	e in taken
ä far	o hot	u cup	sh she	ə = i in pencil
e let	ō open	u̇ put	th thin	o in lemon
ē equal	ô order	ü rule	₮н then	u in circus
ėr term			zh measure	

land wards (land′wərdz), landward. *adv.*

lane (lān), **1** path between hedges, walls, or fences. **2** a narrow country road or city street. **3** any narrow way: *The bride and groom walked down a lane formed by two lines of wedding guests.* **4** course or route used by cars, ships, or aircraft going in the same direction. **5** bowling alley. *n.*

lang., language.

lan guage (lang′gwij), **1** human speech, spoken or written: *Civilization would be impossible without language.* **2** the speech used by one nation, tribe, or other similar large group of people: *the French language, the Navajo language.* **3** form, style, or kind of language; manner of expression: *poetic language.* **4** wording or words: *The lawyer explained to us very carefully the language of the contract.* **5** the special terms used by a science, art, or profession, or by a class of persons: *the language of chemistry.* **6** system of words, numbers, symbols, and abbreviations that stand for information and instructions in a computer. **7** the expression of thoughts and feelings otherwise than by words: *sign language.* **8** the study of language or languages; linguistics. *n.* [*Language* came into English about 700 years ago from French *langage,* and can be traced back to Latin *lingua,* meaning "the tongue, language."]

language arts, course of study in elementary schools and high schools that includes reading, spelling, speech, composition, and other subjects that develop skill in using language.

lan guid (lang′gwid), **1** feeling weak; without energy; drooping: *A hot, sticky day makes a person languid.* **2** without interest or enthusiasm; indifferent: *The lazy child felt too languid to do anything. adj.* —**lan′guid ly,** *adv.* —**lan′guid ness,** *n.*

lan guish (lang′gwish), **1** grow weak; become weary; lose energy; droop: *The flowers languished from lack of water.* **2** become weak or wasted through pain, hunger, etc.; suffer under any unfavorable conditions: *Wild animals often languish in captivity.* **3** droop with longing; pine with love or grief: *The refugees languished for the homeland they had been forced to leave. v.* —**lan′guish er,** *n.*

lan guor (lang′gər), **1** lack of energy; weakness; weariness: *A long illness caused my languor.* **2** lack of interest or enthusiasm; indifference. **3** softness or tenderness of mood. **4** quietness; stillness: *the languor of a summer afternoon.* **5** lack of activity; sluggishness. *n.*

lan guor ous (lang′gər əs), languid; listless. *adj.*

lank (langk), **1** long and thin; slender: *a lank child, lank*

landslide
(def. 2)

grasses. **2** straight and flat; not curly or wavy: *lank locks of hair. adj.* —**lank′ly,** *adv.* —**lank′ness,** *n.*

lank i ly (lang′kə lē), in a lanky condition or form. *adv.*

lank i ness (lang′kē nis), condition of being lanky. *n.*

lank y (lang′kē), awkwardly long and thin; tall and ungraceful: *a lanky teenager. adj.,* **lank i er, lank i est.**

lan o lin (lan′l ən), fatty substance obtained from the natural coating on wool fibers, used in cosmetics, ointments, shoe polish, etc. *n.* [*Lanolin* comes from Latin *lana,* meaning "wool," and *oleum,* meaning "oil."]

Lan sing (lan′sing), capital of Michigan, in the S part. *n.*

lantern

lan tern (lan′tərn), case to protect a light from wind, rain, etc. A lantern has sides of glass, paper, or some other material through which the light can shine. *n.* [*Lantern* came into English about 700 years ago from French *lanterne,* and can be traced back to Greek *lampein,* meaning "to shine."]

lan tha num (lan′thə nəm), a metallic element which occurs in various minerals. It is easily shaped and is used in making alloys. *n.*

lan yard (lan′yərd), **1** a short rope or cord used on ships to fasten rigging. **2** a loose cord around the neck on which to hang a knife, whistle, etc. **3** a short cord with a hook at one end, used in firing certain kinds of cannon. *n.*

La os (lā′os *or* lä′ōs), country in SE Asia, west of Vietnam. *Capital:* Vientiane. See **Indochina** for map. *n.*

La o tian (lā ō′shən), **1** of Laos, its people, or their language. **2** person born or living in Laos. 1 *adj.,* 2 *n.*

lap[1] (lap), **1** the front part from the waist to the knees of a person sitting down, with the clothing that covers it: *I held the baby on my lap.* **2** a loosely hanging edge of clothing; flap. *n.*

in the lap of luxury, in luxurious circumstances.

lap[2] (lap), **1** lay or lie together, one partly over or beside another; overlap: *We lapped shingles on the roof.* **2** the part that laps over. **3** amount that a part laps over. **4** extend out beyond a limit: *The reign of Elizabeth I (queen of England from 1558 to 1603) lapped over into the 1600's.* **5** to wind or wrap; fold: *Lap this edge over that.* **6** one time around a racetrack: *Who won the first lap of the race?* **7** part of any course traveled: *The last lap of our all-day hike was the toughest.* 1,4,5 *v.,* **lapped, lap ping;** 2,3,6,7 *n.*

lap[3] (lap), **1** drink by lifting up with the tongue: *Cats and dogs lap water.* **2** move or beat gently with a lapping sound; splash gently: *Little waves lapped against the boat.* **3** act of lapping: *With one lap of the tongue the bear finished the honey.* **4** sound of lapping: *The lap of the waves against a boat put me to sleep.* 1,2 *v.,* **lapped, lap ping;** 3,4 *n.* —**lap′per,** *n.*

lap up, take in eagerly or greedily; devour: *The scouts were so hungry after the long hike that they lapped up their*

dinners. *The children lapped up the tales about frontier adventures.*

La Paz (lä päs′), one of the two capitals of Bolivia, in the W part. Sucre is the other capital.

lap dog, a small pet dog.

la pel (lə pel′), either of the two front parts of a coat folded back just below the collar. *n.*

lap ful (lap′fül), as much as a lap can hold. *n., pl.* **lap-fuls** or **laps ful.**

lap i dar y (lap′ə der′ē), person who cuts, polishes, or engraves precious stones. *n., pl.* **lap i dar ies.**

lap is laz u li (lap′is laz′yə lī), **1** a deep-blue, semiprecious stone used for an ornament. **2** deep blue.

Lap land (lap′land′), region in N Norway, N Sweden, N Finland, and NW Soviet Union. *n.*

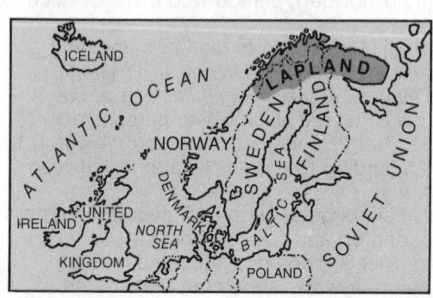

Lap land er (lap′lan′dər), person born or living in Lapland. *n.*

Lapp (lap), **1** one of a group of people that live in Lapland. The Lapps are small in stature with short, broad heads. **2** language of the Lapps. *n.*

lapse (laps), **1** a slight mistake or error: *a lapse of the tongue because of carelessness, a lapse of memory.* **2** make a slight mistake or error. **3** a slipping by; a passing away: *A minute is a short lapse of time.* **4** slip by; pass away: *His interest in the dull story soon lapsed.* **5** a slipping back; sinking down; slipping into a lower condition: *War is a lapse into savage ways.* **6** slip back; sink down: *The abandoned house lapsed into disrepair.* **7** a falling or passing into any state: *a lapse into silence.* **8** fall or pass into any state: *Our discussion lapsed into silence.* **9** the ending of a right or privilege because not renewed, not used, or otherwise neglected: *the lapse of a lease.* **10** end in this way: *My driver's license lapsed when I failed to renew it.* 1,3,5,7,9 *n.,* 2,4,6,8,10 *v.,* **lapsed, laps ing.** [*Lapse* is from Latin *lapsus,* originally meaning "a fall, a slipping," which comes from *labi,* meaning "to fall, slip."]

lapwing
about 1 ft. (30 cm.) long

lap wing (lap′wing′), a crested bird, a kind of plover of Europe, Asia, and northern Africa, that has a slow, irregular flight and a peculiar, wailing cry. *n.*

Lar a mie (lar′ə mē), city in SE Wyoming. *n.*

lar board (lär′bərd), **1** the left or port side of a ship. **2** on the left side of a ship. 1 *n.,* 2 *adj.*

lar ce nous (lär′sə nəs), **1** characterized by larceny; guilty of larceny: *Burglary is a larcenous offense.*

2 thievish: *Blue jays are known for their larcenous habits.* *adj.*

lar ce ny (lär′sə nē), the unlawful taking and using of the personal property of another person; theft. *n., pl.* **lar ce nies.** [*Larceny* came into English about 600 years ago from French *larcin*, and can be traced back to Latin *latro*, meaning "a bandit, a hired soldier."]

larch (lärch), **1** tree related to the pine, with small woody cones and needles that fall off in autumn. **2** the strong, tough wood of this tree. *n., pl.* **larch es.**

lard (lärd), **1** the fat of pigs or hogs, melted down for use in cooking: *The cook uses lard in making pies.* **2** put lard on or in; grease: *Lard the pan well.* **3** give variety to; enrich: *The speaker larded his speech with jokes and stories.* 1 *n.*, 2,3 *v.* —**lard′like′,** *adj.*

lar der (lär′dər), **1** place where food is kept; pantry. **2** supply of food. *n.*

large (lärj), **1** of more than the usual size, amount, or number; big: *America is a large country. A hundred thousand dollars is a large sum of money.* **2** having much scope or range; broad: *a person of large experience. adj.,* **larg er, larg est.** —**large′ness,** *n.*

at large, 1 at liberty; free: *Is the escaped prisoner still at large?* **2** as a whole; altogether: *The people at large want peace.* **3** representing the whole of a state or district, not merely one division of it: *a congresswoman at large.*

large heart ed (lärj′här′tid), generous; liberal. *adj.*

large intestine, the lower part of the intestines into which the small intestine discharges food that has not been digested. It is a wide tube in which water is absorbed and wastes are eliminated.

large ly (lärj′lē), to a great extent; mainly: *This region consists largely of desert. adv.*

large-scale (lärj′skāl′), **1** involving many persons or things; great; extensive: *The great Chicago fire of 1871 was a large-scale disaster.* **2** made or drawn to a large scale: *This large-scale map shows many details. adj.*

lar gess or **lar gesse** (lär′jis), **1** generous giving. **2** a generous gift or gifts. *n.*

larg ish (lär′jish), rather large. *adj.*

lar go (lär′gō), in music: **1** slow and dignified; stately. **2** in a slow and dignified manner. **3** a slow, stately passage or piece of music. 1 *adj.,* 2 *adv.,* 3 *n., pl.* **lar gos.** [*Largo* was borrowed from Italian *largo,* which came from Latin *largus,* meaning "large, abundant."]

lar i at (lar′ē ət), a long rope with a noose at the end, used for catching horses and cattle; lasso. *n.* [*Lariat* comes from Spanish *la reata,* meaning "the rope."]

lark[1] (lärk), **1** a small songbird of Europe, Asia, America, and northern Africa with brown feathers and long hind claws. The skylark is one kind. Larks often sing while soaring in the air. **2** any of several similar songbirds in America, such as the meadowlark. *n.*

lark[2] (lärk), **1** something that is good fun; a merry or gay time; frolic: *What a lark we had at the circus!* **2** have fun; play; frolic. 1 *n.,* 2 *v.*

lark spur (lärk′spėr′), plant with clusters of blue, pink, or white flowers on tall stalks. *n.*

lar va (lär′və), **1** the wormlike early form of an insect from the time it leaves the egg until it becomes a pupa. A caterpillar is the larva of a butterfly or moth. A grub is the larva of a beetle. The silkworm is a larva. **2** an immature form of certain animals that is different in structure from the adult form and must undergo a change or metamorphosis to become like the parent. A tadpole is the larva of a frog or toad. *n., pl.* **lar vae** (lär′vē), **lar vas.** [See **Word History.**]

lar val (lär′vəl), **1** of or having to do with larvae. **2** in the form of a larva. *adj.*

lar yn gi tis (lar′ən jī′tis), inflammation of the larynx,

a hat	**i** it	**oi** oil	**ch** child	a in about
ā age	**ī** ice	**ou** out	**ng** long	e in taken
ä far	**o** hot	**u** cup	**sh** she	ə = { i in pencil
e let	**ō** open	**u̇** put	**th** thin	o in lemon
ē equal	**ô** order	**ü** rule	**ŧH** then	u in circus
ėr term			**zh** measure	

usually accompanied by hoarseness. *n.*

lar ynx (lar′ingks), the upper end of the windpipe, where the vocal cords are; voice box. *n., pl.* **la ryn ges** (lə rin′jēz), **lar ynx es.**

la sa gna (lə zä′nyə), dish consisting of chopped meat, cheese, and tomato sauce, baked with layers of wide noodles. *n.* [*Lasagna* was borrowed from Italian *lasagna,* and can be traced back to Greek *lasanon,* meaning "a utensil, a cooking pot."]

La Salle (lə sal′), **Robert Cavelier, Sieur de,** 1643-1687, Frenchman who explored the Mississippi and Ohio rivers.

las civ i ous (lə siv′ē əs), feeling, showing, or causing physical desire or lust. *adj.*

la ser (lā′zər), device that produces a very narrow and intense beam of light of only one wavelength going in only one direction. Laser beams are used to cut or melt hard materials, remove diseased body tissues, transmit television signals, etc. *n.* [*Laser* comes from the words *light amplification by stimulated emission of radiation.* It was formed by using the first letter of these words except the prepositions.]

lash[1] (lash), **1** the part of a whip that is not the handle: *The leather lash cut the side of the horse.* **2** a stroke or blow with a whip: *The driver gave his horse a lash.* **3** strike with a whip; flog: *The driver of the team lashed her horses on.* **4** beat back and forth: *The lion lashed its tail. The wind lashes the sails.* **5** a sudden, swift movement: *the lash of an animal's tail.* **6** strike violently; hit: *The rain lashed against the windows.* **7** attack severely in words; scold sharply: *In her speech she lashed out at corrupt politicians.* **8** eyelash. 1,2,5,8 *n., pl.* **lash es;** 3,4,6,7 *v.* —**lash′er,** *n.*

lash[2] (lash), tie or fasten with a rope or cord: *We lashed logs together to make a raft. v.*

lash ing (lash′ing), rope or cord, used in tying or fastening. *n.*

lass (las), a girl or young woman. *n., pl.* **lass es.**

las sie (las′ē), girl; lass. *n.*

WORD HISTORY

larva

Larva comes from Latin *larva,* meaning "a ghost, a mask." It was called this because this stage of an insect's life was thought to be "a mask" of its later form.

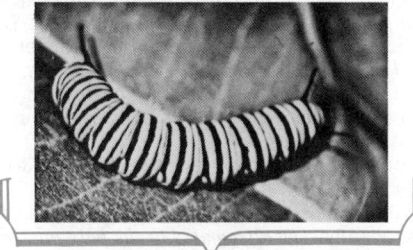

las si tude (las′ə tüd *or* las′ə tyüd), lack of energy; a feeling of weakness; weariness: *a period of renewed excitement after an interval of lassitude. n.*

las so (las′ō *or* la sü′), **1** a long rope with a running noose at one end, used for catching horses and cattle; lariat. **2** catch with a lasso. 1 *n., pl.* **las sos** *or* **las soes;** 2 *v.* [*Lasso* is from Spanish *lazo,* which came from Latin *laqueus,* meaning "a noose."]

last[1] (last), **1** coming after all others; being at the end; final: *the last page of the book. Z is the last letter of the alphabet; A is the first.* **2** after all others; at the end; finally: *He came last in the line.* **3** latest: *When did you see her last?* **4** most unlikely: *Fighting is the last thing I would do.* **5** person or thing that comes after all others: *He was the last in the line.* **6** end: *You have not heard the last of this.* 1,4 *adj.,* 2,3 *adv.,* 5,6 *n.*

at last, at the end; after a long time; finally: *At last the baby fell asleep.*

breathe one's last, die.

last[2] (last), **1** go on; hold out; continue to be; endure: *The storm lasted three days. Can you last through the race? How long will our money last?* **2** continue in good condition, force, etc.: *I hope these shoes last a year. v.*

last[3] (last), block shaped like a person's foot, on which shoes and boots are formed or repaired. *n.*

last ing (las′ting), existing for a long time; permanent: *Their thrilling experiences during the long voyage had a lasting effect on them. adj.* —**last′ing ly,** *adv.*

last ly (last′lē), in conclusion; finally: *Lastly, I want to thank all of you for your help. adv.*

last-min ute (last′min′it), at the latest possible time; just before it is too late: *last-minute shoppers. adj.*

last quarter, 1 period of time between the second half moon and the new moon. **2** phase of the moon represented by the half moon after the full moon.

last straw, last of a series of troublesome things that finally causes a collapse, outburst, etc.

Last Supper, supper of Jesus and His disciples on the evening before He was crucified; Lord's Supper.

last word, 1 last thing said. **2** authority to make the final decision. **3** INFORMAL. the latest thing. **4** INFORMAL. thing that cannot be improved.

Las Ve gas (läs vā′gəs), city in SE Nevada. [*Las Vegas* comes from Spanish *las vegas,* meaning "the meadows." The site was called this because it originally consisted of fertile meadows.]

lat., latitude.

Lat., Latin.

latch (lach), **1** a catch for fastening a door, gate, or window, often one not needing a key. A latch consists of a movable piece of metal or wood that fits into a notch or opening. **2** fasten with a latch: *Latch and bar the door.* 1 *n., pl.* **latch es;** 2 *v.*

latch key (lach′kē′), key used to draw back or unfasten the latch on a door. *n., pl.* **latch keys.**

late (lāt), **1** after the usual or proper time: *We had a late dinner last night* (adj.). *He worked late* (adv.). **2** near the end: *She reached success late in life* (adj.). *It rained late in the afternoon* (adv.). **3** not long past; recent: *How much damage was done by the late storm?* **4** recently dead: *The late Mary Lee was a good citizen.* **5** gone out of or retired from office: *The late president is still working actively.* **6** recently but no longer: *Jane Smith, late of Boston.* 1-5 *adj.,* **lat er** *or* **lat ter, lat est** *or* **last;** 1,2,6 *adv.,* **lat er, lat est** *or* **last.** —**late′ness,** *n.*

of late, a short time ago; lately; recently: *I haven't seen them of late.*

late com er (lāt′kum′ər), person or group that has arrived late or recently: *The latecomers to the play missed part of the first act. n.*

lateen sails

la teen sail (la tēn′), a triangular sail held up by a long yard on a short mast.

late ly (lāt′lē), a little while ago; not long ago; recently: *He has not been looking well lately. adv.*

la tent (lāt′nt), present but not active; hidden: *The power of a seed to grow into a plant remains latent if it is not planted. adj.* —**la′tent ly,** *adv.*

lat er al (lat′ər əl), of the side; at the side; from the side; toward the side: *A lateral fin of a fish grows from its side. A lateral pass in football is thrown toward the side of the field. adj.*

lat er al ly (lat′ər ə lē), in a lateral direction; at the side; sideways. *adv.*

la tex (lā′teks), a milky liquid found in milkweed, poppies, and plants yielding rubber. It hardens in the air, and is used to make chicle, rubber, and other products. *n., pl.* **lat i ces** (lat′ə sēz′), **la tex es.**

lath (lath), **1** a thin, narrow strip of wood used with others like it to form a support for the plaster of a wall or ceiling. **2** a wire cloth or sheet metal with holes in it, used in place of laths. *n., pl.* **laths** (laᴛHz *or* laths).

lathe

lathe (lāᴛH), machine for holding pieces of wood, metal, etc., and turning them rapidly against a cutting tool which shapes them. *n.*

lath er (laᴛH′ər), **1** foam made from soap and water. **2** put lather on: *He lathers his face before shaving.* **3** form a lather: *This soap lathers well.* **4** foam formed in sweating: *the lather on a horse after a race.* 1,4 *n.,* 2,3 *v.*

lath ing (lath′ing), laths collectively. *n.*

lath work (lath′wėrk′), lathing. *n.*

Lat in (lat′n), **1** language of the ancient Romans, used in written form by scholars through the Middle Ages. It is still used in official documents of the Roman Catholic Church. **2** of Latin; in Latin: *Latin poetry, Latin grammar, a Latin scholar.* **3** member of any of the peoples whose languages came from Latin. The Italians, French, Spanish, Portuguese, and Romanians are Latins. **4** of these peoples or their languages. 1,3 *n.,* 2,4 *adj.*

Latin America, South America, Central America, Mexico, and most of the West Indies. The languages spoken in Latin America are Spanish, Portuguese, and French, all of which came from Latin.

Lat in-A mer i can (lat′n ə mer′ə kən), of or having to do with Latin America. *adj.*

Latin American, person born or living in Latin America.

La ti no (la tē′nō *or* lä tē′nō), Latin American. *n., pl.* **La ti nos,** *adj.*

lat ish (lā′tish), rather late. *adj., adv.*

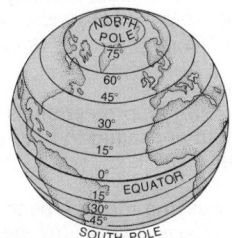

latitude (def. 1)
circles of latitude

lat i tude (lat′ə tüd *or* lat′ə tyüd), **1** distance north or south of the equator, measured in degrees. A degree of latitude is about 69 miles (111 kilometers). **2** place or region having a certain latitude: *Polar bears live in the cold latitudes.* **3** room to act or think; freedom from narrow rules; scope: *We were allowed much latitude in choosing our bedtimes. n.*

lat ter (lat′ər), **1** the second of two: *Canada and the United States are in North America; the former lies north of the latter.* **2** more recent; nearer the end; later: *Friday comes in the latter part of the week. adj.,* one of the comparative forms of **late.**

Lat ter-day Saint (lat′ər dā′), Mormon.

lat ter ly (lat′ər lē), at a recent time; lately. *adv.*

lat tice (lat′is), **1** structure of crossed wooden or metal strips with open spaces between them. **2** furnish with a lattice: *The windows are latticed with iron bars.* **3** window, gate, etc., having a lattice. **4** form into a lattice: *The cook latticed strips of dough across the pie.* 1,3 *n.,* 2,4 *v.,* **lat ticed, lat tic ing.** —**lat′tice like′,** *adj.*

lat tice work (lat′is wėrk′), **1** a lattice. **2** lattices: *Many old New Orleans houses are decorated with lattice work of wrought iron. n.*

Lat vi a (lat′vē ə), Soviet republic in N Europe, on the Baltic Sea. *Capital:* Riga. *n.* —**Lat′vi an,** *adj., n.*

laud (lôd), praise highly; commend: *Our teacher lauded our efforts to raise money for the new library. v.* —**laud′er,** *n.*

laud a ble (lô′də bəl), deserving praise; commendable: *Her desire to help her mother in the store is laudable. adj.* —**laud′a ble ness,** *n.* —**laud′a bly,** *adv.*

lau da num (lôd′n əm), solution of opium in alcohol, used to lessen pain. *n.*

laud a to ry (lô′də tôr′ē), expressing praise; extolling. *adj.*

laugh (laf), **1** make the sounds and movements of the face and body that show one is happy or amused: *We all laughed at the joke.* **2** act or sound of laughing: *a hearty laugh.* **3** drive, put, bring, etc., by or with laughing: *The children laughed their tears away.* 1,3 *v.,* 2 *n.* —**laugh′er,** *n.*

have the last laugh, get the better of (someone) after appearing to lose: *In the race between the hare and the tortoise, the tortoise had the last laugh.*

laugh at, make fun of; ridicule: *They laughed at me for believing in ghosts.*

laugh a ble (laf′ə bəl), causing laughter; amusing; funny: *a laughable mistake. adj.* —**laugh′a ble ness,** *n.* —**laugh′a bly,** *adv.*

laugh ing (laf′ing). **no laughing matter,** matter that is serious. *adj.*

laughing gas, nitrous oxide.

laughing jackass, kookaburra.

laugh ing stock (laf′ing stok′), person or thing that is made fun of. *n.*

laugh ter (laf′tər), **1** sound of laughing: *Laughter filled the room.* **2** action of laughing: *The clown's antics brought forth laughter from the children. n.*

launch[1] (lônch), **1** cause to slide into the water; set afloat: *The new ship was launched from the supports on which it was built.* **2** push out or put forth into the air: *launch a plane from an aircraft carrier. The satellite was launched in a rocket.* **3** act of launching a rocket, missile, aircraft, ship, etc.: *The launch of the first space vehicle was a historic event.* **4** set going; set out; start: *Our friends launched us in business by lending us money. The traveler launched into a long description of her voyage.* **5** send out; throw; hurl: *He used a slingshot to launch pebbles into the air. I launched a wild challenge at my opponent.* **6** burst; plunge: *The rebels launched into a violent attack on their government.* 1,2,4-6 *v.,* 3 *n., pl.* **launch es.** [*Launch*[1] came into English about 600 years ago from French *lanchier,* meaning "to throw a lance," and can be traced back to Latin *lancea,* meaning "a lance."] —**launch′a ble,** *adj.* —**launch′er,** *n.*

launch[2] (lônch), **1** an open motorboat used for pleasure trips, for ferrying passengers, etc. **2** the largest boat carried by a warship. *n., pl.* **launch es.** [*Launch*[2] comes from Spanish and Portuguese *lancha,* meaning "a kind of long boat," and can be traced back to Malay *lanchār,* meaning "fast."]

launch pad, launching pad.

launching pad

launching pad, surface or platform on which a rocket or missile is prepared for launching and from which it is launched.

laun der (lôn′dər), **1** wash and iron (clothes, tablecloths, towels, etc.). **2** be able to be washed; stand washing: *Cotton materials usually launder well. v.* [*Launder* comes from Middle English *lander,* meaning "one who washes," and can be traced back to Latin *lavare,* meaning "to wash."] —**laun′der a ble,** *adj.* —**laun′der er,** *n.*

laun dress (lôn′dris), woman whose work is washing and ironing clothes, tablecloths, towels, etc. *n., pl.* **laun dress es.**

Laun dro mat (lôn′drə mat), trademark for a self-service laundry consisting of coin-operated washing machines and dryers. *n.*

laun dry (lôn′drē), **1** room or building where clothes, tablecloths, towels, etc., are washed and ironed. **2** clothes, tablecloths, towels, etc., washed or to be washed. *n., pl.* **laun dries.**

laun dry man (lôn′drē mən), person who works in or for a laundry: *Our laundryman collects and delivers our laundry every Monday. n., pl.* **laun dry men.**

lau re ate (lôr′ē it), poet laureate. *n.*

laurel (def. 2)

lau rel (lôr′əl), **1** a small evergreen tree of southern Europe, with smooth, shiny leaves; bay. **2** its leaves. The ancient Greeks and Romans made wreaths of laurel to put on the heads of persons they wished to honor. **3** any tree or shrub related to the laurel. **4** mountain laurel. **5 laurels**, *pl.* **a** high honor; fame. **b** victory. *n.*

look to one's laurels, guard one's reputation or record from rivals: *You will have to look to your laurels unless you study harder.*

rest on one's laurels, be satisfied with the honors that one has already won or the achievements one has already attained: *Instead of resting on her laurels, she went on to further success.*

la va (lä′və *or* lav′ə), **1** hot, melted rock flowing from a volcano. **2** rock formed by the cooling of this melted rock. Some lavas are hard and glassy; others are light and porous. *n.* [*Lava* was borrowed from Italian *lava,* and can be traced back to Latin *labi,* meaning "to fall, slide."]

lava bed, layer or surface of lava.

lava field, a large area of cooled lava.

lav a to ry (lav′ə tôr′ē), **1** bowl or basin to wash in. **2** bathroom; toilet. *n., pl.* **lav a to ries.**

lave (lāv), OLD USE. **1** wash, bathe. **2** wash or flow against. *v.,* **laved, lav ing.**

lav en der (lav′ən dər), **1** pale-purple. **2** a pale purple. **3** a small shrub with spikes of fragrant, pale-purple flowers, yielding an oil much used in perfumes. **4** its dried flowers, leaves, and stalks, used to perfume or preserve linens or clothes. **1** *adj.,* **2-4** *n.*

la ver (lā′vər), OLD USE. bowl to wash in. *n.*

lav ish (lav′ish), **1** very free in giving or spending; extravagant: *A very rich person can be lavish with money.* **2** very abundant; more than is needed: *a lavish helping of dessert.* **3** give or spend very freely or too freely: *We lavished kindness on our sick friend.* **1,2** *adj.,* **3** *v.* —**lav′ish er,** *n.* —**lav′ish ly,** *adv.* —**lav′ish ment,** *n.* —**lav′ish ness,** *n.*

law (lô), **1** rule or regulation made by a country, state, etc., for all the people who live there: *a traffic law. Good citizens obey the laws.* **2** system of such rules formed to protect society: *English law is different from French law.* **3** the study of such a system of rules; the profession of a lawyer: *My cousin is planning a career in law.* **4** controlling influence of these rules: *The police maintain law and*

order. **5** system of enforcement of the rules: *courts of law.* **6** all the rules concerned with a particular subject: *commercial law, criminal law.* **7** any rule that must be obeyed: *the laws of hospitality.* **8** statement of what always occurs under certain conditions: *the law of gravitation. Scientists study the laws of nature.* **9 the Law,** the first five books of the Old Testament, containing the Mosaic law. *n.*

lay down the law, 1 give orders that must be obeyed: *There is no official to lay down the law on this question.* **2** give a scolding: *The teacher laid down the law to the noisy class.*

read law, study to be a lawyer.

take the law into one's own hands, protect one's rights or punish a crime without appealing to courts of law: *In the early days of the American West, settlers often took the law into their own hands.*

law-a bid ing (lô′ə bī′ding), obeying the law; peaceful and orderly: *As a law-abiding citizen, I don't litter. adj.*

law break er (lô′brā′kər), person who breaks the law. *n.*

law court, court of law.

law ful (lô′fəl), **1** according to law; done as the law directs: *lawful arrest.* **2** allowed by law; rightful: *lawful demands. adj.* —**law′ful ly,** *adv.* —**law′ful ness,** *n.*

law giv er (lô′giv′ər), person who prepares and puts into effect a system of laws for a people. *n.*

law less (lô′lis), **1** paying no attention to the law; breaking the law: *A thief leads a lawless life.* **2** having no laws: *In pioneer days much of the American West was lawless.* **3** hard to control; disorderly; unruly: *a wild and lawless sea. adj.* —**law′less ly,** *adv.* —**law′less ness,** *n.*

law mak er (lô′mā′kər), person who helps make the laws of a country; member of a legislature, congress, or parliament; legislator. *n.*

law mak ing (lô′mā′king), **1** having the duty and power of making laws; legislative: *Congress is a lawmaking body.* **2** the making of laws; legislation. **1** *adj.,* **2** *n.*

law man (lô′mən), a law enforcement officer. *n., pl.* **law men.**

lawn[1] (lôn), piece of land covered with grass kept closely cut, especially near or around a house. *n.*

lawn[2] (lôn), a kind of thin, sheer linen or cotton cloth. *n.*

lawn bowling, game played on a lawn by rolling a ball as close as possible to a smaller ball at the other end of the lawn.

lawn mower, machine with revolving blades for cutting the grass on a lawn.

lawn tennis, tennis, especially when played on a grass court.

law ren ci um (lô ren′sē əm), a short-lived radioactive element produced artificially from californium. *n.*

law suit (lô′süt′), case in a court of law started by one person to claim something from another; claim brought before a court of law to obtain justice. *n.*

law yer (lô′yər), person whose profession is giving advice about the laws or acting for others in a court of law. *n.*

lax (laks), **1** not tight or firm; slack: *The package was tied so loosely that the cord was lax.* **2** not strict; careless: *Don't become lax about the schedule for doing your homework.* **3** not exact; vague. *adj.* —**lax′ly,** *adv.* —**lax′ness,** *n.*

lax a tive (lak′sə tiv), **1** a medicine that makes the bowels move. **2** making the bowels move. **1** *n.,* **2** *adj.* —**lax′a tive ly,** *adv.* —**lax′a tive ness,** *n.*

lax i ty (lak′sə tē), lax condition or quality. *n.*

lay[1] (lā), **1** place in a certain position; put down: *Lay your hat on the table.* **2** bring down; beat down: *A storm laid the crops low.* **3** place in a lying-down position: *Lay the baby down gently.* **4** place or set: *Lay your hand on* *your heart. The British laid a tax on tea. The scene of this story is laid in New York.* **5** put: *Lay aside that book for me. The horse laid its ears back.* **6** put in place: *lay bricks. They laid the carpet on the floor.* **7** put into a certain state or condition: *lay a wound open.* **8** put down as a bet; offer as a bet; wager: *I lay five dollars that she won't come.* **9** make quiet or make disappear: *lay a ghost.* **10** blame; attribute: *I laid my failure on my lack of effort.* **11** give forth; produce (an egg or eggs): *Birds, fish, and reptiles lay eggs. All the hens were laying well.* **12** apply oneself vigorously: *The rowers laid to their oars. v.,* **laid, lay ing.**

lay about, hit out on all sides: *Attacked by thieves, the merchant laid about with his walking stick.*

lay aside, lay away, or **lay by,** put away for future use; save: *I laid away a dollar a week to buy a new bicycle.*

lay down, 1 declare; state: *The umpire laid down the conditions for settling the dispute.* **2** give; sacrifice: *lay down one's life for the cause of liberty.*

lay for, stay hidden ready to attack.

lay in, put aside for the future; provide: *The trapper laid in enough supplies for the winter.*

lay into, 1 beat; thrash: *She laid into the vicious dog with a stick.* **2** INFORMAL. scold: *My parents laid into me for not doing my homework.*

lay off, 1 put out of work for a time: *During the slack season many workers were laid off.* **2** mark off: *The coach laid off the boundaries of the tennis court.* **3** INFORMAL. stop teasing or interfering with: *Lay off me! I'm trying to study.*

lay of the land, 1 the nature of the place; the position of hills, water, woods, etc. **2** situation; circumstances.

lay oneself out, make a big effort; take great pains: *He laid himself out to be agreeable.*

lay open, 1 make bare; expose: *The captured spy laid open to us the whole scheme of the attack.* **2** make an opening in; wound.

lay out, 1 spread out: *Supper was laid out on the table.* **2** arrange; plan: *The road was laid out but not yet paved.* **3** pay out; spend: *I had to lay out a lot of money for my new bicycle.* **4** prepare (a dead body) for burial.

lay over, stop for a time in a place: *It was raining so hard one day on our trip that we laid over until the rain stopped.*

lay to, head into the wind and stand still: *The ship lay to until the fog lifted.*

lay up, 1 put away for future use: *After the sailing season was over we laid our boat up for the winter.* **2** cause to stay in bed or indoors because of illness: *I was laid up with a bad cold last week.*

lay² (lā), past tense of **lie².** *I took a long walk and then lay down for a rest. v.*

lay³ (lā), **1** of the people of a church not belonging to the clergy. A lay sermon is one given by a person who is not a clergyman. **2** of the people who do not belong to a particular profession: *I am not a doctor, but my lay opinion is that you have the flu. adj.*

lay⁴ (lā), **1** poem to be sung, especially one that tells a story or legend in simple verse form. **2** song; tune. *n.*

lay er (lā′ər), **1** one thickness or fold: *the layer of clothing next to the skin, a layer of clay between two layers of sand.* **2** person or thing that lays: *a pipe layer. That hen is a champion layer.* **3** branch of a plant bent down and partly covered by earth so that it will take root. **4** spread by layers. **5** form (new plants) by layers. 1-3 *n.,* 4,5 *v.*

layer cake, cake made in layers put together with frosting or filling.

lay ette (lā et′), set of clothes and bedding for a newborn baby. *n.*

lay man (lā′mən), **1** member of a church who is not a

clergyman: *The priest and several laymen planned the church budget.* **2** person who is not a member of a particular profession: *It is hard for most laymen to understand doctors' prescriptions. n., pl.* **lay men.**

lay off (lā′ôf′), **1** a dismissing of workers temporarily. **2** time during which the workers are out of work. *n.*

lay out (lā′out′), **1** arrangement; plan: *This map shows the layout of the camp.* **2** a plan or design for an advertisement, book, etc. **3** thing laid or spread out; display. *n.*

lay o ver (lā′ō′vər), a stopping for a time in a place: *After a twenty-minute layover in Chicago we flew on to Los Angeles. n.*

Laz ar us (laz′ər əs), **1** (in the Bible) the brother of Mary and Martha, whom Jesus raised from the dead. **2 Emma,** 1849-1887, American poet. *n.*

laze (lāz), be lazy or idle. *v.,* **lazed, laz ing.**

la zi ly (lā′zə lē), in a lazy manner. *adv.*

la zi ness (lā′zē nis), dislike of work; unwillingness to work or be active; being lazy. *n.*

la zy (lā′zē), **1** not willing to work or be active: *He lost his job because he was lazy.* **2** moving slowly; not very active: *A lazy stream winds through the meadow. adj.,* **la zi er, la zi est.**

la zy bones (lā′zē bōnz′), INFORMAL. a very lazy person. *n.*

lb., pound. *pl.* **lb.** or **lbs.** [The abbreviation *lb.* stands for the Latin word *libra.* This was the word for the ancient Roman pound of twelve ounces. It originally meant "a balance, weight."]

l.c., lower case.

Ld., 1 limited. **2** lord.

lea (lē), a grassy field; meadow. *n.*

leach (lēch), **1** run water through slowly; filter. **2** dissolve out by running water through slowly: *Potash is leached from wood ashes and used to make soap.* **3** lose soluble parts when water passes through. *v.* —**leach′a ble,** *adj.* —**leach′er,** *n.*

lead¹ (lēd), **1** show the way by going along with or in front of: *She led the horses to water.* **2** be first among: *She leads the class in spelling.* **3** guidance or direction; leadership: *The scientists followed the lead of the director of the expedition.* **4** guide or direct in action, policy, opinion, etc.; influence; persuade: *Such actions lead us to distrust them.* **5** be a way or road: *Hard work leads to success.* **6** pass or spend (time) in some special way: *He leads a quiet life in the country.* **7** go first; begin a game or other activity: *You may lead this time.* **8** be chief of; command; direct: *A general leads an army. She leads the community orchestra. I led the singing.* **9** place of leader; place in front: *She always takes the lead when we plan to do anything.* **10** right to go or begin first: *It is your lead this time.* **11** the principal part in a play. **12** person who plays this part. **13** amount that one is ahead: *I had a narrow lead in the race.* **14** a guiding indication: *He was not sure where to look for the information, but the librarian gave him several good leads.* **15** the opening paragraph in a newspaper or magazine article. A lead often summarizes the information in the body of the article. 1,2,4-8 *v.,* **led, lead ing;** 3,9-15 *n.*

lead off, begin; start.

lead on, mislead.

lead up to, prepare the way for.

a hat	**i** it	**oi** oil	**ch** child	a in about	
ā age	**ī** ice	**ou** out	**ng** long	e in taken	
ä far	**o** hot	**u** cup	**sh** she	ə = i in pencil	
e let	**ō** open	**u̇** put	**th** thin	o in lemon	
ē equal	**ô** order	**ü** rule	**ᵀʜ** then	u in circus	
ėr term			**zh** measure		

lead² (led), **1** a soft, heavy, bluish-gray metallic element which is used to make pipe, radiation shields, etc. **2** made of lead: *a lead pipe.* **3** bullets; shot: *a hail of lead.* **4** a long, thin piece of graphite used in pencils. **5** weight on a line used to find out the depth of water; plumb. **6** to cover, frame, or weight with lead. 1,3-5 *n.,* 2 *adj.,* 6 *v.*

lead en (led′n), **1** made of lead: *a leaden coffin.* **2** hard to lift or move; heavy: *leaden arms tired from working.* **3** dull; gloomy. **4** bluish-gray: *Do you suppose those leaden clouds may mean snow? adj.* —**lead′en ly,** *adv.* —**lead′en ness,** *n.*

lead er (lē′dər), person who leads, or is well fitted to lead: *an orchestra leader. That girl is a born leader. n.* —**lead′er less,** *adj.*

lead er ship (lē′dər ship), **1** condition of being a leader. **2** ability to lead: *Leadership is a great asset to an officer.* **3** guidance or direction: *Our group needs some leadership. n.*

lead ing (lē′ding), **1** showing the way; guiding; directing: *to ask someone a leading question.* **2** most important; chief; principal: *She has the leading role in the play. adj.*

lead off (led′ôf′ *or* led′of′), **1** act of beginning or starting something. **2** (in baseball) the first player of the batting order or the first to come to bat in any inning. **3** beginning or leading off. 1,2 *n.,* 3 *adj.*

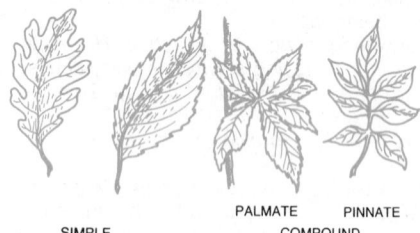

SIMPLE PALMATE PINNATE COMPOUND

leaf (def. 1)—several types of leaves

leaf (lēf), **1** one of the thin, usually flat, green parts of a tree or other plant that grow on the stem or grow up from the roots. **2** put forth leaves: *The trees along the river leaf earlier than those on the hill.* **3** sheet of paper. Each side of a leaf is called a page. **4** turn the pages: *to leaf through a book.* **5** a very thin sheet of metal, etc.: *gold leaf.* **6** a flat, movable piece in the top of a table: *We put two extra leaves in the table for the party.* 1,3,5,6 *n.,* pl. **leaves;** 2,4 *v.* —**leaf′like′,** *adj.*

turn over a new leaf, start all over again; try to do or be better in the future: *I promised to turn over a new leaf and study harder.*

leaf age (lē′fij), leaves; foliage. *n.*

leaf less (lēf′lis), having no leaves. *adj.* —**leaf′less ness,** *n.*

leaf let (lēf′lit), **1** a small, flat or folded sheet of printed matter: *advertising leaflets.* **2** a small or young leaf. **3** one of the separate blades or divisions of a compound leaf. *n.*

leaf y (lē′fē), **1** having many leaves; covered with leaves. **2** resembling a leaf. *adj.,* **leaf i er, leaf i est.** —**leaf′i ness,** *n.*

league¹ (lēg), **1** a union of persons, parties, or nations formed to help one another. **2** unite in a league; form a union. **3** association of sports clubs or teams: *a baseball league.* 1,3 *n.,* 2 *v.,* **leagued, lea guing.** [*League¹* came into English about 500 years ago from French *ligue,* and can be traced back to Latin *ligare,* meaning "to bind, tie."]

in league, associated by agreement; allied.

league² (lēg), an old unit for measuring length or distance, usually about 3 miles (5 kilometers). *n.* [*League²* is from Middle English *leuge,* which came from Latin *leuga.*]

League of Nations, organization intended to promote cooperation among nations and to maintain peace. It was established in 1920 and disbanded in 1946.

lea guer (lē′gər), member of a league. *n.*

leak (lēk), **1** hole or crack not meant to be there that lets something in or out: *a leak in the roof.* **2** go in or out through a hole or crack, or in ways suggesting a hole or crack: *The gas leaked out.* **3** let something in or out which is meant to stay where it is: *My boat leaks and lets water in. That pipe leaks gas.* **4** leakage: *a leak of water, a leak of information.* **5** become known gradually: *The secret leaked out.* 1,4 *n.,* 2,3,5 *v.* —**leak′er,** *n.* —**leak′less,** *adj.*

leak age (lē′kij), **1** a leaking; entrance or escape by a leak. **2** that which leaks in or out. **3** amount of leaking: *a leakage of a pailful an hour. n.*

Lea key (lē′kē), **1 Louis,** 1903-1972, British anthropologist and paleontologist, born in Kenya. **2 Mary Nicol,** born 1913, British anthropologist, wife of Louis Leakey. *n.*

leak i ness (lē′kē nis), leaky condition. *n.*

leak y (lē′kē), having a leak or leaks; leaking. *adj.,* **leak i er, leak i est.**

leal (lēl), SCOTTISH. loyal. *adj.*

lean¹ (lēn), **1** stand slanting, not upright; bend: *The small tree leans over in the wind.* **2** rest the body sloping or slanting against something for support: *Lean against me.* **3** set or put in a leaning position: *Lean the ladder against the wall.* **4** act of leaning; inclination. **5** depend; rely: *lean on a friend's advice.* **6** be inclined; bend: *lean toward the candidate running for reelection.* 1-3,5,6 *v.,* **leaned** or **leant, lean ing;** 4 *n.*

lean² (lēn), **1** not fat; thin: *a lean and hungry stray dog.* **2** meat having little fat. **3** producing little; scant: *a lean harvest, a lean year for business.* 1,3 *adj.,* 2 *n.* —**lean′ness,** *n.*

lean ing (lē′ning), tendency; inclination. *n.*

leant (lent), leaned; a past tense and a past participle of **lean¹.** *v.*

lean-to (lēn′tü′), **1** a small building attached to another, with a roof sloping downward from the side of the larger building. **2** having supports or a roof so arranged: *a lean-to shed.* **3** a crude shelter built against a tree or post. It is usually open on one side. 1,3 *n.,* pl. **lean-tos;** 2 *adj.*

leap (lēp), **1** a jump or spring. **2** thing to be jumped. **3** distance covered by a jump. **4** to jump: *That frog leaps very high.* **5** to jump over: *He leaped the wall.* **6** cause to leap: *She leaped her horse over fences and ditches.* **7** pass, come, rise, etc., as if with a leap or bound: *An idea leaped to her mind.* 1-3 *n.,* 4-7 *v.,* **leaped** or **leapt, leap ing.** —**leap′er,** *n.*

leap frog (lēp′frog′), **1** game in which players take turns jumping over another player who is bending over. **2** jump (over) as in this game. 1 *n.,* 2 *v.,* **leap frogged, leap frog ging.** —**leap′frog′ger,** *n.*

leapt (lept *or* lēpt), leaped; a past tense and a past participle of **leap.** *v.*

leap year, year having 366 days. The extra day is February 29. A year is a leap year if its number can be divided exactly by four, except years at the end of a century, which must be exactly divisible by 400. The years 1980 and 2000 are leap years; 1981 and 1900 are not.

learn (lėrn), **1** gain knowledge or skill: *Some children learn slowly.* **2** memorize: *learn a poem by heart.* **3** find out; come to know: *He learned that ¹/₄ + ¹/₄ = ¹/₂.* **4** find out about; gain knowledge of: *She is learning science and social studies.* **5** become able by study or practice: *In school we learn to read. v.,* **learned** or **learnt, learn ing.**

learn ed (lėr′nid), having, showing, or requiring much

knowledge; scholarly: *a learned professor. adj.*
—**learn′ed ly,** *adv.* —**learn′ed ness,** *n.*

learn er (lėr′nər), **1** person who is learning. **2** beginner. *n.*

learn ing (lėr′ning), **1** the gaining of knowledge or skill. **2** possession of knowledge gained by study; scholarship: *men and women of great learning.* **3** knowledge. *n.*

learnt (lėrnt), learned; a past tense and a past participle of **learn.** *v.*

lease (lēs), **1** the right to use property for a certain length of time by paying rent for it. **2** a written statement saying for how long a certain property is rented and how much money shall be paid for it. **3** the property held by a lease. **4** length of time for which a lease is made. **5** give a lease on. **6** to rent: *We have leased an apartment for one year.* 1-4 *n.,* 5,6 *v.,* **leased, leas ing.** [*Lease* came into English about 500 years ago from French *les,* which comes from *lesser,* meaning "to let, let loose," and can be traced back to Latin *laxus,* meaning "loose."]
—**leas′a ble,** *adj.* —**leas′er,** *n.*

leash (lēsh), **1** a strap or chain for holding an animal in check: *He led the dog on a leash.* **2** fasten or hold in with a leash; control: *He leashed his anger and did not say a harsh word.* 1 *n., pl.* **leash es;** 2 *v.*
hold in leash, control.

least (lēst), **1** less than any other; smallest; slightest: *Ten cents is a little money; five cents is less; one cent is least.* **2** smallest amount; smallest thing: *The least you can do is to thank them.* **3** to the smallest extent, amount, or degree: *She liked that book least of all.* 1 *adj.,* 2 *n.,* 3 *adv.*
at least or **at the least, 1** at the lowest estimate: *The temperature was at least 95 degrees yesterday.* **2** at any rate; in any case: *He may have been late, but at least he came.*
not in the least, not at all.

least ways (lēst′wāz′), INFORMAL. leastwise. *adv.*
least wise (lēst′wīz′), INFORMAL. at least; at any rate. *adv.*

leath er (leṪH′ər), **1** material made from the skins of animals by removing the hair and then tanning them: *Shoes are usually made of leather.* **2** made of leather: *leather gloves.* 1 *n.,* 2 *adj.*

Leath er ette (leṪH′ə ret′), trademark for imitation leather, made of plastic, paper, or cloth. *n.*
leath ern (leṪH′ərn), made of leather. *adj.*
leath er y (leṪH′ər ē), like leather; tough: *leathery skin. adj.*

leave[1] (lēv), **1** go away: *We leave tonight.* **2** go away from: *They left the room. He has left his home and friends and is living in San Francisco.* **3** stop living in, belonging to, or working at or for: *leave the country, leave one's job.* **4** go without taking; let stay behind: *I left a book on the table.* **5** let stay (in a certain condition): *leave the dishes unwashed. I was left alone as before. The story left him unmoved.* **6** let alone: *The potatoes must be left to boil for half an hour.* **7** give (to family, friends, charity) when one dies: *She left a fortune to her children.* **8** give or hand over (to someone else) to do: *I left the driving to my sister.* **9** not attend to: *I shall leave my homework until tomorrow. v.,* **left, leav ing.** —**leav′er,** *n.*
leave off, stop: *Continue the story from where I left off.*
leave out, not do, say, or put in; omit: *She left out two words when she read the sentence.*

leave[2] (lēv), **1** permission; consent: *They gave him leave to go.* **2** permission to be absent from duty. A **leave of absence** is an official permission to be absent from one's work, school, or military duty. **3** length of time for which one has a leave of absence: *Our annual leave is thirty days. n.*
on leave, absent with permission.
take leave of, say good-by to.

leave[3] (lēv), put forth leaves; leaf: *Trees leave in the spring. v.,* **leaved, leav ing.**

leav en (lev′ən), **1** any substance, such as yeast, that will cause fermentation and raise dough. **2** raise with a substance that causes fermentation; make (dough) light or lighter. **3** an influence which, spreading silently and strongly, changes conditions or opinions. **4** spread through and transform. 1,3 *n.,* 2,4 *v.* [*Leaven* came into English over 600 years ago from French *levain,* and can be traced back to Latin *levis,* meaning "light in weight." See **Word Family.**] —**leav′en less,** *adj.*

WORD FAMILY

leaven

Below are words related to *leaven.* They can all be traced back to the Latin word *levis* (le′wis), meaning "light in weight."

alleviate	legerdemain	levity
carnival	levee	levy
elevate	lever	relief

leav en ing (lev′ə ning), thing that leavens. *n.*
leaves (lēvz), plural of **leaf.** *n.*
leave-tak ing (lēv′tā′king), act of taking leave; saying good-by. *n.*
leav ings (lē′vingz), things left; leftovers; remnants. *n.pl.*
Leb a nese (leb′ə nēz′), **1** of Lebanon or its people. **2** person born or living in Lebanon. 1 *adj.,* 2 *n., pl.* **Leb a nese.**
Leb a non (leb′ə nən), country in the Middle East, at the E end of the Mediterranean. *Capital:* Beirut. *n.*
lech er ous (lech′ər əs), full of lust; lewd. *adj.* —**lech′er ous ly,** *adv.* —**lech′er ous ness,** *n.*
lech er y (lech′ər ē), lustful behavior; lewdness. *n.*
lec i thin (les′ə thən), a fatty substance found in plant and animal tissues. Lecithin is extracted from egg yolk, soybeans, and corn. It is used in candy, drugs, paints, etc. *n.*
lec tern (lek′tərn), **1** a reading desk in a church, especially the desk from which the lessons are read at daily prayer. **2** a reading desk or stand. *n.*

lectern (def. 2)

lec ture (lek′chər), **1** a planned talk on a chosen subject; such a talk written down or printed; speech. **2** give a lecture: *The explorer lectured on life in the Arctic.* **3** a scolding: *My parents give me a lecture when I come home late.* **4** scold; reprove. 1,3 *n.*, 2,4 *v.*, **lec tured, lec tur ing.**

lec tur er (lek′chər ər), person who lectures. *n.*

led (led), past tense and past participle of **lead**[1]. *She led her younger brother across the street. We were led through the cave by an experienced guide. v.*

ledge (lej), **1** a narrow shelf: *a window ledge.* **2** shelf or ridge of rock. *n.*

ledg er (lej′ər), book of accounts in which a business keeps a record of all money transactions. *n.*

lee (lē), **1** a shelter. **2** side or part sheltered or away from the wind: *The wind was so fierce that we ran to the lee of the house.* **3** sheltered from the wind: *the lee side of a ship.* 1,2 *n.*, 3 *adj.*

Lee (lē), **Robert E.**, 1807-1870, Confederate general in the Civil War. Lee surrendered to Grant at Appomattox on April 9, 1865. *n.*

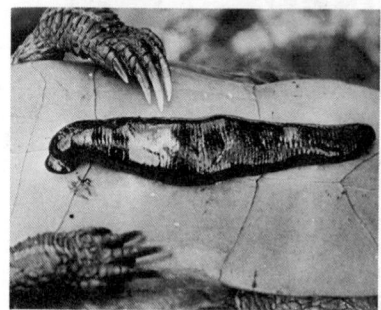

leech (def. 1)—clinging to the underside of a turtle

leech (lēch), **1** worm living in freshwater ponds and streams that sucks the blood of animals. Doctors used to use leeches to suck blood from sick people. **2** person who tries persistently to get money and favors from others, without doing anything to earn them; parasite. *n.*, *pl.* **leech es.**

Leeds (lēdz), city in N England. *n.*

leek (lēk), vegetable somewhat like an onion, but with larger leaves, a smaller bulb shaped like a cylinder, and a milder flavor. *n.*

leer (lir), **1** a sly, nasty look to the side; evil glance. **2** give a sly, evil glance. 1 *n.*, 2 *v.* —**leer′ing ly**, *adv.*

leer y (lir′ē), INFORMAL. suspicious; wary: *We are leery of his advice. adj.*, **leer i er, leer i est.** —**leer′i ly**, *adv.* —**leer′i ness**, *n.*

lees (lēz), dregs; sediment. *n.pl.*

Leeu wen hoek (lā′vən hùk), **Anton van**, 1632-1723, Dutch scientist who was the first to study blood cells and tiny organisms through magnifying lenses. *n.*

lee ward (lē′wərd *or* lü′ərd), **1** on the side away from the wind. **2** the side away from the wind; lee. **3** in the direction toward which the wind is blowing. 1,3 *adj.*, *adv.*, 2 *n.*

Lee ward Islands (lē′wərd), the N part of the Lesser Antilles in the West Indies.

lee way (lē′wā′), **1** the sideways movement of a ship to leeward, out of its course. **2** extra space at the side; more (time, money, etc.) than needed; margin of safety: *By leaving 20 minutes early, I allowed myself a good deal of leeway. n.*

left[1] (left), **1** belonging to the side of the less used hand (in most people); of the side that is turned west when

the main side is turned north: *the left hand.* **2** on this side when viewed from in front: *Take a left turn at the next light.* **3** on or to the left side: *Turn left.* **4** the left side or hand: *I sat at her left.* **5** part of a lawmaking body consisting of the more liberal or radical groups. **6** having liberal or radical ideas in politics. 1,2,6 *adj.*, 3 *adv.*, 4,5 *n.* [*Left*[1] comes from Old English *lyft*, meaning "weak." It came to have this meaning because the left hand is weaker than the right hand in most people.]

left[2] (left), past tense and past participle of **leave**[1]. *I left my hat in the hall. Milk is left at our door. v.*

left field, (in baseball) the section of the outfield beyond third base.

left-hand (left′hand′), **1** on or to the left. **2** of, for, or with the left hand. *adj.*

left-hand ed (left′han′did), **1** using the left hand more easily and readily than the right. **2** done with the left hand. **3** made to be used with the left hand. **4** turning from right to left: *a left-handed screw.* **5** doubtful or insincere: *a left-handed compliment.* **6** toward the left; with the left hand. 1-5 *adj.*, 6 *adv.* —**left′-hand′ed ly**, *adv.*

left ist (lef′tist), **1** person who has liberal or radical ideas in politics. **2** member of a liberal or radical political organization. **3** having liberal or radical ideas. 1,2 *n.*, 3 *adj.*

left o ver (left′ō′vər), **1** thing that is left. Scraps of food from a meal are leftovers. **2** that is left; remaining: *I made some sandwiches with the leftover meat.* 1 *n.*, 2 *adj.*

left wing, the liberal or radical members, especially of a political party.

left-wing (left′wing′), belonging to or like the left wing. *adj.* —**left-wing er** (left′wing′ər), *n.*

left y (lef′tē), INFORMAL. a left-handed person. *n.*, *pl.* **left ies.**

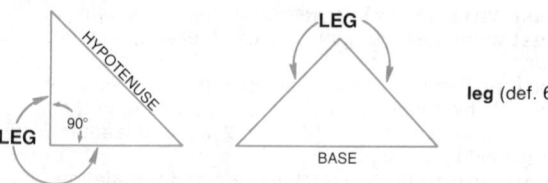

leg (def. 6)

leg (leg), **1** one of the limbs on which people and animals stand and walk. **2** part of a garment that covers a leg: *I fell and tore my pants' leg.* **3** anything shaped or used like a leg; any support that is much longer than it is wide: *a table leg.* **4** one of the parts or stages of any course: *the last leg of a trip.* **5** INFORMAL. walk or run: *We could not get a ride, so we had to leg it.* **6** either of the two sides of a right triangle that is not the hypotenuse. 1-4,6 *n.*, 5 *v.*, **legged, leg ging.** —**leg′like′**, *adj.*

on one's last legs, about to fail, collapse, or die.

pull one's leg, INFORMAL. fool, trick, or make fun of one.

shake a leg, hurry up.

leg., 1 legal. **2** legislative.

leg a cy (leg′ə sē), **1** money or other property left to a person by the will of someone who has died. **2** something that has been handed down from an ancestor or predecessor. *n.*, *pl.* **leg a cies.** [*Legacy* comes from a medieval Latin word *legatia*, and can be traced back to Latin *legem*, meaning "law."]

le gal (lē′gəl), **1** of law: *legal knowledge.* **2** of lawyers: *legal advice.* **3** according to law; lawful: *Hunting is legal only during certain seasons. adj.*

le gal i ty (li gal′ə tē), accordance with law; lawfulness. *n.*, *pl.* **le gal i ties.**

le gal i za tion (lē′gə lə zā′shən), act of legalizing. *n.*

le gal ize (lē′gə līz), make legal; authorize by law; sanction. *v.*, **le gal ized, le gal iz ing.**

le gal ly (lē′gə lē), **1** in a legal manner. **2** according to law: *They are legally responsible for their child's debts. adv.*

legal tender, money that must, by law, be accepted in payment of debts.

leg ate (leg′it), ambassador or representative, especially a representative of the pope. *n.*

leg a tee (leg′ə tē′), person to whom a legacy is left. *n.*

le ga tion (li gā′shən), **1** the diplomatic representative of a country and his or her staff of assistants. A legation ranks next below an embassy. **2** the official residence, offices, etc., of such a representative in a foreign country. *n.*

le ga to (li gä′tō), in music: **1** smooth and connected; without breaks between successive tones. **2** in a smooth and connected manner. **1** *adj.,* **2** *adv.* [*Legato* is from Italian *legato,* also meaning "bound, tied," which came from Latin *ligare,* meaning "to bind, tie."]

leg end (lej′ənd), **1** story coming down from the past, which may be based on actual people and events but is not regarded as historically true: *The stories about King Arthur and his knights of the Round Table are legends.* **2** such stories as a group. **3** what is written on a coin or medal: *Read the legend on a five-cent piece.* **4** words accompanying a picture or diagram: *The legend underneath the picture identified the woman as Queen Elizabeth I. n.* [*Legend* is from a medieval Latin word *legenda,* which came from Latin *legenda,* meaning "(things) to be read," which is from *legere,* meaning "to read."]

leg end ar y (lej′ən der′ē), of a legend or legends; like a legend; not historical: *Robin Hood is a legendary person. adj.*

leg end ry (lej′ən drē), legends collectively. *n.*

leg er de main (lej′ər də mān′), **1** sleight of hand; conjuring tricks. **2** trickery. *n.* [*Legerdemain* came into English over 500 years ago from French *leger de main,* meaning "light of hand, quick of hand." French *leger* comes from Latin *levis,* and French *main* comes from Latin *manus.*]

leg gings (leg′ingz), extra outer coverings of cloth or leather for the legs, for use out of doors. *n.pl.*

leg gy (leg′ē), **1** having long legs. **2** having awkwardly long legs. *adj.,* **leg gi er, leg gi est.** —**leg′gi ness,** *n.*

leg horn (leg′hôrn *or* leg′ərn), **1** hat made of fine, smooth, plaited straw. **2 Leghorn,** a rather small, domestic fowl which produces large numbers of eggs. *n.*

leg i bil i ty (lej′ə bil′ə tē), legible condition or quality; clearness of print or writing. *n.*

leg i ble (lej′ə bəl), **1** able to be read. **2** easy to read; plain and clear: *legible handwriting. adj.* [*Legible* is from Latin *legibilis,* which comes from *legere,* meaning "to read." See **Word Family.**]

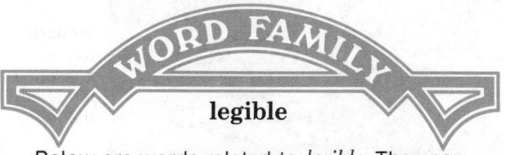

legible

Below are words related to *legible.* They can all be traced back to the Latin word *legere* (le′ge re), meaning "to read, choose, select."

coil	intellect	lesson
collect	intelligent	lignite
cull	intelligible	neglect
diligent	lecture	negligence
elect	legend	recollect
eligible	legion	sacrilege
elite	legume	select

le gion (lē′jən), **1** a division in the ancient Roman army containing several thousand foot soldiers and several hundred horsemen. **2** a large body of soldiers; army. **3** a great many; very large number: *Legions of grasshoppers destroyed the crops. n.*

le gion ar y (lē′jə ner′ē), **1** of or belonging to a legion. **2** member of a legion. **1** *adj.,* **2** *n., pl.* **le gion ar ies.**

leg is late (lej′ə slāt), **1** make laws: *Congress legislates for the United States.* **2** force or bring about by legislation: *The council legislated new standards for pollution control. v.,* **leg is lat ed, leg is lat ing.**

leg is la tion (lej′ə slā′shən), **1** the making of laws: *Congress has the power of legislation.* **2** the laws made: *Important legislation is reported in today's newspaper. n.*

leg is la tive (lej′ə slā′tiv), **1** having to do with making laws: *legislative reforms.* **2** having the duty and power of making laws: *The British Parliament is a legislative body.* **3** ordered by law or as it is by law: *a legislative decree. adj.* —**leg′is la′tive ly,** *adv.*

leg is la tor (lej′ə slā′tər), member of a legislative body; lawmaker. Senators and Representatives are legislators. *n.*

leg is la ture (lej′ə slā′chər), group of persons that has the duty and power of making laws for a state or country. Each state of the United States has a legislature. *n.*

le git (lə jit′), SLANG. legitimate. *adj.*

le git i ma cy (lə jit′ə mə sē), a being legitimate or lawful; being recognized as lawful or proper. *n.*

le git i mate (lə jit′ə mit), **1** allowed or admitted by law; rightful; lawful: *a legitimate title or right, a legitimate ruler.* **2** valid; logical; acceptable: *Sickness is a legitimate reason for being absent from school.* **3** born of parents who are married to each other. *adj.* —**le git′i mate ly,** *adv.*

le git i mize (lə jit′ə mīz), make or declare to be legitimate. *v.,* **le git i mized, le git i miz ing.**

leg less (leg′lis), having no legs; without legs. *adj.*

leg ume (leg′yüm *or* li gyüm′), plant which bears pods containing a number of seeds. Beans and peas are legumes. Legumes can absorb nitrogen from the air. *n.* [*Legume* comes from French *légume,* and can be traced back to Latin *legere,* meaning "to choose."]

le gu mi nous (li gyü′mə nəs), **1** of or bearing legumes. **2** of or belonging to the same group of plants as beans and peas. *adj.*

leg warm ers (leg′wôr′mərz), coverings for the legs, usually knitted and worn for exercise or dancing, that start at the ankles and extend to or above the knees. *n.pl.*

Le Ha vre (lə hä′vrə), seaport in N France.

lei (lā), wreath of flowers, leaves, etc., worn as an ornament around the neck or on the head. *n., pl.* **leis.**

Leip zig (līp′sig), city in S East Germany. *n.*

lei sure (lē′zhər), **1** time free from required work in which you may rest, amuse yourself, and do the things you like to do: *She's been too busy to have much leisure.* **2** free; not busy: *leisure hours.* **1** *n.,* **2** *adj.*

at one's leisure, when one has leisure; at one's convenience: *Let me hear from you at your leisure.*

lei sure ly (lē′zhər lē), without hurry; taking plenty of time: *a leisurely stroll in the park* (adj.). *He walked leisurely across the street* (adv.). *adj., adv.* —**lei′sure li ness,** *n.*

lem ming (lem′ing), a small, mouselike, arctic rodent,

having a short tail and furry feet. When food is scarce, lemmings sometimes migrate in large groups. *n.*

lem on (lem′ən), **1** a sour, light-yellow citrus fruit that grows on a thorny tree in warm climates. **2** pale-yellow. **3** a pale yellow. **4** flavored with lemon. **5** SLANG. something or someone that is worthless or unpleasant. 1,3,5 *n.*, 2,4 *adj.* [*Lemon* came into English about 600 years ago from French *limon*, and can be traced back to Persian *līmūn*.] —**lem′on like′,** *adj.*

lem on ade (lem′ə nād′), a drink made of lemon juice, sugar, and water. *n.*

le mur (lē′mər), a small mammal somewhat like a monkey, but having a foxlike face and woolly fur. Lemurs are found mainly in Madagascar. They live in trees and are active chiefly at night. *n.*

WORD HISTORY

lemur

Lemur comes from Latin *lemures*, meaning "ghosts." Lemurs were called this both because they are active at night and because the face suggests a ghost.

about 3 ft. (1 m.) long with tail

lend (lend), **1** let another have or use for a time: *Will you lend me your bicycle for an hour?* **2** give the use of (money) for a fixed or specified amount of payment: *Banks lend money and charge interest.* **3** make a loan or loans: *A person who borrows should be willing to lend.* **4** give for a time; add; contribute: *The Red Cross lends aid in time of disaster.* *v.,* **lent, lend ing.** —**lend′er,** *n.*

lend itself to or **lend oneself to,** help or be suitable for.

length (lengkth *or* length), **1** how long a thing is; what a thing measures from end to end; the longest way a thing can be measured: *the length of a room, an animal eight inches in length.* **2** how long something lasts or goes on: *the length of a visit, the length of a book.* **3** distance: *The length of this race is one kilometer.* **4** a long stretch or extent: *It's been quite a length of time since our last meeting.* **5** piece of cloth, etc., of a given length: *a length of rope.* *n.*

at full length, with the body stretched out flat: *The snake lay at full length on the rock, sunning itself.*

at length, 1 at last; finally: *At length, after many delays, the meeting started.* **2** with all the details; in full: *She told of her adventures at length.*

go to any length, do everything possible: *I will go to any length to help you.*

keep at arm's length, discourage from becoming friendly.

length en (lengk′thən *or* leng′thən), make or become longer: *A tailor can lengthen trousers. Your legs lengthen as you grow.* *v.*

length i ly (lengk′thə lē *or* leng′thə lē), in a lengthy manner. *adv.*

length i ness (lengk′thē nis *or* leng′thē nis), lengthy condition or quality. *n.*

length ways (lengkth′wāz′ *or* length′wāz′), lengthwise. *adv., adj.*

length wise (lengkth′wīz′ *or* length′wīz′), in the direction of the length: *I cut the cloth lengthwise (adv.). The tailor made a lengthwise cut (adj.).* *adv., adj.*

length y (lengk′thē *or* leng′thē), long; too long: *His directions were so lengthy that everybody lost interest. adj.,* **length i er, length i est.**

len ience (lē′nyəns), leniency. *n.*

len ien cy (lē′nyən sē), lenient quality; mildness; gentleness; mercy. *n.*

len ient (lē′nyənt), mild or gentle; not harsh or stern; merciful: *a lenient judge, a lenient punishment. adj.*

Len in (len′ən), Nikolai, 1870-1924, Russian Communist leader, the founder of the Soviet government and its first premier, from 1918 to 1924. *n.*

Len in grad (len′ən grad), seaport in NW Soviet Union, on the Gulf of Finland. It was formerly called **St. Petersburg** and later **Petrograd.** *n.*

len i ty (len′ə tē), leniency. *n., pl.* **len i ties.**

lens (lenz), **1** a curved piece of glass or other transparent material which brings closer together or sends wider apart the rays of light passing through it. The lens of a camera forms images on film. The lenses of a telescope make distant objects look larger and nearer. **2** the part of the eye that focuses light rays upon the retina. *n., pl.* **lens es.**

lent (lent), past tense and past participle of **lend.** *I lent you my pencil. He had lent me his eraser.* *v.*

Lent (lent), the forty weekdays between Ash Wednesday and Easter, observed in many Christian churches as a time for fasting and repenting of sins. *n.*

lent en or **Lent en** (len′tən), of Lent; during Lent; suitable for Lent. *adj.*

len til (len′tl), a small, flat, beanlike seed which is eaten as a vegetable. Lentils are cooked like peas and are often eaten in soup. *n.*

Le o nar do da Vin ci (lā′ə när′dō də vin′chē). See **da Vinci.**

le o nine (lē′ə nīn), of, or like a lion. *adj.*

leopard
about
8 ft. (2.5 m.)
long with
the tail

leop ard (lep′ərd), a large, fierce cat of Africa and Asia, having a dull-yellowish fur spotted with black. Some leopards are black and may be called panthers. *n.* [*Leopard* came into English about 700 years ago from French *leupart*, and can be traced back to Greek *leōn*, meaning "lion," and *pardos*, meaning "leopard, panther."]

Lé o pold ville (lē′ə pōld vil′), former name of **Kinshasa.** *n.*

leotards

a hat	**i** it	**oi** oil	**ch** child	a in about
ā age	**ī** ice	**ou** out	**ng** long	e in taken
ä far	**o** hot	**u** cup	**sh** she	ə = { i in pencil
e let	**ō** open	**ù** put	**th** thin	o in lemon
ē equal	**ô** order	**ü** rule	**ŦH** then	u in circus
ėr term			**zh** measure	

afraid lest they should come too late to save us. conj.

le o tard (lē′ə tärd). Usually, **leotards,** *pl.* a tight-fitting one-piece garment, with or without sleeves. Dancers, gymnasts, etc., wear leotards. *n.*

lep er (lep′ər), person who has leprosy. *n.*

lep re chaun (lep′rə kôn), (in Irish legends) an elf resembling a little old man, believed to possess hidden gold. *n.*

lep ro sy (lep′rə sē), disease caused by certain rod-shaped bacteria that attack the skin and nerves, causing lumps or spots which may become ulcers; Hansen's disease. If not treated, the injury to the nerves results in numbness, paralysis, and deformity. *n.*

lep rous (lep′rəs), **1** having leprosy: *a leprous person.* **2** of or like leprosy: *white, leprous scabs. adj.*

les bi an or **Les bi an** (lez′bē ən), **1** a woman who shows sexual feelings for another woman. **2** having to do with a lesbian or lesbians. 1 *n.,* 2 *adj.*

le sion (lē′zhən), **1** an injury; hurt. **2** an abnormal change in the structure of an organ or body tissue, caused by disease or injury. *n.*

Le so tho (lə sō′tō), country in S Africa, a member of the Commonwealth of Nations. It is entirely surrounded by the Republic of South Africa. *Capital:* Maseru. See **South Africa** for map. *n.*

less (les), **1** smaller: *of less width, less importance.* **2** not so much; not so much of: *to have less rain, to put on less butter, to eat less meat.* **3** lower in age, rank, or importance: *no less a person than the President.* **4** a smaller amount or quantity: *could do no less, weigh less than before. I won't take less than $5.* **5** to a smaller extent or degree; not so; not so well: *less known, less important.* **6** with (something) taken away; without; minus: *five less two, a coat less one sleeve.* 1-3 *adj.,* 4 *n.,* 5 *adv.,* 6 *prep.*

-less, *suffix forming adjectives.* **1** (*added to nouns*) without a ____; that has no ____: *Homeless = without a home.* **2** (*added to verbs*) that does not ____: *Ceaseless = that does not cease.* **3** (*added to verbs*) that cannot be ____ed: *Countless = that cannot be counted.*

les see (le sē′), person to whom a lease is granted. *n.*

les sen (les′n), **1** grow less: *The fever lessened during the night.* **2** make less; decrease. *v.*

less er (les′ər), **1** less; smaller. **2** the less important of two. *adj.*

les son (les′n), **1** something to be learned or taught; something that has been learned or taught: *Children study many different lessons in school.* **2** unit of learning or teaching; what is to be studied or taught at one time: *Tomorrow we take the tenth lesson.* **3** an instructive experience, serving to encourage or warn: *The accident taught me a lesson: always look before you leap.* **4** a selection from the Bible, read as part of a church service. *n.*

les sor (les′ôr), person who grants a lease. *n.*

lest (lest), **1** for fear that: *Be careful lest you fall from that tree.* **2** that (after words meaning fear, danger, etc.): *I was*

let[1] (let), **1** not stop from doing or having something; allow; permit: *Let the dog have a bone.* **2** allow to pass, go, or come: *They let the visitor on board the ship.* **3** allow to run out: *Doctors used to let some of the blood of their fever patients.* **4** hire out; rent: *That woman lets rooms to students.* **5** Let is used in giving suggestions and commands: *"Let's go home" means "I suggest that we go home." Let all of us do our duty.* **6** suppose; assume: *Let the two lines be parallel. v.,* **let, let ting.**

let down, 1 lower: *We let the box down from the roof.* **2** slow up: *As their interest in the work wore off, they began to let down.* **3** disappoint: *Don't let us down today; we're counting on you to win.*

let in, permit to enter; admit: *Let in some fresh air.*

let off, allow to go free; excuse from punishment, etc.: *I was let off with a warning to do better in the future.*

let on, INFORMAL. **1** allow to be known; reveal one's knowledge of: *He didn't let on that he knew their secret.* **2** make believe; pretend: *She let on that she didn't see me.*

let out, 1 permit to go out. **2** make larger: *Let out the hem on this skirt.* **3** dismiss or be dismissed: *School lets out at three o'clock.* **4** rent: *Has the room been let out yet?*

let up, INFORMAL. stop; pause: *They refused to let up in the fight.*

let[2] (let), interference with the ball in tennis and similar games, especially a serve that hits the net and must be played over. *n.*

-let, *suffix added to nouns to form other nouns.* **1** little ____: *Booklet = a little book.* **2** band worn around the ____: *Anklet = band worn around the ankle.*

let down (let′doun′), **1** a slowing up. **2** disappointment: *Losing the contest was a letdown for me. n.*

le thal (lē′thəl), causing death; deadly: *lethal weapons, a lethal dose of a drug. adj.* —**le′thal ly,** *adv.*

le thar gic (lə thär′jik), **1** unnaturally drowsy; sluggish; dull: *A hot, humid day makes most people feel lethargic.* **2** producing lethargy. *adj.* —**le thar′gi cal ly,** *adv.*

leth ar gy (leth′ər jē), **1** drowsy dullness; lack of energy; sluggish inactivity. **2** a state of unconsciousness resembling deep sleep. *n., pl.* **leth ar gies.** [*Lethargy* can be traced back to Greek *lēthē,* meaning "forgetfulness," *a-,* meaning "not," and *ergon,* meaning "work."]

let's (lets), let us.

let ter (let′ər), **1** a mark or sign that stands for any one of the sounds that make up words. There are 26 letters in our alphabet. **2** mark with letters: *Please letter a new sign.* **3** a written or printed message: *He told me about his vacation in a letter.* **4** exact wording; actual terms: *They kept the letter of the law but not the spirit.* **5** a block of type bearing a letter, used in printing. **6** the initial of a school, college, or other institution, given as an award or trophy to members of a sports team, etc. It is usually made of cloth and sewn to a garment. **7 letters,** *pl.* literature: *a man of letters.* 1,3-7 *n.,* 2 *v.*

to the letter, very exactly; just as one has been told: *I carried out your orders to the letter.*

letter carrier, person who collects and delivers mail; mailman; postman.

let ter head (let′ər hed′), **1** words printed at the top of a sheet of paper, usually a name and address. **2** a sheet of paper so printed. *n.*

let ter ing (let′ər ing), **1** letters drawn, painted, or stamped. **2** act of making letters. *n.*

let ter-per fect (let′ər pèr′fikt), **1** knowing one's part or lesson perfectly: *My speech was letter-perfect.* **2** correct in every detail: *letter-perfect copies. adj.*

let tuce (let′is), the large, crisp, green leaves of a garden plant, used in salad. *n.*

WORD HISTORY

lettuce

Lettuce came into English about 700 years ago from French *laitues,* and can be traced back to Latin *lactis,* meaning "milk." It was called this because of the milky juice of the plant.

let up (let′up′), INFORMAL. a stop or pause. *n.*

leu co cyte (lü′kə sīt), white blood cell. *n.*

leu ke mi a (lü kē′mē ə), a form of cancer, characterized by a large excess of white blood cells in the blood. *n.*

Le vant (lə vant′), the region about the E Mediterranean from Greece to Egypt, especially Syria, Lebanon, and Israel. *n.*

Le van tine (lə van′tən), **1** of the Levant. **2** person or ship of the Levant. 1 *adj.,* 2 *n.*

lev ee (lev′ē), **1** a bank built to keep a river from overflowing: *There are levees in many places along the lower Mississippi River.* **2** a landing place for boats. *n.*

level (def. 4)
If the surface is level, an air bubble stays at the center of a glass tube containing liquid (as in middle tube above). If the surface is not level, the bubble moves to one side.

lev el (lev′əl), **1** having the same height everywhere; flat; even: *a level floor.* **2** of equal height, importance, etc.: *The table is level with the sill of the window.* **3** something that is level; level or flat surface, tract of land, etc. **4** an instrument for showing whether a surface is level. **5** a level position or condition. **6** make level; put on the same level: *level the ground with a bulldozer.* **7** lay low; bring to the level of the ground: *The tornado leveled every house in the valley.* **8** raise and hold level for shooting; aim: *She leveled her rifle at the target.* **9** height: *The flood rose to a level of 60 feet.* **10** stage of learning, achievement, etc.; position; rank: *They told me that my work is not up to a professional level.* **11** remove or reduce (differences, etc.). **12** well-balanced; sensible: *a level head.* 1,2, 12 *adj.,* 3-5,9,10 *n.,* 6-8,11 *v.,* **lev eled, lev el ing** *or* **lev elled, lev el ling.** —**lev′el er, lev′el ler,** *n.* —**lev′el ly,** *adv.* —**lev′el ness,** *n.*

level off, 1 come to an equilibrium; even off; steady.

2 return (an aircraft) to a horizontal position in landing, or after a climb or dive.

on the level, INFORMAL. fair and straightforward; honest; legitimate.

lev el head ed (lev′əl hed′id), having good common sense or good judgment; sensible. *adj.* —**lev′el head′ed ness,** *n.*

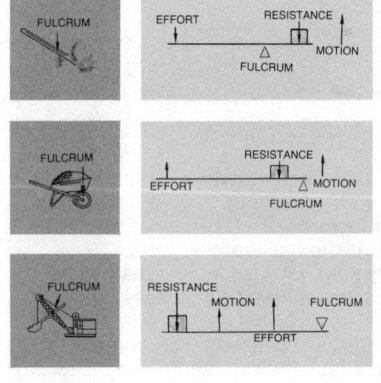

levers (def. 1)

first-class lever: fulcrum between effort and resistance; motion in direction opposite effort

second-class lever: resistance between effort and fulcrum; motion in same direction as effort

third-class lever: effort between resistance and fulcrum; motion in same direction as effort

lev er (lev′ər *or* lē′vər), **1** bar which turns on a fixed support called the fulcrum and is used to transmit effort and motion. It is a simple machine. **2** any bar working on an axis or support: *the gearshift lever of an automobile. n.* [*Lever* came into English about 700 years ago from French *leveor,* and can be traced back to Latin *levis,* meaning "light in weight."] —**lev′er like′,** *adj.*

lev er age (lev′ər ij *or* lē′vər ij), **1** action of a lever. **2** advantage or power gained by using a lever. **3** increased power of action. *n.*

Le vi (lē′vī), (in the Bible) a son of Jacob and ancestor of the Levites. *n.*

le vi a than (lə vī′ə thən), **1** (in the Bible) a huge sea animal. **2** any great and powerful person or thing. *n.*

Le vi's (lē′vīz), trademark for tight-fitting, heavy blue denim trousers reinforced at strain points with copper rivets or extra stitching. *n.pl.*

lev i tate (lev′ə tāt), rise or float in the air. *v.,* **lev i tat ed, lev i tat ing.** —**lev′i ta′tion,** *n.*

Le vite (lē′vīt), member of the tribe descended from Levi, from which assistants to the Jewish priests were chosen. *n.*

Le vit i cus (lə vit′ə kəs), the third book of the Old Testament, containing the laws for the priests and Levites and the ritual for Jewish ceremonies. *n.*

lev i ty (lev′ə tē), lightness of mind, character, or behavior; lack of proper seriousness or earnestness: *Giggling in class shows levity. n., pl.* **lev i ties.**

lev y (lev′ē), **1** order to be paid: *The government levies taxes to pay its expenses.* **2** money collected by authority or force. **3** draft (citizens) for an army: *When war threatened, the government levied a large number of soldiers from each state.* **4** undertake or begin; wage: *to levy war against the enemy.* **5** citizens drafted for an army. 1,3,4 *v.,* **lev ied, lev y ing;** 2,5 *n., pl.* **lev ies.**

lewd (lüd), not decent; obscene: *lewd stories. adj.* —**lewd′ly,** *adv.* —**lewd′ness,** *n.*

Lew is (lü′is), **1** Meriwether, 1774-1809, American explorer of the American northwest together with William Clark. **2** Sinclair, 1885-1951, American novelist. *n.*

lex i cog ra pher (lek′sə kog′rə fər), writer or maker of a dictionary. *n.*

lex i cog ra phy (lek′sə kog′rə fē), the writing or making of dictionaries. *n.*

lex i con (lek′sə kən), dictionary, especially of Greek, Latin, or Hebrew. *n.* [*Lexicon* is from Greek *lexikon,* which also meant "of words," and can be traced back to *legein,* meaning "to say, speak."]

Lex ing ton (lek′sing tən), **1** town in E Massachusetts where the first battle of the Revolutionary War was fought on April 19, 1775. **2** city in N Kentucky. *n.*

Ley den jar (līd′n), device for storing an electric charge, consisting essentially of a glass jar lined inside and outside with tin or aluminum foil and sealed with a stopper containing a metal rod connected to the foil.

LF, L.F., or **l.f.,** low frequency.

l.f., 1 left field. **2** left fielder.

l.h., (in music) left hand.

Lha sa (lä′sə), capital of Tibet, in the S part. *n.*

Li, symbol for lithium.

L.I., Long Island.

li a bil i ty (lī′ə bil′ə tē), **1** state of being liable: *liability to disease, liability for a debt.* **2** debt. **3** something that is to one's disadvantage: *Her poor handwriting was a liability in spelling classes. n., pl.* **li a bil i ties.**

li a ble (lī′ə bəl), **1** likely; unpleasantly likely: *That glass is liable to break. You are liable to slip on ice.* **2** in danger of having, doing, etc.: *We are all liable to diseases.* **3** responsible; under obligation; bound by law to pay: *The Postal Service is not liable for damage to a parcel unless it is insured. adj.*

li ai son (lē′ā zon′ *or* lē ā′zon), connection between military units to secure proper cooperation. *n.*

li a na (lē ä′nə *or* lē an′ə), a climbing plant or vine, especially one of those having woody stems that twine around the trunks of trees of tropical forests. *n., pl.* **li a nas.**

li ar (lī′ər), person who tells lies; person who says what is not true. *n.*

lib., 1 librarian. **2** library.

li bel (lī′bəl), **1** a written or published statement that is likely to harm the reputation of the person about whom it is made; false or damaging statement. **2** write or publish such a statement about. **3** act or crime of writing or publishing such a statement. **1,3** *n.,* **2** *v.,* **li beled, li bel ing** or **li belled, li bel ling.**

li bel er or **li bel ler** (lī′bə lər), person who libels another. *n.*

li bel ous or **li bel lous** (lī′bə ləs), **1** containing a libel: *a libelous communication.* **2** spreading libels: *a libelous tongue. adj.*

lib er al (lib′ər əl), **1** giving or given freely; generous: *a liberal giver, a liberal donation.* **2** plentiful; abundant: *There was a liberal supply of food at the party.* **3** not narrow in one's ideas; broad-minded; tolerant: *a liberal thinker.* **4** not limited; broad. A liberal education develops the mind broadly by including courses in the liberal arts. **5** favoring progress and reforms. **6** person favorable to progress and reforms. **7** Often, **Liberal.** of or belonging to a political party that favors progress and reforms. **1-5,7** *adj.,* **6** *n.* —**lib′er al ly,** *adv.* —**lib′er al ness,** *n.*

liberal arts, subjects studied for culture rather than for immediate practical use. Literature, languages, history, and philosophy are some of the liberal arts.

lib er al ism (lib′ər ə liz′əm), liberal views or opinions; belief in progress and reforms. *n.*

lib er al i ty (lib′ə ral′ə tē), **1** generous act or behavior; generosity. **2** tolerant and progressive nature; broadmindedness. *n., pl.* **lib e ral i ties.**

lib er al i za tion (lib′ər ə lə zā′shən), a making or becoming liberal. *n.*

lib er al ize (lib′ər ə līz), make or become liberal. *v.,* **lib er al ized, lib er al iz ing.** —**lib′er al iz′er,** *n.*

lib e rate (lib′ə rāt′), set free: *liberate political prisoners. v.,* **lib e rat ed, lib e rat ing.**

a hat	**i** it	**oi** oil	**ch** child	a in about
ā age	**ī** ice	**ou** out	**ng** long	e in taken
ä far	**o** hot	**u** cup	**sh** she	ə = i in pencil
e let	**ō** open	**u̇** put	**th** thin	o in lemon
ē equal	**ô** order	**ü** rule	**ᴛʜ** then	u in circus
ėr term			**zh** measure	

lib e ra tion (lib′ə rā′shən), a setting or a being set free. *n.*

lib e ra tor (lib′ə rā′tər), person who sets free; deliverer. *n.*

Li ber i a (lī bir′ē ə), country in W Africa, first settled by freed American Negro slaves in 1822. *Capital:* Monrovia. See **Nigeria** for map. *n.* —**Li ber′i an,** *adj., n.*

lib er tar i an (lib′ər ter′ē ən), person who advocates liberty, especially in thought or conduct. *n.*

lib er tine (lib′ər tēn′), person without moral restraints; immoral or licentious person. *n.*

lib er ty (lib′ər tē), **1** condition of being free; freedom; independence: *The American colonies won their liberty.* **2** right or power to do as one pleases; power or opportunity to do something: *liberty of speech.* **3** permission granted to a sailor to go ashore. **4** right of being in, using, etc.: *We give our dog the liberty of the yard.* **5** too great freedom: *The author took liberties with the facts to make the story more interesting. n., pl.* **lib er ties.** [*Liberty* came into English about 600 years ago from French *liberté,* and can be traced back to Latin *liber,* meaning "free."]

at liberty, 1 free: *The escaped lion is still at liberty.* **2** allowed; permitted: *You are at liberty to make any choice you please.* **3** not busy: *The doctor will see us as soon as she is at liberty.*

Liberty Bell, bell that was rung at Philadelphia on July 8, 1776, when the Continental Congress passed the Declaration of Independence. It is regarded as a symbol of liberty.

li brar i an (lī brer′ē ən), **1** person in charge of a library. **2** person trained for work in a library. *n.*

li brar y (lī′brer′ē), **1** collection of books, magazines, films, recordings, etc., either public or private. **2** room or building where such a collection is kept for public use and borrowing. **3** room in a home where books are kept. *n., pl.* **li brar ies.**

li bret tist (lə bret′ist), writer of a libretto. *n.*

li bret to (lə bret′ō), **1** the words of an opera or other long musical composition. **2** book containing the words. *n., pl.* **li bret tos, li bret ti** (lə bret′ē).

Li bre ville (lē′brə vil), capital of Gabon, in the NW part. *n.*

Lib y a (lib′ē ə), country in N Africa, west of Egypt. *Capital:* Tripoli. See **Algeria** for map. *n.* —**Lib′y an,** *adj., n.*

lice (līs), plural of **louse.** *n.*

li cence (lī′sns), license. *n., v.,* **li cenced, li cenc ing.**

li cense (lī′sns), **1** permission given by law to do something: *A license to drive an automobile is issued by the state.* **2** paper, card, plate, etc., showing such permission: *The policeman asked the reckless driver for her license.* **3** give a license to; permit by law: *A doctor is licensed to practice medicine.* **4** fact or condition of being allowed to do something. **5** freedom of action, speech, thought, etc., that is permitted or conceded. **Poetic license** is the freedom from rules that is permitted in poetry and other arts. **6** too much liberty of action; lack of proper control; abuse of liberty. **1,2,4-6** *n.,* **3** *v.,* **li censed, li cens ing.** —**li′cens a ble,** *adj.* —**li′cens er,** *n.*

li cen tious (lī sen′shəs), unrestrained in sexual activities; immoral. *adj.* —**li cen′tious ly,** *adv.*

lichen on a tree trunk

li chen (lī′kən), a flowerless plant that looks somewhat like moss and consists of a fungus and an alga growing together as one plant. Lichens grow in patches on rocks, trees, and other surfaces. They are gray, yellow, brown, black, or greenish in color. *n.*

lick (lik), **1** pass the tongue over: *lick a stamp.* **2** lap up with the tongue: *The cat licked the milk.* **3** a stroke of the tongue over something: *He gave the ice-cream cone a big lick.* **4** pass about or play over like a tongue: *The flames were licking the roof of the burning house.* **5** place where natural salt is found and where animals go to lick it up. **6** INFORMAL. a blow: *Though I lost the fight, I got in a few good licks.* **7** INFORMAL. to beat or thrash. **8** INFORMAL. to defeat in a fight, etc.; conquer: *I licked him at chess.* **9** a small quantity: *She didn't do a lick of work.* 1,2,4,7,8 *v.,* 3,5,6,9 *n.* —**lick′er,** *n.*

lick e ty-split (lik′ə tē split′), INFORMAL. at full speed; headlong; rapidly: *A frightened rabbit ran lickety-split into the bushes. adv.*

lick ing (lik′ing), INFORMAL. a beating; a whipping. *n.*

lic or ice (lik′ər is *or* lik′ər ish), **1** the sweet-tasting, dried root of a European plant. **2** the plant. **3** a black substance obtained from the root, used in medicine and candy. **4** candy flavored with this substance. *n.* [*Licorice* can be traced back to Greek *glykys,* meaning "sweet," and *rhiza,* meaning "root."]

lid (lid), **1** a movable cover; top: *a jar lid.* **2** eyelid. **3** SLANG. hat or cap. *n.*

lid ded (lid′id), having a lid; covered with a lid. *adj.*

lid less (lid′lis), having no lid or lids. *adj.*

lie¹ (lī), **1** something said that is not true; something that is not true said to deceive: *I went to school today; saying I didn't is a lie.* **2** speak falsely; tell a lie: *He says that he has never lied, but I think he is lying when he says it.* **3** give a false impression; mislead: *That clock must be lying; it isn't noon yet.* 1 *n.,* 2,3 *v.,* **lied, ly ing.**

give the lie to, 1 call a liar; accuse of lying. **2** show to be false: *Her actions gave the lie to her statement.*

lie² (lī), **1** have one's body in a flat position along the ground or other surface: *lie on the grass, lie in bed.* **2** assume such a position: *lie down on the couch.* **3** rest (on a surface): *The book was lying on the table.* **4** be kept or stay in a given state: *lie idle, lie hidden, lie unused.* **5** be; be placed: *a road that lies among trees, a ship lying offshore at anchor. The lake lies to the south of us.* **6** exist; be found to be: *The cure for ignorance lies in education. v.,* **lay, lain, ly ing.**

lie in, be confined in childbirth.

lie over, be left waiting until a later time.

lie to, (of a ship, etc.) come almost to a stop, facing the wind: *During the storm, the sailing ship lay to.*

take (something) lying down, yield to (something); not stand up to (something).

Liech ten stein (lik′tən stīn), small country between W

Austria and E Switzerland. *Capital:* Vaduz. *n.*

lied (lēd), past tense and past participle of **lie**¹. *That girl lied about her work. She has lied before. v.*

lie detector, device that records the physical reaction of an emotion, used especially to determine whether a person is lying.

liege (lēj), in the Middle Ages: **1** lord having a right to the homage and loyal service of his vassals. **2** having a right to the homage and loyal service of vassals. **3** vassal obliged to give homage and loyal service to his lord. **4** obliged to give homage and loyal service to a lord. 1,3 *n.,* 2,4 *adj.*

liege lord, a feudal lord.

liege man (lēj′mən), **1** vassal. **2** a faithful follower. *n., pl.* **liege men.**

lien (lēn), (in law) a claim on the property of another for payment of a debt: *The garage owner has a lien upon my automobile until I pay his bill. n.*

lieu (lü). **in lieu of,** in place of; instead of. *n.*

Lieut., Lieutenant.

lieu ten an cy (lü ten′ən sē), rank, commission, or authority of a lieutenant. *n., pl.* **lieu ten an cies.**

lieu ten ant (lü ten′ənt), **1** person who acts in the place of someone higher in authority: *The scoutmaster used the two boys as his lieutenants.* **2** (in the army, air force, or Marine Corps) a first lieutenant or a second lieutenant. **3** (in the navy) an officer ranking next below a lieutenant commander and next above a lieutenant junior grade. **4** a police officer, usually ranking next below a captain and next above a sergeant. *n.*

lieutenant colonel, (in the army, air force, or Marine Corps) an officer ranking next below a colonel and next above a major.

lieutenant commander, (in the navy) an officer ranking next below a commander and next above a lieutenant.

lieutenant general, (in the army, air force, or Marine Corps) an officer ranking next below a general and next above a major general.

lieutenant governor, (in the United States) a public official next in rank to the governor of a state, who takes the governor's place when necessary.

lieutenant junior grade, (in the navy) an officer ranking next below a lieutenant and next above an ensign.

life (līf), **1** a living or being alive. People, animals, and plants have life. Rocks and minerals do not. Life is shown by growing and reproducing. **2** time of being alive: *During her life she was an outstanding doctor.* **3** time of existence or action of inanimate things: *a machine's life, a lease's life.* **4** a living being; person: *Five lives were lost.* **5** living things: *The desert island had almost no animal or vegetable life.* **6** way of living: *a dull life, a country life.* **7** account of a person's life: *Several lives of Lincoln have been written.* **8** spirit; vigor: *Put more life into your work. n., pl.* **lives.**

for dear life, to save one's life.

life belt, a life preserver made like a belt.

life blood (līf′blud′), **1** blood necessary to life. **2** source of strength and energy. *n.*

life boat (līf′bōt′), a strong boat specially built for saving lives at sea or along the coast. *n.*

life buoy, a life preserver.

life guard (līf′gärd′), person employed at a beach or pool to help in case of accident or danger to bathers. *n.*

life insurance, insurance by which a specified sum of money is paid to the insured person's survivors at the death of that person. Life insurance is bought by the payment of regular premiums.

life jacket, a sleeveless, canvas jacket filled with a

light material such as kapok, or with air, worn as a life preserver.

life less (līf′lis), **1** without life: *a lifeless planet.* **2** dead: *a lifeless body.* **3** dull: *a lifeless party. adj.* —**life′less ly,** *adv.* —**life′less ness,** *n.*

life like (līf′līk′), like life; looking as if alive: *a lifelike portrait. adj.* —**life′like′ness,** *n.*

life line (līf′līn′), **1** rope for saving life, such as one thrown to a person in the water. **2** a diver's signaling line. **3** anything that helps to maintain something that cannot exist by itself, as a remote military position, etc. *n.*

life long (līf′lông′), lasting all one's life: *a lifelong friendship. adj.*

life preserver, a wide belt, jacket, circular tube, etc., usually made of plastic or cork, to keep a person afloat in the water.

life raft

life raft, raft for saving lives in a shipwreck or the wreck of an aircraft at sea.

life sav er (līf′sā′vər), **1** person who saves people from drowning. **2** any lifesaving person or thing. *n.*

life sav ing (līf′sā′ving), **1** a saving of people's lives; keeping people from drowning. **2** designed or used to save people's lives. **1** *n.,* **2** *adj.*

life-size (līf′sīz′), as big as the living person, animal, etc.: *a life-size statue. adj.*

life-sized (līf′sīzd′), life-size. *adj.*

life style (līf′stīl′), a person's or group's characteristic manner of living; one's style of life. *n.*

life-sup port system (līf′sə pôrt′), equipment necessary to maintain human life where a normal environment is lacking. A spacecraft's life-support system enables the crew to live outside the earth's atmosphere.

life time (līf′tīm′), time of being alive; period during which a life lasts: *My grandparents have seen many changes during their lifetime. n.*

life work (līf′werk′), work that takes or lasts a whole lifetime; main work in life. *n.*

lift (lift), **1** raise into the air; raise up higher; take up; pick up: *Please help me lift this heavy box.* **2** raise in rank, condition, estimation, etc.; elevate; exalt. **3** an elevating influence or effect: *The promotion gave her a lift.* **4** rise and go; go away: *The fog lifted at dawn.* **5** go up; be raised: *This window will not lift.* **6** act of lifting: *the lift of a helping hand.* **7** distance through which a thing is lifted. **8** a helping hand: *Give me a lift with this job.* **9** a ride in a vehicle given to a traveler on foot; free ride: *Can you give the children a lift to school?* **10** INFORMAL. pick or take up; steal: *lift things from a store.* **11** elevator. **12** one of the layers of leather in the heel of a shoe. **13** the quantity or weight that can be lifted at one time: *A lift of fifty pounds is all I can manage.* **1,2,4,5,10** *v.,* **3,6-9,11-13** *n.* —**lift′a ble,** *adj.* —**lift′er,** *n.*

lift off (lift′ôf′), the firing or launching of a rocket. *n.*

lig a ment (lig′ə mənt), band of strong tissue which connects bones or holds organs of the body in place. *n.* [*Ligament* is from Latin *ligamentum,* meaning "a band, bandage," which comes from *ligare,* meaning "to bind, tie." See **Word Family.**]

lig a ture (lig′ə chùr *or* lig′ə chər), **1** anything used to bind or tie up; band, bandage, cord, etc. **2** thread, wire, etc., used by surgeons to tie up a bleeding artery or vein. **3** two or three letters joined in printing. Æ and *ffl* are ligatures. **4** bind or tie up with a ligature. **1-3** *n.,* **4** *v.,* **lig a tured, lig a tur ing.**

light[1] (līt), **1** that by which we see; form of radiant energy that acts on the retina of the eye. Light consists of electromagnetic waves that travel at about 186,282 miles (299,728 kilometers) per second. **2** having light. **3** thing that gives light. The sun, a lamp, or a lighthouse is called a light. **4** supply of light: *A tall building cuts off our light.* **5** cause to give light: *She lighted the lamp.* **6** give light to; provide with light: *The room is lighted by six windows.* **7** bright; clear: *It was a moonlit night as light as day.* **8** brightness; clearness; illumination; particular case of this: *a strong or dim light.* **9** a bright part: *light and shade in a painting.* **10** make bright or clear: *Her face was lighted by a smile.* **11** show the way by means of a light: *Here is a candle to light you to bed.* **12** become light: *The sky lights up at dawn.* **13** daytime: *The baker gets up before light.* **14** dawn. **15** pale in color; approaching white: *light hair, light blue.* **16** window or other means of letting in light. **17** thing with which to start something burning: *He wanted a light for his cigar.* **18** set fire to: *She lighted the candles.* **19** take fire: *Matches light when you strike them.* **20** knowledge; information: *We need more light on this subject.* **21** public knowledge; open view: *The reporter brought to light graft in the city government.* **22** aspect in which a thing is viewed: *The principal put the matter in the right light.* **23** shining model or example: *Louis Pasteur is one of the leading lights of science because of his work on the causes of disease.* **1,3,4,8,9,13,14,16,17,20-23** *n.,* **2,7,15** *adj.,* **5,6,10-12,18,19** *v.,* **light ed** or **lit, light ing.**

in the light of, because of; considering: *In the light of all these facts, what you did was completely right.*

see the light or **see the light of day, 1** be born. **2** be made public. **3** get the right idea.

shed light on or **throw light on,** make clear; explain.

light[2] (līt), **1** easy to carry; not heavy: *a light load.* **2** having little weight for its size: *Feathers are light.* **3** having less than usual weight: *light summer clothing.* **4** less than usual in amount, force, etc.: *a light sleep, a light rain, a light meal.* **5** easy to do or bear; not hard or severe: *light punishment, a light task.* **6** not looking heavy;

WORD FAMILY

ligament

Below are words related to *ligament.* They can all be traced back to the Latin word *ligare* (li gä′re), meaning "to bind, tie."

alliance	legato	obligate
alloy	liable	oblige
ally	liaison	rally[1]
furl	lien	rely
league[1]	ligature	self-reliant

graceful; delicate: *a light bridge, light carving.* **7** moving easily; nimble: *a light step.* **8** cheerfully careless; gay: *a light laugh.* **9** not serious enough; fickle: *a light mind, light of purpose.* **10** aiming to entertain; not serious: *light reading.* **11** not important: *light losses.* **12** porous; sandy: *a light soil.* **13** that has risen properly; not soggy: *light dough.* **14** lightly armed or equipped: *light infantry.* **15** lightly. 1-14 *adj.*, 15 *adv.*

light in the head, 1 dizzy. **2** silly; foolish.

make light of, treat as of little importance.

light³ (līt), **1** come down to the ground; alight: *light from a horse.* **2** come down from flight: *A bird lighted on the branch.* **3** come by chance: *Her eye lighted upon a coin in the road. v.,* **light ed** or **lit, light ing.**

light into, INFORMAL. **1** attack. **2** scold.

light out, INFORMAL. leave suddenly; go away quickly.

light bulb, incandescent lamp.

light en¹ (līt′n), **1** make or become brighter; brighten: *Dawn lightens the sky. Her face lightened.* **2** flash with lightning: *It was thundering and lightening outside. v.* —**light′en er,** *n.*

light en² (līt′n), **1** reduce the load of; make or become lighter: *Your help lightened our work.* **2** make or become more cheerful: *The good news lightened our hearts. v.* —**light′en er,** *n.*

light er¹ (lī′tər), thing or person that starts something burning. *n.*

light er² (lī′tər), **1** a flat-bottomed barge used for loading and unloading ships. **2** carry (goods) in such a barge. 1 *n.*, 2 *v.*

light face (līt′fās′), printing type that has thin, light lines. This sentence is in lightface. *n.*

light-foot ed (līt′fut′id), stepping lightly. *adj.* —**light′-foot′ed ly,** *adv.* —**light′-foot′ed ness,** *n.*

light-head ed (līt′hed′id), **1** dizzy; giddy; out of one's head: *The sick man was light-headed from fever.* **2** empty-headed; silly; thoughtless: *That frivolous, light-headed crowd thinks of nothing but parties and games. adj.* —**light′-head′ed ly,** *adv.* —**light′-head′ed ness,** *n.*

light heart ed (līt′här′tid), without worry; carefree; cheerful; gay. *adj.* —**light′heart′ed ly,** *adv.* —**light′heart′ed ness,** *n.*

light heavyweight, boxer who weighs more than 160 pounds (73 kilograms) and less than 175 pounds (79 kilograms).

lighthouse

light house (līt′hous′), tower or framework with a bright light that shines far over the water. It is often located at a dangerous place to warn and guide ships. *n., pl.* **light hous es** (līt′hou′ziz).

light ing (lī′ting), **1** a giving of light; providing with light. **2** way in which lights are arranged. *n.*

light ly (līt′lē), **1** with little weight or force: *Cares rested lightly on her.* **2** to a small degree or extent; not much: *lightly clad.* **3** in an airy way: *flags floating lightly.* **4** quickly; easily: *She jumped lightly aside.* **5** cheerfully:

take bad news lightly. **6** indifferently; in a slighting way: *speak lightly of a person.* **7** thoughtlessly; carelessly; frivolously: *behave lightly. adv.*

light-mind ed (līt′mīn′did), empty-headed; thoughtless; frivolous. *adj.* —**light′-mind′ed ly,** *adv.* —**light′-mind′ed ness,** *n.*

light ness¹ (līt′nis), **1** brightness; clearness. **2** paleness; whitishness. *n.*

light ness² (līt′nis), **1** a being light; not being heavy: *The lightness of this load is a relief after the heavy one I was carrying.* **2** a being gay or cheerful: *lightness of spirits.* **3** lack of proper seriousness: *Such lightness of conduct is out of place in a courtroom. n.*

light ning (līt′ning), flash of light in the sky caused by a discharge of electricity between clouds, or between a cloud and the earth's surface. The sound that it makes is thunder. *n.*

lightning bug, firefly.

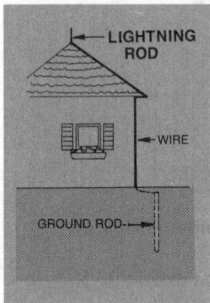

lightning rod

Lightning which strikes the rod is conducted down a heavy wire and grounded through a metal rod.

lightning rod, a metal rod fixed on a building or ship to conduct lightning into the earth or water.

light pen, device like a pen which produces an electrical signal when it is pointed at light. It is used for directing a computer to add, change, or remove information shown on its display screen.

light ship (līt′ship′), ship with a bright light, anchored at a dangerous place to warn ships away. *n.*

light weight (līt′wāt′), **1** person or thing of less than average weight. **2** light in weight. **3** boxer who weighs more than 126 pounds (57 kilograms) and less than 135 pounds (61 kilograms). 1,3 *n.*, 2 *adj.*

light-year (līt′yir′), unit of length used to measure astronomical distances. It is equal to the distance that light travels in one year, about six trillion (6,000,000,000,000) miles (ten trillion kilometers). *n.*

lig nite (lig′nīt), a dark-brown coal, often having a woody texture. *n.* [*Lignite* was borrowed from French *lignite,* which came from Latin *lignum,* meaning "wood."]

lik a ble (lī′kə bəl), having qualities that win goodwill or friendship; popular; pleasing: *the most likable boy in school. adj.* Also, **likeable.** —**lik′a ble ness,** *n.*

like¹ (līk), **1** resembling something or each other; similar to: *Our house is like theirs. I never saw anything like it.* **2** in the same way as; as well as: *sing like a bird.* **3** of the same form, kind, amount, etc.; the same or almost the same; similar: *drawing, painting, or like arts. Her aunt promised her $10 if she could earn a like sum.* **4** such as one would expect of; characteristic of: *Isn't it just like him to be late?* **5** in the right condition for: *I feel like working.* **6** giving promise of: *It looks like rain.* **7** person or thing like another; counterpart or equal: *We shall not see her like again.* **8** INFORMAL. as if: *He acted like he was afraid.* **9** INFORMAL. as: *It was like she said it was.* 1,2,4-6 *prep.,* 3 *adj.,* 7 *n.,* 8,9 *conj.*

and the like, 1 and so forth: *He studied music, painting, and the like.* **2** and other like things: *At the zoo we saw* *lions, tigers, bears, zebras, and the like.*

like² (līk), **1** be pleased with; be satisfied with: *My cat likes milk.* **2** have a kindly or friendly feeling for: *to like a person.* **3** wish for; wish: *I'd like more time to finish this. Come whenever you like.* **4 likes,** pl. liking; preference: *You know all my likes and dislikes.* 1-3 v., **liked, liking;** 4 n.

-like, suffix added to nouns to form adjectives. **1** like: *Wolflike = like a wolf.* **2** like that of; characteristic of: *Childlike = like that of a child.*

like a ble (lī′kə bəl), likable. adj. —**like′a ble ness,** n.

like li hood (līk′lē hüd), probability: *Is there any likelihood of rain today?* n.

like ly (līk′lē), **1** probable: *One likely result of this heavy rain is the rising of the river.* **2** probably: *He will very likely be home all day.* **3** to be expected: *It is likely to be hot in August.* **4** suitable: *Is this a likely place to fish?* **5** promising: *a likely student.* 1,3-5 adj., **like li er, like li est;** 2 adv.

like-mind ed (līk′mīn′did), **1** in agreement or accord. **2** thinking along the same lines. adj.

lik en (lī′kən), represent as like; compare. v.

like ness (līk′nis), **1** a resembling; being alike: *The girl's likeness to her aunt was striking.* **2** something that is like; copy; picture: *This photograph is a good likeness of him.* **3** appearance; shape: *I watched a large cloud assume the likeness of a sailing ship.* n., pl. **like ness es.**

like wise (līk′wīz′), **1** the same: *See what I do. Now you do likewise.* **2** also; moreover; too: *I must go home now, and you likewise.* adv.

lik ing (lī′king), kindly feeling; preference; fondness: *a liking for apples, a liking for children.* n.

li lac (lī′lək or lī′lak), **1** shrub with clusters of tiny, fragrant, pale pinkish-purple or white flowers. **2** a pale pinkish purple. **3** pale pinkish-purple. 1,2 n., 3 adj. [Lilac came into English about 350 years ago from French *lilac,* and can be traced back to Sanskrit *nīla,* meaning "dark blue."]

lilt (lilt), **1** sing or play (a tune) in a light, tripping manner. **2** a lively song or tune with a swing. **3** a lively, springing movement: *She walks with a lilt.* 1 v., 2,3 n. —**lilt′ing ly,** adv.

lil y (lil′ē), **1** plant that grows from a bulb. Its flowers are usually large, bell-shaped, and showy, and are often divided into six parts. The white lily is a symbol of purity. **2** like a white lily; pure and lovely. **3** any of various related or similar plants, such as the calla lily or water lily. 1,3 n., pl. **lil ies;** 2 adj. —**lil′y like′,** adj.

lily of the valley, plant having tiny, sweet-smelling, bell-shaped, white flowers arranged up and down a single flower stem. pl. **lilies of the valley.**

Li ma (lē′mə), capital of Peru, in the W part. n.

li ma bean (lī′mə), a broad, flat, pale-green bean, used as a vegetable. [The *lima bean* gets its name from *Lima.* It was called this because it first grew in this area.]

limb (lim), **1** leg, arm, or wing. **2** a large branch: *They sawed the dead limb off the tree.* n. —**limb′less,** adj.

lim ber (lim′bər), **1** bending easily; flexible: *A piano player should have limber fingers.* **2** make or become limber: *He is stiff when he begins to skate, but limbers up quickly.* 1 adj., 2 v. —**lim′ber ly,** adv. —**lim′ber ness,** n.

lim bo (lim′bō), **1** Often, **Limbo.** (in the belief of Roman Catholics) a region for souls of people who die unbaptized but who do not deserve the punishment of sinners. **2** place for persons and things forgotten, cast aside, or out of date: *The belief that the earth is flat belongs to the limbo of outworn ideas.* n., pl. **lim bos.**

Lim burg er (lim′bèr′gər), a soft cheese having a strong smell. n.

lime¹ (līm), **1** a solid, white compound of calcium and oxygen obtained by burning limestone, shells, bone,

a hat	**i** it	**oi** oil	**ch** child	a in about
ā age	**ī** ice	**ou** out	**ng** long	e in taken
ä far	**o** hot	**u** cup	**sh** she	**ə =** i in pencil
e let	**ō** open	**u̇** put	**th** thin	o in lemon
ē equal	**ô** order	**ü** rule	**ᴛʜ** then	u in circus
ėr term			**zh** measure	

etc.; quicklime; calcium oxide. Lime is used in making mortar and on fields to improve the soil. **2** put lime on. 1 n., 2 v., **limed, lim ing.** —**lime′less,** adj.

lime² (līm), a juicy, greenish-yellow citrus fruit of a tree grown in warm climates. Limes are smaller and sourer than lemons. n.

lime³ (līm), the linden tree. n.

lime ade (līm′ād′ or līm′ād′), drink made of lime juice, sugar, and water. n.

lime light (līm′līt′), **1** a strong light produced by heating lime in a flame, formerly used in theaters to light up certain persons or objects and draw attention to them. **2** center of public attention and interest: *Some people are never happy unless they are in the limelight.* n. —**lime′light′er,** n.

lim er ick (lim′ər ik), kind of humorous verse of five lines. n.

LIMERICK

There was a young lady from Lynn
Who was so exceedingly thin
    That when she essayed
    To drink lemonade
She slid down the straw and fell in.

lime stone (līm′stōn′), rock made mostly of calcium carbonate, used for building and for making lime. Marble is a kind of limestone. n.

lime wa ter (līm′wô′tər or līm′wot′ər), solution of slaked lime in water. It is used to counteract excess acid in the digestive tract. n.

lim it (lim′it), **1** farthest point or edge; where something ends or must end: *the limit of one's vision, the limit of one's patience.* **2 limits,** pl. boundary; bounds: *Keep within the limits of the school grounds.* **3** set a limit to; restrict: *We must limit the expense to $10.* 1,2 n., 3 v. —**lim′it a ble,** adj. —**lim′it er,** n.

lim i ta tion (lim′ə tā′shən), **1** a limiting or a being limited. **2** that which limits; limiting rule or circumstance; restriction; boundary. n.

lim it ed (lim′ə tid), **1** kept within limits; restricted: *a limited space, a limited number.* **2** traveling fast and making only a few stops: *a limited train or bus.* **3** train or bus that travels fast and makes only a few stops. 1,2 adj., 3 n. —**lim′it ed ly,** adv. —**lim′it ed ness,** n.

lim it less (lim′it lis), without limits; boundless; infinite. adj. —**lim′it less ly,** adv. —**lim′it less ness,** n.

limn (lim), **1** paint (a picture). **2** portray in words. v.

lim ou sine (lim′ə zēn′ or lim′ə zēn′), a closed automobile, seating from three to five passengers inside, with a driver's seat separated from the passengers by a partition. n.

limp¹ (limp), **1** a lame step or walk. **2** walk with a limp: *After falling down the stairs, she limped for several days.* 1 n., 2 v. —**limp′er,** n. —**limp′ing ly,** adv.

limp² (limp), not at all stiff or firm; ready to bend or droop: *Spaghetti gets limp when it is cooked. I am so tired I feel as limp as a rag.* adj. —**limp′ly,** adv. —**limp′ness,** n.

lim pet (lim′pit), a small shellfish that clings to rocks and other objects, used for bait and sometimes for food. *n.*

lim pid (lim′pid), clear or transparent: *a spring of limpid water, limpid eyes. adj.* —**lim′pid ly,** *adv.*

lim pid i ty (lim pid′ə tē), limpid quality or condition. *n.*

lim y (lī′mē), of, containing, or resembling lime. *adj.*, **lim i er, lim i est.**

lin., 1 lineal. 2 linear.

linch pin (linch′pin′), pin inserted through a hole in the end of an axle to keep the wheel on. *n.*

Lin coln (ling′kən), **1** Abraham, 1809-1865, the 16th president of the United States, from 1861 to 1865. **2** capital of Nebraska, in the SE part. *n.*

Lind bergh (lind′bėrg′), **Charles Augustus,** 1902-1974, American aviator who made the first solo flight across the Atlantic, in 1927. *n.*

lin den (lin′dən), tree with heart-shaped leaves and clusters of small, sweet-smelling, yellowish flowers; lime. It is often used for shade and ornament. *n.*

line[1] (līn), **1** piece of rope, cord, or wire: *a telegraph line.* **2** a cord for measuring, making level, etc. A plumb line is used to see if a wall is vertical or to find the depth of water. **3** a long narrow mark: *Draw two lines along the margin.* **4** anything that is like a long narrow mark: *the lines in your face.* **5** mark with lines: *Please line your paper with a pencil and ruler.* **6** cover with lines: *a face lined with age.* **7** a straight line: *The lower edges of the two pictures are about on a line.* **8** (in mathematics) the path traced by a moving point. It has length, but no thickness. **9** the use of lines in drawing: *a picture in line, clearness of line in an artist's work.* **10 lines,** pl. outline; contour: *a ship of fine lines.* **11** an edge or boundary: *the line between Texas and Mexico.* **12** row of persons or things: *a line of cars.* **13** arrange in line: *Line your shoes along the edge of the shelf.* **14** arrange a line along; form a line along: *Trees lined the road for a mile.* **15** a row of words on a page or in a column: *a column of 40 lines.* **16** a short letter; note: *Drop me a line.* **17** a connected series of persons or things following one another in time: *The Stuarts were a line of English kings.* **18** family or lineage: *of noble line.* **19** a course, track, or direction: *a railroad line, the line of march of an army.* **20** a certain way of doing: *Please proceed on these lines till further notice.* **21** (in warfare) a front row of trenches or other defenses. **22** formation of soldiers or ships placed side by side. **23** wire or system of wires connecting points or stations in a telegraph or telephone system. **24** any rope, wire, pipe, hose, etc., running from one point to another. **25** a single track of railroad. **26** one branch of a system of transportation: *the main line of a railroad.* **27** a whole system of transportation or conveyance: *the Grand Trunk Line.* **28** a branch of business; kind of activity: *the dry-goods line. This is not my line.* **29** a kind or branch of goods: *Her store carries the best line of shoes in town.* **30** a single verse of poetry. **31 lines,** pl. words that an actor speaks in a play: *forget one's lines.* **32** in football: **a** line of scrimmage. **b** players along the line of scrimmage at the start of a play. Usually the offensive team has seven players in the line, and the defensive team has four. **33** INFORMAL. talk, usually intended to deceive or confuse: *The burglar tried to hand the police a line.* **34** one of the horizontal lines that make a staff in music. 1-4,7-12,15-34 *n.*, 5,6,13,14 *v.*, **lined, lin ing.** —**line′less,** *adj.* —**line′like′,** *adj.*

all along the line, at every point; everywhere: *This car has given us trouble all along the line.*

bring into line, cause to agree or conform.

come into line, agree; conform.

down the line, the whole way; as far as possible; to the end.

draw a line or **draw the line,** set a limit.

get a line on or **have a line on,** INFORMAL. get or have information about.

in line, 1 in alignment: *The children are all in line.* **2** in agreement: *This plan is in line with their thinking.*

line out, 1 (in baseball) hit a line drive which is caught. **2** draw a line or lines to indicate an outline.

line up, form a line; form into a line: *Cars were lined up along the road.*

on a line, even; level.

out of line, 1 in disagreement. **2** uncalled-for; not suitable or proper.

read between the lines, get more from the words than they say; find a hidden meaning.

toe the line, conform to a certain standard of duty, conduct, etc.

line[2] (līn), **1** put a layer of paper, cloth, felt, etc., inside of (a dress, hat, box, etc.). **2** fill: *line one's pockets with money.* **3** serve as a lining for: *This piece of silk would line your coat very nicely. v.,* **lined, lin ing.**

lin e age (lin′ē ij), **1** descent in a direct line from an ancestor. **2** family or origin. *n.*

line[1]
(defs. 1, 3, 5, 12, and 23)

lin e al (lin′ē əl), **1** in the direct line of descent: *She is a lineal descendant of her grandmother.* **2** of or like a line. *adj.* —**lin′e al ly,** *adv.*

lin e a ment (lin′ē ə mənt), part or feature, especially a part or feature of a face with attention to its outline. *n.*

lin e ar (lin′ē ər), **1** of or in a line or lines. **2** made of lines; making use of lines: *linear designs.* **3** of length: *An inch is a linear measure.* **4** like a line; long and narrow: *A pine tree has linear leaves. adj.* —**lin′e ar ly,** *adv.*

line back er (līn′bak′ər), (in football) a defensive player whose position is directly behind the line. *n.*

line drawing, drawing done completely in lines, including the shading, often made to be engraved.

line drive, baseball hit so that it goes in almost a straight line, usually close to the ground; liner.

lineman (def. 1)

a hat	i it	oi oil	ch child	(a in about
ā age	ī ice	ou out	ng long	e in taken
ä far	o hot	u cup	sh she	ə = { i in pencil
e let	ō open	ů put	th thin	o in lemon
ē equal	ô order	ü rule	ŦH then	u in circus
ėr term			zh measure	

joins or connects as a link does: *a cuff link, a link in a chain of evidence.* **3** join as a link does; unite or connect: *Don't try to link me with this scheme.* 1,2 *n.*, 3 *v.*

link age (ling′kij), **1** a linking or a being linked. **2** arrangement or system of links. *n.*

linking verb, verb with little or no meaning of its own, used to connect a subject with a predicate adjective or a predicate noun. In "The trees are maples," *are* is a linking verb. *Am, are, is,* and *seem* are linking verbs.

links (lingks), a golf course. *n.pl.*

lin net (lin′it), a small songbird of Europe, Asia, and Africa. *n.*

li no le um (lə nō′lē əm), **1** a floor covering made by putting a hard surface of ground cork mixed with linseed oil on a canvas or burlap back. **2** any similar floor covering. *n.* [*Linoleum* comes from Latin *linum,* meaning "flax," and *oleum,* meaning "oil."]

lin seed (lin′sēd′), the seed of flax. *n.*

linseed oil, a yellowish oil obtained by pressing linseed. It is used in making paints, printing inks, and linoleum.

lin sey-wool sey (lin′zē wůl′zē), a strong, coarse fabric made of linen and wool or of cotton and wool. *n., pl.* **lin sey-wool seys.**

lint (lint), **1** tiny bits of thread or fluff of any material. **2** the soft down or fleecy material obtained by scraping linen. Formerly, lint was put on wounds to keep out air and dirt. *n.* —**lint′less,** *adj.*

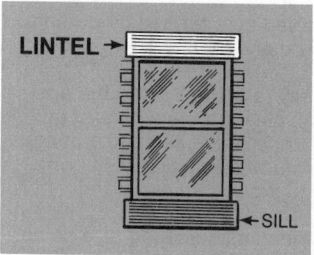

lin tel (lin′tl), a horizontal beam or stone above a door or window to support the structure above it. *n.*

lint y (lin′tē), **1** full of or marked with lint. **2** like lint. *adj.,* **lint i er, lint i est.**

li on (lī′ən), **1** a large, strong, flesh-eating cat, with a dull-yellowish coat, found in Africa and southern Asia. The male has a full, flowing mane of coarse hair. **2** a very brave or strong person. **3** a famous person. *n.* —**li′on like′,** *adj.*

lion (def. 1)
about 3 ft. (1 m.) high
at the shoulder

line man (līn′mən), **1** person who sets up or repairs telegraph, telephone, or electric wires; linesman. **2** (in football) a player in the line; a center, guard, tackle, or end. **3** person who inspects railroad tracks. **4** person who carries the line in surveying. *n., pl.* **line men.**

lin en (lin′ən), **1** cloth or thread made from flax. **2** articles made of linen or some substitute. Tablecloths, napkins, sheets, towels, and shirts are all called linen. **3** made of linen. 1,2 *n.,* 3 *adj.*

line of duty, performance of duty or service, especially military duty: *The guard was injured in the line of duty.*

line of fire, path of a bullet, shell, etc.

line of scrimmage, (in football) an imaginary line running across the field at any point where the ball is placed; scrimmage line.

lin er[1] (lī′nər), **1** ship or airplane belonging to a transportation system. **2** person or thing that makes lines. **3** line drive. *n.*

lin er[2] (lī′nər), **1** person who lines or fits a lining to anything. **2** something that serves as a lining. *n.*

line segment, any section between two points on a line; segment.

lines man (līnz′mən), **1** lineman. **2** (in certain games) person who watches the lines which mark out the field, court, etc., and assists the umpire. *n., pl.* **lines men.**

line up or **line-up** (līn′up′), **1** formation of persons or things into a line. A police lineup is an arrangement of a group of persons for identification. **2** list of the players who will take part or are taking part in a game of football, baseball, etc. *n.*

ling (ling), a food fish of the North Atlantic related to the cod. *n., pl.* **ling** or **lings.**

lin ger (ling′gər), stay on; go slowly, as if unwilling to leave: *He lingered after the others had left. v.*

lin ge rie (lan′zhə rē′ *or* län′zhə rā′), women's underwear, nightgowns, etc. *n.*

lin go (ling′gō), INFORMAL. language or talk that sounds strange or is not understood: *baseball lingo. n., pl.* **lingoes.**

lin guist (ling′gwist), **1** an expert in languages or linguistics. **2** person skilled in a number of languages. *n.*

lin guis tic (ling gwis′tik), having to do with language or the study of languages. *adj.* —**lin guis′ti cal ly,** *adv.*

lin guis tics (ling gwis′tiks), science of language; comparative study of languages. *n.*

lin i ment (lin′ə mənt), a soothing liquid which is rubbed on the skin to relieve the pain of sore muscles, sprains, bruises, etc. *n.*

lin ing (lī′ning), layer of material covering the inner surface of something: *the lining of a coat. n.*

link (lingk), **1** any ring or loop of a chain. **2** anything that

li on ess (lī′ə nis), a female lion. *n., pl.* **li on ess es.**
li on heart ed (lī′ən här′tid), brave; courageous. *adj.*
—**li′on heart′ed ly,** *adv.* —**li′on heart′ed ness,** *n.*
li on ize (lī′ə nīz), treat as very important. *v.,* **li on ized, li on iz ing.** —**li′on i za′tion,** *n.*
lion's share, the biggest or best part.
lip (lip), **1** either of the two fleshy, movable edges of the mouth. **2** the folding or bent-out edge of any opening: *the lip of a pitcher.* **3** not heartfelt or deep, but just on the surface: *He gives lip service to the idea, but never practices it.* 1,2 *n.,* 3 *adj.* —**lip′like′,** *adj.*
keep a stiff upper lip, be brave and firm; show no fear or discouragement.
lip less (lip′lis), having no lips. *adj.*
lip py (lip′ē), SLANG. impertinent. *adj.*
lip-read (lip′rēd′), understand speech by watching the movements of the speaker's lips. *v.,* **lip-read** (lip′red′), **lip-read ing.** —**lip′-read′er,** *n.*
lip reading, understanding of speech by watching the movements of the speaker's lips.
lip stick (lip′stik′), a small stick of a waxlike cosmetic, used for coloring the lips. *n.*
liq., **1** liquid. **2** liquor.
liq ue fac tion (lik′wə fak′shən), **1** process of changing into a liquid. **2** liquefied condition. *n.*
liq ue fy (lik′wə fī), change into a liquid; make or become liquid. *v.,* **liq ue fied, liq ue fy ing.** —**liq′ue fi′a ble,** *adj.* —**liq′ue fi′er,** *n.*
li queur (li kėr′), a strong, sweet, highly flavored alcoholic liquor. *n.*
liq uid (lik′wid), **1** substance that is not a solid or a gas; substance that flows freely like water. Mercury is a liquid at room temperature. **2** in the form of a liquid; melted: *liquid soap, butter heated until it is liquid.* **3** clear and bright like water. **4** clear and smooth-flowing in sound: *the liquid notes of a bird.* **5** easily turned into cash: *United States bonds are a liquid investment.* 1 *n.,* 2-5 *adj.* —**liq′uid ly,** *adv.* —**liq′uid ness,** *n.*
liquid air, an intensely cold liquid formed by putting air under very great pressure and then cooling it. It is used as a refrigerant.
liq ui date (lik′wə dāt), **1** pay (a debt). **2** settle the accounts of (a business, etc.); clear up the affairs of (a bankrupt). **3** get rid of (an undesirable person or thing): *The Russian Revolution liquidated the nobility.* **4** kill ruthlessly; exterminate. *v.,* **liq ui dat ed, liq ui dat ing.** —**liq′ui da′tor,** *n.*
liq ui da tion (lik′wə dā′shən), a liquidating or a being liquidated. *n.*
li quid i ty (li kwid′ə tē), liquid condition or quality. *n.*
liquid measure, system for measuring liquids. In the United States:

4 gills	=	1 pint
2 pints	=	1 quart
4 quarts	=	1 gallon
31½ gallons	=	1 barrel
2 barrels (63 gallons)	=	1 hogshead.

liquid oxygen, an intensely cold liquid formed by putting oxygen under very great pressure and then cooling it; lox. It is used as a rocket fuel.
liq uor (lik′ər), **1** an alcoholic drink, such as brandy, gin, rum, or whiskey. **2** any liquid, especially a liquid in which food is packaged, canned, or cooked: *Pickles are put up in a salty liquor. n.*
lir a (lir′ə), **1** the unit of money in Italy. **2** coin or piece of paper money worth a lira. *n., pl.* **lir e** (lir′ā), **lir as.**
Lis bon (liz′bən), capital of Portugal, in the SW part. *n.*
lisle (līl), **1** a fine, strong, linen or cotton thread, used for making stockings, gloves, etc. **2** made of lisle: *lisle stockings.* 1 *n.,* 2 *adj.*

lisp (lisp), **1** use the sound of *th* in *thin* and *then* instead of the sound of *s* or the sound of *z* in speaking: *A person who lisps might say, "Thing a thong" for "Sing a song."* **2** act, habit, or sound of saying a *th* sound for *s* and *z: He spoke with a lisp.* **3** speak imperfectly: *Young children sometimes lisp when they are learning to talk.* 1,3 *v.,* 2 *n.*
lis some or **lis som** (lis′əm), bending easily; lithe; limber; supple. *adj.* —**lis′some ly,** *adv.* —**lis′some ness,** *n.*
list¹ (list), **1** series of names, numbers, words, or phrases: *a shopping list.* **2** make a list of; enter in a list: *A dictionary lists words in alphabetical order.* 1 *n.,* 2 *v.*
list² (list), **1** a tipping to one side; tilt: *the list of a ship.* **2** tip to one side; tilt: *The sinking ship was listing so that water lapped its decks.* 1 *n.,* 2 *v.*
list³ (list), OLD USE. listen; listen to. *v.*
lis ten (lis′n), **1** try to hear; attend with the ears so as to hear: *She listened for the sound of a car. I like to listen to music.* **2** give heed (to advice, temptation, etc.); pay attention. *v.* —**lis′ten er,** *n.*
listen in, **1** listen to others talking on a telephone: *I listened in on the extension to hear what they were saying.* **2** listen to the radio: *Listen in next week for the exciting conclusion of our story.*
Lis ter (lis′tər), **Joseph,** 1827-1912, English surgeon. He was the first to use antiseptic methods in performing operations. *n.*
list less (list′lis), seeming too tired to care about anything; not interested in things; not caring to be active: *a dull and listless mood. adj.* —**list′less ly,** *adv.*
lists (lists), place where knights fought in tournaments. *n.pl.*
enter the lists, join in a contest; take part in a fight, argument, etc.
Liszt (list), **Franz,** 1811-1886, Hungarian composer and pianist. *n.*
lit¹ (lit), lighted; a past tense and a past participle of **light¹.** *v.*
lit² (lit), lighted; a past tense and a past participle of **light³.** *v.*
lit., **1** liter. **2** literature.
lit a ny (lit′n ē), prayer consisting of a series of requests and responses said by the minister or priest and the congregation in turn. *n., pl.* **lit a nies.**
li ter (lē′tər), a unit for measuring volume, especially of liquids, in the metric system; 1.0567 quarts liquid measure, or .908 quart dry measure. A liter is the volume of 1000 cubic centimeters. *n.* Also, **litre.** [*Liter* comes from French *litre,* which is from a medieval Latin word *litra,* meaning "a liquid measure," which came from Greek *litra,* meaning "a pound of twelve ounces."]
lit er a cy (lit′ər ə sē), **1** ability to read and write. **2** having understanding of the essentials of a particular area of knowledge: *computer literacy. n.*
lit er al (lit′ər əl), **1** following the exact words of the original: *a literal translation.* **2** taking words in their usual meaning, without exaggeration or imagination; matter-of-fact: *the literal meaning of a phrase, a literal type of mind.* **3** true to fact: *a literal account. adj.*
lit er al ly (lit′ər ə lē), **1** word for word; without exaggeration or imagination: *Write the story literally as it happened.* **2** actually: *The earthquake literally destroyed hundreds of houses. adv.*
lit e rar y (lit′ə rer′ē), **1** having to do with literature. **2** knowing much about literature. **3** engaged in literature as a profession. *adj.* —**lit′e rar′i ly,** *adv.*
lit er ate (lit′ər it), **1** able to read and write. **2** person who can read and write. **3** acquainted with literature; educated. **4** having understanding of the essentials of a particular area of knowledge: *courses designed to make students literate in science.* 1,3,4 *adj.,* 2 *n.*

lit er a ture (lit′ər ə chu̇r *or* lit′ər ə chər), **1** writings of a period or of a country, especially those kept alive by their beauty of style or thought: *Shakespeare is a great name in English literature.* **2** all the books and articles on a subject: *the literature of stamp collecting.* **3** writing books as a profession. **4** the study of literature: *I shall take literature and mathematics this spring.* **5** INFORMAL. printed matter of any kind: *election campaign literature.* n.

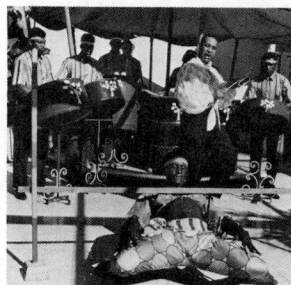

lithe
The **lithe** dancer moved under the bar without touching it.

lithe (līᴛʜ), bending easily; supple: *lithe of body, a lithe willow.* adj. **—lithe′ly,** adv. **—lithe′ness,** n.

lith i um (lith′ē əm), a soft, silver-white metallic element which occurs in various minerals. Lithium is the lightest of all metals. n.

lith o graph (lith′ə graf), **1** print made from a flat stone or metal plate on which the picture, design, etc., is made with a greasy material that will hold printing ink. The rest of the surface is made ink-repellent with water. **2** to print from such a stone or plate. **1** n., **2** v.

li thog ra pher (li thog′rə fər), person who makes lithographs. n.

li thog ra phy (li thog′rə fē), art or process of making lithographs. n.

lith o sphere (lith′ə sfir), the solid part of the earth not including the air and water. n.

Lith u a ni a (lith′ü ā′nē ə), Soviet republic in N Europe, on the Baltic Sea. n. **—Lith′u a′ni an,** adj., n.

lit i gant (lit′ə gənt), person engaged in a lawsuit. n.

lit i ga tion (lit′ə gā′shən), **1** a carrying on a lawsuit. **2** a going to law. **3** a lawsuit or legal proceeding. n.

lit mus (lit′məs), a blue dye obtained from lichens, used in litmus paper as a chemical indicator. n.

litmus paper, paper treated with litmus. Blue litmus paper turns red when put into acid; red litmus paper turns blue when put into alkali.

li tre (lē′tər), liter. n.

lit ter (lit′ər), **1** little bits left around in disorder; things scattered about: *He picked up the litter.* **2** leave odds and ends lying around; scatter things about; make untidy: *You have littered the room with your papers.* **3** the young animals produced at one time: *a litter of puppies.* **4** give birth to (young animals). **5** straw, hay, etc., used as bedding for animals. **6** stretcher for carrying a sick or wounded person. **7** framework to be carried on men's shoulders or by beasts of burden, with a couch usually enclosed by curtains. **1,3,5-7** n., **2,4** v.

lit ter bug (lit′ər bug′), person who throws trash along a highway or sidewalk, in a park, etc. n.

lit tle (lit′l), **1** not big or large; small. A grain of sand or the head of a pin is little. **2** not long in time or in distance; short: *Wait a little while and I'll go a little way with you.* **3** not much; small in number, amount, degree, or importance: *A very sick child has little strength and can eat only a little food.* **4** mean; narrow-minded: *the pettiness of little minds.* **5** a small amount: *She had a big box of candy but gave her sister only a little.* **6** a short time or distance: *Move a little to the left.* **7** to a small extent: *The teacher*

read from an interesting book that was little known to us. **8** not at all: *Little do they know what I plan to do.* **1-4** adj., less or less er, least; or lit tler, lit tlest; **5,6** n., **7,8** adv., less, least. **—lit′tle ness,** n.

little by little, by a small amount at a time; slowly; gradually.

make little of, treat or represent as of little importance.

not a little, much; very: *We were not a little upset by the accident.*

think little of, not value much; consider as unimportant or worthless.

Little America, camp near the South Pole established by Admiral Richard E. Byrd in 1929. See **Antarctica** for map.

Little Bear, Ursa Minor.

Little Dipper, group of seven bright stars in the constellation Ursa Minor.

Little League, a group of baseball teams organized for children from eight to twelve years of age.

Little Rock, capital of Arkansas, in the central part.

li tur gic (lə tėr′jik), liturgical. adj.

li tur gi cal (lə tėr′jə kəl), **1** of liturgies. **2** used in liturgies. adj. **—li tur′gi cal ly,** adv.

lit ur gy (lit′ər jē), a form of public worship. Different churches use different liturgies. n., pl. **lit ur gies.** [*Liturgy* can be traced back to Greek *laos,* meaning "people," and *ergon,* meaning "work."]

liv a ble (liv′ə bəl), **1** fit to live in: *a livable house.* **2** easy to live with: *a livable person.* **3** worth living; endurable. adj. **—liv′a ble ness,** n.

live[1] (liv), **1** have life; be alive; exist: *All creatures have an equal right to live.* **2** remain alive: *She lived until the following year.* **3** last; endure: *His good name will live forever.* **4** keep up life: *Most of us live by working.* **5** feed or subsist: *Lions live upon other animals.* **6** dwell: *live in the country. Who lives in this house?* **7** pass (life): *live a life of ease, live well.* **8** carry out or show in life: *live one's ideals.* **9** have a rich and full life. v., **lived, liv ing.**

live down, live so worthily that (some fault or sin of the past) is overlooked or forgotten.

live up to, act according to; do (what is expected or promised).

live[2] (līv), **1** having life; alive: *a live dog.* **2** burning or glowing: *live coals.* **3** full of energy or activity: *a live person.* **4** of present interest; up-to-date: *a live question.* **5** still in use or to be used: *live steam.* **6** carrying an electric current: *a live wire.* **7** loaded: *a live cartridge.* **8** not recorded on tape or film; broadcast during the actual performance: *a live television show.* adj.

live li hood (līv′lē hu̇d), means of keeping alive; what is needed to support life; a living: *write for a livelihood. She earns her livelihood by working as an editor.* n.

live li ness (līv′lē nis), lively quality or condition. n.

live long (liv′lông′), whole; whole length of; whole; entire: *She is busy the livelong day.* adj.

live ly (līv′lē), **1** full of life and spirit; active; vigorous: *A good night's sleep made us all lively again.* **2** exciting: *We had a lively time during the hurricane.* **3** bright; vivid: *lively colors.* **4** cheerful; gay: *a lively conversation.* **5** bouncing well and quickly: *a lively tennis ball.* **6** in a lively manner. **1-5** adj., **live li er, live li est; 6** adv. **—live′li ly,** adv.

liv en (līv′ən), **1** put life into; cheer up. **2** become more lively; brighten: *As he grew well, his spirits began to liven again.* *v.*

live oak (līv), an evergreen oak of the southern United States.

liv er[1] (liv′ər), **1** the large, reddish-brown organ that makes bile and helps the body absorb food. The liver frees the blood of its waste matter and changes sugar into glycogen. **2** the liver of an animal used as food. *n.*

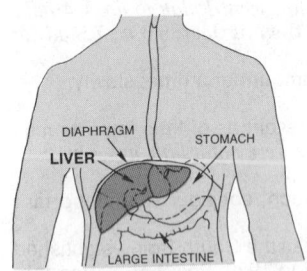

liver[1] (def. 1)

DIAPHRAGM
STOMACH
LIVER
LARGE INTESTINE

liv er[2] (liv′ər), person who lives. *n.*

liv er ied (liv′ər ēd), clothed in livery. *adj.*

Liv er pool (liv′ər pül), seaport city in W England. *n.*

liv er wort (liv′ər wėrt′), **1** plant that grows mostly on damp ground, the trunks of trees, etc. Liverworts are somewhat like mosses. **2** hepatica. *n.*

liv er wurst (liv′ər wėrst′), sausage consisting largely of liver. *n.*

liv er y (liv′ər ē), **1** any uniform provided for servants, or adopted by any group or profession: *a chauffeur in green livery.* **2** the feeding, stabling, and care of horses for pay. **3** the hiring out of horses and carriages. **4** the keeping of cars, boats, bicycles, etc., for hire. **5** livery stable. *n., pl.* **liv er ies.**

livery stable, stable where horses are taken care of for pay or hired out.

lives (līvz), plural of **life.** *n.*

live stock (līv′stok′), farm animals. Cows, horses, sheep, and pigs are livestock. *n.*

live wire (līv), **1** INFORMAL. an energetic, wide-awake person. **2** wire in which an electric current is flowing.

liv id (liv′id), **1** having a dull-bluish or grayish color, as from a bruise: *livid marks on an arm.* **2** very pale: *livid with shock.* **3** flushed; reddish: *livid with rage.* **4** very angry: *Their insults made me livid.* *adj.* —**liv′id ly,** *adv.*

liv ing (liv′ing), **1** having life; being alive: *a living plant.* **2** condition of being alive: *The young people were filled with the joy of living.* **3** means of keeping alive; livelihood: *work for a living.* **4** manner of life: *healthful living.* **5** full of life; vigorous; strong; active: *a living faith.* **6** in actual existence; still in use; alive: *a living language.* **7** true to life; vivid; lifelike: *a picture which is the living image of a person.* **8** of life; for living in: *the poor living conditions in the slums.* **9** sufficient to live on: *a living wage.* **10** of human beings: *within living memory.* **1,5-10** *adj.,* **2-4** *n.* —**liv′ing ly,** *adv.* —**liv′ing ness,** *n.*

living room, room for general family use; sitting room.

Liv ing stone (liv′ing stən), **David,** 1813-1873, Scottish missionary and explorer in Africa. *n.*

Liv y (liv′ē), 59 B.C.-A.D. 17, Roman historian. *n.*

liz ard (liz′ərd), reptile with a long body, long tail, movable eyelids, and usually four legs. Some lizards have no legs and look much like snakes. The iguana, chameleon, and horned toad are lizards. *n.* —**liz′ard like′,** *adj.*

lla ma (lä′mə), a South American mammal that chews the cud and has woolly hair. It is somewhat like a camel, but smaller and without a hump. Llamas are used as beasts of burden. *n., pl.* **lla mas** or **lla ma.**

lla no (lä′nō), (in Spanish America) a broad, treeless, grassy plain. *n., pl.* **lla nos.** [*Llano* was borrowed from Spanish *llano,* which came from Latin *planum,* meaning "level, plain."]

lo (lō), look! see! behold! *interj.*

load (lōd), **1** what one is carrying; burden: *The cart has a load of hay. That's a load off my mind.* **2** amount that usually is carried: *Send us four loads of sand.* **3** place on or in something for conveyance; heap or pile on: *load grain.* **4** put in or put on whatever is to be carried: *load a car, load a ship. She loaded the camera with film.* **5** take on a load: *The ship loaded in five days.* **6** burden; oppress: *load the mind with worries.* **7** supply amply or in excess: *They loaded the singer with compliments.* **8 loads,** *pl.* INFORMAL. a great quantity or number. **9** the weight supported by a structure or part. **10** the total amount of power supplied by a dynamo, generator, or other source of electricity in a given time. **11** one charge of powder and shot for a gun. **12** put a charge in (a gun): *The frontiersman loaded his musket with powder and shot.* **1,2,8-11** *n.,* **3-7,12** *v.* —**load′er,** *n.*

load ed (lō′did), INFORMAL. full of meaning and implications: *a loaded question. adj.*

load star (lōd′stär′), lodestar. *n.*

load stone (lōd′stōn′), lodestone. *n.*

loaf[1] (lōf), **1** bread shaped and baked as one piece. **2** anything like a loaf in shape. Meat loaf is meat chopped and mixed with other things and then baked. *n., pl.* **loaves.**

loaf[2] (lōf), spend time idly; do nothing: *I can loaf all day Saturday. v.*

loaf er (lō′fər), **1** person who loafs; idler. **2 Loafer,** trademark for a shoe resembling a moccasin, but with sole and heel stitched to the upper. *n.*

loam (lōm), rich, fertile earth in which decaying leaves and other plant matter are mixed with clay and sand. *n.*

loam y (lō′mē), of or like loam. *adj.*

loan (lōn), **1** a lending: *She asked for a loan of his pen.* **2** anything that is lent, especially money: *He asked his brother for a small loan.* **3** make a loan; lend: *Her friend loaned her the money.* **1,2** *n.,* **3** *v.*

loath (lōth), unwilling or reluctant: *They were loath to admit that they were wrong. adj.* —**loath′ness,** *n.*

loathe (lōTH), feel strong dislike and disgust for; abhor; hate: *We loathe rotten food or a nasty smell. v.,* **loathed, loath ing.** —**loath′ing ly,** *adv.*

loath ing (lō′ṮHing), strong dislike and disgust; intense aversion. *n.*

loath some (lōṮH′səm), making one feel sick; disgusting: *a loathsome odor. adj.* —**loath′some ly,** *adv.* —**loath′some ness,** *n.*

loaves (lōvz), plural of **loaf**[1]. *n.*

lob (lob), **1** a tennis ball hit in a high arc, usually to the back of the opponent's court. **2** hit (a tennis ball) in a high arc, usually to the back of an opponent's court. **3** throw (a cricket ball) with a slow underhand movement. **1** *n.,* **2,3** *v.,* **lobbed, lob bing.**

lob by (lob′ē), **1** entrance hall; passageway: *the lobby of a theater. A hotel lobby usually has chairs and couches to sit on.* **2** person or persons that try to influence members of a lawmaking body. **3** try to influence the members of a lawmaking body: *The conservation group lobbied to outlaw the use of certain traps by hunters.* **1,2** *n., pl.* **lob bies; 3** *v.,* **lob bied, lob by ing.** —**lob′by er,** *n.*

lob by ist (lob′ē ist), person who tries to influence members of a lawmaking body. *n.*

lobe (lōb), a rounded projecting part. The lobe of the ear is the lower rounded end. *n.*

lobed (lōbd), having a lobe or lobes. *adj.*

lo bel ia (lō bē′lyə), plant with small blue, red, yellow, purple, or white flowers. *n., pl.* **lo bel ias.**

lob lol ly (lob′lol′ē), **1** a pine tree of the southern United States that has a thick bark, long needles, and cones with spiny tips. **2** its coarse wood, used for lumber. *n., pl.* **lob lol lies.**

lobster (def. 1)—about 1 to 2 ft. (30 to 60 cm.) long with the claws

lob ster (lob′stər), **1** a large shellfish having five pairs of legs, with large claws on the front pair. Its shell turns a bright red when boiled. **2** its flesh, used as food. *n.*

lobster pot, trap to catch lobsters.

lo cal (lō′kəl), **1** of a place; of a certain place or places: *the local doctor, local self-government, local news.* **2** of just one part of the body: *a local pain, local disease, local application of a remedy.* **3** making all, or almost all, stops: *a local train.* **4** train, bus, etc., that stops at all, or almost all, of the stations on its route. **5** branch or chapter of a labor union, fraternity, etc. 1-3 *adj.*, 4,5 *n.*

lo cale (lō kal′), a place, especially with reference to events or circumstances connected with it: *The locale of the movie is California in 1849. n.*

lo cal ism (lō′kə liz′əm), a local expression, custom, etc. *n.*

lo cal i ty (lō kal′ə tē), one place and the places near it; region, district, or neighborhood: *I know few people in the locality of Boston. n., pl.* **lo cal i ties.**

lo cal i za tion (lō′kə lə zā′shən), a localizing or a being localized. *n.*

lo cal ize (lō′kə līz), make local; fix in; assign, or limit to a particular place or locality: *The infection seemed to be localized in the foot. v.,* **lo cal ized, lo cal iz ing.**

lo cal ly (lō′kə lē), in a local manner; with regard to place; in one place; in a number of places, but not widely: *Outbreaks of the disease occurred locally. adv.*

lo cate (lō′kāt), **1** establish in a place: *They located their new store on Second Avenue.* **2** establish oneself in a place: *Early settlers located where there was water.* **3** find out the exact position of: *We followed the stream until we located its source.* **4** to state or show the position of: *Can you locate Africa on the globe?* **5** establish the boundaries or rights of: *locate a claim. v.,* **lo cat ed, lo cat ing.** —**lo′cat er, lo′ca tor,** *n.*

be located, be situated; lie: *Albany is located on the Hudson River.*

lo ca tion (lō kā′shən), **1** a locating or a being located: *The scouts argued about the location of the camp.* **2** position or place: *The camp was in a bad location as there was no water near it.* **3** plot of ground marked out by boundaries; lot: *a mining location. n.*

loc. cit., in the place cited.

loch (lok), SCOTTISH. **1** lake: *Loch Lomond.* **2** arm of the sea partly shut in by land. *n.*

Loch Ness (lok′ nes′), a long, narrow and very deep lake in N Scotland. The **Loch Ness Monster,** a large sea animal, is believed by some people to live in the lake.

lo ci (lō′sī), plural of **locus.** *n.*

lock[1] (lok), **1** a means of fastening doors, boxes, etc., consisting of a bolt and usually needing a key of special shape to open it: *The front door of most houses has a lock.* **2** fasten with a lock: *Lock and bar the door.* **3** shut (something in or out or up): *We lock up jewels in a safe.* **4** hold

fast: *The ship was locked in ice. The secret will be locked in my heart forever.* **5** an enclosed section of a canal or dock in which the level of the water can be changed by letting water in or out, to raise or lower ships. **6** the part of a gun by means of which it is fired. **7** join, fit, jam, or link together: *The girls locked arms and walked down the street together.* **8** a kind of hold in wrestling. 1,5,6,8 *n.,* 2-4,7 *v.* —**lock′a ble,** *adj.*

lock out, refuse to give work to employees until they accept the employer's terms.

lock[1] (def. 5)
Locks in a canal allow ships to go from one level of water to another. If the ship enters at the lower level, the gates are closed and water is pumped in to make the level equal with the water above the lock. For ships going the other way, the process is reversed.

lock[2] (lok), **1** curl of hair. **2** portion of hair, wool, flax, etc. **3 locks,** *pl.* the hair of the head: *The child has curly locks. n.*

lock er (lok′ər), **1** a chest, small closet, cupboard, or other compartment that can be locked. **2** a refrigerated compartment for storing frozen foods. *n.*

lock et (lok′it), a small, ornamental case for holding a picture of someone or a lock of hair. A locket is usually worn around the neck on a chain. *n.*

lock jaw (lok′jô′), a form of tetanus in which the jaws become firmly closed. *n.*

lock out (lok′out′), the refusal of an employer to furnish work to employees, used as a means of making them accept the employer's terms. *n.*

lock smith (lok′smith′), person who makes or repairs locks. *n.*

lock up (lok′up′), jail. *n.*

lo co mo tion (lō′kə mō′shən), act or power of moving from place to place. Walking, swimming, and flying are common forms of locomotion. *n.*

lo co mo tive (lō′kə mō′tiv), **1** engine that moves from place to place on its own power, used to pull railroad trains. **2** moving from place to place: *locomotive bacteria.* **3** having to do with the power to move from place to place. 1 *n.,* 2,3 *adj.*

lo cus (lō′kəs), **1** place or locality. **2** (in mathematics) the set of all the points, and only those points, that satisfy a given condition. The locus of all the points which are equidistant from a given point is the surface of a sphere. *n., pl.* **lo ci.**

lo cust (lō′kəst), **1** any of various kinds of grasshoppers which migrate in great swarms, often destroying crops along the way. **2** cicada. **3** tree with small rounded leaflets and clusters of sweet-smelling, white or rose-colored flowers. *n.*

lo cu tion (lō kyü′shən), **1** style of speech. **2** form of expression. *n.*

lode (lōd), a vein of metal ore: *The miners struck a rich lode of copper. n.*

lode star (lōd′stär′), **1** star that shows the way. **2** the North Star. **3** a guide. *n.* Also, **loadstar.**

lode stone (lōd′stōn′), **1** piece of magnetite that attracts iron and steel. It is a natural magnet. **2** something that attracts: *Gold was the lodestone that drew people to Alaska. n.* Also, **loadstone.**

lodge (loj), **1** live in a place for a time: *We lodged in motels on our trip.* **2** supply with a place to live in or sleep in for a time: *Can you lodge us for the weekend?* **3** a place to live in; a house, especially a small or temporary house: *My aunt rents a lodge in the mountains for the summer.* **4** live in a rented room in another's house: *We are merely lodging at present.* **5** get caught or stay in a place without falling or going further: *My kite lodged in the branches of a big tree.* **6** put or send into a particular place: *The archer lodged an arrow in the trunk of the tree.* **7** put before some authority: *We lodged a complaint with the police.* **8** branch of a secret society. **9** the place where it meets. **10** the den of an animal, such as a beaver or an otter. 1,2,4-7 *v.,* **lodged, lodg ing;** 3,8-10 *n.* —**lodge′a ble,** *adj.*

lodg er (loj′ər), person who lives in a rented room in another's house. *n.*

lodg ing (loj′ing), **1** place where one is living only for a time: *a lodging for the night.* **2 lodgings,** *pl.* a rented room or rooms in a house, not in a hotel. *n.*

lodg ment (loj′mənt), **1** act of lodging. **2** condition of being lodged: *the lodgment of a claim against a company.* **3** something lodged or deposited: *a lodgment of earth on a ledge of rock. n.*

lo ess (lō′is), a yellowish-brown loam, usually deposited by the wind. *n.*

loft (lôft), **1** space just below the roof in a cabin; attic. **2** room under the roof of a barn: *This loft is full of hay.* **3** gallery in a church or hall: *a choir loft.* **4** an upper floor of a business building or warehouse. **5** hit or throw (an object) high up. 1-4 *n.,* 5 *v.* [*Loft* came into English about 1000 years ago from Icelandic *lopt,* meaning "air, sky, loft."] —**loft′less,** *adj.*

loft i ly (lôf′tə lē), in a lofty manner. *adv.*

loft i ness (lôf′tē nis), lofty quality or condition. *n.*

loft y (lôf′tē), **1** very high: *lofty mountains.* **2** exalted; dignified; grand: *lofty aims.* **3** proud; haughty: *a lofty contempt for others. adj.,* **loft i er, loft i est.**

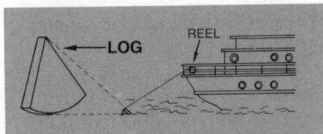

log (def. 8)—trailing in the water behind a ship. The length of line that runs off the reel in a given time indicates the approximate speed of the ship.

log (lôg), **1** a length of wood just as it comes from the tree. **2** made of logs: *a log house.* **3** to cut down trees, cut them into logs, and get them out of the forest. **4** cut (trees) into logs. **5** the daily record of a ship's voyage. **6** enter in a ship's log. **7** record of an airplane trip, performance of an engine, etc. **8** a float for measuring the speed of a ship. 1,5,7,8 *n.,* 2 *adj.,* 3,4,6 *v.,* **logged, logging.** —**log′like′,** *adj.*

lo gan ber ry (lō′gən ber′ē), a large, purplish-red fruit of a plant which is a cross between a blackberry and a red raspberry. *n., pl.* **lo gan ber ries.**

lo ga rithm (lô′gə riϮн′əm), the power to which a fixed number or base (usually 10) must be raised in order to produce a given number. If the fixed number or base is 10, the logarithm of 1000 is 3; the logarithm of 10,000 is 4; the logarithm of 100,000 is 5. *n.*

log book (lôg′bůk′), **1** book in which a daily record of a

ship's voyage is kept. **2** a book for records of an airplane's trip. **3** journal of travel. *n.*

loge (lōzh), **1** box in a theater or opera house. **2** seating area in a theater, made up of the first few rows on the ground floor or in the lowest balcony. *n.*

log ger (lô′gər), **1** person whose work is logging. **2** machine for loading or hauling logs. *n.*

log ger head (lô′gər hed′), **1** a stupid person. **2** a large sea turtle of the Atlantic. *n.*

log gia (loj′ə), gallery or arcade open to the air on at least one side. *n., pl.* **log gias.**

log ging (lô′ging), work of cutting down trees, sawing them into logs, and moving the logs out of the forest. *n.*

log ic (loj′ik), **1** science of proof and of reasoning. **2** use of argument; reasoning. **3** sound sense; reason: *There is much logic in what you say. n.*

log i cal (loj′ə kəl), **1** of logic; according to the principles of logic: *logical reasoning.* **2** reasonable; reasonably expected: *An upset stomach is a logical result of overeating.* **3** reasoning correctly: *a logical person, a clear and logical mind. adj.* —**log′i cal ly,** *adv.* —**log′i cal ness,** *n.*

lo gi cian (lō jish′ən), an expert in logic. *n.*

lo gis tic (lō jis′tik), of logistics. *adj.*

lo gis tics (lō jis′tiks), the planning and carrying out of any complex or large-scale operation, especially one of military movement, evacuation, and supply. *n.*

LO GO (lō′gō), computer programming language designed to be usable by children. *n.*

log roll ing (lôg′rō′ling), **1** a giving of political aid in return for a like favor. **2** act of rolling logs, especially by treading on them. *n.*

lo gy (lō′gē), heavy, sluggish, or dull. *adj.,* **lo gi er, lo gi est.** —**lo′gi ly,** *adv.* —**lo′gi ness,** *n.*

-logy, *combining form.* **1** study or science of: *Biology = the science of life.* **2** words, discussion, or writing: *Phraseology = arrangement of words.* [The form *-logy* comes from Greek *logos,* meaning "word."]

loin (loin), **1** Usually, **loins,** *pl.* the part of the body of an animal or human being between the ribs and the hipbones. The loins are on both sides of the backbone and nearer to it than the flanks are. **2** a piece of meat from this part of an animal: *a loin of pork. n.*
gird up one's loins, get ready for action.

loin cloth (loin′klôth′), piece of cloth worn around the hips and between the thighs. *n., pl.* **loin cloths** (loin′klôϮнz′ or loin′klôths′).

Loire (lwär), river flowing from S France into the Bay of Biscay. See **Rhine** for map. *n.*

loi ter (loi′tər), **1** linger idly; stop and play along the way: *She loitered along the street, looking into all the store windows.* **2** spend (time) idly: *loiter the hours away. v.* —**loi′ter er,** *n.* —**loi′ter ing ly,** *adv.*

Lo ki (lō′kē), (in Norse myths) the god of destruction. *n.*

loll (lol), **1** recline or lean in a lazy manner: *loll on a sofa.* **2** hang loosely or droop: *A dog's tongue lolls out in hot weather.* **3** allow to hang or droop: *The dog lolled out its tongue. v.* —**loll′er,** *n.* —**loll′ing ly,** *adv.*

lol li pop or **lol ly pop** (lol′ē pop), piece of hard candy, usually on the end of a small stick. *n.*

Lom bard y (lom′bər dē), region in N Italy. *n.*

Lo mé (lô mā′), capital of Togo, in the SW part. *n.*

Lo mond (lō′mənd), **Loch,** lake in S central Scotland. *n.*

lon., longitude.

Lon don (lun′dən), **1** capital of the United Kingdom of Great Britain and Northern Ireland, in SE England, on the Thames. London is one of the largest cities in the world. **2 Jack,** 1876-1916, American writer of novels and short stories. *n.*

lone (lōn), **1** without others; alone; solitary; single: *The lone traveler was glad to reach home.* **2** lonesome; lonely:

They lived a lone life after their children grew up and moved away. **3** standing apart; isolated: *a lone house. adj.* **—lone′ness,** *n.*

lone li ness (lōn′lē nis), a being lonely; solitude. *n.*

lone ly (lōn′lē), **1** feeling oneself alone and longing for company or friends: *He was lonely while his brother was away.* **2** without many people: *a lonely road.* **3** alone; isolated: *a lonely tree. adj.,* **lone li er, lone li est. —lone′li ly,** *adv.*

lone some (lōn′səm), **1** feeling lonely: *I was lonesome while you were away.* **2** making one feel lonely: *a lonesome journey.* **3** unfrequented; desolate: *a lonesome road.* **4** solitary: *One lonesome pine stood in the yard. adj.,* **lonesom er, lone som est. —lone′some ly,** *adv.* **—lone′-some ness,** *n.*

long¹ (lông), **1** that measures much from end to end: *An inch is short; a mile is long. A year is a long time. I read a long story.* **2** in length: *My table is three feet long.* **3** having a long narrow shape: *a long board.* **4** a long time: *Summer will come before long.* **5** for a long time: *I can't stay long.* **6** for its whole length: *all summer long, all day long.* **7** at a point of time far distant from the time indicated: *long before, long since.* **8** (of vowels or syllables) taking a comparatively long time to speak. A vowel like *a* in *late, e* in *be,* or *o* in *note* is a long vowel. 1-3,8 *adj.,* **long er** (lông′gər), **long est** (lông′gist); 4 *n.,* 5-7 *adv.* **—long′ly,** *adv.*

as long as or **so long as,** provided that.

long² (lông), wish very much; desire greatly: *long for one's family, long to see a good friend. v.*

long., longitude.

long boat (lông′bōt′), the largest boat carried by a sailing ship. *n.*

long bow (lông′bō′), a large bow drawn by hand, for shooting a long, feathered arrow. *n.*

long distance, operator or exchange that takes care of long-distance calls.

long-dis tance (lông′dis′təns), **1** of telephone service between distant places. **2** from or covering a great distance: *long-distance trucking, a long-distance race.* **3** call by long distance. 1,2 *adj.,* 3 *v.,* **long-dis tanced, long-dis tanc ing.**

lon gev i ty (lon jev′ə tē), long life: *A good diet promotes longevity. n.*

Long fel low (lông′fel′ō), Henry Wadsworth, 1807-1882, American poet. *n.*

long hand (lông′hand′), ordinary writing, not shorthand or typewriting. *n.*

longhorn

long horn (lông′hôrn′), one of a breed of cattle with very long horns, formerly common in the southwestern United States. *n.*

long house, a large, rectangular dwelling of certain North American Indians, especially the Iroquois. Many families lived together in one long house.

a hat	i it	oi oil	ch child	a in about
ā age	ī ice	ou out	ng long	e in taken
ä far	o hot	u cup	sh she	ə = i in pencil
e let	ō open	u̇ put	th thin	o in lemon
ē equal	ô order	ü rule	ᵺ then	u in circus
ėr term			zh measure	

long ing (lông′ing), **1** earnest desire: *a longing for home.* **2** having or showing earnest desire: *a child's longing look at a window full of toys.* 1 *n.,* 2 *adj.* **—long′ing ly,** *adv.* **—long′ing ness,** *n.*

long ish (lông′ish), somewhat long. *adj.*

Long Island, large island south of Connecticut. It is part of New York State.

Long Island Sound, long, narrow strip of water between Connecticut and Long Island. It is an inlet of the Atlantic.

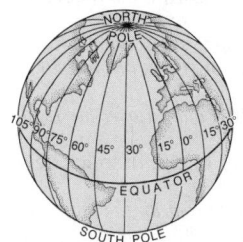

longitude
circles of longitude

lon gi tude (lon′jə tüd *or* lon′jə tyüd), distance east or west on the earth's surface, measured in degrees from a certain meridian, usually the one through Greenwich, England. *n.*

lon gi tu di nal (lon′jə tüd′n əl *or* lon′jə tyüd′n əl), **1** of length; in length: *longitudinal measurements.* **2** running lengthwise: *The flag of the United States has longitudinal stripes.* **3** of longitude: *The longitudinal difference between New York and Seattle is about 50 degrees. adj.*

lon gi tu di nal ly (lon′jə tüd′n ə lē *or* lon′jə tyüd′n ə lē), **1** lengthwise. **2** according to longitude. *adv.*

long jump, broad jump.

long-lived (lông′līvd′ *or* lông′livd′), living or lasting a long time. *adj.* **—long′-lived ness,** *n.*

long-play ing record (lông′plā′ing), a phonograph record playing at 33¹⁄₃ revolutions per minute. A long-playing record 12 inches in diameter provides about 25 minutes of sound on each side.

long-range (lông′rānj′), **1** looking ahead; future: *long-range plans.* **2** able to go a great distance: *a long-range ballistic missile. adj.*

long shore man (lông′shôr′mən), person whose work is loading and unloading ships. *n., pl.* **long shore men.**

long shot, an attempt at something difficult.
not by a long shot, not at all.

long stand ing (lông′stan′ding), having lasted for a long time: *a longstanding feud. adj.*

long-suf fer ing (lông′suf′ər ing), enduring trouble, pain, or injury long and patiently. *adj.* **—long′-suf′fer ing ly,** *adv.*

long-wind ed (lông′win′did), talking or writing at great length; tiresome: *a long-winded speaker, a long-winded magazine article. adj.* **—long′-wind′ed ly,** *adv.* **—long′-wind′ed ness,** *n.*

look (lu̇k), **1** turn the eyes; see; try to see: *Look at the pictures.* **2** look hard; stare: *look questioningly.* **3** search: *I looked through the drawer to see if I could find my keys.* **4** a glance; seeing: *He took a quick look at the magazine.* **5** have a view; face: *Our house looks upon a garden.* **6** expect; anticipate: *I have been looking to hear from you.*

7 seem; appear: *She looks pale.* **8** appearance; aspect: *A deserted house has a desolate look.* **9** show how one feels by one's appearance: *He said nothing but looked his disappointment.* **10 looks,** pl. personal appearance: *He has his mother's good looks.* 1-3,5-7,9 *v.*, 4,8,10 *n.* **—look′er,** *n.*

look after, attend to; take care of: *He looked after the younger children.*

look alive, hurry up! be quick!

look at, examine; pay attention to: *You must look at all the facts.*

look back, think about the past; recollect.

look down on, despise; scorn.

look for, expect: *We'll look for you tonight.*

look forward to, expect with pleasure; be eager for.

look in, make a short visit.

look into, examine; inspect.

look on, 1 watch without taking part: *The teacher conducted the experiment while we looked on.* **2** regard; consider: *I look on her as a very able person.*

look oneself, seem like oneself; seem well.

look out, be careful; watch out: *Look out for cars as you cross the street.*

look over, examine; inspect: *I looked over my report for spelling errors.*

look to, 1 attend to; take care of. **2** turn to for help. **3** look forward to; expect.

look up, 1 refer to; find: *She looked up the unfamiliar word in a dictionary.* **2** call on; visit: *Look me up when you come to town.* **3** INFORMAL. get better; improve: *Things are looking up for me since I got the new job.*

look upon, regard; consider.

look up to, respect; admire.

looking glass, mirror.

look out (lůk′out′), **1** a sharp watch for someone to come or for something to happen: *Keep a lookout for Mother.* **2** place from which to watch. A crow's-nest is a lookout. **3** the person who has the duty of watching: *The lookout cried, "Land ho!"* **4** INFORMAL. thing to be cared for or worried about. *n.*

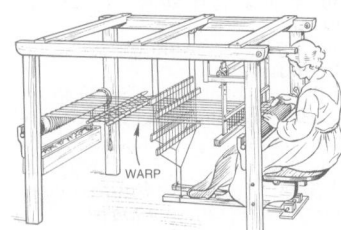

loom[1]—To make cloth, the weaver passes the shuttle carrying the thread of the woof through the threads of the warp. Foot pedals raise and lower alternate warp threads.

loom[1] (lüm), frame or machine for weaving cloth. *n.*

loom[2] (lüm), appear dimly or vaguely as a large, threatening shape: *A large iceberg loomed through the thick, gray fog. War loomed ahead. v.*

loon (lün), a large, web-footed diving bird that eats fish. Loons have a loud, wild cry. *n.*

loon
about 2¹/₂ ft. (75 cm.) long

loon y (lü′nē), INFORMAL. crazy, foolish, or silly. *adj.*, **loon i er, loon i est. —loon′i ness,** *n.*

loop (lüp), **1** the part of a curved string, ribbon, bent wire, etc., that crosses itself. **2** thing, bend, course, or motion shaped like this. In writing, *b* and *g* and *h* and *l* have loops. *The road makes a wide loop around the lake.* **3** a fastening or ornament formed of cord, etc., bent and crossed. **4** make a loop of. **5** make loops in. **6** fasten with a loop: *She looped the sail to the mast with a rope.* **7** encircle with a loop. **8** form a loop or loops. **9** a turn like the letter *ℓ*, especially one made by an airplane. **10** a set of instructions that a computer carries out repeatedly. 1-3,9,10 *n.*, 4-8 *v.* **—loop′er,** *n.*

loop hole (lüp′hōl′), **1** a small opening in a wall for looking through, for letting in air, or for firing through at an enemy outside. **2** a means of escape: *The clever lawyer found a loophole in the law to save his client. n.*

loose (lüs), **1** not fastened: *a loose thread.* **2** not tight: *loose clothing.* **3** not firmly set or fastened in: *a loose tooth.* **4** not bound together: *loose papers.* **5** not put up in a box, can, etc.: *loose coffee.* **6** not shut in or up; free: *The dog has been loose all night.* **7** not pressed close together: *loose earth, cloth with a loose weave.* **8** not strict, close, or exact: *a loose translation from another language, a loose account of the accident.* **9** careless about morals or conduct: *a loose character.* **10** set free; let go: *With an effort I loosed my arm from her grip.* **11** make loose; untie; unfasten: *loose a knot.* **12** in a loose manner. 1-9 *adj.,* **loos er, loos est;** 10,11 *v.,* **loosed, loos ing;** 12 *adv.* **—loose′ly,** *adv.* **—loose′ness,** *n.*

break loose, run away; free oneself.

let loose, set loose, or **turn loose,** set free; let go; release.

loose-joint ed (lüs′join′tid), able to move very freely. *adj.*

loose-leaf (lüs′lēf′), having pages or sheets that can be taken out and replaced: *a loose-leaf notebook. adj.*

loos en (lü′sn), **1** make loose or looser; untie; unfasten: *After our feast we had to loosen our belts.* **2** become loose or looser: *My clothes loosened as I lost weight. v.*

loot (lüt), **1** plunder; rob: *The burglar looted the jewelry store.* **2** things taken in plundering; spoils; booty: *loot taken by soldiers from a captured town, burglar's loot.* 1 *v.,* 2 *n.* **—loot′er,** *n.*

lop[1] (lop), **1** cut; cut off. **2** cut branches or twigs from. *v.,* **lopped, lop′ping. —lop′per,** *n.*

lop[2] (lop), **1** hang loosely; droop. **2** flop. **3** hanging loosely; drooping. 1,2 *v.,* **lopped, lop ping;** 3 *adj.*

lope (lōp), **1** to run with a long, easy stride: *The horse loped along the trail in an easy gallop.* **2** a long, easy stride. 1 *v.,* **loped, lop ing;** 2 *n.* **—lop′er,** *n.*

lop-eared (lop′ird′), having ears that hang loosely or droop: *a lop-eared dog. adj.*

lop sid ed (lop′sī′did), larger or heavier on one side than the other; leaning to one side. *adj.* **—lop′sid′ed ly,** *adv.* **—lop′sid′ed ness,** *n.*

lo qua cious (lō kwā′shəs), talking much; fond of talking. *adj.* **—lo qua′cious ly,** *adv.* **—lo qua′cious ness,** *n.*

lo quac i ty (lō kwas′ə tē), inclination to talk a great deal; talkativeness. *n.*

lord (lôrd), **1** ruler, master, or chief; person who has the power. **2** rule proudly or absolutely. **3** a feudal superior. **4 Lord, a** God. **b** Christ: *the year of our Lord.* **5** (in Great Britain) a man of any of certain high ranks. **6 Lord, a** title used in writing or speaking about noblemen of certain high ranks in Great Britain: *Lord Tennyson.* **b** title given by courtesy to men of certain ranks in Great Britain: *the Lord Chief Justice, the Lord Mayor of London.* **7 the Lords, a** House of Lords. **b** members of the House of Lords. 1,3-7 *n.,* 2 *v.* [*Lord* is from Old English *hlāford,* originally meaning "one who guards the loaf of bread" or "master of the house," which comes from *hlāf*, meaning "loaf," and *weard*, meaning "keeper, guard."]

lord it over, domineer over: *She was the oldest and lorded it over the rest of us.*

lord ly (lôrd′lē), **1** like a lord; suitable for a lord; grand; magnificent. **2** haughty; insolent; scornful: *lordly airs.* *adj.,* **lord li er, lord li est. —lord′li ness,** *n.*

lord ship (lôrd′ship), **1** rank or position of a lord. **2 Lordship,** title used in speaking to or of a man having the rank of Lord: *your Lordship, his Lordship.* *n.*

Lord's Prayer, (in the Bible) the prayer given by Jesus to His disciples which begins with the words "Our Father Who art in Heaven."

Lord's Supper, 1 Last Supper. **2** Holy Communion.

lore (lôr), **1** facts and stories about a certain subject: *fairy lore, bird lore, Irish lore.* **2** learning; knowledge. *n.*

lor gnette (lôr nyet′), eyeglasses or opera glasses mounted on a handle. *n.*

Lor raine (lə rān′), region in NE France, formerly part of Alsace-Lorraine. *n.*

lor ry (lôr′ē), BRITISH. a motor truck. *n., pl.* **lor ries.**

Los An ge les (lôs an′jə ləs *or* lôs an′jə lēz′), the principal city in S California and the third largest city in the United States.

lose (lüz), **1** not have any longer; have taken away from one by accident, carelessness, parting, death, etc.: *lose a finger, lose a friend, lose one's life.* **2** be unable to find: *lose a book.* **3** fail to keep, preserve, or maintain; cease to have: *lose patience, lose your temper.* **4** fail to follow with eye, hearing, mind, etc.: *lose a few words of what was said.* **5** fail to have, get, catch, etc.: *lose a sale.* **6** fail to win: *lose the prize.* **7** be defeated: *Our team lost.* **8** bring to destruction; ruin: *The ship and its crew were lost.* **9** spend or let go by without any result; waste: *lose an opportunity, lose time waiting.* **10** be or become worse off in money, in numbers, etc.: *lose at poker, lose heavily in a battle.* **11** cause the loss of: *Delay lost the battle.* **12** cause to lose: *That one act of misconduct lost me my job.* *v.,* **lost, los ing. —los′a ble,** *adj.*

lose oneself, 1 let oneself go astray; become bewildered. **2** become absorbed.

los er (lü′zər), **1** person or thing that loses or suffers loss. *Our team was the loser.* **2** INFORMAL. person or thing that loses consistently, or fails; failure: *a born loser.* **3** person who loses (in the manner indicated): *a poor loser, a good loser.* *n.*

los ing (lü′zing), **1** not able to win or be won: *You are playing a losing game if you cheat on exams.* **2 losings,** *pl.* losses. **1** *adj.,* **2** *n.*

loss (lôs), **1** losing or having lost something: *Loss of one's health is serious but the loss of a pencil is not.* **2** person or thing lost: *Her house was a complete loss to the fire.* **3** harm or disadvantage caused by losing something; value of the thing lost: *The loss from the fire was $10,000.* **4** a defeat: *Our team had two losses and one tie out of ten games played.* *n., pl.* **loss es.**

at a loss, not sure; puzzled; uncertain; in difficulty: *The embarrassed child was at a loss as to how to act.*

lost (lôst), **1** past tense and past participle of **lose.** *I lost my new pen. I had already lost my ruler.* **2** no longer possessed or kept: *lost friends.* **3** no longer to be found; missing: *lost articles.* **4** not won: *a lost battle.* **5** hopeless: *a lost cause.* **6** not used to good purpose; wasted: *lost time.* **7** destroyed or ruined: *a lost soul.* **8** bewildered: *a lost expression.* **1** *v.,* **2-8** *adj.* **—lost′ness,** *n.*

be lost on, have no effect on; fail to influence.

lost in, completely absorbed or interested in: *He was lost in a book and failed to hear us come in.*

lost to, insensible to: *They were having such a good time*

that they were lost to all sense of responsibility.

lot (lot), **1** a number of persons or things considered as a group; collection: *This lot of oranges is better than the last.* **2** Often, **lots,** *pl.* INFORMAL. a great many; a great deal: *a lot of books, lots of money. I have a lot of marbles.* **3** a plot of ground: *Her house is between two empty lots.* **4** a portion or part: *I divided the fruit into ten lots.* **5** one of a set of objects, such as bits of paper, wood, etc., used to decide something by chance: *We drew lots to see who should be captain.* **6** such a method of deciding: *It was settled by lot.* **7** choice made in this way: *The lot fell to me.* **8** what one gets by lot; one's share or portion. **9** one's fate or fortune: *It was his lot later to become president.* **10** a great deal; much: *I feel a lot better.* **1-9** *n.,* **10** *adv.*

lo tion (lō′shən), a liquid medicine or cosmetic which is applied to the skin. Lotions are used to relieve pain, to heal, to cleanse, or to benefit the skin. *n.*

lot ter y (lot′ər ē), a scheme for distributing prizes by lot or chance. In a lottery a large number of tickets are sold, some of which draw prizes. *n., pl.* **lot ter ies.**

lo tus (lō′təs), **1** kind of water lily that grows in Egypt and Asia. **2** (in Greek legends) a plant whose fruit was supposed to cause a dreamy mental state in which one forgets real life. *n., pl.* **lo tus es.**

loud (loud), **1** making a great sound; not quiet or soft: *a loud voice, a loud noise.* **2** resounding; noisy: *loud music, a loud place to study.* **3** in a loud manner: *The hunter called long and loud.* **4** clamorous; insistent: *be loud in demands.* **5** INFORMAL. showy in dress or manner: *loud clothes.* **1,2, 4,5** *adj.,* **3** *adv.* **—loud′ly,** *adv.* **—loud′ness,** *n.*

loud speak er (loud′spē′kər), device for making sounds louder, especially in a radio or phonograph. *n.*

Lou is XIV (lü′ē), 1638-1715, king of France from 1643 to 1715. He was called "Louis the Great."

Louis XVI, 1754-1793, king of France from 1774 to 1792. He was beheaded during the French Revolution.

Lou i si an a (lü ē′zē an′ə), one of the south central states of the United States. *Abbreviation:* La. or LA *Capital:* Baton Rouge. *n.* [*Louisiana* comes from French *Louisiane*, originally the name of the entire Mississippi valley. The French explorer La Salle named it in honor of his king, *Louis XIV*.] **—Lou i′si an′i an, Lou i′si an′an,** *adj., n.*

Louisiana Purchase, large region that the United States bought from France in 1803. It extended from the Mississippi River to the Rocky Mountains and from Canada to the Gulf of Mexico.

Louisiana Purchase
shown by darker area on a modern map

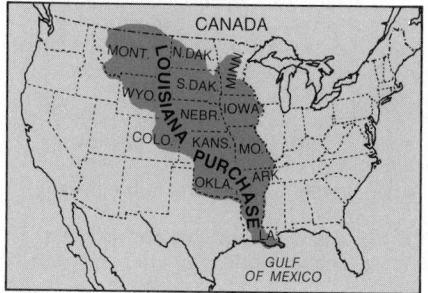

Lou is ville (lü′ē vil), city in N Kentucky, on the Ohio River. *n.*

lounge (lounj), **1** stand, stroll, sit, or lie at ease in a lazy way: *He lounged in an old chair.* **2** pass time lazily or at one's ease. **3** a comfortable and informal room in which one can lounge and be at ease: *a theater lounge.* **4** a couch or sofa. 1,2 *v.*, **lounged, loung ing;** 3,4 *n.* —**loung′er,** *n.*

louse (def. 1)
about ¹/₈ in. (3 mm.) long

louse (lous), **1** a small, wingless insect that infests the hair or skin of people and animals and sucks their blood. **2** any of various other insects that infest and bite birds and a few other animals. **3 louse up,** SLANG. spoil; get (something) all confused or in a mess: *louse up a deal.* 1,2 *n.*, *pl.* **lice;** 3 *v.*, **loused, lous ing.**

lous y (lou′zē), **1** infested with lice. **2** SLANG. bad; poor; of low quality. *adj.*, **lous i er, lous i est.** —**lous′i ly,** *adv.* —**lous′i ness,** *n.*

lout (lout), an awkward, stupid person; boor. *n.*

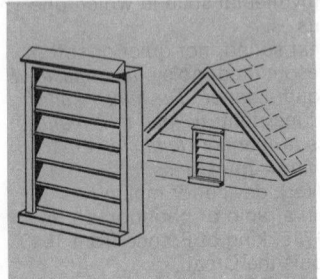

louvers
left, def. 1;
right, def. 2

lou ver (lü′vər), **1** any of several overlapping horizontal boards or strips of wood set at a slant in a window or other opening, so as to keep out rain, but provide ventilation and light. **2** window or other opening covered with these boards. *n.*

Lou vre (lü′vrə), a famous museum in Paris, formerly a palace of the kings of France. *n.*

lov a ble (luv′ə bəl), worthy of being loved; endearing: *She was a most lovable person, always kind and thoughtful. adj.* Also, **loveable.** —**lov′a ble ness,** *n.*

lov a bly (luv′ə blē), in a lovable manner. *adj.*

love (luv), **1** a warm and tender liking; deep feeling of fondness and friendship; great affection or devotion: *love of one's family, love for a sweetheart.* **2** have such a warm liking or deep feeling for: *We love our parents. I love my country.* **3** person who is loved; sweetheart. **4** a strong liking: *a love of books.* **5** like very much; take great pleasure in: *She loves music.* **6** a score of zero in tennis. 1,3,4,6 *n.*, 2,5 *v.*, **loved, lov ing.**

fall in love, begin to love; come to feel love.

make love, caress, kiss, etc., as lovers do; pay loving attention; woo.

love a ble (luv′ə bəl), lovable. *adj.* —**love′a ble ness,** *n.* —**love′a bly,** *adv.*

love bird (luv′bėrd′), a small parrot that shows great affection for its mate. They are often kept in cages as pets. *n.*

love less (luv′lis), without love; not loved. *adj.* —**love′less ly,** *adv.* —**love′less ness,** *n.*

love li ness (luv′lē nis), beauty. *n.*

love lorn (luv′lôrn′), suffering because of love; forsaken by the person whom one loves. *adj.* —**love′lorn′ness,** *n.*

love ly (luv′lē), **1** beautiful or endearing in appearance or character; lovable: *They are the loveliest children we know.* **2** INFORMAL. very pleasing; delightful: *We had a lovely holiday. adj.,* **love li er, love li est.**

lov er (luv′ər), **1** person who is in love with another. **2** person having a strong liking: *a lover of books. n.* —**lov′er like′,** *adj.*

love seat, seat or small sofa for two persons.

love sick (luv′sik′), languishing because of love. *adj.* —**love′sick′ness,** *n.*

lov ing (luv′ing), feeling or showing love; affectionate; fond. *adj.* —**lov′ing ly,** *adv.* —**lov′ing ness,** *n.*

loving cup, a large cup with handles, awarded as a trophy.

lov ing-kind ness (luv′ing kīnd′nis), kindness coming from love: *the loving-kindness of one's parents. n.*

low¹ (lō), **1** not high or tall; short: *low walls. This footstool is very low.* **2** near the ground; close to the earth: *a low shelf, a low jump.* **3** of humble rank; lowly: *to rise rapidly from a low position as clerk to president of the company.* **4** less than usual in amount, degree, force, value, etc.; small: *a low price, low temperature, low speed.* **5** nearly used up: *Our supply of coal is very low.* **6** unfavorable; poor: *I have a low opinion of their work.* **7** mean; coarse; vulgar: *low company.* **8** feeble; weak: *a low state of health.* **9** deep in pitch: *a low note.* **10** not loud; soft: *a low whisper.* **11** at or to a low point, place, rank, amount, degree, price, pitch, etc.: *The sun sank low. Supplies are running low.* **12** arrangement of gears to give the lowest speed and the greatest power. **13** a low point, level, position, etc.: *Many stocks fell to new lows after the bad news was received.* 1-10 *adj.*, 11 *adv.*, 12,13 *n.* —**low′ness,** *n.*

lay low, 1 knock down: *The boxer laid low his opponent.* **2** kill.

lie low, stay hidden; keep still: *The robbers lay low for a time.*

low² (lō), **1** make the sound of a cow; moo. **2** the sound a cow makes; mooing. 1 *v.*, 2 *n.*

low brow (lō′brou′), INFORMAL. **1** person who is not cultured or intellectual. **2** of or suitable for a lowbrow. 1 *n.*, 2 *adj.*

Low Countries, the Netherlands, Belgium, and Luxembourg.

low down (lō′doun′), SLANG. actual facts or truth: *She gave me the lowdown on several confusing rumors that I had heard. n.*

low-down (lō′doun′), INFORMAL. low; mean; contemptible: *Selling me a broken radio was a low-down trick. adj.*

low er¹ (lō′ər), **1** let down or haul down: *We lower the flag at night.* **2** make lower: *lower the volume of a radio.* **3** sink; become lower: *The sun lowered slowly.* **4** bring down in rank, station, or estimation; degrade; dishonor. **5** more low: *Prices were lower last year than this.* 1-4 *v.*, 5 *adj.*, *adv.* —**low′er a ble,** *adj.*

low er² (lou′ər), **1** (of the sky, weather, etc.) look dark and threatening. **2** frown; scowl. **3** a frown; scowl. 1,2 *v.*, 3 *n.*

Low er California (lō′ər), a narrow peninsula in NW Mexico, south of California.

lower case, small letters, not capitals.

low er-case (lō′ər kās′), (in printing) in small letters, not capitals. *adj.*

lower house or **Lower House,** the larger and more representative branch of a lawmaking body that has two branches, made up of members usually elected by popular vote. The House of Representatives is the lower house of Congress.

low er most (lō′ər mōst), lowest. *adj.*

lower world, 1 hell; Hades. **2** earth.

low land (lō′lənd), **1** country or region that is lower and flatter than the neighboring country. **2 Lowlands,** *pl.* a low, flat region in S and E Scotland. *n.*

low land er (lō′lən dər), **1** person born or living in a lowland. **2 Lowlander,** person born or living in the Lowlands of Scotland. *n.*

low li ness (lō′lē nis), humbleness of feeling or behavior; humble station in life. *n.*

low ly (lō′lē), **1** low in rank, station, position, or development: *a lowly clerk, a lowly job.* **2** modest in feeling, behavior, or condition; humble; meek: *He held a lowly opinion of himself.* **3** humbly; meekly. **1,2** *adj.,* **low li er, low li est; 3** *adv.*

low-pitched (lō′picht′), **1** of low tone or sound; deep. **2** having little slope. *adj.*

low profile, a moderate attitude or position, deliberately chosen in order to avoid notice. **—low′-pro′file,** *adj.*

low-spir it ed (lō′spir′ə tid), sad; depressed. *adj.* **—low′-spir′it ed ly,** *adv.* **—low′-spir′it ed ness,** *n.*

low spirits, sadness; depression.

low tide, 1 the lowest level of the tide. **2** time when the tide is lowest.

lox[1] (loks), salmon preserved in salt, then soaked in fresh water before being eaten. *n.* [*Lox*[1] comes from Yiddish *laks.*]

lox[2] (loks), liquid oxygen. *n.* [*Lox*[2] comes from the words *liquid oxygen.* It was formed by using the first letter of *liquid* and the first two letters of *oxygen.*]

loy al (loi′əl), **1** true and faithful to love, promise, or duty. **2** faithful to one's king, government, or country. *adj.* **—loy′al ly,** *adv.* **—loy′al ness,** *n.*

loy al ist (loi′ə list), person who supports the ruler or the existing government, especially in time of revolt. *n.*

loy al ty (loi′əl tē), loyal feeling or behavior; faithfulness. *n., pl.* **loy al ties.**

Loy o la (loi ō′lə), **Ignatius of,** 1491-1556, Spanish soldier, priest, and saint, founder of the Jesuit order. *n.*

loz enge (loz′inj), **1** design or figure shaped like this: ◇; diamond; rhombus. **2** a small tablet of any shape used as medicine or candy. Cough drops are sometimes called lozenges. *n.*

LP, trademark for a long-playing record.

Lr, symbol for lawrencium.

LSD, an extremely powerful drug which produces hallucinations and distorted perceptions.

Lt., Lieutenant.

Ltd. or **ltd.,** limited.

Lu, symbol for lutetium.

Lu an da (lü än′də), capital of Angola, on the Atlantic. *n.*

Lu ang Pra bang (lü äng′ prä bäng′), city in Laos, formerly the royal capital, in the N part.

lu au (lü′ou), a Hawaiian feast, generally held outdoors, with roast pig as the main dish. *n.*

lub ber (lub′ər), **1** a big, clumsy, stupid fellow. **2** a clumsy sailor. *n.*

lu bri cant (lü′brə kənt), oil, grease, etc., for putting on parts of machines that slide or move against one another, to make them smooth and slippery so that they will work easily. *n.*

lu bri cate (lü′brə kāt), **1** make machinery smooth, slippery, and easy to work by putting on oil, grease, etc. **2** make slippery or smooth. *v.,* **lu bri cat ed, lu bri cat ing. —lu′bri ca′tor,** *n.*

lu bri ca tion (lü′brə kā′shən), a lubricating or a being lubricated. *n.*

lu cent (lü′snt), **1** bright or shining; luminous. **2** letting the light through; clear. *adj.* **—lu′cent ly,** *adv.*

lu cid (lü′sid), **1** easy to follow or understand: *A good explanation is lucid.* **2** sane: *An insane person sometimes has lucid intervals.* **3** clear; transparent: *a lucid stream.* **4** shining; bright. *adj.* **—lu′cid ly,** *adv.* **—lu′cid ness,** *n.*

lu cid i ty (lü sid′ə tē), lucid quality or condition. *n.*

Lu ci fer (lü′sə fər), the chief rebel angel who was cast out of heaven; Satan; the Devil.

Lu cite (lü′sīt), trademark for a clear plastic compound used instead of glass for airplane windows, lenses, etc. *n.*

luck (luk), **1** something which seems to happen or come to one by chance; chance; fortune: *Luck favored me, and I won.* **2** good luck: *She gave me a penny for luck. n.*

in luck, having good luck; lucky: *I am in luck today; I found a quarter.*

luck out, INFORMAL. be successful in a difficult situation because of good luck.

out of luck, having bad luck; unlucky.

luck i ly (luk′ə lē), by good luck; fortunately. *adv.*

luck i ness (luk′ē nis), quality or condition of being lucky. *n.*

luck less (luk′lis), having or bringing bad luck; unlucky. *adj.* **—luck′less ly,** *adv.* **—luck′less ness,** *n.*

luck y (luk′ē), having or bringing good luck: *a lucky day, a lucky meeting. adj.,* **luck i er, luck i est. —luck′i ness,** *n.*

lu cra tive (lü′krə tiv), bringing in money; profitable. *adj.* **—lu′cra tive ly,** *adv.* **—lu′cra tive ness,** *n.*

lu cre (lü′kər), money considered as bad or degrading. *n.*

ludicrous
He wore a **ludicrous** revolving hat with various attachments on it.

lu di crous (lü′də krəs), amusingly absurd; ridiculous: *the ludicrous acts of a clown. adj.* **—lu′di crous ly,** *adv.*

luff (luf), **1** turn the bow of a ship toward the wind. **2** act of turning the bow of a ship toward the wind. **3** the forward edge of a fore-and-aft sail. **1** *v.,* **2,3** *n.*

lug[1] (lug), pull along or carry with effort; drag: *We lugged the rug to the yard to clean it. v.,* **lugged, lug ging.**

lug[2] (lug), a projecting part used to hold or grip something. *n.*

lug[3] (lug), lugsail. *n.*

luge (lüzh), **1** a racing sled, used by one or two persons. **2** race on a luge. **1** *n.,* **2** *v.,* **luged, lug ing** or **luge ing. —lug′er,** *n.*

lug gage (lug′ij), baggage. *n.* **—lug′gage less,** *adj.*

lugger

lug ger (lug′ər), boat with lugsails. *n.*

lug sail (lug′sāl′ *or* lug′səl), a four-cornered sail held by a yard that slants across the mast. *n.*

lu gu bri ous (lü gü′brē əs *or* lü gyü′brē əs), too sad; overly mournful: *the lugubrious howl of a dog. adj.* —**lu gu′bri ous ly,** *adv.* —**lu gu′bri ous ness,** *n.*

lug worm (lug′wėrm′), kind of worm that burrows in sand along the seashore. *n.*

Luke (lük), **1** (in the Bible) a physician who was the companion of the apostle Paul. **2** the third book of the New Testament. It tells the story of the life of Jesus. *n.*

luke warm (lük′wôrm′), **1** neither hot nor cold; moderately warm. **2** showing little enthusiasm; half-hearted: *a lukewarm greeting. adj.* —**luke′warm′ly,** *adv.* —**luke′-warm′ness,** *n.*

lull (lul), **1** soothe with sounds or caresses; cause to sleep: *The soft music lulled me to sleep.* **2** make or become calm or more nearly calm; quiet: *Their confidence lulled my fears. The wind lulled.* **3** period of less noise or violence; brief calm: *a lull in a storm.* 1,2 *v.,* 3 *n.* —**lull′ing-ly,** *adv.*

lul la by (lul′ə bī), song for singing to a child in a cradle; soft song to lull a baby to sleep. *n., pl.* **lul la bies.**

lu lu (lü′lü), SLANG. an unusual person or thing: *The thunderstorm was a lulu. n.*

lum ba go (lum bā′gō), pain in the muscles of the small of the back and in the loins. *n.*

lum bar (lum′bər), of the loin or loins: *the lumbar region. adj.*

lum ber[1] (lum′bər), **1** timber that has been roughly cut into boards, planks, etc., and prepared for use. **2** cut and prepare lumber. 1 *n.,* 2 *v.* —**lum′ber er,** *n.* —**lum′ber-less,** *adj.*

lum ber[2] (lum′bər), move along heavily and noisily; roll along with difficulty: *The old truck lumbered down the road. v.*

lum ber ing[1] (lum′bər ing), business of cutting and preparing timber for use. *n.*

lum ber ing[2] (lum′bər ing), moving along heavily, noisily, or with difficulty. *adj.* —**lum′ber ing ly,** *adv.*

lum ber jack (lum′bər jak′), person whose work is cutting down trees and sending the logs to the sawmill; woodsman; logger. *n.*

lum ber man (lum′bər mən), **1** lumberjack. **2** person who prepares lumber or buys and sells lumber. *n., pl.* **lum ber men.**

lum ber yard (lum′bər yärd′), place where lumber is stored and sold. *n.*

lu mi nar y (lü′mə ner′ē), **1** a heavenly body that gives or reflects light. **2** a famous person. *n., pl.* **lu mi nar ies.**

lu mi nes cence (lü′mə nes′ns), the giving out of light without much heat, at a temperature below that of in-candescent bodies. Luminescence includes phosphorescence and fluorescence. *n.*

lu mi nes cent (lü′mə nes′nt), giving out light without much heat. Fireflies and fluorescent lamps are luminescent. *adj.*

lu mi nos i ty (lü′mə nos′ə tē), **1** luminous quality or condition. **2** something luminous. *n., pl.* **lu mi nos i ties.**

lu mi nous (lü′mə nəs), **1** shining by its own light: *The sun and stars are luminous bodies.* **2** full of light; bright: *a luminous sunset.* **3** easily understood; clear; enlightening. *adj.* —**lu′mi nous ly,** *adv.* —**lu′mi nous ness,** *n.*

lump[1] (lump), **1** a small, solid mass of no particular shape: *a lump of coal.* **2** a swelling; bump: *a lump on the head.* **3** form into a lump or lumps: *The cornstarch lumped because we cooked it too fast.* **4** in lumps; in a lump: *lump coal, lump sugar.* **5** put together; deal with in a mass or as a whole: *We will lump all our expenses.* **6** not in parts; whole: *I was given a lump sum of money for all of my living expenses.* 1,2 *n.,* 3,5 *v.,* 4,6 *adj.*

a lump in the throat, feeling of inability to swallow, caused by pity, sorrow, or other strong emotion.

lump[2] (lump), INFORMAL. put up with; endure: *If you don't like it, you can lump it. v.*

lump i ness (lum′pē nis), a being lumpy or full of lumps. *n.*

lump ish (lum′pish), **1** like a lump; heavy and clumsy. **2** dull; stupid. *adj.* —**lump′ish ly,** *adv.* —**lump′ish-ness,** *n.*

lump y (lum′pē), **1** full of lumps: *lumpy gravy.* **2** covered with lumps: *lumpy ground. adj.,* **lump i er, lump i est.** —**lump′i ly,** *adv.*

lu na cy (lü′nə sē), **1** insanity. **2** extreme folly. *n., pl.* **lu na cies.**

lu nar (lü′nər), **1** of the moon. **2** like the moon. *adj.*

lunar module, an independent part of a spacecraft, which carries astronauts from the moon-orbiting craft to the surface of the moon and back.

lunar month, the period of one complete revolution of the moon around the earth; the interval between one new moon and the next; about 29¹/₂ days.

lu na tic (lü′nə tik), **1** an insane person. **2** insane. **3** for insane people: *a lunatic asylum.* **4** extremely foolish; idiotic: *a lunatic search for buried treasure.* 1 *n.,* 2-4 *adj.*

WORD HISTORY

lunatic

Lunatic is from Latin *lunaticus,* which comes from *luna,* meaning "moon." It got this meaning because it was once thought that insanity was caused by changes of the moon.

lunch (lunch), **1** a light meal between breakfast and dinner: *We usually have lunch at noon.* **2** food for a lunch. **3** eat lunch. 1,2 *n., pl.* **lunch es;** 3 *v.* —**lunch′er,** *n.* —**lunch′less,** *adj.*

lunch eon (lun′chən), **1** lunch. **2** a formal lunch. *n.* —**lunch′eon less,** *adj.*

lunch eon ette (lun′chə net′), restaurant in which light meals are served. *n.*

lunch room (lunch′rüm′ *or* lunch′rùm′), **1** restaurant in which light meals are served. **2** room in a school, factory, etc., where light meals are served. *n.*

lunch time (lunch′tīm′), time at which lunch is eaten or served. *n.*

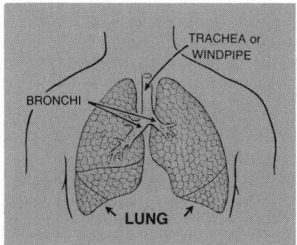

lung (lung), either one of a pair of saclike, spongy organs in the chest of human beings and certain other animals that breathe air. Lungs give the blood the oxygen it needs, and relieve it of carbon dioxide. *n.* —**lung′like′**, *adj.*

lunge (lunj), **1** any sudden forward movement, such as a thrust with a sword or other weapon. **2** move suddenly forward; thrust: *The dog lunged at the stranger.* 1 *n.,* 2 *v.,* **lunged, lung ing.** —**lung′er,** *n.*

lung fish (lung′fish′), fish having a lunglike sac in addition to gills, enabling it to obtain oxygen both in and out of the water. Lungfishes are found in Australia, Africa, and South America. *n., pl.* **lung fish es** or **lung fish.**

lu pine or **lu pin** (lü′pən), plant related to the pea, with long spikes of flowers, clusters of hairy leaflets, and flat pods with bean-shaped seeds. *n.*

lurch[1] (lėrch), **1** a sudden leaning or roll to one side, like that of a ship, a car, or a staggering person: *The boat gave a lurch and upset.* **2** make a lurch; stagger: *The injured animal lurched forward.* 1 *n., pl.* **lurch es;** 2 *v.*

lurch[2] (lėrch). **leave in the lurch,** leave in a helpless condition or difficult situation. *n.*

lure (lür), **1** power of attracting or fascinating; charm; allure; attraction: *Many people feel the lure of the sea.* **2** lead away or into something by arousing desire; attract; tempt: *Bees are lured by the scent of flowers.* **3** a decoy or bait, especially an artificial bait used in fishing. **4** attract with a bait: *We lured the rat into a trap.* 1,3 *n.,* 2,4 *v.,* **lured, lur ing.** —**lur′er,** *n.*

lur id (lür′id), **1** lighted up with a red or fiery glare: *The sky was lurid with the flames of the burning city.* **2** glaring in brightness or color: *a lurid red.* **3** terrible; sensational; startling: *lurid crimes. adj.* —**lur′id ly,** *adv.* —**lur′-id ness,** *n.*

lurk (lėrk), **1** stay about without arousing attention; wait out of sight; be hidden: *A tiger was lurking in the jungle.* **2** move about in a secret and sly manner: *Several people were seen lurking near the house before it was robbed. v.* —**lurk′er,** *n.*

Lu sa ka (lü sä′kə), capital of Zambia, in the central part. *n.*

lus cious (lush′əs), **1** delicious; richly sweet: *a luscious peach.* **2** very pleasing to taste, smell, hear, see, or feel: *a luscious garden. adj.* —**lus′cious ly,** *adv.* —**lus′cious-ness,** *n.*

lush (lush), **1** tender and juicy; growing thick and green: *Lush grass grows along the river banks.* **2** characterized by abundant growth; producing abundantly. **3** luxurious. *adj.* —**lush′ly,** *adv.* —**lush′ness,** *n.*

lust (lust), **1** strong desire. **2** strong sexual desire. **3** have a strong desire: *lust after money and power.* 1,2 *n.,* 3 *v.* —**lust′er,** *n.*

lus ter (lus′tər), **1** a bright shine on the surface: *the luster of pearls.* **2** brightness: *the luster in the eyes of a happy child.* **3** fame; glory; brilliance: *Many prizes added luster to the artist's reputation.* **4** a shiny, metallic, often iridescent surface on pottery or china. *n.* Also, **lustre.** —**lus′ter-less,** *adj.*

lust ful (lust′fəl), full of lust or desire; lewd. *adj.*

—**lust′ful ly,** *adv.* —**lust′ful ness,** *n.*

lust i ly (lus′tə lē), in a lusty manner; vigorously; heartily. *adv.*

lust i ness (lus′tē nis), a being lusty; vigor. *n.*

lus tre (lus′tər), luster. *n.* —**lus′tre less,** *adj.*

lus trous (lus′trəs), having luster; shining; glossy: *lustrous satin. adj.* —**lus′trous ly,** *adv.* —**lus′trous ness,** *n.*

lust y (lus′tē), strong and healthy; full of vigor: *a lusty athlete. adj.,* **lust i er, lust i est.**

lute

lute (lüt), a musical instrument, much used in the 1500's and 1600's, having a pear-shaped body and usually six pairs of strings. It is played by plucking the strings. *n.*

lu te ti um or **lu te ci um** (lü tē′shē əm), a metallic element which usually occurs in nature with ytterbium. *n.*

Lu ther (lü′thər), **Martin,** 1483-1546, leader of the Protestant Reformation in Germany. *n.*

Lu ther an (lü′thər ən), **1** having to do with Luther or the church that was named for him. **2** member of the Lutheran Church. 1 *adj.,* 2 *n.*

Lux em bourg or **Lux em burg** (luk′səm bėrg′), **1** small country in W Europe, bordered by West Germany, France, and Belgium. See **Gaul** for map. **2** its capital. *n.*

lux ur i ance (lug zhúr′ē əns *or* luk shúr′ē əns), luxuriant growth or productiveness; rich abundance. *n.*

lux ur i ant (lug zhúr′ē ənt *or* luk shúr′ē ənt), **1** growing thick and green. **2** producing abundantly. **3** rich in ornament. *adj.* —**lux ur′i ant ly,** *adv.*

lux ur i ate (lug zhúr′ē āt *or* luk shúr′ē āt), **1** indulge in luxury. **2** take great delight: *The campers planned to luxuriate in hot baths when they came home.* **3** grow very abundantly. *v.,* **lux ur i at ed, lux ur i at ing.**

lux ur i ous (lug zhúr′ē əs *or* luk shúr′ē əs), **1** fond of luxury; tending toward luxury; self-indulgent: *a luxurious taste for fine food.* **2** giving luxury; very comfortable and beautiful: *Some theaters are luxurious. adj.* —**lux ur′i ous-ly,** *adv.* —**lux ur′i ous ness,** *n.*

lux ur y (luk′shər ē *or* lug′zhər ē), **1** comforts and beauties of life beyond what is really necessary. **2** use of the best and most costly food, clothes, houses, furniture, and amusements: *The movie star was accustomed to luxury.* **3** thing that one enjoys, usually something choice and costly: *luxuries such as fine paintings.* **4** thing pleasant but not necessary: *Candy is a luxury.* **5** providing lavish comfort and enjoyment; luxurious: *a luxury hotel.* 1-4 *n.,* *pl.* **lux ur ies;** 5 *adj.*

Lu zon (lü zon′), chief island of the Philippines. *n.*

-ly¹, *suffix added to adjectives to form adverbs.* **1** in a _____ manner: *Cheerfully = in a cheerful manner.* **2** in _____ ways or respects: *Financially = in financial respects.* **3** to a _____ degree or extent: *Greatly = to a great degree.* **4** in, to, or from a _____ direction: *Northerly = to or from the north.* **5** in a _____ place: *Thirdly = in the third place.* **6** at a _____ time: *Recently = at a recent time.*

-ly², *suffix added to nouns to form adjectives.* **1** like a _____: *Ghostly = like a ghost.* **2** like that of a _____; characteristic of a _____: *Brotherly = like that of a brother.* **3** suited to a _____; fit or proper for a _____: *Gentlemanly = suited to a gentleman.* **4** of each or every _____; occurring once per _____: *Monthly = of every month.*

ly ce um (lī sē′əm), **1** lecture hall; place where lectures are given. **2** an association for instruction and entertainment through lectures, debates, and concerts. *n.*

Lyd i a (lid′ē ə), ancient country in W Asia Minor, famous for its wealth and luxury. See **Persia** for map. *n.* —**Lyd′i an,** *adj., n.*

lye (lī), any of several strong alkaline solutions used in making soap and in cleaning. *n.*

ly ing¹ (lī′ing), **1** a telling a lie; habit of telling lies. **2** false; untruthful. **3** present participle of **lie¹.** *I was not lying; I told the truth.* 1 *n.,* 2 *adj.,* 3 *v.* —**ly′ing ly,** *adv.*

ly ing² (lī′ing), present participle of **lie².** *I was lying on the ground. v.*

lymph (limf), a nearly colorless liquid in the tissues of the body, filtered from the blood. Lymph bathes and nourishes the tissues. *n.*

lym phat ic (lim fat′ik), **1** of lymph; carrying lymph. **2** sluggish; pale; lacking energy. *adj.*

lymphatic vessel, tube or canal through which lymph is carried from different parts of the body.

lymph node or **lymph gland,** any of the small oval bodies occurring along the paths of the lymphatic vessels. Lymph nodes filter out harmful microorganisms from the lymph.

lymph o cyte (lim′fə sīt), a type of white blood cell, produced by lymph tissues. *n.*

lymph oid (lim′foid), of lymph, lymphocytes, or lymph tissue. *adj.*

lynch (linch), put (an accused person) to death, usually by hanging, without a lawful trial: *The angry mob lynched an innocent man. v.* —**lynch′er,** *n.*

lynx (lingks), wildcat of the northern United States and Canada with a short tail, rather long legs, and tufts of hair at the ends of its ears. *n., pl.* **lynx es** or **lynx.** —**lynx′like′,** *adj.*

lynx-eyed (lingks′īd′), having sharp eyes or keen sight. *adj.*

ly on naise (lī′ə nāz′), fried with pieces of onions: *lyonnaise potatoes. adj.*

Ly ons (lī′ənz or lē ôn′), city in E central France, on the Rhone River. *n.*

Ly ra (lī′rə), a small northern constellation that was thought of as arranged in the shape of a lyre. It contains the star Vega. *n.* Also, **Lyre.**

lyre (def. 1)

lyre (līr), **1** an ancient stringed musical instrument somewhat like a small harp. **2 Lyre,** Lyra. *n.*

lyre bird (līr′bėrd′), an Australian bird. The male has a long tail that is lyre-shaped when spread. *n.*

lyr ic (lir′ik), **1** a short poem expressing personal emotion. A love poem, a patriotic song, a lament, and a hymn might all be lyrics. **2** having to do with such poems: *a lyric poet.* **3** characterized by a spontaneous expression of feeling. **4** of or suitable for singing. **5** Usually, **lyrics,** *pl.* the words for a song. 1,5 *n.,* 2-4 *adj.*

lyr i cal (lir′ə kəl), **1** emotional; poetic: *She became almost lyrical when she described the scenery.* **2** lyric. *adj.* —**lyr′i cal ly,** *adv.*

lyr i cism (lir′ə siz′əm), lyric character, form, or expression. *n.*

lyr i cist (lir′ə sist), **1** person who writes the words for a song; writer of lyrics. **2** a lyric poet. *n.*

ly sin (lī′sn), antibody that can dissolve bacteria, red blood cells, and other cellular elements. *n.*

lynx
about 3 ft. (1 m.)
long with the tail

Mm

a hat	**i** it	**oi** oil	**ch** child	⎧ a in about
ā age	**ī** ice	**ou** out	**ng** long	⎪ e in taken
ä far	**o** hot	**u** cup	**sh** she	ə = ⎨ i in pencil
e let	**ō** open	**ů** put	**th** thin	⎪ o in lemon
ē equal	**ô** order	**ü** rule	**ŦH** then	⎩ u in circus
ėr term			**zh** measure	

M or **m** (em), **1** the 13th letter of the English alphabet. **2** the Roman numeral for 1000. *n., pl.* **M's** or **m's.**

m., **1** meter or meters. **2** mile or miles. **3** minute or minutes.

M., **1** Monday. **2** Monsieur.

ma (mä), INFORMAL. mamma; mother. *n., pl.* **mas.**

MA, Massachusetts (used with postal Zip Code).

M.A., Master of Arts. Also, **A.M.**

ma'am (mam), madam. *n.*

ma ca bre (mə kä′brə or mə kä′bər), gruesome; horrible; ghastly. *adj.*

ma cad am (mə kad′əm), **1** small, broken stones. Layers of macadam are rolled until solid and smooth to make roads. **2** road or pavement made of this. *n.*

ma cad am ize (mə kad′ə mīz), make or cover (a road) with macadam. *v.,* **ma cad am ized, ma cad am iz ing.** **—ma cad′am i za′tion,** *n.*

ma caque (mə käk′), a short-tailed monkey of Asia, the East Indies, and North Africa. *n.*

machete
used to cut
sugar cane

mac a ro ni (mak′ə rō′nē), flour paste that has been dried, usually in the form of hollow tubes, to be cooked for food. *n., pl.* **mac a ro nis** or **mac a ro nies.**

mac a roon (mak′ə rün′), a very sweet cookie, made of whites of eggs, sugar, and ground almonds or coconut. *n.*

Mac Ar thur (mək är′thər), **Douglas,** 1880-1964, American general in World War II and the Korean War. *n.*

ma caw (mə kô′), a large parrot of South and Central America, with a long tail, brilliant feathers, and a harsh voice. *n.*

Mac beth (mək beth′), **1** play by Shakespeare. **2** the principal character in this play, who murders his king and becomes king himself. His wife, Lady Macbeth, helps him do this. *n.*

mace¹ (mās), **1** a club with a heavy metal head, often spiked, used as a weapon in the Middle Ages. **2** staff carried by or before an official as a symbol of authority. *n.*

mace² (mās), spice made from the dried outer covering of nutmegs. *n.*

Mac e don (mas′ə don), Macedonia. *n.*

Mac e do ni a (mas′ə dō′nē ə), ancient country in SE Europe, north of Greece. Macedonia now forms parts of Yugoslavia, Bulgaria, and Greece. See **Etruria** for map. *n.* **—Mac′e do′ni an,** *adj., n.*

mac e rate (mas′ə rāt′), **1** soften or separate the parts of a substance by soaking for some time. Flowers are macerated to extract their perfume. **2** become or cause to become thin. *v.,* **mac e rat ed, mac e rat ing. —mac′e ra′tion,** *n.* **—mac′e ra′tor,** *n.*

Mach (mäk), Mach number. *n.*

mach., **1** machine. **2** machinery.

macaque
about 2 ft. (60 cm.)
long with tail

ma chet e (mə shet′ē or mə chet′ē), a large, heavy knife, used as a tool and weapon in South America, Central America, and the West Indies. *n.*

Mach i a vel li (mak′ē ə vel′ē), **Niccolò,** 1469-1527, Italian statesman and writer who advised rulers to use craft and deceit to maintain their authority. *n.*

Mach i a vel li an (mak′ē ə vel′ē ən), **1** of Machiavelli or his political theory. **2** characterized by subtle or unscrupulous cunning; crafty. *adj.*

mach i nate (mak′ə nāt), contrive or devise artfully or with evil purpose; plot; intrigue. *v.,* **mach i nat ed, mach i nat ing. —mach′i na′tor,** *n.*

mach i na tion (mak′ə nā′shən), **1** evil or artful plotting; scheming against authority. **2** Usually, **machinations,** *pl.* an evil plot; secret or cunning scheme: *The election of our candidate was almost prevented by the machinations of the opponent. n.*

macaw
about 2 ft. (60 cm.) long

ma chine (mə shēn′), **1** arrangement of fixed and moving parts for doing work, each part having some special function: *Sewing machines and washing machines make housework easier.* **2** of a machine or machines: *the machine age, machine action.* **3** make or finish with a machine: *The steel was machined to exact specifications.* **4** by or with a machine, not by hand: *machine printing.* **5** device for applying force or changing its direction. Levers and pulleys are simple machines. **6** automobile. **7** airplane. **8** person or group that acts without thinking. **9** group of people controlling an organization: *a political*

machine. 1,5-9 *n.*, 2,4 *adj.*, 3 *v.*, **ma chined, ma chin ing.** [*Machine* came into English about 400 years ago from French *machine,* and can be traced back to Greek *mēchanē,* meaning "device."] —**ma chin′a ble, ma chine′a ble,** *adj.* —**ma chine′like′,** *adj.*

machine gun, gun that fires ammunition automatically and can keep up a rapid fire of bullets.

ma chine-gun (mə shēn′gun′), fire at with a machine gun. *v.*, **ma chine-gunned, ma chine-gun ning.**

machine language, computer programming language written with only the binary digits 0 and 1. A computer can use a machine language directly, while other computer languages must be translated into this form.

ma chin er y (mə shē′nər ē), 1 machines: *A factory contains much machinery.* 2 the parts or works of a machine: *The machinery of a typewriter should be kept clean.* 3 any combination of persons or things by which something is kept going or something is done: *Police officers, judges, courts, and prisons are the machinery of the law.* *n., pl.* **ma chin er ies.**

machine shop, workshop where machines or parts of machines are made or repaired.

machine tool, a power-driven tool or machine used to form metal into desired shapes by cutting, hammering, squeezing, etc.

ma chin ist (mə shē′nist), 1 a skilled worker with machine tools. 2 person who makes and repairs machinery. *n.*

ma chis mo (mä chēz′mō), manliness, especially when strong or aggressive in nature; excessive concern over one's manliness. *n.*

Mach number (mäk), number expressing the ratio of the speed of an object to the speed of sound in the same medium. An aircraft traveling at the speed of sound has a Mach number of 1; at twice the speed of sound its Mach number is 2. Also, **Mach.**

ma cho (mä′chō), 1 a strong, virile man. 2 machismo. *n., pl.* **ma chos** for 1.

mac in tosh (mak′ən tosh), mackintosh. *n., pl.* **mac in tosh es.**

mack er el (mak′ər əl), a saltwater food fish of the northern Atlantic. *n., pl.* **mack er el** or **mack er els.**

mackerel sky, sky spotted with small, white, fleecy clouds.

Mack i nac (mak′ə nô), **Straits of,** strait connecting Lake Michigan and Lake Huron. *n.*

mack i naw (mak′ə nô), 1 kind of short coat made of heavy woolen cloth. 2 kind of thick woolen blanket, often with bars of color, used in the northern and western United States and Canada. *n.*

mack in tosh (mak′ən tosh), 1 a waterproof coat; raincoat. 2 waterproof cloth. *n., pl.* **mack in tosh es.** Also, **macintosh.** [*Mackintosh* was named for Charles *Macintosh,* 1766-1843, a Scottish inventor.]

mac ra mé or **mac ra me** (mak′rə mā), a coarse lace or fringe made by knotting thread or cord in patterns. *n.*

mac ro bi ot ic (mak′rō bī ot′ik), of a diet that is intended to prolong life, based on brown rice and other organic foods, fish, etc., but not including foods such as meat and eggs: *a macrobiotic lunch.* *adj.*

mac ro cosm (mak′rə koz′əm), the universe. *n.*

ma cron (mā′kron), a straight, horizontal line (¯) placed over a vowel to show that it is pronounced as a long vowel. EXAMPLES: cāme, bē. *n.*

mad (mad), 1 out of one's mind; crazy; insane. 2 very angry; furious: *The insult made me mad.* 3 much excited; wild: *The dog made mad efforts to catch up with the automobile.* 4 foolish; unwise: *a mad undertaking.* 5 blindly and unreasonably fond: *She is mad about skiing.* 6 wildly gay or merry: *Tomorrow will be the maddest, merriest day*

of the year. 7 having rabies. A mad dog often foams at the mouth and may bite people. *adj.*, **mad der, mad dest.** [*Mad* comes from Old English (*ge*)*mæded,* meaning "rendered insane."] —**mad′ly,** *adv.*

like mad, furiously; very hard, fast, etc.: *I ran like mad to catch the train.*

Mad a gas car (mad′ə gas′kər), island country in the Indian Ocean, east of S Africa. *Capital:* Antananarivo. *n.*

mad am (mad′əm), a polite title used in writing or speaking to any woman: *Good day, madam.* *n., pl.* **mad ams** or **mes dames.**

mad ame (mad′əm *or* mä däm′), FRENCH. Mrs.; madam. *n., pl.* **mes dames.**

mad cap (mad′kap′), 1 person who goes ahead and carries out wild ideas without stopping to think first. 2 wild; hasty. 1 *n.*, 2 *adj.*

mad den (mad′n), make or become mad: *The crowd was maddened by the umpire's decision.* *v.*

mad den ing (mad′n ing), very annoying; irritating: *maddening delays.* *adj.* —**mad′den ing ly,** *adv.*

made (mād), 1 past tense and past participle of **make.** *The cook made the cake. It was made of flour, milk, butter, eggs, and sugar.* 2 built; formed: *a strongly made swing.* 1 *v.*, 2 *adj.*

Ma deir a (mə dir′ə), 1 group of Portuguese islands in the Atlantic, west of N Africa. 2 the most important island of this group. 3 Often, **madeira.** kind of wine made there. *n.*

mad e moi selle (mad′ə mə zel′), FRENCH. Miss. *n., pl.* **mes de moi selles.**

made-to-or der (mād′tû ôr′dər), made according to the buyer's wishes. *adj.*

made-up (mād′up′), 1 not real; invented; imaginary: *a made-up story.* 2 painted, powdered, etc., with cosmetics: *made-up lips.* *adj.*

mad house (mad′hous′), 1 asylum for insane people. 2 place of uproar and confusion: *The arena was a madhouse after the home team won the championship game.* *n., pl.* **mad hous es** (mad′hou′ziz).

Mad i son (mad′ə sən), 1 **James,** 1751-1836, the fourth president of the United States, from 1809 to 1817. He had an important part in drawing up the Constitution of the United States. 2 capital of Wisconsin, in the S part. *n.*

mad man (mad′man′), an insane man; crazy person. *n., pl.* **mad men.**

mad ness (mad′nis), 1 a being crazy; insane condition; loss of one's mind. 2 great anger; rage; fury: *In his madness he kicked the fence post.* 3 folly: *It would be madness to try to sail a boat in this storm.* *n.*

Ma don na (mə don′ə), 1 Mary, the mother of Jesus. 2 Also, **madonna.** picture or statue of her. *n., pl.* **Ma don nas** or **ma don nas** for 2.

mad ras (mad′rəs *or* mə dras′), a closely woven cotton cloth, used for shirts, dresses, etc. *n.* [This cloth was named for *Madras,* where it was first produced.]

Ma dras (mə dras′), seaport in SE India. *n.*

Ma drid (mə drid′), capital of Spain, in the central part. *n.*

mad ri gal (mad′rə gəl), 1 a short poem, often about love, that can be set to music. 2 song with parts for several voices, usually sung without instrumental accompaniment. *n.*

mael strom (māl′strəm), 1 a great or turbulent whirlpool. 2 **Maelstrom,** a dangerous whirlpool off the NW coast of Norway. 3 a violent confusion of feelings, ideas, or conditions. *n.*

maes tro (mī′strō), 1 a great composer, teacher, or conductor of music. 2 master of any art. *n., pl.* **maes tros.**

Ma fi a or **ma fi a** (mä′fē ə), 1 a secret organization of criminals supposed to control underworld activities in various parts of the world. **2** a secret Sicilian society hostile to the law and engaging in terrorist activities. *n.*

mag a zine (mag′ə zēn′ *or* mag′ə zēn′), **1** a publication issued at regular intervals, especially weekly or monthly, which contains stories, articles, photographs, etc., by various contributors. **2** room in a fort or warship for storing gunpowder and other explosives. **3** a building for storing gunpowder, guns, food, or other military supplies. **4** place in a repeating or automatic gun from which cartridges are fed into the firing chamber. **5** place for holding a roll or reel of film in a camera or projector. *n.*

WORD HISTORY

magazine

Magazine came into English about 400 years ago from French *magazin*, and can be traced back to Arabic *makhzan*, meaning "storehouse."

Ma gel lan (mə jel′ən), **1** Ferdinand, 1480?-1521, Portuguese navigator. His ship was the first to sail around the world, though he himself was killed soon after he had explored the Philippine Islands. **2 Strait of,** strait at the S tip of South America. *n.*

ma gen ta (mə jen′tə), **1** a purplish-red dye. **2** purplish-red. **3** a purplish red. 1,3 *n.,* 2 *adj.*

mag got (mag′ət), the legless, wormlike larva of various kinds of flies. Maggots usually live in decaying matter. *n.*

Ma gi (mā′jī), (in the Bible) the Three Wise Men who followed the star to Bethlehem and brought gifts to the infant Jesus. *n.pl.* of **Magus.**

mag ic (maj′ik), **1** the pretended art of using secret charms, spirits, etc., to make unnatural things happen: *The fairy's magic changed the brothers into swans.* **2** done by magic or as if by magic: *A magic palace stood in place of their hut.* **3** something that produces results as if by magic; mysterious influence; unexplained power: *the magic of music.* **4** art or skill of creating illusions, especially by sleight of hand. 1,3,4 *n.,* 2 *adj.* [*Magic* is from Latin *magice,* which came from Greek *magikē technē,* meaning "magical art."]

mag i cal (maj′ə kəl), done by magic or as if by magic: *a magical effect. adj.* —**mag′i cal ly,** *adv.*

ma gi cian (mə jish′ən), **1** person skilled in the use of magic: *The wicked magician cast a spell over the princess.* **2** person who entertains by magic tricks: *The magician pulled—not one, but three rabbits out of his hat! n.*

magic lantern, an early type of projector for showing photographic slides on a screen.

Magic Marker, trademark for a marking and drawing pen with a broad felt tip.

mag is ter i al (maj′ə stir′ē əl), **1** of a magistrate; suited to a magistrate: *A judge has magisterial rank.* **2** showing authority: *The principal spoke with a magisterial voice.* **3** imperious; domineering; overbearing: *He paced up and down with a magisterial stride. adj.*

mag is trate (maj′ə strāt), **1** a government official who has power to apply the law and put it in force. The President is the chief magistrate of the United States. **2** judge in a minor court. A justice of the peace is a magistrate. *n.*

mag ma (mag′mə), the molten material beneath the earth's crust from which igneous rock is formed. *n.*

Mag na Char ta or **Mag na Car ta** (mag′nə

kär′tə), the great charter which the English barons forcibly secured from King John in 1215. The Magna Charta provided a basis for guaranteeing the personal and political liberties of the people of England, and placed the king under the rule of the law.

mag na nim i ty (mag′nə nim′ə tē), magnanimous nature or quality; nobility of soul or mind: *show magnanimity by forgiving someone who harmed you. n.*

mag nan i mous (mag nan′ə məs), noble in soul or mind; generous in forgiving; free from mean feelings or acts: *She has a magnanimous attitude toward her children when they misbehave. adj.* —**mag nan′i mous ly,** *adv.*

mag nate (mag′nāt), an important, powerful, or prominent person: *a railroad magnate. n.*

mag ne sia (mag nē′zhə), a white, tasteless powder, used in medicine as an antacid and a laxative, and in industry in making fertilizers and heat-resistant building materials. *n.*

mag ne si um (mag nē′zhē əm), a light, silver-white metallic element that burns with a dazzling white light. Magnesium is used in photography, fireworks, and metal alloys. *n.*

mag net (mag′nit), **1** stone or piece of metal that has the property, either natural or induced, of attracting iron or steel. A lodestone is a natural magnet. **2** anything that attracts: *The rabbits in our backyard were a magnet that attracted all the children in the neighborhood. n.* [*Magnet* is from Latin *magneta,* which came from Greek *Magnēs,* meaning "of Magnesia," an ancient region in Thessaly. The Greek word was used in the phrase *Magnēs lithos,* meaning "stone of Magnesia."]

mag net ic (mag net′ik), **1** having the properties of a magnet: *the magnetic needle of a compass.* **2** of or producing magnetism: *a magnetic circuit.* **3** of or having to do with the earth's magnetism: *the magnetic meridian.* **4** capable of being magnetized or of being attracted by a magnet: *magnetic nickel.* **5** very attractive: *He has a magnetic personality. adj.* —**mag net′i cal ly,** *adv.*

magnetic field, space around a magnet or electric current in which its magnetic force is felt.

magnetic needle, a slender bar of magnetized steel used as a compass. When mounted so that it turns easily, it points approximately north and south toward the earth's Magnetic Poles.

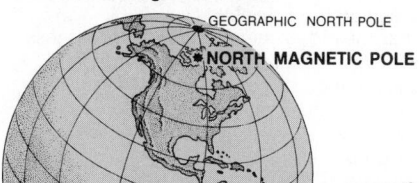

magnetic pole (def. 2)

magnetic pole, 1 one of the two poles of a magnet. **2 Magnetic Pole,** one of the two points on the earth's surface toward which a compass needle points. The **North Magnetic Pole** is in the Arctic; the **South Magnetic Pole** is in Antarctica.

magnetic tape, plastic or paper tape, coated with iron oxide, on which sounds or images can be recorded.

mag net ism (mag′nə tiz′əm), **1** properties or qualities of a magnet; the showing of magnetic properties: *the* *magnetism of iron and steel.* **2** branch of physics dealing with magnets and magnetic properties. **3** power to attract or charm: *A person with magnetism has many friends and admirers. n.*

mag net ite (mag′nə tīt), an important iron ore that is strongly attracted by a magnet. *n.*

mag net ize (mag′nə tīz), **1** give the properties or qualities of a magnet to: *You can magnetize a needle by rubbing it with a magnet.* **2** attract or influence (a person): *Her stirring speech magnetized the audience. v.,* **mag net ized, mag net iz ing.** —**mag′net i za′tion,** *n.*

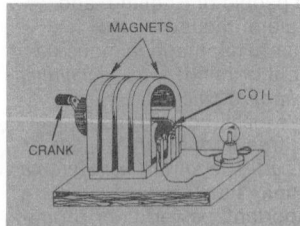

magneto
The coil is turned rapidly by means of the crank. Electricity is produced in the coil as it moves through the magnetic field of a series of magnets.

mag ne to (mag nē′tō), a small electric generator which uses a magnetic field to produce an electric current. In some internal-combustion engines, a magneto supplies an electric spark to explode the gasoline vapor. *n., pl.* **mag ne tos.**

magnet school, school with special programs in certain subjects, that are designed to attract students from all parts of a city or district.

mag ni fi ca tion (mag′nə fə kā′shən), act of magnifying. *n.*

mag nif i cence (mag nif′ə səns), richness of material, color, and ornament; grand beauty; splendor: *We were dazzled by the magnificence of the mountain scenery. n.*

mag nif i cent (mag nif′ə sənt), richly colored or decorated; splendid; grand; stately: *a magnificent palace, a magnificent view of the mountains. adj.* —**mag nif′i cently,** *adv.*

mag ni fi er (mag′nə fī′ər), **1** one that magnifies. **2** magnifying glass. *n.*

mag ni fy (mag′nə fī), **1** cause to look larger than the real size; increase the apparent size of an object: *A microscope magnifies bacteria so that they can be seen and studied.* **2** make too much of; go beyond the truth in telling: *Was the fish really that big, or are you magnifying its size? v.,* **mag ni fied, mag ni fy ing.**

magnifying glass, lens or combination of lenses that causes things to look larger than they really are.

mag nil o quence (mag nil′ə kwəns), use of big and unusual words and elaborate phrases. *n.*

mag nil o quent (mag nil′ə kwənt), using big and unusual words and elaborate phrases. *adj.*

mag ni tude (mag′nə tüd *or* mag′nə tyüd), **1** greatness of size: *the height, strength, and magnitude of a building.* **2** great importance, effect, or consequence: *The war brought problems of very great magnitude to many nations.* **3** measure of brightness of a star. Stars of the first magnitude are the brightest. *n.*

mag nol ia (mag nō′lyə), any of several trees or shrubs of North America and Asia, having large white, yellow, pink, or purplish flowers. *n., pl.* **mag nol ias.**

mag pie (mag′pī), **1** a black-and-white bird that chatters a great deal. It has a long tail and short wings and is related to the jays. **2** person who chatters. *n.*

Ma gus (mā′gəs), one of the Magi. *n., pl.* **Ma gi.**

Mag yar (mag′yär), **1** member of the chief group of people living in Hungary. **2** their language; Hungarian. **3** of the Magyars or their language. 1,2 *n.,* 3 *adj.*

ma ha ra ja (mä′hə rä′jə), formerly, a ruling prince in

India, especially one who ruled a state. *n., pl.* **ma ha ra jas.**

ma ha ra jah (mä′hə rä′jə), maharaja. *n.*

ma ha ra nee (mä′hə rä′nē), **1** wife of a maharaja. **2** formerly, a ruling princess in India, especially one who ruled a state. *n.*

ma ha ra ni (mä′hə rä′nē), maharanee. *n., pl.* **ma ha ra nis.**

ma hat ma (mə hät′mə), a wise and holy person, especially in India. *n., pl.* **ma hat mas.** [*Mahatma* is from Sanskrit *mahātman,* which comes from *mahā,* meaning "great," and *ātman,* meaning "soul."]

Ma hi can (mə hē′kən), Mohican. *n., pl.* **Ma hi can** *or* **Ma hi cans.**

mah-jongg *or* **mah-jong** (mä′jong′), game of Chinese origin played by four people with many small tiles resembling dominoes. Each player tries to form winning combinations by drawing or discarding. *n.*

ma hog a ny (mə hog′ə nē), **1** any of several large tropical American trees which yield a hard, reddish-brown wood. **2** its wood, used in making furniture. **3** made of mahogany: *a mahogany chest of drawers.* **4** dark reddish-brown. **5** a dark reddish brown. 1,2,5 *n., pl.* **ma hog a nies;** 3,4 *adj.*

Ma hom et (mə hom′it), Mohammed. *n.*

Ma hom et an (mə hom′ə tən), Mohammedan. *adj., n.*

ma hout (mə hout′), (in the East Indies) the keeper and driver of an elephant. *n.*

maid (mād), **1** a young unmarried woman; girl. **2** an unmarried woman. **3** a woman servant. *n.*

maid en (mād′n), **1** a young unmarried woman; maid; girl. **2** of a maiden: *maiden grace.* **3** unmarried: *a maiden aunt.* **4** first: *a ship's maiden voyage, the senator's maiden speech in the Senate.* 1 *n.,* 2-4 *adj.* [*Maiden* comes from Old English *mægden.*]

maid en hair (mād′n her′ *or* mād′n har′), fern with very slender stalks and delicate, finely divided fronds. *n.*

maid en hood (mād′n hud), condition or time of being a maiden. *n.*

maid en ly (mād′n lē), of, like, or suited to a maiden. *adj.* —**maid′en li ness,** *n.*

maiden name, a woman's surname before marriage.

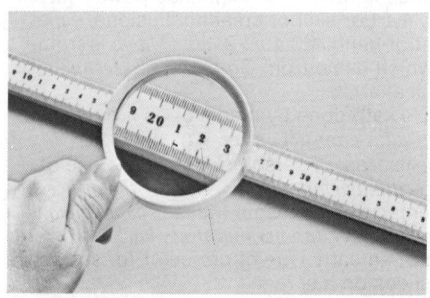

magnifying glass

maid of honor, 1 an unmarried woman who is the chief attendant of the bride at a wedding. **2** an unmarried noble lady who attends a queen or princess. *pl.* **maids of honor.**

maid serv ant (mād′sėr′vənt), a woman servant. *n.*

mail¹ (māl), **1** letters, postcards, papers, parcels, etc., to be sent by post. **2** system by which such mail is sent, managed by the Postal Service: *You can pay most bills by mail.* **3** all that comes by one post or delivery: *Has the mail come yet?* **4** send by mail; put in a mailbox: *Should I mail that letter for you?* **5** of or for mail. 1-3 *n.,* 4 *v.,* 5 *adj.* [*Mail¹* came into English about 700 years ago from French *male,* meaning "wallet, bag."] —**mail′a ble,** *adj.*

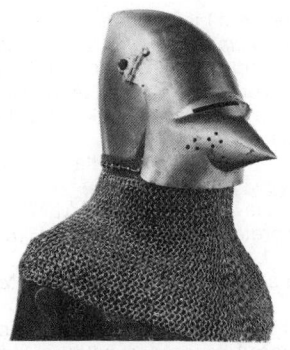

mail²
used in the 1400's

a hat	**i** it	**oi** oil	**ch** child	(**a** in about
ā age	**ī** ice	**ou** out	**ng** long	{ **e** in taken
ä far	**o** hot	**u** cup	**sh** she	**ə** = { **i** in pencil
e let	**ō** open	**u̇** put	**th** thin	{ **o** in lemon
ē equal	**ô** order	**ü** rule	**ᴛʜ** then	(**u** in circus
ėr term			**zh** measure	

mail² (māl), a flexible armor made of metal rings or small loops of chain linked together, or of overlapping plates, for protecting the body against arrows, spears, etc. *n.* [*Mail²* came into English about 600 years ago from French *maille,* which came from Latin *macula,* meaning "a mesh."] —**mail′less,** *adj.*

mail box (māl′boks′), **1** a public box from which mail is collected. **2** a private box to which mail is delivered. *n., pl.* **mail box es.**

mail carrier, person who carries or delivers mail; mailman; postman.

Mail gram (māl′gram), **1** trademark for a speedy electronic message service which transmits a message to a local post office for regular mail delivery on the next business day. **2** a message sent by this service. *n.*

mail man (māl′man′), mail carrier. *n., pl.* **mail men.**

mail order, order for goods sent by mail.

maim (mām), cut off or make useless an arm, leg, ear, etc.; disable: *His foot was maimed in the accident. v.*

main (mān), **1** most important; largest: *the main dish at dinner, the main street of town.* **2** a large pipe or conductor which carries water, gas, sewage, or electricity to or from smaller branches: *When the water main broke, our street was flooded.* **3** the open sea; ocean: *Our fleet will sail the main.* **4** exerted to the utmost; full; sheer: *I moved the piano by main strength.* **1,4** *adj.,* **2,3** *n.*

in the main, for the most part; chiefly; mostly: *Her grades are excellent in the main.*

main clause, independent clause.

Maine (mān), one of the northeastern states of the United States. *Abbreviation:* Me. or ME *Capital:* Augusta. *n.*

main frame (mān′frām′), a large computer, not portable, needing a cabinet to hold it. *n.*

main land (mān′land′ *or* mān′lənd), the main part of a continent or country, apart from outlying islands and peninsulas. *n.*

main ly (mān′lē), for the most part; chiefly; mostly: *Our garden is mainly vegetables. adv.*

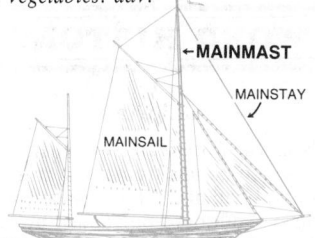

←MAINMAST

MAINSTAY

MAINSAIL

main mast (mān′mast′ *or* mān′məst), the principal mast of a ship. *n.*

main sail (mān′sāl′ *or* mān′səl), the largest sail of a ship on the mainmast. *n.*

main sheet (mān′shēt′), rope or tackle that controls the angle at which the mainsail is set. *n.*

main spring (mān′spring′), **1** the principal spring in a clock or watch that is wound. **2** the main cause, motive, or influence. *n.*

main stay (mān′stā′), **1** rope or wire supporting the mainmast. **2** main support: *Loyal friends are a person's mainstay in time of trouble. n.*

main stream (mān′strēm′), a main course or direction in the development of an idea, institution, etc. *n.*

main tain (mān tān′), **1** keep; keep up; carry on: *maintain a business, maintain a family.* **2** support, uphold, or defend: *maintain an opinion.* **3** keep supplied, equipped, or in repair: *The company employs people to maintain the machinery.* **4** declare to be true: *He maintains that he is innocent.* **5** affirm; assert against opposition: *He maintains his innocence. v.* —**main tain′a ble,** *adj.*

main te nance (mān′tə nəns), **1** a maintaining: *Maintenance of quiet is necessary in a hospital.* **2** a being maintained; support: *A government collects taxes to pay for its maintenance.* **3** a keeping in good repair. **4** enough to support life; means of living: *Their small farm barely provides a maintenance. n.*

maintenance (def. 3)
She was skilled in automobile **maintenance.**

main top (mān′top′), platform on the mainmast. *n.*

maize (māz), **1** corn; Indian corn. **2** the color of ripe corn; yellow. *n.* [*Maize* is from Spanish *maíz,* which came from Arawak *mahiz.* Arawak was an Indian language of the Caribbean region.]

Maj., Major.

ma jes tic (mə jes′tik), of or having majesty; grand; noble; dignified; stately. *adj.* —**ma jes′ti cal ly,** *adv.*

ma jes ti cal (mə jes′tə kəl), majestic. *adj.*

maj es ty (maj′ə stē), **1** royal dignity; stately appearance; nobility: *the majesty of the starry heavens, the great majesty of the Grand Canyon.* **2** supreme power or authority: *Judges uphold the majesty of the law.* **3 Majesty,** title used in speaking to or of a king, queen, emperor, empress, etc.: *Your Majesty, His Majesty, Her Majesty. n., pl.* **maj es ties.**

Maj. Gen., Major General.

ma jor (mā′jər), **1** more important; larger; greater: *Take the major share of the profits.* **2** officer in the army, air force, or marines ranking next below a lieutenant colonel and next above a major. **3** in music: **a** greater by a half step than the corresponding minor interval: *a major chord.* **b** noting a scale or key having half steps after the third and seventh tones: *the C major scale or key.* **c** a major scale, key, chord, interval, etc. **4** subject or course of study to which a student gives most time and attention: *Her major is mathematics.* **5** have or take as a major subject of study: *to major in mathematics.* 1,3a,b *adj.*, 2,3c,4 *n.*, 5 *v.*

ma jor-do mo (mā′jər dō′mō), **1** man in charge of a royal or noble household. **2** butler; steward. *n., pl.* **ma jor-do mos.**

ma jor ette (mā′jə ret′), drum majorette. *n.*

major general, officer in the army, air force, or marines ranking next below a lieutenant general and next above a brigadier general.

ma jor i ty (mə jôr′ə tē), **1** the larger number or part; more than half: *A majority of the children chose red covers for the books they had made.* **2** the number by which the votes on one side are more than those on the other: *He had 18 votes, and she had 12; so he had a majority of 6.* **3** the legal age of responsibility. Under the varying laws of the states of the United States, a person reaches his or her majority at the age of 18 in some states, at 21 in others. *n., pl.* **ma jor i ties.**

major league, either of the two chief leagues in American professional baseball.

make (māk), **1** bring into being; put together; build; form; shape: *make a new coat, make a fire, make jelly.* **2** way in which a thing is made; style; build; character: *Do you like the make of that coat?* **3** kind; brand: *What make of car is this?* **4** have the qualities needed for: *Wood makes a good fire.* **5** cause; bring about: *make trouble, make a noise, make peace.* **6** cause to; force to: *We made them go home.* **7** cause to be or become; cause oneself to be: *make a room warm, make a fool of oneself.* **8** turn out to be; become: *He will make a good legislator.* **9** get ready for use; arrange: *I make my own bed.* **10** get; obtain; acquire; earn: *make a fortune, make one's living.* **11** do; perform: *make a speech, make an attempt, make a mistake.* **12** amount to; add up to; count as: *Two and two make four.* **13** think of as; figure to be: *I make the distance across the room 5 meters.* **14** reach; arrive at: *The ship made port.* **15** go; travel: *Some airplanes can make 600 miles an hour.* **16** cause the success of: *One successful book made the young author.* **17** INFORMAL. get on; get a place on: *She made the tennis team.* 1,4-17 *v.*, **made, mak ing;** 2,3 *n.* [Make comes from Old English *macian*.] —**mak′a ble, make′a ble,** *adj.*

make after, follow; chase; pursue.

make away with, 1 get rid of. **2** kill. **3** steal: *The treasurer made away with the club's funds.*

make believe, pretend: *She liked to make believe she was an airplane pilot.*

make fast, attach firmly.

make for, 1 go toward: *Make for the hills!* **2** help bring about; favor: *The new facts made for the prisoner's acquittal.*

make it, SLANG. succeed.

make off, leave suddenly.

make off with, steal: *They made off with the neighbor's car.*

make out, 1 write out: *I made out a shopping list.* **2** show to be; try to prove: *That makes me out most selfish.* **3** understand: *The boy had a hard time making out the problem.* **4** see with difficulty: *I can barely make out three ships near the horizon.* **5** INFORMAL. get along; manage: *We must try to make out with what we have.*

make over, 1 alter; make different: *I had to make over my costume because it was too big.* **2** hand over; transfer ownership of: *Grandfather made over the farm to mother.*

make up, 1 put together: *make up cloth into a shirt.* **2** invent: *make up a story.* **3** settle (a dispute); reconcile: *make up one's differences.* **4** give or do in place of: *I took a shortcut to make up for lost time.* **5** become friends again after a quarrel: *There we were, quarreling and making up by turns.* **6** put rouge, lipstick, powder, etc., on the face.

7 arrange (type, pictures, etc.) in the pages of a book, paper, or magazine: *make up a page of type.* **8** decide: *make up one's mind.* **9** compose; constitute: *Children made up the audience.* **10** do (work missed) or take (a test or an examination missed) at a later time. **11** take (a test, course, etc., failed) again.

make up to, try to get the friendship of; flatter: *We all made up to the new boy the first day.*

make-be lieve (māk′bi lēv′), **1** pretense: *Elves live in the land of make-believe.* **2** pretended: *Some children have make-believe playmates.* 1 *n.*, 2 *adj.*

mak er (mā′kər), **1** person or thing that makes. **2 Maker,** God. *n.*

make shift (māk′shift′), **1** something used for a time instead of the right thing; temporary substitute: *When the lights went out, we used candles as a makeshift.* **2** used for a time instead of the right thing: *makeshift awnings.* 1 *n.*, 2 *adj.*

make up or **make-up** (māk′up′), **1** way of being put together. **2** nature; disposition: *a nervous makeup.* **3** way in which an actor is dressed and painted to look the part. **4** rouge, lipstick, powder, etc., put on the face; cosmetics. **5** arrangement of type, pictures, etc., in a book, paper, or magazine. **6** special examination taken by a student who has missed or failed the original one. *n.*

mal-, *combining form.* bad or badly; poor or poorly: *Mal-adjusted = badly adjusted.* [The form *mal-* is from French *mal-*, which came from Latin *malus,* meaning "bad," and *male,* meaning "badly."]

Mal a bo (mal′ə bō), capital of Equatorial Guinea. *n.*

Mal a chi (mal′ə kī), **1** Hebrew prophet who lived about 450 B.C. **2** the last book of the Old Testament. *n.*

mal a chite (mal′ə kīt), a green mineral that is an ore of copper and is used for ornamental articles. *n.*

mal ad just ed (mal′ə jus′tid), badly adjusted; not in a healthy relation with one's environment. *adj.*

mal ad just ment (mal′ə just′mənt), a bad adjustment. *n.*

mal a droit (mal′ə droit′), unskillful; awkward; clumsy. *adj.* —**mal′a droit′ly,** *adv.* —**mal′a droit′ness,** *n.*

mal a dy (mal′ə dē), **1** any bodily disorder or disease: *Cancer and malaria are serious maladies.* **2** any unwholesome or disordered condition: *Poverty and slums are social maladies.* *n., pl.* **mal a dies.**

Mál a ga (mal′ə gə), province in S Spain. *n.*

ma lar i a (mə ler′ē ə *or* mə lar′ē ə), disease characterized by periodic chills, fever, and sweating. Malaria is caused by tiny one-celled animals in the blood and is transmitted by the bite of certain mosquitoes which have bitten infected persons. *n.*

WORD HISTORY

malaria

Malaria was borrowed from Italian *malaria,* which comes from *mala aria,* meaning "bad air." The disease was formerly thought to be caused by polluted air.

ma lar i al (mə ler′ē əl *or* mə lar′ē əl), **1** having malaria. **2** of or like malaria. *adj.*

Ma la wi (mə lä′wē), country in SE Africa, a member of the Commonwealth of Nations. *Capital:* Lilongwe. See

South Africa for map. *n.* —**Ma la′wi an,** *adj., n.*

Ma lay (mā′lā), **1** member of the people of the Malay Peninsula and nearby islands. **2** their language. **3** of the Malays or their language. 1,2 *n.,* 3 *adj.*

Ma lay a (mə lā′ə), **1** Malay Peninsula. **2** former country on the Malay Peninsula, now part of Malaysia. *n.* —**Ma lay′an,** *adj., n.*

Malay Archipelago, group of islands between SE Asia and Australia; East Indies; Indonesia.

Malay Peninsula, peninsula in SE Asia, north of Sumatra; Malaya.

Ma lay sia (mə lā′zhə), country consisting of Sabah, Sarawak, Malaya, and many small islands of the Malay Archipelago, a member of the Commonwealth of Nations. *Capital:* Kuala Lumpur. *n.* —**Ma lay′sian,** *adj., n.*

mal con tent (mal′kən tent′), **1** discontented. **2** a discontented person; rebellious person. 1 *adj.,* 2 *n.*

Mal dive Islands (mal′dīv), group of islands in the Indian Ocean.

Mal dives (mal′dīvz), **the,** country in the Indian Ocean southwest of Ceylon, consisting of the Maldive Islands. *Capital:* Malé. *n.*

male (māl), **1** man or boy. **2** of men or boys. **3** belonging to the sex that can fertilize eggs and father young. Bucks, bulls, and roosters are male animals. **4** animal belonging to this sex. **5** (of a plant) having stamens but not pistils. **6** plant bearing only flowers with stamens. 1,4,6 *n.,* 2,3,5 *adj.* —**male′ness,** *n.*

Ma lé or **Ma le** (mä′lā), capital of the Maldives. *n.*

mal e dic tion (mal′ə dik′shən), a curse. *n.*

mal e fac tion (mal′ə fak′shən), an evil deed; crime. *n.*

mal e fac tor (mal′ə fak′tər), a criminal; evildoer. *n.*

ma lev o lence (mə lev′ə ləns), the wish that evil may happen to others; ill will; spite. *n.*

ma lev o lent (mə lev′ə lənt), wishing evil to happen to others; showing ill will; spiteful. *adj.* —**ma lev′o lent ly,** *adv.*

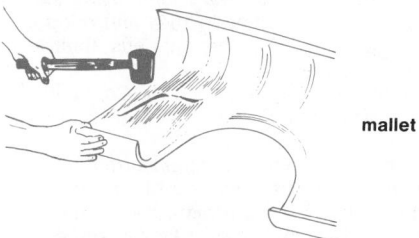

mallet

mal fea sance (mal fē′zns), official misconduct; violation of a public trust or duty: *A judge who accepts a bribe is guilty of malfeasance. n.*

mal for ma tion (mal′fôr mā′shən), bad shape; faulty structure: *A hunchback has a spine malformation. n.*

mal formed (mal fôrmd′), badly shaped; having a faulty structure. *adj.*

mal func tion (mal′fungk′shən), **1** an improper functioning; failure to work or perform: *a malfunction in a machine.* **2** function badly; work or perform improperly. 1 *n.,* 2 *v.*

Ma li (mä′lē), country in W Africa, south of Algeria. *Capital:* Bamako. See **Algeria** for map. *n.* —**Ma′li an,** *adj., n.*

mal ice (mal′is), active ill will; wish to hurt or make suffer; spite: *Lincoln asked the people to act "with malice toward none, with charity for all." n.*

ma li cious (mə lish′əs), showing ill will; wishing to hurt or make suffer; spiteful: *That story is malicious gossip. adj.* —**ma li′cious ly,** *adv.* —**ma li′cious ness,** *n.*

ma lign (mə līn′), **1** speak evil of; slander: *You malign an honest person when you call that person a liar.* **2** evil; injuri-

ous: *Gambling can have a malign influence.* **3** hateful; malicious. 1 *v.,* 2,3 *adj.* —**ma lign′er,** *n.* —**ma lign′ly,** *adv.*

ma lig nance (mə lig′nəns), malignancy. *n.*

ma lig nan cy (mə lig′nən sē), **1** malignant quality or tendency. **2** something malignant, as a tumor. *n., pl.* **ma lig nan cies.**

ma lig nant (mə lig′nənt), **1** very evil, hateful, or malicious. **2** very harmful or dangerous; deadly: *A cancer is a malignant growth. adj.* —**ma lig′nant ly,** *adv.*

ma lig ni ty (mə lig′nə tē), **1** great malice; extreme hate or ill will. **2** great harmfulness; dangerous quality; deadliness. *n., pl.* **ma lig ni ties.**

ma lin ger (mə ling′gər), pretend to be sick in order to escape work or duty; shirk. *v.* —**ma lin′ger er,** *n.*

mall (môl), **1** a shaded walk; public walk or promenade. **2** a central walk in a shopping center. **3** shopping center. *n.*

mal lard (mal′ərd), a wild duck of Europe, northern Asia, and North America. The male has a greenish-black head and a white band around its neck. *n., pl.* **mal lards** or **mal lard.**

mal le a bil i ty (mal′ē ə bil′ə tē), malleable quality or condition: *Manganese increases the malleability of steel. n.*

mal le a ble (mal′ē ə bəl), **1** able to be hammered, rolled, or extended into various shapes without being broken. Gold, silver, copper, and tin are malleable; they can be beaten into thin sheets. **2** adaptable; yielding: *A malleable person can adjust to changed plans. adj.* —**mal′le a ble ness,** *n.*

mal let (mal′it), a hammer, usually with a wooden head. Specially shaped mallets are used to play croquet and polo. *n.*

mal low (mal′ō), plant with purple, pink, or white five-petaled flowers, and hairy leaves and stems. *n.*

malm sey (mäm′zē), kind of strong, sweet wine. *n.*

mal nour ished (mal nėr′isht), improperly nourished: *The stray cat looked malnourished. adj.*

mal nu tri tion (mal′nü trish′ən *or* mal′nyü trish′ən), a poorly nourished condition. People suffer from malnutrition because of eating wrong kinds of food as well as from lack of food. *n.*

mal o dor ous (mal ō′dər əs), smelling bad. *adj.* —**mal o′dor ous ly,** *adv.* —**mal o′dor ous ness,** *n.*

mal prac tice (mal prak′tis), **1** criminal neglect or wrong treatment of a patient by a doctor. **2** wrong practice or conduct in any official or professional position; misconduct. *n.*

malt (môlt), **1** barley or other grain soaked in water until it sprouts, and then dried and aged. Malt has a sweet taste and is used in making beer and ale. **2** malted milk. *n.* [*Malt* comes from Old English *mealt.*]

Mal ta (môl′tə), **1** island in the Mediterranean, south of Sicily. **2** country including Malta and smaller islands nearby, a member of the Commonwealth of Nations. *Capital:* Valletta. *n.*

mal ted (môl′tid), malted milk. *n.*

malted milk, drink prepared by mixing a powder made of dried milk, malted barley, and wheat flour with milk, flavoring, and often ice cream.

Mal tese (môl tēz′), **1** person born or living in Malta. **2** language of Malta. **3** of Malta, its people, or their language. 1,2 *n., pl.* **Mal tese** for 1; 3 *adj.*

Maltese cat, a short-haired, bluish-gray cat.

Maltese cross, a cross with four equal arms resembling arrowheads pointed toward the center.

mal tose (môl′tōs), a white, crystalline sugar made by the action of various enzymes on starch. It is formed in the body during digestion and is produced commercially for use in making beer, ale, etc. *n.*

mal treat (mal trēt′), treat roughly or cruelly; abuse: *maltreat animals, maltreat a fine automobile. v.*

mal treat ment (mal trēt′mənt), rough or cruel treatment; abuse. *n.*

ma ma (mä′mə), mother. *n., pl.* **ma mas.**

mam ma (mä′mə), mother. *n., pl.* **mam mas.**

mam mal (mam′əl), any of a group of warm-blooded animals with a backbone, the females of which secrete milk from mammary glands to nourish their young. Human beings, horses, dogs, lions, bats, and whales are all mammals. *n.* [*Mammal* can be traced back to Latin *mamma,* meaning "breast."]

mam ma li an (ma mā′lē ən), of mammals. *adj.*

mam mar y   gland (mam′ər ē), gland in the breast of mammals, enlarged in females and capable of producing milk.

mam mon or **Mam mon** (mam′ən), riches thought of as an evil; greed for wealth. *n.*

mam moth (mam′əth), **1** a very large, extinct kind of elephant with a hairy skin and long, curved tusks. **2** huge; gigantic: *a mammoth undertaking.* 1 *n.,* 2 *adj.*

mam my (mam′ē), mama; mother. *n., pl.* **mam mies.**

man (man), **1** an adult male person. When a boy grows up, he becomes a man. **2** human being; person: *No man can be certain of the future.* **3** the human race: *Man has existed for thousands of years.* **4** a male follower, servant, or employee: *Robin Hood and his merry men.* **5** husband: *man and wife.* **6** one of the pieces used in games such as chess and checkers. **7** supply with a crew: *We can man ten ships.* **8** serve or operate; get ready to operate: *Man the guns.* 1-6 *n., pl.* **men;** 7,8 *v.,* **manned, man ning.** [*Man* comes from Old English *mann,* meaning "human being, adult male."] —**man′less,** *adj.*

as one man, with complete agreement.

be one's own man, 1 be free to do as one pleases. **2** have complete control of oneself.

to a man, without an exception; all: *We accepted the idea to a man.*

Man (man), **Isle of,** small island in the Irish Sea, west of N England. See **British Isles** for map. *n.*

Man., Manitoba.

man a cle (man′ə kəl), **1** Usually, **manacles,** *pl.* fetter for the hands; handcuff. **2** put manacles on: *to manacle a prisoner.* **3** restrain; hamper. 1 *n.,* 2,3 *v.,* **man a cled, man a cling.**

man age (man′ij), **1** to guide or handle with skill or authority; control; direct: *manage a business, manage a horse.* **2** succeed in accomplishing; contrive; arrange: *I shall manage to keep warm.* **3** get along: *manage on one's allowance. v.,* **man aged, man ag ing.** [*Manage* comes from Italian *maneggiare,* meaning "to handle, or train (horses)," which can be traced back to Latin *manus,* meaning "hand." See **Word Family.**]

man age a ble (man′ə jə bəl), able to be managed. *adj.*

man age ment (man′ij mənt), **1** a managing or handling; control; direction: *Bad management caused the bank's failure.* **2** persons that manage a business or an institution: *a dispute between labor and management. n.*

man ag er (man′ə jər), person who manages, especially one who manages a business: *She is the manager of the department store. n.*

man a ger i al (man′ə jir′ē əl), of a manager; of management: *Executives are given managerial training. adj.*

Ma na gua (mə nä′gwə), capital of Nicaragua, in the W part. *n.*

Ma na ma (mə nä′mə), capital of Bahrein. *n.*

man-at-arms (man′ət ärmz′), **1** soldier. **2** a heavily armed soldier on horseback. *n., pl.* **men-at-arms.**

manatee—about 8 to 13 ft. (2.5 to 4 m.) long

man a tee (man′ə tē′), a large sea mammal with two flippers and a flat, oval tail; sea cow. Manatees live in warm, shallow water near coasts. *n.*

Man ches ter (man′ches′tər), a city in W England, important in textile manufacturing. *n.*

mammoth (def. 1) about 10 ft. (3 m.) high at the shoulder

Man chu (man′chü), **1** member of a people living in Manchuria, who conquered China in 1644 and ruled it until 1912. **2** their language. **3** of the Manchus, their country, or their language. 1,2 *n.,* 3 *adj.*

Man chur i a (man chùr′ē ə), region in NE China, including several provinces of China. *n.* —**Man chur′i an,** *adj., n.*

Man da lay (man′də lā′), city in central Burma. *n.*

man dar in (man′dər ən), **1** an official of high rank under the Chinese empire. **2 Mandarin,** the main dialect of the Chinese language, spoken by officials, and educated people. **3** a small, sweet, spicy citrus fruit with a thin, orange-colored, very loose peel and segments that separate easily. *n.*

man date (man′dāt), **1** an order or command, especially

WORD FAMILY

manage

Below are words related to *manage.* They can all be traced back to the Latin word *manus* (mä′nùs), meaning "hand."

command	maintain	manipulate
commandeer	manacle	manual
commando	mandate	manufacture
commendable	maneuver	manure
demand	manicure	manuscript
emancipate	manifest	recommend

a legal order from a higher court or official to a lower one. **2** the expressed will of voters to their representative. **3** authority given to one nation by a group of nations to manage the government and affairs of a territory. **4** put (a territory) under the management of another nation. **5** a mandated territory. 1-3,5 *n.*, 4 *v.*, **man dat ed, man dat ing.**

man da to ry (man′də tôr′ē), of or containing a command; commanded; required. *adj.*

man di ble (man′də bəl), **1** one of a pair of mouth parts in insects for seizing and biting: *The ant grasped the dead fly with its mandibles.* **2** either part of a bird's beak. **3** a jaw, especially the lower jaw. *n.*

mandolin

man do lin (man′də lin′ *or* man′dl ən), a musical instrument with a pear-shaped body and four to six pairs of metal strings. It is played with a pick. *n.*

man drake (man′drāk), herb related to the nightshade. It has a very short stem and a thick, often forked root thought to resemble the human form. Mandrake roots were formerly used in medicine. *n.*

man drill (man′drəl), a large, fierce baboon of western Africa. The face of the male mandrill is marked with blue and scarlet. *n.*

mane (mān), the long, heavy hair growing on the back of or around the neck of a horse, lion, etc. *n.*

Ma net (mä nā′), Édouard, 1832-1883, French painter. *n.*

ma neu ver (mə nü′vər), **1** a planned movement of troops or warships: *Every year the army and navy hold maneuvers for practice.* **2** perform or cause troops to perform maneuvers. **3** a skillful plan or movement; clever trick: *When we refused to use his idea, he tried to force it on us by a series of maneuvers.* **4** plan skillfully; use clever tricks; scheme: *A scheming person is always maneuvering for some advantage.* **5** to force by skillful plans; get by clever tricks: *She maneuvered her lazy sister out of bed.* **6** move or manipulate skillfully: *I maneuvered the car through the heavy traffic with ease.* 1,3 *n.*, 2,4-6 *v.* Also, **manoeuvre.** [*Maneuver* comes from French *manœuvre*, and can be traced back to Latin *manus*, meaning "hand," and *operare*, meaning "to work."] —**ma neu′ver er**, *n.*

ma neu ver a bil i ty (mə nü′vər ə bil′ə tē), quality or power of being maneuverable. *n.*

ma neu ver a ble (mə nü′vər ə bəl), able to be maneuvered. *adj.*

man ful (man′fəl), manly. *adj.* —**man′ful ly**, *adv.*

man ga nese (mang′gə nēz′), a hard, brittle, grayish-white metallic element. Manganese is used chiefly in making alloys of steel, in fertilizers, paints, insecticides, and industrial chemicals. *n.*

mange (mānj), a skin disease of animals, marked by scabs and loss of hair. It is caused by parasitic mites. *n.*

man ger (mān′jər), box or trough in which hay or other food can be placed for horses or cows to eat. *n.* [*Manger* came into English about 600 years ago from French

a hat	i it	oi oil	ch child	a in about
ā age	ī ice	ou out	ng long	e in taken
ä far	o hot	u cup	sh she	ə = i in pencil
e let	ō open	u̇ put	th thin	o in lemon
ē equal	ô order	ü rule	ŦH then	u in circus
ėr term			zh measure	

mangeoire, and can be traced back to Latin *manducare*, meaning "to chew."]

mang i ness (mān′jē nis), mangy quality or condition. *n.*

man gle[1] (mang′gəl), **1** cut or tear roughly: *The two cats bit and clawed until both were much mangled.* **2** spoil; ruin: *The song was too difficult for the children and they mangled it badly.* *v.*, **man gled, man gling.** —**man′gler,** *n.*

man gle[2] (mang′gəl), **1** machine with rollers for pressing and smoothing sheets, towels, and other flat things after washing. **2** press or smooth in a mangle. 1 *n.*, 2 *v.*, **man gled, man gling.** —**man′gler,** *n.*

man go (mang′gō), the slightly sour, juicy, oval fruit of a tropical tree. Mangoes have a thick, yellowish-red rind and are eaten ripe or are pickled when green. *n., pl.* **man goes** or **man gos.**

man grove (mang′grōv), a tropical tree or shrub having branches that send down many roots which look like additional trunks. Mangroves grow in swamps and along river banks. *n.*

mang y (mān′jē), **1** having the mange; caused by the mange; with the hair falling out. **2** shabby and dirty: *a mangy dog. adj.*, **mang i er, mang i est.** —**mang′i ly,** *adv.*

man han dle (man′han′dl), treat roughly; pull or push about. *v.*, **man han dled, man han dling.**

Man hat tan (man hat′n), island on which the chief business section of New York City is located. It is a borough of New York City. *n.*

man hole (man′hōl′), hole through which a worker can enter a sewer, steam boiler, etc., to inspect or repair it. *n.*

man hood (man′hu̇d), **1** condition or time of being a man: *The boy was about to enter manhood.* **2** character or qualities of a man. **3** men as a group: *the manhood of the United States. n.*

man-hour (man′our′), hour of work by one person, used as a time unit in industry. *n.*

ma ni a (mā′nē ə), **1** kind of mental illness characterized by great excitement, excessive activity, and sometimes violence. **2** unusual or unreasonable fondness; craze: *a mania for dancing. n., pl.* **ma ni as.**

ma ni ac (mā′nē ak), **1** an insane person who is violent or destructive. **2** violently insane. 1 *n.*, 2 *adj.*

ma ni a cal (mə nī′ə kəl), violently insane. *adj.*

man ic (man′ik *or* mā′nik), **1** of or like mania. **2** suffering from mania. *adj.*

man i cure (man′ə kyu̇r), **1** to care for (the fingernails and hands); trim, clean, and polish (the fingernails). **2** the care of the hands; trimming, cleaning, and polishing of fingernails. 1 *v.*, **man i cured, man i cur ing;** 2 *n.*

man i cur ist (man′ə kyu̇r′ist), person whose work is manicuring. *n.*

man i fest (man′ə fest), **1** apparent to the eye or to the mind; plain; clear: *The error was manifest.* **2** show plainly; reveal; display. **3** a list of cargo of a ship or aircraft. 1 *adj.*, 2 *v.*, 3 *n.* —**man′i fest′er,** *n.* —**man′i fest′ly,** *adv.*

man i fes ta tion (man′ə fə stā′shən), a showing; an act that shows or proves: *Entering the burning building was a manifestation of courage. n.*

man i fes to (man′ə fes′tō), a public declaration of intentions, purposes, or motives by an important person or group; proclamation. *n., pl.* **man i fes toes** or **man i fes tos.**

man i fold (man′ə fōld), **1** of many kinds; many and various: *manifold duties.* **2** having many parts or forms: *a manifold way to control prices.* **3** pipe with several openings for connection with other pipes. The exhaust manifold on a car connects the cylinders in the engine with the exhaust pipe. 1,2 *adj.* 3 *n.* —**man′i fold′ly,** *adv.*

man i kin (man′ə kən), **1** a little man; dwarf. **2** mannequin. *n.* Also, **mannikin.**

ma nil a (mə nil′ə), Manila paper. *n.* Also, **manilla.**

Ma nil a (mə nil′ə), capital of the Philippines, on the island of Luzon. *n.*

Manila paper, a strong, brown or brownish-yellow wrapping paper.

ma nil la (mə nil′ə), Manila paper. *n.*

man i oc (man′ē ok), cassava. *n.*

ma nip u late (mə nip′yə lāt), **1** handle or treat, especially with skill: *She manipulated the controls of the airplane.* **2** manage by clever use of personal influence, especially unfair influence: *He manipulated the class so that he was elected president instead of his more qualified opponent.* **3** to change for one's own purpose or advantage; treat unfairly or dishonestly: *The bookkeeper manipulated the company's accounts to conceal her theft.* *v.,* **ma nip u lat ed, ma nip u lat ing.**

ma nip u la tion (mə nip′yə lā′shən), **1** skillful handling or treatment. **2** clever use of influence. **3** a change made for one's own advantage. *n.*

ma nip u la tor (mə nip′yə lā′tər), person who manipulates. *n.*

man i to (man′ə tō), spirit worshiped by Algonquian Indians as a force of nature with supernatural powers. *n., pl.* **man i tos.** Also, **manitou.**

Man i to ba (man′ə tō′bə), **1** province in S Canada. *Capital:* Winnipeg. **2 Lake,** lake in S Manitoba. *n.* —**Man′i to′ban,** *adj., n.*

man i tou (man′ə tü), manito. *n., pl.* **man i tous.**

man kind (man′kīnd′ *for 1;* man′kīnd′ *for 2*), **1** the human race. **2** men as a group. *n.*

man like (man′līk′), **1** like a man. **2** suitable for a man. *adj.*

man li ness (man′lē nis), manly quality or behavior. *n.*

man ly (man′lē), **1** having qualities traditionally admired in a man: *a manly show of strength.* **2** suitable for a man; masculine: *Boxing is a manly sport. adj.,* **man li er, man li est.**

man-made (man′mād′), made by people; not natural; artificial: *a man-made satellite. adj.*

Mann (man *for 1;* män *for 2*), **1 Horace,** 1796-1859, American educator. He established the first school for training teachers in the United States. **2 Thomas,** 1875-1955, German novelist. *n.*

man na (man′ə), **1** (in the Bible) the food miraculously supplied to the Israelites in the wilderness. **2** food for the soul or mind. **3** a much needed thing that is unexpectedly supplied: *Her inheritance was manna from heaven. n.*

manned (mand), occupied or controlled by one or more persons: *a manned space vehicle. adj.*

man ne quin (man′ə kən), **1** woman whose work is wearing new clothes to show them to customers. **2** a model or figure of a person used by tailors, artists, stores, etc. *n.* Also, **manikin, mannikin.**

man ner (man′ər), **1** way of doing, being done, or happening: *We went to school in the usual manner.* **2** way or style of acting or behaving: *She has a kind manner.* **3 manners,** *pl.* polite ways of behaving: *People with manners say "Please" and "Thank you."* **4** kind or kinds: *We saw all manner of birds in the forest. n.*

by all manner of means, most certainly.

by no manner of means, not at all; under no circumstances.

in a manner of speaking, as one might say; so to speak.

man nered (man′ərd), affected; artificial; having many mannerisms: *a mannered style of writing. adj.*

man ner ism (man′ə riz′əm), **1** too much use of some manner in speaking, writing, or behaving. **2** an odd trick or habit; peculiar way of acting. *n.*

man ner ly (man′ər lē), **1** having or showing good manners; polite. **2** politely. 1 *adj.,* 2 *adv.* —**man′ner li ness,** *n.*

man ni kin (man′ə kən), **1** manikin. **2** mannequin. *n.*

man nish (man′ish), (of a woman) having qualities or characteristics traditionally considered to be masculine. *adj.* —**man′nish ly,** *adv.* —**man′nish ness,** *n.*

ma noeu vre (mə nü′vər), maneuver. *n., v.,* **ma noeu vred, ma noeu vring.**

man-of-war (man′əv wôr′), warship of a type used in former times. *n., pl.* **men-of-war.**

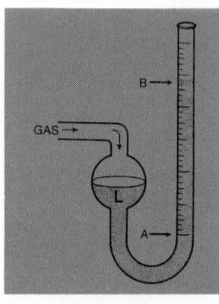

manometer—Gas enters tube at left. Its pressure on liquid L is measured by height of column AB.

ma nom e ter (mə nom′ə tər), instrument for measuring the pressure of gases or vapors. *n.*

man or (man′ər), **1** (in the Middle Ages) a feudal estate, part of which was set aside for the lord and the rest divided among the peasants, who paid the owner rent in goods, services, or money. If the lord sold the manor, the peasants or serfs were sold with it. **2** a large estate. **3** the main house or mansion of an estate. *n.* [*Manor* came into English about 700 years ago from French *manoir,* meaning "a dwelling," and can be traced back to Latin *manere,* meaning "to stay."]

ma no ri al (mə nôr′ē əl), of or like a manor. *adj.*

man pow er (man′pou′ər), **1** power supplied by human physical labor. **2** strength thought of in terms of the number of persons needed or available: *a country's industrial manpower. n.*

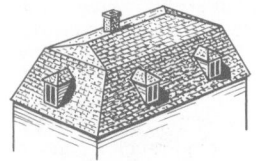

mansard (def. 1)

man sard (man′särd), **1** roof with two slopes on each side. **2** the story under such a roof. *n.* [*Mansard* was named for François *Mansard,* 1598-1666, a French architect.]

manse (mans), a minister's house; parsonage. *n.*

man serv ant (man′sér′vənt), a male servant. *n., pl.* **men serv ants.**

man sion (man′shən), a large house; stately residence. *n.*

man slaugh ter (man′slô′tər), **1** the killing of a human being. **2** (in law) the killing of a person unlawfully but without deliberate intent: *The charge against the prisoner was changed from murder to manslaughter. n.*

man tel (man′tl), **1** shelf above a fireplace. **2** the decorative framework around a fireplace: *a mantel of tile. n.*

man tel piece (man′tl pēs′), mantel (def. 1). *n.*

man til la (man tē′yə *or* man til′ə), a veil or scarf, often of lace, covering the hair and falling over the shoulders. Spanish and Latin-American women sometimes wear mantillas. *n., pl.* **man til las.**

man tis (man′tis), insect that holds its forelegs doubled up as if praying; praying mantis. It eats other insects. *n., pl.* **man tis es, man tes** (man′tēz).

mantis

Mantis comes from Greek *mantis,* meaning "prophet." The folded front legs of the insect suggested a typical pose of a prophet.

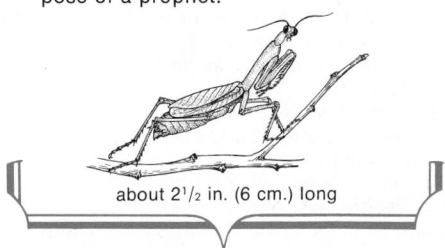

about 2½ in. (6 cm.) long

man tle (man′tl), **1** a loose cloak without sleeves. **2** anything that covers like a mantle: *The ground had a mantle of snow.* **3** to cover with a mantle. **4** redden: *Her cheeks mantled with embarrassment.* **5** a lacelike tube around a flame that gets so hot it glows and gives light. **6** fold of the body wall of a mollusk that lines the shell and secretes the material which forms the shell. **7** the part of the earth beneath the crust and above the core. 1,2,5-7 *n.,* 3,4 *v.,* **man tled, man tling.**

mantle (defs. 1, 2, 5, and 7)

man u al (man′yü əl), **1** of the hands; done with the hands: *manual labor.* **2** a small book that helps its readers to understand and use something; handbook. 1 *adj.,* 2 *n.* —**man′u al ly,** *adv.*

manual training, training in work done with the hands; practice in various arts and crafts, especially in making things out of wood or metal.

manuf., manufacturer.

man u fac ture (man′yə fak′chər), **1** make by hand or by machine. A big factory manufactures goods in large quantities by using machines and dividing the work up among many people. **2** a making of articles by hand or by machine, especially in large quantities. **3** make into something useful: *manufacture steel into rails.* **4** make up; invent: *Tardy students sometimes manufacture excuses.* 1,3,4 *v.,* **man u fac tured, man u fac tur ing;** 2 *n.* —**man′u fac′tur a ble,** *adj.*

man u fac tur er (man′yə fak′chər ər), person or company whose business is manufacturing; owner of a factory. *n.*

ma nure (mə nu̇r′ *or* mə nyu̇r′), **1** substance put in or on the soil to make it rich. Dung or refuse from stables is manure. **2** put manure in or on. 1 *n.,* 2 *v.,* **ma nured, ma nur ing.**

man u script (man′yə skript), book or paper written by hand or with a typewriter. Before printing was invented, all books and papers were handwritten manuscripts. *n.*

Manx (mangks), **1** of the Isle of Man or its people, or the language formerly spoken there. **2** people of the Isle of Man. **3** the extinct Celtic language of the Isle of Man. 1 *adj.,* 2,3 *n.*

Manx cat, kind of domestic cat with short hair and no tail.

man y (men′ē), **1** consisting of a great number; numerous: *many years ago. There are many children in the city.* **2** a great number: *Do you know many of them?* **3** a large number of people or things: *There were many at the dance.* 1 *adj.,* **more, most;** 2,3 *n., pron.* [*Many* comes from Old English *manig.*]

a good many, a fairly large number.

a great many, a very large number.

how many, what number of: *How many days until summer vacation?*

man y-sid ed (men′ē sī′did), **1** having many sides. **2** having many interests or abilities. *adj.*

Ma o ri (mä′ōr ē), **1** member of the Polynesian people who were the original inhabitants of New Zealand. **2** their language. **3** of the Maoris or their language. 1,2 *n., pl.* **Ma o ris;** 3 *adj.*

Ma o Tse-tung (mä′ō dzu′du̇ng′ *or* mou′ tse′tu̇ng′), 1893-1976, Chinese Communist leader, chairman of the Chinese Communist Party from 1945 to 1976.

map (map), **1** a drawing representing the earth's surface or part of it, usually showing countries, cities, rivers, seas, lakes, and mountains. **2** a drawing of the sky or a part of it, showing the position of the stars, etc. **3** make a map of; show on a map. **4** plan; arrange in detail: *Each Monday we map out the week's work.* 1,2 *n.,* 3,4 *v.,* **mapped, map ping.** [*Map* can be traced back to Latin *mappa,* meaning "napkin, cloth." Early maps were drawn on cloth.] —**map′like′,** *adj.* —**map′per,** *n.*

ma ple (mā′pəl), **1** tree grown for shade, ornament, its wood, or its sap. There are many kinds of maples, but all have dry fruits with two wings and opposite leaves. **2** its hard, light-colored wood. **3** flavor of maple sugar or maple syrup. *n.* —**ma′ple like′,** *adj.*

maple leaf, 1 leaf of the maple tree. **2** this leaf as a popular Canadian emblem.

maple sugar, sugar made by boiling maple syrup.

maple syrup, syrup made from the sap of one variety of maple.

Ma pu to (mä pü′tō), capital of Mozambique, in the S part. *n.*

mar (mär), spoil the beauty of; damage; injure; ruin: *The nails in my shoes marred the floor. Weeds mar a garden. v.,* **marred, mar ring.**

mar., 1 marine. **2** maritime. **3** married.

Mar., March.

ma ra ca (mə rä′kə), a percussion instrument consisting of seeds, pebbles, etc., enclosed in a dry gourd and shaken like a rattle. Maracas are usually played in pairs. *n., pl.* **ma ra cas.**

Mar a cai bo (mar′ə kī′bō), **1** seaport in NW Venezuela. **2 Lake,** lake in NW Venezuela. *n.*

mar a schi no cherry (mar′ə skē′nō), cherry preserved in a sweet syrup. It is used to decorate and add flavor to drinks, desserts, etc.

Ma rat (mä rä′), **Jean Paul,** 1743-1793, leader in the French Revolution. *n.*

mar a thon (mar′ə thon), **1** a foot race of 26 miles 385 yards (42.2 kilometers), named after Marathon. **2** any long race or contest. **3 Marathon,** plain in Greece about 25 miles (40 kilometers) northeast of Athens. After the Athenians defeated the Persians there in 490 B.C., a runner ran all the way to Athens with the news of the victory. See **Sparta** for map. *n.*

ma raud (mə rôd′), go about in search of plunder; make raids for booty. *v.* —**ma raud′er,** *n.*

mar ble (mär′bəl), **1** a hard rock formed from limestone by heat and pressure. It may be white or colored and can be polished to a smooth gloss. Marble is used for statues and in buildings. **2** made of marble. **3** like marble; hard, cold, or unfeeling: *a marble heart.* **4** to color in imitation of the patterns in marble: *Binders marble the edges of some books.* **5** a small, usually colored glass ball used in games. **6 marbles,** *pl.* a children's game played with small, usually colored glass balls. Each player uses a larger marble to knock the smaller marbles out of a ring. 1,5,6 *n.,* 2,3 *adj.,* 4 *v.,* **mar bled, mar bling.** —**mar′ble like′,** *adj.*

march (märch), **1** walk as soldiers do, in time and with steps of the same length: *The members of the band marched in the parade to the beat of the drums.* **2** act or fact of marching: *The news of the enemy's march made whole villages flee.* **3** music meant for marching. **4** distance marched: *The camp is a day's march away.* **5** a long, hard walk. **6** walk or go on steadily: *She marched to the front of the room and began her speech.* **7** cause to march or go: *The teacher marched her class out to the playground.* **8** an advance; progress: *History records the march of events.* 1,6,7 *v.,* 2-5,8 *n., pl.* **march es.** —**march′er,** *n.* **steal a march,** gain an advantage without being noticed.

March (märch), the third month of the year. It has 31 days. *n.*

mar chio ness (mär′shə nis), **1** wife or widow of a marquis. **2** woman equal in rank to a marquis. *n., pl.* **mar chio ness es.**

Mar co ni (mär kō′nē), **Guglielmo,** 1874-1937, Italian inventor who perfected the wireless telegraph. *n.*

Mar co Po lo (mär′kō pō′lō), 1254-1324?, Italian merchant who wrote about his travels in Asia.

Mar di gras (mär′dē grä′), the last day before Lent; Shrove Tuesday. It is celebrated in New Orleans and other cities with parades and festivities. [*Mardi gras* comes from French *mardi gras,* originally meaning "fat Tuesday." On the last day before Lent, people typically enjoy a feast.]

mare[1] (mer *or* mar), a female horse, donkey, etc. *n.*

ma re[2] (mär′ē), **1** any of certain dark regions on the surface of the moon. **2** a similar dark region on any planet. *n., pl.* **ma ri a** (mär′ē ə).

mar gar in (mär′jər ən), margarine. *n.*

mar gar ine (mär′jər ən *or* mär′jə rēn′), substitute for butter, made from cottonseed oil, soybean oil, or other vegetable oils; oleomargarine. *n.*

mar gin (mär′jən), **1** an edge or border: *the margin of a lake.* **2** the blank space around the writing or printing on a page: *Do not write in the margin.* **3** an extra amount; amount beyond what is necessary; difference: *We allow a margin of 15 minutes in catching a train. n.*

mar gin al (mär′jə nəl), **1** written or printed in a margin. **2** of, in, or on a margin. **3** barely capable of producing goods, crops, etc., profitably: *marginal land. adj.* —**mar′gin al ly,** *adv.*

mar gue rite (mär′gə rēt′), **1** kind of daisy with white petals and a yellow center. **2** any of several chrysanthemums with daisylike flowers. *n.*

Mar i an a Islands (mar′ē an′ə), group of 15 small islands in the Pacific, east of the Philippines. The largest island, Guam, belongs to the United States. The other islands voted in 1975 to become a self-governing commonwealth under the protection of the United States. See **Melanesia** for map.

Ma rie An toi nette (mə rē′ an′twə net′), 1755-1793, wife of King Louis XVI of France. She was beheaded during the French Revolution.

marigold

mar i gold (mar′ə gōld), plant related to the aster, with yellow, orange, brownish, or red flowers. *n.*

mar i jua na or **mar i hua na** (mar′ə wä′nə), **1** the hemp plant. **2** its dried leaves and flowers. Marijuana is a drug which is sometimes smoked for its effect. *n.*

ma rim ba (mə rim′bə), a musical instrument somewhat like a xylophone. *n., pl.* **ma rim bas.** [*Marimba* is of Bantu origin.]

ma ri na (mə rē′nə), a dock where moorings and supplies are available for small boats. *n., pl.* **ma ri nas.**

mar i nade (mar′ə nād′), a spiced vinegar, wine, etc., used for soaking meat or fish before it is cooked. *n.*

mar i nate (mar′ə nāt), soak in a marinade. *v.,* **mar i nat ed, mar i nat ing.**

ma rine (mə rēn′), **1** of the sea; found in the sea; produced by the sea: *Seals and whales are marine animals.* **2** of shipping; of the navy; for use at sea: *marine law, marine power, marine supplies.* **3** shipping; fleet: *our merchant marine.* **4** soldier formerly serving only at sea, now also serving on land and in the air. **5** Also, **Marine.**

person serving in the Marine Corps. **6 marines,** *pl.* Marine Corps. 1,2 *adj.,* 3-6 *n.*

Marine Corps, a branch of the armed forces of the United States. Its members are trained especially for landing operations. The Marine Corps has its own sea, air, and land units.

mar i ner (mar′ə nər), one who navigates a ship; sailor; seaman. *n.*

mar i o nette (mar′ē ə net′), doll or puppet moved by strings or by the hands, often on a little stage. *n.*

mar i tal (mar′ə təl), of marriage: *marital vows. adj.* —**mar′i tal ly,** *adv.*

mar i time (mar′ə tīm), **1** of the sea; of shipping and sailing: *Ships and sailors are governed by maritime law.* **2** on or near the sea: *Boston is a maritime city.* **3** living near the sea: *Maritime peoples engage in fishing. adj.*

Maritime Provinces, provinces of Canada along the Atlantic coast; New Brunswick, Newfoundland, Nova Scotia, and Prince Edward Island.

mar jor am (mär′jər əm), a fragrant herb related to mint, used as flavoring in cooking. *n.*

mark[1] (märk), **1** trace or impression made by some object on another. A line, dot, spot, stain, or scar is a mark. **2** line or dot to show position: *This mark shows how far you jumped.* **3** the line where a race starts: *On the mark; get set; go.* **4** something that shows what or whose a thing is; sign; indication: *Saying "thank you" is a mark of good manners.* **5** a written or printed stroke or sign: *punctuation marks.* **6** letter or number to show how well one has done; grade or rating: *My mark in arithmetic was B.* **7** give grades to; rate: *The teacher marked our examination papers.* **8** a cross or other sign made in place of a signature by a person who cannot write: *Make your mark here.* **9** make a mark on or put one's name on to show whose a thing is. **10** make a mark on by stamping, cutting, writing, etc.: *Be careful not to mark the table.* **11** put in a pin, make a line, etc., to show where a place is: *Mark all the large cities on this map.* **12** show clearly; manifest: *A tall pine marks the beginning of the trail. A frown marked her displeasure.* **13** something to be aimed at; target; goal: *The empty can was an easy mark.* **14** what is usual, proper, or expected; standard: *A tired person does not feel up to the mark.* **15** influence; impression: *The Industrial Revolution left its mark on society.* **16** distinguish; set off: *Many important inventions mark the last 150 years.* **17** give attention to; notice; observe; see: *Mark my words; their plan will fail.* **18** a tag with a mark on it: *Remove the price mark from your new suit.* **19** put a price mark on; tag. 1-6,8,13-15,18 *n.,* 7,9-12,16,17,19 *v.* [*Mark*[1] comes from Old English *mearc,* meaning "boundary, limit."]

beside the mark, not to the point; not relevant.

hit the mark, 1 succeed in doing what one tried to do. **2** be exactly right.

make one's mark, become well known; succeed.

mark down, 1 write down; note down. **2** mark for sale at a lower price.

mark off or **mark out,** make lines, etc., to show the position of or to separate: *We marked out a tennis court. The hedge marks off one yard from another.*

mark out for, set aside for; select for: *She seemed marked out for success.*

mark up, 1 spoil the appearance of; damage: *Don't mark up the desks.* **2** mark for sale at a higher price.

miss the mark, 1 fail to do what one tried to do. **2** be not exactly right.

of mark, important or famous: *He is a man of mark.*

mark[2] (märk), unit of money in East Germany and West Germany. *n.* [*Mark*[2] comes from German *Mark.*]

Mark (märk), **1** (in the Bible) one of Jesus' twelve apostles. He was one of the four Evangelists and a fellow worker with Paul and Peter. **2** the second book of the New Testament. It tells the story of the life of Jesus. *n.*

Mark Antony. See **Antony.**

mark down (märk′doun′), **1** a decrease in the price of an article. **2** the amount of this decrease. *n.*

marked (märkt), **1** having a mark or marks. **2** very noticeable; very plain; easily recognized: *There are marked differences between apples and oranges.* **3** distinguished or singled out as if by a mark: *Even as a young person she was marked for success. adj.*

mark ed ly (mär′kid lē), in a marked manner or degree; noticeably. *adv.*

mark er (mär′kər), **1** person or thing that marks, especially one who keeps the score in a game. **2** bookmark. *n.*

mar ket (mär′kit), **1** a meeting of people for buying and selling. **2** the people at such a meeting: *Excitement stirred the market.* **3** an open space or covered building where food, cattle, etc., are shown for sale. **4** buy or sell in a market. **5** sell: *The farmers can't market all of their corn.* **6** a store for the sale of food: *a meat market.* **7** chance to sell or buy: *There is always a market for wheat.* **8** the demand (for something); price offered: *The drought created a high market for corn.* **9** center of trade; region in which goods may be sold: *South America is a market for American automobiles.* **10** the stock market. 1-3,6-10 *n.,* 4,5 *v.* —**mar′ket er,** *n.*

be in the market for, be a possible buyer of.

mar ket a bil i ty (mär′kə tə bil′ə tē), quality of being marketable. *n.*

mar ket a ble (mär′kə tə bəl), able to be sold; salable. *adj.*

mar ket place (mär′kət plās′), place where a market is held. *n.*

mark ing (mär′king), **1** mark or marks. **2** arrangement of marks. *n.*

marks man (märks′mən), **1** person who shoots well: *She is noted as a marksman.* **2** person who shoots: *a poor marksman. n., pl.* **marks men.**

marks man ship (märks′mən ship), skill in shooting. *n.*

Mark Twain. See **Twain.**

mark up (märk′up′), **1** an increase in the price of an article. **2** the amount of this increase. **3** percentage or amount added to the cost of an article to determine the selling price. *n.*

mar lin (mär′lən), a large sea fish related to the swordfish and the sailfish. *n., pl.* **mar lins** or **mar lin.**

mar line spike or **mar lin spike** (mär′lən spīk′), a pointed iron implement used by sailors to separate strands of rope in splicing, etc. *n.*

Mar lowe (mär′lō), **Christopher,** 1564-1593, English dramatist and poet. *n.*

mar ma lade (mär′mə lād), a preserve similar to jam, made of oranges or of other fruit. The peel is usually sliced up and boiled with the fruit. *n.* [*Marmalade* comes from Portuguese *marmelada,* and can be traced back to Greek *meli,* meaning "honey," and *melon,* meaning "apple."]

Mar mar a (mär′mər ə), **Sea of,** a small sea between Europe and Asia Minor. It is connected with the Aegean Sea by the Dardanelles and with the Black Sea by the Bosporus. See **Dardanelles** for map. *n.*

---

a hat	i it	oi oil	ch child	a in about
ā age	ī ice	ou out	ng long	e in taken
ä far	o hot	u cup	sh she	ə = i in pencil
e let	ō open	u̇ put	th thin	o in lemon
ē equal	ô order	ü rule	ŦH then	u in circus
ėr term			zh measure	

marmoset—about 16 in. (40 cm.) long with the tail

mar mo set (mär′mə set), a very small monkey with soft, thick fur, that lives in South and Central America. *n.*

mar mot (mär′mət), a gnawing, burrowing animal related to the squirrels, having a thick body and a bushy tail. Woodchucks are marmots. *n.*

Marne (märn), river flowing from NE France into the Seine. *n.*

ma roon[1] (mə rün′), **1** very dark brownish-red. **2** a very dark brownish red. 1 *adj.*, 2 *n.*

maroon[2] (def. 2)—Many were **marooned** during the flood.

ma roon[2] (mə rün′), **1** put (a person) ashore alone in a desolate place: *Pirates used to maroon people on desert islands.* **2** leave in a lonely, helpless position. *v.*

mar quee (mär kē′), a rooflike shelter over an entrance, especially of a theater or hotel. Theater marquees usually display the names of shows being featured. *n.*

mar quess (mär′kwis), BRITISH. marquis. *n.*, *pl.* **mar quess es.**

Mar quette (mär ket′), Father **Jacques,** 1637-1675, French Jesuit missionary who explored part of the Mississippi River and its valley. *n.*

mar quis (mär′kwis *or* mär kē′), a British nobleman ranking below a duke and above an earl. **2** nobleman having a similar rank in certain other countries. *n.*, *pl.* **mar quis es, mar quis** (mär kē′).

mar quise (mär kēz′), marchioness. *n.*

mar riage (mar′ij), **1** a living together as husband and wife; married life: *We wished the bride and groom a happy marriage.* **2** the ceremony of being married; a marrying; wedding. **3** a close union: *The marriage of words and melody in that song was unusually effective. n.*

mar riage a ble (mar′i jə bəl), fit for marriage; old enough to marry: *of marriageable age.* adj. —**mar′riage a ble ness,** *n.*

mar ried (mar′ēd), **1** living together as husband and wife: *a married couple.* **2** having a husband or wife: *a married man.* **3** of marriage; of husbands and wives: *Married life has many rewards.* **4** **marrieds,** *pl.* a married couple. 1-3 *adj.,* 4 *n.*

mar row (mar′ō), **1** the soft tissue that fills the hollow central part of most bones. **2** the inmost or important part: *The icy wind chilled me to the marrow. n.* [Marrow comes from Old English *mearg.*]

mar ry (mar′ē), **1** join as husband and wife: *The minister married them.* **2** take as husband or wife: *She plans to marry him.* **3** become married; take a husband or wife: *She married late in life.* **4** give in marriage: *They have married off all of their children.* **5** bring together in any close union. *v.,* **mar ried, mar ry ing.**

Mars (märz), **1** (in Roman myths) the god of war. The Greeks called him Ares. **2** the planet next beyond the earth. It is the seventh largest planet in the solar system and the fourth in distance from the sun. *n.*

Mar seil laise (mär′sə läz′ *or* mär′sä yez′), the French national anthem, written in 1792 during the French Revolution. *n.*

Mar seilles (mär sā′ *or* mär sālz′), seaport city in SE France, on the Mediterranean. *n.*

marsh (märsh), low land covered at times by water; soft, wet land; swamp. *n., pl.* **marsh es.** —**marsh′like′,** *adj.*

mar shal (mär′shəl), **1** officer of various kinds, especially a police officer. A United States marshal is an officer of a federal court whose duties are like those of a sheriff. **2** chief of police or head of the fire department in some cities. **3** a high officer in an army. A Marshal of France is a general of the highest rank in the French Army. **4** person who arranges the order of march in a parade. **5** arrange in proper order: *marshal facts for a debate.* **6** person in charge of events or ceremonies. 1-4,6 *n.,* 5 *v.,* **mar shaled, mar shal ing** *or* **mar shalled, mar shal ling.**

Mar shall (mär′shəl), **1 George Catlett,** 1880-1959, American general and statesman. **2 John,** 1755-1835, chief justice of the United States Supreme Court from 1801 to 1835. *n.*

Marshall Islands, group of islands in the N Pacific, near the equator, administered by the United States.

marsh gas, methane.

marsh land (märsh′land′), marshy land. *n.*

marsh mal low (märsh′mal′ō *or* märsh′mel′ō), a soft, white, spongy candy, covered with powdered sugar. *n.*

marsh marigold, plant with bright yellow flowers that grows in moist meadows and swamps; cowslip.

marsh y (mär′shē), soft and wet like a marsh: *a marshy field.* adj., **marsh i er, marsh i est.** —**marsh′i ness,** *n.*

mar su pi al (mär sü′pē əl), mammal that carries its young in a pouch. Kangaroos and opossums are marsupials. *n.*

mart (märt), center of trade; market: *New York and London are two great marts of the world. n.*

marten (def. 1) about 2½ ft. (75 cm.) long with the tail

mar ten (märt′n), **1** a slender, meat-eating mammal like a weasel, but larger, valued for its fur. **2** its fur. *n., pl.* **mar tens** *or* **mar ten.**

Martha's Vineyard, island south of Cape Cod. It is part of Massachusetts.

mar tial (mär′shəl), **1** of war; suitable for war: *martial*

music. **2** fond of fighting; warlike: *a martial nation. adj.*
—**mar′tial ly,** *adv.* —**mar′tial ness,** *n.*

martial law, rule by the army in a time of trouble or of war instead of by the ordinary civil authorities.

Mar tian (mär′shən), **1** of the planet Mars. **2** a supposed inhabitant of the planet Mars. 1 *adj.,* 2 *n.*

mar tin (märt′n), any of several swallows with long, pointed wings and a forked tail. The **purple martin** is a large, blue and black martin of North America. *n.*

mar ti net (mär′n et′), person who upholds and enforces very strict discipline. *n.*

GIRTH **MARTINGALE**

mar tin gale (märt′n gāl), strap of a horse's harness that prevents the horse from rising on its hind legs or throwing back its head. *n.*

Mar ti nique (märt′n ēk′), French island in the West Indies. *n.*

mar tyr (mär′tər), **1** person who is put to death or made to suffer greatly because of his or her religion or other beliefs. **2** put (a person) to death or torture because of his or her religion or other beliefs. **3** person who suffers greatly. **4** cause to suffer greatly; torture. 1,3 *n.,* 2,4 *v.*
—**mar′tyr like′,** *adj.*

mar tyr dom (mär′tər dəm), **1** death or suffering of a martyr. **2** great suffering; torment. *n.*

mar tyr ize (mär′tə rīz′), make a martyr of. *v.,* **mar tyr ized, mar tyr iz ing.** —**mar′tyr i za′tion,** *n.*

mar vel (mär′vəl), **1** something wonderful; astonishing thing: *The airplane is one of the marvels of science.* **2** be filled with wonder; be astonished: *I marvel at your boldness. She marveled at the beautiful sunset.* 1 *n.,* 2 *v.,* **mar veled, mar vel ing** or **mar velled, mar vel ling.**

mar vel ous or **mar vel lous** (mär′və ləs), **1** causing wonder; extraordinary. **2** improbable: *Children like tales of marvelous things, like that of Dorothy in Oz.* **3** excellent; splendid; fine: *a marvelous time. adj.* —**mar′vel ous ly, mar′vel lous ly,** *adv.* —**mar′vel ous ness, mar′vel lous ness,** *n.*

Marx (märks), **Karl,** 1818-1883, German writer on economics and advocate of socialism. *n.*

Marx ism (märk′siz′əm), theories of Karl Marx. *n.*

Marx ist (märk′sist), **1** of Marx or his theories. **2** follower of Marx; believer in his theories. 1 *adj.,* 2 *n.*

Mar y (mer′ē *or* mar′ē), (in the Bible) the mother of Jesus. *n.*

Mar y land (mer′ə lənd), one of the southeastern states of the United States. *Abbreviation:* Md. or MD *Capital:* Annapolis. *n.*

Mary Mag da lene (mag′də lēn′), (in the Bible) a woman from whom Jesus cast out seven devils. She is commonly supposed to be the repentant sinner forgiven by Jesus.

Mary, Queen of Scots, 1542-1587, queen of Scotland from 1542 to 1567. She was beheaded by order of her cousin, Queen Elizabeth I.

masc., masculine.

mas car a (ma skar′ə), preparation used for coloring the eyelashes. *n., pl.* **mas car as.**

mas cot (mas′kot), animal, person, or thing supposed to bring good luck. *n.*

mas cu line (mas′kyə lin), **1** of men or boys. **2** like a

a	hat	i	it	oi	oil	ch	child		a in about
ā	age	ī	ice	ou	out	ng	long		e in taken
ä	far	o	hot	u	cup	sh	she	ə =	i in pencil
e	let	ō	open	u̇	put	th	thin		o in lemon
ē	equal	ô	order	ü	rule	ᵺ	then		u in circus
ėr	term					zh	measure		

man; manly. **3** of or belonging to the male sex. **4** (in grammar) of the gender to which nouns and adjectives referring to males belong. *He* is a masculine pronoun; *she* is a feminine pronoun. *adj.* —**mas′cu line ly,** *adv.*
—**mas′cu line ness,** *n.*

mas cu lin i ty (mas′kyə lin′ə tē), masculine quality or condition. *n.*

ma ser (mā′zər), device which amplifies or generates electromagnetic waves, especially microwaves, with great stability and accuracy. Masers are used in long-distance radar and radio astronomy. *n.*

Mas e ru (maz′ə rü′), capital of Lesotho. *n.*

mash (mash), **1** a soft mixture; soft mass. **2** beat into a soft mass; crush to a uniform mass: *I'll mash the potatoes.* **3** a warm mixture of bran or meal and water for horses and other animals. **4** crushed malt or meal soaked in hot water for making beer. **5** crush; smash: *mash a finger with a hammer.* 1,3,4 *n., pl.* **mash es;** 2,5 *v.*
—**mash′er,** *n.*

mask (def. 1) from an island near New Guinea

mask (mask), **1** a covering to hide or protect the face: *The burglar wore a mask.* **2** cover (the face) with a mask. **3** a false face worn for amusement. **4** a masked person. **5** a clay, wax, or plaster likeness of a person's face. **6** a disguise: *She hid her dislike under a mask of friendship.* **7** hide or disguise: *A smile masked his disappointment.* 1,3-6 *n.,* 2,7 *v.* [*Mask* came into English about 400 years ago from French *masque,* and can be traced back to Arabic *maskhara,* meaning "laughingstock."] —**mask′-er,** *n.* —**mask′like′,** *adj.*

masked (maskt), **1** wearing or using a mask: *a masked outlaw.* **2** hidden; secret: *masked treachery. adj.*

masked ball, dance at which masks are worn.

masking tape, a gummed tape used to hold things in place or protect surfaces not to be painted, sprayed, treated, etc.

ma son (mā′sn), **1** person whose work is building with stone, brick, or similar materials. **2 Mason,** Freemason. *n.*

Ma son-Dix on line (mā′sn dik′sən), boundary between Pennsylvania and Maryland, formerly thought of as separating the North and the South of the United States.

ma son ic or **Ma son ic** (mə son′ik), of Masons, or the society of Freemasons. *adj.*

massive (def. 1)—The weight lifter was **massive**.

ma son ry (mā′sn rē), **1** wall, foundation, or part of a building built by a mason; stonework or brickwork. **2** the trade or skill of a mason. *n., pl.* **ma son ries.**

masque (mask), **1** an amateur dramatic entertainment with fine costumes and scenery. Masques were much given in England in the 1500's and 1600's, at court and at the homes of nobles. **2** masked ball; masquerade. *n.*

mas que rade (mas′kə rād′), **1** disguise oneself; go about under false pretenses: *The king masqueraded as a beggar to find out if his people really liked him.* **2** party or dance at which masks and fancy costumes are worn. **3** the costume and mask worn at such a party or dance. **4** take part in a masquerade. **5** false pretense; disguise. 1,4 *v.,* **mas que rad ed, mas que rad ing;** 2,3,5 *n.*

mas que rad er (mas′kə ra′dər), person who masquerades. *n.*

mass[1] (mas), **1** a lump: *a mass of dough.* **2** a large quantity together: *a mass of flowers.* **3** form or collect into a mass; assemble: *She massed the peonies behind the roses. Many people massed in the square.* **4** majority; greater part: *The great mass of the population wants to live in peace.* **5 the masses,** the common people; the working classes; the lower classes of society. **6** of or by many people: *a mass protest.* **7** on a large scale: *mass buying.* **8** bulk or size: *the sheer mass of an iceberg.* **9** the quantity of matter a body contains; the property of a physical body which gives it inertia. The mass of an object is always the same (on earth, in outer space, etc.); its weight, which depends on the force of gravity, can vary. 1,2,4,5,8,9 *n., pl.* **mass es;** 3 *v.,* 6,7 *adj.* [*Mass*[1] came into English about 600 years ago from French *masse,* which came from Latin *massa,* meaning "kneaded dough, lump," which came from Greek *maza,* meaning "barley bread."]
in the mass, as a whole.

Mass or **mass**[2] (mas), **1** the central service of worship in the Roman Catholic Church and in some other churches. The ritual of the Mass consists of Holy Communion and various prayers and ceremonies. **2** music written for certain parts of it. *n., pl.* **Mass es** or **mass es.** [*Mass*[2] is from Old English *mæsse,* and can be traced back to Latin *mittere,* meaning "send."]

Mass., Massachusetts.

Mas sa chu setts (mas′ə chü′sits), one of the northeastern states of the United States. *Abbreviation:* Mass. or MA *Capital:* Boston. *n.*

mas sa cre (mas′ə kər), **1** a pitiless killing of many people or animals. **2** kill (many people or animals) needlessly or cruelly. 1 *n.,* 2 *v.,* **mas sa cred, mas sa cring.** —**mas sa crer** (mas′ə krər), *n.*

mas sage (mə säzh′), **1** a rubbing and kneading of the muscles and joints to increase the circulation of blood: *A thorough massage feels good when you are tired.* **2** give a massage to: *Let me massage your back for you.* 1 *n.,* 2 *v.,* **mas saged, mas sag ing.** [*Massage* was borrowed from

French *massage,* and can be traced back to Arabic *massa,* meaning "to touch, handle."] —**mas sag′er,** *n.*

Mas sa soit (mas′ə soit), 1580?-1661, American Indian chief who was friendly to the Pilgrims. *n.*

mas seur (mə sėr′), man whose work is massaging people. *n.*

mas seuse (mə süs′ *or* mə süz′), woman whose work is massaging people. *n.*

mas sive (mas′iv), **1** big and heavy; large and solid; bulky. **2** giving the impression of being large and broad: *a massive forehead. adj.* —**mas′sive ly,** *adv.* —**mas′sive ness,** *n.*

mass meeting, a large assembly to hear or discuss some matter of common interest.

mass production, the making of goods in large quantities, especially by machinery.

mass y (mas′ē), massive. *adj.,* **mass i er, mass i est.** —**mass′i ness,** *n.*

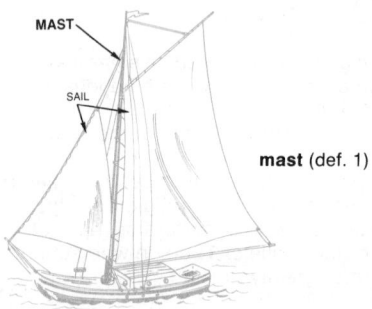

mast (def. 1)

mast (mast), **1** a long pole of wood or metal set upright on a ship to support the sails and rigging. **2** any tall, upright pole: *the mast of a derrick. n.* —**mast′less,** *adj.* —**mast′like′,** *adj.*

before the mast, serving as a common sailor. Such sailors used to sleep in the forward part of the ship.

mas ter (mas′tər), **1** person who has power or authority over others, such as the head of a household, a school, a ship, etc.; the one in control; the owner, employer, or director. **2** a male teacher, especially in private schools: *The master taught his pupils how to read.* **3** title of respect for a boy: *First prize goes to Master Henry Adams.* **4** an expert, such as a great artist or skilled worker; person who knows all there is to know about a subject. **5** picture or painting by a great artist: *an old master.* **6** being master of; of a master; by a master. **7** main; controlling: *a master plan, a master switch.* **8** become master of; conquer; control: *Learn to master your temper.* **9** become expert in; become skillful at; learn: *She has mastered algebra.* **10** person who has taken a degree above bachelor and below doctor at a college or university. 1-5,10 *n.,* 6,7 *adj.,* 8,9 *v.*

mas ter ful (mas′tər fəl), **1** fond of power or authority; domineering. **2** expert or skillful: *a masterful performance. adj.* —**mas′ter ful ly,** *adv.* —**mas′ter ful ness,** *n.*

mas ter ly (mas′tər lē), **1** very skillful; expert: *a masterly argument, a masterly painter.* **2** in an expert or skillful way. 1 *adj.,* 2 *adv.* —**mas′ter li ness,** *n.*

mas ter mind (mas′tər mīnd′), **1** person who plans and supervises a scheme or operation. **2** devise and conduct (a plan of action). 1 *n.,* 2 *v.*

master of ceremonies, person in charge of a ceremony or entertainment who welcomes guests and introduces speakers, performers, etc.

mas ter piece (mas′tər pēs′), **1** anything done or made with wonderful skill; perfect piece of art or workmanship. **2** a person's greatest piece of work. *n.*

mas ter work (mas′tər wėrk′), masterpiece. *n.*

mas ter y (mas′tər ē), **1** power such as a master has; rule; control. **2** the upper hand; victory: *The two teams vied for mastery.* **3** a very great skill or knowledge: *The teacher had a mastery of the subject. n., pl.* **mas ter ies.**

mast head (mast′hed′), **1** top of a ship's mast. A crow's-nest near the masthead of the lower mast is used as a lookout. **2** the part of a newspaper or magazine that gives its name, owner, address, rates, etc. *n.*

mas tic (mas′tik), **1** a yellowish resin obtained from the bark of a small Mediterranean evergreen tree. It is used in making varnish and as an astringent. **2** the tree it comes from. *n.*

mas ti cate (mas′tə kāt), chew. *v.,* **mas ti cat ed, mas ti cat ing.**

mas ti ca tion (mas′tə kā′shən), act of chewing. *n.*

mas tiff (mas′tif), a large, strong dog with a short, thick coat and drooping ears. *n.*

mas to don (mas′tə don), any of a large group of extinct animals much like mammoths and present-day elephants. *n.* [*Mastodon* comes from Greek *mastos*, meaning "breast," and *odōn*, meaning "tooth." The teeth of this animal had raised bumps that looked like nipples.]

mas toid (mas′toid), projection of bone behind the ear. *n.*

mat[1] (mat), **1** piece of coarse fabric made of woven rushes, fiber, straw, rope, etc., used for floor covering, for wiping mud from the shoes, etc. A mat is like a small rug. **2** piece of material to put under a dish, vase, lamp, etc. A mat is put under a hot dish when it is brought to the table. **3** cover with mats. **4** anything growing thickly packed or tangled together: *a mat of weeds.* **5** pack or tangle together like a mat: *The swimmer's wet hair was matted.* **6** a large, thick pad covering part of a floor to protect wrestlers or gymnasts. 1,2,4,6 *n.,* 3,5 *v.,* **mat ted, mat ting.** —**mat′less,** *adj.*

mat[2] (mat), **1** border or background for a picture, used as a frame or placed between the picture and its frame. **2** put a mat around or under. 1 *n.,* 2 *v.,* **mat ted, mat ting.**

matador

mat a dor (mat′ə dôr), the chief performer in a bullfight who kills the bull with a sword. *n.*

match[1] (mach), a short, slender piece of wood or pasteboard tipped with a mixture that catches fire when rubbed on a rough or specially prepared surface. *n., pl.* **match es.**

match[2] (mach), **1** person or thing equal to another or much like another; an equal: *A child is not a match for an adult.* **2** be equal to in a contest: *No one could match the skill of the unknown archer.* **3** two persons or things that are alike or go well together: *Those two horses make a good match.* **4** be alike; go well together: *The rugs and the wallpaper match.* **5** find the equal of or one exactly like: *match a vase so as to have a pair.* **6** make like; fit together. **7** game; contest: *a tennis match.* **8** try (one's skill, strength, etc.) against; oppose: *He matched his strength against his brother's.* **9** marriage. **10** arrange a match for;

marry. **11** person considered as a possible husband or wife. 1,3,7,9,11 *n., pl.* **match es;** 2,4-6,8,10 *v.* —**match′er,** *n.*

match book (mach′bůk′), a folder of safety matches, especially a folder of two rows of safety matches, with a surface for striking at the bottom. *n.*

match less (mach′lis), so great or wonderful that it cannot be equaled: *matchless courage. adj.* —**match′less ly,** *adv.* —**match′less ness,** *n.*

match lock (mach′lok′), an old form of musket fired by lighting the charge of powder with a wick or cord. *n.*

match mak er (mach′mā′kər), **1** person who arranges, or tries to arrange, marriages for others. **2** person who arranges contests, prizefights, races, etc. *n.*

mate[1] (māt), **1** one of a pair: *Where is the mate to this glove?* **2** join in a pair: *Birds mate in the spring.* **3** husband or wife. **4** marry. **5** officer of a ship ranking next below the captain. **6** assistant: *cook's mate.* **7** a petty officer who assists a warrant officer in the United States Navy. **8** companion or fellow worker: *Hand me a hammer, mate.* 1,3,5-8 *n.,* 2,4 *v.,* **mat ed, mat ing.**

mate[2] (māt), checkmate. *n.,v.,* **mat ed, mat ing.**

ma té (mä′tā), kind of tea made from the dried leaves and twigs of a South American holly. Maté is a popular drink in Argentina and Uruguay. *n.* [*Maté* is from Spanish *mate,* which came from Quechua *mati,* meaning "calabash dish."]

ma ter i al (mə tir′ē əl), **1** what a thing is made from or done with: *dress material, building materials, writing materials, the material of which history is made.* **2** of matter or things; physical: *the material world.* **3** of the body: *Food and shelter are material comforts.* **4** leaving out or forgetting the spiritual side of things; worldly: *a material point of view.* **5** that matters; important: *Hard work was a material factor in their success.* 1 *n.,* 2-5 *adj.*

ma ter i al ism (mə tir′ē ə liz′əm), **1** belief that reality is made up of material things only and not of ideas. **2** tendency to care too much for the things of this world and to neglect spiritual needs. *n.*

ma ter i al ist (mə tir′ē ə list), **1** believer in materialism. **2** person who cares too much for the things of this world and neglects spiritual needs. *n.*

ma ter i al is tic (mə tir′ē ə lis′tik), of materialism or materialists. *adj.* —**ma ter′i al is′ti cal ly,** *adv.*

ma ter i al ize (mə tir′ē ə līz), **1** become an actual fact; be realized: *Our plans for the party did not materialize.* **2** appear or cause to appear in material or bodily form: *A spirit materialized from the smoke of the magician's fire. v.,* **ma ter i al ized, ma ter i al iz ing.** —**ma ter′i al i za′tion,** *n.*

ma ter i al ly (mə tir′ē ə lē), **1** with regard to material things; physically: *They improved materially and morally.* **2** considerably; greatly: *The tide helped the progress of the boat materially. adv.*

ma ter i el or **ma té ri el** (mə tir′ē el′), everything used by an army, business, undertaking, etc.; equipment. *n.*

ma ter nal (mə tėr′nl), **1** of or like a mother; motherly. **2** related on the mother's side of the family: *Everyone has two maternal grandparents and two paternal grandparents.* **3** received or inherited from one's mother: *His blue eyes were a maternal inheritance. adj.* —**ma ter′nal ly,** *adv.*

ma ter ni ty (mə tėr′nə tē), **1** motherhood; being a mother. **2** motherliness; qualities of a mother. **3** for a woman soon to have a baby: *maternity clothes.* 1,2 *n.,* 3 *adj.*

math (math), mathematics. *n.*

math e mat i cal (math′ə mat′ə kəl), **1** of mathematics: *Mathematical problems are not always easy.* **2** exact; accurate: *mathematical measurements. adj.*

math e mat i cal ly (math′ə mat′ik lē), **1** according to mathematics. **2** exactly; accurately. *adv.*

math e ma ti cian (math′ə mə tish′ən), an expert in mathematics. *n.*

math e mat ics (math′ə mat′iks), science dealing with the measurement, properties, and relationships of quantities, as expressed in numbers or symbols. Mathematics includes arithmetic, algebra, geometry, calculus, etc. *n.* [*Mathematics* comes from Latin *mathematica,* and can be traced back to Greek *manthanein,* meaning "learn."]

mat i nee (mat′n ā′), a dramatic or musical performance held in the afternoon. *n.*

mat i née (mat′n ā′), matinee. *n., pl.* **mat i nées.**

mat ins (mat′nz), a church service held at dawn or in the morning. *n.pl.*

Ma tisse (mä tēs′), Henri, 1869-1954, French painter. *n.*

ma tri arch (mā′trē ärk), **1** mother who is the ruler of a family or tribe. **2** a highly respected elderly woman. *n.*

ma tri ar chal (mā′trē är′kəl), **1** of or suitable for a matriarch. **2** under the rule of a matriarch: *a matriarchal society. adj.*

ma tri ces (mā′trə sēz′ *or* mat′rə sēz′), a plural of **matrix.** *n.*

ma tric u late (mə trik′yə lāt), enroll as a student; admit to membership and privileges in a college or university by enrolling. *v.,* **ma tric u lat ed, ma tric u lat ing.**

ma tric u la tion (mə trik′yə lā′shən), a matriculating; enrollment as a student or candidate for a degree. *n.*

mat ri mo ni al (mat′rə mō′nē əl), of marriage. *adj.* —**mat′ri mo′ni al ly,** *adv.*

mat ri mo ny (mat′rə mō′nē), marriage. *n., pl.* **mat ri mo nies.**

ma trix (mā′triks *or* mat′riks), that which gives origin or form to something enclosed within it. A mold for a casting or the rock in which gems are embedded is called a matrix. *n., pl.* **ma tri ces** *or* **ma trix es.**

ma tron (mā′trən), **1** wife or widow, especially an older married woman. **2** woman who manages the household matters of a school, hospital, dormitory, or other institution. A police matron has charge of the women in a jail. *n.* [*Matron* is from Latin *matrona,* which comes from *mater,* meaning "mother."]

ma tron ly (mā′trən lē), like a matron; suitable for a matron; dignified. *adj.* —**ma′tron li ness,** *n.*

mat ted (mat′id), **1** formed into a mat; roughly tangled: *a dog's matted hair.* **2** covered with mats or matting. *adj.*

mat ter (mat′ər), **1** what things are made of; material; substance. Matter occupies space, has weight, and can exist as a solid, liquid, or gas. Animals and plants are organic matter; minerals and water are inorganic matter. **2** affair: *business matters, a matter of life and death.* **3** what is said or written, thought of apart from the way in which it appears: *There was very little matter of interest in his speech.* **4** an instance or case; thing or things: *a matter of fact, a matter of record, a matter of accident.* **5** things written or printed: *reading matter. Second-class matter requires less postage than first-class matter.* **6** amount; quantity: *a matter of 20 miles, a matter of two days.* **7** importance; significance: *Let it go since it is of no matter.* **8** be important: *Nothing seems to matter when you are very sick.* **9** something given off from the body, such as pus. 1-7,9 *n.,* 8 *v.*

as a matter of course, as something that is to be expected.

as a matter of fact, in truth; in reality; actually.

for that matter, so far as that is concerned.

no matter, 1 it is not important; let it go. **2** regardless of. **What is the matter?** What is wrong?

Mat ter horn (mat′ər hôrn), mountain peak in the Alps, between Switzerland and Italy, 14,685 feet (4480 meters) high. *n.*

mat ter-of-fact (mat′ər əv fakt′), sticking to facts; not imaginative or fanciful. *adj.* —**mat′ter-of-fact′ly,** *adv.* —**mat′ter-of-fact′ness,** *n.*

Mat thew (math′yü), **1** (in the Bible) one of Jesus' twelve apostles. He was a tax collector who became one of the four Evangelists. **2** the first book of the New Testament. It tells the story of the life of Jesus. *n.*

mat ting (mat′ing), **1** fabric of grass, straw, hemp, or other fiber, for mats, floor covering, wrapping material, etc. **2** mats. *n.*

mat tock (mat′ək), a large tool with a steel head like a pickax, but having a flat blade on one side or flat blades on both sides, used for loosening soil and cutting roots. *n.*

mat tress (mat′ris), a covering of strong cloth stuffed with cotton, foam rubber, or some other material, and sometimes containing springs. It is used on a bed or as a bed. *n., pl.* **mat tress es.** [*Mattress* came into English about 700 years ago from French *materas,* and can be traced back to Arabic *al-maṭraḥ,* meaning "the cushion."]

mat u rate (mach′ù rāt′), mature. *v.,* **mat u rat ed, mat u rat ing.**

mat u ra tion (mach′ù rā′shən), a ripening or maturing. *n.*

ma ture (mə chùr′, mə tùr′, *or* mə tyùr′), **1** ripe or full-grown: *to reach a mature age. Grain is harvested when it is mature.* **2** ripen; come to full growth: *These apples are maturing fast.* **3** bring to full growth. **4** characteristic of full development: *a mature appearance, mature wisdom.* **5** fully worked out; carefully thought out; fully developed: *mature plans.* **6** work out carefully: *She matured her plans for the long trip.* **7** due; payable. **8** fall due: *This note to the bank matured yesterday.* 1,4,5,7 *adj.,* 2,3,6,8 *v.,* —**matured, ma tur ing.** —**ma ture′ly,** *adv.* —**ma ture′ness,** *n.*

ma tur i ty (mə chùr′ə tē, mə tùr′ə tē, *or* mə tyùr′ə tē), **1** full development; ripeness: *to reach maturity at an early age.* **2** condition of being completed or ready: *Our plans have reached maturity.* **3** a falling due; time a note or debt is payable. *n.*

mat zo (mät′sə), a thin piece of unleavened bread, eaten especially during the Jewish holiday of Passover. *n., pl.* **mat zoth** (mät′sōt′), **mat zos.**

maud lin (môd′lən), **1** sentimental in a weak, silly way: *We saw a maudlin movie about two children who lost their dog.* **2** tearfully silly because of drunkenness or excitement. *adj.*

Mau i (mou′ē), the second largest island of Hawaii. *n.*

maul (môl), **1** a very heavy hammer or mallet. **2** beat and pull about; handle roughly: *The lion mauled its keeper badly.* 1 *n.,* 2 *v.* —**maul′er,** *n.*

maul (def. 1)

Mau na Lo a (mou′nə lō′ə), an active volcano on the island of Hawaii, 13,675 feet (4170 meters) high.

maun der (môn′dər), **1** talk in a rambling, foolish way: *People who maunder talk much but say little.* **2** move or act in an aimless, confused manner: *The injured man maundered about in a daze. v.*

Mau ri ta ni a (môr′ə tā′nē ə *or* môr′ə tā′nyə), country in W Africa, on the Atlantic. *Capital:* Nouakchott. *n.* —**Mau′ri ta′ni an,** *adj., n.*

Mau ri tius (mô rish′əs), island country in the Indian Ocean, east of Madagascar. It is a member of the Commonwealth of Nations. *Capital:* Port Louis. See **Sudan** for map. *n.*

mau so le um (mô′sə lē′əm), a large, magnificent tomb. *n., pl.* **mau so le ums, mau so le a** (mô′sə lē′ə).

mauve (mōv), **1** delicate, pale purple. **2** a delicate, pale purple. **1** *adj.,* **2** *n.*

mav er ick (mav′ər ik), **1** calf or other animal not marked with an owner's brand. **2** INFORMAL. person who refuses to affiliate with a regular political party. *n.* [*Maverick* was named for Samuel *Maverick*, 1803-1870, a Texas cattle owner, who did not brand the calves of one of his herds.]

maw (mô), **1** mouth, throat, or gullet, especially of a meat-eating animal. **2** stomach. *n.*

mawk ish (mô′kish), **1** sickening. **2** sickly sentimental; weakly emotional. *adj.* —**mawk′ish ly,** *adv.* —**mawk′ish ness,** *n.*

max., maximum.

max il la (mak sil′ə), jaw or jawbone, especially the upper jawbone in mammals and most vertebrates. *n., pl.* **max il lae** (mak sil′ē), **max il las.**

max il lar y (mak′sə ler′ē), **1** of or having to do with the jaw or jawbone, especially the upper jawbone. **2** maxilla. **1** *adj.,* **2** *n., pl.* **max il lar ies.**

max im (mak′səm), a short rule of conduct; proverb: *"Look before you leap" is a maxim. n.*

Max i mil ian (mak′sə mil′yən), 1832-1867, archduke of Austria, emperor of Mexico from 1864 to 1867. *n.*

max i mize (mak′sə mīz), to increase or magnify to the highest possible amount or degree: *to maximize sales. v.,* **max i mized, max i miz ing.** —**max′i mi za′tion,** *n.* —**max′i miz′er,** *n.*

max i mum (mak′sə məm), **1** the largest or highest amount; greatest possible amount: *Twenty kilometers in a day is the maximum that I can walk.* **2** largest; highest; greatest possible: *The maximum score on this test is 100.* **1** *n., pl.* **max i mums, max i ma** (mak′sə mə). **2** *adj.*

may (mā), **1** be permitted or allowed to: *May I have an apple?* **2** be possible that it will: *It may rain tomorrow.* **3** it is hoped that: *May you prosper. v., past tense* **might.**

May (mā), the fifth month of the year. It has 31 days. *n.*

Ma ya (mī′ə), **1** member of an ancient people of Central America and Mexico. The Mayas had a highly developed culture from about A.D. 350 to about A.D. 800. **2** language of the Mayas. *n., pl.* **Ma yas** *or* **Ma ya** for 1. —**Ma′yan,** *adj., n.*

may be (mā′bē), it may be; possibly; perhaps: *Maybe you'll have better luck next time. adv.*

May Day, the first day of May, often celebrated by crowning a queen of May, dancing around the maypole, etc. In some parts of the world, labor parades and meetings are held on May Day.

may flow er (mā′flou′ər), any of several plants whose flowers blossom in May, especially the trailing arbutus. *n.*

May flow er (mā′flou′ər), ship on which the Pilgrims came to America in 1620. *n.*

may fly (mā′flī), a slender insect, having lacy front wings which are much larger than the hind wings. It dies

a hat	**i** it	**oi** oil	**ch** child	(a in about
ā age	**ī** ice	**ou** out	**ng** long	e in taken
ä far	**o** hot	**u** cup	**sh** she	**ə =** { i in pencil
e let	**ō** open	**u̇** put	**th** thin	o in lemon
ē equal	**ô** order	**ü** rule	**ᵺ** then	(u in circus
ėr term			**zh** measure	

soon after reaching the adult stage. *n., pl.* **may flies.**

may hap (mā′hap), OLD USE. perhaps. *adv.*

may hem (mā′hem), **1** crime of intentionally maiming or injuring a person. **2** needless or intentional damage: *The stampeding cattle caused great mayhem on the ranch. n.*

may n't (mā′ənt), may not.

may on naise (mā′ə nāz′), a salad dressing made of egg yolks, vegetable oil, vinegar or lemon juice, and seasoning, beaten together until thick. *n.*

may or (mā′ər), person at the head of a city or town government; chief official of a city or town. *n.*

may or al ty (mā′ər əl tē *or* mer′əl tē), **1** position of mayor. **2** mayor's term of office. *n., pl.* **may or al ties.**

may pole or **May pole** (mā′pōl′), a high pole decorated with flowers or ribbons, around which merrymakers dance on May Day. *n.*

mayst (māst), OLD USE. may. "Thou mayst" means "you may." *v.*

May time (mā′tīm′), month of May. *n.*

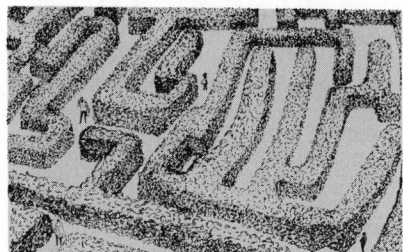

maze
(def. 1)

maze (māz), **1** network of paths through which it is hard to find one's way: *A guide led us through a maze of caves.* **2** confusion; muddle: *I couldn't find what I wanted in the maze of papers on the desk. n.*

ma zur ka (mə zėr′kə *or* mə zúr′kə), **1** a lively Polish dance. **2** music for it. *n., pl.* **ma zur kas.**

ma zour ka (mə zėr′kə *or* mə zúr′kə), mazurka. *n., pl.* **ma zour kas.**

maz y (mā′zē), like a maze; intricate. *adj.,* **maz i er, maz i est.**

M ba bane (əm bä bän′ *or* əm bä bä′nä), capital of Swaziland. *n.*

M.C., Master of Ceremonies.

Mc Clel lan (mə klel′ən), George B., 1826-1885, Union general in the Civil War. *n.*

Mayflower—This boat is a replica of the Mayflower. It is anchored in Plymouth, Massachusetts.

Mc Cor mick (mə kôr′mik), **Cyrus Hall**, 1809-1884, American inventor of harvesting machinery. *n.*

Mc Kin ley (mə kin′lē), **1 William**, 1843-1901, the 25th president of the United States, from 1897 to 1901. **2 Mount,** mountain in central Alaska, 20,320 feet (6194 meters) high. It is the highest peak in North America. *n.*

Md, symbol for mendelevium.

MD, Maryland (used with postal Zip Code).

Md., Maryland.

M.D., Doctor of Medicine.

me (mē). *I* and *me* mean the person speaking. *She said, "Give the dog to me. I like it and it likes me."* *pron.*

ME, Maine (used with postal Zip Code).

Me., Maine.

mead[1] (mēd), OLD USE. meadow. *n.*

mead[2] (mēd), an alcoholic drink made from fermented honey and water. *n.*

mead ow (med′ō), piece of grassy land, especially one used for growing hay or as a pasture. *n.*

mead ow lark (med′ō lärk′), an American songbird having a thick body, short tail, and a yellow breast marked with black. *n.*

mea ger or **mea gre** (mē′gər), **1** poor or scanty: *a meager meal.* **2** thin; lean: *a meager face. adj.* —**mea′ger ly, mea′gre ly,** *adv.* —**mea′ger ness, mea′gre ness,** *n.*

meal[1] (mēl), **1** breakfast, lunch, dinner, supper, or tea. **2** food served or eaten at any one time: *We enjoyed each meal at the hotel. n.*

meal[2] (mēl), **1** coarsely ground grain: *corn meal.* **2** anything ground to a powder. *n.*

meal i ness (mē′lē nis), mealy condition or quality. *n.*

meal time (mēl′tīm′), the usual time for eating a meal. *n.*

meal y (mē′lē), **1** like meal; dry and powdery: *mealy potatoes.* **2** of meal. **3** covered with meal: *the miller's mealy hands.* **4** pale: *a mealy complexion. adj.,* **meal i er, meal i est.**

meal y-mouthed (mē′lē mouᴛʜd′ *or* mē′lē moutht′), unwilling to tell the straight truth in plain words; using soft words insincerely. *adj.*

mean[1] (mēn), **1** have as its thought; signify; import; denote: *What does this word mean?* **2** intend to say or indicate: *"Keep out! That means you!"* **3** have as a purpose; have in mind; intend: *Do you think they mean to come? I mean to have the chops for dinner.* **4** set aside for a definite purpose; destine: *Fate meant us for each other. He was meant to be a priest.* **5** be of a certain importance or value; matter: *Good friends mean a lot to a person. v.,* **meant, mean ing.** [*Mean*[1] comes from Old English *mǣnan,* meaning "to mean, say, tell."]

mean well by, have kindly feelings toward.

mean[2] (mēn), **1** not noble; petty; unkind; small-minded: *It is mean to spread gossip about your friends.* **2** low in quality or grade; poor: *"He is no mean scholar"* means *"he is a good scholar."* **3** low in social position or rank; humble: *A peasant is of mean birth; a queen is of noble birth.* **4** of poor appearance; shabby: *The poor family lived in a mean hut.* **5** stingy or selfish: *A miser is mean about money.* **6** INFORMAL. hard to manage; troublesome; bad-tempered: *a mean horse.* **7** SLANG. excellent; clever; skillful: *to play a mean banjo, play a mean game of tennis. adj.* [*Mean*[2] comes from Old English (ge)*mǣne,* meaning "common."] —**mean′ly,** *adv.*

mean[3] (mēn), **1** halfway between two extremes; average: *Six is the mean number between three and nine.* **2** condition, quality, or course of action halfway between two extremes: *Eight hours is a happy mean between too much sleep and too little.* **3** (in mathematics) quantity having a value intermediate between the values of other quantities, especially the average obtained by dividing the sum

of all the quantities by the total number of quantities: *Six is the mean of three, seven, and eight.* **4 means,** *pl.* **a** what something is done by or the way something is brought about: *We won the game by fair means. Her quick thinking was the means of saving my life.* **b** wealth: *a person of means.* 1 *adj.,* 2-4 *n.* [*Mean*[3] came into English about 600 years ago from French *meien,* and can be traced back to Latin *medius,* meaning "middle."]

by all means, without fail; certainly: *By all means stop in to see us.*

by any means, at all; in any possible way; at any cost.

by means of, by the use of; through; with: *I found my dog by means of a notice in the paper.*

by no means, certainly not; not at all; in no way.

me an der (mē an′dər), **1** follow a winding course: *A brook meanders through the meadow.* **2** a winding course. **3** wander aimlessly: *We meandered through the park.* **4** an aimless wandering. 1,3 *v.,* 2,4 *n.* —**me an′der er,** *n.*

mean ing (mē′ning), **1** that which is meant or intended; significance: *The meaning of the sentence is clear.* **2** that means something; expressive: *a meaning look.* 1 *n.,* 2 *adj.* —**mean′ing ly,** *adv.*

mean ing ful (mē′ning fəl), full of meaning; having much meaning; significant. *adj.* —**mean′ing ful ly,** *adv.* —**mean′ing ful ness,** *n.*

mean ing less (mē′ning lis), without meaning; not making sense; not significant. *adj.* —**mean′ing less ly,** *adv.* —**mean′ing less ness,** *n.*

mean ness (mēn′nis), **1** a being mean in grade or quality; poorness. **2** a being selfish in small things; stinginess. **3** a mean act. *n., pl.* **mean ness es.**

meant (ment), past tense and past participle of **mean**[1]. *She explained what she meant. That sign was meant as a warning. v.*

mean time (mēn′tīm′), **1** time between. **2** in the time between. **3** at the same time. 1 *n.,* 2,3 *adv.*

mean while (mēn′hwīl′), meantime. *n., adv.*

meas., measure.

mea sles (mē′zəlz), **1** a contagious disease caused by a virus, characterized by the symptoms of a bad cold, fever, and a breaking out of small, red spots on the skin. Measles is more common in children than in adults. **2** a less severe disease with a similar breaking out; German measles. *n. sing. or pl.*

mea sly (mē′zlē), **1** of or like measles. **2** having measles. **3** INFORMAL. scanty; meager. *adj.,* **mea sli er, mea sli est.**

meas ur a ble (mezh′ər ə bəl), able to be measured. *adj.* —**meas′ur a ble ness,** *n.*

meas ur a bly (mezh′ər ə blē), to an amount or degree that can be measured; perceptibly: *Your work has improved measurably this semester. adv.*

meas ure (mezh′ər), **1** find the size or amount of (anything); find out how long, wide, deep, large, much, etc., (a thing) is: *We measured the room and found it was 20 feet long and 15 feet wide.* **2** mark off or out (in inches, feet, meters, quarts, liters, etc.): *Measure off 2 yards of silk. Measure out a bushel of potatoes.* **3** compare with a standard or with some other person or thing by estimating, judging, or acting: *I measured my swimming ability with hers by racing her across the pool.* **4** be of a certain size or amount: *Buy some paper that measures 8 by 10 inches.* **5** take measurements; find out size or amount: *Can he measure accurately?* **6** serve as a measure of: *A clock measures time.* **7** size or amount: *His waist measure is 30 inches.* **Short measure** means less than it should be; **full measure** means all it should be. **8** something with which to measure. A yardstick and a quart dipper are common measures. **9** a unit or standard of measure, such as an inch, mile, kilometer, acre, peck, quart, gallon, or liter. **10** any standard of comparison, estimation,

Table of Measures and Weights

Metric System				
	Length	1 millimeter	=	1/1000 meter
		1 centimeter	=	1/100 meter
		1 decimeter	=	1/10 meter
		1 meter	=	{ 10 decimeters / 100 centimeters
		1 decameter	=	10 meters
		1 kilometer	=	1000 meters
	Area	1 square centimeter	=	100 square millimeters
		1 square meter	=	{ 100 square decimeters / 10,000 square centimeters
	Volume or Capacity	1 cubic centimeter	=	1000 cubic millimeters
		1 cubic decimeter	=	1000 cubic centimeters
		1 cubic meter	=	{ 1000 cubic decimeters / 1,000,000 cubic centimeters
		1 milliliter	=	1/1000 liter
		1 liter	=	{ 1 cubic decimeter / 1000 milliliters
	Mass or Weight	1 gram	=	1000 milligrams
		1 kilogram	=	1000 grams
		1 metric ton	=	1000 kilograms
United States System	**Length**	1 foot	=	12 inches
		1 yard	=	{ 3 feet / 36 inches
		1 mile	=	{ 1760 yards / 5280 feet
	Area	1 square foot	=	144 square inches
		1 square yard	=	9 square feet
		1 acre	=	4840 square yards
		1 square mile	=	640 acres
	Volume	1 cubic foot	=	1728 cubic inches
		1 cubic yard	=	27 cubic feet
	Weight	1 pound	=	16 ounces
		1 ton	=	2000 pounds
	Capacity	1 cup	=	8 fluid ounces
		1 pint	=	2 cups
		1 quart	=	2 pints
		1 gallon	=	4 quarts

or judgment. **11** system of measuring: *square measure.* **12** limit; bound: *Her joy knew no measure.* **13** quantity, degree, or proportion: *Carelessness is in large measure responsible for many accidents.* **14** rhythmical movement or arrangement in poetry or music: *the measure in which a poem or song is written.* **15** a bar of music. **16** action meant as means to an end: *What measures shall we take to solve the problem?* **17** a proposed law; a law: *This measure has passed the Senate.* 1-6 *v.,* **meas ured, meas ur ing;** 7-17 *n.* —**meas'ur er,** *n.*

beyond measure, without limit; very greatly; exceedingly: *They were grateful beyond measure.*

for good measure, as something extra.

in a measure, to some degree; partly.

measure up to, meet the standard of: *The movie did not measure up to my expectations.*

take measures, do something; act.

take one's measure, judge one's character.

tread a measure, dance.

meas ured (mezh'ərd), **1** regular; uniform: *measured portions of food.* **2** rhythmical; metrical: *measured lines of poetry.* **3** deliberate and restrained: *measured speech. adj.*

meas ure less (mezh'ər lis), without measure; unlimited; vast: *the measureless universe. adj.*

meas ure ment (mezh'ər mənt), **1** act or fact of measuring; finding the size or amount: *The measurement of length by a yardstick is easy.* **2** size or amount found by measuring: *The measurements of the room are 10 by 15 feet.* **3** system of measuring or of measures: *Metric measurement is used in most countries. n.*

measuring worm, the larva of certain moths; inchworm. It moves by bringing the rear end of its body forward, forming a loop, and then advancing the front end.

meat (mēt), **1** animal flesh used for food. Fish and poultry are not usually called meat. **2** food of any kind: *meat and drink.* **3** part of anything that can be eaten: *The meat of the walnut is tasty.* **4** the essential part or parts: *the meat of an argument, the meat of a book. n.* —**meat'-less,** *adj.*

meat y (mē'tē), **1** like meat. **2** full of meat. **3** full of substance; solid and nourishing: *It was a meaty lesson containing many valuable ideas. adj.,* **meat i er, meat i est.** —**meat'i ly,** *adv.* —**meat'i ness,** *n.*

Mec ca (mek'ə), **1** the religious capital of Saudi Arabia, in the W part. Because Mohammed was born there, Moslems turn toward Mecca when praying and go there on pilgrimages. **2** Also, **mecca. a** place that many people visit or that a person longs to visit. **b** goal of one's desires or ambitions. *n.*

mech., mechanical.

me chan ic (mə kan'ik), worker skilled with tools, especially one who repairs machines: *an automobile mechanic. n.*

me chan i cal (mə kan'ə kəl), **1** of a machine, mechanism, or machinery: *mechanical problems.* **2** made or worked by machinery. **3** like a machine; like that of a machine; automatic; without expression: *The performance was very mechanical.* **4** of or in accordance with the science of mechanics. *adj.*

mechanical drawing, drawing of machines, tools, etc., done to exact scale with rulers, squares, compasses, etc.

me chan i cal ly (mə kan'ik lē), **1** in a mechanical manner: *He greeted us mechanically.* **2** in mechanical respects: *That new engine is mechanically perfect.* **3** toward mechanics: *She is mechanically inclined. adv.*

me chan ics (mə kan'iks), **1** *pl. in form, sing. in use.* branch of physics dealing with the action of forces on solids, liquids, and gases at rest or in motion. **2** *pl. in*

measures
(def. 15)

form, sing. in use. knowledge dealing with machinery. **3** *pl. in form and use.* mechanical part; technique: *The mechanics of playing the piano are easy for some people to acquire. n.*

mech a nism (mek'ə niz'əm), **1** a machine or its working parts: *the mechanism of a watch.* **2** system of parts working together as the parts of a machine do: *The bones and muscles are parts of the mechanism of the body.* **3** means or way by which something is done: *a mechanism for increasing sales. n.*

mech a nis tic (mek'ə nis'tik), **1** of mechanics or mechanical theories. **2** of the belief that everything in the universe is produced by and can be explained by mechanical or material forces. *adj.* —**mech'a nis'ti cal ly,** *adv.*

mech a ni za tion (mek'ə nə zā'shən), a mechanizing or a being mechanized. *n.*

mech a nize (mek'ə nīz), **1** make mechanical. **2** do by machinery, rather than by hand: *Much housework can be mechanized.* **3** replace people or animals by machinery in (a business, farming, etc.). *v.,* **mech a nized, mech a niz ing.** —**mech'a niz'er,** *n.*

med al (med'l), piece of metal like a coin, with a figure or inscription stamped on it: *She won the gold medal for figure skating at the Olympic games. n.*

med al ist (med'l ist), person who has won a medal: *an Olympic gold medalist in gymnastics. n.*

me dal lion (mə dal'yən), **1** a large medal. **2** design, ornament, etc., shaped like a medal. A design on a book or a pattern in lace may be called a medallion. *n.*

med dle (med'l), busy oneself with or in other people's things or affairs without being asked or needed: *Don't meddle with my things. That busybody meddles in everyone's business. v.,* **med dled, med dling.** —**med'dling ly,** *adv.*

med dler (med'lər), person who interferes or meddles. *n.*

med dle some (med'l səm), likely to meddle in other people's affairs; meddling; interfering. *adj.* —**med'dle-some ness,** *n.*

Mede (mēd), person who was born or lived in Media. *n.*

Me de a (mi dē'ə), (in Greek legends) an enchantress who helped Jason win the Golden Fleece. *n.*

me di a (mē'dē ə), **1** a plural of **medium** (defs. 3-5). **2** Often, **the media.** radio, television, newspapers, magazines, and other such means of mass communication: *The media has a great responsibility in the modern world. n.*

Me di a (mē'dē ə), ancient country in SW Asia, south of the Caspian Sea. *n.* —**Me'di an,** *adj., n.*

Media—about 600 B.C., shown by the darker area

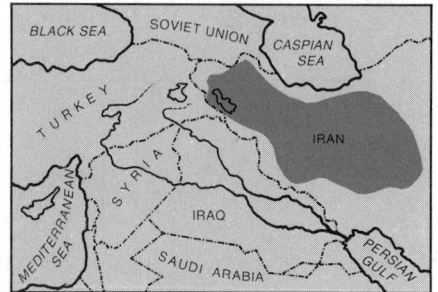

me di ae val (mē′dē ē′vəl *or* med′ē ē′vəl), medieval. *adj.*

me di al (mē′dē əl), **1** in the middle. **2** average; ordinary. *adj.* —**me′di al ly,** *adv.*

me di an (mē′dē ən), **1** in the middle: *the median vein of a leaf.* **2** the middle number of a series: *The median of 1,3,4,8,9 is 4.* **1** *adj.,* **2** *n.* —**me′di an ly,** *adv.*

me di ate (mē′dē āt), **1** come in to help settle a dispute; be a go-between; act in order to bring about an agreement between persons or sides: *The mayor tried to mediate between the bus company and its striking employees.* **2** effect by intervening; settle by intervening: *mediate an agreement, mediate a strike.* *v.,* **me di at ed, me di at ing.** —**me′di ate ly,** *adv.*

me di a tion (mē′dē ā′shən), a mediating; effecting an agreement; friendly intervention. *n.*

me di a tor (mē′dē ā′tər), person who mediates: *a mediator between warring nations. n.*

med ic (med′ik), INFORMAL. **1** physician. **2** a medical student. **3** person who is trained to perform medical services, especially giving first aid in emergencies or in combat. *n.*

Med i caid *or* **med i caid** (med′ə kād′), program that provides medical benefits for needy or disabled persons not covered by social security. It is sponsored by the federal, state, and local governments. *n.*

med i cal (med′ə kəl), of or having to do with healing or with the science and art of medicine: *medical advice, medical schools, medical treatment. adj.* —**med′i cal ly,** *adv.*

me dic a ment (mə dik′ə mənt), medicine. *n.*

Med i care *or* **med i care** (med′ə ker′ *or* med′ə kar′), a government-sponsored program of medical care and hospital services for elderly people covered by social security. *n.*

med i cate (med′ə kāt), **1** treat with medicine: *medicate an infection.* **2** put medicine on or in: *medicate a skin cream.* *v.,* **med i cat ed, med i cat ing.**

med i ca tion (med′ə kā′shən), **1** treatment with medicine. **2** a putting medicine on or in. **3** medicine. *n.*

Med i ci (med′ə chē′), member of a rich, famous, and powerful family of Florence, Italy, during the 1400's and 1500's. The Medici were patrons of many painters, sculptors, and writers. *n., pl.* **Med i ci** *or* **Med i cis.**

me dic i nal (mə dis′n əl), having value as medicine; healing; helping; relieving. *adj.* —**me dic′i nal ly,** *adv.*

med i cine (med′ə sən), **1** substance, such as a drug, used to treat, prevent, or cure disease: *The patient must take this medicine three times a day.* **2** science of treating, preventing, or curing disease; study or practice of maintaining and improving health. **3** any object or ceremony that certain primitive peoples believe has magic power over disease, evil spirits, etc. **4** this power. *n.*

medicine man, man in American Indian tribes who was believed to have close contact with the spirit world, and who was skilled in curing diseases; shaman.

me di e val (mē′dē ē′vəl *or* med′ē ē′vəl), of or belonging to the Middle Ages (the years from about A.D. 500 to about 1450). *adj.* Also, **mediaeval.** —**me′di e′val ly,** *adv.*

Me di na (mə dē′nə), city in W Saudi Arabia. Mohammed's tomb is there. *n.*

me di o cre (mē′dē ō′kər *or* mē′dē ō′kər), neither good nor bad; of average or lower than average quality; ordinary: *a mediocre book, a mediocre poet. adj.* [See **Word History.**]

me di oc ri ty (mē′dē ok′rə tē), **1** quality that is neither good nor bad; mediocre quality. **2** mediocre ability or accomplishment. **3** a mediocre person. *n., pl.* **me di oc ri ties.**

med i tate (med′ə tāt), **1** think quietly; reflect, especially on sacred or solemn objects. **2** think about; consider; plan; intend: *She meditated a subject for her report. v.,* **med i tat ed, med i tat ing.** —**med′i tat′ing ly,** *adv.* —**med′i ta′tor,** *n.*

med i ta tion (med′ə tā′shən), quiet thought; reflection, especially on sacred or solemn subjects. *n.*

med i ta tive (med′ə tā′tiv), fond of meditating; thoughtful. *adj.* —**med′i ta′tive ly,** *adv.* —**med′i ta′tive ness,** *n.*

Med i ter ra ne an (med′ə tə rā′nē ən), **1** of the Mediterranean Sea or the lands around it. **2** Mediterranean Sea. **1** *adj.,* **2** *n.*

Mediterranean Sea, large sea bordered by Europe, Asia, and Africa. See **Roman Empire** for map.

me di um (mē′dē əm), **1** having a middle position, quality, or condition; moderate: *He is of medium height. Cooked eggs can be hard, medium, or soft.* **2** that which is in the middle; neither one extreme nor the other; middle condition: *a happy medium between city and country life.* **3** substance or agent through which anything acts or through which an effect is produced; a means: *Money is a medium of exchange. Copper wire is a medium of electric transmission.* **4** Usually, **media,** *pl.* a means of communication, especially to large numbers of people: *TV, radio, and other media of advertising. Television is a completely different medium from the concert stage.* **5** substance in which something can live; environment: *Water is the medium in which fish live.* **6** person through whom messages from the spirits of the dead are supposedly sent to the living. **1** *adj.,* **2-6** *n., pl.* **me di ums** or also for 3-5 **me di a.** [*Medium* was borrowed from Latin *medium,* another form of *medius,* meaning "middle."]

med ley (med′lē), **1** mixture of things that ordinarily do not belong together. **2** piece of music made up of parts from other pieces. *n., pl.* **med leys.**

me dul la (mi dul′ə), medulla oblongata. *n., pl.* **me dul las, me dul lae** (mi dul′ē′).

medulla ob lon ga ta (ob′long gä′tə), the lowest part of the brain, at the top end of the spinal cord, containing nerve centers which control breathing and other involuntary functions. *pl.* **medulla ob lon ga tas, medullae ob lon ga tae** (ob′long gä′tē).

me du sa (mə dü′sə *or* mə dyü′sə), jellyfish. *n., pl.* **me du sas, me du sae** (mə dü′sē′ *or* mə dyü′sē′).

Me du sa (mə dü′sə *or* mə dyü′sə), (in Greek legends) one of the three Gorgons or horrible monsters with snakes for hair. *n., pl.* **Me du sas.**

meed (mēd), OLD USE. what one deserves or has earned; reward. *n.*

meek (mēk), **1** not easily angered; mild; patient. **2** sub-

a hat	i it	oi oil	ch child	a in about
ā age	ī ice	ou out	ng long	e in taken
ä far	o hot	u cup	sh she	ə = { i in pencil
e let	ō open	u̇ put	th thin	o in lemon
ē equal	ô order	ü rule	ŦH then	u in circus
ėr term			zh measure	

WORD HISTORY

mediocre

Mediocre is from Latin *mediocris,* meaning "halfway up," which comes from *medius,* meaning "middle," and *ocris,* meaning "jagged mountain."

mitting tamely when ordered about or injured by others; too shy or humbled; yielding: *Don't be meek about asking for a promotion.* *adj.* —**meek′ly,** *adv.* —**meek′ness,** *n.*

meer schaum (mir′shəm), **1** a soft, white mineral used to make tobacco pipes. **2** a tobacco pipe made of this material. *n.* [*Meerschaum* comes from German *Meerschaum,* meaning "sea foam."]

meet[1] (mēt), **1** come face to face (with something or someone coming from the other direction): *Our car met another car on a narrow bridge.* **2** come together; come into contact or connection with; join: *Two roads meet near the church. Sword met sword in battle.* **3** keep an appointment with: *Meet me at one o'clock.* **4** be introduced to; become acquainted: *Have you met my sister?* **5** receive and welcome on arrival: *I must go to the station to meet my mother.* **6** be perceived by; be seen or heard by: *There is more to this matter than meets the eye.* **7** fulfill; put an end to; satisfy: *The campers took along enough food to meet their needs for a week.* **8** pay (one's debts, etc.) when due: *I did not have enough money to meet my bills.* **9** fight with; oppose; deal with: *meet an enemy in battle.* **10** face directly: *He met her glance with a smile.* **11** experience: *He met open scorn before he won fame.* **12** assemble: *Congress will meet next month.* **13** a meeting; a gathering: *an athletic meet.* 1-12 *v.,* **met, meet ing;** 13 *n.* —**meet′er,** *n.*

meet with, 1 come across; light upon: *We met with bad weather.* **2** have; get: *The plan met with approval.*

meet[2] (mēt), OLD USE. suitable; proper; fitting: *It is meet that you should help your friends.* *adj.* —**meet′ly,** *adv.*

meet ing (mē′ting), **1** a coming together. **2** a coming together or assembly of people for worship: *a Quaker meeting, a prayer meeting.* **3** any coming together or assembly of people: *The club held a meeting.* **4** place where things meet; junction: *a meeting of roads.* *n.*

meet ing house (mē′ting hous′), a building used for worship; church. *n., pl.* **meet ing hous es** (mē′ting-hou′ziz).

mega-, *combining form.* **1** large: *Megaphone = large horn.* **2** one million: *Megacycle = one million cycles.* [The form *mega-* comes from Greek *megas,* meaning "great."]

meg a cy cle (meg′ə sī′kəl), one million cycles. *n.*

meg a hertz (meg′ə hėrts′), unit of frequency equal to one million hertz, used to express frequency of radio waves. *n., pl.* **meg a hertz.**

megaliths

meg a lith (meg′ə lith), stone of great size, especially in monuments left by people of prehistoric times. *n.*

meg a lo ma ni a (meg′ə lō mā′nē ə), a mental disorder marked by delusions of great personal power, wealth, etc. *n.*

meg a lop o lis (meg′ə lop′ə lis), **1** a large metropolis. **2** a large metropolitan area, often including several cities. *n.*

meg a phone (meg′ə fōn), a large, funnel-shaped horn used to increase the loudness of the voice or the distance at which it can be heard. *n.* [*Megaphone* comes

from Greek *megas,* meaning "great," and *phōnē,* meaning "sound."]

meg a ton (meg′ə tun′), **1** unit of weight equal to one million tons. **2** unit of atomic power equivalent to the energy released by one million tons of the explosive TNT. *n.*

Me ir (me ir′), **Golda,** 1898-1978, prime minister of Israel from 1969 to 1974. *n.*

mel an chol ic (mel′ən kol′ik), melancholy; gloomy. *adj.*

mel an chol y (mel′ən kol′ē), **1** low spirits; sadness; tendency to be sad. **2** sad; gloomy: *a melancholy person.* **3** causing sadness; depressing: *a melancholy scene.* 1 *n.,* 2,3 *adj.*

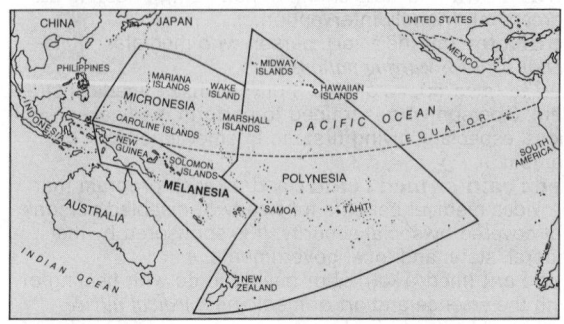

Mel a ne sia (mel′ə nē′zhə), group of islands in the Pacific, northeast of Australia. *n.* —**Mel′a ne′sian,** *adj., n.*

mé lange (mā länzh′), mixture; medley. *n., pl.* **mé langes.**

Mel bourne (mel′bərn), seaport in SE Australia. *n.*

meld (meld), **1** announce and show (cards for a score) in pinochle, etc. **2** act of melding. **3** cards which can be melded. 1 *v.,* 2,3 *n.*

me lee (mā′lā), a confused fight; hand-to-hand fight among a number of fighters. *n.*

mê lée (mā′lā), melee. *n., pl.* **mê lées.**

mel io rate (mē′lyə rāt′), improve. *v.,* **mel io rat ed, mel io rat ing.** —**mel′io ra′tion,** *n.* —**mel′io ra′tor,** *n.*

mel lif lu ous (mə lif′lü əs), sweetly or smoothly flowing: *The actor spoke in a mellifluous voice.* *adj.* —**mel lif′lu ous ly,** *adv.* —**mel lif′lu ous ness,** *n.*

mel low (mel′ō), **1** soft and full-flavored from ripeness; sweet and juicy: *a mellow apple.* **2** fully matured: *mellow wine.* **3** soft and rich: *a violin with a mellow tone, a mellow color.* **4** softened and made wise by age and experience. **5** make or become mellow: *The apples mellowed after we picked them. Time had mellowed his youthful temper.* 1-4 *adj.,* 5 *v.* —**mel′low ly,** *adv.* —**mel′low ness,** *n.*

me lod ic (mə lod′ik), **1** having to do with melody. **2** melodious, *adj.* —**me lod′i cal ly,** *adv.*

me lo di ous (mə lō′dē əs), **1** sweet-sounding; pleasing to the ear; musical: *a melodious voice.* **2** producing melody. *adj.* —**me lo′di ous ly,** *adv.* —**me lo′di ous ness,** *n.*

mel o dra ma (mel′ə drä′mə *or* mel′ə dram′ə), **1** a sensational drama with exaggerated appeal to the emotions and, usually, a happy ending: *Most mystery shows are melodramas.* **2** any sensational writing, speech, or action with exaggerated appeal to the emotions. *n., pl.* **mel o dra mas.**

mel o dra mat ic (mel′ə drə mat′ik), of, like, or suitable for melodrama; sensational and exaggerated. *adj.* —**mel′o dra mat′i cal ly,** *adv.*

mel o dy (mel′ə dē), **1** sweet music; any sweet sound. **2** succession of single tones in music; tune. Most music has melody, harmony, and rhythm. **3** the main tune in music with harmony; the air. *n., pl.* **mel o dies.**

mel on (mel′ən), a large, juicy fruit of a vine much like the pumpkin, squash, and cucumber. Watermelons, cantaloupes, and honeydew melons are different kinds. *n.*

Mel pom e ne (mel pom′ə nē), (in Greek myths) the Muse of tragedy. *n.*

melt (melt), **1** turn into a liquid by applying heat. Ice becomes water when it melts. **2** dissolve: *Sugar melts in water.* **3** disappear or cause to disappear gradually: *The clouds melted away, and the sun came out.* **4** change very gradually; blend; merge: *In the rainbow, the green melts into blue, the blue into violet.* **5** soften: *Their kindness melted her heart.* *v.* —**melt′er,** *n.*

melt down (melt′doun′), accident in a nuclear reactor, involving failure of cooling systems and buildup of heat in the nuclear fuel until it melts through and escapes from its container. *n.*

melting point, temperature at which a solid substance melts. Different substances have different melting points. Tungsten has the highest melting point of all metallic elements.

Mel ville (mel′vil), **Herman,** 1819-1891, American novelist. *n.*

mem ber (mem′bər), **1** person, animal, or thing belonging to a group: *Every member of the family was home for the holidays. The lion is a member of the cat family.* **2** a constituent part of a whole: *a member of an equation, the members of a set.* **3** part or organ of an animal, human body, or plant, especially a leg, arm, or wing. *n.*

mem ber ship (mem′bər ship), **1** fact or state of being a member: *Do you enjoy your membership in the Girl Scouts?* **2** members as a group: *The whole membership was present.* **3** number of members: *Our club has a large membership. n.*

mem brane (mem′brān), **1** a thin, soft sheet or layer of animal tissue, lining or covering some part of the body. **2** a similar layer of vegetable tissue. *n.*

mem bra nous (mem′brə nəs), of or like membrane. *adj.*

me men to (mə men′tō), something serving as a reminder, warning, or remembrance: *These post cards are mementos of our trip abroad. n., pl.* **me men tos** or **me men toes.**

mem o (mem′ō), memorandum, *n., pl.* **mem os.**

mem oir (mem′wär), **1** biography. **2** memoirs, *pl.* **a** record of facts and events written from personal knowledge or special information: *The retired general wrote his memoirs of army life.* **b** record of a person's own life and experiences; autobiography. *n.*

mem o ra bil i a (mem′ər ə bil′ē ə), things or events worth remembering. *n.pl.*

mem o ra ble (mem′ər ə bəl), worth remembering; not to be forgotten; notable: *a memorable occasion. adj.*

mem o ra bly (mem′ər ə blē), in a memorable manner; so as to be remembered. *adv.*

mem o ran da (mem′ə ran′də), a plural of **memorandum.** *n.*

mem o ran dum (mem′ə ran′dəm), **1** a short written statement for future use; note to aid one's memory: *Make a memorandum of the things we'll need for the trip.* **2** an informal letter, note, or report. *n., pl.* **mem o randums** or **mem o ran da.**

me mo ri al (mə môr′ē əl), **1** something that is a reminder of some event or person, such as a statue, an arch or column, a book, or a holiday. **2** helping people to remember some person, thing, or event: *memorial services.* **1** *n.,* **2** *adj.*

Memorial Day, holiday for remembering and honoring members of the United States armed services who have died for their country; Decoration Day. It is celebrated in most states on the last Monday in May.

me mo ri al ize (mə môr′ē ə līz), preserve the memory of; commemorate. *v.,* **me mo ri al ized, me mo ri al iz-**

ing. —**me mo′ri al i za′tion,** *n.* —**me mo′ri al iz′er,** *n.*

mem or i za tion (mem′ər ə zā′shən), act of memorizing. *n.*

mem o rize (mem′ə rīz′), commit to memory; learn by heart: *memorize the alphabet. v.,* **mem o rized, mem o rizing.** —**mem′o riz′er,** *n.*

mem or y (mem′ər ē), **1** ability to remember or keep in the mind: *She will recall when that happened, for she has a good memory.* **2** act of remembering; remembrance: *My memory of the trip is still fresh.* **3** person, thing, or event that is remembered: *I was so young when we moved that our old house is only a vague memory.* **4** all that a person remembers. **5** length of past time that is remembered: *This is the hottest summer within my memory.* **6** part of a computer or computer system in which information and instructions can be stored, temporarily or permanently. *n., pl.* **mem o ries.** [*Memory* came into English about 600 years ago from French *memorie,* and can be traced back to Latin *memor,* meaning "mindful."]

in memory of, to help in remembering; as a reminder of: *I send you this gift in memory of our summer together.*

Mem phis (mem′fis), city in SW Tennessee, on the Mississippi. *n.*

men (men), **1** plural of **man.** **2** human beings; people in general: *"All men are created equal." n.pl.*

men ace (men′is), **1** threat: *In dry weather forest fires are a great menace.* **2** threaten: *Floods menaced the valley towns with destruction.* **1** *n.,* **2** *v.,* **men aced, men ac ing.**

me nag er ie (mə naj′ər ē), **1** a collection of wild animals kept in cages for exhibition. **2** place where such animals are kept. *n.*

mend (mend), **1** put in good condition again; make whole; repair: *mend a road, mend a broken doll, mend stockings.* **2** correct faults; set right; improve: *to mend one's manners.* **3** place that has been mended: *The mend in your shirt scarcely shows.* **4** get back one's health; recover from illness or injury: *My sprained ankle has mended.* **1,2,4** *v.,* **3** *n.* —**mend′a ble,** *adj.* —**mend′er,** *n.*

on the mend, getting better; improving.

men da cious (men dā′shəs), **1** lying; untruthful. **2** false; untrue. *adj.* —**men da′cious ly,** *adv.*

men dac i ty (men das′ə tē), **1** habit of telling lies; untruthfulness. **2** a lie. *n., pl.* **men dac i ties.**

Men del (men′dl), **Gregor,** 1822-1884, Austrian monk and biologist. His investigations of heredity laid the foundations for the science of genetics. *n.*

men de le vi um (men′dl ē′vē əm), a radioactive metallic element, produced artificially from einsteinium. *n.*

Men dels sohn (men′dl sən *or* men′dl sōn), **Felix,** 1809-1847, German composer. *n.*

men di cant (men′də kənt), **1** begging: *Mendicant friars ask alms for charity.* **2** a beggar: *We were surrounded by mendicants asking for money.* **1** *adj.,* **2** *n.*

Men e la us (men′ə lā′əs), (in Greek legends) a king of Sparta, husband of Helen, and brother of Agamemnon. *n.*

men folk (men′fōk′), men. *n.pl.*

men ha den (men hād′n), a sea fish common along the eastern coast of the United States, used for making oil and fertilizer; pogy. *n., pl.* **men ha den.** [*Menhaden* is of Algonquian origin.]

me ni al (mē′nē əl), of or suited to a servant; low; mean:

Pronunciation key

a hat	i it	oi oil	ch child		a in about
ā age	ī ice	ou out	ng long		e in taken
ä far	o hot	u cup	sh she	ə =	i in pencil
e let	ō open	ú put	th thin		o in lemon
ē equal	ô order	ü rule	ᴛʜ then		u in circus
ėr term			zh measure		

Cinderella had to do menial tasks. **2** servant who does the humblest and most unpleasant tasks. 1 *adj.*, 2 *n.* —**me′ni al ly,** *adv.*

men in gi tis (men′in jī′tis), a very serious disease in which the membranes surrounding the brain or spinal cord become inflamed. *n.*

Men non ite (men′ə nīt), member of a Christian church opposed to infant baptism, taking oaths, holding public office, and military service. The Mennonites often wear very plain clothes and live simply. *n.*

men-of-war (men′əv wôr′), plural of **man-of-war.** *n.*

menorah—The center candle is used to light the other candles. One candle is lighted each of the eight days of Hanukkah so that on the last day all nine burn together.

me no rah (mə nôr′ə), candlestick with eight branches used during the Jewish festival of Hanukkah. *n.* [*Menorah* comes from Hebrew *menōrāh.*]

men serv ants (men′sėr′vənts), plural of **manservant.** *n.*

men stru ate (men′strü āt), have a discharge of blood from the uterus, normally at intervals of about four weeks. *v.*, **men stru at ed, men stru at ing.**

men stru a tion (men′strü ā′shən), act or period of menstruating. *n.*

-ment, *suffix added to verbs to form nouns.* **1** act of _____ing: *Enjoyment = act of enjoying. Measurement = act of measuring.* **2** condition of being _____ed: *Amazement = condition of being amazed.* **3** product or result of _____ing: *Pavement = product of paving. Measurement = result of measuring.* **4** means of or instrument for _____ing: *Inducement = means of inducing.*

men tal (men′tl), **1** of the mind: *a mental test, a mental illness.* **2** for the mind; done by the mind: *mental arithmetic.* **3** having a mental disease or disorder: *a mental patient.* **4** for people having mental disease: *a mental hospital. adj.*

mental age, the level of a person's mental development as compared to that of the average person of the same age. A ten-year-old child with a mental age of thirteen has a higher-than-average intelligence.

men tal i ty (men tal′ə tē), **1** mental capacity; mind: *a student with a high mentality.* **2** attitude or outlook: *a mature mentality. n., pl.* **men tal i ties.**

men tal ly (men′tl ē), in the mind; with the mind: *mentally alert. adv.*

men thol (men′thôl), a white, crystalline substance obtained from oil of peppermint, used in medicine. *n.*

men tho lat ed (men′thə lā′tid), **1** containing menthol. **2** treated with menthol. *adj.*

men tion (men′shən), **1** speak about; refer to: *I mentioned your idea to the planning committee.* **2** a short statement; a mentioning; reference: *A mention of the game appeared in the newspaper.* 1 *v.*, 2 *n.* —**men′tion a ble,** *adj.* —**men′tion er,** *n.*

make mention of, speak of; refer to: *She made mention of a book she had read recently.*

not to mention, not even considering; besides.

men tor (men′tər), a wise and trusted adviser. *n.*

Men tor (men′tər), (in Greek legends) a faithful friend of Ulysses and the adviser of Telemachus, Ulysses' son. *n.*

men u (men′yü), **1** list of the food served at a meal; bill of fare. **2** the food served: *Everybody enjoyed the fine menu.* **3** a list of things to choose from, shown by a computer to the user: *You can play any game on the menu. n.*

me ow (mē ou′), **1** sound made by a cat or kitten. **2** make this sound. 1 *n.*, 2 *v.*

Meph i stoph e les (mef′ə stof′ə lēz′), **1** the devil of the Faust legend. **2** a powerful evil spirit; crafty devil. *n.*

mer., meridian.

merc., **1** mercantile. **2** mercury.

mer can tile (mėr′kən til), of merchants or trade; commercial: *a mercantile firm, mercantile law. adj.*

mer ce nar y (mėr′sə ner′ē), **1** working for money only; acting with money as the motive. **2** done for money or gain. **3** soldier serving for pay in a foreign army. 1,2 *adj.*, 3 *n., pl.* **mer ce nar ies.** —**mer′ce nar′i ly,** *adv.*

mer cer (mėr′sər), dealer in cloth. *n.*

mer cer ize (mėr′sə rīz′), treat (cotton thread or cloth) with a chemical solution that strengthens the cotton, makes it hold dyes better, and gives it a silky luster. *v.*, **mer cer ized, mer cer iz ing.** [*Mercerize* was formed from the name of John *Mercer*, 1791-1866, an English calico printer, who patented the process.]

mer chan dise (mėr′chən dīz *or* mėr′chən dīs *for 1;* mėr′chən dīz *for 2,3*), **1** goods for sale; articles bought and sold. **2** buy and sell; trade. **3** to further the sales of (goods and services) by advertising and other methods. 1 *n.*, 2,3 *v.*, **mer chan dised, mer chan dis ing.** —**mer′chan dis′er,** *n.*

mer chant (mėr′chənt), **1** person who buys and sells for profit; trader: *Some merchants do most of their business with foreign countries.* **2** storekeeper. **3** trading; having to do with trade; commercial: *merchant ships.* 1,2 *n.*, 3 *adj.*

mer chant man (mėr′chənt mən), ship used in commerce. *n., pl.* **mer chant men.**

merchant marine, **1** the trading ships of a nation; ships used in commerce. **2** the body of officers and sailors who serve on such ships: *His brother is in the merchant marine.*

mer ci ful (mėr′si fəl), having mercy; showing or feeling mercy; full of mercy. *adj.* —**mer′ci ful ly,** *adv.* —**mer′ci ful ness,** *n.*

mer ci less (mėr′si lis), without mercy; having no mercy; showing no mercy. *adj.* —**mer′ci less ly,** *adv.* —**mer′ci less ness,** *n.*

mer cur i al (mər kyūr′ē əl), **1** sprightly and animated; quick. **2** changeable; fickle. *adj.* —**mer cur′i al ly,** *adv.*

mer cur ic (mər kyūr′ik), (of compounds) containing mercury. *adj.*

Mer cur o chrome (mər kyūr′ə krōm′), trademark for a red liquid containing mercury, used as an antiseptic. *n.*

mer cur y (mėr′kyər ē), **1** a heavy, silver-white, metallic element that is liquid at ordinary temperatures; quicksilver. **2** the column of mercury in a thermometer or barometer. *n., pl.* **mer cur ies.**

Mer cur y (mėr′kyər ē), **1** (in Roman myths) the messenger of the gods. He was the god of commerce, skill of hands, quickness of wit, and eloquence. The Greeks called him Hermes. **2** the smallest planet in the solar system and the one nearest to the sun. *n.*

mer cy (mėr′sē), **1** more kindness than justice requires; kindness beyond what can be claimed or expected: *The judge showed mercy to the young offender.* **2** kindly treatment; pity. **3** something to be thankful for; blessing: *It's a mercy that she wasn't injured in the accident. n., pl.* **mer cies.** [*Mercy* came into English about 700 years ago from French *merci*, which came from Latin *merces*, meaning "reward, wages."]

at the mercy of, in the power of.

mere (mir), nothing else than; only; simple: *The cut was the merest scratch. The mere sight of a dog makes me afraid. adj., superlative* **mer est.**

mere ly (mir′lē), simply; only; and nothing more; and that is all. *adv.*

mer e tri cious (mer′ə trish′əs), attractive in a showy way; alluring by false charms: *meretricious advertising. adj.* —**mer′e tri′cious ly,** *adv.* —**mer′e tri′cious ness,** *n.*

mer gan ser (mər gan′sər), any of several kinds of large, fish-eating ducks with long, slender bills which are hooked at the tip. They often have crested heads. *n., pl.* **mer gan sers** or **mer gan ser.**

merge (mėrj), **1** cause to be swallowed up or absorbed so as to lose its own character or identity; combine or consolidate: *The big company merged various small businesses.* **2** become swallowed up or absorbed in something else: *The twilight merges into darkness. The two railroads merged into one. v.,* **merged, merg ing.** [*Merge* comes from Latin *mergere,* meaning "dip, plunge."]

merg er (mėr′jər), act of merging; combination; consolidation: *One big company was formed by the merger of four small ones. n.*

me rid i an (mə rid′ē ən), **1** an imaginary circle passing through any place on the earth's surface and through the North and South Poles. **2** the half of such a circle from pole to pole. All the places on the same meridian have the same longitude. **3** the highest point: *The meridian of life is the prime of life. n.* [*Meridian* comes from Latin *meridianus,* meaning "of noon," and can be traced back to *medius,* meaning "middle," and *dies,* meaning "day."]

me ringue (mə rang′), **1** a mixture of white of egg and sugar, beaten stiff. Meringue is often spread on pies, puddings, etc., and lightly browned in the oven. **2** a shell made of this mixture and filled with fruit, whipped cream, etc. *n.*

merino (def. 1)
about 2 ft. (60 cm.)
high at the shoulder

me ri no (mə rē′nō), **1** Often, **Merino.** kind of sheep with long, fine wool. **2** a soft, woolen yarn or cloth made from this wool or some substitute. *n., pl.* **me ri nos.**

mer it (mer′it), **1** worth or value; goodness: *Students will be graded according to the merit of their work.* **2** something that deserves praise or reward. **3** deserve: *Your excellent work merits praise.* **4** Usually, **merits,** *pl.* actual facts or qualities, whether good or bad: *The judge will consider the case on its merits.* 1,2,4 *n.,* 3 *v.* —**mer′it less,** *adj.*

mer i to ri ous (mer′ə tôr′ē əs), deserving reward or praise; having merit; worthy: *The student's work at school was meritorious, but not brilliant. adj.* —**mer′i to′ri ous ly,** *adv.* —**mer′i to′ri ous ness,** *n.*

merle or **merl** (mėrl), the common European blackbird. *n.*

Mer lin (mėr′lən), magician who helped King Arthur. *n.*

mer maid (mėr′mād′), an imaginary creature of the sea, with the head and body of a woman, and the tail of a fish. *n.*

mer man (mėr′man′), an imaginary creature of the sea, with the head and body of a man, and the tail of a fish. *n., pl.* **mer men.**

mer ri ly (mer′ə lē), in a merry manner; laughing and gay. *adv.*

Mer ri mac (mer′ə mak), a United States frigate rebuilt with iron armor by the Confederates during the Civil War and renamed the **Virginia.** The Merrimac was the first armored warship. *n.*

Mer ri mack (mer′ə mak), river flowing from central New Hampshire through NE Massachusetts into the Atlantic. *n.*

mer ri ment (mer′ē mənt), laughter and gaiety; fun; mirth; merry enjoyment. *n.*

meridians (def. 2) of longitude

mer ry (mer′ē), **1** laughing and gay; full of fun: *merry talk.* **2** gay; joyful: *a merry holiday. adj.,* **mer ri er, mer ri est.** —**mer′ri ness,** *n.*

make merry, laugh and be gay; have fun.

mer ry-go-round (mer′ē gō round′), **1** set of animal figures and seats on a circular platform that is driven round and round by machinery and that children ride for fun; carrousel. **2** any whirl or rapid round: *The holidays were a merry-go-round of parties. n.*

mer ry mak er (mer′ē mā′kər), person who is being merry; person engaged in merrymaking. *n.*

mer ry mak ing (mer′ē mā′king), **1** laughter and gaiety; fun. **2** gay festival; merry entertainment. **3** gay and full of fun; having a merry time. 1,2 *n.,* 3 *adj.*

me sa (mā′sə), a small, high plateau with a flat top and steep sides, common in dry regions of the western and southwestern United States. *n.*

WORD HISTORY

mesa

Mesa was borrowed from Spanish *mesa,* which came from Latin *mensa,* meaning "table."

mes dames (mā däm′), **1** a plural of **madam. 2** FRENCH. plural of **madame.** *n.*

mes de moi selles (mād mwä zel′), FRENCH. plural of **mademoiselle.** *n.*

mesh (mesh), **1** an open space of a net, sieve, or screen: *This net has half-inch meshes.* **2** cord, wire, etc., used in a net or screen: *We found an old fly swatter made of wire mesh.* **3 meshes,** *pl.* **a** network: *Seaweed was caught in the meshes of the net.* **b** snares: *The spy was entangled in the meshes of his own plot to steal defense secrets.* **4** engage or become engaged. The teeth of a small gear mesh with the teeth of a larger one. 1-3 *n., pl.* **mesh es;** 4 *v.*
in mesh, in gear; fitted together.

mes mer ism (mez′mə riz′əm *or* mes′mə riz′əm), hypnotism. *n.*

mes mer ize (mez′mə rīz′ *or* mes′mə rīz′), hypnotize. *v.,* **mes mer ized, mes mer iz ing.**

mes on (mes′on), a highly unstable particle found in the nucleus of an atom, having a mass greater than that of an electron and less than that of a proton. A meson may have a positive, negative, or neutral charge. *n.*

Mes o po ta mi a (mes′ə pə tä′mē ə), ancient country in SW Asia, between the Tigris and Euphrates rivers. *n.*
—Mes′o po ta′mi an, *adj., n.*

mes o sphere (mes′ə sfir), region of the atmosphere between the stratosphere and the ionosphere, which extends from about 10 to 50 miles (16 to 80 kilometers) above the earth's surface. Most of the ozone in the atmosphere is created in the mesosphere, and there is almost no variation in the temperature. *n.*

Mes o zo ic (mes′ə zō′ik), **1** the geological era before the present era; the age of reptiles. **2** of this era or its rocks. 1 *n.,* 2 *adj.*

me squite (me skēt′), tree or shrub, common in the southwestern United States and Mexico, that often grows in dense clumps or thickets. Its pods furnish a valuable food for cattle. *n.* [*Mesquite* is from Spanish *mezquite,* which came from Nahuatl *mizquitl.*]

mess (mes), **1** a dirty or untidy mass or group of things; dirty or untidy condition: *Please clean up the mess in your room.* **2** make dirty or untidy: *She messed up her book by scribbling in it.* **3** confusion or difficulty: *His business affairs are in a mess.* **4** make a failure of; spoil: *He messed up his chances of winning the race.* **5** an unpleasant or unsuccessful affair or state of affairs: *She made a mess of her final examinations.* **6** group of people who take meals together regularly, especially such a group in the armed forces. **7** meal of such a group: *The officers ate early mess.* **8** take one's meals (with). 1,3,5-7 *n., pl.* **mess es;** 2,4,8 *v.*

mess about *or* **mess around,** be busy without really accomplishing anything.

mes sage (mes′ij), **1** words sent from one person to another: *a telephone message.* **2** an official speech or writing: *the President's message to Congress.* **3** lesson or moral contained in a story, play, speech, etc. *n.*

mes sen ger (mes′n jər), **1** person who carries a message or goes on an errand. **2** a sign that something is coming; forerunner; herald: *Dawn is the messenger of day. n.*

Mes si ah (mə sī′ə), **1** the expected deliverer of the Jewish people. **2** (in Christian use) Jesus. **3** Often, **messiah.** any person hailed as or thought of as a savior. *n.*

Mes si an ic (mes′ē an′ik), **1** of the Messiah. **2** Often, **messianic.** of or like a messiah or savior. *adj.*

mes sieurs (mes′ərz; *French* mā sẏ′), plural of **monsieur.** *n.*

mess kit, a shallow, metal container that includes a fork, spoon, knife, and metal cup, for use by a soldier in the field, a camper, etc.

mess mate (mes′māt′), one of a group of people who eat together regularly. *n.*

Messrs., messieurs, used before names as the plural of **Mr.**: *Messrs. Smith and Jones.*

mess y (mes′ē), in a mess; like a mess; untidy; in disorder; dirty. *adj.,* **mess i er, mess i est. —mess′i ly,** *adv.* **—mess′i ness,** *n.*

mes ti zo (me stē′zō), person of mixed ancestry, especially the child of a Spaniard and an American Indian. *n., pl.* **mes ti zos** or **mes ti zoes.**

met (met), past tense and past participle of **meet**[1]. *They met us this morning. We were met at the gate by our dog. v.*

met a bol ic (met′ə bol′ik), of metabolism. *adj.* **—met′a-bol′i cal ly,** *adv.*

me tab o lism (mə tab′ə liz′əm), process by which all living things turn food into energy and living tissue. In metabolism food is broken down to produce energy, which is then used by the body to build up new cells and tissues, provide heat, and engage in physical activity. Growth and action depend on metabolism. *n.*

met a car pus (met′ə kär′pəs), part of the hand, especially the bones, between the wrist and the fingers. *n., pl.* **met a car pi** (met′ə kär′pī).

met al (met′l), **1** any of a group of chemical elements which usually have a shiny surface, are good conductors of heat and electricity, and can be melted or fused, hammered into thin sheets, or drawn out into wires. Metals form alloys with each other and react with nonmetals to form salts by losing electrons. Iron, gold, sodium, copper, lead, tin, and aluminum are metals. **2** any alloy or fused mixture of these, such as steel, bronze, and brass. **3** made of metal: *a metal container, a metal coin.* **4** mettle. **5** furnish, cover or fit with metal. 1,2,4 *n.,* 3 *adj.,* 5 *v.,* **met aled, met al ing** *or* **met alled, met al ling.**

me tal lic (mə tal′ik), **1** of, containing, or consisting of metal: *a metallic substance.* **2** like metal; characteristic of metal; that suggests metal: *a metallic luster, a metallic voice. adj.*

met al lur gi cal (met′l ėr′jə kəl), of or having to do with metallurgy. *adj.*

met al lur gist (met′l ėr′jist), an expert in metallurgy. *n.*

met al lur gy (met′l ėr′jē), science or art of working with metals, including the study of their properties and structure, the separation and refining of metals from their ores, and the production of alloys. *n.*

met al work (met′l wėrk′), **1** things made out of metal. **2** a making things out of metal. *n.*

met al work ing (met′l wėr′king), act or process of making things out of metal. *n.*

met a mor phic (met′ə môr′fik), **1** characterized by metamorphosis; having to do with change of form. **2** changed in structure by heat, moisture, and pressure. Slate is a metamorphic rock that is formed from shale, a sedimentary rock. *adj.*

met a mor phose (met′ə môr′fōz), change in form; transform: *A caterpillar metamorphoses into a butterfly. v.,* **met a mor phosed, met a mor phos ing.**

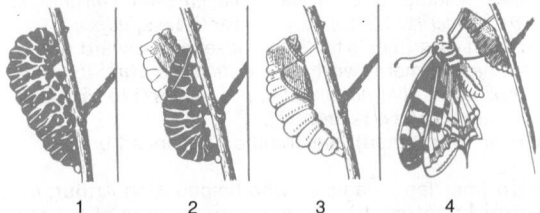

metamorphosis (def. 1) of a butterfly
1 caterpillar before change **2** it sheds skin, exposing chrysalis
3 chrysalis entirely exposed **4** adult emerges from chrysalis

met a mor pho sis (met′ə môr′fə sis), **1** change of form. Tadpoles become frogs by metamorphosis; they lose their tails and grow legs. **2** the changed form. **3** a noticeable or complete change of character, appearance, or condition. *n., pl.* **met a mor pho ses** (met′ə môr′fə sēz′).

met a phor (met′ə fôr), an implied comparison between two different things; a figure of speech in which a word or phrase that ordinarily means one thing is applied to another thing in order to suggest a likeness between the two. "A heart of stone" is a metaphor. *n.*

met a phor i cal (met′ə fôr′ə kəl), using metaphors; figurative. *adj.* —**met′a phor′i cal ly,** *adv.*

met a phys i cal (met′ə fiz′ə kəl), **1** of metaphysics; about the real nature of things. **2** highly abstract; hard to understand. *adj.* —**met′a phys′i cal ly,** *adv.*

met a phys ics (met′ə fiz′iks), branch of philosophy that tries to explain reality and knowledge; the study of the real nature of things. *n.*

met a tar sus (met′ə tär′səs), part of the foot, especially the bones, between the ankle and the toes. *n., pl.* **met a tar si** (met′ə tär′sī).

mete (mēt), give to each person a proper or fair share; distribute; allot: *mete out punishment, mete out praise.* *v.,* **met ed, met ing.**

me te or (mē′tē ər), mass of stone or metal that enters the earth's atmosphere from outer space with enormous speed; shooting star. Meteors become so hot from rushing through the air that they glow and often burn up. *n.*

me te or ic (mē′tē ôr′ik), **1** of meteors: *meteoric dust.* **2** flashing like a meteor; brilliant and soon ended; swift: *a meteoric rise to fame. adj.* —**me′te or′i cal ly,** *adv.*

meteorite

me te o rite (mē′tē ə rīt′), mass of stone or metal that has fallen to the earth from outer space; a fallen meteor. *n.*

me te or o log i cal (mē′tē ər ə loj′ə kəl), of the atmosphere and weather; of meteorology. *adj.* —**me′te or o log′i cal ly,** *adv.*

me te o rol o gist (mē′tē ə rol′ə jist), an expert in meteorology. *n.*

me te o rol o gy (mē′tē ə rol′ə jē), science dealing with the atmosphere and weather. The study of atmospheric conditions, such as winds, moisture, temperature, etc., and forecasts of the weather are part of meteorology. *n.*

me ter[1] (mē′tər), the basic unit of length in the metric system. A meter is equal to 39.37 inches. *n.* Also, **metre.**

me ter[2] (mē′tər), **1** any kind of poetic rhythm; the arrangement of beats or accents in a line of poetry: *The meter of "Jack and Jill went up the hill" is not the meter of "One, two, buckle my shoe."* **2** musical rhythm; the arrangement of beats in music: *Three-fourths meter is waltz time. n.* Also, **metre.**

me ter[3] (mē′tər), device that measures, or measures and records, the amount of gas, water, electricity, etc., used: *an electric meter. n.*

meter maid, woman who issues tickets for violating parking regulations.

meth ane (meth′ān), a colorless, odorless, flammable gas, the simplest of the hydrocarbons; marsh gas. Methane occurs in marshes, oil wells, volcanoes, and coal mines. It is obtained commercially from natural gas. *n.*

me thinks (mi thingks′), OLD USE. it seems to me. *v., past tense* **me thought.**

meth od (meth′əd), **1** way of doing something: *a method of teaching music. Roasting is one method of cooking meat.* **2** order or system in getting things done or in thinking: *If you used more method, you wouldn't waste so much time. n.* —**meth′od less,** *adj.*

me thod i cal (mə thod′ə kəl), **1** done according to a method; systematic; orderly: *a methodical check of one's work.* **2** acting according to a method: *A scientist is usually a methodical person. adj.* —**me thod′i cal ly,** *adv.* —**me thod′i cal ness,** *n.*

Meth od ist (meth′ə dist), **1** member of a church that had its origin in the teachings and work of John Wesley; Wesleyan. **2** of the Methodists. **1** *n.,* **2** *adj.*

me thought (mi thôt′), OLD USE. past tense of **methinks.** *v.*

Me thu se lah (mə thü′zə lə), **1** (in the Bible) a man who lived 969 years. **2** a very old man. *n.*

meth yl alcohol (meth′əl), wood alcohol.

me tic u lous (mə tik′yə ləs), extremely or excessively careful about small details. *adj.* [*Meticulous* is from Latin *meticulosus,* meaning "fearful, timid," which comes from *metus,* meaning "fear."] —**me tic′u lous ly,** *adv.* —**me tic′u lous ness,** *n.*

me tre (mē′tər), BRITISH. meter[1], meter[2], or meter[3]. *n.*

met ric (met′rik), **1** of the meter or the metric system. **2** metrical. *adj.* See **measure** for table.

met ri cal (met′rə kəl), **1** of or written in meter, not in prose; having a regular arrangement of accents: *metrical verse.* **2** of, having to do with, or used in measurement. *adj.* —**met′ri cal ly,** *adv.*

metric system, a decimal system of measurement, one which counts by tens. It is based on the meter as its unit of length, the gram as its unit of mass or weight, and the liter as its unit of volume.

metric ton, unit of weight equal to 1000 kilograms or about 2204.62 pounds avoirdupois.

met ro nome (met′rə nōm), a device that can be adjusted to make loud ticking sounds at different speeds. Metronomes are used especially to mark time for persons practicing on musical instruments. *n.*

me trop o lis (mə trop′ə lis), **1** a large city; important center: *Chicago is a busy metropolis.* **2** the most important city of a country or region: *New York is the metropolis of the United States. n., pl.* **me trop o lis es.** [*Metropolis* can be traced back to Greek *mētēr,* meaning "mother," and *polis,* meaning "city."]

met ro pol i tan (met′rə pol′ə tən), **1** of a large city; belonging to large cities: *metropolitan newspapers.* **2** person who lives in a large city and knows its ways. **3** archbishop presiding over a church province. **1** *adj.,* **2,3** *n.*

metropolitan area, region including a large city and its suburbs.

met tle (met′l), disposition or temperament; spirit; courage. *n.*

on one's mettle, ready to do one's best.

met tle some (met′l səm), full of mettle; spirited; courageous. *adj.*

Mev or **MeV** (mev), a million electron volts, used as a unit for measuring in nuclear physics. *n.*

mew[1] (myü), **1** sound made by a cat or kitten. **2** make this sound: *Our kitten mews when it gets hungry.* **1** *n.,* **2** *v.*

mew[2] (myü), a sea gull; a gull. *n.*

mewl (myül), cry like a baby; whimper. *v.*

mews (myüz), stables built around a court or alley. *n. sing. or pl.*

Mex., 1 Mexican. 2 Mexico.

Mex i can (mek′sə kən), 1 of Mexico or its people. 2 person born or living in Mexico. 1 *adj.*, 2 *n.*

Mexican War, war between the United States and Mexico from 1846 to 1848.

Mex i co (mek′sə kō), 1 country in North America, just south of W United States. *Capital:* Mexico City. 2 **Gulf of,** gulf of the Atlantic, south of the United States and east of Mexico. *n.*

Mexico City, capital of Mexico, in the central part.

me zuz ah (me zủz′ə), a small container holding a parchment scroll inscribed with certain biblical passages and God's name on the outside. It is attached by Jews to the right-hand doorposts of their homes as a symbol of their religion. *n.*

mezuzah

mez za nine (mez′n ēn′), a low story, usually extending above part of the main floor to form a balcony. The lowest balcony in a theater is often called a mezzanine. *n.*

mez zo-so pran o (met′sō sə pran′ō), 1 a voice between soprano and contralto. 2 singer having such a voice. *n., pl.* **mez zo-so pran os.**

Mg, symbol for magnesium.

mg., milligram or milligrams.

Mgr., Manager.

mi (mē), the third note of the musical scale. *n.*

MI, Michigan (used with postal Zip Code).

mi., mile or miles.

Mi am i (mī am′ē), city in SE Florida, famous as a winter resort. *n.*

mi as ma (mī az′mə), a bad-smelling vapor rising from decaying organic matter in swamps. It was formerly supposed to cause disease. *n., pl.* **mi as mas, mi as ma ta** (mī az′mə tə).

mi ca (mī′kə), mineral containing silicon that divides into thin, partly transparent layers; isinglass. Mica is used as an insulator, especially in small electrical appliances such as toasters. *n.* **—mi′ca like′,** *adj.*

Mi cah (mī′kə), 1 Hebrew prophet of the 700's B.C. 2 book of the Old Testament. *n.*

mice (mīs), plural of **mouse.** *n.*

Mich., Michigan.

Mi chael (mī′kəl), **Saint,** (in the Bible) archangel who led the loyal angels in defeating the revolt of Lucifer. *n.*

Mi chel an ge lo (mī′kə lan′jə lō), 1475-1564, Italian sculptor, painter, architect, and poet. *n.*

Mich i gan (mish′ə gən), 1 one of the north central states of the United States. *Abbreviation:* Mich or MI *Capital:* Lansing. 2 **Lake,** one of the five Great Lakes. It is entirely in the United States. *n.*

micro-, *combining form.* 1 small; very small: *Microorganism = a very small organism.* 2 magnifying or enlarging: *Microphone = (instrument) that magnifies sounds.* 3 one

millionth part of: *Microsecond = one millionth part of a second.* [The form *micro-* comes from Greek *mikros,* meaning "small."]

mi crobe (mī′krōb), germ. *n.*

mi cro bi ol o gist (mī′krō bī ol′ə jist), an expert in microbiology. *n.*

mi cro bi ol o gy (mī′krō bī ol′ə jē), science dealing with microorganisms. *n.*

mi cro com pu ter (mī′krō kəm pyü′tər), computer that contains a microprocessor, is therefore comparatively small, and can carry out only one function at a time. Most home computers are microcomputers. *n.*

mi cro cosm (mī′krō koz′əm), 1 a little world; universe in miniature. 2 person or thing thought of as a miniature representation of the universe. *n.*

mi cro film (mī′krō film′), 1 film for making very small photographs of pages of a book, newspapers, records, etc., to preserve them in a very small space. 2 photograph on microfilm. 1 *n.*, 2 *v.*

mi crom e ter (mī krom′ə tər), 1 instrument for measuring very small distances, angles, objects, etc. Certain kinds are used with a microscope or telescope. 2 a micrometer caliper. *n.*

micrometer caliper, a caliper having a screw with a very fine thread, used for very accurate measurement.

mi cron (mī′kron), unit of length equal to one millionth of a meter. *n., pl.* **mi crons, mi cra** (mī′krə).

Mi cro ne sia (mī′krō nē′zhə), group of small islands in the Pacific, east of the Philippines. See **Melanesia** for map. *n.* **—Mi′cro ne′sian,** *adj., n.*

mi cro or gan ism (mī′krō ôr′gə niz′əm), an animal or vegetable organism too small to be seen except with a microscope. Bacteria are microorganisms. *n.*

mi cro phone (mī′krə fōn), instrument for magnifying or transmitting sounds by changing sound waves into an electric current. Radio and television stations use microphones for broadcasting. *n.*

mi cro proc es sor (mī′krō pros′əs ər *or* mī′krō- prō′səs ər), an integrated circuit that functions as a small computer. *n.*

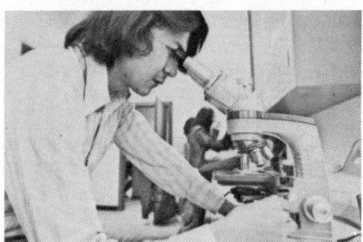

microscope

mi cro scope (mī′krə skōp), instrument with a lens or combination of lenses for making small things look larger. Bacteria, blood cells, and other objects not visible to the naked eye are clearly visible through a microscope. *n.*

mi cro scop ic (mī′krə skop′ik), **1** not able to be seen without using a microscope; tiny: *microscopic germs.* **2** like a microscope; suggesting a microscope: *a microscopic eye for mistakes.* **3** of a microscope; with a microscope: *a microscopic examination of a fly's wing. adj.*

mi cro scop i cal ly (mī′krə skop′ik lē), **1** by the use of a microscope. **2** as if with a microscope; in great detail. *adv.*

mi cros co py (mī kros′kə pē), the use of a microscope; microscopic investigation. *n.*

mi cro sec ond (mī′krō sek′ənd), unit of time equal to one millionth of a second. *n.*

mi cro wave (mī′krō wāv′), an electromagnetic wave, usually having a wavelength ranging from one millimeter to fifty centimeters. *n.*

microwave oven, oven in which food is cooked by the heat produced by microwaves. The microwaves penetrate the food and cook it quickly.

mid[1] (mid), in the middle of; middle. *adj.*

mid[2] or **'mid** (mid), OLD USE. amid. *prep.*

mid-, *combining form.* **1** the middle point or part of: *Midday = the middle part of the day.* **2** of, in, or near the middle of: *Midsummer = in the middle of summer.*

Mid., midshipman.

mid air (mid′er′ *or* mid′ar′), the middle of the air; the air above the ground: *The acrobat made a somersault in midair. n.*

MIDDLE ENGLISH

Middle English developed from Old English and is noted for the addition of many French words, following the Norman Conquest of England in 1066. The majority of these Norman French words were from Latin and have come down to Modern English. Here are a few examples.

	VERBS	NOUNS	ADJECTIVES
Modern English	**complain**	**feast**	**active**
Middle English	*compleynen*	*feste*	*active*
	cry	**envy**	**brief**
	crien	*envie*	*bref*
	judge	**jury**	**certain**
	juggen	*jure*	*certain*
	obey	**siege**	**royal**
	obeien	*sege*	*roial*
	perturb	**soldier**	**violent**
	perturben	*soudier*	*violent*

These two lines, written by Chaucer about 1380, include words from both Old English and French (with the French in italics).

"What folk ben ye, that at myn hoomcominge
Perturben so my *feste* with cryinge?''

Middle English (def. 2)

Mi das (mī′dəs), (in Greek myths) a king of ancient times who had the power to turn everything he touched into gold. *n.* —**Mi′das like′,** *adj.*

mid day (mid′dā′), **1** the middle part of the day; noon. **2** of midday: *a midday meal.* **1** *n.,* **2** *adj.*

mid dle (mid′l), **1** the point or part that is the same distance from each end or side; the center: *the middle of the road.* **2** halfway between; in the center; at the same distance from either end or side: *the middle house in the row.* **3** in between; medium: *a man of middle size.* **4** the middle part of a person's body; waist. **1,4** *n.,* **2,3** *adj.* [*Middle* comes from Old English *middel.*]

middle age, time of life between youth and old age, from about 40 to 65 years of age.

mid dle-aged (mid′l ājd′), between youth and old age; being of middle age. *adj.*

Middle Ages, period in European history between ancient and modern times, from about A.D. 500 to about 1450.

Middle America, the area between the United States and South America. It includes Mexico, Central America, and usually the islands of the West Indies. —**Middle American.**

middle C, the musical note on the first added line below the treble staff and the first above the bass staff. See **clef** for diagram.

middle class, class of people who are socially and economically between the very wealthy class and the class of unskilled laborers and unemployed people. The middle class includes business and professional people, office workers, and many skilled workers.

mid dle-class (mid′l klas′), of or characteristic of the middle class. *adj.*

middle ear, a hollow space between the eardrum and the inner ear. In human beings it contains three small bones which pass on sound waves from the eardrum to the inner ear.

Middle East, region extending from Sudan, Egypt, and Turkey in the west to Iran in the east, and including the countries of SW Asia. Iraq, Israel, Jordan, Syria, and Saudi Arabia are countries in the Middle East. —**Middle Eastern.**

Middle English, 1 period in the development of the English language between Old English and Modern English, lasting from about 1100 to about 1500. **2** language of this period. Chaucer wrote in Middle English.

mid dle man (mid′l man′), **1** trader or merchant who buys goods from the producer and sells them to a retailer or directly to the consumer. **2** person who acts as a go-between for two persons or groups concerned in some matter of business. *n., pl.* **mid dle men.**

middle school, school between elementary school and high school, usually including grades 5 through 9.

mid dle weight (mid′l wāt′), **1** person of average weight. **2** boxer who weighs more than 147 pounds (67 kilograms) and less than 160 pounds (73 kilograms). *n.*

Middle West, part of the United States west of the Appalachian Mountains, east of the Rocky Mountains, and north of the Ohio River and the S boundaries of Missouri and Kansas. Also, **Midwest.**

Middle Western, of the Middle West. Also, **Midwestern.** —**Middle Westerner.**

mid dling (mid′ling), medium in size, quality, grade, etc.; ordinary; average. *adj.* —**mid′dling ly,** *adv.*

mid dy (mid′ē), **1** INFORMAL. midshipman. **2** middy blouse. *n., pl.* **mid dies.**

middy blouse, a loose blouse having a collar with a broad flap at the back, worn by sailors and others.

Mid east (mid′ēst′), Middle East.

Mid east ern (mid′ē′stərn), Middle Eastern. *adj.*

midge (mij), a small two-winged fly; gnat. *n.*

midg et (mij′it), **1** person very much smaller than normal; a tiny person. **2** anything much smaller than the usual size for its type or kind. **3** very small; miniature; diminutive. 1,2 *n.*, 3 *adj.*

mid land (mid′lənd), **1** the middle part of a country; the interior. **2 Midlands,** *pl.* the central part of England. **3** in or of the midland. 1,2 *n.*, 3 *adj.*

mid most (mid′mōst′), in the exact middle; nearest the middle. *adj.*

mid night (mid′nīt′), **1** twelve o'clock at night; the middle of the night. **2** of or at midnight. 1 *n.*, 2 *adj.*

midnight sun, sun seen throughout the day and night in the arctic and antarctic regions during their summers.

mid rib (mid′rib′), the central vein of a leaf. *n.*

mid riff (mid′rif′), the middle portion of the human body. *n.*

mid ship (mid′ship′), in, of, or belonging to the middle part of a ship. *adj.*

mid ship man (mid′ship′mən), **1** student at the United States Naval Academy at Annapolis. **2** a graduate of the British naval schools or an officer of the same rank as such a graduate. **3** (in former times) a boy or young man who assisted the officers of a ship. *n., pl.* **mid ship men.**

midst[1] (midst), **1** the middle part; middle. **2** position or condition of being surrounded, especially by a number of persons: *a traitor in our midst, a stranger in their midst. n.*

in the midst of, 1 in the middle of; among; surrounded by: *in the midst of a forest.* **2** during: *in the midst of a storm.*

midst[2] or **'midst** (midst), amidst; amid. *prep.*

mid stream (mid′strēm′), the middle of a stream. *n.*

mid sum mer (mid′sum′ər), **1** the middle of summer. **2** the time around June 21. **3** in the middle of summer. 1,2 *n.*, 3 *adj.*

mid term (mid′tėrm′), **1** the middle of a school term or of a term of office. **2** taking place or given in the middle of a term: *midterm exams.* **3** examination given in the middle of a school term. 1,3 *n.*, 2 *adj.*

mid way (mid′wā′), **1** in the middle; halfway: *midway between the trees and the lake* (adv.), *a midway position* (adj.). **2** place for games, rides, and other amusements at a fair. 1 *adv., adj.*, 2 *n.*

Midway Islands, group of small islands in the Pacific, belonging to the United States. They are about halfway between the United States and the Philippines. See **Melanesia** for map.

mid week (mid′wēk′), **1** the middle of the week. **2** in the middle of the week. 1 *n.*, 2 *adj.*

Mid west (mid′west′), Middle West. *n.*

Mid west ern (mid′wes′tərn), Middle Western. *adj.*

mid wife (mid′wīf′), person who helps women in childbirth. *n., pl.* **mid wives.**

mid win ter (mid′win′tər), **1** the middle of winter. **2** the time around December 21. **3** in the middle of winter. 1,2 *n.*, 3 *adj.*

mid year (mid′yir′), happening in the middle of the year: *a midyear examination. adj.*

mien (mēn), manner of holding the head and body; way of acting and looking: *have the mien of a judge. n.*

miff (mif), INFORMAL. offend or be offended. *v.*

miffed (mift), offended; irritated: *My friend seemed a little miffed when I didn't accept the invitation. adj.*

might[1] (mīt), past tense of **may.** *Mother said that we might play in the barn. He might have missed the train. v.*

might[2] (mīt), great power; strength: *Work with all your might. n.* **—might′less,** *adj.*

with might and main, with all one's strength.

might i ly (mī′tə lē), **1** in a mighty manner; powerfully; vigorously: *We pushed mightily and freed the car from the*

snowbank. **2** very much; greatly: *We were mightily pleased at winning. adv.*

might i ness (mī′tē nis), power; strength. *n.*

might y (mī′tē), **1** showing strength or power; powerful; strong: *a mighty ruler, mighty force.* **2** very great: *a mighty famine.* **3** INFORMAL. very: *a mighty long time.* 1,2 *adj.*, **might i er, might i est;** 3 *adv.*

mi graine (mī′grān), a severe headache, usually on one side only. *n.* [*Migraine* was borrowed from French *migraine*, and can be traced back to Greek *hēmi-*, meaning "half," and *kranion*, meaning "skull."]

mi grant (mī′grənt), **1** migrating; roving: *a migrant worker.* **2** person, animal, bird, or plant that migrates. 1 *adj.*, 2 *n.*

mi grate (mī′grāt), **1** move from one place to settle in another: *Pioneers from New England migrated to all parts of the United States.* **2** go from one region to another with the change in the seasons: *Most birds migrate to warmer countries in the winter. v.*, **mi grat ed, mi grat ing.** **—mi′gra tor,** *n.*

mi gra tion (mī grā′shən), **1** a migrating. **2** number of people or animals migrating together. *n.*

mi gra to ry (mī′grə tôr′ē), **1** moving from one place to another; migrating: *migratory laborers, migratory birds.* **2** of migration: *the migratory pattern of elephants. adj.*

mi ka do or **Mi ka do** (mə kä′dō), a former title of the emperor of Japan. It is seldom used now except in poetry. *n., pl.* **mi ka dos** or **Mi ka dos.**

mike (mīk), INFORMAL. microphone. *n.*

mil (mil), unit of length equal to .001 of an inch. It is used in measuring the diameter of wires. *n.*

mil., **1** military. **2** militia.

mi la dy or **mi la di** (mi lā′dē), **1** my lady. **2** an English lady. *n., pl.* **mi la dies.**

Mi lan (mi lan′), city in N Italy. *n.*

milch (milch), giving milk; kept for the milk it gives: *a milch cow. adj.*

mild (mīld), **1** gentle or kind: *a mild disposition.* **2** calm; warm; temperate; not harsh or severe: *a mild climate, a mild winter.* **3** soft or sweet to the senses; not sharp, sour, bitter, or strong in taste: *mild cheese, a mild cigar. adj.* **—mild′ly,** *adv.* **—mild′ness,** *n.*

mil dew (mil′dü or mil′dyü), **1** kind of fungus producing a whitish coating or discoloration on plants or on paper, clothes, leather, etc., during damp weather: *Mildew killed the rosebuds in our garden.* **2** the coating or discoloration, or the diseased condition, produced by such a fungus: *Damp clothes left in a pile will show mildew in a few days.* **3** cover or become covered with mildew: *A pile of damp clothes in the closet mildewed.* 1,2 *n.*, 3 *v.*

mile (mīl), **1** unit of distance equal to 5280 feet; statute mile. **2** nautical mile. *n.* [*Mile* is from Old English *mīl*, which came from Latin *mille passus*, meaning "a thousand paces."]

mile age (mī′lij), **1** miles covered or traveled: *Our car's mileage last year was 10,000 miles.* **2** miles traveled per gallon of gasoline: *Do you get good mileage with your car?* **3** length, extent, or distance in miles: *The mileage of a railroad is its total number of miles of roadbed.* **4** an allowance for traveling expenses at so much a mile: *When I use my car for company business, I am given a mileage of 12¢ per mile. n.*

mile post (mīl′pōst′), post set up to show the distance in miles to a certain place or the distance covered. *n.*

mile stone (mīl′stōn′), **1** stone set up to show the distance in miles to a certain place. **2** an important event: *The invention of printing was a milestone in progress. n.*

mi lieu (mē lyu′), surroundings; environment. *n.*

mil i tan cy (mil′ə tən sē), warlike behavior or tendency; militant spirit or policy. *n.*

mil i tant (mil′ə tənt), **1** aggressive; fighting; warlike: *a militant group.* **2** active in serving a cause or in spreading a belief: *a militant conservationist.* **3** a militant person. 1,2 *adj.,* 3 *n.* —**mil′i tant ly,** *adv.* —**mil′i tant ness,** *n.*

mil i tar i ly (mil′ə ter′ə lē), in a military manner. *adv.*

mil i ta rism (mil′ə tə riz′əm), **1** policy of making military organization and power very strong. **2** military spirit and ideals. *n.*

mil i tar ist (mil′ə tər ist), **1** person who believes in a very powerful military organization. **2** an expert in warfare and military matters. *n.*

mil i ta ris tic (mil′ə tə ris′tik), of militarists or militarism. *adj.* —**mil′i ta ris′ti cal ly,** *adv.*

mil i tar i za tion (mil′ə tər ə zā′shən), a militarizing or a being militarized. *n.*

mil i ta rize (mil′ə tə rīz′), **1** make the military organization of (a country) very powerful. **2** fill with military spirit and ideals. *v.,* **mil i ta rized, mil i ta riz ing.**

mil i tar y (mil′ə ter′ē), **1** of armed forces or war: *military training, military history.* **2** done by armed forces: *military maneuvers.* **3** fit for or typical of armed forces: *military discipline.* **4** suitable for war; warlike: *military valor.* **5** **the military,** the armed forces: *an officer of the military.* 1-4 *adj.,* 5 *n.* —**mil′i tar i ly,** *adv.* —**mil′i tar i ness,** *n.*

mil i tate (mil′ə tāt), have or exert force; act; work; operate (against or in favor of): *Bad reviews militated against the success of the play.* *v.,* **mil i tat ed, mil i tat ing.** —**mil′i ta′tion,** *n.*

mi li tia (mə lish′ə), army of citizens who are not regular soldiers but who undergo training for emergency duty or national defense. Every state of the United States has a militia called the National Guard. *n., pl.* **mi li tias.**

mi li tia man (mə lish′ə mən), soldier in the militia. *n., pl.* **mi li tia men.**

milk (milk), **1** the white liquid secreted by female mammals for the nourishment of their young, especially that from cows, which we drink and use in cooking. **2** any kind of liquid resembling this, such as the white juice of a plant, tree, or nut: *the milk of a coconut.* **3** draw milk from (a cow, goat, etc.). **4** drain contents, strength, information, wealth, etc., from; exploit: *The dishonest treasurer milked the club treasury.* 1,2 *n.,* 3,4 *v.* [*Milk* comes from Old English *mioluc, milc.*] —**milk′less,** *adj.*

cry over spilt milk, to waste sorrow or regret on what has happened and cannot be changed.

milk er (mil′kər), **1** person who milks. **2** machine that milks. **3** cow, goat, etc., that gives milk. *n.*

milk i ness (mil′kē nis), condition of being milky or of resembling milk. *n.*

milk maid (milk′mād′), woman who milks cows. *n.*

milk man (milk′man′), person who sells milk or delivers it to customers. *n., pl.* **milk men.**

milk of magnesia, a milk-white medicine, used as a laxative and to counteract acidity.

milk shake, a drink consisting of milk, flavoring, and often ice cream, shaken or beaten until frothy.

milk sop (milk′sop′), a person who lacks courage; coward. *n.*

milk sugar, lactose.

milk tooth, one of the first set of teeth; temporary tooth of a young child or animal.

milk weed (milk′wēd′), plant with white juice that looks like milk. *n.*

milk-white (milk′hwīt′), white as milk. *adj.*

milk y (mil′kē), **1** like milk; white as milk; whitish. **2** of milk; containing milk. *adj.,* **milk i er, milk i est.** —**milk′i ly,** *adv.*

Milky Way, 1 a broad band of faint light that stretches across the sky at night. It is made up of countless stars

too far away to be seen separately without a telescope. **2** the galaxy in which these countless stars are found; Galaxy. The earth, sun, and all the planets around the sun are part of the Milky Way.

mill[1] (mil), **1** machine for grinding grain into flour or meal. **2** a building containing such a machine. **3** grind (grain) into flour or meal. **4** any machine for crushing or grinding: *a coffee mill, a pepper mill.* **5** grind into powder or pulp; grind very fine. **6** a building where manufacturing is done: *Cotton cloth is made in a cotton mill.* **7** cut a series of fine notches or ridges on the edge of (a coin): *A dime is milled.* **8** move in a confused way: *The frightened cattle began to mill around.* 1,2,4,6 *n.,* 3,5,7,8 *v.* —**mill′a ble,** *adj.*

mill[2] (mil), $.001, or ¹/₁₀ of a cent. Mills are used in figuring, but not as coins. *n.*

Mill (mil), **John Stuart,** 1806-1873, English economist and philosopher. *n.*

Mil lay (mə lā′), **Edna St. Vincent,** 1892-1950, American poet. *n.*

mil len ni al (mə len′ē əl), **1** of a thousand years. **2** like that of a millennium; fit for the millennium. *adj.*

mil len ni um (mə len′ē əm), **1** period of a thousand years: *The world is many millenniums old.* **2** (in the Bible) the period of a thousand years during which Christ is expected to reign on earth. **3** period of righteousness and happiness. *n., pl.* **mil len ni ums, mil len ni a** (mə len′ē ə).

mil le pede (mil′ə pēd′), millipede. *n.*

mill er (mil′ər), **1** person who owns or runs a mill, especially a flour mill. **2** moth whose wings look as if they were powdered with flour. *n.*

Mill er (mil′ər), **Arthur,** born 1915, American playwright. *n.*

mil let (mil′it), the very small grain of a kind of cereal grass, grown for food or hay. *n.*

milli-, *combining form.* one thousandth part of: *Milligram = one thousandth part of a gram.* [The form *milli-* comes from Latin *mille,* meaning "one thousand."]

mil li bar (mil′ə bär), unit of atmospheric pressure equal to 1000 dynes per square centimeter. Standard atmospheric pressure at sea level is about 1013 millibars or 14.69 pounds per square inch. *n.*

mil li gram or **mil li gramme** (mil′ə gram), unit of weight or mass equal to ¹/₁₀₀₀ of a gram. *n.*

Mil li kan (mil′ə kən), **Robert A.,** 1868-1953, American physicist. *n.*

mil li li ter or **mil li li tre** (mil′ə lē′tər), unit of volume equal to ¹/₁₀₀₀ of a liter. *n.*

mil li me ter or **mil li me tre** (mil′ə mē′tər), unit of length equal to ¹/₁₀₀₀ of a meter. *n.*

mil li ner (mil′ə nər), person who makes, trims, or sells women's hats. *n.*

mil li ner y (mil′ə ner′ē), **1** women's hats. **2** business of making, trimming, or selling women's hats. *n.*

mil lion (mil′yən), one thousand thousand; 1,000,000. *n., adj.*

mil lion aire (mil′yə ner′ or mil′yə nar′), **1** person whose wealth amounts to a million or more dollars, pounds, francs, etc. **2** a very wealthy person. *n.*

mil lionth (mil′yənth), **1** last in a series of a million. **2** one of a million equal parts. *adj., n.*

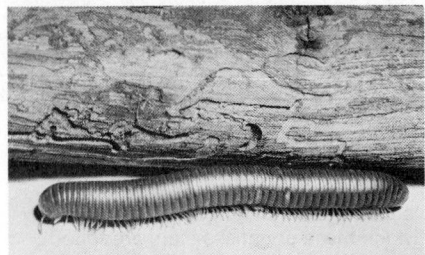
millipede
about life-size

mil li pede (mil′ə pēd′), a small, wormlike animal that has two pairs of legs apiece for most of its many segments. *n.* Also, **millepede.**

mill pond (mil′pond′), pond supplying water to drive a mill wheel. *n.*

mill race (mil′rās′), **1** current of water that drives a mill wheel. **2** channel in which it flows to the mill. *n.*

mill stone (mil′stōn′), **1** either of a pair of round, flat stones for grinding corn, wheat, etc. **2** a heavy burden. **3** anything that grinds or crushes. *n.*

mill wheel, wheel that is turned by water and supplies power for a mill.

Milne (miln), **A. A.,** 1882-1956, English writer of children's verses and stories and of plays. *n.*

mi lord (mi lôrd′), **1** my lord. **2** an English gentleman. *n.*

milque toast (milk′tōst′), an extremely timid person. *n.*

milt (milt), **1** the sperm cells of male fishes with the milky fluid containing them. **2** the reproductive gland in male fishes. *n.*

Mil ton (milt′n), **John,** 1608-1674, English poet. *n.*

Mil wau kee (mil wôk′ē), city in SE Wisconsin, on Lake Michigan. *n.*

mime (def. 4)—The **mime** performed for the passers-by.

mime (mīm), **1** a mimic, jester, or clown. **2** imitate; mimic. **3** pantomime. **4** actor, especially in a pantomime. **5** act in a pantomime; act without using words. 1,3,4 *n.,* 2,5 *v.,* **mimed, mim ing. —mim′er,** *n.*

mim e o graph (mim′ē ə graf), **1** machine for making copies of written or typewritten materials by means of stencils. **2** make (copies) with a mimeograph. 1 *n.,* 2 *v.*

mi met ic (mi met′ik), **1** imitative. **2** make-believe. **3** of or showing mimicry. *adj.* **—mi met′i cal ly,** *adv.*

mim ic (mim′ik), **1** make fun of by imitating: *The children mimicked the babysitter's English accent.* **2** person or thing that imitates. **3** copy closely; imitate: *A parrot can mimic a person's voice.* **4** resemble closely in form, color, etc. **5** not real, but imitated or pretended for some purpose: *We staged a mimic rescue of a drowning victim in our first-aid class.* **6** imitative: *mimic gestures.* 1,3,4 *v.,* **mimicked, mim ick ing;** 2 *n.,* 5,6 *adj.* **—mim′ick er,** *n.*

mim ic ry (mim′ik rē), **1** a mimicking. **2** the close outward resemblance of an animal to its surroundings or to some different animal, especially for protection or concealment. *n., pl.* **mim ic ries.**

mi mo sa (mi mō′sə), tree, shrub, or herb growing in warm regions, and usually having fernlike leaves and heads of small pink, yellow, or white flowers. *n., pl.* **mi mo sas.**

min., 1 minimum. **2** minute or minutes.

min a ret (min′ə ret′), a slender, high tower attached to a Moslem mosque with one or more projecting balconies, from which a crier calls the people to prayer. *n.*

mince (mins), **1** chop up into very small pieces. **2** mincemeat. **3** put on fine airs in speaking or walking. **4** walk with little short steps. 1,3,4 *v.,* **minced, minc ing;** 2 *n.* [*Mince* came into English about 600 years ago from French *mincier,* and can be traced back to Latin *minutum,* meaning "small."] **—minc′er,** *n.*

not to mince matters or **not to mince words,** to speak plainly and frankly.

mince meat (mins′mēt′), mixture of chopped apples, suet, raisins, currants, spices, etc., and sometimes meat, used as a filling for pies. *n.*

mince pie, pie filled with mincemeat.

minc ing (min′sing), **1** putting on a dainty and refined manner: *a mincing voice.* **2** walking with little short steps. *adj.* **—minc′ing ly,** *adv.*

mind (mīnd), **1** the part of a person that knows, remembers, thinks, feels, wishes, wills, etc. **2** mental ability; intelligence; intellect: *have a good mind.* **3** person who has intelligence: *the greatest minds of the period.* **4** reason; sanity: *be out of one's mind.* **5** what one thinks or feels; opinion; view: *change one's mind.* **6** remembrance or recollection; memory: *Keep the rules in mind.* **7** give heed to: *Mind my words!* **8** take notice; observe. **9** be careful concerning: *Mind the step.* **10** take care: *Mind that you come on time.* **11** look after; take care of; tend: *Mind the baby.* **12** obey: *Mind your father and mother.* **13** feel bad about; object to: *Do you mind closing the door for me? Some people don't mind cold weather.* **14** DIALECT. remember. 1-6 *n.,* 7-14 *v.* [*Mind* comes from Old English (*ge*)*mynd,* meaning "memory, thinking."] **—mind′er,** *n.*

bear in mind or **keep in mind,** remember.

be of one mind, have the same opinion; agree.

cross one's mind, occur to one; come into one's thoughts suddenly.

have a mind to, intend to; think of doing.

have in mind, think of; consider.

make up one's mind, decide: *I made up my mind to study harder and get better grades.*

never mind, don't let it trouble you; it does not matter.

on one's mind, in one's mind; in one's thoughts.

put in mind, remind: *Your joke puts me in mind of a joke I heard yesterday.*

set one's mind on, want very much.

to one's mind, in one's opinion; to one's way of thinking.

Min da na o (min′də nä′ō), the second largest island in the Philippines. *n.*

mimic (def. 4)—This insect mimics a twig.

mind-blow ing (mīnd′blō′ing), SLANG. **1** producing or tending to produce hallucinations: *the mind-blowing effects of LSD.* **2** extremely exciting, pleasing, or shocking: *the mind-blowing conclusion of the mystery. adj.*

mind ed (mīn′did), inclined; disposed: *Come a little early, if you are so minded. adj.*

mind ful (mīnd′fəl), **1** having in mind; heedful: *Mindful of your advice, I went slowly.* **2** taking thought; careful: *We had to be mindful of every step we took on the slippery sidewalk. adj.* —**mind′ful ly,** *adv.* —**mind′ful ness,** *n.*

mind less (mīnd′lis), **1** without mind or intelligence; stupid. **2** not taking thought; careless. *adj.* —**mind′less ly,** *adv.* —**mind′less ness,** *n.*

mind's eye, mental view or vision; imagination.

mine[1] (mīn), **1** the one or ones belonging to me: *This book is mine.* **2** OLD USE. my (used only before a vowel or h): *mine eyes.* **1** *pron.,* **2** *adj.*

mine[2] (mīn), **1** a large hole or space dug in the earth to get out ores, precious stones, coal, salt, etc.: *a coal mine, a gold mine.* **2** dig a mine; make a hole or space underground. **3** dig in for coal, gold, etc.: *to mine the earth.* **4** get from a mine: *to mine coal, to mine gold.* **5** to work in a mine. **6** a rich or plentiful source: *The book proved to be a mine of information about radio.* **7** an underground passage in which an explosive is placed to blow up an enemy's forts, etc. **8** make underground passages below. **9** bomb put under water or shallowly buried to blow up enemy troops or equipment. **10** lay mines under: *to mine the mouth of a harbor.* **1,6,7,9** *n.,* **2-5,8,10** *v.,* **mined, min ing.** —**min′a ble, mine′a ble,** *adj.*

min er (mī′nər), person who works in a mine: *a coal miner. n.*

min er al (min′ər əl), **1** substance obtained by mining or digging in the earth. Coal, gold, and mica are minerals. **2** any substance that is neither plant nor animal. Sand is a mineral. **3** of or like a mineral. **4** containing minerals. **1,2** *n.,* **3,4** *adj.*

min er a log i cal (min′ər ə loj′ə kəl), of mineralogy. *adj.*

min er al o gist (min′ə rol′ə jist), an expert in mineralogy. *n.*

min er al o gy (min′ə rol′ə jē), science of minerals. *n.*

mineral water, water containing mineral salts or gases. People drink various mineral waters for their health.

Mi ner va (mə ner′və), (in Roman myths) the goddess of wisdom, the arts, and war. The Greeks called her Athena. *n.*

min e stro ne (min′ə strō′nē), a thick soup containing vegetables, vermicelli, etc. *n.*

min gle (ming′gəl), **1** combine in a mixture; mix; blend: *Two rivers that join mingle their waters.* **2** associate: *I tried to mingle with everyone at a party. v.,* **min gled, min gling.**

mini-, *combining form.* small or short for its kind: *Minibus = a small bus.* [The form *mini-* comes from the word *miniature.*]

min i a ture (min′ē ə chùr *or* min′ə chər), **1** anything represented on a small scale: *In the museum there is a miniature of the ship "Mayflower."* **2** done or made on a very small scale; tiny: *miniature cars, miniature furniture for a dollhouse.* **3** a very small painting, usually a portrait. **1,3** *n.,* **2** *adj.* [*Miniature* comes from Italian *miniatura,* meaning "picture in an illuminated manuscript," and can be traced back to Latin *miniare,* meaning "to paint red."]

min i a tur ize (min′ē ə chə rīz′ *or* min′ə chə rīz′), reduce to a very small size: *to miniaturize electronic devices. v.,* **min i a tur ized, min i a tur iz ing.** —**min′i a tur i za′tion,** *n.*

min i bike (min′ē bīk′), a small motorcycle. *n.*

min i cam (min′ē kam), a miniature camera, especially a television camera. *n.*

min i com put er (min′ē kəm pyü′tər), a small, comparatively inexpensive computer. *n.*

min i mal (min′ə məl), least possible; very small; having to do with a minimum: *minimal damage, a minimal cost. adj.* —**min′i mal ly,** *adv.*

min i mize (min′ə mīz), **1** reduce to the least possible amount or degree: *The polar explorers took every precaution to minimize the dangers of their trip.* **2** to state at the lowest possible estimate; make the least of: *She minimized the work involved in the job in order to get me to do it. v.,* **min i mized, min i miz ing.** —**min′i mi za′tion,** *n.*

min i mum (min′ə məm), **1** the least possible amount; lowest amount: *Each of the children had to drink some milk at breakfast; half a glass was the minimum.* **2** least possible; lowest: *Eighteen is the minimum age for voting in the United States. The workers wanted a minimum wage of $4 an hour.* **1** *n.,* *pl.* **min i mums, min i ma** (min′ə mə); **2** *adj.*

min ing (mī′ning), **1** the working of mines for ores, coal, etc. **2** business of digging coal or ores from mines. **3** the laying of explosive mines. *n.*

min ion (min′yən), **1** servant or follower willing to do whatever is ordered. **2** a darling; a favorite. *n.*

min is ter (min′ə stər), **1** member of the clergy; spiritual guide; pastor. **2** act as a servant or nurse; be of service or aid; be helpful: *minister to a sick person's wants.* **3** person who is given charge of a department of the government: *the Minister of Labor.* **4** person sent to a foreign country to represent his or her own government: *the United States Minister to Switzerland.* **1,3,4** *n.,* **2** *v.* [*Minister* is from Latin *minister,* meaning "servant," which comes from *minus,* meaning "less."]

min is te ri al (min′ə stir′ē əl), **1** of a minister. **2** suited to a minister: *a ministerial manner. adj.*

min is tra tion (min′ə strā′shən), **1** service as a minister of a church. **2** help; aid: *give ministration to the poor. n.*

min is try (min′ə strē), **1** office, duties, or time of service of a minister. **2** ministers of a church; clergy. **3** ministers of a government. **4** a government department under a minister. **5** a ministering or serving. *n.,* *pl.* **min is tries.**

mink (mingk), **1** a small mammal of North America that resembles a weasel and lives in water part of the time. **2** its valuable brown fur. *n.* —**mink′like′,** *adj.*

Minn., Minnesota.

Min ne ap o lis (min′ē ap′ə lis), city in SE Minnesota, on the Mississippi. *n.*

Min ne so ta (min′ə sō′tə), one of the midwestern states of the United States. *Abbreviation:* Minn. *or* MN *Capital:* St. Paul. *n.* —**Min′ne so′tan,** *adj., n.*

min now (min′ō), **1** a very small fresh-water fish related to the carp. **2** any very tiny fish. *n.,* *pl.* **min nows** *or* **min now.**

mi nor (mī′nər), **1** less important; smaller; lesser: *a minor fault. Your paper is good; it contains only a few minor errors.* **2** of a lower rank or order: *a minor poet, a minor political party.* **3** person under the legal age of responsibility (18 or 21 years). **4** in music: **a** less by a half step than the corresponding major interval: *a minor chord.* **b** noting a scale or key whose third tone is minor in relation to the main tone: *the C minor scale or key.* **c** a minor scale, key, chord, interval, etc. **5** subject or course of study to which a student gives less time than a major

a hat	i it	oi oil	ch child	ə = { a in about
ā age	ī ice	ou out	ng long	e in taken
ä far	o hot	u cup	sh she	i in pencil
e let	ō open	u̇ put	th thin	o in lemon
ē equal	ô order	ü rule	ᴛʜ then	u in circus
ėr term			zh measure	

subject: *His minor is French.* **6** have or take as a minor subject of study: *She will minor in French.* 1,2,4a,4b *adj.,* 3,4c,5 *n.,* 6 *v.*

mi nor i ty (mə nôr′ə tē *or* mī nôr′ə tē), **1** the smaller number or part; less than half: *A minority of the voters wanted a tax increase, but the majority defeated it.* **2** a group within a country, state, etc., that differs in race, religion, national origin, etc., from the larger part of the population. **3** condition or time of being under the legal age of responsibility. *n., pl.* **mi nor i ties.**

minor league, any professional baseball league or association other than the major leagues.

Mi nos (mī′nəs), in Greek legends: **1** a king and lawgiver of Crete, the son of Zeus, who became a judge in Hades. **2** his grandson, who built the Labyrinth at Crete and kept the Minotaur in it. *n.*

Minotaur
Theseus battling
the Minotaur

"Theseus Slaying the Minotaur," Antoine Louis Barye.
Courtesy of The Metropolitan Museum of Art

Min o taur (min′ə tôr), (in Greek legends) a monster with a bull's head and a man's body, kept in the Labyrinth at Crete and fed with human flesh. Theseus killed the Minotaur. *n.*

Minsk (minsk), city in W Soviet Union, capital of Byelorussia. *n.*

min strel (min′strəl), **1** singer or musician in the Middle Ages who entertained in the household of a noble or went about singing or reciting poems. **2** member of a minstrel show. *n.*

minstrel show, show or entertainment in which the performers blackened their faces with burnt cork and played music, sang songs, and told jokes. Minstrel shows were very popular until the end of the 1800's.

mint[1] (mint), **1** a sweet-smelling plant used for flavoring. Peppermint and spearmint are kinds of mint. **2** piece of candy flavored with mint. *n.* [*Mint*[1] is from Old English *minte,* which came from Latin *menta.*]

mint[2] (mint), **1** place where money is coined by government authority. **2** to coin (money). **3** a large amount: *A million dollars is a mint of money.* **4** without a blemish; as good as new: *a car in mint condition.* 1,3 *n.,* 2 *v.,* 4 *adj.* [*Mint*[2] is from Old English *mynet,* meaning "coin," which came from Latin *moneta,* meaning "mint, money."]
—**mint′er,** *n.*

min u end (min′yü end), number or quantity from which another is to be subtracted: *In 100 − 23 = 77, the minuend is 100. n.*

min u et (min′yü et′), **1** a slow, stately dance, fashionable in the 1700's. **2** music for it. *n.*

mi nus (mī′nəs), **1** decreased by; less: *5 minus 2 leaves 3.* **2** without; lacking: *a book minus its cover.* **3** less than: *A mark of B minus is not so high as a mark of B.* **4** minus sign. **5** less than zero. 1,2 *prep.,* 3,5 *adj.,* 4 *n., pl.* **minus es.**

minus sign, the sign (−), indicating that the number or quantity following it is to be subtracted, or is a negative number or quantity.

min ute[1] (min′it), **1** one of the 60 equal periods of time that make up an hour; sixty seconds. **2** a short time; instant: *I'll be there in a minute.* **3** an exact point of time: *The minute you see her coming, please tell me.* **4** one sixtieth of a degree. 10°10′ means ten degrees and ten minutes. **5 minutes,** *pl.* a written summary of what happened at a meeting, kept by the secretary. *n.*
up to the minute, up to date.

mi nute[2] (mī nüt′ *or* mī nyüt′), **1** very small; tiny: *a minute speck of dust.* **2** going into or concerned with small details: *minute instructions. adj.* —**mi nute′ly,** *adv.* —**minute′ness,** *n.*

min ute hand (min′it), hand on a clock or watch that indicates minutes. It moves around the whole dial once in an hour.

min ute man (min′it man′), member of the American militia just before and during the Revolutionary War. The minutemen kept themselves ready for military service at a minute's notice. *n., pl.* **min ute men.**

mi nu ti ae (mi nü′shē ē *or* mi nyü′shē ē), very small matters; trifling details. *n.pl.*

minx (mingks), a pert girl. *n., pl.* **minx es.**

mir a cle (mir′ə kəl), **1** a wonderful happening that is contrary to, or independent of, the known laws of nature: *It would be a miracle if we should see the sun stand still in the heavens for an hour.* **2** something marvelous; a wonder: *It was a miracle you weren't hurt in that accident.* **3** a remarkable example: *The teacher was a miracle of patience to put up with the children's racket. n.*

mi rac u lous (mə rak′yə ləs), **1** contrary to, or independent of, the known laws of nature: *The miraculous fountain of youth was supposed to make the old young again.* **2** marvelous; wonderful: *miraculous good fortune. adj.* —**mi rac′u lous ly,** *adv.* —**mi rac′u lous ness,** *n.*

mi rage (mə räzh′), an optical illusion, usually in the desert, at sea, or on a paved road, in which some distant scene appears to be much closer than it actually is. It is caused by the refraction of light rays from the distant scene by air layers of different temperatures. Often what is reflected is seen upside down or as something other than it is. Travelers on the desert may see a mirage of palm trees and water. *n.*

mire (mīr), **1** soft, deep mud; slush. **2** wet, swampy ground; bog. **3** get stuck in mire: *He mired his car and had to go for help.* 1,2 *n.,* 3 *v.,* **mired, mir ing.**

mirk (mėrk), murk. *n.*

mirk y (mėr′kē), murky. *adj.,* **mirk i er, mirk i est.**

mir ror (mir′ər), **1** a piece of glass that reflects images; looking glass. It is coated on one side with silver or aluminum. **2** reflect as a mirror does: *The still water mirrored the trees along the bank.* **3** whatever reflects or gives a true description: *This book is a mirror of the life of the pioneers.* 1,3 *n.,* 2 *v.* —**mir′ror like′,** *adj.*

mirror image, an image in reverse; reflection.

mirth (mėrth), merry fun; being joyous or gay; laughter. *n.*

mirth ful (mėrth′fəl), merry; joyous; gay; laughing. *adj.* —**mirth′ful ly,** *adv.* —**mirth′ful ness,** *n.*

mirth less (mėrth′lis), without mirth; joyless; gloomy. *adj.* —**mirth′less ly,** *adv.* —**mirth′less ness,** *n.*

mir y (mī′rē), **1** muddy; swampy. **2** dirty; filthy. *adj.,* **mir i er, mir i est.** —**mir′i ness,** *n.*

mis-, prefix. **1** bad: *Misgovernment = bad government.* **2** badly: *Misbehave = behave badly.* **3** wrong: *Mispronunciation = wrong pronunciation.* **4** wrongly: *Misapply = apply wrongly.*

mis ad ven ture (mis′əd ven′chər), an unfortunate accident; bad luck; mishap. *n.*

mis an thrope (mis/ən thrōp), person who dislikes or distrusts people in general. *n.*

mis an throp ic (mis/ən throp/ik), of or like a misanthrope. *adj.* —**mis/an throp/i cal ly,** *adv.*

mis an thro py (mis an/thrə pē), hatred, dislike, or distrust of people in general. *n.*

mis ap pli ca tion (mis/ap/lə kā/shən), a misapplying or a being misapplied; wrong application. *n.*

mis ap ply (mis/ə plī/), apply wrongly: *to misapply one's knowledge.* *v.,* **mis ap plied, mis ap ply ing.**

mis ap pre hend (mis/ap/ri hend/), misunderstand. *v.*

mis ap pre hen sion (mis/ap/ri hen/shən), wrong idea; misunderstanding. *n.*

mis ap pro pri ate (mis/ə prō/prē āt), **1** use dishonestly as one's own: *The treasurer misappropriated the club's funds.* **2** put to a wrong use. *v.,* **mis ap pro pri at ed, mis ap pro pri at ing.**

mis ap pro pri a tion (mis/ə prō/prē ā/shən), **1** dishonest use as one's own. **2** any act of putting to a wrong use. *n.*

mis be come (mis/bi kum/), be unbecoming to. *v.,* **mis be came** (mis/bi kām/), **mis be come, mis be com ing.**

mis be have (mis/bi hāv/), behave badly. *v.,* **mis be haved, mis be hav ing.**

mis be hav ior (mis/bi hā/vyər), bad behavior. *n.*

misc., miscellaneous.

mis cal cu late (mis kal/kyə lāt), calculate wrongly or incorrectly. *v.,* **mis cal cu lat ed, mis cal cu lat ing.**

mis cal cu la tion (mis/kal/kyə lā/shən), a wrong or incorrect calculation. *n.*

mis call (mis kôl/), call by a wrong name. *v.*

mis car riage (mis kar/ij), **1** failure: *Because the judge was unfair, that trial resulted in a miscarriage of justice.* **2** birth of a baby before it is able to live. *n.*

mis car ry (mis kar/ē), **1** go wrong; be unsuccessful: *Our plans miscarried, and we could not come.* **2** give birth to a baby before it is able to live. *v.,* **mis car ried, mis car ry ing.**

mis cast (mis kast/), put in a role for which one is not suited. *v.,* **mis cast, mis cast ing.**

mis cel la ne ous (mis/ə lā/nē əs), not all of one kind or nature: *He had a miscellaneous collection of stones, butterflies, stamps, and many other things.* *adj.* —**mis/cel la/ne ous ly,** *adv.* —**mis/cel la/ne ous ness,** *n.*

mis cel la ny (mis/ə lā/nē), **1** a miscellaneous collection; mixture. **2** Also, **miscellanies,** *pl.,* a collection of miscellaneous articles in one book. *n., pl.* **mis cel la nies.**

mis chance (mis chans/), **1** bad luck; misfortune: *By some mischance she didn't receive my telegram.* **2** piece of bad luck; an unlucky accident. *n.*

mis chief (mis/chif), **1** conduct that causes harm or trouble, often unintentionally: *The children were playing with matches, and their mischief resulted in a serious fire.* **2** harm or injury, usually done by some person: *Why are you angry? He did you no mischief.* **3** person who does harm or causes annoyance, often just in fun: *You little mischief! You have hidden my glasses.* **4** merry teasing: *Her eyes were full of mischief.* *n.*

mis chie vous (mis/chə vəs), **1** causing mischief; naughty: *mischievous behavior.* **2** harmful: *mischievous gossip.* **3** full of pranks and teasing fun: *mischievous children. adj.* —**mis/chie vous ly,** *adv.* —**mis/chie vous ness,** *n.*

mis con ceive (mis/kən sēv/), have wrong ideas about; misunderstand. *v.,* **mis con ceived, mis con ceiv ing.** —**mis/con ceiv/er,** *n.*

mis con cep tion (mis/kən sep/shən), a mistaken idea or notion; wrong conception. *n.*

mis con duct (mis kon/dukt *for 1,3;* mis/kən dukt/ *for 2,4*), **1** bad behavior: *The children were punished for their misconduct.* **2** behave badly. **3** bad management: *The mis-*

a hat | **i** it | **oi** oil | **ch** child | a in about
ā age | **ī** ice | **ou** out | **ng** long | e in taken
ä far | **o** hot | **u** cup | **sh** she | ə = i in pencil
e let | **ō** open | **ú** put | **th** thin | o in lemon
ē equal | **ô** order | **ü** rule | **ŦH** then | u in circus
ėr term | | | **zh** measure |

conduct of that business nearly ruined it. **4** manage badly. 1,3 *n.,* 2,4 *v.*

mis con struc tion (mis/kən struk/shən), wrong or mistaken meaning; misunderstanding: *What you said was open to misconstruction. n.*

mis con strue (mis/kən strü/), take in a wrong or mistaken sense; misunderstand: *Shyness is sometimes misconstrued as unfriendliness. v.,* **mis con strued, mis con stru ing.**

mis count (mis kount/ *for 1;* mis/kount/ *for 2*), **1** count wrongly or incorrectly. **2** a wrong or incorrect count. 1 *v.,* 2 *n.*

mis cre ant (mis/krē ənt), a wicked person; villain. *n.*

mis cue (mis kyü/), error; mistake. *n.*

mis deal (mis dēl/ *for 1;* mis/dēl/ *for 2*), **1** deal wrongly at cards. **2** a wrong deal at cards. 1 *v.,* **mis dealt** (mis-delt/), **mis deal ing;** 2 *n.*

mis deed (mis dēd/), a bad act; wicked deed. *n.*

mis de mean or (mis/di mē/nər), **1** a breaking of the law, not so serious as a felony. Disturbing the peace and breaking traffic laws are misdemeanors. **2** a wrong deed. *n.*

mis di rect (mis/də rekt/ *or* mis/dī rekt/), direct wrongly; give wrong directions to. *v.* —**mis/di rec/tion,** *n.*

mis do er (mis dü/ər), wrongdoer. *n.*

mis do ing (mis dü/ing), wrongdoing. *n.*

mi ser (mī/zər), person who loves money for its own sake; one who lives poorly in order to save money and keep it. *n.* [*Miser* comes from Latin *miser,* meaning "wretched, miserable."]

mis er a ble (miz/ər ə bəl), **1** very unhappy or unfortunate; wretched: *The sick child was miserable.* **2** causing trouble or unhappiness: *a miserable cold.* **3** poor; pitiful: *They live in miserable surroundings. adj.* —**mis/er a ble-ness,** *n.*

mis er a bly (miz/ər ə blē), in a miserable manner. *adv.*

mi ser li ness (mī/zər lē nis), condition or quality of being miserly. *n.*

mi ser ly (mī/zər lē), of, like, or suited to a miser; stingy. *adj.*

mis er y (miz/ər ē), **1** a miserable, unhappy state of mind: *Think of the misery of having no home or friends.* **2** poor, mean, miserable circumstances: *a life of misery. n., pl.* **mis er ies.**

mis file (mis fīl/), file incorrectly. *v.,* **mis filed, mis fil-ing.**

mis fire (mis fīr/), **1** fail to fire or explode properly: *The pistol misfired.* **2** failure to discharge or start. **3** go wrong; fail: *I tried to sneak into the movie without paying, but my plan misfired.* 1,3 *v.,* **mis fired, mis fir ing;** 2 *n.*

mis fit (mis/fit/), **1** person who does not fit in a job, a group, etc.; maladjusted person. **2** a bad fit: *Do not buy shoes that are misfits. n.*

mis for tune (mis fôr/chən), **1** bad luck: *She had the misfortune to break her arm.* **2** piece of bad luck; unlucky accident. *n.*

mis giv ing (mis giv/ing), a feeling of doubt, suspicion, or anxiety: *We started off through the storm with some misgivings. n.*

mis gov ern (mis guv/ərn), govern or manage badly. *v.*

mis gov ern ment (mis guv/ərn mənt), bad government or management. *n.*

misnomer (def. 1)—"Smiley" is a **misnomer** for such a grumpy man.

mis guide (mis gīd′), lead into mistakes or wrongdoing; mislead. *v.*, **mis guid ed, mis guid ing.**

mis guid ed (mis gī′did), led into mistakes or wrongdoing; misled: *a misguided person, misguided plans. adj.* —**mis guid′ed ly**, *adv.*

mis han dle (mis han′dl), handle badly; maltreat. *v.*, **mis han dled, mis han dling.**

mis hap (mis′hap), an unlucky accident: *By some mishap the letter went astray. n.*

mish mash (mish′mash′), a confused mixture; hodge-podge; jumble. *n.*

mis in form (mis′in fôrm′), give wrong or misleading information to. *v.*

mis in for ma tion (mis′in fər mā′shən), wrong or misleading information. *n.*

mis in ter pret (mis′in tėr′prit), interpret wrongly; explain wrongly; misunderstand. *v.*

mis in ter pre ta tion (mis′in tėr′prə tā′shən), wrong interpretation; wrong explanation; misunderstanding. *n.*

mis judge (mis juj′), judge wrongly or unjustly: *misjudge distance, misjudge a person's character. v.*, **mis judged, mis judg ing.**

mis judg ment or **mis judge ment** (mis juj′mənt), wrong or unjust judgment. *n.*

mis laid (mis lād′), past tense and past participle of **mislay.** *The boy mislaid his books. I have mislaid my pen. v.*

mis lay (mis lā′), **1** put in a place and then forget where it is; lose temporarily: *I am always mislaying my glasses.* **2** put in an incorrect place. *v.*, **mis laid, mis lay ing.**

mis lead (mis lēd′), **1** cause to go in the wrong direction; lead astray: *Our guide misled us and we got lost.* **2** cause to do wrong; lead into wrongdoing: *Bad companions can mislead a person.* **3** lead to think what is not so; deceive: *Some advertisements are so exaggerated that they mislead people. v.*, **mis led, mis lead ing.**

mis lead ing (mis lē′ding), **1** leading to wrong conclusions; deceiving: *misleading statements in advertising.* **2** causing error or wrongdoing: *Bad advice can be misleading. adj.*

mis led (mis led′), past tense and past participle of **mislead.** *We were misled by the false claims. v.*

mis man age (mis man′ij), manage badly: *If you mismanage the business, you will lose money. v.*, **mis man aged, mis man ag ing.**

mis man age ment (mis man′ij mənt), bad management. *n.*

mis match (mis mach′), **1** match badly or unsuitably. **2** a bad or unsuitable match. 1 *v.*, 2 *n.*, *pl.* **mis match es.**

mis mate (mis māt′), mate unsuitably. *v.*, **mis mat ed, mis mat ing.**

mis name (mis nām′), call by a wrong name. *v.*, **mis named, mis nam ing.**

mis no mer (mis nō′mər), **1** a name that describes wrongly. **2** error in naming. *n.*

mis place (mis plās′), **1** put in the wrong place. **2** put in a place and then forget where it is; mislay: *I have misplaced my pencil.* **3** give (one's love or trust) to the wrong person: *misplace one's confidence in an untrustworthy friend. v.*, **mis placed, mis plac ing.**

mis place ment (mis plās′mənt), a misplacing or a being misplaced. *n.*

mis play (mis plā′), **1** a wrong play. **2** play wrongly: *I misplayed my hand in the card game.* 1 *n.*, 2 *v.*

mis print (mis′print′ for 1; mis print′ for 2), **1** a mistake in printing. **2** to print wrongly. 1 *n.*, 2 *v.*

mis prize (mis prīz′), **1** value too little; slight. **2** despise; scorn. *v.*, **mis prized, mis priz ing.**

mis pro nounce (mis′prə nouns′), pronounce incorrectly. *v.*, **mis pro nounced, mis pro nounc ing.**

mis pro nun ci a tion (mis′prə nun′sē ā′shən), an incorrect pronunciation. *n.*

mis quo ta tion (mis′kwō tā′shən), an incorrect quotation. *n.*

mis quote (mis kwōt′), quote incorrectly. *v.*, **mis quot ed, mis quot ing.**

mis read (mis rēd′), **1** read wrongly. **2** interpret wrongly; misunderstand: *misread a person's intentions. v.*, **mis read** (mis red′), **mis read ing.**

mis rep re sent (mis′rep′ri zent′), represent falsely; give a wrong idea of: *He misrepresented the barren property by claiming it was good farmland. v.*

mis rep re sen ta tion (mis′rep ri zen tā′shən), **1** a false representation: *Tell the truth; do not resort to misrepresentation.* **2** an incorrect story or explanation: *The report is a misrepresentation of the facts in the case. n.*

mis rule (mis rül′), **1** bad or unwise rule; misgovernment. **2** rule badly. 1 *n.*, 2 *v.*, **mis ruled, mis rul ing.**

miss (mis), **1** fail to hit: *I swung at the ball and missed it.* **2** failure to hit or reach: *make more misses than hits.* **3** fail to find, get, or meet: *I set out to meet my father, but in the dark I missed him.* **4** let slip by; not seize: *I missed the chance of a ride to town.* **5** fail to catch: *miss the train.* **6** leave out: *miss a word in reading.* **7** fail to do or answer correctly: *I missed two problems in today's math lesson.* **8** fail to hear or understand: *miss the point of a remark.* **9** fail to keep, do, or be present at: *I missed my music lesson today.* **10** fail to see or notice: *I missed my favorite TV program last night.* **11** escape or avoid: *I barely missed being hit by a car.* **12** notice the absence of; feel keenly the absence of: *I missed you while you were away.* 1,3-12 *v.*, 2 *n.*, *pl.* **miss es.** [*Miss* comes from Old English *missan.*]

A miss is as good as a mile. A close miss has the same effect as a wide miss.

Miss (mis), **1** title put before a girl's or unmarried woman's name: *Miss Brown, the Misses Brown, the Miss Browns.* **2** *miss,* a young unmarried woman; girl. *n.*, *pl.* **Miss es.**

Miss., Mississippi.

mis sal (mis′əl), book containing the prayers, etc., for celebrating Mass throughout the year. *n.*

mis shape (mis shāp′), shape badly; deform. *v.*, **mis shaped, mis shaped** or **mis shap en, mis shap ing.**

mis shap en (mis shā′pən), badly shaped; deformed. *adj.*

mis sile (mis′əl), **1** object that is thrown or shot, such as a stone, an arrow, a bullet, or a lance. **2** a self-propelled rocket or bomb, such as a guided missile. *n.*

miss ing (mis′ing), not found when looked for; lacking; wanting; absent; gone: *One book is missing from the set.* *adj.*

mis sion (mish′ən), **1** a sending or being sent on some special work; errand. An operation by one or more aircraft against the enemy is called a mission. **2** group sent on some special business: *She was one of a mission sent by our government to France.* **3** group of persons sent by a religious organization into other parts of the world to spread its beliefs. **4 missions,** *pl.* an organized effort by a religious group to set up churches, schools, hospitals, etc.: *foreign missions.* **5** business on which a mission is sent: *carry out a mission.* **6** station or headquarters of a religious mission. **7** business or purpose in life; calling: *It seemed to be her mission to help improve living conditions in the city. n.* [*Mission* is from Latin *missionem,* which comes from *mittere,* meaning "to send." See **Word Family.**]

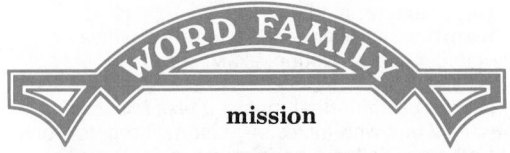

WORD FAMILY

mission

Below are words related to *mission.* They can all be traced back to the Latin word *mittere* (mit′te re), meaning "to send."

admit	emit	omit
commissar	intermission	permission
commissary	intermittent	permit
commission	Mass	premise
commit	mess	promise
compromise	message	remiss
demise	missile	remit
dismiss	missionary	submit
emissary	missive	transmit

mis sion ar y (mish′ə ner′ē), **1** person sent on a religious mission: *Missionaries helped start churches, schools, and hospitals in many places.* **2** person who works to advance some cause or idea. **3** of religious missions or missionaries. **1,2** *n., pl.* **mis sion ar ies; 3** *adj.*

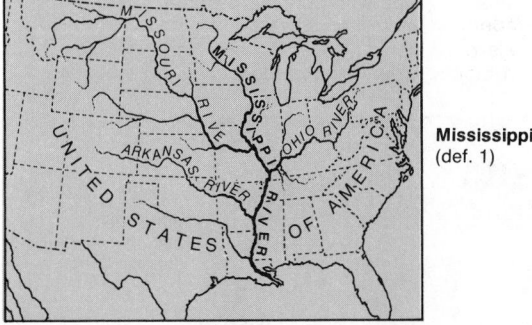

Mississippi (def. 1)

Mis sis sip pi (mis′ə sip′ē), **1** large river in the United States. It flows south from N Minnesota to the Gulf of Mexico. **2** one of the south central states of the United States. *Abbreviation:* Miss. or MS *Capital:* Jackson. *n.*

Mis sis sip pi an (mis′ə sip′ē ən), **1** person born or living in Mississippi. **2** of Mississippi or the Mississippi. **1** *n.,* **2** *adj.*

mis sive (mis′iv), a written message; letter. *n.*

Mis sour i (mə zùr′ē *or* mə zùr′ə), **1** large river in the N

a hat	i it	oi oil	ch child	(a in about
ā age	ī ice	ou out	ng long	e in taken
ä far	o hot	u cup	sh she	ə = { i in pencil
e let	ō open	ù put	th thin	o in lemon
ē equal	ô order	ü rule	ŦH then	u in circus
ėr term			zh measure	

part of the United States, flowing from SW Montana into the Mississippi. **2** one of the midwestern states of the United States. *Abbreviation:* Mo. or MO *Capital:* Jefferson City. *n.* —**Mis sour′i an,** *adj., n.*

mis spell (mis spel′), spell incorrectly. *v.,* **mis spelled** or **mis spelt** (mis spelt′), **mis spell ing.**

mis spell ing (mis spel′ing), an incorrect spelling. *n.*

mis spent (mis spent′), spent foolishly or wrongly; wasted: *a misspent fortune, a misspent life. adj.*

mis state (mis stāt′), state wrongly or incorrectly. *v.,* **mis stat ed, mis stat ing.**

mis state ment (mis stāt′mənt), a wrong or incorrect statement. *n.*

mis step (mis step′), **1** a wrong step. **2** error or slip in conduct. *n.*

mist (mist), **1** cloud of very fine drops of water suspended in the air; haze. **2** come down in mist; rain in very fine drops. **3** anything that dims, blurs, or obscures: *She did not cry, but a mist came over her eyes. A mist of prejudice spoiled his judgment.* **4** become covered with a mist; become dim: *The windows are misting.* **5** cover with a mist; put a mist before; make dim: *Tears misted his eyes.* **1,3** *n.,* **2,4,5** *v.* [*Mist* comes from Old English *mist.*] —**mist′like′,** *adj.*

mis take (mə stāk′), **1** misunderstanding of a thing's use or meaning; error; blunder: *It was a mistake to leave before the snow stopped. I used your towel by mistake.* **2** misunderstand (what is seen or heard). **3** take wrongly; take (to be some other person or thing): *I mistook that stick for a snake.* **1** *n.,* **2,3** *v.,* **mis took, mis tak en, mis tak ing.** —**mis tak′er,** *n.*

mis tak en (mə stā′kən), **1** wrong in opinion; having made a mistake: *I saw I was mistaken and admitted my error.* **2** wrongly judged; wrong; misplaced: *It was a mistaken kindness to give that boy more candy; it will make him sick.* **3** past participle of **mistake.** *I was mistaken for someone else.* **1,2** *adj.,* **3** *v.* —**mis tak′en ly,** *adv.*

Mis ter (mis′tər), **1** Mr., a title put before a man's name or the name of his office: *Mr. Stein, Mr. President.* **2 mister,** INFORMAL. sir. *n.*

mist i ly (mis′tə lē), in a misty manner. *adv.*

mist i ness (mis′tē nis), misty condition. *n.*

mis tle toe (mis′əl tō), plant with small, waxy, white berries that grows as a parasite on trees. It is used as a Christmas decoration. *n.*

mistletoe

mis took (mə stük′), past tense of **mistake.** *I mistook you for your sister yesterday. v.*

mis treat (mis trēt′), treat badly. *v.*

mis treat ment (mis trēt′mənt), bad treatment. *n.*

mis tress (mis′tris), **1** woman who is at the head of a household. **2** woman or country that is in control or can rule: *England was sometimes called mistress of the seas.* **3** woman who has a thorough knowledge or mastery: *She is a complete mistress of the art of cooking.* **4** woman teaching in a school, or at the head of a school, or giving lessons in a special subject: *the dancing mistress.* **5** woman who lives as a wife with a man without being married to him. **6 Mistress,** OLD USE. Mrs., Madam, or Miss. *n., pl.* **mis tress es.**

mis tri al (mis trī′əl), **1** trial in which the jury fails to come to a decision. **2** trial of no effect in law because of some error in the proceedings. *n.*

mis trust (mis trust′), **1** feel no trust or confidence in; distrust; doubt: *I mistrusted my ability to learn to swim.* **2** lack of trust or confidence; suspicion: *He looked with mistrust at the stranger.* **1** *v.,* **2** *n.*

mis trust ful (mis trust′fəl), lacking confidence; distrustful; doubting; suspicious. *adj.* —**mis trust′ful ly,** *adv.* —**mis trust′ful ness,** *n.*

mist y (mis′tē), **1** of or characterized by mist; full of or covered with mist: *misty hills.* **2** as if seen through a mist; vague; indistinct: *a misty form, a misty memory. adj.,* **mist i er, mist i est.**

mis un der stand (mis′un′dər stand′), **1** understand wrongly. **2** take in a wrong sense; give the wrong meaning to. *v.,* **mis un der stood, mis un der stand ing.**

mis un der stand ing (mis′un′dər stan′ding), **1** wrong understanding; failure to understand; mistake as to meaning. **2** disagreement: *After their misunderstanding they scarcely spoke to each other for months. n.*

mis un der stood (mis′un′dər stud′), past tense and past participle of **misunderstand.** *She misunderstood what the teacher said and so did the wrong homework. v.*

mis use (mis yüz′ *for 1,2;* mis yüs′ *for 3*), **1** use for the wrong purpose: *He misuses his knife at the table by lifting food with it.* **2** treat badly; mistreat; abuse: *The children misused their dog by trying to ride on its back.* **3** a wrong use: *I notice a misuse of the word "who" in your letter.* **1,2** *v.,* **mis used, mis us ing; 3** *n.*

mite[1]—about ¹/₁₆ in. (1.5 mm.) long

mite[1] (mīt), a very tiny animal that is related to the spider and has eight legs. It lives in foods, on plants, or on other animals. *n.*

mite[2] (mīt), **1** anything very small; little bit: *I can't eat even a mite of supper.* **2** coin of slight value. **3** a very small child: *What a mite your baby sister is! n.*

mi ter (mī′tər), **1** a tall, pointed, folded cap worn by bishops during sacred ceremonies. **2** kind of joint or corner where two pieces of wood are fitted together at right angles with the ends cut slanting. **3** join thus; prepare (ends of wood) for such joining. The corners of a picture frame are mitered. **1,2** *n.,* **3** *v.* Also, **mitre.**

mit i gate (mit′ə gāt), make or become milder or less harsh; soften. Anger, grief, heat, cold, and other conditions may be mitigated. *v.,* **mit i gat ed, mit i gat ing.**

mit i ga tion (mit′ə gā′shən), a mitigating or a being mitigated. *n.*

mi to sis (mī tō′sis), process by which a cell of a plant or animal divides to form two new cells, each containing the same number of chromosomes as the original cell. *n.*

mi tre (mī′tər), miter. *n., v.,* **mi tred, mi tring.**

mitt (mit), **1** glove with a big pad over the palm and

fingers, used by baseball players: *a catcher's mitt.* **2** mitten. *n.*

mit ten (mit′n), kind of winter glove covering the four fingers together and the thumb separately. *n.*

Mit ter rand (mē tə rän′), **François,** born 1916, president of France since 1981. *n.*

mix (miks), **1** put together; stir well together: *We mix butter, sugar, milk, and flour to make a cake.* **2** prepare by putting different things together: *mix a cake.* **3** join: *mix business and pleasure.* **4** be mixed; blend: *Oil and water do not mix.* **5** associate together; get along together: *She likes people and mixes well in almost any group.* **6** preparation that is already mixed: *a cake mix.* **1-5** *v.,* **mixed** or **mixt** (mikst), **mix ing; 6** *n., pl.* **mix es.**

mix up, 1 confuse: *I was so mixed up that I did very badly on the test.* **2** involve; concern: *They were mixed up in a plot to overthrow the government.*

mixed (mikst), **1** formed of different kinds: *mixed candies.* **2** of or for both sexes: *a mixed chorus. adj.*

mixed bag, mixture; medley.

mixed number, number consisting of a positive or negative integer and a fraction. EXAMPLES: $1\frac{1}{2}$, $16\frac{2}{3}$, $-25\frac{9}{10}$.

mix er (mik′sər), **1** thing that mixes: *a bread mixer, an electric mixer.* **2** one who mixes. A person who gets along well with others is called a good mixer. *n.*

mix ture (miks′chər), **1** a mixing: *The mixture of the paints took almost ten minutes.* **2** mixed condition: *The audience felt a mixture of relief and disappointment.* **3** something that has been mixed; a product of mixing: *Orange is a mixture of yellow and red. n.*

mix-up (miks′up′), confusion; mess. *n.*

miz zen (miz′n), **1** a fore-and-aft sail on a mizzenmast. **2** mizzenmast. *n.*

miz zen mast (miz′n mast′ *or* miz′n məst), mast nearest the stern in a two-masted or three-masted ship. *n.*

ml., milliliter or milliliters.

Mlle., Mademoiselle. *pl.* **Mlles.**

mm., millimeter or millimeters.

Mma ba tho (mä bä′tō), capital of Bophuthatswana. *n.*

Mme., Madame. *pl.* **Mmes.**

Mn, symbol for manganese.

MN, Minnesota (used with postal Zip Code).

mne mon ic (ni mon′ik), **1** aiding the memory. **2** intended to aid the memory. **3** of the memory. *adj.*

Mo, symbol for molybdenum.

MO, Missouri (used with postal Zip Code).

mo., month. *pl.* **mo.** or **mos.**

Mo., Missouri.

M.O., 1 money order. **2** mail order.

miter (def. 1) bishops wearing miters

Mo ab (mō′ab), ancient kingdom in the region east of the Dead Sea and the lower Jordan River in what is now Jordan. See **Judah** for map. *n.*

moan (mōn), **1** a long, low sound of suffering. **2** any similar sound: *the moan of the winter wind.* **3** make moans. **4** utter with a moan: *"I'm so stiff I can't move,"* *she moaned.* **5** complain; grieve: *He was always moaning* *about his bad luck.* 1,2 *n.,* 3-5 *v.* —**moan′ing ly,** *adv.*

moat (mōt), **1** a deep, wide ditch dug around a castle or town in the Middle Ages as a protection against enemies. Moats were usually kept filled with water. **2** a similar ditch used to separate animals in zoos. *n.*

mob (mob), **1** a lawless crowd, easily moved to act without thinking. **2** a large number of people; crowd. **3** to crowd around in curiosity, anger, etc.: *We eagerly mobbed the ice-cream truck the moment it appeared.* **4** attack with violence, as a mob does. **5** the common mass of people. **6** INFORMAL. group of criminals who work together; gang. 1,2,5,6 *n.,* 3,4 *v.,* **mobbed, mobbing.** [*Mob* is short for Latin *mobile vulgus,* meaning "the fickle common people."]

mo bile (mō′bəl *for 1,2;* mō′bēl′ *for 3*), **1** easy to move; movable: *Several mobile classrooms were brought to the crowded school.* **2** moving easily; changing easily: *a face with mobile features, a mobile mind.* **3** pieces of metal, wood, paper, etc., suspended on wires or threads and so balanced as to move in a slight breeze, used for decoration. 1,2 *adj.,* 3 *n.*

Mo bile (mō bēl′), seaport in SW Alabama, on the Gulf of Mexico. *n.*

mobile home, a house trailer, especially a large one set on a more or less permanent site.

mo bil i ty (mō bil′ə tē), a being mobile; ability or readiness to move or be moved. *n.*

mo bi li za tion (mō′bə lə zā′shən), **1** act of mobilizing; calling troops or ships into active military service. **2** condition of being mobilized. *n.*

mo bi lize (mō′bə līz), **1** call (troops or ships) into active military service; organize for war. **2** assemble and prepare for war: *The troops mobilized quickly.* **3** put into motion or active use: *mobilize the wealth of a country.* *v.,* **mo bi lized, mo bi liz ing.**

mob ster (mob′stər), a criminal; gangster. *n.*

moc ca sin (mok′ə sən), **1** a soft leather shoe or sandal without a heel. Moccasins were first made by North American Indians out of deerskin. **2** water moccasin. *n.* [*Moccasin* is of Algonquian origin.]

moccasin flower, a pink or white North American lady's-slipper.

mo cha (mō′kə), **1** a choice variety of coffee originally coming from Arabia. **2** flavored with coffee, or with chocolate and coffee. 1 *n.,* 2 *adj.* [*Mocha* was named for *Mocha,* a seaport in Yemen, where this coffee was shipped from.]

mock (mok), **1** laugh at; make fun of. **2** make fun of by copying or imitating: *My friends mocked the way I hobbled around on my sore foot.* **3** imitate; copy. **4** not real; pretended; copying; imitation: *a mock battle, mock modesty.* **5** an action or speech that mocks; mockery. 1-3 *v.,* 4 *adj.,* 5 *n.* —**mock′er,** *n.* —**mock′ing ly,** *adv.*

mock er y (mok′ər ē), **1** a making fun; ridicule: *Their mockery of my new clothes hurt my feelings.* **2** person or thing to be made fun of. **3** a bad copy or imitation: *Her pretended sorrow was but a mockery of real grief.* **4** a wasted or useless thing; naught: *The unfair trial made a mockery of justice.* *n., pl.* **mock er ies.**

mock ing bird (mok′ing bėrd′), a grayish songbird of the southern United States that imitates the calls of other birds. *n.*

mock orange, syringa.

mod., **1** moderate. **2** moderato. **3** modern.

mo dal (mō′dəl), **1** of or having to do with mode, manner, or form. **2** (in grammar) having to do with the mood of a verb. *adj.* —**mo′dal ly,** *adv.*

mode[1] (mōd), **1** manner or way in which a thing is done: *Riding on a donkey is a slow mode of travel.* **2** (in grammar) mood. **3** (in music) any of various arrangements of the

tones of an octave. *n.* [*Mode*[1] comes from Latin *modus,* meaning "measure, manner."]

mode[2] (mōd), style, fashion, or custom that is current; the way most people are behaving, talking, dressing, etc. *n.* [*Mode*[2] was borrowed from French *mode,* which came from Latin *modus,* meaning "measure, manner."]

mod el (mod′l), **1** a small copy: *a model of a ship or an engine.* **2** figure in clay or wax that is to be copied in marble, bronze, etc.: *a model for a statue.* **3** make, shape, or fashion; design; plan: *to model a horse in clay.* **4** way in which a thing is made; design; style: *Our television set is a new model.* **5** thing or person to be copied or imitated: *Your mother is a fine person; make her your model.* **6** follow as a pattern or example: *Model yourself on your father.* **7** just right or perfect, especially in conduct: *a model child.* **8** serving as a pattern or example: *a model house.* **9** person who poses for artists, photographers, etc. **10** person employed to wear or be photographed in clothing so that customers can see how the clothing looks. **11** be a model: *I modeled for an illustrator.* 1,2,4,5, 9,10 *n.,* 3,6,11 *v.,* **mod eled, mod el ing** *or* **mod elled, mod el ling;** 7,8 *adj.*

mo dem (mō′dem), an electronic device that enables a computer to send or receive information or instructions by telephone lines. *n.*

mod er ate (mod′ər it *for 1-4;* mod′ə rāt′ *for 5,6*), **1** kept or keeping within proper bounds; not extreme: *moderate expenses, moderate styles.* **2** not violent; calm: *moderate in opinion.* **3** not very large or good; fair; medium: *make a moderate profit.* **4** person who holds opinions that are not extreme: *a political moderate.* **5** make or become less extreme or violent: *The wind is moderating.* **6** act as moderator; preside (over). 1-3 *adj.,* 4 *n.,* 5,6 *v.,* **mod er at ed, mod er at ing.** —**mod′er ate ly,** *adv.*

mod e ra tion (mod′ə rā′shən), **1** act of moderating. **2** freedom from excess; proper restraint; temperance: *It is all right to eat candy in moderation.* *n.*

mod e ra to (mod′ə rä′tō), (in music) in moderate time. *adj., adv.*

mod e ra tor (mod′ə rā′tər), a presiding officer; chairman: *the moderator of a panel discussion.* *n.*

mod ern (mod′ərn), **1** of the present time; of times not long past: *Color television is a modern invention.* **2** up-to-date; not old-fashioned: *modern views.* **3** person who has up-to-date ideas and tastes. 1,2 *adj.,* 3 *n.*

Modern English, 1 period in the development of the English language from about 1500 through the present. **2** the English language of this period.

modern history, history from about 1450 to the present time.

mod ern is tic (mod′ər nis′tik), **1** modern. **2** having modern attitudes, methods, or style. *adj.*

mod ern i za tion (mod′ər nə zā′shən), a modernizing or a being modernized; bringing up to present ways or standards. *n.*

mod ern ize (mod′ər nīz), **1** make modern; bring up to present ways or standards. **2** become modern. *v.,* **modern ized, mod ern iz ing.** —**mod′ern iz′er,** *n.*

mod est (mod′ist), **1** not thinking too highly of oneself; not vain; humble: *In spite of many honors, the scientist remained a modest person.* **2** held back by a sense of what is fit and proper; not bold or forward; bashful; shy: *a* *modest child.* **3** not displaying or calling attention to one's body. **4** not too great; not asking too much: *a modest request.* **5** not expensive or showy: *a modest little house. adj.* **—mod′est ly,** *adv.*

mod est y (mod′ə stē), **1** freedom from vanity; being modest or humble. **2** shyness; bashfulness. **3** a not displaying or calling attention to one's body. *n.*

mod i cum (mod′ə kəm), a small or moderate quantity: *Even with a modicum of effort she gets high marks. n.*

mod i fi ca tion (mod′ə fə kā′shən), **1** partial alteration or change: *With these modifications your composition will do for the school paper.* **2** a making less severe or strong; a toning down: *A modification of the workers' demands helped settle the long strike.* **3** limitation of meaning; qualification. **4** a modified form; variety. *n.*

mod i fi er (mod′ə fī′ər), **1** word or group of words that limits the meaning of another word or group of words. In "a very tight coat," the adjective *tight* is a modifier of *coat,* and the adverb *very* is a modifier of *tight.* **2** person or thing that modifies. *n.*

mod i fy (mod′ə fī), **1** change somewhat: *modify the design of an automobile, modify the terms of a lease.* **2** make less; tone down; make less severe or strong: *He has modified his demands.* **3** limit the meaning of; qualify. Adverbs modify verbs, adjectives, and other adverbs. *v.,* **mod i fied, mod i fy ing.** [*Modify* is from Latin *modificare,* meaning "to limit," which comes from *modus,* meaning "measure," and *facere,* meaning "make."]

mod ish (mō′dish), fashionable; stylish. *adj.* **—mod′ish ly,** *adv.* **—mod′ish ness,** *n.*

mod u late (moj′ə lāt), **1** regulate or adjust; soften; tone down. **2** alter (the voice) in pitch, tone, or volume for expression. **3** change from one musical key to another. **4** (in radio or television) change the amplitude or frequency of the carrier waves in accordance with the sound or video signals being sent. *v.,* **mod u lat ed, mod u lat ing.** **—mod′u la′tor,** *n.*

mod u la tion (moj′ə lā′shən), a modulating or a being modulated. *n.*

Mog a di scio (mog′ə dē′shō), capital of Somalia. *n.*

mo hair (mō′her *or* mō′har), **1** cloth made from the long, silky hair of the Angora goat; angora. **2** a similar cloth made of wool and cotton. *n.*

Mo ham med (mō ham′id), A.D. 570?-632, Arab prophet, founder of Islam, the religion of the Moslems. *n.* Also, **Mahomet, Muhammad.**

Mo ham med an (mō ham′ə dən), **1** of Mohammed. **2** Moslem. **3** a Moslem. **1,2** *adj.,* **3** *n.* Also, **Mahometan.**

Mo ham med an ism (mō ham′ə də niz′əm), Islam, the religion of the Moslems. *n.*

Mo hawk (mō′hôk), member of an Iroquois tribe of American Indians formerly living in central New York State. *n., pl.* **Mo hawk** *or* **Mo hawks.**

Mo he gan (mō hē′gən), member of a tribe of American Indians related to the Mohican, formerly living in western Connecticut. *n., pl.* **Mo he gan** *or* **Mo he gans.**

Mo hi can (mō hē′kən), member of a tribe of American Indians formerly living along the Hudson River in New York State. *n., pl.* **Mo hi can** *or* **Mo hi cans.** Also, **Mahican.**

moi e ty (moi′ə tē), **1** half. **2** part: *Only a small moiety of college students win scholarships. n., pl.* **moi e ties.**

moist (moist), slightly wet; damp. *adj.* **—moist′ly,** *adv.* **—moist′ness,** *n.*

mois ten (moi′sn), make or become moist: *His eyes moistened with tears. v.* **—mois′ten er,** *n.*

mois ture (mois′chər), slight wetness; water or other liquid suspended in very small drops in the air or spread on a surface. Dew is moisture that collects at night on the grass. *n.*

Mo ja ve (mō hä′vē), large desert in S California. *n.*

mo lar (mō′lər), tooth with a broad surface for grinding. A person's back teeth are molars. *n.*

mo las ses (mə las′iz), a sweet syrup obtained in the process of making sugar from sugar cane. *n.* [*Molasses* comes from Portuguese *melaco,* and can be traced back to Latin *mellis,* meaning "honey."]

mold¹ (mōld), **1** a hollow shape in which anything is formed, cast, or solidified, such as the mold into which melted metal is poured to harden into shape, or the mold in which gelatin is left to stiffen. **2** the shape or form which is given by a mold: *The molds of ice cream were turkeys and pumpkins.* **3** the model according to which anything is shaped: *Those students are formed in their teacher's mold.* **4** form; shape: *Children mold figures out of clay.* **5** something shaped in a mold: *a mold of pudding.* **6** make or form into shape: *mold dough into loaves to be baked. Her character was molded by the trials she went through.* **7** nature; character: *a person of ambitious mold.* **1-3,5,7** *n.,* **4,6** *v.* Also, **mould.** **—mold′a ble,** *adj.* **—mold′er,** *n.*

mold² (mōld), **1** a woolly or furry fungous growth, often greenish in color, that appears on food and other animal or vegetable substances when they are left too long in a warm, moist place. **2** become covered with mold. **1** *n.,* **2** *v.* Also, **mould.**

mold³ (mōld), loose earth; fine, soft, rich soil. *n.* Also, **mould.**

Mol da vi a (mol dā′vē ə), Soviet republic in SW Soviet Union. *n.*

mold er (mōl′dər), turn into dust by natural decay; waste away; crumble. *v.* Also, **moulder.**

mold i ness (mōl′dē nis), state of being moldy. *n.*

mold ing (mōl′ding), **1** act of shaping: *the molding of dishes from clay.* **2** something molded; a decorative outline used in architecture. **3** a strip, usually of wood, around the upper walls of a room, used to support pictures, to cover electric wires, for decoration etc. *n.* Also, **moulding.**

mold y (mōl′dē), **1** covered with mold: *a moldy crust of bread, moldy cheese.* **2** musty; stale: *a moldy smell. adj.,* **mold i er, mold i est.** Also, **mouldy.**

mole¹ (mōl), a spot on the skin, usually brown, that was there at birth. *n.*

mole²—about 7 in. (18 cm.) long with the tail

mole² (mōl), a small mammal that lives underground most of the time. Moles have dark, velvety fur and very small eyes that cannot see well. *n.* **—mole′like′,** *adj.*

mo lec u lar (mə lek′yə lər), of, caused by, or consisting of molecules. *adj.*

mol e cule (mol′ə kyül), **1** the smallest particle into which an element or compound can be divided without changing its chemical and physical properties. A molecule of an element consists of one or more like atoms. A molecule of a compound consists of two or more different atoms. **2** a very small particle. *n.*

mole hill (mōl′hil′), **1** a small mound or ridge of earth raised up by moles burrowing under the ground. **2** something insignificant. *n.*

mo lest (mə lest′), **1** meddle with and injure; interfere with and trouble; disturb: *It is cruel to molest animals.* **2** interfere with in an indecent manner, especially by making improper sexual advances to women and children. *v.* —**mo lest′er,** *n.*

mo les ta tion (mō′les′tā′shən), a molesting or a being molested; annoying or hostile interference. *n.*

Mol ière (mō lyer′), 1622-1673, French writer of comedies. *n.*

mol li fy (mol′ə fī), soften, especially in temper; appease; mitigate: *I tried to mollify my parents' anger by apologizing. v.,* **mol li fied, mol li fy ing.**

mol lusk or **mol lusc** (mol′əsk), any of a large group of animals having soft bodies not composed of segments, and usually covered with a hard shell. Snails, mussels, oysters, clams, and octopuses are mollusks. *n.*

Mo loch (mō′lok), (in the Bible) a fire god of ancient times. Parents sacrificed their children to Moloch. *n.*

Mo lo kai (mō′lō kī′), the fifth largest island of Hawaii. *n.*

molt (mōlt), **1** shed the feathers, skin, etc., before a new growth. Birds and snakes molt. **2** shed (feathers, skin, etc.): *We saw the snake molt its skin.* **3** act or process of molting. 1,2 *v.,* 3 *n.* Also, **moult.** —**molt′er,** *n.*

mol ten (mōlt′n), **1** made liquid by heat; melted: *molten steel.* **2** made by melting and casting: *a molten image. adj.*

mo lyb de num (mə lib′də nəm), a heavy, hard, grayish metallic element. Molybdenum is much used to strengthen and harden steel. *n.*

mom (mom), INFORMAL. mother. *n.*

mo ment (mō′mənt), **1** a very short space of time; instant: *I'll be with you in a moment.* **2** a particular point of time: *I can't recall her name at the moment.* **3** importance: *Congress is busy on a matter of moment. n.* [*Moment* is from Latin *momentum,* meaning "movement."]

mo men tar i ly (mō′mən ter′ə lē), **1** for a moment: *She hesitated momentarily and then made her decision.* **2** at every moment; from moment to moment: *The danger was increasing momentarily.* **3** at any moment: *He was expecting visitors momentarily. adv.*

mo men tar y (mō′mən ter′ē), lasting only a moment: *a momentary hesitation. adj.* —**mo′men tar′i ness,** *n.*

mo men tous (mō men′təs), very important: *Choosing between peace and war is a momentous decision. adj.*

mo men tum (mō men′təm), **1** the force with which a body moves, equal to the product of its mass and its velocity: *A falling object gains momentum as it falls.* **2** impetus resulting from movement: *The runner's momentum carried him far beyond the finish line. n.*

mom my (mom′ē), INFORMAL. mother. *n., pl.* **mom mies.**

Mon., Monday.

Mon a co (mon′ə kō or mə nä′kō), **1** very small country on the SE coast of France, on the Mediterranean. **2** its capital. *n.* —**Mon′a can,** *adj., n.*

mon arch (mon′ərk), **1** king, queen, emperor, etc.; ruler. **2** person or thing like a monarch: *The tall, solitary pine was monarch of the forest.* **3** a large orange-and-black butterfly. *n.* [See **Word History.**]

mo nar chi cal (mə när′kə kəl), **1** of a monarch or monarchy. **2** favoring a monarchy. *adj.*

mon ar chist (mon′ər kist), person who supports or favors government by a monarch. *n.*

mon ar chy (mon′ər kē), **1** government by a monarch. **2** nation governed by a monarch. *n., pl.* **mon ar chies.**

mon as ter y (mon′ə ster′ē), building or buildings where monks live together. *n., pl.* **mon as ter ies.** [*Monastery* comes from Latin *monasterium,* and can be traced back to Greek *monos,* meaning "alone."]

mo nas tic (mə nas′tik), **1** of monks or nuns: *the monastic vows of chastity, poverty, and obedience.* **2** of monaster-

a hat	**i** it	**oi** oil	**ch** child	a in about
ā age	**ī** ice	**ou** out	**ng** long	e in taken
ä far	**o** hot	**u** cup	**sh** she	ə = { i in pencil
e let	**ō** open	**u̇** put	**th** thin	o in lemon
ē equal	**ô** order	**ü** rule	**ᵮH** then	u in circus
ėr term			**zh** measure	

ies: *monastic architecture.* **3** like that of monks or nuns. **4** monk. 1-3 *adj.,* 4 *n.* —**mo nas′ti cal ly,** *adv.*

mo nas ti cism (mə nas′tə siz′əm), system or condition of living a monastic life. *n.*

Mon dale (mon′dāl), **Walter F.,** born 1928, vice-president of the United States from 1977 to 1981. *n.*

Mon day (mun′dē), the second day of the week; day after Sunday. *n.*

mo ner an (mə nir′ən), any living thing that does not have a cellular nucleus. Bacteria and some algae are monerans. *n.*

Mo net (mō nā′), **Claude,** 1840-1926, French painter. *n.*

mon e tar y (mon′ə ter′ē), **1** of the money of a country: *The monetary unit in the United States is the dollar.* **2** of money: *a monetary reward. adj.* —**mon′e tar′i ly,** *adv.*

mon ey (mun′ē), **1** coins of gold, silver, or other metal, or paper notes which represent these metals, issued by a government for use in buying and selling. **2** any object or material used for buying and selling, such as checks drawn on a bank, gold nuggets, or gold dust. **3** wealth: *He is a man of money. n., pl.* **mon eys** or **mon ies.**

make money, 1 get money. **2** become rich: *My ambition is to make money and retire young.*

WORD HISTORY

money

Money came into English about 700 years ago from French *moneie,* which came from Latin *moneta,* meaning "mint, money," which comes from *Juno Moneta,* meaning "Juno the Protector." In ancient Rome money was coined in the temple of Juno.

mon eyed (mun′ēd), **1** having money; wealthy. **2** consisting of or representing money: *moneyed resources. adj.*

mon ey lend er (mun′ē len′dər), person whose business is lending money at interest. *n.*

money order, order for the payment of a certain sum of money. You can buy a money order at a post office, bank, etc., and send it to a person in another city, who can cash it there.

WORD HISTORY

monarch

Monarch is from Greek *monarchos,* which comes from *monos,* meaning "alone," and *archein,* meaning "to rule."

Mon gol (mong′gəl), **1** member of an Asian people now inhabiting Mongolia and nearby parts of China and Siberia. **2** of this people. **3** a Mongoloid individual. 1,3 *n.,* 2 *adj.*

Mongol Empire
Darker area shows the Empire at its greatest extent in 1294.

Mongol Empire, former empire of the Mongols, which encompassed most of Asia and part of E Europe during the late 1200's.

Mon go li a (mong gō/lē ə), vast region in Asia, south of Siberia. Mongolia includes part of N China and the Mongolian People's Republic. *n.*

Mon go li an (mong gō/lē ən), 1 of Mongolia, the Mongols, or their languages. 2 language or languages of the Mongols or Mongolia. 3 person born or living in Mongolia; Mongol. 4 Mongoloid. 1,4 *adj.*, 2-4 *n.*

Mongolian People's Republic, country in central Asia, north of China and south of the Soviet Union. *Capital:* Ulan Bator.

Mon gol oid (mong/gə loid), 1 of or resembling the Mongols. 2 member of the division of the human race that includes the original inhabitants of the continent of Asia (excluding southwestern Asia and India) and nearby islands, and their descendants throughout the world. 3 of this division of the human race. 1,3 *adj.*, 2 *n.*

mongoose
about 2 ft. (60 cm.) long with the tail

mon goose (mong/güs), a slender, flesh-eating mammal of Asia and Africa that resembles a ferret. It is noted for its ability to kill cobras and other poisonous snakes. *n.*, *pl.* **mon goos es.** [*Mongoose* comes from Marathi *mangūs*. Marathi is a language of western India.]

mon grel (mung/grəl *or* mong/grəl), animal or plant of mixed breed, especially a dog. *n.*

mon ies (mun/ēz), a plural of **money.** *n.*

mon i tor (mon/ə tər), 1 pupil in school with special duties, such as helping to keep order and taking attendance. 2 person who gives advice or warning. 3 **Monitor,** a low, armored warship of the Union, having a big gun in a revolving turret. It fought the Merrimac during the Civil War. 4 a large, flesh-eating lizard of Africa, southern Asia, Australia, and the East Indies. 5 receiver used for checking and listening to radio or television transmissions, telephone messages, etc. 6 television set, or device like a television without a speaker, connected to a computer to show input and output. 7 check and listen to (radio or television transmissions, telephone messages, etc.) by using a receiver. 1-6 *n.*, 7 *v.*

mon i to ry (mon/ə tôr/ē), admonishing; warning: *the monitory growl of a dog. adj.*

monk (mungk), man who gives up all worldly things and enters a monastery to live a life devoted to religion. *n.*

mon key (mung/kē), 1 mammal of the group most closely resembling human beings. 2 one of the smaller mammals in this group, not a chimpanzee, gorilla, or other large ape. It usually has a long tail. 3 person, especially a child, who is full of mischief. 4 INFORMAL. play in a mischievous way; fool; trifle: *Don't monkey with the television.* 1-3 *n., pl.* **mon keys;** 4 *v.* —**mon/key like/,** *adj.* **make a monkey out of,** make a fool of.

mon key shine (mung/kē shīn/), SLANG. a mischievous trick; clownish joke. *n.*

monkey wrench, a wrench with a movable jaw that can be adjusted to fit different sizes of nuts.

monk ish (mung/kish), of a monk or monks; like a monk. *adj.* —**monk/ish ly,** *adv.* —**monk/ish ness,** *n.*

monks hood (mungks/hud/), plant with purple or white hooded flowers. *n.*

mono-, *combining form.* one; a single: *Monosyllable = one syllable. Monotone = a single tone.* [The form *mono-* comes from Greek *monos,* meaning "single."]

mon o chrome (mon/ə krōm), a painting, drawing, etc., in a single color or shades of a single color. *n.*

monocle

mon o cle (mon/ə kəl), eyeglass for one eye. *n.*

mon o cot y le don (mon/ə kot/l ēd/n), a flowering plant with only one cotyledon or seed leaf. Grasses, palms, lilies, and irises are monocotyledons. *n.*

mo nog a my (mə nog/ə mē), practice or condition of being married to only one person at a time. *n.*

mon o gram (mon/ə gram), a person's initials combined in one design. Monograms are used on note paper, table linen, clothing, jewelry, etc. *n.*

monogram

mon o graph (mon/ə graf), book or article, especially a scholarly one, about a particular subject. *n.*

mon o lith (mon/l ith), 1 a single large block of stone. 2 monument, column, statue, etc., formed of a single large block of stone. *n.*

mon o lith ic (mon/l ith/ik), of a monolith; being a monolith. *adj.*

mon o logue or **mon o log** (mon/l ôg), 1 a long speech by one person in a group. 2 entertainment by a single speaker. 3 a play for a single actor. 4 part of a play in which a single actor speaks alone. *n.*

Mo non ga he la (mə non/gə hē/lə), river flowing from N West Virginia which, with the Allegheny River, forms the Ohio River at Pittsburgh. *n.*

mon o plane (mon/ə plān), airplane with only one pair of wings. Most modern airplanes are monoplanes. *n.*

mo nop o list (mə nop/ə list), 1 person who has a monopoly. 2 person who favors monopoly. *n.*

mo nop o lis tic (mə nop′ə lis′tik), **1** that monopolizes. **2** having to do with monopolies or monopolists. *adj.* —**mo nop′o lis′ti cal ly,** *adv.*

mo nop o lize (mə nop′ə līz), **1** have or get exclusive possession or control of: *One company monopolized the production of copper wire.* **2** occupy wholly; keep entirely to oneself. *v.,* **mo nop o lized, mo nop o liz ing.** —**mo nop′o li za′tion,** *n.* —**mo nop′o liz′er,** *n.*

mo nop o ly (mə nop′ə lē), **1** the exclusive control of a commodity or service: *The only milk company in town has a monopoly on milk delivery.* **2** such control granted by a government: *Inventors have a monopoly on their inventions for a certain number of years.* **3** control that, though not exclusive, enables the person or company to fix prices. **4** a commercial product or service that is exclusively controlled or nearly so. **5** person or company that has a monopoly on some commodity or service. **6** the exclusive possession or control of something: *a monopoly on another person's time.* *n., pl.* **mo nop o lies.**

mon o rail (mon′ə rāl), **1** a single rail serving as a complete track. **2** railway in which cars run on a single rail, either balanced on it or suspended from it. *n.*

mon o syl lab ic (mon′ə sə lab′ik), **1** having only one syllable. **2** consisting of a word or words of one syllable: *"No" is a monosyllabic reply.* *adj.* —**mon′o syl lab′i cal ly,** *adv.*

mon o syl la ble (mon′ə sil′ə bəl), word of one syllable. *Yes, no,* and *grand* are monosyllables. *n.*

mon o the ism (mon′ə thē iz′əm), belief that there is only one God. *n.*

mon o the ist (mon′ə thē′ist), believer in only one God. *n.*

mon o the is tic (mon′ə thē is′tik), **1** believing in only one God. **2** having to do with belief in only one God. *adj.*

mon o tone (mon′ə tōn), sameness of tone, style of writing, color, etc.: *Don't read in a monotone; use expression.* *n.*

mo not o nous (mə not′n əs), **1** continuing in the same tone: *She spoke in a monotonous voice.* **2** not varying; without change: *monotonous food.* **3** wearying because of its sameness: *monotonous work.* *adj.* —**mo not′o nous ly,** *adv.* —**mo not′o nous ness,** *n.*

mo not o ny (mə not′n ē), **1** sameness of tone or pitch: *The monotony of the man's voice was irritating.* **2** lack of variety. **3** wearisome sameness. *n., pl.* **mo not o nies.**

mon ox ide (mo nok′sīd), oxide containing one oxygen atom in each molecule. *n.*

Mon roe (mən rō′), **James,** 1758-1831, the fifth president of the United States, from 1817 to 1825. *n.*

Monroe Doctrine, doctrine that European nations should not interfere with American nations or try to acquire more territory in the Western Hemisphere. The Monroe Doctrine was derived from President Monroe's message to Congress on December 2, 1823.

Mon ro vi a (mon rō′vē ə), capital of Liberia, on the Atlantic. *n.*

mon sieur (mə syėr′), FRENCH. Mr.; sir. *n., pl.* **messieurs.**

mon si gnor or **Mon si gnor** (mon sē′nyər), **1** title given to certain dignitaries in the Roman Catholic Church. **2** person having this title. *n.*

mon soon (mon sün′), **1** a seasonal wind of the Indian Ocean and southern Asia. It blows from the southwest from April to October and from the northeast during the rest of the year. **2** the rainy season during which this wind blows from the southwest. *n.* [*Monsoon* is from Dutch *monssoen,* which came from Portuguese *monção,* which came from Arabic *mausim,* meaning "season."]

mon ster (mon′stər), **1** any animal or plant that is very unlike those usually found in nature. A cow with two heads is a monster. **2** an imaginary creature having parts of different animals: *A mermaid is a monster.* **3** an imaginary creature of strange and horrible appearance. **4** person too wicked to be considered human: *a ghastly crime committed by a monster of cruelty.* **5** a huge creature or thing. **6** huge. 1-5 *n.,* 6 *adj.* [*Monster* came into English about 700 years ago from French *monstre,* which came from Latin *monstrum,* meaning "something marvelous, divine warning."]

mon stros i ty (mon stros′ə tē), **1** monster. **2** condition or character of being monstrous. *n., pl.* **mon stros i ties.**

mon strous (mon′strəs), **1** huge; enormous. **2** wrongly formed or shaped; like a monster. **3** so wrong or absurd as to be almost unheard of. **4** shocking; horrible; dreadful. *adj.* —**mon′strous ly,** *adv.* —**mon′strous ness,** *n.*

Mont., Montana.

Mon tan a (mon tan′ə), one of the western states of the United States. *Abbreviation:* Mont. or MT *Capital:* Helena. *n.* —**Mon tan′an,** *adj., n.*

Mont Blanc (môn blän′), the highest mountain in the Alps, between France and Italy, 15,771 feet (4807 meters) high.

Mont calm (mont käm′), **Louis Joseph, Marquis de,** 1712-1759, French general defeated by the English at Quebec. *n.*

Mon te Car lo (mon′tə kär′lō), town in Monaco, noted as a gambling resort.

Mon tes so ri (mon′tə sôr′ē *or* mon′tə sōr′ē), **Maria,** 1870-1952, Italian educator. *n.*

Mon te vi de o (mon′tə vi dā′ō), capital of Uruguay, in the S part. *n.*

Mon te zu ma II (mon′tə zü′mə), 1480?-1520, Aztec emperor of Mexico, from 1502 to 1520, defeated by Cortés.

Mont gom er y (mont gum′ər ē), capital of Alabama, in the central part. *n.*

month (munth), **1** one of the 12 parts into which the year is divided. September, April, June, and November have 30 days; February has 28 days except in leap years, when it has 29; all the other months have 31 days. **2** time from any day of one month to the corresponding day of the next month. **3** lunar month. *n.*

month ly (munth′lē), **1** of a month; for a month; lasting a month: *a monthly supply.* **2** done, happening, payable, etc., once a month: *a monthly meeting.* **3** once a month; every month: *Some magazines come monthly.* **4** magazine published once a month. 1,2 *adj.,* 3 *adv.,* 4 *n., pl.* **monthlies.**

Mon ti cel lo (mon′tə sel′ō *or* mon′tə chel′ō), home of Thomas Jefferson, in central Virginia. *n.*

Mont pel ier (mont pē′lyər), capital of Vermont, in the central part. *n.*

Mon tre al (mon′trē ôl′), large seaport in Quebec, Canada, on the St. Lawrence River. *n.* [*Montreal* is from French *Montréal,* which came from Latin *montem,* meaning "mountain," and *regalis,* meaning "royal."]

mon u ment (mon′yə mənt), **1** something set up to honor a person or an event. A monument may be a building, pillar, arch, statue, tomb, or stone. **2** an enduring or prominent instance: *The Hoover Dam is a monument of engineering.* *n.*

mon u men tal (mon′yə men′tl), **1** of a monument.

a hat	**i** it	**oi** oil	**ch** child	a in about
ā age	**ī** ice	**ou** out	**ng** long	e in taken
ä far	**o** hot	**u** cup	**sh** she	ə = { i in pencil
e let	**ō** open	**u̇** put	**th** thin	o in lemon
ē equal	**ô** order	**ü** rule	**ŦH** then	u in circus
ėr term			**zh** measure	

2 serving as a monument. **3** like a monument. **4** weighty and lasting; important: *The Constitution of the United States is a monumental document.* **5** very great: *monumental ignorance. adj.* —**mon′u men′tal ly,** *adv.*

moo (mü), **1** sound made by a cow. **2** make this sound. **1** *n., pl.* **moos; 2** *v.,* **mooed, moo ing.**

mooch (müch), SLANG. get from another by begging or sponging. *v.* —**mooch′er,** *n.*

mood[1] (müd), state of mind or feeling: *I am in the mood to play now; I don't want to study. n.*

mood[2] (müd), form of a verb which shows whether the act or state it expresses is thought of as a fact, condition, command, etc. In "I am hungry," *am* is in the indicative mood. In "I demand that she answer," *answer* is in the subjunctive mood. In "Open the window," *open* is in the imperative mood. *n.* Also, **mode.**

mood i ly (mü′də lē), in a moody manner. *adv.*

mood i ness (mü′dē nis), moody condition. *n.*

mood y (mü′dē), **1** likely to have changes of mood. **2** often having gloomy moods: *She has been moody ever since she lost her job.* **3** sunk in sadness; gloomy; sullen: *They sat in moody silence. adj.,* **mood i er, mood i est.**

Moog (mōg *or* müg), trademark for an electronic musical instrument with a keyboard, capable of producing great variety of sound. It is often called the **Moog synthesizer.** *n.* [*Moog* is named for Robert A. *Moog,* born 1934, an American engineer who invented the instrument.]

moon (mün), **1** a heavenly body that revolves around the earth once in about 29½ days. It is a natural satellite of the earth and is held in orbit by the earth's gravity. The force of the moon's gravity on the earth causes tides in the oceans. **2** the moon as it looks at a certain period of time in its cycle: *a new moon, a full moon.* **3** the American Indian month of about 29½ days. **4** moonlight. **5** something shaped like the moon in any of its appearances. **6** satellite of any planet: *the moons of Jupiter.* **7** wander about idly or gaze dreamily: *Don't moon when you have work to do.* **1-6** *n.,* **7** *v.* [*Moon* comes from Old English *mōna.*] —**moon′less,** *adj.* —**moon′like′,** *adj.*

moon beam (mün′bēm′), ray of moonlight. *n.*

moon light (mün′līt′), **1** light of the moon. **2** having the light of the moon: *a moonlight night.* **3** while the moon is shining; by night: *a moonlight swim.* **1** *n.,* **2,3** *adj.*

moon lit (mün′lit′), lighted by the moon. *adj.*

moon shine (mün′shīn′), **1** moonlight. **2** empty talk; foolish talk or ideas; nonsense. **3** INFORMAL. intoxicating liquor made unlawfully or smuggled into the country. *n.*

moon stone (mün′stōn′), a whitish, translucent gem with a pearly luster. Moonstone is a variety of feldspar. *n.*

moon struck (mün′struk′), dazed, crazed, or confused. *adj.*

moor[1] (mùr), **1** put or keep (a ship, etc.) in place by means of ropes or chains fastened to the shore or to anchors. **2** fix firmly; secure. **3** tie down or anchor a ship. **4** be made secure by ropes, anchors, etc. *v.*

moor[2] (mùr), an open wasteland, usually covered with heather. *n.*

Moor (mùr), member of a Moslem people of mixed Arab and Berber ancestry, living in northwestern Africa. In the A.D. 700's the Moors invaded and conquered Spain. They were driven out in 1492. *n.*

Moore (mùr *or* môr), **1 Marianne,** 1887-1972, American poet. **2 Thomas,** 1779-1852, Irish poet. *n.*

moor ings (mùr′ingz), **1** ropes, cables, or anchors by which a ship is fastened. **2** place where a ship is moored. *n.pl.*

Moor ish (mùr′ish), of the Moors. *adj.*

moose (müs), a large mammal found in wooded areas of Canada and the northern United States. The male has a large head and broad antlers. It is related to the deer. *n., pl.* **moose.** [*Moose* is of Algonquian origin.]

moot (müt), doubtful or debatable: *a moot point. adj.*

mop (mop), **1** bundle of coarse yarn, rags, or cloth, etc., or a sponge fastened at the end of a stick or handle, for cleaning floors, dishes, etc. **2** wash or wipe up; clean with a mop: *to mop up the floor.* **3** wipe tears or sweat from: *to mop one's brow with one's handkerchief.* **4** a thick head of hair like a mop. **1,4** *n.,* **2,3** *v.,* **mopped, mopping.**

mope (mōp), **1** be dull, silent, and sad. **2** person who is dull, silent, and sad. **1** *v.,* **moped, mop ing; 2** *n.*

moped

mo ped (mō′ped), motorbike which can be pedaled as a bicycle or operated with a motor at up to 30 miles (48 kilometers) an hour. *n.* [*Moped* is a blend of *motor* and *pedal.*]

mop pet (mop′it), a little child. *n.*

mo raine (mə rān′), mass or ridge made of rocks, dirt, etc., that were scraped up and deposited by a glacier. *n.*

mo ral (môr′əl), **1** good in character or conduct; virtuous according to civilized standards of right and wrong; right; just: *a moral act, a moral person.* **2 morals,** *pl.* principles in regard to conduct; character or behavior in matters of right and wrong. **3** capable of understanding right and wrong: *A little baby is not a moral being.* **4** having to do with character or with the difference between right and wrong: *Whether finding should be keeping is a moral question.* **5** lesson, inner meaning, or teaching of a fable, a story, or an event: *The moral of the story was "Look before you leap."* **6** teaching a good lesson; having a good influence. **7** that raises one's morale; inspiring confidence: *We gave moral support to the team by cheering them enthusiastically.* **1,3,4,6,7** *adj.,* **2,5** *n.*

mo rale (mə ral′), moral or mental condition as regards courage, confidence, enthusiasm, etc.: *The morale of the team was low after its defeat. n.*

mo ral ist (môr′ə list), **1** person who teaches, studies, or writes about morals. **2** person who tries to regulate the morals of others. *n.*

mo ral is tic (môr′ə lis′tik), **1** moralizing; teaching the

moose—about 6 ft. (2 m.) high at the shoulder

difference between right and wrong. **2** of or concerned with morals. *adj.* —**mo′ral is′ti cal ly,** *adv.*

mo ral i ty (mə ral′ə tē), **1** the right or wrong of an action: *They spent the evening arguing about the morality of war.* **2** doing right; virtue: *They have high standards of morality.* **3** system of morals; set of rules or principles of conduct. *n., pl.* **mo ral i ties.**

mo ral ize (môr′ə līz), **1** think, talk, or write about questions of right and wrong. **2** point out the lesson or inner meaning of. *v.,* **mo ral ized, mo ral iz ing.** —**mo′ral i za′tion,** *n.* —**mo′ral iz′er,** *n.*

mo ral ly (môr′ə lē), **1** in a moral manner: *to behave morally.* **2** in morals; as to morals: *The king was a good man morally but too easily swayed by his crafty advisers.* **3** from a moral point of view; ethically: *What they did was morally wrong. adv.*

moral victory, defeat that has the effect on the mind that a victory would have.

mo rass (mə ras′), piece of low, soft, wet ground; swamp. *n., pl.* **mo rass es.** [*Morass* comes from Dutch *moeras.*]

mo ra to ri um (môr′ə tôr′ē əm), **1** a legal authorization to delay payments of money due. **2** period during which such authorization is in effect. **3** a temporary stopping of action on any issue. *n., pl.* **mo ra to ri ums, mo ra to ri a** (môr′ə tôr′ē ə).

Mo ra vi a (mô rā′vē ə), region in central Czechoslovakia. *n.* —**Mo ra′vi an,** *adj., n.*

mor bid (môr′bid), **1** not wholesome; unhealthy; sickly: *morbid fancies, a morbid book.* **2** caused by disease; characteristic of disease; diseased: *Cancer is a morbid growth.* **3** horrible; gruesome; grisly: *the morbid details of a murder. adj.* —**mor′bid ly,** *adv.* —**mor′bid ness,** *n.*

mor bid i ty (môr bid′ə tē), **1** morbid condition or quality. **2** proportion of sickness. *n.*

mor dant (môrd′nt), **1** biting; cutting; sarcastic: *The mordant criticism hurt my feelings.* **2** substance that fixes colors in dyeing. **3** acid that eats into metal, used in etching. **1** *adj.,* **2,3** *n.* —**mor′dant ly,** *adv.*

more (môr), **1** greater in amount, degree, or number: *more people, more help. A foot is more than an inch.* **2** a greater or additional amount, degree, or number: *Tell me more about your camping trip. We will need more than two people in order to play this game.* **3** in a higher degree; to a greater extent: *A burn hurts more than a scratch does.* **4** in addition; farther: *Take one step more. Sing once more.* **5** further; additional: *This plant needs more sun.* **6** *More* helps to make the comparative form of most adverbs, and of most adjectives longer than one syllable: *more easily, more truly, more careful. "More common" means "commoner."* **1,5** *adj., comparative of* **much** *and* **many;** **2** *n.,* **3,4,6** *adv., comparative of* **much.**

more or less, 1 somewhat: *Most people are more or less selfish.* **2** about; approximately: *The distance is fifty kilometers more or less.*

More (môr), Sir **Thomas,** 1478-1535, English statesman and author, canonized in 1935. *n.*

more o ver (môr ō′vər), in addition to that; also; besides: *Our field trip was informative; moreover, it was fun. adv.*

mo res (môr′āz), traditional rules and customs of a group of people or a society. They are accepted as right and morally binding. *n.pl.*

Mor gan (môr′gən), **1** Sir **Henry,** 1635?-1688, British buccaneer. **2** **John Pierpont,** 1837-1913, American financier and art collector. *n.*

Mor gan le Fay (môr′gən lə fā′), King Arthur's half sister, a fairy.

morgue (môrg), **1** place in which the bodies of unknown persons found dead are kept until they can be identified

a hat	i it	oi oil	ch child	a in about
ā age	ī ice	ou out	ng long	e in taken
ä far	o hot	u cup	sh she	ə = { i in pencil
e let	ō open	ů put	th thin	o in lemon
ē equal	ô order	ü rule	ŦH then	u in circus
ėr term			zh measure	

and claimed. **2** the reference library in a newspaper office. *n.*

mo ri bund (môr′ə bund), dying. *adj.*

Mor mon (môr′mən), **1** member of the Church of Jesus Christ of Latter-day Saints, founded in 1830 by Joseph Smith. **2** of the Mormons or their religion. **1** *n.,* **2** *adj.*

morn (môrn), OLD USE. morning. *n.*

morn ing (môr′ning), **1** the early part of the day, ending at noon. **2** of or in the morning. **1** *n.,* **2** *adj.*

morn ing-glo ry (môr′ning glôr′ē), a climbing vine that has heart-shaped leaves and funnel-shaped blue, pink, or white flowers which open early in the day. *n., pl.* **morn ing-glo ries.**

morning star, a bright planet, especially Venus, seen in the eastern sky before sunrise.

mo roc co (mə rok′ō), a fine leather made from goatskin, used in binding books. *n., pl.* **mo roc cos.**

Mo roc co (mə rok′ō), country in NW Africa. *Capital:* Rabat. See **Algeria** for map. *n.* —**Mo roc′can,** *adj., n.*

mo ron (môr′on), **1** person born with little mental ability. Morons can learn to read and to do routine tasks, but do not develop beyond a mental age of eight to twelve years. **2** INFORMAL. a very stupid or foolish person. *n.*

Mo ro ni (mō rō′nē), capital of the Comoro Islands. *n.*

mo ron ic (mə ron′ik), of or like a moron. *adj.* —**mo ron′i cal ly,** *adv.*

mo rose (mə rōs′), gloomy; sullen; ill-humored. *adj.* —**mo rose′ly,** *adv.* —**mo rose′ness,** *n.*

mor pheme (môr′fēm), the smallest part of a word that has meaning of its own. Morphemes may be words, prefixes, suffixes, or endings that show inflection. In the word *carelessness,* the morphemes are *care, -less,* and *-ness. n.*

Mor phe us (môr′fē əs *or* môr′fyüs), (in Greek myths) the god of dreams. *n.*

mor phi a (môr′fē ə), morphine. *n.*

mor phine (môr′fēn′), drug made from opium, used to dull pain and to cause sleep. *n.*

mor ris chair (môr′is), armchair with an adjustable back.

morris dance, an old English dance performed by people in fancy costumes.

mor row (môr′ō), **1** the following day or time. **2** OLD USE. morning. *n.*

Morse (môrs), **Samuel F. B.,** 1791-1872, American painter and inventor who made the first telegraph instrument. The Morse code is named after him. *n.*

Morse code, system by which letters, numbers, etc., are represented by dots, dashes, and spaces or by long and short sounds or flashes of light. Morse code is now used mainly in signaling.

mor sel (môr′səl), **1** a small portion of food. **2** piece; fragment. *n.*

mor tal (môr′tl), **1** sure to die sometime. **2** a being that is sure to die sometime. All living creatures are mortals. **3** of human beings; of mortals: *Mortal bodies have many pains and diseases.* **4** human being: *"Lord, what fools these mortals be!"* **5** of death. **6** causing death: *a mortal illness.* **7** to the death: *a mortal enemy, a mortal battle.* **8** very great; deadly: *mortal terror.* **9** (in the Roman Catholic Church) causing death of the soul: *Murder is a mortal sin.* **1,3,5-9** *adj.,* **2,4** *n.*

mor tal i ty (môr tal′ə tē), **1** mortal nature; being sure to die sometime. **2** loss of life on a large scale: *The mortality from automobile accidents is dreadful.* **3** death rate; number of deaths in proportion to population or to a specified part of a population: *The mortality from typhoid fever is decreasing. n., pl.* **mor tal i ties.**

mor tal ly (môr′tl ē), **1** fatally; so as to cause death: *mortally wounded.* **2** very greatly; bitterly; grievously: *She was mortally offended. adv.*

mor tar[1] (môr′tər), mixture of lime, cement, sand, and water, for holding bricks or stones together. *n.*

mortar[2] (def. 1)
three mortars and
two pestles

mor tar[2] (môr′tər), **1** bowl of porcelain, glass, or other very hard material, in which substances may be pounded to a powder with a pestle. **2** a very short cannon for shooting shells or fireworks high into the air. *n.*

mor tar board (môr′tər bôrd′), **1** a flat, square board used by masons to hold mortar while working with it. **2** cap with a close-fitting crown topped by a stiff, flat, cloth-covered square piece from which usually a tassel hangs, worn at graduation exercises and other academic occasions. *n.*

mortarboard (def. 2)

mort gage (môr′gij), **1** a claim on property, given to a person, bank, or firm that has loaned money in case the money is not repaid when due. **2** document that gives such a claim. **3** give a lender a claim to (one's property) in case a debt is not paid when due. **4** put under some obligation; pledge: *Faust mortgaged his soul to the Devil.* 1,2 *n.,* 3,4 *v.,* **mort gaged, mort gag ing.**

mort gag ee (môr′gi jē′), person to whom property is mortgaged. *n.*

mort ga gor or **mort gag er** (môr′gi jər), person who mortgages property. *n.*

mor tice (môr′tis), mortise. *n., v.,* **mor ticed, mor tic ing.**

mor ti cian (môr tish′ən), undertaker. *n.*

mor ti fi ca tion (môr′tə fə kā′shən), **1** a feeling of shame; humiliation: *mortification at having spilled food on the table.* **2** a cause of shame or humiliation. **3** a mortifying or a being mortified: *the mortification of the body by fasting.* **4** death of one part of the body while the rest is alive: *Her leg had to be amputated because moritification had set in. n.*

mor ti fy (môr′tə fī), **1** wound the feelings of; make feel humbled and ashamed; humiliate: *Their bad behavior mortified their parents.* **2** overcome (bodily desires and feelings) by pain and going without things: *The saint mortified her body.* **3** die; decay: *His injured foot has mortified and must be amputated. v.,* **mor ti fied, mor ti fy ing.** **—mor′ti fi′er,** *n.*

mor tise (môr′tis), **1** hole in one piece of wood cut to receive the tenon on another piece so as to form a joint. **2** fasten by a mortise. 1 *n.,* 2 *v.,* **mor tised, mor tis ing.** Also, **mortice.**

mor tu ar y (môr′chü er′ē), **1** a building where the dead are kept until burial or cremation. **2** of death or burial. 1 *n., pl.* **mor tu ar ies;** 2 *adj.*

mos., months.

mo sa ic (mō zā′ik), **1** decoration made of small pieces of stone, glass, wood, etc., of different colors inlaid to form a picture or design. **2** such a picture or design. Mosaics are used in the floors, walls, or ceilings of some fine buildings. **3** formed by, having to do with, or resembling a mosaic. **4** anything like a mosaic: *Her music is a mosaic of folk tunes.* 1,2,4 *n.,* 3 *adj.* [*Mosaic* comes from a medieval Latin word *mosaicus,* meaning "of the Muses, artistic."]

mosaic (def. 2)

Mo sa ic (mō zā′ik), of Moses: *the Mosaic law. adj.*

Mos cow (mos′kou *or* mos′kō), capital of the Soviet Union, in the W part. *n.*

Mo ses (mō′ziz), (in the Bible) the great leader and law-giver of the Hebrews, who led them out of Egypt. *n.*

mo sey (mō′zē), INFORMAL. **1** shuffle along. **2** stroll; saunter. *v.*

Mos lem (moz′ləm), **1** person who believes in and fol-lows the teachings of Mohammed. **2** of Mohammed, his followers, or the religion of Islam. 1 *n., pl.* **Mos lems** or **Mos lem;** 2 *adj.* Also, **Muslim, Muslem.**

mosque (mosk), a Moslem place of worship. *n.*

mo squi to (mə skē′tō), any of various small, slender insects with two wings. The female bites and sucks blood from people and animals, causing itching. One kind of mosquito transmits malaria; another transmits yellow fever. *n., pl.* **mo squi toes** or **mo squi tos.** [*Mosquito* is from Spanish *mosquito,* meaning "little fly," which came from Latin *musca,* meaning "fly."]

moss (môs), very small, soft, green or brown plants that grow close together like a carpet on the ground, on rocks, on trees, etc. *n., pl.* **moss es. —moss′like′,** *adj.*

moss y (mô′sē), **1** covered with moss: *a mossy bank.* **2** like moss: *mossy green. adj.,* **moss i er, moss i est. —moss′i ness,** *n.*

most (mōst), **1** greatest in amount, degree, or number: *The winner gets the most money.* **2** the greatest amount, degree, or number: *He did most of the work. Who gave the most?* **3** in the highest degree; to the greatest extent: *This tooth hurts most. She was most kind to me.* **4** almost all: *Most people like ice cream.* **5** *Most* helps to make the superlative form of almost all adverbs, and of almost all adjectives longer than one syllable: *most easily, most truly, most careful. "Most common" means "commonest."* 1,4 *adj.,* superlative of **much** and **many;** 2 *n.,* 3,5 *adv.,* superlative of **much.**

at most or **at the most,** not more than.

for the most part, mainly; usually.

make the most of, make the best use of.

-most, *suffix forming superlatives of adjectives and adverbs.* greatest in amount, degree, or number, as in *foremost, inmost, topmost, uttermost.*

most ly (mōst'lē), almost all; for the most part; mainly; chiefly. *adv.*

mot (mō), a clever or witty remark. *n.*

mote (mōt), speck of dust. *n.*

mo tel (mō tel'), roadside hotel or group of furnished cottages or cabins providing overnight lodging for motorists. Most motels have parking next to or near the units. *n.* [*Motel* is a blend of *motor* and *hotel.*]

moth (môth), a broad-winged insect very much like a butterfly, but flying mostly at night. Moths are destructive only in the larval stage. One kind lays eggs in cloth, fur, etc., and its larvae eat holes in the material. Some larvae, such as the silkworm, are useful. *n., pl.* **moths** (môᴛʜz *or* môths).

moth ball (môth'bôl'), a small ball of camphor or another strong-smelling substance, used to keep moths away from wool, silk, fur, etc. *n.*

moth-eat en (môth'ēt'n), 1 eaten by moths; having holes made by moths. 2 worn-out. *adj.*

moth er[1] (muᴛʜ'ər), 1 a female parent. 2 take care of; act as mother to: *She mothers her baby sister.* 3 the cause or source of anything. 4 mother superior. 5 of or like a mother: *mother love, the mother church.* 6 person who is like a mother. 7 give birth to; bring forth. 8 native: *our mother tongue, one's mother country.* 1,3,4,6 *n.,* 2,7 *v.,* 5,8 *adj.*

moth er[2] (muᴛʜ'ər), a stringy, sticky substance formed in vinegar or on the surface of liquids that are turning to vinegar. Mother consists of bacteria. *n.*

Mother Goose, the imaginary author of certain old fairy tales and nursery rhymes.

moth er hood (muᴛʜ'ər hud), condition of being a mother. *n.*

moth er-in-law (muᴛʜ'ər in lô'), mother of one's husband or wife. *n., pl.* **moth ers-in-law.**

moth er land (muᴛʜ'ər land'), 1 one's native country. 2 land of one's ancestors. *n.*

moth er less (muᴛʜ'ər lis), having no mother: *a motherless child. adj.*

moth er li ness (muᴛʜ'ər lē nis), motherly quality. *n.*

moth er ly (muᴛʜ'ər lē), 1 of a mother. 2 like a mother; like a mother's; kindly: *a motherly person, motherly love. adj.*

moth er-of-pearl (muᴛʜ'ər əv pėrl'), the hard, smooth, glossy lining of the shell of the pearl oyster and certain other shells. It changes colors as the light changes. It is used to make buttons and ornaments. *n.*

Mother's Day, the second Sunday of May, set apart in the United States and Canada in honor of mothers.

mother superior, woman who is the head of a convent of nuns; mother.

mother tongue, 1 one's native language. 2 an original language to which other languages owe their origin.

moth y (mô'thē), infested by moths; moth-eaten. *adj.,* **moth i er, moth i est.**

mo tif (mō tēf'), 1 a subject for development or treatment in art, literature, or music; a principal idea or feature: *This opera contains a love motif.* 2 a distinctive figure in a design. *n.*

a hat	**i** it	**oi** oil	**ch** child	⎧ a in about
ā age	**ī** ice	**ou** out	**ng** long	⎪ e in taken
ä far	**o** hot	**u** cup	**sh** she	ə = ⎨ i in pencil
e let	**ō** open	**u̇** put	**th** thin	⎪ o in lemon
ē equal	**ô** order	**ü** rule	**ᴛʜ** then	⎩ u in circus
ėr term			**zh** measure	

mo tile (mō'tl), (in biology) moving or able to move by itself. *adj.*

mo tion (mō'shən), 1 change of position or place; movement; moving. Anything is in motion which is not at rest. *Can you feel the motion of the ship?* 2 make a movement, as of the hand or head, to show one's meaning: *He motioned to show us the way.* 3 show (a person) what to do by such a motion: *He motioned me out.* 4 a formal suggestion made in a meeting or court of law, to be voted on: *The motion to adjourn was carried.* 1,4 *n.,* 2,3 *v.*

mo tion less (mō'shən lis), not moving. *adj.* —**mo'tion less ly,** *adv.* —**mo'tion less ness,** *n.*

motion picture, 1 series of pictures projected on a screen in such rapid succession that the viewer gets the impression that the persons and things pictured are moving; moving picture; movie. 2 story or drama told by means of this. —**mo'tion-pic'ture,** *adj.*

mo ti vate (mō'tə vāt), provide with a motive; cause to act. *v.,* **mo ti vat ed, mo ti vat ing.**

mo ti va tion (mō'tə vā'shən), a furnishing with a motive or cause for action. *n.*

mo tive (mō'tiv), 1 thought or feeling that makes one act; moving consideration or reason: *My motive in taking the trip was a wish to travel.* 2 motif. *n.*

mot ley (mot'lē), 1 made up of parts or kinds that are different: *a motley crowd, a motley collection of butterflies, shells, and stamps.* 2 of different colors like a clown's suit. 3 suit of more than one color worn by clowns: *At the costume party he wore motley.* 1,2 *adj.,* 3 *n., pl.* **motleys.**

mo tor (mō'tər), 1 engine that makes a machine go: *an electric motor.* 2 an internal-combustion engine. 3 run by a motor: *a motor vehicle.* 4 having to do with or by means of automobiles: *a motor tour.* 5 to travel by automobile. 6 causing or having to do with motion. Motor nerves arouse muscles to action. 1,2 *n.,* 3,4,6 *adj.,* 5 *v.*

mo tor bike (mō'tər bīk'), INFORMAL. 1 bicycle with an auxiliary motor. 2 motorcycle, especially a small, light one. *n.*

mo tor boat (mō'tər bōt'), boat that is propelled by a motor. *n.*

mo tor cade (mō'tər kād), procession or long line of automobiles. *n.*

mo tor car (mō'tər kär'), automobile. *n.*

mo tor cy cle (mō'tər sī'kəl), 1 a two-wheeled motor vehicle which resembles a bicycle but is heavier and larger. 2 travel by motorcycle. 1 *n.,* 2 *v.,* **mo tor cy cled, mo tor cy cling.**

mo tor cy clist (mō'tər sī'klist), person who rides a motorcycle. *n.*

mo tor ist (mō'tər ist), person who drives or travels in an automobile. *n.*

mo tor ize (mō'tə rīz'), 1 furnish with a motor. 2 supply with motor-driven vehicles in place of horses and horse-drawn vehicles. *v.,* **mo tor ized, mo tor iz ing.** —**mo'tor i za'tion,** *n.*

mo tor man (mō'tər mən), person who runs an electric subway train, streetcar, etc. *n., pl.* **mo tor men.**

motor scooter, a two-wheeled motor vehicle similar to a child's scooter, but having a driver's seat.

motor vehicle, any vehicle run by a motor, which travels on wheels on roads and highways.

mot tle (mot′l), **1** mark with spots or streaks of different colors. **2** a spotted or streaked coloring or pattern. 1 *v.*, **mot tled, mot tling;** 2 *n.*

mot to (mot′ō), **1** a brief sentence adopted as a rule of conduct: *"Think before you speak" is a good motto.* **2** sentence, word, or phrase written or engraved on some object. *n., pl.* **mot toes** or **mot tos.** [*Motto* was borrowed from Italian *motto,* which came from Latin *muttum,* meaning "grunt, word."]

moue (mü), a grimace; pout. *n.*

mould (mōld), mold. *n., v.*

mould er (mōl′dər), molder. *v.*

mould ing (mōl′ding), molding. *n.*

mould y (mōl′dē), moldy. *adj.*, **mould i er, mould i est.**

moult (mōlt), molt. *v., n.*

mound (mound), **1** a bank or heap of earth or stones. **2** heap up: *He mounded the sand.* **3** a small hill. **4** the slightly elevated ground from which a baseball pitcher pitches. 1,3,4 *n.*, 2 *v.*

mount[1] (mount), **1** go up; ascend: *mount stairs.* **2** get up on: *mount a horse, mount a platform.* **3** get on a horse: *The riders mounted quickly.* **4** put on a horse; furnish with a horse. **5** horse provided for riding: *The riding instructor had an excellent mount.* **6** rise; increase; rise in amount: *The cost of living mounts steadily.* **7** put in proper position or order for use: *mount specimens on slides.* **8** have or carry (guns) as a fortress or ship does: *The ship mounts eight guns.* **9** fix in a setting, backing, support, etc.: *mount a picture on cardboard.* **10** a setting; backing; support: *the mount for a picture.* 1-4,6-9 *v.*, 5,10 *n.* [*Mount*[1] came into English about 400 years ago from French *monter,* and can be traced back to Latin *montem,* meaning "mountain."] —**mount′a ble,** *adj.* —**mount′er,** *n.*

mount[2] (mount), mountain; high hill. *Mount* is often used before the names of mountains, as in *Mount Rainier. n.* [*Mount*[2] is from Old English *munt,* which came from Latin *montem,* meaning "mountain."]

moun tain (moun′tən), **1** a very high hill. **2** of mountains: *mountain air.* **3** a very large heap or pile of anything: *a mountain of rubbish.* **4** a huge amount: *She overcame a mountain of difficulties.* 1,3,4 *n.*, 2 *adj.*

make a mountain out of a molehill, give great importance to something which is really insignificant.

moun tain eer (moun′tə nir′), **1** person who lives in the mountains. **2** person skilled in mountain climbing. **3** climb mountains. 1,2 *n.*, 3 *v.*

mountain goats—about 3 ft. (1 m.) high at the shoulder

mountain goat, a white, goatlike antelope of the Rocky Mountains.

mountain laurel, an evergreen shrub with glossy leaves and pale-pink or white flowers.

mountain lion, puma.

moun tain ous (moun′tə nəs), **1** covered with mountain ranges: *mountainous country.* **2** huge: *a mountainous*

wave. *adj.* —**moun′tain ous ly,** *adv.*

mountain range, row of connected mountains; large group of mountains.

mountain sheep, 1 bighorn. **2** any wild sheep living in mountains.

moun tain side (moun′tən sīd′), the slope of a mountain below the summit. *n.*

Mountain Standard Time, the standard time in the Rocky Mountain regions of the United States and Canada. It is seven hours behind Greenwich Time.

moun tain top (moun′tən top′), top or summit of a mountain. *n.*

moun te bank (moun′tə bangk), **1** person who sells quack medicines in public, appealing to the audience by tricks, stories, etc. **2** anybody who tries to deceive people by tricks, stories, etc. *n.*

mount ed (moun′tid), **1** on a horse, mule, bicycle, etc. **2** serving on horseback: *mounted police. adj.*

Mount ie (moun′tē), INFORMAL. member of the Royal Canadian Mounted Police. *n.*

mount ing (moun′ting), support, setting, etc. The mounting of a photograph is the paper or cardboard on which it is pasted. *n.*

Mount Ver non (vėr′nən), home of George Washington in Virginia, on the Potomac River near Washington, D.C.

mourn (môrn), **1** grieve. **2** feel or show grief over: *mourn a lost dog. v.*

mourn er (môr′nər), person who mourns, especially at a funeral. *n.*

mourn ful (môrn′fəl), **1** full of grief; sad; sorrowful: *a mournful voice.* **2** causing sorrow or mourning. *adj.*

mourn ing (môr′ning), **1** the wearing of black or some other color to show sorrow for a person's death. **2** a draping of buildings, flying flags at half-mast, etc., as an outward sign of sorrow for death. **3** clothes or decorations to show sorrow for death. **4** of mourning; used in mourning. 1-3 *n.*, 4 *adj.* —**mourn′ing ly,** *adv.*

mourning dove, a wild dove of North America that has a mournful call.

mouse (mous *for 1,4;* mouz *or* mous *for 2,3*), **1** a small, gnawing rodent with soft fur, a pointed snout, and a long, thin tail. Some kinds of mice are commonly found in houses. Others live in fields and meadows. **2** to hunt for mice; catch mice for food: *Cats and owls go mousing at night.* **3** search as a cat does; move about as if searching. **4** a shy, timid person. **5** box small enough to fit in one hand, connected to a computer by an electric cord. Moving it across a flat surface controls the movement of a pointer on the computer screen. 1,4,5 *n., pl.* **mice;** 2,3 *v.*, **moused, mous ing.** [*Mouse* comes from Old English *mūs.*] —**mouse′like′,** *adj.*

mous er (mou′zər), animal that catches mice. *n.*

mouse trap (mous′trap′), trap for catching mice. *n.*

mous ey (mou′sē), mousy. *adj.*, **mous i er, mous i est.**

mousse (müs), **1** food made with whipped cream, either frozen or stiffened with gelatin: *chocolate mousse.* **2** a foam used to style the hair. *n.*

mous tache (mus′tash *or* mə stash′), mustache. *n.*

mous y (mou′sē), **1** resembling or suggesting a mouse in color, odor, behavior, etc.: *mousy hair.* **2** quiet as a mouse. *adj.*, **mous i er, mous i est.** Also, **mousey.**

mouth (mouth *for 1-3,6;* mouŦH *for 4,5*), **1** the opening through which a person or animal takes in food; space containing the tongue and teeth. **2** an opening suggesting a mouth: *the mouth of a cave, the mouth of a bottle.* **3** a part of a river or the like where its waters are emptied into some other body of water: *the mouth of the Ohio River.* **4** utter (words) in an affected, pompous way: *I dislike actors who mouth their speeches.* **5** seize or rub with the mouth. **6** a grimace: *She made mouths at the cold, greasy food.* 1-3,6 *n., pl.* **mouths** (mouᴛʜz); 4,5 *v.* —**mouth′like′,** *adj.*

down in the mouth, INFORMAL. in low spirits; discouraged.

mouth ful (mouth′fŭl), **1** the amount the mouth can easily hold. **2** what is taken into the mouth at one time. **3** a small amount. *n., pl.* **mouth fuls.**

mouth organ, harmonica.

mouth piece (mouth′pēs′), **1** the part of a pipe, horn, etc., that is placed in or against a person's mouth. **2** person, newspaper, etc., that speaks for others. *n.*

mouth wash (mouth′wosh′ *or* mouth′wôsh′), a mildly antiseptic liquid to cleanse the mouth and teeth. *n.*

mov a ble (mü′və bəl), **1** able to be moved: *Our fingers are movable.* **2** able to be carried from place to place as personal belongings can. **3** changing from one date to another in different years: *Thanksgiving is a movable holiday.* **4** piece of furniture that can be moved to another place. 1-3 *adj.,* 4 *n.* Also, **move able.** —**mov′a ble ness,** *n.* —**mov′a bly,** *adv.*

move (müv), **1** change the place or position of: *Do not move your hand. Move your chair to the other side of the table.* **2** change place or position: *The child moved in her sleep.* **3** change one's place of living: *We move to the country next week.* **4** put or keep in motion; shake; stir: *The wind moves the leaves.* **5** make progress; go: *The train moved slowly.* **6** act of moving; movement. **7** to act: *The government must move in a decisive fashion.* **8** action taken to bring about some result: *His next move was to earn some money.* **9** cause to do something: *What moved you to get up so early?* **10** affect with emotion; excite to tender feeling: *The sad story moved us to tears.* **11** (in games) change to a different square according to rules: *move a pawn in chess.* **12** the moving of a piece in a game: *That was a good move.* **13** a player's turn to move in a game: *It's your move now.* **14** make a formal request, application, or proposal; propose: *Madam Chairman, I move that we adjourn.* **15** cause (the bowels) to empty. **16** be active: *move in the best society.* 1-5,7,9-11,14-16 *v.,* **moved, moving;** 6,8,12,13 *n.* [*Move* came into English about 700 years ago from French *mover,* which came from Latin *movere.* See **Word Family.**]

move in, move oneself, one's family, one's belongings, etc., into a new place to live.

on the move, moving about: *Dolphins are always on the move.*

WORD FAMILY

move

Below are words related to *move.* They can all be traced back to the Latin word *movere* (mō wā′re), meaning "to move."

commotion	mobile	motor
demobilize	motile	movie
demote	motion	promote
emotion	motivate	remote
immobilize	motive	removal

move a ble (mü′və bəl), movable. *adj., n.* —**move′a ble ness,** *n.* —**move′a bly,** *adv.*

move ment (müv′mənt), **1** act or fact of moving: *We run by movements of the legs.* **2** a change in the placing of

a hat	i it	oi oil	ch child	ə = { a in about
ā age	ī ice	ou out	ng long	e in taken
ä far	o hot	u cup	sh she	i in pencil
e let	ō open	u̇ put	th thin	o in lemon
ē equal	ô order	ü rule	ᴛʜ then	u in circus
ėr term			zh measure	

troops or ships. **3** the moving parts of a machine; special group of connected parts that move together. **4** one division of a symphony, sonata, or other long selection: *the second movement of Beethoven's Fifth Symphony.* **5** the efforts and results of a group of people working together to reach a common goal: *the civil rights movement.* **6** an emptying of the bowels. **7** the waste matter emptied from the bowels. *n.*

movement (def. 3) of a watch

mov er (mü′vər), **1** person or thing that moves. **2** person whose occupation is moving furniture, etc., from one house or place to another. *n.*

mov ie (mü′vē), **1** motion picture. **2** theater showing motion pictures. **3** the movies, a showing of motion pictures: *to go to the movies. n.*

mov ing (mü′ving), **1** in motion: *a moving car.* **2** causing action: *She was the moving spirit in planning for the party.* **3** touching; pathetic: *a moving story. adj.* —**mov′ing ly,** *adv.*

moving picture, motion picture.

moving staircase *or* **moving stairway,** escalator.

mow[1] (mō), **1** cut down with a machine or a scythe: *mow grass.* **2** cut down the grass or grain from: *mow a field.* **3** cut down grass, etc.: *We are mowing today.* **4** destroy in large numbers, as if by mowing: *The enemy fire mowed down a platoon of soldiers. v.,* **mowed, mowed** *or* **mown, mowing.**

mow[2] (mou), **1** the place in a barn where hay, grain, or the like is piled or stored. **2** a pile or stack of hay, grain, etc., in a barn. *n.*

mow er (mō′ər), person or thing that mows. *n.*

mown (mōn), mowed; a past participle of **mow**[1]. *v.*

Mo zam bique (mō′zam bēk′), country in SE Africa. *Capital:* Maputo. See **South Africa** for map. *n.*

Mo zart (mōt′särt), Wolfgang Amadeus, 1756-1791, Austrian composer. *n.*

moz za rel la (mot′sə rel′ə), a soft, white, mild Italian cheese. *n.*

m.p., melting point.

MP *or* **M.P., 1** Member of Parliament. **2** Military Police. **3** Mounted Police.

mph *or* **m.p.h.,** miles per hour.

Mr. *or* **Mr** (mis′tər), Mister, a title put in front of a man's name or the name of his position: *Mr. Stern. Mr. President. pl.* **Messrs.**

Mrs. *or* **Mrs** (mis′iz), a title put in front of a married woman's name: *Mrs. Weiss. pl.* **Mmes.**

MS, Mississippi (used with postal Zip Code).

ms., Ms., or MS., manuscript. *pl.* **mss., Mss.,** or **MSS.**

Ms. (miz), a title put in front of a woman's name: *Ms. Karen Hansen. pl.* **Mses.**

M.S. or **M.Sc.,** Master of Science.

Msgr., Monsignor.

M.S.T., Mountain Standard Time.

MT, Montana (used with postal Zip Code).

mt., mountain. *pl.* **mts.**

Mt., Mount: *Mt. Everest. pl.* **Mts.**

M.T., metric ton.

mtg. or **mtge.,** mortgage.

mtn., mountain.

Mu ba rak (mü bär′äk), **Hosni,** born 1928, president of Egypt since October 1981. *n.*

much (much), **1** in great amount or degree: *much money, not much time.* **2** a great amount: *I did not hear much of the talk. Don't eat too much.* **3** to a high degree; greatly: *I was much pleased.* **4** nearly; about: *This is much the same as the other.* 1 *adj.,* **more, most;** 2 *n.,* 3,4 *adv.,* **more, most.** —**much′ness,** *n.*

make much of, pay much attention to or do much for.

not much of a, not a very good: *Fifty dollars a week is not much of a wage.*

too much for, more than a match for.

mu ci lage (myü′sə lij), a sticky, gummy substance used to make things stick together. *n.*

muck (muk), **1** dirt; filth. **2** moist farmyard manure, used as a fertilizer. **3** a heavy, moist, dark soil made up chiefly of decayed plants. *n.*

muck rake (muk′rāk′), hunt for and expose corruption in government, big business, etc. *v.,* **muck raked, muck rak ing.**

muck rak er (muk′rā′kər), person, especially a journalist, who muckrakes. *n.*

muck y (muk′ē), **1** of muck. **2** filthy; dirty. *adj.,* **muck i er, muck i est.**

mu cous (myü′kəs), **1** of or like mucus. **2** containing or secreting mucus. *adj.*

mucous membrane, the mucus-producing lining of the nose, throat, and other cavities of the body that open to the air.

mu cus (myü′kəs), a slimy substance that is produced by and moistens and protects the mucous membranes. *n.*

mud (mud), earth so wet that it is soft and sticky. *n.*

mud di ly (mud′l ē), in a muddy manner. *adv.*

mud dle (mud′l), **1** mix up; get (things) into a mess: *to muddle a piece of work.* **2** think or act in a confused, blundering way: *muddle through a difficulty.* **3** make confused or stupid: *The more you talk, the more you muddle me.* **4** mess; disordered state: *My business affairs are in a muddle.* 1-3 *v.,* **mud dled, mud dling;** 4 *n.*

mud dle head ed (mud′l hed′id), stupid; confused. *adj.*

mud dy (mud′ē), **1** of or like mud: *muddy footprints on the floor.* **2** having much mud; covered with mud: *a muddy road, muddy shoes.* **3** clouded with mud; dull; not pure: *muddy water, a muddy color.* **4** confused; not clear: *muddy thinking.* **5** make muddy; become muddy. 1-4 *adj.,* **mud di er, mud di est;** 5 *v.,* **mud died, mud dy ing.** —**mud′di ness,** *n.*

mu ez zin (myü ez′n), crier who, at certain hours, calls Moslems to prayer. *n.*

muff (muf), **1** a covering of fur or other material for keeping both hands warm. One hand is put in at each end. **2** fail to catch (a ball) when it comes into one's hands. **3** a failure to catch a ball that comes into one's hands: *The catcher's muff allowed the runner to score.* **4** handle awkwardly; bungle. **5** an awkward handling; bungling. 1,3,5 *n.,* 2,4 *v.*

muf fin (muf′ən), a small, round cake made of wheat flour, corn meal, or the like, often without sugar. Muffins are usually served hot and eaten with butter. *n.*

muf fle (muf′əl), **1** wrap or cover up in order to keep warm and dry: *She muffled her throat in a warm scarf.* **2** wrap in something in order to soften or stop the sound: *A bell can be muffled with cloth.* **3** dull or deaden (a sound). *v.,* **muf fled, muf fling.**

muf fler (muf′lər), **1** wrap or scarf worn around the neck for warmth. **2** anything used to deaden sound. An automobile muffler, attached to the exhaust pipe, deadens the sound of the engine's exhaust. *n.*

mug (mug), **1** a heavy china or metal drinking cup with a handle. **2** amount a mug holds: *to drink a mug of milk.* **3** SLANG. face or mouth. **4** attack (a person) from behind, usually to rob. **5** exaggerate one's facial expressions, as in acting; make funny faces or smiles. 1-3 *n.,* 4,5 *v.,* **mugged, mug ging.**

mug ger (mug′ər), person who mugs. *n.*

mug gi ness (mug′ē nis), muggy condition. *n.*

mug gy (mug′ē), warm and humid; damp and close: *The weather was muggy. adj.,* **mug gi er, mug gi est.**

mug wump (mug′wump′), person who is independent in politics. *n.*

Mu ham mad (mù ham′əd), Mohammed. *n.*

mu lat to (mə lat′ō *or* myù lat′ō), person having one white parent and one black parent. *n., pl.* **mu lat toes.**

mul ber ry (mul′ber′ē), **1** tree with small, berrylike fruit that can be eaten. The leaves of one kind are used for feeding silkworms. **2** its sweet, usually dark purple fruit. **3** a dark purplish red. *n., pl.* **mul ber ries.**

mulch (mulch), **1** straw, leaves, sawdust, etc., spread on the ground around trees or plants. Mulch is used to protect the roots from cold or heat, to prevent weed growth and evaporation of moisture from the soil, and to enrich the soil. **2** to cover with straw, leaves, etc. 1 *n., pl.* **mulch es;** 2 *v.*

mulct (mulkt), **1** deprive of something by cunning or deceit; defraud: *He was mulcted of his money by a shrewd trick.* **2** punish (a person) by a fine. **3** a fine; penalty. 1,2 *v.,* 3 *n.*

mule[1] (def. 1)—about 4$\frac{1}{2}$ ft. (1.5 m.) high at the shoulder

mule[1] (myül), **1** offspring of a donkey and a horse. It has the form and size of a horse and the large ears, small hoofs, and tufted tail of a donkey. **2** INFORMAL. a stubborn person. *n.*

mule[2] (myül), kind of slipper that leaves the heel uncovered. *n.*

mule skinner, INFORMAL. muleteer.

mu le teer (myü′lə tir′), driver of mules. *n.*

mul ish (myü′lish), like a mule; stubborn; obstinate. *adj.* —**mul′ish ly,** *adv.* —**mul′ish ness,** *n.*

mull[1] (mul), think about without making much progress; ponder. *v.*

mull² (mul), make (wine, beer, cider, etc.) into a warm drink, adding sugar and spices. *v.*

mul lein or **mul len** (mul′ən), a weed with coarse, woolly leaves and spikes of yellow flowers. *n.*

mul let (mul′it), kind of fish that lives close to shore in warm waters, and is good to eat. There are red mullets and gray mullets. *n.. pl.* **mul lets** or **mul let.**

Mul ro ney (mul rü′nē), (**Martin**) **Brian,** born 1939, prime minister of Canada since 1984. *n.*

multi-, *combining form.* **1** having many or much: *Multicolored = having many colors.* **2** many times over: *Multimillionaire = a millionaire many times over.* [The form *multi-* comes from Latin *multus,* meaning "much, many."]

mul ti col ored (mul′ti kul′ərd), having many colors. *adj.*

mul ti far i ous (mul′tə fer′ē əs *or* mul′tə far′ē əs), **1** having many different parts, elements, forms, etc. **2** many and varied. *adj.* —**mul′ti far′i ous ly,** *adv.*

mul ti lat er al (mul′ti lat′ər əl), **1** having many sides. **2** involving three or more nations. *adj.* —**mul′ti lat′er al ly,** *adv.*

mul ti mil lion aire (mul′ti mil′yə ner′ *or* mul′ti mil′yə nar′), person who owns property worth several millions (of dollars, pounds, francs, etc.); millionaire many times over. *n.*

mul ti ple (mul′tə pəl), **1** of, having, or involving many parts, elements, relations, etc.: *a person of multiple interests.* **2** number that contains another number a certain number of times without a remainder: *12 is a multiple of 3.* **1** *adj.,* **2** *n.*

mul ti pli cand (mul′tə plə kand′), number to be multiplied by another: *In 497 multiplied by 5, the multiplicand is 497. n.*

mul ti pli ca tion (mul′tə plə kā′shən), **1** a multiplying or a being multiplied. **2** operation of multiplying one number by another. *n.*

mul ti plic i ty (mul′tə plis′ə tē), a great many; a large variety: *a multiplicity of interests. n., pl.* **mul ti plic i ties.**

mul ti pli er (mul′tə plī′ər), number by which another number is to be multiplied: *In 83 multiplied by 5, the multiplier is 5. n.*

mul ti ply (mul′tə plī), **1** add (a number) a given number of times: *To multiply 16 by 3 means to add 16 three times, making 48.* **2** increase in number or amount: *My problems multiplied rapidly. v.,* **mul ti plied, mul ti ply ing.**

mul ti ra cial (mul′ti rā′shəl), having a number of races: *a multiracial community. adj.*

mul ti tude (mul′tə tüd *or* mul′tə tyüd), a great many; crowd: *a multitude of difficulties, a multitude of enemies. n.*

mul ti tu di nous (mul′tə tüd′n əs *or* mul′tə tyüd′n əs), forming a multitude; very numerous. *adj.* —**mul′ti tu′di nous ly,** *adv.* —**mul′ti tu′di nous ness,** *n.*

mum¹ (mum), **1** saying nothing; silent: *Keep mum about this; tell no one.* **2** be silent! say nothing! **1** *adj.,* **2** *interj.* **mum's the word,** be silent; say nothing.

mum² (mum), INFORMAL. chrysanthemum. *n.*

mum ble (mum′bəl), **1** speak indistinctly, as a person does when the lips are partly closed. **2** a mumbling: *There was a mumble of protest from the team against the umpire's decision.* **1** *v.,* **mum bled, mum bling;** **2** *n.*

mum ble ty-peg (mum′bəl tē peg′), game in which the players in turn flip a knife from various positions, trying to make it stick in the ground. *n.*

mum mer (mum′ər), **1** person who wears a mask, fancy costume, or disguise for fun: *Six mummers acted in a play at Christmas.* **2** actor. *n.*

mum mer y (mum′ər ē), **1** performance of mummers. **2** a useless or silly show or ceremony. *n., pl.* **mum mer ies.**

mum mi fi ca tion (mum′ə fə kā′shən), act or process of mummifying. *n.*

mum mi fy (mum′ə fī), **1** make into a mummy; make like a mummy. **2** shrivel; dry up. *v.,* **mum mi fied, mum mi fy ing.**

mum my (mum′ē), a dead body preserved from decay. Egyptian mummies have lasted more than 3000 years. *n., pl.* **mum mies.** [*Mummy* comes from a medieval Latin word *mumia,* and can be traced back to Persian *mūm,* meaning "wax." Wax was used in the embalming of the dead.]

mummy—an ancient Egyptian mummy

mumps (mumps), a contagious virus disease marked by swelling of the glands in the neck and difficulty in swallowing. *n.*

mun., municipal.

munch (munch), chew vigorously and steadily; chew noisily: *The horse munched its oats. v.* —**munch′er,** *n.*

mun dane (mun′dān), **1** of this world, not of heaven; earthly. **2** of the universe; of the world. *adj.* —**mun′dane ly,** *adv.*

Mu nich (myü′nik), large city in S West Germany. *n.*

mu nic i pal (myü nis′ə pəl), **1** of or having to do with the affairs of a city or town: *The state police assisted the municipal police.* **2** run by a city, town, or other municipality. *adj.* —**mu nic′i pal ly,** *adv.*

mu nic i pal i ty (myü nis′ə pal′ə tē), city or town having local self-government. *n., pl.* **mu nic i pal i ties.**

mu nif i cence (myü nif′ə səns), very great generosity. *n.*

mu nif i cent (myü nif′ə sənt), extremely generous. *adj.* —**mu nif′i cent ly,** *adv.*

mu ni tion (myü nish′ən), **1** Usually, **munitions,** *pl.* material used in war. Munitions are military supplies, such as guns, ammunition, or bombs. **2** having to do with military supplies: *A munition plant is a factory for making munitions.* **1** *n.,* **2** *adj.*

mur al (myür′əl); **1** on a wall: *A mural painting is painted on a wall of a building.* **2** picture painted on a wall. **1** *adj.,* **2** *n.*

mur der (mėr′dər), **1** the unlawful killing of a human being when it is planned beforehand. **2** an instance of such a crime: *The detective solved the murder.* **3** kill a human being intentionally: *Cain murdered his brother Abel.* **4** do very badly; spoil or ruin: *I really murdered my recital piece.* **1,2** *n.,* **3,4** *v.*

mur der er (mėr′dər ər), person who murders somebody. *n.*

mur der ous (mėr′dər əs), **1** able to kill: *a murderous blow.* **2** ready to murder: *a murderous villain.* **3** causing murder: *a murderous hate. adj.* —**mur′der ous ly,** *adv.* —**mur′der ous ness,** *n.*

murk (mėrk), darkness; gloom: *A light flashed through the murk of the night. n.* Also, **mirk.**

murk i ly (mėr′kə lē), in a murky manner. *adv.*

murk i ness (mėr′kē nis), murky condition. *n.*

murk y (mėr′kē), **1** dark; gloomy: *a murky prison.* **2** very

thick and dark; misty; hazy: *murky smoke. adj.,* **murk i er,
murk i est.**

mur mur (mėr′mər), **1** a soft, low, indistinct sound that
rises and falls a little and goes on without breaks: *the
murmur of a stream, the murmur of voices in another room.*
2 make a soft, low, indistinct sound. **3** a sound in the
heart or lungs, especially an abnormal sound due to a
leaky valve in the heart. **4** say in a murmur: *The shy child
murmured her thanks.* **5** complaint made under the breath,
not aloud. **6** complain under the breath; grumble. **1,3,5**
n., **2,4,6** *v.* —**mur′mur er,** *n.* —**mur′mur ing ly,** *adv.*

mur mur ous (mėr′mər əs), characterized by murmurs;
murmuring. *adj.* —**mur′mur ous ly,** *adv.*

mus., 1 museum. **2** music.

Mus cat (mus′kat), capital of Oman, in the N part. *n.*

mus cle (mus′əl), **1** a body tissue composed of fibers,
each of which is a long cell. The fibers can tighten or
loosen to move parts of the body. **2** a special bundle of
such tissue which moves some particular bone or part.
The biceps muscle bends the arm. **3** strength. *n.*

WORD HISTORY

muscle

Muscle came into English about 400
years ago from French *muscle,* which
came from Latin *musculus,* meaning
"little mouse." Certain muscles appeared to move beneath the surface of
the skin like little mice running.

mus cle-bound (mus′əl bound′), having some of the
muscles enlarged or tight, and lacking normal elasticity,
usually as a result of too much exercise. *adj.*

Mus co vite (mus′kə vīt), Russian. *n., adj.*

Mus co vy (mus′kə vē), OLD USE. Russia. *n.*

mus cu lar (mus′kyə lər), **1** of the muscles; influencing
the muscles: *a muscular strain.* **2** having well-developed
muscles; strong: *a muscular arm.* **3** consisting of muscle.
adj. —**mus′cu lar ly,** *adv.*

muscular dys tro phy (dis′trə fē), a disease in which
the muscles gradually weaken and waste away.

mus cu la ture (mus′kyə lə chúr), system or arrangement of muscles. *n.*

muse (myüz), think in a dreamy way; think; meditate:
The boy spent the whole afternoon in musing. v., **mused,
mus ing.**

Muse (myüz), **1** (in Greek myths) one of the nine goddesses of the fine arts and sciences. **2** Sometimes,
muse. spirit that inspires a poet or composer. *n.*

mu se um (myü zē′əm), a building or rooms where a
collection of objects illustrating science, ancient life, art,
history, or other subjects is kept and displayed. *n.*
[*Museum* was borrowed from Latin *museum,* which came
from Greek *mouseion,* meaning "seat of the Muses."]

mush[1] (mush), **1** corn meal boiled in water or milk. **2** a
soft, thick mass: *After the heavy rain the dirt road turned
to mush. n., pl.* **mush es.**

mush[2] (mush), **1** a journey on foot through snow, driving
a dog sled. **2** to travel in this way. **3** a shout to a team of
sled dogs to start or to speed up. **1** *n., pl.* **mush es; 2** *v.,*
3 *interj.* —**mush′er,** *n.*

mush room (mush′rüm *or* mush′rúm), **1** a small fungus,
shaped like an umbrella, that grows very fast. Some
mushrooms are good to eat; some are poisonous. **2** of or
like a mushroom. **3** grow rapidly: *Their business mush-*

roomed when they opened the new store. **1** *n.,* **2** *adj.,* **3** *v.*

mush y (mush′ē), **1** like mush; pulpy. **2** INFORMAL. weakly
sentimental. *adj.,* **mush i er, mush i est.**

mu sic (myü′zik), **1** art of putting sounds together in
beautiful, pleasing, or interesting arrangements.
2 beautiful, pleasing, or interesting arrangements of
sounds. **3** written or printed signs for tones: *Can you
read music?* **4** any pleasant sound: *the music of a bubbling
brook, the music of the wind. n.*

face the music, INFORMAL. meet trouble boldly or
bravely.

mu si cal (myü′zə kəl), **1** of music: *a musical composer.*
2 sounding beautiful or pleasing; like music: *a musical
voice.* **3** set to music; accompanied by music: *a musical
performance.* **4** fond of music. **5** skilled in music. **6** musical comedy. **1-5** *adj.,* **6** *n.*

musical comedy, play or motion picture with songs,
choruses, and dances.

mu si cale (myü′zə kal′), a social gathering to enjoy
music. *n.*

musical instrument, piano, violin, or other instrument for producing music.

mu si cal ly (myü′zik lē), **1** in a musical manner. **2** in
music: *She is well educated musically. adv.*

music box, box or case containing apparatus for producing music mechanically.

music hall, 1 hall for musical performances. **2** theater
for vaudeville.

mu si cian (myü zish′ən), **1** person skilled in music.
2 person who sings or who plays on a musical instrument, especially as a profession or business: *An orchestra is composed of many musicians.* **3** composer of
music. *n.*

mu si cian ship (myü zish′ən ship), skill in playing, conducting, or composing music; musical ability. *n.*

mu si col o gy (myü′zə kol′ə jē), the systematic study of
music, especially its history, forms, and principles. *n.*

music video, a short musical film on videotape or
videodisc, often a dramatized version of a rock'n'roll
song.

mus ing (myü′zing), **1** meditative. **2** meditation. **1** *adj.,* **2**
n. —**mus′ing ly,** *adv.*

musk (musk), **1** substance with a strong and lasting
odor, used in making perfumes. Musk is found in a
special gland in the male musk deer. **2** a similar substance found in the glands of other animals, such as the
mink and muskrat. **3** odor of musk. *n.*

musk deer, a small, hornless deer of central Asia, the
male of which has a gland containing musk.

mus kel lunge (mus′kə lunj), a very large North American pike. The muskellunge is valued as a food and game
fish. *n., pl.* **mus kel lunge.**

mus ket (mus′kit), kind of old gun used before rifles
were invented. *n.*

mus ket eer (mus′kə tir′), soldier armed with a musket. *n.*

mus ket ry (mus′kə trē), **1** muskets. **2** art of shooting
with muskets or rifles. *n.*

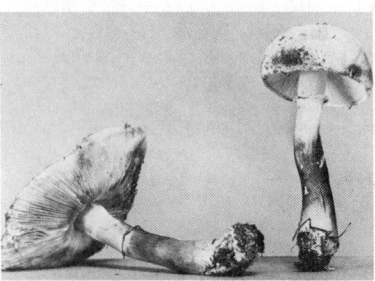

mushrooms
(def. 1)—about
2 to 3 in.
(5 to 7.5 cm.)
high

musk mel on (musk'mel'ən), kind of small, sweet melon with a hard rind and a smell like that of musk. The cantaloupe and honeydew melon are muskmelons. *n.*

musk ox, an arctic mammal having a shaggy coat and a strong, musky smell. It looks like a sheep in some ways and like an ox in others.

muskrat (def. 1) about 22 in. (56 cm.) long with tail

musk rat (musk'rat'), **1** a water rodent of North America somewhat like a rat but larger; water rat. **2** its valuable, dark-brown fur. *n., pl.* **musk rats** or **musk rat.**

musk y (mus'kē), of or like musk; like that of musk: *a musky odor. adj.*, **musk i er, musk i est.** —**musk'i ness,** *n.*

Mus lim or **Mus lem** (muz'ləm), Moslem. *n., adj.*

mus lin (muz'lən), **1** a thin, fine cotton cloth, used for dresses, curtains, etc. **2** a heavier cotton cloth, used for sheets, undergarments, etc. **3** made of muslin: *white muslin curtains.* **1,2** *n.*, **3** *adj.*

muss (mus), **1** put into disorder; rumple: *The child's new outfit was mussed.* **2** INFORMAL. untidy state; mess: *What a muss the room was!* **1** *v.*, **2** *n.*

mus sel (mus'əl), shellfish which resembles a clam. Sea mussels have dark-blue shells and can be eaten. The shells of freshwater mussels are used to make buttons. *n.*

Mus so li ni (mús'ə lē'nē *or* mü'sə lē'nē), **Benito,** 1883-1945, leader of the Italian Fascists and prime minister of Italy from 1922 to 1943. *n.*

Mus sul man (mus'əl mən), a Moslem. *n., pl.* **Mus sulmans.**

muss y (mus'ē), INFORMAL. untidy; messy; rumpled. *adj.*, **muss i er, muss i est.** —**muss'i ly,** *adv.* —**muss'i ness,** *n.*

must (must; *unstressed* məst), **1** be obliged to; be forced to: *You must eat to live.* **2** ought to; should: *I must go home soon. You really must read this story.* **3** be certain or likely to be, do, etc.: *You must be joking. I must seem very rude.* **4** something necessary; obligation: *This rule is a must.* **5** INFORMAL. demanding attention or doing; necessary: *a must item, must legislation.* **1-3** *v., past tense* **must;** **4** *n.*, **5** *adj.*

mus tache (mus'tash *or* mə stash'), **1** hair growing on a man's upper lip. **2** hairs or bristles growing near the mouth of an animal. *n.* Also, **moustache.**

mus tached (mus'tasht *or* mə stasht'), having a mustache. *adj.*

mus ta chio (mə stä'shō), mustache. *n., pl.* **mus tachios.**

mus ta chioed (mə stä'shōd), mustached. *adj.*

mus tang (mus'tang), a small, wild or half-wild horse of the North American plains. *n.*

mus tard (mus'tərd), **1** plant whose seeds have a sharp, hot taste. **2** a yellow powder or paste made from its seeds, used as seasoning. *n.*

mustard plaster, mixture of mustard and water, or of mustard, flour, and water, spread on cloth and applied to the body as medicine.

a hat	**i** it	**oi** oil	**ch** child	a in about
ā age	**ī** ice	**ou** out	**ng** long	e in taken
ä far	**o** hot	**u** cup	**sh** she	ə = { i in pencil
e let	**ō** open	**ù** put	**th** thin	o in lemon
ē equal	**ô** order	**ü** rule	**ŦH** then	u in circus
ėr term			**zh** measure	

mus ter (mus'tər), **1** gather together; assemble; collect. **2** assembly; collection. **3** summon: *muster up courage.* **4** a bringing together of troops or others for review or service: *There was a muster of all the guards.* **5** list of those assembled. **1,3** *v.*, **2,4,5** *n.*

muster out, to discharge.

pass muster, be inspected and approved; meet the required standards.

mus ti ness (mus'tē nis), musty condition or quality. *n.*

must n't (mus'nt), must not.

mus ty (mus'tē), **1** having a smell or taste suggesting mold or damp; moldy: *a musty room, musty crackers.* **2** stale; out-of-date: *musty laws about witches. adj.*, **mus ti er, mus ti est.** —**mus'ti ly,** *adv.*

mu ta ble (myü'tə bəl), **1** liable to change: *mutable customs.* **2** fickle: *a mutable person. adj.* —**mu'ta ble ness,** *n.* —**mu'ta bly,** *adv.*

mu tant (myüt'nt), a new variety of plant or animal resulting from mutation. *n.*

mu tate (myü'tāt), **1** to change. **2** undergo or produce mutation. *v.*, **mu tat ed, mu tat ing.**

mu ta tion (myü tā'shən), **1** a change; alteration. **2** a change within a gene or chromosome resulting in a new feature or character that appears suddenly in animals or plants and can be inherited. **3** such a new feature or character. **4** mutant. *n.* [*Mutation* is from Latin *mutationem,* which comes from *mutare,* meaning "to change."]

mute (myüt), **1** not making any sound; silent: *The little girl stood mute with astonishment.* **2** dumb; unable to speak. **3** person who cannot speak. **4** clip, pad, or other device put on a musical instrument to muffle the sound. **5** put such a device on; muffle the sound of with a mute: *He muted the strings of his violin.* **6** not pronounced. The *e* in *mute* is mute. **1,2,6** *adj.*, **5** *v.*, **mut ed, mut ing.** —**mute'ly,** *adv.* —**mute'ness,** *n.*

mu ti late (myü'tl āt), **1** cut, tear, or break off a limb or other important part of; injure seriously by cutting, tearing, or breaking off some part; maim: *Several passengers were mutilated in the train wreck.* **2** destroy or ruin some part of: *The book was badly mutilated by someone who had torn some pages and written on others. v.*, **mu ti lat ed, mu ti lat ing.** —**mu'ti la'tor,** *n.*

mu ti la tion (myü'tl ā'shən), a mutilating or a being mutilated. *n.*

mu ti neer (myüt'n ir'), person who takes part in a mutiny. *n.*

mu ti nous (myüt'n əs), rebellious: *a mutinous crew. adj.* —**mu'ti nous ly,** *adv.* —**mu'ti nous ness,** *n.*

mu ti ny (myüt'n ē), **1** open rebellion against lawful authority, especially by sailors or soldiers against their officers. **2** take part in a mutiny; rebel. **1** *n., pl.* **mu ti nies;** **2** *v.*, **mu ti nied, mu ti ny ing.**

mutt (mut), SLANG. dog, especially a mongrel. *n.*

mut ter (mut'ər), **1** speak or utter (words) low and indistinctly, with lips partly closed. **2** complain; grumble. **3** a muttering. **4** muttered words: *We heard a mutter of discontent.* **1,2** *v.*, **3,4** *n.* —**mut'ter er,** *n.*

mut ton (mut'n), meat from a sheep: *We had roast mutton for dinner. n.*

mu tu al (myü'chü əl), **1** done, said, felt, etc., by each toward the other; given and received: *mutual promises, mutual dislike. They had mutual affection for each other;*

each liked the others and was liked by them. **2** each to the other: *mutual enemies.* **3** belonging to each of several: *We are happy to have him as our mutual friend. adj.* —**mu′tu al ly,** *adv.*

muz zle (muz′əl), **1** the nose, mouth, and jaws of a four-footed animal. **2** a cover or cage of straps or wires to put over the head and mouth of an animal to keep it from biting or eating. **3** put such a muzzle on. **4** compel (a person) to keep silent about something: *Fear that they might betray friends muzzled them.* **5** the open front part of the barrel of a gun, pistol, etc. 1,2,5 *n.,* 3,4 *v.,* **muz zled, muz zling.** —**muz′zler,** *n.*

MX (em′eks′), an intercontinental ballistic missile equipped with multiple nuclear warheads. *n.* [*MX* comes from *missile* and *experimental.* It was formed from the first letter of *missile* and the second letter of *experimental.*]

my (mī), **1** of me; belonging to me: *My house is around the corner. I learned my lesson.* **2** INFORMAL. exclamation of surprise. 1 *pron.,* 2 *interj.*

my ce li um (mī sē′lē əm), the growing part of a fungus, consisting of interwoven fibers. *n., pl.* **my ce li a** (mī-sē′lē ə).

My ce nae (mī sē′nē), city in the southern part of ancient Greece. *n.*

my col o gy (mī kol′ə jē), branch of botany that deals with fungi. *n.*

my na (mī′nə), any of several Asian starlings that can imitate human speech. *n., pl.* **my nas.**

my nah (mī′nə), myna. *n.*

my o pi a (mī ō′pē ə), near-sightedness. *n.* [*Myopia* is from Greek *myōpia,* which comes from *myein,* meaning "to shut," and *ōps,* meaning "eye."]

my op ic (mī op′ik), near-sighted. *adj.* —**my op′i cal ly,** *adv.*

myr i ad (mir′ē əd), **1** ten thousand. **2** a very great number: *myriads of stars.* **3** countless. 1,2 *n.,* 1,3 *adj.*

myrrh (mėr), a fragrant, gummy substance with a bitter taste, used in medicines, perfumes, and incense. It is obtained from a shrub that grows in Arabia and eastern Africa. *n.*

myr tle (mėr′tl), **1** an evergreen shrub of southern Europe, with shiny leaves, fragrant white flowers, and black berries. **2** periwinkle. *n.*

my self (mī self′), **1** form of *me* or *I* used to make a statement stronger: *I myself will go.* **2** form used instead of *me* or *I* in cases like: *I can cook for myself. I hurt myself.* **3** my real or true self: *I am not myself today. pron.*

mys ter i ous (mi stir′ē əs), **1** full of mystery; hard to explain or understand; secret; hidden. **2** suggesting mystery: *a mysterious look. adj.* —**mys ter′i ous ly,** *adv.*

mys ter y (mis′tər ē), **1** something that is hidden or unknown; secret. **2** secrecy; obscurity. **3** something that is not explained or understood: *the mystery of the migration of birds.* **4** novel, story, etc., about a mysterious event or events which are not explained until the end, so as to keep the reader in suspense. **5** a religious rite, especially one to which only initiated persons are admitted. *n.., pl.* **mys ter ies.** [*Mystery* comes from Latin *mysterium,* and

can be traced back to Greek *mystēs,* meaning "an initiate." The word was called this because only initiates were admitted to "mysteries," or secret rites.]

mystery play, a medieval religious play based on the Bible.

mys tic (mis′tik), **1** mystical. **2** person who believes that truth or God can be known directly through faith, spiritual insight, intuition, etc. 1 *adj.,* 2 *n.*

mys ti cal (mis′tə kəl), **1** having some secret meaning; beyond human understanding; mysterious. **2** spiritually symbolic: *The lamb, the dove, and the wheel are mystical religious symbols.* **3** of or concerned with mystics or mysticism. **4** of or having to do with religious rites, especially those open only to the initiated. *adj.* —**mys′ti cal ly,** *adv.* —**mys′ti cal ness,** *n.*

mys ti cism (mis′tə siz′əm), **1** beliefs or mode of thought of mystics. **2** vague or fuzzy thinking. *n.*

mys ti fi ca tion (mis′tə fə kā′shən), **1** a mystifying or a being mystified; bewilderment; perplexity. **2** something that mystifies. *n.*

mys ti fy (mis′tə fī), **1** bewilder purposely; puzzle; perplex: *The magician's tricks mystified the audience.* **2** make mysterious. *v.,* **mys ti fied, mys ti fy ing.**

myth (mith), **1** legend or story, usually one that attempts to account for something in nature: *The myth of Proserpina is the ancient Roman explanation of summer and winter.* **2** any invented story. **3** an imaginary person or thing: *Her trip to Europe was a myth invented to impress others. n.* [*Myth* comes from Greek *mythos,* meaning "word, story."]

myth., mythology.

myth ic (mith′ik), mythical. *adj.*

mythical (def. 1)—The centaur is a **mythical** beast.

myth i cal (mith′ə kəl), **1** of a myth; like a myth; in myths: *a mythical interpretation of nature, mythical monsters, mythical places.* **2** not real; made-up; imaginary: *His great wealth is merely mythical. adj.* —**myth′i cal ly,** *adv.*

myth o log i cal (mith′ə loj′ə kəl), of mythology: *The phoenix is a mythological bird. adj.* —**myth′o log′i cal ly,** *adv.*

my thol o gy (mi thol′ə jē), **1** a group of myths relating to a particular country or person: *Greek mythology.* **2** study of myths. *n., pl.* **my thol o gies.**

a hat	i it	oi oil	ch child	a in about
ā age	ī ice	ou out	ng long	e in taken
ä far	o hot	u cup	sh she	ə = i in pencil
e let	ō open	ú put	th thin	o in lemon
ē equal	ô order	ü rule	ŦH then	u in circus
ėr term			zh measure	

N or **n** (en), the 14th letter of the English alphabet. *n., pl.* **N's** or **n's.**

n, (in algebra) an indefinite number.

N, symbol for nitrogen.

N or **N., 1** North. **2** Northern.

n., 1 north. **2** northern. **3** noun.

Na, symbol for sodium.

N.A., North America.

NAACP or **N.A.A.C.P.,** National Association for the Advancement of Colored People.

nab (nab), INFORMAL. **1** catch or seize suddenly; grab. **2** arrest: *The police soon nabbed the thief. v.,* **nabbed, nab bing. —nab′ber,** *n.*

na bob (nā′bob), a very rich man. *n.*

na cho (nä′chō), a baked tortilla chip with a topping of cheese, beans, and hot peppers. *n., pl.* **na chos.**

na cre (nā′kər), mother-of-pearl. *n.*

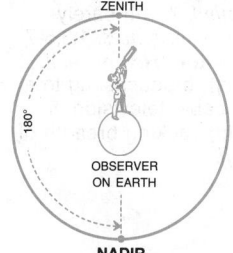

nadir (def. 1)
The nadir, the center of the earth, and the zenith are in a straight line.

na dir (nā′dər), **1** the point in the heavens directly beneath the place where one stands; the point opposite the zenith. **2** the lowest point. *n.* [*Nadir* came into English about 600 years ago from French *nadir,* and can be traced back to Arabic *naẕīr,* meaning "opposite."]

nag¹ (nag), find fault with (a person) all the time; irritate or annoy by peevish complaints; scold: *I will clean up in a minute; please don't nag me. When I am upset I nag at everybody. v.,* **nagged, nag ging. —nag′ger,** *n.*

nag² (nag), **1** INFORMAL. a horse. **2** an old or inferior horse. *n.*

Na ga sa ki (nä′gə sä′kē), seaport in SW Japan, target of the second atomic bomb to be used in war, on August 9, 1945. *n.*

Na hua tl (nä′wä təl), language of the Aztecs, Toltecs, and other American Indians of central Mexico and parts of Central America. *n.*

Na hum (nā′əm), **1** (in the Bible) a Hebrew prophet. **2** book of the Old Testament containing his prophecies. *n.*

nai ad (nā′ad). Also, **Naiad.** (in Greek and Roman myths) a nymph guarding a stream or spring. *n., pl.* **nai ads, nai a des** (nā′ə dēz′).

nail (nāl), **1** a slender piece of metal having a point at one end and usually a flat or rounded head at the other end. Nails are hammered into or through pieces of wood to hold them together. **2** fasten with a nail or nails. **3** hold or keep fixed: *They nailed me to my promise.* **4** INFORMAL. catch; seize. **5** the thin, hard, horny layer on the upper side of the end of a finger or toe. **1,5** *n.,* **2-4** *v.*

hit the nail on the head, guess or understand correctly; say or do something just right.

nail down, find out definitely; make certain; settle finally: *The buyer nailed down the terms of the sale.*

nail set (nāl′set′), tool for driving nails beneath the surface. *n.*

Nai ro bi (nī rō′bē), capital of Kenya, in the SW part. *n.*

na ïve or **na ive** (nä ēv′), simple in nature; like a child; artless; not sophisticated. *adj.* [*Naïve* was borrowed from French *naïve,* and can be traced back to Latin *nasci,* meaning "to be born."] **—na ive′ly, na ive′ly,** *adv.*

na i ve te (nä ē′və tā′), naïveté. *n.*

na ï ve té (nä ē′və tā′), **1** quality of being naïve; unspoiled freshness; artlessness. **2** a naïve action, remark, etc. *n., pl.* **na i ve tés.**

na ked (nā′kid), **1** with no clothes on; nude; bare. **2** not covered; stripped: *naked fields.* **3** not protected; exposed: *a naked sword.* **4** without addition of anything else; plain: *the naked truth. adj.* **—na′ked ly,** *adv.* **—na′ked ness,** *n.*

naked eye, the eye unaided by any glass, telescope, or microscope.

nam by-pam by (nam′bē pam′bē), **1** weakly simple, silly, or sentimental; lacking strength or firmness. **2** a namby-pamby person. **1** *adj.,* **2** *n., pl.* **nam by-pam bies.**

name (nām), **1** word or words by which a person, animal, place, or thing is spoken of or to: *Our dog's name is Shep. "The Corn State" is a name for Iowa.* **2** give a name to: *name a newborn baby.* **3** call by name; mention by name: *Three persons were named in the report.* **4** give the right name for: *Can you name these flowers?* **5** reputation; fame: *get a bad name, make a name for oneself.* **6** mention; speak of; state: *name several reasons.* **7** specify or fix; settle on: *name a price. The class named the day for its party.* **8** choose for some duty or office; nominate; appoint: *He was named for class president.* **9** well-known: *Is this coffee a name brand?* **1,5** *n.,* **2-4,6-8** *v.,* **named, naming; 9** *adj.* **—nam′er,** *n.*

call names, call bad names; swear at; curse.

in name only, supposed to be, but not really so: *a ruler in name only.*

in the name of, 1 for the sake of. **2** acting for: *I ordered the supplies in the name of my supervisor.*

know only by name, know only by hearing about.

to one's name, belonging to one: *I haven't a penny to my name.*

name less (nām′lis), **1** having no name: *a nameless stranger.* **2** not marked with a name: *a nameless grave.* **3** that cannot be named or described: *a strange, nameless longing.* **4** not fit to be mentioned: *nameless crimes.* **5** not named; unknown; obscure: *a book by a nameless writer. adj.* **—name′less ly,** *adv.* **—name′less ness,** *n.*

name ly (nām′lē), that is to say: *The railroad connects two cities—namely, New York and Chicago. adv.*

name sake (nām′sāk′), one having the same name as another, especially one named after another: *My sister, Florence, is the namesake of Florence Nightingale. n.*

Na mib i a (nä mib′ē ə), territory in SW Africa, under the supervision of South Africa. It was formerly called **South-West Africa.** See **South Africa** for map. *n.*

Nan jing (nän′jing′), official spelling of **Nanking.** *n.*

nan keen (nan kēn′), a firm yellow or buff cloth. *n.*

Nan king (nan′king′), city in E China, on the Yangtze

River. It was the capital of China from 1928 to 1937 and from 1946 to 1949. Officially, **Nanjing**. *n.*

nan ny goat (nan′ē), a female goat.

Nan tuck et (nan tuk′it), island south of Cape Cod. It is part of Massachusetts. *n.*

Na o mi (nā ō′mē), (in the Bible) the mother-in-law of Ruth. *n.*

nap[1] (nap), **1** a short sleep: *The baby takes a nap after lunch.* **2** take a short sleep: *Grandfather naps in his armchair.* **3** be off guard; be unprepared: *The test caught me napping.* 1 *n.,* 2,3 *v.,* **napped, nap ping.**

nap[2] (nap), the soft, short, woolly threads or hairs on the surface of cloth: *the nap on velvet. n.* —**nap′less,** *adj.*

na palm (nā′päm′ *or* nā′pälm′), a thickened or jellied gasoline, used for making incendiary bombs and in flamethrowers. *n.*

nape (nāp *or* nap), the back of the neck. *n.*

naph tha (naf′thə *or* nap′thə), a flammable liquid made from petroleum, coal tar, etc., used as fuel and to take spots from clothing. *n., pl.* **naph thas.**

nap kin (nap′kin), **1** piece of cloth or paper used at meals for protecting the clothing or for wiping the lips or fingers. **2** any similar piece, such as a baby's diaper or a small towel. *n.* [*Napkin* comes from Middle English *napekyn,* and can be traced back to Latin *mappa,* meaning "cloth, napkin."]

Na ples (nā′pəlz), seaport on the SW coast of Italy, famous for its beautiful bay. *n.* [*Naples* was borrowed from French *Naples,* and can be traced back to the Greek phrase *nea polis,* meaning "new city." It was called this because it was founded on the site of another ancient city.]

Na po le on I (nə pō′lē ən), 1769-1821, Napoleon Bonaparte, French general who made himself emperor of France in 1804. He conquered a large part of Europe, but was defeated at Waterloo in 1815 and exiled to the island of St. Helena.

Napoleon III, 1808-1873, Louis Napoleon, president of France from 1848 to 1852 and emperor of France from 1852 to 1870. He was the nephew of Napoleon I.

Na po le on ic (nə pō′lē on′ik), of or resembling Napoleon I. *adj.*

nap py (nap′ē), having a nap; shaggy. *adj.,* **nap pi er, nap pi est.** —**nap′pi ness,** *n.*

nar cis sus (när sis′əs), a spring plant with yellow or white flowers and long, slender leaves. It grows from a bulb. Jonquils and daffodils are narcissuses. *n., pl.* **nar cis sus es, nar cis sus, nar cis si** (när sis′ī).

narcissus

Nar cis sus (när sis′əs), (in Greek myths) a beautiful youth who fell in love with his reflection in a spring. He pined away and was changed into the flower narcissus. *n.*

nar cot ic (när kot′ik), **1** any drug that produces drowsiness, sleep, dullness, or an insensible condition, and lessens pain by dulling the nerves. Opium is a powerful narcotic. **2** having the properties and effects of a narcot-

ic. **3** of narcotics or their use. 1 *n.,* 2,3 *adj.* [*Narcotic* came into English about 600 years ago from French *narcotique,* and can be traced back to Greek *narkē,* meaning "numbness."]

Nar ra gan sett Bay (nar′ə gan′sit), bay of the Atlantic, in E Rhode Island.

nar rate (nar′āt *or* na rāt′), tell (a story, etc.); relate. *v.,* **nar rat ed, nar rat ing.** —**nar′rat a ble,** *adj.*

nar ra tion (na rā′shən), **1** act of telling. **2** the form of composition that relates an event or a story. Novels, short stories, histories, and biographies are forms of narration. **3** story or account. *n.*

nar ra tive (nar′ə tiv), **1** story; tale: *Her trip through the Near East made an interesting narrative.* **2** narration; story-telling. **3** that narrates: *"Hiawatha" is a narrative poem.* 1,2 *n.,* 3 *adj.* —**nar′ra tive ly,** *adv.*

nar ra tor (nar′ā tər *or* na rā′tər), person who tells a story. *n.*

nar row (nar′ō), **1** not wide; having little width; less wide than usual for its kind: *a narrow path.* **2 narrows,** *pl.* the narrow part of a river, strait, sound, valley, pass, etc. **3** limited or small in extent, space, amount, range, scope, opportunity, etc.: *a narrow circle of friends.* **4** make or become narrower; decrease in breadth, extent, etc.; limit: *The doctor narrowed his interest to diseases of the throat. The road narrows above the bend.* **5** with little margin; close: *a narrow escape.* **6** lacking breadth of view or sympathy; prejudiced: *a narrow mind.* **7** with barely enough to live on: *live in narrow circumstances.* 1,3,5-7 *adj.,* 2 *n.,* 4 *v.* —**nar′row ly,** *adv.* —**nar′row ness,** *n.*

nar row cast ing (nar′ō kas′ting), broadcasting to a limited, specific audience, as by cable television. *n.*

nar row-mind ed (nar′ō mīn′did), lacking breadth of view or sympathy; prejudiced. *adj.*

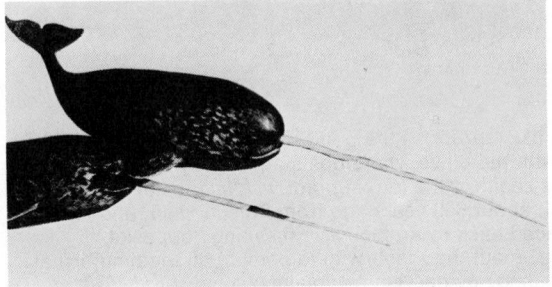

narwhal—head and body up to 16 ft. (5 m.) long
The tusk may be up to 9 ft. (2.7 m.) long.

nar whal (när′hwəl), a large, spotted whale of the arctic seas. The male has a long, twisted tusk extending forward from a tooth in the upper jaw. *n.* [*Narwhal* comes from Danish *narhval,* and can be traced back to Icelandic *nār,* meaning "corpse," and *hvalr,* meaning "whale." It was called this because of its color.]

nar y (ner′ē *or* nar′ē), DIALECT. not: *nary a one. adj.*

NAS A (nas′ə), National Aeronautics and Space Administration (an agency of the United States government set up to direct and aid civilian research and development in aeronautics and aerospace technology). *n.*

na sal (nā′zəl), **1** of, in, or from the nose: *a nasal discharge.* **2** spoken through the nose. *M, n,* and *ng* represent nasal sounds. **3** a nasal sound. 1,2 *adj.,* 3 *n.* —**na′sal ly,** *adv.*

na sal i ty (nā zal′ə tē), nasal quality. *n.*

na sal ize (nā′zə līz), say or speak with a nasal sound. *v.,* **na sal ized, na sal iz ing.** —**na′sal i za′tion,** *n.*

nas cent (nas′nt *or* nā′snt), in the process of coming into existence; just beginning to exist, grow, or develop. *adj.*

Nash ville (nash′vil), capital of Tennessee, in the central part. *n.*

Nas sau (nas′ô), capital of the Bahama Islands. *n.*

Nas ser (nä′sər), **Gamal Abdel,** 1918-1970, chief executive of the Egyptian republic from 1954 to 1970, and president of the United Arab Republic from 1958 to 1970. *n.*

nas ti ly (nas′tl ē), in a nasty manner. *adv.*

nas ti ness (nas′tē nis), **1** disgusting dirtiness; filth. **2** moral filth; vileness. **3** extreme unpleasantness. *n.*

na stur tium (nə stėr′shəm), a garden plant with yellow, orange, or red flowers, and sharp-tasting seeds and leaves. *n.*

nas ty (nas′tē), **1** mean; cruel; hateful: *Several nasty people threw rocks at the birds on the lake.* **2** very unpleasant: *The nasty weather ruined our plans for a picnic.* **3** dirty; filthy: *Dead fish and garbage littered the surface of the nasty creek.* **4** rather serious; bad: *a nasty cut on the hand.* *adj.*, **nas ti er, nas ti est.**

na tal (nā′tl), of one's birth: *Her natal day is September 3.* *adj.* [*Natal* comes from Latin *natalis,* and can be traced back to *nasci,* meaning "to be born." See **Word Family.**]

WORD FAMILY

natal

Below are words related to *natal*. They can all be traced back to the Latin word *nasci* (näs′kē), meaning "to be born."

good-natured	nationality	Noel
innate	native	prenatal
international	natural	puny
naïve	naturalize	renaissance
nation	nature	supernatural

Na tal (nə tal′), province of the Republic of South Africa, on the E coast. *n.*

na tion (nā′shən), **1** people occupying the same country, united under the same government, and usually speaking the same language: *The President appealed to the nation for support of his policies.* **2** a sovereign state; country: *the nations of the West.* **3** a people, race, or tribe; those having the same descent, language, and history: *the Armenian nation.* **4** a North American Indian tribe or federation: *the Sioux nation.* *n.*

na tion al (nash′ə nəl), **1** of a nation; belonging to a whole nation: *national laws, a national disaster.* **2** citizen of a nation: *Many nationals of Canada visit our country.* **1** *adj.,* **2** *n.*

National Guard, the reserve militia of each state of the United States, supported in part by the federal government. The National Guard may be called upon to serve either the state or the federal government in time of emergency.

na tion al ism (nash′ə nə liz′əm), **1** patriotic feelings or efforts. **2** desire and plans for national independence. *n.*

na tion al ist (nash′ə nə list), **1** person who believes in or upholds nationalism. **2** nationalistic. **1** *n.,* **2** *adj.*

Nationalist China, Taiwan; China (def. 2).

na tion al is tic (nash′ə nə lis′tik), of nationalism or nationalists. *adj.* —**na′tion al is′ti cal ly,** *adv.*

na tion al i ty (nash′ə nal′ə tē), **1** nation (def. 1). **2** condition of belonging to a nation. Citizens of the same country have the same nationality. *n., pl.* **na tion al i ties.**

na tion al i za tion (nash′ə nə lə zā′shən), a nationalizing or a being nationalized. *n.*

na tion al ize (nash′ə nə līz), **1** make national. **2** bring (land, industries, railroads, etc.) under the control or ownership of a nation. **3** make into a nation. *v.,* **na tion al ized, na tion al iz ing.** —**na′tion al i za′tion,** *n.*

na tion al ly (nash′ə nə lē), **1** in a national manner; as a nation. **2** throughout the nation: *The program was broadcast nationally.* *adv.*

national park, land kept by the national government for people to enjoy because of its beautiful scenery, historical interest, etc.

National Socialist Party, a fascist political party which ruled Germany from 1933 to 1945, under the leadership of Adolf Hitler; the Nazi party.

na tion wide (nā′shən wīd′), extending throughout the nation: *a nationwide election. adj.*

na tive (nā′tiv), **1** person born in a certain place or country. The natives are the people living in a place, not visitors or foreigners. **2** born in a certain place or country: *People born in New York are native sons and daughters of New York.* **3** belonging to one because of one's birth: *The United States is my native land.* **4** belonging to one because of one's nation or ancestors: *French is his native language.* **5** born in a person; natural: *native ability.* **6** one of the people originally living in a place or country and found there by explorers or settlers. **7** of these people: *native customs.* **8** animal or plant that originated in a place. **9** originating, grown, or produced in a certain place: *Tobacco is native to America.* **10** found pure in nature: *native copper.* **1,6,8** *n.,* **2-5,7,9,10** *adj.* [*Native* came into English about 600 years ago from French *natif,* and can be traced back to Latin *nasci,* meaning "to be born."] —**na′tive ly,** *adv.* —**na′tive ness,** *n.*

Native American, one of the people who have lived in America from long before the time of the first European settlers; American Indian.

na tive-born (nā′tiv bôrn′), born in the place or country indicated: *a native-born American. adj.*

na tiv i ty (nə tiv′ə tē), **1** birth. **2** **the Nativity, a** birth of Christ. **b** Christmas. *n., pl.* **na tiv i ties.**

natl., national.

NA TO (nā′tō), North Atlantic Treaty Organization (an alliance of sixteen non-Communist European and North American nations providing for joint military cooperation). *n.*

nat ti ly (nat′l ē), in a natty manner; with neatness: *nattily dressed. adv.*

nat ti ness (nat′ē nis), natty condition or quality. *n.*

nat ty (nat′ē), trim and tidy; neatly smart in dress or appearance: *a natty outfit. adj.,* **nat ti er, nat ti est.**

nat ur al (nach′ər əl), **1** produced by nature; coming or occurring in the ordinary course of events: *natural feelings and actions, a natural death.* **2** not artificial; not made by human beings: *Coal and oil are natural products.* **3** belonging to the nature one is born with; instinctive; inborn: *natural ability. It is natural for ducks to swim.* **4** in accordance with the nature of things or the circumstances of the case: *a natural conclusion.* **5** instinctively felt to be right and fair: *natural law, natural rights.* **6** like nature; true to nature: *The picture looked natural.* **7** free from affectation or restraint: *a natural manner.* **8** (in mu-

a hat	i it	oi oil	ch child	a in about
ā age	ī ice	ou out	ng long	e in taken
ä far	o hot	u cup	sh she	ə = { i in pencil
e let	ō open	u̇ put	th thin	o in lemon
ē equal	ô order	ü rule	ᴛʜ then	u in circus
ėr term			zh measure	

sic) neither sharp nor flat; not changed in pitch by a sharp or a flat: *C natural.* **9** a natural tone or note. **10** sign (♮) used to cancel the effect of a preceding sharp or flat. **11** INFORMAL. person who is especially suited for something because of inborn talent or ability: *He is a natural on the saxophone.* 1-8 *adj.*, 9-11 *n.* —**nat′ur al ness,** *n.*

natural food, food that is not processed, and to which no preservatives or artificial colorings or flavorings have been added.

natural gas, a combustible gas formed naturally in the earth, consisting primarily of methane. It is used as a fuel.

natural history, the study of animals, plants, minerals, and other things in nature.

nat ur al ist (nach′ər ə list), person who makes a study of animals and plants. *n.*

nat ur al is tic (nach′ər ə lis′tik), of, like, or in accordance with nature. *adj.* —**nat′ur al is′ti cal ly,** *adv.*

nat ur al i za tion (nach′ər ə lə zā′shən), a naturalizing or a being naturalized. *n.*

nat ur al ize (nach′ər ə līz), **1** admit (a foreigner) to citizenship. After living in the United States for a certain number of years, an immigrant can be naturalized after passing a test. **2** adopt (a foreign word or custom): *"Chauffeur" is a French word that has been naturalized in English.* **3** introduce and make at home in another country: *The English oak has become naturalized in parts of Massachusetts.* **4** become like a native. *v.,* **nat ur al ized, nat ur al iz ing.** —**nat′ur al iz′er,** *n.*

nat ur al ly (nach′ər ə lē), **1** in a natural way: *Speak naturally; don't try to imitate someone else.* **2** by nature: *a naturally quiet child.* **3** as might be expected; of course: *She offered me some candy; naturally, I took it. adv.*

natural number, a positive integer. The natural numbers are 1,2,3,4, etc.

natural resources, materials supplied by nature. Minerals, forests, and water power are natural resources.

natural science, any science dealing with the facts of nature or the physical world. Biology, geology, physics, and chemistry are natural sciences.

natural selection, process in nature by which animals and plants best adapted to their environment tend to survive.

na ture (nā′chər), **1** the world; all things except those made by human beings: *the wonders of nature.* **2** Also, **Nature.** all the forces at work throughout the world: *the laws of nature.* **3** the instincts or inborn tendencies that direct behavior: *It is the nature of birds to fly.* **4** life without artificial things: *Wild animals live in a state of nature.* **5** what a thing really is; quality; character: *It is against her nature to be petty.* **6** sort; kind: *books of a scientific nature. n.*

Nau ga hyde (nô′gə hīd), a trademark for a fabric for covering furniture. It is made from vinyl, and resembles leather. *n.*

naught (nôt), **1** nothing. **2** zero; 0. *n.* Also, **nought.** [*Naught* is from Old English *nāwiht,* which comes from *nā,* meaning "no," and *wiht,* meaning "thing."]

naugh ti ly (nô′tə lē), in a naughty manner. *adv.*

naugh ti ness (nô′tē nis), bad behavior; disobedience; mischief. *n.*

naugh ty (nô′tē), **1** bad; not obedient: *a naughty child.* **2** somewhat improper: *a naughty joke. adj.,* **naugh ti er, naugh ti est.**

Na u ru (nä ü′rü), small island country in the S Pacific, northeast of the Solomon Islands. It is a member of the Commonwealth of Nations. *n.*

nau se a (nô′zē ə *or* nô′shə), **1** the feeling that one has when about to vomit. **2** extreme disgust; loathing. *n.*

[*Nausea* comes from Latin *nausea,* which also meant "seasickness," and can be traced back to Greek *naus,* meaning "a ship."]

nau se ate (nô′zē āt *or* nô′shē āt), **1** feel nausea or cause nausea in; make or become sick. **2** cause to feel loathing. *v.,* **nau se at ed, nau se at ing.** —**nau′se at′ing ly,** *adv.*

nau seous (nô′shəs *or* nô′zē əs), **1** causing nausea; sickening. **2** disgusting; loathsome: *The garbage dump was nauseous.* **3** feeling nausea; nauseated. *adj.* —**nau′seous ly,** *adv.* —**nau′seous ness,** *n.*

nau ti cal (nô′tə kəl), of ships, sailors, or navigation. *adj.* [*Nautical* is from Latin *nauticus,* which came from Greek *nautikos,* and can be traced back to *naus,* meaning "a ship." See **Word Family.**] —**nau′ti cal ly,** *adv.*

WORD FAMILY

nautical

Below are words related to *nautical.* They can all be traced back to the Greek word *naus* (nous), meaning "a ship."

aeronautical	nausea	noisy
astronaut	nautilus	
cosmonaut	noise	

nautical mile, unit of distance equal to 6076.11549 feet (1.852 kilometers); geographical mile.

nau ti lus (nô′tl əs), either of two sea animals with a shell. The **pearly nautilus** or **chambered nautilus** has a spiral shell divided into many compartments which have a pearly lining. The **paper nautilus** resembles the octopus and has a thin shell. *n., pl.* **nau ti lus es, nau ti li** (nô′tl ī).

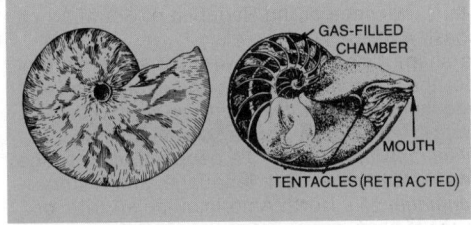

pearly nautilus or **chambered nautilus**
shell to 6 in. (15 cm.) in diameter

nav., 1 naval. **2** navigation.

Nav a ho (nav′ə hō), Navajo. *n., pl.* **Nav a hos** or **Nav a hoes.**

Nav a jo (nav′ə hō), member of a tribe of American Indians living mainly in New Mexico, Arizona, and Utah. *n., pl.* **Nav a jos** or **Nav a joes.**

na val (nā′vəl), **1** of or for warships or the navy: *a naval officer, naval supplies.* **2** having a navy: *a naval power. adj.* —**na′val ly,** *adv.*

Na varre (nə vär′), former kingdom including parts of SW France and N Spain. *n.*

na vel (nā′vəl), the mark or scar in the middle of the surface of the abdomen, where the umbilical cord was attached before birth. *n.*

navel orange, a seedless orange with a small growth at one end shaped somewhat like a navel.

nav i ga bil i ty (nav′ə gə bil′ə tē), condition of being navigable. *n.*

nav i ga ble (nav′ə gə bəl), **1** able to be traveled on by ships: *The Mississippi River is deep enough to be navigable.* **2** able to be steered: *a navigable balloon.* adj. —**nav′i ga ble ness,** n. —**nav′i ga bly,** adv.

nav i gate (nav′ə gāt), **1** sail, manage, or steer (a ship, aircraft, etc.). **2** sail on or over (a sea or river). **3** sail the seas. **4** move, walk, or swim about: *I can barely navigate today.* v., **nav i gat ed, nav i gat ing.** [*Navigate* can be traced back to Latin *navis,* meaning "a ship," and *agere,* meaning "to drive."]

nav i ga tion (nav′ə gā′shən), **1** act or process of navigating. **2** art or science of finding a ship's or an aircraft's position and course. n.

nav i ga tor (nav′ə gā′tər), **1** person who sails the seas. **2** person who has charge of the navigating of a ship or aircraft or who is skilled in navigating. **3** explorer of the seas. n.

na vy (nā′vē), **1** Often, **Navy.** the branch of a nation's armed forces which includes its ships of war, the officers and personnel who run them, and the department that manages them. **2** OLD USE. fleet of ships. **3** a dark blue; navy blue. n., pl. **na vies.**

navy bean, a small, common, white bean, dried for use.

navy blue, a dark blue.

nay (nā), **1** OLD USE. no. **2** not only that, but also: *We are willing, nay, eager to go.* **3** no; a denial or refusal. **4** a negative vote or voter. 1,2 adv., 3,4 n. [*Nay* came into English about 800 years ago, and can be traced back to Icelandic *ne,* meaning "not," and *ei,* meaning "ever."]

Naz a rene (naz′ə rēn′ or naz′ə rēn′), **1** person born or living in Nazareth. **2 the Nazarene,** Jesus. n.

Naz ar eth (naz′ər əth), town in N Israel. It was the childhood home of Jesus. See **Galilee** for map. n.

Naz a rite (naz′ə rīt′), (among the ancient Hebrews) a Jew who had taken certain strict religious vows. n.

Na zi (nä′tsē or nat′sē), **1** member or supporter of the National Socialist Party, a fascist political party in Germany, led by Adolf Hitler. **2** of the Nazis. 1 n., pl. **Na zis;** 2 adj.

Na zi ism (nä′tsē iz′əm or nat′sē iz′əm), Nazism. n.

Na zism (nä′tsiz′əm or nat′siz′əm), the doctrines and practices of the Nazis, including totalitarian government, state control of industry, anti-Semitism, and opposition to communism. n.

Nb, symbol for niobium.

N.B., New Brunswick.

N.B. or **n.b.,** note well; observe carefully.

NBC, National Broadcasting Company.

NC, North Carolina (used with postal Zip Code).

N.C., North Carolina.

Nd, symbol for neodymium.

ND, North Dakota (used with postal Zip Code).

N. Dak. or **N.D.,** North Dakota.

N' dja me na (nə jə mē′nə), capital of Chad, in the S part. n.

Ne, symbol for neon.

NE, Nebraska (used with postal Zip Code).

NE or **N.E., 1** northeast. **2** northeastern.

Ne an der thal (nē an′dər täl or nē an′dər thôl), belonging to a group of prehistoric people who lived in caves in Europe, North Africa, and parts of Asia in the early Stone Age. The **Neanderthal man** had a large, heavy skull and low forehead, a broad, flat nose, and a heavy lower jaw. adj.

Ne a pol i tan (nē′ə pol′ə tən), **1** of Naples. **2** person born or living in Naples. 1 adj., 2 n.

neap tide (nēp), tide that occurs when the difference in height between high and low tide is least; the lowest level of high tide. Neap tide comes twice a month.

near (nir), **1** to or at a short distance; not far; close: *They searched far and near. The holiday season is drawing near.* **2** close by; not distant; less distant: *The post office is quite near.* **3** close to in space, time, condition, etc.: *Our house is near the river.* **4** come or draw near to; approach: *The ship neared the land.* **5** close in feeling; intimate; familiar: *a near friend.* **6** closely related: *a near relative.* **7** all but; almost: *The war lasted near a year.* **8** short; direct: *Go by the nearest route.* **9** by a close margin: *a near escape.* 1,7 adv., 2,5,6,8,9 adj., 3 prep., 4 v. —**near′ness,** n.

come near doing, almost do: *I came near forgetting my glasses.*

near at hand, 1 within easy reach. **2** not far in the future.

near by (nir′bī′), near; close at hand: *a nearby house* (adj.). *They went nearby to visit* (adv.). adj., adv.

Near East, the countries of SW Asia, sometimes including the Balkan States and Egypt. —**Near Eastern.**

near ly (nir′lē), **1** almost: *I nearly missed the train.* **2** closely: *It will cost too much, as nearly as I can figure.* adv.

near sight ed (nir′sī′tid), not able to see far; seeing distinctly at a short distance only. Nearsighted people usually wear glasses. adj. —**near′sight′ed ly,** adv. —**near′sight′ed ness,** n.

neat (nēt), **1** clean and in order: *a neat desk, a neat room, a neat suit.* **2** able and willing to keep things in order: *a neat child.* **3** well-formed; in proportion: *a neat design.* **4** skillful; clever: *a neat trick.* **5** SLANG. wonderful; fine: *It was a neat party.* **6** without anything mixed in it: *He drinks his brandy neat.* adj. [*Neat* came into English about 450 years ago from French *net,* and can be traced back to Latin *nitere,* meaning "to shine."] —**neat′ly,** adv. —**neat′ness,** n.

neath or **'neath** (nēth), OLD USE. beneath. prep.

Ne bo (nē′bō), **Mount,** (in the Bible) the mountain from which Moses looked down upon Canaan, the Promised Land. n.

Nebr. or **Neb.,** Nebraska.

Ne bras ka (nə bras′kə), one of the midwestern states of the United States. *Abbreviation:* Nebr., Neb., or NE *Capital:* Lincoln. n. —**Ne bras′kan,** adj., n.

Neb u chad nez zar (neb′yə kəd nez′ər), died 562 B.C., king of Babylon from 605 to 562 B.C. He twice captured Jerusalem and destroyed it in 586 B.C. n.

Neanderthal man

neb u la (neb′yə lə), a cloudlike cluster of stars or a mass of dust particles and gases which occurs in interstellar space. A nebula may be either dark or illuminated by surrounding stars. *n., pl.* **neb u lae** (neb′yə lē′), **neb u las.**

neb u lar (neb′yə lər), of a nebula or nebulae. *adj.*

neb u lous (neb′yə ləs), **1** hazy; vague; indistinct; confused. **2** cloudlike. **3** of or like a nebula or nebulae. *adj.*

nec es sar i ly (nes′ə ser′ə lē), **1** because of necessity: *Leaves are not necessarily green.* **2** as a necessary result: *War necessarily causes misery and waste. adv.*

nec es sar y (nes′ə ser′ē), **1** needed; having to be done: *a necessary repair.* **2** unavoidable: *Death is a necessary end.* **3** thing impossible to do without: *Food, clothing, and shelter are necessaries of life.* 1,2 *adj.,* 3 *n., pl.* **nec es sar ies.** —**nec′es sar′i ness,** *n.*

ne ces si tate (nə ses′ə tāt), **1** make necessary: *Her broken leg necessitated an operation.* **2** compel; force. *v.,* **ne ces si tat ed, ne ces si tat ing.** —**ne ces′si ta′tion,** *n.*

ne ces si ty (nə ses′ə tē), **1** fact of being necessary; extreme need: *the necessity of eating.* **2** that which cannot be done without; a necessary thing: *Water is a necessity.* **3** that which forces one to act in a certain way: *Necessity often drives people to do disagreeable things.* **4** need; poverty: *a family in great necessity. n., pl.* **ne ces si ties.**

neck (nek), **1** the part of the body that connects the head with the shoulders. **2** the part of a garment that fits the neck: *the neck of a shirt.* **3** any narrow part like a neck: *a neck of land. n.* —**neck′like′,** *adj.*

neck and neck, 1 abreast. **2** running equal or even in a race or contest.

risk one's neck, put oneself in a dangerous position.

neckerchief

neck er chief (nek′ər chif), cloth worn around the neck. *n.*

neck lace (nek′lis), string of jewels, gold, silver, beads, etc., worn around the neck as an ornament. *n.*

neck line (nek′līn′), the line around the neck where a garment ends. *n.*

neck piece (nek′pēs′), a fur scarf. *n.*

neck tie (nek′tī′), a narrow length of cloth worn around the neck, under the collar of a shirt, and tied in front. *n.*

neck wear (nek′wer′ *or* nek′war′), collars, ties, and other articles that are worn around the neck. *n.*

nec ro man cy (nek′rə man′sē), **1** a foretelling of the future by communicating with the dead. **2** magic; sorcery. *n.*

nec tar (nek′tər), **1** (in Greek myths) the drink of the gods. **2** any delicious drink. **3** a sweet liquid found in many flowers. Bees gather nectar and make it into honey. *n.* —**nec′tar like′,** *adj.*

nec ta rine (nek′tə rēn′), kind of peach having no down on its skin. *n.*

nee or **née** (nā), born. *Nee* is placed after the name of a married woman to show her maiden name: *Pam Smith, nee Adams. adj.*

need (nēd), **1** be in want of; be unable to do without; lack: *I need a new hat. Plants need water.* **2** thing wanted

or lacking; that for which a want is felt: *In the jungle their need was fresh water.* **3** lack of a useful or desired thing; want: *Your handwriting shows a need of practice.* **4** situation or time of difficulty: *When I lacked money, my uncle was a friend in need.* **5** lack of money; extreme poverty: *This family's need was so great the children did not have shoes.* **6** must; should; have to; ought to: *You need not go. Need she go?* **7** something that has to be; necessity: *There is no need to hurry.* 1,6 *v.,* 2-5,7 *n.*

have need to, must; should; have to; ought to: *I have need to go to town.*

if need be, if it has to be.

need ful (nēd′fəl), needed; necessary: *a needful change. adj.* —**need′ful ly,** *adv.* —**need′ful ness,** *n.*

need i ness (nēd′ē nis), condition of being needy; poverty; want. *n.*

nee dle (nē′dl), **1** a very slender tool, pointed at one end and with a hole or eye to pass a thread through, used in sewing. **2** a slender rod used in knitting. **3** rod with a hook at one end used in crocheting, etc. **4** a thin steel pointer on a compass or on electrical machinery. **5** a very slender steel tube with a sharp point at one end. It is used at the end of a hypodermic syringe for injecting a liquid beneath the skin, or for withdrawing blood or other bodily fluid. **6** the small, pointed piece of metal, sapphire, or diamond in a phonograph which picks up and transmits the vibrations from the record. **7** the thin, pointed leaf of a fir tree or pine tree. **8** any of various small objects resembling a needle in sharpness: *needles of broken glass, ice, etc.* **9** INFORMAL. vex by repeated sharp prods, gibes, etc.; goad or incite. 1-8 *n.,* 9 *v.,* **nee dled, nee dling.** —**nee′dle like′,** *adj.* —**nee′dler,** *n.*

nee dle point (nē′dl point′), embroidery made on a canvas cloth, usually with woolen yarn. *n.*

need less (nēd′lis), not needed; unnecessary: *It is silly to take a needless risk. adj.* —**need′less ly,** *adv.*

nee dle wom an (nē′dl wüm′ən), **1** woman who is a skillful sewer. **2** woman who earns her living by sewing. *n., pl.* **nee dle wom en.**

nee dle work (nē′dl werk′), work done with a needle; sewing; embroidery. *n.*

need n't (nēd′nt), need not.

need y (nē′dē), very poor; not having enough to live on: *a needy family. adj.,* **need i er, need i est.**

ne'er (ner), OLD USE. never. *adv.*

ne'er-do-well (ner′dü wel′), an irresponsible or good-for-nothing person. *n.*

ne far i ous (ni fer′ē əs *or* ni far′ē əs), very wicked; villainous. *adj.* [*Nefarious* can be traced back to Latin *ne-,* meaning "not," and *fas,* meaning "divine law, right."]

nefarious
We wondered what **nefarious** deeds the villain had in mind.

ne gate (ni gāt′), **1** destroy, nullify, or make ineffective. **2** declare not to exist; deny. *v.*, **ne gat ed, ne gat ing.** —**ne ga′tor, ne gat′er,** *n.*

ne ga tion (ni gā′shən), **1** a denying; denial: *Shaking the head is a sign of negation.* **2** absence or opposite of some positive thing or quality: *Death is the negation of life.* *n.*

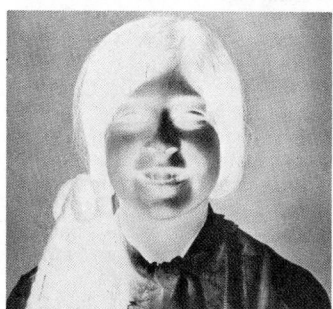

negative (def. 9)

neg a tive (neg′ə tiv), **1** stating that something is not so; saying no: *His answer was negative.* **2** word or statement that says no or denies: *"I won't" is a negative.* **3** the side that says no or argues against a question being debated; side opposing the affirmative. **4** not positive: *Her negative suggestions are not helpful.* **5** less than zero; minus: *−5 is a negative number.* **6** a negative number or quantity. **7** of the kind of electrical charge produced on rubber when it is rubbed with silk. **8** showing the lights and shadows reversed: *the negative image on a photographic plate.* **9** a photographic image in which the lights and shadows are reversed. Prints are made from it. **10** showing the absence of a particular disease, condition, germ, etc. 1,4, 5,7,8,10 *adj.*, 2,3,6,9 *n.* —**neg′a tive ly,** *adv.* —**neg′a tive ness,** *n.*

in the negative, expressing disagreement by saying no; denying.

neg a tiv ism (neg′ə tə viz′əm), tendency to say or do the opposite of what is suggested. *n.*

neg a tiv i ty (neg′ə tiv′ə tē), negative quality or condition. *n.*

ne glect (ni glekt′), **1** give too little care or attention to: *neglect one's health.* **2** leave undone; not attend to: *neglect one's work.* **3** omit; fail: *Don't neglect to water the plants before you leave.* **4** act or fact of neglecting; disregard: *a persistent neglect of duty.* **5** want of attention to what should be done: *That car has been ruined by neglect.* **6** a being neglected: *The children suffered from neglect.* 1-3 *v.*, 4-6 *n.* —**ne glect′er,** *n.* —**ne glect′ing ly,** *adv.*

ne glect ful (ni glekt′fəl), careless; negligent: *neglectful of one's duty.* *adj.* —**ne glect′ful ly,** *adv.*

neg li gee (neg′lə zhā′), a woman's soft, loose dressing gown. *n.*

neg li gence (neg′lə jəns), **1** lack of proper care or attention; neglect: *Negligence was the cause of the accident.* **2** careless conduct; indifference. *n.*

neg li gent (neg′lə jənt), **1** given to neglect; showing neglect; neglectful. **2** careless; indifferent. *adj.* —**neg′li gent ly,** *adv.*

neg li gi ble (neg′lə jə bəl), able to be disregarded: *The loss of ten cents is negligible.* *adj.*

neg li gi bly (neg′lə jə blē), in a quantity or to a degree that can be disregarded. *adv.*

ne go tia bil i ty (ni gō′shə bil′ə tē), condition of being negotiable. *n.*

ne go tia ble (ni gō′shə bəl), **1** able to be negotiated or sold; whose ownership can be transferred: *negotiable securities.* **2** able to be got past or over: *a negotiable path.* *adj.*

ne go ti ate (ni gō′shē āt), **1** talk over and arrange terms; confer; consult: *Both countries negotiated for peace.* **2** arrange for: *They finally negotiated a peace treaty.* **3** get past or over: *The car negotiated the sharp curve easily.* **4** sell. *v.*, **ne go ti at ed, ne go ti at ing.** [*Negotiate* comes from Latin *negotiatum,* meaning "engaged in business," and can be traced back to *neg-,* meaning "not," and *otium,* meaning "ease, leisure."]

ne go ti a tion (ni gō′shē ā′shən), a negotiating; arrangement: *Negotiations for the new school are finished.* *n.*

ne go ti a tor (ni gō′shē ā′tər), person who negotiates. *n.*

Ne gro (nē′grō), **1** member of the division of the human race that includes the original inhabitants of central and southern Africa, and their descendants throughout the world. **2** of this division of the human race. 1 *n., pl.* **Ne groes;** 2 *adj.*

Ne groid (nē′groid), **1** of or related to the Negro race. **2** person belonging to a Negroid people. 1 *adj.*, 2 *n.*

Ne he mi ah (nē′ə mī′ə), **1** Hebrew leader of the 400's B.C. He rebuilt the walls of Jerusalem about 444 B.C. **2** book of the Old Testament describing his achievements. *n.*

Neh ru (nā′rü), **Jawaharlal,** 1889-1964, prime minister of India from 1947 to 1964. *n.*

neigh (nā), **1** sound that a horse makes. **2** make this sound. 1 *n.*, 2 *v.*

neigh bor (nā′bər), **1** someone who lives in the next house or nearby. **2** person or thing that is near another: *The big tree brought down several of its smaller neighbors as it fell.* **3** be near or next to; adjoin: *Canada neighbors the United States.* **4** a fellow human being. 1,2,4 *n.*, 3 *v.* [*Neighbor* is from Old English *nēahgebūr,* which comes from *nēah,* meaning "near," and *gebūr,* meaning "dweller."] —**neigh′bor less,** *adj.*

neigh bor hood (nā′bər hud), **1** region near some place or thing: *She lives in the neighborhood of the mill.* **2** place or district: *Is North Street a good neighborhood?* **3** people living near one another; people of a place: *The whole neighborhood came to the big party.* **4** neighborly feeling or conduct. **5** of a neighborhood: *a neighborhood newspaper.* 1-4 *n.*, 5 *adj.*

in the neighborhood of, INFORMAL. somewhere near; about: *The car cost in the neighborhood of $3500.*

neigh bor ing (nā′bər ing), living or being near; bordering; adjoining; near: *We heard the bird calls from the neighboring woods.* *adj.*

neigh bor li ness (nā′bər lē nis), neighborly disposition or quality. *n.*

neigh bor ly (nā′bər lē), like or befitting a good neighbor; kindly, friendly, or sociable. *adj.*

nei ther (nē′ŦHər *or* nī′ŦHər), **1** not either: *Neither you nor I will go* (*conj.*). *Neither statement is true* (*adj.*). *Neither of the statements is true* (*pron.*). **2** nor yet; nor: *They didn't go; neither did we.* 1,2 *conj.*, 1 *adj.*, 1 *pron.* [*Neither* is from Old English *nāhwæther,* which comes from *nā,* meaning "not," and *hwæther,* meaning "which of two."]

Nel son (nel′sən), Viscount **Horatio,** 1758-1805, British admiral, noted for victories over Napoleon I. *n.*

nem a tode (nem′ə tōd), any of a group of worms with slender round bodies that lack segments; roundworm. The hookworm and the pinworm belong to this group. *n.*

Nem e sis (nem/ə sis), **1** (in Greek myths) the goddess of vengeance. **2 nemesis, a** just punishment for evil deeds. **b** person who punishes another for evil deeds: *Sherlock Holmes was the nemesis of many criminals. n., pl.* **nem e ses** (nem/ə sēz/).

ne o dym i um (nē/ō dim/ē əm), a yellowish metallic element found in various rare minerals. The rose-colored salts of neodymium are used to color glass. *n.*

Ne o lith ic (nē/ə lith/ik), of the latest part of the Stone Age, marked by the beginning of agriculture and the use of polished stone tools. *adj.*

ne on (nē/on), a colorless, odorless gas, forming a very small part of the air. It is a chemical element. Tubes containing neon are used in electric signs, lamps, etc. *n.* [*Neon* comes from Greek *neon,* meaning "new."]

ne o phyte (nē/ə fit), **1** a new convert; one recently admitted to a religious body. **2** beginner; novice. *n.*

ne o prene (nē/ə prēn), a synthetic rubber which resists oil, heat, and harsh weather conditions. It is used in gaskets, shoe soles, gasoline hoses, etc. *n.*

Ne pal (nə pôl/), country between India and Tibet. *Capital:* Katmandu. See **India** for map. *n.*

neph ew (nef/yü), son of one's brother or sister; son of one's brother-in-law or sister-in-law. *n.* [*Nephew* came into English about 700 years ago from French *neveu,* which came from Latin *nepotem,* meaning "grandson, nephew."]

ne phri tis (ni frī/tis), inflammation of the kidneys. *n.*

nep o tism (nep/ə tiz/əm), the showing of favoritism to relatives by someone in power, especially by giving them desirable positions. *n.*

Nep tune (nep/tün *or* nep/tyün), **1** (in Roman myths) the god of the sea. The Greeks called him Poseidon. **2** the fourth largest planet in the solar system and the eighth in distance from the sun. It is visible only through a telescope. *n.*

nep tu ni um (nep tü/nē əm *or* nep tyü/nē əm), a radioactive metallic element which occurs in minute amounts in uranium ore. It is obtained by bombardment of an isotope of uranium with neutrons. *n.*

Ner o (nir/ō), A.D. 37-68, Roman emperor from A.D. 54 to A.D. 68. He was noted for his vices, cruelty, and tyranny. *n.*

nerve (nèrv), **1** fiber or bundle of fibers through which impulses pass between the brain or spinal cord and the eyes, ears, muscles, glands, etc. **2** mental strength; courage: *nerves of steel.* **3** arouse strength or courage in: *The players nerved themselves for the championship game.* **4** INFORMAL. rude boldness; impudence. **5** vein of a leaf. **6** pulp of a tooth. **7 nerves,** *pl.* **a** nervousness. **b** attack of nervousness. 1,2,4-7 *n.,* 3 *v.,* **nerved, nerv ing.**
get on one's nerves, annoy or irritate one.
strain every nerve, exert oneself to the utmost.

nerve cell, 1 neuron. **2** the cell body of a neuron, excluding its fibers.

nerve fiber, any of the threadlike processes or fibers of a neuron; an axon or a dendrite.

nerve less (nèrv/lis), **1** without strength or vigor; feeble; weak. **2** without nervousness; controlled; calm: *be nerveless before an examination. adj.* —**nerve/less ly,** *adv.* —**nerve/less ness,** *n.*

nerve-rack ing *or* **nerve-wrack ing** (nèrv/rak/ing), extremely irritating; causing great annoyance; very trying: *a nerve-racking commotion. adj.*

nerv ous (nèr/vəs), **1** of the nerves: *a nervous disorder, nervous energy.* **2** having easily excited nerves; jumpy: *a nervous, impatient person.* **3** easily excited or upset; restless, uneasy, or timid: *Are you nervous about staying alone at night?* **4** strong; vigorous: *paint with quick, nervous strokes. adj.* —**nerv/ous ly,** *adv.* —**nerv/ous ness,** *n.*

nervous system, the system of nerve fibers, nerve cells, and other nervous tissue in a person or animal by means of which impulses are received and interpreted. The nervous system of animals with backbones includes the brain and spinal cord.

nerv y (nèr/vē), **1** INFORMAL. rude and bold. **2** requiring courage or firmness. **3** nervous. *adj.,* **nerv i er, nerv i est.** —**nerv/i ly,** *adv.* —**nerv/i ness,** *n.*

-ness, *suffix added to adjectives to form nouns.* **1** quality or condition of being ____: *Preparedness = the condition of being prepared.* **2** ____ action; ____ behavior: *Carefulness = careful action; careful behavior.*

nest (nest), **1** structure or place shaped something like a bowl, built by birds out of twigs, straw, etc., as a place in which to lay their eggs and protect their young ones: *a robin's nest.* **2** structure or place used by insects, fishes, turtles, rabbits, etc., for a similar purpose. **3** a snug abode, retreat, or resting place: *He cuddled down in the nest he'd made among the sofa cushions.* **4** a place that swarms (usually with something bad): *a nest of thieves.* **5** the birds, animals, etc., living in a nest. **6** make and use a nest: *The bluebirds are nesting here now.* **7** settle or place in, or as if in, a nest. **8** set or series (often from large to small) such that each fits within another: *a nest of drinking cups.* 1-5,8 *n.,* 6,7 *v.* —**nest/a ble,** *adj.* —**nest/er,** *n.*

nest egg, something, usually a sum of money, saved up as the beginning of a fund or as a reserve.

nes tle (nes/əl), **1** settle oneself comfortably or cozily: *She nestled down into the big chair.* **2** be settled comfortably or cozily; be sheltered: *The little house nestled among the trees.* **3** press close in affection or for comfort: *nestle up to one's mother, nestle a baby in one's arms. v.,* **nestled, nes tling.** —**nes/tler,** *n.*

nest ling (nest/ling), bird too young to leave the nest. *n.*

Nes tor (nes/tər), (in Greek legends) the oldest and wisest of the Greeks at the siege of Troy. *n.*

net¹ (net), **1** an open fabric made of string, cord, or thread, knotted together in such a way as to leave holes regularly arranged. A fish net is used for catching fish. A mosquito net keeps off mosquitoes. A hair net holds the hair in place. **2** anything like a net; set of things that cross each other. **3** a lacelike cloth. **4** a trap or snare: *The suspects were caught in the net of their own lies.* **5** catch in a net: *net a fish.* **6** cover, confine, or protect with a net. **7** make into net: *to net cord.* 1-4 *n.,* 5-7 *v.,* **net ted, net ting.** —**net/like/,** *adj.* —**net/ta ble,** *adj.*

net² (net), **1** remaining after deductions; free from deductions. A net gain or profit is the actual gain after all working expenses have been paid. The net weight of a glass jar of candy is the weight of the candy itself. The net price of a book is the real price, from which no discount can be made. **2** the net weight, profit, price, etc. **3** to gain: *The sale netted me a good profit.* 1 *adj.,* 2 *n.,* 3 *v.,* **net ted, net ting.**

neth er (neŦH/ər), lower. *adj.*

Neth er land er (neŦH/ər lan/dər), Dutchman. *n.*

Neth er lands (neŦH/ər ləndz), **the,** country in NW Europe, west of Germany and north of Belgium; Holland. *Capitals:* The Hague and Amsterdam. See **Prussia** for map. *n.*

Netherlands Antilles, territory of the Netherlands consisting of five islands in the S Caribbean.

neth er most (neŦH/ər mōst), lowest. *adj.*

net ting (net/ing), **1** a netted or meshed material: *wire netting for window screens.* **2** process of making a net. *n.*

net tle (net/l), **1** kind of plant having sharp hairs on the leaves and stems that sting the skin when touched. **2** make angry; irritate; provoke; vex: *Their refusal to help nettled me.* 1 *n.,* 2 *v.,* **net tled, net tling.** —**net/tle like/,** *adj.* —**net/tler,** *n.*

net work (net/wėrk/), **1** any system of lines that cross: *a network of vines, a network of railroads.* **2** group of radio or television stations that work together so that what is broadcast by one may be broadcast by all. **3** any group of people or things connected so that they can work together: *a network of spies, a network of computers.* **4** a netting; net. *n.*

neur al (nur/əl *or* nyur/əl), of a nerve, neuron, or nervous system. *adj.* —**neu/ral ly,** *adv.*

neu ral gia (nu ral/jə *or* nyu ral/jə), a pain, usually sharp, along the course of a nerve. *n.*

neu ri tis (nu rī/tis *or* nyu rī/tis), inflammation of a nerve or nerves. *n.*

neu rol o gist (nu rol/ə jist *or* nyu rol/ə jist), an expert in neurology. *n.*

neu rol o gy (nu rol/ə jē *or* nyu rol/ə jē), study of the nervous system and its diseases. *n.*

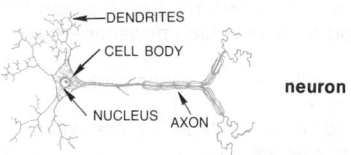

neuron

neur on (nur/on *or* nyur/on), one of the cells of which the brain, spinal cord, and nerves are composed; nerve cell. Neurons conduct impulses. A neuron consists of a cell body containing the nucleus, and usually several branching parts called dendrites and a single longer part called an axon. *n.*

neur one (nur/ōn *or* nyur/ōn), neuron. *n.*

neu ro sis (nu rō/sis *or* nyu rō/sis), any of various mental or emotional disorders, characterized by depression, anxiety, abnormal fears, compulsive behavior, etc. *n., pl.* **neu ro ses** (nu rō/sēz/ *or* nyu rō/sēz/).

neu rot ic (nu rot/ik *or* nyu rot/ik), **1** having or suffering from a neurosis. **2** person having or suffering from a neurosis. **1** *adj.,* **2** *n.* —**neu rot/i cal ly,** *adv.*

neu ter (nü/tər *or* nyü/tər), **1** (in grammar) neither masculine nor feminine. *It* is a neuter pronoun. **2** a neuter word or form. **3** the neuter gender. **4** without sex organs or with sex organs that are not fully developed. Worker bees are neuter. **5** an animal, plant, or insect that is neuter. **1,4** *adj.,* **2,3,5** *n.* [*Neuter* comes from Latin *neuter,* which also means "neither of two."]

neu tral (nü/trəl *or* nyü/trəl), **1** on neither side in a quarrel or war. **2** person or country not taking part in a quarrel or war. **3** of such a country or area: *neutral territory.* **4** neither one thing nor the other; indefinite. **5** having little or no color; grayish. **6** neither acid nor alkaline. **7** (of electricity) neither positive nor negative. **8** position of gears when they do not transmit motion from the engine to the wheels or other working parts. **1,3-7** *adj.,* **2,8** *n.* —**neu/tral ly,** *adv.*

neu tral i ty (nü tral/ə tē *or* nyü tral/ə tē), condition of being neutral; the attitude or policy of a nation that does not take part directly or indirectly in a war between other nations; neutral character or status. *n.*

neu tral i za tion (nü/trə lə zā/shən *or* nyü/trə lə-zā/shən), act of neutralizing. *n.*

neu tral ize (nü/trə līz *or* nyü/trə līz), **1** make neutral; keep war out of: *The city was neutralized so that peace talks could be held there.* **2** make of no effect by some opposite force; counterbalance: *Bases neutralize acids. I neutralized the bright colors in my room by using a tan rug.* *v.,* **neu tral ized, neu tral iz ing.** —**neu/tral i za/tion,** *n.*

neutral vowel, schwa.

neu tri no (nü trē/nō *or* nyü trē/nō), a stable atomic par-

a hat	**i** it	**oi** oil	**ch** child	
ā age	**ī** ice	**ou** out	**ng** long	a in about
ä far	**o** hot	**u** cup	**sh** she	e in taken
e let	**ō** open	**ù** put	**th** thin	ə = i in pencil
ē equal	**ô** order	**ü** rule	**ŦH** then	o in lemon
ėr term			**zh** measure	u in circus

ticle having no electric charge and a mass close to zero. *n., pl.* **neu tri nos.**

neu tron (nü/tron *or* nyü/tron), an atomic particle that is neutral electrically and has about the same mass as a proton. Neutrons occur in the nucleus of all atoms except hydrogen. *n.*

Nev., Nevada.

Ne vad a (nə vad/ə *or* nə vä/də), one of the western states of the United States. *Abbreviation:* Nev. or NV *Capital:* Carson City. *n.* —**Ne vad/an,** *adj., n.*

nev er (nev/ər), **1** not ever; at no time: *I have never been to New York.* **2** in no case; not at all; to no extent or degree: *He will be never the wiser. adv.*

nev er more (nev/ər môr/), never again. *adv.*

nev er the less (nev/ər ŦHə les/), however; nonetheless; for all that; in spite of it: *She was very tired; nevertheless she kept on working. adv.*

new (nü *or* nyü), **1** never having existed before; now first made, thought out, known or heard of, felt, or discovered: *a new invention, a new idea.* **2** lately grown, come, or made; not old: *a new bud.* **3** now first used; not worn or used up: *a new path.* **4** beginning again: *Sunrise marks a new day.* **5** changed or renewed: *to go on with new courage.* **6** not familiar; not yet used: *This is new country to me. She is new to the work.* **7** later; modern; recent: *new dances.* **8** just come; having just reached the position: *a new arrival, a new president.* **9** further; additional; more: *He sought new information on the subject.* **10** newly; recently or lately; freshly: *new-fallen snow, a new-found friend.* **1-9** *adj.,* **10** *adv.* —**new/ness,** *n.*

New Amsterdam, name of New York City when it was a Dutch colonial town.

New ark (nü/ərk *or* nyü/ərk), city in NE New Jersey, near New York City. *n.*

New Bed ford (bed/fərd), seaport in SE Massachusetts, formerly an important whaling port.

new born (nü/bôrn/ *or* nyü/bôrn/), **1** recently or only just born: *a newborn baby.* **2** ready to start a new life; born again. **3** a newborn infant. **1,2** *adj.,* **3** *n., pl.* **newborn, new borns.**

New Bruns wick (brunz/wik), province in SE Canada. *Capital:* Fredericton.

new com er (nü/kum/ər *or* nyü/kum/ər), person who has just come or who came not long ago. *n.*

New Deal, the policies and measures introduced by President Franklin D. Roosevelt in the 1930's as a means of improving the economic and social welfare of the United States.

New Del hi (del/ē), capital of India, in the N part.

new el (nü/əl *or* nyü/əl), the post at the top or bottom of a stairway that supports the railing. *n.*

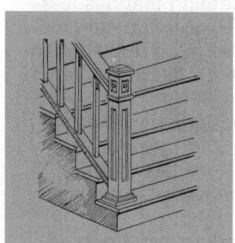

newel

New England, the NE part of the United States. Maine, New Hampshire, Vermont, Massachusetts, Rhode Island, and Connecticut are the New England states.

New Eng land er (ing′glən dər), person born or living in New England.

new fan gled (nü′fang′gəld *or* nyü′fang′gəld), lately come into fashion; of a new kind. *adj.*

Newfoundland (def. 3)—about 27 in. (68.5 cm.) high at the shoulder

New found land (nü′fənd lənd *or* nü found′lənd; nyü′fənd lənd *or* nyü found′lənd), **1** large island in the Atlantic northeast of Nova Scotia. **2** province in E Canada that includes Newfoundland and Labrador. *Capital:* St. John's. **3** a very large, intelligent dog, shaggy and usually black, developed in Newfoundland. *n.*

New Guinea, large island north of Australia; Papua. The W part of New Guinea belongs to Indonesia. The E part is included in the country of Papua New Guinea. See **East Indies** for map.

New Hamp shire (hamp′shər), one of the northeastern states of the United States. *Abbreviation:* N.H. or NH *Capital:* Concord.

New Haven, city in S Connecticut.

New Jersey, one of the northeastern states of the United States. *Abbreviation:* N.J. or NJ *Capital:* Trenton.

New Jerusalem, heaven.

new ly (nü′lē *or* nyü′lē), **1** lately; recently: *newly discovered.* **2** once again; freshly: *a newly painted room. adv.*

new ly wed (nü′lē wed′ *or* nyü′lē wed′), person who has recently become married. *n.*

New Mexico, one of the southwestern states of the United States. *Abbreviation:* N.M., N.Mex., or NM *Capital:* Santa Fe. **—New Mexican.**

new moon, 1 moon when seen as a thin crescent with the hollow side on the left. **2** the moon when its dark side is towards the earth, appearing almost invisible.

New Neth er land (neᴛʜ′ər lənd), former Dutch colony in America, from 1613 to 1664. England captured it in 1664 and divided it into the colonies of New York and New Jersey.

New Or le ans (ôr′lē ənz, ôr lēnz′, *or* ôr′lənz), city in SE Louisiana, near the mouth of the Mississippi River.

news (nüz *or* nyüz), **1** something told as having just happened; information about something that has just happened or will soon happen: *The news that our teacher was leaving made us sad.* **2** a report of a current happening or happenings in a newspaper, on television, radio, etc. *n.* **—news′less,** *adj.*

news boy (nüz′boi′ *or* nyüz′boi′), person who sells or delivers newspapers; paperboy. *n.*

news cast (nüz′kast′ *or* nyüz′kast′), a television or radio broadcast devoted to current events and news bulletins. *n.*

news cast er (nüz′kas′tər *or* nyüz′kas′tər), **1** person who gives the news on a newscast. **2** commentator on the news. *n.*

news let ter (nüz′let′ər *or* nyüz′let′ər), letter or report giving informal or confidential news. Organizations often issue newsletters to members or subscribers. *n.*

news man (nüz′man′ *or* nyüz′man′), **1** person who sells or delivers newspapers. **2** newspaperman. *n., pl.* **newsmen.**

New South Wales, state in SE Australia. *Capital:* Sydney.

news pa per (nüz′pā′pər *or* nyüz′pā′pər), a daily or weekly publication printed on large sheets of paper folded together, telling the news, carrying advertisements, and having stories, pictures, articles, and useful information. *n.*

news pa per man (nüz′pā′pər man′ *or* nyüz′pā′pər-man′), a reporter, editor, or other person who works for a newspaper. *n., pl.* **news pa per men.**

news print (nüz′print′ *or* nyüz′print′), a soft, cheap paper made from wood pulp, on which newspapers are usually printed. *n.*

news reel (nüz′rēl′ *or* nyüz′rēl′), a motion picture showing current events. *n.*

news stand (nüz′stand′ *or* nyüz′stand′), place where newspapers and magazines are sold. *n.*

news wor thy (nüz′wėr′ᴛʜē *or* nyüz′wėr′ᴛʜē), having enough public interest to be printed in a newspaper. *adj.,* **news wor thi er, news wor thi est. —news′-wor′thi ness,** *n.*

news y (nü′zē *or* nyü′zē), INFORMAL. full of news: *a newsy letter. adj.,* **news i er, news i est. —news′i ness,** *n.*

newt (nüt *or* nyüt), a small salamander that lives in water part of the time. *n.*

New Testament, the later part of the Bible, which contains the life and teachings of Christ recorded by His followers, together with their own experiences and teachings.

New ton (nüt′n *or* nyüt′n), Sir **Isaac,** 1642-1727, English scientist and mathematician who discovered the law of gravitation. *n.*

New to ni an (nü tō′nē ən *or* nyü′tō′nē ən), of or by Sir Isaac Newton. *adj.*

New World, the Western Hemisphere; North America and South America.

new-world *or* **New-World** (nü′wėrld′ *or* nyü′wėrld′), of the Western Hemisphere; not of the Old World: *new-world monkeys. adj.*

New Year *or* **New Year's,** January 1; the first day or days of the year.

New Year's Day, January 1, usually observed as a legal holiday.

New York, 1 Often, **New York State.** one of the northeastern states of the United States. *Abbreviation:* N.Y. or NY *Capital:* Albany. **2** Often, **New York City.** seaport in SE New York State, at the mouth of the Hudson River. It is the largest city in the United States.

New York er (yôr′kər), person born or living in New York City or New York State.

New Zea land (zē′lənd), country in the S Pacific, consisting of two main islands and various small ones. It is a member of the Commonwealth of Nations. *Capital:* Wellington. See **Australia** for map.

next (nekst), **1** following at once; nearest: *the next train, the next room.* **2** the first time after this: *When you next come, bring it.* **3** in the place or time or position that is nearest: *I am going to do my arithmetic problems next. Your name comes next.* **4** nearest to: *the house next the church.* **1** *adj.,* **2,3** *adv.,* **4** *prep.*

next to, 1 nearest to. **2** almost; nearly.

next door, 1 in or at the next house, apartment, etc.:

They live next door. **2** very close: *Her requests are next door to commands.*

next-door (nekst/dôr/), in or at the next house: *my next-door neighbor. adj.*

Nez Percé (nez/ pèrs/), member of a North American Indian tribe that formerly lived in Idaho, Oregon, and Washington.

Nfld., Newfoundland.

N.G., National Guard.

NH, New Hampshire (used with postal Zip Code).

N.H., New Hampshire.

Ni, symbol for nickel.

ni a cin (nī/ə sən), nicotinic acid. *n.*

Ni ag ar a (nī ag/rə), **1** short river flowing from Lake Erie into Lake Ontario over Niagara Falls. **2** Niagara Falls. *n.*

Niagara Falls, great waterfall of the Niagara River, on the boundary between the United States and Canada.

Nia mey (nyä/mā), capital of Niger, in the SW part. *n.*

nib (nib), **1** point of a pen. **2** point or tip of anything. **3** beak or bill of a bird. *n.* **—nib/like/,** *adj.*

nib ble (nib/əl), **1** eat away with quick, small bites, as a rabbit or mouse does. **2** bite gently or lightly: *A small fish nibbled at the bait.* **3** a nibbling; small bite. 1,2 *v.,* **nib bled, nib bling;** 3 *n.*

nib bler (nib/lər), person or animal that nibbles. *n.*

Nic a ra gua (nik/ə rä/gwə), country in Central America, north of Costa Rica. *Capital:* Managua. *n.* **—Nic/a ra/guan,** *adj.*

nice (nīs), **1** that is good or pleasing; agreeable; satisfactory: *a nice ride, a nice day.* **2** thoughtful or kind: *He was nice to us.* **3** very fine; minute; subtle: *a nice distinction, a nice shade of meaning.* **4** making very fine distinctions; exact; precise: *a nice ear for music.* **5** delicately skillful; requiring care, skill, or tact: *a nice problem.* **6** exacting; particular; hard to please; fastidious; dainty: *nice in one's habits.* **7** refined; cultured: *nice manners. adj.,* **nic er, nic est. —nice/ly,** *adv.* **—nice/ness,** *n.*

nice and, INFORMAL. pleasantly: *The cabin was nice and cozy.*

Nice (nēs), resort city in SE France, on the Mediterranean. *n.*

ni ce ty (nī/sə tē), **1** exactness; accuracy; delicacy: *Television sets require nicety of adjustment.* **2** a fine point; small distinction; detail: *I play tennis but have not mastered its niceties.* **3** quality of elegance or refinement. **4** something elegant or refined. *n., pl.* **ni ce ties.**

to a nicety, just right: *All the biscuits were browned to a nicety.*

niche (nich), **1** a recess or hollow in a wall for a statue, vase, etc. **2** a suitable place or position; place for which a person is suited: *I have yet to find my niche in the world. n.*

Nich o las (nik/ə ləs), Saint, **1** bishop in Asia Minor in the A.D. 300's. **2** Santa Claus. *n.*

Nicholas II, 1868-1918, the last czar of Russia, from 1894 to 1917, executed during the Russian Revolution.

nick (nik), **1** place where a small bit has been cut or

broken out; notch; groove: *She cut nicks in a stick to keep score.* **2** make a nick or nicks in. 1 *n.,* 2 *v.*

in the nick of time, just at the right moment.

nick el (nik/əl), **1** a hard, silvery-white metallic element found in igneous rocks. It is used in electroplating and is mixed with other metals to make alloys. **2** coin of the United States and Canada equal to five cents. **3** cover or coat with nickel. 1,2 *n.,* 3 *v.,* **nick eled, nick el ing** or **nick elled, nick el ling.**

nickel silver, a white alloy of copper, zinc, and nickel, used for ornaments, utensils, wire, etc.

nick nack (nik/nak/), knickknack. *n.*

nick name (nik/nām/), **1** name added to a person's real name or used instead of it. *"Ed" is a nickname for "Edward." Roy's nickname was "Buzz."* **2** give a nickname to: *They nicknamed the red-haired girl "Rusty."* 1 *n.,* 2 *v.,* **nick named, nick nam ing.**

Nic o si a (nik/ə sē/ə), capital of Cyprus, in the N central part. *n.*

nic o tine (nik/ə tēn/), poison contained in the leaves, roots, and seeds of tobacco. *n.* **—nic/o tine/less,** *adj.*

nic o tin ic acid (nik/ə tin/ik), a vitamin of the vitamin B complex, found especially in lean meat, yeast, liver, and wheat germ; niacin. It is used to treat and prevent pellagra.

niece (nēs), daughter of one's brother or sister; daughter of one's brother-in-law or sister-in-law. *n.* [*Niece* came into English about 700 years ago from French *niece,* and can be traced back to Latin *neptis,* meaning "granddaughter, niece."]

nif ty (nif/tē), INFORMAL. attractive or stylish. *adj.,* **nif ti er, nif ti est.**

Ni ger (nī/jər), **1** country in W Africa north of Nigeria. *Capital:* Niamey. See **Algeria** for map. **2** river in W Africa. *n.*

Ni ger i a (nī jir/ē ə), country in W Africa, a member of the Commonwealth of Nations. *Capital:* Lagos. *n.* **—Ni ger/i an,** *adj., n.*

nig gard (nig/ərd), **1** a stingy person. **2** stingy. 1 *n.,* 2 *adj.*

nig gard li ness (nig/ərd lē nis), niggardly quality; stinginess. *n.*

nig gard ly (nig/ərd lē), **1** stingy. **2** stingily. **3** meanly small or scanty: *a niggardly gift.* 1,3 *adj.,* 2 *adv.*

nig gling (nig/ling), trifling; mean; petty. *adj.*

nigh (nī), **1** near. **2** nearly. 1,2 *adv.,* 1 *adj.,* 1 *prep.*

night (nīt), **1** the time between evening and morning; the time from sunset to sunrise, especially when it is dark. **2** the darkness of night; the dark. **3** sadness of the mind, spirit, or emotions: *"the deep, dark night of the soul."* **4** evening; nightfall. **5** of night. 1-4 *n.,* 5 *adj.*

night cap (nīt/kap/), **1** a cap to be worn in bed. **2** INFORMAL. drink taken just before going to bed. *n.*

night club (nīt/klub/), place for dancing, eating, and entertainment, open only at night. *n.*

night crawler, a large earthworm that comes to the surface of the ground at night.

night dress (nīt/dres/), nightgown. *n.*

night fall (nīt/fôl/), the coming of night; dusk. *n.*

night gown (nīt/goun/), a long, loose garment worn by a woman or child in bed. *n.*

night hawk (nīt/hôk/), **1** bird related to the whippoor-

a hat	i it	oi oil	ch child	
ā age	ī ice	ou out	ng long	a in about
ä far	o hot	u cup	sh she	e in taken
e let	ō open	u̇ put	th thin	ə = i in pencil
ē equal	ô order	ü rule	₮H then	o in lemon
ėr term			zh measure	u in circus

will that flies about at dusk in search of insects. **2** person who often stays up late. *n.*

night ie (nī′tē), INFORMAL. nightgown or nightshirt. *n.* Also, **nighty.**

night in gale (nīt′n gāl), a small, reddish-brown bird of Europe. The male sings sweetly at night as well as in the daytime. *n.* [*Nightingale* is from Old English *nihtegale,* which comes from *niht,* meaning "night," and *galan,* meaning "to sing."]

Night in gale (nīt′n gāl), **Florence,** 1820-1910, English nurse who brought about great improvements in nursing. *n.*

night light, a small light to be kept burning all night.

night long (nīt′lông′), **1** lasting all night. **2** through the whole night. **1** *adj.,* **2** *adv.*

night ly (nīt′lē), **1** done, happening, or appearing every night. **2** every night: *Performances are given nightly except on Sunday.* **3** done, happening, or appearing at night: *nightly dew.* **4** at night; by night: *Many animals come out only nightly.* **1,3** *adj.,* **2,4** *adv.*

night mare (nīt′mer′ *or* nīt′mar′), **1** a very distressing dream. **2** a very distressing experience: *The hurricane was a nightmare. n.*

night mar ish (nīt′mer′ish *or* nīt′mar′ish), like a nightmare; causing fear or anxiety; very distressing: *a nightmarish experience. adj.* —**night′mar′ish ly,** *adv.*

night owl, INFORMAL. person who often stays up late.

night school, school held in the evening for persons who work during the day.

night shade (nīt′shād′), any of various plants related to the potato and the tomato. The black nightshade has white flowers and black berries. Belladonna, or the deadly nightshade, has red flowers and black berries. *n.*

night shirt (nīt′shėrt′), a long, loose shirt worn by a man or boy in bed. *n.*

night stick (nīt′stik′), a police officer's club. *n.*

night time (nīt′tīm′), time between evening and morning. *n.*

night watch, 1 watch or guard kept during the night. **2** person or persons keeping such a watch.

night y (nīt′tē), nightie. *n., pl.* **night ies.**

Ni jin sky (nə jin′skē), **Vaslav,** 1890-1950, great Russian ballet dancer. *n.*

nil (nil), nothing. *n.*

Nile (nīl), river in E Africa flowing north from Lake Victoria through Uganda, Sudan, and Egypt into the Mediterranean Sea. The Nile is the longest river in the world. *n.*

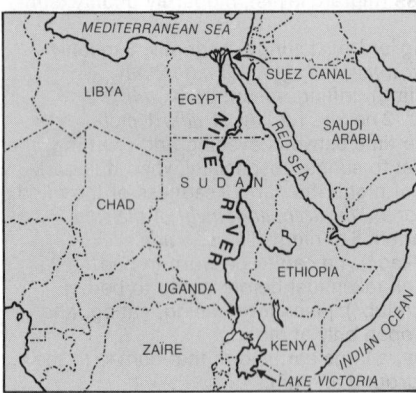

nim ble (nim′bəl), **1** active and surefooted; light and quick; agile: *Goats are nimble in climbing among the rocks.* **2** quick to understand and to reply; clever: *The student had a nimble mind that could quickly come up with solu-*

tions to problems. *adj.,* **nim bler, nim blest.**

nim bly (nim′blē), quickly and lightly. *adv.*

nim bus (nim′bəs), **1** halo. **2** a bright cloud surrounding a god, person, or thing. **3** a low, dark-gray layer of rain or snow clouds. *n., pl.* **nim bus es, nim bi** (nim′bī).

nimbus (def. 2)

Nim rod (nim′rod), **1** (in the Bible) a great hunter. **2** hunter. *n.*

nin com poop (nin′kəm püp), fool; simpleton. *n.*

nine (nīn), **1** one more than eight; 9. **2** set of nine persons or things: *a baseball nine.* **1,2** *n.,* **1** *adj.*

nine fold (nīn′fōld′), nine times as much or as great. *adj., adv.*

nine pins (nīn′pinz′), game in which nine large wooden pins are set up to be bowled over with a ball. *n.*

nine teen (nīn′tēn′), nine more than ten; 19. *n., adj.*

nine teenth (nīn′tēnth′), **1** next after the 18th; last in a series of 19. **2** one of 19 equal parts. **1** *adj.,* **1,2** *n.*

nine ti eth (nīn′tē ith), **1** next after the 89th; last in a series of 90. **2** one of 90 equal parts. **1** *adj.,* **1,2** *n.*

nine ty (nīn′tē), nine times ten; 90. *n., pl.* **nine ties;** *adj.*

Nin e veh (nin′ə və), capital of ancient Assyria. Its ruins are on the Tigris River. *n.*

nin ny (nin′ē), fool. *n., pl.* **nin nies.**

ninth (nīnth), **1** next after the eighth; last in a series of nine. **2** one of nine equal parts. **1** *adj.,* **1,2** *n.*

ni o bi um (nī ō′bē əm), a soft, steel-gray metallic element that is found in nature with tantalum. It is used in stainless steel and in other alloys. *n.*

nip[1] (nip), **1** squeeze tight and suddenly; pinch; bite: *The crab nipped my toe.* **2** a tight squeeze; pinch; sudden bite. **3** take off by biting, pinching, or snipping. **4** hurt at the tips; spoil; injure: *Some of our tomato plants were nipped by frost.* **5** injury caused by frost. **6** have a sharp, biting effect on: *A cold wind nipped our ears.* **7** sharp cold; chill: *There is a nip in the air on a frosty morning.* **8** a small bit. **1,3,4,6** *v.,* **nipped, nip ping; 2,5,7,8** *n.*

nip and tuck, INFORMAL. even in a race or contest.

nip[2] (nip), a small drink. *n.*

nip per (nip′ər), **1** person or thing that nips. **2** a big claw of a lobster or crab. **3** **nippers,** *pl.* pincers, forceps, pliers, or any tool that nips. *n.*

nip ple (nip′əl), **1** a small projection on the breast of a mammal. In females this enlarges to permit offspring to nurse. **2** the rubber cap or mouthpiece of a baby's bottle, through which the baby gets milk and other liquids. **3** anything shaped or used like a nipple. *n.*

Nip pon (ni pon′), Japanese name for **Japan.** *n.*

Nip pon ese (nip′ə nēz′), Japanese. *adj., n., pl.* **Nip pon ese.**

nip py (nip′ē), biting; sharp: *a nippy wind, nippy cheese. adj.,* **nip pi er, nip pi est.**

nir va na *or* **Nir va na** (nir vä′nə), **1** the Buddhist idea of heavenly peace; condition in which the soul is free from all desire and pain. **2** any condition like this; blessed oblivion. *n.*

Ni sei (nē′sā′), person born in the United States or Canada whose parents were Japanese immigrants. *n., pl.* **Ni sei.** [*Nisei* is from Japanese *nisei*, meaning "second generation," which comes from *ni*, meaning "two, second," and *sei*, meaning "generation."]

nit (nit), **1** the egg of a louse or similar insect. **2** a very young louse or similar insect. *n.*

ni ter (nī′tər), **1** potassium nitrate, especially when it occurs naturally as a white salt in the soil and encrusted on rocks; saltpeter. It is used in making gunpowder. **2** sodium nitrate, especially as it occurs in natural deposits. It is used as a fertilizer. *n.* Also, **nitre.**

ni trate (nī′trāt), **1** any salt of nitric acid. **2** potassium nitrate or sodium nitrate when used as fertilizers. *n.*

ni tre (nī′tər), niter. *n.*

ni tric (nī′trik), of or containing nitrogen. *adj.*

nitric acid, a clear, colorless liquid that eats into flesh, clothing, metal, and other substances. It is used in etching and metallurgy and in making dyes and explosives.

ni tro gen (nī′trə jən), a colorless, odorless, tasteless gas which forms about four fifths of the atmosphere. It is a necessary part of all animal and vegetable tissues. *n.*

nitrogen cycle, the circulation of nitrogen and its compounds by living organisms in nature. Nitrogen in the air passes into the soil where it is changed to nitrates by bacteria and used by green plants and then in turn eaten by animals. Decaying plants and animals, and animal waste products, are in turn acted on by bacteria and the nitrogen in them is again made available for circulation.

ni trog e nous (nī troj′ə nəs), containing nitrogen. *adj.*

ni tro glyc er in or **ni tro glyc er ine** (nī′trə glis′ər-ən), an oily, pale yellow, explosive liquid made by treating glycerin with nitric and sulfuric acids. Nitroglycerin is used in making dynamite and in medicine. *n.*

ni trous (nī′trəs), of nitrogen; containing nitrogen. *adj.*

nitrous oxide, a colorless gas that causes laughing and dulls pain. It is sometimes used as an anesthetic; laughing gas.

nit ty (nit′ē), full of nits. *adj.,* **nit ti er, nit ti est.**

nit ty-grit ty (nit′ē grit′ē), SLANG. the basic or fundamental facts: *That's unimportant. Let's forget it and focus on the nitty-gritty of the problem. n.*

nit wit (nit′wit′), INFORMAL. a very stupid person. *n.*

Nix on (nik′sən), Richard Milhous, born 1913, the 37th president of the United States, from 1969 to 1974, vice-president from 1953 to 1961. He was the first president to resign from office. *n.*

NJ, New Jersey (used with postal Zip Code).

N.J., New Jersey.

NM, New Mexico (used with postal Zip Code).

N.M. or **N. Mex.,** New Mexico.

no (nō), **1** word used to indicate that one can't or won't, or that something is wrong; word used to deny, refuse, or disagree: *Will you come? No.* **2** not in any degree; not at all: *He is no better.* **3** not any; not a: *They have no friends.* **4** denial; refusal. **5** a vote against; person voting against: *The noes won.* 1,2 *adv.,* 3 *adj.,* 4,5 *n., pl.* **noes.**

No, symbol for nobelium.

no. or **No.,** number. [The abbreviations *no.* and *No.* stand for the Latin word *numero*, meaning "by number."]

No ah (nō′ə), (in the Bible) a man whom God told to make an ark to save himself, his family, and a pair of each kind of animal from the Flood. *n.*

No bel (nō bel′), **Alfred Bernhard,** 1833-1896, Swedish inventor of dynamite and manufacturer of explosives, founder of the Nobel prizes. *n.*

a hat	**i** it	**oi** oil	**ch** child	⎧ a in about
ā age	**ī** ice	**ou** out	**ng** long	⎪ e in taken
ä far	**o** hot	**u** cup	**sh** she	ə = ⎨ i in pencil
e let	**ō** open	**u̇** put	**th** thin	⎪ o in lemon
ē equal	**ô** order	**ü** rule	**ŦH** then	⎩ u in circus
ėr term			**zh** measure	

no be li um (nō bē′lē əm), a radioactive chemical element produced artificially by bombarding curium with carbon ions. *n.*

Nobel prize, any of five money prizes established by Alfred B. Nobel to be given annually to those persons or organizations who have done outstanding work in physics, chemistry, medicine or physiology, literature, and the promotion of peace. A sixth category, economics, was added in 1969.

no bil i ty (nō bil′ə tē), **1** people of noble rank, title, or birth. Earls, counts, countesses, and marquises belong to the nobility. **2** noble birth; noble rank. **3** noble character. *n., pl.* **no bil i ties.**

no ble (nō′bəl), **1** high and great by birth, rank, or title: *a noble family.* **2** person high and great by birth, rank, or title. **3** high and great in character; showing greatness of mind; good: *a noble person, a noble deed.* **4** excellent; fine; splendid; magnificent: *Niagara Falls is a noble sight.* 1,3,4 *adj.,* **no bler, no blest;** 2 *n.* —**no′ble ness,** *n.*

no ble man (nō′bəl mən), man of noble rank, title, or birth. *n., pl.* **no ble men.**

no ble-mind ed (nō′bəl mīn′did), having noble, pure thoughts; righteous. *adj.* —**no′ble-mind′ed ly,** *adv.* —**no′ble-mind′ed ness,** *n.*

no ble wom an (nō′bəl wu̇m′ən), woman of noble rank, title, or birth. *n., pl.* **no ble wom en.**

no bly (nō′blē), in a noble manner; splendidly; as a noble person would do. *adv.*

no bod y (nō′bod′ē), **1** no one; no person. **2** person of no importance. 1 *pron.,* 2 *n., pl.* **no bod ies.**

noc tur nal (nok tėr′nl), **1** of the night: *Stars are a nocturnal sight.* **2** in the night: *a nocturnal visitor.* **3** active in the night: *The owl is a nocturnal bird.* **4** closed by day, open by night: *a nocturnal flower. adj.* —**noc tur′nal ly,** *adv.*

noc turne (nok′tėrn′), **1** a dreamy or pensive musical piece. **2** a painting of a night scene. *n.*

nod (nod), **1** bow (the head) slightly and raise it again quickly. **2** express by nodding: *I quietly nodded my approval.* **3** a nodding of the head: *She gave us a nod as she passed.* **4** let the head fall forward when sleepy or falling asleep. **5** be sleepy; become careless and dull. **6** droop, bend, or sway back and forth: *Trees nod in the wind.* 1,2,4-6 *v.,* **nod ded, nod ding;** 3 *n.* —**nod′der,** *n.* —**nod′ding ly,** *adv.*

nod al (nō′dl), having to do with nodes; like a node. *adj.*

node (nōd), **1** a knot, knob, or swelling. **2** a joint on a stem where leaves grow out. *n.*

nod u lar (noj′ə lər), having nodules. *adj.*

nod ule (noj′ül), **1** a small knot, knob, or swelling. **2** a small rounded mass or lump: *nodules of pure gold. n.*

No el or **No ël** (nō el′), **1** Christmas. **2** noel or noël, a Christmas song; carol. *n., pl.* **no els** or **no ëls** for 2. [*Noel* comes from French *Noël*, and can be traced back to Latin *nasci*, meaning "to be born."]

nog gin (nog′ən), **1** a small cup or mug. **2** a small drink; ¹/₄ pint. **3** INFORMAL. a person's head. *n.*

no-good (nō′gu̇d′), INFORMAL. **1** a worthless or evil person. **2** not good for anything; worthless: *a no-good villain.* 1 *n.,* 2 *adj.*

no how (nō′hou′), INFORMAL. in no way; not at all. *adv.*

noise (noiz), **1** a sound that is not musical or pleasant;

loud or harsh sound: *The noise kept me awake.* **2** any sound: *the noise of rain on the roof.* **3** din of voices and movements; loud shouting; outcry; clamor: *They made so much noise that they were asked to leave the theater.* **4** spread the news of; tell: *It was noised abroad that the prime minister was ill.* 1-3 *n.,* 4 *v.,* **noised, nois ing.**

WORD HISTORY

noise

Noise came into English about 750 years ago from French *noise,* meaning "uproar, brawl," which came from Latin *nausea,* meaning "seasickness, nausea," and can be traced back to Greek *naus,* meaning "a ship."

noise less (noiz′lis), making no noise; making little noise. *adj.* —**noise′less ly,** *adv.* —**noise′less ness,** *n.*
noise mak er (noiz′mā′kər), **1** person who makes too much noise. **2** thing that makes noise, especially a horn, rattle, etc., used to make noise at a party. *n.*
nois i ly (noi′zə lē), in a noisy manner. *adv.*
nois i ness (noi′zē nis), a being noisy; making a noise. *n.*
noi some (noi′səm), **1** disgusting; offensive; smelling bad: *a noisome slum, a noisome sewer.* **2** harmful; injurious: *a noisome pestilence. adj.* —**noi′some ly,** *adv.* —**noi′some ness,** *n.*
nois y (noi′zē), **1** making much noise: *a noisy crowd, a noisy machine.* **2** full of noise: *a noisy street, the noisy city.* **3** having much noise with it: *a noisy quarrel. adj.,* **nois i er, nois i est.**
nom., nominative.
no mad (nō′mad), **1** member of a tribe which moves from place to place to have food or pasture for its cattle: *Many Arabs are nomads.* **2** wanderer. *n.*
no mad ic (nō mad′ik), of nomads or their life; wandering; roving: *a nomadic people. adj.* —**no mad′i cal ly,** *adv.*
no man's land, 1 the land between opposing lines of trenches in warfare. **2** tract of land to which no one has a valid claim. **3** activity over which no jurisdiction or authority exists.
nom de plume (nom′ də plüm′), a pen name.
Nome (nōm), seaport and mining town in W Alaska, on the Bering Sea. *n.*
no men cla ture (nō′mən klā′chər), set or system of names or terms: *the nomenclature of music. n.*
nom i nal (nom′ə nəl), **1** existing in name only; not real: *The president is the nominal head of our club, but the secretary really runs things.* **2** too small to be considered: *We paid our friend a nominal rent for the cottage—$5 a month. adj.* —**nom′i nal ly,** *adv.*
nom i nate (nom′ə nāt), **1** name as candidate for an office; designate: *William Jennings Bryan was nominated three times for President, but he was never elected.* **2** appoint to an office or duty: *In 1933 Roosevelt nominated the first woman cabinet member in U.S. history. v.,* **nom i nat ed, nom i nat ing.** —**nom′i na tor,** *n.*
nom i na tion (nom′ə nā′shən), **1** a naming as a candidate for office: *The nominations for president of the club were written on the blackboard.* **2** selection for office or duty; appointment to office or duty. **3** a being nominated: *Her friends were pleased by her nomination. n.*
nom i na tive (nom′ə nə tiv), **1** showing the subject of a verb or the words agreeing with the subject. *I, he, she,*

we, and *they* are in the nominative case. **2** the nominative case. **3** a word in that case. *Who* and *I* are nominatives. 1 *adj.,* 2,3 *n.* —**nom′i na tive ly,** *adv.*
nom i nee (nom′ə nē′), person nominated for an office or to be a candidate for election to an office. *n.*
non-, *prefix.* not; not a; opposite of; lack of: *Nonessential = not essential. Nonresident = not a resident. Nonconformity = lack of conformity.*
non ag gres sion (non′ə gresh′ən), a refraining from aggression: *A pact of nonaggression was signed by the two nations. n.*

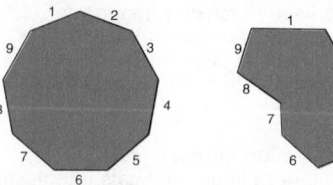

regular nonagon   **irregular nonagon**

non a gon (non′ə gon), a plane figure having nine angles and nine sides. *n.*
non al co hol ic (non′al kə hô′lik), containing no alcohol: *a nonalcoholic drink. adj.*
non break a ble (non brā′kə bəl), not breakable. *adj.*
nonce (nons). **for the nonce,** for the present time or occasion. *n.*
non cha lance (non′shə ləns *or* non′shə läns′), cool unconcern; indifference: *She received the prize with pretended nonchalance. n.*

nonchalant—She was completely **nonchalant** while the others cheered and yelled.

non cha lant (non′shə lənt *or* non′shə länt′), without enthusiasm; coolly unconcerned; indifferent. *adj.* —**non′cha lant ly,** *adv.*
non com bat ant (non′kəm bat′nt *or* non kom′bə tənt), **1** person in the armed forces who takes no part in combat. Surgeons, nurses, chaplains, etc., are noncombatants. **2** not fighting; having civilian status in wartime. 1 *n.,* 2 *adj.*
non com mer cial (non′kə mėr′shəl), not commercial: *a noncommercial airline. adj.*
non com mis sioned (non′kə mish′ənd), without a commission; not commissioned. *adj.*
noncommissioned officer, officer in the armed forces who does not hold a commission or a warrant, especially one with the rank of corporal, sergeant, or petty officer.

non com mit tal (non/kə mit/l), not committing oneself; not saying yes or no: *"I will think it over" is a noncommittal answer. adj.* —**non/com mit/tal ly,** *adv.*

non con duc tor (non/kən duk/tər), substance which does not readily conduct heat, electricity, or sound. *Rubber is a nonconductor of electricity. n.*

non con form ist (non/kən fôr/mist), person who refuses to be bound by or accept the established customs or practices of a social group, business, or church. *n.*

non con form i ty (non/kən fôr/mə tē), lack of conformity; refusal to conform. *n.*

non con ta gious (non/kən tā/jəs), not contagious. *adj.*

non de script (non/də skript), not easily classified; not of any one particular kind: *We drove past a block of nondescript houses. adj.*

none (nun), **1** not any: *We have none of that paper left.* **2** no one; not one: *None of these is a typical case.* **3** no persons or things: *None have arrived.* **4** to no extent; in no way; not at all: *Our supply is none too great.* 1-3 *pron.,* 4 *adv.*

non en ti ty (non en/tə tē), person or thing of little or no importance. *n., pl.* **non en ti ties.**

non es sen tial (non/ə sen/shəl), **1** not essential; not necessary. **2** person or thing not essential. 1 *adj.,* 2 *n.*

none the less (nun/ᴛнə les/), nevertheless. *adv.*

non ex ist ence (non/ig zis/təns), condition of not existing. *n.*

non ex ist ent (non/ig zis/tənt), having no existence. *adj.*

non fat (non/fat/), without the fat content that is normally present: *nonfat milk. adj.*

non fic tion (non fik/shən), writing that is not fiction; form of writing that deals with real people and events rather than imaginary ones. *Biographies and histories are nonfiction. n.*

non fic tion al (non fik/shə nəl), not fictional. *adj.*

non flam ma ble (non flam/ə bəl), that will not catch fire: *a nonflammable paint remover. adj.*

non liv ing (non liv/ing), not living. *adj.*

non met al (non met/l), a chemical element lacking the physical and chemical properties of a metal. *n.*

non me tal lic (non/mə tal/ik), not like a metal. *Carbon, oxygen, sulfur, and nitrogen are nonmetallic elements. adj.*

no-no (nō/nō/),SLANG. something that a person must not do, say, or use: *Telling fibs is a no-no. n.*

non pa reil (non/pə rel/), **1** having no equal. **2** person or thing having no equal. 1 *adj.,* 2 *n.*

non par ti san or **non par ti zan** (non pär/tə zən), not partisan; not supporting, or controlled by, any of the regular political parties: *a nonpartisan voter. adj.*

non pay ment (non pā/mənt), failure to pay or condition of not being paid. *n.*

non plus (non plus/ *or* non/plus), puzzle completely; make unable to say or do anything: *We were nonplused to see two roads leading off to the left where we had expected only one. v.,* **non plused, non plus ing** or **non plussed, non plus sing.** [*Nonplus* comes from the Latin phrase *non plus,* meaning "no further, not more."]

non poi son ous (non poi/zn əs), containing no poison. *adj.*

non pro duc tive (non/prə duk/tiv), **1** not productive. **2** not directly connected with production. *adj.* —**non/- pro duc/tive ly,** *adv.* —**non/pro duc/tive ness,** *n.*

non prof it (non prof/it), not for profit; without profit: *The Salvation Army is a nonprofit organization. adj.*

non res i dent (non rez/ə dənt), **1** living elsewhere; not living in a particular place. **2** not living where official duties require one to live. **3** a nonresident person. 1,2 *adj.,* 3 *n.*

a hat	i it	oi oil	ch child	a in about
ā age	ī ice	ou out	ng long	e in taken
ä far	o hot	u cup	sh she	ə = i in pencil
e let	ō open	u̇ put	th thin	o in lemon
ē equal	ô order	ü rule	ᴛн then	u in circus
ėr term			zh measure	

non re stric tive (non/ri strik/tiv), not restricting or limiting. *adj.*

nonrestrictive clause, (in grammar) any clause which adds descriptive detail but is not an essential part of the sentence in which it appears. EXAMPLE: *My bicycle, which had a flat tire, was stolen today.*

non sched uled (non skej/üld), not operating according to regular schedule: *a nonscheduled flight. adj.*

non sec tar i an (non/sek ter/ē ən), not connected with any religious denomination. *adj.*

non sense (non/sens), **1** words, ideas, or acts without meaning; foolish talk or doings; a plan or suggestion that is foolish: *That tale about the ghost that haunts the old mansion is nonsense.* **2** worthless stuff; junk: *a drawer full of useless gadgets and other nonsense. n.*

non sen si cal (non sen/sə kəl), foolish or absurd. *adj.*

non stop (non/stop/), without stopping: *We took a nonstop flight from Chicago to Paris* (adj.). *I flew nonstop from New York to Denver* (adv.). *adj., adv.*

non un ion (non yü/nyən), **1** not belonging to a trade union. **2** not following trade-union rules. **3** not recognizing or favoring trade unions. *adj.*

non vi o lence (non vī/ə ləns), belief in the use of peaceful methods to achieve any goal; opposition to any form of violence. *n.*

non vi o lent (non vī/ə lənt), not violent; opposing violence: *nonviolent protest. adj.* —**non vi/o lent ly,** *adv.*

noo dle[1] (nü/dl), a mixture of flour, water, and eggs, dried into hard flat strips. *n.* [*Noodle*[1] comes from German *Nudel.*]

noo dle[2] (nü/dl), **1** a very stupid person; fool. **2** SLANG. head. *n.*

nook (núk), **1** a cozy little corner: *a nook facing the fire.* **2** a hidden spot; sheltered place: *There is a wonderful nook in the woods behind our house. n.* —**nook/like/,** *adj.*

noon (nün), **1** 12 o'clock in the daytime; middle of the day. **2** of noon. 1 *n.,* 2 *adj.*

noon day (nün/dā/), noon. *n., adj.*

no one, no person; nobody.

no-one (nō/wun), no one. *pron.*

noon tide (nün/tīd/), noon. *n.*

noon time (nün/tīm/), noon. *n.*

noose (nüs), **1** a loop with a slip knot that tightens as the string or rope is pulled. *Nooses are used especially in lassos and snares.* **2** a snare or bond. **3** catch with a noose; snare. 1,2 *n.,* 3 *v.,* **noosed, noos ing.**

nor (nôr), **1** and no: *We had neither food nor drink left.* **2** neither: *Nor silver nor gold can buy it.* **3** and not: *I have not gone there, nor will I ever go. conj.*

Nor dic (nôr/dik), **1** belonging to or characteristic of the people of northern Europe. **2** a northern European. *Scandinavians are Nordics.* 1 *adj.,* 2 *n.*

Nor folk (nôr/fək), seaport in SE Virginia, near the mouth of Chesapeake Bay. *n.*

norm (nôrm), standard for a certain group; type, model, or pattern: *In arithmetic this class is above the norm for the eighth grade. n.* —**norm/less,** *adj.*

nor mal (nôr/məl), **1** of the usual standard; regular; usual: *The normal temperature of the human body is 98.6 degrees.* **2** the usual state or level: *He is ten pounds above normal for his age.* **3** not diseased, defective, or insane. 1,3 *adj.,* 2 *n.*

nor mal cy (nôr′məl sē), normal condition. *n.*

nor mal i ty (nôr mal′ə tē), normal condition. *n.*

nor mal ize (nôr′mə līz), make normal: *normalize the relations between two countries. v.,* **nor mal ized, nor mal iz ing. —nor′mal i za′tion,** *n.* **—nor′mal iz′er,** *n.*

nor mal ly (nôr′mə lē), in the normal way; regularly; if things are normal: *Children normally begin to lose their baby teeth when they are six years old. adv.*

normal school, school where they are trained to be teachers.

Nor man (nôr′mən), **1** person born or living in Normandy. **2** member of the people descended from the Scandinavians who settled in Normandy in the A.D. 900's and the French who lived there. **3** of the Normans or Normandy. 1,2 *n.,* 3 *adj.*

Norman Conquest, conquest of England by the Normans in 1066, under the leadership of William I.

Nor man dy (nôr′mən dē), region and former province in NW France. *n.*

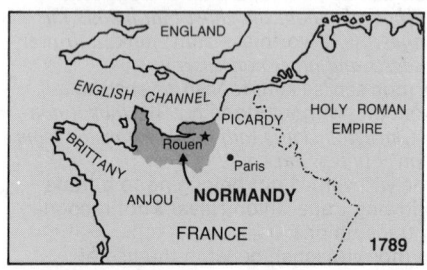

Norse (nôrs), **1** of ancient Scandinavia, its people, or their language. **2** people of ancient Scandinavia; Norsemen; Northmen. **3** language of these people. **4** of Norway or its people. **5** Norwegians. **6** language of Norway. 1,4 *adj.,* 2,5 *n.pl.,* 3,6 *n.sing.*

Norse man (nôrs′mən), one of the Nordic people of ancient Scandinavia. The Norsemen were great sailors and sea fighters. The Vikings were Norsemen. *n., pl.* **Norse men.**

north (nôrth), **1** direction to which a compass needle points; direction to the right as one faces the setting sun. **2** toward the north; farther toward the north: *Drive north for the next mile* (adv.). *We live on the north side of town* (adj.). **3** from the north: *a north wind.* **4** in the north: *the north window of a house.* **5** Also, **North,** the part of any country toward the north. **6 North,** the northern part of the United States; the states north of Maryland, the Ohio River, and Missouri, making up most of the states that formed the Union side in the Civil War. 1,5,6 *n.,* 2 *adv.,* 2-4 *adj.*

north of, further north than: *Canada is north of the United States.*

North America, the northern continent of the Western Hemisphere. The United States, Mexico, and Canada are the three largest countries in North America.

North American, 1 of North America or its people. **2** person born or living in North America.

north bound (nôrth′bound′), going north. *adj.*

North Carolina, one of the southeastern states of the United States. *Abbreviation:* N.C. or NC *Capital:* Raleigh. **—North Carolinian.**

North Dakota, one of the midwestern states of the United States. *Abbreviation:* N. Dak., N.D., or ND *Capital:* Bismarck. **—North Dakotan.**

north east (nôrth′ēst′), **1** halfway between north and east. **2** a northeast direction. **3** a place that is in the northeast part or direction. **4** toward the northeast. **5** from the northeast: *a northeast wind.* **6** in the northeast:

the northeast district. 1,5,6 *adj.,* 2,3 *n.,* 4 *adv.*

north east er (nôrth′ē′stər), wind or storm that blows from the northeast. *n.*

north east er ly (nôrth′ē′stər lē), **1** toward the northeast. **2** from the northeast. *adj., adv.*

north east ern (nôrth′ē′stərn), **1** toward the northeast. **2** from the northeast. **3** of or in the northeast. *adj.*

north er (nôr′ғHər), wind or storm that blows from the north. *n.*

north er ly (nôr′ғHər lē), **1** toward the north: *a northerly exposure.* **2** from the north: *a northerly wind.* **3** wind that blows from the north. 1,2 *adj., adv.,* 3 *n., pl.* **north er lies.**

north ern (nôr′ғHərn), **1** toward the north: *a northern view.* **2** from the north: *a northern breeze.* **3** of or in the north: *northern countries.* **4 Northern,** of or in the northern part of the United States. *adj.*

north ern er (nôr′ғHər nər), **1** person born or living in the north. **2 Northerner,** person born or living in the northern part of the United States. *n.*

Northern Hemisphere, the half of the earth that is north of the equator.

Northern Ireland, self-governing district in NE Ireland that voted not to join the Republic of Ireland and is a part of the United Kingdom of Great Britain and Northern Ireland. *Capital:* Belfast. See **United Kingdom** for map.

northern lights, the aurora borealis.

north ern most (nôr′ғHərn mōst), farthest north. *adj.*

North Island, the northernmost main island of New Zealand.

North Korea, country on the Korean peninsula, north of the 38th parallel. *Capital:* Pyongyang. **—North Korean.**

north land (nôrth′lənd), **1** land in the north; the northern part of a country. **2 Northland,** the northern regions of the world. *n.*

North man (nôrth′mən), Norseman. *n., pl.* **North men.**

North Pole, the northern end of the earth's axis. See **arctic circle** for map.

North Sea, sea that is part of the Atlantic Ocean, east of Great Britain, west of Denmark, and south of Norway. See **Lapland** for map.

North Star, the bright star almost directly above the North Pole, formerly much used as a guide by sailors; Polaris; polestar; lodestar.

North um bri a (nôr thum′brē ə), ancient kingdom in N England. **—North um′bri an,** *adj., n.*

North Vietnam, former country in SE Asia, now part of Vietnam.

north ward (nôrth′wərd), **1** toward the north; north: *I walked northward* (adv.). *The orchard is on the northward slope of the hill* (adj.). **2** a northward part, direction, or point. 1 *adv., adj.,* 2 *n.*

north wards (nôrth′wərdz), northward. *adv.*

north west (nôrth′west′), **1** halfway between north and west. **2** a northwest direction. **3** a place that is in the northwest part or direction. **4** toward the northwest. **5** from the northwest: *a northwest wind.* **6** in the northwest: *The northwest climate is good for wheat.* 1,5,6 *adj.,* 2,3 *n.,* 4 *adv.*

north west er (nôrth′wes′tər), wind or storm that blows from the northwest. *n.*

north west er ly (nôrth′wes′tər lē), **1** toward the northwest. **2** from the northwest. *adj., adv.*

north west ern (nôrth′wes′tərn), **1** toward the northwest. **2** from the northwest. **3** of or in the northwest. **4 Northwestern,** of or in the northwestern part of the United States. *adj.*

Northwest Passage, sea route for ships from the Atlantic to the Pacific along the N coast of North America.

Northwest Territories, division of N Canada, east of the Yukon territory.

Northwest Territory, former name for lands north of the Ohio River and east of the Mississippi River, now forming Ohio, Indiana, Illinois, Michigan, Wisconsin, and part of Minnesota.

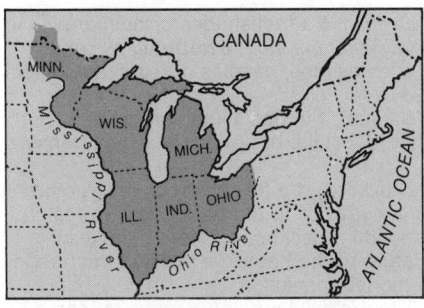

Northwest Territory the darker area

a hat	i it	oi oil	ch child	⎧ a in about
ā age	ī ice	ou out	ng long	e in taken
ä far	o hot	u cup	sh she	ə = ⎨ i in pencil
e let	ō open	u̇ put	th thin	o in lemon
ē equal	ô order	ü rule	ᴛʜ then	⎩ u in circus
ėr term			zh measure	

Nor way (nôr′wā), country in N Europe, west and north of Sweden. *Capital:* Oslo. See **Lapland** for map. *n.*

Nor we gian (nôr wē′jən), **1** of Norway, its people, or their language. **2** person born or living in Norway. **3** language of Norway. 1 *adj.,* 2,3 *n.*

nos. or **Nos.,** numbers.

nose (nōz), **1** the part of the face or head just above the mouth. The nose has openings for breathing and smelling. **2** sense of smell: *A mouse has a good nose for cheese.* **3** discover by smell; smell out. **4** to smell; sniff (at). **5** ability to perceive or detect: *A reporter must have a nose for news.* **6** rub with the nose: *The cat nosed its kittens.* **7** part that stands out, especially the bow of a ship, boat, or airplane. **8** move forward carefully: *The boat nosed along.* **9** search (for); pry (into). 1,2,5,7 *n.,* 3,4,6,8,9 *v.,* **nosed, nos ing.** —**nose′less,** *adj.* —**nose′like′,** *adj.*

count noses, find out how many people are present.

follow one's nose, go straight ahead.

lead by the nose, have complete control over.

look down one's nose at or **turn up one's nose at,** treat with contempt or scorn.

on the nose, SLANG. **1** exactly. **2** solidly.

pay through the nose, pay a great deal too much.

poke one's nose into, pry or meddle in a nosy way: *Our gossipy neighbors were always poking their noses into other people's business.*

under one's nose, in plain sight.

win by a nose, 1 win a horse race by no more than the length of a horse's nose. **2** win by a small margin.

nose bleed (nōz′blēd′), flow of blood from the nose. *n.*

nose cone, the cone-shaped front section of a missile or rocket, made to carry a bomb to a target or instruments or passengers into space. The nose cone is made to withstand high temperatures from friction with air molecules. It usually separates from the rest of the missile or rocket after the fuel runs out.

nose dive, 1 a swift plunge straight downward by an aircraft. **2** a sudden, sharp drop: *The thermometer took a nose dive the first day of winter.*

nose-dive (nōz′dīv′), take a nose dive. *v.,* **nose-dived, nose-div ing.**

nose gay (nōz′gā′), a bunch of flowers; bouquet. *n.*

nos tal gia (no stal′jə), a painful or wistful yearning for one's home, country, city, or for anything far removed in space or time. *n.*

nos tal gic (no stal′jik), feeling or showing nostalgia. *adj.* —**nos tal′gi cal ly,** *adv.*

nos tril (nos′trəl), either of the two openings in the nose. Air is breathed into the lungs, and smells come into the sensitive parts of the nose, through the nostrils.

n. [*Nostril* is from Old English *nosthyrl,* which comes from *nosu,* meaning "nose," and *thyrel,* meaning "a hole."]

nos trum (nos′trəm), **1** medicine made by the person who is selling it; quack remedy; patent medicine. **2** a pet scheme for producing wonderful results; cure-all. *n.* [*Nostrum* comes from Latin *nostrum,* meaning "ours."]

nos y or **nos ey** (nō′zē), INFORMAL. prying or inquisitive. *adj.,* **nos i er, nos i est.** —**nos′i ly,** *adv.* —**nos′i ness,** *n.*

not (not), word that says no; a negative: *not in any way, not to any extent. Six and two are not ten. adv.*

no ta bil i ty (nō′tə bil′ə tē), **1** quality of being notable; distinction. **2** a prominent person. *n., pl.* **no ta bil i ties.**

no ta ble (nō′tə bəl), **1** worthy of notice; striking; remarkable; important: *a notable event, a notable person, a notable book.* **2** person who is notable: *Many notables came to the reception at the White House.* 1 *adj.,* 2 *n.* —**no′ta ble ness,** *n.*

no ta bly (nō′tə blē), **1** in a notable manner; to a notable degree: *Many countries are notably lacking in fertile soil and minerals.* **2** especially; particularly: *Some deserts, notably the Sahara and Death Valley, are extremely hot. adv.*

no ta rize (nō′tə rīz′), certify (a contract, deed, will, etc.). *v.,* **no ta rized, no ta riz ing.** —**no′ta ri za′tion,** *n.*

no tar y (nō′tər ē), notary public. *n., pl.* **no tar ies.** [*Notary* comes from Latin *notarius,* meaning "clerk."]

notary public, a public officer authorized to certify deeds and contracts, to record the fact that a certain person swears that something is true, and to attend to other legal matters. *pl.* **notaries public** or **notary publics.**

no ta tion (nō tā′shən), **1** a set of signs or symbols used to represent numbers, quantities, or other values: *In arithmetic we use the Arabic notation (1, 2, 3, 4, etc.) and sometimes the Roman notation (I, II, III, IV, etc.).* **2** the representing of numbers, quantities, or other values by symbols or signs: *Music has a special system of notation, and so has chemistry.* **3** a note to assist memory; record; jotting: *He made a notation on the margin of the paper.* **4** act of noting. *n.*

notch (noch), **1** a V-shaped nick or cut made in an edge or on a curving surface: *People used to cut notches on a stick to keep count of numbers.* **2** make a notch or notches in. **3** a deep, narrow pass or gap between mountains. **4** INFORMAL. grade; step; degree: *In hot weather we often set the air conditioner several notches higher.* 1,3,4 *n., pl.* **notch es;** 2 *v.*

note (nōt), **1** a short sentence, phrase, or single word written down to remind one of what was in a book, a speech, an agreement, etc.: *Her notes helped her remember what the speaker said. Make a note of that.* **2** write down as a thing to be remembered: *Our class notes the weather daily on a chart.* **3** a comment, remark, or piece of information added concerning a word or a passage in a book, often to help pupils in studying the book: *There are many helpful notes at the back of our chemistry textbook.* **4** a very short letter: *a note of thanks.* **5** a formal letter from one government to another: *England sent a note of protest to France.* **6** promissory note. **7** certificate of a government or bank used as money. **8** piece of paper money. **9** greatness; fame: *a person of note.* **10** observe carefully; give attention to; take notice of: *Now, please note what I do next.* **11** notice; heed; observation. **12** mention specially. **13** in music: **a** a written sign to show the pitch and length of a sound. **b** a single sound of definite pitch made by an instrument or voice: *Sing this note for me.* **c** any one of the black or white keys of a piano: *to strike the wrong note.* **14** a song or call of a bird. **15** a significant sound or way of expression: *There was a note of determination in her voice.* 1,3-9,11,13-15 *n.*, 2,10,12 *v.*, **not ed, not ing.**

compare notes, exchange ideas or opinions.

strike the right note, say or do something suitable.

take note of, take notice of; give attention to; observe.

take notes, write down things to be remembered.

note book (nōt′bùk′), book in which to write notes of things to be learned or remembered. *n.*

not ed (nō′tid), especially noticed; conspicuous; well-known; celebrated; famous: *Samson was noted for his strength. "Little Women" was written by the noted American author Louisa May Alcott. adj.* —**not′ed ly,** *adv.*

note wor thi ness (nōt′wėr′ᴛнē nis), condition or fact of being noteworthy. *n.*

note wor thy (nōt′wėr′ᴛнē), worthy of notice; remarkable: *The first flight across the Atlantic was a noteworthy achievement. adj.* —**note′wor′thi ly,** *adv.*

noth ing (nuth′ing), **1** not anything; no thing: *Nothing arrived by mail.* **2** thing that does not exist: *create a world out of nothing.* **3** thing or person of no importance or value: *Don't worry, it's nothing.* **4** zero; naught. **5** not at all: *She looks nothing like her sister.* 1-4 *n.*, 5 *adv.*

nothing doing, INFORMAL. certainly not; by no means: *You expect me to clean up all this mess? Nothing doing.*

nothing less than, just the same as.

noth ing ness (nuth′ing nis), **1** a being nothing; condition of not existing. **2** a being of no value; worthlessness. *n.*

no tice (nō′tis), **1** attention or heed; observation; awareness: *escape one's notice. A sudden movement caught his notice.* **2** give attention to; observe; see: *I noticed a hole in my sock.* **3** announcement or warning: *The whistle blew to give notice that the boat was about to leave.* **4** a written or printed sign; paper posted in a public place; a large sheet of paper giving information or directions: *We saw a notice of today's motion picture outside the theater.* **5** a telling that one is leaving or must leave rented quarters or a job at a given time: *I gave two weeks' notice when I quit my job.* **6** a written or printed account in a newspaper: *There is a notice in the paper describing the wedding.* 1,3-6 *n.*, 2 *v.*, **no ticed, no tic ing.** [*Notice* came into English about 500 years ago from French *notice,* and can be traced back to Latin *noscere,* meaning "to come to know."] —**no′tic er,** *n.*

serve notice, give warning; announce: *The landlord served notice that the noisy tenants would have to move.*

take notice of, give attention to; observe: *Take no notice of them.*

no tice a ble (nō′ti sə bəl), **1** easily seen or noticed; observable: *The class has made a noticeable improvement in spelling.* **2** worth noticing. *adj.*

no tice a bly (nō′ti sə blē), to a noticeable degree: *It is noticeably cooler in the shade. adv.*

no ti fi ca tion (nō′tə fə kā′shən), **1** a notifying. **2** notice: *We received a notification of the meeting. n.*

no ti fy (nō′tə fī), give notice to; let know; announce to; inform: *Our teacher notified us that there would be a test on Monday. v.*, **no ti fied, no ti fy ing.**

no tion (nō′shən), **1** idea or understanding: *I have no notion of what you mean.* **2** opinion, view, or belief: *One common notion is that red hair means a quick temper.* **3** intention: *He has no notion of risking his money.* **4** inclination or desire; fancy; whim: *She had a sudden notion*

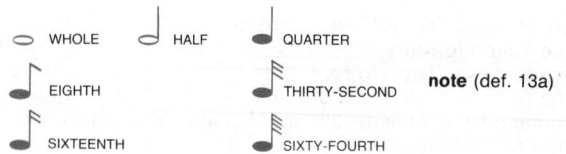

note (def. 13a)

to take a short vacation. **5** a foolish idea or opinion: *Grow oranges in Alaska? What a notion!* **6** **notions,** *pl.* small, useful articles, such as pins, needles, thread, tape, etc. *n.* —**no′tion less,** *adj.*

no tion al (nō′shə nəl), **1** in one's imagination or thought only; not real. **2** full of notions; having strange notions. *adj.*

no to chord (nō′tə kôrd), **1** a flexible, rodlike structure of cells running lengthwise in the back of the lowest forms of animals with a backbone. It forms the main supporting structure of the body. **2** a similar structure in the embryos of higher animals. *n.*

no to ri e ty (nō′tə rī′ə tē), **1** a being famous for something bad; ill fame: *A scandal brings notoriety to those involved in it.* **2** a being widely known. *n.*, *pl.* **no to ri e ties.**

no to ri ous (nō tôr′ē əs), well-known or commonly known, especially because of something bad: *a notorious outlaw. Our neighbors are notorious for giving noisy parties. adj.* —**no to′ri ous ly,** *adv.* —**no to′ri ous ness,** *n.*

Not ting ham (not′ing əm), city in central England. Many of Robin Hood's adventures took place there. *n.*

not with stand ing (not′wiᴛн stan′ding *or* not′with-stan′ding), **1** in spite of: *I bought it notwithstanding the high price.* **2** in spite of the fact that; although: *Notwithstanding there was need for haste, they still delayed.* **3** in spite of it; nevertheless: *It is raining; but I shall go, notwithstanding.* 1 *prep.*, 2 *conj.*, 3 *adv.*

Nouak chott (nwäk shôt′), capital of Mauritania, in the W part. *n.*

nou gat (nü′gət), a kind of soft candy containing nuts. *n.*

nought (nôt), naught. *n.*

noun (noun), **1** word used as the name of a person, place, thing, quality, or event. Words like *Lisa, table, school, bookcase, kindness, skill,* and *party* are nouns. **2** used as a noun. 1 *n.*, 2 *adj.* [*Noun* came into English about 600 years ago from French *noun,* meaning "a name, noun," and can be traced back to Latin *nomen.* See **Word Family.**]

noun

Below are words related to *noun*. They can all be traced back to the Latin word *nomen* (nō′men), meaning "a name, noun."

denomination	nom de plume	nominate
denominator	nomenclature	pronoun
misnomer	nominal	renown

nour ish (nėr′ish), **1** make grow, or keep alive and well, with food; feed; nurture: *Milk is all we need to nourish our small baby.* **2** maintain; foster; support; encourage: *nourish a hope. v.* —**nour′ish a ble,** *adj.* —**nour′ish er,** *n.* —**nour′ish ing ly,** *adv.*

nour ish ing (nėr′ish ing), keeping well-fed and healthy; producing health and growth: *a nourishing diet. adj.*

nour ish ment (nėr/ish mənt), **1** food. **2** a nourishing or a being nourished. *n.*

Nov., November.

no va (nō/və), star that suddenly becomes brighter and then gradually fades back to its normal brightness. *n., pl.* **no vae** (nō/vē/), **no vas.**

No va Sco tia (nō/və skō/shə), province in SE Canada consisting chiefly of a peninsula that extends into the Atlantic. *Capital:* Halifax. —**No/va Sco/tian.**

nov el (nov/əl), **1** of a new kind or nature; strange; new; unfamiliar: *a novel idea, a novel sensation.* **2** story with characters and a plot, long enough to fill one or more volumes. Novels are usually about people, scenes, and happenings such as might be met in real life. 1 *adj.,* 2 *n.*

nov el ette (nov/ə let/), a short novel. *n.*

nov el ist (nov/ə list), writer of novels. *n.*

nov el ty (nov/əl tē), **1** novel character; newness: *After the novelty of ice-skating wore off, we did not want to do it any more.* **2** a new or unusual thing: *Staying up late was a novelty to the children.* **3** novelties, *pl.* small, unusual articles, such as toys or cheap jewelry. *n., pl.* **nov el ties.**

No vem ber (nō vem/bər), the 11th month of the year. It has 30 days. *n.*

no ve na (nō vē/nə), (in the Roman Catholic Church) a devotion for some special purpose, made up of prayers or services on nine successive days. *n., pl.* **no ve nas.**

nov ice (nov/is), **1** one who is new to something; beginner: *Novices are likely to make some mistakes.* **2** person in the period of trial and preparation before becoming a monk or a nun. *n.*

no vi ti ate (nō vish/ē it), **1** the period of trial and preparation in a religious order. **2** the state or period of being a beginner. *n.*

now (nou), **1** at this time: *He is here now. Most people do not believe in ghosts now.* **2** by this time: *She must have reached the city now.* **3** the present; this time: *by now, until now, from now on.* **4** at once: *Do it now!* **5** inasmuch as; now that; since: *Now you mention it, I do remember. Now I am older, I can stay up longer.* **6** as things are; as it is: *I would believe almost anything now.* **7** then; next: *Now you see it; now you don't.* **8** at the time referred to: *The clock now struck three.* **9** a little while ago: *I just now saw him.* **10** *Now* is also used to introduce or emphasize, with little or no change of meaning. *Now what do you mean? Oh, come now!* 1,2,4,6-10 *adv.,* 3 *n.,* 5 *conj.*

now and then or **now and again,** from time to time; once in a while.

NOW (nou), National Organization for Women. *n.*

now a days (nou/ə dāz/), at the present day; in these times: *Nowadays people travel in automobiles rather than carriages. adv.*

no way (nō/wā), in no way; not at all; by no means; nowise: *Noway could we believe the story. adv.*

no way, INFORMAL. certainly not; it is impossible: *"I won't discuss the details. No way!" he insisted.*

no where (nō/hwer or nō/hwar), **1** in no place; at no place; to no place. **2** a nonexistent place. 1 *adv.,* 2 *n.*

nowhere near, INFORMAL. not nearly; not by a long way.

no wise (nō/wīz), noway. *adv.*

nox ious (nok/shəs), very harmful; poisonous: *Clouds of noxious fumes came from the back of the old bus. adj.*

noz zle (noz/əl), a tip put on a hose, pipe, etc., forming an outlet: *A fine spray came from the nozzle. n.*

Np, symbol for neptunium.

N.S., Nova Scotia.

N.T. or **NT,** New Testament.

nth (enth), last in the series 1, 2, 3, 4 . . . n; being of the indefinitely large or small amount denoted by *n. adj.*

to the nth degree, to the utmost: *silly to the nth degree.*

nt. wt., net weight.

a hat	i it	oi oil	ch child	a in about
ā age	ī ice	ou out	ng long	e in taken
ä far	o hot	u cup	sh she	ə = { i in pencil
e let	ō open	u̇ put	th thin	o in lemon
ē equal	ô order	ü rule	ᴛʜ then	u in circus
ėr term			zh measure	

nu ance (nü äns/, nü/äns, nyü äns/, or nyü/äns), **1** shade of expression, meaning, feeling, etc. **2** shade of color or tone. *n.*

nub (nub), **1** part sticking out; knob. **2** lump or small piece. **3** INFORMAL. point or gist of anything. *n.*

nub bin (nub/ən), **1** a small or imperfect ear of corn. **2** an undeveloped fruit. *n.*

nub bly (nub/lē), knobby or lumpy. *adj.,* **nub bli er, nub bli est.**

nub by (nub/ē), nubbly. *adj.,* **nub bi er, nub bi est.**

nu cle ar (nü/klē ər or nyü/klē ər), **1** of nuclei or a nucleus, especially the nucleus of an atom: *nuclear particles.* **2** of atoms, atomic energy, or atomic weapons; atomic: *a nuclear reactor. adj.*

nuclear family, family consisting of father, mother, and child or children living together in one household.

nuclear fission, fission (def. 3).

nuclear fusion, fusion (def. 4).

nuclear physics, branch of physics dealing with the structure of atomic nuclei and the behavior of nuclear particles.

nuclear winter, a theoretical period of intense cold on earth following a nuclear war, in which a blotting out of the sun's rays by dense smoke results in the destruction of plant life, and hence mass starvation of animals and humans.

nu cle ic acid (nü klē/ik or nyü klē/ik), a complex chemical compound, such as deoxyribonucleic acid, found in living cells and viruses. It occurs chiefly in combination with proteins.

nu cle o lus (nü klē/ə ləs or nyü klē/ə ləs), a small, usually round structure found within the nucleus of a cell. *n., pl.* **nu cle o li** (nü klē/ə lī or nyü klē/ə lī).

nu cle on (nü/klē on or nyü/klē on), a proton or a neutron. *n.*

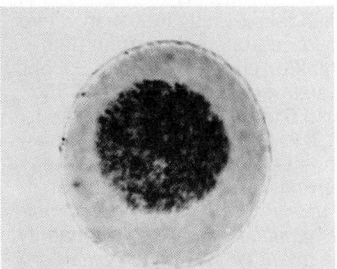

nucleus (def. 4)
nucleus of a
plant cell

nu cle us (nü/klē əs or nyü/klē əs), **1** a central part or thing around which other parts or things are collected. **2** a beginning to which additions are to be made: *Her five-dollar bill became the nucleus of a flourishing bank account.* **3** the central part of an atom, consisting of a proton or protons, neutrons, and other particles. The nucleus carries a positive charge and forms a core around which electrons orbit. **4** mass of specialized protoplasm found in most plant and animal cells, without which the cell cannot grow and divide. *n., pl.* **nu cle i** (nü/klē ī or nyü/klē ī), **nu cle us es.** [*Nucleus* is from Latin *nucleus,* meaning "kernel," which comes from *nucem,* meaning "nut."]

nude (nüd *or* nyüd), **1** naked. **2** a naked figure in painting, sculpture, or photography. 1 *adj.*, 2 *n.*
in the nude, in a naked condition.

nudge (nuj), **1** push slightly; jog with the elbow to attract attention. **2** a slight push or jog. 1 *v.*, nudged, nudg ing; 2 *n.* —**nudg′er,** *n.*

nu di ty (nü′də tē *or* nyü′də tē), a naked condition; nakedness. *n.*

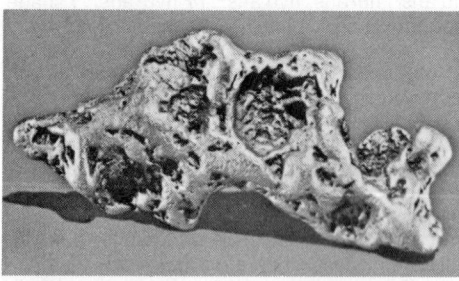
nugget
(def. 1)

nug get (nug′it), **1** valuable lump; lump: *nuggets of gold.* **2** anything valuable: *nuggets of wisdom. n.*

nui sance (nü′sns *or* nyü′sns), thing or person that annoys, troubles, offends, or is disagreeable; annoyance: *Flies are a nuisance. n.*

Nu ku a lo fa (nü′kü ä lō′fä), capital of Tonga. *n.*

null (nul), **1** not binding; of no effect; as if not existing: *A promise obtained by force is legally null.* **2** unimportant; meaningless; empty; valueless. **3** not any; zero. *adj.*
null and void, without legal force or effect; worthless.

nul li fi ca tion (nul′ə fə kā′shən), a nullifying or a being nullified: *the nullification of a treaty. n.*

nul li fy (nul′ə fī), **1** make not binding; render void: *nullify a law.* **2** make of no effect; wipe out; destroy; cancel: *The difficulties of the plan nullify its advantages.* v., **nul li fied, nul li fy ing.** —**nul′li fi′er,** *n.*

null set, empty set.

numb (num), **1** having lost the power of feeling or moving: *My fingers are numb with cold.* **2** make numb. **3** dull the feelings of: *The news numbed us with grief.* 1 *adj.*, 2,3 *v.* —**numb′ly,** *adv.* —**numb′ness,** *n.*

num ber (num′bər), **1** the count or sum of a group of things or persons; amount: *The number of students in our class is twenty.* **2** word that tells exactly how many. Two, fourteen, twenty-six, and one hundred are such numbers. **3** word that tells rank or place in a series. Second, fourteenth, and twenty-sixth are such numbers. **4** find out the number of; count. **5** figure or mark that stands for a number; numeral. 2, 7, and 9 are numbers. **6** mark with a number; give a number to; distinguish with a number: *The pages of this book are numbered.* **7** be or amount to a given number: *The states in the Union number 50. This city numbers a million inhabitants.* **8** quantity, especially a rather large quantity: *We saw a number of birds.* **9** numbers, *pl.* **a** arithmetic. **b** many: *There were numbers who stayed out of school that day.* **c** a being more: *win a battle by force of numbers.* **10** reckon as one of a class or collection: *I number you among my best friends.* **11** a single issue of a magazine: *The May number has an unusually good story.* **12** one of a numbered series, often a particular numeral identifying a person or thing: *a telephone number, a house number.* **13** a single part of a program: *The program consisted of four musical numbers.* **14** fix the number of; limit: *Our old dog's days are numbered.* **15** (in grammar) a word form or ending which shows whether one or more is meant. *Girl, ox,* and *this* are in the singular number; *girls, oxen,* and *these* are in the plural number. 1-3,5,8,9,11-13,15 *n.*, 4,6,7,10,14 *v.*
beyond number, too many to count.

without number, too many to be counted: *stars without number.*

num ber less (num′bər lis), very numerous; too many to count: *There are numberless fish in the sea. adj.*

number line, line divided into equal segments by points corresponding to integers. The points to the right of 0 are positive; those to the left are negative. The set of all the points on the line corresponds to the set of real numbers.

number one, oneself: *to look out for number one.*

num ber-one (num′bər wun′), first in rank; leading: *The book was a number-one best seller. adj.*

Num bers (num′bərz), the fourth book of the Old Testament. It tells about the counting of the Israelites after they left Egypt. *n.*

numb ing (num′ing), causing numbness: *numbing cold. adj.* —**numb′ing ly,** *adv.*

nu mer a ble (nü′mər ə bəl *or* nyü′mər ə bəl), countable. *adj.* —**nu′mer a ble ness,** *n.* —**nu′mer a bly,** *adv.*

nu mer al (nü′mər əl *or* nyü′mər əl), **1** a word, figure, or group of figures standing for a number. One, five, and ten are numerals. 7, 25, and 463 are Arabic numerals. III, VI, and XIX are Roman numerals for 3, 6, and 19. **2** numerals, *pl.* big cloth numbers given by a school for excellence in some sport. They state the year in which the person who wins them will graduate. *n.*

nu me rate (nü′mə rāt′ *or* nyü′mə rāt′), to number, count, or enumerate. *v.*, **nu me rat ed, nu me rat ing.**

nu me ra tion (nü′mə rā′shən *or* nyü′mə rā′shən), **1** a numbering, counting, or enumerating. **2** the reading of numbers expressed in figures. *n.*

nu me ra tor (nü′mə rā′tər *or* nyü′mə rā′tər), number above or to the left of the line in a fraction, which shows how many equal parts of the whole make up the fraction: *In $\frac{3}{8}$, 3 is the numerator and 8 is the denominator. n.*

nu mer i cal (nü mer′ə kəl *or* nyü mer′ə kəl), **1** of a number or numbers; in numbers; by numbers. **2** shown by numbers, not by letters: *10 is a numerical quantity; bx is an algebraic quantity. adj.* —**nu mer′i cal ness,** *n.*

nu mer i cal ly (nü mer′ik lē *or* nyü mer′ik lē), by numbers; in a numerical manner; in numerical respects; so far as numbers are concerned: *The enrollment of our school is numerically larger than theirs. adv.*

nu mer ous (nü′mər əs *or* nyü′mər əs), **1** very many: *The child asked numerous questions.* **2** in great numbers: *He has a numerous acquaintance among politicians. adj.*

nu mis mat ics (nü′miz mat′iks *or* nyü′miz mat′iks), the study or collecting of coins and medals. *n.*

nu mis ma tist (nü miz′mə tist *or* nyü miz′mə tist), an expert in numismatics. *n.*

num skull (num′skul′), a stupid person; blockhead. *n.*

nun (nun), woman who gives up many worldly things and lives a life devoted to religion. Nuns teach, care for the poor and sick, and perform many other duties. *n.*

nun ci o (nun′shē ō), an official representative or ambassador from the pope to a government. *n., pl.* **nun ci os.** [*Nuncio* was borrowed from Italian *nuncio,* which came from Latin *nuntius,* meaning "messenger."]

nun ner y (nun′ər ē), building or buildings where nuns live; convent. *n., pl.* **nun ner ies.**

nup tial (nup′shəl), **1** of marriage or weddings. **2** nuptials, *pl.* a wedding or the wedding ceremony. 1 *adj.*, 2 *n.* —**nup′tial ly,** *adv.*

Nur em berg (nūr′əm bėrg′ *or* nyūr′əm bėrg′), city in SE West Germany. *n.*

nurse (nėrs), **1** person who is trained to take care of the sick, the injured, or the old, especially under a doctor's supervision. **2** be or act as a nurse for sick people; wait on or take care of the sick. **3** cure or try to cure by care: *She nursed a bad cold by going to bed.* **4** woman who cares for and brings up the young children or babies of another person. **5** act as a nurse; have charge of or bring up (another's baby or young child). **6** one who feeds and protects. **7** make grow; nourish; protect: *nurse a plant, nurse a fire, nurse a grudge.* **8** use or treat with special care: *He nursed his sore arm by using it very little.* **9** feed milk to (a baby) at the breast. **10** suck milk from the breast of a mother. 1,4,6 *n.*, 2,3,5,7-10 *v.*, **nursed, nursing.**

nurse maid (nėrs′mād′), girl or woman employed to care for children. *n.*

nurs er y (nėr′sər ē), **1** room set apart for the use and care of babies. **2** a place where babies and small children are cared for during the day: *a day nursery.* **3** piece of ground or place where young trees and plants are raised for transplanting or sale. **4** nursery school. *n., pl.* **nurs er ies.**

nurs er y man (nėr′sər ē mən), person who grows or sells young trees and plants. *n., pl.* **nurs er y men.**

nursery rhyme, a short poem for children. "Sing a Song of Sixpence" is a famous nursery rhyme.

nursery school, school for children not old enough to go to kindergarten.

nursing home, place that is equipped and staffed to care for old people or anyone who needs prolonged nursing care.

nurs ling (nėrs′ling), **1** a baby that is being nursed. **2** any person or thing that is receiving tender care. *n.*

nur ture (nėr′chər), **1** bring up; care for; foster; rear; train: *They nurtured the child as if she were their own.* **2** a bringing up; rearing; training; education: *The two sisters had received very different nurture, one at home and the other at a convent.* **3** nourish: *nurture resentment.* **4** nourishment. 1,3 *v.*, **nur tured, nur tur ing;** 2,4 *n.*

nut (nut), **1** a dry fruit or seed with a hard, woody or leathery shell and a kernel inside which is often good to eat. **2** kernel of a nut. **3** a small, usually metal block which has a threaded hole and screws on to a bolt to hold the bolt in place. **4** SLANG. an odd or silly person. *n.* —**nut′like′,** *adj.*

nut crack er (nut′krak′ər), **1** instrument for cracking the shells of nuts. **2** bird related to the crow which feeds especially on pine seeds. *n.*

nut hatch (nut′hach′), a small, sharp-beaked bird that feeds on small nuts, seeds, and insects. *n., pl.* **nut-hatch es.**

nut meat (nut′mēt′), kernel of a nut. *n.*

nut meg (nut′meg), a hard, spicy seed about as big as a marble, obtained from the fruit of a tree of the East Indies. The seed is grated and used for flavoring food. *n.*

nu tri a (nü′trē ə *or* nyü′trē ə), **1** coypu. **2** its valuable beaverlike fur. *n., pl.* **nu tri as.**

nu tri ent (nü′trē ənt *or* nyü′trē ənt), **1** nourishing. **2** a nourishing substance; food. 1 *adj.*, 2 *n.*

nu tri ment (nü′trə mənt *or* nyü′trə mənt), nourishment; food. *n.*

nymph
(def. 3)
of a
grasshopper

a	hat	i	it	oi	oil	ch	child		a in about
ā	age	ī	ice	ou	out	ng	long		e in taken
ä	far	o	hot	u	cup	sh	she	ə =	i in pencil
e	let	ō	open	ů	put	th	thin		o in lemon
ē	equal	ô	order	ü	rule	ᴛʜ	then		u in circus
ėr	term					zh	measure		

nu tri tion (nü trish′ən *or* nyü trish′ən), **1** food; nourishment: *A balanced diet provides nutrition for your body.* **2** series of processes by which food is used by animals and plants for growth, energy, etc. *n.*

nu tri tion al (nü trish′ə nəl *or* nyü trish′ə nəl), of nutrition. *adj.* —**nu tri′tion al ly,** *adv.*

nutritious—This is a selection of **nutritious** foods.

nu tri tious (nü trish′əs *or* nyü′trish′əs), valuable as food; nourishing: *Eggs are very nutritious. adj.* —**nu tri′tious ly,** *adv.* —**nu tri′tious ness,** *n.*

nu tri tive (nü′trə tiv *or* nyü′trə tiv), **1** of foods and the use of foods. Digestion is part of the nutritive process. **2** nutritious. *adj.* —**nu′tri tive ly,** *adv.*

nuts (nuts), SLANG. crazy: *He's nuts to try a fool stunt like that. adj.*

be nuts about, be very fond of or delighted with: *She's just nuts about water-skiing.*

nut shell (nut′shel′), shell of a nut. *n.*

in a nutshell, in very brief form; in a few words.

nut ting (nut′ing), a looking for nuts; gathering nuts. *n.*

nut ty (nut′ē), **1** containing many nuts: *nutty cake.* **2** like nuts; tasting like nuts. **3** SLANG. odd or silly. **4** SLANG. very interested or enthusiastic. *adj.*, **nut ti er, nut ti est.** —**nut′ti ly,** *adv.* —**nut′ti ness,** *n.*

nuz zle (nuz′əl), **1** poke or rub with the nose; press the nose against: *The horse nuzzled its owner's ear.* **2** nestle; snuggle; cuddle. *v.*, **nuz zled, nuz zling.**

NV, Nevada (used with postal Zip Code).

NW or **N.W.**, **1** northwest. **2** northwestern.

N.W.T., Northwest Territories.

NY, New York (used with postal Zip Code).

N.Y., New York State.

Ny as a land (nī as′ə land′), former British protectorate in SE Africa, now Malawi. *n.*

N.Y.C., New York City.

ny lon (nī′lon), **1** an extremely strong, elastic, and durable synthetic substance, used to make clothing, stockings, bristles, etc. **2 nylons,** *pl.* stockings made of nylon. **3** made of nylon: *nylon carpeting, nylon casters.* 1,2 *n.*, 3 *adj.*

nymph (nimf), **1** (in Greek and Roman myths) a lesser goddess of nature, found in seas, rivers, fountains, hills, woods, or trees. **2** a beautiful or graceful young woman. **3** any of certain insects in the stage of development between the egg and the adult form. It resembles the adult but has no wings. *n.* —**nymph′like′,** *adj.*

N.Z., New Zealand.

Oo

O¹ or **o** (ō), **1** the 15th letter of the English alphabet. **2** zero. *n., pl.* **O's** or **o's.**

O² (ō), oh! *interj.*

o' (ə *or* ō), of: *will-o'-the-wisp. prep.*

O, symbol for oxygen.

O., Ohio.

oaf (ōf), **1** a very stupid person. **2** a clumsy person. *n.* [*Oaf* comes from Icelandic *ālfr*, meaning "elf."]

oaf ish (ō′fish), very stupid; clumsy. *adj.* —**oaf′ish ly,** *adv.* —**oaf′ish ness,** *n.*

O a hu (ō ä′hü), the third largest island of Hawaii. Honolulu, the capital of Hawaii, is on Oahu. *n.*

oak (ōk), **1** tree or shrub found in most parts of the world, with strong, hard, durable wood and nuts called acorns. There are many kinds of oaks. **2** its wood, used in building, for flooring, etc. **3** made of oak wood; oaken: *an oak table.* 1,2 *n.,* 3 *adj.* —**oak′like′,** *adj.*

oak en (ō′kən), made of oak: *the old oaken bucket. adj.*

Oak land (ōk′lənd), city in W California, just east of San Francisco. *n.*

Oak Ridge, city in E Tennessee. Oak Ridge is a research center for studying atomic energy.

oa kum (ō′kəm), a loose fiber obtained by untwisting and picking apart old ropes, used for stopping up the seams or cracks in ships. *n.*

oar (ôr), **1** a long pole with a flat blade at one end, used in rowing. Sometimes an oar is used to steer a boat. **2** use an oar; row. **3** person who rows: *She is the best oar in our crew.* 1,3 *n.,* 2 *v.* —**oar′less,** *adj.* —**oar′like′,** *adj.*

put one's oar in, meddle; interfere.

rest on one's oars, stop working or trying and take a rest.

oar lock (ôr′lok′), a notch or U-shaped support for holding the oar in place while rowing; rowlock. *n.*

oars man (ôrz′mən), **1** person who rows. **2** expert rower, especially a racer. *n., pl.* **oars men.**

obelisk

o a sis (ō ā′sis), **1** a fertile spot in the desert where there is water and some vegetation. **2** any fertile spot in a barren land; any pleasant place in a desolate region. *n., pl.* **o a ses** (ō ā′sēz′).

oat (ōt), **1** Often, **oats,** *pl. or sing.* a tall cereal grass whose seed is used in making oatmeal and as a food for horses. **2 oats,** *pl. or sing.* grains of the oat plant. *n.*

feel one's oats, INFORMAL. **1** be lively or frisky. **2** feel pleased or important and show it.

oat en (ōt′n), **1** made of oats or oatmeal. **2** made of oat straw. *adj.*

oath (ōth), **1** a solemn promise: *The oath bound him to secrecy.* **2** statement that something is true, which God or some holy person or thing is called on to witness. **3** name of God or some holy person or thing used as an exclamation to add force or to express anger. **4** a curse; word used in swearing. *n., pl.* **oaths** (ōⱦHZ *or* ōths).

take oath, make an oath; promise or state solemnly.

under oath, bound by an oath.

oat meal (ōt′mēl′), **1** oats partially ground up and flattened into small flakes. **2** a cooked cereal made from this. *n.*

ob., died.

O ba di ah (ō′bə dī′ə), **1** (in the Bible) a Hebrew prophet. **2** book of the Old Testament containing his prophecies. *n.*

ob dur a cy (ob′dər ə sē *or* ob′dyər ə sē), hardness of heart; stubbornness. *n.*

ob dur ate (ob′dər it *or* ob′dyər it), **1** stubborn or unyielding; obstinate: *an obdurate refusal.* **2** hardened in feelings or heart; not repentant: *an obdurate criminal. adj.* —**ob′dur ate ly,** *adv.* —**ob′dur ate ness,** *n.*

o be di ence (ō bē′dē əns), an obeying; doing what one is told to do; submission to authority or law: *They were strict parents who demanded obedience from their children. He must act in obedience to the judge's order. n.*

o be di ent (ō bē′dē ənt), doing what one is told; willing to obey: *The obedient dog came at its owner's whistle. adj.* —**o be′di ent ly,** *adv.*

o bei sance (ō bā′sns *or* ō bē′sns), **1** movement of the body expressing deep respect; deep bow: *The villagers made obeisance to the queen.* **2** deference; homage: *acts of obeisance. n.*

oarlock

ob e lisk (ob′ə lisk), a tapering, four-sided shaft of stone with a top shaped like a pyramid. *n.*

o bese (ō bēs′), extremely fat. *adj.* [*Obese* is from Latin *obesus,* which comes from *ob-,* meaning "on," and *edere,* meaning "to eat."] —**o bese′ly,** *adv.* —**o bese′ness,** *n.*

o bes i ty (ō bē′sə tē), extreme fatness. *n.*

o bey (ō bā′), **1** do what one is told to do: *The dog obeyed and went home.* **2** follow the orders of: *You must obey the court's decision.* **3** act in accordance with; comply with: *A good citizen obeys the laws.* **4** yield to the control of: *A horse obeys the rein. v.* —**o bey′a ble,** *adj.* —**o bey′er,** *n.* —**o bey′ing ly,** *adv.*

oats (def. 1)

o bi (ōʹbē), a long, broad sash worn by Japanese around the waist of a kimono. *n., pl.* **o bis.**

o bit u ar y (ō bichʹü erʹē), **1** a notice of death, often with a brief account of the person's life. **2** of a death; recording a death: *the obituary notices in the newspaper.* **1** *n., pl.* **o bit u ar ies; 2** *adj.* [*Obituary* comes from a medieval Latin word *obituarius,* which is from *obire* (*mortem*), meaning "to meet (death)," which comes from *ob-,* meaning "toward," and *ire,* meaning "go."]

obj., 1 object. **2** objection. **3** objective.

ob ject (obʹjikt *for 1-4;* əb jektʹ *for 5,6*), **1** something that can be seen or touched; thing: *What is that object by the fence? A dark object moved between me and the door.* **2** person or thing toward which feeling, thought, or action is directed: *an object of study, an object of someone's affection.* **3** thing aimed at; end; purpose; goal: *My object in coming here was to help you.* **4** (in grammar) a word or group of words toward which the action of the verb is directed or to which a preposition expresses some relation. In "He threw the ball to his sister," *ball* is the object of *threw,* and *sister* is the object of *to.* **5** make objections; be opposed; feel dislike: *Many people object to loud noise.* **6** give as a reason against something; bring forward in opposition; oppose: *I objected that it was too cold for camping.* **1-4** *n.,* **5,6** *v.*

ob jec ti fy (əb jekʹtə fī), make objective. *v.,* **ob jec ti fied, ob jec ti fy ing.** —**ob jecʹti fi caʹtion,** *n.*

ob jec tion (əb jekʹshən), **1** something said in objecting; reason or argument against something: *One of his objections to the plan was that it would cost too much.* **2** feeling of disapproval or dislike: *an energetic person with no objection to hard work.* *n.*

ob jec tion a ble (əb jekʹshə nə bəl), **1** likely to be objected to. **2** unpleasant; disagreeable. *adj.* —**ob jecʹtion a ble ness,** *n.* —**ob jecʹtion a bly,** *adv.*

ob jec tive (əb jekʹtiv), **1** something aimed at: *My objective this summer will be learning to play tennis better.* **2** existing outside the mind as an actual object and not merely in the mind as an idea; real. Buildings are objective; ideas are subjective. **3** about outward things, not about the thoughts and feelings of the speaker, writer, painter, etc.; giving facts as they are without a bias toward either side; impersonal: *an objective analysis of a poem or novel. Scientists must be objective in their experiments.* **4** showing the direct object of a verb or the object of a preposition. In "She saw me," *me* is in the objective case. **5** the objective case. **6** word in that case. *Whom* and *me* are objectives. **7** lens or lenses nearest to the thing seen through a telescope, microscope, etc. **1,5-7** *n.,* **2-4** *adj.* —**ob jecʹtive ly,** *adv.* —**ob jecʹtive ness,** *n.*

ob jec tiv i ty (obʹjek tivʹə tē), condition or quality of being objective. *n.*

object lesson, a practical illustration of a principle: *Many accidents are object lessons in the dangers of carelessness.*

ob jec tor (əb jekʹtər), person who objects. *n.*

obl., 1 oblique. **2** oblong.

ob li gate (obʹlə gāt), bind morally or legally; pledge: *A witness in court is obligated to tell the truth. v.,* **ob li gat ed, ob li gat ing.** —**ob li gaʹtor,** *n.*

ob li ga tion (obʹlə gāʹshən), **1** duty under the law; duty due to a promise or contract; duty on account of social relationship or kindness received: *We all have an obligation to our friends. Paying taxes is an obligation which may fall on everybody.* **2** binding power (of a law, promise, sense of duty, etc.): *The one who did the damage is under obligation to pay for it.* **3** a binding legal agreement; bond; contract: *The firm was not able to meet its obligations.* **4** a binding oneself or being bound by oath, prom-

ise, etc., to do something: *It was his obligation to return my favor. n.*

o blig a to ry (ə bligʹə tôrʹē), binding morally or legally; required: *Attendance in school is obligatory. adj.* —**o bligʹa toʹri ly,** *adv.*

o blige (ə blījʹ), **1** bind by a promise, contract, duty, etc.; compel; force: *The law obliges parents to send their children to school.* **2** put under a debt of thanks for some favor or service: *We are very much obliged for your kind offer.* **3** do a favor for: *Kindly oblige me by closing the door. v.,* **o bliged, o blig ing.** —**o bligʹer,** *n.*

o blig ing (ə blīʹjing), willing to do favors; helpful: *Her obliging nature wins friends. adj.* —**o bligʹing ly,** *adv.*

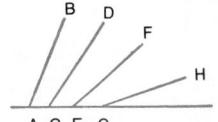

oblique (def. 1)
AB, CD, EF, and GH
are oblique lines.

o blique (ə blēkʹ), **1** not straight up and down; not straight across; slanting. **2** not straightforward; indirect: *She made an oblique reference to her illness, but did not mention it directly. adj.* —**o bliqueʹly,** *adv.* —**o bliqueʹness,** *n.*

oblique angle, any angle that is not a right angle. Acute angles and obtuse angles are oblique angles.

o bliq ui ty (ə blikʹwə tē), **1** indirectness or crookedness of thought or behavior, especially conduct that is not upright and moral. **2** a being oblique. *n., pl.* **o bliq ui ties.**

o blit e rate (ə blitʹə rātʹ), remove all traces of; wipe or blot out; destroy: *The heavy rain obliterated the footprints. v.,* **o blit e rat ed, o blit e rat ing.** [*Obliterate* is from Latin *obliteratum,* meaning "struck out, erased," which comes from *ob literas* (*scribere*), meaning "(draw) through the letters."] —**o blitʹe raʹtor,** *n.*

o blit e ra tion (ə blitʹə rāʹshən), an obliterating or a being obliterated; destruction. *n.*

o bliv i on (ə blivʹē ən), **1** condition of being entirely forgotten: *Many ancient cities have long since passed into oblivion.* **2** forgetfulness: *the oblivion of deep sleep. n.*

o bliv i ous (ə blivʹē əs), forgetful; not mindful: *The book was so interesting that I was oblivious of my surroundings. adj.*

oblongs
(def. 2)

ob long (obʹlông), **1** longer than broad: *an oblong loaf of bread.* **2** rectangle that is not a square. **1** *adj.,* **2** *n.* —**obʹlong ly,** *adv.* —**obʹlong ness,** *n.*

ob lo quy (obʹlə kwē), **1** public reproach; abuse; blame. **2** disgrace; shame. *n., pl.* **ob lo quies.**

ob nox ious (əb nokʹshəs), very disagreeable; offensive;

hateful: *Their rudeness and bad manners made them obnoxious to me. adj.* —**ob nox′ious ly,** *adv.*

o boe (ō′bō), a woodwind instrument in which a thin, high-pitched tone is produced by a double reed. *n.*

WORD HISTORY

oboe

Oboe was borrowed from Italian *oboe,* which came from French *hautbois,* which comes from *haut,* meaning "high," and *bois,* meaning "wood." "High" refers to the pitch of the instrument.

ob scene (əb sēn′), offending modesty or decency; impure; filthy; vile. *adj.* —**ob scene′ly,** *adv.*

ob scen i ty (əb sen′ə tē), 1 obscene quality. 2 obscene language or behavior; an obscene word or act. *n., pl.* **ob scen i ties.**

ob scure (əb skyur′), 1 not clearly expressed; hard to understand; vague: *an obscure passage in a book, an obscure style of writing.* 2 not well known; attracting no notice: *an obscure little village, an obscure poet.* 3 not easily discovered; hidden: *an obscure path, an obscure meaning.* 4 not distinct; not clear: *an obscure shape, obscure sounds.* 5 dark; dim: *an obscure corner.* 6 hide from view; dim; darken: *Clouds obscure the sun.* 1-5 *adj.,* **ob scur er, ob scur est;** 6 *v.,* **ob scured, ob scur ing.** —**ob scure′ly,** *adv.* —**ob scure′ness,** *n.*

ob scur i ty (əb skyur′ə tē), 1 lack of clearness; difficulty in being understood: *The obscurity of the book caused an argument over its meaning.* 2 something obscure; thing hard to understand; point or passage not clearly expressed; doubtful or vague meaning. 3 condition of being unknown: *Lincoln rose from obscurity to fame.* 4 lack of light; dimness: *The dog hid in the obscurity of the thick bushes. n., pl.* **ob scur i ties.**

ob se quies (ob′sə kwēz), funeral rites or ceremonies; a stately funeral. *n.pl.*

ob se qui ous (əb sē′kwē əs), polite or obedient from hope of gain or from fear; servile: *Obsequious courtiers greeted the royal couple. adj.* [*Obsequious* is from Latin *obsequiosus,* and can be traced back to *ob-,* meaning "after," and *sequi,* meaning "follow."] —**ob se′qui ous ly,** *adv.* —**ob se′qui ous ness,** *n.*

ob serv a ble (əb zėr′və bəl), 1 able to be noticed; noticeable; easily seen: *That star is observable on a dark*

night. 2 able to be followed or practiced: *This rule may not be observable. adj.* —**ob serv′a ble ness,** *n.*

ob serv a bly (əb zėr′və blē), so as to be observed; to an observable degree. *adv.*

ob serv ance (əb zėr′vəns), 1 act of observing or keeping laws or customs: *the observance of the Sabbath.* 2 act performed as a sign of worship or respect; religious ceremony. 3 observation. *n.*

ob serv ant (əb zėr′vənt), 1 quick to notice; watchful: *If you are observant in the fields and woods, you will find many flowers that others fail to notice.* 2 careful in observing a law, custom, etc.: *A good driver is observant of the traffic rules. adj.* —**ob serv′ant ly,** *adv.*

ob ser va tion (ob′zər vā′shən), 1 act, habit, or power of seeing and noting: *By trained observation a doctor can tell much about the condition of a patient.* 2 fact or condition of being seen; notice: *The spy avoided observation.* 3 something seen and noted: *During science experiments she kept careful records of her observations.* 4 act of watching for some special purpose; study: *The observation of nature is important in science.* 5 a remark; comment: *"Haste makes waste," was Father's observation when I spilled the milk. n.*

ob ser va tion al (ob′zər vā′shə nəl), of or based on observation: *observational evidence. adj.*

observatory (def. 1)

ob serv a to ry (əb zėr′və tôr′ē), 1 place or building equipped with a telescope for observing the stars and other heavenly bodies. 2 place or building for observing facts or happenings of nature. 3 a high place or building giving a wide view. *n., pl.* **ob serv a to ries.**

obscure (def. 6)
Clouds **obscured** the mountaintops.

ob serve (əb zėrv′), 1 see and note; notice: *I observed nothing strange in her behavior.* 2 examine for some special purpose; study: *An astronomer observes the stars.* 3 to remark; comment: *"Bad weather ahead," she observed.* 4 keep; follow in practice: *observe silence, observe a rule.* 5 show regard for; celebrate: *observe a holiday. v.,* **observed, ob serv ing.**

ob serv er (əb zėr′vər), person who observes. *n.*

ob serv ing (əb zėr′ving), observant; quick to notice. *adj.* —**ob serv′ing ly,** *adv.*

ob sess (əb ses′), fill the mind of; keep the attention of: *I was obsessed with the fear that I might fail. v.*

ob ses sion (əb sesh′ən), **1** an obsessing or a being obsessed; influence of a feeling, idea, or impulse that a person cannot escape. **2** the feeling, idea, or impulse itself. *n.*

ob ses sive (əb ses′iv), having to do with or causing obsession: *an obsessive fear. adj.* —**ob ses′sive ly,** *adv.*

ob sid i an (ob sid′ē ən), a hard, dark, glassy rock that is formed when lava cools. *n.*

ob so les cence (ob′sə les′ns), a passing out of use; getting out of date; becoming obsolete. *n.*

ob so les cent (ob′sə les′nt), passing out of use; tending to become out of date: *an obsolescent machine. adj.*

ob so lete (ob′sə lēt *or* ob′sə lēt′), **1** no longer in use: *"Eft" (meaning again) is an obsolete word. Wooden warships are obsolete.* **2** out of date; old-fashioned: *We still use this machine though it is obsolete. adj.*

ob sta cle (ob′stə kəl), something that stands in the way or stops progress; hindrance: *A fallen tree was an obstacle to traffic. He overcame the obstacle of blindness and became a musician. n.*

ob stet ric (ob stet′rik), having to do with the care of women before, in, and after childbirth. *adj.*

ob stet ri cal (ob stet′rə kəl), obstetric. *adj.*

ob ste tri cian (ob′stə trish′ən), a doctor who specializes in obstetrics. *n.*

ob stet rics (ob stet′riks), branch of medicine concerned with treating women before, in, and after childbirth. *n.* [*Obstetrics* comes from Latin *obstetrica*, which is from *obstetrix*, meaning "midwife," which comes from *ob-*, meaning "by," and *stare*, meaning "to stand."]

ob sti na cy (ob′stə nə sē), a being obstinate; stubbornness. *n., pl.* **ob sti na cies.**

ob sti nate (ob′stə nit), **1** not giving in; stubborn: *They were obstinate and wanted to do everything their own way.* **2** hard to control or treat: *an obstinate cough. adj.* —**ob′sti nate ly,** *adv.* —**ob′sti nate ness,** *n.*

ob strep er ous (əb strep′ər əs), **1** loud or noisy; boisterous: *Many children are naturally obstreperous when playing.* **2** unruly; disorderly. *adj.*

ob struct (əb strukt′), **1** make hard to pass through; block up: *Fallen trees obstruct the road.* **2** be in the way of; hinder: *Trees obstruct our view of the ocean. A shortage of materials obstructed the work of the factory. v.*

ob struc tion (əb struk′shən), **1** thing that obstructs; something in the way; obstacle: *The old path was blocked by such obstructions as boulders and fallen trees. Ignorance is an obstruction to progress.* **2** a blocking or hindering: *the obstruction of justice. n.*

ob struc tion ism (əb struk′shə niz′əm), act or practice of hindering the progress of business in a meeting, legislature, etc. *n.*

ob struc tion ist (əb struk′shə nist), person who hinders (progress, legislation, reform, etc.). *n.*

ob struc tive (əb struk′tiv), tending or serving to obstruct; blocking or hindering. *adj.*

ob tain (əb tān′), **1** get through effort; come to have: *obtain a job one applies for, obtain knowledge through study.* **2** be in use; be customary; prevail: *Different rules obtain in different schools. v.* —**ob tain′er,** *n.*

ob tain a ble (əb tā′nə bəl), able to be obtained. *adj.*

ob trude (əb trüd′), **1** put forward unasked and unwanted; force: *Don't obtrude your opinions on others.* **2** come unasked and unwanted; force oneself; intrude. **3** push out; thrust forward: *A turtle obtrudes its head from its shell. v.,* **ob trud ed, ob trud ing.** —**ob trud′er,** *n.*

ob tru sion (əb trü′zhən), **1** an obtruding. **2** something obtruded. *n.*

ob tru sive (əb trü′siv), inclined to obtrude; putting oneself forward; intrusive. *adj.* —**ob tru′sive ly,** *adv.* —**ob tru′sive ness,** *n.*

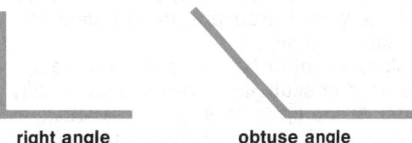

a hat	**i** it	**oi** oil	**ch** child	a in about
ā age	**ī** ice	**ou** out	**ng** long	e in taken
ä far	**o** hot	**u** cup	**sh** she	ə = i in pencil
e let	**ō** open	**ù** put	**th** thin	o in lemon
ē equal	**ô** order	**ü** rule	**ℑH** then	u in circus
ėr term			**zh** measure	

ob tuse (əb tüs′ *or* əb tyüs′), **1** not sharp or acute; blunt. **2** slow in understanding; stupid: *They were too obtuse to take the hint. adj.* —**ob tuse′ly,** *adv.* —**ob tuse′ness,** *n.*

right angle   obtuse angle

obtuse angle, angle larger than a right angle but less than 180 degrees.

ob verse (ob′vėrs′), **1** side of a coin, medal, etc., that has the principal design on it. **2** the face of anything that is meant to be turned toward the observer; front. *n.*

ob vi ate (ob′vē āt), meet and dispose of; clear out of the way; remove: *obviate a difficulty, obviate objections. v.,* **ob vi at ed, ob vi at ing.** —**ob′vi a′tor,** *n.*

ob vi ous (ob′vē əs), easily seen or understood; clear to the eye or mind; not to be doubted; plain: *It is obvious that two plus two make four. adj.* —**ob′vi ous ly,** *adv.* —**ob′vi ous ness,** *n.*

oc a ri na (ok′ə rē′nə), a small wind instrument with finger holes and a mouthpiece like a whistle. It produces a soft sound. *n., pl.* **oc a ri nas.**

WORD HISTORY

ocarina

Ocarina comes from Italian *ocarina*, which also means "little goose," and can be traced back to Latin *avis*, meaning "bird." The instrument was thought to be shaped like a small goose.

oc ca sion (ə kā′zhən), **1** a particular time: *We have met them on several occasions.* **2** a special event: *The jewels were worn only on great occasions.* **3** a good chance; opportunity: *The trip gave us an occasion to get better acquainted.* **4** a cause; reason: *The dog that was the occasion of the quarrel had run away.* **5** to cause; bring about: *His strange behavior occasioned talk.* 1-4 *n.,* 5 *v.*

on occasion, now and then; once in a while.

oc ca sion al (ə kā′zhə nəl), **1** happening or coming now and then, or once in a while: *We had fine weather all through July except for an occasional thunderstorm.* **2** caused by or used for some special time or event: *A piece of occasional music was played at the inauguration.* **3** for use once in a while: *occasional chairs. adj.*

oc ca sion al ly (ə kā′zhə nə lē), at times; now and then; once in a while. *adv.*

Oc ci dent (ok′sə dənt), **1** countries in Europe and America as distinguished from those in Asia; the West. **2 occident,** the west. *n.*

Oc ci den tal (ok′sə den′tl), **1** Western; of the Occident. **2** person born in the West. Europeans are Occidentals. **3 occidental,** western. 1,3 *adj.,* 2 *n.*

oc cip i tal (ok sip′ə təl), of or having to do with the back part of the head or skull. *adj.* —**oc cip′i tal ly,** *adv.*

oc clude (o klüd′), **1** stop up (a passage, pores, etc.); close. **2** shut in, out, or off. **3** meet closely in proper position. The teeth in the upper jaw and those in the lower jaw should occlude. *v.,* **oc clud ed, oc clud ing.**

oc clu sion (ə klü′zhən), an occluding or a being occluded. *n.*

oc cult (ə kult′ *or* ok′ult), **1** beyond the bounds of ordinary knowledge; mysterious. **2** outside the laws of the natural world; magical: *Astrology and alchemy are occult sciences. adj.* —**oc cult′ly,** *adv.* —**oc cult′ness,** *n.*

oc cu pan cy (ok′yə pən sē), occupying; holding (land, houses, etc.) by being in possession: *After five years of occupancy the homesteaders received a title to the land they lived on. n.*

oc cu pant (ok′yə pənt), **1** one that occupies: *The occupants of the car stepped out as I approached.* **2** person in actual possession of a house, estate, office, etc. *n.*

oc cu pa tion (ok′yə pā′shən), **1** work a person does regularly or to earn a living; business; employment; trade: *Caring for the sick is a nurse's occupation.* **2** an occupying or a being occupied; possession: *the occupation of a house by a family, the occupation of a town by the enemy. n.*

oc cu pa tion al (ok′yə pā′shə nəl), of a person's occupation. An occupational hazard or disease is one that results from a person's work or occupation. *adj.*

oc cu pi er (ok′yə pī′ər), one that occupies; occupant. *n.*

oc cu py (ok′yə pī), **1** take up; fill: *The building occupies an entire block. The lessons occupy the morning.* **2** keep busy; engage; employ: *Composing music occupied her attention.* **3** take possession of: *The enemy occupied our fort.* **4** have; hold: *A judge occupies an important position.* **5** live in: *Two families occupy the house next door. v.,* **oc cu pied, oc cu py ing.**

oc cur (ə kėr′), **1** take place; happen: *Storms often occur in winter.* **2** be found; exist: *"E" occurs in print more than any other letter.* **3** come to mind; suggest itself: *Did it occur to you to close the window? v.,* **oc curred, oc cur ring.** [*Occur* is from Latin *occurrere,* which comes from *ob-,* meaning "in the way of," and *currere,* meaning "run."]

oc cur rence (ə kėr′əns), **1** an occurring: *The occurrence of storms delayed our trip.* **2** event; happening: *an unexpected occurrence. n.*

o cean (ō′shən), **1** the great body of salt water that covers almost three fourths of the earth's surface; the sea. **2** any of its four main divisions; the Atlantic, Pacific, Indian, and Arctic oceans. The waters around the Antarctic continent are considered by some to form a separate ocean. *n.* —**o′cean like′,** *adj.*

O ce an i a (ō′shē an′ē ə), **1** islands of the central and south Pacific, north, northeast, and east of Australia. **2** these islands, together with Australasia and the Malay Archipelago. *n.*

o ce an ic (ō′shē an′ik), **1** of the ocean: *oceanic islands.* **2** living in the ocean: *oceanic fish.* **3** like the ocean; wide; vast. *adj.*

o cean og ra pher (ō′shə nog′rə fər), an expert in oceanography. *n.*

o cean og ra phy (ō′shə nog′rə fē), science that deals with oceans and seas, including marine life. *n.*

o ce lot (ō′sə lot *or* os′ə lot), a spotted cat somewhat like a leopard, but smaller, found from Texas through Mexico and into parts of South America. *n.* [*Ocelot* was borrowed from French *ocelot,* which came from Nahuatl *ocelotl.*]

o cher or **o chre** (ō′kər), **1** a yellow, brown, or red earthy mixture containing clay and iron oxide, used as a pigment. **2** a pale brownish yellow. *n.*

o'clock (ə klok′), **1** of the clock; by the clock: *It is one o'clock.* **2** as if on the dial of a clock. 12 o'clock in an airplane is the horizontal direction straight ahead, or the vertical position straight overhead. *adv.*

Oct., October.

octagon
This sign is an octagon.

oc ta gon (ok′tə gon), a plane figure having eight angles and eight sides. *n.*

oc tag o nal (ok tag′ə nəl), having eight angles and eight sides. *adj.* —**oc tag′o nal ly,** *adv.*

oc tane (ok′tān), a colorless, liquid hydrocarbon that occurs in petroleum. High quality gasoline contains more octane than the lower grades. *n.*

oc tave (ok′tiv *or* ok′tāv), **1** interval between a musical tone and another tone having twice or half as many vibrations. From middle C to the C above it is an octave. **2** the eighth tone above or below a given tone, having twice or half as many vibrations per second. **3** series of tones or of keys of an instrument, filling the interval between a tone and its octave. **4** the sounding together of a tone and its octave. **5** group of eight. *n.*

oc tet or **oc tette** (ok tet′), **1** piece of music for eight voices or instruments. **2** group of eight singers or players performing together. **3** any group of eight. *n.*

Oc to ber (ok tō′bər), the tenth month of the year. It has 31 days. *n.*

oc to ge nar i an (ok′tə jə ner′ē ən), **1** person who is 80 years old or between 80 and 90 years old. **2** 80 years old or between 80 and 90 years old. 1 *n.,* 2 *adj.*

oc to pus (ok′tə pəs), **1** a sea animal having a soft body and eight arms with suckers on them; devilfish. It is a mollusk. **2** anything like an octopus. A powerful, grasping organization with far-reaching influence is often called an octopus. *n., pl.* **oc to pus es, oc to pi** (ok′tə pī).

octopus (def. 1)
arm spread from 6 in.
to 20 ft. (15 cm. to 6 m.)

oc u lar (ok′yə lər), **1** of the eye: *an ocular muscle.* **2** received by actual sight; seen: *ocular proof. adj.*

oc u list (ok′yə list), doctor who examines and treats defects and diseases of the eye; ophthalmologist. *n.*

odd (od), **1** left over; extra: *Pay the bill with this money and keep the odd change.* **2** being one of a pair or set of which the rest is missing: *an odd stocking.* **3** occasional: *odd jobs, odd moments.* **4** with some extra: *thirty-odd dollars.* **5** leaving a remainder of 1 when divided by 2: *Three, five, and seven are odd numbers.* **6** having an odd number. **7** strange; peculiar; unusual: *What an odd house; it has no windows. adj.* [Odd came into English about 650 years ago from Icelandic *odda-*.] —**odd′ness,** *n.*

odd ball (od′bôl′), INFORMAL. a very eccentric person. *n.*

odd i ty (od′ə tē), **1** strangeness; peculiarity: *the oddity of wearing a fur coat over a bathing suit.* **2** a strange, unusual, or peculiar person or thing. *n., pl.* **odd i ties.**

odd ly (od′lē), in an odd manner; strangely; unusually. *adv.*

odds (odz), **1** difference in favor of one and against another; advantage. In betting, odds of 3 to 1 mean that 3 will be paid if the bet is lost for every 1 that is received if the bet is won. *The odds are in our favor and we should win.* **2** (in games) an extra allowance given to the weaker side. *n. pl.* or *sing.*

at odds, quarreling; disagreeing: *My sister and brother were often at odds.*

odds and ends, things left over; extra bits; scraps; remnants.

the odds are, the chances are; the probability is: *Since we are a better team, the odds are we will win.*

odds-on (odz′ôn′ or odz′on′), having the odds in one's favor; having a good chance to win in a contest. *adj.*

ode (ōd), a lyric poem full of noble feeling expressed with dignity. It is often addressed to some person or thing. *n.* [Ode was borrowed from Latin *ode*, which came from Greek *ōidē*, meaning "song." See **Word Family.**]

ode

Below are words related to *ode*. They can all be traced back to the Greek word *ōidē* (ō dā′), meaning "song."

| comedy | parody | rhapsody |
| melody | prosody | tragedy |

O der (ō′dər), river flowing from Czechoslovakia through W Poland into the Baltic Sea. *n.*

O des sa (ō des′ə), seaport in SW Soviet Union, on the Black Sea. *n.*

O din (ōd′n), (in Scandinavian myths) the chief god. Odin was the god of wisdom, culture, war, and the dead. The Anglo-Saxons called him Woden. *n.*

o di ous (ō′dē əs), very displeasing; hateful; offensive: *an odious smell, odious lies. adj.* —**o′di ous ly,** *adv.* —**o′di ous ness,** *n.*

o di um (ō′dē əm), **1** hatred; great dislike. **2** reproach; blame: *to bear the odium of having betrayed one's friend. n.*

o dom e ter (ō dom′ə tər), device for measuring distance traveled by a vehicle, by recording the number of revolutions of a wheel. *n.*

o dor (ō′dər), smell or scent: *the odor of roses, the odor of garbage. n.*

o dor if er ous (ō′də rif′ər əs), giving forth an odor, especially a pleasant odor; fragrant: *an odoriferous flower. adj.*

o dor less (ō′dər lis), without any odor: *Water is odorless. adj.*

o dor ous (ō′dər əs), giving forth an odor, especially a pleasant odor; fragrant: *Spices are odorous. adj.* —**o′dor ous ly,** *adv.* —**o′dor ous ness,** *n.*

O dys se us (ō dis′ē əs *or* ō dis′yüs), Ulysses. *n.*

Od ys sey (od′ə sē), **1** a long Greek epic poem describing the ten years of wandering of Ulysses after the Trojan War and his final return home. Homer is supposed to be its author. **2** Also, **odyssey.** any long series of wanderings and adventures. *n., pl.* **Od ys seys.**

Oed i pus (ed′ə pəs *or* ē′də pəs), (in Greek legends) a king who unknowingly killed his father and married his mother. *n.*

o'er (ôr), OLD USE. over. *prep., adv.*

of (ov *or* uv; *unstressed* əv), **1** belonging to: *a friend of my childhood, the news of the day, the driver of the car.* **2** made from: *a house of bricks, castles of sand.* **3** having; containing; with: *a house of six rooms.* **4** having as a quality: *a look of pity, a word of encouragement.* **5** named: *the city of Chicago.* **6** away from; from: *north of Boston, ten minutes of six.* **7** having to do with; in regard to; concerning; about: *think well of someone, be hard of heart, be fifteen years of age.* **8** as a result of having or using; out of; owing to: *expect much of a new medicine, die of a disease.* **9** among: *a friend of mine.* **10** Of connects nouns and adjectives having the meaning of a verb with the noun which would be the object of the verb: *the eating of fruit, the love of truth, in search of a ball, a hall smelling of onions. prep.*

off (ôf), **1** from the usual or correct position, condition, etc.: *I took off my hat.* **2** from; away from: *I jumped off the step. We are miles off the main road.* **3** away; at or to a distance: *go off on a journey. Christmas is only five weeks off.* **4** so as to stop or lessen: *Turn the water off. The game was called off.* **5** not on; not connected: *A button is off his coat (prep.). The electricity is off (adj.).* **6.** without work: *an afternoon off (adv.). He pursues his hobby during off hours (adj.).* **7** in full; wholly: *She cleared off her desk.* **8** in a specified condition in regard to money, property, etc.: *How well off are the Smiths?* **9** not very good; not up to average: *Because I hadn't played in weeks, my tennis game was off.* **10** possible but not likely: *I came on the off chance that I would find you.* **11** on one's way: *The train started and we were off on our trip.* **12** in error; wrong: *Your figures are way off.* **13** seaward from: *The ship anchored off Maine.* 1,3,4,6,7,11 *adv.,* 2,5,13 *prep.,* 5,6,8-10, 12 *adj.*

be off, go away; leave quickly.

off and on, at some times and not at others; now and then: *She has lived in Europe off and on for ten years.*

off with, 1 take off. **2** away with!

off., 1 office. **2** officer. **3** official.

of fal (ô′fəl), **1** the waste parts of an animal killed for food. **2** garbage; refuse. *n.*

off beat (ôf′bēt′), **1** a musical beat with little or no accent. **2** out of the ordinary; unusual; unconventional: *an offbeat play.* 1 *n.,* 2 *adj.*

Of fen bach (ô′fən bäk), **Jacques,** 1819–1880, French composer of light operas. *n.*

---

a hat	**i** it	**oi** oil	**ch** child	a in about
ā age	**ī** ice	**ou** out	**ng** long	e in taken
ä far	**o** hot	**u** cup	**sh** she	ə = { i in pencil
e let	**ō** open	**u̇** put	**th** thin	o in lemon
ē equal	**ô** order	**ü** rule	**ᴛʜ** then	u in circus
ėr term			**zh** measure	

of fence (ə fens′), BRITISH. offense. *n.*

of fend (ə fend′), **1** hurt the feelings of; make angry; displease; pain: *My friend was offended by my laughter.* **2** affect in an unpleasant or disagreeable way. **3** to sin or do wrong: *In what way have I offended? v.* —**of fend′a ble, of fend′i ble,** *adj.*

of fend er (ə fen′dər), **1** person who offends. **2** person who does wrong or breaks a law: *No trespassing; offenders will be prosecuted. n.*

of fense (ə fens′ *for 1-5;* ə fens′ *or* ô′fens *for 6*), **1** a breaking of the law; crime or sin. Offenses against the law are punished by fines or imprisonment. **2** condition of being offended; hurt feelings; anger: *He tried not to cause offense.* **3** act of offending; hurting someone's feelings: *No offense was meant.* **4** something that offends or causes displeasure. **5** act of attacking; attack: *A gun is a weapon of offense.* **6** an attacking team or force. *n.* —**of fense′less,** *adj.* —**of fense′less ly,** *adv.*

give offense, offend.

take offense, be offended.

of fen sive (ə fen′siv), **1** giving offense; irritating; annoying: *"Shut up" is an offensive remark.* **2** unpleasant; disagreeable; disgusting: *Bad eggs have an offensive odor.* **3** used for attack; having to do with attack: *offensive weapons, an offensive war for conquest.* **4** position or attitude of attack: *The army took the offensive.* **5** an attack: *an all-out offensive against polio.* 1-3 *adj.,* 4,5 *n.* —**of fen′sive ly,** *adv.* —**of fen′sive ness,** *n.*

of fer (ô′fər), **1** hold out to be taken or refused; present: *She offered us her help.* **2** be willing if another approves: *They offered to help us.* **3** propose; advance; suggest: *She offered a few ideas to improve the plan.* **4** to present in worship: *offer prayers.* **5** give or show intention; attempt; try: *The thieves offered no resistance to the police.* **6** present itself; occur: *I will come if the opportunity offers.* **7** act of offering: *an offer to sing, an offer of $30,000 for a house.* 1-6 *v.,* 7 *n.* —**of′fer a ble,** *adj.* —**of′fer er, of′fe ror,** *n.*

of fer ing (ô′fər ing), **1** the giving of something as an act of worship. **2** contribution; gift. **3** act of one that offers. *n.*

of fer to ry (ô′fər tôr′ē), **1** collection at a religious service. **2** verses said or the music sung or played while the offering is received. *n., pl.* **of fer to ries.**

off hand (ôf′hand′ *for 1;* ôf′hand′ *for 2-4*), **1** without previous thought or preparation; at once: *The carpenter could not tell offhand how much the work would cost.* **2** done or made offhand: *His offhand remarks were sometimes very wise.* **3** casual; informal. **4** without due courtesy; impolite: *The child's offhand ways angered her parents.* 1 *adv.,* 2-4 *adj.*

off hand ed (ôf′han′did), offhand. *adj.* —**off′hand′ed ly,** *adv.* —**off′hand′ed ness,** *n.*

of fice (ô′fis), **1** place in which the work of a business or profession is done; room or rooms in which to work: *The doctor's office is on the second floor.* **2** position, especially in the public service: *The President holds the highest office in the United States.* **3** duty of one's position; task; job; work: *A teacher's office is teaching.* **4** staff of persons carrying on work in an office: *Half the office is on vacation.* **5** act of kindness or unkindness; attention; service; injury: *Through the good offices of a friend, I was able to get a job.* **6** a religious ceremony or prayer: *the communion office. n.* [*Office* is from Latin *officium,* meaning "service," which comes from *opus,* meaning "work," and *facere,* meaning "do."]

of fice hold er (ô′fis hōl′dər), person who holds a public office; government official. *n.*

of fi cer (ô′fə sər), **1** (in the armed forces) person who commands others, especially a person who holds a commission, such as a major, a general, a captain, or an

admiral. **2** person who holds a public, church, or government office: *a health officer, a police officer.* **3** the president, vice-president, secretary, treasurer, etc., of a club, society, or similiar organization. *n.* —**of′fi cer less,** *adj.*

of fi cial (ə fish′əl), **1** person who holds a public position or who is in charge of some public work or duty: *The mayor is a government official.* **2** person holding office; officer: *bank officials.* **3** of an office or officers: *official duties, an official uniform.* **4** having authority: *An official record is kept of the proceedings of Congress.* **5** suitable for a person in office: *the official dignity of a judge.* 1,2 *n.,* 3-5 *adj.* —**of fi′cial ly,** *adv.*

of fi ci ate (ə fish′ē āt), **1** perform the duties of any office or position: *The president officiates at all club meetings.* **2** perform the duties of a priest, minister, or rabbi: *The rabbi officiated at the bar mitzvah. v.,* **of fi ci at ed, of fi ci at ing.**

of fi cious (ə fish′əs), too ready to offer services or advice; minding other people's business; fond of meddling. *adj.* —**of fi′cious ly,** *adv.* —**of fi′cious ness,** *n.*

off ing (ô′fing), the more distant part of the sea as seen from the shore. *n.*

in the offing, not far off: *trouble in the offing.*

off ish (ô′fish), INFORMAL. inclined to keep aloof; distant and reserved in manner. *adj.* —**off′ish ness,** *n.*

off set (ôf′set′ *for 1,2;* ôf′set′ *for 3-5*), **1** make up for; compensate for: *The better roads offset the greater distance.* **2** set off or balance: *offset a trip to the mountains against a summer job.* **3** something which makes up for something else; compensation: *In tennis, her speed and control were an offset to her lack of strength.* **4** any offshoot. **5** process of printing in which the inked impression is first made on a rubber roller and transferred to the paper, instead of being printed directly on the paper. 1,2 *v.,* **off set, off set ting;** 3-5 *n.*

off shoot (ôf′shüt′), **1** shoot or branch growing out from the main stem of a plant, tree, etc. **2** anything coming, or thought of as coming, from a main part, source, etc.; branch: *an offshoot of a mountain range. n.*

off shore (ôf′shôr′), off or away from the shore: *offshore fisheries (adj.), a wind blowing offshore (adv.). adj., adv.*

off side (ôf′sīd′), (in sports) not on the side allowed by the rules: *According to an official, two linemen were offside before the play began. adj.*

off spring (ôf′spring′), the young of a person, animal, or plant; descendant: *Every one of their offspring had red hair. n., pl.* **off spring** *or* **off springs.**

off stage (ôf′stāj′), away from the part of the stage that the audience can see. *adj.*

off-the-rec ord (ôf′ŦĦə rek′ərd), not intended for publication; not to be repeated publicly or issued as news: *an off-the-record opinion. adj.*

off-the-wall (ôf′ŦĦə wôl′), SLANG. odd; crazy; highly unusual: *an off-the-wall suggestion. adj.*

oft (ôft), OLD USE. often. *adv.*

of ten (ô′fən), in many cases; many times; frequently: *Blame is often misdirected. We come here often. adv.,* **of ten er, of ten est.** —**of′ten ness,** *n.*

of ten times (ô′fən tīmz′), often. *adv.*

oft times (ôft′tīmz′), often. *adv.*

o gle (ō′gəl), **1** look at with desire; make eyes at. **2** an ogling look. 1 *v.,* **o gled, o gling;** 2 *n.*

o gler (ō′glər), person who ogles. *n.*

o gre (ō′gər), **1** (in fairy tales) giant or monster that supposedly eats people. **2** person like such a monster in appearance or character. *n.*

oh *or* **Oh** (ō), word used to express surprise, joy, grief, pain, and other feelings: *Oh, dear me! interj.* Also, **O.**

OH, Ohio (used with postal Zip Code).

O'Hare Airport (ō her′ *or* ō här′), major international and domestic airport in Chicago, Illinois; world's busiest commercial airport.

O hi o (ō hī′ō), one of the north central states of the United States. *Abbreviation:* O. or OH *Capital:* Columbus. *n.* —**O hi′o an,** *adj., n.*

Ohio River, river in the United States, flowing SW from Pittsburgh into the Mississippi River. See **Mississippi River** for map.

ohm (ōm), unit of electrical resistance. A wire in which one volt produces a current of one ampere has a resistance of one ohm. *n.* [Ohm was named for Georg *Ohm*, 1787–1854, a German physicist.]

oil (oil), **1** any of several kinds of thick, fatty or greasy liquids that are lighter than water, burn easily, and are soluble in alcohol, but not in water. Mineral oils, such as kerosene, are used for fuel; animal and vegetable oils, such as olive oil, are used in cooking, medicine, and in many other ways. **2** petroleum. **3** put oil on or in: *oil the squeaky hinges of a door.* **4** oil color. **5** an oil painting. **6** of or for oil: *an oil slick, oil tankers.* 1,2,4,5 *n.,* 3 *v.,* 6 *adj.* **strike oil, 1** find oil by boring a hole in the earth. **2** find something very profitable.

WORD HISTORY

oil

Oil came into English about 700 years ago from French *oile,* which came from Latin *oleum,* meaning "olive oil," and can be traced back to Greek *elaia,* meaning "olive."

oil burner, furnace, ship, etc., that uses oil for fuel.

oil cloth (oil′klôth′), **1** cloth made waterproof by coating it with paint or oil. It is used to cover shelves, tables, etc. **2** piece of this cloth; oilskin: *an oilcloth on a kitchen table. n., pl.* **oil cloths** (oil′klôᴛHz or oil′klôths′).

oil color, 1 paint made by mixing pigment with oil; oil. **2** painting done in such colors. *n.*

oil er (oi′lər), **1** person or thing that oils. **2** can with a long spout used in oiling machinery. *n.*

oil of vitriol, sulfuric acid.

oil painting, 1 picture painted with oil colors. **2** art of painting with oil colors.

oil skin (oil′skin′), **1** cloth treated with oil to make it waterproof. **2** Usually, **oilskins,** *pl.* coat and trousers made of this cloth. *n.*

oil stone (oil′stōn′), any fine-grained stone which is oiled and used for sharpening tools. *n.*

oil well, well drilled in the earth to get oil.

oil y (oi′lē), **1** of oil: *an oily smell.* **2** containing oil: *oily salad dressing.* **3** covered or soaked with oil: *oily rags.* **4** like oil; smooth; slippery. **5** too smooth; suspiciously or disagreeably smooth: *an oily manner. adj.,* **oil i er, oil i est. —oil′i ness,** *n.*

oint ment (oint′mənt), substance made from oil or fat, often containing medicine, used on the skin to heal, soothe, or soften it. Cold cream and salve are ointments. *n.*

O jib wa (ō jib′wä), member of a large tribe of American Indians formerly living around Lake Superior; Chippewa. *n., pl.* **O jib wa** or **O jib was.**

O jib way (ō jib′wä), Ojibwa. *n., pl.* **O jib way** or **O jib ways.**

OK (ō′kā′), INFORMAL. **1** all right; correct; approved: *The new schedule was OK* (adj.). *She's doing OK at work* (adv.).

"OK, OK!" he yelled (interj.). **2** endorse; approve. **3** approval. 1 *adj., adv., interj.,* 2 *v.,* **OK'd, OK'ing;** 3 *n., pl.* **OK's.**

O.K. (ō′kā′), OK. *adj., adv., interj., v.,* **O.K.'d, O.K.'ing;** *n., pl.* **O.K.'s.**

OK, Oklahoma (used with postal Zip Code).

okapi
about 5 ft.
(1.5 m.) high
at the shoulder

o ka pi (ō kä′pē), an African mammal related to the giraffe, but smaller, without spots, and with a much shorter neck. *n., pl.* **o ka pis** or **o ka pi.**

o kay (ō′kā′), INFORMAL. OK. *adj., adv., interj., v., n.*

O'Keeffe (ō kēf′), Georgia, born 1887, American painter. *n.*

O khotsk (ō kotsk′), **Sea of,** sea east of Siberia and north of Japan. *n.*

O kie (ō′kē), INFORMAL. a migrant farm worker, especially one originally from Oklahoma. The word *Okie* is often considered offensive. *n.*

O ki na wa (ō′kə nä′wə), island in the W Pacific belonging to Japan. *n.* —**O′ki na′wan,** *adj., n.*

Okla., Oklahoma.

O kla ho ma (ō′klə hō′mə), one of the southwestern states of the United States. *Abbreviation:* Okla. or OK *Capital:* Oklahoma City. *n.* —**O′kla ho′man,** *adj., n.*

Oklahoma City, capital of Oklahoma, in the central part.

o kra (ō′krə), plant cultivated for its sticky pods, which are used in soups and as a vegetable; gumbo. *n.* [Okra comes from a west African word.]

old (ōld), **1** not young; having existed for a long time; aged: *old people, an old oak tree.* **2** of age; in age: *The baby is ten months old.* **3** not new; not recent; made long ago; ancient: *an old excuse, an old tomb, an old debt, an old family.* **4** much worn by age or use: *old clothes.* **5** looking or seeming old; like an old person in wisdom, feebleness, etc.; mature: *That child is old for her years.* **6** having much experience: *be old in wrongdoing.* **7** of long standing; over a long period of time: *We are old friends.* **8** former: *An old student returned to visit her teacher.* **9** familiar; dear: *good old fellow.* **10** time long ago; the past: *the heroes of old.* **11** the old, old people: *a home for the old.* 1-9 *adj.,* **old er, old est** or **eld er, eldest;** 10,11 *n.* —**old′ness,** *n.*

old age, years of life from about 65 on.

old country, country an emigrant comes from.

old en (ōl′dən), of old; old; ancient: *King Arthur lived in olden times. adj.*

Old English, 1 period in the history of the English language before 1100. **2** language of this period; Anglo-Saxon.

old-fash ioned (ōld′fash′ənd), **1** out of date in style, construction, etc.; of or typical of an old style or time: *an old-fashioned dress.* **2** keeping to old ways, ideas, etc.: *They are very old-fashioned in their ideas. adj.*

Old Glory, flag of the United States; the Stars and Stripes.

old hand, a very skilled or experienced person; expert: *an old hand at skiing.*

old ie (ōl′dē), INFORMAL. something old, popular, or familiar, such as a song or a movie. *n.*

old ish (ōl′dish), somewhat old. *adj.*

old-line (ōld′līn′), **1** keeping to old ideas and ways; conservative. **2** having a long history; established. *adj.*

old maid, 1 woman who has not married and seems unlikely to. **2** a prim, fussy person. **3** a simple card game in which players draw cards from each other's hands to make pairs. The player holding the extra card at the end of the game loses.

old ster (ōld′stər), INFORMAL. an old or older person. *n.*

Old Testament, the earlier part of the Bible, which contains the religious and social laws of the Hebrews, a record of their history, their important literature, and writings of their prophets.

old-time (ōld′tīm′), of former times; like old times. *adj.*

old-tim er (ōld′tī′mər), INFORMAL. person who has long been a resident, member, worker, etc. *n.*

Old World, the Eastern Hemisphere; Europe, Asia, and Africa.

old-world (ōld′wėrld′), **1** Also, **Old-World.** of or having to do with the Eastern Hemisphere; not of the New World: *old-world monkeys.* **2** belonging to or characteristic of a former period: *old-world courtesy. adj.*

o le an der (ō′lē an′dər), a poisonous evergreen shrub with fragrant red, pink, white, or purple flowers. *n.*

o le o (ō′lē ō), oleomargarine. *n.*

o le o mar gar ine (ō′lē ō mär′jər ən *or* ō′lē ō mär′-jə rēn′), a substitute for butter made from vegetable oils; margarine. *n.*

ol fac tor y (ol fak′tər ē), **1** having to do with smelling; of smell. The nose is an olfactory organ. **2** an olfactory organ. 1 *adj.,* 2 *n., pl.* **ol fac tor ies. —ol fac′tor i ly,** *adv.*

ol i garch (ol′ə gärk), one of the rulers in an oligarchy. *n.*

ol i gar chic (ol′ə gär′kik), of an oligarchy; having to do with rule by a few. *adj.*

ol i gar chi cal (ol′ə gär′kə kəl), oligarchic. *adj.*

ol i gar chy (ol′ə gär′kē), **1** form of government in which a few people have the ruling power. **2** country or state having such a government. **3** the ruling few. *n., pl.* **ol i gar chies.**

ol ive (ol′iv), **1** kind of evergreen tree with gray-green leaves that grows in southern Europe and other warm regions. **2** fruit of this tree, with a hard stone and bitter pulp. Olives are eaten green or ripe as a relish and are used to make olive oil. **3** a yellowish green. **4** yellowish-green. **5** a yellowish brown. **6** yellowish-brown. 1-3,5 *n.,* 4,6 *adj.*

olive branch, 1 branch of the olive tree. **2** one or more such branches, used as an emblem or symbol of peace. **3** anything offered as a sign of peace.

olive oil, oil pressed from olives, used in cooking, in medicine, etc.

O lym pi a (ō lim′pē ə), **1** plain in ancient Greece where the Olympic games were held. **2** capital of Washington, in the W part. *n.*

o lym pi ad *or* **O lym pi ad** (ō lim′pē ad), celebration of the modern Olympic games. *n.*

OLD ENGLISH

Old English developed from the Germanic dialects of the Angles, Saxons, and Jutes. Perhaps a quarter of our present English vocabulary goes back to Old English. Since these words include our common verbs and many common nouns and adjectives, they play a more important part in our everyday speech than their number indicates. Here are some examples of Modern English words and the Old English words from which they descended.

	VERBS	NOUNS	ADJECTIVES
Modern English	**eat**	**house**	**fast**
Old English	*etan*	*hūs*	*fæst*
	fight	**land**	**good**
	feohtan	*land*	*gōd*
	go	**meat**	**high**
	gān	*mete*	*hēah*
	sing	**stone**	**merry**
	singan	*stān*	*myrge*
	sit	**water**	**slow**
	sittan	*wæter*	*slāw*

The sentence below is an example of Old English—a law proclaimed by King Ethelbert of Kent about A.D. 560. It tells the amount of the fine for a particular offense. The Old English is followed by a word-for-word "translation," and then the way you might say it in Modern English.

Gif man ōþerne mid fȳste in naso slæhð, III scillinga.
If man other with fist in nose hits, three shillings.
If a man hits another in the nose with his fist, three shillings.

Old English (def. 2)

O lym pi an (ō lim′pē ən), **1** having to do with Olympia in Greece or with Mount Olympus. **2** like a god; heavenly; magnificent; superior: *Olympian calm, Olympian manners.* **3** one of the major Greek gods. **4** contender in the Olympic games. 1,2 *adj.,* 3,4 *n.*

O lym pic (ō lim′pik), **1** of Olympia or Greece. **2** of the Olympic games. **3 Olympics,** *pl.* Olympic games. 1,2 *adj.,* 3 *n.*

Olympic games, 1 contests in athletics, poetry, and music, held every four years by the ancient Greeks in honor of Zeus. **2** modern athletic contests imitating the athletic contests of these games, held once every four years in a different country. Athletes from many nations compete in them.

O lym pus (ō lim′pəs), **Mount,** mountain in NE Greece, which the ancient Greeks believed to be the home of the major Greek gods, 9570 feet (2917 meters) high. *n.*

O ma ha (ō′mə hô *or* ō′mə hä), city in E Nebraska, on the Missouri River. *n.*

O man (ō män′), **1** country in SE Arabia. *Capital:* Muscat. **2 Gulf of,** gulf of the Arabian Sea, between Oman and S Iran. See **Assyria** for map. *n.*

om buds man (om budz′mən), a government official appointed to receive and investigate grievances of citizens against the government. *n., pl.* **om buds men.** [*Ombudsman* was borrowed from Swedish *ombudsman.*]

o meg a (ō meg′ə *or* ō mē′gə), **1** the last letter of the Greek alphabet (Ω or ω). **2** the last of a series; end. *n.*

om e let *or* **om e lette** (om′lit), eggs beaten up with milk or water, fried or baked, and then folded over. *n.*

o men (ō′mən), sign of what is to happen; object or

event that is believed to mean good or bad fortune: *Spilling salt is said to be an omen of bad luck. n.*

om i nous (om′ə nəs), unfavorable; threatening: *Those black clouds look ominous. adj.* —**om′i nous ly,** *adv.* —**om′i nous ness,** *n.*

o mis sion (ō mish′ən), **1** an omitting or a being omitted: *the omission of a paragraph in copying a story.* **2** thing omitted: *Her song was the only omission from the program. n.*

o mit (ō mit′), **1** leave out: *omit a letter in a word.* **2** fail to do; neglect: *They omitted making their beds. v.,* **o mit ted, o mit ting.**

om ni bus (om′nə bus), **1** bus. **2** volume of works by a single author or of similar works by several authors: *an omnibus of detective stories.* **3** covering many things at once: *an omnibus law.* 1,2 *n., pl.* **om ni bus es;** 3 *adj.*

om nip o tence (om nip′ə təns), complete power; unlimited power: *the omnipotence of God. n.*

om nip o tent (om nip′ə tənt), **1** having all power; almighty. **2 the Omnipotent,** God. 1 *adj.,* 2 *n.*

om ni pres ence (om′nə prez′ns), presence everywhere at the same time: *God's omnipresence. n.*

om ni pres ent (om′nə prez′nt), present everywhere at the same time: *the omnipresent God. adj.*

om nis cience (om nish′əns), knowledge of everything; complete or infinite knowledge. *n.*

om nis cient (om nish′ənt), knowing everything; having complete or infinite knowledge. *adj.* —**om nis′cient ly,** *adv.*

om niv or ous (om niv′ər əs), **1** eating every kind of food. **2** eating both animal and vegetable food: *Human beings are omnivorous.* **3** taking in everything; fond of all kinds: *An omnivorous reader reads all kinds of books. adj.* —**om niv′or ous ly,** *adv.* —**om niv′or ous ness,** *n.*

on (ôn *or* on), **1** above and supported by: *The book is on the table.* **2** touching so as to cover, be around, etc.: *a ring on one's finger.* **3** close to: *a house on the shore.* **4** in the direction of; toward: *The protesters marched on the Capitol.* **5** against; upon: *The picture is on the wall.* **6** atop something: *The walls are up, and the roof is on.* **7** to something: *Hold on, or you may fall.* **8** toward something: *Some played; the others looked on.* **9** farther: *March on.* **10** by means of; by the use of: *I just talked to her on the phone.* **11** in the condition of; in the process of; in the way of: *on fire, on purpose, on duty.* **12** in or into a condition, process, manner, action, etc.: *Turn the gas on.* **13** taking place: *The race is on.* **14** in use; operating: *The radio is on.* **15** at the time of; during: *They greeted us on our arrival.* **16** from a time; forward: *later on, from that day on.* **17** concerning; in relation to; in connection with: *a book on animals.* **18** for the purpose of: *I went on an errand.* **19** in addition to: *Defeat on defeat discouraged them.* **20** among: *I am not on the committee.* 1-5,10,11, 15,17-20 *prep.,* 6-9,12,16 *adv.,* 13,14 *adj.*

and so on, and more of the same.

on and off, at some times and not at others; now and then.

on and on, without stopping: *The music played on and on through the entire evening.*

once (wuns), **1** one time: *Read it once more.* **2** a single occasion: *Once is enough.* **3** at some one time in the past; formerly: *a once powerful nation.* **4** even a single time; ever: *if the facts once become known.* **5** when; if ever: *Most people like to swim, once they have learned how.* 1,3,4 *adv.,* 2 *n.,* 5 *conj.*

all at once, suddenly: *All at once the lights went out.*

at once, 1 immediately: *Come at once.* **2** at the same time: *Everyone started shouting at once.*

for once, for one time at least.

once and for all or **once for all,** finally; decisively.

once in a while, not very often; now and then: *We see our cousins once in a while.*

once or twice, a few times.

once upon a time, long ago; once.

once-o ver (wuns′ō′vər), INFORMAL. a short, quick look. *n.*

on com ing (ôn′kum′ing *or* on′kum′ing), **1** approaching or advancing: *oncoming winter.* **2** approach or advance: *the oncoming of the storm.* 1 *adj.,* 2 *n.*

one (wun), **1** the first and lowest whole number; the number 1. **2** being a single unit or individual: *one apple, one dozen.* **3** a single person or thing: *I gave her the one she wanted.* **4** some: *One day you'll be sorry.* **5** some person or thing: *Two of you may go, but one must stay.* **6** any person, standing for people in general: *One must work hard to achieve success.* **7** the same: *All face one way.* **8** the same person or thing: *In Robert Louis Stevenson's story, the kind Dr. Jekyll and the evil Mr. Hyde were one.* **9** joined together; united: *The class was one in its approval.* **10** a certain: *One Maria Serra was elected.* 1,3 *n.,* 2,4, 7,9,10 *adj.,* 5,6,8 *pron.*

all one, 1 exactly the same. **2** making no difference; of no consequence.

at one, in agreement or harmony.

make one, 1 form or be one of a number, assembly, or party. **2** join together; unite in marriage.

one and all, everyone.

one by one, one after another.

one or two, a few.

one another, each other: *They looked at one another.*

O nei da (ō nī′də), member of an Iroquois tribe of American Indians formerly living in New York State. *n., pl.* **O nei da** or **O nei das.**

O'Neill (ō nēl′), **Eugene,** 1888–1953, American playwright. *n.*

one ness (wun′nis), **1** quality of being one in number or the only one of its kind; singleness. **2** quality of being the same in kind; sameness. **3** fact of forming one whole; unity. **4** agreement in mind, feeling, or purpose; harmony. *n.*

on er ous (on′ər əs), hard to take or carry; burdensome. *adj.* —**on′er ous ly,** *adv.* —**on′er ous ness,** *n.*

onerous—Peeling potatoes all day was **onerous** labor.

one self (wun self´), one's own self: *One should not praise oneself. pron.*

be oneself, 1 have full control of one's mind or body. **2** act naturally.

one-sid ed (wun´sī´did), **1** seeing only one side of a question; partial; unfair; prejudiced: *The umpire seemed one-sided in his decisions.* **2** uneven; unequal: *If one team is much better than the other, a game is one-sided.* **3** having but one side. **4** on only one side. *adj.*

one-time (wun´tīm´), of the past; former. *adj.*

one-track (wun´trak´), **1** having only one track. **2** INFOR-MAL. understanding or doing only one thing at a time; narrow: *a one-track mind. adj.*

one-way (wun´wā´), moving or allowing movement in only one direction: *a one-way street, a one-way ticket. adj.*

on go ing (ôn´gō´ing *or* on´gō´ing), continuous; unin-terrupted. *adj.*

on ion (un´yən), vegetable with a bulb eaten raw and used in cooking. Onions have a sharp, strong smell and taste. *n.* **—on´ion like´,** *adj.*

on-line (ôn´līn´ *or* on´līn´), in direct connection with and under the control of a central computer. *adv., adj.*

on look er (ôn´lùk´ər *or* on´lùk´ər), person who watches without taking part; spectator. *n.*

on look ing (ôn´lùk´ing *or* on´lùk´ing), watching; see-ing; noticing. *adj.*

on ly (ōn´lē), **1** by itself or themselves; one and no more; sole or single: *an only child. This is the only road to the cabin.* **2** merely; just: *She sold only two.* **3** and no one else; and nothing more; and that is all: *Only he remained.* **4** except that; but: *She would have started, only it rained.* **5** in a class by itself; best; finest: *He is the only writer for my taste.* **6** but then; it must be added that: *We had camped right beside a stream, only the water was not fit to drink.* **1,5** *adj.,* **2,3** *adv.,* **4,6** *conj.*

if only, I wish: *If only the sun would shine!*

only too, very: *She was only too glad to help us.*

on o mat o poe ia (on´ə mat´ə pē´ə), formation of a name or word by imitating the sound associated with the thing designated, as in *buzz, hum, slap, splash. n.*

On on da ga (on´ən dô´gə), member of an Iroquois tribe of American Indians formerly living in central New York State. *n., pl.* **On on da ga** *or* **On on da gas.**

on rush (ôn´rush´ *or* on´rush´), a very strong or forceful forward rush: *He was knocked down by the onrush of water. n., pl.* **on rush es.**

on set (ôn´set´ *or* on´set´), **1** the beginning or start: *The onset of this disease is gradual.* **2** attack: *The onset of the enemy took us by surprise. n.*

on shore (ôn´shôr´ *or* on´shôr´), toward or on the shore. *adv., adj.*

on side (ôn´sīd´ *or* on´sīd´), (in sports) on the side al-lowed by the rules; not offside. *adj.*

on slaught (ôn´slôt´ *or* on´slôt´), a vigorous attack: *The pirates made an onslaught on the ship. n.*

Ont., Ontario.

On tar i o (on ter´ē ō), **1** province in Canada, north of the Great Lakes. *Capital:* Toronto. **2 Lake,** the smallest of the five Great Lakes. *n.* **—On tar´i an,** *adj., n.*

on to (ôn´tü *or* on´tü), **1** on to; to a position on: *throw a ball onto the roof, get onto a horse.* **2** INFORMAL. familiar with; aware of: *I was soon onto their tricks. prep.*

o nus (ō´nəs), burden; responsibility: *The onus of caring for the invalid fell upon his children. n., pl.* **o nus es.**

on ward (ôn´wərd *or* on´wərd), toward the front; further on; on; forward: *The crowd around the store window began to move onward* (adv.). *An onward movement began* (adj.). *adv., adj.*

on wards (ôn´wərdz *or* on´wərdz), onward. *adv.*

on yx (on´iks), variety of quartz with bands of different colors and shades. Onyx is often dyed and carved to make cameos. *n.*

oo dles (ü´dlz), INFORMAL. large or unlimited quantities; heaps; loads: *oodles of money. n.pl.*

oo mi ak (ü´mē ak), umiak. *n.*

ooze[1] (üz), **1** pass out slowly through small openings; leak out slowly and quietly: *Blood still oozed from the cut. My courage oozed away as I waited.* **2** a slow flow. **3** some-thing that oozes. **1** *v.,* **oozed, ooz ing;** **2,3** *n.*

ooze[2] (üz), a soft mud or slime, especially at the bottom of a pond or river or on the ocean bottom. *n.*

oo zy[1] (ü´zē), oozing. *adj.* **—oo´zi ly,** *adv.*

oo zy[2] (ü´zē), muddy and soft; slimy: *an oozy meadow. adj.,* **oo zi er, oo zi est. —oo´zi ly,** *adv.* **—oo´zi ness,** *n.*

op., opus.

o pac i ty (ō pas´ə tē), a being opaque; darkness. *n.*

o pal (ō´pəl), gem that shows beautiful changes of color. Opals are composed of various forms of silica and are often a milky white. *n.*

o pal esce (ō´pə les´), exhibit a play of colors like that of an opal. *v.,* **o pal esced, o pal esc ing.**

o pal es cence (ō´pə les´ns), a play of colors like that of an opal. *n.*

o pal es cent (ō´pə les´nt), having a play of colors like that of an opal. *adj.*

o paque (ō pāk´), **1** not letting light through; not trans-parent: *A brick wall is opaque.* **2** not shining; dark; dull: *an opaque star, an opaque surface.* **3** obscure; hard to understand. *adj.* **—o paque´ly,** *adv.* **—o paque´ness,** *n.*

ope (ōp), OLD USE. open. *v.,* **oped, op ing;** *adj.*

O PEC (ō´pek), Organization of Petroleum Exporting Countries. *n.*

o pen (ō´pən), **1** not shut; not closed; letting (anyone or anything) in or out: *Open windows let in the fresh air.* **2** not having its door, gate, lid, etc., closed; not shut up: *an open drawer, an open box.* **3** not closed in: *an open field, the open sea, an open car.* **4 the open, a** open or clear space; open country, air, sea, etc.: *sleep out in the open.* **b** public view or knowledge: *The secret is now out in the open.* **5** having spaces or holes: *open ranks, cloth of open texture.* **6** unfilled; not taken: *a position still open.* **7** able to be entered, used, shared, competed for, etc., by all, or by a person or persons mentioned: *an open meeting, an open market. The race is open to anyone under 15.* **8** not covered or protected; exposed: *an open fire, an open jar, open to temptation.* **9** exposed to general view, knowl-edge, etc.; not secret: *open war, open disregard of rules.* **10** ready to listen to new ideas and judge them fairly; not prejudiced: *She has an open mind.* **11** frank and sincere: *an open heart. Please be open with me.* **12** generous; liber-al: *give with an open hand.* **13** make or become open: *Open the window. The door opened.* **14** have an opening or passage: *This door opens into the dining room.* **15** spread out or unfold: *open a book, open a letter.* **16** come apart or burst open: *a crack where the earth had opened. The clouds opened and the sun shone through.* **17** start or set up; es-tablish: *They opened a new store.* **18** begin: *open a debate. School opens today.* **19** free from hindrance, especially from ice: *open water on the lake, a harbor now open.* **1-3, 5-12,19** *adj.,* **4** *n.,* **13-18** *v.* **—o´pen ly,** *adv.*

open to, ready to take; willing to consider.

open up, make or become open; open a way to.

open air, outdoors: *Children like to play in the open air.*

o pen-air (ō´pən er´ *or* ō´pən ar´), outdoor: *an open-air concert. adj.*

o pen-and-shut (ō´pən ən shut´), INFORMAL. simple and direct; obvious; straightforward: *It seemed to be an open-and-shut case of murder. adj.*

o pen er (ō´pə nər), **1** person or thing that opens. **2** the first game of a scheduled series. *n.*

a hat	i it	oi oil	ch child	a in about
ā age	ī ice	ou out	ng long	e in taken
ä far	o hot	u cup	sh she	ə = { i in pencil
e let	ō open	u̇ put	th thin	o in lemon
ē equal	ô order	ü rule	₮H then	u in circus
ėr term			zh measure	

o pen-eyed (ō′pən īd′), **1** having eyes wide open as in wonder. **2** watchful or vigilant; observant. *adj.*

o pen-faced (ō′pən fāst′), having a frank face. *adj.*

o pen hand ed (ō′pən han′did), generous; liberal. *adj.* —**o′pen hand′ed ly,** *adv.* —**o′pen hand′ed ness,** *n.*

o pen-heart (ō′pən härt′), of or referring to a heart that has been stopped and opened by surgery to correct an injury or defect. During the operation, the circulatory function of the heart is carried on by a machine which pumps and oxygenates the blood. *adj.*

o pen heart ed (ō′pən här′tid), free in expressing one's real thoughts, opinions, and feelings; candid; frank; unreserved. *adj.* —**o′pen heart′ed ly,** *adv.* —**o′pen heart′ed ness,** *n.*

o pen-hearth process, (ō′pən härth′), process of making steel in a furnace that reflects the heat from the roof onto the raw material.

open house, 1 party or other social event that is open to all who wish to come. **2** an occasion on which an open house is held: *The High School open house is every other Friday evening.*

o pen ing (ō′pə ning), **1** an open or clear space; gap; hole: *an opening in a wall, an opening in the forest.* **2** the first part; the beginning: *the opening of a story.* **3** first; beginning: *the opening words of his speech.* **4** a formal beginning: *The opening will be at three o'clock tomorrow afternoon.* **5** job that is open or vacant: *an opening for a teller in a bank.* **6** a favorable chance or opportunity: *As soon as I saw an opening, I got up quickly and left the room.* **7** act of making open or fact of becoming open. **1,2,4-7** *n.,* **3** *adj.*

open letter, letter of protest, criticism, or appeal addressed to a person but published in a newspaper, magazine, etc.

o pen-mind ed (ō′pən mīn′did), having or showing a mind open to new arguments or ideas. *adj.*—**o′pen-mind′ed ly,** *adv.* —**o′pen-mind′ed ness,** *n.*

o pen-mouthed (ō′pən mou₮Hd′ *or* ō′pən moutht′), **1** having the mouth open. **2** gaping with surprise or astonishment. **3** having a wide mouth: *an open-mouthed pitcher. adj.*

o pen ness (ō′pən nis), **1** condition of being open. **2** lack of secrecy. **3** frankness. **4** willingness to consider new ideas or arguments. *n.*

open ses a me (ses′ə mē), **1** the magic command that made the door of the robbers' cave fly open in the story of Ali Baba. **2** anything which removes the barriers to entering a restricted place or to reaching a certain goal.

open shop, factory or business that employs both members of labor unions and nonunion workers on equal terms.

o pen work (ō′pən wėrk′), **1** ornamental work with small openings. **2** resembling such ornamental work. **1** *n.,* **2** *adj.*

op er a[1] (op′ər ə), a play in which music is an essential and prominent part, featuring arias, choruses, etc., with orchestral accompaniment. *Tosca, Lohengrin,* and *Carmen* are well-known operas. *n., pl.* **op er as.** [*Opera*[1] was borrowed from Italian *opera,* and can be traced back to Latin *opus,* meaning "work."]

op er a[2] (op′ər ə), a plural of **opus.** *n.*

op er a ble (op′ər ə bəl), **1** able to be operated; in a condition to be used: *The old motorcycle is still operable.* **2** able to be treated by a surgical operation: *It was clear from the X ray that the cancerous growth was operable. adj.*

opera glasses or **opera glass,** small binoculars for use at the opera and in theaters.

op e rate (op′ə rāt′), **1** be at work; run: *The machinery operates night and day.* **2** keep at work; control or manage: *operate an elevator. The company operates three*

factories. **3** produce an effect; work; act: *Several causes operated to bring on the war.* **4** produce a desired effect: *The medicine operated quickly.* **5** do something to the body, usually with instruments, to improve or restore health; perform surgery: *The doctor operated on the damaged lung.* v., **op e rat ed, op e rat ing.**

op e rat ic (op′ə rat′ik), of, in, or like an opera: *an operatic soprano. adj.* —**op′e rat′i cal ly,** *adv.*

operating system, the basic set of programs which controls the working of a computer and enables other programs to be carried out. It controls both information and machinery.

op e ra tion (op′ə rā′shən), **1** a working: *The operation of an airline requires many people.* **2** the way a thing works: *The operation of this machine is simple.* **3** a doing; action; activity: *the operation of organizing an expedition.* **4** something done to the body, usually with instruments, to improve or restore health: *Taking out the tonsils is a common operation.* **5** movements of soldiers, ships, supplies, etc.: *military and naval operations.* **6** (in mathematics) something done to one or more numbers or quantities according to specific rules. Addition, subtraction, multiplication, and division are the four commonest operations in arithmetic. *n.*

in operation, in action or in use.

op e ra tion al (op′ə rā′shə nəl), **1** of operations of any kind. **2** in condition to operate effectively. *adj.*

op er a tive (op′ər ə tiv *or* op′ə rā′tiv), **1** in operation; effective: *the laws operative in a community.* **2** worker; laborer: *The company hired a skilled machine operative.* **3** having to do with work or productiveness: *operative sections of a factory.* **4** detective. **1,3** *adj.,* **2,4** *n.*

op e ra tor (op′ə rā′tər), **1** person who operates. **2** a skilled worker who runs a machine, telephone, telegraph, etc. **3** person who runs a factory, mine, etc. *n.*

op e ret ta (op′ə ret′ə), a short, amusing opera with some spoken dialogue. *n., pl.* **op e ret tas.**

oph thal mol o gist (of′thal mol′ə jist), doctor who specializes in opthalmology; oculist. *n.*

oph thal mol o gy (of′thal mol′ə jē), branch of medicine dealing with the structure, functions, and diseases of the eye. *n.* [*Ophthalmology* comes from Greek *ophthalmos,* meaning "eye," and -*logia,* meaning "study or science of."]

o pi ate (ō′pē it *or* ō′pē āt), **1** any medical preparation that contains opium and so dulls pain or brings sleep. **2** containing opium. **3** anything that quiets. **4** bringing sleep or ease. **1,3** *n.,* **2,4** *adj.*

o pine (ō pīn′), hold or express an opinion; think: *She opined that the book was exciting.* v., **o pined, o pin ing.**

o pin ion (ə pin′yən), **1** what one thinks; belief not so strong as knowledge; judgment: *I try to learn the facts and form my own opinions.* **2** judgment of worth; impression; estimate: *I have a good opinion of her.* **3** a formal judgment by an expert; professional advice: *He wanted the doctor's opinion about the cause of his headache. n.*

o pin ion at ed (ə pin′yə nā′tid), stubborn or conceited with regard to one's opinions; dogmatic: *He is too opinionated to listen to anybody else. adj.* —**o pin′ion at′ed ly,** *adv.* —**o pin′ion at′ed ness,** *n.*

o pi um (ō′pē əm), a powerful drug that causes sleep and eases pain. It is made from a kind of poppy. *n.*

opossum
about 2¹/₂ ft.
(75 cm.) long
with the tail

o pos sum (ə pos′əm), a small mammal that lives in trees and carries its young in a pouch; possum. When it is caught or frightened, it pretends to be dead. The opossum is common in the southern and eastern United States. *n., pl.* **o pos sums** or **o pos sum.** [*Opossum* is of Algonquian origin.]

op po nent (ə pō′nənt), **1** person who is on the other side in a fight, game, or discussion; person fighting, struggling, or speaking against another: *She defeated her opponent in the election.* **2** opposing. **1** *n.,* **2** *adj.*

opportune—The police came at an **opportune** time.

op por tune (op′ər tün′ *or* op′ər tyün′), fortunate or well-chosen; suitable; convenient occasion; favorable. *adj.* [*Opportune* is from Latin *opportunus,* meaning "favorable, driving towards a harbor," which comes from *ob portum* (*veniens*), meaning "(coming) to port."] —**op′por tune′ly,** *adv.* —**op′por-tune′ness,** *n.*

op por tun ism (op′ər tü′niz′əm *or* op′ər tyü′niz′əm), policy or practice of using every opportunity to one's advantage without considering whether such an action is right or wrong. *n.*

op por tun ist (op′ər tü′nist *or* op′ər tyü′nist), person who uses every opportunity to gain advantage, regardless of right or wrong. *n.*

op por tun is tic (op′ər tü nis′tik *or* op′ər tyü nis′tik), of or given to opportunism. *adj.*

op por tu ni ty (op′ər tü′nə tē *or* op′ər tyü′nə tē), a good chance; favorable time; convenient occasion: *I had an opportunity to earn some money baby-sitting. I have had no opportunity to give him your message. n., pl.* **op por tu-ni ties.**

op pose (ə pōz′), **1** be against; be in the way of; act, fight, or struggle against; try to hinder; resist: *Many people opposed building a new highway because of the cost.* **2** put in contrast: *Love is opposed to hate. Night is opposed to day.* *v.,* **op posed, op pos ing.** —**op pos′er,** *n.*

op po site (op′ə zit), **1** placed against; as different in direction as can be; face to face; back to back: *The house straight across the street is opposite to ours.* **2** as different

as can be; just contrary: *North and south are opposite directions. Sour is opposite to sweet.* **3** person or thing as different as can be: *Night is the opposite of day. A saint is the opposite of a sinner.* **4** opposite to: *opposite the church.* **1,2** *adj.,* **3** *n.,* **4** *prep.* —**op′po site ly,** *adv.* —**op′po site-ness,** *n.*

op po si tion (op′ə zish′ən), **1** action against; resist-ance: *There was some opposition to the workers' request for higher wages.* **2** contrast: *His views are in opposition to mine.* **3** Also, **Opposition. a** a political party opposed to the party which is in power. **b** any party or body of oppo-nents. **4** a placing opposite. *n.*

op press (ə pres′), **1** govern harshly; keep down unjustly or by cruelty: *The dictator oppressed the people.* **2** weigh down; lie heavily on; burden: *A sense of trouble ahead oppressed her spirits. v.*

op pres sion (ə presh′ən), **1** cruel or unjust treatment; tyranny; persecution: *Oppression of the poor can lead to revolution. They fought against oppression.* **2** a heavy, weary feeling. *n.*

op pres sive (ə pres′iv), **1** hard to bear; burdensome: *The great heat was oppressive.* **2** harsh; severe; unjust: *Oppressive measures were taken to crush the rebellion. adj.* —**op pres′sive ly,** *adv.* —**op pres′sive ness,** *n.*

op pres sor (ə pres′ər), person who is cruel or unjust. *n.*

op pro bri ous (ə prō′brē əs), **1** expressing scorn, re-proach, or abuse: *Liar and thief are opprobrious names.* **2** disgraceful; shameful; infamous. *adj.* —**op pro′bri-ous ly,** *adv.* —**op pro′bri ous ness,** *n.*

op pro bri um (ə prō′brē əm), disgrace or reproach caused by shameful conduct; infamy; scorn; abuse. *n.*

opt (opt), choose or favor: *The class opted to go on a field trip. v.*

op tic (op′tik), of the eye; of the sense of sight. The **optic nerve** goes from the eye to the brain. *adj.*

op ti cal (op′tə kəl), **1** of the eye or the sense of sight; visual: *an optical illusion. Nearsightedness is an optical defect.* **2** made to assist sight: *Telescopes and microscopes are optical instruments.* **3** of optics. *adj.* —**op′ti cal ly,** *adv.*

op ti cian (op tish′ən), maker or seller of eyeglasses and other optical instruments. *n.*

op tics (op′tiks), science that deals with light and vi-sion. *n.*

op ti mal (op′tə məl), most favorable; best. *adj.* —**op′ti-mal ly,** *adv.*

op ti mism (op′tə miz′əm), **1** tendency to look on the bright side of things. **2** belief that everything will turn out for the best. **3** doctrine that the existing world is the best of all possible worlds. *n.*

op ti mist (op′tə mist), **1** person who looks on the bright side of things. **2** person who believes that everything in life will turn out for the best. *n.*

op ti mis tic (op′tə mis′tik), **1** inclined to look on the bright side of things. **2** hoping for the best: *I am optimis-tic about the chance of continued good weather.* **3** of opti-mism. *adj.* —**op′ti mis′ti cal ly,** *adv.*

op ti mum (op′tə məm), **1** the best or most favorable point, degree, amount, etc., for the purpose. **2** most favorable; best: *optimum security.* **1** *n., pl.* **op ti mums,** **op ti ma** (op′tə mə); **2** *adj.*

op tion (op′shən), **1** right or freedom of choice: *Pupils in our school have the option of taking Spanish, French, or German.* **2** act of choosing: *Where to travel should be left to each person's option.* **3** right to buy or sell something at a certain price within a certain time: *She paid $500 for an option on the land. n.*

op tion al (op′shə nəl), left to one's choice; not re-quired: *Attendance at graduation is optional. adj.* —**op′-tion al ly,** *adv.*

op tom e trist (op tom′ə trist), person skilled in examining the eyes and prescribing eyeglasses. An optometrist is not an M.D. but is legally authorized to do such work. *n.*

op tom e try (op tom′ə trē), measurement of the powers of sight; practice or occupation of testing eyes in order to fit them with glasses. *n.*

op u lence (op′yə ləns), **1** much money or property; wealth; riches. **2** abundance; plenty. *n.*

op u lent (op′yə lənt), **1** having wealth; rich. **2** abundant; plentiful. *adj.* —**op′u lent ly,** *adv.*

o pus (ō′pəs), **1** a musical work or composition: *The orchestra played Beethoven's Symphony No. 5 in C Minor, Opus 67.* **2** any work or composition. *n., pl.* **op er a** or **o pus es.** [*Opus* comes from Latin *opus,* meaning "work." See **Word Family.**]

opus

Below are words related to *opus.* They can all be traced back to the Latin word *opus* (ō′pùs), meaning "work."

cooperate	opera	operation
inoperative	operate	operetta

or (ôr), **1** word used to express a choice or a difference, or to connect words or groups of words of equal importance in a sentence: *You can go or stay. Is it sweet or sour?* **2** and if not; otherwise: *Either eat this or go hungry. Hurry, or you will be late.* **3** that is; being the same as: *an igloo or Eskimo snow house. This is the end or last part.* *conj.*

-or, *suffix added to verbs to form nouns.* person or thing that _____s: *Actor = person who acts. Accelerator = thing that accelerates.*

OR, Oregon (used with postal Zip Code).

o ra cle (ôr′ə kəl), **1** (in ancient times) an answer believed to be given by a god through a priest or priestess to some question. It often had a hidden meaning that was hard to understand. **2** place where the god was believed to give such answers. A famous oracle was at Delphi. **3** the priest, priestess, or other means by which the god's answer was believed to be given. **4** a very wise person. **5** person or thing regarded as a reliable and sure guide. *n.*

o rac u lar (ô rak′yə lər), **1** of or like an oracle. **2** with a hidden meaning that is difficult to make out. **3** very wise. *adj.* —**o rac′u lar ly,** *adv.*

o ral (ôr′əl), **1** using speech; spoken: *An oral agreement is not enough; we must have a written promise.* **2** of the mouth: *The oral opening in an earthworm is small. adj.*

o ral ly (ôr′ə lē), **1** by spoken words. **2** by the mouth. *adv.*

o range (ôr′inj), **1** the round, reddish-yellow, juicy citrus fruit of an evergreen that grows in warm climates. **2** reddish-yellow. **3** a reddish yellow. 1,3 *n.,* 2 *adj.* [*Orange* came into English about 600 years ago from French *orenge,* and can be traced back to Persian *nārang.*]

o range ade (ôr′inj ād′), a drink made of orange juice, sugar, and water. *n.*

orange pekoe, a black tea, made from the young leaves at the tips of the branches.

o rang-ou tang (ô rang′ù tang′), orangutan. *n.*

o rang u tan (ô rang′ù tan′), a large ape of the forests of Borneo and Sumatra, that has very long arms and long, reddish-brown hair. It lives mostly in trees and eats fruits and leaves. *n.* [See **Word History.**]

o rate (ô rāt′), make an oration; talk in a grand manner. *v.,* **o rat ed, o rat ing.**

o ra tion (ô rā′shən), a formal public speech delivered on a special occasion: *the orations of Cicero. n.* [*Oration* is from Latin *orationem,* which comes from *orare,* meaning "pray."]

o ra tor (ôr′ə tər), **1** person who makes an oration. **2** person who can speak very well in public. *n.*

o ra tor i cal (ôr′ə tôr′ə kəl), **1** of orators or oratory: *an oratorical contest.* **2** characteristic of orators or oratory: *She often talks in an oratorical manner. adj.* —**o′ra tor′i cal ly,** *adv.*

o ra to ri o (ôr′ə tôr′ē ō), a musical composition, usually based on a religious theme, for solo voices, chorus, and orchestra. It is dramatic in character but is performed without action, costumes, or scenery. *n., pl.* **o ra to ri os.** [*Oratorio* comes from Italian *oratorio,* which also means "place of prayer," and can be traced back to Latin *orare,* meaning "pray."]

o ra to ry[1] (ôr′ə tôr′ē), **1** skill in public speaking; fine speaking. **2** the art of public speaking. *n.*

o ra to ry[2] (ôr′ə tôr′ē), a small chapel; room set apart for prayer. *n., pl.* **o ra to ries.**

orb (ôrb), **1** anything round like a ball; sphere; globe. **2** sun, moon, planet, or star. **3** the eyeball or eye. *n.*

or bit (ôr′bit), **1** the curved, usually somewhat oval, path of a heavenly body, planet, or satellite about another body in space: *the earth's orbit about the sun, the moon's orbit about the earth, the orbit of a weather satellite about the earth.* **2** the curved path of an electron about the nucleus of an atom. **3** travel in an orbit or go into an orbit around: *Some artificial satellites can orbit the earth in*

WORD HISTORY

orangutan

Orangutan was borrowed from Malay *orangutan,* which comes from *orang,* meaning "man," and *utan,* meaning "of the woods."

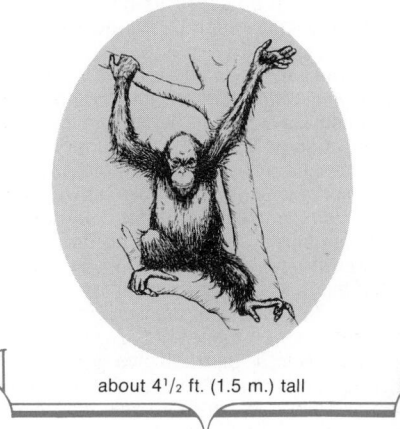

about 4½ ft. (1.5 m.) tall

less than an hour. **4** put into an orbit. **5** the socket in which the eyeball is set. 1,2,5 *n.*, 3,4 *v.*

or bit al (ôr′bə təl), of an orbit. *adj.*

orch., orchestra.

or chard (ôr′chərd), **1** piece of ground on which fruit trees are grown. **2** the trees in an orchard: *The orchard should bear a good crop this year. n.* [*Orchard* is from Old English *ortgeard*, which came from Latin *hortus*, meaning "garden," and Old English *geard*, meaning "yard."]

or ches tra (ôr′kə strə), **1** group of musicians playing together on various stringed, wind, and percussion instruments. Orchestras usually play at concerts, operas, or plays. **2** the violins, cellos, clarinets, and other instruments played together by such a group. **3** the part of a theater just in front of the stage, where the musicians sit to play. **4** the main floor of a theater, especially the part near the front: *Buy two seats in the orchestra. n., pl.* **orches tras.**

or ches tral (ôr kes′trəl), of an orchestra; composed for or performed by an orchestra. *adj.* —**or ches′tral ly,** *adv.*

or ches trate (ôr′kə strāt), compose or arrange (music) for performance by an orchestra. *v.*, **or ches trat ed, or ches trat ing.** —**or′ches tra′tor,** *n.*

or ches tra tion (ôr′kə strā′shən), arrangement of music for an orchestra. *n.*

orchid (def. 1)

or chid (ôr′kid), **1** any of a group of plants with beautiful flowers with three petals that often have unusual shapes and colors. **2** light-purple. **3** a light purple. 1,3 *n.*, 2 *adj.*

or dain (ôr dān′), **1** pass as a law; order; fix; decide; appoint: *The law ordains that all citizens shall have equal rights.* **2** appoint or consecrate officially as a member of the clergy. *v.* —**or dain′a ble,** *adj.* —**or dain′er,** *n.*

or deal (ôr dēl′), **1** a severe test or experience: *I dreaded the ordeal of going to the dentist.* **2** (in early times) an effort to decide the guilt or innocence of an accused person by making that person do something dangerous like holding fire or taking poison. The idea was that God would not let an innocent person be harmed by such danger. *n.*

or der (ôr′dər), **1** the way one thing follows another: *in order of size, in alphabetical order, to copy them in order.* **2** condition in which every part or piece is in its right place: *put a room in order.* **3** put in proper condition; arrange: *order one's affairs.* **4** condition; state: *My affairs are in good order.* **5** the way the world works; way things happen: *the order of nature.* **6** state or condition of things in which the law is obeyed and there is no trouble: *keep order. Order was established after the riot.* **7** principles and rules by which a meeting is run. **8** a command; telling what to do: *Troops are expected to obey orders.* **9** tell what to do; give an order to; command; bid: *The teacher ordered the noisy students to be quiet.* **10** give orders or directions: *Please order for me.* **11** a paper saying that money is to be given or paid, or that something is to be handed over: *a postal money order.* **12** a spoken or writ-

ten request for goods that one wants to buy or receive: *I gave the grocer an order for two dozen eggs, a loaf of bread, and two cans of tomatoes.* **13** goods so requested: *When will you be able to deliver my order?* **14** give an order for: *order a sandwich. We need to order milk, eggs, and bread from the grocer.* **15** decide; will: *The gods ordered it otherwise.* **16** kind or sort: *have ability of a high order.* **17** group of related animals or plants ranking below a class and above a family. The rose family, the pea family, and several others belong to one order. **18** a social rank, grade, or class: *all orders of society.* **19** rank or position in the church: *the order of bishops.* **20** a society of monks, friars, or nuns: *the Franciscan order.* **21** society to which one is admitted as an honor: *the Order of the Golden Fleece.* **22** a modern fraternal organization: *the Order of Masons.* **23** the badge worn by those belonging to an honorary order. **24** any of several styles of columns and architecture: *the Doric, Ionic, and Corinthian orders of Greek architecture.* **25** a regular form of worship for a given occasion. **26** portion or serving of food served in a restaurant, etc. 1,2,4-8,11-13,16-26 *n.*, 3,9,10,14,15 *v.* [*Order* came into English about 600 years ago from French *ordre*, which came from Latin *ordinem*, meaning "row, rank, series."] —**or′der er,** *n.*

by order, according to an order given by the proper person: *The bank was closed by order of the governor.*

call to order, ask to be quiet and start work: *The chairperson called the meeting to order.*

in order, 1 in the right arrangement or condition. **2** working right. **3** allowed by the rules.

in order that, so that; with the purpose that.

in order to, as a means to; with a view to; for the purpose of: *She worked hard in order to win the prize.*

in short order, quickly: *The broken window was replaced in short order.*

on order, having been ordered but not yet received.

on the order of, somewhat like; similar to.

order about or **order around,** send here and there; tell to do this and that.

out of order, 1 in the wrong arrangement or condition. **2** not working right. **3** against the rules.

take (holy) orders, become ordained as a Christian minister or priest.

to order, according to the buyer's wishes or needs.

ordered pair, (in mathematics) any two numbers written in a special order with one first and the other second. (2,5) is an ordered pair.

or der li ness (ôr′dər lē nis), orderly condition or behavior. *n.*

or der ly (ôr′dər lē), **1** in order; with regular arrangement, method, or system: *an orderly arrangement of dishes on shelves, an orderly mind.* **2** keeping order; well-behaved or regulated: *an orderly class.* **3** soldier who attends a superior officer to carry orders and perform other duties. **4** a hospital attendant who keep things clean and in order. 1,2 *adj.*, 3,4 *n.*, *pl.* **or der lies.**

or di nal number (ôrd′n əl), number that shows order or position in a series. First, second, third, etc., are ordinal numbers; one, two, three, etc., are cardinal numbers.

or di nance (ôrd′n əns), rule or law made by authority; decree: *a city ordinance that outlaws firecrackers. n.*

or di nar i ly (ôrd′n er′ə lē), **1** usually; regularly; normally: *We ordinarily go to the movies on Saturday.* **2** to the usual extent. *adv.*

or di nar i ness (ôrd′n er′ē nis), ordinary quality or condition; commonness. *n.*

or di nar y (ôrd′n er′ē), **1** according to habit or custom; usual; regular; normal: *an ordinary day's work. My ordinary lunch is a sandwich.* **2** not special; common; everyday; average: *an ordinary person, an ordinary situation.*

3 somewhat below the average: *The speaker was ordinary and tiresome. adj.*

out of the ordinary, not regular or customary; unusual; extraordinary.

or di na tion (ôrd/n ā/shən), **1** act or ceremony of making a person a member of the clergy. **2** a being made a member of the clergy. *n.*

ord nance (ôrd/nəns), **1** cannon or artillery. **2** military weapons of all kinds. *n.*

ore (ôr), mineral or rock containing enough of a metal or metals to make mining it profitable. The ore may be found in its natural state or combined with other substances. *n.* [*Ore* comes from Old English *ār,* meaning "brass."]

Ore. or **Oreg.,** Oregon.

o reg a no (ə reg/ə nō), an aromatic herb whose leaves are used for seasoning food. *n.*

O re gon (ôr/ə gon *or* ôr/ə gən), one of the Pacific states of the United States. *Abbreviation:* Ore., Oreg., or OR *Capital:* Salem. *n.* **—O re go ni an** (ôr/ə gō/nē ən), *adj., n.*

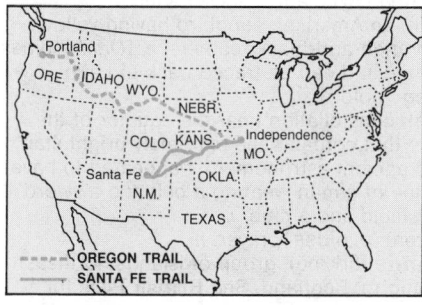

Oregon Trail, trail from Missouri northwest into Oregon, much used by early pioneers and settlers in the 1800's.

O res tes (ô res/tēz), (in Greek legends) the son of Agamemnon and Clytemnestra, who killed his mother because she had murdered his father. *n.*

organ (def. 1)

or gan (ôr/gən), **1** a musical instrument that has pipes of different lengths and often several sets of keys. The tones are produced by air being blown through the pipes by a bellows. **2** a similar instrument with one or more sets of keys but without pipes. The tones are produced by electronic devices. **3** any of various other musical instruments, such as a hand organ or a reed organ. **4** any part of an animal or plant that is composed of various tissues organized to perform some particular function. The eyes, stomach, heart, and lungs are organs of the body. Stamens and pistils are organs of flowers. **5** means of action; instrument: *A court is an organ of government.* **6** a newspaper or magazine that speaks for

and gives the views of a political party or some other organization. *n.*

or gan dy or **or gan die** (ôr/gən dē/), a fine, thin, stiff muslin, used for dresses, curtains, etc. *n., pl.* **or gandies.**

organ grinder, person who plays a hand organ by turning a crank.

or gan ic (ôr gan/ik), **1** of the bodily organs; affecting the structure of an organ: *an organic disease.* **2** of or obtained from plants or animals: *organic fertilizer.* **3** grown by using decaying plant and animal matter instead of artificial fertilizers: *organic foods.* **4** (in chemistry) of compounds containing carbon; containing carbon. Starch is an organic compound. Organic chemistry deals with carbon compounds found in food, fuels, etc. **5** made up of related parts, but being a unit; coordinated: *The United States is an organic whole made up of 50 states. adj.* **—or gan/i cal ly,** *adv.*

or gan ism (ôr/gə niz/əm), **1** a living body made up of separate parts, such as cells, tissues, and organs, which work together to carry on the various processes of life; an individual animal or plant. **2** a whole made up of related parts that work together. Human society, or any community, may be spoken of as a social organism. *n.*

or gan ist (ôr/gə nist), person who plays an organ: *a church organist. n.*

or gan i za tion (ôr/gə nə zā/shən), **1** group of persons united for some purpose. Churches, clubs, and political parties are organizations. **2** an organizing; grouping and arranging parts to form a whole: *The organization of a big picnic takes time and thought.* **3** the way in which a thing's parts are arranged to work together: *The organization of the human body is very complicated. n.*

or gan i za tion al (ôr/gə nə zā/shə nəl), of organization. *adj.* **—or/gan i za/tion al ly,** *adv.*

or gan ize (ôr/gə nīz), **1** put into working order; get together and arrange: *We helped our teacher organize a trip to the city zoo.* **2** combine in a company, political party, labor union, etc.: *organize the truckers. v.,* **or gan ized, or gan iz ing. —or/gan iz/a ble,** *adj.*

or gan iz er (ôr/gə nī/zər), person who organizes or brings elements or parts together. *n.*

or gy (ôr/jē), **1** a wild, drunken revel. **2 orgies,** *pl.* secret rites or ceremonies in the worship of certain Greek and Roman gods, especially the god of wine, celebrated with drinking, wild dancing, and singing. *n., pl.* **or gies.**

o ri el (ôr/ē əl), a bay window projecting from the outer face of a wall. *n.*

oriel

o ri ent (ôr′ē ənt *for 1,2;* ôr′ē ent *for 3,4),* **1** the east. **2 the Orient,** the East; Eastern countries. China and Japan are important nations of the Orient. The Orient usually includes Asia and countries east and southeast of the Mediterranean. **3** to place so as to face any indicated direction: *The building is oriented north and south.* **4** bring into the right relationship with surroundings; adjust to a new situation: *I had to orient myself on coming to a new city. The college has a program to orient freshman students.* 1,2 *n.,* 3,4 *v.*

WORD HISTORY

orient

Orient is from Latin *orientem,* meaning "the East, rising," which comes from *oriri,* meaning "rise." The rising sun appears in the eastern sky.

O ri en tal (ôr′ē en′tl), **1** Eastern; of the Orient: *Oriental customs.* **2** person born or living in the East, especially the Far East. **3** person whose ancestors came from the Far East. This meaning of *Oriental* is often considered offensive. 1 *adj.,* 2,3 *n.*

o ri en tal ist or **O ri en tal ist** (ôr′ē en′tl ist), person skilled in Oriental languages, literature, history, etc. *n.*

o ri en tate (ôr′ē en tāt), orient. *v.,* **o ri en tat ed, o ri en tat ing.**

o ri en ta tion (ôr′ē en tā′shən), **1** an orienting or a being oriented. **2** a bringing into the right relationship with surroundings; adjustment to a new situation: *the orientation of freshman students. n.*

o ri fice (ôr′ə fis), an opening or hole; mouth: *the orifice of a tube or pipe. n.* [*Orifice* is from Latin *orificium,* which comes from *oris,* meaning "mouth," and *facere,* meaning "make."]

orig., **1** origin. **2** original.

origami

o ri ga mi (ôr′ə gä′mē), the Japanese art of folding paper to make decorative objects, such as birds, animals, and flowers. *n.*

o ri gin (ôr′ə jin), **1** thing from which anything comes; starting point; source; beginning: *the origin of a quarrel, the origin of a disease.* **2** parentage, ancestry, or birth: *He is of Mexican origin.* **3** (in mathematics) the point where the horizontal and vertical axes cross in a system of coordinates. *n.*

o rig i nal (ə rij′ə nəl), **1** of the beginning; first; earliest: *They were the original owners of that house. The hat has been marked down from its original price.* **2** new; fresh; novel: *It is hard to plan original games for a party.* **3** able to do, make, or think something new; inventive: *a very original writer.* **4** not copied, imitated, or translated from something else: *She wrote an original poem.* **5** thing from

which another is copied, imitated, or translated: *The original of this picture is in Rome.* 1-4 *adj.,* 5 *n.*

o rig i nal i ty (ə rij′ə nal′ə tē), **1** ability to do, make, or think up something new. **2** freshness; novelty. **3** a being original. *n.*

o rig i nal ly (ə rij′ə nə lē), **1** by origin: *a plant originally African.* **2** at first; in the first place: *Though originally the house was small, rooms have been added.* **3** in a fresh or novel manner: *We want this room decorated originally. adv.*

o rig i nate (ə rij′ə nāt), **1** cause to be; invent: *originate a new style of painting.* **2** come into being; begin; arise: *Where did that story originate? v.,* **o rig i nat ed, o rig i nat ing.**

o rig i na tion (ə rij′ə nā′shən), an originating; origin. *n.*

o rig i na tive (ə rij′ə nā′tiv), having originality; inventive; creative. *adj.* **—o rig′i na′tive ly,** *adv.*

o rig i na tor (ə rij′ə nā′tər), person who originates; inventor. *n.*

O ri no co (ôr′ə nō′kō), large river in South America, flowing through Venezuela into the Atlantic. *n.*

o ri ole (ôr′ē ōl), an American songbird having yellow-and-black or orange-and-black feathers. *n.* [*Oriole* comes from French *oriol,* and can be traced back to Latin *aurum,* meaning "gold."]

O ri on (ô rī′ən), constellation near the equator of the celestial sphere that contains the extremely bright star Betelgeuse. To ancient astronomers it appeared to have the rough outline of a man wearing a belt and a sword and holding a shield and a club. *n.*

o ri son (ôr′ə zən), OLD USE. prayer. *n.*

Ork ney Islands (ôrk′nē), group of islands northeast of, and belonging to, Scotland. See **British Isles** for map.

Or lé ans (ôr′lē ənz), city in central France. *n.*

Or lon (ôr′lon), trademark for a light-weight synthetic fiber that resists sun, rain, and acids. It is used for clothing, sails, awnings, etc. *n.*

or na ment (ôr′nə mənt *for 1;* ôr′nə ment *for 2),* **1** something pretty or decorative; something to add beauty; adornment; decoration: *Lace, jewels, vases, and statues are ornaments.* **2** add beauty to; make more pleasing or attractive; adorn; decorate. 1 *n.,* 2 *v.*

or na men tal (ôr′nə men′tl), **1** of or for ornament; used as an ornament: *ornamental plants.* **2** decorative: *ornamental designs in wallpaper. adj.* **—or′na men′tal ly,** *adv.*

or na men ta tion (ôr′nə men tā′shən), **1** an ornamenting or a being ornamented. **2** decorations; ornaments. *n.*

or nate (ôr nāt′), much adorned; much ornamented: *an ornate vase. adj.* **—or nate′ly,** *adv.* **—or nate′ness,** *n.*

or ner y (ôr′nər ē), INFORMAL. mean in disposition: *an ornery horse. adj.,* **or ner i er, or ner i est.** **—or′ner i ness,** *n.*

or ni tho log i cal (ôr′nə thə loj′ə kəl), dealing with birds. *adj.* **—or′ni tho log′i cal ly,** *adv.*

or ni thol o gist (ôr′nə thol′ə jist), an expert in ornithology. *n.*

or ni thol o gy (ôr′nə thol′ə jē), branch of zoology dealing with the study of birds. *n.*

or phan (ôr′fən), **1** child whose parents are dead; child whose father or mother is dead. **2** of or for such a child or children: *an orphan asylum.* **3** without a father or mother or both. **4** make an orphan of: *The war orphaned him at an early age.* 1 *n.,* 2,3 *adj.,* 4 *v.*

or phan age (ôr′fə nij), home for orphans. *n.*

Or phe us (ôr′fē əs *or* ôr′fyüs), (in Greek myths) a musician who played his lyre so sweetly that animals and even trees and rocks followed him. *n.*

or tho don tia (ôr′thə don′chə), orthondontics. *n.*

or tho don tics (ôr′thə don′tiks), branch of dentistry that deals with straightening and adjusting teeth. *n.*

or tho don tist (ôr′thə don′tist), dentist who specializes in orthodontics. *n.*

or tho dox (ôr′thə doks), **1** generally accepted, especially in religion. **2** having generally accepted views or opinions, especially in religion; adhering to established customs and traditions: *an orthodox Methodist, an orthodox Jew.* **3** approved by convention; usual; customary: *the orthodox Thanksgiving dinner of turkey. adj.*

Orthodox Church, Eastern Church.

or tho dox y (ôr′thə dok′sē), the holding of generally accepted beliefs; orthodox practice, especially in religion; being orthodox. *n., pl.* **or tho dox ies.**

or tho graph ic (ôr′thə graf′ik), **1** having to do with orthography. **2** correct in spelling. *adj.* —**or′tho graph′i cal ly,** *adv.*

or thog ra phy (ôr thog′rə fē), **1** correct spelling; spelling considered as right or wrong. **2** art of spelling; study of spelling. *n., pl.* **or thog ra phies.**

or tho pe dics or or tho pae dics (ôr′thə pē′diks), branch of medicine that deals with the deformities and diseases of bones and joints. *n.*

or tho pe dist or or tho pae dist (ôr′thə pē′dist), physician who specializes in orthopedics. *n.*

Or well (ôr′wel), **George,** 1903-1950, English novelist and essayist. *n.*

-ory, *suffix forming adjectives and nouns.* **1** _____ing: *Contradictory = contradicting.* **2** of _____ion; characterized by _____ion: *Illusory = of illusion. Compulsory = characterized by compulsion.* **3** serving to _____: *Preparatory = serving to prepare.* **4** tending to _____; inclined to _____: *Conciliatory = inclined to conciliate.* **5** place or establishment for _____ing: *Depository = place for depositing.*

o ryx (ôr′iks), an African antelope with long, nearly straight horns. *n., pl.* **o ryx es** or **o ryx.**

Os, symbol for osmium.

O sage (ō′sāj), member of a tribe of American Indians, who originally lived in the region of the Arkansas and Missouri rivers. *n., pl.* **O sage** or **O sag es.**

O sa ka (ō sä′kə), large city and seaport in S Japan. *n.*

os cil late (os′l āt), **1** swing to and fro like a pendulum; move to and fro between two points. **2** vary between opinions, purposes, etc. *v.,* **os cil lat ed, os cil lat ing.**

os cil la tion (os′l ā′shən), **1** a swinging to and fro like a pendulum. **2** a single swing of a vibrating body: *Each oscillation of the pendulum takes one second.* **3** the variation of a quantity from one limit to another, as the voltage of an alternating current. *n.*

os cil la tor (os′l ā′tər), **1** person or thing that oscillates. **2** device which converts direct current into an alternating current of a particular frequency. The oscillator in a radio transmitting apparatus is a vacuum tube which produces the carrier wave for a radio signal. *n.*

os cil lo scope (ə sil′ə skōp), instrument for showing the oscillations of a changing voltage or current on the fluorescent screen of a cathode-ray tube. *n.*

os cu late (os′kyə lāt), to kiss. *v.,* **os cu lat ed, os cu lat ing.**

os cu la tion (os′kyə lā′shən), **1** act of kissing. **2** kiss. *n.*

O si ris (ō sī′ris), one of the chief gods of ancient Egypt, ruler of the lower world and judge of the dead. He represented good and productivity and is identified with the Nile. *n.*

Os lo (oz′lō), capital of Norway, in the SE part. *n.*

os mi um (oz′mē əm), a hard, heavy, bluish-white, metallic element which occurs with platinum and iridium. Osmium is the heaviest or densest known element and is used for electric-light filaments and phonograph needles. *n.*

os mo sis (oz mō′sis), **1** the tendency of two fluids of different strengths that are separated by a membrane to go through it and become mixed. Osmosis is the chief means by which the body absorbs food. Fluid in the tissues moves into the blood vessels by osmosis. **2** a gradual, often unconscious, absorbing of facts, theories, ideas, etc.: *to learn by osmosis. n.*

os mot ic (oz mot′ik), of osmosis. *adj.* —**os mot′i cal ly,** *adv.*

os prey (os′prē), a large hawk that feeds on fish; fish hawk. *n., pl.* **os preys.**

WORD HISTORY

osprey

Osprey is from Latin *ossifraga*, which comes from *ossis,* meaning "bone," and *frangere,* meaning "to break." The bird was believed to drop carcass bones from a height in order to break them and reach the marrow inside.

wingspread up to 6 ft. (2 m.)

os si fi ca tion (os′ə fə kā′shən), process of changing or being changed into bone. *n.*

os si fy (os′ə fī), **1** change into bone; become bone: *The soft parts of a baby's skull ossify as the baby grows older.* **2** harden like bone; make or become fixed, hardhearted, or very conservative. *v.,* **os si fied, os si fy ing.** —**os′si fi er,** *n.*

os ten si ble (o sten′sə bəl), according to appearances; apparent; pretended; professed: *My ostensible purpose for going to the library was to study, but I was really reading magazines. adj.* [*Ostensible* is from Latin *ostensum,* meaning "shown," which comes from *ob-,* meaning "toward," and *tendere,* meaning "to stretch."]

os ten si bly (o sten′sə blē), on the face of it; as openly stated or shown; apparently: *Though ostensibly studying, I was really drawing. adv.*

os ten ta tion (os′ten tā′shən), a showing off; display intended to impress others: *the ostentation of a newly rich family. n.*

os ten ta tious (os′ten tā′shəs), **1** done for display; intended to attract notice: *ostentatious jewels.* **2** showing off; liking to attract notice. *adj.* **—os/ten ta/tious ly,** *adv.* **—os/ten ta/tious ness,** *n.*

os te o path (os/tē ə path), person who specializes in osteopathy. *n.*

os te o path ic (os/tē ə path/ik), of osteopathy. *adj.* **—os/te o path/i cal ly,** *adv.*

os te op a thy (os/tē op/ə thē), treatment of diseases by manipulating the bones and muscles. Osteopathy also includes other types of medical and physical therapy. *n.*

ost ler (os/lər), hostler. *n.*

ost mark (ôst/märk/), unit of money in East Germany. *n.*

os tra cism (os/trə siz/əm), **1** banishment from one's native country. **2** a being shut out from society, from favor, from privileges, or from association with others. *n.*

os tra cize (os/trə sīz), **1** condemn to leave a country; banish. The ancient Greeks ostracized an unpopular citizen by public vote. **2** shut out from society, from favor, from privileges, etc.: *The cheater was ostracized.* *v.,* **ostra cized, os tra ciz ing.** [*Ostracize* is from Greek *ostrakizein,* which comes from *ostrakon,* meaning "tile." The vote to ostracize was written on a small tile.] **—os/tra ciz/a ble,** *adj.* **—os/tra ci za/tion,** *n.* **—os/tra ciz/er,** *n.*

ostrich
up to 8 ft. (2.5 m.) tall

os trich (ôs/trich), a large African and Arabian bird that can run swiftly but cannot fly. Ostriches have two toes and are the largest of existing birds. They have large feathers or plumes which were much used as ornaments. *n., pl.* **os trich es.**

O.T. or **OT,** Old Testament.

O thel lo (ə thel/ō), **1** play by Shakespeare. **2** the principal character in this play, a brave but jealous Moor who kills his wife after being falsely persuaded that she is not true to him. *n.*

oth er (uꞇн/ər), **1** remaining: *He is here, but the other students are gone.* **2** additional or further: *I have no other place to go.* **3** not the same as one or more already mentioned: *Come some other day.* **4** different: *I would not have you other than you are.* **5** the other one; not the same ones: *Each praises the other.* **6** other person or thing: *There are others to be considered.* **7** in any different way; otherwise: *I could not do other than I did.* 1-4 *adj.,* 5,6 *pron.,* 7 *adv.*

every other day, every second; alternate: *We buy milk every other day.*

of all others, more than all others.

the other day (night, etc.), recently.

oth er wise (uꞇн/ər wīz/), **1** in a different way; differently: *I could not do otherwise.* **2** different: *It might have been otherwise.* **3** in other ways: *It is windy, but otherwise a very nice day.* **4** under other circumstances; in a different condition: *She reminded me of what I would otherwise have forgotten.* **5** or else; if not: *Come at once; otherwise you will be too late.* 1,3,4 *adv.,* 2 *adj.,* 5 *conj.*

Ot ta wa (ot/ə wə), capital of Canada, in SE Ontario. *n.*

ot ter (ot/ər), **1** a water mammal related to the weasels, that has webbed toes with claws and is a good swimmer. **2** its thick, glossy, brown fur. *n., pl.* **ot ters** or **ot ter.**

ot to man (ot/ə mən), **1** a low, cushioned seat without back or arms. **2** a cushioned footstool. *n., pl.* **ot to mans.**

Ot to man (ot/ə mən), **1** Turk. **2** Turkish. **1** *n., pl.* **Ot to mans; 2** *adj.*

Ottoman Empire, a former Turkish empire which occupied Asia Minor and parts of northern Africa, southeastern Europe, and southwestern Asia in the middle 1500's.

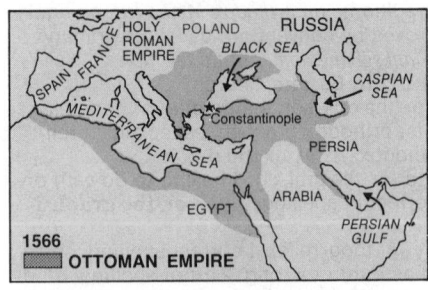

Oua ga dou gou (wä gə dü/gü), capital of Burkina Faso, in the central part. *n.*

ouch (ouch), exclamation of sudden pain. *interj.*

ought[1] (ôt), **1** have a duty; be obliged: *You ought to obey your parents.* **2** be right or suitable: *Cruelty and bullying ought not to be allowed.* **3** be wise: *I ought to go before it rains.* **4** be expected: *At your age you ought to know better.* **5** be very likely: *It ought to be a fine day tomorrow.* *v.*

ought[2] (ôt), aught; anything. *n.*

ought n't (ôt/nt), ought not.

ounce (ouns), **1** unit of weight, $1/16$ of a pound in avoirdupois, and $1/12$ of a pound in troy weight. **2** unit of volume for liquids; fluid ounce. 16 ounces = 1 pint. **3** a little bit; very small amount: *"An ounce of prevention is worth a pound of cure."* *n.* [*Ounce* came into English about 600 years ago from French *unce,* which came from Latin *uncia,* meaning "a twelfth part," and can be traced back to *unus,* meaning "one."]

our (our), of us; belonging to us: *We need our coats now.* *adj.*

Our Father, the Lord's Prayer.

Our Lady, the Virgin Mary.

ours (ourz), the one or ones belonging to us: *This garden is ours. Ours is a large house.* *pron.*

our self (our self/), myself. *Ourself* is used by an author, king, judge, etc. *"We will ourself reward the victor,"* said the queen. *pron.*

our selves (our selvz/), **1** form of *we* or *us* used to make a statement stronger: *We ourselves will do the work.* **2** form used instead of *we* or *us* in cases like: *We cook for ourselves.* **3** our real or true selves: *We weren't ourselves when we said that.* *pron.pl.*

-ous, suffix added to nouns to form adjectives. **1** having; having much; full of: *Famous = having much fame. Joyous = full of joy.* **2** characterized by: *Zealous = characterized by zeal.* **3** having the nature of: *Villainous = having the nature of a villain.* **4** like: *Thunderous = like thunder.*

otter (def. 1)
up to 4 ft.
(1 m.) long
with the tail

oust (oust), force out; drive out: *The sparrows have ousted the bluebirds from their nest. v.* [*Oust* comes from French *ouster,* and can be traced back to Latin *ob-,* meaning "against," and *stare,* meaning "to stand."]

oust er (ou′stər), an ousting, especially an illegal forcing out. *n.*

out (out), **1** away; forth: *The water will rush out. Spread the rug out.* **2** not in use, action, control, or fashion: *The fire is out. Election results show the present mayor is out. That style is out this year. The Democrats are in, the Republicans out.* **3** not at home; away from one's office, work, etc.: *My mother is out just now.* **4** (in baseball) not successful in reaching base or advancing from one base to another: *The outfielder caught the fly and the batter was out.* **5** a being out or putting out in baseball: *An inning lasts until three outs are made.* **6** from the usual place, condition, position, etc.: *Put the light out. I turned all my pockets out.* **7** at a money loss: *be out ten dollars.* **8** forth from; out of: *He went out the door.* **9** into the open; made public; made known; into being; so as to be seen: *The secret is out now. Her new book is out. Many flowers were coming out.* **10** to or at an end: *Let them fight it out.* **11** out along: *Drive out Second Street.* **12** go or come out; be disclosed: *The truth will out.* **13** aloud; plainly: *Speak out so that all can hear.* **14** completely; effectively: *fit out a boat.* **15** so as to project or extend: *stand out.* **16** to others: *let out rooms. Give out the books.* **17** from among others: *Pick out an apple for me.* **18** a defense or excuse: *have an out for stealing.* **19** external; exterior; outer; outlying: *an out island.* 1,3,6,7,9,10,13-17 *adv.,* 2,4,19 *adj.,* 5,18 *n.,* 8,11 *prep.,* 12 *v.*

at outs or **on the outs,** quarreling; disagreeing.

out and away, by far.

out for, looking for; trying to get: *He is out for the best deal he can get.*

out of, 1 from within: *He came out of the house.* **2** not within: *He is out of town.* **3** away from; beyond: *forty miles out of Atlanta. She was out of sight.* **4** not having; without: *She is out of work. We are out of coffee.* **5** so as to take away: *I was cheated out of my money.* **6** from: *His hat was made out of silk.* **7** from among: *We picked our puppy out of that litter.* **8** because of: *I went out of curiosity.*

out to, eagerly trying to.

out-, *prefix.* **1** outward; forth; away: *Outbound = outward bound. Outburst = a bursting forth.* **2** outside; at a distance: *Outlying = lying outside.* **3** more than or longer than: *Outlive = live longer than.* **4** better than: *Outdo = do better than.*

out-and-out (out′n out′), thorough; complete: *an out-and-out defeat. adj.*

out bal ance (out bal′əns), outweigh. *v.,* **out bal anced, out bal anc ing.**

out bid (out bid′), bid higher than (someone else). *v.,* **out bid, out bid** or **out bid den, out bid ding.**

out board (out′bôrd′), outside the hull of a ship or boat. *adj., adv.*

outboard motor, a gasoline motor, often portable, attached to the outside of the stern of a boat or canoe.

out bound (out′bound′), outward bound: *an outbound ship, outbound flights. adj.*

out brave (out brāv′), **1** face bravely. **2** be braver than. *v.,* **out braved, out brav ing.**

out break (out′brāk′), **1** a breaking out: *outbreaks of anger.* **2** a riot; public disturbance. *n.*

out build ing (out′bil′ding), a shed or building built against or near a main building: *Barns are outbuildings on a farm. n.*

out burst (out′bèrst′), a bursting forth: *an outburst of laughter, an outburst of smoke. n.*

out cast (out′kast′), **1** person or animal cast out from

home and friends: *The criminal was an outcast of society.* **2** being an outcast; homeless; friendless. 1 *n.,* 2 *adj.*

out class (out klas′), be of higher class than; be much better than. *v.*

out come (out′kum′), a result; consequence: *the outcome of a race. n.*

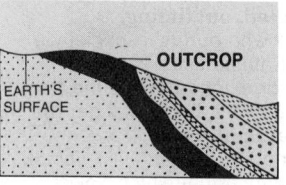

outcrop (def. 2)

out crop (out′krop′ for 1,2; out krop′ for 3), **1** a coming to the surface of the earth: *the outcrop of a vein of coal.* **2** part that comes to the surface: *The outcrop that we found proved to be very rich in gold.* **3** come to the surface; appear. 1,2 *n.,* 3 *v.,* **out cropped, out crop ping.**

out cry (out′krī′), **1** a crying out; sudden cry or scream. **2** a great noise or clamor. *n., pl.* **out cries.**

out date (out dāt′), put out-of-date; make old-fashioned. *v.,* **out dat ed, out dat ing.**

out dat ed (out dā′tid), out-of-date; old-fashioned. *adj.*

out did (out did′), past tense of **outdo.** *She outdid the others in diving. v.*

out dis tance (out dis′təns), leave behind; outstrip: *The winner outdistanced all the other runners in the race. v.,* **out dis tanced, out dis tanc ing.**

out do (out dü′), do more or better than; surpass: *He can outdo the others in running. v.,* **out did, out done, out doing.**

out done (out dun′), past participle of **outdo.** *She has outdone her previous track record. v.*

out door (out′dôr′), done, used, or living outdoors: *outdoor games, an outdoor meal. adj.*

out doors (out′dôrz′), **1** out in the open air; not indoors or in the house: *Let's go outdoors to play.* **2** the world outside of houses; the open air: *We must protect the wildlife of the great outdoors.* 1 *adv.,* 2 *n.*

outboard motor

out er (ou′tər), on the outside; farther out: *Shingles are used as an outer covering for many roofs. adj.* **—out′er ness,** *n.*

out er most (ou′tər mōst), farthest out. *adj.*

outer space, 1 space beyond the earth's atmosphere:

The moon is in outer space. **2** space beyond the solar system.

out field (out′fēld′), **1** the part of the baseball field beyond the diamond or infield. **2** the three players in the outfield. *n.*

out field er (out′fēl′dər), a baseball player stationed in the outfield. *n.*

out fight (out fīt′), fight better than; surpass in a fight. *v.,* **out fought** (out fôt′), **out fight ing.**

out fit (out′fit′), **1** all the articles necessary for any undertaking or purpose: *a skiing outfit.* **2** a set of clothes of which each item is chosen to match or complement the others. **3** furnish with everything necessary for any purpose; equip: *She outfitted herself for camp.* **4** group working together, such as a military unit, business organization, etc. **1,2,4** *n.,* **3** *v.,* **out fit ted, out fit ting.**

out fit ter (out′fit′ər), person who outfits, especially a dealer in outfits for traveling, athletic sports, etc. *n.*

out flank (out flangk′), **1** go or extend beyond the flank of (an opposing army, etc.); turn the flank of. **2** get the better of; circumvent. *v.* —**out flank′er,** *n.*

out flow (out′flō′), **1** a flowing out: *the outflow from a waterpipe, an outflow of sympathy.* **2** that which flows out. *n.*

out gen er al (out jen′ər əl), be a better general than; get the better of by superior strategy. *v.,* **out gen er aled, out gen er al ing** or **out gen er alled, out gen er al ling.**

out go (out′gō′), what goes out; what is paid out; amount that is spent. *n., pl.* **out goes.**

out go ing (out′gō′ing), **1** outward bound; departing: *outgoing steamships.* **2** friendly and helpful to others; sociable: *a very outgoing person. adj.*

out grow (out grō′), **1** grow too large for: *outgrow one's clothes.* **2** grow beyond or away from; get rid of by growing older: *outgrow early friends, outgrow a babyish habit.* **3** grow faster or taller than: *This variety of tomato will outgrow most other kinds. By the time he was ten, he had outgrown his older brother. v.,* **out grew** (out grü′), **out grown** (out grōn′), **out grow ing.**

out growth (out′grōth′), **1** a natural development, product, or result: *This big store is an outgrowth of a little shop.* **2** offshoot; something that has grown out: *A corn is an outgrowth on a toe.* **3** a growing out or forth: *the outgrowth of new leaves in the spring. n.*

out guess (out ges′), be too clever for; get the better of. *v.*

out house (out′hous′), **1** an outdoor toilet. **2** outbuilding. *n., pl.* **out hous es** (out′hou′ziz).

out ing (ou′ting), a short pleasure trip; walk or airing; holiday spent outdoors away from home: *On Sunday the family went on an outing to the beach. n.*

out land er (out′lan′dər), foreigner. *n.*

out land ish (out lan′dish), not familiar; odd; strange or ridiculous: *an outlandish hat. adj.* —**out land′ish ly,** *adv.*

outlandish—The actor wore an **outlandish** costume.

out last (out last′), last longer than. *v.*

out law (out′lô′), **1** a lawless person; criminal. **2** person outside the protection of the law; exile; outcast. **3** make or declare illegal: *outlaw gambling.* **4** deprive of legal force. An outlawed debt is one that cannot be collected because it has been due too long. **1,2** *n.,* **3,4** *v.* [*Outlaw* is from Old English *ūtlaga,* which came from Icelandic *ūt,* meaning "out," and *lög,* meaning "law."]

out lay (out′lā for 1,2; out lā′ for 3), **1** a laying out money; spending; expense: *a large outlay for clothing.* **2** the amount spent: *an outlay of eleven dollars.* **3** expend: *outlay money in improvements.* **1,2** *n.,* **3** *v.,* **out laid, out laying.**

out let (out′let), **1** means or place of letting out or getting out; way out; vent; opening; exit: *the outlet of a lake, an outlet for one's energies.* **2** market for a product. **3** point in an electric circuit where an electric plug may be inserted to receive power. An outlet is usually set in a wall. *n.*

out line (out′līn′), **1** line that shows the shape of an object; line that bounds a figure: *We saw the outlines of the mountains against the evening sky. The outline of Italy suggests a boot.* **2** a drawing or style of drawing that gives only outer lines: *Make an outline of the scene before you paint it.* **3** draw the outer line of: *Outline a map of America.* **4** a general plan; rough draft: *Make an outline before trying to write a composition. The teacher gave a brief outline of the work planned for the term.* **5** give a plan of; sketch: *She outlined their trip abroad.* **1,2,4** *n.,* **3,5** *v.,* **out lined, out lin ing.**

in outline, 1 with only the outline shown. **2** with only the main features.

out live (out liv′), live or last longer than; survive; outlast: *She outlived her older sister. The idea was good once, but it has outlived its usefulness. v.,* **out lived, out liv ing.**

out look (out′lùk′), **1** what one sees on looking out; view: *The room has a pleasant outlook.* **2** what seems likely to happen; prospect: *The outlook for our picnic is not very good; it looks as if it will rain.* **3** way of thinking about things; attitude of mind; point of view: *a cheerful outlook on life.* **4** lookout; place to watch from. *n.*

out ly ing (out′lī′ing), lying outside the boundary; far from the center; remote: *an outlying suburb of the city. adj.*

out ma neu ver (out′mə nü′vər), outdo in maneuvering; get the better of by maneuvering. *v.*

out match (out mach′), surpass; outdo. *v.*

out mod ed (out mō′did), out-of-date. *adj.*

out most (out′mōst), farthest out. *adj.*

out num ber (out num′bər), be more than; exceed in number: *They outnumbered us three to one. v.*

out-of-bounds (out′əv boundz′), outside the boundary line; out of play: *an out-of-bounds ball (adj.). He kicked the ball out-of-bounds (adv.). adj., adv.*

out-of-date (out′əv dāt′), not in present use; old-fashioned: *A horse and buggy is an out-of-date method of transportation. adj.* —**out′-of-date′ness,** *n.*

out-of-door (out′əv dôr′), outdoor. *adj.*

out-of-doors (out′əv dôrz′), **1** outdoor. **2** outdoors. **1** *adj.,* **2** *n., adv.*

out-of-the-way (out′əv ᴛнə wā′), **1** seldom visited; remote; unfrequented; secluded: *an out-of-the-way cottage.* **2** seldom met with; unusual: *out-of-the-way bits of information. adj.*

out pa tient (out′pā′shənt), patient receiving treatment at a hospital but not staying there. *n.*

out play (out plā′), play better than. *v.*

out post (out′pōst′), **1** a guard, or small number of soldiers, placed at some distance from an army or camp to prevent surprise attacks. **2** place where they are stationed. **3** a settlement or village in an outlying place: *a frontier outpost. n.*

out pour ing (out′pôr′ing), **1** a pouring out. **2** anything that is poured out. **3** an outburst: *an outpouring of grief. n.*

out put (out′pu̇t′), **1** put out; produce; deliver. **2** what is put out; amount produced; product or yield: *the daily output of automobiles.* **3** a putting forth: *With a sudden output of effort we moved the rock.* **4** information put out or produced by a computer. 1 *v.,* **out put, out put ting;** 2-4 *n.*

out rage (out′rāj), **1** an act showing no regard for the rights or feelings of others; overturning of the rights of others by force; act of violence; offense; insult: *The tyrant was guilty of many outrages.* **2** offend greatly; do violence to; insult: *The British government outraged the colonists by taxing them unfairly.* **3** break (the law, a rule of morality, etc.) openly; treat as nothing at all: *He outraged all rules of politeness by insulting his guests.* 1 *n.,* 2,3 *v.,* **out raged, out rag ing.** [*Outrage* came into English about 700 years ago from French *outrage,* meaning "a going beyond proper behavior," and can be traced back to Latin *ultra,* meaning "beyond."]

out ra geous (out rā′jəs), very bad or insulting; shocking: *outrageous language. adj.* —**out ra′geous ly,** *adv.* —**out ra′geous ness,** *n.*

out ran (out ran′), past tense of **outrun.** *She outran me easily. v.*

out rank (out rangk′), rank higher than: *A captain outranks a lieutenant. v.*

out reach (out rēch′), **1** reach beyond. **2** stretch out; extend. *v.*

out ride (out rīd′), ride faster, better, or farther than. *v.,* **out rode, out rid den, out rid ing.**

outrigger (def. 1)
on a sailboat

out rig ger (out′rig′ər), **1** framework extending outward from the side of a light boat or canoe and ending in a float. It keeps the boat from turning over. **2** boat equipped with brackets extending outward from either side to hold oarlocks. *n.*

out right (out′rīt′), **1** not gradually; altogether; entirely: *We paid for our car outright.* **2** without restraint; openly: *I laughed outright.* **3** complete; thorough: *an outright criminal, an outright lie.* **4** downright; straightforward; direct: *an outright refusal.* **5** at once; on the spot. 1,2,5 *adv.,* 3,4 *adj.* —**out′right′ness,** *n.*

out run (out run′), **1** run faster than: *She can outrun her older sister.* **2** leave behind; run beyond; pass the limits of: *This month's expenses have outrun our budget. v.,* **out ran, out run, out run ning.**

out sell (out sel′), **1** outdo in selling; sell more than: *He outsold every salesperson in the company last year.* **2** be sold in greater quantity than: *This brand outsells the other brands on the market. v.,* **out sold** (out sōld′), **out sell ing.**

out set (out′set′), a setting out; start; beginning: *At the outset, it looked like a nice day. n.*

out shine (out shīn′), **1** shine more brightly than. **2** be more brilliant or excellent than; surpass. *v.,* **out shone** (out shōn′), **out shin ing.**

out shoot (out shüt′), **1** shoot better or farther than. **2** shoot beyond. *v.,* **out shot** (out shot′), **out shoot ing.**

out side (out′sīd′; *for 5,6 also* out′sīd′), **1** the side or surface that is out; outer part: *polish the outside of a car, the outside of a house.* **2** on the outside; of or nearer the outside: *the outside leaves.* **3** on or to the outside; outdoors: *Run outside and play.* **4** space that is beyond or not inside. **5** INFORMAL. with the exception (of): *Outside of him, none of us liked the play.* **6** out of; beyond the limits of: *Stay outside the house. That is outside my plans.* **7** not belonging to a certain group, set, district, etc.: *Outside people tried to get control of the business.* **8** highest; largest; reaching the utmost limit: *an outside estimate of the cost.* **9** barely possible; very slight: *The team has an outside chance to win.* 1,4 *n.,* 2,7-9 *adj.,* 3 *adv.,* 5,6 *prep.* **at the outside,** at the utmost limit: *I can do it in a week, at the outside.*

out sid er (out′sī′dər), person not belonging to a particular group, set, company, party, district, etc. *n.*

out size (out′sīz′), larger than the usual size. *adj.*

out sized (out′sīzd′), outsize. *adj.*

out skirts (out′skėrts′), the outer parts or edges of a town, district, etc., or of a subject of discussion; outlying parts: *We have a farm on the outskirts of town. n.pl.*

out smart (out smärt′), outdo in cleverness. *v.*

out spo ken (out′spō′kən), not reserved; frank: *an outspoken person, outspoken criticism. adj.* —**out′spo′ken ly,** *adv.* —**out′spo′ken ness,** *n.*

out spread (out′spred′ *for 1;* out spred′ *for 2*), **1** spread out; extended: *an eagle with outspread wings.* **2** to spread out; extend. 1 *adj.,* 2 *v.,* **out spread, out spread ing.**

out stand ing (out stan′ding), **1** standing out from others; well-known; important: *an outstanding student.* **2** unpaid: *outstanding debts.* **3** standing out; projecting. *adj.* —**out stand′ing ly,** *adv.* —**out stand′ing ness,** *n.*

out stay (out stā′), stay longer than. *v.*

out stretched (out′strecht′), stretched out; extended: *He welcomed his old friend with outstretched arms. adj.*

out strip (out strip′), **1** go faster than; leave behind in a race: *A horse can outstrip a human being.* **2** do better than; excel: *She can outstrip most of her classmates in mathematics. v.,* **out stripped, out strip ping.**

out ward (out′wərd), **1** going toward the outside; turned toward the outside: *an outward motion. She gave one outward glance.* **2** toward the outside; away: *A porch extends outward from the house.* **3** outer: *to all outward appearances.* **4** on the outside: *I turned the coat with the lining outward.* **5** that can be seen; plain to see: *outward behavior.* 1,3,5 *adj.,* 2,4 *adv.* —**out′ward ness,** *n.*

out ward ly (out′wərd lē), **1** on the outside or outer surface. **2** in appearance: *Though frightened, she remained outwardly calm. adv.*

out wards (out′wərdz), outward. *adv.*

out wear (out wer′ *or* out wār′), **1** wear longer than. **2** wear out: *outwear someone's patience.* **3** outgrow. *v.,* **out wore** (out wôr′), **out worn, out wear ing.**

out weigh (out wā′), **1** weigh more than. **2** exceed in value, importance, influence, etc.: *The advantages of the plan outweigh its disadvantages. v.*

out wit (out wit′), get the better of by being more intelligent; be too clever for: *She usually outwits me and wins at checkers. v.,* **out wit ted, out wit ting.**

out work (out wėrk′), surpass in working; work harder or faster than. *v.* —**out′work′er,** *n.*

out worn (out′wôrn′ *for 1,2;* out wôrn′ *for 3),* **1** worn out: *outworn clothes.* **2** out-of-date; outgrown: *outworn habits.* **3** past participle of **outwear.** *I have outworn the coat I bought last year.* 1,2 *adj.,* 3 *v.*

oval (def. 1) **ovals** (def. 2)

o val (ō′vəl), **1** shaped like an egg. **2** shaped like an ellipse. **3** something having an oval shape. 1,2 *adj.,* 3 *n.* —**o′val ly,** *adv.* —**o′val ness,** *n.*

o var y (ō′vər ē), **1** the organ of a female animal in which eggs are produced. **2** the enlarged lower part of the pistil of a flowering plant, enclosing the young seeds. *n., pl.* **o var ies.**

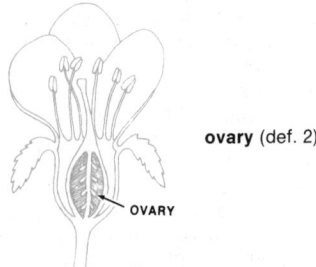

ovary (def. 2)

OVARY

o vate (ō′vāt), egg-shaped: *an ovate leaf. adj.* —**o′vate ly,** *adv.*

o va tion (ō vā′shən), an enthusiastic public welcome; burst of loud clapping or cheering: *The soprano received a great ovation. n.* —**o va′tion al,** *adj.*

o ven (uv′ən), **1** an enclosed space usually in a stove, for baking, roasting, and sometimes broiling food. **2** a small furnace for heating or drying pottery; kiln. *n.* —**ov′en like′,** *adj.*

ov en bird (uv′ən bėrd′), any of various birds that build nests with dome-shaped roofs. *n.*

o ver (ō′vər), **1** above in place or position: *the roof over one's head* (prep.), *the cliff hung over* (adv.). **2** above in authority, power, etc.: *We have a captain over us.* **3** above and to the other side of; across: *leap over a wall. Can you climb over that hill?* **4** across a space or distance: *Come over to my house.* **5** down; out and down (from an edge or from an upright position): *If you go too near the edge, you may fall over.* **6** out and down from; down from the edge of: *The ball rolled over the side of the porch.* **7** so as to cover the surface, or affect the whole surface: *Cover the tar over with sand until it has hardened.* **8** about or upon, so as to cover: *Spread the canvas over the new cement.* **9** at all or various places on; on; upon: *a blanket lying over a bed. A blush came over her face. Farms were scattered over the valley.* **10** here and there on or in; round about; all through: *We shall travel over Europe.* **11** from end to end of; along: *We drove over the new thruway.* **12** from beginning to end: *read a newspaper over.* **13** again: *I had to write my paper over.* **14** during: *We were out of town over the weekend.* **15** at an end: *The play is over.* **16** about; concerning; in connection with: *He is worried over his health.* **17** more than; beyond: *It costs*

over ten dollars. **18** by means of: *They spoke over the telephone.* **19** in excess or addition; too; more; besides: *I ate two apples and had one left over.* **20** so as to bring the upper side or end down or under; upside down: *turn over a page.* **21** surplus; extra: *There was a copy for everyone and three copies over.* **22** on the other side; at some distance: *over in Europe, over by the hill.* 1-3,6,8-11,14, 16-18 *prep.,* 1,4,5,7,12,13,19,20,22 *adv.,* 15,21 *adj.*

over again, once more: *Let's do that over again.*

over and above, besides; in addition to: *We had repairs to pay for over and above the cost of the car.*

over and over, again and again: *Practice the song over and over until you do it right.*

over with, INFORMAL. done; finished.

over-, *prefix.* **1** above: *Overhead = above the head.* **2** higher in rank; superior: *Overlord = superior lord.* **3** across: *Overseas = across the seas.* **4** too; too much; too long, etc.: *Overcrowded = too crowded. Overburden = burden too much.* **5** above normal; extra: *Oversize = above normal size. Overtime = extra time.* **6** being above; worn as an outer covering: *Overcoat = coat that is worn as an outer covering.*

o ver act (ō′vər akt′), act to excess; overdo in acting; act (a part) in an exaggerated manner. *v.*

o ver ac tive (ō′vər ak′tiv), too active; active to too high a degree: *overactive youngsters. adj.* —**o′ver ac′tive ness,** *n.*

o ver all (ō′vər ôl′), **1** from one end to the other: *an overall measurement.* **2** including everything: *an overall estimate. adj.*

o ver alls (ō′vər ôlz′), loose trousers with a piece covering the chest. Overalls are usually worn over clothes to keep them clean. *n.pl.*

o ver anx ious (ō′vər angk′shəs), too anxious. *adj.* —**o′ver anx′ious ly,** *adv.* —**o′ver anx′ious ness,** *n.*

o ver arch (ō′vər ärch′), arch over; span with or like an arch: *The street was overarched by elm trees. v.*

o ver arm (ō′vər ärm′), with the arm raised above the shoulder; overhand. *adj.*

o ver ate (ō′vər āt′), past tense of **overeat.** *I have a stomach ache because I overate. v.*

o ver awe (ō′vər ô′), overcome or restrain with awe: *Eclipses of the sun overawed primitive peoples. v.,* **o ver awed, o ver aw ing.**

o ver bal ance (ō′vər bal′əns), **1** be greater than in weight, importance, value, etc.: *The gains overbalanced the losses.* **2** cause to lose balance: *As I leaned over the side, my weight overbalanced the canoe and it upset. v.,* **o ver bal anced, o ver bal anc ing.**

o ver bear (ō′vər ber′ *or* ō′vər bar′), **1** overcome by weight or force; oppress; master: *My friends overbore all my objections.* **2** bear down by weight or force; overthrow; upset. *v.,* **o ver bore, o ver borne, o ver bear ing.**

o ver bear ing (ō′vər ber′ing *or* ō′vər bar′ing), inclined to dictate; forcing others to one's own will; masterful; domineering: *Promoted too quickly, the young executive became overbearing. adj.* —**o′ver bear′ing ly,** *adv.* —**o′ver bear′ing ness,** *n.*

over bid (ō′vər bid′), **1** bid more than the value of a thing. **2** outbid. **3** bid too high. *v.,* **o ver bid, o ver bid** *or* **o ver bid den** (ō′vər bid′n), **o ver bid ding.**

o ver board (ō′vər bôrd′), from a ship or boat into the water: *to fall overboard. adv.*

go overboard, go too far in an effort because of extreme enthusiasm.

throw overboard, 1 throw into the water. **2** INFORMAL. get rid of; give up; abandon; discard.

o ver bold (ō′vər bōld′), too bold. *adj.* —**o′ver bold′ly,** *adv.* —**o′ver bold′ness,** *n.*

o ver bore (ō′vər bôr′), past tense of **overbear.** *v.*

o ver borne (ō′vər bôrn′), past participle of **over-bear.** *v.*

o ver bur den (ō′vər bėrd′n), load with too great a bur-den. *v.*

o ver came (ō′vər kām′), past tense of **overcome.** *I finally overcame my fear. v.*

overcast (def. 3)

o ver cast (ō′vər kast′), **1** cloudy or dark; gloomy: *The sky was overcast before the storm.* **2** cover or be covered with clouds or darkness. **3** sew over and through (the edges of a seam) with long stitches to prevent raveling. 1 *adj.*, 2,3 *v.*, **o ver cast, o ver cast ing.**

o ver charge (ō′vər chärj′ for 1,3; ō′vər chärj′ for 2), **1** charge too high a price: *The grocer overcharged you for the eggs.* **2** a charge that is too great. **3** load too heavily; fill too full: *The overcharged old musket burst.* 1,3 *v.*; 2 *n.* **o ver charged, o ver charg ing;** 2 *n.* **—o′ver charg′er,** *n.*

o ver cloud (ō′vər kloud′), **1** cloud over or become clouded over; darken. **2** make or become gloomy. *v.*

o ver coat (ō′vər kōt′), an outer coat worn over the regular clothing for warmth in cold weather. *n.*

o ver come (ō′vər kum′), **1** get the better of; win the victory over; conquer; defeat: *overcome an enemy, overcome difficulties.* **2** make weak or helpless: *Weariness overcame her and she fell asleep. v.,* **o ver came, o ver come, o ver com ing.**

o ver con fi dent (ō′vər kon′fə dənt), too confident. *adj.* **—o′ver con′fi dent ly,** *adv.*

o ver cooked (ō′vər kükt′), cooked too much or too long. *adj.*

o ver crowd (ō′vər kroud′), crowd too much; put in too much or too many. *v.*

o ver de vel op (ō′vər di vel′əp), develop too much or too long. If a photograph is overdeveloped, it is too dark. *v.* **—o′ver de vel′op ment,** *n.*

o ver did (ō′vər did′), past tense of **overdo.** *v.*

o ver do (ō′vər dü′), **1** do or attempt to do too much: *When getting over an illness, you mustn't overdo.* **2** exaggerate: *The funny scenes in the play were overdone.* **3** cook too much: *The vegetables were overdone.* **4** exhaust; tire. *v.,* **o ver did, o ver done, o ver do ing. —o′ver-do′er,** *n.*

o ver done (ō′vər dun′), past participle of **overdo.** *v.*

o ver dose (ō′vər dōs′ for 1; ō′vər dōs′ for 2), **1** too big a dose. **2** give too large a dose to. 1 *n.*, 2 *v.*, **o ver dosed, o ver dos ing.**

o ver draft (ō′vər draft′), **1** an overdrawing of an account, especially a bank account. **2** amount of the excess. *n.*

o ver draw (ō′vər drô′), **1** write a check or checks against (a bank account) for more money than is in one's account. **2** exaggerate: *The characters in the book were greatly overdrawn. v.,* **o ver drew** (ō′vər drü′), **o ver-drawn** (ō′vər drôn′), **o ver draw ing.**

o ver dress (ō′vər dres′), to dress too elaborately. *v.*

o ver drive (ō′vər drīv′), an arrangement of gears in an automobile that produces greater speed while using less power than when the car is in high. *n.*

o ver due (ō′vər dü′ *or* ō′vər dyü′), more than due; due some time ago but not yet arrived, paid, etc.: *The train is overdue. This bill is overdue. adj.*

o ver eat (ō′vər ēt′), eat too much. *v.,* **o ver ate, o ver-eat en, o ver eat ing.**

o ver eat en (ō′vər ēt′n), past participle of **overeat.** *Nearly everyone has overeaten at the picnic. v.*

o ver em pha size (ō′vər em′fə sīz), give too much force or emphasis to; stress too much. *v.,* **o ver em pha-sized, o ver em pha siz ing.**

o ver es ti mate (ō′vər es′tə māt for 1; ō′vər es′tə mit for 2), **1** to estimate at too high a value, amount, rate, etc. **2** an estimate that is too high. 1 *v.,* **o ver es ti mat-ed, o ver es ti mat ing;** 2 *n.* **—o′ver es′ti ma′tion,** *n.*

o ver ex pose (ō′vər ek spōz′), **1** expose too much. **2** (in photography) expose (a film or negative) too long to light. *v.,* **o ver ex posed, o ver ex pos ing.**

o ver ex po sure (ō′vər ek spō′zhər), too much or too long an exposure. *n.*

o ver feed (ō′vər fēd′), feed too much. *v.,* **o ver fed** (ō′vər fed′), **o ver feed ing.**

o ver flow (ō′vər flō′ for 1-6; ō′vər flō′ for 7,8), **1** to flow over the bounds: *Rivers often overflow in the spring.* **2** to cover or flood: *The river overflowed my garden.* **3** have the contents flowing over: *My cup is overflowing.* **4** flow over the top of: *The milk overflowed the cup.* **5** extend out beyond; be too many for: *The crowd overflowed the room and filled the hall.* **6** be very abundant: *an overflowing harvest, overflowing kindness.* **7** an overflowing; excess. **8** outlet or container for overflowing liquid. 1-6 *v.,* **o ver-flowed, o ver flown** (ō′vər flōn′), **o ver flow ing;** 7,8 *n.*

o ver grew (ō′vər grü′), past tense of **overgrow.** *Vines overgrew the wall. v.*

o ver grow (ō′vər grō′), **1** grow over: *The wall is over-grown with vines.* **2** grow too fast; become too big. *v.,* **o ver grew, o ver grown, o ver grow ing.**

o ver grown (ō′vər grōn′), **1** grown too big: *an over-grown child.* **2** past participle of **overgrow.** *The vines have overgrown the wall.* 1 *adj.,* 2 *v.*

o ver growth (ō′vər grōth′), **1** too much growth. **2** growth overspreading or covering something. *n.*

o ver hand (ō′vər hand′), **1** with the hand raised above the shoulder: *an overhand throw* (adj.), *pitch overhand* (adv.). **2** with the knuckles upward. *adj., adv.*

o ver hang (ō′vər hang′ for 1; ō′vər hang′ for 2,3), **1** hang over; project over: *Trees overhang the street to form an arch of branches.* **2** a hanging over. **3** something that projects: *The overhang of the roof shaded the bush.* 1 *v.,* **o ver hung, o ver hang ing;** 2,3 *n.*

o ver haul (ō′vər hôl′ for 1,2; ō′vər hôl′ for 3), **1** examine thoroughly so as to make any repairs or changes that are needed: *Once a year we overhaul our boat.* **2** gain upon; overtake: *The pirate's ship was overhauling ours.* **3** an overhauling. 1,2 *v.,* 3 *n.*

o ver head (ō′vər hed′ for 1; ō′vər hed′ for 2,3), **1** over the head; on high; above: *the stars overhead.* **2** placed above; placed high up: *overhead wires.* **3** general expenses of running a business, such as rent, lighting, heating, taxes, repairs. 1 *adv.,* 2 *adj.,* 3 *n.*

o ver hear (ō′vər hir′), hear when one is not meant to hear: *They spoke so loud that I could not help overhearing. v.,* **o ver heard, o ver hear ing.**

o ver heard (ō′vər hėrd′), past tense and past participle of **overhear**. *I overheard what you told her.* v.

o ver heat (ō′vər hēt′), heat too much. v.

o ver hung (ō′vər hung′ *for 1*; ō′vər hung′ *for 2*), **1** hung from above: *an overhung door.* **2** past tense and past participle of **overhang**. *A big awning overhung the sidewalk.* 1 adj., 2 v.

o ver in dulge (ō′vər in dulj′), indulge too much. v., **o ver in dulged, o ver in dulg ing**.

o ver joy (ō′vər joi′), make very joyful. v.

o ver joyed (ō′vər joid′), very joyful; filled with joy; delighted. adj.

o ver kill (ō′vər kil′ *for 1*; ō′vər kill′ *for 2,3*), **1** destroy with greater force or damage than necessary. **2** act or process of overkilling. **3** capacity of a force or weapon to cause greater destruction than necessary. 1 v., 2,3 n.

o ver laid (ō′vər lād′), past tense and past participle of **overlay**[1]. *The workers overlaid the dome with gold. The iron had become overlaid with rust.* v.

o ver lain (ō′vər lān′), past participle of **overlie**. v.

o ver land (ō′vər land′), on land; by land: *travel overland from New York to Florida* (adv.), *an overland route* (adj.). adv., adj.

o ver lap (ō′vər lap′ *for 1*; ō′vər lap′ *for 2,3*), **1** lap over; cover and extend beyond: *Shingles are laid to overlap each other.* **2** a lapping over. **3** part that overlaps. 1 v., 2,3 n., **o ver lapped, o ver lap ping**.

o ver lay[1] (ō′vər lā′ *for 1,2*; ō′vər lā′ *for 3*), **1** lay or place (one thing) over or upon another. **2** put a coating over the surface of; finish with a layer or applied decoration of something: *wood overlaid with gold.* **3** something laid over something else; layer or decoration; covering. 1,2 v., **o ver laid, o ver lay ing**; 3 n.

o ver lay[2] (ō′vər lā′), past tense of **overlie**. v.

o ver leap (ō′vər lēp′), leap over; pass beyond: *Her joy overleaped all bounds.* v., **o ver leaped** or **o ver leapt** (ō′vər lept′), **o ver leap ing**.

o ver lie (ō′vər lī′), lie over; lie upon. v., **o ver lay, o ver lain, o ver ly ing**.

o ver load (ō′vər lōd′ *for 1*; ō′vər lōd′ *for 2*), **1** load too heavily: *overload a boat.* **2** too great a load: *The overload of electric current blew the fuse.* 1 v., 2 n.

o ver look (ō′vər lùk′ *for 1-3*; ō′vər lùk′ *for 4*), **1** fail to see: *overlook a bill.* **2** pay no attention to; excuse: *I will overlook your bad behavior this time.* **3** have a view of from above; be higher than: *This high window overlooks half the city.* **4** a high place from which scenery or points of interest may be viewed. 1-3 v., 4 n.

o ver lord (ō′vər lôrd′), person who is lord over another lord or other lords: *The duke was the overlord of barons and knights who held land from him.* n.

o ver ly (ō′vər lē), overmuch; excessively; too. adv.

o ver mas ter (ō′vər mas′tər), overcome; overpower. v. —**o′ver mas′ter ing ly**, adv.

o ver match (ō′vər mach′), be more than a match for; surpass. v.

o ver much (ō′vər much′), too much. adj., adv., n.

o ver night (ō′vər nīt′ *for 1,4,5*; ō′vər nīt′ *for 2,3*), **1** during the night: *stay overnight.* **2** done, occurring, etc., during the night: *an overnight stop.* **3** for the night: *overnight guests. An overnight bag contains articles needed for one night's stay.* **4** on the night before: *Preparations were made overnight for an early start.* **5** at once; immediately; in a very short time: *Change will not come overnight.* 1,4,5 adv., 2,3 adj.

o ver pass (ō′vər pas′), bridge over a road, railroad, canal, etc. n., pl. **o ver pass es**.

o ver pay (ō′vər pā′), **1** pay too much. **2** pay more than (an amount due). v., **o ver paid** (ō′vər pād′), **o ver pay ing**. —**o′ver pay′ment**, n.

o ver play (ō′vər plā′), play (a part, etc.) in an exaggerated manner. v.

o ver pow er (ō′vər pou′ər), **1** overcome or conquer; master; overwhelm: *overpower one's enemies. Several people were overpowered by the heat.* **2** be much greater or stronger than: *The wind brought a terrible smell which overpowered all others.* v. —**o′ver pow′er ing ly**, adv.

o ver pro duc tion (ō′vər prə duk′shən), production of more than is needed or more than can be sold. n.

o ver ran (ō′vər ran′), past tense of **overrun**. v.

o ver rate (ō′vər rāt′), rate or estimate too highly: *I overrated my strength and soon had to ask for help.* v., **o ver rat ed, o ver rat ing**.

o ver reach (ō′vər rēch′), **1** reach over or beyond. **2** reach too far. v. —**o′ver reach′er**, n. **overreach oneself**, **1** fail or miss by trying for too much. **2** fail by being too crafty or tricky.

o ver ride (ō′vər rīd′), **1** act in spite of: *override advice or objections.* **2** prevail over: *The new rule overrides all previous ones.* **3** ride over; trample on. v., **o ver rode** (ō′vər rōd′), **o ver rid den** (ō′vər rid′n), **o ver rid ing**.

o ver ripe (ō′vər rīp′), too ripe; more than ripe. adj.

o ver rule (ō′vər rül′), **1** rule or decide against (a plea, argument, objection, etc.); set aside: *The president overruled my plan.* **2** prevail over; be stronger than: *I was overruled by the majority.* v., **o ver ruled, o ver rul ing**.

o ver run (ō′vər run′), **1** spread over and spoil or harm in some way, as weeds, insects, disease, or invading troops do. **2** spread over: *Vines overran the wall.* **3** run or go beyond; exceed: *The TV show overran its time limit.* v., **o ver ran, o ver run, o ver run ning**.

o ver saw (ō′vər sô′), past tense of **oversee**. v.

o ver sea (ō′vər sē′ *for adv.*; ō′vər sē′ *for adj.*), overseas. adv., adj.

o ver seas (ō′vər sēz′ *for 1*; ō′vər sēz′ *for 2,3*), **1** across the sea; beyond the sea; abroad: *travel overseas.* **2** done, used, or serving overseas: *overseas service.* **3** of countries across the sea; foreign: *overseas trade.* 1 adv., 2,3 adj.

o ver see (ō′vər sē′), look after and direct (work or workers); supervise; manage: *oversee a factory.* v., **o ver saw, o ver seen** (ō′vər sēn′), **o ver see ing**.

o ver se er (ō′vər sē′ər), person who oversees others or their work. n.

o ver shad ow (ō′vər shad′ō), **1** be more important than: *Preparations for the school play soon overshadowed other activities.* **2** cast a shadow over; make dark or gloomy. v.

o ver shoe (ō′vər shü′), a waterproof shoe or boot, often made of rubber, worn over another shoe to keep the foot dry and warm. n.

o ver shoot (ō′vər shüt′), **1** shoot over, higher than, or beyond. **2** go over, higher than, or beyond. **3** go too far. v., **o ver shot, o ver shoot ing**.

o ver shot (ō′vər shot′ *for 1,2*; ō′vər shot′ *for 3*), **1** having the upper jaw projecting beyond the lower. **2** driven by water flowing over from above. **3** past tense and past participle of **overshoot**. 1,2 adj., 3 v.

o ver sight (ō′vər sīt′), **1** failure to notice or think of something: *Through an oversight, the kitten got no supper last night.* **2** watchful care: *to work under a teacher's oversight and direction.* n.

o ver size (ō′vər sīz′), too big; larger than the proper or usual size. adj.

o ver sized (ō′vər sīzd′), oversize. adj.

o ver sleep (ō′vər slēp′), sleep beyond (a certain hour); sleep too long. v., **o ver slept, o ver sleep ing**.

o ver slept (ō′vər slept′), past tense and past participle of **oversleep**. *I overslept and missed the bus. I have overslept three days in a row.* v.

o ver spread (ō′vər spred′), spread over: *Ivy overspread* *the old cabin. v.*, **o ver spread, o ver spread ing.**

o ver state (ō′vər stāt′), state too strongly; exaggerate. *v.*, **o ver stat ed, o ver stat ing.**

o ver state ment (ō′vər stāt′mənt), too strong a statement; exaggeration. *n.*

o ver stay (ō′vər stā′), stay beyond the time of. *v.*

o ver step (ō′vər step′), go beyond; exceed. *v.*, **o ver stepped, o ver step ping.**

o ver stock (ō′vər stok′ *for 1;* ō′vər stok′ *for 2*), **1** supply with more than is needed. **2** too great a supply. 1 *v.*, 2 *n.*

o ver stuffed (ō′vər stuft′), **1** stuffed too full. **2** made soft and comfortable by thick padding: *overstuffed furniture. adj.*

o ver sup ply (ō′vər sə plī′ *for 1;* ō′vər sə plī′ *for 2*), **1** supply with more than is needed. **2** too great a supply. 1 *v.*, **o ver sup plied, o ver sup ply ing;** 2 *n., pl.* **o ver sup plies.**

o vert (ō′vėrt′ *or* ō vėrt′), open or public; evident; not hidden: *Hitting someone is an overt act. adj.* —**o′vert ly,** *adv.*

o ver take (ō′vər tāk′), **1** come up with; catch up to: *I ran and overtook my friends.* **2** come upon suddenly: *A storm overtook the children. v.*, **o ver took, o ver tak en, o ver tak ing.**

o ver tak en (ō′vər tā′kən), past participle of **overtake.** *v.*

o ver tax (ō′vər taks′), **1** tax too heavily. **2** put too heavy a burden on. *v.* —**o′ver tax a′tion,** *n.*

o ver threw (ō′vər thrü′), past tense of **overthrow.** *v.*

o ver throw (ō′vər thrō′ *for 1-4;* ō′vər thrō′ *for 5*), **1** take away the power of; defeat: *overthrow a government.* **2** put an end to; destroy: *overthrow slavery.* **3** to overturn; upset; knock down. **4** throw (a ball) past the place for which it is intended. **5** a defeat; upset: *the overthrow of the government.* 1-4 *v.*, **o ver threw, o ver thrown, o ver throw ing;** 5 *n.* —**o′ver throw′er,** *n.*

o ver thrown (ō′vər thrōn′), past participle of **overthrow.** *v.*

o ver time (ō′vər tīm′), **1** extra time; time beyond the regular hours. **2** wages for this period. **3** beyond the regular hours: *to work overtime.* **4** of or for overtime: *overtime work.* 1,2 *n.*, 3 *adv.*, 4 *adj.*

o ver tone (ō′vər tōn′), **1** a fainter and higher musical tone heard along with the main or fundamental tone; harmonic. **2** hint or suggestion of something felt, believed, etc.: *an overtone of anger. n.*

o ver took (ō′vər tùk′), past tense of **overtake.** *v.*

o ver top (ō′vər top′), **1** rise above; be higher than: *The new building will overtop all the others.* **2** surpass; excel. *v.*, **o ver topped, o ver top ping.**

o ver ture (ō′vər chər), **1** proposal or offer: *The enemy is making overtures for peace.* **2** a musical composition played by the orchestra as an introduction to an opera, oratorio, or other long musical composition. *n.* [*Overture* came into English about 600 years ago from French *overture,* which came from Latin *apertura,* meaning "opening."]

o ver turn (ō′vər tėrn′ *for 1-3;* ō′vər tėrn′ *for 4*), **1** turn upside down. **2** upset; fall down; fall over: *The boat overturned.* **3** make fall down; overthrow; defeat; destroy the power of: *The rebels overturned the government.* **4** an overturning. 1-3 *v.*, 4 *n.*

o ver use (ō′vər yüz′ *for 1,2;* ō′vər yüs′ *for 3*), **1** use too much. **2** use too hard or too often. **3** too much or too hard use. 1,2 *v.*, **o ver used, o ver us ing;** 3 *n.*

o ver ween ing (ō′vər wē′ning), thinking too much of oneself; conceited; self-confident; presumptuous. *adj.*

o ver weight (ō′vər wāt′ *for 1,2;* ō′vər wāt′ *for 3*), **1** having too much weight: *overweight for one's height.*

2 too much weight. **3** overburden: *a small child overweighted with heavy schoolbooks.* 1 *adj.*, 2 *n.*, 3 *v.*

o ver whelm (ō′vər hwelm′), **1** overcome completely; crush: *overwhelm with grief.* **2** cover completely as a flood would: *A great wave overwhelmed the boat. v.*

o ver whelm ing (ō′vər hwel′ming), too many, too great, or too much to be resisted; overpowering: *an overwhelming majority of votes. adj.* —**o′ver whelm′ing ly,** *adv.* —**o′ver whelm′ing ness,** *n.*

o ver work (ō′vər wėrk′ *for 1,3;* ō′vər wėrk′ *for 2,4*), **1** too much or too hard work: *exhausted from overwork.* **2** work too hard or too long. **3** extra work. **4** to use to excess. 1,3 *n.*, 2,4 *v.*, **o ver worked, o ver work ing.**

o ver wrought (ō′vər rôt′), **1** wearied or exhausted by too much work or excitement; greatly excited: *overwrought nerves.* **2** too elaborate. *adj.*

o vi duct (ō′və dukt′), tube through which the ovum or egg passes from the ovary. *n.*

o vip ar ous (ō vip′ər əs), producing eggs that are hatched after leaving the body. Birds are oviparous. *adj.*

o vi pos i tor (ō′və poz′ə tər), (in certain female insects) an organ at the end of the abdomen, by which eggs are deposited. *n.*

o void (ō′void), **1** egg-shaped. **2** an egg-shaped object. 1 *adj.*, 2 *n.*

o vu late (ō′vyə lāt′ *or* ov′yə lāt′), discharge or give off a mature egg cell from the ovary. *v.*, **o vu lat ed, o vu lat ing.**

o vu la tion (ō′vyə lā′shən *or* ov′yə lā′shən), the discharging or giving off mature egg cells from the ovary. *n.*

o vule (ō′vyül), **1** a small ovum, especially when immature or unfertilized. **2** part of a plant that develops into a seed. *n.*

o vum (ō′vəm), a female reproductive cell produced in the ovary; egg. After the ovum is fertilized, a new organism or embryo develops. *n., pl.* **o va** (ō′və).

owe (ō), **1** have to pay; be in debt for: *I owe the grocer $10.* **2** be in debt: *I am always owing for something.* **3** be obliged or indebted for: *I owe a great deal to my parents. v.*, **owed, ow ing.**

ow ing (ō′ing), due; owed: *pay what is owing. adj.*

owing to, on account of; because of; as a result of: *Owing to the bad weather, we canceled our trip.*

owl (oul), bird with a big head, big eyes, and a short, hooked beak. Owls hunt mice and small birds at night. Some kinds have tufts of feathers on their heads, called "horns" or "ears." *n.* —**owl′like′,** *adj.*

owl—about 2 ft. (60 cm.) tall

a hat	i it	oi oil	ch child	a in about
ā age	ī ice	ou out	ng long	e in taken
ä far	o hot	u cup	sh she	ə = i in pencil
e let	ō open	ù put	th thin	o in lemon
ē equal	ô order	ü rule	ŦH then	u in circus
ėr term			zh measure	

owl et (ouʹlit), **1** a young owl. **2** a small owl. *n.*

owl ish (ouʹlish), like an owl; like an owl's: *owlish eyes, an owlish look of wisdom. adj.* —**owlʹish ly,** *adv.* —**owlʹish ness,** *n.*

own (ōn), **1** have or possess: *They own much land.* **2** of oneself or itself; belonging to oneself or itself: *We have our own troubles. The house is her own.* **3** acknowledge; admit; confess: *own to one's guilt. I own you are right.* 1,3 *v.,* 2 *adj.*

come into one's own, 1 get what belongs to one. **2** get the success or credit that one deserves.

hold one's own, keep one's position; not be forced back.

of one's own, belonging to oneself.

on one's own, not ruled or directed by someone else.

own up, confess fully: *own up to a crime.*

own er (ōʹnər), one who owns: *Who is the owner of this dog? n.* —**ownʹer less,** *adj.*

own er ship (ōʹnər ship), condition of being an owner; the possessing (of something); right of possession: *He claimed ownership of the abandoned car. n.*

ox (oks), **1** the full-grown male of domestic cattle, that has been castrated and is used for farm work or for beef. **2** any of the group of mammals that chew their cud and have horns and cloven hoofs. Domestic cattle, buffaloes, and bison belong to this group. *n., pl.* **ox en.** —**oxʹlikeʹ,** *adj.*

ox bow (oksʹbōʹ), **1** a U-shaped piece of wood placed under and around the neck of an ox, with the upper ends inserted in the bar of the yoke. **2** a U-shaped bend in a river. *n.*

ox cart (oksʹkärtʹ), cart drawn by oxen. *n.*

ox en (okʹsən), plural of **ox.** *n.*

ox ford (okʹsfərd), **1** kind of low shoe, laced over the instep. **2** kind of cotton or rayon cloth used for shirts, blouses, and other garments. *n.*

oxfords (def. 1)

Ox ford (okʹsfərd), **1** city in S England. **2** the very old and famous English university located there. *n.*

ox i da tion (okʹsə dāʹshən), **1** an oxidizing; the combining of oxygen with another element to form one or more new substances. Burning is one kind of oxidation. **2** a being oxidized. *n.*

ox ide (okʹsīd), compound of oxygen with another element or radical. *n.*

ox i dize (okʹsə dīz), combine or cause to combine with oxygen: *Fuel oxidizes rapidly, producing heat. Water oxidizes some metals, producing rust. v.,* **ox i dized, ox i diz ing.** —**oxʹi dizʹa ble,** *adj.* —**oxʹi di zaʹtion,** *n.* —**oxʹi dizʹer,** *n.*

ox y a cet y lene (okʹsē ə setʹl ēnʹ), using a mixture of oxygen and acetylene. An oxyacetylene torch is used for welding or cutting metals. *adj.*

ox y gen (okʹsə jən), a colorless, odorless gas that forms about one fifth of the atmosphere. Oxygen is a chemical element present in combined form in water, carbon dioxide, iron ore, and many other substances. Animals and plants cannot live, and fire will not burn, without oxygen. *n.*

ox y gen ate (okʹsə jə nāt), treat or combine with oxygen. *v.,* **ox y gen at ed, ox y gen at ing.** —**oxʹy gen aʹtion,** *n.* —**oxʹy gen aʹtor,** *n.*

ox y gen ize (okʹsə jə nīz), oxygenate. *v.,* **ox y gen ized, ox y gen iz ing.** —**oxʹy gen izʹa ble,** *adj.* —**oxʹy genizʹer,** *n.*

oxygen mask, device worn over the nose and mouth through which oxygen is supplied from an attached container. Oxygen masks are used by aviators at high altitudes, by firefighters, by submarine crews, etc.

oxygen tent, a small, usually transparent tent which is supplied with a constant, regulated flow of oxygen. It is placed over the head and shoulders of a patient who has difficulty breathing.

o yez (ōʹyes), hear! attend! a cry uttered, usually three times, by a public or court crier to command silence and attention before a proclamation is made. *interj., n.*

oys ter (oiʹstər), shellfish having a rough, irregular shell in two halves. Oysters are found in shallow water along seacoasts. Many kinds are good to eat and some kinds yield pearls. *n.*

oyster bed, a place where oysters breed or are cultivated.

oz., ounce. *pl.* **oz.** or **ozs.**

O zark Mountains (ōʹzärk), a low mountain range in S Missouri, N Arkansas, and E Oklahoma.

O zarks (ōʹzärks), the Ozark Mountains. *n.pl.*

o zone (ōʹzōn), **1** form of oxygen with a sharp, pungent odor, produced by electricity and present in the air, especially after a thunderstorm. It is a strong oxidizing agent and is produced commercially for use in bleaching, in sterilizing water, etc. **2** INFORMAL. pure air that is refreshing. *n.* [*Ozone* is from German *Ozon,* which came from Greek *ozein,* meaning "to smell."]

Pp

a hat	**i** it	**oi** oil	**ch** child	a in about
ā age	**ī** ice	**ou** out	**ng** long	e in taken
ä far	**o** hot	**u** cup	**sh** she	**ə** = { i in pencil
e let	**ō** open	**u̇** put	**th** thin	o in lemon
ē equal	**ô** order	**ü** rule	**ŦH** then	u in circus
ėr term			**zh** measure	

P or **p** (pē), the 16th letter of the English alphabet. *n., pl.* **P's** or **p's.**

P, symbol for phosphorus.

p., **1** page. **2** participle.

pa (pä), INFORMAL. papa; father. *n.*

Pa, symbol for protactinium.

PA, Pennsylvania (used with postal Zip Code).

Pa., Pennsylvania.

PAC (pak), Political Action Committee (committee formed by a corporation, labor union, trade association, etc., that collects money from its members and gives it to political candidates that it wishes to see elected). *n.*

Pac., Pacific.

pace (pās), **1** a step. **2** walk with regular steps: *The tiger paced up and down its cage.* **3** walk over with regular steps: *pace the floor.* **4** the length of a step in walking; about 2¹/₂ feet (76 centimeters): *There were perhaps ten paces between me and the bear.* **5** measure by paces: *We paced off the distance and found it to be 72 paces.* **6** way of stepping. The walk, trot, and canter are some of the paces of the horse. **7** a particular pace of some horses in which the feet on the same side are lifted and put down together. **8** move at a pace: *Some horses are trained to pace.* **9** rate or speed: *walk at a fast pace.* **10** set the pace for: *A motorboat will pace the rowing crew.* 1,4,6,7,9 *n.,* 2,3,5,8,10 *v.,* **paced, pac ing.**

keep pace with, keep up with; go as fast as.

put one through one's paces, try one out; find out what one can do.

set the pace, 1 set an example of speed for others to keep up with. **2** be an example for others to follow.

pace mak er (pās/mā/kər), **1** person, animal, or thing that sets the pace. **2** an electronic device implanted in the chest wall to maintain or restore the normal rhythm of the heartbeat. *n.*

pac er (pā/sər), **1** person or thing that paces. **2** horse that lifts and puts down the feet on the same side together. *n.*

pa chi si (pə chē/zē), game somewhat like backgammon, played on a cross-shaped board. *n.*

pach y derm (pak/ə dėrm/), a thick-skinned mammal with hoofs. The elephant, hippopotamus, and rhinoceros are pachyderms. *n.*

pa cif ic (pə sif/ik), **1** loving peace; not warlike: *The Quakers are a pacific people.* **2** peaceful; calm; quiet: *pacific weather.* *adj.* **—pa cif/i cal ly,** *adv.*

Pa cif ic (pə sif/ik), **1** ocean west of North and South America. It extends to Asia and Australia. **2** of the Pacific Ocean. **3** on, in, over, or near the Pacific Ocean: *Pacific air routes.* **4** of or on the Pacific coast of the United States: *California is one of the Pacific states.* 1 *n.,* 2-4 *adj.*

pac i fi ca tion (pas/ə fə kā/shən), a pacifying; making peaceful; being in a state of peace. *n.*

Pacific Standard Time, the standard time in the westernmost parts of the continental United States and Canada, excluding most of Alaska. It is eight hours behind Greenwich Time.

pac i fi er (pas/ə fī/ər), **1** person or thing that pacifies. **2** a rubber or plastic nipple or ring given to a baby to suck. *n.*

pac i fism (pas/ə fiz/əm), the principle or policy of universal peace; settlement of all differences between na-

tions by peaceful means; opposition to war. *n.*

pac i fist (pas/ə fist), person who is opposed to war and favors settling all disputes between nations by peaceful means. *n.*

pac i fy (pas/ə fī), **1** make peaceful; quiet down: *pacify angry demonstrators, pacify a crying baby.* **2** bring under control; subdue: *pacify a rebellious region.* *v.,* **pac i fied, pac i fy ing.** [*Pacify* can be traced back to Latin *pax,* meaning "peace," and *facere,* meaning "to make."]

pack[1] (pak), **1** bundle of things wrapped up or tied together for carrying: *The hiker carried a pack on her back.* **2** put things together in a bundle, box, bale, etc.: *Pack your clothes in this bag.* **3** put into a container to be sold or stored: *Meat, fish, and vegetables are often packed in cans.* **4** fill with things; put one's things into: *Pack your trunk.* **5** press or crowd closely together: *A hundred people were packed into one small room.* **6** fill (a space) with all that it will hold: *pack a small theater with a large audience.* **7** a set; lot; a number together: *a pack of thieves, a pack of nonsense, a pack of lies.* **8** a number of animals of the same kind hunting together: *Wolves hunt in packs; lions hunt alone.* **9** a complete set of playing cards, usually 52. **10** a large area of floating pieces of ice pushed together: *A ship forced its way through the pack.* **11** make tight with something that water, steam, air, etc., cannot leak through: *The plumber packed the pipe joint with string.* **12** INFORMAL. carry: *pack a gun.* 1,7-10 *n.,* 2-6,11,12 *v.* **—pack/a ble,** *adj.*

pack off, send away: *The child was packed off to bed.*

send packing, send away in a hurry.

pack[2] (pak), arrange unfairly. To pack a jury is to fill it with those who will favor one side. *v.*

pachyderms

pack age (pak′ij), **1** bundle of things packed or wrapped together; box with things packed in it; parcel. **2** put in a package. 1 *n.*, 2 *v.*, **pack aged, pack ag ing.**

pack animal, animal used for carrying loads or packs.

pack er (pak′ər), person or company that packs meat, fruit, vegetables, etc., to be sold to wholesalers. *n.*

pack et (pak′it), **1** a small package; parcel: *a packet of letters.* **2** packet boat. *n.*

packet boat, boat that carries mail, passengers, and goods regularly on a fixed route.

pack ing (pak′ing), **1** material used to keep water, steam, etc., from leaking through. **2** material placed around goods to protect them from damage in shipment, storage, etc. **3** business of preparing and packing meat, fish, fruit, vegetables, etc., to be sold. *n.*

packing house, place where foods are prepared and packed to be sold.

pack rat, a large North American rat with a bushy tail, that carries away bits of food, clothing, small tools, etc., and hides them in its nest.

pact (pakt), agreement; compact: *The three nations signed a peace pact. n.* [*Pact* came into English about 550 years ago from French *pact*, and can be traced back to Latin *pacisci*, meaning "to make an agreement."]

pad[1] (pad), **1** a soft mass used for comfort, protection, or stuffing; cushion: *The baby's carriage has a pad.* **2** fill with something soft; stuff: *pad a chair.* **3** one of the cushion-like parts on the bottom side of the feet of dogs, foxes, and some other animals. **4** foot of a dog, fox, etc. **5** the large floating leaf of the water lily. **6** number of sheets of paper fastened along one edge; tablet. **7** cloth soaked with ink to use with a rubber stamp. **8** use words just to fill space: *I padded my report so that it would fill the required 10 pages.* **9** launching pad: *The rocket rose from the pad.* **10** SLANG. room, house, or apartment: *My pad is on the third floor.* 1,3-7,9,10 *n.*, 2,8 *v.*, **pad ded, pad ding.**

pad[2] (pad), **1** go on foot; walk; tramp; trudge. **2** walk or trot softly: *a wolf padding through the forest.* **3** a dull sound, as of footsteps on the ground. 1,2 *v.*, **pad ded, pad ding;** 3 *n.*

pad ding (pad′ing), **1** material used to pad with, such as cotton or foam rubber. **2** words used just to fill space in making a speech or a written paper longer. *n.*

pad dle[1] (pad′l), **1** a short, lightweight oar with a broad blade at one end or both ends, usually held with both hands in rowing a boat or canoe. **2** row (a boat or canoe) with a paddle or paddles. **3** one of the broad boards fixed around a water wheel or a paddle wheel to push, or be pushed by, the water. **4** a broad piece of wood with a handle at one end, used for stirring, for mixing, etc. **5** a paddle-shaped wooden implement with a short handle, used to hit the ball in table tennis. **6** beat with a paddle; spank. **7** an electronic device used to control video games and computer games. It is a flat handle containing a wheel and a button. 1,3-5,7 *n.*, 2,6 *v.*, **pad dled, pad dling.**

pad dle[2] (pad′l), move the hands or feet about in water: *Children love to paddle at the beach. v.*, **pad dled, pad dling. —pad′dler,** *n.*

pad dler (pad′lər), person who paddles a canoe or boat. *n.*

paddle wheel, wheel with paddles fixed around it for propelling a ship over the water.

pad dock (pad′ək), **1** a small, enclosed field near a stable or house, used for exercising animals or as a pasture. **2** pen at a race track where horses are saddled before a race. *n.*

pad dy (pad′ē), flooded area with raised banks around its sides, for growing rice. *n.*, *pl.* **pad dies.** [*Paddy* comes from Malay *padi.*]

paddy wagon, SLANG. patrol wagon.

Pad e rew ski (pad′ə ref′skē), Ignace Jan, 1860-1941, Polish pianist, composer, and statesman. *n.*

pad lock (pad′lok′), **1** a lock that can be put on and removed. It hangs by a curved bar, hinged at one end and snapped shut at the other. **2** fasten with a padlock. 1 *n.*, 2 *v.*

pa dre (pä′drā), father. It is used as a name for a priest, especially in regions where Spanish, Portuguese, or Italian is spoken. *n.* [*Padre* was borrowed from Spanish, Portuguese, or Italian *padre*, which came from Latin *pater*.]

pae an (pē′ən), song of praise, joy, or triumph. *n.*

pa gan (pā′gən), **1** person who is not a Christian, Jew, or Moslem; one who worships many gods or no god; a heathen. The ancient Greeks and Romans were pagans. **2** of pagans; heathen: *pagan customs.* **3** person who has no religion. 1,3 *n.*, 2 *adj.*

Pag a ni ni (pag′ə nē′nē), Nicolò, 1782-1840, Italian violinist. *n.*

pa gan ism (pā′gə niz′əm), **1** a pagan attitude toward religion or morality. **2** the beliefs and practices of pagans. **3** condition of being a pagan. *n.*

pa gan ize (pā′gə nīz), make or become pagan. *v.*, **pa gan ized, pa gan iz ing. —pa′gan i za′tion,** *n.*

page[1] (pāj), **1** one side of a leaf or sheet of paper: *a page in this book.* **2** the print or writing on one side of a leaf. **3** a record: *the pages of history.* **4** a happening or time considered as part of history: *The settling of the West is an exciting page in American history.* **5** number the pages of. 1-4 *n.*, 5 *v.*, **paged, pag ing.** [*Page*[1] came into English about 400 years ago from French *page*, and can be traced back to Latin *pagina.*]

page[2] (pāj), **1** person who runs errands or delivers messages. Pages at hotels usually wear uniforms. **2** try to find (a person) at a hotel, club, etc., by having his or her name called out. **3** a youth who attends a person of rank. **4** a youth who was preparing to be a knight. 1,3,4 *n.*, 2 *v.*, **paged, pag ing.** [*Page*[2] came into English about 700 years ago from French *page*, and perhaps can be traced back to Greek *paidos*, meaning "child, boy."]

pag eant (paj′ənt), **1** an elaborate spectacle; procession in costume; pomp; display; show: *The coronation of a new ruler is always a splendid pageant.* **2** a public entertainment that represents scenes from history, legend, or the like: *Our school gave a pageant about the Pilgrims. n.*

pag eant ry (paj′ən trē), **1** a splendid show; gorgeous display; pomp. **2** mere show; empty display. *n.*, *pl.* **pageant ries.**

pag er (pā′jər), a small, portable, electronic radio device that pages a person by means of a beeping sound or a voice message. *n.*

pag i nate (paj′ə nāt), mark the number of pages of. *v.*, **pag i nat ed, pag i nat ing. —pag′i na′tion,** *n.*

paddle wheel

pagoda

a hat	i it	oi oil	ch child	a in about
ā age	ī ice	ou out	ng long	e in taken
ä far	o hot	u cup	sh she	ə = { i in pencil
e let	ō open	u̇ put	th thin	o in lemon
ē equal	ô order	ü rule	ŦH then	u in circus
ėr term			zh measure	

pa go da (pə gō′də), temple having many stories, with a roof curving upward from each story. There are pagodas in India, China, and Japan. *n., pl.* **pa go das.** [*Pagoda* is from Portuguese *pagode,* which came from Sanskrit *bhagavati,* meaning "goddess."]

paid (pād), **1** receiving money; hired: *a paid worker, a paid informer.* **2** past tense and past participle of **pay.** *I paid my bills. These bills have been paid.* 1 *adj.,* 2 *v.*

pail (pāl), **1** a round container for carrying liquids, etc.; bucket: *a milk pail.* **2** the amount a pail holds; pailful. *n.*

pail ful (pāl′fu̇l), amount that fills a pail. *n., pl.* **pail fuls.**

pain (pān), **1** a feeling of being hurt; suffering: *A cut gives pain. The death of one we love causes pain.* **2** cause to suffer; give pain: *Does your tooth pain you?* 1 *n.,* 2 *v.*

on pain of or **under pain of,** with the punishment or penalty of unless a certain thing is done: *The traitor was ordered to leave the country on pain of death.*

take pains, be careful: *I took pains to be neat with my book report.*

Paine (pān), **Thomas,** 1737-1809, American writer on politics and religion, born in England. *n.*

pained (pānd), **1** hurt, distressed, grieved, etc.: *I am greatly pained to learn of your refusal.* **2** expressing or showing pain: *a pained look. adj.*

pain ful (pān′fəl), **1** causing pain; unpleasant; hurting: *a painful illness, a painful duty.* **2** difficult. *adj.* —**pain′ful ly,** *adv.* —**pain′ful ness,** *n.*

pain less (pān′lis), without pain; causing no pain. *adj.* —**pain′less ly,** *adv.* —**pain′less ness,** *n.*

pains tak ing (pānz′tā′king), very careful; particular; scrupulous: *a painstaking painter. adj.* —**pains′tak′ing ly,** *adv.* —**pains′tak′ing ness,** *n.*

paint (pānt), **1** substance consisting of solid coloring matter or pigment mixed with a liquid, that can be spread on a surface to make a layer or film of white, black, or colored matter. **2** cover or decorate with paint: *paint a house.* **3** use paint. **4** represent (an object) in colors: *The artist painted animals.* **5** make pictures. **6** picture vividly in words. **7** coloring matter put on the face or body. **8** put on like paint: *paint iodine on a cut.* 1,7 *n.,* 2-6,8 *v.* —**paint′less,** *adj.*

paint brush (pānt′brush′), brush for putting on paint. *n., pl.* **paint brush es.**

paint er[1] (pān′tər), **1** person who paints pictures; artist. **2** person who paints houses, woodwork, etc. *n.*

paint er[2] (pān′tər), a rope, usually fastened to the bow of a boat, for tying it to a ship, pier, etc. *n.*

paint er[3] (pān′tər), puma. *n.*

paint ing (pān′ting), **1** something painted; picture. **2** act of one who paints. *n.*

pair (per *or* par), **1** a set of two; two that go together: *a pair of shoes, a pair of horses.* **2** arrange or be arranged in pairs: *The gloves were neatly paired in a drawer.* **3** a single thing consisting of two parts that cannot be used separately: *a pair of scissors, a pair of trousers.* **4** man and woman who are married or are engaged to be married. **5** join in love and marriage. **6** two animals that are mated. **7** to mate. **8** two cards of the same value in different suits, considered as a unit in one's hand: *a pair of sixes.* 1,3,4,6,8 *n., pl.* **pairs** or (*sometimes after a numeral*) **pair;** 2,5,7 *v.* [*Pair* came into English about 700 years ago from French *paire,* and can be traced back to Latin *par,* meaning "equal."]

pair off, arrange in pairs; form into pairs.

pais ley (pāz′lē), having a detailed and colorful pattern: *a paisley shirt. adj.*

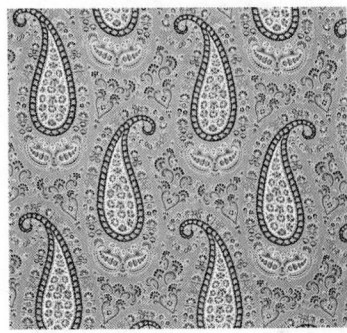

paisley—cloth with a paisley design

Pai ute (pī yüt′ *or* pī′yüt), **1** member of a tribe of American Indians living in Utah. **2** language of this tribe. *n., pl.* **Pai ute** or **Pai utes.**

pa ja mas (pə jä′məz *or* pə jam′əz), garments to sleep or lounge in consisting of a shirt and loose trousers. *n.pl.* Also, **pyjamas.**

Pak i stan (pak′ə stan), country in S Asia, west of India. *Capital:* Islamabad. See **India** for map. *n.*

Pak i stan i (pak′ə stan′ē), **1** person born or living in Pakistan. **2** of Pakistan. 1 *n., pl.* **Pak i stan is** or **Pak i stan i;** 2 *adj.*

pal (pal), **1** a close friend; playmate; comrade. **2** to associate as pals. 1 *n.,* 2 *v.,* **palled, pal ling.**

pal., paleontology.

Pal., Palestine.

pal ace (pal′is), **1** the official home of a king, queen, bishop, or some other ruler. **2** a very fine house or building. *n.* [*Palace* came into English about 700 years ago from French *palais,* and can be traced back to Latin *Palatium,* meaning "the Palatine Hill" in Rome, where the emperor's palace was located.] —**pal′ace like′,** *adj.*

pal an quin or **pal an keen** (pal′ən kēn′), a covered couch carried by poles resting on the shoulders of four or six men, formerly used in the Orient. *n.*

pal at a bil i ty (pal′ə tə bil′ə tē), palatable quality or condition. *n.*

pal at a ble (pal′ə tə bəl), **1** agreeable to the taste; pleasing: *That was a most palatable lunch.* **2** agreeable to the mind or feelings; acceptable. *adj.* —**pal′at a ble ness,** *n.*

pal at a bly (pal′ə tə blē), in a palatable manner; agreeably. *adv.*

pal ate (pal′it), **1** the roof of the mouth. The bony part in front is the hard palate, and the fleshy part in back is the soft palate. **2** sense of taste: *The new flavor pleased my palate. n.* —**pal′ate less,** *adj.* —**pal′ate like′,** *adj.*

pa la tial (pə lā′shəl), like a palace; fit for a palace; magnificent: *a palatial apartment. adj.* —**pa la′tial ly,** *adv.* —**pa la′tial ness,** *n.*

pa lav er (pə lav′ər), **1** a parley or conference, especially between travelers and local people of the area being visited. **2** smooth, persuading talk; flattery. **3** talk fluently and flatteringly. **1,2** *n.,* **3** *v.* —**pa lav′er er,** *n.*

pale[1] (pāl), **1** without much color; whitish: *When you have been ill, your face is sometimes pale.* **2** not bright; dim: *pale blue. The bright stars are surrounded by hundreds of pale ones.* **3** turn pale: *Her face paled at the bad news.* **1,2** *adj.,* **pal er, pal est; 3** *v.,* **paled, pal ing.** [*Pale*[1] came into English about 700 years ago from French *pale,* and can be traced back to Latin *pallere,* meaning "to be pale."] —**pale′ly,** *adv.*

pale[2] (pāl), **1** a long, narrow board, pointed at the top, used for fences. **2** boundary: *Criminals are outside the pale of civilized society.* **3** build a fence around; enclose with pales. **1,2** *n.,* **3** *v.,* **paled, pal ing.** [*Pale*[2] came into English about 650 years ago from French *pal,* and can be traced back to Latin *palus,* meaning "a stake."]

pale face (pāl′fās′), a white person. The American Indians are said to have called white people palefaces. *n.*

pale ness (pāl′nis), condition of being pale. *n.*

Pa le o lith ic (pā′lē ə lith′ik), of the earliest part of the Stone Age. Paleolithic tools were crudely chipped out of stone. *adj.*

pa le on tol o gist (pā′lē on tol′ə jist), an expert in paleontology. *n.*

pa le on tol o gy (pā′lē on tol′ə jē), science of the forms of life existing in prehistoric time, as represented by fossil animals and plants. *n.*

Pa le o zo ic (pā′lē ə zō′ik), **1** the geological era whose fossils represent early forms of life. Fishes, insects, and reptiles developed during the Paleozoic. **2** of this era or its rocks. **1** *n.,* **2** *adj.*

Pal es tine (pal′ə stīn), region in SW Asia between the Mediterranean Sea and the Jordan River. The name has been applied since ancient times to the land of the Jews. Palestine is often called the Holy Land and in the Bible is called Canaan. It is now divided chiefly between Israel and Jordan. *n.* —**Pal′es tin′i an,** *adj., n.*

pal ette (pal′it), **1** a thin board, usually oval or oblong, with a thumb hole at one end, used by painters to lay and mix colors on. **2** set of colors on this board. *n.* [See **Word History.**] —**pal′ette like′,** *adj.*

pal frey (pôl′frē), OLD USE. a gentle riding horse, especially one used by women. *n., pl.* **pal freys.**

pal in drome (pal′in drōm), word, verse, or sentence which reads the same backward or forward. *Madam* and *radar* are palindromes; "Madam, I'm Adam" is a palindrome. *n.*

pal ing (pā′ling), **1** fence of pales. **2** pale in a fence. *n.*

pal i sade (pal′ə sād′), **1** a long, strong, wooden stake pointed at the top end. **2** a fence of stakes set firmly in the ground to enclose or defend. **3** furnish or surround with a palisade. **4** palisades, *pl.* line of high, steep cliffs. **1,2,4** *n.,* **3** *v.,* **pal i sad ed, pal i sad ing.**

pall[1] (pôl), **1** a heavy cloth of black, purple, or white velvet spread over a coffin, a hearse, or a tomb. **2** a dark, gloomy covering: *A thick pall of smoke shut out the sun from the city. n.* —**pall′-like′,** *adj.*

pall[2] (pôl), become distasteful or very tiresome because there has been too much of something: *Even the most tasty food palls if it is served every day. v.*

pal la di um (pə lā′dē əm), a soft, light, silver-white metallic element which occurs in nature with platinum. Palladium is used in making scientific instruments, in alloys with precious metals such as gold and silver, and as a catalyst. *n.*

Pal las (pal′əs), (in Greek myths) a name of Athena. *n.*

pall bear er (pôl′ber′ər *or* pôl′bar′ər), one of the men who walk with or carry the coffin at a funeral. *n.*

pal let (pal′it), bed of straw; poor bed. *n.*

pal li ate (pal′ē āt), **1** lessen without curing: *palliate a disease.* **2** make appear less serious; excuse: *palliate a fault. v.,* **pal li at ed, pal li at ing.** —**pal′li a′tion,** *n.*

pal li a tive (pal′ē ā′tiv), **1** useful to lessen or soften; excusing. **2** something that lessens, softens, or excuses. **1** *adj.,* **2** *n.* —**pal′li a′tive ly,** *adv.*

pal lid (pal′id), lacking color; pale: *a pallid face. adj.* —**pal′lid ly,** *adv.* —**pal′lid ness,** *n.*

pal lor (pal′ər), lack of color from fear, illness, death, etc.; paleness. *n.*

palm[1] (päm), **1** the inside of the hand between the wrist and the fingers. **2** the width of a hand; 3 to 4 inches. **3** the part of a glove covering the palm. **4** conceal in the hand: *The magician palmed the nickel.* **1-3** *n.,* **4** *v.* —**palm′er,** *n.*

palm off, pass off or get accepted by tricks, fraud, or false representation.

palm[2] (päm), **1** any of a group of trees or shrubs which grow in warm climates. Most palms have tall trunks, no branches, and many large leaves at the top. **2** leaf or stalk of leaves of a palm tree, used as a symbol of victory or triumph. **3** victory; triumph. *n.* —**palm′like′,** *adj.*

bear off the palm or **carry off the palm,** be the victor; win: *She bore off the palm both in tennis and swimming.*

pal mate (pal′māt), shaped like a hand with the fingers spread out: *a palmate leaf. adj.* —**pal′mate ly,** *adv.*

pal met to (pal met′ō), kind of palm with fan-shaped leaves, abundant on the southeastern coast of the United States. *n., pl.* **pal met tos** or **pal met toes.** [*Palmetto* comes from Spanish *palmito,* and can be traced back to Latin *palma,* meaning "palm tree, palm of the hand."]

WORD HISTORY

palette

Palette comes from French *palette,* which originally meant "a small spade," and can be traced back to Latin *pala,* meaning "a spade." It was called this because of its shape.

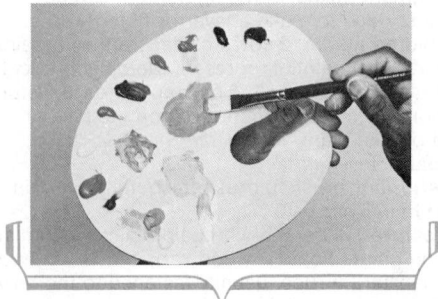

---

palm ist (pä′mist), person who claims to be able to tell fortunes by examining the palm of the hand. *n.*

palm is try (pä′mə strē), the supposed art of telling a person's fortune from lines and marks in the palm of the hand. *n.*

Palm Sunday, the Sunday before Easter Sunday.

palm y (pä′mē), **1** abounding in palms; shaded by palms. **2** flourishing; prosperous; glorious: *palmy days of peace. adj.,* **palm i er, palm i est.**

pal o mi no (pal′ə mē′nō), a cream-colored or golden-tan horse of Arabian stock. Its mane and tail are usually lighter colored. *n., pl.* **pal o mi nos.**

WORD HISTORY

palomino

Palomino is from Spanish *palomino,* which also means "a young dove," and can be traced back to Latin *palumbes,* meaning "a kind of dove." The horse was called this because of its color.

pal pa ble (pal′pə bəl), **1** readily seen or heard and recognized; obvious: *a palpable error.* **2** able to be felt by touching; tangible. *adj.* **—pal′pa ble ness,** *n.*

pal pa bly (pal′pə blē), **1** plainly; obviously. **2** to the touch. *adv.*

pal pate (pal′pāt), examine by touch, especially in medical diagnosis. *v.,* **pal pat ed, pal pat ing. —pal pa′-tion,** *n.*

pal pi tate (pal′pə tāt), **1** beat very rapidly; throb: *Your heart palpitates when you are excited.* **2** quiver; tremble: *His entire body palpitated with terror. v.,* **pal pi tat ed, pal pi tat ing. —pal′pi tat′ing ly,** *adv.*

pal pi ta tion (pal′pə tā′shən), **1** a very rapid beating of the heart; throb. **2** a quivering; trembling. *n.*

pal sied (pôl′zēd), **1** having palsy; paralyzed. **2** shaking; trembling. *adj.*

pal sy (pôl′zē), **1** paralysis, especially a form of paralysis occurring late in life, characterized by trembling and muscular weakness. **2** afflict with palsy; paralyze. **1** *n., pl.* **pal sies; 2** *v.,* **pal sied, pal sy ing.**

pal tri ness (pôl′trē nis), very slight value; meanness. *n.*

pal try (pôl′trē), almost worthless; trifling; petty; mean: *Pay no attention to paltry gossip. We sold our old, broken-down car for a paltry sum of money. adj.,* **pal tri er, pal tri est. —pal′tri ly,** *adv.*

pam pas (pam′pəz), the vast, grassy, treeless plains of South America, especially in Argentina. *n.pl.* [*Pampas* was borrowed from Spanish *pampas,* which came from Quechua *pampa,* meaning "a plain."]

pam per (pam′pər), indulge too much; allow too many privileges: *pamper a child, pamper a sick person, pamper one's appetite. v.* **—pam′per er,** *n.*

pam phlet (pam′flit), booklet in paper covers. It often deals with a question of current interest. *n.*

pam phlet eer (pam′flə tir′), **1** writer of pamphlets. **2** write and issue pamphlets. **1** *n.,* **2** *v.*

pan (pan), **1** dish for cooking and other household uses, usually broad, shallow, and with no cover: *pots and pans.* **2** anything like this. Gold and other metals are sometimes obtained by washing ore in pans. The dishes on a pair of scales are called pans. **3** cook in a pan. **4** wash (gravel, sand, etc.) in a pan to separate the gold. **5** (in old-fashioned guns) the hollow part of the lock that held a little gunpowder to set the gun off. **6** INFORMAL. criticize severely: *The drama critic panned the new play.* **1,2,5** *n.,* **3,4,6** *v.,* **panned, pan ning.**

pan out, INFORMAL. turn out; work out: *Her scheme panned out well.*

a hat	i it	oi oil	ch child	ə = { a in about
ā age	ī ice	ou out	ng long	e in taken
ä far	o hot	u cup	sh she	i in pencil
e let	ō open	ů put	th thin	o in lemon
ē equal	ô order	ü rule	ŦH then	u in circus
ėr term			zh measure	

Pan (pan), (in Greek myths) the god of forests, pastures, flocks, and shepherds. Pan is described as a man with the legs, horns, and ears of a goat. *n.*

Pan., Panama.

pan-, *combining form.* of all; all; entirely: *Pan-American = of all the Americas. Panchromatic = (sensitive to) light of all colors.* [The form *pan-* comes from Greek *pan,* meaning "all."]

pan a ce a (pan′ə sē′ə), a remedy for all diseases or ills; cure-all. *n., pl.* **pan a ce as.** [*Panacea* was borrowed from Latin *panacea,* and can be traced back to Greek *pan,* meaning "all," and *akos,* meaning "a cure."]

Pan a ma (pan′ə mä), **1 Isthmus of,** a narrow neck of land which connects North America with South America. **2** country on the Isthmus of Panama, on either side of the Canal Zone. **3** its capital, a seaport on the Bay of Panama. **4 Bay of,** bay of the Pacific on the S coast of the Isthmus of Panama. **5 panama,** a fine hat woven from the young leaves of a palmlike plant of Central and South America. *n., pl.* **pan a mas** for 5. [The *panama* (hat) is from Spanish *panamá,* which gets its name from *Panamá,* meaning "Panama." The hats were called this because, although made in Ecuador, they were sold in Panama and shipped from there.]

Panama Canal, canal cut across the Isthmus of Panama to connect the Atlantic and Pacific oceans. It was built and formerly controlled by the United States.

Panama Canal Zone. See **Canal Zone.**

Pan a ma ni an (pan′ə mā′nē ən), **1** of Panama. **2** person born or living in Panama. **1** *adj.,* **2** *n.*

Pan-A mer i can (pan′ə mer′ə kən), of all the people or countries of North, Central, and South America. *adj.*

pan cake (pan′kāk′), a thin, flat cake made of batter and fried in a pan or on a griddle. *n.*

pan chro mat ic (pan′krō mat′ik), sensitive to light of all colors: *a panchromatic photographic film. adj.*

pan cre as (pan′krē əs), a large gland near the stomach that secretes insulin into the blood and **pancreatic juice,** a digestive juice which contains various enzymes, into the small intestine. The pancreas of animals when used for food is called sweetbread. *n.* [*Pancreas* is from Greek *pankreas,* which comes from *pan,* meaning "all," and *kreas,* meaning "flesh."]

pan cre at ic (pan′krē at′ik), of the pancreas: *pancreatic secretions. adj.*

pan da (pan′də), **1** a bearlike mammal of Tibet and parts of southern and southwestern China, mostly white with black legs, often called the **giant panda. 2** a reddish-

panda (def. 1) about 5 ft. (1.5 m.) long

brown mammal somewhat like a raccoon, that lives in the Himalayas, often called the **lesser panda.** *n., pl.* **pan das.** [*Panda* was borrowed from French *panda*, which came from the animal's name in Nepal.]

pan de mo ni um (pan/də mō/nē əm), **1** wild uproar or confusion. **2** place of wild disorder or lawless confusion. *n.*

pan der (pan/dər), **1** person who helps other people indulge low desires, passions, or vices. **2** act as a pander; supply material or opportunity for vices: *The newspaper pandered to people's liking for sensational stories.* **1** *n.,* **2** *v.* **—pan/der er,** *n.* **—pan/der ing ly,** *adv.*

Pan do ra (pan dôr/ə), (in Greek myths) the first woman, created by the gods. Curiosity led her to open a box (**Pandora's box**) and thus let out many evils and ills into the world. *n.*

pane (pān), a single sheet of glass in a division of a window, a door, or a sash: *Hailstones and gusts of wind broke several panes of glass.* *n.* **—pane/less,** *adj.*

pan el (pan/l), **1** a strip or surface that is different in some way from what is around it. A panel is often sunk below or raised above the rest, and used for a decoration. Panels may be in a door or other woodwork, on large pieces of furniture, or made as parts of a dress. **2** arrange in panels; furnish or decorate with panels: *Her dining room was paneled with oak.* **3** picture, photograph, or design much longer than wide. **4** list of persons called as jurors; the members of a jury. **5** group formed for discussion: *A panel of experts gave its opinion on ways to solve the traffic problem.* **6** board containing the instruments, controls, or indicators used in operating an automobile, aircraft, computer, or other mechanism. **1,3-6** *n.,* **2** *v.*

panel discussion, the discussion of a particular issue by a selected group of people.

pan el ing (pan/l ing), **1** wood or other material for panels. **2** panels applied as decoration. *n.*

pan el ist (pan/l ist), person who takes part in a panel discussion. *n.*

pang (pang), **1** a sudden, short, sharp pain: *the pangs of a toothache.* **2** a sudden feeling: *A pang of pity moved his heart.* *n.*

pan han dle (pan/han/dl), **1** handle of a pan. **2** a narrow strip of land projecting like a handle: *the Texas panhandle.* **3** INFORMAL. beg, especially in the streets. **1,2** *n.,* **3** *v.,* **pan han dled, pan han dling. —pan/han/-dler,** *n.*

pan ic (pan/ik), **1** a fear spreading through a multitude of people so that they lose control of themselves; unreasoning fear: *When the theater caught fire, there was a panic. When four banks failed in one day, there was a panic among merchants.* **2** caused by panic; showing panic; unreasoning: *panic terror, panic haste.* **3** affect or be affected with panic: *The audience panicked when the fire broke out.* **1** *n.,* **2** *adj.,* **3** *v.,* **pan icked, pan ick ing.**

pan ick y (pan/ə kē), **1** caused by panic: *panicky haste.* **2** showing panic: *panicky actions.* **3** like panic: *panicky feelings.* **4** liable to lose self-control and have a panic. *adj.*

pan ic-strick en (pan/ik strik/ən), frightened out of one's wits; demoralized by fear. *adj.*

pan ni er (pan/ē ər), basket, especially one of a pair of considerable size to be slung across the shoulders or across the back of a beast of burden. *n.*

pan o ply (pan/ə plē), **1** a complete suit of armor. **2** magnificent covering or display: *The queen wore a panoply of jewels.* *n., pl.* **pan o plies.**

pan o ram a (pan/ə ram/ə), **1** a wide, unbroken view of a surrounding region: *a panorama of beach and sea.* **2** a complete survey of some subject: *a panorama of history.*

3 picture of a landscape or other scene, often shown as if seen from a central point; picture unrolled a part at a time and made to pass continuously before the spectators. **4** a continuously passing or changing scene: *the panorama of city life.* *n., pl.* **pan o ram as.** [*Panorama* can be traced back to Greek *pan*, meaning "all," and *horan*, meaning "to see."]

pan o ram ic (pan/ə ram/ik), of or like a panorama: *a panoramic view.* *adj.* **—pan/o ram/i cal ly,** *adv.*

panpipe

pan pipe (pan/pīp/), an early musical instrument made of reeds or tubes of different lengths, fastened together side by side, in order of their length. The reeds or tubes were closed at one end and the player blew across their open tops. *n.*

pan sy (pan/zē), a flower somewhat like a violet but much larger and having flat, velvety petals, usually of several colors. *n., pl.* **pan sies.**

pant (pant), **1** breathe hard and quickly: *She is panting from playing tennis.* **2** a short, quick breath. **3** speak with short, quick breaths: *"Hurry, hurry," he panted.* **4** long eagerly: *I am just panting for my turn.* **1,3,4** *v.,* **2** *n.* **—pant/ing ly,** *adv.*

pan ta lets or **pan ta lettes** (pan/tl ets/), long underpants extending to the ankles, formerly worn by women and girls. *n.pl.*

pan ta loons (pan/tl ünz/), tight-fitting trousers. *n.pl.*

pan the ism (pan/thē iz/əm), belief that God and the universe are the same; doctrine that God is an expression of the physical forces of nature. *n.*

pan the ist (pan/thē ist), believer in pantheism. *n.*

pan the is tic (pan/thē is/tik), of pantheism or pantheists. *adj.* **—pan/the is/ti cal ly,** *adv.*

Pan the on (pan/thē on), temple for all the gods, built at Rome about 27 B.C. and later used as a Christian church. *n.* [*Pantheon* can be traced back to Greek *pan*, meaning "all," and *theos*, meaning "god."]

pan ther (pan/thər), **1** leopard, especially a black leopard. **2** puma. **3** jaguar. *n., pl.* **pan thers** or **pan ther.**

pan ties (pan/tēz), kind of underpants worn by women or children. *n.pl.*

pan to mime (pan/tə mīm), **1** a play without words, in which the actors express themselves by gestures. **2** gestures without words. **3** express by gestures. **1,2** *n.,* **3** *v.,* **pan to mimed, pan to mim ing.**

pan try (pan/trē), a small room in which food, dishes, silverware, or table linen is kept. *n., pl.* **pan tries.**

pants (pants), **1** trousers. **2** underpants. *n.pl.*

pant suit (pant/süt/), a woman's or girl's suit consisting of a jacket and trousers. *n.*

pan ty hose (pan/tē hōz/), undergarment that combines panties and stockings. *n.*

pap (pap), **1** soft food for infants or invalids. **2** ideas or facts watered down in order to appear easier or more interesting. *n.* **—pap/like/,** *adj.*

pa pa (pä/pə), father; daddy. *n.*

pa pa cy (pā′pə sē), **1** position, rank, or authority of the pope. **2** time during which a pope rules. **3** all the popes. *n., pl.* **pa pa cies.**

pa pal (pā′pəl), **1** of the pope: *a papal letter.* **2** of the papacy. **3** of the Roman Catholic Church. *adj.* —**pa′pal ly,** *adv.*

pa paw (pô′pô), **1** the oblong, yellowish fruit of a small North American tree, which is good to eat. **2** papaya. *n.* Also, **pawpaw.**

pa pa ya (pə pä′yə), the fruit of a palmlike tropical American tree. Papayas look somewhat like melons, have yellowish pulp, and are good to eat. *n., pl.* **pa pa yas.** [*Papaya* was borrowed from Spanish *papaya,* which probably came from an American Indian word of the Caribbean region.]

pa per (pā′pər), **1** a material used for writing, printing, drawing, wrapping packages, and covering walls. Paper is made in thin sheets from wood pulp, rags, etc. **2** piece or sheet of paper. **3** piece or sheet of paper with writing or printing on it; document: *Important papers were stolen.* **4** papers, *pl.* documents telling who or what one is. **5** wrapper, container, or sheet of paper containing something: *a paper of pins.* **6** newspaper. **7** article; essay: *The professor read a paper on the teaching of English.* **8** a written promise to pay money; note. **9** made of paper: *paper dolls, paper money.* **10** like paper; thin: *almonds with paper shells.* **11** wallpaper. **12** cover with wallpaper: *paper a room.* 1-8,11 *n.,* 9,10 *adj.,* 12 *v.* [*Paper* came into English about 650 years ago from French *papier,* and can be traced back to Greek *papyros,* meaning "papyrus."] —**pa′per er,** *n.* —**pa′per like′,** *adj.*

on paper, 1 in writing or print. **2** in theory.

pa per back (pā′pər bak′), book with a paper binding or cover, usually sold at a low price. *n.*

pa per boy (pā′pər boi′), person who delivers or sells newspapers; newsboy. *n.*

paper clip, a flat, bent piece of wire forming a clip to hold papers together.

pa per hang er (pā′pər hang′ər), person whose business is to cover walls with wallpaper. *n.*

paper money, money made of paper, not metal. A dollar bill is paper money.

pa per weight (pā′pər wāt′), a small, heavy object put on papers to keep them from being scattered. *n.*

pa pier-mâ ché (pā′per mə shā′), **1** a paper pulp mixed with some stiffener and molded when moist. It becomes hard and strong when dry. **2** made of papier-mâché. 1 *n.,* 2 *adj.*

pa pil la (pə pil′ə), a small, nipplelike projection having to do with the senses of touch, taste, or smell: *the papillae on the tongue. n., pl.* **pa pil lae** (pə pil′ē).

pa poose or **pap poose** (pa püs′), an American Indian baby. The use of this word is often considered offensive. *n.*

pa pri ka (pa prē′kə *or* pap′rə kə), the ground, dried fruit of certain mild red peppers, used as a seasoning in food. *n., pl.* **pa pri kas.** [*Paprika* was borrowed from Hungarian *paprika,* and can be traced back to Greek *peperi,* meaning "pepper."]

Pap u a (pap′yü ə), New Guinea. *n.* —**Pap′u an,** *adj., n.*

Papua New Guinea, country consisting of the E part of the island of New Guinea and many nearby islands. It is a member of the Commonwealth of Nations. *Capital:* Port Moresby.

pa py rus (pə pī′rəs), **1** a tall water plant from which the ancient Egyptians, Greeks, and Romans made a kind of paper to write on. **2** a writing material made from the pith of papyrus plants. **3** an ancient record written on papyrus. *n., pl.* **pa py ri** (pə pī′rī).

par (pär), **1** an equal level; equality: *The gains and losses*

are about on a par. He is quite on a par with his sister in intelligence. **2** an average or normal amount, degree, or condition: *A sick person feels below par.* **3** average; normal. **4** the value of a bond, a note, a share of stock, etc., that is printed on it; face value: *That stock is selling above par.* **5** of or at par. **6** (in golf) a score which is used as a standard for a particular hole or course and which represents the number of strokes that will be taken if the hole or course is played well. Par is based on the length and difficulty of the hole or course. 1,2,4,6 *n.,* 3,5 *adj.*

par., 1 paragraph. **2** parallel.

par a ble (par′ə bəl), a brief story used to teach some truth or moral lesson: *The teacher explained the parable. n.*

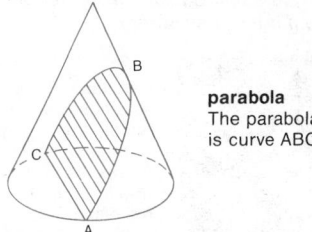

parabola
The parabola
is curve ABC.

pa rab o la (pə rab′ə lə), a plane curve formed by the intersection of a cone with a plane parallel to a side of the cone. *n., pl.* **pa rab o las.**

par a chute (par′ə shüt), **1** apparatus shaped like an umbrella and made of nylon or silk, used in descending gradually through the air from a great height. **2** come down by, or as if by, a parachute: *The pilot of the burning plane parachuted safely to the ground.* **3** convey by a parachute. 1 *n.,* 2,3 *v.,* **par a chut ed, par a chut ing.** —**par′a chut′er,** *n.*

par a chut ist (par′ə shü′tist), person who uses a parachute or is skilled in making descents with a parachute. *n.*

pa rade (pə rād′), **1** a march for display; procession: *The circus had a parade.* **2** to march through with display: *The performers and animals paraded the streets.* **3** to march in procession; walk proudly as if in a parade. **4** group of people walking for display or pleasure. **5** a great show or display: *The modest man did not make a parade of his wealth.* **6** make a great show of: *parade one's wealth.* **7** a military display or review of troops. **8** come together in military order for review or inspection. **9** assemble (troops) for review. **10** the place used for the regular parade of troops. 1,4,5,7,10 *n.,* 2,3,6,8,9 *v.* **pa rad ed, pa rad ing.** —**pa rad′er,** *n.*

par a digm (par′ə dim *or* par′ə dīm), **1** pattern; example. **2** example of a noun, verb, pronoun, etc., in all its inflections. *n.*

par a dise (par′ə dīs), **1** heaven. **2** place or condition of great happiness: *The summer camp was a paradise for her.* **3** place of great beauty. **4** Also, **Paradise.** the garden of Eden. *n.*

par a dox (par′ə doks), **1** statement that may be true but seems to say two opposite things: *"More haste, less speed"* and *"The child is father to the man"* are paradoxes. **2** statement that is false because it says two opposite things. **3** person or thing that seems to be full of contradictions. *n., pl.* **par a dox es.**

par a dox i cal (par/ə dok/sə kəl), of paradoxes; having to do with a paradox. *adj.* —**par/a dox/i cal ly,** *adv.* —**par/a dox/i cal ness,** *n.*

par af fin (par/ə fin), **1** a white, tasteless, waxy substance, used for making candles and for sealing jars of jelly or jam. It is obtained chiefly from crude petroleum. **2** treat with paraffin. 1 *n.,* 2 *v.*

par a gon (par/ə gon), model of excellence or perfection. *n.*

par a graph (par/ə graf), **1** group of sentences relating to the same idea or topic and forming a distinct part of a chapter, letter, or other piece of writing. Paragraphs usually begin on a new line and are indented. **2** divide into paragraphs. **3** a separate note or item of news in a newspaper. **4** write paragraphs about. **5** sign (¶) used to show where a paragraph begins or should begin. It is used mostly in correcting written work. 1,3,5 *n.,* 2,4 *v.*

Par a guay (par/ə gwā *or* par/ə gwī), **1** country in central South America, bordered by Bolivia, Brazil, and Argentina. *Capital:* Asunción. See **Brazil** for map. **2** river in central South America. *n.* —**Par/a guay/an,** *adj., n.*

par a keet (par/ə kēt), a small parrot with a slender body and a long tail. *n.* Also, **parrakeet.**

parallax—Viewed from A, C appears to be the middle tree in a group of three trees. From B, C appears to be a single tree in front of the cabin.

par al lax (par/ə laks), the apparent change in the position of an object when it is seen from two different points which are not on a direct line with the object. Parallax is used in surveying, astronomy, etc., to determine distances of objects. *n.*

par al lel (par/ə lel), **1** at or being the same distance apart everywhere, like the two rails of a railroad track. **2** be at the same distance from throughout the length: *The street parallels the railroad.* **3** a parallel line or surface. **4** any of the imaginary circles around the earth parallel to the equator, marking degrees of latitude. **5** comparison to show likeness: *draw a parallel between this winter and last winter.* **6** compare in order to show likeness. **7** find a case which is similar or parallel to: *Can you parallel that for friendliness?* **8** similar; corresponding: *parallel customs in different countries.* **9** thing like or similar to another: *Her experience was an interesting parallel to ours.* **10** be like; be similar to: *Your story closely parallels his.* 1,8 *adj.,* 2,6,7,10 *v.,* **par al leled, par al lel ing** or **par al lelled, par al lel ling;** 3-5,9 *n.*

parallel bars, a pair of raised bars horizontal to the ground, used in gymnastics to develop the muscles of the arms, chest, etc.

par al lel ism (par/ə lel/iz/əm), **1** a being parallel. **2** likeness; similarity; correspondence; agreement. *n.*

par al lel o gram (par/ə lel/ə gram), a four-sided plane figure whose opposite sides are parallel and equal. *n.*

par a lyse (par/ə līz), paralyze. *v.,* **par a lysed, par a lysing.**

pa ral y sis (pə ral/ə sis), **1** a lessening or loss of the power of motion or sensation in any part of the body: *Polio can cause paralysis.* **2** condition of powerlessness or helpless inactivity; crippling: *The war caused a paralysis of trade. n., pl.* **pa ral y ses** (pə ral/ə sēz/).

par a lyt ic (par/ə lit/ik), **1** of paralysis; having paralysis. **2** person who has paralysis. 1 *adj.,* 2 *n.* —**par/a lyt/i cal ly,** *adv.*

paralyze (def. 2) For days after the snowstorm, traffic was **paralyzed.**

par a lyze (par/ə līz), **1** affect with a lessening or loss of the power of motion or feeling: *The patient's arm was paralyzed.* **2** make powerless or helpless; stun: *Fear paralyzed my mind. v.,* **par a lyzed, par a lyz ing.** Also, **paralyse.** —**par/a lyz/er,** *n.* —**par/a lyz/ing ly,** *adv.*

Par a mar i bo (par/ə mar/ə bō), capital of Suriname, in the N part. *n.*

par a me ci um (par/ə mē/shē əm), an extremely small one-celled animal shaped like a slender slipper and having a groove along one side leading into an open mouth. Paramecia move by means of cilia and live in fresh water. *n., pl.* **par a me ci a** (par/ə mē/shē ə). [*Paramecium* can be traced back to Greek *para,* meaning "beside, near," and *mēkos,* meaning "length."]

par a med ic (par/ə med/ik), person who assists a doctor or gives medical treatment at the scene of an emergency. *n.*

par a mount (par/ə mount), chief in importance; above others; supreme: *Truth is of paramount importance. adj.* —**par/a mount/ly,** *adv.*

parallel (def. 1) The tractor made **parallel** lines as it moved across the field.

par a noi a (par/ə noi/ə), **1** a mental disorder characterized by feelings of persecution. **2** an irrational distrust of others. *n.*

par a noid (par/ə noid), **1** like or tending toward paranoia. **2** having the characteristics of paranoia. **3** a person suffering from paranoia. 1,2 *adj.,* 3 *n.*

parallelograms

par a pet (par/ə pet), **1** a low wall or mound of stone, earth, etc., to protect soldiers. **2** a low wall at the edge of a balcony, roof, bridge, etc. *n.* [*Parapet* is from Italian *parapetto,* which comes from Italian *parare,* meaning "to defend," and *petto,* meaning "chest."]

par a pher nal ia (par/ə fər nā/lyə), **1** personal belongings: *My paraphernalia are ready to be shipped.* **2** equipment; outfit: *A photographer's paraphernalia includes cameras, film, lenses, lights, tripods, etc. n.pl. or sing.*

par a phrase (par′ə frāz), **1** state the meaning of (a passage) in other words. **2** an expression of the meaning of a passage in other words. **1** *v.*, **par a phrased, par a phras ing; 2** *n.* —**par′a phras′a ble,** *adj.*

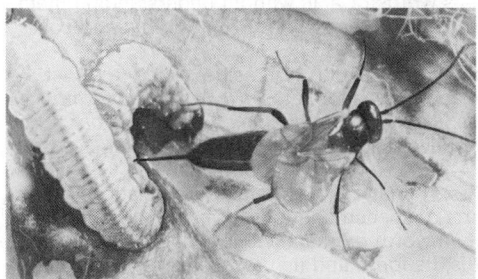

parasite (def. 1)—This wasp, shown here injecting an egg into a weevil larva, is a parasite. When the egg hatches, the wasp larva eats the weevil larva.

par a site (par′ə sīt), **1** animal or plant that lives on or in another which it harms by taking away nourishment. Lice and tapeworms are parasites on animals. Mistletoe is a parasite on oak trees. **2** person who lives on others without making any useful and fitting return; hanger-on. *n.*

par a sit ic (par′ə sit′ik), of or like a parasite; living on others. *adj.* —**par′a sit′i cal ly,** *adv.* —**par′a sit′i cal ness,** *n.*

par a sol (par′ə sôl), a light umbrella used as a protection from the sun. *n.*

par a thy roid glands (par′ə thī′roid), small glands in or near the thyroid gland. Their secretion, which enables the body to use calcium, is necessary for life.

par a troop er (par′ə trü′pər), soldier trained to use a parachute for descent from an aircraft into a battle area. *n.*

par boil (pär′boil′), boil till partly cooked: *parboil beans before baking them. v.*

par cel (pär′səl), **1** bundle of things wrapped or packed together; package: *She had her arms filled with parcels of gifts.* **2** piece: *a parcel of land.* **3** lot; pack: *The peddler had a whole parcel of odds and ends in his sack.* **4** make into a parcel; put up in parcels. 1-3 *n.,* 4 *v.,* **par celed, par cel ing** or **par celled, par cel ling.**

parcel out, divide into, or distribute in, portions.

parcel post, branch of the postal service which carries parcels.

parch (pärch), **1** make or become hot and dry or thirsty: *I am parched with the heat.* **2** dry by heating; roast slightly: *Corn is sometimes parched. v.* —**parch′a ble,** *adj.* —**parch′ing ly,** *adv.*

parch ment (pärch′mənt), **1** the skin of sheep or goats, prepared for use as a writing material. **2** manuscript or document written on parchment. **3** paper that looks like parchment. *n.* —**parch′ment like′,** *adj.*

par don (pärd′n), **1** a passing over an offense without punishment; forgiveness. **2** forgive: *Grandmother pardoned the mischievous children.* **3** excuse or toleration: *I beg your pardon, but I missed your last remark.* **4** set free from punishment: *The governor pardoned the prisoner.* **5** a setting free from punishment. **6** a legal document setting a person free from punishment. 1,3,5,6 *n.,* 2,4 *v.* —**par′don er,** *n.* —**par′don less,** *adj.*

par don a ble (pärd′n ə bəl), able to be pardoned; excusable. *adj.* —**par′don a ble ness,** *n.* —**par′don a bly,** *adv.*

pare (per *or* par), **1** cut, trim, or shave off the outer part

a hat   **i** it   **oi** oil   **ch** child   (a in about
ā age   **ī** ice   **ou** out   **ng** long   e in taken
ä far   **o** hot   **u** cup   **sh** she   ə = { i in pencil
e let   **ō** open   **ù** put   **th** thin   o in lemon
ē equal   **ô** order   **ü** rule   **ŦH** then   u in circus
ėr term   **zh** measure

of; peel: *pare an apple, pare one's toenails.* **2** cut away little by little: *pare down expenses. v.,* **pared, par ing.**

par e go ric (par′ə gôr′ik), a soothing medicine containing camphor and a very little opium. *n.*

paren., parenthesis.

par ent (per′ənt *or* par′ənt), **1** father or mother. **2** any animal or plant that produces offspring. **3** source; cause: *Too much leisure can be the parent of mischief. n.* [*Parent* came into English about 550 years ago from French *parent,* and can be traced back to Latin *parere,* meaning "to bring forth, bear."] —**par′ent like′,** *adj.*

par ent age (per′ən tij *or* par′ən tij), descent from parents; family line; ancestry. *n.*

pa ren tal (pə ren′tl), of a parent or parents; like a parent's: *parental advice. adj.* —**pa ren′tal ly,** *adv.*

pa ren the sis (pə ren′thə sis), **1** word, phrase, sentence, etc., inserted within a sentence to explain or qualify something. **2** either or both of two curved lines ( ) used to set off such an expression. *n., pl.* **pa ren the ses** (pə ren′thə sēz′).

par en thet ic (par′ən thet′ik), **1** serving or helping to explain; qualifying. **2** enclosed in parentheses. **3** using parentheses. *adj.* —**par′en thet′i cal ly,** *adv.*

par en thet i cal (par′ən thet′ə kəl), parenthetic. *adj.*

par ent hood (per′ənt hùd *or* par′ənt hùd), condition of being a parent. *n.*

par fait (pär fā′), **1** ice cream with syrup or crushed fruit and whipped cream, served in a tall glass. **2** a rich ice cream containing eggs and whipped cream. *n.*

pa ri ah (pə rī′ə), outcast. *n.*

par ing (per′ing *or* par′ing), the part pared off; skin; rind: *apple parings. n.*

Par is (par′is), **1** capital and largest city of France, in the N part. Paris is on the Seine River. **2** (in Greek legends) a son of Priam, king of Troy. The kidnaping of Helen by Paris was the cause of the Trojan War. *n.*

par ish (par′ish), **1** district that has its own church and clergyman. **2** people of a parish. **3** members of the congregation of a particular church. **4** (in Louisiana) a county. *n.*

pa rish ion er (pə rish′ə nər), member of a parish. *n.*

Pa ri sian (pə rizh′ən), **1** of Paris or its people. **2** person born or living in Paris. 1 *adj.,* 2 *n.*

par i ty (par′ə tē), similarity or close correspondence with regard to state, position, condition, value, quality, degree, etc.; equality. *n.*

park (pärk), **1** land set apart for the pleasure of the public: *Many cities have beautiful parks.* **2** land set apart for wild animals: *a deer park.* **3** grounds around a fine house. **4** leave (an automobile, etc.) for a time in a certain place: *Park your car here.* 1-3 *n.,* 4 *v.* —**park′er,** *n.* —**park′like′,** *adj.*

par ka (pär′kə), **1** a fur jacket with a hood, worn in Alaska and northeastern Asia. **2** jacket with a hood. *n., pl.* **par kas.**

parking lot, an open area used for parking automobiles and other vehicles, often for a fee.

park way (pärk′wā′), a broad road with spaces planted with grass, trees, etc. *n.*

par lance (pär′ləns), way of speaking; talk; language: *legal parlance. n.*

par ley (pär′lē), **1** conference or informal talk to discuss terms or matters in dispute: *The general held a parley with the enemy about exchanging prisoners.* **2** discuss matters, especially with an enemy. 1 *n., pl.* **par leys;** 2 *v.* —**par′-ley er,** *n.*

par lia ment (pär′lə mənt), **1** council or congress that is the highest lawmaking body in some countries. **2 Parliament, a** the national lawmaking body of Great Britain, consisting of the House of Lords and the House of Commons. **b** the national lawmaking body of Canada, consisting of the Senate and the House of Commons. **c** the lawmaking body of a country or colony having the British system of government. *n.*

par lia men tar i an (pär′lə men tar′ē ən), person skilled in parliamentary procedure or debate. *n.*

par lia men tar y (pär′lə men′tər ē), **1** of a parliament: *parliamentary authority.* **2** done by a parliament: *parliamentary statutes.* **3** according to the rules and customs of a parliament or other lawmaking body: *The United States Congress functions in accordance with the rules of parliamentary procedure.* **4** having a parliament: *a parliamentary form of government. adj.* —**par′lia men′tar i ly,** *adv.*

par lor (pär′lər), **1** room for receiving or entertaining guests; sitting room. **2** room or suite of rooms used for various commercial purposes, requiring special or elaborate decoration, fittings, etc.: *a funeral parlor, a beauty parlor. n.*

parlor car, a railroad passenger car for day travel, with more comfortable seats than a coach.

pa ro chi al (pə rō′kē əl), **1** of or in a parish: *parochial calls, a parochial church.* **2** narrow; limited: *a parochial viewpoint. adj.* —**pa ro′chi al ly,** *adv.* —**pa ro′chi al ness,** *n.*

parochial school, school maintained by a church or a religious organization.

par o dy (par′ə dē), **1** a humorous imitation of a serious writing. A parody follows the form of the original, but often changes its sense to nonsense, thus making fun of the writer's characteristics. **2** make fun of by imitating; make a parody on. 1 *n., pl.* **par o dies;** 2 *v.,* **par o died, par o dy ing.** —**par′o di a ble,** *adj.*

pa role (pə rōl′), **1** conditional release from prison or jail before the full term is served. **2** give a conditional release from jail or prison before the full term is served: *The prisoner was paroled after serving two years of a three-year sentence.* 1 *n.,* 2 *v.,* **pa roled, pa rol ing.** —**pa rol′a ble,** *adj.*

par ox ysm (par′ək siz′əm), **1** a sudden, severe attack of the symptoms of a disease, usually recurring periodically: *a paroxysm of coughing.* **2** a sudden outburst of emotion or activity: *a paroxysm of rage. n.*

parquet
(defs. 1 and 2)

par quet (pär kā′ *or* pär ket′), **1** an inlaid wooden flooring. **2** made of parquet: *parquet floors.* **3** the main floor of a theater; orchestra. 1,3 *n.,* 2 *adj.*

par quet ry (pär′kə trē), mosaic of wood used for floors, wainscoting, etc. *n., pl.* **par quet ries.**

par ra keet (par′ə kēt), parakeet. *n.*

par ri cide (par′ə sīd), **1** the crime of killing one's parent or parents. **2** person who commits this crime. *n.*

par rot (par′ət), **1** bird with a stout, hooked bill and often with bright-colored feathers. Some parrots can imitate sounds and repeat words and sentences. **2** person who repeats words or acts without understanding them. **3** repeat without understanding. 1,2 *n.,* 3 *v.* —**par′rot-like′,** *adj.*

par ry (par′ē), **1** ward off; turn aside; evade (a thrust, stroke, weapon, question, etc.): *He parried the sword with his dagger. She parried our question by asking us one.* **2** act of parrying; avoiding. 1 *v.,* **par ried, par ry ing;** 2 *n., pl.* **par ries.** —**par′ri a ble,** *adj.* —**par′ri er,** *n.*

parse (pärs), **1** analyze (a sentence) grammatically, telling its parts of speech and their uses in the sentence. **2** describe (a word) grammatically, telling what part of speech it is, its form, and its use in a sentence. *v.,* **parsed, pars ing.** —**pars′a ble,** *adj.* —**pars′er,** *n.*

Par see or **Par si** (pär′sē), member of a Zoroastrian sect in India, descended from Persians who settled there in the A.D. 700's. *n.*

par si mo ni ous (pär′sə mō′nē əs), too economical; stingy. *adj.* —**par′si mo′ni ous ly,** *adv.* —**par′si mo′ni ous ness,** *n.*

par si mo ny (pär′sə mō′nē), extreme economy; stinginess. *n.*

par sley (pär′slē), a garden plant with finely divided, fragrant leaves. Parsley is used to flavor food and to trim platters of meat, fish, etc. *n., pl.* **par sleys.** —**par′sley-like′,** *adj.*

par snip (pär′snip), the long, tapering, whitish root of a garden plant, eaten as a vegetable. It is related to the carrot. *n.*

par son (pär′sən), **1** minister in charge of a parish. **2** any clergyman; minister. *n.*

par son age (pär′sə nij), house provided for a minister by a church. *n.*

part (pärt), **1** something less than the whole; not all: *He ate part of an apple.* **2** each of several equal quantities into which a whole may be divided; fraction: *A dime is a tenth part of a dollar.* **3** thing that helps to make up a whole: *A radio has many parts.* **4** share: *I had no part in the mischief.* **5** side in a dispute or contest: *She always takes her sister's part.* **6** character in a play, motion picture, etc.; role: *He played the part of Hamlet.* **7** the words spoken by a character: *She spoke the part of the heroine in our play.* **8** divide into two or more pieces. **9** force apart; divide: *Several mounted police parted the crowd.* **10** go apart; separate: *The friends parted in anger.* **11** a dividing line left in combing one's hair. **12** comb (the hair) away from a dividing line. **13** one of the voices or instruments in a piece of music: *the tenor part, the violin part.* **14** the music for it. **15** less than the whole: *part Irish.* **16** in some measure or degree; partly. **17 parts,** *pl.* **a** ability; talent: *a man of parts.* **b** regions; districts; places: *She has traveled much in foreign parts.* 1-7,11,13,14,17 *n.,* 8-10,12 *v.,* 15 *adj.,* 16 *adv.*

for one's part, as far as one is concerned.

for the most part, mostly: *The plan was for the most part successful.*

in good part, in a friendly or gracious way.

in part, in some measure or degree; to some extent; partly.

on the part of one or **on one's part, 1** as far as one is concerned. **2** by one.

part and parcel, a necessary part.

part from, go away from; leave.

part with, give up; let go.

take part, take or have a share.

par take (pär tāk′), **1** eat or drink some; take some: *We are eating lunch. Will you partake?* **2** take or have a share. *v.,* **par took, par tak en, par tak ing.** —**par tak′a ble,** *adj.* —**par tak′er,** *n.*

partake of, 1 take some; have a share in: *Will you partake of this cake?* **2** have to some extent the nature or character of: *Her graciousness partakes of condescension.*

par tak en (pär tā′kən), past participle of **partake.** *v.*

part ed (pär′tid), divided into parts; severed; cloven. *adj.* —**part′ed ness,** *n.*

Par the non (pär′thə non), temple of Athena on the Acropolis in Athens, regarded as the finest example of Doric architecture. *n.*

par tial (pär′shəl), **1** not complete; not total: *My parents made a partial payment on our new car.* **2** inclined to favor one side more than another; favoring unfairly: *Parents should not be partial to any one of their children.* **3** having a liking for; favorably inclined: *I am partial to sports. adj.* —**par′tial ness,** *n.*

par ti al i ty (pär′shē al′ə tē), **1** the favoring of one more than another or others; favorable prejudice; being partial. **2** a particular liking; fondness; preference; bent: *a partiality for word games. n., pl.* **par ti al i ties.**

par tial ly (pär′shə lē), **1** in part; not generally or totally; partly. **2** in a partial manner; with undue bias. *adv.*

par tic i pant (pär tis′ə pənt), person who shares or participates. *n.*

par tic i pate (pär tis′ə pāt), have a share; take part: *The teacher participated in the children's games. v.,* **par tic i pat ed, par tic i pat ing.** [*Participate* can be traced back to Latin *partem,* meaning "a part, share," and *capere,* meaning "to take."] —**par tic′i pat′ing ly,** *adv.*

par tic i pa tion (pär tis′ə pā′shən), a participating; taking part. *n.*

par tic i pa tor (pär tis′ə pā′tər), person who participates. *n.*

par ti cip i al (pär′tə sip′ē əl), of or resembling a participle. We often use participial adjectives (a *masked* man, a *becoming* dress) and participial nouns (in *cutting* ice, the fatigue of *marching*). *adj.* —**par′ti cip′i al ly,** *adv.*

par ti ci ple (pär′tə sip′əl), a verb form that retains all the attributes of a verb, such as tense, voice, power to take an object, and modification by adverbs, but may be used as an adjective. EXAMPLES: the students *writing* sentences at the blackboard, the people *waiting* for a train, the *stolen* silver, the boy *having missed* the bus. In these phrases, *writing* and *waiting* are present participles; *stolen* and *having missed* are past participles. *n.*

par ti cle (pär′tə kəl), **1** a very little bit: *I got a particle of dust in my eye.* **2** any of the extremely small units of matter of which all atoms are composed, such as the electron, proton, and neutron. **3** prefix or suffix. *Un-* and *-ment* are particles. **4** preposition, conjunction, article, or interjection. *In, if, an,* and *ah* are particles. *n.*

particle accelerator, any of several machines, such as the betatron and cyclotron, that greatly increase the speed and energy of protons, electrons, and other atomic particles and direct them in a steady stream at a target; accelerator. The accelerated particles are used to bombard the nuclei of atoms, causing the nuclei to release new particles.

par ti-col ored (pär′tē kul′ərd), colored differently in different parts: *a parti-colored shirt. adj.*

par tic u lar (pər tik′yə lər), **1** apart from others; considered separately; single: *That particular chair is already sold.* **2** belonging to some one person, thing, group, occasion, etc.: *His particular task is to care for the dog.* **3** different from others; unusual; special: *This vacation was of particular importance to her, for she was going to Brazil. He is a particular friend of mine.* **4** hard to please;

a hat	i it	oi oil	ch child	a in about
ā age	ī ice	ou out	ng long	e in taken
ä far	o hot	u cup	sh she	ə = i in pencil
e let	ō open	u̇ put	th thin	o in lemon
ē equal	ô order	ü rule	ŦH then	u in circus
ėr term			zh measure	

wanting everything to be just right; very careful: *She is very particular; nothing but the best will do.* **5** an individual part; item; point: *All the particulars of the accident are now known.* 1-4 *adj.,* 5 *n.*

in particular, especially: *We strolled around, going nowhere in particular.*

par tic u lar i ty (pər tik′yə lar′ə tē), **1** detailed quality; minuteness. **2** special carefulness. **3** attentiveness to details. **4** a particular feature or trait. *n., pl.* **par tic u lar i ties.**

par tic u lar i za tion (pər tik′yə lər ə zā′shən), act of particularizing. *n.*

par tic u lar ize (pər tik′yə lə rīz′), **1** mention particularly; treat in detail. **2** mention individually; state or discuss in detail. *v.,* **par tic u lar ized, par tic u lar iz ing.** —**par tic′u lar iz′er,** *n.*

par tic u lar ly (pər tik′yə lər lē), **1** in a high degree; especially: *I am particularly fond of her. He mentioned that point particularly.* **2** in a particular manner; in detail; in all its parts; minutely: *The inspector examined the machine particularly. adv.*

part ing (pär′ting), **1** a going away; taking leave; departure: *The friends were sad at parting.* **2** given, taken, done, etc., at parting: *a parting request.* **3** departing. **4** dividing; separating. **5** division; separation. 1,5 *n.,* 2-4 *adj.*

par ti san (pär′tə zən), **1** a strong supporter of a person, party, or cause; one whose support is based on feeling rather than on reasoning. **2** member of light, irregular troops; guerrilla. **3** of or like a partisan: *There are often partisan favors in politics.* 1,2 *n.,* 3 *adj.*

par ti san ship (pär′tə zən ship), **1** strong loyalty to a party or cause. **2** a taking sides. *n.*

par ti tion (pär tish′ən), **1** division into parts: *the partition of a person's estate after death.* **2** divide into parts: *partition a territory into three states, partition a house into rooms.* **3** wall between rooms, etc. **4** separate by a partition. 1,3 *n.,* 2,4 *v.* —**par ti′tion er,** *n.* —**par ti′tion ment,** *n.*

part ly (pärt′lē), in part; in some measure or degree: *You are partly to blame. adv.*

part ner (pärt′nər), **1** one who shares: *My sister was the partner of my walks.* **2** member of a company or firm who shares the risks and profits of the business. **3** wife or husband. **4** companion in a dance. **5** player on the same team or side in a game. *n.* —**part′ner less,** *adj.*

part ner ship (pärt′nər ship), **1** a being a partner; joint interest; association: *a business partnership, the partnership of marriage.* **2** company or firm with two or more members who share in the risks and profits of the business: *a law partnership.* **3** the contract that creates such a relation. *n.*

part of speech, any of the classes into which words are divided according to their use or function in sentences. The traditional parts of speech are the noun, pronoun, adjective, verb, adverb, preposition, conjunction, and interjection.

par took (pär tu̇k′), past tense of **partake.** *We partook of food and drink. v.*

par tridge (pär′trij), **1** any of several game birds of Europe, Asia, and Africa belonging to the same family as the quail and pheasant. **2** any of several similar birds of the United States, such as the ruffed grouse and the quail or bobwhite. *n., pl.* **par tridg es** or **par tridge.**

part song, song with parts in simple harmony for two or more voices, especially one meant to be sung without an accompaniment.

part-time (pärt′tīm′), for part of the usual time: *A part-time job helped her finish college. adj.*

par tu ri tion (pär′tù rish′ən *or* pär′tyù rish′ən), childbirth. *n.*

par ty (pär′tē), **1** a gathering of a group of people to have a good time together: *On her birthday she had a party and invited her friends.* **2** group of people doing something together: *a dinner party, a scouting party of three soldiers.* **3** group of people organized to gain political influence and control: *the Democratic Party.* **4** of a party of people: *They have strong party loyalties.* **5** one who takes part in, aids, or knows about: *He was a party to our secret.* **6** each of the persons or sides in a contract, lawsuit, etc. **7** INFORMAL. person: *The party you were calling is on the telephone now.* 1-3,5-7 *n., pl.* **par ties;** 4 *adj.*

Pas a de na (pas′ə dē′nə), city in SW California, near Los Angeles. *n.*

Pas cal[1] (pa skal′), **Blaise**, 1623-1662, French philosopher, mathematician, and physicist. *n.*

PAS CAL or **Pas cal**[2] (pa skal′ *or* pas′kəl), computer programming language designed to be used in teaching programming and to make programs easier to understand and check. *n.*

pa sha (pə shä′), a former title used after the name of Turkish civil or military officials of high rank. *n., pl.* **pa shas.**

pass (pas), **1** go by; move past: *The parade passed. We passed the big truck. Many people pass our house every day.* **2** move on; go: *The days pass quickly. The salesman passed from house to house.* **3** go from one to another: *The property passed from the father to the daughter. Hot words passed during their quarrel.* **4** hand from one to another; hand around: *Please pass the butter.* **5** get through or by: *The ship passed the channel.* **6** go across or over: *The horse passed the stream.* **7** to move: *Pass your hand over the velvet and feel how soft it is.* **8** go away; depart. **9** be successful in (an examination, a course, etc.): *She passed French.* **10** success in an examination, etc.; passing an examination but without honors. **11** act of passing; passage. **12** cause or allow to go through something; sanction or approve: *The inspector passed the item after examining it.* **13** ratify or enact: *pass a bill or law.* **14** be approved by (a lawmaking body, etc.): *The new law passed the city council.* **15** come to an end; die: *The king passed in peace.* **16** go beyond; exceed; surpass: *That strange story passes belief.* **17** use or spend: *We passed the days pleasantly.* **18** to change: *Water passes from a liquid to a solid state when it freezes.* **19** take place; happen: *Tell me all that passed.* **20** be accepted for or as: *She could pass for twenty.* **21** express; pronounce: *A judge passes sentence on guilty persons.* **22** give a judgment or opinion: *Please pass upon this question.* **23** go without notice: *They were rude, but I let it pass.* **24** a note, license, etc., permitting one to do something: *They needed a pass to enter the fort.* **25** free ticket: *She won a pass to the circus.* **26** state; condition: *Things have come to a strange pass when children give orders to their parents.* **27** motion of the hand or hands. **28** a narrow road, path, way, channel, etc.: *A pass crosses the mountains.* **29** throw (the ball) to another player in basketball, football, etc. **30** a throw of the ball to another player in basketball, football, etc. **31** (in card playing) refrain from bidding or playing a hand. **32** a thrust in fencing. 1-9,12-23,29,31 *v.,* 10,11,24-28,30,32 *n., pl.* **pass es.** —**pass′er,** *n.* —**pass′less,** *adj.*

bring to pass, to cause to be; accomplish.

come to pass, take place; happen.

pass away, come to an end; die.

pass off, use trickery or dishonesty to get something accepted as something else.

pass on, to die.

pass out, 1 give out; distribute. **2** INFORMAL. faint; lose consciousness.

pass over, fail to notice; overlook; disregard.

pass up, give up; renounce: *pass up a chance to go to college.*

pass., 1 passenger. **2** passive.

pass a ble (pas′ə bəl), **1** fairly good; moderate: *a passable knowledge of geography.* **2** able to be traveled over or crossed: *a passable road, a passable river. adj.*

pass a bly (pas′ə blē), fairly; moderately. *adv.*

pas sage (pas′ij), **1** hall or way through a building; passageway. **2** means of passing; way through: *open a passage through a crowd.* **3** right, liberty, or leave to pass: *The guard refused us passage.* **4** a passing: *the passage of time.* **5** piece from a speech, writing, or musical composition: *a passage from the Bible.* **6** a going across; voyage: *We had a stormy passage across the Atlantic.* **7** ticket that entitles the holder to transportation, especially by boat: *obtain passage for Europe.* **8** a making into law by a favoring vote of a legislature: *the passage of a bill. n.*

pas sage way (pas′ij wā′), way along which one can pass. Halls and alleys are passageways. *n.*

pass book (pas′bůk′), bankbook. *n.*

pas sé (pa sā′), out of date. *adj.*

pas sen ger (pas′n jər), traveler in an aircraft, bus, ship, train, etc., usually one that pays a fare. *n.*

passenger pigeons
about 16 in.
(40 cm.) long

passenger pigeon, kind of wild pigeon of North America, now extinct, that flew in very large flocks.

pass er-by (pas′ər bī′), one that passes by. *n., pl.* **pass-ers-by.**

pass ing (pas′ing), **1** going by; moving past: *a passing train.* **2** act of one that passes; a going by; a departure. **3** done or given in passing: *a passing smile.* **4** not lasting; fleeting: *a passing fancy.* **5** allowing one to pass an examination or test: *75 will be a passing mark.* **6** means or place of passing. **7** death: *the passing of a great leader.* 1,3-5 *adj.,* 2,6,7 *n.* —**pass′ing ly,** *adv.* —**pass′ing ness,** *n.*

in passing, by the way; incidentally.

pas sion (pash′ən), **1** very strong feeling: *Hate and fear are passions.* **2** violent anger; rage: *He flew into a passion.* **3** love between a man and a woman. **4** very strong liking: *She has a passion for music.* **5** thing for which a strong liking is felt: *Music is her passion.* **6 the Passion, a** the sufferings of Jesus on the Cross or after the Last Supper. **b** story of these sufferings in the Bible. *n.* [*Passion* came into English about 800 years ago from French *passion,* and can be traced back to Latin *pati,* meaning "to suffer."] —**pas′sion less,** *adj.*

pas sion ate (pash′ə nit), **1** having or showing strong feelings: *She has always been a passionate believer in human rights.* **2** easily moved to a fit or mood of some emotion, especially to anger. **3** resulting from strong feeling: *He made a passionate speech against death sentences. adj.* —**pas′sion ate ly,** *adv.* —**pas′sion ate ness,** *n.*

passion play or **Passion Play,** play representing the sufferings and death of Jesus.

pas sive (pas′iv), **1** being acted on without itself acting; not acting in return: *a passive mind, a passive disposition.* **2** not resisting; yielding or submitting to the will of another: *The children gave passive obedience to their strict parents.* **3** (in grammar) showing the subject as acted on. In "The race was won by her," *was won* is in the passive voice. **4** a verb form in the passive voice. 1-3 *adj.,* 4 *n.* —**pas′sive ly,** *adv.* —**pas′sive ness,** *n.*

pas siv i ty (pa siv′ə tē), a being passive; lack of action or resistance. *n.*

pass key (pas′kē′), **1** key for opening several locks. **2** a private key. *n., pl.* **pass keys.**

Pass o ver (pas′ō′vər), an annual Jewish holiday in memory of the escape of the Hebrews from Egypt, where they had been slaves. *n.*

pass port (pas′pôrt), **1** paper or book giving official permission to travel abroad, under the protection of one's own government. **2** anything that gives one admission or acceptance: *A sense of curiosity can be a passport to knowledge. n.* [*Passport* came into English about 500 years ago from French *passeport,* which comes from *passer,* meaning "to pass," and *port,* meaning "a harbor."] —**pass′port less,** *adj.*

pass word (pas′wėrd′), a secret word that allows a person who says it to pass a guard. *n.*

past (past), **1** gone by; ended: *Summer is past. Our troubles are past.* **2** just gone by: *the past year, the past century.* **3** time gone by; time before; what has happened: *forget the past. History is a study of the past.* **4** a past life or history: *He cannot change his past.* **5** beyond; farther on than: *The arrow went past the mark.* **6** after; later than: *It is past noon.* **7** so as to pass by or beyond: *The cars sped past.* **8** beyond in number, amount, or degree. **9** beyond the ability, range, scope, etc., of: *absurd fancies that are past belief.* **10** having served a term in office: *a past president.* **11** the past tense or a verb form in it. 1,2,10 *adj.,* 3,4,11 *n.,* 5,6,8,9 *prep.,* 7 *adv.*

pas ta (pä′stə), dough made of wheat flour, water, salt, and sometimes milk or eggs and shaped into various forms. Macaroni, spaghetti, and ravioli are kinds of pasta. *n.*

paste (pāst), **1** mixture, such as flour and water boiled together, that will stick paper together. **2** to stick with paste. **3** dough for pastry. **4** a soft, doughlike food: *liver paste.* **5** a hard, glassy material used in making imitations of precious stones. **6** SLANG. hit with a hard, sharp blow. 1,3-5 *n.,* 2,6 *v.,* **past ed, past ing.** —**past′er,** *n.*

paste board (pāst′bôrd′), a stiff material made of sheets of paper pasted together or of paper pulp pressed and dried. *n.*

pas tel (pa stel′), **1** kind of chalklike crayon used in drawing. **2** a drawing made with such crayons. **3** a soft, pale shade of some color. **4** soft and pale: *pastel pink, pastel shades.* 1-3 *n.,* 4 *adj.*

pas tern (pas′tərn), the part of a horse's foot between the fetlock and the hoof. *n.*

Pas teur (pa stėr′), **Louis,** 1822-1895, French chemist who invented a way of preventing rabies and of keeping milk from spoiling. *n.*

pas teur i za tion (pas′chər ə zā′shən), **1** process of pasteurizing. **2** fact or condition of being pasteurized. *n.*

pas teur ize (pas′chə rīz′), heat (milk, wine, beer, etc.)

a hat	i it	oi oil	ch child	a in about
ā age	ī ice	ou out	ng long	e in taken
ä far	o hot	u cup	sh she	ə = { i in pencil
e let	ō open	u̇ put	th thin	o in lemon
ē equal	ô order	ü rule	ᵗʜ then	u in circus
ėr term			zh measure	

to a high enough temperature and for a long enough time to destroy harmful bacteria. When milk is pasteurized, it is heated to about 145 degrees Fahrenheit (63 degrees Celsius) for not less than 30 minutes, then chilled quickly to 50 degrees Fahrenheit (10 degrees Celsius) or less. *v.,* **pas teur ized, pas teur iz ing.** —**pas′teur iz′er,** *n.*

pas time (pas′tīm′), a pleasant way of passing time; amusement; recreation. Games and sports are pastimes. *n.*

past i ness (pā′stē nis), pasty quality, condition, or consistency. *n.*

pas tor (pas′tər), minister in charge of a church; spiritual guide. *n.* —**pas′tor less,** *adj.* —**pas′tor like′,** *adj.*

pastoral (def. 1)

pas tor al (pas′tər əl), **1** of shepherds or country life: *The pastoral villagers graze their sheep on the hillsides.* **2** play, poem, or picture dealing with shepherds or country life. **3** simple or naturally beautiful like the country: *a pastoral landscape.* **4** of a pastor: *a pastoral letter.* 1,3,4 *adj.,* 2 *n.* —**pas′tor al ly,** *adv.*

pas tor ate (pas′tər it), **1** position or duties of a pastor. **2** term of service of a pastor. **3** pastors as a group. *n.*

past participle, participle that indicates time gone by, or a former action or condition. *Played* in "She has played all day," and *thrown* in "The ball should have been thrown to me" are past participles.

pas tra mi (pə strä′mē), a smoked and well-seasoned cut of beef, especially a shoulder cut. *n.* [*Pastrami* was borrowed from Yiddish *pastrami,* which came from Romanian *pastrama.*]

pas try (pā′strē), **1** pies, tarts, or other baked food made with dough rich in butter or other shortening. **2** the dough for such food. *n., pl.* **pas tries.**

past tense, **1** tense expressing time gone by, or a former action or condition. **2** a verb form in the past tense.

pas tur age (pas′chər ij), **1** the growing grass and other plants for cattle, sheep, or horses to feed on. **2** pasture land. *n.*

pas ture (pas′chər), **1** a grassy field or hillside; grasslands on which cattle, sheep, or horses can feed. **2** grass and other growing plants: *These lands afford good pasture.* **3** put (cattle, sheep, etc.) out to pasture. **4** feed on (growing grass, etc.). 1,2 *n.,* 3,4 *v.,* **pas tured, pas tur ing.** [*Pasture* came into English about 700 years ago from French *pasture,* and can be traced back to Latin *pascere,* meaning "to feed."]

past y[1] (pā′stē), **1** like paste. **2** pale. **3** flabby. *adj.,* **past i er, past i est.**

pas ty[2] (pas′tē), pie filled with meat, fish, etc.: *a venison pasty. n., pl.* **pas ties.**

pat (pat), **1** strike or tap lightly with something flat: *He patted the dough into a flat cake.* **2** to tap with the hand as a sign of sympathy, approval, or affection: *pat a dog.* **3** a light stroke or tap with the hand or with something flat. **4** sound made by patting. **5** a small mass, especially of butter. **6** apt; suitable; to the point: *a pat reply.* 1,2 *v.,* **pat ted, pat ting;** 3-5 *n.,* 6 *adj.,* **pat ter, pat test.** —**pat′ly,** *adv.* —**pat′ness,** *n.*

have pat or **have down pat,** INFORMAL. have perfectly; know thoroughly.

pat on the back, praise; compliment.

stand pat, hold to things as they are and refuse to change.

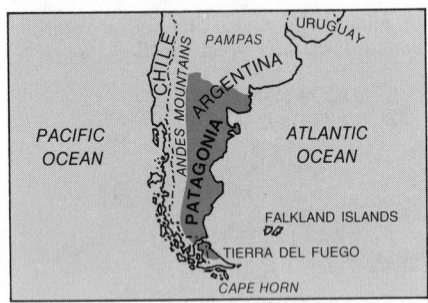

Pat a go ni a (pat′ə gō′nē ə), region in the extreme south of South America. The larger part of Patagonia is in Argentina; the rest is in Chile. *n.* —**Pat′a go′ni an,** *adj., n.*

patch (pach), **1** piece put on to mend a hole or a tear. **2** piece of cloth, etc., put over a wound or a sore. **3** a pad over a hurt eye to protect it. **4** a small bit of black cloth women used to wear on their faces to show off their fair skin. **5** put patches on; mend; protect or adorn with a patch or patches. **6** a small, uneven spot: *a patch of brown on the skin.* **7** piece of ground: *a garden patch.* **8** scrap or bit of cloth left over. **9** make by joining patches or pieces together: *patch a quilt.* **10** piece together; make hastily. 1-4,6-8 *n., pl.* **patch es;** 5,9,10 *v.* —**patch′er,** *n.* —**patch′less,** *adj.*

patch up, 1 put an end to; settle: *patch up a quarrel.* **2** make right hastily or for a time: *patch up a leaking faucet.*

patch work (pach′wėrk′), **1** pieces of cloth of various colors or shapes sewed together: *I made a cover of patchwork for the old cushion.* **2** made of such pieces of cloth. **3** anything with a patchwork design: *From the airplane, we saw a patchwork of fields and woods.* 1,3 *n.,* 2 *adj.*

patch y (pach′ē), **1** abounding in or characterized by patches. **2** occurring in, forming, or resembling patches. *adj.,* **patch i er, patch i est.** —**patch′i ly,** *adv.* —**patch′i ness,** *n.*

pate (pāt), top of the head; head: *a bald pate. n.*

pa tel la (pə tel′ə), kneecap. *n., pl.* **pa tel las, pa tel lae** (pə tel′ē).

pat ent (pat′nt *for 1-5;* pāt′nt *or* pat′nt *for 6*), **1** a government document which gives a person or company sole rights to make, use, or sell a new invention for a certain number of years. **2** given or protected by a patent. **3** get a patent for: *She patented her new invention.* **4** invention that is patented. **5** an official document from a government giving a right or privilege. **6** open to view or knowledge; evident; plain: *It is patent that cats dislike dogs.* 1,4,5 *n.,* 2,6 *adj.,* 3 *v.* —**pat′ent a ble,** *adj.*

pat ent ee (pat′n tē′), person to whom a patent is granted. *n.*

pat ent leather (pat′nt), leather with a very glossy, smooth surface, usually black.

pa tent ly (pāt′nt lē *or* pat′nt lē), plainly or openly; clearly; obviously. *adv.*

pat ent medicine (pat′nt), **1** any medicine that may be purchased without a doctor's prescription. **2** medicine sold by a company which has a patent on its manufacture and trade name.

Patent Office, government office that issues patents.

pa ter nal (pə tėr′nl), **1** of or like a father; fatherly. **2** related on the father's side of the family: *Everyone has two paternal grandparents and two maternal grandparents.* **3** derived or inherited from one's father: *Her blue eyes were a paternal inheritance. adj.* —**pa ter′nal ly,** *adv.*

pa ter nal ism (pə tėr′nl iz′əm), principle or practice of managing the affairs of a country or group of people as a father manages the affairs of his children. *n.*

pa ter nal is tic (pə tėr′nl is′tik), characterized by paternalism. *adj.* —**pa ter′nal is′ti cal ly,** *adv.*

pa ter ni ty (pə tėr′nə tē), **1** a being a father; fatherhood. **2** paternal origin: *King Arthur's paternity was unknown. n.*

pat er nos ter (pat′ər nos′tər *or* pā′tər nos′tər), the Lord's Prayer, especially in Latin. *n.*

path (path), **1** way made by people or animals walking. It is usually too narrow for automobiles or wagons. **2** way made to walk upon or to ride horses, bicycles, etc.: *a garden path.* **3** line along which a person or thing moves; route; track: *The moon has a regular path through the sky.* **4** way of acting or behaving; way of life: *paths of glory, paths of ease. n., pl.* **paths** (paᴛʜz *or* paths).

pa thet ic (pə thet′ik), arousing pity; pitiful: *The stray dog was a pathetic sight. adj.* —**pa thet′i cal ly,** *adv.*

pathetic
Homeless and unemployed, he was a **pathetic** sight.

path find er (path′fīn′dər), one who finds a path or way, as through a wilderness. *n.*

path less (path′lis), having no path through or across it: *a pathless mountain. adj.*

path o gen (path′ə jən), anything capable of producing disease, especially a living microorganism or virus. *n.*

path o gen ic (path′ə jen′ik), producing disease. *adj.*

path o log ic (path′ə loj′ik), pathological. *adj.*

path o log i cal (path′ə loj′ə kəl), **1** of pathology; dealing with diseases or concerned with diseases: *pathological studies.* **2** due to disease or accompanying a physical disease or mental disorder: *a pathological heart condition, a pathological liar. adj.* —**path o log′i cal ly,** *adv.*

pa thol o gist (pa thol′ə jist), an expert in pathology. *n.*

pa thol o gy (pa thol′ə jē), **1** study of the causes and nature of diseases. **2** unhealthy conditions caused by a disease. *n., pl.* **pa thol o gies.**

pa thos (pā′thos), quality in speech, writing, music,

events, or a scene that arouses pity or sadness. *n.*

path way (path'wā'), path. *n.*

pa tience (pā'shəns), **1** willingness to put up with waiting, pain, trouble, etc.; calm endurance of anything that annoys, troubles, or hurts: *The cat watched the mouse hole with patience.* **2** long, hard work; steady effort. *n.*

pa tient (pā'shənt), **1** having or showing patience. **2** person who is being treated by a doctor. **1** *adj.,* **2** *n.* —**pa'tient ly,** *adv.* —**pa'tient ness,** *n.*

pat i o (pat'ē ō), **1** an inner court or yard open to the sky, found especially in houses of Spanish or Spanish-American design. **2** terrace for outdoor eating, lounging, etc. *n., pl.* **pat i os.**

pat ois (pat'wä), dialect spoken by the common people of a district: *the patois of the French Canadians. n., pl.* **pat ois** (pat'wäz).

pa tri arch (pā'trē ärk), **1** father who is the ruler of a family or tribe. **2** a highly respected elderly man. **3** bishop of the highest rank in the Eastern Church and the Roman Catholic Church. *n.*

pa tri ar chal (pā'trē är'kəl), **1** of or suitable for a patriarch. **2** under the rule of a patriarch: *a patriarchal church. adj.*

pa tri cian (pə trish'ən), **1** member of the nobility of ancient Rome. **2** a noble; aristocrat. **3** of high social rank; aristocratic. **4** suitable for an aristocrat. **1,2** *n.,* **3,4** *adj.*

Pat rick (pat'rik), **Saint,** A.D. 389?-461?, British missionary and bishop who converted Ireland to Christianity. He is the patron saint of Ireland. *n.*

pat ri mo ni al (pat'rə mō'nē əl), having to do with a patrimony; inherited from one's father or ancestors. *adj.*

pat ri mo ny (pat'rə mō'nē), **1** property inherited from one's father or ancestors. **2** property belonging to a church, monastery, or convent. **3** any heritage. *n., pl.* **pat ri mo nies.**

pa tri ot (pā'trē ət), person who loves and loyally supports his or her country. *n.* [*Patriot* came into English about 400 years ago from French *patriote,* and can be traced back to Greek *patēr,* meaning "father."]

pa tri ot ic (pā'trē ot'ik), **1** loving one's country. **2** showing love and loyal support of one's own country. *adj.* —**pa'tri ot'i cal ly,** *adv.*

pa tri ot ism (pā'trē ə tiz'əm), love and loyal support of one's country. *n.*

pa trol (pə trōl'), **1** go around in an area watching and guarding in order to protect life and property: *The police patrolled once every hour.* **2** go around (a town, camp, etc.) to watch or guard. **3** a going of the rounds to watch or guard. **4** persons who patrol: *The patrol was changed at midnight.* **5** group of soldiers, ships, or airplanes, sent to find out all they can about the enemy. **6** unit of eight boy or girl scouts. **1,2** *v.,* **pa trolled, pa trol ling; 3-6** *n.* —**pa trol'ler,** *n.*

patrol car, automobile used by the police to patrol an area.

pa trol man (pə trōl'mən), policeman who patrols a certain district. *n., pl.* **pa trol men.**

patrol wagon, a closed wagon or truck used by the police for carrying prisoners.

pa trol wom an (pə trōl'wùm'ən), policewoman who patrols a certain district. *n., pl.* **pa trol wom en.**

pa tron (pā'trən), **1** one who buys regularly at a given store or goes regularly to a certain restaurant, hotel, etc. **2** person who gives approval and support to some person, art, cause, or undertaking: *a patron of artists.* **3** a guardian saint or god; protector. **4** guarding; protecting: *a patron saint.* **1-3** *n.,* **4** *adj.* —**pa'tron less,** *adj.*

pa tron age (pā'trə nij *or* pat'rə nij), **1** regular business given to a store, hotel, etc., by customers. **2** favor, encouragement, or support given by a patron. **3** conde-

scending favor: *an air of patronage.* **4** power to give jobs or favors: *the patronage of a governor, a mayor, or a member of Congress.* **5** political jobs or favors. *n.*

pa tron ize (pā'trə nīz *or* pat'rə nīz), **1** be a regular customer of; give regular business to: *We patronize our neighborhood stores.* **2** act as a patron toward; support or protect: *patronize the ballet.* **3** treat in a condescending way: *We dislike to have anyone patronize us. v.,* **pa tron ized, pa tron iz ing.** —**pa'tron iz'a ble,** *adj.* —**pa'tron iz'er,** *n.* —**pa'tron iz'ing ly,** *adv.*

pa troon (pə trün'), landowner who had certain privileges under the old Dutch governments of New York and New Jersey. A patroon usually owned a large amount of land. *n.* [*Patroon* was borrowed from Dutch *patroon,* which came from Latin *patronus,* meaning "patron."]

pat sy (pat'sē), SLANG. an easy victim or scapegoat. *n., pl.* **pat sies.**

pat ter[1] (pat'ər), **1** make rapid taps: *The rain patters on a windowpane. Bare feet patter along the hard floor.* **2** series of quick taps or the sound they make: *the patter of rain, the patter of little feet.* **1** *v.,* **2** *n.*

pat ter[2] (pat'ər), **1** rapid and easy talk: *a magician's patter.* **2** talk or say rapidly and easily, without much thought: *patter a prayer.* **1** *n.,* **2** *v.* —**pat'ter er,** *n.*

pat tern (pat'ərn), **1** arrangement of forms and colors; design: *the pattern of a wallpaper, a pattern of polka dots.* **2** a model or guide for something to be made: *I used a paper pattern in cutting the cloth for my coat.* **3** a fine example; model to be followed: *He was a pattern of generosity.* **4** make according to a pattern: *Pattern yourself after your mother.* **5** any arrangement: *behavior pattern, a speech pattern.* **1-3,5** *n.,* **4** *v.* —**pat'tern less,** *adj.*

pat ty (pat'ē), **1** a hollow form of pastry filled with chicken, oysters, etc. **2** a small, round, flat piece of food or candy. *n., pl.* **pat ties.**

pau ci ty (pô'sə tē), **1** a small number; fewness. **2** a small amount; scarcity; lack. *n.*

Paul (pôl), **Saint,** died A.D. 67?, apostle who started Christian groups in many countries and wrote many of the books in the New Testament. *n.*

Paul VI, 1897-1978, pope from 1963 to 1978.

paunch (pônch), **1** belly; stomach. **2** a large, bulging belly. *n.*

paunch y (pôn'chē), having a big paunch. *adj.,* **paunch i er, paunch i est.** —**paunch'i ness,** *n.*

pau per (pô'pər), a very poor person; person supported by charity. *n.*

pau per ize (pô'pə rīz'), make a pauper of. *v.,* **pau per ized, pau per iz ing.** —**pau'per i za'tion,** *n.*

pause (pôz), **1** stop for a time; wait: *I paused for a moment to look in a store window.* **2** a brief stop or rest: *After a pause for lunch the employees returned to work. After a short pause I went on reading.* **3** dwell; linger: *pause upon a word.* **4** a sign (⌣ *or* ⌢) above or below a musical note or rest, meaning that it is to be held for a longer time. **1,3** *v.,* **paused, paus ing; 2,4** *n.* —**paus'er,** *n.* —**paus'ing ly,** *adv.*

pave (pāv), **1** cover (a street, sidewalk, etc.) with a pavement: *pave a road with concrete.* **2** make smooth or easy; prepare: *The invention paved the way for new discoveries. v.,* **paved, pav ing.** —**pav'er,** *n.*

pave ment (pāv'mənt), **1** a covering or surface for

streets, sidewalks, etc., made of asphalt, concrete, gravel, stones, etc. **2** a paved road. *n.*

pa vil ion (pə vil′yən), **1** a light building, usually somewhat open, used for shelter, pleasure, etc.: *a bathing pavilion.* **2** a large tent with a floor raised on posts. **3** part of a building higher and more decorated than the rest. **4** one of a group of buildings forming a hospital. **5** any building that houses an exhibition at a fair. *n.*

pav ing (pā′ving), **1** material for pavement. **2** pavement. *n.*

Pav lov (pav′lov or päv′lôf), **Ivan,** 1849-1936, Russian physiologist famous for his studies of the digestive glands and of the reflexes. *n.*

paw (pô), **1** foot of a four-footed animal having claws. **2** strike or scrape with the paws or feet: *The cat pawed the mouse. The horse pawed the ground, eager to be going again.* **3** INFORMAL. handle awkwardly, roughly, or in too familiar a manner: *Stop pawing the tomatoes; you'll bruise them.* **1** *n.,* **2,3** *v.* —**paw′er,** *n.*

pawn[1] (pôn), **1** leave (something) with another person as security that borrowed money will be repaid; pledge: *I pawned my watch to buy food until I could get work.* **2** something left as security. **1** *v.,* **2** *n.* —**pawn′a ble,** *adj.*

pawn[2] (pôn), **1** (in chess) one of the 16 pieces of lowest value. **2** an unimportant person or thing used by someone to gain some advantage. *n.*

pawn bro ker (pôn′brō′kər), person who lends money at interest on articles that are left with him as security for the loan. *n.*

Paw nee (pô nē′), member of an American Indian tribe that once lived in Nebraska and Kansas, and now lives in Oklahoma. *n., pl.* **Paw nee** or **Paw nees.**

pawn shop (pôn′shop′), pawnbroker's shop. *n.*

paw paw (pô′pô), papaw. *n.*

pay (pā), **1** give money to for things, work, etc.: *He paid the doctor.* **2** money given for things or work: *She gets her pay every Friday.* **3** give money for: *Pay your fare. Pay your debts.* **4** give what is due: *She owes it and must pay.* **5** to return for favors or hurts; reward or punish: *He paid them for their insults by causing them trouble.* **6** a return for favors or hurts: *Dislike is the pay for being mean.* **7** give; offer; make: *pay attention, pay a visit.* **8** be worthwhile: *It pays me to keep that stock. It pays to be polite.* **9** yield as a return: *That stock pays me four percent.* **10** let out (a rope, etc.). **11** containing a device for receiving money for use: *a pay telephone.* **1,3-5,7-10** *v.,* **paid** (or **payed** for 10), **pay ing; 2,6** *n.,* **11** *adj.*

in the pay of, paid by and working for: *The spy was in the pay of a foreign state.*

pay back, 1 return borrowed money. **2** give the same treatment as received: *I hope to be able to pay back her help.*

pay off, 1 give all the money that is owed; pay in full. **2** get even with; get revenge on.

pay up, pay; pay in full.

pay a ble (pā′ə bəl), **1** required to be paid; due: *I must spend $100 soon on bills payable.* **2** that may be paid. *adj.*

pay check (pā′chek′), check given in payment of wages or salary. *n.*

pay day (pā′dā′), day on which wages are paid. *n.*

pay ee (pā ē′), person to whom money is paid or is to be paid. *n.*

pay er (pā′ər), person who pays or is to pay. *n.*

pay load (pā′lōd′), load carried by a vehicle. Passengers are the payload of a bus, train, or airplane. The payload of a rocket is contained in the nose cone, and may be instruments, cargo, or astronauts. The payload of a missile is the warhead. *n.*

pay mas ter (pā′mas′tər), person whose job is to pay wages. *n.*

pavilion
(def. 1)

pay ment (pā′mənt), **1** a paying. **2** amount paid: *a monthly payment of $10.* **3** pay: *The pleasure of helping you is payment enought for me.* **4** reward or punishment. *n.*

pay off (pā′ôf′), **1** a paying of wages. **2** time of such payment. **3** returns from an enterprise, action, etc. **4** INFORMAL. climax (of a story, situation, etc.). *n.*

pay roll (pā′rōl′), **1** list of persons to be paid and the amount that each one is to receive. **2** the total amount to be paid to them. *n.*

Pb, symbol for lead.

PBS, Public Broadcasting Service.

PC (pē′sē′), personal computer; a moderately priced microcomputer, designed to fit on a table or desk top and to be used for various personal, business, and home uses. *n.*

Pd, symbol for palladium.

pd., paid.

pea (pē), one of the round seeds eaten as a vegetable, that are inside the long green pod of a garden plant. *n., pl.* **peas** or **pease.**

as like as two peas, exactly alike.

peace (pēs), **1** freedom from strife of any kind; condition of quiet, order, and security: *peace in the family.* **2** freedom from war: *work for world peace.* **3** agreement between enemies to end war: *to sign the peace.* **4** quiet; calm; stillness: *peace of mind. We enjoy the peace of the country. n.* [*Peace* came into English over 800 years ago from French *pais,* which came from Latin *pax.* See **Word Family.**]

at peace, 1 not in a state of war. **2** not quarreling. **3** in a state of quietness; quiet; peaceful.

hold one's peace or **keep one's peace,** be silent.

WORD FAMILY

peace

Below are words related to *peace.* They can all be traced back to the Latin word *pax* (päks), meaning "peace."

appease	pacifier	pacify
Pacific	pacifist	pay

peace a ble (pē′sə bəl), **1** liking peace; keeping peace: *Peaceable people keep out of quarrels.* **2** peaceful. *adj.*

peace a bly (pē′sə blē), in a peaceable manner. *adv.*

Peace Corps, agency of the United States government, established in 1961, which sends trained volunteers to help underdeveloped countries.

peace ful (pēs′fəl), **1** full of peace; quiet; calm: *It was peaceful in the mountains.* **2** liking peace; keeping peace: *peaceful neighbors.* **3** of or having to do with peace: *settle a dispute by peaceful means. adj.* —**peace′ful ly,** *adv.* —**peace′ful ness,** *n.*

peace mak er (pēs′mā′kər), person who makes peace. *n.*

peace pipe

a hat	**i** it	**oi** oil	**ch** child	a in about
ā age	**ī** ice	**ou** out	**ng** long	e in taken
ä far	**o** hot	**u** cup	**sh** she	ə = { i in pencil
e let	**ō** open	**u̇** put	**th** thin	o in lemon
ē equal	**ô** order	**ü** rule	**ᵺ** then	u in circus
ėr term			**zh** measure	

peace pipe, pipe smoked by American Indians as a token or pledge of peace.

peace time (pēs′tīm′), **1** a time of peace. **2** of a time of peace. 1 *n.,* 2 *adj.*

peach (pēch), **1** a juicy, nearly round fruit having downy skin and a rough stone or pit. Peaches grow on trees in temperate climates. **2** a yellowish pink. **3** yellowish-pink. **4** SLANG. an attractive or excellent person or thing. 1,2,4 *n., pl.* **peach es;** 3 *adj.* —**peach′like′,** *adj.*

peach y (pē′chē), SLANG. fine; wonderful. *adj.,* **peach i er, peach i est.** —**peach′i ness,** *n.*

pea cock (pē′kok′), a large bird with beautiful green, blue, and gold feathers. The tail feathers of the male have spots like eyes on them and may be spread out and held upright like a fan. *n., pl.* **pea cocks** or **pea cock.**

peacock blue, greenish blue.

pea green, light green.

pea hen (pē′hen′), a female peacock. *n.*

pea jacket, a short coat of thick woolen cloth, worn by sailors.

peak (pēk), **1** the pointed top of a mountain or hill: *snowy peaks.* **2** mountain that stands alone: *Pikes Peak.* **3** any pointed end or top: *the peak of a roof.* **4** the highest point: *She has reached the peak of her profession.* **5** the front part or the brim of a cap, which stands out. **6** the narrow part of a ship's hold, at either end. *n.*

peaked[1] (pēkt), having a peak; pointed: *a peaked hat. adj.*

peak ed[2] (pē′kid), sickly in appearance; wan; thin. *adj.*

peal (pēl), **1** a loud, long sound: *a peal of thunder.* **2** the loud ringing of bells. **3** set of bells; chimes. **4** sound out in a peal; ring: *The bells pealed forth their message of joy.* 1-3 *n.,* 4 *v.*

pea nut (pē′nut′), **1** the large, nutlike seed of a plant related to the pea. Peanuts are contained in pods that ripen underground. They are roasted and used as food or pressed to get an oil for cooking. **2 peanuts,** *pl.* IN-FORMAL. **a** something of little or no value. **b** a relatively small amount of money. *n.*

peanut butter, food made of roasted peanuts ground until soft and smooth. It is spread on bread, crackers, etc.

peanut oil, oil pressed from peanuts, used especially in cooking and in margarine.

pear (per *or* par), a sweet, juicy, yellowish fruit rounded at one end and smaller toward the stem end. Pears grow on trees and are good to eat. *n.*

pearl (pėrl), **1** a white or nearly white gem that has a soft shine like satin. Pearls are formed inside the shell of a kind of oyster, or other similar shellfish. **2** thing that looks like a pearl, such as a dewdrop or a tear. **3** a very fine one of its kind: *His writings contain many pearls of wisdom.* **4** a very pale, clear, bluish gray. **5** very pale, clear bluish-gray. **6** mother-of-pearl. 1-4,6 *n.,* 5 *adj.* —**pearl′like′,** *adj.*

pearl gray, a soft, pale, bluish gray.

Pearl Harbor, United States naval base near Honolu-lu, Hawaii. A Japanese attack on it on December 7, 1941, was the immediate cause of American entry into World War II.

pearl y (pėr′lē), like a pearl in color or luster: *pearly teeth. adj.,* **pearl i er, pearl i est.** —**pearl′i ness,** *n.*

Pear y (pir′ē), Robert Edwin, 1856-1920, American naval officer and arctic explorer. *n.*

peas ant (pez′nt), **1** farmer of the working class in Europe. **2** of peasants: *peasant labor.* 1 *n.,* 2 *adj.*

peas ant ry (pez′n trē), peasants. *n.*

pease (pēz), a plural of **pea.** *n.*

peat (pēt), kind of turf made of partly rotted moss and plants found in bogs. It is dried and used as fuel in Ireland and Great Britain. *n.* —**peat′like′,** *adj.*

peat moss, kind of moss from which peat has formed or may form. It is dried and used as fertilizer.

peb ble (peb′əl), **1** a small stone, usually worn smooth and round by being rolled about by water. **2** pave with pebbles: *pebble a walk.* 1 *n.,* 2 *v.,* **peb bled, peb bling.** —**peb′ble like′,** *adj.*

peb bly (peb′lē), having many pebbles; covered with pebbles: *The pebbly beach hurt our bare feet. adj.,* **peb bli er, peb bli est.**

pe can (pi kän′ *or* pi kan′), an olive-shaped nut with a smooth, thin shell, that grows on a kind of hickory tree common in the southern United States. It is good to eat. *n.*

pec ca dil lo (pek′ə dil′ō), a slight sin or fault. *n., pl.* **pec ca dil loes** or **pec ca dil los.** [*Peccadillo* comes from Spanish *pecadillo,* and can be traced back to Latin *peccare,* meaning "to sin."]

peanut (def. 1) Peanut pods can be seen attached to the roots.

peccary about 3 ft. (1 m.) long

pec car y (pek′ər ē), a hoofed mammal resembling a pig, found in South America and as far north as Texas. *n., pl.* **pec car ies** or **pec car y.**

peck[1] (pek), **1** strike at and pick up with the beak or a pointed tool: *The hen pecked corn.* **2** stroke made with the beak or a pointed tool: *The hen gave me a peck.* **3** make by striking with the beak or a pointed tool: *Woodpeckers*

peck holes in trees. **4** hole or mark made by pecking.
5 make a pecking motion. **6** INFORMAL. a stiff, unwilling
kiss. 1,3,5 *v.*, 2,4,6 *n.*

peck at, 1 try to peck. **2** INFORMAL. eat only a little, bit by
bit: *Because she is not feeling well, she just pecks at her
food.* **3** keep criticizing.

peck[2] (pek), **1** measure of capacity for grain, fruit, vegetables, and other dry things, equal to 8 quarts or one
fourth of a bushel: *a peck of beans, a peck of potatoes.*
2 container holding just a peck, to measure with. **3** a
great deal: *a peck of trouble. n.*

pec tin (pek′tən), substance that occurs in ripe fruits
and makes fruit jelly stiff. *n.*

pec tor al (pek′tər əl), of, in, or on the breast or chest.
adj.

pe cul iar (pi kyü′lyər), **1** strange; odd; unusual: *It was
peculiar that the fish market had no fish last Friday. A
clock without any hands looks rather peculiar.* **2** belonging
to one area, person, or thing and not to another; special: *a type of pottery peculiar to the ancient Egyptians. adj.*
—**pe cul′iar ly,** *adv.*

pe cu li ar i ty (pi kyü′lē ar′ə tē), **1** a being peculiar;
strangeness; oddness; unusualness: *We noticed the peculiarity of her manner at once.* **2** some little thing that is
strange or odd: *One of his peculiarities is that his eyes are
not the same color.* **3** a peculiar or characteristic quality.
n., pl. **pe cu li ar i ties.**

pe cu ni ar y (pi kyü′nē er′ē), of money; in the form of
money. *adj.*

ped a gog (ped′ə gog), pedagogue. *n.*

ped a gog ic (ped′ə goj′ik), of teachers or teaching; of
pedagogy. *adj.* —**ped′a gog′i cal ly,** *adv.*

ped a gog i cal (ped′ə goj′ə kəl), pedagogic. *adj.*

ped a gogue (ped′ə gog), **1** teacher of children. **2** a dull,
narrow-minded teacher; pedant. *n.* Also, **pedagog.** [*Pedagogue* can be traced back to Greek *paidos,* meaning
"child," and *agein,* meaning "to lead."]

ped a go gy (ped′ə gō′jē), science or art of teaching. *n.*

ped al (ped′l), **1** lever worked by the foot; the part on
which the foot is placed to move any kind of machinery.
Organs and pianos have pedals for changing the tone.
The two pedals of a bicycle, pushed down one after the
other, make it go. **2** work or use the pedals of; move by
pedals: *He pedaled his bicycle slowly up the hill.* 1 *n.*, 2 *v.*,
ped aled, ped al ing or **ped alled, ped al ling.**

ped ant (ped′nt), **1** person who makes an unnecessary
or tiresome display of knowledge. **2** a dull, narrow-
minded teacher or scholar. *n.*

pe dan tic (pi dan′tik), **1** displaying one's knowledge
more than is necessary. **2** scholarly in a dull and narrow
way. *adj.* —**pe dan′ti cal ly,** *adv.*

pedantic (def. 1)

That touchdown reminds
me — in England, "football"
means soccer; their game
called "Rugby" is like
our football, but....

ped ant ry (ped′n trē), **1** an unnecessary or tiresome
display of knowledge. **2** overemphasis on rules, details,
etc., especially in learning. *n., pl.* **ped ant ries.**

ped dle (ped′l), **1** carry from place to place and sell: *The
farmer peddled fruit from house to house.* **2** sell or deal out
in small quantities: *peddle gossip.* **3** travel about with
things to sell. *v.*, **ped dled, ped dling.**

ped dler (ped′lər), person who travels about selling
things carried in a pack or in a cart. *n.*

ped es tal (ped′i stəl), **1** base on which a column or a
statue stands. **2** base of a tall vase, lamp, etc. **3** any base;
support; foundation. *n.*

place on a pedestal or **put on a pedestal,** accord a
very high place to; idolize.

pe des tri an (pə des′trē ən), **1** person who goes on
foot; walker: *Pedestrians have to watch for automobiles
turning corners.* **2** going on foot; walking. **3** without imagination; dull; slow: *a pedestrian style of writing.* 1 *n.*, 2,3
adj.

pe di at ric (pē′dē at′rik), of or having to do with pediatrics. *adj.*

pe di a tri cian (pē′dē ə trish′ən), doctor who specializes in pediatrics. *n.*

pe di at rics (pē′dē at′riks), branch of medicine dealing
with children's diseases and the care of babies and children. *n.* [*Pediatrics* comes from Greek *paidos,* meaning
"child," and *iasthai,* meaning "to heal, cure."]

ped i cab (ped′ə kab′), a three-wheeled vehicle with a
roofed cab for one or two passengers, operated by the
driver, who pedals it. It is used especially in the Far
East. *n.*

ped i cel (ped′ə səl), a small stalk or stalklike part. *n.*

ped i gree (ped′ə grē′), **1** list of ancestors of a person or
animal; family tree. **2** ancestry; line of descent. *n.*

ped i greed (ped′ə grēd′), having a known pedigree:
*Her dog is pedigreed. Horses, cows, dogs, and other ani-
mals of known and recorded ancestry are called pedigreed stock. adj.*

ped i ment (ped′ə mənt), **1** the low triangular part on
the front of buildings in the Greek style. A pediment is
like a gable. **2** any similar decorative part on a building,
door, bookcase, etc. *n.* [*Pediment* comes from earlier
periment, which may be a different form of *pyramid.*]

pe dom e ter (pi dom′ə tər), instrument for recording
the number of steps taken and thus measuring the distance traveled. *n.*

WORD HISTORY

pedometer

Pedometer is from French *pédomètre,*
which came from Latin *pedem,* meaning "foot," and Greek *metron,* meaning
"a measure."

pe dun cle (pi dung′kəl), stalk; stem; stalklike part. *n.*

peek (pēk), **1** look quickly and slyly; peep: *You must not
peek while you are counting in hide-and-seek.* **2** a quick, sly
look. 1 *v.*, 2 *n.*

peel (pēl), **1** the rind or outer covering of fruit, etc. **2** to
strip the skin, rind, or bark from: *to peel an orange.*
3 strip: *I peeled the tape off my hand.* **4** come off: *When I
was sunburned, my skin peeled. The paint on the shed is
peeling.* 1 *n.*, 2-4 *v.* —**peel′a ble,** *adj.* —**peel′er,** *n.*

keep one's eyes peeled, INFORMAL. be on the alert.

peel ing (pē′ling), part peeled off or pared off. *n.*

peep[1] (pēp), **1** look through a small or narrow hole or crack. **2** a look through a hole or crack; little look: *take a peep into the pantry.* **3** look when no one knows it. **4** a secret look: *take a peep at the presents.* **5** look out, as if peeping; come partly out: *Violets peeped among the leaves.* **6** the first looking or coming out: *at the peep of day.* 1,3,5 *v.*, 2,4,6 *n.*

peep[2] (pēp), **1** the cry of a young bird or chicken; a sound like a chirp or squeak. **2** make such a sound; chirp. 1 *n.*, 2 *v.*

peep er[1] (pē′pər), INFORMAL. eye.

peep er[2] (pē′pər), **1** person or thing that peeps. **2** any of certain frogs that make peeping noises. *n.*

peep hole (pēp′hōl′), hole through which one may peep. *n.*

peer[1] (pir), **1** person of the same rank, ability, etc., as another; equal: *He is so fine a man that it would be hard to find his peer.* **2** man belonging to the nobility, especially a British nobleman having the rank of duke, marquis, earl, count, viscount, or baron. *n.* [*Peer*[1] came into English about 700 years ago from French *per*, which came from Latin *par*, meaning "equal."]

peer[2] (pir), **1** look closely to see clearly, as a near-sighted person does: *She peered at the tag to read the price.* **2** come out slightly; peep out: *The sun was peering from behind a cloud. v.* [*Peer*[2] may be a different form of *appear.*]

peer age (pir′ij), **1** rank or dignity of a peer. **2** peers of a country. **3** book giving a list of peers of a country and their family histories. *n.*

peer ess (pir′is), **1** wife or widow of a peer. **2** woman having the rank of peer in her own right. *n., pl.* **peer ess es.**

peer less (pir′lis), without an equal; matchless: *His peerless performance won him a prize. adj.* —**peer′less ly,** *adv.* —**peer′less ness,** *n.*

peeve (pēv), INFORMAL. **1** make peevish. **2** an annoyance. 1 *v.*, **peeved, peev ing;** 2 *n.*

pee vish (pē′vish), feeling cross; fretful; complaining: *A peevish child is unhappy and makes others unhappy. adj.* —**pee′vish ly,** *adv.* —**pee′vish ness,** *n.*

pee wee (pē′wē), **1** a very small person or thing. **2** pewee. *n.*

peg (peg), **1** pin or small bolt of wood, metal, etc., used to fasten parts together, to hang things on, to stop a hole, to make fast a rope or string, to mark the score in a game, etc. **2** fasten or hold with pegs: *peg down a tent.* **3** mark with pegs. **4** work hard: *I pegged away at my studies so that I would get high marks.* **5** step; degree: *Her work is several pegs above yours.* **6** INFORMAL. a hard throw of a ball, especially in baseball. **7** INFORMAL. throw hard: *peg the ball to the shortstop.* 1,5,6 *n.*, 2-4,7 *v.*, **pegged, peg ging.** —**peg′less,** *adj.* —**peg′like′,** *adj.*

take down a peg, lower the pride of; humble.

Peg a sus (peg′ə səs), (in Greek myths) a horse with wings, the steed of the Muses. *n.*

peg board (peg′bôrd′), board with evenly spaced holes in which pegs or hooks are inserted to hold tools, displays, etc. *n.*

P.E.I., Prince Edward Island.

Pei ping (pā′ping′ *or* bā′ping′), former name of **Peking,** from 1928 to 1949. *n.*

Pe kin ese (pē′kə nēz′), Pekingese. *n., pl.* **Pe kin ese.**

Pe king (pē′king′), capital of China, in the NE part. *n.* Officially, **Beijing.**

Pe king ese (pē′kə nēz′ *or* pē′king ēz′), a small dog with long hair and a broad, flat face. *n., pl.* **Pe king ese.** Also, **Pekinese.**

pe koe (pē′kō), kind of black tea, made from leaves picked while very young. *n.*

pelf (pelf), money or riches, thought of as bad or degrading. *n.*

pel i can (pel′ə kən), a very large, fish-eating water bird with a huge bill and a pouch on the underside of the bill for scooping up fish. *n.*

pelican about 4 ft. (1 m.) long. Pelicans bring food up from their stomachs to their pouches for their young to eat.

pel lag ra (pə lag′rə), disease marked by inflammation and scaling of the skin, nervousness, and sometimes mental disorders. It is caused by a lack of nicotinic acid in the diet. *n.*

pel let (pel′it), **1** a little ball of mud, paper, food, medicine, etc.; pill. **2** bullet. *n.* —**pel′let like′,** *adj.*

pell-mell or **pell mell** (pel′mel′), **1** in a rushing, tumbling mass or crowd: *The children dashed pell-mell down the beach and into the waves.* **2** in headlong haste. **3** headlong; tumultuous. 1,2 *adv.*, 3 *adj.*

pel lu cid (pə lü′sid), **1** transparent; clear: *a pellucid stream.* **2** clearly expressed; easy to understand: *pellucid language. adj.* —**pel lu′cid ly,** *adv.* —**pel lu′cid ness,** *n.*

Pel o pon ne sian (pel′ə pə nē′shən), **1** of the Peloponnesus or its people. **2** person born or living in the Peloponnesus. 1 *adj.*, 2 *n.*

Pel o pon ne sus (pel′ə pə nē′səs), peninsula that constitutes the S part of Greece. *n.*

pelt[1] (pelt), **1** throw things at; attack; assail: *Children were pelting each other with snowballs.* **2** beat heavily: *The rain came pelting down.* **3** to throw: *The clouds pelted rain upon us.* **4** a blow from something thrown. 1-3 *v.*, 4 *n.*

pelt[2] (pelt), skin of a sheep, goat, or small fur-bearing animal, before it is tanned. *n.* —**pelt′less,** *adj.*

pel vic (pel′vik), of the pelvis. *adj.*

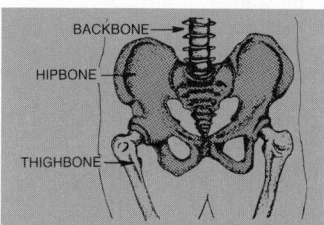

BACKBONE
HIPBONE
THIGHBONE

pelvis (def. 2)

pel vis (pel′vis), **1** the basin-shaped cavity formed by the hipbones and the end of the backbone. **2** bones forming this cavity. *n., pl.* **pel vis es, pel ves** (pel′vēz). [*Pelvis* comes from Latin *pelvis*, meaning "a basin."]

Pem ba (pem′bə), island off E Africa. It is part of Tanzania. *n.*

pem mi can or **pem i can** (pem′ə kən), dried meat pounded into a paste with melted fat. *n.*

pen[1] (pen), **1** instrument used for writing or drawing with ink. Most pens are either ballpoint pens or fountain pens. **2** style of writing; writing. **3** write: *I penned a brief note.* 1,2 *n.,* 3 *v.,* **penned, pen ning.** —**pen′like′,** *adj.*

WORD HISTORY

pen[1]

Pen[1] came into English about 700 years ago from French *penne,* which came from Latin *penna,* meaning "a feather." It was called this because the first pens were made from quills or feathers.

---

pen[2] (pen), **1** a small, closed yard for cows, sheep, pigs, chickens, etc. **2** enclosure for keeping a baby, a dog, etc., confined. **3** shut in a pen. **4** shut in; confine closely: *The fox was penned in a corner with no way of escape.* 1,2 *n.,* 3,4 *v.,* **penned** or **pent, pen ning.** [*Pen*[2] comes from Old English *penn.*] —**pen′like′,** *adj.*

pen[3] (pen), SLANG. penitentiary. *n.*

pe nal (pē′nl), **1** of, having to do with, or given as punishment: *penal laws, penal labor.* **2** liable to be punished: *Robbery is a penal offense.* *adj.* —**pe′nal ly,** *adv.*

pe nal ize (pē′nl īz), **1** declare punishable by law or by rule; set a penalty for: *Speeding on city streets is penalized. Fouls are penalized in many games.* **2** inflict a penalty on; punish: *Our football team was penalized five yards.* *v.,* **pe nal ized, pe nal iz ing.** —**pe′nal iz′a ble,** *adj.* —**pe′nal i za′tion,** *n.*

pen al ty (pen′l tē), **1** punishment imposed by law: *The penalty for speeding is usually a fine.* **2** disadvantage imposed on a side or player for breaking the rules of some game or contest. **3** disadvantage attached to some act or condition: *the penalties of being poor.* *n., pl.* **pen al ties.**

pen ance (pen′əns), **1** punishment borne to show sorrow for sin, to make up for a wrong done, and to obtain pardon for sin. **2** any act done to show that one is sorry or repents. *n.*

pence (pens), a plural of **penny** (defs. 2 and 3). *n.*

pen chant (pen′chənt), a strong taste or liking; inclination: *a penchant for taking long walks. n.*

pen cil (pen′səl), **1** instrument used for writing or drawing, made of a slender rod of graphite encased in wood or in a metal tube. **2** mark or write with a pencil. **3** stick of coloring matter. 1,3 *n.,* 2 *v.,* **pen ciled, pen cil ing** or **pen cilled, pen cil ling.** —**pen′cil er, pen′cil ler,** *n.* —**pen′cil like′,** *adj.*

pend ant (pen′dənt), **1** a hanging ornament, such as a locket. **2** pendent. 1 *n.,* 2 *adj.*

pend ent (pen′dənt), **1** hanging: *the pendent branches of a willow.* **2** overhanging. **3** pending. *adj.* —**pen′dent ly,** *adv.*

pend ing (pen′ding), **1** waiting to be decided or settled: *while the agreement was pending.* **2** while waiting for; until: *Pending your return, we'll get everything ready.* **3** during: *pending the investigation.* **4** likely to happen soon; threatening; about to occur. 1,4 *adj.,* 2,3 *prep.*

pen du lous (pen′jə ləs), **1** hanging loosely: *The oriole builds a pendulous nest.* **2** swinging. *adj.* —**pen′du lous ly,** *adv.* —**pen′du lous ness,** *n.*

pen du lum (pen′jə ləm), weight hung from a fixed point so that it is free to swing to and fro. The movement of the works of a tall clock is often timed by a pendulum. *n.*

Pe nel o pe (pə nel′ə pē), (in Greek legends) the faithful wife of Ulysses. She waited twenty years for his return, meanwhile rejecting many suitors. *n.*

pen e tra bil i ty (pen′ə trə bil′ə tē), capability of being penetrated. *n.*

pen e tra ble (pen′ə trə bəl), able to be penetrated. *adj.* —**pen′e tra ble ness,** *n.* —**pen′e tra bly,** *adv.*

pen e trate (pen′ə trāt), **1** get into or through: *The bullet penetrated this wall, and two inches into the one beyond.* **2** pierce through; make a way: *Our eyes could not penetrate the darkness. Even where the trees were thickest, the sunshine penetrated.* **3** soak through; spread through: *The rain penetrated our clothes. The odor penetrated the whole house.* **4** see into; understand: *I could not penetrate the mystery. v.,* **pen e trat ed, pen e trat ing.** —**pen′e tra′tor,** *n.*

pen e trat ing (pen′ə trā′ting), **1** sharp; piercing. **2** having an acute mind; understanding thoroughly. *adj.* —**pen′e trat′ing ly,** *adv.*

pen e tra tion (pen′ə trā′shən), **1** act or power of penetrating. **2** sharpness of intellect; insight. *n.*

pen e tra tive (pen′ə trā′tiv), penetrating; piercing; acute; keen. *adj.* —**pen′e tra′tive ly,** *adv.* —**pen′e tra′tive ness,** *n.*

pen guin (pen′gwin), a web-footed sea bird that has black and white plumage and wings like flippers, which it uses for diving and swimming, not for flying. Penguins live in Antarctica and other cold areas of the Southern Hemisphere. *n.*

penguin
about 3 ft.
(1 m.) tall

pen i cil lin (pen′ə sil′ən), antibiotic made from a penicillium mold, used to treat diseases caused by certain bacteria. *n.*

pen i cil li um (pen′ə sil′ē əm), any of a certain kind of fungi. The mold on cheese is a penicillium. *n., pl.* **pen i cil li ums, pen i cil li a** (pen′ə sil′ē ə).

pe nin su la (pə nin′sə lə *or* pə nin′syə lə), piece of land almost surrounded by water, or extending far out into the water. Florida is a peninsula. *n., pl.* **pe nin su las.** [*Peninsula* can be traced back to Latin *paene,* meaning "almost," and *insula,* meaning "an island."]

pe nin su lar (pə nin′sə lər *or* pə nin′syə lər), **1** like a peninsula. **2** in or of a peninsula. *adj.*

pe nis (pē′nis), the sex organ of a male animal. Urine leaves the body of male mammals through the penis. *n., pl.* **pe nis es, pe nes** (pē′nēz).

pen i tence (pen′ə təns), sorrow for sinning or doing wrong; repentance. *n.*

pen i tent (pen′ə tənt), **1** sorry for sinning or doing wrong; repenting: *The penitent child promised never to cheat again.* **2** person who is sorry for sin, especially one who confesses and does penance under the direction of a church. 1 *adj.,* 2 *n.* —**pen′i tent ly,** *adv.*

pen i ten tial (pen′ə ten′chəl), of or about penitence or penance. *adj.* —**pen′i ten′tial ly,** *adv.*

pen i ten tiar y (pen′ə ten′chər ē), **1** prison for criminals, especially a state or federal prison. **2** making one liable to punishment in a prison: *a penitentiary offense.* **1** *n., pl.* **pen i ten tiar ies; 2** *adj.*

pen knife (pen′nīf′), a small pocketknife. *n., pl.* **penknives** (pen′nīvz′).

pen man (pen′mən), **1** writer. **2** person whose handwriting is good. *n., pl.* **pen men.**

pen man ship (pen′mən ship), writing with pen, pencil, etc.; handwriting. *n.*

Penn (pen), **William,** 1644-1718, English Quaker who founded the colony of Pennsylvania. *n.*

Penn. or **Penna.,** Pennsylvania.

pen name, name used by a writer instead of his or her real name; pseudonym.

pen nant (pen′ənt), **1** flag, usually long and narrow, used on ships, in signaling, as a school banner, etc. **2** flag that indicates championship, especially of a professional baseball league season. *n.*

pen ni less (pen′ē lis), without a cent of money; very poor: *I've lost all my money and now I'm penniless. adj.* —**pen′ni less ly,** *adv.* —**pen′ni less ness,** *n.*

pen non (pen′ən), **1** a long, usually triangular flag, originally carried on the lance of a knight. **2** any flag or banner. *n.*

Penn syl van ia (pen′səl vā′nyə), one of the northeastern states of the United States. *Abbreviation:* Pa. or PA *Capital:* Harrisburg. *n.* —**Penn′syl van′ian,** *adj., n.*

Pennsylvania Dutch, 1 the descendants of immigrants of the 1600's and 1700's to southeastern Pennsylvania from southern Germany and Switzerland. **2** dialect of German with English intermixed, spoken by them.

pen ny (pen′ē), **1** cent. 100 pennies = 1 dollar. **2** a British coin. One hundred pennies make one pound. **3** a former British coin equal to one twelfth of a shilling. Until 1971, 240 pennies made one pound. *n., pl.* **pen nies** (or **pence** for 2 and 3). [*Penny* comes from Old English *pending.*]

a pretty penny, INFORMAL. a large sum of money.

pen ny weight (pen′ē wāt′), 24 grains or ¹/₂₀ of an ounce in troy weight. *n.*

pen ny-wise (pen′ē wīz′), saving in regard to small sums. *adj.*

penny-wise and pound-foolish, saving in small expenses and wasteful in big ones.

pen ny worth (pen′ē wėrth′), **1** as much as can be bought for a penny. **2** a small amount: *Give me a pennyworth of advice. n.*

Pe nob scot (pə nob′skot), **1** river flowing from NW Maine into the Atlantic. **2** member of an American Indian tribe formerly living near this river. *n., pl.* **Pe nob scots** or **Pe nob scot** for 2.

pen pal, person with whom one corresponds regularly, often in another country and without ever having met.

pen sion (pen′shən), **1** a regular payment to a person which is not wages. A pension is paid by an employer to a person who is retired or disabled. **2** give a pension to: *The company pensioned several employees who were sixtyfive years old.* **1** *n.,* **2** *v.* —**pen′sion a ble,** *adj.* —**pen′sionless,** *adj.*

pen sion er (pen′shə nər), person who receives a pension. *n.*

pen sive (pen′siv), thoughtful in a serious or sad way. *adj.* —**pen′sive ly,** *adv.* —**pen′sive ness,** *n.*

pent (pent), **1** closely shut in; confined: *pent in the house all winter.* **2** penned; a past tense and a past participle of **pen²**. **1** *adj.,* **2** *v.*

pen ta gon (pen′tə gon), **1** a plane figure having five sides and five angles. **2 the Pentagon,** a five-sided building that is the headquarters of the Department of

a hat	i it	oi oil	ch child	a in about
ā age	ī ice	ou out	ng long	e in taken
ä far	o hot	u cup	sh she	ə = { i in pencil
e let	ō open	u̇ put	th thin	o in lemon
ē equal	ô order	ü rule	ŦH then	u in circus
ėr term			zh measure	

Defense of the United States. It is in Arlington, Virginia. *n.* [*Pentagon* can be traced back to Greek *pente,* meaning "five," and *gōnia,* meaning "angle."]

pen tag o nal (pen tag′ə nəl), having five sides and five angles. *adj.*

pen tam e ter (pen tam′ə tər), line of poetry having five feet or measures. EXAMPLE: "A lit′ | tle learn′ | ing is′ | a dan′ | g'rous thing′." *n.*

Pen ta teuch (pen′tə tük *or* pen′tə tyük), the first five books of the Old Testament; Genesis, Exodus, Leviticus, Numbers, and Deuteronomy. *n.*

pen tath lon (pen tath′lən), an athletic contest consisting of five different events entered by each contestant. *n.* [*Pentathlon* can be traced back to Greek *pente,* meaning "five," and *athlon,* meaning "a contest."]

Pen te cost (pen′tə kôst), **1** the seventh Sunday after Easter; Whitsunday. Pentecost is a Christian festival in memory of the descent of the Holy Ghost upon the apostles. **2** Shavuot. *n.*

pent house (pent′hous′), apartment or house built on the top of a building. *n., pl.* **pent hous es** (pent′hou′ziz).

pent-up (pent′up′), shut up; closely confined: *Her pent-up anger could no longer be restrained, and she walked out, slamming the door. adj.*

pe num bra (pi num′brə), the partial shadow outside of the complete shadow formed by the sun, moon, etc., during an eclipse. *n., pl.* **pe num brae** (pi num′brē), **penum bras.**

pe nur i ous (pi nu̇r′ē əs *or* pi nyu̇r′ē əs), mean about spending or giving money; stingy. *adj.* —**pe nur′i ously,** *adv.* —**pe nur′i ous ness,** *n.*

pen ur y (pen′yər ē), very great poverty. *n.*

pe on (pē′on), **1** (in Spanish America) a person doing work that requires little skill. **2** (in the southwestern United States and Mexico) a worker held for service to work off a debt. *n.*

pe on age (pē′ə nij), **1** condition or service of a peon. **2** practice of holding persons to work off debts. *n.*

pe o ny (pē′ə nē), garden plant with large, showy red, pink, or white flowers. *n., pl.* **pe o nies.**

peo ple (pē′pəl), **1** men, women, and children; persons: *There were ten people present.* **2** race; nation: *the peoples of Asia, the American people.* **3** body of citizens of a state; the public. **4** persons of a place, class, or group: *city people, Southern people.* **5** the common people; lower classes: *The French nobles oppressed the people.* **6** persons in relation to a superior: *a queen and her people.* **7** family; relatives: *He spends his holidays with his people.* **8** fill with

pensive

pentagon
(def. 1)

people; populate: *Immigrants from many nations peopled the New World.* 1-7 *n., pl.* **peo ple** (or **peo ples** for 2); 8 *v.,* **peo pled, peo pling.**

Pe o ri a (pē ôr/ē ə), city in central Illinois. *n.*

pep (pep), **1** spirit; energy; vim. **2 pep up,** fill or inspire with energy, etc.; put new life into. 1 *n.,* 2 *v.,* **pepped, pep ping.** [*Pep* was shortened from *pepper.*]

pep per (pep/ər), **1** a seasoning with a hot, spicy taste, made from the berries of a tropical plant and used for soups, meats, vegetables, etc. **Black pepper** is made from whole berries; **white pepper** is made from husked berries. **2** any of several hollow, mild or hot, red or green vegetables with many seeds. They are eaten raw, cooked, pickled, or dried and ground for use as seasoning in food. **3** season or sprinkle with pepper. **4** sprinkle thickly: *His face is peppered with freckles.* **5** hit with small objects sent thick and fast: *We peppered them with snowballs.* 1,2 *n.,* 3-5 *v.* [*Pepper* comes from Old English *pipor,* and can be traced back to Greek *peperi.*]

pep per corn (pep/ər kôrn/), one of the dried berries that are ground up to make pepper. *n.*

pep per mint (pep/ər mint), **1** herb grown for its oil, used in medicine and in candy. **2** this oil. **3** candy flavored with peppermint oil. *n.*

pep pe ro ni (pep/ə rō/nē), a very highly spiced Italian sausage. *n., pl.* **pep pe ro nis** or **pep pe ro ni.**

pep per y (pep/ər ē), **1** full of pepper; like pepper. **2** hot; sharp. **3** having a hot temper; easily made angry. **4** angry and sharp: *peppery words.* adj. —**pep/per i ly,** *adv.*

pep py (pep/ē), INFORMAL. full of pep; energetic; lively. *adj.,* **pep pi er, pep pi est.** —**pep/pi ly,** *adv.*

pep sin (pep/sən), **1** enzyme in the gastric juice of the stomach that helps to digest meat, eggs, cheese, and other proteins. **2** medicine to help digestion, containing this enzyme. *n.*

pep talk, INFORMAL. speech or short talk designed to fill or inspire with energy or enthusiasm.

per (pər; *stressed* pèr), **1** for each; for every: *a pint of milk per child, ten cents per pound.* **2** by means of; by; through: *I send this per my son.* prep.

per., **1** period. **2** person.

per ad ven ture (pèr/əd ven/chər), OLD USE. maybe; perhaps. *adv.*

per am bu late (pə ram/byə lāt), **1** walk through. **2** walk or travel about; stroll. **3** walk through and examine. *v.,* **per am bu lat ed, per am bu lat ing.** —**per am/bu la/tion,** *n.*

per am bu la tor (pə ram/byə lā/tər), BRITISH. a baby's carriage. *n.*

per an num (pər an/əm), per year; for each year; yearly: *Her salary was $10,000 per annum.*

per cale (pər kāl/), a closely woven cotton cloth with a smooth finish. *n.* [*Percale* was borrowed from French *percale,* which came from Persian *pargāla.*]

per cap i ta (pər kap/ə tə), for each person: *a poor country with a low per capita income.*

per ceive (pər sēv/), **1** be aware of through the senses; see, hear, taste, smell, or feel: *Did you perceive the colors of that bird?* **2** take in with the mind; observe: *I soon perceived that I could not make them change their minds.* *v.,* **per ceived, per ceiv ing.** —**per ceiv/a ble,** adj. —**per ceiv/a bly,** *adv.* —**per ceiv/er,** *n.*

per cent (pər sent/), **1** parts in each hundred; hundredths. 5 percent is 5 of each 100, or ⁵/₁₀₀ of the whole. **2** percentage: *A large percent of the state's apple crop was ruined.* *n.*

per cent, percent.

per cent age (pər sen/tij), **1** rate or proportion of each hundred; part of each hundred; percent: *What percentage of children were absent?* **2** part or proportion: *A large per-*

centage *of schoolbooks now have pictures.* **3** allowance, commission, discount, rate of interest, etc., figured by percent. *n.*

per cep ti ble (pər sep/tə bəl), able to be perceived: *The other ship was barely perceptible in the fog.* adj.

per cep ti bly (pər sep/tə blē), in a perceptible way or amount; to a perceptible degree. *adv.*

per cep tion (pər sep/shən), **1** act of perceiving: *His perception of the change came in a flash.* **2** power of perceiving: *a keen perception.* **3** the understanding that is the result of perceiving: *She had a clear perception of the problem, and soon solved it.* *n.*

per cep tive (pər sep/tiv), able to perceive; intelligent: *a perceptive audience.* adj. —**per cep/tive ly,** *adv.* —**per cep/tive ness,** *n.*

perch¹ (pėrch), **1** a bar, branch, or anything else on which a bird can come to rest. **2** alight and rest; sit: *A robin perched on our porch railing.* **3** a rather high seat or position. **4** sit rather high: *I perched on a stool.* **5** to place high up: *a village perched high among the hills.* 1,3 *n., pl.* **perch es;** 2,4,5 *v.* —**perch/er,** *n.*

perch² (pėrch), **1** a small freshwater fish, used for food. **2** a similar saltwater fish. *n., pl.* **perch es** or **perch.**

per chance (pər chans/), perhaps. *adv.*

per co late (pėr/kə lāt), **1** drip or drain through small holes or spaces: *Let the coffee percolate for seven minutes.* **2** filter through; permeate: *Water percolates sand.* *v.,* **per co lat ed, per co lat ing.** —**per/co la/tion,** *n.*

per co la tor (pėr/kə lā/tər), kind of coffeepot in which boiling water drains over and over again through ground coffee. *n.*

per cus sion (pər kush/ən), **1** the striking of one body against another with force; stroke; blow. **2** shock made by the striking of one body against another with force; impact. **3** the striking of sound upon the ear. *n.*

percussion cap, a small cap containing powder. When struck, it explodes and sets off a larger charge.

percussion instrument, a musical instrument played by striking it, such as a drum or cymbal.

per di em (pər dē/əm), per day; for each day: *Rental of the boat per diem was $10.*

per di tion (pər dish/ən), **1** loss of one's soul and the joys of heaven. **2** hell. *n.*

per e gri na tion (per/ə grə nā/shən), a journey; travel. *n.*

per e grine (per/ə grən), a large, swift, powerful falcon, the kind preferred for falconry. *n.*

pe remp tor i ly (pə remp/tər ə lē), in a peremptory manner. *adv.*

pe remp tor y (pə remp/tər ē), **1** leaving no choice; decisive; final; absolute: *a peremptory decree.* **2** allowing no denial or refusal: *a peremptory command.* **3** harsh in manner; dictatorial: *a peremptory teacher.* adj. —**pe remp/tor i ness,** *n.*

pe ren ni al (pə ren/ē əl), **1** lasting through the whole year: *a perennial stream.* **2** lasting for a very long time; enduring: *the perennial beauty of the hills.* **3** living more than two years: *perennial garden plants.* **4** a perennial plant. Roses are perennials. 1-3 adj., 4 *n.* —**per en/ni al ly,** *adv.*

Per es (per/ez or pə rez/), **Shimon,** born 1923, Israeli political leader, prime minister of Israel, alternating with Yitzhak Shamir, since 1984. *n.*

per fect (pėr/fikt *for 1,3-5,7,8;* pər fekt/ *for 2,6*), **1** without defect; not spoiled at any point; faultless: *a perfect spelling paper, a perfect apple, a perfect life.* **2** remove all faults from; make perfect; add the finishing touches to: *perfect an invention. The artist was perfecting his picture.* **3** completely skilled; expert: *a perfect golfer.* **4** having all its parts; whole; complete: *The set was perfect; noth-*

ing was missing or broken. **5** exact: *a perfect copy, a perfect circle.* **6** carry through; complete: *perfect a plan.* **7** entire; utter; absolute: *a perfect stranger.* **8** (in grammar) showing an action or event completed at the time of speaking or at the time spoken of. Three perfect tenses in English are: **present perfect,** *I have eaten;* **past perfect,** *I had eaten;* and **future perfect,** *I will have eaten.* 1,3–5,7,8 *adj.,* 2,6 *v.* —**per fect′er,** *n.* —**per′fect ness,** *n.*

per fect i bil i ty (pər fek′tə bil′ə tē), capability of becoming, or being made, perfect. *n.*

per fect i ble (pər fek′tə bəl), capable of becoming, or being made, perfect. *adj.*

per fec tion (pər fek′shən), **1** perfect condition; highest excellence; faultlessness. **2** a perfect person or thing. **3** a making complete or perfect: *Perfection of our plans will take another week. n.*
to perfection, perfectly: *She played the difficult violin concerto to perfection.*

per fec tion ist (pər fek′shə nist), person who is not content with anything that is not perfect or nearly perfect. *n.*

per fect ly (pėr′fikt lē), in a perfect manner; fully or faultlessly. *adv.*

per fid i ous (pər fid′ē əs), deliberately faithless; treacherous. *adj.* —**per fid′i ous ly,** *adv.* —**per fid′i ous ness,** *n.*

per fi dy (pėr′fə dē), a being false to a trust; base treachery; a breaking faith. *n., pl.* **per fi dies.**

per fo rate (pėr′fə rāt′), **1** make a hole or holes through: *Bullets perforated the target.* **2** make a row or rows of holes through: *Sheets of postage stamps are perforated. v.,* **per fo rat ed, per fo rat ing.** —**per′fo ra′tor,** *n.*

per fo ra tion (pėr′fə rā′shən), **1** hole bored or punched through something: *the perforations in the top of a salt shaker.* **2** a perforating or a being perforated. *n.*

per force (pər fôrs′), by necessity; necessarily. *adv.*

per form (pər fôrm′), **1** do: *Perform your duties well.* **2** put into effect; carry out: *The surgeon performed an operation.* **3** go through; render: *perform a piece of music.* **4** act, play, sing, or do tricks in public: *The performing dog danced on its hind legs. v.* —**per form′a ble,** *adj.*

per form ance (pər fôr′məns), **1** carrying out; doing; performing: *in the performance of one's regular duties, the efficient performance of an automobile.* **2** thing performed; act; deed: *The child's kicks and screams made a disgraceful performance.* **3** the giving of a play, concert, circus, or other show: *The performance is at 8 o'clock. n.*

per form er (pər fôr′mər), person who performs, especially one who performs for the entertainment of others. *n.*

per fume (pėr′fyüm *or* pər fyüm′ *for 1,3;* pər fyüm′ *for 2,4*), **1** liquid having a sweet smell. **2** put a sweet-smelling liquid on. **3** a sweet smell; fragrance: *the perfume of flowers.* **4** give a sweet smell to; fill with sweet odor: *Flowers perfumed the air.* 1,3 *n.,* 2,4 *v.,* **per fumed, per fum ing.**

WORD HISTORY

perfume

Perfume came into English about 450 years ago from French *parfum,* and can be traced back to Latin *per,* meaning "through," and *fumus,* meaning "smoke."

a hat	**i** it	**oi** oil	**ch** child	a in about
ā age	**ī** ice	**ou** out	**ng** long	e in taken
ä far	**o** hot	**u** cup	**sh** she	ə = i in pencil
e let	**ō** open	**u̇** put	**th** thin	o in lemon
ē equal	**ô** order	**ü** rule	**ŦH** then	u in circus
ėr term			**zh** measure	

per fum er y (pər fyü′mər ē), **1** perfume or perfumes. **2** business of making or selling perfumes. *n., pl.* **per fum er ies.**

per func tor i ly (pər fungk′tər ə lē), in a perfunctory manner. *adv.*

per func tor y (pər fungk′tər ē), **1** done merely for the sake of getting rid of the duty; done from force of habit; mechanical; indifferent: *I gave my room a perfunctory cleaning.* **2** acting in a perfunctory way: *The new clerk was perfunctory; she did not really care about her work. adj.* —**per func′tor i ness,** *n.*

perh., perhaps.

per haps (pər haps′), it may be; maybe; possibly: *Perhaps a letter will come to you today. adv.*

Per i cles (per′ə klēz′), 490?–429 B.C., Athenian statesman, orator, and military commander. *n.*

per i gee (per′ə jē), point closest to the earth in the orbit of the moon or any other earth satellite. *n.*

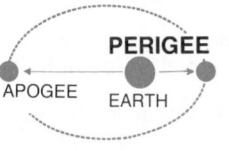

PERIGEE
APOGEE EARTH

perigee—the moon, in orbit around the earth, shown at perigee and apogee

SUN APHELION
PERIHELION

perihelion—a planet, in orbit around the sun, at perihelion and aphelion

per i he lion (per′ə hē′lyən), point closest to the sun in the orbit of a planet or comet. *n., pl.* **per i he lia** (per′ə hē′lyə), **per i he lions.**

per il (per′əl), **1** chance of harm; danger: *This bridge is not safe; cross it at your peril.* **2** put in danger. 1 *n.,* 2 *v.,* **per iled, per il ing** *or* **per illed, per il ling.**

per il ous (per′ə ləs), full of peril; dangerous. *adj.* —**per′il ous ly,** *adv.* —**per′il ous ness,** *n.*

perilous—He got himself into a **perilous** situation.

pe rim e ter (pə rim′ə tər), **1** the outer boundary of a figure or area: *the perimeter of a circle, the perimeter of a garden.* **2** distance around such a boundary. The perimeter of a square equals four times the length of one side. *n.*

per i od (pir′ē əd), **1** portion of time: *He visited us for a short period.* **2** portion of time marked off by events that happen again and again; time after which the same things begin to happen again: *A month, from new moon to new moon, is a period.* **3** a certain series of years: *the period of World War II.* **4** portion of a game during which there is actual play. **5** one of the portions of time into which a school day is divided. **6** dot (.) marking the end of a declarative sentence or showing an abbreviation. EXAMPLES: Mr., Dec. **7** one of the divisions of time into which a geological era is divided. **8** the time of menstruating; menstruation. *n.*

per i od ic (pir′ē od′ik), **1** occurring, appearing, or done again and again at regular intervals: *periodic attacks of malaria. The coming of the new moon is a periodic event.* **2** happening every now and then: *a periodic fit of clearing up one's desk. adj.*

per i od i cal (pir′ē od′ə kəl), **1** magazine that appears regularly. **2** of periodicals. **3** published at regular intervals, less often than daily. **4** periodic. 1 *n.*, 2-4 *adj.*

per i od i cal ly (pir′ē od′ik lē), **1** at regular intervals. **2** every now and then. *adv.*

periodic table, table in which the chemical elements, arranged in the order of their atomic numbers, are shown in related groups.

per i pa tet ic (per′ə pə tet′ik), walking about; traveling from place to place. *adj.* —**per′i pa tet′i cal ly,** *adv.*

pe riph er al (pə rif′ər əl), **1** of, situated in, or forming an outside boundary: *the peripheral areas of the city.* **2** a separate device connected to and used with a computer. 1 *adj.*, 2 *n.* —**pe riph′er al ly,** *adv.*

pe riph er y (pə rif′ər ē), an outside boundary. The periphery of a circle is its circumference. *n., pl.* **pe riph er ies.**

per i scope (per′ə skōp), instrument that allows those in a submarine or trench to obtain a view of the surface. It is a tube with an arrangement of prisms or mirrors that reflect light rays down the tube. *n.*

per ish (per′ish), be destroyed; die: *Three people perished in the fire. Flowers perish when frost comes. v.*

per ish a ble (per′i shə bəl), **1** liable to spoil or decay: *Fruit is perishable.* **2** Usually, **perishables,** *pl.* something perishable. 1 *adj.*, 2 *n.* —**per′ish a ble ness,** *n.* —**per′ish a bly,** *adv.*

per i stal sis (per′ə stôl′sis *or* per′ə stal′sis), the wavelike contractions of the alimentary canal or other tubular organ by which its contents are moved onward. *n., pl.* **per i stal ses** (per′ə stôl′sēz *or* per′ə stal′sēz).

per i to ne um (per′ə tə nē′əm), membrane that lines the walls of the abdomen and covers the organs in it. *n., pl.* **per i to ne a** (per′ə tə nē′ə), **per i to ne ums.**

per i to ni tis (per′ə tə nī′tis), inflammation of the peritoneum. *n.*

per i wig (per′ə wig), wig. *n.*

per i win kle[1] (per′ē wing′kəl), a low, trailing evergreen plant with blue flowers; myrtle. *n.*

per i win kle[2] (per′ē wing′kəl), a sea snail with a thick shell, used for food in Europe. *n.*

per jure (per′jər), make (oneself) guilty of perjury. *v.,* **per jured, per jur ing.**

perjure oneself, swear falsely; lie under oath: *The witness perjured himself by lying about what he did on the night of the crime.*

per jur er (per′jər ər), person who commits perjury. *n.*

per jur y (per′jər ē), act of swearing that something is true which one knows to be false. *n., pl.* **per jur ies.**

perk (perk), **1** raise smartly or briskly: *The dog perked its ears when it heard its owner's voice.* **2** make trim or smart: *They are perked out in their best clothes. v.*

perk up, brighten up; become lively and vigorous: *The birds perked up as the sun rose over the hill.*

perk y (per′kē), smart; brisk; saucy; pert: *a perky squirrel. adj.,* **perk i er, perk i est.** —**perk′i ly,** *adv.*

perm., permanent.

per ma nence (per′mə nəns), a being permanent; lasting quality or condition. *n.*

per ma nen cy (per′mə nən sē), permanence. *n.*

per ma nent (per′mə nənt), **1** intended to last; not for a short time only; lasting: *a permanent filling in a tooth. After doing odd jobs for a week, I got a permanent position as salesclerk.* **2** INFORMAL. permanent wave. 1 *adj.,* 2 *n.* —**per′ma nent ly,** *adv.*

per ma nent-press (per′mə nənt pres′), treated by a chemical process so that creases and pleats are permanently set, resisting wrinkles: *permanent-press fabrics. adj.*

permanent wave, wave put in the hair by a special process so as to last several months; permanent.

per me a bil i ty (per′mē ə bil′ə tē), a being permeable. *n.*

per me a ble (per′mē ə bəl), able to be permeated: *A sponge is permeable by water. adj.* —**per′me a bly,** *adv.*

per me ate (per′mē āt), **1** spread through the whole of; pass through: *Smoke permeated the house.* **2** penetrate: *Water will easily permeate cotton. v.,* **per me at ed, per me at ing.** —**per′me a′tion,** *n.* —**per′me a′tor,** *n.*

per mis si ble (pər mis′ə bəl), permitted; allowable. *adj.* —**per mis′si ble ness,** *n.* —**per mis′si bly,** *adv.*

per mis sion (pər mish′ən), consent; leave: *I asked the teacher's permission to go early. My sister gave me her permission to use her camera. n.*

per mis sive (pər mis′iv), not forbidding; tending to permit: *a permissive attitude, permissive parents. adj.* —**per mis′sive ly,** *adv.* —**per mis′sive ness,** *n.*

per mit (pər mit′ *for 1,2;* per′mit *or* pər mit′ *for 3*), **1** let; allow: *My parents will not permit me to stay up late. The law does not permit smoking in this store.* **2** give leave or opportunity: *I will go on Monday, if the weather permits.* **3** a formal written order giving permission to do something: *Have you a permit to fish in this lake?* 1,2 *v.,* **per mit ted, per mit ting;** 3 *n.* —**per mit′ter,** *n.*

per ni cious (pər nish′əs), that will destroy or ruin; causing great harm or damage; injurious: *Taking drugs is a pernicious habit. adj.* —**per ni′cious ly,** *adv.* —**per ni′cious ness,** *n.*

per o ra tion (per′ə rā′shən), the last part of an oration or discussion. It sums up what has been said. *n.*

pe rox ide (pə rok′sīd), **1** oxide that contains the greatest possible proportion of oxygen. **2** hydrogen peroxide. *n.*

per pen dic u lar (per′pən dik′yə lər), **1** standing straight up; vertical; upright: *a perpendicular cliff.* **2** at right angles. One line is perpendicular to another when it makes a square corner with another. The floor of a room is perpendicular to the side walls and parallel to the ceiling. **3** a perpendicular line or plane. 1,2 *adj.,* 3 *n.* —**per′pen dic′u lar ly,** *adv.*

per pe trate (per′pə trāt), do or commit (a crime, fraud, trick, or anything bad or foolish): *They were both arrested for perpetrating a robbery. v.,* **per pe trat ed, per pe trat ing.**

per pe tra tion (per′pə trā′shən), **1** act of perpetrating. **2** something perpetrated. *n.*

per pe tra tor (per′pə trā′tər), person who perpetrates or does something bad or foolish. *n.*

per pet u al (pər pech′ü əl), **1** lasting forever; eternal: *the perpetual hills.* **2** lasting throughout life: *a perpetual income.* **3** never ceasing; continuous: *a perpetual stream of visitors. adj.*

per pet u al ly (pər pech′ü ə lē), forever. *adv.*

per pet u ate (pər pech′ü āt), make perpetual; keep from being forgotten: *a monument built to perpetuate the memory of a famous person. v.,* **per pet u at ed, per pet u at ing.** —**per pet′u a′tor,** *n.*

per pet u a tion (pər pech′ü ā′shən), a perpetuating or a being perpetuated. *n.*

per pe tu i ty (pér′pə tü′ə tē *or* pér′pə tyü′ə tē), a being perpetual; existence forever. *n., pl.* **per pe tu i ties. in perpetuity,** forever.

per plex (pər pleks′), trouble with doubt; puzzle; confuse; bewilder: *This problem even perplexed the teacher.* *v.* —**per plex′ed ly,** *adv.* —**per plex′ing ly,** *adv.*

per plex i ty (pər plek′sə tē), 1 perplexed condition; being puzzled; a not knowing what to do or how to act; confusion: *My perplexity was so great that I asked many persons for advice.* 2 something that perplexes: *There are many perplexities in such a complicated job.* *n., pl.* **perplex i ties.**

per qui site (pér′kwə zit), anything received for work besides the regular pay: *The company pays medical benefits as a perquisite.* *n.*

Per ry (per′ē), **Matthew C.,** 1794–1858, American naval officer. He arranged a treaty between the United States and Japan which opened Japan to American trade. *n.*

per se (pər sā′), by itself; in itself.

per se cute (pér′sə kyüt), 1 treat badly; do harm to again and again; oppress: *That gang persecutes the children by attacking them on their way home.* 2 treat badly because of one's principles or beliefs: *Christians were persecuted in ancient Rome.* 3 annoy; harass: *persecuted by silly questions.* *v.,* **per se cut ed, per se cut ing.**

per se cu tion (pér′sə kyü′shən), 1 a persecuting: *The gang's persecution of the children was cruel.* 2 a being persecuted: *The children's persecution by the gang made them afraid to walk home.* *n.*

per se cu tor (pér′sə kyü′tər), person who persecutes. *n.*

Per seph o ne (pər sef′ə nē), (in Greek myths) the daughter of Zeus and Demeter, made queen of the lower world by Pluto. The Romans called her Proserpina. *n.*

Per se us (pér′sē əs), 1 (in Greek legends) a hero who slew Medusa and rescued Andromeda from a sea monster. 2 a northern constellation near Taurus. *n.*

per se ver ance (pér′sə vir′əns), a sticking to a purpose or an aim; never giving up what one has set out to do: *By perseverance I finally learned to swim.* *n.*

per se vere (pér′sə vir′), continue steadily in doing something hard; persist. *v.,* **per se vered, per se ver ing.** —**per′se ver′ing ly,** *adv.*

Per shing (pér′shing), **John Joseph,** 1860–1948, general in command of the United States Army in World War I. *n.*

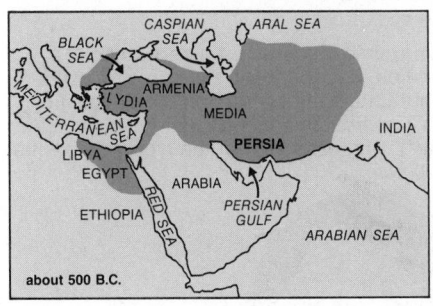

Persia (def. 2) Darker area indicates the empire at its greatest extent.

Per sia (pér′zhə), 1 former name of **Iran.** 2 ancient empire in W and SW Asia. *n.*

Per sian (pér′zhən), 1 of Persia, its people, or their language. 2 person born or living in Persia. 3 language of Persia. 1 *adj.,* 2,3 *n.*

Persian Gulf, gulf of the Arabian Sea, between Iran and Saudi Arabia.

per sim mon (pər sim′ən), the yellowish-orange, plum-

like fruit of a North American tree. Persimmons are very bitter when green, but sweet and good to eat when very ripe. *n.*

per sist (pər sist′), 1 continue firmly; refuse to stop or be changed: *She persists in reading at the dinner table.* 2 remain in existence; last; stay: *On the tops of very high mountains snow persists throughout the year.* 3 say again and again; maintain: *He persisted that he was innocent of the crime.* *v.*

per sist ence (pər sis′təns), 1 a being persistent: *the persistence of a fly buzzing around one's head.* 2 a continuing existence: *the persistence of a cough.* *n.*

per sist en cy (pər sis′tən sē), persistence. *n.*

per sist ent (pər sis′tənt), 1 not giving up, especially in the face of dislike, disapproval, or difficulties; persisting: *a persistent worker, a persistent salesperson.* 2 going on; continuing; lasting: *a persistent headache that lasted for days.* *adj.* —**per sist′ent ly,** *adv.*

per son (pér′sən), 1 man, woman, or child; human being: *Any person who wishes may come to the fair.* 2 the human body: *The person of the queen was well guarded.* 3 bodily appearance: *He kept his person neat and trim.* 4 (in grammar) a form of pronouns or verbs used to show the person speaking, the person spoken to, or the person or thing spoken of. *I* and *we* are used for the first person; *you,* for the second person; *he, she, it,* and *they,* for the third person. *n.*

in person, with or by one's own action or presence; personally: *The author will appear in person.*

per son a ble (pér′sə nə bəl), having a pleasing appearance; good-looking; attractive. *adj.* —**per′son a ble ness,** *n.* —**per′son a bly,** *adv.*

per son age (pér′sə nij), 1 person of importance. 2 person. 3 character in a book or play. *n.*

per son al (pér′sə nəl), 1 of a person; individual; private: *a personal letter, a personal matter.* 2 done in person; directly by oneself, not through others or by letter or phone: *a personal visit.* 3 of the body or bodily appearance: *personal beauty, personal charm.* 4 about or against a person or persons: *personal remarks, personal abuse.* 5 (in grammar) showing person. *I, we, you, he, she, it,* and *they* are personal pronouns. 6 (in law) of property that can be moved, such as furniture and clothing, as contrasted with real property, such as land and buildings. 7 a short paragraph in a newspaper about a particular person or persons. 1-6 *adj.,* 7 *n.*

per son al i ty (pér′sə nal′ə tē), 1 the personal or individual quality that makes one person be different or act differently from another: *A baby two weeks old does not have much personality.* 2 pleasing or attractive qualities of a person: *The boy is developing a personality.* 3 **person-alities,** *pl.* remarks made about or against some particular person: *Please refrain from personalities and stick to the issues.* 4 a well-known person; personage: *personalities of the entertainment world. n., pl.* **per son al i ties.**

per son al ly (pér′sə nə lē), 1 in person; not by the aid of others: *The owner of this store deals personally with customers.* 2 as far as oneself is concerned: *Personally, I like apples better than oranges.* 3 as a person: *I don't know her personally, but I've been told she is a talented writer.* 4 as being meant for oneself: *Don't take what I said personally; I didn't intend to insult you.* *adv.*

personification (def. 2)

per son i fi ca tion (pėr son'ə fə kā'shən), **1** a striking example; embodiment; type: *A miser is the personification of greed.* **2** a representing as a person. Uncle Sam, Cupid, Justice, and Father Time are personifications. **3** figure of speech in which a lifeless thing or quality is spoken of as if alive. EXAMPLES: The music sobbed. Duty calls us. *n.*

per son i fy (pėr son'ə fī), **1** be a type of; embody: *The Rockefellers personify wealth.* **2** regard or represent as a person. We personify time and nature when we refer to *Father Time* and *Mother Nature. v.,* **per son i fied, per son i fy ing. —per son'i fi'er,** *n.*

per son nel (pėr'sə nel'), persons employed in any work, business, or service. *n.*

per spec tive (pėr spek'tiv), **1** art of picturing objects on a flat surface so as to give the appearance of distance. **2** drawn so as to show the proper perspective: *a perspective drawing.* **3** effect of distance on the appearance of objects. **4** effect of the distance of events upon the mind: *Perspective makes many happenings of last year seem less important.* **5** a view of things or facts in which they are in the right relations. **6** a view in front; distant view: *a perspective of lakes and hills.* 1,3-6, *n.,* 2 *adj.* **—per spec'tive ly,** *adv.*

per spi ca cious (pėr'spə kā'shəs), keen in observing and understanding; discerning. *adj.*

per spi cac i ty (pėr'spə kas'ə tē), keen perception; wisdom and understanding in dealing with people or with facts; discernment. *n.*

per spi cu i ty (pėr'spə kyü'ə tē), ease in being understood; clearness in expression. *n.*

per spic u ous (pėr spik'yü əs), easily understood; clear: *a perspicuous argument. adj.* **—per spic'u ous ly,** *adv.* **—per spic'u ous ness,** *n.*

per spi ra tion (pėr'spə rā'shən), **1** sweat: *The runner's forehead was damp with perspiration.* **2** sweating. *n.*

per spire (pėr spīr'), to sweat: *The room was so hot I began to perspire. v.,* **per spired, per spir ing.**

per suade (pėr swād'), win over to do or believe; make willing or sure by urging or arguing: *I knew I should*

study, but he persuaded me to go to the movies. We persuaded her that she was wrong. v., **per suad ed, per suad ing. —per suad'er,** *n.*

per sua sion (pėr swā'zhən), **1** a persuading: *All our attempts at persuasion were useless; she would not come with us.* **2** power of persuading. **3** firm belief; conviction: *different political persuasions.* **4** religious belief or denomination: *All Christians are not of the same persuasion.* n.

per sua sive (pėr swā'siv), able, intended, or fitted to persuade: *The salesman had a very persuasive way of talking. adj.* **—per sua'sive ly,** *adv.* **—per sua'sive ness,** *n.*

pert (pėrt), **1** too forward or free in speech or action; saucy; bold: *a pert reply.* **2** stylish; jaunty: *a pert outfit. adj.* **—pert'ly,** *adv.* **—pert'ness,** *n.*

per tain (pėr tān'), **1** belong or be connected as a part or possession: *We own the house and the land pertaining to it.* **2** have to do with; be related; refer: *My question pertains to yesterday's homework.* **3** be appropriate: *We had turkey and everything else that pertains to Thanksgiving. v.*

Perth (pėrth), city in SW Australia. *n.*

per ti na cious (pėrt'n ā'shəs), holding firmly to a purpose, action, or opinion; very persistent. *adj.*

per ti nac i ty (pėrt'n as'ə tē), great persistence; holding firmly to a purpose, action, or opinion. *n.*

per ti nence (pėrt'n əns), a being to the point; fitness; relevance: *The pertinence of the girl's replies showed that she was alert and intelligent. n.*

per ti nent (pėrt'n ənt), having to do with what is being considered; relating to the matter in hand; to the point; relevant: *If your question is pertinent, I will answer it. adj.*

per turb (pėr tėrb'), disturb greatly; make uneasy or troubled: *My parents were perturbed by my grades. v.*

perspective (def. 3)
The lines in the middle of the street seem to meet at the horizon because of perspective.

per tur ba tion (pėr'tər bā'shən), **1** a perturbing. **2** a perturbed condition. *n.*

Pe ru (pə rü'), mountainous country on the W coast of South America. *Capital:* Lima. See **Brazil** for map. *n.*

pe ruke (pə rük'), wig, especially of the type worn in the 1600's and 1700's. *n.*

peruke

pe rus al (pə rü′zəl), a perusing; reading: *the perusal of a letter.* *n.*

pe ruse (pə rüz′), read, especially thoroughly and carefully: *peruse the newspaper at breakfast.* *v.*, **pe rused, pe rus ing.** [*Peruse* comes from Middle English *perusen*, meaning "to use up, go through one by one," and can be traced back to Latin *per*, meaning "through," and *uti*, meaning "to use."] —**pe rus′er,** *n.*

Pe ru vi an (pə rü′vē ən), **1** of Peru or its people. **2** person born or living in Peru. **1** *adj.*, **2** *n.*

Peruvian bark, cinchona.

per vade (pər vād′), go or spread throughout; be throughout: *The odor of pines pervades the air.* *v.*, **per vad ed, per vad ing.** —**per vad′er,** *n.*

per va sive (pər vā′siv), **1** tending to pervade. **2** having power to pervade. *adj.* —**per va′sive ly,** *adv.* —**per va′sive ness,** *n.*

per verse (pər vėrs′), **1** contrary and willful; stubborn: *The perverse child did just what we told him not to do.* **2** persistent in wrong. **3** morally wrong; wicked. **4** not correct; wrong: *perverse reasoning.* *adj.* —**per verse′ly,** *adv.* —**per verse′ness,** *n.*

per ver sion (pər vėr′zhən), **1** a turning or being turned to what is wrong; a change to what is unnatural, abnormal, or wrong: *A tendency to eat sand is a perversion of appetite.* **2** abnormal sexual behavior. *n.*

per ver si ty (pər vėr′sə tē), **1** quality of being perverse. **2** perverse character or conduct. **3** a perverse act. *n.*, *pl.* **per ver si ties.**

per vert (pər vėrt′ for 1-3; pėr′vėrt′ for 4), **1** lead or turn from what is true, desirable, good, or morally right; corrupt: *pervert the cause of justice.* **2** give a wrong meaning to: *pervert a friendly remark and make it into an insult.* **3** use for wrong purposes or in a wrong way: *pervert one's talents.* **4** a perverted person, especially one whose sexual behavior is abnormal. **1-3** *v.*, **4** *n.* —**per vert′ed ly,** *adv.* —**per vert′er,** *n.*

pes ky (pes′kē), INFORMAL. troublesome; annoying: *a pesky cold, pesky mosquitoes.* *adj.*, **pes ki er, pes ki est.** —**pes′ki ly,** *adv.* —**pes′ki ness,** *n.*

pe so (pā′sō), **1** unit of money in various countries of Latin America and in the Philippines. 100 centavos make a peso. **2** coin or piece of paper money equal to 100 centavos. *n.*, *pl.* **pe sos.** [*Peso* comes from Spanish *peso*, which also means "weight," and can be traced back to Latin *pendere*, meaning "to weigh."]

pes si mism (pes′ə miz′əm), **1** tendency to look on the dark side of things or to see all the difficulties and disadvantages. **2** belief that things naturally tend to evil, or that the evil in life outweighs the good. *n.*

pes si mist (pes′ə mist), **1** person inclined to look on the dark side of things or to see all the difficulties and disadvantages. **2** person who believes that things naturally tend to evil, or that the evil in life outweighs the good. *n.*

pes si mis tic (pes′ə mis′tik), **1** inclined to look on the dark side of things or to see all the difficulties and disadvantages. **2** expecting the worst: *I was pessimistic about passing the test because I hadn't studied.* **3** of or characterized by pessimism. *adj.* —**pes′si mis′ti cal ly,** *adv.*

pest (pest), thing or person that causes trouble, injuries, or destruction; nuisance: *Flies and mosquitoes are pests. Whining children are pests.* *n.*

pes ter (pes′tər), annoy; trouble; vex: *Flies pester us. Don't pester me with foolish questions.* *v.*

pes ti cide (pes′tə sīd), substance used to kill pests, such as mosquitoes. *n.*

pes tif er ous (pe stif′ər əs), bringing disease or infection: *Rats are pestiferous.* *adj.* —**pes tif′er ous ly,** *adv.*

a	hat	i	it	oi	oil	ch	child		a in about
ā	age	ī	ice	ou	out	ng	long		e in taken
ä	far	o	hot	u	cup	sh	she	ə =	i in pencil
e	let	ō	open	u̇	put	th	thin		o in lemon
ē	equal	ô	order	ü	rule	ŦH	then		u in circus
ėr	term					zh	measure		

pes ti lence (pes′tl əns), any disease that spreads rapidly, often causing many deaths. Smallpox, yellow fever, and plague are pestilences. *n.*

pes ti lent (pes′tl ənt), **1** often causing death: *Smallpox is a pestilent disease.* **2** harmful to morals; destroying peace: *the pestilent effects of war.* *adj.*

pes ti len tial (pes′tl en′shəl), **1** of or like a pestilence. **2** causing or likely to cause pestilence. **3** morally harmful. *adj.* —**pes′ti len′tial ly,** *adv.*

pes tle (pes′əl), tool for pounding or crushing substances into powder in a mortar. *n.*

pet[1] (pet), **1** animal kept as a favorite and treated with affection. **2** treated as a pet: *a pet rabbit.* **3** treat as a pet; touch lovingly and gently; stroke or pat: *She is petting the kitten.* **4** a darling or favorite: *teacher's pet.* **5** favorite: *a pet chair, a pet theory.* **6** showing affection: *a pet name.* **1,4** *n.*, **2,5,6** *adj.*, **3** *v.*, **pet ted, pet ting.**

pet[2] (pet), fit of being cross or peevish: *When he didn't get his way, he jumped on his bicycle and rode off in a pet.* *n.*

pet al (pet′l), one of the parts of a flower that are usually colored; one of the leaves of a corolla. A daisy has many petals. *n.* —**pet′al like′,** *adj.*

pet aled or **pet alled** (pet′ld), having petals: *six-petaled.* *adj.*

pet cock (pet′kok′), a small faucet or valve in a pipe or cylinder, for reducing pressure or draining liquids. *n.*

Pe ter (pē′tər), **1** Saint, died A.D. 67?, one of Jesus' twelve apostles. He was also called Simon or Simon Peter. **2** either of two books in the New Testament that bear his name. *n.*

Peter I, 1672-1725, czar of Russia from 1682 to 1725. He was called "Peter the Great."

pet i ole (pet′ē ōl), the slender stalk by which a leaf is attached to the stem. *n.*

pe tite (pə tēt′), of small size; little; tiny: *a petite young woman.* *adj.*

pe ti tion (pə tish′ən), **1** a formal request to someone in authority for some privilege, right, or benefit: *The people on our street signed a petition asking the city council for a new sidewalk.* **2** ask earnestly; make a formal request to: *They petitioned the mayor to use his influence with the city council.* **3** prayer. **4** pray. **1,3** *n.*, **2,4** *v.* —**pe ti′tion er,** *n.*

pet it jury (pet′ē), group of 12 persons chosen to decide a case in court.

Pe trarch (pē′trärk), 1304-1374, Italian poet, famous for his sonnets. *n.*

pet rel (pet′rəl), any of various sea birds, especially the storm petrel. *n.*

petrel
storm petrel
about 5¹/₂ in.
(14 cm.) long

Pe tri dish (pē/trē), a shallow, circular glass dish with a loose cover, used in the preparation of cultures of bacteria.

pet ri fy (pet/rə fī), 1 turn into stone; change (plant or animal matter) into a substance like stone. 2 paralyze with fear, horror, or surprise: *The bird was petrified as the snake came near.* v., **pet ri fied, pet ri fy ing.**

Pet ro grad (pet/rə grad), former capital of Russia, now called **Leningrad.** n.

pet rol (pet/rəl), BRITISH. gasoline. n.

pe tro le um (pə trō/lē əm), a dark, oily, flammable liquid found in the earth's crust, consisting mainly of a mixture of various hydrocarbons. Gasoline, kerosene, and many other products are made from petroleum. n. [*Petroleum* comes from a medieval Latin word *petroleum*, and can be traced back to Greek *petra*, meaning "a rock," and Latin *oleum*, meaning "oil."]

pet ti coat (pet/ē kōt), skirt worn beneath a dress or outer skirt by women and girls. n.

pet ti ness (pet/ē nis), smallness; meanness; petty nature or behavior. n.

pet tish (pet/ish), peevish; cross: *a pettish child.* adj.

pet ty (pet/ē), 1 having little importance or value; small: *Don't let petty disturbances upset you.* 2 mean; narrow-minded: *A gossip is a petty person.* 3 lower in rank or importance; subordinate: *a petty official.* adj., **pet ti er, pet ti est. —pet/ti ly,** adv.

petty cash, 1 small sums of money spent or received. 2 sum of money kept on hand to pay small expenses.

petty officer, a noncommissioned officer in the navy.

pet u lance (pech/ə ləns), a being peevish; bad humor; being irritated by trifles. n.

pet u lant (pech/ə lənt), likely to have little fits of bad temper; irritable over trifles; peevish. adj.

pe tun ia (pə tü/nyə or pə tyü/nyə), a common garden plant that has white, pink, red, or purple flowers shaped like funnels. n., pl. **pe tun ias.**

pew (pyü), bench in a church for people to sit on, fastened to the floor and with a back. n.

pe wee (pē/wē), any of several small American birds with an olive-colored or gray back. A pewee's call sounds somewhat like its name. n. Also, **peewee.**

pew ter (pyü/tər), 1 alloy of tin with lead, copper, or other metals. 2 dishes or other utensils made of this. 3 made of pewter: *a pewter mug.* 1,2 n., 3 adj.

Pfc., Pfc, or **PFC,** private first class.

PG, Parental Guidance (a rating for a motion picture that is recommended for everyone, but with parental guidance for young people).

pg. or **pg,** page.

Pg. or **Pg,** 1 Portugal. 2 Portuguese.

PG-13, Parental Guidance under 13 (a rating between PG and R for a motion picture that is recommended for everyone, but with parental guidance for young people under 13).

pha e ton (fā/ə tən), a light, four-wheeled carriage with or without a top. n.

pha lan ges (fə lan/jēz), the bones of the fingers and toes. n.pl.

pha lanx (fā/langks), 1 (in ancient Greece) a special battle formation of infantry fighting in close ranks with their shields joined and long spears overlapping each other. 2 a compact or closely massed body of persons, animals, or things: *A phalanx of sheep blocked the road.* 3 number of persons united for a common purpose. n., pl. **phalanx es.**

phan tasm (fan/taz/əm), 1 thing seen only in one's imagination; unreal fancy: *the phantasms of a dream.* 2 a deceiving likeness (of something). n.

phan ta sy (fan/tə sē), fantasy. n., pl. **phan ta sies.**

phan tom (fan/təm), 1 image in the mind which seems to be real: *phantoms of a dream.* 2 a vague, dim, or shadowy appearance; ghost. 3 like a ghost; unreal: *a phantom ship.* 4 mere show; appearance with no substance: *a phantom of a government.* 1,2,4 n., 3 adj.

phar aoh or **Phar aoh** (fer/ō), any of the kings of ancient Egypt. n. [*Pharaoh* comes from Latin *Pharao,* and can be traced back to an Egyptian word meaning "a great house."]

Phar i see (far/ə sē), 1 member of a Jewish sect at the time of Jesus that was very strict in keeping to tradition and the laws of its religion. 2 **pharisee,** person who makes a show of religion rather than following its spirit; hypocrite. n.

phar ma ceu tic (fär/mə sü/tik), pharmaceutical. adj., n.

phar ma ceu ti cal (fär/mə sü/tə kəl), 1 of pharmacy. 2 a medicinal drug. 1 adj., 2 n.

phar ma cist (fär/mə sist), person licensed to fill prescriptions; druggist. n.

phar ma col o gy (fär/mə kol/ə jē), science of drugs, their preparation, uses, and effects. n.

phar ma cy (fär/mə sē), 1 place where drugs and medicines are prepared or sold; drugstore. 2 preparation and dispensing of drugs and medicines; occupation of a druggist. n., pl. **phar ma cies.**

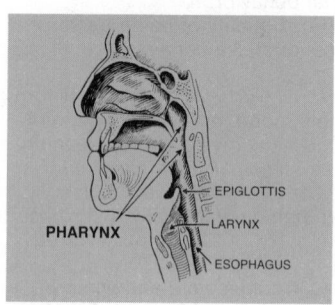

phar ynx (far/ingks), cavity at the back of the mouth where the passages to the nose, lungs, and stomach begin. n., pl. **phar ynx es, pha ryn ges** (fə rin/jēz).

phase (fāz), 1 one of the changing states or stages of development of a person or thing: *At present his voice is changing; that is a phase all boys go through.* 2 one side, part, or view (of a subject): *What phase of arithmetic are you studying now?* 3 the shape of the moon or of a planet as it is seen from the earth at a particular time. n.

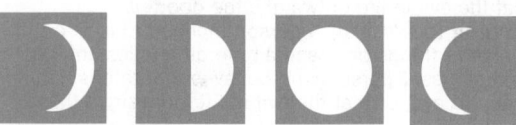

phase (def. 3)—phases of the moon

Ph.B., Bachelor of Philosophy.

Ph.D., Doctor of Philosophy.

pheas ant (fez/nt), a large game bird with brightly colored feathers in the male, and long, pointed tail feathers. Pheasants are native to Asia but now live in many parts of Europe and America. n., pl. **pheas ants** or **pheas ant.**

phe nix (fē/niks), phoenix. n., pl. **phe nix es.**

phe nol (fē/nol or fē/nōl), carbolic acid. n.

phe nom e na (fə nom/ə nə), a plural of **phenomenon.** n.

phe nom e nal (fə nom/ə nəl), 1 extraordinary: *a phenomenal memory.* 2 of or like a phenomenon or phenomena. adj. —**phe nom/e nal ly,** adv.

phenomenon (def. 1)
Lightning is
an electrical
phenomenon.

a hat	**i** it	**oi** oil	**ch** child	⎧ a in about
ā age	**ī** ice	**ou** out	**ng** long	⎪ e in taken
ä far	**o** hot	**u** cup	**sh** she	ə = ⎨ i in pencil
e let	**ō** open	**ů** put	**th** thin	⎪ o in lemon
ē equal	**ô** order	**ü** rule	**ŦH** then	⎩ u in circus
ėr term			**zh** measure	

phe nom e non (fə nom/ə non), **1** fact, event, or circumstance that can be observed. **2** any sign or symptom: *Fever and inflammation are phenomena of disease.*
3 something or someone extraordinary or remarkable: *The Grand Canyon is a phenomenon of nature. The fond parents think their child is a phenomenon. n., pl.* **phe nom e na** (or **phe nom e nons** for 3). [*Phenomenon* comes from Latin *phaenomenon,* and can be traced back to Greek *phainein,* meaning "to show." See **Word Family.**]
phi al (fī/əl), vial. *n.*
Phid i as (fid/ē əs), 500?–432? B.C., Greek sculptor. *n.*
Phila., Philadelphia.
Phil a del phi a (fil/ə del/fē ə), city in SE Pennsylvania, on the Delaware River. *n.* [*Philadelphia* can be traced back to Greek *philos,* meaning "loving," and *adelphos,* meaning "brother."]
phil an throp ic (fil/ən throp/ik), charitable; benevolent; kindly: *a philanthropic nature. adj.* —**phil/an throp/i cal ly,** *adv.*
phil an throp i cal (fil/ən throp/ə kəl), philanthropic. *adj.*
phi lan thro pist (fə lan/thrə pist), person who practices philanthropy, especially by giving sizable donations of money to worthy causes. *n.*
phi lan thro py (fə lan/thrə pē), **1** love of humanity shown by practical kindness and helpfulness: *The charity appealed to philanthropy.* **2** thing that benefits humanity; a philanthropic agency, enterprise, gift, act, etc.: *A hospital is a useful philanthropy. n., pl.* **phi lan thro pies.**
phi lat e list (fə lat/l ist), collector of postage stamps, postmarks, etc. *n.*
phi lat e ly (fə lat/l ē), the collecting, arranging, and study of postage stamps, stamped envelopes, post cards, etc. *n.*
phil har mon ic (fil/här mon/ik), **1** devoted to music; loving music: *A musical club is often called a philharmonic society.* **2** symphony orchestra: *The New York Philharmonic gave a concert last night.* 1 *adj.,* 2 *n.*
Phil ip (fil/əp), (in the Bible) one of Jesus' twelve apostles. *n.*
Phil ip pine (fil/ə pēn/), of the Philippines or its inhabitants; Filipino. *adj.*
Philippine Islands, Philippines.
Phil ip pines (fil/ə pēnz/), country in the W Pacific, southeast of China and northeast of Borneo, consisting of over 7000 islands. The Philippines were governed by the United States from 1898 until 1946. *Capital:* Manila. See **East Indies** for map. *n. sing. or pl.*
Phil is tine (fil/ə stēn/ *or* fə lis/tən), **1** (in the Bible) one of the warlike people in southwestern Palestine who fought the Israelites many times. **2** of the Philistines. **3** Also, **philistine. a** person who is commonplace in ideas and tastes. **b** lacking culture; commonplace. 1,3a *n.,* 2,3b *adj.*
phil o den dron (fil/ə den/drən), a climbing, evergreen plant with smooth, shiny leaves, often grown as a house plant. *n.*

phil o log i cal (fil/ə loj/ə kəl), of philology. *adj.* —**phil/o log/i cal ly,** *adv.*
phi lol o gist (fə lol/ə jist), an expert in philology. *n.*
phi lol o gy (fə lol/ə jē), **1** the study of the historical development of language. **2** the study of literary and other records. *n.*

WORD FAMILY

phenomenon

Below are words related to *phenomenon.* They can all be traced back to the Greek word *phainein* (fī/nän), meaning "to show."

diaphanous	fancy	phantasm
emphasis	fantastic	phantom
emphatic	fantasy	phase
Epiphany	pant	phenomenal

phi los o pher (fə los/ə fər), **1** person who studies philosophy a great deal. **2** author or founder of a system of philosophy. **3** person who is calm and reasonable under hard conditions, accepting life and making the best of it. *n.*
phil o soph ic (fil/ə sof/ik), philosophical. *adj.*
phil o soph i cal (fil/ə sof/ə kəl), **1** of philosophy or philosophers. **2** knowing much about philosophy. **3** devoted to philosophy. **4** wise; calm; reasonable. *adj.* —**phil/o soph/i cal ly,** *adv.*
phi los o phize (fə los/ə fīz), think or reason as a philosopher does; try to understand and explain things: *The old woman philosophized about life and death. v.,* **phi los o phized, phi los o phiz ing.** —**phi los/o phiz/er,** *n.*
phi los o phy (fə los/ə fē), **1** the study of the truth or principles underlying all real knowledge; study of the most general causes and principles of the universe.
2 explanation or theory of the universe, especially the particular explanation or system of a philosopher: *the philosophy of Plato.* **3** system for guiding life. **4** the general principles of a particular subject or field of activity: *the philosophy of history, the army's military philosophy.* **5** a calm and reasonable attitude; accepting things as they are and making the best of them. *n., pl.* **phi los o phies.**
phil ter or **phil tre** (fil/tər), drug or magic potion which is supposed to make a person fall in love. *n.*

philodendrons—three varieties

phlegm (flem), the thick mucus discharged into the mouth and throat during a cold or other respiratory disease. *n.*

phleg mat ic (fleg mat′ik), 1 sluggish; indifferent. 2 cool; calm: *My parents are phlegmatic; they never seem to get excited about anything. adj.* —**phleg mat′i cal ly,** *adv.*

phlo em (flō′em), tissue in a plant or tree through which the sap containing dissolved food materials passes downward to the stems and roots. *n.*

phlox (floks), a common garden plant with clusters of showy flowers in various colors. *n., pl.* **phlox es.**

Phnom Penh (pə nôm′ pen′), capital of Cambodia, in the S part.

pho bi a (fō′bē ə), a deep, irrational fear of a certain thing or group of things: *a phobia about snakes. n., pl.* **pho bi as.**

phoe be (fē′bē), a small North American bird with a grayish-brown back, a yellowish-white breast, and a low crest on the head. *n.*

Phoe be (fē′bē), 1 (in Greek myths) the goddess of the moon. Phoebe was also called Artemis by the Greeks and Diana by the Romans. 2 the moon. *n.*

Phoe bus (fē′bəs), 1 (in Greek myths) Apollo, the god of the sun. 2 the sun. *n.*

Phoe ni cia (fə nish′ə), ancient country on the Mediterranean Sea, in the region of Lebanon, W Syria, and N Israel. It was famous for its traders. *n.*

Phoe ni cian (fə nish′ən), 1 of Phoenicia, its people, or their language. 2 one of the people of Phoenicia. 3 language of Phoenicia. 1 *adj.,* 2,3 *n.*

phoe nix (fē′niks), a mythical bird, the only one of its kind, said to live 500 or 600 years, to burn itself on a funeral pile, and to rise again from the ashes, fresh and beautiful, for another long life. *n., pl.* **phoe nix es.** Also, **phenix.**

Phoe nix (fē′niks), capital of Arizona, in the central part. *n.*

WORD HISTORY

Phoenix

The name *Phoenix* comes from *phoenix,* which can be traced back to Greek *phoinix.* Since traces of an ancient American Indian settlement were found at the site, the new inhabitants hoped that it would rise again like the phoenix and become a great city.

phone (fōn), INFORMAL. telephone. *n., v.,* **phoned, phon ing.**

pho neme (fō′nēm), any one of a set of speech sounds by which the words of a language are distinguished one from another; the smallest meaningful unit of speech in a language. The words *cat* and *bat* are distinguished by their initial phonemes /k/ and /b/. *n.*

pho net ic (fə net′ik), 1 of sounds made with the voice. Phonetic exercises are drills in pronunciation. 2 representing sounds made with the voice. Systems of phonetic spelling spell words as they are pronounced and represent the same sound by the same letter. Phonetic symbols are marks used to show pronunciation. We use ᴛʜ as the phonetic symbol for the sound of *th* in *the* or *then.* 3 of phonetics. *adj.*

pho net i cal ly (fə net′ik lē), in a phonetic manner; as regards the sound and not the spelling of words. *adv.*

pho net ics (fə net′iks), science dealing with sounds made in speech and the art of pronunciation. *n.*

phon ic (fon′ik), 1 of sound. 2 of sounds made in speech; phonetic. *adj.*

phon ics (fon′iks), simplified phonetics for teaching reading. *n.*

phono-, *combining form.* sound: *Phonograph =* (*instrument*) *that reproduces sound.* [The form *phono-* comes from Greek *phōnē.*]

pho no graph (fō′nə graf), instrument that reproduces sounds from phonograph records; record player. *n.*

pho no graph ic (fō′nə graf′ik), of a phonograph. *adj.* —**pho′no graph′i cal ly,** *adv.*

phonograph needle, needle (def. 6).

phonograph record, record (def. 5).

pho ny (fō′nē), INFORMAL. 1 not genuine; counterfeit; fake. 2 a fake; pretender. 1 *adj.,* **pho ni er, pho ni est;** 2 *n., pl.* **pho nies.** —**pho′ni ly,** *adv.* —**pho′ni ness,** *n.*

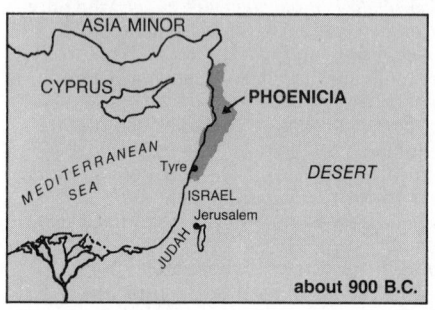

phos phate (fos′fāt), 1 any salt of phosphoric acid. Bread contains phosphates. 2 fertilizer containing such salts. 3 a drink of carbonated water flavored with fruit syrup, and containing a little phosphoric acid. *n.*

phos phor (fos′fər), substance which gives off light when exposed to certain types of energy, such as ultraviolet rays or X rays. Phosphor is widely used in fluorescent lamps and television tubes. *n.*

phos pho res cence (fos′fə res′ns), 1 act or process of giving out light without burning or by very slow burning that seems not to give out heat: *the phosphorescence of fireflies.* 2 light given out in this way. *n.*

phos pho res cent (fos′fə res′nt), showing phosphorescence. *adj.*

phos phor ic (fo sfôr′ik), of or containing phosphorus. *adj.*

phosphoric acid, a colorless, odorless acid containing phosphorus, used in making fertilizers.

phos phor ous (fos′fər əs), having to do with or containing phosphorus. *adj.*

phos phor us (fos′fər əs), a nonmetallic element whose most common form is a yellow or white, poisonous, waxy substance which burns slowly at ordinary temperatures and glows in the dark. *n.* [*Phosphorus* can be traced back to Greek *phōs,* meaning "light," and *pherein,* meaning "to bring."]

pho to (fō′tō), INFORMAL. a photograph. *n., pl.* **pho tos.**

photo-, *combining form.* 1 light: *Photography = the recording of images with light.* 2 photograph: *Photogenic = likely to look well in a photograph.* [The form *photo-* comes from Greek *phōtos,* meaning "light."]

pho to cop y (fō′tō kop′ē), 1 a photographic copy or reproduction of something written, typed, or drawn. 2 produce a photocopy of. 1 *n., pl.* **pho to cop ies;** 2 *v.,* **pho to cop ied, pho to cop y ing.**

pho to e lec tric (fō′tō i lek′trik), having to do with the electricity or electrical effects produced by the action of light. *adj.*

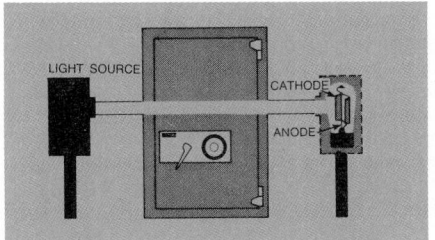

photoelectric cell in a burglar alarm. When light strikes the cathode of the photoelectric cell, it emits electrons which flow to the anode. Interrupting the light beam causes an interruption of this flow which triggers the alarm.

photoelectric cell, vacuum tube that varies the flow of current according to the amount of light reaching its sensitive element; electric eye. Variations or interruptions of the light can start machines to work that open doors, set off alarms, etc.

pho to gen ic (fō/tə jen/ik), having characteristics that photograph very well: *a photogenic face. adj.*

pho to graph (fō/tə graf), **1** picture made with a camera. A photograph is made by the action of light rays from the thing pictured passing through the lens of the camera onto the film. **2** take a photograph of. **3** look (clear, unnatural, etc.) in a photograph: *I do not photograph well.* 1 *n.,* 2-3 *v.*

pho tog ra pher (fə tog/rə fər), **1** person who takes photographs. **2** person whose business is taking photographs. *n.*

pho to graph ic (fō/tə graf/ik), **1** of or like photography: *photographic accuracy.* **2** used in or produced by photography: *a photographic record of a trip. adj.*

pho tog ra phy (fə tog/rə fē), the taking of photographs. *n.*

pho ton (fō/ton), a quantum of radiant energy, moving as a unit with the velocity of light. *n.*

pho to syn the sis (fō/tō sin/thə sis), process by which plant cells make carbohydrates from carbon dioxide and water in the presence of chlorophyll and light, and release oxygen as a by-product. *n.*

pho tot ro pism (fō to/trə piz/əm), tendency of plants to turn in response to light. *n.*

phrase (frāz), **1** combination of words: *Would you please speak in simple phrases so that we can understand you?* **2** expression often used: *"Run out" is a common phrase for "come to an end."* **3** a short, striking expression. EXAMPLES: A Fair Deal. A war to end wars. Liberty or death. **4** express in a particular way: *I tried to phrase my excuse politely.* **5** group of words not containing a subject and predicate. EXAMPLES: in the house; coming by the church; to eat too fast. **6** division of a piece of music, usually several measures in length. 1-3,5,6 *n.,* 4 *v.,* **phrased, phras ing. —phras/er,** *n.*

phra se ol o gy (frā/zē ol/ə jē), selection and arrangement of words; the particular way in which thoughts are expressed in language: *scientific phraseology. n., pl.* **phra se ol o gies.**

phre nol o gy (fri nol/ə jē), **1** theory that the shape of the skull shows what sort of mind and character a person has. **2** practice of reading character from the shape of the skull. *n.*

Phryg i a (frij/ē ə), ancient country in the central and NW part of Asia Minor. See **Troy** for map. *n.* **—Phryg/i an,** *adj., n.*

phy lum (fī/ləm), a primary group of the animal or vegetable kingdom, consisting of one or more classes. The animals or plants in a phylum are thought to be related by descent from a common ancestral form. *n., pl.* **phy la** (fī/lə).

phys., 1 physical. **2** physician. **3** physics.

phys ed or **phys. ed.** (fiz/ ed/), physical education.

phys ic (fiz/ik), **1** medicine, especially one that acts as a laxative. **2** give a medicine or laxative to. 1 *n.,* 2 *v.,* **phys icked, phys ick ing.**

phys i cal (fiz/ə kəl), **1** of the body: *physical exercise, physical strength, a physical disability.* **2** of matter; material: *The tide is a physical force.* **3** according to the laws of nature: *It is a physical impossibility for the sun to rise in the west.* **4** of the science of physics. *adj.* **—phys/i cal ly,** *adv.*

physical change, a change in which the shape or form of a substance becomes different but the nature of the substance stays the same. A change from a liquid to a solid, as when water freezes into ice, is a physical change.

physical education, instruction in how to exercise and take care of the body, especially as a course at a school or college.

physical geography, branch of geography that deals with the natural features of the earth's surface, such as land forms, climate, winds, and ocean currents.

physical therapy, treatment of diseases and defects by physical remedies, such as exercise and massage, rather than by drugs; physiotherapy.

phy si cian (fə zish/ən), doctor of medicine. *n.*

phys i cist (fiz/ə sist), an expert in physics. *n.*

phys ics (fiz/iks), science that deals with matter and energy and the relationships between them. Physics includes the study of mechanics, heat, light, sound, electricity, magnetism, and atomic energy. *n.*

phys i og no my (fiz/ē og/nə mē), **1** kind of features or type of face one has; one's face: *a ruddy physiognomy.* **2** art of estimating character from the features of the face or the form of the body. **3** the general aspect or looks of a countryside, a situation, etc.: *the rugged physiognomy of northern Scotland. n., pl.* **phys i og no mies.**

phys i o log i cal (fiz/ē ə loj/ə kəl), of physiology: *Digestion is a physiological process. adj.*

phys i ol o gist (fiz/ē ol/ə jist), an expert in physiology. *n.*

phys i ol o gy (fiz/ē ol/ə jē), **1** branch of biology dealing with the normal functions of living things or their parts: *animal physiology, plant physiology.* **2** all the functions and activities of a living organism or of one of its parts. *n.*

phys i o ther a py (fiz/ē ō ther/ə pē), physical therapy. *n.*

phy sique (fə zēk/), bodily structure or development; body: *The swimmer had a strong physique. n.*

pi (pī), the Greek letter π, used as the symbol for the ratio of the circumference of any circle to its diameter. π = 3.141592 +. *n., pl.* **pis.**

P.I., Philippine Islands.

pi a nis si mo (pē/ə nis/ə mō), in music: **1** very soft. **2** very softly. 1 *adj.,* 2 *adv.* [Pianissimo was borrowed from Italian *pianissimo*, which comes from *piano*, meaning "soft."]

pi an ist (pē an/ist *or* pē/ə nist), person who plays the piano. *n.*

pi an o[1] (pē an′ō), a large musical instrument whose tones come from many wires. The wires are sounded by hammers that are worked by striking keys on a keyboard. *n., pl.* **pi an os.**

WORD HISTORY

piano[1]

Piano[1] was borrowed from Italian *piano,* which was shortened from *pianoforte,* which comes from the words *piano e forte,* meaning "soft and loud."

---

pi an o[2] (pē an′ō), in music: **1** soft. **2** softly. 1 *adj.,* 2 *adv.* [*Piano*[2] was borrowed from Italian *piano,* which came from Latin *planus,* meaning "plain, flat."]

pi an o for te (pē an′ə fôr′tē), piano[1]. *n.*

pi az za (pē az′ə *for 1;* pē ät′sə *or* pē az′ə *for 2),* **1** a large porch along one or more sides of a house. **2** an open public square in Italian towns. *n., pl.* **pi az zas.**

pi ca (pī′kə), **1** size of type, 12 point.

This sentence is in pica.

2 this size used as a measure; about ¹/₆ inch. *n., pl.* **pi cas.**

Pic ar dy (pik′ər dē), region in N France. See **Normandy** for map. *n.*

Pi cas so (pi kä′sō), **Pablo,** 1881-1973, Spanish painter and sculptor, *n.*

pic a yune (pik′ə yün′), small; petty; mean: *picayune criticism. adj.*

pic ca lil li (pik′ə lil′ē), relish made of chopped pickles, onions, tomatoes, hot spices, etc. *n., pl.* **pic ca lil lis.**

pic co lo (pik′ə lō), a small, shrill flute, sounding an octave higher than an ordinary flute. *n., pl.* **pic co los.**

WORD HISTORY

piccolo

Piccolo was borrowed from Italian *piccolo,* which comes from the phrase *piccolo flauto,* meaning "small flute."

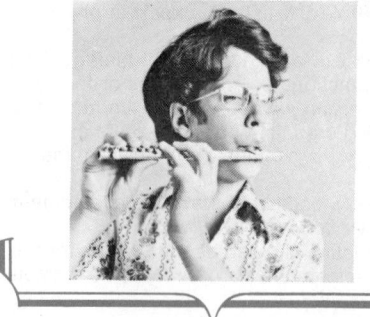

pick[1] (pik), **1** choose out of a number or quantity; select: *I picked a winning horse at the races.* **2** choice; selection: *This red rose is my pick.* **3** the best or most desirable part: *We got a high price for the pick of our peaches.* **4** pull away with the fingers; gather: *We pick fruit and flowers.* **5** use something pointed to remove things from: *pick one's*

teeth, pick a bone. **6** open with a pointed instrument, wire, etc.: *The burglar picked the lock on the garage.* **7** steal the contents of: *In the crowded waiting room I didn't feel the hand that picked my pocket.* **8** prepare for use by removing feathers, waste parts, etc.: *pick a chicken.* **9** pluck at with the fingers or a plectrum: *play a banjo by picking its strings.* **10** thing held in the fingers and used to pull on the strings of a musical instrument; plectrum. **11** seek and find occasion for; seek and find: *pick a quarrel, pick flaws.* 1,4-9,11 *v.,* 2,3,10 *n.*

pick at, 1 pull on with the fingers, etc.: *She picked at the scab on her finger.* **2** eat only a little at a time: *The bird picks at the bread.*

pick off, shoot one at a time.

pick on, INFORMAL. **1** find fault with: *The teacher picked on him for always being late.* **2** annoy; tease: *My older brother and sister always pick on me.*

pick out, 1 choose with care; select: *Pick out a coat you will like to wear.* **2** distinguish (a thing) from surroundings: *Can you pick me out in this group picture?*

pick up, 1 take up: *She picked up the hammer.* **2** get by chance: *pick up a bargain.* **3** learn without being taught: *He picks up games easily.* **4** take up into a vehicle or ship: *The bus picked up passengers at every other corner.* **5** recover; improve: *He seemed to pick up quickly after his fever went down.* **6** go faster; increase in speed. **7** succeed in seeing, hearing, etc.: *She picked up a radio broadcast from Paris.* **8** INFORMAL. become acquainted with without being introduced. **9** tidy up; put in order: *pick up a room.*

pick[2] (pik), **1** pickax. **2** a sharp-pointed tool. Ice is broken into pieces with a pick. *n.*

pick a back (pik′ə bak′), piggyback. *adv.*

pickax

pick ax or **pick axe** (pik′aks′), tool with a heavy metal bar, pointed at one or both ends, attached through the center to a wooden handle; pick. It is used for breaking up dirt, rocks, etc. *n., pl.* **pick ax es.**

pick er (pik′ər), **1** person who gathers, picks, or collects. **2** tool for picking anything. *n.*

pick er el (pik′ər əl), a freshwater fish with a long, narrow pointed head, used for food. It is a kind of pike. *n., pl.* **pick er els** or **pick er el.**

pick et (pik′it), **1** a pointed stake or peg placed upright to make a fence, to tie a horse to, etc. **2** enclose with pickets; fence. **3** tie to a picket: *picket a horse.* **4** a small body of troops, or a single soldier, posted at some place to watch for the enemy and guard against surprise attacks. **5** person stationed by a labor union near a factory, store, etc., where there is a strike. Pickets try to prevent employees from working or customers from buying. **6** person who takes part in a public demonstration or boycott to support a cause. **7** station as pickets. **8** station pickets at or near: *picket a factory.* **9** act as a picket. 1,4-6 *n.,* 2,3,7-9 *v.* —**pick′et er,** *n.*

picket fence, fence made of pickets.

pick ings (pik′ingz), **1** amount picked. **2** things left over; scraps. *n.pl.*

pick le (pik′əl), **1** salt water, vinegar, or other liquid in which meat and vegetables can be preserved. **2** cucumber preserved in pickle. **3** any other vegetable preserved in pickle. **4** preserve in pickle: *We pickled several quarts of beets yesterday.* **5** INFORMAL. trouble; difficulty: *I got in a bad pickle today.* 1-3,5 *n.*, 4 *v.*, **pick led, pick ling.** [*Pickle* comes from Dutch *pekel.*]

pick pock et (pik′pok′it), person who steals from people's pockets. *n.*

pick up (pik′up′), **1** a picking up: *the daily pickup of mail.* **2** INFORMAL. a getting better; improvement: *a pickup in business, a pickup in one's health.* **3** acceleration; going faster; increase in speed. **4** device that transforms into electrical current the vibrations set up in a phonograph needle by variations in the grooves of a record. **5** reception of sounds or images in radio or television and their conversion into electric waves for broadcasting. **6** apparatus for such reception or the place where it occurs. **7** a small, light truck with an open back, used for light hauling. *n.*

pick y (pik′ē), INFORMAL. **1** choosy; particular: *Some customers are very picky when it comes to selecting shoes.* **2** finding fault about trifles; nagging: *The driving instructor was picky about details, but he taught me a lot about driving in highway traffic.* adj., **pick i er, pick i est.** —**pick′i ly,** *adv.* —**pick′i ness,** *n.*

pic nic (pik′nik), **1** a pleasure trip with a meal in the open air. **2** go on such a trip: *Our family often picnics at the beach.* **3** eat in picnic style. 1 *n.*, 2,3 *v.*, **pic nicked, pic nick ing.**

pic nick er (pik′ni kər), person who picnics. *n.*

Pict (pikt), member of an ancient people formerly living in Scotland, especially northern Scotland, between A.D. 200's and 900's. *n.*

OX   WINDOW   WEAPONS FENCE   POST   EYE

pictographs

pic to graph (pik′tə graf), picture used as a sign or symbol. *n.*

pic to ri al (pik tôr′ē əl), **1** of or about pictures; expressed in pictures. **2** illustrated by pictures: *a pictorial history, a pictorial magazine.* **3** of painters or painting: *pictorial skill. adj.* —**pic to′ri al ly,** *adv.*

pic ture (pik′chər), **1** a drawing, painting, portrait, or photograph; a print of any of these: *The book contains a good picture of a tiger.* **2** scene: *The trees and brook make a lovely picture.* **3** something beautiful: *The old castle was a picture in the bright sunlight.* **4** draw, paint, etc.; make into a picture: *The artist pictured life in the old West.* **5** image; likeness: *He is the picture of his father. She was the picture of happiness.* **6** form a picture of in the mind; imagine: *It is hard to picture life a hundred years ago.* **7** a mental image; idea: *have a clear picture of the problem.* **8** a vivid description. **9** show by words; describe vividly: *The speaker pictured the suffering of the poor.* **10** a motion picture. **11** image on a television set. **12** state of affairs; condition; situation: *the employment picture.* 1-3,5,7,8,10-12 *n.*, 4,6,9 *v.*, **pic tured, pic tur ing.** [*Picture* is from Latin *pictura*, which comes from *pingere*, meaning "to paint."]

pic tur esque (pik′chə resk′), **1** quaint or interesting enough to be used as the subject of a picture. **2** making a picture for the mind; vivid: *picturesque language. adj.* —**pic′tur esque′ly,** *adv.* —**pic′tur esque′ness,** *n.*

picture tube, a cathode-ray tube that has a screen at one end on which images are reproduced.

pidg in English (pij′ən), one of several forms of English, with simplified grammatical structure and often a

a	hat	i	it	oi	oil	ch	child		a in about
ā	age	ī	ice	ou	out	ng	long		e in taken
ä	far	o	hot	u	cup	sh	she	ə =	i in pencil
e	let	ō	open	u̇	put	th	thin		o in lemon
ē	equal	ô	order	ü	rule	ᴛʜ	then		u in circus
ėr	term					zh	measure		

mixed vocabulary, used as a language of trade in western Africa, Australia, Melanesia, and China.

pie (pī), fruit, meat, etc., enclosed in pastry and baked: *apple pie, chicken pie. n.*

pie bald (pī′bôld′), **1** spotted in two colors, especially black and white. **2** a piebald horse. 1 *adj.*, 2 *n.*

piece (pēs), **1** one of the parts into which a thing is divided or broken; bit: *The cup broke in pieces.* **2** portion; limited part; small quantity: *a piece of land containing two acres, a piece of bread.* **3** a single thing of a set or class: *This set of china has 144 pieces.* **4** a single composition in an art: *a piece of music.* **5** coin: *A nickel is a five-cent piece.* **6** example; instance: *That silly story is a piece of nonsense.* **7** quantity in which goods are made: *cloth sold only by the piece.* **8** the amount of work done: *paid by the piece.* **9** gun; cannon. **10** make or repair by adding or joining pieces: *piece a quilt.* **11** join the pieces of. 1-9 *n.*, 10,11 *v.*, **pieced, piec ing.** —**piec′er,** *n.*

go to pieces, 1 fall apart; break up: *Another ship had gone to pieces on the rocks.* **2** break down; collapse: *When her business failed, she went completely to pieces.*

of a piece, of the same kind; in keeping: *That plan is of a piece with the rest of their silly suggestions.*

piece of one's mind, a scolding: *I gave them a piece of my mind for coming late again.*

piece meal (pēs′mēl′), **1** piece by piece; a little at a time: *work done piecemeal.* **2** piece from piece; to pieces; into fragments: *The lamb was torn piecemeal by the wolves.* **3** done piece by piece. 1,2 *adv.*, 3 *adj.*

piece of eight, an old Spanish peso, used during the Spanish colonization of America. It corresponded to the United States dollar.

piece work (pēs′wėrk′), work paid for by the amount done, not by the time it takes. *n.*

pie crust (pī′krust′), pastry used for the bottom or top of a pie. *n.*

pied (pīd), having patches of two or more colors; many-colored. *adj.*

Pied mont (pēd′mont), **1** plateau in the United States between the Appalachian Mountains and the lowland along the Atlantic coast. The Piedmont extends over parts of New Jersey, Pennsylvania, Delaware, New York, Maryland, Virginia, North Carolina, South Carolina, Georgia, and Alabama. **2** region in NW Italy. *n.*

pier (pir), **1** structure supported on columns extending into the water, used as a walk or a landing place for ships. **2** breakwater. **3** one of the solid supports on which

picturesque (def. 1) The painting was of a **picturesque** old windmill.

the arches of a bridge rest; pillar. **4** the solid part of a wall between windows, doors, etc. *n.*

pierce (pirs), **1** make a hole in; bore into or through: *A nail pierced the tire of our car.* **2** go into; go through: *A tunnel pierces the mountain.* **3** force a way through or into: *A sharp cry pierced the air.* **4** make a way through with the eye or mind: *pierce a disguise, pierce a mystery.* **5** affect sharply with some feeling: *a heart pierced with grief.* *v.,* **pierced, pierc ing.** —**pierce′a ble,** *adj.* —**pierc′er,** *n.*

Pierce (pirs), **Franklin,** 1804-1869, the 14th president of the United States, from 1853 to 1857. *n.*

pierc ing (pir′sing), that pierces; penetrating; sharp; keen: *piercing cold, a piercing look.* *adj.* —**pierc′ing ly,** *adv.*

Pierre (pir), capital of South Dakota, in the central part. *n.*

pi e ty (pī′ə tē), **1** a being pious; reverence for God; devotion to religion; holiness; goodness. **2** dutiful regard for one's parents. **3** a pious act, remark, belief, etc. *n., pl.* **pi e ties.**

pif fle (pif′əl), INFORMAL. silly talk; nonsense. *n.*

pig (pig), **1** a four-footed mammal with a stout, heavy body, cloven hoofs, and a broad snout; hog; swine. Domesticated pigs are raised for their meat. **2** a young pig. **3** pork. **4** INFORMAL. person who seems or acts like a pig; one who is greedy, dirty, dull, sullen, or stubborn. *n.* —**pig′like′,** *adj.*

pig eon (pij′ən), any of a group of birds with thick bodies and short tails and legs, including doves and many varieties of domestic pigeons. *n.*

pig eon hole (pij′ən hōl′), **1** a small place built, usually as one of a series, for a pigeon to nest in. **2** one of a set of boxlike compartments for holding papers and other articles in a desk, a cabinet, etc. **3** put in a pigeonhole; put away. **4** classify and lay aside in memory where one can refer to it. **5** put aside with the idea of dismissing, forgetting, or neglecting: *The city council pigeonholed the people's request for a new park.* **1,2** *n.,* **3-5** *v.,* **pig eon holed, pig eon hol ing.**

pig eon-toed (pij′ən tōd′), having the toes or feet turned inward. *adj.*

pig gish (pig′ish), **1** very selfish; greedy. **2** dirty; filthy. *adj.* —**pig′gish ly,** *adv.* —**pig′gish ness,** *n.*

pig gy (pig′ē), a little pig. *n., pl.* **pig gies.**

pig gy back (pig′ē bak′), on the back: *a piggyback ride. Flatcars often take trucks piggyback from one place to another.* *adj., adv.* Also, **pickaback.**

piggy bank, **1** a small container in the shape of a pig, with a slot in the top for coins. **2** any coin bank.

pig-head ed (pig′hed′id), stupidly obstinate or stubborn. *adj.* —**pig′-head′ed ly,** *adv.* —**pig′-head′ed ness,** *n.*

pig iron, crude iron as it first comes from the blast furnace or smelter. It is used to make steel, cast iron, and wrought iron. [*Pig iron was called this because the crude iron was originally cast into oblong masses called pigs.*]

pig let (pig′lit), a little pig. *n.*

pig ment (pig′mənt), **1** a coloring matter, especially a powdered dry substance. Paint and dyes are made by mixing pigments with liquid. **2** substance that occurs in and colors the tissues of an animal or plant. The color of a person's hair, skin, and eyes is due to pigment. *n.*

pig men ta tion (pig′mən tā′shən), deposit of coloring matter in the tissue of a living animal or plant. Freckles are spots of pigmentation. *n.*

pig my (pig′mē), pygmy. *n., pl.* **pig mies;** *adj.*

pig pen (pig′pen′), **1** pen where pigs are kept. **2** a filthy place. *n.*

pig skin (pig′skin′), **1** the skin of a pig. **2** leather made from it. **3** INFORMAL. a football. *n.*

pig sty (pig′stī′), pigpen. *n., pl.* **pig sties.**

pig tail (pig′tāl′), braid of hair hanging from the back of the head. *n.*

pike¹ (pīk), a long, wooden shaft with a sharp-pointed metal head; spear. Foot soldiers used to carry pikes. *n.*

pike² (pīk), a sharp point; spike. *n.*

pike³ (pīk), any of a group of large, slender, freshwater fish of the Northern Hemisphere, having a long, pointed head. The muskellunge and pickerel are pikes. *n., pl.* **pikes** or **pike.**

pike⁴ (pīk), turnpike. *n.*

pik er (pī′kər), SLANG. **1** person who does things in a small or cheap way. **2** a stingy person. *n.*

Pikes Peak (pīks), mountain of the Rocky Mountains in central Colorado, 14,110 feet (4301 meters) high.

pike staff (pīk′staf′), staff or shaft of a pike or spear. *n., pl.* **pike staves** (pīk′stāvz′).

pi las ter (pə las′tər), a rectangular pillar, especially when not standing alone, but supporting a part of a wall from which it projects a little. *n.*

Pi late (pī′lət), **Pontius,** Roman governor who, from A.D. 26 to 36?, ruled over Judea in Palestine. During his rule Jesus was crucified. *n.*

pile¹ (pīl), **1** many things lying one upon another in a more or less orderly way: *a pile of wood.* **2** a mass like a hill or mound: *a pile of dirt.* **3** make into a pile; heap up; stack: *The campers piled the extra wood in a corner.* **4** gather or rise in piles: *Snow piled against the fences.* **5** INFORMAL. a large amount: *I have a pile of work to do.* **6** cover with large amounts: *pile a plate with food.* **7** go in a confused, rushing crowd or group: *pile out of a bus, pile into a car.* **8** reactor. **1,2,5,8** *n.,* **3,4,6,7** *v.,* **piled, pil ing.**

pile² (pīl), a heavy beam driven upright into the earth, often under water, to help support a bridge, wharf, building, etc. *n.*

pile³ (pīl), **1** a soft, thick nap on velvet, plush, and many carpets: *The pile of that rug is almost half an inch long.* **2** a soft, fine hair or down. *n.*

pile driver, machine for driving down piles or stakes, usually a tall framework in which a heavy weight is raised and then allowed to fall upon the pile.

pil fer (pil′fər), steal in small quantities; steal: *The children pilfered apples from the neighbor's orchard.* *v.*

pil grim (pil′grəm), **1** person who goes on a journey to a sacred or holy place as an act of religious devotion. In the Middle Ages, many people went as pilgrims to Jerusalem and to holy places in Europe. **2** traveler; wanderer. **3** **Pilgrim,** one of the Puritan settlers of Plymouth Colony in 1620. *n.*

WORD HISTORY

pilgrim

Pilgrim came into English about 800 years ago from French *pelerin,* and can be traced back to Latin *per,* meaning "through," and *agrum,* meaning "territory, field."

pil grim age (pil′grə mij), **1** a pilgrim's journey; a journey to some sacred place as an act of religious devotion. **2** a long journey. *n.*

pil ing (pī′ling), **1** piles or heavy beams driven into the ground. **2** structure made of piles. *n.*

pill (pil), **1** medicine made up into a small pellet, tablet, or capsule to be swallowed whole. **2 the pill,** pill taken by women to prevent pregnancy. *n.*

pil lage (pil′ij), **1** rob with violence; plunder: *Pirates pillaged the towns along the coast.* **2** plunder; robbery. **1** *v.*, **pil laged, pil lag ing; 2** *n.* —**pil′lag er,** *n.*

pil lar (pil′ər), **1** a slender, upright structure; column. Pillars are usually made of stone, wood, or metal and used as supports or ornaments for a building. Sometimes a pillar stands alone as a monument. **2** anything slender and upright like a pillar. **3** an important support or supporter: *a pillar of society, a pillar of the church.* *n.* **from pillar to post,** from one thing or place to another without any definite purpose.

pill box (pil′boks′), **1** a small box, usually shallow and often round, for holding pills. **2** a small, low fortress with thick, concrete walls and roof, equipped with machine guns and other weapons. *n., pl.* **pill box es.**

pil lion (pil′yən), pad attached behind a saddle for a person to sit on. *n.*

pillory (def. 1)

pil lor y (pil′ər ē), **1** frame of wood with holes through which a person's head and hands were put. The pillory was formerly used as a punishment, being set up in a public place where the crowd could make fun of the offender. **2** put in the pillory. **3** expose to public ridicule, contempt, or abuse: *The newspapers pilloried the unpopular mayor.* **1** *n., pl.* **pil lor ies; 2,3** *v.*, **pil lor ied, pil lor ying.**

pil low (pil′ō), **1** bag or case filled with feathers, down, or other soft material, usually used to support the head when resting or sleeping. **2** rest on a pillow. **3** be a pillow for: *He lay with his arm pillowing his head.* **1** *n.*, **2,3** *v.*

pil low case (pil′ō kās′), a cloth cover pulled over a pillow. *n.*

pil low slip (pil′ō slip′), pillowcase. *n.*

pi lot (pī′lət), **1** person who steers a ship or boat. **2** person trained to steer ships in or out of a harbor or through dangerous waters. A ship takes on a pilot before coming into a strange harbor. **3** person who operates the controls of an aircraft or spacecraft in flight. **4** act as the pilot of; steer: *to pilot an airplane.* **5** a guide; leader. **6** to guide; lead: *The manager piloted us through the big factory.* **1-3,5** *n.*, **4,6** *v.* [Pilot came into English about 450 years ago from French *pilote*, which came from Italian *pilota*, and can be traced back to Greek *pēdon*, meaning "an oar."] —**pi′lot less,** *adj.*

pi lot house (pī′lət hous′), an enclosed place on the deck of a ship, sheltering the steering wheel and pilot; wheelhouse. *n., pl.* **pi lot hous es** (pī′lət hou′ziz).

pilot light, a small flame kept burning all the time and used to light a main burner whenever desired. Gas stoves and gas water heaters have pilot lights.

pi men to (pə men′tō), pimiento. *n., pl.* **pi men tos.**

pi mien to (pə men′tō *or* pi myen′tō), kind of sweet pepper, used as a vegetable, relish, and stuffing for green olives. *n., pl.* **pi mien tos.**

pim per nel (pim′pər nel), plant having small scarlet,

a hat	i it	oi oil	ch child	⎧ a in about
ā age	ī ice	ou out	ng long	e in taken
ä far	o hot	u cup	sh she	ə = ⎨ i in pencil
e let	ō open	ů put	th thin	o in lemon
ē equal	ô order	ü rule	ŦH then	⎩ u in circus
ėr term			zh measure	

purple, blue, or white flowers that close in bad weather. *n.*

pim ple (pim′pəl), a small, inflamed swelling of the skin. *n.* —**pim′ple like′,** *adj.*

pim pled (pim′pəld), pimply. *adj.*

pim ply (pim′plē), having pimples. *adj.*, **pim pli er, pim pli est.**

pin (pin), **1** a short, slender piece of wire with a point at one end and a head at the other, for fastening things together. **2** badge with a pin or clasp to fasten it to the clothing: *She wore her class pin.* **3** brooch. **4** peg made of wood, metal, or plastic, used to fasten things together, hold something, hang things on, etc. **5** any of various fastenings, such as a clothespin or safety pin. **6** fasten with a pin or pins; put a pin through. **7** hold fast in one position: *When the tree fell, it pinned the bear to the ground.* **8** a bottle-shaped piece of wood used in bowling. **1-5,8** *n.*, **6,7** *v.*, **pinned, pin ning.** —**pin′like′,** *adj.*

on pins and needles, very anxious or uneasy.

pin down, hold or bind to an undertaking or pledge.

pin on, fix (blame, responsibility, etc.) on: *You're not going to pin the blame on me!*

pin a fore (pin′ə fôr′), **1** a child's apron that covers most of the dress. **2** a light dress without sleeves. *n.*

pi ña ta (pē nyä′tə), pot filled with candy, fruit, etc., hung at Christmastime in Mexico and other Latin-American countries above the heads of blindfolded children. They are given chances to break the pot to get what it contains. *n., pl.* **pi ña tas.**

pin ball (pin′bôl′), game in which a ball is propelled by a spring so that it rolls down a slanting board. Points are scored when the ball strikes or passes through various pegs, bumpers, and alleys. *n.*

pince-nez (pans′nā′ *or* pins′nā′), eyeglasses kept in place by a spring that clips onto the bridge of the nose. *n., pl.* **pince-nez** (pans′nāz′ *or* pins′nāz′).

WORD HISTORY

pince-nez

Pince-nez was borrowed from French *pince-nez*, which is from *pincer*, meaning "to pinch," and *nez*, meaning "nose," which came from Latin *nasus.*

pincers
(def. 2)
of a
crab

pin cers (pin′sərz), **1** tool for gripping and holding tight, made like scissors but with jaws instead of blades. **2** the large claw or pair of claws of crabs, lobsters, etc., which are used to grip and hold the prey. *n. pl. or sing.* Also, **pinchers.**

pinch (pinch), **1** squeeze between two hard edges; squeeze with thumb and forefinger: *pinch a baby's cheek playfully.* **2** act of pinching; a squeeze between two hard edges. **3** press so as to hurt; squeeze: *These new shoes pinch my feet.* **4** sharp pressure that hurts; squeeze: *the pinch of tight shoes.* **5** sharp discomfort or distress: *the pinch of cold.* **6** cause to shrink or become thin: *a face pinched by hunger.* **7** time of special need; emergency: *I will help you in a pinch.* **8** as much as can be taken up with the tips of finger and thumb: *a pinch of salt.* **9** be stingy; be stingy with: *The miser even pinched pennies.* **10** SLANG. to arrest. **11** SLANG. an arrest. **12** SLANG. to steal: *The grocer caught them pinching apples.* **13** SLANG. a stealing. 1,3,6,9,10,12 *v.*, 2,4,5,7,8,11,13 *n.*, *pl.* **pinch es.** —**pinch′er,** *n.*

pinch ers (pin′chərz), pincers. *n. pl. or sing.*

pinch-hit (pinch′hit′), **1** (in baseball) to bat for another player, especially when a hit is badly needed. **2** take another's place in an emergency. *v.*, **pinch-hit,** **pinch-hit ting.**

pinch hitter, one who pinch-hits for another.

pin cush ion (pin′kush′ən), a small cushion to stick pins in until they are needed. *n.*

pine¹ (pīn), **1** any of a group of evergreen trees that have cones and clusters of needle-shaped leaves. Pines are valuable for timber, turpentine, resin, tar, etc. **2** the wood of any of these trees. *n.* [Pine¹ is from Old English *pīn,* which came from Latin *pinus.*]

pine² (pīn), **1** long eagerly; yearn: *The homesick children pined to see their parents.* **2** waste away with pain, hunger, grief, or desire. *v.*, **pined, pin ing.** [Pine² comes from Old English *pīnian,* meaning "to torture, torment," and can be traced back to Greek *poinē,* meaning "penalty, punishment."] —**pin′er,** *n.*

pine ap ple (pīn′ap′əl), the large, juicy fruit of a tropical plant with slender, stiff leaves. Pineapples look something like big pine cones. *n.*

pine y (pī′nē), piny. *adj.*, **pin i er, pin i est.**

pin feath er (pin′feᴛн′ər), an undeveloped feather, especially one just breaking through the skin, that looks like a small stub.

Ping-Pong (ping′pong′), trademark for table tennis. *n.*

pin head (pin′hed′), **1** the head of a pin. **2** something very small or worthless. **3** SLANG. person who has little intelligence. *n.*

pin hole (pin′hōl′), **1** hole made by or as if by a pin. **2** hole for a pin or peg to go in. *n.*

pin ion¹ (pin′yən), **1** the last joint of a bird's wing. **2** a wing. **3** any one of the stiff flying feathers of the wing. **4** cut off or tie the pinions of (a bird) to prevent flying. **5** bind the arms of; bind (to something); bind: *The bank robbers pinioned the guard's arms.* 1-3 *n.*, 4,5 *v.*

pin ion² (pin′yən), a small gear with teeth that fit into those of a larger gear or rack. *n.*

pink¹ (pingk), **1** the color obtained by mixing red with white; light or pale red. **2** having this color. **3** the highest degree or condition: *The athlete was in the pink of health.* **4** a garden plant with spicy-smelling flowers of various colors, mostly white, pink, and red. A carnation is a variety of pink. 1,3,4 *n.*, 2 *adj.* —**pink′ness,** *n.*

pink² (pingk), **1** prick or pierce with a sword, spear, or dagger. **2** cut the edge of (cloth) in small notches to prevent raveling. **3** decorate with small, round holes. *v.*

pink eye (pingk′ī′), a contagious disease that causes inflammation of the membrane that forms the inner surface of the eyelids and covers the eyeball. *n.*

pink ie (ping′kē), the smallest finger. *n.* Also, **pinky.**

pinking shears, shears for cutting the edges of cloth in small notches to prevent raveling.

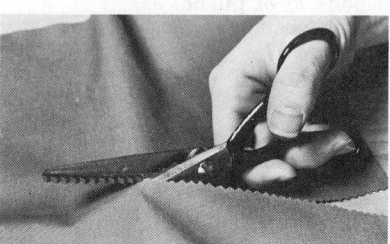

pinking shears

pink ish (ping′kish), somewhat pink. *adj.*

pink y (ping′kē), pinkie. *n.*, *pl.* **pink ies.**

pin money, a small amount of money used to buy extra things for one's own use.

pin na cle (pin′ə kəl), **1** a high peak or point of rock. **2** the highest point: *at the pinnacle of one's fame.* **3** a slender turret or spire. *n.*

pin nate (pin′āt), **1** like a feather. **2** (of a leaf) having leaflets on each side of a stalk. *adj.* —**pin′nate ly,** *adv.*

pi noch le or **pi noc le** (pē′nuk′əl), game played with a double deck of all cards from the nine to the ace. There are 48 cards in the deck. *n.*

piñ on (pin′yən *or* pē′nyōn), pine, especially of the Rocky Mountain region, producing large, nutlike seeds which are good to eat. *n.*, *pl.* **piñ ons.** [*Piñon* comes from Spanish *piñon,* and can be traced back to Latin *pinus,* meaning "pine tree."]

pin point (pin′point′), **1** the point of a pin. **2** aim at accurately; determine precisely. **3** extremely accurate or precise: *pinpoint bombing.* 1 *n.*, 2 *v.*, 3 *adj.*

pint (pīnt), unit of measure for liquids and dry things, equal to ¹/₂ quart; 2 cups; 16 fluid ounces. *n.*

pin to (pin′tō), **1** spotted in two or more colors; pied. **2** a spotted, white and black or white and brown horse. 1 *adj.*, 2 *n.*, *pl.* **pin tos.** [*Pinto* was borrowed from American Spanish *pinto,* and can be traced back to Latin *pingere,* meaning "to paint."]

pin wheel (pin′hwēl′), **1** toy made of a wheel fastened to a stick by a pin so that it revolves in the wind. **2** kind of firework that revolves when lighted. *n.*

pin worm (pin′wėrm′), a small, threadlike worm which sometimes inhabits the large intestine of human beings, especially children. *n.*

pin y (pī′nē), **1** abounding in or covered with pine trees: *piny mountains.* **2** of or suggesting pine trees: *a piny odor. adj.*, **pin i er, pin i est.** Also, **piney.**

pi o neer (pī′ə nir′), **1** person who settles in a part of a country, preparing it for others: *The pioneers of the American West included trappers, explorers, and farming families.* **2** person who goes first, or does something first, and so prepares a way for others: *a pioneer in medical science.*

3 prepare or open up for others; take the lead in doing: *Astronauts are pioneering in exploring outer space.* 1,2 *n.,* 3 *v.*

pi ous (pī′əs), **1** having or showing reverence for God; religious. **2** done under pretense of religion or of serving a good cause: *a pious fraud. adj.* —**pi′ous ly,** *adv.* —**pi′ous ness,** *n.*

pip[1] (pip), seed of an apple, orange, etc. *n.*

pip[2] (pip), a contagious disease of birds that causes the secretion of thick mucus in the mouth and throat. *n.*

pip[3] (pip), one of the spots on playing cards, dominoes, or dice. *n.*

pipe (pīp), **1** tube through which a liquid or gas flows. **2** carry by means of a pipe or pipes. **3** supply with pipes: *Our street is being piped for gas.* **4** tube with a bowl of clay, wood, or other material at one end, for smoking. **5** a musical instrument with a single tube into which the player blows. **6 pipes,** *pl.* **a** set of musical tubes: *the pipes of Pan.* **b** bagpipe. **7** play on a pipe. **8** any one of the tubes in an organ. **9** make a shrill noise; sing in a shrill voice. **10** a shrill sound, voice, or song: *the pipe of the lark.* 1,4-6,8,10 *n.,* 2,3,7,9 *v.,* **piped, pip ing.** —**pipe′- like′,** *adj.*

pipe down, SLANG. be quiet; shut up.

pipe line (pīp′līn′), **1** line of pipes for carrying oil or other liquids, usually over a considerable distance. **2** source of information, usually secret. *n.*

pip er (pī′pər), person who plays on a pipe or bag-pipe. *n.*

pay the piper, pay for one's pleasure; bear the conse-quences.

pi pette (pī pet′ *or* pi pet′), a slender pipe or tube for transferring or measuring small quantities of liquids. Liquid sucked into a tube is retained by closing the top end; then, when the top of the tube is uncovered, the liquid flows from the bottom end. *n.*

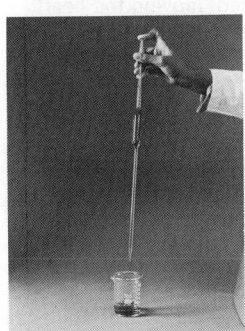

pipette

pip ing (pī′ping), **1** a shrill sound: *the piping of frogs in the spring.* **2** shrill: *a high, piping voice.* **3** pipes: *lead piping.* **4** music of pipes. **5** a narrow band of material, sometimes containing a cord, used for trimming along edges and seams. 1,3-5 *n.,* 2 *adj.*

piping hot, so hot as to hiss; very hot; boiling: *The tea is piping hot.*

pip it (pip′it), a small, brownish bird, somewhat like a lark, that sings while flying. *n.*

pip pin (pip′ən), any of several kinds of apple: *a yellow pippin. n.*

pi quan cy (pē′kən sē), **1** quality of exciting the mind pleasantly. **2** quality of exciting the appetite, being odd to the taste, or pleasantly sharp. *n.*

pi quant (pē′kənt), **1** stimulating to the mind, interest, etc.: *a piquant bit of news, a piquant face.* **2** pleasantly sharp; stimulating to the taste: *a piquant sauce. adj.* —**pi′quant ly,** *adv.* —**pi′quant ness,** *n.*

pique (pēk), **1** a feeling of anger at being slighted;

a hat	**i** it	**oi** oil	**ch** child	a in about
ā age	**ī** ice	**ou** out	**ng** long	e in taken
ä far	**o** hot	**u** cup	**sh** she	ə = i in pencil
e let	**ō** open	**ů** put	**th** thin	o in lemon
ē equal	**ô** order	**ü** rule	**ŦH** then	u in circus
ėr term			**zh** measure	

wounded pride: *In a pique, the couple left the party.* **2** cause a feeling of anger in; wound the pride of: *It piqued her that we had a secret she did not share.* **3** arouse; stir up: *Our curiosity was piqued by the locked trunk.* 1 *n.,* 2,3 *v.,* **piqued, pi quing.**

pique oneself on, feel proud about.

pi qué (pi kā′), fabric of cotton, rayon, or silk, with nar-row ribs or raised stripes. *n.*

pi ra cy (pī′rə sē), **1** robbery on the sea. **2** act of publish-ing or using a book, play, invention, etc., without per-mission. *n., pl.* **pi ra cies.**

piranha—about 15 in. (38 cm.) long

pi ra nha (pi rä′nyə), a small South American fish that attacks human beings and other large mammals. *n., pl.* **pi ra nhas** or **pi ra nha.**

pi rate (pī′rit), **1** person who attacks and robs ships; robber on the sea; buccaneer. **2** be a pirate; plunder; rob. **3** publish or use without the author's, inventor's, or owner's permission. 1 *n.,* 2,3 *v.,* **pi rat ed, pi rat ing.** —**pi′rate like′,** *adj.*

pi rat i cal (pī rat′ə kəl), of pirates; like pirates; like pira-cy. *adj.* —**pi rat′i cal ly,** *adv.*

pir ou ette (pir′ü et′), **1** a whirling about on one foot or on the toes, as in dancing. **2** whirl in this way. 1 *n.,* 2 *v.,* **pir ou et ted, pir ou et ting.**

Pi sa (pē′zə), city in NW Italy, famous for its leaning tower. *n.*

pis ta chi o (pi stä′shē ō *or* pi stash′ē ō), **1** the greenish, almond-flavored nut of a small tree related to sumac. **2** a light green. **3** light-green. 1,2 *n., pl.* **pis ta chi os;** 3 *adj.* [*Pistachio* comes from Italian *pistacchio,* and can be traced back to Persian *pistah.*]

pis til (pis′tl), the part of a flower that produces seeds. It consists, when complete, of an ovary, a style, and a stigma. *n.*

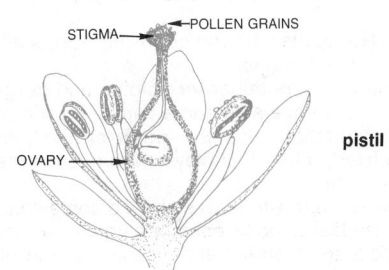

STIGMA
POLLEN GRAINS
OVARY
pistil

pis tol (pis′tl), a small, short gun held and fired with one hand. *n.*

pis ton (pis′tən), a short cylinder, or a flat, round piece of wood or metal, fitting closely inside a tube or hollow cylinder in which it is moved back and forth, often by the force of exploding vapor or steam. Pistons are used in pumps, engines, compressors, etc. *n.*

piston ring, a metal ring fitted in a groove around a piston to ensure a tight fit against the cylinder wall.

piston rod, a rod by which a piston transmits or receives motion.

pit[1] (pit), **1** a natural hole in the ground. **2** hole dug deep into the earth. A mine or the shaft of a mine is a pit. **3** a hollow place on the surface of anything: *the pit of the stomach.* **4** a little hollow place or scar, such as is left by smallpox. **5** to mark with small pits or scars. **6** a covered hole used as a trap for wild animals. **7** place where dogs or cocks are made to fight. **8** set to fight or compete; match: *She was pitted against her friend in the last round of the tennis match.* **9 the pit,** hell. **10 the pits,** SLANG. some thing, place, or situation thought to be utterly bad: *The movie was the pits.* 1-4,6,7,9,10 *n.,* 5,8 *v.,* **pit ted, pit ting.** [*Pit*[1] is from Old English *pytt,* which came from Latin *puteus,* meaning "a pit, a well."]

pit[2] (pit), **1** the hard seed of a cherry, peach, plum, date, etc.; stone. **2** remove pits from (fruit). 1 *n.,* 2 *v.,* **pit ted, pit ting.** [*Pit*[2] comes from Dutch *pit,* meaning "kernel."]

pi ta (pē′tä *or* pē′tə), a flat, round bread eaten in the Middle East. *n.* [*Pita* was borrowed from Hebrew *pita.*]

pit a pat (pit′ə pat′), pitter-patter. *n.*

pitch[1] (pich), **1** throw or fling; hurl; toss: *They were pitching horseshoes.* **2** (in baseball) throw (the ball) to the batter. **3** act of pitching; a throw or toss: *The first pitch was a strike.* **4** fix firmly in the ground; set up: *pitch a tent.* **5** fall or plunge forward: *I lost my balance and pitched down the stairs.* **6** plunge with the bow rising and then falling: *The ship pitched about in the storm.* **7** set at a certain point, degree, or level. **8** determine the key of (a tune). **9** point; position; degree: *She reached the lowest pitch of bad fortune.* **10** degree of highness or lowness of a sound. Notes in music with a low pitch have a slower rate of vibration than those with a high pitch. **11** slope downward; incline; dip. **12** INFORMAL. a talk, argument, offer, plan, etc., used to persuade, as in selling: *make a strong sales pitch.* **13** amount of slope: *a road with a steep pitch.* 1,2,4-8,11 *v.,* 3,9,10,12,13 *n., pl.* **pitch es.**

pitch in, INFORMAL. work vigorously: *All of us pitched in, and the job was soon finished.*

pitch[2] (pich), **1** thick, black, sticky substance made from tar or turpentine, used to fill the seams of wooden ships, to cover roofs, to make pavements, etc. **2** cover with pitch. **3** resin from certain evergreen trees. 1,3 *n., pl.* **pitch es;** 2 *v.* —**pitch′like′,** *adj.*

pitch-black (pich′blak′), very black or dark. *adj.*

pitch blende (pich′blend′), mineral consisting largely of an oxide of uranium, occurring in black, pitchlike masses. It is a source of radium, uranium, and actinium. *n.*

pitch-dark (pich′därk′), pitch-black. *adj.* —**pitch′-dark′ness,** *n.*

pitched battle, battle with the opposing troops arranged in definite positions.

pitch er[1] (pich′ər), **1** container for holding and pouring liquids, with a lip on one side and a handle on the other. **2** amount that a pitcher holds. *n.* —**pitch′er like′,** *adj.*

pitch er[2] (pich′ər), a baseball player who pitches the ball to the batter. *n.*

pitcher plant, plant with leaves shaped somewhat like a pitcher. These leaves often contain a liquid secretion in which insects are captured and digested by the plant.

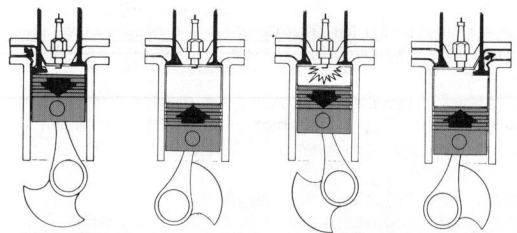

piston—The drawing shows how an automobile piston (shown in blue) moves inside a cylinder. A spark causes the gasoline vapor to explode and drive the piston.

pitch fork (pich′fôrk′), a large fork with a long handle, for lifting and throwing hay, etc.; hayfork. *n.*

pitch man (pich′man′), INFORMAL. person who makes a sales pitch. *n., pl.* **pitch men.**

pitch pipe, a small musical pipe having one or more notes, used to give the pitch for singing or for tuning an instrument.

pitch y (pich′ē), **1** full of pitch. **2** like pitch; sticky. **3** black. *adj.,* **pitch i er, pitch i est.** —**pitch′i ness,** *n.*

pit e ous (pit′ē əs), to be pitied; moving the heart; deserving pity: *A starving person is a piteous sight. adj.* —**pit′e ous ly,** *adv.* —**pit′e ous ness,** *n.*

pit fall (pit′fôl′), **1** a hidden pit to catch animals in. **2** any trap or hidden danger. *n.*

pith (pith), **1** the central, spongy tissue in the stems of certain plants. **2** a similar tissue found in other parts of plants, as that lining the skin of an orange. **3** the soft inner substance of a bone, feather, etc. **4** the important or essential part: *the pith of a speech. n.*

pith y (pith′ē), **1** full of substance, meaning, force, or vigor: *pithy phrases, a pithy speaker.* **2** of or like pith. **3** having much pith: *a pithy orange. adj.,* **pith i er, pith i est.** —**pith′i ly,** *adv.* —**pith′i ness,** *n.*

pit i a ble (pit′ē ə bəl), **1** to be pitied; moving the heart; deserving pity. **2** deserving contempt; mean; to be scorned: *Their half-hearted attempts to help with the work were pitiable. adj.* —**pit′i a ble ness,** *n.*

pit i a bly (pit′ē ə blē), in a pitiable manner; to a pitiable degree. *adv.*

pit i ful (pit′i fəl), **1** to be pitied; moving the heart; deserving pity: *The rabbit caught in the trap was a pitiful sight.* **2** feeling or showing pity; feeling sorrow for the trouble of others. **3** deserving contempt; mean; to be scorned: *a pitiful excuse. adj.* —**pit′i ful ly,** *adv.*

pit i less (pit′ē lis), without pity or mercy. *adj.* —**pit′i less ly,** *adv.*

Pitt (pit), **William,** 1759-1806, prime minister of England from 1783 to 1801 and from 1804 to 1806. *n.*

pit tance (pit′ns), **1** a small allowance of money. **2** a small amount or share. *n.*

pit ter-pat ter (pit′ər pat′ər), a quick succession of light beats or taps; pitapat: *the pitter-patter of rain, the pitter-patter of a child's steps. n.*

pitcher plant

Pitts burgh (pits/bėrg/), city in SW Pennsylvania, a center of the iron and steel industry. *n.*

pi tu i tar y (pə tü/ə ter/ē *or* pə tyü/ə ter/ē), **1** the pituitary gland. **2** of the pituitary gland. 1 *n., pl.* **pi tu i tar ies.** 2 *adj.*

pituitary gland, a small, oval endocrine gland situated at the base of the brain. It secretes hormones that promote growth, stimulate other glands, and regulate many bodily functions.

pit viper, any of a family of poisonous snakes having perforated fangs and a pit between the eye and nostril, including rattlesnakes, water moccasins, copperheads, and bushmasters.

pit y (pit/ē), **1** sorrow for another's suffering or distress; feeling for the sorrows of others; sympathy. **2** feel pity for: *I pitied the sobbing child.* **3** cause for pity or regret; thing to be sorry for: *It is a pity to be kept in the house in good weather.* 1,3 *n., pl.* **pit ies;** 2 *v.,* **pit ied, pit y ing.**

have pity on or **take pity on,** show pity for.

Pi us XII (pī/əs), 1876-1958, pope from 1939 to 1958.

piv ot (piv/ət), **1** shaft, pin, or point on which something turns. **2** mount on, attach by, or provide with a pivot. **3** turn on a pivot: *pivot on one's heel.* **4** a turn on a pivot or as if on a pivot: *With a quick pivot he threw the ball to his teammate.* **5** that on which something turns, hinges, or depends; central point: *the pivot of one's hopes.* 1,4,5 *n.,* 2,3 *v.*

piv ot al (piv/ə təl), **1** of, having to do with, or serving as a pivot. **2** being that on which something turns, hinges, or depends; very important. *adj.* —**piv/ot al ly,** *adv.*

pix el (pik/səl), any one of the many tiny points, each able to be bright or dark, that make up an electronic image. *n.*

pix y or **pix ie** (pik/sē), fairy or elf. *n., pl.* **pix ies.**

Pi zar ro (pi zär/ō), **Francisco,** 1471?-1541, Spanish conqueror of Peru. *n.*

piz za (pēt/sə), a spicy Italian dish made by baking a large flat layer of bread dough covered with cheese, tomato sauce, herbs, etc. *n., pl.* **piz zas.**

piz ze ri a (pēt/sə rē/ə), restaurant or bakery where pizzas are baked and sold. *n., pl.* **piz ze ri as.**

pkg., package.

pl., 1 place. **2** plural.

pla ca ble (plā/kə bəl), that may be placated. *adj.*

plac ard (plak/ärd), **1** notice to be posted in a public place; poster. **2** put placards on or in: *The circus placarded the city with advertisements.* 1 *n.,* 2 *v.*

pla cate (plā/kāt *or* plak/āt), soothe or satisfy the anger of; make peaceful; appease: *placate a person one has offended.* *v.,* **pla cat ed, pla cat ing.** —**pla/cat er,** *n.*

place (plās), **1** the part of space occupied by a person or thing. **2** city, town, village, district, etc.: *What place do you come from?* **3** building or spot used for a certain purpose: *A store or office is a place of business.* **4** house; house and grounds; dwelling: *Her parents have a beautiful place in the country.* **5** part or spot in a body or surface: *a sore place on one's foot. The dentist filled the decayed place in the tooth.* **6** the proper or natural position: *books in place on shelves. There is a time and place for everything.* **7** rank; position; way of life: *She won first place in the essay contest. They have a high place in society.* **8** position in time; part of time occupied by an event: *The performance went too slowly in several places.* **9** (in arithmetic) position of a figure in a number or series: *in the third decimal place.* **10** space or seat for a person: *We took our places at the table.* **11** put (in a spot, position, condition, or relation): *The orphan was placed in a good home. The people placed confidence in their leader.* **12** give the place, position, or condition of; identify: *I remember his name, but I cannot place him.* **13** finish among the leaders in a race or competition: *I failed to place in the first race and was eliminated.* **14** situation; post or office; official employment or position: *get a place in a store.* **15** appoint (a person) to a post or office; find a situation, etc., for. **16** duty; business: *It is not her place to find fault.* **17** a step or point in order of proceeding: *In the first place, the room is too small; in the second place, it is too dirty.* **18** a short street or court: *Waverley Place.* 1-10, 14,16-18 *n.,* 11-13,15 *v.,* **placed, plac ing.**

give place, 1 make room. **2** yield; give in: *My anger gave place to remorse.*

in place, 1 in the proper or usual place; in the original place. **2** fitting, appropriate, or timely.

in place of, instead of: *Use water in place of milk in that recipe.*

know one's place, act according to one's position in life.

out of place, 1 not in the proper or usual place. **2** unsuitable.

take place, happen; occur.

place kick, the kicking of a ball placed or held on the ground in football, soccer, etc.

place mat, a mat of linen, plastic, paper, etc., put under a person's plate or table setting.

place ment (plās/mənt), **1** a placing or a being placed; location; arrangement. **2** the finding of work or a job for a person. **3** a placing of a football on the ground for a place kick. *n.*

pla cen ta (plə sen/tə), organ in most mammals by which the fetus is attached to the wall of the uterus and nourished. *n.*

plac er (plas/ər), deposit of sand, gravel, or earth in the bed of a stream, containing particles of gold or other valuable minerals. *n.*

place value, the value which a figure has because of its place in a number. In 438, the place values of the figures are 4×100, 3×10, and 8×1.

plac id (plas/id), pleasantly calm or peaceful; quiet: *a placid lake, a placid temper.* *adj.* —**plac/id ly,** *adv.*

pla cid i ty (plə sid/ə tē), calmness; peace; tranquillity. *n.*

plack et (plak/it), an opening or slit in a garment, especially at the top of a skirt, to make it easy to put on. *n.*

pla gia rism (plā/jə riz/əm), act of plagiarizing. *n.*

pla giar ist (plā/jər ist), person who plagiarizes. *n.*

pla gia rize (plā/jə rīz/), take and use as one's own (the thoughts, writings, etc., of another), especially to take and use (a passage, plot, etc.) from the work of another writer. *v.,* **pla gia rized, pla gia riz ing.**

plague (plāg), **1** a very dangerous disease that spreads rapidly and often causes death. It occurs in several forms, one of which is bubonic plague. **2** any epidemic disease; pestilence. **3** punishment thought to be sent from God. **4** cause to suffer from a plague. **5** thing or person that torments, vexes, annoys, troubles, offends, or is disagreeable. **6** vex; annoy; bother: *The people of the colony were plagued with high taxes.* 1-3,5 *n.,* 4,6 *v.,* **plagued, pla guing.** —**pla/guer,** *n.*

pla guy or **pla guey** (plā/gē), INFORMAL. **1** troublesome; annoying. **2** annoyingly. 1 *adj.,* 2 *adv.*

plaice (plās), **1** a European flatfish that is important for food. **2** any of various American flatfishes or flounders. *n., pl.* **plaice** or **plaic es.**

Pronunciation key

a hat	**i** it	**oi** oil	**ch** child		a in about	
ā age	**ī** ice	**ou** out	**ng** long		e in taken	
ä far	**o** hot	**u** cup	**sh** she	ə =	i in pencil	
e let	**ō** open	**u̇** put	**th** thin		o in lemon	
ē equal	**ô** order	**ü** rule	**ᴛʜ** then		u in circus	
ėr term			**zh** measure			

plaid (plad), **1** a long piece of woolen cloth, usually having a pattern of checks or stripes in many colors, worn over one shoulder by the Scottish Highlanders. **2** any cloth with a pattern of checks or crisscross stripes. **3** a pattern of this kind. **4** having a pattern of checks or crisscross stripes: *a plaid dress.* 1-3 *n.,* 4 *adj.*

plain (plān), **1** easy to understand; easily seen or heard; clear: *The meaning is plain.* **2** in a plain manner; clearly. **3** without ornament or decoration; simple: *a plain dress.* **4** without figured pattern, varied weave, or variegated color: *a plain blue fabric.* **5** not rich or highly seasoned: *plain food.* **6** common; ordinary; simple in manner: *They were plain, hard-working people.* **7** not pretty or handsome. **8** frank; honest; sincere: *plain speech.* **9** flat; level; smooth: *plain ground.* **10** a flat stretch of land; prairie: *Cattle and horses wandered over the plains.* 1,3-9 *adj.,* 2 *adv.,* 10 *n.* —**plain′ly,** *adv.* —**plain′ness,** *n.*

plains man (plānz′mən), person who lives on the plains. *n., pl.* **plains men.**

plain-spo ken (plān′spō′kən), plain or frank in speech. *adj.*

plaint (plānt), **1** complaint. **2** OLD USE. lament. *n.*

plain tiff (plān′tif), person who begins a lawsuit: *The plaintiff accused the defendant of fraud. n.*

plain tive (plān′tiv), mournful; sad: *a plaintive song. adj.* —**plain′tive ly,** *adv.* —**plain′tive ness,** *n.*

plait (plāt *or* plat), **1** a braid of hair, ribbon, etc.: *She wore her hair in a plait.* **2** to braid: *She plaits her hair.* **3** a pleat. **4** to pleat. 1,3 *n.,* 2,4 *v.*

plan (plan), **1** way of making or doing something that has been worked out beforehand; scheme of action: *Our summer plans were upset by Dad's illness.* **2** think out beforehand how (something) is to be made or done; design, scheme, or devise: *plan a trip.* **3** have in mind as a purpose; intend. **4** a drawing or diagram to show how a garden, a floor of a house, etc., is arranged. **5** make a drawing or diagram of. 1,4 *n.,* 2,3,5 *v.,* **planned, planning.**

plane[1] (plān), **1** any flat or level surface. **2** flat; level. **3** level; grade: *Try to keep your work on a high plane.* **4** airplane. **5** surface such that if any two points on it are joined by a straight line, the line will be contained wholly in the surface. **6** of or having to do with figures wholly in a plane: *plane geometry.* 1,3-5 *n.,* 2,6 *adj.*

plane[2] (plān), **1** tool with a blade for smoothing or shaping wood. **2** smooth (wood) with a plane. **3** remove with a plane. 1 *n.,* 2,3 *v.,* **planed, planing.**

plan er (plā′nər), person or thing that planes, especially a machine for planing wood or for finishing flat surfaces on metal. *n.*

plan et (plan′it), **1** one of the heavenly bodies (except comets and meteors) that move around the sun in nearly circular paths. Mercury, Venus, the earth, Mars, Jupiter, Saturn, Uranus, Neptune, and Pluto are planets. **2** any similar body revolving around a star other than the sun. *n.* [*Planet* came into English about 700 years ago from French *planete,* and can be traced back to Greek *planasthai,* meaning "to wander."] —**plan′et like′,** *adj.*

plan e tar i um (plan′ə ter′ē əm *or* plan′ə tar′ē əm), **1** apparatus that shows the movements of the sun, moon, planets, and stars by projecting lights on the inside of a dome. **2** room or building with such an apparatus. *n., pl.* **plan e tar i ums, plan e tar i a** (plan′ə ter′ē ə *or* plan′ə tar′ē ə).

plan e tar y (plan′ə ter′ē), of a planet. *adj.*

plan et oid (plan′ə toid), asteroid. *n.*

plane tree, the sycamore tree of America.

plank (plangk), **1** a long, flat piece of sawed timber thicker than a board. **2** cover or furnish with planks. **3** cook on a board: *Steak is sometimes planked.* **4** article or

plaid (def. 1)

feature of the platform of a political party or other organization. 1,4 *n.,* 2,3 *v.*

plank down, INFORMAL. put down or pay then and there: *He planked down the package. She planked down her money.*

walk the plank, be put to death by being forced to walk off a plank extending from a ship's side over the water. Pirates used to make their prisoners do this.

plank ton (plangk′tən), the small animal and plant organisms that float or drift in water, especially at or near the surface. *n.* [*Plankton* comes from German *Plankton,* and can be traced back to Greek *plazesthai,* meaning "to wander, drift."]

plan ner (plan′ər), person who plans. *n.*

plant (plant), **1** any living thing that is not an animal. Plants lack a nervous system and sense organs, and are unable to move about by themselves. Plants containing chlorophyll manufacture their own food. Trees, shrubs, herbs, fungi, algae, etc., are plants. **2** a living thing that has leaves, roots, and a soft stem, and is small in contrast with a tree or shrub: *a tomato plant, a house plant.* **3** put or set in the ground to grow: *She planted sunflower seeds in the backyard.* **4** furnish; stock; put seed in: *He planted his garden with beans.* **5** set firmly; put; place: *The boy planted his feet far apart.* **6** establish or set up (a colony, city, etc.); settle. **7** put in or instill (principles, doctrines, ideas, etc.): *Parents try to plant ideals in their children.* **8** the buildings, machinery, etc., used in manufacturing some article. 1,2,8 *n.,* 3-7 *v.* —**plant′like′,** *adj.*

Plan tag e net (plan taj′ə nit), member of the royal family that ruled England from 1154 to 1485. *n.*

plan tain[1] (plan′tən), **1** kind of large banana. **2** plant that it grows on. *n.*

plan tain[2] (plan′tən), a common weed with large, spreading leaves close to the ground and long, slender spikes carrying flowers and seeds. *n.*

plan ta tion (plan tā′shən), **1** a large farm or estate, especially in a tropical or semitropical region, on which cotton, tobacco, sugar cane, rubber trees, etc., are grown. The work on a plantation is done by laborers who live there. **2** a large group of trees or other plants that have been planted: *a rubber plantation. n.*

plant er (plan′tər), **1** person who owns or runs a plantation. **2** machine for planting: *a corn planter.* **3** person who plants. **4** a box, stand, or other holder, usually decorative, for plants. *n.*

plant louse, aphid.

plaque (plak), **1** an ornamental tablet of metal, porcelain, etc. **2** a platelike ornament or badge. **3** a thin film of saliva and food particles which forms on the surface of the teeth. *n.*

plash (plash), splash. *v., n.*

plasm (plaz′əm), plasma. *n.*

plas ma (plaz′mə), the clear, almost colorless, liquid part of blood or lymph, in which the corpuscles or blood cells float. *n.*

plas ter (plas′tər), **1** a soft mixture of lime, sand, and water that hardens as it dries, used for covering walls or ceilings. **2** cover (walls, ceilings, etc.) with plaster. **3** spread with anything thickly: *Her shoes were plastered with mud.* **4** make smooth and flat: *He plastered his hair down.* **5** a medical preparation consisting of some substance spread on cloth, that will stick to the body and protect cuts, relieve pain, etc. 1,5 *n.*, 2-4 *v.* —**plas′ter like′**, *adj.*

plas ter board (plas′tər bôrd′), a large, flat board made of a layer of plaster between two layers of heavy paper and used to cover walls and partitions. *n.*

plas ter er (plas′tər ər), person who plasters walls, etc. *n.*

plas ter ing (plas′tər ing), covering of plaster on walls, etc. *n.*

plaster of Paris, mixture of powdered gypsum and water, which hardens quickly. It is used for making molds, cheap statuary, casts, etc.

plas tic (plas′tik), **1** any of a large group of substances made chemically from materials such as coal, water, and limestone, and molded by heat, pressure, etc., into various forms, such as sheets, fibers, and bottles. Nylon, vinyl, and many cellulose products are plastics. **2** made of plastic: *a plastic bottle.* **3** easily molded or shaped: *Clay, wax, and plaster are plastic substances.* **4** molding or giving shape to material: *Sculpture is a plastic art.* 1 *n.*, 2-4 *adj.* —**plas′ti cal ly**, *adv.*

plas tic i ty (pla stis′ə tē), plastic quality. *n.*

plas ti cize (plas′tə sīz), make or become plastic. *v.*, **plas ti cized, plas ti ciz ing.**

plastic surgery, surgery that restores or improves the outer appearance of the body. —**plastic surgeon.**

plat (plat), **1** a map, chart, or plan. **2** map out in detail; chart; plan. **3** a small piece of ground; plot. 1,3 *n.*, 2 *v.*, **plat ted, plat ting.**

plate (plāt), **1** dish, usually round, that is almost flat. Our food is served on plates. **2** contents of such a dish: *a small plate of stew.* **3** something having the shape of a plate: *A plate is passed in church to receive the collection.* **4** dishes and food served to one person at a meal. **5** dishes and utensils made of or covered with a thin layer of silver or gold. **6** cover with a thin layer of silver, gold, or other metal. **7** a thin, flat sheet or piece of metal: *The warship was covered with steel plates.* **8** cover with metal plates for protection. **9** a thin, flat piece of metal on which something is engraved. Plates are used for printing pictures. **10** something printed from such a piece of metal, especially a full-page illustration printed on special paper. **11** a metal copy of a page of type. **12** a thin sheet of glass or metal coated with chemicals that

platitude (def. 1)
There, my good man, a penny— and mind you don't spend it— **a penny saved is a penny earned.**

are sensitive to light. Plates are sometimes used in taking photographs. **13** piece of metal, plastic, or other firm material with false teeth set into it. **14 the plate,** home plate. **15** a thin cut of beef from the lower end of the ribs. **16** the positive electrode in a vacuum tube. 1-5,7,9-16 *n.*, 6,8 *v.*, **plat ed, plat ing.** [*Plate* came into English about 700 years ago from French *plate*, originally meaning "flat," and can be traced back to Greek *platys*, meaning "broad, flat." See **Word Family.**] —**plate′ like′**, *adj.*

plate

Below are words related to *plate*. They can all be traced back to the Greek word *platys* (plä tüs′), meaning "broad, flat."

commonplace	plaice	platitude
displace	plateau	platter
misplace	platform	platypus
piazza	platinum	plaza
place		

pla teau (pla tō′), **1** plain in the mountains or at a height considerably above sea level; large, high plain; tableland. **2** a level, especially the level at which something is stabilized for a period. *n.*, *pl.* **pla teaus, pla teaux** (pla tōz′).

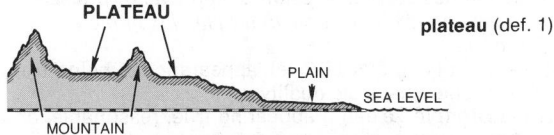

PLATEAU

PLAIN

SEA LEVEL

MOUNTAIN

plateau (def. 1)

plate ful (plāt′fu̇l), as much as a plate will hold. *n.*, *pl.* **plate fuls.**

plate glass, thick and very clear glass made in smooth, polished sheets, used for large windowpanes, mirrors, etc.

plate let (plāt′lit), one of many small disks which float in the blood plasma and are involved in blood clotting. *n.*

plat form (plat′fôrm), **1** a raised level surface. There usually is a platform beside the track at a railroad station. A hall usually has a platform for speakers. **2** plan of action or statement of principles of a group. A political party has a platform made up of planks. *n.*

plat ing (plā′ting), a thin layer of silver, gold, or other metal. *n.*

plat i num (plat′n əm), a heavy, silver-white, metallic element with a very high melting point. Platinum is a precious metal which is resistant to acid and does not tarnish easily. It is used in chemical and industrial equipment and in jewelry. *n.*

plat i tude (plat′ə tüd *or* plat′ə tyüd), **1** a dull or commonplace remark, especially one given out solemnly as if it were fresh and important: *"Better late than never" is a platitude.* **2** flatness; triteness; dullness. *n.*

Pla to (plā′tō), 427?-347? B.C., Greek philosopher who was the pupil of Socrates and the teacher of Aristotle. *n.*

Pla ton ic (plə ton′ik), **1** of or having to do with Plato or his philosophy. **2** Also, **platonic.** friendly but not like a lover. *adj.* —**pla ton′i cal ly,** *adv.*

pla toon (plə tün′), **1** a military unit made up of two or more squads, usually commanded by a lieutenant. Several platoons make up a company. **2** a small group. *n.*

Platte (plat), river flowing from central Nebraska into the Missouri River. *n.*

plat ter (plat′ər), a large, shallow dish for holding or serving food, especially meat and fish. *n.*

plat y pus (plat′ə pəs), a small water mammal of Australia and Tasmania that lays eggs and has webbed feet and a bill somewhat like a duck's; duckbilled platypus. *n., pl.* **plat y pus es, plat y pi** (plat′ə pī).

WORD HISTORY

platypus

Platypus is from Greek *platypous,* meaning "flat-footed," which comes from *platys,* meaning "broad, flat," and *pous,* meaning "foot." The animal was called this because its webbed feet are broad.

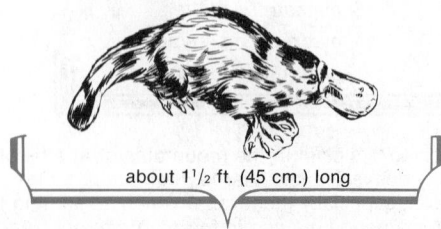

about 1½ ft. (45 cm.) long

plau dit (plô′dit). Usually, **plaudits,** *pl.* round of applause; enthusiastic expression of approval or praise: *The actress bowed in response to the plaudits of the audience. n.*

plau si bil i ty (plô′zə bil′ə tē), appearance of being true or reasonable; plausible quality. *n.*

plau si ble (plô′zə bəl), **1** appearing true, reasonable, or fair. **2** apparently worthy of confidence but often not really so: *a plausible liar. adj.* —**plau′si bly,** *adv.*

play (plā), **1** something done to amuse oneself; fun; sport; recreation: *The children are happy at play.* **2** have fun; do something in sport: *The kitten plays with its tail. He played a joke on his sister.* **3** take part in (a game): *Children play tag and ball.* **4** take part in a game against: *Our team played the sixth-grade team.* **5** a turn, move, or act in a game: *It is your play next.* **6** put into action in a game: *Play your ten of hearts.* **7** act of carrying on a game: *Play was slow in the first half of the game.* **8** a story written for or presented as a dramatic performance; drama: *"Peter Pan" is a charming play.* **9** act a part; act the part of (a character in a play, etc.). **10** act in a specified way: *play sick, play fair, play the fool.* **11** action; operation; working: *foul play, fair play. They brought all their strength into play to move the rock.* **12** make believe; pretend in fun: *Let's play the hammock is a boat.* **13** make music; produce (music) on an instrument. **14** perform on (a musical instrument): *play a piano.* **15** cause to produce recorded or broadcast sound: *play a record, play the radio.* **16** move lightly or quickly: *A breeze played on the water.* **17** a light, quick movement: *the play of sunlight on leaves, the play of color in an opal.* **18** freedom for action,

movement, etc.: *The children gave their fancies full play in telling what they could do with a million dollars.* **19** cause to act, move, or work; direct (on, over, along): *play a hose on a burning building.* **20** act carelessly; do foolish things: *Don't play with matches.* **21** gambling. **22** gamble or bet on: *He plays the horses.* 1,5,7,8,11,17,18,21 *n.*, 2-4,6,9,10,12-16,19,20,22 *v.*

play down, make light of; understate.

played out, 1 exhausted. **2** finished; done with.

play off, 1 play an additional game or match in order to decide (a draw or tie). **2** pit (one person or thing against another), especially for one's own advantage.

play on or **play upon,** take advantage of; make use of: *We played on our friend's good nature, too often making her the victim of our jokes.*

play out, play to the end; bring to an end.

play up, make the most of; exploit.

play up to, INFORMAL. try to get the favor of; flatter: *play up to a celebrity.*

play a ble (plā′ə bəl), **1** able to be played. **2** fit to be played on. *adj.*

play bill (plā′bil′), **1** a handbill or placard announcing a play. **2** program of a play. *n.*

play boy (plā′boi′), man whose chief interest is in having a good time. *n.*

play er (plā′ər), **1** person who plays. **2** actor in a theater. **3** musician. **4** thing or device that plays. *n.*

player piano, piano played by machinery, rather than by a person.

play fel low (plā′fel′ō), playmate. *n.*

play ful (plā′fəl), **1** full of fun; fond of playing: *a playful puppy.* **2** joking; not serious: *a playful remark. adj.* —**play′ful ly,** *adv.* —**play′ful ness,** *n.*

play go er (plā′gō′ər), person who goes often to the theater. *n.*

play ground (plā′ground′), place for outdoor play. *n.*

play house (plā′hous′), **1** a small house for a child to play in. **2** dollhouse. **3** theater. *n., pl.* **play hous es** (plā′hou′ziz).

playing card, card used in playing games like bridge, poker, and pinochle, usually being one of a set of 52 cards including 4 suits (spades, hearts, diamonds, and clubs) of 13 cards each.

play let (plā′lit), a short play. *n.*

play mate (plā′māt′), person who plays with another. *n.*

play-off (plā′ôf′), an extra game or round played to settle a tie. *n.*

play on words, pun.

play pen (plā′pen′), a small folding pen for a baby or young child to play in. *n.*

play room (plā′rüm′ or plā′rùm′), room for children to play in. *n.*

play thing (plā′thing′), thing to play with; toy. *n.*

play time (plā′tīm′), time for playing. *n.*

play wright (plā′rīt′), writer of plays; dramatist. *n.*

plaz a (plaz′ə or plä′zə), a public square in a city or town. *n., pl.* **plaz as.** [*Plaza* was borrowed from Spanish *plaza,* which came from Latin *platea,* meaning "broad street," and can be traced back to Greek *platys,* meaning "broad, flat."]

plea (plē), **1** request or appeal; an asking: *a plea for help.* **2** an excuse or defense: *The man's plea was that he did not see the signal.* **3** answer made by a defendant to a charge in a court of law. *n.*

plead (plēd), **1** offer reasons for or against; argue. **2** ask earnestly; make an earnest appeal: *When the rent was due, the poor family pleaded for more time.* **3** offer as an excuse: *The woman who stole pleaded poverty.* **4** speak for or against in a court of law: *He had a good lawyer to plead his case.* **5** answer to a charge in a court of law:

The defendant pleaded guilty. v., **plead ed** or **pled, plead-ing.** —**plead′a ble,** adj. —**plead′ing ly,** adv.

plead er (plē′dər), person who pleads, especially in a court of law. n.

pleas ant (plez′nt), **1** that pleases; giving pleasure; agreeable: *a pleasant swim on a hot day.* **2** easy to get along with; friendly. **3** fair; not stormy. adj. —**pleas′ant ly,** adv. —**pleas′ant ness,** n.

pleas ant ry (plez′n trē), **1** a good-natured joke; witty remark. **2** joking. n., pl. **pleas ant ries.**

please (plēz), **1** be agreeable to: *Toys please children.* **2** be agreeable: *Such a fine meal cannot fail to please.* **3** wish; think fit: *Do what you please.* **4** be the will of: *May it please the court to show mercy.* **5** be so kind as to (now used merely as a polite addition to requests or commands): *Please come here.* v., **pleased, pleas ing.**

be pleased, 1 be moved to pleasure. **2** be disposed; like; choose.

if you please, if you like; with your permission.

pleas ing (plē′zing), giving pleasure; pleasant: *a pleasing smile, a very well-mannered and pleasing young person.* adj. —**pleas′ing ly,** adv. —**pleas′ing ness,** n.

pleas ur a ble (plezh′ər ə bəl), pleasant; agreeable. adj. —**pleas′ur a ble ness,** n. —**pleas′ur a bly,** adv.

pleas ure (plezh′ər), **1** a feeling of being pleased; enjoyment; delight; joy: *The child's pleasure in the gift was good to see.* **2** something that pleases; cause of joy or delight: *It would be a pleasure to see you again.* **3** anything that amuses; sport; play: *She takes her pleasure in riding and hunting.* **4** one's will, desire, or choice: *What is your pleasure in this matter?* n.

pleat (plēt), **1** a flat, usually narrow, fold made in cloth by doubling it on itself. **2** fold or arrange in pleats: *a pleated skirt.* **1** n., **2** v. —**pleat′er,** n.

ple be ian (pli bē′ən), **1** of the common people; common; vulgar. **2** one of the common people. **3** of the lower class of citizens in ancient Rome. **4** member of this class. **1,3** adj., **2,4** n. [Plebeian is from Latin *plebeius,* which comes from *plebs,* meaning "the common people."]

pleb i scite (pleb′ə sīt), a direct vote by the qualified voters of a country, state, etc., on some important question. n.

plec trum (plek′trəm), a small piece of plastic, metal, etc., used for plucking the strings of a guitar, mandolin, etc.; pick. n., pl. **plec trums, plec tra** (plek′trə).

pled (pled), pleaded; a past tense and past participle of **plead.** v.

pledge (plej), **1** a solemn promise: *They made a pledge to give money to charity.* **2** promise solemnly: *We pledge allegiance to the flag.* **3** cause to promise solemnly; bind by a promise: *pledge hearers to secrecy.* **4** something given to another as a guarantee of good faith or of a future action; security: *She left the jewelry as a pledge for the loan.* **5** give as security. **6** condition of being held as security: *jewelry put in pledge.* **7** drink a health to; drink in honor of (someone) and wish (that person) well: *The nobles rose from the banquet table to pledge the queen.* **8** the drinking of a health or toast. **9** something given to show favor or love, or as a promise of something to come; sign; token. **1,4,6,8,9** n., **2,3,5,7** v., **pledged, pledg ing.** —**pledg′er, pledg′or,** n.

Ple ia des (plē′ə dēz′), cluster of several hundred stars in the constellation Taurus. Six of these stars can normally be seen with the naked eye. n.pl.

ple nar y (plē′nər ē or plen′ər ē), not lacking in any way; full; complete; absolute: *an ambassador with plenary power.* adj.

plen i po ten ti ar y (plen′ə pə ten′shē er′ē), **1** a diplomatic agent having full power or authority. **2** having or

a hat	i it	oi oil	ch child	a in about
ā age	ī ice	ou out	ng long	e in taken
ä far	o hot	u cup	sh she	ə = { i in pencil
e let	ō open	u̇ put	th thin	o in lemon
ē equal	ô order	ü rule	ᵺ then	u in circus
ėr term			zh measure	

giving full power and authority. The United States has either an ambassador or a minister plenipotentiary in every important foreign country. **1** n., **plen i po ten ti ar ies; 2** adj.

plen i tude (plen′ə tüd or plen′ə tyüd), fullness; completeness; abundance. n.

plen te ous (plen′tē əs), plentiful. adj. —**plen′te ous ly,** adv. —**plen′te ous ness,** n.

plen ti ful (plen′ti fəl), more than enough; ample; abundant: *a plentiful supply of food.* adj. —**plen′ti ful ly,** adv. —**plen′ti ful ness,** n.

plen ty (plen′tē), **1** a full supply; all that one needs; a large enough number or quantity: *You have plenty of time to catch the train.* **2** quality or condition of being plentiful; abundance: *years of peace and plenty.* n.

plesiosaur—about 50 ft. (15 m.) long

ple si o saur (plē′sē ə sôr′), any of an order of large sea reptiles of the Mesozoic era, now extinct, that had a long neck and flippers instead of legs. n.

pleth or a (pleth′ər ə), excessive fullness; too much; superabundance: *a plethora of words, a plethora of food.* n.

pleu ra (plu̇r′ə), a thin membrane covering each lung and lining the chest cavity. n., pl. **pleur ae** (plu̇r′ē).

pleur al (plu̇r′əl), of the pleura. adj.

pleur i sy (plu̇r′ə sē), inflammation of the pleura, often marked by fever, chest pains, and difficulty in breathing. n.

plex us (plek′səs), network of nerve fibers or blood vessels. The solar plexus is a collection of nerves behind the stomach. n., pl. **plex us es** or **plex us.**

pli a bil i ty (plī′ə bil′ə tē), pliable condition or quality. n.

pli a ble (plī′ə bəl), **1** easily bent; flexible; supple: *Willow twigs are pliable.* **2** easily influenced; yielding: *He is too pliable to be a good leader.* adj. —**pli′a ble ness,** n.

pli an cy (plī′ən sē), pliant condition or quality. n.

pli ant (plī′ənt), **1** bending easily; flexible; supple: *pliant leather.* **2** easily influenced; yielding: *a pliant nature.* **3** changing easily to fit different conditions; adaptable. adj. —**pli′ant ly,** adv.

pli ers (plī′ərz), small pincers with long jaws for bending or cutting wire, holding small objects, etc. n. pl. or sing.

plight[1] (plīt), condition or situation, usually bad: *He was in a sad plight when he became ill and had no money.* n.

plight[2] (plīt), promise solemnly; pledge: *plight one's loyalty.* v.

plinth (plinth), **1** the lower, square part of the base of a column. **2** a square base of a pedestal. n.

plod (plod), **1** walk heavily; trudge: *The hikers plodded wearily along the road.* **2** proceed in a slow or dull way; work patiently with effort: *I plodded away at the lessons until I learned them.* *v.,* **plod ded, plod ding.**

plod der (plod′ər), person who plods, especially one who works hard but slowly. *n.*

plop (plop), **1** sound like that of a flat object striking water without a splash. **2** make such a sound. 1 *n.,* 2 *v.,* **plopped, plop ping.** [*Plop* comes from an imitation of the sound.]

plot (plot), **1** a secret plan, especially to do something wrong: *They formed a plot to rob the bank.* **2** plan secretly with others; plan: *The rebels plotted against the government.* **3** plan or main story of a play, novel, poem, etc.: *I like plots filled with action and adventure.* **4** a small piece of ground: *a garden plot.* **5** map; diagram. **6** make a map or diagram of: *The pilot plotted the plane's course.* **7** mark the position of (something) on a map or diagram: *The nurse plotted the patient's temperature on a chart over several days.* 1,3-5 *n.,* 2,6,7 *v.,* **plot ted, plot ting.**

plot ter (plot′ər), **1** person who plots. **2** an electronic device that draws pictures or diagrams on paper, controlled by a computer. *n.*

plough (plou), plow. *n., v.*

plough boy (plou′boi′), plowboy. *n.*

plough man (plou′mən), plowman. *n., pl.* **plough men.**

plough share (plou′sher′ or plou′shar′), plowshare. *n.*

plov er (pluv′ər or plō′vər), a shore bird with a short tail and bill, and long, pointed wings. *n., pl.* **plov ers** or **plov er.**

WORD HISTORY

plover

Plover came into English about 650 years ago from French *plover,* and can be traced back to Latin *pluere,* meaning "to rain." The bird may have been called this because its cry is supposed to indicate the approach of rain.

plow (plou), **1** a farm implement used for cutting the soil and turning it over. **2** turn up the soil of with a plow: *plow a field.* **3** snowplow. **4** use a plow. **5** move through anything as a plow does; advance slowly and with effort: *The ship plowed through the waves.* 1,3 *n.,* 2,4,5 *v.* Also, **plough.** —**plow′a ble,** *adj.* —**plow′er,** *n.*

plow boy (plou′boi′), boy who guides a plow or the horses drawing a plow. *n.* Also, **ploughboy.**

plow man (plou′mən), **1** person who guides a plow. **2** a farm worker. *n., pl.* **plowmen.** Also, **ploughman.**

plow share (plou′sher′ or plou′shar′), blade of a plow; the part of a plow that cuts the soil. *n.* Also, **plough-share.**

pluck (pluk), **1** pull off; pick: *He plucked flowers in the garden.* **2** pull at; pull; tug; jerk: *She plucked at the loose threads of her coat.* **3** act of picking or pulling. **4** pull on (the strings of a musical instrument). **5** pull off the feathers or hair from: *pluck a chicken.* **6** courage: *The cat showed pluck in fighting the dog.* 1,2,4,5 *v.,* 3,6 *n.*

pluck i ly (pluk′ə lē), in a plucky manner; with courage or spirit. *adv.*

pluck i ness (pluk′ē nis), character of being plucky; pluck; courage. *n.*

pluck y (pluk′ē), having or showing courage: *a plucky dog. adj.,* **pluck i er, pluck i est.**

plug (plug), **1** piece of wood or other substance used to stop up a hole. **2** stop up or fill with a plug. **3** device to make an electrical connection. Some plugs screw into sockets; others have prongs. **4** spark plug. **5** cake of pressed tobacco; piece of this cut off for chewing. **6** SLANG. hit; shoot. **7** INFORMAL. work steadily; plod: *We plugged away at our typewriters.* **8** INFORMAL. recommend or advertise, especially on a radio or television program: *plug a new product.* **9** INFORMAL. advertisement or recommendation, especially on a radio or television program. **10** INFORMAL. a worn-out or inferior horse. 1,3-5,9,10 *n.,* 2,6-8 *v.,* **plugged, plug ging.** —**plug′ger,** *n.*

plug in, make an electrical connection by inserting a plug.

plum (plum), **1** a roundish, juicy fruit with a smooth skin and a stone or pit. Plums grow on trees. There are purple, red, green, and yellow plums. **2** raisin in a pudding, cake, etc. **3** something very good or desirable: *Her new job is a fine plum.* **4** a dark, bluish purple. **5** dark bluish-purple. 1-4 *n.,* 5 *adj.* —**plum′like′,** *adj.*

plum age (plü′mij), feathers of a bird: *A parrot has bright plumage. n.*

plumb (plum), **1** a small weight hung on the end of a line, used to find the depth of water or to see if a wall is vertical; lead. **2** to test or adjust by a plumb line; sound: *Our line was not long enough to plumb the depths of the lake.* **3** vertical. **4** get to the bottom of: *No one could plumb the deep mystery.* **5** INFORMAL. completely; thoroughly: *That horse is plumb worn out.* 1 *n.,* 2,4 *v.,* 3 *adj.,* 5 *adv.* [*Plumb* came into English about 700 years ago, and can be traced back to Latin *plumbum,* meaning "lead (the element)."]

out of plumb or **off plumb,** not vertical.

plumb, out of plumb
This bell tower is **out of plumb.**

plumb er (plum′ər), person whose work is putting in and repairing water pipes and fixtures in buildings: *When the water pipe froze, we sent for a plumber. n.*

plumb ing (plum′ing), **1** work or trade of a plumber. **2** the water pipes and fixtures in a building: *bathroom plumbing. n.*

plumb line, line with a plumb at the end, used to find the depth of water or to see if a wall is vertical.

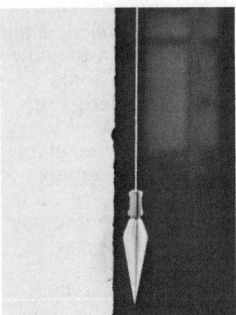

plumb line

plume (plüm), **1** a large, long feather; feather. **2** a feather, bunch of feathers, or tuft of hair worn as an ornament on a hat, helmet, etc. **3** furnish with plumes. **4** smooth or arrange the feathers of: *The eagle plumed its wing.* 1,2 *n.,* 3,4 *v.,* **plumed, plum ing.**

plum met (plum′it), plunge; drop: *to plummet into the sea. v.*

plump[1] (plump), **1** pleasantly round and full: *plump cheeks.* **2** make or become plump: *Plump the pillows on your bed.* 1 *adj.,* 2 *v.* —**plump′ness,** *n.*

plump[2] (plump), **1** fall or drop heavily or suddenly: *All out of breath, she plumped down on a chair.* **2** a sudden plunge; heavy fall. **3** sound made by a plunge or fall. **4** heavily or suddenly: *He ran plump into me.* 1 *v.,* 2,3 *n.,* 4 *adv.*
   plump for, give one's complete support to; champion vigorously: *plump for lower taxes.*

plum pudding, a rich, boiled or steamed pudding containing raisins, currants, spices, etc.

plum y (plü′mē), **1** having plumes or feathers. **2** adorned with a plume or plumes. **3** like a plume; feathery. *adj.*

plun der (plun′dər), **1** rob by force: *The pirates entered the harbor and began to plunder the town.* **2** things taken in plundering; booty; loot: *They carried off the plunder in their ships.* **3** act of robbing by force: *In olden times soldiers often gained great wealth by plunder of a conquered city.* 1 *v.,* 2,3 *n.* [*Plunder* comes from German *plündern.*] —**plun′der er,** *n.*

plunge (plunj), **1** throw or thrust with force into a liquid, place, or condition: *plunge one's hand into water, plunge the world into war.* **2** throw oneself (into water, danger, a fight, etc.): *She plunged into the lake to save the drowning swimmer.* **3** rush; dash: *The runner plunged ahead five yards.* **4** a jump or thrust; a dive: *a sudden plunge into the sea.* **5** pitch suddenly and violently: *The ship plunged about in the storm.* 1-3,5 *v.,* **plunged, plung ing;** 4 *n.*

plung er (plun′jər), **1** person or thing that plunges. **2** part of a machine, such as a piston in a pump, that acts with a plunging motion. **3** a rubber suction cup on a long stick, used for unplugging drains and toilets that are stopped up. *n.*

plunk (plungk), **1** pluck (a banjo, guitar, etc.). **2** make a sudden twanging sound like the plucking of a stringed musical instrument; twang. **3** put, drop, etc., heavily or suddenly. **4** act or sound of plunking. 1-3 *v.,* 4 *n.*

plur., plural.

plur al (plùr′əl), **1** more than one in number: *"Girl" is singular; "girls" is plural.* **2** showing more than one in number: *the plural ending -s, the plural noun "fishes."* **3** the plural number in grammar. *Books* is the plural of *book; men,* of *man; are,* of *is; we,* of *I; these,* of *this.* **4** a word in the plural number. 1,2 *adj.,* 3,4 *n.*

plu ral i ty (plù ral′ə tē), **1** difference between the number of votes received by the winner of an election and the number received by the next highest candidate. **2** the greater number; the majority. **3** state or fact of being plural. *n., pl.* **plu ral i ties.**

plur al ize (plùr′ə līz), make plural; express in the plural form. *v.,* **plur al ized, plur al iz ing.** —**plur′al i za′tion,** *n.*

plur al ly (plùr′ə lē), in the plural number; so as to express or imply more than one. *adv.*

plus (plus), **1** added to: *3 plus 2 equals 5.* **2** and also: *The work of an engineer requires intelligence plus experience.* **3** and more: *a grade average of B plus.* **4** plus sign. **5** INFORMAL. additional; extra: *a plus value.* 1,2 *prep.,* 3,5 *adj.,* 4 *n.*

plush (plush), **1** fabric like velvet but thicker and softer. **2** INFORMAL. luxurious; expensive; stylish: *a plush office.* 1 *n.,* 2 *adj.*

a hat	i it	oi oil	ch child	⎧ a in about
ā age	ī ice	ou out	ng long	⎪ e in taken
ä far	o hot	u cup	sh she	ə = ⎨ i in pencil
e let	ō open	u̇ put	th thin	⎪ o in lemon
ē equal	ô order	ü rule	ᵀʜ then	⎩ u in circus
ėr term			zh measure	

plush y (plush′ē), of or like plush. *adj.,* **plush i er, plush i est.**

plus sign, the sign (+), indicating that the number or quantity following is to be added, or is a positive number or quantity.

Plu to (plü′tō), **1** (in Greek and Roman myths) the god of the region of the dead. **2** the eighth largest planet in the solar system and the farthest from the sun. *n.*

plu toc ra cy (plü tok′rə sē), **1** government in which the rich rule. **2** a ruling class of wealthy people. *n., pl.* **plu toc ra cies.**

plu to crat (plü′tə krat), **1** person who has power or influence because of wealth. **2** a wealthy person. *n.*

plu to ni um (plü tō′nē əm), a radioactive metallic element produced artificially from uranium and found in minute quantities in pitchblende and other uranium ores. It is used as a source of energy in nuclear reactors and bombs. *n.*

plu vi al (plü′vē əl), **1** of rain. **2** caused by rain. *adj.*

ply[1] (plī), **1** work with; use: *The dressmaker plies her needle.* **2** keep up work on; work away at or on: *to ply one's trade. We plied the water with our oars.* **3** urge again and again: *She plied me with questions to make me tell her what was in the package.* **4** supply with in a pressing manner: *ply a person with food or drink. v.,* **plied, ply ing.**

ply[2] (plī), thickness, fold, or twist. *n., pl.* **plies.**

Plym outh (plim′əth), **1** seaport in SW England, on the English Channel. **2** town in SE Massachusetts. *n.*

Plymouth Colony, the settlement established by the Pilgrims in 1620, on the site of Plymouth, Massachusetts.

Plymouth Rock, 1 rock at Plymouth, Massachusetts, on which the Pilgrims are said to have landed in 1620. **2** an American breed of chicken kept for the production of meat and eggs.

ply wood (plī′wùd′), board or boards made of several thin layers of wood glued together. *n.*

Pm, symbol for promethium.

p.m. or **P.M.,** the time from noon to midnight: *School ends at 3 p.m.* [The abbreviations *p.m.* and *P.M.* stand for the Latin phrase *post meridiem,* meaning "after noon."]

pneu mat ic (nü mat′ik *or* nyü mat′ik), **1** filled with air; containing air: *a pneumatic tire.* **2** worked by air: *a pneumatic drill.* **3** of air and other gases. *adj.*

pneu mo nia (nü mō′nyə *or* nyü mō′nyə), an infectious disease that causes inflammation of the lungs and often a high fever and a hard, dry cough. It often follows a bad cold or other disease. Pneumonia in both lungs is called **double pneumonia.** *n.*

Po (pō), river flowing from NW Italy into the Adriatic Sea. See **Rhine** for map. *n.*

Po, symbol for polonium.

P.O. or **p.o.,** post office.

poach[1] (pōch), **1** trespass on (another's land), especially to hunt or fish. **2** take (game or fish) without any right. *v.*

poach[2] (pōch), cook (an egg) by breaking it into gently boiling water. *v.*

poach er (pō′chər), person who hunts or fishes on another's land without any right. *n.*

Po ca hon tas (pō′kə hon′təs), 1595?-1617, American Indian who in her childhood is said to have saved the life of Captain John Smith. *n.*

pock (pok), pimple, mark, or pit on the skin, caused by smallpox and certain other diseases. *n.*

pock et (pok′it), **1** a small bag sewed into clothing for carrying money or other small articles. **2** put in one's pocket. **3** meant to be carried in a pocket: *a pocket handkerchief.* **4** small enough to go in a pocket: *a pocket camera.* **5** a hollow place; enclosed place: *a pocket of infection.* **6** bag at the corner or side of a pool or billiard table. **7** hole in the earth containing gold or other ore: *The miner struck a pocket of silver.* **8** hold back; suppress; hide: *I pocketed my pride and said nothing.* **9** take secretly or dishonestly: *Our partner pocketed the profits.* **10** air pocket. 1,5-7,10 *n.,* 2,8,9 *v.,* 3,4 *adj.* —**pock′et like′,** *adj.*
be out of pocket, spend or lose money.

pock et book (pok′it bùk′), **1** a woman's purse. **2** wallet; billfold. **3** a person's supply of money; income: *This coat is too expensive for my pocketbook. n.*

pock et ful (pok′it fúl′), as much as a pocket will hold. *n., pl.* **pock et fuls.**

pock et knife (pok′it nīf′), a small knife with one or more blades that fold into the handle. *n., pl.* **pock et knives** (pok′it nīvz′).

pock et-size (pok′it sīz′), small enough to go in a pocket: *a pocket-size camera. adj.*

pocket veto, method of vetoing a bill that can be used by the President of the United States on a bill presented for signing within ten days of the end of a session of Congress. If the President does not sign the bill before Congress adjourns, it does not become a law.

pock mark (pok′märk′), mark or pit on the skin; pock. *n.*

pock marked (pok′märkt′), marked with pocks. *adj.*

pock y (pok′ē), marked with pocks. *adj.,* **pock i er, pock i est.**

pod (pod), **1** the shell or case in which plants like beans and peas grow their seeds. **2** produce pods. 1 *n.,* 2 *v.,* **pod ded, pod ding.**

p.o.d., pay on delivery.

po di um (pō′dē əm), a raised platform. The conductor of an orchestra or a speaker before an audience often stands on a podium. *n., pl.* **po di ums, po di a** (pō′dē ə). [*Podium* was borrowed from Latin *podium,* and can be traced back to Greek *podos,* meaning "foot."]

Poe (pō), **Edgar Allan,** 1809-1849, American poet, critic, and writer of tales. *n.*

POE or **P.O.E., 1** port of embarkation. **2** port of entry.

po em (pō′əm), **1** arrangement of words in lines having rhythm or a regularly repeated accent and, often, rhyme; composition in verse. **2** any composition showing great beauty or nobility of language or thought. *n.*

po e sy (pō′ə sē), OLD USE. poetry. *n.*

po et (pō′it), person who writes poetry. Emily Dickinson and Walt Whitman were poets. *n.* [*Poet* came into English about 700 years ago from French *poete,* and can be traced back to Greek *poiein,* meaning "to make, do, compose."]

po et ic (pō et′ik), **1** of poems or poets. **2** suitable for poems or poets. *Alas, o'er,* and *blithe* are poetic words. **3** showing beautiful or noble language, imagery, or thought: *poetic fancies. adj.* —**po et′i cal ly,** *adv.*

po et i cal (pō et′ə kəl), poetic. *adj.*

poetic justice, ideal justice, with virtue being suitably rewarded and wickedness properly punished, as shown often in poems, plays, and stories.

poet laureate, 1 (in Great Britain) a poet appointed by the king or queen to write poems in celebration of court and national events. **2** any poet regarded as the best or most typical of a country or region. *pl.* **poets laureate** or **poet laureates.**

po et ry (pō′i trē), **1** poems: *a collection of poetry.* **2** art of writing poems: *Our class is studying the masters of English poetry.* **3** poetic quality; poetic spirit or feeling. *n.*

po go stick (pō′gō), toy consisting of a stick that contains a spring, and has footrests near the bottom and a handle at the top. One can hop from place to place by jumping up and down on the footrests, while holding the handle.

pogo stick

po grom (pō grom′), an organized massacre of a particular ethnic group, especially of Jews. *n.*

po gy (pō′gē), menhaden. *n., pl.* **po gies** or **po gy.**

poi (poi), a Hawaiian food made of taro root that is baked, pounded, moistened, and fermented. *n.*

poign an cy (poi′nyən sē), a being poignant; sharpness; piercing quality: *poignancy of suffering. n.*

poign ant (poi′nyənt), **1** very painful; piercing: *poignant suffering.* **2** keen; intense: *a subject of poignant interest, a poignant delight. adj.* [*Poignant* came from English about 600 years ago from French *poignant,* and can be traced back to Latin *pungere,* meaning "to pierce, prick."] —**poign′ant ly,** *adv.*

poin set ti a (poin set′ē ə), a tropical plant having a small, greenish-yellow flower surrounded by large, scarlet or white leaves that look like petals. Poinsettias are much used as Christmas decorations. *n., pl.* **poin set ti as.** [*Poinsettia* was named for Joel R. *Poinsett,* 1779-1851, an American diplomat in Mexico, who introduced the plant in the United States.]

point (point), **1** a sharp end; something having a sharp end: *the point of a needle.* **2** a tiny round mark; a punctuation mark; dot: *A period is a point. Use a point to set off decimals.* **3** (in mathematics) something that has position without length or width. Two lines meet or cross at a point. **4** a place; spot: *Stop at this point.* **5** any particular or definite position, condition, or time; degree; stage: *boiling point, freezing point.* **6** item; detail: *He answered my questions point by point.* **7** a distinguishing mark or quality: *Courage and endurance were her good points.* **8** the main idea or purpose; important or essential thing: *I missed the point of the joke.* **9** a particular aim, end, or purpose: *What's the point of rushing?* **10** direct (a finger, weapon, etc.); aim: *Point the arrow at the target.* **11** indicate position or direction, or direct attention with, or as if with, the finger: *He pointed the way to the village over the hills.* **12** (of a dog) show the presence of game by standing rigid and looking toward it. **13** have a specified direction: *The road sign points north.* **14** any of the 32 positions indicating direction marked at the circumference of the card of a compass. North, south, east, and west are the four main, or cardinal, points of the compass. **15** piece of land with a sharp end sticking out into the water; cape. **16** unit of scoring or measuring: *We won the game by three points. The price of that stock has gone up a point.* 1-9,14-16 *n.,* 10-13 *v.* [*Point* came into English about 750 years ago from French *point,* and can be traced back to Latin *pungere,* meaning "to pierce, prick." See **Word Family.**]

at the point of, in the act of; very near to: *at the point of leaving.*

beside the point, having nothing to do with the subject; not appropriate.

in point, pertinent: *a case in point.*

make a point of, insist upon: *He made a point of arriving on time.*

on the point of, just about (to do); on the verge of: *She was on the point of going out when a neighbor came in.*

point off, mark off with points or dots.

point out, show or call attention to: *Please point out my mistakes.*

stretch a point, 1 exceed the reasonable limit. **2** make an exception.

to the point, appropriate to the subject at hand; apt: *His speech was brief and to the point.*

point-blank (point'blangk' for *1,2,4;* point'blangk' for *3,5*), **1** aimed straight at the mark. **2** close enough for aim to be taken in this way: *I fired the gun from point-blank range.* **3** straight at the mark: *to fire point-blank.* **4** plain and blunt; direct: *a point-blank question.* **5** plainly and bluntly; directly: *She gave excuses, but her friend refused point-blank.* *1,2,4 adj., 3,5 adv.*

point ed (poin'tid), **1** having a point or points: *a pointed roof.* **2** sharp; piercing: *a pointed wit.* **3** directed; aimed: *a pointed remark.* **4** emphatic: *She showed me pointed attention. adj.* —**point'ed ly,** *adv.* —**point'ed ness,** *n.*

point er (poin'tər), **1** person or thing that points. **2** a long, tapering stick used in pointing things out on a map, blackboard, etc. **3** hand of a clock, meter, etc. **4** a short-haired hunting dog trained to show where game is by standing still with its head and body pointing toward it. **5** INFORMAL. hint; suggestion: *She gave him some pointers on improving his tennis.* **6 Pointers,** *pl.* the two stars in the Big Dipper which point to the North Star in the Little Dipper. *n.*

point less (point'lis), **1** without a point: *a pointless sword.* **2** without meaning or purpose: *a pointless question. adj.* —**point'less ly,** *adv.* —**point'less ness,** *n.*

point of view, 1 position from which one looks at something. **2** attitude of mind: *Happy people and sad people have different points of view toward life.*

poise (poiz), **1** mental balance, composure, or self-possession: *He has perfect poise and never seems embarrassed.* **2** the way in which the body, head, etc., are held; carriage: *Poise yourself on your toes.* **3** balance. **4** hang supported or suspended. **5** hold or carry evenly or steadily: *The waiter poised the tray on his hand.* *1,2 n., 3-5 v.,* **poised, pois ing.**

poi son (poi'zn), **1** substance very dangerous to life and health. Arsenic and lead are both poisons. **2** kill or harm by poison. **3** put poison in or on. **4** poisonous. **5** anything dangerous or deadly: *the poison of hate.* **6** have a dangerous or harmful effect on: *poison the mind with lies.* *1,5 n., 2,3,6 v., 4 adj.* [*Poison* came into English about 750 years ago from French *poison,* and can be traced back to Latin *potare,* meaning "to drink."] —**poi'son er,** *n.*

poison ivy, a shrub or climbing plant that looks like ivy, with glossy green compound leaves of three leaflets each, that causes a painful rash on most people if they touch it.

poison oak, 1 kind of poison ivy that grows as a shrub. **2** poison sumac.

poi son ous (poi'zn əs), **1** containing poison; very harmful to life and health: *The rattlesnake's bite is poisonous.* **2** having a dangerous or harmful effect: *a poisonous lie. adj.* —**poi'son ous ly,** *adv.* —**poi'son ous ness,** *n.*

a	hat	i	it	oi	oil	ch	child		a in about
ā	age	ī	ice	ou	out	ng	long		e in taken
ä	far	o	hot	u	cup	sh	she	ə = {	i in pencil
e	let	ō	open	ů	put	th	thin		o in lemon
ē	equal	ô	order	ü	rule	ᴛʜ	then		u in circus
ėr	term					zh	measure		

WORD FAMILY

point

Below are words related to *point.* They can all be traced back to the Latin word *pungere* (pùng'ge re), meaning "to pierce, to prick."

appoint	expunge	punctuate
compunction	poignant	puncture
counterpane	pounce	pungent
counterpoint	punch[1]	standpoint
disappoint	punctual	viewpoint

poison sumac, shrub growing in swamps that has leaves composed of seven to thirteen leaflets and white berrylike fruit. It causes a severe rash on most people if they touch it.

poke[1] (pōk), **1** push against with something pointed; prod: *She poked me in the ribs with her elbow.* **2** thrust; push: *The dog poked its head out of the car window.* **3** a poking; thrust; push. **4** search; grope; pry. **5** make by poking: *She poked a hole in the paper.* **6** go lazily; loiter. **7** a slow, lazy person. **8** INFORMAL. hit with the fist; punch: *poke someone in the nose.* **9** INFORMAL. a blow with the fist; a punch. *1,2,4-6,8 v.,* **poked, pok ing;** *3,7,9 n.*

poke[2] (pōk), DIALECT. bag; sack. *n.*

poke[3] (pōk), bonnet or hat with a large brim in front. *n.*

poke[3]

pok er[1] (pō'kər), a metal rod for stirring a fire. *n.*

pok er[2] (pō'kər), a card game in which the players bet on the value of the cards that they hold in their hands. *n.*

pok y or **pok ey** (pō'kē), **1** moving or acting slowly; puttering; slow; dull. **2** small and cramped; confined; mean. *adj.,* **pok i er, pok i est.**

Pol., 1 Poland. **2** Polish.

Po land (pō'lənd), country in central Europe between East Germany and the Soviet Union. *Capital:* Warsaw. See **Prussia** for map. *n.*

po lar (pō'lər), **1** of or near the North or South Pole: *It is very cold in the polar regions.* **2** of the poles of a magnet, electric battery, etc. **3** opposite in character, like the poles of a magnet: *Love and hatred are polar feelings or attitudes. adj.*

polar bear, a large, white bear of the arctic regions.

Po lar is (pō ler'is *or* pō lar'is), the North Star. *n.*

po lar i ty (pō lar'ə tē), **1** the possession of two opposed poles. A magnet or battery has polarity. **2** a positive or negative polar condition, as in electricity. **3** possession of two opposite or contrasted principles or tendencies. *n., pl.* **po lar i ties.**

po lar ize (pō′lə rīz′), give polarity to. *v.,* **po lar ized, po lar iz ing.** —**po′lar iz′a ble,** *adj.* —**po′lar iz′er,** *n.*

Po la roid (pō′lə roid′), trademark for a thin, transparent material that absorbs part of the light passing through it. It is used in sunglasses, filters for cameras, etc., to reduce glare. *n.*

pol der (pōl′dər), tract of lowland reclaimed from the sea or other body of water and protected by dikes. *n.*

pole¹ (pōl), **1** a long, slender piece of wood, etc.: *a telephone pole.* **2** make (a boat) go with a pole. **1** *n.,* **2** *v.,* **poled, pol ing.** [*Pole¹* is from Old English *pāl,* which came from Latin *palus,* meaning "a stake."]

pole² (pōl), **1** either end of the earth's axis. The North Pole and the South Pole are opposite each other. **2** either end of the axis of any sphere. **3** either of two parts where opposite forces are strongest. A magnet or battery has both a positive pole and a negative pole. *n.* [*Pole²* is from Latin *polus,* which came from Greek *polos.*]

Pole (pōl), person born or living in Poland. *n.*

polecat (def. 1) about 2¹/₂ ft. (75 cm.) long with the tail

pole cat (pōl′kat′), **1** a small, dark-brown, meat-eating European mammal related to the weasel, that can emit a very disagreeable odor; fitch. **2** skunk. *n.* [*Polecat* is from Middle English *polcat,* which came from French *poule,* meaning "fowl," and Middle English *cat,* meaning "cat." The animal may have been called this because it eats fowl.]

po lem ic (pə lem′ik), **1** a disputing discussion; controversy; argument. **2** of controversy or disagreement; of dispute. **1** *n.,* **2** *adj.* —**po lem′i cal ly,** *adv.*

pole star (pōl′stär′), **1** the North Star. **2** a guiding principle; guide. *n.*

pole vault, a jump or leap over a high, horizontal bar by using a long pole.

po lice (pə lēs′), **1** persons whose duty is keeping order and arresting people who break the law. **2** department of government that keeps order and arrests persons who break the law. **3** keep order in: *police the streets.* **4** the cleaning and keeping in order of a military camp, area, etc., or those who do it. **5** keep (a military camp, area, etc.) clean and in order. **1,2,4** *n.,* **3,5** *v.,* **po liced, po lic ing.**

police dog, 1 German shepherd. **2** any dog trained to work with policemen.

po lice man (pə lēs′mən), member of the police. *n., pl.* **po lice men.**

po lice wom an (pə lēs′wùm′ən), woman who is a member of the police. *n., pl.* **po lice wom en.**

pol i cy¹ (pol′ə sē), **1** plan of action; way of management: *It is a poor policy to promise more than you can do. The candidates explained their policies.* **2** practical wisdom; prudence. *n., pl.* **pol i cies.** [*Policy¹* came into English about 600 years ago from French *policie,* and can be traced back to Greek *polis,* meaning "city."]

pol i cy² (pol′ə sē), a written agreement about insurance: *My fire insurance policy states that I shall receive $40,000 if my house burns down. n., pl.* **pol i cies.** [*Policy²*

came into English over 400 years ago from French *police,* and can be traced back to Greek *apo,* meaning "from," and *deiknynai,* meaning "to show."]

po li o (pō′lē ō), a severe infectious, virus disease that destroys nervous tissue in the spinal cord, causing fever, paralysis of various muscles, and sometimes death; infantile paralysis; poliomyelitis. Before a vaccine was developed to control it, it attacked children especially, often leaving them crippled. *n.*

po li o my e li tis (pō′lē ō mī′ə lī′tis), polio. *n.*

pol ish (pol′ish), **1** make smooth and shiny: *polish shoes.* **2** become smooth and shiny; take on a polish. **3** substance used to give smoothness or shine: *silver polish.* **4** put into a better condition; improve; refine: *polish one's French.* **5** polished condition; smoothness; refinement: *The polish of the furniture reflected our faces like a mirror. Travel with polite people gave polish to his manners.* **1,2,4** *v.,* **3,5** *n., pl.* **pol ish es.** —**pol′ish er,** *n.*

Pol ish (pō′lish), **1** of Poland, its people, or their language. **2** language of Poland. **1** *adj.,* **2** *n.*

po lite (pə līt′), **1** having or showing good manners; behaving properly: *The polite girl gave the old woman her seat on the bus.* **2** refined; elegant: *He tried to learn all the customs of polite society. adj.,* **po lit er, po lit est.** —**po lite′ly,** *adv.* —**po lite′ness,** *n.*

pol i tic (pol′ə tik), **1** wise in looking out for one's own interests; prudent: *A politic person tries not to offend people.* **2** scheming; crafty. **3** political: *The state is a body politic. adj.* —**pol′i tic ly,** *adv.*

po lit i cal (pə lit′ə kəl), **1** of or concerned with politics. **2** having to do with citizens or government: *Treason is a political offense.* **3** of politicians or their methods: *a political party. adj.* —**po lit′i cal ly,** *adv.*

political science, science of the principles and conduct of government. —**political scientist.**

pol i ti cian (pol′ə tish′ən), **1** person who gives much time to political affairs; person who is experienced in politics. **2** person active in politics chiefly for personal or party profit. **3** person holding a political office. *n.*

pol i tics (pol′ə tiks), **1** management of political affairs; the science and art of government: *Our senior senator has been engaged in politics for many years.* **2** political principles or opinions: *My parents' politics are strongly against rule by any one person.* **3** political methods or maneuvers. *n. sing. or pl.*

pol i ty (pol′ə tē), **1** government. **2** a particular form or system of government. **3** community with a government; state. *n., pl.* **pol i ties.**

Polk (pōk), **James Knox,** 1795-1849, the 11th president of the United States, from 1845 to 1849. *n.*

pol ka (pōl′kə *or* pō′kə), **1** a kind of lively dance. **2** music for it. *n.* [*Polka* was borrowed from Czech *polka.*]

pol ka dot (pō′kə), dot or round spot repeated to form a pattern on cloth.

poll (pōl), **1** a voting; collection of votes: *The class had a poll to decide where it would have its picnic.* **2** number of votes cast. **3** **polls,** *pl.* place where votes are cast and counted: *The polls will be open all day.* **4** list of persons, especially a list of voters. **5** receive at an election: *The mayor polled a record vote.* **6** vote; cast (a vote). **7** take or register the votes of: *to poll a village.* **8** a survey of public opinion concerning a particular subject. **9** the head, especially the part of it on which the hair grows. **1-4,8,9** *n.,* **5-7** *v.* —**poll′er,** *n.*

pol len (pol′ən), a fine, yellowish powder released from the anthers of flowers. Grains of pollen carried to the pistils of flowers fertilize them. *n.*

pol li nate (pol′ə nāt), carry pollen from anthers to pistils of; shed pollen on. Many flowers are pollinated by bees. *v.,* **pol li nat ed, pol li nat ing.**

pollination
of cactus flowers. The dove's beak carries the pollen from anther to pistil.

a hat	i it	oi oil	ch child	(a in about
ā age	ī ice	ou out	ng long	e in taken
ä far	o hot	u cup	sh she	ə = { i in pencil
e let	ō open	u̇ put	th thin	o in lemon
ē equal	ô order	ü rule	ŦH then	(u in circus
ėr term			zh measure	

pol li na tion (pol′ə nā′shən), a carrying pollen to the pistils of flowers. *n.*

pol li wog (pol′ē wog), tadpole. *n.* Also, **pollywog.**

poll tax, a tax on every adult citizen, especially as a prerequisite to the right to vote in public elections.

pol lu tant (pə lüt′nt), something that pollutes. *n.*

pol lute (pə lüt′), make dirty; defile: *The water at the beach was polluted by refuse. v.,* **pol lut ed, pol lut ing.**

pol lu tion (pə lü′shən), **1** the dirtying of any part of the environment, especially with waste material. **2** anything that dirties the environment, especially waste material: *pollution in the air. n.*

Pol lux (pol′əks), (in Greek and Roman myths) one of the twin sons of Zeus. Pollux was immortal; his brother, Castor, was mortal. *n.*

pol ly wog (pol′ē wog), polliwog. *n.*

po lo (pō′lō), game like hockey, played on horseback with long-handled mallets and a wooden ball. *n.* [*Polo* may come from Tibetan *pulu,* meaning "a ball," used in playing the game.]

Po lo (pō′lō), **Marco.** See **Marco Polo.** *n.*

pol o naise (pol′ə nāz′ *or* pō′lə nāz′), **1** a slow, stately dance in three-quarter time. **2** music for it. *n.* [*Polonaise* comes from French *polonaise,* which also means "Polish." The dance was called this because it originated in Poland.]

po lo ni um (pə lō′nē əm), a radioactive metallic element found in pitchblende. *n.*

poly-, *combining form.* many; more than one: *Polygon = (plane figure having) many angles. Polysyllable = (word with) more than one syllable.* [The form *poly-* comes from Greek *polys,* meaning "much, many."]

pol y es ter (pol′ē es′tər), any of a large group of synthetic resins used in making paints, synthetic fibers, films, and plastics. *n.*

po lyg a mous (pə lig′ə məs), having more than one wife or more than one husband at the same time. *adj.*

po lyg a my (pə lig′ə mē), practice or condition of being married to more than one person at the same time. *n.*

pol y glot (pol′ē glot), **1** knowing several languages. **2** person who knows several languages. **3** written in several languages. 1,3 *adj.,* 2 *n.*

pol y gon (pol′ē gon), a closed plane figure with three or more sides and angles. *n.* [See **Word History.**]

po lyg o nal (pə lig′ə nəl), of a polygon. *adj.*

pol y he dron (pol′ē hē′drən), a solid figure having four or more faces. *n., pl.* **pol y he drons** *or* **pol y he dra** (pol′ē hē′drə).

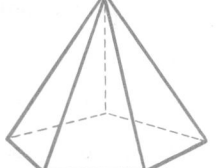

polyhedron

pol y mer (pol′ə mər), a chemical compound in which each molecule is made up of many small molecules strung together. Nylon and cellulose are polymers. *n.*

Pol y ne sia (pol′ə nē′zhə), group of many small islands in the Pacific, east of Micronesia and Melanesia. See **Melanesia** for map. *n.*

Pol y ne sian (pol′ə nē′zhən), **1** member of the division of the human race that includes the original inhabitants of islands in the Pacific from Hawaii south to New Zealand, and their descendants throughout the world. **2** of this division of the human race. **3** the languages of Polynesia, including Maori, Hawaiian, etc. **4** of Polynesia, its people, or their languages. 1,3 *n.,* 2,4 *adj.*

pol yp (pol′ip), a small water animal with a tubular body and a mouth at one end surrounded by fingerlike tentacles to gather in food. Polyps often grow in colonies, with their bases connected. Corals and sea anemones are polyps. *n.* [*Polyp* can be traced back to Greek *polys,* meaning "much, many," and *pous,* meaning "foot."]

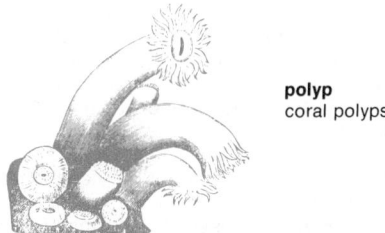

polyp
coral polyps

pol y syl lab ic (pol′ē sə lab′ik), having more than three syllables. *adj.* —**pol′y syl lab′i cal ly,** *adv.*

pol y syl la ble (pol′ē sil′ə bəl), word of more than three syllables. *Politician* is a polysyllable, and so is *possibility. n.*

pol y tech nic (pol′ē tek′nik), of or dealing with many crafts or sciences: *a polytechnic school. adj.*

pol y the ism (pol′ē thē iz′əm), belief in more than one god. The religion of the ancient Greeks was polytheism. *n.*

pol y u re thane (pol′ē yu̇r′ə thān), any of several synthetic substances that are made in the form of foam, fibers, resins, etc. It is used to make cushions, insulating material, and various kinds of molded products. *n.*

WORD HISTORY

polygon

Polygon can be traced back to Greek *polys,* meaning "much, many," and *gōnia,* meaning "angle."

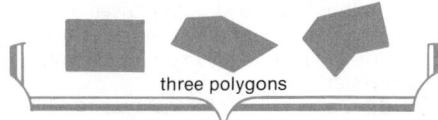

three polygons

po made (pə mād′), a perfumed ointment for the scalp and hair. *n.*

pome gran ate (pom′gran′it), **1** the reddish-yellow fruit of a small tree. It has thick skin, and red pulp and seeds having a pleasant, slightly sour taste. *n.*

pom mel (pum′əl *or* pom′əl), **1** part of a saddle that sticks up at the front. **2** a rounded knob on the hilt of a sword, dagger, etc. **3** pummel. 1,2 *n.,* 3 *v.,*

pomp (pomp), stately or showy display; splendor; magnificence: *The new ruler was crowned with great pomp. n.*

pom pa dour (pom′pə dôr), arrangement of hair in which it is puffed high over the forehead or brushed straight up and back from the forehead. *n.*

Pom pei an (pom pā′ən), of Pompeii or its people. *adj.*

Pom peii (pom pā′), city in ancient Italy, which was buried by an eruption of Mount Vesuvius in A.D. 79. Its ruins have been partly laid bare by excavation. *n.*

Pom pey (pom′pē), 106-48 B.C., Roman general and statesman. *n.*

pom pon (pom′pon), **1** an ornamental tuft or ball of feathers, silk, etc., worn on a hat, dress, or on shoes. **2** kind of chrysanthemum or dahlia with very small, rounded flowers. *n.*

pom pos i ty (pom pos′ə tē), **1** pompous quality. **2** pompous show of self-importance. *n., pl.* **pom pos i ties.**

pom pous (pom′pəs), **1** trying to seem magnificent; fond of display; acting proudly; self-important: *The leader of the band bowed in a pompous manner.* **2** characterized by pomp; splendid; magnificent; stately. *adj.* —**pom′pous ly,** *adv.* —**pom′pous ness,** *n.*

Ponce de Le ón (pons′ də lē′ən), **Juan,** 1460?-1521, Spanish explorer and soldier who was the first European to explore Florida.

pon cho (pon′chō), a large piece of cloth, often waterproof, with a slit in the middle for the head to go through. Ponchos are worn in South America as cloaks. Waterproof ponchos are used in the armed forces and by hikers and campers. *n., pl.* **pon chos.**

pond (pond), body of still water, smaller than a lake. *n.*

pon der (pon′dər), consider carefully; think over: *ponder a problem. v.* —**pon′der er,** *n.*

pon der o sa pine (pon′də rō′sə), a tall pine tree of western North America, valuable for its lumber.

pon der ous (pon′dər əs), **1** very heavy. **2** heavy and clumsy: *A hippopotamus is ponderous.* **3** dull; tiresome: *The speaker talked in a ponderous way. adj.* —**pon′der ous ly,** *adv.* —**pon′der ous ness,** *n.*

pond lily, water lily.

pone (pōn), DIALECT. corn bread, popular in the southern United States. *n.*

pon gee (pon jē′), fabric made of soft silk, usually left in natural brownish-yellow color. *n.*

pon iard (pon′yərd), dagger. *n.*

pons Va ro li i (ponz′ və rō′lē ī), band of nerve fibers in the brain, just above the medulla oblongata, which connects various parts of the brain.

pon tiff (pon′tif), **1** the pope. **2** bishop. **3** a high priest; chief priest. *n.*

pon tif i cal (pon tif′ə kəl), of a pope or bishop. *adj.* —**pon tif′i cal ly,** *adv.*

pon tif i cate (pon tif′ə kāt), behave or speak pompously. *v.,* **pon tif i cat ed, pon tif i cat ing.**

pon toon (pon tün′), **1** a low, flat-bottomed boat. **2** such a boat, or some other floating structure, used as one of the supports of a temporary bridge. **3** either of two boat-shaped parts of an airplane, used for landing on or taking off from water. *n.*

pontoon bridge, a temporary bridge supported by low, flat-bottomed boats or other floating structures.

po ny (pō′nē), kind of small horse. Ponies are usually less than 5 feet (1.5 meters) tall at the shoulder. *n., pl.* **po nies.**

pony express, system of carrying letters and small packages in the western United States in 1860 and 1861 by relays of men riding fast ponies or horses.

pompadour

po ny tail (pō′nē tāl′), a hair style in which the hair is pulled back and tied, with the ends falling free from where the hair is gathered. *n.*

pooch (püch), SLANG. dog. *n., pl.* **pooch es.**

poo dle (pü′dl), dog with thick, curly hair that is often clipped and shaved in an elaborate manner. *n.*

pooh (pü), exclamation of contempt: *Pooh! You don't dare jump. interj.*

pooh-pooh (pü′pü′ *or* pü′pü′), express contempt for; make light of. *v.*

pool¹ (pül), **1** tank of water to swim or bathe in: *a swimming pool.* **2** a small body of still water; small pond: *a wading pool.* **3** a still, deep place in a stream. **4** puddle: *a pool of grease under a car. n.*

pool² (pül), **1** game played with 16 hard balls on a special table with six pockets. The players try to drive numbered balls into the pockets with long sticks called cues. **2** put (things or money) together for common advantage: *We plan to pool our savings for a year so that we can buy a boat.* **3** system or arrangement in which money, vehicles, or other things are put together by different people, so that they all may benefit: *The hikers put all their food and money in a pool.* **4** group of people, usually having the same skills, who are drawn upon as needed: *the labor pool.* **5** persons who form a pool. **6** stake played for in some games. 1,3-6 *n.,* 2 *v.*

pool room (pül′rüm′ *or* pül′rùm′), room or place in which the game of pool is played. *n.*

poop (püp), **1** deck at the stern above the ordinary deck, often forming the roof of a cabin. **2** stern of a ship. *n.*

poor (pùr), **1** having few things or nothing; lacking money or property; needy: *He was so poor that he could not afford to buy a warm coat.* **2** the poor, persons who are needy. **3** not good in quality; lacking something needed: *poor soil, a poor crop, poor health.* **4** needing pity; unfortunate: *This poor child is hurt.* 1,3,4 *adj.,* 2 *n.* [*Poor* came into English about 800 years ago from French *povre,* which came from Latin *pauper.*] —**poor′ness,** *n.*

poor house (pùr′hous′), formerly, a house in which paupers lived at public expense. *n., pl.* **poor hous es** (pùr′hou′ziz).

poor ish (pùr′ish), somewhat poor. *adj.*

poor ly (pùr′lē), in a poor manner; not enough; badly; meanly: *A desert is poorly supplied with water. The student did poorly on the test. adv.*

pop¹ (pop), **1** make a short, quick, explosive sound: *The firecrackers popped in bunches.* **2** a short, quick, explosive sound: *the pop of a cork.* **3** burst open or cause to burst open with such a sound: *The chestnuts were popping in the fire. He popped the balloon.* **4** move, go, or come suddenly or unexpectedly: *Our neighbor popped in for a short call.* **5** thrust or put suddenly: *She popped her head out through the window.* **6** fire a gun or pistol; shoot. **7** a shot from a gun, etc. **8** bulge: *The surprise made her eyes pop out.* **9** (in baseball) hit a short, high ball over the infield. **10** a nonalcoholic carbonated drink: *strawberry pop.* 1,3-6,8,9 *v.*, **popped, pop ping;** 2,7,10 *n.*

pop² (pop), INFORMAL. papa; father. *n.*

pop³ (pop), INFORMAL. popular: *pop songs. adj.*

pop., **1** popular. **2** population.

pop corn (pop′kôrn′), **1** kind of corn, the kernels of which burst open and puff out when heated. **2** the white, puffed-out kernels. *n.*

pope or **Pope** (pōp), the supreme head of the Roman Catholic Church: *the last three popes, the Pope. n.*

pop gun (pop′gun′), a toy gun that shoots with a popping sound. *n.*

porcupine
about 2½ ft.
(75 cm.) long
with the tail

pop in jay (pop′in jā), a vain, overly talkative, conceited person. *n.*

pop lar (pop′lər), **1** any of several trees that grow very rapidly and produce light, soft wood. The cottonwood and the aspen are two kinds of poplars. **2** wood of such a tree. *n.*

pop lin (pop′lən), a ribbed fabric, made of silk, wool, cotton, or rayon, and used for making dresses, curtains, etc. *n.*

pop o ver (pop′ō′vər), a very light and hollow muffin. *n.*

pop py (pop′ē), plant with delicate, showy red, yellow, or white flowers. Opium is made from one kind of poppy. *n., pl.* **pop pies.**

pop py cock (pop′ē kok′), INFORMAL. nonsense; bosh. *n., interj.*

poppy seed, seed of the poppy, used in baking as a flavoring.

Pop si cle (pop′sə kəl), a trademark for flavored, sweetened ice that is molded onto a stick. *n.*

pop u lace (pop′yə lis), the common people. *n.*

pop u lar (pop′yə lər), **1** liked by most people: *a popular song.* **2** liked by acquaintances or associates: *Her ability and good nature make her the most popular girl in the class.* **3** of the people; by the people; representing the people: *a popular election. The United States has a popular government.* **4** widespread among many people; common: *It is a popular belief that black cats bring bad luck.* **5** suited to or intended for ordinary people: *popular prices, books on popular science. adj.*

pop u lar i ty (pop′yə lar′ə tē), fact or condition of being liked by most people. *n.*

pop u lar ize (pop′yə lə rīz′), make popular. *v.*, **pop u lar ized, pop u lar iz ing.** —**pop′u lar i za′tion,** *n.* —**pop′u lar iz′er,** *n.*

pop u lar ly (pop′yə lər lē), **1** in a popular manner. **2** by the people; in general. *adv.*

pop u late (pop′yə lāt), **1** live in; inhabit: *This city is densely populated.* **2** furnish with inhabitants: *Europe helped populate America. v.,* **pop u lat ed, pop u lat ing.**

pop u la tion (pop′yə lā′shən), **1** people of a city, country, or district. **2** the number of people. **3** part of the inhabitants distinguished in any way from the rest: *the urban population.* **4** act or process of furnishing with inhabitants. *n.*

pop u lous (pop′yə ləs), full of people; having many people per square mile. *adj.* —**pop′u lous ly,** *adv.* —**pop′u lous ness,** *n.*

por ce lain (pôr′sə lin), very fine earthenware; china: *Teacups are often made of porcelain. n.*

porch (pôrch), **1** a covered entrance to a building. **2** a long, often open, structure along one or more sides of a house; veranda. *n., pl.* **porch es.**

por cu pine (pôr′kyə pīn), rodent covered with spines or quills. *n.*

pore¹ (pôr), study or think over carefully or earnestly: *pore over a book, pore over a problem. v.,* **pored, por ing.**

pore² (pôr), a very small opening. Sweat comes through the pores in the skin. *n.*

por gy (pôr′gē), a saltwater food fish of Mediterranean and Atlantic waters. *n., pl.* **por gies** or **por gy.**

pork (pôrk), meat of a pig or hog used for food. *n.*

pork er (pôr′kər), pig, especially one fattened to eat. *n.*

por nog ra phy (pôr nog′rə fē), obscene writings or pictures. *n.*

po ros i ty (pô ros′ə tē), porous quality or condition. *n.*

po rous (pôr′əs), full of pores or tiny holes through which water, air, etc., can pass: *Cloth is porous. Aluminum is not porous. adj.* —**po′rous ness,** *n.*

por phyr y (pôr′fər ē), any igneous rock in which large crystals are scattered through a mass of finer-grained minerals. *n., pl.* **por phyr ies.**

por poise (pôr′pəs), **1** a sea mammal with a blunt, rounded snout. Porpoises are related to the whale, and live in groups in the northern Atlantic and Pacific. **2** any of several other small sea mammals, especially the dolphin. *n., pl.* **por pois es** or **por poise.**

por ridge (pôr′ij), food made of oatmeal or other cereal boiled in water or milk until it thickens. *n.* [*Porridge* is a different form of *pottage.*]

por rin ger (pôr′ən jər), a small dish from which soup, porridge, bread and milk, etc., can be eaten. *n.*

port¹ (pôrt), **1** place where ships and boats can be sheltered from storms; harbor. **2** place where ships and boats can load and unload; city or town by a harbor: *New York, Baltimore, and San Francisco are important American ports. n.*

port² (pôrt), **1** porthole. **2** opening in a cylinder or pipe for steam, air, water, etc., to pass through. *n.*

port³ (pôrt), **1** the left side of a ship, boat, or aircraft when facing forward. **2** on the left side of a ship, boat, or aircraft. 1 *n.,* 2 *adj.*

port⁴ (pôrt), a strong, sweet, dark-red wine. *n.*

Port., **1** Portugal. **2** Portuguese.

port a ble (pôr′tə bəl), capable of being carried; easily carried: *a portable typewriter, a portable radio. adj.*

por tage (pôr′tij), **1** a carrying of boats, provisions, etc., overland from one river, lake, etc., to another. **2** place over which this is done. **3** cost of carrying. *n.*

por tal (pôr′tl), door, gate, or entrance, usually an imposing one. *n.*

Port-au-Prince (pôrt′ō prins′), seaport and capital of Haiti, in the S part. *n.*

port cul lis (pôrt kul′is), a strong gate or grating of iron sliding up and down in grooves, used to close the gateway of an ancient castle or fortress. *n., pl.* **port cul lis es.**

por tend (pôr tend′), indicate beforehand; give warning of: *Black clouds portend a storm. v.*

por tent (pôr′tent), a warning, usually of coming evil; sign; omen: *The black clouds were a portent of bad weather. n.*

por ten tous (pôr ten′təs), **1** indicating evil to come; ominous; threatening. **2** amazing; extraordinary. *adj.* —**por ten′tous ly,** *adv.* —**por ten′tous ness,** *n.*

por ter[1] (pôr′tər), **1** person employed to carry loads or baggage: *Give your bags to the porter.* **2** attendant in a parlor car or sleeping car of a railway train. *n.* [*Porter*[1] came into English about 600 years ago from French *porteur*, and can be traced back to Latin *portare*, meaning "to carry."]

por ter[2] (pôr′tər), **1** doorman. **2** janitor. *n.* [*Porter*[2] came into English about 700 years ago from French *portier*, and can be traced back to Latin *porta*, meaning "a gate."]

por ter[3] (pôr′tər), a heavy, dark-brown beer. *n.*

Por ter (pôr′tər), **Katherine Anne,** 1890-1980, American short-story writer and novelist. *n.*

por ter house (pôr′tər hous′), a choice beefsteak containing the tenderloin. *n.*

porterhouse steak, porterhouse.

port fo li o (pôrt fō′lē ō), **1** a portable case for loose papers, drawings, etc.; briefcase. **2** position and duties of a cabinet member or a minister of state: *The Secretary of Defense resigned his portfolio.* **3** holdings in the form of stocks, bonds, etc. *n., pl.* **port fo li os.**

port hole (pôrt′hōl′), **1** opening in a ship's side to let in light and air. **2** opening in a ship, wall, etc., through which to shoot. *n.*

Por tia (pôr′shə), heroine in Shakespeare's *The Merchant of Venice*, who acts as a lawyer. *n.*

portico

por ti co (pôr′tə kō), roof supported by columns, forming a porch or a covered walk. *n., pl.* **por ti coes** or **por ti cos.**

por tiere (pôr tyer′), curtain hung at a doorway. *n.*

por tière (pôr tyer′), portiere. *n., pl.* **por tières.**

por tion (pôr′shən), **1** a part or share: *A portion of each school day is devoted to arithmetic.* **2** quantity of food served for one person: *I can't eat such a large portion.* **3** divide into parts or shares: *The money was portioned out among the children.* **4** dowry. 1,2,4 *n.,* 3 *v.*

Port land (pôrt′lənd), **1** seaport in SW Maine. **2** seaport in NW Oregon. *n.*

port li ness (pôrt′lē nis), portly condition. *n.*

Port Lou is (lü′is *or* lü′ē), capital of Mauritius, in the NW part.

port ly (pôrt′lē), **1** having a large body; stout. **2** stately; dignified. *adj.,* **port li er, port li est.**

port man teau (pôrt man′tō), a stiff, oblong traveling bag with two compartments opening like a book. *n., pl.* **port man teaus** *or* **port man teaux** (pôrt man′tōz).

Port Mores by (môrz′bē), capital of Papua New Guinea, in SE New Guinea.

Port of Spain, Port-of-Spain.

Port-of-Spain (pôrt′əv spān′), capital of Trinidad and Tobago, a seaport in NW Trinidad. *n.*

Por to-No vo (pôr′tō nō′vō), capital of Benin, in the S part. *n.*

Por to Ri co (pôr′tō rē′kō), former name of **Puerto Rico.**

por trait (pôr′trit *or* pôr′trāt), **1** picture of a person, especially of the face. **2** picture in words; description. *n.*

por trai ture (pôr′trə chùr), **1** act of portraying. **2** portrait. *n.*

por tray (pôr trā′), **1** make a likeness of in a drawing or painting; make a picture of: *portray a historical scene.* **2** picture in words; describe: *The book "Black Beauty" portrays the life of a horse.* **3** act the part of in a play or motion picture: *He portrayed a clerk. v.* —**por tray′er,** *n.*

por tray al (pôr trā′əl), **1** a portraying by drawing or in words. **2** a picture or description. *n.*

Por tu gal (pôr′chə gəl), country in SW Europe, west of Spain. *Capital:* Lisbon. See **Castile** for map. *n.*

Por tu guese (pôr′chə gēz′), **1** of Portugal, its people, or their language. **2** person born or living in Portugal. **3** language of Portugal. 1 *adj.,* 2,3 *n., pl.* **Por tu guese.**

pos., **1** positive. **2** possessive.

pose[1] (pōz), **1** position of the body; way of holding the body: *a natural pose, a pose taken in exercising.* **2** hold a position: *He posed an hour for his portrait.* **3** put in a certain position: *The photographer posed her before taking her picture.* **4** attitude assumed for effect; pretense; affectation: *Her interest in other people is quite real; it is not just a pose.* **5** put on an attitude for effect; make a false pretense: *They posed as a rich couple although they had little money.* **6** put forward for discussion; state: *pose a question.* 1,4 *n.,* 2,3,5,6 *v.,* **posed, pos ing.**

pose[2] (pōz), puzzle completely. *v.,* **posed, pos ing.**

Po sei don (pə sīd′n), (in Greek myths) the god of the sea. The Romans called him Neptune. *n.*

pos er (pō′zər), person who poses. *n.*

posh (posh), INFORMAL. elegant or fine in appearance; stylish. *adj.*

po si tion (pə zish′ən), **1** place where a thing or person is: *The flowers grew in a sheltered position behind the house.* **2** way of being placed: *Sit in a more comfortable position.* **3** proper place: *The band got into position to march in the parade.* **4** condition with reference to place or circumstances: *I maneuvered for position before shooting the basketball. Your careless remark put me in an awkward position.* **5** job: *He has a position in a bank.* **6** rank or standing, especially high standing: *She was raised to the position of manager.* **7** way of thinking; set of opinions: *What is your position on this question?* **8** to place in a certain position: *The photographer positioned the tall students behind the shorter ones.* 1-7 *n.,* 8 *v.*

pos i tive (poz′ə tiv), **1** permitting no question; without doubt; sure: *positive proof.* **2** too sure; too confident: *A positive manner annoys some people.* **3** definite; emphatic: *"No. I will not," was his positive refusal.* **4** showing agreement or approval: *a positive answer to a question.* **5** the simple form of an adjective or adverb, as distinct from the comparative and superlative. *Fast* is the positive; *faster* is the comparative; *fastest* is the superlative. **6** of

a hat	**i** it	**oi** oil	**ch** child		a in about
ā age	**ī** ice	**ou** out	**ng** long		e in taken
ä far	**o** hot	**u** cup	**sh** she	**ə** =	i in pencil
e let	**ō** open	**ù** put	**th** thin		o in lemon
ē equal	**ô** order	**ü** rule	**ŦH** then		u in circus
èr term			**zh** measure		

the simple form of an adjective or adverb. **7** showing that a particular disease, condition, germ, etc., is present. **8** able definitely to do or add something; practical: *Don't just make criticisms; give us some positive help.* **9** of the kind of electrical charge produced by rubbing glass with silk. **10** greater than zero; plus: *Five above zero is a positive quantity.* **11** a positive degree or quantity. **12** (in photography) having the lines and shadows in the same position as in the original subject: *a positive image.* **13** print made from a photographic film or plate. 1-4, 6-10,12 *adj.*, 5,11,13 *n.* —**pos′i tive ness,** *n.*

pos i tive ly (poz′ə tiv lē), **1** in a positive way: *The audience reacted positively to the play.* **2** to a great extreme; absolutely: *I was positively furious at them for being so rude. adv.*

pos se (pos′ē), group of citizens called together by a sheriff to help maintain law and order. *n.*

pos sess (pə zes′), **1** have as belonging to one; own: *My aunt possessed great intelligence and determination.* **2** hold as property; hold; occupy. **3** control; influence strongly: *She was possessed by the desire to be rich.* **4** control by an evil spirit: *He fought like one possessed. v.*

pos ses sion (pə zesh′ən), **1** a possessing; holding: *I have in my possession the books you thought you'd lost.* **2** ownership: *On her 21st birthday she came into possession of 50 thousand dollars.* **3** thing possessed; property: *Please move your possessions from my room.* **4** territory under the rule of a country: *Guam is a possession of the United States.* **5** domination by a particular feeling, idea, evil spirit, etc. **6** self-control. *n.*

pos ses sive (pə zes′iv), **1** showing possession. *My, your, his,* and *our* are in the possessive case because they indicate who possesses or owns. **2** the possessive case. **3** word in this case. In "your book," *your* is a possessive. **4** desirous of ownership: *a possessive nature.* 1,4 *adj.*, 2,3 *n.* —**pos ses′sive ly,** *adv.* —**pos ses′sive ness,** *n.*

pos ses sor (pə zes′ər), person who possesses; owner; holder. *n.*

pos si bil i ty (pos′ə bil′ə tē), **1** a being possible: *There is a possibility that the train may be late.* **2** a possible thing, person, or event: *A whole week of rain is a possibility. n., pl.* **pos si bil i ties.**

pos si ble (pos′ə bəl), **1** capable of being, being done, or happening: *It is possible to cure tuberculosis. Space travel is now possible.* **2** not known to be true, but perhaps true: *It is possible that they left without us.* **3** capable of being done or chosen properly: *the only possible action, the only possible candidate. adj.*

pos si bly (pos′ə blē), **1** by any possibility; no matter what happens: *I cannot possibly go.* **2** perhaps: *Possibly you are right. adv.*

pos sum (pos′əm), opossum. *n., pl.* **pos sums** or **possum.**

play possum, put on a false appearance; pretend.

post¹ (pōst), **1** piece of timber, iron, etc., firmly set up, usually to support something else: *the posts of a door, a hitching post.* **2** fasten (a notice) up in a place where it can easily be seen: *The list of winners will be posted soon.* **3** make known by, or as if by, a posted notice; make public: *post a reward.* **4** put (a name) in a list that is published or posted up: *Her train is posted as on time.* **5** put up notices warning people to keep out of: *That farmer posts his land.* 1 *n.*, 2-5 *v.*

post² (pōst), **1** the place where a soldier, police officer, etc., is stationed; place where one is supposed to be when on duty: *When the fire alarm sounded, they all rushed to their posts.* **2** a place where soldiers are stationed; military station; fort. **3** to station at a post: *They posted guards at the door.* **4** job or position: *the post of secretary, a diplomatic post.* **5** trading post. 1,2,4,5 *n.*, 3 *v.*

post³ (pōst), **1** an established system for carrying letters, papers, packages, etc.; the mail: *I shall send the package by post.* **2** a single delivery of mail: *this morning's post.* **3** send by post; mail: *post a letter.* **4** one of a series of fixed stations along a route that furnished relays of horses and riders for carrying the mail. **5** travel with haste; hurry. **6** supply with up-to-date information; inform: *to be well posted on current events.* 1,2,4 *n.*, 3,5,6 *v.*

post-, *prefix.* after in time; later: *Postscript = something written later. Postwar = after the war.*

post age (pō′stij), amount paid on anything sent by mail. *n.*

postage stamp, stamp (def. 1).

post al (pō′stəl), having to do with mail and post offices: *postal rules. adj.*

postal card, post card.

Postal Service, an independent agency of the United States government that provides mail services, sells postage stamps, etc. It replaced the U.S. Post Office Department in 1971.

post card (pōst′kärd′), post card. *n.*

post card, small card for sending a message by mail. Some post cards have a picture on one side.

post chaise, a hired carriage that was used for traveling before there were railroads.

post er (pō′stər), a large printed sheet or notice put up on a wall. *n.*

pos ter i or (po stir′ē ər), **1** situated behind; back; rear; hind. **2** coming after; later. *adj.*

pos ter i ty (po ster′ə tē), **1** generations of the future: *Posterity may travel to distant planets.* **2** anyone's children, and their children, and their children, and so on and on; all of a person's descendants. *n.*

pos tern (pō′stərn *or* pos′tərn), a small back door or gate, especially one in a castle or fort. *n.*

post grad u ate (pōst graj′ü it), **1** student who continues studying in college or at school after graduation. **2** taking a course of study after graduation. **3** of or for postgraduates: *postgraduate courses.* 1 *n.*, 2,3 *adj.*

post haste (pōst′hāst′), very speedily; in great haste. *adv.*

post hu mous (pos′chə məs), **1** happening after death: *posthumous fame.* **2** published after the death of the author: *a posthumous book.* **3** born after the death of the father: *a posthumous child. adj.* —**post′hu mous ly,** *adv.*

pos til ion *or* **pos til lion** (pō stil′yən *or* po stil′yən), person who guides a team of horses drawing a carriage by riding the left-hand horse. *n.*

post man (pōst′mən), mail carrier. *n., pl.* **post men.**

post mark (pōst′märk′), **1** an official mark stamped on mail to cancel the postage stamp and record the place and date of mailing. **2** to stamp with a postmark. 1 *n.*, 2 *v.*

post mas ter (pōst′mas′tər), person in charge of a post office. *n.*

postmaster general, **1** person at the head of the postal system of a country. **2** Postmaster General, the chief executive officer of the Postal Service. *pl.* **postmasters general.**

post mis tress (pōst′mis′tris), woman in charge of a post office. *n., pl.* **post mis tress es.**

post-mor tem (pōst′môr′təm), **1** after death: *A post-*

mortem examination showed that he had died of natural causes. 2 autopsy. 1 *adj.,* 2 *n.* [*Post-mortem comes from the Latin phrase post mortem, meaning "after death."*]

post office, 1 place where mail is handled and postage stamps are sold. 2 Often, **Post Office.** the former government department in charge of mail, replaced by the Postal Service in 1971.

post paid (pōst′pād′), with the postage paid for. *adj.*

post pone (pōst pōn′), put off till later; put off to a later time; delay: *The picnic was postponed because of rain.* *v.,* **post poned, post pon ing.** —**post pon′er,** *n.*

post pone ment (pōst pōn′mənt), a putting off till later; a putting off to a later time; delay: *The postponement of the picnic disappointed the children.* *n.*

post road, 1 road or route over which mail is or was carried. 2 road with stations which furnished horses.

post script (pōst′skript), 1 addition to a letter, written after the writer's name has been signed. 2 a supplementary part added to any composition or literary work. *n.*

pos tu late (pos′chə lit *for 1;* pos′chə lāt *for 2,3*), 1 something taken for granted or assumed as a basis for reasoning; fundamental principle; necessary condition: *One postulate of plane geometry is that a straight line is the shortest distance between any two points.* 2 assume without proof; take for granted: *Geometry postulates certain things as a basis for its reasoning.* 3 require; demand; claim. 1 *n.,* 2,3 *v.,* **pos tu lat ed, pos tu lat ing.** —**pos′tu la′tion,** *n.*

pos ture (pos′chər), 1 position of the body; way of holding the body: *Good posture is important to health.* 2 take a certain position: *The dancer postured before the mirror, bending and twisting her body.* 3 condition; situation; state: *In the present posture of public affairs it is difficult to predict what will happen.* 1,3 *n.,* 2 *v.,* **pos tured, pos tur ing.** —**pos′tur er,** *n.*

post war (pōst′wôr′), after the war. *adj.*

po sy (pō′zē), 1 flower. 2 bunch of flowers; bouquet. *n., pl.* **po sies.**

pot (pot), 1 kind of vessel or dish. There are many different kinds and shapes of pots. They are made of iron, aluminum, earthenware, and other substances. A pot may hold food or drink or contain earth for flowers to grow in. 2 amount a pot can hold: *He ate a small pot of beans.* 3 put into a pot: *pot young tomato plants.* 4 cook and preserve in a pot. 5 take a potshot at; shoot. 1,2 *n.,* 3-5 *v.,* **pot ted, pot ting.** —**pot′like′,** *adj.*

go to pot, go to ruin.

po ta ble (pō′tə bəl), 1 fit or suitable for drinking. 2 Usually, **potables,** *pl.* anything drinkable. 1 *adj.,* 2 *n.*

pot ash (pot′ash′), any of several substances containing potassium made from various minerals, wood ashes, etc., used in making soap, fertilizers, and glass. *n.*

po tas si um (pə tas′ē əm), a soft, silver-white, metallic element, occurring in nature only in compounds. Potassium is one of the most abundant elements in the earth's crust, and is essential for the growth of plants. *n.* [*Potassium is from potash, which comes from pot ashes.*]

potassium hydroxide, a white, solid substance which releases great heat when it dissolves in water; caustic potash. It is used in bleaching, in making liquid soaps, and in medicine.

potassium nitrate, a white or colorless crystalline compound, produced from sodium nitrate and another potassium compound; niter; saltpeter. It is used in explosives, fertilizers, medicine, and meat preservatives.

po ta tion (pō tā′shən), 1 act of drinking. 2 a drink, especially of alcoholic liquor. *n.*

po ta to (pə tā′tō), 1 a round or oval, hard, starchy vegetable with a thin skin; Irish potato; white potato. It is one of the most widely used vegetables. Potatoes grow underground. 2 sweet potato. *n., pl.* **po ta toes.**

potato chip, a thin slice of potato fried in deep fat.

pot bel lied (pot′bel′ēd), 1 having a potbelly. 2 shaped like a potbelly: *a potbellied stove. adj.*

pot bel ly (pot′bel′ē), a bulging belly. *n., pl.* **pot bel lies.**

po ten cy (pōt′n sē), power; strength: *the potency of an argument, the potency of a drug. n., pl.* **po ten cies.**

po tent (pōt′nt), having great power; powerful; strong: *a potent remedy for a disease, potent reasons. adj.* —**po′tent ly,** *adv.*

po ten tate (pōt′n tāt), 1 person having great power. 2 ruler. Kings, queens, and emperors are potentates. *n.*

po ten tial (pə ten′shəl), 1 possible as opposed to actual; capable of coming into being or action: *There is a potential danger of being bitten when playing with a strange dog.* 2 something potential; possibility. 3 (in grammar) expressing possibility by the use of *may, might, can, could,* etc.: *the potential mood of a verb.* 4 amount of electrification of a point with reference to some standard. A current of high potential is used in transmitting electric power over long distances. 1,3 *adj.,* 2,4 *n.* —**po ten′tial ly,** *adv.*

potential energy, energy which a body has because of its position or structure. A coiled spring or a raised weight has potential energy.

po ten ti al i ty (pə ten′shē al′ə tē), 1 potential condition or quality; possible power. 2 something potential; possibility. *n., pl.* **po ten ti al i ties.**

pot ful (pot′fùl), as much as a pot can hold. *n., pl.* **pot fuls.**

poth er (poᴛʜ′ər), confusion; disturbance; fuss. *n.*

pot herb (pot′ėrb′ *or* pot′hėrb′), 1 any plant whose leaves and stems are boiled for use as a vegetable, such as spinach. 2 plant used as seasoning in cooking, such as sage. *n.*

pot hold er (pot′hōl′dər), a thick pad of cloth or other material for handling hot pots, lids, etc. *n.*

pot hole (pot′hōl′), 1 a deep, round hole, especially one made in the rocky bed of a river by stones and gravel being spun around in the current. 2 depression or hollow part forming a defect in the surface of a street or road. *n.*

pot hook (pot′hùk′), 1 hook for hanging a pot over an open fire. 2 rod with a hook for lifting hot pots. *n.*

po tion (pō′shən), a drink, especially one that is used as a medicine or poison, or in magic. *n.*

pot luck (pot′luk′), whatever food happens to be ready or on hand for a meal: *Come and take potluck with me. n.*

Po to mac (pə tō′mək), river flowing from E West Virginia between Maryland and Virginia, into Chesapeake Bay. Washington, D.C., is on the Potomac River. *n.*

pot pie (pot′pī′), 1 a baked meat pie. 2 a stew with dumplings. *n.*

pot pour ri (pō′pù rē′), 1 medley or mixture: *a potpourri of Italian, French, and Austrian folk songs.* 2 a fragrant mixture of dried flower petals and spices. *n.*

WORD HISTORY

potpourri

Potpourri, which originally meant "a stew," comes from the French phrase *pot pourri,* originally meaning "rotten pot."

pot roast, beef browned in a pot and cooked slowly with only a little water.

pot sherd (pot′shėrd′), a broken piece of earthenware. *n.*

pot shot (pot′shot′), **1** a quick shot fired at something from close range without careful aim. **2** Often, **potshots,** *pl.* criticism, usually made in a careless manner. *n.* [The shot was called this because it was fired at game merely to get food for the pot, with little regard to skill or the rules of sport.]

pot tage (pot′ij), a thick soup. *n.*

potter[1]
fashioning a pot on a rotating potter's wheel

pot ter[1] (pot′ər), person who makes pottery. *n.*

pot ter[2] (pot′ər), to putter. *v.* —**pot′ter er,** *n.*

potter's field, piece of public ground set aside for the burial of people who die without friends or money.

potter's wheel, a rotating horizontal disk upon which clay is molded into dishes, etc.

pot ter y (pot′ər ē), **1** pots, dishes, vases, etc., made from clay and hardened by heat. **2** art or business of making them. **3** place where such pots, dishes, vases, etc., are made. *n., pl.* **pot ter ies.**

pouch (pouch), **1** bag or sack: *a tobacco pouch.* **2** a baglike fold of skin. A kangaroo carries its young in a pouch. **3** put into a pouch. **4** form a pouch. 1,2 *n., pl.* **pouch es;** 3,4 *v.* —**pouch′like′,** *adj.*

pouch y (pou′chē), having pouches; like a pouch; baggy. *adj.* **pouch i er, pouch i est.**

poul tice (pōl′tis), **1** a soft, moist mass of mustard, herbs, etc., applied to the body as a medicine. **2** put a poultice on. 1 *n.,* 2 *v.,* **poul ticed, poul tic ing.**

poul try (pōl′trē), birds such as chickens, turkeys, geese, ducks, etc., raised for their meat or eggs. *n.*

pounce (pouns), **1** come down with a rush and seize something: *The cat pounced upon the mouse.* **2** dash, come, or jump suddenly: *The actor pounced onto the stage.* **3** a sudden swoop or pouncing. 1,2 *v.,* **pounced, pouncing;** 3 *n.*

pound[1] (pound), **1** unit of weight equal to 16 ounces in avoirdupois and 12 ounces in troy weight. **2** pound sterling. **3** unit of money of Israel, Egypt, and certain other countries. *n., pl.* **pounds** or **pound.**

pound[2] (pound), **1** hit hard again and again; hit heavily: *She pounded the door with her fist.* **2** beat hard; throb: *After running fast you can feel your heart pound.* **3** make into a powder or pulp by pounding: *They pounded the grains of corn into meal.* **4** move with a pounding sound: *We pounded down the hill to catch the bus.* **5** a heavy blow, or its sound. 1-4 *v.,* 5 *n.*

pound[3] (pound), **1** an enclosed place in which to keep stray animals: *a dog or cat pound.* **2** enclosure for keeping, confining, or trapping animals or fish. *n.*

pound-fool ish (pound′fü′lish), foolish or careless in regard to large sums of money. *adj.*

pound sterling, unit of money of Great Britain. Since February 1971, 1 pound = 100 pence. Formerly, 1 pound = 240 pence. £1 means one pound. The pound sterling is worth almost two dollars.

pour (pôr), **1** flow or cause to flow in a steady stream: *I poured the milk from the bottle. The crowd poured out of the theater.* **2** make known freely or without reserve: *pour out one's grief.* **3** rain heavily. **4** a heavy rain; downpour. 1-3 *v.,* 4 *n.* —**pour′er,** *n.*

pout (pout), **1** thrust or push out the lips, as a displeased or sulky child does. **2** a pushing out of the lips when displeased or sulky. 1 *v.,* 2 *n.*

pout er (pou′tər), kind of domestic pigeon that puffs out its crop. *n.*

pov er ty (pov′ər tē), **1** condition of being poor: *Their tattered clothing and broken furniture indicated their poverty.* **2** lack of what is needed; poor quality: *The poverty of the soil makes the crops small.* **3** a small amount; fewness: *A boring person's talk shows poverty of ideas. n.*

pov er ty-strick en (pov′ər tē strik′ən), extremely poor. *adj.*

POW, prisoner of war.

pow der (pou′dər), **1** a solid reduced to dust by pounding, crushing, or grinding. **2** make into or become powder: *The soil powdered in the heat.* **3** some special kind of powder: *face powder, bath powder.* **4** sprinkle or cover with powder. **5** sprinkle: *The ground was powdered with snow.* **6** put powder on (the face, body, etc.): *powder one's nose.* **7** gunpowder. 1,3,7 *n.,* 2,4-6 *v.* —**pow′der er,** *n.*

powder blue, a light blue.

powder horn

powder horn, case made of an animal's horn for carrying gunpowder.

powder puff, a soft puff or pad for applying powder to the skin.

powder room, lavatory for women, especially one with a dressing table.

pow der y (pou′dər ē), **1** of or like powder; in the form of powder. **2** easily made into powder. **3** sprinkled or covered with powder. *adj.*

pow er (pou′ər), **1** strength or force; might: *Penicillin is a medicine of great power.* **2** ability to do or act: *I will give you all the help in my power.* **3** particular ability: *He has great powers of concentration.* **4** authority; influence; control; right: *Congress has power to declare war.* **5** person, thing, body, or nation having authority or influence: *Five powers held a peace conference.* **6** energy or force that can do work: *Running water produces power to run mills.* **7** provide with power or energy: *a boat powered by an outboard motor.* **8** operated by a motor; equipped with its own motor: *a power drill.* **9** product of a number multiplied by itself one or more times: *16 is the 4th power of 2* $(2 \times 2 \times 2 \times 2 = 16)$. **10** capacity of an instrument to magnify. An object seen through a microscope with a power of ten looks ten times its actual size. 1-6,9,10 *n.,* 7 *v.,* 8 *adj.*

in power, having control or authority.

the powers that be, those who have control or authority.

pow er boat (pou′ər bōt′), boat propelled by an engine on board; motorboat. *n.*

pow er ful (pou′ər fəl), having great power or force; mighty; strong: *a powerful person, a powerful medicine, a powerful argument, a powerful nation. adj.* **—pow′er ful ly,** *adv.*

pow er house (pou′ər hous′), **1** a building containing boilers, engines, generators, etc., for producing electric power. **2** INFORMAL. a powerful, energetic, or highly effective person or group. *n., pl.* **pow er hous es** (pou′ər-hou′ziz).

pow er less (pou′ər lis), without power; helpless: *The mouse was powerless in the cat's claws. adj.* **—pow′er less ly,** *adv.* **—pow′er less ness,** *n.*

power of attorney, a written statement giving one person legal power to act for another.

power saw, saw worked by a motor, not by hand.

power shovel, machine for digging operated by an engine, especially a diesel or gasoline engine.

Pow ha tan (pou′ə tan′), 1550?-1618, Indian chief in Virginia. *n.*

pow wow (pou′wou′), **1** an American Indian ceremony, usually accompanied by magic, feasting, and dancing, performed for the cure of disease, success in hunting, etc. **2** council or conference of or with American Indians. **3** INFORMAL. any conference or meeting. **4** hold a pow-wow; confer. 1-3 *n.,* 4 *v.*

pox (poks), any disease that covers the body or parts of the body with sores, such as chicken pox or smallpox. *n.*

pp., 1 pages. **2** past participle.

p.p., 1 parcel post. **2** past participle. **3** postpaid.

ppr. or **p.pr.,** present participle.

Pr, symbol for praseodymium.

pr., 1 pair. **2** price.

PR, 1 Puerto Rico (used with postal Zip Code). **2** proportional representation. **3** public relations.

P.R., Puerto Rico.

prac ti ca bil i ty (prak′tə kə bil′ə tē), quality of being practicable. *n.*

prac ti ca ble (prak′tə kə bəl), able to be done; capable of being put into practice: *a practicable idea. adj.*

prac ti ca bly (prak′tə kə blē), in a practicable manner. *adv.*

prac ti cal (prak′tə kəl), **1** of action or practice rather than thought or theory: *Earning a living is a practical matter.* **2** fit for actual practice: *a practical plan.* **3** useful: *An outdoor swimming pool is more practical in Florida than in Minnesota.* **4** having good sense: *A practical person does not spend time and money foolishly.* **5** engaged in actual practice or work: *A practical farmer works a farm.* **6** being such in effect; virtual: *So many of our players were injured that our victory was a practical defeat. adj.* **—prac′ti cal ness,** *n.*

prairie dog
about 15 in. (38 cm.) long with the tail

prac ti cal i ty (prak′tə kal′ə tē), **1** quality of being practical; practical usefulness; practical habit of mind. **2** a practical matter. *n., pl.* **prac ti cal i ties.**

practical joke, trick or prank played on a person. **—practical joker.**

practical joke

prac ti cal ly (prak′tik lē), **1** so far as the results will be; in effect; really. **2** almost; nearly: *Our house is around the corner, so we are practically home.* **3** in a practical way; in a useful way. *adv.*

practical nurse, person whose occupation is to care for the sick, but who does not have the hospital training or diploma of a registered nurse.

prac tice (prak′tis), **1** action done many times over for skill: *Practice makes perfect.* **2** skill gained by experience or exercise: *They were out of practice at batting.* **3** do (some act) again and again to learn to do it well: *She practiced pitching the ball. I practice on the piano every day.* **4** action or process of doing or being something: *Your plan is good in theory, but not in actual practice.* **5** follow, observe, or use day after day; make a custom of; do usually: *Practice what you preach. We should practice kindness to others.* **6** the usual way; custom: *It is the practice at the factory to blow a whistle at noon.* **7** work at or follow as a profession, art, or occupation: *practice medicine.* **8** the working at or following of a profession or occupation: *She is engaged in the practice of law.* **9** business of a doctor or lawyer: *The old doctor sold his practice.* 1,2,4,6,8,9 *n.,* 3,5,7 *v.,* **prac ticed, prac tic ing.** Also, **practise. —prac′tic er,** *n.*

prac ticed or **prac tised** (prak′tist), experienced; skilled; expert: *Years of study have made him a practiced musician. adj.*

prac tise (prak′tis), practice. *v.,* **prac tised, prac tis ing.**

prac ti tion er (prak tish′ə nər), person engaged in the practice of a profession. *n.*

prae tor (prē′tər), magistrate or judge in ancient Rome. A praetor ranked next below a consul. *n.*

prae to ri an (prē tôr′ē ən), **1** of a praetor. **2** Often, **Praetorian.** of the bodyguard of a Roman commander or emperor. **3** Often, **Praetorian.** soldier of the bodyguard of a Roman commander or emperor. 1,2 *adj.,* 3 *n.*

prag mat ic (prag mat′ik), concerned with practical results or values; viewing things in a matter-of-fact way. *adj.* **—prag mat′i cal ly,** *adv.*

Prague (präg), capital and largest city of Czechoslovakia, in the W part. *n.*

Pra ia (prä′yə), capital of Cape Verde Islands. *n.*

prair ie (prer′ē), a large area of level or rolling land with grass but few or no trees. *n.*

prairie chicken, either of two brown, black, and white grouse that live on the prairies of North America.

prairie dog, a burrowing animal like a woodchuck but smaller, found on the Great Plains and in the Rocky Mountain region. Prairie dogs bark.

prairie schooner, a large covered wagon used in crossing the plains of North America before the railroads were built.

prairie wolf, coyote.

praise (prāz), **1** a saying that a thing or person is good; words that tell the worth or value of a thing or person. **2** express approval or admiration of: *Everyone praised the winning team for its fine play.* **3** to worship in words or song: *praise God.* **4** words or song worshiping God. 1,4 *n.,* 2,3 *v.,* **praised, prais ing.** —**prais′er,** *n.*

sing the praises of, praise with enthusiasm.

praise wor thy (prāz′wėr′ᵺē), worthy of praise; deserving approval. *adj.* —**praise′wor′thi ly,** *adv.* —**praise′wor′thi ness,** *n.*

pra line (prä′lēn′ *or* prā′lēn′), a small cake of brown candy made of brown or maple sugar and nuts, usually pecans or almonds. *n.*

prance (prans), **1** spring about on the hind legs: *Horses prance when they feel lively.* **2** ride on a horse doing this. **3** move gaily or proudly: *The children pranced about in their new Halloween costumes.* **4** a prancing. 1-3 *v.,* **pranced, pranc ing;** 4 *n.* —**pranc′er,** *n.* —**pranc′ing ly,** *adv.*

prank (prangk), piece of mischief; playful trick: *On April Fools' Day people often play pranks on each other.* *n.*

prank ish (prang′kish), **1** full of pranks; fond of pranks. **2** like a prank. *adj.* —**prank′ish ly,** *adv.* —**prank′ish ness,** *n.*

prank ster (prangk′stər), person who plays pranks. *n.*

pra se o dym i um (prā′zē ō dim′ē əm), a yellowish-white metallic element which occurs with neodymium. Its green salts are used to tint glass. *n.*

prate (prāt), talk a great deal in a foolish way. *v.,* **prat ed, prat ing.** —**prat′er,** *n.* —**prat′ing ly,** *adv.*

prat tle (prat′l), **1** tell freely and carelessly, as some children do. **2** talk in a foolish way; babble. **3** childish or foolish talk. **4** sounds like baby talk; babble: *the prattle of a brook.* 1,2 *v.,* **prat tled, prat tling;** 3,4 *n.* —**prat′tler,** *n.*

prawn (prôn), any of several shellfish used for food. Prawns are much like shrimps but larger. *n.*

pray (prā), **1** ask from God; speak to God in worship: *They prayed for God's help.* **2** ask earnestly for: *pray one's forgiveness.* **3** please: *Pray come with me.* *v.* —**pray′er,** *n.*

prayer (prer *or* prar), **1** act of praying. **2** thing prayed for: *Our prayers were granted.* **3** form of words to be used in praying: *the Lord's Prayer.* **4** form of worship. **5** an earnest or humble request. *n.*

prayer book, book of prayers.

prayer ful (prer′fəl *or* prar′fəl), having the habit of praying often; devout. *adj.* —**prayer′ful ly,** *adv.* —**prayer′ful ness,** *n.*

praying mantis, mantis.

pre-, *prefix.* **1** before: *Prewar = before the war.* **2** beforehand; in advance: *Preview = view beforehand. Prepay = pay in advance.*

preach (prēch), **1** speak on a religious subject; deliver (a sermon). **2** make known by preaching; proclaim: *preach the gospel.* **3** recommend strongly; urge: *The coach was always preaching exercise and fresh air. Practice what you preach.* **4** give earnest advice: *preach about good manners. v.*

preach er (prē′chər), person who preaches; member of the clergy; minister. *n.*

preach y (prē′chē), INFORMAL. **1** inclined to preach. **2** suggestive of preaching. *adj.,* **preach i er, preach i est.** —**preach′i ness,** *n.*

pre am ble (prē′am′bəl), introduction to a speech or a writing. The reasons for a law and its general purpose are often stated in a preamble. *n.* [*Preamble* came into English about 600 years ago from French *preambule,* and

can be traced back to Latin *prae,* meaning "before," and *ambulare,* meaning "to walk."]

pre ar range (prē′ə rānj′), arrange beforehand. *v.,* **pre ar ranged, pre ar rang ing.** —**pre′ar range′ment,** *n.*

prec., preceding.

pre car i ous (pri ker′ē əs *or* pri kar′ē əs), not safe or secure; uncertain; dangerous; risky: *A racing-car driver leads a precarious life. His hold on the branch was precarious. adj.* —**pre car′i ous ly,** *adv.* —**pre car′i ous ness,** *n.*

pre cau tion (pri kô′shən), **1** care taken beforehand; thing done beforehand to ward off evil or secure good results: *Locking doors is a precaution against thieves.* **2** a taking care beforehand: *Proper precaution is wise. n.*

pre cau tion ar y (pri kô′shə ner′ē), of or using precaution: *She took precautionary measures to avoid the flu. adj.*

pre cede (prē sēd′), **1** go or come before: *A precedes B in the alphabet. The band preceded the floats in the parade.* **2** be higher than in rank or importance: *A major precedes a captain. v.,* **pre ced ed, pre ced ing.**

prec e dence (pres′ə dəns *or* pri sēd′ns), **1** act or fact of preceding; a going or coming before in time or order. **2** higher position or rank; greater importance: *This work takes precedence over all other work.* **3** right to precede others in ceremonies or social affairs; social superiority: *A Senator takes precedence over a Representative. n.*

prec e dent (pres′ə dənt *for 1;* pri sēd′nt *or* pres′ə dənt *for 2),* **1** action that may serve as an example or reason for a later action: *A decision of a court often serves as a precedent in other courts. Last year's school picnic set a precedent for having one this year.* **2** preceding. 1 *n.,* 2 *adj.*

pre ced ing (prē sē′ding), going or coming before; previous: *Turn back and look for the answer on the preceding page. adj.*

pre cept (prē′sept), rule of action or behavior; guiding principal: *"If at first you don't succeed, try, try again" is a familiar precept. n.*

pre cep tor (pri sep′tər), instructor; teacher. *n.*

pre cinct (prē′singkt), **1** a part or district of a city: *an election precinct, a police precinct.* **2** space within a boundary: *Do not leave the school precincts during school hours. n.*

pre cious (presh′əs), **1** having great value; worth much; valuable. Gold, platinum, and silver are often called the precious metals. Diamonds, rubies, and sapphires are precious stones. **2** much loved; dear: *a precious child.* **3** too nice; overly refined: *precious language.* **4** very great: *a precious mess.* **5** INFORMAL. very: *precious little money.* 1-4 *adj.,* 5 *adv.* —**pre′cious ly,** *adv.* —**pre′cious ness,** *n.*

prec i pice (pres′ə pis), a very steep or almost vertical face of rock; cliff or steep mountainside. *n.* [*Precipice* comes from Latin *praecipitium,* and can be traced back to Latin *prae,* meaning "before," and *caput,* meaning "head."]

pre cip i tate (pri sip′ə tāt *for 1,3,4,6;* pri sip′ə tit *or* pri sip′ə tāt *for 2,5),* **1** hasten the beginning of; bring about suddenly: *precipitate an argument.* **2** with great haste and force; plunging or rushing; hasty; rash: *a precipitate action.* **3** throw headlong; hurl: *precipitate oneself into a struggle.* **4** separate (a substance) out from a solution as a solid. **5** substance separated out from a solution as a solid. **6** condense (water vapor) from the air in

---

a hat	i it	oi oil	ch child	a in about
ā age	ī ice	ou out	ng long	e in taken
ä far	o hot	u cup	sh she	ə = { i in pencil
e let	ō open	u̇ put	th thin	o in lemon
ē equal	ô order	ü rule	ᵺ then	u in circus
ėr term			zh measure	

the form of rain, dew, snow, etc. 1,3,4,6 *v.*, **pre cip i tat ed, pre cip i tat ing;** 2 *adj.* 5 *n.* —**pre cip′i tate ly,** *adv.* —**pre cip′i tate ness,** *n.* —**pre cip′i ta′tor,** *n.*

pre cip i ta tion (pri sip′ə tā′shən), **1** act or condition of precipitating; a throwing down or falling headlong. **2** a sudden bringing on: *the precipitation of a quarrel, the precipitation of a war without warning.* **3** unwise or rash rapidity; sudden haste. **4** the separating out of a substance from a solution as a solid. **5** the depositing of moisture in the form of rain, dew, snow, etc. **6** something that is precipitated, such as rain, dew, or snow. *n.*

pre cip i tous (pri sip′ə təs), **1** like a precipice; very steep: *precipitous cliffs.* **2** hasty; rash. *adj.* —**pre cip′i tous ly,** *adv.* —**pre cip′i tous ness,** *n.*

pre cise (pri sīs′), **1** very definite or correct; exact; accurate: *The directions they gave were so precise that we found our way easily. The precise sum was 34 cents.* **2** very careful: *precise handwriting. She is precise in her work.* **3** strict: *We had precise orders to come home by nine o'clock. adj.* —**pre cise′ly,** *adv.* —**pre cise′ness,** *n.*

pre ci sion (pri sizh′ən), a being exact; accuracy: *the precision of a machine, to speak with precision. n.*

pre clude (pri klüd′), shut out; make impossible; prevent: *The heavy thunderstorm precluded our going to the beach. v.*, **pre clud ed, pre clud ing.**

pre co cious (pri kō′shəs), developed earlier than usual in knowledge, skill, etc.: *This very precocious child could read well at the age of four. adj.* —**pre co′cious ly,** *adv.* —**pre co′cious ness,** *n.*

pre coc i ty (pri kos′ə tē), precocious development; early maturity: *Mozart's precocity was extraordinary, for when he was only five years old, he began to compose music. n.*

pre con ceived (prē′kən sēvd′), formed beforehand: *The beauty of the scenery surpassed all our preconceived notions. adj.*

preconception

pre con cep tion (prē′kən sep′shən), idea or opinion formed beforehand. *n.*

pre con cert ed (prē′kən sėr′tid), arranged beforehand: *At a preconcerted signal we sang "Happy Birthday." adj.*

pre cur sor (pri kėr′sər), forerunner: *A severe cold may be the precursor of pneumonia. n.*

pred., predicate.

pre date (prē dāt′), **1** be or happen before; precede; antedate: *Radio predated television.* **2** give an earlier date to: *predate a check. v.*, **pre dat ed, pre dat ing.**

pred a tor (pred′ə tər), animal or person that is predatory. *n.*

pred a to ry (pred′ə tôr′ē), **1** living by preying upon other animals. Lions and tigers are predatory animals.

Hawks and owls are predatory birds. **2** inclined to plundering or robbery: *Predatory pirates infested the seas. adj.*

pred e ces sor (pred′ə ses′ər), person holding a position or office before another. *n.*

pre des ti na tion (prē des′tə nā′shən), **1** an ordaining beforehand; destiny; fate. **2** action of God in deciding beforehand what shall happen; doctrine that by God's decree certain souls will be saved and others lost. *n.*

pre des tine (prē des′tən), determine or settle beforehand; foreordain. *v.*, **pre des tined, pre des tin ing.**

pre de ter mine (prē′di tėr′mən), determine or decide beforehand: *to predetermine profits. We met at the predetermined time. v.*, **pre de ter mined, pre de ter min ing.** —**pre′de ter′mi na′tion,** *n.*

pre dic a ment (pri dik′ə mənt), an unpleasant, difficult, or bad situation: *She was in a predicament when she missed the last train home. n.*

pred i cate (pred′ə kit *for 1,2;* pred′ə kāt *for 3-5*), **1** (in grammar) the word or words expressing what is said about the subject. EXAMPLES: Dogs *bark.* The dogs *dug holes.* The dogs *are beagles.* **2** (in grammar) belonging to the predicate. In "Horses are strong." *strong* is a **predicate adjective.** In "The dogs are beagles," *beagles* is a **predicate noun. 3** found or base (a statement, action, etc.) on something. **4** declare, assert, or affirm to be real or true: *Most religions predicate life after death.* **5** declare to be an attribute or quality (of some person or thing): *We predicate faithfulness of friends.* 1 *n.,* 2 *adj.,* 3-5 *v.,* **pred i cat ed, pred i cat ing.**

pre dict (pri dikt′), tell beforehand; prophesy; forecast: *The Weather Service predicts rain for tomorrow. v.*

pre dict a ble (pri dik′tə bəl), able to be predicted. *adj.*

pre dict a bly (pri dik′tə blē), in a predictable manner. *adv.*

pre dic tion (pri dik′shən), **1** act of predicting. **2** thing predicted; prophecy; forecast: *The offical predictions about the weather often come true. n.*

pre di lec tion (prē′də lek′shən *or* pred′ə lek′shən), a liking; preference. *n.*

pre dis pose (prē′dis pōz′), give an inclination or tendency to; make liable or susceptible: *A cold predisposes a person to other diseases. v.*, **pre dis posed, pre dis pos ing.**

pre dis po si tion (prē′dis′pə zish′ən), a being predisposed; inclination or tendency: *a predisposition to look on the dark side of things. n.*

pre dom i nance (pri dom′ə nəns), a being predominant: *the predominance of weeds in a deserted garden. n.*

pre dom i nant (pri dom′ə nənt), **1** having more power, authority, or influence than others; superior: *The United States is the predominant nation in the Western Hemisphere today.* **2** most noticeable; prevailing: *Red was the predominant color in the fabric. adj.* —**pre dom′i nant ly,** *adv.*

pre dom i nate (pri dom′ə nāt), be greater in power, strength, influence, or numbers: *Sunny days predominate over rainy days in desert regions. v.*, **pre dom i nat ed, pre dom i nat ing.**

pre em i nence *or* **pre-em i nence** (prē em′ə nəns), a being outstanding or preeminent; superiority: *the preeminence of an Olympic skier. n.*

pre em i nent *or* **pre-em i nent** (prē em′ə nənt), standing out above all others; superior to others. *adj.* —**pre em′i nent ly, pre-em′i nent ly,** *adv.*

pre empt *or* **pre-empt** (prē empt′), **1** secure before someone else can; acquire beforehand: *preempt the most comfortable chair.* **2** take over; replace: *A special feature preempted the regular TV program.* **3** settle on (land) with the right to buy it before others. *v.*

preen (prēn), **1** smooth or arrange (the feathers) with the beak. **2** dress or groom (oneself) carefully. *v.*

pre ex ist or **pre-ex ist** (prē/ig zist/), exist beforehand, or before something else. *v.*

pre ex ist ence or **pre-ex ist ence** (prē/ig zis/təns), previous existence. *n.*

pre ex ist ent or **pre-ex ist ent** (prē/ig zis/tənt), existing previously. *adj.*

pref., 1 preface. 2 preferred. 3 prefix.

pre fab (prē/fab/), something prefabricated, especially a house. *n.*

pre fab ri cate (prē fab/rə kāt), make all standardized parts of (a building, house, etc.) at a factory. The erection of a prefabricated house requires merely the assembling of the various sections. *v.*, **pre fab ri cat ed, pre fab ri cat ing.** —**pre/fab ri ca/tion,** *n.*

pref ace (pref/is), 1 introduction to a book, writing, or speech: *My history book has a preface written by the author.* 2 introduce by written or spoken remarks; give a preface to. 3 be a preface to; begin. 1 *n.*, 2,3 *v.*, **prefaced, pref ac ing.**

WORD HISTORY

preface

Preface came into English about 600 years ago from French *preface*, and can be traced back to Latin *prae*, meaning "before," and *fari*, meaning "to speak."

pref a to ry (pref/ə tôr/ē), of or like a preface; made as a preface; introductory; preliminary. *adj.* —**pref/a to/ri ly,** *adv.*

pre fect (prē/fekt), 1 (in ancient Rome) the title of various military and civil officers. 2 the chief administrative official of a department of France. *n.*

pre fer (pri fėr/), 1 like better; choose rather: *I will come later, if you prefer. She prefers swimming to fishing.* 2 put forward or present, especially a charge against someone for consideration in a court of law: *The policeman preferred charges of speeding against the driver. v.*, **pre ferred, pre fer ring.** —**pre fer/rer,** *n.*

pref er a ble (pref/ər ə bəl), to be preferred; more desirable. *adj.* —**pref/er a ble ness,** *n.*

pref er a bly (pref/ər ə blē), by choice: *She needs an assistant, preferably one who is a college graduate. adv.*

pref er ence (pref/ər əns), 1 act or attitude of preferring; liking better: *My preference is for beef rather than lamb.* 2 thing preferred; first choice: *My preference in reading is a mystery story.* 3 the favoring of one above another: *A teacher should not show preference for any student. n.*

pref e ren tial (pref/ə ren/shəl), of, giving, or receiving preference: *preferential treatment. adj.* —**pref/e ren/tial ly,** *adv.*

pre fer ment (pri fėr/mənt), advancement; promotion: *seek preferment in one's job. n.*

pre fig ure (prē fig/yər), 1 represent beforehand by a figure or type: *In one painting of Christ, His shadow is that of a cross, prefiguring the Crucifixion.* 2 imagine to oneself beforehand. *v.*, **pre fig ured, pre fig ur ing.** —**pre fig/ure ment,** *n.*

pre fix (prē/fiks for 1; prē fiks/ for 2), 1 syllable, syllables, or word put at the beginning of a word to change its meaning or to make another word, as *pre-* in *prepaid, under-* in *underline, dis-* in *disappear, un-* in *unlike,* and *re-* in *redo.* 2 put before: *We prefix Mr. to a man's name.* 1 *n.*, *pl.* **pre fix es;** 2 *v.*

prefabricate—A wall, **prefabricated** in a factory, is lowered into place.

preg nan cy (preg/nən sē), pregnant quality or condition. *n., pl.* **preg nan cies.**

preg nant (preg/nənt), 1 having one or more offspring developing in the womb; soon to have a baby. 2 filled; full: *words pregnant with meaning.* 3 abounding with ideas; fertile; inventive: *a pregnant mind.* 4 meaningful; significant: *a pregnant pause. adj.* —**preg/nant ly,** *adv.*

pre hen sile (pri hen/səl), adapted for seizing, grasping, or holding on. Many monkeys have prehensile tails. *adj.*

prehensile
The woolly monkey has a prehensile tail.

pre his to ric (prē/hi stôr/ik), of or belonging to times before histories were written: *Prehistoric peoples used stone tools. adj.* —**pre/his to/ri cal ly,** *adv.*

pre his to ri cal (prē/hi stôr/ə kəl), prehistoric. *adj.*

pre judge (prē juj/), judge beforehand; judge without knowing all the facts. *v.*, **pre judged, pre judg ing.** —**pre judg/ment, pre judge/ment,** *n.*

prej u dice (prej/ə dis), 1 opinion formed without taking time and care to judge fairly: *a prejudice against foreigners.* 2 cause a prejudice in; fill with prejudice: *One unfortunate experience prejudiced him against all lawyers.* 3 harm or injury: *I will do nothing to the prejudice of my cousin in this matter.* 4 to harm or injure. 1,3 *n.*, 2,4 *v.*, **prej u diced, prej u dic ing.**

prej u di cial (prej/ə dish/əl), causing prejudice or disadvantage; hurtful: *acting in a manner prejudicial to others. adj.* —**prej/u di/cial ly,** *adv.*

prel ate (prel/it), clergyman of high rank, such as a bishop. *n.*

prelim., preliminary.

pre lim i nar y (pri lim/ə ner/ē), 1 coming before the main business; leading to something more important:

After the preliminary song, the speaker of the day gave an address. **2** a preliminary step; something preparatory: *An examination is a preliminary to entering that school.* **1** *adj.,* **2** *n., pl.* **pre lim i nar ies.**

prel ude (prel´yüd *or* prē´lüd), **1** anything serving as an introduction: *The German invasion of Poland was a prelude to World War II.* **2** in music: **a** a composition, or part of it, that introduces another composition or part. **b** an independent instrumental composition, usually short. *n.*

pre ma ture (prē´mə chùr´, prē´mə tùr´, *or* prē´mə tyùr´), before the proper time; too soon: *Their arrival an hour before the party began was premature. adj.*

pre med i cal (prē med´ə kəl), preparing for the study of medicine: *a premedical student, a premedical course. adj.*

pre med i tate (prē med´ə tāt), consider or plan beforehand: *premeditate a move in chess. The murder was premeditated. v.,* **pre med i tat ed, pre med i tat ing.**

pre med i ta tion (prē´med ə tā´shən), previous planning. *n.*

pre mier (pri mir´ *for 1;* prē´mē ər *for 2,3*), **1** prime minister. **2** first in rank; chief. **3** first in time; earliest. **1** *n.,* **2,3** *adj.*

pre miere (pri mir´ *or* prə myer´), **1** a first public performance: *the premiere of a new play.* **2** premier; first. **1** *n.,* **2** *adj.* [*Premiere* comes from French *première,* and can be traced back to Latin *primus,* meaning "first."]

prem ise (prem´is *for 1,2;* prem´is *or* pri mīz´ *for 3*), **1** (in logic) a statement assumed to be true and used to draw a conclusion. EXAMPLE: Major premise: Children should go to school. Minor premise: They are children. Conclusion: They should go to school. **2 premises,** *pl.* **a** a house or building with its grounds. **b** (in law) things mentioned previously, such as the names of the parties concerned, a description of the property, etc. **c** (in law) the property forming the subject of a document. **3** set forth as an introduction; mention beforehand. **1,2** *n.,* **3** *v.,* **premised, pre mis ing.**

pre mi um (prē´mē əm), **1** a reward, especially one given as an incentive to buy; prize: *Some magazines give premiums for obtaining new subscriptions.* **2** something more than the ordinary price or wages. **3** money paid for insurance: *I pay premiums on my life insurance four times a year.* **4** unusual or unfair value: *put too high a premium on neatness. n.*

at a premium, at more than the usual value or price: *Tickets for the concert were scarce and selling at a premium.*

pre mo lar (prē mō´lər), bicuspid. *n.*

pre mo ni tion (prē´mə nish´ən), a forewarning: *a vague premonition of disaster. n.*

pre mon i to ry (pri mon´ə tôr´ē), giving warning beforehand. *adj.*

pre na tal (prē nā´tl), previous to birth: *A woman soon to have a baby requires prenatal care. adj.*

pre oc cu pa tion (prē ok´yə pā´shən), **1** act of preoccupying. **2** condition of being preoccupied; absorption. *n.*

pre oc cu pied (prē ok´yə pīd), absorbed. *adj.*

pre oc cu py (prē ok´yə pī), **1** take up all the attention of; absorb: *The problem of how to pay her debts preoccupied her mind.* **2** occupy beforehand; take possession of before others: *Our favorite seats had been preoccupied. v.,* **pre oc cu pied, pre oc cu py ing. —pre oc´cu pi er,** *n.*

pre or dain (prē´ôr dān´), decide or settle beforehand; foreordain. *v.*

prep (prep), INFORMAL. preparatory: *a prep school. adj.*

prep., preposition.

pre paid (prē pād´), past tense and past participle of **prepay.** *Send this shipment prepaid. v.*

prep a ra tion (prep´ə rā´shən), **1** a preparing; making ready: *I sharpened the knife in preparation for carving the*

meat. **2** a being ready. **3** thing done to get ready: *He made thorough preparations for his trip by carefully planning which routes to take.* **4** a specially made medicine or food or mixture of any kind. *n.*

pre par a to ry (pri par´ə tôr´ē), **1** of or for preparation; making ready; preparing. Preparatory schools fit pupils for college. **2** as an introduction; preliminary: *preparatory remarks. adj.* **—pre par´a to´ri ly,** *adv.*

pre pare (pri per´ *or* pri par´), **1** make ready; get ready: *prepare lessons, prepare dinner.* **2** make by a special process: *prepare aluminum from bauxite. v.,* **pre pared, pre par ing. —pre par´er,** *n.*

pre par ed ness (pri per´id nis *or* pri par´id nis), **1** a being prepared; readiness. **2** having adequate military forces and defenses to meet threats or outbreaks of war. *n.*

pre pay (prē pā´), pay or pay for in advance. *v.,* **pre paid, pre pay ing.**

pre pay ment (prē pā´mənt), payment in advance. *n.*

pre pon der ance (pri pon´dər əns), **1** greater number; greater weight; greater power or influence. **2** a being the chief or most important element: *the preponderance of oaks in these woods. n.*

pre pon der ant (pri pon´dər ənt), **1** weighing more; being stronger or more numerous; having more power or influence. **2** most important; chief: *Lush vegetation is the preponderant characteristic of the jungle. adj.*

prep o si tion (prep´ə zish´ən), word that expresses some relation to a noun, pronoun, phrase, or clause which follows it. *With, for, by,* and *in* are prepositions in the sentence "A man *with* vegetables *for* sale walked *by* our house *in* the morning." *n.*

prep o si tion al (prep´ə zish´ə nəl), **1** having to do with a preposition: *a prepositional phrase.* **2** having the nature or function of a preposition. *adj.*

pre pos sess ing (prē´pə zes´ing), making a favorable impression; attractive; pleasing: *In my old, ragged work clothes, my appearance was not very prepossessing. adj.*

pre pos ter ous (pri pos´tər əs), contrary to nature, reason, or common sense; absurd; senseless; foolish: *That the moon is made of green cheese is a preposterous notion. adj.* **—pre pos´ter ous ly,** *adv.* **—pre pos´ter ous ness,** *n.*

prep pie *or* **prep py** (prep´ē), SLANG. **1** student or graduate of a preparatory school. **2** of or like that of preppies, especially in regard to clothes or behavior: *preppie fashions.* **1** *n., pl.* **prep pies;** **2** *adj.,* **prep pi er, prep pi est.**

pre quel (prē´kwəl), book, motion picture, TV show, or the like, in which the story or events take place before those of an earlier work. *n.* [*Prequel* comes from *pre-* and the last four letters of *sequel.*]

pre req ui site (prē rek´wə zit), **1** something required beforehand: *The completion of a high-school course is the usual prerequisite to college work.* **2** required beforehand. **1** *n.,* **2** *adj.*

pre rog a tive (pri rog´ə tiv), right or privilege that nobody else has: *The government has the prerogative of coining money. n.*

pres., present.

Pres., **1** Presbyterian. **2** President.

pres age (pres´ij *for 1,3;* pres´ij *or* pri sāj´ *for 2,4*), **1** a sign felt as a warning; omen. **2** give warning of; predict: *Some people think that a circle around the moon presages a storm.* **3** a feeling that something is about to happen. **4** have or give a prophetic impression of. **1,3** *n.,* **2,4** *v.,* **pre saged, pre sag ing. —pre sag´er,** *n.*

pres by ter (prez´bə tər), **1** a minister or a lay elder in the Presbyterian Church. **2** a minister or a priest in the Episcopal Church. *n.*

Pres by ter i an (prez´bə tir´ē ən), **1** of or belonging to a Protestant denomination or church governed by elected presbyters or elders all of equal rank. **2** member of a Presbyterian church. **1** *adj.*, **2** *n.*

Pres by ter i an ism (prez/bə tir/ē ə niz/əm), **1** system of church government by elders all (including ministers) of equal rank. **2** beliefs of Presbyterian churches. *n.*

pre school (prē/skül/), before the age of going to regular school: *preschool training, preschool children. adj.*

pre sci ence (prē/shē əns), knowledge of things before they exist or happen; foreknowledge; foresight: *Some people believe that animals have an instinctive prescience of the approach of danger. n.*

pre sci ent (prē/shē ənt), knowing beforehand; foreseeing. *adj.* —**pre/sci ent ly,** *adv.*

pre scribe (pri skrīb/), **1** lay down as a rule to be followed; order; direct: *Good citizens do what the laws prescribe.* **2** order as a medicine or treatment: *The doctor prescribed penicillin.* **3** give medical advice; issue a prescription. *v.*, **pre scribed, pre scrib ing.** —**pre scrib/er,** *n.*

pre scrip tion (pri skrip/shən), **1** order; direction. **2** a written direction or order for preparing and using a medicine: *a prescription for a cough.* **3** the medicine. *n.*

pre scrip tive (pri skrip/tiv), **1** prescribing. **2** established by law or custom. *adj.* —**pre scrip/tive ly,** *adv.* —**pre scrip/tive ness,** *n.*

pres ence (prez/ns), **1** a being present in a place: *I just learned of her presence in the city.* **2** a place where a person is: *The messenger was admitted to the king's presence.* **3** appearance; bearing: *The queen is a person of noble presence.* **4** something present, especially a ghost, spirit, or the like. *n.*

in the presence of, in the sight or company of: *I signed my name in the presence of two witnesses.*

presence of mind, ability to think calmly and quickly under stress.

pres ent[1] (prez/nt), **1** being in the place or thing in question; at hand, not absent: *Every member of the class was present. Oxygen is present in the air.* **2** at this time; being or occurring now: *the present government, present prices.* **3** the time being; this time; now: *That is enough for the present.* **4** the present tense or a verb form in that tense. **1,2** *adj.*, **3,4** *n.*

pre sent[2] (pri zent/ for 1,3-8; prez/nt for 2), **1** give: *They presented flowers to their teacher.* **2** thing given; gift: *a birthday present.* **3** offer formally; offer: *The host presented the sandwiches to each guest.* **4** make acquainted; bring (a person) before somebody; introduce: *She was presented at court. Miss Smith, may I present Mr. Brown?* **5** offer to view or notice: *The new library presents a fine appearance.* **6** bring before the public: *Our class presented a play.* **7** set forth in words; offer: *The speaker presented arguments for his side.* **8** hand in; send in: *The grocer presented his bill.* **1,3-8** *v.*, **2** *n.* —**pre sent/er,** *n.*

present with, give to: *Our class presented the school with a picture.*

pre sent a ble (pri zen/tə bəl), **1** fit to be seen: *to make a house presentable for company.* **2** suitable in appearance, dress, manners, etc., for being introduced into society or company. **3** suitable to be offered or given. *adj.* —**pre sent/a ble ness,** *n.* —**pre sent/a bly,** *adv.*

pres en ta tion (prez/n tā/shən or prē/zen tā/shən), **1** act of giving; delivering: *the presentation of a gift.* **2** the gift that is presented. **3** a bringing forward; offering to be considered: *the presentation of a plan.* **4** an offering to be seen; showing; exhibition: *the presentation of a play or a motion picture.* **5** a formal introduction: *the presentation of a lady to the queen. n.*

pres ent-day (prez/nt dā/), of the present time. *adj.*

pre sen ti ment (pri zen/tə mənt), a feeling or impression that something is about to happen; vague sense of approaching misfortune; foreboding. *n.*

pres ent ly (prez/nt lē), **1** before long; soon: *I will do the dishes presently.* **2** at the present time; at this time; now: *He is presently in sixth grade. adv.*

pre sent ment (pri zent/mənt), **1** a bringing forward; offering to be considered. **2** a showing; offering to be seen. **3** something brought forward or shown. *n.*

present participle, participle that indicates time that is now. In "Singing merrily, we turn our steps toward home," *singing* is a present participle.

present tense, 1 tense that expresses time that is now. **2** a verb form in the present tense.

pres er va tion (prez/ər vā/shən), **1** a preserving; keeping safe: *Doctors work for the preservation of our health.* **2** a being preserved; being kept safe: *Egyptian mummies have been in a state of preservation for thousands of years. n.*

pre serv a tive (pri zėr/və tiv), **1** any substance that will prevent decay or injury: *Paint is a preservative for wood surfaces. Salt is a preservative for meat.* **2** capable of preserving. **1** *n.*, **2** *adj.*

pre serve (pri zėrv/), **1** keep from harm or change; keep safe; protect. **2** keep up; maintain. **3** keep from spoiling: *Ice helps to preserve food.* **4** prepare (food) to keep it from spoiling. Boiling with sugar, salting, smoking, and pickling are different ways of preserving food. **5** preserves, *pl.* fruit cooked with sugar and sealed from the air: *plum preserves.* **6** a place where wild animals, fish, or trees and plants are protected: *People are not allowed to hunt in that preserve.* **1-4** *v.*, **pre served, pre serv ing; 5,6** *n.* —**pre serv/a ble,** *adj.*

pre serv er (pri zėr/vər), person or thing that saves and protects from danger. Life preservers help to save people from drowning. *n.*

pre set (prē set/), set in advance: *The missile's course was preset before it was launched. v.*, **pre set, pre set ting.**

pre side (pri zīd/), **1** hold the place of authority; have charge of a meeting: *preside at an election.* **2** have authority; have control: *The manager presides over the business of this store. v.*, **pre sid ed, pre sid ing.** —**pre sid/er,** *n.*

pres i den cy (prez/ə dən sē), **1** office of president: *She was elected to the presidency of the Junior Club.* **2** time in which a president is in office: *The United States entered World War II during the presidency of Franklin D. Roosevelt. n., pl.* **pres i den cies.**

pres i dent (prez/ə dənt), **1** the chief officer of a company, college, society, club, etc. **2** Often, **President.** the highest executive officer of a republic. *n.*

pres i dent-e lect (prez/ə dənt i lekt/), president who has been elected but not yet inaugurated. *n.*

pres i den tial (prez/ə den/shəl), of or having to do with a president or presidency: *a presidential election, a presidential candidate. adj.* —**pres/i den/tial ly,** *adv.*

Presidents' Day, the third Monday in February, celebrated as a holiday in some states to commemorate the birthdays of Abraham Lincoln and George Washington.

press[1] (pres), **1** use force or weight steadily against; push with steady force: *Press the button to ring the bell.* **2** squeeze out; squeeze: *press apples for cider. Press all the juice from the oranges.* **3** make smooth; flatten: *Press clothes with an iron.* **4** clasp; hug: *I pressed the puppy to* *me.* **5** a pressing; pressure; push: *The press of many duties keeps her very busy.* **6** machine for pressing: *an ironing press.* **7** a printing press. **8** establishment for printing books, etc. **9** the business of printing newspapers and magazines: *Many editors, writers, and printers work for the press.* **10** newspapers, magazines, radio, and television, and the people who report for them: *The fire was reported by the press.* **11** push forward; keep pushing: *I pressed on in spite of the strong wind.* **12** urge onward; cause to hurry. **13** a crowd; throng: *The little boy was lost in the press.* **14** to crowd; throng: *The people pressed about the famous actor.* **15** keep asking (somebody) earnestly; urge: *We pressed our guest to stay until the snow stopped.* **16** compel; force. **17** harass; oppress; trouble. **18** cupboard or closet for clothes, books, etc. 1-4,11,12,14-17 *v.*, 5-10,13,18 *n.*, *pl.* **press es.** —**press'a ble,** *adj.*

go to press, begin to be printed: *The newspaper goes to press at midnight.*

press² (pres), force into service, usually naval or military. Naval officers used to visit towns and merchant ships to press men for the fleet. *v.*

press agent, agent in charge of publicity for a person, organization, etc.; publicist.

press ing (pres'ing), requiring immediate action or attention; urgent: *A person with a broken leg is in pressing need of a doctor's help. She left town quickly on some pressing business. adj.* —**press'ing ly,** *adv.*

pres sure (presh'ər), **1** the continued action of a weight or force: *The small box was flattened by the pressure of the heavy book on it.* **2** force per unit of area: *There is a pressure of 27 pounds to the square inch in this tire.* **3** a state of trouble or strain: *working under pressure.* **4** a compelling force or influence: *I was under pressure from the others to change my mind.* **5** force or urge by exerting pressure: *The car dealer tried to pressure my parents into buying a car.* **6** need for prompt or decisive action; urgency: *the pressure of business.* 1-4,6 *n.*, 5 *v.*, **pres sured, pres sur ing.** —**pres'sure less,** *adj.*

pressure cooker, an airtight container for cooking with steam under pressure.

pres sur ize (presh'ə rīz'), keep the atmospheric pressure inside (the cabin of an aircraft) at a normal level in spite of the altitude. *v.*, **pres sur ized, pres sur iz ing.** —**pres'sur i za'tion,** *n.* —**pres'sur iz'er,** *n.*

pres tige (pre stēzh'), reputation, influence, or distinction based on what is known about one's abilities, achievements, opportunities, associations, etc.: *Her prestige rose when her classmates learned that she could ski.* *n.*

pres ti gious (pre stij'əs), having prestige. *adj.*

pres to (pres'tō), in music: **1** very quickly. **2** very quick. **3** a very quick part in a piece of music. 1 *adv.*, 2 *adj.*, 3 *n.*, *pl.* **pres tos.** [*Presto* was borrowed from Italian *presto,* which came from Latin *praesto,* meaning "ready."]

pre sum a ble (pri zü'mə bəl), able to be presumed or taken for granted; probable; likely: *the presumable cause of the accident. adj.*

pre sum a bly (pri zü'mə blē), probably. *adv.*

pre sume (pri züm'), **1** take for granted without proving; suppose: *You'll play out of doors, I presume, if there is sunshine. The law presumes innocence until guilt is proved.* **2** take upon oneself; venture; dare: *May I presume to tell you you are wrong?* **3** take an unfair advantage: *Don't presume on his good nature by borrowing from him every week.* **4** act with improper boldness; take liberties: *It would be presuming to camp in a farmer's field without permission. v.*, **pre sumed, pre sum ing.** —**pre sum'er,** *n.*

pre sum ed ly (pri zü'mid lē), presumably. *adv.*

pre sump tion (pri zump'shən), **1** unpleasant boldness: *It is presumption to go to a party when one has not been invited.* **2** thing taken for granted: *Since she took the coat,*

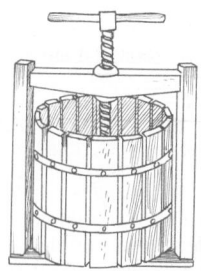

press¹ (def. 6)
for making cider

the presumption was that it was hers. **3** cause or reason for presuming; probability. **4** act of presuming. *n.*

pre sump tive (pri zump'tiv), **1** based on likelihood; presumed: *a presumptive title to an estate.* **2** giving ground for presumption or belief: *Their running away was regarded as presumptive evidence of their guilt. adj.* —**pre sump'tive ly,** *adv.*

pre sump tu ous (pri zump'chü əs), acting without permission; too bold; forward. *adj.* —**pre sump'tu ous ly,** *adv.* —**pre sump'tu ous ness,** *n.*

pre sup pose (prē'sə pōz'), **1** take for granted in advance; assume beforehand: *Let's presuppose that we will be going and make some plans for the trip.* **2** require as a condition; imply: *A debate presupposes debaters. v.*, **pre sup posed, pre sup pos ing.**

pre sup po si tion (prē'sup ə zish'ən), **1** a presupposing. **2** thing presupposed: *The detective acted upon the presupposition that the thief knew the value of the jewels. n.*

pre teen or **pre-teen** (prē'tēn'), **1** person younger than 13, especially one about 10 to 12 years of age. **2** of, for, or characteristic of a preteen or preteens: *preteen styles.* **3** being a preteen or preteens: *preteen children.* 1 *n.*, 2,3 *adj.*

pre tence (prē'tens or pri tens'), pretense. *n.*

pre tend (pri tend'), **1** make believe: *Let's pretend that we are grown-ups.* **2** claim falsely: *I pretended to like the meal so that my host would be pleased.* **3** claim falsely to have: *She pretended illness.* **4** claim: *I don't pretend to be a musician.* **5** lay claim: *The Scottish king pretended to the English throne. v.*

pre tend ed (pri ten'did), claimed falsely; asserted falsely. *adj.* —**pre tend'ed ly,** *adv.*

pre tend er (pri ten'dər), **1** person who pretends. **2** person who lays claim, especially falsely, to a title or throne. *n.*

pre tense (prē'tens or pri tens'), **1** make-believe; pretending: *My anger was all pretense.* **2** a false appearance: *Under pretense of dropping a pencil, she looked at a classmate's test.* **3** a false claim: *She made a pretense of knowing our secret.* **4** a claim: *I make no pretense to a talent for art.* **5** a showing off; display: *a manner free from pretense. n.* Also, **pretence.**

pre ten sion (pri ten'shən), **1** a claim: *The young prince has pretensions to the throne.* **2** a putting forward of a claim; laying claim to. **3** a doing things for show or to make a fine appearance; showy display: *We were annoyed by the pretensions of our wealthy neighbor. n.*

pre ten tious (pri ten'shəs), **1** making claims to excellence or importance: *a pretentious person, a pretentious book.* **2** doing things for show or to make a fine appearance: *a pretentious style of entertaining guests. adj.* —**pre ten'tious ly,** *adv.* —**pre ten'tious ness,** *n.*

pret er it or **pret er ite** (pret'ər it), in grammar: **1** a verb form that expresses occurrence in the past; past tense. EXAMPLES: *Obeyed* is the preterit of *obey; spoke,* of *speak;* and *saw,* of *see.* **2** expressing past time. 1 *n.*, 2 *adj.*

pre ter nat ur al (prē'tər nach'ər əl), **1** out of the ordinary course of nature; abnormal. **2** due to something above or beyond nature; supernatural. *adj.* —**pre′ter-nat′ur al ly,** *adv.*

pre text (prē′tekst), a false reason concealing the real reason; misleading excuse; pretense: *He did not go, on the pretext of being too tired.* *n.*

Pre to ri a (pri tôr′ē ə), administrative capital of the Republic of South Africa, in the NE part. *n.*

pret ti fy (prit′ə fī), make artificially pretty. *v.*, **pret ti-fied, pret ti fy ing.** —**pret′ti fi ca′tion,** *n.*

pret ti ly (prit′ə lē), in a pretty manner; pleasingly. *adv.*

pret ti ness (prit′ē nis), state or quality of being pretty; pleasing appearance. *n.*

pret ty (prit′ē), **1** pleasing to the eye, ear, etc.: *a pretty face, a pretty dress, a pretty tune.* **2** not at all pleasing: *This is a pretty mess, indeed.* **3** fairly; rather: *It is pretty late.* 1,2 *adj.*, **pret ti er, pret ti est;** 3 *adv.*

sitting pretty, in an advantageous position: *They certainly are sitting pretty since they made all that money.*

WORD HISTORY

pretty

Pretty is from Old English *prættig,* meaning "cunning, tricky," which comes from *prætt,* meaning "a trick."

pret zel (pret′səl), a crisp cracker, usually in the form of a knot or stick, salted on the outside. *n.* [*Pretzel* comes from German *Brezel,* and can be traced back to Greek *brachys,* meaning "short."]

pre vail (pri vāl′), **1** exist in many places; be in general use: *Making resolutions on New Year's Day is a custom that still prevails.* **2** be the most usual or strongest: *Sadness prevailed in our minds.* **3** be the stronger; gain the victory; succeed: *prevail against an enemy. Reason prevailed over emotion.* *v.* —**pre vail′er,** *n.*

prevail on or **prevail upon,** persuade: *Can I prevail upon you to stay?*

pre vail ing (pri vā′ling), **1** in general use; common: *a prevailing style. The prevailing summer winds here are from the west.* **2** that prevails; having superior force or influence; victorious. *adj.* —**pre vail′ing ly,** *adv.*

prev a lence (prev′ə ləns), widespread occurrence; general use: *the prevalence of automobiles.* *n.*

prev a lent (prev′ə lənt), in general use; widespread; common: *Colds are prevalent in the winter. adj.* —**prev′a-lent ly,** *adv.*

pre var i cate (pri var′ə kāt), turn aside from the truth in speech or action; lie. *v.*, **pre var i cat ed, pre var i cat-ing.**

pre var i ca tion (pri var′ə kā′shən), a prevaricating; turning aside from the truth. *n.*

pre var i ca tor (pri var′ə kā′tər), person who turns aside from the truth in speech or action. *n.*

pre vent (pri vent′), **1** keep (from): *Illness prevented him from working.* **2** keep from happening: *Rain prevented the game.* **3** hinder: *Doctors try to prevent diseases from spreading by treating them.* *v.* —**pre vent′er,** *n.*

pre vent a ble or **pre vent i ble** (pri ven′tə bəl), able to be prevented. *adj.*

pre ven tion (pri ven′shən), **1** a preventing: *the prevention of fire.* **2** something that prevents. *n.*

pre ven tive (pri ven′tiv), **1** able to prevent or hinder: *preventive measures against disease.* **2** something that prevents: *Vaccination is a preventive against smallpox.* 1 *adj.*,

2 *n.* —**pre ven′tive ly,** *adv.* —**pre ven′tive ness,** *n.*

pre view (prē′vyü′), **1** a previous view, inspection, survey, etc.: *a preview of things to come.* **2** to view beforehand. **3** an advance showing of scenes from a motion picture, play, television program, etc. 1,3 *n.*, 2 *v.*

pre vi ous (prē′vē əs), **1** coming or being before; earlier: *She did better in the previous lesson.* **2** INFORMAL. quick; hasty: *Don't be too previous about refusing. adj.* —**pre′-vi ous ly,** *adv.* —**pre′vi ous ness,** *n.*

previous to, before: *Previous to her departure he gave a party for her.*

pre war (prē′wôr′), before the war. *adj.*

prey (prā), **1** animal hunted and killed for food by another animal: *Mice and birds are the prey of cats.* **2** habit of hunting and killing other animals for food: *Hawks are birds of prey.* **3** person or thing injured; victim: *to be a prey to fear, to be a prey to disease.* **4** **prey on** or **prey upon, a** hunt or kill for food: *Cats prey upon mice.* **b** be a strain upon; injure; irritate: *Worry about debts preys on her mind.* **c** rob; plunder. 1-3 *n.*, 4 *v.* —**prey′er,** *n.*

Pri am (prī′əm), (in Greek legends) the king of Troy at the time of the Trojan War. *n.*

price (prīs), **1** the amount for which a thing is sold or can be bought; the cost to the buyer: *The price of this hat is $10.* **2** put a price on; set the price of: *The hat was priced at $10.* **3** ask the price of; find out the price of: *Mother is pricing cars.* **4** reward offered for the capture of a person alive or dead: *Every member of the gang has a price on his head.* **5** what must be given, done, undergone, etc., to obtain a thing; amount paid for any result: *The Pilgrims paid a heavy price for staying in America, for half of them died during the first winter.* **6** value; worth: *a diamond of great price.* 1,4-6 *n.*, 2,3 *v.*, **priced, pric ing.** [*Price* came into English about 750 years ago from French *pris,* which came from Latin *pretium.*] —**price′a-ble,** *adj.* —**pric′er,** *n.*

at any price, at any cost, no matter how great: *We wanted to win at any price.*

beyond price or **without price,** so valuable that it cannot be bought, or be given a value in money.

price less (prīs′lis), beyond price; extremely valuable: *Many museums have collections of priceless works of art. adj.* —**price′less ness,** *n.*

prick (prik), **1** a sharp point. **2** a little hole or mark made by a sharp point. **3** make a little hole or mark on with a sharp point: *I pricked my finger on a thorn.* **4** a pain like that made by a sharp point: *the prick of conscience.* **5** act of pricking. **6** to point upwards; raise or erect: *The dog pricked up its ears at the noise.* **7** OLD USE. ride fast; spur. 1,2,4,5 *n.*, 3,6,7 *v.* [*Prick* comes from Old English *prica.*] —**prick′er,** *n.* —**prick′ing ly,** *adv.*

prick le (prik′əl), **1** a small, sharp point; thorn; spine. **2** feel a prickly or smarting sensation: *My skin prickled as I listened to the scary story.* **3** such a sensation. **4** cause such a sensation. 1,3 *n.*, 2,4 *v.*, **prick led, prick ling.**

prick li ness (prik′lē nis), prickly condition or quality. *n.*

prick ly (prik′lē), **1** having many sharp points or thorns: *a prickly rosebush, the prickly porcupine.* **2** sharp and stinging; itching; smarting: *Heat sometimes causes a prickly rash on the skin. adj.*, **prick li er, prick li est.**

prickly heat, a red, itching rash on the skin caused by inflammation of the sweat glands.

a hat	i it	oi oil	ch child	ə = { a in about
ā age	ī ice	ou out	ng long	e in taken
ä far	o hot	u cup	sh she	i in pencil
e let	ō open	u̇ put	th thin	o in lemon
ē equal	ô order	ü rule	ŦH then	u in circus
ėr term			zh measure	

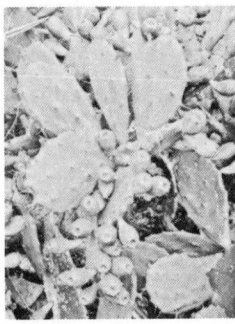

prickly pear
(defs. 1 and 2)

prickly pear, 1 a pear-shaped fruit of a certain kind of cactus. It is good to eat. **2** plant that it grows on.

pride (prīd), **1** a high opinion of one's own worth or possessions: *Pride in our city should make us help to keep it clean.* **2** pleasure or satisfaction in something concerned with oneself: *to take pride in a hard job well done.* **3** something that one is proud of: *Their children are their great pride.* **4** too high an opinion of oneself; scorn of others; haughtiness: *Pride goes before a fall.* **5 pride oneself on,** be proud of: *I pride myself on being punctual.* 1-4 *n.*, 5 *v.*, **prid ed, prid ing.**

pride ful (prīd′fəl), proud. *adj.* —**pride′ful ly,** *adv.*

priest (prēst), **1** clergyman or minister of a Christian church. **2** a special servant of a god, who performs certain public religious acts: *priests of Apollo. n.* [Priest comes from Old English *prēost,* and can be traced back to Greek *presbys,* meaning "an old man."]

priest ess (prē′stis), woman who serves at an altar or in sacred rites: *a priestess of Diana. n., pl.* **priest ess es.**

priest hood (prēst′hùd), **1** position or rank of priest: *He was admitted to the priesthood.* **2** priests as a group: *the priesthood of Spain. n.*

priest ly (prēst′lē), **1** of a priest. **2** like a priest; suitable for a priest. *adj.,* **priest li er, priest li est.** —**priest′li ness,** *n.*

prig (prig), person who is too particular about speech and manners, and prides himself or herself on being better than others. *n.*

prig gish (prig′ish), too particular about doing right in things that show outwardly; priding oneself on being better than others. *adj.* —**prig′gish ly,** *adv.* —**prig′gish ness,** *n.*

prim (prim), stiffly precise, neat, proper, or formal. *adj.,* **prim mer, prim mest.** —**prim′ly,** *adv.* —**prim′ness,** *n.*

pri ma cy (prī′mə sē), **1** a being first in order, rank, importance, etc. **2** the position of a bishop of highest rank. *n., pl.* **pri ma cies.**

pri ma don na (prē′mə don′ə), **1** the principal woman singer in an opera. **2** a temperamental person. [*Prima donna* comes from Italian *prima donna,* which originally meant "first lady."]

pri mal (prī′məl), **1** of early times; first; primeval. **2** chief; fundamental. *adj.* —**pri′mal ly,** *adv.*

pri mar i ly (prī′mer′ə lē *or* prī mer′ə lē), **1** above all; chiefly; principally: *The scientist was primarily interested in physics.* **2** at first; originally. *adv.*

pri mar y (prī′mer′ē), **1** first in time or order; original; fundamental: *the primary causes of unemployment.* **2** first in importance; chief: *A balanced diet is primary to good health.* **3** anything that is first in order, rank, or importance. **4** an election in which members of a political party choose candidates for office. Primaries are held before the regular election. 1,2 *adj.,* 3,4 *n., pl.* **pri mar ies.** —**pri′mar′i ness,** *n.*

primary accent, 1 the strongest accent in the pronunciation of a word. **2** mark (′) used to show this.

primary color, any of a group of pigments or colors which, when mixed together, yield all other colors. Red, yellow, and blue are the primary colors in pigments. In light they are red, green, and blue.

primary school, the first three or four grades of elementary school.

pri mate (prī′māt *for 1;* prī′mit *or* prī′māt *for 2*), **1** one of a group of mammals that have very advanced brains, and hands with thumbs that can grasp things. Primates are the most highly developed mammals. Apes, monkeys, and human beings are primates. **2** archbishop or bishop ranking above all other bishops in a country or church province. *n.*

prime[1] (prīm), **1** first in rank; chief: *The town's prime need is a new school.* **2** first in time or order; primary: *the prime causes of pollution.* **3** first in quality; first-rate; excellent: *prime ribs of beef.* **4** prime number. 1-3 *adj.,* 4 *n.* —**prime′ness,** *n.*

prime[2] (prīm), **1** the best part; best time; best condition: *be in the prime of life.* **2** the first part; beginning. *n.*

prime[3] (prīm), **1** prepare by putting something in or on. **2** supply (a gun) with powder. **3** cover (a surface) with a first coat of paint or oil so that the finishing coat of paint will not soak in. **4** equip (a person) with information, words, etc.: *prime a person with a speech.* **5** pour water into (a pump) to start action. *v.,* **primed, prim ing.**

prime meridian, meridian from which the longitude east and west is measured. It passes through Greenwich, England, and its longitude is 0 degrees.

prime minister, the chief minister in certain governments; premier. The prime minister is the head of the cabinet.

prime number, integer not exactly divisible by any integer other than itself and 1; prime. 2, 3, 5, 7, and 11 are prime numbers; 4, 6, and 9 are composite numbers.

prim er[1] (prim′ər), **1** a first book in reading. **2** a first book; beginner's book: *a primer of statistics. n.*

prim er[2] (prī′mər), **1** person or thing that primes. **2** cap or cylinder containing a little gunpowder, used for firing a charge. *n.*

prime time, the hours during the evening, usually considered to be from 6 to 11 p.m., when the greatest number of people are tuned in to television or radio.

pri me val (prī mē′vəl), **1** of the first age or ages, especially of the world: *In its primeval state the earth was without any forms of life.* **2** ancient: *primeval forests untouched by the ax. adj.* —**pri me′val ly,** *adv.*

prim ing (prī′ming), **1** powder or other material used to set fire to an explosive. **2** a first coat of paint, oil, etc. *n.*

prim i tive (prim′ə tiv), **1** of early times; of long ago: *Primitive people often lived in caves.* **2** very simple; such as people had early in human history: *A primitive way of making fire is by rubbing two sticks together.* **3** artist belonging to an early period. **4** work of art by such an artist. **5** person living in a primitive society or in primitive times. 1,2 *adj.,* 3-5 *n.* —**prim′i tive ly,** *adv.* —**prim′i tive ness,** *n.*

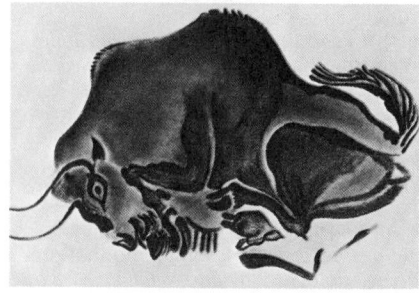

primitive
(def. 1)
Primitive cave dwellers drew this picture on a cave wall.

pri mo gen i ture (prī/mə jen/ə chùr or prī/mə jen/ə-chər), **1** fact of being the first-born among the children of the same parents. **2** the right or rule by which the eldest son inherits his father's land and buildings; inheritance by the first-born. *n.*

pri mor di al (prī môr/dē əl), **1** existing at the very beginning; primitive. **2** original; elementary. *adj.* —**pri-mor/di al ly,** *adv.*

primp (primp), dress (oneself) with excessive care; dress carefully. *v.*

prim rose (prim/rōz/), **1** a plant with showy, bell-shaped or funnel-shaped flowers of various colors. There are many kinds of primroses. *n.*

primrose path, a pleasant way; path of pleasure.

prin., principal.

prince (prins), **1** son of a king or queen; son of a king's or queen's son. **2** sovereign. **3** ruler of a small state or country. **4** the English equivalent of certain titles of nobility of varying importance or rank in other countries. **5** the greatest or best of a group; chief: *a merchant prince. n.* [*Prince* came into English about 750 years ago from French *prince,* and can be traced back to Latin *primus,* meaning "first," and *capere,* meaning "to take."]

prince dom (prins/dəm), **1** lands ruled by a prince. **2** title or rank of a prince. *n.*

Prince Edward Island, province in E Canada consisting of an island in the Gulf of St. Lawrence, just north of Nova Scotia. *Capital:* Charlottetown.

prince ly (prins/lē), **1** of a prince or his rank; royal. **2** like a prince; noble. **3** fit for a prince; magnificent: *Some actors earn princely salaries. adj.,* **prince li er, prince li est.** —**prince/li ness,** *n.*

Prince of Wales, title given to the eldest son, or heir apparent, of the British sovereign.

prince royal, the oldest son of a king or queen.

prin cess (prin/ses or prin/sis), **1** daughter of a king or queen; daughter of a king's or queen's son. **2** wife or widow of a prince. **3** woman having the rank of a prince. *n., pl.* **prin cess es.** —**prin/cess like/,** *adj.*

princess royal, the oldest daughter of a king or queen.

prin ci pal (prin/sə pəl), **1** most important; main; chief: *Chicago is the principal city of Illinois.* **2** a chief person; one who gives orders. **3** the head, or one of the heads, of an elementary or secondary school. **4** sum of money on which interest is paid. **5** money, property, or investments from which income or interest is received. **1** *adj.,* **2-5** *n.*

prin ci pal i ty (prin/sə pal/ə tē), **1** a small state or country ruled by a prince. **2** the country from which a prince gets his title. *n., pl.* **prin ci pal i ties.**

prin ci pal ly (prin/sə pə lē), for the most part; above all; chiefly; mainly. *adv.*

principal parts, the main parts of a verb, from which the rest can be derived. In English the principal parts are the present infinitive, past tense, and past participle. These parts, plus the present participle, are shown for many verbs in this dictionary. EXAMPLES: go, went, gone; do, did, done; drive, drove, driven; push, pushed, pushed.

prin ci ple (prin/sə pəl), **1** a truth that is a foundation for other truths: *the principles of democratic government.* **2** a fundamental belief: *religious principles.* **3** a rule of action or conduct: *I make it a principle to save some money each week.* **4** uprightness; honor: *a person of principle.* **5** a rule of science explaining how things act: *the principle by which a machine works. n.*

on principle, 1 according to a certain principle. **2** for reasons of right conduct.

print (print), **1** use type, plates, etc., to stamp in ink or

dye (letters, words, pictures, etc.) on paper or the like. **2** stamp letters, words, etc., on (paper or the like) with type, etc., and ink or dye. **3** cause to be printed; publish: *print books. Most newspapers are printed daily.* **4** words, letters, etc., in ink stamped by type: *This book has clear print.* **5** make words or letters the way they look in print instead of in writing: *Print your name clearly. Most children learn to print before learning to write.* **6** mark (cloth, paper, etc.) with patterns or designs: *This machine prints wallpaper.* **7** cloth with a pattern printed on it: *This print will make a nice shirt.* **8** a picture or design printed from an engraved plate, block, etc. **9** produce (marks or figures) by pressure; stamp; impress. **10** a mark made by pressing or stamping: *the print of a foot.* **11** something that prints; stamp; die. **12** something that has been marked or shaped by pressing or stamping: *a print of butter.* **13** photograph produced from a negative. **14** produce a photograph by transmission of light through a negative. **1-3,5,6,9,14** *v.,* **4,7,8,10,11-13** *n.*

in print, 1 in printed form. **2** (of books, etc.) still available for purchase from the publisher.

out of print, no longer sold by the publisher.

print a ble (prin/tə bəl), **1** capable of being printed. **2** fit to be printed. *adj.*

printed circuit, (in electronics) circuit in which the parts or connections are printed, painted, or sprayed on an insulating surface with conducting materials such as silver, or an oxide of silver.

print er (prin/tər), **1** person whose business or work is printing or setting type. **2** machine that prints, controlled by a computer. *n.*

print ing (prin/ting), **1** the producing of books, newspapers, etc., by stamping in ink or dye from movable type, plates, etc. **2** printed words, letters, etc. **3** all the copies printed at one time. **4** letters made like those in print. *n.*

printing press, machine for printing from movable type, plates, etc.

print out (print/out/), the printed output of a computer. *n.*

pri or[1] (prī/ər), coming before; earlier: *I can't go with you because I have a prior engagement. adj.*

prior to, coming before in time, order, or importance; earlier than; before.

pri or[2] (prī/ər), head of a priory or monastery for men. Priors usually rank below abbots. *n.*

pri or ess (prī/ər is), head of a convent or priory for women. Prioresses usually rank below abbesses. *n., pl.* **pri or ess es.**

pri or i ty (prī ôr/ə tē), **1** a coming before in order or importance: *Fire engines and ambulances have priority over other traffic.* **2** a being earlier in time: *Their claim to the land has priority because they were the first to live on it.* **3** a governmental rating giving preference to persons or things in order of their importance to national defense or other essential affairs of state. *n., pl.* **pri or i ties.**

pri or y (prī/ər ē), a religious house governed by a prior or prioress. A priory is often, but not necessarily, dependent on an abbey. *n., pl.* **pri or ies.**

prism (priz/əm), **1** a solid figure whose bases or ends have the same size and shape and are parallel to one another, and each of whose sides has two pairs of parallel edges. A six-sided pencil before it is sharpened has

prism (def. 2)
refracting, or
bending, light

the shape of one kind of prism. **2** a transparent solid object, often of glass, having the shape of a prism, usually with three-sided ends. Prisms can refract or reflect light, or separate white light into the colors of the spectrum. *n.*

pris mat ic (priz mat′ik), **1** of or like a prism. **2** formed by a transparent prism. **3** varied in color; brilliant. *adj.* —**pris mat′i cal ly,** *adv.*

prismatic colors, the seven colors formed when white light is passed through a prism; red, orange, yellow, green, blue, indigo, and violet. These are the colors of the spectrum.

pris on (priz′n), **1** a public building in which criminals are confined: *The burglar was put in prison.* **2** any place where a person or animal is shut up unwillingly: *The small apartment was a prison to the big dog.* n. [*Prison* came into English about 850 years ago from French *prison,* and can be traced back to Latin *prehendere,* meaning "to seize, grasp."] —**pris′on like′,** *adj.*

pris on er (priz′n ər), **1** person who is under arrest or held in a jail or prison. **2** person who is confined unwillingly, or who is not free to move. **3** person taken by the enemy in war. *n.*

pris sy (pris′ē), INFORMAL. **1** too precise and fussy. **2** too easily shocked. *adj.,* **pris si er, pris si est.** —**pris′si ly,** *adv.* —**pris′si ness,** *n.*

pris tine (pris′tēn′), as it was in its earliest time or state; original; primitive: *The ancient paintings had kept their pristine freshness. adj.* —**pris′tine ly,** *adv.*

prith ee (priᴛн′ē), OLD USE. I pray thee; I ask you. *interj.*

pri va cy (prī′və sē), **1** condition of being private; being away from others: *in the privacy of one's home.* **2** absence of publicity; secrecy: *He told me his reasons in strict privacy. n., pl.* **pri va cies.**

pri vate (prī′vit), **1** not for the public; for just a few special people or for one: *a private road, a private house, a private letter.* **2** not public; individual; personal: *the private life of a famous person, my private opinion.* **3** confidential; secret: *News reached her through private channels.* **4** secluded: *some private corner.* **5** having no public office: *a private citizen.* **6** soldier or marine of the lowest rank: *The private was promoted to corporal.* 1-5 *adj.,* 6 *n.* —**pri′vate ly,** *adv.* —**pri′vate ness,** *n.*

in private, 1 not publicly: *My parents spoke to the principal in private.* **2** secretly: *We met in private to plan his surprise birthday party.*

private enterprise, free enterprise.

pri va teer (prī′və tir′), **1** an armed ship owned by private persons and holding a government commission to attack and capture enemy ships. **2** commander or one of the crew of a privateer. **3** cruise as a privateer. 1,2 *n.,* 3 *v.*

private first class, soldier or marine ranking next below a corporal and next above a private.

pri va tion (prī vā′shən), **1** lack of the comforts or of the necessities of life: *Many people were hungry and homeless because of privation during the war.* **2** a being deprived; loss; absence: *suffer from the privation of love. n.*

priv et (priv′it), any of several shrubs much used for hedges. Some are evergreen. *n.*

priv i lege (priv′ə lij), a special right, advantage, or favor: *My sister has the privilege of driving the family car. n.*

priv i leged (priv′ə lijd), having some privilege or privileges: *The nobility of Europe was a privileged class. adj.*

priv i ly (priv′ə lē), in a private manner; secretly. *adv.*

priv y (priv′ē), **1** private. **2** OLD USE. secret; hidden. **3** a small outhouse used as a toilet. 1,2 *adj.,* 3 *n., pl.* **priv ies.**
privy to, having secret or private knowledge of.

privy council, group of personal advisers to a ruler. —**privy councilor.**

prize¹ (prīz), **1** a reward won after trying against other people: *Prizes will be given for the three best stories.* **2** given as a prize. **3** that has won a prize. **4** worthy of a prize: *prize vegetables.* **5** a reward worth working for. 1,5 *n.,* 2-4 *adj.*

prize² (prīz), thing or person captured in war, especially an enemy's ship and its cargo taken at sea. *n.*

prize³ (prīz), **1** value highly: *She prizes her new bicycle.* **2** estimate the value of. *v.,* **prized, priz ing.**

prize fight (prīz′fīt′), a boxing match between prizefighters. *n.*

prize fight er (prīz′fī′tər), person who fights or boxes for money. *n.*

prize fight ing (prīz′fī′ting), boxing for money. *n.*

pro¹ (prō), **1** in favor of; for. **2** a reason in favor of. The pros and cons of a question are the arguments for and against it. 1 *adv.,* 2 *n., pl.* **pros.**

pro² (prō), INFORMAL. professional. *n., pl.* **pros;** *adj.*

prob., 1 probable. **2** problem.

prob a bil i ty (prob′ə bil′ə tē), **1** quality or fact of being likely or probable; good chance: *There is a probability of rain today.* **2** something likely to happen: *A storm is a probability for tomorrow. n., pl.* **prob a bil i ties.**
in all probability, probably.

prob a ble (prob′ə bəl), **1** likely to happen: *Cooler weather is probable after this shower.* **2** likely to be true: *Something I ate is the probable cause of my upset stomach. adj.*

prob a bly (prob′ə blē), more likely than not. *adv.*

pro bate (prō′bāt), **1** the official proving of a will as genuine. **2** of or concerned with the probating of wills: *a probate court.* **3** prove by legal process the genuineness of (a will). 1 *n.,* 2 *adj.,* 3 *v.,* **pro bat ed, pro bat ing.**

pro ba tion (prō bā′shən), **1** trial or testing of conduct, character, qualifications, etc.: *He was admitted to the sixth grade on probation.* **2** the system of letting convicted lawbreakers go free under supervision without receiving the punishment which they are sentenced to unless there is a further offense. *n.*

pro ba tion er (prō bā′shə nər), person who is on probation. *n.*

probation officer, officer appointed to supervise offenders who have been placed on probation.

probe (prōb), **1** search into; examine thoroughly; investigate: *I probed my memory for her name.* **2** search; penetrate: *probe into the causes of crime.* **3** a thorough examination; investigation: *a probe into juvenile delinquency.* **4** investigation, usually by a lawmaking body, in an effort to discover evidences of law violation. **5** a slender instrument for exploring something. A doctor or dentist uses a probe to explore the depth or direction of a wound or cavity. A Geiger counter uses a probe to detect the amount of radiation in radioactive matter, such as a rock. **6** spacecraft carrying scientific instruments to record or report back information about planets, etc.: *a lunar probe.* **7** the launching of such a spacecraft. **8** examine with a probe. 1,2,8 *v.,* **probed, prob ing;** 3-7 *n.* —**probe′a ble,** *adj.* —**prob′er,** *n.* —**prob′ing ly,** *adv.*

pro bi ty (prō′bə tē), high principle; uprightness; honesty. *n.*

prob lem (prob′ləm), **1** a question, especially a difficult question: *How to do away with poverty is a problem that concerns the government.* **2** a matter of doubt or difficulty: *The president of a large company has to deal with many problems.* **3** something to be worked out: *a problem in arithmetic.* **4** that causes difficulty: *a problem child.* 1-3 *n.*, 4 *adj.*

prob lem at ic (prob′lə mat′ik), having the nature of a problem; doubtful; uncertain; questionable: *What the weather will be is often problematic. adj.*

prob lem i cal (prob′lə mat′ə kəl), problematic. *adj.*

pro bos cis (prō bos′is), **1** an elephant's trunk. **2** a long, flexible snout, like that of the tapir. **3** the tubelike mouth parts of some insects, such as flies or mosquitoes, developed for piercing or sucking. *n., pl.* **pro bos cis es.** [*Proboscis* was borrowed from Latin *proboscis*, which can be traced back to Greek *pro*, meaning "before," and *boskein*, meaning "to feed."]

proc., process.

pro ce dur al (prə sē′jər əl), of procedure. *adj.*

pro ce dure (prə sē′jər), **1** way of proceeding; method of doing things: *What is your procedure in making bread?* **2** the customary manners or ways of conducting business: *parliamentary procedure, legal procedure. n.*

pro ceed (prə sēd′), **1** go on after having stopped; move forward: *Please proceed with your story. The train proceeded down the track.* **2** carry on any activity: *I proceeded to light the fire.* **3** come forth; issue; go out; emanate: *Heat proceeds from fire. v.* —**pro ceed′er,** *n.*

pro ceed ing (prə sē′ding), **1** what is done; action; conduct. **2** **proceedings,** *pl.* **a** action in a case in a court of law. **b** record of what was done at the meetings of a society, club, etc. *n.*

pro ceeds (prō′sēdz′), money obtained from a sale, etc.: *The proceeds from the school play will be used to buy a new curtain for the stage. n.pl.*

proc ess (pros′es *or* prō′ses), **1** set of actions or changes in a special order: *By what process is cloth made from wool?* **2** treat or prepare by some special method: *This cloth has been processed to make it waterproof.* **3** part that grows out or sticks out: *the process of a bone.* **4** a written command or summons to appear in a court of law. 1,3,4 *n., pl.* **proc ess es;** 2 *v.*

in process, in the course or condition of being done: *The author has just finished one book and has another in process.*

pro ces sion (prə sesh′ən), **1** something that moves forward; persons marching or riding: *A funeral procession filled the street.* **2** an orderly moving forward: *We formed lines to march in procession onto the platform. n.*

pro ces sion al (prə sesh′ə nəl), **1** of a procession. **2** used or sung in a procession: *a processional hymn.* **3** processional music: *The choir marched in singing the processional.* **4** book containing hymns, etc., for use in religious processions. 1,2 *adj.*, 3,4 *n.*

proc es sor (pros′es ər *or* pro′ses ər), **1** person or thing that processes. **2** the central processing unit of a computer, especially the part of this unit in which data are examined, compared, changed, and the like. *n.*

process server, person who serves summonses, subpoenas, etc.

pro claim (prə klām′), make known publicly and officially; declare publicly: *proclaim a holiday. The congresswoman proclaimed that she would run for reelection. v.*

proc la ma tion (prok′lə mā′shən), an official, public announcement: *a proclamation ending the war. n.*

pro cliv i ty (prō kliv′ə tē), tendency; inclination. *n., pl.* **pro cliv i ties.**

a hat	**i** it	**oi** oil	**ch** child	⎧ a in about
ā age	**ī** ice	**ou** out	**ng** long	⎪ e in taken
ä far	**o** hot	**u** cup	**sh** she	ə = ⎨ i in pencil
e let	**ō** open	**ù** put	**th** thin	⎪ o in lemon
ē equal	**ô** order	**ü** rule	**ŦH** then	⎩ u in circus
ėr term			**zh** measure	

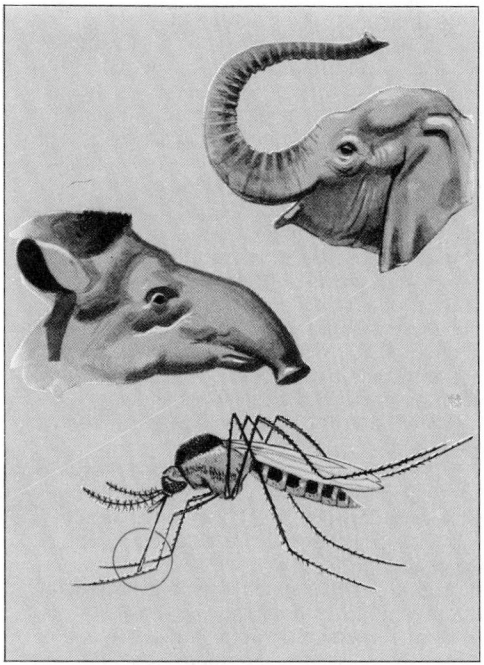

proboscis (defs. 1, 2, and 3)

pro con sul (prō kon′səl), governor or military commander of an ancient Roman province with duties and powers like a consul's. *n.*

pro cras ti nate (prō kras′tə nāt), put things off until later; delay. *v.*, **pro cras ti nat ed, pro cras ti nat ing.**

pro cras ti na tion (prō kras′tə nā′shən), act or habit of putting things off till later; delay. *n.*

pro cras ti na tor (prō kras′tə nā′tər), person who procrastinates. *n.*

pro cre a tion (prō′krē ā′shən), the producing of offspring; reproduction; begetting. *n.*

proc tor (prok′tər), **1** officer in a university or school who keeps good order. **2** serve as a proctor at (an examination). 1 *n.*, 2 *v.* [*Proctor* was shortened from *procurator*, which can be traced back to Latin *pro*, meaning "for," and *cura*, meaning "care."]

proc u ra tor (prok′yə rā′tər), **1** person employed to manage the affairs of another or to act for another; agent. **2** a financial agent or administrator in an ancient Roman province. *n.*

pro cure (prə kyùr′), **1** get by care or effort; obtain; secure: *procure a job in a bank. It is hard to procure water in a desert.* **2** bring about; cause: *The lawyer procured the prisoner's release. v.*, **pro cured, pro cur ing.** —**pro cur′a ble,** *adj.*

pro cure ment (prə kyùr′mənt), act of procuring. *n.*

prod (prod), **1** poke or jab with something pointed: *prod an animal with a stick.* **2** stir up; urge on: *My parents prodded me to clean my room.* **3** a poke; thrust: *That prod in the ribs hurt.* **4** a sharp-pointed stick; goad. **5** words, actions, or feelings that prod. 1,2 *v.*, **prod ded, prod ding;** 3-5 *n.* —**prod′der,** *n.*

prod i gal (prod′ə gəl), **1** spending too much; wasting money or other resources; wasteful: *America has been prodigal of its forests.* **2** abundant; lavish. **3** person who is wasteful or extravagant; spendthrift: *The repentant prodigal was welcomed back home.* 1,2 *adj.,* 3 *n.*

prod i gal i ty (prod′ə gal′ə tē), **1** wasteful or reckless extravagance. **2** rich abundance; profuseness. *n., pl.* **prod i gal i ties.**

pro di gious (prə dij′əs), **1** very great; huge; vast: *The ocean contains a prodigious amount of water.* **2** wonderful; marvelous. *adj.* —**pro di′gious ly,** *adv.* —**pro di′gious ness,** *n.*

prod i gy (prod′ə jē), **1** a marvel; wonder. An infant prodigy is a child remarkably brilliant in some respect. **2** a wonderful sign or omen: *The brilliant comet seemed a prodigy to all who saw it. n., pl.* **prod i gies.**

pro duce (prə düs′ *or* prə dyüs′ *for 1-6;* prod′üs, prod′yüs, prō′düs, *or* prō′dyüs *for 7*), **1** bring into existence; make: *This factory produces stoves.* **2** bring about; cause: *Hard work produces success.* **3** bring forth or yield offspring, crops, products, dividends, interest, etc. **4** bring forth; supply; create; yield: *Hens produce eggs.* **5** bring forward; show: *Produce your proof.* **6** bring (a play, motion picture, etc.) before the public: *Our class produced a play.* **7** farm products, especially fruits and vegetables. 1-6 *v.,* **pro duced, pro duc ing;** 7 *n.* —**pro duc′i ble, pro duc′a ble,** *adj.*

pro duc er (prə dü′sər *or* prə dyü′sər), **1** one that produces, especially a person who grows or manufactures things that are used by others. **2** person in charge of presenting a play, a motion picture, or a television or radio show. *n.*

prod uct (prod′əkt), **1** that which is produced; result of work or of growth: *factory products, farm products.* **2** number or quantity resulting from multiplying two or more numbers together: *40 is the product of 8 and 5. n.*

pro duc tion (prə duk′shən), **1** act of producing; creation; manufacture: *the production of automobiles.* **2** something produced: *the yearly production of a farm.* **3** amount produced: *a decline in production. n.*

pro duc tive (prə duk′tiv), **1** producing much; fertile: *a productive farm, a productive writer.* **2** producing food or other articles of commerce: *Farming is productive labor.* **3** having good results: *Efforts to resolve the dispute were very productive. adj.* —**pro duc′tive ly,** *adv.* —**pro duc′tive ness,** *n.*

pro duc tiv i ty (prō′duk tiv′ə tē), power to produce; productiveness. *n.*

pro em (prō′em), introduction; preface. *n.*

prof. or Prof., professor.

prof a na tion (prof′ə nā′shən), act of showing contempt or disregard toward something holy; treatment of something sacred as it should not be treated. *n.*

pro fane (prə fān′), **1** with contempt or disregard for God or holy things: *a profane person, profane language.* **2** treat (holy things) with contempt or disregard: *Soldiers profaned the church when they stabled their horses in it.* **3** put to wrong or unworthy use. **4** not sacred; worldly: *profane literature.* 1,4 *adj.,* 2,3 *v.,* **pro faned, pro fan ing.** [*Profane can be traced back to Latin pro, meaning "before," and fanum, meaning "temple, shrine."*] —**pro fane′ly,** *adv.* —**pro fane′ness,** *n.* —**pro fan′er,** *n.*

pro fan i ty (prə fan′ə tē), **1** use of profane language; swearing. **2** a being profane; lack of reverence. *n., pl.* **pro fan i ties.**

pro fess (prə fes′), **1** lay claim to; claim: *I don't profess to be an expert in chemistry.* **2** declare one's belief in: *Christians profess the Christian religion.* **3** declare openly: *He professed his loyalty to the United States.* **4** have as one's business or profession: *profess law. v.*

pro fessed (prə fest′), **1** stated or acknowledged; openly declared: *a professed Christian, a professed candidate for office.* **2** alleged or pretended: *accused by one's professed friends. adj.*

pro fes sion (prə fesh′ən), **1** an occupation requiring special education, such as law, medicine, teaching, or the ministry. **2** the people engaged in such an occupation: *the medical profession.* **3** act of professing; open declaration: *a profession of friendship.* **4** declaration of belief in a religion. *n.*

pro fes sion al (prə fesh′ə nəl), **1** of a profession; appropriate to a profession: *Our doctor has a professional seriousness unlike her ordinary joking manner.* **2** engaged in a profession: *A lawyer or a doctor is a professional person.* **3** making a business or trade of something which others do for pleasure: *a professional ballplayer, professional musicians.* **4** person who does this. **5** undertaken or engaged in by professionals rather than amateurs: *a professional ball game.* 1-3,5 *adj.,* 4 *n.* —**pro fes′sion al ly,** *adv.*

pro fes sion al ize (prə fesh′ə nə līz), make or become professional. *v.,* **pro fes sion al ized, pro fes sion al iz ing.** —**pro fes′sion al i za′tion,** *n.*

pro fes sor (prə fes′ər), **1** teacher of the highest rank in a college or university. **2** teacher. *n.*

pro fes so ri al (prō′fə sôr′ē əl *or* prof′ə sôr′ē əl), of or characteristic of a professor. *adj.* —**pro′fes so′ri al ly,** *adv.*

pro fes sor ship (prə fes′ər ship), position or rank of a professor. *n.*

prof fer (prof′ər), **1** offer for acceptance; present; tender: *We proffered our regrets at having to leave so early.* **2** an offer made: *Her proffer of advice was accepted.* 1 *v.,* 2 *n.* —**prof′fer er,** *n.*

pro fi cien cy (prə fish′ən sē), a being proficient; knowledge; skill; advanced state of expertness. *n., pl.* **pro fi cien cies.**

pro fi cient (prə fish′ənt), advanced in any art, science, or subject; skilled; expert: *to be proficient in mathematics. adj.* —**pro fi′cient ly,** *adv.* —**pro fi′cient ness,** *n.*

pro file (prō′fīl), **1** a side view, especially of the human face. **2** outline. **3** a concise description of a person's abilities, personality, or career. *n.*

profile (def. 1)
of Queen Victoria

prof it (prof′it), **1** the gain from a business; what is left when the cost of goods and of carrying on the business is subtracted from the amount of money taken in: *The profits in this business are not large.* **2** make a gain from business; make a profit. **3** advantage; benefit: *What profit is there in worrying?* **4** get advantage; gain; benefit: *profit from one's mistakes.* **5** be an advantage or benefit (to). 1,3 *n.,* 2,4,5 *v.* —**prof′it er,** *n.*

prof it a ble (prof′ə tə bəl), **1** yielding a financial profit: *The sale held by the Girl Scouts was very profitable.* **2** giving a gain or benefit; useful: *We spent a profitable afternoon in the library. adj.* —**prof′it a ble ness,** *n.*

prof it a bly (prof′ə tə blē), with profit. *adv.*

prof it eer (prof′ə tir′), **1** person who makes an unfair profit by charging excessive prices for scarce goods. **2** seek or make such unfair profits. 1 *n.,* 2 *v.*

prof it less (prof′it lis), without profit. *adj.* —**prof′it less-ly,** *adv.* —**prof′it less ness,** *n.*

profit sharing, the sharing of profits between employer and employees.

prof li ga cy (prof′lə gə sē), **1** great wickedness; vice. **2** reckless extravagance. *n.*

prof li gate (prof′lə git), **1** very wicked; shamelessly bad. **2** recklessly extravagant. **3** person who is very wicked or extravagant. 1,2 *adj.,* 3 *n.* —**prof′li gate ly,** *adv.*

pro found (prə found′), **1** very deep: *a profound sigh, a profound sleep.* **2** deeply felt; very great: *profound despair, profound sympathy.* **3** going far deeper than what is easily understood; having or showing great knowledge or understanding: *a profound book, a profound thinker. adj.* —**pro found′ly,** *adv.* —**pro found′ness,** *n.*

pro fun di ty (prə fun′də tē), **1** a being profound; great depth. **2** a very deep thing or place. *n., pl.* **pro fun di-ties.**

pro fuse (prə fyüs′), **1** very abundant: *profuse thanks.* **2** spending or giving freely; lavish; extravagant: *He was profuse in his praise of the book. adj.* —**pro fuse′ly,** *adv.* —**pro fuse′ness,** *n.*

pro fu sion (prə fyü′zhən), **1** great abundance: *a profusion of books, a profusion of roses.* **2** extravagance; lavishness. *n.*

pro gen i tor (prō jen′ə tər), ancestor in the direct line; forefather. *n.*

prog e ny (proj′ə nē), children or offspring; descendants. *n., pl.* **prog e nies.**

prog no sis (prog nō′sis), **1** forecast of the probable course of a disease. **2** estimate of what will probably happen. *n., pl.* **prog no ses** (prog nō′sēz′).

prog nos ti cate (prog nos′tə kāt), predict from facts; forecast. *v.,* **prog nos ti cat ed, prog nos ti cat ing.** —**prog nos′ti ca′tion,** *n.* —**prog nos′ti ca′tor,** *n.*

pro gram (prō′gram), **1** list of items or events set down in order with a list of the performers. There are concert programs, theater programs, and programs of a meeting. **2** items making up an entertainment: *The entire program was delightful.* **3** a broadcast on radio or television: *a news program.* **4** plan of what is to be done: *a school program, a business program, a government program.* **5** set of instructions for an electronic computer or other automatic machine outlining the steps to be performed by the machine in a specific operation. **6** arrange or enter in a program. **7** draw up a program or plan for. **8** prepare a set of instructions for (a computer or other automatic machine). **9** series of statements and questions to each of which a student is required to respond before going on to the next and usually more difficult level. **10** arrange a series of statements and questions in such a sequence: *programmed instruction.* 1-5,9 *n.,* 6-8,10 *v.,* **pro grammed, pro gram ming** or **pro gramed, pro gram ing.**

pro gramme (prō′gram), program. *n., v.,* **pro grammed, pro gram ming.**

pro gram mer or **pro gram er** (prō′gram′ər), person who prepares a program or programs. *n.*

prog ress (prog′res *for 1,3;* prə gres′ *for 2,4*), **1** an advance or growth; development; improvement: *the progress of science, showing rapid progress in one's studies.* **2** get better; advance; develop: *We progress in learning step by step.* **3** a moving forward; going ahead: *make rapid progress on a journey.* **4** move forward; go ahead: *The building of the new school progressed quickly during the summer.* 1,3 *n.,* 2,4 *v.*

pro gres sion (prə gresh′ən), **1** a progressing; a moving forward; going ahead: *Creeping is a slow method of progression.* **2** (in mathematics) series of numbers in which there is always the same relation between a num-

ber and the one after it. 2, 4, 6, 8, 10 are in arithmetical progression. 2, 4, 8, 16, 32 are in geometric progression. *n.*

pro gres sive (prə gres′iv), **1** making progress; advancing to something better; improving: *a progressive nation.* **2** favoring progress; wanting improvement or reform in government, business, etc. **3** person who favors improvement and reform in government, religion, or business. **4** moving forward; developing: *a progressive disease.* 1,2,4 *adj.,* 3 *n.* —**pro gres′sive ly,** *adv.* —**pro gres′sive-ness,** *n.*

pro hib it (prō hib′it), **1** forbid by law or authority: *Picking flowers in this park is prohibited.* **2** prevent: *Rainy weather and fog prohibited flying. v.* —**pro hib′it er, pro hib′i tor,** *n.*

pro hi bi tion (prō′ə bish′ən), **1** act of prohibiting: *The prohibition of swimming in the city's reservoirs is sensible.* **2** law or order that prohibits. **3** law or laws against making or selling alcoholic liquors. National prohibition existed in the United States between 1920 and 1933. *n.*

pro hib i tive (prō hib′ə tiv), enough to prohibit or prevent something: *prohibitive costs. adj.* —**pro hib′i tive ly,** *adv.* —**pro hib′i tive ness,** *n.*

proj ect (proj′ekt *for 1,3,7,8;* prə jekt′ *for 2,4-6*), **1** a plan; scheme: *a project for slum clearance.* **2** to plan; scheme: *to project a tax decrease.* **3** an undertaking; enterprise. **4** throw or cast forward: *A cannon projects shells.* **5** cause to fall on a surface: *Motion pictures are projected on the screen. The tree projects a shadow on the grass.* **6** stick out: *The rocky point projects far into the water.* **7** a special assignment planned and carried out by a student, a group of students, or an entire class. **8** group of apartment buildings built and run as a unit, especially with government support. 1,3,7,8 *n.,* 2,4-6 *v.* —**pro ject′a ble,** *adj.* —**pro ject′ing ly,** *adv.*

pro jec tile (prə jek′təl), any object that is thrown, hurled, or shot, such as a stone or bullet. *n.*

pro jec tion (prə jek′shən), **1** part that projects or sticks out: *rocky projections on the face of a cliff.* **2** a sticking out. **3** a throwing or casting forward: *the projection of a shell from a cannon, the projection of a photographic image on a screen.* **4** representation on a flat surface of all or part of the surface of the earth. *n.*

pro jec tor (prə jek′tər), apparatus for projecting an image on a screen. *n.*

Pro ko fiev (prō kô′fyef), **Sergei Sergeyevich,** 1891-1953, Russian composer. *n.*

pro le tar i an (prō′lə ter′ē ən *or* prō′lə tar′ē ən), **1** of or belonging to the proletariat. **2** person belonging to the proletariat. 1 *adj.,* 2 *n.*

pro le tar i at (prō′lə ter′ē ət *or* prō′lə tar′ē ət), the working class, especially industrial workers working for wages. *n.*

pro lif e rate (prō lif′ə rāt′), **1** grow or produce by multiplication of parts: *The bacteria proliferated in a favorable environment.* **2** multiply; spread: *Suburbs around many major cities have proliferated. v.,* **pro lif e rat ed, pro lif e-rat ing.**

pro lif ic (prə lif′ik), **1** producing many offspring: *Rabbits are prolific.* **2** producing much: *a prolific garden, a prolific imagination, a prolific writer. adj.* —**pro lif′i cal ly,** *adv.* —**pro lif′ic ness,** *n.*

a hat	i it	oi oil	ch child	a in about
ā age	ī ice	ou out	ng long	e in taken
ä far	o hot	u cup	sh she	ə = i in pencil
e let	ō open	u̇ put	th thin	o in lemon
ē equal	ô order	ü rule	ᵺ then	u in circus
ėr term			zh measure	

pro logue or **pro log** (prō′lôg), **1** introduction to a novel, poem, or other literary work. **2** speech or poem addressed to the audience by one of the actors at the beginning of a play. **3** any introductory act or event. *n.*

pro long (prə lông′), make longer; extend; stretch; protract: *prolong a visit. Good care may prolong a sick person's life. v.* —**pro long′a ble,** *adj.* —**pro long′er,** *n.*

pro lon ga tion (prō′lông gā′shən), **1** lengthening in time or space; extension: *the prolongation of a discussion.* **2** added part: *The playroom was built as a prolongation of the garage. n.*

prom (prom), INFORMAL. a formal dance given by a college or high-school class. *n.*

prom e nade (prom′ə nād′ or prom′ə näd′), **1** a walk for pleasure or for show: *a promenade in the park.* **2** walk about or up and down for pleasure or for show: *We promenaded back and forth on the ship's deck.* **3** a public place for such a walk: *Atlantic City has a famous promenade along the beach.* **4** a formal dance. **5** a march of all the guests at the opening of a formal dance. 1,3-5 *n.,* 2 *v.,* **prom e nad ed, prom e nad ing.** —**prom′e nad′er,** *n.*

Pro me the us (prə mē′thē əs or prə mē′thüs), (in Greek myths) one of the Titans. He stole fire from heaven and taught people its use. Zeus punished him by chaining him to a rock. *n.*

pro me thi um (prə mē′thē əm), a radioactive metallic element which is a product of the fission of uranium, thorium, and plutonium. *n.*

prom i nence (prom′ə nəns), **1** a being prominent: *the prominence of Jefferson as a statesman, the prominence of football as a sport.* **2** something that juts out or projects, especially upward. A hill is a prominence. **3** cloud of gas which erupts from the sun and is seen as either a projection from, or a dark spot on, the surface of the sun. *n.*

prom i nent (prom′ə nənt), **1** well-known or important; distinguished: *a prominent citizen.* **2** easy to see: *I hung the picture in a prominent place in the living room.* **3** standing out; projecting: *Some insects have prominent eyes. adj.* —**prom′i nent ly,** *adv.*

prom is cu i ty (prom′i skyü′ə tē), fact or condition of being promiscuous. *n.*

pro mis cu ous (prə mis′kyü əs), **1** making no distinctions; not discriminating; careless: *Doctors warn about the promiscuous use of drugs.* **2** having sexual relations with many persons. **3** mixed and in disorder: *a promiscuous collection of notes. adj.* —**pro mis′cu ous ly,** *adv.* —**pro mis′cu ous ness,** *n.*

prom ise (prom′is), **1** words said or written, binding a person to do or not to do something: *You can count on her to keep her promise.* **2** give one's word; make a promise: *They promised to stay till we came.* **3** make a promise of: *to promise help.* **4** indication of what may be expected: *The clouds give promise of rain.* **5** that which gives hope of success: *a young scholar who shows promise.* **6** give hope; give hope of: *The rainbow promises fair weather.* 1,4,5 *n.,* 2,3,6 *v.,* **prom ised, prom is ing.** —**prom′is er,** *n.*

Promised Land, 1 (in the Bible) the country promised by God to Abraham and his descendants; Canaan. **2 promised land,** a place or condition of expected happiness: *America is a promised land for many immigrants.* **3** heaven.

prom is ing (prom′ə sing), likely to turn out well; hopeful: *a promising beginning. The young pianist has a great deal of talent and is very promising. adj.* —**prom′is ing ly,** *adv.*

prom is so ry note (prom′ə sôr′ē), a written promise to pay a stated sum of money to a certain person at a certain time.

prom on to ry (prom′ən tôr′ē), a high point of land extending from the coast into the water; headland. *n., pl.*

prom on to ries. [*Promontory* is from Latin *promonturium,* which comes from *pro-,* meaning "forward," and *montem,* meaning "mountain."]

pro mote (prə mōt′), **1** raise in rank, condition, or importance: *Pupils who pass the test will be promoted to the next higher grade.* **2** help to grow or develop; help to success: *A kindly feeling toward other countries will promote peace.* **3** help to organize; start: *Several bankers promoted the new company.* **4** further the sale of (an article) by advertising. *v.,* **pro mot ed, pro mot ing.** —**pro mot′a ble,** *adj.*

pro mot er (prə mō′tər), **1** person or thing that encourages or furthers something: *a promoter of energy conservation.* **2** person who organizes new companies and secures capital for them. *n.*

pro mo tion (prə mō′shən), **1** an advance in rank or importance: *The clerk was given a promotion and an increase in salary.* **2** helping to grow or develop; a helping along to success: *They are active in the promotion of better health care.* **3** a helping to organize; starting: *It took much time and money for the promotion of the new company. n.*

pro mo tion al (prə mō′shə nəl), of or used in the promotion of a person, product, or enterprise: *promotional pamphlets. adj.*

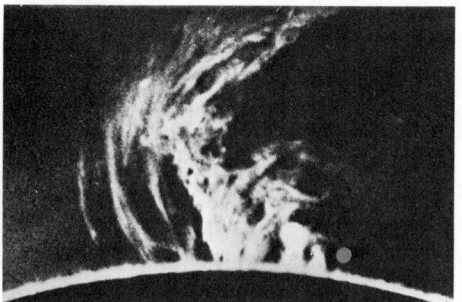

prominence (def. 3)—The size of the prominence is compared with the size of the earth (colored ball at the right).

prompt (prompt), **1** ready and willing; on time; quick: *Be prompt to obey.* **2** done at once; made without delay: *I expect a prompt answer.* **3** cause (someone) to do something: *Her curiosity prompted her to ask questions.* **4** give rise to; suggest; inspire: *A kind thought prompted the gift.* **5** remind (a learner, speaker, actor, etc.) of the words or actions needed: *Please prompt me if I forget my lines.* 1,2 *adj.,* 3-5 *v.* —**prompt′ly,** *adv.* —**prompt′ness,** *n.*

prompt er (promp′tər), person who tells actors, speakers, etc., what to say when they forget. *n.*

prom ul gate (prom′əl gāt or prō mul′gāt), proclaim formally; announce officially: *The king promulgated a decree. v.,* **prom ul gat ed, prom ul gat ing.**

prom ul ga tion (prom′əl gā′shən or prō′mul gā′shən), a promulgating or a being promulgated. *n.*

pron., 1 pronoun. **2** pronunciation.

prone (prōn), **1** inclined or disposed; liable: *He is prone to forget to do his chores.* **2** lying face down: *be prone on the bed.* **3** lying flat: *fall prone on the ground. adj.*

promontory

prong (prông), one of the pointed ends of a fork, antler, etc. *n.*

pronged (prôngd), having prongs. *adj.*

prong horn (prông′hôrn′), mammal resembling an antelope, found on the plains of western North America. *n.*, *pl.* **prong horns** or **prong horn.**

pronghorn
about 3 ft. (1 m.)
high at the shoulder

pro noun (prō′noun), word used to indicate without naming; word used instead of a noun. In "John did not like to go because he was sick," *he* is a pronoun used in the second part of the sentence to avoid repeating *John. n.*

pronouns

pro nounce (prə nouns′), **1** make the sounds of; speak: *Pronounce your words clearly.* **2** declare (a person or thing) to be: *The doctor pronounced her cured.* **3** declare solemnly or positively: *The judge pronounced sentence on the prisoner. v.*, **pro nounced, pro nounc ing.** —**pronounce′a ble,** *adj.* —**pro nounc′er,** *n.*

pro nounced (prə nounst′), strongly marked; emphatic; decided: *She has pronounced opinions on politics. adj.*

pro nounce ment (prə nouns′mənt), **1** a formal statement; declaration. **2** opinion; decision. *n.*

pron to (pron′tō), INFORMAL. promptly; quickly: *They got the job done pronto. adv.*

pro nun ci a tion (prə nun′sē ā′shən), **1** way of pronouncing. This book gives the pronunciation of each main word. **2** a making the sounds of words; speaking. *n.*

proof (prüf), **1** way or means of showing beyond doubt the truth of something: *Is what you say a guess or have you proof?* **2** establishment of the truth of anything. **3** act of testing; trial: *That box looks big enough; but let us put it to the proof.* **4** a trial impression printed from type. A book is first printed in proof so that errors can be corrected. **5** a trial print of an etching, photographic negative, etc. **6** of tested value against something; capable of resisting or withstanding: *This fabric is wrinkle-proof.* 1-5 *n.*, 6 *adj.*

a hat	**i** it	**oi** oil	**ch** child	
ā age	**ī** ice	**ou** out	**ng** long	a in about
ä far	**o** hot	**u** cup	**sh** she	e in taken
e let	**ō** open	**ủ** put	**th** thin	ə = i in pencil
ē equal	**ô** order	**ü** rule	**ŦH** then	o in lemon
ėr term			**zh** measure	u in circus

proof read (prüf′rēd′), read and mark errors to be corrected. *v.*, **proof read** (prüf′red′), **proof read ing.** —**proof′read′er,** *n.*

prop[1] (prop), **1** hold up by placing a support under or against: *Prop the clothesline with a stick. He was propped up in bed with pillows.* **2** support; sustain: *prop a failing cause.* **3** thing or person used to support another: *I used the book as a prop behind my painting.* 1,2 *v.*, **propped, prop ping;** 3 *n.*

prop[2] (prop), property (def. 5). *n.*

prop[3] (prop), INFORMAL. an airplane propeller. *n.*

prop a gan da (prop′ə gan′də), **1** systematic efforts to spread opinions or beliefs; any plan or method for spreading opinions or beliefs: *Propaganda is most effective when there is no freedom of the press.* **2** the opinions or beliefs thus spread: *During the war, the enemy spread false propaganda about us. n.*

prop a gan dist (prop′ə gan′dist), **1** person who gives time or effort to the spreading of some opinion or belief. **2** of propaganda or propagandists. 1 *n.*, 2 *adj.*

prop a gan dize (prop′ə gan′dīz), **1** propagate or spread (opinions or beliefs) by propaganda. **2** carry on propaganda. *v.*, **prop a gan dized, prop a gan diz ing.**

prop a gate (prop′ə gāt), **1** produce offspring; reproduce: *Trees propagate themselves by seeds.* **2** cause to increase in number by the production of young: *Cows and sheep are propagated on farms.* **3** spread (news or knowledge): *The scientist propagated his new theory about life in outer space.* **4** pass on; send further: *Sound is propagated by vibrations. v.*, **prop a gat ed, prop a gat ing.**

prop a ga tion (prop′ə gā′shən), **1** the breeding of plants or animals: *Our propagation of poppies is by seed, and of roses by cuttings.* **2** spreading; getting more widely believed; making more widely known: *the propagation of the principles of science.* **3** passing on; sending further; extending: *the propagation of an earthquake shock. n.*

pro pane (prō′pān), a heavy, colorless, flammable gas, a hydrocarbon. Propane occurs in crude petroleum and is used as a fuel, refrigerant, or solvent. *n.*

pro pel (prə pel′), drive forward; force ahead: *propel a boat by oars, a person propelled by ambition. v.*, **propelled, pro pel ling.** —**pro pel′la ble,** *adj.*

pro pel lant (prə pel′ənt), substance that propels, especially the fuel of a rocket. *n.*

pro pel lent (prə pel′ənt), **1** propelling; driving forward. **2** thing or person that propels. 1 *adj.*, 2 *n.*

pro pel ler (prə pel′ər), device consisting of a revolving hub with blades, for propelling boats and aircraft. *n.*

propeller
of a ship

pro pen si ty (prə pen′sə tē), a natural inclination or bent; leaning: *a propensity for athletics. n., pl.* **pro pen si ties.**

prop er (prop′ər), **1** right for the occasion; fitting: *Night is the proper time to sleep.* **2** strictly so called; in the strict sense of the word: *Puerto Rico is not part of the United States proper.* **3** decent; respectable: *proper conduct.* **4** belonging to one or a few; not common to all. *Mary Jones and John Jones are proper names. adj.* —**prop′er ness,** *n.*

proper fraction, fraction less than 1. EXAMPLES: ²/₃, ¹/₈, ³/₄, and ¹⁹⁹/₂₀₀.

prop er ly (prop′ər lē), **1** in a proper, correct, or fitting manner: *Eat properly.* **2** rightly; justly: *An honest person is properly indignant at the offer of a bribe.* **3** strictly: *Properly speaking, a whale is not a fish. adv.*

proper noun, noun naming a particular person, place, or thing. *Jane, George, Chicago,* and *Monday* are proper nouns. *Girl, boy, city,* and *day* are common nouns.

prop er ty (prop′ər tē), **1** thing or things owned; possession or possessions: *This house is that man's property. That book is my property; please return it to me.* **2** ownership. **3** piece of land or real estate: *She owns property out West.* **4** quality or power belonging specially to something: *Soap has the property of removing dirt. Copper has several important properties.* **5** any piece of furniture or small article (everything except scenery and clothes) used in staging a play or a motion-picture or television scene; prop. *n., pl.* **prop er ties.** —**prop′er ty less,** *adj.*

proph e cy (prof′ə sē), **1** a telling what will happen; foretelling future events. **2** thing told about the future. **3** a divinely inspired utterance, revelation, writing, etc. *n., pl.* **proph e cies.**

proph e sy (prof′ə sī), **1** tell what will happen; foretell; predict: *The fortuneteller prophesied that I would have good luck in the future.* **2** speak when or as if inspired by God. *v.,* **proph e sied, proph e sy ing.** —**proph′e si′er,** *n.*

proph et (prof′it), **1** person who tells what will happen: *Don't be a bad-luck prophet.* **2** a religious leader who speaks as the voice of God: *Jeremiah was a prophet of the Old Testament. n.* [*Prophet* can be traced back to Greek *pro,* meaning "before," and *phanai,* meaning "to speak."]

pro phet ic (prə fet′ik), **1** belonging to a prophet; such as a prophet has: *prophetic power.* **2** giving warning of what is to happen; foretelling: *Thunder is prophetic of showers. adj.* —**pro phet′i cal ly,** *adv.*

pro phy lac tic (prō′fə lak′tik), **1** protecting from disease. **2** medicine or measure that protects against disease. **3** any contraceptive device. **1** *adj.,* **2,3** *n.*

pro pin qui ty (prō ping′kwə tē), nearness in place, especially personal nearness. *n.*

pro pi ti ate (prə pish′ē āt), prevent or reduce the anger of; win the favor of. *v.,* **pro pi ti at ed, pro pi ti at ing.** —**pro pi′ti a′tion,** *n.* —**pro pi′ti a′tor,** *n.*

pro pi tious (prə pish′əs), **1** holding well; favorable: *propitious weather for our trip.* **2** favorably inclined; gracious. *adj.* —**pro pi′tious ly,** *adv.* —**pro pi′tious ness,** *n.*

pro po nent (prə pō′nənt), person who supports something; advocate. *n.*

pro por tion (prə pôr′shən), **1** relation of two things in magnitude; size, number, amount, or degree compared to another: *Each girl's pay will be in proportion to the work she does. Mix water and orange juice in the proportions of three to one by adding three measures of water to every measure of orange juice.* **2** a proper relation between parts: *The dog's short legs were not in proportion to its long body.* **3** fit (one thing to another) so that they go together: *The designs in that rug are well proportioned.* **4** adjust in proper proportion or relation: *to proportion correctly the*

various ingredients of a recipe. **5** part; share: *A large proportion of Nevada is desert.* **6** statement of equality between two ratios. EXAMPLE: 4 is to 2 as 10 is to 5. **7 proportions,** *pl.* **a** size; extent: *She left an art collection of considerable proportions.* **b** dimensions: *The dining room of the castle had the proportions of our entire apartment.* **1,2,5-7** *n.,* **3,4** *v.* —**pro por′tion ment,** *n.*

pro por tion al (prə pôr′shə nəl), in the proper proportion; corresponding: *The pay will be proportional to the amount of time put in. adj.* —**pro por′tion al ly,** *adv.*

pro por tion ate (prə pôr′shə nit), in the proper proportion: *The money earned by the fair was really not proportionate to the effort we put into it. adj.* —**pro por′tion ate ness,** *n.*

pro por tion ate ly (prə pôr′shə nit lē), in proportion: *The money the children earned was divided proportionately to the time each worked. adv.*

pro pos al (prə pō′zəl), **1** what is proposed; plan, scheme, or suggestion: *The club will now hear this member's proposal.* **2** an offer of marriage. **3** act of proposing: *Proposal is easier than performance. n.*

pro pose (prə pōz′), **1** put forward; suggest: *I propose that we take turns at the swing.* **2** present (the name of someone) for an office: *I am proposing Jack for president.* **3** intend; plan: *She proposes to save half of all she earns.* **4** make an offer of marriage. *v.,* **pro posed, pro pos ing.**

prop o si tion (prop′ə zish′ən), **1** what is offered to be considered; proposal: *The corporation presented a proposition to buy several smaller businesses.* **2** statement. EXAMPLE: "All men are created equal." **3** statement that is to be proved true. EXAMPLE: Resolved: that our school should have a bank. **4** problem to be solved: *a proposition in geometry. n.*

pro pound (prə pound′), put forward; propose: *propound a theory, propound a riddle. v.* —**pro pound′er,** *n.*

pro pri e tar y (prə prī′ə ter′ē), **1** of a proprietor or owner: *a proprietary interest in a business.* **2** owned by a private person or company: *a proprietary business.* **3** manufactured and sold by the holder of a patent, trademark, or copyright: *proprietary medicines. adj.*

pro pri e tor (prə prī′ə tər), owner. *n.*

pro pri e tor ship (prə prī′ə tər ship), ownership. *n.*

pro pri e ty (prə prī′ə tē), **1** quality of being proper; fitness. **2** proper behavior: *She acted with propriety.* **3 proprieties,** *pl.* the customs and rules of proper behavior: *The proprieties require that we use good table manners. n., pl.* **pro pri e ties.**

pro pul sion (prə pul′shən), **1** a driving forward or onward. **2** a propelling force or impulse: *Most large aircraft are powered by propulsion of jet engines. n.*

pro rate (prō rāt′ or prō′rāt′), divide proportionally: *I prorated the money according to the number of days each had worked. v.,* **pro rat ed, pro rat ing.** —**pro rat′a ble,** *adj.* —**pro ra′tion,** *n.*

pro sa ic (prō zā′ik), like prose; matter-of-fact; ordinary; not exciting. *adj.* —**pro sa′i cal ly,** *adv.*

prosaic—Washing dishes is a **prosaic** task.

pro scribe (prō skrīb′), **1** prohibit as wrong or danger-ous; talk against; condemn: *Some religions proscribe dancing, drinking, and card playing.* **2** banish; outlaw. *v.,* **pro scribed, pro scrib ing.** —**pro scrib′a ble,** *adj.* —**pro scrib′er,** *n.*

pro scrip tion (prō skrip′shən), a proscribing or a being proscribed; banishment; outlawry. *n.*

prose (prōz), **1** the ordinary form of spoken or written language; plain language not arranged in verses. **2** of prose; in prose. 1 *n.,* 2 *adj.*

pros e cute (pros′ə kyüt), **1** bring before a court of law: *Reckless drivers will be prosecuted.* **2** bring a case before a court of law. **3** carry out; follow up: *The fire department started an inquiry into the cause of the fire, and prosecuted it for several weeks.* **4** carry on (a business or occupation). *v.,* **pros e cut ed, pros e cut ing.**

pros e cu tion (pros′ə kyü′shən), **1** the carrying on of a lawsuit: *The prosecution will be abandoned if the stolen money is returned.* **2** side that starts action against anoth-er in a court of law. The prosecution makes certain charges against the defense. **3** a carrying out; following up: *the prosecution of a plan. n.*

pros e cu tor (pros′ə kyü′tər), **1** the lawyer who takes charge of the government's side of a case against an accused person. **2** person who starts legal proceedings against another person: *Who is the prosecutor in this case? n.*

pros e lyte (pros′ə līt), **1** person who has changed from one opinion, religious belief, etc., to another. **2** to con-vert from one opinion, religious belief, etc., to another. 1 *n.,* 2 *v.,* **pros e lyt ed, pros e lyt ing.** —**pros′e lyt′er,** *n.*

pros e lyt ize (pros′ə lə tīz), make converts; proselyte. *v.,* **pros e lyt ized, pros e lyt iz ing.** —**pros′e lyt iz′er,** *n.*

Pro ser pi na (prō sėr′pə nə), (in Roman myths) the daughter of Jupiter and Ceres. The Greeks called her Persephone. *n.*

pros o dy (pros′ə dē), the science of poetic meters and versification. *n.*

pros pect (pros′pekt), **1** thing expected or looked for-ward to: *The prospects from our gardens are good this year.* **2** act of looking forward; expectation: *The prospect of a vacation is pleasant.* **3** outlook for the future. **4** view; scene: *The prospect from the mountain was breathtaking.* **5** to search or look: *prospect for gold.* **6** person who may become a customer, buyer, candidate, etc.: *The salesman called on several prospects.* 1-4,6 *n.,* 5 *v.* —**pros′pect less,** *adj.*

pro spec tive (prə spek′tiv), **1** likely to happen; proba-ble; expected: *a prospective client, a prospective raise in pay.* **2** looking forward in time; future. *adj.* —**pro spec′-tive ly,** *adv.*

pros pec tor (pros′pek tər), person who explores or ex-amines a region, searching for gold, silver, oil, uranium, etc., or other valuable resources. *n.*

pro spec tus (prə spek′təs), a printed statement de-scribing and advertising something. *n., pl.* **pro spec-tus es.**

pros per (pros′pər), **1** be successful; have good fortune; flourish: *Our business prospered.* **2** make successful. *v.*

pros per i ty (pro sper′ə tē), prosperous condition; good fortune; success: *a time of peace and prosperity. n.*

pros per ous (pros′pər əs), **1** doing well; successful; thriving; fortunate: *a prosperous merchant.* **2** favorable; helpful: *prosperous weather for growing wheat. adj.* —**pros′per ous ly,** *adv.* —**pros′per ous ness,** *n.*

pros ti tute (pros′tə tüt *or* pros′tə tyüt), **1** person who has sexual relations with others for money. **2** person who does base things for money. **3** put to an unworthy or base use: *to prostitute artistic skills.* 1,2 *n.,* 3 *v.,* **pros-ti tut ed, pros ti tut ing.**

a hat	**i** it	**oi** oil	**ch** child	a in about
ā age	**ī** ice	**ou** out	**ng** long	e in taken
ä far	**o** hot	**u** cup	**sh** she	ə = { i in pencil
e let	**ō** open	**u̇** put	**th** thin	o in lemon
ē equal	**ô** order	**ü** rule	**ᴛʜ** then	u in circus
ėr term			**zh** measure	

pros ti tu tion (pros′tə tü′shən *or* pros′tə tyü′shən), the use of one's body, honor, talents, etc., in a base way. *n.*

pros trate (pros′trāt), **1** lay down flat; cast down: *The captives prostrated themselves before the conqueror.* **2** lying flat with face downward: *They were humbly prostrate in prayer.* **3** lying flat: *He stumbled and fell prostrate on the floor.* **4** make very weak or helpless; exhaust: *Sickness often prostrates people.* **5** helpless; overcome: *They were prostrate with grief.* 1,4 *v.,* **pros trat ed, pros trat ing;** 2,3,5 *adj.*

pros tra tion (pro strā′shən), **1** act of prostrating; bow-ing down low or lying face down before a ruler, before idols, or before God. Prostration is an act of submission, of respect, or of worship. **2** a being very much worn out or used up in body or mind; exhaustion. *n.*

pros y (prō′zē), like prose; commonplace; dull; tire-some. *adj.,* **pros i er, pros i est.** —**pros′i ly,** *adv.* —**pros′i ness,** *n.*

pro tac tin i um (prō′tak tin′ē əm), a very rare, heavy, radioactive metallic element which occurs in pitch-blende. It disintegrates to form actinium. *n.*

pro tag o nist (prō tag′ə nist), the main character in a play, story, or novel. *n.*

pro tect (prə tekt′), shield from harm or danger; shelter; defend; guard: *Proper food protects a person's health. v.* —**pro tect′ing ly,** *adv.*

pro tec tion (prə tek′shən), **1** act of protecting; condi-tion of being kept from harm; defense: *We have a large dog for protection.* **2** thing or person that prevents dam-age: *A hat is protection from the sun. n.*

pro tec tive (prə tek′tiv), **1** being a defense; protecting: *the hard protective covering of a turtle.* **2** preventing injury to those around: *a protective device on a machine. adj.* —**pro tec′tive ly,** *adv.* —**pro tec′tive ness,** *n.*

protective coloration, a coloring some animals have that makes them hard to distinguish from the things they live among, or that makes them resemble a harmful or distasteful animal, and so protects them from their ene-mies.

pro tec tor (prə tek′tər), person or thing that protects; defender. *n.*

pro tec tor ate (prə tek′tər it), **1** a weak country under the protection and partial control of a strong country. **2** such protection and control. *n.*

pro té gé (prō′tə zhā), person who has been taken under the protection or kindly care of a friend or patron. *n., pl.* **pro té gés.**

WORD HISTORY

protégé

Protégé comes from French *protégé,* which also means "protected," and can be traced back to Latin *pro,* mean-ing "before," and *tegere,* meaning "to cover."

pro tein (prō′tēn), one of the substances containing nitrogen which are a necessary part of the cells of animals and plants. Meat, milk, cheese, eggs, and beans contain protein. Protein is built up of amino acids. *n.*

pro test (prō′test *for 1,4;* prə test′ *for 2,3,5*), **1** statement that denies or objects strongly: *They yielded only after protest.* **2** make objections; object: *I protested against having to wash the dishes.* **3** object to: *protest an umpire's decision.* **4** expressing objection against some condition: *a protest movement.* **5** declare solemnly; assert: *The accused speeder protested her innocence.* 1 *n.,* 2,3,5 *v.,* 4 *adj.*
under protest, unwillingly; objecting.

Prot es tant (prot′ə stənt), **1** member of any of certain Christian churches which split off from the Roman Catholic Church during the Reformation of the 1500's or developed thereafter. Lutherans, Baptists, Presbyterians, Methodists, Quakers, and many others are Protestants. **2** of Protestants or their religion. 1 *n.,* 2 *adj.*

Protestant Episcopal Church, a church in the United States that has about the same principles and beliefs as the Church of England.

Prot es tant ism (prot′ə stən tiz′əm), **1** the religion of Protestants. **2** their principles and beliefs. **3** Protestants or Protestant churches as a group. *n.*

prot es ta tion (prot′ə stā′shən), **1** a solemn declaration; protesting. **2** a protest. *n.*

pro tes ter (prō′tes′tər *or* prə tes′tər), a person who protests, especially in a determined, public way against governmental policies. *n.*

pro tist (prō′tist), any living thing that has characteristics of both animals and plants, or of neither. Protists have definite nuclei and are usually one-celled. Amebas and many algae are protists. *n., pl.* **pro tists, pro tis ta** (prō tis′tə).

proto-, *combining form.* first in time: *Prototype = the first type in time.* [The form *proto-* comes from Greek *prōtos.*]

pro to col (prō′tə kol), rules of etiquette of the diplomatic corps. *n.*

pro ton (prō′ton), a tiny particle in the nucleus of the atom, carrying one unit of positive electricity. Protons have a mass about 1,836 times that of an electron. *n.* [*Proton* comes from Greek *prōton,* meaning "first."]

pro to plasm (prō′tə plaz′əm), the mixture of proteins, fats, and many other complex substances suspended in water which forms the living matter of all plant and animal cells; the substance that is the basis of life. *n.*

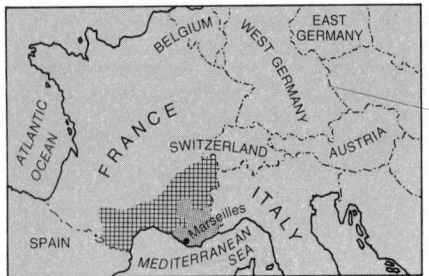

Provence—Smaller area of shading shows Provence in 1225. Larger area of shading to left and above shows the additional territory it occupied while a Roman province in 50 B.C.

pro to plas mic (prō′tə plaz′mik), of or having to do with protoplasm. *adj.*
pro to type (prō′tə tīp), the first or original type or model of anything that is designed or constructed. *n.*
pro to zo an (prō′tə zō′ən), any of a group of microscopic, one-celled animals. Amebas and paramecia are

protozoans. *n., pl.* **pro to zo ans, pro to zo a** (prō′tə-zō′ə).

pro tract (prō trakt′), draw out; lengthen in time: *a protracted visit.* *v.* —**pro tract′i ble,** *adj.*

pro trac tion (prō trak′shən), act of drawing out; extension. *n.*

pro trac tor (prō trak′tər), instrument for drawing or measuring angles. *n.*

protractor

pro trude (prō trüd′), **1** thrust forth; stick out: *The turtle protruded its head.* **2** be thrust forth; project: *teeth that protrude too far.* *v.,* **pro trud ed, pro trud ing.**

pro tru sion (prō trü′zhən), **1** a sticking out: *Bending your arm causes a protrusion of the elbow.* **2** something that sticks out; projection: *A protrusion of rock gave us shelter from the storm.* *n.*

pro tu ber ance (prō tü′bər əns *or* prō tyü′bər əns), part that sticks out; bulge; swelling: *The protuberance in the coat pocket turned out to be a crumpled scarf.* *n.*

pro tu ber ant (prō tü′bər ənt *or* prō tyü′bər ənt), bulging out; sticking out; prominent. *adj.*

proud (proud), **1** thinking well of oneself. **2** feeling or showing pleasure or satisfaction: *I am proud to call him my friend.* **3** having respect for oneself, one's position, or one's character: *The family was too proud to ask for charity.* **4** thinking too well of oneself; haughty; arrogant. **5** very pleasing to one's feelings or one's pride: *It was a proud moment for her when she was awarded the scholarship.* **6** grand; magnificent: *The big ship was a proud sight.* *adj.* —**proud′ly,** *adv.* —**proud′ness,** *n.*
proud of, thinking well of; being well satisfied with.

prove (prüv), **1** show that (a thing) is true and right: *Prove your statement.* **2** turn out; be found to be: *This book proved interesting.* **3** try out; test: *prove a new product.* *v.,* **proved, proved** *or* **prov en, prov ing.** —**prov′a ble,** *adj.* —**prov′a bly,** *adv.* —**prov′er,** *n.*

prov en (prü′vən), proved; a past participle of **prove.** *v.*

Pro ven çal (prō′vən säl′), **1** of Provence, its people, or their language. **2** person born or living in Provence. **3** language of Provence. In its medieval form, it was widely known in Europe as one of the principal languages of the troubadours. 1 *adj.,* 2,3 *n.*

Pro vence (prô väns′), part of SE France, famous during the Middle Ages for chivalry and poetry. *n.*

prototype
The **prototype** of a new car was unveiled.

prov en der (prov′ən dər), **1** dry food for animals, such as hay or corn. **2** INFORMAL. food. *n.*

prov erb (prov′ėrb′), a short, wise saying used for a long time by many people. "Haste makes waste" is a proverb. *n.* —**prov′erb like′**, *adj.*

a hat	**i** it	**oi** oil	**ch** child	a in about
ā age	**ī** ice	**ou** out	**ng** long	e in taken
ä far	**o** hot	**u** cup	**sh** she	ə = i in pencil
e let	**ō** open	**u̇** put	**th** thin	o in lemon
ē equal	**ô** order	**ü** rule	**ŦH** then	u in circus
ėr term			**zh** measure	

proverbs

A stitch in time saves nine.

A SOFT ANSWER TURNETH AWAY WRATH.

A penny saved is a penny earned.

The early bird catches the worm.

Strike while the iron is hot.

CHARITY BEGINS AT HOME.

pro ver bi al (prə vėr′bē əl), **1** of proverbs; expressed in a proverb; like a proverb: *proverbial wisdom, a proverbial saying.* **2** having become a proverb: *the proverbial stitch in time.* **3** well-known: *the proverbial loyalty of dogs. adj.* —**pro ver′bi al ly**, *adv.*

Prov erbs (prov′ėrbz′), book of the Old Testament made up of sayings of the wise men of Israel. *n.*

pro vide (prə vīd′), **1** give what is needed or wanted; supply; furnish: *Sheep provide us with wool.* **2** take care for the future: *provide for old age.* **3** arrange in advance; state as a condition beforehand: *Our club's rules provide that dues must be paid monthly.* **4** get ready; prepare beforehand: *They provided a good dinner. v.,* **pro vid ed, pro vid ing.** —**pro vid′a ble**, *adj.*

pro vid ed (prə vī′did), on the condition that; if: *I will go provided my friends can go also. conj.*

prov i dence (prov′ə dəns), **1** God's care and help: *Trusting in providence, the Pilgrims sailed for the unknown world.* **2** **Providence**, God. **3** care for the future; good management: *Greater providence on my part would have kept me out of debt. n.*

Prov i dence (prov′ə dəns), capital of Rhode Island, in the NE part. *n.*

prov i dent (prov′ə dənt), having or showing foresight; careful in providing for the future: *Provident people save money for the future. adj.* —**prov′i dent ly**, *adv.* —**prov′i dent ness**, *n.*

prov i den tial (prov′ə den′shəl), **1** fortunate: *Our delay seemed providential, for the train we had planned to take was wrecked.* **2** of or proceeding from God's care: *providential help. adj.* —**prov′i den′tial ly**, *adv.*

pro vid er (prə vī′dər), person or thing that provides. *n.*

pro vid ing (prə vī′ding), on the condition that; if: *I shall go providing it doesn't rain. conj.*

prov ince (prov′əns), **1** one of the main divisions of a country. Canada is made up of provinces instead of states. **2** **the provinces**, part of a country outside the capital or the largest cities: *I was accustomed to city life and did not like living in the provinces.* **3** proper work or activity: *Physics is not within the province of Grade 5.* **4** division; department: *the province of science, the province of literature.* **5** an ancient Roman territory outside Italy, ruled by a Roman governor. *n.*

pro vin cial (prə vin′shəl), **1** of a province: *provincial government.* **2** person born or living in a province. **3** belonging or peculiar to some particular province or provinces rather than to the whole country; local: *provincial English, provincial customs.* **4** having the manners, speech, dress, point of view, etc., of people living in a province. **5** lacking refinement or polish; narrow: *a provincial point of view.* **6** a provincial person. 1,3-5 *adj.,* 2,6 *n.* —**pro vin′cial ly**, *adv.*

pro vin cial ism (prə vin′shə liz′əm), **1** provincial manners, habit of thought, etc. **2** narrow-mindedness. **3** word, expression, or way of pronunciation peculiar to a district of a country. *Reckon* for *think* is a provincialism. *n.*

pro vi sion (prə vizh′ən), **1** statement making a condition: *A provision of the lease is that the rent must be paid promptly.* **2** act of providing; preparation: *They made provision for their children's education.* **3** care taken for the future; arrangement made beforehand: *There is a provision for making the building larger if necessary.* **4** that which is made ready; supply; stock, especially of food; food. **5** **provisions,** pl. a supply of food and drinks: *They took plenty of provisions on their trip.* **6** to supply with provisions: *The cabin was well provisioned with canned goods.* 1-5 *n.,* 6 *v.* —**pro vi′sion er**, *n.* —**pro vi′sion less**, *adj.*

pro vi sion al (prə vizh′ə nəl), for the time being; temporary: *a provisional agreement, a provisional governor. adj.*

pro vi so (prə vī′zō), statement making a condition; requirement; provision. *n., pl.* **pro vi sos** or **pro vi soes.**

prov o ca tion (prov′ə kā′shən), **1** a provoking. **2** something that stirs one up; cause of anger: *Their insults were a provocation. n.*

pro voc a tive (prə vok′ə tiv), **1** irritating; vexing. **2** tending or serving to call forth action, thought, laughter, anger, etc.: *a provocative remark. adj.* —**pro voc′a tive ly**, *adv.* —**pro voc′a tive ness**, *n.*

pro voke (prə vōk′), **1** make angry; vex: *She provoked him by her teasing.* **2** stir up; excite: *An insult provokes a person to anger.* **3** call forth; bring about; start into action; cause: *The President's speech provoked much discussion. v.,* **pro voked, pro vok ing.**

pro vok ing (prə vō′king), causing anger; irritating. *adj.* —**pro vok′ing ly**, *adv.*

prov ost (prō′vōst), **1** a high administrative officer in some colleges and universities. **2** head or dean of the clergymen assigned to a cathedral. *n.*

pro vost marshal (prō′vō), **1** (in the army) an officer acting as head of police in a camp or district, and charged with the maintenance of order, etc. **2** (in the navy) an officer charged with the safekeeping of prisoners until their trial by court-martial.

prow (prou), **1** the front part of a ship or boat; bow. **2** the pointed front part of anything that sticks forward: *the prow of an aircraft. n.*

prowess (def. 3)
They were famous for their **prowess** at figure skating.

prow ess (prou′is), **1** bravery; daring. **2** brave or daring acts. **3** unusual skill or ability. *n.*

prowl (proul), **1** go about slowly and secretly hunting for something to eat or steal: *Many wild animals prowl at night.* **2** wander: *He got up and prowled about his room.* **3** a prowling: *It was only a wild animal on its nightly prowl.* 1,2 *v.,* 3 *n.* —**prowl′er,** *n.* —**prowl′ing ly,** *adv.*
on the prowl, prowling about.

prox i mate (prok′sə mit), **1** next; nearest. **2** near the exact amount; approximate. *adj.* —**prox′i mate ly,** *adv.*

prox im i ty (prok sim′ə tē), nearness; closeness. *n.*

prox y (prok′sē), **1** the action of a person having the authority to do something for another person. In marriage by proxy, someone takes the place of the absent bride or bridegroom during the ceremony. **2** a person having this kind of authority; agent, substitute. **3** an official document that gives a person this authority. *n., pl.* **prox ies.**

prs., pairs.

prude (prüd), person who is too proper or too modest; person who puts on extremely proper or modest airs. *n.* —**prude′like,** *adj.*

pru dence (prüd′ns), **1** wise thought before acting; good judgment. **2** good management; economy. *n.*

pru dent (prüd′nt), planning carefully ahead of time; sensible; discreet: *My prudent friend saves part of her wages. adj.* —**pru′dent ly,** *adv.*

pru den tial (prü den′shəl), of, marked by, or showing prudence. *adj.* —**pru den′tial ly,** *adv.*

prud er y (prü′dər ē), **1** extreme modesty or propriety, especially when not genuine. **2** a prudish act or remark. *n., pl.* **prud er ies.**

Prud hoe Bay (prü′dō), town in N Alaska, on the Arctic Ocean. The Alaska Pipeline begins there.

prud ish (prü′dish), like a prude; extremely proper or modest; too modest. *adj.* —**prud′ish ly,** *adv.* —**prud′ish ness,** *n.*

prune[1] (prün), kind of sweet plum that is dried. *n.*

prune[2] (prün), **1** cut out useless or undesirable parts from: *The editor pruned the writer's manuscript.* **2** cut unnecessary or undesirable twigs or branches from (a bush, tree, etc.): *prune fruit trees or grape vines.* **3** cut off or out: *Prune all the dead branches. v.,* **pruned, prun ing.** —**prun′a ble,** *adj.* —**prun′er,** *n.*

Prus sia (prush′ə), former duchy and kingdom in N Europe which became the most important state in the confederation of German states united by Bismarck in 1871. *n.* —**Prus′sian,** *adj., n.*

pry[1] (prī), look with curiosity; peep: *pry into another's private affairs. v.,* **pried, pry ing.**

pry[2] (prī), **1** raise or move by force: *pry up a stone.* **2** lever for prying. **3** get with much effort: *We finally pried the secret out of him.* 1,3 *v.,* **pried, pry ing;** 2 *n., pl.* **pries.**

pry ing (prī′ing), looking or searching too curiously; unpleasantly inquisitive. *adj.* —**pry′ing ly,** *adv.*

P.S., **1** postscript. **2** Public School.

psalm (säm), **1** a sacred song or poem. **2 Psalm,** any of the 150 sacred songs or hymns that together form a book of the Old Testament. *n.*

psalm ist (sä′mist), **1** author of a psalm or psalms. **2 the Psalmist,** King David, who according to tradition wrote many of the Psalms. *n.*

Psalms (sämz), book of the Old Testament consisting of 150 psalms. *n.*

Psal ter (sôl′tər), **1** the book of Psalms. **2** version of the Psalms for use in religious services. **3** a prayer book containing such a version. *n.*

psal ter y (sôl′tər ē), an ancient musical instrument played by plucking the strings. *n., pl.* **psal ter ies.**

pseu do (sü′dō), not genuine; false; pretended: *a pseudo religion, pseudo anger. adj.*

pseu do nym (süd′n im), name used by an author instead of his or her real name; pen name. Mark Twain is a pseudonym for Samuel Langhorne Clemens. *n.* [*Pseudonym* can be traced back to Greek *pseudēs,* meaning "false," and *onyma,* meaning "a name."]

pshaw (shô), exclamation expressing impatience, contempt, or dislike. *interj.*

PST, Pacific Standard Time.

psy che (sī′kē), **1** the human soul or spirit. **2** the mind. **3 Psyche,** (in Greek and Roman myths) the human soul or spirit pictured as a beautiful young woman, usually with butterfly wings. Psyche was loved by Cupid (Eros) and was made immortal. *n.*

psy che del ic (sī′kə del′ik), revealing new areas of consciousness, often accompanied by hallucinations or mental disorders: *psychedelic drugs. adj.*

psy chi at ric (sī′kē at′rik), of the treatment of mental and emotional disorders. *adj.* —**psy′chi at′ri cal ly,** *adv.*

psy chi a trist (sī kī′ə trist), doctor who treats mental and emotional disorders. *n.*

psy chi a try (sī kī′ə trē), study and treatment of mental and emotional disorders. *n.*

psy chic (sī′kik), **1** of the soul or mind; mental: *illness due to psychic causes.* **2** outside the known laws of physics; supernatural. **3** especially affected by psychic influences. *adj.* —**psy′chi cal ly,** *adv.*

psy chi cal (sī′kə kəl), psychic. *adj.*

psycho-, *combining form.* mental; of the mind: *Psychotherapy = mental therapy. Psychoanalysis = analysis of the mind.* [The form *psycho-* comes from Greek *psychē,* meaning "mind, life, soul."]

psy cho a nal y sis (sī′kō ə nal′ə sis), method of psychotherapy that examines a person's mind to discover the unconscious desires, fears, anxieties, etc., which produce mental and emotional disorders. *n.*

psy cho an a lyst (sī′kō an′l ist), person who practices psychoanalysis. *n.*

psy cho an a lyze (sī′kō an′l īz), treat by psychoanalysis. *v.,* **psy cho an a lyzed, psy cho an a lyz ing.**

Prussia
Shading to right shows the duchy of Prussia in 1648. Shading to left shows the additional territory in the kingdom of Prussia in 1871.

psy cho log i cal (sī/kə loj/ə kəl), **1** of the mind. Memories and dreams are psychological processes. **2** of psychology: *a psychological problem. adj.*

psy cho log i cal ly (sī/kə loj/ik lē), **1** in a psychological manner. **2** in psychological respects. *adv.*

psychological moment, 1 the very moment to get the desired effect in the mind. **2** the critical moment.

psy chol o gist (sī kol/ə jist), an expert in psychology. *n.*

psy chol o gy (sī kol/ə jē), **1** science of the mind. Psychology tries to explain why people act, think, and feel as they do. **2** the mental states and processes of a person or persons; mental nature and behavior: *The long illness had a bad effect on the patient's psychology. n., pl.* **psy chol o gies.**

psy cho path (sī/kə path), person having a mental or personality disorder, especially one characterized by immoral or criminal behavior. *n.*

psy cho path ic (sī/kə path/ik), of or like a psychopath. *adj.*

psy cho sis (sī kō/sis), any severe form of mental disorder which seriously disrupts normal behavior and social functioning. *n., pl.* **psy cho ses** (sī kō/sēz/).

psy cho ther a py (sī/kō ther/ə pē), treatment of mental or emotional disorders by psychological means. *n.*

psy chot ic (sī kot/ik), **1** of, having, or caused by a psychosis. **2** a psychotic person. **1** *adj.,* **2** *n.* —**psy chot/i cal ly,** *adv.*

Pt, symbol for platinum.

pt., 1 past tense. **2** pint or pints.

P.T.A., Parent-Teacher Association.

ptarmigan
about 13 in.
(33 cm.) long

ptar mi gan (tär/mə gən), any of several kinds of grouse that have feathered feet and are found in mountainous and cold regions. *n., pl.* **ptar mi gans** or **ptar mi gan.**

PT boat, a small, fast motorboat which carries torpedoes, depth bombs, etc.

pter o dac tyl (ter/ə dak/təl), an extinct flying reptile that had wings somewhat like a bat's. *n.*

Ptol e ma ic (tol/ə mā/ik), of the astronomer Ptolemy. The **Ptolemaic system** of astronomy taught that the earth was the fixed center of the universe and that the sun, moon, and other heavenly bodies moved around it. *adj.*

Ptol e my (tol/ə mē), **Claudius,** Greek mathematician, astronomer, and geographer at Alexandria. He lived in the A.D. 100's. *n.*

pto maine (tō/mān), any of several chemical compounds produced by bacteria in decaying matter. Improperly canned foods may contain ptomaines. Some ptomaines are poisonous. *n.*

Pu, symbol for plutonium.

pub (pub), BRITISH. saloon; tavern. *n.*

pu ber ty (pyü/bər tē), age at which a person is first able to produce offspring; the physical beginning of manhood and womanhood. Puberty comes at about 14 in boys and about 12 in girls. *n.*

pu bic (pyü/bik), of or in the region of the front part of the pelvis. *adj.*

pub lic (pub/lik), **1** of the people as a whole: *public affairs, public buildings.* **2** the people in general; all the people: *inform the public.* **3** done, made, acting, etc., for the people as a whole: *public relief.* **4** open to all the people; serving all the people: *a public park, public meetings.* **5** of or engaged in the affairs or service of the people: *a public official.* **6** known to many or all; not private: *The fact became public.* **7** a particular section of the people: *A popular actor has a large public.* **1,3-6** *adj.,* **2,7** *n.* —**pub/lic ness,** *n.*

in public, not in private or secretly; publicly; openly: *to stand up in public for what you believe.*

public address system, apparatus made up of one or more microphones, amplifiers, and loudspeakers for making sounds audible to a large audience, as on a street or in an auditorium.

pub li can (pub/lə kən), **1** BRITISH. keeper of a pub. **2** a tax collector of ancient Rome. *n.*

pub li ca tion (pub/lə kā/shən), **1** book, newspaper, or magazine; anything that is published. **2** the printing and selling of books, newspapers, magazines, etc. **3** a making known; a being made known; public announcement: *There is prompt publication of any important news over the radio. n.*

public house, BRITISH. saloon; tavern.

pub li cist (pub/lə sist), **1** person skilled or trained in law or in public affairs. **2** writer on law, politics, or public affairs. **3** press agent. *n.*

pub lic i ty (pub lis/ə tē), **1** public notice: *the publicity that actors desire.* **2** measures used for getting, or the process of getting, public notice: *I worked on the publicity for the concert.* **3** articles, announcements, etc., used to get public notice: *write publicity. n.*

pub li cize (pub/lə sīz), give publicity to. *v.,* **pub li cized, pub li ciz ing.**

pub lic ly (pub/lik lē), **1** in a public manner; openly. **2** by the public. *adv.*

pterodactyl
wingspread about
20 ft. (6 m.)

public opinion, opinion of the people in a country, community, etc.: *make a survey of public opinion.*

public relations, 1 activities of an organization, institution, or individual done to create or keep a favorable public image. **2** the business of such activities: *to work in public relations.*

public school, 1 (in the United States) a free school maintained by taxes. **2** (in Great Britain) a private boarding school.

public servant, person who works for the government.

pub lic-spir it ed (pub/lik spir/ə tid), having or showing an unselfish desire for the public good. *adj.*

public utility, company formed or chartered to render essential services to the public, such as a company furnishing electricity, gas, or water, or an airline, a railroad, a bus line, etc.

public works, things built by the government at public expense and for public use, such as roads, docks, canals, and waterworks.

pub lish (pub′lish), **1** prepare and offer (a book, paper, map, piece of music, etc.) for sale or distribution. **2** make publicly or generally known: *Don't publish the faults of your friends. v.* —**pub′lish a ble,** *adj.*

pub lish er (pub′li shər), person or company whose business is to publish books, newspapers, magazines, etc.: *Look at the bottom of the title page of this book for the publisher's name. n.*

Puc ci ni (pü chē′nē), **Giacomo,** 1858-1924, Italian composer of operas. *n.*

puck[1] (puk), a rubber disk used in the game of ice hockey. *n.*

puck[2] (puk), **1** a mischievous fairy; elf. **2 Puck,** a mischievous fairy in English folklore. *n.*

puck er (puk′ər), **1** draw into wrinkles or irregular folds: *pucker one's brow, pucker cloth in sewing. My lips puckered as I tasted the sour grapefruit.* **2** an irregular fold; wrinkle: *There are puckers at the shoulders of this ill-fitting coat.* **1** *v.,* **2** *n.* —**puck′er er,** *n.*

puck ish (puk′ish), mischievous; impish: *a puckish twinkling of the eyes. adj.* —**puck′ish ly,** *adv.* —**puck′ish ness,** *n.*

pud ding (pùd′ing), a soft cooked food, usually sweet: *rice pudding. n.*

pud dle (pud′l), **1** a small pool of water, especially dirty water: *a puddle of rain water.* **2** a small pool of any liquid: *a puddle of ink. n.*

pudg i ness (puj′ē nis), condition of being short and fat. *n.*

pudg y (puj′ē), short and fat or thick: *a child's pudgy hand, a pudgy face. adj.,* **pudg i er, pudg i est.** —**pudg′i ly,** *adv.*

pueblo
(def. 1)

pueb lo (pweb′lō), **1** an Indian village built of adobe and stone. There were once many pueblos in the southwestern United States. **2 Pueblo,** member of any of a group of Indian tribes in the southwestern United States and northern Mexico living in such villages. *n., pl.* **pueb los** for 1; **Pueb lo** or **Pueb los** for 2.

pu er ile (pyü′ər əl), foolish for a grown person to say or do; childish. *adj.* —**pu′er ile ly,** *adv.*

Puer to Ri co (pwer′tō rē′kō), island in the E part of the West Indies. Puerto Rico is a self-governing commonwealth under the protection of the United States. *Abbreviation:* P.R. or PR *Capital:* San Juan. See **Caribbean Sea** for map. Formerly, **Porto Rico.** [*Puerto Rico* was borrowed from Spanish *Puerto Rico,* which comes from the phrase *puerto rico,* meaning "rich port." Originally this was the name of the capital, but later it came to be used for the entire island.] —**Puer′to Ri′can.**

puff (puf), **1** to blow with short, quick blasts: *The bellows*

puffed on the fire. **2** a short, quick blast: *A puff of wind blew away the letter.* **3** breathe quick and hard: *She puffed as she climbed the stairs.* **4** give out puffs; move with puffs: *The engine puffed out of the station.* **5** smoke: *puff a cigar.* **6** swell with air or pride: *puff out one's cheeks. He puffed out his chest when the teacher praised his work.* **7** act or process of swelling. **8** a soft, round mass: *a puff of hair, a puff of cotton.* **9** a small pad for putting powder on the skin. **10** a light pastry filled with whipped cream, jam, etc.: *a cream puff.* **11** praise in exaggerated language: *puff someone to the skies.* 1,3-6,11 *v.,* 2,7-10 *n.*

puff adder, a large and very poisonous African snake that puffs up its body when excited.

puff ball (puf′bôl′), a ball-shaped fungus somewhat like a mushroom. A ripe puffball gives off a cloud of tiny spores when suddenly broken. *n.*

puff er (puf′ər), any of various fishes capable of inflating the body. *n.*

puffin
about 14 in.
(35.5 cm.) long

puf fin (puf′ən), a sea bird of northern waters that has a thick body, a large head, and a bill of several colors. *n.*

puff i ness (puf′ē nis), puffy condition or quality. *n.*

puff y (puf′ē), **1** puffed out; swollen: *My eyes were puffy from crying.* **2** coming in puffs. *adj.,* **puff i er, puff i est.**

pug (pug), **1** a small, heavy-bodied dog with a curly tail and a short nose on a wide, wrinkled face. **2** pug nose. *n.*

Pu get Sound (pyü′jit), a long narrow bay of the Pacific in NW Washington.

pu gi lism (pyü′jə liz′əm), art or sport of boxing. *n.*

pu gi list (pyü′jə list), boxer. *n.*

pu gi lis tic (pyü′jə lis′tik), of boxing. *adj.*

pug na cious (pug nā′shəs), having the habit of fighting; fond of fighting; quarrelsome. *adj.* —**pug na′cious ly,** *adv.* —**pug na′cious ness,** *n.*

pugnacious—The **pugnacious** taxi driver shouted at the driver whose car was stalled.

pug nac i ty (pug nas′ə tē), fondness for fighting; quarrelsomeness. *n.*

pug nose, a short, turned-up nose.

pu is sance (pyü′ə səns *or* pwis′ns), power; might; strength. *n.*

pu is sant (pyü′ə sənt *or* pwis′nt), powerful; mighty; strong. *adj.* —**pu′is sant ly,** *adv.*

puke (pyük), INFORMAL. vomit. *n., v.,* **puked, puk ing.**

Pu las ki (pů las′kē), Count **Casimir,** 1748-1779, Polish nobleman who was a general in the American Revolutionary army. *n.*

pule (pyül), cry in a thin voice, as a sick child does; whimper; whine. *v.,* **puled, pul ing.**

Pu litz er prize (pyü′lit sər *or* půl′it sər), any of various annual awards for high achievement in American journalism, literature, music, and the arts. [This prize is named for Joseph *Pulitzer,* 1847-1911, an American journalist and newspaper publisher, who established it.]

pull (půl), **1** move (something) by grasping it and drawing toward oneself: *Pull the door open; don't push it.* **2** move, usually with effort or force: *pull a sled uphill.* **3** take hold of and tug: *pull a person's hair. She pulled at my sleeve to get my attention.* **4** take hold of and draw out with the fingers or a clutching tool held with the fingers: *She pulled out the nails with the claw of a hammer. The dentist decided to pull my bad tooth.* **5** move; go: *A strange car pulled into our driveway.* **6** pick; pluck: *pull flowers.* **7** tear; rip: *The baby pulled the toy to pieces.* **8** stretch too far; strain: *I pulled a muscle in my leg while skiing.* **9** row: *Pull for the shore as fast as you can.* **10** act of pulling; tug: *The boy gave a pull at the rope.* **11** effort of pulling: *It was a hard pull to get up the hill.* **12** handle, rope, ring, or other thing to pull by: *a bell pull, a curtain pull.* **13** force that attracts: *magnetic pull.* **14** INFORMAL. carry through; perform: *Don't pull any tricks.* **15** INFORMAL. influence; advantage: *use political pull to get a job.* 1-9,14 *v.,* 10-13,15 *n.* —**pull′er,** *n.*

pull down, demolish; destroy: *pull down an old building.*

pull for, INFORMAL. give help to.

pull in, arrive: *They pulled in this morning.*

pull off, INFORMAL. do successfully; succeed in.

pull oneself together, gather one's faculties, energy, etc.

pull out, leave: *What time does the train pull out? It pulled out of the station an hour ago.*

pull over, bring a vehicle to the side of the road or street and stop: *When our tire started going flat, we had to pull over and change it.*

pull through, get through a difficult or dangerous situation.

pull up, bring or come to a halt; stop.

pul let (půl′it), a young hen, usually less than a year old. *n.*

pul ley (půl′ē), **1** wheel with a grooved rim in which a rope can run and so change the direction of a pull. It is a simple machine and is used to raise weights. **2** set of such wheels used to increase the power applied. *n., pl.* **pul leys.**

Pull man (půl′mən), **1** sleeping car. **2** parlor car. *n.*

Pullman car, Pullman.

pull o ver (půl′ō′vər), sweater or shirt put on by pulling it over the head. *n.*

pul mo nar y (půl′mə ner′ē), of the lungs. Pneumonia is a pulmonary disease. *adj.*

puma
about 8 ft. (2.5 m.)
long with tail

pulp (pulp), **1** the soft, fleshy part of any fruit or vegetable. **2** the soft inner part of a tooth, containing blood vessels and nerves. **3** any soft, wet mass. Paper is made from wood ground to a pulp. **4** reduce to pulp. 1-3 *n.,* 4 *v.* —**pulp′less,** *adj.* —**pulp′like′,** *adj.*

pul pit (půl′pit), **1** platform or raised structure in a church from which the minister preaches. **2** preachers or preachings: *the influence of the pulpit. n.* —**pul′pit less,** *adj.*

pulp wood (pulp′wůd′), any soft wood suitable for reducing to pulp to make paper. *n.*

pulp y (pul′pē), of pulp; like pulp; fleshy; soft. *adj.,* **pulp i er, pulp i est.** —**pulp′i ly,** *adv.* —**pulp′i ness,** *n.*

pul sate (pul′sāt), **1** beat; throb: *The patient's heart was pulsating rapidly.* **2** vibrate; quiver. *v.,* **pul sat ed, pul sating.**

pul sa tion (pul sā′shən), **1** a beating; throbbing. **2** a beat; throb. **3** vibration; quiver. *n.*

pulse[1] (puls), **1** the regular beating of the arteries caused by the rush of blood into them after each contraction of the heart. By feeling a person's pulse in the artery of the wrist, one can count the number of times the heart beats each minute. **2** any regular, measured beat: *the pulse in music, the pulse of an engine.* **3** beat; throb; vibrate: *My heart pulsed with excitement.* **4** feeling; sentiment: *the pulse of the nation.* 1,2,4 *n.,* 3 *v.,* **pulsed, puls ing.** [*Pulse*[1] came into English about 650 years ago from French *pouls,* and can be traced back to Latin *pellere,* meaning "to beat, strike."] —**pulse′less,** *adj.*

pulse[2] (puls), **1** the seeds of a group of plants, such as peas, beans, and lentils, used as food. **2** plant that yields such seeds. *n.* [*Pulse*[2] came into English about 600 years ago from French *pols,* which came from Latin *puls,* meaning "porridge."]

pul ve rize (pul′və rīz′), **1** grind to powder or dust. **2** become dust. **3** break to pieces; demolish: *pulverize an enemy force by bombardment, pulverize the hopes of the people. v.,* **pul ve rized, pul ve riz ing.** —**pul′ve riz′a ble,** *adj.* —**pul′ve ri za′tion,** *n.* —**pul′ve riz′er,** *n.*

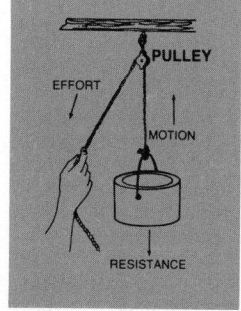
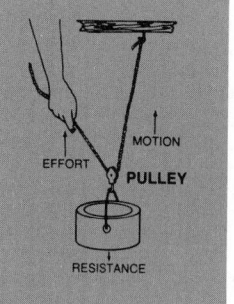

pulley (def. 1)—two types of pulleys

pu ma (pyü′mə), a large, tawny wildcat found in many parts of North and South America; cougar; mountain lion; panther. *n., pl.* **pu mas.**

pum ice (pum′is), a light, porous, glassy lava used for cleaning, smoothing, and polishing. *n.*

pum mel (pum′əl), strike or beat; beat with the fists. *v.,* **pum meled** *or* **pum melled, pum mel ing** *or* **pum melling.** Also, **pommel.**

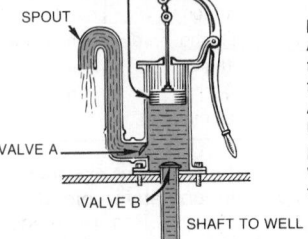

pump¹ (def. 1)
As the handle is raised, the plunger moves downward forcing water through valve A and out the spout. As the handle is pushed down, the plunger moves upward pulling water up through valve B from the shaft.

pump¹ (pump), **1** machine for forcing liquids or gases into or out of things: *a water pump, an oil pump.* **2** move (liquids, air, etc.) by a pump: *Pump water from the well into a pail.* **3** blow air into: *Pump up the car's tires.* **4** remove water, etc., from by a pump: *Pump the well dry.* **5** draw or force as if from a pump: *pump air into one's lungs.* **6** move by, or as if by, a pump handle: *to pump a person's hand.* **7** get information out of; try to get information out of: *Don't let them pump you.* 1 *n.,* 2-7 *v.* —**pump′a ble,** *adj.* —**pump′er,** *n.* —**pump′less,** *adj.*

pump² (pump), a low shoe with a thin sole and no fasteners. *n.*

pum per nick el (pum′pər nik′əl), a heavy, dark, slightly sour bread made from whole, coarse rye. *n.*

pump kin (pump′kin *or* pung′kin), the large, roundish, orange-yellow fruit of a trailing vine, used for making pies, as a vegetable, and for jack-o'-lanterns. *n.*

pun (pun), **1** a humorous use of a word where it can have different meanings; play on words. **2** make puns. 1 *n.,* 2 *v.,* **punned, pun ning.**

punch¹ (punch), **1** hit with the fist: *to punch someone on the arm.* **2** a quick thrust or blow with the fist. **3** tool for making holes. **4** tool or apparatus for piercing or stamping materials, impressing a design, etc. **5** pierce, cut, stamp, or make with a punch: *to punch metal. The conductor punched our tickets.* **6** to herd or drive cattle: *to punch cows.* 1,5,6 *v.,* 2-4 *n., pl.* **punch es.** —**punch′er,** *n.*

punch² (punch), drink made of different liquids, often fruit juices or carbonated beverages, mixed together. *n., pl.* **punch es.**

Punch (punch), a hook-nosed, hunchbacked doll who quarrels violently with his wife Judy in the puppet show *Punch and Judy. n.*

pleased as Punch, very much pleased.

punch card, card on which information is recorded by means of holes punched according to a code, for use in processing data by machine, electronic computer, etc.

punch line, the line or sentence in a story, play, or drama which makes or enforces the point.

punch y (pun′chē), INFORMAL. (of a boxer) uncoordinated in movement or speech because of brain concussion. *adj.,* **punch i er, punch i est.**

punc til i o (pungk til′ē ō), **1** a little point or detail of honor, conduct, ceremony, etc.: *I did not neglect the least punctilio.* **2** care in attending to such little points. *n., pl.* **punc til i os.**

punc til i ous (pungk til′ē əs), **1** very careful and exact: *punctilious in obeying orders, a punctilious concern about neatness.* **2** paying strict attention to details of conduct and ceremony. *adj.* —**punc til′i ous ly,** *adv.* —**punc til′i ous ness,** *n.*

punc tu al (pungk′chü əl), on time; prompt: *She is punctual to the minute. adj.* —**punc′tu al ly,** *adv.* —**punc′tu al ness,** *n.*

punc tu al i ty (pungk′chü al′ə tē), a being on time; promptness. *n.*

punc tu ate (pungk′chü āt), **1** use periods, commas, and

other marks in writing or printing to help make the meaning clear. **2** put punctuation marks in. **3** interrupt now and then: *a speech punctuated with cheers.* **4** give point or emphasis to: *She punctuated her remarks with gestures. v.,* **punc tu at ed, punc tu at ing.** —**punc′tu a′tor,** *n.*

punc tu a tion (pungk′chü ā′shən), **1** use of periods, commas, and other marks to help make the meaning of a sentence clear. Punctuation does for writing and printing what pauses and changes of voice do for speech. **2** punctuation marks. *n.*

punctuation mark, mark used in writing or printing to help make the meaning clear. Periods, commas, question marks, colons, etc., are punctuation marks.

punc ture (pungk′chər), **1** hole made by something pointed. **2** make such a hole in. **3** have or get a puncture. **4** act or process of puncturing. **5** reduce, spoil, or destroy as if by a puncture. 1,4 *n.,* 2,3,5 *v.,* **punc tured, punc tur ing.** —**punc′tur a ble,** *adj.* —**punc′ture less,** *adj.* —**punc′tur er,** *n.*

pun (def. 1)
by
Benjamin Franklin

pun dit (pun′dit), a very learned person; expert; authority. *n.*

pun gen cy (pun′jən sē), sharpness (of taste, smell, feeling, etc.): *the pungency of pepper, the pungency of wit. n.*

pun gent (pun′jənt), **1** sharply affecting the organs of taste and smell: *a pungent pickle, the pungent smell of burning leaves.* **2** sharp; biting: *pungent criticism.* **3** stimulating to the mind; keen; lively: *a pungent wit. adj.* —**pun′gent ly,** *adv.*

pu ni ness (pyü′nē nis), puny condition. *n.*

pun ish (pun′ish), **1** cause pain, loss, or discomfort to for some fault or offense: *punish criminals for wrongdoing.* **2** cause pain, loss, or discomfort for: *The law punishes crimes.* **3** deal with severely, roughly, or greedily: *punish a car by very fast driving. v.* —**pun′ish er,** *n.*

pun ish a ble (pun′i shə bəl), **1** liable to punishment. **2** deserving punishment. *adj.*

pun ish ment (pun′ish mənt), **1** a punishing or a being punished. **2** pain, suffering, or loss: *Her punishment for stealing was a year in prison.* **3** severe or rough treatment. *n.*

pu ni tive (pyü′nə tiv), **1** of punishment: *punitive laws.* **2** inflicting punishment: *The judge imposed a punitive sentence on the prisoner. adj.* —**pu′ni tive ly,** *adv.* —**pu′ni tive ness,** *n.*

punk¹ (pungk), **1** a preparation that burns very slowly. A stick of punk is used to light fireworks. **2** decayed wood used as tinder. *n.*

punk[2] (pungk), SLANG. **1** poor or bad in quality. **2** a young hoodlum. **3** a young, inexperienced person. 1 *adj.*, 2,3 *n.*

pun ster (pun′stər), person fond of making puns. *n.*

punt (punt), **1** a shallow, flat-bottomed boat with square ends, usually moved by pushing with a pole against the bottom of a river, etc. **2** propel (a boat) by pushing with a pole against the bottom of a river, pond, etc. **3** use a punt; travel by punt. **4** kick (a football) before it touches the ground after dropping it from the hands. **5** such a kick. 1,5 *n.*, 2-4 *v.* —**punt′er**, *n.*

pu ny (pyü′nē), **1** of less than usual size and strength; small and weak. **2** petty; not important. *adj.*, **pu ni er**, **pu ni est.**

pup (pup), **1** a young dog; puppy. **2** a young fox, wolf, seal, etc. *n.*

pu pa (pyü′pə), **1** stage between the larva and the adult in the development of many insects. **2** insect in this stage. Most pupae are inactive and some, such as those of many moths, are enclosed in a tough case or cocoon. *n.*, *pl.* **pu pae** (pyü′pē), **pu pas.** [*Pupa* comes from Latin *pupa*, meaning "girl, doll." The *pupa* was called this because it looks somewhat like the adult insect.]

pu pal (pyü′pəl), of or in the form of a pupa. *adj.*

pu pate (pyü′pāt), become a pupa. *v.*, **pu pat ed, pu pat ing.** —**pu pa′tion**, *n.*

pu pil[1] (pyü′pəl), person who is learning in school or being taught by someone. *n.*

pu pil[2] (pyü′pəl), the opening in the center of the iris of the eye which looks like a black spot. The pupil is the only place where light can enter the eye. The size of the pupil is regulated by the expansion and contraction of the iris. *n.*

pup pet (pup′it), **1** figure made to look like a person or animal and moved by wires, strings, or the hands. **2** anybody who is not independent, waits to be told how to act, and does what somebody else says. *n.* —**pup′pet like′**, *adj.*

puppet show, play performed with puppets on a small stage.

pup py (pup′ē), a young dog. *n.*, *pl.* **pup pies.**

WORD HISTORY

puppy

Puppy came into English about 500 years ago from French *poupée*, meaning "a doll," which came from Latin *pupa*.

pup tent, a small, low tent, usually for one or two persons.

pur blind (pėr′blīnd), **1** nearly blind. **2** slow to understand. *adj.* —**pur′blind′ly**, *adv.* —**pur′blind′ness**, *n.*

pur chas a ble (pėr′chə sə bəl), able to be bought. *adj.*

pur chase (pėr′chəs), **1** get by paying a price; buy: *We purchased a new car.* **2** a buying: *the purchase of a new car.* **3** thing bought: *That hat was a good purchase.* **4** get in return for something: *purchase safety at the cost of happiness.* **5** a firm hold to help move something or to keep from slipping: *Wind the rope twice around the tree to get a better purchase.* 1,4 *v.*, **pur chased, pur chas ing;** 2,3,5 *n.*

pur chas er (pėr′chə sər), buyer. *n.*

pure (pyur), **1** not mixed with anything else; unadulterated; genuine: *pure gold.* **2** perfectly clean; spotless: *pure*

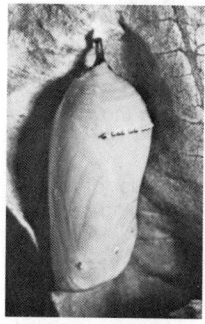

pupa (def. 2) of a butterfly

hands. **3** perfect; correct; without defects: *speak pure French.* **4** nothing else than; mere; sheer: *pure accident.* **5** with no evil; without sin; chaste: *a pure mind.* **6** concerned with theory rather than practical use; not applied; abstract: *pure mathematics.* *adj.*, **pur er, pur est.** —**pure′ness**, *n.*

pure bred (pyur′bred′), of pure breed or stock; having ancestors known to have all belonged to one breed: *purebred Holstein cows. adj.*

pu rée (pyu̇ rā′ *or* pyu̇r′ā), **1** food boiled to a pulp and pushed through a sieve. **2** a thick soup. **3** make into a purée. 1,2 *n.*, *pl.* **pu rées;** 3 *v.*, **pu réed, pu rée ing.**

pure ly (pyur′lē), **1** in a pure manner. **2** exclusively; entirely. **3** merely. **4** innocently; chastely. *adv.*

pur ga tive (pėr′gə tiv), **1** medicine that causes emptying of the bowels. Castor oil is a purgative. **2** purging; cleansing. 1 *n.*, 2 *adj.*

pur ga to ri al (pėr′gə tôr′ē əl), of, like, or having to do with purgatory. *adj.*

pur ga to ry (pėr′gə tôr′ē), **1** (in Roman Catholic belief) a temporary condition or place in which the souls of those who have died repenting are purified from sin by punishment. **2** any condition or place of temporary suffering or punishment. *n.*, *pl.* **pur ga to ries.**

purge (pėrj), **1** wash away all that is not clean; make clean. **2** a purging. **3** clear of any undesired thing or person: *purge a city of dishonest officials.* **4** elimination of undesired persons from a nation or party. **5** empty (the bowels). **6** medicine that purges. 1,3,5 *v.*, **purged, purging;** 2,4,6 *n.* —**purge′a ble**, *adj.* —**purg′er**, *n.*

pur i fi ca tion (pyur′ə fə kā′shən), a purifying or a being purified. *n.*

pur i fi er (pyur′ə fī′ər), person or thing that purifies. *n.*

pur i fy (pyur′ə fī), **1** make pure: *Filters are used to purify water.* **2** become pure. *v.*, **pur i fied, pur i fy ing.**

Pur im (pyur′im *or* pu̇r′im), a Jewish holiday, celebrated each year in February or March. It celebrates Esther's saving of the Jews from a massacre. *n.*

pur ist (pyur′ist), person who is very careful or too careful about purity in language. A purist dislikes slang and all expressions that are not formally correct. *n.*

Pur i tan (pyur′ə tən), **1** member of a group in the Church of England during the 1500's and 1600's who wanted simpler forms of worship and stricter morals. Many Puritans settled in New England. **2** of the Puritans. **3** puritan, person who is very strict in morals and religion. 1,3 *n.*, 2 *adj.*

pur i tan ic (pyur′ə tan′ik), puritanical. *adj.*

Pur i tan i cal (pyùr/ə tan/ə kəl), **1** having to do with or like the Puritans. **2** puritanical, of or like a puritan; very strict or too strict in morals or religion. *adj.*

Pur i tan ism (pyùr/ə tə niz/əm), **1** the principles and practices of the Puritans. **2** puritanism, puritanical behavior or principles. *n.*

pur i ty (pyùr/ə tē), **1** freedom from dirt or mixture; clearness; cleanness: *the purity of drinking water.* **2** freedom from evil; innocence: *a person of goodness and purity.* **3** careful correctness: *purity of style. n., pl.* **pur i-ties.**

purl¹ (pèrl), **1** flow with rippling motions and a murmuring sound: *A shallow brook purls.* **2** a purling motion or sound. 1 *v.,* 2 *n.*

purl² (pèrl), knit with inverted stitches. *v.*

pur lieu (pèr/lü), **1** piece of land on the border of a forest. **2** any bordering, neighboring, or outlying region or district. *n.*

pur loin (pər loin/), steal. *v.* **—pur loin/er,** *n.*

pur ple (pèr/pəl), **1** a dark color made by mixing red and blue. **2** of this color. **3** crimson. This was the ancient meaning of purple. **4** purple cloth or clothing, especially as worn by emperors, kings, etc., to indicate high rank. **5** imperial, royal, or high rank. A prince is born to the purple. **6** imperial; royal. **7** make or become purple. 1,3-5 *n.,* 2,3,6 *adj.,* 7 *v.,* **pur pled, pur pling.**

Purple Heart, medal awarded to members of the armed forces of the United States for wounds received in action against an enemy or as a result of enemy action.

pur plish (pèr/plish), somewhat purple. *adj.*

pur port (pər pôrt/ *for 1,2;* pèr/pôrt *for 3*), **1** to claim or profess: *The document purported to be official.* **2** have as its main idea; mean: *a statement purporting certain facts.* **3** meaning; main idea: *The purport of the letter was that they could not come.* 1,2 *v.,* 3 *n.* **—pur port/ed ly,** *adv.*

pur pose (pèr/pəs), **1** something one has in mind to get or do; plan; aim; intention. **2** object or end for which a thing is made, done, used, etc. **3** to plan; aim; intend. 1,2 *n.,* 3 *v.,* **pur posed, pur pos ing.**

on purpose, with a purpose; not by accident: *He tripped me on purpose.*

to good purpose, with good results.

to little purpose or **to no purpose,** with few or no results.

pur pose ful (pèr/pəs fəl), having a purpose. *adj.* **—pur/pose ful ly,** *adv.* **—pur/pose ful ness,** *n.*

pur pose less (pèr/pəs lis), lacking a purpose. *adj.* **—pur/pose less ly,** *adv.* **—pur/pose less ness,** *n.*

pur pose ly (pèr/pəs lē), on purpose; intentionally: *Did you leave the door open purposely? adv.*

purr (pèr), **1** a low, murmuring sound, such as a cat makes when pleased. **2** make this sound. 1 *n.,* 2 *v.*

purse (pèrs), **1** a small bag or container to hold small change, usually carried in a handbag or pocket. **2** handbag. **3** money; resources; treasury. **4** sum of money: *A purse was made up for the victims of the fire.* **5** draw together; press into folds or wrinkles: *She pursed her lips and frowned.* 1-4 *n.,* 5 *v.,* **pursed, purs ing.**

purs er (pèr/sər), a ship's officer who keeps accounts, pays wages, and attends to other matters of business. The purser is responsible for the welfare of passengers. *n.*

pur su ance (pər sü/əns), a following; carrying out; pursuit: *In pursuance of her duty, the lifeguard risked her life. n.*

pur su ant (pər sü/ənt), following; carrying out; according. *adj.*

pursuant to, following; acting according to; in accordance with.

pur sue (pər sü/), **1** follow to catch or kill; chase: *The dogs pursued the rabbit.* **2** proceed along; follow: *He pursued a wise course by taking no chances.* **3** strive for; try to get; seek: *pursue pleasure.* **4** carry on; keep on with: *She pursued the study of botany for four years.* **5** continue to annoy or trouble: *pursue a teacher with questions. v.,* **pursued, pur su ing. —pur su/a ble,** *adj.*

pur su er (pər sü/ər), person who pursues. *n.*

pur suit (pər süt/), **1** a pursuing; chase: *The dog is in pursuit of the cat.* **2** that which one does, as a profession, business, recreation, etc.; occupation: *Fishing is her favorite pursuit; reading is mine. n.*

pur vey (pər vā/), supply (food or provisions); provide; furnish: *purvey meat for an army, purvey for a royal household. v.*

pur vey ance (pər vā/əns), **1** a purveying. **2** provisions; supplies. *n.*

pur vey or (pər vā/ər), **1** person who supplies provisions: *a purveyor of fine foods and meats.* **2** person who supplies anything: *a purveyor of gossip. n.*

pus (pus), a thick, yellowish-white fluid formed in sores, abscesses, and other infected tissues in the body. It consists of white blood cells, bacteria, etc. *n.* **—pus/-like/,** *adj.*

push (pùsh), **1** move (something) away by pressing against it: *Push the door; don't pull it.* **2** press hard: *We pushed with all our might.* **3** thrust: *Trees push their roots down into the ground.* **4** go forward by force: *We pushed through the crowd.* **5** make go forward; urge: *Please push this job and get it done this week.* **6** extend: *The railroad pushed its tracks across the prairie.* **7** urge the use, sale, etc., of. **8** INFORMAL. force; energy; power to succeed: *She has plenty of push.* **9** a pushing: *Give the door a push.* **10** hard effort; determined advance. 1-7 *v.,* 8-10 *n., pl.* **push es.**

push around, INFORMAL. treat roughly or with contempt; bully.

push off, move from shore: *We pushed off in the boat.*

push on, keep going; proceed.

pushcart of a root beer vendor

push cart (pùsh/kärt/), a light cart pushed by hand. *n.*

push er (pùsh/ər), **1** person or thing that pushes. **2** INFORMAL. person who sells drugs illegally. *n.*

push o ver (pùsh/ō/vər), SLANG. **1** something very easy to do. **2** person very easy to beat in a contest. *n.*

push up (pùsh/up/), exercise done by lying face down and raising the body with the arms while keeping the back straight and the toes on the ground. *n.*

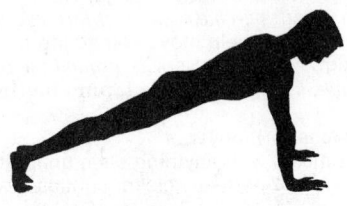

pushup

push y (push/ē), forward; aggressive. *adj.*, **push i er, push i est.** —**push/i ly,** *adv.* —**push/i ness,** *n.*

pu sil la nim i ty (pyü/sə lə nim/ə tē), cowardliness; timidity. *n.*

pu sil lan i mous (pyü/sə lan/ə məs), cowardly; fainthearted; timid: *pusillanimous conduct. n.* —**pu/sil lan/i mous ly,** *adv.*

puss (pus), cat. *n., pl.* **puss es.** —**puss/like/,** *adj.*

puss y (pus/ē), 1 cat. 2 catkin. *n., pl.* **puss ies.**

puss y foot (pus/ē fut/), INFORMAL. 1 move softly and cautiously to avoid being seen. 2 be cautious and timid about revealing one's opinions or committing oneself. *v.*

pussy willow, a small American willow with silky catkins.

pus tule (pus/chul), a small, pus-filled bump on the skin. *n.*

put (put), 1 cause to be in some place or position; place; lay: *I put sugar in my tea. Put away your toys. Put on your hat.* 2 cause to be in some state, condition, position, relation, etc.: *Put your room in order. We put our house on the market.* 3 express: *The teacher puts things clearly.* 4 set at a particular place, point, amount, etc., in a scale of estimation; appraise: *He puts the distance at five miles.* 5 apply: *I put my writing skill to good use.* 6 impose: *put a tax on gasoline.* 7 throw or cast (a heavy metal ball) from the hand placed close to the shoulder: *to put the shot. v.*, **put, put ting.**

put about, (of a ship) change direction.

put across, INFORMAL. 1 carry out successfully. 2 get accepted or understood: *He could not put across his point of view to the audience.*

put away or **put by,** save for future use.

put down, 1 put an end to; suppress: *The rebellion was quickly put down.* 2 write down. 3 slight or belittle; snub.

put forth, 1 grow; sprout; issue: *put forth buds.* 2 use fully; exert: *put forth effort.*

put forward, propose or submit for consideration, deliberation, etc.

put in, 1 spend (time) as specified: *put in a full day of work.* 2 enter a place for safety, supplies, etc.: *The ship put in at Singapore.* 3 make a claim, plea, or offer: *put in for a loan.*

put off, 1 lay aside; postpone: *We put off our meeting for a week.* 2 cause to wait: *She refused to be put off any longer.* 3 offend: *His sarcastic ways put people off.*

put on, 1 present on a stage; produce: *The class put on a play.* 2 take on or add to oneself: *put on weight.* 3 assume or take on, especially as a pretense: *I put on an air of innocence.* 4 apply or exert: *put on pressure.*

put out, 1 extinguish; make an end to; destroy: *put out a fire, put out one's eye.* 2 go; turn; proceed: *The ship put out to sea.* 3 offend; provoke. 4 cause to be out in a game. 5 publish.

put over, INFORMAL. 1 carry out successfully. 2 do or carry out by trickery: *put over a fraud.*

put through, carry out successfully.

put to it, force to a course; put in difficulty.

put up, 1 offer: *put up a house for sale.* 2 give or show: *put up a brave front.* 3 build: *put up a monument.* 4 lay aside (work). 5 propose for election or adoption: *His name was put up for president of the club.* 6 pack up or preserve (fruit, etc.). 7 give lodging or food to.

put upon, impose upon; take advantage of; victimize.

put up to, stir up; incite: *put someone up to mischief.*

put up with, bear with patience; tolerate.

put-down (put/doun/), INFORMAL. 1 a slighting or belittling of a person or thing. 2 comment or reply intended to snub or belittle. *n.*

put-on (put/ôn/ or put/on/), 1 assumed; affected; pretended: *a put-on air of innocence.* 2 a pretense or affecta-

a hat	i it	oi oil	ch child	a in about
ā age	ī ice	ou out	ng long	e in taken
ä far	o hot	u cup	sh she	ə = { i in pencil
e let	ō open	u̇ put	th thin	o in lemon
ē equal	ô order	ü rule	∓H then	u in circus
ėr term			zh measure	

tion: *Those tears were a put-on.* 3 SLANG. joke or trick played for fun on someone; practical joke. 1 *adj.*, 2,3 *n.*

pu tre fac tion (pyü/trə fak/shən), a putrefying; decay; rotting. *n.*

pu tre fy (pyü/trə fī), break down by the action of bacteria and fungi, producing bad-smelling gases; rot; decay: *The meat putrefied because it was not refrigerated. v.*, **pu tre fied, pu tre fy ing.** —**pu/tre fi/a ble,** *adj.* —**pu/tre fi/er,** *n.*

pu trid (pyü/trid), 1 decaying; rotten: *putrid meat.* 2 characteristic of putrefying matter; foul: *a putrid odor. adj.* —**pu/trid ly,** *adv.* —**pu/trid ness,** *n.*

putt (put), 1 strike (a golf ball) gently and carefully in an effort to make it roll into the hole. 2 the stroke itself. 1 *v.*, 2 *n.*

put tee (put/ē or pu tē/), 1 a long, narrow strip of cloth wound around the leg from ankle to knee, worn by sportsmen, soldiers, etc. 2 gaiter of cloth or leather reaching from ankle to knee, worn by soldiers, riders, etc. *n.*

put ter[1] (put/ər), keep busy in an aimless or useless way: *I like to putter in the garden. v.* Also, **potter.** —**put/ter er,** *n.* —**put/ter ing ly,** *adv.*

putt er[2] (put/ər), 1 person who putts. 2 a golf club used in putting. *n.*

put ter[3] (put/ər), person or thing that puts. *n.*

putt ing green (put/ing), the very smooth turf around the hole into which a player putts a golf ball.

put ty (put/ē), 1 a soft mixture of powdered chalk and linseed oil, used for fastening panes of glass in window frames, etc. 2 stop up or cover with putty: *We puttied the holes in the woodwork.* 1 *n., pl.* **put ties;** 2 *v.*, **put tied, put ty ing.** —**put/ti er,** *n.*

puz zle (puz/əl), 1 a hard problem: *How to get all my things into one trunk is a puzzle.* 2 problem or task to be done for fun: *This puzzle has seven pieces of wood you fit together.* 3 make unable to answer, solve, or understand something; perplex: *How the cat got out puzzled us.* 4 be perplexed. 5 exercise one's mind on something hard: *They puzzled over their arithmetic.* 1,2 *n.*, 3-5 *v.*, **puz zled, puz zling.** —**puz/zled ly,** *adv.* —**puz/zling ly,** *adv.*

puzzle out, find out by thinking or trying hard: *puzzle out the meaning of a sentence.*

puz zle ment (puz/əl mənt), puzzled condition. *n.*

puz zler (puz/lər), person or thing that puzzles. *n.*

Pvt., Private.

PWA or **P.W.A.,** Public Works Administration.

---

put, put up with
The dog **put up with** the veterinarian's examination.

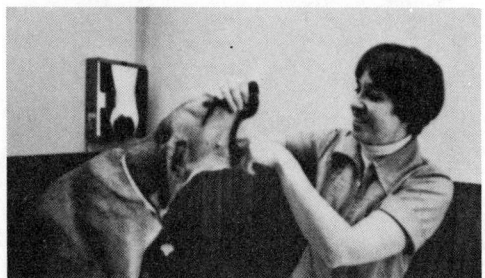

pyg my (pig′mē), **1 Pygmy,** one of a group of people of equatorial Africa who are less than five feet tall. **2** of the Pygmies. **3** a very small person; dwarf. **4** very small: *a pygmy marmoset.* 1,3 *n., pl.* **pyg mies;** 2,4 *adj.* Also, **pigmy.**

py ja mas (pə jä′məz *or* pə jam′əz), BRITISH. pajamas. *n.pl.*

py lon (pī′lon), **1** post or tower for guiding aviators. **2** a tall steel framework used to carry high-tension wires across country. **3** one of a pair of high supporting structures that marks an entrance at either end of a bridge. **4** gateway, particularly to an ancient Egyptian temple, usually consisting of two huge towers. *n.*

py lo ric (pī lôr′ik), of the pylorus. *adj.*

py lo rus (pī lôr′əs), the opening that leads from the stomach into the intestine. *n., pl.* **py lo ri** (pī lôr′ī′).

Pyong yang (pyong′yäng′), capital of North Korea, in the SW part. *n.*

py or rhe a or **py or rhoe a** (pī′ə rē′ə), disease of the gums in which pockets of pus form about the teeth, the gums shrink, and the teeth become loose. *n.*

py or rhe al or **py or rhoe al** (pī′ə rē′əl), of pyorrhea. *adj.*

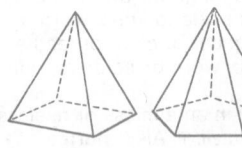

pyramid (def. 1)
two types of pyramids

pyr a mid (pir′ə mid), **1** a solid figure having a polygon for a base and triangular sides which meet in a point. **2** anything having the form of a pyramid: *a pyramid of stones.* **3** be or put in the form of a pyramid. **4** raise or increase (costs, wages, etc.) gradually. **5 Pyramids,** *pl.* the huge, massive stone pyramids, serving as royal tombs, built by the ancient Egyptians. 1,2,5 *n.,* 3,4 *v.* —**pyr′a mid like′,** *adj.*

Pyramids (def. 5)

py ram i dal (pə ram′ə dəl), shaped like a pyramid. *adj.* —**py ram′i dal ly,** *adv.*

pyre (pīr), pile of wood for burning a dead body. *n.*

Pyr e ne an (pir′ə nē′ən), of the Pyrenees. *adj.*

pylon (def. 2)

Pyr e nees (pir′ə nēz′), mountain range between France and Spain. *n.pl.*

Py rex (pī′reks), trademark for a kind of glassware that will not break when heated. *n.*

py rite (pī′rīt), **1** a yellow mineral, a compound of iron and sulfur, which is often mistaken for gold; fool's gold. It is used to make sulfuric acid. **2 pyrites,** *pl.* any of various compounds of sulfur and a metal, such as tin pyrites, an ore of tin. *n.*

py ro ma ni a (pī′rə mā′nē ə), an uncontrollable desire to set things on fire. *n.*

py ro ma ni ac (pī′rə mā′nē ak), person with an uncontrollable desire to set things on fire. *n.*

py ro tech nic (pī′rə tek′nik), **1** of fireworks: *a pyrotechnic display.* **2** resembling fireworks; brilliant; sensational: *pyrotechnic eloquence. adj.*

py ro tech ni cal (pī′rə tek′nə kəl), pyrotechnic. *adj.* —**py′ro tech′ni cal ly,** *adv.*

py ro tech nics (pī′rə tek′niks), **1** the making of fireworks. **2** use of fireworks. **3** display of fireworks. **4** a brilliant or sensational display. *n.*

Pyr rhic victory (pir′ik), victory won at too great cost.

Py thag or as (pə thag′ər əs), 582?-500? B.C., Greek philosopher, religious teacher, and mathematician. *n.*

Py thag o re an (pə thag′ə rē′ən), **1** of Pythagoras, his teachings, or his followers. **2** a follower of Pythagoras. 1 *adj.,* 2 *n.*

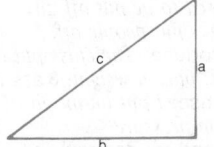

Pythagorean theorem
$c^2 = a^2 + b^2$

Pythagorean theorem, theorem that the square of the hypotenuse of a right triangle equals the sum of the squares of the other two sides.

Pyth i as (pith′ē əs), (in Roman legends) a man famous for his devoted friendship with Damon. *n.*

py thon (pī′thon), a very large snake of Asia, Africa, and Australia that is related to the boa and kills its prey by squeezing. *n.*

Qq

a hat	**i** it	**oi** oil	**ch** child	a in about
ā age	**ī** ice	**ou** out	**ng** long	e in taken
ä far	**o** hot	**u** cup	**sh** she　**ə** =	i in pencil
e let	**ō** open	**u̇** put	**th** thin	o in lemon
ē equal	**ô** order	**ü** rule	**ŦH** then	u in circus
ėr term			**zh** measure	

Q or **q** (kyü), the 17th letter of the English alphabet. *Q* is followed by *u* in most English words. *n., pl.* **Q's** or **q's.**

Qad da fi (kä dä′fē), **Muammar al-,** born 1942, Libyan political leader since 1970. *n.* Also, **Khadafy.**

Qa tar (kä′tär), country in E Arabia. *Capital:* Doha. *n.*

Q.E.D., which was to be proved. [The abbreviation *Q.E.D.* stands for the Latin words *quod erat demonstrandum.*]

qt., quart. *pl.* **qt.** or **qts.**

quack[1] (kwak), **1** the sound a duck makes. **2** make such a sound. 1 *n.,* 2 *v.*

quack[2] (kwak), **1** a dishonest person who pretends to be a doctor. **2** an ignorant pretender to knowledge or skill of any sort. **3** used by quacks: *quack medicine.* **4** not genuine: *a quack doctor.* 1,2 *n.,* 3,4 *adj.*

quad ran gle (kwod′rang′gəl), **1** a four-sided space or court wholly or nearly surrounded by buildings: *the quadrangle of a palace, a college quadrangle.* **2** buildings around a quadrangle. **3** a plane figure with four angles and four sides; quadrilateral. *n.*

qua dran gu lar (kwo drang′gyə lər), like a quadrangle; having four corners or angles. *adj.*

quad rant (kwod′rənt), **1** quarter of the circumference of a circle; arc of 90 degrees. **2** the area contained by such an arc and two radii drawn perpendicular to each other. **3** one of the four parts into which a plane is divided by two perpendicular lines. **4** instrument with a scale of 90 degrees, used in astronomy, navigation, and surveying for measuring altitudes. *n.*

quadrants
left, (def. 1)
of a circumference;
right, (def. 2)
of a circle

quad ra phon ic (kwod′rə fon′ik), of or referring to the recording or the reproduction of sound, using four separate channels instead of two as in ordinary stereo transmission. *adj.*

qua drat ic (kwo drat′ik), **1** of or like a square. **2** of an equation in which one or more of the terms is squared. $x^2 + 3x + 2 = 12$ is a quadratic equation. *adj.*

qua dren ni al (kwo dren′ē əl), **1** occurring every four years: *The United States has a quadrennial presidential election.* **2** of or for four years. *adj.* —**qua dren′ni al ly,** *adv.*

quadrilateral (def. 2)
several kinds of quadrilaterals

quad ri lat er al (kwod′rə lat′ər əl), **1** having four sides and four angles. **2** a plane figure having four sides and four angles. 1 *adj.,* 2 *n.*

qua drille (kwo dril′), **1** a square dance for four couples that usually has five parts or movements. **2** music for such a dance. *n.*

quad ru ped (kwod′rə ped), animal that has four feet. *n.*

qua dru ple (kwo drü′pəl), **1** consisting of four parts; including four parts or parties; fourfold: *a quadruple agreement.* **2** four times; four times as great. **3** number, amount, etc., four times as great as another: *80 is the quadruple of 20.* **4** make or become four times as great. 1,2 *adj.,* 2 *adv.,* 3 *n.,* 4 *v.,* **qua dru pled, qua dru pling.**

qua dru plet (kwo drü′plit), **1** one of four children born at the same time of the same mother. **2** any group or combination of four. *n.*

quaff (kwäf *or* kwaf), drink in large swallows; drink freely. *v.* —**quaff′er,** *n.*

quag mire (kwag′mīr′), **1** soft, muddy ground; boggy or miry place. **2** a difficult situation. *n.*

quail[1] or bobwhite
about 10 in. (25 cm.)
long

quail[1] (kwāl), any of various plump game birds belonging to the same family as the pheasant, especially the bobwhite. *n., pl.* **quails** or **quail.** —**quail′like′,** *adj.*

quail[2] (kwāl), be afraid; lose courage; shrink back in fear: *quail at the sight of a rattlesnake. v.*

quaint (kwānt), strange or odd in an interesting, pleasing, or amusing way: *Old photographs seem quaint to us today. adj.* —**quaint′ly,** *adv.* —**quaint′ness,** *n.*

quake (kwāk), **1** shake; tremble: *I quaked with fear.* **2** a shaking; trembling. **3** earthquake. 1 *v.,* **quaked, quaking;** 2,3 *n.* —**quak′er,** *n.* —**quak′ing ly,** *adv.*

Quak er (kwā′kər), member of a Christian group called the Society of Friends. Quakers favor simple religious services and are opposed to war and to taking oaths. *n.*

qual i fi ca tion (kwol′ə fə kā′shən), **1** that which makes a person fit for a job, task, office, etc.: *A knowledge of trails is one qualification for a guide.* **2** that which limits, changes, or makes less free and full: *His enjoyment of the trip had one qualification; his friends could not enjoy it, too.* **3** modification; limitation; restriction: *The statement was made without any qualification. n.*

qual i fied (kwol′ə fīd), **1** having the desirable or required qualifications; fitted; competent: *A qualified airplane pilot must have good eyesight and hold a license to fly.* **2** modified; limited: *His qualified answer was, "I will go, but only if you will come with me." adj.*

qual i fi er (kwol′ə fī′ər), **1** person or thing that qualifies. **2** word that limits or modifies the meaning of another word. Adjectives and adverbs are qualifiers. *n.*

qual i fy (kwol′ə fī), **1** make fit or competent: *qualify oneself for a job.* **2** become fit; show oneself fit: *qualify for a* *driver's license.* **3** make less strong; change somewhat; limit; modify: *Qualify your statement that dogs are loyal by adding "usually."* **4** limit or modify the meaning of: *Adverbs qualify verbs.* *v.*, **qual i fied, qual i fy ing.**

qual i ta tive (kwol'ə tā'tiv), concerned with quality or qualities: *The qualitative facts about food have to do with vitamin content and nutritional value.* *adj.*

qualitative analysis, a testing of a substance or mixture to find out what its chemical constituents are.

qual i ty (kwol'ə tē), **1** something special about a person or object that makes it what it is; characteristic; attribute: *One quality of iron is hardness; one quality of sugar is sweetness. She has many fine qualities.* **2** nature, kind, or character of something: *the quality of a sound, the refreshing quality of a drink.* **3** grade of excellence; degree of worth: *food of poor quality.* **4** fineness; merit; excellence: *Look for quality rather than quantity.* **5** high rank; good or high social position: *people of quality.* *n.*, *pl.* **qual i ties.** [*Quality* came into English about 700 years ago from French *qualite,* and can be traced back to Latin *qualis,* meaning "of what sort."] —**qual'i ty less,** *adj.*

qualm (kwäm *or* kwälm), **1** a sudden disturbing feeling in the mind; uneasiness; misgiving; doubt: *I tried the test with some qualms.* **2** disturbance or scruple of conscience: *I had no qualms about neglecting my work on such a sunny day.* **3** a momentary feeling of faintness or nausea. *n.*

quan dar y (kwon'dər ē), state of perplexity or uncertainty; dilemma. *n.*, *pl.* **quan dar ies.**

quan ti ta tive (kwon'tə tā'tiv), **1** concerned with quantity or quantities. **2** that can be measured. *adj.* —**quan'ti ta'tive ly,** *adv.* —**quan'ti ta'tive ness,** *n.*

quantitative analysis, a testing of a substance or mixture to find out the amounts and proportions of its chemical constituents.

quan ti ty (kwon'tə tē), **1** number; amount: *Use equal quantities of nuts and raisins in the cake.* **2** a large amount; large number: *The baker buys flour in quantity. She owns quantities of books.* **3** (in mathematics) figure or symbol which represents something having size, amount, extent, etc. *n.*, *pl.* **quan ti ties.**

quan tum (kwon'təm), (in physics) the basic unit of radiant energy; the smallest amount of energy capable of existing independently. Light and heat are given off and absorbed in quanta. *n.*, *pl.* **quan ta** (kwon'tə). [*Quantum* comes from Latin *quantum,* meaning "how much."]

quantum theory, theory that whenever radiant energy is transferred, the transfer occurs in pulsations rather than continuously, and that the amount transferred during each pulsation is a definite amount or quantum.

quar an tine (kwôr'ən tēn'), **1** keep (a person, animal, plant, ship, etc.) away from others for a time to prevent the spread of an infectious disease: *People with smallpox were quarantined.* **2** condition of being quarantined: *The ship was in quarantine because several of the crew had smallpox.* **3** detention, isolation, and other measures taken to prevent the spread of an infectious disease. **4** place or time in which people, animals, plants, ships, etc., are held until it is sure that they have no infectious diseases, insect pests, etc. 1 *v.*, **quar an tined, quar an tin ing;** 2-4 *n.* —**quar'an tin'a ble,** *adj.*

quar rel (kwôr'əl), **1** an angry dispute; a fight with words: *The children had a quarrel over the division of the candy.* **2** fight with words; dispute or disagree angrily: *The two friends quarreled and now they don't speak to each other.* **3** cause for a dispute or disagreement; reason for breaking off friendly relations: *A bully likes to pick quarrels.* **4** find fault: *It is useless to quarrel with fate, because one has no control over it.* 1,3 *n.*, 2,4 *v.*, **quar-**

reled, quar rel ing *or* **quar relled, quar rel ling.** [*Quarrel* came into English about 650 years ago from French *querele,* and can be traced back to Latin *queri,* meaning "to complain."] —**quar'rel er, quar'rel ler,** *n.*

quar rel some (kwôr'əl səm), too ready to quarrel; fond of fighting and disputing: *A quarrelsome child has few friends. adj.* —**quar'rel some ness,** *n.*

quar ry[1] (kwôr'ē), **1** place where stone is dug, cut, or blasted out for use in building. **2** obtain from a quarry: *She watched the workers quarry out a huge block of stone.* 1 *n.*, *pl.* **quar ries;** 2 *v.*, **quar ried, quar ry ing.** [*Quarry*[1] is from a medieval Latin word *quadraria,* which came from Latin *quadrum,* meaning "a square."] —**quar'ri er,** *n.*

quar ry[2] (kwôr'ē), animal chased in a hunt; game; prey. *n.*, *pl.* **quar ries.** [*Quarry*[2] came into English about 650 years ago from French *cuiree,* which can be traced back to Latin *corium,* meaning "skin, hide."]

quart (kwôrt), **1** measure of capacity for liquids, equal to one fourth of a gallon: *a quart of milk.* **2** measure of capacity for dry things, equal to one eighth of a peck: *a quart of berries. n.*

quar ter (kwôr'tər), **1** one fourth; half of a half; one of four equal or corresponding parts: *a quarter of an apple. A quarter of an hour is 15 minutes.* **2** divide into fourths: *She quartered the apple.* **3** coin of the United States and Canada equal to 25 cents. Four quarters make one dollar. **4** one of four equal periods of play in football, basketball, soccer, etc. **5** one fourth of a year; 3 months: *Many savings banks pay interest every quarter.* **6** one of the four periods of the moon, lasting about 7 days each. **7** being one of four equal parts; being equal to only about one fourth of full measure. **8** point of the compass; direction: *From what quarter did the wind blow?* **9** region; place; section: *the French quarter, visit a distant quarter of the globe.* **10 quarters,** *pl.* place to live or stay: *The circus has its winter quarters in the South.* **11** give a place to live in: *Soldiers were quartered in all the houses of the town.* **12** mercy shown in sparing the life of a defeated enemy: *The pirates gave no quarter to their victims.* **13** one of the four legs of an animal, with its adjoining parts. 1,3-6,8-10,12,13 *n.*, 2,11 *v.*, 7 *adj.* —**quar'ter er,** *n.* **at close quarters,** very close together; almost touching: *The cars had to pass at close quarters on the narrow road.*

quar ter back (kwôr'tər bak'), an offensive back who stands directly behind the center in football. He begins each play by handing the ball to a running back, passing it to a teammate, or running with it himself. *n.*

quar ter deck (kwôr'tər dek'), part of the upper deck between the mainmast and the stern, used especially by the officers of a ship. *n.*

quarter horse, a strong horse originally bred for racing on quarter-mile tracks, now used for herding cattle, playing polo, and riding.

quar ter ly (kwôr'tər lē), **1** happening, done, etc., four times a year: *to make quarterly payments on one's insurance.* **2** once each quarter of a year: *to pay one's insurance premiums quarterly.* **3** magazine published every three months. 1 *adj.*, 2 *adv.*, 3 *n.*, *pl.* **quar ter lies.**

quar ter mas ter (kwôr'tər mas'tər), **1** (in the army) an officer who has charge of providing quarters, clothing, fuel, transportation, etc., for troops. **2** (in the navy) a petty officer who has charge of the steering, the compasses, signals, etc., on a ship. *n.*

quarter note, (in music) a note played for one fourth as long a time as a whole note.

quar ter staff (kwôr'tər staf'), an old English weapon consisting of a stout pole 6 to 8 feet long, tipped with iron. *n.*, *pl.* **quar ter staves** (kwôr'tər stāvz').

quar tet *or* **quar tette** (kwôr tet'), **1** group of four singers or players performing together. **2** piece of music for four voices or instruments. **3** any group of four. *n.*

quar to (kwôr′tō), **1** the page size (usually about 9 by 12 inches) of a book in which each leaf is one fourth of a whole sheet of paper. **2** having this size. **3** book having this size. 1,3 *n., pl.* **quar tos;** 2 *adj.*

quartz
common quartz crystals

quartz (kwôrts), a very hard mineral composed of silica and found in many different types of rocks, such as sandstone and granite. Crystals of pure quartz are colorless and transparent. Colored varieties of quartz include flint, jasper, agate, and amethyst. *n.*

quartz ite (kwôrt′sīt), a granular rock consisting of compressed sandstone. *n.*

qua sar (kwā′sär), a heavenly body which looks like a star, but which radiates as much energy as a galaxy. Quasars are believed to be exploding galaxies. *n.* [*Quasar* comes from the words *quasi-stellar radio source.* It was formed by using the first four letters of *quasi* and the last two letters of *stellar.*]

quash[1] (kwosh), put down completely; crush: *quash a revolt. v.*

quash[2] (kwosh), make void; annul: *The judge quashed the charges against the defendant. v.*

qua si (kwā′zī, kwā′sī, *or* kwä′sē), **1** seeming; not real; halfway: *quasi humor.* **2** seemingly; not really; partly; almost: *a quasi-official statement.* 1 *adj.,* 2 *adv.*

quat rain (kwot′rān), stanza or poem of four lines. *n.*

qua ver (kwā′vər), **1** shake; tremble: *The old man's voice quavered.* **2** sing or say in trembling tones. **3** a shaking or trembling, especially of the voice. **4** trill in singing or in playing on a musical instrument. 1,2,4 *v.,* 3 *n.*

quay (kē), a solid landing place for ships, often built of stone. *n.*

quay

Que., Quebec.

quea si ly (kwē′zə lē), in a queasy manner. *adv.*

quea si ness (kwē′zē nis), **1** nausea. **2** uneasiness. **3** squeamishness. *n.*

quea sy (kwē′zē), **1** inclined to nausea; easily upset: *a queasy stomach.* **2** tending to unsettle the stomach. **3** un-

easy; uncomfortable. *adj.,* **quea si er, quea si est.**

Que bec (kwi bek′), **1** province in E Canada. **2** its capital, on the St. Lawrence River. *n.*

que bra cho (kā brä′chō), a South American tree with very hard wood. The wood and sometimes the bark are used in tanning and dyeing. *n., pl.* **que bra chos.**

Quech ua (kech′wä), **1** an Indian of the chief tribal group in the Inca Empire. **2** the language of the Quechuas. Dialects of Quechua are spoken today in parts of Peru, Ecuador, Bolivia, Argentina, and Chile. *n., pl.* **Quech uas** *or* **Quech ua** for 1. —**Quech′uan,** *adj., n.*

queen (kwēn), **1** wife of a king. **2** woman who rules a country and its people. **3** woman who is very important, stately, or beautiful: *the queen of society.* **4** a fully developed female in a colony of bees, ants, etc., that lays eggs. There is usually only one queen in a hive of bees. **5** a playing card bearing a picture of a queen. **6** the most powerful piece in chess. It can move in any straight or diagonal row. *n.* [*Queen* comes from Old English *cwēn.*]

Queen Anne's lace

Queen Anne's lace, a wild variety of the carrot, having lacy clusters of small, white flowers. [*Queen Anne's lace* was named for *Queen Anne,* 1665-1714, queen of Great Britain and Ireland.]

queen ly (kwēn′lē), **1** of a queen; fit for a queen: *queenly rank or majesty.* **2** like a queen; like a queen's: *queenly dignity.* **3** in a queenly manner; as a queen does: 1,2 *adj.,* **queen li er, queen li est;** 3 *adv.* —**queen′li ness,** *n.*

queen mother, widow of a former king and mother of a reigning king or queen.

Queens (kwēnz), borough of New York City, on Long Island, east of Brooklyn. *n.*

queen-size (kwēn′sīz′), larger or longer than others of its kind, but smaller than king-size: *a queen-size mattress. adj.*

Queens land (kwēnz′lənd), state in E Australia. *n.*

queer (kwir), **1** not usual or normal; strange; odd; peculiar: *That was a queer remark for him to make.* **2** not well; faint; giddy: *The motion of the ship made him feel queer.* **3** SLANG. spoil; ruin. 1,2 *adj.,* 3 *v.* —**queer′ly,** *adv.*

quell (kwel), put down; subdue: *quell a riot.*

quench (kwench), **1** put an end to; stop: *quench one's thirst.* **2** drown out; put out: *Water quenched the fire. v.*

quer u lous (kwer′ə ləs), complaining; fretful; peevish: *Some people are very querulous when they are sick. adj.*

quer y (kwir′ē), **1** a question; inquiry. **2** ask; ask about; inquire into. **3** express doubt about. **4** the sign (?) put after a question or used to express doubt about something written or printed. 1,4 *n., pl.* **quer ies;** 2,3 *v.,* **queried, quer y ing.** —**quer′i er,** *n.* —**quer′y ly,** *adv.*

quest (kwest), **1** a search or hunt: *She went to the library in quest of something to read.* **2** search or seek for; hunt. **3** expedition of knights: *There are many stories about the quests of King Arthur's knights.* 1,3 *n.,* 2 *v.* —**quest′er,** *n.*

ques tion (kwes′chən), **1** thing asked in order to get information; inquiry: *The teacher answered the children's questions about the story.* **2** ask in order to find out; seek information from: *Then the teacher questioned the children about what happened in the story.* **3** matter of doubt or dispute; controversy: *A question arose about the ownership of the property.* **4** to doubt; dispute: *question the truth of a story.* **5** matter to be talked over, investigated, considered, etc.; problem: *What is the question you have raised?* **6** proposal to be voted on: *The president asked if the club members were ready for the question.* **7** an asking: *to examine by question and answer.* 1,3,5-7 *n.,* 2,4 *v.* [*Question* came into English about 700 years ago from French *question,* and can be traced back to Latin *quaerere,* meaning "to ask, seek." See **Word Family.**] —**ques′tion er,** *n.*

beg the question, take for granted the very thing being argued about.

beside the question, off the subject.

beyond question, without a doubt; not to be disputed: *The statements in that book are true beyond question.*

call in question, dispute; challenge: *My honesty was called in question when they suggested I had cheated on the test.*

in question, 1 under consideration or discussion. **2** in dispute.

out of the question, not to be considered; impossible.

without question, without a doubt; not to be disputed: *That is without question a beautiful sunset.*

WORD FAMILY

question

Below are words related to *question.* They can all be traced back to the Latin word *quaerere* (kwī′re re), meaning "to seek, ask."

acquire	inquest	query
acquisition	inquire	quest
acquisitive	inquiry	questionnaire
conquer	inquisition	request
conquest	inquisitive	require
exquisite	prerequisite	requisition

ques tion a ble (kwes′chə nə bəl), **1** open to question or dispute; doubtful; uncertain: *a questionable statement.* **2** of doubtful propriety or morality: *questionable behavior.* *adj.* —**ques′tion a ble ness.** *n.*

ques tion a bly (kwes′chə nə blē), in a questionable manner; doubtfully. *adv.*

ques tion ing ly (kwes′chə ning lē), as one who questions; in a questioning manner. *adv.*

question mark, mark (?) put after a question in writing or printing; interrogation mark.

ques tion naire (kwes′chə ner′ or kwes′chə när′), a written or printed list of questions used to gather information, to obtain a sampling of opinion, etc. *n.*

quet zal (ket säl′), a Central American bird having brilliant golden-green and scarlet plumage. The male has long, flowing tail feathers. *n.*

queue (kyü), **1** braid of hair hanging down from the back of the head. **2** a line of people, automobiles, etc.: *There was a long queue in front of the theater.* **3** form or stand in a long line. 1,2 *n.,* 3 *v.,* **queued, queu ing** or **queue ing.** Also, **cue.** [*Queue* was borrowed from French *queue,* which came from Latin *cauda,* meaning "a tail."]

quib ble (kwib′əl), **1** an unfair and petty evasion of the point or truth by using words with a double meaning: *a legal quibble.* **2** evade the point or the truth by twisting the meaning of words. 1 *n.,* 2 *v.,* **quib bled, quib bling.**

quib bler (kwib′lər), person who quibbles. *n.*

quick (kwik), **1** fast and sudden; swift: *The cat made a quick jump. Many weeds have a quick growth.* **2** coming soon; prompt: *a quick reply.* **3** not patient; hasty: *a quick temper.* **4** acting quickly; ready; lively: *a quick wit.* **5** understanding or learning fast: *a child who is quick in school.* **6** quickly. **7** tender, sensitive flesh, especially the flesh under a fingernail or toenail: *bite one's nails down to the quick.* **8** the tender, sensitive part of one's feelings: *Their insults cut me to the quick.* 1-5 *adj.,* 6 *adv.,* 7,8 *n.* [*Quick* comes from Old English *cwic,* meaning "alive."]

quick en (kwik′ən), **1** move more quickly; hasten: *Quicken your pace.* **2** stir up; make alive: *quicken hot ashes into flames. Reading adventure stories quickens my imagination.* **3** become more active or alive: *Her pulse quickened. v.*

quick-freeze (kwik′frēz′), subject (food) to rapid freezing to prepare it for storing at freezing temperatures. *v.,* **quick-froze** (kwik′frōz′), **quick-fro zen** (kwik′frō′zn), **quick-freez ing.**

quick lime (kwik′līm′), lime[1]. *n.*

quick ly (kwik′lē), rapidly; with haste; very soon. *adv.*

quick sand (kwik′sand′), a very deep, soft, wet sand that will not hold up a person's weight. Quicksand may swallow up people and animals. *n.*

quick sil ver (kwik′sil′vər), mercury. *n.*

quick step (kwik′step′), **1** step used in marching in quick time. **2** a lively dance step. **3** music in a brisk march rhythm. *n.*

quick-tem pered (kwik′tem′pərd), easily angered. *adj.*

quick-wit ted (kwik′wit′id), having a quick mind; clever. *adj.* —**quick′-wit′ted ly,** *adv.*

quid[1] (kwid), **1** piece to be chewed. **2** bite of chewing tobacco. *n.*

quid[2] (kwid), BRITISH SLANG. one pound, or 100 pence. *n., pl.* **quid** or **quids.**

qui es cence (kwī es′ns), absence of activity; quietness; stillness. *n.*

qui es cent (kwī es′nt), inactive; quiet; still. *adj.*

qui et (kwī′ət), **1** making no sound; with little or no noise: *quiet footsteps, a quiet room.* **2** moving very little; still: *a quiet river.* **3** at rest; not busy: *a quiet evening at home.* **4** peaceful; gentle: *quiet manners, a quiet person.* **5** state of rest; stillness; absence of motion or noise. **6** freedom from disturbance; peace: *to read in quiet.* **7** make or become more quiet: *Soft words quieted the frightened child. The wind quieted down.* **8** not showy or bright: *Gray is a quiet color.* 1-4,8 *adj.,* 5,6 *n.,* 7 *v.* —**qui′et er,** *n.* —**qui′et ly,** *adv.* —**qui′et ness,** *n.*

qui e tude (kwī′ə tüd or kwī′ə tyüd), quietness; stillness; calmness. *n.*

quill (kwil), **1** a large, stiff feather. **2** the hollow stem of a feather. **3** anything made from the hollow stem of a feather, such as a pen, a toothpick, or an instrument for plucking the strings of a musical instrument. **4** a stiff, sharp hair or spine like the end of a feather. A porcupine has quills on its back. *n.* —**quill′-like′,** *adj.*

quilt (kwilt), **1** cover for a bed, usually made of two pieces of cloth with a soft pad between, held in place by stitching. **2** make quilts. **3** stitch together with a soft lining: *quilt a bathrobe.* 1 *n.,* 2,3 *v.* —**quilt′er,** *n.*

quilt ing (kwil′ting), **1** quilted work. **2** material for making quilts; a stout fabric so woven as to appear quilted. *n.*

quince (kwins), the hard, yellowish, acid, pear-shaped fruit of a small tree, used for preserves and jelly. *n.*

qui nine (kwī′nīn), a bitter drug made from the bark of a cinchona tree, used in treating malaria and fevers. *n.*

quin sy (kwin′zē), tonsillitis with pus; a very sore throat with an abscess in the tonsils. *n.*

quin tes sence (kwin tes′ns), **1** the purest form of some quality; pure essence. **2** the most perfect example of something: *The ballerina was the quintessence of grace. n.*

quin tet or **quin tette** (kwin tet′), **1** group of five singers or players performing together. **2** piece of music for five voices or instruments. **3** any group of five. *n.*

quin tu plet (kwin tup′lit, kwin tü′plit, *or* kwin tyü′plit), **1** one of five children born at the same time of the same mother. **2** any group or combination of five. *n.*

quip (kwip), **1** a clever or witty saying. **2** make quips. 1 *n.,* 2 *v.,* **quipped, quip ping.**

qui pu (kē′pü *or* kwip′ü), cord with knotted strings or threads of various colors, used by the ancient Peruvians to record events, keep accounts, and send messages. *n.*

quire (kwīr), 24 or 25 sheets of paper of the same sort and size. *n.*

quirk (kwėrk), **1** a peculiar way of acting: *Each person has his own quirks.* **2** a sudden twist or turn: *a quirk of fate, a mental quirk. n.*

quirt (kwėrt), a riding whip with a short, stout handle and a lash of braided leather. *n.*

quis ling (kwiz′ling), person who treacherously helps to prepare the way for enemy occupation of his own country. *n.*

quit (kwit), **1** stop: *They quit work at five.* **2** leave: *quit one's job. He quit college after one year.* **3** pay back; pay off (a debt). **4** free; clear; rid: *I gave them money to be quit of them.* 1-3 *v.,* **quit** or **quit ted, quit ting;** 4 *adj.*

quit claim (kwit′klām′), **1** the giving up of a claim. **2** document stating that somebody gives up a claim. **3** give up claim to (a possession, etc.). 1,2 *n.,* 3 *v.*

quite (kwīt), **1** completely; entirely: *a hat quite out of fashion. I am quite alone.* **2** actually; really; positively: *quite the thing.* **3** very; rather; somewhat: *quite pretty. It is quite hot. adv.*

Qui to (kē′tō), capital of Ecuador, in the N part. *n.*

quit rent (kwit′rent′), rent paid in money, instead of services rendered, under a feudal system. *n.*

quits (kwits), even or on equal terms by having given or paid back something: *We each won a game, so we are quits. adj.*

call it quits, abandon an attempt to do something: *The roads were so icy we called it quits and drove home.*

quit tance (kwit′ns), **1** a release from debt or obligation. **2** the paper certifying this; a receipt. **3** a getting back at somebody. *n.*

quit ter (kwit′ər), INFORMAL. person who shirks or gives up easily. *n.*

quiv er[1] (kwiv′ər), **1** to shake; shiver; tremble: *The dog quivered with excitement.* **2** a quivering; shaking or trembling: *A quiver of his mouth showed that he was about to cry.* 1 *v.,* 2 *n.* —**quiv′er er,** *n.* —**quiv′er ing ly,** *adv.*

quiv er[2] (kwiv′ər), case to hold arrows. *n.*

Qui xo te (kē hō′tē *or* kwik′sət), **Don.** See **Don Quixote.** *n.*

quix ot ic (kwik sot′ik), **1** resembling Don Quixote; extravagantly chivalrous or romantic. **2** visionary; not practical. *adj.* —**quix ot′i cal ly,** *adv.*

quiz (kwiz), **1** a short or informal test: *Each week the*

a hat	**i** it	**oi** oil	**ch** child	a in about
ā age	**ī** ice	**ou** out	**ng** long	e in taken
ä far	**o** hot	**u** cup	**sh** she	ə = i in pencil
e let	**ō** open	**u̇** put	**th** thin	o in lemon
ē equal	**ô** order	**ü** rule	**ŦH** then	u in circus
ėr term			**zh** measure	

teacher gives us a quiz in social studies. **2** give such a test to: *quiz a class in spelling.* **3** to question; interrogate: *The lawyer quizzed the witness.* **4** a questioning. 1,4 *n., pl.* **quiz zes;** 2,3 *v.,* **quizzed, quiz zing.** —**quiz′za ble,** *adj.*

quiz show, a radio or television program in which contestants are asked questions and win prizes if they answer correctly.

quiz zi cal (kwiz′ə kəl), **1** teasing; mocking: *a quizzical smile.* **2** questioning; baffled: *She had a quizzical expression on her face.* **3** odd; comical. *adj.* —**quiz′zi cal ly,** *adv.*

quoin (koin *or* kwoin), **1** an outside angle or corner of a wall or building. **2** a stone forming an outside angle of a wall; cornerstone. *n.*

quoit (kwoit), **1** a heavy, flattish iron or rope ring thrown to encircle a peg stuck in the ground or to come as close to it as possible. **2 quoits,** *pl.* game so played. *n.*

Quon set hut (kwon′sit), a prefabricated metal building shaped like a half cylinder.

quo rum (kwôr′əm), number of members of any society or assembly that must be present if the business done is to be legal or binding. *n.* [*Quorum* comes from Latin *quorum,* meaning "of whom."]

quo ta (kwō′tə), the share of a total due from or to a particular district, state, person, etc.: *Each member of the club was given a quota of tickets to sell. n., pl.* **quo tas.**

quot a ble (kwō′tə bəl), **1** able to be quoted. **2** suitable for quoting. *adj.* —**quot′a ble ness,** *n.* —**quot′a bly,** *adv.*

quo ta tion (kwō tā′shən), **1** somebody's words repeated exactly by another person; passage quoted from a book, speech, etc.: *From what author does this quotation come?* **2** a quoting: *Quotation is a habit of some teachers.* **3** the current price of a stock, commodity, etc.: *today's market quotation on wheat. n.*

quotation mark, one of a pair of marks used to indicate the beginning and end of a quotation. For an ordinary quotation use these marks (" "). For a quotation within another quotation use these (' ').

quote (kwōt), **1** repeat the exact words of; give words or passages from: *Our teacher often quotes Shakespeare.* **2** repeat exactly the words of another or a passage from a book: *She quoted from the senator's speech.* **3** bring forward as an example or authority: *Judges quote various cases in support of their opinions.* **4** give (a price): *quote a price on a house up for sale.* **5** quotation. **6** a quotation mark. 1-4 *v.,* **quot ed, quot ing;** 5,6 *n.* —**quot′er,** *n.*

quoth (kwōth), OLD USE. said. *v.*

quo tient (kwō′shənt), number arrived at by dividing one number by another. In $26 \div 2 = 13$, 13 is the quotient. *n.*

q.v., which see. [The abbreviation *q.v.* comes from the Latin words *quod vide.*]

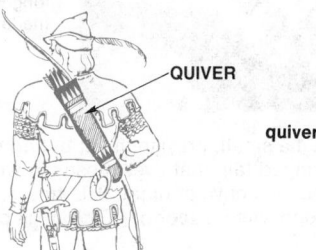

quiver[2]

Rr

R or **r** (är), the 18th letter of the English alphabet. *n., pl.* **R's** or **r's.**

the three R's, reading, writing, and arithmetic.

R, Restricted (a rating for a motion picture that is not recommended for people under the age of 17, except when accompanied by a parent or guardian).

r., 1 radius. **2** railroad. **3** roentgen.

R., 1 Rabbi. **2** Railroad. **3** Republican. **4** River. **5** Royal.

Ra (rä), the Egyptian sun god and supreme deity, typically represented as a man with the head of a hawk bearing the sun on his head. *n.*

Ra, symbol for radium.

R.A., 1 Rear Admiral. **2** Royal Academy.

Ra bat (rə bät′), capital of Morocco, in the NW part. *n.*

rab bi (rab′ī), teacher of the Jewish law and religion; leader of a Jewish congregation. *n., pl.* **rab bis** or **rabbies.** [*Rabbi* comes from Hebrew *rabbī,* meaning "my master."]

rab bin i cal (rə bin′ə kəl), of rabbis, their learning, teachings, etc. *adj.* —**rab bin′i cal ly,** *adv.*

rab bit (rab′it), **1** a small burrowing mammal with soft fur, long ears, long hind legs, and a short, fluffy tail. Rabbits are similar to hares, but smaller. **2** its fur. *n.* —**rab′bit like′,** *adj.*

rabbit ears, INFORMAL. a small, indoor television antenna with two adjustable, lightweight rods that may be set in a V shape. In this position, the upright rods resemble a rabbit's ears.

rab ble (rab′əl), **1** a disorderly crowd; mob. **2 the rabble,** the lower classes: *The nobles scorned the rabble. n.*

rab id (rab′id), **1** unreasonably extreme; fanatical; violent: *The rebels are rabid idealists.* **2** furious; raging: *rabid with anger.* **3** having rabies; mad: *a rabid dog. adj.* [*Rabid* is from Latin *rabidus,* which comes from *rabere,* meaning "to rave, be mad."] —**rab′id ly,** *adv.* —**rab′id ness,** *n.*

ra bies (rā′bēz), a virus disease that attacks the central nervous system of warm-blooded animals, causing mental disturbance, muscular spasms, and paralysis; hydrophobia. The disease is usually transmitted by the bite of a rabid animal, and is fatal unless treated with serum. *n.* [*Rabies* is from Latin *rabies,* meaning "rage, madness," which comes from *rabere,* meaning "to rave, be mad."]

raccoon
(def. 1)
up to 32 in.
(81 cm.)
long with
the tail

rac coon (ra kün′), **1** a small, grayish, meat-eating mammal with a bushy, ringed tail, that lives mostly in wooded areas near water, and is active at night. **2** its fur. *n., pl.* **rac coons** or **rac coon.** Also, **racoon.** [*Raccoon* is of Algonquian origin.]

race[1] (rās), **1** contest of speed, as in running, driving, riding, sailing, etc.: *a dog race, a car race.* **2** engage in a contest of speed. **3** run or cause to run in a race with: *I'll race you to the corner.* **4** any contest that suggests a race: *a political race.* **5** run, move, or go swiftly. **6** cause to run, move, or go swiftly. **7** run (an engine) at high speed when the gears are in neutral position. **8** a strong or fast current of water. 1,4,8 *n.,* 2,3,5-7 *v.,* **raced, racing.** [*Race*[1] came into English about 700 years ago from Icelandic *rās,* meaning "a running, a strong current."]

race[2] (rās), **1** a great division of all human beings that passes on certain physical characteristics from one generation to another. **2** group of persons, animals, or plants having the same ancestors, far back in the past: *the human race, the canine race.* **3** group of people of the same kind: *the brave race of pioneers. n.* [*Race*[2] came into English about 450 years ago from French *rasse,* which came from Italian *razza.*]

race course (rās′kôrs′), racetrack. *n.*

race horse (rās′hôrs′), horse for racing. *n.*

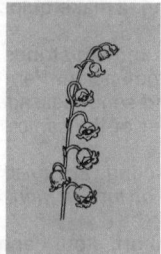

raceme
of lily of the valley

ra ceme (rā sēm′ or rə sēm′), a simple flower cluster having its flowers on nearly equal stalks along a stem. The lily of the valley has a raceme. *n.*

rac er (rā′sər), **1** person, animal, boat, automobile, etc., that takes part in races. **2** any of various North American snakes that can move very rapidly. The blacksnake is a racer. *n.*

race track (rās′trak′), track laid out for racing, usually circular or oval. *n.*

Ra chel (rā′chəl), (in the Bible) the favorite wife of Jacob, and the mother of Joseph and Benjamin. *n.*

Rach ma ni noff (räk mä′ni nôf), **Sergei,** 1873-1943, Russian pianist and composer. *n.*

ra cial (rā′shəl), **1** of a race: *racial traits.* **2** of or involving races: *racial discrimination. adj.* —**ra′cial ly,** *adv.*

rac i ness (rā′sē nis), vigor, liveliness. *n.*

rac ism (rā′siz′əm), **1** belief that a particular race, especially one's own, is superior to other races. **2** discrimination or prejudice against a race or races based on this belief. *n.*

rac ist (rā′sist), **1** a person who believes in, supports, or practices racism. **2** of racism. 1 *n.,* 2 *adj.*

rack[1] (rak), **1** a frame with bars, shelves, or pegs to hold, arrange, or keep things on: *a tool rack, a baggage rack.* **2** framework set on a wagon for carrying hay, straw, etc. **3** instrument once used for torturing people by stretching them. **4** hurt very much: *racked with grief. A toothache racked my jaw.* **5** stretch; strain. **6** bar with pegs or teeth on one edge, into which teeth on the rim of a wheel or pinion can fit. 1-3,6 *n.,* 4,5 *v.* —**rack′er,** *n.*

on the rack, in great pain; suffering very much.

rack up, INFORMAL. score: *rack up three runs in the ninth inning.*

rack[2] (rak). **rack and ruin,** ruin; destruction: *Over the years, the vacant house went to rack and ruin. n.*

rack et[1] (rak′it), **1** loud noise; loud talk; din. **2** INFORMAL. scheme for getting money from people through bribery, threats of violence, and other illegal means. *n.* [*Racket*[1] is probably from an earlier English slang word meaning "kind of fraud."]

rack et² (rak′it), **1** an oval wooden or metal frame strung with netting and with a handle of various lengths, used to hit the ball in tennis, squash, badminton, racquetball, etc. **2** paddle¹ (def. 5). *n. Also,* **racquet.** [*Racket²* came into English about 400 years ago from French *raquette,* which came from Arabic *rāḥa,* meaning "palm of the hand."] —**rack′et like′,** *adj.*

rack et eer (rak′ə tir′), **1** person who gets money from people through bribery, threats of violence, and other illegal means. **2** get money in this way. **1** *n.,* **2** *v.*

ra coon (ra kün′), raccoon. *n., pl.* **ra coons** *or* **ra coon.**

rac quet (rak′it), racket². *n.* —**rac′quet like′,** *adj.*

rac quet ball (rak′it bôl′), game played in a four-walled court with a hollow, rubber ball and a short-handled racket. *n.*

rac y (rā′sē), **1** vigorous; lively: *a racy discussion.* **2** suggestive of indecency; somewhat improper: *a racy story. adj.,* **rac i er, rac i est.** —**rac′i ly,** *adv.*

ra dar (rā′där), instrument for determining the distance, direction, speed, etc., of unseen objects by the reflection of radio waves. *n.* [*Radar* comes from the words *radio detecting and ranging.* It was formed from the first two letters of *radio* and the first letter of the words *detecting, and, ranging.*]

radial (def. 1)
a radial pattern

ra di al (rā′dē əl), **1** of or like radii or rays. **2** arranged like or in radii or rays. *adj.* —**ra′di al ly,** *adv.*

radial tire, a tire that has its inner fabric cords at right angles to the line of the tread, for greater tire strength.

ra di ance (rā′dē əns), vivid brightness: *the radiance of the sun, the radiance of a smile. n.*

ra di an cy (rā′dē ən sē), radiance. *n.*

ra di ant (rā′dē ənt), **1** shining; bright; beaming: *a radiant smile.* **2** sending out rays of light or heat: *The sun is a radiant body.* **3** sent off in rays from some source; radiated: *radiant heat. adj.* —**ra′di ant ly,** *adv.*

radiant energy, energy in the form of waves, especially electromagnetic waves. Heat, light, X rays, and radio waves are forms of radiant energy.

ra di ate (rā′dē āt), **1** give out rays of: *The sun radiates light and heat.* **2** issue in rays: *Heat radiates from those hot steam pipes.* **3** give out; send forth: *Her face radiates joy.* **4** spread out from a center: *Roads radiate from the city in every direction. v.,* **ra di at ed, ra di at ing.**

ra di a tion (rā′dē ā′shən), **1** act or process of giving out light, heat, or other radiant energy. **2** energy radiated: *That radiator does not provide enough radiation for so large a room.* **3** particles or electromagnetic waves given off by the atoms and molecules of a radioactive substance as a result of nuclear decay. Some radiations from atoms are alpha particles, beta particles, gamma rays, and neutrons. Radiation is harmful to living tissue. *n.* —**ra′di a′tion less,** *adj.*

ra di a tor (rā′dē ā′tər), **1** a heating device consisting of a set of pipes through which steam or hot water circulates. **2** device for cooling water. The radiator of an automobile gives off heat very fast and so cools the water circulating inside it. *n.*

rad i cal (rad′ə kəl), **1** going to the root; fundamental: *To lose weight, I had to make radical changes in my eating habits.* **2** favoring extreme changes or reforms; extreme. **3** person who favors extreme changes or reforms, especially in politics; person with extreme opinions. **4** atom or group of atoms acting as a unit in chemical reactions. A carbonate molecule (CO_3) is a radical in sodium carbonate (Na_2CO_3), becoming part of that compound without undergoing change, as if it were a single element instead of two. **5** radical sign. **1,2** *adj.,* **3-5** *n.* [*Radical* is from Latin *radicalis,* meaning "having roots, rooted," which comes from *radix,* meaning "root of a plant."] —**rad′i cal ly,** *adv.* —**rad′i cal ness,** *n.*

rad i cal ism (rad′ə kə liz′əm), principles or practices of radicals; support or advocacy of extreme changes or reforms, especially in politics. *n.*

radical sign, a mathematical sign ($\sqrt{}$) put before a number or expression to show that a root of it is to be found by calculation. $\sqrt{16}$ = the square root of 16 = 4. $\sqrt[3]{27}$ = the cube root of 27 = 3.

ra di i (rā′dē ī), a plural of radius. *n.*

ra di o (rā′dē ō), **1** the sending and receiving of sound or television signals by means of electromagnetic waves without the use of connecting wires between sender and receiver. **2** apparatus for sending or receiving and making audible the sound signals sent in this way. **3** of, used in, or sent by radio: *a radio set, radio programs.* **4** transmit or send out by radio: *The ship radioed a call for help.* **5** business of broadcasting by radio: *He left acting and got a job in radio.* **1,2,5** *n., pl.* **ra di os** for 2; **3** *adj.,* **4** *v.,* **ra di oed, ra di o ing.**

radio-, *combining form.* **1** radiation; radiant energy: *Radioactivity = property of giving off radiation.* **2** radio; by radio: *Radiogram = message sent by radio.* **3** radioactive: *Radiocarbon = radioactive carbon.* [The form *radio-* comes from Latin *radius,* meaning "ray."]

ra di o ac tive (rā′dē ō ak′tiv), of, having, or caused by radioactivity. Radium, uranium, and thorium are radioactive metallic elements. *adj.* —**ra′di o ac′tive ly,** *adv.*

ra di o ac tiv i ty (rā′dē ō ak tiv′ə tē), **1** the property, exhibited by certain elements, of giving off radiation in the form of alpha particles, beta particles, or gamma rays as the result of nuclear decay. **2** the radiation given off. *n.*

radio astronomy, branch of astronomy dealing with the detection of objects in space by means of radio waves that these objects give off. It enables observers to study heavenly bodies beyond the range of ordinary telescopes. —**radio astronomer.**

ra di o car bon (rā′dē ō kär′bən), a radioactive isotope of carbon, especially carbon 14. *n.*

radio frequency, any electromagnetic wave frequency suitable for radio or television broadcasting, usually above 10,000 cycles per second.

ra di o gram (rā′dē ō gram′), message transmitted by radio. *n.*

ra di o i so tope (rā′dē ō ī′sə tōp), a radioactive isotope. Artificially produced radioisotopes are widely used in medical research and treatment. *n.*

ra di ol o gist (rā′dē ol′ə jist), an expert in radiology. *n.*

ra di ol o gy (rā′dē ol′ə jē), science dealing with X rays or the rays from radioactive substances, especially for medical diagnosis or treatment. *n.*

radiometer
Each vane has a black side and a white side. The black side absorbs more light, so the vanes spin clockwise. The brighter the light, the faster the spin.

ra di om e ter (rā′dē om′ə tər), instrument for detecting and measuring radiant energy. *n.*

ra di o sonde (rā′dē ō sond), instrument carried into the atmosphere by a balloon from which it descends by parachute, automatically reporting data on atmospheric conditions to observers on the ground by means of a small radio transmitter. *n.*

radio telescope, device consisting of a radio receiver and a very large, bowl-shaped antenna for detecting radio waves given out by objects in outer space.

radio wave, an electromagnetic wave within the radio frequencies.

rad ish (rad′ish), the small, crisp, red or white root of a garden plant. Radishes are eaten raw as a relish and in salads. *n., pl.* **rad ish es.** —**rad′ish like′,** *adj.*

ra di um (rā′dē əm), a radioactive metallic element found in very small amounts in uranium ores such as pitchblende. Radium is very unstable and gives off alpha particles and gamma rays in breaking down in successive forms into radon, polonium, and, finally, lead. Radium is used in treating cancer and in making luminous paint. *n.*

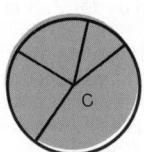

radius (def. 1)
Each line from C (center) is a radius.

ra di us (rā′dē əs), **1** a line segment going straight from the center to the outside of a circle or a sphere. Any spoke in a wheel is a radius. **2** the length of such a line segment: *The radius of the circle is 6 centimeters.* **3** a circular area measured by the length of its radius: *The explosion could be heard within a radius of ten miles.* **4** the thicker, shorter bone of the forearm, on the same side as the thumb. *n., pl.* **ra di i** or **ra di us es.** [*Radius* comes from Latin *radius,* meaning "ray, spoke of a wheel."]

ra don (rā′don), a heavy radioactive gas formed by the decay of radium. It is a chemical element. *n.*

rad waste (rad′wāst′), radioactive waste material, such as discharged nuclear fuel. *n.*

raf fi a (raf′ē ə), fiber from the leaf stalks of a kind of palm tree growing on Madagascar, used in making baskets, mats, etc. *n.* [*Raffia* comes from a Malagasy word. Malagasy is a language spoken in Madagascar.]

raf fle (raf′əl), **1** sale in which many people each pay a small sum for a chance to win a prize. **2** sell (an article) by a raffle. **1** *n.,* **2** *v.,* **raf fled, raf fling.** —**raf′fler,** *n.*

raft[1] (raft), logs or boards fastened together to make a floating platform: *We crossed the stream on a raft. n.*

raft[2] (raft), INFORMAL. a large number; abundance: *a raft of troubles. n.*

raft er (raf′tər), a slanting beam of a roof. *n.*

rag[1] (rag), **1** a torn or waste piece of cloth: *Use a clean rag to rub this mirror bright.* **2 rags,** *pl.* clothing that is torn and in tatters. **3** a small piece of cloth. **4** made from rags: *a rag doll, a rag rug.* **1-3** *n.,* **4** *adj.* —**rag′like′,** *adj.*

rag[2] (rag), SLANG. **1** scold. **2** tease; play jokes on. *v.,* **ragged, rag ging.**

rag a muf fin (rag′ə muf′ən), a dirty, ragged person, especially a child. *n.*

rage (rāj), **1** violent anger: *a voice quivering with rage.* **2** be furious with anger. **3** talk or act violently; move, proceed, or continue with great violence: *Keep your temper; don't rage. A storm is raging.* **4** what everybody wants for a short time; the fashion: *Red ties were all the rage last season.* **1,4** *n.,* **2,3** *v.,* **raged, rag ing.** —**rag′ing ly,** *adv.*

rag ged (rag′id), **1** worn or torn into rags. **2** wearing torn or badly worn-out clothing: *a ragged beggar.* **3** not straight and tidy; rough: *an old dog's ragged coat.* **4** having loose shreds or bits: *a ragged wound.* **5** having rough or sharp points; uneven; jagged: *ragged rocks. adj.* —**rag′ged ly,** *adv.* —**rag′ged ness,** *n.*

rag lan (rag′lən), having sleeves cut so as to continue up to the collar: *a raglan topcoat. adj.*

rag man (rag′man′), person who gathers, buys, or sells rags, old newspapers, etc. *n., pl.* **rag men.**

ra gout (ra gü′), a highly seasoned stew of meat and vegetables. *n.* [*Ragout* is from French *ragoût,* which comes from *ragoûter,* meaning "restore the appetite," and can be traced back to Latin *re-,* meaning "back," *ad-,* meaning "to," and *gustare,* meaning "to taste."]

rag time (rag′tīm′), **1** musical rhythm with accents falling at unusual places. **2** form of jazz using this rhythm. *n.*

rag weed (rag′wēd′), a coarse weed whose pollen is one of the most common causes of hay fever. *n.*

rah (rä), hurrah. *interj., n.*

raid (rād), **1** a sudden attack: *The pirates planned a raid on the harbor.* **2** attack suddenly: *The enemy raided our camp.* **3** an entering and seizing what is inside: *The hungry girls made a raid on the refrigerator.* **4** force a way into; enter and seize what is in: *The police raided the gambling house.* **1,3** *n.,* **2,4** *v.* —**raid′er,** *n.*

rail[1] (rāl), **1** bar of wood or of metal. There are stair rails, fence rails, rails protecting monuments, etc. **2** one of a pair of steel bars laid parallel on crossties as a track for a train, subway train, etc. **3** railroad: *ship freight by rail.* **4** enclose with bars or a fence: *to rail off a space for horses.* **1-3** *n.,* **4** *v.*

rail[2] (rāl), complain bitterly; use violent and reproachful language: *rail at one's hard luck. v.* —**rail′er,** *n.*

rail[3] (rāl), a small bird with short wings and tail, narrow body, long toes, and a harsh cry. It lives in marshes and swamps. *n., pl.* **rails** or **rail.**

rail ing (rā′ling), rail used as a guard or support on a stairway or platform; handrail. *n.*

rail ler y (rā′lər ē), good-humored ridicule; joking; teasing. *n., pl.* **rail ler ies.**

rail road (rāl′rōd′), **1** road or track with parallel steel rails on which the wheels of the cars go. Engines pull trains on railroads. **2** tracks, stations, trains, and other property of a system of transportation that uses rails, together with the people who manage them. **3** to work on a railroad. **4** INFORMAL. carry out or cause quickly, in an unfair way: *Several council members tried to railroad the*

RAFTER   RAFTER

new bill through without full debate. **5** INFORMAL. send (a person) to prison on false evidence, without a fair trail, etc.: *The prisoner claimed that she was railroaded.* 1,2 *n.*, 3-5 *v.* —**rail′road′er**, *n.*

rail way (rāl′wā′), **1** railroad. **2** track made of rails. *n.* —**rail′way′less**, *adj.*

rai ment (rā′mənt), OLD USE. clothing; garments. *n.*

rain (rān), **1** water falling in drops from the clouds. Rain is formed from moisture condensed from water vapor in the atmosphere. *The rain spattered the windows.* **2** the fall of such drops: *a hard rain.* **3** to fall in drops of water: *It rained all day.* **4** a thick, fast fall of anything: *a rain of bullets.* **5** fall like rain: *Sparks rained down from the burning roof.* **6** send like rain: *The crowd rained confetti on the parade.* 1,2,4 *n.*, 3,5,6 *v.* —**rain′less**, *adj.*

rain out, to postpone or cancel because of rain: *Today's game was rained out, and will be played tomorrow as part of a doubleheader.*

rain bow (rān′bō′), **1** bow or arch of colored light seen sometimes in the sky opposite the sun, or in mist or spray. A rainbow shows all the colors of the spectrum: red, orange, yellow, green, blue, indigo, and violet. **2** having many colors like a rainbow. 1 *n.*, 2 *adj.* —**rain′bow′like′**, *adj.*

rain coat (rān′kōt′), a waterproof coat worn for protection from rain. *n.*

rain drop (rān′drop′), drop of rain. *n.*

rain fall (rān′fôl′), **1** shower of rain. **2** amount of water in the form of rain, sleet, or snow that falls within a given time and area: *The yearly rainfall in New York is much greater than that in Arizona.* *n.*

rain forest, a very dense forest in a region where rain is very heavy throughout the year. Rain forests are usually in tropical areas.

Rai nier (rə nir′), **Mount,** mountain in W Washington, 14,408 feet (4392 meters) high. *n.*

rain i ness (rā′nē nis), a rainy condition. *n.*

rain proof (rān′prüf′), not letting rain through; waterproof. *adj.*

rain storm (rān′stôrm′), storm with much rain. *n.*

rain y (rā′nē), **1** having rain; having much rain: *The weather was gloomy, dark, and rainy.* **2** bringing rain: *The sky is filled with dark, rainy clouds.* **3** wet with rain: *rainy streets.* *adj.*, **rain i er, rain i est.** —**rain′i ly**, *adv.*

rainy day, a possible time of greater need in the future: *to save money for a rainy day.*

raise (rāz), **1** lift up; put up: *raise the flag. Children in school raise their hands to answer a question.* **2** cause to rise: *The automobile raised a cloud of dust. Dough for bread is raised by yeast.* **3** put or take into a higher position; make higher or nobler: *raise a clerk to manager.* **4** increase in degree, amount, price, pay, etc.: *raise the rent, raise one's courage.* **5** an increase in amount, price, pay, etc.: *a raise in pay.* **6** gather together; collect; manage to get: *raise funds for a hospital.* **7** breed; grow: *The farmer raises crops and cattle.* **8** bring about; cause: *A funny remark raises a laugh.* **9** build; create; produce; start; set up: *raise a monument to a famous person, raise a skyscraper.* **10** rouse; stir up: *The dog raised a rabbit from the underbrush.* **11** bring up; rear: *Parents raise their children.* **12** bring back to life: *raise the dead.* **13** put an end to: *The soldiers raised the siege of the fort by driving away the enemy.* 1-4,6-13 *v.*, raised, rais ing; 5 *n.* —**rais′a ble, raise′a ble**, *adj.*

rais er (rā′zər), person who grows or raises things: *a cattle raiser.* *n.*

rai sin (rā′zn), a sweet, dried grape. *n.*

ra ja (rä′jə), rajah. *n.*, *pl.* **ra jas.**

ra jah (rä′jə), ruler or chief in India, Java, Borneo, etc. *n.*

rake¹ (rāk), **1** a long-handled tool having a bar at one

a hat	**i** it	**oi** oil	**ch** child	a in about
ā age	**ī** ice	**ou** out	**ng** long	e in taken
ä far	**o** hot	**u** cup	**sh** she	ə = { i in pencil
e let	**ō** open	**ù** put	**th** thin	o in lemon
ē equal	**ô** order	**ü** rule	**ᵺ** then	u in circus
ėr term			**zh** measure	

end with teeth in it. A rake is used for smoothing the soil or gathering together loose leaves, hay, straw, etc. **2** move with a rake: *Rake the leaves off the grass.* **3** make clear, clean, smooth, etc., with a rake, or as if with a rake: *Rake the yard.* **4** search carefully: *I raked the want ads, hoping to find a bicycle for sale.* **5** fire guns along the length of (a ship, line of soldiers, etc.). 1 *n.*, 2-5 *v.*, raked, rak ing.

rake² (rāk), person who shamelessly indulges in vice; immoral or dissolute person. *n.*

rak ish¹ (rā′kish), **1** smart; jaunty; dashing: *a hat set at a rakish angle.* **2** suggesting dash and speed: *They own a rakish boat. adj.* —**rak′ish ly**, *adv.* —**rak′ish ness**, *n.*

rak ish² (rā′kish), like a rake; immoral; dissolute. *adj.*

Ra leigh (rô′lē), **1** Sir **Walter,** 1552?-1618, English soldier, explorer, statesman, and author. **2** capital of North Carolina, in the central part. *n.*

ral ly¹ (ral′ē), **1** bring together, especially to get in order again: *The commander was able to rally the fleeing troops.* **2** come or bring together in a body for a common purpose or action: *The people rallied to rebuild the dike before the river flooded their homes.* **3** come to help a person, party, or cause: *She rallied to the side of her injured friend.* **4** recover health and strength: *My sick friend has begun to rally.* **5** a rallying; recovery. **6** a mass meeting or assembly for a common purpose or action: *a political rally.* 1-4 *v.*, ral lied, ral ly ing; 5,6 *n.*, *pl.* **ral lies.**

ral ly² (ral′ē), make fun of good-naturedly; tease: *We rallied our friend on her forgetfulness. v.*, ral lied, ral ly ing.

ram (ram), **1** a male sheep. **2** butt against; strike head on; strike violently: *One ship rammed the other ship.* **3** push hard; drive down or in by heavy blows. **4** machine or part of a machine that strikes heavy blows. The ram on a pile driver is the weight that drives the piles into the ground. **5** battering ram. 1,4,5 *n.*, 2,3 *v.*, rammed, ram ming. [*Ram* comes from Old English *ramm.*]

RAM (ram), random access memory (a form of temporary computer memory in which all data are equally available. Data can be put into or taken from such memory at any time.) *n.*

ram ble (ram′bəl), **1** wander about: *We rambled here and there through the woods.* **2** a walk for pleasure, not to go to any special place. **3** talk or write about first one thing and then another with no useful connections. **4** spread irregularly in various directions: *Vines rambled over the wall.* 1,3,4 *v.*, ram bled, ram bling; 2 *n.*

ram bler (ram′blər), **1** person or thing that rambles. **2** a climbing rose with clusters of small red, yellow, or white flowers. *n.*

ram bling (ram′bling), **1** wandering about. **2** going from one thing to another with no useful connections: *a rambling speech.* **3** extending irregularly in various directions; not planned in an orderly way: *a rambling old farmhouse. adj.* —**ram′bling ly**, *adv.*

ram bunc tious (ram bungk′shəs), wild and noisy; boisterous. *adj.* —**ram bunc′tious ly**, *adv.*

Ram e ses (ram′ə sēz), Ramses. *n.*

ram i fi ca tion (ram′ə fə kā′shən), **1** a dividing or spreading out into branches or parts. **2** manner or result of branching; branch; part; subdivision. *n.*

ram i fy (ram′ə fī), divide or spread out into branches or parts resembling branches. *v.*, ram i fied, ram i fy ing.

ramp (ramp), a sloping way connecting two different levels of a building, road, etc.; slope. *n.*

ram page (ram′pāj *for 1;* ram pāj′ *for 2*), **1** fit of rushing wildly about; spell of violent behavior; wild outbreak. **2** rush wildly about; behave violently; rage. 1 *n.*, 2 *v.*, **ram paged, ram pag ing.**

rampage (def. 1)—The sheep went on a **rampage.**

ram pant (ram′pənt), **1** growing without any check. **2** passing beyond restraint or usual limits; unchecked: *Looting was rampant during the riot.* **3** angry; excited; violent. **4** (in heraldry) standing up on the hind legs. *adj.* —**ram′pant ly,** *adv.*

rampant (def. 1)
The vines ran **rampant**
over everything.

ram part (ram′pärt), **1** a wide bank of earth, often with a wall on top, built around a fort to help defend it. **2** anything that defends; defense; protection. *n.*

ram rod (ram′rod′), **1** rod for ramming down the charge in a gun that is loaded from the muzzle. **2** rod for cleaning the barrel of a gun. *n.*

Ram ses (ram′sēz), the name of several kings of ancient Egypt. *n.* Also, **Rameses.**

ram shack le (ram′shak′əl), loose and shaky; likely to come apart. *adj.*

ran (ran), past tense of **run.** *The dog ran after the cat. v.*

ranch (ranch), **1** a large farm with grazing land, used for raising cattle, sheep, or horses. **2** any farm, especially one used to raise one kind of animal or crop: *a chicken ranch, a fruit ranch.* **3** to work on a ranch; manage a ranch. 1,2 *n.*, 3 *v.* [*Ranch comes from Spanish rancho.*]

ranch er (ran′chər), person who owns, manages, or works on a ranch. *n.*

ran cid (ran′sid), **1** stale; spoiled: *rancid butter.* **2** tasting or smelling like stale fat or butter: *a rancid odor. adj.* —**ran′cid ly,** *adv.* —**ran′cid ness,** *n.*

ran cor (rang′kər), bitter resentment or ill will; extreme hatred or spite. *n.*

ran cor ous (rang′kər əs), spiteful; bitterly malicious. *adj.* —**ran′cor ous ly,** *adv.* —**ran′cor ous ness,** *n.*

ran dom (ran′dəm), by chance; with no plan; haphazard: *a random guess, random questions, pick a random number. adj.* —**ran′dom ly,** *adv.* —**ran′dom ness,** *n.*
at random, by chance; with no plan or purpose: *She took a book at random from the shelf.*

rang (rang), past tense of **ring².** *The telephone rang. v.*

range (rānj), **1** distance between certain limits; extent: *a range of prices from $5 to $25, the range of hearing.* **2** vary within certain limits: *prices ranging from $5 to $10.* **3** distance a gun can shoot. **4** a place to practice shooting. **5** land for grazing. **6** wander; rove; roam: *Dinosaurs once ranged the earth. Our talk ranged over many subjects.* **7** row or line of mountains: *Mount Rainier is in the Cascade Range.* **8** row; line: *ranges of books in perfect order.* **9** put in a row or rows: *Range the books by size.* **10** put in groups or classes. **11** put in line on someone's side: *The nobles ranged themselves with the king.* **12** district in which certain plants or animals live. **13** run in a line; extend: *a boundary ranging east and west.* **14** be found; occur: *a plant ranging from Canada to Mexico.* **15** a stove for cooking. 1,3-5,7,8,12,15 *n.*, 2,6,9-11,13,14 *v.*, **ranged, ranging.**

rang er (rān′jər), **1** person employed to guard a tract of forest. **2** one of a body of armed troops employed in ranging over a region to police it. **3** person or thing that ranges; rover. *n.*

Ran goon (rang gün′), capital and chief port of Burma, in the S part. *n.*

rang y (rān′jē), slender and long-limbed: *a rangy horse. adj.,* **rang i er, rang i est.** —**rang′i ness,** *n.*

rank¹ (rangk), **1** row or line, especially of soldiers, placed side by side. **2 ranks,** *pl.* **a** army; soldiers. **b** rank and file. **c** formation: *open ranks, close ranks.* **3** arrange in a row or line. **4** position; grade; class: *the rank of colonel.* **5** high position: *A duchess is a woman of rank.* **6** have a certain rank: *rank high in a spelling test.* **7** put in some special order in a list: *Rank the states in the order of size.* 1,2,4,5 *n.*, 3,6,7 *v.* —**rank′er,** *n.*

rank² (rangk), **1** growing in a thick, coarse way: *a rank growth of weeds.* **2** producing a dense and coarse growth: *rank swampland.* **3** having a strong, bad smell or taste: *rank meat, rank tobacco.* **4** strongly marked; extreme: *rank ingratitude, rank nonsense. adj.* —**rank′ly,** *adv.* —**rank′ness,** *n.*

rank and file, 1 common soldiers, especially those with the rank of corporal or below; ranks. **2** common people.

rank ing (rang′king), of highest standing; leading; foremost: *the ranking U.S. Senator. adj.*

ran kle (rang′kəl), cause soreness or pain; continue to irritate: *The memory of the insult rankled in my mind. v.,* **ran kled, ran kling.**

ramshackle—**Ramshackle** houses covered the hillside.

ran sack (ran′sak), **1** search thoroughly through: *A thief ransacked the house for jewelry.* **2** rob; plunder: *The invading army ransacked the city and carried off its treasure. v.* [*Ransack came into English about 700 years ago from Icelandic rannsaka.*] —**ran′sack er,** *n.*

ran som (ran′səm), **1** price paid or demanded before a captive is set free: *The robbers held the travelers for ransom.* **2** obtain the release of (a captive) by paying a price: *They ransomed the kidnaped child.* **3** a ransoming. 1,3 *n.*, 2 *v.* —**ran′som er,** *n.*

rant (rant), **1** speak wildly, extravagantly, violently, or noisily. **2** extravagant, violent, or noisy speech. 1 *v.*, 2 *n.* —**rant′er,** *n.*

rap[1] (rap), **1** a quick, light blow; a light, sharp knock: *a rap at the door.* **2** knock sharply; tap: *The chairman rapped on the table for order.* **3** say sharply: *rap out an answer.* **4** SLANG. punishment; blame: *Although his friends were also involved, he took the rap for the broken window.* 1,4 *n.*, 2,3 *v.*, **rapped, rap ping.**

rap[2] (rap), INFORMAL. the least bit: *I don't care a rap.* *n.*

rap[3] (rap), SLANG. **1** conversation; talk. **2** talk together in an informal way. 1 *n.*, 2 *v.*, **rapped, rap ping.**

ra pa cious (rə pā′shəs), **1** seizing by force; plundering: *rapacious pirates.* **2** grasping; greedy: *a rapacious miser.* **3** living by the capture of prey; predatory: *rapacious birds. adj.* —**ra pa′cious ly,** *adv.* —**ra pa′cious ness,** *n.*

ra pac i ty (rə pas′ə tē), rapacious spirit, action, or practice; greed. *n.*

rape[1] (rāp), **1** crime of having sexual intercourse with a woman or girl against her will, usually by using force. **2** commit rape on. **3** a seizing and carrying off by force. 1,3 *n.*, 2 *v.*, **raped, rap ing.**

rape[2] (rāp), plant whose leaves are used as food for sheep and hogs. Rape seeds yield an oil that is used as a lubricant. *n.*

Raph a el (raf′ē əl *or* rā′fē əl), 1483-1520, Italian painter. *n.*

rap id (rap′id), **1** moving, acting, or doing with speed; very quick; swift: *a rapid worker.* **2 rapids,** *pl.* part of a river's course where the water rushes quickly, often over rocks near the surface: *The boat overturned in the rapids.* 1 *adj.*, 2 *n.* —**rap′id ly,** *adv.* —**rap′id ness,** *n.*

rap id-fire (rap′id fīr′), **1** firing shots in quick succession. **2** ready and quick; occurring in quick succession: *rapid-fire commands. adj.*

ra pid i ty (rə pid′ə tē), swiftness; speed. *n.*

ra pi er (rā′pē ər), a long and light sword used for thrusting. *n.* —**ra′pi er like′,** *adj.*

rap port (ra pôr′ *or* ra pôrt′), **1** relation; connection. **2** agreement; harmony. *n.*

rap scal lion (rap skal′yən), rascal; rogue; scamp. *n.*

rapt (rapt), **1** lost in delight. **2** so busy thinking of or enjoying one thing that one does not know what else is happening: *Rapt in my work, I did not hear the doorbell.* **3** showing a rapt condition; caused by a rapt condition: *a rapt smile, in rapt attention. adj.* —**rapt′ly,** *adv.* —**rapt′ness,** *n.*

rap ture (rap′chər), a strong feeling that absorbs the mind; very great joy: *In rapture the child gazed at the toys in the shop window. n.*

rap tur ous (rap′chər əs), full of rapture; expressing or feeling rapture. *adj.* —**rap′tur ous ly,** *adv.* —**rap′tur ous ness,** *n.*

rare[1] (rer *or* rar), **1** seldom seen or found: *Storks and peacocks are rare birds in the United States.* **2** not happening often; unusual: *Snow is rare in Florida.* **3** unusually good or great: *Edison had rare powers as an inventor.* **4** thin; not dense: *The higher we go above the earth, the rarer the air is. adj.,* **rar er, rar est.** [*Rare*[1] comes from Latin *rarus.*] —**rare′ness,** *n.*

rare[2] (rer *or* rar), not cooked much: *a rare steak. adj.,* **rar er, rar est.** [*Rare*[2] comes from Old English *hrēr.*] —**rare′ness,** *n.*

rare bit (rer′bit *or* rar′bit), Welsh rabbit. *n.*

rar e fy (rer′ə fī *or* rar′ə fī), **1** make or become less dense: *The air on high mountains is rarefied.* **2** refine; purify. *v.*, **rar e fied, rar e fy ing.**

rare ly (rer′lē *or* rar′lē), seldom; not often. *adv.*

rar ing (rer′ing *or* rar′ing), INFORMAL. very eager: *raring to go, raring for a fight. adj.*

rar i ty (rer′ə tē *or* rar′ə tē), **1** something rare: *A person over a hundred years old is a rarity.* **2** fewness; scarcity: *The rarity of diamonds makes them valuable.* **3** lack of density; thinness: *The rarity of the air in the mountains is bad for some people. n., pl.* **rar i ties.**

ras cal (ras′kəl), **1** a bad, dishonest person. **2** a mischievous person. *n.*

ras cal i ty (ra skal′ə tē), rascally character, conduct, or act. *n., pl.* **ras cal i ties.**

ras cal ly (ras′kə lē), mean; dishonest; bad: *a rascally trick. adj.*

rash[1] (rash), too hasty; careless; reckless; taking too much risk: *It is rash to cross the street without looking both ways. adj.* —**rash′ly,** *adv.* —**rash′ness,** *n.*

rash[2] (rash), **1** a breaking out with many small red spots on the skin. Scarlet fever causes a rash. **2** outbreak: *a rash of bank robberies. n., pl.* **rash es.**

rash er (rash′ər), a thin slice of bacon or ham for frying or broiling. *n.*

rasp (rasp), **1** make a harsh, grating sound: *The file rasped as she worked.* **2** a harsh, grating sound: *the rasp of crickets, a rasp in a person's voice.* **3** utter with a grating sound: *rasp out a command.* **4** affect harshly; irritate; grate on: *Their constant squabbling began to rasp my nerves.* **5** scrape with a rough surface or tool. **6** a coarse file with pointed teeth. 1,3-5 *v.*, 2,6 *n.*

rasp ber ry (raz′ber′ē), **1** a small fruit that grows on bushes. It is usually red or black, but some kinds are white or yellow. **2** SLANG. sound of disapproval made with the tongue and lips. *n., pl.* **rasp ber ries.**

rat (rat), **1** a long-tailed rodent like a mouse but larger. Rats are gray, black, brown, or white. **2** hunt for rats; catch rats. **3** SLANG. a low, mean, disloyal person. **4** SLANG. turn informer against one's associates; squeal. 1,3 *n.*, 2,4 *v.*, **rat ted, rat ting.** —**rat′like′,** *adj.*

smell a rat, suspect a trick or scheme.

ra tan (ra tan′), rattan. *n.*

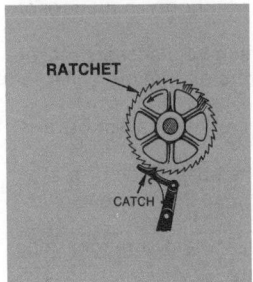

ratchet (def. 1)

ratch et (rach′it), **1** wheel or bar with teeth that come against a catch so that motion is permitted in one direction but not in the other. **2** the catch. **3** the entire device, wheel and catch or bar and catch. *n.*

rate[1] (rāt), **1** quantity, amount, or degree measured in proportion to something else: *The rate of interest is 6 cents on the dollar. The car was going at the rate of 40 miles an hour.* **2** price: *We pay the regular rate.* **3** put a value on: *We rated the house as worth $30,000.* **4** consider; regard: *He was rated as one of the richest men in* *town.* **5** class; grade; rating: *first rate, second rate.* **6** put in a certain class or grade: *rate a baseball player.* **7** be regarded; be classed; rank: *She rates high as a musician.* **8** INFORMAL. be worthy of: *She rates the best seat in the house.* 1,2,5 *n.,* 3,4,6-8 *v.,* **rat ed, rat ing.**

at any rate, in any case; under any circumstances; anyway.

rate² (rāt), scold. *v.,* **rat ed, rat ing.**

rath er (raŦH′ər), **1** more readily; more willingly: *I would rather go today than tomorrow.* **2** more properly or justly; with better reason: *This is rather for your parents to decide than for you.* **3** more truly: *It was late Monday night or, rather, early Tuesday morning.* **4** to some extent; somewhat; more than a little: *After working so long she was rather tired.* **5** on the contrary: *The lesson wasn't difficult to do; rather, it was easy. adv.*

rat i fi ca tion (rat′ə fə kā′shən), confirmation; approval: *the ratification of a treaty by the Senate. n.*

rat i fy (rat′ə fī), confirm; approve; sanction; authorize: *The Senate ratified the treaty. v.,* **rat i fied, rat i fy ing.**

rat ing (rā′ting), **1** class; grade. **2** position in a class or grade: *The judges gave the gymnast a high rating. n.*

ra ti o (rā′shē ō), **1** relation between two quantities expressed as a quotient. "They have sheep and cows in the ratio of 10 to 3" means that they have ten sheep for every three cows. **2** quotient expressing this relation. The ratio between two quantities is the number of times one contains the other. The ratio of 10 to 3 is written as 10:3, 10/3, 10÷3, or ¹⁰/₃. The ratios of 3 to 5 and 6 to 10 are the same. *n., pl.* **ra ti os.**

ra tion (rash′ən *or* rā′shən), **1** a fixed allowance of food; the daily allowance of food for a person or animal. **2** portion of anything dealt out; share; allotment: *rations of sugar.* **3** allow only certain amounts to: *ration citizens when supplies are scarce.* **4** distribute in limited amounts: *Food was rationed to the public during the war.* **5** supply with rations: *ration an army.* 1,2 *n.,* 3-5 *v.* [*Ration* was borrowed from French *ration,* which came from Latin *rationem,* meaning "reckoning, judgment."]

ra tion al (rash′ə nəl), **1** reasoned out; sensible; reasonable: *When very angry, people seldom act in a rational way.* **2** able to think and reason clearly: *Human beings are rational animals.* **3** of reason; based on reasoning: *There is a rational explanation for thunder and lightning. adj.* —**ra′tion al ly,** *adv.*

ra tion ale (rash′ə nal′), the fundamental reason. *n.*

ra tion al ism (rash′ə nə liz′əm), principle or habit of accepting reason as the supreme authority in matters of opinion, belief, or conduct. *n.*

ra tion al ist (rash′ə nə list), person who accepts reason as the supreme authority in matters of opinion, belief, or conduct. *n.*

ra·tion al is tic (rash′ə nə lis′tik), of rationalism or rationalists. *adj.*

ra tion al i ty (rash′ə nal′ə tē), the possession of reason; reasonableness: *That man is odd in some ways, but no one doubts his rationality. n.*

ra tion al i za tion (rash′ə nə lə zā′shən), a rationalizing or a being rationalized. *n.*

ra tion al ize (rash′ə nə līz), **1** make rational or conformable to reason. **2** treat or explain in a rational manner. **3** find (often unconsciously) an explanation or excuse for: *I rationalized drinking two sodas by thinking "I must eat enough to keep up my strength."* **4** find excuses for one's desires. *v.,* **ra tion al ized, ra tion al iz ing.** —**ra′tion al iz′er,** *n.*

rational number, any number that can be expressed as an integer or as a ratio between two integers, excluding zero as a denominator. 2, 5, and ¹/₂ are rational numbers.

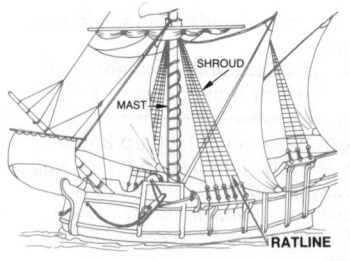

RATLINE

rat line *or* **rat lin** (rat′lən), one of the small ropes that cross the shrouds of a ship, used as steps for going aloft. *n.*

rat tan (ra tan′), **1** kind of climbing palm with a very long stem. **2** stems of such palm trees, used for wickerwork, canes, etc. *n.* Also, **ratan.** [*Rattan* comes from Malay *rotan.*]

rat ter (rat′ər), one that catches rats: *Our terrier is a good ratter. n.*

rat tle (rat′l), **1** make or cause to make a number of short, sharp sounds: *The window rattled in the wind. He rattled the dishes.* **2** a number of short, sharp sounds: *the rattle of empty bottles.* **3** move with short, sharp sounds: *The old car rattled down the street.* **4** toy, instrument, etc., that makes a noise when it is shaken: *The baby shook the rattle.* **5** series of horny pieces at the end of a rattlesnake's tail. **6** talk or say quickly, on and on. **7** confuse; upset: *I was so rattled that I forgot my speech.* 1,3,6,7 *v.,* **rat tled, rat tling;** 2,4,5 *n.*

rat tler (rat′lər), rattlesnake. *n.*

rat tle snake (rat′l snāk′), a poisonous American snake with a thick body and a broad, triangular head, that makes a rattling or buzzing noise with its tail. *n.*

rat tle trap (rat′l trap′), **1** a rattling, rickety wagon or other vehicle. **2** any shaky, rattling object. *n.*

rat ty (rat′ē), **1** of rats; like rats: *a ratty odor.* **2** full of rats: *a ratty cellar.* **3** SLANG. poor; shabby: *a ratty apartment.* **4** SLANG. mean: *That was a ratty thing to do. adj.,* **rat ti er, rat ti est.**

rau cous (rô′kəs), hoarse; harsh-sounding: *the raucous caw of a crow. adj.* —**rau′cous ly,** *adv.* —**rau′cous ness,** *n.*

rav age (rav′ij), **1** damage greatly; lay waste; destroy: *The forest was ravaged by fire.* **2** violence; destruction; great damage: *the ravages of war.* 1 *v.,* **rav aged, rav ag ing;** 2 *n.* —**rav′ag er,** *n.*

rave (rāv), **1** talk wildly. An excited, angry person may rave. **2** talk with much enthusiasm: *They raved about the food.* **3** howl; roar; rage: *The wind raved about the lighthouse.* **4** a raving; frenzy or great excitement. 1-3 *v.,* **raved, rav ing;** 4 *n.*

rav el (rav′əl), separate into threads; fray: *The sweater has raveled at the elbow. v.,* **rav eled, rav el ing** *or* **rav elled, rav el ling.** [*Ravel* comes from Dutch *ravelen.*]

Ra vel (rə vel′), Maurice, 1875-1937, French composer. *n.*

rav el ing *or* **rav el ling** (rav′ə ling), a thread drawn from a woven or knitted fabric. *n.*

ra ven (rā′vən), **1** a large, black bird like a crow, but larger. **2** deep, glossy black: *raven hair.* 1 *n.,* 2 *adj.*

rav en ing (rav′ə ning), ravenous. *adj.*

rav en ous (rav′ə nəs), **1** very hungry. **2** greedy. *adj.* —**rav′en ous ly,** *adv.* —**rav′en ous ness,** *n.*

ra vine (rə vēn′), a long, deep, narrow valley eroded by running water. *n.*

rav ing (rā′ving), **1** that raves; delirious; frenzied; raging. **2** INFORMAL. remarkable; extraordinary: *a raving beauty. adj.* —**rav′ing ly,** *adv.*

rav i o li (rav′ē ō′lē), small, square pieces of dough filled with chopped meat, cheese, etc., and cooked by boiling in water. It is usually served with a tomato sauce. *n. sing. or pl.* [*Ravioli* was borrowed from Italian *ravioli*, and can be traced back to Latin *rapa*, meaning "turnip."]

rav ish (rav′ish), **1** fill with great delight; enrapture. **2** carry off by force. **3** rape. *v.* —**rav′ish er**, *n.*

rav ish ing (rav′i shing), very delightful; enchanting: *jewels of ravishing beauty. adj.* —**rav′ish ing ly**, *adv.*

raw (rô), **1** not cooked: *raw oysters, raw meat.* **2** in the natural state; not manufactured, treated, or prepared: *raw materials. Raw milk has not been pasteurized.* **3** not experienced; not trained: *a raw recruit.* **4** with the skin off; sore: *a raw spot on a horse where the harness rubbed.* **5** damp and cold: *raw weather.* **6** INFORMAL. harsh; unfair: *a raw deal. adj.* —**raw′ly**, *adv.* —**raw′ness**, *n.*

raw boned (rô′bōnd′), having little flesh on the bones; gaunt. *adj.*

raw hide (rô′hīd′), **1** the untanned skin of cattle. **2** rope or whip made of this. *n.*

raw material, substance in its natural state; anything that can be manufactured, treated, or prepared to make it more useful or increase its value. Coal, iron ore, petroleum, cotton, and animal hides are raw materials.

ray[1] (rā), **1** a line or beam of light: *rays of the sun.* **2** a line or stream of radiant energy in the form of heat, light, etc.: *the invisible rays of the spectrum.* **3** a thin line like a ray, coming out from a center. **4** part like a ray. The petals of a daisy and the arms of a starfish are rays. **5** a slight trace; faint gleam: *Not a ray of hope pierced our gloom.* **6** half-line. *n.*

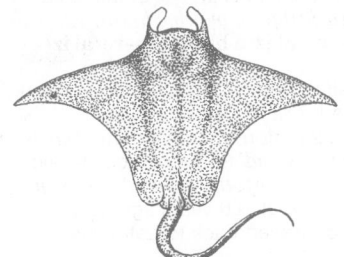

ray[2]
This species may be up to 20 ft. (6 m.) across.

ray[2] (rā), a fish with a broad, flat body and very broad fins. It is related to the shark. *n.*

ray on (rā′on), **1** fiber or fabric made from cellulose treated with chemicals. Rayon is used to make lightweight clothing, automobile tires, etc. **2** made of rayon: *a rayon sweater.* **1** *n.,* **2** *adj.*

raze (rāz), tear down; destroy completely. *v.,* **razed, raz ing.**

raze
The old building was being **razed.**

a hat	**i** it	**oi** oil	**ch** child	a in about
ā age	**ī** ice	**ou** out	**ng** long	e in taken
ä far	**o** hot	**u** cup	**sh** she	**ə =** i in pencil
e let	**ō** open	**u̇** put	**th** thin	o in lemon
ē equal	**ô** order	**ü** rule	**ŦH** then	u in circus
èr term			**zh** measure	

ra zor (rā′zər), tool with one or more blades for shaving. *n.*

razz (raz), SLANG. **1** laugh at; make fun of. **2** strong disapproval; derision. **3** express disapproval of; boo: *The angry crowd razzed the umpire.* **1,3** *v.,* **2** *n.* [*Razz* is short for *razzberry,* a different form of *raspberry,* meaning "sound of disapproval."]

Rb, symbol for rubidium.

R.C., 1 Red Cross. **2** Roman Catholic.

rd., 1 road. **2** rod or rods.

Rd., Road.

R.D., Rural Delivery.

re[1] (rā), the second tone of the musical scale. *n.*

re[2] (rē), with reference to; in the matter or case of; about; concerning: *re your letter of the 7th. prep.*

Re, symbol for rhenium.

re-, *prefix.* **1** again; anew; once more: *Reappear = appear again.* **2** back: *Repay = pay back.*

reach (rēch), **1** get to; come to; arrive at: *reach the top of a hill, reach the end of a book, reach an agreement.* **2** stretch out or hold out an arm or a hand: *I reached in the dark and turned on the lights.* **3** extend in space, time, influence, etc.: *The power of Rome reached to the ends of the known world. The radio reaches millions.* **4** touch: *The anchor reached bottom. I can reach to the top of the wall.* **5** move to touch or seize something; try to get: *I reached for the rope.* **6** get at; influence: *The speaker reached the hearts of the audience.* **7** take or pass with the hand: *Please reach me the newspaper.* **8** get in touch with (someone): *I could not reach you by telephone.* **9** a stretching out; reaching: *By a long reach, the drowning man grasped the rope.* **10** extent or distance of reaching: *Food and water were left within reach of the sick dog.* **11** range; power; capacity: *The difficult lesson was beyond my reach.* **12** a continuous stretch or extent: *vast reaches of snow in the Antarctic.* **1-8** *v.,* **9-12** *n., pl.* **reach es.** —**reach′a ble**, *adj.*

re act (rē akt′), **1** act back; have an effect on the one that is acting: *Unkindness often reacts on the unkind person.* **2** act in response: *Dogs react to kindness by showing affection.* **3** act chemically. Acids react on metals. *v.*

react against, act unfavorably toward or take an unfavorable attitude toward: *Some individuals react against fads.*

re ac tion (rē ak′shən), **1** action in response to some influence or force: *Our reaction to a joke is to laugh. The doctor observed carefully the patient's reactions to certain tests.* **2** action in the opposite direction: *Fever is a common reaction from a chill.* **3** the chemical change of one or more substances resulting in the formation of one or more additional substances. The reaction between nitrogen and hydrogen produces ammonia. **4** a political tendency toward a previous, usually more conservative, state of affairs. *n.*

re ac tion ar y (rē ak′shə ner′ē), **1** having to do with or favoring a return to a previous, usually more conservative, state of affairs: *The bad results of the revolution brought about a reactionary feeling.* **2** person who favors a return to a previous state of affairs, especially in politics. **1** *adj.,* **2** *n., pl.* **re ac tion ar ies.**

re ac ti vate (rē ak′tə vāt), make active again; restore to active service. *v.,* **re ac ti vat ed, re ac ti vat ing.**

re ac tor (rē ak′tər), apparatus for the release of atomic energy by a controlled chain reaction; pile. Reactors consist of layers of fissionable material, such as uranium, spaced with moderators, such as graphite and heavy water. *n.*

read[1] (rēd), **1** get the meaning of (writing or print): *read a book. The blind read by touching special raised print with their fingertips.* **2** learn from writing or print: *I read of the event in the paper.* **3** speak (printed or written words); say aloud the words one sees or touches: *Read this story to me.* **4** show by letters, figures, signs, etc.: *The thermometer reads 70 degrees.* **5** be worded in a certain way: *This line reads differently in the first edition.* **6** study: *read law.* **7** get the meaning of; understand: *I read what you are trying to tell me.* **8** give the meaning of; interpret: *A prophet reads the future.* **9** introduce (something not expressed or directly indicated) by one's manner of understanding or interpreting: *read a hostile intent in a friendly letter. v.,* **read** (red), **read ing.**

read into, interpret in a certain way, often attributing more than intended: *He read into the remark an insult.*

read[2] (red), **1** having knowledge gained by reading; informed: *She is widely read in history.* **2** past tense and past participle of **read**[1]. *I read that book last year. They have read it too.* **1** *adj.,* **2** *v.*

read a bil i ty (rē′də bil′ə tē), readable quality. *n.*

read a ble (rē′də bəl), **1** easy to read; interesting. **2** capable of being read. *adj.* —**read′a ble ness,** *n.*

read er (rē′dər), **1** person who reads. **2** book for learning and practicing reading. *n.*

read i ly (red′l ē), **1** quickly; promptly; without delay: *The eager student answered readily.* **2** easily; without difficulty: *readily accessible.* **3** willingly. *adv.*

read i ness (red′ē nis), **1** a being ready; preparedness. **2** quickness; promptness. **3** ease; facility. **4** willingness. *n.*

read ing (rē′ding), **1** act or process of getting the meaning of writing or printing. **2** a speaking out loud of written or printed words; public recital. **3** written or printed matter read or to be read. **4** amount shown by letters, figures, or signs on the scale of an instrument: *The reading of the thermometer was 96 degrees.* **5** interpretation: *Each actor gave the lines a different reading.* **6** used in or for reading: *reading glasses.* **1-5** *n.,* **6** *adj.*

re ad just (rē′ə just′), adjust again; arrange again. *v.*

re ad just ment (rē′ə just′mənt), a readjusting. *n.*

read y (red′ē), **1** prepared for action or use at once; prepared: *Dinner is ready. We are ready for the test.* **2** willing: *I am ready to forget our disagreement.* **3** quick; prompt: *a ready welcome, a ready wit.* **4** apt; likely; liable: *She is too ready to find fault.* **5** easy to get at; immediately available: *ready money.* **6** make ready; prepare: *The expedition readied itself during the summer.* **7** condition or position of being prepared for action: *The soldiers walked down the road with their guns at the ready.* **1-5** *adj.,* **read i er, read i est;** **6** *v.,* **read ied, read y ing; 7** *n.*

read y-made (red′ē mād′), ready for immediate use; made for anybody who will buy; not made to order: *Department stores sell ready-made clothes. adj.*

re af firm (rē′ə fėrm′), affirm again or anew. *v.*

Rea gan (rā′gən), **Ronald Wilson,** born 1911, the fortieth president of the United States, since 1981. *n.*

re a gent (rē ā′jənt), substance used to detect, measure, or produce other substances by the chemical reactions it causes. *n.*

re al[1] (rē′əl), **1** existing as a fact; not imagined or made up; actual; true: *a real experience, the real reason.* **2** genuine: *a real diamond.* **3** (in law) of immovable property. Lands and houses are called real property. **4** INFORMAL. very; extremely: *It was real kind of you to come.* **1-3** *adj.,* **4** *adv.* [*Real*[1] is from Latin *realis,* which comes from *res, rei,* meaning "matter, thing." See **Word Family.**]

re al[2] (rē′əl *or* rä äl′), a former small silver coin of Spain and Spanish America, worth about 12½ cents. *n., pl.* **re als, re a les** (rä ä′lās). [*Real*[2] comes from Spanish *real* (*de plata*), meaning "royal (coin of silver)."]

real estate, land together with the buildings, fences, trees, water, minerals, etc., that belong with it.

re al ism (rē′ə liz′əm), **1** thought and action based on realities: *Her realism caused her to dislike fanciful schemes.* **2** (in art and literature) the picturing of life as it actually is. *n.*

re al ist (rē′ə list), **1** person interested in what is real and practical rather than what is imaginary or theoretical. **2** artist or writer who represents things as they are in real life. *n.*

re al is tic (rē′ə lis′tik), **1** like the real thing; lifelike. **2** (in art and literature) representing life as it actually is. **3** seeing things as they really are; practical. *adj.* —**re′al is′ti cal ly,** *adv.*

re al i ty (rē al′ə tē), **1** actual existence; true state of affairs: *Ghosts have no place in reality.* **2** a real thing; actual fact: *Slaughter and destruction are terrible realities of war. n., pl.* **re al i ties.**

in reality, really; actually; in fact; truly: *They thought I was serious, but in reality I was joking.*

re al i za tion (rē′ə lə zā′shən), **1** a realizing or a being realized: *the realization of your hopes.* **2** clear understanding; full awareness; perception: *The explorers had a realization of the dangers that they must face. n.*

re al ize (rē′ə līz), **1** understand clearly; be fully aware of: *I realize how hard you worked.* **2** make real; bring into actual existence: *Her uncle's present made it possible for her to realize her dream of going to college.* **3** obtain as a return or profit: *I realized $50 from mowing lawns. v.,* **re al ized, re al iz ing.** —**re′al iz′a ble,** *adj.* —**re′al iz′er,** *n.*

re al ly (rē′ə lē), **1** actually; truly; in fact: *Try to see things as they really are.* **2** indeed: *Oh, really? adv.*

realm (relm), **1** kingdom. **2** region; range; extent: *This is beyond the realm of my understanding.* **3** a particular field of something: *the realm of biology, the realm of poetry. n.* [*Realm* came into English about 700 years ago from French *realme,* and can be traced back to Latin *regere,* meaning "to rule."]

real number, any rational or irrational number.

Re al tor (rē′əl tər), a real-estate agent who is a member of the National Association of Realtors. *n.*

re al ty (rē′əl tē), real estate. *n., pl.* **re al ties.**

ream[1] (rēm), **1** 480, 500, or 516 sheets of paper of the same size and quality. **2** a very large quantity: *ream upon ream of nonsense. n.* [*Ream*[1] came into English about 600 years ago from French *raime,* which came from Arabic *razma,* meaning "bundle."]

ream[2] (rēm), **1** enlarge or shape (a hole). **2** remove with a reamer. *v.* [*Ream*[2] comes from Middle English *reamen.*]

WORD FAMILY

real[1]

Below are words related to *real*[1]. They can all be traced back to Latin *res, rei* (räs, re′ē), meaning "thing."

reality	realty	republican
realize	rebus	surrealism
Realtor	republic	unrealistic

reamer (def. 1)
attached to an electric drill

a hat	i it	oi oil	ch child	a in about
ā age	ī ice	ou out	ng long	e in taken
ä far	o hot	u cup	sh she	i in pencil
e let	ō open	u̇ put	th thin	o in lemon
ē equal	ô order	ü rule	ᴛʜ then	u in circus
ėr term			zh measure	

ə = { ... }

ream er (rē′mər), **1** tool for enlarging or shaping a hole. **2** utensil for squeezing the juice out of oranges, lemons, etc. *n.*

reap (rēp), **1** cut (grain). **2** gather (a crop). **3** cut grain or gather a crop from: *reap fields.* **4** get as a return or reward: *Kind acts often reap happy smiles. v.*

reap er (rē′pər), person or machine that cuts grain or gathers a crop. *n.*

re ap pear (rē′ə pir′), appear again. *v.*

re ap pear ance (rē′ə pir′əns), a reappearing. *n.*

rear[1] (rir), **1** the back part; back: *the rear of the house.* **2** at the back; in the back: *Leave by the rear door of the bus.* **3** the last part of an army, fleet, etc. 1,3 *n.*, 2 *adj.* [*Rear*[1] probably was shortened from *rearguard,* which came into English about 500 years ago from French *rereguarde,* which comes from *rer,* meaning "back," and *guarde,* meaning "a guard."]

bring up the rear, move onward as the rear part; come last in order.

rear[2] (rir), **1** make grow; help to grow; bring up: *They reared their children to respect other people.* **2** to breed (livestock). **3** set up; build: *The Romans reared temples to their gods.* **4** raise; lift up: *The snake reared its head.* **5** (of an animal) rise on the hind legs; rise: *The horse reared and threw its rider. v.* [*Rear*[2] comes from Old English *rǣran,* meaning "to raise."]

rear admiral, a naval officer ranking next above a captain and next below a vice-admiral.

re arm (rē ärm′), **1** arm again; arm oneself again. **2** supply with new or better weapons. *v.*

re ar ma ment (rē är′mə mənt), rearming. *n.*

re ar range (rē′ə rānj′), **1** arrange in a new or different way: *They rearranged the living room furniture for the party.* **2** arrange again: *I had to rearrange my papers after the wind blew them on the floor. v.*, **re ar ranged, re ar rang ing.**

re ar range ment (rē′ə rānj′mənt), a new or different arrangement. *n.*

rear ward (rir′wərd), toward or in the rear. *adv., adj.*

rear wards (rir′wərdz), rearward. *adv.*

rea son (rē′zn), **1** cause or motive for an action, feeling, etc.: *I have my own reasons for doing this.* **2** justification; explanation: *What is your reason for being so late?* **3** ability or power to think: *The poor man has lost his reason.* **4** think logically; think things out: *Most animals can't reason.* **5** draw conclusions or inferences from facts or premises: *I reasoned that their alibi couldn't be true.* **6** right thinking; common sense. **7** consider; discuss; argue: *Reason with him and try to make him change his mind.* 1-3,6 *n.*, 4,5,7 *v.* —**rea′son er,** *n.*

bring to reason, cause to be reasonable: *The stubborn child was at last brought to reason.*

by reason of, on account of; because of: *School was dismissed by reason of the teachers' conference.*

in reason or **within reason,** within reasonable and sensible limits: *I will do anything in reason.*

stand to reason, be reasonable and sensible: *It stands to reason that you can't do your best if you're tired.*

rea son a ble (rē′zn ə bəl), **1** according to reason; sensible; not foolish. **2** not asking too much; fair; just. **3** not high in price; inexpensive: *a reasonable price.* **4** able to reason. *adj.* —**rea′son a ble ness,** *n.*

rea son a bly (rē′zn ə blē), in a reasonable manner; with reason. *adv.*

rea son ing (rē′zn ing), **1** process of drawing conclusions from facts or premises. **2** reasons; arguments. *n.*

re as sem ble (rē′ə sem′bəl), come or bring together again. *v.*, **re as sem bled, re as sem bling.**

re as sur ance (rē′ə shu̇r′əns), **1** new or fresh assurance. **2** restoration of courage or confidence. *n.*

re as sure (rē′ə shu̇r′), **1** restore to confidence: *The crew's calmness during the storm reassured the passengers.* **2** assure again or anew. *v.*, **re as sured, re as sur ing.** —**re′as sur′ing ly,** *adv.*

re a wak en (rē′ə wā′kən), awaken again or anew. *v.*

re bate (rē′bāt), **1** return of part of money paid; partial refund; discount. **2** to return part of money paid. 1 *n.*, 2 *v.*, **re bat ed, re bat ing.** —**re′bat er,** *n.*

Re bec ca (ri bek′ə), (in the Bible) the wife of Isaac, and the mother of Esau and Jacob.

reb el (reb′əl for 1,2; ri bel′ for 3,4), **1** person who resists or fights against authority instead of obeying: *The rebels armed themselves against the government.* **2** defying law or authority: *a rebel army.* **3** resist or fight against law or authority: *Unfair taxes made the colonists rebel.* **4** feel a great dislike or opposition: *We rebelled at having to stay in on so fine a day.* 1 *n.*, 2 *adj.*, 3,4 *v.*, **re belled, re belling.**

re bel lion (ri bel′yən), **1** armed resistance or fight against one's government; revolt. **2** resistance or fight against any power or restriction. *n.*

re bel lious (ri bel′yəs), **1** defying authority; acting like a rebel; mutinous: *a rebellious army.* **2** hard to manage; hard to treat; disobedient: *a rebellious child. adj.* —**re bel′lious ly,** *adv.* —**re bel′lious ness,** *n.*

re bind (rē bīnd′), bind again or anew: *This book with the broken back needs rebinding. v.*, **re bound, re bind ing.**

re birth (rē′bėrth′ or rē bėrth′), a new birth; being born again: *a rebirth of national pride. n.*

re born (rē bôrn′), born again. *adj.*

re bound[1] (ri bound′ for 1; rē′bound′ or ri bound′ for 2), **1** to spring back. **2** a springing back: *In handball, you hit the ball on the rebound.* 1 *v.*, 2 *n.*

re bound[2] (rē bound′), past tense and past participle of **rebind.** *Send this book to be rebound. v.*

re buff (ri buf′), **1** a blunt or sudden check to a person who makes advances, offers help, makes a request, etc.: *Her offer to help him met with the rebuff, "Let me alone."* **2** give a rebuff to: *The friendly dog was rebuffed by a kick.* 1 *n.*, 2 *v.*

re build (rē bild′), build again or anew. *v.*, **re built, re build ing.**

re built (rē bilt′), past tense and past participle of **rebuild.** *v.*

re buke (ri byük′), **1** express disapproval of; reprove. **2** expression of disapproval; scolding: *The child feared the teacher's rebuke.* 1 *v.*, **re buked, re buk ing;** 2 *n.* —**re buk′er,** *n.* —**re buk′ing ly,** *adv.*

re bus (rē′bəs), representation of a word or phrase by pictures suggesting the syllables or words. A picture of a cat on a log is a rebus for catalog. *n., pl.* **re bus es.** [*Rebus* is from Latin *rebus*, meaning "by means of objects," which comes from *res*, meaning "thing, object."]

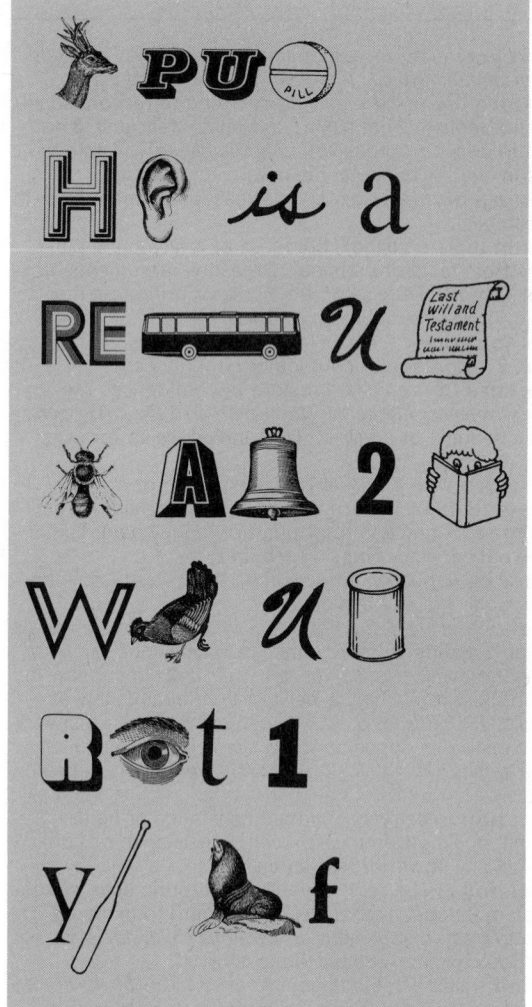

rebus—The solution to this rebus is printed upside down.

Dear pupil,
Here is a rebus you will be able to read.
When you can, write one yourself.

re but (ri but′), oppose by evidence on the other side or by argument; try to disprove: *rebut the argument of the other team in a debate. v.,* **re but ted, re but ting.** —**re-but′ta ble,** *adj.* —**re but′ter,** *n.*

re but tal (ri but′l), a rebutting. *n.*

rec., 1 receipt. 2 recipe. 3 record. 4 recreation.

re cal ci trance (ri kal′sə trəns), refusal to submit, conform, or comply. *n.*

re cal ci trant (ri kal′sə trənt), resisting authority or control; disobedient: *The recalcitrant patient would not take the medicine. adj.* [*Recalcitrant* is from Latin *recalcitrantem,* meaning "kicking back," which comes from *re-,* meaning "back," and *calcem,* meaning "heel."]

re call (ri kôl′ for *1,3,5;* ri kôl′ or rē′kôl′ for *2,4,6,7*), 1 call back to mind; remember: *I can recall stories told to me when I was a small child.* 2 a recalling to mind. 3 call

back; order back: *The ambassador was recalled.* 4 a calling back; ordering back. 5 take back; withdraw: *The order has been given and cannot be recalled.* 6 a taking back; revocation; annulment. 7 call back (a vehicle) in order to replace or repair a defective part. 8 the calling back of a vehicle in order to replace or repair a defective part. 9 procedure by which the people can vote to remove a public official before his or her term has expired. *1,3,5,7 v., 2,4,6,8,9 n.*

re cant (ri kant′), 1 take back formally or publicly; withdraw or renounce (a statement, opinion, purpose, etc.): *The reporter recanted the story when evidence proved it was false.* 2 renounce an opinion or allegiance: *The rebels knew there would be war, yet they would not recant. v.*

re can ta tion (rē′kan tā′shən), a recanting; a public or formal renouncing. *n.*

re ca pit u late (rē′kə pich′ə lāt), repeat or recite the main points of; tell briefly; sum up. *v.,* **re ca pit u lat ed, re ca pit u lat ing.** —**re′ca pit′u la′tor,** *n.*

re ca pit u la tion (rē′kə pich′ə lā′shən), a brief statement of the main points; summary. *n.*

re cap ture (rē kap′chər), 1 capture again; have again. 2 to recall: *The picture album recaptured the past. v.,* **re-cap tured, re cap tur ing.**

re cast (rē kast′), 1 cast again or anew: *recast a bell.* 2 make over; remodel: *recast a sentence. v.,* **re cast, re-cast ing.**

recd. or **rec'd.,** received.

re cede (ri sēd′), 1 go backward; move backward; withdraw: *When the tide receded we dug for clams.* 2 slope backward: *a chin that recedes. v.,* **re ced ed, re ced ing.**

re ceipt (ri sēt′), 1 a written statement that money, a package, a letter, etc., has been received. 2 write on (a bill, etc.) that something has been received or paid for: *Pay the bill and ask the grocer to receipt it.* 3 **receipts,** *pl.* money received; amount or quantity received: *Our expenses were less than our receipts.* 4 a receiving or a being received: *On receipt of the news he went home.* 5 recipe. *1,3,4,5 n., 2 v.*

re ceiv a ble (ri sē′və bəl), 1 fit for acceptance: *Gold is receivable all over the world.* 2 on which payment is to be received. Bills receivable is the opposite of bills payable. *adj.*

re ceive (ri sēv′), 1 take (something offered or sent); take into one's hands or possession: *receive gifts.* 2 be given; get: *receive a letter from home.* 3 take; support; bear; hold: *The boat received a heavy load.* 4 take or let into the mind; accept: *receive new ideas.* 5 experience; suffer; endure: *receive a blow.* 6 let into one's house, society, etc.: *The people of the neighborhood were glad to receive the new couple.* 7 change electromagnetic waves into sound or picture signals: *Our television receives well with the new antenna. v.,* **re ceived, re ceiv ing.**

re ceiv er (ri sē′vər), 1 person who receives. 2 thing that receives: *Public telephones have coin receivers for nickels, dimes, and quarters.* 3 the part of a telephone held to the ear. 4 device that changes electromagnetic waves into sound or picture signals: *a radio or television receiver.* 5 one appointed by law to take charge of the property of others: *He will act as receiver for the bankrupt firm. n.*

re ceiv er ship (ri sē′vər ship), 1 position of a receiver in charge of the property of others. 2 condition of being in the control of a receiver. *n.*

re cent (rē′snt), 1 done or made not long ago: *recent events.* 2 not long past; modern: *a recent period in history. adj.* —**re′cent ly,** *adv.* —**re′cent ness,** *n.*

re cep ta cle (ri sep′tə kəl), any container or place used to put things in to keep them conveniently. Bags, baskets, and vaults are all receptacles. *n.*

re cep tion (ri sep′shən), 1 a receiving or a being received: *calm reception of bad news. Her reception as a club member pleased her.* **2** manner of receiving: *a warm reception.* **3** a gathering to receive and welcome people: *Our school gave a reception for our new principal.* **4** quality of the sound reproduced in a radio or of the sound and picture in a television receiver: *Reception was poor because we were so far from the transmitter.* *n.*

re cep tion ist (ri sep′shə nist), person employed to receive callers: *a receptionist in a doctor's office.* *n.*

re cep tive (ri sep′tiv), able, quick, or willing to receive ideas, suggestions, impressions, etc. *adj.* —**re cep′tive ly,** *adv.* —**re cep′tive ness,** *n.*

re cep tiv i ty (rē′sep tiv′ə tē), ability or readiness to receive. *n.*

re cep tor (ri sep′tər), cell or group of cells sensitive to stimuli; sense organ. *n.*

re cess (rē′ses *or* ri ses′ *for 1,3,5;* ri ses′ *for 2,4*), **1** time during which work stops: *There will be a short recess before the next meeting.* **2** take a recess: *The convention recessed until afternoon.* **3** part in a wall set back from the rest; alcove; niche. **4** put in a recess; set back. **5** an inner place or part; quiet, secluded place: *the recesses of a cave, the recesses of one's secret thoughts.* 1,3,5 *n.,* 2,4 *v.*

re ces sion (ri sesh′ən), **1** a going backward; moving or sloping backward; withdrawal. **2** period of temporary business reduction, shorter and less extreme than a depression. *n.*

re ces sion al (ri sesh′ə nəl), hymn or piece of music sung or played while the clergy and the choir leave the church at the end of a service. *n.*

re ces sive (ri ses′iv), likely to go back; receding. *adj.* —**re ces′sive ly,** *adv.* —**re ces′sive ness,** *n.*

re charge (rē chärj′), to charge again or anew: *recharge a battery.* *v.,* **re charged, re charg ing.**

rec i pe (res′ə pē), **1** set of directions for preparing something to eat: *Give me your recipe for cookies.* **2** set of directions for doing or preparing anything: *a recipe for happiness.* *n.*

re cip i ent (ri sip′ē ənt), person or thing that receives something: *The recipients of the prizes had their names printed in the paper.* *n.*

re cip ro cal (ri sip′rə kəl), **1** in return: *Although she gave me a present, she expected no reciprocal gift from me.* **2** existing on both sides; mutual: *reciprocal liking, reciprocal distrust.* **3** (in grammar) expressing mutual action or relation. In "The two children like each other," *each other* is a reciprocal pronoun. **4** number so related to another that when multiplied together they give 1: *3 is the reciprocal of ¹/₃, and ¹/₃ is the reciprocal of 3.* 1-3 *adj.,* 4 *n.* —**re cip′ro cal ly,** *adv.*

re cip ro cate (ri sip′rə kāt), **1** give, do, feel, or show in return: *She likes me, and I reciprocate her liking.* **2** interchange: *to reciprocate favors.* **3** move or cause to move with an alternating backward and forward motion. *v.,* **re cip ro cat ed, re cip ro cat ing.**

re cip ro ca tion (ri sip′rə kā′shən), a reciprocating; return: *a reciprocation of a favor received.* *n.*

rec i proc i ty (res′ə pros′ə tē), **1** reciprocal state; mutual action. **2** a mutual exchange, especially an exchange of special privileges in regard to trade between two countries. *n., pl.* **rec i proc i ties.**

re cit al (ri sī′tl), **1** a reciting; telling facts in detail: *I hope that my lengthy recital of my problems hasn't bored you.* **2** story; account. **3** a musical entertainment, given usually by a single performer: *My music teacher will give a piano recital Tuesday afternoon.* *n.*

rec i ta tion (res′ə tā′shən), **1** a reciting; a telling of facts in detail. **2** a reciting of a prepared lesson by pupils before a teacher. **3** a repeating of something from memory. **4** piece repeated from memory. *n.*

rec i ta tive (res′ə tə tēv′), **1** passage, part, or piece of music which is sung with the rhythm and phrasing of ordinary speech. Operas often contain long recitatives. **2** this style of singing. *n.*

re cite (ri sīt′), **1** say over; repeat: *He can recite that poem from memory.* **2** say part of a lesson; answer a teacher's questions. **3** give an account of in detail: *She recited the day's adventures.* *v.,* **re cit ed, re cit ing.** —**re cit′er,** *n.*

reck less (rek′lis), rash; heedless; careless: *Reckless driving causes many automobile accidents.* *adj.* —**reck′less ly,** *adv.* —**reck′less ness,** *n.*

reck on (rek′ən), **1** find the number or value of; count: *Reckon the cost before you decide.* **2** consider; judge; account: *He is reckoned the best speller in the class.* **3** INFORMAL. think; suppose. **4** depend; rely: *You can reckon on our help.* **5** settle; settle accounts. *v.* **reckon with,** take into consideration.

reck on ing (rek′ə ning), **1** method of computing; count; calculation: *By my reckoning we are miles from home.* **2** settlement of an account: *a day of reckoning.* **3** bill, especially at an inn or tavern. **4** calculation of the position of a ship. *n.*

re claim (ri klām′), **1** bring back to or put into a useful, good condition: *The farmer reclaimed the swamp by draining it.* **2** get from discarded things: *to reclaim rubber from old tires.* **3** demand or ask for the return of: *We reclaimed our luggage at the end of the trip.* *v.* [Reclaim came into English about 700 years ago from French *reclamer,* meaning "call back," and can be traced back to Latin *re-,* meaning "back," and *clamare,* meaning "cry out."] —**re claim′a ble,** *adj.* —**re claim′er,** *n.*

rec la ma tion (rek′lə mā′shən), restoration to a useful, good condition: *the reclamation of deserts by irrigation.* *n.*

re cline (ri klīn′), lean back; lie or lay down: *recline on a couch.* *v.,* **re clined, re clin ing.**

rec luse (rek′lüs *or* ri klüs′), person who lives shut up or withdrawn from the world. *n.*

rec og ni tion (rek′əg nish′ən), **1** a knowing again; recognizing. **2** a being recognized: *By a good disguise he escaped recognition.* **3** acknowledgment: *We insisted on complete recognition of our rights.* **4** favorable notice; acceptance: *The author soon won recognition from the public.* *n.*

rec og niz a ble (rek′əg nī′zə bəl), able to be recognized. *adj.* —**rec′og niz′a bly,** *adv.*

rec og nize (rek′əg nīz), **1** know again: *You have grown so much that I scarcely recognized you.* **2** identify: *recognize a person from a description.* **3** acknowledge acquaintance with; greet: *recognize a person on the street.* **4** acknowledge; accept; admit: *They recognized and did their duty.* **5** take notice of: *The delegate waited till the chairman recognized her.* **6** show appreciation of. **7** acknowledge and agree to deal with: *For some years other nations did not recognize the new government.* *v.,* **rec og nized, rec og niz ing.**

re coil (ri koil′ *for 1,2;* ri koil′ *or* rē′koil *for 3*), **1** draw back; shrink back: *Most people would recoil at seeing a snake in the path.* **2** spring back: *The gun recoiled after I fired it.* **3** a drawing or springing back. 1,2 *v.,* 3 *n.*

rec ol lect (rek′ə lekt′), call back to mind; remember. *v.*

re-col lect (rē′kə lekt′), **1** collect again. **2** recover control of (oneself). *v.*

rec ol lec tion (rek′ə lek′shən), **1** act or power of calling back to mind. **2** memory; remembrance: *This has been the hottest summer within my recollection.* **3** thing remembered. *n.*

re com bi nant DNA (ri com′bə nənt), DNA from different types of living cells that has been divided and recombined to produce new forms of life.

re com bine (rē′kəm bīn′), to combine again or anew. *v.,* **re com bined, re com bin ing.**

re com mence (rē′kə mens′), begin again or anew. *v.,* **re com menced, re com menc ing.**

rec om mend (rek′ə mend′), **1** speak in favor of; suggest favorably: *The teacher recommended him for the job. Can you recommend a good adventure story?* **2** advise: *The doctor recommended that the patient stay in bed.* **3** make pleasing or attractive: *The location of the camp recommends it as a summer home. v.* —**rec′om mend′a ble,** *adj.*

rec om men da tion (rek′ə men dā′shən), **1** act of recommending. **2** anything that recommends a person or thing. **3** words of advice or praise. **4** thing recommended. *n.*

rec om pense (rek′əm pens), **1** pay (a person); pay back; reward: *The travelers recompensed the man who so carefully directed them.* **2** make a fair return for (an action, anything lost, damage done, or hurt received): *The insurance company recompensed her for the loss of her car.* **3** payment; reward. **4** return; amends: *She received $2000 in recompense for the loss of her car.* 1,2 *v.,* **rec om pensed, rec om pens ing;** 3,4 *n.*

rec on cile (rek′ən sīl), **1** make friends again: *The children had quarreled but were soon reconciled.* **2** settle (a quarrel or difference): *The teacher reconciled the dispute between the two pupils.* **3** make agree; bring into harmony: *It is impossible to reconcile that story with the facts.* **4** make satisfied; make no longer opposed: *It is hard to reconcile oneself to being sick a long time. v.,* **rec on ciled, rec on cil ing.** —**rec′on cile′ment,** *n.* —**rec′on cil′er,** *n.*

rec on cil i a tion (rek′ən sil′ē ā′shən), **1** a bringing together again in friendship. **2** settlement or adjustment of disagreements or differences: *a reconciliation of opposite points of view. n.*

re con di tion (rē′kən dish′ən), restore to a good or satisfactory condition by repairing, making over, etc.: *recondition an old car. v.*

re con firm (rē′kən ferm′), confirm anew. *v.* —**re con′fir ma′tion,** *n.*

re con nais sance (ri kon′ə səns), examination or survey, especially for military purposes. *n.*

rec on noi ter (rek′ə noi′tər *or* rē′kə noi′tər), **1** approach and examine or observe in order to learn something: *Our scouts will reconnoiter the enemy's position before we attack.* **2** approach a place and make a first survey of it: *It seemed wise to reconnoiter before entering the town. v.* —**rec′on noi′ter er,** *n.*

rec on noi tre (rek′ə noi′tər *or* rē′kə noi′tər), reconnoiter. *v.,* **rec on noi tred, rec on noi tring.** —**rec′on noi′trer,** *n.*

re con sid er (rē′kən sid′ər), consider again: *The assembly voted to reconsider a bill. v.* —**re′con sid′er a′tion,** *n.*

re con struct (rē′kən strukt′), construct again; rebuild; make over. *v.*

re con struc tion (rē′kən struk′shən), **1** act of reconstructing. **2** thing reconstructed. **3 Reconstruction, a** process by which the southern states after the Civil War were reorganized and their relations with the national government were reestablished. **b** period when this was done, from 1865 to 1877. *n.*

re cord (ri kôrd′ *for* 1,2,6; rek′ərd *for* 3-5,7-10), **1** set down in writing so as to keep for future use: *Listen to the speaker and record what she says.* **2** put in some per-

manent form; keep for remembrance: *We record history in books.* **3** the thing written or kept. **4** an official written account: *The secretary kept a record of what was done at the meeting.* **5** a thin, flat disk, usually of vinyl or other plastic, with narrow grooves on its surface, used on a phonograph. Variations in the grooves of the record are picked up by the needle of a phonograph and transformed into audible sound. **6** put (music, words, or sounds) on such a disk or on specially treated tape. **7** the known facts about what a person, group, etc., has done: *She has a fine record at school.* **8** the best yet done; best amount, rate, or speed yet reached: *Who holds the record for the high jump?* **9** making or affording a record: *a record wheat crop.* **10** a recording or a being recorded: *What happened is a matter of record.* 1,2,6 *v.,* 3-5,7,8,10 *n.,* 9 *adj.* [*Record* came into English about 700 years ago from French *recorder,* which came from Latin *recordari,* meaning "remember, call to mind," which comes from *re-,* meaning "back," and *cordis,* meaning "heart."] —**re cord′a ble,** *adj.*

break a record, make a better record.

off the record, not to be recorded or quoted.

on record, recorded.

recorder (def. 4)

re cord er (ri kôr′dər), **1** person whose business is to make and keep records. **2** machine or part of a machine that records. The recorder of a cash register adds up and prints the amount of sales made. **3** tape recorder. **4** a wooden musical instrument with a tone somewhat like a flute. *n.*

re cord ing (ri kôr′ding), a phonograph record or a plastic tape used in a tape recorder. *n.*

record player, phonograph.

re count[1] (ri kount′), tell in detail; give an account of: *He recounted all the happenings of the day. v.*

re count[2] *or* **re-count** (rē kount′ *for* 1; rē′kount′ *for* 2), **1** count again: *I recounted the money to make certain it was the right amount.* **2** a second count: *to make a recount of the votes.* 1 *v.,* 2 *n.*

re coup (ri küp′), **1** make up for: *recoup one's losses.* **2** repay: *I will recoup you for any money you spend. v.* —**re coup′a ble,** *adj.* —**re coup′ment,** *n.*

re course (rē′kôrs *or* ri kôrs′), **1** an appealing; turning for help or protection: *Our recourse in illness is to a doctor.* **2** person or thing appealed to or turned to for help or protection: *His only recourse in trouble was his family. n.*

have recourse to, appeal to; turn to for help: *When we do not know what a word means, we have recourse to a dictionary.*

re cov er (ri kuv′ər), **1** get back (something lost, taken away, or stolen): *recover one's temper or health, recover a lost purse.* **2** make up for (something lost or damaged): *recover lost time.* **3** get well; get back to a normal condition: *She is recovering from a cold.* **4** get back to the proper position or condition: *He started to fall but recovered himself.* **5** regain in usable form; reclaim. Many useful substances are now recovered from materials that used to be thrown away. *v.* —**re cov′er a ble,** *adj.* —**re cov′er er,** *n.*

re-cov er (rē kuv′ər), put a new cover on: *We had our couch re-covered. v.*

re cov er y (ri kuv′ər ē), **1** a coming back to health or normal condition: *recovery from a fever.* **2** a getting back something that was lost, taken away, stolen, or sent out: *the recovery of a space capsule.* **3** a getting back to a proper position or condition: *She started to fall, but made a quick recovery. n., pl.* **re cov er ies.**

recovery room, room used in a hospital to treat patients recovering immediately after an operation or childbirth.

rec re ate (rek′rē āt), take recreation. *v.,* **rec re at ed, rec re at ing.** —**rec′re a′tor,** *n.*

re-cre ate (rē′krē āt′), create anew. *v.,* **re-cre at ed, re-cre at ing.**

rec re a tion (rek′rē ā′shən), play or amusement. Walking, gardening, and reading are quiet forms of recreation. *n.*

rec re a tion al (rek′rē ā′shə nəl), of or used for recreation: *recreational opportunities, recreational areas. adj.*

re crim i nate (ri krim′ə nāt), accuse (someone) in return: *He said she had lied, and she recriminated by saying he had lied too. v.,* **re crim i nat ed, re crim i nat ing.** —**re crim′i na′tor,** *n.*

re crim i na tion (ri krim′ə nā′shən), an accusing in return; counter accusation: *The quarreling children indulged in many recriminations, blaming each other for the argument. n.*

re cross (rē krôs′), cross again. *v.*

re cru des cent (rē′krü des′nt), breaking out anew. *adj.*

re cruit (ri krüt′), **1** a newly enlisted soldier, sailor, etc. **2** get (people) to join an army, navy, etc. **3** a new member of any group or class: *The Nature Club needs recruits.* **4** get by enrolling, hiring, etc.: *recruit new members, recruit volunteers.* 1,3 *n.,* 2,4 *v.* —**re cruit′er,** *n.* —**re cruit′a ble,** *adj.*

re cruit ment (ri krüt′mənt), act or business of recruiting. *n.*

rec. sec., recording secretary.

rect., **1** receipt. **2** rectangle.

rec tal (rek′təl), of the rectum. *adj.* —**rec′tal ly,** *adv.*

rectangle
three rectangles

rec tan gle (rek′tang′gəl), a four-sided plane figure with four right angles. *n.*

rec tan gu lar (rek tang′gyə lər), shaped like a rectangle. *adj.* —**rec tan′gu lar ly,** *adv.*

rec ti fy (rek′tə fī), **1** make right; put right; adjust; remedy: *The storekeeper admitted his mistake and was willing to rectify it.* **2** purify or refine: *rectify a liquor by distilling it several times. v.,* **rec ti fied, rec ti fy ing.** —**rec′ti fi′a ble,** *adj.*

rec ti tude (rek′tə tüd *or* rek′tə tyüd), upright conduct or character; honesty; righteousness. *n.*

rec tor (rek′tər), **1** clergyman in the Protestant Episcopal Church or the Church of England who has charge of a parish. **2** priest in the Roman Catholic Church who has charge of a congregation or religious house. **3** the head

of some schools, colleges, and universities. *n.*

rec to ry (rek′tər ē), a rector's house. *n., pl.* **rec tor ies.**

rec tum (rek′təm), the lowest part of the large intestine. *n., pl.* **rec tums, rec ta** (rek′tə).

re cum bent (ri kum′bənt), lying down; reclining; leaning. *adj.* —**re cum′bent ly,** *adv.*

recumbent
The lion assumed a **recumbent** posture.

re cu pe rate (ri kyü′pə rāt′ *or* ri kü′pə rāt′), **1** recover from sickness, exhaustion, loss, etc.: *It took us a few days to recuperate after the long trip.* **2** get back; regain: *She recuperated gradually everything she had lost. v.,* **re cu pe rat ed, re cu pe rat ing.** —**re cu′pe ra′tor,** *n.*

re cu pe ra tion (ri kyü′pə rā′shən *or* ri kü′pə rā′shən), recovery from sickness, exhaustion, loss, etc. *n.*

re cur (ri kėr′), **1** come up again; occur again; be repeated: *Leap year recurs every four years.* **2** return in thought or speech: *Old memories often recurred to her. He recurred to the matter of cost. v.,* **re curred, re cur ring.**

re cur rence (ri kėr′əns), occurrence again; repetition; return: *prevent the recurrence of a mistake. n.*

re cur rent (ri kėr′ənt), occurring again; repeated; recurring: *recurrent attacks of hay fever. adj.*

re curve (rē kėrv′), curve back; bend back. *v.,* **re curved, re curv ing.**

re cy cle (rē sī′kəl), to process or treat (something) in order that it may be used again. Paper, aluminum, and glass products are commonly recycled. *v.,* **re cy cled, re cy cling.**

red (red), **1** the color of blood or of a ruby. **2** having the color of blood or of a ruby: *red paint, a red light, red ink.* **3** being like or suggesting the color of blood: *red hair, a red fox.* **4** a red pigment or dye. **5** a red or reddish person, animal, or thing. **6 Red, a** a Communist or, sometimes, any extreme radical. Revolutionaries, socialists, and anarchists are often called Reds. **b** Communist or extremely radical. 1,4-6a *n.,* 2,3,6b *adj.* —**red′ly,** *adv.*

in the red, in debt; losing money.

see red, INFORMAL. become very angry.

red bird (red′bėrd′), any of several birds with red feathers, such as the cardinal and the scarlet tanager. *n.*

red blood cell, cell in the blood, formed in bone marrow and containing hemoglobin, that carries oxygen from the lungs to various parts of the body; red corpuscle.

red-blood ed (red′blud′id), full of life and spirit; vigorous. *adj.*

red breast (red′brest′), robin. *n.*

red cap (red′kap′), porter at a railroad or bus station whose uniform usually includes a red cap. *n.*

red cell, red blood cell.

red coat (red′kōt′), (in former times) a British soldier. *n.*

red corpuscle, red blood cell.

Red Cross, an international organization to care for the sick and wounded in war, and to relieve suffering caused by floods, fire, diseases, and other calamities. Its badge is a red cross on a white background.

red deer, 1 deer native to the forests of Europe and Asia, and formerly very abundant in England. **2** the common deer of America in its summer coat.

red den (red′n), **1** make or become red. **2** blush. *v.*

red dish (red′ish), somewhat red. *adj.* **—red′dish-ness,** *n.*

re dec o rate (rē dek′ə rāt′), decorate again or anew, especially by painting or papering a room, etc. *v.,* **re dec o rat ed, re dec o rat ing.**

re ded i cate (rē ded′ə kāt), dedicate anew. *v.,* **re ded i cat ed, re ded i cat ing. —re′ded i ca′tion,** *n.*

re deem (ri dēm′), **1** buy back: *The property on which money was lent was redeemed when the loan was paid back.* **2** pay off: *We redeemed the mortgage.* **3** make up for; balance: *A very good feature will sometimes redeem several bad ones.* **4** carry out; make good; fulfill: *We redeem a promise by doing what we said we would.* **5** set free; rescue; save; liberate; deliver; release: *redeemed from sin. v.*

re deem a ble (ri dē′mə bəl), **1** able to be redeemed. **2** that will be redeemed or paid: *bonds redeemable in 1978. adj.* **—re deem′a bly,** *adv.*

re deem er (ri dē′mər), **1** person who redeems. **2** Redeemer, Jesus. *n.*

re demp tion (ri demp′shən), **1** a buying back; paying off. **2** a ransom. **3** deliverance; rescue. **4** deliverance from sin; salvation. *n.*

red-hand ed (red′han′did), in the very act of crime, mischief, etc.: *be caught red-handed in a robbery. adj.* **—red′-hand′ed ly,** *adv.*

red head (red′hed′), person having red hair. *n.*

red head ed (red′hed′id), having red hair. *adj.*

red herring, something used to draw attention away from the real issue.

red-hot (red′hot′), **1** red with heat; very hot: *a red-hot iron.* **2** very enthusiastic; excited; violent: *a red-hot fanatic.* **3** fresh from the source: *red-hot rumors. adj.*

re di rect (rē′də rekt′ *or* rē′dī rekt′), direct again or anew. *v.* **—re′di rec′tion,** *n.*

re dis cov er (rē′dis kuv′ər), discover again or anew. *v.*

red-let ter (red′let′ər), memorable; especially happy: *Graduation is a red-letter day in one's life. adj.*

red line (red′līn′), to discriminate against by refusing to make, or by charging unreasonably high rates for, mortgage loans: *to redline a neighborhood. v.,* **red lined, red lin ing.**

red ness (red′nis), quality of being red; red color. *n.*

re do (rē dü′), do again; do over. *v.,* **re did** (rē did′), **re done** (rē dun′), **re do ing.**

red o lent (red′l ənt), **1** having a pleasant smell; fragrant. **2** smelling strongly; giving off an odor: *a house redolent of fresh paint.* **3** suggesting thoughts or feelings: *Rome is a city redolent of history. adj.* **—red′o lent ly,** *adv.*

re dou ble (rē dub′əl), **1** double again. **2** increase greatly; double: *The swimmer redoubled her speed as she neared the finish line.* **3** double back: *The fox redoubled on its trail to escape the hunters. v.,* **re dou bled, re dou bling.**

re doubt (ri dout′), a small fort standing alone. *n.*

re doubt a ble (ri dou′tə bəl), causing fear or dread: *a redoubtable warrior, a redoubtable debater. adj.* **—re doubt′a bly,** *adv.*

re dound (ri dound′), come back as a result; contribute: *The courage of the pioneers redounds to the glory of the nation. v.*

red pepper, 1 cayenne. **2** any of several varieties of pepper that have hollow, mild or hot fruits which are red when ripe.

re dress (ri dres′ *for 1;* rē′dres *or* ri dres′ *for 2*), **1** set right; repair; remedy: *King Arthur tried to redress wrongs in his kingdom.* **2** a setting right; reparation; relief: *Anyone who has been injured deserves redress.* 1 *v.,* 2 *n.*

Red Sea, narrow sea between the Arabian peninsula and Africa. It is part of the Indian Ocean and is connected with the Mediterranean Sea by the Suez Canal. See **Sudan** for map.

red skin (red′skin′), a North American Indian. The word *redskin* is often considered offensive. *n.*

red start (red′stärt′), **1** a fly-catching warbler of America. **2** a small European bird with a reddish tail. *n.*

red tape, too much attention to details and forms.

re duce (ri düs′ *or* ri dyüs′), **1** make less; make smaller; decrease: *We have reduced expenses this year. She is trying to reduce her weight.* **2** become less in weight: *His doctor advised him to reduce.* **3** bring down; lower: *The family's misfortunes reduced them to poverty. The major was reduced to the rank of captain.* **4** change to another form: *The chalk was reduced to powder. Reduce that statement to writing. If you reduce 3 lbs. 7 oz. to ounces, you have 55 ounces.* **5** bring to a certain state, form, or condition: *The teacher soon reduced the noisy class to order. I was reduced to tears by the cruel words.* **6** conquer; subdue: *The army reduced the fort by a sudden attack.* **7** remove oxygen from. *v.,* **re duced, re duc ing.**

re duc er (ri dü′sər *or* ri dyü′sər), person or thing that reduces. *n.*

re duc i ble (ri dü′sə bəl *or* ri dyü′sə bəl), able to be reduced: *⁴⁄₈ is reducible to ¹⁄₂. adj.* **—re duc′i bly,** *adv.*

re duc tion (ri duk′shən), **1** a reducing or a being reduced: *a reduction of ten pounds in weight. Failure to obey orders caused the corporal's reduction to the rank of private.* **2** amount by which a thing is reduced: *The reduction in cost was $5.* **3** form of something produced by reducing; copy of something on a smaller scale. *n.*

re dun dance (ri dun′dəns), redundancy. *n.*

That's the tenth successive, consecutive strikeout in a row, one right after another!

redundancy (def. 3)

re dun dan cy (ri dun′dən sē), **1** more than is needed. **2** a redundant thing, part, or amount. **3** the use of too many words for the same idea. *n., pl.* **re dun dan cies.**

re dun dant (ri dun′dənt), **1** not needed; extra: *a redundant word.* **2** using too many words for the same idea; wordy: *The use of "two" in the phrase "the two twins" is redundant. adj.* [*Redundant* is from Latin *redundantem,* meaning "overflowing," which comes from *re-,* meaning "back," and *unda,* meaning "a wave."]

re du pli cate (ri dü′plə kāt *or* ri dyü′plə kāt), to double; repeat. *v.,* **re du pli cat ed, re du pli cat ing.**

red wing (red′wing′), red-winged blackbird. *n.*

red-winged blackbird (red′wingd′), a North American blackbird. The male has a scarlet patch on each wing.

red wood (red′wu̇d′), **1** a very large evergreen sequoia tree of California and Oregon coastal regions. Redwoods are the tallest living trees, some reaching a height of over 300 feet (91 meters). **2** its brownish-red wood. *n.*

re ech o or **re-ech o** (rē ek′ō), to echo back: *The house reechoes children's laughter. The thunder reechoed far behind. v.*

reed (rēd), **1** a kind of tall grass with a hollow, jointed stalk that grows in wet places. **2** such a stalk. **3** anything made from the stalk of a reed, such as a pipe to blow on or an arrow. **4** a thin piece of wood, metal, or plastic in a musical instrument that produces sound when a current of air moves it. *n.*

reed instrument, a musical instrument that produces sound by means of a vibrating reed or reeds. Oboes, clarinets, and saxophones are reed instruments.

reed organ, a musical instrument producing tones by means of small metal reeds and played by keys.

reed y (rē′dē), **1** full of reeds: *a reedy pond.* **2** made of a reed or reeds. **3** like a reed or reeds: *reedy grass.* **4** sounding like a reed instrument: *a thin, reedy voice. adj.,* **reed i er, reed i est.** —**reed′i ly,** *adv.*

reef¹ (rēf), a narrow ridge of rocks, sand, or coral at or near the surface of the water: *The ship was wrecked on a hidden reef. n.*

reef² (rēf), **1** the part of a sail that can be rolled or folded up to reduce the area exposed to the wind. **2** reduce the area of (a sail) by rolling or folding up a part of it. **1** *n.,* **2** *v.*

reek (rēk), **1** a strong, unpleasant smell: *We noticed the reek of cooking cabbage as we entered the hall.* **2** send out a strong, unpleasant smell: *The beach reeks of dead fish.* **1** *n.,* **2** *v.* —**reek′ing ly,** *adv.*

reel¹ (rēl), **1** roller or spool for winding yarn, a fishline, rope, wire, etc. **2** something wound on a reel: *two reels of motion-picture film.* **3** to wind on a reel. **4** draw with a reel or by winding: *She reeled in a fish.* **1,2** *n.,* **3,4** *v.* —**reel′er,** *n.*

reel off, say, write, or make in a quick, easy way: *She can reel off stories by the hour.*

reel² (rēl), **1** sway, swing, or rock under a blow or shock: *She reeled when the ball struck her.* **2** sway in standing or walking: *The dazed boy reeled down the street.* **3** be in a whirl; be dizzy: *My head was reeling after the fast dance.* **4** a reeling or staggering movement. **5** become unsteady; waver: *The platoon reeled when the enemy attacked.* **1-3,5** *v.,* **4** *n.*

reel³ (rēl), **1** a lively dance. One kind is the Virginia reel. **2** music for it. *n.*

re e lect or **re-e lect** (rē′i lekt′), elect again. *v.*

re e lec tion or **re-e lec tion** (rē′i lek′shən), election again; election for a second time. *n.*

re en force (rē′en fôrs′), reinforce. *v.,* **re en forced, re en forc ing.** —**re′en forc′er,** *n.*

re-en force (rē′en fôrs′), reinforce. *v.,* **re-en forced, re-en forc ing.** —**re′-en forc′er,** *n.*

re en force ment or **re-en force ment** (rē′en fôrs′mənt), reinforcement. *n.*

re en list or **re-en list** (rē′en list′), enlist again or for an additional term. *v.*

re en list ment or **re-en list ment** (rē′en list′mənt), act or fact of reenlisting. *n.*

re en ter or **re-en ter** (rē en′tər), enter again; go in again: *reenter a room, reenter public life. v.*

a hat	**i** it	**oi** oil	**ch** child	a in about
ā age	**ī** ice	**ou** out	**ng** long	e in taken
ä far	**o** hot	**u** cup	**sh** she	ə = i in pencil
e let	**ō** open	**u̇** put	**th** thin	o in lemon
ē equal	**ô** order	**ü** rule	**ᵀH** then	u in circus
ėr term			**zh** measure	

re en try (rē en′trē), an entering again or returning, especially of a rocket or spacecraft into the earth's atmosphere after flight into outer space. *n., pl.* **re en tries.**

re-en try (rē en′trē), reentry. *n., pl.* **re-en tries.**

re es tab lish or **re-es tab lish** (rē′ə stab′lish), establish again; restore. *v.*

re es tab lish ment or **re-es tab lish ment** (rē′ə-stab′lish mənt), an establishing; restoration. *n.*

re ex am i na tion or **re-ex am i na tion** (rē′eg-zam′ə nā′shən), a second or renewed examination. *n.*

re ex am ine (rē′eg zam′ən), examine again. *v.,* **re ex am ined, re ex am in ing.** —**re′ex am′in er,** *n.*

re-ex am ine (rē′eg zam′ən), reexamine. *v.,* **re-ex am ined, re-ex am in ing.** —**re′-ex am′in er,** *n.*

ref (ref), INFORMAL. referee. *n.*

ref., **1** referee. **2** reference. **3** referred.

re fec tor y (ri fek′tər ē), a room for meals, especially in a monastery, convent, or school. *n., pl.* **re fec tor ies.**

re fer (ri fėr′), **1** send or direct for information, help, or action: *Our teacher refers us to many good books.* **2** hand over; submit: *Let's refer the dispute to the umpire.* **3** turn for information or help: *A person refers to a dictionary to find the meaning of words.* **4** direct attention to or speak about: *The speaker referred to the Bible.* **5** assign to or think of as caused by: *They referred their failure to bad luck.* **6** relate; apply: *The rule refers only to special cases. v.,* **re ferred, re fer ring.** —**re fer′rer,** *n.*

ref e ree (ref′ə rē′), **1** a judge of play in certain games and sports: *a football referee.* **2** person to whom something is referred for decision or settlement. **3** act as referee; act as referee in. **1,2** *n.,* **3** *v.,* **ref e reed, ref e ree ing.**

ref er ence (ref′ər əns), **1** a referring or a being referred. **2** direction of the attention: *The report contained many references to newspaper articles.* **3** statement referred to: *You will find that reference on page 16.* **4** used for information or help: *A dictionary is a reference book.* **5** person who can give information about another person's character or ability: *He gave his principal as a reference.* **6** statement about someone's character or ability: *When she left the company, she received an excellent reference from her boss.* **7** relation; respect; regard: *This test is to be taken by all pupils without reference to age or grade.* **1-3,5-7** *n.,* **4** *adj.*

in reference to or **with reference to,** about; concerning.

make reference to, mention: *Don't make any reference to the bad news.*

ref e ren dum (ref′ə ren′dəm), **1** process of submitting a bill already passed by the lawmaking body to the direct vote of the citizens for approval or rejection. **2** the submitting of any matter to a direct vote. *n., pl.* **ref e ren dums, ref e ren da** (ref′ə ren′də).

re fer ral (ri fėr′əl), **1** a referring. **2** person who is referred. *n.*

re fill (rē fil′ *for 1;* rē′fil′ *for 2*), **1** fill again. **2** something to refill with: *a refill for a pen.* **1** *v.,* **2** *n.*

re fine (ri fīn′), **1** make or become pure: *Sugar, oil, and metals are refined before being used.* **2** make or become fine, polished, or cultivated: *refine one's way of speaking.* **3** make very fine, subtle, or exact. *v.,* **re fined, re fin ing.**

refine on or **refine upon,** **1** improve. **2** excel.

re fined (ri fīnd/), **1** freed from impurities; made pure: *refined sugar.* **2** free from coarseness, crudeness, or vulgarity; well-bred: *refined tastes, a refined voice, refined manners. adj.*

re fine ment (ri fīn/mənt), **1** fineness of feeling, taste, manners, or language: *Good manners and correct speech are marks of refinement.* **2** act or result of refining: *Gasoline is produced by the refinement of petroleum.* **3** improvement. *n.*

re fin er (ri fī/nər), person or thing that refines. *n.*

re fin er y (ri fī/nər ē), a building and machinery for purifying petroleum, sugar, or other things. *n., pl.* **re fin er ies.**

re fin ish (rē fin/ish), give (wood, metal, etc.) a new finish. *v.* —**re fin/ish er,** *n.*

re fit (rē fit/), fit, prepare, or equip for use again: *The old ship was refitted for the voyage. v.,* **re fit ted, re fit ting.**

refl., **1** reflex. **2** reflexive.

re flect (ri flekt/), **1** turn back or throw back (light, heat, sound, etc.): *The sidewalks reflect heat on a hot day.* **2** give back a likeness or image of: *The sky was reflected in the still pond.* **3** reproduce or show like a mirror: *The newspaper reflected the owner's opinions.* **4** think carefully: *Take time to reflect before making a decision.* **5** cast blame, reproach, or discredit: *The children's spoiled behavior reflected on their parents.* **6** serve to cast or bring: *A kind act reflects credit on the person who does it. v.* —**re flect/ing ly,** *adv.*

re flec tion (ri flek/shən), **1** a reflecting or a being reflected. **2** something reflected. **3** likeness; image: *You can see your reflection in a mirror.* **4** careful thinking: *On reflection, the plan seemed too dangerous.* **5** idea or remark resulting from careful thinking. **6** remark or action that casts blame or discredit. **7** blame; discredit. *n.* —**re flec/tion less,** *adj.*

re flec tive (ri flek/tiv), **1** able to reflect; reflecting: *the reflective surface of polished metal.* **2** thoughtful: *The judge had a reflective look. adj.* —**re flec/tive ly,** *adv.* —**re flec/tive ness,** *n.*

re flec tor (ri flek/tər), **1** any thing, surface, or device that reflects light, heat, sound, etc., especially a piece of glass or metal, usually concave, for reflecting light in a required direction. **2** a telescope with a concave mirror which reflects and focuses light. *n.*

re flex (rē/fleks), **1** an involuntary action in direct response to a stimulation of some nerve cells. Sneezing, vomiting, and shivering are reflexes. **2** not voluntary; not controlled by the will; coming as a direct response to a stimulation of some sensory nerve cells. Yawning is a reflex action. **1** *n., pl.* **re flex es; 2** *adj.* —**re/flex ly,** *adv.*

re flex ive (ri flek/siv), **1** (in grammar) expressing an action that refers back to the subject. **2** a reflexive verb or pronoun. In "I hurt myself," *hurt* and *myself* are reflexives. **1** *adj.,* **2** *n.* —**re flex/ive ly,** *adv.* —**re flex/ive ness,** *n.*

re flux (rē/fluks), a flowing back; ebb of a tide. *n.*

re fo rest (rē fôr/ist), replant with trees. *v.*

re fo rest a tion (rē/fôr ə stā/shən), a replanting or a being replanted with trees. *n.*

re form (ri fôrm/), **1** make better; improve by removing faults: *Some prisons try to reform criminals instead of just punishing them.* **2** become better: *They promised to reform if given another chance.* **3** a change intended to improve conditions; improvement: *The new government made many reforms.* **1,2** *v.,* **3** *n.* —**re form/a ble,** *adj.*

re-form (rē fôrm/), **1** form again. **2** take a new shape. *v.*

ref or ma tion (ref/ər mā/shən), **1** a reforming or a being reformed; change for the better; improvement. **2 Reformation,** the religious movement in Europe in the 1500's that aimed at reform within the Roman Catholic Church but led to the establishment of Protestant churches. *n.*

re form a to ry (ri fôr/mə tôr/ē), **1** an institution for reforming young offenders against the laws; prison for young criminals. **2** serving to reform; intended to reform. **1** *n., pl.* **re form a to ries; 2** *adj.*

re form er (ri fôr/mər), person who reforms, or tries to reform, some state of affairs, custom, etc.; supporter of reforms. *n.*

reflect (def. 3)
Her face **reflected** pride in her achievements.

re form ist (ri fôr/mist), a reformer. *n.*

reform school, reformatory.

re fract (ri frakt/), bend (a ray, waves, etc.) from a straight course. Water refracts light. *v.* —**re fract/a ble,** *adj.* —**re fract/ed ly,** *adv.*

refract
Because water refracts light, the ruler appears bent.

re frac tion (ri frak/shən), the turning or bending of a ray of light, sound waves, a stream of electrons, etc., when passing from one medium into another of different density. *n.*

re frac tive (ri frak/tiv), refracting; having power to refract. *adj.*

re frac tor i ly (ri frak/tər ə lē), stubbornly; obstinately. *adv.*

re frac tor i ness (ri frak/tər ē nis), refractory quality or condition. *n.*

re frac tor y (ri frak/tər ē), **1** hard to manage; stubborn; obstinate: *Mules are refractory.* **2** not yielding readily to treatment: *She had a refractory cough.* **3** hard to melt, reduce, or work: *refractory ores. adj.* —**re frac/tor i ly,** *adv.* —**re frac/tor i ness,** *n.*

re frain¹ (ri frān/), hold oneself back: *Refrain from wrongdoing. v.* [*Refrain¹* came into English about 600 years ago from French *refrener,* which came from Latin *refrenare,* meaning "refrain, furnish with a bridle."] —**re frain/ment,** *n.*

re frain² (ri frān/), phrase or verse repeated regularly in a song or poem. In "The Star-Spangled Banner" the refrain is "O'er the land of the free and the home of the brave." *n.* [*Refrain*[2] came into English about 600 years ago from French *refrain*, which can be traced back to *re-*, meaning "back," and *frangere*, meaning "to break."]

re fresh (ri fresh′), make fresh again; freshen up; renew: *His bath refreshed him. She refreshed her memory by a glance at the book. v.*

re fresh er (ri fresh′ər), helping to renew knowledge or abilities, or to bring a person new needed knowledge: *take a refresher course in French. adj.*

re fresh ing (ri fresh′ing), 1 able to refresh: *Cool drinks are refreshing on a warm day.* 2 welcome as a pleasing change. *adj.* —**re fresh′ing ly,** *adv.*

re fresh ment (ri fresh′mənt), 1 a refreshing or a being refreshed. 2 thing that refreshes. 3 **refreshments,** *pl.* food or drink: *Cake and lemonade were the refreshments at our party. n.*

re fried beans (rē′frīd′), frijoles that have been cooked until soft, fried, then fried again after being mashed.

re frig er ant (ri frij′ər ənt), something that cools. Ice is a refrigerant. *n.*

re frig e rate (ri frij′ə rāt′), make or keep (food, etc.) cold or cool: *Milk, meat, and ice cream must be refrigerated to prevent spoiling. v.,* **re frig e rat ed, re frig e rat ing.**

re frig e ra tion (ri frij′ə rā′shən), act or process of cooling or keeping cold. *n.*

re frig e ra tor (ri frij′ə rā′tər), box, room, etc., that keeps foods and other items cool, usually by mechanical means. *n.*

re fu el (rē fyü′əl), 1 supply with fuel again. 2 take on a fresh supply of fuel. *v.,* **re fu eled, re fu el ing** or **re fu elled, re fu el ling.**

ref uge (ref′yüj), shelter or protection from danger or trouble; safety: *The cat took refuge in a tree. n.*

ref u gee (ref′yə jē′ or ref′yə jē′), person who flees for refuge or safety, especially to a foreign country, in time of persecution, war, or disaster: *The homeless refugees from the flooded town were helped by the Red Cross. Many refugees came from Europe to America. n.*

re ful gent (ri ful′jənt), shining brightly; radiant; splendid: *a refulgent sunrise. adj.* —**re ful′gent ly,** *adv.*

re fund (ri fund′ *for 1;* rē′fund *for 2,3*), 1 pay back: *If these shoes do not wear well, the shop will refund your money.* 2 a return of money paid. 3 the money paid back. 1 *v.,* 2,3 *n.* [*Refund* is from Latin *refundere,* meaning "to pour back, give back," which comes from *re-,* meaning "back," and *fundere,* meaning "to pour."] —**re fund′a ble,** *adj.* —**re fund′er,** *n.*

re fur bish (rē fér′bish), polish up again; do up anew; brighten; renovate: *refurbish an old house. v.* —**re fur′-bish ment,** *n.*

re fus al (ri fyü′zəl), 1 act of refusing: *a refusal to lend money.* 2 the right to refuse or take a thing before it is offered to others: *Please give me first refusal if you decide to sell your car. n.*

re fuse[1] (ri fyüz′), 1 say no to; decline to accept; reject: *He refuses the offer. They refused to go with me, so I went by myself.* 2 say no: *She is free to refuse.* 3 say one will not do it, give it, etc.: *refuse to obey. v.,* **re fused, re fus ing.** —**re fus′a ble,** *adj.* —**re fus′er,** *n.*

ref use[2] (ref′yüs), useless stuff; waste; rubbish: *The street-cleaning department took away all refuse from the streets. n.*

ref u ta tion (ref′yə tā′shən), disproof of a claim, opinion, or argument. *n.*

re fute (ri fyüt′), show (a claim, opinion, or argument) to be false or incorrect; prove wrong; disprove: *He refuted the rumors with facts. v.,* **re fut ed, re fut ing.** —**re fut′-er,** *n.*

re gain (ri gān′), 1 get again; recover: *regain health.* 2 get back to; reach again: *You can regain the main road by turning left two miles ahead. v.* —**re gain′a ble,** *adj.*

re gal (rē′gəl), 1 belonging to a king or queen; royal: *regal power.* 2 fit for a king or queen; stately; splendid; magnificent: *a regal banquet. adj.* —**re′gal ly,** *adv.*

re gale (ri gāl′), 1 entertain agreeably; delight with something pleasing: *Grandmother regaled us with stories about her childhood.* 2 entertain with a choice meal; feast. *v.,* **re galed, re gal ing.** —**re gale′ment,** *n.*

re ga li a (ri gā′lē ə), 1 the emblems of royalty. Crowns and scepters are regalia. 2 the emblems or decorations of any society or order. 3 clothes, especially fine clothes: *in party regalia. n.pl.*

re gard (ri gärd′), 1 think of; consider: *Our school band is regarded as the best in the state.* 2 show thought or consideration for; care for; respect: *regard the rights of others.* 3 take notice of; heed: *regard all traffic laws.* 4 consideration; thought; care: *Have regard for the feelings of others.* 5 look at; look closely at; watch: *The cat regarded me anxiously when I picked up her kittens.* 6 a steady look; gaze: *The shoplifter soon found himself the object of the store owner's stern regard.* 7 esteem; favor; good opinion: *He has high regard for your ability.* 8 **re-gards,** *pl.* good wishes; an expression of esteem: *She sends her regards.* 9 point; particular matter: *You are wrong in this regard.* 1-3,5 *v.,* 4,6-9 *n.* —**re gard′a ble,** *adj.*

as regards, with respect to; concerning: *As regards money, I have enough.*

in regard to or **with regard to,** relating to; concerning; about; regarding: *The teacher spoke to me in regard to being late.*

without regard to, not considering.

re gard ful (ri gärd′fəl), heedful or observant; mindful. *adj.* —**re gard′ful ly,** *adv.* —**re gard′ful ness,** *n.*

re gard ing (ri gär′ding), with regard to; concerning; about: *A letter regarding the field trip was sent to parents. prep.*

re gard less (ri gärd′lis), 1 with no heed; careless: *Regardless of the danger, they crossed the thin ice.* 2 in spite of what happens: *We plan to leave on Monday, and we will leave then, regardless.* 1 *adj.,* 2 *adv.* —**re gard′less ly,** *adv.* —**re gard′less ness,** *n.*

re gat ta (ri gat′ə), a boat race or a series of boat races. *n., pl.* **re gat tas.**

re gen cy (rē′jən sē), 1 the position, office, or function of a regent or group of regents: *The Queen Mother held the regency till the young king became of age.* 2 a body of regents. 3 a government consisting of regents. 4 the time during which there is a regency. *n., pl.* **re gen cies.**

re gen e rate (ri jen′ə rāt′ *for 1,2,4;* ri jen′ər it *for 3*), 1 give a new and better spiritual life to; improve the moral condition of. 2 put new life and spirit into. 3 born again spiritually; formed anew morally. 4 grow again; form (new tissue, a new part, etc.) to replace what is lost: *If a young crab loses a claw, it will often regenerate a new one.* 1,2,4 *v.,* **re gen e rat ed, re gen e rat ing;** 3 *adj.* —**re gen′e ra′tor,** *n.*

re gen e ra tion (ri jen′ə rā′shən), a regenerating or a being regenerated. *n.*

re gen e ra tive (ri jen′ə rā′tiv), tending to regenerate; regenerating. *adj.*

re gent (rē′jənt), **1** person who rules when the regular ruler is absent, disabled, or too young: *The Queen will be the regent till her son grows up.* **2** member of a governing board. Many universities have boards of regents. *n.* [*Regent* is from Latin *regentem,* meaning "ruling," which comes from *regere,* meaning "to rule." See **Word Family.**]

regent

Below are words related to *regent.* They can all be traced back to the Latin word *regere* (re′ge re), meaning "to rule."

correct	erect	regiment
direct	irregular	region
directive	rectify	regular
director	rector	regulate
directory	redress	regulatory
dress	regime	rule

re gime or **ré gime** (ri zhēm′ *or* rā zhēm′), **1** system of government or rule: *the Communist regime in China.* **2** regimen. *n.*

reg i men (rej′ə men), a set of rules or habits of diet, exercise, or manner of living, intended to improve health, reduce weight, etc.: *The baby's regimen includes two naps a day. n.*

reg i ment (rej′ə mənt *for 1;* rej′ə ment *for 2*), **1** a military unit made up of several battalions or squadrons, usually commanded by a colonel. It is smaller than a brigade. **2** treat in a strict or uniform manner: *A dictatorship regiments its citizens.* 1 *n.,* 2 *v.*

reg i men tal (rej′ə men′tl), **1** of a regiment. **2** regimentals, *pl.* a military uniform. 1 *adj.,* 2 *n.* —**reg′i men′tal ly,** *adv.*

reg i men ta tion (rej′ə men tā′shən), **1** formation into organized or uniform groups. **2** a making uniform. **3** subjection to control. *n.*

Re gi na (ri jī′nə), city in S Canada, capital of the province of Saskatchewan. *n.*

re gion (rē′jən), **1** a large part of the earth's surface: *the region of the equator.* **2** any place, space, or area: *a mountainous region.* **3** a part of the body: *the region of the heart.* **4** a field of thought or action; sphere: *the region of the imagination. n.*

re gion al (rē′jə nəl), of or in a particular region: *a regional storm. adj.* —**re′gion al ly,** *adv.*

reg is ter (rej′ə stər), **1** write in a list or record: *Register the names of the new members.* **2** have one's name written in a list or record: *Citizens must register before they can vote.* **3** a list or record: *a register of class attendance.* **4** book in which a list or record is kept: *a hotel register.* **5** have (a letter, parcel, etc.) recorded in a post office, paying extra postage for special care in delivery: *She registered the letter containing the check.* **6** thing that records. A cash register shows the amount of money taken in. **7** indicate; record: *The thermometer registers 90 degrees.* **8** show (surprise, joy, anger, etc.) by the expression on one's face or by actions. **9** the range of a voice or an instrument. **10** an opening in a wall or floor with a device to regulate the amount of heated or cooled air that passes through. 1,2,5,7,8 *v.,* 3,4,6,9,10 *n.*

registered nurse, a graduate nurse licensed by state authority to practice nursing.

reg is trant (rej′ə strənt), person who registers. *n.*

reg is trar (rej′ə strär), official who keeps a register; official recorder. *n.*

reg is tra tion (rej′ə strā′shən), **1** act of registering. **2** an entry in a register. **3** number of people registered: *Registration for camp is higher than last year.* **4** a legal document showing proof that some person or thing has been registered: *an automobile registration. n.*

reg is try (rej′ə strē), **1** a registering; registration. **2** place where a register is kept; office of registration. **3** book in which a list or record is kept; register. *n., pl.* **reg is tries.**

re gress (ri gres′), go back; move in a backward direction. *v.*

re gres sion (ri gresh′ən), act of going back; backward movement. *n.*

re gres sive (ri gres′iv), showing regression. *adj.* —**re gres′sive ly,** *adv.* —**re gres′sive ness,** *n.*

re gret (ri gret′), **1** feel sorry for or about: *We regretted his absence.* **2** feel sorry; mourn: *He wrote regretting that he could not visit us.* **3** the feeling of being sorry; sense of loss; sorrow: *With regret she remembered her forgotten promise.* **4** regrets, *pl.* a polite reply declining an invitation: *She could not come to the party, but she sent regrets.* 1,2 *v.,* **re gret ted, re gret ting;** 3,4 *n.* —**re gret′ter,** *n.*

re gret ful (ri gret′fəl), feeling or expressing regret; sorrowful; sorry. *adj.* —**re gret′ful ly,** *adv.* —**re gret′ful ness,** *n.*

re gret ta ble (ri gret′ə bəl), deserving or giving cause for regret. *adj.*

re gret ta bly (ri gret′ə blē), with regret; regretfully. *adv.*

reg u lar (reg′yə lər), **1** fixed by custom or rule; usual; normal: *Six o'clock was her regular hour of rising.* **2** following some rule or principle; according to rule: *A period is the regular ending for a sentence.* **3** coming, acting, or done again and again at the same time: *I make regular visits to the dentist.* **4** steady; habitual: *A regular customer trades often at the same store.* **5** even in size, spacing, or speed; well-balanced: *regular features, regular teeth, regular breathing.* **6** symmetrical. **7** orderly; methodical: *He leads a regular life.* **8** properly fitted or trained: *The regular cook in our school cafeteria is sick.* **9** (of a word) having the usual endings; inflected in the usual way. "Ask" is a regular verb. **10** INFORMAL. thorough; complete: *a regular bore.* **11** INFORMAL. fine; agreeable: *He's a regular fellow.* **12** member of a regularly paid group of any kind: *The fire department was made up of regulars and volunteers.* **13** of or belonging to the permanent army of a country. 1-11,13 *adj.,* 12 *n.*

reg u lar i ty (reg′yə lar′ə tē), a being regular; order; system; steadiness. *n.*

reg u lar ize (reg′yə lə rīz′), make regular. *v.,* **reg u lar ized, reg u lar iz ing.** —**reg′u lar i za′tion,** *n.*

reg u lar ly (reg′yə lər lē), **1** in a regular manner. **2** at regular times. *adv.*

reg u late (reg′yə lāt), **1** control by rule, principle, or system: *The government regulates the coining of money.* **2** put in condition to work properly: *My watch is losing time; I will have to have it regulated.* **3** keep at some standard: *This instrument regulates the temperature of the room. v.,* **reg u lat ed, reg u lat ing.**

reg u la tion (reg′yə lā′shən), **1** control by rule, principle, or system. **2** rule; law: *traffic regulations.* **3** required by some rule; standard: *Soldiers wear a regulation uniform.* **4** usual; ordinary. 1,2 *n.,* 3,4 *adj.*

reg u la tive (reg′yə lā′tiv), regulating. *adj.* —**reg′u la′tive ly,** *adv.*

reg u la tor (reg′yə lā′tər), **1** person or thing that regulates. **2** device in a clock or watch for causing it to go faster or slower. *n.*

reg u la to ry (reg′yə lə tôr′ē), regulating. *adj.*

re gur gi tate (rē gėr′jə tāt), **1** (of liquids, gases, undigested foods, etc.) rush, surge, or flow back. **2** throw up; vomit: *regurgitate food from the stomach. v.,* **re gur gi tat ed, re gur gi tat ing.**

re gur gi ta tion (rē gėr′jə tā′shən), act of regurgitating. *n.*

re ha bil i tate (rē′hə bil′ə tāt), **1** restore to a good condition; make over in a new form: *The old neighborhood is to be rehabilitated.* **2** restore to former standing, rank, rights, privileges, reputation, etc.: *The former criminal was rehabilitated and became a respected citizen. v.,* **re ha bil i tat ed, re ha bil i tat ing.**

re ha bil i ta tion (rē′hə bil′ə tā′shən), restoration to a good condition or to a former standing. *n.*

re hash (rē hash′ *for 1;* rē′hash *for 2*), **1** deal with again; work up (old material) in a new or different form: *The question has been rehashed again and again.* **2** a rehashing; a putting something old into a new or different form: *That play is simply a rehash of an old movie.* 1 *v.,* 2 *n.*

re hears al (ri hėr′səl), a rehearsing; performance beforehand for practice or drill. *n.*

re hearse (ri hėrs′), **1** practice (a play, part, etc.) for a public performance: *We rehearsed our parts for the school play.* **2** drill or train (a person, etc.) by repetition. *v.,* **re hearsed, re hears ing.** [*Rehearse* came into English about 700 years ago from French *rehercier,* meaning "rake over."] —**re hears′er,** *n.*

Rehn quist (ren′kwist), **William,** born 1924, chief justice of the United States Supreme Court since 1986. *n.*

Reich (rīk), Germany as a state; the German nation. *n.*

reign (rān), **1** period of power of a ruler: *Queen Victoria's reign lasted sixty-four years.* **2** to rule: *A king reigns over his kingdom.* **3** act of ruling; royal power; rule: *The reign of a wise ruler benefits a country.* **4** exist everywhere; prevail: *On a still night silence reigns.* **5** existence everywhere; prevalence: *the reign of technology in this century.* 1,3,5 *n.,* 2,4 *v.*

re im burse (rē′im bėrs′), pay back; repay. You reimburse a person for expenses made for you. *v.,* **re im bursed, re im burs ing.** [*Reimburse* can be traced back to Latin *re-,* meaning "back," *in-,* meaning "into," and *bursa,* meaning "purse."] —**re′im burs′a ble,** *adj.*

re im burse ment (rē′im bėrs′mənt), a paying back; repayment (for expenses, loss, etc.). *n.*

Reims (rēmz), city in NE France. Nearly all the French kings were crowned in its cathedral. *n.* Also, **Rheims.**

rein (rān), **1** a long, narrow strap or line fastened to the bit of a bridle, by which to guide and control an animal. **2** check or pull with reins. **3** a means of control and direction: *seize the reins of government.* **4** guide and control: *Rein your tongue.* 1,3 *n.,* 2,4 *v.*

draw rein, 1 tighten the reins. **2** slow down; stop.

give rein to, let move or act freely, without guidance or control: *give rein to one's feelings.*

take the reins, assume control: *When the President was ill, the Vice-President took the reins of government.*

re in car nate (rē′in kär′nāt), give a new body to (a soul). *v.,* **re in car nat ed, re in car nat ing.**

re in car na tion (rē′in kär nā′shən), rebirth of the soul in a new body. *n.*

rein deer (rān′dir′), a kind of large deer with branching antlers that lives in northern regions. It is used to pull sleighs and also for meat, milk, and hides. *n., pl.* **reindeer.** [*Reindeer* came into English about 600 years ago from Icelandic *hreindyri.*]

re in force (rē′in fôrs′), **1** strengthen with new force or materials: *reinforce an army, reinforce a bridge.* **2** strengthen: *reinforce an argument, reinforce a plea, reinforce a supply. v.,* **re in forced, re in forc ing.** Also, **reenforce** or **re-enforce.** —**re′in forc′er,** *n.*

re in force ment (rē′in fôrs′mənt), **1** a reinforcing or a being reinforced. **2** something that reinforces. **3** **reinforcements,** *pl.* extra soldiers, warships, planes, etc.: *Reinforcements were sent to the battlefront. n.* Also, **reenforcement** or **re-enforcement.**

re in state (rē′in stāt′), put back in a former position or condition; establish again. *v.,* **re in stat ed, re in stat ing.**

re in state ment (rē′in stāt′mənt), a putting back in a former position or condition; establishing again. *n.*

re in ter pret (rē′in tėr′prit), interpret anew. *v.*

re it e rate (rē it′ə rāt′), say or do several times; repeat again and again: *The teacher reiterated his request for order. v.,* **re it e rat ed, re it e rat ing.**

re it e ra tion (rē it′ə rā′shən), a reiterating; repetition. *n.*

re ject (ri jekt′ *for 1,2;* rē′jekt *for 3*), **1** refuse to take: *She rejected our help. He tried to join the army but was rejected because of poor health.* **2** throw away as useless or unsatisfactory: *Reject all apples with soft spots.* **3** a rejected person or thing. 1,2 *v.,* 3 *n.* —**re ject′er,** *n.*

re jec tion (ri jek′shən), **1** a rejecting or a being rejected: *The inspector ordered the rejection of the faulty parts.* **2** thing rejected: *All rejections by the inspector were destroyed at once. n.*

re joice (ri jois′), be glad; be filled with joy: *She rejoiced at our success. v.,* **re joiced, re joic ing.** —**re joic′er,** *n.*

re joic ing (ri joi′sing), the feeling or expression of joy. *n.*

re join¹ (rē join′), **1** join again; unite again: *rejoin a broken plate.* **2** join the company of again: *I will rejoin my family in April. v.*

re join² (ri join′), answer; reply: *"Come with me!" "Not on your life," he rejoined. v.*

re join der (ri join′dər), an answer to a reply; response: *a debater's rejoinder. n.*

re ju ve nate (ri jü′və nāt), make young or vigorous again; give youthful qualities to: *The long vacation rejuvenated her. v.,* **re ju ve nat ed, re ju ve nat ing.**

re ju ve na tion (ri jü′və nā′shən), restoration to youth, youthful appearance, vigor, etc. *n.*

re kin dle (rē kin′dl), set on fire again; kindle anew. *v.,* **re kin dled, re kin dling.**

rel., 1 relating. **2** relative.

re-laid (rē lād′), past tense and past participle of **re-lay.** *The pavement on our street has just been re-laid. v.*

re lapse (ri laps′), **1** fall or slip back into a former state or way of acting: *After one cry of surprise she relapsed into silence.* **2** a falling or slipping back into a former state or way of acting: *He seemed to be getting over his illness but*

reindeer
about 4 ft. (1.2 m.)
high at the shoulder

had a relapse. **1** *v.,* **re lapsed, re laps ing; 2** *n.* **—re-laps′er,** *n.*

re late (ri lāt′), **1** give an account of; tell: *The traveler related her adventures.* **2** connect in thought or meaning: *"Better" and "best" are related to "good."* **3** be connected in any way: *We are interested in what relates to ourselves.* *v.,* **re lat ed, re lat ing.** [*Relate* is from Latin *relatum,* meaning "brought back, related," which comes from *re-,* meaning "back," and *latum,* meaning "brought."] **—re-lat′er,** *n.*

re lat ed (ri lā′tid), **1** connected in any way. **2** belonging to the same family; connected by a common origin: *Cousins are related. adj.* **—re lat′ed ness,** *n.*

re la tion (ri lā′shən), **1** connection in thought or meaning: *Your answer has no relation to the question.* **2** connection by family ties of blood or marriage; relationship: *What relation are you to her?* **3** person who belongs to the same family as another; relative. **4 relations,** *pl.* dealings between persons, groups, countries, etc.: *international relations. Our firm has business relations with their firm.* **5** act of telling; account: *We enjoyed the relation of the traveler's adventures. n.*

in relation to or **with relation to,** in reference to; in regard to; about; concerning: *We must plan in relation to the future.*

re la tion ship (ri lā′shən ship), **1** connection: *What is the relationship of clouds to rain?* **2** condition of belonging to the same family. *n.*

rel a tive (rel′ə tiv), **1** person who belongs to the same family as another, such as father, brother, aunt, nephew, or cousin. **2** related or compared to each other: *We discussed the relative characteristics of snakes and lizards.* **3** depending for meaning on a relation to something else: *East is a relative term; for example, Chicago is east of California but west of New York.* **4** referring to a person or thing mentioned. In *"The man who wanted it is gone," who* is a relative pronoun, and *who wanted it* is a relative clause. **5** a relative pronoun. *Who, which, what,* and *that* are relatives. **1,5** *n.,* **2-4** *adj.* **—rel′a tive ness,** *n.*

relative to, 1 about; concerning: *They asked me some questions relative to my plans for the summer.* **2** in proportion to; in comparison with; for: *She is strong relative to her size.*

relative humidity, the ratio between the amount of water vapor present in the air and the greatest amount the air could contain at the same temperature.

rel a tive ly (rel′ə tiv lē), in relation to something else; comparatively: *You are relatively tall for your age. adv.*

rel a tiv i ty (rel′ə tiv′ə tē), **1** a being relative. **2** theory dealing with the physical laws which govern matter, space, time, and motion, expressed in certain equations by Albert Einstein. According to it, mass and energy are interchangeable. *n.*

re lax (ri laks′), **1** loosen up; make or become less stiff or firm: *Relax when you dance.* **2** make or become less strict or severe; lessen in force: *Discipline is relaxed on the last day of school.* **3** relieve or be relieved from work or effort; give or take recreation or amusement: *Take a vacation and relax.* **4** weaken: *Don't relax your efforts because the tests are over. v.* [*Relax* is from Latin *relaxare,* which comes from *re-,* meaning "back," and *laxus,* meaning "loose."] **—re lax′er,** *n.*

re lax a tion (rē′lak sā′shən), **1** a loosening: *the relaxation of the muscles.* **2** a lessening of strictness, severity, force, etc.: *the relaxation of discipline over the holidays.* **3** relief from work or effort; recreation; amusement: *Walking and reading are relaxations.* **4** condition of being relaxed. *n.*

re lay (rē′lā *for 1,3-5;* rē′lā *or* ri lā′ *for 2*), **1** a fresh supply: *New relays of men were sent to the battlefront.*

2 take and carry farther: *relay a message.* **3** a relay race. **4** one part of a relay race. **5** an electromagnetic device with a weak current which acts as a switch for a circuit with a stronger current. Relays are used in equipment for transmitting telegraph and telephone messages. **1,3-5** *n.,* **2** *v.*

re-lay (rē lā′), lay again: *That floor must be re-laid. v.,* **re-laid, re-lay ing.**

relay race—The runner on the left is finishing his part of the race. While still running, he hands a thin, metal rod to his teammate on the right.

re lay race (rē′lā), race in which each member of a team runs, swims, etc., only a certain part of the distance.

re lease (ri lēs′), **1** let go: *Release the catch and the box will open.* **2** let loose; set free: *She released him from his promise.* **3** relieve: *I will be released from duty at seven o'clock.* **4** a letting go; setting free: *The end of the war brought the release of the prisoners.* **5** freedom; relief: *This medicine will give you release from pain.* **6** part of a machine that sets other parts free to move. **7** the legal surrender of a right, estate, etc., to another. **8** give up (legal right, claim, etc.). **9** document that does this. **10** permit to be published, shown, sold, etc. **11** permission for publication, exhibition, sale, etc. **12** article, statement, etc., distributed for publication. **1-3,8,10** *v.,* **re leased, re leas ing; 4-7,9,11,12** *n.*

rel e gate (rel′ə gāt), **1** put away, usually to a lower position or condition: *She relegated the broken chair to the basement.* **2** hand over (a matter, task, etc.). *v.,* **rel e gat ed, rel e gat ing.** **—rel′e ga′tion,** *n.*

re lent (ri lent′), become less harsh; be more tender and merciful: *After I pleaded for hours, my parents relented and let me go on the trip. v.*

re lent less (ri lent′lis), without pity; not relenting; unyielding; harsh: *The storm raged with relentless fury. adj.* **—re lent′less ly,** *adv.* **—re lent′less ness,** *n.*

rel e vance (rel′ə vəns), a being relevant. *n.*

rel e van cy (rel′ə vən sē), relevance. *n.*

rel e vant (rel′ə vənt), bearing upon or connected with the matter in hand; to the point: *relevant questions. adj.* **—rel′e vant ly,** *adv.*

re li a bil i ty (ri lī′ə bil′ə tē), quality of being reliable; trustworthiness; dependability: *We bought our washing machine from that store because it has a reputation for reliability. n.*

re li a ble (ri lī′ə bəl), worthy of trust; able to be depended on: *Send her to the bank for the money; she is reliable. adj.* **—re li′a ble ness,** *n.*

re li a bly (ri lī′ə blē), in a reliable manner; to a reliable extent or degree. *adv.*

re li ance (ri lī′əns), **1** trust or dependence: *an unhealthy reliance on other people's opinions.* **2** confidence. *n.*

re li ant (ri lī′ənt), **1** trusting or depending; relying. **2** confident. **3** relying on oneself. *adj.* **—re li′ant ly,** *adv.*

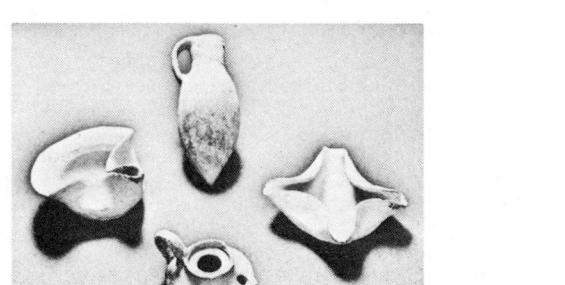

relic (def. 1)—These relics found in Israel are more than 3000 years old. At the top is a jar; the three pieces below are oil lamps.

rel ic (rel′ik), **1** thing left from the past: *This ruined bridge is a relic of the Civil War.* **2** something belonging to a holy person, kept as a sacred memorial. **3** object having interest because of its age or its associations with the past; keepsake; souvenir. *n.*

re lief (ri lēf′), **1** the lessening of, or freeing from, a pain, burden, difficulty, etc.: *His relief from pain came as the medicine began to work.* **2** something that lessens or frees from pain, burden, difficulty, etc.; aid; help: *Relief was sent to the people made homeless by the tornado.* **3** help given to poor people. **4** something that makes a pleasing change or lessens strain. **5** freedom from a post of duty: *The nurse was on duty all day, with only two hours' relief.* **6** change of persons on duty. **7** persons who relieve others from duty; person who does this: *The watchman's relief arrives at seven.* **8** projection of figures or designs from a surface in sculpture, drawing, or painting. **9** figure or design standing out from the surface from which it is cut, shaped, or stamped. **10** the appearance of standing out from a surface, given to a drawing or painting by the use of shading, color, etc. **11** differences in height between the summits and lowlands of a region. *n.*

in relief, standing out from a surface.

on relief, receiving money to live on from public funds.

relief (def. 8)

relief map, map that shows the different heights of a surface by using shading, colors, etc., or solid materials such as clay.

re lieve (ri lēv′), **1** make less; make easier; reduce the pain or trouble of: *Aspirin will relieve a headache. We telephoned to relieve our parents' uneasiness.* **2** set free: *Your coming relieves me of the job of writing a long letter.* **3** free (a person on duty) by taking his or her place. **4** bring aid to; help: *Food and medicine were sent to relieve the flood victims.* **5** give variety or a pleasing change to: *The new red couch will relieve the drabness of the room.* *v.,* **re lieved, re liev ing. —re liev′a ble,** *adj.*

re liev er (ri lē′vər), something that relieves. *n.*

re li gion (ri lij′ən), **1** belief in and worship of God or gods. **2** a particular system of faith and worship: *the Christian religion, the Moslem religion.* *n.*

re li gi os i ty (ri lij′ē os′ə tē), **1** religious feeling or sentiment; piety. **2** affectation of religious feeling. *n.*

re li gious (ri lij′əs), **1** of or connected with religion: *religious meetings, religious books, religious differences.* **2** much interested in religion; devoted to religion: *He is very religious and often goes to church to pray.* **3** monk, nun, friar, etc.; member of a religious order: *There are sixty religious teaching in this school.* **4** very careful; strict; scrupulous: *I gave religious attention to the doctor's orders.* **1,2,4** *adj.,* **3** *n., pl.* **re li gious. —re li′gious ly,** *adv.* **—re li′gious ness,** *n.*

re lin quish (ri ling′kwish), give up; let go: *The small dog relinquished his bone to the big dog.* *v.* **—re lin′quish er,** *n.*

re lin quish ment (ri ling′kwish mənt), a giving up; surrender. *n.*

rel ish (rel′ish), **1** a pleasant taste; good flavor: *Hunger gives relish to simple food.* **2** something to add flavor to food. Olives and pickles are relishes. **3** liking; appetite; enjoyment: *The hungry girl ate with great relish. The teacher has no relish for old jokes.* **4** like the taste of; like; enjoy: *That cat relishes cream. We did not relish the prospect of a long winter.* **1-3** *n.,* **4** *v.* **—rel′ish a ble,** *adj.* **—rel′ish ing ly,** *adv.*

re live (rē liv′), live over or through again. *v.,* **re lived, re liv ing. —re liv′a ble,** *adj.*

re load (rē lōd′), load again. *v.*

re lo cate (rē lō′kāt), locate or settle anew; move to a new place. *v.,* **re lo cat ed, re lo cat ing. —re′lo ca′tion,** *n.*

re luc tance (ri luk′təns), **1** a reluctant feeling or action; unwillingness: *She took part in the game with reluctance.* **2** slowness in action because of unwillingness. *n.*

re luc tant (ri luk′tənt), **1** unwilling; showing unwillingness: *The teacher led the reluctant student to the principal.* **2** slow to act because unwilling: *I am reluctant to go out in very cold weather.* *adj.* **—re luc′tant ly,** *adv.*

re ly (ri lī′), depend or trust: *Rely on your own efforts. I relied upon your promise.* *v.,* **re lied, re ly ing.**

re main (ri mān′), **1** continue in a place; stay: *We shall remain at the seashore till October.* **2** continue; last; keep on: *The town remains the same year after year.* **3** be left: *A few apples remain on the trees. If you take 2 from 5, 3 remains.* **4 remains,** *pl.* **a** what is left: *The remains of the meal were fed to the dog.* **b** a dead body: *Washington's remains are buried at Mount Vernon.* **1-3** *v.,* **4** *n.*

re main der (ri mān′dər), **1** the part left over; the rest: *After studying an hour, she spent the remainder of the afternoon playing.* **2** in arithmetic: **a** number left over after subtracting one number from another. In $9 - 2$, the remainder is 7. **b** number left over after dividing one number by another. In $14 \div 3$, the quotient is 4 with a remainder of 2. *n.*

re make (rē māk′), make anew; make over. *v.,* **re made** (rē mād′), **re mak ing.**

re mand (ri mand′), **1** send back. **2** send back (a prisoner or an accused person) into custody. **3** a remanding. **1,2** *v.,* **3** *n.*

re mark (ri märk′), **1** say in a few words; state; comment: *She remarked that it was a beautiful day.* **2** something said in a few words; short statement: *The president made a few remarks.* **3** notice; observe: *Did you remark that strange cloud?* **4** act of noticing; observation. 1,3 *v.*, 2,4 *n.* —**re mark′er,** *n.*

re mark a ble (ri mär′kə bəl), worthy of notice; unusual: *He has a remarkable memory. adj.* —**re mark′a ble-ness,** *n.*

re mark a bly (ri mär′kə blē), notably; unusually: *The day of the blizzard was remarkably cold. adv.*

re mar riage (rē mar′ij), any marriage after one's first marriage. *n.*

re mar ry (rē mar′ē), marry again. *v.*, **re mar ried, re-mar ry ing.**

re match (rē′mach′), a second or subsequent match between two opponents, teams, etc. *n.*

Rem brandt (rem′brant), 1606-1669, Dutch painter and etcher. *n.*

re me di a ble (ri mē′dē ə bəl), able to be remedied or cured. *adj.* —**re me′di a ble ness,** *n.* —**re me′di a bly,** *adv.*

re me di al (ri mē′dē əl), remedying; curing; helping; re-lieving. *adj.* —**re me′di al ly,** *adv.*

rem e dy (rem′ə dē), **1** a means of removing or relieving diseases or any bad condition; cure: *Aspirin is used as a remedy for headaches.* **2** put right; make right; cure: *A nap remedied my weariness.* 1 *n.; pl.* **rem e dies;** 2 *v.,* **rem e-died, rem e dy ing.** [*Remedy* is from Latin *remedium,* which comes from *re-,* meaning "again," and *mederi,* meaning "heal."]

re mem ber (ri mem′bər), **1** call back to mind: *I can't remember that man's name.* **2** have (something) return to the mind: *Then I remembered where I was.* **3** keep in mind; take care not to forget: *Remember me when I am gone.* **4** keep in mind as deserving a reward, gift, etc.: *Uncle remembered us in his will.* **5** mention (a person) as sending friendly greetings: *She asked to be remembered to you. v.* —**re mem′ber a ble,** *adj.* —**re mem′ber er,** *n.*

re mem brance (ri mem′brəns), **1** power to remember; act of remembering; memory: *I hold my old friend in fond remembrance.* **2** any thing or action that makes one re-member a person; souvenir; keepsake. **3** **remem-brances,** *pl.* greetings: *Give my remembrances to your sister. n.*

re mind (ri mīnd′), make (one) think of something; cause to remember: *This picture reminds me of a story I heard. v.*

re mind er (ri mīn′dər), something to help one remem-ber. *n.*

Rem ing ton (rem′ing tən), Frederic, 1861-1909, American painter and sculptor. *n.*

rem i nisce (rem′ə nis′), talk or think about past experi-ences or events. *v.,* **rem i nisced, rem i nisc ing.**

rem i nis cence (rem′ə nis′ns), **1** a remembering; recall-ing past persons, events, etc. **2** Often, **reminiscences,** *pl.* account of something remembered; recollection: *child-hood reminiscences. n.*

rem i nis cent (rem′ə nis′nt), **1** recalling past persons, events, etc.: *reminiscent talk.* **2** awakening memories of something else; suggestive: *a manner reminiscent of a statelier age. adj.* —**rem′i nis′cent ly,** *adv.*

re miss (ri mis′), careless or slack in doing what one has to do; negligent: *to be remiss in one's duties. adj.* —**re-miss′ly,** *adv.* —**re miss′ness,** *n.*

re mis sion (ri mish′ən), **1** a letting off (from debt, pun-ishment, etc.): *The bankrupt sought remission of his debts.* **2** pardon; forgiveness: *remission of sins.* **3** a lessening (of pain, force, labor, etc.): *The storm continued without remission. n.*

re mit (ri mit′), **1** send money to a person or place: *En-closed is our bill; please remit.* **2** send (money due): *Please*

remit $50. **3** refrain from carrying out; cancel: *The gover-nor is remitting the prisoner's sentence.* **4** pardon; forgive: *the power to remit sins.* **5** make less; decrease: *After we had rowed the boat into calm water, we remitted our efforts. v.,* **re mit ted, re mit ting.**

re mit tance (ri mit′ns), **1** a sending money to someone. **2** the money that is sent. *n.*

re mit ter (ri mit′ər), person or thing that remits. *n.*

rem nant (rem′nənt), **1** a small part left: *This town has only a remnant of its former population.* **2** piece of cloth, ribbon, lace, etc., left after the rest has been used or sold. *n.*

re mod el (rē mod′l), make over; change or alter: *The old barn was remodeled into a house. v.,* **re mod eled, re mod el ing** or **re mod elled, re mod el ling.**

re mon strance (ri mon′strəns), act of remonstrating; protest; complaint. *n.*

re mon strate (ri mon′strāt), speak, reason, or plead in complaint or protest: *The teacher remonstrated with the class about their unruly behavior. v.,* **re mon strat ed, re-mon strat ing.** —**re′mon stra′tion,** *n.* —**re mon′stra-tor,** *n.*

re morse (ri môrs′), deep, painful regret for having done wrong: *I felt remorse for hurting her feelings, so I apolo-gized. n.* [*Remorse* is from a medieval Latin word *remor-sum,* meaning "tormented, bit again," which comes from Latin *re-,* meaning "back," and *mordere,* meaning "to bite."]

re morse ful (ri môrs′fəl), feeling or expressing re-morse. *adj.* —**re morse′ful ly,** *adv.* —**re morse′ful-ness,** *n.*

re morse less (ri môrs′lis), **1** without remorse. **2** pitiless; cruel: *a remorseless killer. adj.* —**re morse′less ly,** *adv.* —**re morse′less ness,** *n.*

re mote (ri mōt′), **1** far away; far off: *The North Pole is a remote part of the world.* **2** out of the way; secluded: *Mail comes to this remote village only once a week.* **3** distant: *He is a remote relative.* **4** slight; faint: *I haven't the remotest idea what you mean. adj.,* **re mot er, re mot est.** —**re-mote′ly,** *adv.* —**re mote′ness,** *n.*

remote control, control from a distance of a machine, operation, etc., usually by electrical impulses or radio signals: *Some model airplanes can be flown by remote control.*

re mov a ble (ri mü′və bəl), able to be removed. *adj.* —**re mov′a ble ness,** *n.* —**re mov′a bly,** *adv.*

re mov al (ri mü′vəl), **1** a removing; taking away: *After the removal of the soup, fish was served.* **2** a change of place: *The store announced its removal to larger quarters.* **3** dismissal from an office or position. *n.*

re move (ri müv′), **1** move from a place or position; take off; take away: *Remove your hat.* **2** get rid of; put an end to: *An experiment removed all our doubt about the fact that water is made up of two gases.* **3** dismiss from an office or position: *The mayor removed the chief of police for failing to do his duty.* **4** go away; move away. **5** step or degree of distance: *At every remove the mountain seemed smaller.* 1-4 *v.,* **re moved, re mov ing;** 5 *n.*

re mov er (ri mü′vər), something that removes: *a bottle of ink remover. n.*

re mu ne rate (ri myü′nə rāt′), pay for work, services, trouble, etc.; reward: *The club remunerated the speaker. v.,* **re mu ne rat ed, re mu ne rat ing.** —**re mu′ne ra′tor,** *n.*

re mu ne ra tion (ri myü′nə rā′shən), a reward; pay; payment. *n.*

re mu ne ra tive (ri myü′nə rā′tiv), paying; profitable. *adj.* —**re mu′ne ra′tive ly,** *adv.* —**re mu ne ra′tive-ness,** *n.*

Re mus (rē′məs), (in Roman legends) the twin brother of Romulus, the founder of Rome. *n.*

ren ais sance (ren′ə säns′ *or* ren′ə säns), **1** a new birth; revival. **2 the Renaissance, a** the great revival of art and learning in Europe during the 1300's, 1400's, and 1500's. **b** the period of time when this revival occurred. **3 Renaissance,** of the Renaissance or its style of art, architecture, etc. 1,2 *n.,* 3 *adj.*

renaissance (def. 3)—a Renaissance cathedral.

re nal (rē′nl), of, having to do with, or located near the kidneys. *adj.*

re name (rē nām′), give a new name to; name again. *v.,* **re named, re nam ing.**

re nas cence (ri nas′ns *or* ri nā′sns), **1** a new birth; revival; renewal: *a renascence of religion.* **2 Renascence,** the Renaissance. *n.*

re nas cent (ri nas′nt *or* ri nā′snt), being born again; reviving. *adj.*

rend (rend), **1** pull apart violently; tear: *Wolves will rend a lamb in pieces.* **2** split: *Lightning rent the tree.* **3** disturb violently: *She was rent by a wish to keep the money she found and the knowledge that she ought to return it.* **4** remove with force or violence. *v.,* **rent, rend ing.**

ren der (ren′dər), **1** cause to become; make: *Fright rendered me speechless.* **2** give; do: *render judgment. She rendered us a great service by her help.* **3** hand in; report: *The treasurer rendered an account of all the money spent.* **4** give in return: *Render thanks for your blessings.* **5** pay as due: *The conquered people rendered tribute to the conqueror.* **6** bring out the meaning of; represent: *The actor rendered the part of the villain well.* **7** play or sing (music). **8** change from one language to another; translate: *She rendered a French poem into English.* **9** melt (fat, etc.); clarify or extract by melting. *Fat from hogs is rendered for lard. v.*

ren dez vous (rän′də vü), **1** an appointment or engagement to meet at a fixed place or time; meeting by agreement. **2** a meeting place; gathering place: *The family's favorite rendezvous was the garden.* **3** place agreed on for a meeting at a certain time, especially of troops or ships. **4** a meeting at a fixed place or time: *the rendezvous of a lunar module and the command ship.* **5** meet at a rendezvous. 1-4 *n., pl.* **ren dez vous** (rän′də vüz); 5 *v.,* **ren dezvoused** (rän′də vüd), **ren dez vous ing** (rän′də vü′ing). [*Rendezvous* comes from French *rendez-vous,* meaning "present yourself!"]

ren di tion (ren dish′ən), **1** act of rendering. **2** the rendering of a dramatic part, music, etc., so as to bring out the meaning. **3** translation. *n.*

ren e gade (ren′ə gād), **1** deserter from a religious faith, a political party, etc.; traitor. **2** like a traitor; deserting; disloyal. 1 *n.,* 2 *adj.*

re nege (ri nig′), **1** fail to play a card of the same suit as that first played, although one is able to do so. It is against the rules of card games to renege. **2** back out; fail to follow up: *renege on a promise. v.,* **re neged, re neg ing. —re neg′er,** *n.*

a hat	**i** it	**oi** oil	**ch** child	⎧ a in about
ā age	**ī** ice	**ou** out	**ng** long	⎪ e in taken
ä far	**o** hot	**u** cup	**sh** she	ə = ⎨ i in pencil
e let	**ō** open	**u̇** put	**th** thin	⎪ o in lemon
ē equal	**ô** order	**ü** rule	**ᵺ** then	⎩ u in circus
ėr term			**zh** measure	

re new (ri nü′ *or* ri nyü′), **1** make new again; make like new; restore: *Rain renews the greenness of the fields.* **2** begin again; get again; say, do, or give again: *He renewed his efforts to open the window.* **3** replace by new material or a new thing of the same sort; fill again: *The well renews itself no matter how much water is taken away.* **4** give or get for a new period: *We renewed our lease for another year. v.* **—re new′er,** *n.*

re new a ble (ri nü′ə bəl *or* ri nyü′ə bəl), able to be renewed: *a renewable contract. adj.* **—re new′a bly,** *adv.*

re new al (ri nü′əl *or* ri nyü′əl), a renewing or a being renewed: *When hot weather comes there will be a renewal of interest in swimming. n.*

ren net (ren′it), substance containing rennin, obtained from the stomach lining of a calf or other cud-chewing mammal, used for making cheese and junket. *n.*

ren nin (ren′ən), enzyme in the gastric juice that coagulates or curdles milk. *n.*

Re no (rē′nō), city in W Nevada. *n.*

Ren oir (ren′wär), **Pierre Auguste,** 1841-1919, French painter. *n.*

re nounce (ri nouns′), **1** declare that one gives up; give up entirely; give up: *He renounces his claim to the money.* **2** cast off; refuse to recognize as one's own: *The people renounced the dictator. v.,* **re nounced, re nounc ing.** **—re nounce′ment,** *n.*

ren o vate (ren′ə vāt), make new again; make like new; restore to good condition: *renovate a house. v.,* **ren o vat ed, ren o vat ing.**

ren o va tion (ren′ə vā′shən), restoration to good condition; renewal. *n.*

ren o va tor (ren′ə vā′tər), person or thing that renovates. *n.*

re nown (ri noun′), fame: *A doctor who finds a cure for a disease wins renown. n.*

re nowned (ri nound′), famous. *adj.*

rent¹ (rent), **1** a regular payment for the use of property. **2** pay at regular times for the use of (property): *We rent a house from them.* **3** receive regular pay for the use of (property): *They rent several other houses.* **4** be leased or let for rent: *This apartment rents for $300 a month.* 1 *n.,* 2-4 *v.* **—rent′a ble,** *adj.* **—rent′er,** *n.*

for rent, available in return for rent paid: *That vacant apartment is for rent.*

rent² (rent), **1** a torn place; tear; split. **2** torn; split. **3** past tense and past participle of **rend.** *The tree was rent by the wind.* 1 *n.,* 2 *adj.,* 3 *v.*

rent al (ren′tl), **1** amount received or paid as rent: *The yearly rental of her house is $3000.* **2** something rented. **3** having to do with or collecting rent: *a rental agent.* 1,2 *n.,* 3 *adj.*

re nun ci a tion (ri nun′sē ā′shən), a giving up of a right, title, possession, etc.; a renouncing. *n.*

re o pen (rē ō′pən), **1** open again: *School will reopen in September.* **2** discuss again or further: *The matter is settled and cannot be reopened. v.*

re or gan i za tion (rē ôr′gə nə zā′shən), a reorganizing or a being reorganized. *n.*

re or gan ize (rē ôr′gə nīz), organize anew; form again; arrange in a new way: *Classes will be reorganized after the first four weeks. v.,* **re or gan ized, re or gan iz ing. —re or′gan iz′er,** *n.*

Rep., 1 Republic. **2** Republican.

re paid (ri pād/), past tense and past participle of **re-pay.** *She repaid the money she had borrowed. All debts should be repaid. v.*

re pair[1] (ri per/ *or* ri par/), **1** put in good condition again; mend: *He repairs shoes.* **2** act or work of repairing. **3** Often, **repairs,** *pl.* instance or piece of repairing: *Repairs on the school building are made during the summer.* **4** condition fit to be used: *The state keeps the roads in repair.* **5** condition for use: *The house was in bad repair.* **6** make up for: *How can I repair the harm done?* 1,6 *v.,* 2-5. *n.* —**re pair/er,** *n.*

re pair[2] (ri per/ *or* ri par/), go (to a place): *After dinner we repaired to the porch. v.*

re pair a ble (ri per/ə bəl *or* ri par/ə bəl), able to be repaired. *adj.*

re pair man (ri per/man/ *or* ri par/man/), person whose work is repairing. *n., pl.* **re pair men.**

rep a ra ble (rep/ər ə bəl), able to be repaired or remedied. *adj.* —**rep/ar a bly,** *adv.*

rep a ra tion (rep/ə rā/shən), **1** a giving of satisfaction or compensation for wrong or injury done. **2 reparations,** *pl.* compensation for wrong or injury, especially payments made by a defeated country for the devastation of territory during war: *England and France demanded reparations from Germany after World War I. n.*

rep ar tee (rep/ər tē/), **1** witty reply or replies. **2** cleverness and wit in making replies. *n.*

re past (ri past/), meal; food: *A light repast was served at the party. n.*

re pa tri ate (rē pā/trē āt), send back or restore to one's own country: *After peace was declared, refugees and prisoners of war were repatriated. v.,* **re pa tri at ed, re pa tri at ing.**

re pa tri a tion (rē pā/trē ā/shən), restoration to one's own country. *n.*

re pay (ri pā/), **1** pay back; give back: *He tried to repay the money he had borrowed.* **2** make return for: *No thanks can repay such kindness.* **3** make return to: *The student's success repaid the teacher for her efforts. v.,* **re paid, re pay ing.**

re pay ment (ri pā/mənt), payment in return for something. *n.*

re peal (ri pēl/), **1** take back; withdraw; do away with: *The law was finally repealed.* **2** act of repealing; withdrawal; abolition: *She voted for the repeal of that law.* 1 *v.,* 2 *n.* —**re peal/a ble,** *adj.* —**re peal/er,** *n.*

re peat (ri pēt/), **1** do or make again: *repeat an error.* **2** say again: *repeat a word for emphasis.* **3** say over; recite: *He can repeat many poems from memory.* **4** say after another says: *Repeat the oath after me.* **5** tell to another or others: *I promised not to repeat the secret.* **6** a repeating. **7** thing repeated. **8** passage in music to be repeated. 1-5 *v.,* 6-8 *n.* —**re peat/a ble,** *adj.* —**re peat/er,** *n.*

repeat oneself, say what one has already said.

re peat ed (ri pē/tid), said, done, or made more than once: *Her repeated efforts at last won success. adj.* —**re peat/ed ly,** *adv.*

re pel (ri pel/), **1** force back; drive back; drive away: *They repelled the enemy. We can repel bad thoughts.* **2** keep off or out; fail to mix with: *Oil and water repel each other. This tent repels moisture.* **3** force apart or away by some inherent force: *The positive poles of two magnets repel each other.* **4** be displeasing to; cause disgust in: *Spiders and worms repel me.* **5** reject: *They repelled his offer of a loan. v.,* **re pelled, re pel ling.**

re pel lent (ri pel/ənt), **1** disagreeable or distasteful; unattractive: *a person with a cold, repellent manner. Cheating is repellent to most people.* **2** repelling; driving back. **3** anything that repels: *We sprayed ourselves with insect repellent before the picnic.* 1,2 *adj.,* 3 *n.* —**re pel/lent ly,** *adv.*

re pent (ri pent/), **1** feel sorry for having done wrong and seek forgiveness: *The thief repented.* **2** feel sorry for; regret: *They bought a white rug and repented their choice. v.* —**re pent/er,** *n.*

re pent ance (ri pen/təns), sorrow for having done wrong; regret. *n.*

re pent ant (ri pen/tənt), repenting; feeling regret; sorry for wrongdoing: *a repentant criminal. adj.* —**re pent/ant ly,** *adv.*

re per cus sion (rē/pər kush/ən), **1** an indirect influence or reaction from an event: *repercussions of war.* **2** sound flung back; echo. **3** a springing back; rebound; recoil: *the repercussion of a cannon. n.*

rep er toire (rep/ər twär), the list of plays, operas, parts, pieces, etc., that a company, an actor, a musician, or a singer is prepared to perform. *n.*

rep er to ry (rep/ər tôr/ē), **1** repertoire. **2** store or stock of things ready for use. *n., pl.* **rep er to ries.**

rep e ti tion (rep/ə tish/ən), **1** a repeating; doing again; saying again: *Repetition helps learning.* **2** thing repeated; repeated occurrence. *n.*

rep e ti tious (rep/ə tish/əs), full of repetitions; repeating in a tiresome way. *adj.* —**rep/e ti/tious ly,** *adv.* —**rep/e ti/tious ness,** *n.*

re pet i tive (ri pet/ə tiv), of or characterized by repetition. *adj.* —**re pet/i tive ly,** *adv.* —**re pet/i tive ness,** *n.*

re place (ri plās/), **1** fill or take the place of: *A substitute replaced our teacher.* **2** get another in place of: *I will replace the cup I broke.* **3** put back; put in place again: *Replace the books on the shelf. v.,* **re placed, re plac ing.** —**re place/a ble,** *adj.*

re place ment (ri plās/mənt), **1** a replacing or a being replaced: *the replacement of steam locomotives by diesel engines.* **2** something or someone that replaces. *n.*

re play (rē plā/ *for 1;* rē/plā/ *for 2,3*), **1** play (a match, game, etc.) again. **2** a match or game played again. **3** a rerun of the videotape of a play, or portion of a game that is being televised: *We saw the touchdown again on the replay.* 1 *v.,* 2,3 *n.*

re plen ish (ri plen/ish), fill again; provide a new supply for: *Once our natural resources are used up we cannot replenish them. v.* —**re plen/ish er,** *n.*

re plen ish ment (ri plen/ish mənt), **1** a replenishing or a being replenished. **2** a fresh supply. *n.*

re plete (ri plēt/), abundantly supplied; filled: *The tour of London was replete with unexpected thrills. adj.* —**re plete/ness,** *n.*

re ple tion (ri plē/shən), a being replete; fullness. *n.*

replica
a replica of
a Viking ship

rep li ca (rep/lə kə), copy; reproduction: *There is a replica of the Mayflower in Plymouth, Massachusetts. n., pl.* **rep li cas.** [*Replica* was borrowed from Italian *replica,* and can be traced back to Latin *re-,* meaning "back," and *plicare,* meaning "to fold."]

re ply (ri plī′), **1** answer by words or action; respond: *She replied with a shout. The enemy replied to the attack with heavy gunfire.* **2** act of replying; response: *I didn't hear your reply to the question.* 1 *v.,* **re plied, re ply ing;** 2 *n., pl.* **re plies.**

re port (ri pôrt′), **1** an account of something seen, heard, read, done, or considered. **2** an account officially or formally expressed, generally in writing: *a committee report.* **3** make a report; give an account of something; announce or state: *Our treasurer reports that all dues are paid up.* **4** repeat (what one has heard, seen, etc.); bring back an account of; describe; tell: *The radio reports the news and weather. The divers reported the treasures they had found in the sunken ship.* **5** present oneself; appear: *Report for work at 9 a.m.* **6** announce as a wrongdoer; denounce: *report someone to the police.* **7** the sound of a shot or an explosion: *the report of a gun.* **8** common talk; rumor: *Report has it that our neighbors are leaving town.* **9** reputation: *a just man of good report.* 1,2,7-9 *n.,* 3-6 *v.* —**re port′a ble,** *adj.*

report card, a report sent regularly by a school to parents or guardians, indicating the quality of a student's work.

re port ed ly (ri pôr′tid lē), according to reports: *A new school is reportedly going to be built next year. adv.*

re port er (ri pôr′tər), **1** person who reports. **2** person who gathers news for a newspaper, magazine, radio or television station, etc. *n.*

re pose¹ (ri pōz′), **1** rest or sleep: *Do not disturb her repose.* **2** lie at rest: *The cat reposed upon the cushion.* **3** lay to rest: *Repose yourself in the hammock.* **4** quietness; ease: *repose of manner.* **5** peace; calmness: *the repose of the country.* 1,4,5 *n.,* 2,3 *v.,* **re posed, re pos ing.**

re pose² (ri pōz′), put; place: *We repose complete confidence in his honesty. v.,* **re posed, re pos ing.**

re pos i to ry (ri poz′ə tôr′ē), place or container where things are stored or kept: *The box was a repository for old magazines. n., pl.* **re pos i to ries.**

re pos sess (rē′pə zes′), possess again; get possession of again. *v.*

rep re hend (rep′ri hend′), reprove or blame. *v.*

rep re hen si ble (rep′ri hen′sə bəl), deserving reproof or blame: *Cheating is a reprehensible act. adj.*

rep re hen si bly (rep′ri hen′sə blē), in a reprehensible manner. *adv.*

rep re sent (rep′ri zent′), **1** stand for; be a sign or symbol of: *The 50 stars in our flag represent the 50 states.* **2** act in place of; speak and act for: *We chose a committee to represent us.* **3** act the part of: *Each child will represent an animal at the party.* **4** show in a picture, statue, carving, etc.; give a likeness of; portray: *This painting represents the seasons.* **5** be a type of; be an example of: *A raft represents a very simple kind of boat.* **6** describe; set forth: *He represented the plan as safe, but it was not. v.* —**rep′re sent′a ble,** *adj.*

rep re sen ta tion (rep′ri zen tā′shən), **1** act of representing. **2** condition or fact of being represented: *"Taxation without representation is tyranny."* **3** representatives considered as a group. **4** likeness; picture; model. **5** performance of a play; presentation: *A representation of the story "Little Women" will be given today.* **6** account; statement: *They deceived us by false representations. n.*

rep re sen ta tion al (rep′ri zen tā′shə nəl), of representation. *adj.*

rep re sent a tive (rep′ri zen′tə tiv), **1** person appointed or elected to act or speak for others: *She is the club's representative at the convention.* **2 Representative,** member of the House of Representatives. **3** having its citizens represented by chosen persons: *a representative government.* **4** representing: *Images representative of ani-*

mals were made by the children. **5** a typical example; type: *The tiger is a representative of the cat family.* **6** serving as an example of; typical: *Oak and maple are representative American hardwoods.* 1,2,5 *n.,* 3,4,6 *adj.* —**rep′re sent′a tive ly,** *adv.* —**rep′re sent′a tive ness,** *n.*

re press (ri pres′), **1** prevent from acting; check: *She repressed an impulse to cough.* **2** keep down; put down; suppress: *repress a revolt. v.* —**re press′er,** *n.*

re pres sion (ri presh′ən), **1** act of repressing: *The repression of a laugh made him choke.* **2** condition of being repressed: *Repression made the people revolt against the government. n.*

re pres sive (ri pres′iv), tending to repress; having power to repress. *adj.*

re prieve (ri prēv′), **1** postpone the punishment of (a person), especially the execution of (a person condemned to death). **2** a delay in carrying out a punishment, especially of the death penalty. **3** the order giving authority for such delay. **4** temporary relief from any evil or trouble. **5** give such relief to. 1,5 *v.,* **re prieved, re priev ing;** 2-4 *n.*

rep ri mand (rep′rə mand), **1** a severe or formal reproof. **2** reprove severely or formally: *The captain was reprimanded and demoted.* 1 *n.,* 2 *v.* [Reprimand is from French *réprimande,* which came from Latin *reprimenda,* meaning "to be repressed," which comes from *re-,* meaning "back," and *premere,* meaning "to press."]

re print (rē print′ for 1; rē′print′ for 2), **1** print again; print a new impression of. **2** a reprinting; a new impression of printed work. 1 *v.,* 2 *n.* —**re print′er,** *n.*

re pris al (ri prī′zəl), injury done in return for injury, especially by one nation to another. *n.*

re proach (ri prōch′), **1** blame or censure: *Their conduct is above reproach.* **2** to blame; censure: *They reproached me for being late.* **3** a cause of blame or disgrace: *That run-down building is a reproach to the owners.* **4** expression of blame, censure, or disapproval. 1,3,4 *n., pl.* **re proach es;** 2 *v.* [Reproach came into English about 500 years ago from French *reproche,* and can be traced back to Latin *re-,* meaning "again," and *prope,* meaning "near."] —**re proach′a ble,** *adj.* —**re proach′er,** *n.* —**re proach′ing ly,** *adv.* —**re proach′less,** *adj.*

re proach ful (ri prōch′fəl), full of reproach; expressing reproach. *adj.* —**re proach′ful ly,** *adv.* —**re proach′ful ness,** *n.*

rep ro bate (rep′rə bāt), **1** a very wicked or unprincipled person; scoundrel. **2** very wicked; unprincipled. 1 *n.,* 2 *adj.*

rep ro ba tion (rep′rə bā′shən), disapproval; condemnation; censure. *n.*

re pro duce (rē′prə düs′ or rē′prə dyüs′), **1** produce again; make or create anew: *The painting was destroyed and can never be reproduced.* **2** make a copy of: *Can you reproduce my handwriting?* **3** produce offspring: *Most plants reproduce by seeds. v.,* **re pro duced, re pro duc ing.** —**re′pro duc′er,** *n.*

re pro duc i ble (rē′prə dü′sə bəl or rē′prə dyü′sə bəl), that can be reproduced. *adj.*

re pro duc tion (rē′prə duk′shən), **1** a reproducing or a being reproduced: *the reproduction of sounds.* **2** a copy. **3** process by which animals and plants produce offspring. *n.*

a hat	i it	oi oil	ch child	(a in about
ā age	ī ice	ou out	ng long	e in taken
ä far	o hot	u cup	sh she	ə = { i in pencil
e let	ō open	u̇ put	th thin	o in lemon
ē equal	ô order	ü rule	ŦH then	u in circus
ėr term			zh measure	

re pro duc tive (rē′prə duk′tiv), **1** capable of reproducing. **2** for or concerned with reproduction. *adj.* —**re′pro-duc′tive ly,** *adv.* —**re′pro duc′tive ness,** *n.*

re proof (ri prüf′), words of blame or disapproval; rebuke. *n.*

re prove (ri prüv′), show disapproval of; find fault with; scold: *I reproved the children for teasing the cat. v.,* **re-proved, re prov ing.** —**re prov′er,** *n.* —**re prov′ing ly,** *adv.*

rep tile (rep′təl), **1** any of a group of cold-blooded animals having a backbone and usually covered with horny plates or scales. Reptiles creep or crawl. Snakes, lizards, turtles, alligators, and crocodiles are reptiles. **2** of or like a reptile; crawling; creeping. **3** a low, mean person. **1,3** *n.,* **2** *adj.*

WORD HISTORY

reptile

Reptile was borrowed from Latin *reptile*, which comes from *repere*, meaning "to crawl."

rep til i an (rep til′ē ən), **1** of reptiles. **2** like a reptile; base; mean. **3** a reptile. **1,2** *adj.,* **3** *n.*

re pub lic (ri pub′lik), nation or state in which the citizens elect representatives to manage the government, which is usually headed by a president. The United States and Mexico are republics. *n.*

re pub li can (ri pub′lə kən), **1** of a republic; like that of a republic: *Many countries have a republican form of government.* **2** person who favors a republic. **3 Republican, a** of the Republican Party. **b** member of the Republican Party. **1,3a** *adj.,* **2,3b** *n.*

Republican Party, one of the two main political parties in the United States. The other is the Democratic Party.

re pu di ate (ri pyü′dē āt), **1** refuse to accept; reject: *repudiate a rumor.* **2** refuse to acknowledge or pay: *repudiate a debt.* **3** cast off; disown: *repudiate a son. v.,* **re-pu di at ed, re pu di at ing.** —**re pu′di a′tor,** *n.*

re pu di a tion (ri pyü′dē ā′shən), a repudiating or a being repudiated. *n.*

re pug nance (ri pug′nəns), strong dislike, distaste, or aversion: *Some people feel a repugnance for snakes. n.*

re pug nant (ri pug′nənt), disagreeable or offensive; distasteful: *a repugnant smell, a repugnant duty. adj.* —**re-pug′nant ly,** *adv.*

re·pulse (ri puls′), **1** drive back; repel: *Our soldiers repulsed the enemy.* **2** a driving or a being driven back: *After the second repulse, the enemy surrendered.* **3** refuse to accept; reject: *She repulsed my invitation.* **4** refusal; rejection: *Her repulse was quite unexpected.* **1,3** *v.,* **re pulsed, re puls ing; 2,4** *n.*

re pul sion (ri pul′shən), **1** strong dislike or aversion. **2** a repelling or a being repelled; repulse. *n.*

re pul sive (ri pul′siv), **1** causing strong dislike or aversion: *the repulsive smell of a skunk.* **2** tending to drive back or repel. *adj.* —**re pul′sive ly,** *adv.* —**re pul′sive-ness,** *n.*

rep u ta ble (rep′yə tə bəl), having a good reputation; well thought of; respectable: *a reputable citizen. adj.*

rep u ta bly (rep′yə tə blē), in a reputable manner; respectably: *They conduct their business reputably. adv.*

rep u ta tion (rep′yə tā′shən), **1** what people think and say the character of a person or thing is; character in

the opinion of others; name; repute: *This store has an excellent reputation for fair dealing. He has the reputation of being very bright.* **2** good name; good reputation: *Cheating at the game ruined that player's reputation.* **3** fame: *an international reputation.*

re pute (ri pyüt′), **1** reputation: *This is a district of bad repute because of the crime here.* **2** suppose to be; consider; suppose: *They are reputed to be quite rich.* **1** *n.,* **2** *v.,* **re put ed, re put ing.**

re put ed (ri pyü′tid), accounted or supposed to be such: *the reputed author of a book. adj.* —**re put′ed ly,** *adv.*

re quest (ri kwest′), **1** ask for; ask as a favor: *She requested a loan from the bank.* **2** ask: *He requested her to go with him.* **3** act of asking: *a request for help.* **4** what is asked for: *He granted my request.* **1,2** *v.,* **3,4** *n.*

by request, in response to a request.

req ui em or **Req ui em** (rek′wē əm), **1** Mass for the dead; musical church service for the dead. **2** music for it. *n.*

re quire (ri kwīr′), **1** have need for; need; want: *We shall require more help.* **2** to command; order; demand: *The rules require us all to be present. v.,* **re quired, re quir ing.**

re quire ment (ri kwīr′mənt), **1** a need; thing needed: *Patience is a requirement in teaching.* **2** a demand; thing demanded: *fulfill the requirements for graduation. n.*

req ui site (rek′wə zit), **1** required by circumstances; needed; necessary; essential; indispensable: *the qualities requisite for a leader, the number of votes requisite for election.* **2** thing needed; requirement: *Food and air are requisites for life.* **1** *adj.,* **2** *n.*

req ui si tion (rek′wə zish′ən), **1** a demand made, especially a formal, written demand: *The principal signed a requisition for new books.* **2** to demand or take by authority: *requisition supplies.* **3** make demands upon: *The hospital requisitioned the city for more funds.* **4** state of being required for use or called into service: *The car was in constant requisition for errands.* **1,4** *n.,* **2,3** *v.*

re quite (ri kwīt′), pay back; make return for: *requite kindness with love. v.,* **re quit ed, re quit ing.** —**re-quit′er,** *n.*

re read (rē rēd′), read again or anew: *reread a good book. v.,* **re read** (rē red′), **re read ing.**

re route (rē rüt′ or rē rout′), send by a new or different route. *v.,* **re rout ed, re rout ing.**

re run (rē run′ *for 1;* rē′run′ *for 2,3*), **1** run again. **2** a running again. **3** a television program or motion-picture film that is shown again. **1** *v.,* **re ran, re run ning; 2,3** *n.*

re sale (rē′sāl′), act of selling again: *the resale of a house. n.*

re scind (ri sind′), deprive of force; repeal; cancel: *rescind a law. v.* —**re scind′a ble,** *adj.* —**re scind′er,** *n.*

res cue (res′kyü), **1** save from danger, capture, harm, etc.; free; deliver: *rescue someone from drowning.* **2** a saving or freeing from danger, capture, harm, etc.: *The fireman was praised for his brave rescue of the children. A dog was chasing our cat when your sister came to the rescue.* **1** *v.,* **res cued, res cu ing; 2** *n.*

res cu er (res′kyü ər), one that rescues. *n.*

re search (ri sèrch′ or rē′sèrch′), **1** a careful hunting for facts or truth; inquiry; investigation: *cancer research.* **2** to hunt for facts or truth; inquire; investigate. **1** *n., pl.* **re-search es; 2** *v.*

re search er (ri sèr′chər or rē′sèr′chər), person who does research; investigator. *n.*

re sem blance (ri zem′bləns), similar appearance; likeness: *Twins often show great resemblance. n.*

re sem ble (ri zem′bəl), be like; be similar to; have likeness to in form, figure, or qualities: *An orange resembles a grapefruit. v.,* **re sem bled, re sem bling.**

re sent (ri zent′), feel injured and angry at; feel indignation at: *I resented being called lazy.* *v.*

re sent ful (ri zent′fəl), feeling resentment; injured and angry; showing resentment. *adj.* —**re sent′ful ly**, *adv.*

re sent ment (ri zent′mənt), the feeling that one has at being injured or insulted; indignation: *Everyone feels resentment at being treated unfairly.* *n.*

res er va tion (rez′ər vā′shən), **1** a keeping back; hiding in part; something not expressed: *She didn't mention it, but she had reservations about their plan.* **2** a limiting condition: *We accepted the plan with reservations plainly stated.* **3** land set aside by the government for a special purpose: *an Indian reservation.* **4** arrangement to keep a thing for a person; securing of accommodations, etc., in advance: *make a reservation for a room in a hotel.* *n.*

re serve (ri zėrv′), **1** keep back; hold back: *Mother reserved judgment until she had heard both sides of the argument.* **2** set apart: *He reserves his evenings to spend them with his family.* **3** save for use later: *Reserve enough money for your fare home.* **4** the actual cash in a bank or assets that can be turned into cash quickly. Banks must keep a reserve of money. **5 reserves**, *pl.* soldiers or sailors not in active service but ready to serve when needed. **6** public land set apart for a special purpose: *a forest reserve.* **7** anything kept back for future use; store: *a reserve of food or energy.* **8** a keeping back or holding back; reservation: *You may speak before her without reserve.* **9** fact, state, or condition of being kept, set apart, or saved for use later: *keep money in reserve.* **10** to set aside for the use of a particular person or persons: *reserve a table at a restaurant.* **11** kept in reserve; forming a reserve: *a reserve stock, a reserve force.* **12** a keeping one's thoughts, feelings, and affairs to oneself; self-restraint in action or speech; lack of friendliness. **13** a silent manner that keeps people from making friends easily. 1-3,10 *v.*, **re served, re serv ing;** 4-9,12,13 *n.*, 11 *adj.* —**re serv′er**, *n.*

re served (ri zėrvd′), **1** kept in reserve; kept by special arrangement: *a reserved seat.* **2** set apart. **3** self-restrained in action or speech. **4** disposed to keep to oneself: *A reserved person does not make friends easily.* *adj.*

re serv ed ly (ri zėr′vid lē), in a reserved manner; with reserve. *adv.*

re serv ist (ri zėr′vist), member of the reserves; soldier or sailor not in active service but available if needed. *n.*

reservoir
(def. 1)

res er voir (rez′ər vwär), **1** place where water is collected and stored for use: *This reservoir supplies the entire city.* **2** anything to hold a liquid: *A fountain pen has an ink reservoir.* **3** place where anything is collected and stored: *Her mind was a reservoir of facts.* **4** a great supply: *a reservoir of weapons.* *n.*

re set (rē set′), set again: *The diamonds were reset in platinum. My broken arm had to be reset.* *v.,* **re set, re setting.**

re side (ri zīd′), **1** live (in or at a place) for a long time; dwell: *This family has resided in our town for 100 years.* **2** be; exist: *The power to declare war resides in Congress.* *v.,* **re sid ed, re sid ing.** —**re sid′er**, *n.*

res i dence (rez′ə dəns), **1** the place where a person lives; house; home; abode: *The President's residence is the White House in Washington, D.C.* **2** a residing; living; dwelling: *Long residence in France made them very fond of the French.* **3** period of residing in a place: *They spent a residence of ten years in France.* *n.*

res i dent (rez′ə dənt), **1** person living in a place permanently; dweller: *The residents of the town are proud of their new library.* **2** staying; dwelling in a place: *Resident owners live on their property.* **3** living in a place while on duty or doing active work: *She is a resident physician at the hospital.* **4** physician practicing in a hospital after completing internship. 1,4 *n.*, 2,3 *adj.*

res i den tial (rez′ə den′shəl), **1** of or suitable for homes or residences: *They live in a large residential district outside the city.* **2** having to do with residence: *The city is considering the adoption of a residential requirement for all city employees to live within the city limits.* *adj.* —**res′i den′tial ly**, *adv.*

re sid u al (ri zij′ü əl), of, or forming a residue; remaining; left over. *adj.* —**re sid′u al ly**, *adv.*

res i due (rez′ə dü *or* rez′ə dyü), what remains after a part is taken; remainder: *His will directed that after the payment of all debts the residue of his property should go to his children. The syrup dried up, leaving a sticky residue.* *n.*

re sign (ri zīn′), give up a job, position, etc.; renounce: *I resigned my position on the school paper.* *v.*

resign oneself, submit quietly; adapt oneself without complaint; yield: *He had to resign himself to a week in bed when he hurt his back.*

res ig na tion (rez′ig nā′shən), **1** act of resigning: *There have been two resignations from the committee.* **2** a written statement giving notice that one resigns. **3** patient acceptance; quiet submission: *bear pain with resignation.* *n.*

re signed (ri zīnd′), accepting what comes without complaint. *adj.*

re sign ed ly (ri zī′nid lē), in a resigned manner. *adv.*

re sil i ence (ri zil′ē əns), **1** power of springing back; elasticity; resilient quality or nature: *Rubber has resilience.* **2** power of recovering quickly; buoyancy; cheerfulness. *n.*

re sil i en cy (ri zil′ē ən sē), resilience. *n.*

re sil i ent (ri zil′ē ənt), **1** springing back; returning to the original form or position after being bent, compressed, or stretched: *resilient steel, resilient turf.* **2** recovering quickly; buoyant; cheerful: *a resilient nature that throws off trouble. adj.* —**re sil′i ent ly**, *adv.*

res in (rez′n), a sticky, yellow or brown substance that flows from certain plants and trees, especially the pine and fir. It is also derived chemically and is used in medicine, varnish, plastics, etc. *n.* —**res′in like′**, *adj.*

res in ous (rez′n əs), of, like, or containing resin. *adj.*

re sist (ri zist′), **1** act against; strive against; oppose: *The window resisted all efforts to open it.* **2** strive successfully against; keep from: *I could not resist laughing.* **3** withstand the action or effect of (an acid, storm, etc.): *A healthy body resists disease.* *v.* —**re sist′er**, *n.*

re sist ance (ri zis′təns), **1** act of resisting: *The bank* *clerk made no resistance to the robbers.* **2** power to resist: *Some people have very little resistance to colds.* **3** thing or act that resists; opposing force; opposition: *An airplane can overcome the resistance of the air and go in the desired direction, while a balloon just drifts.* **4 Resistance,** people who secretly organize and fight for their freedom in a country occupied and controlled by a foreign power: *the French Resistance in World War II.* **5** property of a conductor that opposes the passage of an electric current and changes electric energy into heat. *Copper has a low resistance. n.*

re sist ant (ri zis′tənt), resisting. *adj.*

re sist less (ri zist′lis), that cannot be resisted. *adj.* —**re sist′less ly,** *adv.* —**re sist′less ness,** *n.*

re sis tor (ri zis′tər), conductor used to control voltage in an electric circuit, etc., because of its resistance. *n.*

res o lute (rez′ə lüt), having a fixed resolve; determined; firm: *be resolute against all opposition. She was resolute in her attempt to climb to the top of the mountain. adj.* —**res′o lute′ly,** *adv.* —**res′o lute′ness,** *n.*

res o lu tion (rez′ə lü′shən), **1** thing decided on; thing determined: *We made a resolution to get up early.* **2** act of resolving or determining. **3** power of holding firmly to a purpose; determination: *The pioneers' resolution overcame many hardships.* **4** a formal expression of opinion: *The club passed a resolution thanking the teacher for his help.* **5** a breaking into parts. **6** act or result of solving; solution: *resolution of a problem. n.*

re solve (ri zolv′), **1** make up one's mind; determine; decide: *I resolved to do better work in the future.* **2** thing determined on; thing decided: *He kept his resolve to do better.* **3** firmness in carrying out a purpose; determination: *Helen Keller was a woman of resolve.* **4** decide by vote: *It was resolved that our class should have a picnic.* **5** answer and explain; solve: *The letter resolved our doubts.* **6** break into parts; break up: *Some chemical compounds resolve when heated.* **7** change: *The assembly resolved itself into a committee.* 1,4-7 *v.,* 2,3 *n.* —**re solv′a ble,** *adj.* —**re solv′er,** *n.*

re solved (ri zolvd′), determined; firm; resolute. *adj.*

res o nance (rez′n əns), **1** resounding quality; a being resonant: *the resonance of an organ.* **2** a reinforcing and prolonging of sound by reflection or by vibration of other objects. *The hollow body of a guitar gives it resonance. n.*

res o nant (rez′n ənt), **1** resounding; continuing to sound; echoing. **2** tending to increase or prolong sounds. *adj.* —**res′o nant ly,** *adv.*

re sort (ri zôrt′), **1** go often; go: *Many people resort to the beaches in hot weather.* **2** place people go to, usually for recreation: *There are many summer resorts in the mountains.* **3** turn for help: *The parents resorted to punishment to make the child obey.* **4** act of turning for help: *The resort to force is forbidden in this school.* **5** person or thing turned to for help: *Friends are the best resort in trouble.* 1,3 *v.,* 2,4,5 *n.* —**re sort′er,** *n.*

re sound (ri zound′), **1** give back sound; echo: *The hills resounded when we shouted.* **2** sound loudly: *TV's resound from every apartment.* **3** be filled with sound: *The room resounded with the children's shouts.* **4** be much talked about: *The fame of the first flight across the Atlantic resounded all over the world. v.* —**re sound′ing ly,** *adv.*

re source (ri sôrs′ *or* rē′sôrs), **1** any supply that will meet a need. *We have resources of money, of knowledge, of strength, etc.* **2 resources,** *pl.* the actual and potential wealth of a country: *natural resources, human resources.* **3** any means of getting success or getting out of trouble: *Climbing a tree is a cat's resource when chased by a dog.* **4** skill in meeting difficulties, getting out of trouble, etc. *n.*

re source ful (ri sôrs′fəl), good at thinking of ways to do things; quick-witted: *The resourceful children mowed lawns to earn money to buy a new bicycle. adj.* —**re source′ful ly,** *adv.* —**re source′ful ness,** *n.*

re spect (ri spekt′), **1** high regard; honor; esteem: *The children always showed great respect for their grandparents.* **2** feel or show honor or esteem for: *We respect an honest person.* **3** consideration; care; regard: *Show respect for other people's property.* **4** show consideration for; care for: *Respect the ideas and feelings of others.* **5 respects,** *pl.* expressions of respect; regards: *We must pay our respects to the governor.* **6** feature; point; matter; detail: *The plan is unwise in many respects.* **7** relation; reference: *We must plan with respect to the future.* 1,3,5-7 *n.,* 2,4 *v.* [*Respect* is from Latin *respectus,* meaning "regard," which comes from *re-,* meaning "back," and *specere,* meaning "to look."] —**re spect′er,** *n.*

re spect a bil i ty (ri spek′tə bil′ə tē), **1** quality or condition of being respectable. **2** respectable social standing. *n., pl.* **re spect a bil i ties.**

re spect a ble (ri spek′tə bəl), **1** worthy of respect; having a good reputation; honest and decent: *They are very respectable people.* **2** fairly good; moderate in size or quality: *His record in school was respectable but not brilliant.* **3** good enough to use; fit to be seen: *respectable clothes. adj.*

re spect a bly (ri spek′tə blē), in a respectable manner. *adv.*

re spect ful (ri spekt′fəl), showing respect; considerate and polite. *adj.* —**re spect′ful ly,** *adv.* —**re spect′ful ness,** *n.*

re spect ing (ri spek′ting), regarding; about; concerning: *A discussion arose respecting the merits of different automobiles. prep.*

re spec tive (ri spek′tiv), belonging to each; particular; individual: *The classes went to their respective rooms. adj.*

re spec tive ly (ri spek′tiv lē), as regards each of several persons or things in turn or in the order mentioned: *Pat, José, and Kathy are 16, 18, and 20 years old, respectively. adv.*

re spell (rē spel′), spell over again, especially in a phonetic alphabet. *v.*

res pi ra tion (res′pə rā′shən), **1** act of inhaling and exhaling; breathing: *A bad cold can make respiration difficult.* **2** the process by which an animal or plant secures oxygen from the air or water, distributes it, combines it with substances in the tissues, and gives off carbon dioxide. *n.*

res pi ra tor (res′pə rā′tər), device used to help a person to breathe. *Respirators are used in giving artificial respiration. n.*

res pir a to ry (res′pər ə tôr′ē), having to do with or used for respiration. *The lungs are respiratory organs. adj.*

re spire (ri spīr′), inhale and exhale; breathe. *v.,* **re spired, re spir ing.**

res pite (res′pit), **1** time of relief and rest; lull: *A thick cloud brought a respite from the glare of the sun.* **2** a putting off; delay, especially in carrying out a sentence of death; reprieve. *n.*

re splend ence (ri splen′dəns), great brightness; gorgeous appearance; splendor. *n.*

re splend ent (ri splen′dənt), very bright; shining; splendid: *a gown resplendent with jewels, a face resplendent with joy. adj.* —**re splend′ent ly,** *adv.*

re spond (ri spond′), **1** answer; reply: *He responded to the question.* **2** act in answer; react: *A dog responds to kind treatment by loving its owner. v.*

re sponse (ri spons′), **1** an answer by word or act: *Her response to my letter was prompt. She laughed in response* *to his joke.* **2** words said or sung by the congregation or choir in answer to the minister. **3** the reaction of body or mind to a stimulus. *n.*

re·spon·si·bil·i·ty (ri spon′sə bil′ə tē), **1** a being responsible; obligation: *a highly developed sense of responsibility.* **2** thing for which one is responsible: *Keeping my room clean and feeding the cat are my responsibilities. n., pl.* **re·spon·si·bil·i·ties.**

re·spon·si·ble (ri spon′sə bəl), **1** obliged or expected to account for; accountable; answerable: *You are responsible for the care of your schoolbooks.* **2** deserving credit or blame: *Rain was responsible for the small attendance.* **3** trustworthy; reliable: *Choose a responsible person to take care of the money.* **4** involving obligation or duties: *The presidency is a very responsible position. adj.* **—re·spon′si·ble ness,** *n.*

re·spon·si·bly (ri spon′sə blē), in a responsible manner. *adv.*

re·spon·sive (ri spon′siv), **1** making answer; responding: *a responsive glance.* **2** easily moved; responding readily: *a responsive nature.* **3** using or containing responses: *responsive reading in church in which minister and congregation read in turn. adj.* **—re·spon′sive·ly,** *adv.* **—re·spon′sive ness,** *n.*

rest¹ (rest), **1** state of quiet and ease; sleep: *a good night's rest.* **2** be still or quiet; sleep: *Lie down and rest.* **3** ease after work or effort: *The swimmer left the pool for a short rest.* **4** freedom from anything that tires, troubles, disturbs, or pains; peace: *The medicine gave the patient some rest from pain.* **5** be free from work, effort, care, trouble, etc.: *Some people like to rest on weekends.* **6** absence of motion; stillness: *The ball came to rest at her feet.* **7** give rest to; refresh by rest: *Stop and rest your horse.* **8** to place or be placed for support; lie; lay; lean: *He rested his rake against the fence. The roof of the porch rests on columns.* **9** a support; something to lean on: *a rest for a billiard cue.* **10** be fixed; look: *Our eyes rested on the open book.* **11** be at ease: *Don't let her rest until she promises to visit us.* **12** be or become inactive; let remain inactive: *Let the matter rest.* **13** base or be based; rely; trust; depend: *Our hope rests on you.* **14** be found; be present; lie: *In a democracy, government rests with the people.* **15** place for resting: *a travelers' rest.* **16** in music: **a** a silence of definite length between notes. **b** a mark to show such a silence. **17** (in reading) a pause. **18** death; the grave. **19** be dead; lie in the grave: *The old man rests with his ancestors.* **1,3,4,6,9,15-18** *n.,* **2,5,7,8,10-14,19** *v.*
lay to rest, bury: *Lay a body to rest.*

WHOLE　HALF　QUARTER　EIGHTH　SIXTEENTH

rest¹ (def. 16b)—different types of rests

rest² (rest), **1** what is left; those that are left: *The sun was out in the morning but it rained for the rest of the day. One horse was running ahead of the rest.* **2** continue to be; remain: *You may rest assured that I will keep my promise. The final decision rests with you.* **1** *n.,* **2** *v.*

re·state (rē stāt′), **1** state again or anew. **2** state in a new way. *v.,* **re·stat·ed, re·stat·ing.**

re·state·ment (rē stāt′mənt), **1** act of stating again. **2** statement made again. **3** a new statement. *n.*

res·tau·rant (res′tər ənt *or* res′tə ränt′), place to buy and eat a meal. *n.* [*Restaurant* was borrowed from French *restaurant,* and can be traced back to Latin *restaurare,* meaning "restore."]

rest·ful (rest′fəl), **1** full of rest; giving rest: *He had a restful nap.* **2** quiet; peaceful. *adj.* **—rest′ful·ly,** *adv.* **—rest′ful ness,** *n.*

a hat	**i** it	**oi** oil	**ch** child	a in about
ā age	**ī** ice	**ou** out	**ng** long	e in taken
ä far	**o** hot	**u** cup	**sh** she	ə = i in pencil
e let	**ō** open	** u̇** put	**th** thin	o in lemon
ē equal	**ô** order	**ü** rule	**ŦH** then	u in circus
ėr term			**zh** measure	

res·ti·tu·tion (res′tə tü′shən *or* res′tə tyü′shən), **1** the giving back of what has been lost or taken away. **2** act of making good any loss, damage, or injury: *It is only fair that those who do the damage should make restitution. n.*

res·tive (res′tiv), **1** restless; uneasy: *a restive audience.* **2** hard to manage: *a restive child.* **3** refusing to go ahead; balky: *a restive mule. adj.* **—res′tive·ly,** *adv.* **—res′tive·ness,** *n.*

rest·less (rest′lis), **1** unable to rest; uneasy: *The dog seemed restless, as if it sensed some danger.* **2** without rest or sleep; not restful: *The sick child passed a restless night.* **3** rarely or never still or quiet; always moving: *Some nervous people are very restless. adj.* **—rest′less·ly,** *adv.* **—rest′less·ness,** *n.*

res·to·ra·tion (res′tə rā′shən), **1** a restoring or a being restored; bringing back to a former condition: *the restoration of health.* **2** something restored: *The house was a restoration of a colonial mansion. n.*

re·stor·a·tive (ri stôr′ə tiv), capable of restoring; tending to restore health or strength: *a restorative medicine. adj.* **—re·stor′a·tive·ly,** *adv.*

re·store (ri stôr′), **1** bring back; establish again: *The police restored order.* **2** bring back to a former condition or to a normal condition: *The old house has been restored.* **3** give back; put back: *The boy restored the money he had found to its owner. v.,* **re·stored, re·stor·ing.** **—re·stor′a·ble,** *adj.*

re·stor·er (ri stôr′ər), person or thing that restores. *n.*

re·strain (ri strān′), hold back; keep down; keep in check; keep within limits: *I could not restrain my curiosity to see what was in the box. We restrained the excited dog when guests came. v.* **—re·strain′a·ble,** *adj.* **—re·strain′ed·ly,** *adv.* **—re·strain′er,** *n.*

re·straint (ri strānt′), **1** a restraining or a being restrained: *Violent people sometimes need restraint.* **2** means of restraining. **3** tendency to restrain natural feeling; reserve: *She was very angry, but she spoke with restraint. n.*

re·strict (ri strikt′), keep within limits; confine: *Our club membership is restricted to twelve. v.*

re·strict·ed (ri strik′tid), **1** limited; kept within limits: *She is on a very restricted diet, and can have no sweets.* **2** having restrictions or limiting rules: *Factories may not be built in this restricted residential section. adj.* **—re·strict′ed·ly,** *adv.*

re·stric·tion (ri strik′shən), **1** something that restricts; limiting condition or rule: *The restrictions on the use of the playground are: No fighting; no damaging property.* **2** a restricting or a being restricted: *This park is open to the public without restriction. n.*

re·stric·tive (ri strik′tiv), restricting; limiting: *Restrictive laws limit the amount of pollution the factory can produce. adj.* **—re·stric′tive·ly,** *adv.* **—re·stric′tive·ness,** *n.*

restrictive clause, a subordinate clause that qualifies the noun it modifies so definitely that it cannot be left out without changing the meaning of the sentence. EXAMPLE: *All employees who have been with this firm for five years will receive bonuses.*

rest room, lavatory in a public building.

re·sult (ri zult′), **1** that which happens because of something; what is caused; outcome: *The result of the fall was a broken leg.* **2** good or useful effect: *The new medicine got results.* **3** be a result; follow as a consequence: *Sickness* often results from eating too much. **4** have as a result; end: *Eating too much often results in sickness.* **5** quantity, value, etc., obtained by calculation. 1,2,5 *n.*, 3,4 *v.* [*Result* is from Latin *resultare*, meaning "to rebound," which comes from *re-*, meaning "back," and *salire*, meaning "to spring."]

re sult ant (ri zult′nt), resulting. *adj.*

re sume (ri züm′), **1** begin again; go on: *Resume reading where we left off.* **2** get or take again: *Those standing may resume their seats. v.*, **re sumed, re sum ing.** —**re sum′a ble**, *adj.*

rés u mé (rez′ə mā′), summary: *a résumé of one's education and job experience. n.*

re sump tion (ri zump′shən), a resuming: *the resumption of duties after absence. n.*

re sur gence (ri sėr′jəns), a rising again: *resurgence of interest. n.*

res ur rect (rez′ə rekt′), **1** raise from the dead; bring back to life. **2** bring back to sight, use, etc.: *resurrect an old custom. v.*

reticulate
This giraffe has reticulate markings.

res ur rec tion (rez′ə rek′shən), **1** a coming to life again; rising from the dead. **2 Resurrection,** the rising again of Jesus after His death and burial. **3** restoration from decay, disuse, etc.; revival. *n.*

re sus ci tate (ri sus′ə tāt), bring or come back to life or consciousness; revive: *The doctor resuscitated the man who was overcome by gas. v.*, **re sus ci tat ed, re sus ci tat ing.**

re sus ci ta tion (ri sus′ə tā′shən), restoration to life or consciousness. *n.*

re sus ci ta tor (ri sus′ə tā′tər), device used to revive persons overcome by gas, water in the lungs, etc. It produces artificial respiration by forcing air or oxygen into the lungs through a tight-fitting mask or cup attached to the victim's face. *n.*

re tail (rē′tāl), **1** sale of goods in small quantities directly to the consumer: *Our grocer buys at wholesale and sells at retail.* **2** in small quantities: *The wholesale price of this coat is $40; the retail price is $60.* **3** selling in small quantities: *the retail trade, a retail merchant.* **4** sell or be sold in small quantities. 1 *n.*, 2,3 *adj.*, 4 *v.*

re tail er (rē′tā lər), a retail merchant or dealer. *n.*

re tain (ri tān′), **1** continue to have or hold; keep: *A china teapot retains heat for quite a long time. Our baseball team retained a lead throughout the game.* **2** keep in mind; remember: *She retained the tune but not the words of the song.* **3** employ by payment of a fee: *I retained a very good lawyer. v.*

re tain er[1] (ri tā′nər), **1** person who serves a person of rank; vassal; attendant; follower: *The queen had many retainers.* **2** a metal wire used to hold teeth in place after they have been straightened by the wearing of braces. *n.*

re tain er[2] (ri tā′nər), fee paid to secure services: *This lawyer receives a retainer before he begins work on a case. n.*

re take (rē tāk′ *for 1,2;* rē′tāk′ *for 3*), **1** take again. **2** take back. **3** a retaking: *a retake of a scene in a motion picture.* 1,2 *v.*, **re took, re tak en** (rē tā′kən), **re tak ing;** 3 *n.*

re tal i ate (ri tal′ē āt), pay back wrong, injury, etc.; return like for like, usually to return evil for evil: *If we insult them, they will retaliate. v.*, **re tal i at ed, re tal i at ing.**

re tal i a tion (ri tal′ē ā′shən), a paying back of a wrong, injury, etc.; return of evil for evil. *n.*

re tal i a to ry (ri tal′ē ə tôr′ē), returning like for like, especially evil for evil. *adj.*

re tard (ri tärd′), make slow; delay the progress of; keep back; hinder: *Lack of education retards progress. v.* —**re tard′er,** *n.*

re tar da tion (rē′tär dā′shən), **1** act of retarding. **2** that which retards; hindrance. *n.*

re tard ed (ri tär′did), slow in mental development; backward. *adj.*

retch (rech), make efforts to vomit. *v.* [*Retch* comes from Old English *hrǣcan*, meaning "clear the throat."]

ret'd., returned.

re tell (rē tel′), tell again. *v.*, **re told, re tell ing.**

re ten tion (ri ten′shən), **1** a retaining or a being retained. **2** power to retain. **3** ability to remember. *n.*

re ten tive (ri ten′tiv), **1** able to hold or keep: *a material retentive of moisture.* **2** able to remember easily: *a retentive memory. adj.* —**re ten′tive ly,** *adv.* —**re ten′tive ness,** *n.*

ret i cence (ret′ə səns), tendency to be silent or say little; reserve in speech. *n.*

ret i cent (ret′ə sənt), disposed to keep silent or say little; reserved in speech. *adj.* —**ret′i cent ly,** *adv.*

re tic u late (ri tik′yə lit *or* ri tik′yə lāt), covered with a network. Reticulate leaves have the veins arranged like the threads of a net. *adj.* —**re tic′u late ly,** *adv.*

ret i na (ret′n ə), layer of cells at the back of the eyeball that is sensitive to light and receives the images of things looked at. *n., pl.* **ret i nas, ret i nae** (ret′n ē′).

ret i nal (ret′n əl), of or on the retina. *adj.*

ret i nue (ret′n ü *or* ret′n yü), group of attendants or retainers; a following: *The king's retinue accompanied him. n.*

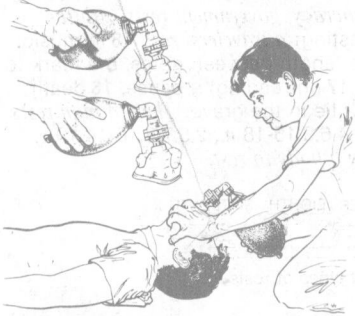

resuscitator
Squeezing and releasing the bag forces air into the lungs.

re tire (ri tīr′), **1** give up an office, occupation, etc., especially because of old age: *Our teachers retire at 65.* **2** remove from an office, occupation, etc. **3** go away, especially to a place which is more quiet or private: *They retired to the country.* **4** withdraw; draw back; send back: *The government retires worn or torn dollar bills from use.* **5** go back; retreat: *The enemy retired before the advance of our troops.* **6** go to bed: *We retire early.* **7** withdraw from circulation and pay off (bonds, loans, etc.). **8** put out (a batter, side, etc.) in baseball and cricket. *v.*, **re tired, re tir ing.**

re tired (ri tīrd′), **1** withdrawn from one's occupation: *a retired accountant.* **2** secluded; shut off; hidden: *a retired spot. adj.*

re tire ment (ri tīr′mənt), **1** a retiring or a being retired;

withdrawal: *The teacher's retirement was regretted by the school.* **2** a quiet way or place of living: *She lives in retirement in the country. n.*

re tir ing (ri tī′ring), shrinking from society or publicity; reserved; shy: *a retiring nature. adj.* —**re tir′ing ly,** *adv.* —**re tir′ing ness,** *n.*

re told (rē tōld′), past tense and past participle of **retell.** *I then retold the story for the newcomers. v.*

re took (rē tük′), past tense of **retake.** *The photographer retook my picture. v.*

re tool (rē tül′), change the tools, machinery, designs, etc., in a plant to make new models or products. *v.*

re tort[1] (ri tôrt′), **1** reply quickly or sharply: *"It's none of your business," I retorted.* **2** a sharp or witty reply: *"Why are your teeth so sharp?" asked Red Ridinghood. "The better to eat you with," was the wolf's retort.* **3** return in kind; turn back on: *I told her what I thought of her, and she retorted insult for insult.* 1,3 *v.,* 2 *n.*

re tort[2] (ri tôrt′), container used for distilling or separating substances by heat. *n.*

re touch (rē tuch′), change or improve (a photographic negative, painting, etc.) by making slight changes with a brush, pencil, etc. *v.* —**re touch′er,** *n.*

re trace (ri trās′), go back over: *We retraced our steps to where we started. v.,* **re traced, re trac ing.** —**re trace′a ble,** *adj.*

re tract (ri trakt′), **1** draw back or in: *The kitten retracted her claws and purred when I petted it.* **2** withdraw; take back: *retract an offer. v.* —**re tract′a ble,** *adj.*

re trac tion (ri trak′shən), **1** a drawing or a being drawn back or in. **2** a taking back; withdrawal of a promise, statement, etc.: *The newspaper published a retraction of the inaccurate report about the actress. n.*

re tread (rē tred′ *for 1;* rē′tred′ *for 2*), **1** put a new tread on. **2** a tire that has been retreaded. 1 *v.,* 2 *n.*

re treat (ri trēt′), **1** go back; move back; withdraw: *The enemy retreated before the advance of our soldiers.* **2** act of going back or withdrawing: *The army's retreat was orderly.* **3** a signal for retreat: *The drums beat a retreat.* **4** a signal on a bugle or drum, given at sunset during the lowering of the flag. **5** a safe, quiet place; place of rest or refuge. **6** a retirement, or period of retirement, by a group of people for religious exercises, meditation, etc.: *The monks conducted a retreat.* 1 *v.,* 2-6 *n.*

beat a retreat, run away; retreat: *We dropped the apples and beat a hasty retreat when the farmer chased us.*

re trench (ri trench′), cut down or reduce expenses, etc.: *In hard times, we must retrench to keep out of debt. v.*

re trench ment (ri trench′mənt), a cutting down or reduction of expenses, etc. *n.*

re tri al (rē trī′əl), a second trial; new trial. *n.*

ret ri bu tion (ret′rə byü′shən), a deserved punishment; return for wrongdoing. *n.*

re trib u tive (ri trib′yə tiv), paying back; bringing or inflicting punishment in return for wrongdoing. *adj.*

re triev al (ri trē′vəl), act of retrieving; recovery. *n.*

re trieve (ri trēv′), **1** get again; recover: *retrieve a lost pocketbook.* **2** bring back to a former or better condition; restore: *retrieve one's fortunes.* **3** make good; make amends for; repair: *retrieve a mistake, retrieve a loss.* **4** find and bring to a person: *A dog can be trained to retrieve game. v.,* **re trieved, re triev ing.** —**re triev′a ble,** *adj.*

re triev er (ri trē′vər), dog trained to find killed or wounded game and bring it to a hunter. *n.*

retro-, *combining form.* backward; back: *Retroactive = acting back. Retrospection = act of looking back.* [The form *retro-* comes from Latin *retro.*]

ret ro ac tive (ret′rō ak′tiv), acting back; having an effect on what is past. A retroactive law applies to events

a hat	i it	oi oil	ch child	⎧ a in about
ā age	ī ice	ou out	ng long	⎪ e in taken
ä far	o hot	u cup	sh she	ə = ⎨ i in pencil
e let	ō open	ů put	th thin	⎪ o in lemon
ē equal	ô order	ü rule	ŦH then	⎩ u in circus
ėr term			zh measure	

that occurred before the law was passed. *adj.* —**ret′ro ac′tive ly,** *adv.*

ret ro grade (ret′rə grād), **1** moving backward; retreating. **2** move or go backward. **3** becoming worse. **4** fall back toward a worse condition; grow worse; decline. 1,3 *adj.,* 2,4 *v.,* **ret ro grad ed, ret ro grad ing.**

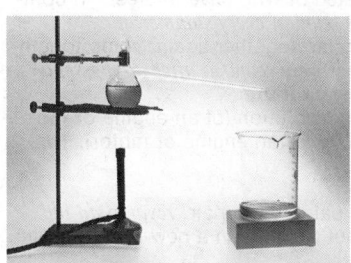

retort[2]
The retort is on the left.

ret ro gress (ret′rə gres *or* ret′rə gres′), **1** move backward; go back. **2** become worse. *v.*

ret ro gres sion (ret′rə gresh′ən), **1** a backward movement. **2** a becoming worse; falling off; decline. *n.*

ret ro rock et (ret′rō rok′it), a small rocket at the front of a rocket or spacecraft. It produces thrust opposite to the motion of the spacecraft in order to reduce speed for landing or for reentry. *n.*

ret ro spect (ret′rə spekt), survey of past time, events, etc.; thinking about the past. *n.*

in retrospect, when looking back: *She saw, in retrospect, that the problem could have been avoided.*

ret ro spec tion (ret′rə spek′shən), a looking back on things past; survey of past events or experiences. *n.*

ret ro spec tive (ret′rə spek′tiv), **1** looking back on things past; surveying past events or experiences. **2** applying to the past; retroactive. *adj.* —**ret′ro spec′tive ly,** *adv.*

re turn (ri tėrn′), **1** go back; come back: *Return home at once. My cousin will return this summer.* **2** a going or coming back; happening again: *We look forward all winter to our return to the country. We wish you many happy returns of your birthday.* **3** bring, give, send, put, or pay back: *Return that book to the library. I left a message for her to return my telephone call.* **4** a bringing, giving, sending, putting, or paying back: *Such bad behavior was a poor return for kindness.* **5** thing returned. **6** Often, **returns,** *pl.* profit; amount received: *The returns from the sale were more than a hundred dollars.* **7** yield: *The concert returned about $50 over expenses.* **8** a report; an account: *election returns. I must make out my income-tax return.*

retriever
2 ft. (60 cm.) high at the shoulder

9 report or announce officially: *The jury returned a verdict of guilty.* **10** to reply; answer: *"No!" she returned crossly.* **11** of or for a return: *a return ticket.* **12** sent, given, done, etc., in return: *a return game.* 1,3,7,9,10 *v.*, 2,4-6,8 *n.*, 11,12 *adj.*

in return, as a return; to return something: *If you let me use your skates, I'll lend you my skis in return.*

re turn a ble (ri tėr′nə bəl), **1** able to be returned. **2** meant or required to be returned. *adj.*

re turn ee (ri tėr′nē′), person who has returned, especially one who has returned from military service abroad. *n.*

re un ion (rē yü′nyən), **1** a coming together again: *the reunion of parted friends.* **2** a social gathering of persons who have been separated or who have interests in common: *We have a family reunion every summer. n.*

re u nite (rē′yü nīt′), bring together again; come together again: *The two friends were reunited after a long separation. v.*, **re u nit ed, re u nit ing.**

rev (rev), INFORMAL. **1** a revolution (of an engine or motor). **2** increase the speed of (an engine or motor). 1 *n.*, 2 *v.*, **revved, rev ving.**

Rev., Reverend.

re vamp (rē vamp′), **1** patch up; repair: *revamp an old car.* **2** take apart and put together in a new form: *revamp plans. v.*

re veal (ri vēl′), **1** make known: *Never reveal my secret.* **2** display; show: *Her smile revealed her even teeth. v.* —**re veal′a ble,** *adj.* —**re veal′er,** *n.*

rev eil le (rev′ə lē), a signal on a bugle or drum to waken soldiers or sailors in the morning. *n.*

rev el (rev′əl), **1** take great pleasure: *The children revel in country life.* **2** a noisy good time; merrymaking: *Christmas revels with feasting and dancing were common in England.* 3 make merry. 1,3 *v.*, 2 *n.* —**rev′el er,** *n.*

rev e la tion (rev′ə lā′shən), **1** act of making known: *We all waited for the revelation of the winner's name.* **2** the thing made known: *Her true nature was a revelation to me.* **3 Revelation,** the last book of the New Testament, supposed to have been written by the apostle John. *n.*

rev el ry (rev′əl rē), boisterous reveling or festivity; noisy merrymaking. *n.*, *pl.* **rev el ries.**

re venge (ri venj′), **1** harm done in return for a wrong; vengeance; returning evil for evil: *a blow struck in revenge.* **2** desire for vengeance. **3** do harm in return for. **4** a chance to win in a return game after losing a game. 1,2,4 *n.*, 3 *v.*, **re venged, re veng ing.**

be revenged or **revenge oneself,** get revenge.

re venge ful (ri venj′fəl), feeling or showing a strong desire for revenge. *adj.* —**re venge′ful ly,** *adv.* —**re venge′ful ness,** *n.*

rev e nue (rev′ə nü *or* rev′ə nyü), money coming in; income: *The government gets revenue from taxes. n.*

re ver be rate (ri vėr′bə rāt′), echo back: *The deep, rumbling sound of the organ reverberated in the church. v.*, **re ver be rat ed, re ver be rat ing.** [*Reverberate* is from Latin *reverberatum,* meaning "beaten back," which comes from *re-,* meaning "back," and *verber,* meaning "a blow, whip."]

re ver be ra tion (ri vėr′bə rā′shən), an echoing back of sound; echo. *n.*

re vere (ri vir′), love and respect deeply; honor greatly; show reverence for: *We revere sacred things. People revered the saint. v.*, **re vered, re ver ing.**

Re vere (ri vir′), Paul, 1735-1818, American patriot. He is famous for his night ride through eastern Massachusetts to warn colonists of the approach of British troops in 1775. *n.*

rev er ence (rev′ər əns), **1** a feeling of deep respect, mixed with wonder, awe, and love. **2** regard with rever-

ence; revere. 1 *n.*, 2 *v.*, **rev er enced, rev er enc ing.**

rev er end (rev′ər ənd), **1** worthy of great respect. **2 Reverend,** title for members of the clergy: *the Reverend Thomas A. Johnson. adj.*

rev er ent (rev′ər ənt), feeling reverence; showing reverence: *a reverent prayer. adj.* —**rev′er ent ly,** *adv.*

rev e ren tial (rev′ə ren′shəl), reverent. *adj.*

rev er ie (rev′ər ē), dreamy thoughts; dreamy thinking of pleasant things: *He loved to indulge in reveries about the future. n.* Also, **revery.**

re ver sal (ri vėr′səl), change to the opposite; a reversing or a being reversed. *n.*

re verse (ri vėrs′), **1** the opposite or contrary: *She did the reverse of what I suggested.* **2** turned backward; opposite or contrary in position or direction: *the reverse side of a phonograph record.* **3** the back: *His name is on the reverse of the medal.* **4** acting in a manner opposite or contrary to that which is usual. **5** causing an opposite or backward movement. **6** turn the other way; turn inside out; turn upside down: *Reverse that hose; don't point it at me.* **7** an opposite or contrary motion or direction: *a reverse in dancing.* **8** arrangement of gears that reverses the movement of machinery: *Put the car in reverse and back up.* **9** change to the opposite; repeal: *The Supreme Court reversed the lower court's decision.* **10** a change to bad fortune; check; defeat: *He used to be rich, but he met with reverses.* 1,3,7,8,10 *n.*, 2,4,5 *adj.*, 6,9 *v.*, **re versed, re vers ing.** —**re verse′ly,** *adv.*

re vers i ble (ri vėr′sə bəl), **1** able to be reversed; able to reverse. **2** (of a fabric, etc.) finished on both sides so that it can be worn with either side showing. *adj.*

re ver sion (ri vėr′zhən), return to a former condition, practice, belief, etc.; return. *n.*

re vert (ri vėrt′), go back; return: *My thoughts reverted to the last time that I had seen her. v.* [*Revert* is from Latin *revertere,* which comes from *re-,* meaning "back," and *vertere,* meaning "to turn." See **Word Family.**]

revert

Below are words related to *revert.* They can all be traced back to the Latin word *vertere* (wer′te re), meaning "to turn."

adversary	diversify	traverse
adverse	diversion	universal
adversity	divert	universe
advertise	extrovert	university
averse	introvert	varsity
aversion	inverse	versatile
avert	invert	verse
controversy	invertebrate	version
conversation	perverse	versus
converse[1]	pervert	vertebra
converse[2]	prose	vertex
convert	reverse	vertical
convertible	subversive	vertigo
diverse	transverse	vortex

rev er y (rev′ər ē), reverie. *n.*, *pl.* **rev er ies.**

re view (ri vyü′), **1** study again; look at again: *Review today's lesson for tomorrow.* **2** a studying again: *Before the examinations we have a review of the term's work.* **3** look back on: *Before falling asleep, she reviewed the day's happenings.* **4** a looking back on; survey: *a review of recent events.* **5** examine again; look at with care; examine: *A*

superior court may review decisions of a lower court.
6 examination; inspection: *A review of the troops will be held during the general's visit to the camp.* **7** inspect formally: *The admiral reviewed the fleet.* **8** an account of a book, play, etc., giving its merits and faults: *Did that movie get good reviews?* **9** examine to give an account of: *She reviews books for a living.* 1,3,5,7,9 *v.,* 2,4,6,8 *n.*

re view er (ri vyü′ər), **1** person who reviews. **2** person who writes articles discussing books, plays, etc. *n.*

re vile (ri vīl′), call bad names; abuse with words: *The pedestrian reviled the reckless driver.* *v.,* **re viled, re vil ing.**

re vise (ri vīz′), **1** read carefully in order to correct; look over and change; examine and improve: *She has revised her essay to make it read better.* **2** change; alter: *revise one's opinion.* *v.,* **re vised, re vis ing.**

re vis er (ri vī′zər), person who revises a manuscript, book, etc. *n.*

re vi sion (ri vizh′ən), **1** act or work of revising. **2** a revised form: *a revision of a book. n.*

re viv al (ri vī′vəl), **1** a bringing or coming back to life or consciousness. **2** restoration to vigor or health. **3** a bringing or coming back to style, use, activity, etc.: *the revival of an old musical.* **4** an awakening or increase of interest in religion. **5** special services or efforts made to awaken or increase interest in religion. *n.*

re vive (ri vīv′), **1** bring back or come back to life or consciousness: *revive a half-drowned person. The half-drowned swimmer revived.* **2** bring or come back to a fresh, lively condition: *Flowers revive in water.* **3** make or become fresh; restore: *Hot cocoa revived the cold, tired hikers.* **4** bring back or come back to notice, use, fashion, memory, activity, etc.: *An old play is sometimes revived on the stage.* *v.,* **re vived, re viv ing.** —**re viv′er,** *n.*

rev o ca ble (rev′ə kə bəl), able to be repealed, canceled, or withdrawn. *adj.*

rev o ca tion (rev′ə kā′shən), a repeal; a canceling; withdrawal: *the revocation of a law. n.*

re voke (ri vōk′), take back; repeal; cancel; withdraw: *revoke a driver's license.* *v.,* **re voked, re vok ing.**

re volt (ri vōlt′), **1** act or state of rebelling: *The town is in revolt.* **2** turn away from and fight against a leader; rise against the government's authority: *The people revolted against the dictator.* **3** turn away with disgust: *revolt at a bad smell.* **4** cause to feel disgust: *Senseless cruelty revolts me.* 1 *n.,* 2-4 *v.* —**re volt′er,** *n.*

re volt ing (ri vōl′ting), disgusting; repulsive: *a revolting odor. adj.* —**re volt′ing ly,** *adv.*

rev o lu tion (rev′ə lü′shən), **1** a complete overthrow of an established government or political system: *The American Revolution gave independence to the colonies.* **2** a complete change: *The automobile caused a revolution in ways of traveling.* **3** movement in a circle or curve around some point: *One revolution of the earth around the sun takes a year.* **4** act or fact of turning round a center or axis; rotation: *The wheel of the motor turns at a rate of more than one thousand revolutions per minute.* **5** time or distance of one revolution. *n.*

rev o lu tion ar y (rev′ə lü′shə ner′ē), **1** of a revolution; connected with a revolution. **2** bringing or causing great changes: *Radio and television were two revolutionary inventions of this century.* **3** revolutionist. 1,2 *adj.,* 3 *n., pl.* **rev o lu tion ar ies.**

Revolutionary War, the war from 1775 to 1783 by which the thirteen American colonies won independence from England; American Revolution.

rev o lu tion ist (rev′ə lü′shə nist), person who advocates, or takes part in, a revolution. *n.*

rev o lu tion ize (rev′ə lü′shə nīz), change completely; produce a very great change in: *The automobile, radio, television, and the computer have revolutionized people's*

lives. v., **rev o lu tion ized, rev o lu tion iz ing.**

re volve (ri volv′), **1** move in a circle; move in a curve round a point: *The moon revolves around the earth.* **2** turn round a center or axis; rotate: *The wheels of a moving car revolve.* **3** cause to move round. *v.,* **re volved, re volving.** —**re volv′a ble,** *adj.*

revolver

re volv er (ri vol′vər), pistol that can be fired several times without being loaded again. It has a revolving cylinder in which the cartridges are contained. *n.*

re vue (ri vyü′), a theatrical entertainment with singing, dancing, parodies of recent plays, humorous treatments of happenings and fads of the year, etc. *n.*

re vul sion (ri vul′shən), a sudden, violent change or reaction, especially of disgust: *Friendship turned to revulsion when I realized their dishonesty. n.* [*Revulsion* is from Latin *revulsionem,* which comes from *re-,* meaning "back," and *vellere,* meaning "to tear away."]

re ward (ri wôrd′), **1** return made for something done. **2** a money payment given or offered for capture of criminals, the return of lost property, etc. **3** give a reward to. **4** give a reward for. 1,2 *n.,* 3,4 *v.*

re ward ing (ri wôr′ding), giving or likely to give a feeling of reward; satisfying: *a rewarding activity. adj.*

re word (rē wėrd′), put into other words. *v.*

re work (rē wėrk′), work over again; revise. *v.*

re write (rē rīt′), write again; write in a different form; revise. *v.,* **re wrote** (rē rōt′), **re writ ten** (rē rit′n), **re writ ing.**

Reye's syndrome (rīz *or* rāz), a rare and often fatal disease that afflicts primarily children, usually occurs after a viral infection, and can damage the liver, brain, and kidneys. [*Reye's syndrome* was named for R.D.K. *Reye,* 1912-1977, an Australian pathologist, one of the first to describe it in 1963.]

Rey kja vik (rā′kyə vēk′), capital of Iceland, in the SW part. *n.*

Reyn ard (ren′ərd *or* rā′närd), fox who is the main character in a group of medieval fables about animals. *n.*

Reyn olds (ren′ldz), Sir **Joshua,** 1723-1792, English portrait painter. *n.*

Rf, symbol for rutherfordium.

R.F.D., Rural Free Delivery.

r.h., 1 relative humidity. **2** (in music) right hand.

Rh, symbol for rhodium.

rhap sod i cal (rap sod′ə kəl), of or characteristic of rhapsody; extravagantly enthusiastic; ecstatic. *adj.*

rhap so dy (rap′sə dē), **1** extravagant enthusiasm in speech or writing: *go into rhapsodies over a present.* **2** (in music) an instrumental composition irregular in form: *Liszt's Hungarian rhapsodies. n., pl.* **rhap so dies.** [*Rhapsody* is from Greek *rhapsōidia,* meaning "a verse composition," which comes from *rhaptein,* meaning "to stitch," and *ōidē,* meaning "song, ode."]

rhea
about 5 ft. (1.5 m.) tall

rhe a (rē′ə), a large bird of South America that is much like the ostrich, but is smaller and has three toes instead of two. *n., pl.* **rhe as.**

Rhe a (rē′ə), (in Greek myths) the mother of Zeus, Hera, Poseidon, and other important Greek gods. *n.*

Rheims (rēmz), Reims. *n.*

Rhen ish (ren′ish), of the Rhine River or the regions near it. *adj.*

rhe ni um (rē′nē əm), a rare, hard, grayish metallic element with a very high melting point, used in making alloys. *n.*

rhe o stat (rē′ə stat), instrument for regulating the strength of an electric current by introducing different amounts of resistance into the circuit. *n.*

rhe sus (rē′səs), a small, yellowish-brown monkey with a short tail, found in India. It is often used in medical research. *n.*

rhet or ic (ret′ər ik), **1** art of using words effectively in speaking or writing. **2** book about this art. **3** mere display in language. *n.*

rhe to ri cal (ri tôr′ə kəl), **1** of or using rhetoric. **2** intended especially for display; artificial. **3** oratorical. *adj.* —**rhe to′ri cal ly,** *adv.*

rhetorical question, question asked only for effect, not for information. EXAMPLE: "Who can tell whether or not life exists on other planets?"

rhet o ri cian (ret′ə rish′ən), **1** person skilled in rhetoric. **2** person given to display in language. *n.*

rheum (rüm), a watery discharge, such as mucus, tears, or saliva. *n.*

rheu mat ic (rü mat′ik), **1** of rheumatism. **2** having rheumatism; liable to have rheumatism. **3** caused by rheumatism. **4** person who has rheumatism. 1-3 *adj.,* 4 *n.* —**rheu mat′i cal ly,** *adv.*

rheumatic fever, disease more common among children than among adults, characterized by fever, pains in the joints, and often damage to the heart.

rheu ma tism (rü′mə tiz′əm), **1** disease with inflammation, swelling, and stiffness of the joints. **2** rheumatic fever. *n.*

rheum y (rü′mē), **1** full of rheum. **2** causing rheum; damp and cold. *adj.,* **rheum i er, rheum i est.**

Rh factor, an antigen found in the red blood cells of most people. Blood containing this substance (**Rh positive**) does not combine favorably with blood lacking it (**Rh negative**).

Rhine (rīn), river flowing from central Switzerland through West Germany and the Netherlands into the North Sea. *n.*

Rhine land (rīn′land′), **1** the region along the Rhine. **2** the part of West Germany west of the Rhine. *n.*

rhine stone (rīn′stōn′), an imitation diamond, made of glass or paste. *n.* [*Rhinestone* is a translation of French *caillou de Rhin,* which literally means "pebble of the Rhine."]

rhi no (rī′nō), rhinoceros. *n., pl.* **rhi nos** or **rhi no.**

rhi noc er os (rī nos′ər əs), a large, thick-skinned mammal of Africa and Asia with one or two upright horns on the snout. Rhinoceroses eat grass and other plants. *n., pl.* **rhi noc er os es** or **rhi noc er os.**

WORD HISTORY

rhinoceros

Rhinoceros is from Greek *rhinokerōs,* which comes from *rhinos,* meaning "nose," and *keras,* meaning "horn."

about 5¹/₂ ft. (1.6 m.) high at the shoulder

rhi zome (rī′zōm), a rootlike underground stem which sends out roots below and leafy shoots above; rootstock. *n.*

Rhode Island (rōd), one of the northeastern states of the United States. Rhode Island is the smallest state. *Abbreviation:* R.I. or RI *Capital:* Providence.

Rhodes (rōdz), **1** Greek island in the Aegean Sea. See **Troy** for map. **2 Cecil John,** 1853-1902, British colonial statesman and administrator in South Africa. *n.*

Rho de sia (rō dē′zhə), former name of **Zimbabwe.** *n.* —**Rho de′sian,** *adj., n.*

rho di um (rō′dē əm), a silver-white metallic element found chiefly in platinum ores. It is resistant to acids, and is used for plating silverware, jewelry, etc. *n.*

rho do den dron (rō′də den′drən), an evergreen shrub with leathery leaves and large pink, purple, or white flowers. *n.*

rhom bus (rom′bəs), parallelogram with equal sides, usually having two obtuse angles and two acute angles. *n., pl.* **rhom bus es, rhom bi** (rom′bī).

rhombuses

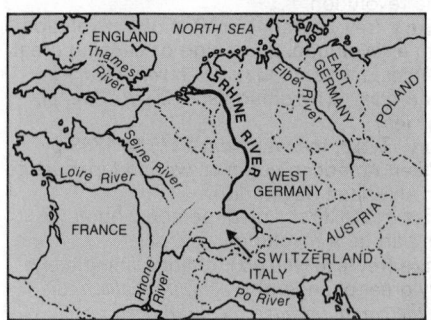

Rhine

Rhone or **Rhône** (rōn), river flowing from S Switzerland through SE France into the Mediterranean Sea. See **Rhine** for map. *n.*

rhu barb (rü′bärb), **1** the sour stalks of a garden plant with very large leaves, used for making sauce, pies, etc. **2** SLANG. a violent argument or protest. *n.*

rhyme (rīm), **1** sound alike in the last part: *"Long" and "song" rhyme. "Go to bed" rhymes with "sleepyhead."* **2** word or line having the same last sound as another: *"Cat" is a rhyme for "mat."* **3** verses or poetry with some of the lines ending in similar sounds. **4** agreement in the final sounds of words or lines. **5** put or make into rhyme: *rhyme a translation.* **6** make rhymes. **7** use (a word) with another that rhymes with it: *rhyme "love" and "dove."* 1,5-7 *v.*, **rhymed, rhym ing;** 2-4 *n.* Also, **rime.**
without rhyme or reason, having no system or sense.

rhym er (rī′mər), person who makes rhymes. *n.*

rhythm (riŦH′əm), **1** movement with a regular repetition of a beat, accent, rise and fall, or the like: *the rhythm of dancing, the rhythm of the tides, the rhythm of one's heartbeats.* **2** repetition of an accent; arrangement of beats in a line of poetry or in a piece of music. *n.*

rhyth mic (riŦH′mik), rhythmical. *adj.*

rhyth mi cal (riŦH′mə kəl), having rhythm; of or having to do with rhythm: *the rhythmical sound of the music. adj.*
—**rhyth′mi cal ly,** *adv.*

RI, Rhode Island (used with postal Zip Code).

R.I., Rhode Island.

ri a ta (rē ä′tə), lariat. *n.*

rib (rib), **1** one of the curved bones extending from the backbone around the heart and lungs to the front of the body. **2** something like a rib. The curved timbers in a ship's frame are called ribs. The thick vein of a leaf is also called a rib. An umbrella has ribs. **3** furnish or strengthen with ribs. **4** ridge in cloth, knitting, etc. **5** a cut of meat containing a rib: *a rib of beef.* **6** mark with riblike ridges. **7** INFORMAL. to tease. 1,2,4,5 *n.*, 3,6,7 *v.*, **ribbed, rib bing.** [*Rib* comes from Old English *ribb.*]
—**rib′ber,** *n.* —**rib′like′,** *adj.*

rib ald (rib′əld), offensive in speech; coarsely mocking; irreverent; indecent; obscene: *a ribald story. adj.*

rib ald ry (rib′əl drē), ribald language. *n., pl.* **rib ald ries.**

ribbed (ribd), having ribs or ridges: *ribbed cloth. adj.*

rib bon (rib′ən), **1** a strip or band of silk, satin, velvet, etc. Bows for the hair, belts, and badges are often made of ribbon. **2** anything like such a strip: *a typewriter ribbon. The flag was torn to ribbons by the severe windstorm. n.*
—**rib′bon like′,** *adj.*

rib boned (rib′ənd), decorated with ribbons; tied with a ribbon. *adj.*

ri bo fla vin (rī′bō flā′vən), a constituent of the vitamin B complex that promotes growth and is present in liver, eggs, milk, spinach, etc. It is sometimes called vitamin G or B_2. *n.*

ri bo nu cle ic acid (rī′bō nü klē′ik *or* rī′bō nyü klē′ik), a complex chemical compound found in the cytoplasm and sometimes in the nuclei of all living cells. It plays an important part in making proteins.

rice (rīs), **1** the starchy grain of a kind of cereal grass, or the plant that it grows on. Rice is grown in warm climates and is an important food in India, China, and Japan. **2** press (food) through a sieve so that it looks like rice: *to rice potatoes.* 1,2 *n.*, 3 *v.*, **riced, ric ing.**

rice bird (rīs′bėrd′), (in the southern United States) a bobolink. *n.*

rich (rich), **1** having much money, land, goods, etc.: *a rich person.* **2 the rich,** rich people. **3** well supplied; abounding: *a country rich in oil.* **4** producing much; fertile: *rich soil, a rich mine.* **5** having great worth; valuable:

a rich harvest, rich advice. **6** costly; elegant: *rich dress, rich jewels, rich carpets.* **7** containing plenty of butter, eggs, flavoring, etc.: *a rich fruit cake.* **8** (of colors, sounds, smells, etc.) deep; full; vivid: *a rich red, a rich tone.* **9** INFORMAL. very amusing; ridiculous. 1,3-9 *adj.*, 2 *n.* —**rich′ly,** *adv.* —**rich′ness,** *n.*

Rich ard I (rich′ərd), 1157-1199, king of England from 1189 to 1199. He was called "Richard the Lion-Hearted."

Rich e lieu (rish′ə lü), 1585-1642, French cardinal and statesman who virtually controlled France from 1624 to 1642. *n.*

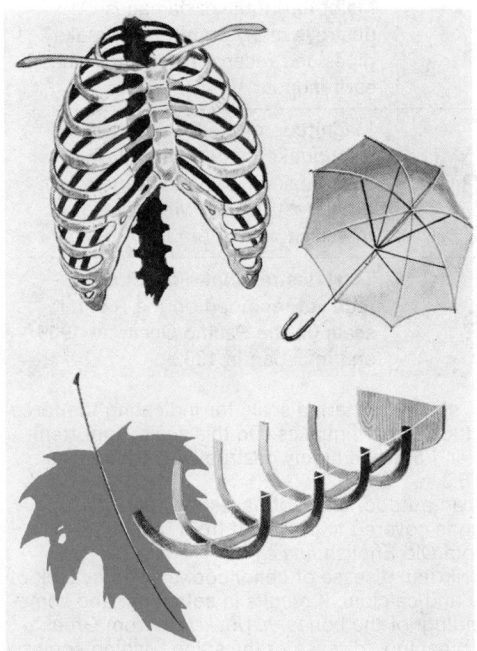

rib (defs. 1 and 2)

rich es (rich′iz), much money, land, goods, etc.; abundance of property; wealth. *n.pl.*

Rich mond (rich′mənd), capital of Virginia, in the E part. *n.*

rice (def. 1)

a hat	**i** it	**oi** oil	**ch** child	a in about
ā age	**ī** ice	**ou** out	**ng** long	e in taken
ä far	**o** hot	**u** cup	**sh** she	ə = i in pencil
e let	**ō** open	**u̇** put	**th** thin	o in lemon
ē equal	**ô** order	**ü** rule	**ŦH** then	u in circus
ėr term			**zh** measure	

Richter Scale

(Each whole number equals 10 times the magnitude of the previous whole number. Thus, a magnitude of 6 is 1000 times greater than a magnitude of 3.)

Magnitude	Effects
0–3	Can be detected only by instruments
3	Usually felt by people near the center of the earthquake
4.5	Felt up to 20 miles (32 km.) from the center; may crack walls and windows
6	Destructive over a 20-mile radius
7.5	Major earthquake; damages or destroys many structures, breaks pipes and reservoirs; faults in the earth appear
8.3	Magnitude of the San Francisco earthquake in 1906 (the Alaska earthquake in 1964 measured 8.4); great destruction, with fissures in the earth 40 in. (1 m.) across
8.9	Total destruction; highest magnitude yet recorded on the Richter scale (in the Pacific Ocean in 1906 and in Japan in 1933)

Rich ter scale (rik′tər), a scale for indicating the force or magnitude of earthquakes. On this scale, light tremors register 1.5, while highly destructive earthquakes measure 8.3.

rick (rik), an outdoor stack of hay, straw, etc., especially one which is covered to protect it from rain. *n.* [*Rick* comes from Old English *hrēac.*]

rick ets (rik′its), disease of childhood, caused by lack of vitamin D and calcium. It results in softening, and sometimes bending, of the bones. *n.* [*Rickets* is from Greek *rhakhitis*, meaning "disease of the spine," which comes from *rhachis*, meaning "backbone."]

rick et y (rik′ə tē), 1 liable to fall or break down; shaky; weak: *a rickety old chair.* 2 having rickets; suffering from rickets. 3 feeble in the joints. *adj.* —**rick′et i ness,** *n.*

rick sha (rik′shô), jinrikisha. *n., pl.* **rick shas.**

rick shaw (rik′shô), jinrikisha. *n.*

ric o chet (rik′ə shā′), 1 the skipping or jumping motion of an object as it goes along a flat surface: *the ricochet of a stone thrown along the surface of water.* 2 move with a skipping or jumping motion: *The bullets struck the ground and ricocheted through the grass.* 1 *n.,* 2 *v.,* **ric o cheted** (rik′ə shād′), **ric o chet ing** (rik′ə shā′ing).

rid[1] (rid), make free: *What will rid a house of mice? v.,* **rid** or **rid ded, rid ding.**

be rid of, be freed from.

get rid of, 1 get free from: *I can't get rid of this cold.* 2 do away with: *Poison will get rid of the rats in the barn.*

rid[2] (rid), OLD USE. a past tense and a past participle of **ride.** *v.*

rid dance (rid′ns), a clearing away or out; removal. *n.*

good riddance, exclamation expressing relief that something or somebody has been removed.

rid den (rid′n), past participle of **ride.** *I had ridden my horse all day. v.*

rid dle[1] (rid′l), 1 a puzzling question, statement, problem, etc. EXAMPLE: When is a door not a door? ANSWER: When it is ajar. 2 person or thing that is hard to understand, explain, etc. 3 speak in riddles. 4 solve a riddle or question. 1,2 *n.,* 3,4 *v.,* **rid dled, rid dling.** —**rid′dler,** *n.*

rid dle[2] (rid′l), 1 pierce with holes: *Insects had riddled the old tree stump.* 2 damage or weaken as if by making many holes in: *The witness's testimony was riddled with lies. v.,* **rid dled, rid dling.**

ride (rīd), 1 sit on a horse and make it go. 2 sit on something and make it go: *ride a camel, ride a bicycle.* 3 be carried along by anything: *ride on a train, ride in a car.* 4 ride over, along, or through. 5 be carried on: *The eagle rides the winds.* 6 a trip on horseback, in an automobile, on a train, etc.: *We took a ride into the country.* 7 move or float on the water: *The ship rode into port.* 8 lie at anchor. 9 INFORMAL. make fun of; tease. 10 cause to ride; carry: *She rode her little sister piggyback.* 11 control, dominate, or tyrannize over: *be ridden by foolish fears.* 1-5,7-11 *v.,* **rode, rid den, rid ing;** 6 *n.* —**rid′a ble, ride′a ble,** *adj.*

let ride, leave undisturbed or inactive: *Let the matter ride until later.*

ride down, 1 knock down. **2** overcome. **3** overtake by riding.

ride out, endure successfully: *The small boat rode out the storm without damage.*

rid er (rī′dər), 1 person who rides: *a horseback rider.* 2 anything added to a record, document, legislative bill, or statement after it was supposed to be complete. *n.* —**rid′er less,** *adj.*

ridge (rij), 1 the long and narrow upper part of something: *the ridge of an animal's back.* 2 the line where two sloping surfaces meet: *the ridge of a roof.* 3 a long, narrow chain of hills or mountains: *the Blue Ridge of the Appalachian Mountains.* 4 any raised narrow strip: *the ridges on corduroy cloth, the ridges in plowed ground.* 5 to form or make into ridges. 6 to cover with ridges; mark with ridges. 1-4 *n.,* 5,6 *v.,* **ridged, ridg ing.**

ridge pole (rij′pōl′), the horizontal timber along the top of a roof or tent; rooftree. *n.*

rid i cule (rid′ə kyül), 1 laugh at; make fun of: *People once ridiculed the Wright brothers' invention.* 2 laughter in mockery; words or actions that make fun of somebody or something: *I was very hurt by the ridicule of my classmates.* 1 *v.,* **rid i culed, rid i cul ing;** 2 *n.* [*Ridicule* is from Latin *ridiculum,* which comes from *ridere,* meaning "to laugh."] —**rid′i cul er,** *n.*

ri dic u lous (ri dik′yə ləs), deserving ridicule; absurd; laughable: *It would be ridiculous to walk backward all the time. adj.* —**ri dic′u lous ly,** *adv.* —**ri dic′u lous ness,** *n.*

ridiculous
Her wig rose to a **ridiculous** height.

rife (rīf), **1** happening often; common; numerous; widespread: *Noise is rife in the big city.* **2** well supplied; full; abounding: *Our town was rife with rumors that the bank had no funds. adj.* —**rife′ly,** *adv.*

riff raff (rif′raf′), **1** disreputable people. **2** trash; rubbish. *n.*

ri fle[1] (rī′fəl), **1** gun with spiral grooves in its long barrel which spin or rotate the bullet as it is shot. A rifle is usually fired from the shoulder. **2** cut such grooves in (a gun). 1 *n.,* 2 *v.,* **ri fled, ri fling.**

ri fle[2] (rī′fəl), search and rob; ransack and rob. *v.,* **ri fled, ri fling.** —**ri′fler,** *n.*

ri fle man (rī′fəl mən), **1** soldier armed with a rifle. **2** person skilled in the use of a rifle. *n., pl.* **ri fle men.**

rift (rift), **1** a split; break; crack: *The sun shone through a rift in the clouds.* **2** to split; break open. 1 *n.,* 2 *v.*

rig (rig), **1** fit out (a ship) with masts, sails, and ropes. **2** the arrangement of masts, sails, ropes, etc., on a ship. A schooner has a fore-and-aft rig; that is, the sails are set lengthwise on the ship. **3** outfit; equipment: *a camper's rig, an oil-drilling rig.* **4** equip; fit out: *rig out a football team with uniforms.* **5** INFORMAL. to dress: *On Halloween the children rig themselves up in funny clothes.* **6** INFORMAL. set of clothes; costume: *His rig consisted of a silk hat and overalls.* **7** get ready for use. **8** put together in a hurry or by using odds and ends: *The girls rigged up a tent with a rope and a blanket.* **9** arrange in an unfair way: *The race was rigged.* **10** INFORMAL. carriage, with its horse or horses. 1,4,5,7-9 *v.,* **rigged, rig ging;** 2,3,6,10 *n.*

Ri ga (rē′gə), **1** seaport on the Baltic Sea and capital of Latvia. **2** Gulf of, gulf on the Baltic Sea. *n.*

rig ger (rig′ər), person who rigs. *n.*

rig ging (rig′ing), **1** ropes, chains, and cables, used to support and work the masts, yards, sails, etc., on a ship. **2** equipment used for a specific purpose. *n.*

right (rīt), **1** agreeing with what is good, just, or lawful: *She did the right thing when she told the truth.* **2** in a way that is good, just, or lawful: *He acted right when he told the truth.* **3** that which is right, just, good, or true: *Do right, not wrong.* **4** a just claim; something that is due to a person: *Each member of the club has a right to vote. I demand my rights.* **5** correct; true: *the right answer.* **6** correctly; truly: *She guessed right.* **7** proper; suitable; fitting: *Learn to say the right thing at the right time.* **8** properly; well: *It's faster to do a job right the first time.* **9** in good condition; well: *I don't feel right; I think I'm getting the flu.* **10** meant to be seen; most important: *the right side of cloth.* **11** make correct; set right: *right a wrong.* **12** do justice to: *right the oppressed.* **13** fair treatment; justice. **14** get or put into proper position: *The ship righted as the wave passed. We righted the sailboat.* **15** opposite of left; belonging to the side that is turned east when the main side is turned north. Most people eat, write, and work with their right hands. **16** on this side when viewed from the front: *Make a right turn at the corner.* **17** on or to the right side: *Turn right.* **18** the right side or hand: *Please sit on my right.* **19** exactly; just; precisely: *Your cap is right where you left it.* **20** at once; immediately: *Stop playing right now.* **21** very: *the Right Honorable Lord Mayor.* **22** DIALECT. extremely: *I am right glad to see you.* **23** in a straight line; directly: *Look me right in the eye.* **24** straight: *a right line.* **25** completely: *My hat was knocked right off.* **26** part of a lawmaking body consisting of the conservative or reactionary political groups. **27** having conservative or reactionary ideas in politics. **28** OLD USE. rightful; real. 1,5,7,9,10,15,16,24,27, 28 *adj.,* 2,6,8,17,19-23,25 *adv.,* 3,4,13,18,26 *n.,* 11,12,14 *v.* [*Right* comes from Old English *riht.*] —**right′er,** *n.* —**right′ness,** *n.*

by right or **by rights,** properly; rightly; correctly.

---

a hat	**i** it	**oi** oil	**ch** child	a in about
ā age	**ī** ice	**ou** out	**ng** long	e in taken
ä far	**o** hot	**u** cup	**sh** she	ə = i in pencil
e let	**ō** open	**ú** put	**th** thin	o in lemon
ē equal	**ô** order	**ü** rule	**ᵮн** then	u in circus
ėr term			**zh** measure	

in the right, right.

right about! turn in the opposite direction.

right away or **right off,** at once; immediately: *I'll do it right away.*

right on, SLANG. exactly right, correct, or true.

to rights, INFORMAL. in or into proper condition, order, etc.

right angle, an angle that is formed by a line perpendicular to another line; angle of 90 degrees. The angles in a square are right angles.

right angles

right-an gled (rīt′ang′gəld), containing a right angle or right angles; rectangular. *adj.*

right eous (rī′chəs), **1** doing right; virtuous; behaving justly: *a righteous person.* **2** proper; just; right: *righteous indignation. adj.* —**right′eous ly,** *adv.* —**right′eous-ness,** *n.*

right field, (in baseball) the section of the outfield beyond first base.

right ful (rīt′fəl), **1** according to law; by rights: *the rightful owner of this dog.* **2** just and right; proper. *adj.* —**right′ful ly,** *adv.* —**right′ful ness,** *n.*

right-hand (rīt′hand′), **1** on or to the right. **2** of, for, or with the right hand. **3** most helpful or useful: *He is the scoutmaster's right-hand man. adj.*

right-hand ed (rīt′han′did), **1** using the right hand more easily and readily than the left. **2** done with the right hand. **3** made to be used with the right hand. **4** turning from left to right: *a right-handed screw.* **5** toward the right; with the right hand. 1-4 *adj.,* 5 *adv.* —**right′-hand′ed ly,** *adv.* —**right′-hand′ed ness,** *n.*

right ist (rī′tist), **1** person who has conservative or reactionary ideas in politics. **2** member of a conservative or reactionary political organization. **3** having conservative or reactionary ideas. 1,2 *n.,* 3 *adj.*

right ly (rīt′lē), **1** in a just manner; fairly. **2** correctly: *She guessed rightly that it would rain.* **3** properly; suitably. *adv.*

right of way, **1** the right to go first, especially the right of a vehicle to cross in front of another. **2** the right to pass over another's property.

right triangle, triangle with one right angle.

right ward (rīt′wərd), on or toward the right. *adj., adv.*

right wards (rīt′wərdz), rightward. *adv.*

right wing, the conservative or reactionary members, especially of a political party.

rig id (rij′id), **1** not bending; stiff; firm: *Hold your arm rigid.* **2** not changing; strict: *a rigid belief, a rigid rule. adj.* —**rig′id ly,** *adv.* —**rig′id ness,** *n.*

ri gid i ty (ri jid′ə tē), **1** stiffness; firmness. **2** strictness; severity. *n.*

rig ma role (rig′mə rōl′), foolish talk or activity; words or action without meaning; nonsense. *n.*

rig or (rig′ər), **1** strictness; severity: *The new recruits were trained with great rigor.* **2** harshness: *endure the rigors of a* long, cold winter. **3** logical exactness: *the rigor of scientific method.* n.

rig or ous (rig′ər əs), **1** severe; strict: *the rigorous discipline in the army.* **2** harsh: *a rigorous climate.* **3** thoroughly logical and scientific; exact: *the rigorous methods of science.* adj. —**rig′or ous ly,** adv. —**rig′or ous ness,** n.

rile (rīl), INFORMAL. disturb; irritate; annoy greatly: *If you criticize them, it will just rile them up, and we'll never get the job done.* v., **riled, ril ing.**

Ri ley (rī′lē), **James Whitcomb,** 1849-1916, American poet. n.

rill (ril), a tiny stream; little brook. n.

rim (rim), **1** an edge, border, or margin on or around anything: *the rim of a wheel, the rim of a cup.* **2** form a rim around; put a rim around: *Wild flowers and grasses rimmed the little pool.* 1 n., 2 v., **rimmed, rim ming.** —**rim′less,** adj.

rime¹ (rīm), rhyme. v., **rimed, rim ing;** n.

rime² (rīm), **1** white frost; hoarfrost. **2** cover with rime. 1 n., 2 v., **rimed, rim ing.**

Rim sky-Kor sa kov (rim′skē kôr′sə kôf), **Nikolay,** 1844-1908, Russian composer. n.

rim y (rī′mē), covered with rime; frosty. adj., **rim i er, rim i est.**

rind (rīnd), the firm outer covering of oranges, melons, cheeses, etc. n.

ring¹ (ring), **1** a circle: *You can tell the age of a tree by counting the number of rings in its wood; one ring grows every year. We danced in a ring.* **2** a thin circle of metal or other material: *a napkin ring, a wedding ring, a key ring.* **3** persons or things arranged in a circle. **4** the outer edge or border of a coin, plate, wheel, or anything round. **5** put a ring around; enclose; form a circle around. **6** toss a horseshoe, ring, etc., over: *He ringed the post.* **7** put a ring in the nose of (an animal). **8** form a ring or rings. **9** an enclosed space (for races or games): *a circus ring, a ring for a fight.* **10** prizefighting. **11** group of people combined for a selfish or bad purpose: *A ring of corrupt politicians controlled the city.* 1-4,9-11 n., 5-8 v., **ringed, ring ing.** —**ring′like′,** adj.

run rings around, INFORMAL. surpass with great ease; beat easily.

ring² (ring), **1** give forth a clear sound, as a bell does: *Did the telephone ring?* **2** cause to give forth a clear ringing sound: *Ring the bell.* **3** cause a bell to sound: *Did you ring?* **4** make (a sound) by ringing: *The bells rang a joyous peal.* **5** a sound of a bell: *Did you hear a ring?* **6** a sound like that of a bell: *On a cold night we can hear the ring of skates on ice.* **7** announce or proclaim by bells; usher; conduct: *Ring out the old year; ring in the new.* **8** proclaim or repeat loudly everywhere: *ring a person's praises.* **9** resound; sound loudly: *The room rang with shouts of laughter.* **10** to echo; give back sound: *The mountains rang with the roll of thunder.* **11** be filled with report or talk. **12** sound: *His words rang true.* **13** have a sensation as of sounds of bells; hear inner sounds: *My ears ring.* **14** a characteristic sound or quality: *a ring of sincerity.* **15** call up on a telephone: *I'll ring you tomorrow.* **16** a call on the telephone. 1-4,7-13,15 v., **rang, rung, ring ing;** 5,6,14,16 n.

ring for, summon by a bell.

ring off, end a telephone call.

ring up, record (a specific amount) on a cash register.

ringed (ringd), **1** having or wearing a ring or rings. **2** marked or decorated with a ring or rings. **3** surrounded by a ring or rings. **4** formed of or with rings; ringlike. adj.

ring er (ring′ər), **1** person or thing that rings; device for ringing a bell. **2** SLANG. person or thing very much like another. n.

ring lead er (ring′lē′dər), person who leads others in

opposition to authority or law: *the ringleaders of the mutiny.* n.

ring let (ring′lit), **1** curl: *The baby's hair was in ringlets.* **2** a little ring: *Drops of rain made ringlets in the pond.* n.

ring side (ring′sīd′), **1** a place just outside the ring at a circus, prizefight, etc. **2** a place affording a close view. n.

ring worm (ring′wėrm′), any of several contagious skin diseases caused by fungi. One kind appears in the form of ring-shaped patches. Athlete's foot is a common type of ringworm. n.

rink (def. 1)—a hockey rink

rink (ringk), **1** sheet of ice for skating. **2** a smooth floor for roller-skating. n.

rinse (rins), **1** wash with clean water: *Rinse all the soap out of your hair after you wash it.* **2** wash lightly: *Rinse your mouth with warm water.* **3** a rinsing: *Give the clothes a final rinse in cold water.* **4** a liquid preparation used after shampooing to add color or luster to the hair. 1,2 v., **rinsed, rins ing;** 3,4 n. [Rinse came into English about 600 years ago from French *reïncier,* and can be traced back to Latin *recentem,* meaning "recent, fresh."]

Ri o de Ja nei ro (rē′ō dā zhə ner′ō), seaport on the SE coast of Brazil.

Ri o Grande (rē′ō grand′ or rē′ō gran′dē), river forming part of the boundary between the United States and Mexico.

ri ot (rī′ət), **1** a wild, violent public disturbance; disorder caused by an unruly crowd or mob: *a riot in a prison.* **2** behave in a wild, disorderly way. **3** to have a noisy good time. **4** a bright display: *The garden was a riot of color.* **5** INFORMAL. a very amusing person or performance: *She was a riot at the party.* 1,4,5 n., 2,3 v. —**ri′ot er,** n.

read the riot act, give orders for disturbance to cease.

run riot, 1 act without restraint; run wild. **2** grow wildly or luxuriantly.

ri ot ous (rī′ə təs), **1** taking part in a riot. **2** boisterous; disorderly: *Sounds of riotous glee came from the playhouse.* adj. —**ri′ot ous ly,** adv. —**ri′ot ous ness,** n.

rip¹ (rip), **1** cut roughly; tear apart; tear off: *Rip the cover off this box.* **2** become torn apart. **3** cut or pull out (the threads in the seams of a garment). **4** a torn place, especially a seam burst in a garment: *Please sew up this rip in my sleeve.* **5** saw (wood) along the grain, not across the grain. **6** INFORMAL. move fast or violently. 1-3,5,6 v., **ripped, rip ping;** 4 n.

rip off, SLANG. steal: *rip off an expensive camera.*

rip² (rip), **1** a stretch of rough water made by opposing currents meeting. **2** a swift current made by the tide. n.

rip cord (rip′kôrd′), cord which is pulled to open a parachute. n.

rip current, a strong, narrow surface current which flows rapidly away from the shore; riptide.

ripe (rīp), **1** full-grown and ready to be gathered and eaten: *ripe fruit.* **2** fully developed; mature: *a ripe cheese,* *ripe in knowledge.* **3** ready: *That country is ripe for revolt.* **4** advanced in years: *the ripe age of 75. adj.,* **rip er, ripest. —ripe′ly,** *adv.* **—ripe′ness,** *n.*

rip en (rī′pən), become or make ripe. *v.* **—rip′en er,** *n.*

rip-off (rip′ôf′), SLANG. **1** theft. **2** something that exploits or cheats. *n.*

rip per (rip′ər), **1** person who rips. **2** tool for ripping. *n.*

ripple (def. 2)

rip ple (rip′əl), **1** a very little wave: *Throw a stone into still water and watch the ripples spread in rings.* **2** anything that seems like a tiny wave: *ripples in the sand.* **3** a sound that reminds one of little waves: *a ripple of laughter in the crowd.* **4** make a sound like rippling water. **5** form or have ripples. **6** make ripples on: *A breeze rippled the quiet waters.* 1-3 *n.,* 4-6 *v.,* **rip pled, rip pling. —rip′pler,** *n.*

rip saw (rip′sô′), saw for cutting wood along the grain, not across the grain. *n.*

rip tide (rip′tīd′), rip current. *n.*

Rip Van Win kle (rip′ van wing′kəl), hero of a story by Washington Irving who falls asleep and wakes twenty years later to find everything changed.

rise (rīz), **1** get up from a lying, sitting, or kneeling position; stand up: *Please rise from your seat when you recite.* **2** get up from sleep or rest: *I rise at 7 every morning.* **3** go up; come up; move up; ascend: *The curtain rose on the first act of the play. Mercury rises in a thermometer on a hot day.* **4** go higher; increase: *Prices are rising. My anger rose at that remark.* **5** a going up; a going higher: *a rise in prices. We watched the rise of the balloon.* **6** an advance in rank, power, etc. **7** to advance in importance, rank, etc.: *He rose from clerk to president of the company.* **8** to slope upward: *Hills rise in the distance.* **9** an upward slope: *The rise of that hill is gradual.* **10** piece of rising or high ground; hill: *The house is situated on a rise.* **11** the vertical height of a step, slope, arch, etc. **12** come above the horizon: *The sun rises in the morning.* **13** start; begin: *The river rises from a spring. Quarrels often rise from trifles.* **14** come into being or action: *The wind rose rapidly.* **15** origin; beginning; start: *the rise of a river, the rise of a storm, the rise of a new problem.* **16** become more cheerful; improve: *Our spirits rose at the good news.* **17** to revolt; rebel: *The people rose against the government.* **18** grow larger and lighter: *Yeast makes dough rise.* **19** come to life again: *Christ is risen.* 1-4,7,8,12-14,16-19 *v.,* **rose, ris en, ris ing;** 5,6,9-11,15 *n.* [*Rise* comes from Old English *rīsan.*]

get a rise out of, INFORMAL. get an emotional reaction from: *My teasing got a rise out of them.*

give rise to, bring about; start; begin; cause: *Their sudden wealth gave rise to rumors about where the money came from.*

rise to, be equal to; be able to deal with: *They rose to the occasion.*

ris en (riz′n), past participle of **rise.** *They had risen before dawn. v.*

a hat	i it	oi oil	ch child	a in about
ā age	ī ice	ou out	ng long	e in taken
ä far	o hot	u cup	sh she	ə = { i in pencil
e let	ō open	ù put	th thin	o in lemon
ē equal	ô order	ü rule	ᴛʜ then	u in circus
ėr term			zh measure	

ris er (rī′zər), **1** person or thing that rises: *an early riser.* **2** the vertical part of a step. *n.*

ris i ble (riz′ə bəl), **1** able or inclined to laugh. **2** of laughter; used in laughter. **3** amusing; funny. *adj.*

risk (risk), **1** chance of harm or loss; danger: *If you drive carefully, there is no risk of being fined.* **2** expose to the chance of harm or loss: *You risk your neck trying to climb that tree.* **3** take the risk of: *She risked defeat in running against the popular candidate.* 1 *n.,* 2,3 *v.*

run a risk or **take a risk,** expose oneself to the chance of harm or loss.

risk y (ris′kē), full of risk; dangerous. *adj.,* **risk i er, risk i est. —risk′i ly,** *adv.* **—risk′i ness,** *n.*

rit. or **ritard.,** ritardando.

ri tar dan do (rē′tär dän′dō), in music: **1** becoming gradually slower. **2** gradually more slowly. **3** movement or passage in which the tempo gradually becomes slower. 1 *adj.,* 2 *adv.,* 3 *n.*

rite (rīt), a solemn ceremony. Most churches have rites for baptism, marriage, and burial. Secret societies have their special rites. *n.*

rit u al (rich′ü əl), **1** a form or system of rites. The rites of baptism, marriage, and burial are parts of the ritual of most churches. Secret societies have a ritual for initiating new members. **2** of rites; done as a rite: *a ritual dance, ritual laws.* **3** any regularly followed routine. 1,3 *n.,* 2 *adj.* **—rit′u al ly,** *adv.*

rit u al ism (rich′ü ə liz′əm), fondness for ritual; insistence upon ritual. *n.*

ritz y (rit′sē), SLANG. stylish; smart. *adj.,* **ritz i er, ritz i est.**

ri val (rī′vəl), **1** person who wants and tries to get the same thing as another or who tries to equal or do better than another; competitor: *The two girls were rivals for the same class office. They were also rivals in sports.* **2** wanting the same thing as another; trying to equal or outdo another; competing: *The rival supermarkets both cut their prices.* **3** try to equal or outdo; compete with: *The stores rival each other in beautiful window displays.* **4** equal; match: *The sunset rivaled the sunrise in beauty.* **5** thing that will bear comparison with something else; equal; match. 1,5 *n.,* 2 *adj.,* 3,4 *v.,* **ri valed, ri val ing** or **ri valled, ri val ling.**

WORD HISTORY

rival

Rival is from Latin *rivalis,* meaning "one who uses the same stream as another," which comes from *rivus,* meaning "stream."

ri val ry (rī′vəl rē), effort to obtain something another person wants; competition: *There is rivalry among business firms for trade. n., pl.* **ri val ries.**

rive (rīv), tear apart; split. *v.,* **rived, rived** or **riv en, riv ing.**

riv en (riv′ən), torn apart; split. *adj.*

riv er (riv′ər), **1** a large, natural stream of water that flows into a lake, ocean, etc. **2** any abundant stream or flow: *rivers of lava. n.*

riv er bank (riv′ər bangk′), the ground bordering a river. *n.*

river basin, land that is drained by a river and its tributaries.

riv er side (riv′ər sīd′), the bank of a river: *We walked along the riverside. n.*

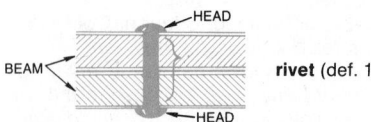

BEAM · HEAD · HEAD · **rivet** (def. 1)

riv et (riv′it), **1** a metal bolt with a head at one end, the other end being hammered into a head after insertion. Rivets fasten heavy steel beams together. **2** fasten with a rivet or rivets. **3** fasten firmly; fix firmly: *Their eyes were riveted on the speaker.* 1 *n.,* 2,3 *v.* —**riv′et er,** *n.*

Riv i er a (riv′ē er′ə), section of SE France and NW Italy along the Mediterranean Sea, famous as a resort. *n.*

riv u let (riv′yə lit), a very small stream. *n.*

Ri yadh (ri yäd′), capital of Saudi Arabia, in the central part. Mecca is the religious capital. *n.*

rm., 1 ream. **2** room. *pl.* **rms.**

Rn, symbol for radon.

R.N., 1 registered nurse. **2** Royal Navy.

RNA, ribonucleic acid.

roach[1] (rōch), cockroach. *n., pl.* **roach es.**

roach[2] (rōch), a silvery European freshwater fish related to the carp. *n., pl.* **roach es** or **roach.**

road (rōd), **1** a way between places; way made for automobiles, trucks, etc., to travel on: *the road from New York to Boston.* **2** a way or course: *the road to ruin, a road to peace.* **3** railroad. **4** Also, **roads,** *pl.* roadstead. *n.* [*Road* comes from Old English *rād,* meaning "a riding, journey."]

on the road, traveling, especially in order to sell something.

road bed (rōd′bed′), foundation for a road or for railroad tracks. *n.*

road block (rōd′blok′), an obstacle. *n.*

road hog, INFORMAL. person who uses more of the road than is necessary, especially by driving in the center of the road.

road map, map for automobile travel, showing the roads in a region and the distances between cities and towns.

road run ner (rōd′run′ər), a long-tailed bird of the deserts of the southwestern United States that is related to the cuckoo. It is noted for its ability to run quickly. *n.*

road side (rōd′sīd′), **1** the side of a road: *Flowers grew along the roadside.* **2** beside a road: *a roadside inn.* 1 *n.,* 2 *adj.*

road stead (rōd′sted), a place near the shore where ships may anchor; road. *n.*

road ster (rōd′stər), an open automobile with a single wide seat. *n.*

road way (rōd′wā′), **1** road. **2** the part of a road used by wheeled vehicles: *Do not walk in the roadway. n.*

roam (rōm), **1** go about with no special plan or aim; wander: *roam through the fields.* **2** wander over. *v.*

roan (rōn), **1** yellowish- or reddish-brown sprinkled with gray or white. **2** horse or other animal of a roan color. **3** a roan color. 1 *adj.,* 2,3 *n.*

roar (rôr), **1** make a loud, deep sound; make a loud noise: *The lion roared. The wind roared at the windows.* **2** a loud, deep sound; loud noise: *the roar of the cannon, a*

roar of laughter. **3** utter loudly: *roar out an order.* **4** laugh loudly: *The audience roared at the clown.* 1,3,4 *v.,* 2 *n.*

roast (rōst), **1** cook by dry heat; bake: *We roasted meat and potatoes.* **2** piece of baked meat; piece of meat to be roasted. **3** an informal outdoor meal, at which some food is cooked over an open fire: *a wiener roast.* **4** roasted: *roast beef, roast pork.* **5** prepare by heating: *roast coffee, roast a metal ore.* **6** make or become very hot. **7** INFORMAL. make fun of; ridicule. 1,5-7 *v.,* 2,3 *n.,* 4 *adj.*

roast er (rō′stər), **1** pan used in roasting. **2** something fit to be roasted. *n.*

rob (rob), **1** take away from by force or threats; steal from; plunder; pillage: *Bandits robbed the bank of thousands of dollars.* **2** steal: *Some girls robbed fruit from the orchard.* **3** take away some characteristic; keep from having or doing: *The disease has robbed him of his strength. v.,* **robbed, robbing.**

rob ber (rob′ər), person who robs; thief. *n.*

rob ber y (rob′ər ē), act of robbing; theft; stealing: *a bank robbery. n., pl.* **rob ber ies.**

robe (rōb), **1** a long, loose outer garment: *The priests wore robes.* **2** garment that shows rank, office, etc.: *a judge's robe, the queen's robes of state.* **3** a covering or wrap: *a beach robe.* **4** put a robe on; dress. **5** bathrobe or dressing gown. 1-3,5 *n.,* 4 *v.,* **robed, rob ing.**

rob in (rob′ən), **1** a large American thrush with a reddish breast. **2** a small European thrush with an orange breast. *n.* [This bird got its name from *Robin,* a nickname for *Robert.*]

Robin Hood, (in English legends) an outlaw who robbed the rich but gave money to the poor.

Rob in son Crusoe (rob′ən sən). See **Crusoe.**

ro bot (rō′bot *or* rō′bət), **1** machine with moving parts and sensing devices controlled by a computer. Computer programs enable a robot to carry out complex series of tasks repeatedly, without human supervision, and to change tasks with a change of programs. Robots are sometimes built to resemble human beings, though they can be of any shape and size. **2** person who acts or works in a dull, mechanical way. *n.*

WORD HISTORY

robot

Robot was borrowed from Czech *robot,* which comes from *robota,* meaning "work."

ro bot ics (rō bot′iks), the study, design, manufacture, and use of robots: *a professor of robotics. n.*

ro bust (rō bust′ *or* rō′bust), strong and healthy; sturdy: *a robust person, a robust mind. adj.* [*Robust* is from Latin *robustus,* meaning "firm, oaken," which comes from *robur,* meaning "oak."] —**ro bust′ly,** *adv.*

roc (rok), (in Arabian legend) a bird having such enormous size and strength that it could carry off an elephant. *n.*

Ro cham beau (rō shäm bō′), **Count de,** 1725-1807, commander of the French forces sent to help the American army in the Revolutionary War. *n.*

Roch es ter (roch′es′tər), city in W New York State. *n.*

rock[1] (rok), **1** a large mass of stone: *The ship was wrecked on the rocks.* **2** any piece of stone; a stone: *I threw a rock in the lake.* **3** the mass of mineral matter of which the earth's crust is made. **4** a particular layer or kind of such matter. **5** something firm like a rock; support; defense: *The Lord is my rock. n.* —**rock′like′,** *adj.* **on the rocks, 1** wrecked; ruined. **2** INFORMAL. bankrupt.

rock[2] (rok), **1** move backward or forward, or from side to side; sway: *The waves rocked the ship.* **2** put (to sleep, rest, etc.) with swaying movements: *I rocked the baby to sleep.* **3** a rocking movement. **4** a kind of popular music, originally called rock'n'roll, with a strong beat and a simple, often repeated, melody. **1,2** *v.,* **3,4** *n.*

rock bottom, the very bottom; lowest level.

rock candy, sugar in the form of large, hard crystals.

Rock e fel ler (rok′ə fel′ər), **1 John D(avison),** 1839-1937, American capitalist and philanthropist. **2** his grandson, **Nelson Aldrich,** 1908-1979, vice-president of the United States from 1974 to 1977. *n.*

rock er (rok′ər), **1** one of the curved pieces on which a cradle, rocking chair, etc., rocks. **2** rocking chair. *n.*

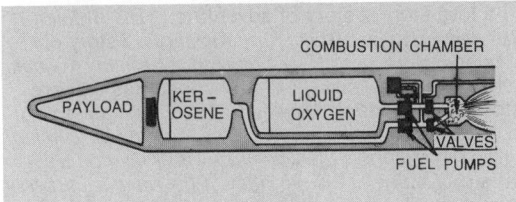

rocket (def. 1) which uses liquid fuel

rock et (rok′it), **1** device consisting of a tube open at one end in which an explosive or fuel is rapidly burned. The burning explosive or fuel creates gases that escape from the open end and force the tube and whatever is attached to it upward or forward. Some rockets, used for fireworks and signaling, shoot up high in the air and explode into showers of sparks or stars. Larger rockets are used in weapons or to carry capsules and satellites into outer space. **2** spacecraft, missile, etc., propelled by such a device. **3** go like a rocket; rise very fast; skyrocket: *rocket across the finish line in a race. The author rocketed to fame when her book was published.* **1,2** *n.,* **3** *v.*

rocket launcher, device consisting of a tube or cluster of tubes from which rockets are launched.

rock et ry (rok′ə trē), the science of building, using, and firing rockets. *n.*

Rock ies (rok′ēz), Rocky Mountains. *n.pl.*

rock i ness (rok′ē nis), a being shaky; weakness. *n.*

rocking chair, chair mounted on rockers, or on springs, so that it can rock back and forth; rocker.

rocking horse, a toy horse on rockers for children to ride.

rock 'n' roll (rok′ən rōl′), kind of popular music with a strong beat and simple melody. *n.*

rock-ribbed (rok′ribd′), **1** having ridges of rock. **2** unyielding; rigid. *adj.*

rock salt, common salt as it occurs in the earth in large crystals; halite. Rock salt is often used to melt ice on roads and sidewalks.

rock wool, woollike fibers made from rock or slag and used for insulation and soundproofing.

rock y[1] (rok′ē), **1** full of rocks: *a rocky shore.* **2** made of rock. **3** like rock; hard; firm: *rocky determination. adj.,* **rock i er, rock i est.**

rock y[2] (rok′ē), **1** likely to rock; shaky: *That table is a bit rocky; put a piece of wood under the short leg.* **2** INFORMAL. sickish; weak; dizzy. *adj.,* **rock i er, rock i est.** —**rock′i ly,** *adv.*

Rocky Mountains, chief group of mountain ranges in W North America; the Rockies. They extend from Alaska to New Mexico.

Rocky Mountain sheep, bighorn.

rococo (def. 2) a room with rococo decoration and furniture

ro co co (rō kō′kō), **1** style of architecture and decoration with elaborate ornamentation, combining shellwork, scrolls, foliage, etc., much used in the 1700's. **2** of this style. **1** *n.,* **2** *adj.*

rod (rod), **1** a thin, straight bar of metal, wood, or plastic. **2** a stick used to beat or punish. **3** punishment. **4** fishing rod. **5** unit of length equal to $5\frac{1}{2}$ yards or $16\frac{1}{2}$ feet. A square rod is $30\frac{1}{4}$ square yards or $272\frac{1}{4}$ square feet. **6** staff or wand carried as a symbol of one's position. *n.* —**rod′like′,** *adj.*

spare the rod, fail to punish.

rode (rōd), past tense of **ride.** *We rode ten miles yesterday. v.*

ro dent (rōd′nt), **1** any of a group of mammals with large front teeth especially adapted for gnawing. Rats, mice, and squirrels are rodents. **2** gnawing. **1** *n.,* **2** *adj.* [*Rodent* comes from Latin *rodentem,* meaning "gnawing."]

ro de o (rō′dē ō *or* rō dā′ō), **1** a contest or exhibition of skill in roping cattle, riding horses and steers, etc. **2** (in the western United States) the driving of cattle together. *n., pl.* **ro de os.** [*Rodeo* was borrowed from Spanish *rodeo,* which comes from *rodear,* meaning "go around," and can be traced back to Latin *rota,* meaning "wheel."]

Ro din (rō dan'), **Auguste,** 1840-1917, French sculptor. *n.*

roe[1] (rō), a small deer of Europe and Asia, with forked antlers. *n., pl.* **roes** or **roe.**

roe[2] (rō), fish eggs. *n.*

roe buck (rō'buk'), a male roe deer. *n.*

roent gen (rent'gən), measure of radiation intensity in X rays and gamma rays. *n.*

Roent gen (rent'gən), **Wilhelm Konrad,** 1845-1923, German physicist who discovered X rays. *n.*

rog er (roj'ər), INFORMAL. O.K.; message received and understood. *interj.*

rogue (rōg), **1** dishonest or unprincipled person; rascal. **2** a mischievous person: *The little rogue has his grandpa's glasses on.* **3** animal with a savage nature that lives apart from the herd. *n.*

ro guer y (rō'gər ē), **1** conduct of rogues. **2** playful mischief. *n., pl.* **ro guer ies.**

rogues' gallery, collection kept by the police of photographs of known criminals.

ro guish (rō'gish), **1** having to do with or like rogues; dishonest; rascally. **2** playfully mischievous: *She had a roguish twinkle in her eyes. adj.* —**ro'guish ly,** *adv.*

roil (roil), **1** make (water, etc.) muddy by stirring up sediment. **2** disturb; irritate; vex. *v.*

rois ter (roi'stər), be boisterous: swagger. *v.*

rois ter ous (rois'tər əs), noisy; boisterous. *adj.*

Ro land (rō'lənd), the most famous of Charlemagne's knights. *n.*

role or **rôle** (rōl), **1** an actor's part in a play, motion picture, etc.: *She played the leading role in the school play.* **2** a part played in real life: *He had the role of mediator in the recent strike. n. [Role comes from French rôle,* meaning "a roll (of paper)," and can be traced back to Latin *rota,* meaning "wheel." An actor's part was written on a roll of paper.]

roll (rōl), **1** move along by turning over and over: *The ball rolled away. The child rolled a wheel.* **2** turn round and round on itself or on something else; wrap; be wrapped round: *She rolled herself up in a blanket. Roll the string into a ball.* **3** something rolled up: *rolls of paper, a roll of carpet.* **4** a rounded or rolled-up mass: *a roll of cookie dough.* **5** move or be moved on wheels or rollers: *roll a bicycle. The car rolled along.* **6** move smoothly; sweep along: *Waves roll in on the beach.* **7** move with a side-to-side motion: *roll one's eyes. The ocean liner rolled in the waves.* **8** act of rolling; motion from side to side: *The ship's roll made many people sick.* **9** rise and fall again and again: *rolling country, rolling waves.* **10** make flat or smooth with a roller; spread out with a rolling pin, etc.: *Roll the dough thin for these cookies.* **11** make deep, loud sounds: *Thunder rolls.* **12** a deep, loud sound: *the roll of thunder.* **13** beat (a drum) with rapid, continuous strokes. **14** a rapid, continuous beating on a drum. **15** trill: *roll one's r's.* **16** a list of names; record; list: *I will call the roll to find out who is absent.* **17** a kind of bread or cake: *a sweet roll.* 1,2,5-7,9-11,13,15 *v.,* 3,4,8,12,14,16,17 *n. [Roll* came into English about 600 years ago from French *roller,* and can be traced back to Latin *rota,* meaning "wheel."]

roll up, pile up; increase: *Bills roll up fast.*

roll call, the calling of a list of names, as of soldiers, pupils, etc., to find out who is present.

roll er (rō'lər), **1** thing that rolls; cylinder on which something is rolled along or rolled up. The shades for many windows are raised and lowered on rollers. **2** cylinder of metal, stone, wood, etc., used for smoothing, pressing, crushing, etc.: *A heavy roller was used to smooth the tennis court.* **3** a long, swelling wave: *Huge rollers broke on the sandy beach. n.*

roller bearing, a bearing in which the shaft turns on rollers to lessen friction.

roller coaster, railway for amusement, consisting of inclined tracks along which small cars roll and make sudden drops and turns.

roller skate, a shoe or metal base with four small wheels, used for skating on a floor, sidewalk, or other surface; skate.

roll er-skate (rō'lər skāt'), move on roller skates. *v.,* **roll er-skat ed, roller-skat ing.**

rol lick ing (rol'ə king), frolicking; jolly; lively: *I had a rollicking good time at the picnic. adj.*

rolling mill, 1 factory where metal is rolled into sheets and bars. **2** machine for doing this.

rolling pin, cylinder of wood, plastic, or glass with a handle at each end, for rolling out dough.

rolling stock, the locomotives and cars of a railroad.

ro ly-po ly (rō'lē pō'lē), **1** short and plump: *a roly-poly child.* **2** a short, plump person or animal. **1** *adj.,* **2** *n., pl.* **ro ly-po lies.**

ROM (rom), read-only memory (computer memory containing data that can be copied but not changed or erased). *n.*

Rom., 1 Roman. **2** Romance. **3** Romania. **4** Romans (book of the New Testament).

Ro man (rō'mən), **1** of ancient or modern Rome or its people. **2** person born or living in Rome. **3** citizen of ancient Rome. **4** of the Roman Catholic Church. **5 roman, a** the style of type most used in printing and typewriting. This sentence is in roman. **b** of or in roman type. 1,4,5b *adj.,* 2,3,5a *n.*

Roman Catholic, 1 of or belonging to the Christian church that recognizes the pope as the supreme head. **2** member of this church.

ro mance (rō mans' *or* rō'mans *for 1-6;* rō mans' *for 7,8*), **1** a love story. **2** story of adventure: *"The Arabian Nights" and "Treasure Island" are romances.* **3** story or poem telling of heroes: *Have you read the romances about King Arthur and his knights?* **4** real happenings that are like stories of heroes and are full of love, excitement, or noble deeds: *The children dreamed of traveling in search of romance. The explorer's life was filled with romance.* **5** a love affair: *"Cinderella" is the story of the romance between a beautiful girl and a prince.* **6** a made-up story: *Nobody believes the romances she tells about her adventures.* **7** make up stories: *Some children romance because of their lively imaginations.* **8** think or talk in a romantic way. 1-6 *n.,* 7,8 *v.,* **ro manced, ro manc ing.** —**ro manc'er,** *n.*

Romance languages, French, Italian, Spanish, Portuguese, Romanian, and other languages that came from Latin, the language of the Romans.

Roman Empire, empire of ancient Rome lasting from 27 B.C. to A.D. 395. It was divided into the **Eastern Roman Empire** (A.D. 395-1453) and the **Western Roman Empire** (A.D. 395-476).

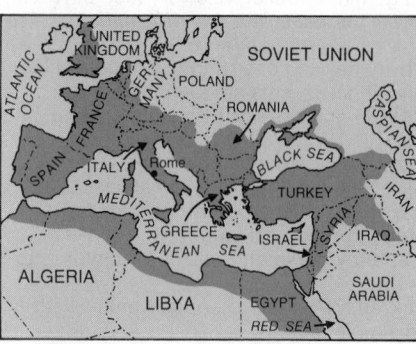

Roman Empire
The darker area shows the Empire at its greatest extent in A.D. 117.

a hat	i it	oi oil	ch child	a in about
ā age	ī ice	ou out	ng long	e in taken
ä far	o hot	u cup	sh she	ə = i in pencil
e let	ō open	ù put	th thin	o in lemon
ē equal	ô order	ü rule	ᴛʜ then	u in circus
ėr term			zh measure	

Romanesque (def. 1)

Ro man esque (rō′mə nesk′), **1** style of architecture developed in Europe during the early Middle Ages before the Gothic period. Romanesque used round arches and vaults. **2** of or in this style of architecture. 1 *n.*, 2 *adj.*

Ro ma ni a (rō mā′nē ə), country in SE Europe. *Capital:* Bucharest. See **Balkan States** for map. *n.* Also, **Rumania** or **Roumania.** —**Ro ma′ni an,** *n., adj.*

Roman nose

Roman nose, nose that has a prominent bridge.

Roman numerals, numerals like XXIII, LVI, and MDCCLX, used by the ancient Romans in numbering. In this system I = 1, V = 5, X = 10, L = 50, C = 100, D = 500, and M = 1000.

Ro mans (rō′mənz), book of the New Testament, an epistle by Saint Paul to the Christians of Rome. *n.*

ro man tic (rō man′tik), **1** characteristic of romances or romance; appealing to fancy and the imagination: *romantic tales of love and adventure, a romantic life in exotic lands.* **2** interested in adventure and love; having ideas or feelings suited to romance: *The old couple reminisced about the days of their courtship, when they were young and romantic.* **3** suited to a romance: *The orchestra played soft, romantic music.* **4** of romanticism in literature, art, and music. **5** not based on fact; fanciful; imaginary; unreal. **6** not customary or practical; fantastic; extravagant; quixotic: *romantic illusion.* **7** a romanticist. **8** a romantic person. 1-6 *adj.*, 7,8 *n.* —**ro man′ti cal ly,** *adv.*

ro man ti cism (rō man′tə siz′əm), a style of literature, art, and music especially widespread in the 1800's. Romanticism allows freedom of form and stresses strong feeling, imagination, and love of nature. *n.*

ro man ti cist (rō man′tə sist), follower of romanticism in literature, art, or music. Wordsworth and Schubert were romanticists. *n.*

ro man ti cize (rō man′tə sīz), make romantic; give a romantic character to. *v.*, **ro man ti cized, ro man ti ciz ing.** —**ro man′ti ci za′tion,** *n.*

Rom a ny (rom′ə nē), **1** gypsy. **2** language of the gyp-

sies. **3** of the gypsies, their customs, or their language. 1,2 *n., pl.* **Rom a nies** for 1; 3 *adj.*

Rome (rōm), **1** capital of Italy, on the Tiber River. The headquarters of the pope and the Roman Catholic Church are in Vatican City, an independent state within Rome. **2** an ancient city in the same place, the capital of the Roman Empire. It was captured by the barbarians in A.D. 410. **3** the ancient Roman republic or the ancient Roman Empire. *n.*

Ro me o (rō′mē ō), hero of Shakespeare's play *Romeo and Juliet. n.*

romp (romp), **1** play in a rough, boisterous way; rush, tumble, and punch in play. **2** a rough, lively play or frolic: *A pillow fight is a romp.* 1 *v.*, 2 *n.* —**romp′er,** *n.*

romp ers (rom′pərz), a loose outer garment, worn by young children at play. *n.pl.*

Rom u lus (rom′yə ləs), (in Roman legends) the founder and first king of Rome. He and his twin brother, Remus, abandoned as infants, were nourished by a wolf. *n.*

rood (rüd), **1** 40 square rods; one fourth of an acre. **2** cross or crucifix. *n.*

roof (rüf *or* rùf), **1** the top covering of a building. **2** something like it: *the roof of a cave, the roof of the mouth.* **3** cover with a roof; form a roof over: *Tall trees roofed the road through the woods.* 1,2 *n.*, 3 *v.* [*Roof* comes from Old English *hrōf.*] —**roof′like′,** *adj.*

raise the roof, INFORMAL. make a disturbance; create an uproar or confusion.

roof er (rü′fər *or* rùf′ər), person who makes or repairs roofs. *n.*

roof ing (rü′fing *or* rùf′ing), material used for roofs. Shingles are a common roofing for houses. *n.*

roof less (rüf′lis *or* rùf′lis), **1** having no roof. **2** having no shelter. *adj.*

roof tree (rüf′trē′ *or* rùf′trē′), ridgepole. *n.*

rook[1] (rùk), **1** a European bird resembling a crow, that often nests in trees near buildings. **2** to cheat. 1 *n.*, 2 *v.* [*Rook*[1] comes from Old English *hrōc.*]

rook[2] (rùk), piece in the game of chess; castle. A rook can move in a straight line across any number of unoccupied squares. *n.* [*Rook*[2] came into English about 600 years ago from French *roc,* and can be traced back to Persian *rukh.*]

rook er y (rùk′ər ē), **1** a breeding place of rooks; colony of rooks. **2** a breeding place or colony where other birds or animals are crowded together: *a rookery of seals. n., pl.* **rook er ies.**

rook ie (rùk′ē), INFORMAL. **1** an inexperienced recruit. **2** beginner; novice. **3** a new player on an athletic team, especially a professional baseball player in his first season. *n.*

room (rüm *or* rùm), **1** a part of a house, or other building, with walls of its own. **2** people in a room: *The whole room laughed.* **3** space occupied by, or available for, something: *The street was so crowded that the cars did not have room to move. There is room for one more in the automobile.* **4** opportunity: *There is room for improvement in his work.* **5** occupy a room; live in a room: *Three girls from our town roomed together at college.* **6** provide with a room. **7 rooms,** *pl.* lodgings. 1-4,7 *n.*, 5,6 *v.*

room er (rü′mər *or* rùm′ər), person who lives in a rented room or rooms in another's house; lodger. *n.*

room ful (rüm′fül *or* rüm′fül), **1** enough to fill a room. **2** people or things in a room. *n., pl.* **room fuls.**

room i ness (rü′mē nis *or* rüm′ē nis), ample space; abundance of room. *n.*

rooming house, house with rooms to rent.

room mate (rüm′māt′ *or* rüm′māt′), person who shares a room with another or others. *n.*

room y (rü′mē *or* rüm′ē), having plenty of room; large; spacious. *adj.*, **room i er, room i est. —room′i ly,** *adv.*

Roo se velt (rō′zə velt), **1** (**Anna**) **Eleanor,** 1884-1962, American author and stateswoman, wife of Franklin Delano Roosevelt. **2 Franklin Delano,** 1882-1945, the 32nd president of the United States, from 1933 to 1945. **3 Theodore,** 1858-1919, the 26th president of the United States, from 1901 to 1909. *n.*

roost (rüst), **1** bar, pole, or perch on which birds rest or sleep. **2** sit as birds do on a roost; settle for the night. **3** place for birds to rest or sleep. **4** place to rest or stay in: *a robber's roost in the mountains.* 1,3,4 *n.,* 2 *v.*

come home to roost, come back so as to harm the doer or user; backfire; boomerang.

rule the roost, INFORMAL. be master.

roost er (rü′stər), a full-grown male chicken. *n.*

root[1] (rüt *or* rüt), **1** the part of a plant that grows downward, usually into the ground, to hold the plant in place, absorb water and mineral foods from the soil, and often to store food material. **2** any underground part of a plant. **3** something like a root in shape, position, use, etc.: *the root of a tooth, the roots of the hair.* **4** a part from which other things grow and develop; cause; source: *"The love of money is the root of all evil."* **5** send out roots and begin to grow; become fixed in the ground: *Some plants root more quickly than others.* **6** fix firmly: *He was rooted to the spot by surprise.* **7** become firmly fixed. **8** pull, tear, or dig (up, out, etc.) by the roots; get completely rid of. **9** the essential part; base. **10 roots,** *pl.* feeling of having ties to a particular place, people, or culture; awareness of the source of one's origins. **11** quantity that produces another quantity when multi-

plied by itself a certain number of times. 2 is the square root of 4 and the cube root of 8 ($2 \times 2 = 4$, $2 \times 2 \times 2 = 8$). **12** word from which other words are made. *Room* is the root of *roominess, roomer, roommate,* and *roomy.* 1-4,9-12 *n.,* 5-8 *v.*

take root, 1 send out roots and begin to grow. **2** become firmly fixed.

root[2] (rüt *or* rüt), **1** dig with the snout: *The pigs rooted up the garden.* **2** rummage: *She rooted through the closet looking for her old shoes.* *v.* **—root′er,** *n.*

root[3] (rüt *or* rüt), INFORMAL. cheer or support a team, candidate, etc., enthusiastically. *v.* **—root′er,** *n.*

root beer, a soft drink flavored with the juice of the roots of certain plants, such as sarsaparilla, sassafras, etc.

root ed (rü′tid *or* rüt′id), **1** having roots. **2** having taken root; firmly fixed: *a deeply rooted belief. adj.*

root hair, a hairlike outgrowth from the root of a plant. Root hairs absorb water and dissolved minerals from the soil.

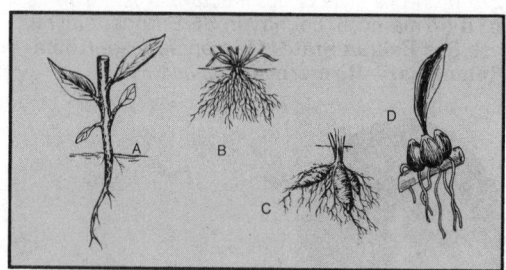

root[1] (def. 1)—the four main types:
A, taproot; B, fibrous roots;
C, storage roots; D, aerial roots

root less (rüt′lis *or* rüt′lis), without a root or roots; not rooted. *adj.*

root stock (rüt′stok′ *or* rüt′stok′), rhizome. *n.*

rope (rōp), **1** a strong, thick line or cord made by twisting smaller cords together. **2** tie, bind, or fasten with a rope. **3** enclose or mark off with a rope. **4** a lasso. **5** catch (a horse, calf, etc.) with a lasso. **6** a number of things twisted or strung together: *a rope of pearls, a rope of onions.* **7** cord or noose for hanging a person. **8** a sticky, stringy mass: *Molasses candy forms a rope.* **9** form a sticky, stringy mass; become ropy: *Cook the syrup until it ropes.* 1,4,6-8 *n.,* 2,3,5,9 *v.,* **roped, rop ing.**

know the ropes, INFORMAL. know about a business or activity.

rope in, INFORMAL. get or lead in by tricking.

the end of one's rope, the end of one's resources, activities, etc.

rop er (rō′pər), **1** person who makes ropes. **2** person who uses a lasso. *n.*

rop y (rō′pē), **1** forming sticky threads; stringy: *a ropy syrup.* **2** like a rope or ropes. *adj.,* **rop i er, rop i est.**

ro sar y (rō′zər ē), **1** string of beads for keeping count in saying a series of prayers. **2** a series of prayers. *n., pl.* **ro sar ies.** [*Rosary* comes from a medieval Latin word *rosarium,* also meaning "wreath of roses," and can be traced back to Latin *rosa,* meaning "rose[1]." In the Middle Ages, a wreath of roses often crowned images of the Virgin Mary.]

rose[1] (rōz), **1** flower that grows on a bush with thorny stems. Roses are red, pink, white, or yellow and usually smell very sweet. **2** any of various related or similar plants or flowers. **3** pinkish-red. **4** a pinkish red. **5** something shaped like a rose or suggesting a rose, such as a rosette. 1,2,4,5 *n.,* 3 *adj.* **—rose′like′,** *adj.*

rose[2] (rōz), past tense of **rise.** *The cat rose slowly. v.*

rose[1] (def. 2)—The peach, apple, plum, strawberry, raspberry, and cherry all belong to the rose family.

ro se ate (rō′zē it *or* rō′zē āt), **1** rose-colored; rosy. **2** cheerful; optimistic. *adj.* —**ro′se ate ly,** *adv.*

rose bud (rōz′bud′), the bud of a rose. *n.*

rose bush (rōz′bush′), shrub or vine bearing roses. *n.*, *pl.* **rose bush es.**

rose-col ored (rōz′kul′ərd), **1** pinkish-red. **2** bright; cheerful. *adj.*

rose mar y (rōz′mer′ē *or* rōz′mar′ē), a fragrant evergreen shrub whose leaves are used in making perfume and in seasoning food. *n.*, *pl.* **rose mar ies.**

rosettes
used in architecture

ro sette (rō zet′), an ornament shaped like a rose. Rosettes are often made of ribbon. Carved or molded rosettes are used in architecture. *n.*

rose water, water made fragrant with oil of roses.

rose wood (rōz′wud′), **1** a beautiful reddish wood used in fine furniture. **2** any of the tropical trees that it comes from. *n.*

Rosh Ha sha nah (rosh′ hə shä′nə), the Jewish New Year. It usually occurs in September.

ros i ly (rō′zə lē), **1** with a rosy tinge or color. **2** brightly; cheerfully. *adv.*

ros in (roz′n), **1** a hard, yellow substance that remains when turpentine is evaporated from pine resin. Rosin is rubbed on violin bows and on the shoes of acrobats and ballet dancers to keep them from slipping. **2** to cover or rub with rosin. **1** *n.*, **2** *v.*

ros i ness (rō′zē nis), rosy color. *n.*

Ross (rôs), **Betsy,** 1752-1836, American woman who is said to have made the first American flag. *n.*

ros ter (ros′tər), **1** list giving each person's name and duties. **2** any list. *n.*

ros trum (ros′trəm), platform for public speaking. *n.*, *pl.* **ros trums, ros tra** (ros′trə).

ros y (rō′zē), **1** like a rose; rose-red; pinkish-red. **2** bright; cheerful: *a rosy future. adj.*, **ros i er, ros i est.**

rot (rot), **1** become rotten; decay; spoil: *So much rain will make the fruit rot.* **2** cause to decay. **3** process of rotting; decay. **4** any of various diseases of plants and animals, especially sheep. **5** lose vigor; degenerate. **6** INFORMAL. nonsense; rubbish. **1,2,5** *v.*, **rot ted, rot ting; 3,4,6** *n.*

ro tar y (rō′tər ē), **1** turning like a top or a wheel; rotating. **2** having parts that rotate. **3** traffic circle. **1,2** *adj.*, **3** *n.*, *pl.* **ro tar ies.**

rotary engine, Wankel engine.

ro tate (rō′tāt), **1** move around a center or axis; turn in a circle; revolve. Wheels, tops, and the earth rotate. **2** change in a regular order; take turns or cause to take turns: *The officials will rotate as chairman. Farmers rotate crops. v.,* **ro tat ed, ro tat ing.** [*Rotate* is from Latin *rotatum,* meaning "rotated," which comes from *rota,* meaning "wheel." See **Word Family.**]

ro ta tion (rō tā′shən), **1** a turning round a center or axis; turning in a circle; revolving: *the rotation of a top. The earth's rotation causes night and day.* **2** a change in a regular order. *n.*

in rotation, in turn; in regular succession.

rotation of crops, the varying from year to year of crops grown in the same field to keep the soil from losing its fertility.

ro ta tor (rō′tā tər), person or thing that rotates. *n.*

ro ta to ry (rō′tə tôr′ē), **1** turning like a top or wheel; rotating. **2** causing rotation: *a rotatory muscle. adj.*

a hat	i it	oi oil	ch child	a in about
ā age	ī ice	ou out	ng long	e in taken
ä far	o hot	u cup	sh she	ə = i in pencil
e let	ō open	u̇ put	th thin	o in lemon
ē equal	ô order	ü rule	ŦH then	u in circus
ėr term			zh measure	

R.O.T.C., Reserve Officers' Training Corps.

rote (rōt), a set, mechanical way of doing things. *n.*

by rote, by memory without thought of the meaning: *to learn a lesson by rote.*

ro tis ser ie (rō tis′ər ē), an electric appliance with a spit for roasting food, rotated by an electric motor. *n.*

ro to gra vure (rō′tə grə vyùr′), **1** process of printing from an engraved copper cylinder on which the pictures, letters, etc., have been depressed instead of raised. **2** a print or section of a newspaper made by this process. *n.*

ro tor (rō′tər), **1** the rotating part of a machine or apparatus. **2** system of rotating blades by which a helicopter is able to fly. *n.*

rotor (def. 2)

rot ten (rot′n), **1** decayed or spoiled: *a rotten egg.* **2** foul; disgusting: *a rotten smell.* **3** unsound; weak: *rotten ice, rotten beams.* **4** corrupt; dishonest: *rotten government.* **5** bad; nasty: *rotten luck, to feel rotten. adj.* —**rot′ten ly,** *adv.* —**rot′ten ness,** *n.*

Rot ter dam (rot′ər dam′), seaport in SW Netherlands. *n.*

ro tund (rō tund′), **1** round or plump: *a rotund face.* **2** sounding rich and full; full-toned: *a rotund voice. adj.* —**ro tund′ly,** *adv.* —**ro tund′ness,** *n.*

ro tun da (rō tun′də), a round building or room, especially one with a dome: *The Capitol in Washington has a large rotunda. n.*, *pl.* **ro tun das.**

ro tun di ty (rō tun′də tē), **1** roundness or plumpness. **2** something round. **3** rounded fullness of tone. *n.*, *pl.* **ro tun di ties.**

rou ble (rü′bəl), ruble. *n.*

Rou en (rü än′), city in N France, on the Seine River, famous for its cathedral. Joan of Arc was burned at the stake in Rouen in 1431. *n.*

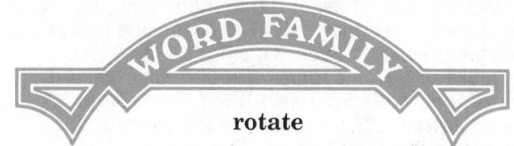

WORD FAMILY

rotate

Below are words related to *rotate*. They can all be traced back to the Latin word *rota* (rō′tä), meaning "wheel."

control	roll	rotogravure
enroll	roller	rotor
rodeo	roly-poly	roulette
role	rotary	rowel

rouge (rüzh), **1** a red or pink powder, paste, or liquid for coloring the cheeks or lips. **2** to color with rouge. **3** a red powder, chiefly an oxide of iron, used for polishing metal, jewels, etc. 1,3 *n.*, 2 *v.*, **rouged, roug ing.**

rough (ruf), **1** not smooth; not level; not even: *rough boards, the rough bark of an oak tree, a rough, rocky hill.* **2** stormy: *rough weather, a rough sea.* **3** likely to hurt others; not gentle; harsh; rude: *rough manners.* **4** without luxury and ease: *She led a rough life at her summer camp.* **5** without polish or fine finish: *rough diamonds.* **6** not completed or perfected; done as a first try; without details: *a rough drawing, a rough idea.* **7** coarse and tangled: *rough fur.* **8** a coarse, violent person. **9** INFORMAL. unpleasant; hard; severe: *She had a rough time in the hospital.* **10** make rough; roughen. **11** treat roughly: *The angry mob roughed up the suspected traitor.* **12** shape or sketch roughly: *rough out a plan.* **13** in a rough manner; roughly: *Those older children play too rough for me.* **14** ground where there is long grass, etc., on a golf course. 1-7,9 *adj.*, 8,14 *n.*, 10-12 *v.*, 13 *adv.* —**rough′ness,** *n.*

in the rough, not polished or refined; coarse; crude.
rough it, live without comforts and conveniences.

rough age (ruf′ij), **1** rough or coarse material. **2** the coarser parts or kinds of food which stimulate the movement of food and waste products through the intestines. Bran, fruit skins, and certain fruits are roughage. *n.*

rough en (ruf′ən), make or become rough. *v.*

rough-hew (ruf′hyü′), hew (timber, stone, etc.) roughly; shape roughly without smoothing or finishing. *v.*, **rough-hewed, rough-hewed** or **rough-hewn, rough-hew ing.**

rough house (ruf′hous′), INFORMAL. **1** rough play; rowdy conduct; disorderly behavior. **2** act in a rough, disorderly way. 1 *n.*, 2 *v.*, **rough housed, rough housing.**

rough ly (ruf′lē), **1** in a rough manner. **2** approximately: *From her house to mine is roughly two miles. adv.*

rough neck (ruf′nek′), INFORMAL. a rough, coarse person. *n.*

rough shod (ruf′shod′), having horseshoes with sharp calks to prevent slipping. *adj.*

ride roughshod over, domineer over; show no consideration for; treat roughly.

rou lette (rü let′), **1** a gambling game in which the players bet on which numbered section of a revolving wheel a small ball will come to rest in. **2** a small wheel with sharp teeth for making lines of marks, dots, or perforations: *a roulette for perforating sheets of postage stamps. n.*

Rou ma ni a (rü mā′nē ə), Romania. *n.* —**Rou ma′ni an,** *adj., n.*

round (round), **1** shaped like a ball, a circle, or a tree trunk; having a circular or curved outline: *Oranges are round. A ring is round. Most candles are round.* **2** anything shaped like a ball, a circle, or a tree trunk; thing that is circular, curved, cylindrical, etc. The rungs of a ladder are sometimes called rounds. **3** plump: *a short, round figure.* **4** make or become round: *The carpenter rounded the corners of the table.* **5** around: *Wheels go round (adv.).* *They built a fence round the yard (prep.).* **6** go around; make a turn to the other side of: *The car rounded the corner at high speed.* **7** Often, **rounds,** *pl.* a fixed course ending where it begins: *The watchman makes his rounds of the building every hour.* **8** movement in a circle or about an axis: *the earth's yearly round.* **9** series (of duties, events, etc.); routine: *a round of pleasures.* **10** section of a game or sport: *a round in a boxing match.* **11** a complete game or unit: *a round of golf.* **12** discharge of guns by a group of soldiers at the same time. **13** bullets, powder, etc., for one such discharge, or for a single shot: *Three*

rounds of ammunition were left in the rifle. **14** an act that a number of people do together: *a round of applause, a round of cheers.* **15** round dance. **16** a short song sung by several persons or groups beginning one after the other. "Row, Row, Row Your Boat" is a round. **17** full; complete; large: *a round dozen, a good round sum of money.* **18** change a number to the nearest hundredth, tenth, ten, hundred, etc. 7578 rounded to the nearest hundred would be 7600. **19** plainly expressed; frank; blunt: *I was scolded in good round terms for being so late.* **20** with a full tone: *a mellow, round voice.* **21** spoken with the lips rounded: *O is a round vowel.* **22** utter (a vowel) with a small circular opening of the lips. **23** a cut of beef just above the hind leg and below the rump. 1,3,17,19-21 *adj.*, 2,7-16,23 *n.*, 4,6,18,22 *v.*, 5 *adv.*, 5 *prep.* —**round′ness,** *n.*

in the round, 1 in a form of sculpture in which the figures are apart from any background. **2** having seats all around a central stage: *theater in the round.*
round off or **round out, 1** make or become round. **2** finish; complete.
round up, drive or bring together: *The cowboys rounded up the cattle.*

round a bout (round′ə bout′), not straight; indirect: *a roundabout route, speak in a roundabout way. adj.*

roun de lay (roun′dl ā), song in which a phrase or a line is repeated again and again. *n.*

round house (round′hous′), **1** a circular building for storing or repairing locomotives. It is built about a platform that turns around. **2** cabin on the after part of a ship's quarterdeck. *n., pl.* **round hous es** (round′hou′ziz).

round ish (roun′dish), somewhat round. *adj.*

round ly (round′lē), **1** in a round manner; in a circle, curve, globe, etc. **2** plainly; bluntly; severely: *scold roundly.* **3** fully; completely. *adv.*

round number, a number in even tens, hundreds, thousands, etc. 3874 in round numbers would be 3900 or 4000.

round-shoul dered (round′shōl′dərd), having the shoulders bent forward. *adj.*

round table, 1 group of persons assembled for an informal discussion, etc. **2 Round Table, a** table around which King Arthur and his knights sat. **b** King Arthur and his knights.

round trip, trip to a place and back again.

round up (round′up′), **1** act of driving or bringing cattle together from long distances. **2** the people and horses that do this. **3** any similar gathering: *a roundup of old friends. n.*

round worm (round′wėrm′), any of a group of worms that have long, round bodies and live in soil or water, or are parasites in animals and plants; nematode. The hookworm is a roundworm. *n.*

rouse (rouz), wake up; stir up; arouse: *I was roused by the ring of the telephone. The dogs roused a deer from the bushes. She was roused to anger by the insult. v.*, **roused, rous ing.** —**rous′er,** *n.*

rous ing (rou′zing), stirring; vigorous; brisk: *a rousing speech. adj.* —**rous′ing ly,** *adv.*

Rous seau (rü sō′), **Jean Jacques,** 1712-1778, French philosopher who wrote about government and education. *n.*

roust a bout (roust′ə bout′), an unskilled laborer on a wharf, a ship, a ranch, in a circus, etc. *n.*

rout[1] (rout), **1** flight of a defeated army in disorder: *The enemy's retreat soon became a rout.* **2** put to flight in disorder: *rout an enemy.* **3** a complete defeat. **4** defeat completely: *The baseball team routed its opponents by a score of ten to one.* 1,3 *n.*, 2,4 *v.*

a hat	**i** it	**oi** oil	**ch** child	a in about
ā age	**ī** ice	**ou** out	**ng** long	e in taken
ä far	**o** hot	**u** cup	**sh** she	ə = i in pencil
e let	**ō** open	**u̇** put	**th** thin	o in lemon
ē equal	**ô** order	**ü** rule	**ŦH** then	u in circus
ėr term			**zh** measure	

rout[2] (rout), **1** dig (out); get by searching. **2** put (out); force (out): *be routed out of bed at five o'clock.* **3** dig with the snout: *The pigs were routing for nuts under the trees.* **4** hollow out; scoop out; gouge. *v.*

route (rüt *or* rout), **1** way to go; road: *Will you go to the coast by the northern route?* **2** arrange the route for: *The automobile club routed us on our vacation to Canada.* **3** send by a certain route: *The signs routed us around the construction work and over a side road.* **4** a fixed, regular course or area assigned to a person making deliveries, sales, etc.: *a newspaper route, a milk route.* 1,4 *n.,* 2,3 *v.,* **rout ed, rout ing.** [*Route* came into English about 700 years ago from French *route,* which came from Latin *rupta* (*via*), meaning "(a way) opened up," which comes from *rumpere,* meaning "to break."]

rou tine (rü tēn′), **1** a fixed, regular method of doing things; habitual doing of the same things in the same way: *Getting up and going to bed are parts of your daily routine.* **2** using routine: *routine methods, a routine operation.* **3** average or ordinary; run-of-the-mill: *a routine show with routine performances.* **4** a set of instructions that directs a computer to perform a certain task or group of tasks. 1,4 *n.,* 2,3 *adj.* —**rou tine′ly,** *adv.*

rou tin ize (rü tē′nīz), make habitual. *v.,* **rou tin ized, rou tin iz ing.** —**rou tin′i za′tion,** *n.*

rove (rōv), wander about; wander; roam; ramble; range: *She loved to rove through the fields and woods. v.,* **roved, rov ing.**

rov er[1] (rō′vər), person who roves; wanderer. *n.*

ro ver[2] (rō′vər), **1** pirate. **2** a pirate ship. *n.*

row[1] (rō), **1** line of people or things: *The children stood in a row. Corn is planted in rows.* **2** street with a line of buildings on either side. *n.*

hard row to hoe, a difficult thing to do.

row[2] (rō), **1** use oars to move a boat: *We rowed across the lake.* **2** cause (a boat) to move by the use of oars. **3** carry in a rowboat: *I rowed them to shore.* **4** trip in a rowboat: *It's only a short row to the island.* 1-3 *v.,* 4 *n.* —**row′er,** *n.*

row[3] (rou), a noisy quarrel or disturbance; squabble: *The three children had a row over the bicycle. n.*

row boat (rō′bōt′), boat moved by oars. *n.*

row di ness (rou′dē nis), a being rowdy; disorderliness. *n.*

row dy (rou′dē), **1** a rough, disorderly, quarrelsome person. **2** rough; disorderly; quarrelsome. 1 *n., pl.* **row dies;** 2 *adj.* **row di er, row di est.** —**row′di ly,** *adv.*

row dy ish (rou′dē ish), like a rowdy; rough and disorderly; quarrelsome. *adj.*

row dy ism (rou′dē iz′əm), disorderly, quarrelsome conduct; rough, noisy behavior. *n.*

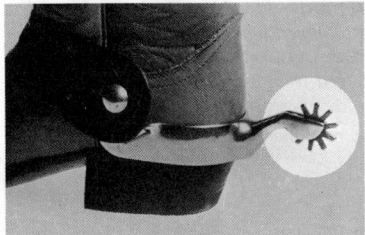

rowel

row el (rou′əl), a small wheel with sharp points, attached to the end of a spur. *n.*

row lock (rō′lok′), oarlock. *n.*

roy al (roi′əl), **1** of kings and queens: *the royal family.* **2** belonging to a king or queen: *royal power, a royal palace.* **3** from or by a king or queen: *a royal command.* **4** of a kingdom: *a royal army or navy.* **5** appropriate for a king or queen; splendid: *a royal welcome, a royal feast.*

6 like a king or queen; noble; majestic: *The lion is a royal beast. adj.* —**roy′al ly,** *adv.*

roy al ist (roi′ə list), **1** supporter of a king or queen or of a royal government. The royalists supported the British king during the Revolutionary War. **2** of royalists: *royalist principles, a royalist party.* 1 *n.,* 2 *adj.*

roy al ty (roi′əl tē), **1** a royal person or royal persons. Kings, queens, princes, and princesses are royalty. **2** rank or dignity of a king or queen; royal power: *The crown is the symbol of royalty.* **3** kingly or queenly nature; royal quality; nobility. **4** a share of the receipts or profits paid to an owner of a patent or copyright; payment for the use of any of various rights. Authors receive royalties from the publishers of their books. *n., pl.* **roy al ties.**

rpm *or* **r.p.m.,** revolutions per minute.

rps *or* **r.p.s.,** revolutions per second.

rpt., report.

R.R., railroad.

R.S.V.P. *or* **r.s.v.p.,** please answer.

rt., right.

rte., route.

Rt. Hon., Right Honorable.

Rt. Rev., Right Reverend.

Ru, symbol for ruthenium.

rub (rub), **1** move one thing back and forth against another: *Rub your hands to warm them. He rubbed soap on his hands.* **2** push and press along the surface of: *Please rub my sore back. That door rubs on the floor.* **3** make or bring by rubbing: *rub silver bright.* **4** clean, smooth, or polish by moving one thing firmly against another: *Rub the silver with a soft cloth.* **5** act of rubbing: *Give the silver a rub with the polish.* **6** thing that hurts the feelings: *He didn't like her mean rub at his slowness.* **7** irritate or make sore by rubbing: *The new shoe rubbed his heel, causing a blister.* **8** difficulty: *The rub is that we all want the last piece of pie.* 1-4,7 *v.,* **rubbed, rub bing;** 5,6,8 *n.*

rub down, rub (the body); massage.

rub it in, INFORMAL. keep on mentioning something unpleasant.

rub off, remove or be removed by rubbing: *Rub off the dust on your sleeve. Ink rubs off easily with this eraser.*

rub the wrong way, annoy; irritate.

rub ber[1] (rub′ər), **1** an elastic substance obtained from the milky juice of certain tropical plants, or produced artificially by a chemical process. Rubber will not let air or water through. **2** something made from this substance, such as a rubber band or eraser. **3** rubbers, *pl.* low-cut overshoes made of rubber. **4** made of rubber: *a rubber tire.* 1-3 *n.,* 4 *adj.* —**rub′ber like′,** *adj.*

rub ber[2] (rub′ər), **1** series of two games out of three or three games out of five won by the same side. **2** the deciding game in such a series: *If each side has won two games, the fifth game will be the rubber. n.*

rubber band, a circular strip of rubber, used to hold things together.

rub ber ize (rub′ə rīz′), cover or treat with rubber: *rubberized cloth. v.,* **rub ber ized, rub ber iz ing.**

rubber stamp, 1 stamp made of rubber, used with ink for printing dates, signatures, etc. **2** INFORMAL. person or group that approves or endorses something without thought or without power to refuse.

rub ber y (rub′ər ē), like rubber; elastic; tough. *adj.*

rub bish (rub′ish), **1** worthless or useless stuff; waste; trash: *Pick up the rubbish and burn it.* **2** silly words and thoughts; nonsense: *Gossip is often a lot of rubbish.* *n.*

rub bish y (rub′i shē), **1** full of or covered with rubbish. **2** of or like rubbish; trashy. *adj.*

rub ble (rub′əl), **1** rough broken stones, bricks, etc.: *the rubble left by an explosion or an earthquake.* **2** masonry made of this: *The house was built of rubble and plaster.* *n.*

rub down (rub′doun′), a massage. *n.*

ru bel la (rü bel′ə), German measles. *n.*

Ru bens (rü′bənz), **Peter Paul,** 1577-1640, Flemish painter. *n.*

ru bi cund (rü′bə kund), reddish; ruddy: *The jolly captain had a rubicund face.* *adj.*

ru bid i um (rü bid′ē əm), a soft, silver-white, metallic element which reacts violently in water and burns spontaneously in air. *n.*

ru ble (rü′bəl), **1** unit of money in the Soviet Union. 100 kopecks make one ruble. **2** silver coin or piece of paper money worth one ruble. *n.* Also, **rouble.**

ru bric (rü′brik), **1** title or heading of a chapter, a law, etc., written or printed in red or in special lettering. **2** direction for the conducting of religious services inserted in a prayer book, ritual, etc. *n.*

ru by (rü′bē), **1** a clear, hard, deep-red precious stone. Rubies are a variety of corundum. **2** deep, glowing red: *ruby lips, ruby wine.* **3** a deep, glowing red. 1,3 *n., pl.* **ru bies;** 2 *adj.* —**ru′by like′,** *adj.*

ruck sack (ruk′sak′), knapsack. *n.*

ruck us (ruk′əs), INFORMAL. a noisy disturbance or uproar; row. *n., pl.* **ruck us es.**

rudder
(def. 1, left;
def. 2, right)

rud der (rud′ər), **1** a flat piece of wood or metal hinged vertically to the rear end of a boat or ship and used to steer it. **2** a similar piece on an aircraft. *n.*

rud di ness (rud′ē nis), quality or state of being ruddy; redness. *n.*

rud dy (rud′ē), **1** red or reddish: *the ruddy glow of a fire.* **2** having a fresh, healthy, red look: *ruddy cheeks.* *adj.,* **rud di er, rud di est.** —**rud′di ly,** *adv.*

rude (rüd), **1** not courteous; impolite: *It is rude to stare at people.* **2** roughly made or done; without finish or polish; coarse: *We made a rude bed from the branches of evergreen trees.* **3** rough in manner or behavior; violent; harsh: *The rude hands of the dogcatcher seized the dog. I had a rude shock when I discovered that my bicycle was gone.* **4** not having learned much; rather wild; barbarous: *a rude, primitive culture.* *adj.,* **rud er, rud est.** —**rude′ly,** *adv.* —**rude′ness,** *n.*

ru di ment (rü′də mənt), **1** part to be learned first; beginning: *the rudiments of grammar.* **2** something in an early stage: *the rudiments of wings on a baby chick.* *n.* [*Rudiment* is from Latin *rudimentum*, which comes from *rudis*, meaning "rude, ignorant."]

ru di men tar y (rü′də men′tər ē), **1** to be learned or studied first; elementary: *It is almost impossible to learn multiplication without knowing the rudimentary steps of addition.* **2** in an early stage of development; undeveloped: *rudimentary wings.* *adj.* —**ru′di men′tar i ly,** *adv.*

rue[1] (rü), **1** be sorry for; regret: *She will rue the day she left school.* **2** sorrow; regret. 1 *v.,* **rued, ru ing;** 2 *n.*

rue[2] (rü), a strong-smelling, woody plant with yellow flowers and bitter leaves. *n.*

rue ful (rü′fəl), **1** sorrowful; unhappy; mournful: *a rueful expression.* **2** causing sorrow or pity: *a rueful sight.* *adj.* —**rue′ful ly,** *adv.* —**rue′ful ness,** *n.*

ruff (def. 1)

ruff (ruf), **1** a deep frill, stiff enough to stand out, worn around the neck by men and women in the 1500's and 1600's. **2** a collarlike growth of long or specially marked feathers or hairs on the neck of a bird or other animal. *n.*

ruffed (ruft), having a ruff. *adj.*

ruffed grouse, a North American game bird with a tuft of feathers on each side of the neck and a fan-shaped tail.

ruf fi an (ruf′ē ən), a rough, brutal, or cruel person; bully; hoodlum. *n.*

ruf fle (ruf′əl), **1** destroy the smoothness of; make rough or uneven: *A breeze ruffled the lake. The chicken ruffled its feathers when the dog barked.* **2** a strip of cloth, ribbon, or lace gathered along one edge and used for trimming. **3** gather into a ruffle. **4** become ruffled: *The flag ruffled in the breeze.* **5** disturb; annoy: *Nothing can ruffle her calm temper.* 1,3-5 *v.,* **ruf fled, ruf fling;** 2 *n.*

rug (rug), **1** a piece of thick, heavy fabric, used as a floor covering: *a rag rug, a fur rug.* Rugs usually cover only part of a room's floor. **2** a thick, warm cloth used as covering: *The coachman wrapped a rug around his legs.* *n.*

Rug by (rug′bē), **1** a famous English school for boys. **2** an English form of the game of football. *n.*

rug ged (rug′id), **1** covered with rough edges; rough and uneven: *rugged ground, rugged rocks.* **2** able to do and endure much; sturdy; hardy: *Pioneers were rugged people.* **3** strong and irregular: *rugged features.* **4** harsh; stern; severe: *rugged times.* **5** rude; unpolished; unrefined: *rugged manners.* **6** stormy: *rugged weather.* *adj.* —**rug′ged ly,** *adv.*

rugged (def. 1)—a rugged mountain landscape

Ruhr (rür), **1** river in West Germany flowing into the Rhine. **2** a rich mining and industrial region along this river. *n.*

ru in (rü′ən), **1** Often, **ruins,** *pl.* that which is left after destruction, decay, or downfall, especially a building, wall, etc., that has fallen to pieces: *the ruins of an ancient city.* **2** very great damage; destruction; overthrow; decay: *The ruin of property caused by the earthquake was enormous. Her enemies planned the queen's ruin.* **3** condition of destruction, decay, or downfall: *The house had gone to ruin from neglect.* **4** cause of destruction, decay, or downfall: *Reckless spending will be your ruin.* **5** bring to ruin; destroy; spoil: *Rain ruined our picnic.* **6** make bankrupt. 1-4 *n.,* 5,6 *v.* —**ru′in er,** *n.*

ru in a tion (rü′ə nā′shən), ruin; destruction; downfall. *n.*

ru in ous (rü′ə nəs), **1** bringing ruin; causing destruction: *ruinous expense, a ruinous war.* **2** fallen into ruins; ruined: *a building in a ruinous condition. adj.* —**ru′in ous ly,** *adv.* —**ru′in ous ness,** *n.*

rule (rül), **1** statement of what to do and not to do; a principle governing conduct, action, arrangement, etc.; law: *the rules of a club, to obey the rules of the game, the rules of the road.* **2** make a rule; decide. **3** make a formal decision: *The judge ruled against them.* **4** to control, govern, or manage: *The majority rules in a democracy.* **5** control; government: *In a democracy the people have the rule.* **6** period of power of a ruler; reign: *The Revolutionary War took place during the rule of George III.* **7** a regular method; thing that usually happens or is done; what is usually true: *Fair weather is the rule in Arizona.* **8** prevail in; dominate: *Wit rules all her poems.* **9** ruler (def. 2). **10** mark with lines: *I used a ruler to rule the paper.* 1,5-7,9 *n.,* 2-4,8,10 *v.,* **ruled, rul ing.**

as a rule, normally; generally.

rule out, decide against; exclude.

rule of thumb, 1 rule based on experience or practice rather than on scientific knowledge. **2** a rough, practical method of procedure.

rul er (rü′lər), **1** person who rules or governs. Kings and queens are rulers. **2** a straight strip of wood, metal, etc., often marked in inches or centimeters, used in drawing lines or in measuring. *n.*

rul ing (rü′ling), **1** decision of a judge or court: *a ruling on a point of law.* **2** that rules; governing; controlling: *the ruling class.* **3** predominating; prevalent; chief: *a ruling passion.* 1 *n.,* 2,3 *adj.* —**rul′ing ly,** *adv.*

rum (rum), **1** an alcoholic liquor made from sugar cane, molasses, etc. **2** any alcoholic liquor. *n.*

Ru ma ni a (rü mā′nē ə), Romania. *n.* —**Ru ma′ni an,** *adj., n.*

rum ba (rum′bə), **1** a lively ballroom dance that originated in Cuba. **2** music for this dance. *n., pl.* **rum bas.**

rum ble (rum′bəl), **1** make a deep, heavy, continuous sound. **2** a deep, heavy, continuous sound: *We heard the far-off rumble of thunder.* **3** move with such a sound: *The train rumbled through the station.* 1,3 *v.,* **rum bled, rumbling;** 2 *n.*

rumble seat, an extra, outside seat for two in the back of some coupes and roadsters.

ru mi nant (rü′mə nənt), **1** animal that chews the cud. Cows, sheep, and camels are ruminants. **2** belonging to the group of ruminants. **3** meditative; reflective. 1 *n.,* 2,3 *adj.* —**ru′mi nant ly,** *adv.*

ru mi nate (rü′mə nāt), **1** chew the cud. **2** chew again: *A cow ruminates its food.* **3** think or ponder; meditate; reflect: *She ruminated on the strange events of the past week. v.,* **ru mi nat ed, ru mi nat ing.** —**ru′mi na′tor,** *n.*

ru mi na tion (rü′mə nā′shən), **1** a chewing of the cud. **2** meditation; reflection. *n.*

ru mi na tive (rü′mə nā′tiv), meditative. *adj.* —**ru′mi na′tive ly,** *adv.*

rum mage (rum′ij), **1** search thoroughly by moving things about: *I rummaged three drawers before I found my gloves.* **2** search in a disorderly way: *He rummaged in the drawer for a sheet of paper.* **3** pull from among other things; bring to light: *She rummaged change from the bottom of her purse.* **4** a thorough search in which things are moved about. 1-3 *v.,* **rum maged, rum mag ing;** 4 *n.*

rummage sale, sale of odds and ends, old clothing, etc., usually held to raise money for charity.

rum my (rum′ē), a kind of card game in which points are scored by forming sets of three or four cards of the same rank or sequences of three or more cards of the same suit. *n.*

ru mor (rü′mər), **1** story or statement talked of as news without any proof that it is true: *The rumor spread that a new school would be built here.* **2** vague, general talk: *Rumor has it that the new girl went to school in France.* **3** tell or spread by rumor: *It was rumored that the government was going to increase taxes.* 1,2 *n.,* 3 *v.*

rump (rump), **1** the hind part of the body of an animal, where the legs join the back. **2** a cut of beef from this part. *n.*

rum ple (rum′pəl), **1** crumple; crush; wrinkle: *a rumpled sheet of paper.* **2** tousle; disorder: *The wind rumpled my hair.* **3** a wrinkle; crease. 1,2 *v.,* **rum pled, rumpling;** 3 *n.*

rum pus (rum′pəs), INFORMAL. a noisy disturbance or uproar; row. *n., pl.* **rum pus es.**

run (run), **1** go by moving the legs quickly; go faster than walking: *A horse can run faster than a person.* **2** go in a hurry; hasten: *Run for help.* **3** make a quick trip: *Let's run over to the lake for the weekend.* **4** escape; flee: *Run for your life.* **5** cause to run; cause to move: *run a horse up and down a track.* **6** do by running: *run a race, run errands.* **7** keep going; go; move: *This train runs from Kansas City to St. Louis. Does your watch run well?* **8** go on; proceed: *Prices of hats run as high as $50.* **9** creep; trail; climb: *Vines run up the sides of the chimney.* **10** pass or cause to pass quickly: *The thought ran through my mind that I might forget my speech. She ran her eyes over the old notes before discarding them.* **11** stretch; extend: *Shelves run along the walls. A fence runs around the yard. The road runs from New York to Atlanta.* **12** drive; force; thrust: *He ran a splinter into his hand.* **13** flow with; flow: *Blood runs from a cut. The streets ran oil after an oil truck overturned.* **14** discharge fluid, mucus, or pus: *My nose runs whenever I have a cold.* **15** get; become: *Never run into debt. The well ran dry.* **16** have a specified character, quality, form, size, etc.: *That suit runs large.* **17** spread: *The color ran when the shirt was washed.* **18** continue; last: *a lease to run two years. The play ran for a whole season.* **19** take part in a race or contest. **20** be a candidate for election: *run for class president.* **21** expose oneself to: *run the risk of catching cold.* **22** move easily, freely, or smoothly; keep operating: *A rope runs in a pulley. The engine ran all day without overheating.* **23** cause to move easily, freely, or smoothly; cause to keep operating: *run a machine.* **24** be worded or expressed: *How does the first verse run?* **25** act of running: *When the bell rang we set out at a run.* **26** spell or period of causing (a machine, etc.)

---

a hat	**i** it	**oi** oil	**ch** child	⎧ a in about
ā age	**ī** ice	**ou** out	**ng** long	e in taken
ä far	**o** hot	**u** cup	**sh** she	ə = ⎨ i in pencil
e let	**ō** open	** u̇** put	**th** thin	o in lemon
ē equal	**ô** order	**ü** rule	**ᴛʜ** then	⎩ u in circus
ėr term			**zh** measure	

to operate; amount of anything produced in such a period: *During a run of eight hours the factory produced a run of 100 cars.* **27** a trip: *The train makes a run of one hundred miles in two hours.* **28** to conduct; manage: *run a business.* **29** unit of score in baseball or cricket. **30** time; period; spell: *a run of wet weather, a run of bad luck.* **31** succession of performances: *This play has had a run of two years.* **32** onward movement; progress; course; trend: *the run of events.* **33** a sudden demand or series of demands: *a run on the bank to draw out money.* **34** (in music) a rapid succession of tones. **35** kind or class: *the usual run of children's books.* **36** free use: *The guests were given the run of the house.* **37** go without restraint: *The children were allowed to run about the streets.* **38** flow or rush of water; small stream. **39** number of fish moving together: *a run of salmon.* **40** stretch of ground or enclosed space for animals: *a dog run, a chicken run.* **41** drop stitches; ravel: *Nylon stockings often run.* **42** a place where stitches have slipped out or become undone: *a run in a stocking.* **43** sew by pushing a needle in and out with even stitches in a line. **44** get past or through: *Enemy ships tried to run the blockade.* **45** publish (an advertisement, story, etc.) in a newspaper, magazine, etc.: *She ran an ad in the evening paper.* 1-24,28,37, 41,43-45 *v.,* **ran, run, run ning;** 25-27,29-36,38-40,42 *n.*
a run for one's money, 1 strong competition. **2** satisfaction for one's expenditures, efforts, etc.: *The travel agent promised to give the tourists a run for their money.*
in the long run, on the whole; in the end.
on the run, 1 hurrying. **2** in retreat or rout; fleeing.
run across, meet or find by chance: *I ran across several old photographs in the attic.*
run away with, win easily over others: *He ran away with every prize in the tournament.*
run down, 1 stop working or going: *The clock has run down.* **2** to chase till caught: *The fox ran down the hare.* **3** knock down by running against. **4** speak evil against.
run for it, run for safety.
run in, 1 SLANG. arrest and put in jail. **2** pay a short visit.
run into, 1 meet by chance. **2** crash into; collide with.
run off, to print: *to run off 1000 copies for a first edition.*
run out, come to an end: *After three minutes his time ran out on the telephone call.*
run out of, use up; have no more.
run out on, 1 leave suddenly; desert: *My friends didn't run out on me when I was having a difficult time.* **2** back out of; not be faithful to: *They ran out on their promise to help me.*
run over, 1 ride or drive over: *The car ran over some glass.* **2** overflow. **3** go through quickly.
run through, 1 use up, spend, or consume rapidly or recklessly. **2** pierce. **3** to review or rehearse: *The teacher ran though the homework assignment a second time.*
run up, 1 make quickly: *The team ran up a big lead in the first quarter.* **2** collect; accumulate: *Don't run up a big bill.*
run a bout (run′ə bout′), **1** a light, open automobile or carriage with a single seat. **2** a small motorboat. *n.*
run a round (run′ə round′), INFORMAL. avoidance or postponement of action, especially in regard to a request. *n.*
run a way (run′ə wā′), **1** person, horse, etc., that runs away. **2** a running away. **3** running with nobody to guide or stop it; out of control: *a runaway horse.* **4** done by runaways: *a runaway marriage.* **5** easily won: *a runaway victory.* 1,2 *n.,* 3-5 *adj.*
run down (run′doun′), an account; summary: *The reporter gave a brief rundown of the week's news.* *n.*
run-down (run′doun′), **1** tired; sick. **2** falling to pieces; partly ruined: *a run-down old building.* **3** that has stopped going or working. *adj.*

rune (rün), **1** any letter of an ancient Germanic alphabet. **2** a mark, verse, or saying which is believed to have some mysterious, magic meaning. *n.*
rung[1] (rung), past participle of **ring**[2]. *The bell has rung. v.*
rung[2] (rung), **1** a round rod or bar used as a step of a ladder. **2** crosspiece set between the legs of a chair or as part of the back or arm of a chair. *n.*
ru nic (rü′nik), consisting of runes; written in runes; marked with runes. *adj.*
run-in (run′in′), INFORMAL. a sharp disagreement; argument; quarrel. *n.*
run let (run′lit), runnel. *n.*
run nel (run′l), a small stream or brook. *n.*

runner (def. 7) of a strawberry plant

run ner (run′ər), **1** person, animal, or thing that runs; racer. **2** (in baseball) a player on the team at bat who either is on base or is running to the next base. **3** messenger: *a runner for a bank.* **4** one of the narrow pieces on which a sleigh, sled, or ice skate slides. **5** a long, narrow strip: *We have a runner of carpet in our hall.* **6** person or ship that tries to evade somebody; smuggler: *a blockade runner.* **7** a slender stem that takes root along the ground, thus producing new plants. Strawberry plants spread by runners. *n.*
run ner-up (run′ər up′), player or team that takes second place in a contest. *n.*
run ning (run′ing), **1** act of a person, animal, or thing that runs. **2** flowing: *running water.* **3** going or carried on continuously: *a running commentary.* **4** following in succession: *for three nights running.* **5** performed with or during a run: *a running leap.* 1 *n.,* 2,3,5 *adj.,* 4 *adv.*
be in the running, have a chance to win.
be out of the running, have no chance to win.
running board, a metal step or footboard attached below the door on some cars and trucks.
running knot, slipknot.
running mate, candidate in an election who is paired with another candidate from the same political party running for a more important office.
run ny (run′ē), that runs: *a runny nose. adj.,* **run ni er, run ni est.**
Run ny mede (run′ē mēd′), meadow near London where King John granted the Magna Charta in 1215. *n.*
run off (run′ôf′), **1** something that runs off, such as rain that flows from the land in streams. **2** a final, deciding race or contest. *n.*
run-of-the-mill (run′əv ᴛʜə mil′), average or commonplace; ordinary. *adj.*
run-on entry (run′ôn′ *or* run′on′), a dictionary entry which is not defined. It is formed by adding a common suffix to a defined entry and appears in heavy type at the end of that entry. The run-on entry **rusher** appears at the end of the entry **rush**[1].
runt (runt), animal, person, or plant which is smaller than the usual size. *n.*
runt y (run′tē), unusually small. *adj.,* **runt i er, runt i est. —runt′i ness,** *n.*
run way (run′wā′), **1** a paved strip at an airport on which aircraft land and take off. **2** way, track, groove, trough, etc., along which something moves, slides, etc. *n.*

ru pee (rü pē′), unit of money in India, Pakistan, and certain other countries. *n.* [*Rupee* is from Hindustani *rūpiyah,* which came from Sanskrit *rūpya,* meaning "silver."]

rup ture (rup′chər), **1** a breaking or a being broken: *the rupture of a blood vessel.* **2** a breaking off of friendly relations. **3** break off; burst; break. **4** hernia. **5** affect with or suffer hernia. 1,2,4 *n.,* 3,5 *v.,* **rup tured, rup tur ing.** [*Rupture* is from Latin *ruptura,* which comes from *rumpere,* meaning "to break." See **Word Family.**]

WORD FAMILY

rupture

Below are words related to *rupture.* They can all be traced back to the Latin word *rumpere* (rùm′pe re), meaning "to break."

abrupt	erupt	route
corrupt	interrupt	routine
disrupt	rout[1]	

rural—rural life in the late 1800's.

rur al (rür′əl), in the country; belonging to the country; like that of the country: *Rural life is quiet. adj.* —**rur′al ly,** *adv.*

rural delivery or **rural free delivery,** free delivery of mail in country districts by regular carriers.

ruse (rüz *or* rüs), scheme to mislead others; trick. *n.*

rush[1] (rush), **1** move with speed or force: *The river rushed past. We rushed to the station.* **2** send, push, or force with speed or haste: *Rush this order, please.* **3** go or act with speed or haste: *They rush into things without knowing anything about them.* **4** to attack with much speed and force: *The soldiers rushed the enemy.* **5** act of rushing; dash: *The rush of the flood swept everything before it.* **6** busy haste; hurry: *the rush of city life.* **7** a great or sudden effort of many people to go somewhere or get something: *a gold rush. The Christmas rush is hard on clerks.* **8** eager demand; pressure: *a rush for tickets to a play. A sudden rush of business kept her working hard.* **9** requiring haste: *A rush order must be filled at once.* 1-4 *v.,* 5-8 *n.,* pl. **rush es;** 9 *adj.* —**rush′er,** *n.*

rush[2] (rush), **1** a grasslike plant with a hollow stem, that grows in wet soil or marshy places. **2** stem of such a plant, used for making chair seats, baskets, floor mats, etc. *n., pl.* **rush es.** —**rush′like′,** *adj.*

rush hour, time of day when traffic is heaviest or when trains, buses, etc., are most crowded.

Rush more (rush′môr′), **Mount,** mountain in the Black

Hills of South Dakota. Huge heads of Washington, Jefferson, Lincoln, and Theodore Roosevelt are carved on its side. *n.*

rush y (rush′ē), **1** abounding with rushes; covered with rushes. **2** made of rushes. *adj.,* **rush i er, rush i est.**

rusk (rusk), **1** piece of bread or cake toasted in the oven. **2** kind of light, soft, sweet biscuit. *n.*

Russ., 1 Russia. **2** Russian.

Rus sell (rus′əl), **Bertrand,** 1872-1970, British philosopher, mathematician, and writer. *n.*

rus set (rus′it), **1** yellowish-brown or reddish-brown. **2** a yellowish brown or a reddish brown. **3** kind of winter apple with a rough, brownish skin. 1 *adj.,* 2,3 *n.*

Rus sia (rush′ə), **1** the Soviet Union. **2** former country in E Europe and NW Asia. It now forms a large part of the Soviet Union. Before 1917 it was part of an empire ruled by a czar. *n.*

Rus sian (rush′ən), **1** of Russia, its people, or their language. **2** person born or living in Russia. **3** the chief language of Russia. 1 *adj.,* 2,3 *n.*

Russian Revolution, revolution which overthrew the government of Nicholas II in 1917, and later that year established the Bolshevik government under Lenin.

Russian Soviet Federated Socialist Republic, the largest republic in the Soviet Union, occupying three fourths of the country's area.

rust (rust), **1** the reddish-brown or orange coating that forms on iron or steel which is exposed to air or moisture. **2** cover or become covered with rust: *Don't let the tools rust by leaving them out in the rain. The rain rusted the tools.* **3** spoil by not using. **4** become spoiled by not being used: *Don't let your mind rust during vacation.* **5** a plant disease that spots leaves and stems. **6** any fungus that produces this disease: *wheat rust.* **7** reddish-brown or orange. **8** a reddish brown or orange. 1,5,6,8 *n.,* 2-4 *v.,* 7 *adj.* [*Rust* comes from Old English *rūst.*] —**rust′less,** *adj.*

rus tic (rus′tik), **1** belonging to the country; suitable for the country; rural. **2** simple; plain: *Their rustic speech and ways made them feel uncomfortable in the royal palace.* **3** rough; awkward. **4** a country person. **5** made of branches with the bark still on them: *rustic furniture, a rustic fence.* 1-3,5 *adj.,* 4 *n.* —**rus′ti cal ly,** *adv.*

rus ti cate (rus′tə kāt), **1** go to the country; stay in the country. **2** send to the country. *v.,* **rus ti cat ed, rus ti cat ing.** —**rus′ti ca′tion,** *n.* —**rus′ti ca′tor,** *n.*

rus tic i ty (rus′tis′ə tē), **1** rustic quality, characteristic, or peculiarity. **2** rural life. **3** awkwardness; ignorance. *n., pl.* **rus tic i ties.**

rust i ly (rus′tl ē), in a rusty manner. *adv.*

rust i ness (rus′tē nis), rusty condition. *n.*

rus tle (rus′əl), **1** a light, soft sound of things gently rubbing together. **2** make or cause to make this sound: *The leaves rustled in the breeze. The wind rustled the papers.* **3** INFORMAL. steal (cattle, horses, etc.). 1 *n.,* 2,3 *v.,* **rus tled, rus tling.**

rustle up, 1 gather; find. **2** get ready; prepare: *The cook rustled up some food.*

rus tler (rus′lər), INFORMAL. a cattle thief. *n.*

rust proof (rust′prüf′), resisting rust. *adj.*

rust y (rus′tē), **1** covered with rust; rusted: *a rusty knife.* **2** made by rust: *a rusty stain, a rusty spot.* **3** colored like rust. **4** no longer good or effective from lack of use or practice: *She hadn't played tennis for months, so her game was rusty. adj.,* **rust i er, rust i est.**

rut (rut), **1** a track made in the ground by wheels. **2** make ruts in. **3** a fixed or established way of acting: *He was so set in his ways that everyone said he was in a rut.* 1,3 *n.,* 2 *v.,* **rut ted, rut ting.**

ru ta ba ga (rü′tə bā′gə), kind of large, yellow or white turnip. *n., pl.* **ru ta ba gas.** [*Rutabaga* comes from Swedish *rotabagge.*]

Ruth (rüth), **1** (in the Bible) a widow who was very devoted to her mother-in-law, Naomi. Ruth left her native land of Moab to go with Naomi to Bethlehem. **2** book of the Old Testament about her. **3 George Herman,** 1895-1948, American baseball player. He was better known as Babe Ruth. *n.*

ru the ni um (rü thē′nē əm), a brittle, white, metallic element which is found in platinum ores. *n.*

Ruth er ford (ruᴛн′ər fərd), **Ernest,** 1871-1937, British physicist, born in New Zealand, who developed the basic theories of nuclear physics. *n.*

ruth er ford i um (ruᴛн′ər fôr′dē əm), proposed name for a radioactive metallic element, produced artificially from californium. *n.*

ruth less (rüth′lis), having no pity; showing no mercy; cruel. *adj.* —**ruth′less ly,** *adv.* —**ruth′less ness,** *n.*

RV, recreational vehicle.

R.V., Revised Version.

Rwan da (rü än′də), country in central Africa, north of Burundi. *Capital:* Kigali. See **Congo** for map. *n.*

-ry, *suffix forming nouns from other nouns.* **1** occupation or work of a ___: *Dentistry = occupation or work of a dentist.* **2** act of a ___: *Mimicry = act of a mimic.* **3** condition of a ___: *Rivalry = condition of a rival.* **4** group or collection of ___s: *Jewelry = collection of jewels.*

Ry., railway.

rye (rī), **1** a hardy annual plant widely grown in cold regions. Rye is a grass. **2** its seeds or grain, used for making flour, as food for livestock, and in making whiskey. **3** made from rye grain or flour: *rye bread.* **4** whiskey made from rye. 1,2,4 *n.,* 3 *adj.*

Ss

a hat	i it	oi oil	ch child	a in about
ā age	ī ice	ou out	ng long	e in taken
ä far	o hot	u cup	sh she	ə = { i in pencil
e let	ō open	u̇ put	th thin	o in lemon
ē equal	ô order	ü rule	₮ʜ then	u in circus
ėr term			zh measure	

S or **s** (es), **1** the 19th letter of the English alphabet. **2** anything shaped like an S: *The road curved in a big S. n., pl.* **S's** or **s's.**

S, symbol for sulfur.

S or **S., 1** Saint. **2** Saturday. **3** September. **4** south. **5** southern. **6** Sunday.

s., 1 second. **2** shilling or shillings. **3** singular. **4** son. **5** south. **6** southern.

S.A., 1 South Africa. **2** South America.

Saar (sär *or* zär), **1** river flowing from NE France into West Germany. **2** state in West Germany, along the Saar River. *n.*

Sa bah (sä′bə), state in N Borneo, a part of Malaysia. *n.*

Sab bath (sab′əth), day of the week used for rest and worship. Sunday is the Sabbath for most Christians; Saturday is the Jewish Sabbath. *n.* [*Sabbath* can be traced back to Hebrew *shabbāth.*]

sab bat ic (sə bat′ik), sabbatical. *adj.*

sab bat i cal (sə bat′ə kəl), **1** of or suitable for the Sabbath. **2** of or for a rest from work. Once in seven years some teachers have a sabbatical leave for rest, study, or travel. *adj.*

sa ber (sā′bər), a heavy sword, usually slightly curved, having a single cutting edge. *n.* Also, **sabre.** [*Saber* comes from French *sabre,* and can be traced back to Hungarian *szabni,* meaning "to cut."]

saber-toothed tiger about 7 ft. (2 m.) long with the tail

sa ber-toothed tiger (sā′bər tütht′), a large, prehistoric mammal somewhat like a tiger. Its upper canine teeth were very long and curved.

Sa bin (sā′bən), **Albert Bruce,** born 1906, American scientist who developed a vaccine against polio that can be taken by mouth. *n.*

sa ble (sā′bəl), **1** a small, flesh-eating mammal valued for its dark-brown, glossy fur. It is in the same group of animals as the weasel. **2** its fur. Sable is one of the most costly furs. *n.*

sab o tage (sab′ə täzh), **1** damage done by enemy agents or sympathizers, by civilians of a conquered nation, etc. **2** damage done to work, tools, machinery, etc., by workers as an attack or threat against an employer. **3** damage or destroy deliberately: *to sabotage an ammunition plant.* **1,2** *n.,* **3** *v.,* **sab o taged, sab o tag ing.**

sab o teur (sab′ə tèr′), person who sabotages. *n.*

sa bra (sä′brə), Israeli born and living in Israel.

sa bre (sā′bər), saber. *n.*

sac (sak), a part like a bag in an animal or plant, often one containing liquids. *n.* [*Sac* is from Latin *saccus,* meaning "bag," which comes from Hebrew *saq.*] —**sac′like′,** *adj.*

Sac (sak *or* sôk), Sauk. *n., pl.* **Sac** or **Sacs.**

Sac a ja we a or **Sac a ga we a** (sak′ə jə wē′ə), 1787?-1812?, American Indian guide and interpreter. She ac-

companied the Lewis and Clark expedition to the American northwest. *n.*

sac char in (sak′ər ən), a very sweet substance gotten from coal tar, used as a substitute for sugar. It has no food value. *n.* [*Saccharin* comes from a medieval Latin word *saccharum,* meaning "sugar," and can be traced back to Sanskrit *śarkarā,* which originally meant "gravel, grit."]

sac char ine (sak′ər ən), **1** overly sweet; sugary: *a saccharine smile.* **2** of or like sugar. **3** saccharin. **1,2** *adj.,* **3** *n.* —**sac′char ine ly,** *adv.*

sac er do tal (sas′ər dō′tl), of priests or the priesthood; priestly. *adj.* —**sac′er do′tal ly,** *adv.*

sa chem (sā′chəm), (among some North American Indians) the chief of a tribe or confederation. *n.*

sa chet (sa shā′ *or* sash′ā), a small bag or pad containing perfumed powder, placed among articles of clothing. *n.*

sack¹ (sak), **1** a large bag made of coarse cloth. Sacks are used for holding grain, flour, potatoes, and coal. **2** such a bag with what is in it: *He bought two sacks of corn.* **3** amount that a sack will hold: *We burned two sacks of coal.* **4** any bag with what is in it: *a sack of candy.* **5** put into a sack or sacks: *to sack grain or salt.* **6** a loose coat: *a knitted sack for a baby.* **7** dismiss from a job; fire. **8** SLANG. bed. **1-4,6,8** *n.,* **5,7** *v.* [*Sack¹* comes from Old English *sacc,* and can be traced back to Hebrew *saq,* meaning "bag."] —**sack′like′,** *adj.*

sack out, SLANG. go to bed.

sack² (sak), **1** plunder (a captured city). **2** a plundering of a captured city: *the sack of Rome by the barbarians.* **1** *v.,* **2** *n.* [*Sack²* came into English about 400 years ago from the French phrase *mettre à sac,* meaning "put to the sack, plunder."] —**sack′er,** *n.*

sack³ (sak), sherry or other strong, light-colored wine. *n.* [*Sack³* came into English about 400 years ago from the French phrase *vin sec,* meaning "dry wine."]

sack cloth (sak′klôth′), **1** coarse cloth for making sacks. **2** coarse cloth worn as a sign of mourning or penance. *n.*

sack ful (sak′fu̇l), enough to fill a sack. *n., pl.* **sack fuls.**

sack ing (sak′ing), coarse cloth for making sacks. *n.*

sac ra ment (sak′rə mənt), **1** (in Christian churches) any of certain religious ceremonies. Baptism and the Eucharist are sacraments. **2** Often, **Sacrament.** the Eucharist; Holy Communion. *n.*

sac ra men tal (sak′rə men′tl), **1** of or having to do with a sacrament; used in a sacrament: *sacramental wine. adj.* —**sac′ra men′tal ly,** *adv.*

Sac ra men to (sak′rə men′tō), capital of California, in the central part. *n.*

sa cred (sā′krid), **1** belonging to or dedicated to God; holy: *the sacred altar, a sacred building.* **2** connected with religion; religious: *sacred writings, sacred music.* **3** worthy of reverence: *the sacred memory of a dead hero.* **4** not to be violated or disregarded: *a sacred promise. adj.* —**sa′cred ly,** *adv.* —**sa′cred ness,** *n.*

sac ri fice (sak′rə fīs), **1** act of offering to a god. **2** the thing offered: *The ancient Hebrews killed animals on the altars as sacrifices to God.* **3** give or offer to a god: *They sacrificed oxen, sheep, and doves.* **4** a giving up of one thing for another: *Our teacher does not approve of any* *sacrifice of studies to sports.* **5** give up: *sacrifice one's life for another, sacrifice business for pleasure.* **6** loss from selling something below its value: *They sold their house at a sacrifice because they needed the money.* **7** sell at a loss. **8** (in baseball) a bunt that helps a base runner to advance, or a fly that allows a base runner to score, although the batter is put out. 1,2,4,6,8 *n.*, 3,5,7 *v.*, **sac ri ficed, sac ri fic ing. —sac'ri fic'er,** *n.*

sac ri fi cial (sak/rə fish/əl), having to do with or used in a sacrifice: *sacrificial rites. adj.* **—sac'ri fi'cial ly,** *adv.*

sac ri lege (sak/rə lij), an intentional injury to anything sacred; disrespectful treatment of anyone or anything sacred: *Robbing the church was a sacrilege. n.*

sac ri le gious (sak/rə lij/əs), injurious or insulting to sacred persons or things. *adj.* **—sac'ri le'gious ly,** *adv.*

sac ris tan (sak/ri stən), person in charge of the sacred vessels, robes, etc., of a church. *n.*

sac ris ty (sak/ri stē), place where the sacred vessels, robes, etc., of a church are kept. *n., pl.* **sac ris ties.**

sac ro sanct (sak/rō sangkt), very holy; very sacred. *adj.*

sa crum (sā/krəm), bone at the lower end of the spine, made by the joining of several vertebrae, forming the back of the pelvis. *n., pl.* **sa cra** (sā/krə), **sa crums.**

sad (sad), **1** not happy; full of sorrow: *You feel sad if your best friend goes away.* **2** causing sorrow: *a sad accident.* **3** extremely bad: *a sad state of affairs. adj.,* **sad der, saddest.** [*Sad* comes from Old English *sæd,* meaning "satisfied."] **—sad'ly,** *adv.* **—sad'ness,** *n.*

Sa dat (sä dät/), Anwar, 1918-1981, president of Egypt from 1970 to 1981. *n.*

sad den (sad/n), make or become sad: *Her face saddened at the news. v.*

sad dle (sad/l), **1** seat for a rider on a horse's back, on a bicycle, etc. **2** thing shaped like a saddle. A ridge between two mountain peaks is called a saddle. **3** put a saddle on. **4** to burden: *He is saddled with too many jobs.* **5** a cut of mutton, venison, lamb, etc., consisting of both loins and the back portion between them. 1,2,5 *n.,* 3,4 *v.,* **sad dled, sad dling.**
in the saddle, in a position of control.

sad dle bag (sad/l bag/), one of a pair of bags laid over an animal's back behind the saddle, or over the rear fender of a bicycle or motorcycle. *n.*

saddle horse, horse for riding.

sad dler (sad/lər), person who makes or sells saddles and harnesses. *n.*

saddle shoes

saddle shoe, a low shoe, usually white, with the instep crossed by a band of leather of a different color.

sa dism (sā/diz/əm *or* sad/iz/əm), **1** practice of a person who gets pleasure from hurting someone else. **2** an unnatural love of cruelty. *n.* [*Sadism* comes from French *sadisme.* It was formed from the name of the Marquis de Sade, 1740-1814, who described such practices in his writings.]

sa dist (sā/dist *or* sad/ist), **1** person who gets pleasure from hurting someone else. **2** person having an unnatural love of cruelty. *n.*

sa dis tic (sə dis/tik), cruel; showing cruelty: *a sadistic villain. adj.* **—sa dis'ti cal ly,** *adv.*

sa fa ri (sə fär/ē), **1** journey or hunting expedition in eastern Africa. **2** any long trip or expedition. *n., pl.* **sa fa ris.** [*Safari* was borrowed from Swahili *safari,* which came from Arabic *safar,* meaning "a journey."]

safe (sāf), **1** free from harm or danger: *Keep money in a safe place.* **2** not harmed: *He returned from war safe and sound.* **3** out of danger; secure: *We feel safe with the dog in the house.* **4** not able to harm or injure: *Several wild dogs were locked up safe in the truck.* **5** careful: *a safe guess, a safe move.* **6** that can be depended on: *a safe guide.* **7** a steel or iron box for money, jewels, papers, etc. **8** (in baseball) reaching a base without being out. 1-6,8 *adj.,* **saf er, saf est;** 7 *n.* **—safe'ly,** *adv.* **—safe'ness,** *n.*

safe-con duct (sāf/kon/dukt), **1** privilege of passing safely through a region, especially in time of war: *At the start of the war, neutrals were given safe-conduct out of the country.* **2** paper granting this privilege. *n.*

safe-de pos it box (sāf/di poz/it), box for storing valuable things, especially in a bank vault. *n.*

safe guard (sāf/gärd/), **1** keep safe; guard against hurt or danger; protect: *Pure food laws safeguard our health.* **2** protection; defense: *Keeping clean is a safeguard against disease.* 1 *v.,* 2 *n.*

safe keep ing (sāf/kē/ping), protection; keeping safe; care. *n.*

safe ty (sāf/tē), **1** a being safe; freedom from harm or danger: *A bank assures safety for your money. You can cross the street in safety when the green light is on.* **2** device to prevent injury or accident. A gun cannot be fired if the safety is on. *n., pl.* **safe ties.**

safety belt, seat belt.

safety glass, glass that resists shattering, made of two or more layers of glass joined together by a layer of transparent plastic.

safety pin, pin bent back on itself to form a spring and having a guard that covers the point and prevents accidental unfastening.

safety valve, 1 valve in a steam boiler, etc., that opens and lets steam or fluid escape when the pressure becomes too great. Pressure cookers have a safety valve. **2** something that helps a person get rid of anger, nervousness, etc., in a harmless way.

saf flow er (saf/lou/ər), plant like a thistle, with large flower heads. Its seeds yield an oil used for cooking. *n.*

saf fron (saf/rən), **1** an autumn crocus with purple flowers having orange-yellow stigmas. **2** an orange-yellow coloring matter obtained from the dried stigmas of this crocus. Saffron is used to color and flavor candy, drinks, etc. **3** an orange yellow. **4** orange-yellow. 1-3 *n.,* 4 *adj.* [*Saffron* can be traced back to Arabic *za'farān.*]

sag (sag), **1** to sink under weight or pressure; bend down in the middle, as a rope, beam, cable, plank, etc. **2** hang down unevenly: *Your dress sags in the back.* **3** become less firm or elastic; yield through weakness, weariness, or lack of effort; droop; sink: *Our courage sagged.* **4** act, state, or degree of sagging. **5** place where anything sags. 1-3 *v.,* **sagged, sag ging;** 4,5 *n.*

sa ga (sä/gə), **1** a Norse or Icelandic story of heroic deeds, written between the 1100's and the 1300's. **2** any story of heroic deeds. *n., pl.* **sa gas.**

sa ga cious (sə gā/shəs), wise in a keen, practical way; shrewd. *adj.* **—sa ga'cious ly,** *adv.* **—sa ga'cious ness,** *n.*

sa gac i ty (sə gas/ə tē), keen, sound judgment; mental acuteness; shrewdness: *The lawyer displayed sagacity in questioning the witnesses. n.*

sag a more (sag/ə môr), (among some North American Indians) a chief or great man, sometimes below a sachem. *n.*

sage[1] (sāj), **1** showing wisdom or good judgment: *a sage* *reply.* **2** wise: *The queen surrounded herself with sage advisers.* **3** wise-looking; grave; solemn: *Owls are sage birds.* **4** a very wise man: *The sage gave advice to his king.* 1-3 *adj.*, **sag er, sag est;** 4 *n.* [*Sage*[1] came into English about 700 years ago from French *sage,* and can be traced back to Latin *sapere,* meaning "to be wise."]

sage[2] (sāj), **1** a small shrub which is an herb related to mint. Its gray-green leaves are used to season food. **2** sagebrush. *n.* [*Sage*[2] came into English about 600 years ago from French *sauge,* and can be traced back to Latin *salvia,* meaning "a healing plant."]

sage brush (sāj′brush′), a grayish shrub that smells like sage, common on the dry plains of western North America. *n.*

sa go (sā′gō), **1** a starchy food used in making puddings, etc. **2** an East Indian palm tree from whose soft center this starchy food is made. *n., pl.* **sa gos.** [*Sago* comes from Malay *sāgū.*]

saguaros

sa gua ro (sə gwär′ō), a very tall, branching cactus of Arizona and neighboring regions. *n., pl.* **sa gua ros.**

Sa har a (sə her′ə *or* sə har′ə), the world's largest desert, in N Africa. See **Sudan** for map. *n.* —**Sa har′an,** *adj., n.*

sa hib (sä′ib), sir; master (in colonial India, a term of respect used to or about Europeans). *n.*

said (sed), **1** past tense and past participle of **say.** *He said he would come. They had said "No" every time.* **2** named or mentioned before: *the said witness, the said sum of money.* 1 *v.,* 2 *adj.*

Sai gon (sī gon′), former name of **Ho Chi Minh City.** *n.*

sail (sāl), **1** piece of cloth attached to the rigging of a ship to catch the wind and make the ship move through the water. **2** something like a sail, such as the part of an arm of a windmill that catches the wind. **3** trip on a boat with sails or on any other vessel: *Let's go for a sail.* **4** to travel on water by the action of wind on sails. **5** to travel on a steamboat, etc. **6** move smoothly like a ship with sails: *The eagle sailed by. The duchess sailed into the room.* **7** sail upon, over, or through: *sail the seas.* **8** manage a ship or boat: *The girls are learning to sail.* **9** begin a trip by water: *We sail at 2 p.m.* 1-3 *n.,* 4-9 *v.* —**sail′like′,** *adj.*

sail into, INFORMAL. **1** attack; beat. **2** criticize; scold: *She sailed into us for being late.*

set sail, begin a trip by water.

under sail, with the sails spread out.

sail board (sāl′bôrd′), surfboard to which a mast and a handheld sail are attached by a universal joint. Speed and direction are controlled by moving the sail. *n.*

sail boat (sāl′bōt′), boat that is moved by a sail or sails. Schooners and sloops are kinds of sailboats. *n.*

sail cloth (sāl′klôth′), canvas used for making sails. *n., pl.* **sail cloths** (sāl′klôᴛʜz′ *or* sāl′klôths′).

sail fish (sāl′fish′), a large, saltwater fish that has a

a hat	**i** it	**oi** oil	**ch** child	(a in about
ā age	**ī** ice	**ou** out	**ng** long	e in taken
ä far	**o** hot	**u** cup	**sh** she	ə = i in pencil
e let	**ō** open	**u̇** put	**th** thin	o in lemon
ē equal	**ô** order	**ü** rule	**ᴛʜ** then	(u in circus
ėr term			**zh** measure	

long, high fin on its back. It is related to the swordfish. *n., pl.* **sail fish es** *or* **sail fish.**

sail ing (sā′ling), **1** act of a person or thing that sails. **2** art of operating a ship; navigation. *n.*

sail or (sā′lər), **1** person whose work is handling a boat or other vessel. **2** member of a ship's crew who is not an officer. **3** a flat-brimmed straw hat modeled after the kind of hat sailors used to wear long ago. *n.*

sail or ly (sā′lər lē), like or suitable for a sailor. *adj.*

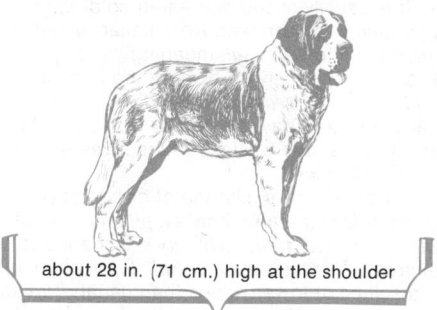
sailplane soaring over the trees

sail plane (sāl′plān′), a lightweight glider. Its very long wings enable it to fly by taking advantage of rising air currents. *n.*

saint (sānt), **1** a very holy person. **2** person who has gone to heaven. **3** person declared a saint by the Roman Catholic Church. **4** person who is very humble, patient, etc., like a saint. *n.* —**saint′like′,** *adj.*

Saint. For names of saints look under the Christian name, and for other entries beginning with "Saint" look under the **St.** words.

Saint Ber nard (bər närd′), a big, brown-and-white dog with a large head. This dog was first bred by monks to rescue travelers lost in the Swiss Alps.

WORD HISTORY

Saint Bernard

This dog gets its name from the monastery of *St. Bernard* in the Swiss Alps. The monks there developed this breed to help find travelers lost in the snow.

about 28 in. (71 cm.) high at the shoulder

saint ed (sān′tid), **1** declared to be a saint. **2** thought of as a saint; gone to heaven. **3** sacred; very holy; saintly. *adj.*

saint hood (sānt′hu̇d), character or status of a saint. *n.*

saint li ness (sānt′lē nis), piety; holiness. *n.*

saint ly (sānt′lē), like a saint; very holy; very good. *adj.,* **saint li er, saint li est.**

Saint Patrick's Day, March 17. It is an Irish national holiday.

saint ship (sānt′ship), sainthood. *n.*

Saint Valentine's Day, February 14, day on which valentines are exchanged.

saith (seth), OLD USE. says. *v.*

sake (sāk), **1** cause; account; interest: *Put yourself to no trouble for our sakes.* **2** purpose; end: *We moved to the country for the sake of peace and quiet. n.* [*Sake* comes from Old English *sacu.*]

sa laam (sə läm′), **1** a greeting that means "Peace," used especially in Moslem countries. **2** a very low bow, with the palm of the right hand placed on the forehead. **3** greet with a salaam. 1,2 *n.,* 3 *v.*

sal a bil i ty (sā/lə bil/ə tē), salable condition or quality. *n.*

sal a ble (sā/lə bəl), fit to be sold; easily sold. *adj.* Also, **saleable.**

sa la cious (sə lā/shəs), **1** obscene; indecent. **2** lustful; lewd. *adj.* —**sa la/cious ly,** *adv.* —**sa la/cious ness,** *n.*

sal ad (sal/əd), raw green vegetables, such as lettuce, cabbage, and celery, served with a dressing. Often cold meat, fish, eggs, cooked vegetables, or fruits are used along with, or instead of, the raw green vegetables. *n.*

salad days, days of youthful inexperience.

salad dressing, sauce used in or on a salad.

salamander—about 5 in. (13 cm.) long

sal a man der (sal/ə man/dər), animal shaped like a lizard, but related to frogs and toads. Salamanders have moist, smooth skin and live in water or in damp places. *n.*

sa la mi (sə lä/mē), kind of thick sausage, often flavored with garlic. It is usually sliced and eaten cold. *n., pl.* **sa la mis.** [*Salami* was borrowed from Italian *salami,* and can be traced back to Latin *sal,* meaning "salt."]

sal ar ied (sal/ər ēd), receiving or bringing in a salary: *a salaried employee, a salaried position. adj.*

sal ar y (sal/ər ē), fixed pay for regular work. Teachers, government officials, and business executives receive salaries. *n., pl.* **sal ar ies.**

sale (sāl), **1** act of selling; exchange of goods or property for money: *the sale of a house.* **2 sales,** *pl.* amount sold: *Today's sales were larger than yesterday's.* **3** chance to sell; demand; market: *There is almost no sale for washboards anymore.* **4** a selling at lower prices than usual: *This store is having a sale on suits.* **5** an auction. **6 sales,** *pl.* busi-

ness of selling: *His first job was in sales. n.*

for sale, to be sold: *There are several houses in the neighborhood for sale, but none for rent.*

on sale, for sale at lower prices than usual: *The grocer has coffee on sale.*

sale a ble (sā/lə bəl), salable. *adj.*

Sa lem (sā/ləm), **1** seaport in NE Massachusetts, settled in 1626. **2** capital of Oregon, in the NW part. *n.*

sales clerk (sālz′klėrk′), person whose work is selling in a store. *n.*

sales la dy (sālz′lā′dē), saleswoman. *n., pl.* **sales la dies.**

sales man (sālz′mən), person whose work is selling. *n., pl.* **sales men.**

sales man ship (sālz′mən ship), **1** work of a salesman. **2** ability at selling. *n.*

sales per son (sālz′pėr′sən), person whose work is selling, especially in a store. *n.*

sales tax, tax based on the amount received for articles sold.

sales wom an (sālz′wu̇m′ən), woman whose work is selling, especially in a store. *n., pl.* **sales wom en.**

sal i cyl ic acid (sal/ə sil/ik), a white, crystalline powder used as a mild antiseptic and preservative, and in making aspirin.

sa li ent (sā/lē ənt), **1** standing out; easily seen or noticed; prominent; striking: *the salient points in a speech. Sharp mountain peaks were salient features in the landscape.* **2** part of a fortification or line of trenches that sticks out toward the enemy. 1 *adj.,* 2 *n.* [*Salient* comes from Latin *salientem,* meaning "leaping."] —**sa/li ent ly,** *adv.*

sa line (sā/lēn′), **1** of salt; like salt; salty. **2** containing common salt or any other salts: *a saline solution.* **3** solution with a high concentration of salt, used in medical examinations and treatment. 1,2 *adj.,* 3 *n.*

sa lin i ty (sə lin/ə tē), saline condition or quality; saltiness. *n.*

Salis bur y (sôlz/ber/ē), **1** city in S England. A famous cathedral is located there. **2** former name of **Harare.** *n.*

sa li va (sə lī/və), liquid produced by glands in the mouth to keep it moist, help in chewing, and start digestion. *n.*

sal i var y (sal/ə ver/ē), of or producing saliva: *the salivary glands. adj.*

sal i vate (sal/ə vāt), produce saliva. *v.,* **sal i vat ed, sal i vat ing.** —**sal/i va/tion,** *n.*

Salk (sôlk), **Jonas Edward,** born 1914, American scientist who developed the Salk vaccine. *n.*

Salk vaccine, vaccine containing dead polio viruses which cause the body to produce antibodies. It protects against infection from live polio viruses.

sal low (sal/ō), having a sickly, yellowish color or complexion. *adj.* —**sal/low ness,** *n.*

sal ly (sal/ē), **1** rush forth suddenly; go out; set out briskly: *We sallied forth at dawn.* **2** a sudden rushing forth: *The men in the fort made a brave sally and returned with many prisoners.* **3** a going forth; trip; excursion. **4** a witty remark: *She continued her story undisturbed by the merry sallies of her hearers.* 1 *v.,* **sal lied, sal ly ing;** 2-4 *n., pl.* **sal lies.** —**sal/li er,** *n.*

salm on (sam/ən), **1** a large saltwater and freshwater food fish with silvery scales and yellowish-pink flesh. It is common in the northern Atlantic and northern Pacific near the mouths of large rivers which it swims up in order to spawn. **2** a yellowish pink. **3** yellowish-pink. 1,2 *n., pl.* **salm ons** or **salm on;** 3 *adj.* —**salm/on like′,** *adj.*

sa lon (sə lon′), **1** a large room for receiving or entertaining guests. **2** a gathering of distinguished persons in such a room. **3** place used to exhibit works of art. **4** a fashionable or stylish shop. *n.*

sa loon (sə lün′), **1** place where alcoholic drinks are sold and drunk; tavern. **2** a large room for general or public use: *The ship's passengers ate in the dining saloon. n.*

sal soda (sal), sodium carbonate.

salt (sôlt), **1** a white substance found in the earth and in sea water; sodium chloride. Salt is used to season and preserve food. **2** containing salt: *salt water.* **3** tasting like salt; salty: *food that is too salt.* **4** mix or sprinkle with salt. **5** cure or preserve with salt. **6** cured or preserved with salt. **7** flooded with or growing in salt water: *salt marshes, salt grass.* **8** season; make pungent: *conversation salted with wit.* **9** that which gives liveliness, piquancy, or pungency to anything. **10 salts,** *pl.* **a** a medicine that causes movement of the bowels. **b** smelling salts. **11** a chemical compound derived from an acid by replacing the hydrogen in the acid wholly or partly by a metal or a radical. Sodium bicarbonate is a salt. **12** INFORMAL. sailor. 1,9-12 *n.,* 2,3,6,7 *adj.,* 4,5,8 *v.* [*Salt* comes from Old English *salt.*] —**salt′er,** *n.* —**salt′like′,** *adj.* —**salt′ness,** *n.*

salt away or **salt down, 1** pack with salt to preserve: *The fish were salted down in a barrel.* **2** INFORMAL. store away: *She salted away money for her old age.*

salt of the earth, the best people.

worth one's salt, worth one's support, wages, etc.

salt cel lar (sôlt′sel′ər), shaker or dish for holding salt, used on the table. *n.*

salt ine (sôl tēn′), a thin, crisp, salted cracker. *n.*

salt i ness (sôl′tē nis), salty condition or quality. *n.*

Salt Lake City, capital of Utah, in the N part.

salt lick, place where natural salt is found on the surface of the ground and where animals go to lick it up.

salt pe ter or **salt pe tre** (sôlt′pē′tər), **1** naturally occuring potassium nitrate; niter. **2** sodium nitrate. **Chile saltpeter** is a naturally occurring form of sodium nitrate and is used as a fertilizer. *n.*

salt shak er (sôlt′shā′kər), holder for salt, with holes in the top through which the salt is sprinkled. *n.*

salt wa ter (sôlt′wô′tər or sôlt′wot′ər), **1** consisting of or containing salt water: *a saltwater solution.* **2** living in the sea or in water like sea water: *saltwater fish.* **3** working on the sea: *a saltwater fisherman. adj.*

salt y (sôl′tē), **1** containing salt; tasting of salt. Sweat and tears are salty. **2** to the point; witty and a bit improper: *a salty remark. adj.,* **salt i er, salt i est.** —**salt′i ly,** *adv.* —**salt′i ness,** *n.*

sa lu bri ous (sə lü′brē əs), healthful: *a salubrious diet. adj.* —**sa lu′bri ous ly,** *adv.* —**sa lu′bri ous ness,** *n.*

sal u tar y (sal′yə ter′ē), **1** beneficial: *The teacher gave the boy salutary advice.* **2** good for the health; wholesome: *Walking is a salutary exercise. adj.* —**sal′u tar′i ly,** *adv.* —**sal′u tar′i ness,** *n.*

sal u ta tion (sal′yə tā′shən), **1** a greeting; saluting: *The man raised his hand in salutation.* **2** something said, written, or done to salute. You begin a letter with a salutation, such as "Dear Sir" or "My Dear Mrs. Jones." *A formal bow was her parting salutation. n.*

sa lu ta to ri an (sə lü′tə tôr′ē ən), student who gives the address of welcome at the graduation of a class. The salutatorian is often the student who ranks second in his or her class. *n.*

sa lu ta to ry (sə lü′tə tôr′ē), **1** expressing greeting; welcoming. **2** an opening address welcoming guests at the graduation of a class. 1 *adj.,* 2 *n., pl.* **sa lu ta to ries.**

sa lute (sə lüt′), **1** to honor in a formal manner by raising the hand to the head, by firing guns, by dipping flags, etc.: *We salute the flag every day at school. The soldier saluted the officer.* **2** meet with kind words, a bow, a kiss,

etc.; greet: *The old gentleman walked along the avenue saluting his friends.* **3** act of saluting; sign of welcome, farewell, or honor: *The queen gracefully acknowledged the salutes of the crowd.* **4** make a salute. **5** position of the hand, gun, etc., in saluting. 1,2,4 *v.,* **sa lut ed, sa lut ing;** 3,5 *n.* —**sa lut′er,** *n.*

Sal va dor (sal′və dôr). See El Salvador. *n.*

sal vage (sal′vij), **1** act of saving a ship or its cargo from wreck, capture, etc. **2** payment for saving it. **3** rescue of property from fire, flood, shipwreck, etc. **4** save from fire, flood, shipwreck, etc. **5** property salvaged: *the salvage from a shipwreck, the salvage from a fire.* 1-3,5 *n.,* 4 *v.,* **sal vaged, sal vag ing.** —**sal′vage a ble,** *adj.* —**sal′vag er,** *n.*

sal va tion (sal vā′shən), **1** a saving or a being saved. **2** person or thing that saves. **3** a saving of the soul; deliverance from sin and from punishment for sin. *n.*

Salvation Army, organization to spread religion and help the poor, founded in England in 1865 by William Booth.

salve (sav), **1** a soft, greasy ointment put on wounds and sores to soothe or heal them. **2** put salve on. **3** something soothing; balm: *The kind words were a salve to his hurt feelings.* **4** soothe; smooth over: *She salved her conscience by the thought that her lie harmed no one.* 1,3 *n.,* 2,4 *v.,* **salved, salv ing.**

sal ver (sal′vər), tray. *n.*

sal vo (sal′vō), **1** the firing of several guns at the same time as a broadside or as a salute. **2** round of cheers or applause. *n., pl.* **sal vos** or **sal voes.**

Salz burg (sôlz′berg′), city in W Austria. Annual music festivals are held there. *n.*

S. Am., South America.

Sa mar i a (sə mer′ē ə), **1** district in the N part of ancient Palestine, now in Jordan. **2** chief city of this district. See **Galilee** for map. *n.*

Sa mar i tan (sə mar′ə tən), **1** person born or living in Samaria. **2** person who helps another in trouble or distress; Good Samaritan. *n.*

sa mar i um (sə mer′ē əm or sə mar′ē əm), a metallic element that is hard, brittle, and grayish-white. It is used in nuclear reactors. *n.*

same (sām), **1** not another; identical: *We came back the same way we went.* **2** just alike; not different: *His name and mine are the same.* **3** unchanged: *It is the same beautiful place.* **4** just spoken of: *We were talking about my aunt. This same aunt will be visiting us next week.* **5** the same person or thing. **6 the same,** in the same manner: *"Sea" and "see" are pronounced the same.* 1-4 *adj.,* 5 *pron.,* 6 *adv.*

all the same, notwithstanding; nevertheless.

just the same, 1 in the same manner. **2** nevertheless.

same ness (sām′nis), **1** state of being the same; exact likeness. **2** lack of variety; tiresomeness. *n.*

sam i sen (sam′ə sen), a Japanese instrument like a guitar, having three strings and played by plucking the strings. *n.*

Sa mo a (sə mō′ə), group of islands in the S Pacific. Several of these islands (**American Samoa**) belong to the United States and the rest make up the independent country of **Western Samoa.** See **Melanesia** for map. *n.* —**Sa mo′an,** *adj., n.*

samovar

sam o var (sam′ə vär), a metal urn used for heating water for tea. *n.* [*Samovar* was borrowed from Russian *samovar.*]

sam pan (sam′pan), a type of small boat used in China, Japan, etc. A sampan is sculled by one or more oars at the stern; it usually has a single sail and a cabin made of mats. *n.* [*Sampan* comes from Chinese *san pan.*]

sam ple (sam′pəl), **1** part to show what the rest is like; one thing to show what the others are like: *Here are some samples of drapery material for you to choose from.* **2** serving as an example: *a sample copy.* **3** take a part of; test a part of: *We sampled the cake and found it very good.* **1** *n.,* **2** *adj.,* **3** *v.,* **sam pled, sam pling.**

sam pler¹ (sam′plər), person who samples. *n.*

sam pler² (sam′plər), piece of cloth embroidered to show skill in needlework. *n.*

sam pling (sam′pling), **1** act or process of taking samples. **2** something taken or serving as a sample. *n.*

Sam son (sam′sən), **1** (in the Bible) a man who had very great strength. He was one of the judges of Israel. **2** any very strong man. *n.*

Sam u el (sam′yü əl), **1** a Hebrew leader, judge, and prophet of the 1000's B.C. **2** either of two books in the Old Testament named after Samuel. *n.*

sam u rai (sam′ù rī′), **1** the military class in feudal Japan, consisting of the retainers of the great nobles. **2** member of this class. *n., pl.* **sam u rai.**

Sa n'a (sä nä′), capital of Yemen. *n.*

San An dre as Fault (san än drā′əs), a large break in the earth's crust located in California. It is a center of earthquake activity.

San An to ni o (san an tō′nē ō), city in S Texas. The Alamo is there.

san a to ri um (san′ə tôr′ē əm), place for treatment of the sick or those recovering from illness. People who are suffering from a sickness that takes a long time to cure, like tuberculosis, often go to sanatoriums. *n., pl.* **san a to ri ums, san a to ri a** (san′ə tôr′ē ə). Also, **sanitarium.**

sanc ti fy (sangk′tə fī), **1** make holy; make free from sin. **2** set apart as sacred; observe as holy: *"Lord, sanctify this our offering to Thy use."* **3** make right; justify or sanction: *a custom sanctified by law. v.,* **sanc ti fied, sanc ti fy ing. —sanc′ti fi′a ble,** *adj.* **—sanc′ti fi′er,** *n.*

sanc ti mo ni ous (sangk′tə mō′nē əs), making a show of holiness; putting on airs of sanctity. *adj.* **—sanc′ti mo′ni ous ly,** *adv.* **—sanc′ti mo′ni ous ness,** *n.*

sanc tion (sangk′shən), **1** permission with authority; support; approval: *You need the owner's sanction to cross this property.* **2** authorize; approve; allow: *Her conscience does not sanction stealing.* **1** *n.,* **2** *v.* **—sanc′tion a ble,** *adj.*

sanc ti ty (sangk′tə tē), **1** holiness; saintliness; godliness. **2** sacredness; holy character: *the sanctity of a church, the sanctity of the home. n.*

sanc tu ar y (sangk′chü er′ē), **1** a sacred place. A church is a sanctuary. **2** part of a church around the altar. **3** place of refuge or protection: *a wildlife sanctuary.*

4 refuge or protection: *The cabin provided sanctuary from the rain. n., pl.* **sanc tu ar ies.**

sanc tum (sangk′təm), **1** a sacred place. **2** a private room or office where a person can be undisturbed. *n., pl.* **sanc tums, sanc ta** (sangk′tə).

sand (sand), **1** tiny grains of worn-down or disintegrated rock: *the sands of the desert, the sands of the seashore.* **2** spread sand over: *The highway department sanded the icy road.* **3** smooth or polish with sand, sandpaper, etc.: *to sand the edges of a piece of wood.* **1** *n.,* **2,3** *v.*

san dal (san′dl), **1** kind of shoe made of a sole fastened to the foot by straps. **2** any of various kinds of open shoes, slippers, etc. *n.*

san dal wood (san′dl wùd′), **1** the fragrant wood of certain trees of Asia, used for making boxes, fans, etc., and burned as incense. **2** any of the trees it comes from. *n.*

sand bag (sand′bag′), **1** bag filled with sand. Sandbags are used to hold back floods and as ballast on balloons. **2** furnish with sandbags. **3** a small bag of sand used as a club. **4** hit or stun with or as if with a sandbag. **1,3** *n.,* **2,4** *v.,* **sand bagged, sand bag ging. —sand′bag′ger,** *n.*

sand bank (sand′bangk′), ridge of sand. *n.*

sand bar (sand′bär′), ridge of sand in a river or along a shore, formed by the action of tides or currents. *n.*

sand blast (sand′blast′), **1** blast of air or steam containing sand, used to clean, grind, cut, or decorate hard surfaces, such as glass, stone, or metal. **2** use a sandblast on; clean, grind, cut, or decorate by a sandblast. **1** *n.,* **2** *v.* **—sand′blast′er,** *n.*

sand box (sand′boks′), box for holding sand, especially for children to play in. *n., pl.* **sand box es.**

Sand burg (sand′bėrg′), **Carl,** 1878-1967, American poet and biographer. *n.*

sand dollar, a small, flat, round sea animal that lives on sandy bottoms of the ocean. It is a kind of sea urchin.

sand er (san′dər), person or machine that sands or sandpapers. *n.*

San Di e go (san dē ā′gō), seaport in SW California.

sand lot (sand′lot′), of or about games or sports, especially baseball, played in vacant lots. *adj.*

sand man (sand′man′), (in stories) a man who makes children sleepy by sprinkling sand on their eyes. *n.*

sand pa per (sand′pā′pər), **1** a strong paper with a layer of sand or similar substance glued on it, used for smoothing, cleaning, or polishing. **2** smooth, clean, or polish with sandpaper. **1** *n.,* **2** *v.*

sandpiper—about 9 in. (23 cm.) long

sand pip er (sand′pī′pər), a small bird with a long bill, living on sandy shores. *n.*

sand stone (sand′stōn′), kind of rock formed mostly of sand and used in building. Sandstone is a sedimentary rock. *n.*

sand storm (sand′stôrm′), windstorm that carries along clouds of sand. *n.*

sand wich (sand′wich), **1** two or more slices of bread with meat, jelly, cheese, or some other filling between them. **2** put or squeeze in (between): *He was sandwiched between two large boxes.* 1 *n., pl.* **sand wich es;** 2 *v.*

WORD HISTORY

sandwich

Sandwich was named for the fourth Earl of *Sandwich,* 1718-1792, a British official who supposedly invented it so that he would not have to leave a card game to eat.

sand y (san′dē), **1** containing sand; consisting of sand: *sandy soil.* **2** covered with sand: *Most of the shore is rocky, but there is a sandy beach.* **3** yellowish-red: *She has sandy hair. adj.,* **sand i er, sand i est.** —**sand′i ness,** *n.*

sane (sān), **1** having a healthy mind; normal; sound; rational. **2** having or showing good sense; sensible: *A driver with a sane attitude doesn't take chances. adj.,* **san er, san est.** —**sane′ly,** *adv.* —**sane′ness,** *n.*

San for ized (san′fə rīzd′), trademark for fabrics that are pre-shrunk by a special process before they are made into articles of clothing. *adj.*

San Fran cis co (san frən sis′kō), large seaport in W California.

San Francisco Bay, bay of the Pacific on which San Francisco and Oakland, California, are located.

sang (sang), a past tense of **sing.** *The bird sang. v.*

san gui nar y (sang′gwə ner′ē), **1** bloody. **2** bloodthirsty. *adj.* —**san′gui nar′i ly,** *adv.* —**san′gui nar′i ness,** *n.*

san guine (sang′gwən), **1** naturally cheerful and hopeful: *a sanguine disposition.* **2** confident; hopeful: *sanguine of success.* **3** having a healthy red color; ruddy: *a sanguine complexion. adj.* —**san′guine ly,** *adv.*

san i tar i um (san′ə ter′ē əm), sanatorium. *n., pl.* **san i tar i ums, san i tar i a** (san′ə ter′ē ə).

san i tar y (san′ə ter′ē), **1** of or having to do with health; favorable to health; preventing disease: *sanitary regulations in a hospital.* **2** free from dirt and filth: *Food should be kept in a sanitary place. adj.* —**san′i tar′i ly,** *adv.* —**san′i tar′i ness,** *n.*

san i ta tion (san′ə tā′shən), the working out and practical application of sanitary measures. Disposal of sewage and government inspection of milk, meat, and other foods are important parts of sanitation. *n.*

san i ty (san′ə tē), **1** soundness of mind; mental health. **2** soundness of judgment; sensibleness. *n.*

San Jo sé (san hō zā′), capital of Costa Rica, in the central part.

San Juan (san wän′), seaport and capital of Puerto Rico, in the NE part.

sank (sangk), a past tense of **sink.** *The ship sank. v.*

San Ma ri no (san mə rē′nō), **1** tiny country in N Italy. **2** its capital.

sans (sanz), without. *prep.*

San Sal va dor (san sal′və dôr), **1** island of the central Bahamas, the first land seen by Columbus. **2** capital of El Salvador, in the central part.

San skrit (san′skrit), the ancient literary language of India. *n.*

San ta (san′tə *for 1;* san′tə *or* sän′tä *for 2*), **1** Santa Claus. **2** a Spanish or an Italian word meaning *holy* or *saint,* used in combinations, as in *Santa Maria.* 1 *n.,* 2 *adj.*

San ta An na (san′tə an′ə *or* sän′tä ä′nä), **Antonio López de,** 1795-1876, Mexican general and politician. His army defeated the Texans at the Alamo.

San ta Claus (san′tə klôz′), the saint of Christmas giving; Saint Nicholas. He is pictured as a fat, jolly, old man with a white beard, dressed in a fur-trimmed red suit.

San ta Fe (san′tə fā′), capital of New Mexico, in the N part.

Santa Fe Trail, an early trade route between Independence, Missouri, and Santa Fe, New Mexico. See **Oregon Trail** for map.

San ta Ma ri a (san′tə mə rē′ə), flagship of Columbus on his voyage of 1492.

San ti a go (san′tē ä′gō), capital of Chile, in the central part. *n.*

San to Do min go (san′tō də ming′gō), capital of the Dominican Republic, in the S part. It was established in 1496 and was the first town founded by Europeans in the Western Hemisphere.

São Pau lo (soun pou′lu̇), large city in S Brazil.

São To mé (soun tü me′), capital of São Tomé e Príncipe.

São To mé e Prín ci pe (soun tü me′ e prēn′sē pə), country made up of two islands off W Africa. *Capital:* São Tomé.

sap[1] (sap), **1** liquid that circulates through a plant, carrying water, food, etc., as blood does in animals. Rising sap carries water and minerals from the roots; sap traveling downward carries sugar, gums, resins, etc. Maple syrup is made from the sap of some maple trees. **2** SLANG. a fool. *n.*

sap[2] (sap), **1** dig under or wear away the foundation of: *The walls of the boathouse had been sapped by the waves.* **2** weaken; use up: *The extreme heat sapped our strength. v.,* **sapped, sap ping.**

sa pi ence (sā′pē əns), wisdom. *n.*

sa pi ent (sā′pē ənt), wise; sage. *adj.* —**sa′pi ent ly,** *adv.*

sap less (sap′lis), **1** without sap; withered. **2** without energy or vigor. *adj.* —**sap′less ness,** *n.*

sap ling (sap′ling), a young tree. *n.*

sa po dil la (sap′ə dil′ə), a large evergreen tree of tropical America that yields chicle and bears large berries tasting like pears. *n., pl.* **sa po dil las.**

sa pon i fy (sə pon′ə fī), **1** make (a fat or oil) into soap by treating with an alkali. **2** become soap. *v.,* **sa pon i fied, sa pon i fy ing.** —**sa pon′i fi′a ble,** *adj.* —**sa pon′i fi′er,** *n.*

sap phire (saf′īr), **1** a clear, hard, usually blue, precious stone. Sapphires are a variety of corundum. **2** bright-blue. **3** a bright blue. 1,3 *n.,* 2 *adj.*

sap py (sap′ē), **1** full of sap; juicy. **2** SLANG. silly; foolish. *adj.,* **sap pi er, sap pi est.** —**sap′pi ness,** *n.*

sap ro phyte (sap′rō fit), any plant that lives on decaying organic matter. Certain fungi are saprophytes. *n.* [*Saprophyte* comes from Greek *sapros,* meaning "rotten," and *phyton,* meaning "plant."]

sap suck er (sap′suk′ər), a small American woodpecker that feeds on the sap of trees. *n.*

sap wood (sap′wu̇d′), the soft, new, living wood between the bark and the hard inner wood of most trees. *n.*

Sar a cen (sar′ə sən), **1** an Arab. **2** a Moslem at the time of the Crusades. **3** of the Saracens. 1,2 *n.,* 3 *adj.*

Sar ah (ser/ə), (in the Bible) the wife of Abraham and the mother of Isaac. *n.*

sa ran (sə ran/), a plastic produced as a fiber, film, or molded form and highly resistant to damage and soiling. It is used especially to package food. *n.*

sa ra pe (sə rä/pē), serape. *n.*

Sa ra wak (sə rä/wäk), state in N Borneo, a member of the Federation of Malaysia. *n.*

sar casm (sär/kaz/əm), **1** a sneering or cutting remark; ironical taunt. **2** act of making fun of a person to hurt his feelings; harsh or bitter irony: *"How unselfish you are!" said the little girl in sarcasm as her sister took the biggest piece of cake. n.* [*Sarcasm* comes from Greek *sarkazein,* meaning "to sneer, to strip off flesh."]

sar cas tic (sär kas/tik), using sarcasm; sneering; cutting: *"Don't hurry!" was my brother's sarcastic comment as I slowly dressed. adj.* —**sar cas/ti cal ly,** *adv.*

sar coph a gus (sär kof/ə gəs), a stone coffin, especially an ornamental one. *n., pl.* **sar coph a gi** (sär kof/ə jī), **sar coph a gus es.**

sar dine (sär dēn/), a young or small herring or related fish, often preserved in oil for food. *n., pl.* **sar dines** or **sar dine.**

packed like sardines, very much crowded.

Sar din i a (sär din/ē ə), large Italian island in the Mediterranean Sea, west of Italy. See **Castile** for map. *n.* —**Sar din/i an,** *adj., n.*

sar don ic (sär don/ik), bitterly sarcastic, scornful, or mocking: *a sardonic laugh. adj.* —**sar don/i cal ly,** *adv.*

sa ri (sär/ē), a long piece of cotton or silk worn wound around the body with one end thrown over the head or shoulder. It is the outer garment of Hindu women. *n., pl.* **sa ris.** [*Sari* comes from Hindi *sārī.*]

sari

sa rong (sə rông/), a rectangular piece of cloth, usually a brightly colored, printed material, worn as a skirt by men and women in the East Indies. *n.* [*Sarong* comes from Malay *sārung.*]

sar sa pa ril la (sas/pə ril/ə *or* sär/sə pə ril/ə), **1** a tropical American climbing or trailing plant. **2** its dried root, used for flavoring. **3** a cooling drink flavored with this root. *n., pl.* **sar sa pa ril las.** [*Sarsaparilla* comes from Spanish *zarzaparrilla.*]

sar to ri al (sär tôr/ē əl), of tailors or their work: *His clothes were a sartorial triumph. adj.* —**sar to/ri al ly,** *adv.*

sash[1] (sash), a long, broad strip of cloth or ribbon, worn as an ornament round the waist or over one shoulder. *n., pl.* **sash es.**

sash[2] (sash), frame which holds the glass in a window or door. *n., pl.* **sash es.**

sa shay (sa shā/), INFORMAL. glide, move, or go about. *v.*

sa shi mi (sä shē/mē), a Japanese dish consisting of thin slices of raw fish, usually dipped in a sauce and eaten as an appetizer. *n.* [*Sashimi* was borrowed from Japanese *sashimi.*]

Sask., Saskatchewan.

Sa skatch e wan (sa skach/ə won), province in S Canada. *Capital:* Regina. *n.*

sass (sas), INFORMAL. **1** rudeness; back talk; impudence. **2** be rude or disrespectful to: *The little girl sassed her mother.* 1 *n.,* 2 *v.*

sas sa fras (sas/ə fras), **1** a slender American tree that has fragrant, yellow flowers and bluish-black fruit. **2** the dried bark of its root, used in medicine, tea, candy, soft drinks, etc. *n.*

sas sy (sas/ē), rude. *adj.,* **sas si er, sas si est.**

sat (sat), past tense and past participle of **sit.** *Yesterday I sat in a train all day. The cat has sat at that mouse hole for hours. v.*

Sat., Saturday.

Sa tan (sāt/n), the evil spirit; the enemy of goodness; the Devil. *n.* [*Satan* can be traced back to Hebrew *sātān,* meaning "enemy."]

sa tan ic or **Sa tan ic** (sā tan/ik *or* sə tan/ik), of Satan; like Satan; like that of Satan; very wicked. *adj.*

satch el (sach/əl), a small bag for carrying clothes, books, etc.; handbag. *n.*

sate (sāt), **1** satisfy fully (any appetite or desire): *A long drink sated his thirst.* **2** supply with more than enough, so as to weary or disgust. *v.,* **sat ed, sat ing.**

sa teen (sa tēn/), a cotton cloth made to imitate satin. *n.*

satellite
(def. 2)

sat el lite (sat/l īt), **1** a heavenly body that revolves around a planet, especially around one of the nine major planets of the solar system. The moon is a satellite of the earth. **2** an artificial object launched by rocket into an orbit around the earth or other heavenly body. **3** country that is supposedly independent but actually is controlled by a more powerful country, especially a country controlled by the Soviet Union. *n.* [*Satellite* comes from Latin *satellitem,* meaning "attendant."]

sa ti ate (sā/shē āt), **1** feed fully; satisfy fully. **2** supply with too much; weary or disgust with too much: *She was so satiated with bananas that she would not even look at one. v.,* **sa ti at ed, sa ti at ing.** —**sa/ti a/tion,** *n.*

sat in (sat/n), **1** a silk, rayon, nylon, or cotton cloth with one very smooth, glossy side. **2** of or like satin; smooth and glossy. 1 *n.,* 2 *adj.*

sat in y (sat/n ē), like satin in smoothness and gloss. *adj.*

sat ire (sat/īr), **1** the use of sarcasm, irony, or wit, to attack or ridicule a habit, idea, custom, etc. **2** poem, essay, story, etc., that attacks or ridicules in this way. *n.*

sa tir ic (sə tir/ik), satirical. *adj.*

sa tir i cal (sə tir/ə kəl), of satire; containing satire; fond of using satire. *adj.* —**sa tir/i cal ly,** *adv.*

sat i rist (sat/ə rist), writer of satires; person who uses satire. *n.*

sat i rize (sat/ə rīz/), attack with satire; criticize with mockery; seek to improve by ridicule. *v.,* **sat i rized, sat-**

i riz ing. —sat′i riz′a ble, *adj.* —sat′i ri za′tion, *n.* —sat′i riz′er, *n.*

sat is fac tion (sat′i sfak′shən), **1** a satisfying; fulfillment: *The satisfaction of hunger requires food.* **2** condition of being satisfied, or pleased and contented: *She felt satisfaction at winning a prize.* **3** anything that makes us feel pleased or contented: *It is a great satisfaction to have things turn out just the way you want.* **4** payment of debt; discharge of an obligation; making up for wrong or injury done. *n.*

give satisfaction, 1 satisfy. **2** fight a duel because of an insult.

sat is fac tor i ly (sat′i sfak′tər ə lē), in a satisfactory manner. *adv.*

sat is fac tor y (sat′i sfak′tər ē), satisfying; good enough to satisfy; pleasing or adequate. *adj.* —sat′is fac′tor i ness, *n.*

sat is fy (sat′i sfī), **1** give enough to; fulfill (desires, hopes, demands, etc.); put an end to (needs, wants, etc.): *He satisfied his hunger with a sandwich and milk.* **2** make contented; please: *Are you satisfied now?* **3** pay; make right: *After the accident he satisfied all claims for the damage he had caused.* **4** set free from doubt; convince: *I am satisfied that it was an accident.* *v.,* **sat is fied, sat is fy ing.** —sat′is fi′a ble, *adj.* —sat′is fi′er, *n.* —sat′is fy′ing ly, *adv.*

sat u rate (sach′ə rāt′), **1** soak thoroughly; fill full: *During the fog, the air was saturated with moisture. The rain had saturated us by the time we had walked all the way home.* **2** cause (a substance) to unite with the greatest possible amount of another substance. A saturated solution of sugar or salt is one that cannot dissolve any more sugar or salt. *v.,* **sat u rat ed, sat u rat ing.** —sat′u rat′er, sat′u ra′tor, *n.*

sat u rat ed fat (sach′ə rā′tid), solid or semisolid animal fat, such as butter or lard.

sat u ra tion (sach′ə rā′shən), **1** act or process of saturating. **2** fact of being saturated; saturated condition. Saturation of a salt solution occurs when no more salt will dissolve in the water. *n.*

Sat ur day (sat′ər dē), the seventh day of the week, following Friday. *n.*

Sat urn (sat′ərn), **1** (in Roman myths) the god of agriculture. Saturn ruled during a golden age. **2** the second largest planet in the solar system and the sixth in distance from the sun. Saturn is encircled by a system of rings made up of tiny particles of matter. *n.*

Sat ur na li a (sat′ər nā′lē ə), the ancient Roman festival of Saturn, celebrated in December with much feasting and merrymaking. *n. pl. or sing.*

sat ur nine (sat′ər nīn), gloomy; grave; taciturn. *adj.*

sa tyr (sā′tər *or* sat′ər), (in Greek myths) a deity of the woods, part man and part goat or horse. *n.* —sa′tyr like′, *adj.*

sauce (sôs), **1** something, usually a liquid, served with or on food to make it taste better. We eat cranberry sauce with turkey, mint sauce with lamb, egg sauce with fish, and many different sauces with puddings. **2** stewed fruit. **3** prepare with sauce; season. **4** give interest or flavor to. **5** rudeness: *Don't give me any sauce!* **1,2,5** *n.,* **3,4** *v.,* **sauced, sauc ing.** —sauce′less, *adj.*

sauce pan (sôs′pan′), a small pan with a handle, used for stewing, boiling, etc. *n.*

sau cer (sô′sər), **1** a shallow dish to set a cup on. **2** something round and shallow like a saucer. *n.* —sau′cer like′, *adj.*

sau ci ly (sô′sə lē), in a saucy manner. *adv.*

sau ci ness (sô′sē nis), rudeness. *n.*

sau cy (sô′sē), showing lack of respect; rude: *saucy language or conduct. adj.,* **sau ci er, sau ci est.**

Sa u di (sä ü′dē), **1** of Saudi Arabia. **2** person born or living in Saudi Arabia. **1** *adj.,* **2** *n., pl.* **Sa u dis.**

Saudi Arabia, country in central Arabia. *Capitals:* Riyadh and Mecca. See **Assyria** for map. —**Saudi Arabian.**

sauer kraut (sour′krout′), cabbage cut fine, salted, and allowed to sour. *n.* [*Sauerkraut* is from German *Sauerkraut,* which comes from *sauer,* meaning "sour," and *Kraut,* meaning "cabbage."]

Sauk (sôk), member of a tribe of American Indians formerly living in Michigan and Wisconsin. *n., pl.* **Sauk** or **Sauks.** Also, **Sac.**

Saul (sôl), in the Bible: **1** the first king of Israel. **2** the original name of the apostle Paul. *n.*

sau na (sou′nə), **1** a steam bath in which the steam is produced by water thrown on hot stones. **2** building or room used for such a steam bath. *n., pl.* **sau nas.** [*Sauna* was borrowed from Finnish *sauna.*]

saun ter (sôn′tər), **1** walk along slowly and happily; stroll: *People sauntered through the park on summer evenings.* **2** a stroll. **1** *v.,* **2** *n.* —**saun′ter er,** *n.*

sau sage (sô′sij), chopped pork, beef, or other meats, seasoned and usually stuffed into a very thin casing. *n.* —**sau′sage like′,** *adj.*

sau té (sō tā′ *or* sô tā′), **1** cooked or browned in a little fat. **2** dish of food cooked or browned in a little fat. **3** fry quickly in a little fat. **1** *adj.,* **2** *n.,* **3** *v.,* **sau téed, sau té ing.**

sav age (sav′ij), **1** member of a primitive, uncivilized people. **2** not civilized; barbarous: *savage customs.* **3** fierce; cruel; ready to fight; brutal: *a savage dog.* **4** a fierce, brutal, or cruel person. **5** wild or rugged: *savage mountain scenery.* **1,4** *n.,* **2,3,5** *adj.* [*Savage* came into English about 700 years ago from French *sauvage,* and can be traced back to Latin *silva,* meaning "forest."] —**sav′age ly,** *adv.* —**sav′age ness,** *n.*

satyr

Sav age (sav′ij), **Augusta,** 1910-1962, American sculptor. *n.*

sav age ry (sav′ij rē), **1** a being fierce; cruelty; brutality. **2** wildness. **3** an uncivilized condition. *n., pl.* **sav age ries.**

sa van na (sə van′ə), a grassy plain with few or no trees, especially one in the southern United States or near the tropics. *n., pl.* **sa van nas.** [*Savanna* comes from Spanish *sabana.*]

sa van nah (sə van′ə), savanna. *n.*

Sa van nah (sə van′ə), seaport in E Georgia. *n.*

---

a	hat	i	it	oi	oil	ch	child		a in about
ā	age	ī	ice	ou	out	ng	long		e in taken
ä	far	o	hot	u	cup	sh	she	ə =	i in pencil
e	let	ō	open	ů	put	th	thin		o in lemon
ē	equal	ô	order	ü	rule	₮н	then		u in circus
ėr	term					zh	measure		

save[1] (sāv), **1** make or keep safe; rescue or protect from harm, danger, loss, etc.; rescue: *The dog saved the child's life. We covered the plants with straw to save them from the frost.* **2** lay aside; store up: *save money. I save pieces of string.* **3** keep from spending or wasting: *We took the shortcut to save time.* **4** avoid expense or waste: *She saves in every way she can.* **5** make less; prevent: *save work, save trouble.* **6** treat carefully to keep in good condition: *Save your strength for the big race.* **7** prevent the loss of: *Another goal will save the game.* **8** set free from sin and its results. *v.*, **saved, sav ing.** —**sav′a ble, save′a ble,** *adj.*

save[2] (sāv), except; but: *He works every day save Sunday. prep.*

sav er (sā′vər), person or thing that saves: *A washing machine is a saver of time and strength. n.*

sav ing (sā′ving), **1** tending to save up money; avoiding waste; economical. **2** way of saving money, time, etc.: *It will be a saving to take this shortcut.* **3** act of preserving, rescuing, etc. **4** that which is saved. **5** savings, *pl.* money saved. **6** with the exception of; save; except: *Saving a few crackers, we had eaten nothing all day.* **7** with all due respect to or for. **8** compensating; redeeming. **9** except: *The pens are the same saving one has red ink and the other blue.* 1,8 *adj.*, 2-5 *n.*, 6,7 *prep.*, 9 *conj.*

savings account, account in a savings bank.

savings bank, bank which accepts money only for savings and investment and which pays interest on all deposits.

savings bond, bond issued by the United States government to help pay its expenses. Savings bonds can be cashed with interest after a certain time.

sav ior or **sav iour** (sā′vyər), person who saves or rescues. *n.*

Sav ior or **Sav iour** (sā′vyər), Jesus Christ. *n.*

sa vor (sā′vər), **1** a taste or smell; flavor: *The soup has a savor of onion.* **2** enjoy the taste or smell of; enjoy very much: *He savored the soup.* **3** to taste or smell (of): *That sauce savors of lemon.* **4** give flavor to; season. **5** a distinctive quality; noticeable trace: *There was a savor of humor in her conversation.* **6** have the quality or nature (of): *The plot savored of mystery.* 1,5 *n.*, 2-4,6 *v.* —**sa′vor er,** *n.* —**sa′vor ing ly,** *adv.* —**sa′vor less,** *adj.*

sa vor y[1] (sā′vər ē), **1** pleasing in taste or smell: *the savory smell of roasting turkey.* **2** morally pleasing; agreeable. *adj.*, **sa vor i er, sa vor i est.**

sa vor y[2] (sā′vər ē), a fragrant herb related to mint, used for seasoning food. *n.*, *pl.* **sa vor ies.**

Sa voy (sə voi′), region in SE France. *n.*

sav vy (sav′ē), SLANG. **1** know; understand. **2** understanding; intelligence; sense: *a person with savvy.* 1 *v.*, **sav vied, sav vy ing;** 2 *n.*

saw[1] (sô), **1** tool for cutting, made of a thin blade with sharp teeth on the edge. **2** a machine with such a tool for cutting. **3** cut with a saw: *to saw wood.* **4** make with a saw: *Boards are sawed from logs.* **5** use a saw: *Can you saw straight?* **6** be sawed: *Pine saws more easily than oak.* 1,2 *n.*, 3-6 *v.*, **sawed, sawed** or **sawn, saw ing.** —**saw′er,** *n.* —**saw′like′,** *adj.*

saw[2] (sô), past tense of **see**[1]. *I saw a robin yesterday. v.*

saw[3] (sô), a wise saying; proverb: *"A stitch in time saves nine" is a familiar saw. n.*

saw buck (sô′buk′), **1** sawhorse. **2** SLANG. a ten-dollar bill. *n.*

saw dust (sô′dust′), particles of wood made by sawing. *n.*

sawed-off (sôd′ôf′), **1** having one end sawed or cut off: *a sawed-off shotgun.* **2** SLANG. small in size; short. *adj.*

saw horse (sô′hôrs′), frame for holding wood that is being sawed. *n.*

saw mill (sô′mil′), **1** a building where machines saw timber into planks, boards, etc. **2** a machine for such sawing. *n.*

sawn (sôn), sawed; a past participle of **saw**[1]. *v.*

saw yer (sô′yər), man whose work is sawing timber. *n.*

sax (saks), saxophone. *n.*, *pl.* **sax es.**

sax i frage (sak′sə frij), plant with white, pink, purple, or yellow flowers. Saxifrage is often grown in rock gardens. *n.*

Sax on (sak′sən), **1** member of a Germanic tribe that, with the Angles and Jutes, conquered England in the A.D. 400's and 500's. **2** language of the Saxons. **3** of the Saxons or their language: *Saxon laws.* **4** Anglo-Saxon. 1,2,4 *n.*, 3,4 *adj.*

saxophone

sax o phone (sak′sə fōn), a woodwind instrument having a curved metal body with keys for the fingers and a mouthpiece with a single reed. *n.* [*Saxophone* was formed in French from the name of its Belgian inventor, Adolphe *Sax,* 1814-1894, and Greek *phōnē,* meaning "sound."]

sax o phon ist (sak′sə fō′nist), a saxophone player. *n.*

say (sā), **1** speak; utter: *What did you say? "Thank you," she said.* **2** put into words; express; declare: *Say what you think.* **3** recite; repeat: *Say your prayers.* **4** about; approximately: *You can learn to dance in, say, ten lessons.* **5** express an opinion: *It is hard to say which shirt is nicer.* **6** chance to say something: *If you have all had your say, we will vote on the matter.* **7** power; authority: *Who has the final say in this matter?* 1-3,5 *v.*, **said, say ing;** 4 *adv.*, 6,7 *n.* —**say′er,** *n.*

that is to say, that is; in other words.

say ing (sā′ing), **1** something said; statement. **2** proverb: *"Haste makes waste" is a saying. n.*

go without saying, be too obvious to need mention.

says (sez), a present tense of **say.** *He says he'll be late. v.*

say-so (sā′sō′), **1** one's mere word: *Do you believe that, just on his say-so?* **2** authority or power to decide. *n.*, *pl.* **say-sos.**

Sb, symbol for antimony.

Sc, symbol for scandium.

SC, South Carolina (used with postal Zip Code).

S.C., South Carolina.

scab (skab), **1** the crust that forms over a sore or wound as it heals: *A scab started to form on my scraped knee.* **2** become covered with a scab. **3** INFORMAL. worker who will not join a labor union or who takes a striker's job. 1,3 *n.*, 2 *v.*, **scabbed, scab bing.** —**scab′like′,** *adj.*

scab bard (skab′ərd), a sheath or case for the blade of a sword, dagger, etc. *n.*

scab by (skab′ē), covered with scabs. *adj.*, **scab bi er, scab bi est.** —**scab′bi ly,** *adv.* —**scab′bi ness,** *n.*

sca bies (skā′bēz), disease of the skin caused by mites that live under the skin and cause itching. *n.*

scads (skadz), INFORMAL. a large quantity. *n.pl.*

scaf fold (skaf′əld), **1** a temporary structure for holding workers and materials. **2** a raised platform on which criminals are put to death. **3** any raised framework. *n.*

scaf fold ing (skaf′əl ding), **1** scaffold. **2** materials for scaffolds. *n.*

scal a wag (skal′ə wag), a dishonorable person; scamp; rascal. *n.*

scald (skôld), **1** to burn with hot liquid or steam: *I scalded myself with hot grease.* **2** a burn caused by hot liquid or steam: *The scald on his hand came from lifting a pot cover carelessly.* **3** pour boiling liquid over; use boiling liquid on: *Scald the dishes before drying them.* **4** heat almost to boiling, but not quite: *Scald the milk.* **5** to burn as if with boiling water. 1,3-5 *v.*, 2 *n.*

scale[1] (skāl), **1** the dish or pan of a balance. **2** Usually, **scales,** *pl.* balance; instrument for weighing: *She weighed some meat on the scales.* **3** weigh: *I scale 65 pounds.* **4** weigh in scales; measure; compare. 1,2 *n.*, 3,4 *v.*, **scaled, scal ing.** [*Scale*[1] came into English about 700 years ago from Icelandic *skal.*]

tip the scales, 1 have as one's weight; weigh: *to tip the scales at 100 pounds.* **2** give greater importance or influence to one side than another; decide: *The new treaty tipped the scales in favor of peace.*

turn the scales, decide.

scale[2] (skāl), **1** one of the thin, flat, hard plates forming the outer covering of some fishes, snakes, and lizards. **2** a thin layer like a scale: *My sunburn caused my skin to peel off in scales.* **3** remove scales from: *She scaled the fish with a knife.* **4** come off in scales: *The paint is scaling off the house.* **5** one of the parts that cover a bud or other plant part. **6** scale insect. 1,2,5,6 *n.*, 3,4 *v.*, **scaled, scaling.** [*Scale*[2] came into English about 600 years ago from French *escale,* meaning "scale, husk."] —**scal′a ble,** *adj.* —**scale′less,** *adj.* —**scale′like′,** *adj.*

scale[3] (skāl), **1** series of steps or degrees; scheme of graded amounts: *The salary scale for this job ranges from $8000 to $10,000 a year.* **2** series of marks made along a line at regular distances to use in measuring: *A thermometer has a scale.* **3** an instrument marked in this way, used for measuring. **4** the size of a plan, map, drawing, or model compared with what it represents: *This map is drawn to the scale of one inch for each 100 miles.* **5** relative size or extent: *That rich family entertains on a large scale.* **6** system of numbering: *The decimal scale counts by tens, as in cents, dimes, dollars.* **7** reduce by a certain amount in relation to other amounts: *To draw this map, mileage was scaled down to one inch for each 100 miles.* **8** (in music) a series of tones ascending or descending in pitch according to fixed intervals: *She practices scales on the piano.* **9** climb: *They scaled the wall by ladders.* **10** make according to a scale. 1-6,8 *n.*, 7,9,10 *v.*, **scaled, scal ing.** [*Scale*[3] comes from Latin *scalae,* meaning "ladder."]

scale insect, any of various small insects that feed on and often destroy plants by piercing them and sucking the sap. The females have the body and eggs covered by a scale or shield formed by a secretion from the body.

sca lene (skā lēn′ *or* skā′lēn′), (of a triangle) having three sides unequal. *adj.*

scal i ness (skā′lē nis), scaly quality or condition. *n.*

scal lion (skal′yən), **1** a young onion that has no large, distinct bulb. **2** leek. *n.*

scallop (def. 1)   **scallop** (def. 3)

scal lop (skol′əp *or* skal′əp), **1** shellfish somewhat like a clam, with a rounded, fan-shaped shell. In some kinds the large muscle that opens and closes the shell is good to eat. **2** bake with sauce and bread crumbs in a dish; escallop: *scalloped oysters.* **3** one of a series of curves on the edge of anything: *This plate has scallops.* **4** make such curves on: *scallop a quilt.* 1,3 *n.*, 2,4 *v.* Also, **scollop.**

scalp (skalp), **1** the skin on the top and back of the head, usually covered with hair. **2** part of this skin, formerly kept as a token of victory. **3** cut or tear the scalp from. 1,2 *n.*, 3 *v.*

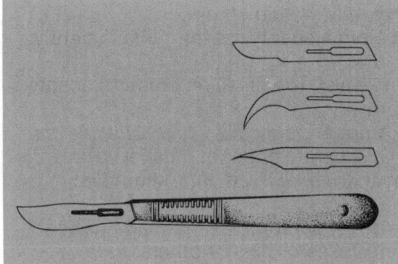

scalpel
with
interchangeable
blades

scal pel (skal′pəl), a small, straight knife used by surgeons. *n.*

scal y (skā′lē), **1** covered with scales; having scales like a fish: *This iron pipe is scaly with rust.* **2** suggesting scales. *adj.*, **scal i er, scal i est.**

scam (skam), SLANG. a clever but dishonest trick; fraud. *n.*

scamp (skamp), a dishonorable person; rascal; rogue. *n.*

scam per (skam′pər), **1** run quickly: *The mice scampered away when the cat came.* **2** a quick run: *Let the dog out for a scamper.* 1 *v.*, 2 *n.*

scan (skan), **1** look at closely; examine with care: *You should scan every word in the contract before you sign it.* **2** glance at; look over hastily. **3** mark off (lines of poetry) into feet. EXAMPLE: Sing′ a | song′ of | six′pence. **4** read or recite (poetry), marking off the lines into feet. **5** (in television) expose bits of a surface in rapid succession to beams of electrons in order to transmit a picture. **6** examine automatically by using a device such as a scanner. **7** the picture or other information provided by a scanner: *a brain scan.* 1-6 *v.*, scanned, scan ning; 7 *n.*

scan dal (skan′dl), **1** a shameful action, condition, or event that brings disgrace or shocks public opinion: *It was a scandal for the city treasurer to take tax money for personal use.* **2** damage to reputation; disgrace. **3** public talk about a person which will hurt that person's reputation; evil gossip; slander. *n.*

scan dal ize (skan′dl īz), offend by doing something thought to be wrong or improper; shock: *Our great-grandparents would be scandalized by many of the things we do today.* *v.,* **scan dal ized, scan dal iz ing.** —**scan′dal i za′tion,** *n.*

scan dal ous (skan′dl əs), **1** bringing disgrace; shameful; shocking: *scandalous behavior.* **2** spreading scandal or slander: *a scandalous piece of gossip.* *adj.* —**scan′dal ous ly,** *adv.* —**scan′dal ous ness,** *n.*

Scan di na vi a (skan′də nā′vē ə), **1** region of NW Europe that includes Norway, Sweden, Denmark, and sometimes Finland and Iceland. **2** peninsula on which Norway and Sweden are located. *n.*

Scan di na vi an (skan′də nā′vē ən), **1** of Scandinavia, its people, or their languages. **2** person born or living in Scandinavia. **3** languages of Scandinavia, both modern and historical. Scandinavian includes Danish, Icelandic, Norwegian, and Swedish. **1** *adj.,* **2,3** *n.*

scan di um (skan′dē əm), a gray, metallic element found in many minerals in Scandinavia. *n.*

scan ner (skan′ər), device which examines automatically, especially one which passes a beam of electrons or radiation over a surface. *n.*

scan sion (skan′shən), the marking off of lines of poetry into feet; scanning. In the oral scansion of poetry, a reader stresses the accented syllables heavily. *n.*

scant (skant), **1** not enough in size or quantity: *Her coat was short and scant.* **2** barely enough; barely full; bare: *Use a scant cup of butter in the cake. You have a scant hour in which to pack.* **3** make scant; cut down; limit; stint: *Don't scant the butter if you want a rich cake.* **1,2** *adj.,* **3** *v.* —**scant′ly,** *adv.* —**scant′ness,** *n.*

scant i ly (skan′tl ē), in a scanty manner; insufficiently. *adv.*

scant i ness (skan′tē nis), too small an amount; scanty quality or condition. *n.*

scant y (skan′tē), **1** not enough: *His scanty clothing did not keep out the cold.* **2** barely enough; meager: *The drought caused a very scanty harvest.* *adj.,* **scant i er, scant i est.**

scape goat (skāp′gōt′), person or thing made to bear the blame for the mistakes or sins of others. *n.*

scap u la (skap′yə lə), shoulder blade. *n., pl.* **scap u lae** (skap′yə lē), **scap u las.**

scar (skär), **1** the mark left by a healed cut, wound, burn, or sore: *My vaccination scar is small.* **2** any mark like this: *See the scars your shoes have made on the chair. War leaves many deep scars on the minds of those who endure it. A fallen leaf leaves a scar where it joined the stem.* **3** mark with a scar: *He scarred the wood with the hammer when he missed the nail.* **4** form a scar; heal: *The wound is scarring quite well.* **1,2** *n.,* **3,4** *v.,* **scarred, scar ring.** —**scar′less,** *adj.*

scar ab (skar′əb), **1** any of a large group or beetles, especially the sacred beetle of the ancient Egyptians. **2** an image of this beetle. Scarabs were much used in ancient Egypt as charms or ornaments. *n.*

scarce (skers *or* skars), **1** hard to get; rare: *Water is becoming scarce in some parts of the country.* **2** scarcely. **1** *adj.,* **scarc er, scarc est; 2** *adv.* —**scarce′ness,** *n.*
make oneself scarce, 1 go away. **2** stay away.

scarce ly (skers′lē *or* skars′lē), **1** not quite; barely: *We could scarcely see the ship through the fog.* **2** decidedly not: *She can scarcely have said that.* *adv.*

scar ci ty (sker′sə tē *or* skar′sə tē), too small a supply; lack; rarity: *There is a scarcity of nurses.* *n., pl.* **scar ci ties.**

scare (sker *or* skar), **1** make or become afraid; frighten: *We were scared and ran away. Courageous people don't scare easily.* **2** a fright. **3** a widespread state of fright or panic: *a bomb scare at the airport.* **4** frighten (away); drive off: *The watchdog scared away the robber by barking.* **1,4** *v.,* **scared, scar ing; 2,3** *n.* —**scar′er,** *n.* —**scar′ing ly,** *adv.*
scare up, INFORMAL. get; raise: *scare up a few extra blankets on a cold night.*

scare crow (sker′krō′ *or* skar′krō′), **1** figure of a person dressed in old clothes, set in a field to frighten birds away from crops. **2** person, usually skinny, dressed in ragged clothes. **3** anything that fools people into being frightened. *n.*

scarf (skärf), **1** a long, broad strip of silk, lace, etc., worn about the neck, shoulders, head, or waist. **2** a long strip of linen, etc., used as a cover for a bureau, table, piano, etc. *n., pl.* **scarfs** *or* **scarves.** —**scarf′less,** *adj.* —**scarf′like′,** *adj.*

scar i ly (sker′ə lē *or* skar′ə lē), INFORMAL. in a scary manner. *adv.*

scar i ness (sker′ē nis *or* skar′ē nis), INFORMAL. scary feeling or condition. *n.*

scar la ti na (skär′lə tē′nə), scarlet fever, especially a mild form of the disease. *n.*

scar let (skär′lit), **1** a very bright red. Scarlet is much lighter than crimson. **2** very bright red. **1** *n.,* **2** *adj.*

scarlet fever, a very contagious disease that affects chiefly children, causing a scarlet rash, sore throat, and fever.

scarlet tanager, a colorful songbird of eastern North America; redbird. The male has black wings and tail and a scarlet body.

scarves (skärvz), a plural of **scarf.** *n.*

scar y (sker′ē *or* skar′ē), INFORMAL. **1** causing fright or alarm: *scary sounds, a scary movie.* **2** easily frightened. *adj.,* **scar i er, scar i est.**

scat (skat), INFORMAL. **1** exclamation used to drive away an animal. **2** go away, especially in a hurry. **1** *interj.,* **2** *v.,* **scat ted, scat ting.**

scath ing (skā′ᴛʜing), bitterly severe: *scathing criticism.* *adj.* —**scath′ing ly,** *adv.*

scat ter (skat′ər), **1** throw here and there; sprinkle: *I scattered salt on the sidewalk to melt the ice.* **2** separate and drive off in different directions: *The police scattered the disorderly crowd.* **3** separate and go in different directions: *The chickens scattered in fright when the truck honked at them.* *v.* —**scat′ter er,** *n.*

scat ter brain (skat′ər brān′), a thoughtless, flighty person. *n.*

scat ter brained (skat′ər brānd′), not able to think steadily; flighty; thoughtless. *adj.*

scat ter ing (skat′ər ing), a small amount or number occurring here and there. *n.*

scatter rug, a small rug.

scav enge (skav′ənj), pick over (discarded objects) for things to use or sell. *v.,* **scav enged, scav eng ing.**

scav en ger (skav′ən jər), **1** animal that feeds on decaying animal or plant matter. Vultures and jackals are scavengers. **2** person who searches through discarded objects for something of value. *n.*

sce nar i o (si ner′ē ō *or* si nar′ē ō), **1** the outline of a motion picture, giving the main facts about the scenes, persons, and acting. **2** the outline of any play, opera, etc. *n., pl.* **sce nar i os.**

sce nar ist (si ner′ist *or* si nar′ist), person who writes scenarios. *n.*

scene (sēn), **1** the time, place, circumstances, etc., of a play or story: *The scene of the novel is laid in Virginia during the Civil War.* **2** the place where anything is carried on or takes place: *the scene of an accident.* **3** the painted screens, hangings, etc., used in a theater to represent places: *The scene represents a city street.* **4** part of an act of a play: *The queen comes to the castle in Act I, Scene 2.* **5** a particular incident of a play: *The scene in which the detective reveals the name of the murderer is the highlight of the play.* **6** action, incident, situation, etc., occurring in reality or represented in literature or art: *He has painted a series of pictures called "Scenes of My Boyhood."* **7** view; picture: *The white sailboats in the blue water made a pretty scene.* **8** show of strong feeling in front of others; exhibition; display: *The child kicked, screamed, and made a dreadful scene. n.*

behind the scenes, 1 out of sight of the audience. **2** not publicly; privately; secretly.

WORD HISTORY

scene

Scene came into English about 400 years ago from French *scene*, and can be traced back to Greek *skēnē*, which originally meant "tent in the theater where actors changed costumes."

scen er y (sē′nər ē), **1** the general appearance of a place; the natural features of a landscape: *She enjoys mountain scenery very much.* **2** the painted hangings, screens, etc., used in a theater to represent places: *The scenery pictures a garden in the moonlight. n., pl.* **scen er ies.**

scen ic (sē′nik *or* sen′ik), **1** of natural scenery: *The scenic splendors of Yellowstone Park are famous.* **2** having much fine scenery: *a scenic highway.* **3** of stage scenery or stage effects: *The production of the musical comedy was a scenic triumph. adj.* —**scen′i cal ly,** *adv.*

scenic (def. 2) a scenic view in the Swiss Alps

scent (sent), **1** a smell: *The scent of roses filled the air.* **2** to smell: *The dog scented a rabbit and ran off after it.* **3** sense of smell: *Bloodhounds have a keen scent.* **4** hunt by using the sense of smell: *The dog scented about till it found the trail.* **5** smell left in passing: *The dogs followed the fox by the scent.* **6** means by which a thing or a person can be traced: *The police are on the scent of the thieves.* **7** have a suspicion of; be aware of: *I scent a trick in their offer.* **8** a

a hat	i it	oi oil	ch child	
ā age	ī ice	ou out	ng long	a in about
ä far	o hot	u cup	sh she	e in taken
e let	ō open	u̇ put	th thin	ə = i in pencil
ē equal	ô order	ü rule	ŦH then	o in lemon
ėr term			zh measure	u in circus

perfume: *She used too much scent.* **9** fill with odor; perfume: *The bouquet of lilacs scented the entire room.* 1,3,5, 6,8 *n.*, 2,4,7,9 *v.* —**scent′less,** *adj.*

scep ter (sep′tər), the rod or staff carried by a ruler as a symbol of royal power or authority. *n.* Also, **sceptre.**

scep tic (skep′tik), skeptic. *n.*

scep ti cal (skep′tə kəl), skeptical. *adj.*

scep ti cism (skep′tə siz′əm), skepticism. *n.*

scep tre (sep′tər), scepter. *n.*

sch., 1 school. **2** schooner.

sched ule (skej′ül), **1** a written or printed statement of details; list: *A timetable is a schedule of the coming and going of trains. The teacher posted the schedule of classes.* **2** make a schedule of; enter in a schedule. **3** to plan or arrange (something) for a definite time or date: *Schedule the convention for the fall.* **4** the time fixed for doing something, arrival at a place, etc.: *The bus was an hour behind schedule.* 1,4 *n.*, 2,3 *v.*, **sched uled, sched ul ing.**

sche mat ic (skē mat′ik), having the nature of a diagram, plan, or scheme. *adj.* —**sche mat′i cal ly,** *adv.*

sche ma tize (skē′mə tīz), arrange according to a scheme or formula. *v.*, **sche ma tized, sche ma tiz ing.** —**sche′ma ti za′tion,** *n.*

scheme (skēm), **1** program of action; plan: *He has a scheme for extracting salt from seawater.* **2** a plot: *a scheme to cheat the government.* **3** devise plans, especially underhanded or evil ones; plot: *They schemed to bring the jewels into the country without paying duty.* **4** system of connected things, parts, thoughts, etc.: *The color scheme of the room is blue and gold.* 1,2,4 *n.*, 3 *v.*, **schemed, schem ing.** —**scheme′less,** *adj.*

schem er (skē′mər), person who plans or plots. *n.*

schem ing (skē′ming), making tricky schemes; crafty. *adj.* —**schem′ing ly,** *adv.*

scher zo (sker′tsō), a light or playful movement of a sonata or symphony. *n., pl.* **scher zos, scher zi** (sker′tsē).

Schick test (shik), a test to determine if a person is immune to diphtheria, made by injecting a very small amount of diphtheria toxin under the skin. [The *Schick test* was named for Béla *Schick*, 1877-1967, an American doctor born in Hungary, who developed it.]

schism (siz′əm), division into hostile groups, especially division because of some difference of opinion about religion. *n.*

schist (shist), kind of rock composed chiefly of mica, that splits easily into layers. Schist is a metamorphic rock. *n.*

Schlie mann (shlē′män), **Heinrich,** 1822-1890, German archaeologist who discovered and excavated the site of ancient Troy. *n.*

schol ar (skol′ər), **1** a learned person; person having much knowledge: *The professor was a famous scholar.* **2** pupil at school; learner. **3** student who is given a scholarship. *n.*

schol ar ly (skol′ər lē), **1** of a scholar; fit for a scholar; like that of a scholar: *scholarly habits.* **2** having much knowledge; learned. **3** fond of learning; studious. **4** thorough and orderly in methods of study: *a scholarly book. adj.* —**schol′ar li ness,** *n.*

schol ar ship (skol′ər ship), **1** possession of knowledge gained by study; quality of learning and knowledge.

2 money or other aid given to help a student continue his or her studies: *The college offered her a scholarship of one thousand dollars. n.*

scho las tic (skə las′tik), of schools, scholars, or education; academic: *scholastic methods, scholastic life. adj.* —**scho las′ti cal ly**, *adv.*

school[1] (skül), **1** place for teaching and learning: *Children go to school to study.* **2** learning in school; instruction: *Most children start school when they are about five years old.* **3** regular meetings of teachers and pupils for teaching and learning: *We attend school every day.* **4** the time or period of such meetings: *to stay after school.* **5** pupils who are taught and their teachers: *The entire school was present.* **6** group of people holding the same beliefs or opinions: *the Dutch school of painting.* **7** a particular department or group in a university: *a medical school, a law school.* **8** teach; train; discipline: *School yourself to control your temper.* **9** of a school or schools. 1-7 *n.*, 8 *v.*, 9 *adj.* [*School*[1] is from Old English *scōl*, which came from Latin *schola*. *Schola* is from Greek *scholē*, which originally meant "leisure." People who were at leisure had time for discussion, lectures, and, later, school.] —**school′a ble**, *adj.* —**school′less**, *adj.* —**school′like′**, *adj.*

school[2] (skül), **1** a large number of the same kind of fish or water animals swimming together: *a school of mackerel.* **2** swim together in a school. 1 *n.*, 2 *v.* [*School*[2] came into English about 600 years ago from Dutch *schōle*, meaning "large group."]

school age, 1 age at which a child begins to go to school. **2** years during which going to school is compulsory or customary.

school board, a group of people or committee managing the public schools of a community.

school book (skül′būk′), book for study in schools; textbook. *n.*

school boy (skül′boi′), boy attending school. *n.*

school bus, bus that carries children to and from school.

school child (skül′chīld′), schoolboy or schoolgirl. *n.*, *pl.* **school chil dren** (skül′chil′drən).

school girl (skül′gėrl′), girl attending school. *n.*

school house (skül′hous′), building used as a school. *n.*, *pl.* **school hous es** (skül′hou′ziz).

school ing (skü′ling), instruction in school; education received at school. *n.*

school marm (skül′märm′), INFORMAL. schoolmistress. *n.*

school mas ter (skül′mas′tər), man who teaches in a school, or is its principal. *n.*

school mate (skül′māt′), companion at school. *n.*

school mis tress (skül′mis′tris), woman who teaches in a school, or is its principal. *n.*, *pl.* **school mis tress es.**

school room (skül′rüm *or* skül′rùm′), room in which pupils are taught. *n.*

school teach er (skül′tē′chər), person who teaches in a school. *n.*

school work (skül′wėrk′), a student's lessons and assignments. *n.*

school yard (skül′yärd′), piece of ground around or near a school, used for play, games, etc. *n.*

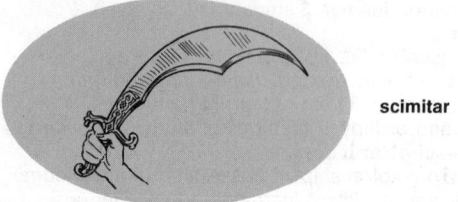
scimitar

school year, part of the year during which a school is in session.

schoon er (skü′nər), **1** ship with two or more masts and fore-and-aft sails. **2** prairie schooner. *n.*

schooner
(def. 1)

schot tische (shot′ish), **1** a dance somewhat like the polka but slower, popular in the 1800's. **2** music for it. *n.* [*Schottische* comes from the German phrase *der schottische Tanz,* meaning "the Scottish dance."]

Schu bert (shü′bərt), **Franz,** 1797-1828, Austrian composer. *n.*

Schu mann (shü′män), **Robert,** 1810-1856, German composer. *n.*

schwa (shwä), an unstressed vowel sound such as *a* in *about* or *u* in *circus,* represented by the symbol ə. *n.*, *pl.* **schwas.** [*Schwa* comes from German *Schwa,* which came from Hebrew *shəwa,* meaning "a silent vowel."]

Schwei tzer (shwī′tsər), **Albert,** 1875-1965, Alsatian physician, philosopher, musician, and missionary in Africa. *n.*

sci., 1 science. **2** scientific.

sci at i ca (sī at′ə kə), pain in a sciatic nerve and its branches. *n.*

sci at ic nerve (sī at′ik), a large nerve which extends from the lower back down the back part of the thigh and leg.

sci ence (sī′əns), **1** knowledge based on observed facts and tested truths arranged in an orderly system: *the laws of science.* **2** branch of such knowledge. Chemistry and physics are physical sciences. Zoology and botany are biological sciences. Economics and sociology are social sciences. **3** skill based on training and practice; technique: *the science of judo, the science of sailing. n.* [*Science* came into English about 600 years ago from French *science,* which came from Latin *scientia,* meaning "knowledge."]

science fair, group of school exhibits prepared by students, each demonstrating a scientific principle, process, development, etc.

science fiction, story or novel that combines science and fantasy. Science fiction deals with life in the future, in other galaxies, etc., but makes much use of the latest discoveries of science and technology.

sci en tif ic (sī′ən tif′ik), **1** using the facts and laws of science: *a scientific method, scientific farming.* **2** of science; used in science: *scientific books. adj.* —**sci′en tif′i cal ly**, *adv.*

sci en tist (sī′ən tist), **1** person who has expert knowledge of some branch of science. Persons specially trained in and familiar with the facts and laws of such fields of knowledge as biology, chemistry, mathematics, physics, geology, and astronomy are scientists. **2 Scientist,** Christian Scientist. *n.*

scim i tar *or* **scim i ter** (sim′ə tər), a short, curved sword used by Turks, Persians, and other Oriental peoples. *n.*

scin til la (sin til′ə), a spark; particle; trace: *not a scintilla of truth. n.*

scin til late (sin′tl āt), to sparkle; flash: *The snow scintillates in the sun like diamonds. Brilliant wit scintillates. v.,*

scin til lat ed, scin til lat ing. —**scin′til lat′ing ly,** *adv.*
—**scin′til la′tor,** *n.*

scin til la tion (sin′tl ā′shən), **1** a sparkling; flashing.
2 a spark; flash. *n.*

sci on (sī′ən), **1** bud or branch cut for grafting or planting. **2** descendant; heir: *the scion of a wealthy family. n.*

scis sors (siz′ərz), tool or instrument for cutting that has
two sharp blades so fastened that their edges slide
against each other. *n. pl. or sing.*

scler a (sklir′ə), the tough, white outer membrane of the
eyeball. *n.*

scle rot ic coat (sklə rot′ik), sclera.

scoff (skôf), **1** make fun to show one does not believe
something; mock: *We scoffed at the idea of swimming in
three inches of water.* **2** mocking words or acts. **3** something ridiculed or mocked. 1 *v.,* 2,3 *n.* —**scoff′er,** *n.*
—**scoff′ing ly,** *adv.*

scold (skōld), **1** find fault with; blame with angry words:
She scolded the painters for doing such a poor job. **2** find
fault; talk angrily: *Don't scold so much.* **3** person who
scolds. 1,2 *v.,* 3 *n.* —**scold′a ble,** *adj.* —**scold′er,** *n.*
—**scold′ing ly,** *adv.*

scol lop (skol′əp), scallop. *n., v.*

sconce (skons), a bracket projecting from a wall, used
to hold a candle or other light. *n.*

scone (skōn), a thick, flat, round cake cooked on a
griddle or in an oven. Some scones taste much like
bread; some are like buns. *n.*

scoop (sküp), **1** tool like a small shovel, having a short
handle and a deep, hollow part for dipping out or shoveling up things. A kitchen utensil to take out flour, sugar, etc., is a scoop. A cuplike scoop is used to dish up
ice cream. **2** the part of a dredge, power shovel, etc.,
that takes up or holds coal, sand, etc. **3** amount taken up
at one time by a scoop: *Use two scoops of flour and one
of sugar.* **4** act of taking up. **5** take up or out with a
scoop, or as a scoop does: *Scoop out a quart of grain.
The children scooped up the snow with their hands to make
snowballs.* **6** hollow out; dig out; make by scooping: *The
children scooped holes in the sand.* **7** INFORMAL. the publishing or broadcasting of a piece of news before a rival
newspaper, magazine, or television station does.
8 INFORMAL. the piece of news. **9** INFORMAL. publish or
broadcast a piece of news before (a rival newspaper,
magazine, or television station). 1-4,7,8 *n.,* 5,6,9 *v.*
—**scoop′er,** *n.* —**scoop′ing ly,** *adv.*

scoop ful (sküp′fùl), enough to fill a scoop. *n., pl.*
scoop fuls.

scoot (süt), INFORMAL. **1** go quickly; dart: *He scooted out
the door.* **2** act of scooting. 1 *v.,* 2 *n.*

scoot er (sü′tər), **1** a child's vehicle consisting of a
footboard between two wheels, one in front of the other,
steered by a long, upright handlebar. It is moved by
pushing one foot against the ground. **2** motor scooter.
3 sailboat with runners, for use on either water or ice. *n.*

scope (skōp), **1** distance the mind can reach; extent of
view: *Very hard words are not within the scope of a child's
understanding.* **2** the area over which any activity extends:
This is not within the scope of our investigation. n.
—**scope′less,** *adj.*

-scope, *combining form.* instrument for viewing, examining, or observing: *Telescope = instrument for viewing distant objects. Stethoscope = instrument for examining the
lungs and heart. Microscope = instrument for observing very
small things.* [See **Word History.**]

scorch (skôrch), **1** burn slightly; burn on the outside:
*The cake tastes scorched. He scorched his shirt while he was
ironing it.* **2** a slight burn. **3** dry up; wither: *The grass is
scorched by so much hot sunshine.* 1,3 *v.,* 2 *n.*
—**scorch′ing ly,** *adv.*

scorch er (skôr′chər), INFORMAL. a very hot day. *n.*

score (skôr), **1** the record of points made in a game,
contest, or test: *The score was 9 to 2 in favor of our
school. He had nearly a perfect score on the history exam.*
2 make as points in a game, contest, or test: *score two
runs in the second inning. She scored 85 per cent on the
final exam.* **3** make points; succeed. **4** keep a record of
the number of points made in a game, contest, or test:
The teacher will appoint some pupil to score for both sides.
5 make as an addition to the score; gain; win: *She scored
five points for our team. He scored a great success in the
school play.* **6** group or set of twenty; twenty: *A score or
more came to the meeting.* **7** **scores,** pl. a large number:
Scores died in the epidemic. **8** a written or printed piece of
music arranged for different instruments or voices: *She
was studying the score of the symphony she was learning to
conduct.* **9** arrange (a piece of music) for different instruments or voices: *score a sonata for piano and strings.* **10** a
cut; scratch; stroke; mark; line: *The carpenter used a nail
to make a score on the board.* **11** to cut; scratch; mark;
line: *Mistakes are scored in red ink. Moving the furniture
across the floor scores the polish.* **12** an account; reason;
ground: *Don't worry on that score.* **13** the score, INFOR-
MAL. the truth about anything or things in general; the
facts: *Our new classmate doesn't know the score yet.* 1,6-8,
10,12,13 *n.,* 2-5,9,11 *v.,* **scored, scor ing.**

pay off a score or **settle a score,** get even for an injury
or wrong: *She had an old score to settle with them.*

score board (skôr′bôrd′), a large board on which the
scores of a sporting event are posted. *n.*

score card (skôr′kärd′), card on which to record the
score of a game, especially while it is being played. *n.*

score keep er (skôr′kē′pər), person who keeps
score. *n.*

score less (skôr′lis), having no score: *The game ended in
a scoreless tie. adj.*

scor er (skôr′ər), **1** scorekeeper. **2** person who makes a
score in a game, contest, or test. *n.*

scorn (skôrn), **1** look down upon; think of as mean or
low; despise: *Most people scorn tattletales.* **2** reject or refuse as low or wrong: *The judge scorned to take a bribe.*
3 a feeling that a person, animal, or act is mean or low;
contempt: *Most pupils feel scorn for those who cheat.*
4 person, animal, or thing that is scorned or despised:
*The team that had lost ten games in a row was the scorn of
the football fans.* 1,2 *v.,* 3,4 *n.* —**scorn′er,** *n.* —**scorn′-
ing ly,** *adv.*

scorn ful (skôrn′fəl), showing contempt; mocking; full
of scorn: *They spoke of our old car in a scornful way. adj.*
—**scorn′ful ly,** *adv.* —**scorn′ful ness,** *n.*

WORD HISTORY

-scope

The form *-scope* is from Greek *-skopion,*
which comes from *skopein,* meaning
"to look at."

a	hat	i	it	oi	oil	ch	child		a in about
ā	age	ī	ice	ou	out	ng	long		e in taken
ä	far	o	hot	u	cup	sh	she	ə =	i in pencil
e	let	ō	open	ù	put	th	thin		o in lemon
ē	equal	ô	order	ü	rule	ŦH	then		u in circus
ėr	term					zh	measure		

scorpion
about 4 in.
(10 cm.) long

scor pi on (skôr′pē ən), a small animal belonging to the same group as the spider and having a poisonous sting at the end of its tail. *n.*

Scot (skot), person born or living in Scotland. *n.*

scotch (skoch), **1** stamp on; make harmless. **2** to cut or gash. *v.*

Scotch (skoch), **1** whiskey made in Scotland. **2** Scottish. The word *Scottish* should be used when referring to the people of Scotland or their customs. The word *Scotch* is often considered offensive. **1** *n.sing.,* **2** *n.pl.,* **2** *adj.*

Scotch man (skoch′mən), Scotsman. The use of *Scotchman* is often considered offensive. *n., pl.* **Scotch-men.**

Scotch tape, trademark for a very thin, transparent or opaque adhesive tape used for mending, sealing, etc.

scot-free (skot′frē′), free from punishment, loss, or injury: *One of the two speeding drivers was fined, but the other got off scot-free. adj.*

Scot land (skot′lənd), division of Great Britain north of England; the land of the Scottish people. *Capital:* Edinburgh. See **United Kingdom** for map. *n.*

Scotland Yard, 1 headquarters of the London police. **2** the London police, especially the department that does detective work.

Scots (skots), **1** of Scotland; Scottish. **2** the people of Scotland. **1** *adj.,* **2** *n.pl.*

Scots man (skots′mən), man born or living in Scotland. *n., pl.* **Scots men.**

Scott (skot), Sir **Walter,** 1771-1832, Scottish novelist and poet. *n.*

Scot tish (skot′ish), **1** of Scotland, its people, or their language: *Scottish industry.* **2** the people of Scotland. **3** form of English spoken by the people of Scotland. **1** *adj.,* **2** *n.pl.,* **3** *n.sing.*

Scottish terrier
about 10 in.
(25 cm.) high at
the shoulder

Scottish terrier, one of a breed of short-legged terriers with rough, wiry hair and pointed, standing ears.

scoun drel (skoun′drəl), a wicked person without honor or good principles; villain; rascal: *The scoundrels who set fire to the barn have been caught. n.*

scour[1] (skour), **1** clean or polish by hard rubbing: *I scoured the sink with cleanser.* **2** remove dirt and grease from (anything) by rubbing. **3** make clear by flowing through or over: *The stream had scoured a channel.* **4** clean; cleanse. **5** act of scouring. **1-4** *v.,* **5** *n.* **—scour′-er,** *n.*

scour[2] (skour), **1** move quickly over: *They scoured the countryside for the lost dog.* **2** go rapidly in search or pursuit. *v.*

scourge (skėrj), **1** a whip. **2** any means of punishment. **3** to whip; punish. **4** some thing or person that causes great trouble or misfortune. Formerly, an outbreak of disease was called a scourge. **5** trouble very much; afflict. **1,2,4** *n.,* **3,5** *v.,* **scourged, scourg ing. —scourg′er,** *n.* **—scourg′ing ly,** *adv.*

scout[1] (skout), **1** person sent to find out what the enemy is doing. A scout usually wears a uniform; a spy does not. **2** thing that acts as a scout. Some ships and airplanes are scouts. **3** act as a scout; hunt around to find something: *Go and scout for firewood for the picnic.* **4** person who is sent out to get information. **5** observe or examine to get information. **6** act of scouting. **7** person belonging to the Boy Scouts or Girl Scouts. **8** INFORMAL. fellow; person: *He's a good scout.* **1,2,4,6-8** *n.,* **3,5** *v.* **—scout′er,** *n.*

scout[2] (skout), refuse to believe in; reject with scorn: *She scouted the idea of a dog with two tails. v.*

scout ing (skou′ting), activities of scouts. *n.*

Scouting USA, Boy Scouts of America.

scout mas ter (skout′mas′tər), adult in charge of a troop or band of Boy Scouts. *n.*

scow (skou), a large, flat-bottomed boat used to carry freight, sand, etc. *n.* [*Scow* comes from Dutch *schouw.*]

scowl (skoul), **1** look angry or sullen by lowering the eyebrows; frown: *She scowled at the man who stepped on her toes.* **2** an angry, sullen look; frown. **1** *v.,* **2** *n.* **—scowl′er,** *n.* **—scowl′ing ly,** *adv.*

scrab ble (skrab′əl), **1** scratch or scrape about with hands, claws, etc.; scramble. **2** to scrawl; scribble. **3** a scraping; scramble. **1,2** *v.,* **scrab bled, scrab bling; 3** *n.* **—scrab′bler,** *n.*

scrag (skrag), **1** a lean, skinny person or animal. An old bony horse is a scrag. **2** the lean, bony end of a neck of veal or mutton. **3** SLANG. neck. **4** SLANG. wring the neck of; hang. **1-3** *n.,* **4** *v.,* **scragged, scrag ging.**

scrag gly (skrag′lē), rough or irregular; ragged. *adj.,* **scrag gli er, scrag gli est.**

scrag gy (skrag′ē), **1** having little flesh; lean; thin. **2** scraggly. *adj.,* **scrag gi er, scrag gi est. —scrag′gi ly,** *adv.* **—scrag′gi ness,** *n.*

scram (skram), SLANG. go at once. *v.,* **scrammed, scram ming.**

scram ble (skram′bəl), **1** make one's way by climbing, crawling, etc.: *The girls scrambled up the steep, rocky hill.* **2** a climb or walk over rough ground: *It was a long scramble through bushes and over rocks to the top of the hill.* **3** struggle with others for something: *The players scrambled to get the ball.* **4** a struggle to possess: *the scramble for wealth and power.* **5** any disorderly struggle or activity; scrambling: *The pile of boys on the football seemed a wild scramble of arms and legs.* **6** mix together in a confused way. **7** cook (eggs) with the whites and yolks mixed together. **8** change (an electronic signal) so that a special receiver is needed to understand transmitted messages. Government agencies sometimes scramble signals that carry secret information. **9** send aircraft into the air quickly to intercept enemy aircraft. **1,3,6-9** *v.,* **scram bled, scram bling; 2,4,5** *n.* **—scram′bler,** *n.*

scrap[1] (skrap), **1** a small piece; little bit; small part left over: *The cook gave some scraps of meat to the dog. Put the scraps of paper in the wastebasket.* **2** old metal fit only to be melted and used again. **3** make into scraps; break up: *The army scrapped the old tanks.* **4** throw aside as useless or worn out. **5** in the form of scraps: *scrap metal.* **1,2** *n.,* **3,4** *v.,* **scrapped, scrap ping; 5** *adj.* **—scrap′-ping ly,** *adv.*

scrap² (skrap), INFORMAL. **1** a fight, quarrel, or struggle. **2** to fight, quarrel, or struggle: *Those two dogs are always scrapping.* 1 *n.,* 2 *v.,* **scrapped, scrap ping.**

scrap book (skrap′bùk′), book in which pictures or clippings are pasted and kept. *n.*

scrape (skrāp), **1** rub with something sharp or rough; make smooth or clean by doing this: *Scrape your muddy shoes with this old knife.* **2** remove by rubbing with something sharp or rough: *We need to scrape the peeling paint off the house before we repaint it.* **3** scratch or graze by rubbing against something rough: *She fell and scraped her knee on the sidewalk.* **4** act of scraping. **5** a scraped place. **6** rub with a harsh sound; rub harshly: *The branch of the tree scraped against the window.* **7** give a harsh sound; grate. **8** a harsh, grating sound: *the scrape of the bow of a violin.* **9** collect by scraping or with difficulty: *I was so hungry I scraped every crumb from my plate. I've finally scraped together enough money to buy a bicycle.* **10** position hard to get out of; difficulty: *Children often get into scrapes.* **11** to bow with a drawing back of the foot. 1-3,6,7,9,11 *v.,* **scraped, scrap ing;** 4,5,8,10 *n.* —**scrap′a ble,** *adj.*

scrape through, get through with difficulty: *I barely scraped through the examination.*

scrap er (skrā′pər), instrument or tool for scraping: *We removed the loose paint with a scraper.* *n.*

scrap iron, broken or waste pieces of old iron to be melted and used again.

scrap per (skrap′ər), INFORMAL. person who scraps or fights. *n.*

scratch (skrach), **1** break, mark, or cut slightly with something sharp or rough: *Your feet have scratched the chair.* **2** mark made by scratching: *There are deep scratches on this desk.* **3** tear or dig with the nails or claws: *The cat scratched me.* **4** a very slight cut: *That scratch on your hand will soon be well.* **5** rub or scrape to relieve itching: *Don't scratch your mosquito bites.* **6** rub with a harsh noise; rub: *I scratched the match on the rock.* **7** sound of scratching: *the scratch of a pen.* **8** write in a hurry or carelessly. **9** any act of scratching. **10** scrape out; strike out; draw a line through. **11** withdraw (a horse, candidate, etc.) from a race or contest. **12** the starting place of a race or contest. **13** for quick notes, a first draft, etc.: *scratch paper.* **14** collected by chance: *a scratch football team.* 1,3,5,6,8,10,11 *v.,* 2,4,7,9,12 *n., pl.* **scratch es;** 13,14 *adj.* —**scratch′er,** *n.*

from scratch, with no advantages; without help.
up to scratch, up to standard; in good condition.

scratch y (skrach′ē), **1** that scratches, scrapes, or grates: *a scratchy pen.* **2** consisting of mere scratches: *It was only a quick, scratchy drawing.* *adj.,* **scratch i er, scratch i est.** —**scratch′i ly,** *adv.* —**scratch′i ness,** *n.*

scrawl (skrôl), **1** write or draw poorly or carelessly. **2** poor, careless handwriting. **3** something scrawled, such as a hastily or badly written letter or note. 1 *v.,* 2,3 *n.* —**scrawl′er,** *n.*

scrawl y (skrô′lē), awkwardly written or drawn. *adj.,* **scrawl i er, scrawl i est.** —**scrawl′i ness,** *n.*

scraw ny (skrô′nē), having little flesh; lean; thin; skinny: *Turkeys have scrawny necks.* *adj.,* **scraw ni er, scraw ni est.** —**scraw′ni ness,** *n.*

scream (skrēm), **1** make a loud, sharp, piercing cry. People scream in fright, in anger, and in excitement. **2** a loud, sharp, piercing cry. **3** utter loudly. **4** something or someone extremely funny. 1,3 *v.,* 2,4 *n.* —**scream′er,** *n.*

scream ing (skrē′ming), **1** crying out; screeching. **2** evoking screams of laughter: *a screaming comedy.* **3** startling: *screaming headlines, screaming colors.* *adj.* —**scream′ing ly,** *adv.*

screech (skrēch), **1** cry out sharply in a high voice; shriek. **2** a shrill, harsh scream. 1 *v.,* 2 *n., pl.* **screech es.**

screech owl, a small owl with hornlike tufts of feathers and a wavering cry.

screen (skrēn), **1** a covered frame that hides, protects, or separates: *We keep the trunk behind a screen.* **2** wire woven together with small openings in between: *We have screens at our windows to keep out flies.* **3** an ornamental partition. **4** anything like a screen: *A screen of trees hides our house from the road.* **5** shelter, protect, or hide with, or as with, a screen: *screen a porch. She screened her eyes from the sun with her hand. The lawyer tried to screen his client from the reporters.* **6** a glass surface on which television pictures, computer information, radar images, etc., appear. **7** information shown by a computer at a particular moment. **8** a flat, white surface on which motion pictures or slides are shown. **9** show (a motion picture) on a screen. **10** to photograph with a motion-picture camera. **11** motion pictures; films. **12** sieve for sifting sand, gravel, coal, seed, etc. **13** sift with a screen or as with a screen: *screen sand. Some government agencies screen their employees for loyalty.* 1-4,6-8,11,12 *n.,* 5,9,10,13, *v.*

screen play (skrēn′plā′), a motion-picture story in manuscript form, including the dialogue, descriptions of scenes, action, camera directions, etc. *n.*

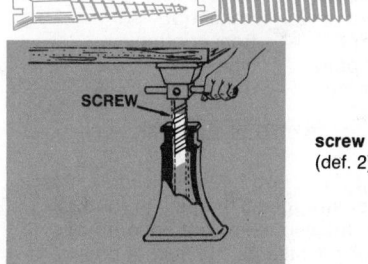

screw (def. 1)
two types

screw
(def. 2)

screw (skrü), **1** device for holding or fastening objects. It consists of a metal cylinder with a ridge twisted evenly round its length and often a groove across the head. **2** cylinder with an inclined plane wound around it and fitting into a threaded, cylindrical hole. It is a simple machine. Screws are used in jacks to lift heavy loads. **3** anything that turns like a screw or looks like one. **4** a turn of a screw; screwing motion. **5** to turn as one turns a screw; twist: *Screw the lid on the jar.* **6** twist out of shape: *His face was screwed up with fear.* **7** fasten or tighten with a screw or screws: *The carpenter screwed the hinges to the door.* **8** to force, press, or stretch tight by using screws. **9** get by force or pressure to tell, give up, etc.: *screw money out of someone.* **10** gather for an effort: *Screw up your courage and dive.* **11** propeller that moves a boat or ship. 1-4,11 *n.,* 5-10 *v.* —**screw′like′,** *adj.*

have a screw loose, SLANG. be crazy.

put the screws on, use pressure or force to get something.

screw ball (skrü′bôl′), **1** SLANG. an eccentric person. **2** SLANG. eccentric; erratic: *a screwball idea.* **3** (in baseball) a pitch thrown with a spin opposite to that of a curve. 1,3 *n.,* 2 *adj.*

a hat	i it	oi oil	ch child		a in about
ā age	ī ice	ou out	ng long		e in taken
ä far	o hot	u cup	sh she	ə =	i in pencil
e let	ō open	ù put	th thin		o in lemon
ē equal	ô order	ü rule	ŦH then		u in circus
ėr term			zh measure		

screw driv er (skrü′drī/vər), tool for putting in or taking out screws by turning them. *n.*

screw propeller, a revolving hub with radiating blades for propelling a steamship, aircraft, etc.

scrib ble (skrib′əl), **1** write or draw carelessly or hastily. **2** make marks that do not mean anything. **3** something scribbled. 1,2 *v.,* **scrib bled, scrib bling;** 3 *n.*

scrib bler (skrib′lər), **1** person who scribbles. **2** author who has little or no importance. *n.*

scribe (skrīb), **1** person who copies manuscripts. Before printing was invented, there were many scribes. **2** (in ancient times) a teacher of the Jewish law. **3** writer; author. **4** a public clerk or secretary. *n.* [*Scribe* is from Latin *scriba,* meaning "an official writer," which came from *scribere,* meaning "to write." See **Word Family.**]

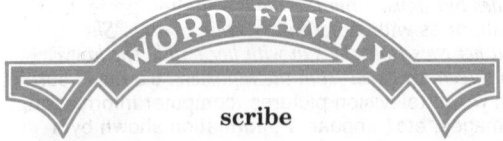

scribe

Below are words related to *scribe.* They can all be traced back to the Latin word *scribere* (skrē′be re), meaning "to write."

ascribe	nondescript	scrivener
circumscribe	postscript	shrive
conscript	prescribe	subscribe
conscription	prescription	subscriber
describe	prescriptive	subscript
description	proscribe	subscription
descriptive	proscription	superscript
descriptively	scribble	superscription
indescribable	scribbler	transcribe
indescribably	scrip	transcript
inscribe	script	transcription
inscription	scriptural	typescript
manuscript	Scripture	unscriptural

scrim mage (skrim′ij), **1** a rough fight or struggle. **2** take part in a rough fight or struggle. **3** the play in football that takes place when the two teams are lined up and the ball is snapped back. **4** take part in such a play. **5** football playing for practice: *an hour of scrimmage between the first and second teams.* 1,3,5 *n.,* 2,4 *v.,* **scrim maged, scrim mag ing.** [*Scrimmage* is a different form of *skirmish.*] —**scrim′mag er,** *n.*

scrimmage line, line of scrimmage.

scrimp (skrimp), **1** be sparing of; be very economical; stint; skimp: *Many parents have to scrimp to keep their children in school.* **2** treat stingily or very economically. *v.*

scrimp y (skrim′pē), too small; too little; scanty. *adj.,* **scrimp i er, scrimp i est.** —**scrimp′i ly,** *adv.* —**scrimp′i ness,** *n.*

scrip (skrip), **1** receipt showing a right to something. **2** paper money issued for temporary use in a time of emergency. *n.*

script (skript), **1** written letters, figures, signs, etc.; handwriting: *German script.* **2** a style of printing that looks like handwriting. **3** manuscript of a play, motion picture, radio or television broadcast, etc. *n.*

scrip tur al or **Scrip tur al** (skrip′chər əl), of the Scriptures; according to the Scriptures; based on the Scriptures. *adj.* —**scrip′tur al ly,** *adv.*

Scrip ture (skrip′chər), **1** the Bible. **2** the **Scriptures** or **the Holy Scriptures,** the Bible. **3** **scripture,** any sacred writing. *n.*

scrive ner (skriv′nər), OLD USE. a public writer of letters or documents for others; clerk; notary. *n.*

scrod (skrod), a young cod, especially one split for cooking. *n.*

scrof u la (skrof′yə lə), a form of tuberculosis that causes a swelling of the lymph nodes in the neck. *n.*

scroll (def. 1)

scroll (skrōl), **1** roll of parchment or paper, especially one with writing on it. **2** ornament resembling a partly unrolled sheet of paper, or having a spiral or coiled form. **3** move across a computer screen in a horizontal or vertical direction. To show a new line of text when the screen is full, the text scrolls upward to make room for the line. 1,2 *n.,* 3 *v.*

Scrooge (skrüj), the old miser in Dickens's story *A Christmas Carol. n.*

scro tum (skrō′təm), pouch that contains the testicles. *n., pl.* **scro ta** (skrō′tə), **scro tums.**

scrounge (skrounj), INFORMAL. **1** search about for what one can find. **2** beg; get by begging: *scrounge a meal. v.,* **scrounged, scroung ing.** —**scroung′er,** *n.*

scrub[1] (skrub), **1** rub hard; wash or clean by rubbing: *I scrubbed the floor with a brush and soap.* **2** a scrubbing: *Give your hands a good scrub.* **3** cancel; reject: *scrub a rocket launch.* 1,3 *v.,* **scrubbed, scrub bing;** 2 *n.*

scrub[2] (skrub), **1** low, stunted trees or shrubs. **2** anything small, or below the usual size: *The stray we found was a little scrub of a dog.* **3** small; poor; inferior: *scrub pine.* A scrub ball team is made up of inferior, substitute, or untrained players. **4** player not on the regular or varsity team. 1,2,4 *n.,* 3 *adj.*

scrub by (skrub′ē), **1** below the usual size; low; stunted; small: *scrubby trees.* **2** covered with low, stunted trees or shrubs. **3** shabby: *scrubby old clothes. adj.,* **scrub bi er, scrub bi est.** —**scrub′bi ness,** *n.*

scruff (skruf), the skin at the back of the neck; back of the neck. *n.*

scrump tious (skrump′shəs), INFORMAL. very pleasing or satisfying, especially to the taste or smell; delightful: *scrumptious pastries. adj.* —**scrump′tious ly,** *adv.*

scrunch (skrunch), **1** crunch; crush; crumple; squeeze. **2** the noise made by scrunching. 1 *v.,* 2 *n.*

scru ple (skrü′pəl), **1** a feeling of doubt about what one ought to do: *No scruple ever holds her back from prompt action.* **2** a feeling of uneasiness that keeps a person from doing something: *He has scruples about playing cards for money.* **3** hesitate or be unwilling (to do something): *A dishonest person does not scruple to deceive others.* **4** measure of apothecaries' weight equal to 20 grains. Three scruples make 1 dram. 1,2,4 *n.,* 3 *v.,* **scrupled, scru pling.**

scru pu lous (skrü′pyə ləs), **1** very careful to do what is right. **2** attending thoroughly to details; very careful: *We tried to pay scrupulous attention to our orders. adj.* —**scru′pu lous ly,** *adv.* —**scru′pu lous ness,** *n.*

scru ti nize (skrüt′n īz), examine closely; inspect carefully: *The jeweler scrutinized the diamond for flaws. v.,* **scru ti nized, scru ti niz ing.** —**scru′ti niz′er,** *n.*

scru ti ny (skrüt′n ē), close examination; careful inspection: *His work looks all right, but it will not bear scrutiny. n.*

scu ba (skü′bə), **1** portable equipment for breathing underwater, used in skin diving. It consists of one or more tanks of compressed air strapped to the diver's back, a hose and mouthpiece with valves to regulate the air, and a glass face mask. **2** using or consisting of such equipment: *scuba diving, scuba gear.* **1** *n.,* **2** *adj.* [*Scuba* comes from the words *self contained underwater breathing apparatus.* It was formed by using the first letter of each of those words.]

scud (skud), **1** run or move swiftly: *Clouds scud across the sky when there is a high wind.* **2** clouds or spray driven by the wind. **1** *v.,* **scud ded, scud ding;** **2** *n.*

scuff (skuf), **1** walk without lifting the feet; shuffle. **2** wear or injure the surface of by hard use: *scuff one's shoes.* **3** act of scuffing. **1,2** *v.,* **3** *n.*

scuf fle (skuf′əl), **1** to struggle or fight in a rough, confused manner: *The two children scuffled and fell down.* **2** a confused, rough struggle or fight: *I lost my hat in the scuffle.* **3** to shuffle. **4** a shuffling. **1,3** *v.,* **scuf fled, scuffling;** **2,4** *n.* —**scuf′fler,** *n.* —**scuf′fling ly,** *adv.*

scull (skul), **1** oar worked with a side twist over the end of a boat to make it go. **2** one of a pair of oars used, one on each side, by a single rower. **3** propel (a boat) by a scull or by sculls. **4** a light racing boat for one or more rowers. **1,2,4** *n.,* **3** *v.* —**scull′er,** *n.*

scul ler y (skul′ər ē), a small room where the dirty, rough work of a kitchen is done. *n., pl.* **scul ler ies.**

scul lion (skul′yən), OLD USE. servant who does the dirty, rough work in a kitchen. *n.*

sculpt (skulpt), to sculpture or make sculptures: *The class is learning to sculpt in clay. v.*

sculp tor (skulp′tər), person who makes figures by carving, modeling, casting, etc.; artist in sculpture. Sculptors work in marble, wood, bronze, etc. *n.*

sculp tress (skulp′tris), a woman sculptor. *n., pl.* **sculptress es.**

sculp tur al (skulp′chər əl), of sculpture; like sculpture. *adj.* —**sculp′tur al ly,** *adv.*

sculpture (def. 3)
a sculpture by
Michelangelo

sculp ture (skulp′chər), **1** the art of making figures by carving, modeling, casting, etc. Sculpture includes the cutting of statues from blocks of marble, stone, or wood, casting in bronze, and modeling in clay or wax. **2** make figures this way. **3** sculptured work; piece of such work. **4** cover or ornament with sculpture. **1,3** *n.,* **2,4** *v.,* **sculptured, sculp tur ing.**

sculp tured (skulp′chərd), covered or ornamented with sculpture. *adj.*

scum (skum), **1** a thin layer that rises to the top of a

liquid: *Green scum floated on the top of the pond.* **2** undesirable person or persons. *n.*

scum my (skum′ē), **1** consisting of or containing scum. **2** low; worthless. *adj.,* **scum mi er, scum mi est.**

scup per (skup′ər), an opening in the side of a ship to let water run off the deck. *n.*

scurf (skèrf), **1** small scales of dead skin. Dandruff is a kind of scurf. **2** any scaly matter on a surface. *n.* —**scurf′like′,** *adj.*

scur ri lous (skèr′ə ləs), coarsely joking; using foul and abusive language: *scurrilous accusations. adj.* —**scur′ri lous ly,** *adv.* —**scur′ri lous ness,** *n.*

scur ry (skèr′ē), **1** run quickly; scamper; hurry: *We could hear the mice scurry about in the walls.* **2** a hasty running; hurrying: *With much fuss and scurry, they at last got started.* **1** *v.,* **scur ried, scur ry ing;** **2** *n., pl.* **scur ries.**

scur vy (skèr′vē), **1** disease caused by a lack of vitamin C in the diet. It causes swollen and bleeding gums, extreme weakness, and bruises on the skin. Scurvy used to be common among sailors who had no citrus fruits or leafy green vegetables to eat. **2** mean; contemptible; base: *a scurvy trick.* **1** *n.,* **2** *adj.,* **scur vi er, scur vi est.** —**scur′vi ly,** *adv.* —**scur′vi ness,** *n.*

scut tle¹ (skut′l), kind of bucket for holding or carrying coal. *n.* [*Scuttle¹* is from Old English *scutel,* which comes from Latin *scutella,* meaning "platter."]

scut tle² (skut′l), scamper; scurry: *The dogs scuttled off into the woods. v.,* **scut tled, scut tling.** [*Scuttle²* is another form of the old word *scuddle,* meaning "to run away hastily."] —**scut′tler,** *n.*

scut tle³ (skut′l), **1** an opening in the deck or side of a ship, with a lid or cover. **2** an opening in a wall or roof, with a lid or cover. **3** the lid or cover for any such opening. **4** cut a hole or holes through the bottom or sides of (a ship) to sink it: *The crew scuttled the old ship after its last voyage.* **1-3** *n.,* **4** *v.,* **scut tled, scut tling.** [*Scuttle³* came into English about 500 years ago, perhaps from French *escoutille,* meaning "hatchway."]

Scyl la (sil′ə), **1** a dangerous rock supposedly located off the southwestern tip of Italy, opposite the whirlpool Charybdis. **2** (in Greek myths) a monster with six heads and twelve feet that lived on this rock and snatched sailors from ships. *n.*

between Scylla and Charybdis, between two dangers, one of which must be met.

scythe (sīŦH), **1** a long, slightly curved blade on a long handle, for cutting grass, etc. **2** cut or mow with a scythe. **1** *n.,* **2** *v.,* **scythed, scyth ing.**

SD, South Dakota (used with postal Zip Code).

S. Dak. or **S.D.,** South Dakota.

SDI, Strategic Defense Initiative.

Se, symbol for selenium.

SE or **S.E., 1** southeast. **2** southeastern.

sea (sē), **1** the great body of salt water that covers almost three fourths of the earth's surface; the ocean. **2** any large body of salt water, smaller than an ocean, partly or wholly enclosed by land: *the North Sea, the Mediterranean Sea.* **3** a large lake of fresh water: *the Sea of Galilee.* **4** a large, heavy wave: *A high sea swept away the ship's masts.* **5** the swell of the ocean: *a heavy sea.* **6** an overwhelming amount or number: *a sea of trouble.* **7** a broad expanse: *a sea of faces.* **8** of, on, or from the sea; marine: *a sea* *animal, a sea route, a sea breeze.* **9** Often, **Sea.** one of the dark, flat plains of the moon once thought to be seas; mare: *the Sea of Tranquility.* 1-7,9 *n., pl.* **seas;** 8 *adj.*

at sea, 1 out on the sea: *We were at sea out of sight of land for ten days.* **2** puzzled; confused: *I can't understand this problem; I'm all at sea.*

follow the sea, be a sailor.

go to sea, 1 become a sailor. **2** begin a voyage.

put to sea, begin a voyage.

sea anemone
commonly about 2 to 4 in. (5 to 10 cm.) in diameter

sea anemone, a small, flowerlike sea animal with a fleshy, cylindrical body and a mouth surrounded by many brightly colored tentacles. It is a kind of polyp.

sea bird, any bird that lives on or near the sea. The petrel is a sea bird.

sea board (sē′bôrd′), land bordering on the sea; seacoast: *New York City is on the Atlantic seaboard. n.*

sea breeze, breeze blowing from the sea toward the land.

sea coast (sē′kōst′), land along the sea; coast: *the seacoast of Maine. n.*

sea cow, any of several large plant-eating sea mammals with two flippers and a flat tail. The manatee is one kind of sea cow.

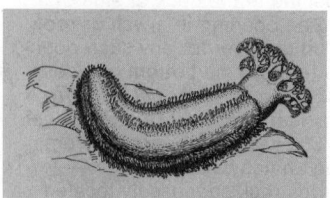

sea cucumber
about 10 in. (25 cm.) long

sea cucumber, a small, spiny sea animal which has a flexible body that resembles a cucumber.

sea dog, sailor, especially one with long experience.

sea far er (sē′fer′ər *or* sē′far′ər), **1** sailor. **2** traveler on the sea. *n.*

sea far ing (sē′fer′ing *or* sē′far′ing), **1** going, traveling, or working on the sea: *a hardy seafaring people.* **2** business or calling of a sailor. 1 *adj.,* 2 *n.*

sea food (sē′füd′), saltwater fish and shellfish that are good to eat. *n.*

sea girt (sē′gėrt′), surrounded by the sea. *adj.*

sea go ing (sē′gō′ing), **1** going by sea; seafaring. **2** fit for going to sea: *a seagoing merchant ship. adj.*

sea green, light bluish green.

sea gull, any gull, especially one living on or near the sea.

sea horse, 1 a small fish with a head suggesting that of a horse and with a tail that can grasp things. **2** walrus. **3** (in old stories) a sea animal supposed to be half horse and half fish.

seal[1] (sēl), **1** design stamped on a piece of wax or other soft material to show ownership or authenticity. The seal of the United States is attached to important government papers. **2** stamp for marking things with such a design: *a seal with one's initials on it.* **3** piece of wax, paper, metal, etc., on which the design is stamped. **4** mark (a document) with a seal to certify it or make it binding: *The treaty was signed and sealed by both governments.* **5** close tightly; shut; fasten: *Seal the letter before mailing it. Her promise sealed her lips.* **6** thing that fastens or closes something tightly. **7** something that secures; pledge: *under seal of secrecy.* **8** something that settles or determines: *the seal of authority.* **9** settle; determine: *The judge's decision sealed the prisoner's fate.* **10** give a sign that (a thing) is true: *They sealed their bargain by shaking hands.* **11** a special kind of stamp: *Christmas seals, Easter seals.* 1-3,6-8,11 *n.,* 4,5,9,10 *v.* [*Seal*[1] came into English about 700 years ago from French *seel,* and can be traced back to Latin *signum,* meaning "a sign."] —**seal′a ble,** *adj.* —**seal′er,** *n.*

set one's seal to, approve.

seal[2] (sēl), **1** a flesh-eating sea mammal with large flippers, living usually in cold regions. **2** its skin or fur; sealskin. **3** hunt seals. 1,2 *n., pl.* **seals** *or* **seal;** 3 *v.* [*Seal*[2] comes from Old English *seolh.*] —**seal′like′,** *adj.*

sea legs, legs accustomed to walking steadily on a rolling or pitching ship.

seal er (sē′lər), **1** person who hunts seals. **2** ship used for hunting seals. *n.*

sea level, level of the surface of the sea, especially when halfway between mean high and low water. Mountains, plains, ocean beds, etc., are measured as so many feet above or below sea level.

sealing wax, a hard, brittle substance made of resin and shellac. It becomes soft when heated and is used for sealing letters, packages, etc.

sea lion, a large seal of the Pacific coast.

seal skin (sēl′skin′), **1** skin or fur of the seal, prepared for use. **2** garment made of this fur. *n.*

seam (def. 5)—Her face was **seamed** by age.

seam (sēm), **1** line formed by sewing two pieces of cloth, canvas, leather, etc., together: *the seams of a coat, the seams of a sail.* **2** any line where edges join: *The seams of the boat must be filled in if they leak.* **3** sew the seam of; join with a seam. **4** any mark or line like a seam: *The old sword cut had left a seam in his face.* **5** mark (the face, etc.) with wrinkles, scars, etc. **6** layer; stratum: *a seam of coal.* 1,2,4,6 *n.,* 3,5 *v.* —**seam′er,** *n.*

sea horse (def. 1)
up to 12 in. (30 cm.) long

sea man (sē′mən), **1** sailor. **2** (in the navy) any sailor ranking below a petty officer. *n., pl.* **sea men.**

sea man ship (sē′mən ship), skill in managing a ship. *n.*

sea mew, sea gull.

seam less (sēm′lis), without a seam or seams: *seamless stockings, seamless shoes. adj.* —**seam′less ly,** *adv.* —**seam′less ness,** *n.*

seam stress (sēm′stris), woman whose work is sewing. *n., pl.* **seam stress es.**

seam y (sē′mē), worst; least pleasant: *The police often see the seamy side of life. adj.,* **seam i er, seam i est.** —**seam′i ness,** *n.*

sé ance (sā′äns), a meeting of people trying to communicate with spirits of the dead by the help of a medium. *n., pl.* **sé anc es.** [*Séance* comes from French *séance,* meaning "a sitting, session."]

seaplane

sea plane (sē′plān′), airplane that takes off from and lands on water, especially one which has floats instead of wheels. *n.*

sea port (sē′pôrt′), port or harbor on the seacoast; city or town with a harbor that ships can reach from the sea: *San Francisco and New Orleans are seaports. n.*

sear (sir), **1** burn or char the surface of: *The cook seared the roast to seal in its juice. The hot iron seared my hand.* **2** dry up; wither: *The hot sun seared the grain.* **3** OLD USE. dried up; withered; sere. 1,2 *v.,* 3 *adj.*

search (sėrch), **1** try to find by looking; seek; look for (something): *We searched all day for the lost cat.* **2** look through; go over carefully; examine, especially for something concealed: *The police searched the prisoners to see if they had weapons.* **3** act of searching; examination: *She found her book after a long search.* 1,2 *v.,* 3 *n., pl.* **search es.** —**search′a ble,** *adj.* —**search′er,** *n.*

in search of, trying to find; looking for: *The children went in search of their lost dog.*

search out, find by searching: *She searched out all the facts in the case.*

WORD HISTORY

search

Search came into English about 600 years ago from French *cerchier,* and can be traced back to Latin *circus,* meaning "circle." People often go about in circles to look for something.

search ing (sėr′ching), **1** examining carefully; thorough: *a searching look, a searching examination.* **2** piercing; sharp: *a searching wind. adj.* —**search′ing ly,** *adv.* —**search′ing ness,** *n.*

search light (sėrch′līt′), **1** device that can throw a very bright beam of light in any direction desired. **2** the beam of light thrown by this device. *n.*

search warrant, a written court order authorizing the search of a house or building for stolen goods, criminals, illegal narcotics, etc.

sea rover, 1 pirate. **2** a pirate ship.

sea shell (sē′shel′), shell of any sea animal, especially a mollusk such as an oyster, a conch, etc. *n.*

sea shore (sē′shôr′), land at the edge of a sea; shore. *n.*

sea sick (sē′sik′), sick because of a ship's motion. *adj.*

sea sick ness (sē′sik′nis), sickness caused by a ship's motion. *n.*

sea side (sē′sīd′), seashore. *n.*

sea son (sē′zn), **1** one of the four periods of the year; spring, summer, autumn, or winter. **2** any period of time marked by something special: *a holiday season, the harvest season.* **3** improve the flavor of: *season soup with salt.* **4** give interest or character to: *season conversation with wit.* **5** make or become fit for use by a period of keeping or treatment: *Wood is seasoned for building by drying and hardening it.* **6** accustom; make used: *Soldiers are seasoned to battle by experience in war.* **7** make less severe; soften: *Season justice with mercy.* 1,2 *n.,* 3-7 *v.* [*Season* came into English about 700 years ago from French *seison,* which came from Latin *sationem,* meaning "a sowing." The narrow meaning of the season for sowing came to be used for any of the four seasons.]

for a season, for a time.

in good season, early enough.

in season, 1 at the right or proper time. **2** in the time or condition for eating, hunting, etc.: *Cherries are in season in June.*

out of season, not in season.

sea son a ble (sē′zn ə bəl), **1** suitable to the season: *Hot weather is seasonable in July.* **2** coming at the right or proper time: *Our business would have failed without your seasonable advice. adj.* —**sea′son a ble ness,** *n.*

sea son a bly (sē′zn ə blē), in due time or season; at the right moment; early enough: *to sow or plant seasonably. adv.*

sea son al (sē′zn əl), having to do with the seasons; depending on a season; happening at regular intervals: *seasonal variations in the weather, a seasonal business, a seasonal worker. adj.* —**sea′son al ly,** *adv.*

sea son ing (sē′zn ing), **1** something that gives a better flavor. Salt, pepper, and herbs are seasonings. **2** something that gives interest or character: *We like conversation with a seasoning of humor. n.*

season ticket, ticket or pass entitling the holder to certain privileges for the season or for a specified period.

seat (sēt), **1** thing to sit on. Chairs, benches, and stools are seats. **2** place to sit. **3** place in which one has the right to sit. If a person has a seat in Congress or a seat in the stock exchange, it means that person is a member. **4** that part of a chair, bench, stool, etc., on which one sits: *This bench has a broken seat.* **5** that part of the body on which one sits, or the clothing covering it: *The seat of her jeans was patched.* **6** manner of sitting on horseback: *That rider has a good seat.* **7** to set or place

on a seat: *seat a person on a chair, seat oneself at the piano.* **8** have or provide seats for (a specified number): *Our school assembly seats one thousand pupils.* **9** put a seat on (a chair, trousers, etc.). **10** an established place or center: *A university is a seat of learning. The seat of our government is in Washington, D.C.* **11** residence; home: *The family seat of the Howards is in Sussex, England.* 1-6,10,11 *n.,* 7-9 *v.* —**seat′er,** *n.* —**seat′less,** *adj.*
be seated, 1 sit down. **2** be sitting. **3** be situated.
seat belt, belt or set of belts fastened to the seat or frame of an automobile or airplane. It helps hold the occupant in the seat in case of a crash, jolt, bump, etc.
Se at tle (sē at′l), seaport in W Washington, on Puget Sound. *n.*

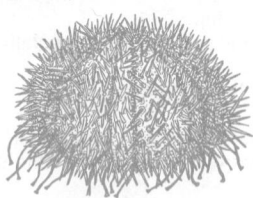

sea urchin
about 3 in. (7.5 cm.)
in diameter

sea urchin, a small, round sea animal with a spiny shell; echinus.
sea wall, a strong wall or embankment made to prevent the waves from wearing away the shore, to act as a breakwater, etc.
sea ward (sē′wərd), **1** toward the sea: *a seaward breeze* (*adj.*). *Our house faces seaward* (*adv.*). **2** direction toward the sea: *The island lies a mile to seaward.* 1 *adj., adv.,* 2 *n.*
sea wards (sē′wərdz), seaward. *adv.*
sea wa ter (sē′wô′tər *or* sē′wot′ər), the salt water of the sea or ocean. *n.*
sea way (sē′wā′), **1** an inland waterway that is deep enough to permit ocean shipping: *Ocean-going freighters reach Detroit by passing through the St. Lawrence Seaway.* **2** a route over the sea. *n.*
sea weed (sē′wēd′), any plant or plants growing in the sea. *n.*
sea wor thy (sē′wėr′ᵺē), fit for sailing on the sea; able to stand storms at sea: *a seaworthy ship. adj.*
—**sea′wor′thi ness,** *n.*
se ba ceous gland (si bā′shəs), gland in an inner layer of the skin that supplies oil to the skin and hair.
sec., **1** second or seconds. **2** secretary. **3** section or sections.
se cant (sē′kənt), in geometry: **1** a straight line that intersects a curve at two or more points. **2** intersecting: *a secant plane.* 1 *n.,* 2 *adj.*
se cede (si sēd′), withdraw formally from an organization. *v.,* **se ced ed, se ced ing.** [*Secede* is from Latin *secedere,* which comes from *se-,* meaning "apart," and *cedere,* meaning "to go."] —**se ced′er,** *n.*
se ces sion (si sesh′ən), **1** a formal withdrawing from an organization. **2** Also, **Secession.** the seceding of the eleven Southern states from the Union in 1860-1861, which resulted in the Civil War. *n.*
se ces sion ist (si sesh′ə nist), **1** person who favors secession. **2** person who secedes. *n.*
se clude (si klüd′), keep apart from company; shut off from others: *He secludes himself and sees only his close friends. v.,* **se clud ed, se clud ing.**
se clud ed (si klü′did), shut off from others; undisturbed: *a secluded cottage in the woods. adj.* —**se clud′ed ly,** *adv.* —**se clud′ed ness,** *n.*
se clu sion (si klü′zhən), **1** a secluding or a being secluded; retirement: *She lives in seclusion apart from her friends.* **2** a secluded place. *n.*
sec ond[1] (sek′ənd), **1** next after the first: *the second seat*

from the front, the second prize.* **2** below the first; inferior: *the second officer on a ship, cloth of second quality.*
3 another; other: *Please give me a second chance.* **4** in the second group, division, rank, etc.; secondly: *I finished second in the tennis finals.* **5** person or thing that is second. **6 seconds,** *pl.* goods below first quality: *These stockings are seconds and have some slight defects.*
7 person who supports or aids another; backer: *The prizefighter had a second.* **8** express approval of; back up; support: *second another person's idea. One member made a motion to adjourn the meeting, and another seconded it.*
9 rendering a part lower in pitch: *second soprano.* 1-3,9 *adj.,* 4 *adv.,* 5-7 *n.,* 8 *v.* —**sec′ond er,** *n.*
sec ond[2] (sek′ənd), **1** one of the 60 very short equal periods of time that make up a minute; $\frac{1}{60}$ of a minute; $\frac{1}{3600}$ of an hour. **2** a very short time; instant; moment. **3** $\frac{1}{3600}$ of a degree of an angle. 12° 10′ 30″ means 12 degrees, 10 minutes, 30 seconds. *n.*
sec ond ar i ly (sek′ən der′ə lē), in a secondary manner. *adv.*
sec ond ar y (sek′ən der′ē), **1** next after the first in order, place, time, or importance: *A secondary industry uses products of other industries as its raw materials.* **2** not main or chief; having less importance: *Reading fast is secondary to reading well.* **3** not original; derived: *a secondary source of the report. adj.* —**sec′ond ar′i ness,** *n.*
secondary accent, 1 an accent that is weaker than the strongest accent in the pronunciation of a word but stronger than no accent. The second syllable of *ab bre′vi a′tion* has a secondary accent. **2** mark (′) used to show this.
secondary school, high school.
sec ond-class (sek′ənd klas′), **1** of the class next after the first: *second-class mail.* **2** by the next-to-the-best and less expensive passenger accommodations offered by ship, airplane, or train: *We could afford only to travel second-class.* **3** of inferior grade or quality. 1,3 *adj.,* 2 *adv.*
second hand, hand on a clock or watch, pointing to the seconds. It moves around the whole dial once in a minute.
sec ond hand (sek′ənd hand′), **1** not original; obtained from another: *secondhand information.* **2** not new; used already by someone else: *secondhand clothes.* **3** dealing in used goods: *a secondhand bookshop.* **4** from other than the original source; not firsthand: *The information came to us secondhand.* 1-3 *adj.,* 4 *adv.*
second lieutenant, a commissioned officer in the army, air force, or marines having the lowest rank, next below a first lieutenant.
sec ond ly (sek′ənd lē), in the second place. *adv.*
second nature, habit, quality, knowledge, etc., acquired and had for so long that it seems to be almost a part of a person's nature.
second person, form of a pronoun or verb used to refer to the person spoken to. *You* and *yours* are pronouns of the second person.
sec ond-rate (sek′ənd rāt′), **1** rated as second-class. **2** inferior: *a second-rate performance. adj.*
se cre cy (sē′krə sē), **1** condition of being secret or of being kept secret. **2** ability to keep things secret. **3** tendency to conceal; lack of frankness: *maintain secrecy as to one's plans. n., pl.* **se cre cies.**
se cret (sē′krit), **1** kept from the knowledge of others: *a secret errand, a secret formula, a secret weapon.* **2** known only to a few: *a secret society, a secret sign.* **3** kept from sight; hidden: *a secret drawer.* **4** working or acting in secret: *secret police.* **5** something secret or hidden: *Can you keep a secret?* **6** a hidden cause or reason: *the secret of her success, the secret of his charm.* 1-4 *adj.,* 5,6 *n.*
—**se′cret ly,** *adv.* —**se′cret ness,** *n.*

in secret, in private; not openly; secretly.

secret agent, agent of a government secret service.

sec re tar i al (sek′rə ter′ē əl), of a secretary; having to do with a secretary: *I learned to do stenography, typewriting, and other secretarial work. adj.*

sec re tar i at (sek′rə ter′ē it), **1** office or position of secretary or secretary-general. **2** the department or administrative unit controlled by a secretary or secretary-general: *the secretariat of the United Nations. n.*

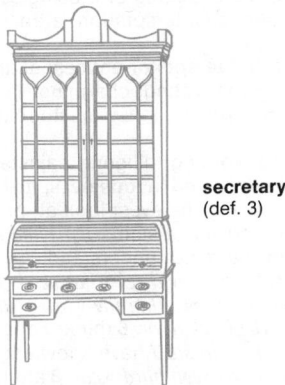

secretary
(def. 3)

sec re tar y (sek′rə ter′ē), **1** person who writes letters, keeps records, etc., for a person, company, club, etc.: *Our club has a secretary who keeps the minutes of the meeting.* **2** person who has charge of a department of the government or similar organization. The Secretary of the Treasury is the head of the Treasury Department. **3** a writing desk with a set of drawers and often with shelves for books. *n., pl.* **sec re tar ies.** [*Secretary* is from Latin *secretarius,* meaning "a confidential officer," which comes from *secretum,* meaning "a secret."]

sec re tar y-gen er al (sek′rə ter′ē jen′ər əl), the chief secretary; the administrative head of a secretariat: *the secretary-general of the United Nations. n., pl.* **sec re tar ies-gen er al.**

se crete (si krēt′), **1** produce and discharge: *Glands in the mouth secrete saliva.* **2** keep secret; hide. *v.,* **se cret ed, se cret ing.**

se cre tion (si krē′shən), **1** substance that is secreted by some part of an animal or plant: *Bile is the secretion of the liver.* **2** a producing and discharging of such a substance. **3** a concealing; hiding. *n.*

se cre tive (sē′krə tiv *or si* krē′tiv *for 1;* si krē′tiv *for 2),* **1** having the habit of secrecy; not frank and open. **2** causing or aiding secretion. *adj.* —**se′cre tive ly,** *adv.* —**se′cre tive ness,** *n.*

secret service, **1** branch of a government that makes secret investigations. **2** **Secret Service,** branch of the United States Treasury Department concerned with discovering and preventing counterfeiting, with protecting the President, etc.

sect (sekt), group of people having the same principles, beliefs, or opinions: *a religious sect. n.*

sect., section.

sec tar i an (sek ter′ē ən), **1** of a sect; denominational. **2** characteristic of one sect only; strongly prejudiced in favor of a certain sect. *adj.* —**sec tar′i an ly,** *adv.*

sec tion (sek′shən), **1** a part separated or cut off; part; division; slice: *Divide the cake into sections. Her section of the family estate was larger than her brother's.* **2** division of a book: *Study sections 10 to 16 of Chapter V for tomorrow's lesson.* **3** part of a country, city, etc.; region or district: *The city has a business section and a residential section.* **4** act of cutting. **5** cut or divide into sections:

---

section an orange. **6** a representation of a thing as it would appear if cut straight through. **7** area of land one mile square; 640 acres. A township usually contains 36 sections. 1-4,6,7 *n.,* 5 *v.* [*Section* is from Latin *sectionem,* which comes from *secare,* meaning "to cut."]

sec tion al (sek′shə nəl), **1** having to do with a particular section; regional or local: *sectional interests, sectional prejudices.* **2** made of sections: *a sectional bookcase. adj.* —**sec′tion al ly,** *adv.*

sec tion al ism (sek′shə nə liz′əm), too great regard for sectional interests; sectional prejudice or hatred. *n.*

sec tor (sek′tər), **1** the part of a circle between two radii and the included arc. **2** an area that a military unit is responsible for defending. **3** any section, zone, or quarter. **4** divide into sectors; provide with sectors. 1-3 *n.,* 4 *v.*

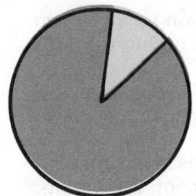

sector (def. 1)
the lighter, shaded
area

sec u lar (sek′yə lər), **1** not religious or sacred; worldly: *secular music, a secular education.* **2** living in the world; not belonging to a religious order: *the secular clergy, a secular priest. adj.* —**sec′u lar ly,** *adv.*

sec u lar ize (sek′yə lə rīz′), make secular or worldly; separate from religious connection or influence. *v.,* **sec u lar ized, sec u lar iz ing.** —**sec′u lar i za′tion,** *n.* —**sec′u lar iz′er,** *n.*

se cure (si kyůr′), **1** safe against loss, attack, escape, etc.: *keep a vicious dog secure on a chain. This is a secure hiding place. Land in a growing city is a secure investment.* **2** make safe; protect: *Every loan was secured by bonds or mortgages. We must secure against the dangers of the coming storm.* **3** sure; certain; that can be counted on: *We know in advance that our victory is secure.* **4** make (something) sure or certain; ensure. **5** free from care or fear: *They hoped for a secure old age.* **6** firmly fastened; not liable to give way: *a secure lock. The boards of this bridge do not look secure.* **7** make firm or fast: *Secure the locks on the windows.* **8** get; obtain: *Secure your tickets early.* 1,3,5, 6 *adj.,* 2,4,7,8 *v.,* **se cured, se cur ing.** [*Secure* is from Latin *securus,* which comes from *se-,* meaning "without," and *cura,* meaning "care."] —**se cur′a ble,** *adj.* —**se cure′ly,** *adv.* —**se cure′ment,** *n.* —**se cure′ness,** *n.* —**se cur′er,** *n.*

se cur i ty (si kyůr′ə tē), **1** freedom from danger, care, or fear; feeling or condition of being safe: *We swam with a sense of security because we knew the lifeguard was nearby.* **2** something that secures or makes safe: *Rubber soles on shoes are a security against slipping. Her watchdog is a security against burglars.* **3** something given as a pledge that a person will fulfill some duty, promise, etc.: *A life-insurance policy may serve as security for a loan.* **4** Usually, **securities,** *pl.* bond or stock certificates: *These railroad securities can be sold for $5000.* **5** person who agrees to be responsible for another. *n., pl.* **se cur i ties.**

Security Council, council in the United Nations consisting of five permanent members and ten rotating members, concerned with maintaining world peace.

secy. or **sec'y.,** secretary.

se dan (si dan'), **1** a closed automobile with a front and back seat, seating four or more persons. **2** sedan chair. *n.*

Se dan (si dan'), town in NE France. Prussia defeated France there in 1870. *n.*

sedan chair

sedan chair, a covered chair carried on poles by two bearers. Sedan chairs were much used during the 1600's and 1700's.

se date (si dāt'), quiet; calm; serious: *I was very sedate as a child and often preferred reading to playing. adj.* —**se date'ly,** *adv.* —**se date'ness,** *n.*

sed a tive (sed'ə tiv), **1** medicine that lessens pain or excitement. **2** lessening pain or excitement. **3** soothing; calming. **1** *n.,* **2,3** *adj.*

sed en tar y (sed'n ter'ē), **1** used to sitting still much of the time: *Sedentary people get little physical exercise.* **2** keeping one sitting still much of the time: *Bookkeeping is a sedentary occupation. adj.* [*Sedentary* is from Latin *sedentarius,* which comes from *sedentem,* meaning "sitting."] —**sed'en tar'i ly,** *adv.* —**sed'en tar'i ness,** *n.*

sedge (sej), a grasslike plant that grows chiefly in wet places. *n.*

sedg y (sej'ē), **1** abounding in or covered with sedge; bordered with sedge: *a sedgy brook.* **2** like sedge. *adj.,* **sedg i er, sedg i est.**

sed i ment (sed'ə mənt), **1** matter that settles to the bottom of a liquid. **2** (in geology) earth, stones, etc., deposited by water, wind, or ice: *When glaciers melt, they leave behind much sediment. n.*

sedimentary (def. 2)
a sedimentary rock

sed i men tar y (sed'ə men'tər ē), **1** of sediment; having to do with sediment. **2** (in geology) formed by the depositing of sediment. Shale is a sedimentary rock. *adj.*

sed i men ta tion (sed'ə men tā'shən), a depositing of sediment. *n.*

se di tion (si dish'ən), speech or action causing discontent or rebellion against the government; an arousing to discontent or rebellion. *n.*

se di tious (si dish'əs), **1** stirring up discontent or rebellion. **2** taking part in sedition; guilty of sedition. **3** having

to do with sedition. *adj.* —**se di'tious ly,** *adv.* —**se di'tious ness,** *n.*

se duce (si düs' *or* si dyüs'), **1** tempt to wrongdoing; persuade to do wrong: *Benedict Arnold, seduced by offers of money, betrayed his country to the enemy.* **2** lead away from virtue; lead astray; beguile. *v.,* **se duced, se duc ing.** —**se duc'i ble,** *adj.* —**se duc'ing ly,** *adv.*

se duc er (si dü'sər *or* si dyü'sər), person who seduces. *n.*

se duc tion (si duk'shən), **1** a seducing or a being seduced. **2** something that seduces; temptation; attraction. *n.*

se duc tive (si duk'tiv), **1** that tempts or entices; alluring: *a very seductive offer.* **2** captivating; charming: *a seductive smile. adj.* —**se duc'tive ly,** *adv.* —**se duc'tive ness,** *n.*

sed u lous (sej'ə ləs), hard-working; diligent; painstaking. *adj.* —**sed'u lous ly,** *adv.* —**sed'u lous ness,** *n.*

see[1] (sē), **1** be aware of by using the eyes; look at: *See that black cloud.* **2** have the power of sight: *The blind do not see.* **3** be aware of with the mind; understand: *I see what you mean.* **4** find out; learn: *I will see what needs to be done.* **5** take care; make sure: *See that the work is done properly. See that you lock the back door.* **6** think; consider: *You may go if you see fit to do so.* **7** have knowledge or experience of: *That coat has seen hard wear.* **8** attend; escort; go with: *My parents will see you home.* **9** have a talk with; call on; meet: *She wishes to see you alone. I went to see a friend.* **10** receive a visit from: *He is too ill to see anyone.* **11** visit; attend: *We saw the World's Fair. v.,* **saw, seen, see ing.** [*See*[1] is from Old English *sēon.*] —**see'a ble,** *adj.*

see into, understand the real character or hidden purpose of.

see off, go with (someone) to the starting place of a journey.

see out, go through with; finish.

see through, 1 understand the real character or hidden purpose of. **2** go through with; finish. **3** watch over or help through: *Friends saw her through her time of illness.*

see to, look after; take care of.

see[2] (sē), **1** position or authority of a bishop. **2** district under a bishop's authority; diocese; bishopric. *n.* [*See*[2] came into English about 700 years ago from French *sie,* which came from Latin *sedes,* meaning "seat."]

seed (sēd), **1** the part of a plant from which another plant like it can grow. A seed consists of a protective outer skin or coat which encloses the embryo that will become the new plant and a supply of food for its growth. **2** bulb, sprout, or any part of a plant from which a new plant will grow. **3** of or containing seeds; used for seeds. **4** sow with seeds; scatter seeds over: *They seeded the field with corn. Dandelions seed themselves.* **5** produce seeds; shed seeds. **6** remove the seeds from: *seed raisins.* **7** source or beginning of anything: *seeds of trouble.* **8** children; descendants: *The Jews are the seed of Abraham.* **1,2,7,8** *n., pl.* **seeds** or **seed;** **3** *adj.,* **4-6** *v.* —**seed'like',** *adj.*

go to seed, 1 come to the time of yielding seeds: *Dandelions go to seed when their heads turn white.* **2** come to the end of vigor, usefulness, prosperity, etc.: *After the mines closed, the miners left and the town went to seed.*

seed case (sēd'kās'), any pod, capsule, or other dry, hollow fruit that contains seeds. *n.*

seed er (sē'dər), **1** person who seeds. **2** machine or device for planting seeds. **3** machine or device for removing seeds. *n.*

seed i ly (sē'də lē), shabbily. *adv.*

seed i ness (sē'dē nis), seedy condition. *n.*

seed less (sēd'lis), without seeds: *seedless grapes. adj.*

seed ling (sēd′ling), **1** a young plant grown from a seed. **2** a young tree less than three feet high. *n.*

seed pearl, a very small pearl.

seed plant, any plant that bears seeds. Most seed plants have flowers and produce seeds in fruits; some, such as the pines, form seeds on cones.

seeds man (sēdz′mən), **1** sower of seed. **2** dealer in seed. *n., pl.* **seeds men.**

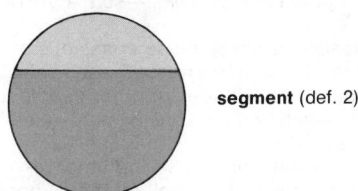

segment (def. 2)

seed y (sē′dē), **1** full of seed. **2** gone to seed. **3** shabby; no longer fresh or new: *seedy clothes. adj.,* **seed i er, seed i est.**

see ing (sē′ing), **1** in view of the fact; considering: *Seeing that it is 10 o'clock, we will wait no longer.* **2** ability to see; sight. 1 *conj.,* 2 *n.*

seek (sēk), **1** try to find; look for; hunt; search: *seek for something lost. We are seeking a new home.* **2** try to get: *Friends sought her advice. Some people seek wealth.* **3** try; attempt: *We seek to make peace with our enemies. v.,* **sought, seek ing.** [Seek comes from Old English *sēcan.*] **—seek′er,** *n.*

seem (sēm), **1** look like; appear to be: *This apple seemed good but was rotten inside. He seemed a very old man. Does this room seem hot to you?* **2** appear to oneself: *I still seem to hear the music.* **3** appear to exist: *There seems no need to wait longer.* **4** appear to be true or to be the case: *It seems likely to rain. This, it seems, is your idea of cleaning a room. v.*

seem ing (sē′ming), **1** apparent; appearing to be: *a seeming advantage.* **2** appearance: *It was worse in its seeming than in reality.* 1 *adj.,* 2 *n.* **—seem′ing ly,** *adv.* **—seem′ing ness,** *n.*

seem li ness (sēm′lē nis), fitness; suitability; propriety; decorum. *n.*

seem ly (sēm′lē), **1** suitable; proper: *Some old people do not consider modern dances seemly.* **2** properly; becomingly; fittingly: *Try to behave seemly.* 1 *adj.,* **seem li er, seem li est;** 2 *adv.*

seen (sēn), past participle of see[1]. *Have you seen Father? v.*

seep (sēp), to ooze, trickle, or leak: *Water seeps through sand. v.*

seep age (sē′pij), **1** a seeping; slow leakage. **2** moisture or liquid that seeps: *two feet of seepage in the cellar. n.*

seer (sir), person who foresees or foretells future events; prophet. *n.*

seer suck er (sir′suk′ər), cloth with alternate stripes of plain and crinkled material. *n.* [Seersucker comes from Persian *shīr o shakkar,* meaning "striped linen cloth."]

see saw (sē′sô′), **1** plank resting on a support near its middle so the ends can move up and down; teeter-totter. **2** a children's game in which the children sit at opposite ends of such a plank and move alternately up and down. **3** move up and down on such a plank: *The two children seesawed in the playground for some time.* **4** to move up and down or back and forth. **5** moving up and down or back and forth. **6** movement up and down or back and forth: *the seesaw of a storm-tossed ship.* 1,2,6 *n.,* 3,4 *v.,* 5 *adj.*

seethe (sēᴛʜ), **1** be excited; be disturbed: *She seethed with anger at being unjustly fired from her job.* **2** bubble

a hat	**i** it	**oi** oil	**ch** child	a in about
ā age	**ī** ice	**ou** out	**ng** long	e in taken
ä far	**o** hot	**u** cup	**sh** she	ə = i in pencil
e let	**ō** open	**u̇** put	**th** thin	o in lemon
ē equal	**ô** order	**ü** rule	**ᴛʜ** then	u in circus
ėr term			**zh** measure	

and foam: *Water seethed under the falls. v.,* **seethed, seeth ing.** **—seeth′ing ly,** *adv.*

seg ment (seg′mənt), **1** piece or part cut, marked, or broken off; division; section: *A tangerine is easily pulled apart into its segments.* **2** (in geometry) part of a circle cut off by a straight line. **3** line segment. **4** divide into segments. 1-3 *n.,* 4 *v.*

seg re gate (seg′rə gāt), **1** to separate from others; set apart; isolate: *The doctor segregated the child sick with mumps to protect the other patients.* **2** to separate from the rest and collect in one place. **3** to separate or keep apart one racial group from another or from the rest of society by maintaining separate schools, separate public facilities, etc. *v.,* **seg re gat ed, seg re gat ing.**

WORD HISTORY

segregate

Segregate is from Latin *segregatum,* meaning "segregated," which comes from *se-,* meaning "apart from," and *gregem,* meaning "herd."

seg re ga tion (seg′rə gā′shən), **1** separation from others; a setting apart; isolation. **2** separation of one racial group from another or from the rest of society, especially in schools, housing, etc. *n.*

seg re ga tion ist (seg′rə gā′shə nist), person who believes in or practices racial segregation. *n.*

seine (def. 1)

seine (sān), **1** a fishing net that hangs straight down in the water. It has floats at the upper edge and sinkers at the lower. **2** fish or catch fish with a seine. 1 *n.,* 2 *v.,* **seined, sein ing.** **—sein′er,** *n.*

Seine (sān *or* sen), river flowing from E France into the English Channel. Paris is on the Seine. See **Rhine** for map. *n.*

seis mic (sīz′mik), **1** of earthquakes: *a seismic detector.* **2** caused by an earthquake: *seismic sea waves. adj.*

seis mo graph (sīz′mə graf), instrument for recording the direction, intensity, and duration of earthquakes. *n.* [Seismograph comes from Greek *seismos,* meaning "earthquake," and the combining form *-graph.*]

seize (sēz), **1** take hold of suddenly; clutch; grasp: *In fright I seized her arm.* **2** take possession of by force: *The rebels seized the palace.* **3** take prisoner; arrest; catch: *seize someone wanted for murder.* **4** take possession of or come upon suddenly: *A fever seized him.* **5** take possession of by legal authority: *seize smuggled goods.* **6** grasp with the mind: *seize an idea.* *v.,* **seized, seiz ing.**

seize on or **seize upon,** **1** take hold of suddenly. **2** take possession of.

sei zure (sē′zhər), **1** act of seizing. **2** condition of being seized. **3** a sudden attack of disease: *an epileptic seizure. n.*

sel dom (sel′dəm), not often; rarely: *I am seldom ill. adv.*

se lect (si lekt′), **1** pick out; choose: *Select the book you want.* **2** picked as best; chosen specially: *She was one of a select group of skiers going to the Olympics.* **3** choice; superior: *That store carries a very select line of merchandise.* **4** careful in choosing; particular as to friends, company, etc.: *She belongs to a very select club.* **1** *v.,* **2-4** *adj.* —**se lect′ly,** *adv.* —**se lect′ness,** *n.*

se lec tion (si lek′shən), **1** act of selecting; choice: *His selection of a hat took a long time. The shop offered a very good selection of hats.* **2** person, thing, or group chosen: *The plain blue hat was her selection. n.*

se lec tive (si lek′tiv), **1** having the power to select; selecting. **2** having to do with selection. *adj.* —**se lec′tive ly,** *adv.* —**se lec′tive ness,** *n.*

selective service, compulsory military service of persons selected from the general population according to age, physical fitness, etc.

se lec tiv i ty (si lek′tiv′ə tē), quality of being selective. *n.*

se lect man (si lekt′mən), member of a board of town officers in New England, chosen each year to manage the town's public affairs. *n., pl.* **se lect men.**

se lec tor (si lek′tər), **1** person who selects. **2** a mechanical or electrical device that selects. *n.*

Se le ne (sə lē′nē), (in Greek myths) the goddess of the moon. The Romans called her Luna. *n.*

se le ni um (sə lē′nē əm), a nonmetallic element found with sulfur in various ores. It is used in photoelectric cells. *n.*

self (self), **1** one's own person: *his very self.* **2** one's own welfare or interests: *A selfish person puts self first.* **3** nature or character of a person or thing: *She is not her old self.* **4** myself; himself; herself; yourself: *a check made payable to self.* **1-3** *n.,* **4** *pron., pl.* **selves.**

self-, *prefix.* **1** of or over oneself: *Self-conscious = conscious of oneself. Self-control = control over oneself.* **2** by or in oneself or itself: *Self-inflicted = inflicted by oneself. Self-evident = evident in itself.* **3** to or for oneself: *Self-addressed = addressed to oneself.* **4** automatic; automatically: *Self-winding = winding automatically.*

self-act ing (self′ak′ting), working of itself: *a self-acting machine. adj.*

self-ad dressed (self′ə drest′), addressed to oneself: *a self-addressed envelope. adj.*

self-ap point ed (self′ə poin′tid), appointed by oneself, not by anyone else: *a self-appointed leader. adj.*

self-as ser tion (self′ə sėr′shən), insistence on one's own wishes, opinions, claims, etc. *n.*

self-as ser tive (self′ə sėr′tiv), putting oneself forward; insisting on one's own wishes, opinions, etc. *adj.* —**self′-as ser′tive ly,** *adv.* —**self′-as ser′tive ness,** *n.*

self-as sur ance (self′ə shur′əns), self-confidence. *n.*

self-as sured (self′ə shurd′), self-confident; sure of oneself. *adj.* —**self′-as sured′ness,** *n.*

self-cen tered (self′sen′tərd), **1** occupied with one's own interests and affairs. **2** selfish. *adj.* —**self′-cen′tered ly,** *adv.* —**self′-cen′tered ness,** *n.*

self-com mand (self′kə mand′), control of oneself. *n.*

self-com pla cent (self′kəm plā′snt), pleased with oneself; self-satisfied. *adj.* —**self′-com pla′cent ly,** *adv.*

self-con ceit (self′kən sēt′), conceit; too much pride in oneself or one's ability. *n.*

self-con fi dence (self′kon′fə dəns), belief in one's own ability, power, judgment, etc.; confidence in oneself. *n.*

self-con fi dent (self′kon′fə dənt), believing in one's own ability, power, judgment, etc. *adj.* —**self′-con′fi dent ly,** *adv.*

self-con scious (self′kon′shəs), made conscious of how one appears to others; embarrassed, especially by the presence, opinions, or attitudes of other people toward one; shy. *adj.* —**self′-con′scious ly,** *adv.* —**self′-con′scious ness,** *n.*

self-con tained (self′kən tānd′), **1** saying little; reserved. **2** containing in oneself or itself all that is necessary. *adj.*

self-con trol (self′kən trōl′), control of one's actions, feelings, etc. *n.*

self-de feat ing (self′di fē′ting), defeating oneself or itself; contrary to one's own purpose or interests. *adj.*

self-de fense (self′di fens′), defense of one's own person, property, reputation, etc. *n.*

self-de ni al (self′di nī′əl), sacrifice of one's own desires and interests; going without things one wants. *n.*

self-de ny ing (self′di nī′ing), unselfish; sacrificing one's own wishes and interests. *adj.*

self-de ter mi na tion (self′di tėr′mə nā′shən), **1** a choosing for oneself, without the help or interference of others. **2** the deciding by the people of a nation what form of government they shall have, without reference to the wishes of any other nation. *n.*

self-dis ci pline (self′dis′ə plin), careful control and training of oneself. *n.*

self-ed u cat ed (self′ej′ə kā′tid), self-taught; educated by one's own efforts. *adj.*

self-em ployed (self′em ploid′), not employed by others; working for oneself. Doctors, lawyers, and farmers are usually self-employed. *adj.*

self-es teem (self′e stēm′), **1** thinking well of oneself; self-respect. **2** thinking too well of oneself; conceit. *n.*

self-ev i dent (self′ev′ə dənt), evident in itself; needing no proof. *adj.* —**self′-ev′i dent ly,** *adv.*

self-ex plan a to ry (self′ek splan′ə tôr′ē), explaining itself; needing no explanation; obvious. *adj.*

self-ex pres sion (self′ek spresh′ən), expression of one's personality. *n.*

self-gov ern ing (self′guv′ər ning), ruling itself: *a self-governing territory. adj.*

self-gov ern ment (self′guv′ərn mənt), **1** government of a group by its own members: *self-government through elected representatives.* **2** self-control. *n.*

self-help (self′help′), a helping oneself; getting along without assistance from others. *n.*

self-im age (self′im′ij), the conception one has of oneself, of one's abilities and ambitions, etc.; one's idea of one's true self. *n.*

self-im por tance (self′im pôrt′ns), a having or showing too high an opinion of one's own importance; conceit; behavior showing conceit. *n.*

self-im por tant (self′im pôrt′nt), having or showing too high an opinion of one's own importance. *adj.*

self-im posed (self′im pōzd′), imposed on oneself by oneself: *a self-imposed task. adj.*

self-im prove ment (self′im prüv′mənt), improvement of one's character, mind, etc., by one's own efforts. *n.*

self-in dul gence (self′in dul′jəns), satisfaction of one's own desires, passions, etc., with too little regard for the welfare of others. *n.*

self-in dul gent (self′in dul′jənt), characterized by self-indulgence. *adj.* —**self′-in dul′gent ly,** *adv.*

self-in flict ed (self′in flik′tid), inflicted on oneself by oneself: *a self-inflicted wound. adj.*

self-in ter est (self′in′tər ist), **1** interest in one's own welfare with too little care for the welfare of others; selfishness. **2** personal advantage. *n.*

self ish (sel′fish), **1** caring too much for oneself; caring too little for others. Selfish people put their own interests first. **2** showing care solely or chiefly for oneself: *selfish motives. adj.* —**self′ish ly,** *adv.* —**self′ish ness,** *n.*

self less (self′lis), having no regard or thought for self; unselfish. *adj.* —**self′less ly,** *adv.* —**self′less ness,** *n.*

self-love (self′luv′), **1** love of oneself; selfishness. **2** conceit. *n.*

self-made (self′mād′), **1** made by oneself. **2** successful through one's own efforts. *adj.*

self-pit y (self′pit′ē), pity for oneself. *n.*

self-por trait (self′pôr′trit *or* self′pôr′trāt), portrait of oneself made by oneself. *n.*

self-pos sessed (self′pə zest′), having or showing control of one's feelings and actions; not excited, embarrassed, or confused; calm. *adj.*

self-pos ses sion (self′pə zesh′ən), control of one's feelings and actions; composure; calmness. *n.*

self-pres er va tion (self′prez′ər vā′shən), preservation of oneself from harm or destruction. *n.*

self-pro pelled (self′prə peld′), propelled by an engine, motor, etc., within itself: *a self-propelled missile. adj.*

self-reg is ter ing (self′rej′ə stər ing), registering automatically. *adj.*

self-re li ance (self′ri lī′əns), reliance on one's own acts, abilities, etc. *n.*

self-re li ant (self′ri lī′ənt), having or showing self-reliance. *adj.* —**self′-re li′ant ly,** *adv.*

self-re proach (self′ri prōch′), blame by one's own conscience. *n.*

self-re spect (self′ri spekt′), respect for oneself; proper pride. *n.*

self-re spect ing (self′ri spek′ting), having self-respect; properly proud. *adj.*

self-re strained (self′ri strānd′), showing self-control. *adj.*

self-re straint (self′ri strānt′), self-control. *n.*

self-right eous (self′rī′chəs), thinking that one is more moral than others; thinking that one is very good and pleasing to God. *adj.* —**self′-right′eous ly,** *adv.* —**self′-right′eous ness,** *n.*

self-rule (self′rül′), self-government. *n.*

self-sac ri fice (self′sak′rə fīs), sacrifice of one's own interests and desires, for one's duty, another's welfare, etc. *n.*

self-sac ri fic ing (self′sak′rə fī′sing), unselfish; giving up things for someone else. *adj.*

self same (self′sām′), very same: *We study the selfsame books that you do. adj.* —**self′same′ness,** *n.*

self-sat is fac tion (self′sat′is fak′shən), satisfaction with oneself or one's achievements. *n.*

self-sat is fied (self′sat′i sfīd), pleased with oneself or one's achievements. *adj.*

self-seek er (self′sē′kər), person who seeks his or her own interests too much. *n.*

self-seek ing (self′sē′king), **1** seeking to advance one's own interests too much; selfish. **2** selfishness. **1** *adj.,* **2** *n.*

self-serv ice (self′sėr′vis), act or process of serving oneself in a restaurant, store, etc. *n.*

self-styled (self′stīld′), called by oneself: *a self-styled leader whom no one follows. adj.*

self-suf fi cien cy (self′sə fish′ən sē), **1** ability to supply one's own needs. **2** conceit; self-assurance. *n.*

a hat	i it	oi oil	ch child	a in about
ā age	ī ice	ou out	ng long	e in taken
ä far	o hot	u cup	sh she	ə = { i in pencil
e let	ō open	u̇ put	th thin	o in lemon
ē equal	ô order	ü rule	ŦH then	u in circus
ėr term			zh measure	

self-suf fi cient (self′sə fish′ənt), **1** asking no help; independent. **2** having too much confidence in one's own resources, power, etc.; conceited. *adj.*

self-sup port ing (self′sə pôr′ting), earning one's expenses; getting along without help. *adj.*

self-sus tain ing (self′sə stā′ning), self-supporting. *adj.*

self-taught (self′tôt′), taught by oneself without aid from others. *adj.*

self-will (self′wil′), insistence on having one's own way. *n.*

self-willed (self′wild′), insisting on having one's own way; objecting to doing what others ask or command. *adj.*

self-wind ing (self′wīn′ding), winding itself. A self-winding watch winds itself by the movements of the person wearing it. *adj.*

sell (sel), **1** to exchange for money or other payment: *sell a house.* **2** deal in; keep for sale: *The butcher sells meat.* **3** be given in exchange; be on sale; be sold: *Strawberries sell at a high price in January.* **4** give up; betray: *The traitor sold his country for money.* **5** cause to be accepted, approved, or adopted by methods characteristic of salesmanship: *sell an idea to the public.* **6** win acceptance, approval, or adoption: *I believe that her idea will sell. v.,* **sold, sell ing.** —**sell′a ble,** *adj.*

sell out, 1 sell all that one has of; get rid of by selling. **2** INFORMAL. betray by a secret bargain.

sell er (sel′ər), **1** person who sells: *The stock exchange was filled with sellers of stocks.* **2** thing considered with reference to its sale: *This book is a good seller. n.*

sel vage *or* **sel vedge** (sel′vij), the edge of a woven fabric finished off to prevent raveling. *n.*

selves (selvz), plural of **self.** *She had two selves—one that liked to save money and one that liked to spend it. n., pron.*

se man tic (sə man′tik), **1** having to do with the meanings of words. **2** having to do with semantics. *adj.* —**se man′ti cal ly,** *adv.*

se man tics (sə man′tiks), the scientific study of the meanings, and the development of meanings, of words. *n.* [*Semantics* comes from French *sémantique,* and can be traced back to Greek *sēma,* meaning "sign."]

sem a phore (sem′ə fôr), **1** device for signaling, especially a post with a movable arm, or a set of colored lights, for controlling railroad traffic. **2** a system of hand signals, using a flag held in each hand. **3** to signal in either of these ways. **1,2** *n.,* **3** *v.,* **sem a phored, sem a-phor ing.**

semaphore (def. 2)

sem blance (sem′bləns), **1** outward appearance: *Their story had the semblance of truth but was really false.* **2** likeness: *These clouds have the semblance of a huge head.* *n.*

se men (sē′mən), a whitish fluid containing the male reproductive cells. *n.* [*Semen* comes from Latin *semen*, meaning "seed."]

se mes ter (sə mes′tər), a division, often one half, of a school year. *n.*

semi-, *prefix.* **1** half: *Semicircle = half a circle.* **2** partly; incompletely: *Semiskilled = partly skilled.* **3** twice. Semi_____ly means in each half of a _____, or twice in a _____: *Semimonthly = every half month, or twice a month.*

sem i an nu al (sem′ē an′yü əl), **1** occurring every half year. **2** lasting a half year. *adj.* —**sem′i an′nu al ly,** *adv.*

sem i ar id (sem′ē ar′id), having very little rainfall. *adj.*

sem i au to mat ic (sem′ē ô′tə mat′ik), **1** partly automatic; self-acting in some part of its operation. **2** gun like an automatic but requiring a press of the trigger to fire each shot. **1** *adj.,* **2** *n.* —**sem′i au′to mat′i cal ly,** *adv.*

sem i cir cle (sem′i sėr′kəl), half a circle: *We sat in a semicircle around the fire.* *n.*

sem i cir cu lar (sem′i sėr′kyə lər), having the form of half a circle. *adj.* —**sem′i cir′cu lar ly,** *adv.*

semicircular canal, any of three curved, tubelike canals in the inner ear that help to maintain balance. *n.*

sem i co lon (sem′i kō′lən), mark of punctuation (;) that shows a separation not so complete as that shown by a period but more so than that shown by a comma. EXAMPLE: We arrived later than we had intended; consequently there was little time left for swimming. *n.*

sem i con duc tor (sem′i kən duk′tər), a mineral substance, such as silicon, that conducts electricity better than an insulator but not so well as a metal. Semiconductors can convert alternating current into direct current and amplify weak electric signals. Transistors are made primarily of semiconductors. *n.*

sem i con scious (sem′i kon′shəs), half conscious; not fully conscious. *adj.* —**sem′i con′scious ly,** *adv.* —**sem′i con′scious ness,** *n.*

sem i fi nal (sem′i fī′nl), **1** of or having to do with the two games, matches, or rounds, that come before the final one in a tournament. **2** Often, **semifinals,** *pl.* one of these two games. **1** *adj.,* **2** *n.*

sem i fi nal ist (sem′i fī′nl ist), contestant in the semifinal game, match, or round. *n.*

sem i liq uid (sem′i lik′wid), **1** partly liquid. **2** a partly liquid substance. **1** *adj.,* **2** *n.*

sem i month ly (sem′i munth′lē), **1** occurring or appearing twice a month. **2** twice a month. **3** magazine or newspaper published twice a month. **1** *adj.,* **2** *adv.,* **3** *n., pl.* **sem i month lies.**

sem i nal (sem′ə nəl), **1** of semen or seed. **2** like seed; having the possibility of future development: *a seminal idea. adj.* —**sem′i nal ly,** *adv.*

sem i nar (sem′ə när), **1** group of students engaged in discussion and original research under the guidance of a professor. **2** meeting in class of such a group. *n.*

sem i nar y (sem′ə ner′ē), **1** school or college for training students to be priests, ministers, rabbis, etc. **2** academy or boarding school, especially for young women. *n., pl.* **sem i nar ies.**

Sem i nole (sem′ə nōl), member of a tribe of North American Indians that settled in Florida in the 1700's. Most of this tribe now lives in Oklahoma, while a few hundred remain in the Florida Everglades. *n., pl.* **Sem i nole** or **Sem i noles.**

sem i of fi cial (sem′ē ə fish′əl), partly official; having some degree of authority. *adj.* —**sem′i of fi′cial ly,** *adv.*

sem i pre cious (sem′i presh′əs), having some value; somewhat precious. Garnets are semiprecious stones. They are less valuable than diamonds, which are precious stones. *adj.*

sem i skilled (sem′i skild′), partly skilled. *adj.*

sem i sol id (sem′i sol′id), **1** partly solid. **2** a partly solid substance. **1** *adj.,* **2** *n.*

Sem ite (sem′īt), member of a group of ancient and modern peoples speaking any of the Semitic languages. The ancient Hebrews, Phoenicians, and Assyrians were Semites. Arabs and Jews are sometimes called Semites. *n.*

Se mit ic (sə mit′ik), **1** of the Semites or their languages. **2** group of languages including Hebrew, Arabic, Aramaic, Phoenician, and Assyrian. **1** *adj.,* **2** *n.*

sem i tone (sem′i tōn′), (in music) half step; half tone. *n.*

sem i trail er (sem′i trā′lər), type of truck trailer having wheels only at the rear, the front end being supported by the tractor. *n.*

sem i trop i cal (sem′i trop′ə kəl), halfway between tropical and temperate: *The climate of Florida is semitropical. adj.* —**sem′i trop′i cal ly,** *adv.*

sem i week ly (sem′i wēk′lē), **1** occurring or appearing twice a week. **2** twice a week. **3** newspaper or magazine published twice a week. **1** *adj.,* **2** *adv.,* **3** *n., pl.* **sem i week lies.**

Sen. or **sen., 1** Senate. **2** Senator.

sen ate (sen′it), **1** a governing or lawmaking assembly. The highest council of state in ancient Rome was called the senate. **2** the upper and smaller branch of an assembly that makes laws. **3 Senate, a** the upper house of Congress or of a state legislature. **b** the upper house of the legislature of certain other countries, such as Canada and Australia. *n.*

WORD HISTORY

senate

Senate is from Latin *senatus*, which comes from *senex,* meaning "an old man." The original Roman senate was called this because it was composed of a group of old men.

sen a tor (sen′ə tər), member of a senate. *n.*

sen a to ri al (sen′ə tôr′ē əl), **1** of or suitable for a senator or senators. **2** made up of senators: *a senatorial fact-finding committee.* **3** entitled to elect a senator: *a senatorial district. adj.* —**sen′a to′ri al ly,** *adv.*

sen a tor ship (sen′ə tər ship′), position, duties, etc., of a senator. *n.*

send (send), **1** cause to go from one place to another: *send a child on an errand, send someone for a doctor.* **2** cause to be carried: *send a letter, send news.* **3** cause to come, occur, or be: *Send help at once. May God send peace.* **4** drive; impel; throw: *send a ball. The volcano sent clouds of smoke into the air. v.,* **sent, send ing.** [*Send* comes from Old English *sendan.*] —**send′a ble,** *adj.* —**send′er,** *n.*

send-off (send′ôf′), INFORMAL. **1** a friendly demonstration in honor of a person setting out on a journey, course, career, etc. **2** a start (favorable or unfavorable) given to a person or thing. *n.*

Sen e ca[1] (sen′ə kə), **Lucius Annaeus,** 4? B.C.-A.D. 65, Roman philosopher. He also wrote tragedies. *n.*

Sen e ca[2] (sen′ə kə), member of the largest tribe of Iroquois Indians, formerly living in western New York State. *n., pl.* **Sen e ca** or **Sen e cas.**

Sen e gal (sen′ə gôl′), country in W Africa, on the Atlantic, a member of the French Community. *Capital:* Dakar. See **Nigeria** for map. *n.*

sen es chal (sen′ə shəl), steward in charge of a royal palace or nobleman's estate in the Middle Ages. Seneschals often had the powers of judges or generals. *n.*

se nile (sē′nīl), **1** of old age. **2** showing the loss of mental and physical ability that can occur in old age. **3** caused by old age. *adj.* —**se′nile ly,** *adv.*

se nil i ty (sə nil′ə tē), **1** old age. **2** weakness of old age. *n.*

sen ior (sē′nyər), **1** the older (used of a father whose son has the same given name): *John Parker, Senior, is the father of John Parker, Junior.* **2** older or elder: *a senior citizen.* **3** an older person: *She is her sister's senior by two years.* **4** of higher position or standing; higher in rank or longer in service: *a senior officer. Mr. Stein is the senior member of the firm of Stein and Marino.* **5** person of higher position or standing; person of higher rank or longer service. **6** student who is a member of the graduating class of a high school or college. **7** of the last year of high school or college: *the senior class, the senior prom.* 1,2,4,7 *adj.,* 3,5,6 *n.*

senior high school, school attended after junior high school. It usually has grades 10, 11, and 12.

sen ior i ty (sē nyôr′ə tē), **1** a being greater in age or standing; a being older: *He felt that two years' seniority gave him the right to advise his sister.* **2** right to come before others because of length of service: *She has seniority because she has worked here longer than anyone else.* *n., pl.* **sen ior i ties.**

sen na (sen′ə), the dried leaves of cassia plants. Senna is used as a laxative. *n.* [*Senna* comes from Arabic *sanā.*]

se ñor (sā nyôr′), SPANISH. **1** Mr. or sir. **2** a gentleman. *n., pl.* **se ño res** (sā nyōr′ās).

se ño ra (sā nyōr′ä), SPANISH. **1** Mrs. or Madam. **2** a lady. *n., pl.* **se ño ras.**

se ño ri ta (sā′nyō rē′tä), SPANISH. **1** Miss. **2** a young lady. *n., pl.* **se ño ri tas.**

sen sa tion (sen sā′shən), **1** action of the senses; power to see, hear, feel, taste, smell, etc.: *An unconscious person is without sensation. Blindness is the loss of the sensation of sight.* **2** feeling: *Ice gives a sensation of coldness.* **3** strong or excited feeling: *The announcement of peace caused a sensation throughout the nation. n.* —**sen sa′tion less,** *adj.*

sen sa tion al (sen sā′shə nəl), **1** arousing strong or excited feeling: *The outfielder's sensational catch made the crowd cheer wildly.* **2** trying to arouse strong or excited feeling: *a sensational newspaper story.* **3** of the senses; having to do with sensation. *adj.* —**sen sa′tion al ly,** *adv.*

sen sa tion al ism (sen sā′shə nə liz′əm), sensational methods, writing, language, etc., aimed at arousing strong or excited feeling. *n.*

sense (sens), **1** power of an organism to know what happens outside itself. Sight, hearing, touch, taste, and smell are senses. *A dog has a keen sense of smell.* **2** feeling: *The extra lock on the door gives us a sense of security.* **3** be aware; feel; understand: *I sensed that he was tired.* **4** understanding; appreciation: *He has a delightful sense of humor.* **5** Usually, **senses,** *pl.* normal, sound condition of mind: *They must be out of their senses to climb that steep cliff.* **6** judgment; intelligence: *She had the good sense to stay out of the argument. Common sense would have prevented the accident.* **7** meaning: *What sense does the word have in this sentence?* 1,2,4-7 *n.,* 3 *v.,* **sensed, sens ing.**

in a sense, in some respects; to some degree.

a hat	i it	oi oil	ch child	a in about
ā age	ī ice	ou out	ng long	e in taken
ä far	o hot	u cup	sh she	ə = i in pencil
e let	ō open	u̇ put	th thin	o in lemon
ē equal	ô order	ü rule	ᴛʜ then	u in circus
ėr term			zh measure	

make sense, have a meaning; be understandable; be reasonable: *The statement "Cow cat bless Monday" doesn't make sense.*

sense less (sens′lis), **1** unconscious: *A hard blow on the head knocked him senseless.* **2** foolish; stupid: *a senseless idea.* **3** meaningless: *senseless words. adj.* —**sense′less ly,** *adv.* —**sense′less ness,** *n.*

sense organ, eye, ear, or other part of the body by which a person or an animal receives sensations of heat, colors, sounds, smells, etc.; receptor.

sen si bil i ty (sen′sə bil′ə tē), **1** ability to feel or perceive: *Some drugs lessen a person's sensibilities.* **2** sensitiveness: *a sensibility to the beauties of nature.* **3** Usually, **sensibilities,** *pl.* sensitive or refined feelings. **4** tendency to feel hurt or offended too easily. *n., pl.* **sen si bil i ties.**

sen si ble (sen′sə bəl), **1** having or showing good sense or judgment; wise: *She is too sensible to do anything foolish.* **2** aware; conscious: *I am sensible of your kindness.* **3** that can be noticed: *There is a sensible difference between yellow and orange.* **4** able to be perceived by the senses. **5** sensitive. *adj.* —**sen′si ble ness,** *n.*

sen si bly (sen′sə blē), **1** in a sensible manner; with good sense. **2** so as to be felt. *adv.*

sen si tive (sen′sə tiv), **1** receiving impressions readily: *The eye is sensitive to light.* **2** easily affected or influenced: *The mercury in the thermometer is sensitive to changes in temperature. Sensitive people are quickly touched by something beautiful or sad.* **3** easily hurt or offended: *to be sensitive about one's weight. adj.* —**sen′si tive ly,** *adv.* —**sen′si tive ness,** *n.*

sen si tiv i ty (sen′sə tiv′ə tē), condition, quality, or degree of being sensitive. *n., pl.* **sen si tiv i ties.**

sen si tize (sen′sə tīz), make sensitive. Camera films have been sensitized to light. *v.,* **sen si tized, sen si tiz ing.** —**sen′si ti za′tion,** *n.* —**sen′si tiz′er,** *n.*

sen sor (sen′sər), a sensing device that reacts to heat, light, pressure, etc., and transmits a signal to control or measure some operation. *n.*

sen sor y (sen′sər ē), of sensation or the senses. The eyes and ears are sensory organs. *adj.*

sen su al (sen′shü əl), **1** having to do with the bodily senses rather than with the mind or soul: *Gluttons derive sensual pleasure from eating.* **2** caring too much for the pleasures of the senses. *adj.* —**sen′su al ly,** *adv.*

sen su al i ty (sen′shü al′ə tē), **1** sensual nature. **2** too much indulgence in the pleasures of the senses. *n., pl.* **sen su al i ties.**

sen su ous (sen′shü əs), **1** of or derived from the senses; having an effect on the senses; perceived by the senses: *the sensuous thrill of a warm bath, a sensuous love of color.* **2** enjoying the pleasures of the senses. *adj.* —**sen′su ous ly,** *adv.* —**sen′su ous ness,** *n.*

sent (sent), past tense and past participle of **send.** *They sent the trunks last week. She was sent on an errand. v.*

sen tence (sen′təns), **1** group of words that is grammatically complete and expresses a statement, request, command, exclamation, etc. "Boys and girls" is not a sentence. "The boys are here" is a sentence. **2** group of mathematical symbols that expresses a complete idea or a requirement. $4 + 2 = 6$ is a closed sentence expressing a complete idea. $X + 2 = 6$ is an open sentence expressing a requirement. **3** decision by a judge on the punishment of a criminal. **4** the punishment itself. **5** pronounce punishment on: *The judge sentenced her to a year in prison.* 1-4 *n.,* 5 *v.,* **sen tenced, sen tenc ing.** —**sen′tenc er,** *n.*

sen ten tious (sen ten′shəs), **1** full of meaning; saying much in few words. **2** inclined to give advice in a self-righteous way. **3** inclined to make wise sayings; speaking in proverbs. *adj.* —**sen ten′tious ly,** *adv.* —**sen ten′tious ness,** *n.*

sen tient (sen′shənt), able to feel; having feeling: *sentient beings. adj.* —**sen′tient ly,** *adv.*

sen ti ment (sen′tə mənt), **1** mixture of thought and feeling. Admiration, patriotism, and loyalty are sentiments. **2** feeling, especially refined or tender feeling: *Her letter expressed sentiments of friendship and sympathy.* **3** thought or saying that expresses feeling. **4** a mental attitude. **5** a personal opinion. *n.*

sen ti men tal (sen′tə men′tl), **1** having or showing much tender feeling: *sentimental poetry.* **2** likely to act from feelings rather than from logical thinking; having too much sentiment. **3** of sentiment; dependent on sentiment: *These old family photographs have sentimental value.* *adj.* —**sen′ti men′tal ly,** *adv.*

sen ti men tal ism (sen′tə men′tl iz′əm), sentimentality. *n.*

sen ti men tal ist (sen′tə men′tl ist), a sentimental person; one who indulges in sentimentality. *n.*

sen ti men tal i ty (sen′tə men tal′ə tē), **1** tendency to be influenced by sentiment rather than reason. **2** too much indulgence in sentiment. **3** feeling expressed too openly or emotionally. *n., pl.* **sen ti men tal i ties.**

sen ti men tal ize (sen′tə men′tl īz), **1** indulge in sentiment. **2** make sentimental. **3** be sentimental about. *v.,* **sen ti men tal ized, sen ti men tal iz ing.** —**sen′ti men′tal i za′tion,** *n.* —**sen′ti men′tal iz′er,** *n.*

sen ti nel (sen′tə nəl), person stationed to keep watch and guard against surprise attacks. *n.* [*Sentinel* is from French *sentinelle,* which comes from Italian *sentinella,* and can be traced back to Latin *sentire,* meaning "to perceive, to feel."]
stand sentinel, act as a sentinel; keep watch.

sen try (sen′trē), soldier stationed at a post to keep watch and guard against surprise attacks; sentinel. *n., pl.* **sen tries.**
stand sentry, keep watch; guard: *The sheepdog stood sentry over the sleeping flock.*

sentry box, a small building for sheltering a sentry.

Seoul (sōl), capital of South Korea, in the NW part. *n.*

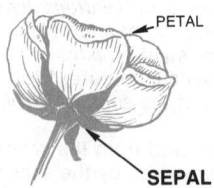

se pal (sē′pəl), one of the leaflike parts which make up the calyx of a flower. The sepals are usually green and cover the unopened bud. In a carnation, the sepals make a green cup at the base of the flower. In a tulip, the sepals are colored in the same way as the petals. *n.*

sep ar a ble (sep′ər ə bəl), able to be separated. *adj.* —**sep′ar a ble ness,** *n.* —**sep′ar a bly,** *adv.*

sep a rate (sep′ə rāt′ *for 1-5;* sep′ər it *for 6-8*), **1** keep apart; be between; divide: *The Atlantic Ocean separates America from Europe.* **2** divide into parts or groups: *sepa-*

rate a tangle of yarn. **3** draw, come, or go apart: *After school the children separated in all directions. The rope separated under the strain.* **4** live apart. A husband and wife may separate by agreement or by order of a court. **5** put apart; take away: *Separate your books from his.* **6** apart from others: *in a separate room.* **7** divided; not joined: *separate seats, separate questions.* **8** individual; single: *the separate parts of a machine.* 1-5 *v.,* **sep a rat ed, sep a rat ing;** 6-8 *adj.* —**sep′ar ate ly,** *adv.* —**sep′ar ate ness,** *n.*

sep a ra tion (sep′ə rā′shən), **1** a separating; dividing; taking apart. **2** a being apart; being separated: *The friends were glad to meet after so long a separation.* **3** line or point of separating: *We now come to the separation of the two branches of the river.* **4** the living apart of husband and wife by agreement or by order of a court. *n.*

sep a ra tist (sep′ər ə tist), member of a group that separates or withdraws from a larger group. *n.*

sep a ra tor (sep′ə rā′tər), person or thing that separates, especially a machine for separating the cream from milk, wheat from chaff or dirt, etc. *n.*

se pi a (sē′pē ə), **1** a dark-brown pigment prepared from the inky liquid produced by cuttlefish. **2** a dark brown. **3** dark-brown. **4** done in tones of brown: *a sepia print.* 1,2 *n., pl.* **se pi as;** 3,4 *adj.* [*Sepia* comes from Greek *sēpia,* meaning "cuttlefish."] —**se′pi a like′,** *adj.*

Sept., September.

Sep tem ber (sep tem′bər), the ninth month of the year. It has 30 days. *n.*

sep tic (sep′tik), **1** causing infection or rot. **2** caused by infection or rot. *adj.* [*Septic* is from Greek *sēptikos,* which comes from *sēpein,* meaning "to rot."] —**sep′ti cal ly,** *adv.*

septic tank, an underground concrete or steel container for household sewage. Bacteria in the sewage break it down, while the liquid flows out through pipes into the soil.

sep tum (sep′təm), a dividing wall; partition. There is a septum of bone and cartilage between the nostrils. The inside of a green pepper is divided into chambers by septa. *n., pl.* **sep ta** (sep′tə). [*Septum* is from Latin *saeptum,* meaning "a fence."]

sep ul cher (sep′əl kər), place of burial; tomb; grave. *n.* Also, **sepulchre.**

se pul chral (sə pul′krəl), **1** of sepulchers or burial: *sepulchral ceremonies.* **2** deep and gloomy; dismal; suggesting a tomb: *sepulchral darkness. adj.* —**se pul′chral ly,** *adv.*

sep ul chre (sep′əl kər), sepulcher. *n.*

se quel (sē′kwəl), **1** something that follows as a result of some earlier happening; result of something; outcome: *Among the sequels of the party were many stomach aches.* **2** a complete story continuing an earlier one about the same people: *Louisa May Alcott's book "Little Men" is a sequel to her "Little Women." n.*

se quence (sē′kwəns), **1** the coming of one thing after another; succession; order of succession: *Arrange the names in alphabetical sequence.* **2** a connected series: *a sequence of lessons on one subject. n.*

se quen tial (si kwen′shəl), forming a sequence or connected series. *adj.* —**se quen′tial ly,** *adv.*

se ques ter (si kwes′tər), **1** remove or withdraw from public use or from public view: *The author sequestered herself in a seaside cottage while she worked on her new book.* **2** take away (property) for a time from an owner until a debt is paid or some claim is satisfied. **3** seize by authority; take and keep: *The soldiers sequestered food from the people they conquered. v.*

se ques tra tion (sē′kwə strā′shən), **1** the seizing and holding of property until legal claims are satisfied.

2 forcible or authorized seizure; confiscation. **3** separation or withdrawal from others; seclusion. *n.*

se quin (sē′kwən), a small spangle used to ornament dresses, scarfs, etc. *n.*

se quoi a (si kwoi′ə), **1** redwood. **2** giant sequoia. *n., pl.* **se quoi as.** [The *sequoia* was named in honor of *Sequoya*.]

Se quoy a or **Se quoy ah** (si kwoi′ə), 1770?-1843, American Indian leader who invented an alphabet for the Cherokee language. *n.*

se ragl io (sə ral′yō), harem. *n., pl.* **se ragl ios.**

se ra pe (sə rä′pē), shawl or blanket, often having bright colors, worn in Mexico and other Latin-American countries. *n.* Also, **sarape.** [*Serape* comes from Mexican Spanish *sarape*.]

ser aph (ser′əf), one of the highest order of angels. *n., pl.* **ser aphs** or **ser a phim.**

se raph ic (sə raf′ik), **1** of seraphs. **2** like a seraph; angelic. *adj.* —**se raph′i cal ly,** *adv.*

ser a phim (ser′ə fim), a plural of **seraph.** *n.*

Serb (sėrb), person born or living in Serbia. *n.*

Ser bi a (sėr′bē ə), former kingdom in SE Europe, now part of Yugoslavia. *n.* —**Ser′bi an,** *adj., n.*

Ser bo-Cro a tian (sėr′bō krō ā′shən), **1** the Slavic language of Serbia and Croatia in Yugoslavia. **2** of this language. 1 *n.,* 2 *adj.*

sere (sir), OLD USE. dried; withered. *adj.* Also, **sear.**

ser e nade (ser′ə nād′), **1** music played or sung outdoors at night, especially by a lover under his sweetheart's window. **2** piece of music suitable for such a performance. **3** sing or play a serenade (to). 1,2 *n.,* 3 *v.,* **ser e nad ed, ser e nad ing.** —**ser′e nad′er,** *n.*

se rene (sə rēn′), **1** peaceful; calm: *serene happiness, a serene smile.* **2** not cloudy; clear; bright: *a serene sky. adj.* —**se rene′ly,** *adv.* —**se rene′ness,** *n.*

se ren i ty (sə ren′ə tē), **1** peace and quiet; calmness. **2** clearness; brightness. *n.*

serf (sėrf), **1** (in the feudal system) slave who could not be sold off the land, but passed from one owner to another with the land. **2** person treated almost like a slave; person who is mistreated, underpaid, etc. *n.* —**serf′like′,** *adj.*

serf dom (sėrf′dəm), **1** condition of a serf. **2** custom of having serfs. Serfdom existed all over Europe in the Middle Ages and lasted in Russia till the middle of the 1800's. *n.*

serge (sėrj), kind of cloth woven with slanting ridges in it. *n.*

ser geant (sär′jənt), **1** (in the army and marine corps) a noncommissioned officer ranking next above a corporal. **2** (in the air force) a noncommissioned officer ranking above an airman. **3** a police officer ranking next above an ordinary policeman and next below a captain or lieutenant. *n.* [*Sergeant* came into English about 700 years ago, in the meaning "servant," from French *sergent*, which came from Latin *servientem*, meaning "serving."]

sergeant at arms, officer who keeps order in a legislature, court of law, etc. *pl.* **sergeants at arms.**

sergt., sergeant.

ser i al (sir′ē əl), **1** story published, broadcast, or televised one part at a time. **2** of a series; arranged in a series; making a series: *Place volumes 1 to 5 on the shelf in serial order.* 1 *n.,* 2 *adj.*

ser i al ize (sir′ē ə līz), publish, broadcast, or televise in a series of installments. *v.,* **ser i al ized, ser i al iz ing.** —**ser′i al i za′tion,** *n.*

ser i al ly (sir′ē ə lē), in a series; as a serial. *adv.*

serial number, number given to one of a series of persons, articles, etc., as a means of easy identification. Every dollar bill has a serial number.

a hat	i it	oi oil	ch child	a in about
ā age	ī ice	ou out	ng long	e in taken
ä far	o hot	u cup	sh she	ə = i in pencil
e let	ō open	u̇ put	th thin	o in lemon
ē equal	ô order	ü rule	ᵺ then	u in circus
ėr term			zh measure	

ser ies (sir′ēz), **1** number of similar things in a row: *A series of rooms opened off the long hall.* **2** number of things placed one after another: *Our names were listed in an alphabetical series.* **3** number of things or events coming one after the other: *A series of rainy days spoiled their vacation.* **4** a television program shown at a regular time. *n., pl.* **ser ies.**

ser i ous (sir′ē əs), **1** showing deep thought or purpose; thoughtful; grave: *a serious manner, a serious face.* **2** in earnest; not fooling; sincere: *Are you joking or are you serious?* **3** needing thought; important: *Choice of one's lifework is a serious matter.* **4** important because it may do much harm; dangerous: *The patient was in serious condition. adj.* —**ser′i ous ly,** *adv.* —**ser′i ous ness,** *n.*

ser mon (sėr′mən), **1** a public talk on religion or something connected with religion, usually given by a member of the clergy. **2** a serious talk about conduct or duty; moral lecture: *After the guests left, the children got a sermon on their bad table manners. n.* —**ser′mon less,** *adj.*

ser mon ize (sėr′mə nīz), give a sermon; preach. *v.,* **ser mon ized, ser mon iz ing.** —**ser′mon iz′er,** *n.*

Sermon on the Mount, (in the Bible) Jesus' sermon to His disciples which presents His basic teachings.

ser ous (sir′əs), **1** of or producing serum. **2** like serum; watery. Tears are drops of a serous fluid. *adj.* —**ser′ous ness,** *n.*

ser pent (sėr′pənt), **1** snake, especially a big snake. **2** a sly, treacherous person. *n.* [*Serpent* can be traced back to Latin *serpentem*, which originally meant "a creeping thing."]

ser pen tine (sėr′pən tēn′ or sėr′pən tīn), **1** of or like a serpent. **2** winding; twisting: *the serpentine course of a creek. adj.*

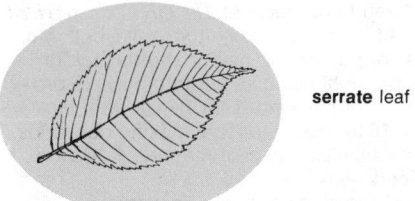

serrate leaf

ser rate (ser′āt), notched like the edge of a saw; toothed. *adj.*

ser rat ed (ser′ā tid), serrate. *adj.*

ser ried (ser′ēd), crowded closely together. *adj.*

ser um (sir′əm), **1** the clear, pale-yellow, watery part that separates from blood when it clots. **2** liquid used to prevent or cure a disease, usually obtained from the blood of an animal that has been made immune to the disease. Polio vaccine is a serum. **3** any watery liquid in animals. Lymph is a serum. *n., pl.* **ser ums, ser a** (sir′ə).

serv ant (sėr′vənt), **1** person employed in a household, such as a cook or maid. **2** public servant. **3** person devoted to any service: *a servant of God. n.* —**serv′ant less,** *adj.* —**serv′ant like′,** *adj.*

serve (sėrv), **1** work for; give service to: *serve a worthwhile cause, serve customers in a store.* **2** give service; perform duties: *She served as a counselor. My cousin served three years in the navy.* **3** to honor and obey; worship: *serve God.* **4** wait on at table; bring food or drink to: *The waiter served us.* **5** put (food or drink) on the table: *Serve crackers with the soup. Dinner is served.* **6** supply with something needed; supply; furnish: *The dairy serves us with milk.* **7** supply enough for: *One pie will serve six persons.* **8** be useful; be what is needed; be used: *Boxes served as seats.* **9** be useful to; fulfill: *This will serve my purpose.* **10** pass; spend: *The thief served a term in prison.* **11** deliver; present: *She was served with a notice to appear in court.* **12** in tennis, badminton, volleyball, etc.: **a** put (the ball or shuttlecock) in play by hitting it. **b** act or way of serving a ball or shuttlecock. **c** a player's turn to serve. 1-12a *v.,* **served, serv ing;** 12b,c *n.* [*Serve* came into English about 700 years ago from French *servir,* meaning "to serve," which can be traced back to Latin *servus,* meaning "a slave."] —**serv′a ble, serve′a ble,** *adj.*

serve one right, be just what one deserves: *If you cheat, it serves you right to be punished.*

serv er (sėr′vər), **1** person who serves. **2** tray for dishes. *n.*

serv ice (sėr′vis), **1** helpful act or acts; aid; a being useful to others: *They performed many services for their community.* **2** business or system that supplies something useful or necessary: *a secretarial service. Bus service was good.* **3** occupation or employment as a servant: *go into domestic service.* **4** Usually, **services,** *pl.* **a** performance of duties: *She no longer needs the services of a doctor.* **b** work in the service of others; useful labor: *We pay for services such as repairs, maintenance, and utilities.* **5** advantage; benefit; use: *This coat has given me great service. Every available vehicle was pressed into service.* **6** department of government or public employment, or the persons engaged in it: *the diplomatic service.* **7** the armed forces: *We entered the service together.* **8** duty in the armed forces: *He was on active service during the war.* **9** Often, **services,** *pl.* a religious meeting, ritual, or ceremony: *They attend services on Friday evening. The marriage service was performed at the home of the bride.* **10** manner of serving food or the food served: *The service in this restaurant is excellent.* **11** set of dishes, etc.: *a solid silver tea service.* **12** (in law) the serving of a process or writ upon a person. **13** make fit for service; keep fit for service: *The mechanic serviced our automobile.* **14** in tennis, badminton, volleyball, etc.: **a** act or manner of putting the ball or shuttlecock in play. **b** the ball or shuttlecock as put into play. **15** provide with a service of any kind: *Only two trains a day service the town.* **16** for use by people making deliveries, household servants, etc.: *a service entrance.* 1-12,14 *n.,* 13,15 *v.,* **serv iced, serv ic ing;** 16 *adj.*

at one's service, ready to do what one wants.

of service, helpful; useful.

serv ice a ble (sėr′vi sə bəl), **1** useful for a long time; able to stand much use: *We want to buy a serviceable second-hand car.* **2** capable of giving good service; useful. *adj.* —**serv′ice a bly,** *adv.*

serv ice man (sėr′vis man′), **1** member of the armed forces. **2** person who maintains or repairs machinery or some kind of equipment: *an automobile serviceman. n., pl.* **serv ice men.**

service station, filling station.

ser vile (sėr′vəl), **1** like that of slaves; fit for a slave; mean; base: *servile flattery.* **2** of slaves: *a servile revolt, servile work. adj.* —**ser′vile ly,** *adv.* —**ser′vile ness,** *n.*

ser vil i ty (sėr′vil′ə tē), attitude or behavior fit for a slave; servile yielding. *n., pl.* **ser vil i ties.**

serv ing (sėr′ving), portion of food served to a person at one time; helping. *n.*

ser vi tor (sėr′və tər), servant; attendant. *n.*

ser vi tude (sėr′və tüd *or* sėr′və tyüd), **1** slavery; bond-

age. **2** forced labor as punishment: *The criminal was sentenced to five years' servitude. n.*

ses a me (ses′ə mē), **1** the seeds of a tropical plant, used in bread, candy, and other foods, and in making an oil used in cooking. **2** plant producing these seeds. *n.*

ses sion (sesh′ən), **1** a sitting or meeting of a court, council, legislature, etc.: *a session of Congress.* **2** a series of such sittings. **3** term or period of such sittings: *This year's session of Congress was unusually long.* **4** a meeting: *an important session with the manager.* **5** a single, continuous course or a period of lessons: *Our school has two sessions, one in the morning and one in the afternoon. n.*

in session, meeting: *The teachers were in session all Saturday morning. Congress is now in session.*

set (set), **1** put in some place; put; place: *Set the box on its end.* **2** put in the right place, position, or condition; put in proper order; arrange: *The doctor set my broken leg. Set the clock. Set the table for dinner.* **3** cause to be; put in some condition or relation: *Their friendliness set me at ease. The prisoner was set free.* **4** fix; arrange; appoint: *set the rules of a contest. The teacher set a time limit for the examination.* **5** fixed or appointed beforehand; established: *a set time, set rules.* **6** prepared; ready: *They are all set to try again.* **7** provide for others to follow: *set a good example.* **8** put in a fixed, rigid, or settled state: *She set her jaw in determination.* **9** fixed; rigid: *a set smile.* **10** make or become firm or hard: *Jelly sets as it cools.* **11** put in a frame or other thing that holds: *set a diamond in gold.* **12** go down; sink: *The sun sets in the west.* **13** number of things or persons belonging together; group; outfit: *a set of dishes.* **14** scenery of a play or for a motion picture. **15** device for receiving radio or television signals that turns them into sounds and pictures. **16** way a thing is put or placed; form; shape: *His jaw had a stubborn set.* **17** direction; tendency; course; drift: *The set of opinion was toward building a new bridge.* **18** turn in a particular direction; direct: *to set one's feet homeward.* **19** begin to move; start: *She set to work.* **20** (in music) adapt; fit: *set words of a poem to music.* **21** put (a hen) to sit on eggs to hatch them; place (eggs) under a hen to be hatched. **22** (of a hen) sit on eggs. **23** act or manner of setting. **24** stubbornly fixed; obstinate: *They are set in their ways.* **25** group of games in tennis. One side must win six games and at least two more than the other side. **26** a young plant: *onion sets.* **27** (in mathematics) a collection of numbers, points, objects, or other elements which are distinguished from all other elements by specific common properties. *The numbers from 0 to 10 form a set, and any number in this set is a member of the set.* 1-4,7,8,10-12,18-22 *v.,* **set, set ting;** 5,6,9,24 *adj.,* 13-17,23,25-27 *n.*

set about, start work upon; begin: *set about one's business.*

set against, 1 make unfriendly toward. **2** balance; compare.

set aside, 1 put to one side. **2** put by for later use. **3** discard, dismiss, or leave out; reject; annul: *Sometimes a higher court sets aside the decision in a lawsuit.*

set back, stop; hinder; check: *Road repairs were set back by bad weather.*

set down, 1 deposit or let alight; put down: *set down a suitcase. The bus set us down near town.* **2** put down in writing or printing. **3** consider; regard: *set a person down as a gossip.* **4** assign; attribute: *Your failure in the test can be set down to too much haste.*

set forth, 1 make known; express; declare: *set forth one's opinions on a subject.* **2** start to go: *set forth on a trip.*

set in, begin: *Winter set in early.*

set off, 1 explode: *set off a string of firecrackers.* **2** start to go: *set off for home.* **3** increase or heighten by contrast:

The green dress set off her red hair. **4** mark off; separate from the others: *One sentence was set off from the rest by quotation marks.*

set on or **set upon, 1** attack: *The dog set on us.* **2** urge to attack.

set out, 1 start to go: *They set out on the hike with plenty of water.* **2** spread out to show, sell, or use: *set out a flag, set out goods for sale.* **3** to plant: *set out tomato plants in the spring.*

set to, 1 begin: *set to work.* **2** begin fighting: *The children set to.*

set up, 1 build: *set up a monument.* **2** begin; start. **3** put up; raise in place, position, power, pride, etc.: *They set him up above his rivals.* **4** claim; pretend: *set up to be honest.* **5** plan, prepare, or establish: *set up a business deal.*

set back (set′bak′), a check to progress; reverse: *The team suffered a setback when its best player became sick. n.*

settee

set tee (se tē′), sofa or long bench with a back and, usually, arms. *n.*

set ter (set′ər), **1** person or thing that sets: *a setter of type, a setter of jewels.* **2** a long-haired hunting dog, trained to stand motionless and point its nose toward the game that it scents. *n.*

setter (def. 2)—2 ft. (60 cm.) high at shoulder

set ting (set′ing), **1** frame or other thing in which something is set. The mounting of a jewel is its setting. **2** scenery of a play. **3** place, time, etc., of a play or story. **4** surroundings; background: *a scenic mountain setting.* **5** music composed to go with a story, poem, etc. **6** the eggs that a hen sets on for hatching. **7** act of a person or thing that sets. **8** dishes or cutlery required to set one place at a table: *a wedding present of six settings of china. n.*

set tle[1] (set′l), **1** determine; decide; agree (upon): *settle an argument. They settled on a time for leaving.* **2** put or be put in order; arrange: *I must settle all my affairs before going away for the winter.* **3** pay; arrange payment of: *She settled a bill before leaving town. Let us settle up our expenses for the trip.* **4** take up residence (in a new country

or place): *settle in New York.* **5** establish colonies in; colonize: *The English settled New England.* **6** set or be set in a fairly permanent position, place, or way of life: *We are settled in our new home.* **7** come to rest in a particular place; become set or fixed: *A heavy fog settled over the airport. My cold settled in my chest.* **8** place in or come to a desired or comfortable position: *The cat settled itself in the chair.* **9** make or become quiet: *A vacation will settle your nerves.* **10** go down; sink: *Our house has settled four inches since it was built.* **11** (of liquid) make or become clear: *A beaten egg or cold water will settle coffee. v.,* **set tled, set tling.** [*Settle*[1] is from Old English *setlan,* which comes from *setl,* meaning "a sitting place."] —**set′tle a ble,** *adj.*

settle down, 1 live a more regular life. **2** direct steady effort or attention. **3** calm down; become quiet: *settle down for a nap.*

settle upon or **settle on,** give (property, etc.) to by law: *She settled one thousand dollars a year upon her housekeeper.*

set tle[2] (set′l), a long bench, usually with arms and a high back. *n.* [*Settle*[2] comes from Old English *setl,* meaning "a sitting place."]

set tle ment (set′l mənt), **1** a settling or a being settled. **2** a putting in order; arrangement: *No settlement of the dispute is possible unless each side yields some point.* **3** payment: *Settlement of all claims against the company will be made shortly.* **4** the settling of persons in a new country: *The settlement of the English along the Atlantic coast gave England claim to that section.* **5** colony: *England had many settlements along the Atlantic coast.* **6** group of buildings and the people living in them: *Ships brought supplies to the scattered settlements of the colonists.* **7** place in a poor, neglected neighborhood where work for its improvement is carried on. **8** the settling of property upon someone: *The will provided that each heir would get a settlement of $20,000. n.*

settlement house, settlement (def. 7).

set tler (set′lər), person who settles in a new country. *n.*

set up (set′up′), **1** arrangement of apparatus, machinery, etc. **2** arrangement of an organization. *n.*

Seuss (süs), **Dr.,** the pen name of Theodor Geisel. *n.*

sev en (sev′ən), one more than six; 7. *n., adj.*

sev en fold (sev′ən fōld′), **1** seven times as much or as many. **2** having seven parts. **3** seven times as much or as often. **1,3** *adv.,* **1,2** *adj.*

setting (def. 1)

seven seas, all the seas and oceans of the world, traditionally believed to be the Arctic, Antarctic, N Atlantic, S Atlantic, N Pacific, S Pacific, and Indian oceans: *to sail the seven seas.*

sev en teen (sev′ən tēn′), seven more than ten; 17. *n., adj.*

sev en teenth (sev′ən tēnth′), **1** next after the 16th; last in a series of 17. **2** one of 17 equal parts. *adj., n.*

sev enth (sev′ənth), **1** next after the sixth; last in a series of 7. **2** one of 7 equal parts. *adj., n.*

sev en ti eth (sev′ən tē ith), **1** next after the 69th; last in a series of 70. **2** one of 70 equal parts. *adj., n.*

sev en ty (sev′ən tē), seven times ten; 70. *n., pl.* **sev en ties;** *adj.*

Seven Wonders of the World, the seven most remarkable structures of ancient times: the Pyramids of Egypt, the hanging gardens of Babylon, the 40-foot-high statue of Zeus by Phidias at Olympia, the temple of Artemis at Ephesus, the Colossus of Rhodes, the 140-foot-high mausoleum at a city in southwestern Asia Minor, and the 400-foot-high lighthouse at Alexandria.

sev er (sev′ər), **1** cut apart; cut off: *I severed the rope with a knife.* **2** part; divide; separate: *The rope severed and the swing fell down.* **3** break off: *The two countries severed friendly relations. v.*

sev er al (sev′ər əl), **1** more than two or three but not many; some; a few: *gain several pounds (adj.). Several have given their consent (n.).* **2** individual; different: *The children went their several ways after school.* 1,2 *adj.,* 1 *n.*

sev er al ly (sev′ər ə lē), separately; singly; individually: *Consider these points, first severally and then collectively. adv.*

sev er ance (sev′ər əns), **1** a severing or being severed; separation; division. **2** a breaking off: *the severance of diplomatic relations between two countries. n.*

se vere (sə vir′), **1** very strict; stern; harsh: *The judge gave the criminal a severe sentence.* **2** sharp or violent: *a severe headache, a severe storm.* **3** serious; grave: *a severe illness.* **4** very plain or simple; without ornament: *severe black clothes.* **5** difficult: *a series of severe tests. adj.,* **se ver er, se ver est.** —**se vere′ly,** *adv.* —**se vere′ness,** *n.*

se ver i ty (sə ver′ə tē), **1** strictness; sternness; harshness: *the severity of a punishment.* **2** sharpness or violence: *the severity of storms, the severity of pain, the severity of grief.* **3** simplicity of style or taste; plainness: *the severity of a modern steel and glass building.* **4** seriousness. *n., pl.* **se ver i ties.**

Se ville (sə vil′), city in SW Spain. *n.*

sew (sō), **1** work with needle and thread. **2** fasten with stitches: *sew on a button, sew a hem on a sewing machine.* **3** close with stitches: *The doctor sewed up the wound. v.,* **sewed, sewed** or **sewn, sew ing.** [*Sew* comes from Old English *siwan.*] —**sew′a ble,** *adj.*

sew age (sü′ij), the waste matter that passes through sewers. *n.*

Sew ard (sü′ərd), **William Henry,** 1801-1872, American statesman. He was secretary of state from 1861 to 1869. *n.*

sew er[1] (sü′ər), an underground pipe or channel for carrying off waste water and refuse. *n.* —**sew′er less,** *adj.* —**sew′er like′,** *adj.*

sew er[2] (sō′ər), person or thing that sews. *n.*

sew er age (sü′ər ij), **1** removal of waste matter by sewers. **2** system of sewers. **3** the waste matter that passes through sewers; sewage. *n.*

sew ing (sō′ing), **1** work done with a needle and thread. **2** something to be sewed. **3** for sewing; used in sewing: *a sewing room.* 1,2 *n.,* 3 *adj.*

sewing machine, machine for sewing or stitching cloth, etc.

sewn (sōn), sewed; a past participle of **sew.** *I've sewn on the buttons. v.*

sex (seks), **1** one of the two divisions, male or female, of human beings or animals, as determined by their func-

tion in reproduction. **2** the character of being male or female: *People were admitted without regard to age or sex.* **3** sexual intercourse. *n., pl.* **sex es** for 1.

sex chromosome, either of a pair of chromosomes, the X chromosome or the Y chromosome, which determine sex.

sex gland, gonad.

sex ism (sek′siz′əm), discrimination or prejudice against a sex or member of a sex, especially the female sex. *n.*

sex ist (sek′sist), of sexism: *sexist attitudes. adj.*

sex less (seks′lis), without sex or the characteristics of sex. *adj.* —**sex′less ly,** *adv.* —**sex′less ness,** *n.*

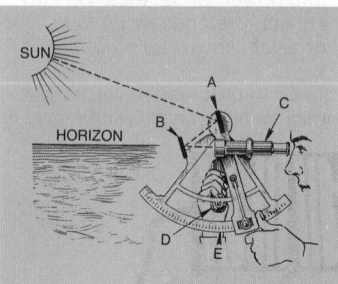

sextant
A, mirror; B, mirror; C, telescope; D, handle; E, graduated arm

sex tant (sek′stənt), instrument used by navigators, surveyors, etc., for measuring the angular distance between two objects. Sextants are used at sea to measure the altitude of the sun, a star, etc., in order to determine latitude and longitude. *n.*

sex tet or **sex tette** (sek stet′), **1** piece of music for six voices or instruments. **2** group of six singers or players performing together. **3** any group of six. *n.*

sex ton (sek′stən), person who takes care of a church building, rings the church bell, arranges burials, etc. *n.*

sex u al (sek′shü əl), of sex or the sexes: *sexual development. adj.* —**sex′u al ly,** *adv.*

sexual intercourse, the uniting of male and female sexual organs.

Sey chelles (sā shelz′), country consisting of a group of islands in the Indian Ocean, off E Africa. *Capital:* Victoria. *n. pl. or sing.*

s.g., specific gravity.

Sgt., Sergeant.

shab bi ly (shab′ə lē), in a shabby manner. *adv.*

shab bi ness (shab′ē nis), shabby condition or quality. *n.*

shab by (shab′ē), **1** much worn: *This old suit looks shabby.* **2** wearing old or much worn clothes: *a shabby beggar.* **3** poor or neglected; run-down: *a shabby old house.* **4** not generous; mean; unfair: *a shabby way to treat a friend. adj.,* **shab bi er, shab bi est.**

shack (shak), **1** a roughly built hut or cabin: *We built a shack of old boards in the backyard.* **2** house in bad condition: *Those run-down shacks are being torn down to make way for new housing. n.*

shack le (shak′əl), **1** a metal band fastened around the ankle or wrist of a prisoner, slave, etc. Shackles are usually fastened to each other, the wall, the floor, etc., by chains. **2 shackles,** *pl.* chains; fetters. **3** link fastening together the two rings for the ankles and wrists of a prisoner. **4** put shackles on. **5** Also, **shackles,** *pl.* anything that prevents freedom of action, thought, etc.: *to remove the shackles of poverty. Ignorance and fear are shackles of the mind.* **6** restrain; hamper. **7** thing for fastening or coupling. 1-3,5,7 *n.,* 4,6 *v.,* **shack led, shack ling.** —**shack′ler,** *n.*

Shack le ton (shak′əl tən), Sir **Ernest,** 1874-1922, British antarctic explorer. *n.*

shad (shad), a saltwater food fish related to the herring. Shad are common along the northern Atlantic coast and go up rivers in the spring to spawn. *n., pl.* **shad** or **shads.**

shade (shād), **1** a partly dark place, not in the sunshine: *We sat in the shade of a big tree.* **2** a slight darkness or coolness given by something that cuts off light: *Leafy trees cast shade.* **3** something that shuts out light: *Pull down the shades of the windows.* **4** keep light from: *A big hat shades the eyes.* **5** lightness or darkness of color: *silks in all shades of blue.* **6** the dark part of a picture. **7** make darker than the rest; use black or color to give the effect of shade in a picture. **8** a very small difference; little bit: *a shade too long, many shades of opinion.* **9** show very small differences; change little by little: *This scarf shades from deep rose to pale pink.* **10** ghost; spirit: *the shades of departed heroes.* **11 the shades,** darkness of evening or night. 1-3,5,6,8,10,11 *n.,* 4,7,9 *v.,* **shad ed, shad ing.** —**shade′less,** *adj.*
in the shade, in or into a condition of being unknown or unnoticed.

shad i ness (shā′dē nis), shady quality or condition. *n.*

shad ing (shā′ding), **1** a covering from the light. **2** use of black or color to give the effect of shade or depth in a picture. **3** a slight variation or difference of color, character, etc. *n.*

shad ow (shad′ō), **1** shade made by some person, animal, or thing. Sometimes one's shadow is much longer than one's actual height, and sometimes much shorter. **2** darkness; partial shade: *Don't turn on the light; we like to sit in the shadow.* **3** the dark part of a place or picture. **4** cast a shadow on. **5** a little bit; small degree; slight suggestion: *They were innocent beyond the shadow of a doubt.* **6** ghost. **7** a faint image: *You look worn to a shadow.* **8** anything that is unreal or imaginary even though it seems to be real. **9** follow closely and secretly: *The detective shadowed the suspect.* **10** person who follows another closely and secretly, as a detective. **11** a constant companion; follower. **12** sadness; gloom. **13** make sad or gloomy. 1-3,5-8,10-12 *n.,* 4,9,13 *v.* —**shad′ow er,** *n.* —**shad′ow less,** *adj.* —**shad′ow like′,** *adj.*

shad ow box ing (shad′ō bok′sing), boxing with an imaginary opponent for exercise or training. *n.*

shad ow y (shad′ə wē), **1** having much shadow or shade; shady: *We were glad to leave the hot sun and come into the cool, shadowy room.* **2** like a shadow; dim, faint, or slight: *We saw a shadowy outline on the window curtain.* *adj.* —**shad′ow i ness,** *n.*

shad y (shā′dē), **1** in the shade; shaded. **2** giving shade. **3** of doubtful honesty, character, etc.: *I hear they were involved in a shady business deal.* *adj.,* **shad i er, shad i est.** —**shad′i ly,** *adv.*

shaft (shaft), **1** bar which supports turning parts in a machine or which transmits motion from one part of the machine to another. **2** a deep passage sunk in the earth. The entrance to a mine is called a shaft. **3** a passage that is like a well; long, narrow space: *an elevator shaft.* **4** the long, slender stem of an arrow, spear, etc. **5** arrow; spear. **6** something aimed at a person like an arrow or spear: *shafts of ridicule.* **7** ray or beam of light. **8** one of the two wooden poles between which a horse is harnessed to a carriage, etc. **9** the main part of a column. **10** the long, straight handle of a hammer, ax, golf club, etc. *n.* [*Shaft* comes from Old English *sceaft.*] —**shaft′less,** *adj.* —**shaft′like′,** *adj.*

shag (shag), **1** rough, matted hair, wool, etc. **2** the long, rough nap of some kinds of cloth or rugs. **3** cloth having such a nap. *n.* —**shag′like′,** *adj.*

shag bark (shag′bärk′), a hickory tree whose rough bark peels off in long strips. *n.*

a hat	i it	oi oil	ch child	⎧ a in about
ā age	ī ice	ou out	ng long	⎪ e in taken
ä far	o hot	u cup	sh she	ə = ⎨ i in pencil
e let	ō open	u̇ put	th thin	⎪ o in lemon
ē equal	ô order	ü rule	ᴛʜ then	⎩ u in circus
ėr term			zh measure	

shag gy (shag′ē), **1** covered with a thick, rough mass of hair, wool, etc.: *a shaggy dog.* **2** long, thick, and rough: *shaggy eyebrows.* **3** untidy in appearance, especially needing a haircut or shave. **4** having a long, rough nap; of coarse texture: *a shaggy felt hat.* *adj.,* **shag gi er, shag gi est.** —**shag′gi ly,** *adv.* —**shag′gi ness,** *n.*

Shah or **shah** (shä), title of the former rulers of Iran. *n.*

shake (shāk), **1** move quickly backward and forward, up and down, or from side to side: *shake a rug. The baby shook the rattle. The branches of the old tree shook in the wind.* **2** bring, throw, force, rouse, scatter, etc., by or as if by movement: *shake snow off one's clothes.* **3** clasp (hands) in greeting, congratulating, etc., another: *shake hands.* **4** tremble: *The kitten was shaking with cold.* **5** make tremble: *The explosion shook the town.* **6** disturb; make less firm: *His lie shook my faith in his honesty.* **7** act or fact of shaking: *A shake of the head was her answer.* **8 the shakes,** a trembling caused by chills or fear. **9** INFORMAL. get rid of: *Can't you shake your little cousin?* 1-6,9 *v.,* **shook, shak en, shak ing;** 7,8 *n.* —**shak′a ble, shake′a ble,** *adj.*
no great shakes, INFORMAL. not unusual, extraordinary, or important.
shake down, 1 bring or throw down by shaking. **2** cause to settle down. **3** bring into working order. **4** SLANG. get money from dishonestly.
shake off, get rid of.
shake up, 1 shake hard: *Shake up a mixture of oil and vinegar for the salad.* **2** make a sudden and complete change in; reorganize completely: *The new manager shook up her office staff.* **3** to jar in body or nerves: *I was much shaken up by the experience.*

shak en (shā′kən), past participle of **shake.** *v.*

shak er (shā′kər), **1** person who shakes something. **2** machine or utensil used in shaking. **3** container for pepper, salt, etc., having a top with holes in it. **4 Shaker,** member of an American religious sect, called this from movements of the body forming part of their worship. *n.*

shafts (def. 1)

Shake speare (shāk′spir), **William,** 1564-1616, English poet and dramatist. *n.*

Shake spear i an or **Shake spear e an** (shāk spir′ē ən), of Shakespeare or his works. *adj.*

shake-up (shāk′up′), a sudden and complete change: *The mayor resigned during a shake-up in the government. n.*

shak i ly (shā′kə lē), in a shaky manner. *adv.*

shak i ness (shā′kē nis), shaky condition. *n.*

shako

shak o (shak′ō or shā′kō), a high, stiff military hat with a plume or other ornament. *n., pl.* **shak os.** [*Shako* comes from Hungarian *csákó,* meaning "peaked."]

shak y (shā′kē), **1** shaking: *a shaky voice.* **2** liable to break down; weak: *a shaky porch.* **3** not to be depended on; not reliable: *a shaky bank, a shaky knowledge of history. adj.,* **shak i er, shak i est.**

shale (shāl), rock formed from hardened clay or mud in thin layers which split easily. *n.* —**shale′like′,** *adj.*

shall (shal; *unstressed* shəl), *Shall* is used to express future time, command, obligation, and necessity. *We shall come soon. You shall go to the party, I promise you. Shall I drink the milk? I shall miss you. v., past tense* **should.**

shal lop (shal′əp), a small, light, open boat with sail or oars. *n.*

shal lot (shə lot′), a small bulb much like an onion, often used for seasoning cooked foods. *n.*

shal low (shal′ō), **1** not deep: *shallow water, a shallow dish.* **2** lacking depth of thought, knowledge, feeling, etc.: *a shallow mind.* **3** Usually, **shallows,** *pl.* a shallow place: *Children splashed in the shallows of the pond.* 1,2 *adj.,* 3 *n.* —**shal′low ly,** *adv.* —**shal′low ness,** *n.*

shalt (shalt), OLD USE. shall. "Thou shalt" means "You shall." *v.*

sham (sham), **1** pretense; fraud: *Their claim to be descended from royalty is a sham.* **2** false; pretended; imitation: *a sham battle fought for practice, sham antiques.* **3** pretend: *He shammed sickness so he wouldn't have to work.* **4** person who is not what he or she pretends to be; fraud. 1,4 *n.,* 2 *adj.,* 3 *v.,* **shammed, sham ming.**

sha man (shä′mən, shā′mən, *or* sham′ən), **1** man in American Indian tribes who was believed to have close contact with the spirit world, and who was skilled in curing diseases; medicine man. **2** a similar man in certain other societies. *n.*

sham ble (sham′bəl), **1** walk awkwardly or unsteadily: *The exhausted hikers shambled into camp.* **2** an awkward or unsteady walk. 1 *v.,* **sham bled, sham bling;** 2 *n.*

sham bles (sham′bəlz), **1** confusion; mess; general disorder: *to make a shambles of a clean room.* **2** place of butchery or of great bloodshed. *n. pl. or sing.*

shame (shām), **1** a painful feeling of having done something wrong, improper, or silly: *to blush with shame.* **2** cause to feel shame: *My silly mistake shamed me.* **3** drive or force by shame: *She was shamed into cleaning her room after guests saw it.* **4** a disgrace; dishonor: *bring shame to one's family.* **5** bring disgrace upon: *to shame one's family.* **6** fact to be sorry about; a pity: *It is a shame to be so wasteful.* **7** person or thing to be ashamed of; cause of disgrace. 1,4,6,7 *n.,* 2,3,5 *v.,* **shamed, sham ing.** —**sham′a ble, shame′a ble,** *adj.*

for shame!, shame on you!

put to shame, 1 disgrace; make ashamed. **2** surpass;

make dim by comparison: *Your careful work has put the rest of us to shame.*

shame faced (shām′fāst′), **1** showing shame and embarrassment. **2** bashful; shy. *adj.* —**shame′fac′ed ly,** *adv.*

shame ful (shām′fəl), causing shame; bringing disgrace. *adj.* —**shame′ful ly,** *adv.* —**shame′ful ness,** *n.*

shame less (shām′lis), **1** without shame. **2** not modest. *adj.* —**shame′less ly,** *adv.* —**shame′less ness,** *n.*

Sha mir (shä mir′), **Yit zhak,** born 1915, Israeli political leader, prime minister of Israel since 1983, alternating with Shimon Peres since 1984. *n.*

sham poo (sham pü′), **1** wash (the hair, the scalp, a rug, etc.) with a soapy or oily preparation. **2** a washing of the hair, the scalp, a rug, etc., with such a preparation. **3** the preparation used in this way. 1 *v.,* **sham pooed, sham poo ing;** 2,3 *n., pl.* **sham poos.** [*Shampoo* comes from Hindustani *chāmpō,* meaning "press, squeeze."]

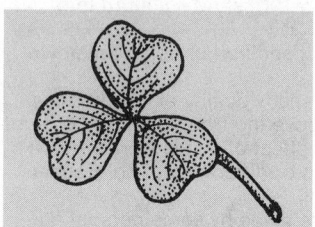

shamrock (def. 1)

sham rock (sham′rok), **1** a bright-green leaf composed of three parts. The shamrock is the national emblem of Ireland. **2** plant, such as white clover, that has leaves like this. *n.* [*Shamrock* comes from Irish *seamróg,* meaning "little clover."]

shang hai (shang′hī), **1** make unconscious by drugs, liquor, etc., and put on a ship to serve as a sailor. **2** force to do something by trickery or force. *v.,* **shanghaied, shang hai ing.**

Shang hai (shang′hī′), seaport in E China. *n.*

shank (shangk), **1** the part of the leg between the knee and the ankle. **2** the corresponding part in animals. **3** cut of meat from the upper part of the leg of an animal. **4** the whole leg. **5** any part like a leg, stem, or shaft. The shank of a fishhook is the straight part between the hook and the loop. *n.*

Shan non (shan′ən), river flowing from N Republic of Ireland southwest into the Atlantic. It is the most important river in Ireland. *n.*

shan't (shant), shall not.

shan tung (shan′tung *or* shan tung′), a silk, rayon, or cotton fabric having a rough, uneven surface. *n.*

Shan tung (shan′tung′), **1** province in NE China. **2** peninsula in the E part of this province. *n.*

shan ty[1] (shan′tē), a roughly built hut or cabin. *n., pl.* **shan ties.** —**shan′ty like′,** *adj.*

shan ty[2] (shan′tē), chantey. *n., pl.* **shan ties.**

shape (shāp), **1** the outward contour or outline; form; figure; appearance: *the shape of a triangle. A white shape stood at his bedside. A witch was supposed to take the shape of a cat or a bat.* **2** to form into a shape; mold: *The child shapes clay into balls. She shaped a clever reply.* **3** assume form; develop; take shape: *Her plan is shaping well.* **4** adapt in form: *That hat is shaped to your head.* **5** condition: *Athletes exercise to keep themselves in good shape.* **6** definite form; proper arrangement; order: *Take time to get your thoughts into shape.* **7** to plan; devise; direct: *to shape one's course in life.* 1,5,6 *n.,* 2-4,7 *v.,* **shaped, shap ing.** —**shap′a ble, shape′a ble,** *adj.*

shape up, 1 take on a certain form or appearance; develop. **2** show a certain tendency. **3** INFORMAL. behave properly; do what is expected.

take shape, have or take on a definite form.

shape less (shāp′lis), **1** without definite shape: *He wore a shapeless old hat.* **2** having an unattractive shape: *a shapeless figure. adj.* —**shape′less ly,** *adv.* —**shape′less ness,** *n.*

shape li ness (shāp′lē nis), shapely condition. *n.*

shape ly (shāp′lē), having a pleasing shape; well-formed. *adj.,* **shape li er, shape li est.**

shard (shärd), piece of broken earthenware or pottery. *n.*

share[1] (sher *or* shar), **1** part belonging to one individual; portion; part: *Do your share of the work. Each of the heirs was left an equal share of the property.* **2** each of the equal parts into which the ownership of a company or corporation is divided: *The ownership of this railroad is divided into several million shares.* **3** use together; enjoy together; have in common: *The sisters share the same room.* **4** divide into parts, each taking a part: *The child shared his candy with his sister.* **5** have a share; take part: *Everyone shared in making the picnic a success.* 1,2 *n.,* 3-5 *v.,* **shared, shar ing.** —**shar′a ble, share′a ble,** *adj.* —**shar′er,** *n.*
go shares, to share in something.

share[2] (sher *or* shar), plowshare. *n.*

share crop (sher′krop′ *or* shar′krop′), farm as a sharecropper. *v.,* **share cropped, share crop ping.**

share crop per (sher′krop′ər *or* shar′krop′ər), person who farms land for the owner in return for part of the crops. *n.*

share hold er (sher′hōl′dər *or* shar′hōl′dər), person owning shares of stock: *The railroad has many thousands of shareholders. n.*

shark[1] (shärk), a flesh-eating fish that generally is large and ferocious and lives in warm seas. Sharks are valued for their hides, flesh, and liver oil, and are sometimes dangerous to human beings. *n.* —**shark′like′,** *adj.*

shark[2] (shärk), a dishonest person who preys on others. *n.* [*Shark*[2] probably comes from German *Schurke,* meaning "scoundrel."]

sharp (shärp), **1** having a thin cutting edge or a fine point: *a sharp knife, a sharp pencil.* **2** having a point; not rounded: *a sharp nose, a sharp corner on a box.* **3** with a sudden change of direction: *a sharp turn.* **4** very cold: *sharp weather, a sharp morning.* **5** severe; biting: *sharp words.* **6** feeling somewhat like a cut or prick; affecting the senses keenly: *a sharp taste, a sharp noise, a sharp pain.* **7** clear; distinct: *the sharp contrast between black and white.* **8** quick; brisk: *a sharp walk, a sharp run.* **9** fierce; violent: *a sharp struggle.* **10** keen; eager: *a sharp desire, a sharp appetite.* **11** being aware of things quickly: *a sharp eye, sharp ears.* **12** watchful; wide-awake: *keep a sharp watch.* **13** quick in mind; shrewd; clever: *a sharp boy, a sharp lawyer, sharp at a bargain.* **14** promptly; exactly: *Come at one o'clock sharp.* **15** high in pitch; shrill: *a sharp voice.* **16** in music: **a** above the true pitch: *sing sharp.* **b** one half step or half tone above natural pitch: *Play a C sharp.* **c** such a tone or note. **d** sign (#) that shows such a tone. **e** (of a key) having sharps in the signature. **f** to raise in pitch. **17** in a sharp manner; in an alert manner; keenly: *Look sharp!* **18** suddenly: *pull a horse up sharp.* **19** SLANG. attractive; stylish. 1-13,15,16b,e, 19 *adj.,* 14,16a, 17,18 *adv.,* 16c,d *n.,* 16f *v.* —**sharp′ly,** *adv.* —**sharp′ness,** *n.*

sharp en (shär′pən), **1** make sharp: *sharpen a pencil. Sharpen your wits.* **2** become sharp. *v.* —**sharp′en er,** *n.*

sharp shoot er (shärp′shü′tər), person who shoots very well, especially with a rifle. *n.*

sharp-sight ed (shärp′sī′tid), **1** having sharp sight. **2** sharp-witted: *a sharp-sighted move. adj.*

sharp-wit ted (shärp′wit′id), having or showing a quick, keen mind. *adj.*

a hat	**i** it	**oi** oil	**ch** child	⎧ a in about
ā age	**ī** ice	**ou** out	**ng** long	⎪ e in taken
ä far	**o** hot	**u** cup	**sh** she	ə = ⎨ i in pencil
e let	**ō** open	**u̇** put	**th** thin	⎪ o in lemon
ē equal	**ô** order	**ü** rule	**ᴛʜ** then	⎩ u in circus
ėr term			**zh** measure	

shat ter (shat′ər), **1** break into pieces: *A stone shattered the window. The glass shattered.* **2** disturb greatly; destroy: *Her hopes were shattered. The great mental strain shattered his mind. v.*

shave (shāv), **1** remove hair with a razor; cut hair from (the face, chin, etc.) with a razor: *Father shaves every day. The actor shaved his head in order to portray a bald man.* **2** the cutting off of hair with a razor. **3** cut off (hair) with a razor. **4** cut off in thin slices: *She shaved the chocolate.* **5** cut very close. **6** come very close to; graze: *The car shaved the corner.* **7** a narrow miss or escape: *The car missed us, but it was a close shave.* 1,3-6 *v.,* **shaved, shaved** or **shav en, shav ing;** 2,7 *n.* [*Shave* comes from Old English *sceafan.*] —**shav′a ble, shave′a ble,** *adj.*

shav en (shā′vən), **1** shaved. **2** closely cut. **3** shaved; a past participle of **shave.** 1,2 *adj.,* 3 *v.*

shav er (shā′vər), **1** person who shaves. **2** instrument for shaving. **3** INFORMAL. youngster; small boy. *n.*

shav ing (shā′ving), **1** a very thin piece or slice. Shavings of wood are cut off by a plane. **2** act or process of cutting hair from the face, chin, etc., with a razor. *n.*

Sha vu ot (shä vü′ōt *or* shə vü′ōs), a Jewish festival observed about seven weeks after Passover, celebrating the harvest and the giving of the law to Moses; Pentecost. *n.*

Shaw (shô), **George Bernard,** 1856-1950, British dramatist, critic, novelist, and social reformer, born in Ireland. *n.*

shawl (shôl), a square or oblong piece of cloth to be worn about the shoulders or head. *n.* [*Shawl* comes from Persian *shāl.*] —**shawl′less,** *adj.* —**shawl′like′,** *adj.*

Shaw nee (shô nē′), member of a tribe of American Indians formerly living in eastern North America, especially Ohio, Tennessee, and South Carolina, and now living in Oklahoma. *n., pl.* **Shaw nee** or **Shaw nees.**

shay (shā), a light carriage; chaise. *n.*

she (shē), **1** girl, woman, or female animal spoken about or mentioned before: *My sister says she likes to read and her reading helps her in school.* **2** anything thought of as female and spoken about or mentioned before: *She was a fine old ship.* **3** a female: *Is the baby a he or a she?* 1,2 *pron., pl.* **they;** 3 *n.*

sheaf (shēf), bundle of things of the same sort: *a sheaf of wheat, a sheaf of arrows. n., pl.* **sheaves.** —**sheaf′like′,** *adj.*

shear (shir), **1** cut with shears or scissors. **2** cut the wool or fleece from. **3** cut close; cut off; cut. **4** to strip or

shear (def. 2)—shearing sheep

deprive as if by cutting: *The assembly had been shorn of its legislative powers.* *v.,* **sheared, sheared** or **shorn, shear ing.** —**shear′er,** *n.*

shears (shirz), **1** large scissors: *barber's shears.* **2** any cutting instrument resembling scissors: *grass shears, tin shears. n.pl.*

sheath (shēth), **1** case or covering for the blade of a sword, knife, etc. **2** any similar covering, especially on an animal or plant. *n., pl.* **sheaths** (shēᴛʜz *or* shēths). —**sheath′less,** *adj.* —**sheath′like′,** *adj.*

sheathe (shēᴛʜ), **1** put (a sword, etc.) into a sheath. **2** enclose in a case or covering: *a mummy sheathed in linen. The doors were sheathed in metal.* *v.,* **sheathed, sheath ing.** —**sheath′er,** *n.*

sheath ing (shē′ᴛʜing), casing; covering. The first covering of boards on a house is sheathing. *n.*

sheave (shēv), gather and tie into a sheaf or sheaves. *v.,* **sheaved, sheav ing.**

sheaves (shēvz), plural of **sheaf.** *n.*

She ba (shē′bə), **1** an ancient country in S Arabia. **2 Queen of,** (in the Bible) a queen who visited Solomon to learn of his great wisdom. *n.*

shed¹ (shed), a building used for shelter, storage, etc., usually having only one story: *a wagon shed, a train shed. n.* —**shed′like′,** *adj.*

shed² (shed), **1** pour out; let flow: *shed tears.* **2** cast off; let drop or fall: *The snake sheds its skin. The umbrella sheds water.* **3** get rid of: *shed one's worries, shed one's fears.* **4** scatter abroad; give forth: *The sun sheds light. Flowers shed perfume.* *v.,* **shed, shed ding.** —**shed′a ble, shed′da ble,** *adj.* —**shed′der,** *n.*

shed blood, destroy life; kill.

she'd (shēd; *unstressed* shid), **1** she had. **2** she would.

sheen (shēn), brightness; luster. Satin and polished silver have a sheen. *n.*

sheep (shēp), **1** mammal with a thick coat and hoofs that chews its cud. Sheep are related to goats and are raised for wool, meat, and skin. **2** person who is timid, weak, or stupid. *n., pl.* **sheep.** [*Sheep* comes from Old English *scēap.*] —**sheep′like′,** *adj.*

make sheep's eyes, give a longing, loving look.

sheep cote (shēp′kōt′), sheepfold. *n.*

sheep dog, collie or other dog trained to help a shepherd watch and tend sheep.

sheep fold (shēp′fōld′), pen or covered shelter for sheep. *n.*

sheep herd er (shēp′hėr′dər), person who watches and tends large numbers of sheep while they are grazing on unfenced land. *n.*

sheep ish (shē′pish), **1** awkwardly bashful or embarrassed: *a sheepish smile.* **2** like a sheep; timid; weak; stupid. *adj.* —**sheep′ish ly,** *adv.* —**sheep′ish ness,** *n.*

sheep skin (shēp′skin′), **1** skin of a sheep, especially with the wool on it. **2** leather or parchment made from the skin of a sheep. **3** INFORMAL. diploma. *n.*

sheer¹ (shir), **1** very thin; almost transparent: *Those sheer curtains will let the light through.* **2** unmixed with anything else; complete: *sheer nonsense, sheer weariness.* **3** straight up and down; very steep: *From the top of the wall it was a sheer drop of 100 feet to the water below. adj.* —**sheer′ness,** *n.*

sheer² (shir), turn from a course; turn aside; swerve: *The speeding car sheered away from the curb. v.*

sheer ly (shir′lē), absolutely; thoroughly; quite. *adv.*

sheet¹ (shēt), **1** a large piece of cotton, linen, or other cloth used to sleep on or under. **2** a broad, thin piece of anything: *a sheet of glass.* **3** a single piece of paper. **4** a broad, flat surface: *a sheet of water.* **5** cover with a sheet: *The windshield was sheeted with ice.* 1-4 *n.,* 5 *v.* —**sheet′less,** *adj.* —**sheet′like′,** *adj.*

sheet² (shēt), rope that controls the angle at which a sail is set. *n.*

sheet ing (shē′ting), cotton, linen, or other cloth for bed sheets. *n.*

sheet lighting, heat lightning.

sheet metal, metal in thin, flat pieces.

sheet music, music printed on unbound sheets of paper.

Shef field (shef′ēld), city in central England, famous for the manufacture of cutlery. *n.*

sheik or **sheikh** (shēk *or* shāk), an Arab chief or head of a family, village, or tribe. *n.*

shek el (shek′əl), **1** an ancient silver coin of the Hebrews that weighed about half an ounce. **2** an ancient unit of weight originating in Babylonia, equal to about half an ounce. *n.*

shel drake (shel′drāk′), **1** any of various large ducks of Europe and Asia. **2** merganser. *n., pl.* **shel drakes** or **shel drake.**

shelf (shelf), **1** a thin, flat piece of wood, metal, stone, etc., fastened to a wall or frame to hold things, such as books, dishes, etc. **2** anything like a shelf: *The ship hit a shelf of coral. n., pl.* **shelves.** —**shelf′like′,** *adj.*

on the shelf, put aside as no longer useful or desirable.

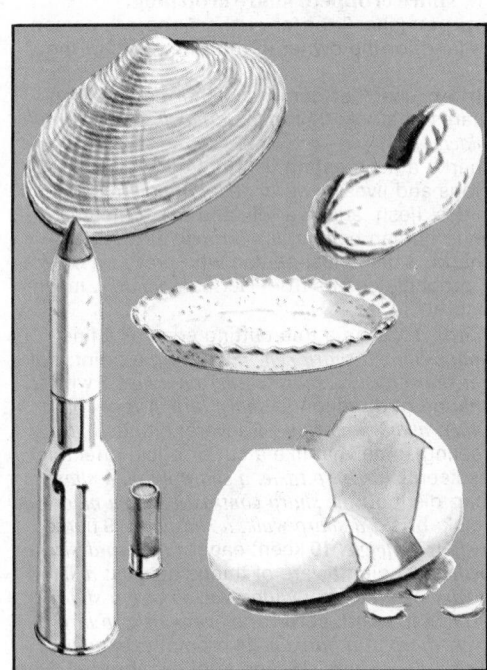

shell (defs. 1, 2, 3, 7, 8, and 9)

shell (shel), **1** the hard outside covering of certain animals. Oysters, turtles, and beetles all have shells. **2** the hard outside covering of a nut, seed, fruit, etc. **3** the hard outside covering of an egg. **4** tortoise shell as used in combs or ornaments. **5** take out of a shell: *shell peas.* **6** separate (grains of corn) from the cob. **7** something like a shell. The framework of a house, a very light racing boat, and a hollow case of pastry are called shells. **8** cartridge used in a rifle or shotgun. **9** a metal case filled with explosives that is fired by artillery and explodes either in the air or when it strikes something. **10** fire cannon at; bombard with shells: *The enemy shelled the town.* 1-4,7-9 *n.,* 5,6,10 *v.* —**shell′-like′,** *adj.*

come out of one's shell, stop being shy or reserved; join in conversation, etc., with others.

shell out, INFORMAL. hand over (money); pay out: *We had to shell out five dollars for the movie.*

she'll (shēl; *unstressed* shil), **1** she shall. **2** she will.

shel lac (shə lak′), **1** liquid that gives a smooth, shiny appearance to wood, metal, etc. Shellac is made from a sticky substance containing resin that is dissolved in alcohol. **2** put this liquid on; cover with this liquid. **3** INFORMAL. defeat completely. **1** *n.,* **2,3** *v.,* **shel lacked, shel lack ing.**

Shel ley (shel′ē), **1 Mary Wollstonecraft,** 1797-1851, English novelist, wife of Percy Bysshe Shelley. **2 Percy Bysshe** (bish), 1792-1822, English poet. *n.*

shell fish (shel′fish′), a water animal having a shell. Oysters, clams, crabs, and lobsters are shellfish. *n., pl.* **shell fish es** or **shell fish.**

shell shock, a nervous or mental disorder resulting from the strain of war.

shel ter (shel′tər), **1** something that covers or protects from weather, danger, or attack: *Trees are a shelter from the sun.* **2** protect; shield; hide: *shelter a fugitive.* **3** protection; refuge: *We took shelter from the storm in a barn.* **1,3** *n.,* **2** *v.* —**shel′ter er,** *n.* —**shel′ter less,** *adj.*

shelve (shelv), **1** put on a shelf: *to shelve the books in a library.* **2** lay aside: *Let us shelve that argument.* *v.,* **shelved, shelv ing.** —**shelv′er,** *n.*

shelves (shelvz), plural of **shelf.** *n.*

shelv ing (shel′ving), **1** wood, metal, etc., for shelves: *I ordered 40 feet of pine shelving.* **2** shelves. *n.*

Shen an do ah (shen′ən dō′ə), river flowing through N Virginia into the Potomac River. *n.*

she nan i gans (shə nan′ə gənz), INFORMAL. mischief or trickery. *n.pl.*

She ol (shē′ōl), a Hebrew name for the abode of the dead. *n.*

shep herd (shep′ərd), **1** person who takes care of sheep. **2** take care of: *to shepherd a flock.* **3** guide; direct: *The teacher shepherded the children safely out of the burning building.* **4** a spiritual guide; pastor. **1,4** *n.,* **2,3** *v.* —**shep′herd less,** *adj.* —**shep′herd like′,** *adj.*

shep herd ess (shep′ər dis), woman who takes care of sheep. *n., pl.* **shep herd ess es.**

sher bet (shėr′bət), a frozen dessert made of fruit juice, sugar, and water or milk. *n.* [*Sherbet* is from Turkish *şerbet,* which came from Arabic *sharbat,* meaning "a drink."]

Sher i dan (sher′ə dən), **Philip Henry,** 1831-1888, Union general in the Civil War. *n.*

sher iff (sher′if), the most important law-enforcing officer of a county. A sheriff appoints deputies who help to keep order in the county. *n.* [*Sheriff* is from Old English *scīrgerēfa,* which comes from *scīr,* meaning "shire," and *gerēfa,* meaning "a local official."]

Sher lock Holmes (shėr′lok). See **Holmes.**

Sher man (shėr′mən), **William Tecumseh,** 1820-1891, Union general in the Civil War. *n.*

sher ry (sher′ē), a strong wine. It varies in color from pale yellow to brown. *n., pl.* **sher ries.**

Sher wood Forest (shėr′wùd), a royal forest near Nottingham, where Robin Hood and his men are said to have lived.

she's (shēz; *unstressed* shiz), **1** she is. **2** she has.

Shet land Islands (shet′lənd), group of British islands northeast of Scotland. See **British Isles** for map.

Shetland pony, a small, sturdy, rough-coated pony. [This pony got its name from the *Shetland Islands,* where it was originally bred.]

Shetland sheep dog, a long-haired working dog resembling a small collie, originally from the Shetland Islands.

shib bo leth (shib′ə lith), any test word, watchword, or

pet phrase of a political party, a class, sect, etc. *n.*

shied (shīd), past tense and past participle of **shy².** *The horse shied and threw the rider. It had never shied like that before.* *v.*

shield (shēld), **1** piece of armor carried on the arm to protect the body in battle. **2** anything used to protect: *I turned up my collar as a shield against the cold wind.* **3** something shaped like a shield. **4** be a shield to; protect; defend: *They shielded me from unjust punishment.* **1-3** *n.,* **4** *v.* —**shield′less,** *adj.* —**shield′like′,** *adj.*

shift (shift), **1** to move or change from one place, position, person, sound, etc., to another: *The wind has shifted to the southeast. I shifted the heavy bag from one hand to the other. Don't try to shift the blame to someone else.* **2** a change of direction, position, attitude, etc.: *a shift of the wind, a shift in policy.* **3** group of workers who work during the same period of time: *She is on the night shift this week.* **4** time during which such a group works. **5** way of getting on; scheme; trick: *The child tried every shift to avoid going to bed.* **6** manage to get along; contrive: *I left home at an early age and had to shift for myself.* **7** change the position of (the gears of an automobile). **1,6,7** *v.,* **2-5** *n.* —**shift′a ble,** *adj.* —**shift′er,** *n.* —**shift′ing ly,** *adv.*

make shift, 1 manage to get along; do as well as one can. **2** manage with effort or difficulty.

shift i ly (shif′tə lē), in a shifty manner. *adv.*

shift i ness (shif′tē nis), character or quality of being shifty. *n.*

shift less (shift′lis), lazy; inefficient. *adj.* —**shift′less ly,** *adv.* —**shift′less ness,** *n.*

shift y (shif′tē), not straightforward; tricky: *shifty eyes, a shifty person. adj.,* **shift i er, shift i est.**

shil le lagh or **shil la lah** (shə lā′lē *or* shə lā′lə), IRISH. a stick to hit with; cudgel. *n.* [The *shillelagh* gets its name from *Shillelagh,* a town in Ireland.]

shil ling (shil′ing), **1** a former unit of money in Great Britain equal to 12 pence or ¹/₂₀ of a pound. **2** a British coin equal to one shilling. *n.*

shil ly-shal ly (shil′ē shal′ē), **1** wavering; hesitating; undecided. **2** be undecided; hesitate. **3** inability to decide; hesitation. **1** *adj.,* **2** *v.,* **shil ly-shal lied, shil ly-shal ly ing; 3** *n., pl.* **shil ly-shal lies.**

shim mer (shim′ər), **1** gleam faintly: *Both the sea and the sand shimmered in the moonlight.* **2** a faint gleam or shine: *The pearls have a beautiful shimmer.* **1** *v.,* **2** *n.* —**shim′mer ing ly,** *adv.*

shim mer y (shim′ər ē), shimmering; gleaming softly. *adj.*

shim my (shim′ē), **1** an unusual shaking or vibration: *a*

Shetland pony
32 to 46 in.
(81 to 117 cm.)
high at the shoulder

dangerous shimmy of a ladder. **2** to shake; vibrate. 1 *n., pl.* **shim mies; 2** *v.,* **shim mied, shim my ing.**

shin (shin), **1** the front part of the leg from the knee to the ankle. **2** climb by clasping or holding fast with the hands or arms and legs and drawing oneself up: *I shinned up the tree.* 1 *n.,* 2 *v.,* **shinned, shin ning.**

shin bone (shin′bōn′), the inner and thicker of the two bones of the leg between the knee and the ankle; tibia. *n.*

shin dig (shin′dig), INFORMAL. a merry or noisy dance, party, etc. *n.*

shine (shīn), **1** send out light; be bright with light; reflect light; glow: *The sun shines. His face is shining with soap and water.* **2** light; brightness: *the shine of a lamp.* **3** luster; polish: *the shine of a new penny.* **4** fair weather; sunshine: *He goes to school rain or shine.* **5** do very well; be brilliant; excel: *She shines at sports.* **6** make bright; polish: *shine shoes.* **7** polish put on shoes. **8** cause to shine: *shine a light.* 1,5,6,8 *v.,* **shone** (or **shined** especially for 6), **shining;** 2-4,7 *n.* —**shine′less,** *adj.*

shine up to, SLANG. try to please and get the friendship of.

take a shine to, SLANG. become fond of; like.

shin er (shī′nər), **1** person or thing that shines. **2** a small American freshwater fish with glistening scales. It is related to the carp. **3** SLANG. black eye. *n.*

shin gle[1] (shing′gəl), **1** a thin piece of asbestos, wood, etc., used to cover roofs, walls, etc. Shingles are laid in overlapping rows with the thicker ends showing. **2** cover with shingles: *shingle a roof.* **3** a small signboard, especially one outside a doctor's or lawyer's office. **4** cut (the hair) short. **5** a short haircut. 1,3,5 *n.,* 2,4 *v.,* **shin gled, shin gling.** —**shin′gler,** *n.*

shin gle[2] (shing′gəl), loose stones or pebbles that lie on the seashore; coarse gravel. *n.*

shin gles (shing′gəlz), a virus disease that causes pain in certain nerves and an outbreak of spots and blisters on the skin in the area of the affected nerves. *n. sing. or pl.* [*Shingles* can be traced back to Latin *cingulus,* meaning "girdle." The blisters frequently appear as a ring or line around the waist.]

shin i ness (shī′nē nis), shiny character or condition; sheen. *n.*

shin ing (shī′ning), glowing; brilliant; outstanding: *a shining star, a shining career.* *adj.* —**shin′ing ly,** *adv.*

shin ny[1] (shin′ē), **1** a simple kind of hockey, played with a ball or the clubs curved at one end. **2** play shinny. 1 *n., pl.* **shin nies; 2** *v.,* **shin nied, shin ny ing.**

shin ny[2] (shin′ē), climb by holding tight with the arms and legs and drawing oneself up: *shinny up a tree.* *v.,* **shin nied, shin ny ing.**

shin splints, pain and inflammation of muscles in the lower legs, caused by overexercise, as in running or rapid walking on a hard surface.

Shin to (shin′tō), the native religion of Japan, primarily a system of nature worship and ancestor worship. *n.* [*Shinto* is from Japanese *shintō,* which came from Chinese *shin tao,* meaning "way of the gods."]

Shin to ism (shin′tō iz′əm), the Shinto religion. *n.*

shin y (shī′nē), **1** shining; bright: *a shiny new penny.* **2** worn to a glossy smoothness: *a coat shiny from hard wear.* *adj.,* **shin i er, shin i est.** —**shin′i ly,** *adv.*

ship (ship), **1** any large vessel for travel on water, such as a steamship, frigate, or galley. **2** a large sailing vessel, especially one with three masts and a bowsprit. **3** an airship, airplane, spacecraft, etc. **4** officers and crew of a ship. **5** travel on a ship, especially as a member of the crew; sail: *He shipped as a cook.* **6** send or carry from one place to another by a ship, train, truck, etc.: *Did you ship it by express or by freight?* **7** INFORMAL. send off; get rid

of. **8** take in (water) over the side, as a boat does when the waves break over it. **9** fix in a ship or boat in its proper place for use: *ship a rudder.* 1-4 *n.,* 5-9 *v.,* **shipped, ship ping.** —**ship′less,** *adj.*

when one's ship comes home or **when one's ship comes in,** when one's fortune is made; when one has money.

-ship, *suffix forming nouns from other nouns.* **1** office, position, or occupation of ____: *Governorship = office of governor. Authorship = occupation of an author.* **2** quality or condition of being ____: *Partnership = condition of being a partner.* **3** act, power, or skill of ____: *Craftsmanship = skill of a craftsman.*

ship biscuit, hardtack.

ship board (ship′bôrd′). **on shipboard,** on or inside a ship. *n.*

ship build er (ship′bil′dər), person who designs or builds ships. *n.*

ship build ing (ship′bil′ding), the designing or building of ships. *n.*

ship load (ship′lōd′), a full load for a ship. *n.*

ship mas ter (ship′mas′tər), master, commander, or captain of a ship. *n.*

ship mate (ship′māt′), a fellow sailor on a ship. *n.*

ship ment (ship′mənt), **1** act of shipping goods: *A thousand boxes of oranges were ready for shipment.* **2** goods sent at one time to a person or company: *We received two shipments of boxes from the factory.* *n.*

ship own er (ship′ō′nər), person who owns a ship or ships. *n.*

ship per (ship′ər), person who ships goods. *n.*

ship ping (ship′ing), **1** the act or business of sending goods by water, rail, etc. **2** ships, especially ships of a nation, city, or business: *Much of the world's shipping passes through the Panama Canal each year.* *n.*

ship shape (ship′shāp′), in good order; trim. *adj.*

ship's papers, the documents giving information as to the ship's nationality, owner, etc., which every ship must carry.

ship worm (ship′wėrm′), a long, wormlike sea animal covered with a shell. Shipworms burrow into the timbers of ships and wharves. *n.*

ship wreck (ship′rek′), **1** destruction or loss of a ship: *Only two people were saved from the shipwreck.* **2** a wrecked ship. **3** destruction; ruin: *The shipwreck of her plans discouraged her.* **4** wreck, ruin, or destroy. **5** suffer shipwreck. 1-3 *n.,* 4,5 *v.*

Shinto—The temple gate is the Shinto symbol.

ship yard (ship′yärd′), place near the water where ships are built or repaired. *n.*

shire (shīr), one of the counties into which Great Britain is divided, especially one whose name ends in *-shire: Yorkshire. n.*

shirk (shėrk), avoid or get out of doing (work, a duty, etc.): *You will lose your job if you continue to shirk your responsibilities.* *v.* —**shirk′er,** *n.*

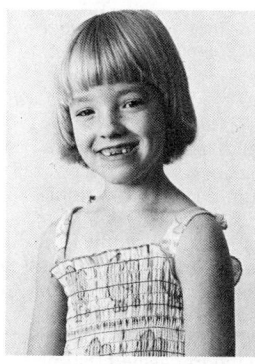

shirr (def. 1)
The top of her
dress was **shirred.**

shirr (shėr), **1** draw up or gather (cloth) on parallel threads. **2** a shirred arrangement of cloth, etc. **3** bake (eggs) in a shallow dish with butter, etc. 1,3 *v.*, 2 *n.*

shirt (shėrt), **1** garment for the upper part of the body. **2** undershirt. *n.* —**shirt′less,** *adj.* —**shirt′like′,** *adj.*

keep one's shirt on, SLANG. stay calm; keep one's temper.

shirt ing (shėr′ting), cloth used for making shirts. *n.*

shirt waist (shėrt′wāst′), **1** a woman's or girl's shirtlike blouse, worn with a separate skirt. **2** a one-piece dress with a shirtlike top. *n.*

shish ke bab (shish′ kə bob′), small pieces of seasoned meat, and sometimes tomatoes and onions, roasted and served on a skewer.

Shiv a (shē′və), one of three chief Hindu divinities, called "the Destroyer." *n.*

shiv er[1] (shiv′ər), **1** shake with cold, fear, etc.: *I crept shivering into bed.* **2** a shaking from cold, fear, etc. 1 *v.*, 2 *n.* —**shiv′er er,** *n.* —**shiv′er ing ly,** *adv.*

shiv er[2] (shiv′ər), **1** break into small pieces: *I shivered the mirror with a hammer.* **2** a small piece; splinter: *There were shivers of glass on the floor.* 1 *v.*, 2 *n.*

shiv er y (shiv′ər ē), **1** quivering from cold, fear, etc.; shivering. **2** chilly. **3** causing shivers: *a shivery experience.* *adj.*

shoal[1] (shōl), **1** place in a sea, lake, or stream where the water is shallow. **2** sandbank or sandbar that makes the water shallow, especially one which can be seen at low tide: *The ship was wrecked on the shoals.* **3** shallow. **4** become shallow. 1,2 *n.*, 3 *adj.*, 4 *v.*

shoal[2] (shōl), **1** a large number; crowd: *We saw a shoal of fish in the water.* **2** form into a shoal; crowd together. 1 *n.*, 2 *v.*

shoat (shōt), a young pig that no longer suckles. *n.* Also, **shote.**

shock[1] (shok), **1** a sudden, violent shake, blow, or crash: *Earthquake shocks are often felt in Japan.* **2** a sudden, violent, or upsetting disturbance: *Her death was a great shock to her family.* **3** cause to feel surprise, horror, or disgust: *That child's bad language shocks everyone.* **4** condition of physical collapse or depression, together with a sudden drop in blood pressure, often resulting in unconsciousness. Shock may set in after a severe injury, great loss of blood, or a sudden emotional disturbance. **5** disturbance produced by an electric current passing through the body. **6** give an electric shock to. 1,2,4,5 *n.*, 3,6 *v.* —**shock′a ble,** *adj.* —**shock′er,** *n.* —**shock′like′,** *adj.*

shock[2] (shok), **1** group of cornstalks or bundles of grain set up on end together in order to dry. **2** make into shocks. 1 *n.*, 2 *v.* —**shock′er,** *n.*

shock[3] (shok), a thick, bushy mass: *a shock of red hair.* *n.*

shock ab sorb er (ab sôr′bər), device consisting of springs, hydraulic pistons, etc., used on automobiles, airplanes, etc., to absorb the force of sudden impacts.

shock ing (shok′ing), **1** causing intense and painful surprise: *shocking news.* **2** offensive; disgusting; revolting: *a shocking sight.* *adj.* —**shock′ing ly,** *adv.*

shock troops, troops chosen and specially trained for making attacks.

shock wave, disturbance of the atmosphere created by the movement of an aircraft, rocket, etc., at a velocity greater than that of sound.

shod (shod), past tense and past participle of **shoe.** *The blacksmith shod the horses. They had never been shod before.* *v.*

shod i ly (shod′l ē), in a shoddy manner. *adv.*

shod i ness (shod′ē nis), shoddy quality or condition. *n.*

shod dy (shod′ē), **1** of inferior quality: *shoddy furniture.* **2** mean; shabby: *a shoddy trick.* *adj.*, **shod di er, shod di est.**

shoe (shü), **1** an outer covering for a person's foot. Shoes are made of leather, vinyl, etc. **2** thing like a shoe in shape or use. **3** a horseshoe. **4** the part of a brake that presses on a wheel to slow it down or stop it. **5** furnish with a shoe or shoes: *A blacksmith shoes horses. Her feet were shod with silver slippers.* **6** protect or arm at the point; edge or face with metal: *a stick shod with steel.* 1-4 *n.*, 5,6 *v.*, **shod, shoe ing.** [*Shoe* comes from Old English *scōh.*] —**shoe′less,** *adj.*

in another's shoes, in another's place, situation, or circumstances.

shoe horn (shü′hôrn′), a curved piece of metal, horn, etc., used to help slip a shoe more easily over the heel. *n.*

shoe lace (shü′lās′), cord, braid, or leather strip for fastening a shoe. *n.*

shoe mak er (shü′mā′kər), person who makes or mends shoes. *n.*

shoe string (shü′string′), **1** shoelace. **2** a very small amount of money used to start or carry on a business, investment, etc.: *The company was formed on a shoestring.* *n.*

shoe tree, a device shaped like a foot, placed in a shoe to keep it in shape or to stretch it.

sho far (shō′fär *or* shō′fər), a ram's horn sounded during certain Jewish religious services, especially on Rosh Hashanah and Yom Kippur. *n., pl.* **sho froth** (shō′frōs *or* shō frōt′). [*Shofar* comes from Hebrew *shōphār.*]

shone (shōn), a past tense and a past participle of **shine.** *The sun shone all last week. It has not shone since.* *v.*

shoo (shü), **1** an exclamation used to scare away hens, birds, etc. **2** scare or drive away by calling "Shoo!": *Shoo those flies away from the sugar.* 1 *interj.*, 2 *v.*, **shooed, shoo ing.**

shook (shůk), past tense of **shake.** *They shook hands.* *v.*

shoot (shüt), **1** hit, wound, or kill with a bullet, arrow, etc.: *He shot a rabbit.* **2** send swiftly: *A bow shoots an arrow. She shot question after question at us.* **3** fire or use (a gun, etc.): *shoot a rifle. They shoot at the target.* **4** send a bullet: *This gun shoots straight.* **5** a trip, party, or contest for shooting. **6** move suddenly and swiftly: *A car shot by us. Flames shot up from the burning house.* **7** pass quickly along, through, over, or under: *Only a shallow boat can shoot this stretch of rapids.* **8** go sharply through part of the body: *Pain shot up her arm from her hurt finger.* **9** come forth from the ground; grow; grow rapidly: *Buds shoot forth in the spring.* **10** a new part growing out; young branch: *The rosebush is putting out new shoots.* **11** take (a picture) with a camera; photograph. **12** project sharply: *a cape that shoots out into the sea.* **13** a sloping trough for conveying coal, grain, etc., to a lower level; chute. **14** vary with some different color, etc.: *The fabric was shot with threads of gold.* **15** send (a ball, puck, marble, etc.) toward the goal, pocket, etc. 1-4,6-9,11,12,14,15 *v.*, **shot, shoot ing;** 5,10,13 *n.* —**shoot′er,** *n.*

shooting star, meteor seen falling or darting through the sky at night.

shop (shop), **1** place where things are sold; store: *a small dress shop.* **2** visit stores to look at or to buy things: *We shopped all morning for a coat.* **3** place where things are made or repaired: *He works in a carpenter's shop.* **4** place where a certain kind of work is done: *We got our hair cut at a barber shop.* **5** schoolroom equipped for woodworking, auto repair, metalworking, printing, and other skills. **6** course offering instruction in these skills. 1,3-6 *n.*, 2 *v.*, **shopped, shop ping.**

set up shop, start work or business.

talk shop, talk about one's work or occupation.

shop keep er (shop′kē′pər), person who owns or manages a shop or store. *n.*

shop lift (shop′lift′), steal goods from a store while pretending to be a customer. *v.* —**shop′lift′er,** *n.*

shop lift ing (shop′lif′ting), a stealing of goods from a store while pretending to be a customer. *n.*

shop per (shop′ər), person who visits stores to look at or buy things. *n.*

shop ping (shop′ing), act of visiting stores to look at or to buy things: *We usually do our shopping on Saturday morning. n.*

shopping center, group of stores built as a unit on or near a main road, especially in a suburban or new community. Most shopping centers have large areas for parking automobiles.

shop talk (shop′tôk′), talk about one's work or occupation, especially outside of working hours. *n.*

shop worn (shop′wôrn′), soiled or damaged by being displayed or handled in a store. *adj.*

shore¹ (shôr), **1** the land at the edge of a sea, lake, etc. **2** land: *After so many months at sea, it was good to be on shore again. n.*

off shore, in or on the water, not far from the shore.

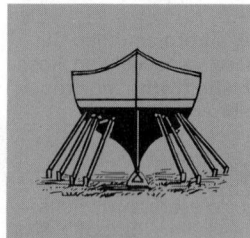

shore² (def. 1)
shores supporting
a ship frame

shore² (shôr), **1** a prop placed against or beneath something to support it. **2** to prop up or support with shores. 1 *n.*, 2 *v.*, **shored, shor ing.**

shore bird, any bird that is often on the shores of seas, inlets, lakes, etc.

shore leave, leave for a member of a ship's crew to go ashore.

shore line (shôr′līn′), line where shore and water meet. *n.*

shore ward (shôr′wərd), toward the shore: *The winds blew shoreward* (*adv.*). *We felt the shoreward breeze* (*adj.*). *adv., adj.*

shorn (shôrn), **1** a past participle of **shear.** *The sheep was shorn of its wool.* **2** sheared. 1 *v.*, 2 *adj.*

short (shôrt), **1** not long; of small extent from end to end: *a short distance, a short time, a short street.* **2** not tall: *a short man, short grass.* **3** not coming up to the right amount, measure, standard, etc.: *I would like to buy this, but I'm short a dime.* **4** not having enough; scanty: *The prisoners were kept on short allowance of food.* **5** so brief as to be rude: *She was so short with me that I felt hurt.* **6** failing to reach the point aimed at: *I threw the ball short.* **7** in a short manner; abruptly; suddenly: *The horse stopped short.* **8** breaking or crumbling easily; crisp or crumbly. Pastry is made short with butter or other shortening. **9** (of vowels or syllables) taking a comparatively short time to speak. The vowels are short in *fat, net, pin, not, up.* **10** shorts, *pl.* **a** short, loose trousers reaching to above the knees. Shorts are worn by men, women, or children in hot weather or when playing tennis, running races, etc. **b** a similar men's or boys' undergarment. **11** a short circuit. **12** to short-circuit. 1-5,8,9 *adj.*, 6,7 *adv.*, 10,11 *n.*, 12 *v.* [*Short* comes from Old English *sceort.*] —**short′ness,** *n.*

cut short, end suddenly; interrupt: *Sickness cut short my vacation.*

fall short, 1 fail to reach. **2** be insufficient.

for short, in order to make shorter: *Robert was called Rob for short.*

in short, briefly.

run short, 1 not have enough. **2** not be enough.

short for, a shortened form of: *The word "phone" is short for "telephone."*

short of, 1 not up to; less than: *Nothing short of your best work will satisfy me.* **2** not having enough of. **3** on the near side of.

short age (shôr′tij), too small an amount; lack; deficiency: *The nation had a serious shortage of grain due to poor crops. n.*

short bread (shôrt′bred′), a rich cake or cookie that crumbles easily. *n.*

short cake (shôrt′kāk′), **1** cake made of rich biscuit dough and shortening, covered or filled with berries or other fruit. **2** a sweet cake filled with fruit. *n.*

short-change (shôrt′chānj′), **1** give less than the right change to. **2** cheat: *be short-changed in getting an education. v.*, **short-changed, short-chang ing.** —**short′-chang′er,** *n.*

short circuit, a side circuit of electricity like that formed when insulation wears off wires which touch each other or another conductor. A short circuit may cause a fire unless it blows a fuse or activates a circuit breaker.

short-cir cuit (shôrt′sėr′kit), **1** make a short circuit in. **2** make a short circuit. *v.*

short com ing (shôrt′kum′ing), flaw in one's character or conduct; fault; defect: *Rudeness is one of her shortcomings. n.*

short cut (shôrt′kut′), a less distant or quicker way. *n.*

short en (shôrt′n), **1** make shorter; cut off: *The new highway shortens the trip. I've had my coat shortened.* **2** become shorter: *The days shorten in November in this country.* **3** make rich with butter, lard, etc.: *shorten a cake. v.* —**short′en er,** *n.*

short en ing (shôrt′n ing), **1** butter, lard, or other fat, used to make pastry, cake, etc., crisp or crumbly. **2** act of a person or thing that shortens. *n.*

short hand (shôrt′hand′), **1** method of rapid writing which uses symbols for abbreviations in place of letters,

a hat	**i** it	**oi** oil	**ch** child		a in about
ā age	**ī** ice	**ou** out	**ng** long		e in taken
ä far	**o** hot	**u** cup	**sh** she	**ə** =	i in pencil
e let	**ō** open	**u̇** put	**th** thin		o in lemon
ē equal	**ô** order	**ü** rule	**ŦH** then		u in circus
ėr term			**zh** measure		

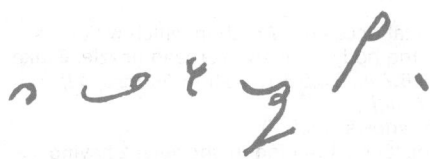

shorthand (def. 2) for "Your letter was received today." (Gregg system)

words, phrases, etc.; stenography. **2** writing in such symbols. *n.*

short-hand ed (shôrt′han′did), not having enough workers, helpers, etc. *adj.*

short horn (shôrt′hôrn′), breed of cattle with short horns, raised for beef. *n.*

short ish (shôr′tish), rather short. *adj.*

short-lived (shôrt′līvd′ *or* shôrt′livd′), living only a short time; lasting a short time. *adj.* —**short′-lived′ness,** *n.*

short ly (shôrt′lē), **1** in a short time; before long; soon: *I will be with you shortly.* **2** in a few words; briefly. **3** briefly and rudely; curtly. *adv.*

short-range (shôrt′rānj′), not reaching far in time or distance; not long-range: *a short-range forecast. adj.*

short shrift, little or no consideration, mercy, or delay in dealing with a person or problem: *Violators of these new regulations will get short shrift.*

short sight ed (shôrt′sī′tid), **1** nearsighted. **2** lacking in foresight; not prudent. *adj.* —**short′sight′ed ly,** *adv.* —**short′sight′ed ness,** *n.*

short stop (shôrt′stop′), a baseball player stationed between second and third base. *n.*

short story, a prose story which usually describes a single event, has a limited number of characters, and is much shorter than a novel.

short-tem pered (shôrt′tem′pərd), easily made angry; quick-tempered. *adj.*

short wave (shôrt′wāv′), **1** a radio wave having a wavelength of 60 meters or less. **2** transmit by short waves. **1** *n.,* **2** *v.,* **short waved, short wav ing.**

short-wind ed (shôrt′win′did), getting out of breath very easily; having difficulty in breathing. *adj.*

Sho sho ne (shō shō′nē) Shoshoni. *n., pl.* **Sho sho ne** *or* **Sho sho nes.**

Sho sho ni (shō shō′nē), member of a tribe of American Indians of Wyoming, Idaho, Utah, Colorado, and Nevada. *n., pl.* **Sho sho ni** *or* **Sho sho nis.**

Shos ta ko vich (shos′tə kō′vich), **Dimitri,** 1906-1975, Russian composer. *n.*

shot[1] (shot), **1** discharge of a gun or cannon: *We heard two shots.* **2** act of shooting. **3** tiny balls of lead, steel, etc., fired from a shotgun. **4** a single ball of lead, steel, etc., for a gun or cannon. **5** an attempt to hit by shooting: *That was a good shot, and it hit the mark.* **6** the distance a weapon can shoot; range: *We were within rifle shot of the fort.* **7** person who shoots: *She is a good shot.* **8** something like a shot. An aimed throw or stroke in a game is sometimes called a shot. **9** injection of a vaccine or drug: *a polio shot, a tetanus shot.* **10** a remark aimed at some person or thing. **11** an attempt; try: *take a shot at the job.* **12** a heavy metal ball used in the shot-put. **13** picture taken with a camera; motion-picture record of a scene. **14** INFORMAL. a drink, usually a jigger, of alcoholic liquor. *n., pl.* **shots** (*or* **shot** for 3). —**shot′less,** *adj.* —**shot′like′,** *adj.*

shot through with, full of: *a composition shot through with errors.*

shot[2] (shot), **1** past tense and past participle of **shoot.** *I shot the gun.* **2** woven so as to show a play of colors: *blue silk shot with gold.* **3** INFORMAL. that has been used up, worn out, or ruined. **1** *v.,* **2,3** *adj.*

shote (shōt), shoat. *n.*

shot gun (shot′gun′), gun with no grooves in its barrel, for firing cartridges filled with small shot. *n.*

shot-put (shot′pu̇t′), contest in which a person sends a heavy metal ball through the air as far as possible with one push. *n.*

should (shu̇d), **1** past tense of **shall.** "I said that I should come next week" means that I said, "I shall come next week." **2** ought to: *You should try to make fewer mistakes.* **3** *Should* is used to express uncertainty. *If it should rain, I won't go.* **4** *Should* is used in speaking of something which might have happened but did not. *I should have gone if you had asked me.* **5** *Should* is used to express a condition or reason for something. *He was pardoned on the condition that he should leave the country. v.*

shoul der (shōl′dər), **1** the part of the body to which an arm, foreleg, or wing is attached. **2** the part of a garment that covers a shoulder. **3 shoulders,** *pl.* the two shoulders and the part of the back between them: *The man carried a trunk on his shoulders.* **4** cut of meat consisting of an upper foreleg and its adjoining parts. **5** take upon or support with the shoulder or shoulders: *shoulder a pack.* **6** bear (a burden, blame, etc.); assume (responsibility, expense, etc.): *She shouldered the responsibility of sending her niece to college.* **7** something that sticks out like a shoulder: *the shoulder of a hill.* **8** edge of a road, often unpaved. **9** push with the shoulders: *shoulder one's way through a crowd.* **1-4,7,8** *n.,* **5,6,9** *v.* [*Shoulder* comes from Old English *sculdor.*] —**shoul′der like′,** *adj.*

put one's shoulder to the wheel, make a great effort.

shoulder to shoulder, **1** side by side; together. **2** with united effort.

straight from the shoulder, frankly; directly.

turn a cold shoulder to, show dislike for; shun; avoid.

shoulder blade, the flat, triangular bone of either shoulder, in the upper back; scapula.

shoulder strap, **1** strap worn over the shoulder to hold a garment up. **2** an ornamental strip fastened on the shoulder of an officer's uniform to show rank.

should n't (shu̇d′nt), should not.

shout (shout), **1** call or cry loudly and vigorously: *I shouted for help when the boat sank. Somebody shouted, "Fire!" The crowd shouted with laughter.* **2** a loud, vigorous call or cry: *Shouts of joy rang through the halls.* **3** express by a shout or shouts. **1,3** *v.,* **2** *n.* —**shout′er,** *n.* —**shout′ing ly,** *adv.*

shout down, to silence by very loud talk.

shove (shuv), **1** move forward or along by the application of force from behind; push: *She shoved the bookcase into place.* **2** push roughly or rudely; jostle: *Someone shoved me out of the line. The people shoved to get on the crowded bus.* **3** a push: *We gave the boat a shove which sent it far out into the water.* **1,2** *v.,* **shoved, shov ing;** **3** *n.* —**shov′er,** *n.*

shove off, **1** push away from the shore; row away. **2** INFORMAL. leave a place; start on one's way.

shov el (shuv′əl), **1** tool with a broad blade or scoop attached to a long handle, used to lift and throw loose matter: *a coal shovel, a snow shovel.* **2** lift and throw with a shovel: *They shoveled the sand into the truck.* **3** make with a shovel: *They shoveled a path through the snow.* **4** a shovelful. **5** throw or lift as if with a shovel: *The hungry* *child greedily shoveled the food into her mouth.* 1,4 *n.,* 2,3,5 *v.,* **shov eled, shov el ing** or **shov elled, shov el ling.**

shov el er (shuv′ə lər), **1** person or thing that shovels. **2** kind of freshwater duck with a broad, flat bill. *n.*

shov el ful (shuv′əl fůl), as much as a shovel can hold. *n., pl.* **shov el fuls.**

show (shō), **1** let be seen; put in sight; display: *She showed me her rock collection.* **2** reveal; manifest; disclose: *show great energy, show signs of fear.* **3** be in sight; appear; be seen: *Anger showed in his face.* **4** point out: *They showed us the way to town.* **5** direct; guide: *Show them out.* **6** make clear; explain. **7** make clear to; explain to: *Show us how to do the problem.* **8** prove: *She showed that it was true.* **9** grant; give: *show mercy, show favor.* **10** a display: *The jewels made a fine show.* **11** a display for effect: *He put on a show of learning to impress us.* **12** any kind of public exhibition or display: *We are going to the flower show and to the automobile show.* **13** a play, motion picture, etc., or a performance of one of these: *The late show starts at 11:00.* **14** a showing: *The club voted by a show of hands.* **15** appearance: *There is some show of truth in his excuse.* **16** false appearance; pretense: *hide one's dislike by a show of friendship.* **17** object of scorn; something odd; queer sight: *Don't make a show of yourself.* **18** INFORMAL. operation or undertaking: *They are running the whole show.* 1-9 *v.,* **showed, shown** or **showed, show ing;** 10-18 *n.* —**show′a ble,** *adj.* —**show′er,** *n.* —**show′less,** *adj.*

for show, for effect; to attract attention.

show off, make a show (of); display (one's good points, etc.): *The toddler liked to show off his new shoes.*

show up, 1 expose. **2** stand out. **3** put in an appearance.

show bill

show bill, poster, placard, or the like, advertising a show.

show boat (shō′bōt′), a river steamboat with a theater for plays. Showboats carry their own actors and make frequent stops to give performances. *n.*

show business, the industry or world of entertainment.

show case (shō′kās′), **1** a glass case to display and protect articles in a store, museum, etc. **2** any display or exhibit. *n.*

show down (shō′doun′), a meeting face to face in order to settle an issue or dispute: *The showdown between the mayor and the council over the new budget resulted in a welcome compromise.* *n.*

show er (shou′ər), **1** a short fall of rain. **2** rain for a short time. **3** wet with a shower; spray; sprinkle. **4** anything like a fall of rain: *a shower of hail, a shower of tears, a shower of sparks from an engine.* **5** send in a steady stream; pour down: *Her rich aunt showered gifts upon her.* **6** party for giving presents to a woman about to be married or on

some other special occasion. **7** bath in which water pours down on the body from an overhead nozzle. **8** take such a bath. 1,4,6,7 *n.,* 2,3,5,8 *v.* —**show′er less,** *adj.* —**show′er like′,** *adj.*

shower bath, shower (def. 7).

show er y (shou′ər ē), **1** raining in showers. **2** having many showers. **3** like a shower. *adj.* —**show′er i ness,** *n.*

show i ly (shō′ə lē), in a showy manner. *adv.*

show i ness (shō′ē nis), quality of being showy; display. *n.*

show ing (shō′ing), **1** show; display; exhibition: *a current showing of paintings.* **2** manner of appearance or performance: *make a good showing.* *n.*

show man (shō′mən), **1** person who manages a show. **2** person skilled in presenting things in a dramatic and exciting way. *n., pl.* **show men.**

show man ship (shō′mən ship), skill or practice of a showman. *n.*

shown (shōn), a past participle of **show.** *We were shown many tricks by the magician.* *v.*

show-off (shō′ôf′), person who shows off by always trying to attract attention: *That athlete is a terrible show-off.* *n.*

show piece (shō′pēs′), anything displayed as an outstanding example of its kind. *n.*

show room (shō′rüm′ *or* shō′rům′), room used for the display of goods or merchandise. *n.*

show window, window in the front of a store, where things are shown for sale.

show y (shō′ē), **1** making a display; likely to attract attention; striking: *Peacocks are showy birds.* **2** too bright and flashy to be in good taste. **3** making a display to impress others; doing things to attract attention. *adj.,* **show i er, show i est.**

shpt., shipment.

shrank (shrangk), a past tense of **shrink.** *My shirt shrank in the wash.* *v.*

shrap nel (shrap′nəl), **1** shell filled with fragments of metal and powder, set to explode in midair and scatter the fragments over a wide area. **2** metal fragments of an exploding shell. *n.* [*Shrapnel* was named for Henry *Shrapnel,* 1761-1842, a British army officer who invented it.]

shred (shred), **1** a very small piece torn off or cut off; very narrow strip; scrap: *The wind tore the sail to shreds.* **2** bit; fragment; particle: *There's not a shred of evidence that he took the money.* **3** tear or cut into small pieces: *He shredded the lettuce for the salad.* 1,2 *n.,* 3 *v.,* **shred ded** or **shred, shred ding.** —**shred′der,** *n.* —**shred′less,** *adj.,* —**shred′like′,** *adj.*

shrew (def. 2) about 6 in. (15 cm.) long with the tail

shrew (shrü), **1** a bad-tempered, quarrelsome woman. **2** a mouselike mammal with a long snout and brownish fur. Shrews eat insects and worms. *n.* —**shrew′like′,** *adj.*

shrewd (shrüd), having a sharp mind; showing a keen wit; clever; keen; sharp: *She is a shrewd lawyer.* *adj.* —**shrewd′ly,** *adv.* —**shrewd′ness,** *n.*

shrew ish (shrü′ish), scolding or bad-tempered. *adj.* —**shrew′ish ly**, *adv.* —**shrew′ish ness**, *n.*

shriek (shrēk), **1** a loud, sharp, shrill sound: *We heard the shriek of the engine's whistle.* **2** make a loud, sharp, shrill sound. People sometimes shriek because of terror, anger, pain, or amusement. **3** utter loudly and shrilly. 1 *n.*, 2,3 *v.* —**shriek′er**, *n.* —**shriek′ing ly**, *adv.*

shrift (shrift), OLD USE. confession of one's sins to a priest, followed by the granting of forgiveness by the priest. *n.*

shrike (shrīk), songbird with a strong, hooked beak that feeds on large insects, frogs, and sometimes on other birds. *n.*

shrill (shril), **1** having a high pitch; high and sharp in sound; piercing: *Crickets, locusts, and katydids make shrill noises.* **2** make a piercing sound; sound sharply. 1 *adj.*, 2 *v.* —**shrill′ness**, *n.*

shril ly (shril′ē), in shrill tones. *adv.*

shrimp (shrimp), **1** a small, long-tailed shellfish with long feelers and five pairs of legs. Some shrimps are used for food. **2** a small, short, or insignificant person. *n., pl.* **shrimps** (or **shrimp** for 1). —**shrimp′like′**, *adj.*

shrine (shrīn), **1** a sacred place; place where sacred things are kept. A shrine may be the tomb of a saint, an altar in a church, or a box holding a holy object. **2** any place or object sacred because of its history; something sacred because of memories connected with it: *America sometimes is called freedom's shrine. Shakespeare's birthplace is visited as a shrine. n.* —**shrine′like′**, *adj.*

shrink (shringk), **1** draw back: *The dog shrank from the whip. That shy girl shrinks from meeting strangers.* **2** become smaller: *My wool sweater shrank when it was washed. When his influence shrank, his wealth also decreased.* **3** make smaller; cause to contract: *Hot water shrinks wool.* **4** SLANG. psychiatrist. 1-3 *v.*, **shrank** or **shrunk, shrunk** or **shrunk en, shrink ing;** 4 *n.* —**shrink′a ble**, *adj.* —**shrink′er**, *n.* —**shrink′ing ly**, *adv.*

shrink age (shring′kij), **1** act or process of shrinking. **2** the amount or degree of shrinking: *a shrinkage of two inches in the length of a sleeve. n.*

shrive (shrīv), OLD USE. **1** hear the confession of and grant absolution to. **2** make confession. *v.*, **shrove** or **shrived, shriv en** or **shrived, shriv ing.**

shriv el (shriv′əl), dry up; wither; shrink and wrinkle: *The hot sunshine shriveled the grass. v.*, **shriv eled, shriv el ing** or **shriv elled, shriv el ling.**

shriv en (shriv′ən), OLD USE. a past participle of **shrive.** *v.*

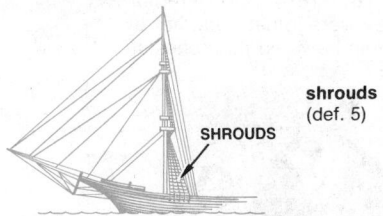

shrouds
(def. 5)

SHROUDS

shroud (shroud), **1** cloth or garment in which a dead person is wrapped or dressed for burial. **2** to wrap or dress for burial. **3** something that covers, conceals, or veils: *The fog was a shroud over the city.* **4** cover; conceal; veil: *plans shrouded in secrecy.* **5** a rope from a mast to the side of a ship. Shrouds help support the mast. 1,3,5 *n.*, 2,4 *v.* —**shroud′less**, *adj.* —**shroud′like′**, *adj.*

shrove (shrōv), OLD USE. a past tense of **shrive.** *v.*

Shrove Tuesday, the day before Ash Wednesday; last day before Lent.

shrub (shrub), a woody plant smaller than a tree, usually with many separate stems starting from or near the ground; bush. *n.* —**shrub′less**, *adj.* —**shrub′like′**, *adj.*

shrub ber y (shrub′ər ē), group of shrubs. *n.*

shrub by (shrub′ē), **1** like shrubs. **2** covered with shrubs. **3** consisting of shrubs. *adj.*, **shrub bi er, shrub bi est.** —**shrub′bi ness**, *n.*

shrug (shrug), **1** raise (the shoulders) as an expression of dislike, doubt, indifference, or impatience: *He merely shrugged his shoulders when we asked for directions. She shrugged and walked away.* **2** a raising of the shoulders in this way: *A shrug was her only reply.* 1 *v.*, **shrugged, shrug ging;** 2 *n.*

shrunk (shrungk), a past tense and past participle of **shrink.** *These socks have shrunk and I can't get them on. v.*

shrunk en (shrung′kən), **1** grown smaller; shriveled: *a shrunken fortune.* **2** shrunk; a past participle of **shrink.** 1 *adj.*, 2 *v.*

shuck (shuk), **1** a husk; pod. **2** remove the husks from: *shuck corn.* **3** take off; remove: *She likes to shuck her shoes when she's indoors.* 1 *n.*, 2,3 *v.* —**shuck′er**, *n.*

shud der (shud′ər), **1** tremble with horror, fear, cold, etc.: *shudder at a ghastly sight.* **2** a trembling; quivering. 1 *v.*, 2 *n.* —**shud′der ing ly**, *adv.*

shuf fle (shuf′əl), **1** walk without lifting the feet: *We shuffled slowly along the slippery sidewalk.* **2** scrape or drag (the feet). **3** a scraping or dragging movement of the feet. **4** mix (cards, etc.) so as to change the order. **5** a mixing of cards. **6** the right or turn to mix (cards). **7** push about; thrust or throw with clumsy haste: *Instead of cleaning his room, he shuffled everything into a drawer.* **8** move this way and that: *shuffle a stack of papers.* **9** movement this way and that: *After a hasty shuffle through his papers, the speaker began to talk.* **10** unfair act; trick: *Through some legal shuffle she secured a new trial.* 1,2,4,7,8 *v.*, **shuf fled, shuf fling;** 3,5,6,9,10 *n.* —**shuf′-fler**, *n.*

shuffle off, get rid of.

shuf fle board (shuf′əl bôrd′), game in which players use long sticks to push large disks along a flat surface to various numbered spaces. *n.*

shun (shun), keep away from; avoid: *She shuns housework. v.*, **shunned, shun ning.** —**shun′ner**, *n.*

shunt (shunt), **1** move out of the way; turn aside. **2** a turning aside; shift. **3** sidetrack; put aside; get rid of. **4** switch (a train) from one track to another. **5** a railroad switch. **6** wire joining two points in an electric circuit and forming a path through which a part of the current may pass. Shunts are used to regulate the amount of current passing through the main circuit. **7** carry (a part of a current) by means of a shunt. 1,3,4,7 *v.*, 2,5,6 *n.* —**shunt′er**, *n.*

shush (shush), hush. *v., n., pl.* **shush es;** *interj.*

shut (shut), **1** close (a container or opening) by pushing or pulling a lid, door, or some part into place: *shut a box, shut a door, shut a window.* **2** close (the eyes, a knife, a book, etc.) by bringing parts together: *Shut your mouth.* **3** close tight; close securely; close doors or other openings of: *shut a house for the summer.* **4** become closed; be closed. **5** keep (from going out); enclose; confine: *The canary was shut in its cage. v.*, **shut, shut ting.**

shut down, 1 close (a factory or the like) for a time; stop work. **2** settle down so as to cover or envelop. **3** put a stop or check on.

shut in, keep from going out.

shut off, turn off; close; obstruct; check; bar: *Shut off the radio.*

shut out, 1 keep from coming in: *The curtains shut out the light. Shut the dog out of this room.* **2** defeat (a team) without allowing it to score.

shut up, 1 shut the doors and windows of. **2** INFORMAL. stop talking. **3** keep from going out.

shut down (shut′doun′), a shutting down; closing of a factory, or the like, for a time. *n.*

shut-in (shut′in′), **1** kept in; held in; confined. **2** person who is kept from going out by sickness, weakness, etc. 1 *adj.*, 2 *n.*

shut out (shut′out′), the defeat of a team without allowing it to score. *n.*

shut ter (shut′ər), **1** a movable cover for a window. **2** a movable cover, slide, etc., for closing an opening. The device that opens and closes in front of the lens of a camera is the shutter. **3** put a shutter or shutters on or over: *As the hurricane approached, we hurried to shutter the windows.* 1,2 *n.*, 3 *v.* —**shut′ter less,** *adj.*

shut tle (shut′l), **1** device used in weaving that carries the thread back and forth across the piece being woven. **2** the sliding holder for the lower thread in a sewing machine, which moves back and forth once for each stitch. **3** move quickly to and fro. **4** bus, train, airplane, etc., that runs back and forth regularly over a short distance. 1,2,4 *n.*, 3 *v.*, **shut tled, shut tling.**

shut tle cock (shut′l kok′), the rounded object hit back and forth in the game of badminton; bird. A shuttlecock was originally a cork with feathers stuck in one end, but now is often made of plastic. *n.*

shy[1] (shī), **1** uncomfortable in company; bashful: *He is shy and dislikes parties.* **2** easily frightened away; timid: *A deer is a shy animal.* **3** start back or aside suddenly: *The horse shied at the newspaper blowing along the ground.* **4** draw back; shrink: *I shied in fright when the dog snarled at me.* **5** not having enough; short; lacking: *The store is shy on children's clothing. I am shy of cash this week.* 1,2,5 *adj.*, **shy er, shy est** or **shi er, shi est;** 3,4 *v.*, **shied, shying.** —**shy′er,** *n.* —**shy′ly,** *adv.* —**shy′ness,** *n.*

fight shy of, keep away from; avoid.

shy[2] (shī), **1** to throw; fling: *The boy shied a stone at the tree.* **2** a throw; fling. 1 *v.*, **shied, shy ing;** 2 *n.*, *pl.* **shies.**

Shy lock (shī′lok), **1** the harsh and pitiless moneylender in Shakespeare's play *The Merchant of Venice.* **2** a greedy moneylender or creditor. *n.*

si (sē), ti. *n.*

Si, symbol for silicon.

Si am (sī am′), former name of **Thailand.** *n.*

Si a mese (sī′ə mēz′), Thai. *adj.*, *n.*, *pl.* **Si a mese.**

Siamese cat, a short-haired, blue-eyed cat, usually with a light tan body and dark face, ears, feet, and tail.

Siamese twins, any twins who are born joined together. [See **Word History.**]

Si be li us (sə bā′lē əs), **Jean,** 1865-1957, Finnish composer. *n.*

Si ber i a (sī bir′ē ə), region in N Asia, extending from the Ural Mountains to the Pacific. It is part of the Soviet Union. *n.* —**Si ber′i an,** *adj.*, *n.*

Siberian husky, a strong, medium-sized, arctic sled dog that has a thick coat and a bushy tail which curves over the back; husky.

sib i lant (sib′ə lənt), **1** hissing. **2** a hissing sound, letter, or symbol. *S* and *sh* are sibilants. 1 *adj.*, 2 *n.* —**sib′i lant ly,** *adv.*

sib ling (sib′ling), brother or sister. An only child has no siblings. *n.*

sib yl (sib′əl), **1** woman that the ancient Greeks and Romans believed could see into and tell about the future. **2** woman who is believed able to see into and tell about the future; a woman prophet. *n.*

sic (sik), **1** set upon or attack (chiefly used as a command to a dog). **2** incite to set upon or attack: *sic a dog on a stranger.* *v.*, **sicked, sick ing.** Also, **sick.**

Si cil ian (sə sil′yən), **1** of Sicily or its people. **2** person born or living in Sicily. 1 *adj.*, 2 *n.*

Sic i ly (sis′ə lē), island near the SW tip of Italy, belonging to Italy since 1860. It is the largest island in the Mediterranean. See **Adriatic Sea** for map. *n.*

sick[1] (sik), **1** in poor health; having some disease; ill. **2** inclined to vomit; feeling nausea; vomiting. **3** for a sick person; connected with sickness: *sick pay.* **4 the sick,** sick people: *The sick need special care.* **5** weary; tired: *I'm sick of school.* **6** disgusted: *Your constant fighting makes me sick.* **7** affected with sorrow or longing: *sick at heart.* 1-3,5-7 *adj.*, 4 *n.*

sick[2] (sik), sic. *v.*

sick bay, a place on a ship used as a hospital.

sick bed (sik′bed′), bed of a sick person. *n.*

sick en (sik′ən), make or become sick: *The sight of blood sickened him. The bird sickened when kept in the cage.* *v.* —**sick′en er,** *n.*

sick en ing (sik′ə ning), making sick; causing nausea, faintness, disgust, or loathing. *adj.* —**sick′en ing ly,** *adv.*

sick ish (sik′ish), **1** somewhat sick. **2** somewhat sickening. *adj.* —**sick′ish ly,** *adv.* —**sick′ish ness,** *n.*

sick le (sik′əl), tool consisting of a short, curved blade on a short handle, for cutting grass, etc. *n.* [*Sickle* comes from Old English *sicol.*]

sickle cell anemia, an inherited blood disease in which the normally round red blood cells become sickle-shaped. These cells prevent oxygen from getting to body tissues.

sick li ness (sik′lē nis), the state or fact of being sickly; ill health. *n.*

sick ly (sik′lē), **1** often sick; not strong; not healthy. **2** of or caused by sickness: *Her skin is a sickly yellow.* **3** causing sickness: *a sickly climate.* **4** faint; weak; pale: *a sickly glow.* *adj.*, **sick li er, sick li est.**

WORD HISTORY

Siamese twins

This term comes from the twins, Eng and Chang, 1811-1874, who were born in *Siam.* They were joined together by a band of flesh between their chests.

sick ness (sik′nis), **1** an abnormal, unhealthy condition; disease; illness. **2** nausea; vomiting. *n., pl.* **sick ness es.**

sick room (sik′rüm′ *or* sik′rüm′), room in which a sick person is cared for. *n.*

side (sīd), **1** a surface or line bounding a thing: *the sides of a square, a side of a box.* **2** one of the two surfaces of an object that is not the front, back, top, or bottom: *There is a door at the side of the house.* **3** either of the two surfaces of paper, cloth, etc.: *Write only on one side of the paper.* **4** a particular surface: *the side of the moon turned toward the earth.* **5** the slope of a hill or bank. **6** either the right or the left part of a thing; either part or region beyond a central line: *the east side of a city, our side of the street.* **7** either the right or the left part of the body: *I felt a sharp pain in my side.* **8** an aspect or view of someone or something: *the better side of one's nature, the bright side of a difficulty.* **9** group of persons who stand up for their beliefs, opinions, ways of doing things, etc., against another group: *Both sides are ready for the contest. The children chose sides for a game of softball.* **10** the position, course, or part of one person or party against another: *It is pleasant to be on the winning side.* **11** part of a family; line of descent: *He is English on his mother's side and Polish on his father's side.* **12** at one side; on one side: *the side aisles of a theater, a side door.* **13** from one side: *a side view.* **14** toward one side: *a side glance.* **15** less important: *a side issue.* **16 side with**, take the part of; agree with: *The sisters always side with each other.* 1-11 *n.,* 12-15 *adj.,* 16 *v.,* **sid ed, sid ing. —side′less,** *adj.*

by one's side, near one.

on the side, in addition to one's ordinary duties.

side by side, beside one another.

split one's sides, laugh very hard.

take sides, place oneself with one person or group against another.

side arm (sīd′ärm′), throwing or thrown from the side with the arm at waist height; not overhand or underhand: *a sidearm pitch. adj.*

side arms, sword, revolver, bayonet, etc., carried at the side or in the belt.

side board (sīd′bôrd′), a low cabinet with drawers and shelves for holding silver and linen, and space on top for dishes; buffet. *n.*

side burns (sīd′bėrnz′), whiskers in front of the ears, especially when the chin is shaved. *n.pl.*

WORD HISTORY

sideburns

Sideburns is a different form of *burnsides*, which were named for Ambrose E. Burnside, 1824-1881, a Union general in the Civil War, who wore such whiskers.

a hat	i it	oi oil	ch child	a in about
ā age	ī ice	ou out	ng long	e in taken
ä far	o hot	u cup	sh she ə =	i in pencil
e let	ō open	u̇ put	th thin	o in lemon
ē equal	ô order	ü rule	₮н then	u in circus
ėr term			zh measure	

side effect, a secondary effect or reaction, usually undesirable or unpleasant: *Many drugs produce side effects on some people.*

side light (sīd′līt′), **1** light coming from the side. **2** incidental information about a subject: *amusing sidelights in a biography. n.*

side line (sīd′līn′), **1** a line at the side of something. **2** line that marks the limit of play on the side of the field in football, etc. **3 sidelines,** *pl.* space just outside these lines: *watch a game from the sidelines.* **4** an additional line of goods, business, or activity. **5** put on the sidelines; make inactive. 1-4 *n.,* 5 *v.,* **side lined, side lining.**

side long (sīd′lông′), to one side; toward the side: *a sidelong glance (adj.). He glanced sidelong at me (adv.). adj., adv.*

side piece (sīd′pēs′), piece forming a side or part of a side, or fixed by the side, of something. *n.*

si der e al (sī dir′ē əl), **1** of the stars. **2** measured by the apparent motion of the stars: *sidereal time. adj.* **—si der′e al ly,** *adv.*

side sad dle (sīd′sad′l), **1** a woman's saddle so made that both of the rider's legs are on the same side of the horse. **2** with both legs on the same side of the horse: *ride sidesaddle.* 1 *n.,* 2 *adv.*

side show (sīd′shō′), a small show in connection with a principal one: *the sideshows of a circus. n.*

side step (sīd′step′), **1** step aside. **2** get away from; avoid: *She would never sidestep a responsibility. v.,* **side stepped, side step ping. —side′step′per,** *n.*

side swipe (sīd′swīp′), **1** hit with a sweeping blow along the side. **2** a sweeping blow along the side. 1 *v.,* **side swiped, side swip ing;** 2 *n.* **—side′swip′er,** *n.*

side track (sīd′trak′), **1** a railroad siding. **2** switch (a train, etc.) to a sidetrack. **3** put aside; turn aside: *Don't sidetrack me with pointless questions.* 1 *n.,* 2,3 *v.*

side walk (sīd′wôk′), place to walk at the side of a street, usually paved. *n.*

side way (sīd′wā′), sideways. *adv., adj.*

side ways (sīd′wāz′), **1** to one side; toward one side: *walk sideways.* **2** from one side: *a sideways glimpse.* **3** with one side toward the front: *stand sideways, place a book sideways on a shelf. adv., adj.*

side wise (sīd′wīz′), sideways. *adv., adj.*

sid ing (sī′ding), **1** a short railroad track to which cars can be switched from a main track. **2** boards, shingles, etc., forming the outside walls of a wooden building. *n.*

si dle (sī′dl), **1** move sideways. **2** move sideways slowly so as not to attract attention: *The child shyly sidled up to the visitor. v.,* **si dled, si dling. —si′dling ly,** *adv.*

siege (sēj), **1** the surrounding of a fortified place by an army trying to capture it: *Troy was under a siege for ten years.* **2** any long or persistent effort to overcome resistance; any long-continued attack: *a siege of illness. n.*

lay siege to, 1 besiege: *The Greeks laid siege to Troy.* **2** attempt to win or get by long and persistent effort.

Sieg fried (sēg′frēd), (in German legends) a hero who killed a dragon and won a treasure. *n.*

si en na (sē en′ə), **1** mixture of clay and iron oxide, used as a pigment. In its natural state, it is yellowish-brown and is called **raw sienna.** After heating, it becomes reddish-brown and is called **burnt sienna. 2** a yellowish brown or a reddish brown. *n.*

WORD HISTORY

sierra

Sierra was borrowed from Spanish *sierra*, which came from Latin *serra*, meaning "a saw."

si er ra (sē er′ə), chain of hills or mountains whose peaks suggest the teeth of a saw. *n., pl.* **si er ras.** [See **Word History.**]

Si er ra Le o ne (sē er′ə lē ō′nē), country on the W coast of Africa, a member of the Commonwealth of Nations. *Capital:* Freetown. —**Si er′ra Le o′ne an.**

Si er ra Ne vad a (sē er′ə nə vad′ə *or* sē er′ə nə-vä′də), a mountain range in E California.

si es ta (sē es′tə), a nap or rest taken at noon or in the afternoon. *n., pl.* **si es tas.** [*Siesta* was borrowed from Spanish *siesta.*]

sieve (siv), **1** utensil having holes that let liquids and smaller pieces pass through, but not the larger pieces: *Shaking flour through a sieve removes lumps.* **2** put through a sieve. 1 *n.,* 2 *v.,* **sieved, siev ing. —sieve′like′,** *adj.*

sift (sift), **1** separate large pieces from small by shaking in a sieve: *Sift the gravel and put the larger stones in another pile.* **2** put through a sieve: *Sift sugar on the top of the cake.* **3** use a sieve. **4** fall through, or as if through, a sieve: *The snow sifted softly down.* **5** examine very carefully: *sift all available evidence.* *v.* —**sift′er,** *n.*

sig., **1** signal. **2** signature.

Sig., signor.

sigh (sī), **1** let out a very long, deep breath because one is sad, tired, relieved, etc.: *We heard her sigh.* **2** act or sound of sighing: *a sigh of regret, a sigh of relief.* **3** say or express with a sigh. **4** make a sound like a sigh: *The wind sighed in the treetops.* **5** wish very much; long: *He sighed for home.* **6** show grief by sighing: *sigh over one's unhappy fate.* 1-3,6 *v.,* 2 *n.* —**sigh′er,** *n.* —**sigh′less,** *adj.* —**sigh′like′,** *adj.*

sight (sīt), **1** power of seeing; vision: *Birds have better sight than dogs.* **2** act or fact of seeing; look: *love at first sight.* **3** range of seeing: *Land was in sight.* **4** thing seen; view; glimpse: *I can't stand the sight of blood.* **5** something worth seeing: *see the sights of the city. Niagara Falls is one of the sights of the world.* **6** something that looks bad or odd: *Your room is a sight.* **7** see: *The lifeboat drifted for several days before the survivors sighted land.* **8** device to guide the eye in taking aim or observing: *the sights on a rifle.* **9** the aim or observation taken by such devices. **10** look at through sights; point to; aim at; aim: *I sighted carefully, then I fired at the target.* **11** way of looking or thinking; regard; opinion: *This is very important in his sight.* 1-6,8,9,11 *n.,* 7,10 *v.* —**sight′a ble,** *adj.* —**sight′er,** *n.*

at sight or **on sight,** as soon as seen: *She reads music at sight.*

catch sight of, see: *I caught sight of him.*

know by sight, know sufficiently to recognize when seen.

out of sight of, 1 where one cannot see: *Our ship was out of sight of land for several weeks.* **2** where one cannot be seen by: *out of sight of the neighbors.*

sight ed (sī′tid), **1** able to see: *a sighted person.* **2 the sighted,** people who are able to see. 1 *adj.,* 2 *n.*

sight ing (sī′ting), a seeing; being seen: *The newspaper reported a UFO sighting.* *n.*

sight less (sīt′lis), blind. *adj.* —**sight′less ly,** *adv.* —**sight′less ness,** *n.*

sight ly (sīt′lē), **1** pleasing to the sight. **2** affording a fine view. *adj.,* **sight li er, sight li est.** —**sight′li ness,** *n.*

sight see ing (sīt′sē′ing), **1** a going around to see objects or places of interest: *a weekend of sightseeing.* **2** that goes around to see objects or places of interest: *a sightseeing tour.* 1 *n.,* 2 *adj.*

sight se er (sīt′sē′ər), person who goes around to see objects or places of interest. *n.*

sign (sīn), **1** any mark or thing used to mean, represent, or point out something: *The signs for addition, subtraction, multiplication, and division are $+, -, \times, \div$.* **2** put one's name on; write one's name. A person signs a letter, a note promising to pay a debt, a check, etc. We sign for telegrams, parcels, etc. **3** write: *Sign your initials here.* **4** hire by a written agreement: *sign a new player.* **5** accept employment: *They signed for three years.* **6** motion or gesture used to mean, represent, or point out something: *A nod is a sign of agreement. She made the sign of the cross.* **7** an inscribed board, space, etc., serving for advertisement, information, etc.: *See the sign over the door. The sign reads, "Keep off the grass."* **8** indication: *There are no signs of life about the house.* **9** indication of a coming event; omen: *The robin is a sign of spring. Ancient people viewed comets as signs of evil.* **10** a trace: *The hunter found signs of deer.* **11** any of the twelve divisions of the zodiac, each named for a constellation and each denoted by a special symbol. 1,6,7-11 *n.,* 2-5 *v.* —**sign′er,** *n.*

sign off, stop broadcasting.

sign up, enlist, join, etc., by written agreement: *sign up as a new member.*

sig nal (sig′nəl), **1** a sign giving notice, warning, or pointing out something: *A red light is a signal of danger. A siren is used as a fire signal. The raising of the flag was a signal to advance.* **2** a wave, current, impulse, etc., that carries sounds and images in communications by radio, television, etc. **3** make a signal or signals to: *She signaled the car to stop by raising her hand.* **4** make known by a signal or signals: *A bell signals the end of a school period.* **5** used as a signal or in signaling: *a signal flag.* **6** remarkable; striking; notable: *The airplane was a signal invention.* 1,2 *n.,* 3,4 *v.,* 5,6 *adj.* —**sig′nal er, sig′nal ler,** *n.*

sig nal ize (sig′nə līz), make stand out; make notable: *Many great inventions signalize the last 150 years.* *v.,* **sig nal ized, sig nal iz ing.**

sig nal ly (sig′nə lē), in a remarkable manner; strikingly; notably. *adv.*

sig nal man (sig′nəl mən *or* sig′nəl man′), person in charge of the signals on a railroad, in the army or navy, etc. *n., pl.* **sig nal men.**

sig na ture (sig′nə chər), **1** a person's name written by that person. **2** act of writing one's name. **3** signs printed at the beginning of a staff to show the key and time of a piece of music. **4** music, sound effects, etc., used to identify a performer or a radio or television program. *n.*

sign board (sīn/bôrd/), board having a sign, notice, advertisement, inscription, etc., on it. *n.*

sig net (sig/nit), a small seal used to stamp documents: *The order was sealed with the king's signet. n.*

sig nif i cance (sig nif/ə kəns), **1** importance; consequence: *The President wanted to see him on a matter of significance. **2** meaning: *She did not understand the significance of my nod. n.*

sig nif i cant (sig nif/ə kənt), **1** full of meaning; important; of consequence: *July 4, 1776, is a significant date for Americans.* **2** having or expressing a hidden meaning: *A significant nod from his friend warned him to stop talking. adj.* —**sig nif/i cant ly,** *adv.*

sig ni fi ca tion (sig/nə fə kā/shən), a meaning; sense. *n.*

sig ni fy (sig/nə fī), **1** be a sign of; mean: *"Oh!" signifies surprise.* **2** make known by signs, words, or actions: *He signified his consent with a nod.* **3** have importance; be of consequence; matter: *What a fool says does not signify. v.,* **sig ni fied, sig ni fy ing.** —**sig/ni fi/er,** *n.*

sign language

 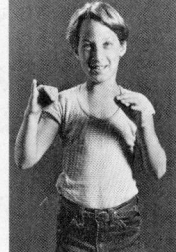 

"The rain   is raining   on the umbrellas."

sign language, language in which motions, especially of the hands, stand for words, ideas, etc.

si gnor (sē/nyôr), ITALIAN. **1** Mr. or sir. **2** a gentleman. *n., pl.* **si gno ri** (sē nyôr/ē).

si gno ra (sē nyôr/ə), ITALIAN. **1** Mrs. or madam. **2** a lady. *n., pl.* **si gno re** (sē nyôr/ā).

si gno ri na (sē/nyə rē/nə), ITALIAN. **1** Miss. **2** a young lady. *n., pl.* **si gno ri ne** (sē/nyə rē/nā).

sign post (sīn/pōst/), post having signs, notices, or directions on it; guidepost. *n.*

Sikh (sēk), member of a religious sect of northwestern India. Sikhs are famous as fighters. *n.*

Sik kim (sik/əm), state of India in the Himalayas, between Tibet and India. It was formerly an independent country. *n.*

si lage (sī/lij), green fodder for winter feeding of farm animals, preserved and stored in a silo or other airtight chamber; ensilage. *n.*

si lence (sī/ləns), **1** absence of sound or noise; stillness: *The teacher asked for silence.* **2** a keeping still: not talking: *Silence gives consent.* **3** a not mentioning: *Mother passed over our foolish remarks in silence.* **4** stop the speech or noise of; make silent; quiet: *Please silence that barking dog.* **5** make silent by restraint; repress: *to silence the press, to silence an uprising.* **6** keep still! be still! 1-3 *n.,* 4,5 *v.,* **si lenced, si lenc ing;** 6 *interj.*

si len cer (sī/lən sər), device which muffles the sound of a gun. *n.*

si lent (sī/lənt), **1** quiet; still; noiseless: *a silent house, the silent hills.* **2** not speaking; saying little or nothing: *The stranger was silent about her early life. Pupils must be silent during the study hour.* **3** not spoken; not said out loud: *a silent prayer. The "e" in "time" is a silent letter.* **4** not active; taking no open or active part. A silent partner in

a business has no share in managing the business. *adj.* —**si/lent ly,** *adv.* —**si/lent ness,** *n.*

Si le sia (sə lē/shə *or* sī lē/shə), region in central Europe most of which is now in Poland and Czechoslovakia. *n.* —**Si le/sian,** *adj., n.*

sil hou ette (sil/ü et/), **1** an outline portrait cut out of a black paper or filled in with some single color. **2** a dark image outlined against a lighter background. **3** show in outline: *The mountain was silhouetted against the sky.* 1,2 *n.,* 3 *v.,* **sil hou et ted, sil hou et ting.**

sil i ca (sil/ə kə), a hard, white or colorless substance. Flint, quartz, and sand are forms of silica. *n., pl.* **sil i cas.**

sil i cate (sil/ə kit *or* sil/ə kāt), compound containing silicon with oxygen and a metal. Mica, soapstone, asbestos, and feldspar are silicates. *n.*

sil i con (sil/ə kən), element found only combined with other elements, chiefly with oxygen in silica. Silicon has the properties of both a metal and a nonmetal. Next to oxygen, it is the most abundant element in nature. *n.*

sil i cone (sil/ə kōn), an organic compound which can resist extreme heat and cold. Silicones are used for lubricants, varnishes, and insulators. *n.*

silk (silk), **1** a fine, soft fiber spun by silkworms to form their cocoons. **2** thread or cloth made from this fiber. **3** garment of such material. **4** fiber like silk, produced by spiders, etc. **5** anything like silk: *corn silk.* **6** of or like silk: *She sewed the silk dress with silk thread.* 1-5 *n.,* 6 *adj.* —**silk/like/,** *adj.*

silk en (sil/kən), **1** made of silk: *The king wore silken robes.* **2** like silk; smooth, soft, and glossy: *silken hair. adj.*

silk i ness (sil/kē nis), silky condition or quality. *n.*

silk worm (silk/wėrm/), caterpillar that spins silk to form a cocoon, especially the larva of a moth that feeds on mulberry leaves. *n.*

silk y (sil/kē), of or like silk; smooth, soft, and glossy; silken: *A kitten has silky fur. adj.,* **silk i er, silk i est.** —**silk/i ly,** *adv.*

sill (sil), **1** piece of wood or stone across the bottom of a door or window frame. **2** a large, wooden beam on which the wall of a house, etc., rests. *n.* —**sill/-like/,** *adj.*

sil li ness (sil/ē nis), **1** a being silly; foolishness. **2** a silly act, thing, etc. *n., pl.* **sil li ness es.**

sil ly (sil/ē), **1** without sense or reason; foolish: *Baby talk is silly.* **2** INFORMAL. stunned; dazed. **3** a foolish person. 1,2 *adj.,* **sil li er, sil li est;** 3 *n., pl.* **sil lies.** —**sil/li ly,** *adv.*

si lo (sī/lō), **1** an airtight building or pit in which green fodder for farm animals is preserved. **2** a vertical under-

silo
(def. 1)

ground shaft for housing and launching missiles, rockets, etc. *n., pl.* **si los.** [*Silo* comes from Spanish *silo,* meaning "a storage pit for grain."]

silt (silt), **1** very fine particles of earth carried by moving water and deposited as sediment: *The harbor is being choked up with silt.* **2** fill or choke up with silt. **1** *n.,* **2** *v.* —**sil ta′tion,** *n.*

silt y (sil′tē), of silt; like silt; full of silt. *adj.,* **silt i er, silt i est.**

sil van (sil′vən), sylvan. *adj.*

sil ver (sil′vər), **1** a shining white, precious metallic element that can be hammered into very thin sheets or drawn out into very fine wire. Silver conducts heat and electricity better than any other substance. It is also used to make coins, jewelry, spoons, dishes, etc. **2** coins made from this or a similar metal: *a pocketful of silver.* **3** utensils or dishes made of or plated with silver; silverware: *table silver.* **4** something like silver. **5** made of or plated with silver: *a silver spoon.* **6** of silver. **7** cover or coat with silver or something like silver: *silver glass to make a mirror.* **8** the color of silver. **9** having the color of silver: *a silver slipper.* **10** make or become the color of silver: *Moonlight silvered the lake. The old lady's hair had silvered.* **11** having a clear ringing sound like that of silver dropped on a hard surface. **1-4,8** *n.,* **5,6,9,11** *adj.,* **7,10** *v.* —**sil′ver er,** *n.* —**sil′ver like′,** *adj.*

silver lining, the brighter side of a sad or unfortunate situation.

sil ver smith (sil′vər smith′), person who makes articles of silver. *n.*

sil ver-tongued (sil′vər tungd′), eloquent. *adj.*

sil ver ware (sil′vər wer′ *or* sil′vər war′), silver things; utensils or dishes made of or plated with silver. *n.*

sil ver y (sil′vər ē), like silver; like that of silver: *Moonbeams are silvery. The bell has a silvery sound. adj.* —**sil′ver i ness,** *n.*

sim., 1 similar. **2** simile.

sim i an (sim′ē ən), **1** apelike or monkeylike. **2** an ape; monkey. **1** *adj.,* **2** *n.*

sim i lar (sim′ə lər), **1** much the same; alike; like: *A creek and a brook are similar.* **2** (in geometry) having the same shape: *similar triangles. adj.* —**sim′i lar ly,** *adv.*

sim i lar i ty (sim′ə lar′ə tē), **1** a being similar; likeness; resemblance. **2 similarities,** *pl.* points of resemblance. *n., pl.* **sim i lar i ties.**

sim i le (sim′ə lē′), a statement that one thing is like another. EXAMPLES: a face like marble, as brave as a lion. *n.*

si mil i tude (sə mil′ə tüd *or* sə mil′ə tyüd), a being similar; likeness; resemblance. *n.*

sim mer (sim′ər), **1** make a murmuring sound while boiling gently: *The kettle simmered on the stove.* **2** keep at or just below the boiling point; boil gently: *Simmer the milk, do not boil it. The soup should simmer for a few hours to improve its taste.* **3** process of cooking at or just below the boiling point: *Do not let the soup cook faster than at a simmer.* **4** be on the point of just breaking out: *simmering rebellion. He simmered with anger, but said nothing.* **1,2,4** *v.,* **3** *n.* —**sim′mer ing ly,** *adv.*

simmer down, 1 cool off; calm down. **2** (of a liquid) reduce in quantity through continued simmering.

Si mon Peter (sī′mən). See **Peter, Saint.**

si mo ny (sī′mə nē *or* sim′ə nē), act of buying and selling sacred things, especially positions or promotion in the church. *n.*

si moom (sə müm′), a hot, suffocating, sand-laden wind of the deserts of Arabia, Syria, and northern Africa. *n.* [*Simoom* comes from Arabic *samūm.*]

si moon (sə mün′), simoom. *n.*

sim per (sim′pər), **1** smile in a silly, affected way. **2** a

silly, affected smile. **1** *v.,* **2** *n.* —**sim′per er,** *n.* —**sim′per ing ly,** *adv.*

sim ple (sim′pəl), **1** easy to do or understand: *a simple problem. This book is in simple language.* **2** not divided into parts; single; not compound. An oak leaf is a simple leaf. "John called his dog" is a simple sentence. **3** having few parts; not complex; elementary: *a simple one-celled animal.* **4** with nothing added; bare; mere: *My answer is the simple truth.* **5** without ornament; not rich or showy; plain: *simple food, simple clothing.* **6** not affected; not showing off; natural: *She has a pleasant, simple manner.* **7** honest; sincere: *a simple heart.* **8** not subtle; not sophisticated; innocent; artless: *a simple child.* **9** common; ordinary: *a simple citizen.* **10** humble: *His parents were simple people.* **11** weak in mind; dull: *The neighbors called him simple. adj.,* **sim pler, sim plest.** —**sim′ple ness,** *n.*

simple fraction, fraction having a whole number in both the numerator and the denominator. EXAMPLES: $1/3$, $3/4$, $219/125$.

sim ple-heart ed (sim′pəl här′tid), **1** having or showing a simple, unaffected nature. **2** guileless; sincere. *adj.*

simple machines
a screw, an inclined plane, and a pulley

simple machine, a basic mechanical device which increases force or changes its direction. The lever, wedge, pulley, wheel and axle, inclined plane, and screw are simple machines. Many parts of more complicated machines are based on these.

sim ple-mind ed (sim′pəl mīn′did), **1** without awareness of conventions; artless; inexperienced. **2** ignorant; foolish. **3** feeble-minded. *adj.* —**sim′ple-mind′ed ly,** *adv.* —**sim′ple-mind′ed ness,** *n.*

simple sentence, sentence consisting of one main clause. EXAMPLE: This book is a dictionary.

sim ple ton (sim′pəl tən), a silly person; fool. *n.*

sim plic i ty (sim plis′ə tē), **1** a being simple. **2** freedom from difficulty; clearness: *The simplicity of that book makes it suitable for children.* **3** plainness: *A room in a hospital should be furnished with simplicity.* **4** absence of show or pretense; sincerity. **5** lack of shrewdness; dullness: *Their simplicity made them easily fooled.* *n., pl.* **simplic i ties.**

sim pli fi ca tion (sim′plə fə kā′shən), **1** a making simpler or a being made simpler. **2** a change to a simpler form. *n.*

sim pli fy (sim′plə fī), make simple or simpler; make plainer or easier: *"Tho" is a simplified spelling of "though."* *v.,* **sim pli fied, sim pli fy ing.** —**sim′pli fi′er,** *n.*

sim ply (sim′plē), **1** in a simple manner. **2** without much ornament; without pretense or affectation; plainly: *The nurse was simply dressed.* **3** merely; only: *The baby did not simply cry; he yelled.* **4** absolutely: *simply perfect, simply hopeless.* *adv.*

sim u late (sim′yə lāt), **1** put on a false appearance of; pretend; feign: *She simulated interest to please her friend.* **2** act like; look like; imitate: *Certain insects simulate flowers or leaves.* *v.,* **sim u lat ed, sim u lat ing.** —**sim′u la′tor,** *n.*

sim u la tion (sim′yə lā′shən), **1** a putting on a false appearance; pretense; feigning. **2** an acting or looking like; imitation: *a harmless insect's simulation of a poisonous one.* *n.*

si mul cast (sī′məl kast′), transmit a program over radio and television simultaneously. *v.,* **si mul cast** or **si mul cast ed, si mul cast ing.** [*Simulcast* is a blend of *simultaneous* and *broadcast.*]

si mul ta ne ous (sī′məl tā′nē əs), existing, done, or happening at the same time: *The two simultaneous shots sounded like one.* *adj.* —**si′mul ta′ne ous ness,** *n.*

si mul ta ne ous ly (sī′məl tā′nē əs lē), at once; at the same time; together. *adv.*

sin (sin), **1** a breaking of the law of God on purpose. **2** break the law of God; be a sinner. **3** wrongdoing of any kind; immoral act. Lying, stealing, dishonesty, and cruelty are sins. **4** do wrong. **1,3** *n.,* **2,4** *v.,* **sinned, sin ning. sin,** sine.

Si nai (sī′nī), **1** Mount, (in the Bible) the mountain where God gave the Ten Commandments to Moses. It is thought to be located in the S part of the Sinai peninsula. **2** triangular peninsula in NE Egypt, between the Mediterranean Sea and the N end of the Red Sea. *n.*

Sin bad (sin′bad), sailor in *The Arabian Nights* who went on seven extraordinary voyages. *n.*

since (sins), **1** from a past time till now: *The sun has been up since five.* **2** after the time that; from the time when: *He has been home only once since he went to New York.* **3** after: *She has worked hard since she left school.* **4** at any time between (some past time or event and the present): *We have not seen them since Saturday.* **5** from then till now: *I caught cold last Saturday and have been in bed ever since.* **6** at some time between then and now: *At first she refused the position, but since has accepted.* **7** before now; ago: *I heard that old joke long since.* **8** because: *Since you feel tired, you should rest.* **1,4** *prep.,* **2,3,8** *conj.,* **5-7** *adv.*

sin cere (sin sir′), free from pretense or deceit; genuine; real; honest: *sincere thanks. I made a sincere effort to pass my exams.* *adj.,* **sin cer er, sin cer est.** —**sin cere′ly,** *adv.* —**sin cere′ness,** *n.*

sin cer i ty (sin ser′ə tē), freedom from pretense or deceit; honesty. *n., pl.* **sin cer i ties.**

sine (sīn), the ratio of the length of the side opposite an acute angle of a right triangle to the length of the hypotenuse. *n.*

si ne cure (sī′nə kyúr *or* sin′ə kyúr), an extremely easy job requiring little or no work and usually paying well. *n.*

sin ew (sin′yü), **1** tendon. **2** strength; energy. **3** Often, **sinews,** *pl.* means of strength; source of power: *Men and money are the sinews of war.* *n.* —**sin′ew less,** *adj.*

sin ew y (sin′yü ē), **1** having strong sinews; strong; powerful: *A wrestler has sinewy arms.* **2** vigorous; forcible. **3** like sinews; having sinews; tough; stringy. *adj.* —**sin′ew i ness,** *n.*

sin ful (sin′fəl), full of sin; wicked; wrong; immoral; evil: *a sinful person, a sinful act.* *adj.* —**sin′ful ly,** *adv.* —**sin′ful ness,** *n.*

sing (sing), **1** make music with the voice: *She sings folk songs.* **2** make pleasant musical sounds: *Birds sing.* **3** speak musically: *He almost seemed to sing his lines from the play.* **4** bring, send, put, etc., with or by singing: *Sing the baby to sleep.* **5** tell in song or poetry: *Poets sang of Camelot.* **6** proclaim: *sing a person's praises.* **7** make a ringing, whistling, humming, or buzzing sound: *The teakettle sang on the stove.* **8** a singing, especially in a group: *We went to a community sing.* **1-7** *v.,* **sang** or **sung, sung, sing ing;** **8** *n.* —**sing′a ble,** *adj.* —**sing′ing ly,** *adv.*

sing out, call loudly; shout.

sing., singular.

Sing a pore (sing′ə pôr), **1** island country off the S tip of the Malay Peninsula, a member of the Commonwealth of Nations. See **Indochina** for map. **2** its capital, on the S coast. *n.*

singe (sinj), **1** burn a little; scorch. **2** a slight burn. **3** burn the ends or edges of: *The fire flared up and singed my hair.* **4** remove by a slight burning: *The cook singed the feathers from the chicken.* **1,3,4** *v.,* **singed, singe ing;** **2** *n.* —**sing′er,** *n.* —**singe′ing ly,** *adv.*

sing er (sing′ər), person or bird that sings: *Our canary is a fine singer.* *n.*

sin gle (sing′gəl), **1** one and no more; only one: *Please give me a single piece of paper.* **2** for only one; individual: *The sisters share one room with two single beds in it.* **3** not married: *a single man.* **4** having only one on each side: *The knights engaged in single combat.* **5 singles,** *pl.* game of tennis, etc., played with only one person on each side: *She likes to play singles rather than doubles.* **6** pick from among others: *The teacher singled us out for praise.* **7** a single thing or person. **8** in baseball: **a** a hit that allows the batter to reach first base only. **b** make such a hit. **9** having only one set of petals. Most cultivated roses have double flowers with many petals; wild roses have single flowers with five petals. **10** sincere; honest; genuine: *She showed single devotion to her work.* **1-4,9,10** *adj.,* **5,7,8a** *n.,* **6,8b** *v.,* **sin gled, sin gling.** —**sin′gle ness,** *n.*

sin gle-breast ed (sing′gəl bres′tid), overlapping across the breast just enough to fasten with one row of buttons: *a suit with a single-breasted jacket.* *adj.*

single file, line of persons or things arranged one behind another: *We walked along the narrow trail in single file.*

sin gle-hand ed (sing′gəl han′did), **1** without help from others. **2** using, requiring, or managed by only one hand

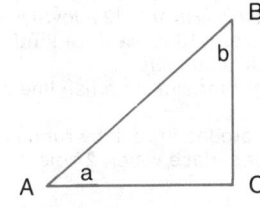

sine of angle a = BC/AB;
sine of angle b = AC/AB.

or only one person: *a single-handed catch. a single-handed saw.* 1 *adj., adv.,* 2 *adj.* —**sin′gle-hand′ed ly,** *adv.* —**sin′gle-hand′ed ness,** *n.*

sin gle-heart ed (sing′gəl här′tid), 1 free from deceit; sincere. 2 having only one purpose. *adj.* —**sin′gle-heart′ed ly,** *adv.* —**sin′gle-heart′ed ness,** *n.*

sin gle-mind ed (sing′gəl mīn′did), 1 having only one purpose in mind. 2 sincere; straightforward. *adj.* —**sin′gle-mind′ed ly,** *adv.* —**sin′gle-mind′ed ness,** *n.*

sin gle tree (sing′gəl trē′), whiffletree. *n.*

sin gly (sing′glē), 1 by itself; individually; separately: *Let us consider each point singly.* 2 one by one; one at a time: *Misfortunes never come singly.* 3 by one's own efforts; without help. *adv.*

sing song (sing′sông′), 1 a monotonous, up-and-down rhythm. 2 a monotonous tone or sound in speaking. 3 monotonous in rhythm: *a singsong recitation of the multiplication table.* 1,2 *n.,* 3 *adj.*

sin gu lar (sing′gyə lər), 1 extraordinary; unusual: *a person of singular ability. a story of singular interest.* 2 strange; odd; peculiar: *The detectives were greatly puzzled by the singular nature of the crime.* 3 being the only one of its kind: *an event singular in history.* 4 one in number. *Boy* is singular; *boys* is plural. 5 the singular number in grammar. *Ox* is the singular of *oxen.* 6 a word in the singular number. 1-4 *adj.,* 5,6 *n.* —**sin′gu lar ly,** *adv.*

sin gu lar i ty (sing′gyə lar′ə tē), 1 oddness; strangeness; unusualness: *The singularity of their speech and clothing attracted much attention.* 2 something singular; peculiarity; oddity: *One of the giraffe's singularities is the length of its neck. n., pl.* **sin gu lar i ties.**

sin is ter (sin′ə stər), 1 showing ill will; threatening: *a sinister rumor. a sinister look.* 2 bad; evil; dishonest: *a sinister plan. adj.* —**sin′is ter ly,** *adv.* —**sin′is ter ness,** *n.*

WORD HISTORY

sinister

Sinister comes from Latin *sinister,* which originally meant "left, on the left side." Later, it came to mean "unlucky" because of the belief that omens seen on the left side were unlucky.

sink (singk), 1 go down; fall slowly; go lower and lower: *sink to the floor in a faint. I sank into a chair.* 2 make go down; make fall: *Lack of rain sank the water level.* 3 go under: *The ship sank.* 4 make go under: *The submarine sank two ships.* 5 make or become lower, weaker, or less in degree or volume: *The wind has sunk down. Her voice sank to a whisper.* 6 pass gradually (into a state of sleep, silence, etc.): *to sink to rest.* 7 go deeply: *Let the lesson sink into your mind.* 8 make go deep: *The men are sinking a well.* 9 become worse: *My spirits sank.* 10 invest (money), especially unprofitably: *We sank $20 in a machine that we never used.* 11 a shallow basin or tub with a drainpipe: *The dishes are in the kitchen sink.* 12 a low-lying inland area where water collects. 1-10 *v.,* **sank** or **sunk, sunk, sink ing;** 11,12 *n.* —**sink′a ble,** *adj.*

sink er (sing′kər), a lead weight for sinking a fish line or net. *n.*

sink hole (singk′hōl′), 1 hole eroded in rock by running water and acting as a drain for surface water. 2 hole where water collects. *n.*

sin less (sin′lis), without sin. *adj.* —**sin′less ly,** *adv.* —**sin′less ness,** *n.*

sin ner (sin′ər), person who sins or does wrong. *n.*

sin u os i ty (sin′yü os′ə tē), 1 sinuous form or character; a winding. 2 curve; bend; turn. *n., pl.* **sin u os i ties.**

sin u ous (sin′yü əs), 1 having many curves or turns; winding: *The motion of a snake is sinuous.* 2 indirect; devious; untrustworthy. *adj.* —**sin′u ous ly,** *adv.* —**sin′u ous ness,** *n.*

si nus (sī′nəs), cavity in a bone, especially one of the cavities in the bones of the skull that connect with the nasal cavity. *n., pl.* **si nus es.**

si nus i tis (sī′nə sī′tis), inflammation of one of the sinuses of the head. *n.*

Si on (sī′ən), Zion. *n.*

Sioux (sü), 1 an American Indian tribe living on the plains of the northern United States and southern Canada. 2 the language of this tribe. *n., pl.* **Sioux** (sü *or* süz) for 1.

sip (sip), 1 drink little by little: *We sipped our tea.* 2 a very small drink: *She took a sip.* 3 act of sipping. 1 *v.,* **sipped, sip ping;** 2,3 *n.* —**sip′per,** *n.*

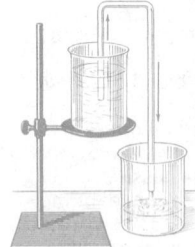

siphon (def. 1)—The arrows show the direction of flow of the liquid.

si phon (sī′fən), 1 a bent tube through which liquid can be drawn from one container into another at a lower level by atmospheric pressure. 2 draw off or pass through a siphon: *They siphoned a gallon of gasoline from their car to ours.* 3 bottle for soda water with a tube through which the liquid is forced out by the pressure of the gas in the bottle. 4 a tube-shaped organ of some animals, such as certain shellfish, for drawing in and expelling water. 1,3,4 *n.,* 2 *v.* Also, **syphon.** —**si′phon-less,** *adj.* —**si′phon like′,** *adj.*

sir (sér; *unstressed* sər), 1 a polite title used in writing or speaking to any man. 2 **Sir,** the title of a knight or baronet: *Sir Walter Scott. n.*

sire (sīr), 1 a male ancestor; forefather. 2 male parent; father: *Lightning was the sire of the racehorse Danger.* 3 be the father of: *Lightning sired Danger.* 4 title of respect used formerly to a great noble and now to a king: *"Good morning, Sire," said the attendant to the king.* 1,2,4 *n.,* 3 *v.,* **sired, sir ing.**

si ren (sī′rən), 1 kind of whistle that makes a loud, piercing sound: *We heard the sirens of the fire engines.* 2 (in Greek myths) any of a group of nymphs who, by their sweet singing, lured sailors to destruction upon the rocks. 3 woman who lures, tempts, or entices. 4 of a siren; tempting; charming. 1-3 *n.,* 4 *adj.* —**si′ren like′,** *adj.*

Sir i us (sir′ē əs), the brightest star in the sky; Dog Star. *n.*

sir loin (sér′loin), cut of beef from the part of the loin in front of the rump. *n.*

si roc co (sə rok′ō), 1 a hot, dry, dust-laden wind blowing from northern Africa across the Mediterranean Sea and southern Europe. 2 any hot, unpleasant wind. *n., pl.* **si roc cos.**

sir rah (sir′ə), OLD USE. fellow, used to address men and boys when speaking contemptuously, angrily, impatiently, etc. *n.*

sir up (sir′əp *or* sėr′əp), syrup. *n.*

sir up y (sir′ə pē *or* sėr′ə pē), syrupy. *adj.*

sis (sis), INFORMAL. sister. *n.*

sis al (sis′əl *or* sī′səl), **1** a strong, white fiber, used for making rope, twine, etc. **2** plant that it comes from. *n.* [*Sisal* was named after a port in Mexico, where the fiber was shipped from.]

sisal hemp, sisal.

sis sy (sis′ē), **1** sister. **2** boy or man who behaves in an unmanly way. **3** a weak or cowardly person. *n., pl.* **sissies.**

sis ter (sis′tər), **1** daughter of the same parents. A girl is a sister to the other children of her parents. **2** a close friend or companion. **3** a female member of the same union, club, religious organization, etc. **4** member of a religious order of women; nun: *Sisters of Charity. n.* —**sis′ter less,** *adj.* —**sis′ter like′,** *adj.*

sis ter hood (sis′tər hůd), **1** bond between sisters; feeling of sister for sister. **2** persons joined as sisters; association of women with some common aim or characteristic. *n.*

sis ter-in-law (sis′tər in lô′), **1** sister of one's husband or wife. **2** wife of one's brother. *n., pl.* **sis ters-in-law.**

sis ter li ness (sis′tər lē nis), sisterly affection or sympathy. *n.*

sis ter ly (sis′tər lē), **1** of a sister: *sisterly traits.* **2** like a sister; very friendly; kindly: *sisterly interest. adj.*

Sis tine Chapel (sis′tēn′), chapel in the Vatican. It is decorated with frescoes by Michelangelo and other great artists.

sit (sit), **1** rest on the lower part of the body with the weight off the feet: *She sat in a chair.* **2** cause to sit; seat: *The woman sat the little boy in his stroller.* **3** sit on: *He sat his horse well.* **4** have place or position: *The clock has sat on that shelf for years.* **5** have a seat in an assembly, etc.; be a member of a council: *sit in Congress.* **6** hold a session: *The court sits next month.* **7** place oneself in a position for having one's picture made; pose: *sit for a portrait.* **8** be in a state of rest; remain inactive: *He did not join in the game; he just sat on the sidelines.* **9** press or weigh: *His responsibilities sit heavy on his mind.* **10** perch: *The birds were sitting on the fence rail.* **11** brood: *The hen will sit until the eggs are ready to hatch.* **12** baby-sit: *I sit for the family next door.* **13** to fit: *The coat sits well. v.,* **sat, sit ting.**

sit down, take a seat; put oneself in a sitting position.

sit in, 1 take part (in a game, conference, etc.). **2** take part in a sit-in.

sit on or **sit upon, 1** sit in judgment or council on. **2** have a seat on (a jury, etc.).

sit out, 1 remain seated during (a dance). **2** stay through (a performance, etc.).

sit up, 1 raise the body to a sitting position. **2** keep such a position. **3** stay up instead of going to bed.

si tar (si tär′), a musical instrument of India, with a long neck and strings. It is played with a pick. *n.*

sit-down strike (sit′doun′), strike in which the workers stay in the factory, store, etc., without working until their demands are met or an agreement is reached.

site (sīt), position or place (of anything); location: *The site for the new school has not yet been chosen. n.*

sit-in (sit′in′), form of protest in which a group of people enter and remain seated for a long period of time in a public place. Sit-ins are organized to protest racial discrimination, government policies, etc. *n.*

Sit ka (sit′kə), town in SE Alaska. *n.*

sit ter (sit′ər), baby-sitter. *n.*

sit ting (sit′ing), **1** meeting or session of a court of law,

legislature, etc. **2** time of remaining seated: *She read five chapters at one sitting. n.*

Sitting Bull, 1834?-1890, Sioux Indian chief who defeated Custer in 1876.

sitting duck, an easy target or mark.

sitting room, parlor; living room.

sit u ate (sich′ü āt), place or locate. *v.,* **sit u at ed, sit u at ing.**

sit u at ed (sich′ü ā′tid), **1** placed; located: *New York is a favorably situated city.* **2** in a certain financial or social position: *The doctor was quite well situated. adj.*

sit u a tion (sich′ü ā′shən), **1** circumstances; case; condition: *act calmly in a difficult situation.* **2** place to work; job; position: *She is trying to find a good situation.* **3** site; location; place: *Our house has a beautiful situation on a hill. n.*

sit-up (sit′up′), exercise done by lying on the back with the hands behind the head, legs extended, and then sitting up without raising the feet. *n.*

six (siks), one more than five; 6. *n., pl.* **six es;** *adj.*

at sixes and sevens, 1 in confusion. **2** in disagreement.

Six Nations, federation of Iroquois Indian tribes. The Tuscarora tribe of Iroquois in 1722 joined the original confederacy of Iroquois tribes called the Five Nations.

six-pack (siks′pak′), a cardboard container holding six bottles, cans, or other items sold as a unit. *n.*

six pence (siks′pəns), **1** six British pennies; six pence. **2** a former British coin of this value. *n.*

six-shoot er (siks′shü′tər), INFORMAL. revolver that can fire six shots without being reloaded. *n.*

six teen (sik′stēn′), six more than ten; 16. *n., adj.*

six teenth (sik′stēnth′), **1** next after the 15th; last in a series of 16. **2** one of 16 equal parts. *adj., n.*

sixteenth note, (in music) a note played for one sixteenth as long a time as a whole note.

sixth (siksth), **1** next after the fifth; last in a series of 6. **2** one of 6 equal parts. *adj., n.*

sixth sense, an unusual power of perception; intuition.

sitars

six ti eth (sik′stē ith), **1** next after the 59th; last in a series of 60. **2** one of 60 equal parts. *adj., n.*

six ty (sik′stē), six times ten; 60. *n., pl.* **six ties;** *adj.*

siz a ble (sī′zə bəl), fairly large. *adj.* Also, **sizeable.** —**siz′a ble ness,** *n.* —**siz′a bly,** *adv.*

size¹ (sīz), **1** amount of surface or space a thing takes up: *The two boys are of the same size.* **2** extent; amount; magnitude: *the size of an industry.* **3** one of a series of measures: *His shoes are size 10.* **4** arrange according to size or in sizes: *Will you size these nails?* 1-3 *n.*, 4 *v.*, **sized, siz ing.**

of a size, of the same size.

size up, form an opinion of; estimate.

size² (sīz), **1** preparation made from glue, starch, or other sticky material. It is used to glaze paper, cover plastered walls, stiffen cloth, etc. **2** to coat or treat with size. 1 *n.*, 2 *v.*, **sized, siz ing.**

size a ble (sī′zə bəl), sizable. *adj.* —**size′a ble ness,** *n.* —**size′a bly,** *adv.*

siz zle (siz′əl), **1** make a hissing sound, as fat does when it is frying or burning. **2** a hissing sound. 1 *v.*, **siz zled, siz zling;** 2 *n.*

S.J. or **SJ,** Society of Jesus.

skate¹ (skāt), **1** a frame with a blade fixed to a shoe or that can be fastened to a shoe so that a person can glide over ice. **2** roller skate. **3** glide or move along on skates. 1,2 *n.*, 3 *v.*, **skat ed, skat ing.** [*Skate*¹ comes from Dutch *schaats.*]

skate² (skāt), a broad, flat fish, usually having a pointed snout. It is a kind of ray. *n.*, *pl.* **skates** or **skate.** [*Skate*² came into English about 600 years ago from Icelandic *skata.*]

skate board (skāt′bôrd′), a narrow board resembling a surfboard, with roller-skate wheels attached to each end, used for gliding or moving on any hard surface. *n.*

skat er (skā′tər), person who skates. *n.*

skeet (skēt), sport of shooting at targets, called clay pigeons, which are flung in the air at angles similar to those taken by a bird in flight. *n.*

skeins of yarn

skein (skān), a small, coiled bundle of yarn or thread. There are 120 yards in a skein of cotton yarn. *n.*

skel e tal (skel′ə təl), of or like a skeleton; attached to a skeleton. *adj.* —**skel′e tal ly,** *adv.*

skel e ton (skel′ə tən), **1** the framework of bones in a body that supports the muscles, organs, etc. **2** frame: *the steel skeleton of a building.* **3** the basic features or elements; outline: *the skeleton of a poem.* *n.* [*Skeleton* comes from the Greek phrase *skeleton sōma,* meaning "a dried-up body."] —**skel′e ton like′,** *adj.*

skeleton in the closet, a secret source of embarrassment, grief, or shame, especially to a family.

skeleton key, key made to open many locks.

skep tic (skep′tik), **1** person who questions the truth of theories or apparent facts; doubter. **2** person who doubts the truth of religious doctrines. *n.* Also, **sceptic.**

skep ti cal (skep′tə kəl), of or like a skeptic; inclined to doubt; not believing easily. *adj.* Also, **sceptical.** —**skep′ti cal ly,** *adv.*

skep ti cism (skep′tə siz′əm), skeptical attitude; doubt; unbelief. *n.* Also, **scepticism.**

sketch (skech), **1** a rough, quickly done drawing, painting, or design. **2** make a sketch of; draw roughly. **3** make sketches: *He sketches in his free time.* **4** outline; plan. **5** a short description, story, play, etc. 1,4,5 *n.*, *pl.* **sketch es;** 2,3 *v.* —**sketch′er,** *n.*

sketch book (skech′bük′), book to draw or paint sketches in. *n.*

sketch y (skech′ē), **1** like a sketch; having or giving only outlines or main features. **2** incomplete; slight; imperfect: *The first news bulletins gave only a sketchy account of the disaster.* *adj.*, **sketch i er, sketch i est.** —**sketch′i ly,** *adv.* —**sketch′i ness,** *n.*

skew (skyü), **1** twisted to one side; slanting. **2** a slant. **3** to slant. 1 *adj.*, 2 *n.*, 3 *v.* —**skew′ness,** *n.*

skew er (skyü′ər), **1** a long pin of wood or metal stuck through meat to hold it together while it is cooking. **2** fasten with a skewer or skewers. **3** pierce with or as if with a skewer. 1 *n.*, 2,3 *v.* —**skew′er er,** *n.*

ski (skē), **1** one of a pair of long, slender pieces of hard wood, plastic, or metal, that can be fastened to the shoes or boots to enable a person to glide over snow. **2** glide over the snow on skis. 1 *n.*, *pl.* **skis** or **ski;** 2 *v.*, **skied, ski ing.** [*Ski* was borrowed from Norwegian *ski.*] —**ski′a ble,** *adj.* —**ski′er,** *n.*

skid (skid), **1** to slip or slide sideways while moving: *The car skidded on the slippery road.* **2** a slip or slide while moving: *The car went into a skid on the icy road.* **3** piece of wood or metal to prevent a wheel from turning. **4** slide along without turning, as a wheel does when held by a skid. **5** timber, frame, etc., on which something rests, or on which something heavy may slide. **6** to slide along on a skid or skids. 1,4,6 *v.*, **skid ded, skid ding;** 2,3,5 *n.* —**skid′der,** *n.* —**skid′ding ly,** *adv.*

on the skids, SLANG. headed for dismissal, failure, or other disaster.

skies (skīz), plural of **sky.** *n.*

skiff (skif), **1** a light rowboat. **2** a small, light boat with a mast for a single triangular sail. *n.*

ski ing (skē′ing), act or sport of gliding over snow on skis. *n.*

skil ful (skil′fəl), skillful. *adj.* —**skil′ful ly,** *adv.* —**skil′ful ness,** *n.*

skill (skil), **1** ability gained by practice, knowledge, etc.; expertness: *The trained teacher managed the children with skill.* **2** ability to do things well with one's body or tools: *It takes skill to tune a piano.* **3** an art or craft: *master the carpenter's skill.* *n.* —**skill′-less, skill′less,** *adj.*

skilled (skild), **1** having skill; trained; experienced: *A carpenter is a skilled worker.* **2** showing skill; requiring skill: *Bricklaying is skilled labor.* *adj.*

skil let (skil′it), a shallow pan with a long handle, used for frying. *n.*

skill ful (skil′fəl), **1** having skill; expert: *a skillful surgeon.* **2** showing skill: *a skillful piece of bricklaying.* *adj.* Also, **skilful.** —**skill′ful ly,** *adv.* —**skill′ful ness,** *n.*

skim (skim), **1** remove from the top: *I skimmed the fat from the soup.* **2** take something from the top of: *skim milk by taking off the cream.* **3** move lightly over: *The*

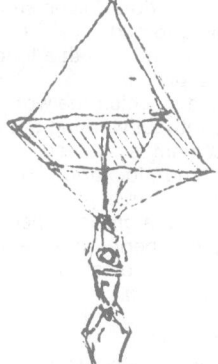

sketch (def. 1) drawn by Leonardo da Vinci in the 1400's. He believed this device would enable human beings to fall from great heights without injury.

pebble I threw skimmed the surface of the water. **4** glide along: *The swallows were skimming by.* **5** send skimming: *We made a contest to see who could skim a flat stone over the water the farthest.* **6** read hastily or carelessly; read with omissions: *It took me an hour to skim the book.* *v.,* **skimmed, skim ming.**

skim mer (skim′ər), **1** a shallow ladle full of holes, with a long handle. It is used in skimming liquids. **2** a sea bird that skims along the surface of water to get food. *n.*

skim milk or **skimmed milk,** milk from which the cream has been removed.

skimp (skimp), **1** supply in too small an amount: *Don't skimp the butter in making a cake.* **2** be very saving or economical: *She had to skimp to send her children to college.* **3** do imperfectly: *She is always skimping on her assignments.* *v.*

skimp y (skim′pē), scanty; not enough: *I was hungry all afternoon after my skimpy lunch.* *adj.,* **skimp i er, skimp i est.** —**skimp′i ly,** *adv.* —**skimp′i ness,** *n.*

skin (skin), **1** the outer layer of tissue of the body in persons and animals, especially when soft and flexible: *Cows have thick skins.* **2** a hide; pelt: *The skin of a calf makes soft leather.* **3** any outer surface layer, as the rind of a fruit, a sausage casing, etc. **4** take the skin off: *He skinned his knees when he fell. The hunter skinned the deer.* **5** container made of skin for holding liquids. **6** SLANG. to swindle of money, etc.; cheat. 1-3,5 *n.,* 4,6 *v.,* **skinned, skin ning.** —**skin′like′,** *adj.*

by the skin of one's teeth, very narrowly; barely.

save one's skin, escape without harm.

skin-deep (skin′dēp′), no deeper than the skin; shallow; slight. *adj.*

skin-dive (skin′dīv′), engage in skin diving. *v.,* **skin-dived, skin-div ing.**

skin diver

skin diver, person engaged in skin diving.

skin diving, sport of swimming under water, equipped with a face mask, rubber flippers, and often a portable breathing device.

skin flint (skin′flint′), a mean, stingy person. *n.*

skin less (skin′lis), having no skin: *skinless frankfurters.* *adj.*

skin ner (skin′ər), **1** person who skins. **2** person who prepares or deals in skins, furs, etc. *n.*

skin ny (skin′ē), very thin; very lean. *adj.,* **skin ni er, skin ni est.** —**skin′ni ness,** *n.*

skip (skip), **1** leap lightly; spring; jump: *The children skipped down the street.* **2** leap lightly over: *children skipping rope.* **3** a light spring, jump, or leap: *The child gave a skip of joy.* **4** go or send bounding along a surface: *we liked to skip stones on the lake.* **5** pass over; omit: *I skipped the questions I couldn't answer.* **6** a passing over; omission. **7** advance in school by being promoted one or more grades ahead of the next regular grade. **8** INFORMAL. leave in a hurry: *They skipped town to avoid paying their bills.* 1,2,4,5,7,8 *v.,* **skipped, skip ping;** 3,6 *n.*

skip jack (skip′jak′), any of various fishes that sometimes leap out of the water, such as a variety of tuna. *n., pl.* **skip jacks** or **skip jack.**

skip per (skip′ər), **1** captain of a ship, especially of a small trading or fishing boat. **2** any captain or leader. *n.*

skir mish (skėr′mish), **1** a slight fight between small groups: *The children had a skirmish over whose turn it was.* **2** a slight conflict, argument, contest, etc. **3** take part in a skirmish. 1,2 *n., pl.* **skir mish es;** 3 *v.* —**skir′mish er,** *n.*

skirt (skėrt), **1** the part of a dress that hangs from the waist. **2** a woman's or girl's garment that hangs from the waist. **3** something like a skirt: *A skirt covered the legs of the chair.* **4** border; edge: *The rabbits fed at the skirts of the field.* **5** the outer part of a place, group of people, etc. **6** pass along the border or edge; pass along the border or edge of: *We skirted the swamp.* 1-5 *n.,* 6 *v.*

skit (skit), a short sketch that contains humor or satire: *a television skit. n.*

skit ter (skit′ər), move lightly or quickly; skim or skip along a surface. *v.*

skit tish (skit′ish), **1** apt to start, jump, or run; easily frightened: *a skittish horse.* **2** fickle; changeable: *a skittish wind.* **3** shy and timid; coy: *a skittish child.* *adj.* —**skit′tish ly,** *adv.* —**skit′tish ness,** *n.*

skit tles (skit′lz), game in which the players try to knock down nine wooden pins by rolling balls or throwing wooden disks at them. *n.*

skoal (skōl), a Scandinavian word used in making a toast. It means "Hail" or "May you prosper." *n., interj.*

skul dug ger y (skul dug′ər ē), trickery; dishonesty. *n.*

skulk (skulk), **1** keep out of sight to avoid danger, work, duty, etc.; hide or lurk in a cowardly way. **2** move in a stealthy, sneaking way: *The wolf was skulking near the sheep.* *v.* —**skulk′er,** *n.* —**skulk′ing ly,** *adv.*

skull (skul), the bony framework of the head and face in human beings and other animals with backbones. The skull encloses and protects the brain. *n.*

skull and crossbones, picture of a human skull above two crossed bones. It was often used on pirates' flags as a symbol of death, and it is now sometimes used on labels of poisonous drugs, etc.

skull cap (skul′kap′), a close-fitting cap without a brim. *n.*

skunk (def. 1) about 2 ft. (60 cm.) long with the tail

skunk (skungk), **1** a black, bushy-tailed mammal of North America, usually with white stripes along its back. It is about the size of a cat. When frightened or attacked, skunks squirt a spray of liquid with a very strong, unpleasant smell from a pair of glands near the tail. **2** fur of this animal, used on coats, etc. **3** INFORMAL. a mean, contemptible person. **4** SLANG. defeat utterly, as in an unequal contest where one side is held scoreless. *n.* [*Skunk* is of Algonquian origin.]

sky (skī), **1** the space high above the earth, appearing as a great arch or dome covering the world; the region of the clouds or the upper air; the heavens: *a cloudy sky.* **2** heaven. *n., pl.* **skies.**

out of a clear sky, suddenly; unexpectedly.

to the skies, very highly: *to praise someone to the skies.*

sky blue, a clear, soft blue. —**sky′-blue′,** *adj.*

sky div ing (skī′dī′ving), act or sport of diving from an airplane and dropping for a great distance before releasing a parachute. *n.*

sky-high (skī′hī′), very high. *adv., adj.*

sky jack (skī′jak′), **1** hijack (an airplane), especially to a foreign country. **2** a hijacking of an airplane. 1 *v.,* 2 *n.* —**sky′jack′er,** *n.*

Sky lab (skī′lab′), the first U.S. space station. It was launched May 14, 1973, and fell to earth July 11, 1979. *n.*

sky lark (skī′lärk′), **1** a common European lark, a small bird that sings very sweetly as it flies toward the sky. **2** to play; frolic. 1 *n.,* 2 *v.*

sky light (skī′līt′), window in a roof or ceiling. *n.*

sky line (skī′līn′), **1** line at which earth and sky seem to meet; horizon. **2** outline of buildings, mountains, trees, etc., as seen against the sky: *New York City has a remarkable skyline. n.*

skyline (def. 2)

sky rock et (skī′rok′it), **1** firework that goes up high in the air and bursts into a shower of stars, sparks, etc. **2** act like a skyrocket; rise suddenly and make a brilliant show: *The movie star skyrocketed to fame.* **3** rise much and quickly: *The price of beef skyrocketed during the shortage.* 1 *n.,* 2,3 *v.*

sky scrap er (skī′skrā′pər), a very tall building. *n.*

sky ward (skī′wərd), toward the sky. *adv., adj.*

sky wards (skī′wərdz), skyward. *adv.*

sky writ ing (skī′rī′ting), the tracing of words, etc., against the sky from an airplane. Smoke or some similar substance is used. *n.*

slab (slab), a broad, flat, thick piece (of stone, wood, meat, etc.): *a slab of cheese as big as my hand. This sidewalk is made of slabs of concrete. n.*

slack (slak), **1** not tight or firm; loose: *a slack rope.* **2** part that hangs loose: *Pull in the slack of the rope.* **3** careless: *a slack worker.* **4** slow: *The horse was moving at a slack pace.* **5** not active; not brisk; dull: *Business is slack at this season.* **6** a dull season; quiet period. **7** make or become slack; let up: *He slacked his pace so we could catch up. The breeze slacked.* 1,3-5 *adj.,* 2,6 *n.,* 7 *v.* —**slack′ly,** *adv.* —**slack′ness,** *n.*

slack off, 1 loosen. **2** lessen one's efforts.

slack up, slow down; go more slowly.

slack en (slak′ən), **1** make or become slower: *Don't slacken your efforts till the work is done. Their business*

always slackens in the winter. **2** make or become looser: *Slacken the rope. The rope slackened as the wave sent the boat toward the pier. v.*

slack er (slak′ər), person who shirks work or evades duty. *n.*

slacks (slaks), trousers for casual wear. *n.pl.*

slag (slag), **1** the rough, hard waste left after metal is separated from ore by melting. **2** a light, spongy lava. *n.*

slain (slān), past participle of **slay.** *The sheep were slain by the wolves. v.*

slake (slāk), **1** satisfy (thirst, revenge, wrath, etc.): *We slaked our thirst at the spring.* **2** change lime to slaked lime by leaving it in the moist air or putting water on it. *v.,* **slaked, slak ing.**

slaked lime, a white powder obtained by exposing lime to moist air or by putting water on lime; calcium hydroxide. Plaster contains slaked lime and sand.

slalom—He won the men's slalom.

sla lom (slä′ləm *or* slal′əm), (in skiing) a zigzag race downhill. *n.* [*Slalom* is borrowed from Norwegian *slalom,* which comes from *slad,* meaning "bent," and *lom,* meaning "trail."]

slam (slam), **1** shut with force and noise; close with a bang: *She slammed the window down. The door slammed.* **2** throw, push, hit, or move hard with force: *That car slammed into a truck.* **3** a violent and noisy closing, striking, etc.; bang: *I threw my books down with a slam.* **4** INFORMAL. criticize harshly. **5** the winning of 12 (**little slam** or **small slam**) or all 13 (**grand slam**) tricks in the game of bridge. 1,2,4 *v.,* **slammed, slam ming;** 3,5 *n.*

slan der (slan′dər), **1** a false spoken statement meant to harm a person's reputation: *The candidate for mayor accused his opponent of slander.* **2** talk falsely about. **3** the spreading of false reports: *Malicious slander had caused some people to doubt the mayor's honesty.* 1,3 *n.,* 2 *v.* —**slan′der er,** *n.*

slan der ous (slan′dər əs), **1** containing a slander. **2** speaking or spreading slanders. *adj.* —**slan′der ous ly,** *adv.* —**slan′der ous ness,** *n.*

slang (slang), **1** words, phrases, meanings, etc., not accepted as good English when speaking or writing formal English. Slang is often very vivid and expressive and is used in familiar talk between friends but is not usually appropriate in school themes. Slang is mostly made up of new words or meanings that are popular for only a short time. *Goof* and *on the skids* are slang. **2** special talk of a particular class of people. *Shake a leg* is a slang expression for *hurry up. n.*

slang y (slang′ē), **1** containing slang; full of slang. **2** using much slang. *adj.,* **slang i er, slang i est.** —**slang′i ly,** *adv.* —**slang′i ness,** *n.*

slant (slant), **1** to slope: *Most handwriting slants to the right. The carpenters slanted the roof to allow water to run off.* **2** a slanting or oblique direction or position; slope: *The roof has a sharp slant.* **3** sloping: *A lean-to has a slant* *roof.* **4** way of regarding something; mental attitude. 1 *v.,* 2,4 *n.,* 3 *adj.*

slant ing (slan′ting), sloping: *a slanting roof. adj.*

slant ways (slant′wāz′), slantwise. *adv.*

slant wise (slant′wīz′), **1** in a slanting manner; obliquely. **2** slanting; oblique. 1 *adv.,* 2 *adj.*

slap (slap), **1** a blow with the open hand or with something flat. **2** strike with the open hand or with something flat: *I slapped the table with my hand.* **3** sound made by a slapping. **4** put, dash, or cast with force: *She slapped the book down angrily.* 1,3 *n.,* 2,4 *v.,* **slapped, slap ping.**

slap dash (slap′dash′), **1** hastily and carelessly. **2** hasty and careless. **3** hasty, careless action, methods, or work. 1 *adv.,* 2 *adj.,* 3 *n.*

slap shot, (in hockey) a fast shot made with a swinging stroke of the stick at the puck.

slap stick (slap′stik′), **1** comedy full of rough play. **2** full of rough play. In slapstick comedy, the actors knock each other around, throw pies at each other, etc., to make people laugh. 1 *n.,* 2 *adj.*

slash (slash), **1** to cut with a sweeping stroke of a sword, knife, etc.; gash: *I slashed the bark off the tree with my knife.* **2** make a slashing stroke: *She slashed at the vines growing across the path with her knife.* **3** a sweeping, slashing stroke: *the slash of a sword, the slash of the rain.* **4** a cut or wound made by such a stroke. **5** to cut or slit to let a different cloth or color show through. **6** whip severely; lash. **7** criticize sharply, severely, or unkindly: *The critics slashed the new play.* **8** cut down sharply; reduce a great deal: *My salary was slashed when business became bad.* **9** a sharp cutting down; great reduction: *a slash in prices.* 1,2,5-8 *v.,* 3,4,9 *n., pl.* **slash es. —slash′-er,** *n.*

slat (slat), a long, thin, narrow piece of wood or metal. *n.*

slate (slāt), **1** a fine-grained, bluish-gray rock that splits easily into thin, smooth layers. Slate is used to cover roofs and for blackboards. **2** a thin piece of this rock. Schoolchildren used to write on slates, but now they use paper. **3** to cover with slate. **4** a dark, bluish gray. **5** dark bluish-gray. **6** list of candidates, officers, etc., to be considered for appointment, nomination, election, etc. **7** put on such a list: *She is slated for nomination to the office of class president.* 1,2,4,6 *n.,* 3,7 *v.,* **slat ed, slat ing;** 5 *adj.* **—slate′like′,** *adj.*

a clean slate, a record not marred by mistakes or faults: *to start again with a clean slate.*

slat tern (slat′ərn), woman who is dirty, careless, or untidy in her dress, her ways, her housekeeping, etc. *n.*

slat tern ly (slat′ərn lē), like a slattern; slovenly; untidy. *adj.* **—slat′tern li ness,** *n.*

slat y (slā′tē), **1** of or like slate. **2** slate-colored. *adj.,* **slat i er, slat i est.**

slaugh ter (slô′tər), **1** the killing of an animal or animals for food; butchering: *the slaughter of a steer, to fatten hogs for slaughter.* **2** brutal killing; much or needless killing: *The battle resulted in a frightful slaughter.* **3** kill an animal or animals for food; butcher: *Millions of cattle are slaughtered every year in the stockyards.* **4** kill brutally; massacre. 1,2 *n.,* 3,4 *v.* **—slaugh′ter er,** *n.*

slaugh ter house (slô′tər hous′), place where animals are killed for food. *n., pl.* **slaugh ter hous es** (slô′tər-hou′ziz).

Slav (släv), **1** member of a group of peoples in eastern, southeastern, and central Europe whose languages are related. Russians, Poles, Czechs, Slovaks, Slovenes, Bulgarians, and Yugoslavs are Slavs. **2** of Slavs; Slavic. 1 *n.,* 2 *adj.*

slave (slāv), **1** person who is owned by another. **2** person who is controlled or ruled by some desire, habit, or influence: *a slave to drugs, a slave to one's emotions.*

3 person who works like a slave. **4** work like a slave: *We slaved all day long cleaning our house.* **5** of slaves; done by slaves: *slave labor.* 1-3 *n.,* 4 *v.,* **slaved, slav ing;** 5 *adj.* **—slave′like′,** *adj.*

slave driver, 1 overseer of slaves. **2** a harsh supervisor.

slave hold er (slāv′hōl′dər), owner of slaves. *n.*

slave hold ing (slāv′hōl′ding), **1** owning slaves. **2** the owning of slaves. 1 *adj.,* 2 *n.*

slav er[1] (slā′vər), **1** dealer in slaves. **2** ship used in the slave trade. *n.*

slav er[2] (slav′ər), **1** let saliva run from the mouth. **2** saliva running from the mouth. 1 *v.,* 2 *n.*

slav er y (slā′vər ē), **1** condition of being a slave. **2** custom of owning slaves. Where slavery is permitted, certain people own other people. **3** condition like that of a slave. **4** hard work like that of a slave. *n.*

slave trade, the business of obtaining and selling slaves.

Slav ic (slä′vik), **1** of the Slavs or their languages. **2** language or group of languages spoken by the Slavs. 1 *adj.,* 2 *n.*

slav ish (slā′vish), **1** weakly submitting; like slaves; fit for slaves: *their slavish obedience.* **2** lacking originality and independence: *a slavish reproduction. adj.* **—slav′ish ly,** *adv.* **—slav′ish ness,** *n.*

slaw (slô), coleslaw. *n.*

slay (slā), kill with violence: *Jack slew the giant. v.,* **slew, slain, slay ing. —slay′er,** *n.*

slea zi ness (slē′zē nis), sleazy quality. *n.*

slea zy (slē′zē), **1** flimsy and poor: *sleazy cloth.* **2** in poor condition; disreputable: *a sleazy hotel. adj.,* **slea zi er, slea zi est. —slea′zi ly,** *adv.*

sled (sled), **1** framework mounted on runners for use on snow or ice. Sleds pulled by dogs are common in the Arctic. **2** ride or carry on a sled. 1 *n.,* 2 *v.,* **sled ded, sled ding. —sled′der,** *n.*

sled ding (sled′ing), a riding or coasting on a sled: *two months of good sledding.*

hard sledding, unfavorable conditions; difficult going: *The bill will have hard sledding before the legislature passes it.*

sledge[1] (slej), **1** a heavy sled or sleigh, usually pulled by horses, etc. **2** carry on or ride in a sledge. 1 *n.,* 2 *v.,* **sledged, sledg ing.** [*Sledge*[1] comes from Dutch *sleedse.*]

sledge[2] (slej), sledgehammer. *n.*

sledge ham mer (slej′ham′ər), a large, heavy hammer, usually swung with both hands. *n.*

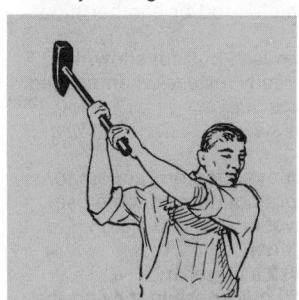

sledgehammer

sleek (slēk), **1** soft and glossy; smooth: *sleek hair.*
2 having smooth, soft skin, hair, fur, etc.: *a sleek cat.*
3 smooth of manners and speech: *a sleek salesclerk.*
4 having clean lines; trim: *a sleek jet plane.* **5** to smooth or make smooth: *He sleeked down his hair.* 1-4 *adj.,* 5 *v.*
[*Sleek* is a different form of *slick.*] —**sleek′ly,** *adv.*
—**sleek′ness,** *n.*

sleep (slēp), **1** to rest body and mind; be without ordinary thought or movement: *We sleep at night.* **2** a rest of body and mind occurring naturally and regularly: *Most people need eight hours of sleep a day.* **3** be in a condition like sleep: *The seeds sleep in the ground all winter.*
4 condition like sleep. The last sleep means death. 1,3 *v.,* **slept, sleep ing;** 2,4 *n.* —**sleep′like′,** *adj.*

sleep away, pass or spend in sleeping: *I slept away the whole morning.*

sleep off, get rid of by sleeping: *She was sleeping off a headache.*

sleep er (slē′pər), **1** person or thing that sleeps: *a sound sleeper. The noise woke the sleepers.* **2** a railroad sleeping car. **3** a heavy horizontal beam used as a support. *n.*

sleep i ly (slē′pə lē), in a sleepy manner. *adv.*

sleep i ness (slē′pē nis), sleepy quality or condition. *n.*

sleep ing (slē′ping), **1** sleep. **2** that sleeps. **3** used for sleeping on or in: *sleeping quarters.* 1 *n.,* 2,3 *adj.*

sleeping bag, a warmly lined bag made of nylon, Dacron, down, etc., to sleep in outdoors.

sleeping car, a railroad car with berths for passengers to sleep in; Pullman.

sleeping sickness 1 disease common in Africa and carried by the tsetse fly, causing fever, inflammation of the brain, weakness, sleepiness, and usually death. **2** a virus disease marked by inflammation of the brain, weakness, and extreme drowsiness.

sleep less (slēp′lis), **1** without sleep; restless: *a hot, sleepless night.* **2** watchful; wide-awake. **3** always moving or acting. *adj.* —**sleep′less ly,** *adv.* —**sleep′less ness,** *n.*

sleep walk er (slēp′wô′kər), person who walks about while asleep. *n.*

sleep walk ing (slēp′wô′king), act of walking while asleep. *n.*

sleep y (slē′pē), **1** ready to go to sleep; inclined to sleep: *He never gets enough rest and is always sleepy.* **2** not active; quiet: *a sleepy little mountain town.* *adj.,* **sleep i er, sleep i est.**

sleep y head (slē′pē hed′), a sleepy, drowsy, or lazy person. *n.*

sleet (slēt), **1** partly frozen rain; snow or hail mixed with rain. Sleet forms when rain falls through a layer of cold air. **2** come down in sleet: *It sleeted; then it snowed; then it rained.* 1 *n.,* 2 *v.*

sleet y (slē′tē), of or like sleet; characterized by sleet: *a dismal and sleety morning. adj.,* **sleet i er, sleet i est.**
—**sleet′i ness,** *n.*

sleeve (slēv), **1** the part of a garment that covers the arm: *The sleeves of her coat were too long and hung down over her hands.* **2** tube into which a rod or another tube fits. *n.*

laugh up one's sleeve, be amused but not show it.

up one's sleeve, in reserve; ready for use when needed.

sleeved (slēvd), having sleeves. *adj.*

sleeve less (slēv′lis), without sleeves: *a sleeveless summer dress. adj.*

sleigh (slā), **1** carriage or cart mounted on runners for use on ice or snow. In northern countries people use sleighs in the winter. **2** to travel or ride in a sleigh. 1 *n.,* 2 *v.* [*Sleigh* comes from Dutch *slee.*]

sleight (slīt), **1** skill, dexterity. **2** a clever trick. *n.*

sleight of hand, 1 skill and quickness in moving the hands. **2** tricks or skill of a modern magician; juggling.

slen der (slen′dər), **1** long and thin; not big around; slim: *a slender child. A pencil is a slender piece of wood.*
2 slight; small; scanty: *a slender meal, a slender income, a slender hope. adj.* —**slen′der ly,** *adv.* —**slen′der ness,** *n.*

slept (slept), past tense and past participle of **sleep.** *The child slept soundly. I haven't slept well for weeks. v.*

sleuth (slüth), INFORMAL. detective. *n.* [*Sleuth* came into English over 700 years ago from Icelandic *slōth,* meaning "a trail."]

slew[1] (slü), past tense of **slay.** *Jack slew the giant. v.*

slew[2] (slü), **1** to turn; swing; twist: *She slewed the front wheels sharply to avoid hitting the dog. The car suddenly slewed to the left.* **2** a turn; swing; twist. 1 *v.,* 2 *n.* Also, **slue.**

slew[3] (slü), slough[1] (def. 2). *n.*

slew[4] (slü), INFORMAL. a lot; large number or amount: *The new girl quickly gained a slew of friends. n.* Also, **slue.**

slice (slīs), **1** a thin, flat, broad piece cut from something: *a slice of bread, meat, or cake.* **2** cut into slices: *slice the bread. We ate sliced peaches.* **3** cut (off) as a slice. **4** cut through or across: *The boat sliced the waves.* **5** (in sports) hit (a ball) so that it curves to one's right if hit right-handed. 1 *n.,* 2-5 *v.,* **sliced, slic ing.**

slic er (slī′sər), **1** tool or machine that slices: *a meat slicer.* **2** person who slices. *n.*

slick (slik), **1** soft and glossy; smooth: *slick hair.* **2** make sleek or smooth: *He slicked down his hair.* **3** slippery; greasy: *a road slick with ice or mud.* **4** a smooth place or spot. Oil makes a slick on the surface of water. **5** clever; ingenious. **6** sly; tricky. **7** smooth of speech, manners, etc. 1,3,5-7 *adj.,* 2 *v.,* 4 *n.* —**slick′ly,** *adv.* —**slick′ness,** *n.*

slick er (slik′ər), **1** a long, loose, waterproof coat, made of oilskin or the like. **2** an unpleasantly smooth, tricky person: *a city slicker. n.*

slid (slid), past tense and a past participle of **slide.** *The minutes slid by. v.*

slid den (slid′n), slid; a past participle of **slide.** *v.*

slide (slīd), **1** move smoothly along a surface: *The bureau drawers slide in and out.* **2** move easily, quietly, or secretly: *I hid by sliding behind the door.* **3** to slip as when losing one's foothold: *The car slid into the ditch.* **4** pass by degrees; slip: *They slid into bad habits.* **5** pass or put quietly or secretly: *I slid the letter into my pocket.* **6** act of sliding: *The children each take a slide in turn.* **7** a smooth surface for sliding on: *The frozen brook makes a good slide.* **8** track, rail, etc., on which something slides. **9** something that slides or that works by sliding. **10** mass of earth, snow, etc., sliding down: *The slide cut off the valley from the rest of the world.* **11** the sliding down of such a mass: *The slide was felt at the other end of the valley.* **12** a small, thin sheet of glass on which objects are placed in order to look at them under a microscope. **13** a small transparent photograph made of film or glass. Slides are put in a projector and shown on a screen. 1-5 *v.,* **slid, slid** or **slid den, slid ing;** 6-13 *n.*

let slide, neglect; not bother about: *They let their business slide until they were bankrupt.*

sleigh (def. 1)—The **sleighs** raced over the icy road.

slide fastener, zipper.
slide projector, instrument for projecting onto a screen the images on photographic slides.
slide rule, ruler with a sliding section in the center, both parts marked with scales, used for making rapid mathematical calculations.

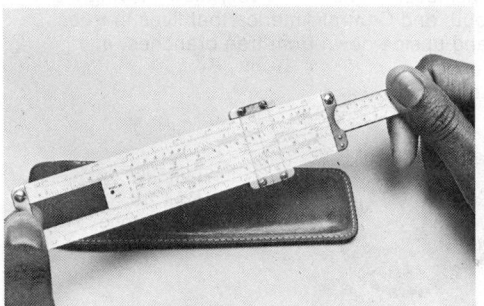

slide rule

a hat	i it	oi oil	ch child		a in about
ā age	ī ice	ou out	ng long		e in taken
ä far	o hot	u cup	sh she	ə =	i in pencil
e let	ō open	u̇ put	th thin		o in lemon
ē equal	ô order	ü rule	ŦH then		u in circus
ėr term			zh measure		

slight (slīt), **1** not much; not important; small: *I have a slight headache.* **2** not big around; slender: *a slight figure.* **3** treat as of little value; pay too little attention to; neglect: *They often slight their work. I felt slighted because I was not asked to the party.* **4** slighting treatment; act of neglect: *The unpopular student suffered many slights in school.* **1,2** *adj.,* **3** *v.,* **4** *n.* —**slight′ness,** *n.*
slight ing (slī′ting), that slights: *a slighting remark. adj.* —**slight′ing ly,** *adv.*
slight ly (slīt′lē), **1** in a slight manner. **2** to a slight degree; somewhat; a little: *I knew him slightly. adv.*
sli ly (slī′lē), slyly. *adv.*
slim (slim), **1** slender; thin: *He was very slim, being 6 feet tall and weighing only 130 pounds.* **2** small; slight; weak: *We had a slim attendance at the football game because of the rain. The invalid's chances for getting well were very slim.* **3** make or become slim or slender: *slim down one's weight with a rigid diet.* **1,2** *adj.,* **slim mer, slim mest;** **3** *v.,* **slimmed, slim ming.** —**slim′ly,** *adv.* —**slim′ness,** *n.*
slime (slīm), **1** soft, sticky mud or something like it: *Her shoes were covered with slime from the swamp.* **2** a sticky substance given off by snails, snakes, fish, etc. **3** disgusting filth. *n.*
slim y (slī′mē), **1** covered with slime: *The pond is too slimy to swim in.* **2** of or like slime. **3** disgusting; filthy. *adj.,* **slim i er, slim i est.** —**slim′i ly,** *adv.* —**slim′i ness,** *n.*

sling (def. 6)

sling (sling), **1** strip of leather with a string fastened to each end, for throwing stones. **2** a slingshot. **3** throw with a sling. **4** throw; cast; hurl; fling: *I slung the bag of oats into the truck.* **5** a hanging loop of cloth fastened around the neck to support an injured arm. **6** loop of rope, band, chain, etc., by which heavy objects are lifted, carried, or held: *We lowered the heavy boxes over the railing with a sling.* **7** raise, lower, etc., with a sling. **8** hang in a sling; hang so as to swing loosely: *I carried*

the bag slung over my shoulder. **1,2,5,6** *n.,* **3,4,7,8** *v.,* **slung, sling ing.** —**sling′er,** *n.*
sling shot (sling′shot′), a Y-shaped stick with a band of rubber between its prongs, used to shoot pebbles, etc. *n.*
slink (slingk), move in a sneaking, guilty manner; sneak: *After stealing the meat, the dog slunk away. v.,* **slunk, slink ing.**
slip[1] (slip), **1** go or move smoothly, quietly, easily, or quickly: *She slipped out of the room. Time slips by.* **2** slide; move out of place: *The knife slipped and cut his finger.* **3** slide suddenly without wanting to: *He slipped on the icy sidewalk.* **4** act or fact of slipping: *Her broken leg resulted from a slip on a banana peel.* **5** cause to slip; put, pass, or draw smoothly, quietly, or secretly: *I slipped back the bolt on the door. I slipped the ring from my finger. Slip the note into her hand.* **6** put or take (something) easily or quickly: *Slip on your coat and come with us. Slip off your shoes.* **7** pillowcase. **8** a sleeveless garment worn under a dress. **9** pass without notice; pass through neglect; escape: *Don't let this opportunity slip.* **10** get loose from; get away from; escape from: *The dog has slipped its collar. Your name has slipped my mind.* **11** fall off; decline: *Sales are slipping.* **12** make a mistake or error: *I slipped when I mailed the wrong letter.* **13** mistake; error: *He makes slips in pronouncing words. That remark was a slip of the tongue.* **14** space for ships between wharves or in a dock. **1-3,5, 6,9-12** *v.,* **slipped, slip ping;** **4,7,8,13,14** *n.*
let slip, tell without meaning to: *They talked too much and let the secret slip.*
slip one over on, INFORMAL. get the advantage of, especially by trickery: *The fox slipped one over on the hounds and got away.*
slip out, become known.
slip up, make a mistake or error: *I must have slipped up somewhere when I did the problem, because my answer is wrong.*
slip[2] (slip), **1** a small, narrow strip of paper, wood, etc.: *The teacher passed out slips of paper for us to write our names on.* **2** a young, slender person: *He is just a slip of a boy.* **3** a small branch or twig cut from a plant, used to grow a new plant: *She has promised us slips from her rosebush.* **4** cut branches from (a plant) to grow new plants; take (a part) from a plant. **1-3** *n.,* **4** *v.,* **slipped, slip ping.**
slip cov er (slip′kuv′ər), a removable cloth or plastic cover for a chair, sofa, etc. *n.*
slip knot (slip′not′), knot made to slip along the rope or cord around which it is made; running knot. *n.*
slip o ver (slip′ō′vər), pullover. *n.*
slip per (slip′ər), a light, low shoe that is slipped on easily: *dancing slippers, bedroom slippers. n.* —**slip′per less,** *adj.*
slip pered (slip′ərd), wearing slippers. *adj.*
slip per i ness (slip′ər ē nis), slippery quality or condition. *n.*
slip per y (slip′ər ē), **1** causing or likely to cause slipping: *The steps are slippery with ice.* **2** slipping away easily: *Wet soap is slippery.* **3** not to be depended on; tricky. *adj.,* **slip per i er, slip per i est.**
slip shod (slip′shod′), careless in dress, habits, speech, etc.; untidy; slovenly. *adj.*

slip-up (slip′up′), INFORMAL. mistake; error: *Do this job right, with no slip-ups. n.*

slit (slit), **1** cut or tear in a straight line; make a long, straight cut or tear in: *slit cloth into strips, slit a skirt to make a pocket.* **2** a straight, narrow cut, tear, or opening: *a slit in a bag, the slit in a mailbox.* **1** *v.,* **slit, slit ting; 2** *n.* —**slit′like′,** *adj.* —**slit′ter,** *n.*

slith er (sliᴛʜ′ər), **1** slide down or along a surface, especially unsteadily: *Rocks slithered down the side of the hill.* **2** go with a sliding motion: *The snake slithered into the weeds.* **3** a slithering movement; a slide. 1,2 *v.,* 3 *n.*

sliv er (sliv′ər), **1** a long, thin piece that has been split off, broken off, or cut off; splinter. **2** split or break into slivers. 1 *n.,* 2 *v.*

slob (slob), INFORMAL. a dirty, untidy, or clumsy person. *n.* [*Slob* comes from Irish *slab*, meaning "mud."]

slob ber (slob′ər), **1** let liquid run out from the mouth; drool. **2** saliva or other liquid running out from the mouth. **3** speak in a silly, sentimental way. 1,3 *v.,* 2 *n.* —**slob′ber er,** *n.*

slob ber y (slob′ər ē), **1** slobbering. **2** disagreeably wet; sloppy. *adj.*

sloe (slō), **1** a dark-purple, plumlike fruit. **2** the thorny shrub that it grows on. *n.*

slog (slog), **1** plod heavily. **2** work hard (at something). *v.,* **slogged, slog ging.** —**slog′ger,** *n.*

slo gan (slō′gən), word or phrase used by a business, club, political party, etc., to advertise its purpose; motto: *"Service with a smile" was the store's slogan. n.*

WORD HISTORY

slogan

Slogan is from Gaelic *sluagh-ghairm.* In Gaelic, *sluagh* means "army" and *gairm* means "a cry, a shout."

---

sloop (slüp), sailboat having one mast, a mainsail, a jib, and sometimes other sails. *n.* [*Sloop* comes from Dutch *sloep.*]

slop (slop), **1** spill liquid upon; spill; splash: *She slopped water on me.* **2** liquid carelessly spilled or splashed about. **3** Often, **slops,** *pl.* dirty water; liquid garbage: *kitchen slops.* **4** a thin, liquid mud or slush. **5** splash through mud, slush, or water. **6** weak, liquid food, such as gruel. 1,5 *v.,* **slopped, slop ping;** 2-4,6 *n.*

slop over, INFORMAL. show too much feeling, enthusiasm, etc.

slope (slōp), **1** go up or down at an angle; slant: *a sloping roof. The land slopes toward the sea.* **2** any line, surface, land, etc., that goes up or down at an angle: *If you roll a ball up a slope, it will roll down again.* **3** amount of slant: *The floor of the theater has a slope of four feet from back to front.* 1 *v.,* **sloped, slop ing;** 2,3 *n.* —**slop′er,** *n.*

slop pi ly (slop′ə lē), in a sloppy manner. *adv.*

slop pi ness (slop′ē nis), sloppy quality or condition. *n.*

slop py (slop′ē), **1** very wet; slushy: *sloppy ground, sloppy weather.* **2** careless; slovenly: *do sloppy work, use sloppy English.* **3** INFORMAL. weak; silly: *sloppy sentiment. adj.,* **slop pi er, slop pi est.**

slosh (slosh), splash in slush, mud, or water: *She sloshed around in the bathtub and got the floor all wet. v.* [*Slosh* may be a blend of *slop* and *slush.*]

slot (slot), **1** a small, narrow opening or depression: *Put a dime in the slot to get candy from this machine.* **2** make a slot or slots in. 1 *n.,* 2 *v.,* **slot ted, slot ting.**

slot car, a plastic, toy racing car built to exact scale, electrically driven over a slotted track, and operated by a hand-held, remote control.

sloth (slôth *or* slōth), **1** unwillingness to work or exert oneself; laziness; idleness. **2** a very slow-moving mammal of South and Central America that lives in trees. Sloths hang upside down from tree branches. *n.*

sloth (def. 2) about 2 ft. (60 cm.) long

sloth ful (slôth′fəl *or* slōth′fəl), unwilling to work or exert oneself; lazy; idle. *adj.* —**sloth′ful ly,** *adv.* —**sloth′ful ness,** *n.*

slot machine, machine that is worked by dropping a coin into a slot. Some slot machines are vending machines that sell peanuts, candy, etc.; others are used for gambling.

slouch (slouch), **1** stand, sit, walk, or move in an awkward, drooping manner: *The weary traveler slouched along.* **2** a bending forward of head and shoulders; awkward, drooping way of standing, sitting, or walking. **3** droop or bend downward: *I slouched my shoulders.* **4** an awkward, careless, or inefficient person. 1,3 *v.,* 2,4 *n., pl.* **slouch es.** —**slouch′er,** *n.*

slouch hat, a soft hat, usually with a soft brim that bends down easily.

slouch y (slou′chē), slouching awkwardly; carelessly untidy. *adj.,* **slouch i er, slouch i est.** —**slouch′i ly,** *adv.* —**slouch′i ness,** *n.*

slough¹ (slou *for 1;* slü *for 2*), **1** a soft, deep, muddy place. **2** a swampy place; marshy inlet; slew; slue. *n.*

sloop

slough² (sluf), **1** the old skin shed or cast off by a snake. **2** drop off; throw off; shed or cast: *slough a heavy pack. I finally sloughed off my bad habits.* **3** be shed or cast; drop or fall: *A scab sloughs off when new skin takes its place.* **4** anything that has been or can be shed or cast off: *As people become civilized, they cast off the slough of primitive ways.* 1,4 *n.,* 2,3 *v.*

Slo vak (slō′vak), **1** member of a Slavic people living in E Czechoslovakia. The Slovaks are related to the Bohemians and the Moravians. **2** their language. **3** of Slovakia, its people, or their language: *Slovak writers.* 1,2 *n.,* 3 *adj.*

Slo va ki a (slō vä′kē ə), region in E Czechoslovakia. *n.* —**Slo va′ki an,** *adj., n.*

slov en (sluv′ən), person who is untidy, dirty, or careless in dress, appearance, habits, work, etc. *n.*

Slo vene (slō/vēn/), **1** member of a Slavic people living in NW Yugoslavia. The Slovenes are related to the Croats and Serbians. **2** their language. *n.*

Slo ve ni a (slō vē/nē ə), region in NW Yugoslavia. *n.* —**Slo ve/ni an,** *adj., n.*

slov en li ness (sluv/ən lē nis), lack of neatness; carelessness in appearance, dress, habits, work, etc. *n.*

slov en ly (sluv/ən lē), **1** untidy, dirty, or careless in appearance, dress, habits, work, etc. **2** in a slovenly manner. 1 *adj.,* **slov en li er, slov en li est;** 2 *adv.*

slow (slō), **1** taking a long time; taking longer than usual; not fast or quick: *a slow journey. She is slow to anger.* **2** behind time; running at less than proper speed: *This train is usually slow.* **3** indicating time earlier than the correct time: *That clock is slow.* **4** causing a low or lower rate of speed: *a slow track.* **5** make slow or slower; reduce the speed of: *slow down a car.* **6** become slow; go slower: *Slow up when you drive through a town.* **7** in a slow manner: *Drive slow past a school.* **8** sluggish; inactive: *Business is slow.* **9** dull; not interesting: *a slow party.* **10** not quick to understand: *a slow pupil.* 1-4,8-10 *adj.,* 5,6 *v.,* 7 *adv.* —**slow/ly,** *adv.* —**slow/ness,** *n.*

slow ish (slō/ish), rather slow. *adj.*

slow-mo tion (slō/mō/shən), showing action at much less than its actual speed: *slow-motion photography. adj.*

slow poke (slō/pōk/), INFORMAL. a very slow person or thing. *n.*

sludge (sluj), **1** soft mud; mire; slush. **2** a soft, thick, muddy mixture, deposit, sediment, etc. **3** small broken pieces of floating ice: *In winter there is sludge on the sea near the shore. n.*

sludg y (sluj/ē), made up of sludge; slushy. *adj.,* **sludg i er, sludg i est.**

slue[1] (slü), slew[2]. *v.,* **slued, slu ing;** *n.*

slue[2] (slü), slough[1] (def. 2). *n.*

slue[3] (slü), slew[4]. *n.*

slug[1] (slug), **1** a slow-moving animal like a snail, without a shell or with only a partially developed shell. Slugs live mostly in forests, gardens, and damp places feeding on plants. **2** caterpillar or other larva that looks like a slug. **3** any slow-moving person, animal, wagon, etc. **4** piece of lead or other metal for firing from a gun. **5** a round metal piece or counterfeit coin inserted in a coin-operated machine instead of a genuine coin. **6** strip of metal used to space lines of type. A slug is more than $1/16$ of an inch in thickness. *n.*

slug[2] (slug), INFORMAL. **1** hit hard with the fist or with a baseball bat; hit hard. **2** a hard blow with the fist. 1 *v.,* **slugged, slug ging;** 2 *n.*

slug gard (slug/ərd), a lazy, idle person. *n.*

slug ger (slug/ər), INFORMAL. a person who slugs or hits hard, especially a boxer who punches very hard, or a home-run hitter in baseball. *n.*

slug gish (slug/ish), **1** slow-moving; not active; lacking energy or vigor: *When I stay up late, I am often sluggish the next day.* **2** moving slowly; having little motion: *The stream was so sluggish that I could hardly tell which way it flowed. adj.* —**slug/gish ly,** *adv.* —**slug/gish ness,** *n.*

sluice (slüs), **1** structure with a gate for holding back or controlling the water of a canal, river, or lake. **2** gate that holds back or controls the flow of water. When the water behind a dam gets too high, the sluices are opened. **3** let out or draw off (water) by opening a sluice. **4** flush or cleanse with a rush of water; pour or throw water over. **5** a long, sloping trough through which water flows, used to wash gold from sand, dirt, or gravel. **6** channel for carrying off overflow or surplus water. 1,2,5,6 *n.,* 3,4 *v.,* **sluiced, sluic ing.**

slum (slum), **1** Often, **slums,** *pl.* a run-down, overcrowded part of a city or town. Poverty, dirt, and unhealthy living conditions are common in the slums. **2** go into or visit the slums. 1 *n.,* 2 *v.,* **slummed, slum ming.** —**slum/mer,** *n.*

slum ber (slum/bər), **1** to sleep lightly; doze. **2** a light sleep: *He awoke from his slumber.* **3** pass in sleep: *The baby slumbers away the hours.* **4** be inactive: *The volcano had slumbered for years.* **5** an inactive state or condition. 1,3,4 *v.,* 2,5 *n.* —**slum/ber er,** *n.*

slum ber ous (slum/bər əs), **1** sleepy; heavy with drowsiness: *slumberous eyelids.* **2** causing or inducing sleep. *adj.* —**slum/ber ous ly,** *adv.*

slum brous (slum/brəs), slumberous. *adj.* —**slum/brous ly,** *adv.*

slump (slump), **1** drop heavily; fall suddenly: *The thin air made me so faint that I slumped to the ground.* **2** move, walk, sit, etc., in a drooping manner; slouch: *The bored students slumped in their seats.* **3** a heavy or sudden fall; collapse. **4** a great or sudden decline: *a slump in prices.* 1,2 *v.,* 3,4 *n.*

slung (slung), past tense and past participle of **sling.** *They slung some stones and ran away. The girl had slung her laundry bag over her shoulder. v.*

slunk (slungk), past tense and past participle of **slink.** *The dog slunk away ashamed. v.*

slur (slėr), **1** pass lightly over; go through hurriedly or in a careless way: *They slurred over their team's poor performance last year, thinking only of today's game.* **2** pronounce indistinctly: *Many persons slur "how do you do."* **3** a slurred pronunciation, sound, etc. **4** sing or play (two or more tones of different pitch) without a break; run together in a smooth, connected manner. **5** a slurring of tones. **6** a curved mark (⌢) (⌣) indicating this. **7** a blot or stain (upon reputation); insulting or slighting remark: *a slur on a person's good name.* **8** harm the reputation of; insult; slight. 1,2,4,8 *v.,* **slurred, slur ring;** 3,5-7 *n.*

slush (slush), **1** partly melted snow; snow and water mixed. **2** soft mud. **3** silly, sentimental talk, writing, etc. *n.*

slush i ness (slush/ē nis), slushy condition or quality. *n.*

slush y (slush/ē), **1** having much slush. **2** of or like slush. *adj.,* **slush i er, slush i est.**

slut (slut), **1** a dirty, untidy woman. **2** a sexually immoral woman. *n.*

sly (slī), **1** able to fool, trick, or deceive; cunning; crafty; tricky; wily: *someone as sly as a fox. The sly cat stole the meat while the cook's back was turned.* **2** playfully mischievous or knowing: *a sly wink. Waiting for the surprise party to begin, the children exchanged many sly looks and smiles.* **3** acting secretly or stealthily. *adj.,* **sly er, sly est** or **sli er, sli est.** —**sly/ness,** *n.*

on the sly, in a sly way.

sly ly (slī/lē), in a sly manner. *adv.* Also, **slily.**

Sm, symbol for samarium.

S.M. or **SM, 1** Master of Science. **2** Sergeant Major.

smack[1] (smak), **1** a slight taste or flavor: *The sauce had a smack of nutmeg.* **2** trace; suggestion: *The old sailor still had a smack of the sea about him.* **3** have a smack: *The immigrant talked in a way that smacked of the old country.* 1,2 *n.,* 3 *v.*

smack[2] (smak), **1** open (the lips) quickly so as to make a sharp sound: *She smacked her lips at the thought of cake.* **2** a smacking movement of the lips. **3** the sharp sound made in this way. **4** kiss loudly. **5** to slap: *She smacked the*

a hat	i it	oi oil	ch child	⎧ a in about
ā age	ī ice	ou out	ng long	⎪ e in taken
ä far	o hot	u cup	sh she	ə = ⎨ i in pencil
e let	ō open	ů put	th thin	⎪ o in lemon
ē equal	ô order	ü rule	ŦH then	⎩ u in circus
ėr term			zh measure	

horse on its rump. **6** a loud kiss or slap. **7** directly; square-
ly: *He fell smack on his face.* 1,4,5 *v.,* 2,3,6 *n.,* 7 *adv.*
smack³ (smak), **1** a small sailboat with one mast. **2** a
fishing boat with a well for keeping fish alive. *n.*
small (smôl), **1** not large; little; not large as compared
with other things of the same kind: *A cottage is a small
house.* **2** not great in amount, degree, extent, duration,
value, strength, etc.: *a small dose, small hope of success.
The cent is our smallest coin.* **3** not important: *This is only
a small matter.* **4** not prominent; of low social position;
humble; poor: *Both great and small people mourned the
President's death.* **5** having little land, capital, etc.; doing
business on a limited scale: *a small farmer. They own a
small business.* **6** having little strength; gentle; soft; low: *a
small voice.* **7** mean; petty: *A person with a small nature is
not generous.* **8** (of letters) not capital. **9** a small, slender,
or narrow part: *the small of the back.* 1-8 *adj.,* 9 *n.* [*Small*
comes from Old English *smæl.*] —**small'ness,** *n.*
feel small, be ashamed or humiliated.
small arms, weapons easily carried by a person, such
as rifles or revolvers.
small change, 1 coins of small value, such as nickels,
dimes, etc. **2** anything small and unimportant.
small fry, 1 young children. **2** people or things having
little importance.
small hours, the early hours in the morning.
small intestine, the slender part of the intestines, extending from the stomach to the large intestine. It is a
long, winding tube that receives partly digested food
from the stomach. The small intestine completes the
digestion of food and sends it into the blood.
small ish (smô'lish), rather small. *adj.*
small letter, an ordinary letter, not a capital.
small-mind ed (smôl'mïn'did), narrow-minded; petty;
mean. *adj.* —**small'-mind'ed ly,** *adv.* —**small'-mind'edness,** *n.*
small pox (smôl'poks'), a very contagious virus disease that causes fever and red spots on the skin. These
spots often leave permanent scars called pocks. Vaccination prevents smallpox. *n.*
small talk, conversation about unimportant matters;
chitchat.
smart (smärt), **1** feel sharp pain: *Her eyes smarted.*
2 cause sharp pain: *The cut smarts.* **3** a sharp pain: *The
smart of the wound kept me awake.* **4** feel distress or irritation: *I smarted from the scolding.* **5** sharp; severe: *He gave
the horse a smart blow.* **6** keen; active; lively: *They walked
home at a smart pace.* **7** clever; bright: *a smart student.*
8 fresh and neat; in good order: *the smart uniforms of the
band-members.* **9** stylish; fashionable: *some smart new
clothes.* **10** in a smart manner; cleverly. 1,2,4 *v.,* 3 *n.,* 5-9
adj., 10 *adv.* —**smart'ly,** *adv.* —**smart'ness,** *n.*
smart al eck (al'ik), INFORMAL. a conceited, obnoxious
person.
smart en (smärt'n), **1** improve in appearance; brighten.
2 make or become brisker. *v.*
smash (smash), **1** break into pieces with violence and
noise: *smash a dish, smash a window with a stone.*
2 destroy; shatter; ruin: *smash a person's hopes.* **3** be broken to pieces: *The dishes smashed on the floor.* **4** become
ruined. **5** rush violently; crash: *The car smashed into a
tree.* **6** a violent crash or collision: *Two cars were involved
in the smash.* **7** act or sound of smashing: *the smash of
broken glass.* **8** a crushing defeat; disaster. **9** INFORMAL. a
highly successful performance or production; great hit:
a theatrical smash. **10** INFORMAL. highly successful: *a
smash Broadway musical.* 1-5 *v.,* 6-9 *n., pl.* **smash es;** 10
adj. —**smash'er,** *n.*
smash ing (smash'ing), INFORMAL. wonderful; fine. *adj.*
—**smash'ing ly,** *adv.*

smash-up (smash'up'), **1** a bad collision; wreck. **2** a
great misfortune; disaster. *n.*
smat ter ing (smat'ər ing), very slight knowledge: *a
smattering of French. n.*
smear (smir), **1** cover or stain with anything sticky,
greasy, or dirty: *I smeared my fingers with jam.* **2** rub or
spread (oil, grease, paint, etc.). **3** a mark or stain left by
smearing: *There are smears of paint on the wallpaper.*
4 receive a mark or stain; be smeared: *Wet paint smears
easily.* **5** harm; soil; spoil: *smear a person's good reputation.* **6** act of smearing. 1,2,4,5 *v.,* 3,6 *n.*
smell (smel), **1** perceive by breathing in through the
nose: *Can you smell the smoke?* **2** sense of smelling: *Smell
is keener in dogs than in people.* **3** use this sense: *We smell
with our noses.* **4** sniff at: *pick up a rose and smell it. The
dog smelled the strange man's legs.* **5** quality in a thing that
affects the sense of smell; odor: *The smell of burning
rubber is not pleasant.* **6** give out a smell: *The garden
smelled of roses.* **7** give out a bad smell; have a bad smell:
That dirty, wet dog smells. **8** find a trace or suggestion of:
We smelled trouble. **9** have the smell (of); have the trace
(of): *The plan smells of trickery.* **10** act of smelling: *Have a
smell of this rose.* 1,3,4,6-9 *v.,* **smelled** or **smelt, smelling;** 2,5,10 *n.* —**smell'er,** *n.*
smelling salts, a form of ammonia breathed in to relieve faintness, headaches, etc.
smell y (smel'ē), having or giving out a strong or unpleasant smell: *Rotten fish are smelly. adj.,* **smell i er,
smell i est.** —**smell'i ness,** *n.*
smelt¹ (smelt), **1** melt (ore) in order to get the metal out
of it. **2** get (metal) from ore by melting. **3** refine (impure
metal) by melting. *v.*
smelt² (smelt), a small, saltwater or freshwater food fish
with silvery scales. *n., pl.* **smelts** or **smelt.**
smelt³ (smelt), smelled: a past tense and a past participle of **smell.** *v.*
smelt er (smel'tər), **1** person whose work or business is
smelting ores or metals. **2** place where ores or metals
are smelted. **3** furnace for smelting ores. *n.*
smidg en, smidg eon, or **smidg in** (smij'ən), INFOR-
MAL. a tiny bit: *There isn't a smidgen of truth in this
rumor. n.*
smile (smīl), **1** look pleased or amused; show pleasure,
favor, kindness, amusement, etc., by an upward curve of
the mouth. **2** show scorn, disapproval, etc., by a curve of
the mouth: *She smiled bitterly.* **3** bring, put, drive, etc., by
smiling: *Smile your tears away.* **4** give (a smile): *She smiled
a sunny smile.* **5** express by a smile: *He smiled consent.*
6 act of smiling: *a friendly smile, a smile of pity.* **7** to look
upon or regard with favor: *Good fortune always smiled at
her.* **8** a favoring look or regard. 1-5,7 *v.,* **smiled, smiling;** 6,8 *n.* —**smil'er,** *n.* —**smil'ing ly,** *adv.*
smirch (smėrch), **1** make dirty; soil with soot, dirt, dust,
dishonor, disgrace, etc. **2** a dirty mark; blot; stain. 1 *v.,* 2
n., pl. **smirch es.**
smirk (smėrk), **1** smile in an affected, silly, or self-satisfied way. **2** an affected, silly, or self-satisfied smile. 1 *v.,*
2 *n.*
smite (smīt), strike hard; hit hard; strike: *The hero smote
the giant with his sword. I was smitten with curiosity about
the forbidden room. v.,* **smote, smit ten** or **smote, smit-
ing.** —**smit'er,** *n.*
smith (smith), **1** worker in metal, especially iron.
2 blacksmith. *n.*
Smith (smith), **1** Captain **John,** 1580-1631, English explorer and early settler in Virginia. **2 Joseph,** 1805-1844,
American who founded the Mormon Church. *n.*
smith e reens (smiᴛʜ'ə rēnz'), INFORMAL. small pieces;
bits: *smash a chair into smithereens. n.pl.*
smith y (smith'ē), workshop of a smith, especially a

blacksmith: *"Under a spreading chestnut tree the village smithy stands."* n., pl. **smith ies.**

smit ten (smit′n), **1** hard hit; struck: *sudden sparks from smitten steel.* **2** a past participle of **smite.** *The country was smitten with a famine.* 1 adj., 2 v.

smock (smok), **1** a loose outer garment worn to protect clothing. **2** ornament (a smock, dress, etc.) with smocking. 1 n., 2 v.

smocking

smock ing (smok′ing), a honeycomb pattern formed by lines of stitches crossing each other diagonally and gathering the material, used to ornament smocks, dresses, etc. n.

smog (smog), mixture of smoke and fog in the air: *Automobile exhaust fumes were blamed as one of the major causes of smog.* n. [*Smog* is a blend of *smoke* and *fog.*]

smog gy (smog′ē), full of smog. adj.

smoke (smōk), **1** the mixture of gases and particles of carbon that can be seen rising in a cloud from anything burning. **2** something like this. **3** give off smoke or steam, or something like it: *The fireplace smokes. The turkey was brought smoking hot to the table.* **4** draw the smoke from (a cigarette, cigar, pipe, etc.) into the mouth and puff it out again. **5** something that is smoked; cigarette, cigar, pipe, etc. **6** act or period of smoking tobacco. **7** cure (meat, fish, etc.) by exposing to smoke. People smoke fish to preserve them. 1,2,5,6 n., 3,4,7 v., **smoked, smok ing.** [*Smoke* comes from Old English *smoca.*] —**smoke′like′,** adj.

smoke out, 1 drive out by smoke: *We tried to smoke the woodchuck out of its hole.* **2** find out and make known: *smoke out a plot.*

smoke house (smōk′hous′), building or place in which meat, fish, etc., are treated with smoke to keep them from spoiling. n., pl. **smoke hous es** (smōk′hou′ziz).

smoke jumper, a forester trained to parachute into areas difficult to reach in order to fight fires.

smoke less (smōk′lis), making no smoke; having little smoke: *smokeless powder.* adj.

smok er (smō′kər), **1** person who smokes tobacco. **2** a railroad car or a part of it where smoking is allowed. **3** an informal gathering of men. n.

smoke screen, mass of thick smoke used to hide troops, ships, airplanes, etc., from the enemy.

smoke stack (smōk′stak′), **1** a tall chimney. **2** pipe that discharges smoke: *the smokestack of a steamship.* n.

smok i ness (smō′kē nis), smoky condition. n.

smok y (smō′kē), **1** giving off much smoke: *a smoky fire.* **2** full of smoke. **3** darkened or stained with smoke. **4** like smoke or suggesting smoke: *a smoky gray, a smoky taste.* adj., **smok i er, smok i est.** —**smok′i ly,** adv.

smol der (smōl′dər), **1** burn and smoke without flame: *The campfire smoldered for hours after the blaze died down.* **2** a slow, smoky burning without flame; smoldering fire. **3** exist or continue in a barely hidden condition: *The people's discontent smoldered for years before it broke out into open rebellion.* **4** show barely hidden feeling: *I smol-*

dered with anger and nearly shouted out that the charges against me were all lies. 1,3,4 v., 2 n. Also, **smoulder.**

smooth (smüŦH), **1** having an even surface, like glass, silk, or still water; flat; level: *smooth stones.* **2** free from unevenness or roughness: *smooth sailing, a smooth voyage.* **3** without lumps: *smooth sauce.* **4** make smooth or smoother; make flat, even, or level: *Smooth this dress with a hot iron. He smoothed out the ball of crushed paper and read it.* **5** without trouble or difficulty; easy: *a smooth course of affairs.* **6** make easy: *Her tact smoothed the way to an agreement.* **7** calm; serene: *a smooth temper.* **8** polished; pleasant; polite: *That salesclerk is a smooth talker.* **9** not harsh in sound or taste: *smooth verses, smooth wine.* **10** make less harsh or crude; polish or refine (writing, manners, etc.). **11** in a smooth manner. 1-3,5,7-9 adj., 4,6,10 v., 11 adv. —**smooth′ly,** adv. —**smooth′ness,** n.

smooth away, get rid of (troubles, difficulties, etc.): *He smoothed away all objections to the plan.*

smooth down, calm; soothe: *She smoothed down her friend's temper.*

smooth over, make (something) seem less wrong, unpleasant, or noticeable: *The teacher tried to smooth over the differences between the two students who always quarreled with each other.*

smooth bore (smüŦH′bôr′), gun without grooves in its barrel. A shotgun is a smoothbore. n.

smooth en (smü′ŦHən), make or become smooth or smoother. v.

smooth-faced (smüŦH′fāst′), **1** having a smooth face or surface. **2** agreeable in speech and manner: *a smooth-faced hypocrite.* adj.

smooth-tongued (smüŦH′tungd′), speaking smoothly; agreeable. adj.

smor gas bord (smôr′gəs bôrd), a buffet meal with a large variety of meats, salads, hors d'oeuvres, etc. n. [*Smorgasbord* comes from Swedish *smörgåsbord,* which comes from *smörgås,* meaning "bread and butter," and *bord,* meaning "table."]

smote (smōt), a past tense and past participle of **smite.** *The blacksmith smote the horseshoe with a hammer.* v.

smoth er (smuŦH′ər), **1** make unable to get air; kill by keeping air from: *The gas almost smothered the coal miners but they got out in time.* **2** be unable to breathe freely; suffocate: *We are smothering in this stuffy room.* **3** cover thickly: *In the fall the grass is smothered with leaves.* **4** deaden or put out by covering thickly: *The fire is smothered by ashes.* **5** keep back; check; suppress: *He smothered a sharp reply. Her smothered anger finally broke out.* **6** cloud of dust, smoke, spray, etc. 1-5 v., 6 n. —**smoth′er er,** n.

smoul der (smōl′dər), smolder. v., n.

smudge (smuj), **1** a dirty mark; smear. **2** mark with dirty streaks; smear: *The child's drawing was smudged.* **3** a smoky fire made to drive away insects or to protect fruit and plants from frost. 1,3 n., 2 v., **smudged, smudg ing.**

smudge pot, pot or stove in which oil or other fuel is burned to produce a smoky fire.

smudg y (smuj′ē), smudged; marked with smudges. adj., **smudg i er, smudg i est.** —**smudg′i ly,** adv. —**smudg′i ness,** n.

smug (smug), too pleased with one's own goodness,

cleverness, respectability, etc.; self-satisfied; complacent: *Nothing disturbs the smug beliefs of some prim, narrow-minded people.* adj., **smug ger, smug gest.** —**smug′ly,** adv. —**smug′ness,** n.

smug gle (smug′əl), **1** bring into or take out of a country secretly and against the law, especially without payment of legal duties. **2** bring, take, put, etc., secretly: *I tried to smuggle my puppy into the house.* v., **smug gled, smug gling.**

smug gler (smug′lər), **1** person who smuggles. **2** ship used in smuggling. n.

smut (smut), **1** a bit or bits of soot, dirt, etc. **2** to soil or be soiled with smut: *smut one's hands with coal.* **3** a dirty mark; smudge. **4** indecent, obscene talk or writing. **5** a plant disease in which the grain is replaced by black, dustlike spores. **6** fungus producing this disease. 1,3-6 n., 2 v., **smut ted, smut ting.**

smut ty (smut′ē), **1** soiled with smut; dirty or sooty. **2** indecent; nasty; obscene. **3** (of plants) having the disease smut. adj., **smut ti er, smut ti est.** —**smut′ti ly,** adv. —**smut′ti ness,** n.

Smyr na (smėr′nə), former name of **Izmir.** n.

Sn, symbol for tin.

snack (snak), **1** a light meal, especially one eaten between regular meals. **2** to eat a light meal. 1 n., 2 v.

snaf fle (snaf′əl), **1** a slender, jointed bit used on a bridle. **2** control or manage by a snaffle. 1 n., 2 v., **snaf fled, snaf fling.**

snag (snag), **1** tree or branch held fast in a river or lake. Snags are dangerous to boats. **2** any sharp or rough projecting point, such as the broken end of a branch. **3** run or catch on a snag: *She snagged her sweater on a nail.* **4** a tear made by snagging. **5** a hidden or unexpected obstacle: *Our plans hit a snag.* **6** hinder. 1,2,4,5 n., 3,6 v., **snagged, snag ging.** —**snag′like′,** adj.

snag gle tooth (snag′əl tüth′), an uneven, broken or projecting tooth. n., pl. **snag gle teeth.**

snag gy (snag′ē), **1** having snags. **2** projecting sharply or roughly. adj., **snag gi er, snag gi est.**

snail (snāl), **1** a small, soft-bodied animal that crawls very slowly. Most snails have spiral shells on their backs into which they can move for protection. **2** a lazy, slow-moving person. n. —**snail′like′,** adj.

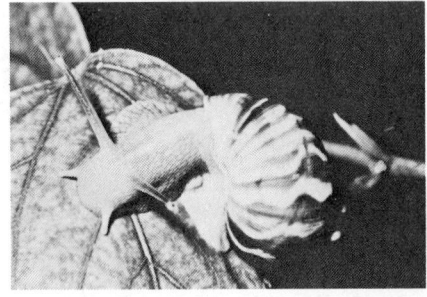

snail (def. 1) about 2 in. (5 cm.) long

snake (snāk), **1** a long, slender, crawling reptile without limbs. A few snakes are poisonous. **2** a sly, treacherous person. **3** a long, flexible, metal tool used by plumbers to clean out a drain. **4** move, wind, or curve like a snake: *The narrow road snaked through the mountains.* 1-3 n., 4 v., **snaked, snak ing.** [*Snake* comes from Old English *snaca.*] —**snake′like′,** adj.

snake skin (snāk′skin′), **1** skin of a snake. **2** leather made from it. n.

snak y (snā′kē), **1** of a snake or snakes. **2** like a snake; twisting; winding. **3** having many snakes. **4** sly; venomous; treacherous. adj., **snak i er, snak i est.** —**snak′i ly,** adv. —**snak′i ness,** n.

snap (snap), **1** make or cause to make a sudden, sharp sound: *This wood snaps as it burns. The teacher snapped her fingers to get our attention.* **2** a quick, sharp sound: *The box shut with a snap.* **3** move, shut, catch, etc., with a snap: *The latch snapped.* **4** break suddenly or sharply: *The violin string snapped because it was fastened too tight.* **5** a sudden breaking or the sound of breaking: *One snap made the knife useless.* **6** make a sudden, quick bite or snatch: *The turtle snapped at the child's hand. The dog snapped up the meat.* **7** seize suddenly: *to snap up a bargain. I snapped at the chance to visit my uncle.* **8** a quick, sudden bite or snatch: *The dog made a snap at a fly.* **9** speak quickly and sharply: *Don't snap at him; he doesn't understand what you want.* **10** move quickly and sharply: *The soldiers snapped to attention.* **11** a quick, sharp way: *She moves with snap and energy.* **12** a short spell of cold weather. **13** made or done suddenly: *A snap judgment is likely to be wrong.* **14** fastener; clasp: *Several of the snaps of your dress are unfastened.* **15** a thin, crisp cooky: *a chocolate snap.* **16** snapshot. **17** take a snapshot of. **18** INFORMAL. an easy job, piece of work, etc. **19** INFORMAL. easy. **20** (in football) pass back (the ball) to begin a play. 1,3,4,6,7,9,10,17,20 v., **snapped, snap ping;** 2,5,8,11,12,14-16,18 n., 13,19 adj.

snap out of it, INFORMAL. change one's attitude or habit suddenly: *He was in a bad mood one minute, but then he snapped out of it and started to laugh.*

snap drag on (snap′drag′ən), a garden plant with spikes of showy flowers of crimson, purple, white, yellow, etc. n.

snap per (snap′ər), **1** person or thing that snaps. **2** snapping turtle. **3** any of several large fish of tropical seas used for food, especially the **red snapper** of the Gulf of Mexico. n.

snapping turtle—up to 18½ in. (47 cm.) long

snapping turtle, a large American freshwater turtle that has powerful jaws with which it snaps at its prey.

snap pish (snap′ish), **1** apt to snap. **2** quick and sharp in speech or manner; impatient. adj. —**snap′pish ly,** adv. —**snap′pish ness,** n.

snap py (snap′ē), **1** snappish; sharp. **2** snapping or crackling in sound: *a snappy fire.* **3** INFORMAL. having snap, smartness, pungency, etc.; crispy; lively: *snappy cheese, a snappy sports jacket.* adj., **snap pi er, snap pi est.** —**snap′pi ly,** adv. —**snap′pi ness,** n.

snap shot (snap′shot′), photograph taken quickly with a small camera. n.

snare[1] (sner or snar), **1** noose for catching small animals and birds: *They made snares to catch rabbits.* **2** catch with a snare: *One day they snared a skunk.* **3** a trap: *Flattery is a snare in which fools are caught.* **4** to trap. 1,3 n., 2,4 v., **snared, snar ing.**

snare[2] (sner or snar), one of the strings of wire or gut stretched across the bottom of a snare drum. n.

a hat	i it	oi oil	ch child	a in about
ā age	ī ice	ou out	ng long	e in taken
ä far	o hot	u cup	sh she	ə = i in pencil
e let	ō open	u̇ put	th thin	o in lemon
ē equal	ô order	ü rule	ᴛ̵ʜ then	u in circus
ėr term			zh measure	

snare drum

snare drum, a small drum with strings of wire or gut stretched across the bottom to make a rattling sound.

snarl¹ (snärl), **1** growl sharply and show one's teeth: *The dog snarled at the stranger.* **2** a sharp, angry growl. **3** say or express with a snarl; speak harshly in a sharp, angry tone: *snarl a nasty threat.* **4** a sharp, angry tone or remark: *A snarl was her only reply.* 1,3 *v.,* 2,4 *n.* —**snarl′er,** *n.* —**snarl′ing ly,** *adv.*

snarl² (snärl), **1** a tangle: *I combed the snarls out of my hair.* **2** confusion: *Their legal affairs were in a snarl.* **3** to tangle or become tangled: *The kitten snarled the yarn by playing with it. Her hair snarls easily.* **4** confuse. 1,2 *n.,* 3,4 *v.*

snatch (snach), **1** seize suddenly; grasp hastily: *The hawk snatched the chicken and flew away.* **2** act of snatching: *The girl made a snatch at the ball.* **3** take suddenly: *He snatched off his hat and bowed.* **4** a short time: *She had a snatch of sleep sitting in her chair.* **5** a small amount; bit; scrap: *We heard snatches of their conversation as they raised their voices from time to time.* 1,3 *v.,* 2,4,5 *n., pl.* **snatch es.** —**snatch′er,** *n.*

snatch at, 1 try to seize or grasp: *He snatched at the rail.* **2** take advantage of eagerly: *She snatched at the chance to travel.*

snaz zy (snaz′ē), SLANG. fancy; flashy: *a snazzy suit. adj.,* **snaz zi er, snaz zi est.**

sneak (snēk), **1** move in a stealthy, sly way: *The man sneaked about the barn watching for a chance to steal the horse.* **2** get, put, pass, etc., in a stealthy, sly way: *They sneaked the puppy into the house.* **3** act like a thief or a person who is ashamed to be seen: *He sneaked in by the back way.* **4** person who sneaks; a sneaking, cowardly person. **5** stealthy; underhand; sneaking: *a sneak thief, a sneak attack.* 1-3 *v.,* 4 *n.,* 5 *adj.*

sneak er (snē′kər), **1** sneakers, *pl.* light canvas shoes with rubber soles, used for games, sports, etc. **2** person that sneaks; sneak. *n.*

sneak i ly (snē′kə lē), in a sneaky manner. *adv.*

sneak i ness (snē′kē nis), sneaky character or quality. *n.*

sneak ing (snē′king), **1** cowardly; underhand; concealed. **2** that one cannot justify or does not like to confess: *She had a sneaking suspicion that they knew she had broken the vase. adj.* —**sneak′ing ly,** *adv.*

sneak y (snē′kē), like a person ashamed to be seen. *adj.,* **sneak i er, sneak i est.**

sneer (snir), **1** show scorn or contempt by looks or words: *The students sneered at the sentimentality of the poem.* **2** a look or words expressing scorn or contempt: *She feared sneers more than blows.* **3** say or express with scorn or contempt: *"Bah!" he sneered with a curl of his lip.* 1,3 *v.,* 2 *n.* —**sneer′er,** *n.* —**sneer′ing ly,** *adv.*

sneeze (snēz), **1** force air suddenly and violently through the nose and mouth by an involuntary spasm. A person with a cold often sneezes. *The pepper made her sneeze.* **2** a sudden, violent forcing of air through the nose and mouth. 1 *v.,* sneezed, sneez ing: 2 *n.* —**sneez′er,** *n.*

sneeze at, INFORMAL. treat with contempt; despise; scorn: *Ten dollars is not a sum to be sneezed at.*

snick er (snik′ər), **1** a half-suppressed and often disrespectful laugh; sly or silly laugh; giggle. **2** laugh in this way. 1 *n.,* 2 *v.* Also, **snigger.**

snide (snīd), mean or spiteful in a sly way: *a snide remark. adj.,* —**snid er, snid est.** —**snide′ness,** *n.*

sniff (snif), **1** draw air through the nose in short, quick breaths that can be heard: *The man who had a cold was sniffing.* **2** smell with sniffs: *The dog sniffed suspiciously at the stranger.* **3** try the smell of: *I sniffed the medicine before taking a spoonful of it.* **4** draw in through the nose with the breath: *He sniffed steam to clear his head.* **5** act or sound of sniffing: *He cleared his nose with a loud sniff.* **6** show contempt by sniffing: *sniff at an inexpensive gift.* **7** suspect; detect: *sniff a plot, sniff danger.* **8** a single breathing in of something; breath. 1-4,6,7 *v.,* 5,8 *n.* —**sniff′er,** *n.*

snif fle (snif′əl), **1** sniff again and again as one does from a cold in the head or in trying to stop crying. **2** act or sound of sniffling. **3** the sniffles, a slight cold in the head. 1 *v.,* snif fled, snif fling; 2,3 *n.* —**snif′fler,** *n.*

snig ger (snig′ər), snicker. *n., v.*

snip (snip), **1** cut with a small, quick stroke or series of strokes with scissors: *I snipped the thread.* **2** act of snipping: *With a few snips I cut out the picture.* **3** a small piece cut off: *Pick up the snips of cloth and thread from the floor.* **4** snips, *pl.* hand shears for cutting metal. **5** INFORMAL. a small or unimportant person. 1 *v.,* snipped, snip ping; 2-5 *n.* —**snip′per,** *n.*

snipe (snīp), **1** a marsh bird with a long bill. **2** hunt for snipe. **3** shoot at an enemy one at a time from a hidden place. 1 *n., pl.* **snipes** or **snipe;** 2,3 *v.,* **sniped, snip ing.**

snip er (snī′pər), person who shoots at someone from a hidden place; a hidden sharpshooter. *n.*

snip pet (snip′it), a small piece snipped off; bit; scrap; fragment. *n.*

snip py (snip′ē), INFORMAL. **1** sharp; curt. **2** haughty; disdainful. *adj.,* **snip pi er, snip pi est.** —**snip′pi ly,** *adv.* —**snip′pi ness,** *n.*

snitch¹ (snich), SLANG. snatch; steal. *v.* —**snitch′er,** *n.*

snitch² (snich), SLANG. **1** be an informer; tell tales. **2** informer. 1 *v.,* 2 *n., pl.* **snitch es.** —**snitch′er,** *n.*

sniv el (sniv′əl), **1** cry with sniffling. **2** put on a show of grief; whine. **3** run at the nose; sniffle. *v.,* **sniv eled, sniv el ing** or **sniv elled, sniv el ling.** —**sniv′el er, sniv′el ler,** *n.*

snob (snob), person who cares too much for rank, wealth, position, etc., and too little for real merit; person who tries too hard to please superiors and ignores inferiors. *n.*

snob ber y (snob′ər ē), snobbishness. *n., pl.* **snob ber ies.**

snob bish (snob′ish), of or like a snob; looking down on those in a lower position. *adj.* —**snob′bish ly,** *adv.* —**snob′bish ness,** *n.*

snood (snüd), net or bag worn over a woman's hair. A snood may be a part of a hat. *n.*

snoop (snüp), INFORMAL. **1** go about in a sneaking, prying way; prowl; pry: *Our neighbor snoops into everybody's business.* **2** person who snoops. 1 *v.,* 2 *n.* [*Snoop* comes

from Dutch *snoepen*, meaning "to eat in secret."]
—**snoop′er,** *n.*

snoot y (snü′tē), INFORMAL. snobbish; conceited. *adj.,*
snoot i er, snoot i est. —snoot′i ly, *adv.* —**snoot′i-
ness,** *n.*

snooze (snüz), INFORMAL. **1** take a nap; sleep; doze: *The
dog snoozed on the porch in the sun.* **2** a nap; doze. **1** *v.,*
snoozed, snooz ing; 2 *n.* —**snooz′er,** *n.*

snore (snôr), **1** breathe during sleep with a harsh rough
sound: *The child had a stuffy nose and snored all night.*
2 sound made in snoring. **1** *v.,* **snored, snor ing; 2** *n.*
—**snor′er,** *n.*

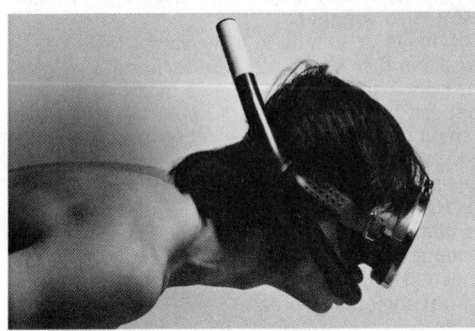

snorkel
(def. 2)

snor kel (snôr′kəl), **1** pair of metal tubes for taking air in
and letting gases out. This device allows submarines to
remain under water for a very long time. It is like a
periscope in shape. **2** a curved tube which enables
swimmers to breathe under water while swimming near
the surface. *n.* [*Snorkel* comes from German *Schnorchel.*]

snort (snôrt), **1** force the breath violently through the
nose with a loud, harsh sound: *The horse snorted.* **2** make
a sound like this: *The engine snorted.* **3** act or sound of
snorting. **4** show contempt, defiance, anger, etc., by
snorting. **5** say or express with a snort: *"Indeed!" snorted
my aunt.* **1,2,4,5** *v.,* **3** *n.* —**snort′er,** *n.*

snout (snout), **1** the part of an animal's head that sticks
forward and contains the nose, mouth, and jaws. Pigs,
dogs, and crocodiles have snouts. **2** anything like an
animal's snout, such as a nozzle. *n.* —**snout′less,** *adj.*
—**snout′like′,** *adj.*

snow (snō), **1** water vapor frozen into crystals that fall to
earth in soft, white flakes and often spread upon it as a
white layer. Rain falls in summer; snow falls in winter.
2 a fall of snow. **3** fall as snow: *to snow all day.* **4** let fall
or scatter as snow. **1,2** *n.,* **3,4** *v.* [*Snow* comes from Old
English *snāw.*] —**snow′less,** *adj.* —**snow′like′,** *adj.*

snow in, shut in by snow: *The mountain village was
snowed in for almost a week after the blizzard.*

snow under, 1 cover with snow: *The houses were snowed
under by the blizzard.* **2** overwhelm: *He is snowed under
with work.*

snow ball (snō′bôl′), **1** ball made of snow pressed together. **2** throw balls of snow at: *The children snowballed
each other.* **3** shrub with white flowers in large clusters
like balls. **4** grow quickly in size, like a rolling snowball:
*The number of signers of the petition for a new school
snowballed.* **1,3** *n.,* **2,4** *v.*

snow bank (snō′bangk′), large mass or drift of snow,
especially at the side of a road. *n.*

snow bird (snō′bėrd′), any of several small birds that
are seen in the winter months. Juncos are snowbirds. *n.*

snow-blind (snō′blīnd′), affected with snow blindness.
adj.

snow blindness, temporary blindness caused by the
reflection of sunlight from snow or ice.

snow bound (snō′bound′), shut in by snow; snowed in.
adj.

snow bunting, a small, white finch with black and
brownish markings that lives in cold regions.

snow capped (snō′kapt′), having its top covered with
snow: *a snowcapped mountain. adj.*

snow drift (snō′drift′), **1** mass or bank of snow piled up
by the wind. **2** snow driven before the wind. *n.*

snow drop (snō′drop′), a small plant with white flowers
that blooms early in the spring. *n.*

snow fall (snō′fôl′), **1** a fall of snow. **2** amount of snow
falling within a certain time and area: *The snowfall in that
one storm was 16 inches. n.*

snowflakes
(magnified
many times)

snow flake (snō′flāk′), a small, feathery crystal of
snow. *n.*

snow line, line on mountains above which there is
always snow.

snow man (snō′man′), snow made into a figure somewhat like that of a person. *n., pl.* **snow men.**

snowmobiles
(def. 1)

snow mo bile (snō′mō bēl), **1** tractor or other vehicle
for use in snow. Some snowmobiles have skis or run-
ners in front. **2** travel by snowmobile. **1** *n.,* **2** *v.,* **snow-
mo biled, snow mo bil ing.** —**snow′mo bil′er,** *n.*

snow plow (snō′plou′), machine for clearing away
snow from streets, railroad tracks, etc. *n.*

snow shoe (snō′shü′), **1** a light, wooden frame with
strips of leather stretched across it. Trappers in the far
North wear snowshoes on their feet to keep from sinking

snowshoe (def. 1)—hunters on snowshoes

a hat	i it	oi oil	ch child		a in about
ā age	ī ice	ou out	ng long		e in taken
ä far	o hot	u cup	sh she	ə =	i in pencil
e let	ō open	u̇ put	th thin		o in lemon
ē equal	ô order	ü rule	ᴛʜ then		u in circus
ėr term			zh measure		

in deep, soft snow. **2** walk or travel on snowshoes. **1** *n.,* **2** *v.,* **snow shoed, snow shoe ing.**

snow slide (snō′slīd′), the sliding down of a mass of snow on a steep slope. *n.*

snow storm (snō′stôrm′), storm with much snow. *n.*

snow-white (snō′hwīt′), white as snow. *adj.*

snow y (snō′ē), **1** having snow: *a snowy day.* **2** covered with snow: *a snowy roof.* **3** like snow; white as snow: *The old woman has snowy hair. adj.,* **snow i er, snow i est.** —**snow′i ly,** *adv.* —**snow′i ness,** *n.*

snub (snub), **1** treat coldly, scornfully, or with contempt: *snub one's neighbors by ignoring them.* **2** cold, scornful, or disdainful treatment. **3** check or stop (a rope or cable running out) suddenly. **4** a sudden check or stop. **5** short and turned up at the tip: *a snub nose.* **1,3** *v.,* **snubbed, snub bing; 2,4** *n.,* **5** *adj.*

snub-nosed (snub′nōzd′), having a snub nose. *adj.*

snuck (snuk), INFORMAL. sneaked; a past tense and past participle of **sneak.** *v.*

snuff¹ (snuf), **1** draw in through the nose; draw up into the nose. **2** sniff; smell: *The dog snuffed at the track of the fox.* **3** powdered tobacco taken into the nose. **1,2** *v.,* **3** *n.* —**snuff′er,** *n.*

up to snuff, INFORMAL. in perfect order or condition; as good as expected.

snuff² (snuf), **1** cut or pinch off the burned wick of. **2** put out (a candle); extinguish. *v.* —**snuff′er,** *n.*

snuff out, put an end to suddenly and completely; wipe out: *The new dictator snuffed out the people's hopes for freedom.*

snuff box (snuf′boks′), a very small box for holding snuff. *n., pl.* **snuff box es.**

snuff ers (snuf′ərz), small tongs for taking off burned wick or putting out the light of a candle. *n.pl.*

snuf fle (snuf′əl), **1** breathe noisily through the nose like a person with a cold in the head. **2** act or sound of breathing in this way. **3 the snuffles,** a cold in the head. **1** *v.,* **snuf fled, snuf fling; 2,3** *n.* —**snuf′fler,** *n.*

snug (snug), **1** comfortable and warm; sheltered; cozy: *The cat has found a snug corner behind the stove.* **2** neat; trim; compact: *The cabins on the boat are snug.* **3** fitting closely: *That coat is a little too snug.* **4** in a snug manner. **1-3** *adj.,* **snug ger, snug gest; 4** *adv.* —**snug′ly,** *adv.* —**snug′ness,** *n.*

snug gle (snug′əl), lie or press closely for warmth or comfort or from affection; nestle; cuddle. *v.,* **snug gled, snug gling.**

so¹ (sō), **1** in that way; in the same way or degree; as shown: *Hold your pen so. Do not walk so fast.* **2** as stated; true: *Is that really so?* **3** in such a way; to such a degree: *He is not so tall as his brother.* **4** very: *You are so kind.* **5** very much: *My head aches so.* **6** for that reason; accordingly; therefore: *The dog seemed hungry; so we fed it.* **7** with the result that; in order that: *Go away so I can rest.* **8** with the purpose or intention that: *I did the work so you would not need to.* **9** likewise; also: *She likes dogs; so do I.* **10** *So* is sometimes used alone to ask a question or to exclaim. *So! late again! The train is late. So?* **11** more or less: *a pound or so.* **1,3-6,9** *adv.,* **2** *adj.,* **7,8** *conj.,* **10** *interj.,* **11** *pron.*

so as, with the result or purpose: *I go to bed early so as to get enough sleep.*

so that, with the result or purpose that: *The boy studies so that he will do well.*

so² (sō), sol. *n.*

so., **1** south. **2** southern.

So., **1** South. **2** Southern.

soak (sōk), **1** make or become very wet; wet through: *The rain soaked my clothes.* **2** let remain in water or other liquid until wet clear through: *Soak the clothes all night*

before you wash them. **3** make its way; enter; go: *Water will soak through the earth.* **4** act or process of soaking: *Give the clothes a long soak.* **5** INFORMAL. make pay too much; charge or tax heavily: *I was soaked in the deal.* **1-3,5** *v.,* **4** *n.* —**soak′er,** *n.*

soak up, **1** absorb: *The sponge soaked up the water.* **2** take into the mind: *soak up knowledge.*

so-and-so (sō′ən sō′), some person or thing not named. *n., pl.* **so-and-sos.**

soap (sōp), **1** substance used for washing, usually made of a fat and lye. **2** rub with soap: *Soap your hands well.* **1** *n.,* **2** *v.* [*Soap* comes from Old English *sāpe.*] —**soap′less,** *adj.* —**soap′like′,** *adj.*

soap box (sōp′boks′), an empty box used as a temporary platform by speakers addressing gatherings on the street. *n., pl.* **soap box es.**

soap stone (sōp′stōn′), a soft rock that feels somewhat like soap, used for griddles, hearths, etc. *n.*

soap suds (sōp′sudz′), bubbles and foam made with soap and water. *n.pl.*

soap y (sō′pē), **1** covered with soap or soapsuds. **2** containing soap: *soapy water.* **3** of or like soap: *The water has a soapy taste. adj.,* **soap i er, soap i est.** —**soap′i ly,** *adv.* —**soap′i ness,** *n.*

soar (sôr), **1** fly at a great height; fly upward: *The eagle soared without flapping its wings.* **2** rise beyond what is common and ordinary: *Prices are soaring. Her hope soared when she heard that she was a finalist in the contest. v.*

sob (sob), **1** cry or sigh with short, quick breaths: *"I have lost my penny," the child sobbed. She sobbed herself to sleep.* **2** a catching of short, quick breaths because of grief, etc. **3** make a sound like this: *The wind sobbed.* **4** a sound like this. **5** say or express with short, quick breaths: *sob out a sad story.* **1,3,5** *v.,* **sobbed, sob bing; 2,4** *n.*

so ber (sō′bər), **1** not drunk. **2** temperate; moderate: *The Puritans led sober, hard-working lives.* **3** quiet; serious; solemn: *He looked sober at the thought of missing the picnic.* **4** calm; sensible; free from exaggeration: *sober facts. The judge's sober opinion was not influenced by prejudice or strong feeling.* **5** make or become sober: *Seeing the car accident sobered us all. The class sobered as the teacher came into the room.* **6** quiet in color: *He was dressed in sober gray.* **1-4,6** *adj.,* **5** *v.* —**so′ber ly,** *adv.* —**so′ber ness,** *n.*

so ber-mind ed (sō′bər mīn′did), having or showing a sober mind or self-control; sensible. *adj.*

so bri e ty (sə brī′ə tē), **1** soberness. **2** temperance in the use of strong drink. **3** moderation. **4** quietness; seriousness. *n.*

so bri quet (sō′brə kā), nickname. *n.* Also, **soubriquet.**

soc., **1** social. **2** society.

Soc., **1** Socialist. **2** Society.

so-called (sō′kôld′), called so, but really not so; called so improperly or incorrectly: *Her so-called friend hasn't even written to her. adj.*

soc cer (sok′ər), game played with a round ball between two teams of eleven players each. The players may strike the ball with any part of the body except the hands and arms. Only the goalkeeper may touch the ball with the hands and arms. Players score by knocking the ball into a net cage at either end of the field. *n.*

so ci a bil i ty (sō/shə bil/ə tē), sociable disposition; friendly behavior. *n.*

so cia ble (sō/shə bəl), **1** liking company; friendly: *They are a sociable family and entertain a great deal.* **2** marked by conversation and companionship: *We had a sociable afternoon together.* **3** an informal social gathering. 1,2 *adj.,* 3 *n.*

so cia bly (sō/shə blē), in a sociable manner; familiarly. *adv.*

so cial (sō/shəl), **1** of or dealing with human beings in their relations to each other; having to do with the life of human beings in a community or society: *social conditions, social problems.* Schools and hospitals are social institutions. **2** living, or liking to live, with others: *People are social beings.* **3** for companionship or friendliness; having to do with companionship or friendliness: *a social club.* **4** liking company: *She has a social nature.* **5** connected with fashionable society: *They are the social leaders in our town.* **6** a social gathering or party. **7** (of animals) living together in organized communities. Ants and bees are social insects. 1-5,7 *adj.,* 6 *n.* [*Social* is from Latin *socialis,* which comes from *socius,* meaning "companion." See **Word Family.**]

social

Below are words related to *social.* They can all be traced back to the Latin word *socius* (sō/ki ús), meaning "companion, ally."

antisocial	sociability	society
associate	socialism	sociological
association	socialite	sociology
dissociate	socialize	unsociable

so cial ism (sō/shə liz/əm), **1** theory or system of social organization by which the major means of production and distribution are owned, managed, or controlled by the government, by associations of workers, or by the community as a whole. **2** a political movement supporting or associated with this system. *n.*

so cial ist (sō/shə list), **1** person who favors or supports socialism. **2** socialistic. **3 Socialist,** member of a Socialist Party. **4 Socialist,** of a Socialist Party. 1,3 *n.,* 2,4 *adj.*

so cial is tic (sō/shə lis/tik), **1** of socialism or socialists. **2** favoring or supporting socialism. *adj.* —**so/cial is/ti cal ly,** *adv.*

Socialist Party, a political party which supports socialism.

so cial ite (sō/shə līt), member of the fashionable society of a community. *n.*

so cial i za tion (sō/shə lə zā/shən), a socializing or a being socialized. *n.*

so cial ize (sō/shə līz), **1** be social or sociable: *He has never learned to socialize with his fellow workers.* **2** establish or regulate in accordance with socialism. **3** make social; make fit for living with others. *v.,* **so cial ized, so cial iz ing.** —**so/cial iz/er,** *n.*

so cial ly (sō/shə lē), **1** in a social way or manner; in relation to other people. **2** as a member of society or of a social group: *He is an able man, but socially he is a failure. adv.*

social science, study of people, their activities, their customs, and their institutions in relationship to other people. History, sociology, economics, geography, and civics are social sciences.

social security, system of federal old-age pensions and medical care for retired persons and their dependents. The program is financed by the government, the employee, and the employer.

social service, social work.

social studies, course of study in elementary schools and high schools that includes history, civics, economics, geography, and other subjects in the social sciences.

social work, work directed toward the betterment of social conditions in a community. Social work includes such services as free medical clinics, counseling for families, and recreational activities for underprivileged children.

social worker, person who does social work.

so ci e ty (sə sī/ə tē), **1** group of persons joined together for a common purpose or by a common interest: *a debating society, a legal society.* A club, a fraternity, a lodge, or an association may be called a society. **2** all the people; human beings living together as a group: *Society must work hard for world peace.* **3** the people of any particular time or place: *20th-century society. American society, the lower and middle classes of industrial society.* **4** the activities and customs of society or of a particular society: *Magic plays an important part in primitive society.* **5** company; companionship: *I enjoy their society.* **6** fashionable people or their doings: *Her parents are leaders of society. n., pl.* **so ci e ties.**

Society Islands, group of French islands in the S Pacific that includes Tahiti.

Society of Friends, the Quakers.

Society of Jesus, the religious order of the Jesuits.

so ci o log i cal (sō/sē ə loj/ə kəl), **1** of human society or problems relating to it: *Unemployment is a sociological problem.* **2** of sociology. *adj.* —**so/ci o log/i cal ly,** *adv.*

so ci ol o gist (sō/sē ol/ə jist), an expert in sociology. *n.*

so ci ol o gy (sō/sē ol/ə jē), study of the nature, origin, and development of human society and community life; science of society. Sociology deals with social conditions, such as crime and poverty, and social institutions, such as marriage, the family, and the school. *n.*

sock[1] (sok), a short, close-fitting, knitted covering for the foot and leg, especially one that reaches about halfway to the knee. *n.* —**sock/less,** *adj.* —**sock/like/,** *adj.*

sock[2] (sok), SLANG. **1** strike or hit hard. **2** a hard blow. 1 *v.,* 2 *n.*

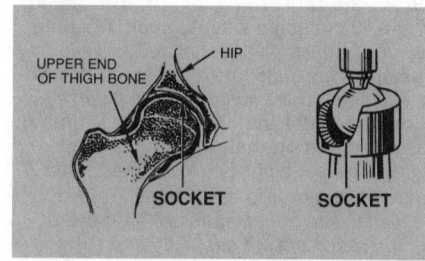

sock et (sok/it), a hollow part or piece for receiving and holding something. A candlestick has a socket in which to set a candle. A person's eyes are set in sockets. An electric lamp has a socket into which a bulb is screwed. *n.*

Soc ra tes (sok/rə tēz/), 469?-399 B.C., Athenian philosopher whose teachings were written down by his disciple Plato. *n.*

So crat ic (sō krat/ik), of Socrates, his philosophy, followers, etc. *adj.*

sod (def. 2)—They lived in a house made of **sod.**

a hat	i it	oi oil	ch child	a in about
ā age	ī ice	ou out	ng long	e in taken
ä far	o hot	u cup	sh she	ə = { i in pencil
e let	ō open	u̇ put	th thin	o in lemon
ē equal	ô order	ü rule	̵FH then	u in circus
ėr term			zh measure	

sod (sod), **1** ground covered with grass. **2** piece or layer of this containing the grass and its roots. **3** to cover with sods: *We had the bare spots of our lawn sodded.* 1,2 *n.,* 3 *v.,* **sod ded, sod ding.**

so da (sō′də), **1** any of several chemical substances containing sodium, such as sodium bicarbonate or baking soda, sodium carbonate or sal soda, and sodium hydroxide or caustic soda. **2** soda water. **3** soda water flavored with fruit juice or syrup, and often containing ice cream. *n., pl.* **so das.**

soda fountain, counter with places for holding soda water, flavored syrups, ice cream, etc.

so dal i ty (sō dal′ə tē), **1** fellowship; friendship. **2** (in the Roman Catholic Church) a lay society with religious or charitable purposes. *n., pl.* **so dal i ties.**

soda pop, a nonalcoholic carbonated drink.

soda water, water charged with carbon dioxide to make it bubble and fizz, often served with the addition of syrup, ice cream, etc.

sod den (sod′n), **1** soaked through: *The girl's clothes were sodden with rain.* **2** heavy and moist: *This bread is sodden because it was not baked well. adj.* —**sod′den ly,** *adv.*

so di um (sō′dē əm), a soft, silver-white, metallic element which reacts violently with water. It occurs in nature only in combination with other elements. Salt and soda contain sodium. *n.*

sodium bicarbonate, a powdery, white, crystalline substance used in baking, medicine, manufacturing, etc.; baking soda; bicarbonate of soda. It is a source of carbon dioxide.

sodium carbonate, a white crystalline powder used for softening water, making soap and glass, and in medicine and photography; sal soda.

sodium chloride, salt (def. 1).

sodium fluoride, a crystalline substance used in the fluoridation of water and in treating certain forms of tooth decay.

sodium hydroxide, a white solid that is a strong, corrosive alkali; caustic soda. It is used in making soap and as a bleaching agent.

sodium nitrate, a colorless, crystalline compound used in making fertilizer, explosives, etc., and as a preservative in meats; niter; saltpeter.

Sod om (sod′əm), (in the Bible) a wicked city destroyed, together with Gomorrah, by fire from heaven. *n.*

so fa (sō′fə), a long, upholstered seat or couch having a back and arms. *n., pl.* **so fas.** [*Sofa* comes from Arabic *suffah,* meaning ''bench.'']

So fi a (sō fē′ə), capital of Bulgaria, in the W part. *n.*

soft (sôft), **1** not hard; not stiff; yielding easily to touch: *a soft pillow. Feathers, cotton, and wool are soft.* **2** not hard compared with other things of the same sort: *Pine is softer than oak. Copper and lead are softer than steel.* **3** pleasant to the touch; not rough or coarse; smooth: *the soft fur of a kitten, soft silk.* **4** not loud: *a soft voice.*

5 quietly pleasant; mild; not harsh: *a soft spring morning, soft words, the soft light of candles.* **6** gentle; kind; tender: *a soft heart, soft eyes.* **7** weak; out of condition; not fit: *become soft from idleness and luxury.* **8** softly; quietly; gently. **9** free from minerals that keep soap from forming suds: *Soft water is easy to wash with.* **10** having a more or less hissing sound. The *c* is soft in *city* and hard in *corn*; *g* is soft in *gentle* and hard in *get*. **11** easy; easy-going: *a soft job, a soft person.* 1-7,9-11 *adj.,* 8 *adv.* —**soft′ly,** *adv.* —**soft′ness,** *n.*

soft ball (sôft′bôl′), **1** a kind of baseball that is played on a smaller field, with a larger and softer ball, and lighter bats. A softball must be pitched underhand. **2** the ball used in this game. *n.*

soft-boiled (sôft′boild′), (of an egg) boiled only a little so that the yolk is still soft. *adj.*

soft coal, bituminous coal.

soft drink, drink that does not contain alcohol.

soft en (sôf′ən), make or become soft: *Hand lotion softens the skin. Soap softens in water. v.* —**soft′en er,** *n.*

soft heart ed (sôft′här′tid), gentle; kind; tender. *adj.* —**soft′heart′ed ly,** *adv.* —**soft′heart′ed ness,** *n.*

soft palate, the fleshy back part of the roof of the mouth.

soft-spo ken (sôft′spō′kən), **1** speaking with a soft voice. **2** spoken softly: *a soft-spoken reply. adj.*

soft ware (sôft′wer′ *or* sôft′war′), instructions for a computer or computer system; programs. *n.*

soft wood (sôft′wu̇d′), **1** the soft, easily cut wood of such trees as pine, fir, hemlock, and redwood. **2** any of such trees, having needles, or lacking broad leaves. **3** made of such wood: *softwood furniture.* 1,2 *n.,* 3 *adj.*

soft y (sôf′tē), INFORMAL. a soft, silly, or weak person. *n., pl.* **soft ies.**

sog gi ness (sog′ē nis), soggy condition. *n.*

sog gy (sog′ē), **1** thoroughly wet; soaked: *The wash on the line was soggy from the rain.* **2** damp and heavy: *soggy bread. adj.,* **sog gi er, sog gi est.** —**sog′gi ly,** *adv.*

soil¹ (soil), **1** ground; earth; dirt. **2** land; country: *This is my native soil. n.*

soil² (soil), **1** make or become dirty: *I soiled my clean clothes. White shirts soil easily.* **2** to disgrace; dishonor: *False rumors can soil one's good name. v.*

WORD HISTORY

soil²

Soil² came into English about 700 years ago from French *soillier*, meaning ''to soil,'' and can be traced back to Latin *sus*, meaning ''pig.''

soil less (soil′lis), without soil. *adj.*

soi ree (swä rā′), an evening party or social gathering. *n., pl.* **soi rees.**

soi rée (swä rā′), soiree. *n., pl.* **soi rées.**

so journ (sō′jėrn′ *or* sō jėrn′ *for 1;* sō′jėrn′ *for 2*),
1 stay for a time: *The Israelites sojourned in the land of
Egypt.* **2** a brief stay; a stay that is not permanent: *During
his sojourn in Africa he learned much about tribal customs.*
1 *v.*, 2 *n.* —**so′journ′er**, *n.*

sol (sōl), the fifth tone of the musical scale. *n.* Also, **so.**

sol., **1** soluble. **2** solution.

sol ace (sol′is), **1** comfort or relief: *She found solace from
her troubles in music.* **2** to comfort or relieve; cheer: *He
solaced himself with a book.* 1 *n.*, 2 *v.*, **sol aced, sol ac ing.**
—**sol′ac er**, *n.*

so lar (sō′lər), **1** of the sun: *solar energy, a solar eclipse.*
2 measured or determined by the earth's motion in relation to the sun: *solar time.* **3** working by means of the
sun's light or heat. A solar battery traps sunlight and
converts it into electrical energy. *adj.*

solar collectors on the roof of a building

solar collector, device for collecting heat from sunlight. It usually consists of glass panels over a black
surface with a space between for liquid or air to flow
and remove heat.

so lar i um (sə ler′ē əm), room, porch, etc., where people can lie or sit in the sun. *n., pl.* **so lar i a** (sə ler′ē ə),
so lar i ums.

solar plex us (plek′səs), network of nerves situated at
the upper part of the abdomen, behind the stomach and
in front of the aorta.

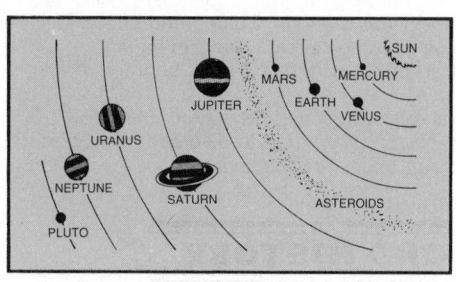

solar system

solar system, the sun and all the planets, satellites,
comets, etc., that revolve around it.

solar year, the period of time required for the earth to
make one revolution around the sun. It lasts about 365¹/₄
days.

sold (sōld), past tense and past participle of **sell.** *She
sold her car a week ago. She has sold it to a friend. v.*

sol der (sod′ər), **1** metal or alloy that can be melted and
used for joining or mending metal surfaces, parts, etc.
2 fasten, mend, or join with such a metal or alloy: *She
soldered the broken wires together.* 1 *n.*, 2 *v.* —**sol′der a-
ble,** *adj.* —**sol′der er,** *n.* —**sol′der less,** *adj.*

sol dier (sōl′jər), **1** person who serves in an army. **2** an
enlisted man or woman in the army who is not a com-

missioned officer. **3** person who serves in any cause:
Christian soldiers. **4** act or serve as a soldier. 1-3 *n.*, 4 *v.*
[*Soldier* came into English about 700 years ago from
French *soldier,* and can be traced back to Latin *solidus,*
the name of a Roman gold coin. Soldiers were called
this because they served in an army for pay.]

sol dier ly (sōl′jər lē), like a soldier; like that of a soldier. *adj.* —**sol′dier li ness,** *n.*

soldier of fortune, person serving or ready to serve
as a soldier under any government for money, adventure, or pleasure.

sole[1] (sōl), **1** one and only; single: *He was the sole heir to
the fortune when his aunt died.* **2** only: *We three were the
sole survivors from the wreck.* **3** of or for only one person
or group and not others; exclusive: *the sole right of use.*
adj. —**sole′ness,** *n.*

sole[2] (sōl), **1** the bottom or undersurface of the foot.
2 bottom of a shoe, slipper, boot, etc. **3** put a sole on: *I
must have my shoes soled.* 1,2 *n.*, 3 *v.*, **soled, sol ing.**
—**sole′less,** *adj.*

sole[3] (sōl), any of various flatfishes. European sole is
valued highly as food. *n., pl.* **soles** *or* **sole.**

sol e cism (sol′ə siz′əm), **1** mistake in using words: *"I
done it"* is a solecism. **2** mistake in social behavior;
breach of good manners or etiquette. *n.*

sole ly (sōl′lē), **1** as the only one or ones; alone: *You will
be solely responsible for providing the lunch.* **2** only: *Bananas grow outdoors solely in warm climates. adv.*

sol emn (sol′əm), **1** serious; grave; earnest: *to speak in a
solemn voice. I gave my solemn promise to do better.*
2 causing serious or grave thoughts: *The organ played
solemn music.* **3** done with form and ceremony: *a solemn
procession.* **4** connected with religion; sacred. **5** gloomy;
dark; somber in color. *adj.* —**sol′emn ly,** *adv.* —**sol′-
emn ness,** *n.*

so lem ni ty (sə lem′nə tē), **1** solemn feeling; seriousness; impressiveness: *The solemnity of the occasion was
felt even by the children.* **2** a solemn, formal ceremony:
Passover is observed with solemnities. n., pl. **so lem ni ties.**

sol em nize (sol′əm nīz), **1** observe with ceremonies:
*Christian churches solemnize the resurrection of Christ at
Easter.* **2** hold or perform (a ceremony or service): *The
marriage was solemnized in the temple.* **3** make serious or
grave. *v.,* **sol em nized, sol em niz ing.** —**sol′em ni-
za′tion,** *n.* —**sol′em niz′er,** *n.*

so le noid (sō′lə noid), a spiral or cylindrical coil of wire
that acts like a magnet when an electric current passes
through it. It is used in automobile starters and other
electromagnetic switches. *n.*

so lic it (sə lis′it), **1** ask earnestly; try to get: *The new
business is soliciting trade through newspaper advertising.*
2 make appeals or requests: *solicit for contributions to the
Red Cross. v.*

so lic i ta tion (sə lis′ə tā′shən), a soliciting; earnest request; urging. *n.*

so lic i tor (sə lis′ə tər), **1** person who entreats or requests. **2** lawyer. In England a solicitor prepares a case
and gives advice, but can plead a case only in a lower
court. **3** lawyer for a town, city, state, etc. *n.*

so lic i tous (sə lis′ə təs), **1** showing care or concern;
anxious; concerned: *Parents are solicitous for their children's progress in school.* **2** desirous; eager: *solicitous to
please. adj.* —**so lic′i tous ly,** *adv.* —**so lic′i tous ness,** *n.*

so lic i tude (sə lis′ə tüd *or* sə lis′ə tyüd), anxious care;
anxiety; concern. *n.*

sol id (sol′id), **1** substance that is not a liquid or a gas.
Iron, wood, and ice are solids. **2** in the form of a solid;
not liquid: *After I had my tooth pulled I couldn't eat solid
food.* **3** not hollow: *A bar of iron is solid; a pipe is hollow.*
4 strongly put together; hard; firm: *They were glad to*

leave the boat and put their feet on *solid ground.* **5** alike throughout: *The cloth is a solid blue.* **6** firmly united: *The country was solid for peace.* **7** real; serious: *Chemistry and physics are solid subjects.* **8** able to be depended on: *a solid citizen.* **9** having good judgment; sound; sensible; intelligent: *a solid book by a solid thinker.* **10** whole; entire: *I spent a solid hour on my arithmetic.* **11** undivided; continuous: *a solid row of houses.* **12** having length, breadth, and thickness. **13** body that has length, breadth, and thickness. A cube is a solid. 1,13 *n.*, 2-12 *adj.*
—**sol′id ly,** *adv.* —**sol′id ness,** *n.*

sol i dar i ty (sol′ə dar′ə tē), unity or fellowship arising from common responsibilities and interests. *n.*

solid geometry, branch of mathematics that deals with objects having the three dimensions of length, breadth, and thickness.

so lid i fi ca tion (sə lid′ə fə kā′shən), a solidifying or a being solidified. *n.*

so lid i fy (sə lid′ə fī), **1** make or become solid; harden: *The melted butter solidified as it cooled.* **2** unite firmly. *v.*, **so lid i fied, so lid i fy ing.** —**so lid′i fi′a ble,** *adj.* —**so lid′i fi′er,** *n.*

so lid i ty (sə lid′ə tē), condition or quality of being solid; firmness or hardness; substantial quality: *the solidity of marble or steel, the solidity of a person's character.* *n.*

sol id-state (sol′id stāt′), made with transistors, printed circuits, etc. Tiny solid-state devices have replaced larger parts, such as vacuum tubes, in many radios, television sets, and other appliances. *adj.*

so lil o quize (sə lil′ə kwīz), **1** talk to oneself. **2** speak a soliloquy. *v.*, **so lil o quized, so lil o quiz ing.** —**so lil′o-quiz′er,** *n.*

so lil o quy (sə lil′ə kwē), **1** a talking to oneself. **2** speech made by an actor to himself or herself. It reveals the actor's thoughts and feelings to the audience, but not to the other characters in the play. *n., pl.* **so lil o quies.**

sol i taire (sol′ə ter or sol′ə tar), **1** any card game played by one person. **2** diamond or other gem set by itself. *n.*

solitary (def. 2)—He took a **solitary** walk through the park.

sol i tar y (sol′ə ter′ē), **1** alone; single; only: *A solitary rider was seen in the distance.* **2** without companions; away from people; lonely. *adj.* —**sol′i tar′i ly,** *adv.* —**sol′i tar′i ness,** *n.*

sol i tude (sol′ə tüd or sol′ə tyüd), **1** a being alone: *He likes company and hates solitude.* **2** a lonely place: *This forest is a solitude.* **3** loneliness. *n.*

so lo (sō′lō), **1** piece of music for one voice or instrument: *She sang three solos.* **2** arranged for and performed by one voice or instrument: *a solo part.* **3** without a partner, teacher, etc.; alone: *a solo flight across the ocean, a solo dance.* **4** anything done without a partner, teacher, etc. **5** make a flight alone in an airplane. 1,4 *n., pl.* **so los**

or **so li** (sō′lē); 2,3 *adj.*, 5 *v.*, **so loed, so lo ing.** [*Solo* comes from Italian *solo,* meaning "alone."]

so lo ist (sō′lō ist), person who sings or plays a solo or solos. *n.*

Sol o mon (sol′ə mən), **1** king of Israel who lived in the 900's B.C. Solomon was a son of David and was famous for his wisdom, and for the great temple which he had built in Jerusalem. **2** man of great wisdom. *n.*

Solomon Islands, island country consisting of many small islands in the S Pacific, northeast of Australia. It is a member of the Commonwealth of Nations. *Capital:* Honiara. See Australia for map.

So lon (sō′lən or sō′lon), **1** 638?-558? B.C., wise Athenian lawgiver. **2** a wise man; sage. *n.*

so long, INFORMAL. good-by; farewell.

sol stice (sol′stis), either of the two times in the year when the sun appears to be farthest north or south in the heavens. In the Northern Hemisphere, June 21 or 22, the **summer solstice,** is the longest day of the year and December 21 or 22, the **winter solstice,** is the shortest. *n.*

sol u bil i ty (sol′yə bil′ə tē), quality that some substances have of dissolving or being dissolved easily: *the solubility of sugar in water.* *n.*

sol u ble (sol′yə bəl), **1** capable of being dissolved: *Salt is soluble in water.* **2** capable of being solved: *soluble puzzles. This problem is soluble.* *adj.* —**sol′u ble ness,** *n.*

sol ute (sol′yüt or sō′lüt), one of the substances, usually the smaller amount, in a solution: *Salt is a solute in seawater.* *n.*

so lu tion (sə lü′shən), **1** the solving of a problem: *That problem was hard; its solution required many hours.* **2** explanation: *The police are seeking a solution of the crime.* **3** mixture formed by combining a solid, liquid, or gas with another solid, liquid, or gas so that the molecules of each are evenly distributed: *Salt and water form a solution.* **4** the forming of such a mixture: *the solution of a gas in a liquid.* **5** (in mathematics) any number which makes an open sentence a true statement. *n.*

solution set, the set which contains all the solutions of an equation or inequality.

solv a ble (sol′və bəl), capable of being solved. *adj.* —**solv′a ble ness,** *n.*

solve (solv), find the answer to; clear up; explain: *The detective solved the mystery. He has solved all the problems in the lesson.* *v.*, **solved, solv ing.** —**solv′er,** *n.*

sol ven cy (sol′vən sē), ability to pay all one owes. *n., pl.* **sol ven cies.**

sol vent (sol′vənt), **1** able to pay all one owes: *A bankrupt firm is not solvent.* **2** able to dissolve: *Gasoline is a solvent liquid that removes grease spots.* **3** substance, usually a liquid, that can dissolve other substances: *Water is a solvent of sugar and salt.* 1,2 *adj.*, 3 *n.*

So ma li a (sə mä′lyə), country in E Africa. *Capital:* Mogadiscio. *n.*

so mat ic (sō mat′ik), having to do with the body. *adj.*

somatic cell, any cell of an animal or plant, except a germ cell.

som ber or **som bre** (som′bər), **1** having deep shadows; dark; gloomy: *A cloudy winter day is somber. It was a somber room with dark furniture and heavy black hangings.* **2** melancholy; gloomy; dismal: *His losses made him*

very somber. adj. —**som′ber ly, som′bre ly,** *adv.*
—**som′ber ness, som′bre ness,** *n.*

som brer o (som brer′ō), a broad-brimmed hat worn in the southwestern United States, Mexico, and Spain. *n.,* *pl.* **som brer os.** [*Sombrero* was borrowed from Spanish *sombrero,* which comes from *sombra,* meaning "shade." The wide hat gives shade to the wearer.]

some (sum), **1** certain or particular, but not known or named: *Some dogs are larger than others.* **2** a number of: *Ask some friends to help you. I left the city some years ago.* **3** a quantity of: *Drink some milk.* **4** a certain number or quantity: *She ate some and gave the rest away.* **5** a; any: *Can't you find some kind person who will help you?* **6** about: *Some twenty people asked for work.* **7** INFORMAL. uncommonly big, bad, etc.; remarkable: *That was some storm!* 1-3,5,7 *adj.,* 4 *pron.,* 6 *adv.*

-some[1], *suffix forming adjectives.* **1** (*added to verbs*) tending to____: *Meddlesome = tending to meddle.* **2** (*added to nouns*) *causing*____: *Troublesome = causing trouble.* **3** (*added to adjectives*) ____ *to a considerable degree: Lonesome = lone to a considerable degree.*

-some[2], *suffix added to numbers.* group of ____: *Twosome = group of two. Foursome = group of four.*

some bod y (sum′bod′ē), **1** person not known or named; some person; someone: *Somebody has taken my pen.* **2** person of importance: *She acts as if she were somebody since she won the prize.* 1 *pron.,* 2 *n.,* *pl.* **some bod ies.**

some day (sum′dā), at some future time. *adv.*

some how (sum′hou), in a way not known or not stated; in one way or another: *I'll finish this work somehow. adv.*

some one (sum′wun), some person; somebody: *Someone is coming. pron.*

some place (sum′plās), in or to some place; somewhere. *adv.*

som er sault (sum′ər sôlt), **1** a roll or jump, turning the heels over the head. **2** roll or jump, turning the heels over the head. 1 *n.,* 2 *v.*

som er set (sum′ər set), somersault. *n., v.*

some thing (sum′thing), **1** some thing; a particular thing not named or known: *I'm sure I've forgotten something. She has something on her mind.* **2** a certain amount or quantity; a part; a little: *There is something of his father in his smile. Something yet of doubt remains.* **3** somewhat; to some extent or degree: *She is something like her father.* **4** thing or person of some value or importance: *He thinks he's something.* 1,2,4 *n.,* 3 *adv.*

some time (sum′tīm), **1** at one time or another: *Come to see me sometime.* **2** at an indefinite point of time: *It happened sometime last May.* **3** former: *a sometime pupil of our school.* 1,2 *adv.,* 3 *adj.*

some times (sum′tīmz), now and then; at times: *She comes to visit sometimes. adv.*

some way (sum′wā), in some way. *adv.*

some what (sum′hwot), **1** to some extent or degree; slightly: *My hat is somewhat like yours.* **2** some part; some amount: *The large gift came as somewhat of a surprise.* 1 *adv.,* 2 *n.*

some where (sum′hwer *or* sum′hwar), **1** in or to some place; in or to one place or another: *She lives somewhere in the neighborhood.* **2** at some time: *It happened somewhere in the last century. adv.*

som nam bu lism (som nam′byə liz′əm), sleepwalking. *n.*

som nam bu list (som nam′byə list), sleepwalker. *n.*

som no lence (som′nə ləns), sleepiness; drowsiness. *n.*

som no lent (som′nə lənt), **1** sleepy; drowsy. **2** tending to produce sleep: *The music had a somnolent effect. adj.* —**som′no lent ly,** *adv.*

son (sun), **1** a male child. A boy or man is the son of his

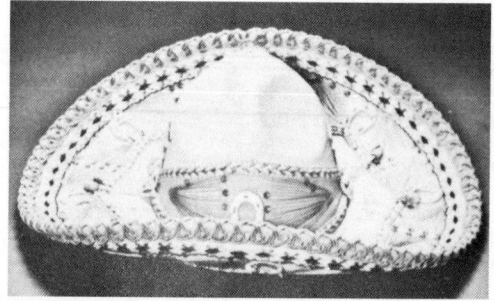

sombrero

father and mother. **2** a male descendant. **3** the Son, Jesus Christ. *n.* [*Son* comes from Old English *sunu.*] —**son′less,** *adj.* —**son′like′,** *adj.*

so nar (sō′när), device for finding the depth of water or for detecting and locating underwater objects. Sonar sends sound waves into water, which return when they strike the bottom or any object. *n.* [*Sonar* comes from the words *sound navigation ranging.* It was formed from the first two letters of *sound* and *navigation* and the first letter of *ranging.*]

so na ta (sə nä′tə), piece of music for one or two instruments, having three or four movements in contrasted rhythms but related keys. *n., pl.* **so na tas.** [*Sonata* was borrowed from Italian *sonata,* and can be traced back to Latin *sonus,* meaning "a sound."]

song (sông), **1** something to sing; a short poem set to music. **2** music to fit a poem; singing: *The canary burst into song.* **3** poetry that has a musical sound. **4** any sound like singing: *the cricket's song, the song of the teakettle. n.* —**song′like′,** *adj.*

for a song, very cheap: *buy things for a song.*

song bird (sông′bėrd′), bird that sings. *n.*

song ful (sông′fəl), full of song; musical; melodious. *adj.* —**song′ful ly,** *adv.* —**song′ful ness,** *n.*

song less (sông′lis), not able to sing. *adj.* —**song′less ly,** *adv.* —**song′less ness,** *n.*

Song of Solomon, The, book of the Old Testament.

Song of Songs, Song of Solomon.

song writ er (sông′rī′tər), composer of popular songs or tunes. *n.*

son ic (son′ik), **1** of sound waves. **2** having to do with the rate at which sound travels in air. At sea level the rate is 1087 feet (331 meters) per second. *adj.* —**son′i cal ly,** *adv.*

sonic barrier, a sudden increase in air resistance met by an aircraft or projectile as it nears the speed of sound; sound barrier.

sonic boom, a very loud noise caused by shock waves that are produced by an aircraft moving faster than the speed of sound. As the shock waves move down and touch the earth's surface, they produce explosive sounds.

son-in-law (sun′in lô′), husband of one's daughter. *n., pl.* **sons-in-law.**

son net (son′it), poem having 14 lines with a fixed measure and a formal arrangement of rhymes. *n.* —**son′net like′,** *adj.*

son net eer (son′ə tir′), writer of sonnets. *n.*

son ny (sun′ē), little son. *Sonny* is used as a pet name, or as a way of speaking to a little boy. *n.*

so nor i ty (sə nôr′ə tē), sonorous quality or condition. *n.*

so no rous (sə nôr′əs), **1** giving out or having a deep, loud sound: *a big, sonorous church bell.* **2** full and rich in sound. **3** having an impressive sound; high-sounding: *sonorous phrases, a sonorous style. adj.* —**so no′rous ly,** *adv.* —**so no′rous ness,** *n.*

soon (sün), **1** in a short time; before long: *I will see you again soon.* **2** before the usual or expected time; early: *Why have you come so soon?* **3** promptly; quickly: *As soon as I hear, I will let you know.* **4** readily; willingly: *I would as soon die as have to go through such a terrible experience again. adv.*

soot (sut *or* süt), a black substance in the smoke from burning coal, wood, oil, etc. Soot makes smoke dark and collects on the inside of chimneys. *n.*

sooth (süth), OLD USE. truth. *n.*

soothe (süŦH), **1** quiet; calm; comfort: *The mother soothed the crying child.* **2** make less painful; relieve; ease: *Heat soothes some aches; cold soothes others. v.,* **soothed, sooth ing. —sooth'er,** *n.*

sooth ing (sü'ŦHing), that soothes: *soothing words, soothing syrup. adj.* **—sooth'ing ly,** *adv.* **—sooth'ing ness,** *n.*

sooth say er (süth'sā'ər), person who claims to foretell the future; person who makes prophecies or predictions. *n.*

sooth say ing (süth'sā'ing), the foretelling of future events; prediction or prophecy. *n.*

soot y (sut'ē *or* sü'tē), **1** covered or blackened with soot. **2** dark-brown or black; dark-colored. *adj.,* **soot i er, soot i est. —soot'i ly,** *adv.* **—soot'i ness,** *n.*

sop (sop), **1** piece of food dipped or soaked in milk, broth, etc. **2** dip or soak: *to sop bread in milk.* **3** something given to soothe or quiet; bribe. **4** take up (water, etc.); wipe; mop: *Please sop up that water with a cloth.* **5** soak thoroughly; drench. 1,3 *n.,* 2,4,5 *v.,* **sopped, sop ping.**

sopping wet, soaked; drenched.

sop., soprano.

soph ist (sof'ist), a clever but misleading reasoner. *n.*

so phis ti cate (sə fis'tə kāt *for 1;* sə fis'tə kāt *or* sə fis'tə kit *for 2*), **1** make experienced in worldly ways. **2** a sophisticated person. 1 *v.,* **so phis ti cat ed, so phis ti cat ing;** 2 *n.*

so phis ti cat ed (sə fis'tə kā'tid), **1** experienced in worldly ways; changed from natural simplicity. **2** very complex and advanced in design: *sophisticated laboratory equipment. adj.* **—so phis'ti cat'ed ly,** *adv.*

so phis ti ca tion (sə fis'tə kā'shən), a lessening or loss of naturalness, simplicity, or frankness; worldly experience or ideas; artificial ways. *n.*

soph ist ry (sof'ə strē), **1** unsound reasoning. **2** a clever but misleading argument. *n., pl.* **soph ist ries.**

Soph o cles (sof'ə klēz'), 495?-406? B.C., Greek writer of tragedies. *n.*

soph o more (sof'ə môr), student in the second year of high school or college. *n.*

soph o mor ic (sof'ə môr'ik), of or like a sophomore. *adj.*

so po rif ic (sō'pə rif'ik *or* sop'ə rif'ik), **1** causing or tending to cause sleep. **2** sleepy; drowsy. **3** drug that causes sleep. 1,2 *adj.,* 3 *n.*

sop ping (sop'ing), soaked; drenched. *adj.*

sop py (sop'ē), soaked; very wet; rainy: *soppy ground, soppy weather. adj.,* **sop pi er, sop pi est. —sop'pi ness,** *n.*

so pran o (sə pran'ō), **1** the highest singing voice in women and boys. **2** singer with such a voice. **3** part for such a voice or for a corresponding instrument. **4** instrument playing such a part. **5** of or for a soprano. 1-4 *n., pl.* **so pran os;** 5 *adj.* [*Soprano* was borrowed from Italian *soprano,* and can be traced back to Latin *supra,* meaning "above."]

sor cer er (sôr'sər ər), person who practices magic, especially with the supposed aid of evil spirits; wizard; magician. *n.*

sor cer ess (sôr'sər is), woman who practices magic, es-

pecially with the supposed aid of evil spirits; witch. *n., pl.* **sor cer ess es.**

sor cer y (sôr'sər ē), magic performed with the supposed aid of evil spirits; witchcraft: *The prince had been changed into a lion by sorcery. n., pl.* **sor cer ies.**

sor did (sôr'did), **1** dirty; filthy: *a sordid back street, a sordid shack.* **2** mean; low; base: *sordid crimes. adj.* **—sor'did ly,** *adv.* **—sor'did ness,** *n.*

sore (sôr), **1** causing sharp or continuous pain; painful; aching; tender; smarting: *a sore throat, a sore finger.* **2** a painful place on the body where the skin or flesh is broken or bruised. **3** sad; distressed: *The suffering of her friend made her heart sore.* **4** INFORMAL. angry; vexed: *He is sore at missing the game.* **5** causing misery, anger, or offense; vexing: *Their defeat is a sore subject with the members of the team.* **6** cause of pain, sorrow, sadness, anger, offense, etc. **7** severe; distressing: *Your going away is a sore grief to us.* 1,3-5,7 *adj.,* **sor er, sor est;** 2,6 *n.* **—sore'ly,** *adv.* **—sore'ness,** *n.*

sor ghum (sôr'gəm), **1** any of a group of tall plants which resemble corn. One kind of sorghum has a sweet juice used for making molasses or syrup. Some kinds provide food for livestock either by their grain or as hay, and others furnish material for brushes or brooms. **2** molasses or syrup made from a sorghum plant. *n.*

so ro ri ty (sə rôr'ə tē), club or society of women or girls, especially at a college. *n., pl.* **so ro ri ties.**

sor rel[1] (sôr'əl), **1** reddish-brown. **2** a reddish brown. **3** a horse having this color. 1 *adj.,* 2,3 *n.*

sor rel[2] (sôr'əl), any of several plants with sour leaves. *n.*

sor ri ly (sôr'ə lē), in a sorry manner. *adv.*

sor ri ness (sôr'ē nis), condition or feeling of being sorry. *n.*

sor row (sor'ō), **1** grief, sadness, or regret: *He felt sorrow at the loss of his kitten. He expressed sorrow at his mistake.* **2** cause of grief, sadness, or regret; trouble; suffering; misfortune: *Her sorrows have aged her.* **3** feel or show grief, sadness, or regret; be sad; feel sorry; grieve: *She sorrowed over the lost money.* 1,2 *n.,* 3 *v.* **—sor'row er,** *n.* **—sor'row less,** *adj.*

sor row ful (sor'ə fəl), **1** full of sorrow; feeling sorrow; sad: *A funeral is a sorrowful occasion.* **2** showing sorrow. **3** causing sorrow. *adj.* **—sor'row ful ly,** *adv.* **—sor'row ful ness,** *n.*

sor ry (sor'ē), **1** feeling pity, regret, sympathy; sad: *I am sorry that you are sick. We are sorry that we cannot come to the party.* **2** wretched; poor; pitiful: *The ragged, hungry child was a sorry sight. adj.,* **sor ri er, sor ri est.** [*Sorry* comes from Old English *sārig.*]

sort (sôrt), **1** kind or class; type: *What sort of work does he do? I like this sort of candy best.* **2** character; quality; nature: *materials of an inferior sort.* **3** person or thing of a certain kind or quality: *He is a good sort.* **4** arrange by kinds or classes; arrange in order: *Sort these cards according to their colors.* **5** separate from others; put: *sort out the best apples for eating.* 1-3 *n.,* 4,5 *v.* **—sort'a ble,** *adj.* **—sort'er,** *n.*

of sorts, of a poor or mediocre quality.

out of sorts, ill, cross, or uncomfortable.

sort of, INFORMAL. somewhat; rather: *In spite of her faults I sort of like her.*

---

sor tie (sôr′tē), **1** a sudden rushing forth of troops from a besieged fort, town, castle, etc., to attack the besiegers. **2** a single flight of an aircraft attacking an enemy. *n.*

S O S (es′ō′es′), **1** signal of distress consisting of the letters *s o s* of the international Morse code (. . . --- . . .), used in wireless telegraphy by ships, aircraft, etc. **2** any urgent call for help.

so-so (sō′sō′), **1** neither very good nor very bad; fairly good: *The speech was only so-so, but we enjoyed the singing that followed.* **2** in a passable or indifferent manner; tolerably: *"How is he doing his work?" "So-so."* **1** *adj.,* **2** *adv.*

sot (sot), person made stupid and foolish by drinking too much alcoholic liquor; drunkard. *n.*

sot tish (sot′ish), of or like a sot. *adj.* —**sot′tish ly,** *adv.*

sou (sü), a former French coin, worth 5 centimes or ¹/₂₀ of a franc. *n.*

sou bri quet (sü′brə kā), sobriquet. *n.*

Sou dan (sü dan′), Sudan. *n.*

souf flé (sü flā′), a frothy baked dish, usually made light by beaten eggs: *cheese soufflé. n., pl.* **souf flés.** [*Soufflé* was borrowed from French *soufflé.*]

sough (suf *or* sou), **1** make a rustling or murmuring sound: *The pines soughed when the wind blew.* **2** a rustling or murmuring sound. **1** *v.,* **2** *n.*

sought (sôt), past tense and past participle of **seek.** *For days she sought a job. They were sought and found. v.*

soul (sōl), **1** the spiritual part of a human being, regarded as the source of thought, feeling, and action, and considered as separate from the body. **2** energy of mind or feelings; spirit: *She puts her whole soul into her work.* **3** cause of inspiration and energy: *Florence Nightingale was the soul of the movement to reform nursing.* **4** the essential part: *Brevity is the soul of wit.* **5** a distinctive emotional or spiritual quality associated with black American culture, especially as expressed through music. **6** person: *Don't tell a soul.* **7** embodiment: *the soul of grace. n.*

soul ful (sōl′fəl), **1** full of feeling; deeply emotional: *soulful music.* **2** expressing or suggesting deep feeling: *a soulful sigh. adj.* —**soul′ful ly,** *adv.* —**soul′ful ness,** *n.*

soul less (sōl′lis), having no soul; without spirit or noble feelings. *adj.* —**soul′less ly,** *adv.*

sound¹ (sound), **1** what is or can be heard; sensation produced in the organs of hearing by vibrations transmitted by the air or some other medium: *the sound of music, the sound of thunder.* **2** energy in the form of vibrations causing this sensation. Sound travels through air in waves about 1087 feet (331 meters) per second. **3** distance within which a noise may be heard. **4** one of the simple elements that make up speech: *a vowel sound.* **5** make a sound or noise: *The wind sounds like an animal howling.* **6** pronounce: *Sound each syllable.* **7** be pronounced: *"Rough" and "ruff" sound just alike.* **8** cause to sound: *"Sound the trumpets; beat the drums."* **9** to order or direct by a sound: *Sound the retreat.* **10** make known; announce; utter: *The trumpets sounded the call to battle. Everyone sounded her praises.* **11** seem: *That excuse sounds peculiar.* **12** effect produced on the mind by what is heard: *a warning sound, a strange sound.* **1-4,12** *n.,* **5-11** *v.*

within sound, near enough to hear.

sound² (sound), **1** free from disease; healthy: *a sound body and mind.* **2** free from injury, decay, or defect: *sound walls, a sound ship, sound fruit.* **3** strong; safe; secure: *a sound business firm.* **4** solid: *sound roof supports.* **5** correct; right; reasonable; reliable: *sound advice, sound arguments.* **6** morally good; honest; upright: *sound values.* **7** deep; heavy; profound: *a sound sleep.* **8** thorough; complete: *a sound whipping.* **9** deeply; thoroughly: *sleep long and sound.* **1-8** *adj.,* **9** *adv.*

sound³ (sound), **1** to measure the depth of (water) by letting down a weight fastened on the end of a line. **2** try to find out the views of; test; examine: *We sounded them on the subject of a picnic.* **3** go quickly toward the bottom; dive: *The whale sounded. v.*

sound⁴ (sound), **1** a long, narrow strip of water, larger than a strait, joining two larger bodies of water or separating an island from the mainland: *Long Island Sound.* **2** inlet or arm of the sea: *Puget Sound.* **3** sac in fishes containing air or gas that helps them float. *n.*

sound barrier, sonic barrier.

sound er (soun′dər), person or thing that measures the depth of water. *n.*

sound ing¹ (soun′ding), **1** making a sound. **2** resounding. *adj.* —**sound′ing ly,** *adv.*

sound ing² (soun′ding), **1** act of measuring the depth of water with a sounding line. **2** the depth of water found by this means. **3** soundings, *pl.* **a** depths of water found by using a sounding line. **b** water not more than 600 feet (183 meters) deep, which can be measured by an ordinary sounding line. *n.*

sounding board, 1 a thin piece of wood on a violin, piano, etc. The sounding board vibrates and increases the fullness of the instrument's tone. **2** structure used to direct sound outward toward an audience. **3** means or way of bringing opinion to public attention.

sounding line, line having a weight fastened to the end, used to measure the depth of water.

sound less¹ (sound′lis), without sound; making no sound: *soundless steps. adj.* —**sound′less ly,** *adv.*

sound less² (sound′lis), so deep that the bottom cannot be reached: *the soundless depths of the ocean. adj.*

sound ly (sound′lē), **1** deeply; heavily: *The tired child slept soundly.* **2** vigorously; thoroughly: *He scolded us soundly.* **3** with good judgment: *to make a decision soundly. adv.*

sound ness (sound′nis), **1** good health: *soundness of body and mind.* **2** freedom from weakness or defect. **3** good judgment; correctness and reliability: *We have confidence in our doctor's soundness. n.*

sound proof (sound′prüf′), **1** not letting sound pass through: *a soundproof room or ceiling.* **2** make soundproof: *The halls at school are soundproofed.* **1** *adj.,* **2** *v.*

sound track, a recording of the sounds of words, music, etc., made along one edge of a motion-picture film.

soup (süp), a liquid food made by boiling meat, vegetables, fish, etc. *n.*

in the soup, in difficulty.

soup up, SLANG. to increase the horsepower of (an engine, automobile, etc.).

soup y (sü′pē), like soup. *adj.,* **soup i er, soup i est.**

sour (sour), **1** having a taste like vinegar or lemon juice; sharp and biting; acid: *This green fruit is sour.* **2** fermented; spoiled: *sour milk.* **3** having a sour or rank smell. **4** disagreeable; bad-tempered; peevish: *a sour face, a sour remark.* **5** unusually acid: *sour soil.* **6** make or become sour; turn sour: *The milk soured while it stood in the hot sun.* **7** make or become peevish, bad-tempered, or disagreeable. **1-5** *adj.,* **6,7** *v.* —**sour′ly,** *adv.* —**sour′ness,** *n.*

source (sôrs), **1** person or place from which anything comes or is obtained: *The newspaper gets news from many sources. Mines are the chief source of diamonds.* **2** beginning of a brook or river; fountain; spring. *n.* [*Source* came into English about 600 years ago from French *sourse,* and can be traced back to Latin *surgere,* meaning "to rise."]

sour cream, a thick cream that has soured, but has a pleasant taste. It is used on baked potatoes, and in cooking.

sour dough (sour′dō′), **1** prospector or pioneer in Alaska or Canada. **2** fermented dough saved from one baking to start fermentation in the next. *n.*

sour grapes, a pretending that you dislike something because you cannot have it.

Sou sa (sü′zə), **John Philip,** 1854-1932, American conductor and composer of band music. *n.*

souse (sous), **1** plunge into liquid; throw liquid over; soak in a liquid. **2** a plunging into a liquid; drenching. **3** soak in vinegar, brine, etc.; pickle. **4** liquid used for pickling. **5** something soaked or pickled in brine, especially the head, ears, and feet of a pig. 1,3 *v.,* **soused, sous ing;** 2,4,5 *n.*

south (south), **1** direction to the left as one faces the setting sun; direction just opposite north. **2** toward the south; farther toward the south: *drive south (adv.), the south side of town (adj.).* **3** from the south: *a south wind.* **4** in the south: *the south window.* **5** Also, **South.** the part of any country toward the south. **6 South,** the southern part of the United States; the states south of Pennsylvania, the Ohio River, and Missouri, making up most of the states that formed the Confederate side in the Civil War. 1,5,6 *n.,* 2-4 *adj.,* 2 *adv.* [*South* comes from Old English *sūth.*]

south of, further south than: *New York is south of Boston.*

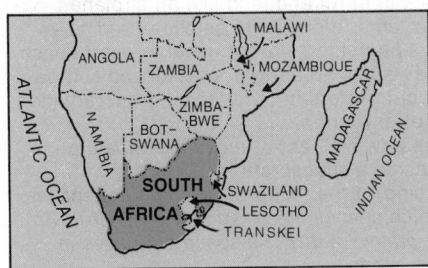

South Africa, Republic of, country in S Africa, formerly called **Union of South Africa.** *Capitals:* Pretoria and Cape Town.

South African, 1 of or having to do with the Republic of South Africa. **2** person born or living in the Republic of South Africa.

South African Dutch, Afrikaans.

South America, continent in the Western Hemisphere southeast of North America.

South American, 1 of or having to do with South America or its people. **2** person born or living in South America.

South amp ton (sou thamp′tən), seaport in S England. *n.*

South Bend, city in N Indiana.

south bound (south′bound′), going south. *adj.*

South Carolina, one of the southeastern states of the

southwester (def. 2)

a hat	**i** it	**oi** oil	**ch** child	a in about
ā age	**ī** ice	**ou** out	**ng** long	e in taken
ä far	**o** hot	**u** cup	**sh** she	ə = { i in pencil
e let	**ō** open	**u̇** put	**th** thin	o in lemon
ē equal	**ô** order	**ü** rule	**ᴛʜ** then	u in circus
ėr term			**zh** measure	

United States. *Abbreviation:* S.C. or SC *Capital:* Columbia. —**South Carolinian.**

South Dakota, one of the midwestern states of the United States. *Abbreviation:* S.Dak., S.D., or SD *Capital:* Pierre. —**South Dakotan.**

south east (south′ēst′), **1** halfway between south and east. **2** a southeast direction. **3** a place that is in the southeast part or direction. **4** toward the southeast. **5** from the southeast: *a southeast wind.* **6** in the southeast. 1,5,6 *adj.,* 2,3 *n.,* 4 *adv.*

south east er (south′ē′stər), wind or storm from the southeast. *n.*

south east er ly (south′ē′stər lē), **1** toward the southeast. **2** from the southeast. *adj., adv.*

south east ern (south′ē′stərn), **1** toward the southeast. **2** from the southeast. **3** of or in the southeast. *adj.*

south er ly (suᴛʜ′ər lē), **1** toward the south: *a southerly exposure.* **2** from the south: *a southerly wind.* **3** wind that blows from the south. 1,2 *adj., adv.,* 3 *n., pl.* **south er lies.**

south ern (suᴛʜ′ərn), **1** toward the south: *a southern view.* **2** from the south: *a southern breeze.* **3** of or in the south: *southern countries.* **4 Southern,** of or in the southern part of the United States. *adj.*

Southern Cross, group of four bright stars in the form of a cross, visible in the Southern Hemisphere.

south ern er (suᴛʜ′ər nər), **1** person born or living in the south. **2 Southerner,** person born or living in the southern part of the United States. *n.*

Southern Hemisphere, the half of the earth that is south of the equator.

south ern most (suᴛʜ′ərn mōst), farthest south. *adj.*

Southern Yemen, country in SW Arabia. *Capital:* Aden.

South Korea, country in the S part of the Korean peninsula. It is the area south of the 38th parallel. *Capital:* Seoul. —**South Korean.**

south land (south′lənd *or* south′land′), land in the south; southern part of a country. *n.*

south paw (south′pô′), INFORMAL. **1** a left-handed baseball pitcher. **2** any left-handed person. **3** left-handed. 1,2 *n.,* 3 *adj.*

South Pole, the southern end of the earth's axis.

South Sea Islands, islands in the S Pacific.

South Vietnam, former country in SE Asia, now part of Vietnam.

south ward (south′wərd), **1** toward the south; south: *She walked southward (adv.). The orchard is on the southward slope of the hill (adj.).* **2** a southward part, direction, or point. 1 *adv., adj.,* 2 *n.*

south wards (south′wərds), southward. *adv.*

south west (south′west′), **1** halfway between south and west. **2** a southwest direction. **3** a place that is in the southwest part or direction. **4** toward the southwest. **5** from the southwest: *a southwest wind.* **6** in the southwest. 1,5,6 *adj.,* 2,3 *n.,* 4 *adv.*

South-West Africa (south′west′), former name of **Namibia.**

south west er (south′wes′tər *for 1;* sou′wes′tər *for 2*), **1** wind or storm from the southwest. **2** a waterproof hat with a broad brim behind to protect the neck, worn especially by sailors. *n.* Also, **sou'wester.**

south west er ly (south′wes′tər lē), **1** toward the south-west. **2** from the southwest. *adj., adv.*

south west ern (south′wes′tərn), **1** toward the south-west. **2** from the southwest. **3** of or in the southwest. **4 Southwestern,** of or in the southwestern part of the United States. *adj.*

sou ve nir (sü′və nir′ *or* sü′və nir), something given or kept for remembrance; a remembrance; keepsake: *She bought a pair of moccasins as a souvenir of her trip out West. n.* [*Souvenir* comes from French *souvenir,* which originally meant "to remember," and can be traced back to Latin *sub-,* meaning "up from under," and *venire,* meaning "to come."]

sou'west er (sou′wes′tər), southwester. *n.*

sov er eign (sov′rən), **1** supreme ruler; king or queen; monarch. Queen Victoria was the sovereign of Great Britain from 1837 to 1901. **2** having supreme rank, pow-er, or authority: *a sovereign prince, a sovereign court.* **3** independent of the control of other governments: *When the thirteen colonies won the Revolutionary War, America became a sovereign nation.* **4** above all others; supreme; greatest: *Character is of sovereign importance.* **5** very excellent or powerful: *a sovereign cure for colds.* **6** a British gold coin, worth 20 shillings, or one pound. 1,6 *n.,* 2-5 *adj.* —**sov′er eign ly,** *adv.*

sov er eign ty (sov′rən tē), **1** supreme power or authori-ty: *The French Revolution rejected the sovereignty of the king.* **2** freedom from outside control; independence in exercising power or authority: *Countries that are satellites lack full sovereignty.* **3** state, territory, community, etc., that is independent or sovereign. **4** the rank, power, or jurisdiction of a sovereign. *n., pl.* **sov er eign ties.**

so vi et (sō′vē et), **1** any of the governing councils or assemblies of the Soviet Union, including town soviets and village soviets as well as the **Supreme Soviet,** the national legislative body. **2** of or having to do with sovi-ets. **3 Soviet,** of or having to do with the Soviet Union. 1 *n.,* 2,3 *adj.* [*Soviet* comes from Russian *sovet,* meaning "council."]

Soviet Russia, 1 the Russian Soviet Federated Social-ist Republic, the largest republic in the Soviet Union. **2** Soviet Union.

Soviet Union, the Union of Soviet Socialist Republics, a union of fifteen republics in E Europe and W and N Asia, the largest of which is the Russian Soviet Federat-ed Socialist Republic. The European part is often called Russia; Siberia comprises most of the Asian part. *Capi-tal:* Moscow. See **Ural Mountains** for map.

sow¹ (sō), **1** scatter (seed) on the ground; plant (seed): *He sows more wheat than oats.* **2** plant seed in: *They sowed the field with oats.* **3** scatter (anything); spread abroad: *The rebels sowed discontent among the people. v.,* **sowed, sown** or **sowed, sow ing.** —**sow′er,** *n.*

sow² (sou), a fully grown female pig. *n.*

sow bug (sou), wood louse.

sown (sōn), a past participle of **sow**¹. *The field had been sown with oats. v.*

sox (soks), socks (stockings). *n.pl.*

soy (soi), **1** a Chinese and Japanese sauce for fish, meat, etc., made from fermented soybeans. **2** soybean. *n.*

soy a (soi′ə), soy. *n.*

soy bean (soi′bēn′), bean native to Asia, now grown in North America and other parts of the world. Soybeans are an important protein-rich food. The oil is removed and used in margarine, paints, etc. The remaining meal is fed to livestock or made into flour. *n.*

sp., 1 special. **2** species. **3** spelling.

Sp., 1 Spain. **2** Spaniard. **3** Spanish.

spa (spä), **1** a mineral spring. **2** town, locality, or resort where there is a mineral spring or springs. *n., pl.* **spas.**

space (spās), **1** the unlimited room or area which ex-tends in all directions and in which all things exist: *The earth moves through space.* **2** limited place or room: *The brick will fill a space 2½ by 4 by 8 inches. Is there space in the car for another person?* **3** extent or area of ground, surface, etc.: *The trees covered acres of space.* **4** outer space: *the conquest and exploration of space, a rocket launched into space.* **5** of or having to do with outer space: *space travel.* **6** distance: *The road is bad for a space of ten miles.* **7** length of time: *The flowers died in the space of a day.* **8** (in music) one of the intervals between the lines of a staff. **9** fix the space or spaces of; divide into spaces. **10** separate by spaces: *Space your words evenly when you write.* 1-4,6-8 *n.,* 5 *adj.,* 9,10 *v.,* **spaced, spac-ing.**

space age, the current period in history, as marked by the advances made in the exploration of outer space. —**space′-age′,** *adj.*

space craft (spās′kraft′), vehicle used for flight in outer space. *n., pl.* **space craft.**

space heater, a small gas or electric heater, often port-able, for warming a room or a portion of a room.

space man (spās′mən), astronaut. *n., pl.* **space men.**

space ship (spās′ship′), spacecraft. *n.*

space shuttle, a reusable winged spacecraft, designed to be launched into orbit around the earth by a rocket, but to glide back to earth and land like an airplane.

space station, an artificial earth satellite used as an observatory or a launching site for travel in outer space.

space suit (spās′süt′), an airtight, pressurized suit de-signed to protect travelers in outer space from radiation, heat, and lack of oxygen. *n.*

space walk (spās′wôk′), act of moving or floating in space while outside a spacecraft. *n.*

spac ing (spā′sing), **1** the fixing or arranging of spaces. **2** manner in which spaces are arranged: *even, close, or open spacing in printed matter.* **3** a space or spaces in printing or other work. *n.*

spa cious (spā′shəs), containing much space; with plenty of room; vast: *The rooms were bright and spacious. adj.* —**spa′cious ly,** *adv.* —**spa′cious ness,** *n.*

spade¹ (spād), **1** tool for digging, having an iron blade which can be pressed into the ground with the foot, and a long handle with a grip or crosspiece at the top. **2** dig with a spade: *Spade up the garden.* 1 *n.,* 2 *v.,* **spad ed, spad ing.** [*Spade*¹ comes from Old English *spadu.*]

call a spade a spade, call a thing by its real name; speak plainly and frankly.

spade² (spād), **1** figure shaped like this:♠. **2** a playing card marked with one or more black figures like this. **3 spades,** *pl.* suit of such playing cards. *n.* [*Spade*² comes from Italian *spada,* and can be traced back to Greek *spathē,* meaning "broad blade."]

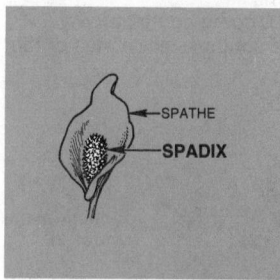

spa dix (spā′diks), spike composed of minute flowers on a fleshy stem. A spadix is usually enclosed in a spathe, as in the jack-in-the-pulpit and the calla lily. *n., pl.* **spa dix es, spa di ces** (spā dī′sēz).

spa ghet ti (spə get′ē), long, slender sticks made of the same mixture of flour and water as macaroni. Spaghetti is thinner than macaroni and not hollow. It is cooked by boiling in water. *n.*

WORD HISTORY

spaghetti

Spaghetti comes from Italian *spaghetti,* which originally meant "thin strings."

Spain (spān), country in SW Europe. *Capital:* Madrid. See **Roman Empire** for map. *n.*

spake (spāk), OLD USE. spoke; a past tense of **speak.** *v.*

span¹ (span), **1** part between two supports: *The bridge crossed the river in a single span.* **2** distance between two supports: *The arch had a fifty-foot span.* **3** a short space of time: *His span of life is nearly over.* **4** extend over: *A bridge spanned the river.* **5** measure by the hand spread out: *This post can be spanned by one's two hands.* **6** the distance between the tip of the thumb and the tip of the little finger when the hand is spread out; about 9 inches. 1-3,6 *n.,* 4,5 *v.,* **spanned, span ning.**

span² (span), pair of horses or other animals harnessed and driven together. *n.*

span gle (spang′gəl), **1** a small piece of glittering metal used for decoration: *The costume was covered with spangles.* **2** any small, bright bit: *This rock shows spangles of gold.* **3** decorate with spangles: *The costume was spangled with gold.* **4** sprinkle with small, bright bits: *The sky is spangled with stars.* 1,2 *n.,* 3,4 *v.,* **span gled, span gling.**

Span iard (span′yərd), person born or living in Spain. *n.*

span iel (span′yəl), **1** a small or medium-sized dog with long, silky hair and drooping ears. **2** person who yields too much to others. *n.* —**span′iel like′,** *adj.*

WORD HISTORY

spaniel

Spaniel came into English about 600 years ago from French *espagneul,* which originally meant "Spanish," which came from Latin *Hispania,* meaning "Spain." The dog was called this because it first came from Spain.

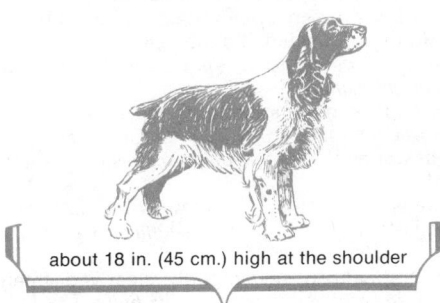

about 18 in. (45 cm.) high at the shoulder

a hat	i it	oi oil	ch child	a in about
ā age	ī ice	ou out	ng long	e in taken
ä far	o hot	u cup	sh she	ə = i in pencil
e let	ō open	ů put	th thin	o in lemon
ē equal	ô order	ü rule	₮н then	u in circus
ėr term			zh measure	

Span ish (span′ish), **1** of Spain, its people, or their language: *Spanish literature.* **2** the people of Spain. **3** the language of Spain. It is also the language of most Latin-American countries. 1 *adj.,* 2 *n.pl.,* 3 *n.sing.*

Spanish America, countries and islands south and southeast of the United States, in which the principal language is Spanish.

Spanish American, person born or living in a Spanish-American country.

Span ish-A mer i can, (span′ish ə mer′ə kən),**1** of Spain and America, or Spain and the United States. **2** of the parts of America where Spanish is the principal language. *adj.*

Spanish-American War, war between Spain and the United States in 1898, fought chiefly in Cuba and the Philippines.

Spanish Main, 1 (formerly) the NW coast of South America, from which Spanish ships used to sail with gold for Spain. **2** (in later use) the Caribbean Sea.

Spanish moss

Spanish moss, a mosslike plant that grows on the branches of certain trees, from which it hangs in gray streamers. It is found in the southern United States and tropical America.

spank (spangk), **1** strike with the open hand or a flat object: *I spanked the naughty child.* **2** a blow with the open hand or a flat object. 1 *v.,* 2 *n.*

spank ing (spang′king), **1** a striking with the open hand or a flat object. **2** blowing briskly: *a spanking breeze.* **3** unusually fine, great, large, etc.: *a spanking team of horses.* 1 *n.,* 2,3 *adj.*

spar¹ (spär), **1** a stout pole used to support or extend the sails of a ship; mast, yard, gaff, boom, etc., of a ship. **2** provide (a ship) with spars. 1 *n.,* 2 *v.,* **sparred, spar ring.**

spar² (spär), **1** make motions of attack and defense with the arms and fists; box. **2** argue: *Two people were sparring about who would win the election.* *v.,* **sparred, spar ring.**

spar³ (spär), any of various shiny minerals, such as feldspar, that split into flakes easily. *n.*

spare (sper *or* spar), **1** show mercy to; refrain from harming or destroying: *spare a conquered enemy. Her quick wit spares nobody, not even herself.* **2** make (a person, etc.) free from labor, pain, etc.: *We walked up the hill to spare the horse. I did the work to spare you the trouble.* **3** get along without; do without: *Mother couldn't spare the* *car; so father and I had to take the bus.* **4** use in small quantities or not at all; be saving of: *to spare no expense.* **5** free for other use: *spare time.* **6** extra; in reserve: *a spare tire.* **7** a spare thing, part, tire, etc. **8** thin; lean: *Lincoln was a tall, spare man.* **9** small in quantity; meager; scanty: *I'm still hungry after that spare meal.* **10** the knocking down of all the pins with two rolls of a bowling ball. 1-4 *v.*, **spared, spar ing;** 5,6,8,9 *adj.*, **spar er, spar est;** 7,10 *n.* —**spare′a ble,** *adj.* —**spare′ness,** *n.* —**spar′er,** *n.*

spare ly (sper′lē *or* spar′lē), not amply or fully; sparingly; scantily; sparsely. *adv.*

spare ribs (sper′ribs′ *or* spar′ribs′), ribs of pork having less meat than the ribs near the loins. *n.pl.*

spar ing (sper′ing *or* spar′ing), avoiding waste; economical; frugal: *a sparing use of sugar. adj.* —**spar′ing ly,** *adv.* —**spar′ing ness,** *n.*

spark (spärk), **1** a small bit of fire: *The burning wood threw off sparks.* **2** flash given off when electricity jumps across an open space. An electric spark ignites the gasoline vapor in the engine of an automobile. **3** a bright flash; gleam; sparkle: *We saw a spark of light through the trees.* **4** to flash; gleam; sparkle. **5** a small amount: *I haven't a spark of interest in the plan.* **6** a glittering bit: *The moving sparks we saw were fireflies.* **7** send out small bits of fire; produce sparks. **8** stir to activity; stimulate: *spark a revolt, spark one's teammates.* 1-3,5,6 *n.*, 4,7,8 *v.* —**spark′less,** *adj.*

spar kle (spär′kəl), **1** send out little sparks: *The fireworks sparkled.* **2** a little spark. **3** to shine; glitter; flash; gleam: *The diamonds sparkled.* **4** a shine; glitter; flash: *the sparkle of someone's eyes.* **5** be brilliant; be lively: *Wit sparkles.* **6** brilliance; liveliness. **7** bubble. Ginger ale and champagne sparkle. 1,3,5,7 *v.*, **spar kled, spar kling;** 2,4,6 *n.*

spar kler (spär′klər), **1** firework that sends out little sparks. **2** a sparkling gem, especially a diamond. *n.*

spar kling (spär′kling), **1** shining; glittering: *sparkling stars.* **2** brilliant: *She has a sparkling wit.* **3** bubbling: *sparkling drinks. adj.*

spark plug, device in the cylinder of a gasoline engine by which the mixture of gasoline and air is ignited by an electric spark.

spar row (spar′ō), any of various small, usually brownish songbirds common in North and South America but also found in Europe, Asia, and Africa. Sparrows are finches. *n.* [*Sparrow* comes from Old English *spearwa.*] —**spar′row like′,** *adj.*

sparrow hawk, a small hawk which feeds on birds, insects, and other small animals.

sparse (spärs), **1** thinly scattered; occurring here and there: *a sparse population, sparse hair.* **2** scanty; meager: *a sparse diet. adj.*, **spars er, spars est.** —**sparse′ly,** *adv.* —**sparse′ness,** *n.*

spar si ty (spär′sə tē), sparse or scattered condition; sparseness. *n.*

Spar ta (spär′tə), one of the most important cities in ancient Greece, famous for its soldiers. *n.*

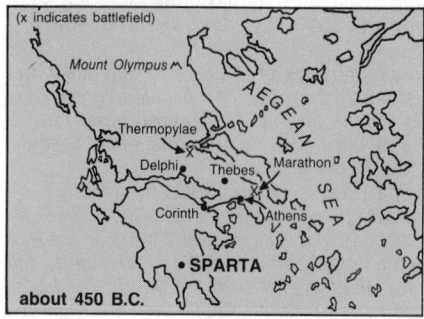

Spar tan (spär′tn), **1** of Sparta or its people. **2** person who was born or lived in Sparta. The Spartans were noted for living simply, saying little, being brave, and enduring pain without complaining. **3** like the Spartans; simple, frugal, and severe. **4** person who is like the Spartans. 1,3 *adj.*, 2,4 *n.* —**Spar′tan ly,** *adv.*

spasm (spaz′əm), **1** a sudden, abnormal, involuntary contraction of a muscle or muscles. **2** any sudden, brief fit or spell of unusual energy or activity: *a spasm of temper, a spasm of industry. n.*

spas mod ic (spaz mod′ik), **1** having to do with spasms; resembling a spasm: *a spasmodic cough.* **2** occurring very irregularly: *a spasmodic interest in reading.* **3** having or showing bursts of excitement. *adj.* —**spas mod′i cal ly,** *adv.*

spas tic (spas′tik), **1** of or characterized by spasms. **2** person suffering from a form of paralysis marked by muscle spasms and jerky movements. 1 *adj.*, 2 *n.* —**spas′ti cal ly,** *adv.*

spat[1] (spat), **1** a slight quarrel. **2** quarrel slightly. 1 *n.*, 2 *v.*, **spat ted, spat ting.**

spat[2] (spat), a past tense and a past participle of **spit**[1]. *The cat spat at the dog. v.*

spat[3] (spat). Usually, **spats,** *pl.* a short outer covering worn over the top part of the shoe and reaching just above the ankle. *n.*

spathe (spāᴛʜ), a large leaf, often resembling a petal, that encloses a flower cluster. The calla lily has a white spathe around a yellow flower cluster. *n.*

spa tial (spā′shəl), **1** of space. **2** existing in space. *adj.* —**spa′tial ly,** *adv.*

spat ter (spat′ər), **1** to scatter or dash in drops or particles: *spatter mud.* **2** to fall in drops or particles: *Rain spatters on the sidewalk.* **3** to strike in a shower; strike in a number of places: *Bullets spattered the wall.* **4** act or sound of spattering: *We listened to the spatter of rain on the roof.* **5** a splash or spot. 1-3 *v.*, 4,5 *n.* —**spat′ter ing ly,** *adv.*

spat u la (spach′ə lə), tool with a broad, flat, flexible blade, used for mixing drugs, spreading paints or frostings, etc. *n.*, *pl.* **spat u las.**

spav ined (spav′ənd), (of horses) having a disease in which a bony swelling forms at the hock, causing lameness. *adj.*

spawn (spôn), **1** the eggs of fish, frogs, shellfish, etc. **2** the young newly hatched from such eggs. **3** bring forth; give birth to. **4** offspring, especially a large number of offspring. 1,2,4 *n.*, 3 *v.* —**spawn′er,** *n.*

spay (spā), remove the ovaries of (a female animal). *v.*

S.P.C.A., Society for the Prevention of Cruelty to Animals.

speak (spēk), **1** say words; talk: *speak clearly.* **2** make a speech: *Who is going to speak at the meeting?* **3** make known; tell; express; say: *Speak the truth.* **4** use (a language): *Do you speak French?* **5** express an idea, feeling, etc.; communicate: *Actions speak louder than words.* **6** make sounds: *The cannon spoke. v.*, **spoke, spo ken, speak ing.** —**speak′a ble,** *adj.*

so to speak, to speak in such a manner; to use that expression: *He has a chance to win the race; he is, so to speak, still in the running.*

speak for, 1 speak in the interest of; represent: *Why don't you speak for yourself instead of having others speak for you?* **2** ask or apply for: *We ought to speak for reserved seats ahead of time.*

speak of, refer to; mention: *She spoke of this matter to me. Speaking of school, how do you like the new gym? I have no complaints to speak of.*

speak out or **speak up,** speak loudly, clearly, or freely: *No one dared to speak out against the big bully. The chil-*

dren all spoke up in favor of the teacher's suggestion to have a party.

speak well for, give a favorable idea of; be evidence in favor of: *Her behavior speaks well for her.*

speak er (spē′kər), **1** person who speaks. **2** Also, **Speaker.** person who presides over a legislative assembly. The Speaker of the House of Representatives is its presiding officer. **3** loudspeaker. *n.*

speak ing (spē′king), **1** act, utterance, or discourse of a person who speaks. **2** used in, suited to, or involving speech: *the speaking voice, within speaking distance, a speaking part in a play.* **3** permitting conversation: *a speaking acquaintance with a person.* **4** highly expressive: *speaking eyes.* **5** lifelike: *a speaking likeness.* **1** *n.*, **2-5** *adj.*

spear¹ (spir), **1** weapon with a long shaft and a sharp-pointed head. **2** pierce with a spear: *I speared a fish.* **3** pierce or stab with anything sharp: *spear string beans with a fork.* **1** *n.*, **2,3** *v.* —**spear′er,** *n.*

spear² (spir), sprout or shoot of a plant: *a spear of grass. n.*

spear head (spir′hed′), **1** the sharp-pointed striking end of a spear. **2** part that is first in an attack, undertaking, etc. **3** lead or clear the way for; head: *He commanded the regiment which spearheaded the assault on the fort. Our group spearheaded the efforts to clean the lake.* **1,2** *n.*, **3** *v.*

spear man (spir′mən), soldier armed with a spear. *n.*, *pl.* **spear men.**

spear mint (spir′mint′), a fragrant herb grown for its oil which is used for flavoring. *n.*

spec., special.

spe cial (spesh′əl), **1** of a particular kind; distinct from others; not general: *This desk has a special lock. Have you any special color in mind for your new coat?* **2** more than ordinary; unusual; exceptional: *Today's topic is of special interest.* **3** for a particular person, thing, purpose, etc.: *The railroad ran special trains on holidays. Send the letter by a special messenger.* **4** a special train, car, bus, etc. **5** a specially featured product or service. **6** a television show produced especially for a single broadcast. **7** held in high regard; great; chief: *a special friend.* **1-3,7** *adj.*, **4-6** *n.*

special delivery, the delivery of a letter or package for an additional fee, by a special messenger rather than by the regular mail carrier.

spe cial ist (spesh′ə list), **1** person who pursues one particular branch of study, business, etc. A heart specialist is a doctor who treats diseases of the heart. **2** (in the U.S. Army) a soldier with administrative or technical duties, ranking below a corporal and above a private. *n.*

spe cial i za tion (spesh′ə lə zā′shən), a specializing or a being specialized. *n.*

spe cial ize (spesh′ə līz), **1** pursue some special branch of study, work, etc.: *Some doctors specialize in treating heart disease.* **2** adapt to a special function or condition: *Lungs and gills are specialized for breathing.* **3** develop in a special way: *Animals and plants are specialized to fit their surroundings.* *v.,* **spe cial ized, spe cial iz ing.**

spe cial ly (spesh′ə lē), in a special manner or degree; particularly; unusually. *adv.*

spe cial ty (spesh′əl tē), **1** a special study, line of work, profession, trade, etc.: *American history is the specialty of my social studies teacher.* **2** product, article, etc., to which special attention is given: *This store makes a specialty of children's clothes.* **3** special character or quality. **4** a special or particular characteristic; peculiarity. *n., pl.* **spe cial ties.**

spe cie (spē′shē), money in the form of coins; metal money. Silver dollars are specie. *n.*

spe cies (spē′shēz), **1** group of animals or plants that have certain permanent characteristics in common and

a hat
ā age
ä far
e let
ē equal
ėr term

i it
ī ice
o hot
ō open
ô order

oi oil
ou out
u cup
u̇ put
ü rule

ch child
ng long
sh she
th thin
ᵺH then
zh measure

ə = {
a in about
e in taken
i in pencil
o in lemon
u in circus
}

are able to interbreed. A species ranks next below a genus and may be divided into several varieties, races, or breeds. Wheat is a species of grass. The lion is one species of cat. **2** kind; sort; distinct kind or sort: *There are many species of advertisements.* **3 the species,** the human race. *n., pl.* **spe cies.** [*Species* is from Latin *species,* meaning "kind, sort, appearance." See **Word Family.**]

species

Below are words related to *species.* They can all be traced back to the Latin word *species* (spe′ki ās), meaning "kind, sort, appearance."

allspice	specialize	specification
especially	specialty	specify
special	specie	specious
specialist	specific	spice

spe cif ic (spi sif′ik), **1** definite; precise; particular: *There was no specific reason for the quarrel.* **2** characteristic (of); peculiar (to): *Feathers are a feature specific to birds.* **3** curing some particular disease. **4** a cure for some particular disease: *Vitamin C is a specific for scurvy.* **5** produced by some special cause. **6** of or having to do with a species: *the specific name of a plant.* **1-3,5,6** *adj.*, **4** *n.*

spe cif i cal ly (spi sif′ik lē), in a specific manner; definitely; particularly: *The doctor told her specifically not to eat eggs. adv.*

spec i fi ca tion (spes′ə fə kā′shən), **1** act of specifying; definite mention; detailed statement of particulars: *She made careful specification as to the kinds of cake and candy for her party.* **2** Usually, **specifications,** *pl.* a detailed description of the dimensions, materials, etc., for a building, road, dam, boat, etc. **3** something specified; particular item, article, etc. *n.*

specific gravity, the ratio of the weight of a given volume of any substance to that of the same volume of some other substance taken as a standard, water being used for solids and liquids, and hydrogen or air for gases. The specific gravity of gold is 19 because any volume of gold weighs 19 times as much as the same volume of water.

spec i fic i ty (spes′ə fis′ə tē), specific quality. *n.*

spec i fy (spes′ə fī), **1** mention or name definitely: *Did you specify any particular time for us to call?* **2** include in the specifications: *He delivered the paper as specified. v.,* **spec i fied, spec i fy ing.** —**spec′i fi′er,** *n.*

spec i men (spes′ə mən), one of a group or class taken to show what the others are like; sample: *He collects specimens of all kinds of rocks and minerals. The statue was a fine specimen of Greek sculpture. n.*

spe cious (spē′shəs), seeming desirable, reasonable, or

probable, but not really so; apparently good, but without real merit: *The teacher saw through that specious excuse. adj.* —**spe′cious ly,** *adv.* —**spe′cious ness,** *n.*

speck (spek), **1** a small spot; stain: *Can you clean the specks off this wallpaper?* **2** a tiny bit; particle: *I have a speck in my eye.* **3** mark with specks: *His shirt was specked with ink.* 1,2 *n.,* 3 *v.* —**speck′less,** *adj.*

speck le (spek′əl), **1** a small spot or mark: *This hen is gray with white speckles.* **2** mark with speckles: *The shirt was speckled with paint.* 1 *n.,* 2 *v.,* **speck led, speck ling.**

spec ta cle (spek′tə kəl), **1** thing to look at; sight: *The children at play among the flowers made a charming spectacle. A quarrel is an unpleasant spectacle.* **2** a public show or display: *The big parade was a fine spectacle.* **3** **spectacles,** *pl.* eyeglasses. *n.*

spec tac u lar (spek tak′yə lər), **1** making a great display: *the spectacular eruption of a volcano.* **2** having to do with a spectacle or show. **3** a spectacular display. **4** a lengthy motion picture or television show, usually produced on a lavish scale. 1,2 *adj.,* 3,4 *n.* —**spec tac′u lar ly,** *adv.*

spec ta tor (spek′tā tər), person who looks on without taking part: *There were many spectators at the game. n.*

spec ter (spek′tər), **1** ghost. **2** thing causing terror or dread: *the grim specter of war. n.* Also, **spectre.**

spec tral (spek′trəl), **1** of or like a specter; ghostly: *the spectral form of a ship on a foggy sea.* **2** of or produced by the spectrum: *spectral colors. adj.* —**spec′tral ly,** *adv.* —**spec′tral ness,** *n.*

spec tre (spek′tər), specter. *n.*

spec tro scope (spek′trə skōp), instrument for producing and examining the spectrum of a ray from any source. The spectrum produced by passing a light ray through a prism can be examined to determine the composition of the source of the ray. *n.*

spec trum (spek′trəm), the band of colors formed when a beam of light is passed through a prism or broken up by some other means. A rainbow has all the colors of the spectrum: red, orange, yellow, green, blue, indigo, and violet. *n., pl.* **spec tra** (spek′trə), **spec trums.**

spec u late (spek′yə lāt), **1** think carefully; reflect; meditate; consider: *The philosopher speculated about time and space.* **2** to guess; conjecture: *She tried to speculate about the possible winner.* **3** buy or sell when there is a large risk, with the hope of making a profit from future price changes: *He became poor after speculating in what turned out to be worthless oil wells. v.,* **spec u lat ed, spec u lat ing.**

spec u la tion (spek′yə lā′shən), **1** careful thought; reflection: *speculations about the nature of the universe.* **2** a guessing; notion: *Our estimates of the cost were based on speculation.* **3** a buying or selling when there is a large risk, with the hope of making a profit from future price changes: *Her speculations in the stock market made her a thousand dollars. n.*

spec u la tive (spek′yə lā′tiv), **1** carefully thoughtful; reflective. **2** theoretical rather than practical. **3** of or involving buying or selling at a large risk. *adj.* —**spec′u la′tive ly,** *adv.* —**spec′u la′tive ness,** *n.*

spec u la tor (spek′yə lā′tər), person who speculates, usually in business. A ticket speculator buys tickets for shows, games, etc., in advance, hoping to sell them later at a higher price. *n.*

sped (sped), a past tense and a past participle of **speed.** *The police car sped down the road. v.*

speech (spēch), **1** act of speaking; talk. **2** power of speaking: *Animals lack speech.* **3** manner of speaking: *I could tell by their speech that they were from the South.* **4** what is said; the words spoken: *We made the usual farewell speeches.* **5** a public talk: *Our Congresswoman gave a fine speech.* **6** language: *The native speech of most Americans is English. n., pl.* **speech es.**

speech i fy (spē′chə fī), INFORMAL. make a speech or speeches. *v.,* **speech i fied, speech i fy ing.** —**speech′i fi′er,** *n.*

speech less (spēch′lis), **1** not able to speak: *He was speechless with anger.* **2** silent: *Her frown gave a speechless message. adj.* —**speech′less ly,** *adv.* —**speech′less ness,** *n.*

speed (spēd), **1** swift or rapid movement: *the amazing speed with which a cat jumps on a mouse.* **2** go fast: *The boat sped over the water.* **3** make go fast: *Let's all help speed the work.* **4** rate of movement: *The children ran at full speed.* **5** go faster than is safe or lawful: *The car was caught speeding near the school zone.* **6** arrangement of gears to give a certain rate of movement. An automobile usually has three speeds forward and one backward. **7** help forward; promote: *speed an undertaking.* **8** OLD USE. good luck; success. 1,4,6,8 *n.,* 2,3,5,7 *v.,* **sped** or **speed ed, speed ing.** [*Speed comes from Old English spēd.*]

speed up, go or cause to go faster; increase in speed.

speed boat (spēd′bōt′), motorboat built to go fast. *n.*

speed er (spē′dər), person who drives an automobile at a higher speed than is safe or lawful. *n.*

speed i ly (spē′dl ē), quickly; with speed; soon. *adv.*

speed i ness (spē′dē nis), speedy quality; quickness; rapidity. *n.*

speed om e ter (spē dom′ə tər), instrument to indicate the speed of an automobile or other vehicle, and often the distance traveled. *n.*

speed up (spēd′up′), an increase in speed. *n.*

speed way (spēd′wā′), a road or track for automobile or motorcycle racing. *n.*

speed well (spēd′wel), any of various low plants with small blue, purple, pink, or white flowers. *n.*

speed y (spē′dē), moving, going, or acting with speed; fast; rapid; quick; swift: *speedy workers, a speedy decision. adj.,* **speed i er, speed i est.**

spe le ol o gy (spē′lē ol′ə jē), the scientific study of caves. *n.*

spell¹ (spel), **1** write or say the letters of (a word) in order: *Some words are easy to spell.* **2** spell words: *We learn to spell in school.* **3** make up or form (a word): *C-a-t spells cat.* **4** mean: *These clouds spell a storm. Delay spells danger.* **5** read with difficulty: *If you have to spell out each sentence in the story, you'll never understand what it is about. v.,* **spelled** or **spelt, spell ing.** —**spell′a ble,** *adj.*

spell out, explain carefully, step by step, and in detail: *We asked him to spell out his plan for raising more money.*

spell² (spel), **1** word or set of words supposed to have magic power. **2** magic influence; fascination; charm: *A spell of mystery seemed to hang over the old castle. We were under the spell of the beautiful music. n.* —**spell′-like′,** *adj.*

cast a spell on, put under the influence of a spell; fascinate.

under a spell, controlled by a spell; fascinated; spellbound: *The adventure story held the children under a spell.*

spell³ (spel), **1** period of work or duty: *The rower's spell at the oars was half an hour.* **2** period or time of anything: *The child has spells of coughing. There was a long spell of rainy weather in August.* **3** a brief period: *rest for a spell.* **4** to work in place of (another person) for a while: *I'll spell you at cutting the grass.* **5** give a time of rest to. **6** relief of one person by another in doing something. 1-3,6 *n.,* 4,5 *v.,* **spelled, spell ing.**

spell bind (spel′bīnd′), make spellbound; fascinate; enchant. *v.,* **spell bound, spell bind ing.**

spell bind er (spel′bīn′dər), speaker who can hold listeners spellbound. *n.*

spell bound (spel′bound′), too interested to move; fascinated; enchanted: *The children were spellbound by the circus performance. adj.*

spell er (spel′ər), **1** person who spells words. **2** book for teaching spelling. *n.*

spell ing (spel′ing), **1** the writing or saying of the letters of a word in order: *He is good at spelling.* **2** the way a word is spelled: *"Ax" has two spellings, "ax" and "axe." n.*

spelling bee, a spelling contest.

spelt (spelt), spelled; a past tense and a past participle of **spell**[1]. *v.*

spe lunk er (spi lung′kər), person who explores and maps caves. *n.* [*Spelunker* comes from Latin *spelunca*, meaning "cave."]

spend (spend), **1** pay out: *She spent ten dollars shopping for food today.* **2** pay out money: *Earn before you spend.* **3** use; use up: *Don't spend any more time on that lesson.* **4** pass: *She spent last summer at the seashore.* **5** wear out: *The storm has spent its force.* **6** to waste; squander: *He spent his fortune on horse racing. v.,* **spent, spend ing.** —**spend′a ble,** *adj.* —**spend′er,** *n.*

spend thrift (spend′thrift′), **1** person who wastes money. **2** extravagant with money; wasteful. 1 *n.,* 2 *adj.*

Spen ser (spen′sər), **Edmund,** 1552?-1599, English poet, author of *The Faerie Queene. n.*

spent (spent), **1** past tense and past participle of **spend.** *Saturday was spent in playing. How have you spent your time today?* **2** used up. **3** worn out; tired: *a spent swimmer, a spent horse.* 1 *v.,* 2,3 *adj.*

sperm (spėrm), **1** sperm cell. **2** semen. *n.*

sper ma cet i (spėr′mə set′ē *or* spėr′mə sē′tē), a whitish, waxy substance obtained from the oil in the head of the sperm whale and used in making fine candles, ointments, cosmetics, etc. *n.*

sperm cell, a male reproductive cell; sperm. A sperm cell unites with an ovum to fertilize it.

sperm whale—up to 60 ft. (18 m.) long

sperm whale, a large, square-headed, toothed whale that is valuable for its oil.

spew (spyü), **1** throw out; cast forth; vomit. **2** something that is spewed; vomit. 1 *v.,* 2 *n.* Also, **spue.** —**spew′er,** *n.*

sp. gr., specific gravity.

sphere (sfir), **1** a round solid figure. Every point on the surface of a sphere is the same distance from the center. **2** ball or globe. The sun, moon, earth, and stars are spheres. **3** place or surroundings in which a person or thing exists, acts, works, etc.: *The woman's sphere today includes both home and business.* **4** range; extent; region: *England's sphere of influence.* **5** a place, position, or rank in society: *the sphere of the aristocracy. n.*

spher i cal (sfir′ə kəl *or* sfer′ə kəl), **1** shaped like a sphere. **2** of a sphere or spheres. *adj.*

spher i cal ly (sfir′ik lē *or* sfer′ik lē), **1** in the form of a sphere, or of part of a sphere. **2** so as to be spherical. *adv.*

spher oid (sfir′oid), object or geometric figure shaped somewhat like a sphere, but not perfectly round. *n.*

sphinc ter (sfingk′tər), a ringlike muscle that surrounds an opening or passage of the body, and can contract to close it. *n.*

sphinx (def. 1)
The Great Sphinx

sphinx (sfingks), **1** statue of a lion's body with the head of a man, ram, or hawk. There are many sphinxes in Egypt. The **Great Sphinx** is a huge statue with a man's head and a lion's body, near Cairo. **2 Sphinx,** (in Greek myths) a monster with the head of a woman, the body of a lion, and wings. The Sphinx proposed a riddle to every passer-by and killed those unable to guess it. **3** a puzzling or mysterious person. *n., pl.* **sphinx es.**

spice (spīs), **1** any of various seasonings obtained from plants and used to flavor food. Pepper, cinnamon, cloves, ginger, and nutmeg are common spices. **2** put spice in; season: *spiced peaches.* **3** something that adds flavor or interest: *"Variety is the spice of life."* **4** add flavor or interest to: *The principal spiced her speech with stories and jokes.* 1,3 *n.,* 2,4 *v.,* **spiced, spic ing.**

spic i ness (spī′sē nis), spicy flavor or smell. *n.*

spick-and-span (spik′ən span′), neat and clean; spruce or smart; fresh; new: *a spick-and-span room. adj.*

spic ule (spik′yül), **1** a small, slender, sharp-pointed piece, usually bony or crystalline. **2** such a piece in a sponge. *n.*

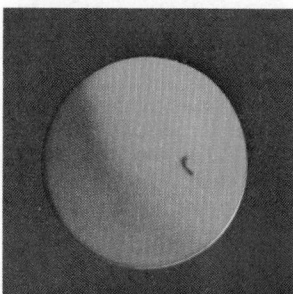

sphere
(def. 1)

spic y (spī′sē), **1** flavored with spice: *The cookies were rich and spicy.* **2** like spice: *Those apples have a spicy smell and taste.* **3** lively; spirited: *spicy conversation full of gossip.* **4** somewhat improper. *adj.,* **spic i er, spic i est.** —**spic′i ly,** *adv.*

spi der (spī′dər), **1** a small animal with eight legs, no wings, and a body divided into two parts. Spiders are arachnids. Many spiders spin webs to catch insects for food. **2** something like or suggesting a spider. *n.* [*Spider* comes from Old English *spīthra.*] **—spi′der like′,** *adj.*
spider web, web spun by a spider.
spi der y (spī′dər ē), **1** long and thin like a spider's legs. **2** suggesting a spider web. *adj.*
spied (spīd), past tense and past participle of **spy.** *He spied his friend in the crowd. Who had spied on us? v.*
spi er (spī′ər), a spy. *n.*
spiff y (spif′ē), SLANG. smart; neat; trim: *a spiffy new suit. adj.,* **spiff i er, spiff i est. —spiff′i ly,** *adv.*
spig ot (spig′ət), **1** faucet. **2** peg or plug used to stop the small hole of a cask, barrel, or keg; bung. *n.*
spike¹ (spīk), **1** a large, strong nail. **2** fasten with spikes: *The work crew laid the track by spiking the rails to the ties.* **3** a sharp-pointed piece or part: *Ballplayers wear shoes with spikes.* **4** provide with spikes: *Runners wear spiked shoes to keep from slipping.* **5** pierce or injure with a spike. **6** make (a cannon) useless by driving a spike into the opening where the powder is set off. **7** put an end or stop to; make useless; block: *The mayor spiked the talk of an increase in taxes.* **1,3** *n.,* **2,4-7** *v.,* **spiked, spik ing. —spike′like′,** *adj.*

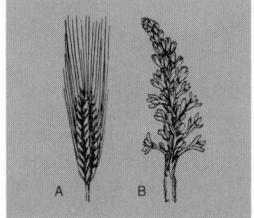
spike²
(A, def. 1)
(B, def. 2)

spike² (spīk), **1** ear of grain. **2** a long, pointed flower cluster. *n.*
spike nard (spīk′nərd *or* spīk′närd), **1** a sweet-smelling ointment used by the ancients. **2** the fragrant East Indian plant from which it was probably obtained. *n.*
spik y (spī′kē), **1** having spikes; set with sharp, project-ing points. **2** having the shape of a spike. *adj.,* **spik i er, spik i est. —spik′i ly,** *adv.* **—spik′i ness,** *n.*
spill¹ (spil), **1** let (liquid or any loose matter) run or fall: *spill milk or salt.* **2** fall or flow out: *Water spilled from the pail.* **3** shed (blood). **4** INFORMAL. cause to fall from a horse, car, boat, etc.: *The boat upset and spilled all of us into the water.* **5** act of spilling. **6** quantity spilled. **7** INFORMAL. a fall: *She took a bad spill trying to ride that horse.* **8** INFORMAL. make known; tell: *spill a secret.* **1-4,8** *v.,* **spilled** *or* **spilt, spill ing; 5-7** *n.* [*Spill*¹ came from Old English *spillan,* meaning "destroy, waste."] **—spill′er,** *n.*
spill² (spil), a thin piece of wood, or a folded or twisted piece of paper, used to light a candle, pipe, etc. *n.*
spill way (spil′wā′), channel or passage for the escape of surplus water from a dam, river, etc. *n.*
spilt (spilt), spilled; a past tense and a past participle of **spill**¹. *v.*
spin (spin), **1** turn around rapidly: *The wheel spins round.* **2** make turn around rapidly: *The child spun the top.* **3** feel as if one were whirling around; feel dizzy: *My head is spinning.* **4** draw out and twist (cotton, flax, wool, etc.) into thread. **5** make (thread, yarn, etc.) by drawing out and twisting cotton, wool, flax, etc. **6** make (a thread, web, cocoon, etc.) by giving out from the body sticky material that hardens in air. A spider spins a web. **7** draw out; produce; tell: *My grandparents often spin yarns about life on the farm.* **8** act of spinning. **9** a rapid run, ride, drive, etc.: *Get your bicycle and come for a spin with me.*

10 a rapid turning around of an airplane as it falls. **1-7** *v.,* **spun, spin ning; 8-10** *n.*
spin out, make long and slow; draw out; prolong.
spin ach (spin′ich), the green leaves of a garden plant, cooked and eaten as a vegetable, or used uncooked in a salad. *n.*
spi nal (spī′nl), of the backbone. *adj.* **—spi′nal ly,** *adv.*
spinal column, backbone.
spinal cord, the thick, whitish cord of nerve tissue which extends from the brain down through most of the backbone. Nerves branch off from the spinal cord to various parts of the body.

spindle
(def. 1)

spin dle (spin′dl), **1** the rod or pin used in spinning to twist, wind, and hold thread. **2** any rod or pin that turns around, or on which something turns. **3** something shaped like a spindle. **4** grow very long and thin. **1-3** *n.,* **4** *v.,* **spin dled, spin dling.**
spin dle-leg ged (spin′dl leg′id *or* spin′dl legd′), having long, thin legs. *adj.*
spin dle legs (spin′dl legz′), **1** long, thin legs. **2** INFOR-MAL. person with long, thin legs. *n.pl.*
spin dling (spind′ling), spindly. *adj.*
spin dly (spind′lē), very long and slender; too tall and thin: *a spindly plant. adj.,* **spin dli er, spin dli est.**
spin drift (spin′drift′), spray blown or dashed up from the waves. *n.* Also, **spoondrift.**
spine (spīn), **1** backbone. **2** anything like a backbone; long, narrow ridge or support. **3** a stiff, sharp-pointed growth on plants or animals; thorn or something like it. A cactus has spines; so has a porcupine. **4** the support-ing back portion of a book cover. *n.* **—spine′like′,** *adj.*
spined (spīnd), having a spine or spines. *adj.*
spine less (spīn′lis), **1** having no backbone; inverte-brate: *All insects are spineless.* **2** without courage; weak: *a spineless coward.* **3** having no spines: *a spineless cactus. adj.* **—spine′less ly,** *adv.* **—spine′less ness,** *n.*
spin et (spin′it), **1** a compact upright piano. **2** an old-fashioned musical instrument like a small harpsi-chord. *n.*
spin na ker (spin′ə kər), a large, triangular sail which is used as an extra sail when sailing downwind, to increase the speed of a boat. *n.*

spinnaker

spin ner (spin′ər), person, animal, or thing that spins. *n.*

spin ner et (spin′ə ret′), organ by which spiders and certain insect larvae such as silkworms spin their threads. *n.*

spinning jenny, an early type of spinning machine having more than one spindle, whereby one person could spin a number of threads at the same time; jenny.

spinning wheel

spinning wheel, a large wheel with a spindle, arranged for spinning cotton, flax, wool, etc., into thread or yarn.

spin ster (spin′stər), an unmarried woman, especially an older woman. *n.*

spin y (spī′nē), **1** covered with spines; having spines; thorny: *a spiny cactus.* **2** stiff and sharp-pointed; spine-like: *the spiny quills of a porcupine. adj.,* **spin i er, spin i est.** —**spin′i ness,** *n.*

spi ra cle (spī′rə kəl *or* spir′ə kəl), a small opening for breathing. Insects take in air through tiny spiracles. The blowhole of the whale is a spiracle. *n.*

spi rae a (spī rē′ə), a shrub that has clusters of small white, pink, or red flowers with five petals. *n.* Also, **spi rea.**

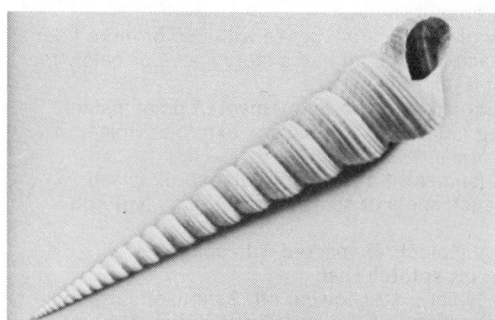

spiral (def. 2)—This shell has a **spiral** shape.

spi ral (spī′rəl), **1** a winding and gradually widening coil. A watch spring is a spiral. The thread of a screw is a spiral. **2** winding; coiled: *a spiral staircase.* **3** move in a spiral: *The flaming airplane spiraled to earth.* **4** form into a spiral. **1** *n.,* **2** *adj.,* **3,4** *v.,* **spi raled, spi ral ing,** or **spi ralled, spi ral ling.** —**spi′ral ly,** *adv.*

spire¹ (spīr), **1** the top part of a tower or steeple that narrows to a point. **2** anything tapering and pointed: *The sunset shone on the rocky spires of the mountains. n.* —**spire′like′,** *adj.*

spire² (spīr), a coil; spiral. *n.*

spi re a (spī rē′ə), spiraea. *n.*

spi ril lum (spī ril′əm), any of a group of bacteria that have spirally twisted forms. *n., pl.* **spi ril la** (spī ril′ə).

spir it (spir′it), **1** the immaterial part of human beings; soul: *Some religions teach that at death the spirit leaves the body.* **2** a human being's moral, religious, or emotional nature: *a worthy spirit.* **3** a supernatural being. God is a

spirit. Ghosts and fairies are spirits. **4** the Spirit, **a** God. **b** the Holy Ghost. **5** Often, **spirits,** *pl.* state of mind; disposition; temper: *She is in good spirits.* **6** person; personality: *She is a brave spirit. He was one of the more active spirits in our town.* **7** feeling that stirs up and rouses: *people with a spirit of progress.* **8** courage; vigor; liveliness: *A race horse must have spirit.* **9** enthusiasm and loyalty. **10** what is really meant as opposed to what is said or written: *The spirit of a law is more important than its words.* **11** the prevailing character, quality, or tendency. **12** Often, **spirits,** *pl.* **a** solution of a volatile substance in alcohol: *spirits of camphor.* **b** strong alcoholic liquor. **13** carry (away or off) secretly: *The child has been spirited away.* **14** of or having to do with spirits or spiritualism: *the spirit world.* **1-12** *n.,* **13** *v.,* **14** *adj.*

out of spirits, sad or gloomy.

spir it ed (spir′ə tid), full of energy and spirit; lively; dashing; brave: *a spirited race horse. adj.* —**spir′it ed ly,** *adv.* —**spir′it ed ness,** *n.*

spir it less (spir′it lis), without spirit or courage; depressed; tame. *adj.*

spir i tu al (spir′ə chü əl), **1** of the spirit or spirits. **2** caring much for things of the spirit or soul. **3** of the church; sacred; religious: *spiritual teachings.* **4** of spirits; supernatural. **5** a religious song which originated among the Negroes of the southern United States. **1-4** *adj.,* **5** *n.* —**spir′i tu al ly,** *adv.* —**spir′i tu al ness,** *n.*

spir i tu al ism (spir′ə chü ə liz′əm), **1** the belief that spirits of the dead communicate with the living, especially through persons called mediums. **2** spiritual quality. *n.*

spir i tu al ist (spir′ə chü ə list), person who believes that the dead communicate with the living. *n.*

spir i tu al i ty (spir′ə chü al′ə tē), devotion to spiritual things; spiritual quality. *n.*

spir i tu al ize (spir′ə chü ə līz), make spiritual. *v.,* **spir i tu al ized, spir i tu al iz ing.** —**spir′i tu al i za′tion,** *n.*

spi ro chete (spī′rə kēt′), any of a group of bacteria that are slender, spiral, and very flexible. *n.*

spi ro gy ra (spī′rə jī′rə), any of a large group of green algae that grow in masses like scum in freshwater ponds. *n., pl.* **spi ro gy ras.**

spirt (spėrt), spurt. *v., n.*

spit¹ (spit), **1** throw out (saliva, bits of food, etc.) from the mouth. **2** hurl: *A gun spits fire. The crew spat curses.* **3** saliva. **4** sound or act of spitting. **5** make a spitting

spire¹ (def. 1)—The cathedral had two tall **spires.**

sound: *The cat spits when angry.* 1,2,5 *v.,* **spat** or **spit, spit ting;** 3,4 *n.*

spit and image, INFORMAL. spitting image.

spit[2] (spit), **1** a sharp-pointed, slender rod or bar on which meat is roasted. **2** run a spit through; pierce; stab: *The cook spitted two rabbits.* **3** a narrow point of land running into the water. 1,3 *n.,* 2 *v.,* **spit ted, spit ting.**

spit ball (spit'bôl'), **1** a small ball of chewed-up paper, used as a missile. **2** (in baseball) an illegal curve thrown by the pitcher after moistening one side of the ball with saliva, grease, etc. *n.*

spite (spīt), **1** ill will; grudge: *He broke my new radio out of spite.* **2** show ill will toward; annoy: *They let the weeds grow in their yard to spite their neighbors.* 1 *n.,* 2 *v.,* **spit ed, spit ing. —spite'less,** *adj.*

in spite of, not prevented by; notwithstanding: *The schools were open in spite of the snowstorm.*

spite ful (spīt'fəl), full of spite; eager to annoy; behaving with ill will: *My spiteful little cousin tore up all my drawings. adj.* **—spite'ful ly,** *adv.* **—spite'ful ness,** *n.*

spit fire (spit'fīr'), person, especially a woman or girl, who has a quick and fiery temper. *n.*

spitting image, INFORMAL. the exact likeness; spit and image: *She is the spitting image of her mother.*

spit tle (spit'l), saliva; spit. *n.*

spit toon (spi tün'), container to spit into; cuspidor. *n.*

spitz (spits), any of various sturdy, small dogs with long hair, pointed nose, and tail curled up over the back. *n.,* *pl.* **spitz es.** [*Spitz comes from German Spitz.*]

splash (splash), **1** cause (water, mud, etc.) to fly about. **2** dash liquid about: *The baby likes to splash in the tub.* **3** dash in scattered masses or drops: *The waves splashed on the beach.* **4** to wet, spatter, or soil: *Our car is all splashed with mud.* **5** act or sound of splashing; splashing: *The splash of the wave knocked him over. The boat upset with a loud splash.* **6** fall, move, or go with a splash or splashes: *He splashed across the brook.* **7** spot of liquid splashed upon a thing: *She had splashes of grease on her clothes.* **8** spot; patch: *The dog is white with brown splashes.* 1-4,6 *v.,* 5,7,8 *n.,* *pl.* **splash es.**

make a splash, attract attention; cause excitement.

splash down (splash'doun'), the landing of a capsule or other spacecraft in the ocean after reentry. *n.*

splash y (splash'ē), **1** making a splash. **2** full of irregular spots or streaks. **3** attracting attention; causing excitement. *adj.,* **splash i er, splash i est. —splash'i ly,** *adv.* **—splash'i ness,** *n.*

splat ter (splat'ər), **1** to splash or spatter. **2** a splash or spatter. 1 *v.,* 2 *n.*

splay (splā), **1** to spread out. **2** wide and flat: *splay feet.* **3** awkward; clumsy. **4** a slanting surface; surface which makes an oblique angle with another. **5** make slanting; bevel. 1,5 *v.,* 2,3 *adj.,* 4 *n.*

splay foot (splā'fút'), a broad, flat foot, especially one turned outward. *n.,* *pl.* **splay feet.**

spleen (splēn), **1** a ductless, glandlike organ located near the stomach, which stores blood and helps filter foreign substances from the blood. **2** bad temper; spite; anger. *n.*

spleen ful (splēn'fəl), irritable; spiteful. *adj.* **—spleen'-ful ly,** *adv.*

splen did (splen'did), **1** brilliant or glorious; magnificent; grand: *a splendid sunset, a splendid palace, splendid jewels, a splendid victory.* **2** very good; fine; excellent: *a splendid chance. adj.* **—splen'did ly,** *adv.* **—splen'did-ness,** *n.*

splen dif er ous (splen dif'ər əs), INFORMAL. splendid. *adj.* **—splen dif'er ous ly,** *adv.* **—splen dif'er ous-ness,** *n.*

splen dor (splen'dər), **1** great brightness; brilliant light:

The sun set in a golden splendor. **2** magnificent show; pomp; glory. *n.*

splen dor ous (splen'dər əs), full of splendor. *adj.*

splice (splīs), **1** join together (ropes) by weaving together ends which have been untwisted. **2** join together (two pieces of timber) by overlapping. **3** join together (film, tape, wire, etc.) by gluing or cementing the ends. **4** a joining of ropes, timbers, film, etc., by splicing: *How neat a splice can you make?* 1-3 *v.,* **spliced, splic ing;** 4 *n.*

splic er (splī'sər), person or thing that splices. *n.*

splint (splint), **1** arrangement of wood, metal, or plaster to hold a broken or dislocated bone in place. **2** a thin strip of wood, such as is used in making baskets. *n.*

splin ter (splin'tər), **1** a thin, sharp piece of wood, bone, glass, etc.: *I have a splinter in my hand. The mirror broke into splinters.* **2** split or break into thin, sharp pieces: *to splinter wood with an ax. The mirror splintered.* 1 *n.,* 2 *v.*

splin ter y (splin'tər ē), **1** apt to splinter: *splintery wood.* **2** rough and jagged, as if from splintering. **3** full of splinters. *adj.*

split (split), **1** to break or cut from end to end, or in layers: *We split the logs into firewood. The baker split the cake and filled it with jelly.* **2** separate into parts; divide: *The huge tree split when it was struck by lightning. We decided to split the cost of the dinner between us.* **3** divide into different groups, factions, parties, etc. **4** division in a group, party, etc.: *There was a split in the club for a time, but harmony was soon restored.* **5** a splitting; break; crack: *Frost caused the split in the rock.* **6** broken or cut from end to end; divided. **7** divide (a molecule or atomic nucleus) into two or more smaller parts. **8** an acrobatic trick of sinking to the floor with the legs spread far apart in opposite directions. **9** SLANG. go away; leave. 1-3,7,9 *v.,* **split, split ting;** 4,5,8 *n.,* 6 *adj.* **—split'ter,** *n.*

split infinitive, infinitive having one or more words between *to* and the verb. EXAMPLE: *Last summer I learned to really enjoy swimming.*

split-lev el (split'lev'əl), house with two or more floor levels, each level about half a story above or below the adjacent level. *n.*

split second, a very brief moment of time; instant.

split ting (split'ing), very severe; extreme; violent: *a splitting headache. adj.*

splotch (sploch), **1** a large, irregular spot; splash. **2** make such spots or splashes on. 1 *n.,* *pl.* **splotch-es;** 2 *v.*

splotch y (sploch'ē), marked with splotches. *adj.,* **splotch i er, splotch i est.**

splurge (splėrj), **1** a showing off. **2** show off. **3** spend extravagantly. 1 *n.,* 2,3 *v.,* **splurged, splurg ing.**

splut ter (splut'ər), **1** talk in a hasty, confused way. People sometimes splutter when they are excited. **2** make spitting or popping noises; sputter: *The baked apples are spluttering in the oven.* **3** a spluttering. 1,2 *v.,* 3 *n.*

spoil (spoil), **1** damage or injure (something) so as to make it unfit or useless; ruin; destroy: *I spoiled two pieces of paper while trying to write a neat letter. The rain spoiled the picnic.* **2** be damaged; become bad or unfit for use: *The fruit spoiled because I kept it too long.* **3** injure the character or disposition of: *That child is being spoiled by too much attention.* **4** Often, **spoils,** *pl.* **a** things taken by force; things won: *The victors returned with the spoils of war.* **b** offices and positions filled by the political party that has won an election. 1-3 *v.,* **spoiled** or **spoilt, spoil-ing;** 4 *n.*

be spoiling for, be longing for (a fight, etc.): *They are both spoiling for a fight.*

spoil a ble (spoi'lə bəl), capable of spoiling. *adj.*

spoil age (spoi'lij), **1** act of spoiling. **2** fact of being spoiled. **3** something spoiled. *n.*

spoil er (spoi'lər), **1** person or thing that spoils. **2** person who takes spoils. *n.*

spoils system, system or practice in which public offices with their salaries and advantages are awarded to supporters of the winning political party.

spoilt (spoilt), spoiled; a past tense and a past participle of **spoil.** *v.*

spoke[1] (spōk), past tense of **speak.** *She spoke about that yesterday. v.*

spoke[2] (spōk), **1** one of the bars extending from the center of a wheel to the rim. **2** rung of a ladder. *n.* [*Spoke*[2] comes from Old English *spāca.*]

spo ken (spō'kən), **1** past participle of **speak.** *They have spoken about coming to visit.* **2** expressed with the mouth; uttered; told: *I usually understand a spoken direction better than a written one.* **3** speaking in a certain way: *a soft-spoken person.* **1** *v.,* **2,3** *adj.*

spokes man (spōks'mən), person who speaks for another or others: *I am the spokesman for my class in the student council. n., pl.* **spokes men.**

spokes per son (spōks'pèr'sən), person who speaks for another or others. *n.*

spokes wom an (spōks'wùm'ən), woman who speaks for another or others. *n., pl.* **spokes wom en.**

spo li a tion (spō'lē ā'shən), a plundering; robbery. *n.*

sponge (spunj), **1** a water animal having a tough, elastic skeleton with many pores. Most sponges live in large colonies on the bottom of the ocean, attached to stones, plants, etc. **2** the soft, light skeleton of any of these animals, used for soaking up water in bathing, cleaning, etc. **3** a similar article made of rubber, plastic, etc. **4** wipe or rub with a wet sponge; make clean or damp in this way: *Sponge up the spilled water. Sponge the mud spots off the car.* **5** absorb. **6** something used like a sponge, such as a pad of gauze used by doctors to absorb blood in surgery. **7** INFORMAL. live or profit at the expense of another in a mean or selfish way: *They are sponging on their relatives instead of working.* **1-3,6** *n.,* **4,5,7** *v.,* **sponged, spong ing. —sponge'like',** *adj.*

throw in the sponge, give up; admit defeat.

sponge cake, a light, spongy cake made with eggs, sugar, flour, etc., but no shortening.

spong er (spun'jər), **1** person or boat engaged in gathering sponges. **2** person who continually lives at the expense of others. *n.*

spon gy (spun'jē), **1** like a sponge; soft, light, and full of holes: *spongy moss, spongy dough.* **2** full of holes: *a spongy rock. adj.,* **spon gi er, spon gi est. —spon'gi ly,** *adv.* **—spon'gi ness,** *n.*

spon sor (spon'sər), **1** person or group that endorses, supports, or is responsible for a person or thing: *the sponsor of a law, the sponsor of a student applying for a scholarship.* **2** person who stands with the parents at an infant's baptism, agreeing to assist in the child's religious upbringing if necessary; godparent. **3** business firm or other organization that pays the costs of a radio or television program advertising its products or services. **4** act as sponsor for. **1-3** *n.,* **4** *v.*

spon sor ship (spon'sər ship), position and duties of a sponsor. *n.*

spon ta ne i ty (spon'tə nē'ə tē), quality, condition, or fact of being spontaneous. *n.*

spon ta ne ous (spon tā'nē əs), **1** caused by natural impulse or desire; not forced or compelled; not planned beforehand: *Both sides burst into spontaneous cheers at the skillful play.* **2** taking place without external cause or help; caused entirely by inner forces: *The eruption of a volcano is spontaneous. adj.* [*Spontaneous* is from Latin *spontaneus,* which comes from *sponte,* meaning "of one's own accord."] **—spon ta'ne ous ly,** *adv.*

a hat	i it	oi oil	ch child	(a in about
ā age	ī ice	ou out	ng long	e in taken
ä far	o hot	u cup	sh she	ə = { i in pencil
e let	ō open	ù put	th thin	o in lemon
ē equal	ô order	ü rule	ᴛʜ then	u in circus
èr term			zh measure	

spontaneous combustion, the bursting into flame of a substance without anyone's having set it on fire. In spontaneous combustion, the heat produced by chemical action within the substance itself causes it to catch on fire.

spoof (spüf), **1** a trick, hoax, or joke. **2** play tricks; make fun of; ridicule. **1** *n.,* **2** *v.*

spook (spük), INFORMAL. **1** ghost. **2** scare; frighten: *The storm spooked the horses.* **1** *n.,* **2** *v.* [*Spook* was borrowed from Dutch *spook.*]

spook y (spü'kē), INFORMAL. like a spook; suited to or suggesting spooks. *adj.,* **spook i er, spook i est. —spook'i ly,** *adv.* **—spook'i ness,** *n.*

spool (spül), **1** cylinder of wood or metal on which thread, wire, etc., is wound. **2** wind on a spool. **1** *n.,* **2** *v.*

spoon (spün), **1** utensil consisting of a small, shallow bowl at the end of a handle. Spoons are used to take up or stir food or drink. **2** take up in a spoon. **3** something shaped like a spoon. **1,3** *n.,* **2** *v.* **—spoon'like',** *adj.*

born with a silver spoon in one's mouth, born lucky or rich.

spoon bill (spün'bil'), a long-legged wading bird that has a long, flat bill with a spoon-shaped tip. *n.*

spoon-feed (spün'fēd'), feed with or as if with a spoon; coddle; pamper. *v.,* **spoon-fed** (spün'fed'), **spoon-feeding.**

spoon ful (spün'fùl), as much as a spoon can hold. *n., pl.* **spoon fuls.**

spoor (spùr), trail of a wild animal; track. *n.* [*Spoor* was borrowed from Afrikaans *spoor.*]

spo rad ic (spə rad'ik), occurring in scattered cases; appearing here and there or now and then: *sporadic outbreaks of scarlet fever. adj.*

spo rad i cal ly (spə rad'ik lē), here and there; now and then. *adv.*

spo ran gi um (spə ran'jē əm), spore case. *n., pl.* **spo ran gi a** (spə ran'jē ə).

spore (spôr), a single cell capable of growing into a new plant or animal. Spores are produced by plants that do not have flowers, such as ferns or molds. *n.*

spore case, case containing spores; sporangium. The little brown spots on the underside of ferns are spore cases.

SPORRAN

spor ran (spôr'ən), a large purse, commonly of fur, hanging from the belt in front of a Scottish Highlands costume. *n.*

sport (spôrt), **1** game, contest, or other pastime requiring some skill and usually involving a certain amount of physical exercise. Baseball and fishing are outdoor sports; bowling and basketball are indoor sports. **2** any pastime or amusement: *They spend Saturdays in sport and play.* **3** amuse oneself; play: *Lambs sport in the fields. The kitten sports with its tail.* **4** of sports; suitable for sports. **5** playful joking; fun: *That was great sport.* **6** ridicule: *The fool's actions were a source of sport to the villagers.* **7** object of jokes and ridicule: *The awkward beginner was the sport of the experienced golfers.* **8** to make fun; jest. **9** sportsman. **10** person who behaves in a fair and honorable manner and is a good loser: *to be a sport.* **11** INFORMAL. to display: *to sport a new hat.* 1,2,5-7,9,10 *n.*, 3,8,11 *v.*, 4 *adj.*

for sport or **in sport,** in fun; as a joke: *She teased her younger sister in sport.*

make sport of, make fun of; laugh at; ridicule: *Don't make sport of me.*

sport ful (spôrt′fəl), playful; sportive. *adj.* —**sport′ful ly,** *adv.* —**sport′ful ness,** *n.*

sport i ly (spôr′tə lē), INFORMAL. in a sporty fashion or manner. *adv.*

sport i ness (spôr′tē nis), INFORMAL. sporty quality or tendency. *n.*

sport ing (spôr′ting), **1** of, interested in, or engaging in sports. **2** playing fair; sportsmanlike: *The loser made a sporting gesture in shaking the winner's hand.* **3** willing to take a chance. **4** involving risk; uncertain: *She took a sporting chance in climbing up the cliff. adj.* —**sport′ing ly,** *adv.*

spor tive (spôr′tiv), playful; merry: *The old dog seemed as sportive as the puppy. adj.* —**spor′tive ly,** *adv.* —**spor′-tive ness,** *n.*

sports (spôrts), of sports; suitable for sports: *sports clothes. adj.*

sports car, a small, low, fast car, usually with two seats and an open top.

sports man (spôrts′mən), **1** person who takes part in sports, especially hunting, fishing, or racing. **2** person who likes sports. **3** person who plays fair and is a good loser. *n., pl.* **sports men.** —**sports′man ly,** *adj.*

sports man like (spôrts′mən līk′), like or suitable for a sportsman; fair and honorable. *adj.*

sports man ship (spôrts′mən ship), **1** qualities or conduct of a sportsman; fair play. **2** ability in sports. *n.*

sports wom an (spôrts′wùm′ən), woman who engages in or is interested in sports. *n., pl.* **sports wom en.**

sport y (spôr′tē), INFORMAL. **1** showy; flashy. **2** smart in dress, appearance, manners, etc. **3** sportsmanlike; sporting. *adj.,* **sport i er, sport i est.**

spot (spot), **1** a small mark or stain that discolors or disfigures: *You have grease spots on your suit. That spot on her arm is a bruise.* **2** a blemish or flaw in character or reputation: *His record is without spot.* **3** a small part unlike the rest: *a blue tie with red spots.* **4** make or become spotted: *The tablecloth was spotted with gravy. This silk spots from water.* **5** a place: *From this spot you can see the ocean.* **6** to place in a certain spot; scatter in various spots: *Lookouts were spotted all along the coast.* **7** ready; on hand: *a spot answer, spot cash.* **8** pick out; find out; recognize: *I spotted my sister in the crowd. The teacher spotted every mistake.* **9** figure or dot on a playing card, domino, or die to show its kind and value. 1-3,5,9 *n.*, 4,6,8 *v.*, **spot ted, spot ting;** 7 *adj.*

hit the spot, INFORMAL. be just right; be satisfactory.

in a spot, in trouble or difficulty.

on the spot, 1 at that very place. **2** at once: *Your orders will be carried out on the spot.* **3** INFORMAL. in an awkward or difficult position: *He put me on the spot by asking a question I could not answer.*

spot cash, money paid just as soon as the goods are delivered or the work is done.

spot check, 1 a brief, rough sampling. **2** a checkup made without warning.

spot less (spot′lis), without a spot: *a spotless white shirt. adj.* —**spot′less ly,** *adv.* —**spot′less ness,** *n.*

spot light (spot′līt′), **1** a spot or circle of bright light thrown upon a particular place or person. **2** lamp that gives such light: *a spotlight in a theater.* **3** light up with a spotlight or spotlights: *At night the baseball field is spotlighted.* **4** public notice; anything that directs attention on a person or thing: *Movie stars are often in the spotlight.* **5** call attention to; give public notice to: *The newspaper article spotlights the growth of the soybean industry.* 1,2,4 *n.*, 3,5 *v.*, **spot light ed** or **spot lit** (spot′lit′), **spot light ing.**

spot ted (spot′id), **1** stained with spots: *a spotted reputation.* **2** marked with spots: *a spotted dog. adj.*

spot ty (spot′ē), **1** having spots; spotted. **2** not of uniform quality; irregular: *Your work is spotty. adj.,* **spot ti er, spot ti est.** —**spot′ti ly,** *adv.* —**spot′ti ness,** *n.*

spouse (spous), husband or wife: *Mr. Smith is Mrs. Smith's spouse, and she is his spouse. n.* —**spouse′less,** *adj.*

spout (spout), **1** throw out (a liquid) in a stream or spray: *The fountain spouted up high. A whale spouts water when it breathes.* **2** flow out with force: *Water spouted from a break in the pipe.* **3** stream; jet: *A spout of water shot up from the hole in the pipe.* **4** pipe for carrying off water: *Rain runs down a spout from our roof to the ground.* **5** tube or lip by which liquid is poured. A teakettle and a coffeepot have spouts. **6** INFORMAL. speak in loud and very emotional tones: *The inexperienced actor spouted his lines.* 1,2,6 *v.*, 3-5 *n.* —**spout′er,** *n.* —**spout′less,** *adj.*

sprain (sprān), **1** injure (the ligaments of a joint) by a sudden twist or wrench: *I sprained my ankle.* **2** injury caused by a sudden twist or wrench: *The sprain took a long time to heal.* 1 *v.*, 2 *n.*

sprang (sprang), a past tense of **spring.** *The hungry tiger sprang at the antelope. v.*

sprat (sprat), a small herring of the Atlantic coast of Europe. *n., pl.* **sprats** or **sprat.**

sprawl (sprôl), **1** lie or sit with the arms and legs spread out, especially ungracefully: *The people sprawled on the beach in their bathing suits.* **2** to spread out in an irregular or awkward manner: *His large handwriting sprawled across the page.* **3** act or position of sprawling. 1,2 *v.*, 3 *n.* [*Sprawl* comes from Old English *sprēawlian.*]

spray[1] (sprā), **1** liquid going through the air in small drops: *We were wet with the sea spray.* **2** something like this: *A spray of bullets hit the target.* **3** instrument that sends a liquid out as spray. **4** scatter spray on; sprinkle: *Spray the apple tree.* 1-3 *n.*, 4 *v.* —**spray′er,** *n.* —**spray′like′,** *adj.*

spray[2] (sprā), a small branch or piece of some plant with its leaves, flowers, or fruit: *a spray of lilacs. n.* —**spray′like′,** *adj.*

spray can, container from which an insecticide, paint, cosmetic, etc., can be released as a spray or mist.

spray gun, device used to spray paint, insecticide, or other liquids.

spread (spred), **1** cover or cause to cover a large or larger area; stretch out; unfold; open out: *to spread rugs on the floor, spread one's arms. The petals spread. The bird spread its wings.* **2** move farther apart: *Spread out your fingers. The rails of the track have spread.* **3** extend; lie: *Fields of corn spread out before us.* **4** scatter; distribute: *She spread the news. She spread grain for the chickens.* **5** cover with a thin layer: *She spread each slice with butter.* **6** put as a thin layer: *He spread jam on his bread.* **7** act of spreading: *to fight the spread of infection, encourage the spread of knowledge.* **8** width; extent; amount of or capacity for spreading: *the spread of a bird's wings.* **9** a covering for a bed or table. **10** set or put food on (a table). **11** INFORMAL. food put on the table; feast. **12** something spread. *Butter and jam are spreads.* **13** advertisement, article, etc., occupying a number of adjoining columns or pages in a magazine or newspaper: *The advertisement was given a three-column spread.* 1-6,10 *v.*, **spread, spread ing;** 7-9,11-13 *n.* **—spread′er,** *n.*

spree (sprē), a short period of excessively engaging in a particular activity: *a drinking spree, a shopping spree. n.*

sprig (sprig), shoot, twig, or small branch: *a sprig of mint. n.*

spright li ness (sprīt′lē nis), liveliness; gaiety. *n.*

spright ly (sprīt′lē), lively; gay: *a sprightly kitten. adj.,* **spright li er, spright li est.** Also, **spritely.**

spring (spring), **1** to leap or jump; rise or move suddenly and lightly: *I sprang to my feet. The dog sprang at the stranger.* **2** a leap or jump: *a spring over the fence.* **3** fly back or away as if by elastic force: *The door sprang shut.* **4** cause to spring; cause to act by a spring: *spring a trap.* **5** an elastic device that returns to its original shape after being pulled or held out of shape. *Beds have wire springs. The spring in a clock makes it go.* **6** elastic quality: *The old man's knees have lost their spring.* **7** season when plants begin to grow; season of the year between winter and summer. **8** of or for spring; coming in spring: *spring showers. Spring wheat is wheat sown in the spring.* **9** a small stream of water flowing naturally from the earth. **10** come from some source; arise; grow: *Plants spring from seeds. A wind has sprung up.* **11** source; beginning; cause. **12** begin to move, act, grow, etc., suddenly; burst forth: *Towns spring up where oil is discovered.* **13** bring out, produce, or make suddenly: *to spring a surprise on someone.* **14** to crack, split, warp, bend, strain, or break: *Frost has sprung the rock wall. Cracks all along the wall showed where it had sprung.* 1,3,4,10,12-14 *v.,* **sprang** or **sprung, sprung, spring ing;** 2,5-7,9,11 *n.,* 8 *adj.* **—spring′er,** *n.*

spring board (spring′bôrd′), **1** a flexible board used to give added spring in diving, jumping, and vaulting. **2** anything that serves as a way to get to something else: *Hard work is often a springboard to success. n.*

spring bok (spring′bok′), a small antelope of South Africa. It leaps almost directly upward when excited or disturbed. *n., pl.* **spring boks** or **spring bok.** [*Springbok* comes from Afrikaans *springbok,* meaning "a springing buck."]

Spring field (spring′fēld′), **1** capital of Illinois, in the central part. **2** city in S Massachusetts. *n.*

spring tide (spring′tīd′), springtime. *n.*

spring tide, the exceptionally high and low tides which come at the time of the new moon or the full moon.

spring time (spring′tīm′), the season of spring. *n.*

spring y (spring′ē), having bounce; elastic: *Her step was springy. adj.,* **spring i er, spring i est. —spring′i ly,** *adv.*

sprin kle (spring′kəl), **1** scatter in drops or tiny bits: *I sprinkled salt on the icy sidewalk.* **2** spray or cover with small drops: *sprinkle flowers with water.* **3** a sprinkling; small quantity: *The cook put a sprinkle of nuts on the cake.* **4** rain a little. **5** a light rain. 1,2,4 *v.,* **sprin kled, sprin kling;** 3,5 *n.*

sprin kler (spring′klər), device for sprinkling water. *n.*

sprin kling (spring′kling), a small quantity or number scattered here and there: *a sprinkling of gray hairs. n.*

sprint (sprint), **1** run at full speed, especially for a short distance. **2** a race or any short spell of running, rowing, etc., at top speed. 1 *v.,* 2 *n.* **—sprint′er,** *n.*

sprit (sprit), a small pole running diagonally from the foot of the mast to the top corner of a fore-and-aft sail, to support and stretch it. *n.*

SPRIT

sprite (sprīt), elf; fairy; goblin. *n.*

sprite ly (sprīt′lē), sprightly. *adj.,* **sprite li er, sprite li est. —sprite′li ness,** *n.*

sprit sail (sprit′sāl′ *or* sprit′səl), sail supported and stretched by a sprit. *n.*

sprocket (defs. 1 and 2) on a bicycle

sprock et (sprok′it), **1** one of a set of projections on the rim of a wheel, arranged so as to fit into the links of a chain. *The sprockets keep the chain from slipping.* **2** Also, **sprocket wheel.** wheel made with sprockets. *n.*

sprout (sprout), **1** begin to grow; shoot forth: *Seeds sprout. Buds sprout in the spring.* **2** cause to grow: *The rain has sprouted the corn.* **3** a shoot of a plant: *The gardener was setting out sprouts.* **4 sprouts,** *pl.* **a** the first stalks of germinating beans, alfalfa seeds, etc., eaten as a vegetable. **b** Brussels sprouts. 1,2 *v.,* 3,4 *n.*

spruce[1] (sprüs), **1** an evergreen tree related to the pine. The spruce has cones and needle-shaped leaves, and is often used as a Christmas tree in America. **2** its wood, used for making paper, boxes, ship masts, etc. *n.*

spruce[2] (sprüs), **1** neat; trim: *You look very spruce in your new suit.* **2** make or become spruce: *Spruce up before you go back to school.* 1 *adj.,* **spruc er, spruc est;** 2 *v.,* **spruced, spruc ing. —spruce′ly,** *adv.* **—spruce′ness,** *n.*

sprung (sprung), a past tense and the past participle of **spring.** *The mouse sprung the trap. The mousetrap was sprung. v.*

spry (sprī), active; lively; nimble: *The spry old woman traveled all over the country. adj.,* **spry er, spry est** or **spri er, spri est. —spry′ly,** *adv.* **—spry′ness,** *n.*

spud (spud), **1** tool with a narrow blade for digging up or cutting the roots of weeds. **2** INFORMAL. potato. *n.*

spue (spyü), spew. *v.*, **spued, spu ing.**

spume (spyüm), **1** frothy matter; foam; froth. **2** to foam or froth. **1** *n.*, **2** *v.*, **spumed, spum ing.**

spum y (spyü′mē), foamy; frothy. *adj.*, **spum i er, spum i est.**

spun (spun), past tense and past participle of **spin.** *The car skidded and spun on the ice. The thread was spun from silk. v.*

spun glass, fiberglass.

spunk (spungk), INFORMAL. courage; spirit: *a little puppy full of spunk. n.*

spunk y (spung′kē), INFORMAL. courageous; brave; spirited: *a spunky person. adj.*, **spunk i er, spunk i est.** —**spunk′i ly,** *adv.* —**spunk′i ness,** *n.*

spun silk, silk waste spun into yarn.

spur (spėr), **1** a spike or a spiked wheel, worn on a rider's heel for urging a horse on. **2** to prick with spurs: *The riders spurred their horses on.* **3** something like a spur; point sticking out. A rooster has spurs on its legs. *A spur of rock stuck out from the hill.* **4** anything that urges on: *Ambition was the spur that made him work.* **5** urge on: *Anger spurred her to speak unkindly.* **6** ridge sticking out from or smaller than the main body of a mountain or mountain range. **7** any short branch: *a spur of a railroad.* **1,3,4,6,7** *n.*, **2,5** *v.*, **spurred, spur ring.** —**spur′like′,** *adj.* **on the spur of the moment,** on a sudden impulse or without previous thought or preparation. **win one's spurs,** make a reputation for oneself or win distinction.

spur i ous (spyur′ē əs), not coming from the right source; not genuine; false; counterfeit: *a spurious document, spurious anger. adj.* —**spur′i ous ly,** *adv.* —**spur′i ous ness,** *n.*

spurn (spėrn), **1** refuse with scorn; scorn: *The judge spurned the bribe.* **2** strike with the foot; kick away. *v.* —**spurn′er,** *n.*

spurred (spėrd), having spurs or a spur: *a spurred boot, spurred feet. adj.*

spurt (spėrt), **1** flow suddenly in a stream or jet; gush out; squirt: *Water spurted from the drinking fountain.* **2** a sudden rushing forth; jet: *a spurt of blood from a cut.* **3** a great increase of effort or activity for a short time: *To win the race he put on a spurt of speed at the end.* **4** put forth great energy for a short time; show great activity for a short time: *The runners spurted near the end of the race.* **1,4** *v.*, **2,3** *n.*

sput nik (sput′nik or sput′nik), any of the artificial earth satellites put into orbit by the Soviet Union. *n.* [*Sputnik* comes from Russian *sputnik,* which originally meant "fellow traveler."]

sput ter (sput′ər), **1** make spitting or popping noises: *fat sputtering in the frying pan. The firecrackers sputtered.* **2** throw out (drops of saliva, bits of food, etc.) in excitement or in talking too fast. **3** say (words or sounds) in haste and confusion. **4** confused talk. **5** a sputtering; sputtering noise. **1-3** *v.*, **4,5** *n.* —**sput′ter er,** *n.* —**sput′ter ing ly,** *adv.*

spu tum (spyü′təm), **1** saliva; spit. **2** mixture of saliva and mucus coughed up and spat out. *n.*, *pl.* **spu ta** (spyü′tə).

spy (spī), **1** person who keeps secret watch on the action of others. **2** person paid by a government to get secret information about another government or country, especially in time of war. **3** keep secret watch: *He saw two men spying on him from behind a tree.* **4** act as a spy; be a spy. The punishment for spying in wartime is death. **5** catch sight of; see: *She was the first to spy the rescue party in the distance.* **1,2** *n.*, *pl.* **spies; 3-5** *v.*, **spied, spy ing.**

spy out, find out by watching secretly or carefully.

spy glass (spī′glas′), a small telescope. *n.*, *pl.* **spy glass es.**

sq., square.

squab (skwob), a very young bird, especially a young pigeon. *n.*

squab ble (skwob′əl), **1** a petty, noisy quarrel: *Children's squabbles annoy their parents.* **2** take part in a petty, noisy quarrel: *I won't squabble over a nickel.* **1** *n.*, **2** *v.*, **squabbled, squab bling.** —**squab′bler,** *n.*

squad (skwod), **1** a military unit usually made up of ten to twelve men. It is the basic unit for drill, inspection, or work. It is usually commanded by a sergeant or a corporal. **2** any small group of persons working together: *A squad of children cleaned up the yard. n.*

squad car, police patrol car which is equipped with a special radio to keep in communication with headquarters.

squad ron (skwod′rən), **1** part of a naval fleet used for special service: *a destroyer squadron.* **2** formation of eight or more airplanes that fly or fight together. **3** any group or formation. *n.*

squal id (skwol′id), very dirty; filthy; wretched: *a squalid tenement. adj.* —**squal′id ly,** *adv.* —**squal′id ness,** *n.*

squall[1] (skwôl), **1** a sudden, violent gust of wind, often with rain, snow, or sleet. **2** undergo or give rise to a squall. **1** *n.*, **2** *v.*

squall[2] (skwôl), **1** cry out loudly; scream violently: *The hungry baby squalled.* **2** a loud, harsh cry: *The parrot's squall was heard all over the house.* **1** *v.*, **2** *n.* —**squall′er,** *n.*

squall y (skwô′lē), having many sudden and violent gusts of wind: *squally weather. adj.*, **squall i er, squall i est.**

squal or (skwol′ər), misery and dirt; filth. *n.*

squan der (skwon′dər), spend foolishly; waste: *squander one's time and money in gambling. v.* —**squan′der er,** *n.*

square (skwer or skwar), **1** a plane figure with four equal sides and four right angles (□). **2** having this shape: *a square box. A block of stone is usually square.* **3** anything having this shape or nearly this shape: *I gave the child a square of chocolate.* **4** having length and width. A square meter is the area of a square whose edges are each one meter long. **5** make square; make rectangular; make cubical: *square a block of granite.* **6** an open space in a city or town bounded by streets on four sides, often planted with grass, trees, etc.: *The library is in the square directly opposite the city hall.* **7** any similar open space, such as at the meeting of streets. **8** of a specified length on each side of a square: *a room ten feet square.* **9** forming a right angle: *a square corner.* **10** bring to the form of a right angle. **11** instrument shaped like a T or an L, used for drawing right angles and testing the squareness of anything. **12** straight; level; even. **13** make straight, level, or even: *square a picture on a wall.* **14** leaving no balance; even: *make accounts square.* **15** adjust; settle: *Let us square our accounts.* **16** agree; conform: *Her acts do not square with her promises.* **17** just; fair; honest: *You will get a square deal at this shop.* **18** satisfying: *a square meal.* **19** product obtained when a number is multiplied by itself: *16 is the square of 4.* **20** multiply (a number) by itself: *25 squared makes 625.* **21** person who is too conventional or old-fashioned. **22** SLANG. too conventional or old-fashioned. **1,3,6,7,11,19,21** *n.*, **2,4,8,9,12,14, 17,18,22** *adj.*, **squar er, squar est; 5,10,13,15,16,20** *v.*, **squared, squar ing.** —**square′ly,** *adv.* —**square′ness,** *n.*

on the square, 1 at right angles. **2** justly; fairly; honestly.

square away, set the sails so that the ship will stay before the wind.

square off, put oneself in a position of defense or attack.

square oneself, INFORMAL. **1** make up for something one has said or done. **2** get even.

square dance, dance done by a set of couples arranged around a square space.

square foot, measure of area one foot long and one foot wide; any area equal to that.

square inch, measure of area one inch long and one inch wide; any area equal to that.

square knot, knot firmly joining two loose ends of rope or cord. Each end is formed into a loop which both encloses and passes through the other.

square measure, system of units, such as square centimeter, square inch, square meter, square mile, used for measuring area.

square-rigged sails on the foremast

square-rigged (skwer′rigd′ or skwar′rigd′), having the principal sails set at right angles across the masts. *adj.*

square-rig ger (skwer′rig′ər or skwar′rig′ər), a square-rigged ship. *n.*

square root, number that produces a given number when multiplied by itself: *The square root of 16 is 4.*

squash[1] (skwosh), **1** press or be pressed until soft or flat; crush: *She squashed the bug. Carry the cream puffs carefully, for they squash easily.* **2** act, fact, or sound of squashing. **3** put an end to; stop by force: *The police quickly squashed the riot.* **4** to crowd; squeeze. **5** either of two games somewhat like handball and tennis, played in a walled court with rackets and a rubber ball. 1,3,4 *v.*, 2,5 *n., pl.* **squash es.** [*Squash*[1] came into English about 400 years ago from French *esquasser*, and can be traced back to Latin *ex-*, meaning "out," and *quassare*, meaning "to press."] —**squash′er,** *n.*

squash[2] (skwosh), the fruit of a trailing garden vine related to the pumpkin and cucumber. Squash is used as a vegetable and has different shapes and colors, usually yellow, green, or white. *n., pl.* **squash** or **squash es.**

WORD HISTORY

squash[2]

Squash[2] was shortened from the earlier spellings *squantersquash* and *isquoutersquash,* which came from Narragansett Indian *askutasquash,* meaning "the green things that may be eaten raw."

a hat	i it	oi oil	ch child	ə =	a in about
ā age	ī ice	ou out	ng long		e in taken
ä far	o hot	u cup	sh she		i in pencil
e let	ō open	ù put	th thin		o in lemon
ē equal	ô order	ü rule	ŦH then		u in circus
ėr term			zh measure		

squash i ness (skwosh′ē nis), a being squashy. *n.*

squash y (skwosh′ē), **1** easily squashed: *The baby liked soft, squashy toys.* **2** soft and wet: *squashy ground.* adj., **squash i er, squash i est.** —**squash′i ly,** *adv.*

squat (skwot), **1** crouch on the heels. **2** sit on the ground or floor with the legs drawn up closely beneath or in front of the body: *The campers squatted around the fire.* **3** crouching: *A squat figure sat in front of the fire.* **4** act of squatting; squatting posture. **5** settle on another's land without title or right. **6** settle on public land to acquire ownership of it. **7** short and thick; low and broad: *a squat man, a squat teapot.* 1,2,5,6 *v.,* **squat ted** or **squat, squat ting;** 3,7 *adj.,* **squat ter, squat test;** 4 *n.* —**squat′ly,** *adv.* —**squat′ness,** *n.*

squat ter (skwot′ər), **1** person who settles on another's land without right. **2** person who settles on public land to gain ownership of it. *n.*

squat ty (skwot′ē), short and thick; squat. *adj.,* **squat ti er, squat ti est.**

squaw (skwô), a North American Indian woman. The word *squaw* is often considered offensive. *n.* [*Squaw* comes from Narragansett Indian *squaws,* meaning "woman."]

squaw fish (skwô′fish′), any of several large, slender carps, common in rivers of the Pacific coast of North America. *n., pl.* **squaw fish es** or **squaw fish.**

squawk (skwôk), **1** make a loud, harsh sound: *Hens and ducks squawk when frightened.* **2** such a sound. **3** SLANG. complain loudly. **4** SLANG. a loud complaint. 1,3 *v.,* 2,4 *n.* —**squawk′er,** *n.*

squeak (skwēk), **1** make a short, sharp, shrill sound: *A mouse squeaks.* **2** such a sound: *We heard the squeak of the rocking chair.* **3** get or pass (by or through) with difficulty: *The Senate will block the bill even if it squeaks through the House of Representatives.* **4** a chance to get by or through; chance of escape: *a narrow squeak.* 1,3 *v.,* 2,4 *n.*

squeak i ly (skwē′kə lē), in a squeaky manner: *to sing squeakily. adv.*

squeak i ness (skwē′kē nis), quality of being squeaky. *n.*

squeak y (skwē′kē), squeaking. *adj.,* **squeak i er, squeak i est.**

squeal (skwēl), **1** make a long, sharp, shrill cry: *A pig squeals when it is hurt.* **2** such a cry. **3** SLANG. turn informer. 1,3 *v.,* 2 *n.* —**squeal′er,** *n.*

squeam ish (skwē′mish), **1** too proper, modest, etc.; easily shocked. **2** slightly sick at one's stomach; nauseated. **3** easily affected with nausea; queasy. *adj.* —**squeam′ish ly,** *adv.* —**squeam′ish ness,** *n.*

squee gee (skwē′jē′), tool consisting of a blade of rubber and a handle, used for removing water from windows after washing, sweeping water from wet decks, etc. *n.*

squeeze (skwēz), **1** press hard; compress: *Don't squeeze the kitten; you'll hurt it.* **2** a squeezing; tight pressure: *a squeeze of the hand. She gave her sister's arm a squeeze.* **3** to hug: *She squeezed her child.* **4** force by pressing: *I can't squeeze another thing into my trunk.* **5** force out by pressure: *squeeze juice from a lemon.* **6** get by pressure, force, or effort: *The dictator squeezed money from the people.* **7** yield to pressure: *Sponges squeeze easily.* **8** force a way: *squeeze through a crowd.* **9** crush; crowd: *Six people squeezed into the little car.* 1,3-9 *v.* **squeezed, squeezing;** 2 *n.* **—squeez′a ble,** *adj.*

squeez er (skwē′zər), device for squeezing juice from fruits or vegetables. *n.*

squelch (skwelch), cause to be silent; crush: *She squelched him with a look of contempt. v.* **—squelch′er,** *n.*

squib (skwib), a short, witty attack in speech or writing; sharp sarcasm. *n.*

squid—this type up to 8 ft. (2.5 m.) long with arms

squid (skwid), a sea animal having ten arms with suckers, and a pair of tail fins. Squids are mollusks and are related to octopuses. *n., pl.* **squids** *or* **squid.**

squig gle (skwig′əl), **1** a wriggly twist or curve. **2** make with twisting or curving lines. **3** twist and turn about; writhe; squirm; wriggle. 1 *n.,* 2,3 *v.* **squig gled, squig gling.** [*Squiggle* is a blend of *squirm* and *wriggle.*]

squint (skwint), **1** to look with the eyes partly closed. **2** a looking with partly closed eyes. **3** a sidelong look; hasty look. **4** to look sideways; look askance. **5** tendency to look sideways or askance. **6** looking sideways; looking askance. **7** be cross-eyed. **8** cross-eyed condition. **9** cross-eyed. 1,4,7 *v.* 2,3,5,8 *n.,* 6,9 *adj.* **—squint′er,** *n.*

squire (skwīr), **1** (in Great Britain) a country gentleman, especially the chief landowner in a district. **2** (in the United States) a justice of the peace or a local judge. **3** a young man of noble family who attended a knight till he himself was made a knight. **4** attendant. **5** attend as squire. **6** a woman's escort. **7** to escort (a woman). 1-4,6 *n.,* 5,7 *v.* **squired, squir ing.**

squirm (skwėrm), **1** turn and twist; writhe: *The restless boy squirmed in his chair. The dog squirmed its way through the hole in the fence.* **2** a wriggle; twist. **3** show great embarrassment, annoyance, confusion, etc. 1,3 *v.,* 2 *n.*

squirm y (skwėr′mē), squirming; wriggling. *adj.,* **squirm i er, squirm i est.**

squir rel (skwėr′əl), **1** a small, bushy-tailed rodent that usually lives in trees. **2** its gray, reddish, or dark-brown fur. *n.* **—squir′rel like′,** *adj.* [See **Word History.**]

squirt (skwėrt), **1** force out (liquid) through a narrow opening: *squirt water through a tube.* **2** come out in a jet or stream: *Water squirted from the hose.* **3** to wet or soak by shooting liquid in a jet or stream: *The elephant squirted me with its trunk.* **4** act of squirting. **5** jet of liquid, etc.: *I soaked her with squirts of water from the hose.* **6** something that squirts. **7** INFORMAL. an insignificant person who is impudent or conceited: *a little squirt of a man.* 1-3 *v.,* 4-7 *n.* **—squirt′er,** *n.*

Sr, symbol for strontium.

Sr., senior.

Sri Lan ka (srē′ läng′kə), country in the Indian Ocean consisting of the island of Ceylon. It is a member of the Commonwealth of Nations. *Capital:* Colombo.

SS or **S.S.,** steamship.

SST, supersonic transport (a large passenger or transport airplane that flies faster than the speed of sound).

St., 1 Saint. **2** Street.

stab (stab), **1** pierce or wound with a pointed weapon. **2** to thrust with a pointed weapon; aim a blow. **3** a thrust or blow made with a pointed weapon. **4** any thrust or sudden, sharp blow. **5** wound made by stabbing. **6** wound sharply or deeply in the feelings: *The parents were stabbed to the heart by their son's ingratitude.* **7** injury to the feelings. **8** an attempt. 1,2,6 *v.* **stabbed, stabbing;** 3-5,7,8 *n.*

stab ber (stab′ər), person or thing that stabs. *n.*

sta bil i ty (stə bil′ə tē), **1** being fixed in position; firmness: *A concrete wall has more stability than a light wooden fence.* **2** permanence. **3** steadfastness of character, purpose, etc.: *the stability of someone who helps a friend in need. n., pl.* **sta bil i ties.**

sta bi li za tion (stā′bə lə zā′shən), a stabilizing or a being stabilized. *n.*

sta bi lize (stā′bə līz), **1** make stable or firm: *stabilize a government.* **2** prevent changes in; hold steady: *stabilize prices.* **3** keep well balanced. *v.,* **sta bi lized, sta bi lizing.**

sta bi liz er (stā′bə lī′zər), **1** person or thing that stabilizes. **2** device for keeping an airplane, ship, etc., steady. *n.*

sta ble¹ (stā′bəl), **1** building where horses or cattle are kept and fed: *I accompanied her to the stable where she took riding lessons.* **2** group of animals housed in such a building. **3** put or keep in a stable. **4** group of race horses belonging to one owner. 1,2,4 *n.,* 3 *v.* **sta bled, stabling. —sta′bler,** *n.*

sta ble² (stā′bəl), **1** not likely to move or change; steadfast; firm; steady: *Concrete reinforced with steel is stable.* **2** lasting without change; permanent. *adj.* **—sta′ble ness,** *n.* **—sta′bly,** *adv.*

stac ca to (stə kä′tō), in music: **1** with breaks between the successive tones; disconnected; abrupt. **2** in a stac-

WORD HISTORY

squirrel

Squirrel came into English about 600 years ago from French *esquirel,* and can be traced back to Greek *skia,* meaning "shadow," and *oura,* meaning "tail." The squirrel was called this because its long, bushy tail curls over its back and seems to keep it in a shadow.

about 18 in. (45 cm.) long with tail

cato manner. **1** *adj.,* **2** *adv.* [*Staccato* was borrowed from Italian *staccato.*]

stack (stak), **1** a large pile of hay, straw, etc. **2** pile of anything: *a stack of wood.* **3** group of three or more rifles arranged with their muzzles together to form a cone or pyramid. **4** pile or arrange in a stack: *stack hay, stack firewood, stack guns.* **5** arrange (playing cards) unfairly. **6** INFORMAL. a large number or quantity: *a stack of people, a stack of compliments.* **7** chimney. **8** rack with shelves for books. **9 stacks,** *pl.* part of a library in which the main collection of books is shelved. 1-3,6-9 *n.,* 4,5 *v.* —**stack′er,** *n.*

sta di um (stā′dē əm), an oval, U-shaped, or round building, usually without a roof. Tiers of seats for spectators surround the playing field. *n.*

staff (staf), **1** a stick, pole, or rod used as a support, as an emblem of office, as a weapon, etc.: *The flag hangs on a staff. The woman leaned on her staff.* **2** something that supports or sustains. Bread is called the staff of life because it will support life. **3** group assisting a chief; group of employees: *Our school has a staff of twenty teachers.* **4** (in the armed forces) group of officers assisting a commanding officer with administration, planning, etc., but without command or combat duties. **5** provide with officers or employees. **6** set of five lines and the four spaces between them on which music is written; stave. 1-4,6 *n., pl.* **staves** or **staffs** for 1 and 2, **staffs** for 3,4,6; 5 *v.*

staff er (staf′ər), member of a staff. *n.*

stags (def. 1)

stag (stag), **1** a full-grown male deer. **2** attended by or for men only: *a stag dinner.* 1 *n.,* 2 *adj.*

stage (stāj), **1** one step or degree in a process; period of development. An insect passes through several stages before it is full-grown. Childhood, adolescence, and adulthood are stages in a person's life. **2** the raised platform in a theater on which the actors perform. **3** the stage, the theater; the drama; actor's profession: *Shakespeare wrote for the stage.* **4** scene of action: *Bunker Hill was the stage of a famous battle.* **5** put on a stage or arrange: *The play was very well staged. Mother had staged a surprise for the children's party by hiring a magician. The angry people staged a riot.* **6** section of a rocket or missile having its own engine and fuel. A three-stage rocket has three engines, one in each stage, which separate one after another from the rocket after the fuel is burned up. **7** stagecoach or bus. **8** place of rest on a journey; regular stopping place. **9** distance between two stopping places on a journey. **10** platform; flooring. 1-4,6-10 *n.,* 5 *v.,* **staged, stag ing.** —**stage′like′,** *adj.*

by easy stages, a little at a time; slowly; often stopping.
on the stage, being an actor or actress.

stage coach (stāj′kōch′), coach pulled by horses and carrying passengers, parcels, and mail over a regular route. *n.*

stage fright, nervous fear of appearing before an audience.

stage hand (stāj′hand′), person whose work is moving scenery, arranging lights, etc., in a theater. *n.*

stage-struck (stāj′struk′), extremely interested in acting; wanting very much to become an actor or actress. *adj.*

stage whisper, a loud whisper on a stage meant for the audience to hear.

stag ger (stag′ər), **1** sway or reel (from weakness, a heavy load, or drunkenness): *I staggered and fell while trying to carry too many books.* **2** make sway or reel: *The blow staggered me for the moment.* **3** a swaying or reeling. **4** become unsteady; waver: *The troops staggered under the severe gunfire.* **5** confuse or astonish greatly: *He was staggered by the news of his friend's death.* **6** arrange in a zigzag order or way. **7** arrange to begin at different times: *Vacations were staggered so that only one person was away at a time.* **8 staggers,** *pl.* in form, *sing.* in use. a nervous disease of horses, cattle, etc., that makes them stagger or fall suddenly. 1,2,4-7 *v.,* 3,8 *n.* —**stag′ger er,** *n.* —**stag′ger ing ly,** *adv.*

stag nant (stag′nənt), **1** not running or flowing: *stagnant air, stagnant water.* **2** foul from standing still: *a stagnant pool of water.* **3** not active; sluggish; dull: *During the summer, business is often stagnant. adj.* —**stag′nant ly,** *adv.*

stag nate (stag′nāt), **1** be stagnant; become stagnant. **2** make stagnant. *v.,* **stag nat ed, stag nat ing.**

stag na tion (stag nā′shən), becoming or making stagnant; stagnant condition. *n.*

staid (stād), having a settled, quiet character; sober; sedate: *We think of the Puritans as staid people. adj.* —**staid′ly,** *adv.* —**staid′ness,** *n.*

stain (stān), **1** to discolor with streaks of dirt, blood, etc.; soil; spot: *Spilled food stained the tablecloth.* **2** a discoloration made by soiling; a spot: *He has ink stains on his shirt.* **3** to spot by wrongdoing or disgrace; dishonor: *His crimes stained the family honor.* **4** mark of disgrace; dishonor: *Her character is without stain.* **5** to color or dye: *He stained the chair green.* **6** a coloring or dye: *She painted the table with a brown stain.* 1,3,5 *v.,* 2,4,6 *n.* —**stain′a ble,** *adj.* —**stain′er,** *n.*

stain less (stān′lis), without stain; spotless. *adj.* —**stain′less ly,** *adv.* —**stain′less ness,** *n.*

stainless steel, steel containing a high percentage of chromium, making it very resistant to rust and corrosion.

stair (ster *or* star), **1** one of a series of steps for going from one level or floor to another. **2** Also, **stairs,** *pl.* set of such steps; stairway: *the top of the stairs. We climbed the winding stair to the tower. n.* —**stair′less,** *adj.* —**stair′like′,** *adj.*

stair case (ster′kās′ *or* star′kās′), flight of stairs with its framework; stairs. *n.*

stair way (ster′wā′ *or* star′wā′), way up and down by stairs; a flight or flights of stairs: *the back stairway. n.*

stair well (ster′wel′ *or* star′wel′), the vertical passage or open space containing the stairs of a building. *n.*

stake¹ (stāk), **1** a stick or post pointed at one end for driving into the ground. **2 the stake, a** post to which a person was tied and then burned to death: *Joan of Arc*

---

was burned at the stake. **b** death by being burned in this way. **3** fasten to a stake or with a stake: *stake down a tent.* **4** mark with stakes; mark the boundaries of: *stake out a mining claim.* 1,2 *n.,* 3,4 *v.,* **staked, stak ing.**

pull up stakes, INFORMAL. move away: *Constant flooding of their land led the farmers to pull up stakes and leave the valley for the highlands.*

stake² (stāk), **1** risk (money or something valuable) on the result of a game or on any chance: *She staked all her money on the black horse.* **2** money risked; what is staked: *They played for high stakes.* **3** Often, **stakes,** *pl.* prize in a race or contest: *The stakes were divided up among the winners.* **4** something to gain or lose; interest; share in a property: *Each of us has a stake in the future of our country.* **5** INFORMAL. assist or back (a person) with money, etc.: *I'll stake you to a dinner if you'll come.* 1,5 *v.,* **staked, stak ing;** 2-4 *n.* —**stak′er,** *n.*

at stake, to be won or lost; risked: *Our friendship is at stake.*

sta lac tite (stə lak′tīt), a formation of lime, shaped like an icicle, hanging from the roof of a cave. It is formed by dripping water that contains lime. *n.*

stalactites and **stalagmites**

sta lag mite (stə lag′mīt), a formation of lime, shaped like a cone, built up on the floor of a cave. It is formed by water dripping from a pistil. *n.*

stale (stāl), **1** not fresh: *stale bread.* **2** no longer new or interesting: *a stale joke.* **3** out of condition: *The horse has gone stale from too much running.* **4** make stale. **5** become stale. 1-3 *adj.,* **stal er, stal est;** 4,5 *v.,* **staled, stal ing.** —**stale′ly,** *adv.* —**stale′ness,** *n.*

stale mate (stāl′māt′), **1** (in chess) a draw which results when you cannot move any of your pieces without putting your own king in check. **2** any position in which no action can be taken; complete standstill. **3** put in such a position; bring to a complete standstill. 1,2 *n.,* 3 *v.,* **stale mat ed, stale mat ing.**

Sta lin (stä′lin), **Joseph,** 1879-1953, Soviet political leader, dictator of the Soviet Union from 1929 to 1953. *n.*

Sta lin grad (stä′lin grad), former name of **Volgo-grad.** *n.*

stalk¹ (stôk), **1** the main stem of a plant. **2** any slender, supporting part of a plant. A flower or a leaf blade may have a stalk. **3** any similar part. The eyes of a crayfish are on stalks. *n.* —**stalk′less,** *adj.* —**stalk′like′,** *adj.*

stalk² (stôk), **1** approach or pursue without being seen or heard: *The hungry lion stalked a zebra.* **2** spread silently and steadily: *Disease stalked through the land.* **3** walk with slow, stiff, or haughty strides: *She became angry and stalked out of the room.* **4** a haughty gait. **5** act of stalking. 1-3 *v.,* 4,5 *n.* —**stalk′a ble,** *adj.* —**stalk′er,** *n.* —**stalk′-ing ly,** *adv.*

stall¹ (stôl), **1** place in a stable for one animal. **2** a small place for selling things: *At the public market different*

things were sold in different stalls under one big roof. **3** seat in the choir of a church. **4** put or keep in a stall: *The horses were safely stalled.* **5** stop or bring to a standstill, usually against one's wish: *The engine stalled. We were stalled in the mud.* **6** a parking space. 1-3,6 *n.,* 4,5 *v.* —**stall′-like′,** *adj.*

stall² (stôl), INFORMAL. **1** pretext to prevent action, the accomplishment of a purpose, etc. **2** to delay. **3** pretend; evade; deceive: *Every time I ask for a raise my boss stalls.* 1 *n.,* 2,3 *v.*

stal lion (stal′yən), a male horse that can be used for breeding. *n.*

stal wart (stôl′wərt), **1** strongly built. **2** strong and brave: *a stalwart knight.* **3** firm; steadfast: *a stalwart refusal.* **4** a stalwart person. 1-3 *adj.,* 4 *n.* [*Stalwart* is from Old English *stǣlwierthe,* meaning "serviceable," which comes from Old English *stathol,* meaning "position," and *wierthe,* meaning "worthy."] —**stal′wart ly,** *adv.* —**stal′wart ness,** *n.*

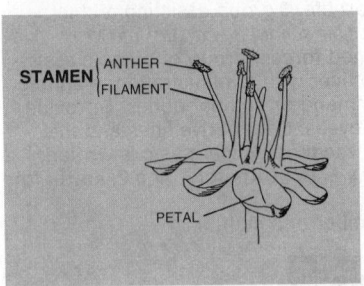

sta men (stā′mən), the part of a flower that contains the pollen. The stamens are surrounded by the petals. A stamen consists of a slender stem or filament which supports the anther. *n., pl.* **sta mens, stam i na** (stam′-ə nə).

stam i na (stam′ə nə), strength; endurance: *physical stamina, moral stamina.* *n.*

stam i nate (stam′ə nit *or* stam′ə nāt), having stamens but no pistils. *adj.*

stam mer (stam′ər), **1** hesitate in speaking; speak haltingly, as from nervousness, embarrassment, or fear. **2** say in this manner: *stammer an excuse.* **3** a stammering; stuttering: *He has a nervous stammer.* 1,2 *v.,* 3 *n.* —**stam′mer er,** *n.* —**stam′mer ing ly,** *adv.*

stamp (stamp), **1** a small piece of paper with a sticky back, put on letters, papers, parcels, etc., to show that a charge for mailing has been paid; postage stamp. **2** a similar piece of paper given to customers as a bonus, to be exchanged for goods; trading stamp. **3** any official mark or label required by law to be affixed to a paper or item to show that a fee, duty, tax, etc., has been paid. **4** put a stamp on: *stamp an official document, stamp a letter.* **5** bring down (one's foot) with force: *He stamped on the spider. He stamped his foot in anger.* **6** act of stamping. **7** pound, crush, trample, or tread: *She stamped out the fire.* **8** fix firmly or deeply: *an event stamped on one's memory.* **9** instrument that cuts, shapes, or impresses a design on (paper, wax, metal, etc.); thing that puts a mark on: *The stamp had her name on it.* **10** to mark with such an instrument: *She stamped the papers with the date.* **11** the mark made by such an instrument. **12** mill or machine that crushes rock, etc. **13** show to be of a certain quality or character; indicate: *Her speech stamps her as an educated woman.* **14** impression; marks: *a face bearing the stamp of suffering.* **15** kind; type: *Men of his stamp are rare.* 1-3,6,9,11,12,14,15 *n.,* 4,5,7,8,10,13 *v.* —**stamp′a-ble,** *adj.* —**stamp′er,** *n.* —**stamp′less,** *adj.*

stam pede (stam pēd′), **1** a sudden scattering or head-

long flight of a frightened herd of cattle, horses, etc.
2 any headlong flight of a large group: *a stampede of a panic-stricken crowd from a burning building.* **3** scatter or flee in a stampede. **4** a general rush: *a stampede to newly discovered gold fields.* **5** make a general rush. **6** cause to stampede. 1,2,4 *n.,* 3,5,6 *v.,* **stam ped ed, stam ped ing.** [*Stampede* comes from Mexican Spanish *estampida.*] —**stam ped′a ble,** *adj.* —**stam ped′er,** *n.* —**stam ped′ing ly,** *adv.*

stance (stans), **1** position of the feet of a player when making a stroke in golf or other games. **2** manner of standing; posture: *an erect stance. n.*

stanch[1] (stänch), **1** stop or check the flow of (blood, etc.). **2** stop the flow of blood from (a wound). *v.* Also, **staunch.** —**stanch′a ble,** *adj.* —**stanch′er,** *n.*

stanch[2] (stänch), staunch[2]. *adj.* —**stanch′ly,** *adv.* —**stanch′ness,** *n.*

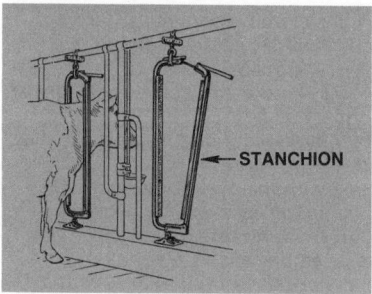

stanchions
for cattle. The closed one permits the cow to move her head but not to get away.

←— STANCHION

stan chion (stan′shən), an upright bar, post, or support (in a window, in a stall for cattle, on a ship, etc.). *n.*

stand (stand), **1** be upright on one's feet: *Don't stand if you are tired; sit down.* **2** have a certain height when upright: *He stands six feet in his socks.* **3** rise to one's feet: *We stood when the guest entered the room.* **4** be set upright; be placed; be located: *The box stands over there. Some food stood on the table.* **5** set upright or in an indicated position, condition, etc.: *Stand the box here.* **6** be in a certain place, rank, scale, etc.: *He stood first in his class.* **7** take or keep a certain position: *"Stand back!" called the policeman to the crowd.* **8** take a way of thinking or acting: *stand for fair play, stand on one's rights.* **9** be in a special condition: *She stands innocent of any wrong. The poor child stands in need of food and clothing. The door stood ajar.* **10** be unchanged; hold good; remain the same: *The rule against being late will stand.* **11** stay in place; last: *The old house has stood for a hundred years.* **12** be submitted to (a trial, test, ordeal, etc.); undergo: *stand a rigid examination.* **13** put up with; tolerate: *I can't stand that singer.* **14** bear; endure; withstand: *cloth that will stand wear. Those plants cannot stand cold and die in winter.* **15** INFORMAL. bear the expense of: *I'll stand you a dinner.* **16** take a certain course: *The ship stood out to sea.* **17** stop moving; halt; stop: *The cars stood and waited for the light to change. "Stand!" cried the sentry.* **18** act of standing. **19** a halt; stop. **20** a stop for defense, resistance, etc.: *We made a last stand against the enemy.* **21** place where a person stands; position: *The usher took her stand near the door.* **22** a moral position: *We took a strong stand against pumping sewage into the lake.* **23** Also, **stands,** *pl.* a raised place where people can sit or stand: *The mayor sat on the reviewing stand at the parade. The crowd in the stands cheered the winning team.* **24** something to put things on or in: *Leave your wet umbrella in the stand in the hall.* **25** stall, booth, table, etc., for a small business: *a newspaper stand.* **26** group of growing trees or plants: *stand of timber.* 1-17 *v.,* **stood, stand ing;** 18-26 *n.*

stand by, 1 be near. **2** help; support: *stand by a friend.* **3** be or get ready for use, action, etc.

stand for, 1 represent; mean: *What does the abbreviation St. stand for?* **2** be on the side of; take the part of; uphold: *Our school stands for fair play.* **3** INFORMAL. put up with: *The teacher said she would not stand for talking during class.*

stand off, keep off; keep away: *stand off an angry crowd.*

stand out, 1 project: *His ears stood out.* **2** be noticeable or prominent: *Certain facts stand out.*

stand over, be left for later consideration, treatment, or settlement.

stand up, 1 get to one's feet: *I stood up and began to speak.* **2** endure; last.

stand up for, take the part of; defend; support: *stand up for a friend.*

stand up to, meet or face boldly.

stan dard (stan′dərd), **1** anything taken as a basis of comparison; model: *Your work is not up to the class standard.* **2** of the accepted or normal size, amount, power, quality, etc.: *the standard rate of pay, a standard gauge.* **3** used as a standard; according to rule: *standard spelling, standard pronunciation.* **4** having recognized excellence or authority: *Use a standard encyclopedia to look up these subjects.* **5** flag, emblem, or symbol: *The dragon was the standard of China.* **6** an upright support: *The floor lamp has a long standard.* 1,5,6 *n.,* 2-4 *adj.*

stan dard i za tion (stan′dər də zā′shən), a standardizing or a being standardized. *n.*

stan dard ize (stan′dər dīz), make standard in size, shape, weight, quality, strength, etc.: *Bicycle tires are standardized. v.,* **stan dard ized, stan dard iz ing.**

standard time, time officially adopted for a region or country.

stand by (stand′bī′), **1** person or thing that can be relied upon; chief support; ready resource. **2** person or thing held in reserve, especially as a possible replacement or substitute. *n., pl.* **stand bys.**

stand-in (stand′in′), **1** person whose work is standing in the place of a motion-picture actor or actress while the lights, camera, etc., are being arranged, or during scenes in which dangerous action occurs. **2** person or thing that takes the place of another; substitute. *n.*

stand ing (stan′ding), **1** position; reputation: *a person of good standing.* **2** duration: *a family feud of long standing.* **3** straight up; erect: *standing timber.* **4** done from an erect position: *a standing jump.* **5** established; permanent: *a standing invitation, a standing army.* **6** not flowing; stagnant: *standing water.* 1,2 *n.,* 3-6 *adj.*

Stan dish (stan′dish), **Miles,** 1584?-1656, the military leader of the colony at Plymouth, Massachusetts. *n.*

stand off ish (stand′ô′fish), reserved; aloof: *A cool, standoffish attitude does not help one make friends. adj.* —**stand′off′ish ly,** *adv.* —**stand′off′ish ness,** *n.*

stand pipe (stand′pīp′), a large, upright pipe or tower to hold water at a height great enough to provide pressure for a water system. *n.*

stand point (stand′point′), point of view; mental attitude. *n.*

stand still (stand′stil′), a complete stop; halt. *n.*

stank (stangk), a past tense of **stink.** *The dead fish stank. v.*

Stan ley (stan/lē), Sir **Henry Morton,** 1841-1904, British explorer in Africa. He found the Scottish missionary, David Livingstone, who had disappeared in Africa. *n.*

Stan ton (stan/tən), **1 Edwin M.,** 1814-1869, American statesman who was Secretary of War during the Civil War. **2 Elizabeth Cady,** 1815-1902, American leader in the movement for women's rights. *n.*

stan za (stan/zə), group of lines of poetry, usually four or more, arranged according to a fixed plan; verse of a poem: *They sang the first and last stanzas of "America."* *n., pl.* **stan zas.** [*Stanza* was borrowed from Italian *stanza.*]

staph y lo coc cus (staf/ə lə kok/əs), any of a group of spherical bacteria that bunch together in irregular masses. *n., pl.* **staph y lo coc ci** (staf/ə lə kok/sī).

WORD HISTORY

staphylococcus

Staphylococcus comes from Greek *staphylē,* meaning "bunch of grapes," and *kokkos,* meaning "a seed, a berry." The bacteria are called this because they form groups that look somewhat like bunches of grapes.

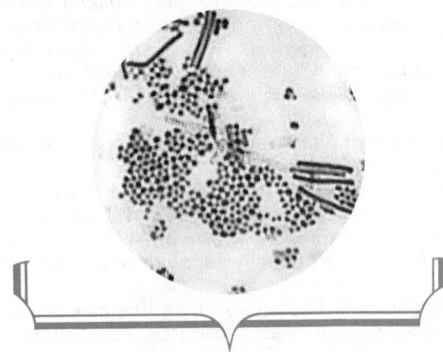

sta ple¹ (stā/pəl), **1** a U-shaped piece of metal with pointed ends. Staples are driven into wood or other material to hold hooks, wiring, insulation, etc. **2** a bent piece of wire used to hold together papers, parts of a book, etc. **3** fasten with a staple or staples. 1,2 *n.,* 3 *v.,* **sta pled, sta pling.**

sta ple² (stā/pəl), **1** the most important or principal article grown or manufactured in a place: *Cotton is the staple in many Southern states.* **2** any major article of commerce or trade; something of recognized quality or in constant demand. **3** chief element or material. **4** most important; principal: *Bread is a staple food.* **5** a raw material. **6** fiber of cotton or wool. **7** regularly produced in large quantities for the market. 1-3,5,6 *n.,* 4,7 *adj.*

sta pler (stā/plər), machine for fastening together papers, parts of a book, etc., with wire staples. *n.*

star (stär), **1** any of the heavenly bodies appearing as bright points in the sky at night. **2** any heavenly body that shines by its own light and is not a comet, meteor, or nebula. Stars are extremely hot bodies of gas which vary in size from smaller than the earth to several million times as large as the sun. **3** a plane figure having five points, or sometimes six, like these: ☆ ☆. **4** thing having or suggesting this shape. **5** asterisk (*). **6** mark with an asterisk. **7** person having brilliant qualities: *an athletic*

star. **8** a famous person in some art, profession, etc., especially one who plays the lead in a performance: *a movie star, an opera star.* **9** chief; best; leading; excellent: *the star player on the team.* **10** be prominent; be a leading performer; excel: *She has starred in many motion pictures.* **11** to present as a star. **12** fate; fortune. 1-5,7,8,12 *n.,* 6,10,11 *v.,* **starred, star ring;** 9 *adj.*

star board (stär/bərd), **1** the right side of a ship, boat, or aircraft when facing forward. **2** on the right side of a ship, boat, or aircraft. 1 *n.,* 2 *adj.*

starch (stärch), **1** a white, tasteless food substance. Potatoes, wheat, rice, and corn contain much starch. **2** preparation of this substance used to stiffen clothes, curtains, etc. **3** stiffen (clothes, curtains, etc.) with starch: *starch curtains.* **4** a stiff, formal manner; stiffness. 1,2,4 *n.,* 3 *v.* —**starch/less,** *adj.* —**starch/like/,** *adj.*

starch i ness (stär/chē nis), starchy condition or quality. *n.*

starch y (stär/chē), **1** like starch; containing starch. **2** stiffened with starch. **3** stiff in manner; formal. *adj.,* **starch i er, starch i est.** —**starch/i ly,** *adv.*

star dom (stär/dəm), **1** a being a star actor or performer. **2** star actors or performers as a group. *n.*

stare (ster *or* star), **1** look long and directly with the eyes wide open: *The children stared at the toys in the window.* **2** a long and direct look with the eyes wide open: *The doll's eyes were set in an unwinking stare.* 1 *v.,* **stared, star ing;** 2 *n.* —**star/er,** *n.* —**star/ing ly,** *adv.*

stare down, confuse or embarrass by staring.

star fish (stär/fish/), a star-shaped sea animal with a flattened body. Starfish are not fish. *n., pl.* **star fish es** or **star fish.**

starfish
about 4 in.
(10 cm.) across

star gaze (stär/gāz/), **1** gaze at the stars. **2** be absent-minded; daydream. *v.,* **star gazed, star gaz ing.**

stark (stärk), **1** downright; complete: *That fool is talking stark nonsense.* **2** entirely; completely: *The boys went swimming stark naked.* **3** stiff: *The dog lay stark in death.* **4** bare; barren; desolate: *a stark landscape.* 1,3,4 *adj.,* 2 *adv.* —**stark/ly,** *adv.* —**stark/ness,** *n.*

star less (stär/lis), without stars; without starlight. *adj.* —**star/less ly,** *adv.* —**star/less ness,** *n.*

star let (stär/lit), a young actress who is being trained for leading roles in motion pictures. *n.*

star light (stär/līt/), light from the stars. *n.*

star like (stär/līk/), **1** shaped like a star: *pattern of star-like snowflakes.* **2** shining like a star. *adj.*

star ling (stär/ling), a common European and American bird with glossy, greenish-black or brownish-black feathers. Starlings nest about buildings and fly in large flocks. *n.*

star lit (stär/lit/), lighted by the stars: *a starlit night. adj.*

starred (stärd), **1** full of or decorated with stars. **2** marked with a star or asterisk. **3** presented as a star actor or performer. *adj.*

star ry (stär/ē), **1** lighted by stars; containing many

stars: *a starry sky.* **2** shining like stars: *starry eyes. adj.,*
star ri er, star ri est. —star′ri ly, *adv.* **—star′ri ness,** *n.*
Stars and Stripes, the flag of the United States.
star-span gled (stär′spang′gəld), sprinkled with stars.
adj.
Star-Spangled Banner, 1 the national anthem of the
United States. The words were composed by Francis
Scott Key during the War of 1812. **2** flag of the United
States; Stars and Stripes.
Star Wars, INFORMAL. Strategic Defense Initiative.
start (stärt), **1** begin to move, go, or act: *The train started
on time.* **2** begin: *start reading a book, start in business,
start at the beginning.* **3** set going; put into action: *start an
automobile, start a fire.* **4** a setting in motion: *We pushed
the car to give the motor a start.* **5** a beginning to move,
go, or act: *see a race from start to finish.* **6** move suddenly: *He started in surprise.* **7** a sudden movement; jerk: *I
awoke with a start.* **8** come, rise, or spring out suddenly:
Tears started from the baby's eyes. **9** a beginning ahead of
others; advantage: *The fox had a mile start over the
hounds.* **10** place, line, etc., where a race begins.
11 rouse: *start a rabbit.* **12** make or become loose: *The
huge waves had started some of the ship's bolts.* 1-3,6,8,
11,12 *v.,* 4,5,7,9,10 *n.*
start in, start out, or **start up,** begin to do something.
start er (stär′tər), **1** person or thing that starts. **2** an
electric motor for starting an internal-combustion engine. **3** person who gives the signal for starting. **4** the
first in a series of things: *This request was only a start-
er. n.*
star tle (stär′tl), **1** frighten suddenly; surprise: *The dog
jumped at the girl and startled her.* **2** move suddenly in fear
or surprise. *v.,* **star tled, star tling. —star′tler,** *n.*
star tling (stärt′ling), surprising; frightening: *startling
tales. adj.* **—star tling ly,** *adv.*
star va tion (stär vā′shən), **1** a starving: *Starvation of
prisoners is barbarous.* **2** suffering from extreme hunger;
being starved: *Starvation caused his death. n.*
starve (stärv), **1** die because of hunger. **2** suffer severely
because of hunger. **3** weaken or kill with hunger: *They
starved the enemy into surrendering.* **4** INFORMAL. feel very
hungry. **5** have a strong desire or craving. *v.,* **starved,
starv ing.** [*Starve* comes from Old English *steorfan,*
meaning "to die."] **—starv′er,** *n.*
starve for, suffer from lack of: *That lonely child is starving for affection.*
starve ling (stärv′ling), person or animal that is suffering from lack of food. *n.*
stash (stash), INFORMAL. hide or put away for safekeeping or future use. *v.*
state (stāt), **1** situation in which a person or thing is;
condition of being: *The house is in a bad state of repair.
He is in a state of poor health.* **2** a particular condition of
mind or feeling: *a state of uncertainty, a state of excitement.* **3** the physical condition of a material with regard
to its structure, composition, or form. A substance may
exist in a solid, liquid, or gaseous state. Ice is water in
a solid state. **4** group of people occupying a given area
and organized under a government; commonwealth;
nation. **5** Often, **State.** one of several organized political
groups of people which together form a nation: *The
state of Alaska is one of the United States.* **6** territory of
a state. **7** the civil government; highest civil authority:
affairs of state. **8** of a state: *a state road, state police.*
9 position in life; rank: *a person of humble state.* **10** tell
in speech or writing; express; say: *State your opinion
of the new school rules.* **11** specify; fix; settle: *to state a
price.* **12** high style of living; dignity; pomp: *The royal
family lived in great state.* **13** with ceremony; of ceremony:

a hat	i it	oi oil	ch child	a in about
ā age	ī ice	ou out	ng long	e in taken
ä far	o hot	u cup	sh she	i in pencil
e let	ō open	u̇ put	th thin	o in lemon
ē equal	ô order	ü rule	ŦH then	u in circus
ėr term			zh measure	

ə = { a in about / e in taken / i in pencil / o in lemon / u in circus }

state occasions, state robes. 1-7,9,12 *n.,* 10,11 *v.,* **stat ed,
stat ing;** 8,13 *adj.* **—stat′a ble, state′a ble,** *adj.*
lie in state, lie in a coffin so as to be seen formally and
publicly before being buried: *The dead queen lay in state.*
stat ed (stā′tid), **1** put into words; said; told: *the stated
facts of a case.* **2** specified; fixed; settled: *School begins
daily at a stated time. adj.*
state hood (stāt′hud), condition of being a state, especially a state of the United States. *n.*
state house or **State house** (stāt′hous′), building in
which the legislature of a state meets; capitol of a
state. *n.*
state less (stāt′lis), not belonging to any country; having
no citizenship or nationality: *a stateless refugee. adj.*
state li ness (stāt′lē nis), stately quality or character. *n.*
state ly (stāt′lē), having dignity; imposing; grand; majestic: *The Capitol at Washington is a stately building. adj.,*
state li er, state li est.
state ment (stāt′mənt), **1** something stated; report;
account: *Her statement was correct.* **2** act of stating; manner of stating something: *The statement of an idea helps
me to remember it.* **3** summary of an account, showing the
amount owed or due: *a bank statement.* **4** a single instruction given to a computer; command. *n.*
Stat en Island (stat′n), island in New York Bay, south
of Manhattan. It is part of New York City.
state room (stāt′rüm′ or stāt′rum′), a private room on a
ship or railroad train. *n.*
state side (stāt′sīd′), from or in the United States: *Americans abroad are happy to receive stateside news. adj.*
states man (stāts′mən), person skilled in the management of public or national affairs. *n., pl.* **states men.**
states man like (stāts′mən līk′), having the qualities of
a statesman. *adj.*
states man ship (stāts′mən ship), the qualities of a
statesman; skill in the management of public or national
affairs. *n.*
states' rights, powers belonging to the individual
states of the United States, under the Constitution. The
doctrine of states' rights holds that all powers which the
Constitution does not specifically delegate to the federal
government and does not specifically deny to the individual states belong to the states.
states wom an (stāts′wum′ən), a woman skilled in the
management of public or national affairs. *n., pl.* **states-
wom en.**
state wide (stāt′wīd′), covering an entire state; over all
of a state. *adj.*
stat ic (stat′ik), **1** at rest; standing still: *Civilization does
not remain static, but changes constantly.* **2** having to do
with bodies at rest or with forces that balance each
other. **3** acting by weight without producing motion: *static pressure.* **4** having to do with stationary electrical
charges. Static electricity can be produced by rubbing a
glass rod with a silk cloth. **5** electrical disturbances in
the air caused by electrical storms, etc. **6** noises and
other interference with radio and television reception
caused by such electrical disturbances. 1-4 *adj.,* 5,6 *n.*
stat ics (stat′iks), branch of mechanics that deals with
bodies at rest or with forces that balance each other. *n.*
sta tion (stā′shən), **1** place to stand in; place which a
person is appointed to occupy in the performance of

some duty; assigned post: *The policeman took his station at the corner.* **2** building or place used for a definite purpose. A place where soldiers live, a harbor for ships, the police headquarters of a district, and a place for raising sheep or cattle are all called stations. **3** a regular stopping place: *She met her at the bus station.* **4** place or equipment for sending out or receiving programs, messages, etc., by radio or television. **5** assign a station to; place: *She stationed herself just outside the main doorway to collect tickets. The soldier was stationed at Fort Hays.* **6** social position; rank: *A serf was a person of humble station in life.* 1-4,6 *n.,* 5 *v.*

sta tion ar y (stā′shə ner′ē), **1** having a fixed station or place; not movable: *A factory engine is stationary.* **2** standing still; not moving: *A parked car is stationary.* **3** not changing in size, number, activity, etc.: *The population of this town has been stationary for ten years at about 5000 people. adj.*

sta tion er (stā′shə nər), person who sells paper, pens, pencils, ink, etc. *n.*

sta tion er y (stā′shə ner′ē), writing materials such as paper, cards, and envelopes. *n.*

sta tion mas ter (stā′shən mas′tər), person in charge of a railroad station. *n.*

station wagon, automobile with a rear door for loading and unloading and seats in the rear that can be folded down, for use as a light truck.

sta tis tic (stə tis′tik), **1** statistical. **2** any value, item, etc., used in statistics: *an important statistic.* 1 *adj.,* 2 *n.*

sta tis ti cal (stə tis′tə kəl), of statistics; consisting of or based on statistics. *adj.*

sta tis ti cal ly (stə tis′tik lē), in a statistical manner; according to statistics. *adv.*

stat is ti cian (stat′ə stish′ən), an expert in statistics; person who prepares statistics. *n.*

sta tis tics (stə tis′tiks), **1** *pl. in form and use.* numerical facts about people, the weather, business conditions, etc. Statistics are collected and classified systematically. **2** *pl. in form, sing. in use.* science of collecting and using such facts. *n.*

stat u ar y (stach′ü er′ē), **1** statues. **2** art of making statues. *n., pl.* **stat u ar ies.**

statue of Moses
by Michelangelo

stat ue (stach′ü), image of a person or animal carved in stone or wood, cast in bronze, or modeled in clay or wax: *Nearly every city has a statue of some famous person. n.* —**stat′ue less,** *adj.* —**stat′ue like′,** *adj.*

Statue of Liberty, a huge statue of a woman holding aloft a lighted torch, given to the United States by France. It stands on an island in New York Bay.

stat u esque (stach′ü esk′), like a statue in dignity, formal grace, or classic beauty. *adj.* —**stat′u esque′ly,** *adv.* —**stat′u esque′ness,** *n.*

stat u ette (stach′ü et′), a small statue. *n.*

stat ure (stach′ər), **1** height: *a young woman of average stature.* **2** physical, mental, or moral growth; accomplishment: *Thomas Jefferson was a man of great stature among his countrymen. n.*

sta tus (stā′təs *or* stat′əs), **1** social or professional standing; position; rank: *to lose status, to seek status. What is her status in the government?* **2** state; condition: *Diplomats are interested in the status of world affairs. n.*

status quo (kwō), the way things are; existing state of affairs.

stat ute (stach′üt), **1** law enacted by a legislative body: *The statutes for the United States are made by Congress.* **2** a formally established rule; law; decree: *the statutes of a university. n.*

statute mile, mile (def. 1).

stat u to ry (stach′ü tôr′ē), **1** having to do with a statute. **2** fixed by statute. **3** punishable by statute. *adj.*

St. Au gus tine (sānt ô′gə stēn′), seacoast city in NE Florida. It is the oldest city in the United States, founded by the Spanish in 1565.

staunch¹ (stônch), stanch¹. *v.*

staunch² (stônch), **1** strong or firm: *staunch walls, a staunch defense.* **2** loyal; steadfast: *staunch friends, a staunch supporter of the law.* **3** watertight: *a staunch boat. adj.* Also, **stanch.** —**staunch′ly,** *adv.* —**staunch′ness,** *n.*

stave (stāv), **1** one of the curved pieces of wood that form the sides of a barrel, tub, etc. **2** stick or staff. **3** break a hole in (a barrel, boat, etc.). **4** become smashed or broken in. **5** verse or stanza of a poem or song. **6** the musical staff. **7** furnish with staves. 1,2,5,6 *n.,* 3,4,7 *v.,* staved *or* stove, stav ing. —**stav′a ble, stave′a ble,** *adj.* —**stave′less,** *adj.*

stave off, put off; keep back; delay or prevent: *The lost campers ate birds' eggs to stave off starvation.*

staves (stāvz), **1** a plural of **staff** (defs. 1 and 2). **2** plural of **stave.** *n.*

stay¹ (stā), **1** continue to be as indicated; remain: *Stay still. The cat stayed out all night. Shall I go or stay?* **2** live for a while; dwell: *She is staying with her aunt for a few weeks.* **3** a staying; a stop; time spent: *a pleasant stay in the country.* **4** stop; halt: *We have no time to stay.* **5** pause; wait: *Time and tide stay for no man.* **6** put an end to for a while; satisfy: *He ate some cheese to stay his hunger.* **7** put off; hold back; delay; restrain; check: *The teacher stayed judgment till he could hear both sides.* **8** a check; restraint: *a stay on one's activity.* **9** a delay in carrying out the order of a court: *The judge granted a stay of execution.* **10** to last; endure: *The runner was unable to stay to the end of the race.* 1,2,4-7,10 *v.,* 3,8,9 *n.* —**stay′a ble,** *adj.* —**stay′er,** *n.*

stay put, INFORMAL. remain where or as placed; remain fixed: *We stayed put in the tent until the rain stopped.*

stay² (stā), **1** a support; prop; brace: *The oldest child was the family's stay.* **2** strengthen mentally or spiritually; fix or rest in dependence or reliance; hold up; support; prop. **3** **stays,** *pl.* corset, especially a stiffened one. 1,3 *n.,* 2 *v.*

stay³ (stā), **1** a strong rope, often of wire, which supports the mast of a ship. **2** any rope or chain attached to something to steady it. **3** support or secure with stays. 1,2 *n.,* 3 *v.*

staying power, power to hold out and not give in even though weakened or tired; power or will to endure.

stay sail (stā′sāl′ *or* stā′səl), a sail fastened on a stay or rope. *n.*

std., standard.

stead (sted), place: *Our regular babysitter could not come, but sent her brother in her stead. n.*

stand in good stead, be of advantage or service to: *Her* *ability to swim stood her in good stead when the boat upset.*

stead fast (sted′fast′), firmly fixed; constant; not moving or changing: *a steadfast friend, a steadfast gaze. adj.* —**stead′fast′ly,** *adv.* —**stead′fast′ness,** *n.*

stead i ly (sted′l ē), in a steady manner; firmly; uniformly. *adv.*

stead i ness (sted′ē nis), steady character, quality, or condition. *n.*

stead y (sted′ē), **1** changing little; uniform; regular: *He is making steady progress at school.* **2** firmly fixed; firm; not swaying or shaking: *This post is steady as a rock. Hold the ladder steady.* **3** not easily excited; calm: *steady nerves.* **4** steadfast; firm: *steady friendship.* **5** having good habits; reliable: *He is a steady young man.* **6** make steady; keep steady: *Steady the ladder while I climb to the roof.* **7** become steady: *Our sails filled as the wind steadied from the east.* **8** INFORMAL. one's regular sweetheart. **1-5** *adj.,* **stead i er, stead i est; 6,7** *v.,* **stead ied, stead y ing; 8** *n.,* *pl.* **stead ies.**

go steady, have an agreement with a person to date only that person.

steak (stāk), **1** slice of meat or fish for broiling or frying. *Steak* often means *beefsteak.* **2** finely ground meat shaped and cooked somewhat like a steak: *hamburger steak. n.*

steal (stēl), **1** take (something) that does not belong to one; take dishonestly: *Robbers stole the money.* **2** take, get, or do secretly: *She stole time from her lessons to read a story.* **3** take, get, or win by art, charm, etc.: *The baby stole our hearts.* **4** move secretly or quietly: *She stole softly out of the house.* **5** act of stealing. **6** INFORMAL. something obtained at a very low cost or with very little effort: *This table is such a bargain it's a steal.* **7** (in baseball) run to (second base, third base, or home plate) as the pitcher throws the ball to the catcher. **1-4,7** *v.,* **stole, sto len, steal ing; 5,6** *n.* —**steal′a ble,** *adj.* —**steal′er,** *n.*

stealth (stelth), secret or sly action: *He obtained the letter by stealth, taking it while nobody was in the room. n.*

stealth i ly (stel′thə lē), in a stealthy manner; secretly; slyly. *adv.*

stealth i ness (stel′thē nis), condition of being stealthy. *n.*

stealth y (stel′thē), done in a secret manner; secret; sly: *The cat crept in a stealthy way toward the bird. adj.,* **stealth i er, stealth i est.**

steam (stēm), **1** the invisible vapor or gas into which water is changed when heated to the boiling point. Steam may be used to heat homes or drive turbines to generate electricity. **2** the white cloud or mist formed by the condensation of this invisible vapor or gas. **3** give off steam: *The cup of coffee was steaming.* **4** become covered with steam: *The windshield had completely steamed up inside the heated car.* **5** rise in the form of steam. **6** move by steam: *The ship steamed off.* **7** cook, soften, or freshen by steam: *The cook steamed the plum pudding.* **8** INFORMAL. power; energy; force: *She has worked hard all day and is running out of steam.* **9** of, using, or consisting of steam; produced or worked by steam: *steam power. Many large office buildings and apartments have steam heat.* **1,2,8** *n.,* **3-7** *v.,* **9** *adj.* [*Steam* comes from Old English *stēam.*] —**steam′less,** *adj.* —**steam′like′,** *adj.*

let off steam, INFORMAL. relieve one's feelings.

steam boat (stēm′bōt′), boat moved by steam. *n.*

steam engine, engine worked by the action of steam under pressure. The steam, generated in a boiler, expands so that it can push a piston in a cylinder. Steam engines were used to drive locomotives, ships, and large machines.

steam er (stē′mər), **1** steamboat or steamship run by steam. **2** container in which something is steamed or kept warm. *n.*

a hat	**i** it	**oi** oil	**ch** child	a in about
ā age	**ī** ice	**ou** out	**ng** long	e in taken
ä far	**o** hot	**u** cup	**sh** she	**ə =** i in pencil
e let	**ō** open	**u̇** put	**th** thin	o in lemon
ē equal	**ô** order	**ü** rule	**TH** then	u in circus
ėr term			**zh** measure	

steam fitter, person who installs and repairs steam pipes, radiators, boilers, etc.

steam iron, an electric iron which releases steam through holes in its undersurface to dampen cloth while pressing it.

steam roll er (stēm′rō′lər), **1** a heavy roller, formerly run by steam but now usually by an internal-combustion engine, used to crush and level materials in making roads. **2** means of crushing opposition. **3** to crush: *to steamroller all political opposition.* **1,2** *n.,* **3** *v.*

steam ship (stēm′ship′), ship moved by steam. *n.*

steam shovel, machine for digging, formerly run by steam but now usually by an internal-combustion engine; power shovel.

steam y (stē′mē), **1** of or like steam: *a steamy vapor.* **2** full of steam; giving off steam; rising in steam: *a steamy room. adj.,* **steam i er, steam i est.** —**steam′i ly,** *adv.* —**steam′i ness,** *n.*

steed (stēd), **1** horse, especially a riding horse. **2** a high-spirited horse. *n.*

steel (stēl), **1** an alloy of iron and carbon. Steel has greater hardness and flexibility than cast iron and is used for tools and machinery. **2** something made from steel, such as a sword, a rod of steel for sharpening knives, etc. **3** like or made of steel. **4** to point, edge, or cover with steel. **5** make hard or strong like steel: *They steeled their hearts against the sufferings of the poor. I tried to steel myself against a possible failure.* **6** steellike hardness or strength: *nerves of steel.* **1,2,6** *n.,* **3** *adj.,* **4,5** *v.* —**steel′less,** *adj.* —**steel′like′,** *adj.*

steel wool, pad of long, fine steel threads used in cleaning or polishing surfaces.

steel work er (stēl′wėr′kər), person who works in a place where steel is made. *n.*

steel works (stēl′wėrks′), place where steel is made. *n. pl. or sing.*

steel y (stē′lē), **1** made of steel. **2** like steel in color, strength, or hardness. *adj.,* **steel i er, steel i est.** —**steel′i ness,** *n.*

steamboats

steel yard (stēl′yärd *or* stil′yərd), scale for weighing, having arms of unequal length. The longer one has a movable weight and is marked in units of weight; the shorter one has a hook for holding the object to be weighed. *n.*

steep[1] (stēp), **1** having a sharp slope; almost straight up and down: *The hill is steep.* **2** too high; unreasonable: *a steep price. adj.* [*Steep*[1] comes from Old English *stēap.*] —**steep′ly,** *adv.* —**steep′ness,** *n.*

steep[2] (stēp), **1** soak: *Let the tea steep in boiling water for five minutes.* **2** involve deeply in something: *to steep oneself in history. v.* [*Steep*[2] comes from Middle English *stepen,* which is probably related to Old English *stēap,* meaning "a bowl."] —**steep′er,** *n.*

steeped in, filled with; absorbed in: *ruins stepped in gloom, a mind steeped in hatred.*

steep en (stē′pən), make or become steep or steeper. *v.*

stee ple (stē′pəl), **1** a high tower on a church. Steeples usually have spires. **2** spire on top of the tower or roof of a church or similar building. *n.* —**stee′ple like′,** *adj.*

stee ple chase (stē′pəl chās′), a horse race over a course having ditches, hedges, and other obstacles. *n.*

stee ple jack (stē′pəl jak′), person who climbs steeples, tall chimneys, or the like, to make repairs, etc. *n.*

steer[1] (stir), **1** guide the course of: *steer a ship, steer a sled, steer an automobile.* **2** be guided: *This car steers easily.* **3** set and follow: *She steered a middle course during the debate, agreeing with speakers on both sides.* **4** direct one's way or course: *Steer away from trouble. Steer for the harbor v.* —**steer′a ble,** *adj.* —**steer′er,** *n.*

steer clear of, keep away from; avoid.

steer[2] (stir), a young male of beef cattle, usually two to four years old, that cannot father young. *n.*

steer age (stir′ij), **1** the part of a passenger ship occupied by passengers traveling at the cheapest rate. **2** act of steering. *n.*

steering wheel, wheel that is turned to steer an automobile, ship, etc.

steers man (stirz′mən), person who steers a boat or ship. *n., pl.* **steers men.**

steg o sau rus (steg′ə sôr′əs), a plant-eating dinosaur of great size, with bony armor in the form of plates and spikes along the back and tail. *n., pl.* **steg o sau ri** (steg′ə sôr′ī). [*Stegosaurus* can be traced back to Greek *stegos,* meaning "roof," and *sauros,* meaning "lizard."]

stein (stīn), a mug for beer. *n.*

WORD HISTORY

stein

Stein was probably shortened from German *Steingut,* meaning "stoneware." In German, *Stein* means "stone" and *Gut* means "goods, ware." A stein is called this because it was originally made of stoneware.

Stein beck (stīn′bek), **John,** 1902-1968, American novelist. *n.*

Stein metz (stīn′mets), **Charles P.,** 1865-1923, American scientist and engineer, born in Germany. *n.*

stel lar (stel′ər), **1** of the stars or a star; like a star. **2** chief: *a stellar role. adj.*

stel late (stel′āt), spreading out like the points of a star; star-shaped. *adj.* —**stel′late ly,** *adv.*

St. El mo's fire (sānt el′mōz), ball of light due to a discharge of atmospheric electricity, often seen on masts of ships, towers, etc. [*St. Elmo's fire* gets its name from *St. Elmo,* a Syrian martyr of the A.D. 200's who was considered a patron saint of sailors.]

stem[1] (stem), **1** the main part of a plant, usually above the ground. The stem supports the branches, leaves, flowers, etc. **2** the part of a flower, a fruit, or a leaf that joins it to the plant or tree. **3** remove the stem from (a leaf, fruit, etc.). **4** anything like the stem of a plant: *the stem of a goblet, the stem of a pipe.* **5** the part of a word to which endings are added and in which changes are made. *Run* is the stem of *running, runner, ran,* etc. **6** the bow or front end of a boat. 1,2,4-6 *n.,* 3 *v.,* **stemmed, stem ming.** —**stem′like′,** *adj.*

from stem to stern, 1 from one end (of a ship) to the other. **2** completely; thoroughly.

stem from, come from; have as a source or cause: *The difficulty stems from their failure to plan properly.*

stem[2] (stem), **1** dam up (a stream, river, etc.); stop; check. **2** make headway or progress against: *When you swim upstream you have to stem the current. v.,* **stemmed, stem ming.**

stem less (stem′lis), having no stem or no visible stem. *adj.*

stemmed (stemd), **1** having a stem. **2** having the stem removed. *adj.*

stench (stench), a very bad smell; stink: *the stench of a garbage dump, the stench of gas. n., pl.* **stench es.**

stegosaurus
about 18 ft.
(5.5 m.) long

sten cil (sten′səl), **1** a thin sheet of metal, paper, etc., having letters or designs cut through it. When it is laid on a surface and ink or color is spread on, these letters or designs are made on the surface. **2** the letters or designs made in this way. **3** mark, paint, or make with a stencil: *to stencil one's name on a box.* 1,2 *n.,* 3 *v.,* **sten ciled, sten cil ing** or **sten cilled, sten cil ling.**

ste nog ra pher (stə nog′rə fər), person whose work is taking dictation in shorthand and transcribing it, usually with a typewriter. *n.*

sten o graph ic (sten′ə graf′ik), **1** of stenography. **2** made by stenography. **3** using stenography. *adj.* —**sten′o graph′i cal ly,** *adv.*

ste nog ra phy (stə nog′rə fē), **1** method of rapid writing that uses symbols, abbreviations, etc.; shorthand. **2** act of writing in such symbols. *n.* [*Stenography* comes from Greek *stenos,* meaning "narrow," and the combining form *-graphy.*]

sten to ri an (sten tôr′ē ən), very loud or powerful in sound: *a stentorian voice. adj.* —**sten to′ri an ly,** *adv.*

step (step), **1** a movement made by lifting the foot and putting it down again in a new position; one motion of the leg in walking, running, dancing, etc. **2** distance covered by one such movement: *We were three steps away when she called us back.* **3** move the legs as in walking, running, dancing, etc.: *Step lively!* **4** a short distance; little way: *The school is only a step from our house.* **5** walk a short distance: *Step this way.* **6** way of walking, dancing, etc.: *a quick step, a dance with fancy steps.* **7** measure (off) by taking steps: *Step off the distance from the door to the window.* **8** put the foot down: *He stepped on a bug.* **9** sound made by putting the foot down: *I hear steps upstairs.* **10** a place for the foot in going up or coming down. A stair or a rung of a ladder is a step. **11** footprint:

I see steps in the mud. **12** action: *the first step toward peace.* **13** a degree in a scale; a grade in rank: *A colonel is three steps above a captain.* **14** stage in a gradual process, operation, etc.: *a step in a chemical experiment, a step in the growth of an insect.* **15** (in music) a degree of the staff or the scale. 1,2,4,6,9-15 *n.*, 3,5,7,8 *v.*, **stepped, step ping. —step′less,** *adj.* **—step′like′,** *adj.*

in step, 1 making one's steps fit those of another person or persons; at a uniform pace with others or in time with music. **2** making one's actions or ideas agree with those of another person or persons; in harmony or agreement.

keep step, move the same leg at the same time that another person does.

out of step, not in step; not at a uniform pace or in harmony with another or others.

step by step, little by little; slowly.

step down, 1 surrender or resign from an office or position. **2** lower by steps or degrees; decrease.

step in, intervene; take part.

step into, come into, acquire, or receive, especially without particular effort or by chance: *step into a fortune.*

step on it, INFORMAL. go faster; hurry up: *Please step on it or we'll be late.*

step out, INFORMAL. go out for entertainment.

step up, raise by steps or degrees; go faster, higher, etc.; increase: *step up the production of automobiles, step up the pressure in a boiler.*

take steps, adopt, put into effect, or carry out measures considered to be necessary, desirable, etc.: *The principal took steps to stop needless absence from school.*

watch one's step, be careful: *Watch your step when you ride down that steep hill on the bicycle.*

step-, *combining form.* related by the remarriage of a parent: *Stepfather = a father related by the remarriage of the mother.* [The form *step-* comes from Old English *stēop.*]

step broth er (step′bruᴛʜ′ər), a stepfather's or stepmother's son by a former marriage. *n.*

step-by-step (step′bī step′), progressing by stages; gradual. *adj.*

step child (step′chīld′), child of one's husband or wife by a former marriage. *n., pl.* **step chil dren** (step′chil′drən).

step daugh ter (step′dô′tər), daughter of one's husband or wife by a former marriage. *n.*

step fa ther (step′fä′ᴛʜər), man who has married one's mother after the death or divorce of one's father. *n.*

step lad der (step′lad′ər), ladder with flat steps instead of rungs. *n.*

step moth er (step′muᴛʜ′ər), woman who has married one's father after the death or divorce of one's mother. *n.*

step par ent (step′per′ənt *or* step′par′ənt), stepfather or stepmother. *n.*

steppe (step), **1** one of the vast, treeless plains in southeastern Europe and in Asia, especially as found in Russia. **2** a vast, treeless plain. *n.* [*Steppe* comes from Russian *step′.*]

step ping stone (step′ing stōn′), **1** stone or one of a line of stones in shallow water, a marshy place, or the like, used in crossing. **2** stone for use in mounting or ascending. **3** anything serving as a means of advancing or rising. *n.*

step sis ter (step′sis′tər), a stepfather's or stepmother's daughter by a former marriage. *n.*

step son (step′sun′), son of one's husband or wife by a former marriage. *n.*

-ster, suffix forming nouns. **1** person who _____s: *Trickster = a person who tricks or cheats.* **2** person who makes _____: *Punster = a person who makes puns.*

a hat	i it	oi oil	ch child		a in about	
ā age	ī ice	ou out	ng long		e in taken	
ä far	o hot	u cup	sh she	ə =	i in pencil	
e let	ō open	u̇ put	th thin		o in lemon	
ē equal	ô order	ü rule	ᴛʜ then		u in circus	
ėr term			zh measure			

ster e o (ster′ē ō *or* stir′ē ō), **1** stereophonic. **2** stereophonic equipment. 1 *adj.*, 2 *n., pl.* **ster e os.**

ster e o phon ic (ster′ē ə fon′ik *or* stir′ē ə fon′ik), giving the effect of lifelike sound by using two or more sets of equipment for recording or broadcasting and two or more sets of receiving equipment. Stereophonic sound has the same effects of depth and direction as the original sound. *adj.* [Stereophonic comes from Greek *stereos,* meaning "solid," and *phōnē,* meaning "sound."] **—ster′e o phon′i cal ly,** *adv.*

ster e op ti con (ster′ē op′tə kən *or* stir′ē op′tə kən), projector arranged to project two images upon a screen so that the image of one object or scene gradually passes into that of another with dissolving effect. *n.*

ster e o scope (ster′ē ə skōp′ *or* stir′ē ə skōp′), instrument through which two pictures of the same object or scene, taken from slightly different angles, are viewed, one by each eye. The object or scene thus viewed appears to have three dimensions. *n.*

ster e o scop ic (ster′ē ə skop′ik *or* stir′ē ə skop′ik), of stereoscopes. *adj.* **—ster′e o scop′i cal ly,** *adv.*

ster e o type (ster′ē ə tīp′ *or* stir′ē ə tīp′), **1** a printing plate cast from a mold. **2** a fixed form, character, image, etc.; something stereotyped; conventional type. Long John Silver, in Stevenson's *Treasure Island,* is the stereotype of a pirate. **3** give a fixed or settled form to. 1,2 *n.* 3 *v.*, **ster e o typed, ster e o typ ing. —ster′e o typ′er,** *n.*

ster e o typed (ster′ē ə tīpt′ *or* stir′ē ə tīpt′), **1** cast in the form of, or printed from, a stereotype. **2** fixed or settled in form; conventional: *"It gives me great pleasure to be with you tonight" is a stereotyped opening for a speech. adj.*

ster ile (ster′əl), **1** free from living germs: *Bandages should always be kept sterile.* **2** not producing seed, offspring, crops, etc.; not fertile; barren: *sterile land, a sterile cow. adj.* **—ster′ile ly,** *adv.* **—ster′ile ness,** *n.*

ste ril i ty (stə ril′ə tē), sterile condition or character; barrenness. *n.*

ster i li za tion (ster′ə lə zā′shən), a sterilizing or a being sterilized: *the sterilization of dishes by boiling them. n.*

ster i lize (ster′ə līz), **1** make free from living germs: *The water had to be sterilized by boiling to make it fit to drink.* **2** make incapable of bearing offspring. *v.,* **ster i lized, ster i liz ing. —ster′i liz′a ble,** *adj.*

ster i liz er (ster′ə lī′zər), any device for killing germs. *n.*

ster ling (ster′ling), **1** of standard quality for silver; containing 92.5 percent pure silver. *Sterling* is stamped on solid silver knives, forks, etc. **2** sterling silver or things made of it. **3** made of sterling silver. **4** genuine; excellent; dependable; reliable: *a person of sterling character.* **5** British money, especially the pound as the standard British monetary unit in international trade: *to pay in sterling.* **6** of British money; payable in British money. 1,3,4,6 *adj.,* 2,5 *n.*

sterling silver, solid silver; silver 92.5 percent pure.

stern¹ (stern), **1** harshly firm; hard; strict: *a stern parent. Our teacher's stern frown silenced us.* **2** very severe; rigorous; harsh: *stern necessity. adj.* **—stern′ly,** *adv.* **—stern′ness,** *n.*

stern² (stern), the rear part of a ship, boat, or aircraft. *n.*

ster nal (ster′nl), of the breastbone or sternum. *adj.*

ster num (stėr′nəm), breastbone. *n.*

steth o scope (steth′ə skōp), instrument used by doctors to hear the sounds produced in the lungs, heart, etc. *n.* [*Stethoscope* is from French *stéthoscope,* which came from Greek *stēthos,* meaning "chest," and *-skopion,* meaning "instrument for viewing."]

stethoscope—veterinarian using a stethoscope

ste ve dore (stē′və dôr), person who loads and unloads ships. *n.* [*Stevedore* comes from Spanish *estibador,* and can be traced back to Latin *stipare,* meaning "to pack together."]

Ste ven son (stē′vən sən), **Robert Louis,** 1850-1894, Scottish author of novels, poems, and essays. *n.*

stew (stü *or* styü), **1** cook by slow boiling: *The cook stewed the chicken for a long time.* **2** food cooked by slow boiling: *beef stew.* **3** INFORMAL. worry; fret. **4** INFORMAL. state of worry; fret: *They were in a stew over their lost luggage.* 1,3 *v.,* 2,4 *n.* —**stew′a ble,** *adj.*

stew ard (stü′ərd *or* styü′ərd), **1** person who has charge of the food and table service for a club, restaurant, etc. **2** man employed on an airplane, a ship, etc., to look after passengers; flight attendant. **3** person who manages another's property or finances. *n.* [*Steward* comes from Old English *stigweard.* In Old English, *stig* meant "hall" and *weard* meant "keeper."]

stew ard ess (stü′ər dis *or* styü′ər dis), woman employed on an airplane, a ship, etc., to look after passengers; flight attendant. *n., pl.* **stew ard ess es.**

stew ard ship (stü′ərd ship *or* styü′ərd ship), position or work of a steward. *n.*

St. George's, capital of Grenada.

St. He le na (sānt hə lē′nə), British island in the S Atlantic. Napoleon I was exiled there from 1815 until his death in 1821.

St. Hel ens (sānt hel′ənz), **Mount,** volcano in the Cascade Range in W Washington. It erupted in 1980, causing great damage. 8364 feet (2549 meters) high.

stick[1] (stik), **1** a long, thin piece of wood: *Put some sticks on the fire.* **2** such a piece of wood shaped for a special use: *a walking stick.* **3** a slender branch or twig of a tree or shrub, especially when cut or broken off. **4** something like a stick in shape: *a stick of candy.* **5** INFORMAL. a stiff, awkward, or stupid person. **6** device used in certain small airplanes to control the ailerons and elevators. **7 the sticks,** *pl.* INFORMAL. the outlying or undeveloped districts; backwoods. *n.* —**stick′like′,** *adj.*

stick[2] (stik), **1** pierce with a pointed instrument; thrust (a point) into; stab: *She stuck a fork into the potato.* **2** kill by stabbing or piercing. **3** fasten by thrusting the point or end into or through something: *He stuck a flower in his buttonhole.* **4** put into a position: *Don't stick your head out of the window.* **5** be thrust; extend: *My arms stick out of my coat sleeves.* **6** fasten; attach: *Stick a stamp on the letter.* **7** keep close: *The puppy stuck to my heels.* **8** be or become fastened; become fixed; be at a standstill: *Our car stuck in the mud. Two pages of the book stuck together.*

9 bring to a stop: *Our work was stuck by the breakdown of the machinery.* **10** hold one's position; hold fast; cling: *She stuck on the horse's back. Let's stick to the task until we've finished it.* **11** puzzle: *That problem in arithmetic stuck me.* **12** SLANG. cheat; swindle. **13** take advantage of; burden: *I got stuck washing dishes when everyone else went out.* *v.,* **stuck, stick ing.** —**stick′a ble,** *adj.*

stick around, INFORMAL. stay or wait nearby.

stick at, hesitate or stop for: *He sticks at nothing to get his own way.*

stick by *or* **stick to,** remain faithful to; refuse to desert: *She sticks by her friends when they need her help.*

stick up, SLANG. hold up; rob.

stick up for, INFORMAL. stand up for; support; defend.

stick er (stik′ər), **1** a gummed label. **2** thorn or bur. *n.*

stick i ly (stik′ə lē), in a sticky manner. *adv.*

stick i ness (stik′ē nis), condition of being sticky. *n.*

stick le (stik′əl), make objections about trifles; contend or insist stubbornly. *v.,* **stick led, stick ling.**

stick le back (stik′əl bak′), a small, scaleless fish with a row of sharp spines on the back. The male builds an elaborate nest for the eggs and guards them carefully. *n., pl.* **stick le backs** *or* **stick le back.**

stick ler (stik′lər), **1** person who contends or insists stubbornly, sometimes over trifles: *a stickler for accuracy.* **2** something that puzzles: *That's a real stickler; I don't know the answer. n.*

stick pin (stik′pin′), pin worn in a necktie for ornament. *n.*

stick up (stik′up′), SLANG. robbery; holdup. *n.*

stick y (stik′ē), **1** apt to stick: *sticky candy.* **2** covered with a layer of material that will stick: *Adhesive tape is sticky.* **3** hot and damp: *sticky weather.* **4** difficult: *a sticky problem. adj.,* **stick i er, stick i est.**

stiff (stif), **1** not easily bent; fixed; rigid: *a stiff collar.* **2** hard to move: *The old hinges on the barn door are stiff.* **3** not able to move easily: *a stiff neck.* **4** not fluid; firm: *The jelly is stiff enough to keep its shape.* **5** not easy or natural in manner; formal: *The magician made a stiff bow to the audience. The novelist writes in a stiff style.* **6** strong: *a stiff breeze.* **7** hard to deal with; hard: *The teacher gave us a stiff test.* **8** more than seems suitable: *a stiff price for a house.* **9** INFORMAL. very much; extremely: *I was scared stiff.* 1-8 *adj.,* 9 *adv.* —**stiff′ly,** *adv.* —**stiff′ness,** *n.*

stiff en (stif′ən), make or become stiff: *The jelly will stiffen as it cools. She stiffened with anger. The wind was stiffening as the storm approached. v.* —**stiff′en er,** *n.*

stiff-necked (stif′nekt′), **1** having a stiff neck. **2** stubborn; obstinate. *adj.* —**stiff′-neck′ed ly,** *adv.*

sti fle (stī′fəl), **1** stop the breath of; smother: *The smoke stifled the firefighters.* **2** be unable to breathe freely: *I am stifling in this close room.* **3** keep back; suppress; stop: *stifle a cry, stifle a yawn, stifle business activity, stifle a rebellion. v.,* **sti fled, sti fling.** —**sti′fler,** *n.*

stig ma (stig′mə), **1** a mark of disgrace or shame; stain or reproach on one's reputation. **2** spot in the skin which bleeds or turns red. **3** the part of the pistil of a plant which receives the pollen. *n., pl.* **stig mas, stig ma ta** (stig′mə tə).

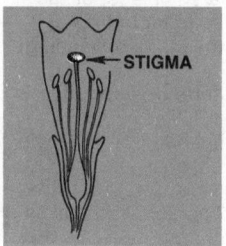

stigma (def. 3)

stig ma tize (stig′mə tīz), set some mark of disgrace upon; reproach; brand: *He always felt that his father's prison record stigmatized both of them.* v., **stig ma tized, stig ma tiz ing.** —**stig′ma ti za′tion,** *n.* —**stig′ma tiz′er,** *n.*

stile (stīl), **1** step or steps for getting over a fence or wall. **2** turnstile. *n.*

sti let to (stə let′ō), dagger with a narrow blade. *n.*, *pl.* **sti let tos** or **sti let toes.** *n.* [*Stiletto* comes from Italian *stiletto*, and can be traced back to Latin *stilus*, meaning "a pointed instrument, a stylus."]

still[1] (stil), **1** staying in the same position or at rest; without motion; motionless: *to stand or lie still. Sit still. The lake is still today.* **2** without noise; quiet: *a still night. The room was so still that you could have heard a pin drop.* **3** make or become calm or quiet: *The father stilled the crying baby. The storm stilled before dawn.* **4** stillness; silence: *in the still of the night.* **5** even; yet: *You can read still better if you try.* **6** and yet; but yet; nevertheless: *Though she liked her other jobs, she still favors this one* (adv.). *He was hungry; still he would not eat* (conj.). **7** even to this time; even to that time: *Was the store still open?* **8** without moving; quietly. **9** OLD USE. always; ever. 1,2 *adj.*, 3 *v.*, 4 *n.*, 5-9 *adv.*, 6 *conj.*

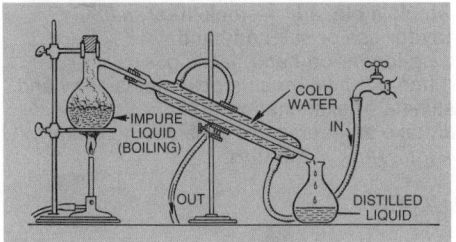

still[2] (def. 1)

still[2] (stil), **1** apparatus for distilling liquids, especially alcoholic liquors. **2** distillery. *n.*

still born (stil′bôrn′), dead when born. *adj.*

still life, a picture of inanimate objects, such as fruit, flowers, pottery, dead animals, etc. —**still′-life′,** *adj.*

still ness (stil′nis), **1** absence of noise; quiet; silence. **2** absence of motion; calm. *n.*

stilt (stilt), **1** one of a pair of poles, each with a support for the foot at some distance above the ground. Stilts are used in walking through shallow water, or by children for amusement. **2** a long post or pole used to support a house, shed, etc., above water, swampland, etc. **3** a wading bird with long, slender legs and bill that lives in marshes. *n.*, *pl.* **stilts** (or **stilt** for 3). —**stilt′like′,** *adj.*

stilt ed (stil′tid), stiffly dignified or formal: *a stilted manner of speaking. adj.* —**stilt′ed ly,** *adv.* —**stilt′ed ness,** *n.*

stim u lant (stim′yə lənt), **1** food, drug, medicine, etc., that temporarily increases the activity of the body or some part of the body. Tea and coffee are stimulants. **2** something that excites, stirs, or stimulates: *Advertising is a stimulant to business.* **3** stimulating. 1,2 *n.*, 3 *adj.*

stim u late (stim′yə lāt), **1** spur on; stir up; rouse to action: *The new factory helped to stimulate the growth of the town.* **2** act as a stimulant or a stimulus. *v.*, **stim u lat ed, stim u lat ing.** —**stim′u lat′er, stim′u la′tor,** *n.*

stim u la tion (stim′yə lā′shən), a stimulating or a being stimulated: *This town needs new industries or some other stimulation to make it grow. n.*

stim u li (stim′yə lī), plural of **stimulus.** *n.*

stim u lus (stim′yə ləs), **1** something that stirs to action or effort: *Ambition is a great stimulus.* **2** something that excites the body or some part of the body to activity: *The doctor used mild electric shocks as a stimulus to keep the patient's heart beating. n.*, *pl.* **stim u li.**

a hat	i it	oi oil	ch child	a in about
ā age	ī ice	ou out	ng long	e in taken
ä far	o hot	u cup	sh she	i in pencil
e let	ō open	u̇ put	th thin	o in lemon
ē equal	ô order	ü rule	ᴛʜ then	u in circus
ėr term			zh measure	

ə =

sting (sting), **1** to prick or wound with a sharp-pointed organ: *A bee stung her.* **2** act of stinging. **3** a wound caused by stinging: *The wasp sting began to swell.* **4** the sharp-pointed organ of an insect, animal, or plant that pricks or wounds and often poisons. **5** pain sharply: *The actor was stung by the insults of the audience.* **6** sharp pain: *The ball team felt the sting of defeat.* **7** cause a feeling like that of a sting: *Mustard stings. The electric spark stung her arm.* **8** drive or stir up as if by a sting: *Their ridicule stung him into making a sharp reply.* **9** SLANG. impose upon; charge too much. **10** INFORMAL. any complicated confidence game, especially one carried out by police out of uniform, or other law enforcement agents, to entrap criminals. 1,5,7-9 *v.*, 2-4,6,10 *n.*

sting er (sting′ər), **1** the part of an insect or animal that stings. **2** anything that stings. *n.*

stin gi ly (stin′jə lē), in a stingy manner. *adv.*

stin gi ness (stin′jē nis), unwillingness to spend or give money. *n.*

sting less (sting′lis), having no sting. *adj.*

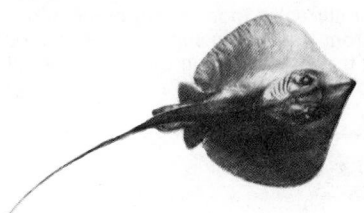

stingray
up to 12 ft.
(3.7 m.) long
with the tail

sting ray (sting′rā′), a large ray that can cause severe wounds with the sharp spines on its tail. *n.*

stin gy (stin′jē), **1** unwilling to spend or give money; not generous: *He tried to save money without being stingy.* **2** scanty; meager. *adj.*, **stin gi er, stin gi est.**

stink (stingk), **1** a very bad smell. **2** have a very bad smell: *Decaying fish stink.* **3** cause to have a very bad smell. **4** have a very bad reputation; be in great disfavor. 1 *n.*, 2-4 *v.*, **stank** or **stunk, stunk, stink ing.** —**stink′er,** *n.*

stink y (sting′kē), stinking. *adj.*, **stink i er, stink i est.**

stint (stint), **1** keep on short allowance; be saving or careful in using or spending; limit: *The parents stinted themselves of food to give it to their children.* **2** a limit; limitation: *a generous person who gives without stint.* **3** be saving; get along on very little. **4** amount or share set aside. **5** task assigned: *She did a stint as a reporter for the local newspaper.* 1,3 *v.*, 2,4,5 *n.* —**stint′er,** *n.* —**stint′ing ly,** *adv.* —**stint′less,** *adj.*

sti pend (stī′pend), fixed or regular pay; salary: *The scholarship winner received a monthly stipend to cover her college expenses. n.*

stip ple (stip′əl), paint, draw, or engrave by using dots or small, light strokes. *v.*, **stip pled, stip pling.**

stip u late (stip′yə lāt), arrange definitely; demand as a condition of agreement: *He stipulated that he should receive a month's vacation every year if he took the job.* v., **stip u lat ed, stip u lat ing.** —**stip′u la′tor,** *n.*

stip u la tion (stip′yə lā′shən), a definite arrangement; agreement; condition in an agreement or bargain: *We* rented the apartment with the stipulation that it should be decorated. n.

stip ule (stip′yül), one of the pair of little leaflike parts at the base of a leaf stem. n.

stir (stėr), **1** set in motion; move: *The wind stirred the leaves.* **2** move about: *No one was stirring in the house.* **3** mix by moving around with a spoon, fork, stick, etc.: *stir sugar into one's tea.* **4** set going; affect strongly; excite: *Don't stir up trouble.* **5** movement: *There was a stir in the bushes where the children were hiding.* **6** excitement: *The news caused a great stir.* **7** act of stirring: *She gave the mixture a hard stir.* 1-4 v., **stirred, stir ring;** 5-7 n.

stir ring (stėr′ing), **1** moving, active, or lively: *stirring times.* **2** rousing; exciting: *a stirring speech.* adj.

stirrup (def. 1)

stir rup (stėr′əp or stir′əp), **1** loop or ring of metal or wood that hangs from a saddle to support a rider's foot. **2** the innermost of the three bones in the middle ear. It looks like a stirrup. n.

WORD HISTORY

stirrup

Stirrup is from Old English *stigrāp.* In Old English, *stige* meant "a climbing" and *rāp* meant "rope."

stitch (stich), **1** one complete movement of a threaded needle through cloth in sewing, or through skin, flesh, etc., in surgery. **2** one complete movement in knitting, crocheting, embroidering, etc. **3** a particular method of taking stitches: *buttonhole stitch.* **4** loop of thread, etc., made by a stitch: *The doctor will take the stitches out of the wound tomorrow.* **5** make stitches in; fasten with stitches: *The tailor stitched a pocket on the new jacket. The doctor stitched the cut.* **6** sew. **7** piece of cloth or clothing: *He hadn't a dry stitch on.* **8** a small bit: *She wouldn't do a stitch of work.* **9** a sudden, sharp pain: *After running, I had a stitch in my side.* 1-4,7-9 n., pl. **stitch es;** 5,6 v.

St. John's (sānt jonz′), **1** capital of Newfoundland, in the SE part. **2** capital of Antigua and Barbuda.

St. Law rence (sānt lôr′əns), **1** river in SE Canada flowing northeast from Lake Ontario into the Gulf of St. Lawrence. **2** Gulf of, arm of the Atlantic Ocean in E Canada.

St. Lawrence Seaway, waterway that links the Great Lakes to the Atlantic Ocean by means of canals and the St. Lawrence River.

St. Lou is (sānt lü′is or sānt lü′ē), city in E Missouri, on the Mississippi River.

St. Lu cia (sānt lü′shə), island country in the West In-

dies, a member of the Commonwealth of Nations. *Capital:* Castries.

stoat (stōt), the ermine in its summer coat of brown. n.

stock (stok), **1** things for use or for sale; supply used as it is needed: *This store keeps a large stock of toys.* **2** livestock: *The farm was sold with all its stock.* **3** furnish with stock; supply: *Our camp is well stocked with everything we need for a short stay.* **4** lay in a supply: *stock up for the winter.* **5** keep regularly for use or for sale: *A toy store stocks toys.* **6** kept on hand regularly: *stock sizes of dresses.* **7** in common use; commonplace; everyday: *The weather is a stock subject of conversation.* **8** shares in a company. **9** heredity or family: *a person of aristocratic stock.* **10** group of closely related animals or plants. **11** part used as a support or handle; part to which other parts are attached: *the wooden stock of a rifle.* **12** raw material: *Rags are used as a stock for making paper.* **13** water in which meat or fish has been cooked, used as a base for soups, sauces, etc. **14** trunk or stump of a tree; main stem of a plant. **15** stem in which a graft is inserted. **16** furnish with livestock: *stock a farm.* **17 the stocks,** an old instrument of punishment consisting of a heavy wooden frame with holes to put a person's feet and sometimes hands through. 1,2,8-15,17 n., 3-5,16 v., 6,7 adj. [*Stock* comes from Old English *stocc,* meaning "stump."] —**stock′a ble,** adj. —**stock′like′,** adj.

in stock, ready for use or sale; on hand.

out of stock, no longer on hand; lacking.

take stock, 1 find out how much stock one has on hand. **2** make an estimate or examination.

take stock in, take an interest in; consider important; trust: *He took little stock in the story.*

the stocks (def. 17)

stock ade (sto kād′), **1** a defensive pen or barrier made of large, strong posts fixed upright in the ground: *A heavy stockade around the cabins protected the pioneers from attack.* **2** protect, fortify, or surround with a stockade. 1 n., 2 v., **stock ad ed, stock ad ing.**

stock boy (stok′boi′), person who puts merchandise on the shelves in stores, supermarkets, etc. n.

stock bro ker (stok′brō′kər), person who buys and sells stocks and bonds for others for a commission. n.

stock car, 1 a standard passenger car modified for racing. **2** a railroad freight car for livestock.

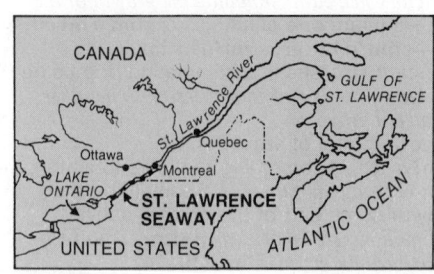

stock company, 1 company whose capital is divided into shares. **2** a theatrical company employed usually at one theater to perform many different plays.

stock exchange, 1 place where stocks and bonds are bought and sold. **2** association of brokers and dealers in stocks and bonds.

stock hold er (stok′hōl′dər), owner of stocks or shares in a company. *n.*

Stock holm (stok′hōm *or* stok′hōlm), seaport and capital of Sweden, in the SE part. *n.*

stock ing (stok′ing), a close-fitting, knitted covering of wool, cotton, silk, nylon, etc., for the foot and leg. *n.*

stocking cap, a close-fitting, knitted cap with a long, pointed end that falls over the back or shoulder, worn for skiing, sledding, etc.

stock man (stok′mən), person who raises livestock. *n., pl.* **stock men.**

stock market, 1 place where stocks and bonds are bought and sold; stock exchange. **2** the buying and selling in such a place. **3** prices of stocks and bonds.

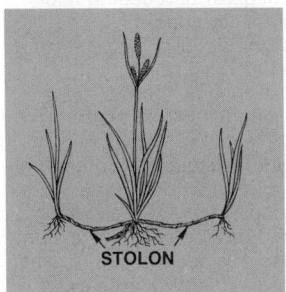

stolon
plant with
two stolons

stock pile (stok′pīl′), **1** a supply of raw materials, essential items, etc., built up and held in reserve for use during a time of emergency or shortage. **2** such a reserve of weapons for warfare. **3** collect or bring together a stockpile. 1,2 *n.,* 3 *v.,* **stock piled, stock pil ing.** —**stock′pil′er,** *n.*

stock room (stok′rüm′ *or* stok′rum′), room where a stock is kept. *n.*

stock-still (stok′stil′), motionless. *adj.*

stock y (stok′ē), having a solid or sturdy form or build; thick for its height: *a stocky little child, a stocky building.* *adj.,* **stock i er, stock i est.** —**stock′i ly,** *adv.* —**stock′i ness,** *n.*

stock yard (stok′yärd′), place with pens and sheds to keep cattle, sheep, hogs, and horses before shipping or slaughtering them. *n.*

stodg y (stoj′ē), **1** dull or uninteresting; tediously commonplace: *a stodgy book.* **2** old-fashioned: *a stodgy attitude.* *adj.,* **stodg i er, stodg i est.** —**stodg′i ly,** *adv.* —**stodg′i ness,** *n.*

sto gie *or* **sto gy** (stō′gē), a long, slender, cheap cigar. *n., pl.* **sto gies.**

sto ic (stō′ik), **1** person who remains calm and self-controlled, and appears to be indifferent to pleasure and pain. **2** stoical. 1 *n.,* 2 *adj.*

sto i cal (stō′ə kəl), like a stoic; self-controlled; indifferent to pleasure and pain. *adj.* —**sto′i cal ly,** *adv.* —**sto′i cal ness,** *n.*

sto i cism (stō′ə siz′əm), patient endurance; indifference to pleasure and pain. *n.*

stoke (stōk), **1** stir up and feed (a fire); tend the fire of (a furnace). **2** tend a fire. *v.,* **stoked, stok ing.**

stoke hold (stōk′hōld′), place in a steamship where the furnaces and boilers are. *n.*

stoke hole (stōk′hōl′), **1** hole through which fuel is put into a furnace. **2** space in front of furnaces where coal

is shoveled in and ashes are taken out. *n.*

stok er (stō′kər), **1** worker who tends the fires of a furnace or boiler. **2** a mechanical device for putting coal in a furnace. *n.* —**stok′er less,** *adj.*

stole[1] (stōl), past tense of **steal.** *They stole my car. v.*

stole[2] (stōl), **1** a narrow strip of silk or other material worn over the shoulders by a clergyman during certain church functions. **2** a woman's collar or scarf of fur or cloth with ends hanging down in front. *n.*

sto len (stō′lən), past participle of **steal.** *The money was not stolen; it was lost. v.*

stol id (stol′id), hard to arouse; not easily excited; showing no emotion; seeming dull. *adj.* —**stol′id ly,** *adv.* —**stol′id ness,** *n.*

sto lid i ty (stə lid′ə tē), stolid quality or condition. *n.*

sto lon (stō′lon), a slender stem along or beneath the ground, that takes root at the tip and grows into a new plant. *n.*

sto ma (stō′mə), a small opening or pore in a plant or animal. A leaf contains many stomata which let water and gases in and out of the plant. *n., pl.* **sto ma ta** *or* **sto mas.**

stom ach (stum′ək), **1** the large muscular bag in the body which receives swallowed food, and digests some of it before passing it on to the intestines. **2** the part of the body containing the stomach; abdomen; belly: *I was hit in the stomach.* **3** appetite. **4** put up with; bear; endure: *She could not stomach such insults.* **5** desire; liking: *I have no stomach for killing harmless creatures.* 1-3,5 *n.,* 4 *v.*

stom ach ful (stum′ək fu̇l), as much as one can put up with. *n., pl.* **stom ach fuls.**

sto ma ta (stō′mə tə *or* stom′ə tə), a plural of **stoma.** *n.*

stomp (stomp), **1** to stamp with the foot. **2** a stomping. 1 *v.,* 2 *n.* —**stomp′er,** *n.* —**stomp′ing ly,** *adv.*

stone (stōn), **1** the hard, mineral material of which rocks are made up. Stone, such as granite and marble, is much used in building. **2** a small piece of rock: *They threw stones into the pond.* **3** piece of rock of definite size, shape, etc., used for a particular purpose: *His grave is marked by a fine stone.* **4** made of stone: *a stone wall, a stone house.* **5** having to do with stone. **6** gem; jewel: *The queen's diamonds were very fine stones.* **7** something hard like a stone, which sometimes forms in the kidneys or gall bladder, causing sickness and pain. **8** throw stones at. **9** kill by throwing stones: *The martyr was stoned as a heretic.* **10** a hard seed: *peach stones.* **11** take stones or seeds out of: *to stone cherries or plums.* **12** made of stoneware or coarse clay. **13** a British measure of weight equal to 14 pounds. 1-3,6,7,10,13 *n., pl.* **stones** (but **stone** for 13); 4,5,12 *adj.,* 8,9,11 *v.,* **stoned, ston ing.** [*Stone* comes from Old English *stān.*] —**ston′a ble,** **stone′a ble,** *adj.* —**ston′er,** *n.* —**stone′like′,** *adj.*

Stone (stōn), Lucy, 1818-1893, American leader in the woman's rights and anti-slavery movements. *n.*

Stone Age, the earliest known period of human culture, in which people used tools and weapons made from stone. It was followed by the Bronze Age.

stone-blind (stōn′blīnd′), totally blind. *adj.*

stone-broke (stōn′brōk′), SLANG. totally without money. *adj.*

stone cut ter (stōn′kut′ər), **1** person who cuts or carves stones. **2** machine for cutting or dressing stone. *n.*

stoned (stōnd), SLANG. drunk from alcohol, or drugged. *adj.*

stone-deaf (stōn′def′), totally deaf. *adj.*

Stone henge (stōn′henj), a prehistoric ruin in southern England, consisting of huge slabs of roughly shaped stone in a circular arrangement. It may have been a kind of observatory used by astronomers. *n.*

Stonehenge

stone ma son (stōn′mā′sn), person who cuts stone or builds walls, etc., of stone. *n.*

stone's throw, a short distance: *We live only a stone's throw from the school.*

stone ware (stōn′wer′ or stōn′war′), a coarse, hard, glazed pottery. *n.*

stone work (stōn′wèrk′), 1 wall, foundation, or other structure made of stone. 2 the part of a building made of stone. *n.*

ston i ly (stō′nə lē), in a stony manner; stiffly; harshly; coldly. *adv.*

ston y (stō′nē), 1 having many stones: *The beach is stony.* 2 hard like stone: *A cruel person has a stony heart.* 3 without expression or feeling: *a stony stare. adj.,* **ston i er, ston i est. —ston′i ness,** *n.*

stood (stůd), past tense and past participle of **stand.** *She stood in the corner for five minutes. I had stood in line all morning to buy tickets to the game. v.*

stooge (stüj), INFORMAL. 1 person on the stage who asks questions of a comedian and is the butt of the comedian's jokes. 2 person who follows and flatters another; hanger-on. *n.*

stool (stül), 1 seat without back or arms. 2 a similar article used to rest the feet on, or to kneel on. *n.* **—stool′like′,** *adj.*

stool pigeon, SLANG. a spy for the police; informer.

stoop¹ (stüp), 1 bend forward: *He stooped to pick up the money. She stooped over her work.* 2 a forward bend: *My uncle walks with a stoop.* 3 carry head and shoulders bent forward: *The old man stoops.* 4 a forward bend of the head and shoulders. 5 lower oneself; descend: *He stooped to cheating.* 1,3,5 *v.,* 2,4 *n.* [*Stoop¹* comes from Old English *stūpian.*] **—stoop′er,** *n.* **—stoop′ing ly,** *adv.*

stoop² (stüp), a porch or platform at the entrance of a house. *n.* [*Stoop²* comes from Dutch *stoep.*]

stop (stop), 1 keep from moving, acting, doing, being, working, etc.: *I stopped the children from teasing the cat. I stopped the clock.* 2 put an end to; interrupt; check: *stop a noise.* 3 stay; halt: *She stopped at the bank for a few minutes.* 4 leave off (moving, acting, doing, being, etc.); come to an end; cease: *The baby stopped crying. The rain is stopping.* 5 close (a hole or opening) by filling (it): *I will stop the rats' holes.* 6 close (a container) with a cork, plug, or other stopper: *stop up a bottle.* 7 block (a way); obstruct: *A big box stops up the doorway.* 8 act of stopping; closing; filling up; blocking; hindering; checking; halting; cessation; stay: *Her sudden stop startled us. The singing came to a stop.* 9 a being stopped. 10 place where

a stop is made: *a bus stop.* 11 thing that stops, such as a block, plug, etc.; obstacle. 12 punctuation mark. 13 a device that controls the pitch of a musical instrument. 14 (in organs) a graduated set of pipes of the same kind, or the knob or handle that controls them. 15 any piece or device that serves to check or control movement or action in a mechanism. 1-7 *v.,* **stopped, stop ping;** 8-15 *n.* **—stop′pa ble,** *adj.* **—stop′less,** *adj.*

stop off, stop for a short stay.

stop over, 1 make a short stay. 2 stop in the course of a trip.

pull out all the stops, do something in the biggest way possible.

put a stop to, stop; end.

stop gap (stop′gap′), thing that fills the place of something lacking; a temporary substitute. *n.*

stop light (stop′līt′), 1 a red light on the rear end of a vehicle, that turns on automatically when the brakes are applied. 2 traffic light. *n.*

stop o ver (stop′ō′vər), a stopping over in the course of a trip, especially with the privilege of proceeding later on the ticket originally issued for the trip. *n.*

stop page (stop′ij), 1 act of stopping: *The foreman called for a stoppage of operations to oil the machinery.* 2 condition of being stopped: *During the work stoppage many workers looked for other jobs.* 3 a block; obstruction. *n.*

stop per (stop′ər), plug or cork for closing a bottle, tube, etc. *n.* **—stop′per less,** *adj.*

stop watch (stop′woch′ or stop′wôch′), watch which has a hand that can be stopped or started at any instant. A stopwatch indicates fractions of a second and is used for timing races and contests. *n., pl.* **stop watch es.**

stor age (stôr′ij), 1 act or fact of storing goods: *the storage of storm windows in summertime.* 2 condition of being stored. Cold storage is used to keep eggs and meat from spoiling. 3 place for storing: *She has put her furniture in storage.* 4 price for storing: *She paid $30 storage on her furniture. n.*

storage battery, battery in which chemical energy is converted into direct-current electrical energy. When the cells of the battery have been discharged they may be charged again by passing a current through them in the direction opposite to that of the flow of current when discharging.

store (stôr), 1 place where goods are kept for sale: *a clothing store.* 2 something put away for use later; supply; stock: *We put up stores of preserves and jellies every year.* 3 to supply or stock. 4 put away for use later; lay up: *The squirrel stores away nuts.* 5 place where supplies are kept for future use; storehouse. 6 put in a warehouse or place used for preserving. 1,2,5 *n.,* 3,4,6 *v.,* **stored, stor ing.** **—stor′a ble,** *adj.* **—stor′er,** *n.*

in store, on hand; in reserve; saved for the future.

set store by, to value; esteem: *She sets great store by her friend's opinions.*

store house (stôr′hous′), 1 place where things are stored; warehouse: *This factory has many storehouses for its products.* 2 person or thing resembling such a place: *A library is a storehouse of information. n., pl.* **store hous es** (stôr′hou′ziz).

store keep er (stôr′kē′pər), person who owns or manages a store or stores. *n.*

store room (stôr′rüm′ or stôr′rům′), room where things are stored. *n.*

sto rey (stôr′ē), story². *n., pl.* **sto reys.**

sto ried¹ (stôr′ēd), celebrated in story or history: *the storied Wild West. adj.*

sto ried² (stôr′ēd), having stories or floors: *a storied tower, a two-storied house. adj.*

stork—about 3 ft. (1 m.) high

a hat	i it	oi oil	ch child	a in about
ā age	ī ice	ou out	ng long	e in taken
ä far	o hot	u cup	sh she	ə = { i in pencil
e let	ō open	u̇ put	th thin	o in lemon
ē equal	ô order	ü rule	ŦH then	u in circus
ėr term			zh measure	

stork (stôrk), a large, long-legged wading bird with a long neck and a long bill. Storks are found in most warm parts of the world. *n.* —**stork′like′**, *adj.*

storm (stôrm), **1** a strong wind often accompanied by rain, snow, hail, or thunder and lightning. A storm blows with a velocity of 64 to 72 miles per hour. **2** a heavy fall of rain, snow, or hail. **3** blow hard; rain; snow; hail. **4** anything like a storm: *a storm of arrows.* **5** a violent outburst or disturbance: *a storm of tears, a storm of angry words.* **6** be violent; rage. **7** rush violently: *He stormed out of the room.* **8** attack violently: *The troops stormed the city.* **9** a violent attack: *The castle was taken by storm.* 1,2,4,5,9 *n.*, 3,6-8 *v.* —**storm′like′**, *adj.*

storm cellar, cellar for shelter during cyclones, tornadoes, etc.

storm center, 1 center of a cyclone, where there is very low air pressure and comparative calm. **2** any center of trouble, tumult, etc.

storm door, an extra door outside of an ordinary door, to keep out snow, cold winds, etc.

storm i ly (stôr′mə lē), in a stormy manner. *adv.*

storm i ness (stôr′mē nis), condition of being stormy. *n.*

storm petrel, a small black-and-white sea bird with long, pointed wings, whose presence is supposed to give warning of a storm. See **petrel** for picture. Also, **stormy petrel.**

storm window, an extra window outside of an ordinary window, to keep out snow, cold winds, etc.

storm y (stôr′mē), **1** having storms; likely to have storms; troubled by storms: *a stormy sea, stormy weather, a stormy night.* **2** rough and disturbed; violent: *They had stormy quarrels.* *adj.*, **storm i er, storm i est.**

stormy petrel, storm petrel.

sto ry[1] (stôr′ē), **1** an account of some happening or group of happenings: *Tell us the story of your life.* **2** such an account, either true or made up, intended to interest the reader or hearer; tale: *fairy stories, stories of adventure.* **3** INFORMAL. falsehood: *That's not true; you're telling stories. n., pl.* **sto ries.** [*Story*[1] came into English about 700 years ago from French *estorie*, and can be traced back to Greek *historia*, meaning "an inquiry, history."] —**sto′ry less,** *adj.*

sto ry[2] (stôr′ē), set of rooms on the same level or floor of a building; one of the structural divisions in the height of a building: *That house has two stories. n., pl.* **stories.** Also, **storey.**

sto ry book (stôr′ē bùk′), **1** book containing one or more stories or tales, especially for children. **2** of or like that of a storybook; romantic; fictional: *a storybook hero, a storybook ending.* 1 *n.*, 2 *adj.*

sto ry tell er (stôr′ē tel′ər), person who tells stories. *n.*

sto ry tell ing (stôr′ē tel′ing), act or art of telling stories. *n.*

stoup (stüp), **1** a drinking cup; flagon; tankard. **2** amount it holds. **3** basin for holy water at the entrance to a church. *n.*

stout (stout), **1** fat and large: *That boy could run faster if he weren't so stout.* **2** strongly built; firm; strong: *The fort has stout walls.* **3** brave; bold: *Robin Hood was a stout fellow.* **4** not yielding; stubborn: *stout resistance.* **5** a strong, dark-brown beer. 1-4 *adj.*, 5 *n.* —**stout′ly,** *adv.* —**stout′ness,** *n.*

stout heart ed (stout′här′tid), having courage; brave; bold. *adj.* —**stout′heart′ed ly,** *adv.* —**stout′heart′ed ness,** *n.*

stove[1] (stōv), apparatus for cooking and heating. There are wood, coal, gas, oil, and electric stoves. *n.*

stove[2] (stōv), staved; a past tense and a past participle of **stave.** *v.*

stove pipe (stōv′pīp′), **1** a metal pipe that carries smoke and gases from a stove to a chimney. **2** INFORMAL. a tall silk hat. *n.*

stow (stō), **1** pack: *stow books in a trunk. The cargo was stowed in the ship's hold.* **2** pack things closely in; fill by packing: *stow a pantry with cans of food. v.* —**stow′a ble,** *adj.* —**stow′er,** *n.*

stow away, hide on a ship, airplane, etc., to get a free passage or to escape secretly.

stow a way (stō′ə wā′), person who hides on a ship, an airplane, etc., to get a free passage or to escape secretly. *n.*

Stowe (stō), **Harriet Beecher,** 1811-1896, American writer, author of *Uncle Tom's Cabin. n.*

St. Paul, capital of Minnesota, in the SE part, on the Mississippi River.

St. Pe ters burg (sānt pē′tərz bėrg′), **1** former capital of Russia, now called **Leningrad. 2** city in W Florida.

strad dle (strad′l), **1** walk, stand, or sit with the legs wide apart. **2** spread (the legs) wide apart. **3** have a leg on each side of (a horse, bicycle, chair, ditch, etc.). **4** stand or lie across; be on both sides of: *A pair of field glasses straddled her nose.* **5** avoid taking sides; attempt to favor both sides (of a question, etc.): *All three political candidates straddled the issue of higher taxes. v.,* **straddled, strad dling.** —**strad′dling ly,** *adv.*

strad dler (strad′lər), person that straddles. *n.*

Strad i var i us (strad′ə ver′ē əs), violin, viola, or cello made by Antonio Stradivari, a famous Italian violin maker who lived from about 1644 to 1737. *n.*

strafe (strāf), **1** (of aircraft) to fly low over enemy troops or positions and attack with machine-gun fire. **2** to shell or bombard heavily. *v.,* **strafed, straf ing.** [*Strafe* comes from the German World War I slogan *Gott strafe England,* meaning "God punish England."] —**straf′er,** *n.*

strag gle (strag′əl), **1** wander in a scattered fashion: *Cows straggled along the lane.* **2** stray from the rest. **3** spread in an irregular, rambling manner: *Vines straggled over the yard. It was a straggling little town. v.,* **straggled, strag gling.** —**strag′gling ly,** *adv.*

strag gler (strag′lər), person or thing that straggles. *n.*

strag gly (strag′lē), spread out in an irregular, rambling way; straggling. *adj.,* **strag gli er, strag gli est.**

straight (strāt), **1** without a bend or curve; not crooked or irregular: *a straight line, a straight path, a straight nose, straight hair.* **2** in a line; directly: *Walk straight. He went straight home.* **3** going in a line; direct: *a straight course,*

a straight throw. **4** frank; honest; upright: *straight conduct, a straight answer.* **5** frankly; honestly; uprightly: *Live straight.* **6** right; correct: *straight thinking, a straight thinker.* **7** in proper order or condition: *Keep your accounts straight. Set the room straight.* **8** showing no emotion, humor, etc.: *I kept a straight face, though I wanted to laugh.* **9** supporting the candidates of one party only: *to vote a straight Republican ticket.* 1,3,4,6-9 *adj.,* 2,5 *adv.* —**straight′ly,** *adv.* —**straight′ness,** *n.*
straight away or **straight off,** at once.

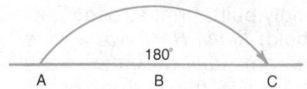

straight angle
ABC is a
straight angle

straight angle, angle of 180 degrees.
straight a way (strāt′ə wā′), **1** a straight course. **2** in a straight course. **3** straightway. 1 *n.,* 2 *adj.,* 3 *adv.*
straight edge (strāt′ej′), strip of wood or metal having one edge accurately straight, used in obtaining or testing straight lines and level surfaces. *n.*
straight en (strāt′n), **1** make straight: *He straightened the bent pin. Straighten your shoulders.* **2** become straight. **3** put in the proper order or condition: *Straighten up your room. We must straighten out our accounts and see how much we owe each other.* *v.* —**straight′en er,** *n.*
straight for ward (strāt′fôr′wərd), **1** honest; frank: *a straightforward answer.* **2** going straight ahead; direct. **3** directly. 1,2 *adj.,* 3 *adv.* —**straight′for′ward ly,** *adv.*
straight way (strāt′wā′), at once; immediately: *I will leave straightway. adv.*
strain[1] (strān), **1** draw tight; stretch: *The weight strained the rope.* **2** pull hard: *The dog strained at its leash.* **3** force or weight that stretches: *The strain on the rope made it break.* **4** stretch as much as possible: *She strained the truth in telling the story.* **5** use to the utmost: *I strained every muscle to lift the rock. She strained her eyes to see.* **6** injure by too much effort or by stretching: *I strained a muscle.* **7** injury caused by too much effort or by stretching: *The injury to his back was only a slight strain.* **8** any severe, trying, or wearing pressure: *the strain of worry. The strain of overwork can make you ill.* **9** effect of such pressure on the body or mind. **10** make a very great effort. **11** press or pour through a strainer: *Strain the soup before serving it. Babies eat strained foods.* **12** part of a piece of music; melody; song. **13** manner or style of doing or speaking: *a playful strain, a poem in a melancholy strain.* 1,2,4-6,10,11 *v.,* 3,7-9,12,13 *n.*
strain[2] (strān), **1** line of descent; stock: *My friend is of Spanish strain.* **2** group of animals or plants from a breed, race, or variety, distinguished from other members of the group by some feature. **3** an inherited quality: *There is a strain of musical talent in that family.* **4** trace or streak: *That horse has a mean strain. n.*
strained (strānd), forced; not natural: *Her greeting was cold and strained. adj.* —**strained′ly,** *adv.*
strain er (strā′nər), object that separates, usually solids from liquids. A filter, a sieve, and a colander are strainers. *n.*
strait (strāt), **1** a narrow channel connecting two larger bodies of water: *The Strait of Gibraltar connects the Mediterranean Sea and the Atlantic Ocean.* **2** OLD USE. narrow; limited; confining. **3** **straits,** *pl.* difficulty; need; distress: *be in desperate straits for money.* 1,3 *n.,* 2 *adj.*
strait en (strāt′n), limit by the lack of something; restrict. *v.*
strait jack et (strāt′jak′it), a strong, tight jacket or coat that binds the arms close to the sides. It keeps a violent person from doing harm.

strait-laced (strāt′lāst′), very strict in matters of conduct; prudish. *adj.* —**strait′-lac′ed ly,** *adv.* —**strait′-lac′ed ness,** *n.*
strand[1] (strand), **1** leave in a helpless position: *She was stranded a thousand miles from home with no money.* **2** run aground; drive on the shore: *The ship was stranded on the rocks.* **3** shore; land bordering a sea, lake, or river. 1,2 *v.,* 3 *n.*
strand[2] (strand), **1** one of the threads, strings, or wires that are twisted together to make a rope or cable. **2** thread or string: *a strand of pearls, a strand of hair. n.*
strange (strānj), **1** unusual; odd; peculiar: *a strange accident, a strange experience. There was a strange quiet throughout the city.* **2** not known, seen, or heard of before; not familiar: *She is moving to a strange place. A strange cat is on our steps.* **3** not used to: *He is strange to the work but will soon learn.* **4** out of place; not at home: *The poor child felt strange in the palace. adj.,* **strang er, strang est.** [*Strange* came into English about 700 years ago from French *estrange,* which came from Latin *extraneus,* meaning "foreign, strange." *Extraneus* comes from *extra,* meaning "outside, beyond."] —**strange′ly,** *adv.* —**strange′ness,** *n.*
stran ger (strān′jər), **1** person not known, seen, or heard of before: *She is a stranger to us.* **2** person or thing new to a place: *I am a stranger in New York.* **3** person who is out of place or not at home in something: *He is no stranger to hard work.* **4** person from another country: *The king received the strangers with kindness. n.*
stran gle (strang′gəl), **1** kill by squeezing the throat to stop the breath. **2** choke: *His high collar seemed to be strangling him. She almost strangled on a piece of meat that caught in her throat.* **3** choke down; suppress; keep back: *I strangled an impulse to cough. v.,* **stran gled, strangling.** —**stran gling ly,** *adv.*
stran gler (strang′glər), person who strangles somebody. *n.*
stran gu la tion (strang′gyə lā′shən), a strangling or a being strangled. *n.*
strap (strap), **1** a narrow strip of leather or other material that bends easily: *She has a strap around her books. Put a strap around the trunk.* **2** a narrow band or strip of cloth: *The general wore shoulder straps.* **3** a narrow strip for fastening things, holding things together, etc.: *The box was strengthened by straps of steel.* **4** fasten with a strap: *We strapped the trunk.* **5** beat with a strap. **6** a strop. **7** sharpen on a strap or strop. 1-3,6 *n.,* 4,5,7 *v.,* **strapped, strapping.** —**strap′pa ble,** *adj.* —**strap′per,** *n.*
strap less (strap′lis), having no strap or straps: *a strapless gown. adj.*
strap ping (strap′ing), INFORMAL. tall, strong, and healthy: *a fine, strapping youngster. adj.*
Stras bourg (stras′bérg′), city in NE France, on the Rhine River. *n.*
stra ta (strā′tə), a plural of **stratum.** *n.*
strat a gem (strat′ə jəm), scheme or trick for deceiving the enemy; trick; trickery: *The spy got into the castle by the stratagem of dressing as a royal guard. n.*
stra te gic (strə tē′jik), **1** of strategy; based on strategy; useful in strategy: *a strategic retreat.* **2** important in strategy: *a strategic link in national defense. adj.* —**stra te′gi cal ly,** *adv.*
Strategic Defense Initiative, program of the United States government to develop a missile-defense system, based chiefly in space, made up of sophisticated rockets, lasers, and other weapons, capable of destroying rockets before they reach their targets.
strat e gist (strat′ə jist), person trained or skilled in strategy: *a military strategist, a chess strategist, a football strategist. n.*

strat e gy (strat′ə jē), **1** science or art of war; planning and directing of large-scale military movements and operations. **2** the skillful planning and management of anything. **3** plan based on strategy: *We need some strategy to win this game. n., pl.* **strat e gies.**

Strat ford-on-A von (strat′fərd on ā′vən), town in central England on the Avon River. It is Shakespeare's birthplace and burial place. *n.*

strat i fi ca tion (strat′ə fə kā′shən), arrangement in layers or strata: *the stratification of society. n.*

strat i fy (strat′ə fī), arrange in layers or strata; form into layers or strata. *v.,* **strat i fied, strat i fy ing.**

strat o sphere (strat′ə sfir *or* strā′tə sfir), region of the atmosphere between the troposphere and the mesosphere, which extends from about 5 to 40 miles (8 to 64 kilometers) above the earth's surface. In the stratosphere, temperature varies little with changes in altitude, and the winds are chiefly horizontal. *n.*

strat o spher ic (strat′ə sfir′ik *or* strat′ə sfer′ik), of the stratosphere. *adj.*

stra tum (strā′təm), **1** layer of material; especially, one of several parallel layers placed one upon another: *In digging the well, they first struck a stratum of sand, then several strata of rock.* **2** social level: *rise from a low stratum to a high stratum of society. n., pl.* **stra ta** *or* **stra tums.**

stratus

stra tus (strā′təs), a low, horizontal layer of gray cloud that spreads over a large area. *n., pl.* **stra ti** (strā′tī).

Strauss (strous), **1 Johann,** 1804-1849, Austrian composer of dance music. **2** his son, **Johann,** 1825-1899, Austrian composer of dance music and light operas. **3 Richard,** 1864-1949, German composer. *n.*

Stra vin sky (strə vin′skē), **Igor,** 1882-1971, American composer, born in Russia. *n.*

straw (strô), **1** the stalks or stems of grain after drying and threshing. Straw is used as bedding for horses and cows, for making hats, and for many other purposes. **2** one such stem or stalk. **3** tube made of waxed paper, plastic, or glass, used for sucking up drinks. **4** made of straw: *a straw hat.* **5** bit; trifle: *He doesn't care a straw.* 1-3,5 *n.,* 4 *adj.* —**straw′less,** *adj.* —**straw′like′,** *adj.*

straw ber ry (strô′ber′ē), the small, juicy, red fruit of a plant that grows close to the ground. Strawberries are good to eat. *n., pl.* **straw ber ries.**

straw man, an imaginary opponent or opposing argument, put up in order to be defeated or refuted.

straw vote, an unofficial vote taken to find out general opinion.

stray (strā), **1** lose one's way; wander; roam: *Our dog has strayed off somewhere.* **2** wandering; lost: *A stray cat is crying at the door.* **3** wanderer; lost animal: *The cat is a stray that we took in.* **4** turn from the right course; go wrong. **5** scattered; here and there: *stray thoughts. The beach was empty except for a few stray swimmers.* 1,4 *v.,* 2,5 *adj.,* 3 *n.* —**stray′er,** *n.*

a hat	i it	oi oil	ch child	a in about
ā age	ī ice	ou out	ng long	e in taken
ä far	o hot	u cup	sh she	ə = i in pencil
e let	ō open	u̇ put	th thin	o in lemon
ē equal	ô order	ü rule	ᴛʜ then	u in circus
ėr term			zh measure	

streak (strēk), **1** a long, thin mark or line: *a streak of dirt on one's face. We saw a streak of lightning.* **2** layer: *Bacon has streaks of fat and streaks of lean.* **3** vein; strain; element: *He has a streak of humor, though he looks very serious.* **4** put long, thin marks or lines on: *The children streaked their faces with water colors.* **5** a brief period; spell: *a streak of luck.* **6** move very fast; go at full speed: *She streaked past the others and over the finish line.* 1-3,5 *n.,* 4,6 *v.* —**streak′er,** *n.* —**streak′like′,** *adj.*

like a streak, INFORMAL. very fast; at full speed: *When her dog saw her, it ran like a streak to greet her.*

streak y (strē′kē), **1** marked with streaks. **2** occurring in streaks. **3** varying; uneven: *These jeans have faded so much that the color is streaky. adj.,* **streak i er, streak i est.** —**streak′i ly,** *adv.* —**streak′i ness,** *n.*

stream (strēm), **1** flow of water in a channel or bed. Small rivers and large brooks are both called streams. *Because of the lack of rain many streams dried up.* **2** any steady flow: *a stream of words, a stream of light, a stream of cars.* **3** to flow: *Tears streamed from her eyes.* **4** move steadily; move swiftly: *People streamed out of the theater.* **5** pour out: *The gash in his arm streamed blood.* **6** be so wet as to drip in a stream: *streaming eyes, a streaming umbrella.* **7** float or wave: *Flags streamed in the wind.* 1,2 *n.,* 3-7 *v.* —**stream′less,** *adj.* —**stream′like′,** *adj.*

stream er (strē′mər), **1** any long, narrow, flowing thing: *Streamers of ribbon hung from the new boat.* **2** a long, narrow flag. *n.*

stream let (strēm′lit), a small stream. *n.*

stream line (strēm′līn′), **1** streamlined. **2** give a streamlined shape to. **3** bring up to date; make more efficient: *streamline an office.* 1 *adj.,* 2,3 *v.,* **stream lined, stream lin ing.**

stream lined (strēm′līnd′), **1** having a shape that offers the least possible resistance to air or water. The fastest automobiles, airplanes, and trains have streamlined bodies. **2** brought up to date; made more efficient: *streamlined methods of production, a streamlined organization. adj.*

street (strēt), **1** road in a city or town, usually with buildings on both sides. **2** place or way for automobiles, wagons, etc., to go: *Be careful in crossing the street.* **3** people who live in the buildings on a street: *The whole street planted new trees. n.* [*Street* is from Old English *strǣt,* which comes from Latin (*via*) *strata,* meaning "paved (road)."] —**street′like′,** *adj.*

street car (strēt′kär′), car that runs on rails in the streets and carries passengers; trolley car. *n.*

streetcar

strength (strengkth), **1** quality of being strong; power; force; vigor: *I do not have the strength to lift that heavy box. I did not have enough strength of mind to refuse. The strength of a dog's love for its master is well known.* **2** power to resist or endure: *the strength of a fort, the strength of a rope.* **3** military force measured in numbers of soldiers, warships, etc.: *an army at full strength.* **4** degree of strength; intensity: *the strength of a beverage. Some flavorings lose their strength in cooking. n.*

on the strength of, relying or depending on; with the support or help of: *They bought the dog on the strength of the children's promise to take care of it.*

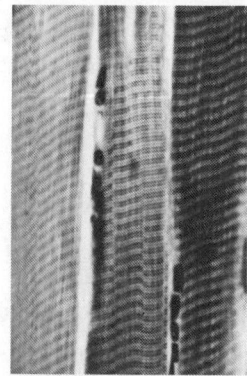
striated
a striated muscle

strength en (strengk'thən), make or grow stronger: *Exercise strengthens muscles. v.* —**strength'en er,** *n.*

stren u ous (stren'yü əs), **1** very active: *We had a strenuous day moving into our new house.* **2** full of energy: *Beavers are strenuous workers.* **3** requiring much energy: *Running is strenuous exercise. adj.* —**stren'u ous ly,** *adv.*

strep (strep), INFORMAL. streptococcus. *n.*

strep throat, a serious throat inflammation caused by a streptococcus, and marked by fever, aching muscles, headache, etc.

strep to coc cus (strep'tə kok'əs), any of a group of spherical bacteria that multiply by dividing in only one direction, usually forming chains. Many serious infections and diseases, such as scarlet fever and rheumatic fever, are caused by streptococci. *n., pl.* **strep to coc ci** (strep'tə kok'sī).

strep to my cin (strep'tō mī'sn), a powerful antibiotic effective against tuberculosis, typhoid fever, and certain other bacterial infections. *n.*

stress (stres), **1** great pressure or force; strain: *the stress of war. The stress on the rope caused it to break.* **2** put pressure upon. **3** great effort. **4** emphasis; importance: *Our teacher lays stress upon punctuation and spelling.* **5** treat as important; emphasize: *Stress the important words of a sentence.* **6** the relative loudness in the pronunciation of syllables, words in a sentence, etc.; accent: *In "zero," the stress is on the first syllable.* **7** pronounce with stress: *"Accept" is stressed on the second syllable.* 1,3,4,6 *n., pl.* **stress es;** 2,5,7 *v.* —**stress'less,** *adj.*

stress ful (stres'fəl), full of stress; subject to strain: *stressful conditions. adj.*

stretch (strech), **1** draw out; extend (one's body, arms, legs, wings, etc.) to full length: *The bird stretched its wings. She stretched herself out on the grass to rest.* **2** extend one's body or limbs: *I stretched out on the couch.* **3** continue over a distance; extend from one place to another; fill space; spread: *The forest stretches for miles. She stretched the hammock from a tree to a pole.* **4** reach out; hold out: *I stretched out my hand for the money.* **5** draw out to greater size: *Stretch the shoe a little.*

6 become longer or wider without breaking: *Rubber stretches.* **7** draw tight; strain: *stretch a guitar string until it breaks.* **8** extend beyond proper limits: *They stretched the law to suit their own purpose.* **9** exaggerate: *stretch the truth.* **10** an unbroken length; extent: *A stretch of sand hills lay between the road and the ocean.* **11** a stretching or a being stretched: *With a sudden stretch he took the cap off the tall boy's head.* **12** capacity for being stretched; extent to which something can be stretched: *The stretch of that bird's wings is two feet.* 1-9 *v.,* 10-12 *n., pl.* **stretch es.** —**stretch'a ble,** *adj.*

stretch er (strech'ər), **1** person or thing. that stretches. **2** canvas stretched on a frame for carrying the sick, wounded, or dead. *n.*

strew (strü), **1** scatter or sprinkle: *She strewed seeds in her garden.* **2** cover with something scattered or sprinkled: *The ground was strewn with leaves. v.,* **strewed, strewed** or **strewn, strew ing.**

strewn (strün), strewed; a past participle of **strew.** *v.*

stri at ed (strī'ā tid), striped; streaked; furrowed. *adj.*

stri a tion (strī ā'shən), striated condition or appearance. *n.*

strick en (strik'ən), **1** hit, wounded, or affected by (a weapon, disease, trouble, sorrow, etc.): *a stricken deer. They fled from the stricken city. The stricken man was taken immediately to a hospital.* **2** struck; a past participle of **strike.** 1 *adj.,* 2 *v.*

stricken in years, old.

strict (strikt), **1** very careful in following a rule or in making others follow it: *The teacher was strict but fair.* **2** harsh; severe: *a strict parent, strict discipline.* **3** exact; precise; accurate: *She told the strict truth.* **4** perfect; complete; absolute: *The secret was told in strict confidence. adj.* —**strict'ly,** *adv.* —**strict'ness,** *n.*

stric ture (strik'chər), **1** an unfavorable criticism; critical remark. **2** an unhealthy narrowing of some duct or tube of the body. *n.*

strid den (strid'n), past participle of **stride.** *She had stridden away angrily. v.*

stride (strīd), **1** walk with long steps: *She strides rapidly, as though always late. I strode the halls of the building, looking for the exit.* **2** pass with one long step: *They strode over the brook.* **3** a long step: *The child could not keep up with his father's stride.* **4** distance covered by a stride. 1,2 *v.,* **strode, strid den, strid ing;** 3,4 *n.* —**strid'er,** *n.* —**strid'ing ly,** *adv.*

hit one's stride, reach one's regular speed or normal activity.

take in one's stride, deal with in one's normal activity; do or take without difficulty, hesitation, or special effort.

stri dence (strīd'ns), a being strident. *n.*

stri den cy (strīd'n sē), stridence. *n.*

stri dent (strīd'nt), making or having a harsh sound; creaking; grating; shrill. *adj.* —**stri'dent ly,** *adv.*

strife (strīf), **1** a quarreling; fighting: *bitter strife between rivals.* **2** a quarrel; fight: *to find out the cause of a strife. n.* —**strife'less,** *adj.*

strike (strīk), **1** hit: *strike a person in anger. Lightning struck the barn. The car struck a fence.* **2** give forth or out; deal: *strike a blow in self-defense.* **3** make by stamping, printing, etc.: *They will strike a medal in memory of the great victory.* **4** set or be set on fire by hitting or rubbing: *strike a match. The match wouldn't strike.* **5** have a strong effect on the mind or feeling of; impress: *The plan strikes me as silly.* **6** to sound: *The clock strikes twelve times at noon. This clock strikes the hour and the half hour.* **7** affect deeply; influence; overcome (by death, disease, suffering, fear, etc.): *They were struck with terror. The town was struck with a flu epidemic.* **8** to attack: *The enemy will strike at dawn. They struck the town by surprise.* **9** an attack: *a* strike by bombers on a target. **10** occur to: *An amusing thought struck her.* **11** find or come upon (ore, oil, water, etc.): *After years of prospecting, the old man finally struck gold.* **12** act or fact of finding rich ore in mining, oil in boring, etc.; sudden success: *He made a rich strike in the Yukon.* **13** stop work to get better pay, shorter hours, etc.: *The coal miners struck when the company refused to improve safety conditions in the mines.* **14** such a stopping of work: *The workers were home for six weeks during the strike last year.* **15** cross; rub: *Strike out the last word. Strike that name off the list.* **16** go; advance: *We walked along the road a mile, then struck out across the fields.* **17** assume: *strike an amusing pose.* **18** make; decide; enter upon: *The employer and the workers have struck an agreement.* **19** lower or take down (a sail, flag, tent, etc.): *The ship struck its flag as a sign of surrender.* **20** act of striking. **21** baseball pitched through the strike zone and not swung at, any pitch that is swung at and missed, or any pitch that is hit foul under the rules of the game. After three strikes, a batter is out. **22** (in bowling) an upsetting of all the pins with the first ball bowled. 1-8,10,11,13,15-19 *v.*, **struck, struck** or **strick en, striking; 9,12,14,20-22** *n.* —**strike′less,** *adj.*

on strike, stopping work to get more pay, shorter hours, etc.: *Most of the workers voted to go on strike.*

strike it rich, 1 find rich ore, oil, etc. **2** have a sudden or unexpected great success.

strike out, 1 cross out; rub out. **2** (in baseball) put out or be put out by three strikes: *The batter struck out. The pitcher struck out six batters.*

strike up, begin: *The two children struck up a friendship.*

strike break er (strīk′brā′kər), person who helps to break up a strike of workers by taking a striker's job or by furnishing persons who will do so. *n.*

strike break ing (strīk′brā′king), forceful measures taken to halt a strike. *n.*

strike out (strīk′out′), in baseball: **1** an out caused by three strikes. **2** a striking out. *n.*

strik er (strī′kər), **1** person or thing that strikes. **2** worker who is on strike: *The union won't accept any settlement that does not greatly improve the working conditions of the strikers. n.*

strike zone, (in baseball) zone or area above home plate, between the batter's knees and armpits, through which a pitch must be thrown to be called a strike.

strik ing (strī′king), **1** attracting attention; very noticeable: *a striking performance by an actor.* **2** on strike: *The striking miners will soon return to work. adj.* —**strik′ing ness,** *n.*

strik ing ly (strī′king lē), in a way that attracts attention: *strikingly handsome. adv.*

string (string), **1** a thick thread; small cord or wire; very thin rope: *The package is tied with red string.* **2** such a thread with things on it: *She wore a string of beads around her neck.* **3** put on a string: *The child is stringing beads.* **4** a special cord or wire for musical instruments, bows, etc.: *the strings of a violin.* **5 strings,** *pl.* violins, cellos, and other stringed instruments. **6** furnish with strings: *She had her tennis racket strung.* **7** anything used for tying: *apron strings.* **8** tie with string or rope; hang with a string or rope: *We dry herbs by stringing them from the rafters in the barn.* **9** extend or stretch from one point to another: *string a cable.* **10** a cordlike part of plants. String beans have little strings connecting the two halves of a pod. **11** remove strings from: *String the beans before cooking them.* **12** form into a string or strings. **13** number of things in a line or row: *A string of cars came down the street.* **14** INFORMAL. condition; proviso: *an offer with strings attached to it.* 1,2,4,5,7,10,13,14 *n.*, 3,6,8,9,11,12 *v.*, **strung, strung** or **stringed, string ing.** [*String* comes

---

a hat	**i** it	**oi** oil	**ch** child	a in about
ā age	**ī** ice	**ou** out	**ng** long	e in taken
ä far	**o** hot	**u** cup	**sh** she	ə = i in pencil
e let	**ō** open	**u̇** put	**th** thin	o in lemon
ē equal	**ô** order	**ü** rule	**ŦH** then	u in circus
ėr term			**zh** measure	

from Old English *streng.*] —**string′less,** *adj.* —**string′-like′,** *adj.*

on a string, under control.

pull strings, 1 direct the actions of others secretly. **2** use secret influence.

string along, INFORMAL. **1** to fool; hoax. **2** go along (with); agree. **3** believe in or trust completely.

string out, INFORMAL. stretch; extend: *The program was strung out too long.*

string bean, the long, green or yellow seed pod of a garden plant, cooked and eaten as a vegetable.

stringed instrument, a musical instrument having strings, played either with a bow or by plucking. A harp, a violin, and a guitar are stringed instruments.

strin gen cy (strin′jən sē), strictness; severity. *n., pl.* **strin gen cies.**

strin gent (strin′jənt), strict; severe: *stringent laws against speeding. adj.* —**strin′gent ly,** *adv.*

string er (string′ər), **1** person or thing that strings. **2** a long, horizontal timber in a building, bridge, railroad track, etc. *n.*

string i ness (string′ē nis), stringy quality or condition. *n.*

string y (string′ē), **1** like a string or strings. **2** forming strings: *a stringy syrup.* **3** having tough fibers: *stringy meat.* **4** lean and sinewy: *He is a boy of about sixteen, tall and stringy. adj.,* **string i er, string i est.**

strip¹ (strip), **1** make bare or naked; undress. **2** take off the covering of: *to strip a log by removing the bark.* **3** remove; pull off: *The birds stripped the fruit from the trees.* **4** rob: *Thieves stripped the house of everything valuable.* **5** take away the titles, rights, etc., of (a person or thing). **6** tear off the teeth of (a gear, etc.). **7** break the thread of (a bolt, nut, etc.). *v.,* **stripped, strip ping.**

strip² (strip), a long, narrow, flat piece (of cloth, paper, bark, etc.). *n.*

stripe (strīp), **1** a long, narrow band of different color, material, etc. The stripes on a uniform show a person's rank. *A tiger has stripes. The American flag has thirteen stripes.* **2** mark with stripes. **3** sort; type: *a man of quite a different stripe.* 1,3 *n.,* 2 *v.,* **striped, strip ing.** —**stripe′less,** *adj.*

striped (strīpt), having stripes; marked with stripes: *Zebras are striped. adj.*

strip ling (strip′ling), boy just coming into manhood; youth; lad. *n.*

strip per (strip′ər), person or thing that strips. *n.*

strive (strīv), **1** try hard; work hard: *strive for self-control. Strive to succeed.* **2** struggle; fight: *The swimmer strove against the tide. v.,* **strove** or **strived, striv en, striv ing.** —**striv′er,** *n.*

striv en (striv′ən), past participle of **strive.** *She has striven hard to make the business a success. v.*

strode (strōd), past tense of **stride.** *He strode into the room. v.*

stroke¹ (strōk), **1** act of striking; blow: *drive in a nail with several strokes of a hammer. The house was hit by a stroke of lightning.* **2** sound made by striking: *the stroke of a bell. We arrived at the stroke of three o'clock.* **3** piece of luck, fortune, etc.: *a stroke of bad luck.* **4** a single complete movement to be made again and again: *He rowed with a strong stroke of the oars. She swims a fast stroke.* **5** movement or mark made by a pen, pencil, brush, etc.: *I write with a heavy down stroke.* **6** a very successful effort; feat: *a stroke of genius.* **7** a single effort; act: *I felt lazy and didn't do a stroke of work all day.* **8** a sudden attack of illness, especially one caused by a blood clot or bleeding in the brain. **9** rower who sets the time for the other oarsmen. **10** be the stroke of: *Who stroked the Yale crew?* 1-9 *n.,* 10 *v.,* **stroked, strok ing.**

stroke² (strōk), **1** move the hand gently over: *She stroked the kitten.* **2** a stroking movement: *to brush away the crumbs with one stroke.* 1 *v.,* **stroked, strok ing;** 2 *n.* —**strok′er,** *n.*

stroll (strōl), **1** take a quiet walk for pleasure; walk. **2** a leisurely walk. **3** go from place to place: *strolling musicians.* 1,3 *v.,* 2 *n.*

stroll er (strō′lər), **1** person who strolls: *There were many strollers in the park.* **2** kind of light baby carriage in which a small child sits erect. *n.*

strong (strông), **1** having much force or power: *A strong person can lift heavy things. A strong wind blew down the trees. A strong nation has many able citizens and great resources.* **2** able to last, endure, resist, etc.: *a strong fort, a strong rope.* **3** not easily influenced or changed; firm: *a strong will.* **4** of great force or effectiveness: *strong arguments.* **5** having a certain number: *A group that is 100 strong has 100 members.* **6** having a particular quality or property in a high degree: *strong perfume, a strong acid. Strong tea has more flavor than weak tea.* **7** containing much alcohol: *a strong drink.* **8** with force; powerfully; vigorously; in a strong manner. 1-7 *adj.,* **strong er** (strông′gər), **strong est** (strông′gəst); 8 *adv.* —**strong′ly,** *adv.* —**strong′ness,** *n.*

strong box (strông′boks′), a strongly made box to hold valuable things: *The diamonds were kept in a strongbox. n., pl.* **strong box es.**

strong hold (strông′hōld′), a strong place; safe place; fort; fortress: *The robbers have a stronghold in the mountains. n.*

stron ti um (stron′shē əm *or* stron′tē əm), a metallic element which occurs only in combination with other elements. It is used in making alloys and in fireworks and signal flares. *n.*

strontium 90, a radioactive isotope of strontium that occurs in the fallout from a nuclear explosion. It is extremely dangerous because it is easily absorbed by the bones and tissues.

strop (strop), **1** a leather strap used for sharpening razors. **2** sharpen on a strop. 1 *n.,* 2 *v.,* **stropped, stropping.**

stro phe (strō′fē), group of lines of poetry; stanza. *n.*

strove (strōv), a past tense of **strive.** *They strove hard, but did not win the game. v.*

struck (struk), past tense and a past participle of **strike.** *The clock struck four. The barn was struck by lightning. v.*

struc tur al (struk′chər əl), **1** used in building. Structural steel is steel made into beams, girders, etc. **2** of structure or structures: *The geologist showed the structural difference in rocks of different ages. adj.*

struc tur al ly (struk′chər ə lē), with regard to structure: *The new library is structurally perfect, but it is not beautiful. adv.*

struc ture (struk′chər), **1** something built; a building or construction. Dams, bridges, and tunnels are very large structures; apartment houses are smaller structures. **2** anything composed of parts arranged together: *The human body is a wonderful structure.* **3** manner of building; way parts are put together; construction: *The structure of the school was excellent.* **4** arrangement of parts, elements, etc.: *the structure of a molecule, the structure of a flower, sentence structure, the structure of a story.* **5** make

into a structure; build; construct: *to structure a sentence.* 1-4 *n.,* 5 *v.,* **struc tured, struc tur ing.** —**struc′ture less,** *adj.*

strug gle (strug′əl), **1** make great efforts with the body; try hard; work hard against difficulties: *The poor have to struggle for a living. The swimmer struggled against the tide. She struggled to keep back her anger.* **2** get, move, or make one's way with great effort: *The old horse struggled to its feet.* **3** great effort; hard work: *It was a struggle for the couple to send their six children to college. Making the baby eat spinach is a struggle.* **4** to fight: *The brave dog struggled fiercely with the large wildcat.* **5** a fighting; conflict: *The struggle between the two enemy countries went on for years.* 1,2,4 *v.,* **strug gled, strug gling;** 3,5 *n.* —**strug′gler,** *n.* —**strug′gling ly,** *adv.*

strum (strum), **1** play by running the fingers lightly or carelessly across the strings or keys: *strum a guitar, strum on the piano.* **2** act of strumming. **3** sound of strumming. 1 *v.,* **strummed, strum ming;** 2,3 *n.*

strum mer (strum′ər), person who strums. *n.*

strum pet (strum′pit), prostitute. *n.*

strung (strung), past tense and a past participle of **string.** *The children strung along after the teacher. The vines had been strung on poles. v.*

strut¹ (strut), **1** walk in a vain, important manner: *The rooster struts about the barnyard.* **2** a strutting walk. 1 *v.,* **strut ted, strut ting;** 2 *n.* —**strut′ter,** *n.*

strut²
struts between beams

strut² (strut), a supporting piece; brace. *n.*

strych nine (strik′nən *or* strik′nīn), a poisonous drug formerly used in medicine in small doses as a tonic or stimulant. *n.* [*Strychnine* can be traced back to Greek *strychnos,* meaning "nightshade."]

Stu art (stü′ərt *or* styü′ərt), **1** the royal family that ruled Scotland from 1371 to 1603, and England and Scotland for most of the period from 1603 to 1714. Charles I and Queen Anne belonged to the house of Stuart. **2 Mary.** See **Mary, Queen of Scots.** *n.*

stub (stub), **1** a short piece that is left: *the stub of a pencil.* **2** the short piece of each leaf in a checkbook, etc., kept as a record. **3** something short and blunt; short, thick piece or part. **4** pen having a short, blunt point. **5** stump of a tree, a broken tooth, etc. **6** strike (one's toe) against something: *I stubbed my toe on a sharp rock.* 1-5 *n.,* 6 *v.,* **stubbed, stub bing.**

stub bi ness (stub′ē nis), stubby condition or form. *n.*

stub ble (stub′əl), **1** the lower ends of stalks of grain left in the ground after the grain is cut: *The stubble hurt the child's bare feet.* **2** any short, rough growth: *He had three days' stubble on his unshaven face. n.*

stub bly (stub′lē), **1** covered with stubble. **2** resembling stubble; bristly: *a stubbly mustache. adj.,* **stub bli er, stub bli est.** —**stub′bli ness,** *n.*

stub born (stub′ərn), **1** fixed in purpose or opinion; not giving in to argument or requests: *The stubborn child refused to listen to reasons for not going out in the rain.* **2** hard to deal with or manage: *a stubborn cough. adj.* —**stub′born ly,** *adv.* —**stub′born ness,** *n.*

stub by (stub′ē), **1** short and thick: *stubby fingers.* **2** short, thick, and stiff: *a stubby beard.* **3** having many stubs or stumps. *adj.,* **stub bi er, stub bi est.**

stuc co (stuk′ō), **1** plaster used for covering walls. One kind is used for covering the outer walls of buildings;

another kind is used for cornices, moldings, and other interior decoration. **2** cover with stucco: *We had our house stuccoed last year.* 1 *n., pl.* **stuc coes** or **stuc cos**; 2 *v.* [*Stucco is borrowed from Italian* stucco.]

stuck (stuk), past tense and past participle of **stick²**. *She stuck her arm out of the car window. We were stuck in the mud. v.*

stuck-up (stuk′up′), INFORMAL. too proud; conceited; haughty. *adj.*

stud¹ (def. 1)
a dog collar
with studs

stud¹ (stud), **1** head of a nail, knob, etc., sticking out from a surface, used especially for ornament. **2** to set with studs or something like studs: *The dagger handle was studded with jewels.* **3** be set or scattered over: *Little islands stud the harbor.* **4** to set like studs; scatter at intervals: *Shocks of corn were studded over the field.* **5** a kind of small button used in men's shirts. **6** an upright post to which boards or laths are nailed in making walls in houses. 1,5,6 *n.*, 2-4 *v.*, **stud ded, stud ding.**

stud² (stud), **1** a male horse or other male animal kept for breeding. **2** collection of horses kept for breeding. *n.*

stu dent (stüd′nt or styüd′nt), **1** person who studies: *She is a student of birds.* **2** person who is studying in a school, college, or university: *That high school has 3000 students. n.* —**stu′dent like′**, *adj.*

stud ied (stud′ēd), carefully planned; done on purpose; deliberate: *What she said to me was a studied insult. adj.* —**stud′ied ly**, *adv.* —**stud′ied ness**, *n.*

stu di o (stü′dē ō or styü′dē ō), **1** workroom of a painter, sculptor, photographer, etc. **2** place where motion pictures are made. **3** place from which a radio or television program is broadcast. *n., pl.* **stu di os.**

studio couch, an upholstered couch, without a back or arms, that can be used as a bed.

stu di ous (stü′dē əs or styü′dē əs), **1** fond of study. **2** showing careful consideration; careful; thoughtful: *He is always studious of other peoples' comfort. The clerk made a studious effort to please customers. adj.* —**stu′di ous ly**, *adv.* —**stu′di ous ness**, *n.*

stud y (stud′ē), **1** effort to learn by reading or thinking: *After an hour's hard study, he knew his lesson.* **2** try to learn: *She studied her spelling lesson for half an hour. I am studying to be a doctor.* **3** a careful examination; investigation: *make a study of the life of Mark Twain.* **4** examine carefully: *We studied the map to find the shortest road home.* **5** subject that is studied; branch of learning; thing investigated or to be investigated. *History, music, and law are studies.* **6** a room for study, reading, writing, etc.: *The author was at work in her study.* **7** piece of writing or work of art that deals in careful detail with one particular subject: *a study of art in Germany.* **8** sketch for a picture, story, etc. **9** consider with care; think out; plan: *The mayor studied ways to cut expenses.* **10** deep thought; reverie: *The judge was absorbed in study about the case.* **11** piece of music intended to develop skill; étude. 1,3,5-8,10,11 *n., pl.* **stud ies**; 2,4,9 *v.*, **stud ied, stud ying.**—**stud′i a ble**, *adj.* —**stud′i er**, *n.*

stuff (stuf), **1** what a thing is made of; material. **2** any woven fabric, especially a woolen or worsted one: *She bought some white stuff for curtains.* **3** thing or things;

substance: *The doctor rubbed some kind of stuff on the burn.* **4** goods; belongings: *He was told to move his stuff out of the room.* **5** worthless material; useless things: *Their attic is full of old stuff.* **6** silly words and thoughts: *a lot of stuff and nonsense.* **7** inward qualities; character: *That girl has good stuff in her.* **8** pack full; fill: *They stuffed the pillows with feathers.* **9** put fraudulent votes in (a ballot box). **10** stop up; block; choke up: *stuff one's ears with cotton. My head is stuffed up by a cold.* **11** fill the skin of (a dead animal) to make it look as it did when alive. **12** fill (a chicken, turkey, etc.) with seasoned bread crumbs, etc., before cooking. **13** force; push; thrust: *She stuffed her clothes into the drawer.* **14** fill too much with food: *After I stuffed myself with candy, I felt sick.* 1-7 *n.*, 8-14 *v.* —**stuff′er**, *n.*

stuffed shirt, INFORMAL. person who tries to seem more important than he really is.

stuff i ly (stuf′ə lē), in a stuffy manner. *adv.*

stuff i ness (stuf′ē nis), stuffy quality or condition. *n.*

stuff ing (stuf′ing), **1** material used to fill or pack something. **2** seasoned bread crumbs, etc., used to stuff a chicken, turkey, fish, etc., before cooking. *n.*

stuff y (stuf′ē), **1** lacking fresh air: *a stuffy room.* **2** lacking freshness or interest; dull: *a stuffy conversation, a stuffy person.* **3** stopped up: *A cold makes one's head feel stuffy. adj.*, **stuff i er, stuff i est.**

stul ti fy (stul′tə fī), to make useless, weak, or foolish; make futile or absurd; frustrate: *stultify a person's efforts or incentive. v.*, **stul ti fied, stul ti fy ing.** —**stul′ti fi ca′tion**, *n.* —**stul′ti fi′er**, *n.*

stum ble (stum′bəl), **1** trip by striking the foot against something: *He stumbled over the stool in the dark kitchen.* **2** walk unsteadily: *The tired hikers stumbled along.* **3** speak, act, etc., in a clumsy or hesitating way: *The actors made many blunders as they stumbled through the play.* **4** make a mistake; do wrong. **5** a wrong act; mistake. **6** come by accident or chance: *While in the country, we stumbled upon some fine antiques.* **7** act of stumbling. 1-4,6 *v.*, **stum bled, stum bling**; 5,7 *n.* —**stum′bler**, *n.*

stumbling block, obstacle; hindrance.

stum bling ly (stum′bling lē), in a clumsy or hesitating way; unsteadily. *adv.*

stump (stump), **1** the lower end of a tree or plant, left after the main part is cut off: *She sat on top of a stump.* **2** anything left after the main or important part is removed: *the stump of a pencil, the stump of a candle. The dog wagged its stump of a tail.* **3** place where a political speech is made. **4** make political speeches in: *The candidates for governor will stump the state.* **5** walk in a stiff, clumsy way. **6** INFORMAL. make unable to answer, do, etc.; cause to be at a loss: *The riddle stumped me.* 1-3 *n.*, 4-6 *v.* —**stump′less**, *adj.* —**stump′like′**, *adj.*

stump y (stum′pē), **1** short and thick: *a stumpy person.* **2** having many stumps: *stumpy ground. adj.*, **stump i er, stump i est.** —**stump′i ly**, *adv.* —**stump′i ness**, *n.*

stun (stun), **1** make senseless; knock unconscious: *He was stunned by the blow.* **2** daze; bewilder; shock; overwhelm: *She was stunned by the news of her friend's death. v.*, **stunned, stun ning.**

stung (stung), past tense and past participle of **sting**. *A wasp stung me. He had been stung on the neck by a hornet. v.*

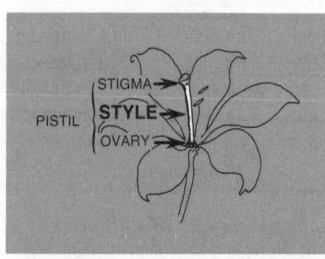

style (def. 10)

stunk (stungk), a past tense and past participle of **stink**. *The garbage stunk. Rotten eggs had stunk up the kitchen. v.*

stun ning (stun′ing), **1** having striking excellence, beauty, etc.; very attractive: *a stunning outfit.* **2** shocking; bewildering: *a stunning blow. adj.* —**stun′ning ly,** *adv.*

stunt[1] (stunt), to check in growth or development: *Lack of proper food stunts a child. v.*

stunt[2] (stunt), feat to attract attention; act showing boldness or skill: *Circus riders perform stunts on horseback. n.*

stu pe fy (stü′pə fī *or* styü′pə fī), **1** make stupid, dull, or senseless: *be stupefied by a drug.* **2** overwhelm with shock or amazement; astound: *They were stupefied by the news of the disaster. v.,* **stu pe fied, stu pe fy ing.**

stu pen dous (stü pen′dəs *or* styü pen′dəs), amazing; marvelous; immense: *Niagara Falls is a stupendous sight. adj.* —**stu pen′dous ly,** *adv.* —**stu pen′dous ness,** *n.*

stu pid (stü′pid *or* styü′pid), **1** not intelligent; dull: *a stupid person, a stupid remark.* **2** not interesting: *a stupid book.* **3** dazed; senseless. *adj.* —**stu′pid ly,** *adv.*

stu pid i ty (stü pid′ə tē *or* styü pid′ə tē), **1** lack of intelligence; dullness. **2** a foolish act, idea, etc. *n., pl.* **stu pid i ties.**

stu por (stü′pər *or* styü′pər), a dazed condition; loss or lessening of the power to feel: *The injured mountain climber lay in a stupor, unable to tell what had happened. n.*

stur di ly (stėr′də lē), in a sturdy manner. *adv.*

stur di ness (stėr′dē nis), sturdy quality or condition; strength; firmness. *n.*

stur dy (stėr′dē), **1** strong; stout: *a sturdy chair.* **2** not yielding; firm: *sturdy defence. adj.,* **stur di er, stur di est.**

sturgeon—up to 14 ft. (4 m.) long

stur geon (stėr′jən), a large food fish whose long body has a tough skin with rows of bony plates. Caviar is made from sturgeon eggs. *n., pl.* **stur geons** *or* **sturgeon.**

stut ter (stut′ər), **1** repeat (the same sound) in an effort to speak. **2** act or habit of stuttering. **1** *v.,* **2** *n.* —**stut′ter er,** *n.* —**stut′ter ing ly,** *adv.*

St. Vin cent and the Gren a dines (sānt vin sənt ənd тнə gren′ə dēnz′), island country in the West Indies, a member of the Commonwealth of Nations. *Capital:* Kingstown.

sty[1] (stī), **1** pen for pigs. **2** any filthy place. *n., pl.* **sties.**

sty[2] (stī), a painful swelling on the edge of the eyelid. A sty is a small boil. *n., pl.* **sties.**

style (stīl), **1** fashion: *Several popular teenagers set the style in dress at the school. My clothes are out of style.* **2** manner; method; way: *the Gothic style of architecture. She learned several styles of swimming.* **3** way of writing or speaking: *Books for children should have a clear, easy style.* **4** good style: *She dresses in style.* **5** excellence of form or expression in literature, speech, art, etc.: *a model of style, a master of literary style.* **6** make in or conform to a given or accepted style; stylize: *Her poem is styled with care.* **7** to design according to a style or fashion: *His suits are styled by a famous designer.* **8** to name; call: *She styles herself a poet.* **9** stylus. **10** the stemlike part of the pistil of a flower. **1-5,9,10** *n.,* **6-8** *v.,* **styled, styling.** —**style′less,** *adj.* —**style′like′,** *adj.* —**styl′er,** *n.*

styl ish (stī′lish), having style; fashionable: *He wears stylish clothes. adj.* —**styl′ish ly,** *adv.* —**styl′ish ness,** *n.*

styl ist (stī′list), **1** writer, speaker, artist, etc., who is considered to be an expert or a master of style. **2** person who designs, arranges, or advises concerning interior decorations, clothes, hair styles, etc. *n.*

sty lis tic (stī lis′tik), of style. *adj.*

sty lis ti cal ly (stī lis′tik lē), with regard to style; in matters of style. *adv.*

styl ize (stī′līz), make or design according to a particular or conventional style. *v.,* **styl ized, styl iz ing.** —**styl′i za′tion,** *n.* —**styl′iz er,** *n.*

sty lus (stī′ləs), **1** a pointed instrument for writing on wax; style. **2** a needlelike point used in making or playing phonograph records. *n., pl.* **sty lus es, sty li** (stī′lī).

sty mie (stī′mē), block completely; hinder; thwart: *His plans were stymied by lack of money. v.,* **sty mied, sty mieing.**

styp tic (stip′tik), **1** able to stop or check bleeding; astringent. **2** something that stops or checks bleeding by contracting the tissue. Alum is a common styptic. **1** *adj.,* **2** *n.*

Sty ro foam (stī′rə fōm′), trademark for a lightweight plastic foam, used to insulate buildings and to make cups, coolers, etc. *n.*

sua sion (swā′zhən), an advising or urging; persuasion. *n.*

sua sive (swā′siv), advising or urging; persuasive. *adj.* —**sua′sive ly,** *adv.* —**sua′sive ness,** *n.*

suave (swäv), smoothly agreeable or polite. *adj.* —**suave′ly,** *adv.* —**suave′ness,** *n.*

sua vi ty (swä′və tē), smoothly agreeable quality of behavior; blandness; smooth politeness. *n.*

sub (sub), **1** substitute. **2** submarine. **3** act as a substitute. **1,2** *n.,* **3** *v.,* **subbed, sub bing.**

sub-, *prefix.* **1** under; below: *Subnormal = below normal.* **2** down; further; again: *Subdivide = divide again.* **3** near; nearly: *Subtropical = nearly tropical.* **4** lower; subordinate: *Subcommittee = a lower or subordinate committee.*

sub., **1** subscription. **2** substitute. **3** suburban.

sub com mit tee (sub′kə mit′ē), a small committee chosen from a larger general committee for some special duty. *n.*

sub com pact (sub′kom′pakt), automobile smaller than a compact, usually having a four-cylinder engine. *n.*

sub con scious (sub kon′shəs), **1** not wholly conscious; existing in the mind but not fully perceived or recognized: *Some students drop out of school not really because they have to go to work, but because of a subconscious fear of failure in school.* **2** thoughts, feelings, etc., that are present in the mind but not fully perceived or recognized. **1** *adj.,* **2** *n.* —**sub con′scious ly,** *adv.*

sub con ti nent (sub kon′tə nənt), a land mass or region that is very large, but smaller than a continent. India is a subcontinent. *n.*

sub cu ta ne ous (sub′kyü tā′nē əs), **1** under the skin:

subcutaneous tissue. **2** placed or performed under the skin: *a subcutaneous injection. adj.* —**sub′cu ta′ne ous ly,** *adv.*

sub di vide (sub′də vīd′ *or* sub′də vīd′), divide again; divide into smaller parts: *A real estate dealer bought the farm and subdivided it into building lots. v.,* **sub di vid ed, sub di vid ing.**

sub di vi sion (sub′də vizh′ən *or* sub′də vizh′ən), **1** division into smaller parts. **2** part of a part. **3** tract of land divided into building lots. *n.*

sub dom i nant (sub dom′ə nənt), the fourth note in a musical scale. F is the subdominant in the key of C. *n.*

sub due (səb dü′ *or* səb dyü′), **1** overcome by superior force; conquer: *The Romans subdued all the peoples of the Mediterranean.* **2** keep down; hold back; suppress: *We subdued a desire to laugh.* **3** tone down; soften: *Pulling down the shades subdued the light in the room. v.,* **sub dued, sub du ing.** —**sub du′a ble,** *adj.* —**sub du′er,** *n.*

sub group (sub′grüp′), a subordinate group; division of a group. *n.*

sub head (sub′hed′), **1** a subordinate heading or title. **2** a subordinate division of a heading or title. *n.*

sub head ing (sub′hed′ing), subhead. *n.*

sub hu man (sub hyü′mən), below the human race; less than human. *adj.*

subj., **1** subject. **2** subjective. **3** subjectively. **4** subjunctive.

sub ject (sub′jikt *for 1-5,8,10-12;* səb jekt′ *for 6,7,9*), **1** something thought about, discussed, investigated, etc.: *The subject for our composition was "An Exciting Moment."* **2** something learned or taught; course of study in some branch of knowledge: *English, science, and arithmetic are some of the subjects we take up in school.* **3** person under the power, control, or influence of another: *The people are the subjects of the king.* **4** bound by loyalty or allegiance (to); obedient to some power or influence: *We are subject to our country's laws.* **5** under some power or influence: *the subject nations of an empire.* **6** bring under some power or influence: *Rome subjected all Italy to its rule.* **7** cause to undergo or experience something: *The school subjected new students to many tests.* **8** likely to have or receive; liable (to suffer from); prone (to): *I am subject to colds. Japan is subject to earthquakes.* **9** make liable (to have or receive); lay open (to); expose: *The location of the island in the middle of the ocean subjected it to frequent hurricanes.* **10** person or thing that undergoes or experiences something: *Rabbits and mice are often subjects for medical experiments.* **11** depending on; on the condition of: *I bought the car subject to your approval.* **12** (in grammar) a word or group of words about which something is said in a sentence. The subject is usually the performer of the action of an active verb or the receiver of the action of a passive verb. *I* is the subject of the following sentences: I see the cat. I am seen by the cat. I can see. 1-3,10,12 *n.,* 4,5,8,11 *adj.,* 6,7,9 *v.*

sub jec tion (səb jek′shən), **1** a bringing under some power or influence; conquering: *The subjection of the rebels took years.* **2** condition of being under some power or influence: *The peasants lived in subjection to the nobility. n.*

sub jec tive (səb jek′tiv), **1** existing in the mind; belonging to the person thinking rather than to the object thought of: *Base your subjective opinions on objective facts.* **2** about the thoughts and feelings of the speaker, writer, painter, etc.; personal: *a subjective poem. adj.* —**sub jec′tive ly,** *adv.* —**sub jec′tive ness,** *n.*

subject matter, **1** something thought about, discussed, studied, written about, etc. **2** what a talk, book, etc., is about, as distinguished from its form or style: *The speaker's subject matter was better than her presentation.*

a hat	i it	oi oil	ch child	a in about
ā age	ī ice	ou out	ng long	e in taken
ä far	o hot	u cup	sh she	ə = i in pencil
e let	ō open	u̇ put	th thin	o in lemon
ē equal	ô order	ü rule	ŦH then	u in circus
ėr term			zh measure	

sub ju gate (sub′jə gāt), subdue; conquer. *v.,* **sub ju gat ed, sub ju gat ing.** —**sub′ju ga′tor,** *n.*

sub ju ga tion (sub′jə gā′shən), conquest; subjection. *n.*

sub junc tive (səb jungk′tiv), **1** (in grammar) referring to a verb form which expresses a state, act, or event as possible, conditional, or dependent, rather than actual. **2** form of a verb which expresses this. In "I insist that he go" and "If I were you," *go* and *were* are subjunctives. **3** mood of such a verb. **1** *adj.,* **2,3** *n.*

sub lease (sub′lēs′ *for 1;* sub lēs′ *or* sub′lēs′ *for 2*), **1** a lease granted by a person on property which that person has leased. **2** give a sublease of. **3** take a sublease of. **1** *n.,* **2,3** *v.,* **sub leased, sub leas ing.**

sub let (sub let′ *or* sub′let′), **1** rent to another (something which has been rented to oneself); give a sublease of: *She sublet her house for the summer.* **2** take a sublease of: *I have sublet an apartment whose tenants went away for the summer.* **3** give part of (a contract) to another: *The contractor for the whole building sublet the contract for the plumbing. v.,* **sub let, sub let ting.**

sub li mate (sub′lə māt), change (an undesirable impulse or trait) into a desirable activity. *v.,* **sub li mat ed, sub li mat ing.**

sub li ma tion (sub′lə mā′shən), act or process of sublimating. *n.*

sub lime (sə blīm′), **1** lofty or elevated in thought, feeling, language, etc.; noble; grand; exalted: *sublime devotion, sublime poetry. Mountain scenery is often sublime.* **2** that which is lofty, noble, exalted, etc.: *the sublime in literature and art.* **1** *adj.,* **2** *n.* —**sub lime′ly,** *adv.* —**sub lime′ness,** *n.*

sub lim i ty (sə blim′ə tē), lofty excellence; grandeur; majesty; exalted state. *n.*

sub ma chine gun (sub′mə shēn′), a lightweight automatic or semiautomatic gun, designed to be fired from the shoulder or hip.

sub ma rine (sub′mə rēn′ *for 1;* sub′mə rēn′ *for 2*), **1** boat that can go under water. Submarines are used in warfare for attacking enemy ships with torpedoes and for launching missiles. **2** under the surface of the sea; underwater: *submarine plants, submarine warfare.* **1** *n.,* **2** *adj.*

sub merge (səb mėrj′), **1** put under water; cover with water: *A big wave submerged us. At high tide this path is submerged.* **2** cover; bury: *His talent was submerged by his shyness.* **3** sink under water; go below the surface: *The submarine submerged to escape attack. v.,* **sub merged, sub merg ing.**

sub mer gence (səb mėr′jəns), a submerging or a being submerged. *n.*

sub merse (səb mėrs′), submerge. *v.,* **sub mersed, sub mers ing.**

sub mers i ble (səb mėr′sə bəl), **1** able to be submerged. **2** a submarine. **1** *adj.,* **2** *n.*

sub mer sion (səb mėr′zhən), a submerging or a being submerged. *n.*

sub mis sion (səb mish′ən), **1** a yielding to the power, control, or authority of another; submitting: *The defeated general showed his submission by giving up his sword.* **2** obedience; humbleness: *They all bowed in submission to the queen's order.* **3** a referring or a being referred to the consideration or judgment of some person or group. *n.*

sub mis sive (səb mis′iv), yielding to the power, control, or authority of another; obedient; humble. *adj.* —**sub mis′sive ly,** *adv.* —**sub mis′sive ness,** *n.*

sub mit (səb mit′), 1 yield to the power, control, or authority of some person or group; surrender; yield: *They submitted to the will of the majority.* 2 refer to the consideration or judgment of some person or group: *The secretary submitted a report of the last meeting.* 3 suggest or urge respectfully: *I submit that more evidence is needed to support the case.* *v.,* **sub mit ted, sub mit ting.**

sub nor mal (sub nôr′məl), below normal: *a subnormal temperature, subnormal intelligence. adj.*

sub or di nate (sə bôrd′n it *for 1-3;* sə bôrd′n āt *for 4*), 1 lower in rank: *In the army, lieutenants are subordinate to captains.* 2 having less importance; secondary; dependent: *An assistant has a subordinate position.* 3 a subordinate person or thing. 4 make subordinate: *He was an agreeable person, who often subordinated his wishes to those of other people.* 1,2 *adj.,* 3 *n.,* 4 *v.,* **sub or di nat ed, sub or di nat ing.** —**sub or′di nate ly,** *adv.* —**sub or′di nate ness,** *n.*

subordinate clause, dependent clause.

sub or di na tion (sə bôrd′n ā′shən), 1 a subordinating or a being subordinated. 2 subordinate position or importance. 3 submission to authority; willingness to obey; obedience. *n.*

sub orn (sə bôrn′), 1 persuade, bribe, or cause (someone) to do an illegal or evil deed. 2 persuade or cause (a witness) to give false testimony in court. *v.* —**sub′or na′tion,** *n.* —**sub orn′er,** *n.*

sub pe na (sə pē′nə), subpoena. *n., pl.* **sub pe nas;** *v.*

sub poe na (sə pē′nə), 1 an official written order commanding a person to appear in a court of law. 2 summon with such an order. 1 *n., pl.* **sub poe nas;** 2 *v.*

sub scribe (səb skrīb′), 1 promise to give or pay (a sum of money): *She subscribed $15 to the hospital fund.* 2 promise to accept and pay for: *We subscribe to a few magazines.* 3 write (one's name) at the end of a document, etc.; show one's consent or approval by signing: *The men who subscribed to the Declaration of Independence are now famous.* 4 give one's consent or approval; agree: *She does not subscribe to my opinion. v.,* **sub scribed, sub scrib ing.**

sub scrib er (səb skrī′bər), person who subscribes: *The magazines make a special offer to new subscribers. n.*

sub script (sub′skript), number, letter, etc., written underneath and to one side of a symbol. In H_2SO_4 the 2 and 4 are subscripts. *n.*

sub scrip tion (səb skrip′shən), 1 a subscribing. 2 money subscribed; contribution: *My subscription to the Fresh Air Fund was $5.* 3 the right to receive something, obtained by paying a certain sum: *Our subscription to the newspaper expires next week.* 4 sum of money raised by a number of persons: *We are raising a subscription for a new hospital. n.*

sub sec tion (sub′sek′shən), part of a section. *n.*

sub se quent (sub′sə kwənt), coming after; following; later: *Subsequent events proved that she was right. adj.* —**sub′se quent ly,** *adv.* —**sub′se quent ness,** *n.*

sub serve (səb sėrv′), to help or assist (a purpose, action, etc.): *Chewing food well subserves digestion. v.,* **sub served, sub serv ing.**

sub ser vi ence (səb sėr′vē əns), tame submission; slavish politeness and obedience; servility. *n.*

sub ser vi ent (səb sėr′vē ənt), 1 tamely submissive; slavishly polite and obedient; servile. 2 useful as a means to help a purpose or end; serviceable. *adj.* —**sub ser′vi ent ly,** *adv.*

sub set (sub′set′), (in mathematics) a set, each of whose members is a member of a second set: *A subset of S is a set every element of which belongs to S. n.*

sub side (səb sīd′), 1 grow less; die down; become less active: *The storm finally subsided. Her fever subsided after she took the medicine.* 2 sink to a lower level: *Several days after the rain stopped, the floodwaters subsided. v.,* **sub sid ed, sub sid ing.**

sub sid ence (səb sīd′ns *or* sub′sə dəns), act or process of subsiding: *the subsidence of a flood. n.*

sub sid i ar y (səb sid′ē er′ē), 1 useful to assist or supplement; auxiliary; supplementary: *The teacher sold books as a subsidiary occupation.* 2 thing or person that assists or supplements. 3 company having over half of its stock owned or controlled by another company: *The bus line was a subsidiary of the railroad.* 4 maintained by a subsidy. 1,4 *adj.,* 2,3 *n., pl.* **sub sid i ar ies.**

sub si dize (sub′sə dīz), aid or assist with a grant of money: *The government subsidizes airlines that carry mail. v.,* **sub si dized, sub si diz ing.** —**sub′si di za′tion,** *n.*

sub si diz er (sub′sə dī′zer), person or group that subsidizes. *n.*

sub si dy (sub′sə dē), grant or contribution of money, especially one made by a government: *a subsidy for education. n., pl.* **sub si dies.**

sub sist (səb sist′), 1 keep alive; live: *The lost hiker subsisted on wild berries for two days.* 2 continue to be; exist: *Many superstitions still subsist. v.*

sub sist ence (səb sis′təns), 1 a keeping alive; living: *Selling papers was his only means of subsistence.* 2 means of keeping alive; livelihood: *The sea provides a subsistence for fishermen.* 3 existence; continuance. *n.*

sub soil (sub′soil′), layer of earth that lies just under the surface soil. *n.*

sub son ic (sub son′ik), 1 of a speed which is less than the speed of sound, about 740 miles (1190 kilometers) per hour at sea level. 2 that moves at a speed slower than the speed of sound: *a subsonic airplane. adj.*

sub stance (sub′stəns), 1 what a thing consists of; matter; material: *Ice and water are the same substance in different forms.* 2 the real, main, or important part of anything: *The substance of an education is its effect on your life, not just learning lessons.* 3 real meaning: *Give the substance of the speech in your own words.* 4 solid quality; body: *Pea soup has more substance than water.* 5 wealth; property: *a person of substance. n.*

sub stand ard (sub stan′dərd), below standard. *adj.*

sub stan tial (səb stan′shəl), 1 having substance; material; real; actual: *People and things are substantial; dreams and ghosts are not.* 2 strong; firm; solid: *The house is substantial enough to last a hundred years.* 3 large; important; ample: *Your work shows substantial improvement.* 4 providing ample or abundant nourishment: *Eat a substantial breakfast.* 5 in the main; in essentials: *The stories told by the two children were in substantial agreement.* 6 well-to-do; wealthy. *adj.*

sub stan tial ly (səb stan′shə lē), 1 essentially; mainly: *This report is substantially correct.* 2 really; actually. 3 strongly; solidly: *a substantially built house. adv.*

sub stan ti ate (səb stan′shē āt), establish by evidence; prove: *substantiate a rumor, substantiate a claim. v.,* **sub stan ti at ed, sub stan ti at ing.**

sub stan ti a tion (səb stan′shē ā′shən), a substantiating or a being substantiated; proof. *n.*

sub stan tive (sub′stən tiv), 1 noun or pronoun; the name of a person or thing. 2 used as a noun. 3 showing or expressing existence: *The verb to be is the substantive verb.* 4 substantial. 1 *n.,* 2-4 *adj.*

sub sta tion (sub′stā′shən), a branch station; subordinate station: *Besides the main post office in our city, there are six substations. n.*

sub sti tute (sub′stə tüt *or* sub′stə tyüt), **1** thing used instead of another; person taking the place of another: *Margarine is a common substitute for butter. A substitute taught us at school today.* **2** put in the place of another: *We substituted brown sugar for molasses in these cookies.* **3** take the place of another: *She substituted for our teacher, who is ill.* **4** put in or taking the place of another: *a substitute teacher.* 1 *n.,* 2,3 *v.,* **sub sti tut ed, sub sti tut ing;** 4 *adj.*

sub sti tu tion (sub′stə tü′shən *or* sub′stə tyü′shən), the use of one thing for another; a putting (one person or thing) in the place of another; a taking the place of another. *n.*

sub stra tum (sub strā′təm), layer lying under another: *Beneath the sandy soil there was a substratum of clay. n., pl.* **sub stra ta** (sub strā′tə), **sub stra tums.**

sub teen (sub′tēn′), boy or girl nearly thirteen years old. *n.*

sub ter fuge (sub′tər fyüj), trick or excuse used to escape something unpleasant: *The child's headache was only a subterfuge to avoid going to school. n.*

sub ter ra ne an (sub′tə rā′nē ən), **1** underground: *A subterranean passage led from the castle to a cave.* **2** carried on secretly; hidden: *subterranean plotting. adj.*

sub ti tle (sub′tī′tl), **1** an additional or secondary title of a book, article, etc. **2** word or words shown on a motion-picture screen, especially as the translation of the words spoken in a foreign-language film; caption. **3** give a subtitle to. 1,2 *n.,* 3 *v.,* **sub ti tled, sub ti tling.**

subtle (def. 2)
She had a **subtle** smile.

sub tle (sut′l), **1** not obvious; delicate; fine: *a subtle odor of perfume. Subtle humor is often hard to understand.* **2** faint; mysterious. **3** keen; quick; acute: *a subtle mind, subtle reasoning.* **4** sly; crafty; tricky: *a subtle scheme to get some money.* **5** skillful; clever; expert: *a subtle worker in gold and silver. adj.,* **sub tler, sub tlest. —sub′tle ness,** *n.*

sub tle ty (sut′l tē), **1** subtle quality. **2** something subtle. *n., pl.* **sub tle ties.**

sub tly (sut′lē *or* sut′l ē), in a subtle manner. *adv.*

sub top ic (sub′top′ik), a secondary or subordinate topic. *n.*

sub to tal (sub tō′tl), **1** not quite total; less than complete. **2** something less than the total. 1 *adj.,* 2 *n.*

sub tract (səb trakt′), take away: *Subtract 2 from 10 and you have 8. v.* **—sub tract′er,** *n.*

sub trac tion (səb trak′shən), act or process of subtracting one number or quantity from another; finding the difference between two numbers or quantities: $10-2 = 8$ *is a simple subtraction. n.*

sub tra hend (sub′trə hend), number or quantity to be subtracted from another: *In* $10-2 = 8$, *the subtrahend is 2. n.*

sub trop i cal (sub trop′ə kəl), **1** bordering on the tropics. **2** nearly tropical. *adj.*

sub urb (sub′ėrb′), district, town, or village just outside or near a city: *Many people who work in the city live in the suburbs. n.*

sub ur ban (sə bėr′bən), **1** of a suburb; in a suburb: *We have excellent suburban train service.* **2** characteristic of a suburb or its inhabitants. *adj.*

sub ur ban ite (sə bėr′bə nīt), person who lives in a suburb. *n.*

sub ver sion (səb vėr′zhən), a subverting or a being subverted; overthrow; destruction. *n.*

sub ver sive (səb vėr′siv), **1** tending to overthrow; destructive; causing ruin: *a subversive organization.* **2** person who seeks to overthrow or weaken (a government, etc.). 1 *adj.,* 2 *n.* **—sub ver′sive ly,** *adv.*

sub vert (səb vėrt′), **1** overthrow (something established or existing); cause the downfall, ruin, or destruction of: *Dictators subvert democracy.* **2** weaken the principles of; corrupt: *subvert a peaceful society. v.* **—sub vert′er,** *n.*

subway
(def. 1)

sub way (sub′wā′), **1** an electric railroad running beneath the surface of the streets in a city. **2** an underground passage. *n.*

suc ceed (sək sēd′), **1** turn out well; do well; have success: *Her plans succeeded.* **2** come next after; follow; take the place of: *John Adams succeeded Washington as President.* **3** come next after another; follow another; take the place of another: *When George VI died, Elizabeth II succeeded to the throne. v.* **—suc ceed′er,** *n.*

suc cess (sək ses′), **1** a favorable result; wished-for ending; good fortune: *Success in school comes from intelligence and work.* **2** the gaining of wealth, position, etc.: *He has had little success in life.* **3** person or thing that succeeds: *The circus was a great success.* **4** result; outcome; fortune: *What success did you have in finding a new apartment? n.*

suc cess ful (sək ses′fəl), having success; ending in success; prosperous; fortunate: *a successful writer, a successful campaign. adj.* **—suc cess′ful ly,** *adv.* **—suc cess′ful ness,** *n.*

suc ces sion (sək sesh′ən), **1** group of things happening one after another; series: *A succession of accidents spoiled our automobile trip.* **2** the coming of one person or thing after another. **3** right of succeeding to an office, property, or rank: *There was a dispute about the rightful succession to the throne.* **4** order or arrangement of persons having such a right of succeeding: *The king's oldest daughter is next in succession to the throne. n.*

in succession, one after another: *We visited our sick friend several days in succession.*

suc ces sive (sək ses′iv), coming one after another; following in order: *It rained for three successive days. adj.* —**suc ces′sive ly,** *adv.* —**suc ces′sive ness,** *n.*

suc ces sor (sək ses′ər), one that follows or suceeds another in office, position, or ownership of property; thing that comes next after another in a series: *John Adams was Washington's successor as President. n.*

suc cinct (sək singkt′), expressed briefly and clearly; concise: *Her letter was succinct with all the main points on one page. adj.* —**suc cinct′ly,** *adv.* —**suc cinct′ness,** *n.*

suc cor (suk′ər), help; aid. *n., v.* Also, BRITISH **succour.** —**suc′cor er,** *n.*

suc co tash (suk′ə tash), kernels of sweet corn and beans, usually lima beans, cooked together. *n.* [*Succotash* comes from Narragansett Indian *msiquatash.*]

suc cour (suk′ər), BRITISH. succor. *n., v.*

suc cu lence (suk′yə ləns), juiciness. *n.*

suc cu lent (suk′yə lənt), juicy: *a succulent peach. adj.* —**suc′cu lent ly,** *adv.*

suc cumb (sə kum′), **1** give way; yield: *I succumbed to temptation and ate the last piece of candy.* **2** die: *She succumbed of old age. v.*

such (such), **1** of that kind; of the same kind or degree: *Such perfect diamonds as those are quite rare. The child had such a fever that she nearly died.* **2** of the kind already spoken of or suggested: *They did not like tea and coffee and such drinks.* **3** so great, so bad, so good, etc.: *He is such a liar. Such weather!* **4** that kind of person or thing: *Take from the blankets such as you need.* 1-3 *adj.,* 4 *pron.*

as such, as being what is indicated or implied: *A friend, as such, deserves understanding.*

such as, 1 similar to; like: *A good friend such as you is rare.* **2** for example: *members of the dog family, such as the wolf and fox.*

suck (suk), **1** draw into the mouth by using the lips and tongue: *Lemonade can be sucked through a straw.* **2** draw liquid from with the mouth: *suck oranges.* **3** draw milk from the breast or a bottle. **4** draw or be drawn by sucking: *He sucked at his pipe.* **5** drink, take, or absorb: *A sponge sucks in water.* **6** hold in the mouth and lick: *The child sucked a lollipop.* **7** act of sucking: *The baby took one suck at the empty bottle and pushed it away.* 1-6 *v.,* 7 *n.*

suck er (suk′ər), **1** animal or thing that sucks. **2** a freshwater fish with large, fleshy lips that suck in food. **3** organ in some animals for sucking or holding fast by a sucking force. **4** shoot growing from an underground stem or root. **5** lollipop. **6** SLANG. person easily deceived. *n.*

suck le (suk′əl), **1** feed with milk from the breast or udder: *The cat suckles her kittens.* **2** suck at the breast or udder. *v.,* **suck led, suck ling.**

suck ling (suk′ling), a very young animal or child, especially one not yet weaned. *n.*

Su cre (sü′krā), one of the two capitals of Bolivia, in the S part. La Paz is the other capital. *n.*

su crose (sü′krōs), ordinary sugar obtained from sugar cane, sugar beets, etc. *n.*

suc tion (suk′shən), **1** process of drawing liquids or gases into a space by sucking out or removing part of the air to produce a vacuum. We draw lemonade through a straw by suction. Vacuum cleaners and some pumps work by suction. **2** the force caused by suction. **3** act or process of sucking. **4** causing a suction; working by suction: *a suction valve.* 1-3 *n.,* 4 *adj.*

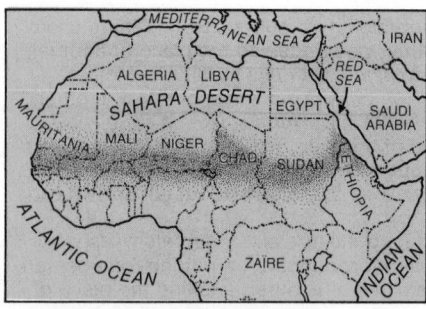

the Sudan (def. 2)—the darker area

Su dan (sü dan′), **1** country in NE Africa. *Capital:* Khartoum. **2 the Sudan,** vast region in Africa, south of the Sahara Desert and extending from the Atlantic Ocean to the Red Sea. *n.* Also, **Soudan.**

Su da nese (süd′n ēz′), **1** of Sudan or the Sudan or their inhabitants. **2** person born or living in Sudan or the Sudan. 1 *adj.,* 2 *n., pl.* **Su da nese.**

sud den (sud′n), **1** happening without warning or notice; not expected: *a sudden stop, a sudden rainstorm, a sudden rise to power.* **2** found or hit upon unexpectedly; abrupt: *There was a sudden turn in the road.* **3** quick; rapid: *The cat made a sudden jump at the mouse. adj.* —**sud′den ness,** *n.*

all of a sudden, in a sudden manner; unexpectedly or quickly.

sud den ly (sud′n lē), in a sudden manner. *adv.*

suds (sudz), **1** soapy water. **2** bubbles and foam on soapy water; soapsuds. *n.pl.*

suds y (sud′zē), full of soapsuds. *adj.,* **suds i er, suds i est.**

sue (sü), **1** start a lawsuit against: *She sued the driver of the car that hit her.* **2** take action in law: *sue for damages.* **3** beg or ask (for); plead: *Messengers came suing for peace. v.,* **sued, su ing.** —**su′a ble,** *adj.* —**su′er,** *n.*

suede or **suède** (swād), **1** a soft leather that has a velvety nap on one or both sides. **2** kind of cloth that has a similar appearance. **3** made of suede: *suede shoes, a suede jacket.* 1,2 *n.,* 3 *adj.*

su et (sü′it), the hard fat around the kidneys and loins of cattle and sheep. Suet is used in cooking and for making tallow. *n.*

su et y (sü′ə tē), **1** like suet. **2** containing suet. *adj.*

Su ez Canal (sü ez′), canal in the NE part of Egypt, connecting the Mediterranean and Red seas. See **Nile** for map.

suf. or **suff.,** suffix.

suf fer (suf′ər), **1** have pain, grief, injury, etc.: *Sick people suffer.* **2** have or feel (pain, grief, etc.): *I suffered sunburn from being at the beach all day.* **3** experience harm, loss, etc.: *His business suffered greatly last year.* **4** allow; permit: *"Suffer the little children to come unto me."* **5** bear with patiently; endure: *I will not suffer such insults. v.* —**suf′-fer er,** *n.*

suf fer a ble (suf′ər ə bəl), able to be endured; bearable. *adj.* —**suf′fer a ble ness,** *n.* —**suf′fer a bly,** *adv.*

suf fer ance (suf′ər əns), permission or consent given only by a failure to object or prevent. *n.*

suf fer ing (suf′ər ing), **1** condition of being in pain: *Hunger causes suffering.* **2** the enduring of pain, trouble, or distress: *the suffering of a poor family. n.*

suf fice (sə fīs′), **1** be enough; be sufficient: *Fifty dollars will suffice to buy that coat.* **2** satisfy; make content: *A small amount of cake sufficed the baby. v.,* **suf ficed, suf fic ing.**

suf fi cien cy (sə fish′ən sē), **1** a sufficient amount; large enough supply: *The ship had a sufficiency of provisions for a voyage of two months.* **2** condition or fact of being sufficient; adequacy; ability. *n., pl.* **suf fi cien cies.**

suf fi cient (sə fish′ənt), as much as is needed; enough: *sufficient proof. They did not have sufficient clothing for winter. adj.* —**suf fi′cient ly,** *adv.*

suf fix (suf′iks *for 1;* sə fiks′ *or* suf′iks *for 2*), **1** syllable or syllables put at the end of a word to change its meaning or to make another word, as *-ly* in *badly, -ness* in *goodness,* and *-ful* in *spoonful.* **2** add at the end; put after. **1** *n., pl.* **suf fix es; 2** *v.*

suf fo cate (suf′ə kāt), **1** kill by stopping the breath. **2** keep from breathing; hinder in breathing. **3** gasp for breath; choke. **4** die for lack of oxygen; be suffocated. **5** smother; suppress. *v.,* **suf fo cat ed, suf fo cat ing.** —**suf′fo cat′ing ly,** *adv.*

suf fo ca tion (suf′ə kā′shən), a suffocating or a being suffocated. *n.*

suf fo ca tive (suf′ə kā′tiv), stifling. *adj.*

suf frage (suf′rij), **1** the right to vote; franchise: *The United States granted suffrage to women in 1920.* **2** a vote, usually in support of a proposal, candidate, etc. **3** a voting; casting of votes. *n.*

suf fra gette (suf′rə jet′), woman advocating suffrage for women. *n.*

suf fra gist (suf′rə jist), person who favors giving suffrage to more people, especially to women. *n.*

suf fuse (sə fyüz′), overspread (with a liquid, dye, etc.): *eyes suffused with tears. At twilight the sky was suffused with glorious color. v.,* **suf fused, suf fus ing.**

sugar maples
being tapped

suf fu sion (sə fyü′zhən), **1** a suffusing or a being suffused. **2** that with which anything is overspread. **3** flush of color. *n.*

sug ar (shug′ər), **1** a sweet substance obtained chiefly from sugar cane or sugar beets and used extensively in food products; sucrose. **2** any of the class of carbohydrates to which this substance belongs. Glucose, lactose, and maltose are sugars. **3** put sugar in; sweeten with sugar: *She sugared her tea.* **4** cover with sugar; sprinkle with sugar: *to sugar doughnuts.* **5** form sugar crystals: *Honey sugars if kept too long.* **6** cause to seem pleasant or agreeable: *He sugared his criticism of the play with some praise for the performers.* **1,2** *n.,* **3-6** *v.* —**sug′ar like′,** *adj.*

WORD HISTORY

sugar

Sugar came into English about 700 years ago from French *sucre,* and can be traced back to Sanskrit *śarkarā,* which originally meant "gravel, grit."

a hat	i it	oi oil	ch child	a in about
ā age	ī ice	ou out	ng long	e in taken
ä far	o hot	u cup	sh she	ə = i in pencil
e let	ō open	u̇ put	th thin	o in lemon
ē equal	ô order	ü rule	ŦH then	u in circus
ėr term			zh measure	

sugar beet, a large beet with a white root that yields sugar.

sugar cane, a very tall grass with a strong, jointed stem and long, flat leaves, growing in warm regions. Sugar cane is the main source of sugar.

sugar cane

sug ar-coat (shug′ər kōt′), **1** cover with sugar. **2** cause to seem more pleasant or agreeable: *to sugar-coat discipline with humor. v.*

sugar loaf, 1 a solid cone-shaped mass of molded sugar. **2** something shaped like a sugar loaf, especially a cone-shaped hill.

sugar maple, a maple tree of eastern North America, highly valued for its hard, tough wood and for its sweet sap, from which maple sugar and maple syrup are made.

sug ar plum (shug′ər plum′), piece of candy; bonbon. *n.*

sug ar y (shug′ər ē), **1** consisting of sugar; like sugar; sweet. **2** outwardly, but not sincerely, pleasant or agreeable: *a sugary greeting. adj.* —**sug′ar i ness,** *n.*

sug gest (səg jest′), **1** bring to mind; call up the thought of: *The thought of summer suggests swimming, tennis, and hot weather.* **2** put forward; propose: *She suggested a swim, and we all agreed.* **3** show in an indirect way; hint: *His yawns suggest that he would like to go to bed. v.* —**sug gest′er,** *n.*

sug gest i bil i ty (səg jes′tə bil′ə tē), quality or condition of being suggestible. *n.*

sug gest i ble (səg jes′tə bəl), **1** capable of being influenced by suggestion. **2** able to be suggested. *adj.*

sug ges tion (səg jes′chən), **1** act of suggesting: *The suggestion of a swim made the children jump with joy.* **2** thing suggested; proposal: *The picnic was an excellent suggestion.* **3** a very small amount; slight trace: *She spoke with just a suggestion of a French accent. n.*

sug ges tive (səg jes′tiv), **1** tending to suggest ideas, acts, or feelings: *The teacher gave an interesting and suggestive list of composition subjects.* **2** tending to suggest something improper or indecent. *adj.* —**sug ges′tive ly,** *adv.* —**sug ges′tive ness,** *n.*

su i cid al (sü′ə sī′dl), **1** of suicide; leading to or causing suicide. **2** ruinous to one's own interests; disastrous to oneself: *It would be suicidal for a store to sell many things below cost. adj.* —**su′i cid′al ly,** *adv.*

su i cide (sü′ə sīd), **1** the killing of oneself on purpose. **2** person who commits suicide. **3** destruction of one's own interests or prospects. *n.*

suit (süt), **1** set of clothes to be worn together. A man's suit consists of a coat, pants, and sometimes a vest. A woman's suit consists of a coat and either a skirt or pants. **2** case in a court of law; application to a court for justice: *He started a suit to collect damages for his injuries.* **3** make suitable; make fit: *to suit the punishment to the crime.* **4** be suitable for; agree with: *A cold climate suits apples and wheat, but not oranges and tea.* **5** be agreeable, convenient, or acceptable to; please; satisfy: *Which date suits you best?* **6** be becoming to: *That blue sweater suits you.* **7** one of the four sets of cards (spades, hearts, diamonds, and clubs) making up a deck. **8** suite (def. 2). 1,2,7,8 *n.*, 3-6 *v.*

follow suit, 1 play a card of the same suit as that first played. **2** follow the example of another.

suit oneself, do as one pleases.

suit a bil i ty (sü′tə bil′ə tē), a being suitable; fitness; appropriateness. *n.*

suit a ble (sü′tə bəl), right for the occasion; fitting; proper: *Plain clothes are suitable for school wear. The park gives the children a suitable playground. adj.* —**suit′a ble ness,** *n.*

suit a bly (sü′tə blē), in a suitable manner; fitly; appropriately. *adv.*

suit case (süt′kās′), a flat, rectangular traveling bag. *n.*

suite (swēt *for 1,3-5;* swēt *or* süt *for 2*), **1** set of connected rooms to be used by one person or family: *They have a suite of rooms at the hotel—a living room, bedroom, and bath.* **2** set of furniture that matches; suit. **3** any set or series of like things. **4** in music: **a** a series of connected instrumental movements: *a suite for strings.* **b** a set of dance tunes. **5** group of attendants: *The queen traveled with a suite of twelve. n.*

sui tor (sü′tər), **1** man who is courting a woman. **2** person bringing suit in a court of law. **3** anyone who sues or petitions. *n.*

su ki ya ki (sü′kē yä′kē *or* skē yä′kē), a Japanese dish consisting mainly of fried meat, onions, and other vegetables. *n.* [*Sukiyaki* is borrowed from Japanese *sukiyaki.*]

Su la we si (sü′lä wä′sē), Celebes. *n.*

sul fa (sul′fə), **1** of a group of drugs derived from sulfanilamide, and used in treating various bacterial infections. **2** a sulfa drug. 1 *adj.,* 2 *n.* Also, **sulpha.**

sul fa nil a mide (sul′fə nil′ə mīd), a white, crystalline substance that is the basis for most of the sulfa drugs. *n.*

sul fate (sul′fāt), any salt of sulfuric acid. *n.* Also, **sulphate.**

sul fide (sul′fīd), any compound of sulfur with another element or radical. *n.* Also, **sulphide.**

sul fur (sul′fər), a light-yellow nonmetallic element that burns easily, producing a stifling odor. Sulfur is common in volcanic regions, occurring in nature in both free and combined forms, and is also in proteins. It is used in making matches, gunpowder, paper pulp, fertilizers, insecticides, etc., and in medicine. *n.* Also, **sulphur.**

sul fur ic (sul fyür′ik), of or containing sulfur. *adj.* Also, **sulphuric.**

sulfuric acid, a heavy, oily, colorless, and very corrosive acid derived from sulfur. Sulfuric acid is used in making explosives and fertilizers, in refining petroleum, and in many other industrial processes.

sul fur ous (sul′fər əs *or* sul′fyər əs), **1** of or containing sulfur. **2** like sulfur; like burning sulfur. **3** of or like the fires of hell; hellish. *adj.* Also, **sulphurous.** —**sul′fur ous ly,** *adv.* —**sul′fur ous ness.** *n.*

sulk (sulk), **1** hold aloof in a sullen manner; be sulky. **2** a sulking; a fit of sulking. **3 the sulks,** bad humor shown by sulking: *The baby seems to have a fit of the sulks.* 1 *v.,* 2,3 *n.*

sulk i ly (sul′kə lē), in a sulky manner; sullenly. *adv.*

sulk i ness (sul′kē nis), sulky behavior; sullenness. *n.*

sulk y (sul′kē), **1** silent and bad-humored because of resentment; sullen: *Some people become sulky when they cannot have their own way.* **2** a light one-horse carriage with two wheels, for one person, now commonly used in trotting races. 1 *adj.,* **sulk i er, sulk i est;** 2 *n., pl.* **sulkies.**

sulky (def. 2)

sul len (sul′ən), **1** silent because of bad humor or anger: *The sullen child refused to answer my question.* **2** gloomy; dismal: *The sullen skies threatened rain. adj.* —**sul′len ly,** *adv.* —**sul′len ness,** *n.*

sul ly (sul′ē), to soil, stain, or tarnish: *Evil gossip sullied the lawyer's reputation. Smog sullied the usually attractive skyline of the city. v.,* **sul lied, sul ly ing.**

sul pha (sul′fə), sulfa. *adj., n.*

sul phate (sul′fāt), sulfate. *n.*

sul phide (sul′fīd), sulfide. *n.*

sul phur (sul′fər), sulfur. *n.*

sul phur ic (sul fyür′ik), sulfuric. *adj.*

sul phur ous (sul′fər əs *or* sul′fyər əs), sulfurous. *adj.*

sul tan (sult′n), ruler of a Moslem country. *n.*

sul tan a (sul tan′ə), **1** wife of a sultan. **2** mother, sister, or daughter of a sultan. *n., pl.* **sul tan as.**

sul tan ate (sult′n āt), **1** position, authority, or period of rule of a sultan. **2** territory ruled over by a sultan. *n.*

sul tri ness (sul′trē nis), sultry condition or quality. *n.*

sul try (sul′trē), **1** hot, close, and moist: *We expect sultry weather during July.* **2** hot or fiery: *a sultry sun, a sultry glance. adj.,* **sul tri er, sul tri est.** —**sul′tri ly,** *adv.*

sum (sum), **1** amount of money: *We paid a large sum for the house.* **2** number or quantity obtained by adding two or more numbers or quantities together: *The sum of 2 and 3 and 4 is 9.* **3** problem in arithmetic: *He can do easy sums in his head, but he has to use pencil and paper for hard ones.* **4** the whole amount; total amount: *The sum of scientific knowledge has increased greatly in this century.* **5** find the total of. 1-4 *n.,* 5 *v.,* **summed, sum ming.**

sum up, express or tell briefly: *Sum up the main points of the lesson in three sentences. The judge summed up the evidence.*

su mac *or* **su mach** (sü′mak *or* shü′mak), **1** any of a group of shrubs or small trees which have divided leaves that turn scarlet in the autumn and clusters of red or white fruit. Some sumacs are poisonous to the touch. **2** the dried leaves of certain kinds of sumac, used in tanning and dyeing. *n.* [*Sumac* can be traced back to Arabic *summaq.*]

Su ma tra (sů mä′trə), large island in Indonesia, off the SE coast of Asia. *n.* —**Su ma′tran,** *adj., n.*

Su mer (sü′mər), ancient region in the valley of the Euphrates River, north of its mouth. See **Babylonia** for map. *n.*

Su mer i an (sü mir′ē ən), **1** of the people of Sumer or their language. **2** person who was born or lived in Sumer. **3** their language. Sumerian is recorded in cuneiform inscriptions. 1 *adj.,* 2,3 *n.*

sum mar i ly (sə mer′ə lē *or* sum′ər ə lē), in a summary manner; briefly; without delay. *adv.*

sum ma rize (sum′ə rīz′), make a summary of; give only the main points of; express briefly: *summarize the story of a book.* *v.,* **sum ma rized, sum ma riz ing.** —**sum′ma ri za′tion,** *n.* —**sum′ma riz′er,** *n.*

sum mar y (sum′ər ē), **1** a brief statement giving the main points: *The history book had a summary at the end of each chapter.* **2** giving only the main points; brief; short. **3** direct and prompt; without delay or formality: *summary vengeance. The governor took summary action to aid the flood victims.* **1** *n., pl.* **sum mar ies;** **2,3** *adj.*

sum ma tion (sə mā′shən), **1** process of finding the sum or total; addition. **2** the total. **3** (in law) the final presentation of facts and arguments by the counsel for each side. *n.*

sum mer (sum′ər), **1** the warmest season of the year; season of the year between spring and autumn. **2** of or for summer; coming in summer: *summer heat, summer clothes.* **3** pass the summer: *to summer at the seashore.* **1** *n.,* **2** *adj.,* **3** *v.* [*Summer* comes from Old English *sumor.*]

sum mer house (sum′ər hous′), building in a park or garden in which to sit in warm weather. Summerhouses often have no walls. *n., pl.* **sum mer hous es** (sum′ər-hou′ziz).

sum mer time (sum′ər tīm′), the summer season. *n.*

sum mer y (sum′ər ē), of or for summer; like summer: *summery heat, a summery day in spring.* *adj.*

sum mit (sum′it), the highest point; top: *the summit of a mountain. The summit of her ambition was to be a doctor.* *n.*

summit meeting, a meeting between heads of governments, especially for the purpose of settling disagreements.

sum mon (sum′ən), **1** to call with authority; order to come; send for: *I was summoned to the principal's office. An urgent phone call summoned me home.* **2** to call together: *summon an assembly.* **3** to order or notify formally to appear before a court of law or judge, especially to answer a charge. **4** stir to action; rouse: *We summoned our courage and entered the deserted house.* *v.* —**sum′mon er,** *n.*

sum mons (sum′ənz), **1** a formal order or notice to appear before a court of law or judge, especially to answer a charge: *I received a summons for speeding.* **2** an urgent call; a summoning command, message, or signal: *I hurried in response to my friend's summons for help.* *n., pl.* **sum mons es.**

sump (sump), pit or reservoir for collecting water or other liquid waste in a basement, factory, mine, etc. *n.*

sump pump, pump which removes liquid from a sump when the liquid reaches a certain level.

sump tu ar y (sump′chü er′ē), having to do with or regulating the spending of money, especially to control extravagance or waste. A law prohibiting any family from owning more than one car would be a sumptuary law. *adj.*

sump tu ous (sump′chü əs), involving great expense; lavish and costly; magnificent; rich: *sumptuous jewels, a sumptuous banquet.* *adj.* —**sump′tu ous ly,** *adv.* —**sump′tu ous ness,** *n.*

Sum ter (sum′tər), **Fort,** fort in the harbor of Charleston, South Carolina. The Civil War began with a Confederate attack on this fort on April 12, 1861. *n.*

sun (sun), **1** the brightest heavenly body in the sky; the star around which the earth and other planets revolve and which supplies them with light and heat. It is a glowing ball of hot gases and is about 93 million miles (150 million kilometers) from the earth. **2** the light and warmth of the sun: *to sit in the sun.* **3** expose to the sun's rays: *The swimmers sunned themselves on the beach.* **4** any heavenly body made up of burning gas and having satellites. Many stars are suns and have planets orbiting around them. **5** something like the sun in brightness or splendor; something that is a source of light, honor, glory, or prosperity. **1,2,4,5** *n.,* **3** *v.,* **sunned, sun ning.**

Sun., Sunday.

sun bath, exposure of the body to the sun's rays or to a sunlamp.

sun bathe (sun′bāтн′), expose oneself to the sun's rays or to a sunlamp. *v.,* **sun bathed, sun bath ing.** —**sun′bath′er,** *n.*

sun beam (sun′bēm′), ray of sunlight: *A sunbeam brightened the child's hair to gold. n.*

sun belt or **Sun belt** (sun′belt′), those areas that form the southern boundaries of the United States, from Virginia to southern California. *n.*

sun bon net (sun′bon′it), a large bonnet that shades the face and neck. *n.*

sun burn (sun′bėrn′), **1** a burning of the skin by the sun's rays or by a sunlamp. A sunburn is often red and painful. **2** burn the skin by the sun's rays or by a sunlamp. **3** become sunburned: *My skin sunburns very quickly.* **1** *n.,* **2,3** *v.,* **sun burned** or **sun burnt, sun burn ing.**

sun burnt (sun′bėrnt′), sunburned; a past tense and a past participle of **sunburn.** *v.*

sun dae (sun′dē), dish of ice cream served with syrup, crushed fruits, nuts, etc., over it. *n.*

Sun day (sun′dē), **1** the first day of the week. **2** of or on Sundays; not everyday or regular; occasional: *a Sunday driver, Sunday painters.* **1** *n.,* **2** *adj.*

Sunday best, INFORMAL. best clothes.

Sunday school, 1 school held on Sunday for teaching religion. **2** its members.

sun der (sun′dər), put asunder; separate; part; sever; split: *Time often sunders friends. v.*

in sunder, apart: *Lightning tore the tree in sunder.*

sundial

sun di al (sun′dī′əl), instrument for telling the time of day by the position of a shadow cast by the sun; dial. The sun strikes an upright pointer, casting a shadow onto a dial indicating the hours. *n.*

sun down (sun′doun′), sunset: *We'll be home by sundown. n.*

sun dries (sun′drēz), sundry things; items not named;

a hat	**i** it	**oi** oil	**ch** child	⎧ a in about
ā age	**ī** ice	**ou** out	**ng** long	⎪ e in taken
ä far	**o** hot	**u** cup	**sh** she	ə = ⎨ i in pencil
e let	**ō** open	**u̇** put	**th** thin	⎪ o in lemon
ē equal	**ô** order	**ü** rule	**тн** then	⎩ u in circus
ėr term			**zh** measure	

odds and ends: *I spent $5.00 for sundries at the drugstore.* *n.pl.*

sun dry (sun′drē), several; various: *From sundry hints, I guessed I was to be given a bicycle for my birthday. adj.*

sun fish (sun′fish′), **1** a large fish with tough flesh that lives in tropical or temperate seas. **2** a small freshwater fish of North America, used for food. Sunfish are related to perch. *n., pl.* **sun fish es** or **sun fish.**

sun flow er (sun′flou′ər), a tall plant related to the aster, having large yellow flowers with brown centers. Its seeds are used as food and to produce oil for cooking. *n.*

sung (sung), a past tense and past participle of **sing.** *Many songs were sung at the concert. v.*

sun glass es (sun′glas′iz), spectacles to protect the eyes from the glare of the sun. They are usually made of colored glass. *n.pl.*

sun gods—left, Apollo, the Greek and Roman sun god; right, Ra, the Egyptian sun god

sun god, god representing the sun. Many different peoples have worshiped sun gods. Apollo and Ra were sun gods.

sunk (sungk), a past tense and past participle of **sink.** *The ship had sunk to the bottom. v.*

sunk en (sung′kən), **1** sunk: *a sunken ship.* **2** submerged; underwater: *a sunken rock.* **3** situated below the general level: *a sunken garden.* **4** fallen in; hollow: *sunken eyes. adj.*

sun lamp (sun′lamp′), lamp for producing ultraviolet rays similar to those in sunlight. *n.*

sun less (sun′lis), without sun; without sunlight: *a rainy, sunless day. adj.*

sun light (sun′līt′), the light of the sun. *n.*

sun lit (sun′lit′), lighted by the sun. *adj.*

sun ny (sun′ē), **1** having much sunshine: *a sunny day.* **2** exposed to, lighted by, or warmed by the direct rays of the sun: *a sunny room.* **3** bright; cheerful; happy: *The baby gave a sunny smile. adj.,* **sun ni er, sun ni est.**

sun parlor, room with many windows to let in sunlight.

sun porch, porch enclosed largely by glass.

sun ray (sun′rā′), sunbeam. *n.*

sun rise (sun′rīz′), **1** the first appearance of the sun above the horizon in the morning. **2** the time when the sun first appears; the beginning of day. **3** the display of light or color in the sky at this time. *n.*

sun room (sun′rüm′ *or* sun′rum′), room with many windows to let in sunlight. *n.*

sun screen (sun′skrēn′), a chemical compound that screens out the ultraviolet rays of the sun, used in skin preparations to prevent sunburn. *n.*

sun set (sun′set′), **1** the last appearance of the sun above the horizon in the evening. **2** the time when the sun last appears; the close of day. **3** the display of light or color in the sky at this time. *n.*

sun shade (sun′shād′), an umbrella, parasol, awning, etc., used to provide protection against the sun. *n.*

sun shine (sun′shīn′), **1** light or rays of the sun. **2** brightness; cheerfulness; happiness. *n.*

sun shin y (sun′shī′nē), **1** having much sunshine. **2** bright; cheerful; happy. *adj.,* **sun shin i er, sun shin i est.**

sun spot (sun′spot′), one of the dark spots that appear from time to time on the surface of the sun. Disturbances of the earth's magnetic field often occur when sunspots appear. *n.*

sun stroke (sun′strōk′), a sudden illness caused by too much or too long an exposure to the sun's rays. Sunstroke results in fever, dry skin, extreme exhaustion, and often loss of consciousness. *n.*

sun tan (sun′tan′), the reddish-brown color of a person's skin tanned by the sun or by a sunlamp. *n.*

sun up (sun′up′), sunrise. *n.*

sun ward (sun′wərd), toward the sun: *I glanced briefly sunward as the cloud cast its shadow (adv.). Apples grow larger on the sunward side of the tree (adj.). adv., adj.*

Sun Yat-sen (sun′ yät′sen′), 1866-1925, Chinese revolutionary leader and statesman, president of China from 1921 to 1922.

sup[1] (sup), eat the evening meal; take supper: *We supped on bread and milk. v.,* **supped, sup ping.**

sup[2] (sup), sip. *v.,* **supped, sup ping;** *n.*

sup., 1 above. **2** superior. **3** superlative. **4** supplement. **5** supplementary.

su per (sü′pər), **1** INFORMAL. superintendent. **2** INFORMAL. a supernumerary. **3** INFORMAL. excellent. 1,2 *n.,* 3 *adj.*

super-, *prefix.* **1** over; above: *Superimpose = impose over or above.* **2** in high proportion; to excess; exceedingly: *Superabundant = abundant to excess.* **3** surpassing: *Supernatural = surpassing the natural.* **4** superior to the ordinary; more than the usual: *Superhuman = superior to the ordinary human.*

su per a bun dance (sü′pər ə bun′dəns), **1** very great abundance: *a superabundance of rain.* **2** a greater amount than is needed. *n.*

su per a bun dant (sü′pər ə bun′dənt), **1** very abundant. **2** more than enough. *adj.*

su perb (su perb′), **1** grand and stately; majestic; magnificent; splendid: *Mountain scenery is superb. The queen's jewels were superb.* **2** rich; elegant: *a superb dinner.* **3** very fine; first-rate; excellent: *The singer gave a superb performance. adj.* **—su perb′ly,** *adv.* **—su perb′ness,** *n.*

su per charge (sü′pər chärj′), increase the power of (an internal-combustion engine) by fitting it with a supercharger. *v.,* **su per charged, su per charg ing.**

su per charg er (sü′pər chär′jər), compressor, pump, or similar device which increases the amount of the fuel vapor forced into the cylinders of an internal-combustion engine. Superchargers are used to increase the power of racing-car and aircraft engines. *n.*

su per cil i ous (sü′pər sil′ē əs), proud, haughty, and contemptuous; disdainful; showing scorn or indifference because of a feeling of superiority: *a supercilious smile, a supercilious stare. adj.* **—su′per cil′i ous ly,** *adv.*

su per com put er (sü′pər kəm pyü′tər), a very powerful, high-speed computer that can perform several hundred million operations a second and work on many aspects of a problem simultaneously. *n.*

su per con duc tor (sü′pər kən duk′tər), metal, such as lead or tin, that can conduct electric current with no resistance at temperatures near absolute zero. *n.*

su per e rog a to ry (sü′pər ə rog′ə tôr′ē), **1** doing more than duty requires. **2** unnecessary; superfluous. *adj.*

su per fi cial (sü'pər fish'əl), **1** of, on, or at the surface: *superficial measurement. His burns were superficial and soon healed.* **2** concerned with or understanding only what is on the surface; not thorough; shallow: *superficial knowledge, a superficial education.* **3** not real or genuine: *a superficial friendship. adj.* —**su'per fi'cial ness,** *n.*

su per fi ci al i ty (sü'pər fish'ē al'ə tē), **1** superficial quality or condition; shallowness. **2** something superficial. *n., pl.* **su per fi ci al i ties.**

su per fi cial ly (sü'pər fish'ə lē), in a superficial manner; on the surface; not thoroughly: *superficially attractive. adv.*

su per fine (sü'pər fīn'), **1** very fine; extra fine. **2** too refined; too nice. *adj.*

su per flu i ty (sü'pər flü'ə tē), **1** a greater amount than is needed; excess: *Our orchard gives us a superfluity of apples.* **2** something not needed: *Luxuries are superfluities. n., pl.* **su per flu i ties.**

su per flu ous (sù pèr'flü əs), **1** more than is needed; excessive; surplus: *In writing telegrams it pays to omit superfluous words.* **2** needless; unnecessary: *A raincoat is superfluous on a clear day. adj.* —**su per'flu ous ly,** *adv.* —**su per'flu ous ness,** *n.*

su per high way (sü'pər hī'wā), highway for fast traveling. Superhighways are often very long and have two or more lanes for traffic in each direction. *n.*

su per hu man (sü'pər hyü'mən), **1** above or beyond what is human: *superhuman beings.* **2** above or beyond ordinary human power, experience, etc.: *With a superhuman burst of speed, the runner set a new Olympic record. adj.* —**su'per hu'man ly,** *adv.*

su per im pose (sü'pər im pōz'), put on top of something else. *v.,* **su per im posed, su per im pos ing.**

su per in tend (sü'pər in tend'), oversee and direct (work or workers); manage (a place, institution, etc.). *v.*

su per in tend ence (sü'pər in ten'dəns), guidance and direction; management. *n.*

su per in tend ent (sü'pər in ten'dənt), person who oversees, directs, or manages; supervisor: *a superintendent of schools, a superintendent of a factory. n.*

su per i or (sə pir'ē ər), **1** above the average; very good; excellent: *superior work in school.* **2** higher in quality; better; greater: *a superior blend of coffee. We lost the baseball game to a superior team.* **3** higher in position, rank, importance, etc.: *a superior officer.* **4** person who is superior: *A captain is a lieutenant's superior.* **5** showing a feeling of being above others; proud: *superior airs, superior manners.* **6** head of a monastery or convent. 1-3,5 *adj.,* 4,6 *n.* —**su per'i or ly,** *adv.*

superior to, 1 higher than; above: *Apes are considered superior to most other animals in intelligence.* **2** better than; greater than: *This restaurant's food is superior to any other.* **3** not giving in to; above yielding to: *A wise person is superior to flattery.*

Su per i or (sə pir'ē ər), **Lake,** the largest of the five Great Lakes. It is the largest body of fresh water in the world. *n.*

su per i or i ty (sə pir'ē ôr'ə tē), superior state or quality: *the superiority of modern ways of traveling over those of olden times. n.*

su per la tive (sə pèr'lə tiv), **1** of the highest kind; above all others; supreme: *superlative skills, superlative wisdom.* **2** person or thing above all others; supreme example. **3** the highest degree of comparison of an adjective or adverb. *Fairest* and *most slowly* are the superlatives of *fair* and *slowly.* **4** showing the highest degree of comparison of an adjective or adverb. *Best* is the superlative form of *good.* 1,4 *adj.,* 2,3 *n.* —**su per'la tive ness,** *n.* **talk in superlatives,** exaggerate.

su per la tive ly (sə pèr'lə tiv lē), to the highest degree; above all others; supremely. *adv.*

su per man (sü'pər man'), person having more than human powers. *n., pl.* **su per men.**

su per mar ket (sü'pər mär'kit), a large store for groceries and household articles in which customers select their purchases from open shelves and pay for them just before leaving. *n.*

su per nal (sù pėr'nl), **1** heavenly; divine. **2** lofty; exalted. *adj.* —**su per'nal ly,** *adv.*

su per nat ur al (sü'pər nach'ər əl), **1** above or beyond what is natural: *supernatural voices. Ghosts are supernatural beings.* **2 the supernatural,** something above or beyond what is natural. 1 *adj.,* 2 *n.* —**su'per nat'ur al ly,** *adv.* —**su'per nat'ur al ness,** *n.*

su per nat ur al ism (sü'pər nach'ər ə liz'əm), **1** supernatural character or agency. **2** belief in the supernatural. *n.*

su per nu me rar y (sü'pər nü'mə rer'ē *or* sü'pər nyü'mə rer'ē), **1** more than the usual or necessary number; extra. **2** an extra person or thing. **3** person who appears on the stage but has no lines to speak: *In addition to the regular actors, there were 20 supernumeraries for the mob scene.* 1 *adj.,* 2,3 *n., pl.* **su per nu me rar ies.**

su per pow er (sü'pər pou'ər), **1** power on an extraordinary or extensive scale. **2** nation so great or strong as a power that its actions and policies greatly affect those of smaller, less powerful nations. *n.*

su per script (sü'pər skript), **1** written above. **2** number, letter, etc., written above and to one side of a symbol. In $a^3 = b^n$ the *3* and the *n* are superscripts. 1 *adj.,* 2 *n.*

su per scrip tion (sü'pər skrip'shən), **1** a writing above, on, or outside of something. **2** something written above or on the outside. **3** address on a letter or parcel. *n.*

su per sede (sü'pər sēd'), **1** take the place of; cause to be set aside; displace: *Electric lights have superseded gaslights.* **2** fill the place of; replace: *A new governor superseded the old one. v.,* **su per sed ed, su per sed ing.**

su per sen si tive (sü'pər sen'sə tiv), extremely or abnormally sensitive. *adj.* —**su'per sen'si tive ly,** *adv.* —**su'per sen'si tive ness,** *n.*

su per son ic (sü'pər son'ik), **1** of sound waves beyond the limit of human ability to hear (above frequencies of 20,000 cycles per second). **2** greater than the speed of sound in air, about 740 miles (1190 kilometers) per hour at sea level. **3** capable of moving at a speed greater than the speed of sound: *supersonic aircraft. adj.* —**su'per son'i cal ly,** *adv.*

su per star (sü'pər stär'), person, often an entertainer or athlete, who is exceptionally successful in his or her field. *n.*

su per sti tion (sü'pər stish'ən), **1** an unreasoning fear of what is unknown or mysterious; unreasoning expectation. **2** belief or practice founded on ignorant fear or mistaken reverence: *A common superstition considers 13 an unlucky number. n.*

su per sti tious (sü'pər stish'əs), full of superstition; likely to believe superstitions; of or caused by superstition: *a superstitious habit, a superstitious belief. adj.* —**su'per sti'tious ly,** *adv.* —**su'per sti'tious ness,** *n.*

su per struc ture (sü'pər struk'chər), **1** structure built on something else. **2** all of a building above the foundation. **3** parts of a ship above the main deck. *n.*

su per vene (sü′pər vēn′), come as something additional or interrupting. *v.*, **su per vened, su per ven ing.**

su per vise (sü′pər vīz), look after and direct (work or workers, a process, etc.); oversee; superintend; manage: *Study halls are supervised by teachers. v.*, **su per vised, su per vis ing.**

su per vi sion (sü′pər vizh′ən), management; direction: *The house was built under the careful supervision of an architect. n.*

su per vi sor (sü′pər vī′zər), person who supervises. *n.*

su per vi so ry (sü′pər vī′zər ē), **1** of a supervisor; having to do with supervision. **2** supervising. *adj.*

su pine (sü pīn′), **1** lying flat on the back: *a supine person.* **2** lazily inactive; listless. *adj.* —**su pine′ly,** *adv.* —**su pine′ness,** *n.*

supp. or **suppl.,** supplement.

sup per (sup′ər), the evening meal; meal eaten early in the evening if dinner is near noon, or late in the evening if dinner is at six or later. *n.* —**sup′per less,** *n.*

sup per time (sup′ər tīm′), the time at which supper is served. *n.*

sup plant (sə plant′), **1** take the place of; displace or set aside: *Machinery has supplanted hand labor in making shoes.* **2** take the place of by unfair methods or by treacherous means: *The prince plotted to supplant the king. v.* —**sup′plan ta′tion,** *n.* —**sup plant′er,** *n.*

sup ple (sup′əl), **1** bending or folding easily: *a supple birch tree, supple leather.* **2** capable of bending easily; moving easily or nimbly: *a supple dancer.* **3** readily adaptable to different ideas, circumstances, people, etc.; yielding: *a supple mind. She gets along well with people because of her supple nature. adj.,* **sup pler, sup plest.** —**sup′ple ly,** *adv.* —**sup′ple ness,** *n.*

sup ple ment (sup′lə mənt *for 1,3;* sup′lə ment *for 2*), **1** something added to complete a thing, or to make it larger or better. Many newspapers and periodicals have supplements that are usually of a special character and issued as an additional feature. **2** supply what is lacking in; add to; complete: *He supplements his diet with vitamin pills.* **3** something added to supply a deficiency: *a diet supplement.* 1,3 *n.,* 2 *v.* —**sup′ple men ta′tion,** *n.*

sup ple men tal (sup′lə men′tl), supplementary. *adj.*

sup ple men tar y (sup′lə men′tər ē), added to supply what is lacking; additional: *The new members of the class received supplementary instruction. adj.*

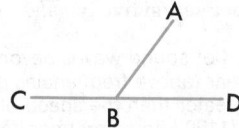

supplementary angle
ABC and ABD are
supplementary angles

supplementary angle, either of two angles which together form an angle of 180 degrees: *A 60-degree angle is the supplementary angle of a 120-degree angle.*

sup pli ant (sup′lē ənt), **1** asking humbly and earnestly: *He sent a suppliant message for help.* **2** person who asks humbly and earnestly: *I knelt as a suppliant before the queen.* 1 *adj.,* 2 *n.* —**sup′pli ant ly,** *adv.*

sup pli cant (sup′lə kənt), suppliant. *n., adj.* —**sup′pli cant ly,** *adv.*

sup pli cate (sup′lə kāt), **1** beg humbly and earnestly: *They supplicated the judge to pardon the prisoner.* **2** pray humbly. *v.,* **sup pli cat ed, sup pli cat ing.** —**sup′pli cat′ing ly,** *adv.* —**sup′pli ca′tor,** *n.*

sup pli ca tion (sup′lə kā′shən), **1** a supplicating. **2** a humble and earnest request or prayer: *Supplications to God arose from many of the people in the besieged town. n.*

sup pli er (sə plī′ər), person or thing that supplies. *n.*

sup ply (sə plī′), **1** provide (what is lacking); furnish: *Many cities supply books for children in school.* **2** quantity ready for use; stock; store: *The school gets its supplies of books, paper, pencils, chalk, etc., from the city. We have a large supply of milk in the refrigerator.* **3** quantity of an article in the market ready for purchase, especially at a given price: *a supply of coffee.* **4 supplies,** *pl.* the food, equipment, etc., necessary for an army, expedition, or the like. **5** satisfy (a want, need, etc.): *There was just enough to supply the demand.* **6** act of supplying. 1,5 *v.,* **sup plied, sup ply ing;** 2-4,6 *n., pl.* **sup plies.**

sup port (sə pôrt′), **1** keep from falling; hold up: *Walls support the roof.* **2** give strength or courage to; keep up; help: *Hope supported us during our troubles.* **3** provide for: *support a large family.* **4** maintain, keep up, or keep going: *This city supports two orchestras.* **5** be in favor of; back; second: *She supports the amendment.* **6** help prove; bear out: *The facts support her claim.* **7** act of supporting: *He spoke in support of the proposal.* **8** condition of being supported: *This argument lacks support.* **9** help or assistance: *They need our financial support.* **10** means of livelihood: *That family lacks support.* **11** person or thing that supports; prop: *The neck is the support of the head.* 1-6 *v.,* 7-11 *n.*

sup port a ble (sə pôr′tə bəl), capable of being supported; bearable or endurable. *adj.* —**sup port′a ble ness,** *n.* —**sup port′a bly,** *adv.*

sup port er (sə pôr′tər), person or thing that supports. *n.*

sup por tive (sə pôr′tiv), providing support; supporting: *supportive evidence. adj.*

sup pose (sə pōz′), **1** consider as possible; take for granted; assume: *Suppose you are late, what excuse will you make?* **2** believe, think, or imagine: *I suppose he will come at noon.* **3** expect: *I'm supposed to be there early. v.,* **sup posed, sup pos ing.** —**sup pos′a ble,** *adj.* —**sup pos′a bly,** *adv.*

sup posed (sə pōzd′), accepted as true; considered as possible or probable; assumed: *The supposed beggar was really a prince. adj.*

sup pos ed ly (sə pō′zid lē), according to what is supposed or was supposed. *adv.*

sup pos ing (sə pō′zing), in the event that; if: *Supposing it rains, shall we go? conj.*

sup po si tion (sup′ə zish′ən), **1** act of supposing. **2** thing supposed; belief; opinion: *The speaker planned her talk on the supposition that her listeners would be schoolchildren. n.*

sup pos i to ry (sə poz′ə tôr′ē), medicine in the form of a cone or cylinder to be put into the rectum or vagina. *n., pl.* **sup pos i to ries.**

sup press (sə pres′), **1** put an end to; stop by force; put down: *suppress a rebellion.* **2** keep in; hold back; keep from appearing: *suppress the news. She suppressed a yawn.* **3** hold in (a feeling, etc.): *suppress a desire.* **4** check the flow of; stop: *suppress bleeding. v.* —**sup press′er, sup pres′sor,** *n.*

sup pres sion (sə presh′ən), **1** a putting down by force or authority; putting an end to: *Troops were used in the suppression of the revolt.* **2** a keeping in; holding back: *The suppression of facts may be as dishonest as the telling of lies. n.*

sup pu rate (sup′yə rāt′), form or discharge pus; fester: *The wound suppurated badly. v.,* **sup pu rat ed, sup pu rat ing.**

su prem a cy (sə prem′ə sē), **1** condition of being supreme. **2** supreme authority or power. *n.*

su preme (sə prēm′), **1** highest in rank or authority: *a supreme ruler.* **2** highest in degree or quality; greatest;

utmost: *supreme disgust, supreme courage. People who die for their country make the supreme sacrifice. adj.* **—supreme′ly,** *adv.* **—su preme′ness,** *n.*

Supreme Being, God.

Supreme Court, 1 the highest court in the United States, which meets at Washington, D.C. It is made up of a chief justice and eight associate justices. **2** the highest court in some states of the United States. **3** a similar court in other countries.

Supt. or **supt.,** superintendent.

sur cease (sər sēs′), OLD USE. end; cessation. *n.*

sur charge (sėr′chärj′ *for 1,4;* sėr′chärj′ *or* sėr′chärj′ *for 2,3,5*), **1** an additional charge, load, or burden; extra charge: *The express company made a surcharge for delivering the trunk outside of the city limits.* **2** to charge extra. **3** overload; overburden: *The mourner's heart was surcharged with grief.* **4** an additional mark printed on a postage stamp to change its value, date, etc. **5** print a surcharge on (a postage stamp). *1,4 n., 2,3,5 v.,* **surcharged, sur charg ing.**

surcoat

sur coat (sėr′kōt′), an outer coat, especially such a coat worn by knights over their armor. *n.*

sure (shůr), **1** free from doubt; certain; having ample reason for belief; confident; positive: *She is sure of success. I am quite sure of their guilt.* **2** to be trusted; safe; reliable: *a sure messenger.* **3** never missing, slipping, etc.; unfailing; unerring: *sure aim, a sure touch.* **4** without any doubt or question: *sure proof.* **5** firm: *to stand on sure ground.* **6** INFORMAL. surely; certainly. *1-5 adj.,* **sur er, sur est;** *6 adv.* **—sure′ness,** *n.*

for sure, certainly; undoubtedly.

to be sure, of course; certainly: *The weather, to be sure, was unfavorable.*

sure fire (shůr′fīr′), INFORMAL. definite; certain: *a sure-fire success. adj.*

sure-foot ed (shůr′fůt′id), not liable to stumble, slip, or fall. *adj.* **—sure′-foot′ed ness,** *n.*

sure ly (shůr′lē), **1** undoubtedly; certainly: *Half a loaf is surely better than none.* **2** without mistake; without missing, slipping, etc.; firmly: *The goat leaped surely from rock to rock. adv.*

sur e ty (shůr′ə tē), **1** security against loss, damage, or failure to do something: *An insurance company gives surety against loss by fire.* **2** person who agrees to be responsible for another: *She was surety for her sister's appearance in court on the day set.* **3** OLD USE. a sure thing; certainty. *n., pl.* **sur e ties.**

surf (sėrf), **1** waves or swell of the sea breaking in a foaming mass on the shore or upon shoals, reefs, etc. **2** the deep pounding or thundering sound of this. **3** ride on the crest of a wave, especially with a surfboard. *1,2 n., 3 v.* **—surf′er,** *n.*

sur face (sėr′fis), **1** the outside of anything: *the surface of a golf ball, the surface of a mountain.* **2** any face or side

of a thing: *A cube has six surfaces.* **3** the outward appearance: *He seems rough, but you will find him very kind below the surface.* **4** of the surface; on the surface; having to do with the surface: *a surface view.* **5** superficial; external: *surface emotions.* **6** put a surface on; make smooth: *surface a road.* **7** rise to the surface: *The submarine surfaced.* *1-3 n., 4,5 adj., 6,7 v.,* **sur faced, sur fac ing. —sur′fac er,** *n.*

surf board (sėrf′bôrd′), a long, narrow board for riding the surf. *n.*

sur feit (sėr′fit), **1** too much; excess: *A surfeit of food makes one sick.* **2** disgust or nausea caused by too much of anything. **3** to feed or supply too much. *1,2 n., 3 v.*

surf ing (sėr′fing), act or sport of riding the surf on a surfboard. *n.*

surg., 1 surgeon. **2** surgery.

surge (sėrj), **1** rise and fall; move like waves: *A great wave surged over us. The crowd surged through the streets.* **2** a swelling wave; sweep or rush of waves: *Our boat was upset by a surge.* **3** something like a wave: *A surge of anger swept over him.* *1 v.,* **surged, surg ing;** *2,3 n.*

sur geon (sėr′jən), doctor who performs operations: *A surgeon removed the patient's ruptured appendix. n.*

sur ger y (sėr′jər ē), **1** art and science of treating diseases, injuries, etc., by operations and instruments: *Malaria can be cured by medicine, but a ruptured appendix requires surgery.* **2** operating room or other area where surgical operations are performed. **3** the work performed by a surgeon; operation. *n., pl.* **sur ger ies** for 2 and 3.

WORD HISTORY

surgery

Surgery came into English about 600 years ago from French *cirurgerie,* and can be traced back to Greek *cheir,* meaning "hand," and *ergon,* meaning "work."

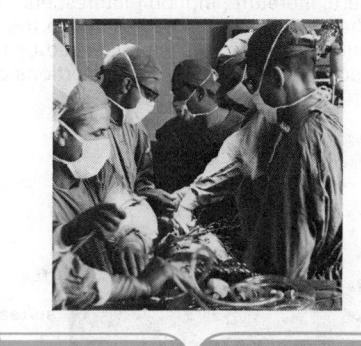

sur gi cal (sėr′jə kəl), **1** of surgery: *a surgical patient.* **2** used in surgery: *surgical instruments.* **3** performed by a surgeon: *a surgical operation. adj.* **—sur′gi cal ly,** *adv.*

Sur i name (sůr′ə nam), country in N South America, on the Atlantic. *Capital:* Paramaribo. See **Brazil** for map. *n.*

a hat	i it	oi oil	ch child		a in about
ā age	ī ice	ou out	ng long		e in taken
ä far	o hot	u cup	sh she	ə =	i in pencil
e let	ō open	ů put	th thin		o in lemon
ē equal	ô order	ü rule	ᴛʜ then		u in circus
ėr term			zh measure		

sur li ness (sėr′lē nis), surly condition or character. *n.*

sur ly (sėr′lē), bad-tempered and unfriendly; rude; gruff: *They got a surly answer from their grouchy neighbor. adj.,* **sur li er, sur li est.**

sur mise (sər mīz′ *for 1;* sər mīz′ *or* sėr′mīz *for 2*), **1** infer or guess: *We surmised that the delay was caused by some accident.* **2** formation of an idea with little or no evidence; a guessing: *Their guilt was a matter of surmise; there was no proof.* 1 *v.,* **sur mised, sur mis ing;** 2 *n.*

sur mount (sər mount′), **1** rise above: *That mountain surmounts all the peaks near it.* **2** be above or on top of: *A statue surmounts the monument.* **3** go up and across: *surmount a hill.* **4** overcome: *She surmounted many difficulties. v.* —**sur mount′a ble,** *adj.*

sur name (sėr′nām′), **1** a last name; family name: *Stein is the surname of Jane Stein.* **2** name added to a person's real name: *William I of England had the surname "the Conqueror."* **3** give an added name to; call by a surname. 1,2 *n.,* 3 *v.,* **sur named, sur nam ing.**

sur pass (sər pas′), **1** do better than; be greater than; excel: *She surpasses her sister in arithmetic.* **2** be too much or too great for; go beyond; exceed: *The beauty of the sunset surpassed description. v.* —**sur pass′a ble,** *adj.* —**sur pass′ing ly,** *adv.*

sur plice (sėr′plis), a broad-sleeved, white gown worn by members of the clergy and choir singers over their other clothes. *n.*

sur plus (sėr′pləs *or* sėr′plus), **1** amount over and above what is needed; extra quantity left over; excess: *The bank keeps a large surplus of money in reserve.* **2** more than is needed; extra; excess: *Surplus wheat and cotton are shipped abroad.* 1 *n.,* 2 *adj.*

sur prise (sər prīz′), **1** the feeling caused by something happening suddenly or unexpectedly; astonishment; wonder: *His face showed surprise at the news.* **2** cause to feel surprised; astonish: *The victory surprised us.* **3** something unexpected: *Our grandparents always have a surprise for us on holidays.* **4** not expected; surprising: *a surprise party, a surprise visit.* **5** catch unprepared; come upon suddenly; attack suddenly: *The enemy surprised the fort.* **6** a catching unprepared; coming upon suddenly; sudden attack: *The fort was captured by surprise.* **7** lead or bring (a person, etc.) unawares: *The news surprised the visitor into tears.* 1,3,6 *n.,* 2,5,7 *v.,* **sur prised, sur pris ing;** 4 *adj.*

sur pris ing (sər prī′zing), causing surprise or wonder: *a surprising recovery. adj.* —**sur pris′ing ly,** *adv.*

sur re al (sə rē′əl), **1** surrealistic. **2** eerie; bizarre. *adj.*

sur re al ism (sə rē′ə liz′əm), a modern movement in painting, sculpture, literature, motion pictures, etc., that tries to show what takes place in dreams and in the subconscious mind. Surrealism is characterized by unusual and unexpected arrangements and distortions of images. *n.*

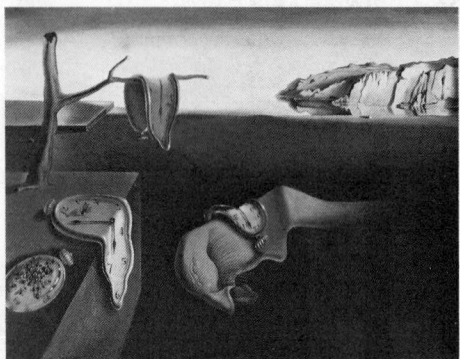

surrealism

sur re al ist (sə rē′ə list), artist or writer who uses surrealism. *n.*

sur re al is tic (sə rē′ə lis′tik), of surrealism or surrealists. *adj.* —**sur re′al is′ti cal ly,** *adv.*

sur ren der (sə ren′dər), **1** give up; give (oneself or itself) up; yield: *The town surrendered to the enemy. They surrendered themselves to bitter grief.* **2** act of surrendering: *The surrender of the town saved it from bombardment.* 1 *v.,* 2 *n.*

sur rep ti tious (sėr′əp tish′əs), **1** stealthy: *a surreptitious look.* **2** secret and unauthorized: *surreptitious meetings. adj.* —**sur′rep ti′tious ly,** *adv.* —**sur′rep ti′tious ness,** *n.*

surrey

sur rey (sėr′ē), a light, four-wheeled carriage having two seats. *n., pl.* **sur reys.** [*Surrey* was named for *Surrey,* a county in England, where the vehicle was first made.]

sur ro gate (sėr′ə gāt *or* sėr′ə git), **1** person or thing that takes the place of another; substitute. **2** serving as a substitute: *The baby-sitter became a surrogate parent to the children.* **3** (in certain states of the United States) a judge having charge of the probate of wills, the administration of estates, etc. 1,3 *n.,* 2 *adj.*

sur round (sə round′), **1** shut in on all sides; be around: *A high fence surrounds the field.* **2** form an enclosure around; encircle: *They surrounded the invalid with every comfort. v.*

sur round ings (sə roun′dingz), surrounding things, conditions, etc.: *The family lived in poor but cheerful surroundings. n.pl.*

sur tax (sėr′taks′), an additional or extra tax on something already taxed. *n., pl.* **sur tax es.**

sur veil lance (sər vā′ləns), **1** watch kept over a person: *The police kept the suspected criminal under close surveillance.* **2** supervision. *n.*

sur vey (sər vā′ *for 1,4;* sėr′vā *or* sər vā′ *for 2,3,5,6*), **1** look over; view; examine: *The buyers surveyed the goods offered for sale.* **2** a general look; view; examination; inspection: *We were pleased with our first survey of the house.* **3** a formal or official inspection, study, poll, etc.: *a survey of public opinion.* **4** to measure for size, shape, position, boundaries, etc.: *They are surveying the land before it is divided into house lots.* **5** a careful measurement: *A survey showed that the northern boundary was not correct.* **6** plan or description of such a measurement: *She pointed out the route of the railroad on the government survey.* 1,4 *v.,* 2,3,5,6 *n., pl.* **sur veys.**

sur vey ing (sər vā′ing), **1** business or act of making surveys of land. **2** mathematical instruction in the principles of making surveys. *n.*

sur vey or (sər vā′ər), person who surveys land. *n.*

sur viv al (sər vī′vəl), **1** act or fact of surviving; continuance of life; living or lasting longer than others. **2** person, thing, custom, belief, etc., that has lasted from an earlier time: *Belief in the evil eye is a survival of ancient magic. n.*

sur vive (sər vīv′), **1** live longer than; remain alive after: *He survived his wife by three years. Only ten of the crew survived the shipwreck.* **2** sustain the effects of and continue to live: *The crops survived the drought.* **3** continue to exist; remain: *These cave paintings have survived for over 15,000 years. v.,* **sur vived, sur viv ing.**

sur vi vor (sər vī′vər), person, animal, or plant that remains alive; thing that continues to exist: *There were two survivors from the plane crash.* n.

sus cep ti bil i ty (sə sep′tə bil′ə tē), **1** quality or state of being susceptible; sensitiveness. **2 susceptibilities,** *pl.* sensitive feelings. n., *pl.* **sus cep ti bil i ties.**

sus cep ti ble (sə sep′tə bəl), easily influenced by feelings or emotions; very sensitive: *Poetry appealed to his susceptible nature.* adj. —**sus cep′ti ble ness,** n. —**sus cep′ti bly,** adv.

susceptible of, capable of receiving, undergoing, or being affected by: *The preliminary plans were susceptible of a great deal of improvement.*

susceptible to, easily affected by; liable to; open to: *Young children are susceptible to many diseases. Vain people are susceptible to flattery.*

sus pect (sə spekt′ *for 1-3;* sus′pekt *for 4;* sus′pekt *or* sə spekt′ *for 5),* **1** imagine to be so; think likely: *The old fox suspected danger and did not touch the trap. I suspect that some accident has delayed her.* **2** believe guilty, false, bad, etc., without proof: *The police suspected them of being shoplifters.* **3** feel no confidence in; doubt: *I suspected the truth of my guest's excuse.* **4** person suspected: *The police have arrested two suspects in connection with the bank robbery.* **5** open to or seen with suspicion. 1-3 *v.,* 4 *n.,* 5 *adj.*

sus pend (sə spend′), **1** hang down by fastening to something above: *The lamp was suspended from the ceiling.* **2** hold in place as if by hanging: *We saw the smoke suspended in the still air.* **3** stop for a while: *We suspended building operations during the winter.* **4** cause (a law, etc.) to be for a time no longer in force. **5** remove or keep for a while from some privilege or job: *They were suspended from school for a week for bad conduct.* **6** keep undecided; put off: *The court suspended judgment till next Monday.* v.

sus pend ers (sə spen′dərz), straps worn over the shoulders to hold up the trousers. n.pl.

sus pense (sə spens′), **1** condition of being uncertain: *The detective story kept me in suspense until the last chapter.* **2** anxious uncertainty; anxiety: *There was an air of suspense in the room as the teacher graded our tests.* n.

sus pen sion (sə spen′shən), **1** a suspending or a being suspended: *the suspension of a driver's license for speeding.* **2** support on which something is suspended. **3** arrangement of springs for supporting the body of an automobile, railroad car, etc. **4** mixture in which very small particles of a solid remain suspended without dissolving. n.

suspension bridge

suspension bridge, bridge having its roadway anchored at each end and suspended on cables or chains between towers.

sus pi cion (sə spish′ən), **1** state of mind of a person

who suspects; act of suspecting: *The real thief tried to turn suspicion toward others.* **2** condition of being suspected. **3** a very small amount; slight trace; suggestion: *She spoke with a suspicion of humor.* n.

above suspicion, not to be suspected: *Don't blame my friend; he is above suspicion.*

on suspicion, because of being suspected: *They were arrested on suspicion of robbery.*

under suspicion, suspected.

sus pi cious (sə spish′əs), **1** causing one to suspect: *a suspicious manner.* **2** feeling suspicion; suspecting: *Our dog is suspicious of strangers.* **3** showing suspicion: *The dog gave a suspicious sniff at my leg.* adj. —**sus pi′cious ly,** adv. —**sus pi′cious ness,** n.

sus pire (sə spīr′), **1** sigh. **2** breathe. v., **sus pired, sus pir ing.**

Sus que han na (sus′kwə han′ə), river flowing from central New York State through Pennsylvania and Maryland into Chesapeake Bay. n.

sus tain (sə stān′), **1** keep up; keep going: *Hope sustains him in his misery.* **2** supply with food, provisions, etc.: *sustain a family.* **3** hold up; support: *Arches sustain the weight of the roof.* **4** bear; endure: *The sea wall sustains the shock of the waves.* **5** suffer; experience: *She sustained a great loss in the death of her parents.* **6** allow; admit; favor: *The court sustained his suit.* **7** agree with; confirm: *The facts sustain her theory.* v. —**sus tain′a ble,** adj. —**sus tain′er,** n.

sus te nance (sus′tə nəns), **1** means of sustaining life; food or provisions: *The lost campers went for two days without sustenance.* **2** means of living; support: *She gave money for the sustenance of the poor.* n.

su ture (sü′chər), **1** the sewing together or joining of two surfaces, especially the edges of a cut or wound. **2** seam formed in sewing up a wound. **3** one of the stitches or fastenings used. **4** unite by suture or in a similar manner. **5** line where two bones, especially of the skull, join. 1-3 *n.,* 4 *v.,* **su tured, su tur ing.**

Su va (sü′və), capital of Fiji. n.

su zer ain (sü′zər in *or* sü′zə rān′), **1** a feudal lord. **2** state or government exercising political control over a dependent state. n.

su zer ain ty (sü′zər in tē *or* sü′zə rān′tē), position or authority of a suzerain. n., *pl.* **su zer ain ties.**

svelte (svelt), slender; lithe: *The countess was tall, svelte, and very pale.* adj. [*Svelte* was borrowed from French *svelte.*]

SW, S.W., or **s.w., 1** southwest. **2** southwestern.

swab (swob), **1** a mop for cleaning decks, floors, etc. **2** a bit of sponge, cloth, or cotton for cleansing some part of the body or for applying medicine to it. **3** a cleaner for the bore of a firearm. **4** clean with a swab; apply a swab to: *swab a person's throat.* 1-3 *n.,* 4 *v.,* **swabbed, swabbing.** Also, **swob.** —**swab′ber,** n.

swad dle (swod′l), bind (a baby) with long, narrow strips of cloth; wrap tightly with clothes, bandages, etc. *v.,* **swad dled, swad dling.**

swaddling clothes, 1 long, narrow strips of cloth for wrapping a newborn infant. **2** long clothes for an infant.

swag (swag), SLANG. things stolen or gotten in a dishonest way. n.

swag ger (swag′ər), **1** walk with a bold, rude, or superior air; strut about or show off in a vain or bragging way: *The actor swaggered onto the stage.* **2** boast or brag noisily. **3** a swaggering way of walking, acting, or speaking. 1,2 *v.,* 3 *n.* —**swag′ger er,** *n.* —**swag′ger ing ly,** *adv.*

Swa hi li (swä hē′lē), a Bantu language containing many Arabic and other foreign words, spoken in much of eastern Africa and parts of Zaïre. *Safari came into English from Swahili.* *n.*

swain (swān), OLD USE. **1** lover. **2** a young man who lives in the country. *n.*

swale (swāl), a low, wet piece of land; low place. *n.*

swal low¹ (swol′ō), **1** take into the stomach through the throat: *We swallow all our food and drink.* **2** perform the act of swallowing: *I cannot swallow.* **3** take in; absorb: *The waves swallowed up the swimmer.* **4** INFORMAL. believe too easily; accept without question or suspicion: *He will swallow any story.* **5** put up with; take meekly; accept without opposing or resisting: *He had to swallow the insult.* **6** take back: *swallow words said in anger.* **7** keep back; keep from expressing: *She swallowed her displeasure and smiled.* **8** a swallowing: *She took the medicine at one swallow.* **9** amount swallowed at one time: *There are only about four swallows of water left in the bottle.* 1-7 *v.,* 8,9 *n.* [*Swallow¹* comes from Old English *swelgan.*] —**swal′low er,** *n.*

swal low² (swol′ō), a small, swift-flying bird with long, pointed wings. Swallows are noted for their regular flights or migrations, in large numbers and over very long distances. Some kinds have deeply forked tails. *n.* [*Swallow²* comes from Old English *swealwe.*]

swal low tail (swol′ō tāl′), **1** a large butterfly having taillike extensions of the hind wings. **2** swallow-tailed coat. *n.*

swal low-tailed coat (swol′ō tāld′), a man's coat with tails, worn at certain formal events.

swam (swam), past tense of **swim.** *We swam all afternoon.* *v.*

swa mi (swä′mē), title of a Hindu religious teacher. *n., pl.* **swa mis.**

swamp (swomp), **1** wet, soft land; marsh: *We will drain the swamp on our farm so that we can plant crops there.* **2** plunge or sink in a swamp or in water: *The horses were swamped in the stream.* **3** fill with water and sink: *Their boat swamped. The wave swamped the boat.* **4** overwhelm or be overwhelmed as by a flood; make or become helpless: *swamped with work. He was swamped with letters asking for money.* 1 *n.,* 2-4 *v.*

swamp land (swomp′land′), tract of land covered by swamps. *n.*

swamp y (swom′pē), **1** like a swamp; soft and wet: *The front yard is swampy from the heavy rain.* **2** containing swamps: *a swampy region.* **3** of swamps. *adj.,* **swamp i er, swamp i est.** —**swamp′i ness,** *n.*

swan (swon), **1** a large, graceful water bird with a long, slender, curving neck. The adult is usually pure white. **2** a sweet singer; poet. *n.* —**swan′like′,** *adj.*

swank (swangk), INFORMAL. stylish; smart; dashing: *a swank new restaurant. adj.*

swank y (swang′kē), INFORMAL. swank. *adj.,* **swank i er, swank i est.** —**swank′i ly,** *adv.* —**swank′i ness,** *n.*

swan's-down (swonz′doun′), **1** the soft feathers of a swan. **2** Also, **swansdown.** a fine, thick, soft cloth made from wool or cotton, used for babies' coats, bathrobes, etc. *n.*

swan song, 1 song which, according to fable, a swan sings as it is about to die. **2** a person's last appearance or last piece of work.

swap (swop), INFORMAL. **1** to exchange, barter, or trade: *The children swapped books.* **2** an exchange, barter, or trade. 1 *v.,* **swapped, swap ping;** 2 *n.* Also, **swop.** [*Swap*

comes from Middle English *swappen,* meaning "to strike." *Swap* probably got its present meaning from the practice of "striking hands" as a sign of agreement in bargaining.] —**swap′per,** *n.*

sward (swôrd), a grassy surface; turf. *n.*

sware (swer *or* swar), OLD USE. swore; a past tense of **swear.** *v.*

swarm (swôrm), **1** group of bees led by a queen that leave a hive and fly off together to start a new colony. **2** fly off together in this way to start a new colony. **3** group of bees settled together in a hive. **4** a large group of insects, animals, people, etc., moving about together: *Swarms of children were playing in the park.* **5** fly or move about in great numbers; be in very great numbers: *The mosquitoes swarmed about us.* **6** be crowded; crowd: *The swamp swarms with mosquitoes. Mosquitoes swarmed the open tent.* 1,3,4 *n.,* 2,5,6 *v.* —**swarm′er,** *n.*

swart (swôrt), dark; swarthy. *adj.*

swarth y (swôr′ŦHē *or* swôr′thē), having a dark skin: *The ship's crew was swarthy from the sun of the tropics. adj.,* **swarth i er, swarth i est.** —**swarth′i ly,** *adv.* —**swarth′i ness,** *n.*

swash (swosh), **1** dash (water, etc.) about; splash. **2** a swashing action or sound: *the swash of waves against a boat.* 1 *v.,* 2 *n., pl.* **swash es.**

swash buck ler (swosh′buk′lər), a swaggering swordsman, bully, or boaster. *n.*

swash buck ling (swosh′buk′ling), swaggering; bullying; boasting: *military swashbuckling (n.), a swashbuckling adventurer (adj.).* *n., adj.*

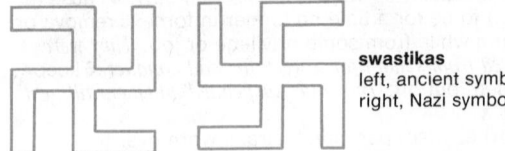

swastikas
left, ancient symbol;
right, Nazi symbol

swas ti ka (swos′tə kə), an ancient symbol or ornament like a cross with the arms bent. Swastikas were thought in early times to bring good luck. The swastika with arms turning clockwise was the symbol of the Nazis in Germany. *n., pl.* **swas ti kas.**

swat (swot), **1** hit sharply or violently: *swat a fly.* **2** a sharp or violent blow. 1 *v.,* **swat ted, swat ting;** 2 *n.* —**swat′ter,** *n.*

swatch (swoch), sample of cloth or other material. *n., pl.* **swatch es.**

swath (swoth), **1** the space covered by a single cut of a scythe or by one cut of a mowing machine. **2** row of grass, grain, etc., cut by a scythe or mowing machine. **3** a strip. *n.* Also, **swathe.**

swathe¹ (swoŦH *or* swāŦH), **1** wrap up closely or fully: *swathed in a blanket.* **2** to bind, wrap, or bandage. **3** a wrapping or bandage. **4** envelop or surround like a wrapping: *White clouds swathed the mountain.* 1,2,4 *v.,* **swathed, swath ing;** 3 *n.*

swathe² (swoŦH *or* swāŦH), swath. *n.*

sway (swā), **1** swing back and forth; rock from side to side, or to one side: *The pail swayed in her hands as she ran.* **2** make move; cause to sway: *The wind swayed the branches.* **3** a swinging back and forth or from side to side: *The sway of the pail caused some water to spill out.* **4** move to one side; turn aside: *The horse swayed left at the crossroads.* **5** to change in opinion or feeling: *Nothing could sway her after she had made up her mind.* **6** to influence, control, or rule: *The speaker's words swayed the audience.* **7** an influence, control, or rule: *The country was under the sway of a dictator.* 1,2,4-6 *v.,* 3,7 *n.* —**sway′-er,** *n.*

swaybacked—The driver had a **swaybacked** horse.

a hat	**i** it	**oi** oil	**ch** child	a in about
ā age	**ī** ice	**ou** out	**ng** long	e in taken
ä far	**o** hot	**u** cup	**sh** she	ə = i in pencil
e let	**ō** open	**u̇** put	**th** thin	o in lemon
ē equal	**ô** order	**ü** rule	**ᴛʜ** then	u in circus
ėr term			**zh** measure	

sway backed (swā′bakt′), having the back sagged or hollowed to an unusual degree. *adj.*

Swa zi land (swä′zē land′), country in SE Africa, a member of the Commonwealth of Nations. *Capital:* Mbabane. *n.*

swear (swer *or* swar), **1** make a solemn statement, appealing to God or some other sacred being or object; take oath: *A witness at a trial is asked, "Do you swear to tell the truth, the whole truth, and nothing but the truth, so help you God?"* **2** to promise on oath or solemnly (to observe or do something); vow; pledge: *The governor swore to uphold the constitution. I swear I will tell no one.* **3** bind by an oath; require to promise or pledge: *Members of the club were sworn to secrecy.* **4** use profane language; curse: *They raged and swore when they were captured.* *v.,* **swore, sworn, swear ing. —swear′er,** *n.*
swear by, 1 name as one's witness in taking an oath. **2** have great confidence in.
swear in, admit to office or service by giving an oath: *to swear in a jury.*
swear off, promise to give up: *to swear off smoking.*
swear out, get by swearing that a certain charge is true: *He swore out a warrant for the arrest of the man who had hit him.*

sweat (swet), **1** moisture coming through the pores of the skin: *After mowing the lawn I wiped the sweat from my face.* **2** give out moisture through the pores of the skin: *We sweated because it was very hot.* **3** cause to sweat: *She sweated her horse by riding it too hard.* **4** get rid of by sweating or as if by sweating: *to sweat off excess weight, to sweat out a hard test.* **5** a fit or condition of sweating: *He was in a cold sweat from fear.* **6** INFORMAL. condition of anxiety, impatience, or anything that might make a person sweat: *We were all in a sweat over the big test.* **7** moisture given out by something or gathered on its surface. **8** give out moisture; collect moisture from the air: *A pitcher of ice water sweats on a hot day.* **9** cause to work hard and under bad conditions: *a company that sweats its workers.* **10** INFORMAL. work very hard. **1,5-7** *n.,* **2-4,8-10** *v.,* **sweat** or **sweat ed, sweat ing.**

sweat er (swet′ər), a knitted garment of wool, nylon, etc., worn on the upper part of the body. *n.*

sweat gland, gland of the skin that secretes sweat. A sweat gland is connected with the surface of the skin by a tube or duct that ends in a pore.

sweat shirt, a heavy pullover with long sleeves, sometimes with a fleece lining, worn especially by athletes to keep warm before and after exercise.

sweat shop (swet′shop′), place where workers are employed at low pay for long hours under bad conditions. *n.*

sweat y (swet′ē), **1** covered or wet with sweat; sweating. **2** causing sweat. **3** laborious. *adj.,* **sweat i er, sweat i est. —sweat′i ly,** *adv.* **—sweat′i ness,** *n.*

Swede (swēd), person born or living in Sweden. *n.*

Swe den (swēd′n), country in N Europe, east and south

of Norway. *Capital:* Stockholm. See **Lapland** for map. *n.*

Swed ish (swē′dish), **1** of Sweden, its people, or their language: *a Swedish movie.* **2** the people of Sweden. **3** language of Sweden. **1** *adj.,* **2** *n.pl.,* **3** *n.sing.*

sweep (swēp), **1** clean or clear (a floor, etc.) with a broom, brush, etc.; use a broom or something like one to remove dirt; brush: *The campers swept the floor of their cabin every morning.* **2** move, drive, or take away with or as with a broom, brush, etc.: *Please sweep the dust into a pan. The wind sweeps the snow into drifts.* **3** remove with a sweeping motion; carry along: *A flood swept away the bridge.* **4** act of sweeping; clearing away; removing: *I made a clean sweep of all my debts.* **5** pass over with a steady movement: *Her fingers swept the strings of the harp. His eyes swept the crowd, looking for his friend.* **6** move swiftly; pass swiftly: *The hawk swept down on the mouse. The wind sweeps over the plain.* **7** a steady, driving motion or swift onward course of something: *the sweep of the wind across the prairie.* **8** move with dignity: *The diplomat swept out of the room.* **9** move or extend in a long course or curve: *The shore sweeps to the south for miles.* **10** a swinging or curving motion: *She cut the tall grass with strong sweeps of the scythe.* **11** a continuous extent; stretch: *The house looks upon a wide sweep of farming country.* **12** a reach; range; extent: *The mountain is beyond the sweep of your eye.* **13** a winning of all the games in a series, match, contest, etc.; complete victory. **14** person who sweeps chimneys, streets, etc. **15** a long oar used to row or steer a boat. **16** a long pole which pivots on a high post and is used to raise or lower a bucket in a well. **1-3,5,6,8,9** *v.,* **swept, sweep ing; 4,7,10-16** *n.*

sweep er (swē′pər), person or thing that sweeps: *a carpet sweeper.* *n.*

sweep ing (swē′ping), **1** passing over a wide space: *Her sweeping glance took in the whole room.* **2** having wide range: *a sweeping victory, a sweeping statement.* **3** sweepings,** *pl.* dust, rubbish, scraps, etc., swept out or up. **1,2** *adj.,* **3** *n.* **—sweep′ing ly,** *adv.*

sweep stake (swēp′stāk′), sweepstakes. *n.*

sweep stakes (swēp′stāks′), **1** system of gambling on horse races, etc. People buy tickets, and the money they pay goes to the holder or holders of winning tickets. **2** the race or contest. **3** prize in such a race or contest. *n.*

sweet (swēt), **1** having a taste like that of sugar or honey: *Pears are much sweeter than lemons.* **2** having a pleasant taste or smell: *Perfume is sweet.* **3** pleasant; agreeable: *a sweet child, a sweet smile, sweet music.* **4** fresh; not sour, salty, bitter, or spoiled: *sweet cream.* **5** a dear; darling. **6** something sweet. **7** sweets,** *pl.* candy or other sweet things. **8** in a sweet manner. **1-4** *adj.,* **5-7** *n.,* **8** *adv.* [*Sweet* comes from Old English *swēte.*] **—sweet′ly,** *adv.* **—sweet′ness,** *n.*

sweet bread (swēt′bred′), the pancreas or thymus of a calf, lamb, etc., used as meat. *n.*

sweet cider, unfermented cider.

sweet corn, kind of corn which is eaten by people, usually when it is young and tender. It may be preserved by canning or freezing.

sweet en (swēt′n), **1** make sweet: *He sweetened his coffee with sugar.* **2** become sweet: *Those pears will sweeten as they ripen.* *v.* **—sweet′en er,** *n.*

swift (def. 5)
about 5 in.
(13 cm.) long

sweet en ing (swēt′n ing), something that sweetens. Sugar is the most common sweetening. *n.*

sweet flag, 1 plant with long, sword-shaped leaves. **2** its fragrant root, used in perfumes and medicines.

sweet heart (swēt′härt′), a loved one; lover. *n.*

sweet ish (swē′tish), somewhat sweet. *adj.*

sweet meats (swēt′mēts′), candied fruits, sugar-covered nuts, etc.; candy; bonbons. *n.pl.*

sweet pea, an annual climbing plant with delicate, fragrant flowers of various colors.

sweet potato, the sweet, thick, yellow or reddish root of a creeping vine grown in warm regions. Sweet potatoes are used as a vegetable or in pies.

sweet-tem pered (swēt′tem′pərd), having a gentle or pleasant nature. *adj.*

sweet tooth, fondness for sweets.

sweet william or **sweet William,** plant related to the pink, with dense, rounded clusters of small flowers of various shades of white and red.

swell (swel), **1** grow or make bigger: *Bread dough swells as it rises. The bee sting had swelled his finger.* **2** be larger or thicker in a particular place; stick out: *A barrel swells in the middle.* **3** increase in amount, degree, force, etc.: *Savings may swell into a fortune.* **4** act of swelling; an increase in amount, degree, force, etc. **5** condition of being swollen. **6** rise or cause to rise above the level: *Rounded hills swell gradually from the plain. Rain swelled the river.* **7** part that rises or swells out. **8** piece of higher ground; rounded hill. **9** a long, unbroken wave or waves: *The boat rocked in the swell.* **10** grow or make louder: *The sound swelled from a murmur to a roar. All joined in to swell the chorus.* **11** become filled with emotion: *to swell with pride.* **12** a swelling tone or sound. **13** in music: **a** a gradual increase in sound followed by a decrease. **b** sign for this (<>). **14** INFORMAL. a fashionable person. **15** INFORMAL. stylish; grand. **16** SLANG. excellent; first-rate. 1-3,6,10,11 *v.*, **swelled, swelled** or **swol len, swell ing;** 4,5,7-9,12-14 *n.*, 15,16 *adj.*

swell head ed (swel′hed′id), INFORMAL. conceited. *adj.* —**swell′head′ed ness,** *n.*

swell ing (swel′ing), an increase in size; swollen part: *There is a swelling on her head where she bumped it. n.*

swel ter (swel′tər), **1** suffer from heat. **2** perspire freely; sweat. **3** a sweltering condition. 1,2 *v.*, 3 *n.*

swept (swept), past tense and past participle of **sweep.** *I swept the room. It was swept clean. v.*

swept-back (swept′bak′), (of the wings of an aircraft) extending outward and sharply backward from the fuselage. *adj.*

swept-back
an airplane
with swept-back
wings

swerve (swėrv), **1** turn aside: *The car swerved sharply to avoid hitting the truck. Nothing could swerve her from reaching her goal.* **2** a turning aside: *The swerve of the ball made it hard to hit.* 1 *v.*, **swerved, swerv ing;** 2 *n.*

swift (swift), **1** moving very fast: *a swift automobile.* **2** coming or happening quickly: *a swift response.* **3** quick, rapid, or prompt to act, etc.: *He is swift to repay a kindness.* **4** in a swift manner. **5** a small bird with long wings. It is related to the hummingbird but looks somewhat like a swallow. 1-3 *adj.*, 4 *adv.*, 5 *n.* —**swift′ly,** *adv.* —**swift′-ness,** *n.*

Swift (swift), **Jonathan,** 1667-1745, English writer of satires, born in Ireland. He is the author of *Gulliver's Travels. n.*

swift-foot ed (swift′fút′id), able to run swiftly. *adj.*

swig (swig), INFORMAL. **1** a big or hearty drink. **2** drink heartily or greedily. 1 *n.*, 2 *v.*, **swigged, swig ging.** —**swig′ger,** *n.*

swill (swil), **1** kitchen refuse, especially when partly liquid; garbage; slops. Swill is sometimes fed to pigs. **2** drink greedily; drink too much. 1 *n.*, 2 *v.*

swim (swim), **1** move along on or in the water by using arms, legs, fins, etc.: *Fish swim. Most boys and girls like to swim.* **2** swim across: *She swam the river.* **3** make swim: *He swam his horse across the stream.* **4** float: *The roast lamb was swimming in gravy.* **5** be overflowed or flooded with: *Her eyes were swimming with tears.* **6** act, time, motion, or distance of swimming: *Her swim had tired her. They had had an hour's swim.* **7** the swim, the current of affairs, activities, etc.: *An active and sociable person likes to be in the swim.* **8** go smoothly; glide: *White clouds swam across the sky.* **9** be dizzy; whirl: *The heat and noise made my head swim.* 1-5,8,9 *v.*, **swam, swum, swim ming;** 6,7 *n.*

swim mer (swim′ər), person or animal that swims. *n.*

swim mer et (swim′ə ret′), an abdominal limb or appendage in many crustaceans, such as lobsters and shrimp. It is used for respiration, for carrying eggs, etc., and usually adapted for swimming. *n.*

swim ming (swim′ing), **1** practice or sport of swimming: *My friend is an expert at both swimming and diving. She is our teacher in swimming.* **2** act of swimming: *Can you reach the island by swimming?* **3** of or for swimming or swimmers: *a swimming teacher, a swimming pool.* **4** dizzy: *a swimming sensation.* 1,2 *n.*, 3,4 *adj.*

swim ming ly (swim′ing lē), with great ease or success: *Everything went swimmingly at our party. adv.*

swim suit (swim′süt′), bathing suit. *n.*

swin dle (swin′dl), **1** cheat; defraud: *Honest storekeepers do not swindle their customers.* **2** get by fraud. **3** a cheating act; fraud. 1,2 *v.*, **swin dled, swin dling;** 3 *n.*

swin dler (swin′dlər), person who cheats or defrauds. *n.*

swine (swīn), **1** a hog or pig. **2** a coarse or beastly person. *n., pl.* **swine.**

swine herd (swīn′hėrd′), person who tends hogs or pigs. *n.*

swing (swing), **1** move back and forth, especially with a regular motion: *The hammock swings. He swings his arms as he walks.* **2** move in a curve: *She swung the automobile around a corner.* **3** act or manner of swinging. **4** a swinging blow: *He brought the hammer down with a long swing.* **5** seat hung from ropes or chains in which one may sit and swing. **6** hang: *We swung the hammock between two trees.* **7** move with a free, swaying motion: *The children came swinging down the street.* **8** a swinging gait or movement; steady, marked rhythm: *The song "Dixie" has a swing.* **9** movement; activity: *It's hard to get into the swing of school after summer vacation.* **10** jazz music with a lively, steady rhythm, in which the players improvise freely on the original melody. **11** INFORMAL. manage successfully: *swing a business deal.* 1,2,6,7,11 *v.,* **swung, swing ing;** 3-5,8-10 *n.* —**swing′er,** *n.*

in full swing, going on actively and completely; without restraint: *By five o'clock the party was in full swing.*

swin ish (swī′nish), **1** very selfish; greedy. **2** dirty; filthy; beastly. *adj.* —**swin′ish ly,** *adv.* —**swin′ish ness,** *n.*

swipe (swīp), **1** INFORMAL. a sweeping stroke; hard blow: *He made two swipes at the golf ball without hitting it.* **2** INFORMAL. to strike with a sweeping blow. **3** SLANG. steal. 1 *n.,* 2,3 *v.,* **swiped, swip ing.**

swirl (swėrl), **1** move or drive along with a twisting motion; whirl: *dust swirling in the air, a stream swirling over rocks. The heat and noise made my head swirl.* **2** a swirling movement; whirl; eddy. **3** to twist or curl: *a lock of hair swirled against the neck.* **4** a twist or curl: *a swirl of whipped cream on top of a sundae.* 1,3 *v.,* 2,4 *n.*

swish (swish), **1** move or cause to move with a thin, light, hissing or brushing sound: *The whip swished through the air. The child swished the stick.* **2** make such a sound: *The long gown swished as she danced across the floor.* **3** a swishing movement or sound: *the swish of little waves on the shore.* 1,2 *v.,* 3 *n., pl.* **swish es.**

Swiss (swis), **1** of Switzerland or its people: *the Swiss lakes.* **2** person born or living in Switzerland. **3** the people of Switzerland. 1 *adj.,* 2 *n.sing.,* 3 *n.pl.*

Swiss cheese, a firm, pale-yellow or whitish cheese with many large holes.

switch (swich), **1** a slender stick used in whipping. **2** to whip or strike: *She switched the horse to make it gallop.* **3** a stroke or lash: *The big dog knocked a vase off the table with a switch of its tail.* **4** move or swing like a switch: *The horse switched its tail to drive off the flies.* **5** device for making or breaking a connection in an electric circuit. **6** pair of movable rails by which a train is shifted from one track to another. **7** to shift or turn by using a switch: *to switch railroad cars from one track to another. Switch off the light.* **8** to change or shift: *switch places. They switched hats.* **9** a change or shift: *a last-minute switch of plans. He lost the election when his supporters made a switch of their votes to the other candidate.* 1,3,5,6,9 *n., pl.* **switch es;** 2,4,7,8 *v.* —**switch′er,** *n.*

switch blade (swich′blād′), pocketknife with a blade that springs out at the push of a button or knob on the handle. *n.*

switch board (swich′bôrd′), panel containing the necessary switches, meters, and other devices for opening, closing, combining, or controlling electric circuits. A telephone switchboard has plugs for connecting one line to another. *n.*

switch-hit ter (swich′hit′ər), a baseball player who bats either right- or left-handed. *n.*

switch man (swich′mən), person in charge of one or more railroad switches. *n., pl.* **switch men.**

Swit zer land (swit′sər lənd), small country in central Europe, north of Italy. *Capital:* Bern. See **Rhine** for map. *n.*

swiv el (swiv′əl), **1** a fastening that allows the thing fastened to turn round freely upon it. **2** a chain link having two parts, one of which turns freely in the other. **3** support on which a chair, gun, etc., can turn round. **4** turn on a swivel. 1-3 *n.,* 4 *v.,* **swiv eled, swiv el ing** or **swiv elled, swiv el ling.**

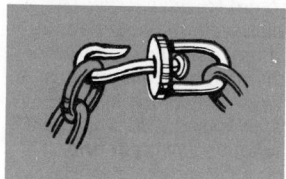

swivel (def. 2)

swivel chair, chair having a seat that turns on a swivel.

swob (swob), swab. *n., v.,* **swobbed, swob bing.** —**swob′ber,** *n.*

swol len (swō′lən), **1** swelled: *a swollen ankle.* **2** swelled; a past participle of **swell.** 1 *adj.,* 2 *v.*

swoon (swün), **1** to faint: *swoon at the sight of blood.* **2** a faint: *Cold water may help to bring someone out of a swoon.* 1 *v.,* 2 *n.* —**swoon′ing ly,** *adv.*

swoop (swüp), **1** come down with a rush, as a hawk does; sweep rapidly down upon in a sudden attack: *Bats swooped down from the roof of the cave.* **2** a rapid downward sweep; sudden, swift descent or attack: *With one swoop the hawk seized the chicken and flew away.* **3** snatch: *The nurse rushed after the running child and swooped him up in her arms.* 1,3 *v.,* 2 *n.* —**swoop′er,** *n.*

swop (swop), swap. *v.,* **swopped, swop ping;** *n.*

sword (sôrd), **1** weapon, usually metal, with a long, sharp blade fixed in a handle or hilt. **2 the sword,** fighting, war, or military power: *Those that live by the sword shall perish by the sword. n.* [*Sword* comes from Old English *sweord.*] —**sword′like′,** *adj.*

at swords' points, very unfriendly.

cross swords, 1 fight. **2** quarrel; dispute.

sword fish (sôrd′fish′), a very large saltwater food fish with a long, swordlike projection from its upper jaw. *n., pl.* **sword fish es** or **sword fish.**

sword play (sôrd′plā′), action, practice, or art of wielding a sword; fencing. *n.*

swords man (sôrdz′mən), **1** person skilled in using a sword. **2** person using a sword. *n., pl.* **swords men.**

swore (swôr), past tense of **swear.** *I swore to keep my friend's secret. v.*

sworn (swôrn), **1** past participle of **swear.** *A solemn oath of loyalty was sworn by all the knights.* **2** having taken an oath; bound by an oath: *There were ten sworn witnesses.* **3** declared, promised, etc., with an oath: *We have her sworn statement.* 1 *v.,* 2,3 *adj.*

swum (swum), past participle of **swim.** *He had never swum before. v.*

swung (swung), past tense and past participle of **swing.** *She swung her arms as she walked. The door had swung open. v.*

syc a more (sik′ə môr′), **1** a tall North American shade tree with broad leaves, small, round fruit, and bark that breaks or peels off in tiny scales; buttonwood; plane tree. **2** a large maple tree of Europe and Asia. **3** a fig tree of Egypt and Syria. *n.*

syc o phant (sik′ə fənt), person who tries to win the favor of important people by flattery. *n.*

Syd ney (sid′nē), the largest city and most important seaport in Australia, in the SE part. *n.*

syl lab ic (sə lab′ik), **1** of or consisting of syllables. **2** forming a separate syllable by itself. The second *l* sound in *little* is syllabic. *adj.* —**syl lab′i cal ly,** *adv.*

syl lab i cate (sə lab′ə kāt), divide into syllables. *v.,* **syl lab i cat ed, syl lab i cat ing.**

syl lab i ca tion (sə lab′ə kā′shən), division into syllables. *n.*

syl lab i fi ca tion (sə lab′ə fə kā′shən), syllabication. *n.*

syl lab i fy (sə lab′ə fī), divide into syllables. *v.,* **syl lab i fied, syl lab i fy ing.**

syl la ble (sil′ə bəl), **1** word or part of a word pronounced as a unit. A syllable usually consists of a vowel alone or a vowel with one or more consonants. The word *syllable* (sil′ə bəl), has three syllables. Certain consonant sounds may be used as a vowel sound in syllables, such as the (l) in *bottle* (bot′l) or the (n) in *hidden* (hid′n). **2** letter or group of letters representing a syllable in writing and printing. A syllable may be separated from other syllables of the word by a space, hyphen, or other mark to show where the word may be divided at the end of a line. *Strength* has only one syllable; *ap prox i mate* has four. *n.*

syl la bus (sil′ə bəs), a brief statement of the main points of a speech, a book, a course of study, etc. *n., pl.* **syl la bus es, syl la bi** (sil′ə bī).

syl lo gism (sil′ə jiz′əm), a form of argument or reasoning, consisting of two statements and a conclusion drawn from them. EXAMPLE: All trees have roots; an oak is a tree; therefore, an oak has roots. *n.*

sylph (silf), **1** a slender, graceful girl or woman. **2** an imaginary spirit of the air. *n.* —**sylph′like′,** *adj.*

syl van (sil′vən), of, in, or having woods: *They lived in a sylvan retreat.* Also, **silvan.**

sym., 1 symmetrical. **2** symphony.

sym bi o sis (sim′bē ō′sis), the association or living together of two unlike organisms for the benefit of each other. Most lichens, which are composed of an alga and a fungus, are examples of symbiosis; the alga provides the food, and the fungus provides water and protection. *n.* [*Symbiosis* comes from Greek *symbiōsis,* meaning "a living together."]

sym bi ot ic (sim′bē ot′ik), of symbiosis; living in symbiosis. *adj.* —**sym′bi ot′i cal ly,** *adv.*

symbols—The lion is the symbol of courage; the lamb, of meekness. The marks +, −, ×, ÷ are symbols for add, subtract, multiply, and divide.

sym bol (sim′bəl), something that stands for or represents something else. *n.*

sym bol ic (sim bol′ik), **1** used as a symbol: *A lily is symbolic of purity.* **2** of a symbol; expressed by a symbol or symbols; using symbols: *Writing is a symbolic form of expression. adj.* —**sym bol′i cal ly,** *adv.*

sym bol i cal (sim bol′ə kəl), symbolic. *adj.*

sym bol ism (sim′bə liz′əm), **1** use of symbols; representation by symbols. **2** system of symbols: *The cross, the crown, the lamb, and the lily are parts of Christian symbolism. n.*

sym bol i za tion (sim′bə lə zā′shən), symbolizing; representation by symbols. *n.*

sym bol ize (sim′bə līz), **1** be a symbol of; stand for; represent: *A dove symbolizes peace.* **2** represent by a symbol or symbols: *The ancient Egyptians symbolized the sun as a boat.* **3** use symbols. *v.,* **sym bol ized, sym bol iz ing.** —**sym′bol iz′er,** *n.*

sym met ric (si met′rik), symmetrical. *adj.*

sym met ri cal (si met′rə kəl), having symmetry; well-proportioned: *symmetrical figures. adj.* —**sym met′ri cal ly,** *adv.*

symmetry (def. 1)—left, radial; right, bilateral

sym me try (sim′ə trē), **1** exact agreement in size, shape, and arrangement of parts on opposite sides of a line or plane, or around a center or axis. **2** pleasing proportions between the parts of a whole; well-balanced arrangement of parts; harmony. *n., pl.* **sym me tries.**

sym pa thet ic (sim′pə thet′ik), **1** having or showing kind feelings toward others; sympathizing: *a sympathetic friend.* **2** approving; agreeing: *The teacher was sympathetic to the class's plan for a trip to the museum.* **3** enjoying the same things and getting along well together. **4** harmonious; agreeable: *a sympathetic environment. adj.*

sym pa thet i cal ly (sim′pə thet′ik lē), in a sympathetic way; with kindness: *The doctor spoke sympathetically while bandaging my leg. adv.*

sym pa thize (sim′pə thīz), **1** feel or show sympathy: *I sympathized with the injured child.* **2** share in or agree with a feeling or opinion: *My parents sympathize with my plan to be a painter. v.,* **sym pa thized, sym pa thiz ing.** —**sym′pa thiz′ing ly,** *adv.*

sym pa thiz er (sim′pə thī′zər), person who sympathizes; person who is favorably inclined toward a particular belief or person. *n.*

sym pa thy (sim′pə thē), **1** a sharing of another's sorrow or trouble: *We feel sympathy for a person who is ill.* **2** agreement in feeling; condition or fact of having the same feeling: *The sympathy between the twins was so great that they always smiled or cried at the same things.* **3** agreement; approval; favor: *I am in sympathy with your plan. n., pl.* **sym pa thies.**

sym phon ic (sim fon′ik), of or like a symphony: *symphonic music. adj.* —**sym phon′i cal ly,** *adv.*

sym pho ny (sim′fə nē), **1** an elaborate musical composition for an orchestra. A symphony usually has three or more movements in different rhythms but related keys. **2** symphony orchestra: *the Chicago Symphony.* **3** harmony of sounds. **4** harmony of colors: *In autumn the woods are a symphony in red, brown, and yellow. n., pl.* **sym phonies.**

symphony orchestra, a large orchestra that plays symphonies, made up of brass, woodwind, percussion, and stringed instruments.

sym po si um (sim pō′zē əm), **1** a meeting or conference for the discussion of some subject: *hold a symposium on science.* **2** a collection of the opinions of several persons on some subject: *This magazine contains a sports symposium. n., pl.* **sym po si ums, sym po si a** (sim pō′zē ə).

symp tom (simp′təm), **1** a sign or indication: *Quaking knees and paleness are symptoms of fear.* **2** a noticeable change in the normal working of the body that indicates or accompanies disease, sickness, etc.: *The doctor made her diagnosis after studying the patient's symptoms. n.*

symp to mat ic (simp′tə mat′ik), being a sign or symptom: *Headaches are sometimes symptomatic of eyestrain. Riots are symptomatic of political or social unrest. adj.*

syn., 1 synonym. **2** synonymous.

syn a gogue (sin′ə gôg), **1** building used by Jews for worship and religious instruction. **2** a Jewish congregation. *n.*

syn apse (si naps′ *or* sin′aps), place where a nerve impulse passes from one nerve cell to another. *n.*

syn chro nize (sing′krə nīz), **1** occur at the same time; agree in time. **2** move or take place at the same rate and exactly together. **3** make agree in time: *synchronize all the clocks in a building. v.,* **syn chro nized, syn chro niz ing.**

syn chro nous (sing′krə nəs), **1** occurring at the same time; simultaneous. **2** going on at the same rate and exactly together: *the synchronous movements of the two dancers. adj.* —**syn′chro nous ly,** *adv.*

syn co pate (sing′kə pāt), (in music) begin (a tone) on an unaccented beat and hold it into an accented one. *v.,* **syn co pat ed, syn co pat ing.** —**syn′co pa′tor,** *n.*

syn co pa tion (sing′kə pā′shən), a syncopating or a being syncopated. *n.*

syn di cate (sin′də kit *for 1,2;* sin′də kāt *for 3-5*), **1** a combination of persons or companies formed to carry out some undertaking, especially one requiring a large capital investment. **2** agency that sells special articles, photographs, etc., to a large number of newspapers or magazines for publication at the same time. **3** combine into a syndicate. **4** manage by a syndicate. **5** publish through a syndicate. **1,2** *n.,* **3-5** *v.,* **syn di cat ed, syn di cat ing.** —**syn′di ca′tor,** *n.*

syn di ca tion (sin′də kā′shən), a syndicating or a being syndicated. *n.*

syn drome (sin′drōm), group of symptoms considered together as characteristic of a particular disease. *n.*

syn fu el (sin′fyü′əl), a fuel made by altering the molecular structure of coal or by treating crops. Gasoline and methane can be produced as synfuels. *n.* [*Synfuel* comes from the phrase *synthetic fuel.*]

syn od (sin′əd), a council of churches or church officials. *n.*

syn o nym (sin′ə nim), word that means the same or nearly the same as another word. "Keen" is a synonym of "sharp." *n.*

syn on y mous (si non′ə məs), having the same or nearly the same meaning. "Little" and "small" are synonymous. *adj.* —**syn on′y mous ly,** *adv.*

syn op sis (si nop′sis), a brief statement giving a general view of some subject, book, play, etc.; summary. *n., pl.* **syn op ses** (si nop′ sēz).

syn tac tic (sin tak′tik), syntactical. *adj.*

syn tac ti cal (sin tak′tə kəl), of syntax; in accordance with the rules of syntax. *adj.* —**syn tac′ti cal ly,** *adv.*

syn tax (sin′taks), **1** way in which the words and phrases of a sentence are arranged to show how they relate to each other. **2** part of grammar dealing with this. *n.*

syn the sis (sin′thə sis), **1** combination of parts or ele-

a hat	i it	oi oil	ch child		a in about
ā age	ī ice	ou out	ng long		e in taken
ä far	o hot	u cup	sh she	ə =	i in pencil
e let	ō open	u̇ put	th thin		o in lemon
ē equal	ô order	ü rule	ᴛʜ then		u in circus
ėr term			zh measure		

ments into a whole: *a synthesis of various cultures in a nation.* **2** formation of a compound from its elements or from simpler compounds, by one or more chemical reactions. *n., pl.* **syn the ses** (sin′thə sēz′).

syn the size (sin′thə sīz), **1** combine into a complex whole. **2** make up by combining parts or elements. **3** treat synthetically. *v.,* **syn the sized, syn the siz ing.**

syn the siz er (sin′thə sī′zər), **1** person or thing that synthesizes. **2** an electronic instrument that can imitate and mix together many types of conventional and ultrasonic sounds. *n.*

syn thet ic (sin thet′ik), **1** having to do with synthesis: *synthetic chemistry.* **2** made artificially by chemical synthesis. Nylon is a synthetic fiber. Many kinds of fabrics, furs, dyes, rubbers, and drugs are synthetic products. **3** not real or genuine; artificial: *synthetic laughter.* **4** synthetics, *pl.* artificially made substances formed by chemical synthesis. Plastics are synthetics. **1-3** *adj.,* **4** *n.* —**syn thet′i cal ly,** *adv.*

syph i lis (sif′ə lis), a contagious disease transmitted by sexual intercourse, that attacks the skin, internal organs, and finally the brain and spinal cord. *n.*

sy phon (sī′fən), siphon. *n., v.*

Syr i a (sir′ē ə), country in W Asia, south of Turkey. *Capital:* Damascus. See **Euphrates** for map. *n.* —**Syr′i an,** *adj., n.*

sy rin ga (sə ring′gə), shrub with fragrant white flowers blooming in early summer; mock orange. *n., pl.* **sy rin gas.**

sy ringe (sə rinj′), **1** a narrow tube fitted with a plunger or rubber bulb for drawing in a quantity of fluid and then forcing it out in a stream. Syringes are used for cleaning wounds, injecting fluids into the body, etc. **2** hypodermic syringe. **3** clean, wash, inject, etc., by means of a syringe. **1,2** *n.,* **3** *v.,* **sy ringed, sy ring ing.**

syr up (sir′əp *or* sėr′əp), a sweet, thick liquid. Sugar boiled with water or fruit juice makes a syrup. A cough syrup contains medicine to relieve coughing. Maple syrup is made from the sap of maple trees. *n.* Also, **sirup.** —**syr′up like′,** *adj.*

syr up y (sir′ə pē *or* sėr′ə pē), like syrup in consistency or sweetness. *adj.* Also, **sirupy.**

sys tem (sis′təm), **1** set of things or parts forming a whole: *a mountain system, a railroad system, the digestive system.* **2** an ordered group of facts, principles, beliefs, etc.: *a system of government, a system of education.* **3** plan, scheme, or method: *a system of classification, a system for betting.* **4** an orderly way of getting things done: *They work by a system, not by chance.* **5** the body as a whole: *Exercise is good for your system. n.*

sys tem at ic (sis′tə mat′ik), **1** according to a system; having a system, method, or plan: *systematic work.* **2** orderly in arranging things or in getting things done: *a systematic person. adj.* —**sys′tem at′i cal ly,** *adv.*

sys tem a tize (sis′tə mə tīz), arrange according to a system; make into a system; make more systematic. *v.,* **sys tem a tized, sys tem a tiz ing.**

sys tem ic (si stem′ik), of or affecting the body as a whole: *a systemic disease. adj.*

sys tol ic pressure (si stol′ik), the blood pressure measured when the heart is contracting to pump blood. Systolic pressure is higher than diastolic pressure.

Tt

T or **t** (tē), the 20th letter of the English alphabet. *n., pl.* **T's** or **t's.**

to a T, exactly; perfectly: *That suits me to a T.*

T (tē), anything shaped like the letter T. *n., pl.* **T's.**

t., 1 teaspoon or teaspoons. **2** temperature. **3** tenor. **4** tense. **5** territory. **6** time. **7** ton or tons.

T., 1 tablespoon or tablespoons. **2** Territory. **3** Testament. **4** ton or tons. **5** Tuesday.

Ta, symbol for tantalum.

TA or **T.A.,** Transit Authority.

tab (tab), **1** a small flap, strap, loop, or piece: *a fur cap with tabs over the ears.* **2** a small extension of or attachment to a card, used for labeling, numbering, coding, etc., in filing. **3** a small metal flap attached to the top of a can so that the top may be easily pulled off. **4** INFOR-MAL. a bill or check: *pick up the tab. n.*

keep tab on or **keep tabs on,** INFORMAL. keep track of; keep watch on; check: *Please keep tabs on the children while I'm out.*

tab ard (tab′ərd), **1** a short, loose coat worn by heralds. **2** mantle worn over armor by knights. *n.*

tab by (tab′ē), **1** a gray or tawny cat with dark stripes. **2** a female cat. *n., pl.* **tab bies.**

WORD HISTORY

tabby

Tabby is from French *tabis,* meaning "striped silk taffeta," which came from Arabic *'attābi.*

tab er nac le (tab′ər nak′əl), **1** place of worship for a large congregation. **2** a Jewish temple. **3 Tabernacle,** the covered, wooden framework carried by the Jews for use as a place of worship during their journey from Egypt to Palestine. **4** recess covered with a canopy and used as a shrine. **5** container for something holy or precious; container for the consecrated bread used in the Mass. *n.*

table (def. 7)

ta ble (tā′bəl), **1** piece of furniture having a smooth, flat top on legs. **2** food put on a table to be eaten: *Our hosts set a good table.* **3** the persons seated at a table, especially at a dinner or for informal discussion: *The whole table joined in the conversation.* **4** a flat surface; plateau. **5** information in a very brief, tabulated form; list: *a table of contents in the front of a book, the multiplication table.* **6** make a list or statement in tabulated form. **7** a thin, flat piece of wood, stone, metal, etc.; tablet: *The Ten Commandments were written on tables of stone.* **8** put on a table. **9** put off discussing (a bill, motion, etc.) until a future time. 1-5,7 *n.,* 6,8,9 *v.,* **ta bled, ta bling.** [*Table* is from Old English *tabule,* which came from Latin *tabula,* meaning "slab for writing or painting."]

turn the tables, reverse conditions or circumstances completely.

tab leau (tab′lō), **1** a striking scene; picture. **2** representation of a picture, statue, scene, etc., by a person or group posing in appropriate costume: *Our school is going to present several tableaux from American history. n., pl.* **tab leaux** (tab′lōz), **tab leaus.**

ta ble cloth (tā′bəl klôth′), cloth for covering a table. *n., pl.* **ta ble cloths** (tā′bəl klôᴛʜz′ *or* tā′bəl klôths′).

ta ble land (tā′bəl land′), a high plain; plateau. *n.*

ta ble spoon (tā′bəl spün′), **1** a large spoon used to serve food. **2** unit of measure in cooking equal to 3 teaspoons or ¹/₂ fluid ounce. *n.*

ta ble spoon ful (tā′bəl spün′fůl), as much as a table-spoon holds. *n., pl.* **ta ble spoon fuls.**

tab let (tab′lit), **1** a thin, flat sheet of stone, wood, ivory, etc., used to write or draw on. The ancient Romans used tablets as we use pads of paper. **2** number of sheets of writing paper fastened together at the edge. **3** a small, flat surface with an inscription: *The Hall of Fame is a building that has many tablets in memory of famous people.* **4** a small, flat piece of medicine, candy, etc.: *aspirin tablets. n.*

table talk, conversation at meals.

table tennis, game played on a large table marked somewhat like a tennis court, using small wooden rackets and a light, hollow ball.

ta ble ware (tā′bəl wer′ *or* tā′bəl war′), dishes, knives, forks, spoons, etc., used at meals. *n.*

tab loid (tab′loid), a newspaper, usually having half the ordinary size newspaper page, that has many pictures and gives the news in short articles. *n.* [*Tabloid* originally was a trademark for drugs concentrated in tablet form.]

ta boo (tə bü′), **1** forbidden by custom or tradition; prohibited; banned. **2** forbid; prohibit; ban. **3** system or act of setting things apart as forbidden; prohibition; ban. The Polynesians have many taboos under which certain things, places, and persons are set apart or prohibited as sacred, unclean, or cursed. 1 *adj.,* 2 *v.,* 3 *n., pl.*

ta boos. Also, **tabu.** [*Taboo* comes from Tongan *tabu.* Tongan is the language spoken in Tonga.]

ta bor (tā′bər), a small drum, used especially by a person playing a pipe or fife as an accompaniment. *n.*

ta bu (tə bü′), taboo. *adj., v., n.*

tab u lar (tab′yə lər), **1** of tables or lists; arranged in lists; written or printed in columns. **2** flat like a table: *a tabular rock. adj.*

tab u late (tab′yə lāt), arrange (facts, figures, etc.) in tables or lists. *v.,* **tab u lat ed, tab u lat ing.**

tab u la tion (tab′yə lā′shən), arrangement in tables or lists. *n.*

tab u la tor (tab′yə lā′tər), person or thing that tabulates. *n.*

ta chom e ter (tə kom′ə tər), instrument for measuring the speed of rotation of a shaft, wheel, etc. *n.*

tac it (tas′it), **1** implied or understood without being openly expressed: *His eating the food was a tacit admission that he liked it.* **2** unspoken; silent: *a tacit prayer. adj.* —**tac′it ly,** *adv.* —**tac′it ness,** *n.*

tac i turn (tas′ə tėrn′), speaking very little; not fond of talking. *adj.* —**tac′i turn′ly,** *adv.*

tac i tur ni ty (tas′ə tėr′nə tē), habit of keeping silent or talking little. *n.*

Tac i tus (tas′ə təs), A.D. 55?-120?, Roman historian. *n.*

tack (tak), **1** a short, sharp-pointed nail or pin having a broad, flat head: *carpet tacks.* **2** fasten with tacks: *She tacked mosquito netting over the windows.* **3** stitch used as a temporary fastening. **4** sew with temporary stitches. **5** attach; add: *He tacked a postscript to the end of the letter.* **6** sail in a zigzag course against the wind: *The ship was tacking, trying to make the harbor.* **7** a zigzag course against the wind. **8** a zigzag movement; one of the movements in a zigzag course. **9** direction in which a ship moves in regard to the position of her sails. When on port tack, a ship has the wind on her left. **10** act of zigzagging; a turn from one direction to the next. **11** course of action or conduct: *Ordering rather than asking her to help was the wrong tack to take.* 1,3,7-11 *n.,* 2,4-6 *v.* —**tack′er,** *n.* —**tack′less,** *adj.*

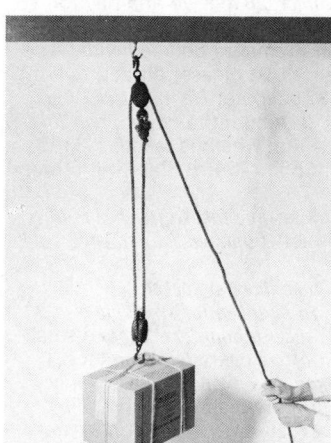

tackle (def. 2)

tack le (tak′əl), **1** equipment; apparatus; gear. Fishing tackle means the rod, line, hooks, etc., used in catching fish. **2** set of ropes and pulleys for lifting, lowering, or moving heavy things. The sails of a ship are raised and moved by tackle. **3** try to deal with: *We have a difficult problem to tackle.* **4** lay hold of; seize: *He tackled the boy who was running away and pulled him to the ground.* **5** (in football) seize and stop, or throw to the ground (an opponent who has the ball). **6** act of tackling. **7** an offen-

a hat	**i** it	**oi** oil	**ch** child	a in about
ā age	**ī** ice	**ou** out	**ng** long	e in taken
ä far	**o** hot	**u** cup	**sh** she	ə = { i in pencil
e let	**ō** open	**u̇** put	**th** thin	o in lemon
ē equal	**ô** order	**ü** rule	**ŦH** then	u in circus
ėr term			**zh** measure	

sive or defensive player between the guard and the end on either side of the line in football. 1,2,6,7 *n.,* 3-5 *v.,* **tack led, tack ling.**

tack y[1] (tak′ē), sticky. *adj.* **tack i er, tack i est.**

tack y[2] (tak′ē), INFORMAL. shabby; dowdy. *adj.,* **tack i er, tack i est.** —**tack′i ly,** *adv.* —**tack′i ness,** *n.*

ta co (tä′kō), tortilla filled with chopped meat, chicken, cheese, etc., and served hot. *n., pl.* **ta cos.**

Ta co ma (tə kō′mə), seaport in W Washington, on Puget Sound. *n.*

tact (takt), ability to say and do the right things; skill in dealing with people or handling difficult situations: *Mother's tact kept her from talking about things likely to be unpleasant to her guests. n.*

tact ful (takt′fəl), **1** having tact: *a tactful person.* **2** showing tact: *a tactful reply. adj.* —**tact′ful ly,** *adv.* —**tact′ful ness,** *n.*

tac tic (tak′tik), **1** detail of military tactics; maneuver. **2** any skillful move; gambit. *n.*

tac ti cal (tak′tə kəl), **1** of tactics; concerning tactics. **2** relating to the disposal of military or naval forces in action against an enemy. **3** characterized by skillful procedure, methods, or expedients. *adj.* —**tac′ti cal ly,** *adv.*

tac ti cian (tak tish′ən), an expert in tactics. *n.*

tac tics (tak′tiks), **1** *pl. in form, sing. in use.* art or science of disposing military or naval forces in action. **2** *pl. in form and use.* the operations themselves: *The tactics of pretending to retreat fooled the enemy.* **3** *pl. in form and use.* procedures to gain advantage or success; methods: *When coaxing failed, they changed their tactics and began to threaten. n.*

tac tile (tak′təl), **1** of touch. **2** having the sense of touch. **3** able to be felt by touch. *adj.*

tact less (takt′lis), **1** without tact: *a tactless person.* **2** showing no tact: *a tactless reply. adj.* —**tact′less ly,** *adv.* —**tact′less ness,** *n.*

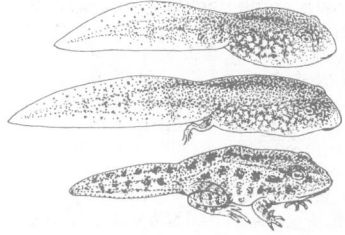

tadpole
three different
stages of growth

tad pole (tad′pōl′), a very young frog or toad in the larval stage when it lives in water and has gills, a long tail, and no limbs. *n.*

taf fe ta (taf′ə tə), **1** a light, stiff silk cloth with a smooth, glossy surface. **2** a similar cloth of linen, rayon, etc. *n., pl.* **taf fe tas.** [*Taffeta* came into English about 600 years ago from French *taffeta,* which came from Persian *tāftah,* meaning "silk, linen."]

taff rail (taf′rāl′), a rail around a ship's stern. *n.*

taf fy (taf′ē), kind of chewy candy made of brown sugar or molasses boiled down, often with butter; toffee: *saltwater taffy. n., pl.* **taf fies.**

Taft (taft), **William Howard,** 1857-1930, the 27th president of the United States, from 1909 to 1913, and chief justice of the Supreme Court, from 1921 to 1930. *n.*

tag¹ (tag), **1** piece of card, paper, leather, etc., to be tied or fastened to something: *a price tag, a name tag.* **2** a metal point at the end of a string. A shoelace has a tag on each end. **3** quotation, moral, etc., added for ornament or effect. **4** the last line or lines of a song, play, actor's speech, etc. **5** furnish with a tag or tags: *All his trunks and suitcases are tagged with his name and address.* **6** INFORMAL. follow closely: *The baby tagged after his sister.* **7** fasten a tag or label onto, especially in order to identify a biological specimen. 1-4 *n.,* 5-7 *v.,* **tagged, tag ging.** —**tag′ger,** *n.* —**tag′like′,** *adj.*

tag² (tag), **1** a children's game in which one player who is "it" chases the others and tries to touch them. The first one touched is then "it" and must chase the others. **2** touch or tap with the hand. **3** in baseball: **a** touch (a base runner) with the ball to make an out. **b** the act of touching a base runner with the ball to make an out. 1,3b *n.,* 2,3a *v.,* **tagged, tag ging.** —**tag′ger,** *n.*

Ta ga log (tä gä′log), **1** member of the chief Malay people in the Philippines. **2** their language. *n., pl.* **Ta ga logs** or **Ta ga log** for 1.

Ta hi ti (tə hē′tē), French island in the S Pacific. See **Melanesia** for map. *n.*

Ta hi tian (tə hē′shən), **1** of Tahiti, its people, or their language. **2** person born or living in Tahiti. **3** the Polynesian language of Tahiti. 1 *adj.,* 2,3 *n.*

Ta hoe (tä′hō), **Lake,** mountain lake in NE California and W Nevada. *n.*

tail (tāl), **1** the part of an animal's body that sticks out beyond the back of the main part. **2** something like an animal's tail: *the tail of a kite.* **3** part at the rear of an airplane. **4** the hind part of anything; back; rear: *the tail of a cart. A crowd of children formed the tail of the procession.* **5 tails,** *pl.* **a** the reverse side of a coin. **b** coat with long tails, worn on formal occasions. **6** at the tail, back, or rear. **7** coming from behind: *a tail wind.* **8** follow close behind; form the tail of: *Children tailed after the parade.* **9** SLANG. follow closely and secretly, especially in order to watch or prevent escaping. 1-5 *n.,* 6,7 *adj.,* 8,9 *v.* [*Tail* comes from Old English *tægel.*] —**tail′like′,** *adj.*

turn tail, run away from danger, trouble, etc.

with one's tail between one's legs, afraid, humiliated, or dejected.

tail board (tāl′bôrd′), tailgate of a truck or wagon. *n.*

tail gate (tāl′gāt′), **1** board at the back end of a wagon, truck, station wagon, etc., that can be let down or removed when loading or unloading. **2** drive a vehicle too close to the one ahead of it. 1 *n.,* 2 *v.,* **tail gat ed, tail gat ing.**

tail less (tāl′lis), having no tail. *adj.* —**tail′less ly,** *adv.*

tail light (tāl′līt′), a warning light, usually red, at the back end of a vehicle. *n.*

tai lor (tā′lər), **1** person whose business is making, altering, or mending clothes. **2** make by tailor's work: *The suit was well tailored.* **3** make or mend clothes. **4** make specially to fit; adjust; adapt. 1 *n.,* 2-4 *v.*

tai lor ing (tā′lər ing), business or work of a tailor. *n.*

tail piece (tāl′pēs′), piece added at or forming the end. *n.*

tail race (tāl′rās′), part of a millrace below the water wheel that leads the water away. *n.*

tail spin (tāl′spin′), a downward movement of an airplane with the nose first and the tail spinning in a circle above. *n.*

tail wind, wind blowing toward the direction in which a ship or aircraft is moving.

taint (tānt), **1** a stain or spot; trace of decay, corruption, or disgrace: *No taint of scandal ever touched the mayor.* **2** a cause of any such condition. **3** give a taint to; spoil:

Flies sometimes taint what they touch. Rumors about taking bribes tainted the judge's reputation. **4** become tainted; decay: *Meat will taint if it is left too long in a warm place.* 1,2 *n.,* 3,4 *v.* [*Taint* came into English about 600 years ago from French *teint,* meaning "dyed," which came from Latin *tingere,* meaning "to dye."] —**taint′less,** *adj.*

Tai pei or **Tai peh** (tī′pā′), capital of Taiwan, in the N part. *n.*

Tai wan (tī′wän′), island country off SE China. Since 1949 it has been the seat of the Chinese nationalist government; Nationalist China. *Capital:* Taipei. See **China** for map. *n.* Also, **Formosa.**

Taj Ma hal (täj′ mə häl′), a famous white marble mausoleum in northern India, built in the 1600's.

take (tāk), **1** lay hold of; grasp: *I took her hand when we crossed the street.* **2** seize; catch; capture: *take a wild animal in a trap.* **3** catch hold; lay hold; have effect: *The fire has taken. The medicine seems to be taking; the fever is going away.* **4** accept: *Take my advice. The man won't take a cent less for the car.* **5** get; receive: *She took the gifts and opened them.* **6** win: *He took first prize.* **7** get; have: *take a seat.* **8** obtain from a source: *Washington, D.C., takes its name from George Washington.* **9** absorb: *Wool takes dye well.* **10** use; make use of: *take medicine. We took a train to Boston.* **11** receive into the body; swallow: *take food, take drink.* **12** indulge in: *take a nap, take a vacation.* **13** submit to; put up with: *take hard punishment.* **14** need; require: *It takes time and patience to learn how to play the guitar.* **15** choose; select: *Take the shortest way home.* **16** remove: *Please take the wastebasket away and empty it.* **17** subtract: *If you take 2 from 7, you have 5.* **18** go with; escort: *Take them home.* **19** lead: *Where will this road take me?* **20** carry: *Take your lunch along.* **21** do; make; obtain by some special method: *Please take my photograph.* **22** write down; record: *take dictation, take minutes at a meeting.* **23** form and hold in mind; feel: *She takes pride in her schoolwork.* **24** find out: *The doctor took my temperature.* **25** understand or suppose: *How did you take his remark? I take it the train was late.* **26** regard; consider: *Let us take an example.* **27** engage; hire; lease: *We have taken a cottage for the summer.* **28** receive and pay for regularly; subscribe for: *take a newspaper.* **29** become affected by: *take cold.* **30** (in grammar) be used with: *A plural noun takes a plural verb.* **31** please; attract; charm: *The song took our fancy.* **32** become: *He took sick.* **33** SLANG. swindle; cheat. **34** amount taken: *a great take of fish.* **35** act of taking. **36** that which is taken. 1-33 *v.,* **took, tak en, tak ing;** 34-36 *n.* —**tak′a ble, take′a ble,** *adj.*

take after, be like; resemble: *She takes after her mother.*

take back, withdraw; retract: *I apologized and took back my rude remark.*

take down, write down: *take down a speech.*

take for, suppose to be: *to be taken for someone else.*

take in, 1 receive; admit: *take in boarders.* **2** make smaller: *Please take in the waist of my pants.* **3** understand. **4** deceive; trick; cheat. **5** include; visit: *take in a show.*

take off, 1 leave the ground or water: *Three airplanes took off at the same time.* **2** rush away: *I took off at the first sign of trouble.* **3** INFORMAL. give an amusing imitation of; mimic.

take on, 1 engage; hire. **2** undertake to deal with: *take on an opponent.* **3** acquire: *take on the appearance of health.* **4** INFORMAL. show great excitement, grief, etc. **5** agree to do; take upon oneself: *I plan to take on more jobs when school lets out this June.*

take over, take the ownership or control of.

take to, 1 form a liking for; become fond of: *We took to one another right away.* **2** go to: *The cat took to the woods and became wild.*

take up, 1 soak up; absorb: *A sponge takes up liquid.*
2 make shorter: *The tailor took up the hem of the dress.*
3 begin; undertake: *He took up piano lessons in the summer:* **4** lift.

take up with, INFORMAL. begin to be friendly with.

tak en (tā′kən), past participle of **take.** *I have taken this toy from the shelf. v.*

take off (tāk′ôf′), **1** the leaving of the ground in flight, as in an aircraft; taking off. **2** the place or point at which one takes off. **3** INFORMAL. an amusing imitation. *n.*

take out (tāk′out′), (of food) intended to be taken away and eaten elsewhere. *adj.*

take o ver (tāk′ō′vər), a taking over; seizure of ownership or control: *a takeover of a country by the military. n.*

tak er (tā′kər), person or thing that takes. *n.*

tak ing (tā′king), **1** attractive or pleasing; winning: *a taking smile.* **2** act of one who takes or condition of being taken. **3** that which is taken. **4 takings,** *pl.* money taken in; receipts. 1 *adj.,* 2-4 *n.*

talc (talk), a soft, smooth mineral, used in making face powder, chalk, etc. *n.* [*Talc* is from a medieval Latin word *talcum,* which came from Arabic *ṭalq.*]

tal cum (tal′kəm), **1** talcum powder. **2** talc. *n.*

talcum powder, powder made of purified white talc, for use on the face and body.

tale (tāl), **1** story, especially a made-up story: *a tale about ghosts. She enjoys reading tales about life in frontier days.* **2** falsehood; lie. **3** piece of gossip or scandal. *n.*

tell tales, spread gossip or scandal.

tale bear er (tāl′ber′ər *or* tāl′bar′ər), person who spreads gossip or scandal. *n.*

tale bear ing (tāl′ber′ing *or* tāl′bar′ing), the spreading of gossip or scandal. *n.*

tal ent (tal′ənt), **1** a special natural ability: *She has a talent for music.* **2** person or persons with talent: *That young singer is a real talent.* **3** an ancient unit of weight or money, varying with time and place. *n.*

tal ent ed (tal′ən tid), having natural ability; gifted: *a talented musician. adj.*

tal is man (tal′i smən), **1** stone, ring, etc., engraved with figures or characters supposed to have magic power; charm. **2** anything that acts as a charm. *n., pl.* **tal is mans.** [*Talisman* was borrowed from French *talisman,* which can be traced back to Greek *telesma,* meaning "initiation into the mysteries."]

talk (tôk), **1** use words to express feelings or ideas; speak: *Baby is learning to talk.* **2** use in speaking: *talk sense. Can you talk French?* **3** exchange words; converse: *They talked for an hour.* **4** the use of words; spoken words; speech; conversation: *The old friends met for a good talk.* **5** an informal speech: *The coach gave the team a talk about the need for more team spirit.* **6** a way of talking: *baby talk.* **7** bring, put, drive, influence, etc., by talk: *We talked them into joining the club.* **8** discuss: *talk politics, talk business.* **9** consult; confer: *talk with one's doctor.* **10** conference; council: *summit talks.* **11** spread ideas by other means than speech: *talk by signs.* **12** spread rumors; gossip: *talk behind someone's back.* **13** gossip or rumor: *There is talk of a quarrel between them.* **14** a subject for talk or gossip: *be the talk of the town.* 1-3,7-9,11,12 *v.,* 4-6,10,13,14 *n.* —**talk′a ble,** *adj.*

talk back, answer rudely or disrespectfully.

talk down to, speak to in a superior tone.

talk over, discuss.

talk a tive (tô′kə tiv), having the habit of talking a great deal; fond of talking. *adj.* —**talk′a tive ness,** *n.*

talk er (tô′kər), **1** person who talks. **2** a talkative person. *n.*

talk ing-to (tô′king tü′), INFORMAL. a scolding. *n., pl.* **talk ing-tos.**

a hat	**i** it	**oi** oil	**ch** child	⎧ a in about
ā age	**ī** ice	**ou** out	**ng** long	⎪ e in taken
ä far	**o** hot	**u** cup	**sh** she	ə = ⎨ i in pencil
e let	**ō** open	**u̇** put	**th** thin	⎪ o in lemon
ē equal	**ô** order	**ü** rule	**ᴛʜ** then	⎩ u in circus
ėr term			**zh** measure	

tall (tôl), **1** higher than the average; having great height: *a tall building.* **2** of the specified height: *two meters tall.* **3** INFORMAL. high or large in amount; extravagant: *a tall price, a tall order.* **4** INFORMAL. hard to believe; exaggerated: *a tall tale. adj.* [*Tall* comes from Old English (*ge*)*tæl,* meaning "prompt, active."] —**tall′ness,** *n.*

Tal la has see (tal′ə has′ē), capital of Florida, in the N part. *n.*

tall ish (tô′lish), rather tall. *adj.*

tal low (tal′ō), the hard fat from sheep, cows, etc., after it has been melted. It is used for making candles, soap, etc. *n.* —**tal′low like′,** *adj.*

tal ly (tal′ē), **1** anything on which a score or account is kept. **2** mark made for a certain number of objects in keeping account. **3** mark on a tally; count up: *tally a score.* **4** account; reckoning; score: *a tally of a game.* **5** (in sports) make scoring points; score: *The hockey team tallied seven goals in their last game.* **6** agree; correspond: *Your account tallies with mine.* 1,2,4 *n., pl.* **tal lies;** 3,5,6 *v.,* **tal lied, tal ly ing.** —**tal′li er,** *n.*

tal ly ho (tal′ē hō′), a hunter's cry on catching sight of the fox. *n., pl.* **tal ly hos;** *interj.*

Tal mud (tal′məd), a collection of sixty-three volumes containing the Jewish civil and canonical law in the form of interpretation and expansion of the teachings of the Old Testament. *n.*

tal on (tal′ən), claw of an animal, especially a bird of prey: *The eagle seized a chicken with its talons. n.*

ta lus (tā′ləs), the main bone of the ankle. *n., pl.* **ta li** (tā′lī).

tam (tam), tam-o′-shanter. *n.*

tam a ble (tā′mə bəl), tameable. *adj.*

ta ma le (tə mä′lē), a Mexican food made of corn meal and minced meat, seasoned with red peppers, wrapped in cornhusks, and roasted or steamed. *n.* [*Tamale* was borrowed from Spanish *tamale,* which came from Nahuatl *tamalli.*]

tam a rack (tam′ə rak′), a North American larch tree which yields strong, heavy timber. *n.*

tam a rind (tam′ə rind′), **1** a tropical tree grown for its wood and fruit. **2** its fruit, a brown pod with juicy, acid pulp, used in foods, drinks, and medicine. *n.* [*Tamarind* comes from Arabic *tamr hindī,* meaning "date of India."]

tam a risk (tam′ə risk′), an ornamental shrub or small tree with slender, feathery branches. *n.*

tam bou rine (tam′bə rēn′), a small, shallow drum with jingling metal disks around the side, played by striking it with the knuckles or by shaking it; timbrel. *n.*

tambourine

tame (tām), **1** taken from the wild state and made obedient: *a tame bear.* **2** without fear; not wild; gentle: *The birds are so tame that they will eat from our hands.* **3** make tame; break in: *The lion was tamed for the circus.* **4** become tame: *White rats tame easily.* **5** deprive of courage; tone down; subdue: *The bad news tamed our spirits.* **6** without spirit; dull: *a tame story. The party was tame because we were sleepy.* 1,2,6 *adj.,* **tam er, tam est;** 3-5 *v.,* **tamed, tam ing. —tame′ly,** *adv.* **—tame′ness,** *n.*

tame a ble (tā′mə bəl), able to be tamed or subdued. *adj.* Also, **tamable. —tame′a ble ness,** *n.*

tame less (tām′lis), never tamed; not able to be tamed. *adj.* **—tame′less ly,** *adv.* **—tame′less ness,** *n.*

tam er (tā′mər), person who tames: *a lion tamer. n.*

tam-o'-shanter

tam-o'-shan ter (tam′ə shan′tər), a soft, woolen cap, originally of Scotland, with a flat, round crown and often with a tassel. *n.* Also, **tam.**

tamp (tamp), **1** pack down: *tamp the earth about a newly planted tree.* **2** (in blasting) fill (the hole containing explosive) with dirt, etc. *v.* **—tamp′er,** *n.*

Tam pa (tam′pə), seaport in W Florida. *n.* **—Tam′pan,** *adj., n.*

tam per (tam′pər), meddle improperly; meddle: *Do not tamper with the lock. v.* **—tam′per er,** *n.*

tan (tan), **1** yellowish-brown: *tan shoes.* **2** the brown color of a person's skin resulting from being in the sun and air: *His arms and legs had a dark tan.* **3** make or become brown by exposure to sun and air: *Sun and wind had tanned her face. If you lie on the beach in the sun you will tan.* **4** make (a hide) into leather by soaking in a special liquid, especially one containing tannin. **5** tanbark. **6** INFORMAL. thrash or beat in punishment. 1 *adj.,* **tanner, tan nest;** 2,5 *n.,* 3,4,6 *v.,* **tanned, tan ning. —tan′na ble,** *adj.*

tan or **tan.,** tangent.

tan a ger (tan′ə jər), any of various small American birds related to the finches. The males are usually brilliantly colored. *n.* [*Tanager* comes from Tupi *tangara.*]

Ta nan a rive (tə nan′ə rēv′), capital of Madagascar, in the central part. *n.*

tan bark (tan′bärk′), crushed bark used in tanning hides. Riding tracks and circus rings are often covered with used tanbark. *n.*

tan dem (tan′dəm), **1** one behind the other: *drive horses tandem.* **2** having animals, seats, parts, etc., arranged one behind the other. **3** two horses harnessed tandem. **4** carriage drawn by two horses so harnessed. **5** Also, **tandem bicycle.** bicycle with two seats, one behind the other. 1 *adv.,* 2 *adj.,* 3-5 *n.*

tang (tang), **1** a strong taste or flavor: *the tang of mustard, the salt tang of sea air.* **2** a slight touch or suggestion; trace. *n.*

Tan gan yi ka (tang′gə nyē′kə), **1** former country in E Africa, now part of Tanzania. **2 Lake,** lake in central Africa. *n.* **—Tan′gan yi′kan,** *adj., n.*

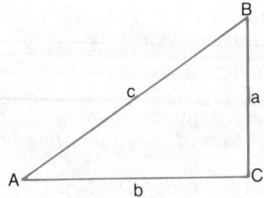

tangent (def. 4)
Triangle ABC is a right triangle in which angle C is the right angle and side c is the hypotenuse;
    the tangent of angle A is a/b
    the tangent of angle B is b/a

tan gent (tan′jənt), **1** in contact; touching. **2** (in geometry) touching a curve or surface at one point but not intersecting. These circles are tangent: ∞. **3** a tangent line, curve, or surface. **4** the ratio of the length of the side opposite an acute angle in a right triangle to the length of the shorter of the other sides. 1,2 *adj.,* 3,4 *n.* [*Tangent* is from Latin *tangentem,* which comes from *tangere,* meaning "to touch." See **Word Family.**]

fly off at a tangent or **go off at a tangent,** change suddenly from one course of action or thought to another.

WORD FAMILY

tangent

Below are words related to *tangent.* They can all be traced back to the Latin word *tangere* (täng′ge re), meaning "to touch."

attain	contiguous	integrity
attainment	intact	tact
contact	integer	tactile
contagious	integral	tangential
contingent	integrate	tangible

tan gen tial (tan jen′shəl), **1** of a tangent. **2** diverging. **3** slightly connected. *adj.* **—tan gen′tial ly,** *adv.*

tan ge rine (tan′jə rēn′), a reddish-orange citrus fruit with a very loose peel and segments that separate easily. It looks like a small orange and is widely grown in the United States. *n.* [*Tangerine* was formed from the name of *Tanger,* French for *Tangier.* The fruit was shipped from this port.]

tan gi bil i ty (tan′jə bil′ə tē), fact or quality of being tangible. *n.*

tan gi ble (tan′jə bəl), **1** capable of being touched or felt by touch: *A chair is a tangible object.* **2** real; actual; definite: *I want tangible evidence, not opinion. adj.* **—tan′gi ble ness,** *n.*

tan gi bly (tan′jə blē), in a tangible manner. *adv.*

Tan gier (tan jir′), seaport in Morocco, on the Strait of Gibraltar. *n.*

tan gle (tang′gəl), **1** twist and twine together in a confused mass: *The kitten had tangled the ball of twine.* **2** a confused or tangled mass: *The climbing vines are all one tangle and need to be pruned and tied up.* **3** involve in something that hampers or obstructs. **4** a bewildering confusion; mess: *a tangle of contradictory statements.* 1,3 *v.,* **tan gled, tan gling;** 2,4 *n.* **—tan′gle ment,** *n.* **—tan′gler,** *n.*

tan go (tang′gō), **1** a Spanish-American dance with long, gliding steps and many figures and poses. **2** music for it. **3** dance the tango. 1,2 *n., pl.* **tan gos;** 3 *v.,* **tan goed, tan go ing.**

tang y (tang′ē), having a tang. *adj.,* **tang i er, tang i est.**

tank (tangk), **1** a large container for liquid or gas: *the gasoline tank of an automobile, a storage tank for water.* **2** put or store in a tank: *The plane tanked up on gas.* **3** a heavily armored combat vehicle carrying machine guns and usually a cannon, moving on an endless track on each side. Tanks can travel over rough ground, fallen trees, and other obstacles. 1,3 *n.*, 2 *v.* [*Tank* is apparently from Hindustani *tankh*, meaning "cistern." The armored vehicle was labeled "tank," in order to hide its actual nature, for reasons of military security.] —**tank′less**, *adj.*

tankard

a hat	i it	oi oil	ch child	⎧ a in about
ā age	ī ice	ou out	ng long	⎪ e in taken
ä far	o hot	u cup	sh she	ə = ⎨ i in pencil
e let	ō open	u̇ put	th thin	⎪ o in lemon
ē equal	ô order	ü rule	ᴛʜ then	⎩ u in circus
ėr term			zh measure	

an alloy in nuclear reactors and in surgical and dental equipment. *n.*

tan ta mount (tan′tə mount), equivalent: *The withdrawal of his statement is tantamount to an apology. adj.*

tan trum (tan′trəm), fit of bad temper or ill humor. *n.*

tantrum—In a violent **tantrum**, he pounded the stool against the desk.

tank ard (tang′kərd), a large drinking mug with a handle and a hinged cover. *n.*

tank car, a railroad car with a tank for carrying liquids or gases.

tank er (tang′kər), ship, airplane, or truck with tanks for carrying oil or other liquid freight. *n.*

tank ful (tangk′fu̇l), as much as a tank will hold. *n., pl.* **tank fuls.**

tank top, clothing for the upper body with wide straps for the shoulders. It is similar to the top of a one-piece bathing suit.

tan ner (tan′ər), person whose work is tanning hides. *n.*

tan ner y (tan′ər ē), place where hides are tanned. *n., pl.* **tan ner ies.**

tan nic acid (tan′ik), tannin.

tan nin (tan′ən), acid obtained from the bark or galls of oaks, etc., and from certain other plants. It is used in tanning, dyeing, making ink, and in medicine. *n.*

tan ning (tan′ing), the converting of hide or skins into leather. *n.*

tan sy (tan′zē), a coarse, strong-smelling, bitter-tasting plant with notched, divided leaves and clusters of small yellow flowers. Tansy was formerly much used in cooking and medicine. *n., pl.* **tan sies.**

tan ta lize (tan′tl īz), torment or tease by keeping something desired in sight but out of reach, or by holding out hopes that are repeatedly disappointed: *They tantalized the hungry dog by pretending to feed it. v.,* **tan ta lized, tan ta liz ing.** —**tan′ta liz′ing ly,** *adv.*

WORD HISTORY

tantalize

Tantalize was formed from the name of *Tantalus,* a king in a Greek myth. After death, his spirit was punished by having to stand in water under branches filled with fruit. When he reached for either fruit or water, they receded from his grasp.

tan ta liz er (tan′tə lī′zər), person or thing that tantalizes. *n.*

tan ta lum (tan′tl əm), a hard, shiny, grayish-white metallic element occurring with niobium in certain rare minerals. It is very resistant to corrosion and is used as

Tan za ni a (tan′zə nē′ə), country in E Africa, a member of the Commonwealth of Nations. It was formed in 1964 by the union of Tanganyika and the adjacent islands of Zanzibar and Pemba. *Capital:* Dodoma. See **Congo** for map. *n.* —**Tan′za ni′an,** *adj., n.*

Tao ism (tou′iz′əm), one of the main religions of China. It teaches natural simplicity and humility as a way to peace and harmony in life. *n.*

Tao ist (tou′ist), 1 believer in Taoism. 2 of or belonging to Taoists or Taoism. 1 *n.,* 2 *adj.*

tap[1] (tap), 1 strike lightly: *Tap him on the shoulder.* 2 cause to strike lightly: *She tapped her foot to the music.* 3 a light blow: *There was a tap at the door.* 4 sound of a light blow. 5 make, put, etc., by light blows: *tap a rhythm, tap time, tap the ashes out of a pipe.* 1,2,5 *v.,* **tapped, tap ping;** 3,4 *n.* —**tap′per,** *n.*

tap[2] (tap), 1 stopper or plug to close a hole in a cask containing liquid. 2 faucet. 3 make a hole in to let out liquid: *tap sugar maples.* 4 draw the plug from: *tap a cask.* 5 let out (liquid) by piercing or by drawing a plug. 6 make (resources, reserves, etc.) accessible; penetrate; open up: *This highway taps a large district.* 7 point in an electric circuit where a connection is or can be made. 8 to wiretap. 9 a wiretap. 10 tool for cutting screw threads on the inner surface of a cylinder or opening. 1,2,7,9,10 *n.,* 3-6,8 *v.,* **tapped, tap ping.** —**tap′per,** *n.*

on tap, 1 ready to be let out of a keg or barrel and served. **2** ready for use; on hand: *I try to keep extra money on tap in case of an emergency.*

tap dance, dance in which the steps are accented by loud taps of the foot, toe, or heel.

tap-dance (tap′dans′), do a tap dance. *v.,* **tap-danced, tap-danc ing.** —**tap′-danc′er,** *n.*

tape (tāp), 1 a long, narrow strip of cloth, paper, plastic, etc.: *adhesive tape.* 2 a long, narrow strip of other material. Surveyors measure with a steel tape. 3 fasten with tape; wrap with tape: *The doctor taped up the wound.*

4 measure with a tape measure. **5** a plastic or paper tape on which sounds or images can be recorded. **6** to record on such a tape: *The parade was taped to show on television in the evening.* **7** strip, string, etc., stretched across a race track at the finish line. 1,2,5,7 *n.*, 3,4,6 *v.*, **taped, tap ing. —tape′less,** *adj.* **—tape′like′,** *adj.* **—tap′er,** *n.*

tape deck, the mechanical part of a tape recorder that is used with a separate amplifier and speaker system.

tape measure, a long strip of cloth or steel marked in inches, feet, etc., for measuring.

ta per (tā′pər), **1** make or become gradually smaller toward one end: *A church spire tapers off to a point.* **2** grow less gradually; diminish: *Their business tapered to nothing as people moved away.* **3** a gradual decrease of force, capacity, etc. **4** a very slender candle. 1,2 *v.*, 3,4 *n.*

tape-re cord (tāp′ri kôrd′), record on a tape recorder. *v.*

tape recorder, machine that records sound magnetically on plastic tape and plays the sound back after it is recorded.

tape recording, 1 the recording of sound on a tape. **2** a tape on which sound has been recorded.

tap es try (tap′ə strē), **1** fabric with pictures or designs woven in it, used to hang on walls, cover furniture, etc. **2** cover with tapestry; cover with a pattern like that of tapestry. 1 *n.*, *pl.* **tap es tries;** 2 *v.*, **tap es tried, tap es- try ing. —tap′es try like′,** *adj.*

tapeworm—up to 30 ft. (9 m.) long

tape worm (tāp′wėrm′), a long, flat worm that lives during its adult stage as a parasite in the intestines of human beings and other animals. *n.*

tap i o ca (tap′ē ō′kə), a starchy food obtained from the root of the cassava plant. It is used for puddings. *n.* [*Tapioca* can be traced back to Tupi *tipioca*.]

tapir
about 3 ft. (1 m.)
high at the shoulder

ta pir (tā′pər), a large piglike mammal of tropical America and southern Asia, having hoofs and a flexible snout. It is related to the horse and rhinoceros. *n.*, *pl.* **ta pirs** or **ta pir.**

tap room (tap′rüm′ *or* tap′rūm′), barroom. *n.*

tap root (tap′rüt′ *or* tap′rūt′), a main root growing downward. *n.*

taps (taps), signal on a bugle or drum to put out lights at night. Taps are also sounded at military funerals. *n.pl.*

tar[1] (tär), **1** a thick, black, sticky substance obtained by the distillation of wood or coal. Tar is used to cover and patch roads, roofs, etc. **2** cover with tar: *tar a roof.* **3** the brownish-black residue from the smoke of cigarettes, cigars, etc., containing by-products produced by the burning of tobacco. 1,3 *n.*, 2 *v.*, **tarred, tar ring. —tar′like′,** *adj.*

tar and feather, pour heated tar on and cover with feathers as a punishment.

tar[2] (tär), sailor. *n.*

tar an tel la (tar′ən tel′ə), **1** a rapid, whirling southern Italian dance in very quick rhythm. **2** music for this dance. *n.*, *pl.* **tar an tel las.**

tarantula
(def. 2)
body 1 to 2 in.
(2.5 to 5 cm.)
long

ta ran tu la (tə ran′chə lə), **1** a large spider of southern Europe with a slightly poisonous bite. **2** any of various large, hairy spiders of the southwestern United States and Central and South America, with a painful but not serious bite. *n.*, *pl.* **ta ran tu las, ta ran tu lae** (tə ran′- chə lē). [*Tarantula* was borrowed from Latin *tarantula*, and can be traced back to *Taranto*, a town in Italy. The spiders were quite common there.]

Ta ra wa (tə rä′wə), capital of Kiribati. It is an atoll in the central Pacific. *n.*

tar di ly (tär′də lē), slowly; late; with delay. *adv.*

tar di ness (tär′dē nis), slowness; lateness. *n.*

tar dy (tär′dē), **1** behind time; late: *I was tardy for school today.* **2** slow: *a tardy reaction. adj.*, **tar di er, tar di est.**

tare[1] (ter *or* tar), (in the Bible) an injurious weed. *n.*

tare[2] (ter *or* tar), deduction made from the gross weight of goods to allow for the weight of the wrapper, box, or conveyance they are in. *n.*

tar get (tär′git), **1** mark for shooting at; thing aimed at. A target is often a circle, but anything may be used as a target. **2** object of abuse, scorn, criticism, etc.: *Their crazy plan was the target of jokes.* **3** any aim one tries to achieve; goal; objective. *n.* **—tar′get less,** *adj.*

tar iff (tar′if), **1** list of duties or taxes on imports or exports. **2** system of duties or taxes on imports or exports. **3** any duty or tax in such a list or system: *There is a very high tariff on imported jewelry.* **4** any table or scale of prices. *n.* [*Tariff* is from Italian *tariffa*, which came from Arabic *ta'rīf*, meaning "information."]

tarn (tärn), a small lake or pool in the mountains. *n.*

tar nish (tär′nish), **1** dull the luster or brightness of: *Salt will tarnish silver.* **2** lose luster or brightness: *The brass doorknobs tarnished.* **3** loss of luster or brightness. **4** a discolored coating, especially on silver. **5** bring disgrace upon (a reputation, one's honor, etc.); sully; taint. 1,2,5 *v.*, 3,4 *n.* **—tar′nish a ble,** *adj.*

ta ro (tär′ō), the starchy root of a plant grown in the Pacific islands and other tropical regions, used as food. *n.*, *pl.* **ta ros.** [*Taro* is of Polynesian origin.]

tar pau lin (tär pô′lən), sheet of canvas, plastic, or other strong waterproof material, used as a protective covering. *n.*

tar pon (tär′pon *or* tär′pən), a large, silver-colored fish found in the warmer parts of the Atlantic Ocean. *n.*, *pl.* **tar pons** or **tar pon.**

tar ry[1] (tar′ē), **1** to delay leaving; remain; stay: *We tarried* another day to see all the sights. **2** be tardy; hesitate: *Why do you tarry so long? v.,* **tar ried, tar ry ing.**

tar ry[2] (tär′ē), **1** of tar; like tar: *a tarry smell.* **2** covered with tar: *a tarry road. adj.,* **tar ri er, tar ri est. —tar′ri ness,** *n.*

tar sal (tär′səl), **1** of the tarsus. **2** one of the bones or cartilages in the ankle. 1 *adj.,* 2 *n.*

tar sus (tär′səs), **1** the ankle. **2** the group of small bones composing it. *n., pl.* **tar si** (tär′sī).

Tar sus (tär′səs), city in S Turkey. It was the home of Saint Paul. *n.*

tart[1] (tärt), **1** having a sour but agreeable taste: *tart apples.* **2** sharp; sarcastic: *a tart reply. adj.* **—tart′ly,** *adv.* **—tart′ness,** *n.*

tart[2] (tärt), pastry filled with cooked fruit, jam, etc. In the United States and Canada, a tart is small and the fruit shows; in England, any fruit pie is a tart. *n.*

tartan (def. 2)

tar tan (tärt′n), **1** a plaid woolen cloth. Each Scottish Highland clan has its own pattern of tartan. **2** the pattern or design itself. **3** any similar plaid design or fabric of silk, cotton, etc. **4** made of tartan. **5** of or like tartan. 1-3 *n.,* 4,5 *adj.*

tar tar (tär′tər), **1** an acid substance present in grape juice and deposited as a reddish crust on the inside of wine casks. After it is purified, this substance is called cream of tartar and is used with sodium bicarbonate to make baking powder. **2** a hard substance formed by the action of saliva on food and deposited as a crust on the teeth. *n.*

Tar tar (tär′tər), **1** member of a group of Mongolians and Turks who invaded Asia and eastern Europe during the Middle Ages. Tartars now live in parts of the Soviet Union and central and western Asia. **2 tartar,** person who has a bad temper. **3** of a Tartar or Tartars. 1,2 *n.,* 3 *adj.* Also, **Tatar** for 1 and 3.

tartar sauce, sauce, usually for fish, made of mayonnaise with chopped pickles, onions, olives, herbs, etc. *n.*

Tar tar us (tär′tər əs), in Greek myths: **1** a place of punishment below Hades. **2** the underworld; Hades. *n.*

Tash kent or **Tash kend** (tash kent′), city in S central Soviet Union. It is the capital of Uzbek. *n.*

task (task), **1** work to be done; piece of work; duty: *His task is to set the table.* **2** burden or strain: *Lifting that trunk tasked me beyond my strength.* 1 *n.,* 2 *v.*

take to task, blame; scold; reprove: *The teacher took the student to task for not studying.*

task force, a temporary group of military units, especially naval units, assigned to one commander for carrying out a specific operation.

task mas ter (task′mas′tər), person who sets tasks for others to do. *n.*

Tasm., Tasmania.

Tas ma ni a (taz mā′nē ə), island off SE Australia. It is a state of Australia. *n.* **—Tas ma′ni an,** *adj., n.*

Tass or **TASS** (tas *or* täs), a government news agency of the Soviet Union. *n.*

tas sel (tas′əl), **1** a hanging bunch of threads, small cords, beads, etc., fastened together at one end. **2** something like this. Corn has tassels. **3** put tassels on. **4** take tassels from. **5** grow tassels: *Corn tassels just before the ears form.* 1,2 *n.,* 3-5 *v.,* **tas seled, tas sel ing** or **tas selled, tas sel ling. —tas′sel er, tas′sel ler,** *n.*

Tas so (tas′ō), Torquato, 1544-1595, Italian poet. *n.*

taste (tāst), **1** what is special about (something) to the sense organs of the mouth; flavor. Sweet, sour, salt, and bitter are four important tastes. **2** try the flavor of (something) by taking a little into the mouth: *The cook tastes everything to see if it is right.* **3** the sense by which the flavor of things is perceived. **4** get the flavor of by the sense of taste: *She tasted almond in the cake.* **5** have a particular flavor: *The soup tastes of onion.* **6** eat or drink a little bit of: *The children barely tasted their breakfast the day they went to the circus.* **7** a little bit; sample: *Take a taste of this cake. The snowstorm will give you a taste of northern winter.* **8** experience; have: *taste freedom.* **9** a liking: *Suit your own taste.* **10** ability to perceive and enjoy what is beautiful and excellent: *My friend has taste in art.* **11** manner or style that shows such ability: *Their house is furnished in excellent taste.* 1,3,7,9-11 *n.,* 2,4-6,8 *v.,* **tast ed, tast ing. —tast′a ble, taste′a ble,** *adj.*

taste bud, any of certain groups of cells, most of which are in the outer layer of the tongue, that are sense organs of taste.

taste ful (tāst′fəl), **1** having good taste; refined. **2** showing or done in good taste: *The room had tasteful furnishings that went well together. adj.* **—taste′ful ly,** *adv.* **—taste′ful ness,** *n.*

taste less (tāst′lis), **1** without taste: *Oatmeal is tasteless and unpleasant if it gets cold.* **2** without good taste; in poor taste. *adj.* **—taste′less ly,** *adv.* **—taste′less ness,** *n.*

tast er (tā′stər), person who tastes, especially one whose work is judging the quality of wine, tea, coffee, etc., by the taste. *n.*

tast i ness (tā′stē nis), INFORMAL. tasty quality or condition. *n.*

tast y (tā′stē), INFORMAL. tasting good; pleasing to the taste. *adj.,* **tast i er, tast i est. —tast′i ly,** *adv.*

tat (tat), make a kind of lace by looping and knotting (threads) with a shuttle. *v.,* **tat ted, tat ting. —tat′ter,** *n.*

Ta tar (tä′tər), Tartar (defs. 1 and 3). *n., adj.*

tat ter (tat′ər), **1** a torn piece; rag: *After the storm the flag hung in tatters upon the mast.* **2 tatters,** *pl.* torn or ragged clothing. **3** tear or wear to pieces; make ragged. 1,2 *n.,* 3 *v.* [*Tatter* came into English about 600 years ago from Icelandic *tötturr,* meaning "rag."]

tat tered (tat′ərd), **1** full of tatters; torn; ragged: *a tattered dress.* **2** wearing torn or ragged clothes. *adj.*

tat ting (tat′ing), **1** process or work of making a kind of lace by looping and knotting cotton or linen thread with a shuttle. **2** lace made in this way. *n.*

tat tle (tat′l), **1** tell tales or secrets. **2** talk or utter foolishly; gossip. **3** idle or foolish talk; gossip; telling tales or secrets. 1,2 *v.,* **tat tled, tat tling;** 3 *n.* **—tat′tling ly,** *adv.*

tat tler (tat′lər), person who tattles; tattletale; telltale. *n.*

tat tle tale (tat′l tāl′), **1** person who tells tales on others; telltale. **2** revealing; telltale. 1 *n.,* 2 *adj.*

tat too[1] (ta tü′), **1** signal on a bugle, drum, etc., calling soldiers or sailors to their quarters at night. **2** series of raps, taps, etc.: *The hail beat a loud tattoo on the window-*

---

a	hat	i	it	oi	oil	ch	child	a in about
ā	age	ī	ice	ou	out	ng	long	e in taken
ä	far	o	hot	u	cup	sh	she	ə = { i in pencil
e	let	ō	open	ú	put	th	thin	o in lemon
ē	equal	ô	order	ü	rule	ŦH	then	u in circus
ėr	term					zh	measure	

pane. n., pl. **tat toos.** [*Tattoo*[1] is from Dutch *taptoe*, which comes from *tap*, meaning "taproom," and *toe*, meaning "pull to, shut."]

tat too[2] (ta tü′), **1** mark (the skin) with designs or patterns by pricking it and putting in colors: *An artist tattooed the sailor's arm with the design of a ship.* **2** the mark or design made by tattooing. 1 *v.,* **tat tooed, tat too ing;** 2 *n., pl.* **tat toos.** [*Tattoo*[2] comes from Polynesian *tatu.*] **—tat too′er,** *n.*

taught (tôt), past tense and past participle of **teach.** *That professor taught my brother. She has taught arithmetic for many years. v.*

taunt (tônt), **1** jeer at; mock; reproach: *My classmates taunted me for being teacher's pet.* **2** a bitter or insulting remark; mocking; jeering. 1 *v.,* 2 *n.* **—taunt′er,** *n.* **—taunt′ing ly,** *adv.*

taupe (tōp), **1** a dark, brownish gray. **2** dark brownish-gray. 1 *n.,* 2 *adj.*

Tau rus (tôr′əs), a northern constellation that was thought of as arranged in the shape of a bull. *n.*

taut (tôt), **1** tightly drawn; tense: *a taut rope.* **2** in neat condition; tidy: *a taut ship. adj.* **—taut′ly,** *adv.* **—taut′ness,** *n.*

tau tol o gy (tô tol′ə jē), a saying a thing over again in other words without adding clearness or force; useless repetition. EXAMPLE: the *modern* college student of *today. n., pl.* **tau tol o gies.**

tav ern (tav′ərn), **1** place where alcoholic drinks are sold and drunk; saloon. **2** inn. *n.* **—tav′ern less,** *adj.*

taw (tô), **1** a fancy marble used for shooting. **2** the line from which the players shoot their marbles. *n.*

taw dri ness (tô′drē nis), tawdry condition or quality. *n.*

taw dry (tô′drē), showy and cheap; gaudy. *adj.,* **tawdri er, taw dri est.** [*Tawdry* is short for (*Sain*)t *Audrey*('s *lace*), which was sold at the fair of Saint Audrey, every October 17th at Ely, England.] **—taw′dri ly,** *adv.*

taw ny (tô′nē), brownish-yellow: *A lion has a tawny coat. adj.,* **taw ni er, taw ni est. —taw′ni ly,** *adv.* **—taw′ni ness,** *n.*

tax (taks), **1** money paid by people for the support of the government and the cost of public works and services; money regularly collected from citizens by their rulers. **2** put a tax on. People who own property are taxed in order to provide clean streets, good roads, protection against crime, and free education. **3** a burden, duty, or demand that oppresses; strain: *Climbing stairs is a tax on a weak heart.* **4** lay a heavy burden on; be hard for: *The work taxed my strength. Reading in a poor light taxes the eyes.* 1,3 *n., pl.* **tax es** for 1; 2,4 *v.* **—tax′er,** *n.* **—tax′ing ly,** *adv.* **—tax′less,** *adj.*

tax a ble (tak′sə bəl), liable to be taxed; subject to taxation: *a taxable income. adj.* **—tax′a ble ness,** *n.*

tax a tion (tak sā′shən), **1** a taxing: *Taxation is necessary to provide roads, schools, and police.* **2** amount people pay for the support of the government; taxes. *n.*

tax i (tak′sē), **1** taxicab. **2** ride in a taxi. **3** (of an aircraft) move slowly on the ground or water. An airplane taxis into position before takeoff. 1 *n., pl.* **tax is** or **tax ies;** 2,3 *v.,* **tax ied, tax i ing** or **tax y ing.**

tax i cab (tak′sē kab′), automobile for hire, usually with an automatic meter to record the amount to be paid. *n.*

tax i der mist (tak′sə dėr′mist), person who practices taxidermy. *n.*

tax i der my (tak′sə dėr′mē), art of preparing the skins of animals and stuffing and mounting them so that they look alive. *n.*

tax i me ter (tak′sē mē′tər), meter of a taxicab. *n.*

tax o nom ic (tak′sə nom′ik), of taxonomy. *adj.* **—tax′o nom′i cal ly,** *adv.*

tax on o my (tak son′ə mē), **1** classification, especially of plant and animal species. **2** branch of science dealing with classification. *n.*

tax pay er (taks′pā′ər), person who pays a tax or is required by law to do so. *n.*

Tay lor (tā′lər), Zachary, 1784-1850, the 12th president of the United States, from 1849 to 1850. *n.*

Tb, symbol for terbium.

TB, T.B., or **t.b.,** tuberculosis.

tbs. or **tbsp.,** tablespoon or tablespoons.

Tc, symbol for technetium.

TC, teachers college.

Tchai kov sky or **Tchai kow sky** (chī kôf′skē), Peter Ilich, 1840-1893, Russian composer. *n.* Also, **Tschaikowsky** or **Tschaikovsky.**

tchr. or **tchr.,** teacher.

TD, (in football) touchdown.

T.D., Treasury Department.

Te, symbol for tellurium.

tea (tē), **1** a common drink made by pouring boiling water over the dried and prepared leaves of a certain shrub. **2** the dried and prepared leaves from which this drink is made. **3** the shrub on which these leaves grow. Tea is raised chiefly in China, Japan, and India. **4** a light meal in the late afternoon or early evening, at which tea is commonly served. The English have afternoon tea. **5** an afternoon reception at which tea is served. **6** drink prepared from some other thing named: *sage tea.* Beef tea is a strong broth made from beef. *n., pl.* **teas.** [*Tea* comes from Chinese *t'e.*] **—tea′less,** *adj.*

tea bag, tea leaves in a little bag of thin cloth or paper for easy removal from the cup or pot after use.

teach (tēch), **1** help to learn; show how to do; make understand: *He is teaching his dog tricks.* **2** give instruction to: *She teaches her classes well.* **3** give lessons in: *He teaches mathematics.* **4** give instruction; act as teacher: *She teaches for a living. v.,* **taught, teach ing.**

teach a bil i ty (tē′chə bil′ə tē), fact or quality of being teachable. *n.*

teach a ble (tē′chə bəl), capable of being taught. *adj.* **—teach′a ble ness,** *n.* **—teach′a bly,** *adv.*

teach er (tē′chər), person who teaches, especially one who teaches in a school. *n.* **—teach′er like′,** *adj.*

teach ing (tē′ching), **1** work or profession of a teacher. **2** act of a person who teaches. **3** what is taught; instruction; precept. *n.*

tea cup (tē′kup′), cup for drinking tea. *n.*

tea cup ful (tē′kup′fùl), as much as a teacup holds, usually four fluid ounces. *n., pl.* **tea cup fuls.**

tea house (tē′hous′), place where tea and other light refreshments are served. There are many teahouses in Japan and China. *n., pl.* **tea hous es** (tē′hou′ziz).

teak (tēk), a large tree of the East Indies with a hard, durable, yellowish-brown wood that is used for furniture, shipbuilding, etc. *n.* [*Teak* is from Portuguese *teca,* which came from Malayalam *tēkka.* Malayalam is a language spoken in southwestern India.]

teak wood (tēk′wùd′), wood of the teak. *n.*

tea ket tle (tē′ket′l), kettle for heating water to make tea, etc. *n.*

teal (tēl), a small wild duck related to the mallard. *n., pl.* **teals** or **teal.**

team (tēm), **1** number of people working or acting together, especially one of the sides in a game or match: *a football team, a debating team.* **2** two or more horses or other animals harnessed together to work. **3** join together in a team: *Everybody teamed up to clean the classroom after the party.* 1,2 *n.,* 3 *v.* **—team′less,** *adj.*

team mate (tēm′māt′), a fellow member of a team. *n.*

team ster (tēm′stər), person whose work is hauling things with a truck or driving a team of horses. *n.*

team work (tēm′wėrk′), the acting together of a number of people to make the work of the group successful and effective: *Football requires teamwork even more than individual skill. n.*

tea pot (tē′pot′), container with a handle and a spout for making and serving tea. *n.*

tear[1] (tir), **1** drop of salty liquid coming from the eye. **2** fill with tears; shed tears. 1 *n.,* 2 *v.*
  in tears, shedding tears; crying: *The baby is in tears because he is hungry.*

tear[2] (ter *or* tar), **1** pull apart by force: *tear a box open. I tore the letter into tiny pieces.* **2** make by pulling apart: *She tore a hole in her jeans.* **3** pull hard; pull violently: *Tear out the page.* **4** cut badly; wound: *The jagged stone tore his skin.* **5** divide; split; rend: *The party was torn by two factions.* **6** remove by effort; force away: *She could not tear herself from that spot.* **7** make miserable; distress: *torn by grief.* **8** become torn: *Lace tears easily.* **9** a torn place: *She has a tear in her jeans.* **10** act or process of tearing: *the wear and tear of a political campaign.* **11** move with great force or haste: *An automobile came tearing down the road.* 1-8,11 *v.,* **tore, torn, tear ing;** 9,10 *n.*
  —**tear′a ble,** *adj.* —**tear′er,** *n.*

tear down, 1 pull down; raze; destroy: *to tear down an old building.* **2** bring about the wreck of; discredit; ruin: *tear down another's reputation.*

tear into, attack or criticize severely.

tear drop (tir′drop′), tear[1]. *n.*

tear ful (tir′fəl), **1** full of tears; weeping. **2** causing tears; sad. *adj.* —**tear′ful ly,** *adv.* —**tear′ful ness,** *n.*

tear gas (tir), gas that irritates the eyes and temporarily blinds them with tears.

tear less (tir′lis), without tears; not crying. *adj.* —**tear′less ly,** *adv.* —**tear′less ness,** *n.*

tea room (tē′rüm′ *or* tē′rüm′), room or shop where tea, coffee, and light meals are served. *n.*

tease (tēz), **1** vex or worry by jokes, questions, requests, etc.; annoy: *The children teased the dog until it snapped at them.* **2** beg: *The child teases for everything he sees.* **3** person who teases. **4** comb out (wool, flax, etc.). **5** comb (hair) toward the head to produce fullness. **6** raise nap on (cloth). 1,2,4-6 *v.,* **teased, teas ing;** 3 *n.*

teas er (tē′zər), **1** person or thing that teases. **2** INFORMAL. an annoying problem; puzzling task. *n.*

teas ing ly (tē′zing lē), in a teasing way. *adv.*

tea spoon (tē′spün′), **1** a small spoon often used to stir tea or coffee. **2** unit of measure in cooking equal to 1/3 tablespoon. *n.*

tea spoon ful (tē′spün′fül), as much as a teaspoon holds. 1 teaspoon = 1/3 tablespoonful. *n., pl.* **tea spoonfuls.**

teat (tēt), nipple of a breast or udder, from which the young suck milk. *n.*

tec or **tec., 1** technical. **2** technician.

tech. or **techn., 1** technical. **2** technician. **3** technology.

tech ne ti um (tek nē′shē əm), a radioactive metallic element produced artificially from uranium or molybdenum. *n.*

tech nic (tek′nik), **1** any technique. **2** technical. 1 *n.,* 2 *adj.*

tech ni cal (tek′nə kəl), **1** of a mechanical or industrial art or applied science: *This technical school trains engineers, chemists, and architects.* **2** of the special facts of a science or art: *"Electrolysis" and "ulna" are technical words.* **3** of technique: *Her singing showed technical skill, but her voice was weak.* **4** by the rules of a certain science, art, game, etc.: *When the boxer was so badly hurt that the fight was stopped, his opponent won by a technical knockout. adj.* —**tech′ni cal ness,** *n.*

tech ni cal i ty (tek′nə kal′ə tē), **1** a technical matter,

point, detail, term, expression, etc.: *Books on engineering contain many technicalities which the ordinary reader does not understand.* **2** technical quality or character. *n., pl.* **tech ni cal i ties.**

tech ni cal ly (tek′nik lē), in a technical manner or respect; in technical terms; in a technical sense. *adv.*

tech ni cian (tek nish′ən), **1** person experienced in the technicalities of a subject. **2** person skilled in the technique of an art. *n.*

Tech ni col or (tek′nə kul′ər), trademark for a process of making colored motion pictures. *n.*

tech nique (tek nēk′), **1** method or ability of an artist's performance, execution, etc.; technical skill: *The pianist's technique was excellent.* **2** a special method or system used to accomplish something. *n.*

tech noc ra cy (tek nok′rə sē), government by technical experts. *n.*

technol., 1 technological. **2** technology.

tech no log i cal (tek′nə loj′ə kəl), of technology; used in technology. *adj.* —**tech′no log′i cal ly,** *adv.*

tech nol o gist (tek nol′ə jist), person skilled in technology. *n.*

tech nol o gy (tek nol′ə jē), science of the mechanical and industrial arts: *I studied engineering at a school of technology. n.*

Te cum seh (tə kum′sə), 1768?-1813, American Indian leader, chief of the Shawnee tribe. *n.*

ted dy bear or **Ted dy bear** (ted′ē), a child's furry toy bear.

WORD HISTORY

teddy bear

The word **teddy** comes from **Teddy,** a nickname for President Theodore Roosevelt. This cartoon shows him refusing to shoot a bear cub when he was hunting. Soon, stuffed toy animals were being sold that came to be known as "teddy bears."

a hat	i it	oi oil	ch child	a in about
ā age	ī ice	ou out	ng long	e in taken
ä far	o hot	u cup	sh she	ə = i in pencil
e let	ō open	ů put	th thin	o in lemon
ē equal	ô order	ü rule	ŦH then	u in circus
ėr term			zh measure	

Te De um (tā dā′əm), **1** a hymn of praise and thanksgiving sung in Roman Catholic and Anglican churches at morning prayers or on special occasions. **2** music for this hymn.

te di ous (tē′dē əs *or* tē′jəs), long and tiring: *A boring talk that you cannot understand is tedious. adj.* —**te′di ous ly,** *adv.* —**te′di ous ness,** *n.*

te di um (tē′dē əm), state of being wearisome; tiresomeness; tediousness. *n.*

tee (tē), **1** a raised place from which a player starts in playing each hole in golf. **2** a short wooden or plastic peg with a concave top on which a golf ball is placed when a player drives. **3** put (a golf ball) on a tee. 1,2 *n.,* 3 *v.,* **teed, tee ing.**

tee off, drive (a golf ball) from a tee.

teem (tēm), be full (of); abound; swarm: *The swamp teemed with mosquitoes. v.* —**teem′er,** *n.*

teem ing (tē′ming), **1** full of; alive with: *ponds teeming with fish.* **2** fruitful: *teeming colonies of bacteria. adj.* —**teem′ing ly,** *adv.* —**teem′ing ness,** *n.*

teen (tēn), **1** teenage: *teen fashions.* **2** teenager. 1 *adj.,* 2 *n.*

-teen, suffix added to numbers. ten more than ____: *Sixteen = ten more than six.*

teen age or **teen-age** (tēn′āj′), **1** of or for a teenager or teenagers: *a teenage club.* **2** in one's teens; being a teenager: *a teenage girl. adj.*

teen aged or **teen-aged** (tēn′ājd′), in one's teens; being a teenager: *a teenaged athlete. adj.*

teen ag er or **teen-ag er** (tēn′ā′jər), person in his or her teens. *n.*

teens (tēnz), the years of life from 13 to 19 inclusive. *n.pl.*

teen sy (tēn′sē), INFORMAL. tiny. *adj.,* **teen si er, teen si est.**

teent sy (tēnt′sē), INFORMAL. tiny. *adj.,* **teent si er, teent si est.**

tee ny (tē′nē), INFORMAL. tiny. *adj.,* **tee ni er, tee ni est.**

tee pee (tē′pē), tepee. *n.*

tee shirt, T-shirt.

tee ter (tē′tər), **1** rock unsteadily; sway. **2** balance on a seesaw. **3** seesaw. 1,2 *v.,* 3 *n.*

tee ter-tot ter (tē′tər tot′ər), seesaw. *n.*

teeth (tēth), plural of **tooth.** *n.* —**teeth′less,** *adj.*

in the teeth of, 1 straight against; in the face of: *We advanced in the teeth of the wind.* **2** in defiance of; in spite of.

teethe (tēⱦH), grow teeth; cut teeth; have teeth grow through the gums: *Babies teethe. v.,* **teethed, teeth ing.**

tee to tal er or **tee to tal ler** (tē tō′tl ər), person who never takes alcoholic liquor. *n.*

Tef lon (tef′lon), trademark for a slippery plastic used for coating kitchen utensils, as a dry lubricant, and in electric insulation. *n.*

Te gu ci gal pa (tā gü′sē gäl′pä), capital of Honduras, in the S part. *n.*

Te he ran or **Te hran** (te′ə ran′), capital of Iran, in the N part. *n.*

tel., 1 telegram. **2** telegraph. **3** telephone.

Tel A viv (tel′ ə vēv′), largest city of Israel, in the W part.

tele-, *combining form.* **1** over a long distance: *Telescope = instrument for looking over a long distance.* **2** television: *Telecast = broadcast over television.* [The form *tele-* comes from Greek *tēle,* meaning "far."]

tel e cast (tel′ə kast′), **1** broadcast by television. **2** a television broadcast. 1 *v.,* **tel e cast** or **tel e cast ed, tel e cast ing;** 2 *n.* —**tel′e cast′er,** *n.*

teleg., 1 telegram. **2** telegraph. **3** telegraphy.

tel e gram (tel′ə gram), message sent by telegraph: *receive a telegram. n.*

tel e graph (tel′ə graf), **1** way of sending coded messages over wires by means of electrical impulses. **2** device used for sending these messages. **3** send a message to (a person, etc.) by telegraph. 1,2 *n.,* 3 *v.*

te leg ra pher (tə leg′rə fər), person who sends and receives messages by telegraph. *n.*

tel e graph ic (tel′ə graf′ik), of the telegraph; sent as a telegram. *adj.* —**tel′e graph′i cal ly,** *adv.*

te leg ra phy (tə leg′rə fē), the making or operating of telegraphs. *n.*

te lem e ter (tə lem′ə tər), **1** device for measuring heat, radiation, etc., and transmitting the information to a distant receiving station. **2** measure and transmit by telemeter. 1 *n.,* 2 *v.*

te lem e try (tə lem′ə trē), the use of telemeters for measuring and transmitting information. *n.*

tel e path ic (tel′ə path′ik), of or by telepathy. *adj.* —**tel′e path′i cal ly,** *adv.*

te lep a thy (tə lep′ə thē), communication of one mind with another without using speech, hearing, sight, or any other sense used normally to communicate. *n.*

tel e phone (tel′ə fōn), **1** apparatus, system, or process for sending sound or speech to a distant point over wires by means of electrical impulses. **2** talk through a telephone; send (a message) by telephone. **3** make a telephone call to. 1 *n.,* 2,3 *v.,* **tel e phoned, tel e phon ing.** —**tel′e phon′er,** *n.*

telephone book or **telephone directory,** list of names, addresses, and telephone numbers of people or businesses with telephones in a certain area.

tel e phon ic (tel′ə fon′ik), of or by the telephone: *telephonic communication. adj.*

te leph o ny (tə lef′ə nē), the making or operating of telephones. *n.*

tel e pho to lens (tel′ə fō′tō), lens used in a camera for producing an enlarged image of a distant object.

tel e scope (tel′ə skōp), **1** instrument for making distant objects appear nearer and larger. The stars are studied by means of telescopes. **2** force or be forced together one inside another like the sliding tubes of some telescopes: *When the two railroad trains crashed into each other, the cars were telescoped.* **3** shorten; condense. 1 *n.,* 2,3 *v.,* **tel e scoped, tel e scop ing.**

WORD HISTORY

telescope

Telescope comes from Greek *tēle,* meaning "far," and *skopein,* meaning "look at."

tel e scop ic (tel′ə skop′ik), **1** of a telescope. **2** obtained or seen by means of a telescope: *a telescopic view of the moon.* **3** visible only through a telescope. **4** far-seeing. **5** consisting of parts that slide one inside another like the tubes of some telescopes. *adj.*

tel e text (tel′ə tekst), system of delivering information, such as stock-market listings, weather reports, etc., by televising it to viewers. A control panel attached to a television set allows viewers to select what is to be shown. *n.*

tel e thon (tel′ə thon), a television program lasting many hours, especially one seeking contributions for a charity, etc. *n.*

tel e type (tel′ə tīp), **1** Teletype, trademark for a tele-typewriter. **2** system of sending signals by Teletype. **3** send (a message) by Teletype. 1,2 *n.*, 3 *v.*, **tel e typed, tel e typ ing.**

tel e type writ er (tel′ə tīp′rī′tər), a telegraphic device which resembles a typewriter, used in sending, receiving, and automatically printing out messages. *n.*

tel e view er (tel′ə vyü′ər), person who watches television. *n.*

tel e vise (tel′ə vīz), send by television: *televise a baseball game.* *v.*, **tel e vised, tel e vis ing.**

tel e vi sion (tel′ə vizh′ən), **1** process of sending and receiving images and sounds over wires or through the air by means of electrical impulses. In television, waves of light and sound are changed into electric waves and transmitted to a receiver where they are changed back into waves of light and sound so that the images can be seen and the sounds heard. **2** the apparatus on which these pictures may be seen. **3** the business of television broadcasting; the television industry. **4** of, used in, or sent by television. 1-3 *n.*, 4 *adj.*

tell (tel), **1** put in words; say: *Tell the truth.* **2** tell to; inform: *Tell us about it.* **3** make known; reveal: *Don't tell where the money is.* **4** recognize; know; distinguish: *He couldn't tell which house it was.* **5** say to; order; command: *Tell her to stop!* **6** say to with force: *I don't like it, I tell you.* **7** count; count one by one: *The nun tells her beads.* **8** have effect or force: *Every blow told.* *v.*, **told, tell ing.**

tell off, 1 count off; count off and detach for some special duty. **2** strike back sharply in words; scold.

tell on, 1 inform on; tell tales about. **2** have a harmful effect on; break down: *The strain told on the man's health.*

Tell (tel), **William,** legendary hero in the Swiss struggle for independence against Austria. He was forced to shoot an apple from his son's head. *n.*

tell er (tel′ər), **1** person who tells: *a teller of tales.* **2** a bank cashier who takes in and gives out money. *n.*

tell ing (tel′ing), having effect or force; striking: *a telling blow.* *adj.*

tell ing ly (tel′ing lē), effectively; forcefully. *adv.*

tell tale (tel′tāl′), **1** person who tells tales on others; person who reveals private or secret matters from ill will. **2** serving to identify; revealing: *a telltale fingerprint.* 1 *n.*, 2 *adj.*

tel lur i um (te lur′ē əm), a silver-white nonmetallic element with some metallic properties. It usually occurs in nature combined with various metals. *n.*

te mer i ty (tə mer′ə tē), reckless boldness; rashness. *n.*

temp., 1 temperature. **2** temporary.

tem per (tem′pər), **1** state of mind; disposition; condition: *a sweet temper. She was in no temper to be kept waiting.* **2** angry state of mind: *fly into a temper. In his temper he slammed the door.* **3** calm state of mind: *I became angry and lost my temper.* **4** soften; moderate: *Temper justice with mercy.* **5** bring or be brought to a proper or desired condition of hardness, toughness, flexibility, etc., by mixing or preparing. A painter tempers colors by

a hat	i it	oi oil	ch child	(a in about
ā age	ī ice	ou out	ng long		e in taken
ä far	o hot	u cup	sh she	ə = { i in pencil
e let	ō open	u̇ put	th thin		o in lemon
ē equal	ô order	ü rule	ŦH then	(u in circus
ėr term			zh measure	

mixing them with oil. Steel is tempered by heating it and cooling it under controlled conditions until it has the proper degree of hardness and flexibility. **6** the degree of hardness, toughness, flexibility, etc., of a substance given by tempering: *The temper of the clay was right for shaping.* 1-3,6 *n.*, 4,5 *v.* —**tem′per a ble,** *adj.*

tem per a ment (tem′pər ə mənt), **1** a person's nature or disposition: *a nervous temperament.* **2** an easily irritated, sensitive nature: *an artist's display of temperament.* *n.*

tem per a men tal (tem′pər ə men′tl), **1** subject to moods and whims; easily irritated; sensitive: *A temperamental person can be hard to live with.* **2** showing a strongly marked individual temperament. *adj.*

tem per ance (tem′pər əns), **1** a being moderate in action, speech, habits, etc.; self-control. **2** a being moderate in the use of alcoholic drinks. **3** the principle and practice of not using alcoholic drinks at all. *n.*

tem per ate (tem′pər it), **1** not very hot and not very cold: *Seattle has a temperate climate.* **2** moderate; using self-control: *She spoke in a temperate manner, not favoring either side especially.* **3** moderate in using alcoholic drinks. *adj.* —**tem′per ate ly,** *adv.* —**tem′per ate ness,** *n.*

NORTH TEMPERATE ZONE SOUTH TEMPERATE ZONE

temperate zone or **Temperate Zone,** the part of the earth's surface between the tropic of Cancer and the arctic circle in the Northern Hemisphere, or the part between the tropic of Capricorn and the antarctic circle in the Southern Hemisphere.

tem per a ture (tem′pər ə chər), **1** degree of heat or cold. The temperature of freezing water is 32 degrees Fahrenheit (0 degrees Celsius). **2** a body temperature higher than normal (98.6 degrees Fahrenheit or 37.0 degrees Celsius); fever: *A sick person may have a temperature.* *n.*

tem pered (tem′pərd), **1** softened or moderated. **2** treated so as to become hard but not too brittle: *The sword was made of tempered steel.* *adj.*

tem pest (tem′pist), **1** a violent windstorm, usually accompanied by rain, hail, or snow: *The tempest drove the ship on the rocks.* **2** a violent disturbance: *a tempest of anger.* *n.*

tem pes tu ous (tem pes′chü əs), **1** stormy: *It was a tempestuous night.* **2** violent: *a tempestuous fit of anger.* *adj.* —**tem pes′tu ous ly,** *adv.* —**tem pes′tu ous ness,** *n.*

Tem plar (tem′plər), member of a medieval religious and military order called Knights Templars. *n.*

tem ple[1] (tem′pəl), **1** building used for the service or worship of a god or gods. **2** Temple, any of three temples in ancient Jerusalem built at different times by the Jews. Solomon built the first Temple. **3** synagogue. **4** building set apart for Christian worship; church. *n.* [*Temple*[1] is from Old English *tempel*, which comes from Latin *templum*.] —**tem′ple like′,** *adj.*

tem ple[2] (tem′pəl), the flattened part on either side of the forehead. *n.* [*Temple*[2] came into English about 600 years ago from French *temple*, which comes from Latin *tempora*, meaning "temples."]

tem po (tem′pō), **1** (in music) the time or rate of movement; proper or characteristic speed of movement: *the correct tempo for a dance tune.* **2** rhythm; characteristic rhythm: *the fast tempo of modern life. n., pl.* **tem pos, tem pi** (tem′pē).

tem por al[1] (tem′pər əl), **1** of time. **2** lasting for a time only. **3** of this life only. **4** not religious or sacred; worldly. *adj.* —**tem′por al ly**, *adv.* —**tem′por al ness**, *n.*

tem por al[2] (tem′pər əl), of the temples or sides of the forehead. *adj.*

tem po rar i ly (tem′pə rer′ə lē), for a short time; for the present: *They are living in a hotel temporarily. adv.*

tem po rar y (tem′pə rer′ē), lasting for a short time only; used for the time being; not permanent: *This is just a temporary job. adj.* —**tem′po rar′i ness**, *n.*

tem po rize (tem′pə rīz′), **1** evade immediate action or decision in order to gain time, avoid trouble, etc. **2** fit one's acts to the time or occasion. *v.,* **tem po rized, tem po riz ing.** —**tem′por i za′tion**, *n.* —**tem′po riz′er**, *n.* —**tem′po riz′ing ly**, *adv.*

tempt (tempt), **1** make or try to make (a person) do something: *Extreme hunger can tempt a person to steal food.* **2** appeal strongly to; attract: *That candy tempts me.* **3** provoke: *It is tempting fate to try to cross the lake in that old boat. v.* —**tempt′a ble**, *adj.*

temp ta tion (temp tā′shən), **1** a tempting: *No temptation could make her break her promise.* **2** a being tempted: *"Lead us not into temptation."* **3** thing that tempts: *Money left carelessly about is a temptation. n.*

tempt er (temp′tər), **1** person who tempts. **2 the Tempter,** the Devil; Satan. *n.*

tempt ing (temp′ting), apt to tempt; alluring; inviting: *a tempting suggestion. adj.* —**tempt′ing ly**, *adv.* —**tempt′ing ness**, *n.*

temp tress (temp′tris), woman who tempts. *n., pl.* **temp tress es.**

ten (ten), **1** one more than nine; 10. **2** set of ten persons or things. 1,2 *n.,* 1 *adj.*

ten., tenor.

ten a ble (ten′ə bəl), able to be held or defended: *a tenable position, a tenable theory. adj.* —**ten′a ble ness**, *n.* —**ten′a bly**, *adv.*

te na cious (ti nā′shəs), **1** holding fast: *the tenacious jaws of a bulldog, a tenacious memory.* **2** stubborn; persistent: *a tenacious salesman.* **3** holding fast together; not easily pulled apart. *adj.* [*Tenacious* is from Latin *tenacem*, meaning "holding fast," which comes from *tenere*, meaning "to hold." See **Word Family.**] —**te na′cious ly**, *adv.* —**te na′cious ness**, *n.*

te nac i ty (ti nas′ə tē), **1** firmness in holding fast. **2** stubbornness; persistence. **3** firmness in holding together; toughness. *n.*

ten an cy (ten′ən sē), **1** condition of being a tenant; an occupying and paying rent for land or buildings. **2** property so held. **3** length of time a tenant occupies a property. *n., pl.* **ten an cies.**

ten ant (ten′ənt), **1** person paying rent for the temporary use of the land or buildings of another person: *That building has apartments for one hundred tenants.* **2** person or thing that occupies: *Wild animals were the only tenants of the forest.* **3** hold or occupy as a tenant; inhabit: *That old house has not been tenanted for many years.* 1,2 *n.,* 3 *v.* —**ten′ant a ble**, *adj.* —**ten′ant like′**, *adj.*

tenant farmer, person who lives on and farms land belonging to another. The owner receives cash or a share of the crops as rent.

ten ant less (ten′ənt lis), without a tenant; vacant. *adj.*

ten ant ry (ten′ən trē), **1** all the tenants on an estate. **2** tenancy. *n., pl.* **ten ant ries.**

Ten Commandments, (in the Bible) the ten rules for living and for worship that God revealed to Moses on Mount Sinai.

tend[1] (tend), **1** be apt; be likely; incline (to): *Fruit tends to decay. Homes tend to use more mechanical appliances now.* **2** move; be directed: *The coastline tends to the south here. v.*

tend[2] (tend), take care of; look after; attend to: *tend the sick. She tends the store for her parents. A shepherd tends a flock. v.*

tend en cy (ten′dən sē), inclination; leaning: *a tendency to fight. Wood has a tendency to swell if it gets wet. n., pl.* **tend en cies.**

ten der[1] (ten′dər), **1** not hard or tough; soft: *tender feet. The meat is tender.* **2** not strong and hardy; delicate: *The leaves in spring are green and tender.* **3** kind; affectionate; loving: *She spoke tender words to the baby.* **4** not rough or crude; gentle: *He patted the dog with tender hands. These young plants need tender care.* **5** young: *She came to live here at the tender age of five.* **6** sensitive; painful; sore: *a tender wound. Automobiles are a tender subject with Dad since his accident.* **7** feeling pain or grief easily: *a tender heart. adj.* —**ten′der ly**, *adv.*

ten der[2] (ten′dər), **1** offer formally: *She tendered her thanks.* **2** a formal offer: *She refused his tender of marriage.* **3** thing offered. Money that must be accepted as payment for a debt is called legal tender. **4** offer (money, goods, etc.) in payment of a debt. 1,4 *v.,* 2,3 *n.* —**ten′der a ble**, *adj.* —**ten′der er**, *n.*

tend er[3] (ten′dər), **1** person or thing that tends another: *a machine tender.* **2** a small boat carried or towed by a ship and used for landing passengers. **3** the car that carries coal and water, attached behind a steam locomotive. *n.*

ten der foot (ten′dər fůt′), INFORMAL. **1** newcomer to the pioneer life of the western United States. **2** person not used to rough living and hardships. **3** an inexperienced person; beginner. **4** a beginning member of the Boy Scouts or Girl Scouts. *n., pl.* **ten der foots, ten der feet** (ten′dər fēt′).

ten der heart ed (ten′dər här′tid), kindly; sympathetic. *adj.* —**ten′der heart′ed ly**, *adv.* —**ten′der heart′ed ness**, *n.*

ten der ize (ten′də rīz′), make soft or tender: *tenderize*

WORD FAMILY

tenacious

Below are words related to *tenacious*. They can all be traced back to the Latin word *tenere* (te nā′re), meaning "to hold."

abstain	entertain	retainer[2]
abstinence	impertinent	sustain
contain	maintain	sustenance
container	maintenance	tenable
content[1]	obtain	tenant
content[2]	pertain	tenement
continent	pertinacity	tenet
continue	pertinent	tenon
continuity	retain	tenor
detain	retainer[1]	tenure
detention		

meat by pounding. *v.*, **ten der ized, ten der iz ing.**
—**ten′der i za′tion,** *n.* —**ten′der iz′er,** *n.*
ten der loin (ten′dər loin′), a tender part of the loin of
beef or pork. *n.*
ten der ness (ten′dər nis), **1** a being tender: *A steak is
judged by its flavor and tenderness.* **2** tender feeling: *He
has a tenderness for cats. n.*

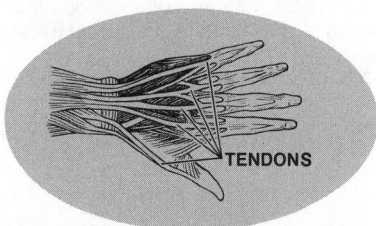

TENDONS

ten don (ten′dən), a tough, strong band or cord of
tissue that joins a muscle to a bone or some other part;
sinew. *n.*
ten dril (ten′drəl), **1** a threadlike part of a climbing plant
that attaches itself to something and helps support the
plant. **2** something similar: *curly tendrils of hair. n.*
ten e ment (ten′ə mənt), **1** a building, especially in a
poor section of a city, divided into sets of rooms occupied by separate families. **2** a dwelling, or part of a
dwelling, occupied by a tenant. *n.*
ten et (ten′it), doctrine, principle, belief, or opinion held
as true. *n.*
ten fold (ten′fōld′), ten times as much or as many. *adj.,
adv.*
Tenn., Tennessee.
Ten nes see (ten′ə sē′), **1** one of the south central
states of the United States. *Abbreviation:* Tenn. or TN
Capital: Nashville. **2** river flowing from E Tennessee into
the Ohio River. *n.* —**Ten′nes se′an, Ten′nes see′an,
adj., n.**
Tennessee Valley Authority, TVA.
ten nis (ten′is), game played by two or four players on a
rectangular court, in which a ball is hit back and forth
over a net with a racket. *n.* [*Tennis* came into English
about 600 years ago from French *tenetz*, meaning
"hold!", and can be traced back to Latin *tenere*, meaning
"to hold."]
Ten ny son (ten′ə sən), **Alfred,** Lord, 1809-1892, English poet. *n.* —**Ten′ny so′ni an,** *adj.*

tenon (def. 1)
Tenon on the right fits
into mortise on the left.

ten on (ten′ən), **1** the end of a piece of wood cut so as
to fit into the mortise in another piece and so form a
joint. **2** cut so as to form a tenon. **3** fit together with
tenon and mortise. 1 *n.*, 2,3 *v.*
ten or (ten′ər), **1** the highest male voice in music. **2** singer with such a voice. **3** part to be sung by such a voice.
4 of or for a tenor. **5** the general tendency; course: *He
found he enjoyed the even tenor of country life.* **6** the general meaning or drift: *I understand French well enough to get
the tenor of her speech.* 1-3,5,6 *n.*, 4 *adj.*
tenor clef, the C clef when the clef symbol is placed
on the fourth line of the staff. See **clef** for diagram.

a hat	**i** it	**oi** oil	**ch** child	⎧ a in about
ā age	**ī** ice	**ou** out	**ng** long	⎪ e in taken
ä far	**o** hot	**u** cup	**sh** she	**ə** = ⎨ i in pencil
e let	**ō** open	**ů** put	**th** thin	⎪ o in lemon
ē equal	**ô** order	**ü** rule	**ŦH** then	⎩ u in circus
ėr term			**zh** measure	

ten pins (ten′pinz′), the game of bowling. *n.*
tense[1] (tens), **1** stretched tight; strained to stiffness: *a
tense rope, a face tense with pain.* **2** stretch tight; stiffen:
She tensed her muscles for the leap. **3** strained; keyed up:
tense nerves, a tense moment. 1,3 *adj.*, **tens er, tens est;** 2
v., **tensed, tens ing.** [*Tense*[1] is from Latin *tensum*, which
comes from *tendere*, meaning "to stretch." See **Word
Family.**] —**tense′ly,** *adv.* —**tense′ness,** *n.*

WORD FAMILY

tense[1]

Below are words related to *tense*[1]. They can
all be traced back to the Latin word *tendere*
(ten′de re), meaning "to stretch."

attend	intend	pretense
attendance	intense	superintend
attention	intensify	tend[1]
contend	intensity	tend[2]
contentious	intent	tendency
distend	ostensible	tender[2]
extend	ostentatious	tensile
extensive	portend	tent
extent	pretend	tenterhook
inattentive		

tense[2] (tens), **1** form of a verb that shows the time of the
action or state expressed by the verb. *I dance* is in the
present tense. *I danced* is in the past tense. *I will dance* is
in the future tense. **2** set of such forms for the various
persons. The present tense of *dance* is: *I dance; you
dance; he, she, or it dances; we dance; you dance; they
dance. n.* [*Tense*[2] came into English about 600 years ago
from French *tens*, meaning "time," which came from
Latin *tempus.*] —**tense′less,** *adj.*
ten sile (ten′səl), **1** of tension: *Steel has great tensile
strength.* **2** able to be stretched. *adj.*
ten sion (ten′shən), **1** a stretching. **2** a stretched condition: *The tension of the bow gives speed to the arrow.*
3 mental strain: *Tension is sometimes brought on by
overwork.* **4** strained condition: *political tension. n.*
—**ten′sion less,** *adj.*
tent (tent), a movable shelter made of cloth or skins
supported by a pole or poles. *n.* —**tent′like′,** *adj.*
ten ta cle (ten′tə kəl), **1** a long, slender, flexible growth
on the head or around the mouth of an animal, used to
touch, hold, or move; feeler. **2** a sensitive, hairlike
growth on a plant. *n.*
ten ta tive (ten′tə tiv), **1** done as a trial or experiment;
experimental: *a tentative plan.* **2** hesitating: *a tentative
laugh. adj.* —**ten′ta tive ly,** *adv.* —**ten′ta tive ness,** *n.*
tent caterpillar, caterpillar that spins a tentlike, silken
web in which it lives. Tent caterpillars feed on leaves
and do great damage to fruit and forest trees.
ten ter (ten′tər), framework on which cloth is stretched
so that it may set or dry evenly without shrinking. *n.*
ten ter hook (ten′tər hůk′), one of the hooks or bent
nails that hold the cloth stretched on a tenter. *n.*
on tenterhooks, in suspense; anxious.

tenth (tenth), **1** next after the ninth; last in a series of 10. **2** one of 10 equal parts: *A dime is a tenth of a dollar.* *adj., n.*

ten u ous (ten′yü əs), **1** thin or slight; slender: *the tenuous thread of a spider's web.* **2** not dense: *The air ten miles above the earth is very tenuous.* **3** having slight importance; not substantial: *She has only a tenuous claim to the property. adj.* —**ten′u ous ly,** *adv.* —**ten′u ous ness,** *n.*

ten ure (ten′yər), **1** a holding or possessing. **2** length of time of holding or possessing: *The tenure of office of the president of our club is one year. n.*

tepee

te pee (tē′pē), tent used by the American Indians of the Great Plains, made of hides sewn together and stretched over poles arranged in the shape of a cone. *n.* Also, **teepee.** [*Tepee comes from Sioux tipi.*]

tep id (tep′id), slightly warm; lukewarm. *adj.* —**tep′id ly,** *adv.* —**tep′id ness,** *n.*

ter., territory.

ter bi um (tėr′bē əm), a metallic element which occurs in certain minerals with yttrium and ytterbium. *n.*

term (tėrm), **1** word or phrase used in connection with some special subject, science, art, or business: *medical terms. "Acid," "base," and "salt" are terms commonly used in chemistry.* **2** any particular word or expression: *a foreign term.* **3** apply a term to; name; call: *He might be termed handsome.* **4** a set period of time; length of time that a thing lasts: *The President's term of office is four years.* **5** one of the periods into which the school year is divided: *Most schools have a fall term and a spring term.* **6 terms,** *pl.* **a** conditions: *The terms of the peace were very hard for the defeated nation.* **b** agreement: *The company and the union could not come to terms.* **c** way of speaking: *She talked about you in very flattering terms.* **d** personal relations: *We are on good terms with our neighbors.* **7** numerator or denominator in a fraction. **8** any part of an algebraic expression separated from the other parts by a plus or minus sign. In $13ax^2 - 2bxy + y$, $13ax^2$, $2bxy$, and y are the terms. 1,2,4-8 *n.*, 3 *v.*

ter mi na ble (tėr′mə nə bəl), able to be ended: *The contract was terminable by either party. adj.*

ter mi nal (tėr′mə nəl), **1** at the end; forming the end part. A terminal flower or bud is one growing at the end of a stem, branch, etc. **2** the end; the end part. A terminal is either end of a railroad line, bus line, airline, or shipping route where sheds, hangars, garages, stations, etc., to handle freight and passengers are located. **3** resulting in death; fatal: *a terminal disease.* **4** device for making an electrical connection: *the terminals of a battery.* **5** device by which a person and a computer may communicate, usually having a keyboard and a printer or a fluorescent screen. 1,3 *adj.*, 2,4,5 *n.* —**ter′mi nal ly,** *adv.*

ter mi nate (tėr′mə nāt), **1** bring to an end; put an end to: *The two lawyers terminated their partnership and each opened a separate office.* **2** come to an end: *The contract*

terminates soon. *v.*, **ter mi nat ed, ter mi nat ing.**

ter mi na tion (tėr′mə nā′shən), an ending; end: *Termination of the contract left both parties free to do business elsewhere. n.*

ter mi nol o gy (tėr′mə nol′ə jē), the special words or terms used in a science, art, business, etc.: *medical terminology. n., pl.* **ter mi nol o gies.**

ter mi nus (tėr′mə nəs), **1** an end of a railroad line, bus line, etc. **2** boundary; goal; end. *n., pl.* **ter mi ni** (tėr′mə nī), **ter mi nus es.**

ter mite (tėr′mīt), an insect with a soft, pale body; white ant. Termites live in colonies somewhat like ants and eat wood, paper, and other material containing cellulose. They are very destructive to buildings, furniture, etc. *n.*

termite
about ¹/₄ in. (6 mm.) long

tern (tėrn), a sea bird related to the gulls but with a more slender body and bill and usually a long, forked tail. *n.*

ter race (ter′is), **1** a paved outdoor space adjoining a house, used for lounging, dining, etc. **2** the flat roof of a house, especially of an Oriental or Spanish house. **3** a row of houses or a short street running along the side or top of a slope: *She lives at 7 Oak Terrace.* **4** a flat, raised level of land with vertical or sloping sides, especially one of a series of such levels placed one above the other. **5** form into a terrace or terraces; furnish with terraces: *to terrace a hillside.* 1-4 *n.*, 5 *v.*, **ter raced, ter rac ing.**

WORD HISTORY

terrace

Terrace came into English about 400 years ago from French *terrace*, meaning "a heap of rubble," and can be traced back to Latin *terra*, meaning "earth."

terrace (def. 4)

ter ra cot ta (ter′ə kot′ə), **1** kind of hard, often unglazed, brownish-red earthenware, used for vases, statuettes, building decorations, etc. **2** a dull brownish red.

ter ra fir ma (ter′ə fėr′mə), solid earth; dry land.

ter rain (te rān′), tract of land, especially considered with respect to its extent and natural features: *the hilly, rocky terrain of the island. n.*

ter ra pin (ter′ə pin), a North American turtle used for food. It lives in fresh water or tidewater. *n.* [*Terrapin* is of Algonquian origin.]

ter rar i um (tə rer′ē əm), a glass enclosure in which plants or small land animals are kept. *n., pl.* **ter rar i ums, ter rar i a** (tə rer′ē ə).

ter res tri al (tə res′trē əl), **1** of the earth; not of the heavens: *this terrestrial globe.* **2** of land, not water: *Islands and continents make up the terrestrial parts of the earth.* **3** living on the ground, not in the air or water or in trees: *Cows, lions, and elephants are terrestrial animals.* **4** growing on land; growing in the ground: *terrestrial plants.* **5** worldly; earthly. *adj.* —**ter res′tri al ly,** *adv.*

ter ri ble (ter′ə bəl), **1** causing great fear; dreadful; awful: *a terrible storm.* **2** distressing; severe: *War causes terrible suffering.* **3** INFORMAL. extremely bad; unpleasant: *a terrible temper. adj.* —**ter′ri ble ness,** *n.*

ter ri bly (ter′ə blē), **1** in a terrible manner; dreadfully: *to be terribly afraid of lightning.* **2** INFORMAL. extremely: *I am terribly sorry I stepped on your toes. adv.*

ter ri er (ter′ē ər), a small, active dog, formerly used to chase prey into its burrow. Some well-known breeds are fox terriers, Irish terriers, and Scottish terriers. *n.* [*Terrier* came into English about 500 years ago from French (*chien*) *terrier,* meaning "burrowing (dog)."]

ter rif ic (tə rif′ik), **1** causing great fear; terrifying: *A terrific earthquake shook Japan.* **2** INFORMAL. very unusual; remarkable; extraordinary: *A terrific hot spell ruined many of the crops.* **3** INFORMAL. very good; wonderful: *She is a terrific tennis player. adj.*

ter rif i cal ly (tə rif′ik lē), in a terrific manner; to a terrific degree. *adv.*

ter ri fy (ter′ə fī), fill with great fear; frighten very much: *Terrified by the sight of the bear, they ran into the cabin. v.,* **ter ri fied, ter ri fy ing.** —**ter′ri fy′ing ly,** *adv.*

ter ri to ri al (ter′ə tôr′ē əl), **1** of territory: *The purchase of Louisiana was a valuable territorial addition to the United States.* **2** of a particular territory or district; restricted to a particular district: *a territorial government. adj.*

ter ri to ry (ter′ə tôr′ē), **1** land; region: *Much territory in the northern part of Africa is desert.* **2** land belonging to a government; land under the rule of a distant government: *Gibraltar is British territory.* **3** region assigned to a salesman or agent. **4** a district not admitted as a state but having its own lawmaking body. Alaska was a territory of the United States until 1958. *n., pl.* **ter ri to ries.**

ter ror (ter′ər), **1** great fear: *The child has a terror of thunder.* **2** cause of great fear: *Pirates were once the terror of the sea. n.*

ter ror ism (ter′ə riz′əm), **1** a terrorizing; use of terror or violence. **2** condition of fear and submission produced by frightening people. *n.*

ter ror ist (ter′ər ist), person who uses or favors terrorism. *n.*

ter ror ize (ter′ə rīz′), **1** fill with terror: *The sight of the growling dog terrorized the little child.* **2** rule or subdue by causing terror. *v.,* **ter ror ized, ter ror iz ing.**

ter ror-strick en (ter′ər strik′ən), terrified. *adj.*

ter ry cloth (ter′ē), a rough cloth made of uncut looped yarn.

terse (tėrs), brief and to the point: *"No" was her terse reply when I asked her to help me with my homework. adj.,* **ters er, ters est.** —**terse′ly,** *adv.* —**terse′ness,** *n.*

a hat	i it	oi oil	ch child	a in about
ā age	ī ice	ou out	ng long	e in taken
ä far	o hot	u cup	sh she	ə = i in pencil
e let	ō open	u̇ put	th thin	o in lemon
ē equal	ô order	ü rule	ᵺ then	u in circus
ėr term			zh measure	

ter ti ar y (tėr′shē er′ē), of the third order, rank, or formation. *adj.*

test (test), **1** examination or trial: *a test in arithmetic, a driver's test.* **2** means of trial: *Trouble is a test of character.* **3** examination of a substance to see what it is or what it contains: *A test showed that the water was pure.* **4** put to a test of any kind; try out: *test a rope for strength. The doctor tested my eyes.* **5** to show a certain result on a test. 1-3 *n.,* 4,5 *v.* [*Test* came into English about 600 years ago from French *test,* meaning "pot, vessel used in assaying," which came from Latin *testum,* meaning "earthen vessel."] —**test′a ble,** *adj.* —**test′er,** *n.*

tes ta ment (tes′tə mənt), **1** written instructions telling what to do with a person's property after the person dies; will. **2 Testament, a** a main division of the Bible; the Old Testament or the New Testament. **b** the New Testament. *n.*

tes tate (tes′tāt), having made and left a valid will. *adj.*

tes ta tor (tes′tā tər), **1** person who makes a will. **2** person who has died leaving a valid will. *n.*

tes ti cle (tes′tə kəl), gland in a male human being or animal that produces the sperm; testis. *n.*

tes ti fy (tes′tə fī), **1** declare or give evidence under oath in a court of law: *The witness testified that the speeding car had crashed into the truck.* **2** give evidence; bear witness: *The excellence of Shakespeare's plays testifies to his genius. v.,* **tes ti fied, tes ti fy ing.**

tes ti ly (tes′tə lē), in a testy manner. *adv.*

tes ti mo ni al (tes′tə mō′nē əl), **1** certificate of character, conduct, qualifications, value, etc.; recommendation: *She received a testimonial from her former employer.* Advertisements of headache remedies sometimes contain testimonials from people who have used them. **2** something given or done to show esteem, admiration, gratitude, etc.: *They collected money for a testimonial to the retiring pastor.* **3** given or done as a testimonial. 1,2 *n.,* 3 *adj.*

tes ti mo ny (tes′tə mō′nē), **1** statement used for evidence or proof: *A witness gave testimony that the defendant was at home all day Sunday.* **2** evidence: *The pupils presented their teacher with a watch in testimony of their respect and affection.* **3** an open declaration or profession of one's faith. *n., pl.* **tes ti mo nies.**

tes ti ness (tes′tē nis), testy quality or condition. *n.*

tes tis (tes′tis), testicle. *n., pl.* **tes tes** (tes′tēz).

test pilot, pilot that tests new or experimental aircraft by subjecting them to greater than normal stress.

test tube, a thin glass tube closed at one end, used in making chemical tests.

test-tube (test′tüb′ *or* test′tyüb′), **1** of or having to do with a test tube: *a test-tube experiment.* **2** conceived in a test tube for later implantation in a uterus: *a test-tube baby. adj.*

tes ty (tes′tē), easily irritated; impatient. *adj.,* **tes ti er, tes ti est.**

tet a nus (tet′n əs), disease caused by certain bacteria usually entering the body through wounds, characterized by violent spasms and stiffness of many muscles, sometimes resulting in death. Tetanus of the jaw muscles is called lockjaw. You can be protected against it by inoculation. *n.*

tête-à-tête (tāt′ə tāt′), **1** two together in private: *They dined tête-à-tête.* **2** of or for two people in private: *a tête-*

à-tête conversation. **3** a private conversation between two people. **1** *adv.,* **2** *adj.,* **3** *n.*

teth er (teᴛн′ər), **1** rope or chain for fastening an animal so that it can graze or move only within a certain limit. **2** fasten with a tether: *tether a horse to a stake.* **1** *n.,* **2** *v.* **at the end of one's tether,** at the end of one's resources or endurance.

teth er ball (teᴛн′ər bôl′), game played by two people with a ball fastened by a cord to the top of a tall post. The object of the game is to hit the ball so as to wind the cord around the post, in one direction or the other. *n.*

Teu ton (tüt′n *or* tyüt′n), **1** a German. **2** person belonging to the group of northern Europeans that speak Germanic languages. **3** member of an ancient Germanic tribe that threatened the Roman republic in the 100's B.C. **4** German. 1-3 *n.,* 4 *adj.*

Teu ton ic (tü ton′ik *or* tyü ton′ik), **1** of the ancient Teutons or their language. **2** Germanic. **3** German. *adj.*

Tex., Texas.

Tex an (tek′sən), **1** of Texas or its people. **2** person born or living in Texas. **1** *adj.,* **2** *n.*

Tex as (tek′səs), one of the southwestern states of the United States. *Abbreviation:* Tex. or TX *Capital:* Austin. *n.*

text (tekst), **1** the main body of reading matter in a book: *This history book contains 300 pages of text and about 50 pages of maps and pictures.* **2** the original words of a writer. **3** a short passage in the Bible: *The minister preached on the text "Judge not, that ye be not judged."* **4** topic; subject: *Town improvement was the speaker's text.* **5** textbook. *n.*

text book (tekst′bùk′), book for regular study by pupils. Most books used in schools are textbooks. *n.*

tex tile (tek′stəl *or* tek′stīl), **1** a woven fabric; cloth: *Beautiful textiles are sold in Paris.* **2** suitable for weaving: *Linen, cotton, silk, nylon, and wool are common textile materials.* **3** material that can be woven. **4** of the making, selling, etc., of textiles: *the textile industry.* 1,3 *n.,* 2,4 *adj.*

tex tu al (teks′chü əl), of the text: *A misprint is a textual error. adj.*

tex ture (teks′chər), **1** arrangement of threads in a woven fabric: *Burlap has a much coarser texture than linen.* **2** arrangement of the parts of anything; structure; makeup: *Velvet has a soft texture. n.*

-th[1], *suffix added to numbers.* number _____ in order or position in a series: *Sixth = number six in order or position in a series.* The suffix -*eth* is used to form numbers like *fiftieth* and *sixtieth.*

-th[2], **1** *suffix forming nouns, usually from verbs.* act or process of _____ing: *Growth = process of growing.* **2** *suffix forming nouns, usually from adjectives.* quality, state, or condition of being _____: *Truth = quality of being true.* [The suffix -*th*[2] comes from Old English -*th, -tho,* or -*thu.*]

Th, symbol for thorium.

Thack er ay (thak′ər ē), **William Makepeace,** 1811-1863, English novelist. *n.*

Thai (tī), **1** of Thailand, its people, or their language. **2** person born or living in Thailand. **3** language of Thailand. **1** *adj.,* 2,3 *n., pl.* **Thais** for 2.

Thai land (tī′land), country in SE Asia. *Capital:* Bangkok. See **Indochina** for map. Formerly called **Siam.** *n.*

thal li um (thal′ē əm), a soft, bluish-white metallic element that occurs in iron and zinc ores and in various minerals. It is highly poisonous and its compounds are used to kill insects, rodents, etc. *n.*

thal lo phyte (thal′ə fīt), any of a large group of plants that have no leaves, stems, or roots. Bacteria, algae, fungi, and lichens are thallophytes. *n.*

Thames (temz), river flowing from S England into the North Sea. London is on the Thames. See **Rhine** for map. *n.*

than (ᴛнan; *unstressed* ᴛнən), **1** in comparison with: *She is taller than her sister.* **2** compared to that which: *You know better than I do.* **3** except; besides: *How else can we come than by train?* 1,2 *conj.,* 1,3 *prep.*

thane (thān), **1** man who ranked between an earl and an ordinary freeman in early England. Thanes held lands of the king or lord and gave military service in return. **2** a Scottish feudal lord. *n.*

thank (thangk), **1** say that one is pleased and grateful for something given or done; express gratitude to: *She thanked her teacher for helping her.* **2 thanks,** *pl.* **a** I thank you. **b** act of thanking; expression of gratitude and pleasure. **c** feeling of kindness received; gratitude: *You have our thanks for everything you have done.* **1** *v.,* **2** *n.* [*Thank* comes from Old English *thanc,* originally meaning "thought."]

have oneself to thank, be to blame: *You have yourself to thank if you eat too much.*

thanks to, owing to; because of: *Thanks to his efforts, the garden is a great success.*

thank ful (thangk′fəl), feeling or expressing thanks; grateful: *He is thankful for good health. adj.* **—thank′ful ly,** *adv.* **—thank′ful ness,** *n.*

thank less (thangk′lis), **1** not feeling or expressing thanks; ungrateful: *The thankless child did not appreciate our gift.* **2** not likely to get thanks; not appreciated: *Giving advice can be a thankless act. adj.* **—thank′less ly,** *adv.* **—thank′less ness,** *n.*

thanks giv ing (thangks giv′ing), **1** a giving of thanks. **2** expression of thanks: *They offered thanksgiving to God for their escape.* **3 Thanksgiving,** Thanksgiving Day. *n.*

Thanksgiving Day, day set apart as a holiday on which to give thanks for past blessings. In the United States, Thanksgiving Day is the fourth Thursday in November.

that (ᴛнat; *unstressed* ᴛнət), **1** *That* is used to point out some one person or thing or idea. We use *this* for the thing nearer us, and *that* for the thing farther away from us. *Do you know that boy? (adj.). Shall we buy this book or that one? (adj.). I like that better (pron.).* **2** *That* is also used to connect a group of words. *I know that 6 and 4 are 10.* **3** *That* is used to show purpose. *Study that you may learn.* **4** *That* is used to show result. *She ran so fast that she was five minutes early.* **5** who; whom; which: *Is he the man that sells dogs? She is the girl that you saw in school. Bring the box that will hold most.* **6** when; at or in which: *It was the day that school began. The year that we went to England was 1964.* **7** to that extent; to such a degree; so: *The baby cannot stay up that long.* **1** *adj., pl.* **those;** 1,5,6 *pron., pl.* **those;** 2-4 *conj.,* 7 *adv.*

that's that, that is settled or decided.

thatch (thach), **1** straw, rushes, palm leaves, etc., used as a roof or covering. **2** to roof or cover with thatch. **1** *n.,* **2** *v.* **—thatch′er,** *n.*

thatch
(def. 2)

Thatch er (thach′ər), **Margaret**, born 1925, British political leader, prime minister of Great Britain since 1979. *n.*

that'll (ŦHat′l), **1** that will. **2** that shall.

that's (ŦHats), that is.

thaw (thô), **1** melt (ice, snow, or anything frozen); free from frost: *The sun will thaw the ice on the streets.* **2** weather above the freezing point (32 degrees Fahrenheit or 0 degrees Celsius): *In January we usually have a thaw.* **3** become free of frost, ice, etc.: *The pond freezes in November and thaws in April.* **4** make or become less stiff and formal in manner; soften: *His shyness thawed under the teacher's kindness.* **1,3,4** *v.,* **2** *n.*

the¹ (ŦHə *or* ŦHi; *stressed* ŦHē), **1** that or those and no others; a certain; a particular: *The dog I saw had no tail. The girl driving the car is my sister.* **2** the well-known; the only: *the Alps.* **3** the best or most important: *the place to dine.* **4** any one of its kind; any: *The dog is a quadruped.* **5** that which is; those which are: *visit the sick, a love of the beautiful. definite article.*

the² (ŦHə *or* ŦHē), in that degree; to that degree: *The later I sit up, the sleepier I become. adv.*

the a ter *or* **the a tre** (thē′ə tər), **1** place where plays are acted or motion pictures are shown. **2** place that looks like a theater in its arrangement of seats: *The surgeon performed an operation before the medical students in the operating theater.* **3** place of action: *France has been the theater for many wars.* **4** plays; writing, acting in, or producing plays; the drama: *She was interested in the theater and tried to write plays herself. n.*

the at ri cal (thē at′rə kəl), **1** of the theater or actors: *theatrical performances, a theatrical company.* **2** suggesting a theater or acting; for display or effect; artificial. **3 theatricals,** *pl.* dramatic performances, especially as given by amateurs. **1,2** *adj.,* **3** *n.* —**the at′ri cal ly,** *adv.*

Thebes (thēbz), **1** important city in ancient Greece. See **Sparta** for map. **2** city in ancient Egypt, on the Nile, formerly a center of Egyptian civilization. *n.*

thee (ŦHē), OLD USE. you. *pron.*

theft (theft), stealing: *The prisoner was jailed for theft. n.*

their (ŦHer *or* ŦHar), of them; belonging to them: *I like their house. adj.*

theirs (ŦHerz *or* ŦHarz), the one or ones belonging to them: *Our house is white; theirs is brown. pron.*

them (ŦHem; *unstressed* ŦHəm), the persons, animals, things, or ideas spoken about: *The books are new; take care of them. pron.*

the mat ic (thē mat′ik), of a theme; having to do with themes. *adj.*

theme (thēm), **1** topic; subject: *The theme of her speech was equal rights for all Americans.* **2** a short written composition: *Our school themes must be written in ink and on white paper.* **3** the principal melody in a piece of music; short melody repeated in different forms. **4** melody used to identify a particular radio or television program. *n.*

them selves (ŦHem selvz′ *or* ŦHəm selvz′), **1** form of *they* or *them* used to make a statement stronger: *The teachers themselves said the test was too hard.* **2** form used instead of *them* in cases like: *They speak for themselves. They hurt themselves sledding down the hill.* **3** their normal or usual selves: *They are ill and are not themselves today. pron.*

then (ŦHen), **1** at that time: *Father talked of his childhood, and recalled that prices were lower then.* **2** that time: *By then we shall know the result of the election.* **3** being at that time; existing then: *the then President.* **4** soon afterwards: *The noise stopped, and then began again.* **5** next in time or place: *First comes spring, then summer.* **6** at another time: *Now one team was ahead and then another.* **7** also; besides: *The circus is too good to miss, and then it costs very little.* **8** in that case; therefore: *If she painted the best*

a hat	i it	oi oil	ch child	⌈a in about
ā age	ī ice	ou out	ng long	e in taken
ä far	o hot	u cup	sh she	ə = ⟨ i in pencil
e let	ō open	u̇ put	th thin	o in lemon
ē equal	ô order	ü rule	ŦH then	⌊u in circus
ėr term			zh measure	

picture, then she should receive the first prize. **1,4-8** *adv.,* **2** *n.,* **3** *adj.*

thence (ŦHens), **1** from that place; from there: *We went to Italy; thence we went to France.* **2** for that reason: *You didn't work, thence you will get no pay.* **3** from that time; from then: *a few years thence. adv.*

thence forth (ŦHens′fôrth′), from then on; from that time forward: *I bought an old guitar and thenceforth began my musical career. adv.*

thence for ward (ŦHens′fôr′wərd), thenceforth. *adv.*

the oc ra cy (thē ok′rə sē), **1** government in which God is recognized as the supreme civil ruler and in which religious authorities rule the state as God's representatives. **2** any government headed by religious authorities. **3** country or state governed by a theocracy. *n., pl.* **the oc ra cies.**

the o crat ic (thē′ə krat′ik), **1** of theocracy. **2** having a theocracy. *adj.*

the o lo gian (thē′ə lō′jən), an expert in theology. *n.*

the o log i cal (thē′ə loj′ə kəl), of theology. A theological school trains people for the ministry. *adj.* —**the′o-log′i cal ly,** *adv.*

the ol o gy (thē ol′ə jē), **1** doctrines concerning God and His relations to human beings and the universe. **2** study of religion and religious beliefs. **3** system of religious beliefs. *n., pl.* **the ol o gies.**

the o rem (thē′ər əm *or* thir′əm), **1** statement or rule in mathematics that has been or is to be proved. EXAMPLE: In an isosceles triangle the angles opposite the equal sides are equal. **2** any statement or rule that can be proved to be true. *n.*

the o ret ic (thē′ə ret′ik), theoretical. *adj.*

the o ret i cal (thē′ə ret′ə kəl), **1** planned or worked out in the mind, not from experience; based on theory, not on fact; limited to theory. **2** dealing with theory only; not practical: *City students can get a theoretical knowledge of farming from textbooks. adj.*

the o ret i cal ly (thē′ə ret′ik lē), in theory; according to theory; in a theoretical manner. *adv.*

the o re ti cian (thē′ər ə tish′ən), an expert in the theory of an art, science, etc. *n.*

the o rist (thē′ər ist), person who theorizes. *n.*

the o rize (thē′ə rīz′), form a theory or theories; speculate. *v.,* **the o rized, the o riz ing.** —**the′o riz′er,** *n.*

the o ry (thē′ər ē *or* thir′ē), **1** an explanation based on observation and reasoning: *According to one scientific theory of life, the more complicated animals developed from the simpler ones.* **2** the principles or methods of a science or art rather than its practice: *the theory of music.* **3** idea or opinion about something: *I think the fire was started by a careless smoker. What is your theory? n., pl.* **the o ries.**

ther a peu tic (ther′ə pyü′tik), having to do with curing or therapy; curative: *Heat has therapeutic value. adj.*

ther a peu tics (ther′ə pyü′tiks), branch of medicine that deals with the treating or curing of disease. *n.*

ther a pist (ther′ə pist), person who specializes in some form of therapy. *n.*

ther a py (ther′ə pē), treatment of diseases or disorders. *n., pl.* **ther a pies.**

there (ŦHer *or* ŦHar; *unstressed* ŦHər), **1** in or at that place: *Sit there. Finish reading the page and stop there.* **2** to or into that place: *We are going there tomorrow.* **3** that

place: *We go to New York first and from there to Boston.*
4 in that matter: *You are mistaken there.* **5** *There* is also used in sentences in which the verb comes before its subject. *There are three new houses on our street. Is there a drugstore near here?* **6** *There* is used to call attention to some person or thing. *There goes the bell.* **7** *There* is also used to express some feeling. *There, there! don't cry.* 1,2,4-6 *adv.,* 3 *n.,* 7 *interj.*

there a bout (ᴛнer′ə bout′ *or* ᴛнar′ə bout′), thereabouts. *adv.*

there a bouts (ᴛнer′ə bouts′ *or* ᴛнar′ə bouts′), **1** near that place: *She lives downtown, on Main Street or thereabouts.* **2** near that time: *He went home in the late afternoon, at 5 o'clock or thereabouts.* **3** near that number or amount: *It was very cold and the temperature fell to zero or thereabouts. adv.*

there af ter (ᴛнer af′tər *or* ᴛнar af′tər), after that; afterward: *He was very ill as a child and was considered delicate thereafter. adv.*

there at (ᴛнer at′ *or* ᴛнar at′), **1** when that happened; at that time. **2** because of that; because of it. **3** at that place; there. *adv.*

there by (ᴛнer bī′ *or* ᴛнar bī′), **1** by means of that; in that way: *He wished to travel and thereby study the customs of other countries.* **2** in connection with that: *She won the game, and thereby hangs a tale.* **3** near there: *A farm lay thereby. adv.*

there'd (ᴛнerd *or* ᴛнard), **1** there had. **2** there would.

there for (ᴛнer fôr′ *or* ᴛнar fôr′), for that; for this; for it: *They promised to give a building for a hospital and the land necessary therefor. adv.*

there fore (ᴛнer′fôr *or* ᴛнar′fôr), for that reason; as a result of that: *She had to work last night and therefore had little time to study. adv.*

there from (ᴛнer from′, ᴛнar from′, ᴛнer frum′, *or* ᴛнar frum′), from that; from this; from it: *He opened his bag and took therefrom an apple. adv.*

there in (ᴛнer in′ *or* ᴛнar in′), **1** in that place; in it: *the oceans and all the creatures therein.* **2** in that matter; in that way: *He is a good worker, but he can't get along with people. Therein lay the problem. adv.*

there'll (ᴛнerl *or* ᴛнarl), **1** there will. **2** there shall.

there of (ᴛнer uv′, ᴛнar uv′, ᴛнer ov′, *or* ᴛнar ov′), **1** of that; of it. **2** from it; from that source. *adv.*

there on (ᴛнer on′ *or* ᴛнar on′), **1** on that; on it: *Before the window was a table. A huge book lay thereon.* **2** immediately after that: *Cinderella's fairy godmother cast a spell; thereon the pumpkin was changed into a coach. adv.*

there's (ᴛнerz *or* ᴛнarz), there is.

The re sa (tə rē′sə), **Saint,** 1515-1582, Spanish nun and mystic. *n.*

there to (ᴛнer tü′ *or* ᴛнar tü′), **1** to that; to it: *The castle stands on a hill, and the road thereto is steep and rough.* **2** in addition to that; also: *The queen gave her faithful servant rich garments and added thereto a bag of gold. adv.*

there to fore (ᴛнer′tə fôr′ *or* ᴛнar′tə fôr′), before that time; until then. *adv.*

there un der (ᴛнer un′dər *or* ᴛнar un′dər), **1** under that; under it. **2** under the authority of that; according to that. *adv.*

there un to (ᴛнer un′tü *or* ᴛнar un′tü), to that; to it. *adv.*

there up on (ᴛнer′ə pon′ *or* ᴛнar′ə pon′), **1** immediately after that: *The clown appeared; thereupon the people clapped.* **2** because of that; therefore: *They planned to rent the old, abandoned house and thereupon remodeled it.* **3** on that; on it: *The knight carried a shield with a cross painted thereupon. adv.*

there with (ᴛнer wiᴛн′, ᴛнar wiᴛн′, ᴛнer with′, *or* ᴛнar with′), **1** with that; with it: *She gave him a rose and a smile therewith.* **2** immediately after that; then: *"Avenge*

me!" said the ghost and therewith disappeared. adv.

ther mal (ᴛнer′məl), **1** of heat. **2** a rising current of warm air. 1 *adj.,* 2 *n.* —**ther′mal ly,** *adv.*

thermo-, *combining form.* heat: *Thermoelectricity = electricity produced by heat.* [The form *thermo-* comes from Greek *thermē.*]

ther mo dy nam ic (ᴛнer′mō dī nam′ik), of thermodynamics; using force due to heat or to the conversion of heat into other forms of energy. *adj.*

ther mo dy nam ics (ᴛнer′mō dī nam′iks), branch of physics that deals with the relations between heat and other forms of energy, and of the conversion of one into the other. *n.*

ther mo e lec tric (ᴛнer′mō i lek′trik), of thermoelectricity. *adj.*

ther mo e lec tric i ty (ᴛнer′mō i lek tris′ə tē), electricity produced directly by heat, especially that produced by a temperature difference between two different metals used as conductors in a circuit. *n.*

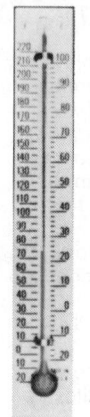

thermometers
two types of thermometers

ther mom e ter (thər mom′ə tər), instrument for measuring temperature. Most thermometers contain mercury or alcohol in a narrow tube. When the temperature outside the tube goes up, the liquid rises by expanding; when the temperature outside the tube goes down, the liquid drops by contracting. *n.* [*Thermometer* comes from Greek *thermē,* meaning "heat," and *metron,* meaning "a measure."]

ther mo nu cle ar (ᴛнer′mō nü′klē ər *or* ᴛнer′mō-nyü′klē ər), of the fusion of atoms (as in the hydrogen bomb) through very high temperature: *a thermonuclear reaction. adj.*

Ther mop y lae (thər mop′ə lē), mountain pass in ancient Greece. In 480 B.C., a small force of Greeks defended it against an army of Persians until most of the Greeks were killed. See **Sparta** for map. *n.*

ther mos (ᴛнer′məs), container made with a vacuum between its inner and outer walls so that its contents remain hot or cold for a long time. *n.*

thermos bottle, thermos.

ther mo stat (ᴛнer′mə stat), an automatic device for regulating temperature. In most thermostats, the expansion and contraction of a metal, liquid, or gas opens and closes an electric circuit connected to a furnace, air conditioner, etc. *n.*

the sau rus (thi sôr′əs), **1** dictionary in which synonyms, antonyms, and other related words are classified under certain headings. **2** any dictionary, encyclopedia, or other book filled with information. *n., pl.* **the sau ri** (thi-sôr′ī) *or* **the sau rus es.** [*Thesaurus* comes from Latin *thesaurus,* meaning "treasure."]

these (ᴛʜēz). *These* is used to point out persons, things, or ideas. *These two problems are hard (adj.). These are my books (pron.).* adj., pron.pl. of **this.**

The se us (thē′sē əs *or* thē′süs), (in Greek legends) the chief hero of Athens. He killed the Minotaur and escaped from Crete with the help of Ariadne. *n.*

the sis (thē′sis), **1** proposition or statement to be proved or to be maintained against objections. **2** a long essay presented by a candidate for a diploma or degree. *n., pl.* **the ses** (thē′sēz′).

Thes pi an (thes′pē ən), **1** having to do with the drama or tragedy. **2** actor or actress. 1 *adj.*, 2 *n.*

Thes pis (thes′pis), Greek poet of the 500's B.C. Traditionally, he was the founder of Greek tragedy. *n.*

Thes sa lo ni ans (thes′ə lō′nē ənz), either of two books of the New Testament written by Saint Paul. *n.*

Thes sa ly (thes′ə lē), district in E Greece. *n.* —**Thes sa li an** (the sā′lē ən), *adj., n.*

The tis (thē′tis), (in Greek legends) a sea nymph who was the mother of Achilles. *n.*

thews (thüz), **1** muscles or sinews. **2** bodily force; might; strength. *n.pl.*

they (ᴛʜā), **1** the persons, animals, things, or ideas spoken about: *I had three books yesterday. Do you know where they are? They are on the table.* **2** some people; any people; persons: *They say we should have a new school.* *pron.pl.*

they'd (ᴛʜād), **1** they had. **2** they would.

they'll (ᴛʜāl), **1** they will. **2** they shall.

they're (ᴛʜer), they are.

they've (ᴛʜāv), they have.

thi a mine or **thi a min** (thī′ə mən), vitamin that promotes growth and prevents and cures beriberi; vitamin B_1. It is found in yeast, meats, whole-grain cereals, and certain vegetables. *n.*

thick (thik), **1** with much space from one side to the opposite side; not thin: *The castle has thick stone walls.* **2** measuring between two opposite sides: *A dime is about one millimeter thick.* **3** set close together; dense: *She has thick hair. It is a thick forest.* **4** many and close together; abundant: *The troops were greeted by bullets thick as hail.* **5** like glue or syrup, not like water: *Thick liquids pour slowly.* **6** not clear; foggy: *The weather was thick and the airports were shut down.* **7** not clear in sound; hoarse: *He had a thick voice because of a cold.* **8** stupid; dull: *I couldn't get it through my thick head.* **9** thickly: *The field was planted so thick with corn that you could hide among the stalks. The cars came thick and fast.* **10** hardest part; place where there is the most danger, activity, etc.: *They were in the thick of the fight.* **11** very friendly; intimate. 1-8,11 *adj.,* 9 *adv.,* 10 *n.*

through thick and thin, in good times and bad.

thick en (thik′ən), **1** make or become thick or thicker: *You thicken gravy with flour. The pudding will thicken as it cools.* **2** become more involved or complicated: *In the second act of the play the plot thickens.* *v.* —**thick′en er,** *n.*

thick et (thik′it), shrubs, bushes, or small trees growing close together: *We crawled into the thicket and hid. n.*

thick head ed (thik′hed′id), stupid; dull. *adj.* —**thick′head ed ness,** *n.*

thick ly (thik′lē), **1** in a thick manner; closely; densely: *Most of New York City is thickly settled.* **2** in great numbers; in abundance: *Weeds grow thickly in the rich soil.* **3** frequently: *The houses came more thickly as we got closer to the city.* **4** in tones that are hoarse or hard to understand. *adv.*

thick ness (thik′nis), **1** quality or state of being thick: *The thickness of the walls shuts out all sounds.* **2** distance between two opposite sides; the third measurement of a solid, not length nor breadth: *The length of the board is*

10 feet, the width 6 inches, the thickness 2 inches. **3** layer: *The pad was made up of three thicknesses of cloth.* *n., pl.* **thick ness es.**

thick set (thik′set′), **1** thickly set: *a thickset hedge.* **2** thick in form or build: *a thickset opera singer.* *adj.*

thick-skinned (thik′skind′), **1** having a thick skin. **2** not sensitive to criticism, rebuff, or the like. *adj.*

thief (thēf), person who steals, especially one who steals secretly and usually without using force: *A thief stole my bicycle from the yard.* *n., pl.* **thieves.**

thieve (thēv), steal. *v.,* **thieved, thiev ing.**

thiev er y (thē′vər ē), stealing; theft. *n., pl.* **thiev er ies.**

thieves (thēvz), plural of **thief.** *n.*

thiev ish (thē′vish), **1** having the habit of stealing; likely to steal. **2** like a thief; sly: *a thievish look.* *adj.*

thigh (thī), part of the leg between the hip and the knee. *n.*

thigh bone (thī′bōn′), bone of the leg between the hip and the knee; femur. *n.*

thimble

thim ble (thim′bəl), a small metal or plastic cap worn on the finger to protect it when pushing the needle in sewing. *n.*

Thim bu (tim′bü), capital of Bhutan, in the W part. *n.*

thin (thin), **1** with little space from one side to the opposite side; not thick: *thin paper, thin wire, thin ice.* **2** having little flesh; slender; lean: *a thin person.* **3** not set close together; scanty: *He has thin hair.* **4** not dense: *The air on the top of high mountains is thin.* **5** few and far apart; not abundant: *The actors played to a thin audience.* **6** like water; not like glue or syrup: *This gravy is too thin.* **7** not deep or strong; having little depth, fullness, or intensity: *a thin color. They heard a shrill, thin voice.* **8** easily seen through; flimsy: *It was a thin excuse that satisfied no one.* **9** make or become thin: *Hunger had thinned their cheeks.* 1-8 *adj.,* **thin ner, thin nest;** 9 *v.,* **thinned, thin ning.** —**thin′ly,** *adv.* —**thin′ness,** *n.*

thine (ᴛʜīn), OLD USE. **1** yours. "It is thine" means "it is yours." **2** your (used only before a vowel or *h*). "Thine eyes" means "your eyes." 1 *pron.,* 2 *adj.*

thing (thing), **1** any object or substance; what one can see or hear or touch or taste or smell: *All the things in the house were burned. Put these things away.* **2 things,** *pl.* **a** personal belongings. **b** clothes: *I packed my things and took the train.* **3** whatever is spoken or thought of; act; deed; fact; event; idea: *It was a good thing to do. A strange thing happened.* **4** matter; affair: *Let's settle this thing between us. How are things going?* **5** person or creature: *I felt sorry for the poor thing.* *n.*

do one's thing, INFORMAL. do the thing that one wants to do, or the thing that one does best.

know a thing or two, be experienced or wise.

make a good thing of, INFORMAL. profit from.

see things, have hallucinations.

think (thingk), **1** have ideas; use the mind: *You must learn to think clearly.* **2** have in the mind: *He thought that he would go.* **3** have an opinion; believe: *Do you think it will rain? Do what you think fit.* **4** reflect: *I want to think before answering that question.* **5** consider: *They think their teacher a genius.* **6** imagine: *You can't think how surprised I was.* **7** expect: *I did not think to find you here.* *v.,* **thought, think ing.** —**think′er,** *n.*

think of, 1 have in mind: *I think of you often.* **2** imagine: *She doesn't like apple pie. Think of that!* **3** remember: *I can't think of his name.*

think out, 1 plan or discover by thinking. **2** solve or understand by thinking. **3** think through to the end.

think over, consider carefully.

think twice, think again before acting; hesitate.

think up, plan or discover by thinking.

thin-skinned (thin′skind′), **1** having a thin skin. **2** sensitive to criticism, reproach, rebuff, etc. *adj.*

third (thėrd), **1** next after the second; last in a series of three: *C is the third letter of the alphabet.* **2** one of three equal parts: *We divided the cake into thirds.* *adj., n.*

third degree, INFORMAL. use of severe treatment by the police to force a person to give information or make a confession.

third ly (thėrd′lē), in the third place. *adv.*

third person, form of a pronoun or verb used to refer to the person spoken of. *He, she, it,* and *they* are pronouns of the third person.

third-rate (thėrd′rāt′), distinctly inferior. *adj.*

thirst (thėrst), **1** a dry, uncomfortable feeling in the mouth or throat caused by having had nothing to drink. **2** desire or need for drink: *She satisfied her thirst with a glass of water.* **3** feel thirst; be thirsty. **4** a strong desire: *a thirst for adventure.* **5** have a strong desire. 1,2,4 *n.,* 3,5 *v.*

thirst i ly (thėr′stə lē), in a thirsty manner. *adv.*

thirst y (thėr′stē), **1** feeling thirst; having thirst: *The dog is thirsty; please give it some water.* **2** without water or moisture; dry: *land as thirsty as a desert. adj.,* **thirst i er, thirst i est.**

thir teen (thėr′tēn′), three more than ten; 13. *n., adj.*

thir teenth (thėr′tēnth′), **1** next after the 12th; last in a series of 13. **2** one of 13 equal parts. *adj., n.*

thir ti eth (thėr′tē ith), **1** next after the 29th; last in a series of 30. **2** one of 30 equal parts: *A day is about one thirtieth of a month. adj., n.*

thir ty (thėr′tē), three times ten; 30. *n., pl.* **thir ties;** *adj.*

thir ty-sec ond note (thėr′tē sek′ənd), (in music) a note played for one thirty-second (¹/₃₂) as long a time as a whole note.

this (ᴛHis), **1** *This* is used to point out some person, thing, or idea as present, or near, or spoken of before. We use *that* for the thing farther away from us and *this* for the thing nearer us. *School begins at eight this year* (*adj.*). *Shall we buy this or that?* (*pron.*). **2** present; near; spoken of: *this minute, this child.* **3** to this degree or extent; so: *You can have this much.* 1,2 *adj., pl.* **these;** 1 *pron., pl.* **these;** 3 *adv.*

this tle (this′əl), plant with a prickly stalk and leaves and usually with purple flowers. *n.* —**this′tle like′,** *adj.*

this tle down (this′əl doun′), downy growth that forms on ripe thistle seeds. *n.*

thith er (thiᴛH′ər), to or toward that place; there. *adv.*

tho or **tho'** (ᴛHō), though. *conj., adv.*

Tho ho yan dou (tō′hō yan′dou), capital of Venda. *n.*

thole (thōl), peg or pin, often one of a pair, on the side of a boat to hold an oar in rowing. *n.*

thole pin (thōl′pin′), thole. *n.*

Thom as (tom′əs), **1** one of Jesus' twelve apostles. He at first doubted the Resurrection. **2 Dylan,** 1914-1953, Welsh poet. *n.*

thong (thông), **1** a narrow strip of leather, especially one used as a fastening. **2** lash of a whip. *n.*

Thor (thôr), (in Scandinavian myths) the god of thunder. *n.*

tho rac ic (thô ras′ik), of the thorax. The thoracic cavity contains the heart and lungs. *adj.*

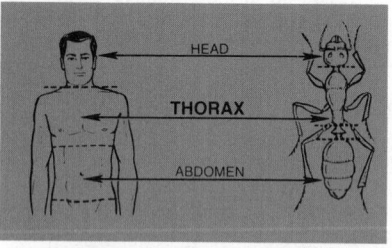

thorax
left, (def. 1)
right, (def. 2)

tho rax (thôr′aks), **1** the part of the body between the neck and the abdomen; chest. **2** the second division of an insect's body, between the head and the abdomen. *n., pl.* **tho rax es, tho ra ces** (thôr′ə sēz′).

Tho reau (thə rō′), **Henry David,** 1817-1862, American author and naturalist. *n.*

tho ri um (thôr′ē əm), a dark-gray, radioactive, metallic element present in certain rare minerals. When thorium is bombarded with neutrons, it changes into a form of uranium which is used as an atomic fuel. *n.*

thorn (thôrn), **1** stiff, sharp-pointed growth on a stem or branch of a tree or other plant: *Roses have thorns.* **2** tree or other plant with thorns: *Thorns sprang up and choked the wheat. n.*

thorn in the flesh or **thorn in the side,** a cause of trouble or annoyance.

thorn y (thôr′nē), **1** full of thorns: *a thorny bush.* **2** troublesome; annoying: *a thorny problem. adj.,* **thorn i er, thorn i est.** —**thorn′i ness,** *n.*

thor ough (thėr′ō), **1** being all that is needed; complete: *Please make a thorough search for the lost money.* **2** doing all that should be done; very careful: *The doctor was very thorough in examining the patient. adj.* —**thor′ough ly,** *adv.* —**thor′ough ness,** *n.*

thor ough bred (thėr′ō bred′), **1** of pure breed or stock. **2** a thoroughbred animal. **3 Thoroughbred,** any race horse of a breed derived from a crossing of domestic English stock with Arabian stock. **4** a well-bred or thoroughly trained person. 1 *adj.,* 2-4 *n.*

thor ough fare (thėr′ō fer′ *or* thėr′ō far′), **1** passage, road, or street open at both ends: *A city street is a public thoroughfare.* **2** a main road; highway. *n.*

thor ough go ing (thėr′ō gō′ing), thorough; complete. *adj.*

those (ᴛHōz). *Those* is used to point out several persons or things. *She owns that dog; the boys own those dogs*

thistle

(adj.). That is his book; those are my books (pron.). adj., pron.pl. of **that.**

thou (ᴛнou), OLD USE. you. *pron. sing.*

though (ᴛнō), **1** in spite of the fact that: *Though it was pouring, no one went indoors.* **2** yet; still; nevertheless: *He is better, though not yet cured.* **3** even supposing that: *Though I fail, I shall try again.* **4** however: *I am sorry about our quarrel; you began it, though.* 1-3 *conj.,* 4 *adv.* Also, **tho** or **tho'.**

as though, as if; as it would be if: *You look as though you were tired.*

thought (thôt), **1** what one thinks; idea; notion: *I would like your thoughts on the subject.* **2** thinking: *Thought helps us solve problems.* **3** care; attention; regard: *Show some thought for others than yourself.* **4** intention: *His thought was to avoid controversy.* **5** a little bit; trifle: *Be a thought more polite.* **6** the characteristic thinking of a particular person, time, or place: *20th-century scientific thought.* **7** past tense and past participle of **think.** *We thought it would snow yesterday.* 1-6 *n.,* 7 *v.*

thought ful (thôt′fəl), **1** full of thought; thinking: *He was thoughtful for a while and then replied, "No."* **2** careful of others; considerate: *She is always thoughtful of her parents.* **3** indicating thought: *a thoughtful expression. adj.* —**thought′ful ly,** *adv.* —**thought′ful ness,** *n.*

thought less (thôt′lis), **1** without thought; doing things without thinking; careless: *Thoughtless drivers cause many automobile accidents.* **2** showing little or no care or regard for others: *It is thoughtless of them to keep us waiting so long. adj.* —**thought′less ly,** *adv.* —**thought′less ness,** *n.*

thou sand (thou′znd), ten hundred; 1000. *n., adj.*

thou sandth (thou′zndth), **1** next after the 999th; last in a series of 1000. **2** one of 1000 equal parts. *adj., n.*

Thrace (thrās), region in the E part of the Balkan Peninsula. In ancient times it was first an independent country and later a Roman province. See **Troy** for map. *n.* —**Thra cian** (thrā′shən), *adj., n.*

thrall (thrôl), **1** person in bondage; slave: *The thralls did the work of the castle.* **2** bondage; slavery: *The witch's spell kept the princess in thrall.*

thrall dom or **thral dom** (thrôl′dəm), bondage; slavery: *A sorcerer held the knight in thralldom. n.*

thrash (thrash), **1** beat as punishment; flog: *I'd like to thrash whoever broke my camera.* **2** move violently; toss: *Unable to sleep, I thrashed about in bed.* **3** thresh (wheat, etc.). *v.*

thrash out, settle by thorough discussion.

thrash er (thrash′ər), **1** a long-tailed North American songbird related to the mockingbird. It is somewhat like a thrush. **2** thresher. *n.*

thread (thred), **1** a fine cord made of strands of cotton, silk, nylon, etc., spun out and twisted together. You sew with thread. **2** pass a thread through: *thread a needle, thread beads onto a string.* **3** something long and slender like a thread: *The spider hung by a thread. A thread of light came through a crack in the door.* **4** form into a thread: *Cook the syrup until it threads.* **5** the main thought that connects the parts of a story, speech, etc.: *Something distracted her and she lost the thread of their conversation.* **6** pass like a thread through; pervade. **7** make one's way through; make (one's way) carefully; go on a winding course: *He threaded his way through the crowd.* **8** the sloping ridge that winds around a bolt, screw, pipe joint, etc. The thread of a nut interlocks with the thread of a bolt. **9** form a thread on (a bolt, screw, pipe joint, etc.). 1,3,5,8 *n.,* 2,4,6,7,9 *v.* —**thread′er,** *n.* —**thread′like′,** *adj.*

thread bare (thred′ber′ or thred′bar′), **1** having the nap worn off; worn so much that the threads show: *a threadbare coat.* **2** wearing clothes worn to the threads; shabby: *a threadbare beggar.* **3** old and worn; stale: *Saying*

"I forgot" is a threadbare excuse. adj.

thread y (thred′ē), **1** consisting of or resembling a thread. **2** fibrous; stringy or viscid. **3** thin and feeble: *a thready pulse.* **4** lacking in fullness: *a thready voice. adj.,* **thread i er, thread i est.**

threat (thret), **1** statement of what will be done to hurt or punish someone: *The teacher's threat to keep us after school stopped our noise.* **2** sign or cause of possible evil or harm: *Those black clouds are a threat of rain. n.*

threat en (thret′n), **1** make a threat; say what will be done to hurt or punish: *The teacher threatened to fail students that did no homework.* **2** utter threats: *They threaten and scold too much.* **3** be a sign or warning of (possible evil or harm): *Black clouds threaten rain.* **4** be a cause of possible evil or harm to: *A flood threatened the city. v.* —**threat′en ing ly,** *adv.*

three (thrē), one more than two; 3. *n., adj.* [*Three* comes from Old English *thrēo.*]

three fold (thrē′fōld′), **1** three times as much or as many. **2** having three parts. 1,2 *adj.,* 1 *adv.*

three pence (thrip′əns), **1** three British pennies; three pence. **2** coin of this value. *n.*

three pen ny (thrip′ə nē), **1** worth three pence. **2** of little worth; cheap; paltry. *adj.*

three score (thrē′skôr′), three times twenty; 60. *adj.*

three some (thrē′səm), group of three people. *n.*

Three Wise Men, the Magi.

thren o dy (thren′ə dē), song of lamentation, especially at a person's death. *n., pl.* **thren o dies.**

thresh (thresh), **1** separate the grain or seeds from (wheat, etc.). Nowadays machines are generally used to thresh grain. **2** toss about; thrash. *v.*

thresh out, settle by thorough discussion.

thresh er (thresh′ər), **1** person or thing that threshes. **2** machine used for separating the grain or seeds from the stalks and other parts of wheat, oats, etc. **3** a large shark with a very long tail; thrasher. *n.*

thresh old (thresh′ōld), **1** piece of wood or stone under a door. **2** doorway. **3** point of entering; beginning point: *The scientist was on the threshold of a great discovery. n.*

threw (thrü), past tense of **throw.** *She threw the ball to me. v.*

thrice (thrīs), three times: *He knocked thrice. adv.*

thrift (thrift), absence of waste; saving; economical management; habit of saving: *By thrift they managed to get along on their small income. A bank account encourages thrift. n.*

thrift i ly (thrif′tə lē), in a thrifty manner; with thrift; economically. *adv.*

thrift i ness (thrif′tē nis), the quality or condition of being thrifty. *n.*

thrift less (thrift′lis), without thrift; wasteful. *adj.*

thrift y (thrif′tē), careful in spending; economical; saving: *a thrifty shopper. adj.,* **thrift i er, thrift i est.**

thrill (thril), **1** a shivering, exciting feeling: *I get a thrill whenever I see a parade.* **2** give a shivering, exciting feeling to: *Stories of adventure thrilled him.* **3** have a shivering, exciting feeling: *The children thrilled at the sight of their presents.* **4** quiver; tremble: *Her voice thrilled with excitement.* 1 *n.,* 2-4 *v.* [*Thrill* comes from Old English *thyrlian,* meaning "pierce."] —**thrill′ing ly,** *adv.*

thrill er (thril′ər), **1** person or thing that thrills. **2** INFOR-

Pronunciation key

a hat	**i** it	**oi** oil	**ch** child			a in about	
ā age	**ī** ice	**ou** out	**ng** long			e in taken	
ä far	**o** hot	**u** cup	**sh** she	**ə** =	{	i in pencil	}
e let	**ō** open	**u̇** put	**th** thin			o in lemon	
ē equal	**ô** order	**ü** rule	**ᴛн** then			u in circus	
ėr term			**zh** measure				

MAL. story, play, or motion picture filled with excitement, suspense, etc. *n.*

thrive (thrīv), be successful; grow rich; grow strong; prosper: *Flowers will not thrive without sunshine.* *v.*, **throve** or **thrived, thrived** or **thriv en** (thriv′ən), **thriving.**

thro or **thro'** (thrü), through. *prep., adv., adj.*

throat (thrōt), 1 the front of the neck. 2 the passage from the mouth to the stomach or the lungs. 3 any narrow passage: *the throat of a mine.* *n.*

throat y (thrō′tē), 1 produced or modified in the throat; guttural: *She had a throaty voice.* 2 low-pitched and resonant: *The engine started with a throaty roar.* *adj.*, **throat i er, throat i est.**

throb (throb), 1 beat rapidly or strongly: *The long climb up the hill made my heart throb. My injured foot throbbed with pain.* 2 a rapid or strong beat: *A throb of pain shot through his head.* 3 beat steadily. 4 a steady beat: *the throb of a pulse.* 1,3 *v.*, **throbbed, throb bing;** 2,4 *n.*

throes (thrōz), 1 great pain; agony: *an animal in its death throes.* 2 a desperate struggle; violent disturbance: *a nation in the throes of revolution.* *n.pl.*

throm bo sis (throm bō′sis), a blood clot in the heart or in a blood vessel that blocks circulation. *n., pl.* **thrombo ses** (throm bō′sēz).

throne (thrōn), 1 chair on which a king, queen, bishop, or other person of high rank sits during ceremonies. 2 power or authority of a king, queen, etc.: *the throne of England. n.*

throng (thrông), 1 a crowd; multitude. 2 to crowd; fill with a crowd: *People thronged the theater to see the famous actress.* 3 come together in a crowd; go or press in large numbers: *The people thronged to see the king.* 1 *n.*, 2,3 *v.*

throt tle (throt′l), 1 valve regulating the flow of gasoline vapor, steam, etc., to an engine. 2 lever, pedal, etc., working such a valve. The throttle of a car is called an accelerator. 3 stop or lessen the speed of (an engine) by closing a throttle: *to throttle a steam engine.* 4 stop the breath of by pressure on the throat; choke; strangle: *The thief throttled the dog to keep it from barking.* 5 check or stop the flow of; suppress: *High tariffs throttle trade between countries.* 1,2 *n.*, 3-5 *v.*, **throt tled, throt tling.** [*Throttle* is from Middle English *throtel,* which comes from *throte,* meaning "throat."] —**throt′tler,** *n.*

through (thrü), 1 from end to end of; from side to side of; between the parts of; from beginning to end of: *march through a town, cut a tunnel through a mountain, drive through a snowstorm.* 2 from end to end; from side to side; between the parts; from beginning to end: *The bullet hit the wall and went through. She read the book all the way through.* 3 here and there in; over; around: *We traveled through New England visiting many old towns.* 4 because of; by reason of: *The family refused help through pride.* 5 by means of: *She became rich through her wise investments.* 6 completely; thoroughly: *He walked home in the rain and was wet through.* 7 going all the way without change: *a through train from New York City to Chicago.* 8 having reached the end of; finished with: *We are through school at three o'clock.* 9 having reached the end; finished: *I am almost through.* 1,3-5,8 *prep.,* 2,6 *adv.,* 7,9 *adj.* Also, **thro, thro',** or **thru.**

through out (thrü out′), 1 all the way through; through all; in every part of: *The Fourth of July is celebrated throughout the United States.* 2 in every part: *The house is well built throughout.* 1 *prep.,* 2 *adv.*

through way (thrü′wā′), thruway. *n.*

throve (thrōv), a past tense of **thrive.** *The plants throve in the rich soil. v.*

throw (thrō), 1 send through the air with force; cast; toss; hurl: *throw a ball. I threw water on the fire.* 2 act of

throwing; a cast, toss, or hurl: *That was a good throw from left field to the catcher.* 3 distance a thing is or may be thrown. 4 bring to the ground: *His horse threw him.* 5 put by force: *throw someone into jail.* 6 put carelessly or in haste: *I threw a coat over my shoulders.* 7 turn, direct, or move, especially quickly: *She threw a glance at us.* 8 move (a lever, etc.) that connects or disconnects parts of a switch, clutch, or other mechanism. 9 INFORMAL. let an opponent win (a race, game, etc.), often for money. 1,4-9 *v.*, **threw, thrown, throw ing;** 2,3 *n.*

throw away, 1 get rid of; discard: *Throw away those old shoes.* 2 waste: *Don't throw away your opportunities.*

throw in, add, especially as a bargain.

throw off, 1 get rid of: *throw off a cold.* 2 give off; emit: *The burning oil threw off thick smoke.* 3 cause to lose: *The fox threw the hounds off its trail by doubling back.*

throw out, 1 get rid of; discard. 2 reject. 3 (in baseball) put out (a base runner) by throwing the ball to a baseman.

throw over, give up; discard; abandon.

throw up, 1 vomit. 2 give up; abandon. 3 build rapidly.

throw a way (thrō′ə wā′), 1 handbill, pamphlet, etc., intended to be thrown away after reading. 2 able to be thrown away or discarded: *a throwaway bottle.* 3 bottle, can, etc., intended to be thrown away after use. 1,3 *n.*, 2 *adj.*

throw back (thrō′bak′), 1 a throwing back. 2 setback or check. 3 reversion to an ancestral type or character: *The white stallion was a throwback to an albino ancestor. n.*

thrown (thrōn), past participle of **throw.** *She has thrown her old toys away. v.*

throw rug, scatter rug.

thru (thrü), through. *prep., adv., adj.*

thrum (thrum), 1 play on a stringed instrument by plucking the strings, especially in an idle or careless way; strum. 2 drum or tap idly with the fingers: *thrum on a table. v.*, **thrummed, thrum ming.**

thrush (thrush), any of a large group of migratory songbirds that includes the robin, the bluebird, the wood thrush, etc. *n., pl.* **thrush es.** —**thrush′like′,** *adj.*

thrust (thrust), 1 push with force: *He thrust his hands into his pockets.* 2 a push with force: *She hid the book behind the pillow with a quick thrust.* 3 stab; pierce: *thrust a knife into an apple.* 4 a stab: *A thrust with the pin broke the balloon.* 5 put forth; extend: *The tree thrust its roots deep into the ground.* 6 an attack. 7 the push exerted by the rotation of a propeller, that causes a ship, airplane, etc., to move. 8 the force driving a rocket or a jet engine forward, caused by the rearward discharge of gases, burning fuels, etc., through the exhaust. 1,3,5 *v.*, **thrust, thrust ing;** 2,4,6-8 *n.* —**thrust′er,** *n.*

thru way (thrü′wā′), an express highway. *n.* Also, **throughway.**

thud (thud), 1 a dull sound. A heavy blow or fall may cause a thud. *The book hit the floor with a thud.* 2 hit, move, or strike with a thud: *The heavy box fell and thudded on the floor.* 1 *n.*, 2 *v.*, **thud ded, thud ding.**

thug (thug), ruffian; hoodlum. *n.* [*Thug* is from Hindi *thag,* which came from Sanskrit *sthaga,* meaning "rogue."]

thu li um (thü′lē əm), a metallic element found in various minerals. An isotope of thulium is used as the radiating element in portable X-ray units. *n.*

thumb (thum), 1 the short, thick finger of the hand. It can be moved against any of the other four fingers to grasp things. 2 part that covers the thumb: *There was a hole in the thumb of my mitten.* 3 soil or wear by handling with the thumbs: *The book was badly thumbed.* 4 turn pages of (a book, etc.) rapidly, reading only portions: *He thumbed the book and gave it back to me.* 5 handle awkwardly. **6** INFORMAL. ask for or get (a free ride) by holding up one's thumb to motorists going in one's direction. 1,2 *n.*, 3-6 *v.* —**thumb′like′,** *adj.*

be all thumbs, be very clumsy, awkward, etc.

thumbs down, sign of disapproval or rejection.

thumbs up, sign of approval or acceptance.

twiddle one's thumbs, do nothing; be idle.

under one's thumb, under one's power or influence: *The younger children were under the bully's thumb.*

thumb nail (thum′nāl′), **1** nail of the thumb. **2** very small or short: *a thumbnail sketch.* 1 *n.*, 2 *adj.*

thumb screw (thum′skrü′), **1** screw made so that its head can be easily turned with the thumb and a finger. **2** an old instrument of torture that squeezed the thumbs. *n.*

thumb tack (thum′tak′), tack with a broad, flat head, that can be pressed into a wall, board, etc., with the thumb. *n.*

thump (thump), **1** strike with something thick and heavy; pound: *She thumped the table with her fist.* **2** a blow with something thick and heavy; heavy knock: *a thump on the head.* **3** the dull sound made by a blow, knock, or fall: *We heard a thump when the book fell.* **4** make a dull sound: *The hammer thumped against the wood.* **5** beat violently: *My heart thumped.* 1,4,5 *v.*, 2,3 *n.* —**thump′er,** *n.*

thun der (thun′dər), **1** the loud noise that accompanies or follows a flash of lightning. It is caused by a disturbance of the air resulting from the discharge of electricity. **2** give forth thunder: *It thundered, but no rain fell.* **3** any noise like thunder: *the thunder of Niagara Falls, a thunder of applause.* **4** make a noise like thunder: *The cannon thundered.* **5** utter very loudly; roar: *thunder a reply.* 1,3 *n.*, 2,4,5 *v.* —**thun′der er,** *n.* —**thun′der ing ly,** *adv.*

thun der bolt (thun′dər bōlt′), **1** a flash of lightning and the thunder that follows it. **2** something sudden, startling, and terrible: *The news of the accident came as a thunderbolt.* *n.*

thun der clap (thun′dər klap′), **1** a loud crash of thunder. **2** something sudden or startling. *n.*

thun der cloud (thun′dər kloud′), a dark, electrically charged cloud that brings thunder and lightning; cumulonimbus. *n.*

thun der head (thun′dər hed′), one of the round, swelling masses of very high clouds that frequently develop into thunderclouds; cumulonimbus. *n.*

thun der ous (thun′dər əs), **1** producing thunder. **2** making a noise like thunder: *The actors received thunderous applause at the end of the play.* *adj.*

thun der show er (thun′dər shou′ər), shower with thunder and lightning. *n.*

thun der storm (thun′dər stôrm′), storm with thunder and lightning. *n.*

thun der struck (thun′dər struk′), overcome, as if hit by a thunderbolt; astonished; amazed: *We were thunderstruck by the terrible news.* *adj.*

Thurs. or **Thur.,** Thursday.

Thurs day (thėrz′dē), the fifth day of the week, following Wednesday. *n.*

thus (THus), **1** in this way; in the way just stated, indicated, etc.; in the following manner: *He spoke thus: "Friends, Romans, Countrymen."* **2** accordingly; consequently; therefore: *We hurried and thus arrived on time.* **3** to this extent or degree; so: *Thus far he is enjoying his studies.* *adv.*

thwack (thwak), **1** strike hard with a stick or something flat. **2** a sharp blow with a stick or something flat. 1 *v.*, 2 *n.* —**thwack′er,** *n.*

thwart (thwôrt), **1** prevent from doing something, particularly by blocking the way; oppose and defeat: *Lack of money thwarted her plans for college.* **2** a seat across a

boat, on which a rower sits. **3** a brace in a canoe. **4** lying across. 1 *v.*, 2,3 *n.*, 4 *adj.* —**thwart′er,** *n.*

thy (THī), OLD USE. your. "Thy name" means "your name." *adj.*

thyme (tīm), a small plant related to the mint. Its sweet-smelling leaves are used for seasoning. *n.*

thy mus (thī′məs), a small, ductless glandlike organ found in young human beings and animals near the base of the neck and disappearing or becoming rudimentary in adults. It is an organ of the immune system. *n.*

thy roid (thī′roid), **1** thyroid gland. **2** medicine made from the thyroid glands of animals, used to treat disorders caused by a deficiency in the thyroid gland. **3** thyroid cartilage. **4** of the thyroid gland or thyroid cartilage. 1-3 *n.*, 4 *adj.*

thyroid cartilage, the principal cartilage of the larynx, which forms the lump called the Adam's apple.

thyroid gland, an important ductless gland in the neck of human beings and animals that secretes thyroxine.

thy rox in (thī rok′sən), thyroxine. *n.*

thy rox ine (thī rok′sēn), hormone secreted by the thyroid gland, which affects growth and metabolism. *n.*

thy self (THī self′), OLD USE. yourself. *pron.*

ti (tē), the seventh tone of the musical scale; si. *n.*

Ti, symbol for titanium.

ti ar a (tē er′ə *or* tē är′ə), **1** band of gold, jewels, flowers, etc., worn around the head as an ornament. **2** the triple crown worn by the pope as a symbol of his position. *n.*, *pl.* **ti ar as.**

Ti ber (tī′bər), river flowing from central Italy through Rome into the Tyrrhenian Sea. *n.*

Ti bet (ti bet′), former country of central Asia, now part of China. Its official Chinese name is **Xizang.** *Capital:* Lhasa. See **Yangtze** for map. *n.*

Ti bet an (ti bet′n), **1** of Tibet, its people, or their language. **2** person born or living in Tibet. **3** language of Tibet, related to Burmese and Thai. 1 *adj.*, 2,3 *n.*

tib i a (tib′ē ə), shinbone. *n.*, *pl.* **tib i ae** (tib′ē ē′), **tib i as.**

tic (tik), a habitual, involuntary twitching of certain muscles, especially those of the face. *n.*

tick[1] (tik), **1** sound made by a clock or watch. **2** make such a sound: *The clock ticked.* **3** a sound like it: *the tick of a moth against a windowpane.* **4** mark off: *The clock ticked away the minutes.* **5** a small mark. We use ✔ or / as a tick. **6** mark with a tick; check: *He ticked off the items one by one.* **7** INFORMAL. to function, work, or go: *What makes that gadget tick?* 1,3,5 *n.*, 2,4,6,7 *v.*

tick[2] (tik), **1** a tiny eight-legged animal, related to the spider, that attaches itself to humans and animals and sucks blood. **2** a wingless insect that sucks blood of certain animals, such as sheep, cattle, or deer. *n.*

tick[2] (def. 1)
about ¼ in. (6 mm.) long

tick³ (tik), the cloth covering of a mattress or pillow. *n.*

tick er (tik′ər), **1** a telegraphic instrument that prints stock-market reports or news on a paper tape. **2** SLANG. the heart. *n.*

ticker tape, a paper tape on which a ticker prints stock-market reports or news.

tick et (tik′it), **1** card or piece of paper that gives its holder a right or privilege: *a ticket to the theater, a rail-road ticket.* **2** INFORMAL. summons to appear in court, given to a person accused of breaking a traffic law: *a ticket for speeding, a parking ticket.* **3** INFORMAL. serve with such a summons. **4** card or piece of paper attached to something to show its price, etc. **5** put a ticket on; mark with a ticket: *All articles in the store are ticketed with the price.* **6** the list of candidates to be voted on that belong to one political party. 1,2,4,6 *n.,* 3,5 *v.* —**tick′et less,** *adj.*

tick ing (tik′ing), a strong cotton or linen cloth, used to cover mattresses and pillows and to make tents and awnings. *n.*

tick le (tik′əl), **1** touch lightly, causing little thrills, shivers, or wriggles: *He tickled the baby's feet and made her laugh.* **2** have a feeling like this; cause to have such a feeling: *My nose tickles.* **3** a tingling or itching feeling. **4** excite pleasantly; amuse: *The story tickled me. The child was tickled with her new toys.* **5** a tickling. 1,2,4 *v.,* **tickled, tick ling;** 3,5 *n.*

tick ler (tik′lər), person or thing that tickles, especially a small feather brush used to tickle the faces of others at a carnival, party, etc. *n.*

tick lish (tik′lish), **1** sensitive to tickling: *The bottoms of the feet are ticklish.* **2** requiring careful handling; delicate; risky: *Telling your friends their faults is a ticklish business.* **3** easily upset; unstable: *A canoe is a ticklish craft.* **4** easily offended: *be ticklish about one's weight. adj.* —**tick′lish ly,** *adv.* —**tick′lish ness,** *n.*

O	O	O
O	X	
	X	X

tick-tack-toe

tick-tack-toe (tik′tak tō′), game in which two players alternately put circles or crosses in a figure of nine squares. The object is to be the first to fill three squares in a row with your mark. *n.*

Ti con de ro ga (tī′kon də rō′gə), village and old fort on Lake Champlain, in NE New York State. *n.*

tid al (tī′dl), of tides; having tides; caused by tides. A tidal river is affected by the ocean's tide. *adj.* —**tid′al ly,** *adv.*

tidal wave, 1 a large wave or sudden increase in the level of water along a shore, caused by unusually strong winds. **2** an enormous, destructive ocean wave which is caused by an underwater earthquake. **3** any great movement or manifestation of feeling, opinion, or the like: *a tidal wave of popular indignation.*

tid bit (tid′bit′), a very pleasing bit of food, news, etc. *n.* Also, **titbit.**

tid dly winks (tid′lē wingks′), game in which the players try to make small colored disks jump from a flat surface into a cup by pressing on their edges with larger disks. *n.*

tide (tīd), **1** the rise and fall of the ocean about every twelve hours, caused by the pull of the moon and the sun: *We go swimming at high tide; at low tide we dig clams.* **2** anything that rises and falls like the tide: *the tide of public opinion.* **3 tide over,** help along for a time: *Her*

savings will tide her over her illness. 1,2 *n.,* 3 *v.,* **tid ed, tid ing.** [*Tide* comes from Old English *tīd,* originally meaning "time."] —**tide′less,** *adj.* —**tide′like′,** *adj.*

turn the tide, change from one condition to the opposite: *A touchdown in the final minute of play turned the tide against us.*

tide land (tīd′land′), land flooded at high tide. *n.*

tide wa ter (tīd′wô′tər *or* tīd′wot′ər), **1** water in rivers, streams, etc., affected by the rise and fall of the tides. **2** low-lying land along a seacoast through which such water flows. **3** of or along tidewater. Tidewater country is land along the seacoast. 1,2 *n.,* 3 *adj.*

ti di ly (tī′dl ē), in a tidy manner; neatly. *adv.*

ti di ness (tī′dē nis), neatness. *n.*

ti dings (tī′dingz), news; information: *joyful tidings. n.pl.*

ti dy (tī′dē), **1** neat and in order: *a tidy room.* **2** put in order; make neat: *I tidied the room. Be sure to tidy up before going out.* **3** INFORMAL. fairly large; considerable: *a tidy sum of money.* 1,3 *adj.,* **ti di er, ti di est;** 2 *v.,* **ti died, ti dy ing.**

tie (tī), **1** fasten with string or the like; bind: *Please tie this package.* **2** arrange to form a bow or knot: *We tied blue and white ribbons on the party favors.* **3** fasten; form a bow: *That ribbon doesn't tie well.* **4** tighten and fasten the string or strings of: *tie one's shoes.* **5** anything connecting or holding together two or more things or parts; link. **6** cord, chain, etc., used for tying. **7** necktie. **8** fasten, join, or connect in any way; make a bond or connection. **9** anything that unites; bond; obligation: *family ties, ties of friendship.* **10** restrain; restrict; limit: *be tied to a steady job.* **11** a heavy piece of timber or iron placed crosswise to form a foundation or support. The rails of a railroad track are fastened to ties about a foot apart. **12** a connecting beam, rod, or the like. **13** equality in points, votes, etc.: *The game ended in a tie, 3 to 3.* **14** a match or contest in which this occurs. **15** make the same score; be equal in points: *The two teams tied.* **16** (in music) a curved line set above or below two notes of the same pitch, indicating that they are to be played or sung as one sustained tone. 1-4,8,10,15 *v.,* **tied, ty ing;** 5-7,9,11-14,16 *n.*

tie down, limit; confine; restrict: *I feel tied down by all these responsibilities.*

tie in, make or have a connection; relate: *How does that statement tie in with what you said yesterday?*

tie up, 1 tie firmly or tightly. **2** wrap up. **3** hinder; stop: *The stalled truck tied up traffic for half an hour.* **4** invest (money) or place (property) in such a way as to make it unavailable for other uses: *All our money was tied up in stocks, so we couldn't buy property.* **5** have one's program

tide (def. 1)
top, a ship at
high tide;
bottom, the same
ship at low tide

full; be very busy, etc.: *I can't go tomorrow; I'm all tied up.*

tie-dye (tī′dī′), dye (cloth) by tying some of the material in knots to prevent the cloth inside from absorbing the dye. *v.,* **tie-dyed, tie-dy ing.**

Tien tsin (tin′tsin′), port city in NE China, near Peking. *n.*

tier (tir), one of a series of rows arranged one above another: *tiers of seats in a football stadium. n.*

Tier ra del Fue go (tyer′ə del fwä′gō), group of islands at the S end of South America. Part belongs to Argentina, part to Chile. See **Patagonia** for map.

tie-up (tī′up′), **1** a stopping of work or action on account of a strike, storm, accident, etc.: *The heavy snowstorm caused a tie-up of traffic.* **2** connection; relation. *n.*

tiff (tif), a little quarrel. *n.*

ti ger (tī′gər), a large, fierce, flesh-eating mammal of Asia, that has dull-yellow fur striped with black. It is related to the cat and the lion. *n.* **—ti′ger like′,** *adj.*

ti ger ish (tī′gər ish), like a tiger; fierce; cruel. *adj.* **—ti′ger ish ly,** *adv.* **—ti′ger ish ness,** *n.*

tiger lily, lily that has dull-orange flowers spotted with black.

tiger moth, moth having spotted or striped wings.

tight (tīt), **1** packed or put together firmly; held firmly; firm: *a tight knot.* **2** closely; securely; firmly: *The rope was tied too tight.* **3** drawn; stretched: *a tight canvas.* **4** close; fitting closely or too closely: *tight clothing.* **5** not letting water, air, or gas in or out: *The tight roof kept rain from leaking in.* **6** hard to deal with or manage; difficult: *A lie got her into a tight spot.* **7** INFORMAL. almost even; close: *It was a tight race.* **8** hard to get; scarce: *Money is tight just now.* **9** strict; severe: *to rule with a tight hand.* **10** INFORMAL. stingy: *They are tight with their money.* 1,3-10 *adj.,* 2 *adv.* [*Tight* came into English about 600 years ago, probably from Icelandic *thēttr,* meaning "watertight."] **—tight′ly,** *adv.* **—tight′ness,** *n.*

sit tight, keep the same position, opinion, etc.

tight en (tīt′n), make or become tight: *He tightened his belt. The rope tightened as I pulled it. v.* **—tight′en er,** *n.*

tight fist ed (tīt′fis′tid), stingy. *adj.*

tight-lipped (tīt′lipt′), **1** keeping the lips firmly together. **2** saying little or nothing. *adj.*

tight rope (tīt′rōp′), rope stretched tight on which acrobats perform. *n.*

tights (tīts), a close-fitting garment, usually covering the lower part of the body and the legs, worn by acrobats, dancers, etc. *n.pl.*

tight wad (tīt′wod′), SLANG. a stingy person. *n.*

ti gress (tī′gris), a female tiger. *n., pl.* **ti gress es.**

Ti gris (tī′gris), river flowing from SE Turkey through Iraq, where it joins the Euphrates River and empties into the Persian Gulf. See **Euphrates** for map. *n.*

tike (tīk), tyke. *n.*

til de (til′də), a diacritical mark (˜) to indicate a special sound. It is used over *n* in Spanish when it is pronounced *ny,* as in *cañón* (kä nyōn′). It is used over certain vowels in Portuguese to indicate that they are nasal, as in *São Paulo* (soun pou′lú). *n.*

tile (tīl), **1** a thin piece of baked clay, stone, plastic, etc. Tiles are used for covering roofs, paving floors, and ornamenting. **2** a baked clay pipe for draining land. **3** put tiles on or in: *to tile a bathroom floor.* 1,2 *n.,* 3 *v.,* **tiled, til ing. —til′er,** *n.* **—tile′like′,** *adj.*

til ing (tī′ling), **1** tiles collectively. **2** the work of covering with tiles. **3** anything consisting of tiles. *n.*

till¹ (til), **1** up to the time of; until: *The child played till eight.* **2** up to the time when; until: *Walk till you come to a white house.* 1 *prep.,* 2 *conj.*

till² (til), cultivate (land); plow: *Farmers till the land. v.*

till³ (til), a small drawer for money under or behind a counter. *n.*

till age (til′ij), **1** cultivation of land. **2** tilled land. *n.*

till er¹ (til′ər), bar or handle used to turn the rudder in steering a boat. *n.*

till er² (til′ər), person who tills land; farmer. *n.*

tilt (tilt), **1** tip or cause to tip; slope; slant; lean: *You tilt your head forward when you bow. This table tilts.* **2** a slope; sloping position; a slant: *This table is on a tilt.* **3** rush, charge, or fight with lances. Knights used to tilt on horseback. **4** a fight on horseback with lances. **5** any dispute or quarrel. 1,3 *v.,* 2,4,5 *n.* **—tilt′a ble,** *adj.*

full tilt, at full speed; with full force: *The car ran full tilt against the tree.*

tilth (tilth), **1** cultivation of land. **2** tilled land. *n.*

tim ber (tim′bər), **1** wood used for building and making things. Houses, ships, and furniture are made from timber. **2** a large piece of wood used in building. Beams and rafters are timbers. **3** growing trees, especially when used to provide wood for building. **4** cover, support, or furnish with timber. 1-3 *n.,* 4 *v.*

tim bered (tim′bərd), **1** made or furnished with timber. **2** covered with growing trees. *adj.*

tim ber land (tim′bər land′), land with trees that are, or will be, useful for timber. *n.*

tim ber line (tim′bər līn′), line on mountains and in polar regions beyond which trees will not grow because of the cold. *n.*

timber wolf
about 3 ft. (1 m.)
high at the shoulder

timber wolf, a large gray, black, or white wolf of northwestern North America.

tim bre (tim′bər), the quality in sounds, regardless of their pitch and volume, by which a certain voice, instrument, etc., can be distinguished from others. Because of differences in timbre, identical notes played on a violin, an oboe, and a trumpet can be distinguished from one another. *n.*

tim brel (tim′brəl), tambourine. *n.*

time (tīm), **1** all the days there have been or ever will be; the past, present, and future. Time is measured in years, months, weeks, days, hours, minutes, and seconds. **2** a part of the past, present, or future: *A minute is a short time.* **3** period of time; epoch: *the time of the Stuarts in England.* **4** a long time: *What a time it took you!* **5** some point in time; a particular point in time: *What time is it? The time the game begins is 2 p.m.* **6** the right part or point of time: *It is time to eat.* **7** occasion: *This time we will succeed.* **8** way of reckoning time: *solar time.* **9** condition of life: *War brings hard times.* **10** an experience during a certain time: *He had a good time at the party.* **11** rate of movement in music or poetry; rhythm: *waltz time, to beat time.* **12** amount of time that one has worked or should work: *Her normal time is 8 hours a day.* **13** the pay for a period of work. **14** leisure: *have time to read.* **15** measure the time of: *time a race.* **16** do at regular times; do in rhythm with; set the time of: *The dancers timed their steps to the music.* **17** choose the moment or occasion for: *He timed his request for a raise so as to catch his boss in a good mood.* **18** of time. **19** provided with a clocklike mechanism so that it will explode or ignite at a given moment: *a time bomb.* **20 times,** *pl.* multiplied by. The sign for this in arithmetic is ×. *Four times three is twelve. Twenty is five times as much as four.* 1-14,20 *n.,* 15-17 *v.,* **timed, tim ing;** 18,19 *adj.*

against time, trying to finish before a certain time: *They were in a race against time in their rescue efforts.*

at the same time, however; nevertheless.

at times, now and then; once in a while.

behind the times, old-fashioned; out-of-date.

bide one's time, wait for a good chance.

for the time being, for the present; for now: *The baby is asleep for the time being.*

from time to time, now and then; once in a while: *From time to time we visit my grandparents.*

in good time, at the right time.

in no time, shortly; before long: *We hurried and arrived home in no time.*

in time, 1 after a while. **2** soon enough: *Will she arrive in time to have dinner with us?* **3** in the right rate of movement in music, dancing, marching, etc.

keep time, 1 (of a watch or clock) go correctly. **2** to measure or record time, rate of speed, etc.: *I kept time at the race with a stopwatch.* **3** to sound or move at the right rate: *The marchers kept time to the music.*

make time, go with speed.

mark time, 1 move the feet as in marching, but without advancing. **2** suspend progress temporarily. **3** go through motions without accomplishing anything.

on time, 1 at the right time; not late; punctual. **2** with time in which to pay; on credit: *She bought a car on time.*

tell time, know what time it is by the clock.

time after time or **time and again,** again and again.

time exposure, 1 exposure of a photographic film for a certain time, longer than a half second. **2** photograph taken in this way.

time-hon ored (tīm′on′ərd), honored because old and established: *Shaking hands is a time-honored custom. adj.*

time keep er (tīm′kē′pər), person or thing that keeps time: *My watch is an excellent timekeeper. n.*

time less (tīm′lis), **1** never ending; eternal. **2** referring to no special time. *adj.* —**time′less ness,** *n.*

time line, a chart consisting of a printed line representing a certain length of time and subdivided into smaller time units, along which historical events are listed in order at the point they occurred. A time line may be either horizontal or vertical.

time li ness (tīm′lē nis), condition of being timely. *n.*

time ly (tīm′lē), at the right time: *The timely arrival of the doctor saved my life. adj.,* **time li er, time li est.**

time piece (tīm′pēs′), clock or watch. *n.*

tim er (tī′mər), **1** device for indicating or recording intervals of time, such as a stopwatch. **2** a clockwork device for indicating when a certain period of time has elapsed: *Many stoves have timers for baking.* **3** any device that au-

tomatically turns something on or off at a preset time. Timers can operate many electrical devices. *n.*

time-shar ing (tīm′shar′ing *or* tīm′sher′ing), system in which a large computer is used by many people, for many jobs, at the same time. The computer shifts back and forth between the different jobs so quickly that it seems to be doing them all at once. *n.*

time ta ble (tīm′tā′bəl), schedule showing the times when trains, buses, airplanes, etc., arrive and depart. *n.*

time worn (tīm′wôrn′), worn by long existence or use. *adj.*

time zone, a geographical region within which the same standard time is used. The world is divided into 24 time zones, beginning and ending at the International Date Line.

tim id (tim′id), easily frightened; shy: *The timid child was afraid of the dark. adj.* —**tim′id ly,** *adv.* —**tim′id ness,** *n.*

ti mid i ty (tə mid′ə tē), a being timid; shyness. *n.*

tim ing (tī′ming), **1** arrangement or regulation of the time or speed of anything to get the greater effect: *the timing of a stroke in tennis, the timing of an actor in responding to a cue, the timing of the release of a new play.* **2** measurement of time: *the timing of a runner. n.*

tim or ous (tim′ər əs), easily frightened; timid: *The timorous rabbit ran away. adj.* —**tim′or ous ly,** *adv.*

timothy

tim o thy (tim′ə thē), kind of coarse grass with long, cylindrical spikes, often grown for hay. *n.* [*Timothy* was named for *Timothy* Hanson, an American farmer who cultivated this grass around 1720.]

Tim o thy (tim′ə thē), **1** a disciple of the apostle Paul. **2** either of the two books of the New Testament written as letters by Paul to Timothy. *n.*

tim pa ni (tim′pə nē), kettledrums. *n.pl.*

tim pa nist (tim′pə nist), person who plays the kettledrums. *n.*

tin (tin), **1** a soft, silver-white metallic element used in plating metals to prevent corrosion and in making alloys such as bronze and pewter. **2** made of tin or tin plate. **3** cover with tin. **4** any can, box, pan, or other container made of or lined with tin; tinware: *a pie tin.* 1,4 *n.,* 2 *adj.,* 3 *v.,* **tinned, tin ning.** [*Tin* comes from Old English *tin.*] —**tin′like′,** *adj.*

tinc ture (tingk′chər), **1** solution of medicine in alcohol: *tincture of iodine.* **2** trace; tinge: *a tincture of amusement in someone's eyes, a tincture of pink in the sky.* **3** give a trace or tinge to: *Everything she says is tinctured with conceit.* 1,2 *n.,* 3 *v.,* **tinc tured, tinc tur ing.**

tin der (tin′dər), **1** anything that catches fire easily. **2** material used to catch fire from a spark. *n.*

tin der box (tin′dər boks′), **1** box for holding tinder, flint, and steel for making a fire. **2** a very flammable thing. *n.,* *pl.* **tin der box es.**

tine (tīn), a sharp projecting point or prong: *the tines of a fork. n.*

tin foil (tin′foil′), a very thin sheet of aluminum, tin, or tin and lead, used as a wrapping for candy, tobacco, etc. *n.*

ting (ting), **1** make or cause to make a clear, ringing sound. **2** such a sound. 1 *v.*, 2 *n.*

tinge (tinj), **1** color slightly: *The dawn sky was tinged with pink.* **2** a slight coloring or tint: *There is a tinge of red in those leaves.* **3** add a trace of some quality to; change slightly: *Sad memories tinged his present joy.* **4** a very small amount; trace: *She likes just a tinge of lemon in her tea.* 1,3 *v.*, **tinged, tinge ing** or **ting ing**; 2,4 *n.*

tin gle (ting′gəl), **1** have or cause a feeling of thrills or a pricking, stinging feeling: *to tingle with excitement.* **2** a pricking, stinging feeling: *The cold caused a tingle in my fingers.* 1 *v.*, **tin gled, tin gling**; 2 *n.* —**tin′gling ly,** *adv.*

tink er (ting′kər), **1** person who mends pots, pans, etc. **2** to mend; patch. **3** work or repair in an unskilled or clumsy way: *The children were tinkering with the clock and broke it.* **4** work or keep busy in a rather useless way: *I was tinkering in my workshop.* 1 *n.*, 2-4 *v.* —**tink′er er,** *n.*

tin kle (ting′kəl), **1** make short, light, ringing sounds: *Little bells tinkle.* **2** cause to tinkle. **3** series of short, light, ringing sounds: *the tinkle of sleigh bells.* 1,2 *v.*, **tin kled, tin kling**; 3 *n.* —**tin′kling ly,** *adv.*

tin kly (ting′klē), full of tinkles; marked by tinkling. *adj.*, **tin kli er, tin kli est.**

tin ny (tin′ē), **1** of tin; containing tin. **2** like tin in looks, sound, or taste: *These sardines have a tinny flavor. adj.*, **tin ni er, tin ni est.** —**tin′ni ly,** *adv.* —**tin′ni ness,** *n.*

tin sel (tin′səl), **1** very thin sheets, strips, or threads of glittering metal or plastic used to trim Christmas trees, costumes, etc. **2** anything showy but having little value. **3** of or like tinsel; showy but not worth much. **4** trim with tinsel. 1,2 *n.*, 3 *adj.*, 4 *v.*, **tin seled, tin sel ing** or **tin selled, tin sel ling.** [*Tinsel* came into English about 400 years ago from French *estincelle,* meaning "spark."]

tin smith (tin′smith′), person who works with tin; maker of tinware. *n.*

tint (tint), **1** variety of a color: *The picture was painted in several tints of blue.* **2** a delicate or pale color. **3** put a tint on; color slightly: *The walls were tinted gray.* 1,2 *n.*, 3 *v.* —**tint′er,** *n.*

Tin to ret to (tin′tə ret′ō), 1518-1594, Venetian painter. *n.*

tin type (tin′tīp′), photograph taken on a sheet of enameled tin or iron. *n.*

tin ware (tin′wer′ or tin′war′), articles made of tin or tin plate. *n.*

ti ny (tī′nē), very small; wee: *a tiny baby. adj.*, **ti ni er, ti ni est.** —**ti′ni ly,** *adv.* —**ti′ni ness,** *n.*

-tion, suffix added to verbs to form nouns. **1** act or process of ____ing: *Addition = act or process of adding.* **2** condition of being ____ed: *Exhaustion = condition of being exhausted.* **3** result of ____ing: *Reflection = result of reflecting.*

tip¹ (tip), **1** the end part; end; point: *the tips of the fingers.* **2** a small piece put on the end of something: *Buy rubber tips to put on the legs of a stool.* **3** put a tip on; furnish with a tip: *spears tipped with steel.* **4** cover or adorn at the tip: *The mountains were tipped with snow.* 1,2 *n.*, 3,4 *v.*, **tipped, tip ping.** —**tip′less,** *adj.*

tip² (tip), **1** slope; slant: *She tipped the table toward her.* **2** a slope; slant: *There is such a tip to that table that everything slips off it.* **3** upset; overturn: *He tipped over his glass of water.* **4** take off (a hat) in greeting: *The old gentleman tipped his hat to a neighbor.* **5** empty out; dump: *She tipped the money in her purse onto the table.* 1,3-5 *v.*, **tipped, tip ping**; 2 *n.* —**tip′pa ble,** *adj.*

tip³ (tip), **1** a small present of money in return for service: *She gave the waiter a tip.* **2** give a small present of

money to: *Did you tip the porter?* **3** piece of secret information: *He had a tip that the black horse would win the race.* **4** a useful hint, suggestion, etc.: *Someone gave me a helpful tip about pitching a tent where the trees would shade it.* **5** hit lightly and sharply; tap. **6** a light, sharp blow; tap. 1,3,4,6 *n.*, 2,5 *v.*, **tipped, tip ping.** —**tip′less,** *adj.* —**tip′pa ble,** *adj.*

tip off, INFORMAL. **1** give secret information to: *They tipped me off about a good bargain.* **2** warn: *Someone tipped off the criminals and they escaped.*

tip-off (tip′ôf′), INFORMAL. **1** piece of secret information. **2** a warning. *n.*

tip per (tip′ər), person who gives a tip or tips. *n.*

tip pet (tip′it), **1** scarf for the neck and shoulders with ends hanging down in front. **2** a long, narrow, hanging part of a hood, sleeve, or scarf. *n.*

tip ple (tip′əl), drink (alcoholic liquor) often. *v.*, **tip pled, tip pling.**

tip pler (tip′lər), a habitual drinker of alcoholic liquor. *n.*

tip si ly (tip′sə lē), in a tipsy manner. *adv.*

tip si ness (tip′sē nis), tipsy condition. *n.*

tip sy (tip′sē), **1** tipping easily; unsteady; tilted. **2** somewhat intoxicated but not thoroughly drunk. *adj.*, **tip si er, tip si est.**

tip toe (tip′tō′), **1** the tips of the toes. **2** walk on one's toes, without using the heels: *She tiptoed quietly up the stairs.* 1 *n.*, 2 *v.*, **tip toed, tip toe ing.**

tip top (tip′top′), **1** the very top; highest point. **2** at the very top or highest point. **3** INFORMAL. first-rate; excellent. 1 *n.*, 2,3 *adj.*

ti rade (tī′rād), **1** a long, vehement speech. **2** a long, scolding speech. *n.* [*Tirade* was borrowed from French *tirade,* which came from Italian *tirata,* meaning "volley."]

Ti ra na (ti rä′nə), capital of Albania, in the central part. *n.*

tire¹ (tīr), **1** to lower or use up the strength of; make weary: *The work tired him.* **2** become weary: *An elderly person may tire easily.* **3** wear down the patience, interest, or appreciation of because of dullness, excess, etc.: *Monotonous filing tired the office worker. v.*, **tired, tir ing.** [*Tire¹* comes from Old English *tēorian.*]

tire² (tīr), a band of rubber around a wheel. Some tires have inner tubes for holding air; others hold the air in the tire itself or are made of solid rubber. *n.* [*Tire²* is apparently short for *attire,* meaning "a covering," which can be traced back to French *a-,* meaning "to," and *tire,* meaning "row, order."]

tired (tīrd), weary; fatigued; exhausted: *I am tired, but I must get back to work. adj.* —**tired′ly,** *adv.* —**tired′ness,** *n.*

tire less (tīr′lis), **1** never becoming tired; requiring little rest: *a tireless worker.* **2** never stopping: *tireless efforts. adj.* —**tire′less ly,** *adv.* —**tire′less ness,** *n.*

tire some (tīr′səm), not interesting; tiring; boring: *a tiresome speech. adj.* —**tire′some ly,** *adv.* —**tire′some ness,** *n.*

Ti rol (tə rōl′ or tī′rōl), region in the Alps, partly in Austria and partly in Italy. *n.* Also, **Tyrol.**

'tis (tiz), it is.

tis sue (tish′ü), **1** substance forming the parts of animals and plants. **2** mass of similar cells which performs a particular function: *brain tissue, muscular tissue, skin* *tissue.* **3** a thin, light cloth: *Her gown was of silk tissue.* **4** web; network: *The whole story was a tissue of lies.* **5** tissue paper. **6** a thin, soft paper that absorbs moisture easily. Tissue is used to wipe the face or the nose. *n.*

tissue paper, a very thin, soft paper, used for wrapping, covering things, making carbon copies of letters, etc.

tit[1] (tit), **1** titmouse. **2** any of certain other small birds. *n.*

tit[2] (tit), nipple; teat. *n.*

tit., title.

Ti tan (tīt′n), **1** (in Greek myths) one of a family of giants who ruled the world before the gods of Mount Olympus. Prometheus and Atlas were Titans. **2** Also, **titan.** person or thing having enormous size, strength, power, etc.; giant. *n.*

ti tan ic (tī tan′ik), having great size, strength, or power; gigantic; huge: *titanic energy. adj.* —**ti tan′i cal ly,** *adv.*

ti ta ni um (tī tā′nē əm), a strong, lightweight, silver-gray metallic element occurring in various minerals. It is highly resistant to corrosion and is used in making steel and other alloys for missiles, jet engines, etc. *n.*

tit bit (tit′bit′), tidbit. *n.*

tit for tat, blow for blow; like for like.

tithe (tīᴛʜ), **1** one tenth. **2** one tenth of one's yearly income, paid for the support of the church. **3** make or pledge such a payment. 1,2 *n.,* 3 *v.,* **tithed, tith ing.** —**tithe′less,** *adj.* —**tith′er,** *n.*

Ti tian (tish′ən), 1477?-1576, Venetian painter. *n.*

tit il late (tit′l āt), **1** excite pleasantly; stimulate agreeably. **2** tickle. *v.,* **tit il lat ed, tit il lat ing.** —**tit′il lat′ing ly,** *adv.*

tit il la tion (tit′l ā′shən), **1** pleasant excitement; agreeable stimulation. **2** a tickling. *n.*

ti tle (tī′tl), **1** the name of a book, poem, picture, song, etc. **2** name showing rank, occupation, or condition in life. King, duke, lord, countess, captain, doctor, professor, Madame, and Miss are titles. **3** call by a title; name. **4** a first-place position; championship: *the tennis title.* **5** a legal right to the possession of property. **6** evidence, especially a document, showing such a right. When a house is sold, the seller gives title to the buyer. **7** a recognized right; claim: *What title does he have to my gratitude?* 1,2,4-7 *n.,* 3 *v.,* **ti tled, ti tling.**

ti tled (tī′tld), having a title: *a titled noble. adj.*

title page, page at the beginning of a book that contains the title, the name of the author and publisher, etc.

tit mouse (tit′mous′), a small bird with a short bill and dull-colored feathers. *n., pl.* **tit mice** (tit′mīs′).

Ti to (tē′tō), **Marshal,** 1892-1980, Yugoslav political leader, president of Yugoslavia from 1953 to 1980. *n.*

tit ter (tit′ər), **1** laugh in a half-restrained manner; giggle. **2** a tittering laugh. 1 *v.,* 2 *n.* —**tit′ter er,** *n.* —**tit′ter ing ly,** *adv.*

tit tle (tit′l), **1** a very little bit; particle; whit. **2** a small stroke or mark over a letter in writing or printing. The dot over an *i* is a tittle. *n.*

tit tle-tat tle (tit′l tat′l), gossip. *n., v.,* **tit tle-tat tled, tit-tle-tat tling.**

tit u lar (tich′ə lər), **1** in title or name only: *He is a titular prince without any power.* **2** of or having a title. *adj.* —**tit′-u lar ly,** *adv.*

tiz zy (tiz′ē), SLANG. a very excited, confused state. *n., pl.* **tiz zies.**

Tl, symbol for thallium.

Tm, symbol for thulium.

tn., ton.

TN, Tennessee (used with postal Zip Code).

TNT or **T.N.T.,** a pale yellow solid used as an explosive; trinitrotoluene.

to (tü; *unstressed* tù *or* tə), **1** in the direction of: *Go to the right.* **2** as far as; until: *rotten to the core, faithful to the end.* **3** for the purpose of; for: *She came to the rescue.* **4** so as to produce, cause, or result in: *To their horror, the beast approached.* **5** into: *She tore the letter to pieces.* **6** along with; with: *We danced to the music.* **7** compared with: *The score was 9 to 5.* **8** in agreement or accordance with: *It is not to my liking.* **9** belonging with; of: *the key to my room.* **10** on; against: *Fasten it to the wall.* **11** about; concerning: *What did he say to that?* **12** in: *four apples to the pound.* **13** *To* is used to show action toward. *Give the book to me. Speak to her.* **14** *To* is used with the infinitive form of verbs. *I like to read. The birds began to sing. "To err is human; to forgive, divine."* **15** forward: *He wore his cap wrong side to.* **16** together; touching; closed: *The door slammed to.* **17** to action or work: *After church we set to.* 1-14 *prep.,* 15-17 *adv.*

to and fro, first one way and then back again; back and forth.

toad
up to 5¹/₂ in. (14 cm.) long

toad (tōd), a small, tailless amphibian somewhat like a frog, living most of the time on land rather than in water. Toads have a rough, brown skin that suggests a lump of earth. *n.* —**toad′less,** *adj.* —**toad′like′,** *adj.*

toad stool (tōd′stül′), mushroom, especially a poisonous mushroom. *n.*

toadstools

toad y (tō′dē), **1** a fawning flatterer. **2** fawn upon; flatter. 1 *n., pl.* **toad ies;** 2 *v.,* **toad ied, toad y ing.**

toast[1] (tōst), **1** slices of bread browned by heat. **2** brown by heat: *We toasted the bread.* **3** heat thoroughly: *He toasted his feet by the fire.* 1 *n.,* 2,3 *v.*

toast[2] (tōst), **1** wish good fortune to before drinking; drink to the health of: *We first toasted our hosts.* **2** act of drinking to the health of a person or thing. **3** person or thing whose health is proposed and drunk: *"The Queen" was the first toast drunk by the officers.* **4** a popular or celebrated person: *the toast of the town.* 1 *v.,* 2-4 *n.*

toast er (tō′stər), an electric appliance for toasting bread. *n.*

toast mas ter (tōst′mas′tər), person who presides at a dinner and introduces the speakers. *n.*

to bac co (tə bak′ō), the prepared leaves of certain related plants, used for smoking or chewing or as snuff. *n., pl.* **to bac cos** or **to bac coes.** [*Tobacco* is from Spanish *tabaco,* which came from a Carib word. Carib is a language spoken in the Caribbean region.]

to bac co nist (tə bak′ə nist), dealer in tobacco. *n.*

To ba go (tə bā′gō), island in the West Indies, near Venezuela, part of the country of Trinidad and Tobago. *n.*

to bog gan (tə bog′ən), 1 a long, narrow, flat sled with its front end curved upward and without runners. 2 slide downhill on such a sled. 1 *n.*, 2 *v.* [*Toboggan* comes from French Canadian *tabagane*, which is of Algonquian origin.] —**to bog′gan er**, *n.*

toc sin (tok′sən), 1 alarm sounded on a bell; warning signal. 2 bell used to sound an alarm. *n.*

to day or **to-day** (tə dā′), 1 this day; the present time: *Today is Wednesday.* 2 on or during this day: *What are you doing today?* 3 at the present time; now: *Pollution is a major problem today.* 1 *n.*, 2,3 *adv.*

tod dle (tod′l), walk with short, unsteady steps, as a baby does. *v.*, **tod dled, tod dling.**

tod dler (tod′lər), child just learning to walk. *n.*

tod dy (tod′ē), drink made of whisky, brandy, etc., with hot water and sugar. *n.*, *pl.* **tod dies.** [*Toddy* comes from Hindustani *tāṛī*.]

to-do (tə dü′), INFORMAL. fuss; bustle: *to make a great to-do over nothing. n., pl.* **to-dos.**

toe (tō), 1 one of the five divisions that end the foot. 2 the part of a stocking, shoe, etc., that covers the toes: *have a hole in the toe of a sock.* 3 the forepart of a foot or hoof. 4 anything like a toe: *the toe and heel of a golf club.* 5 touch or reach with the toes: *toe a line.* 1-4 *n.*, 5 *v.*, **toed, toe ing.** —**toe′less**, *adj.* —**toe′like′**, *adj.*

on one's toes, ready for action; alert.

toe nail (tō′nāl′), the nail growing on a toe. *n.*

tof fee (tô′fē), taffy. *n.*

tof fy (tô′fē), toffee. *n., pl.* **tof fies.**

tog (tog), INFORMAL. 1 **togs,** *pl.* clothes. 2 to clothe; dress. 1 *n.*, 2 *v.*, **togged, tog ging.**

toga

to ga (tō′gə), a loose, outer garment worn in public by citizens of ancient Rome. *n., pl.* **to gas.**

to geth er (tə geṬH′ər), 1 with each other; in company: *They were standing together.* 2 with united action; in cooperation: *to work together for peace.* 3 into one gathering, company, mass, or body: *The principal called the school together.* 4 at the same time: *You cannot have day and night together.* 5 without a stop or break; continuously: *He worked for days together. adv.*

to geth er ness (tə geṬH′ər nis), condition of being close together, especially in family or social activities. *n.*

tog gle (tog′əl), 1 pin, bolt, or rod put through a loop in a rope or a link of a chain to keep it in place, to hold two ropes together, to serve as a hold for the fingers, etc. 2 furnish with a toggle; fasten with a toggle. 1 *n.*, 2 *v.*, **tog gled, tog gling.** —**tog′gler**, *n.*

To go (tō′gō), country in W Africa. *Capital:* Lomé. See **Nigeria** for map. *n.*

toil[1] (toil), 1 hard work; labor: *to succeed after years of*

toil. 2 work hard: *to toil with one's hands for a living.* 3 move with difficulty, pain, or weariness: *Carrying heavy loads, they toiled up the mountain.* 1 *n.*, 2,3 *v.* [*Toil*[1] came into English about 700 years ago from French *toeillier*, meaning "drag about," which came from Latin *tudiculare*, meaning "stir up."] —**toil′er**, *n.*

toil[2] (toil). Often, **toils,** *pl.* net or snare: *The thief was caught in the toils of the law. n.* [*Toil*[2] came into English about 400 years ago from French *toile*, which came from Latin *tela*, meaning "web."]

toi let (toi′lit), 1 bathroom or lavatory. 2 a porcelain bowl with a seat attached and with a drain at the bottom connected to a water tank to flush the bowl clean. Waste matter from the body is disposed of in a toilet. 3 process of dressing. Bathing, combing the hair, and putting on one's clothes are all part of one's toilet. *I made a hurried toilet.* 4 of or for the toilet. Combs and brushes are toilet articles. 1-3 *n.*, 4 *adj.*

toi let ry (toi′lə trē), soap, face powder, perfumery, or other articles for the toilet. *n., pl.* **toi let ries.**

toilet water, a fragrant liquid not so strong as perfume, used after bathing, as a cologne in grooming, etc.

toil some (toil′səm), requiring hard work; laborious; wearisome: *a long, toilsome climb up the mountain. adj.*

to ken (tō′kən), 1 a mark or sign (of something): *His actions are a token of his sincerity.* 2 sign of friendship; keepsake: *She received many birthday tokens.* 3 piece of metal stamped for a higher value than the metal is worth and used for some special purpose, such as bus or subway fare. 4 piece of metal, plastic, etc., indicating a right or privilege: *This token will admit you to the swimming pool.* 5 having only the appearance of; serving as a symbol; nominal; partial: *a token payment, token resistance.* 1-4 *n.*, 5 *adj.*

by the same token, for the same reason; in the same way; moreover.

To ky o or **To ki o** (tō′kē ō), capital of Japan, in the central part. Tokyo is one of the largest cities in the world. *n.*

told (tōld), past tense and past participle of **tell.** *You told me that last week. We were told to wait. v.*

To le do (tə lē′dō), 1 city in NW Ohio. 2 city in central Spain. *n.*

tol er a ble (tol′ər ə bəl), 1 able to be borne or endured; bearable: *The pain has become tolerable.* 2 fairly good: *She is in tolerable health. adj.* —**tol′er a ble ness**, *n.*

tol er a bly (tol′ər ə blē), 1 in a tolerable manner. 2 moderately. *adv.*

tol er ance (tol′ər əns), 1 a willingness to be tolerant; a putting up with people whose opinions or ways differ from one's own. 2 the power of enduring or resisting the action of a drug, poison, etc. 3 action of allowing or permitting: *The principal's tolerance of their bad behavior surprised us. n.*

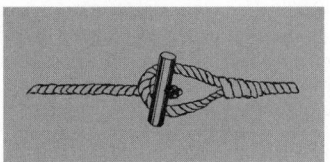

toggle (def. 1)

tol er ant (tol′ər ənt), **1** willing to let other people do as they think best; willing to endure beliefs and actions of which one does not approve: *to be tolerant toward all religious beliefs.* **2** able to endure or resist the action of a drug, poison, etc. *adj.* —**tol′er ant ly,** *adv.*

tol e rate (tol′ə rāt′), **1** allow or permit: *The teacher won't tolerate any disorder.* **2** bear; endure; put up with: *I cannot tolerate loud noises.* **3** endure or resist the action of (a drug, poison, etc.). *v.,* **tol e rat ed, tol e rat ing.** —**tol′e ra′tor,** *n.*

tol e ra tion (tol′ə rā′shən), **1** willingness to put up with beliefs and actions of which one does not approve: *Toleration of dishonest officials encourages corruption.* **2** recognition of the right to worship as one thinks best without loss of civil rights or social privileges; freedom of worship. *n.*

toll[1] (tōl), **1** to sound with single strokes slowly and regularly repeated: *The church bells tolled the President's death.* **2** stroke or sound of a bell being tolled. **3** act or fact of tolling. **4** call, announce, etc., by tolling. 1,4 *v.,* 2,3 *n.*

toll[2] (tōl), **1** tax or fee paid for some right or privilege: *We pay a toll when we use the bridge.* **2** charge for a certain service. There is a toll on long-distance telephone calls. **3** something paid, lost, suffered, etc.: *Automobile accidents take a heavy toll of human lives. n.*

toll booth (tōl′büth′), booth or gate at which tolls are collected before or after going over a bridge, highway, etc. *n., pl.* **toll booths** (tōl′büᴛʜz′ *or* tōl′büths′).

toll gate (tōl′gāt′), tollbooth. *n.*

toll road, road on which tolls are charged; turnpike.

toll way (tōl′wā′), toll road; turnpike. *n.*

Tol stoy (tol′stoi), **Leo,** 1828-1910, Russian novelist. *n.*

Tol tec (tol′tek), **1** member of an ancient people of central Mexico from about A.D. 900 to about A.D. 1200. The Toltecs influenced the cultures of the Aztecs and the Mayas. **2** of the Toltecs or their culture. 1 *n.,* 2 *adj.*

tol u ene (tol′yü ēn), a colorless, flammable liquid obtained from coal tar and petroleum. It is used as a solvent and for making explosives, dyes, etc. *n.*

tol u ol (tol′yü ōl), toluene. *n.*

tom (tom), **1** tomcat. **2** the male of various other animals: *Our Thanksgiving turkey was a tom. n.*

tomahawks

tom a hawk (tom′ə hôk), a light ax used by North American Indians as a weapon and a tool. *n.* [*Tomahawk* is of Algonquian origin.]

to ma to (tə mā′tō *or* tə mä′tō), a juicy, slightly acid, red or yellow fruit, eaten as a vegetable. Tomatoes grow on a spreading, strong-smelling plant with hairy leaves and stems and yellow flowers. *n., pl.* **to ma toes.** [*Tomato* is from Spanish *tomate,* which came from Nahuatl *tomatl.*]

tomb (tüm), grave, vault, mausoleum, etc., for a dead body, often above ground. *n.* —**tomb′less,** *adj.* —**tomb′like′,** *adj.*

tom boy (tom′boi′), girl who likes to play games supposedly suited to boys; boisterous, romping girl. *n.*

tom boy ish (tom′boi′ish), like or resembling a tomboy. *adj.* —**tom′boy′ish ly,** *adv.* —**tom′boy′ish ness,** *n.*

tomb stone (tüm′stōn′), gravestone. *n.*

tom cat (tom′kat′), a male cat. *n.*

tome (tōm), a book, especially a large, heavy book. *n.*

tom fool er y (tom′fü′lər ē), silly behavior; nonsense. *n., pl.* **tom fool er ies.**

to mor row or **to-mor row** (tə môr′ō), **1** the day after today. **2** the near future. **3** on the day after today. **4** very soon. 1,2 *n.,* 3,4 *adv.*

tom tit (tom′tit′), a small bird, especially a titmouse. *n.*

tom-tom (tom′tom′), a drum, usually beaten with the hands, originally used in the East Indies. *n.*

ton (tun), measure of weight equal to 2000 pounds (**short ton**) in the United States and Canada, and 2240 pounds (**long ton**) in Great Britain. A **metric ton** is 1000 kilograms. *n.*

ton al (tō′nl), of tone or tonality. *adj.* —**to′nal ly,** *adv.*

to nal i ty (tō nal′ə tē), **1** in music: **a** sum of relations existing between the tones of a scale or musical system. **b** a key or system of tones. **2** the color scheme of a painting, etc. *n., pl.* **to nal i ties.**

tone (tōn), **1** any sound considered with reference to its quality, pitch, strength, source, etc.: *angry tones, gentle tones, the deep tone of an organ.* **2** quality of sound: *a voice that is soft in tone.* **3** in music: **a** a sound of definite pitch and character. **b** whole step. C and D are one tone apart. **4** manner of speaking or writing: *We disliked their disrespectful tone.* **5** spirit; character; style: *A tone of quiet elegance prevails in their home.* **6** normal, healthy condition; vigor: *Regular exercise will keep your body in tone.* **7** effect of color and of light and shade in a picture: *I like the soft green tone of that painting.* **8** shade of color: *The room is furnished in tones of brown.* **9** harmonize: *This rug tones in well with the wallpaper and furniture.* **10** give a tone to. 1-8 *n.,* 9,10 *v.,* **toned, ton ing.** —**ton′er,** *n.*

tone down, soften: *Tone down your voice.*

tone up, give more sound, color, or vigor to; strengthen: *Bright curtains would tone up this dull room.*

tone less (tōn′lis), **1** without tone; without expression: *a toneless voice, a toneless reading.* **2** (of color) dull. *adj.* —**tone′less ly,** *adv.* —**tone′less ness,** *n.*

Ton ga (tong′gə), island country in the S Pacific, northeast of New Zealand. It is a member of the Commonwealth of Nations. *Capital:* Nukualofa. *n.*

tongs used to pour a liquid

tongs (tôngz), tool with two arms that are joined by a hinge, pivot, or spring, used for seizing, holding, or lifting. *n.pl.*

tongue (tung), **1** the movable fleshy organ in the mouth. The tongue is used in tasting and, by people, for talking. **2** an animal's tongue used as food: *We ate cold tongue and salad.* **3** power of speech: *Have you lost your tongue?* **4** way of speaking; speech; talk: *a flattering tongue.* **5** the language of a people: *the English tongue.* **6** something shaped or used like a tongue: *Tongues of flame leaped* *from the fire.* **7** the strip of leather under the laces of a shoe. *n.* —**tongue′less,** *adj.* —**tongue′like′,** *adj.*

hold one's tongue, keep silent: *"Hold your tongue while I'm speaking!"* he demanded.

on the tip of one's tongue, 1 almost spoken. **2** ready to be spoken.

with tongue in cheek, with sly humor; not to be taken seriously; in a mocking manner: *I spoke with tongue in cheek when I said I enjoyed doing all that homework.*

tongue-tied (tung′tīd′), **1** having the motion of the tongue hindered. **2** unable to speak because of shyness, embarrassment, etc. *adj.*

tongue twister, phrase or sentence that is difficult to say quickly without a mistake.

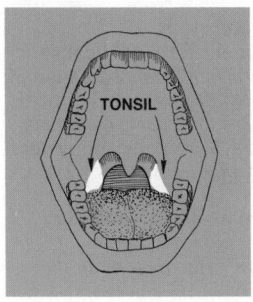

TONGUE TWISTER

Sally's selfish
　selling shellfish,
So Sally's shellfish
　seldom sell.

ton ic (ton′ik), **1** anything that gives strength; medicine to give strength: *Cod-liver oil is a tonic.* **2** restoring to health and vigor; giving strength; bracing: *The mountain air is tonic.* **3** in music: **a** the first note of a scale; keynote. **b** of or based on a keynote: *a tonic chord.* 1,3a *n.,* 2,3b *adj.* —**ton′i cal ly,** *adv.*

to night or **to-night** (tə nīt′), **1** the night of this day; this night: *I am going to bed early tonight.* **2** on or during this night: *Do you think it will snow tonight?* 1 *n.,* 2 *adv.*

ton nage (tun′ij), **1** the carrying capacity of a ship, expressed in units of 100 cubic feet per ton. A ship of 50,000 cubic feet of space or freight has a tonnage of 500 tons. **2** total amount of shipping in tons. **3** duty or tax on ships at so much a ton. **4** weight in tons. *n.*

ton neau (tu nō′), the rear part of an automobile body, with seats for passengers. *n., pl.* **ton neaus, ton neaux** (tu nōz′).

ton sil (ton′səl), either of the two oval masses of lymph tissue on the sides of the throat, just back of the mouth. *n.*

ton sil lec to my (ton′sə lek′tə mē), the surgical removal of the tonsils. *n., pl.* **ton sil lec to mies.**

ton sil li tis (ton′sə lī′tis), inflammation of the tonsils. *n.*

ton so ri al (ton sôr′ē əl), of a barber or the work of a barber. *adj.*

ton sure (ton′shər), **1** a clipping of the hair or shaving of a part or the whole of the head, formerly required of a person entering the priesthood or an order of monks. **2** the shaved part of the head of a priest or monk. *n.*

ton y (tō′nē), SLANG. high-toned; fashionable; stylish. *adj.,* **ton i er, ton i est.**

too (tü), **1** in addition; also; besides: *The dog is hungry, and thirsty too. We, too, are going away.* **2** beyond what is desirable, proper, or right; more than enough: *I ate too much.* **3** very; exceedingly: *I am only too glad to help. adv.*

took (tu̇k), past tense of **take.** *She took the car an hour ago. v.*

tool (tül), **1** a knife, hammer, saw, shovel, or any instrument used in doing work: *Plumbers, mechanics, carpenters, and shoemakers need tools.* **2** person or thing used by another like a tool: *Books are a scholar's tools. He is a tool of the party boss.* **3** a part of a machine that cuts, bores, smooths, etc. **4** use a tool on; work or shape with a tool: *She tooled beautiful designs in the leather with a knife.* **5** ornament with a tool. **6** provide or equip (a factory, etc.) with tools. 1-3 *n.,* 4-6 *v.* —**tool′er,** *n.* —**tool′less,** *adj.*

tool box (tül′boks′), box in which tools and sometimes small parts, accessories, etc., are kept. *n.*

tool mak er (tül′mā′kər), **1** machinist who makes, repairs, and maintains machine tools. **2** any maker of tools: *Prehistoric people were the first toolmakers. n.*

toot (tüt), **1** sound of a horn, whistle, etc. **2** give forth a short blast: *He heard the train whistle toot three times.* **3** sound (a horn, whistle, etc.) in short blasts. 1 *n.,* 2,3 *v.* —**toot′er,** *n.*

tooth (tüth), **1** one of the hard, bonelike parts in the mouth, used for biting and chewing. **2** something like a tooth. Each one of the projecting parts of a comb, rake, or saw is a tooth. **3** cut teeth on the edge of; indent. 1,2 *n., pl.* **teeth;** 3 *v.* —**tooth′like′,** *adj.*

fight tooth and nail, fight fiercely, with all one's force.

tooth ache (tüth′āk′), pain in a tooth or the teeth. *n.*

tooth brush (tüth′brush′), a small brush for cleaning the teeth. *n., pl.* **tooth brush es.**

toothed (tütht *or* tüŦHd), **1** having teeth. **2** notched: *the toothed surface of a gear. adj.*

tooth less (tüth′lis), without teeth. *adj.* —**tooth′less ly,** *adv.* —**tooth′less ness,** *n.*

tooth paste (tüth′pāst′), paste used in cleaning the teeth. *n.*

tooth pick (tüth′pik′), a small, pointed piece of wood, plastic, etc., for removing bits of food from between the teeth. *n.*

tooth pow der (tüth′pou′dər), powder used in cleaning the teeth. *n.*

tooth some (tüth′səm), **1** pleasing to the taste; tasting good. **2** pleasing to the sight; pretty. *adj.* —**tooth′some ly,** *adv.* —**tooth′some ness,** *n.*

top[1] (top), **1** the highest point or part: *the top of a mountain.* **2** the upper part, end, or surface: *the top of a table, a shoe top.* **3** the highest or leading place, rank,

etc.: *She is at the top of her class.* **4** the highest point, pitch, or degree: *They were yelling at the top of their voices.* **5** the best or most important part: *top of the morning.* **6** part of a plant that grows above ground: *Beet tops are somewhat like spinach.* **7** the head: *The toddler was all bundled up from top to toe.* **8** the cover of an automobile, carriage, can, etc. **9** having to do with, situated at, or forming the top: *the top shelf of a cupboard.* **10** highest or greatest: *He received top honors at school. The runners set off at top speed.* **11** put a top on: *I will top the box.* **12** be on top of; be the top of: *A church tops the hill.* **13** reach the top of: *They topped the mountain.* **14** rise high; rise above: *The sun topped the horizon.* **15** be higher or greater than. **16** do better than; outdo; excel: *His story topped all the rest.* **17** remove the top of (a plant, tree, etc.). 1-8 *n.,* 9,10 *adj.,* 11-17 *v.,* **topped, top ping.**
on top, with success; with victory: *We have the best players, so our team will come out on top.*
top off, complete; finish; end.
top[2] (top), toy that spins on a point. *n.*
sleep like a top, sleep soundly.
to paz (tō′paz), a hard mineral that occurs in crystals of various forms and colors. Transparent yellow topaz is used as a gem. *n., pl.* **to paz es.**
top coat (top′kōt′), a lightweight overcoat. *n.*
To pe ka (tə pē′kə), capital of Kansas, in the NE part. *n.*
top gal lant (top′gal′ənt *or* tə gal′ənt), **1** the mast or sail above the topmast; the third section of a mast above the deck. **2** next above the topmast. 1 *n.,* 2 *adj.*

top hat

top hat, a tall, black silk hat worn by men in formal clothes; high hat.
top-heav y (top′hev′ē), too heavy at the top. *adj.* —**top′-heav′i ly,** *adv.* —**top′-heav′i ness,** *n.*
top ic (top′ik), subject that people think, write, or talk about: *Newspapers discuss the topics of the day. I chose women's rights as the topic for my report. n.*
top i cal (top′ə kəl), **1** having to do with topics of the day; of current or local interest. **2** of a topic: *Some books have topical outlines for each chapter. adj.* —**top′i cal ly,** *adv.*
top knot (top′not′), a knot of hair or a tuft of feathers on the top of the head. *n.*
top mast (top′mast′ *or* top′məst), the second section of a mast above the deck. *n.*
top most (top′mōst), highest: *I need a ladder to reach the apples on the topmost branches. adj.*
top-notch (top′noch′), INFORMAL. first-rate; best possible. *adj.*
to pog ra pher (tə pog′rə fər), an expert in topography. *n.*
top o graph ic (top′ə graf′ik), topographical. *adj.*
top o graph i cal (top′ə graf′ə kəl), of topography. A topographical map shows mountains, rivers, etc. *adj.* —**top′o graph′i cal ly,** *adv.*
to pog ra phy (tə pog′rə fē), **1** the accurate and detailed

description or drawing of places or their surface features. **2** the surface features of a place or region. The topography of a region includes hills, valleys, streams, lakes, bridges, tunnels, roads, etc. *n., pl.* **to pog ra phies.** [*Topography* comes from Greek *topos,* meaning "place," and *graphein,* meaning "write."]
top ple (top′əl), **1** fall forward; tumble down: *The chimney toppled over on the roof.* **2** throw over or down; overturn: *The wrestler toppled his opponent. v.,* **top pled, top pling.**
tops (tops), SLANG. of the highest degree in quality, excellence, etc. *adj.*
top sail (top′sāl′ *or* top′səl), the second sail above the deck on a mast. *n.*
top-se cret (top′sē′krit), of the greatest secrecy; highly confidential: *top-secret codes. adj.*
top side (top′sid′), to or on the upper deck: *The crew were all topside. adv.*
top soil (top′soil′), the upper part of the soil; surface soil: *Rich topsoil helps produce good crops. n.*
top sy-tur vy (top′sē tėr′vē), **1** upside down. **2** in confusion or disorder: *On moving day everything in the house was topsy-turvy. adv., adj.* —**top′sy-tur′vi ly,** *adv.* —**top′sy-tur′vi ness,** *n.*
To rah (tôr′ə), **1** the entire body of Jewish law and tradition. **2** the first five books of the Old Testament; the Pentateuch. **3** scroll on which the Pentateuch is written. *n.*

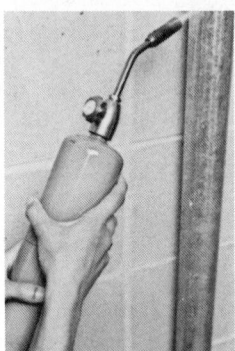

torch (def. 2)
a torch being used to
thaw a frozen pipe

torch (tôrch), **1** light to be carried around or stuck in a holder on a wall. A piece of pine wood or anything that burns easily makes a good torch. **2** device for producing a very hot flame, used especially to burn off paint and to solder or melt metal. **3** BRITISH. flashlight. **4** something thought of as a source of enlightenment: *the torch of civilization. n., pl.* **torch es.** —**torch′less,** *adj.* —**torch′like′,** *adj.*
torch bear er (tôrch′ber′ər *or* tôrch′bar′ər), person who carries a torch. *n.*
torch light (tôrch′lit′), light of a torch or torches. *n.*
tore (tôr), past tense of **tear**[2]. *She tore her jeans on a nail yesterday. v.*
to re a dor (tôr′ē ə dôr′), bullfighter. *n.*
tor ment (tôr ment′ *for* 1,5; tôr′ment *for* 2-4), **1** cause very great pain to: *Headaches tormented him.* **2** a cause of very great pain: *A bad burn can be a torment.* **3** very great pain: *She suffered torments from her toothache.* **4** a cause of very much worry or annoyance. **5** worry or annoy very much: *Don't torment me with silly questions.* 1,5 *v.,* 2-4 *n.* —**tor ment′ing ly,** *adv.*
tor men tor *or* **tor ment er** (tôr men′tər), person or thing that torments. *n.*
torn (tôrn), past participle of **tear**[2]. *He has torn up the plant by the roots. v.*

tornado

tor na do (tôr nā′dō), an extremely violent and destructive whirlwind. A tornado extends down from a mass of dark clouds as a twisting funnel and moves over the land in a narrow path. *n., pl.* **tor na does** or **tor na dos.** —**tor na′do like′,** *adj.*

To ron to (tə ron′tō), city in SE Canada, on Lake Ontario. It is the capital of Ontario. *n.*

tor pe do (tôr pē′dō), **1** a large, cigar-shaped metal tube that contains explosives and travels under water by its own power. Torpedoes may be fired from submarines or torpedo boats or launched from aircraft to blow up enemy ships. **2** attack or destroy with a torpedo. **3** an explosive put on a railroad track which makes a loud noise for a signal when a wheel of the engine runs over it. **4** a firework consisting of an explosive and gravel wrapped in tissue paper. It explodes when it is thrown against something hard. 1,3,4 *n., pl.* **tor pe does;** 2 *v.* [*Torpedo,* originally meaning "electric eel" in English, came from Latin *torpedo,* which originally meant "numbness." The weapon was named for its being shaped something like the eel.] —**tor pe′do like′,** *adj.*

torpedo boat, a small, fast warship used for attacking with torpedoes.

tor pid (tôr′pid), **1** dull, inactive, or sluggish. **2** not moving or feeling. Animals that hibernate become torpid in winter. *adj.* —**tor′pid ly,** *adv.* —**tor′pid ness,** *n.*

tor pid i ty (tôr pid′ə tē), torpid condition. *n.*

tor por (tôr′pər), torpid condition. *n.*

torque (tôrk), force causing rotation. *n.*

tor rent (tôr′ənt), **1** a violent, rushing stream of water: *The mountain torrent dashed over the rock.* **2** a heavy downpour: *The rain came down in torrents during the thunderstorm.* **3** any violent, rushing stream; flood: *a torrent of questions, a torrent of lava.* *n.*

tor ren tial (tô ren′shəl), of, caused by, or like a torrent: *torrential rains, a torrential flow of words.* *adj.* —**tor ren′tial ly,** *adv.*

tor rid (tôr′id), very hot: *July is a torrid month. adj.* —**tor′rid ly,** *adv.* —**tor′rid ness,** *n.*

Torrid Zone, the very warm region between the tropic of Cancer and the tropic of Capricorn; the tropics. The equator divides the Torrid Zone.

tor sion (tôr′shən), **1** act or process of twisting. **2** state of being twisted. **3** the twisting of a body by two equal and opposite forces. *n.*

tor so (tôr′sō), **1** the trunk of the human body. **2** the trunk or body of a statue without any head, arms, or legs. *n., pl.* **tor sos.**

tor til la (tôr tē′yə), a thin, flat, round cake made of corn meal, commonly eaten in Spanish America. It is baked on a flat surface and served hot. *n., pl.* **tor til las.** [*Tortilla* was borrowed from Spanish *tortilla.*]

tor toise (tôr′təs), **1** turtle living only on land, especially in dry regions. Tortoises have stumpy legs and a high, arched shell. **2** any turtle. *n., pl.* **tor tois es** or **tor toise.**

tortoise shell, the mottled yellow-and-brown shell of some turtles. It is much used for combs and ornaments.

tor toise-shell (tôr′təs shel′), **1** made of tortoise shell. **2** mottled or colored like a tortoise shell. *adj.*

tor tu ous (tôr′chü əs), **1** full of twists, turns, or bends; twisting; winding; crooked: *We found the river's course very tortuous.* **2** mentally or morally crooked; not straightforward: *tortuous reasoning. adj.* —**tor′tu ous ly,** *adv.* —**tor′tu ous ness,** *n.*

tor ture (tôr′chər), **1** act of inflicting very severe pain. Torture has been used to make people give evidence about crimes, or to make them confess. **2** very severe pain; agony: *suffer tortures from rheumatism.* **3** cause very severe pain to; torment: *It is cruel to torture animals.* 1,2 *n.,* 3 *v.,* **tor tured, tor tur ing.** —**tor′tur ing ly,** *adv.*

tor tur er (tôr′chər ər), person or thing that tortures; tormentor. *n.*

tor tur ous (tôr′chər əs), full of, involving, or causing torture. *adj.* —**tor′tur ous ly,** *adv.*

To ry (tôr′ē), **1** member of the British political party that favored royal power and the established church and opposed change. Strictly speaking, there is no Tory party in modern Britain, although members of the Conservative party are often called Tories. **2** member of the Conservative party of Canada. **3** an American who favored British rule over the colonies at the time of the Revolutionary War. **4** Also, **tory.** a very conservative person. **5** of Tories. 1-4 *n., pl.* **To ries;** 5 *adj.*

Tos ca ni ni (tos′kə nē′nē), Arturo, 1867-1957, American conductor, born in Italy. *n.*

toss (tôs), **1** throw lightly with the palm upward; cast; fling: *She tossed the ball to me.* **2** throw about; roll or pitch about: *The ship was tossed by the waves. He tossed in bed all night.* **3** lift quickly; throw upward: *She tossed her head.* **4** shake up or about, especially to mix the ingredients: *toss a salad.* **5** throw a coin to decide something by the side that falls upward. **6** a throw; tossing: *A toss of a coin decided who should play first.* 1-5 *v.,* 6 *n., pl.* **toss es.** —**toss′er,** *n.* —**toss′ing ly,** *adv.*

toss off, 1 do or make quickly and easily: *She tossed off a poem.* **2** drink all at once: *He tossed off a glass of milk.*

toss up (tôs′up′), **1** a tossing of a coin to decide something. **2** INFORMAL. an even chance: *It's a tossup as to who will win. n.*

tot (tot), a little child. *n.*

to tal (tō′tl), **1** whole; entire: *The total cost of the house and land will be $25,000.* **2** the whole amount; sum: *Her expenses reached a total of $100.* **3** find the sum of; add: *Total that column of figures.* **4** reach an amount of;

tortoise
(def. 1)
shell up to
10 in. (25 cm.)
long

amount to: *The money spent yearly on chewing gum totals millions of dollars.* **5** complete; absolute; utter: *We were in total darkness.* **6** SLANG. wreck (a vehicle) completely: *The collision totaled both cars.* 1,5 *adj.*, 2 *n.*, 3,4,6 *v.*, **to taled, to tal ing** or **to talled, to tal ling.**

to tal i tar i an (tō tal/ə ter/ē ən *or* tō tal/ə tar/ē ən), **1** of a government controlled by one political group which suppresses all opposition, often with force, and which controls many aspects of people's lives. A totalitarian government usually regulates what goods are produced by industry, what radio or television programs are broadcast, what books the people may read, etc. **2** person in favor of totalitarian principles. 1 *adj.*, 2 *n.*

to tal i tar i an ism (tō tal/ə ter/ē ə niz/əm *or* tō tal/ə-tar/ē ə niz/əm), system, principles, or methods of a totalitarian government. *n.*

to tal i ty (tō tal/ə tē), the total amount; entirety. *n.*, *pl.* **to tal i ties.**

to tal ize (tō/tl īz), make total; combine into a total. *v.*, **to tal ized, to tal iz ing.** —**to/tal iz/er,** *n.*

to tal ly (tō/tl ē), wholly; entirely; completely: *I was totally unprepared. adv.*

tote (tōt), INFORMAL. carry; haul. *v.*, **tot ed, tot ing.** —**tot/er,** *n.*

tote bag, a large handbag similar to a shopping bag, for carrying somewhat bulky objects.

to tem (tō/təm), **1** a natural object, often an animal, taken as the emblem of a tribe, clan, or family. **2** image of such an object. Totems are often carved and painted on poles. *n.* [*Totem* is of Algonquian origin.]

totem pole

totem pole, pole carved and painted with representations of totems, erected by the Indians of the northwestern coast of North America, especially in front of their houses.

tot ter (tot/ər), **1** walk with shaky, unsteady steps: *The baby came tottering across the room.* **2** be unsteady; shake as if about to fall: *The old wall tottered in the gale and fell. v.* —**tot/ter er,** *n.* —**tot/ter ing ly,** *adv.*

tou can (tü/kan), a bright-colored bird of tropical America, with a very large beak. *n.*

touch (tuch), **1** put the hand or some other part of the body on or against: *She touched the soft, furry kitten.* **2** put against; make contact with: *I touched the post with my umbrella.* **3** be against; come against: *Your sleeve is touching the butter.* **4** be in contact: *Our hands touched.* **5** a touching or a being touched: *A bubble bursts at a touch.* **6** the sense by which things are perceived by feeling, handling, or coming against them: *The blind develop a keen touch.* **7** communication or connection: *He always kept in touch with his family while he was overseas.* **8** a slight amount; little bit: *We had a touch of frost. The child has a touch of fever.* **9** a light, delicate stroke with a brush, pencil, pen, etc.: *The artist finished the picture with a few touches.* **10** a detail in any artistic work: *a story with*

charming poetic touches. **11** strike lightly or gently: *touch the strings of a harp.* **12** injure slightly: *The flowers were touched by the frost.* **13** affect with some feeling: *The sad story touched us.* **14** make slightly crazy. **15** have to do with; concern: *The matter touches your interest.* **16** speak of; deal with; refer to; treat lightly: *Our conversation touched many subjects.* **17** handle; use: *He won't touch liquor or tobacco.* **18** reach; come up to: *His head almost touches the ceiling. Nobody in our class can touch her in science.* **19** make a brief stop: *Most ships touch at that port.* **20** act or manner of playing a musical instrument, especially an instrument with a keyboard: *The piano player had an excellent touch.* **21** a distinctive manner or quality: *The work showed an expert's touch.* 1-4,11-19 *v.*, 5-10,20,21 *n.*, *pl.* **touch es.** —**touch/a ble,** *adj.* —**touch/-er,** *n.* —**touch/less,** *adj.*

touch down, land an aircraft: *The pilot touched down at a small airfield.*

touch off, 1 cause to go off; fire. **2** cause to happen.

touch on or **touch upon, 1** mention; treat lightly: *Our conversation touched on many subjects.* **2** come close to.

touch up, change a little; improve: *touch up a photograph.*

touch-and-go (tuch/ən gō/), uncertain; risky. *adj.*

touch down (tuch/doun/), **1** score of six points made in football by putting the ball on the ground behind the opponent's goal line. **2** the landing of an aircraft, especially the moment of first contact with the ground. *n.*

touched (tucht), **1** slightly crazed. **2** stirred emotionally: *She was touched by our concern for her welfare. adj.*

touch football, game with rules similar to those of football except that the player carrying the ball is touched rather than tackled.

touch ing (tuch/ing), **1** arousing tender feeling: *"A Christmas Carol" is a touching story.* **2** concerning; about: *The interviewer asked questions touching my home and school life.* 1 *adj.*, 2 *prep.* —**touch/ing ly,** *adv.*

touch stone (tuch/stōn/), **1** a black stone used to test the purity of gold or silver by the color of the streak made on the stone by rubbing it with the metal. **2** any means of testing; a test: *Adversity is the touchstone of friendship. n.*

touch y (tuch/ē), **1** apt to take offense at trifles; too sensitive: *He is tired and very touchy this afternoon.* **2** requiring skill in handling; ticklish; precarious: *a very touchy situation. adj.*, **touch i er, touch i est.** —**touch/i ly,** *adv.* —**touch/i ness,** *n.*

tough (tuf), **1** bending without breaking: *Leather is tough; cardboard is not.* **2** hard to cut, tear, or chew: *The steak was so tough I couldn't eat it.* **3** strong; hardy: *Donkeys are tough little animals and can carry big loads.* **4** hard; difficult: *Dragging the load uphill was tough work.* **5** hard to influence; stubborn: *a tough customer.* **6** rough; disorderly: *a tough neighborhood.* **7** a rough person: *A gang of toughs attacked them.* 1-6 *adj.*, 7 *n.* —**tough/ly,** *adv.* —**tough/ness,** *n.*

tough en (tuf/ən), make or become tough: *I toughened my muscles by doing exercises. v.* —**tough/en er,** *n.*

Tou louse-Lau trec (tü lüz/lō trek/), **Henri de,** 1864-1901, French painter. *n.*

tou pee (tü pā/), wig or patch of false hair worn by men to cover a bald spot. *n.*

tour (tùr), **1** to travel from place to place: *We toured by bus for a week.* **2** travel through: *Last year they toured Europe.* **3** a long journey: *They made a European tour.* **4** a short journey; a walk around: *Our class made a tour of the old boat.* **5** walk around in: *Our class will tour the museum.* **6** period or turn of military or other activity at a certain place or station: *a soldier on a tour of duty overseas.* 1,2,5 *v.*, 3,4,6 *n.*

on **tour** touring. A show on tour travels around the country giving performances in various places.

tour de force (tür′ də fôrs′), a notable feat of strength, skill, or ingenuity. *pl.* **tours de force** (tür′ də fôrs′).

tour ism (tür′iz′əm), **1** a touring or traveling for pleasure. **2** the business of serving tourists. *n.*

tour ist (tür′ist), **1** person traveling for pleasure. **2** of or for tourists: *tourist accommodations.* **1** *n.,* **2** *adj.*

tour na ment (tėr′nə mənt *or* tür′nə mənt), **1** series of contests testing the skill of many persons in some sport: *a golf tournament.* **2** a medieval contest between two groups of knights on horseback who fought for a prize. *n.*

tour ney (tėr′nē *or* tür′nē), **1** tournament. **2** take part in a tournament. **1** *n., pl.* **tour neys; 2** *v.,* **tour neyed, tour ney ing.**

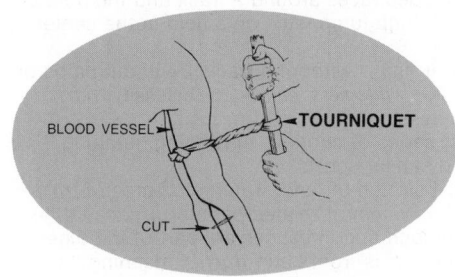

BLOOD VESSEL ←TOURNIQUET

CUT

tour ni quet (tür′nə ket), device for stopping bleeding by compressing a blood vessel, such as a bandage tightened by twisting with a stick, or a pad held down tightly. *n.*

tou sle (tou′zəl), put into disorder; make untidy; muss: *tousled hair.* *v.,* **tou sled, tou sling.**

tout (tout), INFORMAL. **1** try to get (customers, jobs, votes, etc.). **2** praise highly and insistently. *v.*

tow[1] (tō), **1** pull by a rope, chain, etc.: *The tug is towing three barges.* **2** act of towing. **3** condition of being towed: *The launch had the sailboat in tow.* **4** that which is towed: *Each tug had a tow of three barges.* **5** the rope, chain, etc., used for towing. **1** *v.,* **2-5** *n.* **—tow′a ble,** *adj.*

tow[2] (tō), the coarse, broken fibers of flax, hemp, etc., prepared for spinning. *n.*

to ward (tôrd *or* tə wôrd′), **1** in the direction of: *She walked toward the north.* **2** with respect to; regarding; about; concerning: *What is his attitude toward foreign aid?* **3** shortly before; near: *Toward morning the storm ended.* **4** as a help to; for: *Will you give something toward our new hospital?* *prep.*

to wards (tôrdz *or* tə wôrdz′), toward. *prep.*

tow boat (tō′bōt′), a powerful boat with a flat bottom used to tow or push barges on rivers. *n.*

tow el (tou′əl), piece of cloth or paper for wiping and drying something wet. We have hand towels, face towels, and bath towels. *n.*

tow er (tou′ər), **1** a high structure, standing alone or forming part of a church, castle, or other building. Some towers are forts or prisons. **2** defense; protection. **3** rise high up: *The new skyscraper towers over the older buildings.* **1,2** *n.,* **3** *v.* **—tow′er less,** *adj.* **—tow′er like′,** *adj.*

tow er ing (tou′ər ing), **1** very high: *a towering mountain peak.* **2** very great: *Making electricity from atomic power is a towering achievement.* **3** very violent: *a towering rage. adj.*

Tower of London, an ancient palace-fortress of London. The present building dates back to William I. It has been used as a palace, prison, mint, and arsenal.

tow head (tō′hed′), person having very light or pale-yellow hair. *n.*

tow head ed (tō′hed′id), having very light or pale-yellow hair. *adj.*

tow hee (tou′hē *or* tō′hē), a bird of North America with a stout bill, whose cry sounds somewhat like its name; chewink. It is a kind of finch. *n.*

town (toun), **1** a large group of houses and buildings, smaller than a city but larger than a village: *Do you live in a town or in the country?* **2** any large place with many people living in it: *I hear that Boston is a fine town.* **3** the people of a town: *The whole town was having a holiday.* **4** the part of a town or city where the stores and office buildings are: *Let's go into town to see a show. n.* **—town′less,** *adj.*

town crier, (in former times) person who called out the news and made announcements in the streets of a city or town.

town hall, a building used for a town's business.

town meeting, 1 a general meeting of the inhabitants of a town. **2** (in New England) a meeting of the qualified voters of a town for the transaction of public business.

towns folk (tounz′fōk′), the people of a town. *n.pl.*

town ship (toun′ship), **1** part of a county in the United States and Canada having certain powers of government. **2** (in United States surveys of public land) a region or district six miles square, made up of 36 sections. *n.*

towns man (tounz′mən), **1** person who lives in a town. **2** person who lives in one's own town. *n., pl.* **towns men.**

towns peo ple (tounz′pē′pəl), the people of a town. *n.pl.*

tow path (tō′path′), path along the bank of a canal or river for use in towing boats. *n., pl.* **tow paths** (tō′-paŦHz′ *or* tō′paths′).

tox., toxicology.

tox e mi a (tok sē′mē ə), blood poisoning caused by toxins. *n.*

tox ic (tok′sik), **1** of poison; caused by poison: *a toxic illness.* **2** poisonous: *toxic plants. adj.* **—tox′i cal ly,** *adv.*

WORD HISTORY

toxic

Toxic is from Latin *toxicum,* meaning "poison," which came from Greek *to-xikon (pharmakon),* meaning "(poison) for shooting arrows." Early poisons were used on the tips of arrows.

tox ic i ty (tok sis′ə tē), toxic or poisonous quality. *n.*

tox i col o gist (tok′sə kol′ə jist), an expert in toxicology. *n.*

tox i col o gy (tok′sə kol′ə jē), science that deals with poisons, their effects, antidotes, detection, etc. *n.*

tox in (tok′sən), any poison formed by an animal or plant organism as a product of its metabolism. Toxins formed by bacteria cause diseases such as diphtheria and scarlet fever. The body reacts to some toxins by producing antitoxins. *n.*

toy (toi), **1** something for a child to play with; plaything.

2 thing that has little value or importance. **3** of, made as, or like a toy. **4** small or miniature in size: *a toy poodle.* **5** amuse oneself; play; trifle: *I toyed with my pencil.* 1,2 *n.,* 3,4 *adj.,* 5 *v.* —**toy′er,** *n.* —**toy′less,** *adj.* —**toy′like′,** *adj.*

tr., 1 transitive. **2** treasurer.

trace[1] (trās), **1** a mark, sign, or evidence of the former existence of something: *Archaeologists found traces of an ancient city.* **2** footprint or other mark left; track; trail: *We saw traces of rabbits and squirrels on the snow.* **3** follow by means of marks, tracks, or clues: *trace a missing person.* **4** follow the course of: *We traced the river to its source. The Aldens trace their family back to John Alden, one of the Pilgrims.* **5** a very small amount; little bit: *There was a trace of gray in his hair.* **6** mark out; draw: *She traced the plan of our new house.* **7** copy by following the lines of with a pencil or pen: *I put thin paper over the map and traced it.* 1,2,5 *n.,* 3,4,6,7 *v.,* **traced, trac ing.**

trace[2] (trās), either of the two straps, ropes, or chains by which an animal pulls a wagon, carriage, etc. *n.*

trace a ble (trā′sə bəl), able to be traced. *adj.*

trace element, a chemical element used in small amounts by an organism but considered necessary to its proper functioning.

trac er (trā′sər), **1** person or thing that traces. **2** inquiry sent from place to place to trace a missing person, letter, parcel, etc. **3** bullet with a substance in it that burns when the bullet is fired, leaving a trail that can be followed with the eye. **4** substance, such as a radioactive isotope, which can be traced and observed as it passes through a body, plant, or other system in order to study biological processes or chemical reactions within the system. *n.*

trac er y (trā′sər ē), ornamental work or designs consisting of lines. Stonework, carving, and embroidery often have tracery. *n., pl.* **trac er ies.**

tra che a (trā′kē ə), windpipe. *n., pl.* **tra che ae** (trā′kē-ē′), **tra che as.**

tra che ot o my (trā′kē ot′ə mē), a surgical cutting into the trachea. *n., pl.* **tra che ot o mies.**

tra cho ma (trə kō′mə), a contagious inflammation of the eyelids. Trachoma is common in the Orient and sometimes causes blindness. *n.*

trac ing (trā′sing), copy of something made by marking or drawing over it. *n.*

track
(def. 9)

track (trak), **1** a double, parallel line of metal rails for cars to run on: *railroad tracks.* **2** mark or pattern left: *The dirt road showed many automobile tracks.* **3** footprint: *We saw bear tracks near the camp.* **4** follow by means of footprints, marks, smell, etc.: *We tracked the deer and photographed it.* **5** trace in any way: *I will track down her new address.* **6** make footprints or other marks on: *Don't track the floor.* **7** bring (snow or mud) into a place on one's feet: *He tracked mud into the house.* **8** path; trail; road: *A track runs through the woods to the farmhouse.* **9** a course for running or racing. **10** track and field. **11** one of the

endless belts of linked steel plates on which a tank, bulldozer, etc., moves. 1-3,8-11 *n.,* 4-7 *v.* —**track′a ble,** *adj.* —**track′er,** *n.*

in one's tracks, INFORMAL. right where one is: *The squirrel froze in its tracks when it saw us.*

jump the track, leave the rails suddenly; derail without warning.

keep track of, keep within one's sight or attention: *The noise made it difficult to keep track of what was going on.*

lose track of, fail to keep track of: *When on vacation, it is easy to lose track of what day it is.*

make tracks, INFORMAL. go very fast; run away: *We saw a bear and made tracks for home.*

off the track, off the subject; wrong.

on the track, on the subject; right.

track and field, the sports or events of running, jumping, vaulting, throwing, etc., as a group. A track and field meet includes races around a track and the pole vault, shot-put, high jump, etc., on a field in the center of the track.

track less (trak′lis), **1** without a track. **2** without paths or trails: *a trackless wilderness. adj.* —**track′less ly,** *adv.* —**track′less ness,** *n.*

track meet, series of contests in running, jumping, throwing, and similar sports.

tract[1] (trakt), **1** stretch of land, water, etc.; area: *a tract of desert land.* **2** system of related parts or organs in the body. The stomach and intestines are part of the digestive tract. *n.* [*Tract*[1] is from Latin *tractus,* meaning "a drawing out," which comes from *trahere,* meaning "to drag."]

tract[2] (trakt), **1** a little book or pamphlet on a religious or political subject. **2** any little book or pamphlet. *n.* [*Tract*[2] apparently is from Latin *tractatus,* meaning "a handling," which comes from *tractare,* meaning "to handle."]

trac ta ble (trak′tə bəl), **1** easily managed or controlled; easy to deal with; docile: *Dogs are more tractable than mules.* **2** easily handled or worked: *Gold is a tractable metal that can be hammered into thin sheets. adj.* —**trac′ta ble ness,** *n.* —**trac′ta bly,** *adv.*

trac tile (trak′təl), able to be drawn out in length. *adj.*

trac tion (trak′shən), **1** a drawing or pulling or a being drawn. **2** the drawing or pulling of loads along a road, track, etc. **3** kind of power used for this. Electric traction is used on subways and some railroads. **4** friction between a body and the surface on which it moves, enabling the body to move without slipping: *Wheels slip on ice because there is too little traction. n.*

trac tor (trak′tər), **1** a heavy, motor-driven vehicle which moves on wheels or on two endless tracks, used for pulling wagons, plows, etc., along roads or over fields.

tractor (def. 1)

2 a powerful truck having a short body and a cab for the driver, used to pull a freight trailer along a highway. *n.* [*Tractor* is from Latin *tractus*, meaning "drawn, pulled," which comes from *trahere*, meaning "to drag." See **Word Family.**]

WORD FAMILY

tractor

Below are words related to *tractor*. They can all be traced back to the Latin word *trahere* (trä′he re), meaning "to drag."

abstract	intractable	subtract
attract	maltreat	trace¹
attractive	mistreat	trace²
contract	portrait	tract¹
contraction	portray	traction
detract	protract	train
distract	protractor	trait
distraught	retrace	treat
entreat	retract	treatise
extract	retreat	treaty

trade (trād), **1** buying and selling; exchange of goods; commerce: *The United States has much trade with foreign countries.* **2** buy and sell; exchange goods; be in commerce: *Some American companies trade all over the world.* **3** an exchange: *an even trade.* **4** to exchange; make an exchange: *If you don't like your book, I'll trade with you.* **5** a bargain or deal: *I made a good trade.* **6** kind of work; business, especially one requiring skilled mechanical work: *the carpenter's trade.* **7** people in the same kind of work or business: *Carpenters, plumbers, and electricians are members of the building trade.* **8** customers: *That store has a lot of trade.* **9** be a customer: *I have traded at that store for years.* **10 the trades,** the trade winds. 1,3,5-8,10 *n.,* 2,4,9 *v.,* **trad ed, trad ing. —trad′a ble, trade′a ble,** *adj.* **—trade′less,** *adj.*

trade in, give (an automobile, refrigerator, etc.) as payment or part payment for something, especially for a newer model.

trade off, get rid of by trading.

trade on, take advantage of: *trade on one's wealth to gain political influence.*

trade-in (trād′in′), automobile, refrigerator, etc., given or accepted as payment or part payment for something, especially for a newer model. *n.*

trade mark (trād′märk′), **1** a mark, picture, name, word, symbol, design, or letters, used to identify and distinguish a product or merchandise as belonging to a specific manufacturer or seller. A registered trademark is legally protected, and may be used only by the owner. **2** register the trademark of. 1 *n.,* 2 *v.*

trade name, 1 name by which a product is normally called in business or trade. **2** name used by a company to identify a product that it makes or sells, which may be registered as a trademark. **3** name under which a company does business.

trad er (trā′dər), **1** person who trades: *The trappers sold furs to traders.* **2** ship used in trading. *n.*

trade school, school where trades are taught.

trades man (trādz′mən), storekeeper; shopkeeper. *n., pl.* **trades men.**

trades peo ple (trādz′pē′pəl), storekeepers; shopkeepers. *n.pl.*

trade union, 1 association of workers in a trade or

craft to protect and promote their interests. **2** any labor union.

trade wind, wind blowing steadily toward the equator from about 30 degrees north latitude and about 30 degrees south latitude. North of the equator, it blows from the northeast; south of the equator, from the southeast.

trading post, store or station of a trader, especially on the frontier or in unsettled country. Trading posts used to trade food, weapons, clothes, and other articles in exchange for hides and furs.

trading stamp, stamp (def. 2).

tra di tion (trə dish′ən), **1** the handing down of beliefs, opinions, customs, stories, etc., from parents to children. **2** what is handed down in this way: *According to tradition, Betsy Ross made the first American flag. n.*

tra di tion al (trə dish′ə nəl), **1** of tradition. **2** handed down by tradition: *Shaking hands upon meeting is a traditional custom.* **3** according to tradition: *traditional furniture.* **4** customary: *A Memorial Day parade is traditional in almost every town. adj.* **—tra di′tion al ly,** *adv.*

tra duce (trə düs′ *or* trə dyüs′), speak evil of (a person) falsely; slander. *v.,* **tra duced, tra duc ing. —tra-duce′ment,** *n.* **—tra duc′er,** *n.* **—tra duc′ing ly,** *adv.*

Tra fal gar (trə fal′gər), **Cape,** cape in SW Spain, on the Atlantic. In a naval battle near this cape in 1805, Napoleon's fleet was defeated by a British fleet under Nelson. *n.*

traf fic (traf′ik), **1** people, automobiles, wagons, ships, etc., coming and going along a way of travel: *Police control the traffic in large cities.* **2** buying and selling; commerce; trade. **3** carry on trade; buy; sell; exchange: *The traders trafficked with the islanders for ivory.* **4** business done by a railroad line, airline, etc.; number of passengers or amount of freight carried. **5** dealings; association: *Traffic with criminals is dangerous.* **6** have illicit dealings: *to traffic in narcotics.* 1,2,4,5 *n.,* 3,6 *v.,* **traf-ficked, traf fic ing. —traf′fic less,** *adj.*

traffic circle, junction of several roads at which the merging traffic goes around a central circle in one direction only; rotary.

traf fick er (traf′ə kər), person who buys and sells; trader. *n.*

traffic light, set of electric lights used for signaling at a corner or intersection to control traffic; stoplight. Usually a red light ("stop") and a green light ("go") are flashed automatically every so many seconds or minutes.

tra ge di an (trə jē′dē ən), **1** actor in tragedies. **2** writer of tragedies. *n.*

trag e dy (traj′ə dē), **1** a serious play having an unhappy ending. Shakespeare's *Hamlet* is a tragedy. **2** a very sad or terrible happening: *Her sudden death was a tragedy to her friends. n., pl.* **trag e dies.** [*Tragedy* comes from Latin *tragoedia,* and can be traced back to Greek *tragos,* meaning "goat," and *ōidē,* meaning "song."]

trag ic (traj′ik), **1** of tragedy; having to do with tragedy: *a tragic poet.* **2** very sad; dreadful: *a tragic event. adj.*

trag i cal (traj′ə kəl), tragic. *adj.*

trag i cal ly (traj′ik lē), in a tragic manner. *adv.*

trail (trāl), **1** path across a wild or unsettled region: *The hikers followed mountain trails for days.* **2** a track or smell: *The dogs found the trail of the rabbit.* **3** hunt by track or smell: *The dogs trailed the rabbit.* **4** anything that follows along behind: *The car left a trail of dust behind it.* **5** follow along behind; follow: *The dog trailed its master constantly.* **6** pull or be pulled along behind: *The child trailed a toy horse.* **7** grow along: *Poison ivy trailed by the road.* **8** go along slowly: *The children trailed to school.* **9** pass little by little: *Her voice trailed off into silence.* 1,2,4 *n.,* 3,5-9 *v.*

trail blaz er (trāl′blā′zər), person or thing that pioneers or prepares the way to something new. *n.*

trail er (trā′lər), **1** person or animal that follows a trail. **2** vehicle, often large, used for hauling freight. It is usually pulled by a truck. **3** vehicle fitted up for people to live in and usually pulled by an automobile; house on wheels. *n.*

train (trān), **1** a connected line of railroad cars moving along together: *A very long freight train of 100 cars rolled by.* **2** line of people, animals, wagons, trucks, etc., moving along together: *The early settlers crossed the continent by wagon train.* **3** part that hangs down and drags along: *the train of a gown.* **4** group of followers: *the king and his train.* **5** series; succession: *A long train of misfortunes overcame them.* **6** order of succession; sequence: *I lost my train of thought when I was interrupted.* **7** bring up; rear; teach: *They trained their child to be considerate of others.* **8** make skillful by teaching and practice: *Saint Bernard dogs were trained to hunt for travelers lost in the snow.* **9** make fit by exercise and diet: *Runners train for races.* **10** to point; aim: *train cannon upon a fort.* **11** bring into a particular position: *Train the vine around this post.* 1-6 *n.,* 7-11 *v.* —**train′a ble,** *adj.* —**train′less,** *adj.*

train ee (trā nē′), person who is receiving training. *n.*

train er (trā′nər), person who trains: *He is an animal trainer for the circus. n.*

train ing (trā′ning), **1** practical education in some art, profession, etc.: *training for teachers.* **2** development of strength and endurance: *physical training.* **3** good condition maintained by exercise, diet, etc.: *The athlete kept in training by not overeating and not smoking. n.*

train load (trān′lōd′), as much as a train can hold or carry. *n.*

train man (trān′mən), brakeman or railroad worker in a train crew, of lower rank than a conductor. *n., pl.* **train-men.**

traipse (trāps), walk about aimlessly, carelessly, or needlessly: *The children traipsed about, looking for something to do. v.,* **traipsed, traips ing.**

trait (trāt), quality of mind, character, etc.; distinguishing feature; characteristic: *Courage, love of fair play, and common sense are desirable traits. n.*

trai tor (trā′tər), **1** person who betrays his or her country or ruler: *Benedict Arnold became a traitor by helping the British during the Revolutionary War.* **2** person who betrays a trust, duty, friend, etc. *n.*

trai tor ous (trā′tər əs), like a traitor; treacherous; faithless. *adj.* —**trai′tor ous ly,** *adv.* —**trai′tor ous ness,** *n.*

tra jec tor y (trə jek′tər ē), the curved path of a projectile, comet, or planet. *n., pl.* **tra jec tor ies.**

tram (tram), **1** BRITISH. streetcar. **2** truck or car on which loads are carried in mines. *n.* —**tram′less,** *adj.*

tram mel (tram′əl), **1** Usually, **trammels,** *pl.* anything that hinders or restrains: *A large inheritance freed the artist from the trammels of poverty.* **2** hinder; restrain. 1 *n.,* 2 *v.,* **tram meled, tram mel ing** or **tram melled, tram mel ling.**

tramp (tramp), **1** walk heavily: *She tramped across the room in her heavy boots.* **2** step heavily (on): *He tramped on the flowers.* **3** sound of a heavy step: *the tramp of marching feet.* **4** go on foot; walk: *The hikers tramped through the mountains.* **5** a long, steady walk; hike: *The children went on a tramp through the woods.* **6** person who

travels from place to place on foot, living by doing odd jobs, begging, etc. **7** freighter that takes a cargo when and where it can. 1,2,4 *v.,* 3,5-7 *n.* —**tramp′er,** *n.*

tram ple (tram′pəl), **1** tread heavily on; crush: *The herd of wild cattle trampled the farmer's crops.* **2** tread heavily; tramp. **3** treat cruelly, harshly, or scornfully: *The tyrant trampled his subjects and deprived them of all their rights.* **4** act or sound of trampling: *We heard the trample of many feet.* 1-3 *v.,* **tram pled, tram pling;** 4 *n.*

trample on or **trample upon,** treat with scorn, harshness, or cruelty: *to trample on someone's rights.*

trampoline

tram po line (tram′pə lēn′), piece of canvas or other sturdy fabric stretched on a metal frame, used for tumbling, acrobatics, etc. *n.* [*Trampoline* comes from Italian *trampolino.*]

tram way (tram′wā′), BRITISH. track for streetcars. *n.*

trance (def. 1)—The hypnotist placed her in a **trance,** so that she was able to lie completely stiff between the chairs.

trance (trans), **1** state of unconsciousness somewhat like sleep. A person may be in a trance from illness or from hypnosis. Some people can even put themselves into a trance. **2** a dreamy, absorbed condition that is like a trance: *She sat in a trance, thinking of her past life. n.* [*Trance* came into English about 600 years ago from French *transe,* which comes from *transir,* meaning "pass away," and can be traced back to Latin *trans-,* meaning "across," and *ire,* meaning "go."] —**trance′like′,** *adj.*

tran quil (trang′kwəl), calm; peaceful; quiet: *the tranquil morning air. adj.* —**tran′quil ly,** *adv.* —**tran′quil ness,** *n.*

tran quil ize (trang′kwə līz), **1** make calm, peaceful, or quiet. **2** become tranquil. *v.,* **tran quil ized, tran quil iz ing.** —**tran′quil i za′tion,** *n.*

tran quil iz er (trang′kwə lī′zər), any of several drugs that relax muscles, reduce nervous tension, lower blood pressure, etc. *n.*

tran quil li ty or **tran quil i ty** (trang kwil′ə tē), tranquil condition; calmness; peacefulness; quiet. *n.*

trans-, *prefix.* **1** across; over; through; beyond: *Transcon-*

tinental = across the continent. **2** in or to a different place, condition, etc.: *Transplant = plant in another place.*

trans act (tran zakt′), attend to; manage; do; carry on (business): *We transact business with stores all over the country. v.* —**trans ac′tor,** *n.*

trans ac tion (tran zak′shən), **1** the carrying on (of business): *She attends to the transaction of important matters herself.* **2** piece of business: *A record was kept of the firm's latest transaction with the bank.* **3 transactions,** *pl.* record of what was done at the meetings of a society, club, etc. *n.*

Trans Alaska Pipeline (tranz), official name of the **Alaska Pipeline.**

trans at lan tic (tran′sət lan′tik), **1** crossing the Atlantic: *a transatlantic liner, a transatlantic cable.* **2** on the other side of the Atlantic. *adj.* —**trans′at lan′ti cal ly,** *adv.*

tran scend (tran send′), **1** go beyond the limits or powers of; exceed; be above: *The grandeur of Niagara Falls transcends words.* **2** be higher or greater than; surpass; excel: *The speed of airplanes transcends that of any previous form of transportation. v.*

tran scend ence (tran sen′dəns), a being transcendent. *n.*

tran scend ent (tran sen′dənt), surpassing ordinary limits; excelling; superior; extraordinary. *adj.*

tran scen den tal (tran′sen den′tl), going beyond ordinary experience or limits. *adj.*

trans con ti nen tal (tran′skon tə nen′tl), **1** crossing a continent: *a transcontinental railroad.* **2** on the other side of a continent. *adj.*

tran scribe (tran skrīb′), **1** to copy in writing or in typewriting: *The minutes of the meeting were transcribed from the secretary's shorthand notes.* **2** make a recording or phonograph record for broadcasting. *v.*, **tran scribed, tran scrib ing.** —**tran scrib′er,** *n.*

tran script (tran′skript), **1** a written or typewritten copy: *The secretary prepared a transcript of the minutes of the meeting.* **2** copy or reproduction of anything: *The college wanted a transcript of my high-school record. n.*

tran scrip tion (tran skrip′shən), **1** a transcribing; copying. **2** a copy; transcript. **3** arrangement of music, etc., on a record for use in broadcasting. *n.*

tran sept (tran′sept), **1** the shorter part of a cross-shaped church. **2** either end of this part. *n.*

trans fer (tran sfėr′ *or* tran′sfėr′ for 1,2,5; tran′sfėr′ for 3,4,6,7), **1** change or move from one person or place to another; hand over: *The clerk was transferred to another department. Please have my trunks transferred to the Union Station.* **2** convey (a drawing, design, pattern) from one surface to another: *You transfer the embroidery design from the paper to cloth by pressing it with a warm iron.* **3** a transferring or a being transferred. **4** thing transferred; a drawing, pattern, etc., printed from one surface onto another. **5** change from one bus, train, etc., to another. **6** ticket allowing a passenger to change from one bus, train, etc., to another. **7** point or place for transferring. 1,2,5 *v.*, **trans ferred, trans fer ring;** 3,4,6,7 *n.*

trans fer a ble (tran sfėr′ə bəl), able to be transferred. *adj.*

trans fer ence (tran sfėr′əns), a transferring or a being transferred. *n.*

trans fig u ra tion (tran sfig′yə rā′shən), **1** a change in form or appearance; transformation. **2 Transfiguration,** (in the Bible) the change in the appearance of Jesus on the mountain. *n.*

trans fig ure (tran sfig′yər), **1** change in form or appearance; transform: *New paint had transfigured the old house.* **2** change so as to glorify; exalt. *v.*, **trans fig ured, trans fig ur ing.** —**trans fig′ure ment,** *n.*

trans fix (tran sfiks′), **1** pierce through: *The hunter trans-*

fixed the lion with a spear. **2** make motionless (with amazement, terror, etc.). *v.* —**trans fix′ion** (tran sfik′shən).

trans form (tran sfôrm′), **1** change in form or appearance: *The blizzard transformed the bushes into mounds of white.* **2** change in condition, nature, or character: *A tadpole becomes transformed into a frog.* **3** change (one form of energy) into another. A dynamo transforms mechanical energy into electricity. **4** change (an electric current) to a higher or lower voltage, from alternating to direct current, or from direct to alternating current. *v.*

trans for ma tion (tran′sfər mā′shən), a transforming or a being transformed: *the transformation of a caterpillar into a butterfly. n.*

trans form er (tran sfôr′mər), **1** person or thing that transforms. **2** device for changing an alternating current into one of higher or lower voltage. *n.*

trans fuse (tran sfyüz′), transfer (blood) from one person or animal to another. *v.*, **trans fused, trans fus ing.**

trans fu sion (tran sfyü′zhən), transfer of blood from one person or animal to another: *The injured driver was bleeding badly and needed a transfusion. n.*

trans gress (trans gres′), **1** break a law, command, etc.; sin. **2** go beyond (a limit): *Their manners transgress the bounds of good taste. v.*

trans gres sion (trans gresh′ən), a transgressing or a being transgressed: *the transgression of a law, to commit a grave transgression. n.*

trans gres sor (trans gres′ər), person who transgresses; sinner. *n.*

tran sient (tran′shənt), **1** passing soon; fleeting; not lasting: *Joy and sorrow are often transient.* **2** passing through and not staying long: *a transient guest in a hotel.* **3** visitor or boarder who stays for a short time. 1,2 *adj.*, 3 *n.* —**tran′sient ly,** *adv.*

tran sis tor (tran zis′tər), a small electronic device containing semiconductors, which amplifies or controls the flow of electrons in an electric circuit. Transistors are used in radios, television sets, computers, etc. *n.* [*Transistor* is a blend of *transfer* and *resistor.*]

tran sis tor ize (tran zis′tə rīz′), equip or reduce in size with transistors. *v.*, **tran sis tor ized, tran sis tor iz ing.**

transistor radio, a usually small, battery-powered radio equipped with transistors.

tran sit (tran′sit *or* tran′zit), **1** a passing across or through. **2** a carrying or a being carried across or through: *The goods were damaged in transit.* **3** transportation by trains, buses, etc.: *All systems of transit are crowded during the rush hour.* **4** instrument used in surveying to measure angles. *n.*

transit (def. 4)

tran si tion (tran zish′ən), a change or passing from one condition, place, thing, activity, topic, etc., to another: *a transition from poverty to power. Abrupt transitions in a book confuse the reader.* *n.*

tran si tion al (tran zish′ə nəl), of transition; of change from one more or less fixed condition to another. *adj.* —**tran si′tion al ly,** *adv.*

tran si tive (tran′sə tiv), taking a direct object. In "Bring me my coat" and "Raise the window," *bring* and *raise* are transitive verbs. *adj.* —**tran′si tive ly,** *adv.* —**tran′si tive ness,** *n.*

tran si to ry (tran′sə tôr′ē), passing soon or quickly; lasting only a short time: *My distress was transitory; I was soon happy again. adj.* —**tran′si to′ri ly,** *adv.* —**tran′si to′ri ness,** *n.*

Trans kei (tran skā′ *or* tran skī′), country in S Africa. It was formerly part of the Republic of South Africa. See **South Africa** for map. *Capital:* Umtata. *n.*

trans late (tran slāt′ *or* tran′slāt), 1 change from one language into another: *translate a book from French into English.* 2 express (one thing) in terms of another: *translate words into action. v.,* **trans lat ed, trans lat ing.** —**trans lat′a ble,** *adj.*

trans la tion (tran slā′shən), 1 a translating or a being translated: *the translation of the Bible from Hebrew into Latin, the translation of a promise into deed.* 2 result of translating; version. The Latin translation of the Bible is called the Vulgate. *n.*

trans la tor (tran slā′tər *or* tran′slā tər), person who translates. *n.*

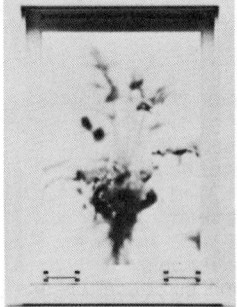

translucent
a plant seen through
translucent glass

transparent
the same plant seen
through transparent glass

trans lu cent (tran slü′snt), letting light through without being transparent: *Frosted glass is translucent. adj.* —**trans lu′cent ly,** *adv.*

trans mi gra tion (tran′smī grā′shən), (in certain religious beliefs) the passing of a soul at death into another body. *n.*

trans mis sion (tran smish′ən), 1 a sending over; passing on; passing along; letting through: *Mosquitoes are the only means of transmission of malaria.* 2 the part of an automobile or other motor vehicle that transmits power from the engine to the rear or front axle by the use of gears. 3 passage through space of electromagnetic waves from the transmitting station to the receiving station: *When transmission is good, even foreign radio stations can be heard.* 4 something transmitted. *n.*

trans mit (tran smit′), 1 send over; pass on; pass along; let through: *I will transmit the money by special messenger. Rats transmit disease.* 2 cause (light, heat, sound, etc.) to pass through a medium. 3 convey (force or movement) from one part of a body or mechanism to another.

4 send out (signals) by means of electromagnetic waves or by wire: *Some station is transmitting every hour of the day.* 5 pass on through inheritance: *One's physical characteristics may be transmitted to one's children. v.,* **trans mit ted, trans mit ting.** —**trans mit′ta ble, trans mit′ti ble,** *adj.*

trans mit ter (tran smit′ər), 1 person or thing that transmits something. 2 that part of a telegraph or telephone by which sound waves are converted to electrical impulses and sent to a receiver. 3 device that sends out signals by means of electromagnetic waves: *Radio and television stations have transmitters. n.*

trans mu ta tion (tran′smyə tā′shən), a change from one nature, substance, or form into another. *n.*

trans mute (tran smyüt′), change from one nature, substance, or form into another: *We can transmute water power into electrical power. v.,* **trans mut ed, trans mut ing.** —**trans mut′a ble,** *adj.* —**trans mut′a bly,** *adv.* —**trans mut′er,** *n.*

tran som (tran′səm), 1 window over a door or other window, usually hinged for opening. 2 a horizontal bar across a window; crossbar separating a door from the window over it. *n.*

tran son ic (tran son′ik), having to do with or moving at a speed immediately below or above the speed of sound. *adj.* Also, **transsonic.**

trans pa cif ic (tran′spə sif′ik), 1 crossing the Pacific. 2 on the other side of the Pacific. *adj.*

trans par en cy (tran sper′ən sē *or* tran spar′ən sē), 1 transparent quality or condition. 2 something transparent. 3 picture, design, or the like, made visible by light shining through from behind. *n., pl.* **trans par en cies.**

trans par ent (tran sper′ənt *or* tran spar′ənt), 1 letting light through so that things on the other side can be distinctly seen: *Window glass is transparent.* 2 easily seen through or detected: *a transparent excuse.* 3 frank; free from pretense or deceit: *a person of transparent honesty. adj.* —**trans par′ent ly,** *adv.* —**trans par′ent ness,** *n.*

tran spi ra tion (tran′spə rā′shən), a transpiring. *n.*

tran spire (tran spīr′), 1 take place; happen: *I heard later what transpired at the meeting.* 2 leak out; become known. 3 pass off or send off moisture in the form of vapor through a membrane or surface, as from the human body or from leaves. *v.,* **tran spired, tran spir ing.** —**tran spir′a ble,** *adj.*

trans plant (tran splant′ *for 1-3;* tran′splant *for 4,5*), 1 plant again in a different place: *We grow the flowers indoors and then transplant them to the garden.* 2 remove from one place to another: *A group of farmers was transplanted to the island by the government.* 3 transfer (skin, an organ, etc.) from one person, animal, or part of the body to another: *transplant a kidney.* 4 the transfer of skin, an organ, etc., from one person, animal, or part of the body to another: *a heart transplant.* 5 something that has been transplanted. 1-3 *v.,* 4,5 *n.* —**trans plant′a ble,** *adj.* —**trans plant′er,** *n.*

trans plan ta tion (tran′splan tā′shən), a transplanting or a being transplanted. *n.*

trans port (tran spôrt′ *for 1,5,7;* tran′spôrt *for 2-4,6*), 1 carry from one place to another: *Wheat is transported from the farms to the mills.* 2 a carrying from one place to another: *Trucks are much used for transport.* 3 ship used to carry troops and supplies. 4 aircraft that transports passengers, mail, freight, etc. 5 carry away by strong feeling: *She was transported with joy by the good news.* 6 a strong feeling: *a transport of rage.* 7 send away to another country as a punishment: *Years ago, England transported many of its criminals to Australia.* 1,5,7 *v.,* 2-4,6 *n.* —**trans port′a ble,** *adj.* —**trans port′er,** *n.*

trans por ta tion (tran′spər tā′shən), 1 a transporting:

The transportation for our trip was arranged by the travel bureau. **2** a being transported. **3** the business of transporting people or goods: *Railroads, trucks, bus lines, and airlines are all engaged in transportation.* **4** means of transport. **5** cost of transport; ticket for transport. **6** a sending away to another country as a punishment. *n.*

trans pose (tran spōz′), **1** change the position or order of; interchange: *Transpose the two colors to make a better design.* **2** change the usual order of (letters, words, or numbers): *I transposed the numbers and mistakenly wrote 19 for 91.* **3** (in music) change the key of. **4** transfer (a term) to the other side of an algebraic equation, changing plus to minus or minus to plus. *v.,* **trans posed, trans pos ing. —trans pos′a ble,** *adj.* **—trans pos′er,** *n.*

trans po si tion (tran′spə zish′ən), **1** a transposing or a being transposed. **2** piece of music transposed into a different key. *n.*

trans ship (tran ship′), transfer from one ship, train, car, etc., to another. *v.,* **trans shipped, trans ship ping.**

trans son ic (tran son′ik), transonic. *adj.*

tran sub stan ti a tion (tran′səb stan′shē ā′shən), **1** a changing of one substance into another. **2** (in Christian theology) the doctrine that the bread and wine of the Holy Communion are changed into the substance of the body and blood of Christ. *n.*

Trans vaal (trans väl′), province of the Republic of South Africa, in the NE part. *n.*

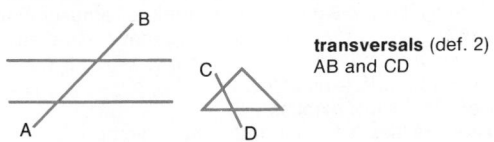

transversals (def. 2) AB and CD

trans ver sal (trans vėr′səl), **1** transverse. **2** line intersecting two or more other lines. 1 *adj.,* 2 *n.* **—transver′sal ly,** *adv.*

trans verse (trans vėrs′), **1** lying across; placed crosswise; crossing from side to side: *transverse beams.* **2** something transverse. 1 *adj.,* 2 *n.* **—trans verse′ly,** *adv.*

Tran syl van ia (tran′səl vā′nyə), region in central and W Romania, formerly part of Hungary. *n.* **—Tran′syl van′ian,** *adj., n.*

trap (trap), **1** thing or means for catching animals. **2** trick or other means for catching someone off guard: *The lawyer set traps to make the witness contradict herself.* **3** catch in a trap: *The bear was trapped.* **4** set traps for animals. **5** trap door. **6** a bend in a drainpipe for holding a small amount of water to prevent the escape of air, sewer gas, etc. **7** a light, two-wheeled carriage. **8** device to throw clay pigeons, etc., into the air to be shot at. **9 traps,** *pl.* drums, cymbals, bells, gongs, etc., used especially in a small band or orchestra. 1,2,5-9 *n.,* 3,4 *v.,* **trapped, trap ping. —trap′like′,** *adj.*

trap door, door in a floor or roof.

tra peze (trə pēz′), a short horizontal bar hung by ropes like a swing, used in gymnasiums and circuses. *n.*

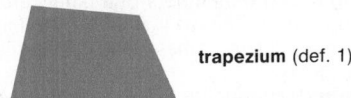

trapezium (def. 1)

tra pe zi um (trə pē′zē əm), **1** a four-sided plane figure having no sides parallel. **2** (in Great Britain) trapezoid (def. 1). *n., pl.* **tra pe zi ums, tra pe zi a** (trə pē′zē ə).

trap e zoid (trap′ə zoid), **1** a four-sided plane figure having two sides parallel and two sides not parallel. **2** (in

Great Britain) trapezium (def. 1). *n.*

trap per (trap′ər), person who traps, especially one who traps wild animals for their furs. *n.*

trap pings (trap′ingz), things worn; ornaments: *He had all the trappings of a cowboy, but he couldn't even ride a horse. n.pl.*

trap shoot er (trap′shü′tər), person who engages in trapshooting. *n.*

trap shoot ing (trap′shü′ting), sport of shooting at clay pigeons or other targets thrown or released from traps into the air. *n.*

trash (trash), **1** broken or torn bits, such as leaves, twigs, husks, etc.: *Rake up the trash in the yard.* **2** worthless stuff; rubbish: *That magazine is trash.* **3** disreputable people; riffraff. *n.* [*Trash* comes from Norwegian *trask.*]

trash y (trash′ē), like or containing trash; worthless. *adj.,* **trash i er, trash i est. —trash′i ly,** *adv.* **—trash′i ness,** *n.*

trau ma (trô′mə *or* trou′mə), **1** a physical wound or an emotional shock; injury. **2** the condition produced by it. *n., pl.* **trau mas, trau ma ta** (trô′mə tə).

trau mat ic (trô mat′ik *or* trou mat′ik), of or produced by a wound, injury, or shock: *a traumatic experience. adj.* **—trau mat′i cal ly,** *adv.*

tra vail (trə vāl′ *or* trav′āl), **1** toil; labor. **2** to toil; labor. **3** trouble; hardship: *It was a time of great travail.* **4** the pains of childbirth. **5** suffer the pains of childbirth. 1,3,4 *n.,* 2,5 *v.*

trav el (trav′əl), **1** go from one place to another; journey: *She is traveling to Europe this summer.* **2** a going in trains, ships, cars, etc., from one place to another; journeying: *She loves travel.* **3 travels,** *pl.* journeys: *"Gulliver's Travels."* **4** go from place to place selling things: *He travels for a large firm.* **5** move; proceed; pass: *Sound travels in waves.* **6** pass through or over: *travel a road.* 1,4-6 *v.,* **trav eled, trav el ing** *or* **trav elled, trav el ling;** 2,3 *n.*

trav eled *or* **trav elled** (trav′əld), **1** that has done much traveling: *a well-traveled friend.* **2** much used by travelers: *a heavily traveled road. adj.*

trav el er *or* **trav el ler** (trav′ə lər), person or thing that travels. *n.*

trav e logue *or* **trav e log** (trav′ə lôg), **1** lecture describing travel, usually accompanied by pictures or films. **2** motion picture depicting travel. *n.*

trav erse (trav′ərs *or* trə vėrs′ for 1; trav′ərs for 2,3), **1** pass across, over, or through: *We traversed the desert by truck.* **2** lying across; being across; transverse. **3** something put or lying across: *We walked over the traverse that lay across the gully.* 1 *v.,* **trav ersed, trav ers ing;** 2 *adj.,* 3 *n.* **—trav ers′a ble,** *adj.* **—trav ers′er,** *n.*

trav es ty (trav′ə stē), **1** an imitation of a serious literary work or subject, done in such a way as to make it seem ridiculous. **2** any treatment or imitation that makes a serious thing seem ridiculous: *A prejudiced judge made the trial a travesty of justice.* **3** make (a serious subject or

trapezoids (def. 1)

matter) ridiculous; imitate in an absurd or grotesque way. 1,2 *n., pl.* **trav es ties;** 3 *v.,* **trav es tied, trav es ty-ing.** [*Travesty* comes from French *travesti,* meaning "disguised," and can be traced back to Latin *trans-,* meaning "over," and *vestire,* meaning "to dress."]

trawl (trôl), 1 a strong net dragged along the bottom of the sea. 2 to fish or catch fish with a net by dragging it along the bottom of the sea. 3 line supported by buoys and having many short lines with baited hooks attached to it. 4 to fish or catch fish with lines supported by buoys. 1,3 *n.,* 2,4 *v.*

trawl er (trô/lər), boat used in trawling. *n.*

tray (trā), 1 a flat, shallow holder or container with a low rim around it: *I carried the dishes on a tray.* 2 tray with dishes of food on it: *a breakfast tray.* 3 a shallow box that fits into a trunk, cabinet, etc.: *Dentists keep many of their instruments in trays. n.*

treach er ous (trech/ər əs), 1 not to be trusted; not faithful; disloyal: *The king was betrayed by treacherous advisers.* 2 having a false appearance of strength, security, etc.; not reliable; deceiving: *Thin ice is treacherous. adj.* —**treach/er ous ly,** *adv.* —**treach/er ous ness,** *n.*

treach er y (trech/ər ē), 1 a breaking of faith; treacherous behavior; deceit. 2 treason. *n., pl.* **treach er ies.**

trea cle (trē/kəl), BRITISH. molasses. *n.*

tread (tred), 1 set the foot down; walk; step: *Don't tread on the flower beds. They trod through the meadow.* 2 set the feet on; walk on or through; step on: *tread the streets.* 3 press under the feet; trample on; crush: *tread grapes.* 4 make, form, or do by walking: *Cattle had trodden a path to the pond.* 5 act or sound of treading: *We heard the tread of marching feet.* 6 way of walking: *He walks with a heavy tread.* 7 the part of stairs or a ladder that a person steps on: *The stair treads were covered with rubber to prevent slipping.* 8 the part of a wheel or tire that presses against the ground, rail, etc. The treads of rubber tires are grooved to improve traction. 1-4 *v.,* **trod, trod den** or **trod, tread ing;** 5-8 *n.* —**tread/er,** *n.*

trea dle (tred/l), 1 lever or pedal worked by the foot to impart motion to a machine: *the treadle of a sewing machine.* 2 work a treadle. 1 *n.,* 2 *v.,* **trea dled, trea-dling.** —**trea/dler,** *n.*

treadmill (def. 1)

tread mill (tred/mil/), 1 device used for exercise or to power a machine by having a person or animal walk or run on a sloping, endless belt. 2 any wearisome or monotonous round of work or of life. *n.*

treas., 1 treasurer. 2 treasury.

trea son (trē/zn), betrayal of one's country or ruler. *Helping the enemies of one's country is treason. n.*

trea son a ble (trē/zn ə bəl), of treason; involving treason; traitorous. *adj.* —**trea/son a ble ness,** *n.* —**trea/-son a bly,** *adv.*

trea son ous (trē/zn əs), treasonable. *adj.* —**trea/son-ous ly,** *adv.*

treas ure (trezh/ər), 1 wealth or riches stored up; valuable things: *The pirates buried their treasure along the coast.* 2 any thing or person that is much loved or valued: *The silver teapot was the old couple's chief treasure.* 3 value highly: *treasure good health.* 4 put away for future use; store up. 1,2 *n.,* 3,4 *v.,* **treas ured, treas ur ing.** —**treas/ur a ble,** *adj.* —**treas/ure less,** *adj.*

treas ur er (trezh/ər ər), person in charge of money. *The treasurer of a club pays its bills. n.*

treas ur y (trezh/ər ē), 1 place where money is kept. 2 money owned; funds: *We voted to pay for the party out of the club treasury.* 3 Also, **Treasury.** department of the government that has charge of the income and expenses of a country. The Treasury of the United States collects federal taxes, mints money, supervises national banks, and prevents counterfeiting. 4 place where treasure is kept. *n., pl.* **treas ur ies.**

treat (trēt), 1 act toward: *The children treated the puppy with care.* 2 think of; consider; regard: *He treated his mistake as a joke.* 3 deal with to relieve or cure: *The dentist is treating my toothache.* 4 deal with to bring about some special result: *treat a metal plate with acid in engraving.* 5 deal with; discuss: *The article treated the subject thoroughly.* 6 express in literature or art: *The author of these books always treats his themes realistically.* 7 entertain with food, drink, or amusement: *treat some friends to ice cream.* 8 gift of food, drink, or amusement: *"This is my treat," she said.* 9 anything that gives pleasure: *Being in the country is a treat to her.* 1-7 *v.,* 8,9 *n.* —**treat/a ble,** *adj.* —**treat/er,** *n.*

treat of, deal with; discuss.

trea tise (trē/tis), a formal and systematic book or writing dealing with some subject. *n.*

treat ment (trēt/mənt), 1 act or process of treating: *My cold won't respond to treatment.* 2 way of treating: *This cat has suffered from bad treatment.* 3 thing done or used to treat a disease, condition, etc. *n.*

trea ty (trē/tē), a formal agreement, especially one between nations, signed and approved by each nation. *n., pl.* **trea ties.** —**trea/ty less,** *adj.*

tre ble (treb/əl), 1 three times: *Her salary is treble mine.* 2 make or become three times as much: *He trebled his money by buying property for $5,000 and selling it for $15,000.* 3 the highest part in music; soprano. 4 voice or instrument that takes this part. 5 of or for the treble. 6 shrill; high-pitched. 1,5,6 *adj.,* 2 *v.,* **tre bled, tre bling;** 3,4 *n.*

treble clef, symbol in music indicating that the pitch of the notes on a staff is above middle C; G clef. See **clef** for diagram.

tre bly (treb/lē), three times. *adv.*

tree (trē), 1 a large plant with a woody trunk and usually having branches and leaves at some distance from the ground. 2 any plant that resembles a tree in form or size. 3 piece or structure often made of wood or resembling a tree, used for some special purpose: *a clothes tree.* 4 anything like a tree. A family tree is a diagram with branches showing how the members of a family are related. 5 chase up a tree: *The cat was treed by a dog.* 1-4 *n.,* 5 *v.,* **treed, tree ing.** [*Tree* comes from Old English *trēo.*] —**tree/like/,** *adj.*

bark up the wrong tree, pursue the wrong object or use the wrong means to get it.

up a tree, INFORMAL. in a difficult position.

tree frog, any of various small, tree-dwelling frogs with adhesive disks or suckers on their toes.

tree less (trē/lis), without trees: *a treeless plain. adj.* —**tree/less ness,** *n.*

tree **toad,** tree frog.

tree top (trē′top′), the top or uppermost part of a tree. *n.*

tre foil (trē′foil), **1** plant having threefold leaves. Clover is a trefoil. **2** ornament like a threefold leaf. *n.*

trek (trek), **1** travel slowly by any means: *The pioneers trekked across the great western plains by covered wagon.* **2** a journey: *It was a long trek over the mountains.* **1** *v.*, **trekked, trek king; 2** *n.* [*Trek* is from Afrikaans *trekken,* which came from Dutch *trekken,* meaning originally "to draw, pull."] —**trek′ker,** *n.*

trel lis (trel′is), frame of light strips of wood or metal crossing one another with open spaces in between, especially one supporting growing vines. *n., pl.* **trel lis es.** —**trel′lis like′,** *adj.*

trem ble (trem′bəl), **1** shake because of fear, excitement, weakness, cold, etc.: *The child's voice trembled with fear.* **2** feel fear, anxiety, etc.: *We trembled for the safety of the trapped miners.* **3** move gently: *The leaves trembled in the breeze.* **4** a trembling: *There was a tremble in her voice as she began to recite.* **1-3** *v.,* **trem bled, trem bling; 4** *n.* —**trem′bler,** *n.* —**trem′bling ly,** *adv.*

trem bly (trem′blē), trembling; tremulous. *adj.,* **trem bli er, trem bli est.**

tre men dous (tri men′dəs), **1** very severe; dreadful; awful: *The army suffered a tremendous defeat.* **2** INFORMAL. very great; enormous: *That is a tremendous house for a family of three.* **3** INFORMAL. extraordinary: *We had a tremendous time at the party.* *adj.* —**tre men′dous ly,** *adv.* —**tre men′dous ness,** *n.*

trem o lo (trem′ə lō), **1** a rapid repetition of musical tones or a rapid alternation of tones, causing a trembling or vibrating effect. **2** device in an organ used to produce this effect. *n., pl.* **trem o los.**

trem or (trem′ər), **1** an involuntary shaking or trembling: *a nervous tremor in the voice.* **2** thrill of emotion or excitement. **3** a shaking or vibrating movement. An earthquake is sometimes called an earth tremor. *n.* —**trem′or less,** *adj.*

trem u lous (trem′yə ləs), **1** trembling; quivering: *The child's voice was tremulous with sobs.* **2** timid; fearful: *He was shy and tremulous in the presence of strangers. adj.* —**trem′u lous ly,** *adv.* —**trem′u lous ness,** *n.*

trench (trench), **1** a long, narrow ditch with earth thrown up in front to protect soldiers. **2** a deep furrow; ditch: *to dig a trench for a sewer pipe.* **3** a long, narrow depression in the ocean floor. **4** dig a trench in. **1-3** *n., pl.* **trench es; 4** *v.*

trench ant (tren′chənt), **1** sharp; keen; cutting: *trenchant wit.* **2** vigorous; effective: *a trenchant policy. adj.* —**trench′ant ly,** *adv.*

trench coat, kind of belted raincoat with straps on the shoulders and cuffs.

trench coat

a hat	i it	oi oil	ch child	(a in about
ā age	ī ice	ou out	ng long	e in taken
ä far	o hot	u cup	sh she	ə = { i in pencil
e let	ō open	u̇ put	th thin	o in lemon
ē equal	ô order	ü rule	ᵀH then	(u in circus
ėr term			zh measure	

trench er (tren′chər), a wooden platter on which meat is served and carved. *n.*

trench er man (tren′chər mən), person who has a hearty appetite; eater. *n., pl.* **trench er men.**

trend (trend), **1** the general direction; course; tendency: *The trend of modern living is away from many old customs.* **2** have a general direction; tend; run: *Modern life trends toward less formal customs.* **1** *n.,* **2** *v.*

Tren ton (tren′tən), capital of New Jersey, in the W part. *n.*

trep i da tion (trep′ə dā′shən), nervous dread; fear; fright. *n.*

tres pass (tres′pəs), **1** go on somebody's property without any right: *We put up "No Trespassing" signs to keep hunters off our land.* **2** go beyond the limits of what is right, proper, or polite: *I won't trespass on your time any longer.* **3** act or fact of trespassing. **4** do wrong; sin. **5** a wrong; a sin. **6** an unlawful act done by force against the person, property, or rights of another. **1,2,4** *v.,* **3,5,6** *n., pl.* **tres pass es.** —**tres′pass er,** *n.*

tress (tres), **1** a lock, curl, or braid of hair. **2 tresses,** *pl.* long, flowing hair: *golden tresses. n.*

trestle (def. 2)

tres tle (tres′əl), **1** framework similar to a sawhorse, used as a support for a table top, platform, etc. **2** a braced framework of timber, steel, etc., used as a bridge to support a road, railroad tracks, etc. *n.*

trey (trā), card, die, or domino with three spots. *n.*

tri-, *prefix.* **1** having three ____: *Triangle = (a figure) having three angles.* **2** three ____s: *Trisect = divide into three parts.* **3** once every three ____: *Trimonthly = once every three months.*

tri ad (trī′ad), **1** group of three, especially of three closely related persons or things. **2** (in music) a chord of three tones. *n.*

tri al (trī′əl), **1** the examining and deciding of a case in court: *The suspect was brought to trial.* **2** process of trying or testing the fitness, truth, strength, or other quality of anything: *The mechanic gave the motor another trial to see if it would start.* **3** for a try or test: *a trial run, a trial model.* **4** condition of being tried or tested: *The new clerk was hired on trial for one month.* **5** trouble; hardship: *The pioneers faced many trials.* **6** cause of trouble or hardship: *be a trial to one's parents.* **7** an attempt to do something; effort. **1,2,4-7** *n.,* **3** *adj.*

trial and error, method of arriving at a desired result by repeated experiments until past errors are eliminated.

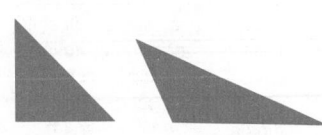

triangles (def. 1)

tri an gle (trī/ang/gəl), **1** a plane figure having three sides and three angles. **2** something shaped like a triangle. **3** a musical instrument consisting of a triangle of steel, open at one corner, that is struck with a steel rod. *n.*

triangle (def. 3)

tri an gu lar (trī ang/gyə lər), shaped like a triangle; three-cornered. *adj.* —**tri an/gu lar ly,** *adv.*

tri ath lete (trī ath/lēt), one who takes part in a triathlon. *n.*

tri ath lon (trī ath/lon), an athletic contest combining a lengthy swim, bicycle ride, and run. *n.* [*Triathlon* comes from *tri-,* meaning "three," and Greek *athlon,* meaning "contest."]

trib al (trī/bəl), of a tribe: *tribal customs. adj.*

tribe (trīb), **1** group of people united by common ancestry and customs, forming a community under a leader or leaders. **2** class or set of people: *a tribe of hungry children. n.*

tribes man (trībz/mən), member of a tribe. *n., pl.* **tribesmen.**

trib u la tion (trib/yə lā/shən), great trouble; severe trial; affliction: *The castaways on the desert island suffered many tribulations. n.*

tri bu nal (tri byü/nl *or* trī byü/nl), **1** court of justice; place of judgment: *They were brought before the tribunal of seven judges for trial.* **2** something by or in which judgment is given; deciding authority: *the tribunal of the polls, the tribunal of the press. n.*

trib une (trib/yün), **1** official in ancient Rome chosen by the plebeians to protect their rights and interests. **2** defender of the people. *n.*

trib u tar y (trib/yə ter/ē), **1** stream that flows into a larger stream or body of water: *The Ohio River is one of the tributaries of the Mississippi River.* **2** flowing into a larger stream or body of water. **3** paying tribute; required to pay tribute. **4** a person or country that pays tribute. 1,4 *n., pl.* **trib u tar ies;** 2,3 *adj.*

trib ute (trib/yüt), **1** money paid by one nation to another for peace or protection or because of some agreement. **2** any forced payment: *The pirates demanded tribute from passing ships.* **3** an acknowledgment of thanks or respect; compliment: *Labor Day is a tribute to workers. n.*

trice (trīs), a very short time; moment; instant: *I'll open the gate in a trice. n.*

tri ceps (trī/seps), the large muscle at the back of the upper arm. It extends or straightens the arm. *n., pl.* **tri ceps** *or* **tri ceps es.**

tri chi na (tri kī/nə), a small, slender worm whose adult form lives in the intestines and whose larva lives in the muscles of human beings, pigs, and some other animals. Trichinae usually get into the human body from pork which is infected with the larvae and is not cooked long enough to destroy them. *n., pl.* **tri chi nae** (tri kī/nē).

trich i no sis (trik/ə nō/sis), disease due to the presence of trichinae, characterized by headache, chills, fever, and soreness of muscles. *n.*

trick (trik), **1** something done to deceive or cheat: *The false message was a trick to get her to leave the house.* **2** deceive; cheat: *We were tricked into buying a stolen sailboat.* **3** feat of skill, as in juggling or sleight of hand; clever act: *We enjoyed the tricks of the trained animals.* **4** the best way of doing or dealing with something: *She knows the trick of restoring old furniture.* **5** piece of mischief; prank: *Hiding my lunch was a mean trick.* **6** play tricks. **7** of, like, or done as a trick or stunt: *trick riding, trick shooting.* **8** a peculiar habit or way of acting: *He has a trick of pulling at his collar.* **9** the cards played in one round of a card game. **10** a turn or period of duty on a job, especially at steering a ship. **11** to dress: *The guests were all tricked up in fancy clothes.* 1,3-5,8-10 *n.,* 2,6,11 *v.,* 7 *adj.* —**trick/er,** *n.* —**trick/ing ly,** *adv.* —**trick/less,** *adj.* **do the trick** or **turn the trick,** do what one wants done.

trick er y (trik/ər ē), use of tricks; deception; cheating. *n., pl.* **trick er ies.**

trick le (trik/əl), **1** flow or cause to flow in drops or in a small stream: *Tears trickled down their cheeks. He trickled water over the flowers.* **2** a small flow or stream. **3** come, go, pass, etc., slowly and unevenly: *An hour before the show people began to trickle into the theater.* 1,3 *v.,* **trickled, trick ling;** 2 *n.* —**trick/ling ly,** *adv.*

trick ster (trik/stər), a cheat; deceiver. *n.*

trick y (trik/ē), **1** full of tricks; deceiving: *A fox is trickier than a sheep.* **2** not doing what is expected; dangerous or difficult to handle: *The back door has a tricky lock. adj.,* **trick i er, trick i est.** —**trick/i ly,** *adv.*

tri col or (trī/kul/ər), **1** having three colors. **2** flag having three colors. The tricolor of France has three equal vertical sections of blue, white, and red. 1 *adj.,* 2 *n.*

tri col ored (trī/kul/ərd), having three colors: *a tricolored flag. adj.*

tri cot (trē/kō), **1** a knitted fabric made by hand or machine. **2** a kind of woolen cloth. *n.*

tri cy cle (trī/sə kəl *or* trī/sik/əl), vehicle having three wheels, worked by pedals. *n.*

tri dent (trīd/nt), a three-pronged spear, especially the spear carried by Neptune, or Poseidon, god of the sea. *n.* [*Trident* is from Latin *tridentem,* which comes from *tri-,* meaning "three," and *dentem,* meaning "tooth."]

tried (trīd), **1** tested by experience or examination; proven: *a person of tried abilities.* **2** past tense and past participle of **try.** *I tried to call you. Have you tried calling again?* 1 *adj.,* 2 *v.*

tri en ni al (trī en/ē əl), **1** lasting three years. **2** occurring every three years. **3** event that occurs every three years. 1,2 *adj.,* 3 *n.*

tries (trīz), **1** plural of **try. 2** the present tense of **try.** *She always tries to do her best.* 1 *n.,* 2 *v.*

tri fle (trī/fəl), **1** thing having little value or importance. **2** a small amount; little bit: *He was a trifle late.* **3** a small amount of money: *The picture cost only a trifle.* **4** talk or act lightly, not seriously: *Don't trifle with serious matters.* **5** handle a thing idly; play or toy (with): *She trifled with her pencil.* **6** spend (time, effort, money, etc.) on things having little value: *They trifled away the whole morning.* 1-3 *n.,* 4-6 *v.,* **tri fled, tri fling.**

tri fler (trī/flər), person who trifles; frivolous, shallow person. *n.*

tri fling (trī'fling), **1** having little value; not important; small: *The friends treated their quarrel as only a trifling matter.* **2** frivolous; shallow. *adj.* —**tri'fling ly**, *adv.* —**tri'fling ness**, *n.*

trig ger (trig'ər), **1** the small lever pulled back by the finger in firing a gun. **2** lever pulled or pressed to release a spring or catch and set some mechanism in action. **3** set off (an explosion): *A spark triggered the explosion.* **4** initiate; start: *trigger an outburst of violence.* **5** anything that sets off or initiates something else. 1,2,5 *n.*, 3,4 *v.* [*Trigger* is from Dutch *trekker*, which comes from *trekken,* meaning "to pull."] —**trig'ger less**, *adj.*

trig o no met ric (trig'ə nə met'rik), of trigonometry. *adj.* —**trig'o no met'ri cal ly**, *adv.*

trig o nom e try (trig'ə nom'ə trē), branch of mathematics that deals with the relations between the sides and angles of triangles and the calculations based on these. *n.*

trill (tril), **1** sing, play, sound, or speak with a tremulous, vibrating sound: *Some birds trill their songs.* **2** act or sound of trilling. **3** a quick alternation of two musical notes either a tone or a half tone apart. **4** in phonetics: **a** a rapid vibration of the lips, the tip of the tongue, or the uvula. **b** sound produced by such a vibration. 1 *v.*, 2-4 *n.*

tril lion (tril'yən), **1** (in the United States and France) 1 followed by 12 zeros; one thousand billions. **2** (in Great Britain) 1 followed by 18 zeros; one million billions. *n., adj.*

tril li um (tril'ē əm), plant with three leaves in a whorl from the center of which rises a single flower. *n.*

tri lo bite (trī'lə bīt), a small marine animal that lived hundreds of millions of years ago. It had a body divided into three vertical lobes and many horizontal segments. Fossil trilobites are widely found in various rocks. *n.*

tril o gy (tril'ə jē), group of three plays, operas, novels, etc., which together form a related series, although each is a complete work in itself. *n., pl.* **tril o gies.**

trim (trim), **1** put in good order; make neat by cutting away parts: *The gardener trimmed the hedge. Would you trim my hair?* **2** remove (parts that are not needed or not neat): *trim dead leaves off plants.* **3** neat; in good condition or order: *a trim room, a trim uniform, a trim athlete.* **4** well designed and maintained: *We saw a trim little sailboat out on the lake.* **5** good condition or order: *get in trim for a race.* **6** condition; order: *That ship is in poor trim for a voyage.* **7** decoration; trimming: *the trim on a coat.* **8** decorate: *The children trimmed the Christmas tree.* **9** balance (a boat, aircraft, etc.) by arranging the load carried. **10** such balance. **11** arrange (the sails) to fit wind and direction. **12** the visible woodwork inside a building, especially that around doors, windows, and other openings. **13** INFORMAL. defeat; beat. 1,2,8,9,11,13 *v.*, trimmed, trim ming; 3,4 *adj.*, trim mer, trim mest; 5-7,10,12 *n.* —**trim'ly**, *adv.* —**trim'ness**, *n.*

trim mer (trim'ər), person or thing that trims. *n.*

trim ming (trim'ing), **1** anything used to trim or decorate; decoration; ornament: *trimming for a shirt.* **2** INFORMAL. a defeat; beating. **3** act of a person or thing that trims. **4** trimmings, *pl.* **a** parts cut away in trimming. **b** everything needed to make something complete and festive: *turkey with all the trimmings. n.*

tri month ly (trī munth'lē), occurring every three months. *adj.*

Trin i dad (trin'ə dad), island in the West Indies, near Venezuela, part of the country of Trinidad and Tobago. *n.*

Trinidad and Tobago, country composed of two islands in the West Indies, a member of the Commonwealth of Nations. *Capital:* Port-of-Spain.

tri ni tro tol u ene (trī nī'trō tol'yü ēn'), TNT. *n.*

trin i ty (trin'ə tē), **1** group of three. **2** a being three. **3 Trinity,** the union of Father, Son, and Holy Ghost in one divine nature. *n., pl.* **trin i ties.**

trin ket (tring'kit), any small fancy article, bit of jewelry, or the like. *n.*

tri o (trē'ō), **1** piece of music for three voices or instruments. **2** group of three singers or players performing together. **3** any group of three. *n., pl.* **tri os.**

trip (trip), **1** a traveling about; journey; voyage: *We took a trip to Europe.* **2** stumble: *He tripped on the stairs.* **3** a loss of footing; stumble; slip. **4** cause to stumble and fall: *The loose board on the stairs tripped her.* **5** make a mistake; do something wrong: *She tripped on that difficult question.* **6** a mistake; blunder. **7** cause to make a mistake or blunder: *The difficult question tripped him.* **8** take light, quick steps: *The children came tripping down the path to meet us.* **9** a light, quick tread; stepping lightly. **10** release or operate suddenly (a catch, clutch, etc.); operate, start, or set free (a mechanism, weight, etc.). **11** a projecting part, catch, or the like for starting or checking some movement. **12** SLANG. hallucination or an instance of increased perception that is experienced while under the influence of LSD or a similar psychedelic drug. **13** SLANG. an exciting experience of any kind. 1,3,6,9,11-13 *n.*, 2,4,5,7,8,10 *v.*, **tripped, trip ping.**

tri par tite (trī pär'tīt), **1** divided into three parts. **2** made or shared by three parties: *a tripartite treaty between Great Britain, the United States, and France. adj.*

tripe (trīp), **1** the walls of the first and second stomachs of an ox, steer, or cow, used as food. **2** INFORMAL. something foolish, worthless, or offensive. *n.*

trip ham mer (trip'ham'ər), a heavy iron or steel block raised by machinery and then tripped by a mechanism and allowed to drop. *n.*

tri ple (trip'əl), **1** three times as much or as many: *a triple portion of cake, to get triple pay.* **2** number or amount that is three times as large: *Nine is the triple of three.* **3** having three parts: *a triple crown.* **4** make or become three times as much or as many: *The number of club members has tripled this year.* **5** hit by which a batter gets to third base in baseball. **6** make such a hit: *The batter tripled in the third inning.* 1,3 *adj.*, 2,5 *n.*, 4,6 *v.*, **tri pled, tri pling.**

trip let (trip'lit), **1** one of three children born at the same time of the same mother. **2** group of three. **3** (in music) group of three notes of equal value to be performed in the time of two. **4** three successive lines of poetry, usually rhyming and equal in length. *n.*

trip li cate (trip'lə kit *for 1,2;* trip'lə kāt *for 3*), **1** triple; threefold. **2** one of three things exactly alike. **3** make threefold; triple. 1 *adj.*, 2 *n.*, 3 *v.*, **trip li cat ed, trip li cat ing.** —**trip'li ca'tion**, *n.*
in triplicate, in three copies exactly alike.

tri ply (trip'lē), in a triple manner; three times. *adv.*

tri pod (trī'pod), **1** a three-legged support or stand for a camera, telescope, etc. **2** stool or other article having three legs. *n.*

Trip o li (trip'ə lē), **1** region in N Africa. It was a Turkish province and later an Italian colony; it is now included in Libya. **2** seaport and capital of Libya, in the NW part. *n.*

trip ping (trip′ing), light and quick. *adj.* —**trip′ping ly,** *adv.*

trip tych (trip′tik), set of three panels side by side, having pictures, carvings, or the like, on them. *n.*

tri reme (trī′rēm′), (in ancient Greece and Rome) a ship, usually a warship, with three rows of oars, one above the other, on each side. *n.*

tri sect (trī sekt′), **1** divide into three parts. **2** divide into three equal parts. *v.* —**tri sec′tion,** *n.* —**tri sec′tor,** *n.*

tri syl lab ic (trī′sə lab′ik), having three syllables. *adj.* —**tri′syl lab′i cal ly,** *adv.*

trite (trīt), worn out by use; no longer interesting; commonplace: *"Cheeks like roses" is a trite expression. adj.,* **trit er, trit est.** [*Trite* comes from Latin *tritum,* meaning "rubbed away."] —**trite′ly,** *adv.* —**trite′ness,** *n.*

Tri ton (trīt′n), (in Greek myths) a sea god having the head and body of a man and the tail of a fish. *n.*

tri umph (trī′umf), **1** victory; success: *final triumph over the enemy. The conquest of outer space is one of the great triumphs of modern science.* **2** gain victory; win success: *Our team triumphed over theirs.* **3** joy because of victory or success: *We welcomed the team home with cheers of triumph.* 1,3 *n.,* 2 *v.* —**tri′umph er,** *n.*

tri um phal (trī um′fəl), of or for a triumph; celebrating a victory: *a triumphal march. adj.*

tri um phant (trī um′fənt), **1** victorious or successful: *a triumphant army.* **2** rejoicing because of victory or success: *The winners spoke in triumphant tones about their skillful play. adj.* —**tri um′phant ly,** *adv.*

tri um vir (trī um′vər), one of three men who shared the same public office in ancient Rome. *n., pl.* **tri um virs, tri um vi ri** (trī um′və rī′).

tri um vir ate (trī um′vər it), **1** government by three persons together. **2** any association of three in office or authority. **3** any group of three. *n.*

triv et (triv′it), a stand or support with three legs or feet. *Trivets are used over fires and under platters. n.*

triv i a (triv′ē ə), things of little or no importance; trifles; trivialities. *n.pl.*

triv i al (triv′ē əl), not important; trifling; insignificant: *Your composition had only a few trivial mistakes. adj.* —**triv′i al ly,** *adv.* —**triv′i al ness,** *n.*

triv i al i ty (triv′ē al′ə tē), **1** trivial quality. **2** a trivial thing, remark, affair, etc.; trifle. *n., pl.* **triv i al i ties.**

triv i al ize (triv′ē ə līz), make trivial. *v.,* **triv i al ized, triv i al iz ing.** —**triv′i al i za′tion,** *n.*

trod (trod), past tense and a past participle of **tread.** *The path was trod by many feet. v.*

trod den (trod′n), a past participle of **tread.** *The cattle had trodden down the corn. v.*

Troi lus (troi′ləs *or* trō′i ləs), (in Greek legends) a son of King Priam of Troy. He was killed by Achilles. *n.*

Tro jan (trō′jən), **1** of Troy or its people. **2** person who was born or lived in Troy. **3** person who shows courage or energy: *They worked like Trojans.* 1 *adj.,* 2,3 *n.*

Trojan horse, (in Greek legends) a huge wooden horse in which the Greeks concealed soldiers and brought them into Troy during the Trojan War.

Trojan War, (in Greek legends) a ten years' war carried on by the Greeks against Troy to get back Helen, wife of King Menelaus of Sparta, who was carried off by Paris, son of King Priam of Troy.

troll[1] (trōl), **1** to fish with a moving line, usually by trailing the line behind the boat near the surface: *I trolled for bass.* **2** sing in succession the parts of a song: *troll a round. v.* —**troll′er,** *n.*

troll[2] (trōl), (in Scandinavian folklore) an ugly dwarf or giant living underground or in caves. *n.*

trol ley (trol′ē), **1** pulley at the end of a pole which moves against a wire to carry electricity to a streetcar or

an electric engine. A **trolley car** or **trolley bus** is a streetcar or bus having such a pulley. **2** basket, carriage, etc., suspended from a pulley which runs on an overhead track. *n., pl.* **trol leys.**

trolley car, streetcar drawing power from an overhead electric wire by means of a trolley.

trombone

trom bone (trom′bōn), a large brass wind instrument with a loud tone, usually with a long, sliding piece for varying the length of the tube. *n.*

trom bon ist (trom′bō nist), person who plays the trombone. *n.*

troop (trüp), **1** group or band of persons: *a troop of children.* **2** a herd, flock, or swarm: *a troop of deer.* **3** a military unit of cavalry, especially an armored cavalry unit, usually commanded by a captain. **4 troops,** *pl.* soldiers: *The government sent troops to put down the revolt.* **5** unit of boy scouts or girl scouts made up of two to four patrols or 16 to 32 members. **6** gather in troops or bands; move together: *The children trooped around the teacher.* **7** walk; go; go away: *The younger children trooped off after the older ones.* 1-5 *n.,* 6,7 *v.*

troop er (trü′pər), **1** soldier in a troop of cavalry. **2** a mounted police officer. The state police of some states are called troopers, because they were originally organized as mounted troops. **3** a cavalry horse. *n.*

troop ship (trüp′ship′), ship used to carry soldiers; transport. *n.*

trophy (def. 1)—She proudly displayed her **trophy.**

tro phy (trō′fē), **1** any prize, cup, etc., awarded to a victorious person or team: *The champion kept her tennis trophies on the mantelpiece.* **2** a spoil or prize of war, hunting, etc.: *The hunter kept the lion's skin and head as trophies.* **3** anything serving as a remembrance. *n., pl.* **tro phies.** —**tro′phy less,** *adj.*

trop ic (trop′ik), **1** either of two imaginary circles around the earth which represent the points farthest north and south at which the sun shines directly overhead. The **tropic of Cancer** is 23.45 degrees north of the equator; the **tropic of Capricorn** is 23.45 degrees south of the equator. **2 tropics** or **Tropics,** *pl.* the regions between and near these circles; the Torrid Zone. The hottest part of the earth is in the tropics. **3** of the tropics; belonging to the Torrid Zone. **1,2** *n.*, **3** *adj.*

trop i cal (trop′ə kəl), of the tropics: *Bananas are tropical fruit. adj.* —**trop′i cal ly,** *adv.*

tropical fish, any of certain small, usually brightly colored fishes native to the tropics, commonly kept in home aquariums.

tro pism (trō′piz′əm), tendency of an animal or plant to turn or move in response to a stimulus. *n.*

trop o sphere (trop′ə sfir), region of the atmosphere between the earth and the stratosphere, extending to about 13 miles (21 kilometers) above the earth's surface. Within the troposphere, there is a steady fall of temperature with increasing altitude. Most cloud formations occur in the troposphere. *n.*

trot (trot), **1** go at a gait between a walk and a run by lifting the right forefoot and the left hind foot at about the same time and then the other two feet in the same way. Horses and some other four-legged animals trot. **2** the motion or gait of trotting. **3** ride or drive at a trot: *The riders trotted home.* **4** run, but not fast: *The child trotted after me.* **5** a brisk, steady movement; a slow running. **1,3,4** *v.*, **trot ted, trot ting; 2,5** *n.*

troth (trôth), OLD USE. **1** faithfulness or fidelity; loyalty. **2** a promise. **3** betrothal. *n., pl.* **troths** (trôths *or* trôŦHz). **plight one's troth, 1** promise to marry. **2** promise to be faithful.

Trot sky (trot′skē), **Leon,** 1879-1940, leader in the Russian Revolution and Soviet minister of war from 1918 to 1925. He was later exiled and was assassinated in Mexico. *n.*

trot ter (trot′ər), horse that trots, especially one bred and trained to trot in a race. *n.*

trou ba dour (trü′bə dôr), one of the lyric poets and composers of southern France, eastern Spain, and northern Italy from the 1000's to the 1200's. The troubadours wrote mainly about love and chivalry. *n.*

trou ble (trub′əl), **1** pain and sorrow; distress; worry; difficulty: *The unruly students made trouble for their teacher.* **2** cause trouble to; disturb: *The lack of business troubled the grocer.* **3** disturbance; disorder: *political troubles.* **4** extra work; bother; effort: *Take the trouble to do careful work.* **5** require extra work or effort of: *May I trouble you to pass the sugar?* **6** to cause oneself inconvenience: *Don't trouble to come to the door; I can let myself in.* **7** a cause of inconvenience: *Is helping me a trouble to you?* **8** ailment; disease: *The patient suffered from heart trouble.* **9** cause pain to; hurt; pain: *A toothache troubled me.* **1,3,4,7,8** *n.*, **2,5,6,9** *v.*, **trou bled, troubling.** —**trou′bler,** *n.* —**trou′bling ly,** *adv.*

trou ble mak er (trub′əl mā′kər), person who often causes trouble for others. *n.*

trou ble shoot er (trub′əl shü′tər), person who discovers and eliminates causes of trouble. *n.*

trou ble some (trub′əl səm), **1** causing trouble; disturbing; annoying: *noisy, troublesome neighbors.* **2** tiresome; difficult: *a troublesome process. adj.* —**trou′ble some ly,** *adv.* —**trou′ble some ness,** *n.*

trou blous (trub′ləs), **1** disturbed; unsettled. **2** troublesome. *adj.* —**trou′blous ly,** *adv.* —**trou′blous ness,** *n.*

trough (trôf), **1** a long, narrow container for holding food or water: *We led our horses to the watering trough.* **2** something shaped like this: *The baker used a trough for kneading dough.* **3** channel for carrying water; gutter: *The wooden trough under the eaves of the house carries off rain water.* **4** a long hollow between two ridges, etc.: *the trough between two waves. n.* —**trough′like′,** *adj.*

trounce (trouns), **1** beat or thrash. **2** defeat in a contest or match: *The victors trounced the losing team. v.*, **trounced, trounc ing.**

troupe (trüp), troop, band, or company, especially a group of actors, singers, or acrobats. *n.*

troup er (trü′pər), **1** member of a theatrical troupe. **2** an experienced actor. *n.*

trou sers (trou′zərz), a two-legged outer garment reaching from the waist to the ankles; pants. *n.pl.* [*Trousers* can be traced back to Scottish Gaelic *triubhas.*]

trous seau (trü′sō *or* trü sō′), a bride's outfit of clothes, linen, etc. *n., pl.* **trous seaux** (trü′sōz *or* trü sōz′), **trousseaus.**

trout (trout), a freshwater food fish related to the salmon. *n., pl.* **trouts** *or* **trout.**

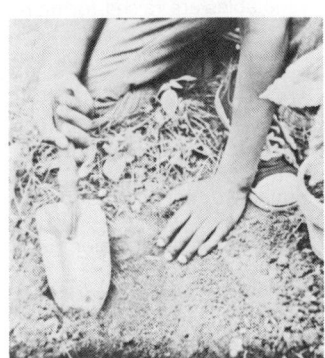

trowel (def. 2)

trow el (trou′əl), **1** tool with a broad, flat blade, used for spreading or smoothing plaster or mortar. **2** tool with a curved blade, used for taking up plants, loosening dirt, etc. **3** spread, smooth, or form with or as if with a trowel. **1,2** *n.*, **3** *v.*, **trow eled, trow el ing** *or* **trow elled, trow el ling.**

troy (troi), **1** in or by troy weight. **2** troy weight. **1** *adj.*, **2** *n.*

Troy (troi), **1** city in the NW part of ancient Asia Minor, scene of the Trojan War. **2** city in E New York State, on the Hudson River. *n.*

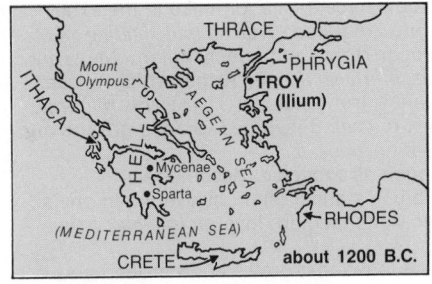

Troy (def. 1)

troy weight, a standard system of weights used for gems and precious metals. One pound troy equals a little over four fifths of an ordinary pound. 12 troy ounces = 1 troy pound.

tru an cy (trü′ən sē), act or habit of playing truant; truant behavior. *n., pl.* **tru an cies.**

tru ant (trü′ənt), **1** student who stays away from school without permission. **2** staying away from school without permission. **3** person who neglects duty. **4** guilty of neglecting duty: *The truant factory worker left the machine running without watching it.* **5** lazy. **6** wandering: *That truant dog won't stay home.* **7** of a truant or truants: *a truant officer.* 1,3 *n.,* 2,4-7 *adj.* **—tru′ant ly,** *adv.*

play truant, 1 stay away from school without permission. **2** stay away from work or duties.

truce (trüs), a stop in fighting; temporary peace: *A truce was declared between the two armies. n.* **—truce′less,** *adj.*

truck[1] (truk), **1** a strongly built motor vehicle for carrying heavy loads. **2** carry on a truck: *truck freight to the warehouse.* **3** drive a truck. **4** frame on small wheels for moving trunks, etc. **5** frame with two or more pairs of wheels for supporting the end of a railroad car, locomotive, etc. 1,4,5 *n.,* 2,3 *v.*

truck[2] (truk), **1** vegetables raised for market. **2** small articles of little value; odds and ends. **3** INFORMAL. rubbish; trash. **4** INFORMAL. dealings: *She has no truck with peddlers. n.*

truck er (truk′ər), **1** person who drives a truck. **2** person whose business is carrying goods, etc., by trucks. *n.*

truck farm, farm where vegetables are raised for market.

truck ing (truk′ing), act or business of carrying goods, etc., on a truck or trucks. *n.*

truck le (truk′əl), give up or submit tamely; be servile: *Some workers got promoted by truckling to superiors and flattering them. v.,* **truck led, truck ling. —truck′ler,** *n.*

truckle bed, trundle bed.

truc u lence (truk′yə ləns), quality or condition of being truculent; fierceness; brutal harshness. *n.*

truc u lent (truk′yə lənt), **1** fierce, savage, or violent: *a truculent villain, a truculent defense of one's rights.* **2** brutally harsh or scathing: *a truculent remark. adj.* **—truc′u lent ly,** *adv.*

Tru deau (trü dō′), **Pierre Elliott,** born 1919, prime minister of Canada from 1968 to 1979 and from 1980 to 1984. *n.*

trudge (truj), **1** go on foot; walk. **2** walk wearily or with effort. **3** a hard or weary walk: *a long trudge up the hill.* 1,2 *v.,* **trudged, trudg ing;** 3 *n.* **—trudg′er,** *n.*

true (trü), **1** agreeing with fact; not false: *It is true that 6 and 4 are 10. The story I told is true; I did not make it up.* **2** real; genuine: *true gold, true kindness.* **3** faithful; loyal: *a true friend, true to your promises.* **4** agreeing with a standard; right; proper; correct; exact; accurate: *a true copy.* **5** representative of the class named: *A sweet potato is not a true potato.* **6** rightful; lawful: *the true heir to the property.* **7** accurately formed, fitted, or placed: *a true angle.* **8** make true; shape, place, or make in the exact position, form, etc., required: *True up that slanting door.* **9** steady in direction, force, etc.; unchanging: *The arrow made a true course through the air.* **10** that which is true. **11** in a true manner; truly; exactly: *Your words ring true.* 1-7,9 *adj.,* **tru er, tru est;** 8 *v.,* **trued, tru ing** or **true ing;** 10 *n.,* 11 *adv.* **—true′ness,** *n.*

come true, happen as expected; become real.

true-blue (trü′blü′), staunch and unwavering in one's faith, beliefs, etc.; unchanging; loyal: *a true-blue friend. adj.*

truf fle (truf′əl), fungus that grows underground and is valued as a food. It resembles a potato in appearance. *n.*

tru ism (trü′iz′əm), statement that almost everybody knows is true, such as "Good health is a blessing." *n.*

tru ly (trü′lē), **1** in a true manner; exactly; rightly; faithfully: *Tell me truly what you think.* **2** in fact; really: *It was truly a beautiful sight. adv.*

Tru man (trü′mən), **Harry S.,** 1884-1972, the 33rd president of the United States, from 1945 to 1953. *n.*

trump[1] (trump), **1** any playing card of a suit that during the play of a hand ranks higher than the other suits.

2 Often, **trumps,** *pl.* the suit itself. **3** take (a trick, card, etc.) with a trump. **4** play a card of the suit that is trump. 1,2 *n.,* 3,4 *v.* **—trump′less,** *adj.*

trump[2] (trump), make (up) to deceive: *trump up false charges against a person. v.*

trumped-up (trumpt′up′), made up to deceive; fabricated: *a trumped-up charge. adj.*

trump er y (trump′ər ē), something showy but without value; worthless ornaments; useless stuff; rubbish; nonsense. *n., pl.* **trump er ies.**

trumpet (def. 1)

trum pet (trum′pit), **1** a brass wind instrument that has a powerful tone, commonly a curved tube with a flaring bell at one end. **2** thing shaped like a trumpet. Ear trumpets were once used to help people who were not able to hear well. **3** blow a trumpet. **4** a sound like that of a trumpet. **5** make a sound like a trumpet: *The elephant trumpeted in fright.* **6** proclaim loudly or widely: *trumpet a story all over town.* 1,2,4 *n.,* 3,5,6 *v.* **—trum′pet less,** *adj.* **—trum′pet like′,** *adj.*

trumpet creeper, bignonia.

trum pet er (trum′pə tər), person who blows a trumpet. *n.*

trumpet vine, bignonia.

trun cate (trung′kāt), **1** cut off a part of. **2** cut off; blunt, as if cut off: *the truncate leaf of the tulip tree.* 1 *v.,* **trun cat ed, trun cat ing;** 2 *adj.* **—trun′cate ly,** *adv.* **—trun ca′tion,** *n.*

trun cheon (trun′chən), a stick cut and shaped for use as a weapon; club: *a policeman's truncheon. n.*

trun dle (trun′dl), **1** roll along; push along: *The worker trundled a wheelbarrow full of cement.* **2** trundle bed. 1 *v.,* **trun dled, trun dling;** 2 *n.* **—trun′dler,** *n.*

trundle bed, a low bed on small wheels; truckle bed. It can be pushed under a regular bed when not in use.

trunk (trungk), **1** the main stem of a tree, as distinct from the branches and the roots. **2** the main part of anything: *the trunk of a column.* **3** main; chief: *a trunk highway.* **4** a big, sturdy box with a hinged lid, for holding clothes, etc., when traveling. **5** an enclosed compartment in an automobile for storing baggage, a spare tire, etc. **6** a human or animal body, not counting the head, arms, and legs. **7** an elephant's snout. **8** trunk line. **9 trunks,** *pl.* very short pants worn by athletes, swimmers, acrobats, etc. 1,2,4-9 *n.,* 3 *adj.* **—trunk′less,** *adj.* **—trunk′like′,** *adj.*

trunk line, 1 the main line of a railroad, canal, etc. **2** any main line, such as the line between telephone exchanges.

truss (trus), **1** tie or fasten; bind: *truss up a prisoner hand and foot. The cook trussed up the chicken before roasting it.* **2** framework of beams or other supports, usually connected in a series of triangles and used to support a roof, bridge, etc. **3** support (a roof, bridge, etc.) with trusses. **4** pad attached to a belt, used to support a hernia. 1,3 *v.*, 2,4 *n.*, *pl.* **truss es. —truss′er,** *n.*

trust (trust), **1** firm belief in the honesty, truthfulness, justice, or power of a person or thing; faith: *Children put trust in their parents.* **2** have faith; believe; rely: *Trust in me.* **3** believe firmly in the honesty, truth, justice, or power of; have faith in: *a person you can trust.* **4** rely on; depend on: *If you can't trust your memory, write things down.* **5** person or thing trusted: *God is our trust.* **6** confident expectation or hope: *Our trust is that she will soon be well.* **7** hope; believe: *I trust you will soon feel better.* **8** something managed for the benefit of another; something committed to one's care: *The house is a trust which she holds for her dead brother's children.* **9** duty or responsibility that a person takes on when given confidence or authority: *Congress has a public trust.* **10** keeping; care: *The will was left in my trust.* **11** managing for an owner. A trust company undertakes to manage property for anyone. **12** commit to the care of; leave without fear: *Can I trust the keys to them?* **13** confidence in the ability or intention of a person to pay at some future time for goods, etc.; business credit: *to sell on trust.* **14** give business credit to: *The butcher will trust us for the meat.* **15** an illegal combination of companies to control the production and price of some commodity and to eliminate or reduce competition: *a steel trust.* **16** of a trust or trusts; held in trust. 1,5,6,8-10,13,15 *n.*, 2-4,7,12,14 *v.*, 11,16 *adj.* [*Trust* came into English about 700 years ago from Icelandic *traust.*] **—trust′a ble,** *adj.* **—trust′er,** *n.*

in trust, as a thing taken charge of for another.

trust to, rely on; depend on: *trust to luck.*

trus tee (tru stē′), person responsible for the property or affairs of another person, a company, or an institution: *A trustee will manage the children's property until they grow up.* *n.*

trus tee ship (tru stē′ship), **1** position of trustee. **2** administration by a country of a trust territory. **3** trust territory. *n.*

trust ful (trust′fəl), ready to confide; ready to have faith; trusting; believing: *The trustful child would lend money to anyone.* *adj.* **—trust′ful ly,** *adv.* **—trust′ful ness,** *n.*

trust fund, money, property, or other valuables held in trust by one person for the benefit of another.

trust ing (trus′ting), trustful. *adj.* **—trust′ing ly,** *adv.* **—trust′ing ness,** *n.*

trust territory, a territory or region administered by a country or countries on behalf of the United Nations.

trust wor thi ness (trust′wėr′ᵬē nis), condition or character of being trustworthy. *n.*

trust wor thy (trust′wėr′ᵬē), able to be depended on; reliable: *a trustworthy person.* *adj.*

trust y (trus′tē), **1** able to be depended on; reliable: *a trusty friend.* **2** a convict who is given special privileges because of good behavior. 1 *adj.*, **trust i er, trust i est;** 2 *n.*, *pl.* **trust ies.** **—trust′i ly,** *adv.* **—trust′i ness,** *n.*

truth (trüth), **1** that which is true: *Tell the truth.* **2** a fixed or established principle, law, etc.; proven doctrine: *a basic scientific truth.* **3** quality or nature of being true, exact, honest, sincere, or loyal. *n.*, *pl.* **truths** (trüᵬz or trüths). **—truth′less,** *adj.*

in truth, truly; really; in fact: *It was in truth a beautiful scene.*

truth ful (trüth′fəl), **1** telling the truth: *He is a truthful boy and will tell exactly what happened.* **2** conforming to truth; agreeing with the facts: *You can count on her for a truthful report.* *adj.* **—truth′ful ly,** *adv.* **—truth′ful ness,** *n.*

try (trī), **1** make an effort; attempt: *I tried to do the work.* **2** attempt to do or accomplish: *It seems easy until you try it.* **3** experiment on or with; make trial of: *Try this candy and see if you like it.* **4** find out about; test: *We try each*

car before we sell it. **5** an attempt; test; experiment: *Each girl had three tries at the high jump.* **6** judge in a court of law: *They were tried and found guilty.* **7** to subject to trials or hardship; afflict: *The pioneers were tried by the severe winter.* **8** put to severe test; strain: *Her carelessness tries my patience.* **9** make pure by melting or boiling: *The lard was tried in a big kettle.* 1-4,6-9 *v.*, **tried, try ing;** 5 *n.*, *pl.* **tries.**

try on, put on to test the fit, looks, etc.: *I tried on several coats.*

try out, 1 test or sample: *Try out this new recipe for apple pie.* **2** undergo a test or trial to determine fitness: *He tried out for the baseball team.*

try ing (trī′ing), hard to endure; annoying: *a trying day, a trying person.* *adj.* **—try′ing ly,** *adv.* **—try′ing ness,** *n.*

try out (trī′out′), INFORMAL. test made to determine fitness for a specific purpose: *Tryouts for the swimming team will start tomorrow.* *n.*

tryp sin (trip′sən), enzyme in the pancreatic juice that aids in the digestion of proteins. *n.*

tryst (trist), **1** appointment to meet at a certain time and place, especially one made by lovers. **2** place of meeting. *n.*

tsar (zär), czar. *n.*

tsa ri na (zä rē′nə), czarina. *n.*, *pl.* **tsa ri nas.**

Tschai kow sky or **Tschai kov sky** (chī kôf′skē), Tchaikovsky. *n.*

tset se fly (tset′sē), an African fly that sucks the blood of mammals and transmits sleeping sickness. [*Tsetse* is of Bantu origin.]

T-shirt (tē′shėrt′), **1** a light, close-fitting knitted shirt with short sleeves and no collar, worn for sports. **2** an undershirt resembling this. *n.* Also, **tee shirt.**

tsp., teaspoon or teaspoons.

T square, a T-shaped ruler used for making parallel lines, etc. The shorter arm slides along the edge of the drawing board, which serves as a guide.

T square

Tu., Tuesday.

tub (tub), **1** a large, open container for washing or bathing. **2** bathtub. **3** INFORMAL. bath: *He takes a cold tub every morning.* **4** a round container for holding butter, lard, etc., originally wooden but now often made of metal or plastic. **5** as much as a tub can hold. **6** INFORMAL. a clumsy, slow boat or ship. *n.* [*Tub* comes from Dutch *tubbe.*] **—tub′like′,** *adj.*

a hat	i it	oi oil	ch child	a in about
ā age	ī ice	ou out	ng long	e in taken
ä far	o hot	u cup	sh she	ə = { i in pencil
e let	ō open	u̇ put	th thin	o in lemon
ē equal	ô order	ü rule	ᴛʜ then	u in circus
ėr term			zh measure	

tuba

tu ba (tü′bə *or* tyü′bə), a large brass wind instrument of low pitch. *n., pl.* **tu bas.**

tub by (tub′ē), shaped like a tub; short and fat. *adj.*, **tub bi er, tub bi est. —tub′bi ness,** *n.*

tube (tüb *or* tyüb), **1** a long pipe of metal, glass, rubber, etc., mostly used to hold or carry liquids or gases. **2** a small cylinder of thin, easily bent metal with a cap that screws on the open end, used for holding toothpaste, paint, etc. **3** inner tube. **4** pipe or tunnel through which something travels: *The railroad runs under the river in a tube.* **5** anything like a tube: *the bronchial tubes.* **6** an electron or vacuum tube. **7 the tube,** INFORMAL. television. *n.* **—tube′like′,** *adj.*

tube less (tüb′lis *or* tyüb′lis), having no inner tube or tubes: *a tubeless tire. adj.*

tu ber (tü′bər *or* tyü′bər), the thick part of an underground stem. A potato is a tuber. *n.* **—tu′ber less,** *adj.*

tu ber cle (tü′bər kəl *or* tyü′bər kəl), **1** a small, rounded swelling or knob on an animal or plant. **2** a swelling caused by tuberculosis. *n.*

tu ber cu lar (tü bėr′kyə lər *or* tyü bėr′kyə lər), **1** having tubercles. **2** of tubercles. **3** having tuberculosis. **4** of tuberculosis: *tubercular symptoms. adj.* **—tu ber′cu lar ly,** *adv.*

tu ber cu lin (tü bėr′kyə lən *or* tyü bėr′kyə lən), a liquid substance prepared from the germ that causes tuberculosis, used to diagnose tuberculosis. *n.*

tu ber cu lo sis (tü bėr′kyə lō′sis *or* tyü bėr′kyə lō′sis), an infectious disease affecting various tissues of the body, but most often the lungs. *n.*

tu ber cu lous (tü bėr′kyə ləs *or* tyü bėr′kyə ləs), tubercular. *adj.* **—tu ber′cu lous ly,** *adv.*

tu ber ous (tü′bər əs *or* tyü′bər əs), **1** bearing tubers. **2** of or like tubers: *a tuberous root.* **3** covered with rounded knobs or swellings. *adj.*

tub ing (tü′bing *or* tyü′bing), **1** material in the form of a tube: *rubber tubing.* **2** tubes collectively. **3** a piece of tube. *n.*

tu bu lar (tü′byə lər *or* tyü′byə lər), **1** shaped like a tube; round and hollow. **2** of a tube or tubes. **3** constructed with or consisting of a number of tubes: *a tubular boiler. adj.* **—tu′bu lar ly,** *adv.*

tu bule (tü′byül *or* tyü′byül), a small tube. *n.*

tuck (tuk), **1** thrust into some narrow space or into some out-of-the-way place: *I tucked the letter into my pocket.* **2** thrust the edge or end of (a garment, covering, etc.) closely into place: *Tuck your shirt in.* **3** cover snugly: *Tuck the children in bed.* **4** pull or gather in a fold or folds: *She tucked up her sleeves before washing her hands.* **5** a fold sewed in a garment: *The pants were too big, so I put a tuck in them.* **6** sew a fold in (a garment) for trimming or to make it shorter or tighter: *The baby's dress was beautifully tucked with tiny stitches.* 1-4,6 *v.,* 5 *n.*

tuck er[1] (tuk′ər), piece of muslin, lace, etc., formerly worn around the neck or over the chest. *n.*

tuck er[2] (tuk′ər), INFORMAL. tire; weary; exhaust: *He was all tuckered out after the long trip. v.*

Tuc son (tü′son), city in S Arizona, famous as a health resort. *n.*

Tu dor (tü′dər *or* tyü′dər), **1** the royal family that ruled England from 1485 to 1603. Henry VIII belonged to the house of Tudor. **2** of the English Gothic style of architecture prevailing during the reign of the Tudor family. It was characterized by flat arches, shallow moldings, and elaborate paneling. 1 *n.,* 2 *adj.*

Tues., Tuesday.

Tues day (tüz′dē *or* tyüz′dē), the third day of the week, following Monday. *n.*

tu fa (tü′fə *or* tyü′fə), any of various porous rocks, especially a form of limestone deposited by springs, etc. *n., pl.* **tu fas.**

tuft (tuft), **1** bunch of feathers, hair, grass, etc., held together at one end: *The goat had a tuft of hair on its chin.* **2** clump of bushes, trees, etc. **3** cluster of threads sewn tightly through a mattress, comforter, etc., so as to keep the padding in place. **4** put tufts on. 1-3 *n.,* 4 *v.* **—tuft′er,** *n.*

tuft ed (tuf′tid), **1** furnished with a tuft or tufts. **2** formed into a tuft or tufts. *adj.*

tug (tug), **1** pull with force or effort; pull hard: *We tugged the boat in to shore. The dog tugged at the rope.* **2** a hard pull: *The baby gave a tug at my hair.* **3** tugboat. **4** tow by a tugboat. **5** trace[2]. 1,4 *v.,* **tugged, tug ging;** 2,3,5 *n.* **—tug′ger,** *n.* **—tug′less,** *adj.*

tug boat (tug′bōt′), a small, powerful boat used to tow or push other boats. *n.*

tug-of-war (tug′əv wôr′ *or* tug′ə wôr′), **1** contest between two teams pulling at the ends of a rope, each trying to drag the other over a line marked between them. **2** any hard struggle: *The rival politicians waged a long tug-of-war for the leadership of their party. n., pl.* **tugs-of-war.**

Tui ler ies (twē′lər ēz), former royal palace in Paris. It was burned in 1871. *n.*

tu i tion (tü ish′ən *or* tyü ish′ən), **1** money paid for instruction: *a $300 increase in college tuition.* **2** teaching or instruction. *n.* **—tu i′tion less,** *adj.*

tu lip (tü′lip *or* tyü′lip), a plant having long, narrow leaves and cup-shaped flowers of various colors. Tulips grow from bulbs and bloom in the spring. *n.*

WORD HISTORY

tulip

Tulip is from Turkish *tülbend,* meaning "turban," which came from Persian *dulband.* The flower was thought to resemble a turban.

tulle (tül), a thin, fine net, usually of silk, used for veils, etc. *n.*

Tul sa (tul′sə), city in NE Oklahoma, on the Arkansas River. *n.*

tum ble (tum′bəl), **1** to fall headlong or in a helpless way: *The child tumbled down the stairs.* **2** a fall by tumbling: *The tumble only bruised the child.* **3** throw over or down; cause to fall: *The strong winds tumbled a tree in our yard.* **4** roll or toss about: *The patient tumbled restlessly in the bed.* **5** move in a hurried or awkward way: *I tumbled out of bed.* **6** perform leaps, springs, somersaults, etc. **7** turn over; rumple; muss: *to tumble bedclothes.* **8** confusion; disorder: *Her desk was a complete tumble of papers.* 1,3-7 *v.*, **tum bled, tum bling**; 2,8 *n.*

tum ble-down (tum′bəl doun′), ready to fall down; not in good condition; dilapidated: *a tumble-down shack in the mountains. adj.*

tum bler (tum′blər), **1** person who performs leaps, springs, etc.; acrobat. **2** a drinking glass without a stem and with a heavy, flat bottom. **3** the contents of such a glass. **4** part in the lock that must be moved from a certain position in order to release the bolt. *n.*

tum ble weed (tum′bəl wēd′), plant growing in the western United States that breaks off from its roots and is blown about by the wind. *n.*

tum brel or **tum bril** (tum′brəl), **1** a two-wheeled cart, especially one used on a farm for hauling and dumping manure. **2** cart that carried prisoners to be executed during the French Revolution. *n.*

tu mes cence (tü mes′ns *or* tyü mes′ns), a swelling; a swollen condition. *n.*

tu mes cent (tü mes′nt *or* tyü mes′nt), becoming swollen; swelling. *adj.*

tu mid (tü′mid *or* tyü′mid), **1** swollen. **2** swollen with big words; pompous. *adj.* —**tu′mid ly,** *adv.* —**tu′mid ness,** *n.*

tum my (tum′ē), INFORMAL. stomach. *n., pl.* **tum mies.**

tu mor (tü′mər *or* tyü′mər), an abnormal growth in or on some part of the body. *n.* —**tu′mor like′,** *adj.*

tu mult (tü′mult *or* tyü′mult), **1** noise or uproar; commotion: *The sailors' voices could not be heard above the tumult of the storm.* **2** a violent disturbance or disorder: *The cry of "Fire! Fire!" caused a tumult in the theater.* **3** a violent disturbance of mind or feeling; confusion or excitement: *The quarrel left her in a tumult. n.*

tu mul tu ous (tü mul′chü əs *or* tyü mul′chü əs), **1** characterized by tumult; very noisy or disorderly; violent: *a tumultuous celebration.* **2** greatly disturbed: *tumultuous emotion.* **3** rough; stormy: *tumultuous ocean waves. adj.* —**tu mul′tu ous ly,** *adv.* —**tu mul′tu ous ness,** *n.*

tun (tun), **1** a large cask for holding liquids. **2** (in former times) a measure of capacity of liquor, equal to 252 gallons. *n.*

tu na (tü′nə), a large sea fish closely related to the mackerel, having coarse, oily flesh that is widely used as food; tunny. *n., pl.* **tu nas** *or* **tu na.** [*Tuna* comes from Spanish *atún,* and can be traced back to Greek *thynnos.*]

tun a ble (tü′nə bəl *or* tyü′nə bəl), **1** able to be tuned. **2** in tune. *adj.* Also, **tuneable.** —**tun′a ble ness,** *n.*

tuna fish, tuna.

tun dra (tun′drə), a vast, level, treeless plain in the arctic regions. The ground beneath its surface is frozen even in summer. Much of Alaska and northern Canada is tundra. *n.* [*Tundra* was borrowed from Russian *tundra.*]

tune (tün *or* tyün), **1** piece of music; an air or melody: *popular tunes.* **2** the proper pitch: *The piano is out of tune. I can't sing in tune.* **3** mood or manner; tone: *They'll soon change their tune.* **4** agreement; harmony: *ideas in tune with the times.* **5** be in tune; be in harmony. **6** adjust to

the proper pitch; put in tune: *tune a piano.* 1-4 *n.,* 5,6 *v.,* **tuned, tun ing.**

to the tune of, INFORMAL. to the amount or extent of.

tune in, adjust a radio or television set to hear or see (what is wanted).

tune out, adjust a radio or television set to get rid of (a signal or interference that is unwanted).

tune up, 1 bring (musical instruments) to the same pitch; put in tune. **2** put (a motor or engine) into the best working order.

tune a ble (tü′nə bəl *or* tyü′nə bəl), tunable. *adj.*

tune ful (tün′fəl *or* tyün′fəl), musical; melodious: *a tuneful song. adj.* —**tune′ful ly,** *adv.* —**tune′ful ness,** *n.*

tune less (tün′lis *or* tyün′lis), without tune; not musical. *adj.* —**tune′less ly,** *adv.*

tun er (tü′nər *or* tyü′nər), **1** person who tunes pianos, organs, or other musical instruments. **2** device for adjusting a radio receiver to accept a given frequency and reject other frequencies. *n.*

tune-up (tün′up′ *or* tyün′up′), series of checks and adjustments and replacement of certain parts of an engine or motor to keep it running well. *n.*

tung sten (tung′stən), a heavy, hard, steel-gray, metallic element found only in certain rare minerals. Tungsten has the highest melting point of all metals. It is used in making steel, electric light bulb filaments, surgical instruments, automobile parts, etc. *n.* [*Tungsten* was borrowed from Swedish *tungsten,* which comes from *tung,* meaning "heavy," and *sten,* meaning "stone."]

tu nic (tü′nik *or* tyü′nik), **1** garment like a shirt or gown, worn by the ancient Greeks and Romans. **2** any garment like this. **3** a short, close-fitting coat worn by soldiers, policemen, etc. *n.*

tuning fork

tuning fork, a small, two-pronged steel instrument used in tuning musical instruments. When struck it vibrates at a fixed, constant, known rate and so makes a musical tone of a certain pitch.

Tu nis (tü′nis *or* tyü′nis), seaport and capital of Tunisia, in the NE part. *n.*

Tu ni sia (tü nē′zhə *or* tyü nē′zhə), country in N Africa. *Capital:* Tunis. See **Algeria** for map. *n.* —**Tu ni′sian,** *adj., n.*

tun nel (tun′l), **1** an underground passage: *Motor traffic passes under the river through a tunnel.* **2** make an underground passage: *The mole tunneled in the ground.* 1 *n.,* 2 *v.* —**tun′nel er,** *n.* —**tun′nel like′,** *adj.*

tun ny (tun′ē), tuna. *n., pl.* **tun nies** *or* **tun ny.**

tu pe lo (tü′pə lō *or* tyü′pə lō), a large North American tree with strong, tough wood, whose flowers are often used by bees in making honey. *n., pl.* **tu pe los.**

Tu pi (tü pē′ *or* tü′pē), **1** member of a group of Indian tribes of Brazil, Paraguay, and Uruguay. **2** language of these tribes. *n., pl.* **Tu pi** or **Tu pis** for 1.

tup pence (tup′əns), two pence. *n.*

tur ban (tėr′bən), **1** scarf wound around the head or around a cap, worn by men in parts of India and in some other countries. **2** any hat or headdress like this. *n.*

turban (def. 1)

tur bid (tėr′bid), **1** not clear; muddy; thick: *a turbid river.* **2** confused; disordered: *a turbid imagination. adj.*

tur bine (tėr′bən *or* tėr′bīn), engine or motor consisting of a wheel with vanes which is made to revolve by the force of water, steam, or air. Turbines are often used to turn generators that produce electric power. *n.*

tur bo jet (tėr′bō jet′), **1** jet engine having a turbine-driven air compressor which supplies a continuous, high-pressure flow of air to the burners. **2** aircraft having such an engine. *n.*

tur bo prop (tėr′bō prop′), **1** adaptation of the turbojet in which a propeller, driven by a shaft from the turbine, provides most of the thrust. Some additional thrust is provided by the ejection of exhaust gases from the rear. **2** aircraft having such an engine. *n.*

tur bot (tėr′bət), a large European flatfish, much valued as food. *n., pl.* **tur bots** or **tur bot.**

tur bu lence (tėr′byə ləns), turbulent condition; disorder: tumult; commotion. *n.*

tur bu lent (tėr′byə lənt), **1** causing disturbance; disorderly; unruly; violent: *a turbulent mob.* **2** stormy; tempestuous: *turbulent weather. adj.* —**tur′bu lent ly,** *adv.*

tu reen (tə rēn′), a deep, covered dish for serving soup, etc. *n.*

turf (tėrf), **1** the upper surface of the soil covered with grass and other small plants, including their roots and the soil clinging to them; sod. **2** piece of this. **3** cover with turf. **4** peat. **5** Usually, **the turf, a** a racetrack for horses. **b** horse racing. 1,2,4,5 *n., pl.* **turfs;** 3 *v.*

Tur ge nev (tùr gā′nyef), **Ivan,** 1818-1883, Russian novelist. *n.*

tur gid (tėr′jid), **1** puffed out; swollen; bloated. **2** using big words and elaborate comparisons; pompous. *adj.*

Turk (tėrk), person born or living in Turkey. *n.*

Tur ke stan (tėr′kə stan′), region in W and central Asia. Part of Turkestan belongs to China, part to the Soviet Union, and part to Afghanistan. *n.*

tur key (tėr′kē), **1** a large North American bird with brown or white feathers and a bare head and neck. It is related to the pheasant. **2** its flesh, used for food. *n., pl.* **tur keys.**

talk turkey, speak in a frank, blunt way.

[The *turkey* was apparently named by confusion with a guinea fowl originally imported by the Portuguese from Africa to Europe by way of *Turkey.*]

Tur key (tėr′kē), country in W Asia and SE Europe.

Capital: Ankara. See **Roman Empire** for map. *n.*

turkey buzzard or **turkey vulture,** vulture of South and Central America and southern United States, having a bare, reddish head and dark plumage.

Turk ish (tėr′kish), **1** of Turkey, its people, or their language. **2** language of the Turks. 1 *adj.,* 2 *n.*

Turkish Empire, Ottoman Empire.

turkish towel, a thick, cotton towel with a long nap made of uncut loops.

tur mer ic (tėr′mər ik), the yellow root of an East Indian plant, used in powdered form as a seasoning or as a yellow dye. *n.*

tur moil (tėr′moil), state of agitation or commotion; disturbance; tumult: *Unexpected guests put us in a turmoil. n.*

turn (tėrn), **1** move round as a wheel does; rotate: *The merry-go-round turned.* **2** cause to move round as a wheel does: *I turned the crank twice.* **3** a motion like that of a wheel: *At each turn the screw goes in further.* **4** move part way around; change from one side to the other: *Turn over on your back.* **5** do by turning; open, close, make lower, higher, tighter, looser, etc., by moving around: *She turned the key in the lock.* **6** take a new direction: *The road turns to the north here.* **7** give a new direction to: *He turned his steps to the north.* **8** a change of direction: *a turn to the left.* **9** place where there is a change in direction: *a turn in the road.* **10** change in direction or position; invert; reverse: *turn a page.* **11** change or transform so as to be; become: *She turned pale.* **12** make or become sour or spoiled: *Warm weather turns milk.* **13** a change in affairs, conditions, or circumstances: *Matters have taken a turn for the worse. The sick child took a turn for the better.* **14** the time at which such a change takes place: *the turn of the year, the turn of a fever.* **15** give form to; make: *He can turn pretty compliments.* **16** change from one language into another: *Turn this sentence into Latin.* **17** a form; style: *a scholarly turn of mind.* **18** change the attitudes of; unsettle: *Too much praise turns his head.* **19** direct (one's thoughts or attention): *He turned his thoughts toward home.* **20** direct thought, eyes, etc.: *turn to God for help.* **21** move to the other side of; go round; get beyond: *She turned the corner.* **22** pass or get beyond (a particular age, time, or amount): *She just turned thirty.* **23** a twist, bend: *Give that rope a few more turns around the tree.* **24** time or chance to do something; opportunity: *My turn comes after yours.* **25** deed; act: *One good turn deserves another.* **26** time or period of work or action: *Take a turn at the oars.* **27** make antagonistic; prejudice: *turn friends against friends.* **28** a walk, drive, or ride: *a turn in the park.* **29** form, work, or make by means of a lathe. **30** make or become sick: *The sight of blood turns my stomach.* **31** become dizzy: *The height made my head turn.* **32** INFORMAL. a nervous shock: *give someone a bad turn.* 1,2,4-7,10-12,15,16,18-22,27,29-31 *v.,* 3,8,9,13,14,17,23-26,28,32 *n.* —**turn′a ble,** *adj.*

at every turn, on every occasion; constantly.

by turns, one after another.

in turn, in proper order.

out of turn, not in proper order.

take turns, act one after another in proper order.

to a turn, to just the right degree: *meat done to a turn.*

turn about or **turn and turn about,** one after another in proper order.

turn down, 1 fold down: *turn down the covers on the bed.* **2** bend downward. **3** place with face downward. **4** refuse: *turn down a plan.* **5** lower by turning something: *turn down the gas.*

turn in, 1 INFORMAL. go to bed: *It's late and I'm going to turn in now.* **2** give or give back. **3** exchange: *turn in an old appliance for a new model.*

turn off, 1 stop the flow of; shut off: *Is the water tap* *turned off?* **2** put out (a light). **3** turn aside. **4** SLANG. cause (a person) to feel displeasure or dislike: *She turns me off with her bragging.*

turn on, 1 start the flow of; put on. **2** put on (a light). **3** attack; resist; oppose: *The dog turned on its pursuer.* **4** depend on: *The success of the picnic turns on the weather.* **5** SLANG. **a** take or use an intoxicating drug. **b** cause (a person) to feel pleasure or liking: *That music turns me on.*

turn out, 1 put out; shut off. **2** drive out. **3** come or go out: *Everyone turned out for the circus.* **4** make; produce. **5** result: *How did the game turn out?* **6** equip; fit out: *be smartly turned out in a new suit.* **7** be found or known: *The rumor turned out to be true.*

turn over, 1 give; hand over; transfer: *turn over a job to someone.* **2** think carefully about; consider in different ways: *turn over an idea in the mind.*

turn to, 1 go to for help. **2** get busy; set to work.

turn up, 1 fold up or over, especially so as to shorten. **2** make (a lamp, etc.) burn stronger. **3** make (a radio, television set, etc.) louder. **4** appear: *An old friend has turned up.* **5** be found; reappear.

turn buck le (tèrn′buk′əl), a short, hollow piece turning on a screw, used to unite and tighten two parts. *n.*

turn coat (tèrn′kōt′), person who changes to another set of beliefs or political party. *n.*

tur nip (tèr′nəp), the large, fleshy, roundish root of a garden plant, eaten as a vegetable. *n.* —**tur′nip like′,** *adj.*

turn key (tèrn′kē′), person in charge of the keys of a prison; keeper of a prison. *n., pl.* **turn keys.**

turn off (tèrn′ôf′ *or* tèrn′of′), **1** place at which a road, path, etc., turns off to another. **2** SLANG. thing that causes displeasure or dislike: *Final exams are a real turnoff. n.*

turn-on (tèrn′ôn′ *or* tèrn′on′), SLANG. thing that is pleasurably exciting: *Music can be a real turn-on. n.*

turn out (tèrn′out′), **1** a gathering of people. **2** output. **3** a wide place in the road, where vehicles can pass. **4** way in which somebody or something is equipped; equipment. *n.*

turn o ver (tèrn′ō′vər), **1** a turning upside down; an overturn; upset. **2** the amount of changing from one job to another: *Employers wish to reduce labor turnover.* **3** the paying out and getting back of the money involved in a business transaction: *The store reduced prices to make a quick turnover.* **4** the total amount of business done in a given time: *She made a profit of $6000 on a turnover of $90,000.* **5** a small pie made by folding half the crust over the filling and upon the other half. *n.*

turn pike (tèrn′pīk′), **1** toll road. **2** road that has, or used to have, a gate where toll is paid. *n.*

turn spit (tèrn′spit′), person or thing that turns a roast of meat on a spit. *n.*

turn stile (tèrn′stīl′), post with bars that turn, set in an entrance or an exit. The bars are turned to let one person through at a time. *n.*

turn ta ble (tèrn′tā′bəl), **1** a revolving platform with a track for turning locomotives around. **2** the round, revolving platform of a phonograph upon which records are placed. *n.*

tur pen tine (tèr′pən tīn), **1** mixture of oil and resin obtained from various cone-bearing trees. **2** an oil distilled from this mixture. Turpentine is used in mixing paints and varnishes, in medicine, etc. *n.*

tur pi tude (tèr′pə tüd *or* tèr′pə tyüd), great wickedness; baseness. *n.*

tur quoise (tèr′koiz *or* tèr′kwoiz), **1** a sky-blue or greenish-blue mineral often used as a gem. **2** a sky blue or greenish blue, like that of the turquoise. **3** sky-blue; greenish-blue. **1,2** *n.,* **3** *adj.* [*Turquoise* came into English

about 600 years ago from French (*pierre*) *turquoise,* meaning "Turkish (stone)."]

tur ret (tèr′it), **1** a small tower, often on the corner of a building. **2** any of various low, rotating armored structures within which guns are mounted, as in a warship or tank. **3** a plastic bubble on the fuselage of some bombers, for machine guns and a gunner. **4** an attachment on a lathe, drill, etc., to hold cutting tools. *n.* —**tur′ret less,** *adj.*

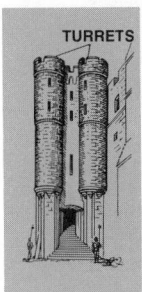

turret
left, (def. 1)
right, (def. 2)

tur ret ed (tèr′ə tid), having a turret or turrets. *adj.*

tur tle (tèr′tl), **1** reptile with a soft, rounded body enclosed in a hard shell into which many kinds can draw their head or legs. Turtles live in fresh water, salt water, or on land; those living on land are often called tortoises. **2** a mark that can be moved about on a computer screen by instructions in LOGO and certain other computer languages. *n.*

turtledove
11 in. (28 cm.)
long

tur tle dove (tèr′tl duv′), kind of small, slender dove, noted for its soft cooing and the affection that the mates seem to have for each other. *n.*

tur tle neck (tèr′tl nek′), **1** a round, high, closely fitting collar on a sweater, etc., usually worn turned down over itself. **2** garment with such a collar. *n.*

Tus can (tus′kən), **1** of Tuscany or its people. **2** person born or living in Tuscany. **3** dialect of Tuscany, regarded as the standard form of Italian. **1** *adj.,* **2,3** *n.*

Tus ca ny (tus′kə nē), district in central Italy. Florence is its chief city. *n.*

Tus ca ro ra (tus′kə rôr′ə), member of a tribe of Iroquois Indians that lived in colonial North Carolina and now live in New York State and Ontario. *n., pl.* **Tus ca ro ra** *or* **Tus ca ro ras.**

tusk (tusk), a very long, pointed, projecting tooth. Elephants, walruses, and wild boars have tusks. *n.*

a hat	i it	oi oil	ch child	a in about
ā age	ī ice	ou out	ng long	e in taken
ä far	o hot	u cup	sh she	i in pencil
e let	ō open	ù put	th thin	o in lemon
ē equal	ô order	ü rule	ŦH then	u in circus
ėr term			zh measure	

tus sle (tus′əl), **1** struggle or wrestle; scuffle: *The boys tussled over the ball.* **2** a vigorous or disorderly conflict; severe struggle or hard contest. 1 *v.,* **tus sled, tus sling;** 2 *n.*

tus sock (tus′ək), a tuft of growing grass or the like. *n.*

tut (tut), exclamation of impatience, contempt, or rebuke. *interj., n.*

Tutankhamun
A gold mask covered the face of the mummy of Tutankhamun.

Tut ankh a mun (tü′tängk ä′mən), died 1350? B.C., king of Egypt from 1358? to 1350? B.C. His tomb, discovered in 1922, contained many treasures. *n.*

tu te lage (tü′tl ij *or* tyü′tl ij), **1** the office or function of a guardian; guardianship; protection. **2** instruction. *n.*

tu tor (tü′tər *or* tyü′tər), **1** a private teacher: *A tutor comes once a week to help me with mathematics.* **2** teach; instruct, especially individually or privately: *She was tutored at home during her long illness.* **3** INFORMAL. be taught by a tutor: *He is tutoring in algebra.* 1 *n.,* 2,3 *v.*

tu to ri al (tü tôr′ē əl *or* tyü tôr′ē əl), **1** of a tutor: *tutorial authority.* **2** using tutors: *the tutorial system. adj.*

tut ti-frut ti (tü′tē frü′tē), **1** a preserve of mixed fruits. **2** ice cream containing a variety of fruits or fruit flavorings. **3** flavored by mixed fruits. 1,2 *n.,* 3 *adj.* [*Tutti-frutti* comes from Italian *tutti frutti,* meaning "all fruits."]

tut-tut (tut′tut′), exclamation of impatience, irritation, etc. *interj., n.*

tux (tuks), INFORMAL. tuxedo. *n., pl.* **tux es.**

tux e do (tuk sē′dō), **1** a man's coat for evening wear, made without tails, usually black with satin lapels. **2** the suit to which such a coat belongs. *n., pl.* **tux e dos** *or* **tux e does.**

TV, television.

TVA, Tennessee Valley Authority (a United States government organization for developing the resources of the Tennessee River valley, started in 1933).

TV dinner, a frozen, prepared meal on a tray of aluminum foil, that is heated in an oven before it is served.

twad dle (twod′l), **1** silly, feeble, tiresome talk or writing. **2** talk or write in a silly, feeble, tiresome way. 1 *n.,* 2 *v.,* **twad dled, twad dling. —twad′dler,** *n.*

twain (twān), OLD USE. two. *n., adj.*

Twain (twān), **Mark,** 1835-1910, American writer, author of *Tom Sawyer* and *Huckleberry Finn.* His real name was Samuel Langhorne Clemens. *n.*

twang (twang), **1** a sharp, ringing sound: *The bow made a twang when she shot the arrow.* **2** make or cause to make a sharp, ringing sound: *The banjos twanged.* **3** a sharp, nasal tone: *the twang of a Maine farmer.* **4** speak with a sharp, nasal tone. 1,3 *n.,* 2,4 *v.*

'twas (twoz *or* twuz), it was: "*'Twas the night before Christmas.*"

tweak (twēk), **1** seize and pull with a sharp jerk and twist: *tweak a person's ear.* **2** a sharp pull and twist. 1 *v.,* 2 *n.*

tweed (twēd), **1** a woolen cloth with a rough surface. Tweed is sometimes made of wool and cotton or synthetic fibers, and usually has two or more colors. **2** suit, etc., made of this cloth. **3 tweeds,** *pl.* clothes made of tweed. *n.*

tweed y (twē′dē), **1** made of or like tweed. **2** given to wearing tweeds. *adj.,* **tweed i er, tweed i est.**

tweet (twēt), **1** the sound made by a bird. **2** utter a tweet or tweets. 1 *n., interj.,* 2 *v.*

tweez ers (twē′zərz), small pincers for pulling out hairs, picking up small objects, etc. *n.pl.*

twelfth (twelfth), **1** next after the 11th; last in a series of 12. **2** one of 12 equal parts. *adj., n.*

twelve (twelv), one more than 11; 12. A year has twelve months. *n., adj.*

twelve month (twelv′munth′), twelve months; a year. *n.*

twen ti eth (twen′tē ith), **1** next after the 19th; last in a series of 20. **2** one of 20 equal parts. *adj., n.*

twen ty (twen′tē), two times ten; 20. *n., pl.* **twen ties;** *adj.*

'twere (twėr), it were.

twice (twīs), **1** two times: *twice a day.* **2** doubly: *twice as much. adv.*

twice-told (twīs′tōld′), **1** told twice. **2** told many times before; trite. *adj.*

twid dle (twid′l), **1** twirl: *twiddle one's pencil.* **2** play with idly. **3** a twirl. 1,2 *v.,* **twid dled, twid dling;** 3 *n.* **—twid′dler,** *n.*

twig (twig), a slender shoot of a tree or other plant; very small branch: *Dry twigs are good to start a fire with. n.* **—twig′less,** *adj.* **—twig′like′,** *adj.*

twi light (twī′līt′), **1** the faint light reflected from the sky before the sun rises and after it sets. **2** the period during which this light is seen, especially from sunset to dark night. **3** condition or period after or before full development, glory, etc. **4** of twilight; like that of twilight: *the twilight hour.* 1-3 *n.,* 4 *adj.*

twill (twil), **1** cloth woven in raised diagonal lines. **2** a diagonal line or pattern formed by such weaving. *n.*

'twill (twil), it will.

twilled (twild), woven in raised diagonal lines. *adj.*

twin (twin), **1** one of two persons born at the same time of the same mother. Twins sometimes look exactly alike. **2** being a twin: *Have you met my twin sister?* **3** one of two persons or things exactly alike. **4** being one of two things very much or exactly alike: *twin beds.* **5** having two like parts. 1,3 *n.,* 2,4,5 *adj.*

twine (twin), **1** a strong thread or string made of two or more strands twisted together. **2** twist together: *She twined holly into wreaths.* **3** wind or wrap around: *The vine twines around the tree.* **4** follow a twisting course; meander. **5** a twisting; twisting together. **6** a twist; twisted thing. 1,5,6 *n.,* 2-4 *v.,* **twined, twin ing. —twine′a ble,** *adj.* **—twin′er,** *n.*

twinge (twinj), **1** a sudden, sharp pain: *a twinge of rheumatism, a twinge of remorse.* **2** feel or affect with such a pain. 1 *n.,* 2 *v.,* **twinged, twing ing.**

twin kle (twing′kəl), **1** shine with quick little gleams: *The stars twinkled. His eyes twinkled when he laughed.* **2** a twinkling; sparkle; gleam: *She has a merry twinkle in her eye.* **3** move quickly: *The dancer's feet twinkled.* **4** a quick motion of the eye; wink; blink. **5** time required for a wink: *in the twinkle of an eye.* 1,3 *v.,* **twin kled, twin kling;** 2,4,5 *n.* **—twin′kler,** *n.*

twin kling (twing′kling), **1** a little, quick gleam. **2** a very brief period; an instant. *n.*

twirl (twėrl), **1** revolve rapidly; spin; whirl. **2** turn round and round idly: *He twirled his umbrella as he walked.* **3** a twirling; spin; whirl; turn: *a twirl in a dance.* 1,2 *v.,* 3 *n.* **—twirl′er,** *n.*

twist (twist), **1** turn with a winding motion; wind: *I twisted the cap off the jar.* **2** wind together: *This rope is twisted from many threads.* **3** turn around: *He twisted in his seat to see what was happening behind him.* **4** give a spiral form to. **5** curve; crook; bend: *to twist a piece of wire into a loop.* **6** a curve; crook; bend: *The path is full of twists.* **7** force out of shape or place: *twist an ankle.* **8** give a wrong meaning to; distort the meaning of: *twist an opposing candidate's words to get votes.* **9** a twisting or a being twisted. **10** anything made by twisting: *a twist of bread.* **11** a thread, cord, or rope made of two or more strands twisted together. **12** a peculiar bias or inclination: *a strange twist of character.* **13** an unexpected variation: *A new twist in the plot kept the audience in suspense.* 1-5,7,8 *v.*, 6,9-13 *n.* —**twist'a ble**, *adj.* —**twist'ing ly**, *adv.*

twist er (twis'tər), INFORMAL. whirlwind; tornado; cyclone. *n.*

twit (twit), **1** jeer at; reproach; taunt; tease: *They twitted me because I could not reach the top shelf.* **2** a reproach; taunt. 1 *v.*, **twit ted, twit ting;** 2 *n.*

twitch (twich), **1** move with a quick jerk: *The cat's paw twitched when I touched it.* **2** a quick, jerky movement of some part of the body. **3** pull with a sudden tug or jerk; pull (at): *She twitched the curtain aside.* **4** a short, sudden pull or jerk: *I felt a twitch at my shirt tail.* 1,3 *v.*, 2,4 *n., pl.* **twitch es.** —**twitch'er**, *n.* —**twitch'ing ly**, *adv.*

twit ter (twit'ər), **1** sound made by birds; chirping. **2** make such a sound: *Birds begin to twitter just before sunrise.* **3** to titter; giggle. **4** a brief or muffled giggle; titter. **5** an excited condition: *My nerves are in a twitter when I have to speak in public.* **6** tremble with excitement. 1,4,5 *n.*, 2,3,6 *v.* —**twit'ter er**, *n.* —**twit'ter ing ly**, *adv.*

two (tü), one more than one; 2. *n., pl.* **twos;** *adj.*
in two, in two parts or pieces.

two-by-four (tü'bī fôr'), **1** measuring two inches, feet, etc., by four inches, feet, etc. **2** piece of lumber four inches wide and two inches thick. Two-by-fours are much used in building. **3** INFORMAL. small; narrow; limited. 1,3 *adj.*, 2 *n.*

two-edged (tü'ejd'), **1** having two edges; cutting both ways: *a two-edged sword.* **2** effective either way. *adj.*

two-faced (tü'fāst'), deceitful; hypocritical. *adj.*

two-fist ed (tü'fis'tid), INFORMAL. strong; vigorous. *adj.*

two fold (tü'fōld'), **1** two times as much or as many; double. **2** having two parts: *a twofold shipment, part coming now and the rest later.* 1,2 *adj.*, 1 *adv.*

two pence (tup'əns), **1** two British pennies; two pence. **2** coin of this value. *n.* Also, **tuppence.**

two pen ny (tup'ə nē), **1** worth twopence. **2** trifling; worthless. *adj.*

two-ply (tü'plī'), having two thicknesses, folds, layers, or strands. *adj.*

two some (tü'səm), group of two people. *n.*

two-step (tü'step'), **1** a dance in march or polka rhythm, performed with sliding steps. **2** music for it. **3** dance the two-step. 1,2 *n.*, 3 *v.*, **two-stepped, two-step ping.**

two-time (tü'tīm'), SLANG. betray or be disloyal to; double-cross. *v.*, **two-timed, two-tim ing.** —**two'-tim'er**, *n.*

'twould (twùd), it would.

two-way (tü'wā'), **1** moving or allowing movement in two directions: *a two-way street.* **2** used in two ways or for two purposes: *A two-way radio receives and transmits messages. adj.*

twp., township.

TX, Texas (used with postal Zip Code).

-ty[1], *suffix added to numbers.* ____ tens; ____ times ten: *Seventy = seven tens, or seven times ten.*

a hat	**i** it	**oi** oil	**ch** child	⌠ a in about
ā age	**ī** ice	**ou** out	**ng** long		e in taken
ä far	**o** hot	**u** cup	**sh** she	ə = ⟨ i in pencil
e let	**ō** open	**ù** put	**th** thin		o in lemon
ē equal	**ô** order	**ü** rule	**ᴛʜ** then	⌡ u in circus
ėr term			**zh** measure	

-ty[2], *suffix added to adjectives to form nouns.* quality, condition, or fact of being ____: *Safety = condition or quality of being safe.* Also, **-ity.**

ty coon (tī kün'), an important businessman. *n.* [*Tycoon* is from Japanese *taikun*, which came from Chinese *tai*, meaning "great," and *kiun*, meaning "lord."]

ty ing (tī'ing), present participle of **tie.** *He is tying his shoes. v.*

tyke (tīk), INFORMAL. a small child. *n.* Also, **tike.**

Ty ler (tī'lər), **John**, 1790-1862, tenth president of the United States, from 1841 to 1845. *n.*

tym pan ic (tim pan'ik), of the eardrum or the middle ear. *adj.*

tympanic membrane, eardrum.

tym pa num (tim'pə nəm), **1** the eardrum. **2** the middle ear. *n., pl.* **tym pa nums, tym pa na** (tim'pə nə).

Tyne (tīn), river in N England, flowing into the North Sea. *n.*

type (tīp), **1** a kind, class, or group having common characteristics: *three types of local government. She is the type of person I like, kind and considerate of others.* **2** person or thing having the characteristics of a kind, class, or group; example; illustration; model; representative; symbol: *The skyscraper is a modern type of building.* **3** the general form, style, or character of some kind, class, or group: *He is above the ordinary type of student.* **4** be a type or symbol of; symbolize; typify. **5** piece of metal or wood having on its upper surface a raised letter for use in printing. **6** collection of such pieces: *set the manuscript for a book in type.* **7** printed letters; typewritten letters: *small or large type.* **8** write with a typewriter; typewrite: *type a letter asking for a job.* **9** find out the type of; classify: *type a person's blood.* 1-3,5-7 *n.*, 4,8,9 *v.*, **typed, typing.** [*Type* is from Latin *typus*, which came from Greek *typos*, meaning "dent, impression."]

type script (tīp'skript'), a typewritten manuscript. *n.*

type set ter (tīp'set'ər), person or machine that sets type for printing. *n.*

type set ting (tīp'set'ing), **1** act of setting type for printing. **2** used or adapted for setting type: *a typesetting machine.* 1 *n.*, 2 *adj.*

type write (tīp'rīt'), write with a typewriter; type: *to typewrite a letter, to know how to typewrite. v.*, **type wrote** (tīp'rōt'), **type writ ten, type writ ing.**

type writ er (tīp'rī'tər), **1** machine for writing which reproduces letters, figures, etc., similar to printed ones. **2** typist. *n.*

type writ ing (tīp'rī'ting), **1** act or art of using a typewriter: *to study typewriting.* **2** work done on a typewriter: *Your typewriting is very accurate. n.*

type writ ten (tīp'rit'n), **1** written with a typewriter: *a typewritten letter.* **2** past participle of **typewrite.** *Your letter was typewritten and mailed yesterday.* 1 *adj.*, 2 *v.*

ty phoid fever (tī'foid), an infectious, often fatal, disease with a high fever and intestinal inflammation. It is caused by bacteria in impure food or water. People can be inoculated against typhoid fever.

ty phoon (tī fün'), hurricane occurring in the western Pacific, chiefly during the period from July to October. *n.* [*Typhoon* comes from Chinese *tai fung*, meaning "big wind."]

ty phus (tī'fəs), an acute, infectious disease with high fever, extreme weakness, and dark-red spots on the skin. It is caused by a microscopic organism carried by fleas, lice, ticks, or mites. *n.*

typ i cal (tip′ə kəl), **1** being a type; representative: *The typical Thanksgiving dinner consists of turkey, cranberry sauce, several vegetables, and mince or pumpkin pie.* **2** of a type; characteristic: *the hospitality typical of frontier people. adj.*

typ i cal ly (tip′ik lē), **1** in a typical manner. **2** to a typical degree. **3** ordinarily. *adv.*

typ i fy (tip′ə fī), **1** be a symbol of: *The Statue of Liberty typifies the American tradition of freedom.* **2** have the common characteristics of: *Daniel Boone typifies the pioneer. v.*, **typ i fied, typ i fy ing.** —**typ′i fi ca′tion,** *n.* —**typ′i-fi′er,** *n.*

typ ist (tī′pist), person operating a typewriter, especially one who does typewriting as a regular occupation. *n.*

ty po (tī′pō), SLANG. a typographical error. *n., pl.* **ty pos.**

ty pog ra pher (tī pog′rə fər), printer. *n.*

ty po graph ic (tī′pə graf′ik), typographical. *adj.*

ty po graph i cal (tī′pə graf′ə kəl), of printing or typing: *"Catt" and "cOw" contain typographical errors. adj.* —**ty′po graph′i cal ly,** *adv.*

ty pog ra phy (tī pog′rə fē), **1** art or process of printing with type; work of setting and arranging type and of printing from it. **2** arrangement, appearance, or style of printed matter. *n.*

Tyr (tir), (in Scandinavian myths) the god of war and victory, son of Odin. *n.*

ty ran nic (tə ran′ik), tyrannical. *adj.*

ty ran ni cal (tə ran′ə kəl), of or like a tyrant; cruel; unjust: *a tyrannical queen. adj.* —**ty ran′ni cal ly,** *adv.*

tyr an nize (tir′ə nīz), **1** use power cruelly or unjustly; oppress: *The feudal lord tyrannized the peasants who farmed his land.* **2** rule as a tyrant. *v.*, **tyr an nized, tyr-an niz ing.** —**tyr′an niz′er,** *n.* —**tyr′an niz′ing ly,** *adv.*

ty ran no sau rus (ti ran′ə sôr′əs), a huge, prehistoric, flesh-eating dinosaur that lived in North America and walked erect on its two hind legs. *n., pl.* **ty ran no sau-rus es.** [See **Word History.**]

tyr an nous (tir′ə nəs), acting like a tyrant; cruel or unjust; tyrannical: *The Stamp Act seemed tyrannous to the colonists. adj.* —**tyr′an nous ly,** *adv.*

tyr an ny (tir′ə nē), **1** cruel or unjust use of power: *Cinderella escaped the tyranny of her stepsisters.* **2** a tyrannical act: *The colonists rebelled against the king's tyrannies.* **3** government by an absolute ruler. *n., pl.* **tyr an nies.**

ty rant (tī′rənt), **1** person who uses power cruelly or unjustly. **2** a cruel or unjust ruler. **3** an absolute ruler, as in ancient Greece. Some tyrants of Greek cities were mild and just rulers. *n.*

Tyre (tīr), ancient seaport in S Phoenicia. It was noted for its wealth and wickedness. See **Phoenicia** for map. *n.*

Tyr i an (tir′ē ən), **1** of Tyre. **2** person who was born or lived in Tyre. **1** *adj.,* **2** *n.*

Tyrian purple, 1 a crimson or purple dye used by the ancient Greeks and Romans. **2** bluish red.

ty ro (tī′rō), beginner in learning anything; novice: *Much practice changed the tyro into an expert. n., pl.* **ty ros.**

Ty rol (tə rōl′ *or* tī′rōl), Tirol. *n.*

Tyr rhe ni an Sea (tə rē′nē ən), part of the Mediterranean Sea lying between Italy and Sicily, Sardinia, and Corsica. *n.*

tzar (zär), czar. *n.*

tza ri na (zä rē′nə), czarina. *n., pl.* **tza ri nas.**

WORD HISTORY

tyrannosaurus

Tyrannosaurus comes from Greek *tyrannos,* meaning "tyrant," and *sauros,* meaning "lizard."

about 19 ft. (5.8 m.) tall

Uu

a hat	i it	oi oil	ch child	⎧ a in about
ā age	ī ice	ou out	ng long	e in taken
ä far	o hot	u cup	sh she	ə = ⎨ i in pencil
e let	ō open	u̇ put	th thin	o in lemon
ē equal	ô order	ü rule	ᴛʜ then	⎩ u in circus
ėr term			zh measure	

U or **u** (yü), **1** the 21st letter of the English alphabet. **2** anything shaped like a U. *n., pl.* **U's** or **u's.**

U, symbol for uranium.

U., University.

u biq ui tous (yü bik/wə təs), being everywhere at the same time; present everywhere. *adj.*

u biq ui ty (yü bik/wə tē), a being everywhere at the same time. *n.*

U-boat (yü/bōt/), a German submarine. *n.*

ud der (ud/ər), the baglike part that hangs down from the belly of a cow, female goat, etc., which contains the milk-producing glands and which has teats through which milk can be drawn. *n.*

UFO (yü/ef ō/), an unidentified, often disklike object, reported seen in the sky over many different parts of the world, especially since about 1947; flying saucer. *n., pl.* **UFOs** or **UFO's.**

u fol o gist (yü fol/ə jist), person engaged in or devoted to ufology. *n.*

u fol o gy (yü fol/ə jē), practice or hobby of tracking unidentified flying objects. *n.* [*Ufology* comes from *UFO* and the combining form *-logy.*]

U gan da (ü gan/də *or* yü gan/də), country in E Africa, a member of the Commonwealth of Nations. *Capital:* Kampala. See **Congo** for map. *n.* —**U gan/dan,** *adj., n.*

ugh (ug *or* u), exclamation of disgust or horror. *interj.*

ug li fy (ug/lə fī), make ugly; disfigure. *v.,* **ug li fied, ug li fy ing.** —**ug/li fi ca/tion,** *n.*

ug li ness (ug/lē nis), ugly quality or appearance. *n.*

ug ly (ug/lē), **1** very unpleasant to look at: *an ugly house.* **2** bad; disagreeable; offensive: *an ugly smell, ugly language.* **3** morally low or offensive; base: *an ugly act of treason.* **4** likely to cause trouble; threatening; dangerous: *an ugly wound, ugly clouds.* **5** bad-tempered; quarrelsome; cross: *an ugly mood. adj.,* **ug li er, ug li est.** [*Ugly* came into English over 700 years ago from Icelandic *uggliger,* meaning "dreadful," which comes from *uggr,* meaning "fear."]

UHF or **uhf,** ultrahigh frequency.

U.K., United Kingdom.

U kraine (yü krān/), republic in SW Soviet Union. *Capital:* Kiev. *n.* —**U krain/i an,** *adj., n.*

u ku le le (yü/kə lā/lē), a small guitar having four strings. *n.* [*Ukulele* comes from Hawaiian *ukulele,* which originally meant "leaping flea."]

U lan Ba tor (ü/län bä/tôr), capital of the Mongolian People's Republic, in the NE part.

ul cer (ul/sər), **1** an open sore on the skin or, within the body, on a mucous membrane. It sometimes discharges pus. **2** a moral sore spot; corrupting influence. *n.*

ul ce rate (ul/sə rāt/), **1** affect or be affected with an ulcer. **2** form or be formed into an ulcer. *v.,* **ul ce rat ed, ul ce rat ing.**

ul ce ra tion (ul/sə rā/shən), **1** an ulcerating or a being ulcerated. **2** an ulcer. *n.*

ul cer ous (ul/sər əs), having or affected with an ulcer or ulcers; like an ulcer. *adj.*

ul na (ul/nə), the thinner, longer bone of the forearm, on the side opposite the thumb. *n., pl.* **ul nae** (ul/nē), **ul nas.** [*Ulna* comes from Latin *ulna,* meaning "an elbow."]

ul ster (ul/stər), a long, loose, heavy overcoat, often belted at the waist. *n.*

Ul ster (ul/stər), former province of Ireland, now forming all of Northern Ireland and part of the Republic of Ireland. *n.*

ult., of the past month: *your order of the 14th ult.*

ul ter i or (ul tir/ē ər), **1** beyond what is seen or expressed; hidden: *an ulterior motive, an ulterior purpose.* **2** more distant; on the farther side. **3** further; later. *adj.*

ul ti mate (ul/tə mit), **1** coming at the end; last; final: *The ultimate result of driving too fast might be a serious accident.* **2** beyond which there is nothing at all; extreme: *the ultimate limits of the universe.* **3** fundamental; basic: *The brain is the ultimate source of ideas.* **4** greatest possible: *To give one's life is to pay the ultimate price.* **5** an ultimate point, result, fact, etc. 1-4 *adj.,* 5 *n.*

ul ti mate ly (ul/tə mit lē), in the end; finally. *adv.*

ul ti ma tum (ul/tə mā/təm), a final offer or demand, given with the threat of severe penalties if refused. *n., pl.* **ul ti ma tums, ul ti ma ta** (ul/tə mā/tə).

ul tra (ul/trə), beyond what is usual; very; excessive; extreme. *adj.*

ultra-, *prefix.* **1** beyond the _____: *Ultraviolet = beyond the violet.* **2** extremely _____: *Ultramodern = extremely modern.* [The prefix *ultra-* comes from Latin *ultra,* meaning "beyond."]

ul tra high frequency (ul/trə hī/), the band of radio frequencies between 300 and 3000 megahertz.

ul tra light (ul/trə līt/), **1** very light in weight. **2** a very lightweight airplane made of aluminum tubing and sailcloth, powered by a small engine, and designed to fly at speeds below 64 miles per hour. 1 *adj.,* 2 *n.*

ul tra ma rine (ul/trə mə rēn/), **1** a deep blue. **2** deep-blue. **3** a blue pigment made from powdered lapis lazuli. **4** imitation of this. 1,3,4 *n.,* 2 *adj.*

ul tra mod ern (ul/trə mod/ərn), extremely modern: *ultramodern furniture. adj.*

ukulele

ul tra son ic (ul/trə son/ik), of sound waves beyond the limit of human hearing. *adj.* —**ul/tra son/i cal ly,** *adv.*

ul tra vi o let (ul/trə vī/ə lit), of the invisible part of the spectrum whose rays have wavelengths shorter than those of the violet end of the visible spectrum. Ultraviolet rays are present in sunlight and are important in healing, forming vitamins, etc. *adj.*

U lys ses (yü lis/ēz), (in Greek legends) a king of Ithaca and hero of the Trojan War, known for his wisdom and shrewdness. Ulysses is the hero of Homer's *Odyssey,* which tells about his adventures. The Greeks called him Odysseus. *n.*

um bel (um′bəl), a flower cluster in which stalks nearly equal in length spring from a common center, as in parsley. *n.*

umbel

Umbel is from Latin *umbella*, meaning "parasol, umbrella," which comes from *umbra*, meaning "shade, shadow." The cluster was called this because its stalks look like the ribs of an umbrella.

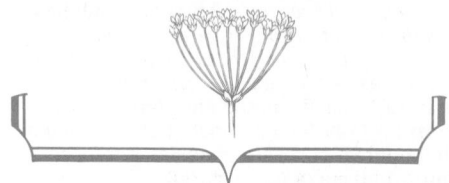

um ber (um′bər), **1** mixture of clay and iron oxide. In its natural state it is a brown pigment called **raw umber**. After heating it becomes dark reddish brown and is called **burnt umber. 2** a brown or reddish brown. **3** brown or reddish-brown. 1,2 *n.*, 3 *adj.*

um bil i cal cord (um bil′ə kəl), a cordlike structure that connects the navel of an embryo or fetus with the placenta of the mother. It carries nourishment to the fetus and carries away waste. [*Umbilical* comes from Latin *umbilicus*, meaning "navel."]

um bra (um′brə), the completely dark shadow cast by the earth, moon, etc., during an eclipse. *n., pl.* **um brae** (um′brē), **um bras.**

um brage (um′brij), suspicion that one has been slighted or injured; feeling offended; resentment. *n.* [*Umbrage* came into English about 550 years ago from French *umbrage,* meaning "shade, shadow," and can be traced back to Latin *umbra.*]
take umbrage, take offense; feel insulted or offended: *take umbrage at the slightest criticism.*

um brel la (um brel′ə), a light, folding frame covered with cloth or plastic, used as a protection against rain or sun. *n., pl.* **um brel las.** [*Umbrella* comes from Italian *ombrella,* and can be traced back to Latin *umbra,* meaning "shade, shadow."] —**um brel′la like′,** *adj.*

u mi ak (ü′mē ak), a large, Eskimo boat made of skins covering a wooden frame and worked with paddles. *n.* [*Umiak* was borrowed from Eskimo *umiak.*]

um pire (um′pīr), **1** person who rules on the plays in a game: *The umpire called the ball a foul.* **2** person chosen to settle a dispute. **3** act as an umpire in (a game, dispute, etc.). 1,2 *n.*, 3 *v.*, **um pired, um pir ing.**

ump teen (ump′tēn′), INFORMAL. a very large number of; countless: *It seemed as if I had umpteen errands to do last weekend. adj.*

Um ta ta (ùm tä′tə), capital of Transkei. *n.*

un-, *prefix.* **1** not _____: *Unchanged = not changed. Unjust = not just.* **2** do the opposite of _____: *Unfasten = do the opposite of fasten.*

UN or **U.N.,** United Nations.

un a bashed (un′ə basht′), not embarrassed, ashamed, or awed. *adj.* —**un′a bash′ed ly,** *adv.*

un a ble (un ā′bəl), not able: *A newborn baby is unable to walk or talk. adj.*

un a bridged (un′ə brijd′), not shortened or condensed; complete: *an unabridged book. adj.*

un ac cent ed (un ak′sen tid), not pronounced with force; not accented. *adj.*

un ac com pa nied (un′ə kum′pə nēd), **1** not accompanied; alone. **2** (in music) without instrumental accompaniment. *adj.*

un ac count a ble (un′ə koun′tə bəl), **1** not able to be accounted for or explained. **2** not responsible: *A wild animal is unaccountable for its actions. adj.*

un ac count a bly (un′ə koun′tə blē), in a manner that cannot be accounted for; strangely. *adv.*

un ac count ed-for (un′ə koun′tid fôr′), not accounted for or explained. *adj.*

un ac cus tomed (un′ə kus′təmd), **1** not accustomed: *Polar bears are unaccustomed to hot weather.* **2** not familiar; unusual; strange: *unaccustomed surroundings. adj.* —**un′ac cus′tomed ness,** *n.*

un ac quaint ed (un′ə kwān′tid), not acquainted. *adj.*

un a dul te rat ed (un′ə dul′tə rā′tid), not adulterated; pure: *unadulterated flour. adj.*

un ad vis ed ly (un′əd vī′zid lē), in an indiscreet manner; without careful consideration; rashly. *adv.*

un af fect ed[1] (un′ə fek′tid), not affected; not influenced. *adj.*

un af fect ed[2] (un′ə fek′tid), simple and natural; straightforward; sincere. *adj.* —**un′af fect′ed ly,** *adv.* —**un′af fect′ed ness,** *n.*

un aid ed (un ā′did), not aided; without help. *adj.*

un al ien a ble (un ā′lyə nə bəl), inalienable. *adj.*

un al ter a ble (un ôl′tər ə bəl), not able to be altered; not changeable. *adj.* —**un al′ter a ble ness,** *n.*

un al ter a bly (un ôl′tər ə blē), in a way that cannot be changed; permanently. *adv.*

un al tered (un ôl′tərd), not altered; unchanged. *adj.*

un-A mer i can (un′ə mer′ə kən), not characteristic of or proper to American traditions, customs, or ideals. *adj.*

u na nim i ty (yü′nə nim′ə tē), complete accord or agreement. *n.*

u nan i mous (yü nan′ə məs), **1** in complete accord or agreement; agreed: *The children were unanimous in their wish to go to the beach.* **2** characterized by or showing complete accord: *She was elected by a unanimous vote. adj.* [*Unanimous* is from Latin *unanimus,* which comes from *unus,* meaning "one," and *animus,* meaning "mind."] —**u nan′i mous ness,** *n.*

u nan i mous ly (yü nan′ə məs lē), with complete agreement; without a single opposing vote. *adv.*

un an swer a ble (un an′sər ə bəl), **1** not able to be answered. **2** not able to be disproved. *adj.* —**un an′swer a bly,** *adv.*

un ap proach a ble (un′ə prō′chə bəl), **1** very hard to

In each of the words below **un** *means not.*

un′a bat′ed	un′ac com′mo dat′ing	un′ad just′a ble	un′al loyed′	un′ap peal′ing
un′ab solved′	un′ac com′plished	un′ad just′ed	un′am big′u ous	un′ap peased′
un′ac a dem′ic	un′ac cred′it ed	un′a dorned′	un′am bi′tious	un ap′pe tiz′ing
un′ac cept′a ble	un′ac knowl′edged	un′ad vis′a ble	un a′mi a ble	un′ap pre′ci at′ed
un′ac cli′mat ed	un′a dapt′a ble	un′a fraid′	un an′i mat′ed	un′ap pre′ci a′tive
un′ac cli′ma tized	un′a dapt′ed	un′al lied′	un′an nounced′	un′ap proached′
		un′al low′a ble	un an′swered	

approach; distant. **2** without an equal; unrivaled. *adj.*
—**un′ap proach′a ble ness,** *n.* —**un′ap proach′a bly,** *adv.*

un arm (un ärm′), disarm. *v.*

un armed (un ärmd′), without weapons: *an unarmed robber. adj.*

un as sum ing (un′ə sü′ming), modest; not putting on airs: *The people of the village were delighted with the duke's unassuming manner. adj.* —**un′as sum′ing ly,** *adv.* —**un′as sum′ing ness,** *n.*

un at tached (un′ə tacht′), **1** not attached. **2** not engaged or married. *adj.*

un at tend ed (un′ə ten′did), **1** without attendants; alone. **2** not accompanied. **3** not taken care of; not attended to. *adj.*

un a vail ing (un′ə vā′ling), not successful; useless: *The dog's efforts to jump the high fence were unavailing. adj.* —**un′a vail′ing ly,** *adv.*

un a void a ble (un′ə voi′də bəl), not able to be avoided: *an unavoidable delay. adj.* —**un′a void′a ble ness,** *n.*

un a void a bly (un′ə voi′də blē), because of something that cannot or could not be avoided or prevented; inevitably. *adv.*

un a ware (un′ə wer′ *or* un′ə wär′), **1** not aware; unconscious: *We were unaware of the approaching storm.* **2** unawares. **1** *adj.,* **2** *adv.* —**un′a ware′ly,** *adv.* —**un′a ware′ness,** *n.*

un a wares (un′ə werz′ *or* un′ə wärz′), **1** without being expected; by surprise: *They caught the burglar unawares.* **2** without knowing; unintentionally: *approach danger unawares. adv.*

un bal anced (un bal′ənst), **1** not balanced. **2** not entirely sane: *an unbalanced mind. adj.*

un bar (un bär′), remove the bars from; unlock. *v.,* **unbarred, un bar ring.**

un bear a ble (un ber′ə bəl *or* un bar′ə bəl), not able to be endured; intolerable: *The pain from a severe toothache is almost unbearable. adj.* —**un bear′a ble ness,** *n.*

un bear a bly (un ber′ə blē *or* un bar′ə blē), in an unbearable manner; intolerably. *adv.*

un beat a ble (un bē′tə bəl), not able to be beaten, overcome, or surpassed. *adj.*

un beat en (un bēt′n), **1** not defeated or surpassed. **2** not trodden; not traveled: *unbeaten paths.* **3** not struck, pounded, or whipped: *unbeaten metal, unbeaten eggs. adj.*

un be com ing (un′bi kum′ing), **1** not becoming; not flattering: *unbecoming clothes.* **2** not fitting; not proper: *unbecoming behavior. adj.* —**un′be com′ing ly,** *adv.* —**un′be com′ing ness,** *n.*

un be known (un′bi nōn′), not known: *He arrived unbeknown to anyone. adj.*

un be knownst (un′bi nōnst′), unbeknown. *adj.*

un be lief (un′bi lēf′), lack of belief; lack of faith. *n.*

un be liev a ble (un′bi lē′və bəl), not believable; incredible: *an unbelievable lie. adj.*

un be liev a bly (un′bi lē′və blē), beyond belief; incredibly: *This piece of pottery is unbelievably old. adv.*

un be liev er (un′bi lē′vər), **1** person who does not believe. **2** person who does not believe in a particular religion. *n.*

un be liev ing (un′bi lē′ving), not believing; doubting.

a hat	i it	oi oil	ch child	(a in about
ā age	ī ice	ou out	ng long	e in taken
ä far	o hot	u cup	sh she	ə = { i in pencil
e let	ō open	u̇ put	th thin	o in lemon
ē equal	ô order	ü rule	ᴛʜ then	(u in circus
ėr term			zh measure	

adj. —**un′be liev′ing ly,** *adv.* —**un′be liev′ing ness,** *n.*

un bend (un bend′), **1** make or become straight; straighten: *unbend the fingers. The wire was hard and would not unbend.* **2** release from strain: *unbend a bow.* **3** relax: *Music helps me unbend after a hard day. v.,* **unbent** or **un bend ed, un bend ing.** —**un bend′a ble,** *adj.*

un bend ing (un ben′ding), **1** not bending or curving; rigid. **2** not yielding; stubborn; firm: *an unbending will. adj.* —**un bend′ing ly,** *adv.* —**un bend′ing ness,** *n.*

un bent (un bent′), a past tense and a past participle of **unbend.** *v.*

un bi ased (un bī′əst), not prejudiced; impartial; fair: *Each member of a jury should be unbiased. adj.* —**un bi′ased ly,** *adv.*

un bid den (un bid′n), **1** not invited: *an unbidden guest.* **2** not commanded. *adj.*

un bind (un bīnd′), release from bonds or restraint; let loose; untie; unfasten. *v.,* **un bound, un bind ing.**

un bleached (un blēcht′), not bleached; not made white by bleaching: *unbleached linen. adj.*

un blem ished (un blem′isht), not blemished; spotless; flawless. *adj.*

un blessed or **un blest** (un blest′), **1** not blessed. **2** unhappy. *adj.*

un blush ing (un blush′ing), **1** not blushing. **2** unabashed; shameless. *adj.* —**un blush′ing ly,** *adv.* —**un blush′ing ness,** *n.*

un bolt (un bōlt′), draw back the bolts of (a door, etc.). *v.*

un bolt ed (un bōl′tid), not bolted or fastened: *an unbolted door. adj.*

un born (un bôrn′), not yet born; still to come; of the future: *unborn generations. adj.*

un bos om (un bu̇z′əm *or* un bü′zəm), reveal; disclose. *v.*

unbosom oneself, tell or reveal one's thoughts, feelings, secrets, etc.

un bound (un bound′), **1** not bound: *Unbound sheets of music were scattered about the room.* **2** past tense and past participle of **unbind.** **1** *adj.,* **2** *v.*

un bound ed (un boun′did), **1** not limited; very great; boundless: *the unbounded reaches of the universe.* **2** not kept within limits; not controlled. *adj.* —**un bound′ed ly,** *adv.* —**un bound′ed ness,** *n.*

un break a ble (un brā′kə bəl), not breakable; not easily broken: *an unbreakable phonograph record. adj.* —**un break′a ble ness,** *n.* —**un break′a bly,** *adv.*

un bri dled (un brī′dld), **1** not having a bridle on. **2** not controlled; not restrained: *unbridled anger. adj.*

un bro ken (un brō′kən), **1** not broken; whole: *an unbroken dish.* **2** not interrupted; continuous: *I had eight hours of unbroken sleep.* **3** not tamed: *an unbroken colt. adj.* —**un bro′ken ly,** *adv.* —**un bro′ken ness,** *n.*

In each of the words below **un** *means not.*

un′ap pro′pri at′ed	un′as signed′	un′au then′ti cat′ed	un′bap tized′
un′ap proved′	un′as sist′ed	un au′thor ized	un barbed′
un ar rest′ed	un′at tain′a ble	un′a vail′a ble	un′be fit′ting
un ar tis′tic	un′at tempt′ed	un′a venged′	un′be trothed′
un′a shamed′	un′at trac′tive	un′a vowed′	un blam′a ble
un asked′	un′au then′tic	un baked′	un blamed′
		un band′aged	un blink′ing
			un blurred′
			un bought′
			un bowed′
			un braced′
			un branched′
			un brand′ed

un buck le (un buk′əl), **1** unfasten the buckle or buckles of. **2** unfasten; detach. *v.*, **un buck led, un buck ling.**

un bur den (un bėrd′n), **1** free from a burden. **2** relieve (one's mind or heart) by talking. *v.*

un busi ness like (un biz′nis līk′), without system and method; not efficient: *unbusinesslike procedures. adj.*

un but ton (un but′n), unfasten the button or buttons of. *v.*

un called-for (un kôld′fôr′), **1** unnecessary and improper: *an uncalled-for remark.* **2** not called for; not requested. *adj.*

un can ni ly (un kan′ə lē), in an uncanny manner. *adv.*

un can ny (un kan′ē), **1** strange and mysterious; weird: *The trees took uncanny shapes in the half darkness.* **2** so far beyond what is normal or expected as to have some special power: *an uncanny knack for solving math problems in her head. adj.* **—un can′ni ness,** *n.*

un cap (un kap′), take the cap, top, or covering off of: *uncap a bottle. v.*, **un capped, un cap ping.**

un cared-for (un kerd′fôr′ *or* un kärd′fôr′), not cared for or looked after; neglected. *adj.*

un cer e mo ni ous (un′ser ə mō′nē əs), **1** not ceremonious; informal. **2** not as courteous as would be expected. *adj.* **—un′cer e mo′ni ous ly,** *adv.*

un cer tain (un sėrt′n), **1** not certain; doubtful: *I came so late that I was uncertain of my welcome.* **2** likely to change; not to be depended on: *This dog has an uncertain temper.* **3** vague; indefinite: *an uncertain shape. adj.*

un cer tain ly (un sėrt′n lē), in an uncertain manner: *He spoke slowly and uncertainly. adv.*

un cer tain ty (un sėrt′n tē), **1** uncertain state or condition; doubt. **2** something uncertain. *n., pl.* **un cer tain ties.**

un chain (un chān′), let loose; set free. *v.*

un change a ble (un chān′jə bəl), not changeable; not able to be changed. *adj.* **—un change′a bly,** *adv.*

un changed (un chānjd′), not changed; the same: *unchanged tradition. adj.*

un char i ta ble (un char′ə tə bəl), not generous; not charitable; severe; harsh. *adj.* **—un char′i ta bly,** *adv.*

un chart ed (un chär′tid), not mapped; not marked on a chart. *adj.*

un chaste (un chāst′), not chaste; not virtuous. *adj.* **—un chaste′ly,** *adv.*

un checked (un chekt′), not checked; not restrained. *adj.*

un chris tian (un kris′chən), **1** not Christian. **2** unworthy of Christians. *adj.* **—un chris′tian ly,** *adv.*

un civ il (un siv′əl), not civil; rude; impolite. *adj.* **—un civ′il ly,** *adv.* **—un civ′il ness,** *n.*

un civ i lized (un siv′ə līzd), not civilized; barbarous; savage. *adj.* **—un civ′i lized′ly,** *adv.* **—un civ′i lized′ness,** *n.*

un clad (un klad′), not dressed; not clothed; naked. *adj.*

un clasp (un klasp′), **1** unfasten. **2** release or be released from a clasp or grasp. *v.*

un cle (ung′kəl), **1** brother of one's father or mother. **2** husband of one's aunt. *n.* [*Uncle* came into English about 700 years ago from French *uncle*, which came from Latin *avunculus*, meaning "one's mother's brother."]

un clean (un klēn′), **1** not clean; dirty; filthy. **2** not pure morally; evil. **3** not ceremonially clean. *adj.* **—un clean′ness,** *n.*

un clean li ness (un klen′lē nis), lack of cleanliness; dirtiness; filthiness. *n.*

un clean ly[1] (un klen′lē), not cleanly; unclean. *adj.*

un clean ly[2] (un klēn′lē), in an unclean manner. *adv.*

un clench (un klench′), open or become opened from a clenched state: *unclench one's fists. v.*

Uncle Sam (sam), the government or people of the United States. Uncle Sam is usually drawn in pictures as a tall, thin man with white chin whiskers, wearing a high hat, a blue swallow-tailed coat, and red-and-white striped pants. [*Uncle Sam* comes from the initials *U.S.*]

un cloak (un klōk′), **1** remove the coat from. **2** reveal; expose. *v.*

un clothed (un klō₮Hd′), not clothed; naked; bare. *adj.*

un coil (un koil′), unwind. *v.*

un com fort a ble (un kum′fər tə bəl), **1** not comfortable. **2** uneasy. **3** causing discomfort; disagreeable. *adj.* **—un com′fort a ble ness,** *n.*

un com fort a bly (un kum′fər tə blē), in a way that is not comfortable; with discomfort and uneasiness; disagreeably. *adv.*

uncommon (def. 1) Our kittens had an **uncommon** guardian.

un com mon (un kom′ən), **1** rare; unusual. **2** remarkable. *adj.* **—un com′mon ness,** *n.*

un com mon ly (un kom′ən lē), **1** rarely; unusually. **2** remarkably; especially: *She is an uncommonly good cook. adv.*

un com mu ni ca tive (un′kə myü′nə kā′tiv), not giving out any information, opinions, etc.; talking little; reserved; reticent. *adj.* **—un′com mu′ni ca′tive ly,** *adv.* **—un′com mu′ni ca′tive ness,** *n.*

un com pro mis ing (un kom′prə mī′zing), unyielding; firm: *An uncompromising person can be hard to deal with. adj.* **—un com′pro mis′ing ly,** *adv.*

un con cern (un′kən sėrn′), lack of concern; lack of interest; freedom from care or anxiety; indifference. *n.*

un con cerned (un′kən sėrnd′), not concerned; not interested; free from care or anxiety; indifferent. *adj.*

In each of the words below **un** *means not.*

un broth′er ly	un caught′	un chewed′	un clut′tered	un′com pan′ion a ble
un bruised′	un ceas′ing	un chiv′al rous	un coat′ed	un′com plain′ing
un brushed′	un cen′sored	un chris′tened	un cocked′	un′com plai′sant
un bur′ied	un cen′sured	un claimed′	un′col lect′ed	un′com plet′ed
un burned′	un chal′lenged	un clas′si fied	un col′ored	un com′pli cat′ed
un burnt′	un chang′ing	un cleaned′	un combed′	un′com pli men′tar y
un can′celed	un chap′e roned	un clear′	un′com bined′	un′com pound′ed
un cap′i tal ized	un charged′	un cleared′	un come′ly	un′com pre hend′ing
un cashed′	un chas′tened	un closed′	un com′fort ed	un com′pro mised
		un cloud′ed	un′com mit′ted	un′con cealed′

un con cern ed ly (un′kən sėr′nid lē), in an uncon-cerned manner; without concern or anxiety. *adv.*

un con di tion al (un′kən dish′ə nəl), without condi-tions; absolute: *The victorious general demanded the unconditional surrender of the enemy. adj.* —**un′con di′-tion al ly**, *adv.*

un con nect ed (un′kə nek′tid), separated; disconnect-ed. *adj.*

un con quer a ble (un kong′kər ə bəl), not able to be conquered. *adj.* —**un con′quer a bly**, *adv.*

un con scion a ble (un kon′shə nə bəl), **1** not influenced or guided by conscience: *an unconscionable liar.* **2** very great; unreasonable: *an unconscionable delay. adj.* —**un-con′scion a bly**, *adv.*

un con scious (un kon′shəs), **1** not conscious; not able to feel or think: *knock unconscious, unconscious from anesthetic.* **2** not aware: *unconscious of being followed, un-conscious of the time.* **3** not done or felt consciously; not purposeful: *unconscious neglect.* **4** thoughts, feelings, etc., that are present in the mind but that one is not directly or fully aware of: *subconscious.* 1-3 *adj.,* 4 *n.* —**un-con′scious ly**, *adv.* —**un con′scious ness**, *n.*

un con sti tu tion al (un′kon stə tü′shə nəl *or* un′kon-stə tyü′shə nəl), contrary to the constitution; not consti-tutional. *adj.* —**un′con sti tu′tion al ly**, *adv.*

un con sti tu tion al i ty (un′kon stə tü′shə nal′ə tē *or* un′kon stə tyü′shə nal′ə tē), a being contrary to the con-stitution. *n.*

un con trol la ble (un′kən trō′lə bəl), not able to be controlled; not able to be checked or restrained: *an uncontrollable temper. adj.*

un con trolled (un′kən trōld′), not controlled; not re-strained. *adj.*

un con ven tion al (un′kən ven′shə nəl), not bound by or conforming to convention, rule, or precedent; free from conventionality. *adj.* —**un′con ven′tion al ly**, *adv.*

un cork (un kôrk′), pull the cork from. *v.*

un count a ble (un koun′tə bəl), not able to be counted; innumerable: *an uncountable number of stars. adj.*

un count ed (un koun′tid), **1** not counted; not reckoned. **2** very many; innumerable. *adj.*

un cou ple (un kup′əl), disconnect; unfasten: *They un-coupled two freight cars. v.,* **un cou pled, un cou pling.**

un cour te ous (un kėr′tē əs), not courteous; impolite; rude. *adj.* —**un cour′te ous ly**, *adv.* —**un cour′te ous-ness**, *n.*

un couth (un küth′), not refined; awkward; clumsy; crude: *uncouth manners, an uncouth person. adj.* [*Uncouth* is from Old English *uncūth*, which comes from *un-,* meaning "not," and *cūth,* meaning "known."] —**un-couth′ly**, *adv.* —**un couth′ness**, *n.*

un cov er (un kuv′ər), **1** remove the cover from. **2** make known; reveal; expose. *v.*

un crowned (un kround′), **1** not crowned; not having yet assumed the crown. **2** having royal power without being king, queen, etc. *adj.*

a hat	**i** it	**oi** oil	**ch** child	a in about
ā age	**ī** ice	**ou** out	**ng** long	e in taken
ä far	**o** hot	**u** cup	**sh** she　ə =	i in pencil
e let	**ō** open	**u̇** put	**th** thin	o in lemon
ē equal	**ô** order	**ü** rule	**ᴛʜ** then	u in circus
ėr term			**zh** measure	

unc tion (ungk′shən), **1** an anointing with oil, ointment, etc., for medical purposes or as a religious rite. **2** the oil, ointment, or the like, used for anointing. **3** something soothing or comforting: *the unction of flattery. n.* [*Unction* is from Latin *unctionem,* which comes from *unguere,* meaning "to anoint."]

unc tu ous (ungk′chü əs), **1** like an oil or ointment in texture; oily; greasy. **2** soothing, sympathetic, and per-suasive. **3** too smooth and oily: *the hypocrite's unctuous manner. adj.* —**unc′tu ous ly**, *adv.* —**unc′tu ous ness**, *n.*

un cul ti vat ed (un kul′tə vā′tid), not cultivated; wild; undeveloped. *adj.*

un curl (un kėrl′), straighten out. *v.*

un cut (un kut′), **1** not cut, gashed, or wounded; not having received a cut: *They were fortunate to walk away from the collision uncut, with only a few bruises.* **2** not fashioned or shaped by cutting: *an uncut diamond.* **3** not shortened: *an uncut version of a movie. adj.*

un daunt ed (un dôn′tid), not afraid; not discouraged; fearless: *The skier was undaunted by the bad fall she suf-fered in the first race. adj.* —**un daunt′ed ly**, *adv.* —**un-daunt′ed ness**, *n.*

un de ceive (un′di sēv′), free (a person) from error, mis-take, or deception. *v.,* **un de ceived, un de ceiv ing.**

un de cid ed (un′di sī′did), **1** not decided; not settled. **2** not having one's mind made up. *adj.* —**un′de cid′ed-ly**, *adv.* —**un′de cid′ed ness**, *n.*

un de fined (un′di find′), **1** not defined or explained. **2** indefinite. *adj.*

un de ni a ble (un′di nī′ə bəl), not able to be denied or disputed; certain. *adj.*

un de ni a bly (un′di nī′ə blē), beyond denial or dispute; certainly. *adv.*

un der (un′dər), **1** below; beneath: *The book fell under the table* (*prep.*). *The swimmer went under* (*adv.*). **2** below the surface of: *under the sea.* **3** in or to a lower place or condition. **4** lower in position, rank, degree, amount, price, etc.: *the under lip.* **5** lower than; lower down than; not so high as: *There is a bruise under your eye.* **6** less than: *It will cost under ten dollars.* **7** during the rule or time of: *England under King John.* **8** according to; be-cause of: *under the law. We cannot join your club under these conditions.* **9** represented by: *under a new name.* **10** required or bound by: *You are not under any obligation to pay for damaged merchandise.* **11** included in a particu-lar group, category, or class: *In this library, books on stamp collecting are listed under philately.* 1,2,5-11 *prep.,* 1,3 *adv.,* 4 *adj.*

In each of the words below **un** means *not.*

un′con fined′	**un′con test′ed**	**un′cor rob′o rat′ed**	**un dam′aged**	**un′de fen′si ble**
un′con firmed′	**un′con tra dict′ed**	**un′cor rupt′ed**	**un damped′**	**un′de filed′**
un′con gealed′	**un′con vert′ed**	**un′cre at′ed**	**un dat′ed**	**un′de layed′**
un′con gen′ial	**un′con vinced′**	**un cred′it ed**	**un daz′zled**	**un′de liv′ered**
un′con gest′ed	**un′con vinc′ing**	**un crit′i cal**	**un′de bat′a ble**	**un′dem o crat′ic**
un con′quered	**un cooked′**	**un crowd′ed**	**un′de cayed′**	**un′de mon′stra ble**
un con′se crat′ed	**un′co op′er a tive**	**un crys′tal lized**	**un′de ceived′**	**un′de mon′stra tive**
un con sid′ered	**un′co or′di nat′ed**	**un cul′tured**	**un′de ci′phered**	**un′de pend′a ble**
un con strained′	**un cor′dial**	**un curbed′**	**un′de clared′**	
un con sumed′	**un corked′**	**un cured′**	**un′de co′rat′ed**	
un′con tam′i nat′ed	**un′cor rect′ed**	**un cur′tained**	**un′de feat′ed**	
		un cut′	**un′de fend′ed**	

under-, *prefix.* **1** below; beneath: *Underline = draw a line below. Underground = beneath the ground.* **2** being beneath; worn beneath: *Underclothes = clothes worn beneath one's outer clothes.* **3** lower in rank; subordinate: *Undersecretary = secretary that is lower in rank.* **4** lower than: *Underbid = bid lower than.* **5** not enough; not sufficiently: *Undernourished = not sufficiently nourished.* **6** below normal: *Underweight = below normal weight.*

un der a chieve (un/dər ə chēv/), (of a student) fail to work at the level of one's ability. *v.,* **un der a chieved, un der a chiev ing.**

un der a chiev er (un/dər ə chē/vər), a student who fails to work at his or her level of ability. *n.*

un der age (un/dər āj/), not of full age; less than the usual or required age. *adj.*

un der arm (un/dər ärm/), **1** situated or placed under the arm; found in or near the armpit: *an underarm scar, an underarm deodorant.* **2** armpit. **3** underhand: *an underarm pitcher (adj.). In softball a pitcher must throw underarm (adv.).* 1,3 *adj.,* 2 *n.,* 3 *adv.*

un der bid (un/dər bid/), make a lower bid than (another): *to underbid a competitor in seeking a contract. v.,* **un der bid, un der bid ding. —un/der bid/der,** *n.*

un der brush (un/dər brush/), shrubs, bushes, and small trees growing under large trees in woods or forests. *n.*

un der clothes (un/dər klōz/ *or* un/dər klōᴛʜz/), underwear. *n.pl.*

un der cloth ing (un/dər klō/ᴛʜing), underwear. *n.*

un der coat (un/dər kōt/), **1** growth of short, fine hair under an animal's outer coat. **2** coat of paint, varnish; etc., applied before the finishing coats. **3** undercoating. *n.*

un der coat ing (un/dər kō/ting), a heavy, tarlike substance sprayed on the underside of an automobile to protect it from water, dirt, salt, etc., on the road. *n.*

un der cov er (un/dər kuv/ər), working or done in secret: *The jeweler was an undercover agent of the police. adj.*

un der cur rent (un/dər ker/ənt), **1** current below the upper currents, or below the surface, of a body of water, air, etc. **2** an underlying tendency: *There was an undercurrent of sadness in her laugh. n.*

un der cut (un/dər kut/ *for 1,3;* un/dər kut/ *for 2*), **1** cut under or beneath; cut away material from so as to leave a portion overhanging. **2** a cut, or a cutting away, underneath. **3** sell or work for less than (another). 1,3 *v.,* **un der cut, un der cut ting;** 2 *n.*

un der de vel oped (un/dər di vel/əpt), **1** not normally developed: *underdeveloped muscles.* **2** poorly or insufficiently developed in production, technology, medicine, standard of living, etc.: *an underdeveloped country. adj.*

un der dog (un/dər dôg/), **1** person having the worst of any struggle; person in an inferior position: *The senator's early experience of poverty made him a champion of the underdog.* **2** contestant considered unlikely to win. *n.*

un der done (un/dər dun/ *or* un/dər dun/), not cooked enough; cooked very little. *adj.*

un der es ti mate (un/dər es/tə māt *for 1;* un/dər es/-tə mit *or* un/dər es/tə māt *for 2*), **1** to estimate at too low a value, amount, rate, etc. **2** an estimate that is too low. 1 *v.,* **un der es ti mat ed, un der es ti mat ing;** 2 *n.*

un der ex pose (un/dər ek spōz/), expose (a film or negative) for too short a time. *v.,* **un der ex posed, un der ex pos ing.**

un der ex po sure (un/dər ek spō/zhər), too little or too short an exposure. Underexposure to light makes a photograph look dim. *n.*

un der feed (un/dər fēd/), feed too little. *v.,* **un der fed** (un/dər fed/), **un der feed ing.**

un der foot (un/dər fút/), **1** under one's foot or feet; on

the ground; underneath. **2** in the way: *The cat is always underfoot when I'm cooking a meal. adv.*

un der gar ment (un/dər gär/mənt), garment worn under an outer garment, especially next to the skin. *n.*

un der go (un/dər gō/), **1** go through; pass through; be subjected to: *The town is undergoing many changes as it grows.* **2** endure; suffer: *The pioneers underwent many hardships. v.,* **un der went, un der gone, un der go ing.**

un der gone (un/dər gôn/), past participle of **undergo.** *The town has undergone many changes. v.*

un der grad u ate (un/dər graj/ü it), **1** student in a college or university who has not yet received a degree. **2** of or for undergraduates. 1 *n.,* 2 *adj.*

un der ground (un/dər ground/ *for 1,5;* un/dər ground/ *for 2-4,6,7*), **1** beneath the surface of the ground: *The mole burrowed underground.* **2** being, working, or used beneath the surface of the ground: *an underground passage.* **3** a place or space beneath the surface of the ground. **4** BRITISH. subway. **5** in or into secrecy or concealment: *The thief went underground after the robbery.* **6** secret: *an underground plot.* **7** a secret organization working against an unpopular government, especially during military occupation: *the French underground during World War II.* 1,5 *adv.,* 2,6 *adj.,* 3,4,7 *n.*

underground railroad, system by which the opponents of slavery secretly helped fugitive slaves to escape to the free states or Canada before the Civil War.

un der growth (un/dər grōth/), underbrush. *n.*

un der hand (un/dər hand/), **1** not open or honest; secret; sly. **2** secretly; slyly. **3** with the hand below the level of the shoulder: *an underhand pitch (adj.), throw a ball underhand (adv.).* 1,3 *adj.,* 2,3 *adv.*

un der hand ed (un/dər han/did), underhand; secret; sly: *an underhanded trick. adj.* **—un/der hand/ed ly,** *adv.*

un der lie (un/dər lī/), **1** lie under; be beneath. **2** be at the basis of; form the foundation of. *v.,* **un der lay** (un/dər lā/), **un der lain** (un/dər lān/), **un der ly ing.**

un der line (un/dər līn/ *or* un/dər līn/), **1** draw a line or lines under: *In writing, we underline titles of books.* **2** make emphatic or more emphatic; emphasize. *v.,* **un der lined, un der lin ing.**

un der ling (un/dər ling), person of lower rank or position; inferior. *n.*

un der ly ing (un/dər lī/ing), **1** lying under or beneath. **2** fundamental; basic; essential. **3** present participle of **underlie.** 1,2 *adj.,* 3 *v.*

un der mine (un/dər mīn/ *or* un/dər mīn/), **1** make a passage or hole under; dig under: *Burrowing animals had undermined the wall.* **2** wear away the foundations of. **3** weaken by secret or unfair means: *Nasty rumors undermined his reputation.* **4** weaken or destroy gradually: *Many severe colds had undermined her health. v.,* **un der mined, un der min ing.**

undermine (def. 2)—Waves had **undermined** the shoreline.

un der most (un/dər mōst), lowest. *adj., adv.*

un der neath (un/dər nēth/), beneath; below; under: *They sat underneath a tree* (prep.). *Someone was pushing underneath* (adv.). *prep., adv.*

un der nour ished (un/dər nėr/isht), not sufficiently nourished. *adj.*

un der nour ish ment (un/dər nėr/ish mənt), lack of nourishment; not having enough food. *n.*

un der pants (un/dər pants/), shorts, panties, etc., worn as an undergarment; drawers. *n.pl.*

un der part (un/dər pärt/), the part of an object, animal, etc., that lies below or underneath. *n.*

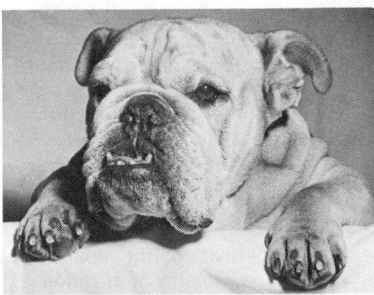

undershot (def. 1)
the undershot jaw
of a bulldog

un der pass (un/dər pas/), passageway underneath; road under railroad tracks or under another road. *n., pl.* **un der pass es.**

un der pay (un/dər pā/), pay too little. *v.,* **un der paid** (un/dər pād/), **un der pay ing. —un/der pay/ment,** *n.*

un der pin ning (un/dər pin/ing), **1** the materials or structure that give support from beneath to a building, wall, etc. **2** a support; prop. *n.*

un der priv i leged (un/dər priv/ə lijd), having fewer advantages than most have, especially because of poverty: *underprivileged children. adj.*

un der rate (un/dər rāt/), to rate or estimate too low; put too low a value on. *v.,* **un der rat ed, un der rat ing.**

un der score (un/dər skôr/ *or* un/dər skôr/), underline. *v.,* **un der scored, un der scor ing.**

un der sea (un/dər sē/ *for 1;* un/dər sē/ *for 2*), **1** being, working, or used beneath the surface of the sea: *an undersea cable, undersea exploration.* **2** underseas. 1 *adj.,* 2 *adv.*

un der seas (un/dər sēz/), beneath the surface of the sea: *Submarines go underseas. adv.*

un der sec re tar y (un/dər sek/rə ter/ē), official ranking just below the secretary in charge of a department of the government. *n., pl.* **un der sec re tar ies.**

understatement (def. 1)

We've had a little rain.

un der sell (un/dər sel/), sell things at a lower price than (another): *This store can undersell other stores because it sells in great volume.* v., **un der sold** (un/dər sōld/), **un der sell ing. —un/der sell/er,** *n.*

un der shirt (un/dər shėrt/), shirt worn next to the skin under other clothing. *n.*

un der shot (un/dər shot/), **1** having the lower jaw projecting beyond the upper. **2** driven by water passing beneath: *an undershot water wheel. adj.*

un der side (un/dər sīd/), surface lying underneath; bottom side. *n.*

un der signed (un/dər sīnd/), **1** signed, or having signed, at the end of a letter or document. **2 the undersigned,** person or persons signing a letter or document. 1 *adj.,* 2 *n.*

un der sized (un/dər sīzd/), smaller than the usual size: *an undersized fish. adj.*

un der skirt (un/dər skėrt/), skirt worn under an outer skirt. *n.*

un der stand (un/dər stand/), **1** get the meaning of: *Now I understand the teacher's question.* **2** get the meaning: *I have told her three times, but she still doesn't understand.* **3** know how to deal with; know well; know: *A good teacher understands children.* **4** be informed; learn: *I understand that she bought a house.* **5** take as a fact; believe: *It is understood that you will come.* **6** take as meaning; interpret: *I understood your comment as approval of the plan.* **7** supply in the mind. In "He hit the tree harder than I," the word *did* is understood after *I. v.,* **un der stood, un der stand ing.**

un der stand a ble (un/dər stan/də bəl), able to be understood. *adj.*

un der stand a bly (un/dər stan/də blē), in a manner that can be understood. *adv.*

un der stand ing (un/dər stan/ding), **1** comprehension; knowledge: *a clear understanding of the problem.* **2** ability to learn and know; intelligence: *a person with limited understanding.* **3** that understands; intelligent and sympathetic: *an understanding reply.* **4** knowledge of each other's meaning and wishes: *True friendship is based on understanding.* **5** a mutual arrangement or agreement: *We have an understanding about the use of the car on Saturdays.* 1,2,4,5 *n.,* 3 *adj.* **—un/der stand/ing ly,** *adv.*

un der state (un/dər stāt/), **1** state too weakly. **2** say less than the full truth about. *v.,* **un der stat ed, un der stat ing.**

un der state ment (un/dər stāt/mənt), **1** statement that expresses a fact too weakly. **2** statement that says less than could be said truly. *n.*

un der stood (un/dər stùd/), past tense and past participle of **understand.** *Have all of you understood today's lesson? I understood what she said. v.*

un der stud y (un/dər stud/ē), **1** person who can act as a substitute for an actor, actress, or any other regular performer. **2** learn (a part) in order to replace the regular performer when necessary. **3** to act as an understudy to. 1 *n., pl.* **un der stud ies;** 2,3 *v.,* **un der stud ied, un der stud y ing.**

un der sur face (un/dər sėr/fis), underside: *the undersurface of a leaf. n.*

un der take (un/dər tāk/), **1** set about; try; attempt: *undertake to reach home before dark.* **2** agree to do; take upon oneself: *I will undertake the feeding of your dogs while you are away.* **3** to promise; guarantee. *v.,* **undertook, un der tak en, un der tak ing.**

un der tak er (un′dər tā′kər), person whose business is preparing the dead for burial and arranging funerals; mortician. *n.*

un der tak ing (un′dər tā′king *for 1,2;* un′dər tā′king *for 3*), **1** something undertaken; task; enterprise. **2** a promise; guarantee. **3** business of preparing the dead for burial and arranging funerals. *n.*

un der-the-count er (un′dər ₮нə koun′tər), hidden and stealthy; unauthorized; illegal. *adj.*

un der tone (un′dər tōn′), **1** a low or very quiet tone: *talk in undertones.* **2** a subdued color; color seen through other colors: *There was an undertone of brown beneath all the gold and crimson of autumn.* **3** something beneath the surface; an underlying quality, condition, or element: *an undertone of sadness in their gaiety. n.*

un der took (un′dər túk′), past tense of **undertake.** *He failed because he undertook more than he could do. v.*

un der tow (un′dər tō′), **1** any strong current below the surface of the water, moving in a direction different from that of the surface current. **2** the backward flow from waves breaking on a beach. *n.*

un der val ue (un′dər val′yü), put too low a value on. *v.,* **un der val ued, un der val u ing. —un′der val′u a′tion,** *n.*

un der wa ter (un′dər wô′tər *or* un′dər wot′ər), **1** below the surface of the water: *an underwater current* (adj.), *to swim underwater* (adv.). **2** made for use under the water: *A submarine is an underwater boat.* 1,2 *adj.,* 1 *adv.*

un der way (un′dər wā′), going on; in motion; in progress: *The construction of the new library is now underway. adv.*

un der wear (un′dər wer′ *or* un′dər war′), clothing worn under one's outer clothes, especially next to the skin; underclothes; underclothing. *n.*

un der weight (un′dər wāt′), **1** having too little weight; below the normal or required weight. **2** weight that is not up to standard. 1 *adj.,* 2 *n.*

un der went (un′dər went′), past tense of **undergo.** *Transportation underwent a great change with the development of the automobile. v.*

un der world (un′dər wérld′), **1** the criminal part of human society. **2** the world of the dead; Hades. *n.*

un der write (un′dər rīt′ *or* un′dər rīt′), **1** insure (property) against loss. **2** sign (an insurance policy), thereby accepting the risk of insuring something against loss. **3** write under (other written matter); sign one's name to (a document, etc.). **4** agree to buy (all the stocks or bonds of a certain issue that are not bought by the public): *The bankers underwrote the steel company's bonds. v.,* **un der wrote** (un′dər rōt′ *or* un′dər rōt′), **un derwrit ten** (un′dər rit′n *or* un′dər rit′n), **un der writ ing.**

un der writ er (un′dər rī′tər), **1** person who underwrites an insurance policy or carries on an insurance business. **2** person who underwrites (usually with others) an issue or issues of stocks or bonds. *n.*

un de sir a ble (un′di zī′rə bəl), **1** objectionable; dis

agreeable: *The drug was taken off the market because it had undesirable effects on users.* **2** an undesirable person or thing: *criminals and other undesirables.* 1 *adj.,* 2 *n.* **—un′de sir′a ble ness,** *n.*

un de sir a bly (un′di zī′rə blē), in an undesirable manner. *adv.*

un de vel oped (un′di vel′əpt), **1** not developed. **2** not fully grown; immature. **3** not put to full use: *undeveloped natural resources of a country. adj.*

un did (un did′), past tense of **undo.** *The fire in the artist's studio undid many years of work. v.*

un dis ci plined (un dis′ə plind), not disciplined; without proper control; untrained. *adj.*

un dis guised (un′dis gīzd′), **1** not disguised. **2** unconcealed; open; plain; frank: *undisguised delight. adj.*

un dis put ed (un′dis pyü′tid), not disputed; not doubted. *adj.* **—un′dis put′ed ly,** *adv.*

un dis tin guish a ble (un′dis ting′gwi shə bəl), not able to be distinguished. *adj.*

un dis tin guished (un′dis ting′gwisht), not distinguished; commonplace. *adj.*

un dis turbed (un′dis tèrbd′), not disturbed; not troubled; calm. *adj.*

un di vid ed (un′də vī′did), not divided; not separated into parts; complete: *Give me your undivided attention. adj.*

un do (un dü′), **1** unfasten; untie: *Please undo the package. I undid the string.* **2** do away with the effect of; cancel or reverse: *The workers mended the road, but a heavy storm undid their work.* **3** bring to ruin; spoil; destroy. *v.,* **un did, un done, un do ing. —un do′er,** *n.*

un do ing (un dü′ing), **1** a bringing to ruin; spoiling; destroying. **2** cause of destruction or ruin: *Gambling was their undoing.* **3** a canceling or reversing the effect of something. **4** an untying; unfastening. *n.*

un done (un dun′), **1** not done; not finished. **2** ruined. **3** untied; unfastened. **4** past participle of **undo.** 1-3 *adj.,* 4 *v.*

un doubt ed (un dou′tid), not doubted; accepted as true. *adj.*

un doubt ed ly (un dou′tid lē), beyond doubt; certainly. *adv.*

un draw (un drô′), draw back or away: *She undrew the curtain. v.,* **un drew** (un drü′), **un drawn** (un drôn′), **undraw ing.**

un dreamed-of (un drēmd′uv′ *or* un drēmd′ov′), never thought of, even in the imagination: *undreamed-of advances in medicine. adj.*

un dreamt-of (un dremt′uv′ *or* un dremt′ov′), undreamed-of. *adj.*

un dress (un dres′), **1** take the clothes off; strip. **2** take off one's clothes. **3** nakedness; nudity: *be caught in a state of undress.* 1,2 *v.,* 3 *n.*

un due (un dü′ *or* un dyü′), **1** not fitting; not right; improper: *make rude, undue remarks to someone.* **2** too great; too much; excessive: *give undue importance to money. adj.*

un du lant (un′jə lənt), waving; wavy. *adj.*

un du late (un′jə lāt), **1** move or cause to move in waves: *undulating water.* **2** have a wavy form or surface:

In each of the words below **un** *means not.*

un′de served′	un′de terred′	un′dip lo mat′ic	un′dis solved′	un doubt′ing
un′de serv′ing	un′de vout′	un′dis cern′i ble	un′dis tin′guish ing	un drained′
un des′ig nat ed	un′dif fe ren′ti at ed	un′dis cern′ing	un′dis tort′ed	un′dra mat′ic
un′de sired′	un′di gest′ed	un′dis charged′	un′dis tract′ed	un draped′
un′de spair′ing	un dig′ni fied	un′dis closed′	un′dis trib′ut ed	un dreamed′
un′de tach′a ble	un′di lut′ed	un′dis cour′aged	un′di ver′si fied	un dreamt′
un′de tect′ed	un′di min′ished	un′dis cov′ered	un′di vulged′	un dressed′
un′de ter′mined	un dimmed′	un′dis crim′i nat′ing	un′do mes′ti cat′ed	un drilled′
		un′dis so′ci at ed	un dou′bled	

undulating hair, an undulating prairie. v., **un du lat ed, un du lat ing.** [*Undulate* is from Latin *undula,* meaning "a small wave," which comes from *unda,* meaning "a wave." See **Word Family.**]

undulate

Below are words related to *undulate.* They can all be traced back to the Latin word *unda* (ùn′dä), meaning "a wave."

abound	inundate	redundant
abundant	redound	surround

un du la tion (un′jə lā′shən), **1** a wavelike motion; undulating. **2** a wavy form. **3** one of a series of wavelike bends, curves, swellings, etc. *n.*

un du ly (un dü′lē *or* un dyü′lē), **1** in an undue manner; improperly. **2** too much; excessively: *unduly harsh. adv.*

un dy ing (un dī′ing), that never dies; deathless; immortal; eternal: *undying fame, undying beauty. adj.* —**un dy′ing ly,** *adv.*

un earned (un ėrnd′), **1** not earned; not gained by labor or service. **2** not deserved: *unearned punishment. adj.*

un earth (un ėrth′), **1** dig up: *unearth a buried city.* **2** find out; discover: *unearth a plot. v.*

un earth ly (un ėrth′lē), **1** not of this world; supernatural. **2** strange; weird; ghostly. *adj.* —**un earth′li ness,** *n.*

un eas i ly (un ē′zə lē), in an uneasy manner; restlessly. *adv.*

un eas i ness (un ē′zē nis), a being uneasy; restlessness. *n.*

un eas y (un ē′zē), **1** restless; disturbed; anxious. **2** not comfortable. **3** not easy in manner; awkward. *adj.,* **un eas i er, un eas i est.**

un ed u cat ed (un ej′ə kā′tid), not educated; not taught or trained. *adj.*

un em ployed (un′em ploid′), **1** not employed; not in use: *an unemployed skill.* **2** not having a job; having no work: *an unemployed person.* **3 the unemployed,** people out of work. **1,2** *adj.,* **3** *n.*

un em ploy ment (un′em ploi′mənt), lack of employment; being out of work. *n.*

un e qual (un ē′kwəl), **1** not the same in amount, size, number, value, degree, or rank: *unequal sums of money.* **2** not fair; one-sided: *an unequal contest.* **3** not enough; not adequate: *Their strength was unequal to the task.* **4** not regular; not even: *unequal vibrations. adj.* —**un e′qual ly,** *adv.* —**un e′qual ness,** *n.*

un e qualed (un ē′kwəld), that has no equal or superior; matchless: *unequaled beauty, unequaled speed. adj.*

un e quiv o cal (un′i kwiv′ə kəl), clear; plain: *an un-*equivocal refusal. *adj.* —**un′e quiv′o cal ly,** *adv.* —**un′-e quiv′o cal ness,** *n.*

un err ing (un ėr′ing *or* un er′ing), making no mistakes; exactly right: *unerring aim. adj.* —**un err′ing ly,** *adv.*

U NES CO *or* **U nes co** (yü nes′kō), United Nations Educational, Scientific, and Cultural Organization. *n.*

un e ven (un ē′vən), **1** not even; not level, flat, or smooth: *uneven ground.* **2** not equal: *an uneven contest.* **3** not uniform or regular; changeable; inconsistent: *Her work is of uneven quality.* **4** leaving a remainder of 1 when divided by 2; odd: *1, 3, 5, 7, and 9 are uneven numbers. adj.* —**un e′ven ly,** *adv.* —**un e′ven ness,** *n.*

un e vent ful (un′i vent′fəl), without important or striking occurrences: *a quiet, uneventful day in the country. adj.* —**un e vent′ful ly,** *adv.*

un ex cep tion a ble (un′ek sep′shə nə bəl), beyond criticism; wholly admirable. *adj.*

un ex pect ed (un′ek spek′tid), not expected: *an unexpected difficulty, an unexpected change in the weather. adj.* —**un ex pect′ed ness,** *n.*

un ex pect ed ly (un′ek spek′tid lē), without being expected; in a way that is not expected; suddenly. *adv.*

un ex per i enced (un′ek spir′ē ənst), inexperienced. *adj.*

un fail ing (un fā′ling), **1** never failing; always ready when needed; loyal: *an unfailing friend.* **2** never running short; endless: *an unfailing supply of water.* **3** sure; certain: *unfailing proof of guilt. adj.* —**un fail′ing ness,** *n.*

un fail ing ly (un fā′ling lē), without fail; always. *adv.*

un fair (un fer′ *or* un far′), not fair; unjust: *an unfair decision. It was unfair of you to trick him. adj.* —**un fair′ly,** *adv.* —**un fair′ness,** *n.*

un faith ful (un fāth′fəl), **1** not faithful; not true to duty or one's promises; faithless. **2** not accurate; not exact: *an unfaithful translation. adj.* —**un faith′ful ly,** *adv.* —**un faith′ful ness,** *n.*

un fal ter ing (un fôl′tər ing), not hesitating; firm; steadfast. *adj.*

un fa mil iar (un′fə mil′yər), **1** not well known; unusual; strange: *That face is unfamiliar to me.* **2** not acquainted: *She is unfamiliar with the Greek language. adj.*

un fa mil iar i ty (un′fə mil′yar′ə tē), lack of familiarity. *n.*

un fas ten (un fas′n), undo; untie; loosen; open. *v.*

un fath om a ble (un faTH′ə mə bəl), **1** too deep to be measured. **2** too mysterious to be understood. *adj.*

un fath omed (un faTH′əmd), **1** not measured. **2** not understood. *adj.*

Pronunciation key

a	hat	i	it	oi	oil	ch	child
ā	age	ī	ice	ou	out	ng	long
ä	far	o	hot	u	cup	sh	she
e	let	ō	open	ù	put	th	thin
ē	equal	ô	order	ü	rule	ŦH	then
ėr	term					zh	measure

ə = { a in about, e in taken, i in pencil, o in lemon, u in circus }

In each of the words below **un** *means not.*

un du′ti ful	un′em phat′ic	un′en joy′a ble	un′ex ag′ge rat′ed	un′ex plod′ed
un dyed′	un′en closed′	un′en light′ened	un′ex celled′	un′ex plored′
un eat′a ble	un′en cum′bered	un en′ter pris′ing	un′ex cep′tion al	un′ex posed′
un eat′en	un′en dan′gered	un′en ter tain′ing	un′ex cit′ed	un′ex pressed′
un′e co nom′ic	un end′ing	un′en thu′si as′tic	un′ex cit′ing	un′ex pres′sive
un′e co nom′i cal	un′en dorsed′	un en′vi a ble	un′ex cused′	un ex′pur gat′ed
un ed′i fy′ing	un en′dur′a ble	un en′vied	un ex′e cut′ed	un′ex tin′guished
un′e lim′i nat′ed	un en′dur′ing	un en′vi ous	un′ex haust′ed	un fad′ed
un′em bar′rassed	un′en force′a ble	un e quipped′	un′ex pend′ed	un fad′ing
un′em bel′lished	un′en forced′	un es sen′tial	un′ex pired′	un fash′ion a ble
un′e mo′tion al	un′en gaged′	un es′ti mat′ed	un′ex plain′a ble	un fas′tened
		un eth′i cal	un′ex plained′	

un fa vor a ble (un fā′vər ə bəl), not favorable; adverse; harmful. *adj.* —**un fa′vor a ble ness,** *n.*

un fa vor a bly (un fā′vər ə blē), in an unfavorable manner. *adv.*

un feel ing (un fē′ling), 1 hardhearted; cruel: *a cold, unfeeling person.* 2 not able to feel; numb. *adj.* —**un feel′ing ly,** *adv.* —**un feel′ing ness,** *n.*

un feigned (un fānd′), not feigned; sincere; real: *unfeigned joy. adj.*

un fin ished (un fin′isht), 1 not finished; not complete: *unfinished homework, an unfinished symphony.* 2 without some special finish; not polished or painted: *unfinished furniture. adj.*

un fit (un fit′), 1 not fit; not suitable. 2 not good enough; unqualified. 3 make unfit; spoil. 1,2 *adj.,* 3 *v.,* **un fit ted, un fit ting.** —**un fit′ly,** *adv.* —**un fit′ness,** *n.*

un fix (un fiks′), 1 loosen; detach; unfasten. 2 unsettle. *v.*

un flag ging (un flag′ing), not weakening or failing: *unflagging strength, unflagging efforts. adj.* —**un flag′ging ly,** *adv.*

un fledged (un flejd′), 1 too young to fly; not having full-grown feathers: *an unfledged crow.* 2 undeveloped; immature; inexperienced. *adj.*

un flinch ing (un flin′ching), not drawing back from difficulty, danger, or pain; firm: *unflinching courage. adj.* —**un flinch′ing ly,** *adv.*

un fold (un fōld′), 1 open the folds of; open up; spread out: *unfold a napkin.* 2 reveal; show; explain: *unfold the plot of a story.* 3 open; develop: *Buds unfold into flowers. v.*

un forced (un fôrst′), 1 not forced; not compelled; willing. 2 natural; spontaneous. *adj.*

un fore seen (un′fôr sēn′), not known beforehand; unexpected. *adj.*

un for get ta ble (un′fər get′ə bəl), unable to be forgotten. *adj.*

un for get ta bly (un′fər get′ə blē), in an unforgettable manner. *adv.*

un formed (un fôrmd′), 1 without definite or regular form; shapeless: *an unformed ball of clay.* 2 undeveloped: *an unformed mind. adj.*

un for tu nate (un fôr′chə nit), 1 not lucky; having bad luck. 2 not suitable; not fitting: *an unfortunate choice of words.* 3 an unfortunate person. 1,2 *adj.,* 3 *n.* —**un for′tu nate ly,** *adv.*

un found ed (un foun′did), without foundation; without reason; baseless: *an unfounded complaint. adj.*

un freeze (un frēz′), 1 thaw; loosen. 2 free from control or restrictions. 3 release (money) for spending. *v.,* **un froze** (un frōz′), **un fro zen** (un frō′zn), **un freez ing.**

un fre quent ed (un′frē kwen′tid), not frequented; seldom visited; rarely used. *adj.*

un friend li ness (un frend′lē nis), a being unfriendly. *n.*

un friend ly (un frend′lē), 1 not friendly; hostile. 2 not favorable. *adj.*

un furl (un fėrl′), spread out; shake out; unfold: *Unfurl the sail. v.*

un fur nished (un fėr′nisht), not furnished; without furniture. *adj.*

un gain li ness (un gān′lē nis), a being ungainly; awkwardness; clumsiness. *n.*

un gain ly (un gān′lē), awkward; clumsy: *Long arms and large hands can give a person an ungainly appearance. adj.*

un gen er ous (un jen′ər əs), not generous; mean. *adj.* —**un gen′er ous ly,** *adv.*

un god li ness (un god′lē nis), lack of godliness; wickedness; sinfulness. *n.*

un god ly (un god′lē), 1 not devout; not religious; impious. 2 wicked; sinful. 3 INFORMAL. very annoying; outrageous; shocking: *an ungodly noise, pay an ungodly price. adj.*

un gov ern a ble (un guv′ər nə bəl), impossible to control; very hard to control or rule; unruly. *adj.* —**un gov′ern a ble ness,** *n.* —**un gov′ern a bly,** *adv.*

un grace ful (un grās′fəl), not graceful; not elegant or beautiful; clumsy; awkward. *adj.* —**un grace′ful ly,** *adv.*

un gra cious (un grā′shəs), 1 not polite; discourteous; rude. 2 unpleasant; disagreeable; displeasing. *adj.* —**un gra′cious ly,** *adv.* —**un gra′cious ness,** *n.*

un grate ful (un grāt′fəl), 1 not grateful; not thankful. 2 unpleasant; disagreeable: *an ungrateful task. adj.* —**un grate′ful ly,** *adv.* —**un grate′ful ness,** *n.*

un ground ed (un groun′did), without foundation; without reasons; unfounded. *adj.*

un grudg ing (un gruj′ing), not grudging; willing; hearty; liberal. *adj.* —**un grudg′ing ly,** *adv.*

un guard ed (un gär′did), 1 not protected: *an unguarded camp.* 2 careless: *In an unguarded moment she gave away the secret. adj.* —**un guard′ed ly,** *adv.*

un guent (ung′gwənt), ointment for sores, burns, etc.; salve. *n.* [*Unguent* is from Latin *unguentum,* which comes from *unguere,* meaning "to anoint."]

un gu late (ung′gyə lit), 1 having hoofs; belonging to the group of animals having hoofs. 2 animal that has hoofs. Horses, cows, sheep, and deer are ungulates. 1 *adj.,* 2 *n.* [*Ungulate* comes from Latin *ungulatus,* and can be traced back to *unguis,* meaning "a nail, hoof."]

un hal lowed (un hal′ōd), not made holy; not sacred. *adj.*

un hand (un hand′), let go; take the hands from; release. *v.*

un hand y (un han′dē), 1 not easy to handle: *an unhandy tool.* 2 not skillful: *an unhandy worker. adj.*

un hap pi ly (un hap′ə lē), 1 not happily: *to live unhappily.* 2 unfortunately: *Unhappily I missed seeing him.* 3 unsuitably. *adv.*

un hap pi ness (un hap′ē nis), 1 a being unhappy; sadness; sorrow. 2 bad luck; ill fortune. *n.*

un hap py (un hap′ē), 1 without gladness; sad; sorrowful: *an unhappy face.* 2 unlucky: *an unhappy accident.* 3 not suitable: *an unhappy selection of colors. adj.,* **un hap pi er, un hap pi est.**

un har ness (un här′nis), take harness off from (a horse, etc.). *v.*

In each of the words below **un** *means not.*

un fazed′	un fil′i al	un′for giv′ing	un gath′ered	un guid′ed
un fea′si ble	un filled′	un′for got′ten	un gen′tle	un ham′pered
un fed′	un fil′tered	un for′mu lat′ed	un gen′tle man ly	un hand′i capped
un fed′e rat ed	un fit′ting	un for′ti fied	un gift′ed	un hand′some
un felt′	un fixed′	un framed′	un glam′or ous	un hanged′
un fem′i nine	un flat′ter ing	un fre′quent	un glazed′	un har′assed
un fenced′	un fla′vored	un fruit′ful	un gov′erned	un hard′ened
un′fer ment′ed	un′for get′ting	un′ful filled′	un grad′ed	un harmed′
un fer′ti lized	un′for giv′a ble	un fun′ny	un′gram mat′i cal	un′har mo′ni ous
un fet′tered	un′for giv′en	un gal′lant	un grat′i fied	un har′nessed
		un gar′nished	un′guar an teed′	un hatched′

un health ful (un helth′fəl), bad for the health. *adj.*
—**un health′ful ly,** *adv.* —**un health′ful ness,** *n.*

un health i ly (un hel′thə lē), in an unhealthy manner. *adv.*

un health i ness (un hel′thē nis), **1** lack of health; sickness. **2** condition causing disease or harmful to health. *n.*

un health y (un hel′thē), **1** not possessing good health; not well: *an unhealthy person.* **2** coming from or showing poor health: *an unhealthy paleness.* **3** hurtful to health; unwholesome: *an unhealthy climate.* **4** morally or mentally harmful: *an unhealthy attitude. adj.,* **un health i er, un health i est.**

un heard (un hèrd′), **1** not listened to; not heard: *unheard melodies.* **2** not given a hearing: *condemn a person unheard. adj.*

un heard-of (un hèrd′uv′ *or* un hèrd′ov′), **1** never heard of; unknown: *Electric stoves were unheard-of 200 years ago.* **2** such as was never known before; unprecedented: *unheard-of prices. adj.*

un heed ed (un hē′did), not heeded; disregarded; unnoticed. *adj.*

un hes i tat ing (un hez′ə tā′ting), prompt; ready. *adj.*
—**un hes′i tat′ing ly,** *adv.*

un hinge (un hinj′), **1** take (a door, etc.) off its hinges. **2** remove the hinges from. **3** separate from something; detach. **4** unsettle; upset: *a mind unhinged by shock. v.,* **un hinged, un hing ing.**

un hitch (un hich′), to free from being hitched; unfasten: *We unhitched the trailer from the car. v.*

un ho ly (un hō′lē), not holy; wicked; sinful. *adj.,* **un ho li er, un ho li est.** —**un ho′li ness,** *n.*

un hook (un hùk′), **1** loosen from a hook. **2** undo by loosening a hook or hooks. **3** become unhooked; become undone. *v.*

un horse (un hôrs′), throw from a horse's back; cause to fall from a horse. *v.,* **un horsed, un hors ing.**

un hur ried (un hèr′ēd), not hurried; without haste; leisurely. *adj.* —**un hur′ried ly,** *adv.*

un hurt (un hèrt′), not hurt; not harmed. *adj.*

uni-, *combining form.* one; single: *Unicellular = having one cell.* [The form *uni-* comes from Latin *unus,* meaning "one."]

u ni cam er al (yü′nə kam′ər əl), having only one house in a lawmaking body. Nebraska has a unicameral legislature. *adj.*

U NI CEF or **U ni cef** (yü′nə sef), United Nations Children's Fund. *n.* [UNICEF comes from the words *United Nations International Children's Emergency Fund,* the original name of the fund. It was formed by using the first letter of each of these words.]

u ni cel lu lar (yü′nə sel′yə lər), having one cell only. The amoeba is a unicellular animal. *adj.*

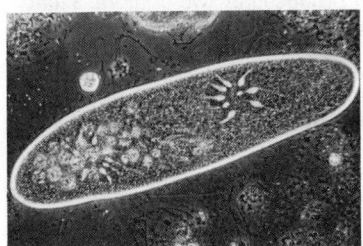

unicellular
a microscopic view
of a unicellular
animal, the paramecium

u ni corn (yü′nə kôrn), an imaginary animal like a horse, but having a single, long horn in the middle of its forehead. *n.*

WORD HISTORY

unicorn

Unicorn came into English about 750 years ago from French *unicorne,* and can be traced back to Latin *unus,* meaning "one," and *cornu,* meaning "horn."

u ni cy cle (yü′nə sī′kəl), vehicle made up of a frame mounted on a single wheel, propelled by pedaling, used especially by acrobats, circus performers, etc. *n.*

unicycles

u ni fi ca tion (yü′nə fə kā′shən), **1** formation into one unit; union: *the unification of many states into one nation.* **2** a making or a being made more alike: *The traffic laws of the different states need unification. n.*

u ni form (yü′nə fôrm), **1** always the same; not changing: *The earth turns at a uniform rate.* **2** all alike; not

---

In each of the words below **un** *means not.*

un healed′	**un heed′ing**	**un′he ro′ic**	**un housed′**	**un′i den′ti fied**
un heat′ed	**un help′ful**	**un hes′i tant**	**un′hy gien′ic**	**un′id i o mat′ic**
un heed′ful	**un her′ald ed**	**un hin′dered**		
		un hon′ored		

varying: *All the bricks have a uniform size.* **3** the distinctive clothes worn by members of a group when on duty, by which they may be recognized as belonging to that group. Soldiers, police officers, and nurses wear uniforms. **4** clothe or furnish with a uniform. 1,2 *adj.*, 3 *n.*, 4 *v.* —**u′ni form′ness,** *n.*

u ni formed (yü′nə fôrmd), wearing a uniform; in uniform: *a uniformed soldier, a uniformed schoolgirl. adj.*

u ni form i ty (yü′nə fôr′mə tē), uniform condition or character; sameness throughout. *n., pl.* **u ni form i ties.**

u ni form ly (yü′nə fôrm′lē), without variation; always; regularly. *adv.*

u ni fy (yü′nə fī), make or form into one; unite: *Several small states were unified into one nation. v.,* **u ni fied, u ni fy ing.** —**u′ni fi′er,** *n.*

u ni lat er al (yü′nə lat′ər əl), of, on, or affecting one side only: *unilateral disarmament. adj.*

un i mag i na ble (un′i maj′ə nə bəl), that cannot be imagined or thought of; inconceivable. *adj.*

un im peach a ble (un′im pē′chə bəl), free from fault, flaw, or error; not to be doubted or questioned: *an unimpeachable fact. adj.* —**un′im peach′a bly,** *adv.*

un im por tance (un′im pôrt′ns), unimportant nature or quality. *n.*

un im por tant (un′im pôrt′nt), not important; insignificant; trifling. *adj.*

un in hab it ed (un′in hab′ə tid), not lived in; without inhabitants: *an uninhabited wilderness. adj.*

un in jured (un in′jərd), not hurt; not damaged. *adj.*

un in spired (un′in spīrd′), not inspired; dull; tiresome: *uninspired writing. adj.*

un in tel li gi ble (un′in tel′jə bəl), not intelligible; not able to be understood: *unintelligible handwriting. adj.*

un in ten tion al (un′in ten′shə nəl), not intentional; not done purposely. *adj.* —**un′in ten′tion al ly,** *adv.*

un in ter est ed (un in′tər ə stid *or* un in′tə res′tid), not interested; paying no attention. *adj.*

un in ter rupt ed (un′in tə rup′tid), without interruption; continuous. *adj.* —**un′in ter rupt′ed ly,** *adv.*

un in vit ed (un′in vī′tid), not invited; without an invitation. *adj.*

un ion (yü′nyən), **1** a uniting or a being united: *The United States was formed by the union of thirteen former British colonies.* **2** group of people, states, etc., united for some special purpose: *The ten provinces of Canada form a union.* **3 the Union, a** the United States of America. **b** those states that supported the federal government of the United States during the Civil War. **4** group of workers joined together to protect and promote their interests; labor union or trade union. **5** marriage. **6** device for connecting parts of machinery or apparatus, especially a piece to join pipes or tubes together; coupling. **7** (in

union (def. 6)
pipe union

mathematics) a set including all the members which belong to either or both of two sets. EXAMPLE: If set A = {1,2,3,4} and set B = {4,5,6}, then the union of the two sets is {1,2,3,4,5,6}. *n.*

un ion ism (yü′nyə niz′əm), **1** principle of union. **2** system, principles, or methods of labor unions. *n.*

un ion ist (yü′nyə nist), **1** person who favors the uniting of certain groups, states, etc. **2 Unionist,** supporter of the federal government of the United States during the Civil War. **3** member of a labor union. *n.*

un ion i za tion (yü′nyə nə za′shən), a unionizing or a being unionized. *n.*

un ion ize (yü′nyə nīz), **1** form into a labor union. **2** organize under a labor union. *v.,* **un ion ized, un ion iz ing.**

Union Jack, the flag of the United Kingdom.

Union of South Africa, former name of the **Republic of South Africa.**

Union of Soviet Socialist Republics, the Soviet Union.

union shop, business establishment that employs only members of a labor union, but may hire nonmembers provided they join the union within a specified period.

u nique (yü nēk′), **1** having no like or equal; being the only one of its kind: *a unique specimen of rock, a unique experience.* **2** INFORMAL. very uncommon or unusual; rare; remarkable: *a rather unique idea. adj.* [*Unique* was borrowed from French *unique,* and can be traced back to Latin *unus,* meaning "one."] —**u nique′ly,** *adv.*

u ni son (yü′nə sən), **1** agreement: *The marchers' feet moved in unison. We spoke in unison.* **2** agreement in pitch of two or more tones, voices, etc.; a sounding together at the same pitch. *n.*

u nit (yü′nit), **1** a single thing or person. **2** any group of things or persons considered as one: *The family is a social unit.* **3** one of the individuals or groups of which a whole is composed: *The body consists of units called cells.* **4** a standard quantity or amount, used as a basis for measuring: *A meter is a unit of length; a gram is a unit of weight.* **5** a special part, division, or section: *the beginning unit of a book.* **6** a part of a machine or other apparatus that has one specific purpose: *the storage unit in an electronic computer.* **7** the smallest whole number; one. *n.* [*Unit* was formed from *unity.*]

U ni tar i an (yü′nə ter′ē ən *or* yü′nə tar′ē ən), **1** Christian who does not accept the doctrine of the Trinity. A Unitarian may follow the moral teachings of Jesus, but does not believe that He was divine. **2** of Unitarians. 1 *n.,* 2 *adj.*

u nite (yü nīt′), join together; make one; become one; combine: *The businesses united to form one company. v.,* **u nit ed, u nit ing.** —**u nit′er,** *n.*

u nit ed (yü nī′tid), **1** made one; joined; combined. **2** having to do with or produced by two or more. **3** that harmonizes or agrees; in concord. *adj.* —**u nit′ed ly,** *adv.*

United Arab E mir ates (ə mir′its), country in E Arabia. *Capital:* Abu Dhabi.

United Arab Republic, former name of Egypt and Syria, from 1958 to 1961, and of Egypt, from 1961 to 1971.

In each of the words below **un** *means not.*

un′il lu′mi nat′ed	**un′in flect′ed**	**un′in struc′tive**	**un′in vit′ing**
un′i mag′i na tive	**un in′flu enced**	**un′in sured′**	**un′in volved′**
un′im paired′	**un′in formed′**	**un in′te grat ed**	**un is′sued**
un′im pas′sioned	**un′im pres′sive**	**un′in hab′it a ble**	**un in tel′li gent**
un′im ped′ed	**un′im proved′**	**un in hib′it ed**	**un in tend′ed**
un′im pos′ing	**un′in cor′po rat′ed**	**un′i ni′ti at′ed**	**un in′ter est ing**
	un′in fect′ed	**un′in struct′ed**	**un′in ven′tive**

United Kingdom, 1 country in NW Europe composed of Great Britain and Northern Ireland. It is a member of the Commonwealth of Nations. *Capital:* London. **2** Great Britain and Ireland from 1801 to 1922.

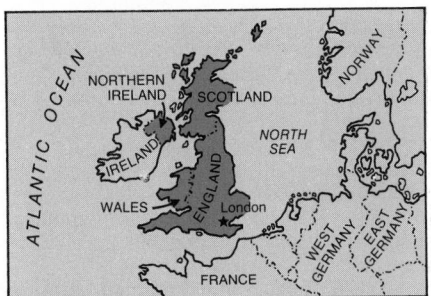

United Kingdom (def. 1)—the darker area

a hat	**i** it	**oi** oil	**ch** child		a in about
ā age	**ī** ice	**ou** out	**ng** long		e in taken
ä far	**o** hot	**u** cup	**sh** she	**ə** =	i in pencil
e let	**ō** open	**u̇** put	**th** thin		o in lemon
ē equal	**ô** order	**ü** rule	**ŦH** then		u in circus
ėr term			**zh** measure		

United Nations, 1 a worldwide organization established in 1945 to promote world peace and economic and social welfare. It has over 150 members. Its headquarters are in New York City. **2** the nations that belong to this organization.

United States, country in North America composed of 50 states and the District of Columbia. It extends from the Atlantic to the Pacific and from the Gulf of Mexico to Canada. Alaska, the 49th state, lies west and northwest of Canada, and Hawaii, the 50th state, is an island group in the Pacific. *Capital:* Washington, D.C.

United States of America, United States.

u ni ty (yü′nə tē), **1** a being united; oneness: *The group's unity of purpose helped it get results.* **2** harmony: *work together in unity.* **3** oneness of effect; choice and arrangement of material (for a composition, book, picture, statue, etc.) to secure a single effect. *n., pl.* **u ni ties.** [*Unity* came into English about 700 years ago from French *unité,* and can be traced back to Latin *unus,* meaning "one." See **Word Family.**]

unity

Below are words related to *unity.* They can all be traced back to the Latin word *unus* (ü′nus), meaning "one."

inch	unicellular	unison
inchworm	unicorn	unit
onion	uniform	unite
ounce	unify	univalve
reunion	unilateral	universal
reunite	union	universe
unanimous	unique	university

univ., 1 universal. **2** university.

u ni valve (yü′nə valv′), any mollusk whose shell consists of one piece. Snails are univalves. *n.*

u ni ver sal (yü′nə vėr′səl), **1** of all; belonging to all; concerning all: *Food is a universal need.* **2** existing everywhere: *The law of gravity is universal. adj.*

U ni ver sal ist (yü′nə vėr′sə list), member of a Christian church holding the belief that all people will finally be saved. *n.*

u ni ver sal i ty (yü′nə vər sal′ə tē), a being universal. *n., pl.* **u ni ver sal i ties.**

universal joint, joint or coupling between two shafts that allows or provides for movement in almost any direction. In an automobile, power is transmitted from the transmission to the drive shaft through a universal joint.

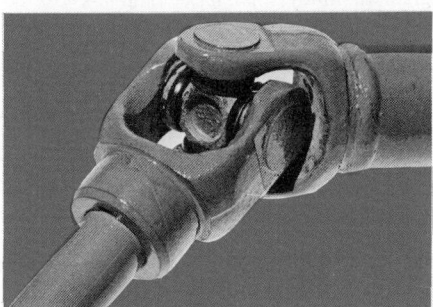

universal joint

u ni ver sal ly (yü′nə vėr′sə lē), **1** in every instance; without exception. **2** everywhere. *adv.*

Universal Product Code, a symbol, made up of a series of short black and white lines, that appears on grocery merchandise. At supermarket checkout counters, an electronic device reads this code symbol, causing a central computer to automatically register the product's price.

Universal Product Code

u ni verse (yü′nə vėrs′), **1** the whole of existing things; everything there is, including all space and matter; the cosmos. *Our world is but a small part of the universe.* **2** (in mathematics and logic) the set of all objects being considered at any one time. The universe might be the set of all natural numbers, the numbers from 0 through 10, all animals, the animals on a farm, etc. *n.* [*Universe* comes from Latin *universum,* which also meant "whole,

univalve, a whelk

bivalve, a clam

turned into one," and can be traced back to *unus*, meaning "one," and *vertere*, meaning "to turn."]

u ni ver si ty (yü/nə vėr/sə tē), institution of learning of the highest grade. A university usually has schools of law, medicine, teaching, business, etc., as well as a college of liberal arts and a graduate school. *n., pl.* **u ni ver si ties.**

un just (un just/), not just; not fair. *adj.* —**un just/ly,** *adv.* —**un just/ness,** *n.*

un jus ti fi a ble (un jus/tə fī/ə bəl), not able to be justified. *adj.*

un kempt (un kempt/), **1** not combed. **2** not properly cared for; neglected; untidy: *unkempt clothes. adj.*

un kind (un kīnd/), not kind; harsh; cruel. *adj.* —**un kind/ness,** *n.*

un kind ly (un kīnd/lē), **1** harsh; unkind. **2** in an unkind way; harshly. **1** *adj.,* **2** *adv.*

un know a ble (un nō/ə bəl), not able to be known. *adj.*

un known (un nōn/), **1** not known; not familiar; strange: *Most of Antarctica was once unknown land.* **2** person or thing that is unknown: *a political unknown. The diver descended into the unknown.* **1** *adj.,* **2** *n.*

un lace (un lās/), undo the laces of. *v.,* **un laced, un lacing.**

un latch (un lach/), unfasten or open by lifting a latch. *v.*

un law ful (un lô/fəl), contrary to the law; against the law; forbidden; illegal. *adj.* —**un law/ful ly,** *adv.* —**un law/ful ness,** *n.*

un lead ed (un led/id), refined from petroleum without the addition of a lead compound that reduces engine knock: *unleaded gasoline. adj.*

un learn (un lėrn/), get rid of (ideas, habits, or tendencies); give up knowledge of; forget. *v.*

un learn ed (un lėr/nid *for 1;* un lėrnd/ *for 2*), **1** not educated; ignorant: *They were unlearned and could not read or write.* **2** not learned; known without being learned: *Swallowing is unlearned behavior. adj.*

un leash (un lēsh/), **1** release from a leash: *She unleashed the dog.* **2** let loose: *unleash one's temper. v.*

un leav ened (un lev/ənd), not leavened. Unleavened bread is made without yeast. *adj.*

un less (ən les/ *or* un les/), if it were not that; if not: *We shall go unless it rains. conj.*

un let tered (un let/ərd), **1** not educated. **2** not able to read or write; illiterate. *adj.*

un like (un līk/), **1** not like; different: *The two problems are quite unlike.* **2** different from: *to act unlike others.* **1** *adj.,* **2** *prep.*

un like li hood (un līk/lē hùd), improbability. *n.*

un like li ness (un līk/lē nis), a being unlikely; improbability. *n.*

un like ly (un līk/lē), **1** not likely; not probable: *He is unlikely to win the race.* **2** not likely to succeed: *an unlikely undertaking. adj.*

un like ness (un līk/nis), a being unlike; difference. *n.*

un lim it ed (un lim/ə tid), **1** without limits; boundless. **2** not restrained; not restricted: *a government of unlimited power. adj.* —**un lim/it ed ness,** *n.*

un load (un lōd/), **1** remove (a load). **2** take the load from. **3** get rid of: *They tried to unload their problems on us.* **4** remove powder, shot, bullets, or shells from (a gun). **5** discharge a cargo: *The ship is unloading. v.* —**un load/er,** *n.*

un lock (un lok/), **1** open the lock of; open (anything firmly closed). **2** disclose; reveal: *Science has unlocked the mystery of the atom.* **3** become open or unfastened. *v.*

un looked-for (un lùkt/fôr/), unexpected; unforeseen. *adj.*

un loose (un lüs/), let loose; set free; release. *v.,* **un loosed, un loos ing.**

un loos en (un lü/sn), unloose; loosen. *v.*

un love ly (un luv/lē), without beauty or charm; unpleasing in appearance; unpleasant; disagreeable. *adj.* —**un love/li ness,** *n.*

un luck i ly (un luk/ə lē), in an unlucky manner; unfortunately. *adv.*

un luck i ness (un luk/ē nis), a being unlucky. *n.*

un luck y (un luk/ē), not lucky; bringing bad luck; unfortunate. *adj.,* **un luck i er, un luck i est.**

un manned (un mand/), without a crew: *an unmanned space flight. adj.*

un man ner ly (un man/ər lē), having bad manners; rude; discourteous. *adj.* —**un man/ner li ness,** *n.*

un mar ried (un mar/ēd), not married; single. *adj.*

un mask (un mask/), **1** remove a mask or disguise: *The guests unmasked at midnight.* **2** take off a mask or disguise from. **3** expose the true character of: *unmask a coward. v.*

un match a ble (un mach/ə bəl), not able to be matched or equaled. *adj.*

un mean ing (un mē/ning), **1** without meaning or significance; meaningless: *unmeaning words.* **2** empty of feeling or thought; without sense or expression; vacant: *an unmeaning stare. adj.* —**un mean/ing ly,** *adv.*

un meas ured (un mezh/ərd), **1** not measured; unlimited; measureless. **2** not restrained; excessive. *adj.*

un men tion a ble (un men/shə nə bəl), not able to be mentioned; not fit to be spoken about. *adj.* —**un men/tion a ble ness,** *n.*

un mer ci ful (un mėr/si fəl), having or showing no mercy; cruel. *adj.* —**un mer/ci ful ly,** *adv.* —**un mer/ci ful ness,** *n.*

un mind ful (un mīnd/fəl), not mindful; heedless; careless: *He went ahead despite our warning and unmindful of the results. adj.* —**un mind/ful ly,** *adv.*

un mis tak a ble (un/mə stā/kə bəl), not able to be mistaken or misunderstood; clear; plain; evident. *adj.* —**un/mis tak/a ble ness,** *n.*

un mis tak a bly (un/mə stā/kə blē), in an unmistakable manner. *adv.*

un mit i gat ed (un mit/ə gā/tid), **1** not softened or lessened: *unmitigated harshness.* **2** unqualified or absolute: *an unmitigated fraud. adj.* —**un mit/i gat ed ly,** *adv.*

un mixed (un mikst/), not mixed; pure. *adj.*

un mo lest ed (un/mə les/tid), not molested; undisturbed. *adj.*

un mo ral (un môr/əl), neither moral nor immoral; not perceiving or involving right and wrong. *adj.* —**un mo/ral ly,** *adv.*

In each of the words below **un** *means not.*

un jus/ti fi/a bly	un li/censed	un loved/	un mar/ket a ble	un mer/it ed
un kept/	un light/ed	un lov/ing	un mar/riage a ble	un/me thod/i cal
un know/ing	un lik/a ble	un mag/ni fied	un mas/tered	un mil/i tar/y
un la/beled	un lined/	un mal/le a ble	un matched/	un min/gled
un la/dy like/	un liq/ue fied	un man/age a ble	un meant/	un/mis tak/en
un laid/	un lit/	un man/ly	un/me chan/i cal	un mod/i fied
un/la ment/ed	un lov/a ble	un/man u fac/tured	un melt/ed	un mod/u lat/ed
		un marked/	un men/tioned	

un moved (un müvd′), **1** not moved; firm. **2** not disturbed; indifferent. *adj.*

un named (un nāmd′), **1** having no name; nameless. **2** not mentioned by name. *adj.*

un nat ur al (un nach′ər əl), **1** not natural; not normal. **2** shocking; horrible. **3** artificial. *adj.* —**un nat′ur al ly,** *adv.* —**un nat′ur al ness,** *n.*

un nec es sar i ly (un nes′ə ser′ə lē), in an unnecessary manner; needlessly. *adv.*

un nec es sar y (un nes′ə ser′ē), not necessary; needless. *adj.* —**un nec′es sar′i ness,** *n.*

un nerve (un nėrv′), deprive of nerve, firmness, or self-control: *The sight of blood unnerves some people.* *v.,* **unnerved, un nerv ing.**

un no ticed (un nō′tist), not noticed; not observed; not receiving any attention. *adj.*

un num bered (un num′bərd), **1** not numbered; not counted. **2** too many to count; innumerable: *There are unnumbered fish in the ocean.* *adj.*

un ob served (un′əb zėrvd′), not observed; not noticed; disregarded. *adj.*

un ob tru sive (un′əb trü′siv), modest; inconspicuous. *adj.* —**un′ob tru′sive ly,** *adv.* —**un′ob tru′sive ness,** *n.*

un oc cu pied (un ok′yə pīd), **1** not occupied; vacant: *an unoccupied room.* **2** not busy; not employed; idle. *adj.*

un of fend ing (un′ə fen′ding), not offending; inoffensive. *adj.*

un of fi cial (un′ə fish′əl), not official. *adj.* —**un′of fi′cial ly,** *adv.*

un or gan ized (un ôr′gə nīzd), **1** not formed into an organized or systematized whole. **2** not organized into labor unions. *adj.*

un pack (un pak′), **1** take out (things packed in a box, trunk, etc.): *I unpacked my clothes.* **2** take things out of: *unpack a trunk.* *v.*

un paid (un pād′), not paid: *unpaid bills for $200.* *adj.*

un pal at a ble (un pal′ə tə bəl), not agreeable to the taste; unpleasant. *adj.* —**un pal′at a ble ness,** *n.*

un par al leled (un par′ə leld), having no parallel; unequaled; matchless: *an unparalleled achievement.* *adj.*

un peg (un peg′), loosen or detach. *v.,* **un pegged, un peg ging.**

un pin (un pin′), take out a pin or pins from; unfasten: *unpin a scarf.* *v.,* **un pinned, un pin ning.**

un pleas ant (un plez′nt), not pleasant; disagreeable. *adj.* —**un pleas′ant ly,** *adv.*

un pleas ant ness (un plez′nt nis), **1** unpleasant quality. **2** something unpleasant. **3** a quarrel. *n.*

un plug (un plug′), **1** remove the plug or stopper from. **2** disconnect by removing the plug from an electric outlet. *v.,* **un plugged, un plug ging.**

a hat	**i** it	**oi** oil	**ch** child		a in about		
ā age	**ī** ice	**ou** out	**ng** long		e in taken		
ä far	**o** hot	**u** cup	**sh** she	**ə** =	i in pencil		
e let	**ō** open	**ù** put	**th** thin		o in lemon		
ē equal	**ô** order	**ü** rule	**ŦH** then		u in circus		
ėr term			**zh** measure				

un pop u lar (un pop′yə lər), not popular; not generally liked; disliked. *adj.* —**un pop′u lar ly,** *adv.*

un pop u lar i ty (un′pop yə lar′ə tē), lack of popularity; being unpopular. *n.*

un prac ticed or **un prac tised** (un prak′tist), **1** not skilled; not expert. **2** not put into practice; not used. *adj.*

un prec e dent ed (un pres′ə den′tid), having no precedent; never done before; never known before: *An unprecedented event took place in 1961, when a human being traveled for the first time in outer space.* *adj.* —**un prec′e dent′ed ly,** *adv.*

un pre dict a ble (un′pri dik′tə bəl), not able to be predicted; uncertain or changeable. *adj.*

un pre dict a bly (un′pri dik′tə blē), in an unpredictable manner. *adv.*

un prej u diced (un prej′ə dist), without prejudice; fair; impartial. *adj.*

un pre med i tat ed (un′prē med′ə tā′tid), not premeditated; not planned in advance. *adj.*

un pre pared (un′pri perd′ or un′pri pard′), **1** not made ready; not worked out ahead: *an unprepared speech.* **2** not ready: *I was unprepared to go.* *adj.*

un pre par ed ness (un′pri per′id nis or un′pri par′-id nis), a being unprepared. *n.*

un pre tend ing (un′pri ten′ding), unpretentious. *adj.*

un pre ten tious (un′pri ten′shəs), not given to or characterized by pretension; modest. *adj.* —**un′pre ten′-tious ly,** *adv.* —**un′pre ten′tious ness,** *n.*

un prin ci pled (un prin′sə pəld), lacking good moral principles; bad. *adj.*

un print a ble (un prin′tə bəl), not fit or proper to be printed. *adj.*

un pro fes sion al (un′prə fesh′ə nəl), contrary to professional etiquette; unbecoming in members of a profession: *It would be unprofessional for doctors to speak publicly of their patients' personal problems.* *adj.* —**un′pro fes′sion al ly,** *adv.*

un prof it a ble (un prof′ə tə bəl), not profitable; producing no gain or advantage. *adj.* —**un prof′it a ble-ness,** *n.*

un prof it a bly (un prof′ə tə blē), in an unprofitable manner; without profit, gain, benefit, advantage, or use. *adv.*

In each of the words below **un** *means not.*

un mo′ti vat′ed	un′ob scured′	un paired′	un′phil o soph′i cal	un′po et′i cal
un mount′ed	un′ob serv′a ble	un par′don a ble	un picked′	un poised′
un mourned′	un par′doned	un pierced′	un′po liced′
un mov′a ble	un′ob serv′ant	un′par lia men′tar y	un pit′ied	un pol′ished
un mov′ing	un′ob serv′ing	un pas′teur ized	un pit′y ing	un′pol lut′ed
un mu′si cal	un′ob struct′ed	un′pa tri ot′ic	un placed′	un pop′u lat′ed
un muz′zled	un′ob tain′a ble	un paved′	un plagued′	un′pre pos sess′ing
un nat′ur al ized	un of′fered	un peace′a ble	un planned′	un pressed′
un nav′i ga ble	un o′pened	un peo′pled	un plant′ed	un′pre vail′ing
un need′ed	un′op posed′	un′per ceived′	un played′	un′pre vent′a ble
un neigh′bor ly	un′or dained′	un′per ceiv′ing	un pleased′	un print′ed
un not′ed	un or′dered	un′per fect′ed	un pleas′ing	un priv′i leged
un no′tice a ble	un′o rig′i nal	un′per plexed′	un pledged′	un′pro duc′tive
un′o beyed′	un or′tho dox	un′per suad′ed	un pli′ant	un′pro faned′
un′ob jec′tion a ble	un′os ten ta′tious	un′per sua′sive	un plowed′	
un′o blig′ing	un owned′	un′per turbed′	un plumbed′	
	un paint′ed	un′phil o soph′ic	un′po et′ic	

un pro nounce a ble (un′prə noun′sə bəl), not able to be pronounced. *adj.*

un pro voked (un′prə vōkt′), not provoked; without provocation. *adj.*

un qual i fied (un kwol′ə fīd), **1** not qualified; not fitted: *They are unqualified for this job.* **2** not modified, limited, or restricted in any way: *unqualified praise.* **3** complete; absolute: *an unqualified failure. adj.* —**un qual′i fied′ly,** *adv.*

un quench a ble (un kwen′chə bəl), not able to be quenched or extinguished: *an unquenchable thirst, un-quenchable zeal. adj.*

un ques tion a ble (un kwes′chə nə bəl), beyond dispute or doubt; certain: *Being tall is an unquestionable advantage to a basketball player. adj.* —**un ques′tion-a ble ness,** *n.*

un ques tion a bly (un kwes′chə nə blē), beyond dispute or doubt; certainly. *adv.*

un ques tioned (un kwes′chənd), not questioned; not disputed. *adj.*

un quote (un kwōt′), to mark the end of a quotation. *v.,* **un quot ed, un quot ing.**

un rav el (un rav′əl), **1** separate the threads of; pull apart: *Can you unravel this tangle of yarn?* **2** come apart: *This sweater is unraveling at the elbow.* **3** bring or come out of a tangled state: *The detective unraveled the mystery. v.,* **un rav eled, un rav el ing** or **un rav elled, un rav-el ling.**

un read (un red′), **1** not read: *an unread book.* **2** not having read much: *an unread person. adj.*

un read y (un red′ē), **1** not ready; not prepared. **2** not prompt or quick; slow. *adj.* —**un read′i ly,** *adv.* —**un-read′i ness,** *n.*

un re al (un rē′əl), not real; imaginary; fanciful. *adj.* —**un re′al ly,** *adv.*

un re al i ty (un′rē al′ə tē), **1** lack of reality; imaginary or fanciful quality. **2** impractical or visionary character or tendency; impracticality. **3** something without reality; something unreal. *n., pl.* **un re al i ties.**

un rea son a ble (un rē′zn ə bəl), **1** not reasonable: *an unreasonable fear of the dark.* **2** not moderate; excessive: *an unreasonable price. adj.* —**un rea′son a ble ness,** *n.*

un rea son a bly (un rē′zn ə blē), **1** in a way that is not reasonable; foolishly. **2** extremely: *August often has some unreasonably hot days. adv.*

un rea son ing (un rē′zn ing), not reasoning; irrational. *adj.* —**un rea′son ing ly,** *adv.*

un re flect ing (un′ri flek′ting), not thinking; thoughtless. *adj.* —**un′re flect′ing ly,** *adv.*

un re lent ing (un′ri len′ting), **1** not yielding to feelings of kindness or compassion; merciless; cruel: *an unrelent-ing enemy.* **2** not slackening or relaxing: *She worked at an unrelenting pace. adj.* —**un′re lent′ing ly,** *adv.* —**un′re-lent′ing ness,** *n.*

un re li a ble (un′ri lī′ə bəl), not reliable; not to be depended on; irresponsible. *adj.* —**un′re li′a bly,** *adv.*

un re mit ting (un′ri mit′ing), never stopping; maintained steadily: *unremitting enthusiasm. adj.* —**un′re-mit′ting ly,** *adv.*

un re served (un′ri zėrvd′), **1** not restrained in action or speech; frank; open. **2** not restricted, limited, or qualified; without reservation. *adj.*

un re serv ed ly (un′ri zėr′vid lē), in an unreserved manner. *adv.*

un rest (un rest′), **1** lack of ease and quiet; restlessness. **2** agitation or disturbance amounting almost to rebellion. *n.*

un re strained (un′ri strānd′), not restrained; not held back; not checked: *unrestrained laughter. adj.* —**un′re-strain′ed ly,** *adv.*

un right eous (un rī′chəs), not righteous; wicked; sinful; unjust. *adj.* —**un right′eous ly,** *adv.* —**un right′-eous ness,** *n.*

un ripe (un rīp′), not ripe; not fully developed; immature. *adj.*

un ri valed or **un ri valled** (un rī′vəld), having no rival; without an equal. *adj.*

un roll (un rōl′), **1** to open or spread out (something rolled). **2** become opened or spread out. **3** lay open; display. *v.*

un ruf fled (un ruf′əld), **1** not ruffled; smooth. **2** not disturbed; calm. *adj.*

un ruled (un rüld′), **1** not kept under control; not governed. **2** not marked with lines: *unruled paper. adj.*

un rul i ness (un rü′lē nis), a being unruly. *n.*

un rul y (un rü′lē), hard to rule or control; ungovernable; disorderly: *an unruly horse, an unruly mob. adj.*

un sad dle (un sad′l), take the saddle off (a horse). *v.,* **un sad dled, un sad dling.**

un safe (un sāf′), not safe; dangerous. *adj.* —**un safe′-ness,** *n.*

un said (un sed′), **1** not said: *Everything I had meant to say remained unsaid.* **2** past tense and past participle of **unsay. 1** *adj.,* **2** *v.*

un san i tar y (un san′ə ter′ē), not sanitary; bad for the health; unhealthful. *adj.* —**un san′i tar′i ness,** *n.*

un sat is fac tor i ly (un′sat i sfak′tər ə lē), in an unsat-isfactory manner. *adv.*

In each of the words below **un** *means not.*

un′pro gres′sive	un quail′ing	un′re cord′ed	un′re pent′ant	un′re voked′
un prom′is ing	un quenched′	un′re deemed′	un′re pent′ing	un′re ward′ed
un prompt′ed	un ques′tion ing	un′re fined′	un′re port′ed	un′re ward′ing
un′pro nounced′	un qui′et	un′re formed′	un′rep re sent′a tive	un rhymed′
un′pro pi′tious	un quot′a ble	un reg′is tered	un′rep re sent′ed	un right′ful
un′pro por′tioned	un raised′	un′reg′u lat′ed	un′re pressed′	un rip′ened
un′pro tect′ed	un ran′somed	un′re lat′ed	un′re proved′	un′ro man′tic
un′pro test′ed	un rat′i fied	un′re laxed′	un′re quit′ed	un saint′ly
un proved′	un read′a ble	un′re lax′ing	un′re signed′	un sal′a ble
un prov′en	un′re al is′tic	un′re lieved′	un′re sist′ed	un sal′ar ied
un′pro vid′ed	un re′al ized	un′re mem′bered	un′re sist′ing	un salt′ed
un′pro vok′ing	un rea′soned	un′re mit′ted	un′re solved′	un sanc′ti fied
un pruned′	un′re ceived′	un′re moved′	un′re spon′sive	un sanc′tioned
un pub′li cized	un′re claimed′	un′re mu′ne ra′tive	un′re strict′ed	un sat′ed
un pub′lished	un rec′og niz′a ble	un′re nowned′	un′re ten′tive	un sa′ti at′ed
un punc′tu al	un rec′og nized	un rent′ed	un′re trieved′	
un pun′ished	un rec′om pensed	un′re paid′	un′re turned′	
un pur′chas a ble	un rec′on ciled	un′re paired′	un′re vealed′	
		un′re pealed′	un′re venged′	

un sat is fac tor y (un′sat i sfak′tər ē), not satisfactory; not good enough to satisfy; inadequate. *adj.*

un sat is fied (un sat′i sfīd), not satisfied; not contented. *adj.*

un sa vor y (un sā′vər ē), 1 tasteless. 2 unpleasant in taste or smell; distasteful: *an unsavory medicine.* 3 morally unpleasant; offensive: *an unsavory act. adj.* —**un sa′vor i ly,** *adv.* —**un sa′vor i ness,** *n.*

un say (un sā′), take back (something said). *v.,* **un said, un say ing.**

un scathed (un skāᵗʜd′), not harmed; uninjured: *She escaped unscathed from the car wreck. adj.*

un schooled (un sküld′), not schooled; not taught; not disciplined. *adj.*

un sci en tif ic (un′sī ən tif′ik), not in accordance with the facts or principles of science: *an unscientific notion. adj.* —**un′sci en tif′i cal ly,** *adv.*

un scram ble (un skram′bəl), change from confusion to order; bring out of a scrambled condition: *After the wind died down, we unscrambled the papers that had blown on the floor. v.,* **un scram bled, un scram bling.**

un screw (un skrü′), 1 take out the screw or screws from. 2 loosen or take off by turning: *unscrew an electric light bulb. v.*

un scru pu lous (un skrü′pyə ləs), not careful about right and wrong; without principles or conscience: *The unscrupulous student cheated on the test. adj.* —**un scru′pu lous ly,** *adv.* —**un scru′pu lous ness,** *n.*

un seal (un sēl′), 1 break or remove the seal of: *unseal a letter.* 2 open: *The threat of punishment unsealed their lips. v.*

un search a ble (un sėr′chə bəl), not to be searched into; that cannot be understood by searching; mysterious. *adj.* —**un search′a bly,** *adv.*

un sea son a ble (un sē′zn ə bəl), 1 not suitable to or characteristic of the season: *an unseasonable heat wave.* 2 coming at the wrong time; not timely: *an unseasonable suggestion. adj.*

un sea son a bly (un sē′zn ə blē), in an unseasonable manner. *adv.*

un seat (un sēt′), 1 displace from a seat. 2 throw (a rider) from a saddle. 3 remove from office: *unseat a member of Congress, unseat a government. v.*

un seem ly (un sēm′lē), not seemly; not suitable; improper: *Laughter is often unseemly in a courtroom. adj.,* **un seem li er, un seem li est.** —**un seem′li ness,** *n.*

un seen (un sēn′), 1 not seen; unnoticed: *an unseen error.* 2 not able to be seen; invisible: *an unseen spirit. adj.*

un self ish (un sel′fish), not selfish; considerate; generous. *adj.* —**un self′ish ly,** *adv.* —**un self′ish ness,** *n.*

un set tle (un set′l), make or become unstable; disturb; shake; weaken: *The shock unsettled his nerves. v.,* **un set tled, un set tling.**

un set tled (un set′ld), 1 not in proper condition or order; disordered; disturbed: *an unsettled mind. Her house is still unsettled.* 2 liable to change; uncertain: *The weather is unsettled.* 3 not adjusted or disposed of: *an unsettled estate, an unsettled bill.* 4 not determined or decided: *an unsettled question.* 5 not populated; uninhabited: *Some parts of the world are still unsettled. adj.*

un shak a ble (un shā′kə bəl), not able to be shaken; firm. *adj.*

un shak en (un shā′kən), not shaken; firm: *an unshaken belief. adj.*

un sheathe (un shēᵀʜ′), draw (a sword, knife, etc.) from a sheath. *v.,* **un sheathed, un sheath ing.**

un shod (un shod′), without shoes. *adj.*

un sight li ness (un sīt′lē nis), a being unsightly; ugliness. *n.*

un sight ly (un sīt′lē), ugly or unpleasant to look at: *an unsightly old shack. adj.*

un skilled (un skild′), 1 not skilled; not trained; not expert: *unskilled workers.* 2 not requiring special skills or training: *unskilled labor. adj.*

un skill ful or **un skil ful** (un skil′fəl), not skillful; lacking in skill; awkward; clumsy. *adj.* —**un skill′ful ly, un skil′ful ly,** *adv.* —**un skill′ful ness, un skil′ful ness,** *n.*

un smil ing (un smī′ling), not smiling; grave; serious. *adj.* —**un smil′ing ly,** *adv.*

un snap (un snap′), unfasten the snap or snaps of. *v.,* **un snapped, un snap ping.**

un snarl (un snärl′), remove the snarls from; untangle. *v.*

un so cia ble (un sō′shə bəl), not sociable; not associating easily with others: *unsociable behavior. adj.* —**un so′cia ble ness,** *n.* —**un so′cia bly,** *adv.*

un so phis ti cat ed (un′sə fis′tə kā′tid), not sophisticated; simple; natural; artless. *adj.*

un sought (un sôt′), not sought; not looked for; not asked for: *unsought advice, an unsought compliment. adj.*

un sound (un sound′), 1 not in good condition; not sound: *unsound walls, an unsound business.* 2 not based on truth or fact; not valid: *an unsound theory.* 3 not deep; not restful; disturbed: *an unsound sleep. adj.* —**un sound′ly,** *adv.* —**un sound′ness,** *n.*

un spar ing (un sper′ing *or* un spar′ing), 1 not sparing; very generous; liberal. 2 not merciful; severe. *adj.* —**un spar′ing ly,** *adv.*

un speak a ble (un spē′kə bəl), 1 not able to be expressed in words; beyond description; indescribable: *unspeakable joy, an unspeakable loss.* 2 extremely bad; bad or objectionable beyond description. *adj.*

un speak a bly (un spē′kə blē), beyond words; extremely: *unspeakably rude. adv.*

a hat	i it	oi oil	ch child	a in about
ā age	ī ice	ou out	ng long	e in taken
ä far	o hot	u cup	sh she	i in pencil
e let	ō open	u̇ put	th thin	o in lemon
ē equal	ô order	ü rule	ᴛʜ then	u in circus
ėr term			zh measure	

ə = { e in taken, i in pencil, o in lemon, u in circus }

In each of the words below **un** *means not.*

un sat′is fy ing	un scrip′tur al	un′se lec′tive	un shed′	un slaked′
un sat′u rat ed	un sealed′	un′self-con′scious	un shelled′	un so′cial
un scaled′	un sea′soned	un′sen ti men′tal	un shel′tered	un soiled′
un scarred′	un sea′wor′thy	un serv′ice a ble	un shield′ed	un sold′
un scent′ed	un sec′ond ed	un set′	un shorn′	un sol′dier ly
un sched′uled	un′se cured′	un shad′ed	un shrink′ing	un′so lic′it ed
un schol′ar ly	un seed′ed	un shad′owed	un sift′ed	un solv′a ble
un scorched′	un see′ing	un shaped′	un sight′ed	un solved′
un scratched′	un seg′ment ed	un shape′ly	un signed′	un sort′ed
un screened′	un seg′re gat′ed	un sharp′ened	un sized′	un sound′ed
		un shav′en	un slacked′	un sown′

un spot ted (un spot/id), not spotted; without spot or stain; pure: *an unspotted reputation. adj.*

un sta ble (un stā/bəl), **1** not firmly fixed; easily moved, shaken, or overthrown. **2** tending to sudden emotional changes; emotionally unsettled. **3** not constant; variable: *an unstable nature.* **4** (of a chemical compound) easily decomposed; readily changing into other compounds. *adj.* —**un sta/ble ness**, *n.* —**un sta/bly**, *adv.*

un stained (un stānd/), not stained; without stain or spot. *adj.*

un stead i ly (un sted/ə lē), in an unsteady manner; without steadiness. *adv.*

un stead y (un sted/ē), **1** not steady; shaky: *an unsteady voice.* **2** likely to change; not reliable: *unsteady winds. adj.,* **un stead i er, un stead i est.** —**un stead/i ness**, *n.*

un strap (un strap/), take off or loosen the strap or straps of (a trunk, box, etc.). *v.,* **un strapped, un strapping.**

un stressed (un strest/), not stressed; unaccented. In *upward,* the second syllable is unstressed. *adj.*

un strung (un strung/), **1** upset or nervous. **2** with strings loose, broken, or missing: *an unstrung guitar. adj.*

un sub stan tial (un/səb stan/shəl), not substantial; flimsy; slight. *adj.* —**un/sub stan/tial ly**, *adv.*

un suc cess ful (un/sək ses/fəl), not successful; without success. *adj.* —**un/suc cess/ful ly**, *adv.*

un suit a ble (un sü/tə bəl), not suitable; unfit. *adj.*

un suit a bly (un sü/tə blē), in an unsuitable manner. *adv.*

un suit ed (un sü/tid), not suited; unfit. *adj.*

un sul lied (un sul/ēd), not sullied; spotless; pure. *adj.*

un sung (un sung/), **1** not sung: *an unsung note.* **2** not honored or celebrated, especially by song or poetry: *unsung heroes. adj.*

un sus pect ed (un/sə spek/tid), **1** not suspected. **2** not thought of: *an unsuspected danger. adj.*

un tan gle (un tang/gəl), **1** take the tangles out of; disentangle. **2** straighten out or clear up (anything confused or perplexing). *v.,* **un tan gled, un tan gling.**

un tapped (un tapt/), (of resources, reserves, etc.) not yet available for use; not used: *untapped mineral wealth. adj.*

un taught (un tôt/), **1** not taught; not educated: *an untaught child.* **2** known without being taught; learned naturally: *untaught wisdom. adj.*

un thank ful (un thangk/fəl), **1** ungrateful. **2** not appreciated; thankless. *adj.* —**un thank/ful ly**, *adv.*

un think a ble (un thing/kə bəl), not able to be imagined; inconceivable. *adj.*

un think ing (un thing/king), **1** thoughtless; careless. **2** showing little or no thought: *blind, unthinking anger. adj.* —**un think/ing ly**, *adv.*

un thought-of (un thôt/uv/ *or* un thôt/ov/), not imagined or considered. *adj.*

un ti di ly (un tī/dl ē), in an untidy manner. *adv.*

un ti di ness (un tī/dē nis), a being untidy. *n.*

un ti dy (un tī/dē), not in order; not neat; slovenly: *an untidy house. adj.,* **un ti di er, un ti di est.**

un tie (un tī/), **1** loosen; unfasten; undo: *untie a knot.* **2** make free; release: *untie a horse. v.,* **un tied, un ty ing.**

un til (un til/), **1** up to the time of: *It was cold from December until April.* **2** up to the time when: *We waited until the sun had set.* **3** before: *She did not leave until morning* (prep.). *He did not come until the meeting was almost over* (conj.). **4** to the degree or place that: *She worked until she was too tired to do more.* 1,3 prep., 2-4 conj.

un time ly (un tīm/lē), **1** at a wrong time or season; unseasonable: *Snow in May is untimely.* **2** too early; too soon: *an untimely death at the age of 18.* 1,2 adj., 2 adv. —**un time/li ness**, *n.*

un tir ing (un tī/ring), that does not tire; tireless: *an untiring runner, untiring efforts to succeed. adj.* —**un tir/ing ly**, *adv.*

un to (un/tü), to: *be faithful unto death. prep.*

un told (un tōld/), **1** not told; not revealed: *an untold secret.* **2** too many to be counted or numbered; countless: *There are untold stars in the sky.* **3** very great; immense: *untold wealth. The tornado did untold damage. adj.*

un touch a ble (un tuch/ə bəl), **1** not able to be touched; out of reach. **2** not to be touched. **3** person of the lowest caste in India, whose touch supposedly defiled members of higher castes. 1,2 adj., 3 n.

un touched (un tucht/), not touched: *The cat left the milk untouched. The miser was untouched by the poor man's story. adj.*

un toward (un tôrd/ *or* un tōrd/), **1** unfavorable; unfortunate: *an untoward wind, an untoward accident.* **2** perverse; stubborn; willful: *The untoward child was hard to manage. adj.* —**un toward/ly**, *adv.*

un trained (un trānd/), not trained; without discipline or education: *The new recruits were completely untrained. adj.*

un tried (un trīd/), not tried; not tested: *an untried plan. adj.*

un trod (un trod/), not trodden. *adj.*

un true (un trü/), **1** not true to the facts; false. **2** not faithful; disloyal. **3** not true to a standard or rule; not exact; inaccurate. *adj.*

un tru ly (un trü/lē), in an untrue manner; falsely. *adv.*

un truth (un trüth/), **1** lack of truth; falsity. **2** a lie; falsehood. *n., pl.* **un truths** (un trüŦHz/ *or* un trüths/).

un truth ful (un trüth/fəl), **1** not truthful; contrary to the truth: *an untruthful rumor.* **2** not telling the truth: *an untruthful person. adj.* —**un truth/ful ly**, *adv.* —**un truth/ful ness**, *n.*

In each of the words below **un** *means not.*

un spe/cial ized	un stint/ed	un/sus pect/ing	un tanned/	un tilled/
un/spe cif/ic	un stint/ing	un/sus pi/cious	un tar/nished	un trace/a ble
un spec/i fied	un stitched/	un/sus tained/	un tast/ed	un traced/
un/spec tac/u lar	un stopped/	un swayed/	un taxed/	un tracked/
un spec/u la/tive	un strained/	un sweet/ened	un teach/a ble	un/trans fer/a ble
un spent/	un strat/i fied	un swept/	un tech/ni cal	un/trans lat/ed
un spir/i tu al	un stud/ied	un swerv/ing	un tem/pered	un trav/eled
un spoiled/	un/sub dued/	un/sym met/ri cal	un ten/a ble	un trav/elled
un spoilt/	un/sub mis/sive	un/sym pa thet/ic	un ten/ant ed	un trav/ersed
un spo/ken	un/sub stan/ti at ed	un/sym pa thiz/ing	un tend/ed	un trimmed/
un sports/man like/	un/sug ges/tive	un/sys tem at/ic	un ter/ri fied	un trod/den
un stamped/	un/sup port/ed	un tact/ful	un test/ed	un trou/bled
un stat/ed	un/sup pressed/	un taint/ed	un thanked/	un trust/wor/thy
un states/man like/	un sure/	un tak/en	un thought/	un turned/
un ster/i lized	un/sur passed/	un tal/ent ed	un thought/ful	
		un tamed/	un thrift/y	

un tu tored (un tü′tərd *or* un tyü′tərd), not tutored; not educated; untaught. *adj.*

un twine (un twīn′), untwist. *v.,* **un twined, un twin ing.**

un twist (un twist′), **1** undo or loosen (something twisted); unravel. **2** become untwisted. *v.*

un used (un yüzd′ *for 1,2; for 3, before the word "to" usually,* un yüst′), **1** not in use; not being used: *an unused room.* **2** never having been used: *unused drinking cups.* **3** not accustomed: *The actor's hands were unused to labor. adj.*

un u su al (un yü′zhü əl), not usual; not ordinary; not in common use; uncommon; rare. *adj.* —**un u′su al ness,** *n.*

un u su al ly (un yü′zhü ə lē), in an unusual manner; uncommonly; rarely. *adv.*

un ut ter a ble (un ut′ər ə bəl), not able to be expressed in words; unspeakable. *adj.*

un ut ter a bly (un ut′ər ə blē), in an unutterable manner; to a degree that cannot be expressed in words; unspeakably. *adv.*

un var nished (un vär′nisht), **1** not varnished. **2** plain; unadorned: *the unvarnished truth. adj.*

un var y ing (un ver′ē ing *or* un var′ē ing), steady; constant. *adj.*

un veil (un vāl′), **1** remove a veil from; disclose; reveal: *The statue was unveiled the day the graduating class presented it to the school.* **2** become unveiled; remove one's veil; reveal oneself. *v.*

un vo cal (un vō′kəl), **1** not vocal. **2** silent; taciturn. *adj.*

un war rant ed (un wôr′ən tid), not authorized or justified: *unwarranted interference. adj.*

un war y (un wer′ē *or* un war′ē), not wary; not cautious; careless; unguarded. *adj.,* **un war i er, un war i est.**

un wel come (un wel′kəm), not welcome; not wanted: *The bees were unwelcome guests at our picnic. adj.*

un well (un wel′), not in good health; ailing; ill; sick. *adj.*

un wept (un wept′), **1** not wept for; not mourned. **2** not shed: *unwept tears. adj.*

un whole some (un hōl′səm), not wholesome; bad for the body or the mind; unhealthy: *a damp, unwholesome climate. A diet consisting mainly of candy is unwholesome. adj.* —**un whole′some ly,** *adv.* —**un whole′some ness,** *n.*

un wield i ness (un wēl′dē nis), a being unwieldy. *n.*

un wield y (un wēl′dē), hard to handle or manage because of size, shape, or weight; bulky and clumsy: *a large, unwieldy package. adj.,* **un wield i er, un wield i est.**

un will ing (un wil′ing), **1** not willing; not consenting. **2** not freely or willingly granted or done: *an unwilling acceptance of more responsibilities. adj.* —**un will′ing ly,** *adv.* —**un will′ing ness,** *n.*

un wind (un wīnd′), **1** wind off or uncoil; take from a spool, ball, etc. **2** become unrolled or uncoiled. **3** relax: *unwind after a hard day. v.,* **un wound, un wind ing.**

un wise (un wīz′), not wise; not showing good judgment; foolish: *It is unwise to delay going to the doctor if you are sick. adj.* —**un wise′ly,** *adv.*

un wit ting (un wit′ing), not knowing; unaware; unconscious; unintentional. *adj.*

un wit ting ly (un wit′ing lē), not knowingly; not intentionally; unconsciously. *adv.*

un wont ed (un wun′tid), not customary; not usual: *unwonted anger. adj.* —**un wont′ed ly,** *adv.* —**un wont′ed ness,** *n.*

un world ly (un wėrld′lē), not caring much for the things of this world, such as money, pleasure, and power. *adj.* —**un world′li ness,** *n.*

un wor thi ness (un wėr′ᴛʜē nis), a being unworthy. *n.*

un wor thy (un wėr′ᴛʜē), **1** not worthy; not deserving: *Such a silly story is unworthy of belief.* **2** unsuitable; unfit; unbecoming: *a remark unworthy of a friend.* **3** base; shameful: *unworthy conduct. adj.,* **un wor thi er, un wor thi est.** —**un wor′thi ly,** *adv.*

un wound (un wound′), past tense and past participle of **unwind.** *v.*

un wrap (un rap′), **1** remove the wrapping from; open. **2** become opened. *v.,* **un wrapped, un wrap ping.**

un writ ten (un rit′n), **1** not written: *an unwritten order.* **2** understood or customary, but not actually expressed in writing: *an unwritten law. adj.*

un yield ing (un yēl′ding), not yielding; not giving way; firm: *succeed because of unyielding determination. adj.*

un yoke (un yōk′), **1** to free from or remove a yoke: *Unyoke the oxen.* **2** to separate; disconnect. *v.,* **un yoked, un yok ing.**

unwieldy
an unwieldy spacesuit

up (up), **1** from a lower to a higher place or condition: *The bird flew up. Prices have gone up.* **2** in a higher place or condition: *We stayed up in the mountains several days* (*adv.*). *The sun is up* (*adj.*). **3** to a higher place on; at a higher place in: *The cat ran up the tree.* **4** along: *They walked up the street.* **5** to, near, or at the upper part of: *We sailed up the river.* **6** going or pointed upward: *an up*

In each of the words below **un** *means not.*

un twist′ed	**un veiled′**	**un war′like′**	**un wed′ded**	**un wor′ried**
un typ′i cal	**un ven′ti lat′ed**	**un washed′**	**un weed′ed**	**un wound′ed**
un us′a ble	**un ver′i fied**	**un wast′ed**	**un wife′ly**	**un wo′ven**
un ut′tered	**un versed′**	**un watched′**	**un wink′ing**	**un wrin′kled**
un vac′ci nat′ed	**un vexed′**	**un wa′ver ing**	**un wit′nessed**	**un wrought′**
un val′ued	**un vis′it ed**	**un weaned′**	**un wom′an ly**	
un van′quished	**un voiced′**	**un wear′y ing**	**un work′a ble**	
un var′ied	**un want′ed**	**un weath′ered**	**un work′man like′**	
		un wed′	**un worn′**	

trend. **7** piece of good luck: *Life has its ups and downs.*
8 out of bed: *Please get up or you will be late* (adv.). *The children were up at dawn* (adj.). **9** thoroughly; completely; entirely: *The house burned up.* **10** at an end; over: *The time is up now.* **11** in or into being or action: *Don't stir up trouble.* **12** to or in an even position; not behind: *catch up in a race, keep up with the times.* **13** into storage or a safe place: *Squirrels lay up nuts for the winter.* **14** at bat in baseball: *She was up four times in the game.* **15** for each one; apiece; each: *The score at the half was ten up.* **16** INFORMAL. put, lift, or get up. **17** to increase: *They upped the price of eggs.* 1,2,8-13,15 *adv.*, 2,6,8,14 *adj.*, 3-5 *prep.*, 7 *n.*, 16,17 *v.*, **upped, up ping.**

on the up and up, INFORMAL. honest; legitimate: *Since all the arrangements were carefully explained, we knew everything was on the up and up.*

up against, INFORMAL. facing as a thing to be dealt with.

up for, 1 a candidate for: *be up for reelection.* **2** on trial in a court of law for: *be up for robbery.*

up till or **up until,** till; until.

up to, 1 about to do; doing: *She is up to some mischief.* **2** equal to; capable of doing: *Do you feel up to going out so soon after being sick?* **3** before (a person) as a duty or task to be done: *It's up to the judge to decide if he is guilty.*

up-and-com ing (up′ən kum′ing), on the way to prominence or success; promising: *an up-and-coming young scientist. adj.*

up beat (up′bēt′), **1** (in music) an unaccented beat in a measure, especially one preceding a downbeat. **2** IN-FORMAL. hopeful; buoyant: *a motion picture with an up-beat ending.* 1 *n.*, 2 *adj.*

up braid (up brād′), find fault with; blame; reprove: *The captain upbraided the guards for falling asleep. v.*

up bring ing (up′bring′ing), care and training given to a child while growing up; bringing-up. *n.*

UPC, Universal Product Code.

up chuck (up′chuk′), INFORMAL. to vomit. *v.*

up com ing (up′kum′ing), forthcoming: *the upcoming semester. adj.*

up coun try (up′kun′trē), in the interior of a country: *an upcountry village* (adj.). *We went fishing upcountry* (adv.). *adj., adv.*

up date (up dāt′), **1** bring up to date. **2** the newest, most up-to-date information or data: *a news update, a computer update.* 1 *v.*, **up dat ed, up dat ing;** 2 *n.*

up draft (up′draft′), an upward movement of air, wind, gas, etc. *n.*

up end (up end′), to set on end; stand on end: *If you upend the box it will take up less space. v.*

up front or **up-front** (up′frunt′), INFORMAL. **1** outspoken; straightforward; direct; candid: *an upfront statement.* **2** in advance: *upfront payments. adj.*

up grade (up′grād′), **1** an upward slope or incline. **2** raise to a higher position, status, rating, etc.: *upgrade a job, upgrade an employee.* 1 *n.*, 2 *v.*, **up grad ed, up grad ing.**

on the upgrade, increasing in strength, power, value, etc.; improving: *Sales have been on the upgrade since the new advertising plans were put into effect.*

up heav al (up hē′vəl), **1** a heaving up or a being heaved up. **2** a sudden or violent agitation; great turmoil: *a flood, earthquake, or other upheaval. n.*

up heave (up hēv′), heave up; lift up: *land upheaved by volcanic forces. v.*, **up heaved, up heav ing.**

up held (up held′), past tense and past participle of **up-hold.** *The higher court upheld the lower court's decision. v.*

up hill (up′hil′ for 1,3; up′hil′ for 2), **1** up the slope of a hill; upward: *an uphill road.* **2** upward: *We walked a mile uphill.* **3** difficult: *an uphill fight.* 1,3 *adj.*, 2 *adv.*

up hold (up hōld′), **1** give support to; confirm: *The prin-*

cipal upheld the teacher's decision. **2** hold up; not let down; support: *We uphold the good name of our school.* **3** sustain on appeal; approve: *The higher court upheld the decision of the lower court. v.*, **up held, up hold ing.**

up hol ster (up hōl′stər), provide (furniture) with coverings, cushions, springs, stuffing, etc. *v.*

up hol ster er (up hōl′stər ər), person whose business is upholstering. *n.*

up hol ster y (up hōl′stər ē), **1** coverings for furniture. **2** business of upholstering. *n., pl.* **up hol ster ies.**

up keep (up′kēp′), **1** maintenance: *the upkeep of a house.* **2** cost of operating and repair: *The upkeep of a yacht is very expensive. n.*

up land (up′lənd), **1** high land. **2** of high land; living or growing on high land: *upland meadows.* 1 *n.*, 2 *adj.*

up lift (up lift′ for 1,3; up′lift′ for 2,4), **1** lift up; raise; elevate. **2** act of lifting up. **3** raise socially or morally. **4** social or moral improvement or effort toward it. 1,3 *v.*, 2,4 *n.* **—up lift′er,** *n.*

up link (up′lingk′), the communications connection for transmission of signals from an earth station to a space-craft or satellite. *n.*

up most (up′mōst), uppermost. *adj.*

up on (ə pôn′ *or* ə pon′), on. *prep.*

up per (up′ər), **1** higher: *the upper lip, the upper floors of an office building.* **2** farther from the sea: *the upper reaches of a river. adj.*

upper case, capital letters.

up per-case (up′ər kās′), (in printing) in capital letters. *adj.*

up per cut (up′ər kut′), (in boxing) a swinging blow directed upward from beneath. *n.*

upper hand, advantage; control: *Do what the doctor says or that cold may get the upper hand.*

upper house or **Upper House,** the smaller and less representative branch of a lawmaking body that has two branches. The House of Lords is the upper house of the British Parliament.

up per most (up′ər mōst), **1** highest; topmost. **2** having the most force or influence; most prominent. **3** in, at, or near the top. **4** first: *The safety of the passengers was uppermost in the pilot's mind.* 1,2 *adj.*, 3,4 *adv.*

Upper Vol ta (vol′tə), former name of **Burkina Faso.**

up pi ty (up′ə tē), INFORMAL. arrogant, self-assertive, or conceited. *adj.* **—up′pi ty ness,** *n.*

up raise (up rāz′), lift up; raise. *v.*, **up raised, up rais-ing.**

up rate (up′rāt′), **1** increase the rate of. **2** increase, as in power or efficiency; improve. *v.*, **up rat ed, up rat ing.**

up right (up′rīt′), **1** standing up straight; erect: *an upright post.* **2** straight up; in a vertical position: *Hold yourself upright.* **3** something standing erect; vertical part or piece. **4** an upright piano. **5** good; honest; righteous: *an upright citizen.* **6** raise to an upright position: *to upright a rowboat.* 1,5 *adj.*, 2 *adv.*, 3,4 *n.*, 6 *v.* **—up′right′ly,** *adv.* **—up′right′ness,** *n.*

upright piano, a rectangular piano having vertical strings behind the keyboard.

up rise (up rīz′), **1** rise up. **2** to slope upward; ascend. *v.*, **up rose, up ris en, up ris ing.**

up ris en (up riz′n), past participle of **uprise.** *v.*

up ris ing (up′rī′zing), a revolt; rebellion: *an uprising in a prison. n.*

up roar (up′rôr′), **1** loud or confused noise: *the uproar following a last-minute touchdown.* **2** a confused, disturbed, or excited state: *the uproar caused by a large tax increase. n.* [*Uproar* comes from Dutch *oproer*, meaning "insurrection, tumult."]

up roar i ous (up rôr′ē əs), **1** making an uproar; noisy and disorderly: *an uproarious crowd.* **2** loud and confused: *uproarious laughter. adj.* —**up roar′i ous ly,** *adv.*

up root (up rüt′ *or* up rut′), **1** tear up by the roots: *The storm uprooted many trees.* **2** tear away, remove, or displace completely: *Many families were uprooted from their homes by the flood.* *v.* —**up root′er,** *n.*

up rose (up rōz′), past tense of **uprise.** *v.*

ups-and-downs (ups′ən dounz′), changes in fortunes; successes and failures: *Her career has had many ups-and-downs. n.pl.*

up set (up set′ *for 1,4,7;* up′set′ *for 2,5,8;* up set′ *or* up′set′ *for 3,6),* **1** tip over; overturn: *He upset his glass of milk. Moving about in a boat may upset it.* **2** a tipping over; overturn. **3** tipped over; overturned. **4** disturb greatly; disorder: *Rain upset our plans for a picnic. The shock upset my nerves.* **5** a great disturbance; disorder. **6** greatly disturbed; disordered: *an upset stomach.* **7** defeat unexpectedly in a contest: *The independent candidate upset the mayor in the election.* **8** an unexpected defeat: *The hockey team suffered an upset.* 1,4,7 *v.,* **up set, up set ting;** 2,5,8 *n.,* 3,6 *adj.* —**up set′er,** *n.*

up shot (up′shot′), conclusion; result: *The upshot of our discussion was a better understanding of one another. n.*

up side (up′sīd′), the upper side. *n.*

upside down, 1 having what should be on top at the bottom: *The pie fell upside down on the floor.* **2** in or into complete disorder: *The children turned the house upside down.*

up side-down cake (up′sīd′doun′), a cake made of batter poured over fruit, baked, and served bottom up.

up stage (up′stāj′), **1** toward or at the back of the stage: *walk upstage (adv.), upstage furniture (adj.).* **2** draw attention away from (an actor) by standing upstage or by forcing him or her to face away from the audience. 1 *adv., adj.,* 2 *v.,* **up staged, up stag ing.**

up stairs (up′sterz′ *or* up′starz′), **1** up the stairs: *The boy ran upstairs.* **2** on or to an upper floor: *She lives upstairs (adv.). He is waiting in an upstairs hall (adj.).* **3** the upper floor or floors: *That small cottage has no upstairs.* **4** INFORMAL. in the mind; mentally: *Something's wrong with him upstairs.* 1,2,4 *adv.,* 2 *adj.,* 3 *n.*

kick upstairs, INFORMAL. promote (a person) to a higher but less powerful or important position.

up stand ing (up stan′ding), **1** standing up; erect: *short, upstanding hair.* **2** honorable: *a fine, upstanding young woman. adj.*

up start (up′stärt′), **1** person who has suddenly risen from a humble position to wealth, power, or importance. **2** a bold, unpleasant, and conceited person. *n.*

up state (up′stāt′), of the part of a state away from and usually north of the principal city: *upstate New York. adj.*

up stream (up′strēm′), against the current of a stream; up a stream: *He swam upstream (adv.). We had an upstream campsite (adj.). adv., adj.*

up surge (up′sėrj′), **1** a rising upward; rise; upturn. **2** surge upward. 1 *n.,* 2 *v.,* **up surged, up surg ing.**

up swing (up′swing′), **1** an upward swing; movement upward. **2** a marked improvement; strong advance. *n.*

up tight (up′tīt′), SLANG. **1** very upset, angry, or worried: *be uptight over losing a job.* **2** having very old-fashioned, traditional, or conventional ideas: *an uptight neighborhood. adj.*

up tilt (up tilt′), tilt up. *v.*

up-to-date (up′tə dāt′), **1** extending to the present time: *an up-to-date record of sales.* **2** keeping up with the times in style, ideas, etc.; modern: *an up-to-date store. adj.*

up town (up′toun′), to or in the upper part or away from the main business section of a town or city: *go uptown (adv.), an uptown store (adj.). adv., adj.*

up turn (up tėrn′ *for 1;* up′tėrn′ *for 2,3),* **1** turn up. **2** an upward turn: *The airplane made a sudden upturn to avoid*

the mountain. **3** an improvement: *As business improved, his income took an upturn.* 1 *v.,* 2,3 *n.*

up turned (up tėrnd′), turned upward. *adj.*

up ward (up′wərd), **1** toward a higher place: *I climbed upward until I reached the apple.* **2** directed or moving toward a higher place; in a higher position: *an upward course, an upward flight.* **3** toward a higher or greater rank, amount, age, etc.: *From ten years of age upward, she had studied French.* **4** above; more: *Children of five years and upward must pay the full fare.* **5** toward the source: *We traced the brook upward.* 1,3-5 *adv.,* 2 *adj.* —**up′ward ly,** *adv.* —**up′ward ness,** *n.*

upward of, more than: *The car will cost upward of $1000.*

up wards (up′wərdz), upward. *adv.*

upwards of, more than; upward of.

up wind (up′wind′), against the wind; in the direction from which the wind is blowing: *upwind flight (adj.), to fly upwind (adv.). adj., adv.*

Ur (ėr), city in ancient Sumer, on the Euphrates River. *n.*

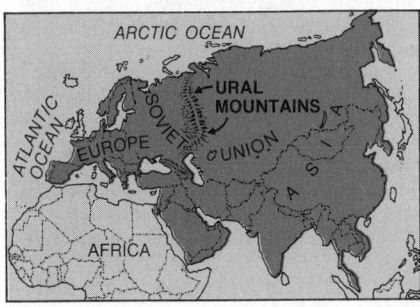

Ur al Mountains (yur′əl), mountain range in W Soviet Union, between Europe and Asia.

Ural River, river flowing south from the Ural Mountains into the Caspian Sea.

Ur als (yur′əlz), Ural Mountains. *n.pl.*

u ra ni um (yu̇ rā′nē əm), a very heavy, white, radioactive metallic element that occurs in pitchblende. Certain isotopes of uranium are used as sources of atomic energy. *n.*

Ur a nus (yur′ə nəs), **1** (in Greek myths) a god who represented heaven. Uranus was the father of the Titans and the Cyclopes. **2** the third largest planet in the solar system and the seventh in distance from the sun. *n.*

ur ban (ėr′bən), **1** of cities or towns: *an urban district, urban planning.* **2** living in a city or cities: *the urban population, urban dwellers.* **3** characteristic of cities: *urban life. adj.* [*Urban* is from Latin *urbanus,* which comes from *urbs,* meaning "city."]

ur bane (ėr bān′), courteous, refined, or elegant: *urbane manners. adj.* —**ur′bane′ly,** *adv.* —**ur′bane′ness,** *n.*

ur ban i ty (ėr′ban′ə tē), courtesy, refinement, or elegance. *n., pl.* **ur ban i ties.**

ur ban i za tion (ėr′bə nə zā′shən), a making or becoming urban. *n.*

ur ban ize (ėr′bə nīz), make or become urban: *urbanize an area. v.,* **ur ban ized, ur ban iz ing.**

urban renewal, improvement of urban areas by removing slums and converting them into attractive living or industrial areas.

ur chin (ėr'chən), **1** a small child. **2** a mischievous child. **3** a poor, ragged child. **4** sea urchin. *n.* [*Urchin* came into English about 700 years ago from French *irechon*, meaning "a hedgehog," and can be traced back to Latin *er.*]

-ure, suffix added to verbs to form nouns. **1** act or fact of _____ing: *Failure = act of failing.* **2** state of being _____ed: *Pleasure = state of being pleased.* **3** result of being _____ed: *Exposure = result of being exposed.* **4** something that _____s: *Legislature = something that legislates.* **5** thing that is _____ed: *Disclosure = thing that is disclosed.*

u re a (yü rē'ə), substance present in the urine of mammals. Urea produced synthetically is used in making adhesives and plastics, in fertilizers, in medicine, etc. *n.*

u re ter (yü rē'tər), duct that carries urine from a kidney to the bladder. *n.*

u re thra (yü rē'thrə), duct through which urine is discharged from the bladder. *n., pl.* **u re thras, u re thrae** (yü rē'thrē).

urge (ėrj), **1** push, force, or drive forward or onward: *The rider urged on his horse with whip and spurs. Hunger urged her to find food.* **2** a driving force or impulse: *I had an urge to see my old friends again.* **3** try to persuade with arguments; ask earnestly: *We urged them to stay.* **4** plead or argue earnestly for; recommend strongly: *The doctor urged a change of climate.* 1,3,4 *v.*, **urged, urg ing;** 2 *n.*

ur gen cy (ėr'jən sē), **1** urgent character; need for immediate action or attention: *Conserving fuel became a matter of great urgency.* **2** insistence: *There was urgency in her voice. n., pl.* **ur gen cies.**

ur gent (ėr'jənt), **1** demanding immediate action or attention; pressing; important: *an urgent duty, an urgent message.* **2** insistent. *adj.* —**ur'gent ly,** *adv.*

ur i nal (yür'ə nəl), **1** container for urine. **2** place for urinating. *n.*

ur i nal y sis (yür'ə nal'ə sis), a chemical analysis of a sample of urine. By means of urinalysis doctors can detect certain diseases, such as diabetes. *n., pl.* **ur i nal y ses** (yür'ə nal'ə sēz').

ur i nar y (yür'ə ner'ē), **1** of urine. **2** of the organs that secrete and discharge urine. *adj.*

ur i nate (yür'ə nāt), discharge urine from the body. *v.*, **ur i nat ed, ur i nat ing.** —**ur'i na'tion,** *n.*

ur ine (yür'ən), the liquid waste product that is excreted by the kidneys. Urine passes through the ureters into the bladder, and is then discharged from the body through the urethra. *n.*

urn (def. 1)

Greek vase—5th century B.C., Athenian, The Metropolitan Museum of Art, Rogers Fund, 1907

urn (ėrn), **1** vase with a foot or pedestal. Urns were used in ancient Greece and Rome to hold the ashes of the dead. **2** a coffeepot or teapot with a faucet, used for making or serving coffee or tea at the table. *n.*

Ur sa Major (ėr'sə), the most prominent northern constellation, shaped somewhat like a bear, and including the stars of the Big Dipper; Great Bear.

Ur sa Minor (ėr'sə), a northern constellation, shaped somewhat like a bear, that includes the stars of the Little Dipper; Little Bear.

Ur u guay (yür'ə gwā *or* yür'ə gwī), country in the SE part of South America. *Capital:* Montevideo. See **Brazil** for map. *n.* —**Ur'u guay'an,** *adj., n.*

us (us; *unstressed* əs). *We* and *us* mean the person speaking plus the person or persons addressed or spoken about: *They often help us. He came with us to the movie. pron.*

U.S., the United States.

U.S.A. or **USA, 1** the United States of America. **2** United States Army.

us a ble (yü'zə bəl), able to be used; fit for use. *adj.* Also, **useable.** —**us'a ble ness,** *n.* —**us'a bly,** *adv.*

USAF or **U.S.A.F.,** United States Air Force.

us age (yü'sij *or* yü'zij), **1** way or manner of using or of being used; treatment: *The car has had rough usage.* **2** a long-continued practice; customary use; habit; custom. **3** the customary way of using words: *The usage of the best speakers and writers determines what is good English. n.*

USCG or **U.S.C.G.,** United States Coast Guard.

use (yüz *for 1-4;* yüs *for 5-12*), **1** put into action or service: *use a knife to cut meat. We use our legs in walking.* **2** act toward; treat: *She used us well.* **3** consume or expend by using: *We have used most of the money. He uses tobacco.* **4** avail oneself of; put to one's own purposes: *May I use your telephone?* **5** a using: *the use of tools.* **6** a being used: *methods long out of use.* **7** usefulness: *a thing of no practical use.* **8** purpose that a thing is used for: *find a new use for something.* **9** way of using: *a proper use of one's time, poor use of a material.* **10** need or occasion for using; necessity; demand: *A camper has use for a hatchet.* **11** power or capacity of using; ability to use: *lose the use of an arm.* **12** right or privilege of using: *have the use of a friend's boat for the summer.* 1-4 *v.*, **used, us ing;** 5-12 *n.* [*Use* came into English about 750 years ago from French *use,* and can be traced back to Latin *uti,* meaning "to use." See **Word Family.**]

have no use for, 1 not need or want. **2** dislike.

in use, being used.

make use of, use; utilize: *She made use of her Spanish while in Mexico.*

put to use, use: *If you can put to use that old bicycle, you may have it.*

used to (yüst'tü *or* yü'stə), **1** accustomed to: *I'm not used to cold weather.* **2** formerly did: *I used to have a car, but now I don't.*

use up, consume or expend entirely: *We have used up our sugar.*

use

Below are words related to *use.* They can all be traced back to the Latin word *uti* (ü'tē), meaning "to use."

abuse	usual	utensil
peruse	usurp	utility
usage	usury	utilize

use a ble (yü'zə bəl), usable. *adj.*

used (yüzd), not new; that has belonged to another or others: *a used car. adj.*

use ful (yüs'fəl), of use; giving service; helpful: *a useful suggestion. He made himself useful about the house. adj.*

use less (yüs′lis), of no use; worthless: *A television set would be useless in a house without electricity. adj.* —**use′less ly,** *adv.* —**use′less ness,** *n.*

us er (yü′zər), one that uses. *n.*

us er-friend ly (yü′zər frend′lē), designed to be easy to use, even by people without training or experience: *The program is so user-friendly, it fixes your mistakes. adj.*

ush er (ush′ər), **1** person who shows people to their seats in a theater, church, etc. **2** to conduct; escort; show: *We ushered the visitors to the door.* 1 *n.,* 2 *v.* [*Usher* came into English about 600 years ago from French *uissier,* and can be traced back to Latin *ostium,* meaning "door."]

usher in, inaugurate; introduce: *a winter ushered in by cold rains.*

USMC or **U.S.M.C.,** United States Marine Corps.

USN or **U.S.N.,** United States Navy.

U.S.S.R. or **USSR,** Union of Soviet Socialist Republics.

u su al (yü′zhü əl), commonly seen, found, or happening; ordinary; customary: *This is our usual spring weather. My usual bedtime is 10 p.m. adj.* [*Usual* comes from Latin *usualis,* and can be traced back to *uti,* meaning "to use."] —**u′su al ness,** *n.*

as usual, in the usual manner; as is customary: *My friend and I met, as usual, on the way to school.*

u su al ly (yü′zhü ə lē), according to what is usual; commonly; ordinarily; customarily: *We usually eat dinner at 6. adv.*

u sur er (yü′zhər ər), person who lends money at an extremely high or unlawful rate of interest. *n.*

u sur i ous (yü zhùr′ē əs), **1** taking extremely high or unlawful interest for the use of money. **2** of usury: *Fifty percent is a usurious rate of interest. adj.* —**u sur′i ous ly,** *adv.* —**u sur′i ous ness,** *n.*

u surp (yü zėrp′), seize and hold (power, position, or authority) by force or without right: *The queen's younger sister tried to usurp the throne. v.* —**u surp′er,** *n.*

u sur pa tion (yü′zər pā′shən), a usurping; the seizing and holding of the place or power of another by force or without right. *n.*

u sur y (yü′zhər ē), **1** the lending of money at an extremely high or unlawful rate of interest. **2** an extremely high or unlawful interest. *n., pl.* **u sur ies.**

UT, Utah (used with postal Zip Code).

Ut., Utah.

U tah (yü′tô *or* yü′tä), one of the western states of the United States. *Abbreviation:* Ut. or UT *Capital:* Salt Lake City. *n.* —**U′tah an,** *adj., n.*

u ten sil (yü ten′səl), **1** container or implement used for practical purposes. Pots and pans are kitchen utensils. **2** instrument or tool used for some special purpose. Pens and pencils are writing utensils. *n.*

u ter us (yü′tər əs), the part of the body in female mammals that holds and nourishes the young till birth; womb. *n., pl.* **u ter i** (yü′tər ī).

a	hat	i	it	oi	oil	ch	child		a in about
ā	age	ī	ice	ou	out	ng	long		e in taken
ä	far	o	hot	u	cup	sh	she	ə =	i in pencil
e	let	ō	open	ù	put	th	thin		o in lemon
ē	equal	ô	order	ü	rule	ᴛʜ	then		u in circus
ėr	term					zh	measure		

u til i tar i an (yü til′ə ter′ē ən), **1** of utility. **2** aiming at usefulness rather than beauty, style, etc. *adj.*

u til i ty (yü til′ə tē), **1** power to satisfy people's needs; usefulness: *They appreciated the utility of their dishwasher.* **2** a useful thing. **3** company that performs a public service; public utility. Railroads, bus lines, and gas and electric companies are utilities. **4** capable of playing more than one role or position: *a utility infielder.* 1-3 *n., pl.* **u til i ties,** 4 *adj.*

u ti li za tion (yü′tl ə zā′shən), a utilizing or a being utilized. *n.*

u ti lize (yü′tl īz), make use of; put to some practical use: *The cook utilized the bones to make soup. v.,* **u ti lized, u ti liz ing.** —**u′ti liz′a ble,** *adj.* —**u′ti liz′er,** *n.*

ut most (ut′mōst), **1** greatest possible; greatest; highest: *A balanced diet is of the utmost importance to health.* **2** most distant; farthest; extreme: *She walked to the utmost edge of the cliff.* **3** the most that is possible; extreme limit: *He enjoyed himself to the utmost.* 1,2 *adj.,* 3 *n.*

u to pi a or **U to pi a** (yü tō′pē ə), **1** an ideal place or condition; a perfect place or way to live. **2** an idealistic system or plan of government with ideal laws and social conditions, that is impractical in actual use. *n.*

u to pi an or **U to pi an** (yü tō′pē ən), **1** of or like a utopia. **2** idealistic but impractical. **3** an idealistic but not always practical reformer; idealist. 1,2 *adj.,* 3 *n.*

ut ter[1] (ut′ər), complete; total; absolute: *utter surprise, utter darkness, utter defeat. adj.*

ut ter[2] (ut′ər), **1** make known; speak; express: *the last words he uttered, utter one's thoughts.* **2** give forth; give out: *He uttered a cry of pain. v.* —**ut′ter a ble,** *adj.*

ut ter ance (ut′ər əns), **1** an uttering; expression in words or sounds: *The child gave utterance to her grief.* **2** way or manner of speaking. **3** something uttered; a spoken word or words. *n.*

ut ter ly (ut′ər lē), completely; totally; absolutely. *adv.*

ut ter most (ut′ər mōst), utmost. *adj., n.*

U-turn (yü′tėrn′), a U-shaped turn made by a motor vehicle in order to reverse its direction. *n.*

UV, ultraviolet.

u vu la (yü′vyə lə), the small piece of flesh hanging down from the soft palate in the back of the mouth. *n., pl.* **u vu las, u vu lae** (yü′vyə lē′). [*Uvula* was borrowed from Latin *uvula,* which comes from *uva,* which also meant "grape." It was called this because of its shape.]

Uz bek (üz′bek), republic of the Soviet Union, in central Asia. *n.*

Vv

V or **v** (vē), **1** the 22nd letter of the English alphabet. **2** anything shaped like a V. **3** the Roman numeral for 5. *n., pl.* **V's** or **v's.**

v, volt.

V, symbol for vanadium.

v., 1 verb. **2** verse. **3** versus. **4** vice-. **5** voice. **6** volume.

VA, Virginia (used with postal Zip Code).

Va., Virginia.

va can cy (vā′kən sē), **1** a being vacant; emptiness. **2** an unoccupied position: *The retirement of two bookkeepers made two vacancies in our office.* **3** a room, space, or apartment for rent; empty space: *a vacancy in the motel, a vacancy in the parking lot.* **4** emptiness of mind. *n., pl.* **va can cies.**

va cant (vā′kənt), **1** not occupied: *a vacant chair, a vacant house.* **2** empty; not filled: *a vacant space.* **3** empty of thought or intelligence: *a vacant smile.* **4** free from work, business, etc.: *vacant time. adj.* —**va′cant ly,** *adv.*

va cate (vā′kāt), go away from and leave empty or unoccupied; make vacant: *They will vacate the house on May 1. v.,* **va cat ed, va cat ing.**

va ca tion (vā kā′shən), **1** freedom from school, business, or other duties: *There is a vacation from school every summer.* **2** take a vacation. **1** *n.,* **2** *v.* —**va ca′tion er,** *n.* —**va ca′tion less,** *adj.*

vac ci nate (vak′sə nāt), inoculate with vaccine. Persons who are vaccinated against whooping cough, tetanus, etc., are made immune to these diseases for several years or longer. *v.,* **vac ci nat ed, vac ci nat ing.**

vac ci na tion (vak′sə nā′shən), **1** act or process of vaccinating: *Vaccination has made smallpox a very rare disease.* **2** scar where vaccine was injected. *n.*

vac cine (vak′sēn′ *or* vak sēn′), a preparation of dead or weakened bacteria or viruses of a particular disease, used to inoculate a person in order to prevent or lessen the effects of that disease. Vaccines work by causing the body to develop antibodies against the disease germs. *n.*

WORD HISTORY

vaccine

Vaccine is from Latin *vaccinus,* meaning "of cows," which comes from *vacca,* meaning "cow." The first vaccine contained cowpox virus.

vac il late (vas′ə lāt), **1** waver in mind or opinion: *I was vacillating between two possible choices.* **2** move first one way and then another; waver. *v.,* **vac il lat ed, vac il lat ing.** —**vac′il lat′ing ly,** *adv.*

vac il la tion (vas′ə lā′shən), **1** a wavering in mind or opinion. **2** unsteadiness; swaying. *n.*

va cu i ty (va kyü′ə tē), **1** emptiness. **2** an empty space; vacuum. **3** emptiness of mind; lack of ideas or intelligence. *n., pl.* **va cu i ties.**

vac u ole (vak′yü ōl), a tiny cavity in the protoplasm of a living cell, containing fluid. *n.*

vac u ous (vak′yü əs), **1** showing no intelligence; stupid. **2** empty. *adj.* —**vac′u ous ly,** *adv.* —**vac′u ous ness,** *n.*

vac u um (vak′yü əm *or* vak′yüm), **1** an empty space without even air in it. **2** an enclosed space from which almost all air or gas has been removed. **3** an empty space; void: *Their child's death left a vacuum in their lives.* **4** vacuum cleaner. **5** clean with a vacuum cleaner: *We vacuum the rugs every week or two.* **1-4** *n., pl.* **vac u ums** or (except for def. 4) **vac u a** (vak′yü ə); **5** *v.*

vacuum bottle, thermos.

vacuum cleaner, apparatus for cleaning carpets, curtains, floors, etc., by suction.

vac u um-packed (vak′yü əm pakt′ *or* vak′yüm pakt′), **1** packed in an airtight container to keep fresh: *vacuum-packed coffee.* **2** having had all or most of the air removed before sealing: *vacuum-packed cans. adj.*

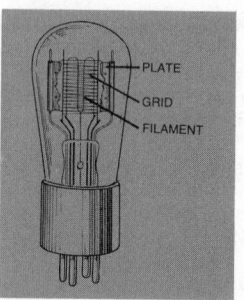

vacuum tube

vacuum tube, a sealed tube from which most of the air has been removed, formerly widely used to control the flow of electric current in radios, television sets, and other electronic devices. In most of these, transistors are now used in place of vacuum tubes.

Va duz (vä′düts), capital of Liechtenstein. *n.*

vag a bond (vag′ə bond), **1** an idle wanderer; wanderer; tramp. **2** wandering: *The gypsies lead a vagabond life.* **1** *n.,* **2** *adj.*

va gar y (və ger′ē *or* vā′gər ē), **1** an odd fancy; extravagant notion: *the vagaries of a dream.* **2** odd action; caprice: *the vagaries of fashion. n., pl.* **va gar ies.**

va gi na (və jī′nə), the passage in female mammals that leads from the uterus to the external genital organs. *n., pl.* **va gi nas.**

va gran cy (vā′grən sē), a wandering idly from place to place without proper means or ability to earn a living: *The tramp was arrested for vagrancy. n., pl.* **va gran cies.**

va grant (vā′grənt), **1** an idle wanderer; tramp. **2** moving in no definite direction or course; wandering. **3** wandering without proper means of earning a living. **1** *n.,* **2,3** *adj.* —**va′grant ly,** *adv.*

vague (vāg), not definite; not clear; not distinct: *In a fog everything looks vague. His vague statement confused them. adj.,* **va guer, va guest.** —**vague′ly,** *adv.* —**vague′ness,** *n.*

vain (vān), **1** having too much pride in one's looks, ability, etc.: *a good-looking but vain person.* **2** of no use; unsuccessful: *I made vain attempts to reach her by telephone.* **3** of no value; empty; worthless: *a vain boast. adj.*

in vain, 1 without effect or success: *My shout for help was in vain, for no one could hear me.* **2** in a disrespectful manner; lightly or irreverently: *The Bible says that one must not take God's name in vain.* —**vain′ness,** *n.*

vain glo ri ous (vān′glôr′ē əs), excessively proud or boastful; extremely vain. *adj.* —**vain′glo′ri ous ly,** *adv.* —**vain′glo′ri ous ness,** *n.*

vain glo ry (vān′glôr′ē), **1** an extreme pride in oneself; boastful vanity. **2** worthless pomp or show. *n.*

vain ly (vān′lē), **1** in vain. **2** with conceit. *adv.*

valance (def. 1)

valance (def. 2)

a hat	i it	oi oil	ch child	⎧ a in about
ā age	ī ice	ou out	ng long	⎪ e in taken
ä far	o hot	u cup	sh she	ə = ⎨ i in pencil
e let	ō open	u̇ put	th thin	⎪ o in lemon
ē equal	ô order	ü rule	ŦH then	⎩ u in circus
ėr term			zh measure	

val ance (val′əns), **1** a short drapery over the top of a window. **2** a short curtain hanging from the frame or canopy of a bed. *n.*

Val dez (val dēz′), seaport in S Alaska. The Alaska Pipeline ends there. *n.*

vale (vāl), valley. *n.*

val e dic tion (val′ə dik′shən), a bidding farewell. *n.*

val e dic to ri an (val′ə dik tôr′ē ən), student who gives the farewell address at the graduating exercises. The valedictorian is usually the student who ranks highest in the class. *n.*

val e dic tor y (val′ə dik′tər ē), **1** a farewell address, especially at the graduating exercises of a school or college. **2** bidding farewell. **1** *n., pl.* **val e dic tor ies; 2** *adj.*

va lence (vā′ləns), the combining capacity of an atom or radical, determined by the number of electrons that an atom will lose, add, or share when it reacts with other atoms. Elements whose atoms lose electrons, such as hydrogen and the metals, have a positive valence. Elements whose atoms add electrons, such as oxygen and other nonmetals, have a negative valence. Oxygen has a negative valence of 2; hydrogen has a positive valence of 1; one atom of oxygen combines with two of hydrogen to form a molecule of water. *n.*

Va len cia (və len′shə), seaport in E Spain. *n.*

Va len ci ennes (və len′sē enz′), a fine lace in which the pattern and background are made together of the same threads. *n.*

val en tine (val′ən tīn), **1** a greeting card or small gift sent on Saint Valentine's Day, February 14. **2** a sweetheart chosen on this day. *n.*

Val en tine (val′ən tīn), **Saint,** Christian martyr of the A.D. 200's. He was beheaded by the Romans on February 14. *n.*

Valentine's Day, Saint Valentine's Day, February 14.

va ler i an (və lir′ē ən), **1** a strong-smelling drug formerly used to quiet the nerves. **2** plant from whose root the drug can be made. Valerian has small pinkish or white flowers and is often grown in gardens. *n.*

val et (val′it *or* val′ā), **1** servant who takes care of a man's clothes and gives him personal service. **2** worker in a hotel who cleans or presses clothes. *n.*

Val hal la (val hal′ə), (in Scandinavian myths) the hall where the souls of heroes slain in battle feast with the god Odin. *n.*

val iance (val′yəns), bravery; valor. *n.*

val iant (val′yənt), brave; courageous: *a valiant soldier, a valiant deed. adj.* —**val′iant ly,** *adv.* —**val′iant ness,** *n.*

val id (val′id), **1** supported by facts or authority; sound or true: *a valid argument.* **2** having legal force; legally binding: *A contract made by an insane person is not valid.* **3** having force; holding good; effective: *Illness is a valid excuse for being absent from school. adj.* —**val′id ly,** *adv.*

val i date (val′ə dāt), **1** make valid; give legal force to: *The farmer's deed validated his claim to the land.* **2** support by facts or authority; confirm. *v.,* **val i dat ed, val i dating.** —**val′i da′tion,** *n.*

va lid i ty (və lid′ə tē), **1** truth or soundness: *the validity*

of an argument, the validity of an excuse. **2** legal soundness or force: *the validity of a contract. n., pl.* **va lid i ties.**

va lise (və lēs′), a traveling bag to hold clothes, etc. *n.*

Val kyr ie (val kir′ē), (in Scandinavian myths) one of the goddesses sent by Odin to ride through the air and hover over battlefields, choosing the heroes who would die in battle and afterward leading them to Valhalla. *n.*

Val let ta (və let′ə), capital of Malta. *n.*

val ley (val′ē), **1** low land between hills or mountains: *Most large valleys have rivers running through them.* **2** a wide region drained by a great river system: *the Mississippi valley. n., pl.* **val leys.**

Valley Forge, village in SE Pennsylvania, in which Washington and his army spent the winter of 1777-1778.

val or (val′ər), bravery; courage. *n.* [*Valor* is from Latin *valor,* meaning "value, courage," which comes from *valere,* meaning "be strong." See **Word Family.**]

WORD FAMILY

valor

Below are words related to *valor.* They can all be traced back to the Latin word *valere* (wä lā′re), meaning "to be strong."

avail	invalid[2]	valence
convalescent	invalidate	valiant
devalue	invaluable	valid
equivalent	prevail	valuable
evaluate	prevalent	value
invalid[1]	valedictorian	

val or ous (val′ər əs), valiant; brave; courageous. *adj.* —**val′or ous ly,** *adv.* —**val′or ous ness,** *n.*

Val pa rai so (val′pə rī′zō), chief seaport of Chile, in the central part. *n.*

val u a ble (val′yü ə bəl *or* val′yə bəl), **1** having value; being worth something: *valuable information, a valuable friend.* **2** worth much money: *a valuable ring.* **3** Usually, **valuables,** *pl.* articles of value: *She keeps her jewelry and other valuables in a safe.* **1,2** *adj.,* **3** *n.* —**val′u a bly,** *adv.*

val u a tion (val′yü ā′shən), **1** value estimated or determined: *The jeweler's valuation of the necklace was $10,000.* **2** an estimating or determining of the value of something. *n.*

val ue (val′yü), **1** the real worth; proper price: *We bought the house for less than its value.* **2** high worth; excellence, usefulness, or importance: *the value of education, the value of milk as a food.* **3** power to buy: *The value of the dollar lessened from 1960 to 1970.* **4** estimate the worth of: *The land is valued at $5000.* **5** estimated worth: *We placed a value of $3000 on our furniture.* **6** think highly of; regard highly: *to value an expert's opinion.* **7** meaning, effect, or force: *the value of a symbol.* **8** number or amount represented by a symbol: *The value of XIV is fourteen.* **9** the relative length of a tone in music indicated by a note. **1-3,5,7-9** *n.,* **4,6** *v.,* **val ued, val u ing.** [*Value* came into English about 600 years ago from French *value,* and can

be traced back to Latin *valere*, meaning "be strong."]
—**val′u er**, *n.*

val ued (val′yüd), **1** having its value estimated or determined. **2** regarded highly. *adj.*

val ue less (val′yə lis), without value; worthless. *adj.*

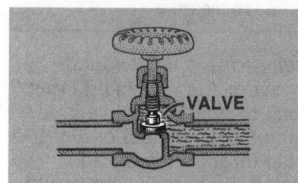

valve (def. 1)

valve (valv), **1** a movable part that controls the flow of a liquid, gas, etc., through a pipe by opening and closing the passage. A faucet contains a valve. **2** part of the body that works like a valve. The valves of the heart are membranes that control the flow of blood into and out of the heart. **3** one of the parts of hinged shells like those of oysters and clams. **4** device in certain brass wind instruments, such as trumpets, French horns, etc., for changing the pitch of the tone by changing the direction and length of the column of air. *n.* [*Valve* comes from Latin *valva*, meaning "one of a pair of folding doors."] —**valve′less**, *adj.* —**valve′like′**, *adj.*

va moose (va müs′), SLANG. go away quickly. *v.*, **va-moosed, va moos ing.**

vamp (vamp), **1** the upper front part of a shoe or boot. **2** furnish with a vamp; repair with a new vamp. 1 *n.*, 2 *v.*

vam pire (vam′pīr), **1** corpse supposed to come to life at night and suck the blood of people while they sleep. **2** person who preys ruthlessly on others. **3** vampire bat. *n.* [*Vampire* was borrowed from French *vampire*, and can be traced back to a Slavic word.]

vampire bat (def. 1) wingspread about 12 in. (30 cm.)

vampire bat, **1** a bat of South and Central America that pierces the skin of animals with its sharp teeth and drinks their blood. **2** any of various other bats incorrectly supposed to drink blood.

van (van), **1** a large, enclosed truck or wagon for moving furniture and household goods. **2** a small, enclosed truck designed for light hauling or for recreational use. *n.*

va na di um (və nā′dē əm), a very hard, silver-white metallic element used in making various strong alloys of steel. *n.*

Van Al len radiation belt (van al′ən), either of two broad bands of intense radiation in outer space that surround the earth, consisting of charged particles which are apparently held by the earth's magnetic field.

Van Bur en (van byúr′ən), **Martin**, 1782-1862, the eighth president of the United States, from 1837 to 1841.

Van cou ver (van kü′vər), **1** seaport in SW Canada. **2** island in the Pacific Ocean, just off the SW coast of Canada. It is part of British Columbia. *n.*

van dal (van′dl), **1** person who destroys or damages beautiful or valuable things on purpose. **2 Vandal**,

member of a Germanic tribe that ravaged Gaul, Spain, and northern Africa. In A.D. 455 the Vandals took Rome. *n.*

van dal ism (van′dl iz′əm), the destroying or damaging of beautiful or valuable things on purpose. *n.*

van dal ize (van′dl īz), destroy willfully or senselessly. *v.*, **van dal ized, van dal iz ing.**

Van Dyck (van dīk′), Vandyke.

vandyke (def. 2)

Van dyke (van dīk′), **1** Sir **Anthony**, 1599-1641, Flemish painter who lived for some years in England. **2 vandyke**, a short, pointed beard. *n.*

vane (vān), **1** a flat piece of metal, or wood, etc., fixed upon a rod in such a way as to move with the wind and indicate its direction; weather vane; weathercock. **2** blade, wing, or similar part attached to an axis, wheel, etc., so as to be acted upon by a current of air or liquid or to produce a current by rotation: *the vanes of a windmill.* **3** the flat, soft part of a feather. *n.*

vane (def. 1)

Van Gogh (van gō′), **Vincent**, 1853-1890, Dutch painter.

van guard (van′gärd′), **1** the front part of an army; soldiers marching ahead of the main part of an army to clear the way and guard against surprise. **2** the foremost or leading position. **3** leaders of a movement. *n.*

va nil la (və nil′ə), a flavoring extract made from the bean of a tropical climbing plant. It is used in candy, ice cream, etc. *n.*

van ish (van′ish), **1** disappear, especially suddenly: *The sun vanished behind a cloud.* **2** pass away; cease to be: *Dinosaurs have vanished from the earth. v.* —**van′ish er**, *n.*

van i ty (van′ə tē), **1** too much pride in one's looks, ability, etc. **2** lack of real value: *the vanity of wealth.* **3** worthless pleasure or display. **4** dressing table. **5** a small case containing face powder and rouge. *n.*, *pl.* **van i ties.**

van quish (vang′kwish), conquer; defeat; overcome. *v.* —**van′quish a ble**, *adj.* —**van′quish er**, *n.*

van tage (van′tij), a better position or condition; advantage. *n.*

Va nu a tu (vä/nü ä/tü), country made up of a group of islands east of Australia. *Capital:* Vila. *n.*

vap id (vap/id), without much life or flavor; tasteless; dull. *adj.* —**vap/id ly**, *adv.* —**vap/id ness**, *n.*

va por (vā/pər), **1** moisture in the air that can be seen, such as steam, fog, mist, etc., usually due to the effect of heat upon a liquid. **2** gas formed from a substance that is usually a liquid or a solid; the gaseous form of a liquid or solid. *n.*

va por i za tion (vā/pər ə zā/shən), a changing or a being changed into vapor. *n.*

va por ize (vā/pə rīz/), change into vapor: *Heat vaporizes water.* *v.*, **va por ized, va por iz ing.**

va por iz er (vā/pə rī/zər), device for converting a liquid into vapor, such as an apparatus that releases steam into a room for medicinal purposes. *n.*

vapor lock, a block in the flow of gasoline in an engine, usually occurring when excessive heat causes bubbles in the fuel line or carburetor.

va por ous (vā/pər əs), **1** full of vapor; misty. **2** like vapor. **3** soon passing; worthless. *adj.* —**va/por ous ly**, *adv.*

va por y (vā/pər ē), vaporous. *adj.*

va quer o (vä ker/ō), (in the southwestern United States) a cowboy, herdsman, or cattle driver. *n.*, *pl.* **va quer os.** [*Vaquero* was borrowed from Spanish *vaquero*, and can be traced back to Latin *vacca*, meaning "cow."]

var., variant.

var i a bil i ty (ver/ē ə bil/ə tē *or* var/ē ə bil/ə tē), **1** changeableness. **2** tendency to vary. *n.*

var i a ble (ver/ē bəl *or* var/ē ə bəl), **1** apt to change; changeable; uncertain: *variable winds. The weather is more variable in New York than it is in California.* **2** that can be varied: *These adjustable curtain rods are of variable length.* **3** thing or quality that varies. **4 a** quantity that can assume any of a given set of values. **b** symbol representing this quantity. 1,2 *adj.*, 3,4 *n.* —**var/i a ble ness**, *n.*

var i a bly (ver/ē ə blē *or* var/ē ə blē), in a variable manner; changeably. *adv.*

var i ance (ver/ē əns *or* var/ē əns), **1** difference; disagreement. **2** a varying; change. *n.*

at variance, in disagreement: *His actions are at variance with his promises.*

var i ant (ver/ē ənt *or* var/ē ənt), **1** varying; different: *"Rime" is a variant spelling of "rhyme."* **2** a different form; a different pronunciation or spelling of the same word. 1 *adj.*, 2 *n.*

var i a tion (ver/ē ā/shən *or* var/ē ā/shən), **1** a varying; change: *variations in color.* **2** amount of change: *There was a variation of 30 degrees in the temperature yesterday.* **3** a varied or changed form. **4** (in music) a tune or theme repeated with changes in rhythm, harmony, etc. *n.*

var i col ored (ver/ē kul/ərd *or* var/ē kul/ərd), having various colors. *adj.*

var i cose (var/ə kōs), abnormally swollen or enlarged: *legs covered with varicose veins. adj.*

var ied (ver/ēd *or* var/ēd), **1** of different kinds; having variety: *a varied assortment of candies.* **2** changed; altered. *adj.* —**var/ied ly**, *adv.*

var i e gat ed (ver/ē ə gā/tid *or* var/ē ə gā/tid), **1** varied in appearance; marked with different colors: *variegated pansies.* **2** having variety. *adj.* —**var/i e gat/ed ly**, *adv.*

va ri e ty (və rī/ə tē), **1** lack of sameness; difference or change: *Variety is the spice of life.* **2** number of different kinds: *This shop has a variety of toys.* **3** kind or sort: *Which varieties of cake did you buy?* **4** division of a species. *n.*, *pl.* **va ri e ties.**

variety show, entertainment featuring different kinds of acts, such as songs, dances, acrobatic feats, and comic skits.

var i ous (ver/ē əs *or* var/ē əs), **1** differing from one another; different: *There have been various opinions as to the best way to raise children.* **2** several; many: *We have looked at various houses, but have decided to buy this one. adj.* —**var/i ous ly**, *adv.* —**var/i ous ness**, *n.*

var mint (vär/mənt), DIALECT. **1** vermin. **2** an objectionable animal or person. *n.*

var nish (vär/nish), **1** a liquid that gives a smooth, glossy appearance to wood, metal, etc. Varnish is often made from substances like resin dissolved in oil or alcohol. **2** the smooth, hard surface made by this liquid when it dries: *The varnish on the table was scratched.* **3** put varnish on. **4** a glossy appearance. **5** a false or deceiving appearance; pretense: *cover one's selfishness with a varnish of good manners.* **6** give a false or deceiving appearance to: *to varnish over the truth with a lie.* 1,2,4,5 *n.*, *pl.* **var nish es;** 3,6 *v.* —**var/nish er**, *n.*

var si ty (vär/sə tē), the most important team in a given sport in a university, college, or school. *n.*, *pl.* **var si ties.**

var y (ver/ē *or* var/ē), **1** make or become different; change: *The driver can vary the speed of an automobile.* **2** be different; differ: *Stars vary in brightness.* *v.*, **var ied, var y ing.** —**var/y ing ly**, *adv.*

vas cu lar (vas/kyə lər), having to do with, made of, or provided with vessels that carry blood, sap, etc. *adj.*

vase

vase (vās), holder or container used for ornament or for holding flowers. *n.* —**vase/like/**, *adj.*

Vas e line (vas/ə lēn/), trademark for a soft, greasy, yellow or whitish substance made from petroleum, used as a healing ointment or as a lubricant. *n.*

vas sal (vas/əl), **1** (in the feudal system) a person who held land from a lord or superior, to whom in return he gave help in war or some other service. A great noble could be a vassal of the king and have many other men as his vassals. **2** like a vassal; like that of a vassal; subordinate: *a vassal nation.* **3** servant. 1,3 *n.*, 2 *adj.*

vas sal age (vas/ə lij), **1** condition of being a vassal. **2** the homage or service due from a vassal to his lord or superior. **3** dependence; servitude. *n.*

vast (vast), very great; immense: *Texas and Alaska cover vast territories. A billion dollars is a vast amount of money.* *adj.* —**vast/ness**, *n.*

vast ly (vast/lē), very greatly; to a vast extent or degree. *adv.*

vast y (vas/tē), vast; immense. *adj.*

vat (vat), a large container for liquids; tank: *a vat of dye.* *n.* [*Vat* comes from Old English *fæt.*]

a hat	i it	oi oil	ch child	a in about
ā age	ī ice	ou out	ng long	e in taken
ä far	o hot	u cup	sh she	ə = i in pencil
e let	ō open	u̇ put	th thin	o in lemon
ē equal	ô order	ü rule	ŦH then	u in circus
ėr term			zh measure	

Vat i can (vat′ə kən), **1** the collection of buildings grouped about the palace of the pope in Rome. **2** the government, office, or authority of the pope. *n.*

Vatican City, an independent state inside the city of Rome. It is ruled by the pope and includes Saint Peter's Church and the Vatican.

vaude ville (vôd′vil *or* vô′də vil), theatrical entertainment featuring a variety of acts. Vaudeville consists of songs, dances, acrobatic feats, short plays, trained animals, etc. *n.*

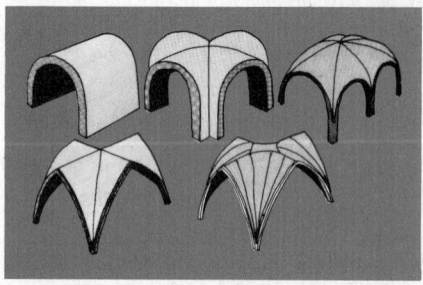

vault¹ (def. 1) different types

vault¹ (vôlt), **1** an arched roof or ceiling; series of arches. **2** an arched space or passage. **3** make in the form of a vault: *The roof was vaulted.* **4** cover with a vault. **5** an underground cellar or storehouse. **6** place for storing valuable things and keeping them safe. Vaults are often made of steel. **7** place for burial. 1,2,5-7 *n.* 3,4 *v.*

vault² (vôlt), **1** jump or leap over by using the hands or a pole: *She vaulted the fence.* **2** act of vaulting. **3** to jump; to leap: *He vaulted over the wall.* 1,3 *v.*, 2 *n.* —**vault′er,** *n.*

vaunt (vônt), boast. *v., n.* —**vaunt′er,** *n.*

vb., **1** verb. **2** verbal.

VCR, videocassette recorder (a recorder that uses videotape to record and play programs, movies, etc., through a television set).

V.D. or **VD,** venereal disease.

veal (vēl), flesh of a calf, used for food. *n.*

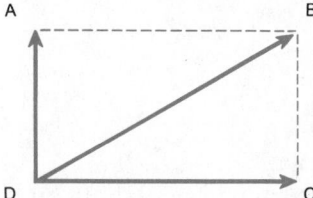

vector
DA and DC are vectors; DB is the resultant.

vec tor (vek′tər), quantity involving direction as well as magnitude, represented by an arrow which shows the direction of the force. The length of the arrow indicates the magnitude of the force. *n.*

veer (vir), **1** change in direction; shift; turn: *The wind veered to the south. The talk veered to ghosts.* **2** change the direction of: *We veered our boat.* **3** a shift; turn: *The car made a sudden veer to the left.* 1,2 *v.*, 3 *n.* —**veer′ing ly,** *adv.*

veer y (vir′ē), thrush of eastern North America with tawny head, back, and tail and a faintly spotted white breast. *n., pl.* **veer ies.**

Ve ga (vē′gə), a bluish-white star, the brightest star in the constellation Lyra. *n.*

veg e ta ble (vej′ə tə bəl), **1** plant whose fruit, seeds, leaves, roots, or other parts are used for food. Peas, corn, lettuce, tomatoes, and beets are vegetables. **2** the part of such a plant which is used for food. **3** any plant. **4** of or like plants: *the vegetable kingdom, vegetable life.* **5** consisting of or made from vegetables: *vegetable soup.* 1-3 *n.*, 4,5 *adj.* [*Vegetable* is from Latin *vegetabilis,*

meaning "refreshing," and can be traced back to *vegetus,* meaning "vigorous."]

veg e tar i an (vej′ə ter′ē ən), **1** person who eats only vegetables but no meat, fish, or other animal products. **2** eating vegetable foods only. **3** containing no meat: *a vegetarian diet.* **4** serving no meat: *a vegetarian restaurant.* **1** *n.* 2-4 *adj.*

veg e tate (vej′ə tāt), **1** grow as plants do. **2** live with very little action or thought. *v.*, **veg e tat ed, veg e tat ing.**

veg e ta tion (vej′ə tā′shən), **1** plant life; growing plants: *There is not much vegetation in deserts.* **2** act or process of vegetating; growth of plants. *n.*

veg e ta tive (vej′ə tā′tiv), **1** growing as plants do. **2** of plants or plant life. **3** having very little action, thought, or feeling. *adj.* —**veg′e ta′tive ly,** *adv.*

ve he mence (vē′ə məns), vehement quality or nature; strong feeling; forcefulness; violence: *The two cousins argued loudly and with vehemence.* *n.*

ve he ment (vē′ə mənt), **1** having or showing strong feeling; caused by strong feeling; eager; passionate. **2** forceful; violent: *vehement quarrels, a vehement burst of energy. adj.* —**ve′he ment ly,** *adv.*

ve hi cle (vē′ə kəl), **1** any means of carrying, conveying, or transporting, such as a car, carriage, cart, wagon, sled, etc. Automobiles and trucks are motor vehicles. Rockets and satellites are space vehicles. **2** a means or medium by which something is communicated, shown, done, etc.: *Language is the vehicle of thought.* **3** (in painting) a liquid into which pigment is mixed to apply color to a surface: *Linseed oil is a vehicle for paint. n.*

ve hic u lar (vi hik′yə lər), of vehicles: *vehicular traffic. adj.*

veil (vāl), **1** piece of very thin material worn to protect or hide the face, or as an ornament. **2** piece of material worn so as to fall over the head and shoulders. **3** cover with a veil: *They veiled their faces.* **4** anything that screens or hides: *a veil of clouds, a veil of deception.* **5** to cover, screen, or hide: *Fog veiled the shore. They veiled their plans in secrecy.* 1,2,4 *n.*, 3,5 *v.* —**veil′like′,** *adj.*

take the veil, become a nun.

vein (vān), **1** one of the blood vessels or tubes that carry blood to the heart from all parts of the body. **2** one of the strands or bundles of vascular tissue forming the principal framework of a leaf. **3** one of the ribs that strengthen the wing of an insect. **4** a crack or seam in rock filled with a deposit, especially of metallic ore: *a vein of copper.* **5** any streak or marking of a different shade or color in wood, marble, etc. **6** a special character or disposition; state of mind; mood: *a vein of cruelty, a joking vein.* **7** cover with veins; mark with veins: *Age had veined his hands.* 1-6 *n.*, 7 *v.* —**vein′like′,** *adj.*

Vel cro (vel′krō), trademark for a kind of fastener, especially for clothing, consisting of two nylon strips. Tiny nylon hooks in one strip attach tightly to tiny loops in the other strip. *n.*

veld or **veldt** (velt), open country in South Africa, having grass or bushes but few trees. *n.*

vel lum (vel′əm), **1** the finest kind of parchment, usually prepared from the skins of calves and lambs, once used instead of paper for books. **2** paper or cloth imitating such parchment. *n.*

ve loc i ty (və los′ə tē), **1** swiftness; quickness: *The car sped by with such velocity that the driver's face was just a blur.* **2** rate of motion; speed: *The velocity of light is about 186,000 miles per second. n., pl.* **ve loc i ties.**

ve lour or **ve lours** (və lùr′), fabric like velvet, usually made of silk, wool, cotton, or rayon. Velour is used for clothing, draperies, upholstery, etc. *n.*

vel vet (vel′vit), **1** cloth with a thick, soft pile, made of silk, rayon, nylon, etc. **2** made of velvet: *a velvet jacket.*

3 like velvet: *Our kitten has soft, velvet paws.* 1 *n.*, 2,3 *adj.*
—**vel′vet like′,** *adj.*

vel vet een (vel′və tēn′), a cotton fabric resembling velvet. *n.*

vel vet y (vel′və tē), smooth and soft like velvet. *adj.*

ve na ca va (vē′nə kā′və), either of two large veins that empty blood from the upper and lower halves of the body into the right auricle of the heart. *pl.* **ve nae ca vae** (vē′nē kā′vē).

ve nal (vē′nl), **1** willing to sell one's services or influence basely; open to bribes; corrupt: *Venal judges are a disgrace to a country.* **2** influenced or obtained by bribery: *venal conduct. adj.* —**ve′nal ly,** *adv.*

vend (vend), sell; peddle: *They were vending popcorn. v.*

Ven da (ven′də), country in S Africa, formerly part of the Republic of South Africa. *Capital:* Thohoyandou. *n.*

vend er (ven′dər), vendor. *n.*

ven det ta (ven det′ə), feud in which a murdered person's relatives try to kill the slayer or the slayer's relatives. *n., pl.* **ven det tas.** [*Vendetta* was borrowed from Italian *vendetta,* which came from Latin *vindicta,* meaning "revenge," and can perhaps be traced back to Latin *vis,* meaning "force, strength," and *dicere,* meaning "to say."]

vending machine, machine from which one obtains candy, stamps, etc., when a coin is dropped in.

ven dor (ven′dər), seller; peddler. *n.* Also, **vender.**

ve neer (və nir′), **1** cover (wood) with a thin layer of finer wood or other material: *The pine desk is veneered with mahogany.* **2** a thin layer of wood or other material used in veneering: *The panel had a veneer of gold and ivory.* **3** cover (anything) with a layer of something else to give an appearance of superior quality. **4** surface appearance or show: *Their treachery was hidden by a veneer of friendship.* 1,3 *v.,* 2,4 *n.* —**ve neer′er,** *n.*

venerable
He was a wise and **venerable** man.

ven er a ble (ven′ər ə bəl), worthy of reverence; deserving respect because of age, character, or importance: *venerable customs. adj.* —**ven′er a bly,** *adv.*

ven e rate (ven′ə rāt′), regard with deep respect; revere: *They venerate their parents' memory. v.,* **ven e rat ed, ven e rat ing.** —**ven′e ra′tor,** *n.*

ven e ra tion (ven′ə rā′shən), deep respect; reverence. *n.*

ve ner e al (və nir′ē əl), of or transmitted by sexual intercourse. Syphilis is a venereal disease. *adj.*

Ve ne tian (və nē′shən), **1** of Venice or its people. **2** person born or living in Venice. 1 *adj.,* 2 *n.*

Venetian blind, a window blind made of many horizontal wooden, steel, or aluminum slats. The blind can be raised and lowered, or the slats can be tilted so that they overlap, to regulate the light that is let in. [The *Venetian blind* was called this because it was widely used in *Venice,* Italy, during the 1600's.]

Ven e zue la (ven′ə zwā′lə *or* ven′ə zwē′lə), country in the N part of South America. *Capital:* Caracas. *n.* —**Ven′e zue′lan,** *adj., n.*

venge ance (ven′jəns), punishment in return for a wrong; revenge: *She swore vengeance against her hateful enemies. n.*

with a vengeance, 1 with great force or violence: *By six o'clock it was raining with a vengeance.* **2** extremely. **3** much more than expected.

venge ful (venj′fəl), feeling or showing a strong desire for vengeance. *adj.* —**venge′ful ly,** *adv.* —**venge′ful ness,** *n.*

ve ni al (vē′nē əl), able to be forgiven; not very wrong; wrong but pardonable. *adj.* —**ve′ni al ly,** *adv.*

Ven ice (ven′is), city on the NE coast of Italy. Venice has many canals in place of streets. *n.*

ven i son (ven′ə sən), the flesh of a deer, used for food; deer meat. *n.*

ven om (ven′əm), **1** the poison of snakes, spiders, etc. **2** spite; malice: *They spoke of their enemies with venom. n.*

ven om ous (ven′ə məs), **1** poisonous: *a venomous snake.* **2** spiteful; malicious. *adj.* —**ven′om ous ly,** *adv.* —**ven′om ous ness,** *n.*

ve nous (vē′nəs), of or in veins: *venous blood. adj.*

vent¹ (vent), **1** hole or opening, especially one serving as an outlet: *He used a pencil to make air vents in the box so the frog could breathe.* **2** outlet; way out; free expression: *Her great energy found vent in hard work. We gave vent to our grief in tears.* **3** let out; express freely: *Don't vent your anger on the dog.* **4** make a vent in. 1,2 *n.,* 3,4 *v.*

vent² (vent), slit in a garment. *n.*

ven ti late (ven′tl āt), **1** change the air in: *We ventilate a room by opening windows.* **2** purify by fresh air: *The lungs ventilate the blood.* **3** make known publicly; discuss openly. *v.,* **ven ti lat ed, ven ti lat ing.** [*Ventilate* is from Latin *ventilatum,* meaning "fanned," which comes from *ventus,* meaning "a wind."]

ven ti la tion (ven′tl ā′shən), **1** change of air; act or process of supplying with fresh air. **2** means of supplying fresh air: *Air conditioning provides ventilation in summer. n.*

ven ti la tor (ven′tl ā′tər), any apparatus or means, such as an opening, an air conditioner, or a fan, for changing or improving the air in an enclosed space. *n.*

ven tral (ven′trəl), abdominal. We call the side of any animal where its belly is the ventral side. *adj.*

ven tri cle (ven′trə kəl), one of the two chambers of the heart that receive the blood from the auricles and force it into the arteries. *n.*

ven tril o quism (ven tril′ə kwiz′əm), art or practice of speaking or uttering sounds with the lips shut or nearly shut so that the voice may seem to come from some source other than the speaker. *n.* [*Ventriloquism* can be traced back to Latin *venter,* meaning "belly," and *loqui,* meaning "speak." It was once thought that a ventriloquist spoke from the stomach.]

ven tril o quist (ven tril′ə kwist), person skilled in ventriloquism. *n.*

ven ture (ven′chər), **1** a risky or daring undertaking: *Our courage was equal to any venture. A lucky venture in oil stock made him rich.* **2** expose to risk or danger: *She* *ventured her life to rescue me.* **3** dare: *No one ventured to interrupt the speaker.* **4** dare to come or go: *We ventured out on the thin ice and fell through.* **5** dare to say or make: *He ventured an objection.* 1 *n.*, 2-5 *v.*, **ven tured, ven tur ing.**

ven ture some (ven′chər səm), **1** inclined to take risks; rash; daring. **2** risky. *adj.* —**ven′ture some ly,** *adv.*

ven tur ous (ven′chər əs), **1** bold; daring; adventurous. **2** risky. *adj.* —**ven′tur ous ly,** *adv.*

Ve nus (vē′nəs), **1** (in Roman myths) the goddess of love and beauty. The Greeks called her Aphrodite. **2** a very beautiful woman. **3** the sixth largest planet in the solar system and the second in distance from the sun. It is the most brilliant planet in the solar system, and the one that comes closest to the earth. *n.*

Ve nus's-fly trap (vē′nə siz flī′trap′), plant with hairy leaves which can fold together to trap and digest insects. *n.*

ve ra cious (və rā′shəs), **1** truthful. **2** true. *adj.* —**ve ra′cious ly,** *adv.* —**ve ra′cious ness,** *n.*

ve rac i ty (və ras′ə tē), **1** truthfulness. **2** truth. **3** correctness; accuracy. *n., pl.* **ve rac i ties.**

veranda

ve ran da (və ran′də), a large porch along one or more sides of a house. *n., pl.* **ve ran das.** [*Veranda* comes from Hindustani *varandā.*]

ve ran dah (və ran′də), veranda. *n.*

verb (vėrb), word that tells what is or what is done; the part of speech that expresses action or being. *Do, go, come, be, sit, think, know,* and *eat* are verbs. *n.* [*Verb* comes from Latin *verbum,* meaning "word."]

ver bal (vėr′bəl), **1** in words; of words: *A description is a verbal picture.* **2** expressed in spoken words; oral: *a verbal message, a verbal promise.* **3** word for word; literal: *a verbal translation from the French.* **4** having to do with a verb. Two common verbal endings are *-ed* and *-ing.* **5** derived from a verb: *a verbal noun.* **6** a noun, adjective, or other word derived from a verb. 1-5 *adj.*, 6 *n.*

ver bal ize (vėr′bə līz), **1** express in words. **2** be wordy. *v.*, **ver bal ized, ver bal iz ing.** —**ver′bal i za′tion,** *n.*

ver bal ly (vėr′bə lē), **1** in spoken words; orally: *Instead of replying verbally, I answered with a nod of my head.* **2** word for word: *The witness reported the conversation verbally.* **3** as a verb: *"Veil" is used verbally in "Fog veiled the shore."* *adv.*

ver ba tim (vər bā′tim), word for word; in exactly the same words: *His speech was printed verbatim in the newspaper* (*adv.*). *The newspaper gave a verbatim report of the speech* (*adj.*). *adv., adj.*

ver be na (vər bē′nə), a garden plant with very long or flattened spikes of flowers having various colors. *n., pl.* **ver be nas.**

ver bi age (vėr′bē ij), use of too many words; abundance of useless words. *n.*

ver bose (vər bōs′), using too many words; wordy. *adj.* —**ver bose′ly,** *adv.* —**ver bose′ness,** *n.*

ver bos i ty (vər bos′ə tē), use of too many words; wordiness. *n.*

ver bo ten (fer bōt′n), a German word meaning absolutely forbidden by authority. *adj.*

ver dant (vėrd′nt), green: *The fields are covered with verdant grass. adj.* —**ver′dant ly,** *adv.*

Verde (vėrd), **Cape.** See **Cape Verde.** *n.*

Ver di (ver′dē), Giuseppe, 1813-1901, Italian composer of operas. *n.*

ver dict (vėr′dikt), **1** the decision of a jury: *The jury returned a verdict of "Not guilty."* **2** any decision or judgment: *the verdict of history. n.*

ver di gris (vėr′də grēs′), **1** a green or bluish coating that forms on brass, copper, or bronze when exposed to the air for long periods of time. **2** a green or bluish-green poisonous compound used in paints and insecticides. *n.*

ver dure (vėr′jər), **1** fresh greenness. **2** a fresh growth of green grass, plants, or leaves. *n.*

verge[1] (vėrj), **1** the point at which something begins or happens; brink: *Their business is on the verge of ruin.* **2** be on the verge; border: *The speech was so poorly prepared that it verged on the ridiculous.* 1 *n.*, 2 *v.*, **verged, verg ing.**

verge[2] (vėrj), tend; incline: *The cook was plump, verging toward fatness. v.*, **verged, verg ing.**

Ver gil (vėr′jəl), 70-19 B.C., Roman poet, author of the *Aeneid. n.* Also, **Virgil.**

ver i fi a ble (ver′ə fī′ə bəl), able to be verified. *adj.* —**ver′i fi′a bly,** *adv.*

ver i fi ca tion (ver′ə fə kā′shən), proof by evidence or testimony; confirmation. *n.*

ver i fy (ver′ə fī), **1** prove to be true; confirm: *The driver's report of the accident was verified by two witnesses.* **2** test the correctness of; check for accuracy: *You can verify the spelling of a word by looking in a dictionary. v.*, **ver i fied, ver i fy ing.** —**ver′i fi′er,** *n.*

ver i ly (ver′ə lē), OLD USE. in truth; truly; really. *adv.*

ver i ta ble (ver′ə tə bəl), true; real; actual. *adj.* —**ver′i ta ble ness,** *n.*

ver i ta bly (ver′ə tə blē), in truth; truly; really; actually. *adv.*

ver i ty (ver′ə tē), **1** truth. **2** a true statement or fact. **3** reality. *n., pl.* **ver i ties.**

ver mi cel li (vėr′mə sel′ē *or* ver′mə chel′ē), a mixture of flour and water like spaghetti but thinner. *n.*

ver mi form (vėr′mə fôrm), shaped like a worm. *adj.*

vermiform appendix, a slender tube, closed at one end, growing out of the large intestine in the lower right-hand part of the abdomen; appendix. Appendicitis is inflammation of the vermiform appendix.

ver mil ion or **ver mil lion** (vər mil′yən), **1** a bright red. **2** bright-red. **3** a bright-red coloring matter. 1,3 *n.*, 2 *adj.*

ver min (vėr′mən), **1** small animals that are troublesome or destructive. Fleas, lice, bedbugs, rats, and mice are vermin. **2** very unpleasant or vile person or persons. *n. pl. or sing.*

Ver mont (vər mont′), one of the northeastern states of the United States. *Abbreviation:* Vt. or VT *Capital:* Montpelier. *n.*

ver mouth (vər müth′), a white wine flavored with wormwood or other herbs and used as a liqueur or in cocktails. *n.*

ver nac u lar (vər nak′yə lər), **1** a native language; language used by the people of a certain country or place. **2** of or in the native language, rather than a literary or learned language. **3** everyday language; informal speech. **4** language of a profession, trade, etc.: *There are many technical words in the vernacular of lawyers.* 1,3,4 *n.*, 2 *adj.*

ver nal (vėr′nl), **1** of spring; coming in spring: *vernal flowers, vernal months.* **2** youthful: *memories from one's vernal days. adj.* —**ver′nal ly,** *adv.*

Verne (vėrn), **Jules,** 1828-1905, French writer of science fiction and adventure stories. *n.*

Ve ro na (və rō′nə), city in N Italy. The story of *Romeo and Juliet* takes place in Verona. *n.*

Ver sailles (ver sī′), **1** city in N France, near Paris. A treaty of peace between the Allies and Germany was signed there after World War I, on June 28, 1919. **2** a large palace there. *n.*

ver sa tile (vėr′sə təl), able to do many things well: *She is a versatile student; she is skilled at science, art, mathematics, English, German, and history. adj.* —**ver′sa tile ly,** *adv.* —**ver′sa tile ness,** *n.*

ver sa til i ty (vėr′sə til′ə tē), ability to do many things well. *n.*

verse (vėrs), **1** lines of words with a regularly repeated accent and often with rhyme; poetry. **2** a single line of poetry. **3** group of such lines: *Sing the first verse of "America."* **4** type of verse; meter: *blank verse, iambic verse.* **5** a short division of a chapter in the Bible. *n.*

versed (vėrst), experienced; practiced; skilled: *Our doctor is well versed in medicine. adj.*

ver si fi ca tion (vėr′sə fə kā′shən), **1** the making of verses. **2** art or theory of making verses. **3** form or style of poetry; metrical structure. *n.*

ver si fi er (vėr′sə fī′ər), person who makes verses. *n.*

ver si fy (vėr′sə fī), **1** write verses. **2** tell in verse. **3** turn (prose) into poetry. *v.,* **ver si fied, ver si fy ing.**

ver sion (vėr′zhən), **1** one particular statement, account, or description: *Each of the three boys gave his own version of the quarrel.* **2** a translation from one language to another: *a version of the Bible.* **3** a special form or variant of something: *I liked the movie version better than the book. n.*

ver sus (vėr′səs), against: *The most exciting game was Harvard versus Yale. prep.*

vert., vertical.

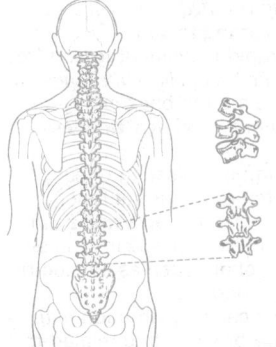

vertebra
Human beings have 33 vertebrae. Three of them are shown in detail.

ver te bra (vėr′tə brə), one of the bones of the backbone. *n., pl.* **ver te brae** (vėr′tə brē), **ver te bras.**

ver te bral (vėr′tə brəl), of a vertebra or the vertebrae. *adj.*

ver te brate (vėr′tə brit *or* vėr′tə brāt), **1** animal that has a backbone. Fishes, amphibians, reptiles, birds, and mammals are vertebrates. **2** having a backbone. **1** *n.,* **2** *adj.*

ver tex (vėr′teks), **1** the highest point; top. **2 a** point opposite the base of a triangle, pyramid, etc. **b** the point where the two sides of an angle meet. *n., pl.* **ver tex es, ver ti ces** (vėr′tə sēz).

ver ti cal (vėr′tə kəl), **1** straight up and down; perpendicular to a level surface; upright. **2** a vertical line, plane,

a hat	**i** it	**oi** oil	**ch** child		a in about	
ā age	**ī** ice	**ou** out	**ng** long		e in taken	
ä far	**o** hot	**u** cup	**sh** she	ə =	i in pencil	
e let	**ō** open	**u̇** put	**th** thin		o in lemon	
ē equal	**ô** order	**ü** rule	**ᴛʜ** then		u in circus	
ėr term			**zh** measure			

direction, position, etc. **1** *adj.,* **2** *n.* —**ver′ti cal ly,** *adv.*

ver ti go (vėr′tə gō), dizziness; giddiness. *n., pl.* **ver ti goes, ver ti gos,** or **ver tig i nes** (vər tij′ə nēz).

verve (vėrv), enthusiasm; energy; vigor; spirit; liveliness. *n.*

ver y (ver′ē), **1** much; greatly; extremely: *The sunshine is very hot in July.* **2** absolutely; exactly: *I stood in the very same place for an hour.* **3** same; identical: *The very people who supported the plan are against it now.* **4** even; mere; sheer: *The very thought of summer vacation makes her happy.* **5** real; true; genuine: *The shrine was said to contain the very bones of the saint.* **6** actual: *caught in the very act of stealing.* **1,2** *adv.,* **3-6** *adj.,* **ver i er, ver i est.** [*Very* came into English about 700 years ago from French *verai,* and can be traced back to Latin *verus,* meaning "true."]

very high frequency, the band of radio frequencies between 30 and 300 megahertz.

ves i cle (ves′ə kəl), a small bladder, cavity, sac, or cyst. A blister is a vesicle in the skin. *n.*

ve sic u lar (və sik′yə lər), of or like a vesicle or vesicles. *adj.* —**ve sic′u lar ly,** *adv.*

ves per (ves′pər), **1** evening. **2 Vesper,** the planet Venus, when it appears as the evening star. **3** of evening. **4** an evening prayer, hymn, or service. **5 vespers** or **Vespers,** *pl.* a church service held in the late afternoon or in the evening; evensong. **6** Sometimes, **Vesper.** of vespers. **1,2,4,5** *n.,* **3,6** *adj.*

Ves puc ci (ve spü′chē), **Amerigo,** 1451-1512, Italian merchant, adventurer, and explorer. America is named after him. *n.*

ves sel (ves′əl), **1** a large boat; ship: *Ocean liners and*

vertebrates (def. 1)

other vessels are usually docked by tugboats. **2** a hollow holder or container. *Cups, bowls, pitchers, bottles, barrels, and tubs are vessels.* **3** tube carrying blood or other fluid. *Veins and arteries are blood vessels. n.*

vest (vest), **1** a short, sleeveless garment worn over a shirt or blouse. **2** clothe or robe. **3** furnish with powers, authority, rights, etc.: *Congress is vested with the power to make laws.* **4** put in the possession or control of a person or persons: *The management of the hospital is vested in a board of trustees.* **1** *n.,* **2-4** *v.* [*Vest* came into English about 500 years ago from French *veste,* which came from Latin *vestis,* meaning "garment."] —**vest′less,** *adj.* —**vest′like′,** *adj.*

Ves ta (ves′tə), (in Roman myths) the goddess of the hearth. A sacred fire was always kept burning in the temple of Vesta. *n.*

ves tal (ves′tl), **1** one of the vestal virgins. **2** virgin. **3** pure; chaste. **1,2** *n.,* **3** *adj.*

vestal virgin, priestess of the Roman goddess Vesta. Six vestal virgins tended an undying fire in honor of Vesta at her temple in Rome.

vest ed (ves′tid), **1** placed in the possession or control of a person or persons; fixed: *vested rights.* **2** clothed or robed, especially in church garments. *adj.*

ves ti bule (ves′tə byül), **1** passage or hall between the outer door and the inside of a building. **2** the enclosed space at the end of a railroad passenger car. *n.*

ves tige (ves′tij), a slight remnant; trace; mark: *They have discovered vestiges of an ancient civilization. n.* [*Vestige* was borrowed from French *vestige,* which came from Latin *vestigium,* meaning "footprint."]

ves tig i al (ve stij′ē əl), remaining as a vestige of something that has disappeared. *adj.* —**ves tig′i al ly,** *adv.*

vest ment (vest′mənt), **1** garment worn by a clergyman in performing sacred duties. **2** garment, especially a robe or gown, worn by an official on a ceremonial occasion. *n.*

ves try (ves′trē), **1** room in a church, where vestments are kept. **2** room in a church or an attached building, used for Sunday school, prayer meetings, etc. **3** a committee that helps manage church business. *n., pl.* **vestries.**

ves try man (ves′trē mən), member of a committee that helps manage church business. *n., pl.* **ves try men.**

ves ture (ves′chər), clothing; garments. *n.*

Ve su vi us (və sü′vē əs), **Mount,** an active volcano near Naples, Italy. During an eruption in A.D. 79 its lava buried the ancient city of Pompeii. 4000 feet (1220 meters) high. *n.*

vet (vet), INFORMAL. **1** veterinarian. **2** veteran. *n.*

vetch (vech), vine of the same family as the pea, grown as food for cattle and sheep. *n., pl.* **vetch es.**

vet er an (vet′ər ən), **1** person who has served in the armed forces. **2** having had much experience in war: *Veteran troops fought side by side with the young soldiers.* **3** person who has had much experience in some position, occupation, etc. **4** grown old in service; experienced: *a veteran teacher.* **1,3** *n.,* **2,4** *adj.*

Veterans Day, November 11, formerly Armistice Day.

vet er i nar i an (vet′ər ə ner′ē ən), doctor or surgeon who treats animals. *n.*

vet er i nar y (vet′ər ə ner′ē), **1** having to do with the medical or surgical treatment of animals. **2** veterinarian. **1** *adj.,* **2** *n., pl.* **vet er i nar ies.**

ve to (vē′tō), **1** the right of the president, governor, etc., to reject bills passed by a lawmaking body: *The President has the power of veto over most bills passed in Congress.* **2** having to do with a veto: *veto power.* **3** the use of this right: *The governor's veto kept the bill from becoming a law.* **4** reject by a veto. **5** refusal of consent; prohibition: *Our*

plan met with a veto from the boss. **6** refuse to consent to: *Her parents vetoed her plan to buy a car.* **1,3,5** *n., pl.* **ve toes;** **2** *adj.,* **4,6** *v.,* **ve toed, ve to ing.** [*Veto* comes from Latin *veto,* meaning "I forbid."]

vex (veks), **1** anger by trifles; annoy; provoke: *It is vexing to have to wait for somebody.* **2** disturb; trouble: *The island is much vexed by storms. v.* —**vex′er,** *n.* —**vex′ing ly,** *adv.*

vex a tion (vek sā′shən), **1** a vexing or a being vexed: *His faced showed his vexation at the delay.* **2** thing that vexes: *Rain on Saturday was a vexation to the children. n.*

vex a tious (vek sā′shəs), vexing; annoying. *adj.* —**vex a′tious ly,** *adv.* —**vex a′tious ness,** *n.*

V.F.W. or **VFW,** Veterans of Foreign Wars.

VHF, V.H.F., or **vhf,** very high frequency.

VI, Virgin Islands (used with postal Zip Code).

v.i. or **vi,** intransitive verb.

V.I., Virgin Islands.

vi a (vī′ə *or* vē′ə), by way of; by a route that passes through: *She is going from New York to Paris via London. prep.*

vi a bil i ty (vī′ə bil′ə tē), quality or condition of being viable. *n.*

vi a ble (vī′ə bəl), **1** able to keep alive: *a viable animal or plant.* **2** fit to live in; livable: *a viable community.* **3** able to be put to use; workable: *a viable program, a viable economy. adj.* —**vi′a bly,** *adv.*

vi a duct (vī′ə dukt), bridge for carrying a road or railroad over a valley, a part of a city, etc. *n.*

vi al (vī′əl), a small glass or plastic bottle for holding medicines or the like; phial. *n.*

vi and (vī′ənd), **1** article of food. **2** **viands,** *pl.* articles of choice food. *n.*

vi bran cy (vī′brən sē), quality or condition of being vibrant. *n.*

vi brant (vī′brənt), **1** vibrating. **2** resounding; resonant. **3** throbbing with vitality, enthusiasm, etc.: *a vibrant personality. adj.* —**vi′brant ly,** *adv.*

vi brate (vī′brāt), **1** move rapidly to and fro: *A piano string vibrates and makes a sound when a key is struck.* **2** cause to swing to and fro; set in motion. **3** be moved; quiver. **4** resound: *The clanging vibrated in her ears. v.,* **vi brat ed, vi brat ing.** —**vi′brat ing ly,** *adv.*

vi bra tion (vī brā′shən), **1** a rapid movement to and fro; quivering motion; vibrating: *The buses shake the house so much that we feel the vibration.* **2** motion back and forth across a position of equilibrium. *n.* —**vi bra′tion less,** *adj.*

vi bra to (vi brä′tō), **1** a vibrating or pulsating effect produced by a wavering in the pitch of a musical tone. **2** with much vibration of tone. **1** *n., pl.* **vi bra tos;** **2** *adv.*

vi bra tor (vī′brā tər), **1** thing that vibrates. **2** instrument causing a vibrating motion or action, such as an electrical device used to massage the body. *n.*

vi bra to ry (vī′brə tôr′ē), of or causing vibration. *adj.*

vi bur num (vī bėr′nəm), shrub or small tree related to the honeysuckle, having showy clusters of white or pinkish flowers. *n.*

vic ar (vik′ər), **1** the minister of a parish or a clergyman who has charge of one chapel in a parish. **2** (in the Roman Catholic Church) a clergyman who represents the pope or a bishop. **3** person acting in place of another; representative. *n.*

vic ar age (vik′ər ij), **1** residence of a vicar. **2** position or duties of a vicar. **3** salary paid to a vicar. *n.*

vi car i ous (vī ker′ē əs), felt by sharing in others' experience: *The invalid received vicarious pleasure from reading travel stories. adj.* —**vi car′i ous ly,** *adv.* —**vi car′i ous ness,** *n.*

vice¹ (vīs), **1** an evil habit or tendency: *Lying and cruelty are vices.* **2** evil; wickedness. **3** a moral fault or defect:

They believe that gambling is a vice. n. —**vice′less,** *adj.*

vice² (vīs), vise. *n.* —**vice′like′,** *adj.*

vice-, *prefix.* substitute; deputy; subordinate: *Vice-president = substitute for the president.*

vice-ad mir al (vīs′ad′mər əl), a naval officer ranking next below an admiral and next above a rear admiral. *n.*

vice-pres i den cy (vīs′prez′ə dən sē), position of vice-president. *n., pl.* **vice-pres i den cies.**

vice-pres i dent (vīs′prez′ə dənt), officer next in rank to the president, who takes the president's place when necessary. If the President of the United States dies or resigns, the Vice-President becomes President. *n.*

vice-pres i den tial (vīs′prez′ə den′shəl), of the vice-president. *adj.*

vice roy (vīs′roi), person ruling a country or province as the deputy of the sovereign. *n.*

vi ce ver sa (vī′sə vėr′sə), the other way round: *John blamed Mary, and vice versa (Mary blamed John).*

vi chys soise (vish′ē swäz′), a creamy potato-and-leek soup, sprinkled with chives and served cold. *n.*

vi cin i ty (və sin′ə tē), **1** region near or about a place; neighborhood; surrounding district: *New York and vicinity.* **2** nearness in place; being close. *n., pl.* **vi cin i ties.**

vi cious (vish′əs), **1** evil; wicked: *The criminal led a vicious life.* **2** having bad habits or a bad disposition; fierce; savage: *a vicious animal.* **3** spiteful; malicious: *vicious gossip.* **4** unpleasantly severe: *a vicious headache.* *adj.* —**vi′cious ly,** *adv.* —**vi′cious ness,** *n.*

vicious circle, two or more undesirable things each of which keeps causing the other.

vi cis si tude (və sis′ə tüd *or* və sis′ə tyüd), change in circumstances, fortune, etc.: *The vicissitudes of life may suddenly make a rich person poor. n.*

vic tim (vik′təm), **1** person or animal sacrificed, injured, or destroyed: *victims of war.* **2** person badly treated or taken advantage of; dupe: *the victim of a swindler. n.*

vic tim ize (vik′tə mīz), **1** make a victim of; cause to suffer. **2** cheat; swindle. *v.,* **vic tim ized, vic tim iz ing.**

vic tor (vik′tər), winner; conqueror. *n.*

vic to ri a (vik tôr′ē ə), a low, four-wheeled carriage with a folding top, a seat for two passengers, and a raised seat in front for the driver. *n., pl.* **vic to ri as.**

victoria

Vic to ri a (vik tôr′ē ə), **1** 1819-1901, queen of Great Britain from 1837 to 1901. **2** capital of British Columbia, in the SW part. **3** capital of Seychelles. **4** state in SE Australia. **5 Lake,** lake in E Africa, bordered by Kenya, Tanzania, and Uganda. See **Nile** for map. *n.*

Vic to ri an (vik tôr′ē ən), **1** of the time of Queen Victoria. **2** person, especially an author, who lived during the reign of Queen Victoria. **3** having characteristics considered typical of Victorians. 1,3 *adj.,* 2 *n.*

vic to ri ous (vik tôr′ē əs), **1** having won a victory; conquering: *a victorious team.* **2** having to do with victory; ending in victory: *a victorious war. adj.*

vic tor y (vik′tər ē), defeat of an enemy or opponent; success in a contest: *The game ended in a victory for our school. n., pl.* **vic tor ies.** —**vic′tor y less,** *adj.*

Vic tro la (vik trō′lə), trademark for a kind of phonograph. *n.*

vict ual (vit′l), **victuals,** *pl.* food or provisions. *n.*

vi cu ña (vi kü′nə), **1** a wild mammal of South America,

related to and resembling a llama, having a soft, delicate wool. **2** cloth made from this wool. *n., pl.* **vi cu ñas** or **vi cu ña.** [*Vicuña* was borrowed from Spanish *vicuña,* which came from a Quechua word.]

vid e o (vid′ē ō), **1** of or used in the transmission or reception of images in television. **2** television. **3** having or using a television screen or screen like that of a television: *a video display of computer information.* 1,3 *adj.,* 2 *n.* [*Video* is from Latin *video,* meaning "I see," which comes from *videre,* meaning "to see." See **Word Family.**]

video

Below are words related to *video.* They can all be traced back to the Latin word *videre* (wi dā′re), meaning "to see."

advice	provide	viewpoint
advise	providence	visa
clairvoyant	purvey	visage
envision	review	visible
envy	revise	vision
evident	supervise	visit
improvident	supervisory	visor
improvise	survey	vista
invisible	view	visual
preview		

vid e o cas sette (vid′ē ō kə set′), a recording on videotape, housed in a cassette. *n.*

vid e o disc (vid′ē ō disk′), disk like a phonograph record on which pictures and sounds can be recorded for playing back through a television set. Videodiscs are also used to store computer data and in video games. *n.*

video display terminal, device for communicating with a computer. It has a screen like that of a television and often has a keyboard.

video game, an electronic game that produces images on a television or display screen, is accompanied by sound, and permits the player to control the action by means of mechanical devices.

vid e o tape (vid′ē ō tāp′), **1** a magnetic tape that records and reproduces both sound and picture for television. **2** to record on videotape. 1 *n.,* 2 *v.,* **vid e o taped, vid e o tap ing.**

vie (vī), strive for superiority; contend in rivalry; compete. *v.,* **vied, vy ing.** —**vi′er,** *n.*

Vi en na (vē en′ə), capital of Austria, in the NE part, on the Danube River. *n.*

Vi en nese (vē′ə nēz′), **1** of Vienna or its people. **2** person born or living in Vienna. 1 *adj.,* 2 *n., pl.* **Vi en nese.**

Vien tiane (vyen tyän′), capital of Laos, in the NW. *n.*

Vi et cong (vē et′kông′), **1** the Communist guerrilla force in South Vietnam during the Vietnam War. **2** member of this force. *n., pl.* **Vi et cong.**

Vi et minh (vē et′min′), a Communist group in Vietnam formed during World War II to promote independence. *n.*

a hat	i it	oi oil	ch child	a in about
ā age	ī ice	ou out	ng long	e in taken
ä far	o hot	u cup	sh she	ə = i in pencil
e let	ō open	u̇ put	th thin	o in lemon
ē equal	ô order	ü rule	ᵀʜ then	u in circus
ėr term			zh measure	

Vi et nam (vē et′näm′), country in SE Asia. From 1954 to 1976 it was divided into two countries, North Vietnam and South Vietnam. *Capital:* Hanoi. See **Indochina** for map. *n.*

Viet Nam, Vietnam.

Vi et nam ese (vē et′nə mēz′), **1** of Vietnam, its people, or their language. **2** person born or living in Vietnam. **3** language of Vietnam. 1 *adj.,* 2,3 *n., pl.* **Vi et nam ese** for 2.

Vietnam War, war between South Vietnam, the United States, and their allies on the one side, and the Vietcong, North Vietnam, and their allies on the other side. The war began about 1957. The United States withdrew from the war in 1973.

view (vyü), **1** act of seeing; sight: *It was our first view of the ocean.* **2** power of seeing; range of the eye: *A ship came into view.* **3** see; look at: *They viewed the scene with pleasure.* **4** look at carefully; inspect. **5** thing seen; scene: *The view from our house is beautiful.* **6** picture of some scene: *Various views of the coast hung on the walls.* **7** a mental picture; an idea: *This book will give you a general view of the way the pioneers lived.* **8** way of looking at or considering a matter; opinion: *What are your views on the subject?* **9** consider; regard: *The plan was viewed favorably.* 1,2,5-8 *n.,* 3,4,9 *v.* —**view′a ble,** *adj.*

in view, 1 in sight: *As the noise grew louder, the airplane came in view.* **2** under consideration: *Keep the teacher's advice in view as you work.* **3** as a purpose or intention. **4** as a hope; as an expectation.

in view of, considering; because of.

on view, to be seen; open for people to see: *The exhibit is on view from 9 a.m. to 5 p.m.*

with a view to, with the purpose or intention of: *She worked hard after school with a view to earning money for a new bicycle.*

view er (vyü′ər), person who views, especially one who views television. *n.*

view less (vyü′lis), **1** without a view: *a viewless window.* **2** without views or opinions. *adj.* —**view′less ly,** *adv.*

view point (vyü′point′), point of view: *A heavy rain that is good from the viewpoint of farmers may be bad from the viewpoint of tourists.* *n.*

vig il (vij′əl), **1** a staying awake for some purpose; act of watching; watch: *All night the parents kept vigil over the sick child.* **2 vigils,** *pl.* prayers, services, etc., on the night before a religious festival. **3** the day and night before a solemn religious festival. *n.*

vig i lance (vij′ə ləns), watchfulness; alertness; caution: *Constant vigilance is necessary in order to avoid accidents in driving.* *n.*

vig i lant (vij′ə lənt), watchful; alert; wide-awake: *The dog kept vigilant guard.* *adj.* —**vig′i lant ly,** *adv.* —**vig′i-lant ness,** *n.*

vig i lan te (vij′ə lan′tē), member of an unauthorized group of citizens organized to maintain order and punish criminals. In the 1800's, committees of vigilantes were common in frontier territories of the United States. *n.*

vig or (vig′ər), **1** active strength or force: *The principal argued with vigor that the new school should have a library.* **2** healthy energy or power: *A person's vigor lessens with old age.* *n.* —**vig′or less,** *adj.*

vig or ous (vig′ər əs), full of vigor; strong and active; energetic; forceful: *a vigorous and lively man. Doctors wage a vigorous war against disease. adj.* —**vig′or ous ly,** *adv.* —**vig′or ous ness,** *n.*

vig our (vig′ər), BRITISH. vigor. *n.*

Vi king or **vi king** (vī′king), one of the Scandinavian seafarers who raided the coasts of Europe during the A.D. 700's, 800's, and 900's. The vikings conquered parts of England, France, Russia, and other countries and explored distant lands that may have included North America. *n.*

Vi la (vē′lə), capital of Vanuatu. *n.*

vile (vīl), **1** very bad; wretched: *The weather was vile—rainy and cold.* **2** foul; disgusting: *A vile smell hung in the air around the garbage dump.* **3** evil; immoral: *a vile crime. adj.,* **vil er, vil est.** —**vile′ly,** *adv.* —**vile′ness,** *n.*

vil i fi ca tion (vil′ə fə kā′shən), a vilifying or a being vilified. *n.*

vil i fy (vil′ə fī), speak evil of; revile; slander. *v.,* **vil i fied, vil i fy ing.** —**vil′i fi′er,** *n.* —**vil′i fy′ing ly,** *adv.*

vil la (vil′ə), a house in the country or suburbs, sometimes at the seashore. A villa is usually a large and elegant residence. *n., pl.* **vil las.** —**vil′la like′,** *adj.*

vil lage (vil′ij), **1** group of houses, usually smaller than a town. **2** the people of a village: *The whole village was out to see the fire.* *n.*

vil lag er (vil′i jər), person who lives in a village. *n.*

vil lain (vil′ən), **1** a very wicked person: *The villain stole the money and cast the blame on a friend.* **2** villein. *n.*

vil lain ous (vil′ə nəs), **1** very wicked. **2** extremely bad; vile. *adj.* —**vil′lain ous ly,** *adv.* —**vil′lain ous ness,** *n.*

vil lain y (vil′ə nē), **1** great wickedness. **2** a wicked act; a crime. *n., pl.* **vil lain ies.**

vil lein (vil′ən), one of a class of half-free peasants in the Middle Ages. A villein was under the control of a lord, but was free in relations with other people. *n.*

vil li (vil′ī), tiny, hairlike parts growing out of the membrane of the small intestine. The villi aid in absorbing certain substances. *n.pl. of* **vil lus** (vil′əs).

vim (vim), force; energy; vigor: *The campers were full of vim after a good night's sleep.* *n.*

Vin ci (vin′chē), **Leonardo da.** See da Vinci. *n.*

vin di cate (vin′də kāt), **1** clear from suspicion, dishonor, or any charge of wrongdoing: *The verdict of "Not guilty" vindicated them.* **2** defend successfully against opposition; uphold; justify: *The heir vindicated her claim to the fortune. v.,* **vin di cat ed, vin di cat ing.** —**vin′di-ca′tor,** *n.*

vin di ca tion (vin′də kā′shən), a vindicating or a being vindicated; defense; justification. *n.*

vin dic tive (vin dik′tiv), **1** bearing a grudge; wanting revenge: *A vindictive person is unforgiving.* **2** showing a strong tendency toward revenge: *a vindictive act. adj.* —**vin dic′tive ly,** *adv.* —**vin dic′tive ness,** *n.*

vine (vīn), **1** plant with a long, slender stem, that grows along the ground or that climbs by attaching itself to a wall, tree, or other support. Melons and pumpkins grow on vines. Ivy is a vine. **2** grapevine. *n.* —**vine′less,** *adj.* —**vine′like′,** *adj.*

vin e gar (vin′ə gər), a sour liquid produced by the fermentation of cider, wine, malt, etc. Vinegar is used in salad dressing and in flavoring or preserving food. *n.* [*Vinegar* came into English about 700 years ago from French *vinaigre,* which comes from *vin,* meaning "wine," and *aigre,* meaning "sour."] —**vin′e gar like′,** *adj.*

vin e gar y (vin′ə gər ē), of or like vinegar; sour: *a vinegary taste, a vinegary disposition. adj.*

vine yard (vin′yərd), a place planted with grapevines. *n.*

vi nous (vī′nəs), of or like wine. *adj.*

vin tage (vin′tij), **1** the wine from a certain crop of grapes: *The finest vintages cost much more than others.* **2** a year's crop of grapes. **3** the season of gathering grapes and making wine. **4** of outstanding quality; choice: *vintage wines.* **5** type of thing fashionable or popular during an earlier season: *a hat of the vintage of 1940.* 1-3,5 *n.,* 4 *adj.*

vint ner (vint′nər), dealer in wine; wine merchant. *n.*

vi nyl (vī′nl), any of various tough synthetic plastics or resins used in floor coverings, toys, molded articles, phonograph records, etc. *n.*

vi ol (vī′əl), **1** any of several stringed musical instruments played with a bow and usually held either on or between the knees while they are played. Viols were used chiefly in the 1500's and 1600's. **2** double bass. *n.*

vi o la (vē ō′lə), a stringed musical instrument like a violin, but somewhat larger and lower in pitch. See **violin** for picture. *n., pl.* **vi o las.**

vi o late (vī′ə lāt), **1** break (a law, rule, agreement, promise, etc.); act contrary to; fail to perform: *Speeding violates the traffic laws.* **2** break in upon; disturb: *The sound of automobile horns violated the usual calm of Sunday morning.* **3** treat with disrespect or contempt: *Vandals violated several grave sites by overturning the tombstones.* *v.,* **vi o lat ed, vi o lat ing.** —**vi′o lat′er,** *n.*

vi o la tion (vī′ə lā′shən), **1** a breaking (of a law, rule, agreement, promise, etc.): *He was fined $10 for his violation of the traffic law.* **2** a breaking in upon; interruption or disturbance. **3** treatment (of a holy thing) with disrespect or contempt. *n.*

vi o la tor (vī′ə lā′tər), person who violates something. *n.*

vi o lence (vī′ə ləns), **1** rough force in action: *She slammed the door with violence.* **2** rough or harmful action or treatment: *The police had to use violence in arresting the murderer.* **3** harm; injury: *It would do violence to her principles to work on Sunday.* **4** strength of action, feeling, etc. *n.*

vi o lent (vī′ə lənt), **1** acting or done with strong, rough force: *a violent blow.* **2** caused by strong, rough force: *a violent death.* **3** showing or caused by very strong feeling, action, etc.: *violent language, a violent rage.* **4** very great; extreme: *a violent pain, violent heat. adj.* —**vi′o lent ly,** *adv.* —**vi′o lent ness,** *n.*

vi o let (vī′ə lit), **1** a small plant with purple, blue, yellow, or white flowers. Many common violets grow wild and bloom in the spring. **2** a bluish purple. Violet is red and blue mixed. **3** bluish-purple. **1,2** *n.,* **3** *adj.*

violin and **viola**
The girl is playing a violin; the boy is playing a viola.

vi o lin (vī′ə lin′), a musical instrument with four strings played with a bow. The violin has the highest pitch of the stringed instruments. *n.*

vi o lin ist (vī′ə lin′ist), person who plays the violin. *n.*

vi ol ist (vē ō′list), person who plays the viola. *n.*

vi o lon cel list (vī′ə lən chel′ist), cellist. *n.*

vi o lon cel lo (vī′ə lən chel′ō), cello. *n., pl.* **vi o lon cel los.**

VIP or **V.I.P.,** INFORMAL. very important person.

vi per (vī′pər), **1** any of various poisonous snakes with a pair of large, hollow fangs and often having a thick, heavy body. **2** a spiteful, treacherous person. *n.* —**vi′per like′,** *adj.*

vi per ous (vī′pər əs), **1** of or like a viper or vipers. **2** spiteful; treacherous. *adj.* —**vi′per ous ly,** *adv.*

vi ra go (və rä′gō), a violent, bad-tempered, or scolding woman. *n., pl.* **vi ra goes** or **vi ra gos.**

a hat	i it	oi oil	ch child	(a in about
ā age	ī ice	ou out	ng long	e in taken
ä far	o hot	u cup	sh she	ə = ⟨ i in pencil
e let	ō open	u̇ put	th thin	o in lemon
ē equal	ô order	ü rule	ᴛн then	(u in circus
ėr term			zh measure	

vi ral (vī′rəl), of or caused by a virus. *adj.* —**vi′ral ly,** *adv.*

vir e o (vir′ē ō), a small, olive-green, North American songbird that eats insects. *n., pl.* **vir e os.**

Vir gil (vėr′jəl), Vergil. *n.*

vir gin (vėr′jən), **1** person who has not had sexual intercourse. **2 the Virgin,** Virgin Mary. **3** of a virgin; suitable for a virgin: *virgin modesty.* **4** pure; spotless. Virgin snow is newly fallen snow. **5** not yet used: *virgin soil, a virgin forest.* **1,2** *n.,* **3-5** *adj.*

virginal
(def. 2)

vir gin al (vėr′jə nəl), **1** of or suitable for a virgin; maidenly. **2** a small harpsichord set in a rectangular box without legs. It was much used in the 1500's and 1600's. **1** *adj.,* **2** *n.* —**vir′gin al ly,** *adv.*

Vir gin ia (vər jin′yə), one of the southeastern states of the United States. *Abbreviation:* Va. or VA *Capital:* Richmond. *n.* —**Vir gin′ian,** *adj., n.*

Virginia creeper, an American climbing plant having leaves with five leaflets and bluish-black berries that are not good to eat; woodbine.

Virginia reel, an American folk dance in which the partners form two lines facing each other and perform a number of dance steps.

Virgin Islands, group of islands in the West Indies, east of Puerto Rico. Several of these islands belong to the United States and the rest (**British Virgin Islands**) are a British territory. *Abbreviation:* V.I. or VI

vir gin i ty (vər jin′ə tē), condition of being a virgin. *n.*

Virgin Mary, the mother of Jesus.

vir ile (vir′əl), **1** of or characteristic of a man; manly; masculine. **2** full of strength or vigor; vigorous; forceful. *adj.*

vi ril i ty (və ril′ə tē), **1** manhood. **2** strength; vigor; forcefulness. *n., pl.* **vi ril i ties.**

vi rol o gist (vī rol′ə jist), an expert in virology. *n.*

vi rol o gy (vī rol′ə jē), science that deals with viruses and virus diseases. *n.*

vir tu al (vėr′chü əl), being something in effect, though not so in name; for all practical purposes; actual; real: *The battle was won with so great a loss of soldiers that it was a virtual defeat. adj.*

vir tu al ly (vėr′chü ə lē), in effect, though not in name; practically: *If you travel by jet plane, New York and Los Angeles are virtually neighbors. adv.*

vir tue (vėr′chü), **1** moral excellence; goodness: *a person of the highest virtue.* **2** a particular moral excellence: *Kindness is a virtue.* **3** a good quality: *She praised the virtues of her small car.* **4** chastity; purity. **5** power to produce good results: *There is little virtue in that medicine. n.*

by virtue of or **in virtue of,** because of; on account of.

vir tu os i ty (vėr′chü os′ə tē), skill of a virtuoso. *n., pl.* **vir tu os i ties.**

vir tu o so (vėr′chü ō′sō), person skilled in the techniques of an art, especially in playing a musical instrument. *n., pl.* **vir tu o sos, vir tu o si** (vėr′chü ō′sē).

vir tu ous (vėr′chü əs), **1** good; moral; righteous: *virtuous conduct, a virtuous life.* **2** chaste; pure: *a virtuous maiden. adj.* —**vir′tu ous ly,** *adv.* —**vir′tu ous ness,** *n.*

vir u lence (vir′yə ləns), **1** quality of being very poisonous or harmful; deadliness: *the virulence of a rattlesnake's bite.* **2** intense bitterness or spite; violent hostility. *n.*

vir u lent (vir′yə lənt), **1** very poisonous or harmful; deadly: *a virulent form of a disease.* **2** intensely bitter or spiteful; violently hostile: *virulent abuse. adj.* —**vir′u lently,** *adv.*

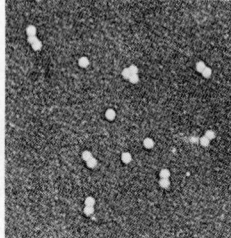

virus—two types of virus, 50,000 times actual size

vi rus (vī′rəs), any of a group of disease-producing agents composed of protein and nucleic acid. Viruses are smaller than any known bacteria and depend on the living tissue of larger cells for their reproduction and growth. Viruses cause rabies, polio, chicken pox, the common cold, and many other diseases. They are so small that they cannot be seen through most microscopes. *n., pl.* **vi rus es.** [*Virus* comes from Latin *virus,* meaning "poison."]

vi sa (vē′zə), an official signature or endorsement upon a passport, showing that it has been examined and approved. A visa is granted by the consul or other representative of the country to which a person wishes to travel. *n., pl.* **vi sas.** [*Visa* was borrowed from French *visa,* which came from Latin (*carta*) *visa,* meaning "(paper) that has been seen, or inspected," and can be traced back to *videre,* meaning "to see."]

vis age (viz′ij), face or appearance: *a grim visage. n.*

vis cer a (vis′ər ə), the soft internal organs of the body. The heart, stomach, liver, intestines, kidneys, etc., are viscera. *n.pl. of* **vis cus** (vis′kəs).

vis cer al (vis′ər əl), of the viscera. *adj.*

vis cid (vis′id), thick like heavy syrup or glue; sticky. *adj.*

vis cos i ty (vi skos′ə tē), condition or quality of being viscous. *n.*

vis count (vī′kount), nobleman ranking next below an earl or count and next above a baron. *n.*

vis count ess (vī′koun tis), **1** wife or widow of a viscount. **2** woman whose rank is equal to that of a viscount. *n., pl.* **vis count ess es.**

vis cous (vis′kəs), thick like heavy syrup or glue; sticky. *adj.* —**vis′cous ly,** *adv.* —**vis′cous ness,** *n.*

vise (vīs), tool having two jaws opened and closed by a screw, used to hold an object firmly while work is being done on it. *n.* Also, **vice.** —**vise′like′,** *adj.*

Vish nu (vish′nü), one of the three chief Hindu divinities, called "the Preserver." *n.*

vis i bil i ty (viz′ə bil′ə tē), **1** condition or quality of being visible: *In a fog the visibility is very poor.* **2** distance at which things are visible: *Fog and rain decreased visibility to about 50 feet. n., pl.* **vis i bil i ties.**

vis i ble (viz′ə bəl), **1** that can be seen: *The shore was barely visible through the fog.* **2** readily evident; apparent; obvious: *The vagrant had no visible means of support. adj.*

vis i bly (viz′ə blē), so as to be visible; plainly; evidently: *After the long hike the children were visibly weary. adv.*

Vis i goth (viz′ə goth), member of the western division of the Goths. The Visigoths sacked Rome in A.D. 410 and eventually settled in France and Spain. *n.*

vi sion (vizh′ən), **1** power of seeing; sense of sight: *I have to wear glasses because my vision is poor.* **2** act or fact of seeing; sight: *The vision of the table loaded with food made our mouths water.* **3** power of perceiving by the imagination or by clear thinking: *a person of great vision.* **4** something seen in the imagination, in a dream, in one's thoughts, etc.: *The gambler had visions of great wealth.* **5** a very beautiful person, scene, etc. *n.* —**vi′sion less,** *adj.*

vi sion ar y (vizh′ə ner′ē), **1** person given to imagining or dreaming; person whose ideas seem impractical; dreamer: *Many great scientists have been visionaries.* **2** not practical; dreamy: *He is a visionary child; he spends hours daydreaming.* **3** not practicable; fanciful: *Fifty years ago people would have regarded plans for an atomic power plant as visionary.* **4** of or belonging to a vision; seen in a vision; imaginary: *The visionary scene faded, and she awoke.* **5** person who sees visions. 1,5 *n., pl.* **vi sion ar ies;** 2-4 *adj.* —**vi′sion ar′i ness,** *n.*

vis it (viz′it), **1** go to see; come to see: *He visited New York.* **2** make a call on or stay with; be a guest of: *She is visiting her aunt.* **3** go or come to see in order to inspect, examine officially, give professional service or treatment to, etc.: *The doctor visited her patients at the hospital. The inspector visits the factory once a month.* **4** a visiting; a call from friendship, for purpose of inspection, examination, professional treatment, etc.: *pay a visit to a friend, a visit to the dentist.* **5** come upon; afflict: *They were visited by many troubles.* **6** send upon; inflict: *visit one's anger on someone.* **7** to talk or chat. 1-3,5-7 *v.,* 4 *n.*

vis it ant (viz′ə tənt), visitor; guest. *n.*

vis i ta tion (viz′ə tā′shən), **1** act of visiting. **2** a visit for the purpose of making an official inspection or examination. A nation at war has the right of visitation of neutral ships; that is, the right to inspect their cargoes. **3** punishment or reward sent by God. *n.*

vis i tor (viz′ə tər), person who visits or is visiting; guest. *n.*

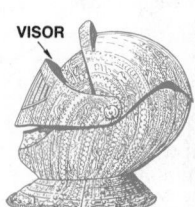

VISOR

visor
left, (def. 1)
right, (def. 2)

vi sor (vī′zər), **1** the movable front part of a helmet, covering the face. **2** the brim of a cap, projecting in front to shade the eyes. **3** shade above a windshield, that can be lowered to shield the eyes from the sun. *n.* Also, **vizor.**

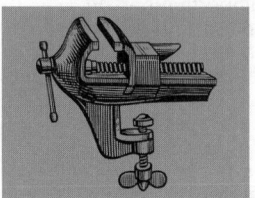

vise

a hat	i it	oi oil	ch child	(a in about
ā age	ī ice	ou out	ng long	e in taken
ä far	o hot	u cup	sh she	ə = { i in pencil
e let	ō open	u̇ put	th thin	o in lemon
ē equal	ô order	ü rule	ŦH then	u in circus
ėr term			zh measure	

vis ta (vis′tə), **1** view seen through a narrow opening or passage: *The opening between the two rows of trees afforded a vista of the lake.* **2** such an opening or passage itself: *a shady vista of elms.* **3** a mental view: *Education should open up new vistas. n., pl.* **vis tas.** [*Vista* was borrowed from Italian *vista,* and can be traced back to Latin *videre,* meaning "to see."] —**vis′ta less,** *adj.*

VISTA (vis′tə), Volunteers in Service to America. *n.*

Vis tu la (vis′chə lə), river flowing through Poland to the Baltic Sea. *n.*

vis u al (vizh′ü əl), **1** of or used in sight or vision: *Being near-sighted is a visual defect. Telescopes and microscopes are visual aids.* **2** received through the sense of sight: *visual impressions.* **3** that can be seen; visible: *the visual parts of the spectrum. adj.* —**vis′u al ly,** *adv.*

vis u al i za tion (vizh′ü ə lə zā′shən), **1** a visualizing or a being visualized. **2** thing visualized. *n.*

vis u al ize (vizh′ü ə līz), **1** form a mental picture of: *visualize the face of an old friend.* **2** make visible. *v.,* **vis u al ized, vis u al iz ing.** —**vis′u al iz′er,** *n.*

vi tal (vī′tl), **1** of life. *Vital statistics give facts about births, deaths, marriages, etc. Growth and decay are vital processes.* **2** necessary to life: *Eating is a vital function. The heart is a vital organ.* **3 vitals,** *pl.* **a** parts or organs necessary to life. *The brain, heart, lungs, and stomach are vitals.* **b** essential parts or features. **4** very important; basic: *a vital question. Pure water is vital to the welfare of a community.* **5** causing death, failure, or ruin: *a vital wound, a vital blow to an industry.* **6** full of life and spirit; lively: *What a vital person she is—never idle, never dull!* 1,2,4-6 *adj.,* 3 *n.* —**vi′tal ly,** *adv.* —**vi′tal ness,** *n.*

vi tal i ty (vī tal′ə tē), **1** vital force; power to live: *One's vitality can be lessened by illness.* **2** power to endure and be active: *Poetry of great vitality is read hundreds of years after it was written.* **3** strength; energy; vigor: *Exercise helps maintain vitality. n., pl.* **vi tal i ties.**

vi tal ize (vī′tl īz), **1** give life to. **2** put vitality into; make more energetic, lively, or enterprising. *v.,* **vi tal ized, vi tal iz ing.** —**vi′tal i za′tion,** *n.*

vi ta min or **vi ta mine** (vī′tə mən), **1** any of certain special substances required for the normal growth and proper nourishment of the body, found especially in milk, butter, raw fruits and vegetables, cod-liver oil, and the outside part of wheat and other grains. Lack of essential vitamins causes such diseases as rickets and scurvy, as well as generally poor health. **2** of or containing vitamins: *a vitamin tablet, a vitamin deficiency.* 1 *n.,* 2 *adj.*

vitamin A, vitamin found in milk, butter, cod-liver oil, egg yolk, liver, green and yellow vegetables, etc. Vitamin A increases the resistance of the body to infection and prevents night blindness.

vitamin B₁, thiamine.

vitamin B₂, riboflavin.

vitamin B complex, group of vitamins including vitamin B₁, vitamin B₂, nicotinic acid, etc., found in high concentration in yeast and liver.

vitamin C, vitamin found in citrus fruits, tomatoes, leafy green vegetables, etc.; ascorbic acid. Vitamin C prevents and cures scurvy.

vitamin D, vitamin found in cod-liver oil, milk, and egg yolk, that is necessary for the growth and health of bones and teeth. Vitamin D prevents rickets.

vitamin E, vitamin found in wheat germ oil, whole grain cereals, lettuce, etc. Vitamin E is used to treat sterility.

vitamin G, riboflavin.

vitamin K, vitamin found in leafy green vegetables, egg yolk, etc., that promotes clotting of the blood.

vi ti ate (vish′ē āt), destroy the legal force or authority of: *The contract was vitiated because one person signed under compulsion. v.,* **vi ti at ed, vi ti at ing.** —**vi′ti a′tion,** *n.* —**vi′ti a′tor,** *n.*

vit re ous (vit′rē əs), of or like glass; glassy. *adj.* —**vit′re ous ness,** *n.*

vitreous humor, the transparent, jellylike substance that fills the eyeball behind the lens.

vit ri fy (vit′rə fī), to change into glass or something like glass, especially by fusion through heat. *v.,* **vit ri fied, vit ri fy ing.** —**vit′ri fi′a ble,** *adj.* —**vit′ri fi ca′tion,** *n.*

vit ri ol (vit′rē əl), **1** sulfuric acid. **2** any of certain sulfates of metals, such as **blue vitriol,** a sulfate of copper, **green vitriol,** a sulfate of iron, or **white vitriol,** a sulfate of zinc. Vitriols are characterized by a glassy appearance. **3** very sharp speech or severe criticism. *n.*

vit ri ol ic (vit′rē ol′ik), **1** of or containing vitriol. **2** bitterly severe; sharp: *vitriolic criticism. adj.*

vi tu pe rate (vī tü′pə rāt′ *or* vī tyü′pə rāt′), scold very severely; find fault with in abusive words; revile. *v.,* **vi tu pe rat ed, vi tu pe rat ing.** —**vi tu′pe ra′tor,** *n.*

vi tu pe ra tion (vī tü′pə rā′shən *or* vī tyü′pə rā′shən), bitter abuse in words; very severe scolding. *n.*

vi tu pe ra tive (vī tü′pə rā′tiv *or* vī tyü′pə rā′tiv), abusive; reviling. *adj.* —**vi tu′pe ra′tive ly,** *adv.*

vi va (vē′və), a Spanish or Italian exclamation of approval, meaning (long) live (the person or thing named). *interj.*

vi va cious (vī vā′shəs *or* vi vā′shəs), lively; sprightly; animated; gay: *a vivacious manner. adj.* —**vi va′cious ly,** *adv.* —**vi va′cious ness,** *n.*

vi vac i ty (vī vas′ə tē *or* vi vas′ə tē), liveliness; sprightliness; animation; gaiety. *n., pl.* **vi vac i ties.**

vive (vēv), a French exclamation of approval, meaning (long) live (the person or thing named). *interj.*

viv id (viv′id), **1** strikingly bright; strong and clear; brilliant: *Dandelions are a vivid yellow.* **2** full of life; lively: *a vivid description of an experience.* **3** strong and distinct: *I have a vivid memory of the fire.* **4** very active or intense: *a vivid imagination. adj.* [*Vivid* is from Latin *vividus,* which comes from *vivere,* meaning "to live."] —**viv′id ly,** *adv.* —**viv′id ness,** *n.*

viv i fy (viv′ə fī), **1** give life or vigor to: *vivify the desert by irrigation.* **2** make vivid; enliven: *vivify an idea with wit. v.,* **viv i fied, viv i fy ing.** —**viv′i fi ca′tion,** *n.* —**viv′i fi′er,** *n.*

vi vip ar ous (vī vip′ər əs), bringing forth living young, rather than eggs. Dogs, cats, cows, and human beings are viviparous. *adj.* —**vi vip′ar ous ly,** *adv.* —**vi vip′ar ous ness,** *n.*

viv i sect (viv′ə sekt), dissect the living body of. *v.*

viv i sec tion (viv′ə sek′shən), act or practice of dissecting or operating on living animals for scientific study or experimentation. *n.*

viv i sec tion ist (viv′ə sek′shə nist), person who favors or defends vivisection. *n.*

vix en (vik′sən), **1** a female fox. **2** a quarrelsome or malicious woman. *n.*

viz., that is to say; namely: *There are four seasons, viz., spring, summer, fall, and winter.*

vi zier or **vi zir** (vi zir′), (in Moslem countries) a high official, such as a minister of state. *n.* [*Vizier* is from

Turkish *vezīr*, which came from Arabic *wazīr*, originally meaning "porter[1]."]

vi zor (vī′zər), visor. *n.* —**vi′zor less,** *adj.*

Vlad i vos tok (vlad′ə vos′tok), seaport on the Sea of Japan in SE Soviet Union. *n.*

vocab., vocabulary.

vo cab u lar y (vō kab′yə ler′ē), **1** the stock of words used by a person or group of people: *Reading will increase your vocabulary. The vocabulary of science has grown tremendously.* **2** collection or list of words, usually in alphabetical order, with their translations or meanings: *There is a vocabulary in the back of our French book. n., pl.* **vo cab u lar ies.** [*Vocabulary* comes from a medieval Latin word *vocabularius,* and can be traced back to Latin *vocare,* meaning "to call." See **Word Family.**]

vocabulary

Below are words related to *vocabulary.* They can all be traced back to the Latin word *vocare* (wō cä′re), meaning "to call."

advocate	equivocate	provocative
avocation	evoke	provoke
avow	invocation	revoke
convocation	invoke	vocation
convoke	irrevocable	vouch
equivocal	provocation	vouchsafe

vo cal (vō′kəl), **1** of the voice: *The tongue is a vocal organ.* **2** made with the voice: *I like vocal music better than instrumental.* **3** having a voice; giving forth sound: *Humans are vocal beings. The zoo was vocal with the roar of the lions.* **4** aroused to speech; inclined to talk freely: *become vocal with indignation. adj.* —**vo′cal ly,** *adv.*

vocal cords, two pairs of membranes in the throat, projecting into the cavity of the larynx. The lower pair can be pulled tight and the passage of breath between them then causes them to vibrate, which produces the sound of the voice.

vo cal ic (vō kal′ik), **1** of or like a vowel sound. **2** having many vowel sounds. *adj.*

vo cal ist (vō′kə list), singer. *n.*

vo cal i za tion (vō′kə lə zā′shən), a vocalizing or a being vocalized. *n.*

vo cal ize (vō′kə līz), **1** use the voice; speak, sing, shout, etc. **2** make vocal; utter: *The dog vocalized its pain in a series of long howls. v.,* **vo cal ized, vo cal iz ing.** —**vo′cal iz′er,** *n.*

vo ca tion (vō kā′shən), **1** occupation, business, profession, or trade: *Architecture is her vocation.* **2** an inner call or summons. *n.* [*Vocation* is from Latin *vocationem,* originally meaning "a calling," which comes from *vocare,* meaning "to call."]

vo ca tion al (vō kā′shə nəl), having to do with some occupation, business, profession, or trade. A vocational school provides training in special trades, such as printing, stenography, or mechanics. *adj.* —**vo ca′tion al ly,** *adv.*

vo cif er ous (vō sif′ər əs), loud and noisy; shouting; clamoring: *a vociferous person, vociferous cheers. adj.* —**vo cif′er ous ly,** *adv.* —**vo cif′er ous ness,** *n.*

vod ka (vod′kə), an alcoholic drink distilled from potatoes, rye, barley, or corn. *n., pl.* **vod kas.** [*Vodka* was

borrowed from Russian *vodka,* which comes from *voda,* meaning "water."]

vogue (vōg), **1** the fashion: *Hoop skirts were in vogue more than 100 years ago.* **2** popularity or acceptance: *That song had a great vogue at one time. n.* [*Vogue* came into English about 400 years ago from French *vogue,* meaning "success, course, a rowing," and can be traced back to Italian *vogare,* meaning "to row."]

voice (vois), **1** sound made through the mouth, especially by people in speaking, singing, shouting, etc.: *The voices of the children could be heard coming from the playground.* **2** power to make sounds through the mouth: *His voice was gone because of a sore throat.* **3** anything like speech or song: *the voice of the wind.* **4** ability as a singer: *She knew she had no voice.* **5** singer: *a choir of fifty voices.* **6** part of a piece of music for one kind of singer or instrument. **7** express; utter: *They voiced their approval of the plan.* **8** expression: *They gave voice to their joy.* **9** an expressed opinion or choice: *His voice was for compromise.* **10** the right to express an opinion or choice: *We have no voice in the matter.* **11** form of a verb that shows whether its subject is active or passive. **12** utter with a sound made by vibration of the vocal cords. *Z* and *v* are voiced; *s* and *f* are not. 1-6,8-11 *n.,* 7,12 *v.,* **voiced, voic ing.**

with one voice, unanimously.

voice box, larynx.

voice less (vois′lis), **1** having no voice; dumb; silent. **2** not voiced. The consonants *p, t,* and *k* are voiceless. *adj.* —**voice′less ly,** *adv.* —**voice′less ness,** *n.*

void (void), **1** an empty space: *The death of his dog left a void in the boy's life.* **2** empty; vacant: *a void space.* **3** without legal force or effect; not binding in law: *A contract made by a twelve-year-old is void.* **4** make of no force or effect in law. **5** to empty out. 1 *n.,* 2,3 *adj.,* 4,5 *v.*

void a ble (voi′də bəl), capable of being voided or given up: *The contract was voidable by either party. adj.*

voile (voil), a very thin cloth with an open weave, used for dresses. *n.*

vol., volume.

vol a tile (vol′ə təl), **1** evaporating rapidly; changing into vapor easily: *Gasoline is volatile.* **2** changing rapidly from one mood or interest to another; fickle: *a volatile disposition. adj.* —**vol′a tile ness,** *n.*

vol a til i ty (vol′ə til′ə tē), volatile quality or condition. *n.*

vol can ic (vol kan′ik), **1** of or caused by a volcano; having to do with volcanoes: *a volcanic eruption.* **2** like a volcano; liable to break out violently: *a volcanic temper. adj.* —**vol can′i cal ly,** *adv.*

volcano (def. 2)

vol ca no (vol kā′nō), **1** an opening in the earth's crust through which steam, ashes, and lava are forced out in periods of activity. **2** a cone-shaped hill or mountain around this opening, built up of the material that is forced out. *n., pl.* **vol ca noes** or **vol ca nos.** [*Volcano* was borrowed from Italian *volcano*, which came from Latin *Vulcanus*, meaning "Vulcan."]

vole (vōl), rodent related to rats and mice, usually of heavier build and having short limbs and tail. *n.*

vole
about 5½ in. (14 cm.)
long with the tail

Vol ga (vol′gə), river in the W Soviet Union, flowing into the Caspian Sea. *n.*

Vol go grad (vol′gə grad), city in SW Soviet Union, on the Volga River. Formerly, **Stalingrad.** *n.*

vo li tion (vō lish′ən), act of willing; decision: *She took on extra work of her own volition. n.*

vol ley (vol′ē), **1** shower of stones, bullets, words, oaths, etc.: *A volley of arrows rained down upon the attacking knights.* **2** the discharge of a number of guns at once. **3** discharge or be discharged in a volley: *Cannon volleyed on all sides.* **4** the hitting or return of a tennis ball before it touches the ground. **5** hit or return (a tennis ball) before it touches the ground. **6** hit a tennis ball back and forth over the net until someone misses or faults. 1,2,4 *n., pl.* **vol leys;** 3,5,6 *v.,* **vol leyed, vol ley ing.** —**vol′ley er,** *n.*

volleyball
(def. 1)

vol ley ball (vol′ē bôl′), **1** game played by two teams of players with a large ball and a high net. The players must hit the ball back and forth over the net with their hands without letting it touch the ground. **2** ball used in this game. *n.*

vols., volumes.

volt (vōlt), unit for measuring electrical force, equal to the amount of energy needed to cause a current of one ampere to flow through a resistance of one ohm. *n.* [*Volt* was formed from the name of Alessandro *Volta*, 1745-1827, an Italian physicist.]

volt age (vōl′tij), strength of electrical force, measured in volts. A current of high voltage is used in transmitting electric power over long distances. *n.*

vol ta ic cell (vol tā′ik), an electric cell consisting of two electrodes connected by a wire and immersed in an electrolyte. An electric current is produced in the wire by a chemical reaction between the electrolyte and the electrodes.

Vol taire (vol ter′ *or* vol tar′), 1694-1778, French writer and philosopher. *n.*

volt me ter (vōlt′mē′tər), instrument for measuring in volts the force between two points in an electric circuit. *n.*

vol u bil i ty (vol′yə bil′ə tē), tendency to talk much; fondness for talking. *n.*

vol u ble (vol′yə bəl), tending to talk much; fond of talking; talkative: *a voluble speaker. adj.* —**vol′u ble ness,** *n.*

vol u bly (vol′yə blē), in a voluble manner. *adv.*

vol ume (vol′yəm), **1** book: *We own a library of five hundred volumes.* **2** book forming part of a set or series: *You can find what you want to know in the ninth volume of this encyclopedia.* **3** space occupied: *The storeroom has a volume of 800 cubic feet.* **4** amount; quantity: *the volume of business at a store. Volumes of smoke poured from the chimneys of the factory.* **5** amount of sound; fullness of tone: *A pipe organ has more volume than a flute. n.* [*Volume* came into English about 600 years ago from French *volume*, which came from Latin *volumen*, meaning "scroll," which comes from *volvere*, meaning "to roll."]

vol u met ric (vol′yə met′rik), of measurement by volume. *adj.* —**vol′u met′ri cal ly,** *adv.*

vo lu mi nous (və lü′mə nəs), **1** forming or filling a large book or many books: *a voluminous report.* **2** writing much: *a voluminous author.* **3** of great size; very bulky; large: *A voluminous cloak covered him from head to foot. adj.* —**vo lu′mi nous ly,** *adv.* —**vo lu′mi nous ness,** *n.*

vol un tar i ly (vol′ən ter′ə lē), of one's own free will; without force or compulsion. *adv.*

vol un tar y (vol′ən ter′ē), **1** acting, done, made, or given of one's own free will; not forced or compelled: *a voluntary confession, a voluntary worker.* **2** done on purpose; intended: *voluntary manslaughter. Voluntary disobedience will be punished.* **3** controlled by the will: *Talking is voluntary; hiccupping is not voluntary. adj.*

vol un teer (vol′ən tir′), **1** person who enters any service by choice; one who is not drafted. Some soldiers are volunteers. **2** person who serves without pay. In some towns, the fire department is made up of volunteers. **3** offer one's services: *She volunteered for the Peace Corps.* **4** to offer of one's own free will: *He volunteered to help.* **5** of or made up of volunteers: *Our village has a volunteer fire department.* **6** serving as a volunteer: *a volunteer fireman.* **7** tell or say voluntarily: *He volunteered the information.* 1,2 *n.,* 3,4,7 *v.,* 5,6 *adj.*

vo lup tu ar y (və lup′chü er′ē), person who cares much for luxurious or sensual pleasures. *n., pl.* **vo lup tu ar ies.**

vo lup tu ous (və lup′chü əs), **1** caring much for the pleasures of the senses. **2** giving pleasure to the senses: *voluptuous music, voluptuous beauty. adj.* —**vo lup′tu ous ly,** *adv.* —**vo lup′tu ous ness,** *n.*

vom it (vom′it), **1** expel the contents of the stomach through the mouth; throw up what has been eaten. **2** the substance thrown up from the stomach. **3** throw out or come out with force: *The chimneys vomited smoke.* 1,3 *v.,* 2 *n.* —**vom′it er,** *n.*

voo doo (vü′dü), **1** religion that came from Africa, made up of mysterious rites and practices that include the use of sorcery and magic. Belief in voodoo still prevails in many parts of the West Indies and some parts of the southern United States. **2** person who practices voodoo. *n., pl.* **voo doos.** [*Voodoo* is from Creole French *voudou*, which came from a west African word.]

voo doo ism (vü′dü iz′əm), voodoo rites or practices. *n.*

vo ra cious (və rā′shəs), **1** eating much; greedy in eating; ravenous: *voracious sharks.* **2** very eager; unable to be satisfied: *He is a voracious reader of history. adj.* —**vo ra′cious ly,** *adv.*

vo rac i ty (və ras′ə tē), a being voracious. *n.*

vor tex (vôr/teks), a whirling mass or movement of water, air, etc., that sucks everything near it toward its center; whirlpool; whirlwind. *n., pl.* **vor tex es, vor ti ces** (vôr/tə sēz).

vote (vōt), **1** a formal expression of a choice on a proposal, motion, candidate for office, etc. A vote can be cast by a ballot or indicated by saying "aye" or "nay," holding up the hand, standing up, or otherwise. In an election the person receiving the most votes is elected. **2** the right to cast or indicate a vote. Children do not have the vote, and adults can lose it by being convicted of certain crimes. **3** ballot or other means by which a vote is cast or indicated: *More than a million votes were counted.* **4** what is expressed or granted by a majority of voters: *a vote of confidence.* **5** votes considered together: *the labor vote, the vote of the people.* **6** give or cast a vote: *I voted for that senator.* **7** support by one's vote: *vote the Republican ticket.* **8** pass, determine, or grant by a vote: *Money for a new school was voted by the board.* **9** declare: *The children all voted the trip a great success.* 1-5 *n.,* 6-9 *v.,* **vot ed, vot ing.**

vote down, defeat by voting against.

vote in, elect.

vot er (vō/tər), **1** person who votes. **2** person who has the right to vote. *n.*

voting machine, machine which records and counts votes in political elections.

vo tive (vō/tiv), promised by a vow; done, given, etc., because of a vow: *He lighted a votive candle. adj.*

vouch (vouch), be responsible; give a guarantee (for): *I can vouch for the truth of the story. v.* [*Vouch* came into English about 600 years ago from French *voucher,* which came from Latin *vocare,* meaning "to call."]

vouch er (vou/chər), written evidence of payment; receipt. Canceled checks returned from one's bank are vouchers. *n.*

vouch safe (vouch sāf/), be willing to grant or give; deign (to do or give): *She vouchsafed no reply to their rude, prying questions. v.,* **vouch safed, vouch saf ing.**

vow (vou), **1** a solemn promise: *a vow of secrecy, marriage vows.* **2** a promise made to God: *a nun's vows.* **3** make a vow: *I vowed never to leave home again.* **4** make a vow to do, give, get, etc.: *vow revenge.* 1,2 *n.,* 3,4 *v.* —**vow/er,** *n.* —**vow/less,** *adj.*

vow el (vou/əl), **1** a voiced speech sound produced by not blocking the breath with the lips, teeth, or tongue. A vowel can form a syllable by itself, as the first syllable of *awful* (ô/fəl). **2** letter that stands for such a sound. *A, e, i, o,* and *u* are vowels. *Y* is sometimes a vowel, as in *bicycle.* **3** of a vowel. *Voluntary* has four vowel sounds; *strength* has only one. 1,2 *n.,* 3 *adj.* [*Vowel* came into English about 600 years ago from French *vouel,* which came from Latin (*littera*) *vocalis,* meaning "sounded (letter)," and can be traced back to *vocem,* meaning "voice."] —**vow/el less,** *adj.* —**vow/el like/,** *adj.*

voy age (voi/ij), **1** a journey by water; cruise: *We had a pleasant voyage to England.* **2** a journey through the air or through space: *the earth's voyage around the sun.* **3** make or take a voyage; go by sea or air: *We voyaged across the Atlantic.* 1,2 *n.,* 3 *v.,* **voy aged, voy ag ing.**

voy ag er (voi/i jər), person who makes a voyage; traveler. *n.*

vo ya geur (vwä yä zhèr/), a French Canadian worker for the early fur-trading companies who transported people and supplies to and from remote places, especially by boat. *n., pl.* **vo ya geurs** (vwä yä zhèrz/).

VP, V.P., or **V.Pres.,** Vice-President.

vs. or **vs, 1** verse. **2** versus.

VT, Vermont (used with postal Zip Code).

Vt., Vermont.

v.t. or **vt,** transitive verb.

Vul can (vul/kən), (in Roman myths) the god of fire and metalworking. *n.*

vul can i za tion (vul/kə nə zā/shən), act or process of vulcanizing. *n.*

vul can ize (vul/kə nīz), treat (rubber) with sulfur and heat to make it more elastic and durable. *v.,* **vul can ized, vul can iz ing.** —**vul/can iz/er,** *n.*

vul gar (vul/gər), **1** showing a lack of good breeding, manners, taste, etc.; not refined; coarse; low: *use vulgar language.* **2** of the common people. *adj.* —**vul/gar ly,** *adv.* —**vul/gar ness,** *n.*

vul gar ism (vul/gə riz/əm), word, phrase, or expression used only in ignorant or coarse speech. In "I disrecollect his name," *disrecollect* is a vulgarism. *n.*

vul gar i ty (vul gar/ə tē), **1** lack of refinement; lack of good breeding, manners, taste, etc.; coarseness. **2** thing done or said that shows vulgarity; vulgar act or word: *Their vulgarities annoyed me. n., pl.* **vul gar i ties.**

vul gar ize (vul/gə rīz/), make vulgar or common; degrade or debase. *v.,* **vul gar ized, vul gar iz ing.** —**vul/gar i za/tion,** *n.* —**vul/gar iz/er,** *n.*

Vul gate (vul/gāt), the Latin translation of the Bible, made about A.D. 405 by Saint Jerome. It is the Bible used by the Roman Catholic Church. *n.*

vul ner a bil i ty (vul/nər ə bil/ə tē), vulnerable quality or condition; a being open to attack or injury. *n.*

vul ner a ble (vul/nər ə bəl), **1** capable of being wounded or injured; open to attack: *The army's retreat left the city vulnerable.* **2** sensitive to criticism, temptations, influences, etc.: *Most people are vulnerable to ridicule. adj.* —**vul/ner a ble ness,** *n.*

vul ner a bly (vul/nər ə blē), in a vulnerable manner. *adv.*

vul pine (vul/pīn), of or like a fox. *adj.*

vultures (def. 1) about 2½ ft. (75 cm.) long

vul ture (vul/chər), **1** a large bird of prey related to eagles, falcons, and hawks, that eats the flesh of dead animals. Vultures usually have featherless heads and necks. **2** a greedy, ruthless person. *n.* —**vul/ture like/,** *adj.*

vul va (vul/və), the external sex organs of the female animal. *n., pl.* **vul vae** (vul/vē), **vul vas.**

vy ing (vī/ing), **1** present participle of **vie.** *Members of the class were vying with each other for a position on the student council.* **2** competing. 1 *v.,* 2 *adj.* —**vy/ing ly,** *adv.*

a hat	**i** it	**oi** oil	**ch** child	⎡ a in about
ā age	**ī** ice	**ou** out	**ng** long	⎢ e in taken
ä far	**o** hot	**u** cup	**sh** she	ə = ⎨ i in pencil
e let	**ō** open	**ù** put	**th** thin	⎢ o in lemon
ē equal	**ô** order	**ü** rule	**ŦH** then	⎣ u in circus
ėr term			**zh** measure	

W or **w** (dub′əl yü), the 23rd letter of the English alphabet. *n., pl.* **W's** or **w's.**

w, watt or watts.

W, 1 west. 2 western. 3 symbol for tungsten.

w., 1 watt or watts. 2 week or weeks. 3 weight. 4 west. 5 western. 6 width.

W., 1 Wales. 2 Wednesday. 3 west. 4 western.

WA, Washington (used with postal Zip Code).

Wa bash (wô′bash), river flowing from W Ohio southwest across Indiana into the Ohio River. *n.*

wab ble (wob′əl), wobble. *v.,* **wab bled, wab bling;** *n.* **—wab′bler,** *n.*

wab bly (wob′lē), wobbly. *adj.,* **wab bli er, wab bli est. —wab′bli ness,** *n.*

WAC or **Wac** (wak), formerly, woman in the United States Army other than a nurse. *n.* [*WAC* comes from the words *Women's Army Corps.* It was formed from the first letter of each of these words.]

wack y (wak′ē), SLANG. odd; crazy; unconventional. *adj.,* **wack i er, wack i est. —wack′i ly,** *adv.* **—wack′i ness,** *n.*

wad (wod), 1 a small, soft mass: *I plugged my ears with wads of cotton.* 2 a tight roll; compact bundle or mass: *a wad of chewing gum.* 3 make into a wad; press into a wad: *I wadded up the paper and threw it away.* 4 a round plug of felt, cardboard, etc., used to hold powder and shot in place in a gun or cartridge. 5 stuff with a wad. 6 hold in place by a wad. 7 fill out with padding; pad. 1,2,4 *n.,* 3,5-7 *v.,* **wad ded, wad ding.**

wad dle (wod′l), 1 walk with short steps and an awkward, swaying motion, as a duck does: *The toddler waddled from the house bundled in his snowsuit.* 2 act of waddling: *He made us laugh by imitating the waddle of a duck.* 3 an awkward, swaying way of walking. 1 *v.,* **waddled, wad dling;** 2,3 *n.* **—wad′dler,** *n.*

wade (wād), 1 walk through water, snow, sand, mud, or anything that hinders free motion. 2 make one's way with difficulty: *Must I wade through that dull book?* 3 cross or pass through by wading: *wade a stream.* *v.,* **wad ed, wad ing.**

wade into, INFORMAL. attack or go to work upon vigorously.

wad er (wā′dər), 1 person or thing that wades. 2 a long-legged bird that wades about in shallow water, searching for food. Cranes, herons, storks, and sandpipers are waders. 3 a high, waterproof boot. *n.*

WAF or **Waf** (waf), formerly, woman in the United States Air Force other than a nurse. *n.* [*WAF* comes from the words *Women in the Air Force.* It was formed from the first letter of *Women, Air,* and *Force.*]

waf er (wā′fər), 1 a very thin cake or biscuit, sometimes flavored or sweetened. 2 the thin, round piece of unleavened bread used in Holy Communion in certain churches, especially the Roman Catholic Church. 3 a thin piece of candy, chocolate, medicine, etc. 4 piece of sticky paper, dried paste, etc., used as a seal or fastening. *n.* **—waf′er like′,** *adj.*

waf fle (wof′əl *or* wô′fəl), a batter cake cooked in a waffle iron until brown and crisp, usually eaten while hot with butter, syrup, etc. *n.* [*Waffle* comes from Dutch *wafel.*]

waffle iron, utensil in which waffles are cooked, consisting of two hinged parts having projections on the inside that make the cakes very thin in places.

waft (waft *or* wäft), 1 carry over water or through air: *The waves wafted the boat to shore.* 2 a breath or puff of air, wind, scent, etc.: *A waft of fresh air came through the open window.* 1 *v.,* 2 *n.* **—waft′er,** *n.*

wag (wag), 1 move from side to side or up and down, especially rapidly and repeatedly: *The dog wagged its tail.* 2 a wagging motion: *She refused with a wag of her head.* 3 person who is fond of making jokes. 1 *v.,* **wagged, wag ging;** 2,3 *n.* **—wag′ger,** *n.*

wage (wāj), 1 Usually, **wages,** *pl. or sing.* **a** amount paid for work: *wages of $200 a week.* **b** something given in return: *"The wages of sin is death."* 2 carry on: *Doctors wage war against disease.* 1 *n.,* 2 *v.,* **waged, wag ing. —wage′less,** *adj.*

wage earner, person who works for wages.

wa ger (wā′jər), 1 make a bet; bet; gamble: *I'll wager the black horse will win the race.* 2 act of betting; bet: *The wager of $10 was promptly paid.* 1 *v.,* 2 *n.* **—wa′ger er,** *n.*

wag ger y (wag′ər ē), 1 act or habit of joking. 2 a joke. *n., pl.* **wag ger ies.**

wag gish (wag′ish), 1 fond of making jokes. 2 characteristic of a wag; funny; humorous: *a waggish remark.* *adj.* **—wag′gish ly,** *adv.* **—wag′gish ness,** *n.*

wag gle (wag′əl), 1 move quickly and repeatedly from side to side; wag. 2 a waggling motion. 1 *v.,* **wag gled, wag gling;** 2 *n.* **—wag′gling ly,** *adv.*

Wag ner (väg′nər), Richard, 1813-1883, German composer. *n.*

wag on (wag′ən), a four-wheeled vehicle, especially one for carrying loads: *a milk wagon.* *n.* [*Wagon* comes from Dutch *wagen.*]

wag on er (wag′ə nər), person who drives a wagon. *n.*

wag on load (wag′ən lōd′), amount that a wagon can hold or carry. *n.*

waif (wāf), 1 a homeless or neglected child. 2 anything without an owner; stray thing, animal, etc. *n.*

wail (wāl), 1 cry loud and long because of grief or pain: *The baby wailed.* 2 a long cry of grief or pain. 3 a sound like such a cry: *the wail of a hungry coyote.* 4 make a mournful sound: *The wind wailed around the old house.* 5 lament; mourn. 1,4,5 *v.,* 2,3 *n.* **—wail′er,** *n.*

wain (wān), OLD USE. wagon. *n.*

wainscot (def. 3)

wain scot (wān′skot *or* wān′skət), 1 a lining of wood, usually in panels, on the walls of a room. 2 line with wood: *a room wainscoted in oak.* 3 the lower part of the wall of a room when it is decorated differently from the upper part. 1,3 *n.,* 2 *v.*

wain scot ing (wān′skō ting *or* wān′skə ting), **1** wainscot. **2** material used for wainscots. *n.*

waist (wāst), **1** the part of the human body between the ribs and the hips. **2** waistline. **3** garment or part of a garment covering the body from the neck or shoulders to the waistline; blouse or bodice. *n.*

waist band (wāst′band′), a band around the waist: *the waistband of a skirt or of a pair of trousers. n.*

waist coat (wāst′kōt *or* wes′kət), BRITISH. a man's vest. *n.*

waist line (wāst′līn′), **1** line around the body at the smallest part of the waist. **2** place of smallest width in a woman's dress between the arms and the knees. **3** line where the waist and skirt of a dress join. *n.*

wait (wāt), **1** stay or stop doing something until someone comes or something happens: *Let's wait in the shade.* **2** act or time of waiting: *I had a long wait at the doctor's office.* **3** look forward; be expecting or ready: *The children wait impatiently for vacation.* **4** be left undone; be put off: *That matter can wait until tomorrow.* **5** INFORMAL. delay or put off: *Wait dinner for me.* **6** act as a servant; change plates, pass food, etc., at table. 1,3-6 *v.,* 2 *n.*
lie in wait, stay hidden ready to attack: *Robbers lay in wait for the caravan.*
wait on *or* **wait upon, 1** be a servant to; serve, especially at the table: *wait on hotel guests.* **2** call on (a superior) to pay a respectful visit: *The victorious general waited upon the king.*

wait er (wā′tər), man who waits on table in a hotel, restaurant, etc. *n.*

wait ing (wā′ting), **1** that waits: *The waiting crowd rushed to get on the bus.* **2** time that one waits. 1 *adj.,* 2 *n.*
in waiting, in attendance on a king, queen, prince, princess, etc.

waiting room, room at a railroad station, doctor's office, etc., for people to wait in.

wai tress (wā′tris), woman who waits on table in a hotel, restaurant, etc. *n., pl.* **wai tress es.**

waive (wāv), **1** give up (a right, claim, etc.); refrain from claiming or pressing; do without; relinquish: *The lawyer waived the privilege of cross-examining the witness.* **2** put aside; defer. *v.,* **waived, waiv ing.**

waiv er (wā′vər), **1** a giving up of a right, claim, etc.; a waiving. **2** a written statement of this: *The injured man signed a waiver of all claims against the railroad. n.*

wake[1] (wāk), **1** stop sleeping: *I usually wake at dawn. She wakes up at seven every morning.* **2** cause to stop sleeping: *The noise of the traffic always wakes the baby. Wake me up early.* **3** be awake; stay awake: *Does she sleep or wake?* **4** become alive or active: *The flowers wake in the spring.* **5** make alive or active: *He needs some interest to wake him up.* **6** an all-night watch kept beside the body of a dead person before its burial. 1-5 *v.,* **waked** or **woke, waked** or **wo ken, wak ing;** 6 *n.*

wake[2] (wāk), **1** track left behind a moving ship. **2** track left behind any moving thing. *n.*
in the wake of, behind; after: *floods coming in the wake of a hurricane.*

wake ful (wāk′fəl), **1** not able to sleep. **2** without sleep. **3** watchful. *adj.* —**wake′ful ly,** *adv.* —**wake′ful ness,** *n.*

Wake Island, small island in the N Pacific, about 2000 miles west of Hawaii, belonging to the United States.

wak en (wā′kən), wake. *v.*

wale (wāl), **1** a streak or ridge made on the skin by a stick or whip; welt. **2** to mark with wales; raise wales on. **3** a ridge in the weave of cloth. 1,3 *n.,* 2 *v.,* **waled, wal ing.**

Wales (wālz), division of Great Britain west of England; the land of the Welsh. *Capital:* Cardiff. See **United Kingdom** for map. *n.*

walk (wôk), **1** go on foot. In walking, a person always has one foot on the ground. *Walk down to the post office with me.* **2** go over, on, or through: *walk the length of a trail.* **3** cause to walk; make go slowly: *The rider walked the horse up the hill.* **4** act of walking, especially for pleasure or exercise: *We went for a walk in the country.* **5** accompany or escort in walking; conduct on foot: *walk a guest to the door.* **6** distance to walk: *It is a long walk from here.* **7** manner or way of walking; gait: *We could tell she was happy from her lively walk.* **8** place for walking; path: *There are many pretty walks in the park.* **9** social position; rank; occupation: *Your walk of life is different from mine.* **10** in baseball: **a** go to first base after the pitcher has thrown four balls. **b** a going to first base after four balls. **c** allow a batter to reach first base by pitching four balls. 1-3,5,10a,10c *v.,* 4,6-9,10b *n.* —**walk′er,** *n.*

walk ie-talk ie (wô′kē tô′kē), a small, portable receiving and transmitting radio set. It is powered by a battery and has an antenna. *n., pl.* **walk ie-talk ies.**

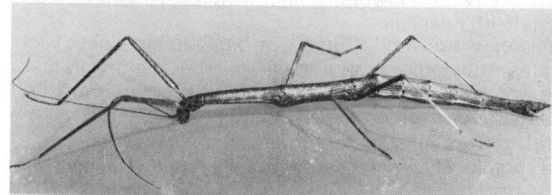

walking stick (def. 2)—up to 6 in. (15 cm.) long

walking stick, 1 cane. **2** any of various insects having a body like a stick or twig.

walk out (wôk′out′), **1** strike of workers. **2** a sudden departure from a room, meeting, etc., usually as a form of protest. *n.*

walk o ver (wôk′ō′vər), an easy victory. *n.*

walk-up (wôk′up′), an apartment house or building having no elevator. *n.*

walk way (wôk′wā′), **1** structure for walking: *an overhead steel walkway.* **2** path; walk. *n.*

wall (wôl), **1** side of a house, room, or other hollow thing. **2** structure of stone, brick, or other material built up to enclose, divide, support, or protect. Cities used to be surrounded by high walls to keep out enemies. **3** something like a wall in looks or use: *a wall of water ten feet high, a wall of ignorance. The mayor met a solid wall of protesters.* **4** enclose, divide, protect, or fill with or as if with a wall: *wall a garden, wall out the noise of the city.* 1-3 *n.,* 4 *v.* —**wall′-less,** *adj.* —**wall′-like′,** *adj.*
drive to the wall, make desperate or helpless: *Poverty drove them to the wall.*

wal la by (wol′ə bē), any of various small kangaroos. Some wallabies are no larger than rabbits. *n., pl.* **wal la bies** or **wal la by.** [*Wallaby* comes from *wolabā,* its native name in Australia.]

wall board (wôl′bôrd′), any building material, such as plasterboard or fiberboard, made by pressing wood pulp, plaster, etc., into large, flat sheets. Wallboard is used instead of wood or plaster to make or cover inside walls. *n.*

wal let (wol′it *or* wô′lit), **1** a small, flat, leather case for carrying paper money, cards, etc., in one's pocket; folding pocketbook; billfold. **2** bag for carrying food and small articles for personal use when on a journey. *n.*

wall eye (wôl′ī′), a walleyed pike. *n.*

wall eyed (wôl′īd′), **1** having eyes that show much white and little color. **2** having one or both eyes turned away from the nose, so as to show much white. **3** having large, staring eyes, as a fish. *adj.* [*Walleyed* came into

English about 600 years ago from Icelandic *vagl-eygr,* which comes from *vagl,* meaning "a speck in the eye," and *auga,* meaning "the eye.")

walleyed pike, a large freshwater fish with large, staring eyes, used for food.

wall flow er (wôl′flou′ər), **1** INFORMAL. person who sits by the wall at a dance instead of dancing. **2** a perennial plant with sweet-smelling yellow, orange, or red flowers, found growing on walls, cliffs, etc. *n.*

wal lop (wol′əp), INFORMAL. **1** beat soundly; thrash. **2** hit very hard; strike with a vigorous blow. **3** a very hard blow: *The wallop knocked me down.* **4** power to hit very hard blows. **5** defeat thoroughly, as in a game. 1,2,5 *v.,* 3,4 *n.* —**wal′lop er,** *n.*

wal low (wol′ō), **1** roll about; flounder: *The pigs wallowed in the mud. The boat wallowed helplessly in the stormy sea.* **2** live contentedly in filth, wickedness, etc. **3** live or delight self-indulgently or luxuriously in some form of pleasure, manner of life, etc.: *wallow in wealth, wallow in sentimentality.* **4** act of wallowing. **5** place where an animal wallows. 1-3 *v.,* 4,5 *n.* —**wal′low er,** *n.*

wall pa per (wôl′pā′pər), **1** paper, usually printed with a pattern in color, for pasting on and covering walls. **2** put wallpaper on. 1 *n.,* 2 *v.*

Wall Street, 1 street in downtown New York City that is the chief financial center of the United States. **2** the money market or the financiers of the United States.

wal nut (wôl′nut), **1** a rather large, almost round nut with a hard, ridged shell and a division between its two halves. The meat of the walnut is eaten by itself, used in cakes and candy, etc. **2** the tree that it grows on. **3** the wood of this tree. Some kinds of walnut are used in making furniture. *n.* [*Walnut* comes from Old English *wealhhnutu,* originally meaning "foreign nut." The nut was called this because it was introduced from southern Europe and therefore was "foreign" to England.]

wal rus (wôl′rəs *or* wol′rəs), a large sea mammal of the arctic regions, resembling a seal but having long tusks. Walruses are hunted for their hides, tusks, and blubber oil. *n., pl.* **wal rus es** *or* **wal rus.**

WORD HISTORY

walrus

Walrus was borrowed from Dutch *walrus,* which comes from *walvisch,* meaning "a whale," and *ros,* meaning "a horse."

up to 11 ft. (3.5 m.) long

waltz (wôlts), **1** a smooth, even, gliding dance with three beats to a measure. **2** music for it. **3** dance a waltz. 1,2 *n., pl.* **waltz es;** 3 *v.* [*Waltz* is from German *Walzer,* which comes from *walzen,* meaning "to roll, dance."]

a hat	i it	oi oil	ch child	a in about
ā age	ī ice	ou out	ng long	e in taken
ä far	o hot	u cup	sh she	ə = i in pencil
e let	ō open	u̇ put	th thin	o in lemon
ē equal	ô order	ü rule	ᵺ then	u in circus
ėr term			zh measure	

wam pum (wom′pəm *or* wôm′pəm), beads made from shells, formerly used by North American Indians as money and for ornament. *n.* [*Wampum* was shortened from *wampumpeag,* which comes from a North American Indian word *wampompeag,* meaning "strings of white shell beads."]

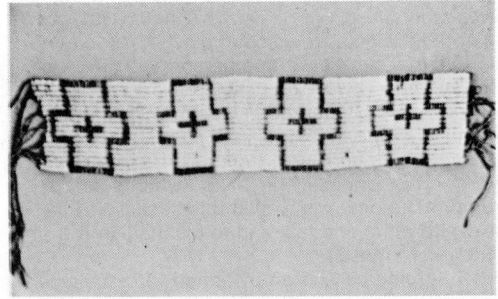

wampum

wan (won), **1** lacking natural color; pale: *Her face looked wan after her long illness.* **2** looking worn or tired; faint; weak: *The sick boy gave the doctor a wan smile.* *adj.,* **wan ner, wan nest.** —**wan′ly,** *adv.* —**wan′ness,** *n.*

wand (wond), a slender stick or rod: *a magician's wand.* *n.*

wan der (won′dər), **1** move here and there without any special purpose: *We wandered around the fair, looking at exhibits.* **2** follow an uncertain or irregular course; meander: *a driver who wanders all over the road.* **3** go from the right way; stray: *The dog wandered off and got lost. The speaker wandered away from the subject.* **4** not be able to think sensibly; be delirious or incoherent: *A high fever sometimes makes a person's mind wander.* *v.* —**wan′der er,** *n.*

wan der lust (won′dər lust′), a strong desire to wander: *Her wanderlust led her all over the world.* *n.*

wane (wān), **1** lose size; become smaller gradually: *The moon wanes after it has become full.* **2** lose power, influence, or importance: *Many great empires have waned.* **3** lose strength or intensity: *The light of day wanes in the evening.* **4** draw to a close: *Summer wanes as autumn approaches.* **5** a waning. 1-4 *v.,* waned, wan ing; 5 *n.* **on the wane,** growing less; waning.

wan gle (wang′gəl), INFORMAL. **1** manage to get by schemes, tricks, persuasion, etc.: *wangle an interview with a TV star.* **2** make one's way through difficulties. *v.,* wan gled, wan gling. —**wan′gler,** *n.*

Wan kel en gine (wong′kəl), an internal-combustion engine with few moving parts. It produces power by the spinning of (usually) two triangular rotors in an oval combustion chamber. [The *Wankel engine* was named for Felix *Wankel,* born in 1902, a German engineer who invented it.]

want (wont *or* wônt), **1** wish for; wish: *We want a new car. I want to become an engineer.* **2** thing desired or needed; desire: *a person having few wants.* **3** be without; lack: *The fund wants half of the sum needed.* **4** condition of being without something desired or needed; a lack: *The plant died from want of water.* **5** to need; require: *Plants want water.* **6** a need: *supply a long-felt want.* **7** a lack of food, clothing, or shelter; great poverty: *Those old people are in want.* **8** need food, clothing, and shelter; be very poor. **9** wish to see, speak to, or use (a person): *Call me if you want me. You are the one we want for the job.* **10** seek after to catch or arrest: *wanted by the police.* 1,3,5,8-10 *v.,* 2,4,6,7 *n.*

want ad, a small notice in a newspaper stating that an employee, an apartment, etc., is wanted.

want ing (won′ting *or* wôn′ting), **1** not found or in evidence; lacking; missing: *One volume of the set is wanting.* **2** without; less; minus: *a year wanting three days.* **3** not satisfactory; not coming up to a standard or need: *The vegetables were weighed and found wanting.* 1,3 *adj.,* 2 *prep.*

wan ton (won′tən), **1** done in a reckless, heartless, or malicious way; done without reason or excuse: *a wanton attack, wanton mischief, wanton cruelty.* **2** not moral; not chaste. **3** not restrained; frolicsome; playful: *a wanton breeze, a wanton mood.* **4** a wanton person. 1-3 *adj.,* 4 *n.* —**wan′ton ly,** *adv.* —**wan′ton ness,** *n.*

wap i ti (wop′ə tē), a large, reddish deer of North America, with long, slender antlers; elk. *n., pl.* **wap i tis** *or* **wap i ti.** [*Wapiti* was borrowed from a North American Indian word *wapiti,* originally meaning "white deer" or "white rump." The deer was called this because of its yellowish-white rump and tail, and to distinguish it from the much darker moose.]

war (wôr), **1** fighting carried on by armed force between nations or parts of a nation. **2** any fighting or struggle; strife; conflict: *Doctors carry on war against disease.* **3** the occupation or art of fighting with weapons: *Soldiers are trained for war.* **4** make war; fight: *to war with an aggressor, to war against poverty.* **5** of war; used in war; caused by war: *war weapons, war crimes, war casualties.* 1-3 *n.,* 4 *v.,* **warred, war ring;** 5 *adj.* —**war′less,** *adj.*

War Between the States, the American Civil War.

war ble (wôr′bəl), **1** sing with trills, quavers, or melodious turns: *Birds warbled in the trees.* **2** make a sound like that of a bird warbling: *The brook warbled over its rocky bed.* **3** a bird's song or a sound like it. 1,2 *v.,* **war bled, war bling;** 3 *n.*

war bler (wôr′blər), **1** any of a large group of small songbirds, often brightly colored. **2** one that warbles; singer. *n.*

war bonnet, a ceremonial headdress set with feathers and often a long trailing piece with feathers, worn by certain North American Indians.

war cry, battle cry.

ward (wôrd), **1** a division of a hospital or prison. **2** district of a city or town. **3** person under the care of a guardian or of a court. *n.*

ward off, keep away; turn aside: *ward off a blow, ward off an illness.*

-ward, *suffix forming adverbs.* in the direction of _____; toward _____: *Homeward* = *in the direction of home. Backward* = *toward the back.* Also, **-wards.**

ward en (wôrd′n), **1** the official in charge of a prison. **2** any official who enforces certain laws and regulations: *an air-raid warden, a fire warden. n.*

ward er (wôr′dər), **1** guard or watchman. **2** BRITISH. warden or jailer. *n.*

ward robe (wôrd′rōb′), **1** stock of clothes: *a spring wardrobe.* **2** room, closet, or piece of furniture for holding clothes. *n.*

-wards, *suffix forming adverbs.* in the direction of _____; toward _____: *Backwards* = *in the direction of or toward the back.* Also, **-ward.**

ware (wer *or* war), **1** Usually, **wares,** *pl.* a manufactured thing; article for sale: *The peddler sold his wares cheap.* **2** kind of manufactured thing or article for sale: *copper ware.* **3** earthenware; pottery: *porcelain ware. n.*

ware house (wer′hous′ *or* war′hous′), place where goods are kept; storehouse. *n., pl.* **ware hous es** (wer′hou′ziz *or* war′hou′ziz).

war fare (wôr′fer′ *or* wôr′far′), war; fighting. *n.*

war head (wôr′hed′), the forward part of a torpedo, missile, etc., that contains the explosive. *n.*

war horse, 1 horse used in war; charger. **2** INFORMAL. person who has taken part in many battles, struggles, etc.; veteran.

war i ly (wer′ə lē *or* war′ə lē), in a wary manner; cautiously; carefully: *The hikers climbed warily up the dangerous path. adv.*

war i ness (wer′ē nis *or* war′ē nis), caution; care. *n.*

war like (wôr′līk′), **1** fit for war; ready for war; fond of war: *a warlike nation.* **2** threatening war; hostile: *a warlike speech. adj.*

war lock (wôr′lok), a male witch; wizard. *n.*

warm (wôrm), **1** more hot than cold; having some heat; giving forth moderate or gentle heat: *a warm fire. She sat in the warm sunshine.* **2** having a feeling of heat: *be warm from running.* **3** able to keep in body heat: *a warm coat.* **4** having or showing affection, enthusiasm, or zeal: *a warm welcome, a warm heart.* **5** easily excited: *a warm temper.* **6** exciting; lively: *a warm dispute.* **7** fresh and strong: *a warm scent.* **8** (in games, treasure hunts, etc.) near what one is searching for. **9** suggesting heat. Red, orange, and yellow are called warm colors. **10** make or become warm: *warm a room.* **11** make or become cheered, interested, friendly, or sympathetic: *The speaker warmed to his subject.* 1-9 *adj.,* 10,11 *v.* —**warm′ly,** *adv.* —**warm′ness,** *n.*

warm up, 1 heat or cook again. **2** make or become more interested, friendly, etc. **3** to practice or exercise for a few minutes before entering a game, contest, etc. **4** run (a machine) before using it until it reaches its normal working condition.

warm-blood ed (wôrm′blud′id), **1** having blood that stays about the same temperature regardless of the air or water around the animal. Birds and mammals are warm-blooded; reptiles, turtles, fishes, etc., are cold-blooded. **2** with much feeling; eager. *adj.*

warm front, the advancing edge of a warm air mass as it passes over and displaces a cooler one.

warm heart ed (wôrm′här′tid), kind; sympathetic; friendly. *adj.*

warming pan, a covered pan with a long handle for holding hot coals, formerly used to warm beds.

war mon ger (wôr′mong′gər), person who is in favor of war or attempts to bring about war. *n.*

warmth (wôrmth), **1** a being warm: *the warmth of the open fire.* **2** warm or friendly feeling: *the warmth of our host's welcome.* **3** liveliness of feelings or emotions; fervor: *She spoke with warmth of the natural beauty of the country. n.*

warm-up (wôrm′up′), **1** practice or exercise taken for a few minutes before entering a game, contest, etc. **2** period of running required for a machine to reach normal working condition before use. *n.*

warn (wôrn), **1** give notice to in advance; put on guard (against danger, evil, harm, etc.): *The children were warned not to speak to strangers.* **2** give notice to; inform: *The whistle warned visitors that the ship was ready to sail. v.*

warn ing (wôr′ning), something that warns; notice given in advance. *n.* —**warn′ing ly,** *adv.*

War of 1812, war between the United States and Great Britain. It lasted from 1812 to 1815.

War of Independence, Revolutionary War.

warp (wôrp), **1** bend or twist out of shape: *This floor has warped so that it is not level.* **2** mislead; pervert: *Prejudice* *warps our judgment.* **3** a bend or twist; distortion. **4** move (a ship, etc.) by ropes fastened to something fixed. **5** the threads running lengthwise in a fabric. The warp is crossed by the woof. **6** a supposed distortion in time or space that enables a person to pass abruptly between two points normally far apart: *a time warp linking the present and 1930.* 1,2,4 *v.*, 3,5,6 *n.* **—warp′er,** *n.*

WARP →

warp (def. 5)

a hat	**i** it	**oi** oil	**ch** child	a in about
ā age	**ī** ice	**ou** out	**ng** long	e in taken
ä far	**o** hot	**u** cup	**sh** she	ə = i in pencil
e let	**ō** open	**ů** put	**th** thin	o in lemon
ē equal	**ô** order	**ü** rule	**ᴛʜ** then	u in circus
ėr term			**zh** measure	

war path (wôr′path′), the way taken by a fighting expedition of North American Indians. *n., pl.* **war paths** (wôr′paᴛʜz′ *or* wôr′paths′).

on the warpath, 1 ready for war. **2** looking for a fight; angry.

war plane (wôr′plān′), airplane used in war. *n.*

war rant (wôr′ənt *or* wor′ənt), **1** that which gives a right; authority: *He had no warrant to tell us how to behave.* **2** a written order giving authority for something: *a warrant to search the house.* **3** authorize: *The law warrants their arrest.* **4** justify: *Nothing warrants such rudeness.* **5** give one's word for; guarantee; promise: *The company warranted the quality of their cameras.* **6** declare positively; certify: *I'll warrant they won't try that again.* 1,2 *n.*, 3-6 *v.*

warrant officer, (in the armed forces) an officer who has received a certificate of appointment, but not a commission, ranking between commissioned officers and enlisted men.

war ran ty (wôr′ən tē *or* wor′ən tē), **1** warrant or authorization. **2** a promise or pledge that something is what it is claimed to be; guarantee: *a warranty of the quality of the goods sold.* *n., pl.* **war ran ties.**

war ren (wôr′ən *or* wor′ən), **1** piece of ground filled with burrows, where rabbits live or are raised. **2** a crowded district or building. *n.*

War ren (wôr′ən *or* wor′ən), **Earl,** 1891-1974, chief justice of the United States Supreme Court from 1953 to 1969. *n.*

war ri or (wôr′ē ər *or* wor′ē ər), person experienced in fighting battles. *n.* [*Warrior* came into English about 700 years ago from French *werreieor*, and can be traced back to *werre*, meaning "war."] **—war′ri or like′,** *adj.*

War saw (wôr′sô), capital and largest city of Poland, in the E part. *n.*

war ship (wôr′ship′), ship armed for war. *n.*

wart (wôrt), **1** a small, hard lump on the skin. **2** a similar lump on a plant. *n.* **—wart′like′,** *adj.*

wart hog, a wild hog of Africa that has two large tusks

wart hog—up to 2¹/₂ ft. (75 cm.) high at the shoulder

and large, wartlike growths on each side of its face.

war time (wôr′tīm′), **1** a time of war. **2** of a time of war. 1 *n.*, 2 *adj.*

war y (wer′ē *or* war′ē), **1** on one's guard against danger, deception, etc.: *a wary fox.* **2** cautious or careful: *give wary answers to a stranger's questions.* *adj.*, **war i er, war i est.**

wary of, cautious or careful about: *Be wary of gossip.*

was (woz *or* wuz; *unstressed* wəz), form of the verb **be** used with *I, he, she, it,* or any singular noun to indicate the past tense. *I was late. Was he late, too? v.*

wash (wosh *or* wôsh), **1** clean with water or other liquid: *wash one's face, wash clothes, wash dishes.* **2** remove (dirt, stains, paint, etc.) by or as by scrubbing with soap and water: *Can you wash that spot out?* **3** wash oneself: *I washed before eating dinner.* **4** wash clothes: *I have to wash today.* **5** make clean or free from guilt, corruption, etc.; purify: *washed from sin.* **6** a washing or a being washed: *This floor needs a good wash.* **7** quantity of clothes washed or to be washed: *Take the wash from the dryer.* **8** undergo washing without damage: *That cloth washes well.* **9** carry or be carried along or away by water or other liquid: *Wood is often washed ashore by the waves.* **10** material carried along by moving water and then deposited as sediment. A delta is formed by the wash of a river. **11** wear (by water or any liquid): *The cliffs are being washed away by the waves.* **12** to flow or beat with a lapping sound: *The waves washed upon the rocks.* **13** motion, rush, or sound of water: *We listened to the wash of the waves against the boat.* **14** make wet: *The flowers are washed with dew.* **15** tract of land sometimes overflowed with water and sometimes left dry; tract of shallow water; fen, marsh, or bog. **16** liquid for a special use: *an eye wash.* **17** waste liquid matter; liquid garbage: *The kitchen wash is given to the pigs.* **18** a thin coating of color or metal. **19** cover with a thin coating of color or of metal: *silver washed with gold.* **20** sift (earth, ore, etc.) by action of water to separate. **21** the rough or broken water left behind a moving ship. **22** disturbance in air made by an airplane or any of its parts. 1-5,8,9,11,12,14,19,20 *v.*, 6,7,10,13,15-18,21,22 *n., pl.* **wash es.**

wash down, 1 wash from top to bottom or from end to end: *wash down the walls of a kitchen.* **2** drink some liquid along with or after solid food to help in swallowing.

wash up, wash one's hands and face, as before eating.

Wash., the state of Washington.

wash a ble (wosh′ə bəl *or* wô′shə bəl), able to be washed without damage: *washable silk. adj.*

wash-and-wear (wosh′ən wer′, wosh′ən war′, wôsh′ən wer′, *or* wôsh′ən war′), specially treated to require little or no ironing after washing and drying: *wash-and-wear fabrics. adj.*

wash ba sin (wosh′bā′sn *or* wôsh′bā′sn), washbowl. *n.*

wash board (wosh′bôrd′ *or* wôsh′bôrd′), a board with ridges on it, used for rubbing the dirt out of clothes. *n.*

wash bowl (wosh′bōl′ *or* wôsh′bōl′), bowl for holding water to wash one's hands and face; washbasin. *n.*

wash cloth (wosh′klôth′ *or* wôsh′klôth′), a small cloth for washing oneself. *n., pl.* **wash cloths** (wosh′klôᴛʜz′, wosh′klôths′, wôsh′klôᴛʜz′, *or* wôsh′klôths′).

washed-out (wosht′out′ *or* wôsht′out′), **1** lacking color; faded. **2** INFORMAL. lacking life, spirit, etc. *adj.*

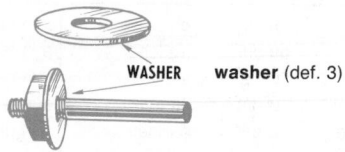

WASHER washer (def. 3)

wash er (wosh′ər *or* wô′shər), **1** person who washes. **2** machine that washes. **3** a flat ring of metal, rubber, leather, etc., used with bolts or nuts, to make joints tight. *n.*

wash ing (wosh′ing *or* wô′shing), **1** a cleaning with water. **2** clothes, etc., washed or to be washed: *send washing to the laundry.* **3** matter removed in washing something: *washings of gold obtained from earth. n.*

washing machine, machine that washes clothes.

Wash ing ton (wosh′ing tən *or* wô′shing tən), **1** capital of the United States, covering the entire District of Columbia. Washington is situated along the Potomac River between Maryland and Virginia. **2** one of the Pacific states of the United States. *Abbreviation:* Wash. *or* WA *Capital:* Olympia. **3 Booker T.,** 1856-1915, American writer and educator who worked for civil rights. **4 George,** 1732-1799, commander in chief of the American army in the Revolutionary War and the first president of the United States, from 1789 to 1797. **5 Martha,** 1731-1802, wife of George Washington. *n.*

wash out (wosh′out′ *or* wôsh′out′), **1** a washing away of earth, a road, etc., by water. **2** the hole or break made by it. **3** INFORMAL. failure; disappointment: *The party was a complete washout. n.*

wash room (wosh′rüm′, wosh′rum′, wôsh′rüm′, *or* wôsh′rum′), room where toilet facilities are provided; lavatory. *n.*

wash stand (wosh′stand′ *or* wôsh′stand′), **1** bowl with pipes and faucets for running water to wash one's hands and face. **2** stand for holding a basin, pitcher, etc., for washing. *n.*

wash tub (wosh′tub′ *or* wôsh′tub′), tub used to wash or soak clothes in. *n.*

was n't (woz′nt *or* wuz′nt), was not.

wasp (wosp *or* wôsp), insect related to the ants and the bees, having a slender body, two pairs of wings, and a powerful sting. Hornets and yellow jackets are kinds of wasps. *n.*

WASP (wosp *or* wôsp), a white Anglo-Saxon Protestant. The use of this term is often considered offensive. *n.*

wasp ish (wos′pish *or* wô′spish), **1** like a wasp; like that of a wasp. **2** bad-tempered; irritable. *adj.* —**wasp′ish ly,** *adv.* —**wasp′ish ness,** *n.*

was sail (wos′əl), **1** a drinking party; revelry with drinking of healths. **2** take part in a wassail; revel. **3** spiced ale or other liquor drunk at a wassail. **4** salutation wishing good health or good luck to a person, used especially in England in former times when drinking a toast. **5** to drink to the health of. 1,3,4 *n.,* 2,5 *v.,* 4 *interj.* [*Wassail* came into English about 800 years ago from Icelandic *ves heill,* meaning "be healthy!"]

wast (wost), OLD USE. were. "Thou wast" means "you were." *v.*

wast age (wā′stij), **1** loss by use, wear, decay, leakage, etc.; waste. **2** amount wasted. *n.*

waste (wāst), **1** make poor use of; spend uselessly; fail to get full value or benefit from: *Though I had much work to do, I wasted my time doing nothing.* **2** poor use; useless spending; failure to get the most out of something: *Buying that suit was a waste of money; it is already starting to wear out.* **3** thrown away as useless or worthless: *waste products,* a pile of *waste* lumber. **4** useless or worthless material; stuff to be thrown away; refuse: *Garbage or*

sewage is *waste.* **5** carrying off or holding refuse: *a waste drain.* **6** left over; not used: *waste food.* **7** stuff that is left over. Bunches of cotton waste are used to clean machinery. **8** bare or wild land; desert; wilderness: *We traveled through treeless wastes.* **9** not cultivated; that is a desert or wilderness; bare; wild. **10** wear down little by little; destroy or lose gradually: *The patient was wasted by disease.* **11** a wearing down little by little; gradual destruction or loss: *Both waste and repair are constantly going on in our bodies.* **12** damage greatly; destroy; spoil; ruin: *The soldiers wasted the enemy's fields.* 1,10,12 *v.,* **wast ed, wast ing;** 2,4,7,8,11 *n.,* 3,5,6,9 *adj.* [*Waste* came into English about 800 years ago from French *waster,* and can be traced back to Latin *vastus,* meaning "vast, waste."]

go to waste, be wasted.

lay waste, damage greatly; destroy; ravage.

waste bas ket (wāst′bas′kit), basket or other container for wastepaper. *n.*

waste ful (wāst′fəl), using or spending too much: *be wasteful of water. adj.* —**waste′ful ly,** *adv.* —**waste′ful ness,** *n.*

waste land (wāst′land′), barren, uncultivated land. *n.*

waste pa per (wāst′pā′pər), paper thrown away or to be thrown away as useless or worthless. *n.*

wast rel (wā′strəl), **1** spendthrift. **2** good-for-nothing. *n.*

watch (woch *or* wôch), **1** look attentively or carefully: *The medical students watched while the surgeon performed the operation.* **2** look at; observe; view: *Let's watch television.* **3** look or wait with care and attention; be very careful: *I watched for a chance to cross the street.* **4** a careful looking; attitude of attention: *Be on the watch for automobiles when you cross the street.* **5** keep guard: *The sentry watched throughout the night.* **6** keep guard over: *The police watched the prisoner.* **7** a protecting; guarding: *She kept watch over the house while we were away.* **8** person or persons kept to guard and protect: *A call for help aroused the night watch.* **9** period of time for guarding: *a watch in the night.* **10** device for telling time, small enough to be carried in a pocket or worn on the wrist. **11** the time of duty of one part of a ship's crew. A watch usually lasts four hours. **12** the part of a ship's crew on duty at the same time. 1-3,5,6 *v.,* 4,7-12 *n., pl.* **watch es.** —**watch′er,** *n.*

watch out, be careful; be on guard: *Watch out for cars when you cross the street.*

watch dog (woch′dôg′ *or* wôch′dôg′), dog kept to guard property. *n.*

watch ful (woch′fəl *or* wôch′fəl), watching carefully; on the lookout; wide-awake: *He is watchful of his health. You should always be watchful for cars when you cross the street. adj.* —**watch′ful ly,** *adv.* —**watch′ful ness,** *n.*

watch mak er (woch′mā′kər *or* wôch′mā′kər), person who makes and repairs watches. *n.*

watch man (woch′mən *or* wôch′mən), person who keeps watch; guard: *A watchman guards the bank at night. n., pl.* **watch men.**

watch tow er (woch′tou′ər *or* wôch′tou′ər), tower from which a watch is kept for enemies, fires, ships, etc. *n.*

watch word (woch′wėrd′ *or* wôch′wėrd′), **1** password: *We gave the watchword, and the sentinel let us pass.* **2** motto; slogan: *"Forward" is our watchword. n.*

wa ter (wô′tər *or* wot′ər), **1** the liquid that fills the oceans, rivers, lakes, and ponds, and falls from the sky as rain. Pure water is a colorless, tasteless, and odorless compound of hydrogen and oxygen. It freezes at 32 degrees Fahrenheit (0 degrees Celsius) and boils at 212 degrees Fahrenheit (100 degrees Celsius). **2** a liquid like water, occurring in or discharged from the body, such as tears, sweat, saliva, urine, serum, etc. **3** any liquid preparation that suggests water: *lavender water.* **4** body of water; sea, lake, river, etc.: *cross the water on a ferry.* **5** to sprinkle or wet with water: *water grass.* **6** supply with water: *Our valley is well watered by rivers and brooks.* **7** weaken by adding water: *It is against the law to sell watered milk.* **8** get or take in a supply of water: *A ship waters before sailing.* **9** fill with water; discharge water: *Her eyes watered. The cake made my mouth water.* **10** of water; holding, storing, or conveying water: *a water jug, a water pipe, a water system.* **11** done or used in or on water: *water sports.* **12** growing or living in or near water: *water plants, water insects.* **13 waters,** *pl.* **a** flowing water. **b** water moving in waves; the sea; the high sea. **c** mineral water. 1-4,13 *n.,* 5-9 *v.,* 10-12 *adj.* [*Water* comes from Old English *wæter.*] —**wa′ter er,** *n.*

above water, out of trouble or difficulty, especially out of financial trouble or difficulty.

by water, on a ship or boat: *travel by water.*

hold water, stand the test; be true, dependable, effective, etc.

throw cold water on, discourage: *My parents threw cold water on my plan to camp alone in the woods.*

tread water, keep oneself from sinking by moving the feet up and down.

water bed, bed with a mattress consisting of a vinyl bag filled with water.

water bird, bird that swims or wades in water.

wa ter buck (wô′tər buk′ *or* wot′ər buk′), an African antelope that frequents rivers, marshes, etc. *n., pl.* **wa ter bucks** or **wa ter buck.**

water buffalo, buffalo of Asia, commonly used to pull loads.

water clock, instrument for measuring time by the flow of water.

water closet, toilet flushed by water.

wa ter col or (wô′tər kul′ər *or* wot′ər kul′ər), **1** paint mixed with water instead of oil. **2** art of painting with watercolors. **3** picture made with watercolors. *n.*

water cooler, any device for cooling water, or for cooling something by means of water.

wa ter course (wô′tər kôrs′ *or* wot′ər kôrs′), **1** stream of water; river; brook. **2** channel or bed of a stream of water: *In the summer many watercourses dry up. n.*

wa ter cress (wô′tər kres′ *or* wot′ər kres′), plant that grows in water and has crisp, pungent leaves which are used for salad and as a garnish. *n.*

wa ter fall (wô′tər fôl′ *or* wot′ər fôl′), fall of water from a high place; cascade or cataract. *n.*

wa ter fowl (wô′tər foul′ *or* wot′ər foul′), a water bird, especially one that swims. *n., pl.* **wa ter fowls** or **wa ter fowl.**

wa ter front (wô′tər frunt′ *or* wot′ər frunt′), land at the water's edge, especially the part of a city beside a river, lake, or harbor. *n.*

Wa ter gate (wô′tər gāt *or* wot′ər gāt), a political scandal involving the 1972 presidential campaign of Richard M. Nixon. It caused President Nixon's resignation in 1974, and resulted in prison terms for many of his aides. *n.* [This scandal was named after *the Watergate,* a set of buildings in Washington, D.C., site of Democratic Party headquarters which was broken into in hope of finding evidence of political wrongdoing.]

water hole, hole in the ground where water collects; small pond; pool.

watering place, 1 resort with springs of mineral water. **2** place where water may be obtained.

wa ter less (wô′tər lis *or* wot′ər lis), using or containing little or no water. *adj.*

water level, the surface level of a body of water: *The water level of the pond rose after the heavy rains.*

a hat	i it	oi oil	ch child	(a in about
ā age	ī ice	ou out	ng long	e in taken
ä far	o hot	u cup	sh she	ə = { i in pencil
e let	ō open	u̇ put	th thin	o in lemon
ē equal	ô order	ü rule	ᴛʜ then	u in circus
ėr term			zh measure	

water lily

water lily, a water plant having flat, floating leaves and showy, fragrant flowers. The flowers of the common American water lily are white, or sometimes pink.

water line, 1 line where the surface of the water touches the side of a ship or boat. **2** any of several lines marked on a ship's hull to show the depth to which it sinks when unloaded, partly loaded, or fully loaded.

water buffaloes—about 5 ft. (1.5 m.) high at the shoulder

wa ter logged (wô′tər lôgd′ *or* wot′ər lôgd′), so full of water that it will barely float. *adj.*

Wa ter loo (wô′tər lü *or* wot′ər lü), **1** small town in Belgium, near Brussels, the site of the battle in which Napoleon I was finally defeated in 1815. **2** any decisive or crushing defeat. *n., pl.* **Wa ter loos** for 2.

water main, a large or main pipe for carrying water.

wa ter mark (wô′tər märk′ *or* wot′ər märk′), **1** a mark showing how high water has risen or how low it has fallen: *the high watermark of a river.* **2** a faint distinguishing design made in some kinds of paper. *n.*

wa ter mel on (wô′tər mel′ən *or* wot′ər mel′ən), a large, juicy melon with red or pink pulp and a hard, green rind. It grows on a vine. *n.*

water moccasin, a large, poisonous snake of the southern United States that lives in swamps and along streams; cottonmouth.

water pistol, a toy pistol that shoots water taken in by suction.

water polo, game played in a swimming pool by two teams of seven swimmers who try to throw or push an inflated ball into the opponent's goal.

water power, the power from flowing or falling water. It can be used to drive machinery and generate electricity.

wa ter proof (wô′tər prüf′ or wot′ər prüf′), **1** able to keep water from coming through; resistant to water: *An umbrella should be waterproof.* **2** make waterproof: *These hiking shoes have been waterproofed.* 1 adj., 2 v.

water rat, 1 rodent that lives on the banks of streams or lakes. **2** muskrat.

wa ter shed (wô′tər shed′ or wot′ər shed′), **1** ridge between the regions drained by two different river systems. On one side of a watershed, rivers and streams flow in one direction; on the other side, they flow in the opposite direction. **2** the region drained by one river system. *n.*

water ski, one of a pair of skis for gliding over water while being towed at the end of a rope by a motorboat.

wa ter-ski (wô′tər skē′ or wot′ər skē′), glide over the water on water skis. *v.,* **wa ter-skied, wa ter-ski ing.** —**wa′ter-ski′er,** *n.*

wa ter spout (wô′tər spout′ or wot′ər spout′), **1** pipe which takes away or discharges water, especially one used to drain water from a roof. **2** a rapidly spinning column or cone of mist, spray, and water, produced by the action of a whirlwind over the ocean or a lake. *n.*

water table, the level below which the ground is saturated with water.

wa ter tight (wô′tər tīt′ or wot′ər tīt′), **1** so tight that no water can get in or out. Large ships are often divided into watertight compartments by watertight partitions. **2** leaving no opening for misunderstanding, criticism, etc.; perfect: *a watertight argument. adj.*

water vapor, water in a gaseous state, especially when fairly diffused, as it is in the air, and below the boiling point, as distinguished from steam.

wa ter way (wô′tər wā′ or wot′ər wā′), **1** river, canal, or other body of water that ships can go on. **2** channel for water. *n.*

water wheel, wheel turned by water and used to do work. The grindstones of grain mills used to be run by water wheels.

wa ter works (wô′tər werks′ or wot′ər werks′), **1** system of pipes, reservoirs, pumps, etc., for supplying a city or town with water. **2** building with machinery for pumping water. *n. pl. or sing.*

wa ter y (wô′tər ē or wot′ər ē), **1** full of water; wet: *watery soil.* **2** indicating rain: *a watery sky.* **3** full of tears; tearful: *watery eyes.* **4** containing too much water: *watery soup.* **5** of water; like water: *a watery discharge.* **6** weak; thin; poor; pale: *a watery blue. adj.,* **wa ter i er, wa ter i est.**

watt (wot), unit of electric power, equal to the flow of one ampere under the pressure of one volt: *My lamp uses 60 watts; my toaster uses 1000 watts. n.* [The *watt* was named for James *Watt.*]

Watt (wot), **James,** 1736-1819, Scottish engineer and inventor who perfected the steam engine. *n.*

watt age (wot′ij), amount of electric power, measured in watts, especially kilowatts. *n.*

watt-hour (wot′our′), unit of electrical energy, equal to the work done by one watt acting for one hour. *n.*

wat tle[1] (wot′l), **1** Also, **wattles,** *pl.* sticks interwoven with twigs or branches; framework of wicker: *a hut built of wattle.* **2** twist or weave together (twigs, branches, etc.). 1 *n.,* 2 *v.*). **wat tled, wat tling.**

wat tle[2] (wot′l), the red flesh hanging down from the throat of a chicken, turkey, etc. *n.*

wave (wāv), **1** a moving ridge or swell of water: *The raft rose and fell on the waves.* **2** any movement like this, especially a movement of particles, by which energy is transferred from one place to another. Light, heat, and sound travel in waves. Waves are usually measured by their length, amplitude, velocity, and frequency. **3** a swell or sudden increase in some condition, emotion, etc.; flood or rush of anything: *A wave of cold weather is sweeping over the country.* **4** move as waves do; move up and down; sway: *The tall grass waved in the breeze.* **5** move back and forth: *wave a flag. Wave your hand.* **6** to signal or direct by moving the hand or an object back and forth: *The stranded motorist waved a passing driver to the side of the road.* **7** a waving: *a wave of the hand.* **8** a curve or series of curves: *waves in a person's hair.* **9** have a wavelike form: *Her hair waves naturally.* **10** give a wavelike form to: *wave one's hair.* 1-3,7,8 *n.,* 4-6,9,10 *v.,* **waved, wav ing.** —**wave′like′,** *adj.*

waterspout (def. 2)

Wave or **WAVE** (wāv), formerly, woman in the United States Navy other than a nurse. *n.* [*Wave* comes from the abbreviation *WAVES,* which stands for *Women Accepted for Volunteer Emergency Service.*]

wave length (wāv′lengkth′ or wāv′length′), distance between one part, such as the crest, of a wave of light, sound, etc., and the next corresponding part. *n.*

wave let (wāv′lit), a little wave. *n.*

wa ver (wā′vər), **1** move back and forth; flutter: *He spoke in a wavering voice.* **2** vary in intensity; flicker: *a wavering light.* **3** be undecided; hesitate: *We are still wavering between a picnic and a trip to the zoo.* **4** become unsteady; begin to give way: *His determination began to waver.* **5** act of wavering. 1-4 *v.,* 5 *n.* —**wa′ver er,** *n.* —**wa′ver ing ly,** *adv.*

wav i ness (wā′vē nis), condition of being wavy. *n.*

wav y (wā′vē), having waves or curves: *wavy hair, a wavy line. adj.,* **wav i er, wav i est.** —**wav′i ly,** *adv.*

wax[1] (waks), **1** a yellowish substance made by bees for constructing their honeycomb. Wax is hard when cold, but can be easily shaped when warm. **2** any substance like this. Most of the wax used for candles, for keeping air from jelly, etc., is really paraffin. **3** substance containing wax for polishing floors, furniture, cars, or the like. **4** rub, stiffen, polish, etc., with wax or something like wax: *We wax the floor once a month.* 1-3 *n., pl.* **wax es** for 2 and 3; 4 *v.* —**wax′like′,** *adj.*

wax[2] (waks), **1** grow bigger and greater; increase: *The moon waxes till it becomes full, and then wanes.* **2** become: *The party waxed merry. v.*

wattle[2]
of a turkey

WATTLE

wax bean, a yellow string bean.

wax en (wak′sən), **1** made of wax. **2** like wax; smooth, soft, and pale: *Her skin was waxen. adj.*

wax i ness (wak′sē nis), condition of being waxy; waxy appearance. *n.*

wax myrtle, a shrub or tree having small berries coated with wax. The bayberry is a wax myrtle.

wax paper, paper coated with paraffin.

wax wing (waks′wing′), a small bird with a showy crest and red markings at the tips of the wings. *n.*

wax work (waks′werk′), **1** figure or figures made of wax. **2 waxworks,** *pl.* exhibition of figures made of wax. *n.*

wax y (wak′sē), **1** like wax. **2** made of wax; containing wax. *adj.,* **wax i er, wax i est.**

way (wā), **1** form or mode of doing; manner; style: *a new way of wearing one's hair.* **2** method; means: *Scientists are finding new ways of preventing disease.* **3** point; feature; respect; detail: *His plan is bad in several ways.* **4** direction: *Look this way.* **5** a coming or going; moving along a course: *Our guide led the way through the museum.* **6** distance: *The sun is a long way off.* **7** means of moving along a course; road; path: *The children found a way through the forest.* **8** space for passing or going ahead: *Automobiles must make way for a fire engine.* **9** habit; custom: *She's always on time; it's her way.* **10** one's wish; will: *Just once I'd like to have my own way.* **11** condition; state: *The patient was in a bad way.* **12** INFORMAL. district; area; region: *They live out our way.* **13** INFORMAL. at or to a (great) distance; far: *The cloud of smoke stretched way out to the pier.* 1-12 *n.,* 13 *adv.*

by the way, 1 while coming or going. **2** in that connection; incidentally.

by way of, 1 by the route of; through. **2** as; for: *By way of an answer he just nodded.*

give way, 1 make way; retreat; yield. **2** break down or fall: *The old bridge gave way.* **3** abandon oneself to emotion: *give way to despair.*

in the way, being an obstacle, hindrance, etc.

make one's way, 1 go. **2** get ahead; succeed.

out of the way, 1 so as not to be an obstacle, hindrance, etc. **2** far from where most people live or go. **3** unusual; strange.

under way, going on; in motion; in progress: *The ship is under way.*

way far er (wā′fer′ər *or* wā′far′ər), traveler. *n.*

way far ing (wā′fer′ing *or* wā′far′ing), traveling. *adj.*

way laid (wā′lād′ *or* wā′lād′), past tense and past participle of **waylay.** *I waylaid her when she entered the meeting. v.*

way lay (wā′lā′ *or* wā′lā′), **1** lie in wait for; attack on the way: *Robin Hood waylaid travelers and robbed them.* **2** stop (a person going somewhere) on the way: *Newspaper reporters waylaid the mayor and asked many questions. v.,* **way laid, way lay ing. —way′lay′er,** *n.*

way-out (wā′out′), INFORMAL. far-out. *adj.*

-ways, *suffix forming adverbs.* **1** in the direction or position of the _____: *Lengthways = in the direction of the length.* **2** in _____ manner: *Anyways = in any manner.*

way side (wā′sīd′), **1** edge of a road or path: *We ate lunch on the wayside.* **2** along the edge of a road or path: *We slept in a wayside inn.* 1 *n.,* 2 *adj.*

way ward (wā′wərd), **1** turning from the right way; disobedient; willful: *The wayward student never did any homework.* **2** irregular; unsteady. *adj.* **—way′ward ly,** *adv.* **—way′ward ness,** *n.*

we (wē), **1** the persons speaking: *We are glad to see you.* **2** the person speaking. An author, a ruler, or a judge sometimes uses *we* to mean *I. pron.pl.*

weak (wēk), **1** that can easily be broken, crushed, overcome, torn, etc.; not strong: *a weak board in the floor, a weak foundation, weak defenses.* **2** not having bodily strength or health: *Long sickness had made the patient weak.* **3** lacking power, authority, force, etc.: *a weak law.* **4** lacking moral strength or firmness: *a weak character.* **5** lacking mental power: *A weak mind is a feeble one.* **6** lacking or poor in amount, volume, loudness, taste, intensity, etc.: *Weak tea has less flavor than strong tea.* **7** lacking or poor in something specified: *She is still a little weak in spelling. adj.* [*Weak* came into English about 700 years ago from Icelandic *veikr.*]

weak en (wē′kən), **1** make weak or weaker: *You can weaken tea by adding water.* **2** become weak or weaker: *We are almost to the top of the mountain; let's not weaken now. v.*

weak fish (wēk′fish′), a spiny-finned saltwater food fish with a tender mouth. *n., pl.* **weak fish es** *or* **weak fish.**

weak ling (wēk′ling), **1** a weak person or animal. **2** weak. 1 *n.,* 2 *adj.*

weak ly (wēk′lē), **1** in a weak manner. **2** weak; feeble; sickly. 1 *adv.,* 2 *adj.,* **weak li er, weak li est.**

weak-mind ed (wēk′mīn′did), **1** having or showing little intelligence; feeble-minded. **2** lacking firmness of mind. *adj.* **—weak′-mind′ed ness,** *n.*

weak ness (wēk′nis), **1** a being weak; lack of power, force, or vigor: *Weakness kept him in bed.* **2** a weak point; slight fault: *Putting things off is her weakness.* **3** a liking that one is a little ashamed of; fondness: *a weakness for sweets. n., pl.* **weak ness es.**

wealth (welth), **1** many valuable possessions; property; riches: *people of wealth, the wealth of a city.* **2** all things that have money value; resources: *The wealth of our country includes its mines and forests as well as its factories.* **3** a large quantity; abundance: *a wealth of hair, a wealth of words. n.*

wealth y (wel′thē), having wealth; rich. *adj.,* **wealth i er, wealth i est. —wealth′i ly,** *adv.* **—wealth′i ness,** *n.*

wean (wēn), **1** accustom (a child or young animal) to food other than its mother's milk. **2** accustom (a person) to do without something; cause to turn away: *wean someone from a bad habit. v.*

weap on (wep′ən), **1** any object or instrument used in fighting. Swords, spears, arrows, clubs, guns, cannons, and shields are weapons. Animals use claws, horns, teeth, and stings as weapons. **2** any means of attack or defense: *Drugs are effective weapons against many diseases. n.*

weap on less (wep′ən lis), having no weapon; unarmed. *adj.*

weap on ry (wep′ən rē), **1** the developing and producing of weapons. **2** weapons. *n.*

wear (wer *or* war), **1** have on the body: *wear a coat, wear a beard, wear black, wear a ring.* **2** have or show: *The empty old house wore an air of sadness.* **3** a wearing or a being worn: *Clothing for summer wear is being shown in the shops.* **4** things worn or to be worn; clothing: *The store sells children's wear.* **5** last long; give good service: *This material wears well. Their friendship wore well.* **6** lasting quality; good service: *There is still much wear in these shoes.* **7** use up; be used up: *The pencil is worn to a stub.* **8** damage from use: *The rug shows wear.* **9** make by rubbing, scraping, washing away, etc.: *Walking wore a*

a hat	i it	oi oil	ch child	⎧ a in about
ā age	ī ice	ou out	ng long	e in taken
ä far	o hot	u cup	sh she	ə = i in pencil
e let	ō open	u̇ put	th thin	o in lemon
ē equal	ô order	ü rule	ᴛH then	⎩ u in circus
ėr term			zh measure	

hole in my shoe. **10** to tire; weary: *They were worn with toil and care.* **11** pass or go gradually: *It became hotter as the day wore on.* 1,2,5,7,9-11 *v.*, **wore, worn, wear ing;** 3,4, 6,8 *n.* —**wear′a ble,** *adj.* —**wear′er,** *n.*

wear down, 1 overcome by persistent effort. **2** reduce in height.

wear off, become less.

wear out, 1 wear or use until no longer fit for use. **2** tire out; weary: *She was worn out by too much work.*

wear i ly (wir′ə lē), in a weary manner: *The tired hikers walked slowly and wearily along the road. adv.*

wear i ness (wir′ē nis), weary condition; tired feeling: *After tramping all day the hikers were overcome with weariness. n.*

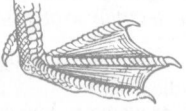
webbed (def. 2)
webbed foot of a duck

wear ing (wer′ing *or* war′ing), exhausting; tiring: *a very wearing trip, a wearing conversation. adj.*

wear i some (wir′ē səm), wearying; tiring; tiresome: *a wearisome tale. adj.*

wear y (wir′ē), **1** worn out; tired: *weary feet, a weary brain.* **2** causing tiredness; tiring: *a weary wait.* **3** having one's patience, tolerance, or liking exhausted. **4** make or become tired: *Walking all day wearied the sightseers.* 1-3 *adj.*, **wear i er, wear i est;** 4 *v.*, **wear ied, wear y ing.** [*Weary* comes from Old English *wērig.*]

wea sel (wē′zəl), **1** a small, flesh-eating mammal related to the mink and skunk, with a long, slender, furry body and short legs. Weasels have keen sight and smell and are known for their quickness and slyness. **2** a cunning, sneaky person. *n.* —**wea′sel like′,** *adj.*

weath er (weŦH′ər), **1** condition of the atmosphere with respect to temperature, moisture, wind, cloudiness, etc.: *hot weather. The weather is very windy today in Chicago.* **2** windy, rainy, or stormy weather: *damage done by the weather.* **3** expose to the weather; wear or discolor by sun, rain, frost, etc.: *Wood turns gray if weathered for a long time.* **4** become discolored or worn by air, rain, sun, frost, etc. **5** go or come through safely: *The ship weathered the storm.* 1,2 *n.*, 3-5 *v.*

under the weather, INFORMAL. sick; ailing.

weath er-beat en (weŦH′ər bēt′n), worn or hardened by the wind, rain, and other forces of the weather: *a seaman's weather-beaten face, a weather-beaten barn. adj.*

weath er cock (weŦH′ər kok′), vane to show which way the wind is blowing, especially one in the shape of a rooster. *n.*

weath er ing (weŦH′ər ing), destructive or discoloring action of air, water, frost, etc., especially on rocks. *n.*

weath er man (weŦH′ər man′), person who forecasts the weather. *n., pl.* **weath er men.**

weath er proof (weŦH′ər prüf′), protected against rain, snow, or wind; able to stand exposure to all kinds of weather. *adj.*

weather strip, a narrow strip of cloth or metal to fill or cover the space between the door or window and the casing, so as to keep out rain, snow, and wind.

weather vane, vane (def. 1).

weave (wēv), **1** form (threads or strips) into a thing or fabric. People weave thread into cloth, straw into hats, and reeds into baskets. **2** make out of thread, strips, or strands of the same material. A spider weaves a web. *She is weaving a rug.* **3** work with a loom. **4** method or pattern of weaving: *Homespun is a cloth of coarse weave.* **5** combine into a whole: *The author wove three plots together into one story.* **6** make by combining parts: *The*

author wove a story from three plots. **7** go by twisting and turning; move with a rocking or swaying motion: *The car ahead was weaving in and out of traffic.* 1-3,5-7 *v.*, **wove, wo ven** or **wove, weav ing;** 4 *n.*

weav er (wē′vər), **1** person who weaves. **2** person whose work is weaving. *n.*

web (web), **1** something woven. The fabric of delicate, silken threads spun by a spider is a web. **2** a whole piece of cloth while being woven or after being taken from the loom. **3** anything like a web, especially something that ensnares or entangles: *a web of lies.* **4** the skin joining the toes of swimming birds and certain other water animals. *n.* —**web′like′,** *adj.*

webbed (webd), **1** formed like a web or with a web. **2** having the toes joined by a web. Ducks have webbed feet. *adj.*

web bing (web′ing), **1** cloth woven into strong strips, used in upholstery and for belts. **2** skin joining the toes, as in a duck's feet. *n.*

web-foot ed (web′fùt′id), having the toes joined by a web. *adj.*

Web ster (web′stər), **1** Daniel, 1782-1852, American statesman and orator. **2** Noah, 1758-1843, American author who wrote the first well-known American dictionary. *n.*

weasel (def. 1)
about 16 in. (40 cm.)
long with the tail

wed (wed), **1** marry. **2** unite. *v.*, **wed ded, wed ded** or **wed, wed ding.**

we'd (wēd), **1** we had. **2** we should. **3** we would.

Wed., Wednesday.

wed ded (wed′id), **1** married. **2** of marriage: *wedded bliss.* **3** united. **4** devoted. *adj.*

wed ding (wed′ing), **1** the marriage ceremony. **2** an anniversary of it. A golden wedding is the fiftieth anniversary of a marriage. *n.*

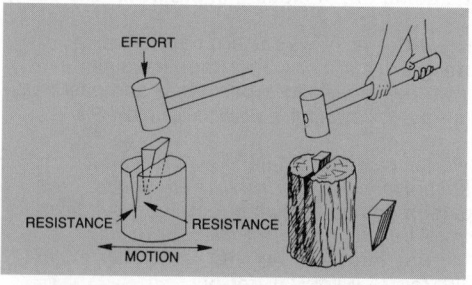
EFFORT

RESISTANCE   RESISTANCE
MOTION

wedge
(def. 1)

wedge (wej), **1** piece of wood or metal in the form of an inclined plane, thick at one end and tapering to a thin edge at the other, used in splitting logs, etc. It is a simple machine. **2** something shaped like a wedge or

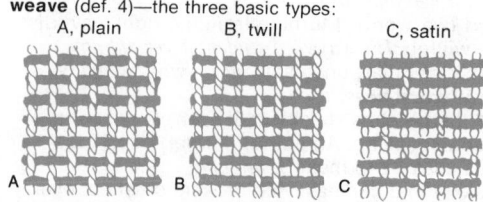
weave (def. 4)—the three basic types:
A, plain   B, twill   C, satin

A   B   C

used like a wedge: *Wild geese fly in a wedge. The quarrel drove a wedge between him and his relatives.* **3** split or separate with a wedge. **4** fasten or tighten with a wedge. **5** thrust or pack in tightly; squeeze: *He wedged himself through the narrow window. The child's foot was wedged between the rocks.* 1,2 *n.*, 3-5 *v.*, **wedged, wedg ing.** —**wedge′like′**, *adj.*

wedg ie (wej′ē), shoe with a thick, wedgelike piece forming the heel. *n.*

Wedg wood (wej′wud′), **Josiah,** 1730-1795, English potter. *n.*

wed lock (wed′lok), married life; marriage. *n.*

Wednes day (wenz′dē), the fourth day of the week, following Tuesday. *n.*

wee (wē), very small; tiny. *adj.*, **we er, we est.** [*Wee* is from Middle English *we,* meaning "a little bit," which came from Old English *wæg,* meaning "a weight."]

weed (wēd), **1** a useless or troublesome plant: *Weeds choked out the vegetables and flowers in the garden.* **2** take weeds out of: *Please weed the garden now.* **3** take out weeds. 1 *n.*, 2,3 *v.* —**weed′less**, *adj.* —**weed′like′**, *adj.*

weed out, remove as useless or worthless.

weeds (wēdz), black mourning garments: *a widow's weeds. n.pl.*

weed er (wē′dər), **1** person who weeds. **2** tool or machine for digging up weeds. *n.*

weed y (wē′dē), **1** full of weeds: *a weedy garden.* **2** of or like weeds. **3** thin and lanky; weak. *adj.*, **weed i er, weed i est.** —**weed′i ly**, *adv.* —**weed′i ness**, *n.*

week (wēk), **1** seven days, one after another. **2** time from Sunday through Saturday: *I am away most of the week but come home on Sunday.* **3** the working days of a seven-day period: *A school week is usually five days. n.*

week day (wēk′dā′), any day of the week except Sunday or (now often) Saturday. *n.*

week end (wēk′end′), **1** Saturday and Sunday as a time for recreation, visiting, etc.: *a weekend in the country.* **2** spend a weekend. 1 *n.*, 2 *v.*

week ly (wēk′lē), **1** of a week; for a week; lasting a week: *a weekly wage of $150.* **2** done or happening once a week: *She writes him a weekly letter.* **3** once each week; every week: *I play tennis weekly.* **4** newspaper or magazine published once a week. 1,2 *adj.*, 3 *adv.*, 4 *n.*, *pl.* **week lies.**

ween y (wē′nē), INFORMAL. very small; little; tiny. *adj.*, **ween i er, ween i est.**

weep (wēp), **1** shed tears; cry: *They wept for joy when they won the award.* **2** let fall or flow in drops; shed: *weep bitter tears.* **3** be very damp; drip. *v.*, **wept, weep ing.**

weep ing (wē′ping), **1** that weeps. **2** having thin, drooping branches: *a weeping willow. adj.* —**weep′ing ly**, *adv.*

weevil—all species less than ¹/₄ in. (6 mm.) long

wee vil (wē′vəl), any of a group of small beetles that have long snouts and feed on plants. The larvae of the weevil feed on and destroy grain, nuts, cotton, fruit, etc. *n.*

weft (weft), woof, in weaving. *n.*

weigh (wā), **1** find out how heavy a thing is: *weigh oneself, weigh a bag of potatoes.* **2** measure by weight: *The grocer weighed out five pounds of potatoes.* **3** have as a measure by weight: *I weigh 110 pounds.* **4** bend by weight; burden: *The boughs of the apple tree are weighed down with fruit. They are weighed down with many troubles.* **5** bear down; be a burden: *Don't let the mistake weigh on your mind.* **6** have importance or influence: *Your excuses will not weigh with us.* **7** balance in the mind; consider carefully: *weigh both sides of an argument.* **8** lift up (an anchor): *The ship weighed anchor and sailed away. v.*

weigh in, find out one's weight before a contest.

weight (wāt), **1** how heavy a thing is: the amount a thing weighs: *The dog's weight is 50 pounds.* **2** force with which a body is attracted to the earth or some other heavenly body: *Gas has hardly any weight.* **3** system of units for expressing weight: *avoirdupois weight.* **4** unit of such a system. **5** piece of metal used in weighing things: *a pound weight.* **6** quantity that has a certain weight: *a half-ounce weight of gold dust.* **7** a heavy thing or mass: *A weight keeps the papers in place.* **8** load; burden: *The pillars support the weight of the roof. Your good news has taken a weight off my mind.* **9** load down; burden: *to be weighted with troubles.* **10** add weight to; put weight on: *They weighted the elevator too heavily.* **11** influence; importance; value: *the weight of public opinion.* 1-8,11 *n.*, 9,10 *v.*

weight i ly (wā′tl ē), in a weighty manner; heavily. *adv.*

weightless (def. 2) Astronauts know what it is like to float in space while in a **weightless** condition.

weight less (wāt′lis), **1** having little or no weight: *weightless snow.* **2** being free from the pull of gravity. *adj.* —**weight′less ly**, *adv.* —**weight′less ness**, *n.*

weight y (wā′tē), **1** heavy. **2** too heavy; burdensome: *weighty responsibilities.* **3** important; serious: *This is indeed a weighty problem. adj.*, **weight i er, weight i est.** —**weight′i ness**, *n.*

weir (wir), **1** dam in a river. **2** fence of stakes or broken branches put in a stream or channel to catch fish. *n.*

weird (wird), **1** unearthly or mysterious; wild; strange: *They were awakened by a weird shriek.* **2** odd; fantastic; queer: *The shadows made weird figures on the wall. adj.* [*Weird* is from Middle English *wird,* which came from Old English *wyrd,* meaning "fate."] —**weird′ly**, *adv.* —**weird′ness**, *n.*

weird o (wir′dō), SLANG. an odd or crazy person. *n.*, *pl.* **weird os.**

wel come (wel′kəm), **1** greet kindly; give a friendly reception to: *We always welcome guests at our house.* **2** a kind or friendly reception: *You will always have a wel-come here.* **3** receive gladly: *We welcome new ideas and suggestions.* **4** gladly received: *a welcome letter, a welcome visitor, a welcome rest.* **5** gladly or freely permitted: *You are welcome to pick the flowers.* **6** free to enjoy courtesies, etc., without obligation (said in response to thanks): *You are quite welcome.* **7** exclamation of friendly greeting: *Welcome, everyone!* 1,3 *v.,* **wel comed, wel com ing;** 2 *n.,* 4-6 *adj.,* 7 *interj.* [*Welcome* is from Old English *wilcuma,* meaning "an agreeable guest."] —**wel′come less,** *adj.* —**wel′come ly,** *adv.* —**wel′come ness,** *n.* —**wel′com-er,** *n.*

wear out one's welcome, visit a person too often or too long.

weld (def. 1)

weld (weld), **1** join (pieces of metal) together by heat-ing the parts that touch to the melting point, so that they can be hammered or pressed together or flow together and become one piece: *She welded the broken rod.* **2** a welded joint. **3** act of welding. **4** unite closely: *Working together welded them into a strong team.* **5** be welded or be capable of being welded: *Steel welds; wood does not.* 1,4,5 *v.,* 2,3 *n.* —**weld′a ble,** *adj.* —**weld′er,** *n.* —**weld′less,** *adj.*

wel fare (wel′fer′ *or* wel′far′), **1** health, happiness, and prosperity; condition of being or doing well: *My uncle asked about the welfare of everyone in our family.* **2** aid provided by the government to poor or needy people. *n.* [*Welfare* comes from the Middle English phrase *wel faren,* meaning "to fare well."]

on welfare, receiving aid from the government because of hardship or need.

welfare state, state whose government provides for the welfare of its citizens through social security, unem-ployment insurance, free medical treatment, etc.

welfare work, work done to improve the conditions of people who need help, carried on by government, pri-vate organizations, or individuals.

wel kin (wel′kən), OLD USE. the sky. *n.*

well¹ (wel), **1** in a satisfactory, favorable, or good man-ner; all right: *The job was well done. Is everything going well at school?* **2** satisfactory; good; right: *It is well you came along.* **3** thoroughly: *Shake the medicine well before taking it. He knew the lesson well.* **4** to a considerable degree; much: *The fair brought in well over a hundred dollars.* **5** fairly; reasonably: *I couldn't very well refuse their request.* **6** in good health: *I am very well.* **7** expression used to show mild surprise or merely to fill in: *Well! Well! Here they are. Well, I'm not sure.* 1,3-5 *adv.,* **bet ter, best;** 2,6 *adj.,* 7 *interj.* —**well′ness,** *n.*

as well, 1 also; besides. **2** equally.

as well as, 1 in addition to; besides. **2** as much as.

well² (wel), **1** hole dug or bored in the ground to get

water, oil, gas, etc.: *I pumped a bucket of water from the well.* **2** spring; fountain; source: *This book is a well of ideas.* **3** something like a well in shape or use. The reser-voir of a fountain pen is a well. **4** shaft for stairs or elevator, extending vertically through the floors of a building. **5** to spring, rise, or gush: *Tears welled up in the child's eyes. Water wells from a spring beneath the rock.* 1-4 *n.,* 5 *v.*

we'll (wēl), **1** we shall. **2** we will.

well-bal anced (wel′bal′ənst), **1** rightly balanced, ad-justed, or regulated: *A well-balanced diet includes plenty of fruit and vegetables.* **2** sensible; sane: *She has a well-balanced outlook on life.* *adj.*

well-be haved (wel′bi hāvd′), showing good manners or conduct. *adj.*

well-be ing (wel′bē′ing), health and happiness; wel-fare. *n.*

well born (wel′bôrn′), belonging to a good family. *adj.*

well-bred (wel′bred′), well brought up; having or showing good manners. *adj.*

well-de fined (wel′di fīnd′), rightly, properly, or defi-nitely marked. *adj.*

well-de vel oped (wel′di vel′əpt), **1** developed or worked out well: *a well-developed plan.* **2** showing good development: *The athlete had a well-developed body.* *adj.*

well-done (wel′dun′), **1** performed well; skillfully done: *a well-done job.* **2** (of meat) thoroughly cooked: *a well-done steak.* *adj.*

well-fed (wel′fed′), showing the result of good feeding; fat; plump. *adj.*

well-fixed (wel′fikst′), INFORMAL. well-to-do. *adj.*

well-formed (wel′fôrmd′), rightly or finely formed; shapely. *adj.*

well-groomed (wel′grümd′ *or* wel′grümd′), well cared for; neat and trim. *adj.*

well-ground ed (wel′groun′did), **1** based on good rea-sons. **2** thoroughly instructed in the fundamental princi-ples of a subject. *adj.*

well-in formed (wel′in fôrmd′), **1** having reliable or full information on a subject. **2** having information on a wide variety of subjects. *adj.*

Wel ling ton (wel′ing tən), **1** first **Duke of,** 1769-1852, British general who defeated Napoleon I at Waterloo in 1815. **2** capital of New Zealand, on the S coast of North Island. *n.*

well-kept (wel′kept′), well cared for; carefully tended. *adj.*

well-knit (wel′nit′), well joined or put together. *adj.*

well-known (wel′nōn′), **1** clearly known; familiar. **2** generally or widely known; famous. *adj.*

well-made (wel′mād′), skillfully made; sturdily built: *a well-made old desk.* *adj.*

well-man nered (wel′man′ərd), having good manners; polite; courteous: *A well-mannered person always remem-bers to say "please."* *adj.*

well-marked (wel′märkt′), clearly marked; distinct. *adj.*

well-mean ing (wel′mē′ning), **1** having good intentions. **2** caused by good intentions. *adj.*

well-nigh (wel′nī′), very nearly; almost. *adv.*

well-off (wel′ôf′), **1** in a good condition or position. **2** fairly rich. *adj.*

well-pre served (wel′pri zėrvd′), showing few signs of age. *adj.*

well-read (wel′red′), having read much; knowing a great deal about books and literature. *adj.*

Wells (welz), **H(erbert) G(eorge),** 1866-1946, English writer of science fiction, history, and essays. *n.*

well spring (wel′spring′), **1** source of a stream or spring; fountainhead. **2** source of supply that never fails; source. *n.*

well-thought-of (wel′thôt′uv′ or wel′thôt′ov′), highly respected; esteemed. *adj.*

well-timed (wel′tīmd′), at the right time; timely. *adj.*

well-to-do (wel′tə dü′), having enough money to live well; prosperous. *adj.*

well-wish er (wel′wish′ər), person who wishes well to a person, cause, etc. *n.*

well-worn (wel′wôrn′), **1** much worn by use. **2** used too much; trite; stale. *adj.*

Welsh (welsh or welch), **1** of Wales, its people, or their Celtic language. **2** the people of Wales. **3** their language. 1 *adj.*, 2 *n.pl.*, 3 *n.sing.* [*Welsh* comes from Old English *Wælisc*, also meaning "foreign." The people were called this because they were not of Anglo-Saxon origin.]

Welsh man (welsh′mən or welch′mən), person born or living in Wales. *n., pl.* **Welsh men.**

Welsh rabbit or **Welsh rarebit,** melted cheese cooked with milk, egg, etc., and poured over toast or crackers; rarebit.

welt (welt), **1** a strip of leather between the upper part and the sole of a shoe. **2** a raised streak or ridge made on the skin by a stick or whip. *n.*

wel ter (wel′tər), **1** roll or tumble about; wallow. **2** a rolling or tumbling about. **3** a surging or confused mass: *All we saw was a welter of arms, legs, and bodies.* **4** confusion; commotion. **5** be drenched. 1,5 *v.*, 2-4 *n.*

wel ter weight (wel′tər wāt′), boxer who weighs more than 135 pounds (61 kilograms) and less than 147 pounds (67 kilograms). *n.*

wen (wen), a harmless saclike growth of the skin, especially on the scalp. *n.*

wench (wench), OLD USE. **1** girl or young woman. **2** a woman servant. *n., pl.* **wench es.**

wend (wend), **1** direct (one's way): *We wended our way home.* **2** go. *v.*, **wend ed** or **went, wend ing.**

went (went), **1** past tense of **go.** *I went home promptly after school.* **2** a past tense amd a past participle of **wend.** *v.*

wept (wept), past tense and past participle of **weep.** *The children wept over the loss of their dog. v.*

were (wėr), **1** form of the verb **be** used with *you, we, they* or any plural noun to indicate the past tense. *The officer's orders were obeyed.* **2** form of **be** used to express something as possible or as a condition but not as an actual thing. *If I were rich, I would help the poor. v.*

we're (wir), we are.

weren't (wėrnt), were not.

were wolf (wir′wůlf′), (in folklore) a person who changes into a wolf at certain times. *n., pl.* **were wolves** (wir′wůlvz′). Also, **werwolf.**

WORD HISTORY

werewolf

Werewolf is from Old English *werwulf,* which comes from *wer,* meaning "man," and *wulf,* meaning "wolf."

wert (wėrt), OLD USE. were. "Thou wert" means "you were." *v.*

wer wolf (wir′wůlf′), werewolf. *n., pl.* **wer wolves** (wir′wůlvz′).

Wes ley (wes′lē), **1 John,** 1703-1791, English clergyman who founded the Methodist Church. **2** his brother, **Charles,** 1707-1788, English clergyman and helper of John. He wrote many hymns. *n.*

a	hat	i	it	oi	oil	ch	child		a in about
ā	age	ī	ice	ou	out	ng	long		e in taken
ä	far	o	hot	u	cup	sh	she	ə =	i in pencil
e	let	ō	open	ů	put	th	thin		o in lemon
ē	equal	ô	order	ü	rule	ŦH	then		u in circus
ėr	term					zh	measure		

Wes ley an (wes′lē ən), member of the church founded by John Wesley; Methodist. *n.*

Wes sex (wes′iks), ancient kingdom in S England from A.D. 500? to 886. *n.*

west (west), **1** direction of the sunset. **2** toward the west; farther toward the west: *We took the west road (adj.). Walk west three blocks (adv.).* **3** from the west: *a warm, west wind.* **4** in the west: *the west wing of a house.* **5** Also, **West.** the part of any country toward the west. **6 West, a** the western part of the United States. **b** the countries in Europe and America as distinguished from those in Asia. 1,5,6 *n.*, 2-4 *adj.*, 2 *adv.*

west of, farther west than: *Kansas is west of Pennsylvania.*

West Berlin, the W part of Berlin belonging to West Germany. It is located in East Germany and separated from East Berlin by a wall.

west bound (west′bound′), going west. *adj.*

west er ly (wes′tər lē), **1** toward the west: *a westerly exposure.* **2** from the west: *a westerly wind.* **3** wind that blows from the west. 1,2 *adj., adv.*, 3 *n., pl.* **west er lies.**

west ern (wes′tərn), **1** toward the west. **2** from the west. **3** of or in the west. **4** story, motion picture, or television show dealing with life in the western part of the United States, especially cowboy life. **5 Western, a** of or in the western part of the United States. **b** of or in the countries of Europe and America. 1-3,5 *adj.*, 4 *n.*

Western Australia, state in W Australia.

west ern er (wes′tər nər), **1** person born or living in the west. **2 Westerner,** person born or living in the western part of the United States. *n.*

Western Hemisphere, the half of the world that includes North and South America.

west ern ize (wes′tər nīz), make western in character, ideas, ways, etc. *v.*, **west ern ized, west ern iz ing.**

west ern most (wes′tərn mōst), farthest west. *adj.*

Western Sahara, country in NW Africa, south of Morocco. *Capital:* El Aaiún.

Western Samoa, country made up of several islands in the S Pacific. It is a member of the Commonwealth of Nations. *Capital:* Apia.

West Germany, country in central Europe, consisting of the part of Germany which came under American, British, and French control at the end of World War II. *Capital:* Bonn. See **Rhine** for map.

West Indian, 1 of the West Indies. **2** person born or living in the West Indies.

West Indies, long chain of islands between Florida and South America; Greater Antilles, Lesser Antilles, and Bahamas.

West Ir i an (ir′ē än), W part of New Guinea, belonging to Indonesia.

West min ster Abbey (west′min′stər), church in London where the kings and queens of Great Britain are crowned and in which many English monarchs and famous people are buried.

West Point, college for training cadets to become officers in the United States Army. It is located on the Hudson River in SE New York State.

West Virginia, one of the southeastern states of the United States. *Abbreviation:* W. Va. or WV *Capital:* Charleston. —**West Virginian.**

west ward (west'wərd), **1** toward the west; west: *We walked westward* (adv.). *The orchard is on the westward slope of the hill* (adj.). **2** a westward part, direction, or point. 1 *adv.*, *adj.*, 2 *n.*

west wards (west'wərdz), westward. *adv.*

wet (wet), **1** covered or soaked with water or other liquid: *wet hands, a wet sponge.* **2** watery: *eyes wet with tears.* **3** not yet dry: *The paint is wet; don't touch it.* **4** make or become wet: *Wet the cloth before you wipe off the window.* **5** water or other liquid. **6** rainy: *wet weather.* **7** wetness; rain: *Come in out of the wet.* **8** INFORMAL. permitting the sale of alcoholic drinks: *a wet town or district.* 1-3,6,8 *adj.*, **wet ter, wet test**; 4 *v.*, **wet** or **wet ted, wet ting**; 5,7 *n.* —**wet'ly**, *adv.* —**wet'ness**, *n.* —**wet'ta ble**, *adj.* —**wet'ter**, *n.*

wet blanket, person or thing that has a discouraging or depressing effect.

wet suit

wet suit, a skin-tight rubber suit worn by skin divers, surfers, sailors, etc.

we've (wēv), we have.

whack (hwak), INFORMAL. **1** a sharp, resounding blow. **2** to strike with such a blow: *The batter whacked the ball out of the park.* **3** trial or attempt: *I'd like to have a whack at parachuting.* 1,3 *n.*, 2 *v.* —**whack'er**, *n.*

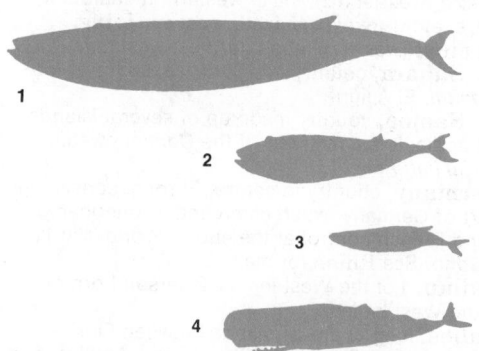

whale[1] (def. 1)
1. blue whale—about 90 ft. (27 m.) long
2. humpback whale—about 45 ft. (13.5 m.) long
3. Minke whale—about 28 ft. (8.5 m.) long
4. sperm whale—about 50 ft. (15 m.) long

whale[1] (hwāl), **1** mammal shaped like a huge fish and living in the sea. Oil from whales used to be burned in lamps. **2** hunt and catch whales. 1 *n.*, *pl.* **whales** or **whale**; 2 *v.*, **whaled, whal ing.** [*Whale*[1] comes from Old English *hwæl.*] —**whale'like'**, *adj.*

a whale of, INFORMAL. a very excellent, big, or impressive kind of: *a whale of a good time.*

whale[2] (hwāl), INFORMAL. whip severely; beat; thrash. *v.*,

whaled, whal ing. [*Whale*[2] may be a different form of *wale*, which comes from Old English *walu*, meaning "mark of a lash, weal[2]."]

whale boat (hwāl'bōt'), a long, narrow rowboat, pointed at both ends, formerly much used in whaling. *n.*

whale bone (hwāl'bōn'), an elastic, horny substance growing in place of teeth in the upper jaw of certain whales; baleen. Thin strips of whalebone were formerly used for stiffening corsets and dresses. *n.*

whal er (hwā'lər), **1** hunter of whales. **2** ship used for hunting and catching whales. *n.*

whal ing (hwā'ling), the hunting and catching of whales. *n.*

wham (hwam), INFORMAL. **1** exclamation or sound as of one thing striking hard against another. **2** hit with a hard, striking sound. 1 *n.*, *interj.*, 2 *v.*, **whammed, wham ming.**

wharf (hwôrf), platform built on the shore or out from the shore, beside which ships can load and unload. *n.*, *pl.* **wharves** or **wharfs.**

wharves (hwôrvz), a plural of **wharf.** *n.*

what (hwot *or* hwut; *unstressed* hwət), **1** *What* is used in asking questions about persons or things. *What is your name?* (pron.). *What time is it?* (adj.). **2** that which: *I know what you mean* (pron.). *Put back what money is left* (adj.). **3** whatever; anything that; any that: *Do what you please* (pron.). *Take what supplies you will need* (adj.). **4** how much; how: *What does it matter?* **5** partly: *What with the wind and rain, our walk was spoiled.* **6** *What* is often used to show surprise, doubt, anger, liking, etc., or to add emphasis. *What a pity!* (adj.). *What happy times!* (adv.). *What! Are you late again?* (interj.). 1-3 *pron.*, 1-3,6 *adj.*, 4-6 *adv.*, 6 *interj.*

and what not, and all kinds of other things: *a collection of buttons, beads, and what not.*

what if, what would happen if: *What if it rains on the day of the game?*

what's what, INFORMAL. the true state of affairs: *to know what's what.*

what e'er (hwot er' *or* hwut er'), whatever. *pron.*, *adj.*

what ev er (hwot ev'ər) *or* hwut ev'ər), **1** anything that: *Do whatever you like.* **2** any that: *Take whatever books you need.* **3** no matter who; at all: *Any person whatever can tell you the way.* **4** no matter what: *Whatever happens, they are safe* (pron.). *Whatever excuse he makes will not be believed* (adj.). **5** *Whatever* is used for emphasis instead of *what. Whatever do you mean?* 1,4,5 *pron.*, 2-4 *adj.*

what not (hwot'not' *or* hwut'not'), a stand with several shelves for books, ornaments, etc. *n.*

what's (hwots *or* hwuts), **1** what is: *What's the latest news?* **2** what has: *What's been going on here lately?*

what so ev er (hwot'sō ev'ər *or* hwut'sō ev'ər), whatever. *pron.*, *adj.*

wheal (hwēl), weal; welt. *n.*

wheat (hwēt), **1** the grain of a common cereal grass, used to make flour. **2** the plant yielding this grain. *n.*

wheat en (hwēt'n), made of wheat: *wheaten flour. adj.*

wheat germ, the tiny germ or embryo of the wheat kernel, separated in the milling of flour and used as a cereal, etc. It is rich in vitamins.

whee dle (hwē'dl), **1** persuade by flattery, smooth words, caresses, etc.; coax: *The children wheedled their parents into letting them go to the picnic.* **2** get by wheedling: *They finally wheedled the secret out of me. v.*, **whee dled, whee dling.** —**whee'dler**, *n.* —**whee'dling ly**, *adv.*

wheel (hwēl), **1** a round frame turning on a pin or shaft in the center. **2** any instrument, machine, apparatus, etc., shaped or moving like a wheel. A ship's wheel is used in steering. Clay is shaped into dishes on a potter's wheel. **3** any force thought of as moving or propelling: *the*

wheels of government. **4 wheels,** *pl.* SLANG. automobile. **5** turn: *The rider wheeled her horse about. I wheeled around suddenly.* **6** move on wheels: *I wheeled the load of bricks on a wheelbarrow.* **7** ride a bicycle. 1-4 *n.,* 5-7 *v.*
—**wheel′less,** *adj.*

at the wheel, 1 at the steering wheel of an automobile. **2** at the wheel of a ship. **3** in control.

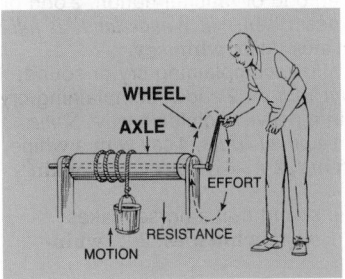

WHEEL
AXLE
EFFORT
RESISTANCE
MOTION

wheel and axle

wheel and axle, axle on which a wheel is fastened, used to lift weights by winding a rope onto the axle as the wheel is turned. It is a simple machine.

wheel bar row (hwēl′bar′ō), a small vehicle with a wheel at one end and two handles at the other, used for carrying loads. *n.*

wheel chair (hwēl′cher′ *or* hwēl′char′), chair mounted on wheels, used especially by invalids. It can be propelled by the person who is sitting in the chair. *n.*

wheeled (hwēld), having a wheel or wheels. *adj.*

wheel house (hwēl′hous′), pilothouse. *n., pl.* **wheelhous es** (hwēl′hou′ziz).

wheel ie (hwē′lē), a stunt in which a moving bicycle, motorcycle, or car is balanced only on its back wheel or wheels. *n.*

wheel wright (hwēl′rīt′), person whose work is making or repairing wheels, carriages, and wagons. *n.*

wheeze (hwēz), **1** breathe with difficulty and a whistling sound. **2** a whistling sound caused by difficult breathing. **3** make a sound like this: *The old engine wheezed.* 1,3 *v.,* **wheezed, wheez ing;** 2 *n.* [*Wheeze* came into English over 500 years ago, probably from Icelandic *hvæsa,* meaning "to hiss."]

wheez y (hwē′zē), wheezing: *The old dog was fat and wheezy. adj.,* **wheez i er, wheez i est.** —**wheez′i ly,** *adv.* —**wheez′i ness,** *n.*

whelks—Shells are 2 to 3 in. (5 to 7.5 cm.) long.

whelk (hwelk), a sea animal with a spiral shell, used for food in Europe. *n.*

whelm (hwelm), overwhelm. *v.*

whelp (hwelp), **1** puppy or cub; young dog, wolf, bear, lion, tiger, or seal. **2** give birth to whelps. **3** an impudent young person. 1,3 *n.,* 2 *v.*

when (hwen), **1** at what time: *When does school close?* **2** at the time that: *Stand up when your name is called.* **3** at

any time that: *The dog comes when it is called.* **4** at which time; and then: *We had just decided to go out for a walk, when it began to rain.* **5** although: *We have only three books when we need five.* **6** what time; which time: *Since when have they had a new car?* **7** the time or occasion: *the when and where of an act.* 1 *adv.,* 2-5 *conj.,* 6 *pron.,* 7 *n.*

whence (hwens), from what place, source, or cause; from where: *Whence do you come? (adv.). They returned to the country whence they came (conj.). adv., conj.*

whence so ev er (hwens′sō ev′ər), from whatever place, source, or cause. *conj.*

when e′er (hwen er′), whenever. *conj., adv.*

when ev er (hwen ev′ər), when; at whatever time; at any time that: *Come whenever you wish (conj.). I'll come whenever possible (adv.). conj., adv.*

when so ev er (hwen′sō ev′ər), whenever; at whatever time. *conj., adv.*

where (hwer *or* hwar), **1** in what place; at what place: *Where do you live? Where is he?* **2** to what place: *Where are you going?* **3** from what place: *Where did you get that story?* **4** what place: *Where did it come from?* **5** in which; at which: *That is the house where I was born.* **6** to which: *I know the place where he is going.* **7** in what way; in what respect: *Where is the harm in trying?* **8** in the place in which; at the place at which: *Your coat is where you left it.* **9** to the place to which: *I will go where you go.* **10** place or scene. 1-3,7 *adv.,* 4,10 *n.,* 5,6,8,9 *conj.*

where a bouts (hwer′ə bouts′ *or* hwar′ə bouts′), **1** where; near what place: *Whereabouts are my books? (adv.). We did not know whereabouts we were (conj.).* **2** place where a person or thing is: *Do you know the whereabouts of the cottage?* 1 *adv., conj.,* 2 *n.*

where as (hwer az′ *or* hwar az′), **1** on the contrary; but; while: *Some children like school, whereas others do not.* **2** considering that; since: *"Whereas the people of the colonies have been grieved and burdened with taxes. . . ." conj.*

where at (hwer at′ *or* hwar at′), at what; at which. *adv., conj.*

where by (hwer bī′ *or* hwar bī′), by what; by which: *There is no other way whereby she can do it. adv., conj.*

where fore (hwer′fôr *or* hwar′fôr), **1** for what reason? why? **2** for which reason; therefore; so. **3** for what reason; why. **4** reason: *I don't want to hear all the whys and wherefores.* 1,2 *adv.,* 3 *conj.,* 4 *n.*

where in (hwer in′ *or* hwar in′), in what; in which; how. *adv., conj.*

where of (hwer uv′, hwar uv′, hwer ov′, *or* hwar ov′), of what; of which; of whom: *I know whereof I speak. adv., conj.*

where on (hwer ôn′, hwar ôn′, hwer on′, *or* hwar on′), on which; on what: *Cottages occupy the land whereon the old farmhouse stood. adv., conj.*

where so ev er (hwer′sō ev′ər *or* hwar′sō ev′ər), wherever. *conj., adv.*

where to (hwer tü′ *or* hwar tü′), **1** to what; to which; where: *They went to the place whereto they had been sent.* **2** for what purpose; why: *Whereto do you mock me? adv., conj.*

where up on (hwer′ə pôn′, hwar′ə pôn′, hwer′ə pon′, *or* hwar′ə pon′), **1** upon what; upon which. **2** at which; after which. *adv., conj.*

wher ev er (hwer ev′ər *or* hwar ev′ər), where; to whatever place; in whatever place: *Sit wherever you like (conj.). Wherever are you going? (adv.). conj., adv.*

where with (hwer wiᴛʜ′, hwar wiᴛʜ′, hwer with′, *or* hwar with′), with what; with which: *Wherewith shall we be fed? adv., conj.*

where with al (hwer′wi ᴛʜôl *or* hwar′wi ᴛʜôl *for 1;* hwer′wi ᴛʜôl′ *or* hwar′wi ᴛʜôl′ *for 2*), **1** means, supplies, or money needed: *Has she the wherewithal to pay for the trip?* **2** OLD USE. wherewith. **1** *n.,* **2** *adv., conj.*

wher ry (hwer′ē), a light, shallow rowboat for carrying passengers and goods on rivers. *n., pl.* **wher ries.**

whet (hwet), **1** sharpen by rubbing: *whet a knife.* **2** make keen or eager; stimulate: *The smell of food whetted my appetite.* **3** act of whetting. **1,2** *v.,* **whet ted, whet ting; 3** *n.* —**whet′ter,** *n.*

wheth er (hweᴛʜ′ər), **1** *Whether* is used in expressing a choice or an alternative. *It matters little whether we go or stay. I do not know whether to work or rest.* **2** either: *Whether sick or well, she is always cheerful.* **3** if: *I asked whether I should finish the work. conj.*

whet stone (hwet′stōn′), stone for sharpening knives or tools. *n.*

whew (hwyü), exclamation of surprise, dismay, etc.: *Whew! it's cold! interj., n.*

whey (hwā), the watery part of milk that separates from the curd when milk sours or when cheese is made. *n.*

which (hwich), **1** *Which* is used in asking questions about persons or things. *Which is the best plan? (pron.). Which book do you want to read? (adj.).* **2** *Which* is also used in connecting a group of words with some word in the sentence. *Read the book which you have (pron.). Be careful which way you turn (adj.).* **3** the one that; any that: *Here are three boxes. Choose which you like best.* **1-3** *pron.,* **1,2** *adj.*

which ev er (hwich ev′ər), **1** any one; any that: *Take whichever you want (pron.). Buy whichever hat you like (adj.).* **2** no matter which: *Whichever you choose will be fine (pron.). Whichever side wins, I shall be satisfied (adj.). pron., adj.*

which so ev er (hwich′sō ev′ər), whichever. *pron., adj.*

whiff (hwif), **1** a slight gust; puff; breath: *A whiff of smoke blew in my face.* **2** a breathing in of an odor, smoke, or gas: *I took a whiff of the rose.* **3** to blow or puff. **1,2** *n.,* **3** *v.*

whif fle tree (hwif′əl trē′), the horizontal crossbar of a carriage or wagon, to which the traces of a harness are fastened; singletree. *n.* Also, **whippletree.**

Whig (hwig), **1** member of a British political party of the late 1600's to early 1800's that favored reforms and opposed the Tory party. The Whig party became the Liberal party. **2** an American who opposed British rule over the colonies at the time of the Revolutionary War. **3** member of a political party in the United States that was formed about 1834 in opposition to the Democratic Party. It was succeeded by the Republican Party about 1855. *n.*

while (hwīl), **1** time; space of time: *He kept us waiting a long while. The mail came a while ago.* **2** the while, during the time: *They danced and sang the while.* **3** during the time that; in the time that: *While I was speaking he said nothing. Summer is pleasant while it lasts.* **4** although: *While I like the color of the hat, I do not like its shape.* **5** pass or spend in some easy, pleasant manner: *The children while away many afternoons on the beach.* **1,2** *n.,* **3,4** *conj.,* **5** *v.,* **whiled, whil ing.**

worth one's while, worth one's time, attention, or effort: *If you help me with the painting, I'll make it worth your while—I'll pay you ten dollars.*

whilst (hwīlst), while. *conj.*

whim (hwim), a sudden fancy or notion: *I had a whim to take a plane somewhere. n.*

whim per (hwim′pər), **1** cry with low, broken sounds, in the way that a sick child or dog does. **2** a whimpering cry. **3** complain in a peevish, childish way; whine. **1,3** *v.,* **2** *n.* —**whim′per er,** *n.* —**whim′per ing ly,** *adv.*

whim sey (hwim′zē), whimsy. *n., pl.* **whim seys.**

whim si cal (hwim′zə kəl), having many odd notions or fancies; fanciful; odd. *adj.* —**whim′si cal ly,** *adv.*

whim sy (hwim′zē), **1** an odd or fanciful notion. **2** odd or fanciful humor; quaintness: *"Alice in Wonderland" is full of whimsy. n., pl.* **whim sies.** Also, **whimsey.**

whine (hwīn), **1** make a low, complaining cry or sound: *The dog whined to go out with us.* **2** a low, complaining cry or sound. **3** complain in a peevish, childish way: *Some people are always whining about trifles.* **4** say with a whine. **1,3,4** *v.,* **whined, whin ing; 2** *n.* —**whin′er,** *n.* —**whin′ing ly,** *adv.*

whin ny (hwin′ē), **1** the sound that a horse makes. **2** make such a sound. **1** *n., pl.* **whin nies; 2** *v.,* **whin nied, whin ny ing.**

whin y (hwī′nē), marked by whining; apt to whine; fretful. *adj.,* **whin i er, whin i est.**

whip (hwip), **1** thing to strike or beat with, usually a stick or handle with a flexible cord at the end. **2** strike or beat with or as with a whip; lash: *whip a horse to make it gallop. Rain whipped the pavement.* **3** a blow or stroke with or as with a whip. **4** move, put, or pull quickly and suddenly: *whip off a coat, whip out a knife. The child whipped behind the tree to hide from us.* **5** INFORMAL. defeat in a fight, contest, etc.: *The mayor whipped his opponent in the election.* **6** beat (cream, eggs, etc.) to a froth. **7** dessert made by beating cream, eggs, etc., into a froth. **8** rouse; incite: *whip up some enthusiasm.* **1,3,7** *n.,* **2,4-6,8** *v.,* **whipped** *or* **whipt, whip ping.** —**whip′like′,** *adj.* —**whip′per,** *n.*

whip hand, 1 the hand that holds the whip in driving. **2** position of control; advantage: *A clever person often gets the whip hand over others.*

whip lash (hwip′lash′), **1** lash of a whip. **2** injury to the neck caused by a sudden jolt that snaps the head backward and then forward. A driver whose car is struck with force from the rear may suffer whiplash. *n., pl.* **whip lash es.**

whip per-snap per (hwip′ər snap′ər), an impudent young person. *n.*

whip pet (hwip′it), a very swift dog that looks somewhat like a small greyhound, often used in racing. *n.*

whip ple tree (hwip′əl trē′), whiffletree. *n.*

whippoorwill
about 10 in. (25 cm.) long

whip poor will (hwip′ər wil′ *or* hwip′ər wil), a North American bird whose call sounds somewhat like its name. It is active at night or twilight. *n.*

whir (hwėr), **1** noise that sounds like whir-r-r: *the whir of machinery.* **2** operate or move with such a noise: *The motor whirs.* **1** *n.,* **2** *v.,* **whirred, whir ring.** Also, **whirr.**

whirl (hwėrl), **1** turn or swing round and round; spin: *The leaves whirled in the wind.* **2** move round and round: *whirl a lasso. We whirled about the room.* **3** move or carry quickly: *We were whirled away in an airplane.* **4** a whirling movement: *The dancer suddenly made a whirl.* **5** feel dizzy or confused. **6** dizzy or confused condition: *My thoughts are in a whirl.* **7** a rapid round of happenings, parties, etc. 1-3,5 *v.,* 4,6,7 *n.* —**whirl′er,** *n.* —**whirl′ing ly,** *adv.*

whirl i gig (hwer′lē gig′), **1** toy that whirls or spins. **2** merry-go-round. **3** anything that whirls. *n.*

whirl pool (hwerl′pül′), current of water whirling round and round rapidly and violently. *n.*

whirl wind (hwerl′wind′), current of air whirling violently round and round; whirling windstorm. *n.*

whirr (hwer), whir. *n., v.*

whisk (hwisk), **1** sweep or brush from a surface: *I whisked the crumbs from the table.* **2** a quick sweep: *I brushed away the dirt with a few whisks of a broom.* **3** move quickly: *The mouse whisked into its hole. I whisked the letter out of sight.* **4** a light, quick movement. **5** beat or whip to a froth. **6** a wire beater for eggs, cream, etc. 1,3,5 *v.,* 2,4,6 *n.*

whisk broom, a small broom for brushing clothes, etc.

whisk er (hwis′kər), **1** one of the hairs growing on a man's face. **2 whiskers,** *pl.* the hair or part of a beard that grows on a man's cheeks. **3** a long, stiff hair growing near the mouth of a cat, rat, etc. *n.* —**whis′ker less,** *adj.*

whisk ered (hwis′kərd), having whiskers. *adj.*

whis key (hwis′kē), a strong alcoholic drink made from grain. Some kinds of whiskey are half alcohol. *n., pl.* **whis keys.** [*Whiskey* was shortened from *whiskybae,* which came from Gaelic *uisge beatha,* originally meaning "water of life."]

whis ky (hwis′kē), whiskey. *n., pl.* **whis kies.**

whis per (hwis′pər), **1** speak very softly and low. **2** a very soft, low, spoken sound. **3** speak to in a whisper. **4** tell secretly or privately: *It is whispered that the business is failing.* **5** something told secretly or privately: *No whisper about his being fired has come to our ears.* **6** make a soft, rustling sound: *The wind whispered in the pines.* **7** a soft, rustling sound: *We could hear the whisper of the leaves.* 1,3,4,6 *v.,* 2,5,7 *n.* —**whis′per er,** *n.* —**whis′per ing ly,** *adv.*

whist (hwist), a card game somewhat like bridge for two pairs of players. *n.*

whis tle (hwis′əl), **1** make a clear, shrill sound by forcing breath through one's teeth or pursing one's lips: *The girl whistled and her dog ran to her quickly.* **2** the sound made by whistling. **3** instrument for making whistling sounds, usually consisting of a tube through which air or steam is blown. **4** blow a whistle: *The traffic officer whistled for the cars to stop. The engineer whistled to warn the people at the train crossing.* **5** produce or utter by whistling: *whistle a tune.* **6** move with a shrill sound: *The wind whistled around the house.* 1,4-6 *v.,* **whis tled, whis tling;** 2,3 *n.* —**whis′tle a ble,** *adj.*

whis tler (hwis′lər), person or thing that whistles. *n.*

Whis tler (hwis′lər), **James Abbott McNeill,** 1834-1903, American painter and etcher. *n.*

whit (hwit), a very small bit: *I don't care a whit what we do. n.*

white (hwit), **1** the color of snow, salt, or the paper on which this book is printed. **2** having or approaching this color: *a white sheet.* **3** white coloring matter. **4** white clothing. **5** part that is white or whitish, such as the albumen surrounding the yolk of an egg or the white part of the eyeball. **6** pale: *They all turned white with fear.* **7** light-colored: *white meat, a white wine.* **8** having a light-colored skin; Caucasian. **9** person who has light-colored skin; Caucasian. **10** silvery; gray: *Grandmother has white hair.* **11** snowy: *the white peaks of the Rockies.* **12** spotless; pure; innocent. 1,3-5,9 *n.,* 2,6-8,10-12 *adj.,* **whit er, whit est.** —**white′ness,** *n.*

a hat	**i** it	**oi** oil	**ch** child	a in about
ā age	**ī** ice	**ou** out	**ng** long	e in taken
ä far	**o** hot	**u** cup	**sh** she	ə = { i in pencil
e let	**ō** open	**u̇** put	**th** thin	o in lemon
ē equal	**ô** order	**ü** rule	**ŦH** then	u in circus
ėr term			**zh** measure	

White (hwit), **E(lwyn) B(rooks),** 1899-1985, American writer of essays, children's stories, and poems. *n.*

white ant, termite.

white blood cell, any colorless blood cell with a nucleus, that destroys disease germs; white corpuscle; leucocyte.

white cap (hwit′kap′), wave with a foaming white crest. *n.*

white cell, white blood cell.

white-col lar (hwit′kol′ər), of clerical, professional, or business work or workers. *adj.*

white corpuscle, white blood cell.

white elephant, anything that is expensive and troublesome to keep and take care of.

white feather, symbol of cowardice.

white fish (hwit′fish′), a food fish with white or silvery sides, found in lakes and streams. *n., pl.* **white fish es** or **white fish.**

white flag, a plain white flag displayed as a sign of truce or surrender.

white frost, hoarfrost.

white gold, alloy of gold and nickel or platinum, sometimes with copper and zinc. White gold looks much like platinum and is used for jewelry.

White hall (hwit′hôl′), **1** street in London, where many government offices are located. **2** the British government or its policies. *n.*

White horse (hwit′hôrs), capital of Yukon territory, in NW Canada. *n.*

white-hot (hwit′hot′), **1** white with heat; extremely hot. **2** extremely angry; passionate, violent, etc. *adj.*

White House, 1 the official residence of the President of the United States, in Washington, D.C. **2** office, authority, opinion, etc., of the President of the United States.

white lie, a lie about some small matter; polite or harmless lie.

white matter, the tissue in the brain and spinal cord that consists chiefly of nerve fibers.

White Mountains, range of the Appalachian Mountains in New Hampshire.

whit en (hwit′n), make or become white: *Sunshine helps to whiten clothes. A person's hair whitens with age. v.*

white oak, an oak tree of eastern North America having light-gray or whitish bark and hard wood.

white potato, another name for the potato.

White Russia, Byelorussia.

White Sea, arm of the Arctic Ocean, in NW Soviet Union.

white wash (hwit′wosh′ *or* hwit′wôsh′), **1** liquid for whitening walls, woodwork, etc. Whitewash is usually made of lime and water. **2** whiten with whitewash. **3** cover up the faults or mistakes of. **4** a covering up of faults or mistakes. **5** INFORMAL. to defeat in a game without a score for the loser. 1,4 *n.,* 2,3,5 *v.* —**white′wash′er,** *n.*

whith er (hwiŦH′ər), to what place; to which place; where. *adv., conj.*

whit ing[1] (hwi′ting), any of several food fishes of the Atlantic Ocean. *n., pl.* **whit ings** or **whit ing.**

whit ing[2] (hwi′ting), a powdered white chalk. Whiting is used in making putty, whitewash, and silver polish. *n.*

whit ish (hwī′tish), somewhat white. *adj.* —**whit′ish-
ness,** *n.*

Whit man (hwit′mən), **Walt,** 1819-1892, American
poet. *n.*

Whit ney (hwit′nē), **1 Eli,** 1765-1825, American who invented the cotton gin. **2 Mount,** peak of the Sierra Nevada mountains, in E California, 14,495 feet (4418
meters) high. It is the highest mountain in the United
States outside Alaska. *n.*

Whit sun day (hwit′sun/dē), the seventh Sunday after
Easter; Pentecost. *n.* [Whitsunday comes from Old English *hwīta Sunnandæg,* originally meaning "white Sunday." It was probably called this because the persons
newly baptized wore white robes on this day.]

Whit sun tide (hwit′sən tīd′), the week beginning with
Whitsunday, especially the first three days. *n.*

Whit ti er (hwit′ē ər), **John Greenleaf,** 1807-1892,
American poet. *n.*

whit tle (hwit′l), **1** to cut shavings or chips from (wood,
etc.) with a knife, usually for fun. **2** shape by whittling;
carve: *The students learned how to whittle animals from
wood. v.,* **whit tled, whit tling.** —**whit′tler,** *n.*
whittle down, cut down little by little: *whittle down
expenses.*

whiz *or* **whizz** (hwiz), **1** a humming or hissing sound.
2 move or rush with such a sound: *An arrow whizzed past
his head.* **3** SLANG. a very clever person; expert. 1,3 *n., pl.*
whiz zes; 2 *v.,* **whizzed, whiz zing.** —**whiz′zer,** *n.*

who (hü), **1** Who is used in asking questions about a
person or persons. *Who goes there? Who is your friend?
Who told you?* **2** Who is also used in connecting a group
of words with some previous word that refers to a person or persons in the sentence. *The girl who spoke is my
best friend. We saw people who were working in the fields.*
3 the person that; any person that; one that: *Who is not
for us is against us. pron.*

whoa (hwō *or* wō), stop! *"Whoa there!" she said to her
horse. interj.*

who'd (hüd), **1** who would. **2** who had.

who ev er (hü ev′ər), **1** who; any person that: *Whoever
wants the book may have it.* **2** no matter who: *Whoever else
leaves you, I won't. pron.*

whole (hōl), **1** having all its parts; complete: *They gave us
a whole set of dishes.* **2** full; entire: *We worked the whole
day. He ate the whole melon.* **3** all of a thing; the total:
Three thirds make a whole. **4** thing complete in itself; a
system: *the complex whole of civilization.* **5** not injured,
broken, or defective: *I came out of the fight with a whole
skin.* **6** in one piece; undivided: *The dog swallowed the
meat whole.* **7** well; healthy. 1,2,5-7 *adj.,* 3,4 *n.* [Whole
comes from Old English *hāl.*] —**whole′ness,** *n.*
on the whole, 1 considering everything. **2** for the most
part.

whole heart ed (hōl′här′tid), earnest; sincere; hearty;
cordial: *The school gave the team its wholehearted support. adj.* —**whole′heart′ed ly,** *adv.*

whole milk, milk from which none of the natural elements have been removed.

whole note, (in music) note to be played four times as
long as a quarter note.

whole number, 1 a number such as 1, 2, 3, 4, 5, etc.,
which is not a fraction or a mixed number; integer. 15
and 106 are whole numbers; $^1/_2$ and $^7/_8$ are fractions; $1^3/_8$
and $23^2/_3$ are mixed numbers.

whole sale (hōl′sāl′), **1** sale of goods in large quantities
at a time, usually to storekeepers or others who will in
turn sell them to users: *Our grocer buys at wholesale and
sells at retail.* **2** in large lots or quantities: *buy something
wholesale (adv.). The wholesale price of this coat is $30; the
retail price is $50 (adj.).* **3** selling in large quantities: *a*

wholesale fruit business. **4** sell or be sold in large quantities: *They wholesale these jackets at $10 each.* **5** general;
extensive: *Avoid wholesale condemnation.* 1 *n.,* 2,3,5 *adj.,*
2 *adv.,* 4 *v.,* **whole saled, whole sal ing.**

whole sal er (hōl′sā′lər), a wholesale merchant. *n.*

whole some (hōl′səm), **1** good for the health; healthful:
Milk is a wholesome food. **2** healthy-looking; suggesting
health: *a clean, wholesome face.* **3** good for the mind or
morals; beneficial: *The students had a wholesome interest
in learning. adj.* —**whole′some ly,** *adv.* —**whole′some-
ness,** *n.*

whole step, (in music) an interval of two half steps,
such as D to E, or F to G.

whole tone, whole step.

whole-wheat (hōl′hwēt′), **1** made of the entire wheat
kernel: *whole-wheat flour.* **2** made from whole-wheat
flour: *whole-wheat bread. adj.*

who'll (hül), **1** who will. **2** who shall.

whol ly (hō′lē), to the whole amount or extent; completely; entirely; totally: *The patient was wholly cured. adv.*

whom (hüm), what person; which person. *Whom is a
form of who. Whom do you like best? He does not know
whom to believe. The girl to whom I spoke is my cousin.
pron.*

whom ev er (hüm′ev′ər), **1** whom; any person whom.
2 no matter whom. *pron.*

whom so ev er (hüm′sō ev′ər), any person whom. *pron.*

whoop (hüp, hüp, hwüp, *or* hwüp), **1** a loud cry or
shout: *The winner gave a whoop of joy.* **2** shout loudly.
3 the loud, gasping sound a person with whooping
cough makes after a fit of coughing. **4** make this noise.
1,3 *n.,* 2,4 *v.*

whooping cough, an infectious disease of children,
and rarely of adults, that causes fits of coughing that
end with a loud, gasping sound.

whooping crane
up to 5 ft. (1.5 m.) tall

whooping crane, a large, white, North American
crane having a loud, raucous cry. It is nearly extinct.

whop per (hwop′ər), INFORMAL. **1** something very large.
2 a big lie. *n.*

whore (hôr), prostitute. *n.*

whorl (hwėrl), **1** circle of leaves or flowers round a stem
of a plant. **2** one of the turns of a spiral shell. **3** anything

whorl (def. 1)
whorl of leaves

whorl (def. 2)
shell with whorls

that circles or turns on or around something else. People can be identified by the whorls of their fingerprints. *n.*

who's (hüz), **1** who is. **2** who has.

whose (hüz), of whom; of which: *The girl whose work got the prize is very talented. Whose book is this? pron.*

who so ev er (hü′sō ev′ər), whoever. *pron.*

whse., warehouse.

why (hwī), **1** for what reason: *Why did the baby cry?* (*adv.*). *He does not know why he lost* (*conj.*). **2** for which; because of which: *That is the reason why I left.* **3** the reason for which: *That is why she raised the question.* **4** reason: *I tried to find out the whys and wherefores of their strange behavior.* **5** *Why* is sometimes used to show surprise, doubt, etc., or just to fill in, without adding any important meaning to what is said. *Why it's all gone! Why, yes, I will if you wish.* 1 *adv.*, 1-3 *conj.*, 4 *n., pl.* **whys;** 5 *interj.*

WI, Wisconsin (used with postal Zip Code).

W.I., West Indies.

Wich i ta (wich′ə tô), city in S Kansas. *n.*

Wichita Falls, city in N Texas.

wick (wik), cord of twisted thread on an oil lamp or candle. When the wick is lit, it draws the oil or melted wax up to be burned. *n.* **—wick′less,** *adj.*

wick ed (wik′id), **1** bad; evil; sinful: *a wicked person, wicked deeds.* **2** mischievous; playfully sly: *a wicked smile.* **3** unpleasant; severe: *A wicked snowstorm swept through the state. adj.* **—wick′ed ly,** *adv.*

wick ed ness (wik′id nis), **1** quality of being wicked. **2** a wicked thing or act. *n., pl.* **wick ed ness es.**

wick er (wik′ər), **1** a slender, easily bent branch or twig. **2** twigs, or any slender, easily bent material, woven together. Wicker is used in making baskets and furniture. **3** made of wicker. 1,2 *n.*, 3 *adj.*

wick er work (wik′ər wėrk′), objects made of wicker. *n.*

wick et (wik′it), **1** (in croquet) a wire arch stuck in the ground to knock the ball through. **2** (in cricket) either of the two sets of sticks that one side tries to hit with the ball. **3** a small window: *Buy your tickets at this wicket.* **4** a small door or gate: *The big door has a wicket in it. n.*

wide (wīd), **1** filling much space from side to side; not narrow; broad: *a wide street. The ship sailed across the wide ocean. They went forth into the wide world.* **2** extending a certain distance from side to side: *The door is three feet wide.* **3** over an extensive space or region: *travel far and wide.* **4** having great range; including many different things: *A trip around the world gives wide experience.* **5** far open: *He stared with wide eyes.* **6** to the full extent; fully: *Open your mouth wide. The gates stand wide open.* **7** far from a named point or object: *The shot was wide of the mark.* 1,2,4,5,7 *adj.*, **wid er, wid est;** 3,6 *adv.* **—wide′ness,** *n.*

wide-a wake (wīd′ə wāk′), **1** with the eyes wide open; fully awake. **2** alert; keen; knowing: *a wide-awake watchdog. adj.* **—wide′-a wake′ness,** *n.*

wide-eyed (wīd′īd′), with the eyes wide open: *The children watched the rabbits with wide-eyed interest. adj.*

wide ly (wīd′lē), to a wide extent: *a person who is widely known, to be widely read, widely opened eyes. adv.*

wid en (wīd′n), make or become wide or wider: *We widened the path through the forest. The river widens as it flows. v.* **—wid′en er,** *n.*

wide spread (wīd′spred′), **1** spread widely: *widespread wings.* **2** spread over a wide space: *a widespread flood.* **3** occurring in many places or among many persons far apart: *a widespread belief. adj.*

widg eon (wij′ən), a wild duck of fresh waters. *n., pl.* **widg eons** or **widg eon.**

widg et (wij′it), INFORMAL. gadget. *n.*

a hat	**i** it	**oi** oil	**ch** child	a in about
ā age	**ī** ice	**ou** out	**ng** long	e in taken
ä far	**o** hot	**u** cup	**sh** she	ə = { i in pencil
e let	**ō** open	**u̇** put	**th** thin	o in lemon
ē equal	**ô** order	**ü** rule	**ᴛʜ** then	u in circus
ėr term			**zh** measure	

wid ow (wid′ō), **1** woman whose husband is dead and who has not married again. **2** make a widow of: *She was widowed when she was only thirty years old.* 1 *n.*, 2 *v.*

wid ow er (wid′ō ər), man whose wife is dead and who has not married again. *n.*

wid ow hood (wid′ō hu̇d), condition or time of being a widow. *n.*

width (width), **1** how wide a thing is; distance across; breadth: *The room is 12 feet in width.* **2** piece of a certain width: *Two widths of cloth will make the curtains. n.*

wield (wēld), hold and use; manage; control: *The worker wielded a hammer. A writer wields the pen. The people wield the power in a democracy. v.* **—wield′a ble,** *adj.* **—wield′er,** *n.*

wield y (wēl′dē), easily controlled or handled; manageable. *adj.,* **wield i er, wield i est.**

wie ner (wē′nər), frankfurter. *n.* [*Wiener* comes from German *Wiener Würstchen,* meaning "Vienna sausage."]

wife (wīf), woman who has a husband; a married woman. *n., pl.* **wives.** [*Wife* comes from Old English *wīf,* which originally meant "woman."] **—wife′less,** *adj.*

wife ly (wīf′lē), of a wife; like a wife. *adj.,* **wife li er, wife li est.** **—wife′li ness,** *n.*

wig (wig), an artificial covering of natural or false hair for the head. *n.*

wig gle (wig′əl), **1** move with short, quick movements from side to side; wriggle: *The puppy wiggled out of my arms.* **2** such a movement. 1 *v.*, **wig gled, wig gling;** 2 *n.*

wig gler (wig′lər), **1** person or thing that wiggles. **2** the larva or pupa of a mosquito. *n.*

wig gly (wig′lē), **1** wiggling. **2** wavy. *adj.,* **wig gli er, wig gli est.**

wig wag (wig′wag′), **1** move back and forth. **2** signal by movements of arms, flags, or lights, according to a code. **3** such signaling. 1,2 *v.*, **wig wagged, wig wagging;** 3 *n.* **—wig′wag′ger,** *n.*

wigwam
Part of the wigwam is cut away to show the framework.

wig wam (wig′wom *or* wig′wôm), hut made of bark, mats, or skins laid over a dome-shaped frame of poles, used by certain North American Indians. *n.* [*Wigwam* comes from its North American Indian name.]

wild (wīld), **1** living or growing in the forests or fields; not tamed; not cultivated: *a wild animal, a wild daisy.* **2** with no people living in it: *the wild region of the far north.* **3 wilds,** *pl.* wild country. **4** not civilized; savage: *He is reading about the wild tribes of ancient times in Europe.* **5** not checked; not restrained: *a wild rush for the ball.* **6** not in proper control or order: *wild hair.* **7** violently excited; frantic: *The injured animal was wild with pain.* **8** violent: *Wild waves came roaring onto the shore.* **9** rash; crazy: *a wild scheme.* **10** far from the mark. **11** in a wild

manner; to a wild degree. 1,2,4-10 *adj.*, 3 *n.*, 11 *adv.*
—**wild′ly,** *adv.* —**wild′ness,** *n.*
run wild, live or grow without restraint.
wild and woolly, rough and uncivilized.
wild boar, a wild hog of Europe, southern Asia, and northern Africa.
wild cat (wīld′kat′), **1** any of several wild animals related to the common cat and similar to it in appearance, but larger. A lynx is one kind of wildcat. **2** not safe; reckless: *We lost all of our money by investing in wildcat stocks.* **3** a fierce fighter. **4** a well drilled for oil or gas in a region where none has been found before. **5** not authorized by proper union officials; precipitated by small groups or local unions: *a wildcat strike.* 1,3,4 *n.*, 2,5 *adj.*
Wilde (wīld), **Oscar,** 1854-1900, British playwright, poet, and novelist, born in Ireland. *n.*
Wil der (wīl′dər), **Thornton,** 1897-1975, American playwright and novelist. *n.*
wil der ness (wīl′dər nis), a wild, uncultivated, or desolate region with no people living in it. *n., pl.* **wil der ness es.**
wild-eyed (wīld′īd′), **1** staring wildly or angrily. **2** senseless; irrational: *wild-eyed notions. adj.*
wild fire (wīld′fīr′), a fire that is hard to put out. *n.*
like wildfire, very rapidly: *The news spread like wildfire.*
wild flow er (wīld′flou′ər), any uncultivated flowering plant that grows in the woods, fields, etc. *n.*
wild flower, wildflower.
wild fowl, birds ordinarily hunted, such as wild ducks or geese, partridges, quails, and pheasants.
wild-goose chase (wīld′güs′), a useless search or attempt; foolish or hopeless quest.
wild life (wīld′līf′), wild animals and plants: *The campers saw many kinds of wildlife. n.*
wild rice, a North American aquatic grass, whose grain is used for food.
wild West, the western United States during pioneer days.
wile (wīl), **1** a trick to deceive; cunning way: *The automobile dealer used many wiles to make a sale.* **2** coax; lure; entice: *The sunshine wiled him away from his work.* 1 *n.*, 2 *v.*, **wiled, wil ing.**
wil ful (wīl′fəl), willful. *adj.* —**wil′ful ness,** *n.*
wil ful ly (wīl′fə lē), willfully. *adv.*
Wil helm II (vil′helm), 1859-1941, last emperor of Germany, from 1888 until he abdicated the throne in 1918. He was known as Kaiser Wilhelm.
wil i ness (wī′lē nis), wily quality; craftiness; slyness. *n.*
will[1] (wil), **1** am going to; is going to; are going to: *I will go shopping tomorrow.* **2** am willing to; is willing to; are willing to: *I will help clean the house if he does.* **3** wish; desire: *We cannot always do as we will.* **4** be able to; can: *The pail will hold four gallons.* **5** must: *Don't argue; you will do it at once!* **6** do often or usually: *She will read for hours at a time. v., past tense* **would.**
will[2] (wil), **1** power of the mind to decide and do: *A good leader must have a strong will.* **2** decide by using this power; use the will: *I willed to keep awake.* **3** influence or try to influence by deliberate control over thought and action: *She willed the person in front of her to turn around.* **4** determine; decide: *Fate has willed it otherwise.* **5** purpose or determination: *the will to live.* **6** wish; desire: *"Thy will be done."* **7** a legal statement or document telling what one wishes to be done with one's property after he or she is dead. **8** give by such a statement: *They willed all their property to their children.* **9** feeling toward another: *Most of us feel good will toward people we like.* 1,5-7,9 *n.*, 2-4,8 *v.*
at will, whenever one wishes.
will ful (wil′fəl), **1** wanting or taking one's own way;

stubborn: *The willful child would not obey.* **2** done on purpose; intended: *willful murder. adj.* Also, **wilful.**
—**will′ful ness,** *n.*
will ful ly (wil′fə lē), **1** by choice; voluntarily. **2** by design; intentionally. **3** selfishly; stubbornly. *adv.* Also, **wilfully.**
Wil liam I (wil′yəm), 1027?-1087, duke of Normandy who conquered England at the battle of Hastings in 1066 and was king of England from 1066 to 1087. He was called "William the Conqueror."
Wil liams (wil′yəmz), **1 Roger,** 1604?-1683, English clergyman who founded Rhode Island. **2 Tennessee,** 1911-1983, American playwright. *n.*
Wil liams burg (wil′yəmz bérg′), city in SE Virginia. It has been restored to look as it did before the Revolutionary War. *n.*
wil lies (wil′ēz), SLANG. spell of nervousness. *n.pl.*
will ing (wil′ing), **1** ready; consenting: *He is willing to wait.* **2** cheerfully ready: *willing obedience. adj.* —**will′ing ly,** *adv.* —**will′ing ness,** *n.*
will-o'-the-wisp (wil′ə ＴＨə wisp′), **1** a flickering light appearing at night over marshy places. It is thought to be caused by combustion of marsh gas. **2** thing that deceives or misleads by luring on: *Any scheme to get rich quickly is likely to be a will-o'-the-wisp. n.*
wil low (wil′ō), tree or shrub with tough, slender branches and narrow leaves. The branches of most willows bend easily and are used to make furniture, baskets, etc. *n.*

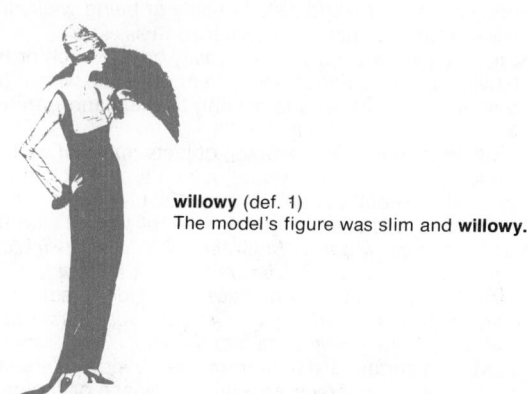

willowy (def. 1)
The model's figure was slim and **willowy.**

wil low y (wil′ō ē), **1** like a willow; slender; supple; graceful. **2** having many willows. *adj.*, **wil low i er, wil low i est.**
will pow er (wil′pou′ər), strength of will; firmness. *n.*
wil ly-nil ly (wil′ē nil′ē), willingly or not; with or against one's wishes. *adv.*
Wil ming ton (wil′ming tən), city in N Delaware, on the Delaware River. *n.*
Wil son (wil′sən), **1 Harold,** born 1916, British statesman, prime minister from 1964 to 1970 and from 1974 to 1976. **2 (Thomas) Woodrow,** 1856-1924, the 28th president of the United States, from 1913 to 1921. **3 Mount,** peak in SW California. One of the largest telescopes in the world is in the observatory on top of Mount Wilson. *n.*
wilt[1] (wilt), **1** become limp and drooping; wither. **2** lose strength, vigor, assurance, etc. **3** cause to wilt. *v.*
wilt[2] (wilt), OLD USE. will[1]. "Thou wilt" means "you will." *v.*
wil y (wī′lē), using subtle tricks to deceive; crafty; cunning; sly: *a wily thief. The wily fox got away. adj.*, **wil i er, wil i est.** —**wil′i ly,** *adv.* —**wil′i ness,** *n.*
wim ble (wim′bəl), tool for boring. *n.*

wimple (def. 1)

wim ple (wim′pəl), **1** cloth for the head arranged in folds about the head, cheeks, chin, and neck, worn sometimes by nuns and formerly by other women. **2** to cover with a wimple. **3** to ripple. **1** *n.,* **2,3** *v.,* **wim pled, wim pling.**

win (win), **1** be successful over others; get victory or success: *We all hope our team will win.* **2** get victory or success in: *He won the race.* **3** INFORMAL. success; victory: *We had four wins and no defeats.* **4** get by effort, ability, or skill; gain: *win fame, win a prize.* **5** gain the favor of; persuade: *The speaker soon won the audience. She has completely won the other scientists over to her opinion.* **6** get to; reach, often by effort: *win the summit of a mountain.* **1,2,4-6** *v.,* **won, win ning; 3** *n.* —**win′na ble,** *adj.*

wince (wins), **1** draw back suddenly; flinch slightly: *I winced when the dentist's drill touched my tooth.* **2** act of wincing: *Seeing the wince, the dentist stopped drilling for a moment.* **1** *v.,* **winced, winc ing; 2** *n.* —**winc′er,** *n.* —**winc′ing ly,** *adv.* —**winc′ing ness,** *n.*

winch (def. 1)

winch (winch), **1** machine for lifting or pulling, turned by hand with a crank or by an engine. The crank is attached to a drum around which rope for hoisting or hauling is wound. **2** lift or pull by using a winch. **1** *n., pl.* **winch es; 2** *v.* —**winch′er,** *n.*

wind¹ (wind), **1** air in motion. The wind varies in force from a slight breeze to a strong gale. **2** a strong wind; gale: *Winds blowing at ninety miles an hour toppled a tree onto our roof.* **3** air filled with some smell: *The deer caught the wind of us and ran off.* **4** follow by scent; smell. **5** power of breathing; breath: *A runner needs good wind.* **6** put out of breath; cause difficulty in breathing: *Walking up the steep hill winded me.* **7 winds,** *pl.* wind instruments. **1-3,5,7** *n.,* **4,6** *v.,* **wind ed, wind ing.**

get wind of, find out about; get a hint of: *Don't let Mother get wind of our plans to have a surprise party on her birthday.*

in the wind, happening; about to happen.

take the wind out of one's sails, take away one's advantage, argument, etc., suddenly or unexpectedly.

wind² (wīnd), **1** move this way and that; go in a crooked way; change direction; turn: *A brook winds through the*

woods. *We wound our way through the narrow streets.* **2** to fold, wrap, or place about something: *She wound her arms around her new puppy.* **3** to cover with something put, wrapped, or folded around: *The patient's arm is wound with bandages.* **4** roll into a ball or on a spool: *We took turns winding yarn. Thread comes wound on spools.* **5** a bend; turn; twist. **6** twist or turn around something: *The vine winds around a pole.* **7** make (some machine) go by turning some part of it: *wind a clock.* **8** be wound: *This clock winds easily.* **1-4,6-8** *v.,* **wound, wind ing; 5** *n.* —**wind′a ble,** *adj.* —**wind′er,** *n.*

wind up, 1 end; settle; conclude. **2** (in baseball) make swinging and twisting movements of the arm and body just before pitching the ball.

wind³ (wind), blow: *wind a fanfare on a trumpet.* *v.,* **wind ed** or **wound, wind ing.**

wind bag (wind′bag′), SLANG. person who talks a great deal but does not say much. *n.*

wind break (wind′brāk′), a shelter from the wind: *The campers pitched their tent next to the stone wall, so the wall would serve as a windbreak.* *n.*

Wind break er (wind′brā′kər), trademark for a short jacket of nylon, wool, etc., with a tight-fitting band at the waist and cuffs. It is worn outdoors. *n.*

wind chill or **wind chill factor,** the estimated cooling effect on exposed human skin of air temperature and wind speed combined. If the air temperature is 10 degrees Fahrenheit and the wind speed is 20 miles per hour, the wind chill is −24 degrees Fahrenheit.

wind fall (wind′fôl′), **1** fruit blown down by the wind. **2** an unexpected piece of good luck. *n.*

wind flow er (wind′flou′ər), anemone. *n.*

wind i ly (win′də lē), in a windy manner. *adv.*

wind i ness (win′dē nis), a being windy. *n.*

wind ing (win′ding), **1** act of one that winds. **2** a bend; turn. **3** bending; turning. **4** something that is wound or coiled. **1,2,4** *n.,* **3** *adj.* —**wind′ing ly,** *adv.* —**wind′ing ness,** *n.*

wind instrument (wind), a musical instrument sounded by blowing air into it. French horns, flutes, and trombones are wind instruments.

wind jam mer (wind′jam′ər), INFORMAL. a sailing ship. *n.*

wind lass (wind′ləs), machine for pulling or lifting things. The windlass is a kind of winch used to hoist water from a well or an anchor out of the water. *n., pl.* **wind lass es.**

WORD HISTORY

windlass

Windlass came into English about 600 years ago from Icelandic *vindāss,* which comes from *vinda,* meaning "to wind, turn," and *āss,* meaning "a pole."

wind less (wind′lis), free from wind; calm. *adj.*

wind mill (wind′mil′), a mill or machine worked by the action of the wind upon a wheel of vanes or sails mounted on a tower. Windmills are mostly used to pump water. *n.*

windmill

win dow (win′dō), **1** an opening to let in light or air set into an outer wall or roof of a building or into a vehicle. **2** an opening like this, with its glass and its wooden or metal frame. Windows may open and shut, or may be fixed in a closed position. *n.* **—win′dow less,** *adj.*

WORD HISTORY

window

Window came into English about 750 years ago from Icelandic *vindauga,* which comes from *vindr,* meaning "the wind," and *auga,* meaning "the eye."

window box, container of wood, metal, or plastic, set on or fastened to a windowsill, in which small plants may be grown.

win dow pane (win′dō pān′), piece of glass in a window. *n.*

win dow-shop (win′dō shop′), look at articles in store windows without going in to buy anything. *v.,* **win dow-shopped, win dow-shop ping.**

win dow sill (win′dō sil′), piece of wood or stone across the bottom of a window. *n.*

wind pipe (wind′pīp′), the passage by which air is carried from the throat to the lungs; trachea. *n.*

wind row (wind′rō′), row of hay raked together to dry before being made into heaps. *n.*

wind shear (wind′shir′), a sudden, powerful shift in wind direction. It is a threat to aircraft that are taking off or landing. *n.*

wind shield (wind′shēld′), sheet of glass, etc., to keep off the wind. Automobiles have windshields. *n.*

wind sock or **wind sleeve** (wind), device somewhat like a large sock, mounted on a pole and open at one end to catch the wind and show its direction.

Wind sor (win′zər), **1** town in S England, where **Windsor Castle,** chief residence of the British sovereign, is located. **2** the family name of the royal house of Great Britain since 1917. *n.*

wind storm (wind′stôrm′), storm with much wind but little or no rain. *n.*

wind surf ing (wind′sėr′fing), surfing on a sailboard; boardsailing. *n.*

wind tunnel (wind), tunnel for testing the effects of wind and air pressure on aircraft, missiles, etc., with air forced through at high speeds.

wind up (wind′up′), **1** a winding up; end; close; conclusion. **2** series of swinging and twisting movements of the arm and body made by a baseball pitcher just before pitching the ball. *n.*

wind ward (wind′wərd), **1** on the side toward the wind. **2** the side toward the wind. **3** in the direction from which the wind is blowing. 1,3 *adj., adv.,* 2 *n.*

Wind ward Islands (wind′wərd), the S part of the Lesser Antilles in the West Indies.

wind y (win′dē), **1** having much wind: *a windy day, the windy deck of a ship, windy weather.* **2** made of wind; empty: *windy talk.* **3** talking a great deal; voluble. *adj.,* **wind i er, wind i est. —wind′i ly,** *adv.* **—wind′i ness,** *n.*

wine (wīn), **1** an alcoholic drink made from the fermented juice of grapes. **2** the fermented juice of other fruits or plants: *currant wine, dandelion wine.* **3** entertain with wine. 1,2 *n.,* 3 *v.,* **wined, win ing. —wine′less,** *adj.*

wing (wing), **1** one of the movable parts of a bird, insect, or bat used in flying, or a corresponding part of a bird or insect that does not fly. Birds have one pair of wings; insects usually have two pairs. **2** anything like a wing in shape or use: *the wings of an airplane.* **3** part that sticks out from the main part or body, especially the part of a building that sticks out sideways from the main part. **4** either of the side portions of an army or fleet ready for battle. **5** either of the spaces to the right or left of the stage in a theater. **6** part of an organization; faction. The liberals of a political group are often called the left wing. **7** an air force unit composed of two or more groups. **8** fly: *The bird wings its way to the south.* **9** make able to fly; give speed to: *Terror winged our steps as the bear drew nearer.* **10** to wound in the wing or arm: *The bullet winged the bird but did not kill it.* 1-7 *n.,* 8-10 *v.* [*Wing* came into English about 800 years ago from Icelandic *vængr.*]
on the wing, in flight.

take wing, fly away: *The bird took wing when the cat came near.*

under the wing of, under the protection of.

winged (wingd *or* wing′id), **1** having wings. **2** swift; rapid: *winged messenger. adj.*

wing span (wing′span′), distance between the wing tips of an airplane. *n.*

wing spread (wing′spred′), distance between the tips of the wings when they are spread. *n.*

wink (wingk), **1** close the eyes and open them again quickly: *The bright light made him wink.* **2** close and open one eye on purpose as a hint or signal: *I winked at my sister to keep still.* **3** a winking. **4** a hint or signal given by winking. **5** twinkle: *The stars winked.* **6** a very short time: *quick as a wink.* 1,2,5 *v.,* 3,4,6 *n.* **—wink′ing ly,** *adv.*

wink at, pretend not to see: *My parents knew I came home past my bedtime last night, but they winked at it.*

win ner (win′ər), person or thing that wins: *The winner of the contest got a prize. n.*

win ning (win′ing), **1** that wins: *a winning team.* **2** charming; attractive: *a very winning smile.* **3 winnings,** *pl.* what is won; money won: *The gamblers pocketed their winnings.* 1,2 *adj.,* 3 *n.* **—win′ning ly,** *adv.*

Win ni peg (win′ə peg), **1** city in S Canada, capital of Manitoba. **2 Lake,** lake in S Canada. *n.*

win now (win′ō), **1** blow off the chaff from (grain); drive or blow away (chaff). **2** sort out; separate; sift: *winnow truth from lies. v.* [*Winnow* is from Old English *windwian,* which comes from *wind,* meaning "the wind."]

win some (win′səm), charming; attractive; pleasing: *a winsome young couple, a winsome smile. adj.* [*Winsome* is from Old English *wynsum,* which comes from *wynn,* meaning "joy."]

win ter (win/tər), **1** the coldest of the four seasons; time of the year between autumn and spring. **2** of winter: *winter clothes, winter weather.* **3** pass the winter: *Robins winter in the south.* **4** keep or feed during winter: *We wintered our cattle in the warm valley.* 1 *n.,* 2 *adj.,* 3,4 *v.*

win ter green (win/tər grēn/), a small evergreen plant of North America with bright-red berries and aromatic leaves. An oil made from its leaves is used in medicine and as a flavoring. *n.*

win ter ize (win/tə rīz/), make (an automobile, etc.) ready for operation or use during the winter. *v.,* **win ter ized, win ter iz ing. —win/ter i za/tion,** *n.*

win ter time (win/tər tīm/), the season of winter. *n.*

win try (win/trē), **1** of winter; like that of winter: *wintry weather, a wintry sky.* **2** not warm or friendly; chilly: *a wintry manner, a wintry smile, a wintry greeting.* *adj.,* **win tri er, win tri est. —win/tri ly,** *adv.* **—win/tri ness,** *n.*

wipe (wīp), **1** rub in order to clean or dry: *Wipe your shoes on the mat. We wiped the dishes with a towel.* **2** take (away, off, or out) by rubbing: *Wipe away your tears. I wiped off the dust.* **3** remove: *The rain wiped away all the footprints.* **4** rub or draw (something) over a surface. **5** act of wiping: *He gave his face a hasty wipe.* 1-4 *v.,* **wiped, wip ing;** 5 *n.*

wipe out, 1 destroy completely: *Whole cities have been wiped out by volcanoes.* **2** kill. **3** SLANG. fall or cause to fall off a surfboard or other sports equipment.

wipe out (wīp/out/), **1** INFORMAL. complete destruction. **2** SLANG. a fall from a surfboard or other sports equipment. *n.*

wip er (wī/pər), thing used for wiping: *a windshield wiper.* *n.*

wire (wīr), **1** metal drawn out into a thin, flexible rod or fine thread. **2** a long piece of such metal used for electrical transmission, as in electric lighting, telephones, and telegraphs. **3** made of or consisting of wire: *a wire fence.* **4** furnish with wire: *wire a house for electricity.* **5** fasten with wire: *She wired the two pieces together.* **6** telegraph: *I sent a message by wire.* **7** to telegraph: *I wired a reply.* **8** telegram: *The news came in a wire.* 1,2,6,8 *n.,* 3 *adj.,* 4,5,7 *v.,* **wired, wir ing. —wire/a ble,** *adj.* **—wire/-like/,** *adj.*

pull wires, INFORMAL. use secret influence to accomplish one's purposes: *She pulled wires to get her son a job.*

wire-haired (wīr/herd/ *or* wīr/hard/), having coarse, stiff hair: *a wire-haired fox terrier.* *adj.*

wire less (wīr/lis), **1** using no wires; transmitting by radio waves instead of by electric wires: *wireless telegraphy.* **2** system of transmission by radio waves without the use of wires. **3** BRITISH. radio. 1 *adj.,* 2,3 *n., pl.* **wire less es. —wire/less ly,** *adv.*

wire tap (wīr/tap/), **1** tap a telephone or telegraph wire secretly in order to record or get information. **2** to record or get by wiretapping: *wiretap a conversation.* **3** a wiretapping. 1,2 *v.,* **wire tapped, wire tap ping;** 3 *n.* **—wire/-tap/per,** *n.*

wir i ness (wī/rē nis), a being wiry. *n.*

wir ing (wī/ring), system of wires to carry an electric current. *n.*

wir y (wī/rē), **1** made of wire. **2** like wire. **3** lean, strong, and tough. *adj.,* **wir i er, wir i est. —wir/i ly,** *adv.*

Wis. *or* **Wisc.,** Wisconsin.

Wis con sin (wi skon/sən), one of the north central states of the United States. *Abbreviation:* Wis., Wisc., or WI *Capital:* Madison. *n.*

wis dom (wiz/dəm), **1** knowledge and good judgment based on experience; being wise. **2** wise conduct; wise words: *Her wisdom guided us.* **3** scholarly knowledge. *n.* [*Wisdom* is from Old English *wīsdōm,* which comes from *wīs,* meaning "wise."] **—wis/dom less,** *adj.*

a hat	i it	oi oil	ch child	(a in about
ā age	ī ice	ou out	ng long	e in taken
ä far	o hot	u cup	sh she	ə = { i in pencil
e let	ō open	ù put	th thin	o in lemon
ē equal	ô order	ü rule	ŦH then	u in circus
ėr term			zh measure	

wisdom tooth, the back tooth on either side of each jaw, ordinarily appearing between the ages of 17 and 25.

wise[1] (wīz), **1** having or showing knowledge and good judgment: *a wise judge, wise plans.* **2** having knowledge or information: *wise in the ways of politics.* *adj.,* **wis er, wis est. —wise/ly,** *adv.*

wise[2] (wīz), way; manner: *I am in no wise interested.* *n.*

-wise, *suffix forming adverbs.* **1** in _____ manner: *Likewise = in a like manner.* **2** in a _____ing manner: *Slantwise = in a slanting manner.* **3** in the characteristic way of a _____: *Clockwise = in the way the hands of a clock go.* **4** in the direction of the _____: *Lengthwise = in the direction of the length.*

wise a cre (wī/zā/kər), person who pretends to know everything; smart aleck. *n.*

wise crack (wīz/krak/), INFORMAL. **1** a snappy comeback; smart remark. **2** make wisecracks. 1 *n.,* 2 *v.* **—wise/crack/er,** *n.*

wise guy, SLANG. person who pretends to know everything; impudent or conceited person.

wish (wish), **1** have a need or longing for; want; desire: *What is it that you wish? They wish to see you urgently.* **2** have a desire; express a hope: *She wished for a telescope.* **3** a wishing or wanting; desire; longing: *I have no wish to be rich.* **4** expression of a wish: *Please give them my best wishes for a happy New Year.* **5** to desire (something) for someone; have or express a hope for: *I wish you a happy New Year.* **6** to request or command: *Do you wish me to come over now?* **7** a request or command: *grant someone's slightest wish.* **8** thing wished for: *She got her wish.* 1,2,5,6 *v.,* 3,4,7,8 *n., pl.* **wish es. —wish/er,** *n.*

wish bone (wish/bōn/), the forked bone in the front of the breastbone in poultry and other birds. *n.*

wish ful (wish/fəl), having or expressing a wish; desiring; desirous: *His boast was only wishful thinking.* *adj.* **—wish/ful ly,** *adv.* **—wish/ful ness,** *n.*

wish y-wash y (wish/ē wosh/ē *or* wish/ē wôsh/ē), **1** thin and weak: *wishy-washy soup with no flavor.* **2** lacking strength of character; indecisive: *a wishy-washy person.* *adj.* **—wish/y-wash/i ly,** *adv.* **—wish/y-wash/i ness,** *n.*

wisp (wisp), **1** a small bundle; small bunch: *a wisp of hay.* **2** a small tuft, lock, or portion of anything; slight bit: *a wisp of hair, a wisp of smoke.* **3** a little thing: *a wisp of a child.* *n.* **—wisp/like/,** *adj.*

wisp y (wis/pē), like a wisp; thin; slight. *adj.,* **wisp i er, wisp i est.**

wist (wist), OLD USE. knew. *v.*

wis ter i a (wi stir/ē ə), a climbing shrub with large, drooping clusters of purple, blue, or white flowers. *n., pl.* **wis ter i as.** [*Wisteria* was named in honor of Caspar *Wistar,* 1761-1818, an American physician.]

wist ful (wist/fəl), longing; yearning: *A child stood looking with wistful eyes at the toys in the window.* *adj.* **—wist/ful ly,** *adv.* **—wist/ful ness,** *n.*

wit (wit), **1** the power to perceive quickly and express cleverly ideas that are unusual, striking, and amusing: *Her wit made even troubles seem amusing.* **2** person with such power: *Mark Twain was a famous wit.* **3** power of understanding; mind or sense: *People with quick wits learn easily. I was out of my wits with fright.* **4** OLD USE. know. 1-3 *n.,* 4 *v.,* **wist, wit ting.**

to wit, that is to say; namely: *To my daughter I leave all I* *own—to wit: my house, what is in it, and the land on which it stands.*

witch (wich), **1** woman supposed to be under the influence of supernatural spirits and to have magic powers which she generally uses to do evil. **2** an ugly old woman. *n., pl.* **witch es.**

witch craft (wich′kraft′), what a witch does or can do; magic power or influence. *n.*

witch doctor, medicine man, especially in certain primitive societies.

witch er y (wich′ər ē), **1** witchcraft; magic. **2** charm; fascination. *n., pl.* **witch er ies.**

witch hazel, 1 shrub or small tree of eastern North America that has yellow flowers in the fall or winter after the leaves have fallen. **2** lotion for cooling and soothing the skin, made from the bark and leaves of this shrub.

witch ing (wich′ing), bewitching; magical; enchanting. *adj.* —**witch′ing ly,** *adv.*

with (wiᴛʜ *or* with). *With shows that persons or things are taken together in some way.* **1** in the company of: *Come with me.* **2** among: *They will mix with the crowd.* **3** having, wearing, carrying, etc.: *He is a man with brains. She received a telegram with good news.* **4** by means of: *The man cut the meat with a knife.* **5** using; showing: *Work with care.* **6** added to: *Do you want sugar with your tea?* **7** in relation to: *They are friendly with us.* **8** in regard to: *We are pleased with the house.* **9** in proportion to: *Her pay increased with her responsibilities.* **10** because of: *The child is shaking with cold.* **11** in the keeping or service of: *Leave the dog with me.* **12** in the region, sphere, experience, opinion, or view of: *High taxes are unpopular with many people.* **13** at the same time as: *With this battle the war ended.* **14** in the same direction as: *The boat floated along with the current.* **15** on the side of; for: *They are with us in our plan.* **16** from: *I hate to part with my favorite things.* **17** against: *The English fought with the Germans.* **18** receiving; having: *I went with his permission.* **19** in spite of: *With all his weight he was not a strong man.* *prep.*

with al (wi ᴛʜôl′ *or* wi thôl′), with it all; as well; besides; also: *I am tired and hungry and hurt withal. adv.*

with draw (wiᴛʜ drô′ *or* with drô′), **1** draw back; draw away: *The dog quickly withdrew his hand from the hot stove. I withdrew from the discussion before it became an argument.* **2** take back; remove: *The owner of the store agreed to withdraw the charge of theft if the robbers returned the money. She withdrew all of her savings from the bank.* **3** go away: *She withdrew from the room. v.,* **withdrew, with drawn, with draw ing. —with draw′a ble,** *adj.* —**with draw′er,** *n.* —**with draw′ing ly,** *adv.*

with draw al (wiᴛʜ drô′əl *or* with drô′əl), a withdrawing or a being withdrawn. *n.*

with drawn (wiᴛʜ drôn′ *or* with drôn′), past participle of **withdraw.** *The goalie was withdrawn from the game because of an injury. v.*

with drew (wiᴛʜ drü′ *or* with drü′), past tense of **withdraw.** *The coach withdrew the player from the game when he was hurt. v.*

with er (wiᴛʜ′ər), **1** lose or cause to lose freshness; make or become dry and lifeless; dry up; fade; shrivel: *The hot sun withers the grass. Flowers wither after they are cut. Age had withered the old woman's face.* **2** cause to feel ashamed or confused: *be withered by a scornful look. v.* —**with′er er,** *n.* —**with′er ing ly,** *adv.*

with ers (wiᴛʜ′ərz), the highest part of a horse's or other animal's back, between the shoulder blades. *n.pl.*

with held (with held′ *or* wiᴛʜ held′), past tense and past participle of **withhold.** *The witness withheld information from the police. Because information had been withheld, the wrong person was charged with the crime. v.*

with hold (with hōld′ *or* wiᴛʜ hōld′), **1** refrain from giv-

ing or granting: *There will be no school play if the principal withholds consent.* **2** hold back; keep back: *Tell the whole story; don't withhold anything. v.,* **with held, with hold ing. —with hold′er,** *n.*

withholding tax, the part of a person's salary or wages deducted for income tax by an employer on behalf of the government.

with in (wiᴛʜ in′ *or* with in′), **1** inside the limits of; not beyond: *The task was within my power. I will guess your weight within five pounds.* **2** in or into the inner part of; inside of: *By the use of X rays, doctors can see within the body.* **3** in or into the inner part; inside: *The house has been painted within and without.* **1,2** *prep.,* **3** *adv.*

with out (wiᴛʜ out′ *or* with out′), **1** with no; not having; free from; lacking: *A cat walks without noise. I drink tea without sugar.* **2** so as to leave out, avoid, or neglect: *She walked past without noticing us.* **3** outside of; beyond: *Children were playing within and without the house.* **4** on the outside; outside: *The house is painted without and within.* **1-3** *prep.,* **4** *adv.*

with stand (with stand′ *or* wiᴛʜ stand′), stand against; hold out against; resist; oppose, especially successfully; endure: *withstand hardships. These heavy shoes will withstand much hard wear. v.,* **with stood, with stand ing.** [*Withstand is from Old English withstandan, which comes from with, meaning "against," and standan, meaning "to stand."*] —**with stand′er,** *n.*

with stood (with stud′ *or* wiᴛʜ stud′), past tense and past participle of **withstand.** *The family withstood many hardships. These shoes have withstood three years of hard wear. v.*

wit less (wit′lis), lacking sense; stupid; foolish: *Crossing the street without looking is a witless thing to do. adj.* —**wit′less ly,** *adv.* —**wit′less ness,** *n.*

wit ness (wit′nis), **1** person who saw something happen; spectator; eyewitness: *There were several witnesses to the accident.* **2** be a witness of; see: *He witnessed the accident.* **3** person who gives evidence or testifies under oath in a court of law. **4** evidence; testimony: *A person who gives false witness in court is guilty of perjury.* **5** testify to; give evidence of: *Her whole manner witnessed her surprise.* **6** person who signs a document to show that he or she saw the maker sign it. **7** sign (a document) as a witness: *witness a will.* **1,3,4,6** *n., pl.* **wit ness es; 2,5,7** *v.* —**wit′ness a ble,** *adj.* —**wit′ness er,** *n.*

bear witness, be evidence; give evidence; testify: *The woman's fingerprints bore witness to her guilt. His blushes bore witness to his great embarrassment.*

wit ti cism (wit′ə siz′əm), a witty remark. *n.*

wit ti ly (wit′ə lē), in a witty manner; with wit. *adv.*

wit ti ness (wit′ē nis), quality or character of being witty. *n.*

wit ting ly (wit′ing lē), knowingly; intentionally. *adv.*

wit ty (wit′ē), full of wit; clever and amusing: *A witty person makes witty remarks. adj.,* **wit ti er, wit ti est.**

wive (wīv), **1** marry a woman. **2** take as a wife. *v.,* **wived, wiv ing.**

wives (wīvz), plural of **wife.** *n.*

wiz ard (wiz′ərd), **1** man supposed to have magic power; magician; sorcerer. **2** INFORMAL. a very clever person; expert: *She is a wizard at mathematics. n.* —**wiz′ard like′,** *adj.*

wiz ard ry (wiz′ər drē), magic skill; magic. *n.*

wiz ened (wiz′nd), dried up; withered; shriveled: *a wizened apple, a wizened face. adj.*

wk., week. *pl.* **wks.**

wo (wō), woe. *n., interj.*

wob ble (wob′əl), **1** move unsteadily from side to side; shake; tremble: *A baby wobbles when it begins to walk alone.* **2** be uncertain, unsteady, or inconstant; waver. **3** a wobbling motion. 1,2 *v.*, **wob bled, wob bling; 3** *n.* Also, **wabble. —wob′bler,** *n.*

wob bly (wob′lē), unsteady; shaky; wavering. *adj.*, **wobbli er, wob bli est.** Also, **wabbly. —wob′bli ness,** *n.*

wo be gone (wō′bi gôn′), woebegone. *adj.*

Wo den (wōd′n), (in Anglo-Saxon myths) the chief god. The Scandinavians called him Odin. *n.*

woe (wō), **1** great grief, trouble, or distress: *the woes of sickness and poverty.* **2** an exclamation of grief, trouble, or distress: *"Woe! woe is me!"* **1** *n.*, **2** *interj.* Also, **wo.**

woe be gone (wō′bi gôn′), looking sad, sorrowful, or wretched. *adj.*

woe ful (wō′fəl), **1** full of woe; sad; sorrowful; wretched: *The lost child had a woeful expression.* **2** pitiful: *a woeful mistake. adj.* **—woe′ful ly,** *adv.* **—woe′ful ness,** *n.*

wo ful (wō′fəl), woeful. *adj.* **—wo′ful ly,** *adv.* **—wo′fulness,** *n.*

woke (wōk), waked; a past tense of **wake**[1]. *She woke before we did. v.*

wo ken (wō′kən), waked; a past participle of **wake**[1]. *I was woken by the sound of bells. v.*

wold (wōld), high, rolling country, bare of woods. *n.*

wolf (wulf), **1** a flesh-eating mammal related to the dog, with a long muzzle, high pointed ears, and a bushy tail. Wolves usually hunt in packs and sometimes kill livestock. **2** a cruel, greedy person. **3** eat greedily: *The starving man wolfed down the food.* **1,2** *n.,* *pl.* **wolves; 3** *v.* **—wolf′like′,** *adj.*

cry wolf, give a false alarm.

keep the wolf from the door, keep safe from hunger or poverty.

Wolfe (wulf), **1 James,** 1727-1759, British general who was killed at the battle of Quebec, in which he defeated the French. **2 Thomas,** 1900-1938, American novelist. *n.*

wolf hound (wulf′hound′), a large dog of any of various breeds once used in hunting wolves. *n.*

wolf ish (wul′fish), **1** like a wolf; savage: *wolfish cruelty.* **2** greedy: *a wolfish appetite. adj.* **—wolf′ish ly,** *adv.* **—wolf′ish ness,** *n.*

wolf ram (wul′frəm), tungsten. *n.*

wolverine
about 3½ ft. (1 m.)
long with the tail

wol ve rine or **wol ve rene** (wul′və rēn′), a heavily built, flesh-eating mammal living in the northern regions of North America. It is related to the weasel and badger. *n.*

wolves (wulvz), plural of **wolf.** *n.*

wom an (wum′ən), **1** an adult female person. When a girl grows up, she becomes a woman. **2** a female servant: *The princess told her woman to wait outside. n., pl.* **wom en.** [*Woman* is from Old English *wīfman,* which comes from *wīf,* meaning "woman, wife," and *man,* meaning "a human being."] **—wom′an less,** *adj.*

wom an hood (wum′ən hud), **1** condition or time of being a woman: *The girl was entering womanhood.*

2 character or qualities of a woman. **3** women as a group: *the womanhood of America. n.*

wom an ish (wum′ə nish), (of a man) having qualities or characteristics traditionally considered to be feminine. *adj.* **—wom′an ish ly,** *adv.* **—wom′an ish ness,** *n.*

wom an kind (wum′ən kind′), women as a group. *n.*

wom an like (wum′ən līk′), **1** like a woman. **2** suitable for a woman. *adj.*

wom an li ness (wum′ən lē nis), womanly quality or behavior. *n.*

wom an ly (wum′ən lē), **1** having qualities traditionally admired in a woman: *a womanly expression of sympathy.* **2** suitable for a woman: *Tennis is as much a womanly as it is a manly sport. adj.*

woman's rights, social, political, and legal rights for women, equal to those of men.

woman suffrage, 1 the political right of women to vote. **2** women's votes.

womb (wüm), the part of the body in female mammals that holds and nourishes the young till birth; uterus. *n.*

wombat
2 to 4 ft.
(60 cm. to 1.2 m.) long

wom bat (wom′bat), a burrowing Australian mammal that looks like a small bear. A female wombat has a pouch for carrying her young. *n.*

wom en (wim′ən), plural of **woman.** *n.*

wom en folk (wim′ən fōk′), women. *n.pl.*

wom en folks (wim′ən fōks′), women. *n.pl.*

Women's Liberation, the efforts of women to achieve equality for women in all areas of life.

won (wun), past tense and past participle of **win.** *Which side won yesterday? We have won four games. v.*

won der (wun′dər), **1** a strange and surprising thing or event: *The Grand Canyon is one of the wonders of the world. It is a wonder that he refused such a good offer.* **2** the feeling caused by what is strange and surprising: *The baby looked with wonder at the snow.* **3** feel wonder: *We wonder at the splendor of the stars.* **4** be surprised or astonished: *I shouldn't wonder if she wins the prize.* **5** be curious; be curious about; wish to know: *I wonder where she has gone.* **1,2** *n.* **3-5** *v.* **—won′der er,** *n.* **—won′dering ly,** *adv.*

won der ful (wun′dər fəl), **1** causing wonder; marvelous; remarkable: *a wonderful adventure.* **2** excellent; splendid; fine: *We had a wonderful time at the party. adj.* **—won′der ful ly,** *adv.* **—won′der ful ness,** *n.*

won der land (wun′dər land′), a land full of wonders. *n.*

won der ment (wun′dər mənt), wonder; surprise: *He stared at the huge bear in wonderment. n.*

won drous (wun′drəs), **1** wonderful. **2** wonderfully. **1** *adj.,* **2** *adv.* **—won′drous ly,** *adv.* **—won′drous ness,** *n.*

wont (wunt), **1** accustomed: *He was wont to read the* *paper at breakfast.* **2** custom; habit: *He rose early, as was his wont.* **1** *adj.,* **2** *n.*

won't (wōnt *or* wunt), will not.

wont ed (wun′tid), accustomed; customary; usual: *The cat was in its wonted place by the stove.* *adj.* —**wont′ed ly,** *adv.* —**wont′ed ness,** *n.*

woo (wü), **1** make love to; seek to marry. **2** seek to win; try to get: *Some people woo fame; some woo wealth.* **3** try to persuade; urge. *v.,* **wooed, woo ing.** —**woo′er,** *n.*

wood (wu̇d), **1** the hard substance beneath the bark of trees and shrubs. **2** trees or parts of trees cut up for use in building houses, making boats and furniture, etc.: *We bought wood to build a playhouse. Put some wood on the fire.* **3** made of wood; wooden: *a wood house.* **4** Often, **woods,** *pl.* **a** a large number of growing trees; small forest: *We walked through the woods behind the farm.* **b** area covered by a forest or forests: *Many campers go to the Maine woods.* **1,2,4** *n.,* **3** *adj.* —**wood′less,** *adj.*
out of the woods, out of danger or difficulty.

wood alcohol, a colorless, poisonous, flammable liquid made by distilling wood; methyl alcohol. It is used as a solvent, fuel, etc., and to make formaldehyde.

wood bine (wu̇d′bīn), **1** honeysuckle. **2** Virginia creeper. *n.*

wood carv er (wu̇d′kär′vər), person who carves figures or other objects from wood. *n.*

woodchuck
about 2 ft. (60 cm.)
long with the tail

wood chuck (wu̇d′chuk′), a small, thick-bodied North American mammal with short legs and a bushy tail; ground hog. It is a kind of marmot. Woodchucks grow fat in summer and sleep in their holes in the ground all winter. *n.*

wood cock (wu̇d′kok′), a small game bird with short legs and a long bill used to probe the ground for worms. *n., pl.* **wood cocks** *or* **wood cock.**

wood craft (wu̇d′kraft′), **1** skill in working with wood. **2** knowledge about how to get food and shelter in the woods; skill in hunting, trapping, finding one's way, etc. *n.*

wood cut (wu̇d′kut′), **1** an engraved block of wood to print from. **2** a print from such a block. *n.*

wood cut ter (wu̇d′kut′ər), person who cuts down trees or chops wood. *n.*

wood ed (wu̇d′id), covered with trees: *The house stood on a wooded hill. adj.*

wood en (wu̇d′n), **1** made of wood. **2** stiff as wood; awkward. **3** dull; stupid. *adj.* —**wood′en ly,** *adv.* —**wood′en ness,** *n.*

wooden horse, Trojan horse.

wood i ness (wu̇′dē nis), woody condition or quality. *n.*

wood land (wu̇d′lənd), **1** land covered with trees. **2** of or living in the woods: *woodland animals.* **1** *n.,* **2** *adj.*

wood louse, a very small animal with a flat, oval body that lives in decaying wood, damp soil, etc.; sow bug. It is a crustacean.

wood man (wu̇d′mən), woodsman. *n., pl.* **wood men.**

wood nymph, nymph that lives in the woods; dryad.

wood peck er (wu̇d′pek′ər), bird with a hard, pointed bill for pecking holes in trees to get insects. The flicker is one kind of woodpecker. *n.*

woodpeckers
about 9 in. (23 cm.) long

wood pile (wu̇d′pīl′), pile of wood, especially wood for fuel. *n.*

wood pulp, pulp made from wood, used in making paper.

wood shed (wu̇d′shed′), shed for storing wood. *n.*

woods man (wu̇dz′mən), **1** person used to life in the woods and skilled in hunting, fishing, trapping, etc. **2** lumberjack. *n., pl.* **woods men.**

woods y (wu̇d′zē), of or like the woods. *adj.,* **woods i er, woods i est.**

wood tar, tar obtained by the distillation of wood, and containing resins, turpentine, etc. It is used as a preservative on wood, rope, etc.

wood thrush, thrush with a white, spotted breast, common in the thickets and woods of eastern North America.

wood wind (wu̇d′wind′), **1** any of a group of wind instruments which were originally made of wood, but are now often made of metal or plastic. Clarinets, flutes, oboes, and bassoons are woodwinds. **2** of woodwinds: *Flutes are in the woodwind section of an orchestra.* **1** *n.,* **2** *adj.*

woodcut (def. 2)

wood work (wu̇d′werk′), things made of wood; wooden parts inside a house, such as doors, stairs, moldings, and the like. *n.*

wood work ing (wu̇d′wer′king), **1** making or shaping things of wood: *She is skilled in woodworking.* **2** of or for woodworking: *woodworking tools.* **1** *n.,* **2** *adj.*

wood y (wu̇d′ē), **1** having many trees; covered with trees: *a woody hillside.* **2** consisting of wood: *the woody* parts of a shrub. **3** like wood: *Turnips become woody when they are old. adj.,* **wood i er, wood i est.**

woof (wüf), **1** the threads running from side to side across a woven fabric. The woof crosses the warp. **2** fabric; cloth; texture. *n.*

wool (wùl), **1** the soft curly hair or fur of sheep and some other animals. **2** short, thick, curly hair. **3** something like wool. **4** yarn, cloth, or garments made of wool: *wear wool in winter.* **5** made of wool. 1-4 *n.,* 5 *adj.*
pull the wool over one's eyes, INFORMAL. deceive or trick one.

wool en (wùl′ən), **1** made of wool: *a woolen suit.* **2** yarn or cloth made of wool. **3 woolens,** *pl.* cloth or clothing made of wool: *I put my woolens in a plastic bag to protect them against moths.* **4** of or having to do with wool or cloth made of wool: *a woolen mill.* 1,4 *adj.,* 2,3 *n.*

wool gath er ing (wùl′gaтн′ər ing), **1** absorption in thinking or day-dreaming; absent-mindedness. **2** inattentive; absent-minded; dreamy. 1 *n.,* 2 *adj.*

wool len (wùl′ən), woolen. *adj., n.*

wool ly (wùl′ē), **1** consisting of wool: *the woolly coat of a sheep.* **2** like wool. **3** covered with wool or something like it. **4** not clear; confused; muddled: *woolly thinking. adj.,* **wool li er, wool li est. —wool′li ness,** *n.*

woolly bear, the hair-covered larva of a tiger moth.

wool y (wùl′ē), woolly. *adj.,* **wool i er, wool i est.**

wooz y (wü′zē or wùz′ē), INFORMAL. muddled; confused. *adj.,* **wooz i er, wooz i est. —wooz′i ly,** *adv.*

Worces ter (wùs′tər), city in central Massachusetts. *n.*

word (werd), **1** a sound or a group of sounds that has meaning and is a unit of speech. We speak words when we talk. **2** the writing or printing that stands for a word: *This page is filled with words.* **3** a short talk: *May I have a word with you?* **4** speech: *He is honest in word and deed.* **5** a brief expression: *The teacher gave us a word of advice.* **6** command; order: *The tyrant's word was law.* **7 the Word,** the Bible. **8** promise: *She kept her word. He is a man of his word.* **9** news: *No word has come from the battle front.* **10 words,** *pl.* angry talk; quarrel; dispute. **11** unit of computer information equal to the number of bits of data that a particular computer can store or process as a unit, so varying from machine to machine. **12** put into words: *She worded her message clearly.* 1-11 *n.,* 12 *v.*
be as good as one's word, keep one's promise.
by word of mouth, by spoken words; orally.
eat one's words, take back what one has said; retract.
in a word, briefly.
take one at one's word, take one's words seriously and act accordingly.
take the words out of one's mouth, say exactly what one was just going to say.
upon my word, 1 expression of surprise. **2** I promise.
word for word, in the exact words.

word book (werd′bùk′), list of words, usually with explanations, etc.; dictionary. *n.*

word history, account or explanation of the origin and history of a word; etymology.

word i ness (wer′dē nis), a being wordy; verbosity. *n.*

word ing (wer′ding), way of saying a thing; choice and use of words: *Careful wording is needed for clearness. n.*

word less (werd′lis), **1** without words; speechless. **2** not put into words; unexpressed. *adj.* **—word′less ly,** *adv.*

word of honor, a solemn promise.

word processing, the editing, storage, and reproduction of words by means of computers and other complex machines.

Words worth (werdz′werth′), **William,** 1770-1850, English poet. *n.*

word y (wer′dē), using too many words; verbose. *adj.,* **word i er, word i est. —word′i ly,** *adv.*

a hat	i it	oi oil	ch child	a in about
ā age	ī ice	ou out	ng long	e in taken
ä far	o hot	u cup	sh she	ə = i in pencil
e let	ō open	ù put	th thin	o in lemon
ē equal	ô order	ü rule	тн then	u in circus
ėr term			zh measure	

wore (wôr), past tense of **wear.** *He wore out his shoes in two months. v.*

work (werk), **1** effort in doing or making something: *Some people like hard work.* **2** something to do; occupation; employment: *My friend is out of work.* **3** something made or done; result of effort: *The artist considers that picture to be her greatest work.* **4** that on which effort is put: *We carried our work out onto the front porch.* **5 works,** *pl.* **a** factory or other place for doing some kind of work. **b** the moving parts of a machine: *the works of a watch.* **c** buildings, bridges, docks, etc. **d** actions: *good works.* **6** labor: *Most people must work to earn money.* **7** work for pay; be employed: *She works at an airplane factory.* **8** put effort on: *They worked their farm with success.* **9** act; operate: *This pump will not work. The plan worked well.* **10** cause to do work: *That company works its employees hard.* **11** make, get, do or bring about by effort: *I worked my way across the room in the dark. She worked her way through college.* **12** move as if with effort: *His face worked as he tried to keep back the tears.* **13** bring about; cause; do: *The plan worked harm.* **14** go slowly or with effort: *The ship worked to windward.* **15** become (up, round, loose, etc.): *The window catch has worked loose.* **16** to form; shape: *He worked a piece of copper into a tray.* **17** move; stir; excite: *Don't work yourself into a temper.* 1-5 *n.,* 6-17 *v.,* **worked, work ing.**
make short work of, deal with quickly.
out of work, having no job.
work in, put in.
work off, get rid of: *work off a debt.*
work on or **work upon,** try to persuade or influence.
work out, 1 plan; develop. **2** solve; find out. **3** give exercise to; practice. **4** result.

work a ble (wer′kə bəl), able to be worked. *adj.*

work a day (wer′kə dā′), of working days; practical; commonplace; ordinary. *adj.* Also, **workday.**

work bench (werk′bench′), a strong, heavy table used by a carpenter, or by anyone who uses tools and materials. *n., pl.* **work bench es.**

work book (werk′bùk′), book containing outlines for the study of some subject, questions to be answered, etc.; book in which a student does written work. *n.*

work day (werk′dā′), **1** day for work; day that is not Sunday or a holiday. **2** part of a day during which work is done. **3** workaday. 1,2 *n.,* 3 *adj.*

work er (wer′kər), **1** person or thing that works. **2** bee, ant, wasp, or other insect that works for its community and usually does not produce offspring. *n.*

work fare (werk′fer′ or werk′far′), a welfare program under which those receiving aid must do assigned work or enlist in a job-training program. *n.*

work horse (werk′hôrs′), **1** horse used for labor, and not for showing, racing, or hunting. **2** a very hard worker. *n.*

work house (werk′hous′), **1** house of correction where petty criminals are kept and made to work. **2** (formerly, in Great Britain) a house where very poor people were lodged and set to work. *n., pl.* **work hous es** (werk′hou′ziz).

work ing (wer′king), **1** method or manner of work; operation; action: *Do you understand the working of this machine?* **2** that works: *The class constructed a working model* *of a helicopter.* **3** of, for, or used in working: *working hours, working clothes.* **4** used to operate with or by: *a working majority.* **5 workings,** *pl.* parts of a mine, quarry, tunnel, etc., where work is being done. 1,5 *n.,* 2-4 *adj.*

working day, workday.

work ing man (wėr′king man′), workman. *n., pl.* **work ing men.**

work man (wėrk′mən), **1** worker. **2** person who works with his or her hands or with machines. *n., pl.* **work men.**

work man like (wėrk′mən līk′), skillful; well-done: *a workmanlike job. adj.*

work man ship (wėrk′mən ship), **1** the art or skill in a worker or the work done: *Good workmanship requires long practice.* **2** quality or manner of work. *n.*

work out (wėrk′out′), **1** exercise; practice: *She had a good workout running around the track before breakfast.* **2** trial; test: *The mechanic gave the car a thorough workout after repairing it. n.*

work room (wėrk′rüm′ *or* wėrk′rùm′), room where work is done. *n.*

work shop (wėrk′shop′), **1** shop or building where work is done. **2** group of people working on or studying a special project. *n.*

work ta ble (wėrk′tā′bəl), table to work at. *n.*

work week (wėrk′wēk′), the part of the week in which work is done, usually Monday through Friday. *n.*

world (wėrld), **1** the earth: *Ships can sail around the world.* **2** all of certain parts, people, or things of the earth: *the insect world, the world of fashion.* **3** all people; the public: *The whole world knows it.* **4** the things of this life and the people devoted to them: *Some monks and nuns live apart from the world.* **5** any planet, especially when considered as inhabited: *alien creatures from another world.* **6** any time, condition, or place of life: *the next world, a better world.* **7** all things; everything; the universe. **8** a great deal; very much; large amount: *Sunshine does children a world of good. n.*

for all the world, 1 for any reason, no matter how great. **2** in every respect; exactly.

world-beat er (wėrld′bē′tər), INFORMAL. a champion. *n.*

world li ness (wėrld′lē nis), worldly ideas, ways, or conduct. *n.*

world ly (wėrld′lē), **1** of this world; not of heaven: *worldly wealth.* **2** caring much for the interests and pleasures of this world. **3** worldly-wise. *adj.,* **world li er, world li est.**

world ly-wise (wėrld′lē wīz′), wise about the ways and affairs of this world. *adj.*

World Series, series of baseball games played each fall between the winners of the two major league championships, to decide the professional championship of the United States.

world's fair, an international exposition with exhibits of arts, crafts, products, etc., from various countries.

World War I, war fought mainly in Europe and the Middle East, from 1914 to 1918. The United States, Great Britain, France, Russia, and their allies were on one side; Germany, Austria-Hungary, and their allies were on the other side.

World War II, war fought in Europe, Asia, Africa, and elsewhere, from 1939 to 1945. The chief conflict was between Great Britain, the United States, France, and the Soviet Union on one side and Germany, Italy, and Japan on the other.

world-wear y (wėrld′wir′ē), weary of this world; tired of living. *adj.*

world wide (wėrld′wīd′), spread throughout the world: *Pollution is becoming a worldwide problem. adj.*

worm (wėrm), **1** a small, slender, crawling or creeping animal. Most worms have soft bodies and no legs. **2** something like a worm in shape or movement, such as the thread of a screw. **3** move like a worm; crawl or creep like a worm: *The children wormed their way under the fence.* **4** get by persistent and secret means: *worm information out of someone, worm the truth from a person.* **5** a weak, disgusting, or pitiful person. **6 worms,** *pl.* disease caused by parasitic worms in the body, especially in the intestines. 1,2,5,6 *n.,* 3,4 *v.* —**worm′like′,** *adj.*

worm-eat en (wėrm′ēt′n), **1** eaten into by worms: *worm-eaten timbers.* **2** worn-out; worthless; out-of-date. *adj.*

worm wood (wėrm′wùd′), **1** a bitter plant used in certain liquors and formerly in medicine. **2** something bitter or extremely unpleasant. *n.*

worm y (wėr′mē), **1** having worms; containing many worms: *wormy apples.* **2** damaged by worms: *wormy wood. adj.,* **worm i er, worm i est.** —**worm′i ness,** *n.*

worn (wôrn), **1** past participle of **wear.** *I have worn these jeans for two years.* **2** damaged by use: *worn rugs.* **3** tired; wearied: *a worn face.* 1 *v.,* 2,3 *adj.*

worn-out (wôrn′out′), **1** used until no longer fit for use. **2** very tired; exhausted. *adj.*

wor ri er (wėr′ē ər), person who worries. *n.*

wor ri some (wėr′ē səm), **1** causing worry. **2** inclined to worry. *adj.* —**wor′ri some ly,** *adv.*

wor ry (wėr′ē), **1** feel anxious; be uneasy: *Don't worry about little things. They will worry if we are late.* **2** make anxious; trouble: *The problem worried me.* **3** anxiety; uneasiness; trouble; care: *Worry kept me awake.* **4** cause of trouble or care: *Parents of a sick child have many worries.* **5** annoy; bother; vex: *Don't worry me right now with so many questions.* **6** seize and shake with the teeth; bite at; snap at: *The cat worried the mouse.* 1,2,5,6 *v.,* **wor ried, wor ry ing;** 3,4 *n., pl.* **wor ries.** —**wor′ri less,** *adj.* —**wor′ry ing ly,** *adv.*

worse (wėrs), **1** less well; more ill: *The patient seems even worse today.* **2** less good; more evil: *Disobedience is bad enough, but lying about it is worse.* **3** in a more severe or evil manner or degree: *It is raining worse than ever today.* **4** that which is worse: *The loss of their property was terrible, but worse followed.* 1,2 *adj.,* 3 *adv.,* 4 *n.*

wors en (wėr′sən), make or become worse. *v.*

wor ship (wėr′ship), **1** great honor and reverence paid to someone or something regarded as sacred: *the worship of God.* **2** pay great honor and reverence to: *to worship God.* **3** religious ceremonies or services in which one expresses such honor and reverence. Prayers and hymns are part of worship. **4** take part in a religious service. **5** great love and admiration; adoration: *hero worship, the worship of wealth.* **6** consider extremely precious; hold very dear; adore: *She worships her mother. A miser worships money.* **7** title used in Great Britain in addressing certain magistrates: *They addressed the judge as "your worship."* 1,3,5,7 *n.,* 2,4,6 *v.* —**wor′ship a ble,** *adj.* —**wor′ship er,** *n.* —**wor′ship ing ly,** *adv.*

wor ship ful (wėr′ship fəl), **1** honorable: *We beg you, worshipful gentlemen, to grant our request.* **2** worshiping: *the worshipful eyes of a dog watching its master. adj.* —**wor′ship ful ly,** *adv.* —**wor′ship ful ness,** *n.*

worst (wėrst), **1** least well; most ill: *This is the worst I've been since I got sick.* **2** least good; most evil: *It is the worst movie I've seen.* **3** in the worst manner or degree: *He acts worst when he's tired.* **4** that which is worst: *Yesterday was bad, but the worst is yet to come.* **5** beat; defeat: *worst one's enemies.* 1,2 *adj.,* 3 *adv.,* 4 *n.,* 5 *v.*

at worst, under the least favorable circumstances.

if worst comes to worst, if the very worst thing happens.

wor sted (wùs′tid *or* wėr′stid), **1** a firmly twisted woolen thread or yarn. **2** made of worsted. **3** cloth made from such thread or yarn. 1,3 *n.,* 2 *adj.*

worth (wėrth), **1** good or important enough for; deserving of: *That book is worth reading. New York is a city worth visiting.* **2** merit; usefulness; importance: *We should read books of real worth.* **3** value: *I got my money's worth out of this coat.* **4** quantity that a certain amount will buy: *I bought a dollar's worth of stamps.* **5** equal in value to: *That book is worth $5.* **6** having property that amounts to: *That man is worth millions.* 1,5,6 *adj.,* 2-4 *n.*

wor thi ly (wėr′ℱə lē), in a worthy manner. *adv.*

wor thi ness (wėr′ℱē nis), quality or condition of being worthy; merit; worth; excellence. *n.*

worth less (wėrth′lis), without worth; good-for-nothing; useless: *Throw those worthless, broken toys away. adj.* —**worth′less ly,** *adv.* —**worth′less ness,** *n.*

worth while (wėrth′hwĭl′), worth time, attention, or effort; having real merit: *This is a worthwhile book; you should read it. adj.* —**worth′while′ness,** *n.*

wor thy (wėr′ℱē), **1** having worth or merit: *Helping the poor is a worthy cause.* **2** deserving; meriting: *Her courage was worthy of high praise.* **3** person of great merit; admirable person: *The Wright brothers stand high among American worthies.* 1,2 *adj.,* **wor thi er, wor thi est;** 3 *n., pl.* **wor thies.**

wot (wot), OLD USE. know. "I wot" means "I know." "He wot" means "He knows." *v.*

would (wud), **1** past tense of **will**[1]. *She said that she would come. They would go in spite of our warning.* **2** *Would* is also used: **a** to express future time: *Would they never go?* **b** to express action done again and again in the past time: *The children would play for hours on the beach.* **c** to express a wish: *I would I were rich.* **d** to make a statement or question sound more polite than *will* sounds: *Would you help us, please?* **e** to express conditions: *If you would only try, you could do it. v.*

would-be (wud′bē′), **1** wishing or pretending to be. **2** intended to be. *adj.*

would n't (wud′nt), would not.

wouldst (wudst), OLD USE. would. "Thou wouldst" means "you would." *v.*

wound[1] (wünd), **1** a hurt or injury caused by cutting, stabbing, shooting, etc.: *a knife wound, a bullet wound.* **2** injure by cutting, stabbing, shooting, etc.; hurt: *The hunter wounded the deer.* **3** any hurt or injury to feelings, reputation, etc.: *The loss of his job was a wound to his pride.* **4** injure in feelings, reputation, etc.: *Her unkind words wounded me.* 1,3 *n.,* 2,4 *v.* —**wound′ing ly,** *adv.*

wound[2] (wound), past tense and past participle of **wind**[2]. *I wound the yarn into a ball. The yarn is wound too tightly. v.*

wound[3] (wound), winded; a past tense and a past participle of **wind**[3]. *v.*

wove (wōv), past tense and a past participle of **weave**. *The spider wove a new web after the first was destroyed. v.*

wo ven (wō′vən), a past participle of **weave**. *This cloth is closely woven. v.*

wow (wou), exclamation of surprise, joy, etc. *interj.*

wpm, words per minute.

wrack (rak), **1** ruin; destruction. **2** seaweed cast ashore. *n.*

wrack and ruin, ruin; destruction: *go to wrack and ruin.*

wraith (rāth), **1** ghost of a person seen shortly before or soon after the person's death. **2** specter; ghost. *n.*

wran gle (rang′gəl), **1** argue or dispute in a noisy or angry way: *The children wrangled about who should wash the dog.* **2** a noisy dispute; angry quarrel. **3** (in the western United States and Canada) to herd or tend (horses, cattle, etc.) on the range. 1,3 *v.,* **wran gled, wran gling;** 2 *n.*

wran gler (rang′glər), **1** person who wrangles. **2** (in the western United States and Canada) a herder in charge of horses, cattle, etc. *n.*

wrap (rap), **1** to cover by winding or folding something around: *She wrapped herself in a shawl.* **2** to wind or fold as a covering: *Wrap a shawl around yourself.* **3** to cover with paper and tie up or fasten: *Have you wrapped his birthday present yet?* **4** to envelop; veil: *The mountain peak is wrapped in clouds. She sat wrapped in thought.* **5** an outer covering. Shawls, scarfs, coats, and furs are wraps. 1-4 *v.,* **wrapped** or **wrapt, wrap ping;** 5 *n.*

wrapped up in, devoted to; thinking mainly of: *She is so wrapped up in her work that we never see her any more.*

wrap up, 1 put on warm outer clothes. **2** INFORMAL. finish; conclude: *Let's wrap up this meeting; it's getting late.*

wrap per (rap′ər), **1** person or thing that wraps. **2** a covering or cover: *Some magazines are mailed in paper wrappers.* **3** a woman's long, loose garment to wear in the house. *n.*

wrap ping (rap′ing), paper, cloth, etc., in which something is wrapped. *n.*

wrapt (rapt), wrapped; a past tense and a past participle of **wrap.** *v.*

wrap-up (rap′up′), INFORMAL. the final item or summary of a news report. *n.*

wrath (rath), very great anger; rage. *n.*

wrath
She seethed with **wrath** and hatred.

wrath ful (rath′fəl), very angry; showing wrath: *The wrathful lion turned on the hunters. Its wrathful eyes flashed. adj.* —**wrath′ful ly,** *adv.* —**wrath′ful ness,** *n.*

wreak (rēk), **1** give expression to; work off (feelings, desires, etc.): *I wreaked my anger on my sister by screaming at her.* **2** inflict (vengeance, punishment, etc.). *v.* —**wreak′er,** *n.*

wreath (rēth), **1** a ring of flowers or leaves twisted together: *There were wreaths in the windows at Christmas.* **2** something suggesting a wreath: *a wreath of smoke. n., pl.* **wreaths** (rēℱℋz). —**wreath′less,** *adj.* —**wreath′like′,** *adj.*

wreathe (rēℱℋ), **1** make into a wreath: *The children wreathed a chain of daisies.* **2** decorate or adorn with wreaths: *The doors of the houses were wreathed with greens.* **3** make a ring around; encircle: *Mist wreathed the*

hills. v., **wreathed, wreath ing. —wreath′er,** *n.*
wreathed in smiles, smiling greatly.

wreck (rek), **1** destruction of a motor vehicle, ship, building, train, or aircraft: *The hurricane caused many wrecks. Reckless driving causes many wrecks on the highway.* **2** any destruction or serious injury: *Heavy rains caused the wreck of many crops.* **3** what is left of anything that has been destroyed or much injured: *The waves cast the wreck of a ship upon the shore.* **4** cause the wreck of; destroy; ruin: *Raccoons wrecked our campsite looking for food.* **5** person who has lost his or her health or money: *She is a wreck from overwork.* 1-3,5 *n.,* 4 *v.*

wreck age (rek′ij), **1** what is left by a wreck or wrecks: *The shore was covered with the wreckage of ships.* **2** a wrecking or a being wrecked: *They felt defeated by the wreckage of their hopes.* *n.*

wreck er (rek′ər), **1** person whose work is tearing down buildings. **2** person, car, train, or machine that removes wrecks. **3** person or ship that recovers wrecked or disabled ships or their cargoes. *n.*

wren (ren), a small songbird with a slender bill and a short tail. Wrens often build their nests near houses. *n.*

Wren (ren), Sir **Christopher,** 1632-1723, English architect. *n.*

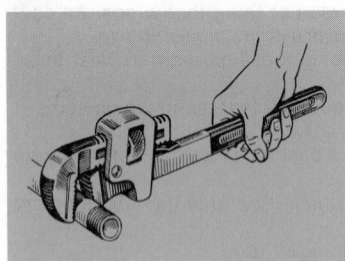

wrench (def. 6)

wrench (rench), **1** a violent twist or twisting pull: *He broke the branch off with a sudden wrench.* **2** twist or pull violently: *He wrenched the knob off when he was trying to open the door. The policeman wrenched the gun out of the man's hand.* **3** injure by twisting: *She wrenched her back doing acrobatics.* **4** injury caused by twisting. **5** source of grief or sorrow: *It was a wrench to leave our old home.* **6** tool for turning nuts, bolts, etc. 1,4-6 *n., pl.* **wrench es;** 2,3 *v.* **—wrench′er,** *n.* **—wrench′ing ly,** *adv.*

wrest (rest), **1** twist, pull, or tear away with force; wrench away: *She wrested the knife from her attacker.* **2** take by force: *An enemy wrested the power from the duke.* **3** obtain by persistence or persuasion; wring: *wrest a secret from someone.* *v.* **—wrest′er,** *n.*

wres tle (res′əl), **1** try to throw or force (an opponent) to the ground. **2** a wrestling match. **3** contend with in wrestling, or as if in wrestling. **4** struggle: *I have been wrestling with this problem for over an hour.* 1,3,4 *v.,* **wres tled, wres tling;** 2 *n.*

wres tler (res′lər), person who wrestles, especially as a sport. *n.*

wres tling (res′ling), sport or contest in which two opponents try to throw or force each other to the ground. The rules for wrestling do not allow using the fists or certain holds on the body. *n.*

wretch (rech), **1** a very unfortunate or unhappy person. **2** a very bad person. *n., pl.* **wretch es.**

wretch ed (rech′id), **1** very unfortunate or unhappy. **2** very unsatisfactory; miserable: *a wretched hut.* **3** very bad: *a wretched traitor. adj.* **—wretch′ed ly,** *adv.* **—wretch′ed ness,** *n.*

wrig gle (rig′əl), **1** twist and turn: *Children wriggle when they are restless.* **2** move by twisting and turning: *The worm wriggled out of my hand when I tried to put it on the*

hook. **3** make one's way by shifts and tricks: *wriggle out of a difficulty.* **4** a wriggling. 1-3 *v.,* **wrig gled, wrig-gling;** 4 *n.* **—wrig′gling ly,** *adv.*

wrig gler (rig′lər), **1** person who wriggles. **2** larva of a mosquito. *n.*

wrig gly (rig′lē), twisting and turning. *adj.,* **wrig gli er, wrig gli est.**

Wright (rīt), **1** Frank Lloyd, 1869-1959, American architect. **2** Orville, 1871-1948, and his brother **Wilbur,** 1867-1912, American inventors, who perfected the airplane and made the world's first flight in a motor-powered plane, in 1903. *n.*

wring (ring), **1** twist with force; squeeze hard: *Wring out your wet bathing suit.* **2** get by twisting or squeezing; force out: *The boy wrung water from his wet bathing suit.* **3** get by force, effort, or persuasion: *wring a secret from someone.* **4** clasp and hold firmly; press: *She wrung her old friend's hand.* **5** cause pain or pity in: *Their poverty wrung our hearts.* **6** twist violently; wrench: *He was so angry he threatened to wring my neck.* **7** a twist or squeeze. 1-6 *v.,* **wrung, wring ing;** 7 *n.*

wring er (ring′ər), machine for squeezing water from wet clothes. *n.*

wrin kle (ring′kəl), **1** an irregular ridge or fold; crease: *The faces of very old people have wrinkles. I must press out the wrinkles in this shirt.* **2** make a wrinkle or wrinkles in: *She wrinkled her forehead.* **3** have wrinkles; acquire wrinkles: *This shirt will not wrinkle.* **4** INFORMAL. useful hint or idea; clever trick: *He knows all the latest wrinkles in style.* 1,4 *n.,* 2,3 *v.,* **wrin kled, wrin kling. —wrin′kle a ble,** *adj.* **—wrin′kle less,** *adj.*

wrin kly (ring′klē), wrinkled. *adj.,* **wrin kli er, wrin kli est.**

wrist (rist), the joint connecting hand and arm. *n.*

wrist watch (rist′woch′ *or* rist′wôch′), a small watch worn on the wrist. *n., pl.* **wrist watch es.**

writ (rit), **1** something written; piece of writing. The Bible is sometimes called Holy Writ. **2** formal order directing a person to do or not to do something: *A writ from the judge ordered the prisoner's release from jail.* **3** OLD USE. written. 1,2 *n.,* 3 *v.*

write (rīt), **1** make letters or words with pen, pencil, or chalk: *You can read and write.* **2** mark with letters or words: *Please write on both sides of the paper.* **3** put down the letters or words of: *Write your name and address.* **4** make up stories, books, etc.; compose: *He writes for the magazines.* **5** be a writer: *Her ambition was to write.* **6** write a letter: *I write to my family every week.* **7** write a letter to: *She wrote her parents that she would be home for New Year's.* **8** show plainly: *Amusement was written on her face. v.,* **wrote, writ ten, writ ing.** [*Write* comes from Old English *wrītan,* originally meaning "to scratch."] **—writ′-a ble,** *adj.*

write down, put into writing.

write off, cancel.

write out, 1 put into writing. **2** write in full.

write up, write a description or account of, especially a full or detailed account of.

writ er (rī′tər), **1** person who writes. **2** person whose occupation is writing; author. *n.*

write-up (rīt′up′), a written description or account. *n.*

writhe (rīᴛʜ), **1** twist and turn; twist about: *writhe in pain. The snake writhed along the branch.* **2** suffer mentally; be very uncomfortable. *v.,* **writhed, writh ing.** **—writh′er,** *n.* **—writh′ing ly,** *adv.*

writ ing (rī′ting), **1** act of making letters or words with pen, pencil, chalk, etc. **2** written form: *Put your ideas in writing.* **3** handwriting: *Your writing is hard to read.* **4** something written; a letter, paper, document, etc. **5** literary work; a book or other literary production: *the* *writings of Benjamin Franklin.* **6** profession or business of a person who writes. *n.*

writ ten (rit′n), past participle of **write.** *He has written a letter. v.*

wrong (rông *or* rong), **1** not right; bad: *Stealing is wrong.* **2** not true; not correct; not what it should be: *give a wrong answer.* **3** not proper; not fit; unsuitable: *Heavy boots would be the wrong thing to wear for tennis.* **4** out of order: *Something is wrong with the car.* **5** in an incorrect way; badly: *They did their homework wrong and had to do it over.* **6** anything not right; wrong thing or action: *Two wrongs do not make a right.* **7** injustice; injury; harm: *You can do an innocent person a wrong by spreading false rumors.* **8** do harm to; treat unfairly; injure: *forgive someone who has wronged you.* **9** not meant to be seen; least important: *the wrong side of cloth.* 1-4,9 *adj.,* 5 *adv.,* 6,7 *n.,* 8 *v.* [*Wrong* came into English about 900 years ago from Icelandic *rangr,* meaning "crooked, unjust."] **—wrong′ly,** *adv.* **—wrong′ness,** *n.*

go wrong, 1 turn out badly: *Everything went wrong today.* **2** stop being good and become bad.

in the wrong, at fault; guilty.

wrong do er (rông′dü′ər *or* rong′dü′ər), person who does wrong. *n.*

wrong do ing (rông′dü′ing *or* rong′dü′ing), a doing wrong; bad acts: *The thief was guilty of wrongdoing. n.*

wrong ful (rông′fəl *or* rong′fəl), **1** wrong. **2** unlawful. *adj.* **—wrong′ful ly,** *adv.* **—wrong′ful ness,** *n.*

wrong head ed (rông′hed′id *or* rong′hed′id), **1** wrong in judgment or opinion. **2** stubborn even when wrong. *adj.* **—wrong′head′ed ly,** *adv.*

wrote (rōt), past tense of **write.** *He wrote his parents a long letter. v.*

wroth (rôth *or* roth), angry. *adj.*

wrought (rôt), **1** made: *a skillfully wrought piece of pottery.* **2** (of metals) formed by hammering. **3** OLD USE. worked; a past tense and a past participle of **work.** 1,2 *adj.,* 3 *v.*

wrought iron, a tough, durable form of iron with little carbon in it. Wrought iron will not break as easily as cast iron.

a hat	i it	oi oil	ch child	a in about
ā age	ī ice	ou out	ng long	e in taken
ä far	o hot	u cup	sh she	ə = i in pencil
e let	ō open	u̇ put	th thin	o in lemon
ē equal	ô order	ü rule	ŦH then	u in circus
ėr term			zh measure	

wrung (rung), past tense and past participle of **wring.** *I wrung out the wet cloth and hung it up. His heart is wrung with pity for the poor. v.*

wry (rī), **1** turned to one side; twisted: *She made a wry face to show her disgust.* **2** ironic: *wry humor. adj.,* **wri er, wri est. —wry′ly,** *adv.* **—wry′ness,** *n.*

wt., weight.

WV, West Virginia (used with postal Zip Code).

W. Va., West Virginia.

WY, Wyoming (used with postal Zip Code).

Wy eth (wī′əth), **Andrew N.,** born 1917, American painter. *n.*

Wyo., Wyoming.

Wy o ming (wī ō′ming), one of the western states of the United States. *Abbreviation:* Wyo. or WY *Capital:* Cheyenne. *n.*

wrought iron
house seen through a wrought iron gate

X or **x** (eks), **1** the 24th letter of the English alphabet. **2** an unknown quantity. **3** a mark in the shape of an X, made instead of a signature by a person who cannot write. **4** a mark that shows a particular place on a map or diagram: *X marks the spot where the gold is supposed to be buried.* **5** the Roman numeral for 10. *n., pl.* **X's** or **x's.**

X, a rating for a motion picture that is restricted to people over the age of 17.

Xa vi er (zā′vē ər *or* zav′ē ər), **Saint Francis,** 1506-1552, Spanish Jesuit missionary in the Far East. *n.*

X chromosome, one of the two chromosomes that determine sex. A fertilized egg cell containing two X chromosomes, one from each parent, develops into a female.

Xe, symbol for xenon.

xe bec (zē′bek), a small, three-masted vessel of the Mediterranean. *n.* [*Xebec* is probably from French *chebec,* and can be traced back to Arabic *shabbāk.*]

xe non (zē′non), a colorless, odorless element which is a gas that forms a very small part of the air. Xenon is used in filling flashbulbs, vacuum tubes, etc. It forms compounds with fluorine and oxygen. *n.* [*Xenon* comes from Greek *xenon.* meaning "strange."]

xen o pho bi a (zen′ə fō′bē ə), fear of foreigners. *n.*

Xen o phon (zen′ə fən), 434?-355? B.C., Greek historian and military leader. *n.*

Xer ox (zir′oks), **1** trademark for a dry process of making copies of letters, etc., by using electrically charged

xylophone

particles instead of ink to make a photographic print. **2** make a copy or copies of by using a Xerox copying machine. 1 *n.,* 2 *v.*

Xerx es (zėrk′sēz′), 519?-465 B.C., king of ancient Persia from 486? to 465 B.C. He tried to conquer Greece but was defeated in 480 B.C. *n.*

Xi zang (shē′zäng′), Chinese name of **Tibet.** *n.*

XL, extra large.

X mas (kris′məs *or* eks′məs), Christmas. *n.*

X ray (def. 2) of a flower

X ray, 1 an electromagnetic ray having an extremely short wavelength, that can go through substances that ordinary rays of light cannot penetrate; Roentgen ray. X rays are formed when a high-speed stream of electrons strikes a target, usually of metal, in a special kind of vacuum tube. X rays are used to locate breaks in bones, bullets lodged in the body, etc., and to diagnose and treat certain diseases. **2** picture made by means of X rays.

X-ray (eks′rā′), **1** examine, photograph, or treat with X rays: *The doctor X-rayed my knee to find out if any bones had been broken by my fall.* **2** of, by, or having to do with X rays: *an X-ray examination of one's teeth.* 1 *v.,* 2 *adj.*

xy lem (zī′ləm *or* zī′lem), the woody part of plants. It consists of tissue through which water and dissolved minerals pass upward from the roots. *n.* [*Xylem* is from German *Xylem,* which came from Greek *xylon,* meaning "wood."]

xy lo phone (zī′lə fōn), a musical instrument consisting of two rows of wooden bars of varying lengths, which are sounded by striking with wooden hammers. *n.* [*Xylophone* comes from Greek *xylon,* meaning "wood," and *phōnē,* meaning "a sound."]

xy lo phon ist (zī′lə fō′nist), person who plays on a xylophone. *n.*

Yy

a hat	**i** it	**oi** oil	**ch** child	a in about
ā age	**ī** ice	**ou** out	**ng** long	e in taken
ä far	**o** hot	**u** cup	**sh** she	**ə** = i in pencil
e let	**ō** open	**u̇** put	**th** thin	o in lemon
ē equal	**ô** order	**ü** rule	**ŦH** then	u in circus
ėr term			**zh** measure	

Y or **y** (wī), **1** the 25th letter of the English alphabet. **2** anything shaped like a Y. *n., pl.* **Y's** or **y's.**

Y, symbol for yttrium.

y., 1 yard or yards. **2** year.

-y¹, *suffix forming adjectives.* **1** (*added to nouns*) full of _____: *Bumpy = full of bumps.* **2** (*added to nouns*) containing _____: *Salty = containing salt.* **3** (*added to nouns*) having _____: *Cloudy = having clouds.* **4** (*added to nouns*) characterized by _____: *Funny = characterized by fun.* **5** (*added to adjectives*) somewhat _____: *Chilly = somewhat chill.* **6** (*added to verbs*) inclined to _____: *Sleepy = inclined to sleep.*

-y², *suffix added to nouns to form nouns.* **1** small _____: *Dolly = a small doll.* **2** dear _____: *Daddy = dear dad.*

-y³, *suffix forming nouns.* **1** (*added to adjectives*) _____ condition or quality: *Jealousy = a jealous condition or quality.* **2** (*added to nouns*) condition or quality of being _____: *Victory = condition or quality of being a victor.* **3** (*added to verbs*) activity of _____ing: *Delivery = activity of delivering. Entreaty = activity of entreating.*

yacht (yot), **1** boat for pleasure trips or for racing. **2** to sail or race on a yacht. 1 *n.,* 2 *v.* [*Yacht* came into English over 400 years ago from Dutch *jaght,* which was shortened from *jaghtschip,* meaning "a chasing ship."]

yacht ing (yot'ing), **1** art of sailing a yacht. **2** pastime of sailing on a yacht. *n.*

yachts man (yots'mən), person who owns or sails a yacht. *n., pl.* **yachts men.**

yack (yak), SLANG. yak². *v.*

yak¹ (yak), a long-haired ox of Tibet and central Asia. The domesticated yak is raised for its meat, milk, and hair and is used as a beast of burden. *n.* [*Yak¹* comes from Tibetan *gyag.*]

yak² (yak), SLANG. talk endlessly and foolishly. *v.,* **yakked, yak king.** Also, **yack.**

Yal ta (yôl'tə), seaport and winter resort in S Crimea, on the Black Sea. *n.*

Ya lu (yä'lü), river in E Asia, between Manchuria and Korea. *n.*

yam (yam), **1** the thick, sweet, orange root of a vine of warm regions, eaten as a vegetable. **2** the sweet potato: *We often have candied yams with ham. n.* [*Yam* comes from Spanish *ñame,* and can be traced back to Senegalese *nyami,* meaning "to eat." Senegalese is a west African language.]

Yang tze (yang'sē'), river flowing from Tibet through China. Officially, **Chang Jiang.** *n.*

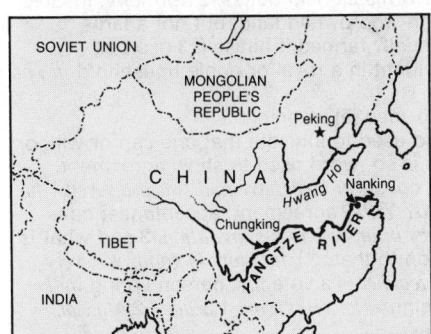

yank (yangk), INFORMAL. **1** to pull with a sudden motion; jerk; tug: *She yanked the weeds out of the flower bed.* **2** a sudden pull; jerk; tug: *She gave the door a yank.* 1 *v.,* 2 *n.*

Yan kee (yang'kē), **1** person born or living in New England. **2** person born or living in the North, especially during the Civil War. **3** person born or living in the United States; American. **4** of Yankees. 1-3 *n.,* 4 *adj.*

Yankee Doo dle (dü'dl), an American song, probably of English origin and taken over by the American soldiers in the Revolutionary War.

Ya oun dé (yä ün dā'), capital of Cameroon. *n.*

yap (yap), **1** a quick, sharp bark; yelp. **2** bark in a quick, sharp way; yelp: *The little dog yapped at every strange person who came to the door.* **3** SLANG. sharp, noisy, or foolish talk. **4** SLANG. talk sharply, noisily, or foolishly. 1,3 *n.,* 2,4 *v.,* **yapped, yap ping. —yap'per,** *n.*

yard¹ (yärd), **1** piece of ground near or around a house, barn, school, etc.: *You can play outside, but you must not leave the yard.* **2** piece of enclosed ground for some special purpose or business: *a chicken yard.* **3** space with tracks where railroad cars are stored, shifted around, etc.: *My cousin works in the railroad yards. n.*

yak
about 5¹/₂ ft. (1.5 m.) high at shoulder

yard² (yärd), **1** unit of length equal to 36 inches; 3 feet: *buy six yards of cloth, run 50 yards.* **2** a beam or pole fastened across a mast, used to support a sail. *n.*

yard age (yär'dij), **1** length in yards. **2** amount measured in yards. *n.*

yard arm (yärd'ärm'), either end of the beam or pole used to support a square sail. *n.*

yard goods, cloth cut to measure and sold by the yard.

yard mas ter (yärd'mas'tər), person in charge of a railroad yard. *n.*

yard stick (yärd'stik'), **1** a stick one yard long, used for measuring. **2** standard of judgment or comparison: *What yardstick do you use to decide whether you've done well? n.*

yar mul ke (yär'məl kə), skullcap worn by Jewish males especially for prayer and ceremonial occasions. *n.*

yarmulke

yarn (yärn), **1** any spun thread, especially that prepared for weaving or knitting: *I'm knitting a scarf from this yarn.* **2** INFORMAL. tale; story: *We took turns making up yarns and telling them.* *n.*

yar row (yar′ō), a common plant with finely divided leaves and flat clusters of white or pink flowers. *n.*

yaw (yô), **1** to turn from a straight course; go unsteadily. **2** (of an aircraft) to turn from a straight course by a motion about its vertical axis. **3** movement from a straight course. 1,2 *v.*, 3 *n.*

yawl (yôl), boat with a large mast near the bow and a small mast near the stern. *n.*

yawn (yôn), **1** open the mouth wide because one is sleepy, tired, or bored. **2** act of doing so. **3** open wide: *The canyon yawned in front of us.* 1,3 *v.*, 2 *n.*

yaws (yôz), a contagious disease of the tropics which produces sores on the skin. *n.*

Yb, symbol for ytterbium.

Y chromosome, one of the two chromosomes that determine sex. A fertilized egg cell containing a Y chromosome develops into a male.

y clept or **y cleped** (i klept′), OLD USE. called; named. *adj.*

yd., yard. *pl.* **yd.** or **yds.**

ye[1] (yē; *unstressed* yi), OLD USE. you. *pron.pl.*

ye[2] (ᴛнē *or* yē), an old way of writing the definite article "the." *definite article.*

yea (yā), **1** yes (used in agreeing with or assenting to something). **2** indeed; truly (used to introduce a sentence or clause). **3** a vote or voter in favor of something. **4** exclamation expressing approval or support (for a person, team, etc.). 1,2 *adv.*, 3 *n.*, 4 *interj.*

yeah (ye, ya, *or* ye′ə), INFORMAL. yes. *adv.*

year (yir), **1** 12 months or 365 days; January 1 to December 31. Leap year has 366 days. **2** 12 months reckoned from any point: *a year from today.* **3** the part of a year spent in a certain activity: *Our school year is 9 months.* **4** period of the earth's revolution around the sun. **5** years, *pl.* age: *young in years but old in experience.* *n.*

year after year, every year.

year by year, with each succeeding year; as years go by.

year in, year out, always; continuously.

year book (yir′bůk′), book or report published every year. Yearbooks often report facts of the year. The graduating class of a school or college usually publishes a yearbook, with pictures of its members. *n.*

year ling (yir′ling), **1** animal one year old. **2** one year old: *a yearling colt.* 1 *n.*, 2 *adj.*

year long (yir′lông′), **1** lasting for a year. **2** lasting for years. *adj.*

year ly (yir′lē), **1** once a year; in every year: *He takes a yearly trip to New York (adj.). That company sends out new calendars to its customers yearly (adv.).* **2** lasting a year: *The earth makes a yearly revolution around the sun.* **3** for a year: *a yearly salary of $12,000.* 1-3 *adj.*, 1 *adv.*

yearn (yėrn), **1** feel a longing or desire; desire earnestly: *I yearned for home.* **2** feel pity; have tender feelings: *Our hearts yearned for the homeless victims of the flood.* *v.*

yearn ing (yėr′ning), earnest or strong desire; longing. *n.* —**yearn′ing ly,** *adv.*

year-round (yir′round′), throughout the year: *She is a year-round resident. adj., adv.*

yeast (yēst), **1** the substance that causes dough for bread to rise and beer to ferment. Yeast consists of many tiny fungi which grow quickly in a liquid containing sugar. **2** any of the fungi which form yeast. **3** yeast cake. **4** foam; froth. *n.* —**yeast′less,** *adj.*

yeast cake, a small block or cake of compressed yeast.

yeast y (yē′stē), **1** of, containing, or resembling yeast. **2** frothy or foamy: *yeasty waves. adj.,* **yeast i er, yeast i est.** —**yeast′i ly,** *adv.* —**yeast′i ness,** *n.*

Yeats (yāts), **William Butler,** 1865-1939, Irish writer of poems, plays, and essays. *n.*

yell (yel), **1** cry out with a strong, loud sound: *I yelled with pain.* **2** a strong, loud cry. **3** say with a yell: *We yelled our good-bys as the bus moved away.* **4** a special shout or cheer used by a school or college to encourage its sports teams. 1,3 *v.*, 2,4 *n.* —**yell′er,** *n.*

yel low (yel′ō), **1** the color of gold, butter, or ripe lemons. **2** having this color. **3** make or become yellow: *Paper yellows with age.* **4** the yolk of an egg, or other thing that is yellow. **5** INFORMAL. cowardly. 1,4 *n.*, 2,5 *adj.*, 3 *v.* —**yel′low ness,** *n.*

yel low bird (yel′ō bėrd′), **1** the goldfinch of America. **2** yellow warbler. **3** any of various other yellow birds. *n.*

yellow fever, a dangerous, infectious disease of warm climates, transmitted by the bite of a certain kind of mosquito; yellow jack. Yellow fever causes high fever and turns the skin yellow. It was once common in some southern parts of the United States.

yel low ham mer (yel′ō ham′ər), a European bunting with a bright-yellow head, neck, and breast. *n.*

yel low ish (yel′ō ish), somewhat yellow. *adj.*

yellow jack, 1 yellow fever. **2** a yellow flag used as a signal of quarantine.

yellow jacket, wasp marked with bright yellow.

Yellow Pages, a section of a telephone directory printed on yellow paper, that lists business services and professional people. Within each classification of business or profession, the names are alphabetized.

Yellow River, Hwang Ho.

Yellow Sea, part of the Pacific Ocean between NE China and Korea. See **China** for map.

Yel low stone (yel′ō stōn′), Yellowstone National Park. *n.*

Yellowstone National Park, a large national park, mostly in NW Wyoming, famous for its scenery, hot springs, and geysers.

yellow warbler, a small, American warbler; yellowbird. The male has yellow plumage, streaked with brown.

yelp (yelp), **1** the quick, sharp bark or cry of a dog, fox, etc. **2** make such a bark or cry. **3** utter with a yelp. 1 *n.*, 2,3 *v.* —**yelp′er,** *n.*

Yem en (yem′ən), **1** country in SW Arabia. *Capital:* San′a. **2** See **Southern Yemen.** *n.*

yen[1] (yen), unit of money of Japan. *n., pl.* **yen.** [*Yen*[1] is from Japanese *en,* which came from Chinese *yüan,* meaning "a round object."]

yen[2] (yen), INFORMAL. **1** a sharp desire or hunger; urgent fancy: *a yen for ice cream, a sudden yen to leave.* **2** have a yen; desire sharply or urgently. 1 *n.*, 2 *v.,* **yenned, yenning.**

yeo man (yō′mən), **1** (in the United States Navy) a petty officer who performs clerical duties. **2** (formerly, in Great Britain) a person who owned land, but not a large amount, and usually farmed it himself. **3** OLD USE. servant or attendant in a royal or noble household. *n., pl.* **yeo men.**

yeo man ry (yō′mən rē), yeomen. *n.*

yes (yes), **1** word used to indicate that one can or will, or that something is so; word used to show agreement, acceptance, or consent: *"Yes, five and two are seven," he said. Will you go? Yes.* **2** agreement; acceptance; consent: *I gave a yes in answer to his invitation.* **3** and what is more; in addition to that: *"Your work is good, yes, very good," said the teacher.* **4** a vote for; person voting in favor of something: *The yeses won.* 1,3 *adv.*, 2,4 *n., pl.* **yes es** or **yes ses.**

a hat	**i** it	**oi** oil	**ch** child		a in about	
ā age	**ī** ice	**ou** out	**ng** long		e in taken	
ä far	**o** hot	**u** cup	**sh** she	**ə =**	i in pencil	
e let	**ō** open	**u̇** put	**th** thin		o in lemon	
ē equal	**ô** order	**ü** rule	**ᵺ** then		u in circus	
ėr term			**zh** measure			

ye shi va (yə shē′və), **1** a Jewish school for higher studies, often a rabbinical seminary. **2** a Jewish elementary or high school in which both religious and secular subjects are taught. *n., pl.* **ye shi vas, ye shi voth** (yeshē′vōt′). [*Yeshiva* comes from Hebrew *yeshībāh*, originally meaning "a sitting."]

yes ter day (yes′tər dē), **1** the day before today: *Yesterday was cold and rainy.* **2** on the day before today. **3** the recent past: *We are often amused by the fashions of yesterday.* **4** recently. 1,3 *n.,* 2,4 *adv.*

yes ter night (yes′tər nīt′), OLD USE. last night; the night before today. *n., adv.*

yes ter year (yes′tər yir′), OLD USE. last year; the year before this. *n., adv.*

yet (yet), **1** up to the present time; thus far: *The work is not yet finished.* **2** at this time; now: *Don't go yet.* **3** at that time; then: *It was not yet dark.* **4** even now; still: *She is doing her homework yet.* **5** sometime: *I may yet get rich.* **6** also; again: *Yet once more I forbid you to go.* **7** moreover: *They won't do it for you nor yet for me.* **8** even: *The judge spoke yet more harshly to the lawbreaker.* **9** nevertheless; however; but: *The story was strange, yet true* (*adv.*). *The work is good, yet it could be better* (*conj.*). 1-9 *adv.,* 9 *conj.*

as yet, up to now.

ye ti or **Ye ti** (ye′tē), Abominable Snowman. *n.*

yew (yü), **1** an evergreen tree native to Europe and Asia. Some kinds of yew are now widely grown in the United States as shrubs. **2** the wood of this tree. Bows for archery used to be made of a kind of yew that grows in England. *n.*

Yid dish (yid′ish), **1** language which developed from a dialect of German. Yiddish contains many Hebrew expressions and is written in Hebrew characters. It is spoken mainly by Jews of eastern and central Europe, and their descendants. **2** of Yiddish. 1 *n.,* 2 *adj.*

yield (yēld), **1** produce: *This land yields good crops. Mines yield ore.* **2** amount yielded; product: *This year's yield from the silver mine was very large.* **3** give in return; bring in: *an investment which yielded a large profit.* **4** give; grant: *Her parents yielded their consent to the plan.* **5** give up; surrender: *The enemy yielded to our soldiers.* **6** give way: *The door yielded to his touch.* **7** give place: *We yield to nobody in love of freedom.* 1,3-7 *v.,* 2 *n.* —**yield′a ble,** *adj.* —**yield′er,** *n.*

yield ing (yēl′ding), not resisting; submissive: *a person with a humble and yielding nature. adj.* —**yield′ing ly,** *adv.*

yip (yip), INFORMAL. **1** (especially of dogs) bark or yelp briskly. **2** a sharp, barking sound. 1 *v.,* **yipped, yipping;** 2 *n.*

yip pee (yip′ē), shout of great joy. *interj.*

Y.M.C.A., Young Men's Christian Association.

Y.M.H.A., Young Men's Hebrew Association.

yo del (yō′dl), **1** sing with frequent changes from the ordinary voice to a forced shrill voice or falsetto and back again, in the manner of mountaineers of Switzerland and the Tirol. **2** act or sound of yodeling. 1 *v.,* **yo deled, yo del ing** or **yo delled, yo del ling;** 2 *n.* —**yo′del er, yo′del ler,** *n.*

yo dle (yō′dl), yodel. *v.,* **yo dled, yo dling;** *n.* —**yo′dler,** *n.*

yo ga or **Yo ga** (yō′gə), **1** system of Hindu religious philosophy that requires intense mental and physical discipline as a means of attaining a state of union with the universal spirit. **2** system of physical exercises and positions used in yoga. *n.*

yo gi (yō′gē), person who practices or follows yoga. *n., pl.* **yo gis.**

yo gurt (yō′gərt), kind of thickened, slightly fermented liquid food made from milk acted upon by bacteria. *n.*

yoke
(defs. 1 and 2)

yoke (yōk), **1** a wooden frame which fits around the necks of two work animals to fasten them together for pulling a plow or vehicle. **2** pair fastened together by a yoke: *The plow was drawn by a yoke of oxen.* **3** any frame connecting two other parts: *I tried to carry two buckets on a yoke, one at each end.* **4** put a yoke on; fasten with a yoke. **5** harness or fasten a work animal or animals to: *The farmer yoked the plow.* **6** part of a garment fitting the neck and shoulders closely. **7** a top piece to a skirt, fitting the hips. **8** something that binds together; bond; tie: *the yoke of marriage.* **9** join; unite: *They are yoked in marriage.* **10** something that holds people in slavery or submission: *Throw off your yoke and be free.* **11** rule; dominion: *The country was under the yoke of a dictator.* 1-3,6-8,10,11 *n.,* 4,5,9 *v.,* **yoked, yok ing.** —**yoke′less,** *adj.*

yo kel (yō′kəl), an awkward or unsophisticated person from the country. *n.*

Yo ko ha ma (yō′kə hä′mə), large seaport in central Japan, near Tokyo. *n.*

yolk (yōk), the yellow part of an egg. *n.* [*Yolk* is from Old English *geolca*, which comes from *geolu*, meaning "yellow."]

Yom Kip pur (yom kip′ər), a Jewish fast day of atonement for sins; Day of Atonement. It occurs ten days after Rosh Hashanah, the Jewish New Year.

yon (yon), OLD USE. yonder. *adj., adv.*

yond (yond), OLD USE. yonder. *adj., adv.*

yon der (yon′dər), **1** within sight, but not near; over there: *Look at that wild duck yonder! The sky is getting black yonder in the west.* **2** being within sight, but not near; situated over there: *On yonder hill stands a ruined castle.* 1 *adv.,* 2 *adj.*

Yon kers (yong′kərz), city just north of New York City. *n.*

yore (yôr). **of yore,** now long since gone; long past: *She told us an old tale about days of yore. n.*

York (yôrk), **1** the royal house of England from 1461 to 1485. Its emblem was a white rose. **2** city in NE England. **3** Yorkshire. *n.*

York shire (yôrk′shər), county in NE England. *n.*

Yorkshire pudding, a batter cake often served with roast beef.

Yorkshire terrier, one of an English breed of small, shaggy dogs with a steel-blue coat, weighing 4 to 8 pounds.

York town (yôrk′toun′), village in SE Virginia, where

Lord Cornwallis surrendered to George Washington in 1781. *n.*

Yo sem i te (yō sem′ə tē), **1** Yosemite National Park. **2** a very deep valley in this park, famous for its waterfalls. *n.*

Yosemite National Park, large national park in E California.

you (yü; *unstressed* yù), **1** the person or persons spoken to: *Are you ready? Then you may go.* **2** one; anybody: *You never can tell. You push this button to get a light.* *pron. sing. or pl.*

you-all (yü′ôl′ *or* yôl), DIALECT. you: *You-all come and see us real soon.* *pron. pl.*

you'd (yüd; *unstressed* yùd), **1** you had. **2** you would.

you'll (yül; *unstressed* yùl), **1** you will. **2** you shall.

young (yung), **1** in the early part of life or growth; not old: *A puppy is a young dog.* **2** young offspring: *An animal will fight to protect its young.* **3** the young, young people. **4** having the looks or qualities of youth or a young person: *She looks and acts young for her age.* **5** of youth; early: *one's young days.* **6** not so old as another or the other: *Young Mr. Jones worked for his father.* **7** in an early stage; not far advanced: *The night was still young when they left the party.* **8** without much experience or practice: *I was too young in the trade to be successful.* 1,4-8 *adj.,* **young er** (yung′gər), **young est** (yung′gist); 2,3 *n.*

with young, pregnant.

Young (yung), **Brigham,** 1801-1877, American Mormon leader. *n.*

young ish (yung′ish), rather young. *adj.*

young ling (yung′ling), **1** a young person, animal, or plant. **2** young; youthful. 1 *n.,* 2 *adj.*

young ster (yung′stər), **1** child: *He is a lively youngster.* **2** a young person: *The old woman was as spry as a youngster.* *n.*

Youngs town (yungz′toun′), city in NE Ohio. *n.*

your (yùr; *unstressed* yər), **1** belonging to you: *Wash your hands.* **2** having to do with you: *We enjoyed your visit.* **3** that you know; well-known; that you speak of; that is spoken of: *your real lover of music, your average voter.* **4** *Your* is used as part of a title. *Your Lordship, Your Ladyship, Your Highness, Your Honor.* *adj.*

you're (yùr; *unstressed* yər), you are.

yours (yùrz), **1** the one or ones belonging to you: *This pencil is yours. My hands are clean; yours are dirty.* **2** at your service: *I am yours to command.* **3** *Yours* is used in closing a letter, just before the signature. *Yours truly, Sincerely yours.* *pron. sing. or pl.*

your self (yùr self′ *or* yər self′), **1** form of *you* used to make a statement stronger: *You yourself know the story is not true.* **2** form used instead of *you* in cases like: *Did you hurt yourself? Ask yourself what you really want.* **3** your real or true self: *Now that your cold is better, you'll feel like yourself again.* *pron., pl.* **yourselves.**

your selves (yùr selvz′ *or* yər selvz′), plural of **yourself.** *You can all see for yourselves that the jar is full.* *pron.*

youth (yüth), **1** fact or quality of being young: *She has all the vigor of youth.* **2** the time between childhood and adulthood. **3** a young man. **4** young people. **5** the first or early stage of anything: *Many of our laws go back to the youth of this country.* *n., pl.* **youths** (yüths *or* yǖᴛHz), **youth.**

youth ful (yüth′fəl), **1** young. **2** of or suitable for youth: *youthful energy, youthful clothing.* **3** having the looks or qualities of youth; fresh; lively: *The old man had a gay and youthful spirit.* *adj.* —**youth′ful ly,** *adv.* —**youth′ful ness,** *n.*

you've (yüv; *unstressed* yùv), you have.

yowl (youl), **1** a long, distressful, or dismal cry; howl. **2** to howl: *That dog is always yowling.* 1 *n.,* 2 *v.*

yo yo (yō′yō), a small toy consisting of a deeply grooved disk which is spun out and reeled in by means of an attached string. *n., pl.* **yo yos.**

yr., year. *pl.* **yr.** *or* **yrs.**

yt ter bi um (i tėr′bē əm), a metallic element which occurs in certain minerals and is used in making special alloys. *n.* [*Ytterbium* gets its name from *Ytterby,* a town in Sweden, where it was discovered.]

yt tri um (it′rē əm), a dark-gray metallic element which occurs in various minerals. It is used in making iron alloys and to remove impurities from metals. *n.*

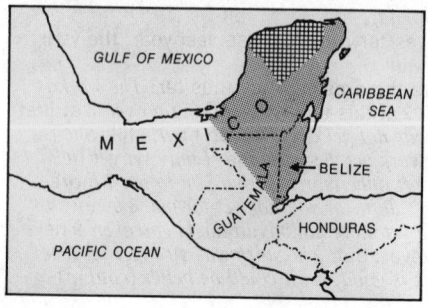

Yucatán (def. 1, all of the darkened area; def. 2, upper darkened area only)

Yu ca tán (yü′kə tan′), **1** peninsula of SE Mexico and N Central America. **2** state in SE Mexico.

yuc ca (yuk′ə), plant found in dry, warm regions of North and Central America, having stiff, narrow leaves at its base and an upright cluster of white, bell-shaped flowers. *n., pl.* **yuc cas.**

yucca

Yu go slav (yü′gō släv′), **1** person born or living in Yugoslavia. **2** of Yugoslavia or its people. 1 *n.,* 2 *adj.* Also, **Jugoslav.**

Yu go sla vi a (yü′gō slä′vē ə), country in SE Europe, on the Adriatic. *Capital:* Belgrade. See **Danube** for map. *n.* Also, **Jugoslavia.** —**Yu′go sla′vi an,** *adj., n.*

Yu kon (yü′kon), **1** river flowing from NW Canada through Alaska into the Bering Sea. **2** territory in NW Canada. *Capital:* Whitehorse. *n.*

yule *or* **Yule** (yül), **1** Christmas. **2** yuletide. *n.*

Yule log, a large log burned at Christmas.

yule tide *or* **Yule tide** (yül′tīd′), Christmastide; the Christmas season. *n.*

yum my (yum′ē), INFORMAL. very pleasing to the senses; delicious; delightful. *adj.,* **yum mi er, yum mi est.**

Yup pie *or* **yup pie** (yup′ē), SLANG. member of the young, middle-class, professional portion of the population. *n.* [*Yuppie* comes from the first letters of the words *young urban professional,* and *-ie,* a form of the suffix *-y*[2].]

Y.W.C.A., Young Women's Christian Association.

Y.W.H.A., Young Women's Hebrew Association.

Zz

a hat	**i** it	**oi** oil	**ch** child		a in about
ā age	**ī** ice	**ou** out	**ng** long		e in taken
ä far	**o** hot	**u** cup	**sh** she	**ə** =	i in pencil
e let	**ō** open	**ù** put	**th** thin		o in lemon
ē equal	**ô** order	**ü** rule	**ŦH** then		u in circus
ėr term			**zh** measure		

Z or **z** (zē), the 26th and last letter of the English alphabet. *n., pl.* **Z's** or **z's.**

Za ïre (zä ir′ *or* zar), **1** country in central Africa. *Capital:* Kinshasa. See **Congo** for map. Formerly called **Democratic Republic of the Congo. 2** Congo (def. 1). *n.*

Zam be zi (zam bē′zē), river flowing through S Africa into the Indian Ocean. *n.*

Zam bi a (zam′bē ə), country in S Africa, a member of the Commonwealth of Nations. *Capital:* Lusaka. See **South Africa** for map. *n.* —**Zam′bi an,** *adj., n.*

za ny (zā′nē), **1** a fool. **2** a clown. **3** clownish; foolish; idiotic. 1,2 *n., pl.* **za nies;** 3 *adj.,* **za ni er, za ni est.**

Zan zi bar (zan′zə bär), island near the E coast of Africa. It is part of Tanzania. *n.*

zap (zap), SLANG. **1** exclamation of surprise, shock, dismay, etc.: *Zap! A home run beat us.* **2** hit hard; beat; defeat; kill. 1 *interj.,* 2 *v.,* **zapped, zap ping.**

zeal (zēl), eager desire or effort; earnest enthusiasm: *work with zeal. n.* [*Zeal* is from Latin *zelus,* which came from Greek *zēlos.*]

Zea land (zē′lənd), the largest island in Denmark, in the E part. Copenhagen is located on it. *n.*

zeal ot (zel′ət), person who shows too much zeal; fanatic. *n.*

zeal ous (zel′əs), full of zeal; eager; earnest; enthusiastic: *We made zealous efforts to clean up the house for the party. adj.* —**zeal′ous ly,** *adv.* —**zeal′ous ness,** *n.*

ze bra (zē′brə), a wild mammal of Africa, related to the horse and donkey but striped with dark bands on white. *n., pl.* **ze bras** or **ze bra.**

zebu
up to 5 ft.
(1.5 m.) high
at shoulder

ze bu (zē′bü *or* zē′byü), a kind of ox with a large hump over the shoulders. The zebu is a domestic animal in Asia and eastern Africa. *n., pl.* **ze bus** or **ze bu.**

Zech a ri ah (zek′ə rī′ə), **1** a Hebrew prophet of the 500's B.C. **2** book of the Old Testament. *n.*

Zen Buddhism (zen), a Japanese form of Buddhism that emphasizes meditation and introspection.

ze nith (zē′nith), **1** the point in the heavens directly overhead. **2** the highest point: *At the zenith of its power Rome dominated the world. n.*

zeph yr (zef′ər), **1** the west wind. **2** any soft, gentle wind; mild breeze. **3** a fine, soft yarn or worsted. *n.*

Zep pe lin or **zep pe lin** (zep′ə lən), a large, rigid, cigar-shaped airship with separate compartments filled with gas. Zeppelins were mostly used in the period between 1914 and 1937. *n.* [The *Zeppelin* was named for Count Ferdinand von *Zeppelin,* 1838-1917, a German general who invented it.]

zer o (zir′ō), **1** the figure or digit 0; naught. **2** point

marked with a zero on the scale of a thermometer, etc. **3** temperature that corresponds to zero on the scale of a thermometer. **4** of or at zero: *The other team's score was zero.* **5** complete absence of quantity; nothing. **6** not any; none at all: *zero visibility in dense fog.* **7** a very low point: *The losing team's spirit sank to zero.* 1-3,5,7 *n., pl.* **zer os** or **zer oes;** 4,6 *adj.* [*Zero* was borrowed from Italian *zero,* which came from Arabic *sifr,* meaning "empty."]

zero in on, 1 get the range of (a target) by adjusting the sights of a firearm, etc. **2** to aim with precision toward (a target).

zero g or **zero gravity,** condition in which the effects of gravity are not felt. In an orbiting spacecraft, zero g is experienced as weightlessness.

zero hour, 1 time set for beginning an attack or other military operation. **2** time set for any important action to begin; crucial moment.

zero population growth, the condition in which a population has stabilized, because the birthrate and death rate have become equal.

zest (zest), **1** keen enjoyment; relish: *The hungry children ate with zest.* **2** a pleasant or exciting quality, flavor, etc.: *Wit gives zest to conversation. n.* —**zest′less,** *adj.*

zest ful (zest′fəl), characterized by zest. *adj.* —**zest′ful ly,** *adv.* —**zest′ful ness,** *n.*

Zeus (züs), (in Greek myths) the chief god, ruler of gods and human beings. The Romans called him Jupiter. *n.*

zig zag (zig′zag′), **1** with short, sharp turns from one side to the other: *to go in a zigzag direction (adj.). The path ran zigzag up the hill (adv.).* **2** move in a zigzag way: *Lightning zigzagged across the sky.* **3** a zigzag line or course. **4** one of the short, sharp turns of a zigzag. 1 *adj., adv.,* 2 *v.,* **zig zagged, zig zag ging;** 3,4 *n.*

zil lion (zil′yən), SLANG. **1** any very large, indefinite number. **2** of such a number; very many. 1 *n.,* 2 *adj.*

Zim ba bwe (zim bä′bwe), country in SE Africa, a member of the Commonwealth of Nations. *Capital:* Harare. See **South Africa** for map. Formerly called **Rhodesia.** *n.* —**Zim ba bwe an** (zim bä′bwē ən), *adj., n.*

zinc (zingk), a bluish-white metallic element that is little affected by air and moisture at ordinary temperatures, but at high temperatures it burns in air with a bright, blue-green flame. Zinc is used as a coating for iron, in alloys such as brass, as a roofing material, in electric batteries, in paint, and in medicine. *n.*

zinc oxide, compound of zinc and oxygen, used in making paint, rubber, glass, cosmetics, and ointments.

zing (zing), **1** a sharp, humming sound. **2** INFORMAL. liveliness; spirit; zest: *a story without zing.* 1,2 *n.,* 1 *interj.*

zin ni a (zin′ē ə), a garden plant grown for its showy

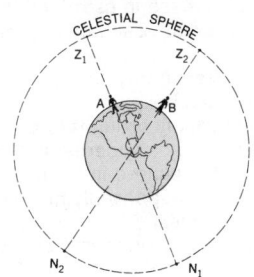

zenith (def. 1)
Observer A has zenith Z_1
and nadir N_1;
Observer B has zenith Z_2
and nadir N_2.

flowers of many colors. *n.* [The *zinnia* was named in honor of Johann G. *Zinn*, 1727-1759, a German botanist.]

Zi on (zī′ən), **1** hill in Jerusalem on which the royal palace and the Temple were built. **2** Israel or the Israelites; the people of Israel. **3** heaven, as the final home of those who are virtuous. **4** the Christian church of God. *n.*

Zi on ism (zī′ə niz′əm), movement that started in the 1800's to set up a Jewish national state in Palestine and that now seeks to help maintain and develop the state of Israel. *n.*

Zi on ist (zī′ə nist), person who supports or favors Zionism. *n.*

Zion National Park, a national park in SW Utah.

zip (zip), **1** fasten or close with a zipper: *zip up one's jacket before going out.* **2** a sudden, brief, hissing sound, as of a flying bullet. **3** make such a sound. **4** INFORMAL. energy or vim. **5** INFORMAL. proceed with energy. 1,3,5 *v.*, **zipped, zip ping;** 2,4 *n.*

Zip Code, 1 Zone Improvement Plan Code (system of numbers, each number of which identifies one of the postal delivery areas into which the United States and its larger cities have been divided). **2** a number in this system. [*Zip* was formed from the first letters of the words *zone improvement plan.*]

zip per (zip′ər), **1** a sliding fastener for clothing, shoes, etc.: *a zipper on a jacket.* **2** fasten or close with a zipper: *Zipper your jacket before you go out.* 1 *n.*, 2 *v.*

zip py (zip′ē), INFORMAL. full of energy; lively; gay. *adj.*, **zip pi er, zip pi est.**

zir con (zėr′kon), a crystalline mineral that occurs in various forms and colors. Transparent zircon is used as a gem. *n.*

zir co ni um (zėr′kō′nē əm), a white metallic element obtained from zircon. Zirconium is used in alloys for wires, filaments, etc., in making steel, and in atomic reactors. *n.*

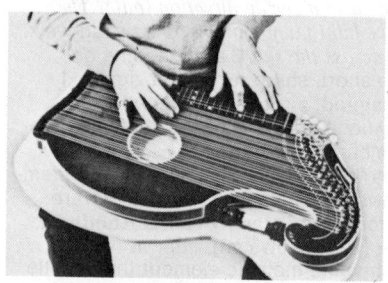

zither

zith er (zith′ər *or* ziŦH′ər), a musical instrument having 30 to 40 strings, played with the fingers and a plectrum. *n.*

Zn, symbol for zinc.

zo di ac (zō′dē ak), **1** an imaginary belt of the heavens extending on both sides of the apparent yearly path of the sun and including the apparent path of the major planets and the moon. The zodiac is divided into 12 equal parts, called signs, named after 12 groups of stars. **2** diagram representing the zodiac, used in astrology. *n.*

zo di a cal (zō dī′ə kəl), **1** of the zodiac. **2** situated in the zodiac. *adj.*

Zo la (zō′lə), Émile, 1840-1902, French novelist. *n.*

zom bi (zom′bē), zombie. *n., pl.* **zom bis.**

zom bie (zom′bē), **1** corpse supposedly brought to a trancelike condition resembling life by a supernatural power. People who practice voodoo believe in zombies. **2** a supernatural power or force that supposedly makes the dead move and act. *n., pl.* **zom bies.**

zon al (zō′nl), **1** of a zone or zones. **2** divided into zones. *adj.* —**zon′al ly,** *adv.*

zone (zōn), **1** any of the five great divisions of the earth's surface, bounded by imaginary lines going around the earth parallel to the equator. **2** any region or area especially considered or set off. A combat zone is a district where fighting is going on. **3** area or district in a city or town under special restrictions as to building. **4** one of the numbered sections into which a large city or metropolitan area is divided in order to speed the sorting and delivery of mail. **5** a circular area or district within which the same rate of postage is charged for parcel post shipments from a particular point. **6** divide into zones: *The city was zoned for factories and residences.* **7** be formed into zones. 1-5 *n.*, 6,7 *v.*, **zoned, zon ing.**

zoo (zü), place where animals are kept and shown; zoological garden. *n., pl.* **zoos.**

zoo-, *combining form.* animal or animals: *Zoology = the science of animals.* [The form *zoo-* comes from Greek *zōion,* meaning "animal."]

zo o log i cal (zō′ə loj′ə kəl), **1** of animals and animal life. **2** having to do with zoology. *adj.* —**zo′o log′i cal ly,** *adv.*

zoological garden, zoo.

zo ol o gist (zō ol′ə jist), an expert in zoology. *n.*

zo ol o gy (zō ol′ə jē), the science of animals; the study of animals and animal life. Zoology is a branch of biology. *n.*

zoom (züm), **1** move suddenly upward: *The airplane zoomed.* **2** an act of zooming; sudden upward flight: *The airplane made a zoom and left the mountain far below.* **3** move or travel with a humming or buzzing sound. 1,3 *v.*, 2 *n.*

zoom lens, type of motion-picture or television camera lens which can be adjusted quickly to take either wide-angle distance shots or close-up shots.

Zo ro as ter (zôr′ō as′tər), Persian religious teacher who lived about 600 B.C. *n.*

Zo ro as tri an (zôr′ō as′trē ən), **1** of Zoroaster or the religion founded by him. **2** person believing in the teachings of Zoroaster. 1 *adj.*, 2 *n.*

Zo ro as tri an ism (zôr′ō as′trē ə niz′əm), religion founded by Zoroaster and practiced in ancient Persia. Zoroastrianism taught that there is an eternal struggle between the powers of light and of darkness. *n.*

zounds (zoundz), OLD USE. oath expressing surprise or anger. *interj.*

Zr, symbol for zirconium.

zuc chi ni (zü kē′nē), kind of dark-green squash shaped like a cucumber. It is eaten as a vegetable. *n., pl.* **zucchi ni** or **zuc chi nis.** [*Zucchini* is from Italian *zucchino,* which comes from *zucca,* meaning "squash, gourd."]

Zui der Zee (zī′dər zē′), a shallow gulf in central Netherlands. It is now closed off from the North Sea by a dike. Also, **Zuyder Zee.**

Zu lu (zü′lü), **1** member of a Bantu people of SE Africa. **2** their language. **3** of this people or their language. 1,2 *n., pl.* **Zu lus** or **Zu lu;** 3 *adj.*

Zu lu land (zü′lü land), territory in NE Natal, in the Republic of South Africa. Zululand is the home of the Zulus. *n.*

Zu ñi (zü′nyē), member of a tribe of Pueblo Indians living in western New Mexico. *n., pl.* **Zu ñi** or **Zu ñis.**

Zur ich (zùr′ik), city in N Switzerland. *n.*

Zuy der Zee (zī′dər zē′), Zuider Zee.

zwie back (swī′bak′ *or* zwī′bak′), kind of bread or cake cut into slices and toasted dry in an oven. *n.* [*Zwieback* is from German *Zwieback,* meaning "a biscuit," which comes from *zwie-,* meaning "twice," and *backen,* meaning "to bake."]

zy gote (zī′gōt), the cell formed by the union of two germ cells or gametes. A fertilized egg is a zygote. *n.*

Picture Credits

How to Use This Dictionary

p. 10	Wide World Photos
p. 13	Scott, Foresman staff photos
p. 14	Katherine Young
p. 24	Baron Hugo van Lawick © National Geographic Society
p. 32	Frederic Remington, *Bronco Buster*, 1905 Courtesy of The Art Institute of Chicago
p. 37 (left)	National Basketball Hall of Fame
p. 37 (right)	Lily Solmssen / Photo Researchers, Inc.

Dictionary

abominable	United Press International
abstract	The Solomon R. Guggenheim Museum, New York / photo by Robert E. Mates
accessible	Aero-Photo
accommodate	Culver Pictures, Inc.
accordion	J. Lochridge
acupuncture	United Press International
adapted	John H. Gerard
adobe	Stewart / Jeroboam, Inc.
adventure	Wide World Photos
adversary	P. A. Southwick / Stock, Boston, Inc.
aerial	Arnold Chalfant
agave	H. Armstrong Roberts
aground	United Press International
air bag	General Motors Corporation
albino	"Paris Match" / Pictorial Parade Inc.
alliteration	Culver Pictures, Inc.
aloof	The Museum of Modern Art Film Stills Archive
American eagle	The National Archives
amphitheater	Art Reference Bureau
anemometer	N.O.A.A.
angelfish	Walter Chandoha
antenna	Turtox-Cambosco, MacMillan Science Company, Chicago
antiquated	National Film Board of Canada
Appaloosa	Appaloosa News
apprehend	The Museum of Modern Art Film Stills Archive
aptitude	Library of Congress
aqueduct	Spanish National Tourist Office
arch	Alinari / Art Reference Bureau
armor	The Metropolitan Museum of Art, The Bashford Dean Memorial Collection. Gift of Helen Fahnestock Hubbard, 1929, in memory of her father, Harris C. Fahnestock
artifact	Courtesy of The Trustees of the British Museum
aster	Gretchen Garner
atom	The University of Chicago
avalanche	U.S.D.A.
baboon	Animals, Animals © Al Szabo
bacteria	Dr. Wyckoff / National Institute of Health
banish	The Museum of Modern Art Film Stills Archive
barley	U.S.D.A.
bathyscaph	United States Navy
bearing	Courtesy of The Timken Company
beeper	Motorola Inc.
bestride	Art Reference Bureau
blimp	Courtesy of the Goodyear Tire and Rubber Company
bloodhound	H. Armstrong Roberts

bloomers	General Research and Humanities Division, The New York Public Library, Astor, Lenox and Tilden Foundation
boll weevil	U.S.D.A.
bow	N.O.A.A.
brand	Courtesy of the Montana State Highway Commission
breakwater	United States Navy
breeches	The Franklin D. Roosevelt Library
bristlecone pine	William S. Stickney / Morton Arboretum
bulldozer	Courtesy of the Caterpillar Tractor Company
burnoose	F. Siteman / Stock, Boston, Inc.
bust	Sculpture by Malvina Hoffman, Courtesy of The Field Museum of Natural History, Chicago
cable	Courtesy of American Telephone and Telegraph
cacao	U.S.D.A.
cactus	U.S.D.A.
Canada goose	Walter Chandoha
cantilever bridge	The Smithsonian Institution
capsule	NASA
carillon	Laura Spelman Rockefeller Memorial Carillon, The University of Chicago Photo by Patricia Evans
cascade	William B. Parker
caterpillar	Lynn M. Stone
cecropia moth	Lynn M. Stone
chairlift	Swiss National Tourist Bureau
chaps	Library of Congress
chassis	General Motors Corporation
château	French Government Tourist Bureau
chipmunk	John H. Gerard
chrysalis	Louis Quitt / Photo Researchers, Inc.
cirrus	NASA
clover	U.S.D.A.
cloverleaf	U.S. Highway Department
coffee bean	U.S.D.A.
colonnade	Raymond V. Schoder, S.J.
combine	Bob Kral / U.S.D.A.
comet	Courtesy of Hale Observatories
commemorative	U.S. Postal Service
compress	Emelio A. Mercado / Jeroboam, Inc.
confinement	Dom Franco / Van Cleve Photography
conflagration	The Bettmann Archive
congest	United Press International
conservatory	Courtesy of the Chicago Park District
console	Joseph Abeles Studio
constrictor	Dade W. Thornton / National Audubon Society / Photo Researchers, Inc.
contortion	Dorka Raynor
contour	U.S.D.A.
converge	National Film Board of Canada
coot	Karl H. Maslowski / Photo Researchers, Inc.
copperhead	John H. Gerard
coral snake	John H. Gerard
corona	NASA
corral	Courtesy of the Montana Historical Society
countenance	Library of Congress
coupe	Courtesy of General Motors Corporation
cowl	Alinari / Art Reference Bureau
coyote	National Film Board of Canada
crater	NASA

crevasse	National Film Board of Canada
crocodile	The New York Zoological Society
crude	National Gallery of Art, Washington, D.C.
cubism	"Still Life with Guitar," Juan Gris National Museum, Kröller-Müller Museum
cumulonimbus	NOAA
curlew	Alexander Lowry / Photo Researchers, Inc.
cutter	"The Road-Winter," N. Currier, 1853 The Harry T. Peters Collection Museum of The City of New York
dam	Ben Glaha / U.S. Department of the Interior
dapper	The Museum of Modern Art Film Stills Archive
date palm	Culver Pictures, Inc.
Dead Sea Scrolls	The Hebrew University of Jerusalem
decoration	Library of Congress
deerskin	Courtesy of The American Museum of Natural History, New York
deformed	Courtesy of the Highland Park Historical Society
delta	G. R. Roberts
derailleur	Courtesy of the Schwinn Bicycle Company
derailment	Culver Pictures, Inc.
derby	Barbara Frankel
desolation	U.S.D.A.
desperado	The Museum of Modern Art Film Stills Archive
destroyer	United States Navy
destructive	NOAA
diamondback	The New York Zoological Society
dingo	The New York Zoological Society
diorama	Courtesy of The Field Museum of Natural History, Chicago
dirigible	United States Navy
discus	United Press International
disk harrow	U.S.D.A.
dispirit	T. Carlson / Stock, Boston, Inc.
distaff	Walter S. Clark, Jr.
Doberman pinscher	Mary Ellen Browning Photo Researchers, Inc.
dodo	Brown Brothers
dome	Abbie Rowe / National Park Service
dory	National Film Board of Canada
doublet	National Portrait Gallery, London
dragonfly	Lynn M. Stone
dromedary	H. Armstrong Roberts
dugout	James McLean
dulcimer	Courtesy of Arkansas Department of Parks and Tourism
dumbbell	"Country Fair Athlete," Camille Bombois, © S.P.A.D.E.M., 1978, Musée National d'Art Moderne, Paris
dunes	Cecil W. Stoughton / National Park Service
dwarf (top)	Courtesy of the Holsten Bonsai Collection, Brooklyn Botanic Garden
dwarf (bottom)	National Film Board of Canada
eagle	John H. Gerard
earthquake	Library of Congress
elation	D. C. Dietz / Stock, Boston, Inc.
electrocardiograph	Courtesy of Lutheran General Hospital, Park Ridge, Ill.
elk	National Film Board of Canada
encroach	U.S.D.A.
encrust	Editorial Photocolor Archives, Inc.

enthrall — Dorka Raynor

entrenchment — Imperial War Museum, London

envelop — Ewing Galloway, New York

epaulet — Brown Brothers

erosion — U.S.D.A.

estuary — G. R. Roberts

everglade — Lynn M. Stone

exhibit — "Staircase of the Old British Museum, Montague House," George Scharf, The Elder, Courtesy of The Trustees of the British Museum

expedition — Photographer, Jonathan Wright © National Geographic Society from their film "Journey to the Outer Limits"

extinct — Culver Pictures, Inc.

facade — Art Reference Bureau

fakir — United Press International

falcon — Arabian American Oil Company

Ferris wheel — Courtesy of The Chicago Historical Society

fife — Library of Congress

fingerprint — Federal Bureau of Investigation

fissure — G. R. Roberts

flipper — Nina Leen

fluoroscope — Courtesy of Lutheran General Hospital, Park Ridge, Ill.

folly — The Bettmann Archive

forge — "Trotting Cracks at the Forge" Currier and Ives, 1869 The Harry T. Peters Collection Museum of The City of New York

forum — Alinari / Editorial Photocolor Archives

frond — Gretchen Garner

funnel — NOAA

furor — United Press International

furrow — F.A.O.

galaxy — © California Institute of Technology & Carnegie Institution of Washington

gall — U.S.D.A.

gambol — Dorka Raynor

gambrel roof — International Harvester Company

gastropod — John H. Gerard

gaunt — "The Old Guitarist," Pablo Picasso, 1903 Helen Birch Bartlett Memorial Collection Courtesy of The Art Institute of Chicago

gazelle — Lynn M. Stone

geodesic dome — Hedrich-Blessing, Chicago

geometric — Courtesy of Museum of the American Indian, Heye Foundation, New York

German shepherd — Walter Chandoha

girder — Ray Ellis / Photo Researchers, Inc.

glacier — U.S. Department of the Interior Geological Survey

glass blowing — Susan McCartney / Photo Researchers, Inc.

glower — E. M. Demjen / Stock, Boston, Inc.

goatee — The Public Archives of Canada

gondola — Dorka Raynor

Gothic — Photographie Giraudon

grandeur — Courtesy of American Airlines

Great Wall of China — Brown Brothers

grebe — Animals, Animals © Harry Engels

grub — George Robinson / U.S.D.A.

gut — United Press International

gymnastic — Wide World Photos

hand organ — Culver Pictures, Inc.

hang glider — Wide World Photos

harp — Musée Instrumental, Brussels, Belgium

harpsichord — The Metropolitan Museum of Art, Crosby Brown Collection

harrow — U.S.D.A.

haycock — National Film Board of Canada

headdress — Philadelphia Museum of Art

heather — A. W. Ambler / National Audubon Society Photo Researchers, Inc.

helmet (left) — NASA

helmet (right) — Iron Helmet from the Anglo-Saxon Period Courtesy of The Trustees of the British Museum

hippopotamus — John Padour

histrionics — Illustrated London News

hogan — Ira Kirschenbaum / Stock, Boston, Inc.

horse — Suburban Trib, photo by Michael Sims

horseshoe crab — Animals, Animals © Perry Shankle

hovercraft — British Rail Hovercraft Ltd.

hurdle — Wide World Photos

hyena — Animals, Animals © Barrett Gallagher

iceberg — U.S. Coast Guard Official Photo

iceboat — William B. Parker

icon — The Byzantine Museum, Athens

idyllic — Dorka Raynor

igloo — National Film Board of Canada

imposing — Brown Brothers

impressionism — "Two Dancers," Edgar Degas, Amy McCormick Memorial, Courtesy of The Art Institute of Chicago

inclement — Wide World Photos

incongruous — The Museum of Modern Art Film Stills Archive

incubator — Reprinted by permission of Michael Reese Hospital and Medical Center, Chicago

infamous — Brown Brothers

interference — Vernon J. Biever

intractable — Shepard Sherbell / USDA Photo

irrigate — Monsanto Company, St. Louis, Missouri

issue — U.S. Postal Service

isthmus — Fairchild Aerial Surveys, Inc.

jai alai — Florida Division of Tourism

jellyfish — Al Giddings / Sea Library TOM STACK & ASSOCIATES

jerkin — Folger Shakespeare Library

jubilation — United Press International

jumbo — Philip Sills

kabuki — Consulate General of Japan at Chicago

kayak — National Film Board of Canada

kiwi — Courtesy of The American Museum of Natural History, Chicago

koala — Walter S. Clark, Jr.

ladybug — Lynn M. Stone

landslide — USDA—Soil Conservation Service

larva — Turtox-Cambosco, MacMillan Science Company, Chicago

launching pad — NASA

leech — Lynwood Chace / Photo Researchers, Inc.

lemur — Animals, Animals © George Roos

leopard — Carlton C. McAvey

leotard — Myron Wood / Photo Researchers, Inc.

lichen — William B. Parker

lineman — American Telephone and Telegraph

lithe — Fritz Menle / Photo Researchers, Inc.

lock — Ewing Galloway, New York

longhorn — "Texas Longhorns," Tom Lea, Courtesy of The Dallas Museum of Fine Arts

loon — National Film Board of Canada

louse — U.S.D.A.

ludicrous — The American Antiquarian Society

lynx — Animals, Animals © Miriam Austerman

macaque — Jen and Des Bartlett

macaw — Jeanne White Audubon-Photo Researchers, Inc.

machete — Victor Englebert / Photo Researchers, Inc.

mail — The Metropolitan Museum of Art, Bashford Dean Memorial Collection, Purchase, 1929, Funds from Various Donors

mammoth — Courtesy of The Field Museum of Natural History, Chicago

maroon — Ron Curbow / Photo Researchers, Inc.

marten — Russ Kinne / Photo Researchers, Inc.

mask — Courtesy of The Field Museum of Natural History, Chicago

massive — United Press International

matador — Walter S. Clark, Jr.

megalith — George Holton / Photo Researchers, Inc.

mesa — G. R. Roberts

millipede — John H. Gerard

mime — Dorka Raynor

mimic — Lynn M. Stone

Minotaur — "Theseus Slaying the Minotaur," Antoine Louis Barye, Courtesy of The Metropolitan Museum of Art, Bequest of John L. Cadwalader, 1914

mistletoe — U.S.D.A.

miter — Ray Ellis / Photo Researchers, Inc.

mole — John H. Gerard

monocle — The Museum of Modern Art Film Stills Archive

moose — National Film Board of Canada

mosaic — Rheinisches Landesmuseum, Trier, West Germany

mountain goat — Dr. Russell Congdon / U.S.D.A.

mummy — Courtesy of The Field Museum of Natural History, Chicago

mushroom — U.S.D.A.

muskrat — John H. Gerard

mythical — Musèi Capitolini, Rome

narcissus — U.S.D.A.

narwhal — Courtesy of The Field Museum of Natural History, Chicago

Neanderthal — Courtesy of The Field Museum of Natural History, Chicago

nefarious — Memory Shop

Newfoundland — Walter Chandoha

nimbus — "Madonna and Child," Jan Gossaert Courtesy of The Art Institute of Chicago

nucleus — A. H. Sparrow and R. F. Smith Brookhaven National Laboratory

nugget — Lee Boltin / Museum of Natural History The Smithsonian Institution

nymph — Animals, Animals © Charles Behnke

oats — U.S.D.A.

obelisk — Ewing Galloway, New York

obscure — James McLean

observatory — Hale Observatories

okapi — George Holton / Photo Researchers, Inc.

opossum — John H. Gerard

opportune — The Museum of Modern Art Film Stills Archive

orchid — Walter Chandoha

osprey — Animals, Animals © Harry Engels

otter	William B. Parker	pushcart	"Root Beer Seller," Nicolino Calyo Museum of The City of New York	sitar	Marilyn Silverstone / Magnum Photos, Inc.
outlandish	Historical Pictures Service	pyramid	Walter S. Clark, Jr.	sketch	Courtesy of Royal Library of Windsor Castle
outrigger	George Holton / Photo Researchers, Inc.	quartz	William B. Parker	skin diver	Russ Kinne / Photo Researchers, Inc.
paddle wheel	Brown Brothers	quay	Dorka Raynor	skyline	Ray Ellis Rapho / Photo Researchers, Inc.
pagoda	Courtesy of the Consulate General of Japan, New York	Queen Anne's lace	Jerome Wexler / Photo Researchers, Inc.	slalom	André Sima National Film Board of Canada
panda	Courtesy of The Smithsonian Institution	raccoon	Lynn M. Stone	sleigh	Library of Congress
parallel	© Foto Georg Gerster Rapho / Photo Researchers, Inc.	rampant	James McLean	snail	Lynn M. Stone
paralyze	The Chicago Historical Society	ramshackle	Paul Almasy	snapping turtle	John H. Gerard
parasite	USDA Photo	raze	T. D. Lovering / Stock, Boston, Inc.	snowflake	N.O.A.A.
passenger pigeon	Watercolor by John J. Audubon, Courtesy of The New-York Historical Society, New York City	recumbent	Sally Anne Thompson / Pictorial Parade	snowmobile	Bill Lingard National Film Board of Canada
		reflect	Richard Stromberg / Media House, Chicago	sod	Courtesy of Nebraska State Historical Society
pastoral	"The Harvesters," Pieter Bruegel, Courtesy of The Metropolitan Museum of Art, Rogers Fund, 1919	relay race	Thomas Hopker / Woodfin Camp	solar collector	Urban Investment and Development Co., Chicago
		relief	Courtesy of The Trustees of the British Museum		
pathetic	Dorothea Lange Collection The Oakland Museum	Renaissance	Alinari / Art Reference Bureau	solitary	Dorka Raynor
peace pipe	Carlton C. McAvey	replica	Culver Pictures, Inc.	southwester	The Bettmann Archive
peanut	Steve Wade / USDA Photo	reservoir	Courtesy of Chicago Bridge & Iron Company	Spanish moss	Hermann Postlethwaite USDA-SCS Photo
peccary	Lynn M. Stone	resuscitator	Courtesy of Puritan-Bennett Corporation		
pelican	Lynn M. Stone	reticulate	Animals, Animals © Karen Tweedy-Holmes	sperm whale	"Capturing a Sperm Whale," Engraving by John Hill, 1835; Courtesy of The New York Historical Society, New York City
penguin	Liaison				
pensive	"The Thinker," A. Rodin The Metropolitan Museum of Art	rhea	Lynn M. Stone	spindle	Dorka Raynor
		rice	U.S.D.A.	spinnaker	Fritz Henle / Photo Researchers, Inc.
perilous	The Museum of Modern Art Film Stills Archive	ridiculous	Orbis Publishing, Ltd.	spire	Library of Congress
		robot	United Press International	squid	Massachusetts Institute of Technology
peruke	Culver Pictures, Inc.	rococo	Avery Memorial Architectural Library Columbia University	squirrel	Animals, Animals © Paula Wright
phenomenon	Noel M. Klein / U.S. Department of Commerce, Weather Bureau			staphylococcus	Eric V. Grave / Photo Researchers, Inc.
		Romanesque	Culver Pictures, Inc.	starfish	William B. Parker
philodendron	USDA Photo	Roman nose	Alinari / Art Reference Bureau	statue	Alinari / Art Reference Bureau
picturesque	Rijksmuseum, Amsterdam	rotor	U.S. Navy Photograph	steamboat	Courtesy of the Museum of The City of New York
pince-nez	Brown Brothers	ruff	Folger Shakespeare Library		
pincers	Lynn M. Stone	rugged	G. R. Roberts	stingray	Courtesy of The Field Museum of Natural History, Chicago
piranha	Courtesy of The Field Museum of Natural History, Chicago	rural	Union Pacific Railroad Museum Collection		
				Stonehenge	Aerofilms
pitcher plant	B. W. Allred / USDA-SCS Photo	saguaro	Josef Muench	stork	Lynn M. Stone
plaid	Tom Hollyman / Photo Researchers, Inc.	sailplane	Bruce Roberts Rapho / Photo Researchers, Inc.	stratus	NOAA
plesiosaur	Charles R. Knight © The Field Museum of Natural History, Chicago			streetcar	The Bettmann Archive
		salamander	Lynn M. Stone	striated	© 1977 Walker England Photo Researchers, Inc.
plumb	H. Armstrong Roberts	sari	Jean-Claude Lejeune		
pollination	USDA Photo	satellite	NASA	sturgeon	T. McHugh / Photo Researchers, Inc.
pompadour	Courtesy of Istituto Geografico de Agostini-Novara	satyr	Culver Pictures, Inc.	subtle	Shostal Associates
		scenic	Dorka Raynor	sugar cane	USDA—Soil Conservation Service
porcupine	Philip F. Allan / USDA-SCS Photo	scorpion	USDA	sugar maple	Marcel Cognac National Film Board of Canada
portico	Courtesy of Virginia State Travel Service	sculpture	Alinari / Art Reference Bureau		
potter	UNITED NATIONS	sea anemone	Naval Photo Center	sundial	The Metropolitan Museum of Art, Gift of Mrs. Stephen D. Tucker, 1903
prairie dog	USDA—Soil Conservation Service	seam	Erich Hartmann / Magnum Photos, Inc.		
prefabricate	James McLean	seaplane	Pierre Gaudard National Film Board of Canada	sun god (left)	Marburg / Art Reference Bureau
prehensile	© Robert C. Hermes / National Audubon Society / Photo Researchers, Inc.			sun god (right)	The Bettmann Archive
		sedan chair	Messrs. Mallett and Son, London	surgery	Lee Balterman
prickly pear	Lynn M. Stone	seine	F.A.O.	surrealism	"The Persistence of Memory," 1931, Salvador Dali, Collection, The Museum of Modern Art, New York
primitive	Courtesy of The American Museum of Natural History, New York	semaphore	The National Archives		
		settee	National Gallery of Art, Washington, D.C.		
prism	Bernice Abbott / Photo Researchers, Inc.	setter	Mary Eleanor Browning Photo Researchers, Inc.	suspension bridge	Gabriel Moulin / Library of Congress
prominence	Mt. Wilson / Palomar			swept-back	William B. Parker
propeller	Newport News Shipbuilding	shako	F. B. Grunzweig / Photo Researchers, Inc.	symmetry (left)	William B. Parker
prosaic	Paul Mathews	shear	Murray Lemmon / USDA	tabby	Ylla / Photo Researchers, Inc.
prototype	United Press International	Shinto	Culver Pictures, Inc.	tapeworm	USDA
prowess	United Press International	show bill	Library of Congress	tarantula	J. McDonald / Bruce Coleman, Inc.
ptarmigan	Lynn M. Stone	shrew	Jerry Hennen	teddy bear	Courtesy of The American Museum of Natural History, New York
pueblo	Emil W. Haury / Courtesy of the Arizona State Museum, The University of Arizona	Siamese twins	United Press International		
		sideburns	Courtesy of The Chicago Historical Society	tepee	Lynn M. Stone
pugnacious	Constantine Manos / Magnum Photos, Inc.			termite	USDA
		sierra	C. G. Maxwell / Photo Researchers, Inc.	terrace	James McLean
pupa	Lynn M. Stone	silo	Jack Schneider / USDA		

thatch	Diane M. Lowe	turtledove	Russ Kinne / Photo Researchers, Inc.	walrus	F. Erize / Bruce Coleman, Inc.
tick	USDA	Tutankhamun	George Holton / Photo Researchers, Inc.	wampum	Courtesy of Museum of the American Indian, Heye Foundation, New York
tide (top, bottom)	Nova Scotia Information Service	uncommon	Keystone Press Agency Inc.		
timber wolf	Karl H. Maslowski Photo Researchers, Inc.	undermine	Paul Sequeira Rapho / Photo Researchers, Inc.	wart hog	New York Zoological Society Photo
				water buffalo	Walter S. Clark, Jr.
timothy	R. L. Stevens / USDA-SCS Photo	undershot	Mary Eleanor Browning Photo Researchers, Inc.	water lily	Lynn M. Stone
toadstool	USDA			waterspout	U.S. Navy Photograph
toga	Alinari / Art Reference Bureau	unicellular	Eric V. Grave / Photo Researchers, Inc.	weevil	USDA
tomahawk	Courtesy of Museum of the American Indian, Heye Foundation, New York	unicorn	French or Flemish, Late XV century, "The Hunt of the Unicorn," VII. Wool and silk with metal threads. From the Château of Verteuil; The Metropolitan Museum of Art, The Cloisters Collection, Gift of John D. Rockefeller, Jr. 1937	weightless	NASA
top hat	Courtesy of The Chicago Historical Society			weld	Courtesy of The Chicago Historical Society
tornado	ESSA			whelk	Lynn M. Stone
tortoise	Lynn M. Stone	unicycle	United Press International	whooping crane	Courtesy of The New York Historical Society
totem pole	National Film Board of Canada	unwieldy	Republic Aviation Corporation		
track	National Film Board of Canada	urn	The Metropolitan Museum of Art, Rogers Fund, 1907	willowy	Reprinted from VOGUE copyright © 1919, 1947 by The Condé Nast Publications Inc.
tractor	Caterpillar Tractor Co.				
trance	The Bettmann Archive	vampire bat	Daniel P. Mannix	windmill	Bill Marr / USDA
transit	Mike West / National Film Board of Canada	vandyke	Culver Pictures, Inc.	wolverine	National Film Board of Canada
		vane	Gordon S. Smith / Photo Researchers, Inc.	woodchuck	John H. Gerard
treadmill	Library of Congress			wrath	James Foote / Photo Researchers, Inc.
trench coat	The Museum of Modern Art Film Stills Archive	venerable	Culver Pictures, Inc.	wrought iron	Andy Rojecki
		veranda	Walter S. Clark, Jr.	X ray	Picker Corporation
trestle	R. Collins Bradley / Sante Fe Railway	virus	Gene M. Milbrath, Department of Plant Pathology, University of Illinois	yak	F.A.O.
trophy	Robert Farbin			yoke	Library of Congress
tulip	Gretchen Garner	volcano	Hugo Brehme Rapho / Photo Researchers, Inc.	yucca	USDA—Soil Conservation Service
turban	Walter S. Clark, Jr.			zebu	Tomalin / Bruce Coleman, Inc.
		vulture	Lynn M. Stone		
		walking stick	USDA		

Student's Reference Section

p. 1074–1076   U.S. Postal Service
p. 1077–1081   U.S. Bureau of Engraving and Printing
p. 1095   NASA and © Association of Universities for Research in Astronomy, Kitt Peak National Observatory

Scott, Foresman staff photos:

abacus, abalone, African violet, agate, amorphous, andiron, appliqué, atomizer, Autoharp, backgammon, bagpipe, balance, balcony, banjo, barometer, bassoon, bellows, bias, binoculars, brooch, browse (left), browse (right), bucksaw, catkin, cat's cradle, cello, chisel, churn, clarinet, cleaver, cog, collate, compass (left), compass (right), concertina, cone, convolution, cornet, cotton, counterclockwise, crane, crowbar, cruet, cylinder, cymbal, daisy, descendant, deterrent, dimple, disparity, double bass, dress, earthenware, emboss, embryo, engage (left), engage (right), English horn, filigree, fleur-de-lis, flute, fly, forehand, fossil, fraternal twins, French horn, fret, fulcrum, fungus, gable, gargoyle, garter snake, gear, geode (left), geode (right), gerbil, gimlet, goblet, gouge, gourd, grand piano, guinea pig, guitar, gull, gyroscope, hacksaw, half nelson, halter, hamster, harmonica, hibachi, hitch, hypodermic syringe, iguana, inflammable, inscription, insignia, instep, insulator, interlace, iris, jack, Jew's harp, jigsaw, kettledrum, kimono, kiosk, knapsack, knocker, lace, ladle, lantern, lathe, lectern, level, lighthouse, lion, magnifying glass, maintenance, mandolin, marigold, Mayflower, menorah (from the collection of Rabbi Hillel Gamoran), meteorite, mezuzah, microscope, moped, mortar, mortarboard, movement, mule, neckerchief, negative, nutritious, oboe, ocarina, octagon, organ, origami, outboard motor, overcast, oxford, paisley, palette, parquet, perspective, piccolo, pinking shears, pipette, plumb line, pogo stick, protractor, put, pylon, radiometer, reamer, recorder, refract, relic (from the collection of Rabbi Hillel Gamoran), rhinoceros, rink, ripple, rowel, saddle shoe, saxophone, scallop (left), scallop (right), sedimentary, setting, shaft, shirr, sign language, skein, slide rule, smocking, snare drum, snorkel, sombrero, sphere, spiral, sprocket, stalactite/stalagmite, stethoscope, stirrup, stud, subway, tackle, tam-o'-shanter, tankard, tartan, telescope, thermometer (left), thermometer (right), tongs, torch, trampoline, translucent, transparent, triangle (bottom), trombone, trowel, trumpet, T square, tuba, tuning fork, ukulele, universal joint, Universal Product Code, univalve (left)/bivalve (right), vase, violin/viola, visor (right), volleyball, wet suit, winch, xylophone, yarmulke, zither

ANSWER KEY

TO

HOW TO USE THIS DICTIONARY

6 **TEACH YOURSELF**
A. Frankenstein   E. -or
B. backgammon   F. etc.
C. Bronx   G. infatuation
D. clavichord   H. Homo sapiens

7 **EXERCISE**
A. 1. Buddy
  2. Craig
  3. Ebenezer
  4. Laura
  5. Una
  6. Wanda
  The class lives in Urbana.

B. perceptible
  percolate
  peremptorily
  perennial
  perfection
  perfectionist
  perfidy
  perhaps
  The state is Illinois.

8 **TEACH YOURSELF**
1. kisser | knight-errant
2. Yes.
3. Yes.
4. (no answer required)
5. page 733
6. pushy | PWA

EXERCISE
1. b.   5. a.
2. a.   6. b.
3. a.   7. b.
4. c.   8. b.

9 **TEACH YOURSELF**
1. fan^2
2. fan^1

EXERCISES
1. a. 2   d. 3
  b. 5   e. 2
  c. 3

2. a. cow^1, cow^2 f. close^1, seal^1
  b. alight^1, alight^2 g. jog^1, pike^4
  c. felt^1, flight^1 h. squash^1, squash^2
  d. grave^2 i. mole^2, scuttle^2
  e. cue^1, cue^2 j. host^1, perch^2

10 **TEACH YOURSELF**
1. *d.*
2. *y* changes to *i.*
3. *e.*
4. *y* changes to *i.*
5. *e.*
6. Because the spelling of *exist* does not change when endings are added.

EXERCISE
1. pen^2 4. possibility   7. scrutinize
2. happy   5. locate   8. mere
3. investigate   6. realize   9. identify

11 **EXERCISE**
1. Ecuador, -ian, -an   5. un-, mar
2. over-, populate   6. non-, aggressive
3. thoughtless, -ly^1 7. destructive, -ness
4. over-, abundant   8. re-, introduce

12 **EXERCISE**
1. No, it's a muscle cramp.
2. No, it's something used to draw attention away from the real issue.
3. No, it's a kind of armor used in the Middle Ages.
4. Yes, it's a public official who has been defeated for reelection and is serving the last part of a term.
5. No, it's a watery liquid in the eye.
6. No, it's a sailor.
7. No, it's a child's game.
8. No, it's a list of students with high grades.

13 **EXERCISES**
A. 1. eye, b.
  2. hair, b.
  3. ear, a.

B. 1. red   4. rub   7. crow^2
  2. shake   5. pedestal   8. quits
  3. tree   6. peel   9. hand

14 *TEST YOURSELF*
1. a. whiz, who   b. whitish | whorl

2. a. top^1 e. let^1
  b. scale^3 f. rest^2
  c. steep^1 g. tip^1
  d. left^2 h. real^1

3. The moose, the oxen, the calves, and the geese were upset by the mice.

4. twiddle his <u>thumbs</u>   on your <u>toes</u>
  rack his <u>brains</u>   lose your <u>head</u>
  had his <u>hands</u> full   made no <u>bones</u> about
  by the <u>skin</u> of his teeth   be all <u>ears</u>
  turned a cold <u>shoulder</u> to   <u>knuckle</u> down
  take to <u>heart</u>   risking his <u>neck</u>
  hold your <u>tongue</u>   keep a stiff upper <u>lip</u>

15 **TEACH YOURSELF**
1. Three sounds.
2. Yes.
3. (f)

16 **TEACH YOURSELF**
sand, circle, silly, city, scene, psalm

EXERCISE

1. cuff	7. dunce	13. sieve
2. knot	8. wreck	14. dance
3. gem	9. sick	15. gym
4. salve	10. gnat	16. prince
5. lodge	11. rack	17. ledge
6. prance	12. calf	18. sock

17 **EXERCISE A**
1. Jane, ate
2. we, eat
3. nice, mice
4. coal, boat, broke

EXERCISE B
1. cards, darts
2. crawl, walk
3. woods, full, wolves
4. who, shoe, soup
5. few, use

18 **TEACH YOURSELF A**
1. loud, crowd, now
2. coin, toy, noise

TEACH YOURSELF B
1. (th)—thin, thought, thrush, thrived, thistles
   (ŦH)—the, that, this
2. (ch)—cheap, arch
   (sh)—shop, shoes
   (zh)—beige

EXERCISE

1. fur	4. sketch	7. moth
2. voice	5. junk	8. scythe
3. owl	6. chef	9. Jeanne

19 **TEACH YOURSELF**
1. two, two
2. three, three

EXERCISE

1. em ploy'	5. ra'di a'tor
2. chick'en	6. so lid'i ty
3. laugh'ing stock'	7. chem'is try
4. pas'sen ger	8. tor na'do

20 **TEACH YOURSELF**

enormous—ou	luncheon—eo	fashion—io
bargain—ai	tortoise—oi	epaulet—au

EXERCISE

authority	marine
accountant	biologist
orchestra	dangerous
clarinetist	mountaineer
aquarium	

21 **TEACH YOURSELF**
1. first sentence—a.
   second sentence—b.

2. first sentence—b.
   second sentence—a.

EXERCISE

1. b	9. a
2. a	10. b
3. a	11. b
4. b	12. a
5. b	13. a
6. a	14. b
7. a	15. b
8. b	16. a

22 *TEST YOURSELF*
1. a. steely   d. who
   b. ferry   e. mammy
   c. mile

2.

23 *TEST YOURSELF*
   Mr. Otis was awakened by a curious noise in the hall, outside his room. It sounded like the clank of metal, and seemed to be coming nearer every moment. He put on his slippers, took a small oblong phial from his dresser, and opened the door. Right in front of him he saw an old man of terrible aspect. Long gray hair fell over his shoulders in matted coils. His garments were of antique cut, and from his wrists and ankles hung heavy manacles and rusty fetters.
ANSWER: long gray hair
   "My dear sir," said Mr. Otis, "I really must insist on your oiling those chains and have brought you for that purpose a small bottle of lubricating oil."
ANSWER: No
   For a moment the Canterville ghost stood quite motionless in natural indignation. Then, dashing the bottle violently upon the polished floor, he fled. On reaching the west wing, he leaned up against a moonbeam to recover his breath. Never, in a brilliant and uninterrupted career of three hundred years, had he been so grossly insulted.
ANSWER: No

25 EXERCISES

1. a. meat-eating   d. one of a kind
   b. make   e. famous person
   c. never known before

2. a. an ideal place or condition *or* a perfect
      place or way to live
   b. of large scope or extent *or* including much
   c. give notice to *or* let know *or* inform
   d. collect little by little *or* pile up *or* gather
   e. the science dealing with the origins,
      development, races, customs, and beliefs of
      human beings
   f. close examination *or* careful inspection
   g. drawn out *or* lengthened in time
   h. not giving in readily *or* firm and unyielding
   i. open forest *or* wild, unsettled land
   j. very important

26 TEACH YOURSELF

1. four noun definitions; three verb definitions
2. noun
3. definition 1
4. definition 7

EXERCISE

1. def. 1, noun
2. def. 4, verb
3. def. 4, verb
4. def. 1, noun
5. def. 3, adjective
6. def. 4, adverb

27 EXERCISE

1. automobile or other vehicle which gets low
   gasoline mileage. Informal.
2. bag; sack. Dialect.
3. fan or devotee. Informal.
4. spoke. Old Use.
5. insincere talk; nonsense; humbug. Slang.
6. would. Old Use.
7. go away; leave. Slang.
8. child. Scottish.

29 EXERCISE

1. French   6. Chinese
2. Old English   7. Narragansett
3. name of an estate   8. Latin, from
   in England   Taranto, Italy
4. Dutch   9. Czech
5. a blend of simul- 10. Spanish,
   taneous and broadcast   Senegalese

30 EXERCISE

1. *legere*, Latin   4. *naus*, Greek
2. *hāl*, Old English   5. *pungere*, Latin
3. *bonus*, Latin   6. *platys*, Greek

31 TEST YOURSELF

1.

2. a. boa   d. crab   g. car
   b. bay   e. coral   h. bar
   c. curly f. boy   i. curl

3. a. the island of Jersey
   b. Marie and Pierre Curie
   c. Damascus, a city in Syria
   d. Conestoga Valley, Pennsylvania
   e. the Countess of Chinchón, wife of a
      Spanish viceroy to Peru
   f. Sylvester Graham, American minister
      and dietary reformer
   g. Rudolf Diesel, German engineer
   h. the fourth Earl of Sandwich
   i. Chihuahua, a city and state in Mexico
   j. Samuel Maverick, Texas cattle owner
   k. Nîmes, a town in France
   l. Queen Anne of Great Britain and Ireland

33 TEACH YOURSELF

1. one way
2. ph
3. gh
4. ow
5. ay; grey; ey

EXERCISE

fascinated   coulees   captured
drawings   mesas
could   mesquite
frontier   cayuse
sketches   Cheyenne
chronicle   khaki
rough   motion
physical   designers
roamed   authentic

36 EXERCISE

hun dred   bal co ny
phys i cal   re trieve
in struc tor   e nough
school   dif fer ent
some thing   ex cit ing
bored   through
de cid ed   spec ta tor
sea son   chil dren
spring   a dults
sud den ly   hand i capped
sur prise   o ver

Student's Reference Section

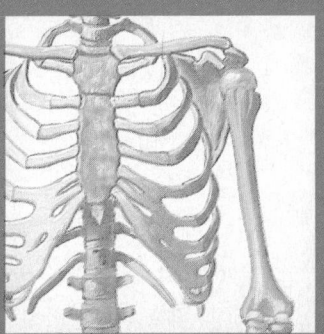

The World

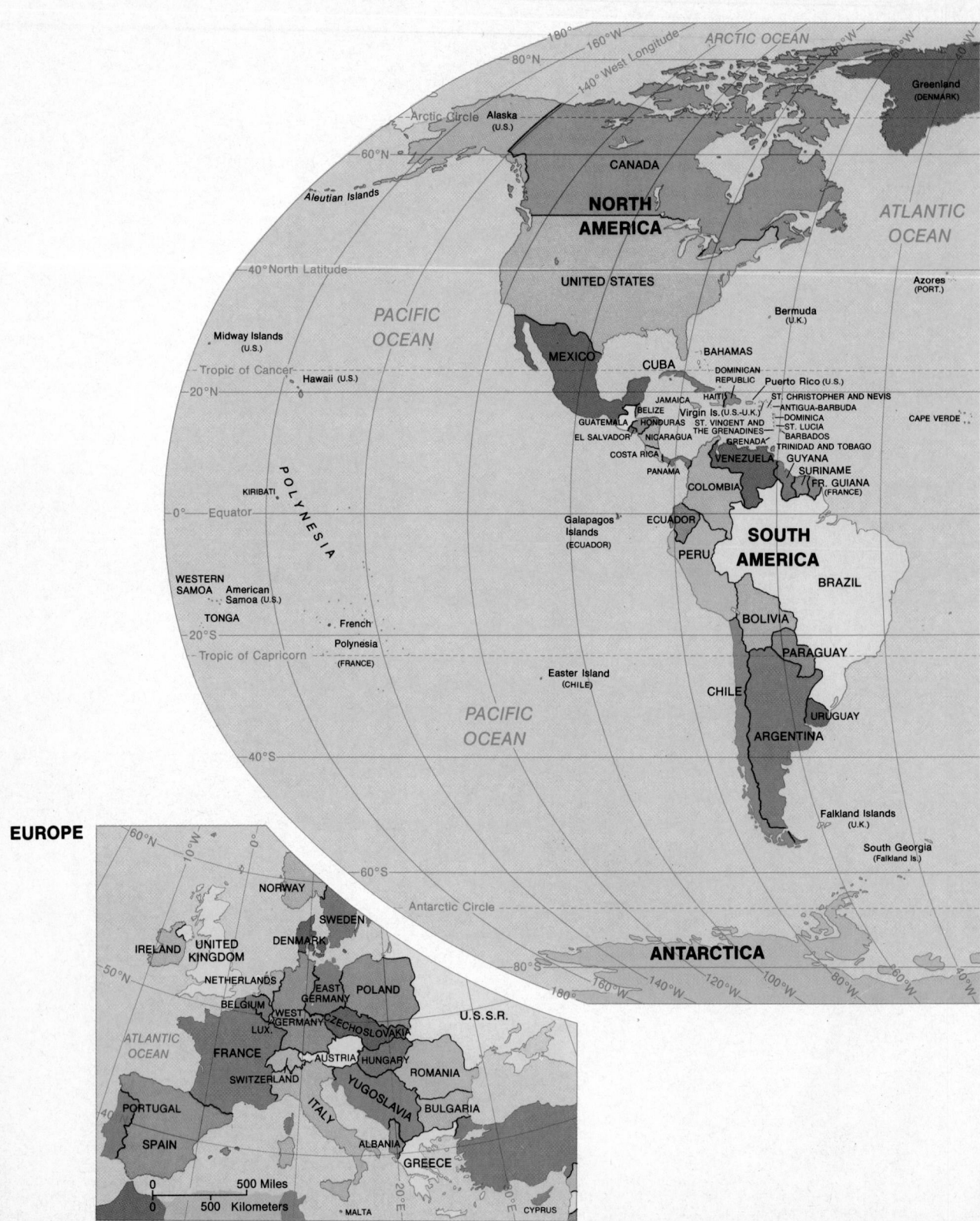

ARCTIC OCEAN

Greenland
(DENMARK)

Arctic Circle   Alaska
(U.S.)

CANADA

**NORTH
AMERICA**

ATLANTIC
OCEAN

Aleutian Islands

40° North Latitude

UNITED STATES

Azores
(PORT.)

PACIFIC
OCEAN

Bermuda
(U.K.)

Midway Islands
(U.S.)

MEXICO   CUBA   BAHAMAS

Tropic of Cancer

Hawaii (U.S.)

20°N

DOMINICAN
REPUBLIC   Puerto Rico (U.S.)

CAPE VERDE

JAMAICA   HAITI   ST. CHRISTOPHER AND NEVIS
BELIZE   Virgin Is. (U.S.-U.K.)   ANTIGUA-BARBUDA
GUATEMALA   HONDURAS   ST. VINCENT AND   DOMINICA
EL SALVADOR   NICARAGUA   THE GRENADINES   ST. LUCIA
COSTA RICA   GRENADA   BARBADOS
PANAMA   TRINIDAD AND TOBAGO
VENEZUELA   GUYANA
COLOMBIA   SURINAME
FR. GUIANA
(FRANCE)

KIRIBATI

0°   Equator

Galapagos
Islands
(ECUADOR)   ECUADOR

**SOUTH
AMERICA**

PERU

BRAZIL

WESTERN
SAMOA   American
Samoa (U.S.)

TONGA

French
Polynesia
(FRANCE)

20°S

Tropic of Capricorn

BOLIVIA

PARAGUAY

Easter Island
(CHILE)

CHILE

URUGUAY

PACIFIC
OCEAN

ARGENTINA

40°S

Falkland Islands
(U.K.)

South Georgia
(Falkland Is.)

60°S

Antarctic Circle

80°S

ANTARCTICA

EUROPE

60°N

NORWAY

SWEDEN

IRELAND   UNITED
KINGDOM   DENMARK

50°N

NETHERLANDS

EAST
GERMANY   POLAND

BELGIUM
WEST
LUX.   GERMANY   CZECHOSLOVAKIA

U.S.S.R.

ATLANTIC
OCEAN

FRANCE

AUSTRIA   HUNGARY

SWITZERLAND

ROMANIA

YUGOSLAVIA

BULGARIA

PORTUGAL

ITALY

ALBANIA

SPAIN

GREECE

500 Miles

0
500 Kilometers

MALTA

CYPRUS

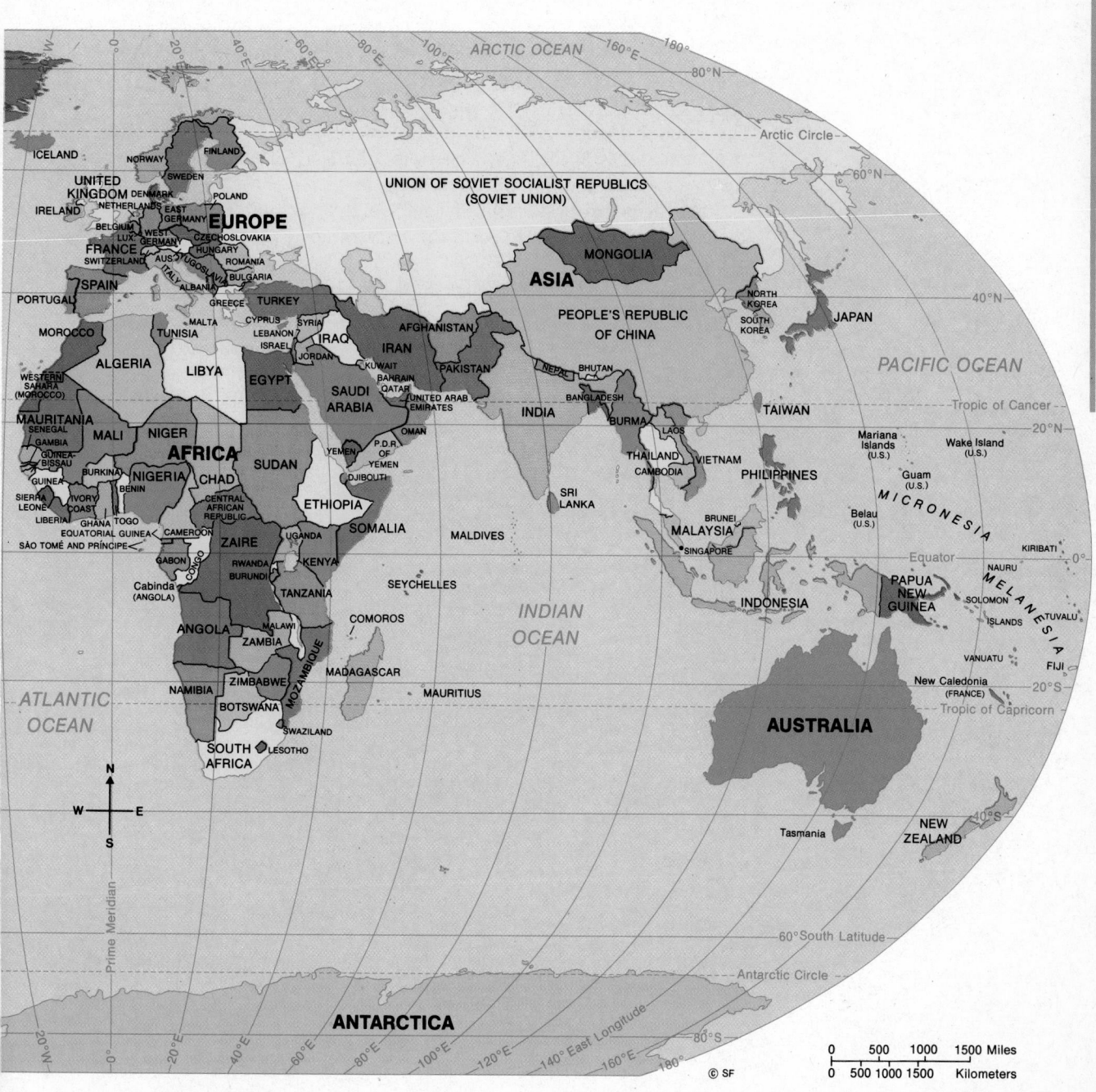

AUS.—AUSTRIA
LUX.—LUXEMBOURG
P.D.R. OF YEMEN—PEOPLE'S DEMOCRATIC REPUBLIC OF YEMEN
PORT.—PORTUGAL
U.K.—UNITED KINGDOM
U.S.—UNITED STATES
U.S.S.R.—UNION OF SOVIET SOCIALIST REPUBLICS

Hemispheres

The equator divides the earth into two equal parts. Everything north of the equator is in the Northern Hemisphere. Everything south of the equator is in the Southern Hemisphere.

A meridian that passes through the North and South poles also divides the earth in half to form the Eastern and Western hemispheres.

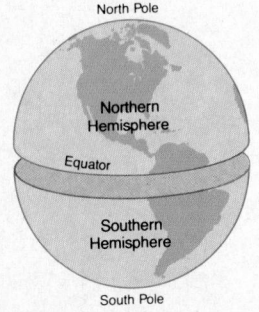

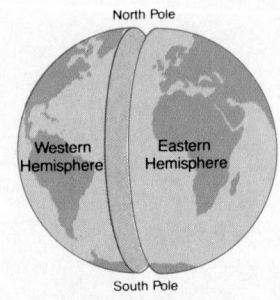

Northern Hemisphere

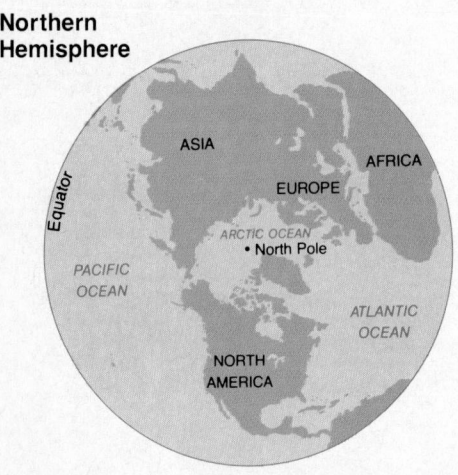

Western Hemisphere

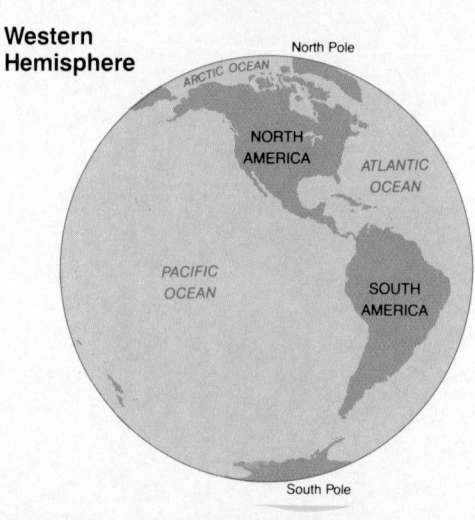

Southern Hemisphere

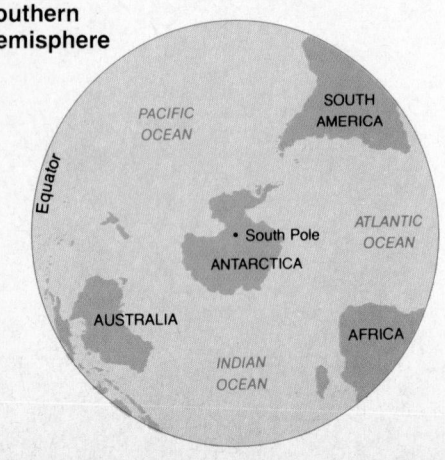

Eastern Hemisphere

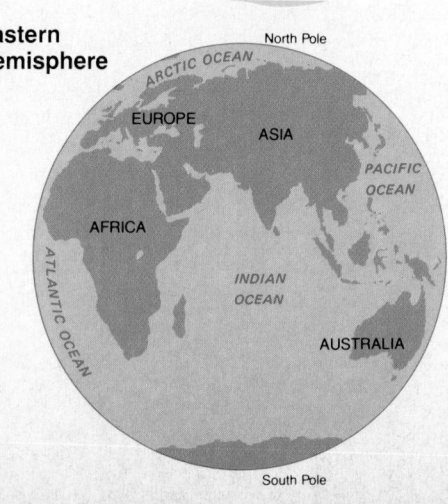

Time Zones

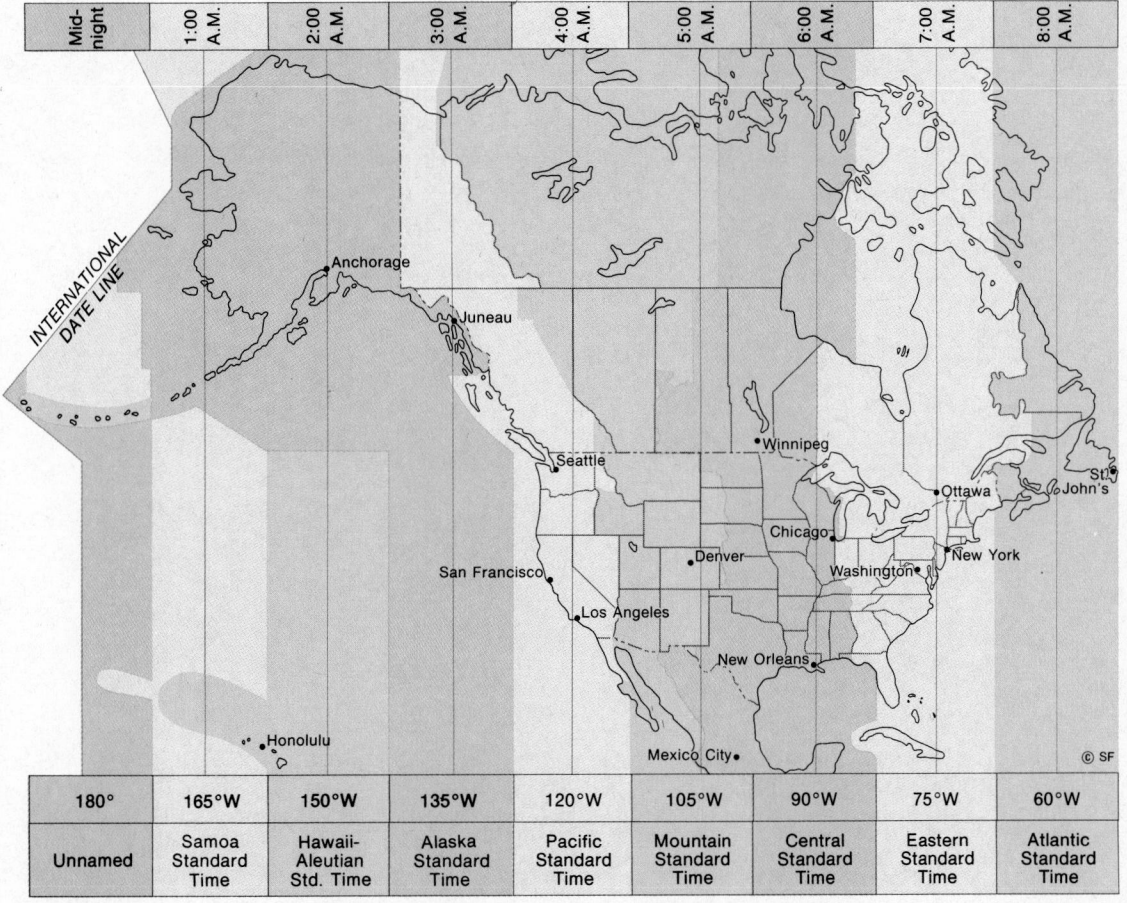

Midnight	1:00 A.M.	2:00 A.M.	3:00 A.M.	4:00 A.M.	5:00 A.M.	6:00 A.M.	7:00 A.M.	8:00 A.M.
180°	165°W	150°W	135°W	120°W	105°W	90°W	75°W	60°W
Unnamed	Samoa Standard Time	Hawaii-Aleutian Std. Time	Alaska Standard Time	Pacific Standard Time	Mountain Standard Time	Central Standard Time	Eastern Standard Time	Atlantic Standard Time

Time zones have been set up to standardize time in the various areas of the United States. Since the earth rotates as it travels around the sun, the sun does not rise and set at the same time in every part of the country. When it is 2 p.m. in Los Angeles, it is 5 p.m. in New York.

The United States did not always have standard time zones. At first each community set its own time by the sun. Then railroads tried to simplify their schedules by setting up a standard time along sections of their routes. But there were many railroads, and many different railroad times. So, in 1883, all the railroads agreed to divide the United States into four time zones.

There are now six time zones in the United States. The time in each zone is one hour different from that in the neighboring zones. Time is earlier in zones to the west, and later in zones to the east. Each zone is centered on a line of longitude. The time at the meridian at the center of the zone is used by all places within the zone.

The United States

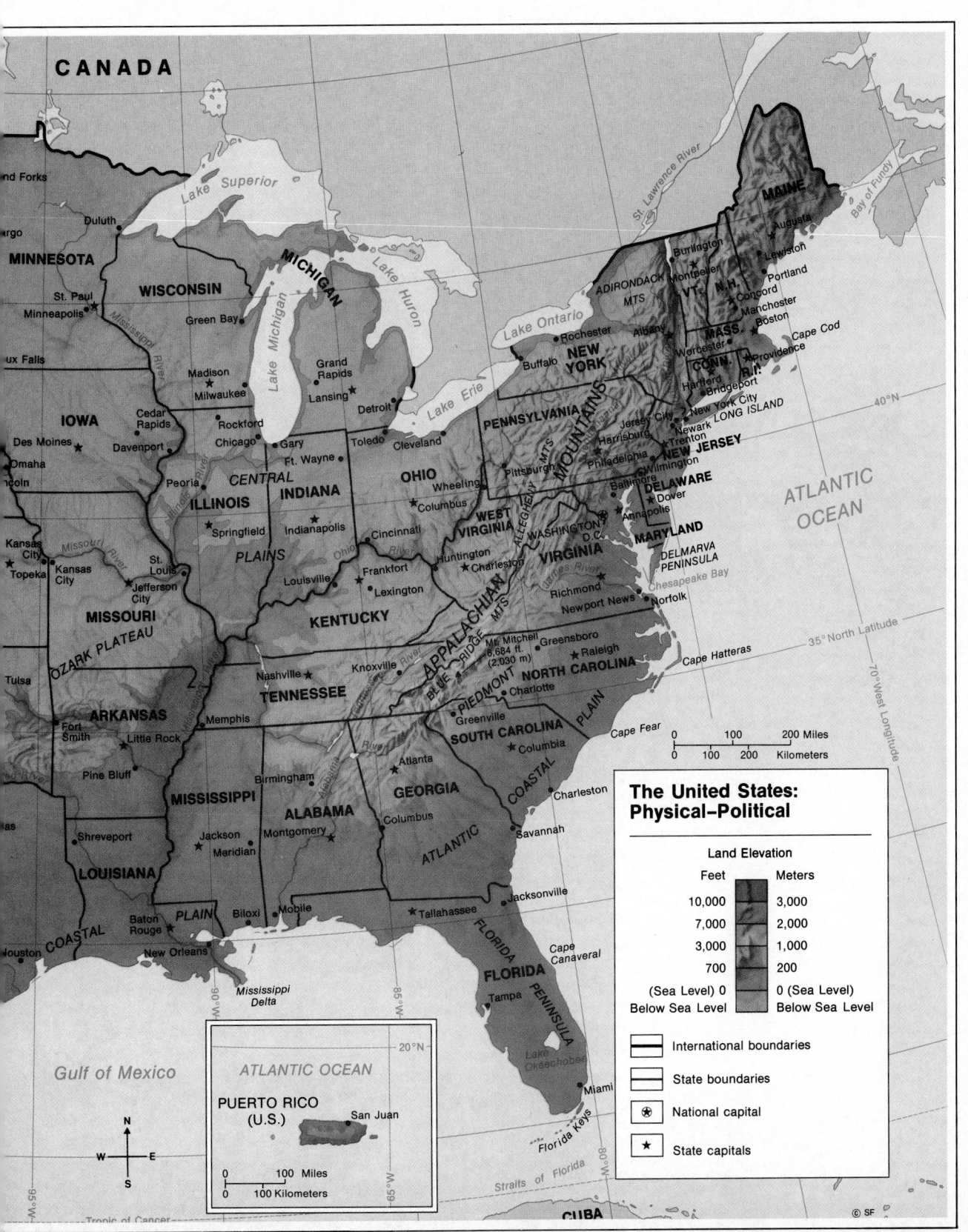

CANADA

MINNESOTA

Lake Superior

nd Forks
Duluth

argo

WISCONSIN

MICHIGAN

Lake Huron

St. Paul
Minneapolis

ux Falls

Green Bay

Lake Michigan

Grand
Rapids

Lake Ontario

ADIRONDACK
MTS

Rochester

MAINE

Augusta

Burlington
Lewiston

VT. N.H.
Montpelier
Concord
Portland

IOWA

Madison
Milwaukee

Lansing

Detroit

Buffalo

NEW
YORK

Albany

MASS.
Worcester

Manchester
Boston
Cape Cod

Des Moines

Cedar
Rapids

Rockford
Chicago

Toledo

Cleveland

Lake Erie

PENNSYLVANIA

CONN. R.I.
Providence
Hartford
Bridgeport

Omaha

Davenport

Gary

Ft. Wayne

New York City
LONG ISLAND

ncoln

Peoria

CENTRAL

INDIANA

OHIO

Wheeling

Pittsburgh

Harrisburg

Jersey City
Newark
Trenton

Philadelphia

NEW JERSEY

ILLINOIS

Springfield

Indianapolis

Columbus

WEST
VIRGINIA

Wilmington

DELAWARE

Baltimore
Dover

Kansas
City

Kansas
City

PLAINS

St.
Louis

Cincinnati

Frankfort

Huntington

WASHINGTON
D.C.

Annapolis

MARYLAND

Topeka

Jefferson
City

Louisville

Lexington

Charleston

VIRGINIA

DELMARVA
PENINSULA

Chesapeake Bay

MISSOURI

KENTUCKY

Richmond

Newport News

Norfolk

OZARK PLATEAU

Tulsa

Nashville

Knoxville

Mt. Mitchell
6,684 ft.
(2,030 m)

Greensboro
Raleigh

Cape Hatteras

ATLANTIC
OCEAN

TENNESSEE

APPALACHIAN
MTS

PIEDMONT

NORTH CAROLINA

Charlotte

ARKANSAS

Fort
Smith

Little Rock

Memphis

Greenville

Columbia

SOUTH CAROLINA

Cape Fear

Pine Bluff

Birmingham

Atlanta

COASTAL

Charleston

MISSISSIPPI

Jackson

Meridian

Montgomery

Columbus

GEORGIA

PLAIN

Savannah

Shreveport

ALABAMA

ATLANTIC

LOUISIANA

Baton
Rouge

Biloxi

Mobile

Jacksonville

Tallahassee

FLORIDA

Cape
Canaveral

ouston

COASTAL

New Orleans

Mississippi
Delta

FLORIDA
PENINSULA

Tampa

Lake
Okeechobee

Miami

Gulf of Mexico

Florida Keys

Straits of Florida

CUBA

The United States: Physical–Political

Land Elevation

Feet		Meters
10,000		3,000
7,000		2,000
3,000		1,000
700		200
(Sea Level) 0		0 (Sea Level)
Below Sea Level		Below Sea Level

International boundaries

State boundaries

⊛ National capital

★ State capitals

ATLANTIC OCEAN

PUERTO RICO
(U.S.)

San Juan

0   100 Miles
0   100 Kilometers

N
W   E
S

0   100   200 Miles
0   100   200 Kilometers

St. Lawrence River

Bay of Fundy

Mississippi River

Missouri River

Ohio River

James River

BLUE RIDGE MTS

ALLEGHENY MTS

40°N

35° North Latitude

70° West Longitude

95°W

90°W

85°W

80°W

65°W

20°N

Tropic of Cancer

© SF

Facts About the 50 States

State	U.S. Postal Service Abbreviation	State Capital	Area in Square Miles	Population	State Nickname	Year Admitted to Union	Order of Admission
Alabama	AL	Montgomery	51,600	3,890,000	Yellowhammer State	1819	22
Alaska	AK	Juneau	586,400	400,000	The Last Frontier	1959	49
Arizona	AZ	Phoenix	113,900	2,718,000	Grand Canyon State	1912	48
Arkansas	AR	Little Rock	53,100	2,286,000	Land of Opportunity	1836	25
California	CA	Sacramento	158,700	23,669,000	Golden State	1850	31
Colorado	CO	Denver	104,200	2,889,000	Centennial State	1876	38
Connecticut	CT	Hartford	5,000	3,108,000	Nutmeg State	1788	5
Delaware	DE	Dover	2,400	595,000	Diamond State	1787	1
Florida	FL	Tallahassee	58,600	9,740,000	Sunshine State	1845	27
Georgia	GA	Atlanta	58,900	5,464,000	Peach State	1788	4
Hawaii	HI	Honolulu	6,400	965,000	Aloha State	1959	50
Idaho	ID	Boise	83,600	944,000	Gem State	1890	43
Illinois	IL	Springfield	56,400	11,418,000	Prairie State	1818	21
Indiana	IN	Indianapolis	36,300	5,490,000	Hoosier State	1816	19
Iowa	IA	Des Moines	56,300	2,913,000	Hawkeye State	1846	29
Kansas	KS	Topeka	82,300	2,363,000	Sunflower State	1861	34
Kentucky	KY	Frankfort	40,400	3,661,000	Bluegrass State	1792	15
Louisiana	LA	Baton Rouge	48,500	4,204,000	Pelican State	1812	18

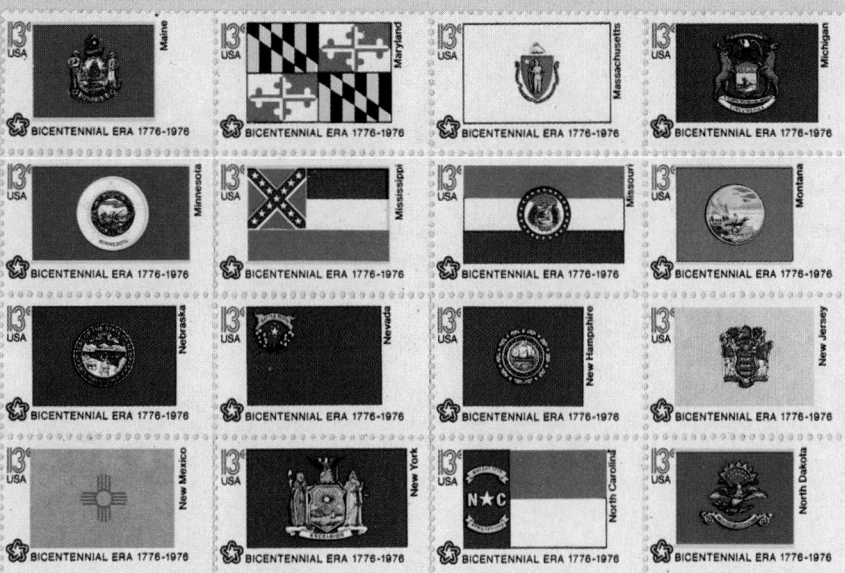

State	U.S. Postal Service Abbreviation	State Capital	Area in Square Miles	Population	State Nickname	Year Admitted to Union	Order of Admission
Maine	ME	Augusta	33,200	1,125,000	Pine Tree State	1820	23
Maryland	MD	Annapolis	10,600	4,216,000	Free State	1788	7
Massachusetts	MA	Boston	8,300	5,737,000	Bay State	1788	6
Michigan	MI	Lansing	58,200	9,258,000	Wolverine State	1837	26
Minnesota	MN	St. Paul	84,100	4,077,000	North Star State	1858	32
Mississippi	MS	Jackson	47,700	2,521,000	Magnolia State	1817	20
Missouri	MO	Jefferson City	69,700	4,917,000	Show Me State	1821	24
Montana	MT	Helena	147,100	787,000	Treasure State	1889	41
Nebraska	NE	Lincoln	77,200	1,570,000	Cornhusker State	1867	37
Nevada	NV	Carson City	110,500	799,000	Silver State	1864	36
New Hampshire	NH	Concord	9,300	921,000	Granite State	1788	9
New Jersey	NJ	Trenton	7,800	7,364,000	Garden State	1787	3
New Mexico	NM	Santa Fe	121,700	1,300,000	Land of Enchantment	1912	47
New York	NY	Albany	49,600	17,557,000	Empire State	1788	11
North Carolina	NC	Raleigh	52,600	5,874,000	Tar Heel State	1789	12
North Dakota	ND	Bismarck	70,700	653,000	Sioux State	1889	39

State	U.S. Postal Service Abbreviation	State Capital	Area in Square Miles	Population	State Nickname	Year Admitted to Union	Order of Admission
Ohio	OH	Columbus	41,200	10,797,000	Buckeye State	1803	17
Oklahoma	OK	Oklahoma City	69,900	3,025,000	Sooner State	1907	46
Oregon	OR	Salem	97,000	2,633,000	Beaver State	1859	33
Pennsylvania	PA	Harrisburg	45,300	11,867,000	Keystone State	1787	2
Rhode Island	RI	Providence	1,200	947,000	Ocean State	1790	13
South Carolina	SC	Columbia	31,100	3,119,000	Palmetto State	1788	8
South Dakota	SD	Pierre	77,000	690,000	Sunshine State	1889	40
Tennessee	TN	Nashville	42,200	4,591,000	Volunteer State	1796	16
Texas	TX	Austin	267,300	14,228,000	Lone Star State	1845	28
Utah	UT	Salt Lake City	85,000	1,461,000	Beehive State	1896	45
Vermont	VT	Montpelier	9,600	511,000	Green Mountain State	1791	14
Virginia	VA	Richmond	40,800	5,346,000	The Old Dominion	1788	10
Washington	WA	Olympia	68,200	4,130,000	Evergreen State	1889	42
West Virginia	WV	Charleston	24,200	1,950,000	Mountain State	1863	35
Wisconsin	WI	Madison	56,200	4,705,000	Badger State	1848	30
Wyoming	WY	Cheyenne	97,900	471,000	Equality State	1890	44

Presidents of the United States

Beneath each President's picture are his name, his age on becoming President, the state where he was born, his birth and death dates, his political party, the name of his vice-president, and the name of his wife.

1.

George Washington, 57
Virginia 1732–1799
In office: 1789–1797
No party affiliation
John Adams
Martha Dandridge Washington

2.

John Adams, 61
Massachusetts 1735–1826
In office: 1797–1801
Federalist
Thomas Jefferson
Abigail Smith Adams

3.

Thomas Jefferson, 57
Virginia 1743–1826
In office: 1801–1809
Democratic-Republican
Aaron Burr; George Clinton
Martha Wayles Jefferson

4.

James Madison, 57
Virginia 1751–1836
In office: 1809–1817
Democratic-Republican
George Clinton; Elbridge Gerry
Dolley Payne Madison

5.

James Monroe, 58
Virginia 1758–1831
In office: 1817–1825
Democratic-Republican
Daniel D. Tompkins
Elizabeth Kortright Monroe

6.

John Quincy Adams, 57
Massachusetts 1767–1848
In office: 1825–1829
Whig
John C. Calhoun
Louisa Johnson Adams

7.

Andrew Jackson, 61
South Carolina 1767–1845
In office: 1829–1837
Democratic; John C. Calhoun;
Martin Van Buren
Rachel Donelson Jackson

8.

Martin Van Buren, 54
New York 1782–1862
In office: 1837–1841
Democratic
Richard M. Johnson
Hannah Hoes Van Buren

9.

William Henry Harrison, 68
Virginia 1773–1841
In office: 1841 (one month)*
Whig
John Tyler
Anna Symmes Harrison

10.

John Tyler, 51
Virginia 1790–1862
In office: 1841–1845
Whig
(No vice-president)
Julia Gardiner Tyler

11.

James K. Polk, 49
North Carolina 1795–1849
In office: 1845–1849
Democratic
George M. Dallas
Sarah Childress Polk

12.

Zachary Taylor, 64
Virginia 1784–1850
In office: 1849–1850*
Whig
Millard Fillmore
Margaret Smith Taylor

13.

Millard Fillmore, 50
New York 1800–1874
In office: 1850–1853
Whig
(No vice-president)
Abigail Powers Fillmore

14.

Franklin Pierce, 48
New Hampshire 1804–1869
In office: 1853–1857
Democratic
William R. King
Jane Appleton Pierce

15.

James Buchanan, 65
Pennsylvania 1791–1868
In office: 1857–1861
Democratic
John C. Breckinridge
Unmarried

*died in office

16.

Abraham Lincoln, 52
Kentucky 1809–1865
In office: 1861–1865**
Republican
Hannibal Hamlin; Andrew Johnson
Mary Todd Lincoln

17.

Andrew Johnson, 56
North Carolina 1808–1875
In office: 1865–1869
Democratic
(No vice-president)
Eliza McCardle Johnson

18.

Ulysses S. Grant, 46
Ohio 1822–1885
In office: 1869–1877
Republican
Schuyler Colfax; Henry Wilson
Julia Dent Grant

19.

Rutherford B. Hayes, 54
Ohio 1822–1893
In office: 1877–1881
Republican
William A. Wheeler
Lucy Webb Hayes

20.

James A. Garfield, 49
Ohio 1831–1881
In office: 1881 (6½ months)**
Republican
Chester A. Arthur
Lucretia Rudolph Garfield

21.

Chester A. Arthur, 50
Vermont 1830–1886
In office: 1881–1885
Republican
(No vice-president)
Ellen Herndon Arthur

22. and 24.

Grover Cleveland, 47
New Jersey 1837–1908
In office: 1885–1889; 1893–1897
Democratic; Thomas Hendricks;
Adlai E. Stevenson
Frances Folsom Cleveland

23.

Benjamin Harrison, 55
Ohio 1833–1901
In office: 1889–1893
Republican
Levi P. Morton
Caroline Scott Harrison

25.

William McKinley, 54
Ohio 1843–1901
In office: 1897–1901**
Republican; Garret A. Hobart;
Theodore Roosevelt
Ida Saxton McKinley

**assassinated

26.

Theodore Roosevelt, 42
New York 1858–1919
In office: 1901–1909
Republican
Charles Warren Fairbanks
Edith Carow Roosevelt

27.

William Howard Taft, 51
Ohio 1857–1930
In office: 1909–1913
Republican
James S. Sherman
Helen Herron Taft

28.

Woodrow Wilson, 56
Virginia 1856–1924
In office: 1913–1921
Democratic
Thomas A. Marshall
Edith Bolling Wilson

29.

Warren G. Harding, 55
Ohio 1865–1923
In office: 1921–1923*
Republican
Calvin Coolidge
Florence Kling Harding

30.

Calvin Coolidge, 51
Vermont 1872–1933
In office: 1923–1929
Republican
Charles G. Dawes
Grace Goodhue Coolidge

31.

Herbert C. Hoover, 54
Iowa 1874–1964
In office: 1929–1933
Republican
Charles Curtis
Lou Henry Hoover

32.

Franklin Delano Roosevelt, 51
New York 1882–1945
In office: 1933–1945*
Democratic; John Garner;
Henry Wallace; Harry S. Truman
Anna Eleanor Roosevelt

33.

Harry S. Truman, 60
Missouri 1884–1972
In office: 1945–1953
Democratic
Alben W. Barkley
Elizabeth (Bess) Wallace Truman

34.

Dwight D. Eisenhower, 62
Texas 1890–1969
In office: 1953–1961
Republican
Richard M. Nixon
Mamie Doud Eisenhower

*died in office

35.

36.

37.

John F. Kennedy, 43
Massachusetts 1917–1963
In office: 1961–1963**
Democratic
Lyndon Baines Johnson
Jacqueline Bouvier Kennedy

Lyndon Baines Johnson, 55
Texas 1908–1973
In office: 1963–1969
Democratic
Hubert H. Humphrey
Claudia (Lady Bird) Taylor Johnson

Richard M. Nixon, 56
California 1913–
In office: 1969–1974***
Republican
Spiro T. Agnew; Gerald R. Ford
Thelma (Pat) Ryan Nixon

38.

39.

40.

Gerald R. Ford, 61
Nebraska 1913–
In office: 1974–1977
Republican
Nelson Rockefeller
Elizabeth (Betty) Bloomer Ford

Jimmy (James E.) Carter, 52
Georgia 1924–
In office: 1977–1981
Democratic
Walter F. Mondale
Rosalynn Smith Carter

Ronald Reagan, 69
Illinois 1911–
In office: 1981–
Republican
George H. Bush
Nancy Davis Reagan

Facts About the Presidency

Qualifications
 at least 35 years old
 a natural-born citizen
 lived in the United States 14 years
Term of Office
 four years, and not more than twice
Inauguration
 January 20 after election
Oath of Office
 "I do solemnly swear (or affirm) that
 I will faithfully execute the office
 of President of the United States,
 and will to the best of my ability,
 preserve, protect, and defend the
 Constitution of the United States."

**assassinated   ***resigned

Time Line of Events in United States History

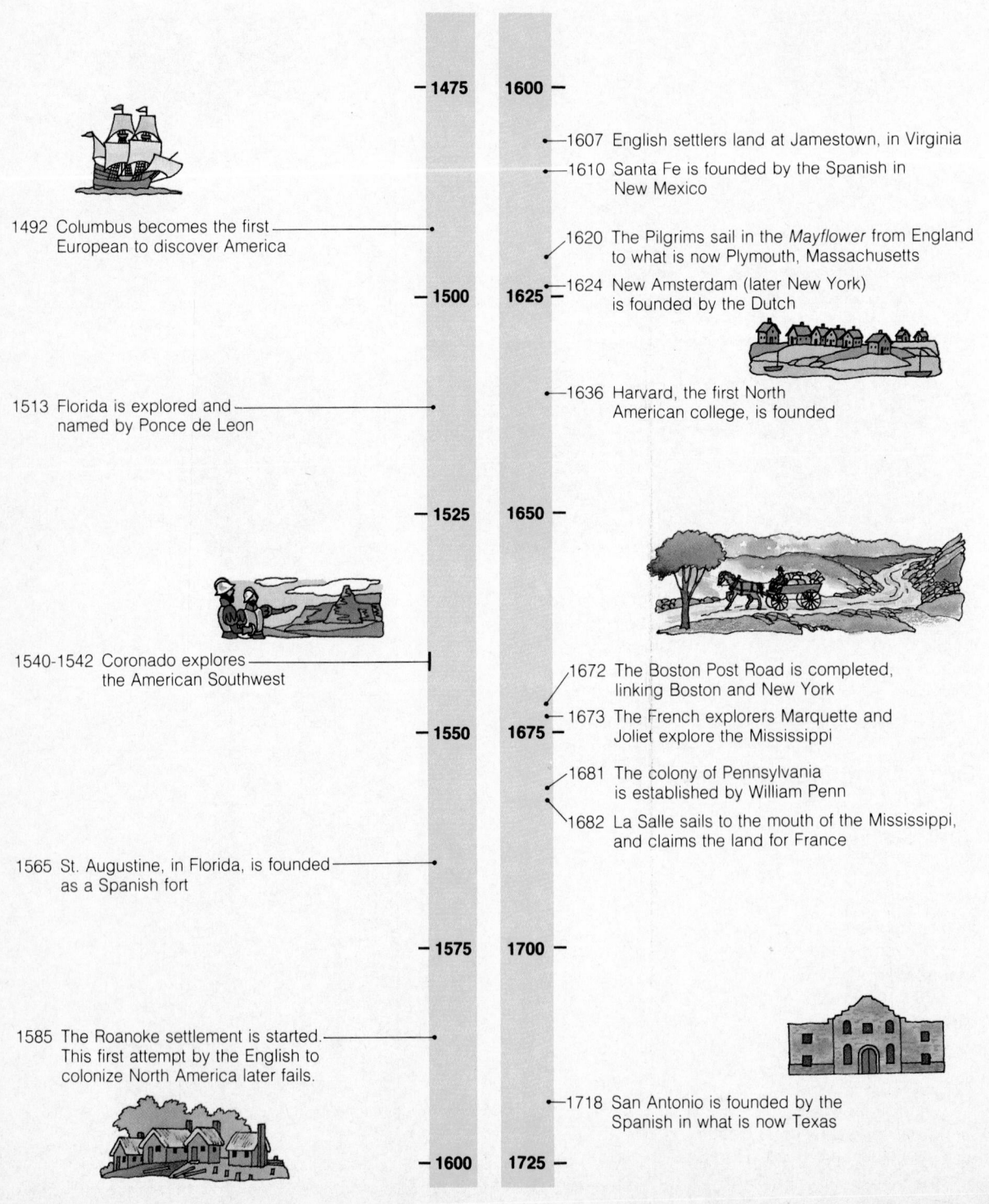

— 1475   1600 —

1492 Columbus becomes the first
       European to discover America

1607 English settlers land at Jamestown, in Virginia

1610 Santa Fe is founded by the Spanish in
       New Mexico

1620 The Pilgrims sail in the *Mayflower* from England
       to what is now Plymouth, Massachusetts

— 1500   1625 —

1624 New Amsterdam (later New York)
       is founded by the Dutch

1513 Florida is explored and
       named by Ponce de Leon

1636 Harvard, the first North
       American college, is founded

— 1525   1650 —

1540-1542 Coronado explores
            the American Southwest

1672 The Boston Post Road is completed,
       linking Boston and New York

1673 The French explorers Marquette and
       Joliet explore the Mississippi

— 1550   1675 —

1681 The colony of Pennsylvania
       is established by William Penn

1682 La Salle sails to the mouth of the Mississippi,
       and claims the land for France

1565 St. Augustine, in Florida, is founded
       as a Spanish fort

— 1575   1700 —

1585 The Roanoke settlement is started.
       This first attempt by the English to
       colonize North America later fails.

1718 San Antonio is founded by the
       Spanish in what is now Texas

— 1600   1725 —

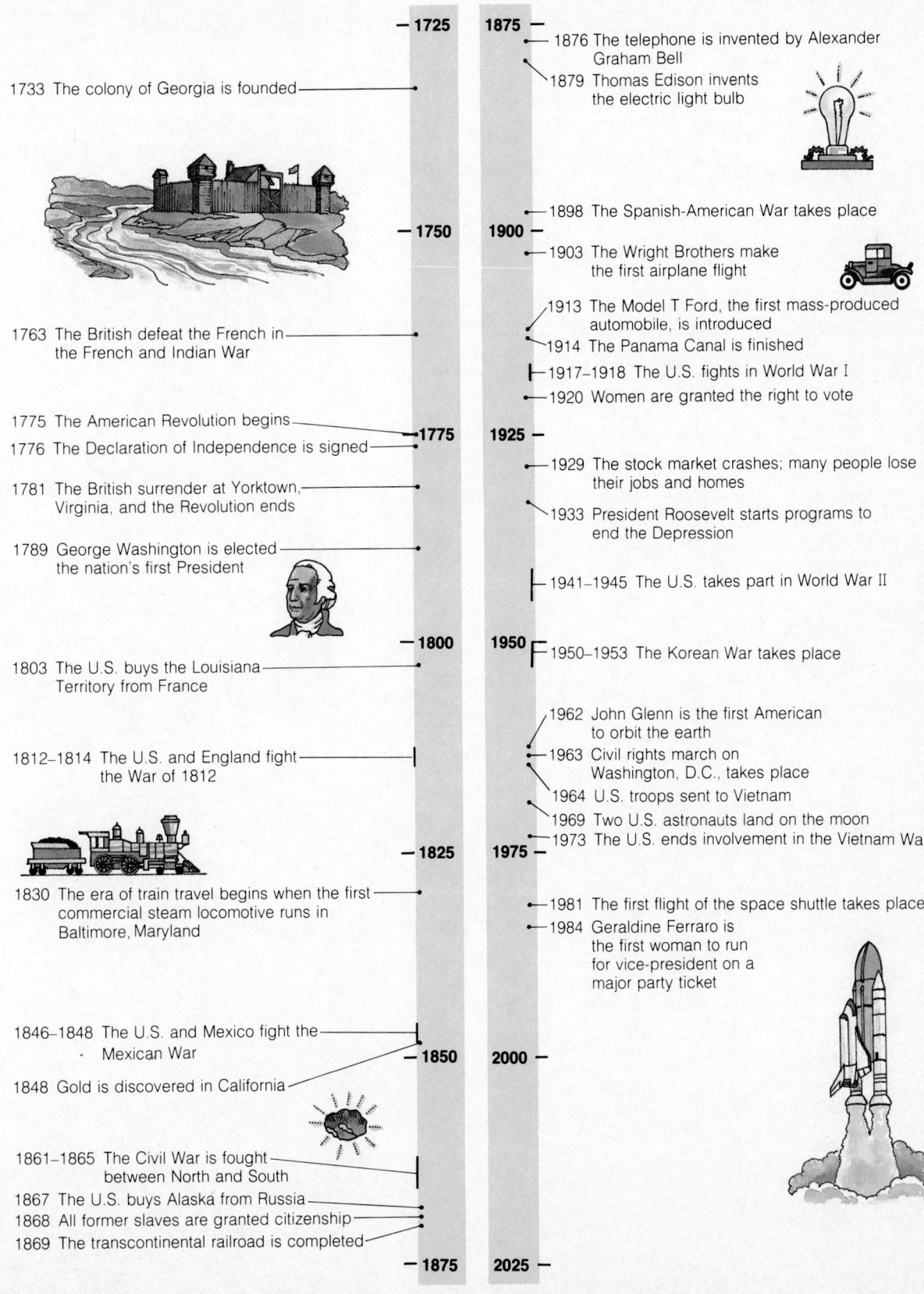

— 1725

1733 The colony of Georgia is founded

— 1750

1763 The British defeat the French in the French and Indian War

1775 The American Revolution begins
1776 The Declaration of Independence is signed
— 1775

1781 The British surrender at Yorktown, Virginia, and the Revolution ends

1789 George Washington is elected the nation's first President

— 1800

1803 The U.S. buys the Louisiana Territory from France

1812–1814 The U.S. and England fight the War of 1812

— 1825

1830 The era of train travel begins when the first commercial steam locomotive runs in Baltimore, Maryland

1846–1848 The U.S. and Mexico fight the Mexican War
— 1850

1848 Gold is discovered in California

1861–1865 The Civil War is fought between North and South

1867 The U.S. buys Alaska from Russia
1868 All former slaves are granted citizenship
1869 The transcontinental railroad is completed

— 1875

1875 —

1876 The telephone is invented by Alexander Graham Bell
1879 Thomas Edison invents the electric light bulb

1898 The Spanish-American War takes place
1900 —
1903 The Wright Brothers make the first airplane flight

1913 The Model T Ford, the first mass-produced automobile, is introduced
1914 The Panama Canal is finished
1917–1918 The U.S. fights in World War I
1920 Women are granted the right to vote

1925 —

1929 The stock market crashes; many people lose their jobs and homes

1933 President Roosevelt starts programs to end the Depression

1941–1945 The U.S. takes part in World War II

1950 —
1950–1953 The Korean War takes place

1962 John Glenn is the first American to orbit the earth
1963 Civil rights march on Washington, D.C., takes place
1964 U.S. troops sent to Vietnam
1969 Two U.S. astronauts land on the moon
1973 The U.S. ends involvement in the Vietnam War
1975 —

1981 The first flight of the space shuttle takes place
1984 Geraldine Ferraro is the first woman to run for vice-president on a major party ticket

2000 —

2025 —

English Words from Other Languages

It may surprise you to learn that most of the words in the English language have come from other languages. These words, from languages all over the world, came into English in various ways.

During its early history, England was invaded by people from other lands. Words from the languages spoken by these invaders became part of the English language. Later, English explorers

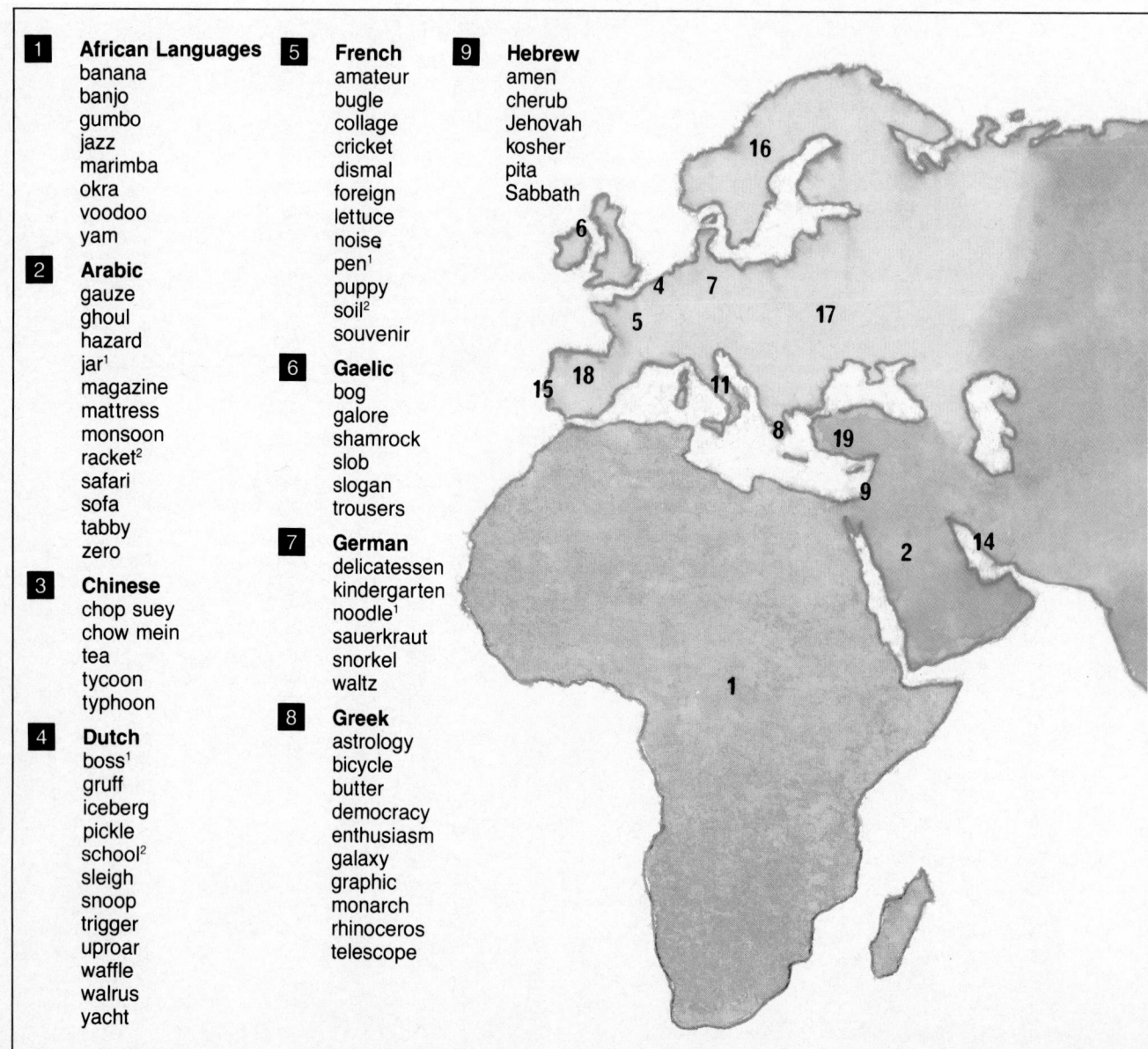

1 **African Languages**
banana
banjo
gumbo
jazz
marimba
okra
voodoo
yam

2 **Arabic**
gauze
ghoul
hazard
jar[1]
magazine
mattress
monsoon
racket[2]
safari
sofa
tabby
zero

3 **Chinese**
chop suey
chow mein
tea
tycoon
typhoon

4 **Dutch**
boss[1]
gruff
iceberg
pickle
school[2]
sleigh
snoop
trigger
uproar
waffle
walrus
yacht

5 **French**
amateur
bugle
collage
cricket
dismal
foreign
lettuce
noise
pen[1]
puppy
soil[2]
souvenir

6 **Gaelic**
bog
galore
shamrock
slob
slogan
trousers

7 **German**
delicatessen
kindergarten
noodle[1]
sauerkraut
snorkel
waltz

8 **Greek**
astrology
bicycle
butter
democracy
enthusiasm
galaxy
graphic
monarch
rhinoceros
telescope

9 **Hebrew**
amen
cherub
Jehovah
kosher
pita
Sabbath

brought back to England words from the lands they visited. Later still, when English colonists settled in other lands, they saw many new and unusual things. They adopted many of the words spoken by the people who were already living there to describe these unfamiliar things.

This borrowing of words from other languages is still going on. At the present time, scientists often borrow words from Latin and ancient Greek to name new scientific developments, inventions, and products.

Here is a small sample of words that have entered English from or through other languages.

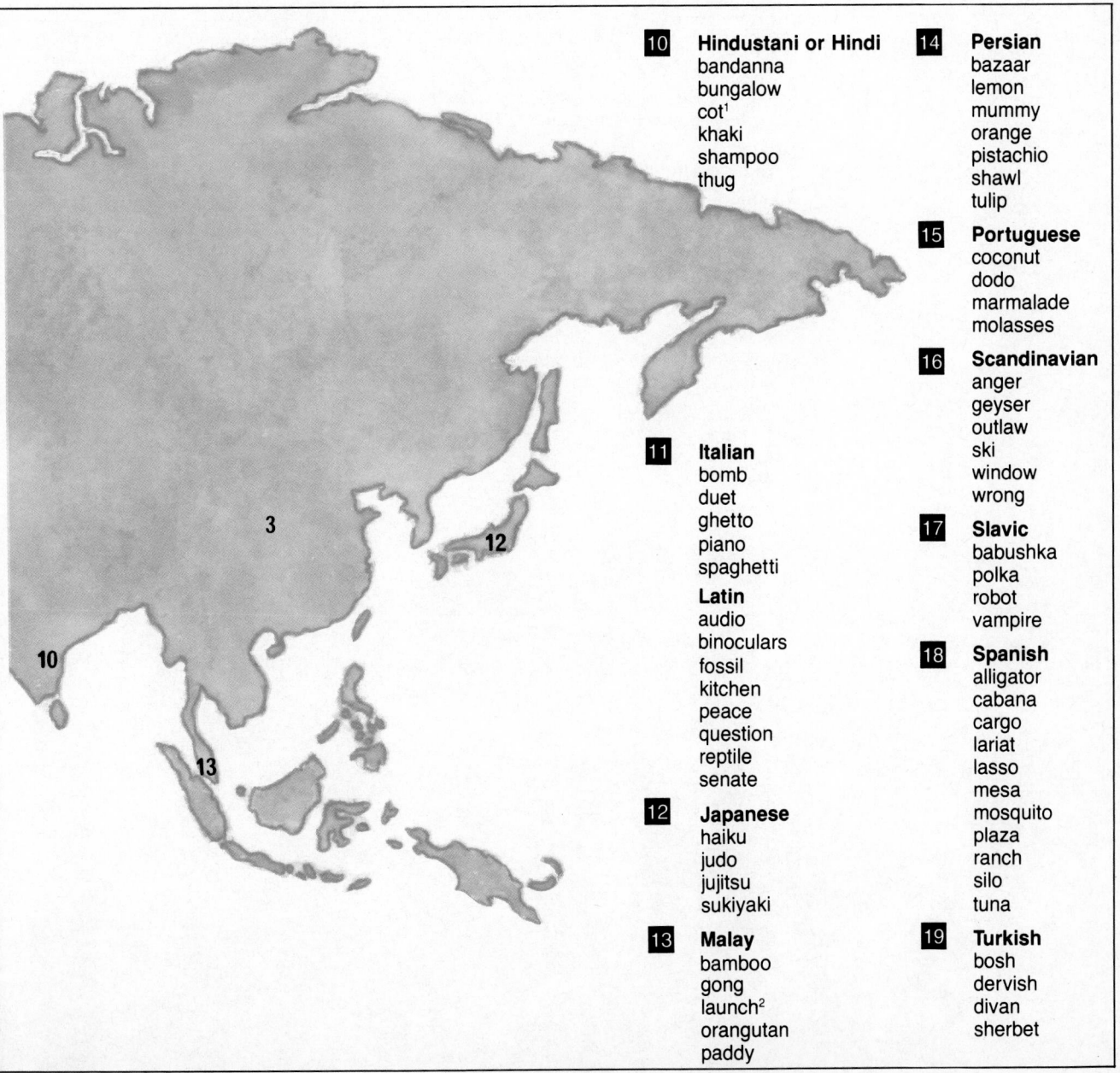

10 Hindustani or Hindi
bandanna
bungalow
cot[1]
khaki
shampoo
thug

11 Italian
bomb
duet
ghetto
piano
spaghetti

Latin
audio
binoculars
fossil
kitchen
peace
question
reptile
senate

12 Japanese
haiku
judo
jujitsu
sukiyaki

13 Malay
bamboo
gong
launch[2]
orangutan
paddy

14 Persian
bazaar
lemon
mummy
orange
pistachio
shawl
tulip

15 Portuguese
coconut
dodo
marmalade
molasses

16 Scandinavian
anger
geyser
outlaw
ski
window
wrong

17 Slavic
babushka
polka
robot
vampire

18 Spanish
alligator
cabana
cargo
lariat
lasso
mesa
mosquito
plaza
ranch
silo
tuna

19 Turkish
bosh
dervish
divan
sherbet

English Words Borrowed from Mexican Spanish

The first explorers of what is today the American Southwest were Spanish. Modern place names, from San Antonio in Texas to San Francisco in California, testify to the Spanish heritage of this vast region. Indeed, before 1836 it was all part of the Republic of Mexico. As English-speaking settlers began to move into the region, they began to borrow and use words from the Spanish speakers they found living there.

Over the years, many kinds of Mexican foods have become popular. *Chocolate* was an early favorite as a hot drink. Spicy *chili* was eaten. Later on, *abalone* became a popular seafood along the Pacific Coast. In more recent years, people all over the United States have learned to eat and enjoy *burritos, enchiladas, nachos, tacos,* and *tamales.*

The Southwest is a rugged, dry land where cattle have been raised for many years. The following sentence contains six words borrowed from Mexican Spanish; look up any of the words in italic type that you don't know:

Out on the open range, where the *coyotes* roam, cattle often *stampeded*, running aimlessly through *mesquite* shrubs until they were herded into a *canyon* by cowboys riding *broncos* and wearing *chaps.*

Other English words borrowed from Mexican Spanish words include *cafeteria, Chicana, Chicano, chicle, macho, mustang, quetzal,* and *serape.*

English Words from Native American Words

Some English words were borrowed directly from American Indian words. When explorers and settlers first came to the New World, they found people here speaking languages different from any they had ever heard. These Europeans began to use the Indian words for the unfamiliar things they saw.

An animal that the Europeans had never seen before roamed the forests of the New World. Instead of making up a name for the animal, they used a word based on the Indian name and called it a moose. A number of names of North and South American animals came into English this way. A few examples of these are *opossum, raccoon, llama, iguana, terrapin,* and *tanager.*

A common vegetable that the Indians grew was taken into English as the word *squash.* American Indians not only helped the early settlers plant their crops, but they gave the newcomers the names for many good things to eat such as *maize, potato, succotash, pecan,* and *hominy.*

There are about 100 words in this dictionary that have come from Native American languages. Many came from Algonquian, a family of related North American Indian languages. Such words as *moccasin, toboggan, skunk,* and *wigwam* are of Algonquian origin. *Tobacco* and *key* (meaning a reef) are from Indian languages of the Caribbean area. *Avocado, chili, tomato,* and *mesquite* come from Nahuatl, an Indian language still spoken by about 800,000 people, most of whom live in Mexico. Words from South American Indian languages include *hammock, alpaca, pampas,* and *tapioca.*

Acronyms

The *Readers' Guide to Periodical Literature,* a reference book that lists magazine articles, had a new heading in its volume for March 1984 to February 1985. The heading was "Yuppies," and nineteen articles on the subject were listed. It was a new heading because the word *yuppie* was a newly formed acronym (a word formed from the first letters or syllables of other words). *Yuppie* means "young urban professional," and it was formed from the first letters of *y*oung *ur*ban *p*rofessional plus the ending *-ie.* The new word was needed to denote the new generation of well-educated and well-paid professionals and their lifestyle.

In the 1960s, computers were being used by more and more people. To make it easier to give instructions to a computer, it was necessary to devise a language made up mainly of simple commands such as PRINT, INPUT, etc. This language was called "*b*eginner's *a*ll-purpose *s*ymbolic *i*nstruction *c*ode." Combining these first letters resulted in the word BASIC, which also suggests the word *basic,* meaning "fundamental."

Many acronyms began as regular abbreviations, and then developed pronunciations of their own. Examples of such words are NATO, AIDS, NASA, and UNICEF.

You can find other examples of words made from other words by looking up the definitions or etymologies of *alnico, lox*[2]*, OPEC, radar, scuba, sonar, UNESCO, WAC, Wave,* and *Zip Code.*

Blends—Words Made by Combining Parts of Other Words

Before the 1800s there were very few blends in English, but in 1872 Lewis Carroll, while writing *Through the Looking Glass*, coined the word *chortle* by cleverly combining the words *chuckle* and sn*ort*. When some or all of the letters of one word are joined with some or all of the letters of another word in this way, we call the new word a *blend*. This contrasts with a true compound word, such as *carfare*, in which all the letters of both the words *car* and *fare* are used in the combination.

Quite a few blends have come into our language since Lewis Carroll's *chortle*, especially in scientific vocabulary. Other blends have been coined from ordinary words that are used in everyday speech.

In the following list, the blend at the left was formed by combining the words given at the right.

Blend	Formed by combining	
bionics	biology	electronics
brunch	breakfast	lunch
camcorder	camera	recorder
Eurasia	Europe	Asia
gasohol	gasoline	alcohol
gerrymander	Gerry	salamander
mailgram	mail	telegram
motel	motor	hotel
pennant	pennon	pendant
prequel	pre-	sequel
quasar	quasi	stellar
radwaste	radioactive	waste
simulcast	simultaneous	broadcast
slosh	slop	slush
smog	smoke	fog
software	soft	hardware
squiggle	squirm	wriggle
transistor	transmitter	resistor
zillion	z	million

Words from People's Names and Place Names

Many English words are derived from the names of real or imaginary people.

These words get their names from mythical figures:

money (from Juno Moneta, a name for the Roman goddess Juno)

museum (from the Muses, the nine Greek goddesses of the fine arts and sciences)

tantalize (from Tantalus, a king in a Greek myth)

volcano (from Vulcan, the Roman god of fire)

These flowers and plants are named for people:

begonia	gardenia	timothy
forsythia	poinsettia	wisteria
fuchsia	Queen Anne's lace	zinnia

Scientific names are often derived from the names of well-known scientists. Some examples are:

ampere	einsteinium	hertz	ohm
curium	fermium	joule	volt
diesel	Fahrenheit	Kelvin	watt

The following names for clothing are derived from the name of the person who originated or popularized the style:

bloomers	derby
cardigan	mackintosh

Frankfurter, bologna, and *tarantula* have something in common. The first two words are, of course, kinds of sausage. But what does a tarantula have in common with sausages?

If you were to look at the word histories for these words you would discover that *frankfurters* were a specialty of Frankfurt, a city in West Germany, and that *bologna* was first made in Bologna, a city in Italy. As you can see, the words *frankfurter* and *bologna* come from the names of places, and so does *tarantula.* This spider got its name from Taranto, a seaport in southern Italy where it is commonly found.

Many other English words are derived from place names. Word histories for the following words of this type can be found in this dictionary:

badminton	denim	jersey	Shetland pony
bayonet	epsom salts	jimsonweed	shillelagh
bungalow	fez	lima bean	spaniel
bunk[2]	gypsy	madras	tangerine
Cheddar	hamburger	mocha	wiener
Chihuahua	indigo	palace	ytterbium
damask	jean	sisal	

Proofreading

Proofreader's Marks

≡	Make a capital letter.	On tuesday I went home.
⊙	Write a period.	The next day I left again
⑦	Write a question mark.	When did you arrive
⑴	Write an exclamation point.	Put that down
∧	Put in a letter or word.	You shouldn't _be_ rude.
℮	Take out a letter or word.	The same goes double for you.
ⓢⓟ	Correct the spelling.	Why are you smileing?
⁋	Indent or start a new paragraph.	⁋ He was only eight.
⌄⌄	Put in quotes.	Mother said, Certainly you may.
⌃	Put in a comma.	John said "No you can't."
/	Make a small letter.	I'll ask my Dad.

Proofreader's Check List

As you look over your written work, ask yourself each of these questions:

· Does each sentence begin with a capital letter?
· Does each sentence end with the correct mark (. ? !)?
· Do all proper nouns begin with a capital letter?
· Are all words spelled correctly?
· Is each new paragraph indented?
· Does each sentence tell one complete thought?

If you can answer yes to all these questions, you're on your way to being a superwriter!

Spelling Rules

The chart below shows words that students your age often misspell. Look them over carefully and try to learn their correct spellings. A number of spelling hints follow to help you remember how to spell the more difficult words.

Words That Are Often Misspelled

accept	dangerous	hamburger	necessary	sense
ache	daughter	height	neighbor	separate
achievement	decided	hospital	neither	sincerely
advice	describe	hundred		something
against	desert		occasion	sometimes
aisle	diamond	instead	occurred	stationary
already	different	interesting	office	sure
although	dining	its	often	surprise
argument	dinosaur	it's	opposite	
assignment	disappear			terrible
		jealous	personal	though
believe	eighth		poison	thought
break	elementary	kitchen	possible	through
breakfast	especially		practice	truly
breathe	except	ladies	prefer	
broke	excited	laid	principle	until
brother	exercise	let's	privilege	unusual
business	experience	library	probably	usually
		license		
calendar	famous	listen	quiet	vegetable
category	favorite	lose	quit	
cemetery	field		quite	weird
challenge	foreign	marriage		which
chose	forest	minute	receive	while
college	forty	muscle	recommend	whole
committee		mysterious	restaurant	witch
cough	government		rhyme	woman
course	grammar		rhythm	writing
	grateful		rough	
	guard			you're

The brother's ache was worse than the daughter's cough.

To make singular nouns possessive add 's.
  Some examples: daughter + 's = daughter's
  brother + 's = brother's

The ladies' diamonds were left in the neighbors' kitchens.

To make plural nouns possessive add '.
  Some examples: ladies + ' = ladies'
  neighbors + ' = neighbors'

To make plurals of words ending in *ch*, *sh*, *x*, *s*, *ss*, *z*, or sometimes *o*, add *-es*.

Some examples: business + es = businesses
witch + es = witches

Some exceptions: radios, pianos

The witches went about their business cooking lizard tongue and potatoes.

To make plurals of nouns ending in a *consonant* and *y*, change the *y* to *i* and add *-es*.

Some examples: category + es = categories
cemetery + es = cemeteries

Some exceptions: Proper nouns, such as in *the two Marys*

The lady asked the ladies to name forty categories of berries.

Words that end in *e* drop the final *e* before adding a suffix that begins with a *vowel*.

Some examples: exercise + ing = exercising
believe + able = believable
decide + ed = decided

Some exceptions: mileage, saleable, traceable

I decided that exercising is more challenging for the experienced.

Words that end in *e* keep the final *e* before adding a suffix beginning with a *consonant*.

Some examples: achieve + ment = achievement
sense + less = senseless
sure + ly = surely

Some exceptions: argument, duly, ninth, wholly

Surely it is senseless to speak too loosely about others.

Words ending in *l* keep the final *l* before adding *-ly*.

Some examples: personal + ly = personally
usual + ly = usually

Some exceptions: Words ending in *ll* drop one *l* before adding *-ly*, as in hilly, fully.

He is usually quiet, especially in the library.

One-syllable words that end in a *consonant* preceded by a single vowel double the final consonant before adding a suffix that begins with a *vowel*.

Some examples: grab + ed = grabbed
shred + ed = shredded
tan + est = tannest

An Exception: mixed

I grabbed the paper and skimmed it quite excitedly.

If a word has more than one syllable and ends in a *consonant* preceded by a single *vowel*, double the consonant only if the final syllable is stressed.

Some examples: occur + ence = occurrence
outwit + ed = outwitted
prefer + ed = preferred, but prefer + ence = preference

I preferred not to describe what had occurred.

The Solar System and the Milky Way

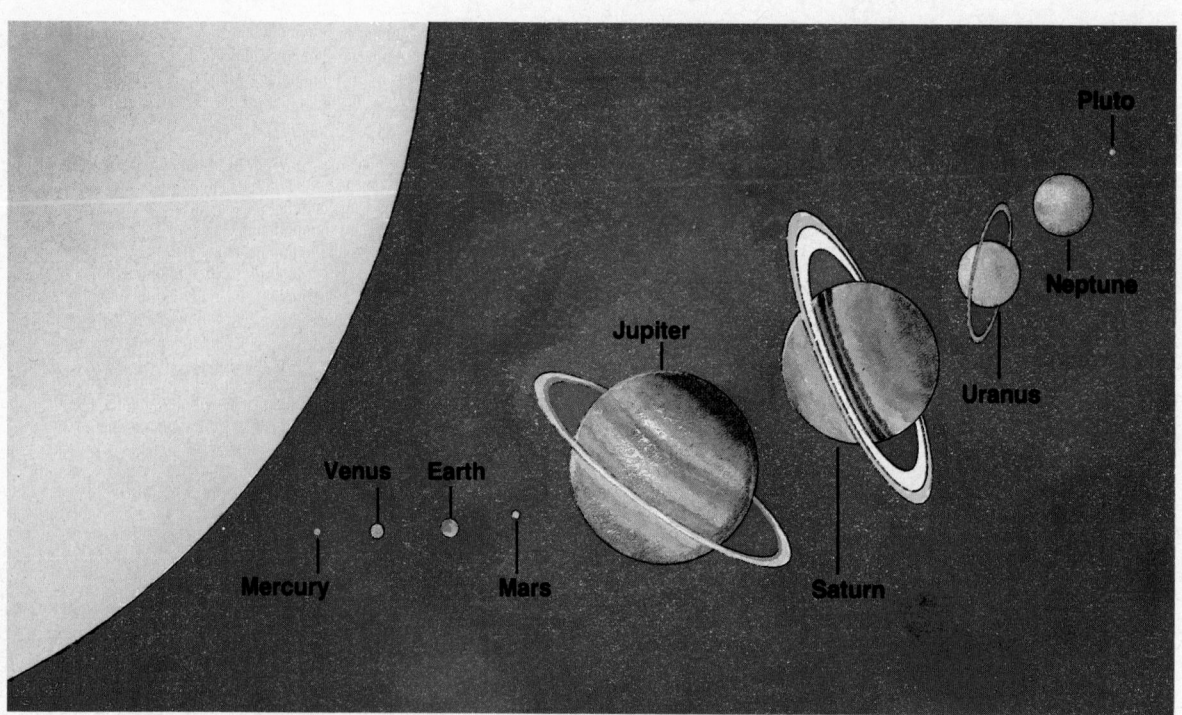

The Solar System

The sun and all of the heavenly bodies that orbit it make up the solar system. Earth is one of nine major planets in the solar system. These planets are shown in the diagram above in order of their distance from the sun. Thousands of minor planets called asteroids also travel around the sun between the orbits of Mars and Jupiter. Comets and meteors are also found in the solar system. More than thirty natural satellites orbit the planets. The moon is the earth's only natural satellite.

The Milky Way

The sun is a star. It is one of a vast group of stars that form our galaxy. A galaxy is a huge cloud of many billions of stars. Galaxies are shaped like disks with a bulge at the center. Since we are inside our galaxy, which is called the Milky Way, we can only see parts of it. The Milky Way is thought to have several arms. Our solar system is located on one of the arms.

Our galaxy is called the Milky Way because the part of it that we can see appears as a broad, milky-white band of light across the night sky.

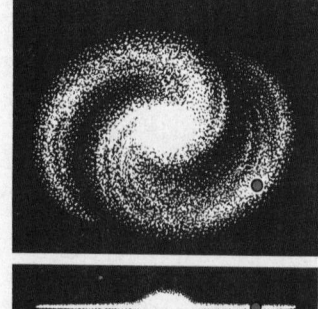

Milky Way Galaxy
above, top view, below, side view. The dot shows the estimated position of the solar system which contains the planet Earth.

Earth's Neighbors
The Other Planets in Our Solar System

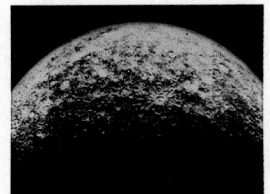

Mercury

Mercury, the planet closest to the sun, has a very hot surface. It is much smaller than Earth and is covered with craters. It is sometimes visible for an hour just after sunset or just before sunrise, but it is never high enough in the sky for us to see well.

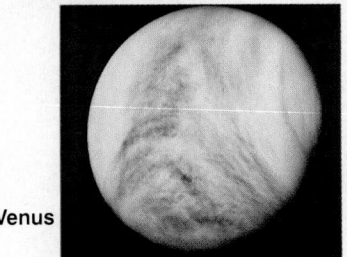

Venus

Venus is the second closest planet to the sun and the closest to Earth. It is the planet most like Earth in terms of size. Venus has a temperature of nearly 850°F (455°C) and a surface pressure 90 times greater than Earth's. It is covered by clouds made of acid and carbon dioxide. Venus is often visible from Earth.

Mars comes after Earth in relation to the sun. Like Earth, it has seasons and is warmer at its equator than at its poles. Average temperatures on Mars are much lower than on Earth. It is thought to have enough water frozen in its soil to support a party of explorers. Mars appears reddish to us because it is covered with red soil.

Mars

Jupiter

Jupiter often gleams brilliantly in the sky at night. It is a giant planet, having a diameter 11 times greater than Earth's. It is covered by bands of thick, colorful clouds, and has a very thin ring. Jupiter's interior is very hot; it puts out more heat than it receives from the sun. It does not have a solid surface like Earth. Jupiter has 16 known moons.

Saturn is the second largest planet, smaller than Jupiter but much larger than Earth. Like Jupiter, it is covered by clouds and has no solid surface. Saturn is surrounded by a series of brilliant light-reflecting rings that extend for thousands of miles. Each ring is made up of ice-covered rocks that vary in size from specks to chunks 10 feet in diameter. Saturn has 23 moons.

Uranus is a dark, icy planet, smaller than Saturn and farther from the sun. It is much colder than either Jupiter or Saturn, seldom rising above 310°F below zero (−192°C). It revolves around the sun in the time equal to 84 Earth years. Uranus has at least nine rings and five moons.

Saturn

Uranus

Neptune, along with Jupiter, Saturn, and Uranus, is one of the four gas giants. Like Uranus, Neptune is about four times the diameter of Earth. Neptune has a thick gaseous atmosphere and a very cold surface—360°F below zero (−220°C). Neptune is known to have two moons.

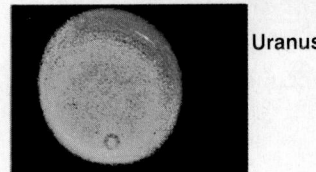

Pluto, the smallest of all the planets, is only slightly larger than our moon. It is considered the farthest planet from the sun, although its orbit sometimes takes it within the orbit of Neptune. Pluto takes almost 250 Earth years to make one trip around the sun. It is known to have one moon.

The photographs above were taken by NASA space probes. Neptune and Pluto are so far away the photographs of them just show small dots.

The Human Skeleton

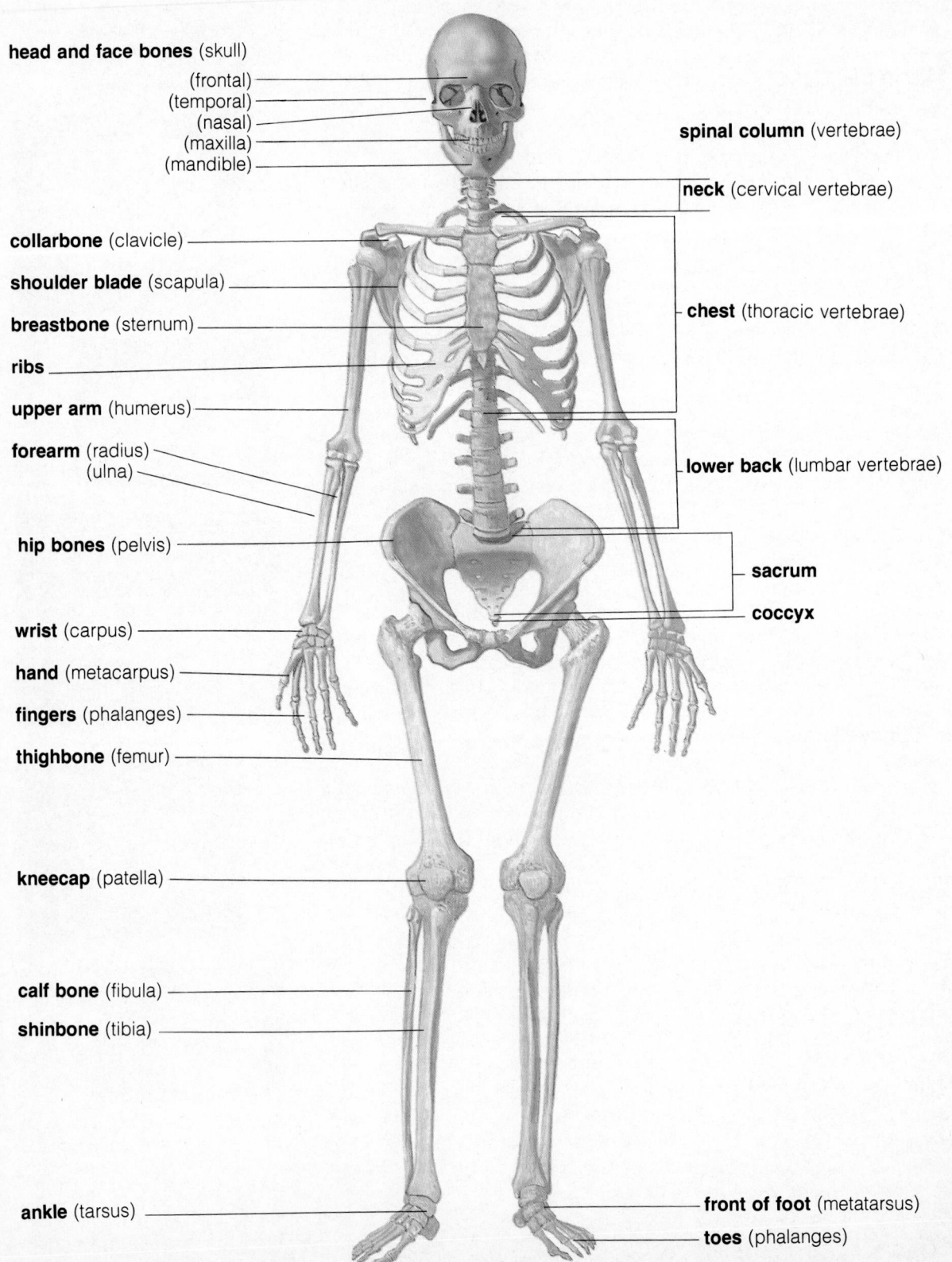

head and face bones (skull)

(frontal)
(temporal)
(nasal)
(maxilla)
(mandible)

spinal column (vertebrae)

neck (cervical vertebrae)

collarbone (clavicle)

shoulder blade (scapula)

breastbone (sternum)

ribs

upper arm (humerus)

forearm (radius)
(ulna)

hip bones (pelvis)

chest (thoracic vertebrae)

lower back (lumbar vertebrae)

sacrum

coccyx

wrist (carpus)

hand (metacarpus)

fingers (phalanges)

thighbone (femur)

kneecap (patella)

calf bone (fibula)

shinbone (tibia)

ankle (tarsus)

front of foot (metatarsus)

toes (phalanges)

Table of Measures and Weights

Metric System

Length	1 millimeter	=	1/1000 meter
	1 centimeter	=	1/100 meter
	1 decimeter	=	1/10 meter
	1 meter	=	{ 10 decimeters { 100 centimeters
	1 decameter	=	10 meters
	1 kilometer	=	1000 meters

Area	1 square centimeter	=	100 square millimeters
	1 square meter	=	{ 100 square decimeters { 10,000 square centimeters

Volume or Capacity	1 cubic centimeter	=	1000 cubic millimeters
	1 cubic decimeter	=	1000 cubic centimeters
	1 cubic meter	=	{ 1000 cubic decimeters { 1,000,000 cubic centimeters
	1 milliliter	=	1/1000 liter
	1 liter	=	{ 1 cubic decimeter { 1000 milliliters

Mass or Weight	1 gram	=	1000 milligrams
	1 kilogram	=	1000 grams
	1 metric ton	=	1000 kilograms

United States System

Length	1 foot	=	12 inches
	1 yard	=	{ 3 feet { 36 inches
	1 mile	=	{ 1760 yards { 5280 feet

Area	1 square foot	=	144 square inches
	1 square yard	=	9 square feet
	1 acre	=	4840 square yards
	1 square mile	=	640 acres

Volume	1 cubic foot	=	1728 cubic inches
	1 cubic yard	=	27 cubic feet

Weight	1 pound	=	16 ounces
	1 ton	=	2000 pounds

Capacity	1 cup	=	8 fluid ounces
	1 pint	=	2 cups
	1 quart	=	2 pints
	1 gallon	=	4 quarts

Metric Conversion Table

To Convert	To	Multiply By	To Convert	To	Multiply By
linear measure			**linear measure**		
centimeters	inches	0.394	inches	centimeters	2.54
meters	feet	3.281	feet	meters	0.3048
meters	yards	1.0936	yards	meters	0.914
kilometers	miles	0.62	miles	kilometers	1.609
square measure			**square measure**		
square centimeters	square inches	0.155	square inches	square centimeters	6.45
square meters	square feet	10.76	square feet	square meters	0.093
square meters	square yards	1.196	square yards	square meters	0.836
hectares	acres	2.471	acres	hectares	0.405
square kilometers	square miles	0.386	square miles	square kilometers	2.59
cubic measure			**cubic measure**		
cubic centimeters	cubic inches	0.061	cubic inches	cubic centimeters	16.387
cubic meters	cubic yards	1.31	cubic yards	cubic meters	0.765
cubic meters	cubic feet	35.315	cubic feet	cubic meters	0.028
liquid measure			**liquid measure**		
milliliters	fluid ounces	0.0338	fluid ounces	milliliters	29.57
liters	fluid ounces	33.814	fluid ounces	liters	0.03
liters	quarts	1.057	quarts	liters	0.946
liters	gallons	0.264	gallons	liters	3.785
dry measure			**dry measure**		
liters	dry quarts	0.908	dry quarts	liters	1.101
liters	pecks	0.114	pecks	liters	8.810
liters	bushels	0.028	bushels	liters	35.24
weight			**weight**		
grams	grains	15.43	grains	grams	0.0648
grams	ounces	0.0353	ounces	grams	28.35
kilograms	pounds	2.2046	pounds	kilograms	0.4536
kilograms	tons	0.001	tons	kilograms	907.18
metric tons	tons	1.102	tons	metric tons	0.907
temperature			**temperature**		
Celsius	Fahrenheit	1.8 then *add* 32	Fahrenheit	Celsius	subtract 32; then *divide* by 1.8

Full pronunciation key

The pronunciation of each word is shown just after the word, in this way:
ab bre vi ate (ə brē′vē āt).

The letters and signs used are pronounced as in the words below.

The mark ′ is placed after a syllable with primary or heavy accent, as in the example above.

The mark ′ after a syllable shows a secondary or lighter accent, as in
ab bre vi a tion (ə brē′vē ā′shən).

a	hat, cap		**p**	paper, cup
ā	age, face		**r**	run, try
ä	father, far		**s**	say, yes
			sh	she, rush
b	bad, rob		**t**	tell, it
ch	child, much		**th**	thin, both
d	did, red		**ŦH**	then, smooth
e	let, best		**u**	cup, butter
ē	equal, be		**u̇**	full, put
ėr	term, learn		**ü**	rule, move
f	fat, if		**v**	very, save
g	go, bag		**w**	will, woman
h	he, how		**y**	young, yet
			z	zero, breeze
			zh	measure, seizure
i	it, pin			
ī	ice, five			
j	jam, enjoy		**ə**	represents:
k	kind, seek			a in about
l	land, coal			e in taken
m	me, am			i in pencil
n	no, in			o in lemon
ng	long, bring			u in circus
o	hot, rock			
ō	open, go			
ô	order, all			
oi	oil, voice			
ou	house, out			